# THE CONCISE CAMBRIDGE ITALIAN DICTIONARY

# THE CONCISE CAMBRIDGE ITALIAN DICTIONARY

COMPILED BY
BARBARA REYNOLDS



CAMBRIDGE UNIVERSITY PRESS

Published by the Syndics of the Cambridge University Press
Bentley House, 200 Euston Road, London NW1 2DB
American Branch: 32 East 57th Street, New York, N.Y. 10022



Library of Congress Catalogue Card Number: 74-77384

ISBN: 0 521 07273 5

First published 1975

Printed in Great Britain
at the University Printing House, Cambridge
(Euan Phillips, University Printer)

To

KERSTIN

# CONTENTS

# INTRODUCTION

This *Concise Italian–English, English–Italian Dictionary*, though compiled chiefly for English-speaking users, is aimed also at meeting the requirements of Italian students of English. The Italian–English section is based on *The Cambridge Italian Dictionary*,[1] which it follows closely in style and conventions. The English–Italian section represents a selection of material compiled in preparation for the English–Italian volume of that publication.

The relationship which the present work bears to these larger compilations has resulted in a width of vocabulary and a richness of exemplifying phrases unusual in a dictionary of this size. The division of the page into three columns, which avoids wasteful blank spaces, has made it possible to provide what is in fact a much longer dictionary than its bulk suggests, and to include in its 800 or so pages many special features.

As in *The Cambridge Italian Dictionary*, care has been taken to indicate the range and limitations of usage, both of vocabulary and of phrases. Style or probable context is suggested by indications in brackets as well as by examples. The specialized terms selected from the parent dictionary cover a wide range: Music, Fine Art, Religion, Philosophy, Science, Technology, Industry, Zoology, Ornithology, Botany, Military, Nautical and Aviation terminology, Law, Social Institutions and other categories. Wherever possible, care has been taken to render such terms by their English equivalents rather than by explanatory definitions. All specialized terms and specialized uses of ordinary words were submitted in the first instance to the specialist responsible for the category in question. This is true of both the English–Italian and the Italian–English section and it may consequently be fairly claimed that specialized vocabulary has here been identified and translated with exceptional precision. To meet the needs of users who read Italian and English classics a proportion of literary words has been included. Obsolete words, however, have been omitted, to make room for a selection of the new colloquial and slang vocabulary which has become part of educated usage, particularly in English.

Americanisms are represented only by terms in general use in English or by distinctions in meaning which may prove helpful to Italian users of the dictionary (e.g. **Fall**, autunno; **homely**, bruttino; **to guess**, credere).

## Arrangement of the Italian–English section

### 1. *Word-list*

The presentation of the word-list is in accordance with the two main principles followed in *The Cambridge Italian Dictionary*: alphabetical sequence and sub-division into head-words and derivatives. For example, the verb **andare** is listed as a head-word, being split into stem

[1] Cambridge University Press, 1962.

and termination by a tilde (-); the derivatives **andamento, andante, andata** (indicated by means of their terminations: **-amento, -ante,-ata**) are entered in alphabetical order in relation to each other, after the infinitive. Adverbs are placed immediately after the adjectives from which they are derived; this sometimes involves breaking the alphabetical sequence in which derivatives are listed. Occasionally, to allow for a wide range of translations of an adjective, the adverb is omitted, on the assumption that the user will be able to select the appropriate translation from the meanings of the adjective. Inclusiveness and the avoidance of the otiose are two criteria which have influenced choice in the compilation of this dictionary.

Accordingly, for economy of space and to give preference to less obvious items, derivatives formed from nouns or adjectives by the addition of diminutive, augmentative, pejorative and other suffixes have been omitted, except for words in which some special use or anomaly is involved.[1]

Homonyms (e.g. **adagio** *adj.* slow, and **adagio** *m.* adage) are listed as separate head-words, distinguished by superior figures, [1], [2] *etc.* Near-homonyms, that is to say, words of widely divergent meaning or use, though of common origin (e.g. **a·bito** *m.* habit, and **a·bito** *m.* clothes) are similarly distinguished. Facility of reference, rather than the rigid application of semantics, has here been the operative criterion.

Under words commanding wide areas of meaning, a system of numbering is used, as in the case of **fare**, where examples are organized in 25 groups of meaning or usage.

## 2. *Grammatical Indications*

A new feature of this dictionary is the Concise Reference Grammar of Italian, which is to be found on pp. xxii–l. This, combined with the Verb Scheme, which has been adapted from *The Cambridge Italian Dictionary*, provides the user with a key to the basic elements of Italian. In addition, the following grammatical indications are to be found in the body of the dictionary.

### (i) *Verbs*

All verbs are entered in the active infinitive form (that is, with the termination **-are, -ere, -ire, -arre,** or **-urre**). The reflexive or passive form (that is, with the termination **-arsi, -ersi, -irsi,** or **-ursi**) is not entered as a head-word, but is to be deduced, where relevant, from the active form. All verbs are indicated as transitive, intransitive, reflexive or reciprocally reflexive; exemplifying phrases are given under the relevant headings. The auxiliaries in use with intransitive verbs are given in brackets at the beginning of the entry. Reflexive constructions in which the pronoun **si** is in the dative are distinguished from those in which it is in the accusative. All verbs are followed by a cipher in square brackets referring to the Verb Scheme, by means of which the user is able to find

[1] For a list of the principal suffixes in Italian, see Concise Reference Grammar, pp. xxxiii–xxxv.

the appropriate conjugation and supply the desired form. A list of verbs showing the prepositions used in construction with infinitives is given on p. lxxvii.

(ii) *Nouns*

The gender of all nouns is shown at the beginning of the entry. All nouns and masculine adjectives ending in **-co** or **-go** form their plural in **-ci** or **-gi** unless otherwise indicated. Nouns which are irregular or anomalous in the formation or use of the plural are shown with appropriate indications.[1]

(iii) *Prepositions*

The contractions of prepositions with the definite article are shown at the beginning of each entry.[2] Since the syntax of prepositions cannot be adequately conveyed without examples, special use has been made of phrases illustrating the differences between English and Italian in this respect. The prepositions used in construction with verbs followed by an infinitive are shown both under the verbs concerned in the body of the dictionary and in a list printed separately at the end of the Verb Scheme.[3]

## 3. *Pronunciation*

A Concise Guide to the Pronunciation of Italian is included on pp. xx–xxi. In addition, the following indications are given in the dictionary.

(i) *Main stress* (*tonic accent*)

Unless otherwise indicated, the main stress falls on the syllable before the last, e.g. **mano, cappello, amico.**

Words ending in a vowel with a written accent bear the main stress on that vowel, e.g. **città, virtù.**

Words in which the main stress falls on any but the last syllable or the syllable before the last, or in which doubt might arise are marked by a mid-point, printed after the stressed vowel or syllable, e.g. **ta.vola, com.pito.**

(ii) *Close and open* **e** *and* **o**

If the stressed vowel is a close **e** or **o**, the indication that this is so (that is, a dot beneath the vowel) also shows that this vowel bears the main stress, e.g. **sẹmplice.** Since unstressed **e** and **o** are always close, only stressed **e** and **o** need to be distinguished in respect of close or open pronunciation.

[1] See also pp. xxiv–xxix of the Concise Reference Grammar.
[1] See also paradigm on p. xxiii.
[3] See p. lxvvii.
[4] The mid-point is sometimes placed after the vowel in a closed syllable, sometimes after the consonant, e.g. **per.dere, sospi.ngere.** The subtle distinction as to pronunciation thereby implied need not concern the average user. The important thing in every case is to give the stressed vowel its full length and quality.

(iii) *Voiced and harsh* **s** *or* **z**

An **s** or **z** pronounced with the voiced or soft sound is marked with a sub-dot, e.g. **roṣa, aẓẓurro.** An **s** or **z** which has no such indication is pronounced with the unvoiced or harsh sound, e.g. **casa, zio.**

(iv) **g** *followed by* **li**

In cases in which **g** followed by **li** is pronounced as in English *glee* rather than as in the Italian definite article *gli*, the **g** is marked by a sub-dot, e.g. **g̣li·cine, g̣lifo.**

(v) *Foreign words*

Foreign words imported into Italian either become Italianized or retain their original pronunciation. In the latter case, an indication is given e.g. (pron. as Fr.).

4. *Typography*

All head-words and terminations of derivatives are printed in bold type in their place of entry. A tilde (⁓) splits the head-word either into stem and termination or into whatever divisions are convenient for the indication of stress. The Italian convention of syllabic division has not been followed in the splitting of head-words and derivatives, but it is observed where it has been necessary to divide Italian words at the end of a line of phrases.[1]

The em-rule or dash (—) stands in every instance for the entire head-word; in phrases, derivatives are represented in Italics by the form in which they are printed in bold type, preceded by a tilde (⁓).

The true hyphen (-) is used in the case of the relatively few Italian words in which it occurs. It is used more sparingly than in English, e.g.

*ex Ministro*, ex-Minister

It is also used to divide Italian words at the end of a line, in accordance with the Italian convention for syllabic division (see below).

Phrases in Italian are printed in Italics; the translations are printed in Roman type.

## ARRANGEMENT OF THE ENGLISH–ITALIAN SECTION

1. *Word-list*

As in the Italian–English section, the alphabetical sequence is modified by the division of head-words by a tilde (⁓) into stem and termination, and derivatives are entered under head-words in alphabetical order to each other. In English this arrangement disturbs the alphabetical order less than in Italian. Any inconvenience caused by the few instances in which

1 The Italian convention differs from the English in that every syllable must begin with a consonant or consonantal group, if there is one, e.g.

**ca-de-re**
**ca-sca-re**

This is in conflict with the division of these verbs into stem and termination:

**cad⁓ere**
**casc⁓are**

displacement does occur is outweighed by the economical use of space, the avoidance of repetitious translations, and the advantage of being able to take in at a glance the relationship of head-words and derivatives. A richer network of meaning can be conveyed by this system than by entering every word in isolation.

Hyphenated words, as distinguished from compound words, are entered separately or, if alphabetical sequence permits, as entries grouped together. Almost all compound words are entered separately; in the case of those which appear as derivatives under a head-word, the termination is preceded by a tilde (~), not a hyphen.

Homonyms and near-homonyms are entered as separate head-words and are distinguished by superior figures, e.g.

**bound**[1], *n.* confine *m.*
**bound**[2] *n.* salto
**bound**[3] *adj.* diretto
**bound**[4] *part.* of **bind,** *q.v.*; *adj.* rilegato

Words which require extensive translation and exemplification and which function as several parts of speech are entered separately according to grammatical categories but are not necessarily distinguished by superior figures, e.g.

**about** *adv.* attorno
**about** *prep.* circa

Under words commanding wide areas of meaning a system of numbering is sometimes used, as in the Italian–English section, to facilitate reference.

## 2. *Grammatical indications*

### (i) *Verbs*

A list of the principal irregular verbs in English is included on pp. lxxviii–lxxx.

All verbs are entered in the infinitive form. The past participles of strong verbs are entered separately if they are used extensively as adjectives. Further guidance as to conjugation may be deduced from exemplifying phrases, which have been selected partly for this purpose. The indication *tr.*, *intr.* or *rfl.* is given after every verb. Examples are grouped in relation to these categories, except where such an arrangement would be wasteful or inconvenient, as when it is necessary to show the use of the verb in combination with various adverbs or prepositions. In such cases, phrases are arranged in the alphabetical order of the first letter of the adverb or preposition, transitive and intransitive uses not being separated (e.g. see under **take** *tr.*).

### (ii) *Nouns*

All nouns are indicated as such by the abbreviation *n.* The gender of Italian nouns given as translations is indicated in this section only when there is likely to be doubt or wherever space has permitted. For the general rules concerning gender in Italian, reference should be made to the Concise Grammar, pp. xxiv–xxix. Gender may also be deduced from exemplifying phrases.

### 3. *Pronunciation*

Since this dictionary has been compiled mainly to meet the needs of English-speaking users, indication of the pronunciation of the English head-words is limited to the mid-point, used in cases where a difference in main stress (tonic accent) affects the meaning or use of two words identical in spelling, e.g.

**absent** *adj.* assente
**abse·nt** *rfl.* assentarsi

### 4. *Typography*

As in the Italian–English section, all head-words and terminations are printed in bold type in their place of entry. A tilde (~) splits the head-word into stem and termination and precedes the termination of the derivative. The em-rule or dash (—) stands in every instance for the entire head-word; in phrases, derivatives are represented in Italics by the form in which they are first entered in bold type, preceded by a tilde.

The true hyphen (-) is used in separate head-words which are normally spelled with a hyphen, and to divide words at the end of a line; in the case of English words, such division is in accordance with the English convention.

Phrases in English are printed in Italics; the translations are printed in Roman type.

### ACKNOWLEDGEMENTS

In the process of selecting material from the two parent compilations, *The Cambridge Italian Dictionary*, Volume I and the forthcoming second volume, I have been assisted by several of my lexicographical colleagues, especially the late Mr R. H. Boothroyd. I also acknowledge with thanks the help of Dr Edward Allam and Dr G. S. Purkis and of Miss Emi Messora and Mr Sergio Sakota. Of the editorial staff of the Cambridge University Press, I owe thanks to Mr Peter Burbidge, who conceived the three-column page, and to Mr Iain White for his help in the final stages of the revision. I wish also to express my gratitude to Mrs Gwen Thimann and to Mrs Luisa Gunning for their secretarial skill and patience.

BARBARA REYNOLDS

1 *January* 1974

# ABBREVIATIONS

*Abbreviations are puzzling, but to puzzle is not their purpose.*
(FOWLER)

*abbrev.* abbreviation
*abl.* ablative
*abs.* absolute
*abstr.* abstract
*acc.* accusative
*adj.* adjective
*admin.* administration
*adv.* adverb
*aeron.* aeronautics
*aesthet.* aesthetics
*agric.* agriculture
*alp.* alpine, relating to alpinists, and mountain climbing
*altern.* alternative, alternatively
*anat.* anatomy
*antiphr.* antiphrasis
*antiq.* in antiquity
*apocop.* apocopated
*appos.* (in) apposition
*archaeol.* archaeology
*archit.* architecture
*art* relating to the visual arts
*artill.* artillery
*astron.* astronomy
*athl.* athletics
*augm.* augmentative
*autom.* automobile engineering
*aux.* auxiliary

*bibl.* biblical
*bibliogr.* bibliography
*biblioph.* bibliophily
*biochem.* biochemistry
*biol.* biology
*bldg.* building
*bookb.* bookbinding
*bootm.* bootmaking
*bot.* botany
*butcher.* butchering
*B.V.M.* Blessed Virgin Mary

*carpen.* carpentry
*C.C.* Italian Civil Code
*C.C.P.* Italian Code of Civil Procedure
*ceram.* ceramics
*cf.* compare
*chem.* chemistry
*chem. eng.* chemical engineering
*cider-m.* cider-making
*cinem.* cinematography
*class.* classical
*clockm.* clockmaking
*colloq.* colloquial
*comm.* commerce
*comp.* comparative
*conj.* conjunction
*conjunct.* conjunctive
*constr.* construction
*contd.* continued
*contempt.* contemptuous
*contr.* contraction, contracted
*corrupn.* corruption
*Cors.* Corsican
*cost.* costume
*C.P.* Italian Penal Code
*C.P.P.* Italian Code of Penal Procedure
*crit.* criticism
*cryst.* crystallography
*cul.* culinary term
*cyt.* cytology

*dat.* dative
*def.* defective
*def. art.* definite article
*deriv(s).* derivative(s)
*derog.* derogatory
*dial.* dialect.
*dim.* diminutive
*disjunct.* disjunctive
*dressm.* dressmaking
*dye.* dyeing

*eccl.* ecclesiastical
*eccl. hist.* ecclesiastical history
*econ.* economics
*Egypt.* Egyptology
*electr.* electricity
*electron.* electronics
*encl.* enclitic
*eng.* engineering
*ent.* entomology
*equestr.* equestrian
*esp.* especially
*etc.* et cetera
*euphem.* euphemism
*excl.* exclamation
*exist.* existentialist
*explos.* explosives
*expr.* expression

*f.* feminine
*fam.* familiar
*fig.* figurative
*finan.* financial, finance
*Florent.* Florentine
*Flor. hist.* Florentine history
*foll.* followed, following
*fortif.* fortifications
*found.* foundry
*Fr.* French
*furn.* furniture

*gen.* genitive
*geneal.* genealogy, genealogical
*geog.* geography
*geol.* geology
*geom.* geometry
*ger.* gerund
*Gk.* Greek
*glass-m.* glass-manufacturing
*govt.* government
*gramm.* grammatical
*gymn.* gymnastics

*herald.* heraldry
*hist.* history, historical
*hortic.* horticulture
*hosp.* hospital
*hunt.* hunting
*hydr.*, *hydraul.* hydraulics
*hydr. eng.* hydraulic engineering

*I.C.* Italian Constitution
*ichth.* ichthyology
*illum.* illumination
*imp.* imperative
*impers.* impersonal
*indecl.* indeclinable
*indef.* indefinite
*indic.* indicative
*industr.* industry
*inf.* infinitive
*infant.* baby language
*intens.* intensive form
*interr.* interrogative
*intr.* intransitive
*iron.* ironical
*Ital. antiq.* Italian antiquity

*joc.* jocular
*journ.* journalism

*km.* kilometre(s)
*knitt.* knitting

*lang.* language
*Lat.* Latin
*leather-m.* leather-manufacturing
*leg.* legal term
*ling.* linguistic(s)
*lit. hist.* literary history
*lit.* literature
*liturg.* liturgy
*log.* logic
*Lomb.* Lombardy

*m.* masculine
*math.* mathematics
*mech.* mechanics
*med.* medical
*mediev.* medieval
*mens.* mensuration
*met.*, *metall.* metallurgy
*meteor.* meteorology
*mfr.* manufacturing
*mil.* military
*mil. comm.* military command
*min.* mining

*miner.* mineralogy
*motor.* motoring
*motorcycl.* motorcycling
*mount.* mountaineering
*ms.* manuscript
*mus.* music
*myth.* mythology

*n.* noun *or* used as a noun
*naut.* nautical
*naut. comm.* nautical command
*naut. hist.* nautical history
*Neap.* Neapolitan
*needle-w.* needle-work
*neg.* negative
*neol.* neologism
*N. Ital.* North Italian
*no.* number
*nos.* numbers
*nom.* nominative
*numis.* numismatics

*obstet.* obstetrics
*onom.* onomatopoeic
*opt.* optics
*orig.* originally
*orn.* ornithology

*paint.* painting
*palaeog.* palaeography
*palaeont.* palaeontology
*paperm.* papermaking
*part.* participle (present or past)
*part. adj.* participle used adjectivally
*partit.* partitive
*patrist.* patristic
*pedagog.* pedagogy
*pejor.* pejorative
*perh.* perhaps
*pers.* person
*pharm.* pharmacy, pharmacology
*philol.* philology
*philos.* philosophy
*phon.* phonetics
*photog.* photography
*phr.* phrase
*phys.* physics
*physiol.* physiology
*Piedm.* Piedmont, Piedmontese
*pl.* plural
*poet.* poetical
*pol.* politics, political
*pol. hist.* political history
*pop.* popular, popularly
*poss.* possessive
*pr.* proper
*pref.* prefix
*prep.* preposition
*prn.* pronoun
*pr. n.* proper noun
*procl.* proclitic
*pron.* pronounced
*prosod.* prosody
*Prov.* Provençal
*provb.* proverb, proverbial
*psychol.* psychology

*q.v.* quod vide

*radiol.* radiology
*recip.* reciprocal
*rel.* religion
*repet.* repetitive
*Repub.* Republic
*rfl.* reflexive
*rhet.* rhetoric
*rlwy.* railway
*Rom.* Roman
*Romagn.* Romagnuolo
*Rom. antiq.* Roman antiquity

*Sard.* Sardinian
*schol.* scholastic
*scient.* scientific
*Scot.* Scottish
*sculp.* sculpture
*seis.* seismology
*shoem.* shoemaking
*Sicil.* Sicilian
*silkb.* silkbreeding
*sim.* similar
*sing.* singular
*sociol.* sociology
*sp.* species
*suff.* suffix

*superl.* superlative
*surg.* surgery
*syll.* syllable

*tailor.* tailoring
*tan.* tanning
*techn.* technical, technology
*teleph.* telephonic
*telev.* television
*text.* textile
*text. ind.* textile industry
*theatr.* theatrical
*theol.* theology
*tr.* transitive
*Tusc.* Tuscan
*typ.* typography

*Umbr.* Umbrian
*usu.* usually

*Ven.* Venetian
*vet.* veterinary
*vulg.* vulgar

*zool.* zoology

# DIACRITIC MARKS

· **Mid-point** Indicates that the main stress (or tonic accent) falls on the preceding syllable, for example **me.dico.** *Note*: in words not marked with the mid-point, the main stress falls on the penultimate syllable, for example **cappello.**

. **Sub-dot** (*a*) Appearing under **e** or **o** indicates that the vowel is close. **e** and **o** are marked thus only when they bear the main stress, since unstressed **e** or **o** is always close. The sub-dot appearing under **e** or **o** therefore serves two purposes: (i) it shows that the vowel so marked bears the main stress; (ii) it shows that the vowel is close, for example **rispọndere** (in which the vowel **o** bears the main stress and is close). Cf. **co.gliere** (in which **o** bears the main stress and is open).

(*b*) Appearing under **s** or **z** indicates that the consonant is soft, for example **roṣa, organiẓẓare.**

(*c*) Appearing under **g** in the group **gli** indicates that the **g** is pronounced as a separate consonant (as in English), for example, **g̣lifo.**

` **Grave accent** This is the only accent used on Italian words in the dictionary and wherever it appears it is part of the word as written in Italian. *Note*: Italian typographers vary as to the style of accentuation they adopt; some use the acute accent for front vowels (close *e*, *i*, and *u*),[1] the grave for back vowels (*a*, open *e*, open *o*); others use the acute accent only for the close *e*. The use of the circumflex over **i**, instead of double *i*, is still found but is tending to become obsolete. In the face of such variation, it has been thought advisable to use only the grave accent, which indicates stress only. If the vowel so marked is close, a sub-dot indicates as much, for example **perchẹ̀.**

^ **Circumflex accent;** ´ **acute accent** These accents are used only on French words in the dictionary.

[A 1], **etc.** See Verb Scheme.

[1] Close *o* never bears a written accent.

# CONCISE GUIDE TO PRONUNCIATION OF ITALIAN

## VOWELS

| | *Near equivalent in English* |
|---|---|
| **a** | A in HAT |
| **e** (open) | E in EGG |
| **e** (close) | A in FATE[1] |
| **i** | EE in FEET |
| **o** (open) | O in DOG |
| **o** (close) | O in SHOW[1] |
| **u** | OO in MOON |
| **iu** | YOU |
| **uo** | OO-O or WO (the O as in DOG) |

## CONSONANTS

Those which differ markedly from English are:

| | |
|---|---|
| **c** before **e** or **i** | CH |
| **g** before **e** or **i** | J |
| **ch** | K |
| **gh** | G in GATE |
| **gli** | LLI in MILLION[2] |
| **gn** | NI in ONION[2] |
| **h** | is silent |
| **r** | is rolled on the tip of the tongue |
| **s** (unvoiced) | S in CASE |
| **s** (voiced) | S in ROSE[3] |
| **sc** before **e** or **i** | SH |
| **sch** | SK |
| **z** (unvoiced) | TS |
| **z** (voiced) | DS[3] |

J, W, X, Y are seldom used in Italian; their pronunciation is approximately as in English, except for J which is pronounced like Italian **i.** Every letter in Italian is sounded separately, except:

**i** before a vowel following **c**, **g** or **p**

| | *Near equivalent in English* |
|---|---|
| **giorno** | JORNO |
| **più** | PEW |
| **ciò** | CHO (O as in DOG) |
| **Giovanni** | JOVANNI |
| **giù** | JEW |

[1] Indicated by a sub-dot when it bears the main stress.
[2] Exceptions are indicated by a dot under the **g**.
[3] Indicated by a sub-dot.

**u** before a vowel

| | |
|---|---|
| **acqua** | AKWA |
| **uopo** | WOPO |
| **quiete** | KWEE-ETAY |

Double consonants are pronounced distinctly, even with a slight pause between the two:

| | |
|---|---|
| **quello** | KWEL-LO |
| **bocca** | BOK-KA |
| **fatto** | FAT-TO |
| **ferro** | FER-RO (as double rolled R, similar to the Scottish R) |

MAIN STRESS (TONIC ACCENT)

The majority of Italian words bear the main stress on the last syllable but one. All words which have a written accent on the final vowel bear the main stress on the last syllable.

**città**
**difficoltà**

In the dictionary, if the main stress falls on any syllable other than the last or the last but one, this is indicated by a mid-point.

**me·dico**
**si·mile**

# CONCISE REFERENCE GRAMMAR OF ITALIAN

## DEFINITE ARTICLE

*Masculine*

| *Singular* | *Plural* |
|---|---|
| il | i |
| l' (before vowel) | gli (before vowel, gn, ps, x, z, s followed by a consonant) |
| lo (before gn, ps, x, z, s followed by a consonant) | gl' (before i) |

*Examples*

| | |
|---|---|
| *il libro* the book | *i libri* the books |
| *l'uomo* the man | *gli uomini* the men |
| *lo zio* the uncle | *gli zii* the uncles |
| *lo scopo* the aim | *gli scopi* the aims |
| *l'inno* the hymn | *gl'inni* the hymns |

*Feminine*

| | |
|---|---|
| la | le |
| l' (before vowel) | l' (before e) |

*Examples*

| | |
|---|---|
| *la casa* the house | *le case* the houses |
| *l'anima* the soul | *le anime* the souls |
| *l'erba* the grass | *l'erbe* the grasses |

The definite article is used in Italian in some contexts in which it is omitted in English and vice versa.

*Examples*

*gli uomini* men
*le donne* women
*l'anno scorso* last year
*la vita* life
*la morte* death
*i fiori* flowers
*per l'Italia* for Italy
*la Francia* France
*alla Germania* to Germany
*dall'Inghilterra* from England

After the preposition **in** the definite article is often omitted, e.g.

*in Italia* in Italy
*in cucina* in the kitchen

The definite article tends to be used before names of persons; it is always used before titles except in the vocative.

*Examples*

*la Rossi* Mrs Rossi, Miss Rossi
*il Marconi* Marconi
*la Duse* Duse
*il Gianni non c'è* Ian isn't here
*il signor Bianchi* Mr White
*la regina Elisabetta* Queen Elizabeth
*il Professor Bruni* Professor Brown
*buon giorno, Professor Bruni* good morning, Professor Brown

The definite article is sometimes used in Italian where an indefinite article is used in English, e.g.

*fa l'avvocato* he is a lawyer
*non fare lo scemo* don't be a fool, *or* don't play the fool

### PREPOSITIONS COMBINED WITH DEFINITE ARTICLE

A definite article preceded by one of the prepositions **a, con, da, di, in, per, su** is combined with it to form one word, as follows:

| | **il** | **l'** | **lo** | **i** | **gli** | **gl'** | **la** | **l'** | **le** |
|---|---|---|---|---|---|---|---|---|---|
| **a** | al | all' | allo | ai | agli | agl' | alla | all' | alle |
| **con** | col | coll' | collo | coi | cogli | cogl' | colla | coll' | colle |
| **da** | dal | dall' | dallo | dai | dagli | dagl' | dalla | dall' | dalle |
| **di** | del | dell' | dello | dei | degli | degl' | della | dell' | delle |
| **in** | nel | nell' | nello | nei | negli | negl' | nella | nell' | nelle |
| **per** | pel | per l' | per lo | pei | per gli | per gl' | per la | per l' | pelle |
| **su** | sul | sull' | sullo | sui | sugli | sugl' | sulla | sull' | sulle |

The prepositions **con** and **per** are not always combined with the definite article, especially in formal use.

### INDEFINITE ARTICLE

*Masculine*

| *Singular* | *Plural or Partitive* |
|---|---|
| un (before consonant or vowel) | dei (before consonant) |
| uno (before gn, ps, x, z, s followed by a consonant) | degli (before vowel, gn, ps, x, z, s followed by a consonant) |
| | degl' (before i) |

*Examples*

| | |
|---|---|
| *un ragazzo* a boy | *dei ragazzi* some boys |
| *un allievo* a pupil | *degli allievi* some pupils |

*uno studente* a student — *degli studenti* some students
*un insetto* an insect — *degl'insetti* some insects

*Feminine*

una — delle
un' (before a vowel) — delle, dell' (before e, optionally)

*Examples*

*una ragazza* a girl — *delle ragazze* some girls
*un'allieva* a girl pupil — *delle allieve* some girl pupils
*un'eccezione* an exception — *delle (dell') eccezioni* some exceptions

The indefinite article is omitted in Italian when a noun in the predicate position is not accompanied by an adjective, e.g.

*è medico* he is a doctor
*è un buon medico* he is a good doctor

It is omitted also after the preposition **da**, used in the sense of *like*, *as*:
*da uomo* like a man

## GENDER AND PLURAL OF NOUNS

### *Nouns ending in* -**o**

The majority of nouns ending in **-o** are masculine. The regular plural ending is **-i**.

*Examples*

*il corpo* the body — *i corpi* the bodies
*il bambino* the child — *i bambini* the children
*il fratello* the brother — *i fratelli* the brothers
*l'albero* the tree — *gli alberi* the trees

*Exceptions*

*la mano* the hand — *le mani* the hands
*l'eco* the echo (*m*. or *f*.) — *gli echi* the echoes (*m*. only)
*l'uomo* the man — *gli uomini* the men

Some nouns ending in -**o** are masculine in the singular and form a feminine plural in -**a**.

*Examples*

*il dito* the finger — *le dita* the fingers
*il grido* the shout — *le grida* the shouts
*l'uovo* the egg — *le uova* the eggs

Nouns ending in -**aio** and -**io** are masculine. The regular plural ending is -**ai** and -**i**.

*Examples*

*il guaio* the sorrow — *i guai* the sorrows
*il fascio* the bundle — *i fasci* the bundles

*Exceptions*

| | |
|---|---|
| *il dio* the god | *gli dei* the gods[1] |
| *il tempio* the temple | *i tempii* [2] the temples |

Some nouns ending in **-aio** or **-io** are masculine in the singular and form a feminine plural in **-aia.**

*Examples*

| | |
|---|---|
| *il paio* the pair | *le paia* the pairs |
| *il braccio* the arm | *le braccia* the arms |
| *il ginocchio* the knee | *le ginocchia* the knees |
| *il centinaio* the hundred | *le centinaia* the hundreds |

Nouns ending in **-aìo** and **-ìo** are masculine. The plural ending is **-aìi, -ìi.**

*Nouns ending in* **-a**

The majority of nouns ending in **-a** are feminine. The regular plural ending is **-e.**

*Examples*

| | |
|---|---|
| *la testa* the head | *le teste* the heads |
| *la gamba* the leg | *le gambe* the legs |
| *la stella* the star | *le stelle* the stars |
| *l'aula* the hall | *le aule* the halls |

Some nouns ending in **-a** denoting male persons are nevertheless feminine in gender.

*Examples*

| | |
|---|---|
| *la guardia* the guard | *le guardie* the guards |
| *la sentinella* the sentinel | *le sentinelle* the sentinels |
| *la guida* the guide | *le guide* the guides |
| *la recluta* the recruit | *le reclute* the recruits |

Some nouns ending in **-a** are masculine. The plural ending of such nouns is **-i.**

*Examples*

| | |
|---|---|
| *il poeta* the poet | *i poeti* the poets |
| *il sistema* the system | *i sistemi* the systems |
| *il problema* the problem | *i problemi* the problems |
| *il tema* the theme | *i temi* the themes |

Nouns ending in **-cia** or **-gia** form a plural in **-ce, -ge.**

*Examples*

| | |
|---|---|
| *la camicia* the shirt | *le camice* the shirts |
| *la valige* the suitcase | *le valige* the suitcases |
| *la ciliegia* the cherry | *le ciliege* the cherries |

[1] This form of the definite article before **dei**, gods, is a unique exception.
[2] To distinguish it from **tempi**, the plural of **tempo**, time.

When the tonic accent (main stress) is on the -**i**, the plural is -**ie**, e.g.

*la bugia* the lie — *le bugie* the lies

Some nouns ending in -**a** can be either masculine or feminine, according to the sex of the person denoted. The collective plural is masculine.

*Examples*

| | |
|---|---|
| *il collega, la collega* the colleague | *i colleghi, le colleghe* the colleagues |

• There are many such nouns ending in -**ista**, corresponding to English -**ist**:

*Examples*

*artista* artist
*autista* driver
*comunista* communist

They can, in theory, be either masculine or feminine. Usage is influenced by social customs in Italy. The plural is -**isti**

### *Nouns ending in* -**à**

All nouns ending in -**à** are feminine and remain unchanged in the plural.

*Examples*

| | |
|---|---|
| *la città* the city | *le città* the cities |
| *la necessità* the necessity | *le necessità* the necessities |
| *la difficoltà* the difficulty | *le difficoltà* the difficulties |
| *la metà* the half | *le metà* the halves |

### *Nouns ending in* -**e**

The majority of nouns ending in -**e** are masculine. The regular plural ending is -**i**.

*Examples*

| | |
|---|---|
| *il giornale* the newspaper | *i giornali* the newspapers |
| *il fiume* the river | *i fiumi* the rivers |
| *il monte* the hill | *i monti* the hills |
| *il prete* the priest | *i preti* the priests |
| *il limone* the lemon | *i limoni* the lemons |
| *il fucile* the rifle | *i fucili* the rifles |
| *il mese* the month | *i mesi* the months |

Nouns ending in -**ante**, -**ente**, -**iere**, -**ore**, representing male performers of an activity, are masculine.

*Examples*

| | |
|---|---|
| *il mercante* the merchant | *i mercanti* the merchants |
| *il presidente* the president | *i presidenti* the presidents |
| *il gondoliere* the gondolier | *i gondolieri* the gondoliers |
| *un autore* an author | *gli autori* the authors |

The feminine forms of such endings are **-antessa, -entessa, -iera, -rice,** but: *amante, m.f.*, lover, *cantante, m.f.*, singer

When nouns ending in **-e** are feminine, the ending in the plural is **-i.**

*Examples*

| | |
|---|---|
| *la notte* the night | *le notti* the nights |
| *la cornice* the frame | *le cornici* the frames |
| *l'attrice* the actress | *le attrici* the actresses |

*Nouns ending in* **-zione, -gione, -ggine, -udine**

All such nouns are feminine; the plural endings are **-zioni, -gioni, -ggini, -udini.**

*Examples*

| | |
|---|---|
| *la nazione* the nation | *le nazioni* the nations |
| *la ragione* the reason | *le ragioni* the reasons |
| *la stupidaggine* stupidity | *le stupidaggini* the stupidities |
| *l'attitudine* the aptitude | *le attitudini* the aptitudes |

*Nouns ending in* **-i**

Most nouns ending in **-i** are feminine and all remain unchanged in the plural.

*Examples*

| | |
|---|---|
| *la crisi* the crisis | *le crisi* the crises |
| *l'oasi* the oasis | *le oasi* the oases |
| *la diocesi* the diocese | *le diocesi* the dioceses |
| *l'analisi* the analysis | *le analisi* the analyses |
| *la tesi* the thesis | *le tesi* the theses |

*Exception*

| | |
|---|---|
| *il brindisi* the toast (drunk) | *i brindisi* the toasts |

*Nouns ending in* **-ì**

All such nouns are masculine and remain unchanged in the plural.

*Examples*

| | |
|---|---|
| *il dì* the day | *i dì* the days |
| *il chicchirichì* the crowing (of a cock) | *i chicchirichì* sounds of crowing |

*Nouns ending in* **-u** *or* **-ù**

Most nouns ending in **-u** or **-ù** are feminine and all remain unchanged in the plural.

*Examples*

| | |
|---|---|
| *la gru* the crane | *le gru* the cranes |
| *la virtù* the virtue | *le virtù* the virtues |
| *il bambù* the bamboo | *i bambù* the bamboo-trees |
| *il soprappiù* the surplus | *i sorpappiù* the surpluses |

*Nouns ending in a consonant and foreign nouns*

Such hours remain unchanged in the plural.

*Examples*

| | |
|---|---|
| *lo zenit* the zenith | *gli zenit* the zeniths |
| *il golf* the cardigan | *i golf* the cardigans |
| *il big* the V.I.P. | *i big* the V.I.P.s |

*Irregular plurals*

Apart from examples already given, the following are irregular in the plural:

| | |
|---|---|
| *il bue* the ox | *i buoi* the oxen |
| *la moglie* the wife | *le mogli* the wives |
| *la specie* the kind | *le specie* the kinds |
| *mille* a thousand | *due mila* two thousand |

*Plurals of nouns ending in* **-ca, -ga, -co, -go**

All feminine nouns ending in **-ca** or **-ga** form a plural which retains the hard sound of the consonant by the insertion of **h** between it and the plural ending **-e.**

*Examples*

| | |
|---|---|
| *l'amica* the woman friend | *le amiche* the women friends |
| *l'oca* the goose | *le oche* the geese |
| *la bottega* the shop | *le botteghe* the shops |

All masculine nouns ending in **-ca** or **-ga** form a plural which retains the hard sound of the consonant by the insertion of **h** between it and the plural ending **-i.**

*Examples*

| | |
|---|---|
| *il monarca* the monarch | *i monarchi* the monarchs |
| *il collega* the colleague | *i colleghi* the colleagues |

All nouns ending in **-co** or **-go** are masculine. Some form a plural which retains the hard sound of the consonant (**-chi, -ghi**); others do not, forming a plural **-ci, -gi.**[1]

*Examples*

| | |
|---|---|
| *lo stomaco* the stomach | *gli stomachi* the stomachs |
| *il medico* the doctor | *i medici* the doctors |
| *l'amico* the friend | *gli amici* the friends |
| *il nemico* the enemy | *i nemici* the enemies |
| *il fico* the fig | *i fichi* the figs |
| *il porco* the pig | *i porci* the pigs |
| *il Greco* the Greek | *i Greci* the Greeks |
| *il castigo* the punishment | *i castighi* the punishments |
| *il fisiologo* the physiologist | *i fisiologi* the physiologists |
| *il catalogo* the catalogue | *i cataloghi* the catalogues |

[1] Most nouns ending in **-go** form a plural in **-ghi**. Many nouns ending in **-co** of which the penultimate syllable bears the main stress form a plural in **-chi**, but there are also many exceptions.

*Gender and plural of compound nouns*

Compound nouns consisting of a finite verb and a noun (usually plural) are masculine. Most of them are invariable in the plural.

*Examples*

| | |
|---|---|
| *un apriscatole* a tin-opener | *gli apriscatole* the tin-openers |
| *lo spaventapasseri* the scarecrow | *glie spaventapasseri* the scarecrows |
| *la cavalcavia* the fly-over | *le cavalcavie* the fly-overs |

Some compound nouns of this kind have two forms in the singular, e.g.

| | |
|---|---|
| *un asciugamano* / *un asciugamani* } a towel | *gli asciugamani* the towels |

Compound nouns consisting of two nouns take their gender from the first noun; some form a plural in the first noun, some in the second.[1]

*Examples*

| | |
|---|---|
| *il capobanda* the ringleader | *i capibanda* the ringleaders |
| *il capocuoco*, the head chef | *i capicuochi*, the head chefs |
| *il capostipite* the head of the clan | *i capostipiti* the heads of the clans |
| *il capolavoro* the master-piece | *i capolavori* the master-pieces |

## ADJECTIVES

Adjectives agree in gender and number with the nouns which they qualify; those used with nouns of more than one gender are put in the masculine plural.

Adjectives ending in **-o** are masculine and form their plural in **-i**. The feminine forms of such adjectives end in **-a** in the singular and **-e** in the plural.

*Examples*

| | |
|---|---|
| *il fiore rosso* the red flower | *i fiori rossi* the red flowers |
| *la casa rossa* the red house | *le case rosse* the red houses |

Adjectives ending in **-e** are both masculine and feminine. The plural ending for both genders is **-i**.

*Examples*

| | |
|---|---|
| *un uomo felice* a happy man | *degli uomini felici* happy men |
| *la donna felice* the happy woman | *le donne felici* the happy women |

Adjectives of colour which are the names of flowers used in apposition do not change in the plural.

*Examples*

| | |
|---|---|
| *un cappello rosa* a pink hat | *i cappelli rosa* the pink hats |

[1] The plurals of such nouns are indicated in the body of the dictionary.

| | |
|---|---|
| *il vestito viola* the violet dress | *i vestiti viola* the violet dresses |

Adjectives of nationality do not begin with a capital letter as in English.

*Examples*

*la lingua italiana* the Italian language
*una ragazza inglese* an English girl

If the adjective is used as a noun, it begins with a capital.

*Examples*

*due Italiani sono arrivati* two Italians have arrived
*noi altri Inglesi* we English

The adjectives **bello, buono, grande** and **santo** have the following forms when used before certain masculine nouns:

**bello**

| | *Singular* | *Plural* |
|---|---|---|
| (before a noun beginning with a consonant) | bel | bei |
| (before a noun beginning with a vowel) | bell' | begli |
| (before a noun beginning with gn, ps, x, z, or s followed by a consonant) | bello | begli |

*Examples*

| | |
|---|---|
| *il bel giardino* the beautiful garden | *i bei giardini* the beautiful gardens |
| *un bell'albero* a beautiful tree | *dei begli alberi* beautiful trees |
| *un bello studio* a beautiful study | *dei begli studi* beautiful studies |

**buono, grande**

| | *Singular* | *Plural* |
|---|---|---|
| (before a noun beginning with a consonant or with a vowel) | buon<br>gran | buoni<br>grandi |
| (before a noun beginning with gn, ps, x, z, or s followed by a consonant) | buono<br>grande | buoni<br>grandi |

*Examples*

| | |
|---|---|
| *un buon libro* a good book | *un gran letto,* a large bed |
| *un buono studente* a good student | *un grande albergo,* a large hotel |

**santo**

| | |
|---|---|
| (before a name beginning with a consonant) | San |
| (before a name beginning with a vowel) | Sant' |
| (before a name beginning with S followed by a consonant) | Santo |

*Examples*

*San Bernardo* St Bernard
*Sant'Antonio* St Anthony
*Santo Stefano* St Stephen

*Order of Adjectives in relation to Nouns*

Adjectives expressing emotion or conveying emphasis usually precede the noun, especially **bello, bravo, buono, grande.**

*Examples*

*che buona idea!* what a good idea!
*una grande città* a large city
*è un bellissimo libro* it is a beautiful book
*una brava ragazza,* a clever girl

The adjective **povero** differs in meaning according to whether it precedes or follows the noun:

*pover'uomo!* poor man!
*un uomo povero* a poor man (who has little money)

Adjectives of nationality, shape, colour and material description follow the noun:

*un libro italiano* an Italian book
*un film francese* a French film
*la bandiera svizzera* the Swiss flag
*una palla rossa* a red ball
*un cappello morbido* a soft hat
*una faccia rotonda* a round face

Adjectives of more than two syllables usually follow the noun, but usage is flexible:

*la vostra gentilissima lettera* your very kind letter
*è un uomo gentilissimo* he is a very nice man
*un ragazzo intelligente* an intelligent boy

*Comparative and superlative forms of adjectives*

The comparative of adjectives is formed by placing **più**, (more), before the adjective; the superlative is formed by placing the definite article before the comparative.

*Examples*

*bello* beautiful
*più bello* more beautiful
*il più bello, la più bella* the most beautiful

When the superlative follows the noun, the definite article is omitted, making it identical in form with the comparative:

*la via più lunga* the longest (*or* the longer) way

Some adjectives have irregular forms of comparison as well as regular forms.

*Examples*

*grande* large
*più grande, maggiore* larger
*il più grande, il maggiore* the largest
*massimo* greatest
*buono* good
*più buono, migliore* better
*ottimo* excellent
*alto* high
*più alto, superiore* higher
*altissimo* highest
*piccolo* small
*più piccolo, minore* smaller
*minimo* smallest, least
*basso* low
*più basso, inferiore* lower
*infimo* lowest
*cattivo* bad
*più cattivo, peggiore* worse
*pessimo* worst

### *Construction of adjectives of comparison*

Nouns and pronouns compared are constructed with **di.**

*Examples*

*la cucina è più piccola della sala da pranzo* the kitchen is smaller than the dining-room
*lui è più forte di me* he is stronger than I am

Adjectives and adverbs compared are constructed with **che.**

*Examples*

*l'aula è più grande che bella* the hall is more large than beautiful
*più presto che mai* faster than ever

### *Adjectives used as nouns*

Adjectives can be used as nouns in two ways:

(i) to denote a person or persons, e.g.

*il geloso* the jealous man
*la brutta* the ugly woman
*gl'infelici* unhappy people
*gli assenti* those absent

(ii) in an abstract or collective sense; in this use the adjective is always masculine; e.g.

*bello* beautiful
*il bello* beauty
*buono* good
*il buono* goodness
*vero* true
*il vero* truth

## ADVERBS

Adverbs are formed by the addition of **-mente** to the feminine singular form of adjectives, e.g.

*sereno* serene
*serenamente* serenely
*semplice* simple
*semplicemente* simply

*Exceptions*

*violento* violent
*violentemente* violently

*tardo* slow, tardy
*tardi* (*adv.*) late

If the adjective ends in **-ale**, the ending of the adverb formed from it is **-almente**, e.g.

*finale* final
*finalmente* finally
*attuale* present-day
*attualmente* at the present time

A few adverbs end in **-one** or **-oni** and function almost as invariable adjectives, e.g.

*ciondolone, ciondoloni* dangling
*penzolone, penzoloni* drooping

Among adverbs not formed from adjectives are:

*bene* well (also used as a noun: *il bene* good)
*male* badly (also used as a noun: *il male* evil)
*presto* quickly
*sempre* always
*spesso* often
*subito* at once

### *Order of adverbs in relation to verbs*

It is usual for the adverb to be placed immediately after the verb, even when there is a direct object, e.g.

*lesse subito il giornale* he read the paper at once
*pulire bene la cucina* to clean the kitchen well
*fa sempre il suo dovere* he always does his duty
*aprì lentamente la porta* he opened the door slowly

## SUFFIXES

Suffixes are added to nouns, proper names, adjectives and to some adverbs. Sometimes the addition of a suffix gives rise to the formation of a new word with an independent meaning or use. In some cases a suffix changes the gender of a noun to which it is added.

*Diminutives*

The suffixes which convey a meaning of smallness can also suggest affection, approval or condescension. Among the most usual diminutive suffixes are: **-ello, -ellino, -etto, -cello, -icello, -icino, -ino, -uccio, -(u)olo, -uzzo.**

*Examples*

| | |
|---|---|
| *campana* | bell |
| *campanello* | little bell |
| *frate* | friar |
| *fratello* | brother |
| *fratellino* | little brother |
| *suora* | nun |
| *sorella* | sister |
| *sorellina* | little sister |
| *piazza* | square (in a town) |
| *piazzetta* | small square |
| *campo* | field |
| *campicello* | little field, small plot |
| *libro* | book |
| *libretto* | (mus.) libretto |
| *libricino* | little book |
| *gatto* | cat |
| *gattino* | kitten |
| *mano* | hand |
| *manina* | little hand |
| *Tonio* | Tony |
| *Tonino* | young Tony |
| *brutto* | ugly |
| *bruttino* | rather ugly |
| *piano* | softly |
| *pianino* | very softly |
| *bene* | well |
| *benino* | very nicely |
| *violone* | double-bass viol |
| *violoncello* | 'cello |
| *Berta* | Bertha |
| *bertuccia* | gossip; ape |
| *figlio* | son |
| *figliuolo* | little son, young son |
| *figlia* | daughter |
| *figliuola* | dear daughter, young daughter |
| *Maria* | Mary |
| *Mariuzza* | Molly |

*Augmentatives*

The suffixes which convey a meaning of largeness can also suggest admiration, or distaste.

The suffix -**one** is masculine; added to a feminine noun, it changes the gender.

*Examples*

*il libro* the book — *il librone* the large book
*la donna* the woman — *il donnone* the large woman
*la casa* the house — *il casone* the large house

The feminine suffix -**ona** is also used.

*Examples*

*pigro* lazy
*il pigrone* the lazy man — *il poltrone* the idle man
*la pigrona* the lazy woman — *la poltrona* the idle woman; the armchair

The suffix -**otto** suggests sizeableness; it can also express contempt, e.g.

*semplice* simple
*sempliciotto* simple-minded
*la sempliciotta* the little fool of a girl

*Pejoratives*

The suffixes -**accio** and -**astro** convey a meaning of dislike or disapproval. Added to adjectives of colour, the suffix -**astro** is equivalent to English -**ish.**

*Examples*

*Lorenzo* Lawrence
*Lorenzaccio* (the suffix gives a sinister or blackguardly meaning to the name)
*ragazzo* boy
*ragazzaccio* naughty boy
*nero* black
*nerastro* blackish
*giallo* yellow
*giallastro* yellowish

*Superlatives*

The suffix -**issimo,** denoting superlative or extreme degree, is added to adjectives and adverbs.

*Examples*

*bene* well
*benissimo* very well
*bello* nice, good
*bellissimo* beautiful, lovely
*povero* poor
*poverissimo* extremely poor

In some instances, mainly for humorous effect, the suffix -**issimo** is added to a noun, e.g.

*bacio* kiss
*bacissimo* long kiss

## DEMONSTRATIVE ADJECTIVES AND PRONOUNS

*questo* this

*quello* that (for changes in form, cf. **bello**)

### *Adjectival use*

*questro libro* this book
*quest'uomo* this man
*questa signora* this lady
*questi studenti* these students
*queste lettere* these letters

*quel ragazzo* that boy
*quell'uovo* that egg
*quella casa* that house
*quegli studiosi* those scholars
*quelle ragazze* those girls

### *Used as pronouns*

*questo* this man, this thing
*questa* this woman, this thing
*questi* these men, these things
*queste* these women, these things

*quello* that man, that thing
*quella* that woman, that thing
*quelli* those men, those things
*quelle* those women, those things

*non questo ma quello* not this one but that
*questi (m.sing.)* this man
*quegli (m.sing.)* that man
*costui* he, this man here
*costei* she, this woman here
*colui* he, that man there
*colei* she, that woman there
*ciò* that
*cioè* that is

## PERSONAL PRONOUNS

### *Nominative*

These pronouns are used only for clarity or emphasis.

*io* I
*tu* thou, you (informal)
*lui* he (informal)
*lei* she (informal)

*egli* he (formal)
*ella* she (formal)

*noi* we
*voi* you (plural; singular, semi-formal)
*loro (m., f.)* they

*essi (m.)* they
*esse (f.)* they

*Lei (m., f.)* you (singular, formal)
*Loro (m., f.)* you (plural, formal)

The last two pronouns are used as a formal mode of address. The accompanying verb is in the 3rd person singular or plural.

*Examples*

*Lei parla inglese* you speak English
*Loro sono Italiani* you are Italians

The modern fashion is to dispense with the capital L of these pronouns; the result is that there is now no distinction between:

*lei* she
*lei* you (singular)

or between:

*loro* they
*loro* you (plural)

### *Disjunctive pronouns*

(used after prepositions or in positions disjoined from the verb)

*me* me
*te* thee, you (informal)
*lui* him
*lei* her, you (formal, *m.*, *f.*)
*noi* us
*voi* you (*pl.*, informal)
*loro* them, you (formal, *m.*, *f.*)

*Examples*

*vieni con me* come with me
*alto come lui* as tall as he is
*più intelligente di voi* more intelligent than you

*Conjunctive pronouns* (direct or indirect objects of verbs, used conjoined with the verb)

| *Direct Object (Accusative)* | *Indirect Object (Dative)* |
|---|---|
| *mi* me | *mi* to me |
| *ti* thee, you (informal) | *ti* to thee, to you (informal) |
| *lo* him, it *m.* | *gli* to him |
| *la* her, it *f.*, you (formal, *m.*, *f.*) | *le* to her, to you (formal, *m.*, *f.*) |
| *ci* us | *ci* to us |
| *vi* you (*pl.*, informal) | *vi* to you (*pl.*, informal) |
| *li* them *m.* | *loro* to them, to you (*pl.*, formal, *m.*, *f.*) |
| *le* them *f.* (*pl.*, formal, *m.*, *f.*) | |

Pronouns of these two groups precede the verb, except **loro.**

*Examples*

*mi colpì* he hit me
*gli diedi il libro* I gave him the book
*disse loro* he said to them

When direct and indirect objects are used together, the indirect object always precedes the direct, and the indirect pronouns undergo the following changes:

| | | |
|---|---|---|
| *mi* | becomes | *me* |
| *ti* | | *te* |
| *gli* | | *glie* (and is joined to the direct object) |
| *le* | | *glie* (and is joined to the direct object) |
| *ci* | | *ce* |
| *vi* | | *ve* |

**loro** always follows the verb.

These changes also occur if the pronoun is followed by **ne** (of it, some).

*Examples*

*mi diede il libro* he gave me the book
*me lo diede* he gave it to me
*gli diedi il libro* I gave him the book
*glielo diedi* I gave it to him
*le dissero la notizia* they told her, you, the news
*gliela dissero* they told it to her, to you
*fece loro la domanda* he asked them, you, the question
*lo diede loro* he gave it to them, to you
*me ne parlò* he spoke of it to me

When conjunctive pronouns are the direct or indirect objects of an infinitive, they follow it and are joined to it as one word, the final **-e** (or, in the case of infinitives ending in **-rre**, the final **-re**) being elided.

*Examples*

*volevo dare il libro a lui* I wanted to give the book to him
*or* *volevo dargli il libro*
*volevo darlo a lui* I wanted to give it to him
*or* *volevo darglielo*
*volevo tradurre il libro* I wanted to translate the book
*volevo tradurlo* I wanted to translate it

### REFLEXIVE PRONOUNS

*mi* myself
*ti* thyself, yourself (informal)
*si* himself, herself, yourself (formal)
*ci* ourselves
*vi* yourselves (informal)
*si* themselves, yourselves (formal)

*As direct object*

*mi diverto* I amuse myself
*si difende* he defends himself
*si lavano* they wash themselves

*As indirect object*

*ti farai male* you will do harm to yourself
*Lei si fa onore* you do yourself honour
*mi lavo le mani* I wash my hands

If a reflexive pronoun used as a direct object is followed by the partitive **ne** (of it, some) and if a reflexive pronoun used as an indirect object is followed by a pronoun used as a direct object, or by the partitive **ne**, the following changes occur: *mi* becomes *me*; *ti*, *te*; *si*, *se*; *ci*, *ce*; *vi*, *ve*.

*Examples*

*mi difendo del pericolo* I defend myself against the danger
*me ne difendo* I defend myself against it
*si diverte dello spettacolo* he enjoys the show
*se ne diverte* he enjoys it
*vi prendete la responsabilità* you take the responsibility on yourselves
*ve la prendete* you take it on yourselves
*si permettono il piacere* they allow themselves the pleasure
*se lo permettono* they allow it to themselves

(N.B. When the reflexive pronoun **si** is changed to **se**, it becomes identical in spelling with **se** meaning 'if'.

*se lo permettono*

can mean *either*:

*they allow it to themselves*

*or*:

*if they permit it*)

*Reciprocal use*

*ci amiamo* we love each other
*si odiano* they hate one another
*vi fate male, l'uno all'altro* you harm each other

*Reflexive construction used as passive*

*il libro si vende* the book is sold
*la chiave non si trova* the key is not found
*i giornali si leggono* the newspapers are read
*un rumore si sente* a noise is heard

## INDEFINITE PRONOUNS

The indefinite pronoun **si** (one, you, we, they) is identical in form with the reflexive pronoun **si** (himself, herself, itself, yourself, themselves, yourselves). Constructions with the indefinite pronoun sometimes overlap in meaning with the passive use of the reflexive construction.

*Examples*

*si dice* one says
*si fa così* one does it this way
*si parla italiano* one speaks Italian
*or* Italian is spoken
*si sente un rumore* one hears a noise
*or* a noise is heard

*se ne parla* people speak of it
*or* it is spoken of

*Other indefinite pronouns*

*uno* one, a person, someone
*qualcuno* somebody, anybody
*nessuno* nobody
*tutti (m.pl.)* everybody, all
*niente* nothing
*qualcosa* } something
*qualche cosa* }
*altri...altri* some...others
*tutti e due* } both
*tutte e due* }

In advertisements, the indefinite pronoun **si** sometimes follows a finite verb and is joined to it.

*Examples*
*cercasi* wanted
*affittasi* to let

In such constructions the tonic accent (main stress) is on the syllable of the verb which normally bears the stress (i.e. in the examples given above:
*cer· casi*
*affit· tasi*).

RELATIVE PRONOUNS

There are two forms of relative pronouns:
(i) *che (m., f., sing., pl.)* who, which, whom
*cui* to whom, to which
*il cui, la cui, i cui, le cui* whose
(ii) *il quale (m.sing.) i quali (m.pl.)* who, which, whom
*la quale (f.sing.) le quali (f.pl.)*

The second form can be contracted with prepositions:
*col quale* with whom, with which
*dalla quale* by whom, from which
*nei quali* in whom, in which
*sulle quali* on whom, on which
*del quale* of whom, whose, of which

*Indefinite relative pronouns*

*chi, colui che* he whom, him whom, anyone who, anyone whom
*chiunque* whoever, whomever
*qualunque* whatever

INTERROGATIVE PRONOUNS

*chi*? who? whom?
*che*? what?

*di chi?* whose?
*che?* which?
*quale? quali?* which?
*quanto?* how much?
*quanti? quante?* how many?

### POSSESSIVE ADJECTIVES

*il mio, la mia, i miei, le mie* my
*il tuo, la tua, i tuoi, le tue* thy, your
*il suo, la sua, i suoi, le sue* his, her, your[1]
*il nostro, la nostra, i nostri, le nostre* our
*il vostro, la vostra, i vostri, le vostre* your
*il loro, la loro, i loro, le loro* their, your[1]

*Examples*

*il mio cappello* my hat
*la tua penna* your pen
*il suo libro* his, her, your book
*i nostri genitori* our parents
*le vostre mani* your hands
*la loro casa* their, your (*pl.*) house

When used with certain nouns denoting relatives, the definite article is omitted:

*mio padre* my father
*tua madre* your mother
*suo fratello* his, her, your brother
*nostra sorella* our sister

But:

*il mio nonno* my grandpa

Even with such nouns, *il loro, la loro, i loro, le loro* retain the definite article:

*i loro fratelli* their, your (*pl.*) brothers
*la loro madre* their, your (*pl.*) mother

When nouns denoting relatives are in the plural or are qualified by an adjective, the definite article of the possessive adjective of all persons is retained.

*Examples*

*i miei fratelli* my brothers
*il nostro caro zio* our dear uncle
*le tue sorelle* your sisters

[1] The formal modes of address, *Lei* and *Loro*, have the corresponding 3rd persons singular and plural forms of the possessive adjective. The convention of using a capital S (*il Suo, la Sua*) and a capital L (*il Loro, la Loro*) is gradually disappearing in modern Italian.

When possessive adjectives are used in the predicate position (e.g. after the verb **to be**), the definite article is omitted.

*Examples*

*il cappello è mio* this hat is mine
*è tuo questo libro?* is this book yours?
*non è nostra la casa* the house is not ours
*questo signore è suo maestro* this gentleman is his teacher

### POSSESSIVE PRONOUNS

Possessive pronouns are identical in form with possessive adjectives. They are distinguished from them by the retention of the definite article in the predicate position.

*Examples*

*questo cappello è il mio* this is the hat which is mine
*quale casa è la sua?* which house is his, hers, yours?
*ecco la tua* here is yours
*la tua lettera è arrivata, la mia, no* your letter has arrived, mine has not

### NUMERALS

*Cardinal*

| | | | | | |
|---|---|---|---|---|---|
| 1 | *uno* | 11 | *undici* | 21 | *ventuno* |
| 2 | *due* | 12 | *dodici* | 22 | *ventidue* |
| 3 | *tre* | 13 | *tredici* | 30 | *trenta* |
| 4 | *quattro* | 14 | *quattordici* | 31 | *trentuno* |
| 5 | *cinque* | 15 | *quindici* | 35 | *trentacinque* |
| 6 | *sei* | 16 | *sedici* | 40 | *quaranta* |
| 7 | *sette* | 17 | *diciassette* | 50 | *cinquanta* |
| 8 | *otto* | 18 | *diciotto* | 60 | *sessanta* |
| 9 | *nove* | 19 | *diciannove* | 70 | *settanta* |
| 10 | *dieci* | 20 | *venti* | 80 | *ottanta* |
| | | 90 | *novanta* | | |
| | | 100 | *cento* | | |
| | | 101 | *centuno* | | |
| | | 103 | *centotre* | | |
| | | 115 | *centoquindici* | | |
| | | 125 | *cento venticinque* | | |
| | | 200 | *duecento* | | |
| | | 250 | *duecento cinquanta* | | |
| | | 300 | *trecento* | | |
| | | 1000 | *mille* | | |
| | | 2000 | *due mila* | | |

**uno** has a feminine form, **una.** Used as an adjective it has the same forms as the indefinite article (*cf.* p. xxiii–xxiv).

**Ventun, trentun,** etc. are invariable, e.g.

*ventun cavalli* twenty-one horses
*trentun ragazze* thirty-one girls

No indefinite article is used before **cento** and **mille**, e.g.

*cento ragazzi* a hundred boys
*mille libri* a thousand books

*Ordinal*

| | | | |
|---|---|---|---|
| 1st | *primo* | 11th | *undecimo, decimo primo* |
| 2nd | *secondo* | 12th | *dodicesimo, duodecimo, decimo secondo* |
| 3rd | *terzo* | 13th | *tredicesimo, decimo terzo* |
| 4th | *quarto* | 14th | *quattordicesimo, decimo quarto* |
| 5th | *quinto* | 15th | *quindicesimo, decimo quinto* |
| 6th | *sesto* | 16th | *sedicesimo, decimo sesto* |
| 7th | *settimo* | 17th | *decimo settimo* |
| 8th | *ottavo* | 18th | *decimo ottavo* |
| 9th | *nono* | 19th | *decimo nono* |
| 10th | *decimo* | 20th | *ventesimo* |

| | |
|---|---|
| 21st | *ventunesimo, ventesimo primo* |
| 30th | *trentesimo* |
| 100th | *centesimo* |
| 101st | *centesimo primo* |
| 115th | *centoquindicesimo* |
| 200th | *duecentesimo* |
| 1000th | *millesimo* |
| 2000th | *duemillesimo* |

Ordinal numerals are declined like other adjectives ending in **-o**. They are used after the names of rulers, etc., with no definite article, e.g.

*Enrico Ottavo* Henry the Eighth
*Pio Nono* Pius the Ninth
*Capitolo Secondo* Chapter Two

*Collective numerals*

*una diecina* about ten
*una ventina* about twenty
*una trentina* about thirty
*una quarantina* about forty
*un centinaio* about a hundred
*due centinaia* about two hundred
*un migliaio* about a thousand
*tre migliaia* about three thousand

## DATES

The definite article precedes the number representing the year, e.g.

*il* 1974 1974
*nel* 1975 in 1975

For the day of the month, except the first, a cardinal number is used, e.g.

*il sedici marzo* the sixteenth of March
*il primo luglio* the first of July
*il cinque maggio* the fifth of May

Centuries are indicated in two ways:

(i) as in English, by the use of ordinal numerals, e.g.

*il secolo decimo nono* the nineteenth century
*il secolo quarto* the fourth century
*il secolo ventesimo* the twentieth century
*il secolo decimo secondo* the twelfth century

(ii) From 1200, by omitting the first number (*mille*) and counting from the second, by which the century is identified; the initial letter is always a capital.

*Examples*

*il Duecento* the thirteenth century
*il Trecento* the fourteenth century
*il Quattrocento* the fifteenth century
*il Cinquecento* the sixteenth century
*il Seicento* the seventeenth century
*il Settecento* the eighteenth century
*l'Ottocento* the nineteenth century
*il Novecento* the twentieth century

These nouns have adjectival forms ending in **-esco**, which are not written with a capital, e.g.

*l'arte quattrocentesca* fifteenth-century art
*gli autori novecenteschi* twentieth-century authors

## VERBS

For conjugations, see VERB SCHEME.

### *Auxiliary verbs*

Transitive verbs (i.e. those which express action and take a direct object) are conjugated in compound tenses with the auxiliary **avere.**

*Examples*

*legge il libro* he reads the book
*ha letto il giornale* he has read the newspaper
*scrivo una lettera* I write a letter
*ho scritto una lettera* I have written a letter
*fanno il loro dovere* they do their duty
*avevano fatto il loro dovere* they had done their duty
*avrebbe chiuso la porta* he would have shut the door

Transitive verbs used absolutely (i.e. without a direct object) are also conjugated with **avere.**

*Examples*

*hai finito?* have you finished?
*abbiamo firmato* we have signed
*ho fatto* I have done (it)
*che cosa hai fatto oggi? ho letto.* what have you done today? I have been reading

Intransitive verbs (i.e. those which do not take a direct object, whether explicit or implied) can express action, motion or being. Those expressing action are conjugated in compound tenses with the auxiliary **avere.**

*Examples*

*ho dormito bene* I have slept well
*ha riso molto* he laughed a lot
*non me ne ha parlato* he has not spoken to me about it
*abbiamo lavorato tanto* we have worked so hard

Intransitive verbs expressing motion are conjugated with **avere** if the idea of motion is closer to action than to being.

*Examples*

*hanno viaggiato molto* they have travelled a great deal
*avevo camminato troppo* I had walked too far
*ha saltato dalla finestra* he has jumped out of the window

Some verbs expressing motion are conjugated either with **avere** or **essere**, according to whether it is closer to action or to being.

*Example*

**correre** to run

If this verb conveys simply the action of running, it is conjugated with **avere**, e.g.

*quanto hai corso!* what a long way you have run!

If destination is indicated, the verb is conjugated with **essere**:[1]

*è corso dal medico* he has run to the doctor
*la ragazza era corsa subito alla mamma* the little girl ran immediately to her mother
*sono corsi tutti a casa* they have all run home

The following verbs expressing motion are always conjugated with **essere: andare, cadere, entrare, partire, passare, uscire, venire.**

*Examples*

*è andato* he has gone
*erano caduti* they had fallen
*siamo entrati* we have entered
*sono partiti* they have departed
*era passato molto tempo* much time had gone by

[1] If a verb is conjugated in compound tenses with **essere**, the past participle agrees with the subject in gender and number.

*siete usciti* you have gone out
*perchè sei venuto*? why have you come?

Intransitive verbs which express being are conjugated with **essere.** The verb **essere** is always conjugated with itself.

*Examples*

*è svenuta* she has fainted
*che cosa è successo*? what has happened?[1]
*il ragazzo è cresciuto* the boy has grown
*sono diventati matti* they have gone mad
*è sembrato strano* it has seemed strange
*è stata ammalata* she has been ill
*dove sei stato*? where have you been?

Reflexive verbs (i.e. those of which the action is reflected back onto the subject, rather than carried forward onto a direct object, as with transitive verbs) are conjugated in compound tenses with the auxiliary **essere.**

*Examples*

*Enrico si è divertito* Henry has amused himself
*mi sono fatto male* I have hurt myself
*ci siamo alzati di buon'ora* we have got up early

*Active and passive voice*

The action of verbs can be conveyed by either the active or the passive voice.

*Examples*

Active: *il maestro punisce l'allievo* the master punishes the boy
Passive: *l'allievo è punito dal maestro* the boy is punished by the master
Active: *il libraio vende il libro* the bookseller sells the book
Passive: *il libro è venduto dal libraio* the book is sold by the bookseller

There are three auxiliaries in use in the passive construction: **essere, venire, andare.**

If **venire** is used, a meaning of habitualness is conveyed.

If **andare** is used, a meaning of obligation is conveyed.

*Examples*

*la parola è pronunciata così* the word is pronounced like this
*la parola viene pronunciata così* the word is usually pronounced like this
*la parola va pronunciata così* the word must be pronounced like this

[1] The phrase **che cosa** is masculine, although the noun **cosa,** used by itself, is feminine.

The reflexive construction is often used to convey the passive:

*il libro è* / *viene* } *venduto* } the book is sold
*il libro si vende*

*Indicative, subjunctive and imperative mood*

*The indicative mood is used*:

(i) in a principal clause, to make a statement.

*Examples*

*vado a scuola* I go to school
*viene ogni sera* he comes every evening
*bisogna farlo* it must be done
*non piove ora* it is not raining now

(ii) In a subordinate clause, to make an unqualified or unrestricted statement.

*Examples*

*quando entrò vide subito che non c'era il fratello* when he entered he saw at once that his brother was not there
*se non è vero, è ben trovato* if it is not true, it is a good invention

*The subjunctive mood is used*:

(i) in a principal clause, to express a wish.

*Examples*

*così sia* so be it
*sia fatta la volontà di Dio* God's will be done
*chi la fa l'aspetti* you must expect tit for tat

(ii) in a subordinate clause which is qualified or restricted or which expresses purpose, supposition, concession, doubt, fear, etc.

*Examples*

*benchè piovesse, uscì* although it was raining, he went out
*l'unica cosa che mi piaccia è il colore* the only thing I like is the colour
*la prima volta che la vedesse, se ne innamorò* the first time he saw her he fell in love with her
*questo è il quadro più bello ch'io abbia mai veduto* this is the most beautiful picture I have ever seen
*lo feci perchè venisse* I did it so that he would come
*aspetta finchè torni la mamma* wait until your mother comes back
*non credo che sia vero* I do not think it is true
*andò via senza che lo vedessi* he went away without my seeing him
*me ne vado a meno che non venga* I shall go unless he comes
*può venire purchè venga subito* he may come provided he comes at once
*per quante volte lo dicesse* however many times he said it

(iii) after **se** (if), when the supposition is unlikely.

*Examples*

*se l'avessi, te lo darei* if I had it, I should give it to you
*se fosse vero, quanto saremmo contenti!* if it were true, how happy we should be!
*sec venisse, sarei molto felice* if he came I should be very happy

But cf.

*se lo fece, dev'essere punito* if he did it, he ought to be punished

(iv) in indirect questions if the main verb is in the past.

*Example*

*domandai se il ragazzo fosse uscito* I asked if the boy had gone out

But cf.

*domando se il ragazzo è uscito* I ask if the boy has gone out
*era* had

*The imperative mood is used:*

To express commands, suggestions, wishes.

*Examples*

*andiamo* let us go
*venga qua* come here
*si accomodi* come in, sit down, make yourself at home
*state zitti* be quiet
*che dica subito il suo parere* let him give him his opinion at once

(*2nd pers. sing.*)

*dammelo* give it to me
*non parlare* don't talk[1]
*non lo toccare* don't touch it
*non ti preoccupare* don't worry

## *Tenses*

*Extended present and imperfect*

Italian, like English, has an extended present and imperfect. It is formed by a gerund, preceded by one of the following auxiliary verbs: **stare, venire, andare.**

*Examples*

*scrivo una lettera* I write a letter
*sto scrivendo una lettera* I am writing a letter
*lo leggo* I read it
*lo vengo leggendo* I am reading it gradually
*se ne accorge* he notices it
*se ne veniva accorgendo* he gradually began to notice it
*grida tutto il giorno* he shouts all day long

[1] The imperative form addressed to the 2nd person singular in the negative, is the infinitive; a direct or indirect object or a reflexive pronoun precedes the infinitive.

*va gridando tutto il giorno* he never stops shouting all day long
*andavamo leggendo Dante* we were reading Dante regularly

Sometimes tenses in Italian convey meanings different from those conveyed by equivalent tenses in English.

*Future tense*

The future is commonly used to convey probability or possibility.

*Examples*

*sarà vero* it is probably true
*se verrà* if he comes
*avrà molti amici* he probably has many friends
*sarà stanca* she is probably tired
*sarà mio fratello che arriva* it is probably my brother who is arriving, that will be my brother

*Perfect tense*

The perfect is used more frequently in Italian than in English. In Tuscan usage, it is restricted to a period of 24 hours preceding the present, but in educated Italian spoken in other regions its use is more extensive.

*Examples*

*vi sono andato stamattina* I went there this morning
*l'ha vista ieri* he saw her yesterday
*l'anno scorso abbiamo visitato Firenze* last year we visited Florence

*Imperfect tense*

The imperfect indicative can be used instead of the past conditional and the pluperfect subjunctive.

*Example*

*Se Lei non fosse venuto, sarei morto di fame* if you had not come, I should have died of hunger

can be rendered also as:

*Se Lei non veniva, morivo di fame*

*Past conditional tense*

The past conditional, when used in a subordinate clause in reported speech, is equivalent to the present conditional in English.

*Examples*

*disse che sarebbe venuto* he said he would come
*mi assicurò che la signora sarebbe tornata* he assured me that the lady would return

*past definite of* **volere, potere** *and* **sapere**

Used in the past definite, these verbs have a meaning of desire, power and ability fulfilled.

*Examples*

Compare:

{ *volevo andare* I wanted to go
{ *volli andare* I insisted on going (and I went)

{ *poteva alzarlo* he was strong enough, he had the ability, to lift it
{ *potè alzarlo* he succeeded in lifting it

{ *non sapeva farlo* he did not know how to do it
{ *non seppe farlo* he failed to do it

*The tenses of* **dovere**

**dovere,** used as an auxiliary, conveys either obligation or probability. The tenses are not always equivalent to those used in English.

*Examples*

(i) *Obligation*

*deve andare* he ought to go, he must go
*ha dovuto studiare molto* he has had to study hard
*doveva partire* it was his duty to depart
*dovrebbe rispondere* he ought to reply
*avrebbe dovuto scrivere* he ought to have written
*dovè (dovette) venire* he was obliged to come, he had to come (and he did)

(ii) *Probability*

*deve arrivare fra poco* he is likely to arrive soon
*dev'essere matto* he must be mad
*dev'essere partito* he must have departed
*doveva trovarsi male* he must have been embarrassed
*devono essere arrivati* they must have arrived
*deve aver scritto* he must have written

# THE VERB SCHEME

In the following pages the user will find a complete survey of Italian conjugations by means of which any verb occurring in the body of the dictionary may be constructed or its various forms recognized. Care has been taken to include models of every type of conjugation, including anomalies presenting only minor orthographical and other variations, since it is on such points that the user is most likely to seek assistance. A reference list of the principal verbs constructed with a preposition before an infinitive will be found at the end of this verb scheme.

### METHOD OF REFERENCE

Every infinitive in current use included in the Italian word-list of the dictionary is followed by a reference in square brackets which consists of one of the upper-case letters A, B, C, or D, followed by a figure, to which may be added one or more of the lower-case letters: s, d, c, etc. For example: **andare** [A8]; **danneggiare** [A3c].

The verbs have been grouped into four main categories, lettered A, B, C, D. Group A comprises the true *-are* verbs and corresponds to what grammarians term the First Conjugation, except that 'fare' and its compounds are not included in it. Group D comprises the *-ire* verbs and corresponds to what some grammarians term the Third and others the Fourth Conjugation. Groups B and C comprise the *-ere* verbs, which have been subdivided arbitrarily according to how much of the conjugation it is necessary to give in full; they correspond to what some grammarians term the Second, and others the Second and Third Conjugations.

### INDICATION OF STRESS

The lower-case letters s, d, and c serve to indicate verbs in which the stress or tonic accent differs from that of the model in certain forms of the present indicative and subjunctive and in the imperative. The lower-case letter 's' (= stress), placed after an upper-case letter and a figure, indicates that the stress falls on the antepenultimate syllable in certain finite forms of the verb. For instance, the verb **abdicare** is given as follows: **abdicare** [A2s]. The indication A2 signifies that the verb is conjugated like the A2 models, **peccare** and **pagare**; the lower-case letter 's' signifies that in the relevant persons of the present indicative and subjunctive and of the imperative, the stress falls on the antepenultimate syllable, for example: **ab·dico, ab·dichi, ab·dica,** etc. If the stressed vowel in question is 'e' or 'o', it is necessary to indicate whether it is open or close in pronunciation. If the vowel is close, a lower-case 'c' (= close) is included in the

reference. For instance, the indication [A2sc] given after the verb **convocare** conveys that in the relevant tenses the tonic or stressed syllable is the ante-penultimate and that the vowel in question is close, for example: **cọnvoco, cọnvochi, cọnvoca,** etc. If no lower-case 'c' is included in the reference, the pronunciation of the stressed vowel is open.

In cases of diphthongization of the stressed vowel (i.e. the change of **e** to **ie** and of **o** to **uo**), a lower-case letter 'd' is included in the reference. (For an instance of such verbs, see paradigm of **muovere**, p. lxxi.) In other cases in which stress falls on the first of two vowels, the vowel in question appears in the reference (in lower-case). For instance, the verb **augurare** has the reference [A1sa]. This indicates that in the relevant tenses the stress is on the vowel 'a' of the antepenultimate syllable, for example; **a·uguro, a·uguri, a·ugura,** etc.

### USE OF THE PARADIGM OR MODEL

It will be found that some paradigms represent unique verbs, whereas others serve as models for many others. When it is desired to conjugate a verb from a model to which reference is made, *remove as much from the end of the infinitive of the verb in question as is identical with the infinitive of the example* and build up the tenses on this basis. For instance, the verb **crẹscere** has the reference [B9c]. On reference to the verb scheme it will be found that the model for B9 is **conọscere.** Removing from the end of the infinitive of **crẹscere** as much as is identical with **conọscere,** we are left with the syllable **crẹ-**, corresponding to the syllables **conọ-** of the model. If it is desired to know, for instance, the 3rd person plural past definite of **crẹscere**, reference to the paradigm shows that the form for **conọscere** is: **conọbbero.** Replacing **crẹ-** for **conọ-**, we obtain the form **crẹbbero.** The lower-case letter 'c' contained in the reference for **crẹscere** (as for **conọscere**) shows that the stressed vowel has the close pronunciation.

## GROUP A

[A1] **mandare**

INDICATIVE

*Present*

| | |
|---|---|
| mando | mandiamo |
| mandi | mandate |
| manda | man·dano |

*Imperfect*

| | |
|---|---|
| mandavo | mandavamo |
| mandavi | mandavate |
| mandava | manda·vano |

*Past definite*

| | |
|---|---|
| manda·i | mandammo |
| mandasti | mandaste |
| mandò | manda·rono |

*Future*

| | |
|---|---|
| manderò | manderẹmo |
| mandera·i | manderẹte |
| manderà | manderanno |

*Conditional*

| | |
|---|---|
| mandere·i | manderẹmmo |
| manderẹsti | manderẹste |
| manderebbe | mandereb·bero |

SUBJUNCTIVE

*Present*

| | |
|---|---|
| mandi | mandiamo |
| mandi | mandiate |
| mandi | man·dino |

*Imperfect*

| | |
|---|---|
| mandassi | mandas·simo |
| mandassi | mandaste |
| mandasse | mandas·sero |

IMPERATIVE

| | |
|---|---|
| — | mandiamo |
| manda | mandate |
| mandi | man·dino |

*Gerund*: mandando

*Present participle*: mandante

*Past participle*: mandato

[A 1 S] **evitare**

| | |
|---|---|
| e·vito | evitiamo |
| e·viti | evitate |
| e·vita | e·vitano |

*Present subjunctive*

| | |
|---|---|
| e·viti | evitiamo |
| e·viti | evitiate |
| e·viti | e·vitino |

*Imperative*

| | |
|---|---|
| — | evitiamo |
| e·vita | evitate |
| e·viti | e·vitino |

All other tenses as A 1.

[A 2] The verbs of this group are conjugated exactly as those in group A 1 except that adjustments have to be made in the spelling to show that the 'hard' sound of *c* or *g* at the end of the stem is retained throughout the conjugation. This means that *h* is inserted in such verbs wherever the termination begins with *e* or *i*. In the following examples only those tenses are given in which these adjustments are necessary. All other tenses are conjugated as in A 1 in every detail.

| **peccare** | **pagare** |
|---|---|

INDICATIVE

*Present*

| | |
|---|---|
| pecco | pago |
| pecchi | paghi |
| pecca | paga |
| pecchiamo | paghiamo |
| peccate | pagate |
| pec·cano | pa·gano |

*Future*

| | |
|---|---|
| peccherò | pagherò |
| pecchera·i | paghera·i |
| peccherà | pagherà |
| peccherẹmo | pagherẹmo |
| peccherẹte | pagherẹte |
| peccheranno | pagheranno |

*Conditional*

| | |
|---|---|
| pecchere·i | paghere·i |
| peccherẹsti | pagherẹsti |
| peccherebbe | pagherebbe |
| peccherẹmmo | pagherẹmmo |
| peccherẹste | pagherẹste |
| pecchereb·bero | paghereb·bero |

SUBJUNCTIVE

*Present*

| | |
|---|---|
| pecchi | paghi |
| pecchi | paghi |
| pecchi | paghi |
| pecchiamo | paghiamo |
| pecchiate | paghiate |
| pec·chino | pa·ghino |

| | |
|---|---|
| — | — |

IMPERATIVE

| | |
|---|---|
| — | — |
| pecca | paga |
| pecchi | paghi |
| pecchiamo | paghiamo |
| peccate | pagate |
| pec·chino | pa·ghino |

[A2s] **abdicare**

*Present indicative*

| | |
|---|---|
| ab·dico | abdichiamo |
| ab·dichi | adbicate |
| ab·dica | ab·dicano |

*Present subjunctive*

| | |
|---|---|
| ab·dichi | abdichiamo |
| ab·dichi | abdichiate |
| ab·dichi | ab·dichino |

*Imperative*

| | |
|---|---|
| — | abdichiamo |
| ab·dica | abdicate |
| ab·dichi | ab·dichino |

All other tenses as A2.

[A2sa] **augurare**

*Present indicative*

| | |
|---|---|
| a·uguro | auguriamo |
| a·uguri | augurate |
| a·ugura | a·ugurano |

*Present subjunctive*

| | |
|---|---|
| a·uguri | auguriamo |
| a·uguri | auguriate |
| a·uguri | a·ugurino |

*Imperative*

| | |
|---|---|
| — | auguriamo |
| a·ugura | augurate |
| a·uguri | a·ugurino |

All other tenses as A1.

[A3] This group comprises verbs having a stem ending in a 'soft' *c* or *g*. This is denoted in the infinitive (i.e. before *a*) by *ci* or *gi*. These verbs are conjugated exactly as those of group A1 except that before terminations beginning with *e* or *i* the orthographical *i* is omitted because it is no longer necessary to show the 'softness' of the *c* or *g*. In the examples only those tenses are given in which these adjustments are necessary. All other tenses are conjugated as in A1 in every detail.

**scacciare** **mangiare**

INDICATIVE

*Present*

| | |
|---|---|
| scaccio | mangio |
| scacci | mangi |
| scaccia | mangia |
| scacciamo | mangiamo |
| scacciate | mangiate |
| scac·ciano | man·giano |

*Future*

| | |
|---|---|
| scaccerò | mangerò |
| scaccera·i | mangera·i |
| scaccerà | mangerà |
| scaccerẹmo | mangerẹmo |
| scaccerẹte | mangerẹte |
| scacceranno | mangeranno |

*Conditional*

| | |
|---|---|
| scaccere·i | mangere·i |
| scaccerẹsti | mangerẹsti |
| scaccerebbe | mangerebbe |
| scaccerẹmmo | mangerẹmmo |
| scaccerẹste | mangerẹste |
| scaccereb·bero | mangereb·bero |

SUBJUNCTIVE

*Present*

| | |
|---|---|
| scacci | mangi |
| scacci | mangi |
| scacci | mangi |
| scacciamo | mangiamo |

| | |
|---|---|
| scacciate | mangiate |
| scac·cino | man·gino |

IMPERATIVE

| | |
|---|---|
| — | — |
| scaccia | mangia |
| scacci | mangi |
| scacciamo | mangiamo |
| scacciate | mangiate |
| scac·cino | man·gino |

[A4] This group comprises verbs having a stem ending in *i* preceded by a consonant other than *c* or *g*, or by a vowel. Such verbs are conjugated as in A1 except that the *i* is omitted before terminations beginning with *i*. In the example, only those tenses are given in which these adjustments are necessary. All other tenses are conjugated as in A1 in every detail.

| **invidiare** | **abbaiare** |
|---|---|

INDICATIVE

*Present*

| | |
|---|---|
| invi·dio | abba·io |
| invidi | abba·i |
| invi·dia | abba·ia |
| invidiamo | abbaiamo |
| invidiate | abbaiate |
| invi·diano | abba·iano |

SUBJUNCTIVE

*Present*

| | |
|---|---|
| invidi | abba·i |
| invidi | abba·i |
| invidi | abba·i |
| invidiamo | abbaiamo |
| invidiate | abbaiate |
| invi·dino | abba·ino |

IMPERATIVE

| | |
|---|---|
| — | — |
| invi·dia | abba·ia |
| invidi | abba·i |
| invidiamo | abbaiamo |
| invidiate | abbaiate |
| invi·dino | abba·ino |

[A5] This group comprises verbs having a stem ending in *-gnare*. Such verbs are conjugated as in A1 except that two forms are permissible in certain tenses. In the example only those tenses are given in which such variation is permissible. All other tenses are conjugated as in A1 in every detail.

**regnare**

INDICATIVE

*Present*

| | |
|---|---|
| ręgno | regniamo *or* regnamo |
| ręgni | regnate |
| ręgna | ręgnano |

SUBJUNCTIVE

*Present*

| | |
|---|---|
| ręgni | regniamo *or* regnamo |
| ręgni | regniate *or* regnate |
| ręgni | ręgnino |

IMPERATIVE

| | |
|---|---|
| — | regniamo |
| ręgna | regnate |
| ręgni | ręgnino |

[A6] This group comprises verbs having a stem ending in *-uare* or *-eare*. Such verbs are conjugated as A1 except that two forms are permissible in certain tenses. In the example only those tenses are given in which such variation is permissible. All other tenses are conjugated as in A1 in every detail.

| **continuare** | **creare** |
|---|---|

INDICATIVE

*Present*

| | |
|---|---|
| conti·nuo | creo |
| conti·nui | crei |
| conti·nua | crea |
| continuiamo *or* continuamo | creiamo *or* creamo |
| continuate | create |
| conti·nuano | cre·ano |

IMPERATIVE

| | |
|---|---|
| conti·nua | crea |
| conti·nui | crei |
| continuiamo *or* continuamo | creiamo |
| continuate | create |
| conti·nuino | cre·ino |

[A7] **andare**

INDICATIVE

*Present*

| | |
|---|---|
| vado, vo | andiamo |
| vai | andate |
| va | vanno |

*Imperfect*

andavo, *etc.* as A1

*Past definite*

anda·i, *etc.* as A1

*Future*

| | |
|---|---|
| andrò | andręmo |
| andra·i | andręte |
| andrà | andranno |

*Conditional*

| | |
|---|---|
| andre·i | andręmmo |
| andręsti | andręste |
| andrebbe | andreb·bero |

SUBJUNCTIVE

*Present*

| | |
|---|---|
| vada | andiamo |
| vada | andiate |
| vada | va·dano |

*Imperfect*: as A1

IMPERATIVE

| | |
|---|---|
| — | andiamo |
| va (vai, va') | andate |
| vada | va·dano |

*Gerund*: andando

*Present participle*: andante

*Past participle*: andato

[A8] **dare**

INDICATIVE

*Present*

| | |
|---|---|
| do | diamo |
| da·i | date |
| da, dà | danno, dànno |

*Imperfect*

| | |
|---|---|
| davo | davamo |
| davi | davate |
| dava | da·vano |

*Past definite*

| | |
|---|---|
| detti, diedi | dęmmo |
| dęsti | dęste |
| dette, diede | det·tero, die·dero |

*Future*

| | |
|---|---|
| darò | daręmo |
| dara·i | daręte |
| darà | daranno |

*Conditional*

| | |
|---|---|
| dare·i | daręmmo |
| daręsti | daręste |
| darebbe | dareb·bero |

SUBJUNCTIVE

*Present*

| | |
|---|---|
| dia | diamo |
| dia | diate |
| dia | di·ano, di·eno |

*Imperfect*

| | |
|---|---|
| dęssi | dęmmo |
| dęssi | dęste |
| dęsse | dęssero |

IMPERATIVE

| | |
|---|---|
| — | diamo |
| da (dai, da') | date |
| dia | di·ano, di·eno |

*Gerund*: dando

*Present participle*: dante

*Past participle*: dato

[A9] **stare**

INDICATIVE

*Present*

| | |
|---|---|
| sto | stiamo |
| stai | state |
| sta | stanno |

*Imperfect*

| | |
|---|---|
| stavo | stavamo |
| stavi | stavate |
| stava | sta·vano |

*Past definite*

| | |
|---|---|
| stetti | stęmmo |
| stęsti | stęste |
| stette | stet·tero |

*Future*

| | |
|---|---|
| starò | starẹmo |
| stara·i | starẹte |
| starà | staranno |

*Conditional*

| | |
|---|---|
| stare·i | starẹmmo |
| starẹsti | starẹste |
| starebbe | stareb·bero |

SUBJUNCTIVE

*Present*

| | |
|---|---|
| sti·a | stiamo |
| sti·a | stiate |
| sti·a | sti·ano |

*Imperfect*

| | |
|---|---|
| stęssi | stęssimo |
| stęssi | stęste |
| stęsse | stęssero |

IMPERATIVE

| | |
|---|---|
| — | stiamo |
| sta (stai, sta') | state |
| stia | sti·ano |

*Gerund*: stando

*Past participle*: stato

## GROUP B

[B1] **temẹre** **vẹndere**

Although these verbs may be said to fall into two classes in that the stress occurs on a different syllable in the infinitive (temẹre, vẹndere), this is the only place in the whole conjugation where such a difference in stress occurs. Such verbs have therefore been classed together, the marking of the infinitive as it occurs in the body of the dictionary being sufficient indication regarding the position of the stress on the infinitive itself.

INDICATIVE

*Present*

| | |
|---|---|
| temo | vẹndo |
| tẹmi | vẹndi |

| | |
|---|---|
| tẹme | vẹnde |
| temiamo | vendiamo |
| temẹte | vendẹte |
| tẹmono | vẹndono |

*Imperfect*

| | |
|---|---|
| temẹvo | vendẹvo |
| temẹvi | vendẹvi |
| temẹva | vendẹva |
| temevamo | vendevamo |
| temevate | vendevate |
| temẹvano | vendẹvano |

*Past definite*

| | |
|---|---|
| temẹi, temetti | vendẹi, vendetti |
| temẹsti | vendẹsti |
| temẹ̀, temette | vendè, vendette |
| temẹmmo | vendẹmmo |
| temẹste | vendẹste |
| temẹrono, temet·tero | vendẹrono, vendet·tero |

*Future*

| | |
|---|---|
| temerò | venderò |
| temera·i | vendera·i |
| temerà | venderà |
| temerẹmo | venderẹmo |
| temerẹte | venderẹte |
| temeranno | venderanno |

*Conditional*

| | |
|---|---|
| temere·i | vendere·i |
| temerẹsti | venderẹsti |
| temerebbe | venderebbe |
| temerẹmmo | venderẹmmo |
| temerẹste | venderẹste |
| temereb·bero | vendereb·bero |

SUBJUNCTIVE

*Present*

| | |
|---|---|
| tẹma | vẹnda |
| tẹma | vẹnda |
| tẹma | vẹnda |
| temiamo | vendiamo |
| temiate | vendiate |
| tẹmano | vẹndano |

*Imperfect*

| | |
|---|---|
| temẹssi | vendẹssi |
| temẹssi | vendẹssi |
| temẹsse | vendẹsse |
| temẹssimo | vendẹssimo |
| temẹste | vendẹste |
| temẹssero | vendẹssero |

IMPERATIVE

| | |
|---|---|
| — | — |
| tẹmi | vẹndi |
| tẹma | vẹnda |
| temiamo | vendiamo |
| temẹte | vendẹte |
| tẹmano | vẹndano |

*Gerund*: temendo vendendo
*Present participle*: temente vendente
*Past participle*: temuto venduto

[B2] **addurre**

*Present*

| | |
|---|---|
| adduco | adduciamo |
| adduci | adducẹte |
| adduce | addu·cono |

*Imperfect*: adducẹvo, *etc.*

*Past definite*:

| | |
|---|---|
| addussi | adducẹmmo |
| adducẹsti | adducẹste |
| addusse | addus·sero |

*Future*: addurrò, *etc.*
*Conditional*: addurrei, *etc.*

SUBJUNCTIVE

*Present*

| | |
|---|---|
| adduca | adduciamo |

| | |
|---|---|
| adduca | adduciate |
| adduca | addu·cano |

*Imperfect*: adducẹssi, *etc.*

IMPERATIVE

| | |
|---|---|
| — | adduciamo |
| adduci | adducẹte |
| adduca | addu·cano |

*Gerund*: adducendo

*Present participle*: adducente

*Past participle*: addọtto

[B 3] **avẹre**

INDICATIVE

*Present*

| | |
|---|---|
| ho | abbiamo |
| hai | avẹte |
| ha | hanno |

*Imperfect*: avẹvo, *etc.*

*Past definite*

| | |
|---|---|
| ebbi | avẹmmo |
| avẹsti | avẹste |
| ebbe | eb·bero |

*Future*: avrò, *etc.*

*Conditional*

| | |
|---|---|
| avre·i | avrẹmmo |
| avrẹsti | avrẹste |
| avrebbe | avreb·bero |

SUBJUNCTIVE

*Present*

| | |
|---|---|
| ab·bia | abbiamo |
| ab·bia | abbiate |
| ab·bia | ab·biano |

*Imperfect*: avẹssi, *etc.*

IMPERATIVE

| | |
|---|---|
| — | abbiamo |
| abbi | abbiate |
| abbia | ab·biano |

*Gerund*: avendo

*Present participle*: avente

*Past participle*: avuto

[B 4] **bẹre** or **bevẹre**

INDICATIVE

*Present*

| | |
|---|---|
| bẹvo | beviamo |
| bẹvi | bevẹte |
| bẹve | bẹvono |

*Imperfect*: bevẹvo, *etc.*

*Past definite*

| | |
|---|---|
| bẹvvi, bevetti | bevẹmmo |
| bevẹsti | bevẹste |
| bẹvve, bevette | bẹvvero, bevet·tero |

*Future*: beverò, *etc.*

*Conditional*: bevere·i, *etc.*

SUBJUNCTIVE

*Present*

| | |
|---|---|
| bẹva | beviamo |
| bẹva | beviate |
| bẹva | bẹvano |

*Imperfect*: bevẹssi, *etc.*

IMPERATIVE

| | |
|---|---|
| — | beviamo |
| bẹvi | bevẹtte |
| bẹva | bẹvano |

*Gerund*: bevendo

*Present participle*: bevente

*Past participle*: bevuto

[B 5] **cadẹre**

As B 1, except past definite, future and conditional as follows:

*Past definite*

| | |
|---|---|
| caddi | cadẹmmo |
| cadẹsti | cadẹste |
| cadde | cad·dero |

*Future*: cadrò, *etc.*

*Conditional*: cadre·i, *etc.*

[B 6] **chiẹdere**

INDICATIVE

*Present*

| | |
|---|---|
| chiẹdo | chiediamo |
| chiẹdi | chiedẹte |
| chiẹde | chiẹdono |

*Past definite*

| | |
|---|---|
| chiẹsi | chiedẹmmo |
| chiedẹsti | chiedẹste |
| chiẹse | chiẹsero |

*Past particle*: chiẹsto

*Past participle*: chiẹsto

Other tenses and forms as for B 1.

[B 7] **co·gliere, corre**

INDICATIVE

*Present*

| | |
|---|---|
| colgo | cogliamo |
| cogli | cogliẹte |
| co·glie | col·gono |

*Imperfect*: cogliẹvo, *etc.*

*Past definite*

| | |
|---|---|
| colsi | cogliẹmmo |
| cogliẹsti | cogliẹste |
| colse | col·sero |

*Future*: coglierò, *etc.*

*Conditional*: cogliere·i, *etc.*

SUBJUNCTIVE

*Present*

| | |
|---|---|
| colga | cogliamo |
| colga | cogliate |
| colga | col·gano |

*Imperfect*: cogliẹssi, *etc.*

IMPERATIVE

| | |
|---|---|
| — | cogliamo |
| cogli (co') | cogliẹte |
| colga | col·gano |

*Gerund*: cogliendo

*Present participle*: cogliente

*Past participle*: colto

[B 8] **cọmpiere**
See D 6.

[B 9] **conọscere**

INDICATIVE

*Present*

| | |
|---|---|
| conọsco | conosciamo |
| conọsci | conoscẹte |
| conọsce | conọscono |

*Imperfect*: conoscẹvo, *etc.*

*Past definite*

| | |
|---|---|
| conọbbi | conoscẹmmo |
| conoscẹsti | conoscẹste |
| conọbbe | conọbbero |

*Future*: conoscerò, *etc.*

*Conditional*: conoscere·i, *etc.*

SUBJUNCTIVE

*Present*

| | |
|---|---|
| conọsca | conosciamo |
| conọsca | conosciate |
| conọsca | conọscano |

*Imperfect*: conoscẹssi, *etc.*

IMPERATIVE

| | |
|---|---|
| — | conosciamo |
| conọsci | conoscẹte |
| conọsca | conọscano |

*Gerund*: conoscendo

*Present participle*: conoscente

*Past participle*: conosciuto

[B 10] **dire**

INDICATIVE

*Present*

| | |
|---|---|
| dico | diciamo |
| dici | dite |
| dice | di·cono |

*Imperfect*: dicẹvo, *etc.*

*Past definite*

| | |
|---|---|
| dissi | dicẹmmo |
| dicẹsti | dicẹste |
| disse | dis·sero |

*Future*: dirò, *etc.*

*Conditional*: dire·i, *etc.*

SUBJUNCTIVE

*Present*

| | |
|---|---|
| dica | diciamo |
| dica | diciate |
| dica | di·cano |

*Imperfect*: dicẹssi, *etc.*

IMPERATIVE

| | |
|---|---|
| — | diciamo |
| di' | dite |
| dica | di·cano |

*Gerund*: dicendo

*Present participle*: dicente

*Past participle*: dẹtto

[B 11] **dolẹre**

INDICATIVE

*Present*

| | |
|---|---|
| dolgo | dogliamo |
| duoli | dolẹte |
| duole | dol·gono |

*Imperfect*: dolẹvo, *etc.*

*Past definite*

| | |
|---|---|
| dolsi | dolẹmmo |
| dolẹsti | dolẹste |
| dolse | dol·sero |

*Future*: dorrò, *etc.*

*Conditional*: dorre·i, *etc.*

SUBJUNCTIVE

*Present*

| | |
|---|---|
| dolga | dogliamo |
| dolga | dogliate |
| dolga | dol·gano |

*Imperfect*: dolẹssi, *etc.*

IMPERATIVE

| | |
|---|---|
| — | dogliamo |
| duoli | dolẹte |
| dolga | dol·gano |

*Gerund*: dolendo

*Present participle*: dolente

*Past participle*: doluto

[B 12] **dovẹre**

INDICATIVE

*Present*

| | |
|---|---|
| devo, debbo, deg·gio | dobbiamo |
| devi | dovẹte |
| deve | de·vono, deb·bono |

*Imperfect*: dovẹvo, *etc.*

*Past definite*

| | |
|---|---|
| dovei, dovetti | dovẹmmo |

| | |
|---|---|
| dovẹsti | dovẹste |
| dovẹ̀, dovette | dovet·tero |

*Future*: dovrò, *etc.*

*Conditional*: dovre·i, *etc.*

SUBJUNCTIVE

*Present*

| | |
|---|---|
| debba deva, deg·gia | dobbiamo |
| debba deva, deg·gia | dobbiate |
| debba deva, deg·gia | deb·bano, de·vano |

*Imperfect*: dovẹssi, *etc.*

*Gerund*: dovendo

*Past principle*: dovuto

[B 13] **es·sere**

INDICATIVE

*Present*

| | |
|---|---|
| sọno | siamo |
| sei | siẹte |
| è | sọno |

*Imperfect*

| | |
|---|---|
| ero | eravamo |
| eri | eravate |
| era | e·rano |

*Past definite*

| | |
|---|---|
| fui | fummo |
| fọsti | fọste |
| fu | fu·rono |

*Future*

| | |
|---|---|
| sarò | sarẹmo |
| sarai | sarẹte |
| sarà | saranno |

*Conditional*

| | |
|---|---|
| sare·i | sarẹmmo |
| sarẹsti | sarẹste |
| sarebbe | sareb·bero |

SUBJUNCTIVE

*Present*

| | |
|---|---|
| sia | siamo |
| sia | siate |
| sia | si·ano |

*Imperfect*

| | |
|---|---|
| fọssi | fọssimo |
| fọssi | fọste |
| fọsse | fọssero |

IMPERATIVE

| | |
|---|---|
| — | siamo |
| sii, si' | siate |
| sia | si·ano |

*Gerund*: essendo

*Present participle*: None

*Past participle*: stato

[B 14] **fare**

INDICATIVE

*Present*

| | |
|---|---|
| faccio, fo | facciamo |
| fai | fate |
| fa | fanno |

*Imperfect*: facẹvo, *etc.*

*Past definite*

| | |
|---|---|
| fẹci | facẹmmo |
| facẹsti | facẹste |
| fẹce | fẹcero |

*Future*: farò, *etc.*

*Conditional*: fare·i, *etc.*

SUBJUNCTIVE

*Present*

| | |
|---|---|
| faccia | facciamo |
| faccia | facciate |
| faccia | fac·ciano |

*Imperfect*

| | |
|---|---|
| facęssi | facęssimo |
| facęssi | facęste |
| facęsse | facęssero |

### IMPERATIVE

| | |
|---|---|
| — | facciamo |
| fa, fai, fa' | fate |
| faccia | fac·ciano |

*Gerund*: facendo

*Present participle*: facente

*Past participle*: fatto

[B15]　**giacęre**

### INDICATIVE
*Present*

| | |
|---|---|
| giaccio | giaciamo |
| giaci | giacęte |
| giace | gia·ciono |

*Imperfect*: giacęvo, *etc.*

*Past definite*

| | |
|---|---|
| giacqui | giacęmmo |
| giacęsti | giacęste |
| giacque | giac·quero |

*Future*: giacerò, *etc.*

*Conditional*: giacere·i, *etc.*

### SUBJUNCTIVE
*Present*

| | |
|---|---|
| giacia | giaciamo |
| giacia | giaciate |
| giacia | gia·ciano |

*Imperfect*: giacęssi, *etc.*

### IMPERATIVE

| | |
|---|---|
| — | giaciamo |
| giaci | giacęte |
| giacia | gia·ciano |

*Gerund*: giacendo

*Present participle*: giacente

*Past participle*: giaciuto

[B16]　**godęre**

As B1, except that future and conditional may be godrò, godre·i, *etc.*, as well as goderò, godere·i, *etc.*

[B17]　**męscere**

As B1 except for alternative in the Present Indicative, as follows:

### INDICATIVE
*Present*

| | |
|---|---|
| męscio, męsco | mesciamo |
| męsci | mescęte |
| męsce | męscono |

[B18]　**na·scere**

### INDICATIVE
*Present*

| | |
|---|---|
| nasco | nasciamo |
| nasci | nascęte |
| nasce | na·scono |

*Imperfect*: nascęvo, *etc.*

*Past definite*

| | |
|---|---|
| nacqui | nascęmmo |
| nascęsti | nascęste |
| nacque | nac·quero |

*Future*: nascerò, *etc.*

*Conditional*: nascere·i, *etc.*

### SUBJUNCTIVE
*Present*

| | |
|---|---|
| nasca | nasciamo |
| nasca | nasciate |
| nasca | na·scano |

*Imperfect*: nascęssi, *etc.*

### IMPERATIVE

| | |
|---|---|
| — | nasciamo |
| nasci | nascęte |
| nasca | na·scano |

*Gerund*: nascendo

*Present participle*: nascente

*Past participle*: nato

[B19] **parẹre**

INDICATIVE

*Present*

| | |
|---|---|
| pa·io | paia·mo |
| pari | parẹte |
| pare | pa·iono |

*Imperfect*: parẹvo, *etc.*

*Past definite*

| | |
|---|---|
| parvi | parẹmmo |
| parẹsti | parẹste |
| parve | par·vero |

*Future*: parrò, *etc.*

*Conditional*: parre·i, *etc.*

SUBJUNCTIVE

*Present*

| | |
|---|---|
| pa·ia | paiamo |
| pa·ia | paiate |
| pa·ia | pa·iano |

*Imperfect*: parẹssi, *etc.*

*Gerund*: parendo

*Past participle*: parso

[B20] **piacẹre**

This is conjugated like B15 except for slight differences (-cc- for -c-) in present indicative and subjunctive.

*Present indicative*

| | |
|---|---|
| piaccio | piacciamo |
| piaci | piacẹte |
| piace | piac·ciono |

*Present subjunctive*

| | |
|---|---|
| piaccia | piacciamo |
| piaccia | piaciate |
| piaccia | piac·ciano |

[B21] **pọrre**

INDICATIVE

*Present*

| | |
|---|---|
| pọngo | poniamo |
| pọni | ponẹte |
| pọne | pọngono |

*Imperfect*: ponẹvo, *etc.*

*Past definite*

| | |
|---|---|
| pọsi | ponẹmmo |
| ponẹsti | ponẹste |
| pọse | pọsero |

*Future*: porrò, *etc.*

*Conditional*: porre·i, *etc.*

SUBJUNCTIVE

*Present*

| | |
|---|---|
| pọnga | poniamo |
| pọnga | poniate |
| pọnga | pọngano |

*Imperfect*: ponẹssi, *etc.*

IMPERATIVE

| | |
|---|---|
| — | poniamo |
| pọni (pon) | ponẹte |
| pọnga | pọngano |

*Gerund*: ponendo

*Present participle*: ponente

*Past participle*: pọsto

[B22] **potẹre**

*Present*

| | |
|---|---|
| posso | possiamo |
| puo·i | potẹte |
| può | pos·sono |

*Imperfect*: potẹvo, *etc.*

*Past definite*

| | |
|---|---|
| potẹi | potẹmmo |
| potẹsti | potẹste |
| potè | potẹrono |

*Future*: potrò, *etc.*

*Conditional*: potre·i, *etc.*

## SUBJUNCTIVE

*Present*

| possa | possiamo |
|-------|----------|
| possa | possiate |
| possa | pos·sano |

*Imperfect*: potęssi, *etc.*

*Gerund*: potendo

*Present participle*: None
[potente, possente, *adjs.* meaning 'powerful']

*Past participle*: potuto

[B23]   **prevedęre**

As B35, except future and conditional as follows:

*Future*: prevederò, *etc.*

*Conditional*: prevedere·i, *etc.*

[B24]   **riavęre**

As B3, but note present indicative forms.

*Present indicative*

| riò | riabbiamo |
|-----|-----------|
| ria·i | riavęte |
| rià | rianno |

[B25]   **rimanęre**

Except for infinitive, like B21.

[B26]   **sapęre**

### INDICATIVE

*Present*

| so | sappiamo |
|----|----------|
| sai | sapęte |
| sa | sanno |

*Imperfect*: sapęvo, *etc.*

*Past definite*

| seppi | sapęmmo |
|-------|---------|
| sapęsti | sapęste |
| seppe | sep·pero |

*Future*: saprò, *etc.*

*Conditional*: sapre·i, *etc.*

## SUBJUNCTIVE

*Present*

| sap·pia | sappiamo |
|---------|----------|
| sap·pia | sappiate |
| sap·pia | sap·piano |

*Imperfect*: sapęssi, *etc.*

### IMPERATIVE

| — | sappiamo |
|---|----------|
| sa | sapęte |
| sap·pia | sap·piano |

*Gerund*: sapendo

*Present participle*: sapiente

*Past participle*: saputo

[B27]   **scęgliere**

### INDICATIVE

*Present*

| scęlgo | scegliamo |
|--------|-----------|
| scęgli | sceglięte |
| scęglie | scęlgono |

*Imperfect*: sceglięvo, *etc.*

*Past definite*

| scęlsi | sceglięmmo |
|--------|------------|
| sceglięsti | sceglięste |
| scęlse | scęlsero |

*Future*: sceglierò, *etc.*

*Conditional*: sceliere·i, *etc.*

### SUBJUNCTIVE

*Present*

| scęlga | scegliamo |
|--------|-----------|
| scęlga | scegliate |
| scęlga | scęlgano |

*Imperfect*: sceglięssi, *etc.*

### IMPERATIVE

| — | scegliamo |
|---|-----------|
| scęgli | sceglięte |
| scęlga | scęlgano |

*Gerund*: scegliendo
*Present participle*: None
*Past participle*: scẹlto

[B28] **sedẹre**

INDICATIVE

*Present*

| | |
|---|---|
| siedo (seggo) | sediamo |
| siedi | sedẹte |
| siede | sie·dono (seg·gono) |

*Imperfect*: sedẹvo, *etc.*
*Past definite*: sedẹi, *or* sedetti, *etc.*
*Future*: sederò, *etc.*
*Conditional*: sedere·i, *etc.*

SUBJUNCTIVE

*Present*

| | |
|---|---|
| sieda, segga | sediamo |
| sieda, segga | sediate |
| sieda, segga | sie·dano, seg·gano |

*Imperfect*: sedẹssi, *etc.*

IMPERATIVE

| | |
|---|---|
| — | sediamo |
| siedi | sedẹte |
| sieda, segga | sie·dano, seg·gano |

*Gerund*: sedendo
*Present participle*: sedente
*Past participle*: seduto

[B29] **soddisfare**

*Present*: As A1 or B14
*All other tenses*: as B14

[B30] **solẹre**

INDICATIVE

*Present*

| | |
|---|---|
| soglio | sogliamo |
| suoli | solẹte |
| suole | so·gliono |

*Imperfect*: solẹvo, *etc.*
*Past definite*: solẹi, *etc.*
*Future*: solerò, *etc.*
*Conditional*: solere·i, *etc.*

SUBJUNCTIVE

*Present*

| | |
|---|---|
| soglia | sogliamo |
| soglia | sogliate |
| soglia | so·gliano |

*Imperfect*: solẹssi, *etc.*
*Gerund*: solendo
*Past participle*: so·lito

[B31] **ṣvel·lere, ṣverre**

INDICATIVE

*Present*

| | |
|---|---|
| ṣvello, ṣvelgo | ṣvelliamo |
| ṣvelli, ṣvelgi | ṣvellẹte |
| ṣvelle, ṣvelge | ṣvel·lono, ṣvel·gono |

*Imperfect*: ṣvellẹvo, *etc.* *or* ṣvelgẹvo, *etc.*

*Past definite*

| | |
|---|---|
| ṣvelsi | ṣvelgẹmmo |
| ṣvellẹsti, svelgẹsti | ṣvellẹste, ṣvelgẹste |
| ṣvelse | ṣvel·sero |

*Future*: ṣvellerò, *etc.* *or* ṣvelgerò, *etc.*
*Conditional*: ṣvellere·i, *etc.* *or* ṣvelgere·i, *etc.*
*Gerund*: ṣvellendo
*Past participle*: ṣvelto

[B32] **tenẹre**

INDICATIVE

*Present*

| | |
|---|---|
| tengo | teniamo |
| tieni | tenẹte |
| tiene | ten·gono |

*Imperfect*: tenẹvo, *etc.*

*Past definite*

| | |
|---|---|
| tẹnni | tenẹmmo |
| tenẹsti | tenẹste |
| tẹnne | tẹnnero |

*Future*: terrò, *etc.*

*Conditional*: terre·i, *etc.*

SUBJUNCTIVE

*Present*

| | |
|---|---|
| tenga | teniamo |
| tenga | teniate |
| tenga | ten·gano |

*Imperfect*: tenẹssi, *etc.*

IMPERATIVE

| | |
|---|---|
| — | teniamo |
| tieni | tenẹte |
| tenga | ten·gano |

*Gerund*: tenendo

*Present participle*: tenente

*Past participle*: tenuto

[B33] **trarre**

INDICATIVE

*Present*

| | |
|---|---|
| traggo | traiamo, tragghiamo |
| trai | traẹte |
| trae | trag·gono |

*Imperfect*: traẹvo, *etc.*

*Past definite*

| | |
|---|---|
| trassi | traẹmmo |
| traẹsti | traẹste |
| trasse | tras·sero |

*Future*: trarrò, *etc.*

*Conditional*: trarre·i, *etc.*

SUBJUNCTIVE

*Present*

| | |
|---|---|
| tragga | traiamo, tragghiamo |
| tragga | traiate |
| tragga | trag·gano |

*Imperfect*: traẹssi, *etc.*

IMPERATIVE

| | |
|---|---|
| — | traiamo |
| trai | traẹte |
| tragga | trag·gano |

*Gerund*: traendo

*Present participle*: traente

*Past participle*: tratto

[B34] **valẹre**

INDICATIVE

*Present*

| | |
|---|---|
| valgo | valiamo, vagliamo |
| vali | valẹte |
| vale | val·gono |

*Imperfect*: valẹvo, *etc.*

*Past definite*

| | |
|---|---|
| valsi | valẹmmo |
| valẹsti | valẹste |
| valse | val·sero |

*Future*: varrò, *etc.*

*Conditional*: varre·i, *etc.*

SUBJUNCTIVE

*Present*

| | |
|---|---|
| valga | valiamo |
| valga | valiate |
| valga | val·gano |

*Imperfect*: valẹssi, *etc.*

IMPERATIVE

| | |
|---|---|
| — | valiamo |
| vali | valęte |
| valga | val·gano |

*Gerund*: valendo

*Present participle*: valente

*Past participle*: valuto, valso

[B35] **vedęre**

INDICATIVE

*Present*

| | |
|---|---|
| vędo vęggo, veg·gio | vediamo, veggiamo |
| vędi | vedęte |
| vęde | vędono, vęggono |

*Imperfect*: vedęvo, *etc.*

*Past definite*

| | |
|---|---|
| vidi | vedęmmo |
| vedęsti | vedęste |
| vide | vi·dero |

*Future*: vedrò, *etc.*

*Conditional*: vedre·i, *etc.*

SUBJUNCTIVE

*Present*

| | |
|---|---|
| vęda vęgga, veg·gia | vediamo |
| vęda, vęgga, veg·gia | vediate |
| vęda, vęgga, veg·gia | vędano, vęggano |

*Imperfect*: vedęssi, *etc.*

IMPERATIVE

| | |
|---|---|
| — | vediamo |
| vędi | vedęte |
| vęda | vędano |

*Gerund*: vedendo

*Present participle*: vedente, veggente

*Past participle*: veduto, visto

[B36] **volęre**

INDICATIVE

*Present*

| | |
|---|---|
| voglio, vo' | vogliamo |
| vuoi | volęte |
| vuole | vogliono |

*Imperfect*: volęvo, *etc.*

*Past definite*

| | |
|---|---|
| volli | volęmmo |
| volęsti | volęste |
| volle | vol·lero |

*Future*: vorrò, *etc.*

*Conditional*: vorre·i, *etc.*

SUBJUNCTIVE

As B30

*Gerund*: volendo

*Present participle*: volente

*Past principle*: voluto

## GROUP C

The verbs given under the letter C., sometimes known as strong verbs, all belong to the *-ere* conjugation. They are conjugated like B1 except for the past participle and the first person singular and third person singular and plural of the past definite. The full conjugation of 'prendere' is here given as an example showing where the irregular forms occur.

[C1] **pren·dere**

*Present*

| | |
|---|---|
| prendo | prendiamo |
| prendi | prendęte |
| prende | pren·dono |

*Imperfect*

| | |
|---|---|
| prendẹvo | prendevamo |
| prendẹvi | prendevate |
| prendẹva | prendẹvano |

*Past definite*

| | |
|---|---|
| prẹsi | prendẹmmo |
| prendẹsti | prendẹste |
| prẹse | prẹsero |

*Future*

| | |
|---|---|
| prenderò | prenderẹmo |
| prendera·i | prenderẹte |
| prenderà | prenderanno |

*Conditional*

| | |
|---|---|
| prendere·i | prenderẹmmo |
| prenderẹsti | prenderẹste |
| prenderebbe | prendereb·bero |

SUBJUNCTIVE

*Present*

| | |
|---|---|
| prenda | prendiamo |
| prenda | prendiate |
| prenda | pren·dano |

*Imperfect*

| | |
|---|---|
| prendẹssi | prendẹssimo |
| prendẹssi | prendẹste |
| prendẹsse | prendẹssero |

IMPERATIVE

| | |
|---|---|
| — | prendiamo |
| prendi | prendẹte |
| prenda | pren·dano |

*Gerund*: prendendo

*Present participle*: prendente

*Past participle*: prẹso

It will be seen from the above that it is sufficient to know the first person singular of the past definite (prẹsi) in order to be able to form the third person singular and plural (prẹse, prẹsero). As the same applies to all verbs of group c, it is only necessary for the infinitive, first person singular past definite and the past participle to be listed in order to give sufficient data for the whole conjugation.

| | *Infinitive* | *1st pers. sing. past def.* | *Past participle* |
|---|---|---|---|
| c1 | pren·dere | prẹsi | prẹso |
| | contundere | contuṣi | contuṣo |
| c2 | fọndere | fuṣi | fuṣo |
| c3 | ri·dere | risi | riso |
| | ar·dere | arsi | arso |
| | persuadẹre | persuaṣi | persuaṣo |
| c4 | emer·gere | emersi | emerso |
| | spar·gere | sparsi | sparso |
| c5 | sor·gere | sorsi | sorto |
| | assur·gere | assursi | assurto |
| | pun·gere | punsi | punto |
| | tor·cere | torsi | torto |
| | vin·cere | vinsi | vinto |
| | vol·gere | volsi | volto |
| | cọrrere | cọrsi | cọrso |
| c6 | distin·guere | distinsi | distinto |

| | Infinitive | 1st pers. sing. past def. | Past participle |
|---|---|---|---|
| C7 | spẹgnere | spensi | spento |
| C8 | assu·mere | assunsi | assunto |
| C9 | redi·mere | redensi | redento |
| C10 | strin·gere | strinsi | strẹtto |
| C11 | rispọndere | risposi | risposto |
| C12 | frig·gere | frissi | fritto |
| | leg·gere | lessi | letto |
| | strug·gere | strussi | strutto |
| | scri·vere | scrissi | scritto |
| C13 | diri·gere | diressi | diretto |
| C14 | invol·gere | involsi | involto, involuto |
| | assol·vere | assolvetti, assolvei, assolsi | assolto, assoluto |
| | asciol·vere | asciolsi | asciolto |
| C15d | cuo·cere | cossi | cotto |
| | muo·vere | mossi | mosso |
| C16 | vivere | vissi | vissuto |
| C17 | prefig·gere | prefissi | prefisso |
| C18 | oppri·mere | oppressi | oppresso |
| C19 | inflet·tere | inflessi | inflesso |
| | conce·dere | concessi | concesso |
| | discu·tere | discussi | discusso |
| C19d | scuo·tere | scossi | scosso |
| C20 | mẹttere | misi | mẹsso |
| C21 | scin·dere | scindetti | scisso |
| | fen·dere | fendetti | fesso |
| C22 | succe·dere | succedetti, successi | succeduto, successo |
| C23 | espel·lere | espulsi | espulso |
| C24 | resi·stere | resistei, resistetti | resistito |
| C25 | span·dere | spandetti | spanto |
| C26 | rọmpere | ruppi | rọtto |
| C27 | pio·vere | piovvi | piovuto |
| C28 | per·dere | perdette, persi | perduto, perso |
| C29 | cer·nere | cernei, cernetti | cernito |
| C30 | contes·sere | contessei | contessuto, contesto |
| C31 | riful·gere | rifulsi | rifulso |
| C32 | redi·gere | redigei | redatto |

*Diphthongization of verbs of Group C*

In the example which follows, only those tenses are given in which dipthongization occurs. In all other tenses, such verbs are conjugated as C1 in every detail.

[C15d] **muo·vere**

INDICATIVE

*Present*

| | |
|---|---|
| muovo | moviamo |
| muovi | movẹte |
| muove | muovono |

SUBJUNCTIVE

*Present*

| | |
|---|---|
| muova | moviamo |
| muova | moviate |
| muova | muovano |

IMPERATIVE

| | |
|---|---|
| — | moviamo |
| muovi | movẹte |
| muova | muovano |

## GROUP D

[D1] **servire**

INDICATIVE

*Present*

| | |
|---|---|
| servo | serviamo |
| servi | servite |
| serve | ser·vono |

*Imperfect*

| | |
|---|---|
| servivo | servivamo |
| servivi | servivate |
| serviva | servi·vano |

*Past definite*

| | |
|---|---|
| servii | servimmo |
| servisti | serviste |
| servì | servi·rono |

*Future*

| | |
|---|---|
| servirò | servirẹmo |
| servira·i | servirẹte |
| servirà | serviranno |

*Conditional*

| | |
|---|---|
| servire·i | servirẹmmo |
| servirẹsti | servirẹste |
| servirebbe | servireb·bero |

SUBJUNCTIVE

*Present*

| | |
|---|---|
| serva | serviamo |
| serva | serviate |
| serva | ser·vano |

*Imperfect*

| | |
|---|---|
| servissi | servis·simo |
| servissi | serviste |
| servisse | servis·sero |

IMPERATIVE

| | |
|---|---|
| — | serviamo |
| servi | servite |
| serva | ser·vano |

*Gerund*: servendo

*Present participle*: serviente (the present participle is usually wanting in verbs of D group, though *adjs.* servente, divertente, etc., exist)

*Past participle*: servito

[D2] **finire**

As D1 except in the present indicative and subjunctive and in the imperative:

*Present indicative*

| | |
|---|---|
| finisco | finiamo |
| finisci | finite |
| finisce | fini·scono |

*Present subjunctive*

| | |
|---|---|
| finisca | finiamo |
| finisca | finiate |
| finisca | fini·scano |

IMPERATIVE

| | |
|---|---|
| — | finiamo |
| finisci | finite |
| finisca | fini·scano |

[D 3] **apparire**

INDICATIVE

*Present*

| | |
|---|---|
| appa·io, apparisco | appaiamo |
| appari, apparisci | apparite |
| appare, apparisce | appa·iono, appari·scono |

*Imperfect*: apparivo, *etc.*

*Past definite*

| | |
|---|---|
| apparii, apparvi, apparsi | apparimmo |
| apparisti | appariste |
| apparì, apparve, apparse | apparirono, apparvero, appar·sero |

*Future*: apparirò, *etc.*

*Conditional*: apparire·i, *etc.*

SUBJUNCTIVE

*Present*

| | |
|---|---|
| appa·ia, apparisca | appaiamo |
| appa·ia, apparisca | appariate |
| appa·ia, apparisca | appa·iano, appari·scano |

*Imperfect*: apparissi, *etc.*

IMPERATIVE

| | |
|---|---|
| — | appaiamo |
| appari, apparisce | apparite |
| appaia, apparisca | appa·iano, appariscano |

*Gerund*: apparendo

*Past participle*: apparito, apparso

[D 4] **assalire**

INDICATIVE

*Present*

| | |
|---|---|
| assalgo | assalghiamo |
| assalì | assalite |
| assale | assal·gono |

*Past definite*

| | |
|---|---|
| assalsi, assalii | assalimmo |
| assalisti | assaliste |
| assalse, assalì | assali·rono, assal·sero |

SUBJUNCTIVE

*Present*

| | |
|---|---|
| assalga | assalghiamo |
| assalga | assalghiate |
| assalga | assal·gano |

IMPERATIVE

| | |
|---|---|
| — | assalghiamo |
| assali | assalite |
| assalga | assal·gano |

All other tenses as D 1.

[D 5] **comparire**

INDICATIVE

*Present*

| | |
|---|---|
| comparisco, compaio | compariamo |

| | |
|---|---|
| comparisci | comparite |
| comparisce, compare | compari·scono, compa·iono |

*Imperfect*: comparivo, *etc.*

*Past definite*

| | |
|---|---|
| comparii, comparsi, comparvi | comparimmo |
| comparisti | compariste |
| comparì, comparse, comparve | compar·vero |

[N.B. The three forms in the singular of this tense are used for different meanings, viz. comparì = he made a good appearance; comparse = he appeared in court; comparve = he made his appearance.]

SUBJUNCTIVE

*Present*

| | |
|---|---|
| comparisca, compa·ia | compariamo |
| comparisca, compa·ia | compariate |
| comparisca, compa·ia | compa·iano |

IMPERATIVE

| | |
|---|---|
| — | compariamo |
| comparisci | comparite |
| comparisca, compa·ia | compa·iano |

*Past participle*: comparso

Other tenses as for D 1.

[D 6] **compire or cọmpiere**

INDICATIVE

*Present*

| | |
|---|---|
| cọmpio, compisco | compiamo |
| cọmpi, compisci | compite |
| cọmpie, compisce | cọmpiono, compi·scono |

SUBJUNCTIVE

*Present*

| | |
|---|---|
| cọmpia, compisca | compiamo |
| cọmpia, compisca | compiate |
| cọmpia, compisca | cọmpiano, compiscano |

*Imperfect*: compissi, *etc. or* compiessi, *etc.*

IMPERATIVE

| | |
|---|---|
| — | compiamo |
| compisci, cọmpi | compite |
| compisca, compia | compiscano, cọmpiano |

*Past participle*: compito, compiuto

Other tenses as D 1.

[D 7] **convertire**

As D 1, but *past participle*: converso, convertito.

[D 8] **coprire**

*Past definite*

| | |
|---|---|
| coprii, copersi | coprimmo |
| copristi | copriste |
| coprì, coperse | copri·rono, coper·sero |

*Past participle*: coperto

Other tenses as D 1.

[D 9] **costruire**

As D 2, except that alternative form of *past definite* is costrussi, etc. and alternative *past participle* is costrutto.

[D 10] **disparire**

*Present indicative*

| | |
|---|---|
| disparisco | — |
| disparisci | disparite |
| disparisce | dispari·scono |

*Past definite*

| | |
|---|---|
| disparii, disparvi | disparimmo |
| disparisti | dispariste |
| disparve | dispar·vero |

Other tenses as D 2.

[D 11] **empire** *or* **ẹmpiere**

*Present indicative*

| | |
|---|---|
| ẹmpio | empiamo |
| ẹmpi | empite |
| ẹmpie | ẹmpiono |

*Present subjunctive*

| | |
|---|---|
| ẹmpia | empiamo |
| ẹmpia | empiate |
| ẹmpia | ẹmpiano |

*Past participle*: empito, empiuto.

Other tenses as D 1.

[D 12] **morire**

INDICATIVE

*Present*

| | |
|---|---|
| m(u)o·io | moriamo |
| m(u)ori | morite |
| m(u)ore | m(u)o·iono |

SUBJUNCTIVE

*Present*

| | |
|---|---|
| m(u)oia | moriamo |
| m(u)oia | moriate |
| m(u)oia | m(u)o·iano |

IMPERATIVE

| | |
|---|---|
| — | moriamo |
| m(u)ori | morite |
| m(u)oia | m(u)o·iano |

*Past participle*: morto

Other tenses as D 1.

[D 13] **salire**

INDICATIVE

*Present*

| | |
|---|---|
| salgo | saliamo |
| sali | salite |
| sale | sal·gono |

SUBJUNCTIVE

*Present*

| | |
|---|---|
| salga | saliamo |
| salga | saliate |
| salga | sal·gano |

IMPERATIVE

| | |
|---|---|
| — | saliamo |
| sali | salite |
| salga | sal·gano |

Other tenses as D 1.

[D 14] **sparire**

*Past definite*

| | |
|---|---|
| sparii, sparvi | sparimmo |
| sparisti, sparvisti | spariste |
| sparì, sparve | spari·rono, spar·vero |

Other tenses as D 2.

[D 15] **udire**

INDICATIVE

*Present*

| | |
|---|---|
| odo | udiamo |
| odi | udite |
| ode | o·dono |

*Imperfect*: udivo, *etc.*

*Past definite*: udii, *etc.*

*Future*: ud(i)rò, *etc.*

*Conditional*: ud(i)re·i, *etc.*

SUBJUNCTIVE

*Present*

| | |
|---|---|
| oda | udiamo |
| oda | udite |
| oda | o·dano |

*Imperfect*: udissi, *etc.*

IMPERATIVE

| | |
|---|---|
| — | udiamo |
| odi | udite |
| oda | o·dano |

*Gerund*: udendo

*Past participle*: udito

[D 16] **uscire**

INDICATIVE

*Present*

| | |
|---|---|
| esco | usciamo |
| esci | uscite |
| esce | e·scono |

SUBJUNCTIVE

*Present*

| | |
|---|---|
| esca | usciamo |
| esca | usciate |
| esca | e·scano |

IMPERATIVE

| | |
|---|---|
| — | usciamo |
| esci | uscite |
| esca | e·scano |

Other tenses as D 1.

[D 17] **venire**

INDICATIVE

*Present*

| | |
|---|---|
| vengo | veniamo |
| vieni | venite |
| viene | ven·gono |

*Imperfect*: venivo, *etc.*

*Past definite*

| | |
|---|---|
| venni | venimmo |
| venisti | veniste |
| venne | ven·nero |

*Future*: verrò, *etc.*

*Conditional*: verre·i, *etc.*

SUBJUNCTIVE

*Present*

| | |
|---|---|
| venga | veniamo |
| venga | veniate |
| venga | ven·gano |

*Imperfect*: venissi, *etc.*

IMPERATIVE

| | |
|---|---|
| — | veniamo |
| vieni | venite |
| venga | ven·gano |

*Gerund*: venendo

*Present participle*: veniente, vegnente

*Past participle*: venuto

**calere** exists only as *infin.* and in *impers.* cale

**cernere** see **discernere**

**consu·mere** as C8, but used only in 1*st*, 3*rd pers. sing.*, 3*rd pers. pl.* of *past def.* and in *past part.*

**controver·tere** as B1, but *pres. indic.* and *pres. subj.* only.

**conver·gere** as B1, but lacks *past part.*

**delin·quere** as B1, but lacks *past part.*

**diri·mere** as B1, but lacks *past part.*

**discer·nere** as B1, but rare except in *infin. pres. indic.*, *pres. subj.*, *imperf.*

**erọmpere** as C26, but lacks *past part.*

**gire** poet., chiefly found in 3*rd pers. sing. imperf.* giva; *past part.* gito.

**investire** as D1, but lacks *pres. part.*

**ire** exists only as *infin.* and *past part.* ito.

**le·dere** as C3, but chiefly in 3*rd pers. sing.* in simple tenses.

**lucẹre** 3*rd pers. sing.*, *pl. pres. indic.* luce, lucono; *imperf.* luceva, lucevano.

**mọlcere** as B1 but chiefly in 3*rd pers. sing.* in simple tenses; lacks *past part.*

**pentire** as D1, but lacks *pres. part.*

**pru·dere** as B1, but lacks *pres. part.*, *past part.*

**rilu·cere** as C1, but lacks *pres. part.*, *past part.*

**stri·dere** as B1, but lacks *past part.*

**ur·gere** as B1, but lacks *past def.* and *past part.*

**ver·tere** as B1, but chiefly in 3*rd pers. sing.* of simple tenses; lacks *past part.*

**vi·gere** as B1, but chiefly in 3*rd pers. sing.* of simple tenses; lacks *past part.*

# LIST OF VERBS SHOWING PREPOSITIONS USED IN CONSTRUCTION WITH AN INFINITIVE[1]

| | |
|---|---|
| abituare | a |
| accettare | di |
| affrettare | a |
| agognare | a |
| aiutare | a |
| ammonire | di |
| ardire | (di) |
| arrischiare | a |
| aspettare | a, per |
| autorizzare | a |
| avvezzare | a |
| avviare | a |
| badare | a, di |
| bramare | a, di |
| cercare | di |
| cessare | a, di |
| cominciare | a |
| concedere | di |
| conchiudere | di |
| condannare | a |
| condurre | a |
| consentire | a, di |
| consigliare | a, di |
| continuare | a |
| contribuire | a |
| costringere | a |
| credere | di |
| dare | a |
| degnare | di |
| deliberare | di |
| desiderare | (di) |
| determinare | a |
| dichiarare | di |
| dimenticare | di |
| disperare | di |
| disporre | a |
| divertire | a |
| domandare | di |
| eccitare | a |
| esercitare | a |
| esitare | a |
| esortare | a |
| figurare | di |
| fingere | di |
| finire | di |
| forzare | a |
| giustificare | di |
| guardare | di |
| imparare | a |
| impedire | di |
| impegnare | a, di |
| imprendere | a |
| incitare | a |
| inclinare | a |
| incoraggiare | a |
| indugiare | a |
| indurre | a |
| insegnare | a |
| intendere | di |
| invitare | a |
| mancare | di |
| meravigliare | di |
| meritare | di |
| mettere | a |
| muovere | a |
| obbligare | a, di |
| occupare | a |
| offrire | di |
| ordinare | di |
| ostinare | a |
| parere | (di) |
| penare | a |
| pensare | a, di |
| pentire | di |
| permettere | di |
| persistere | a |
| persuadere | a, di |
| pervenire | a |
| preferire | (di) |
| prendere | a |
| preparare | a |
| presumere | di |
| pretendere | di |
| principiare | a |
| procurare | di |
| proibire | di |
| promettere | di |
| proporre | di |
| provare | a |
| rassegnare | a |
| ricordare | di |
| ricusare | di |
| rinunziare | a |
| riuscire | a |
| scongiurare | di |
| scusare | di |
| sdegnare | di |
| sedurre | a |
| seguire | a |
| seguitare | a |
| sembrare | (di) |
| servire | a |
| sfidare | a |
| sforzare | a, di |
| smaniare | di |
| smettere | di |
| sollecitare | a |
| sopportare | di |
| sperare | (di) |
| spingere | a |
| spronare | a |
| stabilire | di |
| stentare | a |
| stimolare | a |
| suggerire | di |
| supplicare | a, di |
| tardare | a |
| temere | di |
| tentare | a, di |
| tornare | a |
| valere | a |
| vantare | di |
| vergognare | a |
| vietare | a |

[1] This list is intended only for ready reference. For more detailed guidance the user should consult the relevant entry in the Dictionary. Brackets round a preposition indicate that its use is optional.

**A**, a *f.*, *m.* the vowel A; the letter A; (tel.) — *come Ancona*, A for Andrew; (fig.) beginning.

**a** *prep.* (before another vowel usually **ad**; *contr. with def. art.*: **al, allo, ai, agli, alla, alle**). **1.** Motion towards (to): *andare — scuola*, to go to school; *andiamo — casa*, let's go home; *prendete — destra*, turn to the right. **2.** Place, Position (at, on, in, near, towards, facing): — *casa*, at home; — *letto*, in bed; — *bordo*, on board; *sto — Roma*, I live in Rome; *al sole*, in the sun; *finestra che dà — mezzogiorno*, window facing south. **3.** Distance: — *dieci miglia da Firenze*, ten miles from Florence. **4.** Time (*a*) Moment, point of time (at, on, upon): *alle cinque*, at five o'clock; *alla domenica*, on Sundays; *al giorno d'oggi*, nowadays. (*b*) Interval of time: *oggi — otto*, a week from today; *addio — domani*, goodbye until tomorrow. **5.** Measurement, quantity, price (in, by, for): *misurare — chili*, to measure in kilos; *vendere alla dozzina*, to sell by the dozen; — *buon mercato*, cheaply; *otto ore al giorno*, eight hours a day. **6.** Method, means (with, by): *chiudere — chiave*, to lock; *campare — pane e acqua*, to live on bread and water; — *forza di*, by dint of. **7.** Result, consequence, extent: *ferito — morte*, mortally wounded; — *piena soddisfazione di*, to the complete satisfaction of. **8.** Construction, material, kind, form: *costruire — mattoni*, to build in brick; *mulino — vento*, wind-mill; *cotto al burro*, cooked in butter. **9.** Manner, condition (as, like, in the style of, with, on): *posa — poeta*, he poses as a poet; *una stanza accomodata — biblioteca*, a room fitted up as a library; — *braccia aperte*, with open arms; — *piedi*, on foot; — *poco — poco*, little by little; — *caso*, at random. **10.** Occasion (upon, at, for): — *tali parole*, upon these words; — *prima vista*, at first sight; *destarsi al più piccolo rumore*, to wake at the slightest noise. **11.** Syntactical uses: (i) In Interjections: *al ladro ! al ladro !*, thief! thief!; — *voi*, your turn, over to you. (ii) Followed by an infinitive: (*a*) expressing purpose after verbs of motion: *andò — vedere*, he went to look; *andiamo — vedere*, let's go and see; (*b*) representing a conditional clause: — *parlar così ti farai detestare*, if you talk like that you will get yourself disliked; (*c*) corresponding to an English participle, esp. after **stare**: *stavo — sedere*, I was sitting; *non staranno molto — tornare*, they won't be long getting back; (*d*) with the historic infinitive: *abbaiò il cane, e tutti — fuggire*, the dog barked and off they all went; (*e*) after an adj: *facile — mentire*, given to lying; *bello — vedersi*, lovely to look at; (*f*) with **essere**, replacing a relative clause: *fu egli — dirmelo*, it was he who told me so.

**a·ba-co** *m.* (*pl.* **-chi**, **-ci**) abacus, calculating frame; (archit.) abacus; (math.) graph.

**abate** *m.* abbot; *stare come un padre —*, to be in clover; cleric, abbé.

**abbac-are** (A2 s) *intr.* (*aux.* avere) to compute, to reckon; to let the thoughts wander. **-one** *m.* day-dreamer.

**abbacchiare** [A4] *tr.* to knock down (fruit, nuts) with a pole; (fig.) to humiliate; to bring down (price); to sell off.

**abbac·chio** *m.* young lamb (slaughtered); lamb (on a menu); (fig.) *fare — di*, to sell off.

**abbacin-are** [A1, A1 s] *tr.* to dazzle; to delude; to dim; to outshine. **-ante** *part. adj.* dazzling; fascinating.

**ab·ba-co** *m.* (*pl.* **-chi**) elementary arithmetic book; abacus, calculating frame (also **abaco**).

**abbagli-are** [A4] *tr.* to dazzle; to fascinate; to delude; to astonish; *stile che -a*, flashy style. **-amento** *m.* glare, dazzle; bewilderment. **-ante** *part. adj.* dazzling; fascinating; confusing; *faro anti-abbagliante*, anti-dazzle lamp.

**abba·gl-io** *m.* (*pl.* **-i**) dazzle; glare; blunder, slip; *prendere un —*, to make a mistake; *per —*, by mistake.

**abbagl-ìo** *m.* (*pl.* **-ìi**) continuous dazzle; spots before the eyes.

**abbai-are** [A4] *intr.* (*aux.* avere) to bark; to bay, to howl; *è can che -a ma non morde*, his bark is worse than his bite; (fig.) to shout, to rant. **-ata** *f.*, **-atura** *f.* bark, barking; baying; (fig.) jeering, booing.

**abbaino** *m.* sky-light; garret-window; dormer-window.

**abb-a·io** *m.* (*pl.* **-a·i**) bark, barking.

**abba-ìo** *m.* (*pl.* **-ìi**) prolonged barking, howling.

**abballare** [A1] *tr.* to make up into parcels; to embale, to pack.

**abbandon-are** (A1 c) *tr.* to abandon; to neglect; to forsake; to let go, to loose; *rfl.* to resign oneself; to lose courage; (*prep.* a) to become addicted (to); to indulge (in). **-ato** *part. adj.* abandoned; forsaken; neglected.

**abbandono** *m.* abandon, abandonment, neglect; *lasciare in —*, to abandon; relinquishing.

**abbarbagli-are** [A4] *tr.* to dazzle; to daze. **-ante** *part. adj.* dazzling.

**abbarbic-are** [A2 s] *rfl.*, *intr.* (*aux.* avere) to strike root; to climb, to cling; (of habit, emotion) to take hold. **-ato** *part. adj.* rooted; clinging; (fig.) inveterate; entrenched.

**abbaruff-are** [A1] *tr.* to rumple; to untidy; *recip. rfl.* to come to blows. **-ato** *part. adj.* untidy; dishevelled, ruffled.

**abbass-are** [A1] *tr.* to lower; to diminish; to reduce; — *i fari*, to dip headlights; to degrade, to abase; *intr.* (*aux.* essere) to lessen; to drop; to sink; *rfl.* to humble oneself; to stoop; to slope. **-a·bile** *adj.* adjustable, detachable.

**abbasso** *adv.* down; below; downstairs; downwards; *giù —*, down below; *stanze d' —*, rooms on the ground floor; *excl.* — *!*, down!

**abbastanza** *adv.* enough; rather, somewhat; pretty, fairly.

**abbat·t-ere** [B1] *tr.* to knock down; to reap; to overthrow; to fell; to kill, to destroy; to abate; to dishearten; *rfl.* to lose heart; to collapse; *-ersi in*, to meet by chance, to run into. **-imento** *m.* dejection; prostration; knocking-down; overthrow; abating.

**abbazi·a** *f.* abbey; abbacy; benefice.

**abbellire** [D2] *tr.* to embellish; to adorn; to enhance.

**abbiente** *adj.* prosperous, well-to-do; *n.m.pl. gli abbienti*, the haves; *i non abbienti*, the have-nots.

**abbigli-are** [A4] *tr.* to dress; to adorn; *rfl.* to dress oneself. **-amento** *m.* manner of dressing, style; attire, apparel; *l'industria dell'-amento*, clothing trade; adornment. **-atoio** *m.* dressing-room.

**abbin-are** [A1] *tr.* to couple, to join; to sort into pairs, **-amento** *m.* combining, grouping; joint venture.

**abbisogn-are** [A5 c] *intr.* (*aux.* avere; *prep.* di) to have need (of); *impers.* to be necessary. **-evole**, **-oso** *adj.* needful; needy, in need.

**abbocc-are** [A2 c] *tr.* to seize with the jaws; to bite; — *l'esca*, to swallow the bait (also fig.); to seize with pincers; to grip; *intr.* (*aux.* avere) — *all'amo*, to nibble at the hook **-amento** *m.* parley, talk; conference.

**abbonacci-are** [A3] *tr.* to calm; to placate; *rfl.* to grow calm; (of weather) to turn fine. **-ato** *part. adj.* calm; serene; placated; (of weather) *è -ato*, the wind has dropped.

**abbon-are**[1] [A1] *tr.* to take out a subscription or season-ticket for; *rfl.* (*prep.* a) to subscribe (to); to take a season-ticket (for). **-amento** *m.* subscription; agreement, contract; *tessera d'-amento*, season-ticket. **-ato** *part. adj.* subscribing; subscribed; *n.m.* subscriber; season-ticket holder.

**abbonare**[2] [A1 d] *tr.* to approve; to credit with; to believe of.

**abbond-are** [A1 c] *intr.* (*aux.* essere) to abound, to be plentiful; to be excessive; (*aux.* avere; *prep.* di, in) to abound (in), to have plenty (of). **-ante** *part. adj.* abounding; rich, fertile; abundant, plentiful, copious; *un pasto -ante*, a good meal; *una pioggia -ante*, a heavy fall of rain; *tre miglia -anti*, a good three miles. **-anza** *f.* abundance; plenty; provisions, victuals. **-ẹvole** *adj.* abundant, plentiful.

**abbon-ire** [D2] *tr.* to calm, to pacify; to appease; to cultivate, to improve (land); *tr.*, *intr.* (*aux.* essere) to ripen; to mature; *rfl.* to grow calm; to be placated. **-imẹnto** *m.* improvement (of land); cultivation; brightening (of weather).

**abbord-are** [A1] *tr.* (naut.) to lay (a ship) alongside; to assault, to ram; (fig.) to approach; to open conversation with; — *un argomento*, to broach a subject. **-a·bile** *adj.* approachable; affable; (of a subject) not too difficult. **-o** *m.* (naut.) boarding; (fig.) *di primo -o*, first of all, at first sight; *di facile -o*, affable.

**abborracci-are** [A3] *tr.* to bungle, to botch; to make a rough sketch of. **-ọne** *m.*, **-ọna** *f.* bungler.

**abbotton-are** [A1 c] *tr.* to button up; *rfl.* to button one's clothes; (fig.) to become reserved; to be secretive. **-ato** *part. adj.* buttoned; (fig.) reserved; secretive; taciturn. **-atura** *f.* buttoning; buttons, row of buttons.

**abbozz-are** [A1] *tr.* to sketch, to make a rough draft of; (fig.) — *un sorriso*, to smile faintly. **-atic·cio** *adj.* sketchy, rough; *n.m.* rough outline; badly finished work. **-atura** *f.* rough sketch.

**abbozzo** *m.* rough sketch, outline; *quaderno per abbozzi*, sketch-book; *in —*, in rough.

**abbracci-are** [A3] *tr.* to embrace; to hug; to encircle; to comprise; — *un consiglio*, to follow advice; — *con lo sguardo*, to take in at a glance; *rfl.* (*prep.* a) to cling (to); to twine (round); *recip. rfl.* to embrace each other. **-ata** *f.* embrace, hug; *un'-ata a tutti*, love to all. **-atutto** *m.*, *f. indecl.* busybody.

**abbrac·cio** *m.* embrace, hug.

**abbrancare**[1] [A2] *tr.* to seize (with claws); to grasp, to catch; to steal; *rfl.* (*prep.* a) to seize; *recip. rfl.* to fight tooth and nail.

**abbrancare**[2] [A2] *tr.* to collect in a drove, to herd together.

**abbrevi-are** [A4] *tr.* to abbreviate; to abridge; to shorten; *per -arla*, to cut a long story short. **-aziọne** *f.* abbreviation; abridgement; sign of abbreviation.

**abbricc-are** [A2] *rfl.* to climb, to clamber; (of plants) to twine. **-a·gnolo** *m.* hold (for climbing); (fig.) cavil, pretext.

**abbriv-are** [A1] *intr.* (*aux.* avere) (naut.) to get under way; *abbriva !*, full speed ahead! **-o** *m.* (naut.) way, course, headway; *pigliare l'-o*, to gather way.

**abbronẓ-are** [A1 c] *tr.* to bronze; to scorch; to tan; to toast; *rfl.* to get brown, to become sunburnt. **-ata** *f.*, **-atura** *f.*, bronzing; suntan. **-ato** *part. adj.* sun-tanned; bronzed; tawny.

**abbronẓ-ire** [D2] *intr.* (*aux.* essere) to become sun-tanned. **-ito** *part. adj.* sun-tanned, brown.

**abbrun-are** [A1] *tr.* to darken; to drape with black (for mourning); *rfl.* to grow dark; to put on mourning. **-ato** *part. adj.* darkened; hung with black; *bandiera -ata*, flag at half-mast.

**abbrun-ire** [D2] *tr.* to bronze, to darken; *rfl.*, *intr.* (*aux.* essere) to darken; to become sun-tanned. **-imẹnto** *m.* darkening; discoloration; sun-tan.

**abbrustol-are** [A1 s], **-ire** [D2] *tr.* to toast (bread); to roast (coffee); to over-cook, to burn; to singe. **-acaffè** *m. indecl.* coffee-roasting machine. **-ato, -ito** *part. adj.* toasted, roasted; scorched; *pane -ato*, toast.

**abbrut-ire** [D2] *tr.* to brutalize; to coarsen; to degrade; *rfl.*, *intr.* (*aux.* essere) to become degraded, to sink to the level of a brute. **-ito** *part. adj.* brutal, cruel; brutish.

**abbuiare** [A4] *tr.* to darken; to tarnish; (fig.) to obscure; to hush up; *rfl.* (of weather) to become overcast; (of a person) to lapse into melancholy; (of a countenance) to cloud, to darken; (of sight) to grow dim.

**abbuono** *m.* handicap, advantage, start; (comm.) allowance, discount.

**abburattare** [A1] *tr.* to sieve, to sift, to bolt; — *le parole*, to choose one's words with care.

**abbuzzire** [D2] *tr.* to cram, to stuff; *rfl.* to over-eat, to stuff oneself.

**abdic-are** [A2 s] *tr.* to abdicate; to renounce, to waive; *intr.* (*aux.* avere; *prep.* a) to abdicate. **-atọre** *m.* abdicator, abdicant. **-aziọne** *f.* abdication, abdicating.

**aberr-are** [A1] *intr.* (*aux.* avere) to err; to go astray; to deviate. **-aziọne** *f.* aberration; error.

**abet-e** *m.* (bot.) fir-tree; **-a·ia** *f.* fir-forest; grove of firs. **-ella** *f.* fir pole; scaffold pole. **-ina** *f.* grove of firs; fir pole.

**abiettare** [A1] *rfl.* to become depraved.

**abietto** *adj.* low, vile; abject; lowly.

**abieziọne** *f.* degradation; abjection; lowly estate.

**a·bile** *adj.* able; capable; clever; skilful; talented; suitable; fit; eligible.

**abilit-à** *f.* (*prep.* a, per) ability, aptitude, skill; cleverness, adroitness; permission, facility, access; *fare — a*, to permit. **-are** (A1 s) *tr.* to qualify, to pass; to train; to enable; *rfl.* to become qualified; to train. **-aziọne** *f.* qualification; diploma, certificate; competency.

**abisso** *m.* ocean deep; sea bottom; abyss; gulf; chasm; (fig.) vast quantity.

**abit-are** [A1 s] *tr.* to populate; to inhabit; to occupy; to frequent; *intr.* (*aux.* avere) to dwell, to reside. **-a·bile** *adj.* habitable, inhabitable; *stanze -abili*, living rooms. **-a·colo** *m.* dwelling; (aeron.) *-acolo del pilota*, cockpit. **-ato** *part. adj.* inhabited; *paese molto -ato*, thickly populated country; *n.m.* inhabited district, built-up area; village, hamlet. **-aziọne** *f.* habitation, residence; *crisi delle -azioni*, housing problem.

**a·bito**[1] *m.* habit, custom; tendency.

**a·bit-o**[2] *m.* clothes, costume; gown; — *completo*, suit of clothes; *-i fatti*, ready-made clothes; — *su misura*, suit made to measure. **-ifi·cio** *m.* clothing-firm, clothiers.

**abituale** *adj.* habitual, usual, customary.

**abitu-are** [A6] *tr.* to accustom, to inure; *rfl.* (*prep.* a) to accustom oneself (to); to get used (to). **-ato** *part. adj.* accustomed, inured.

**abitu·dine** *f.* habit, custom; rule, practice; natural disposition, tendency; *per —*, out of habit.

**abituro** *m.* hovel, poor cottage, hut.

**abiur-a** *f.* (eccl.) abjuration. **-ante** *part. adj.* abjuring; *n.m.*, *f.* abjurer. **-are** [A1] *tr.* to abjure; to renounce formally; to forswear.

**ablativo** *adj.* (gramm.) ablative; — *assoluto*, ablative absolute; (colloq.) *essere ridotto all' — assoluto*, to be penniless.

**abluziọne** *f.* washing, purification; ablution.

**abneg-are** [A2] *tr.* to abnegate, to renounce. **-aziọne** *f.* abnegation, renunciation, sacrifice; self-denial.

**abol-ire** [D2] *tr.* to abolish; to annul; to repeal; to abrogate. **-iziọne** *f.* abolition; cessation; repeal. **-izionịsmo** *m.* abolitionism. **-izionista** *m.*, *f.* abolitionist.

**abomin-are** [A1 s] *tr.* to abominate, to detest. **-a·bile** *adj.* abominable, detestable. **-aziọne** *f.* abomination; detestation. **-ẹvole** *adj.* abominable.

**abomi·nio** *m.* shame, disgrace, abomination.

**abori·g-eno, -ene, -ine** *adj.* aboriginal; indigenous, native; *n.m.pl.* aborigines; natives.

**aborr-ire** [D1, D2] *tr.* to abhor; to loathe; *intr.* (*aux.* avere; *prep.*

da) to have a dread (of), to shrink (from), to feel repugnance (for), to abhor. -**ente** *part. adj.* (*prep.* da) abhorring; unwilling, reluctant.
**abort-ire** [D2] *intr.* (*aux.* avere) to have a miscarriage; (fig.) to miscarry, to fail. -**ivo** *adj.* abortive; (fig.) unfinished.
**abra·dere** [C3] *tr.* to abrade.
**abraṣ-ivo** *adj.*, *n.m.* abrasive. -**iọne** *f.* abrasion.
**ab·sid-e, -a** *f.* (archit.) apse.
**absin·tio** *m.* (bot.) wormwood.
**abuṣ-are** [A1] *intr.* (*aux.* avere; *prep.* di) to misuse, to abuse; to over-indulge (in); to take advantage (of); (with *inf.*, *prep.* in) *-a nel bere*, he drinks too much; *rfl.* (*prep.* di) to take advantage (of). -**ivo** *adj.* improper; irregular; excessive. -**o** *m.* abuse; excessive use; misuse; *-o di confidenza*, breach of confidence; *per -o*, improperly, illicitly; without authorization; *fa -o di caffè*, he drinks too much coffee.
**aca·cia** *f.* (bot.) acacia.
**acagiù** *m. indecl.* (bot.) cashew-nut; — *da mobili*, mahogany.
**acanto** *m.* (bot.) acanthus, bear's breech thistle; (archit.) acanthus leaf.
**acca** *f.*, *m.* the letter H; (fig.) a mere nothing; *non vale un'*—, it's not worth a fig; *non ci capisco un'*—, it's all Greek to me.
**accade·mia** *f.* academy; learned society; college, high school; institute.
**accade·m-ico** *adj.* academic; theoretic; *n.m.* academician; student at an academy. -**ista** *m.*, *f.* pupil at an academy.
**accad-ẹre** [B5] *intr.* (*aux.* essere) to happen, to occur; to befall; *accada quel che accada*, come what may; to be opportune; (with *neg.* or *interrog.*) to be of importance, to be necessary; *non accade*, it is not necessary. -**uto** *part. adj.*; *n.m.* event, occurrence; case, accident.
**accagion-are** [A1 c] *tr.* to accuse, to inculpate; (*prep.* di) to charge (with), to blame (on). -**atọre** *m.* accuser.
**accagliare** [A4] *tr.* to curdle; to cause to coagulate; *rfl.*, *intr.* (*aux.* avere) to curdle; to coagulate.
**accalappi-are** [A4] *tr.* to catch, to ensnare; to trick. -**acani** *m. indecl.* dog-catcher.
**accald-are** [A1] *rfl.* to grow warm; to get over-heated; (fig.) to excite oneself. -**ato** *part. adj.* warm, hot; over-heated; (fig.) excited.
**accalorare** [A1 c] *tr.* to excite; to incite; to heat; *rfl.* to excite oneself; to become animated.
**accamp-are** [A1] *tr.* (mil.) to camp; (fig.) to allege, to assert; to marshal, to set forth; *rfl.*, *intr.* (*aux.* avere) to camp; to pitch one's tent; to go camping. -**amẹnto** *m.* camp; camping; camping-site; *il necessario per l'-amento*, camping equipment.
**accan-ire** [D2] *tr.* to enrage; to infuriate; *rfl.* to become enraged; to persist obstinately. -**imẹnto** *m.* rage; obstinacy. -**ito** *part. adj.* enraged; dogged; *un'-ita resistenza*, a stubborn resistance.
**accanto** *adv.* beside, near, by, nearby; *prep. phr.* — *a*, next to, beside.
**accantonare** [A1 c] *tr.* to set aside, to reserve; to pigeon-hole, to shelve.
**accaparr-are** [A1] *tr.* to engage, to book, to secure (by paying a deposit); to hoard; to corner; (fig.) to gain; to seize. -**atọre** *m.* hoarder.
**accapigli-are** [A4] *recip. rfl.* to scuffle, to tear each other's hair; to squabble. -**atura** *f.* scuffling; squabbling.
**accappatọio** *m.* loose wrap; dressing-gown; bath-robe; beach-wrap.
**accappi-are** [A4] *tr.* to catch in a noose, to lasso; (fig.) to ensnare. -**atura** *f.* slip-knot; noose, lasso.
**accappon-are** [A1 c] *tr.* to caponize, to castrate; *rfl.* (of flesh) to creep; *intr.* (*infin.* after *fare*) *racconti che fanno — la pelle*, stories which make one's flesh creep. -**ato** *part. adj.* castrated; *pelle -ata*, goose-flesh.
**accappucci-are** [A3] *tr.* to put a hood on; *rfl.* to put on a hood, to cover one's head. -**ato** *part. adj.* hooded.
**accarezz-are** [A1 c] *tr.* to caress, to fondle; to stroke, to pat; to cherish (illusion, resentment); to flatter. -**ativo** *adj.* amorous; caressing. -**ato** *part. adj.* caressed; cherished; (of a child) indulged, petted. -**ẹvole** *adj.* caressing, soothing; flattering, coaxing; affectionate.
**accartocciare** [A3] *tr.* to twist into a cone; to wrap up; *rfl.* to curl up; to shrivel.
**accasare** [A1] *tr.* to settle, to marry off (a daughter); *rfl.* to marry, to settle down, to set up house.
**accasciare** [A3] *tr.* to weaken; to crush, to dispirit; *rfl.* to collapse; *accasciarsi su una poltrona*, to sink wearily into an armchair; to lose courage.
**accastellare** [A1] *tr.* to pile, to heap up, to build up into a pyramid.
**accatast-are**[1] [A1] *tr.* to heap, to pile up (wood). -**amẹnto** *m.* stacking, piling; stack, pile.
**accatastare**[2] [A1] *tr.* to register (property) for assessment.
**accatt-are** [A1] *tr.* to beg; to borrow; to scrounge; (fig.) — *lodi*, to look for praise; — *pretese*, to seek excuses; *abs.* to go begging; to collect alms; *essere ridotta ad* —, to be reduced to beggary. -**abriga, -abrighe** *m. indecl.* quarrelsome person; mischief-maker; busybody. -**apane** *m. indecl.* beggar, mendicant. -**eri·a** *f.* begging; beggary. -**ọne** *m.* beggar, mendicant; vagrant.
**accatto** *m.* begging; collecting of alms; amount collected; loan; *campar d'*—, to live by begging; *sapienza d'*—, second-hand knowledge; derivation, borrowing.
**accavalci-are** [A3] *tr.* to bestride. -**ọne, -ọni** *adv.* astride.
**accavallare** [A1] *tr.* to superimpose, to cross (one thing over another); — *le gambe*, to cross one's legs; to stagger, to space; *recip. rfl.* to overlap.
**accecare** [A2 d] *tr.* to blind; to dazzle; to block, to stop up; to scratch out; to blur; to darken; *rfl.*, *intr.* (*aux.* essere) to go blind; (of colours) to fade.
**acce·dere** [B1] *intr.* (*aux.* essere; *prep.* a) to accede; to assent, to agree; to approach.
**acceler-are** [A1 s] *tr.*, *abs.* to accelerate, to quicken; to speed up; *rfl.* to become quicker, to hasten. -**ato** *part. adj.* accelerated; quick; *polso -ato*, rapid pulse; *treno -ato*, slow train; *marcia -ata*, quick march. -**aziọne** *f.* acceleration; quickening, speeding-up.
**accen·d-ere** [C1] *tr.* to light, to kindle; to set fire to; (fig.) to inflame, to excite; to switch on; *l'ora d'— le luci*, lighting-up time; *rfl.* to be kindled; to light up; to catch fire; *-ersi in volto*, to blush; *-ersi d'ira*, to fly into a rage. -**ẹvole, -i·bile** *adj.* inflammable, combustible. -**ino** *m.*, -**isi·garo** *m. indecl.* cigarette-lighter. -**itọio** *m.* pilot-burner. -**itọre** *m.* lighter; *-itore automatico*, cigarette-lighter.
**accenn-are** [A1 c] *tr.*, *intr.* (*aux.* avere; *prep.* a) to nod at; to point at, to indicate; to beckon to; to hint at, to allude to; to mention; (with *infin.*, *prep.* a, di); *il tempo -a di calmarsi*, the weather looks like clearing up. -**ato** *part. adj.* indicated; *su -ato*, above-mentioned.
**accẹnno** *m.* indication, hint, allusion; sign; *un — di*, a touch of.
**accensi·bile** *adj.* inflammable; irascible; touchy.
**accensiọne** *f.* ignition, lighting; *candela d'*—, sparking-plug; flush, high colour; (of colours) brightness, vividness.
**accent-are** [A1] *tr.* to mark with an accent; to accentuate; to emphasize. -**ato** *part. adj.* accented; stressed.
**accento** *m.* accent, pronunciation; stress; emphasis; tone (of voice); (written) accent.
**accentr-are** [A1] *tr.* to centralize; to gather; *rfl.* to become central-

ized; to assemble; to centre; *l'attenzione della stampa si -a su*, the attention of the press is focused on.

**accentu-are** [A6] *tr.* to accentuate; to accent; to stress. **-ato** *part. adj.* accentuated, noticeable; stressed. **-azióne** *f.* accentuation; stress, emphasis.

**accerchi-are** [A4c] *tr.* to encircle; to circumvent; to cheat. **-aménto** *m.* encircling; *politica d'-amento*, policy of encirclement; circuit, tour.

**accerpellato** *adj.* pock-marked, scarred.

**accertare** [A1] *tr.* to ascertain, to verify; to check; to assure; *— la mira*, to take careful aim; *rfl.* (*prep.* di) to assure oneself; *accèrtati*, rest assured.

**accéso** *part. adj.* slight, lit, burning; switched on; bright, vivid; *un radicale —*, a violent Radical.

**accessi·bile** *adj.* accessible; approachable; affable; (of ideas) easily understood.

**accesso** *m.* access; entry; admittance; accessibility; *di facile —*, affable; *— d'ira*, access of rage.

**accessó·rio** *m.* accessory; addition; appurtenance; *pl.* fittings; *adj.* supplementary.

**accétta** *f.* hatchet, chopper; battle-axe; adze.

**accett-are** [A1] *tr.* to accept; to approve, to admit; to agree to; to welcome. **-a·bile** *adj.* acceptable, admissible. **-azióne** *f.* acceptance; reception. **-évole** *adj.* acceptable, pleasing.

**accetto** *adj.* acceptable; welcome; gratifying; *è bene — a tutti*, he is universally liked.

**accezióne** *f.* accepted meaning; significance; acceptation.

**acchetare** [A1] *tr.* to quiet; to lull; to quell; *rfl.* to grow quiet; to be appeased.

**acchiapp-are** [A1] *tr.* to catch, to seize; to net; *fare ad -arsi*, to play tig. **-acani** *m. indecl.* dog-catcher. **-afarfalle** *m. indecl.* butterfly-net. **-atóio** *m.* booby-trap; snare.

**acchiocciolare** [A1s] *tr.* to coil up; to wind (a spring) on a cylinder; *rfl.* to curl oneself up.

**acchito** *m.* (billiards) lead; (fig.) *di primo —*, at once, from the outset.

**ac·cia**[1] *f.* spun hemp or flax.

**ac·cia**[2] *f.* axe; battle-axe.

**acciabatt-are** (A1) *tr.* to botch, to cobble; to patch; to bungle. **-óne** *m.*, **-óna** *f.* bungler.

**acciaccare** (A2) *tr.* to crush, to squash, to squeeze together; to pound; to bruise; (fig.) to beat down; to oppress.

**acciac-co** *m.* (*pl.* **-chi**) infirmity; pain; burden; tribulation. **-cóso** *adj.* infirm, ailing.

**acciaiare** [A4] *tr.* to convert (iron) into steel; (fig.) to steel, to harden.

**accia·i-o** *m.* steel. **-eri·a** *f.* steel-works.

**acciarp-are** [A1] *tr.*, *intr.* (*aux.* avere) to bungle, to botch; to bundle together. **-óne** *m.*, **-óna** *f.* bungler.

**accident-e** *m.* misfortune, casualty; apoplectic fit; accident; unforeseen event; *excl. accidente!* (or) *accidenti!*, the devil! **-ale** *adj.* accidental, fortuitous; incidental, not essential; casual. **-ato** *part. adj.* paralysed, suffering from the effects of a stroke; (of ground) uneven, rough.

**acci·di-a** *f.* indolence, sloth; accidie; exasperation; *far venir l'—*, to exasperate. **-óso** *adj.* indolent, slothful.

**accigli-are** [A4] *rfl.* to frown; to knit one's brows. **-ato** *adj.* frowning; glowering; worried-looking.

**accileccare** [A2c] *tr.* to entice; to trick; to make (false) promises to.

**accin·gere** (C5) *tr.* to gird on; *rfl.* (fig.) to gird up one's loins; *accingersi al lavoro*, to set to work.

**accinto** *part. adj.* girt; ready; disposed.

**acciò, acciocché** *conj.* in order that, so that.

**acciottol-are** [A1s] *tr.* to pave with cobbles; to clatter, to rattle. **-ato** *part. adj.* cobbled; *n.m.* cobbled paving. **-atura** *f.* cobbles, cobbled pavement; cobbling. **-ìo** *m.* (*pl.* **-ii**) clatter, rattle, clashing.

**accipigli-are** [A4] *rfl.* to frown. **-ato** *adj.* frowning; scowling.

**acciuffare** [A1] *tr.* to seize by the hair; to lay hold of; *recip. rfl.* to seize each other by the hair.

**acciug-a** *f.* anchovy; *pasta di acciughe*, anchovy paste; *pigiati come acciughe*, packed like sardines. **-ata** *f.* anchovy sauce; anchovies in oil.

**accivett-are** [A1c] *tr.* to lure; (fig.) to charm, to flatter; to flirt with; to allure. **-ato** *adj.* lured; (fig.) shrewd, experienced.

**acclam-are** [A1] *tr.* to acclaim; to cheer; to proclaim; to elect unanimously; to applaud. **-ato** *part. adj.* acclaimed; applauded; *n.m.* hero, idol. **-azióne** *f.* acclamation; applause; *per -azione*, unanimously.

**acclim-are** [A1], **-atare** [A1], **-atizzare** (A1) *tr.* to acclimatize; *rfl.* to acclimatize oneself, to become acclimatized.

**acclin-e, -o** *adj.* sloping downward.

**accliv-e** *adj.* sloping upward. **-ità** *f.* acclivity, ascent, upward slope.

**acclu·dere** [C3] *tr.* (*prep.* a) to enclose (in a letter).

**acclus-a** *f.* letter enclosed. **-o** *part. adj.* enclosed; *n.m.* enclosure.

**accocc-are** [A2] *tr.* to notch; to fit (an arrow) to the bowstring; (fig.) to let fly; *rfl.* (*prep.* a) to stick (to), to become attached (to). **-ato** *part. adj.* notched; *n.m.* notch.

**accoccol-are** [A1s] *rfl.* to squat; to crouch. **-ato** *part. adj.* squatting; crouched.

**accod-are** [A1c] *tr.* to fasten head to tail (of animals walking in line); to arrange in single file; to set in a row; *rfl.* (*prep.* a) to tail after; to tag on, to fall in behind. **-ato** *part. adj.* in single file, tagging along behind.

**acco·gli-ere** [B7] *tr.* to receive, to accept; to contain; to welcome; *— una domanda*, to grant a request. **-ente** *part. adj.* hospitable, welcoming, cordial; comfortable; cosy. **-enza** *f.* reception; welcome; *fare -enza a*, to welcome. **-ménto** *m.* reception; acceptance; granting.

**acco·lito** *m.* (eccl.) acolyte; (fig.) devotee.

**accollare** [A1] *tr.* (*prep.* di) to load; to charge; to yoke; (fig.) to burden, to saddle (with).

**accollo** *m.* weight, burden; (fig.) commitment; contract.

**accolta** *f.* assemblage, assembly, gathering.

**accoltell-are** [A1] *tr.* to knife, to stab. **-atóre** *m.* ruffian, cut-throat.

**accom(m)iat-are** [A1] *tr.* to dismiss, to send away; *rfl.* to say good-bye; *-arsi da*, to take leave of; *recip. rfl.* to part. **-atura** *f.* dismissal; leave-taking, farewell.

**accomod-are** [A1s] *tr.* to fix, to repair; to patch up; to put in order, to tidy; to deck out; to lodge; to reach agreement concerning; *-arla*, to get out of a scrape; *— le uova nel panierino*, to make the most of one's means; (iron. colloq.) to settle, to deal with; *intr.* (*aux.* avere) to be pleasing, to suit; to be convenient; to be obliging; *rfl.* to accommodate oneself; to make oneself comfortable; to take a seat; *s'-i*, do sit down, please come in, please come this way; *recip. rfl.* to come to an agreement. **-a·bile** *adj.* adjustable; alterable; *la cosa è -abile*, the matter can be settled. **-aménto** *m.* agreement; compromise; settlement; adjustment. **-ante** *part. adj.* accommodating; peaceable, easy-going.

**accompagn-are** [A5] *tr.* to accompany; to attend; to wait upon; to escort; to match; to class together; *rfl.* (*prep.* a) to keep company with, to join; *questa salsa s'-a bene con la carne fredda*, this sauce goes well with cold meat; *recip. rfl.* to match, to be in keeping, to go well together

**-amęnto** *m.* accompaniment; procession, retinue, escort. **-atǫre** *m.* companion escort; accompanist. **-atura** *f.* escort; *essere d'-atura,* to match, to suit.

**accomunare** [A1] *tr.* to join, to unite; to share in common; to throw open to all; *rfl.* (*prep.* a, con) to be on equal terms (with); to mingle with.

**acconci-are** [A3 c] *tr.* to arrange, to put in order; to adorn, to attire; (iron. colloq.) to fix. to settle; (fig.) — *le uova nel paniere,* to make the most of one's means; *rfl.* to deck oneself out; to adapt oneself; to compose oneself. **-atura** *f.* arrangement; hair-style; head-dress; attire.

**acconcime** *m.* (usu. *pl.*) minor repairs (of buildings); restoration.

**accǫncio** *adj.* fit, proper, suitable; serviceable; *n.m.* suitability, opportuneness; *venire in* —, to be opportune.

**accondiscęndere** [C1] *intr.* (*aux.* avere; *prep.* a) to yield, to comply; to agree, to admit; to condescend.

**acconsent-ire** [D1] *intr.* (*aux.* avere) to consent; to approve; to assent; *tr.* to allow, to permit. **-imęnto** *m.* consent, approval; assent.

**accontentare** [A1] *tr.* to meet the wishes of, to gratify; to content; *rfl.* (*prep.* di) to be content (with).

**accǫnto** *m.* instalment; part payment; *pagare in* —, to pay on account.

**accoppiare** [A4] *tr.* to couple, to pair; to match; to yoke; to combine; (colloq.) to join in marriage, to hitch.

**accor-are** [A1 d, A1] *tr.* to stab through the heart; (fig.) to grieve, to pierce to the heart; *rfl.* to grieve, to be heart-broken. **-amęnto** *m.* heart-ache; heart-felt sentiment. **-ante** *part. adj.* heart-rending. **-ato** *part. adj.* heart-broken; *una melodia -ata,* a melancholy tune.

**accorci-are** [A3 c] *tr.* to shorten; to abbreviate; to abridge; *rfl.*, *intr.* (*aux.* essere) to become shorter; to shrink. **-ativo** *adj.* reducible; *n.m.* abbreviation; diminutive. **-atǫia** *f.* short cut.

**accord-are** [A1] *tr.* to grant, to accord; to match (colours); (gramm.) to make agree; (mus.) to tune; (radio) to tune; *intr.* (*aux.* essere) to be in tune; *rfl.* *-arsi per,* to agree to; *recip. rfl.* to concur; to agree. **-anza** *f.* agreement, accord. **-atǫre** *m.* tuner (of instruments).

**accordess-are** [A1] *tr.* to twist. **-ato** *part. adj.* twisted; *n.m.* ribbed cloth; corduroy.

**accor·dio, accor·dion** *m.* accordion.

**accordo** *m.* accord, agreement; *essere d'-,* to agree; *andare d'-,* to get on well together; *d'— !,* agreed!; arrangement, convention; *un — commerciale,* a trade agreement; *stare agli accordi,* to stand by the agreement; (mus.) chord; *d'—,* in tune; (gramm.) agreement, concordance; (radio) tuning, syntonization.

**accor·g-ere** [C5] *rfl.* (*prep.* di) to perceive, to notice; to become aware (of). **-imęnto** *m.* perception; shrewdness; expedient, device.

**accǫrrere** [C5 c] *intr.* (*aux.* essere) to run, to run up; to hasten; to run together; to run to help.

**accort-o** *part. adj.* shrewd, wise, sagacious; wary; suspicious; *fare — di,* to caution against; *stare* —, to be on the alert. **-ęzza** *f.* shrewdness, sagacity; alertness.

**accosci-are** [A4] *rfl.* to squat; to crouch. **-ato** *part. adj.* squatting; crouched.

**accost-are** [A1] *tr.* to bring close together, to bring near; to be in close attendance on; to approach; *nessuno l'-a,* no one will have anything to do with him; *intr.* (*aux.* essere) to be close-fitting; *questa porta non -a bene,* this door does not shut properly; (of food) to be sustaining; *rfl.* (*prep.* a) to approach, to draw near; to adhere to (an opinion). **-a·bile** *adj.* approachable; affable. **-ante** *part. adj.* sustaining, restorative; corroborative.

**accosto** *adv.* alongside, near at hand, nearby; *la casa* —, the house next door; *d'—,* close by; *prep.* — *a,* next to, near; *n.m.* supporter; support.

**accostum-are** [A1] *tr.* to accustom; to inure; *rfl.* (*prep.* a) to accustom oneself; to get used (to); to get into the habit (of). **-ato** *part. adj.* accustomed; well-bred; well-mannered.

**accovacciare** [A3] *rfl.* to crouch; to hide; to run into a lair; to curl up (of animals) for sleep.

**accozz-are** [A1] *tr.* to jumble together; to amass; to shuffle (cards); *rfl.* to foregather, to meet; to assemble; to conspire; to clash. **-a·glia** *f.* crowd, medley, hurly-burly. **-amęnto** *m.* jumble, muddle; heap.

**accozzo** *m.* jumble, medley; combination.

**accredit-are** [A1 sc] *tr.* to credit; to confirm; to accredit; *rfl.* to gain credit, to gain ground (of rumour). **-a·bile** *adj.* (comm.) to be credited. **-ato** *part. adj.* accredited; recognized; having credentials; reliable.

**accręsc-ere** [B9 c] *tr.* to increase, to augment, to amplify; *rfl.* to grow, to multiply. **-imęnto** *m.* increase; enlargement.

**accucciare** [A3] *rfl.* (of a dog) to lie down, to curl up for sleep; to crouch; to sit.

**accud-ire** [D2] *intr.* (*aux.* avere; *prep.* a) to attend (to); to be responsible (for). **-ienza** *f.* activity of caretaker, keeper or supervisor.

**accumul-are** [A1 s] *tr.* to accumulate; to heap, to amass; to store; *abs.* to make money. **-a·bile** *adj.* accumulative. **-atǫre** *m.* hoarder; collector; accumulator. **-aziǫne** *f.* accumulation; heap, mass.

**accupire** [D2] *rfl.* to grow sad; to become gloomy.

**accur-ato** *adj.* done with care; thorough; *lavoro* —, careful work, work done diligently; (of a person) meticulous, scrupulous, careful, diligent; tidy, well-groomed. **-atęzza** *f.* diligence, care; thoroughness.

**accuṣa** *f.* charge, accusation.

**accuṣ-are** [A1] *tr.* (*prep.* di) to accuse, to charge; to blame; to acknowledge; to report; to complain of; *il malato -a un dolore al lato sinistro,* the patient complains of a pain on his left side; (at cards) to call; (comm.) — *ricevuta di,* to acknowledge receipt of. **-ata** *f.* (at cards) call, declaration.

**accuṣativo** *adj.* (gramm.) accusative; *n.m.* accusative case.

**ace·falo** *adj.* acephalous; headless; lacking a beginning.

**acerb-o** *adj.* unripe; sour; tart, pungent; immature; green; *n.m.* sour part; sourness; (fig.) immaturity; harshness. **-ęzza** *f.*, **-ità** *f.* unripeness; sourness; (fig.) severity, harshness.

**a·cero** *m.* (bot.) maple-tree.

**acęt-o** *m.* vinegar; *pigliare l'—,* to turn to vinegar, to go sour; (fig.) *pigliare d'—,* to be piqued. **-are** (A1 c) *tr.* to turn to vinegar, to make sour; to season with vinegar. **-ato** *part. adj.* sour; smelling of vinegar. **-ino** *adj.* sour, vinegarish; *n.m.pl.* gherkins; pickels. **-ire** (D2) *intr.* (*aux.* avere) to go sour. **-o·lio** *m.* cruet. **-ǫso** *adj.* acid, sour. **-ume** *m.* acidity, sourness; pickles.

**a·cid-o** *m.* sourness, acidity; (chem.) acid; — *azotico,* nitric acid; *adj.* acid, sour. **-are** (A1 s) *tr.* to etch. **-ęzza** *f.* sourness. **-ità** *f.* acidity. **-ume** *m.* sour matter.

**a·cino** *m.* pip, grape-stone; grape; berry: kernel.

**acme** *f.* acme, highest point.

**acqu-a** *f.* water; rain; *ho preso molt'—,* I've got soaking wet; *che non assorbe l'—,* waterproof; fluid, liquid; waters; sea; current, stream. FIGURATIVE AND PROVERBIAL USE: *innocente come l'—,* as innocent as a newborn babe; *lasciar andar l'— per la sua china,* to let things take their course; *è*

*passata molt'— sotto i ponti*, a lot of water has flowed under the bridges; *portare — al mare*, to carry coals to Newcastle; *rassomigliarsi come due gocce d'—*, to be as like as two peas; *fuggir l'— sotto le grondaie*, out of the frying pan into the fire. **-ata** *f.* sudden storm, squall; cistern. **-a·tico** *adj.* aquatic. **-azzọne** *m.* downpour, cloud-burst. **-erella** *f.*, **-eru·giola** *f.* light shower; fine rain, drizzle. **-olina** *f.* light shower; fine rain, drizzle; flow of saliva; *far venire l'-olina in bocca*, to make one's mouth water. **-ọso** *adj.* watery.

**acquafort-e** *f.* (art) etching; (chem.) acquafortis, nitric acid. **-ista** *m., f.* etcher.

**acqua·io** *m.* kitchen-sink.

**acquapendente** *m.* slope, incline.

**acquaplan-o** *m.* surf-board. **-ista** *m., f.* surf-rider.

**acquara·gia** *f.* turpentine.

**acquattare** [A1] *rfl.* to crouch, to cower; to squat; to hide.

**acquavite** *f.* rough brandy.

**acquedọtto** *m.* aqueduct; waterworks; water company; water main.

**ac·queo** *adj.* aqueous, watery; *vapore —*, steam.

**acquerell-are** [A1] *tr.* to paint in water-colour. **-ista** *m., f.* painter in water-colour. **-o** *m.* water-colour painting.

**acquie·sc-ere** [B1] *intr.* (*aux.* avere; *prep.* a) to acquiesce. **-ente** *part. adj.* acquiescent, resigned. **-enza** *f.* acquiescence.

**acquietare** [A1] *tr.* to quieten; to appease, to placate; *rfl.* to become quiet, to calm oneself; to resign oneself; to be appeased; (of a storm) to die down.

**acquirente** *m., f.* (comm.) purchaser, consumer; client.

**acquist-are** [A1] *tr.* to acquire, to obtain; to buy; (fig.) *— tempo*, to gain time; *— terreno*, to make headway; to win, to gain; to incur; *abs.* to make progress; to succeed. **-a·bile** *adj.* obtainable. **-atọre** *m.* obtainer; buyer.

**acquist-o** *m.* acquisition; purchase; profit, gain, advantage; increase; *far degli -i*, to shop; *— d'occasione*, bargain; *potere d'—*, purchasing power; (comm.) *addetto ufficio -i*, buyer.

**acquitrin-o** *m.* morass; bog, fen, marsh; water oozing from the ground, flush. **-ọso** *adj.* boggy, marshy; sodden.

**acr-e** *adj.* sharp, pungent; sour; bitter; acrid; (fig.) austere; acrimonious. **-e·dine** *f.* sourness; bitterness; severity.

**acrimo·ni-a** *f.* acrimony; harshness; sourness. **-ọso** *adj.* acrimonious.

**acro** *m.* acre.

**acro·b-ata** *m.* acrobat; (fig.) clever, skilful person; one who stunts. **-a·tico** *adj.* acrobatic. **-atịsmo** *m.* acrobatics; *fare dell'-atismo*, to be an acrobat; (fig.) to stunt. **-azi·a** *f.* acrobatics; *-azie di volo*, stunt flying, aerobatics.

**acro·stico** *adj., n.m.* acrostic.

**acu-ire** [D2] *tr.* to sharpen; to make acute; to whet, to stimulate. **-ità** *f.* sharpness; acuteness; alertness. **-itivo** *adj.* stimulating, exciting.

**acu·leo** *m.* sharp point; sting; prickle; thorn; goad; (fig.) incentive; stinging comment, sarcasm.

**acume** *m.* sharpness, acumen; perspicacity; insight.

**acu·stic-o** *adj.* acoustic; *corno —*, ear-trumpet. **-a** *f.* acoustics.

**acut-o** *adj.* pointed, sharp; acute; shrewd; keen, eager; piercing; shrill; *freddo —*, intense cold. **-ẹzza** *f.* acuteness; shrewdness; *-ezza d'ingegno*, insight.

**adagi-are** [A3] *tr.* to set gently down; to make comfortable; to place in a reclining position; *rfl.* to lie down; to stretch oneself out; to make oneself comfortable; *-arsi sugli allori*, to rest on one's laurels. **-a·bile** *adj.* adjustable. **-ato** *part. adj.* comfortable; slow; well-to-do.

**ada·gio**[1] *adv.* slowly; softly, quietly; in a low voice; carefully; (mus.) adagio.

**ada·gio**[2] *m.* adage, proverb.

**adamant-e** *m.* adamant, impregnable hardness; diamond. **-ino** *adj.* adamantine.

**adami·tico** *adj.* pertaining to Adam; primitive; *in costume —*, naked.

**adastare** [A1] *tr.* to incite; to urge; *rfl.* to hurry.

**adatt-are** [A1] *tr.* to adapt, to fit; to adjust; *rfl.* (*prep.* a) to fit; to suit; to resign oneself; *bisogna -arci*, we must make the best of it; to conform (to); *-arsi a qualunque lavoro*, to turn one's hand to any work. **-a·bile** *adj.* adaptable. **-amẹnto** *m.* adaptation, arrangement; modification; *capacità d'-amento*, adaptability. **-azịone** *f.* adaptation.

**adatt-o** *adj.* (*prep.* a) fit (for); qualified; suited; *— al mare*, seaworthy; suitable; proper; disposed. **-ẹzza** *f.* aptness, suitability.

**addare** [A8] *rfl.* (*prep.* di) to perceive, to notice, to become aware of; (*prep.* a) to begin; to be engaged (in); to devote oneself (to).

**addẹbit-o** *m.* accusation, imputation; (comm.) debit entry. **-are** [A1 sc] *tr.* to accuse, to inculpate; (*prep.* di) to charge (with); (*prep.* a) to impute (to); (comm.) to debit.

**addendo** *m.* sum, tot, figures to be added; addition to be made.

**addensare** [A1] *tr.* to thicken; to make dense; to condense; *rfl.* to thicken; to grow dense; to gather, to crowd.

**addent-are** [A1] *tr.* to seize with the teeth; to bite; to dovetail, to mortise, to cog; (fig.) to assail; to censure; to carp at. **-ellare** [A1] *tr.* (archit.) to leave (the end of a wall) toothed. **-ellato** *part. adj.* (archit.) toothed; (fig.) unfinished; *n.m.* (archit.) toothed wall-end; (fig.) pretext; *pl. gli -ellati*, things pertaining, kindred subjects.

**addentrare** [A1 c] *tr.* to thrust, to drive in; to put in; *rfl.* to enter, to penetrate; to study deeply, to become immersed.

**addẹntro** *adv.* inside, within; well in; deeply; *essere — in*, to have inside information about; to be well versed in.

**addestr-are** [A1] *tr.* to train; to instruct; to inure; to discipline; to break in (a horse); *rfl.* (*prep.* a, in) to exercise; to practise; to train oneself; to become skilled. **-amẹnto** *m.* training; instruction; drilling. **-atọre** *m.*, **-atrice** *f.* trainer.

**addẹtto** *adj.* employed, assigned; forming part, belonging; *è — al reparto esportazioni*, he has a job in the export department; given over; occupied; *stanze addette all'amministrazione*, rooms assigned to the management; *n.m.* attaché; *— Stampa*, Press attaché.

**addietro** *adv.* behind; ago, before, previously; *tempo —*, some time ago; *molti anni —*, many years before; *due pagine —*, two pages back; (of a clock) *essere —*, to be slow; *n.m.* rear, hind part; stern; past; *per l'—*, formerly.

**add-i·o** *excl., n.m.* (*pl.* **ii**) goodbye, farewell, adieu; parting; *parola d'—*, parting word; *fare —* to wave good-bye.

**addire** [B10] *tr.* to dedicate, to assign, to allot; *rfl.* (*prep.* a) to be fitting, to be proper; to suit, to be becoming; to be to the taste (of); to dedicate oneself.

**addirittura** *adv.* directly, immediately, without more ado; simply; quite, absolutely; downright, frankly.

**addirizzare** [A1] *tr.* to straighten; to set up; to set right; to remedy; *— le gambe ai cani*, to attempt the impossible; *rfl.* to stand erect.

**additare** [A1] to indicate; to point out; to denote; to be indicative of; to disclose.

**additivo** *adj., n.m.* additive.

**addivenire** [D17] *intr.* (*aux.* essere) to become; to occur; to come (to); *— ad un accordo*, to reach an agreement: to consent (to).

**addizi̩on-e** *f.* addition; total; supplement. **-ale** *adj.* additional, supplementary. **-are** [A1 c] *tr.* to add up; to add; *-are di,* to supplement with; *-are X di Y* to add *Y* to *X.* **-atrice** *f.* adding machine.

**addobb-are** [A1] *tr.* to decorate; to furnish; to garnish; *rfl.* to deck oneself out. **-atọre** *m.,* **-atrice** *f.* decorator, upholsterer. **-o** *m.* ornament; decoration; *pl.* hangings, bunting.

**addolc-ire** [D2] *tr.* to sweeten; (fig.) to soften; to soothe; to alleviate; to civilize; *rfl.* to become sweet; to be appeased; to grow mild; to be assuaged. **-itivo** *adj.* sweetening; soothing; softening.

**addolor-are** [A1 c] *tr.* to grieve, to sadden; to pain; to afflict; *rfl.* (*prep.* di, per) to grieve; to mourn; to regret; to be sorry. **-ato** *part. adj.* sorrowful, grieved; sorry, regretful.

**addo·m-e** *m.* abdomen. **-inale** *adj.* abdominal.

**addomestic-are** [A2 s] *tr.* to tame; to train; to domesticate; to refine; to improve by cultivation; *rfl.* to become tame; to become sociable; *-arsi con,* to get to know, to become friendly with. **-atọre** *m.,* **-atrice** *f.* tamer, trainer.

**addomestichẹvole** *adj.* tameable, capable of being domesticated.

**addorment-are** [A1 c] *tr.* to send to sleep, to make sleepy; — *un bambino con le canzoni,* to sing a child to sleep; to lull; to numb, to deaden; to beguile; *rfl.* to fall asleep; to grow numb; to be inactive; *-arsi sugli allori,* to rest on one's laurels. **-ativo** *adj.* soporific. **-atọre** *m.* bore; *-atore di serpenti,* snake-charmer.

**addoss-are** [A1] *tr.* to put on (clothing); to pile, to heap; to load, to burden; (*prep.* a) to lay (upon); to attribute (to); to entrust (to); — *le spese (a),* to charge expenses (to); *rfl.* (*acc.* of *rfl. prn., prep.* a) to lean against; (*dat.* of *rfl. prn.*) to undertake; *-arsi un debito,* to take over liability for a debt; *recip. rfl.* to stand back to back; to jostle. **-ata** *f.* fitting, trying-on.

**addosso** *prep. adv.* on, upon; on one's back; close up against; *avere* —, to be burdened with; *tirarsi* —, to bring on oneself; *portare* —, to wear; *gli furono subito* —, they fell on him at once; *levarsi i panni d'*—, to undress.

**addottrin-are** [A1] *tr.* to instruct, to teach; to indoctrinate; *rfl.* to learn; to teach oneself; to become learned; (iron.) to learn wisdom. **-atura** *f.* instruction, indoctrination.

**addurre** [B2] *tr.* to allege; to quote; to adduce.

**adeguare** [A6 c] *tr.* to equalize; — *le spese all'entrate,* to keep within one's budget; to smooth out; — *al suolo,* to raze to the ground; *rfl.* (*prep.* a) to become equal (to); to become adjusted.

**adeguato** *adj.* adequate; proportionate; fitting; right, fair; *prezzo* —, reasonable price.

**adempiere** [D11], **ademp-ire** [D11] *tr.* to accomplish; to fulfil; to satisfy; to execute, to put into effect; *intr.* (*aux.* avere; *prep.* a) to fulfil, to carry out; — *ad un impegno,* to meet an obligation; *rfl.* to be fulfilled, to come to pass. **-imẹnto** *m.* fulfilment, realization; accomplishment.

**ader-ire** [D2] *intr.* (*aux.* avere; *prep.* a) to adhere; to be an adherent; to support; to assent (to). **-ente** *adj.* sticking; adhesive; relevant; (of clothes) close-fitting; *n.m.* adherent; supporter. **-enza** *f.* adherence; (motor.) wheel grip; (med.) adhesion; *pl.* connexions, contacts, influence. **-imẹnto** *m.* adherence; assent.

**adescare** [A2 c] *tr.* to lure; to bait; to decoy; (eng.) to prime (a pump).

**adesiọn-e** *f.* adherence; adhesion; *-i ad una società,* members of a society; approval, assent; support; formal acceptance (of an invitation).

**adeṣiv-o** *adj.* adhesive; sticky. **-ità** *f.* adhesiveness.

**ade·spot-a, -o** *adj.* without an owner; anonymous, of unknown authorship.

**addesso** *adv.* now, at the present moment; *è uscito* —, he's just gone out; *uomini d'*—, men of today; *per* —, for the present; — *si spiega !,* so that's it!

**adiac-ente** *adj.* (foll. by *prep.* a) adjacent, adjoining; nearby; contiguous. **-enza** *f.* adjacency; *pl.* vicinity, neighbourhood.

**adibire** [D2] *tr.* to destine; to reserve; to convert; — *una stanza ad uso di cucina,* to convert a room as a kitchen.

**a·dip-e** *m.* fat, corpulence; *adj.* fat, corpulent. **-osità** *f.* adiposity. **-ọso** *adj.* adipose, fat.

**adir-are** [A1] *tr.* to enrage, to anger; to vex; *rfl.* to get angry; to take offence; *recip. rfl.* to quarrel, to fall out. **-ato** *part. adj.* enraged, angry; *fare l'-ato,* to be angry, to sulk.

**a·dito** *m.* entry, entrance; access.

**adocchiare** [A4] *tr.* to set eyes on; to catch a glimpse of; to eye; to covet.

**adolesc-ente** *adj.* adolescent; *n.m.* lad, youth; *f.* adolescent girl. **-enza** *f.* boyhood; girlhood; teenage, teens; adolescence.

**adombrare** [A1 c] *tr.* to shade; to darken; to adumbrate, to outline; *rfl.* (of horses) to shy; (of persons) to take umbrage.

**adont-are** [A1 c] *tr.* to reproach; to offend; *rfl.* to take umbrage. **-ọso** *adj.* touchy.

**adop-erare** [A1 s], **adopr-are** [A1] *tr.* to use, to employ; to engage the services of; to exert, to spend; *rfl.* to exert oneself; *-arsi per,* to work for, to aim at; to strive, to endeavour.

**ador-are** [A1 c] *tr.* to adore; to love passionately; to revere; to worship; *intr.* (*aux.* avere; *prep.* a) to pray to, to pay worship to. **-a·bile** *adj.* adorable, lovable; charming; worthy of worship. **-ante** *part. adj.* adoring; worshipping; *n.m., f.* adorer, worshipper. **-aziọne** *f.* adoration; worship; veneration.

**adorn-are** [A1 c] *tr.* to adorn, to decorate; to embellish, to enhance; *rfl.* to adorn oneself; (fig.) to boast. **-amẹnto** *m.* adornment; ornament; decoration, trimming.

**adọrn-o** *adj.* ornate; adorned, decorated. **-ẹzza** *f.* ornateness.

**adott-are** [A1] *tr.* to adopt; to accept; to have recourse to; — *una decisione,* to take a decision. **-ativo** *adj.,* **-ato** *part. adj.* adopted; adoptive. **-ivo** *adj.* adoptive, by adoption.

**adoziọne** *f.* adoption; *figliuolo d'*—, adopted son; acceptance, choice.

**aduggi-are** [A3] *tr.* to overshadow; to darken; to sully; to sadden; to hinder; to blight; *rfl., intr.* (*aux.* essere) to be darkened; to grow sad; to be stultified; to become embittered. **-ato** *part. adj.* shady, overshadowed; *luogo -ato,* sunless spot.

**adu·glia** *f.* twist, turn; *un'— di cavo,* a coil of a cable.

**adul-are** [A1] *tr.* to adulate; to fawn upon; to flatter; *rfl.* to flatter oneself; to be conceited. **-atọre** *m.,* **-atrice** *f.* flatterer, adulator; *adj.* flattering. **-ato·rio** *adj.* adulatory; complimentary; flattering. **-aziọne** *f.* adulation; flattery.

**adulterare** [A1 s] *tr.* to adulterate; to contaminate; to falsify; to debase; to counterfeit.

**adulte·rio** *m.* adultery.

**adul·ter-o** *m.* adulterer; *adj.* adulterous. **-a** *f.* adulteress. **-ino** *adj.* born of adultery, adulterine.

**adulto** *adj.* adult; advanced; full-grown; *n.m.* adult, grown-up.

**adun-are** [A1] *tr.* to assemble, to gather together; to summon, to muster; to convene; to contain, to comprise; *rfl.* to assemble, to congregate, to combine. **-anza** *f.* assembly, meeting; board; *indire un'-anza,* to call a meeting. **-ata** *f.* gathering, assembly; (mil.) parade, rally; fall-in. **-ato** *part. adj.* gathered together,

assembled; *n.m.pl. gli -ati*, the assembly, those present.

**adun-co** *adj.* (*m.pl.* **-chi**) hooked; curved; crooked; *naso* —, hook nose.

**adunghiare** [A4] *tr.* to claw, to clutch; to seize.

**aduṣ-are** [A1] *tr.* to accustom; *rfl.* to accustom oneself. **-o** *adj.* accustomed.

**adust-o** *adj.* scorched; dried up; sunburnt; sun-drenched; dry, thin, wiry. **-are** [A1] *tr.* to parch, to dry up. **-ẹzza** *f.* dryness; aridity. **-iọne** *f.* burning, scorching; combustibility.

**aer-are** [A1] *tr.* to air, to ventilate, to aerate. **-ag·gio** *m.* ventilation. **-aziọne** *f.* airing, ventilation. **-emoto** *m.* wind-storm, hurricane. **-o·foro** *m.* air-conditioner. **-ọso** *adj.* airy.

**a·ere** *m.* (poet.) air; sky; atmosphere; — *chiaro*, daylight; — *bruno*, night.

**ae·re-o** *adj.* pertaining to air; aerial, ethereal; airy, unsubstantial; *ferrovia -a*, overhead railway; *posta -a*, air mail; *forze -e*, Air Force; *n.m.* aircraft; outdoor aerial.

**aer-odina·mica** *f.* aerodynamics. **-o·dine** *f.* glider. **-o·dromo** *m.* aerodrome. **-ofotografi·a** *f.* air photography. **-ogramma** *m.* air-letter. **-oli·nea** *f.* air-line. **-ona·uta** *m.* pilot. **-ona·utica** *f.* aeronautics; air-force. **-ona·utico** *adj.* aeronautical. **-oplano** *m.* aeroplane. **-oporto** *m.*, **-oscalo** *m.* airport.

**af-a** *f.* sultriness; oppressive heat; breathlessness; tedium; *fare — a*, to suffocate; to bore. **-ọso** *adj.* sultry, suffocating.

**affa·bil-e** *adj.* affable; courteous; kind. **-ità** *f.* affability.

**affaccend-are** [A1] *tr.* to give employment to, to occupy; *rfl.* to be busily occupied, to bustle about; (*prep.* a, dietro a) to busy oneself (with). **-ato** *part. adj.* busy; bustling; fussy. **-ìo** *m.* continual bustling.

**affacchin-are** [A1] *tr.* to overwork; to slave-drive; *rfl.* to labour, to drudge. **-ato** *part. adj.* weary; overworked.

**affacciare** [A3] *tr.* to hold up; to present, to show; *rfl.* to show oneself; to put in an appearance; to stand forth; *affacciarsi alla finestra*, to appear at the window.

**affagott-are** [A1] *tr.* to roll up into a bundle; to make into faggots; *rfl.* to bundle oneself up; to dress carelessly. **-ato** *part. adj.* bundled up; carelessly dressed.

**affaldare** [A1] *tr.* to pleat; to fold; *rfl.* to become wrinkled.

**affam-are** [A1] *tr.* to starve; to reduce to hunger; *intr.* (*aux.* essere) to be hungry. **-ato** *part. adj.* hungry, famished; voracious; *n.m.pl. gli -ati*, the hungry, the poor.

**affann-are** [A1] *tr.* to make breathless; to distress; to vex; to make uneasy; *rfl.* to be breathless; to busy oneself; to do one's utmost; (*prep.* dietro a) to strive after. **-ato** *part. adj.* uneasy; breathless; distressed.

**affann-o** *m.* heavy breathing; panting; palpitation; exertion; anguish; *darsi* —, to take trouble. **-ọne** *m.* (colloq.) busybody, meddler. **-ọso** *adj.* (of breathing) troubled; wearisome; hurried; incessant; anguished; (fig.) feverish.

**affardellare** [A1] *tr.* to tie up into a bundle; to pack; (mil.) — *lo zaino*, to pack one's kit.

**affar-e** *m.* affair, matter; *è — fatto*, that's settled; *un bell'— !*, a nice mess!; *badate ai vostri -i*, mind your own business; bargain; — *di cuore*, love affair; importance; moment; thing, thingummy; *pl.* business; *uomo d'-i*, business man; *-i esteri*, foreign affairs. **-ìo** *m.* bustle, activity. **-iṣmo** *m.* speculation; sharp practice. **-ista** *m.* profiteer, shark. **-ọne** *m.* bargain, good stroke of business.

**affascin-are** [A1 s] *tr.* to enchant, to bewitch; to fascinate; to attract. **-amẹnto** *m.* fascination; seduction; evil eye; enchantment, spell. **-ante** *part. adj.* fascinating; attractive; bewitching. **-atọre** *m.* lady-killer, charmer; sorcerer. **-atrice** *f. femme fatale*; enchantress.

**affastell-are** [A1] *tr.* to tie into bundles; to jumble, to confuse. **-ìo** *m.* confusion, muddle, chaos.

**affatic-are** [A2] *tr.* to fatigue, to weary; to strain; to exhaust; *rfl.* to toil, to strive; to tire. **-ante** *part. adj.* fatiguing; wearisome. **-ato** *part. adj.* tired, weary; exhausted.

**affatto** *adv.* quite, wholly; absolutely; not at all; *niente* —, nothing at all.

**affatturare** [A1] *tr.* to bewitch; to beguile; to delude; to concoct.

**afferm-are** [A1] *tr.* to affirm; to state; to point out; to confirm; *rfl.* to prove oneself; to make a name for oneself. **-ativa** *f.* affirmation; affirmative. **-ativo** *adj.* affirmative; positive. **-aziọne** *f.* affirmation, assertion; achievement, victory; *una -azione personale*, a personal success.

**afferr-are** [A1] *tr.* to take hold of, to grasp; to understand; — *a volo*, to catch on, to be quick in the uptake; *rfl.* (*prep.* a) to get hold (of), to grasp; to cling (to). **-atọio** *m.* pincers, grippers.

**affett-are**[1] [A1] *tr.* to affect, to feign, to simulate; to influence, to have an effect on. **-ato** *part. adj.* affected; mannered, insincere. **-aziọne** *f.* affectation; insincerity.

**affett-are**[2] [A1 c] *tr.* to slice; to cut; *rfl.* to be cut; to be thick enough to cut. **-asalumi** *m. indecl.* sausage-slicing machine. **-ato** *part. adj.* sliced; *n.m.* sliced sausage, salame, ham. **-atọre** *m.* slicer. **-atrice** *f.* slicing machine.

**affetti·bile** *adj.* modifiable, susceptible to modification.

**affett-o**[1] *m.* affection; love; *con* —, with love, (mus.) with feeling; feeling, sentiment; *prendere — a*, to become fond of. **-ivo** *adj.* affective; emotional. **-uọso** *adj.* affectionate, loving; warm-hearted, tender; affecting; *n.m.* (mus.) movement expressing tender feeling.

**affetto**[2] *adj.* liked, loved; *n.m.* favourite; *essere il bene — (a)*, to be well liked (by).

**affetto**[3] *adj.* (*prep.* da) affected (by); suffering (from); afflicted (with).

**affezion-are** [A1 c] *tr.* (*prep.* a) to attach, to bind, to make fond (of); *rfl.* (*prep.* a) to become fond (of); to take a liking (to). **-ato** *part. adj.* affectionate; loving; faithful, devoted; *-ato a*, fond of.

**affeziọne** *f.* affection, love; emotion, feeling; *prezzo d'—*, sentimental value; (med.) disorder, affection.

**affiancare** [A2] *tr.* to place side by side; to flank, to support; to call in the assistance of.

**affiat-are** [A1] *tr.* to harmonize; to train to work together; *rfl.* to adjust oneself; *recip. rfl.* to agree, to fall in with one another; (mus.) to achieve a good ensemble. **-ato** *part. adj.* agreeing, harmonizing; adjusted; *non è ancora molto -ato*, he's still rather new to it; *bene -ati*, working well together.

**affibbi-are** [A6] *tr.* to buckle, to clasp; (fig.) to palm off; — *un colpo*, to deal a blow; — *un soprannome (a)*, to nickname; — *la colpa (a)*, to lay the blame (on); *rfl.* to buckle oneself. **-atọio** *m.* buckle. **-atura** *f.* buckling; buckle, clasp; row of hooks and eyes.

**affid-are** [A1] *tr.* to confide; to commit; to entrust; to assign; — *alla memoria*, to learn by heart; to guarantee; *rfl.* (*prep.* a) to rely (on), to trust (to, in). **-amẹnto** *m.* assurance, guarantee; *dare -amento*, to inspire confidence, to show promise; *fare -amento su*, to rely on. **-anza** *f.* confidence; familiarity, liberty.

**affievolire** [D2] *tr.* to weaken, to enfeeble; to soften; *rfl.*, *intr.* (*aux.* essere) to grow weak; to grow soft; (of sound) to fade away.

**affig·gere** [C17] *tr.* to affix, to post up; to placard; — *i propri*

*sentimenti*, to parade one's feelings; — *gli occhi su*, to stare at; *rfl.* to stop, to stand still; (*prep.* a) to gaze at.

**affil-are**[1] [A1] *tr.* to sharpen, to whet; to taper; to hone; to strop. **-ato** *part. adj.* sharpened, pointed; *lingua -ata*, sharp tongue; *fare il viso -ato*, to grow thin in the face. **-atọio** *m.* sharpener; razor strop.

**affilare**[2] [A1] *tr.* to place in rows (e.g. trees, plants); *rfl.* to form a line.

**affili-are** [A4] *tr.* to affiliate; to associate; *rfl.* to become affiliated, to become a member. **-ato** *part. adj.* affiliated; associated; *n.m.* member, supporter.

**affinare** [A1] *tr.* to refine; to sharpen; to purify; *rfl.* to become refined; to become sharper; (of weather) to set fine.

**affinchẹ̀** *conj.* in order that, so that; — *non*, lest.

**affine**[1] *conj.* (*prep.* di) in order to, for the purpose of, so as to; *affin di bene*, in a good cause.

**affin-e**[2], **-o** *adj.* akin, kindred; alike; bordering; *n.m.* kinsman, relative; *f.* kinswoman; *conoscenti ed -i*, kith and kin. **-ità** *f.* similarity; affinity; relationship, connexion.

**affioch-ire** [D2] *tr.* to make hoarse; to weaken; to dim; *rfl.*, *intr.* (*aux.* essere) to become hoarse; to grow weak; (of light) to grow dim; to burn low; (of sound) to die away. **-ito** *part. adj.* hoarse; faint; weak, dim.

**affior-are**[1] [A1 c] *tr.* to refine (flour). **-ato** *part. adj. pane -ato*, bread made of the finest flour.

**affior-are**[2] [A1 c] *intr.* (*aux.* essere) (naut.) to appear (on the surface); (of a submarine) to surface; (fig.) to crop up; *è -ata una notizia*, the news has come through. **-amẹnto** *m.* apparition; *la crema di -amento*, cream off the top of the milk. **-ato** *part. adj.* barely perceptible, just emerging.

**affiorare**[3] [A1 c] to embroider, etc., with a floral pattern.

**affiss-are** [A1] *tr.* to fix with the eye; — *gli occhi a*, to stare fixedly at; — *la mente a*, to apply one's mind to. **-iọne** *f.* bill-posting; *è proibita l'-ione*, stick no bills.

**affisso** *part. adj.* affixed, attached, fastened; *n.m.* bill, placard, poster; *pl.* fixtures.

**affitt-are** [A1] *tr.* to let; to lease; to hire; to rent; *stanze da —*, rooms to let; *affittasi*, to let. **-aca·mere** *m.*, *f. indecl.* lodging-house keeper; landlord, landlady. **-ante** *m.*, *f.* landlord, landlady; lessee, tenant. **-anza** *f.* tenancy.

**affittire** [D2] *tr.* to thicken, to make thicker; *rfl.*, *intr.* (*aux.* essere) to grow thicker; to grow darker.

**affitto** *m.* rent; hire; lease; *dare in —*, to let out; *prendere in —*, to hire; to rent.

**afflig·g-ere** [C17] *tr.* to afflict; to distress; to vex; *rfl.* to grieve; to distress oneself; to worry. **-ente** *part. adj.* distressing; troublesome, vexatious.

**afflitto** *part. adj.* afflicted; vexed; dejected; sorrowing; — *da*, suffering from; *n.m.* sufferer.

**afflizione** *f.* affliction; suffering; sadness, distress.

**afflu-ire** [D2] *intr.* (*aux.* essere) (of a river) to be a tributary; to flow; to stream; to be in abundance. **-ente** *part. adj.*, *n.m.* tributary, affluent. **-enza** *f.* concourse; influx; abundance, affluence.

**affoc-are**[1] [A2 d] *tr.* to inflame; to set fire to; to make red hot; (fig.) to fire; *rfl.* to become inflamed; to be made red hot; (fig.) to become enraged. **-ato** *part. adj.* red-hot; fiery-red; inflamed; enraged; ardent.

**affoc-are**[2] [A2 d] *tr.* to get in focus, to focus. **-ato** *part. adj.* in focus.

**affog-are** [A2 c] *tr.* to suffocate, to stifle, to choke; to drown; to submerge; to silence; to poach (eggs); *intr.* (*aux.* essere) to drown; to suffocate; to be submerged; *rfl.* to drown oneself; to plunge; to lose oneself. **-ato** *part. adj.* suffocated, drowned; *uovo -ato*, poached egg.

**affollare** [A1] *tr.* to crowd round; to throng; to crush; (fig.) to importune; *rfl.* to flock, to crowd.

**affondare** [A1 c] *tr.* to sink; to send to the bottom; to thrust, to drive in; to embed; *rfl.*, *intr.* (*aux.* essere) to sink; to founder.

**afforestare** [A1] *tr.* to afforest.

**afforzare** [A1] *tr.* to fortify, to strengthen, to reinforce; *rfl.* to gather strength; (mil.) to marshal forces.

**affoss-are** [A1] *tr.* to dig a moat round; to trench; to ditch; to excavate; *rfl.* (of eyes, cheeks) to become hollowed. **-ato** *part. adj.* surrounded by a moat; sunken, hollowed; *occhi -ati*, deep-set eyes.

**affranc-are** [A2] *tr.* to liberate; to exempt; to redeem; to prepay; to stamp, to frank (a letter); *rfl.* to free oneself; to take courage; to gain confidence. **-atrice** *f.* stamping-machine. **-atura** *f.* postage; postage-stamp.

**affranto** *adj.* dejected; overcome; *un cuore —*, a broken heart.

**affratell-are** [A1] *tr.* to unite in comradeship; *rfl.* to fraternize. **-ẹvole** *adj.* fraternizing, friendly.

**affrẹs-co** *m.* (*pl.* **-chi**) (paint.) fresco. **-care** [A2 c] *tr.* to paint in fresco. **-chista** *m.* painter in fresco.

**affrett-are** [A1 c] *tr.* to hurry; to quicken; — *il passo*, to quicken one's pace; to anticipate; *rfl.*, *intr.* (*aux.* avere) to hurry, to make haste; *affrettatevi!*, hurry up! **-ato** *part. adj.* hasty, hurried; careless; (of fruit) forced.

**affront-are** [A1 c] *tr.* to confront; to defy; to face; — *spese*, to meet expenses; — *battaglia*, to give battle; *rfl.* *-arsi di*, to take offence at; *recip. rfl.* to come face to face; to meet in battle.

**affrọnto** *m.* insult, affront.

**affumicare** [A2 s] *tr.* to blacken with smoke; to smoke, to cure (ham, fish); to fumigate.

**affus-are** [A1], **-ellare** [A1], **-olare** [A1 s] *tr.* to make spindle-shaped; to taper.

**affusto** *m.* gun-carriage.

**afor-iṣma, -iṣmo** *m.* aphorism. **-i·stico** *adj.* aphoristic.

**afr-o**[1] *adj.* pungent, sharp (of smell or taste). **-ẹzza** *f.*, **-ọre** *m.* pungency, strong odour. **-ọso** *adj.* strong-smelling.

**afro-**[2] *adj. indecl.* African (in compounds); *rapporti afro-europei*, Afro-European relations.

**afrodisi·aco** *adj.*, *n.m.* aphrodisiac.

**a·gat-a**[1], **-e** *f.* agate.

**agata**[2] *f.* needleful.

**a·gave** *f.* so-called American aloe, frequently planted in Italy.

**agenda** *f.* diary; appointment book; agenda.

**agente** *m.* agent; representative; — *della Questura*, policeman; — *investigativo*, police inspector, detective; — *di cambio*, stock-broker; — *delle tasse*, tax-collector; *adj.* acting, active.

**agenzi·a** *f.* (comm.) agency, branch office; agentship, stewardship; — *di prestiti su pegno*, pawnbroker's; — *di viaggi*, travel agency; — *d'informazioni*, enquiry office; — *di collocamento*, employment agency.

**agevol-are** [A1 sc] *tr.* to facilitate; to assist; to alleviate; to cut through (red tape). **-aziọne** *f.* facilitation; facility; concession.

**agẹvol-e** *adj.* easy; manageable; handy; compliant; affable; quick-witted; fluent; (of clothing) comfortable. **-ẹzza** *f.* facility; fluency; convenience; courtesy; *usare -ezze con*, to treat with consideration.

**agganci-are** [A3] *tr.* to hook; to couple; to hitch. **-atọio** *m.* fastening, catch.

**aggangherare** [A1 s] *tr.* to fasten with hook and eye; to hinge; *rfl.* to be fastened; (fig.) to hold together.

**aggettivo** *m.* adjective; *adj.* adjectival.

**aggett-o** *m.* (bldg.) projection; shoulder; overhang. **-are** [A1] *intr.* (*aux.* essere) to project, jut out.

**aggheronato** *adj.* (of clothing) gored.
**agghiacciare** [A3] *tr.* to congeal; to freeze; to ice; *intr.* (*aux.* essere), *rfl.* to freeze; to turn to ice.
**agghind-are** [A1] *tr.* to dress up; to overdress; *rfl.* to dress oneself up. **-ato** *part. adj.* overdressed; decked out; artificial; *stile -ato*, stilted style.
**ag·gio** *m.* (comm.) premium; interest (on a loan); *fare —*, to command a premium.
**aggiogare** [A2 c] *tr.* to yoke; to subject; to couple (oxen, horses); to link.
**aggiorn-are** [A1 c] *tr.* to fix (a day); to bring up to date; to adjourn; to defer; *intr. impers.* (*aux.* essere) to become daylight; *rfl.* to get up to date; to become modernized. **-ato** *part. adj.* adjourned; up-to-date.
**aggir-are** [A1] *tr.* to revolve; to whirl; to trick; (mil.) to outflank; *rfl.*, *intr.* (*aux.* avere) to revolve; to wander about; (*prep.* su) to have a bearing on, to deal with. **-atọre** *m.* trickster, dodger.
**aggiudic-are** [A2 s] *tr.* to adjudge; to adjudicate; to award. **-aziọne** *f.* adjudication; award.
**aggiun·gere** [C5] *tr.* to add; to subjoin; *rfl.* (*prep.* a) to be added (to); to join.
**aggiunta** *f.* addition, increase; supplement.
**aggiunt-are** [A1] *tr.* to join, to piece together. **-atura** *f.* join, joint. **-ivo** *adj.* additional.
**aggiunto** *part. adj.* added; joined; *n.m.* adjunct; assistant; deputy.
**aggiunziọne** *f.* addition; adding.
**aggiust-are** [A1] *tr.* to adjust, to adapt; to settle; to arrange; to tidy; *— la mira*, to take careful aim; *rfl.* to adjust oneself; to make arrangements. **-ato** *part. adj.* tidy; spruce; precise.
**agglomer-are** [A1 s] *tr.* to agglomerate; *rfl.* to crowd together. **-ato** *part. adj.* agglomerated; crowded; *n.m.* built-up area. **-aziọne** *f.* agglomeration.
**agglutin-are** [A1 s] *tr.*, *rfl.* to agglutinate. **-ante** *adj.* agglutinant; agglutinative; *n.m.* binder, cementing material. **-aziọne** *f.* agglutination.
**aggobbire** [D2] *tr.* to make hunchbacked; *intr.* (*aux.* essere), *rfl.* to become hunchbacked; *— sui libri*, to swot.
**aggomitolare** [A1 s] *tr.* to wind; to make up into a ball; *rfl.* to curl oneself up.
**aggraff-are** [A1], **-iare** [A4], **-ignare** [A5] *tr.* to seize; to catch; to claw.
**aggranch-ire** [D2] *tr.* to numb; *rfl.*, *intr.* (*aux.* essere) to grow numb; to get cramp. **-ito** *part. adj.* numbed; cramped; stiff.
**aggrandire** [D2] *tr.* to aggrandize; to enlarge; to exaggerate; to raise; *rfl.*, *intr.* (*aux.* essere) to increase; to grow powerful; to become elevated.
**aggrappare** [A1] *tr.* to seize, to grasp; to grapple; *rfl.* (*prep.* a) to grasp (at); to cling (to).
**aggrappo** *m.* hold, clutch, grip.
**aggrappol-are** [A1 s] *rfl.* to cluster. **-ato** *part. adj.* clustered, clustering.
**aggraticciare** [A3] *tr.* to intertwine; to twist into trellis-work; *rfl.* to cling; to climb (of plants).
**aggrav-are** [A1] *tr.* to aggravate; to overload; to oppress; *rfl.* to become aggravated; to grow heavy; to lean more heavily. **-ante** *part. adj.* aggravating. **-ato** *part. adj.* aggravated; burdened.
**aggra·vio** *m.* weight; *esser d'— a*, to be a burden upon; wrong; injury; *— fiscale*, tax, duty.
**aggraziare** [A4] *tr.* to make graceful; to make pleasing; to flavour pleasantly; *rfl.* (*acc.* of *prn.*) to ingratiate oneself; (*dat.* of *prn.*) to win over to oneself.
**aggredire** [D2] *tr.* to attack; to assault.
**aggreg-are** [A2] *tr.* to aggregate; to enrol; *rfl.* to become united, joined; (*prep.* a) to join, to enrol (in). **-ativo** *adj.* associative; cohesive. **-ato** *part. adj.* aggregated; associated; *n.m.* aggregate; assemblage; amalgam; *-ato di case*, block of houses; deputy; member.
**aggress-iọne** *f.* aggression; attack. **-ività** *f.* aggressiveness. **-ivo** *adj.* aggressive; *n.m.* weapon. **-ọre** *m.* aggressor, assailant.
**aggrinzire** [D2] *tr.* to wrinkle; to shrivel; *rfl.* to become wrinkled; to shrivel; to ripple.
**aggrond-are** [A1 c] *tr.* *— le ciglia*, to frown. **-ato** *part. adj.* frowning; gloomy; dejected.
**aggroppare**[1] [A1] *tr.* to do up into a knot, to bundle; *rfl.* to amass, to accumulate.
**aggroppare**[2] [A1] *tr.*, *rfl.* to bow, to bend.
**aggrott-are** [A1] *tr.* *— le ciglia*, to frown; to knit the brows. **-amẹnto** *m.* frowning.
**aggrovigli-are** [A4] *tr.* to entangle; *rfl.* to become entangled; to intertwine; to shrink. **-ato** *part. adj.* entangled; intricate; involved; obscure.
**aggrumare** [A1] *tr.* to curdle; *intr.* (*aux.* essere), *rfl.* to clot, to coagulate.
**aggruppare** [A1] *tr.* to gather together; to group; *rfl.* to form groups, to gather together.
**agguagliare** [A4] *tr.* to equalize; to level; to make smooth; to tally; *rfl.* (*prep.* a) to be compared (with); to be equal (to); to emulate.
**agguantare** [A1] *tr.* to catch; to seize to snatch.
**agguato** *m.* ambush; ambuscade trap, snare; *stare in —*, to lie in wait, to be on the alert; *cadere in un —*, to fall into an ambush.
**agguin·dolo** *m.* bobbin, reel.
**aghẹtto** *m.* shoe-lace; boot-lace; tag of a lace.
**agiat-o** *adj.* well-to-do, comfortably off; indolent; unhurried. **-ẹzza** *f.* comfort; competency, comfortable means.
**agi·bil-e** *adj.* practicable, feasible, in working order. **-ità** *f.* feasibility.
**a·gil-e** *adj.* agile, nimble; lithe; alert; skilful. **-ità** *f.* agility.
**agilitare** [A1 s] *tr.* to exercise, to make supple.
**a·gio** *m.* ease; *non trovarsi ad —*, to be ill at ease; comfort; *gli agi della vita*, the comforts of life; time; *se avrò —*, if I have time; *appena avrò un po' d'—*, as soon as I have a little leisure; *a mio —*, at my convenience.
**agire** [D2] *intr.* (*aux.* avere) to act; to behave; *— da*, to act as; to function, to work; to take action; (of a theatrical company) to act, to play.
**agit-are** [A1 s] *tr.* to agitate; to shake; to wave, to stir; (fig.) to stir up; to urge forward; to air (a question); *rfl.* to fidget; to get upset. **-atọre** *m.* agitator; churn. **-aziọne** *f.* agitation; unrest, tumult.
**a·glio** *m.* garlic; (fig.) *mangiar l'—*, to swallow one's rage.
**agnell-o** *m.* lamb; meek and mild individual. **-a** *f.* ewe lamb.
**agnin-a** *f.* lamb's fleece. **-o** *adj.* lamb's, lamb-like.
**agno·stic-o** *adj.*, *n.m.* agnostic. **-ịsmo** *m.* agnosticism.
**ago** *m.* (*pl.* **aghi**) needle; *astuccio per aghi*, needle-case; *cruna d'—*, eye of the needle; bodkin; *— torto*, crochet hook; *— da calza*, knitting-needle; *lavoro d'—*, needlework.
**agognare** [A5 c] *tr.* to covet; to yearn for; *intr.* (*aux.* avere; *prep.* a) to yearn (for).
**agọne**[1] *m.* packing-needle.
**agọn-e**[2] *m.* circus, arena; athletic or gladiatorial combat; contest; *entrare nell'—*, to enter the lists. **-ista** *m.* competitor; combatant. **-i·stica** *f.* athletics. **-i·stico** *adj.* sporting, competitive; athletic.
**agon-i·a** *f.* death struggle; agony; suspense; longing. **-iẓẓare** [A1] *intr.* (*aux.* avere) to be breathing one's last; to suffer anguish.
**a·gor-a** *f.* agora; market-place. **-afobi·a** *f.* (med.) agoraphobia.
**agra·r-ia** *f.* agriculture; science of agriculture. **-io** *adj.* agricultural, agrarian.
**agreste** *adj.* wild, uncultivated; rustic.
**agrest-o** *adj.* sour; *n.m.* kind of grapes which do not ripen; verjuice. **-ino** *adj.* sour; *n.m.* sauce

made from verjuice; unripened grapes.
**agrẹzza** *f.* sourness; bitterness, irascibility.
**agri·colo** *adj.* agricultural.
**agri-coltọre, -cultọre** *m.* farmer; agriculturist. **-coltura, -cultura** *f.* farming; agriculture; tillage.
**agrifo·glio** *m.* (bot.) holly.
**agrigno** *adj.* sour, tart, sharp.
**agrimani** *m.pl.* decorations, trimmings, ornaments.
**agrimens-ọre** *m.* land-surveyor. **-ura** *f.* land-surveying.
**agro**[1] *m.* land round a city; *l'— romano*, the plain surrounding Rome; *l'— pontino*, the Pontine marshes.
**agr-o**[2] *adj.* sour; bitter; acid, tart; severe; *n.m. l'— di limone*, lemon-juice. **-odọlce** *adj., n.m.* bitter-sweet; subacid. **-ọre** *m.* sour taste.
**agro·lo-go** *m.* student of agrarian science. **-gi·a** *f.* agrarian science.
**agro·n-omo** *m.* scientific agriculturist, agronomist. **-omi·a** *f.* agronomy. **-o·mico** *adj.* agronomic.
**agrum-e** *m.* citrus fruit; sour taste; *pl.* citrus fruits. **-ẹto** *m.* land cultivated with citrus fruit-trees. **-icoltura** *f.* citrus cultivation.
**aguc·chi-a** *f.* needle. **-are** [A4] *intr.* (*aux.* avere) to stitch; to sew; to knit.
**aguzz-are** [A1] *tr.* to sharpen; to stimulate; to quicken; *— l'appetito*, to whet the appetite. **-atọre** *m.* sharpener; grinder.
**aguzzo** *adj.* sharp; pointed; whetted; edged.
**a·ia**[1] *f.* threshing-floor; *menar il can per l'—*, to beat about the bush.
**a·ia**[2] *f.* children's nurse; governess.
**aierino** *adj.* airy, of the air; *n.m.* sprite.
**a·io** *m.* tutor.
**ai·re** *m.* (colloq.) impulse; impetus; going; gait; *prendere l'—*, to set off; *dare l'— a*, to set going.
**airọne** *m.* (orn.) heron.
**aitante** *adj.* strong, vigorous; stout, robust.
**aiuola** *f.* flower-bed.
**aiut-are** [A1] *tr.* to help; to assist; *— la barca*, to pull one's weight; *rfl.* to help oneself; to make an effort; (*prep.* di) to avail oneself (of); to make do (with); *recip. rfl.* to help one another. **-ante** *m.* assistant; (mil.) adjutant.
**aiu·to** *m.* help. assistance, aid; *excl. aiuto !*, help!; *chiamare —*, to call for help; assistant; *pl.* aid; (mil.) auxiliaries.
**aizz-are** [A1] *tr.* to instigate, to incite; *— un cane contro*, to set a dog on. **-ọso** *adj.* touchy, excitable.
**al-a** *f.* (*pl.* -i, -e) wing; *apertura d'-i*, wing-span; *star sulle -i*, to hover; *in un batter d'-i*, in a twinkling; fin; tip, edge; line, row; *— di onore*, guard of honour; *far —*, to make way, to fall back. **-ato** *adj.* winged; *n.m.pl. gli -ati*, the birds and winged animals. **-ẹtta** *f.* iron support, bracket; fin; pinion.
**alabard-a** *f.* halberd. **-iere** *m.* halberdier.
**alabastr-o** *m.* alabaster. **-ino** *adj.* alabastrine.
**a·lacr-e, ala·cre** *adj.* active; industrious; willing; brisk. **-ità** *f.* alacrity; eagerness.
**alamaro** *m.* braiding; loop; *pl.* frogs, loops, braided fastenings.
**alambicco** *m.* still, alembic.
**alano** *m.* bulldog; mastiff; boar-hound; wolf-hound.
**alare**[1] *m.* andiron; firedog (usu. *pl.*); trestle.
**alare**[2] [A1] *tr.* to tow, to haul; (naut.) *intr.* (*aux.* avere) to sail close to the wind.
**alba**[1] *f.* day-break; first light; dawn; aubade.
**alba**[2] *f.* (liturg.) alb.
**alba-gi·a** *f.* pride, conceit; haughtiness. **-giọso** *adj.* vain; haughty.
**albata** *f.* aubade, dawn song.
**al·batro**[1] *m.* (bot.) strawberry tree, arbutus-tree.
**al·batro**[2] *m.* (orn.) albatross.
**albeggiare** [A3 c] *intr.* (*aux.* essere), to dawn; to grow white; to tend towards white.
**alber-are** [A1 s] *tr.* to plant with trees; to hoist; (naut.) to step (a mast). **-atura** *f.* plantation of trees; (naut.) masts, yards, spars.
**al·bera, alberella** *f.* (bot.) aspen.
**alberello**[1] *m.* big shrub; small tree.
**alberello**[2] *m.* pot, jar; phial.
**alberẹt-a** *f.*, **-o** *m.* grove of trees; arboretum; plantation of poplars; avenue of poplars.
**alberg-are** [A2] *tr.* to house; to shelter; (fig.) to harbour, to cherish; *intr.* (*aux.* avere) to put up at an inn, to lodge. **-atọre** *m.* hotel-keeper, innkeeper. **-atrice** *f.* landlady.
**alber-gheri·a** *f.* free lodging. **-ghiero** *adj.* relating to hotel-keeping; *l'industria -ghiera*, the hotel industry.
**alber-go** *m.* (*pl.* -ghi) hotel; inn; shelter; abode; hostel; *— diurno*, public baths; *— per la gioventù*, youth hostel; *dare — a*, to give shelter to.
**al·bero** *m.* tree; *— di Natale*, Christmas tree; *— genealogico*, family tree; poplar; wood from the poplar; mast; *— maestro*, mainmast; shaft, spindle, axle, arbor.
**albicocc-a** *f.* apricot. **-o** *m.* apricot tree.
**albin-o** *adj.* albino; whitish; *n.m.* albino. **-ịsmo** *m.* albinism.
**albo** *m.* album; scrap-book; register; *— d'onore*, roll of honour; public notice-board.
**albọre** *m.* whiteness; first light; dawn; *gli albori della civiltà*, the dawn of civilization.
**album-e** *m.* albumen; white of egg. **-ina** *f.* albumin. **-inọso** *adj.* albuminous.
**alburno** *m.* sapwood.
**alchi·m-ia, alchimi·a** *f.* alchemy; (fig.) deception. **-iare** [A4] *tr.* to falsify. **-ista** *m.* alchemist.
**alciọne** *m.* (orn.) kingfisher; halcyon; *giorni dell'—*, halcyon days.
**a·lco-ol** *m.* alcohol; *— denaturato*, methylated spirits. **-o·lico** *adj.* alcoholic; *n.m.pl.* wines and spirits. **-olịsmo** *m.* alcoholism. **-olista** *m., f.* alcoholic.
**alcov-a, alcọva** *f.* alcove, recess; bedchamber.
**alcunchẹ̀** *pron.* anything, something; a little.
**alcun-o** *adj.* (sing.) any (usu. in neg. context); *non vedo -a ragione*, I do not see any reason; *pl.* some, a few; *ha -i buoni quadri*, he has some good pictures; *prn.* (sing.) anyone, anybody (usu. in neg. context); *non c'è — che possa aiutarmi*, there isn't anyone who can help me; *se — mi vedesse*, if anyone should see me; *pl.* some, some people; a few; *adv. alcun poco*, a little, somewhat.
**a·lea** *f.* contingency, risk, hazard; *correr l'—*, to run the risk; game of chance.
**aleggi-are** [A3 c] *intr.* (*aux.* avere) to flutter; to flit; to hover; to quiver; (fig.) to be in the air; *tr.* to have the air of, to suggest. **-ante** *part. adj.* fluttering, quivering; hovering.
**alfa** *m.* Alpha; *dall'— all'omega*, from Alpha to Omega.
**alfa-beto** *m.* alphabet; code; *per —*, in alphabetical order; (colloq.) *perder l'—*, to talk nonsense. **-be·tico** *adj.* alphabetical.
**alfiere** *m.* standard-bearer; ensign; (chess) bishop.
**alfine** *adv.* finally, at last; after all; in the long run.
**alga** *f.* seaweed.
**al·gebr-a** *f.* algebra. **-a·ico, -a·tico** *adj.* algebraical. **-ista** *m.* algebraist.
**aliante** *m.* (aeron.) glider.
**aliare** [A4] *intr.* (*aux.* avere) (poet.) to flutter; to fly; to flit.
**alien-are** [A1] *tr.* to alienate, to turn against; to estrange, to sever; *rfl.* (*dat.* of *prn.*) to lose, to alienate from oneself; *si è -ato l'affetto di tutti*, he has turned everyone against him. **-ato** *part. adj.* alienated; *n.m.* lunatic; *ospizio per -ati*, mental home. **-aziọne** *f.* (leg.) alienation; transfer; mental derangement; (fig.) estrangement. **-ista** *m.* alienist, mental specialist.

**alieno** *adj.* (*prep.* da) averse, disinclined, reluctant; irrelevant; alien.

**aliment-o** *m.* food, nutriment, aliment; (fig.) nourishment, succour; *pl.* (leg.) alimony, maintenance. **-are** *tr.* [A1 c] to feed, to nourish; to support, to maintain; (fig.) to cherish, to entertain (hopes). **-are, -a·rio** *adj.* alimentary; *condotto -are*, alimentary canal; nutritive; *prodotti -ari*, foodstuffs. **-arista** *m.* purveyor of foodstuffs. **-azione** *f.* alimentation; (eng.) feed; supply.

**alise·o** *adj.* (geog.) *venti alisei*, trade winds; *n.m.pl. gli alisei*, trade winds.

**alitare** [A1 s] *intr.* (*aux.* avere) to breathe; to blow softly; *senz'—*, breathlessly, with rapt attention.

**a·lit-o** *m.* breath; exhalation; light breeze; puff; *non ci spira un — di vento*, there's not a breath of wind. **-oso** *adj.* suffering from halitosis.

**allacci-are** [A3] *tr.* to lace; to tie; to leash, to lasso; to connect; *— relazioni commerciali*, to establish business connexions. **-amento** *m.* lacing; link; connexion; (rlwy.) branch-line; ligature. **-atura** *f.* tie, lace, fastening; buttoning.

**allag-are** [A2] *tr.* to inundate, to flood; to overflow; (fig.) to overwhelm. **-ato** *part. adj.* flooded, inundated; under water.

**allamp-anare** [A1 s] *intr.* (*aux.* essere) to grow lean and pale; *— dalla fame*, to be half-starved. **-ato** *part. adj.* lean, emaciated, cadaverous; tall as a lamp-post, gangling.

**allapp-are** [A1] *tr.* to set (one's teeth) on edge; *— la bocca*, to make the mouth dry. **-ante** *part. adj.* sour, pungent.

**allarg-are** [A2] *tr.* to widen; to broaden; to extend; to spread; *rfl.* to become wider, to widen; to spread; (of weather) to improve; *-arsi sopra un argomento*, to enlarge upon a subject; *-arsi con*, to open one's heart to. **-ata** *f.* widening; stretching; *dare un'-ata a*, to stretch.

**allarm-e** *m.* alarm; warning; call to arms; agitation, alarm. **-are** [A1] *tr.* to alarm, to frighten; *rfl.* to be alarmed, to take fright. **-ismo** *m.* alarmist tendencies. **-ista** *m., f.* alarmist.

**all'armi**! *excl.* to arms!

**allato** *adv.* (*prep.* di) beside; near; in comparison (with).

**allatt-are** [A1] *tr.* to give suck to; to feed, to nurse; *intr.* (*aux.* avere) to suck, to suckle. **-atrice** *f.* nursing mother; wet nurse. **-atura** *f.* lactation; suckling, feeding.

**alle-are** [A1] *tr.* to unite, to ally; *rfl.* (*prep.* con) to ally oneself, to form an alliance. **-anza** *f.* alliance; league. **-ato** *part. adj.* allied; *le forze -ate*, the allied forces; *n.m.* ally.

**alleg-are**[1] [A2] *tr.* (leg.) to allege, to assert. **-azione** *f.* (leg.) allegation, assertion, plea, adduction of evidence.

**alleg-are**[2] [A2] *tr.* to alloy; (fig.) *— i denti*, to set one's teeth on edge; to enclose (in a letter); *intr.* (*aux.* avere) (of scissors) to be blunt; (of teeth) to be set on edge (also *rfl.*). **-ata** *f.* letter enclosed. **-ato** *part. adj.* enclosed; *n.m.* enclosure; alloy.

**allegger-ire** [D2] *tr.* (*prep.* di) to lighten; to ease, to relieve (of); *rfl.* to become lighter; to be relieved. **-imento** *m.* lightening; easing; relief.

**alle-gori·a** *f.* allegory. **-go·rico** *adj.* allegorical. **-gorista** *m.* allegorist. **-gorizzare** [A1] to allegorize.

**allegr-o** *adj.* merry; cheerful; gay; lively; *su, allegro!*, cheer up!; (mus.) quick, vivacious; *n.m.* (mus.) an allegro movement. **-ezza** *f.* cheerfulness; joy, gladness; gaiety, merriment. **-i·a** *f.* merriment, gaiety.

**allen-are** [A1 c] *tr.* to invigorate, to strengthen; to train, to coach; *rfl.* to go into training. **-amento** *m.* training; practice; course of instruction. **-atore** *m.* trainer, coach.

**allenire** [D2] *tr.* to weaken, to soften; to alleviate; *rfl.* to grow weak, to lose strength.

**allentare** [A1] *tr.* to slacken; to release; to let slip; *— il passo*, to go more slowly; *rfl., intr.* (*aux.* avere) to slacken; to work loose; to relax; (of a slope) to become less steep.

**aller·g-ico** *adj.* allergic. **-i·a** *f.* allergy.

**allerta** *f.* warning, alert.

**allesso** *adv.* boiled; *n.m.* boiled meat.

**allest-ire** [D2] *tr.* to prepare; to equip, to rig out; (theatr.) *— uno spettacolo*, to put on a show; *rfl.* to prepare oneself; to get fitted out. **-imento** *m.* preparation; (theatr.) *-imento scenico*, scenery, costumes.

**allett-are**[1] [A1] *tr.* to entice; to decoy; to flatter; to delight. **-ante, -ativo** *adj.* alluring; attractive; charming.

**allett-are**[2] [A1] *tr.* (of wind) to lay (crops) on the ground, to flatten; *rfl.* to take to one's bed; (of corn, etc.) to be flattened to the ground. **-ato** *part. adj.* bedridden; (of crops) beaten down.

**allev-are** [A1] *tr.* to breed; to rear; *— api*, to keep bees. **-amento** *m.* breeding; rearing; lactation; *avere un -amento di*, to be a breeder of; *-amento di cavalli*, stud farm. **-ata** *f.* litter. **-atore** *m.* breeder; raiser.

**alleviare** [A4] *tr.* (*prep.* di) to alleviate; to allay; to soothe; *rfl.* to be relieved (of).

**allib-ire** [D2] *intr.* (*aux.* essere) to turn pale; to be dismayed; to be terrified. **-imento** *m.* dismay, consternation.

**allibr-are** [A1] *tr.* to register; to enter, to book. **-atore** *m.* (sport) bookmaker.

**allietare** [A1] *tr.* to cheer, to enliven; to gladden; *rfl.* to rejoice; to make merry.

**alliev-o** *m.* pupil; schoolboy; student; apprentice; nursling; calf; foal. **-a** *f.* schoolgirl.

**alligatore** *m.* (zool.) alligator.

**allignare** [A5] *intr.* (*aux.* essere, avere) to take root; to flourish; to thrive.

**allindare** [A1] *tr.* to make tidy; to adorn; to embellish; *rfl.* to tidy oneself; to adorn oneself.

**allineare** [A6 s] *tr.* to set in line, to line up; *rfl.* to form a line.

**allit(t)era-zione** *f.* alliteration; pun; tongue-twister; play on words. **-tivo** *adj.* alliterative.

**allividire** [D2] *intr.* (*aux.* essere) to become livid; to turn pale.

**allocazione** *f.* (sport) prize-money; stake.

**alloc-co** *m.* (*pl.* **-chi**) (orn.) tawny owl; (colloq.) dolt, simpleton. **-cheri·a** *f.* stupidity. **-chire** [D2] *intr.* to play the fool.

**allocu-tore** *m.* speaker; orator. **-zione** *f.* address, oration; solemn speech; exhortation.

**allo·dola** *f.* (orn.) lark.

**allog-are** [A2] *tr.* to place; to find employment for; to allocate; to assign; *— una figlia*, to marry off a daughter; *— denari*, to lay out money; *rfl.* to find employment, to get placed. **-atore** *m.* lessor, contractor. **-azione** *f.* lease; adjudication of contract work.

**allo·geno** *n.m.* alien-born citizen of a State; (also *adj.*).

**alloggi-are** [A3] *tr.* to give lodging to; to house; to quarter; to billet; *intr.* (*aux.* avere) to lodge. **-amento** *m.* lodging; (mil.) camp; quarters; billet. **-atore** *m.* landlord; lodging-house-keeper. **-atrice** *f.* landlady.

**allog·gio** *m.* board, lodging; *prendere un —*, to take lodgings; *vitto e —*, board residence; *— militare*, billet.

**alloglotto** *adj.* speaking a different language; *n.m.* member of a linguistic minority.

**allo·nimo** *adj.* published under a pseudonym.

**allontan-are** [A1] *tr.* to send away; to dispel; to defer; to estrange; to influence against; *— i sospetti*, to avert suspicion; *rfl.* (*prep.* da) to go away; to draw away; to become aloof; *-arsi dal male*, to renounce evil; *-arsi dall'argomento*, to wander from the subject.

**allọra** *adv.* then, at that moment; in that case; *d'— in poi*, from then on; *d'—*, a moment ago, newly; *— poi !*, if that's the case!...
**allorchẹ̀** *conj.* when, at the time when, whilst; whenever.
**alloro** *m.* (bot.) bay laurel; avocado pear; (fig.) laurel crown; victory, glory.
**allorquando** *conj.* when.
**allucchettare** [A1 c] *tr.* to padlock.
**allucciol-ante, -ato** *adj.* glittering, shimmering; spangled, moiré.
**al·luce** *m.* (anat.) big toe.
**allucin-are** [A1s] *tr.* to hallucinate; to dazzle; to bewilder; *rfl.* to be dazzled; to be deceived. **-ato** *part. adj.* hallucinated; dazzled; *aria -ata*, haunted look; *n.m.* one suffering from hallucinations; madman.
**allu·dere** [C3] *intr.* (*aux.* avere; *prep.* a) to allude (to); to hint (at).
**allume** *m.* alum.
**allumi·ni-o** *m.* aluminium. **-eri·a** *f.* aluminium works.
**allungare** [A2] *tr.* to lengthen; to elongate; to extend, to stretch; *allungami quel libro*, hand me that book; to prolong; to water; to eke out; *— il passo*, to quicken one's pace; *— il muso*, to pull a long face; *rfl.* to grow longer; to stretch oneself; to grow tall; *le giornate si allungano*, the days are drawing out.
**alluṣ-iọne** *f.* allusion, reference; hint; *fare — a*, to have reference to. **-ivo** *adj.* allusive.
**alluvi-ale** *adj.* (geol.) alluvial. **-onato** *adj.* inundated, flooded; *zona -onata*, flood-area; *n.m.pl.* refugees from flood area. **-ọne** *f.* alluvion; alluvium; flood.
**alma** *f.* (poet.) soul; spirit.
**almanac-co** *m.* (*pl.* **-chi**) almanack; calendar; (fig., of a person) an original, an eccentric. **-care** [A2] *intr.* (*aux.* avere) to daydream.
**almẹno** *adv.* at least; as much as.
**almo** *adj.* (poet.) life-giving; benign, kindly; beloved; sublime; fertile.
**alno** *m.* (bot.) alder tree.
**alọne** *m.* halo; aura, effulgence.
**alp-e** *f.* high mountain, alp; pasture; *le Alpi*, the Alps. **-ẹggio** *m.* summer pasture in the mountains. **-estre** *adj.* mountainous; Alpine; wild; *giardino -estre*, rock garden. **-igiano** *m.* inhabitant of alpine regions; mountaineer. **-iniṣmo** *m.* mountaineering. **-ino** *adj.* alpine; *n.m.pl.* Alpine troops. **-ista** *m., f.* mountaineer, mountain-climber.
**alquanto** *adv.* somewhat, rather; considerably; *adj.* much, a good deal (of); *prn.* (*foll. by* di) *— di carne*, a fair amount of meat; *pl.* a good many, several.
**alt** ! *excl.* halt!; *n.m. indecl.* halt, stop.
**altalẹn-a** *f.* seesaw; swing; (fig.) alternation, ups and downs; *fare l'—*, to swing to and fro; (fig.) to alternate. **-are** [A1 c] *intr.* (*aux.* avere), *rfl.* to swing; (fig.) to alternate.
**altare** *m.* altar; (fig.) religion; *— maggiore*, high altar.
**alter-are** *tr.* [A1 s] to alter, to change; to vary; to impair; to counterfeit; to adulterate; *— i fatti*, to misrepresent the facts; *— un testo*, to falsify a text; *— il viso*, to show anger; *rfl.* to be altered; to vary; to be impaired; to become angry. **-aziọne** *f.* alteration; deterioration; falsification; debasement.
**alterc-are** [A2] *intr.* (*aux.* avere) to quarrel; to wrangle. **-aziọne** *f.* altercation; wrangle.
**alter-co** *m.* (*pl.* **-chi**) quarrel, row; *avere un —*, to have a row.
**altern-are** *tr., rfl.* [A1] to alternate. **-ativa** *f.* alternative. **-ativo** *adj.* alternative. **-aziọne** *f.* alternation; rotation; permutation.
**alterno** *adj.* alternate; alternating.
**alter-o** *adj.* proud; haughty, stately. **-ẹzza** *f.* pride; arrogance. **-i·gia** *f.* haughtiness, arrogance; insolence.
**altẹzz-a** *f.* height; hill; grandeur; loftiness; *Altezza*, Highness; (of material) breadth, width; thickness; volume; depth; (geog.) latitude; (fig.) *essere all'— di*, to be equal to, to be on a level with. **-ọso** *adj.* proud, haughty, overbearing.
**alt-imetri·a** *f.* altimetry. **-ime·trico** *adj.* altimetric. **-i·metro** *m.* altimeter.
**altipiano** *m.* (geog.) upland plain.
**altisonante** *adj.* high-sounding; loud-sounding; pompous.
**altis·simo** *adj. superl.* very high; highest; *n.m. l'Altissimo*, the Almighty.
**altitu·dine** *f.* altitude; height.
**alt-o**[1] *adj.* high; elevated; tall; eminent; sublime; difficult; loud; deep; early, medieval; upper; (geog.) northern; (mus.) high; loud; *-a novità*, latest fashion; *ad -a voce*, out loud; *a notte -a*, in the dead of night; *adv.* loudly; aloud; high up; *in —*, on high; *guardare d'— in basso*, to look down one's nose at; *n.m.* height; summit; heaven; deep sea; (mus.) alto voice; *pl. alti e bassi*, ups and downs.
**alto**[2] ! *excl.* (mil.) halt!; *n.m.* halt; *fare —*, to halt.
**altolà** ! *excl.* (mil.) who goes there?; halt!
**altolocato** *adj.* high-ranking, highly placed.
**altomare** *m.* open sea; *in* -, out at sea.
**altoparlant-e** *m.* (*pl.* **-i**) loudspeaker.
**altorilievo** *m.* (sculp.) high-relief.
**altr-esì** *adv.* also, too, likewise, as well. **-ettale** *adj.* similar; another such; equal. **-ettanto** *adj.* as much; as much more; *n.m.* the same; *pl.* as many, so many; *adv.* equally, likewise; so much, as much; *tanti auguri! grazie e — (a voi)*, all the best! thank you and the same to you.
**altri** *indef. prn. indecl.* another person, someone else; anyone; anyone else.
**altrieri** *adv.* the day before yesterday.
**altrimẹnti** *adv.* otherwise; or else; differently.
**altr-o** *adj.* other, different; another; next; more; *non dico —*, I say no more; *volete dell'— caffè ?*, will you have some more coffee?; *nessun —*, nobody else; *quest'-a settimana*, next week; *l'-a settimana*, last week; *-a volta*, previously; *-e volte*, at other times; *n.m. indecl.* another thing; something else; *ben —*, much more than that; *pane, carne, e —*, bread, meat and other things besides; (iron.) *non ci mancava —*, that's the limit; *— è dire, — è fare*, easier said than done; *adv. phrases*: *senz'—*, immediately; without fail; *tutt'—*, far from it, quite the opposite; *— !* (or) *-chè !*, yes, indeed!, rather!; *se non —*, at least; *per —*, moreover; *più che —*, especially; *prn.* someone else; *diventò un —*, he changed completely; *l'un l'—*, each other, one another; *nè l'uno nè l'—*, neither; *pl.* others, other people; *noi -i Inglesi*, we English. **-ọnde** *adv.* elsewhere; *d'-onde*, besides, on the other hand. **-ọve** *adv.* elsewhere.
**altru-i** *prn. indecl. nom., acc., dat., abl.* another person, others; *gen.* another's; of others; *la roba —*, other people's property. **-iṣmo** *m.* altruism. **-ista** *m., f.* altruist. **-i·stico** *adj.* unselfish; altruistic.
**altura** *f.* eminence, rise, high ground.
**alunn-o** *m.* pupil; schoolboy; student; apprentice. **-a** *f.* schoolgirl. **-ato** *m.* apprenticeship.
**alveare** *m.* beehive.
**al·veo** *m.* river-bed; canal; conduit.
**alvo** *m.* belly; *-materno*, womb; (fig.) centre, heart.
**alz-are** [A1] *tr.* to raise; to lift; *— di peso*, to lift bodily; to erect; to heighten; (fig.) to exalt; *— le spalle*, to shrug one's shoulders; *rfl.* to get up; to raise oneself; *-arsi in piedi*, to stand up. **-ata** *f.* raising; rise; rising; *-ata di mani*, show of hands; elevation; *-ata di spalle*, shrug.
**ama·bil-e** *adj.* lovable; amiable; charming, gracious; (of wine) sweet. **-ità** *f.* amiability; sweetness; courtesy.
**ama·ca, a·maca** *f.* hammock.

**amal·gam-a** *m.* amalgam. **-are** [A1 s] *tr.* to amalgamate.

**amanuense** *m.* amanuensis, copyist.

**am-are** [A1] *tr.* to love; to be in love with; to be fond of; to like; to take pleasure in; to want; (of plants) to require; — *meglio*, to prefer; *abs.* to love; to be in love; *recip. rfl.* to love one another. **-ante** *part. adj.* loving; fond; *n.m.* lover; *f.* mistress. **-ata** *f.* lady-love, mistress. **-ato** *part. adj.* loved, beloved; dear; liked; preferred; *n.m.* loved one. **-atọre** *m.* amateur, connoisseur; admirer; lover. **-ato·rio** *adj.* amatory.

**amar-o** *adj.* bitter; biting, sharp; grievous; *mandar giù un boccone —*, to swallow an insult; *una vita -a*, a hard life; *n.m.* bitters; apéritif; gall; (fig.) rancour, resentment; *aver dell'— contro*, to feel bitter towards; *pl.* bitters. **-eggiare** [A3 c] *tr.* to make bitter; (fig.) to embitter; to chagrin; to afflict, to torment; *rfl.* to grieve, to fret, to take things to heart. **-ẹzza** *f.* bitterness; pain; sharpness; rancour. **-itu·dine** *f.* bitterness; grief.

**amaẓ·ẓone** *f.* Amazon; horsewoman; *montare ad —*, to ride side-saddle.

**ambag-e** *f.*, *usu. pl.* circumlocution; evasion, ambages, subterfuge; *senz'-i*, plainly, in a few words; *sing.* circuitous path.

**amba·sci-a** *f.* distress, anguish; difficulty in breathing, breathlessness. **-ato** *part. adj.* anguished, distressed.

**ambasc-iata** *f.* embassy; ambassador's residence; (fig.) commission, negotiation; *fare un'—*, to bring a message. **-iatọre** *m.* ambassador; woman-ambassador; messenger. **-iatrice** *f.* wife of an ambassador, ambassadress. **-eri·a** *f.* representation, embassy.

**ambedue** *prn. pl.*, *indecl.* both.

**ambidestro** *adj.* ambidextrous; (fig.) astute.

**ambient-e** *m.* surroundings, environment; habitat; setting; background; sphere, circle; society, (fig.) atmosphere; enclosed space; *vivere troppo in -i chiusi*, to live too much indoors; room; *appartamento di cinque -i*, five-roomed flat; circumference; surrounding atmosphere; *adj.* surrounding, ambient; *temperatura —*, room temperature. **-are** [A1] *rfl.* to accustom oneself to one's surroundings.

**ambi·gu-o** *adj.* ambiguous; dubious; *persona -a*, person of doubtful reputation. **-ità** *f.* ambiguity, ambiguousness.

**ambilaterale** *adj.* two-sided.

**am·bi-o** *m.* amble; *andare all'—*, to amble; (fig.) *pigliar l'—*, to take oneself off. **-are** [A4] *intr.* (*aux.* avere) to amble. **-atura** *f.* ambling.

**amb-ire** [D2] *tr.* to covet; to hanker after; to aspire towards; *intr.* (*aux.* avere) to be ambitious. **-ito** *part. adj.* desired, coveted; sought after.

**am·bito** *m.* ambit; orbit; precincts; compass; range; *nell'— del possibile*, within the limits of possibility; *questo rientra nel nostro —*, this lies within our competence.

**ambival-ente** *adj.* (psychol.) ambivalent. **-enza** *f.* ambivalence.

**ambiz-iọne** *f.* ambition; desire for success; pretension; eagerness. **-iọso** *adj.* ambitious; aspiring; desirous, eager; proud; *n.m.* ambitious person; careerist.

**ambo** *adj. indecl.* both; *n.m.* pair; (iron.) *un bell'—*, a nice pair (of rogues); double (at lotto).

**ambr-a** *f.* amber; — *grigia*, ambergris; — *nera*, jet. **-ato** *adj.* amber-coloured.

**ambro·si-a** *f.* ambrosia; **-o** *adj.* ambrosial.

**ambul-are** [A1 s] *intr.* (*aux.* avere) to walk; to ambulate; to walk off. **-ante** *adj.* ambulating; itinerant; peripatetic. **-anza** *f.* ambulance; first-aid post, field-hospital. **-ato·rio** *adj.* ambulatory; itinerant; *n.m.* cloister; clinic; health-centre; out-patients' department; surgery.

**amen** *excl.* amen; *n.m.indecl. in un —*, in a twinkling; *e —*, and that's that.

**amen-o** *adj.* droll; amusing; *un capo —*, a funny chap; *un libro —*, an amusing book; entertaining, delightful; agreeable, pleasant; *paesaggio —*, smiling landscape. **-ità** *f.* pleasantness, agreeableness; amenity; pleasantry: urbanity.

**ametista** *f.* amethyst.

**amianto** *m.* asbestos.

**amic-are** [A2] *tr.* to inspire friendly feelings in; to reconcile; *rfl.* (*dat.* of *prn.*) *-arsi uno*, to gain the allegiance of someone; *recip. rfl.* to make friends with one another; to become reconciled.

**amichẹvol-e** *adj.* friendly, amicable; amiable, affable; courteous; *all'—*, as between friends. **-ẹzza** *f.* friendliness; friendly action.

**amici·zia** *f.* friendship; amity; friendliness; *per —*, out of friendship; *stringere — con*, to make friends with; affinity; *in —*, in confidence; *pl.* friends; friendships.

**ami·c-o** *m.* friend; well-wisher; boy-friend; lover; enthusiast; — *del cuore*, bosom friend; *adj.* friendly; pleasing; beloved; propitious; *colori -i*, colours that go well together, **-a** *f.* girl-friend, woman-friend; mistress.

**a·mid-o** *m.* starch; *dare l'— a*, to starch. **-a·ceo**, **-ọso** *adj.* starchy.

**amig·dal-a** *f.* (anat.) tonsil. **-ite** *f.* tonsillitis.

**ammacc-are** [A2] *tr.* to bruise; to dent; to crush; to grind. **-atura** *f.* bruise; dent.

**ammaestr-are** [A1] *tr.* to teach, to instruct; to train; to tame. **-a·bile** *adj.* teachable; docile, manageable. **-amẹnto** *m.* teaching; training; precept; *pl.* upbringing. **-atọre** *m.*, **-atrice** *f.* instructor; trainer; tamer. **-aziọne** *f.* instruction; training.

**ammal-are** [A1] *intr.* (*aux.* essere), *rfl.* to become ill, to fall sick; *-arsi di morbillo*, to catch measles; *tr.* to infect, to make ill. **-ato** *part. adj.* ill, sick, unwell; *n.m.* patient.

**ammali-are** [A4] *tr.* to bewitch, to charm; to enchant; to cast a spell on. **-atọre** *m.* enchanter, sorcerer. **-atrice** *f.* enchantress, sorceress. **-atura** *f.*, **-aziọne** *f.* enchantment; sorcery.

**ammalizi-are** [A4] *tr.* to teach mischief to; to make sly; to sharpen (wits); to dupe; *rfl.*, *intr.* (*aux.* essere) to become sly; to sharpen one's wits. **-ato** *part. adj.* sly, cunning; sharp.

**ammammol-are** [A1 s] *rfl.* to drop off to sleep, to nod. **-ato** *part. adj.* (of eyes) heavy with sleep.

**ammanco** *m.* (comm.) deficit; — *di peso*, underweight.

**ammanettare** [A1 c] *tr.* to handcuff; to manacle, to fetter.

**ammansire** [D2] *tr.* to tame; to domesticate; to appease; to assuage; *rfl.* to be subdued; to become docile.

**ammant-are** [A1] *tr.* to cloak, to mantle; to conceal; *rfl.* to wrap oneself in a cloak; *-arsi di*, to cloak oneself in. **-atura** *f.* mantle, covering, wrap. **-ellare** [A1] *tr.*, *rfl.* to wrap in a mantle.

**ammar-are** *intr.* (*aux.* avere) to alight, to touch down (on water, of a seaplane). **-ag·gio**, **-ata** *f.* alighting (on water).

**ammarr-are** [A1] *tr.* (naut.) to fasten, to moor; *intr.* (*aux.* avere) to moor. **-ag·gio** *m.* (naut.) mooring.

**ammassare** [A1] *tr.* to amass; to pile; *rfl.* to crowd together; to muster.

**ammassicciare** [A3] *tr.* to mass, to pack; *rfl.* to form into a mass, to become solid; (of a cliff, hill) to tower, to overhang.

**ammasso** *m.* mass; bulk; heap.

**ammatt-ire** [D2] *intr.* (*aux.* essere) to go mad; *far —*, to drive mad, to give endless trouble to; *rfl.* to cudgel one's brains; to torment oneself. **-ito** *part. adj.* driven mad, harassed.

**ammatton-are** [A1 c] *tr.* to pave with bricks; **-amẹnto** *m.* brick-paving. **-ato** *part. adj.* paved

with bricks; *n.m.* paving, pavement; brick floor.

**ammazz-are** [A1] *tr.* to kill; to murder; to slay; to slaughter; to bore, to weary; — *il tempo*, to kill time; *rfl.* to kill oneself; to ruin one's health; to wear oneself out; *recip. rfl.* to kill one another. **-amẹnto** *m.* killing, carnage; slaughter; heavy labour. **-ante** *part. adj.* killing; boring. **-ato** *part. adj.* murdered; slaughtered; *n.m.* murdered man. **-atọio** *m.* slaughterhouse; bludgeon; knock-out blow.

**ammenda** *f.* amends; correction; (leg.) fine for lesser crimes (e.g. 'contravvenzioni', misdemeanours).

**ammend-are** [A1] *tr.* to amend; to correct; to make amends for. **-amẹnto** *m.* amending, amendment.

**ammeni·colo** *m.* cavil, pretext; *pl.* sundries; *l'affitto e tutti gli ammenicoli relativi*, the rent and all the other sundry expenses.

**ammẹsso** *part.* of **ammettere,** q.v.; *adj.* admitted; acknowledged; — *che*, supposing that.

**ammẹttere** [C20] *tr.* to admit; to permit; to acknowledge; to receive; — *come cosa stabilita*, to take for granted.

**ammeẓẓare** [A1] *tr.* to halve; to half-fill; to half-empty; to clip (words).

**ammezzire** [D2] *intr.* (*aux.* essere), *rfl.* (of fruit) to go soft, to become over-ripe.

**ammiccare** [A2] *intr.* (*aux.* avere) to wink; to beckon.

**ammic-co** *m.* (*pl.* **-chi**) wink; winking; sign, nod.

**amministr-are** [A1] *tr.* to administer; to manage. **-ativo** *adj.* administrative; *governo -ativo*, caretaker government; *anno -ativo*, financial year. **-atọre** *m.* administrator; manager; director. **-aziọne** *f.* administration; management; directorship; *consiglio di -azione*, board of directors.

**ammira·gli-o** *m.* admiral; *adj. ufficiale* —, flag officer. **-a** *f.* flagship.

**ammir-are** [A1] *tr.* to admire; to gaze at in wonder; *abs.* to marvel. **-a·bile** *adj.* admirable; strange, wondrous. **-ando** *adj.* worthy of admiration. **-ativo** *adj.* admiring. **-ato** *part. adj.* admired; lost in wonder. **-atọre** *m.* admirer; suitor. **-aziọne** *f.* admiration; object of admiration. **-ẹvole** *adj.* admirable.

**ammiss-i·bile** *adj.* admissible; allowable. **-iọne** *f.* admission; admittance.

**ammobi(g)li-are** [A4] *tr.* to furnish. **-amẹnto** *m.* furnishing; furnishings. **-ato** *part. adj.* furnished; *stanze -ate*, furnished rooms.

**ammodernare** [A1] *tr.* to modernize; to bring up to date; to refashion.

**ammodo** *adv.* nicely; properly; with care; *adj. indecl.* nice; good, well-behaved; respectable; circumspect.

**ammogliare** [A4c] *tr.* to find a wife for; (fig.) to match; *rfl.* to take a wife.

**ammollare** [A1] *tr.* to steep, to soak; to soften; to slacken (a rope); to relax, to let go; to land (with), to fob off (with); *intr.* (*aux.* avere) to give way, to yield; *rfl.* to get soaked; to soften; to become loose.

**ammoll-ire** [D2] *tr.* to soften; to mellow; to move (emotionally); to enervate; *rfl.* to become mellow, to grow soft. **-iẹnte** *adj., n.m.* emollient. **-imẹnto** *m.* softening; *-imento senile*, senile decay. **-itivo** *adj., n.m.* emollient.

**ammoni·ac-a** *f.* (chem.) ammonia. **-ato** *adj.* ammoniated.

**ammon-ire** [D2] *tr.* to reprimand; to caution; to advise; to forbid. **-imẹnto** *m.* warning; reproof. **-itọre** *m.* adviser; admonisher. **-ito·rio** *adj.* admonitory. **-iziọne** *f.* admonishment.

**ammontare** [A1c] *tr.* to amass, to accumulate; to pile up; *intr.* (*aux.* essere; *prep.* a) to amount (to); *rfl.* to accumulate; *n.m.* amount, sum.

**ammorbare** [A1] *tr.* to infect, to taint; to foul.

**ammorbidire** [D2] *tr.* to soften; to make supple; *rfl.* to become soft; to ripen.

**ammorsare**[1] [A1] *tr.* to bite; to nibble.

**ammorsare**[2] [A1] *tr.* to bit (a horse).

**ammort-are** [A1] *tr.* (comm.) to redeem, to buy off. **-amẹnto** *m.* depreciation; amortization; *fondo di -amento*, sinking fund; *piano di -amento*, funding scheme.

**ammortire** [D2] *tr.* to deaden; to numb; to parry; to tone down; *intr.* (*aux.* avere), *rfl.* to fade; to faint.

**ammortiẓẓ-are** [A1] *tr* to amortize, to redeem, to buy off. **-atọre** *m.* shock absorber. **-aziọne** *f.* amortization.

**ammorz-are** [A1] *tr.* to extinguish; to weaken; *rfl.* to die down; to grow faint. **-atọre** *m.* buffer, shock absorber.

**ammoscire** [D2] *intr.* (*aux.* essere) to become flabby; to shrivel.

**ammost-are** [A1c] *tr.* to tread, to press (grapes); *rfl., intr.* (*aux.* essere) to ferment. **-atọio** *m.* plunger, winepress.

**ammucchiare** [A4] *tr.* to pile up; to cram; *rfl.* to accumulate.

**ammuff-ire** [D2] *intr.* (*aux.* essere) to grow mouldy; (fig.) — *sui libri*, to pore over books; — *in casa*, to be house-bound. **-ito** *part. adj.* musty, mouldy.

**ammuṣ-are** [A1] *tr.* to nuzzle; *intr.* (*aux.* avere) to sulk, to pout; *rfl.* to sulk; *recip. rfl.* to nuzzle one another. **-ato** *part. adj.* pouting, sulky.

**ammutin-are** [A1s] *intr.* (*aux.* essere), *rfl.* to mutiny; to rebel; *tr.* to excite to revolt. **-ato** *part. adj.* mutinous; seditious; *n.m.* mutineer; rebel.

**ammutol-ire** [D2] *intr.* (*aux.* essere) to become dumb; to be reduced to silence. **-ito** *part. adj.* rendered speechless.

**amneṣi·a** *f.* amnesia, loss of memory.

**amnisti·a** *f.* amnesty; general pardon.

**amo** *m.* fish-hook; (fig.) flattery; lure; *tendere l'—*, to bait the hook; *pigliar l'—*, to swallow the bait.

**amoral-e** *adj.* amoral. **-iṣmo** *m.*, **-ità** *f.* amoralism.

**amọr-e** *m.* love; love personified, Cupid, Eros; affection; fondness; friendship; passion; love-affair; loved one; *con* —, eagerly, lovingly; *per* —, willingly; *per — o per forza*, willy-nilly; *per l'amor di Dio!*, for Heaven's sake!; *per — di brevità*, for the sake of brevity; (bot.) — *nascosto*, columbine. **-ẹvole** *adj.* loving; kind, fond. **-evolẹzza** *f.* love; kindliness. **-ọso** *adj.* loving; affectionate; *con -osa cura*, with loving care; amorous; *lettera -osa*, love-letter; *n.m.* (theatr.) *primo -oso*, juvenile lead.

**amoreggi-are** [A3c] *intr.* (*aux.* avere) to flirt; to philander. **-amẹnto** *m.* flirtation; philandering; gallantry.

**amorfo** *adj.* shapeless, amorphous.

**am·pi-o** *adj.* ample; wide; roomy; liberal, abundant; (of style) diffuse. **-ẹzza** *f.* spaciousness; width; range; capaciousness.

**amplesso** *m.* embrace.

**ampliare** [A4s] *tr.* to enlarge; to extend; *rfl.* to expand; to dilate.

**amplific-are** [A2s] *tr.* to amplify; to extol; to laud to the skies. **-atọre** *m.* amplifier. **-aziọne** *f.* amplification; enlargement; exegesis.

**ampli·fono** *m.* (radio, etc.) pick-up.

**ampl-o** *adj.* wide. **-itu·dine** *f.* amplitude.

**ampọll-a** *f.* phial; ampoule; *pl.* cruet (for oil and vinegar); bubble; blister; electric light bulb. **-iera** *f.* cruet-stand.

**ampollọs-o** *adj.* bombastic, pompous; high-flown. **-ità** *f.* bombast, pomposity.

**amput-are** [A1s] *tr.* to amputate; to perform an amputation upon. **-aziọne** *f.* amputation.

**amuleto** *m.* amulet, charm; talisman.
**anacron-ismo** *m.* anachronism. **-i·stico** *adj.* anachronistic.
**ana·grafe** *f.* register of births, deaths and marriages; register office; census; *capo dell'ufficio d'—*, registrar-general; *ufficio d'—*, registry.
**anagramma** *m.* anagram.
**analfabet-a** *adj.* illiterate; unlettered; *n.m.*, *f.* illiterate person. **-ismo** *m.* illiteracy.
**anal-gesi·a** *f.* analgesia. **-ge·sico** *adj.* analgesic; *n.m.* pain-killer.
**an-a·lisi** *f.indecl.* analysis; test; (telev.) scanning; — *tempi*, time study. **-alista** *m.* analyst; analyser. **-ali·tica** *f.* analytics. **-ali·tico** *adj.* analytic(al).
**analizz-are** [A1] *tr.* to analyse; to examine. **-atore** *m.* analyser, analyst.
**ana·lo-go** *adj.* (*m.pl.* **-ghi**) analogous; like, suitable. **-gi·a** *f.* analogy.
**ananasso** *m.* pineapple.
**an-archi·a** *f.* anarchy; (colloq.) tumult, chaos. **-ar·chico** *adj.* anarchic(al). **-archista** *m.* anarchist.
**anatem-a, ana·tem-a** *m.* anathema, excommunication, curse; accursed thing. **-atizzare** [A1], **-izzare** [A1] *tr.* to anathematize.
**anat-omi·a** *f.* anatomy. **-o·mico** *adj.* anatomic(al); *sala -omica*, dissecting room. **-omista** *m.* anatomist. **-omizzare** [A1] *tr.* to anatomize, to dissect.
**a·natr-a** *f.* (orn.) duck; *m.* — *maschio*, drake. **-are** [A1] *intr.* (*aux.* avere) to quack. **-oc·colo, -otto** *m.* duckling.
**anca** *f.* haunch; hip; thigh; side; drumstick (of a bird); *pl.* (of animals) hindquarters.
**ancella** *f.* (poet.; joc.) handmaid; maidservant.
**ancestrale** *adj.* ancestral.
**anche** *adv.*; *conj.* and, too, also; likewise; still; even; *quand'—*, even though; — *se*, even if; *ce n'è —*, there's some more left; *fosse —*, even if; *nè —*, not even.
**anci·pite** *adj.* amphibious; two-headed; uncertain, dubious.
**ancor-a** *adv.* still; yet; again; once more; more; further; also; *per —*, up to now; *dammene —*, give me some more; — *una settimana*, one week longer; — *una volta*, once more; *ancor più*, even more. **-chè** *conj.*, **-quando** *conj.* although, even if.
**an·cor-a** *f.* (naut.) anchor; *stare sull'—*, to lie at anchor; *salpare l'—*, to weigh anchor; *dar fondo all'—*, to cast anchor. **-ag·gio** *m.* anchorage; berth. **-are** [A1 s] *tr.* to anchor; *rfl.* to come to anchor, to cast anchor.
**andana** *f.* avenue between trees; rope-walk.
**and-are** [A8] *intr.* (*aux.* essere). **1.** To go (locomotion, travel); — *a piedi*, to walk; — *di corsa*, to run; — *in bicicletta*, to cycle; — *in macchina*, to go by car; — *col treno*, to go by train; — *per mare*, to go by sea; — *per terra*, to go by land. **2.** To go away, to set out; *andiamo*, let's go; *andarsene*, to go away, to take one's leave; — *in pensione*, to retire. **3.** To arrive, to reach, to get, to land; — *a fondo di*, to get to the bottom of; — *a un pelo da*, to be a hair's-breadth from; — *sotto un'automobile*, to get run over; — *a gambe all'aria*, to tumble head over heels. **4.** To go about, to proceed, to make one's way; — *a zonzo*, to stroll; — *a braccetto*, to walk arm in arm; — *per i propri affari*, to go about one's business; — *in processione*, to process; — *di notte*, to go about at night; — *per le lunghe*, to be long-drawn-out. **5.** To turn out, to end up, to prove, to go; — *bene*, to turn out well; *com'è -ata?*, how was it, how did you get on?; *com'è -ato a finire?*, what became of him?; — *male*, to go wrong. **6.** To become, to grow, to go; — *a male*, to go bad; — *in aceto*, to turn to vinegar; — *in pezzi*, to fall to pieces; — *in collera*, to lose one's temper; — *per i trenta*, to be getting on for thirty. **7.** To go through it, to suffer; — *per le mani di tutti*, to be abused by all; *ne va di mezzo la vita*, it's a matter of life and death. **8.** To serve, to pass, to do; *può —*, it will do, it will serve; *va bene*, that's all right; to be legal tender; to be valid. **9.** To suit, to fit; — *a pennello*, to suit to a t; — *a genio*, to please; to suit. **10.** To act, to behave; — *cauto*, to act cautiously; — *con le buone*, to be kindly; — *d'accordo*, to get on well together. **11.** To function, to work, to go; — *a elettricità*, to run on electricity; — *in orario*, to run to time; *così va il mondo*, that's the way of the world. **12.** To frequent the company (of), to go (with); — *insieme con*, to keep company with. **13.** To be saleable, to be sold; — *a ruba*, to sell like hot cakes; — *in vendita*, to be put up for sale; *a quanto va il grano?*, what's the price of wheat? **14.** To be needed; *a quest' opera ci andranno molti anni*, it will take many years to finish this work. **15.** To continue, to last; *benone, finchè la va!*, very nice, as long as it lasts! **16.** To be contained, to go (into); *quanto vino può — in questa botte?*, how much wine will this cask hold?; *n.m.* gait, walk; manner, style; *sull'— di*, in imitation of; go, going, pace; *il treno correva a tutt'—*, the train was running at full speed; *a lungo —*, in the long run; *al peggio —*, at the worst. **-amento** *m.* proceeding; course; progress; *l' -amento di casa*, the running of a house. **-ante** *part. adj.* current, instant; *il mese -ante*, the current month; plain, everyday; cheap; easy-going; steady; continuous; (mus.) neither quick nor slow; *adv.* fluently. **-ata** *f.* going, journey; *viaggio di -ata*, outward journey; *biglietto d'-ata e ritorno*, return ticket; *a lunga -ata*, in the long run. **-atura** *f.* gait; pace; way of walking.
**andirivieni** *m. indecl.* coming and going, bustle; labyrinth, maze.
**an·dito** *m.* passage, corridor; gallery.
**androne** *m.* corridor; lobby, entrance-hall; alley.
**aned·d-oto** *m.* anecdote; *pl.* anecdota. **-o·tica** *f.* collection of anecdotes; anecdotage. **-o·tico** *adj.* anecdotal.
**anel-are** [A1] *intr.* (*aux.* avere) to pant; to gasp; *tr.* to long for, to desire. **-ante** *part. adj.* panting, breathless; eager, desirous.
**ane·lito** *m.* panting, gasping; yearning.
**anell-o** *m.* ring; circle, group (of people); — *delle chiavi*, key-ring; — *di fidanzamento*, engagement-ring; — *matrimoniale*, wedding-ring; curl, ringlet; (fig.) (*pl.f. le -a*) link, intermediary; — *di congiunzione*, missing link. **-ato** *adj.* ringed; ring-shaped; (of hair) in ringlets. **-oso** *adj.* looped, in rings.
**an-emi·a** *f.* anaemia. **-e·mico** *adj.* anaemic.
**ane·mone** *m.* (bot.) anemone, windflower; (zool.) — *di mare*, sea anemone.
**anest-esi·a** *f.* anaesthesia. **-esino** *m.dim.* local anaesthetic. **-e·tico** *adj.*, *n.m.* anaesthetic. **-etista** *m.* anaesthetist. **-etizzare** [A1] *tr.* to anaesthetize.
**anfi·bio** *adj.* amphibious; amphibian; *n.m.* amphibian.
**anfi·bo-lo** *adj.* ambiguous. **-logi·a** *f.* ambiguity. **-lo·gico** *adj.* ambiguous.
**anfiteatro** *m.* amphitheatre.
**an·fora** *f.* amphora; jar; water-jar.
**anfratt-o** *m.* winding path; sinuous crevice. **-uosità** *f.* sinuosity; *pl.* winding crevices. **-uoso** *adj.* winding, sinuous.
**angariare** [A4] *tr.* to oppress; to harass; to overtax.
**ange·lic-o** *adj.* angelic. **-ato** *adj.* idealized.
**an·gelo** *m.* angel; cherub; darling; *cantare come un —*, to sing divinely; *è un — di bontà*, he's as good as gold; — *custode*, guardian angel.
**angheri·a** *f.* oppression, tyranny; imposition; heavy taxation.
**anglicano** *adj.* Anglican.
**angl-o** *pref.* Anglo. **-ofili·a** *f.* pro-English feeling. **-o·filo** *m.*

anglophile. **-ofobi·a** *f.* anglophobia, anti-English feeling. **-o·fobo** *m.* anglophobe. **-o·mane** *m., f.* passionate admirer of the English. **-omani·a** *f.* Anglomania. **-osas·sone** *adj.* Anglo-Saxon; English-speaking; *n.m., f.*

**an·gol-o** *m.* corner; nook; angle; *un posto d'–*, a corner seat; *– visuale*, view point. **-are** *adj.* angular; *pietra -are*, corner-stone. **-are** [A1 s] *tr.* to photograph from a certain angle. **-azione** *f.* (cinem.; photog.) angle; (fig.) point of view. **-oso** *adj.* angular; (fig.) touchy.

**ango·sci-a** *f.* anguish; pain; grief. **-are** [A3] *tr.* to distress; to torment; *rfl.* to grieve. **-oso** *adj.* grievous; painful; anguished.

**anguilla** *f.* eel; (fig.) *sguizzare di mano come un'–*, to be as slippery as an eel.

**anguina·ia** *f.* (anat.) groin.

**angu·sti-a** *f.* poverty, penury; anxiety; distress; *— di tempo*, want of time; *essere nelle -e*, to be in difficulties. **-are** [A4] *tr.* to distress; to afflict; *rfl.* to distress oneself; to worry.

**angusto** *adj.* narrow; limited; petty.

**a·nim-a** *f.* soul, spirit, breath of life; *render l'— a Dio*, to give up the ghost; *un'— buona*, a kindly soul; *non c'è — viva*, there's not a soul here; *cavare l'— a*, to pester; ghost, spectre; person; *è un'— lunga*, he's a tall chap; *pl.* inhabitants; *stato d'-e*, register of population; emotions, feeling, heart; *arrivare all'—*, to go to one's heart; *un bene dell'—*, a heartfelt love; courage; animation, zest; *senz'—*, lifeless; centre, core.

**animadversione** *f.* animadversion.

**animal-e** *m.* animal; dumb creature; brute, beast; (fig.) blockhead, imbecile; *adj.* animal, physical; *regno —*, animal kingdom; *funzioni -i*, physical functions. **-esco** *adj.* (*m.pl.* **-eschi**) animal; *istinto -esco*, animal instinct; bestial.

**anim-are** [A1 s] *tr.* to animate; to quicken; to enliven; to encourage; *— il commercio*, to promote trade; *rfl.* to become animated; to grow cheerful; to take courage. **-ato** *part. adj.* animated; vivacious; animate; containing a core; *bastone -ato*, sword-stick. **-azione** *f.* animation; life, activity.

**a·nimo** *m.* mind; heart; tendency; intention; courage; *stato d'—*, mood; *avere in — di*, to intend to; *mettersi in — di*, to make up one's mind to; *aprire l'—*, to speak frankly; *avere — a*, to have the courage to; *farsi —*, to take heart; *d'— gentile*, of a kindly disposition; *mal —*, ill-will; *di buon —*, cheerfully; *mettersi l'— in pace*, to resign oneself; *con — di ucciderlo*, intending to kill him.

**animos-o** *adj.* courageous; spirited; fiery. **-ità** *f.* animosity, animus, rancour.

**anisetta** *f.* aniseed cordial.

**annacqu-are** [A6] *tr.* to water, to dilute; to moderate; to soften. **-ata** *f.* sprinkling; light shower.

**annaffi-are** [A4] *tr.* to water, to sprinkle, to wet. **-atoio** *m.* watering-can.

**annal-i** *m.pl.* annals. **-ista** *m.* annalist.

**annaspare** [A1] *tr.* to wind (thread) on a reel; *intr.* (*aux.* avere) to gesticulate wildly; to puzzle in vain.

**annata** *f.* year, the space of a year; the events of a year; crop; income.

**annebbiare** [A4 c] *tr.* to darken, to obscure; to cloud; to dim; *rfl.* to be obscured; to become foggy; (of sight) to grow dim.

**annegare** [A2 c] *tr.* to drown; *intr.* (*aux.* essere) to drown, to be drowned; *stare per —* to be drowning; *rfl.* to drown oneself.

**annerire** [D2] *tr.* to blacken; to darken; (fig.) to denigrate; *intr.* (*aux.* essere), *rfl.* to become black; to grow dark.

**anness-o** *part. adj.* annexed; attached; included, enclosed; *n.m.* annexe; appendage. **-a** *f.* letter enclosed, enclosure. **-ione** *f.* annexation; addition.

**annet·tere** [C19] *tr.* to annex; to attach; to enclose; *– importanza*, to attribute importance.

**annichil-are** [A1 s], **-ire** [D2] *tr.* to annihilate; to destroy; *rfl.* to be annihilated; to humble oneself, to cringe.

**annidare** [A1] *tr.* to find a nook for; (fig.) to cherish; *rfl.* to nest; to nestle; to lie concealed.

**annientare** [A1] *tr.* to annihilate; to bring to nought; *rfl.* (fig.) to humble oneself; to come to nothing.

**anniversa·rio** *adj., n.m.* anniversary; birthday.

**ann-o** *m.* year; *— bisestile*, leap-year; *Capo d'—*, New Year's Day; *pl.* age; *quanti -i hai?*, how old are you?; *pieno d'-i*, old; *mi par mill'-i di tornare*, I am longing to return; *innanzi gli -i*, before the proper time. **-osità** *f.* age (of plants); life-span (of animals). **-oso** *adj.* full of years, age; *una questione -osa*, an age-old problem.

**annobilire** [D2] *tr.* to ennoble; to adorn; *intr.* (*aux.* essere) to become ennobled.

**annodare** [A1] *tr.* to knot; to tie; to bind; *— le scarpe*, to tie up one's shoes; *— relazioni*, to form connexions; *— un affare*, to clinch an affair; *rfl.* to form a knot; to get entangled.

**annoi-are** [A4] *tr.* to bore; to annoy; to tease; to trouble; to weary; *rfl.* to be bored; to be annoyed; to get weary; *-arsi da morire*, to be bored to death.

**annon-a** *f.* food supply (of a municipality); supply of wheat; *ufficio dell'–*, food office, victualling-board. **-a·rio** *adj.* pertaining to provisions; *leggi -arie*, victualling laws; *carta -aria*, ration card.

**annot-are** [A1] *tr.* to annotate; to note, to jot down; to book. **-azione** *f.* annotation; entry; *-azione in calce*, footnote.

**annottare** [A1] *impers. intr.* (*aux.* essere) to grow dark; (of night) to draw on.

**annoverare** [A1 s] *tr.* to enumerate; to include; to class; to number, to count.

**annual-e** *adj.* annual, yearly; year-long; (bot.) annual; also *n.m.* **-mente** *adv.* annually, yearly; from year to year.

**annua·rio** *m.* year-book; annual, directory; list.

**annu-ire** [D2] *intr.* (*aux.* avere; *prep.* a) to nod in agreement; to assent, to agree; to consent (to). **-ente** *part. adj.* in agreement, consenting. **-enza** *f.* consent; agreement.

**annuità** *f.* annuity.

**annull-are** [A1] *tr.* to annul; to cancel; to undo; to wipe, to wash (of tape-recordings); *recip. rfl.* to cancel out, to cancel each other. **-amento** *m.* annulment; cancellation.

**annumerare** [A1 s] *tr.* to enumerate; to include, to class.

**annunzi-are** [A4] *tr.* to announce; to proclaim; to indicate; to prophesy; *— sui giornali*, to advertise. **-atore** *m.* announcer; harbinger; advertiser; wireless announcer; *angelo -atore*, angel of the Annunciation. **-azione** *f.* (eccl.) Annunciation; Lady Day (25 March).

**annun·zio** *m.* announcement; notice; information; presage; *– pubblicitario*, advertisement.

**an·nuo** *adj.* annual, yearly.

**annus-are** [A1] *tr., abs.* to sniff, to smell; to suspect; to nose out; *– tabacco*, to take snuff. **-ata** *f.*, **-o** *m.* sniff.

**annuvolare** [A1 s] *tr.* to darken, to cloud; to obscure; *intr.* (*aux.* essere), *rfl.* to grow cloudy; to become gloomy.

**ano·dino, anodino** *adj., n.m.* anodyne.

**ano·mal-o** *adj.* anomalous. **-i·a** *f.* anomaly.

**ano·nim-o** *adj.* anonymous; (leg.) *società -a*, limited company; *n.m.* one who is anonymous; *conservare l'–*, to remain anonymous. **-a** *f.* limited company. **-ato** *m.*, **-i·a** *f.* anonymity.

**anormal-e** *adj.* abnormal. **-ità** *f.* abnormality.
**ans-a** *f.* pot-handle; handle; (fig.) pretext, loophole; bend, loop. **-ato** *adj.* with handles.
**ans-are** [A1] *intr.* (*aux.* avere) to pant; to gasp; to breathe heavily. **-ante** *part. adj.* panting, breathless.
**an·si-a** *f.* longing, impatience; anxiety; *vivere in* –, to be on tenterhooks. **-età** *f.* anxiety, trepidation. **-ọso** *adj.* anxious; wistful; desirous.
**an·sim-a** *f.*, **-o** *m.* shortness of breath. **-are** [A1 s] *intr.* (*aux.* avere) to be short of breath. **-ante** *part. adj.* panting, gasping.
**an·sito** *m.* troubled breathing; gasping, panting
**anta**[1] window-frame; door-frame; panel; *ante scorrevoli*, sliding doors.
**anta**[2] *f.* (archit.) anta, pilaster.
**anta**[3] *m.indecl.* termination of numbers from 40 to 90, e.g. *quaranta.*
**anta·cido** *adj.*, *n.m.* antacid.
**antagon-ịsmo** *m.* antagonism; rivalry; contest. **-ista** *m.* antagonist; adversary; rival. **-i·stico** *adj.* antagonistic.
**ante-ce·dere** [C19] *intr.* (*aux.* avere) to precede (in time). **-cedente** *part. adj.* previous, prior, antecedent; foregoing. **-cedenza** *f.* antecedence; priority. **-cessọre** *m.* predecessor; ancestor.
**antedẹtto** *adj.* already mentioned, aforesaid.
**antefatto** *m.* antecedent facts; previous history; all that has occurred before a play begins.
**anteguerra** *m.* pre-war period; *la letteratura d'*—, pre-war literature; *adj. indecl.* pre-war; *prezzi* –, pre-war prices.
**antelucano** *adj.* antelucan; preceding the dawn; *splendori antelucani*, first light.
**antenato** *m.* ancestor, forefather, progenitor.
**antenna** *f.* (naut.) yard; antenna, feeler; aerial.
**antenotato** *adj.* already noted.
**anteporre** [B21] *tr.* to place before; to prefer; to give precedence to.
**anteprima** *f.* private view; preview.
**antera, an·tera** *f.* (bot.) anther.
**anteriọr-e** *adj.* preceding; previous, prior; former; anterior, front, fore; (gramm.) *futuro* —, future perfect. **-ità** *f.* priority; precedence.
**antescritto** *adj.* aforementioned.
**antevịsiọne** *f.* preview.
**anti-**[1] *pref.* against, counter, anti; *adj. indecl.* anti, opposed. **-abbagliante** *adj.* anti-dazzle; *faro -abbagliante*, dipped headlamp. **-a·cido** *adj.* antacid; acid-proof; *n.m.* antacid. **-ae·reo** *adj.* anti-aircraft. **-alcoo·lico** *adj.* teetotal, abstinent, abstemious. **-bio·tico** *adj.*, *n.m.* anti-biotic. **-calca·reo** *m.* water-softener. **-carro** *adj. indecl.* anti-tank; *cannone -carro*, anti-tank gun. **-ciclọne** *m.* anticyclone. **-clericale** *adj.*, *n.m.* anti-clerical. **-concettivo, -concezionale** *adj.*, *n.m.* contraceptive. **-congelante** *adj.*, *n.m.* anti-freeze. **-corpo** *m.* antibody. **-febbrile** *adj.*, *n.m.* febrifuge. **-furto** *adj. indecl.* burglar-proof, thief-proof; *dispositivo -furto*, burglar alarm. **-gelo** *adj.*, *n.m.* anti-freeze. **-ghiac·cio** *m.* (aeron.) de-icer. **-gie·nico** *adj.* unhygienic. **-guerrẹsco** *adj.* anti-war. **-infortuni·stica** *f.* accident prevention. **-manifesto** *m.* counter-manifesto. **-nevral·gico** *adj.* pain-relieving. **-ora·rio** *adj.* anti-clockwise. **-piega, -pigehe** *adj. indecl.* crease-resisting, uncrushable. **-rug·gine** *adj. indecl.* rust-proof; stainless. **-schẹggia** *adj. indecl.* anti-splinter, non-splinterable. **-ṣdrucciolẹvole** *adj.* anti-slip; (of a tyre) anti-skid. **-semi·tico** *adj.* anti-Semitic. **-sepsina** *f.* disinfectant. **-set·tico** *adj.* antiseptic; disinfectant. **-sociale** *adj.* anti-social. **-u·mido** *adj.* damp-resisting. **-velẹno** *m.* antidote.
**anti-**[2] *pref.* ante. **-ca·mera** *f.* antechamber, ante-room; *fare -camera*, to be kept waiting. **-conoscenza** *f.* foreknowledge, prescience. **-cọrte** *f.* courtyard. **-cursọre** *m.* pioneer; precursor. **-datare** [A1] *tr.* to antedate. **-diluviano** *adj.* antediluvian; (joc.) out-moded. **-meridiano** *adj.* antemeridian. **-mẹsso** *adj.* placed before; preferred. **-pasto** *m.* hors-d'œuvre. **-penul·timo** *adj.* antepenultimate. **-porta** *f.* vestibule, entrance-hall. **-vedẹre** [B23] *tr.* to foresee. **-veggenza** *f.* foresight.
**antica·glia** *f.* curiosity, antique; *pl.* junk, lumber; *negozio di anticaglie*, old curiosity shop.
**antichità** *f.* antiquity; ancient times; antique; *pl.* ancient monuments; *negozio di* –, antique shop.
**anticip-are** [A1 s] *tr.* to anticipate; to forestall; to put forward (time or date); to pay in advance; to antedate; *intr.* (*aux.* avere) to arrive before schedule; (of a train) to get in early; (of a watch) to be fast; *rfl.* to gain time, to get ahead of one's schedule. **-aziọne** *f.* anticipation; (comm.) advance.
**anti·cipo** *m.* anticipation; advance (of money); *in* –, in advance, early; *il treno arrivò con un – di sette minuti*, the train got in seven minutes early.
**anti-co** *adj.* (*m.pl.* **-chi**) ancient; long-standing; old-fashioned; obsolete; antique; *all'-ca*, in an old-fashioned way; *in* —, in ancient times; in the old days; *n.m.* antiquity; *pl. gli -chi*, the ancients.
**anti·doto** *m.* antidote; preservative.
**anti·lope** *m.* (zool.) antelope.
**anti-pati·a** *f.* antipathy, dislike. **-pa·tico** *adj.* unpleasant, displeasing; antipathetic.
**anti·pod-e, -o** *m.* one who lives at the Antipodes; *pl.* Antipodes; (fig.) *essere agli -i* (*l'uno all'altro*), to be poles apart.
**antiqua·ri-o** *adj.*, *n.m.* dealer in antiques; antiquarian; antiquary. **-ato** *m.* antiquarian trade; second-hand book-trade.
**antiquato** *adj.* antiquated, old-fashioned; obsolete, archaic.
**antirrino** *m.* (bot.) snapdragon, antirrhinum.
**anti·t-eṣi** *f.indecl.* antithesis. **-e·tico** *adj.* antithetic.
**antologi·a** *f.* anthology.
**antro** *m.* cave, cavern; den, lair; hovel.
**antro-po·fago** *adj.* (*m.pl.* **-po·fagi, -po·faghi**) man-eating, cannibal, anthropophagous; *n.m.* man-eater, cannibal. **-pologi·a** *f.* anthropology. **-polo·gico** *adj.* anthropological. **-po·logo** *m.* (*pl.* **-po·logi, -po·loghi**) anthropologist. **-pomor·fico** *adj.* anthropomorphic. **-pomorfịsmo** *m.* anthropomorphism.
**anulare** *adj.* ring-shaped; *dito* —, ring-finger; annular.
**anzi** *conj.* on the contrary; in fact, indeed; still more; or rather; *fai bene, – benone*, you're doing well, in fact very well; *prep.* before; — *tempo*, before the expected time, early. **-chẹ** *conj.* rather than. **-dẹtto** *adj.* aforesaid, above mentioned. **-tutto** *adv.* above all; first of all.
**anzian-o** *adj.* aged; elderly; senior; retired; former; *n.m.* elder; senior; alderman. **-ità** *f.* seniority; term of office, length of service; *avanzamento ad -ità*, promotion by seniority.
**apati·a** *f.* apathy; indifference; listlessness.
**apa·t-ico** *adj.* apathetic; indifferent; lackadaisical. **-ista** *m.* apathetic individual.
**ape** *f.* (ent.) bee; — *operaia*, worker-bee; – *regina*, queen-bee; *maschio dell'*–, drone; – *da miele*, honey-bee.
**aperiente** *adj.*, *n.m.* aperient.
**aperitivo**[1] *adj.*, *n.m.* (med.) aperient.
**aperitivo**[2] *m.* apéritif; appetizer.
**apert-o** *part. adj.* open; spacious; roomy; obvious, clear; frank, sincere; alert; *all'aria -a*, in the open-air; *adv.* openly, frankly; *n.m.* open space. **-a** *f.* opening; opening time (for shops, etc.). **-amẹnte** *adv.* openly, frankly; clearly, **-ura** *f.* opening; aper-

ture, hole, chink; breach, cleft; width; spread; *-ura alare*, wing span; inauguration; preliminary step; *far qualche -ura*, to make preliminary enquiries; (pol.) approach, overture; (mus.) overture.

**api-a·io** *m.* beekeeper, apiarist. **-a·ria** *f.* apiculture. **-a·rio** *m.* apiary.

**a·pice** *m.* apex; culminating point, height.

**apicult-ore** *m.* beekeeper, apiarist. **-ura** *f.* beekeeping, apiculture.

**a·pio** *m.* celery.

**apo·crifo** *adj.* apocryphal.

**apoft-egma, -emma** *m.* apophthegm, maxim.

**apoge·o**[1] *m.* (astron.) apogee; (fig.) height, summit, climax.

**apoge·o**[2] *m.* land wind.

**apo·lide** *adj.* stateless; *n.m., f.* person without a country, displaced person.

**apoli·tico** *adj.* non-political.

**apolog-i·a** *f.* formal defence (written or spoken); justification; apologia. **-e·tica** *f.* (theol.) apologetics. **-e·tico** *adj.* vindicatory; *scritto -etico*, apologia; *n.m.* apologia. **-ista** *m.* apologist.

**apo·lo-go** *m.* (*m.pl.* **-ghi**) apologue, fable.

**apo-plessi·a** *f.* apoplexy. **-plet·-tico** *adj.* apoplectic(al); *n.m.* sufferer from apoplexy, apoplectic.

**apostași·a** *f.* (rel.; fig.) apostasy.

**apo·stat-a** *m., f.* apostate. **-are** [A1 s] *intr.* (*aux.* avere) to apostatize.

**apo·st-olo** *m.* apostle; propagandist. **-olato** *m.* apostolate. **-o·lico** *adj.* apostolic.

**apo·strof-e** *f.* (rhet.) exclamatory address; (gramm.) apostrophe. **-o** *m.* (gramm.) apostrophe, omission mark.

**apostrofare** [A1 s] *tr., abs.* to apostrophize.

**apoteoși** *f.indecl.* apotheosis; triumph; deification; (fig.) *far l' — di*, to laud to the skies.

**appaciare** [A3] *tr.* to appease.

**appacificare** [A2 s] *tr.* to pacify; to reconcile; *recip. rfl.* to make peace, to become reconciled.

**appadiglionare** [A1 c] *abs.* to pitch a tent; *rfl.* to go under canvas.

**appagare** [A2] *tr.* to satisfy; to content; to satiate; *— la sete*, to quench one's thirst; *rfl.* (*prep.* di) to be satisfied; to rest content.

**appaiare** [A4] *tr.* to pair, to couple; to yoke; to match (colours); *rfl.* to form a pair; (of colours, materials) to match.

**appalt-are** [A1] *tr.* to let out on contract, to undertake on contract; *rfl. -arsi a*, to take out a season-ticket for. **-o** *m.* allocation (of contract); contract.

**appannag·gio** *m.* appanage; Household List; (fig.) prerogative; attribute.

**appannare** [A1] *tr.* to dim, to blur, to mist; to tarnish; to frost (glass); to hood, to clock; *rfl.* to become tarnished; (of sound) to die away; (of sight) to grow dim.

**apparato** *m.* array, display; pomp, magnificence; decoration; *discorso d' —*, ceremonial address; furnishings, fittings; *— scenico*, mise-en-scène, set; apparatus.

**apparatore** *m.* decorator; (theatr.) stage-manager.

**apparecchi-are** [A4 c] *tr.* to prepare; to make ready; *— la tavola*, to lay the table; *rfl.* to prepare oneself; to get ready. **-atore** *m.* decorator. **-atura** *f.* apparatus; equipment, switchgear; preparation.

**apparecchio** *m.* preparation; arrangement; layout; apparatus; machine; *— radio*, wireless set; outfit, equipment, gear; requisites; *apparecchi di guerra*, preparations for war; (aeron.) plane.

**apparentamento** *m.* (neol. pol.) coalition, agreement, political alliance.

**apparentato** *adj.* (neol. pol.) forming a coalition.

**apparigli-are** [A4] *tr.* to pair, to match. **-ato** *part. adj.* paired; (fig.) level, neck and neck.

**appar-ire** [D3] *intr.* (*aux.* essere) to appear; to come into view; to be visible; to result, to turn out; to be apparent. **-ente** *part. adj.* apparent, seeming, ostensible; visible; evident, clear. **-enza** *f.* appearance; guise; aspect; look; form, shape; *l'-enza inganna*, appearances are deceptive; *per salvare l'-enza*, for the sake of appearances; sign, indication; likelihood, probability; *in -enza*, apparently, to all appearance. **-ita** *f.* appearance, coming into view. **-izione** *f.* apparition; phantasm.

**appariscen-te** *adj.* visible; striking, conspicuous; showy; spectacular; *colori -ti*, gaudy colours. **-za** *f.* striking appearance; conspicuousness; gaudiness.

**appartamento** *m.* apartment, flat, living quarters.

**appart-are** [A1] *tr.* to set apart; to put on one side; to separate; *rfl.* to stand aloof; to withdraw; to lead a secluded life. **-ato** *part. adj.* set apart; secluded; solitary; remote.

**apparten-ere** [B32] *intr.* (*aux.* avere, essere; *prep.* a) to belong; to appertain; to be a member (of); to be related (to); to befit, to behove, to be the duty of (also *rfl.*). **-enza** *f., usu. pl.* belongings; accessories; (leg.) appurtenances.

**appassion-are** [A1 c] *tr.* to impassion; to move, to touch; to enamour; *rfl.* (*prep.* a, di, per) to be enamoured (of); *si -a molto alla musica*, he is very fond of music; (*prep.* per, di) to sorrow (over), to be deeply moved (by). **-ato** *part. adj.* passionate; ardent; fond; broken-hearted, stricken; enamoured.

**appass-ire** [D2] *tr.* to dry (fruit) in the sun; *intr.* (*aux.* essere), *rfl.* to fade; to wither; to decay. **-ito** *part. adj.* dried-up; *uva -ita*, raisins; faded, withered.

**appell-are** [A1] *intr.* (*aux.* avere), *rfl.* to appeal; *tr.* to name, to designate; *rfl.* to be called. **-ativo** *adj. nome -ativo*, common noun; *n.m.* designation, name, term. **-azione** *f.* appellation.

**appello** *m.* call; appeal; *fare — a*, to appeal to; *— al popolo*, plebiscite; *fare l'—*, to call the roll; (leg.) appeal; *ricorrere in —*, to appeal.

**appena** *adv.* as soon as; hardly; scarcely, just; with difficulty; almost immediately; *— che*, no sooner...than; *non —*, just as soon as.

**appen·dere** [C1] *tr.* (*prep.* a) to suspend, to hang (on).

**append-ice** *f.* appendix; supplement; (anat.) appendix. **-icite** *f.* appendicitis.

**appesire** [D2] *intr.* (*aux.* essere) to put on weight, to get heavier.

**appestare** [A1] *tr.* to infect; to taint; to pollute; (fig.) to corrupt.

**appet-ire** [D2] *tr.* to hunger for; to desire; to long for; *intr.* (*aux.* essere, avere) to stimulate appetite, to be appetizing. **-ente** *part. adj.* appetizing; hungry for, in need of. **-enza** *f.* appetite; inclination; longing. **-i·bile, -itivo** *adj.* desirable; appetizing.

**appetit-o** *m.* appetite; hunger; inclination; avidity; lust. **-oso** *adj.* appetizing; tempting; attractive; hungry.

**appetto** *prep.* (*foll. by* a) in comparison (with); opposite.

**appiallare** [A1] *tr.* to plane.

**appian-are** [A1] *tr.* to level; to smooth; (fig.) to facilitate; to remove (difficulties). **-atoio** *m.* garden-roller.

**appiastrare** [A1] *tr.* to plaster; to stick; to glue; to daub; *rfl.* to stick (together), to adhere.

**appiattare** [A1] *tr.* to flatten; to conceal, to hide; *rfl.* to crouch in hiding; to cower; to squat; (fig.) to lurk.

**appiattire** [D2] *tr.* to level, to flatten; *rfl.* to become flat; to be levelled.

**appiccafuoco** *m. indecl.* incendiary.

**appicc-are** [A2] *tr.* to attach, to join; to affix; to hang (by the neck); to fasten on; to palm off on; *-arla a*, to play a trick on; to pass on (a disease); *— il fuoco a*, to set fire to; *— lite*, to pick a quarrel; *rfl.* to cling; to hang one-

self; (of fire, disease) to spread. **-a·gnolo** *m.* hook, peg; (fig.) pretext; cavil. **-ante** *part. adj.* adhesive, sticky; clammy; contagious. **-atic·cio** *adj.* sticky; contagious; (fig.) importunate. **-atọia** *f.*, **-atọio** *m.* peg.

**appicci-are** [A3] *tr.* to attach; to kindle; to light; *rfl.* to be kindled. **-ante** *part. adj.* sticky, adhesive; clammy.

**appiccicare** [A2 s] *tr.* (*prep.* a) to paste; to stick; to palm off; (fig.) to tack on; — *uno schiaffo a*, to slap; *intr.* (*aux.* avere) to adhere; to stick; *rfl.* to attach oneself; to cling.

**appic-co** *m.* (*pl.* **-chi**) pretext; foothold.

**appiè** *prep.* (*foll. by* di) at the foot (of); *adv.* below, at the foot.

**appieno** *adv.* fully, completely; thoroughly; quite.

**appigion-are** [A1 c] *tr.* to let; *appigiònasi*, house to let, room to let. **-amẹnto** *m.* letting; rent.

**appi·glio** *m.* foothold, grip; (climbing) hold; pretext; excuse; *dare — a*, to give occasion to.

**appiọmbo** *adv.* perpendicularly; *cascare d'—*, to arrive in the nick of time; *n.m.* plumb-line, perpendicular; aplomb; confidence; balance; (of a dress, etc.) fall, line.

**appiṣolare** [A1 s] *rfl.* to doze, to have forty winks; to feel drowsy.

**applaud-ire** [D1 or D2] *tr.*, *intr.* (*aux.* avere; *prep.* a) to applaud; to clap; to approve; to praise. **-ente** *part. adj.* applauding, admiring, approving. **-ito** *part. adj.* applauded; celebrated, acclaimed.

**appla·uso** *m.* applause; clapping; cheering; approval.

**applic-are** [A1 s] *tr.* to apply; to lay on; to stick; to inflict; *rfl.* to apply oneself; to pay attention; to devote oneself. **-a·bile** *adj.* applicable, appropriate, suitable. **-aziọne** *f.* application; *pl.* appliances.

**appoggi-are** [A3] *tr.* to lean; to rest; — *nelle mani di*, to entrust to; to support; — *una mozione*, to second a motion; *rfl.* (*prep.* a) to lean (against); (*prep.* a, su) to base oneself (upon); to depend (on); to place confidence (in). **-atọio** *m.* support, rest; prop.

**appog·gio** *m.* support; balustrade; buttress; corbel; (fig.) favour; aid.

**appọrre** [B21] *tr.* to affix; — *la firma a*, to sign; to impute, to attribute; *rfl.* to guess, to conjecture; to be in the right.

**apportare** [A1] *tr.* to bring; to carry; to bring about, to cause; — *fortuna*, to bring good luck; to adduce.

**apporto** *m.* contribution; thing brought.

**appo·ṣit-o** *adj.* suitable; apposite; respective; made to order. **-amẹnte** *adv.* appropriately; on purpose.

**appoṣiziọne** *f.* apposition; appending (of signature).

**apposta** *adv.* on purpose; deliberately; wilfully; — *per voi*, just for you; *adj. indecl.* special, specially made.

**appostic·cio** *adj.* false, artificial; fictitious.

**appren·d-ere** [C1] to learn; to hear; to apprehend; to inform; to teach; *rfl.* (*prep. a*) to seize, to apprehend; to take root. **-ente** *n.m.,f.* learner; apprentice; beginner. **-ista** *m.,f.* apprentice; learner. **-istato** *m.* apprenticeship.

**apprens-i·bile** *adj.* capable of being learnt; intelligible. **-iọne** *f.* apprehension; comprehension. **-iva** *f.* power of apprehension. **-ivo** *adj.* capable of learning; apprehensive.

**appressare** [A1] *tr.* to bring near, to move close; *rfl.* to draw near, to approach; to resemble.

**appresso** *adv.* near, close by, at hand; *prep.* in the presence of; in comparison with.

**apprestare** [A1] *tr.* to prepare; to supply.

**apprezz-are** [A1] *tr.* to appreciate; to appraise; to price. **-a·bile** *adj.* appreciable; valuable. **-amẹnto** *m.* appreciation; appraisement.

**approd-are**[1] [A1] *intr.* (*aux.* essere) (naut.) to come alongside, to berth; (fig.) to lead (to), to come (to). **-o** *m.* landing; landing-place.

**approdare**[2] [A1] *intr.* (*aux.* avere; *prep.* a), to be of use, to avail, to serve.

**approfittare** [A1] *rfl.*, *intr.* (*aux.* avere; *prep.* di), to profit (by); to avail oneself (of); — *dell'occasione*, to jump at the chance.

**approfondare** [A1 c] *tr.* to deepen; to investigate thoroughly; to dig down into.

**approfondire** [D2] *tr.* to examine carefully, to get to the bottom of; *rfl.* (*prep.* in) to go deeply (into); to become learned (in).

**approntare** [A1 c] *tr.* to prepare, to make ready.

**appropinquare** [A6] *rfl.* to draw near, to approach; *intr.* (*aux.* essere) to approach.

**appropo·ṣito** *adv.* à propos.

**appropri-are** [A4] *tr.* to adapt; to adjust; — *l'azione alla parola*, to suit the action to the word; *rfl.* (*dat.* of *prn.*) to appropriate; to assimilate. **-ato** *part. adj.* appropriated; appropriate.

**approssim-are** [A1 s] *tr.* to bring near, to place beside; *rfl.* to approach; to approximate. **-ativo** *adj.* approximate; *calcolo -ativo*, rough estimate.

**approv-are** [A1] *tr.* to approve; to confirm. **-ato** *part. adj.* approved; *essere -ato agli esami*, to pass examinations; *elenco dei candidati -ati*, pass-list. **-aziọne** *f.* approval.

**approvvigionare** [A1 c] *tr.* to supply; to stock; to victual; *rfl.* to get in supplies.

**appuntamẹnto** *m.* appointment; *dare — a*, to make an appointment with; *darsi —*, to arrange to meet one another.

**appunt-are** [A1] *tr.* to sharpen, to make pointed; to aim at; — *lo sguardo su*, to fix one's eyes on; to make notes on; to censure; to stitch; to appoint. **-a·bile** *adj.* blameworthy; faulty. **-alapis** *m. indecl.* pencil-sharpener. **-ata** *f.* rough sewing, tacking.

**appunt-o**[1] *m.* note; comment; criticism; *muovere un — a*, to censure; *fare -i a*, to find fault with.

**appunto**[2] *adv.* precisely, exactly; just; *per l'—*, precisely; as it happens; *n.m.* exact point; *stare sull'—*, to be a stickler for accuracy; *adj. indecl.* precise, impeccable.

**appurare** [A1] *tr.* to ascertain, to verify; to wipe out (debt).

**appuzzare** [A1] *tr.* to pollute; to infect; (fig.) to taint, to corrupt.

**apribarat·tolo** *m. indecl.* tin-opener.

**apri-co** *adj.* (*m.pl.* **-chi**) sunny; exposed to the sun; open, airy.

**aprile** *m.* April; *nell'— degli anni*, in the flower of youth; *un pesce d'—*, an April fool.

**apr-ire** [D8] *tr.* to open; to begin; to inaugurate; to expound; to disclose; — *una buca*, to make a hole; — *la radio*, to switch on the wireless; *rfl.* to open; to lead (into); to begin; *-irsi con alcuno*, to confide in someone; to split, to crack; (of weather), to clear up; *intr.* (*aux.* essere) to gap, to gape.

**aprisca·tole** *m. indecl.* tin-opener.

**a·quil-a** *f.* eagle; (fig.) genius, outstanding intellect. **-astro** *m.* osprey. **-ino** *m. dim.* eaglet; *adj.* aquiline. **-otto** *m.* young eagle; (aeron.) learner pilot.

**aquile·gia** *f.* (bot.) columbine.

**aquilọne**[1] *m.* north wind.

**aquilọne**[2] *m.* (orn.) kite.

**ara**[1] *f.* (pagan) altar.

**ara**[2] *f.* are, 100 sq.m.

**ara**[3] *f.* (orn.) macaw.

**a·r-abo** *n.m.* Arab; Arabian; the Arabic language; Arabian steed; *adj.* Arab, Arabian, Arabic; *l'-aba fenice*, the phoenix. **-abẹsco** *adj.* (*m.pl.* **-abẹschi**) Arabic; Arabian; arabesque; *n.m.* Arab; *pl.* arabesques; scribbling; illegible handwriting. **-a·bico** *adj.* Arabian; Arabic.

**ara·chide** *f.* peanut, groundnut.

**aragọsta** *f.* (zool.) sea crayfish,

crawfish, langouste; (pop.) lobster.
**ar-aldo** *m.* herald; forerunner, harbinger. **-al·dica** *f.* heraldry. **-al·dico** *adj.* heraldic.
**aranceto** *m.* orange-grove.
**aran·ci-a** *f.* orange (see also **arancio**); — *mandarina,* mandarin or tangerine orange. **-ata** *f.* orangeade. **-ato** *adj.* orange-coloured, orange. **-o** *m.* (bot.) orange-tree; *fiori d'-o,* orange-blossom; orange; *spremuta d'-o,* orange juice; *adj. indecl.* orange-coloured.
**ar-are** [A1] *tr.* to plough. **-a·bile** *adj.* arable. **-ato** *part. adj.* ploughed; lined, furrowed. **-atore** *m.* ploughman.
**aratro** *m.* plough; (astron.) the Plough, Ursa Major.
**arazz-o** *m.* arras; hanging, tapestry. **-eri·a** *f.* tapestry.
**arbi·trio** *m.* judgment; caprice; absolute power; *fare a proprio* —, to do as one likes; *libero* —, free will.
**ar·bitr-o** *m.* arbiter; referee, umpire; adjudicator; arbitrator. **-ag·gio** *m.* refereeing; umpiring; arbitration. **-are** [A1 s] *intr.* (*aux.* avere) to arbitrate; to assume authority; *tr.* to judge, to consider; (sport) to referee; *rfl.* to take the liberty, to assume the responsibility. **-a·rio** *adj.* arbitrary. **-ato** *m.* arbitration; *part. adj.* arbitrated. **-atore** *m.* arbitrator, judge; one who takes matters into his own hands.
**ar·b-ore** *m., f.* (poet.) tree; mast. **-o·reo** *adj.* arboreal; branching. **-oreto** *m.* arboretum.
**arboscello** *m.* small tree; shrub.
**arbusto** *m.* shrub with woody stems.
**arca** *f.* tomb, sarcophagus; chest, coffer; *l'— di Noè,* Noah's ark.
**arca·ico** *adj.* archaic, obsolete.
**arcaismo** *m.* archaism.
**arc-an·gelo, -an·giolo** *m.* archangel.
**arcano** *adj.* secret; occult; mysterious; *n.m.* mystery, arcanum.
**arc-are** *tr.* to shoot (with bow and arrow). **-ata** *f.* space of a bowshot; arcade; archway; span (of a bridge).
**arca·volo** *m.* great-great-grandfather; ancestor.
**arce** *f.* citadel.
**archeggi-are** [A3 c] *tr.* (mus.) to play (an instrument) with a bow. **-amento** *m.* (mus.) bowing.
**archeggio** *m.* arching, curving; (mus.) bowing.
**arche-ologi·a** *f.* archaeology. **-olo·gico** *adj.* archaeological. **-o·logo** *m.* (*pl.* **-o·logi, -o·loghi**) archaeologist.
**arche·tipo** *m.* archetype; master manuscript; model; *adj.* archetypal.
**archi-** *pref.* equiv. to English arch-. **-mandrita** *m.* (eccl.) archimandrite. **-trave** *m.* (archit.) architrave, lintel.
**architettare** [A1 c] *tr.* (archit.) to make an architectural design of, to build; (fig.) to contrive, to devise; to plot.
**architett-o** *m.* architect; (fig.) creator, author. **-o·nico** *adj.* architectonic, architectural.
**architettura** *f.* architecture.
**archi·v-io** *m.* archive; archives; repository. **-iare** [A4] *tr.* to record, to register; to file. **-ista** *m., f.* archivist; librarian.
**arci-** *pref.* equivalent to English arch-. **-beato** *adj.* blissfully happy. **-dia·cono** *m.* (eccl.) archdeacon. **-duca** *m.* archduke. **-pe·lago** *m.* (*pl.* **-pe·laghi**) archipelago. **-prete** *m.* (eccl.) archpriest, (rural) dean. **-ve·scovo** *m.* archbishop.
**arciere** *m.* archer, bowman.
**arcigno** *adj.* sour, vinegary; harsh; sullen.
**arcione** *m.* saddle-bow; saddle; *inforcar l'—,* to mount into the saddle.
**ar-co** *m.* (*pl.* **-chi**) bow (for shooting); *tiro d'—,* bowshot; archway; curve; arch; (mus.) bow; *pl.* strings (of an orchestra); (theatr.) — *scenico,* proscenium; (geom.) arc; *lampada ad* —, arc lamp.
**arcobaleno** *m.* rainbow, iris; *un — di colori,* all the colours of the rainbow.
**arcola·io** *m.* winder, a circular revolving frame to hold a skein of wool for winding; (fig.) *girare come un* —, to whirl, to reel.
**arcuare** [A6] *tr.* to arch, to curve.
**ardente** *adj.* burning, blazing; passionate; fervid; *febbre* —, high fever.
**ar·d-ere** [C3] *intr.* (*aux.* essere) to burn, to be on fire; to be parched; to rage; to shine; *tr.* to set fire to; (fig.) to inflame. **-ore** *m.* ardour; fervour; heat, warmth.
**arde·sia** *f.* slate; *cava d'—,* slate-quarry.
**ard-ire** [D2] *intr.* (*aux.* avere) to dare; to have the courage to; *abs., tr.* to venture; *n.m.* courage; daring. **-ito** *part. adj.* courageous; daring; *farsi -ito di,* to dare to; *salita -ita,* steep incline.
**ar·du-o** *adj.* arduous; steep, uphill; inaccessible; (poet.) lofty. **-ità** *f.* arduousness, difficulty.
**a·rea** *f.* area; surface; zone; extent; — *fabbricabile,* building plot.
**aren-a** *f.* gravel; soil, earth; arena; stadium. **-are** (naut.) *intr.* (*aux.* essere), *rfl.* to run aground; to be stranded; (fig.) to be shelved. **-ato** *part. adj.* stranded; aground; (fig.) shelved; at a standstill. **-oso** *adj.* sandy, full of sand; arid; shifting; unstable.
**ar·gano** *m.* capstan; winch, windlass; *a forza d'argani,* with a great effort.
**argent-are** [A1] *tr.* to silver-plate, **-a·rio** *m.* silversmith; *adj.* like silver; silvery. **-ato** *part. adj.* silvered; silver-plated; argent. **-atore** *m.* silversmith. **-eri·a** *f.* silver plate. **-iera** *f.* silver mine. **-iere** *m.* silversmith. **-i·fero** *adj.* argentiferous. **-ino** *adj.* silvery; argentine.
**argen·teo** *adj.* silvery; like silver; (of a voice) bell-like.
**argento** *m.* silver; silver plate; silver colour, whiteness; white hair; *d'—* silvery; *pl.* silverware.
**argentovivo** *m.* quicksilver, mercury.
**argill-a** *f.* clay; — *cotta,* terracotta. **-oso** *adj.* clayey, loamy.
**ar·gin-e** *m.* embankment; dyke; causeway; (fig.) obstacle, barrier; *rompere ogni* —, to break all bounds; — *traverso,* dam. **-are** [A1 s] *tr.* to dam; to embank; (fig.) to stem; to check. **-atura** *f.* embankment; dykes.
**argoment-are** [A1 c] *tr., abs.* to argue; to reason; to infer, to conclude. **-ativo** *adj.* explanatory, expository. **-atore** *m.* arguer, reasoner; *adj.* reasoning. **-azione** *f.* formal reasoning; argument.
**argomento** *m.* summary, exposition, synopsis; theme, subject-matter; topic; reason, proof; indication.
**arguire** [D2] *tr.* to infer, to deduce; to argue.
**argut-o** *adj.* quick-witted, sharp; witty; *occhio* —, shrewd glance; (of sound) acute, strident. **-ezza** *f.* sharpness, keenness; subtlety; wit.
**argu·zia** *f.* witticism, jest; shrewdness; sharpness.
**a·ri-a** *f.* air; *colpo d'—,* sudden chill; *corrente d'—,* draught; *sacca d'—,* air-lock; *impermeabile all'—,* air-tight; *castelli in* —, castles in Spain; (mus.) aria; air, melody, tune; manner, air, demeanour; *darsi delle -e,* to put on airs; appearance, aspect; *giudicare ad* —, to judge by appearances. **-oso** *adj.* airy, well aired; graceful; pretentious; (mus.) tuneful.
**a·rid-o** *adj.* arid, dry; parched; *n.m.* aridity; *pl.* dry goods, grain, etc. **-ità** *f.* aridity.
**arieggiare** [A3 c] *tr.* to air, to ventilate; to resemble; *intr.* (*aux.* avere; *prep.* a) to imitate, to assume the manner (of).
**ariete** *m.* ram.
**aringa** *f.* herring; — *affumicata,* kipper.
**aristo-cra·tico** *adj.* aristocratic; *n.m.* aristocrat. **-crazi·a** *f.* aristocracy, nobility; haughtiness, condescension.
**aritme·tic-a** *f.* arithmetic; *l'— non è un'opinione,* facts are facts. **-o** *adj.* arithmetical; *n.m.* arithmetician.
**arlecchino** *m.* harlequin, clown.

**arma** *f.* (*pl.* **armi, arme**) branch, arm (of a service); *di che — è soldato?*, what arm is he in?; regiment; service (army, navy, air force).

**armacollo** *adv. phr. ad* —, slung diagonally across the shoulders.

**arma·dio** *m.* wardrobe; cupboard.

**armaiuo·lo** *m.* armourer; gunsmith.

**arm-are** [A1] *tr.* to arm; to enlist; to recruit; to man; to fortify; to reinforce (concrete); to store (a ship); *rfl.* to take up arms; (fig.) *-arsi di coraggio*, to take courage. **-amẹnto** *m.* armament; arming. **-ata** *f.* fleet; armada; army. **-ato** *part. adj.* armed; *a mano -ata*, by force; armoured; strengthened; *carro -ato*, tank; furnished, equipped; *cemento -ato*, reinforced concrete. **-atọre** *m.* (mil.) fitter-out; shipowner.

**arm-e** *f.* (*pl.* **-i**) weapon; instrument of war; bayonet; sword; *— da fuoco*, firearm; *le -i*, the armed forces; *il porto d' -i*, licence to carry firearms.

**armeggiare** [A3 c] *intr.* (*aux.* avere) to fight; to brandish weapons; (fig.) to bustle; to manoeuvre.

**armẹggio** *m.* (naut.) armament, equipment.

**armeggìo** *m.* manoeuvring; bustling.

**armẹnt-o** *m.* herd, flock; drove; *greggi e -i*, sheep and cattle. **-iere** *m.* herdsman.

**armerì·a** *f.* museum of arms; armoury; arsenal.

**armiere** *m.* gunner.

**armi·gero** *adj.* pugnacious, bellicose; martial, brave; *n.m.* arms bearer; shield bearer.

**armisti·zio** *m.* armistice.

**armo** *m.* (naut.) fitting out stores; crew (of a yacht); (sport) rowing crew.

**armonì·a** *f.* harmony; chord; agreement; *in — con*, in keeping with.

**armo·nic-a** *f.* (mus.) harmonica, mouth organ; harmonic, overtone. **-o** *adj.* (mus.) harmonic; (fig.) harmonious; *n.m.* (mus.) harmonic.

**armo·nio** *m.* harmonium.

**armoniọso** *adj.* harmonious; tuneful; proportionate.

**armonizzare** [A1] *tr.* (mus.) to harmonize, to furnish with harmony; (fig.) to attune; to match (colours); to make agree; *intr.* (*aux.* avere) (mus.) to harmonize; to be attuned.

**arnẹs-e** *m.* tool, implement; *borsa degli -i*, tool-kit; attire, dress; *male in —*, poorly dressed; (joc.) individual, type; *un triste —*, a bad lot.

**ar·ni-a** *f.* beehive. **-a·io** *m.* apiary.

**arniọne** *m.* (butcher) kidney.

**arom-a** *m.* aroma, fragrance; *pl.* spices; aromatic herbs. **-a·tico** *adj.* aromatic; fragrant; savoury. **-atizzare** [A1] *tr.* to spice.

**arp-a** *f.* (mus.) harp. **-eggiare** [A3 c] *intr.* (*aux.* avere) (mus.) to play the harp. **-eg·gio** *m.* (mus.) arpeggio. **-eggío** *m.* strumming. **-icordo** *m.* (mus.) spinet, harpsichord. **-ista** *m., f.* harpist.

**arpì·a** *f.* (myth.) harpy; (fig.) hag.

**arpicare** [A2 s] *rfl.* to climb, to clamber; to scramble up; *intr.* (*aux.* avere) *— col cervello*, to rack one's brains.

**arpiọne** *m.* hook; grapnel; hinge.

**arpọne** *m.* harpoon.

**arra** *f.* token; (comm.) pledge; guarantee; payment on account.

**arrabbiare** [A4] *rfl.* to fly into a passion; to get angry; (of dogs) to catch rabies; *intr.* (*aux.* essere) to rage; *non lo fate —*, don't annoy him.

**arrampicare** [A2 s] *rfl.* (*prep.* a, su) to climb, to clamber, to scramble; (of plants) to climb, to twine.

**arranc-are** [A2] *intr.* (*aux.* avere) to drag oneself along; to trudge; to hobble; to limp. **-ato** *adj.* lame, limping.

**arrangiare** [A3] *tr.* (colloq.) to adjust, to arrange; (mus.) to arrange; *rfl.* to improvise; to make shift; *arràngiati*, do the best you can (by fair means or foul).

**arraspare** [A1] *tr.* to rasp; to file; (fig.) to steal.

**arrecare** [A2] *tr.* to occasion, to cause; to cite; to bring.

**arred-are** [A1] *tr.* to furnish; to equip; to fit out. **-amẹnto** *m.* equipping, fitting out; equipment; rigging; interior decoration; *pl.* fittings, soft furnishings. **-o** *m.* (often *pl.*) fittings, furnishings, equipment.

**arren·d-ere** [C1] *rfl.* to surrender; to yield; to give way; to be flexible. **-ẹvole** *adj.* pliant; biddable.

**arrestare** [A1] *tr.* to arrest; to stop; to detain; *rfl.* to stop, to halt.

**arresto** *m.* (leg.) arrest; detention; *essere agli arresti*, to be under arrest; stop; delay; standstill.

**arretare** [A1] *tr.* to net, to snare.

**arretr-are** [A1] *tr.* to move back, to push back; *rfl., intr.* (*aux.* essere, avere) to withdraw; to recoil; to fall behind. **-ato** *part. adj.* behindhand; in arrears; *numero -ato*, back number; backward; *area -ata*, depressed area; *n.m.* back number; (comm.) *in -ato*, in arrears.

**arricchire** [D2] *tr.* to enrich; to endow; to embellish; *intr.* (*aux.* essere), *rfl.* to prosper, to thrive; to be enriched.

**arricci-are** [A3] *tr.* to curl; *-arsi i capelli*, to curl one's hair; *— la fronte*, to frown; *rfl.* (of hair) to be curly; to bristle.

**arri·dere** [C3] *intr.* (*aux.* avere; *prep.* a) to smile (upon); to be propitious (to), to favour.

**arring-a** *f.* harangue; address; speech. **-are** [A2] *tr.* to harangue; to exhort; *intr.* (*aux.* avere) to make a speech.

**arrin-go** *m.* (*pl.* **-ghi**) lists; arena; fight, contest.

**arrischi-are** [A4] *tr.* to risk, to venture, to hazard; *— la pelle*, to risk one's life; *abs.* to dare; *rfl.* to venture, to run risks. **-ato** *part. adj.* risky, hazardous; bold, rash.

**arriv-are** [A1] *intr.* (*aux.* essere; *prep.* a) to arrive (at); to reach; to amount (to); to manage (to), to succeed (in); to be sufficient; to go as far (as); *abs.* to arrive; *— a proposito*, to arrive at the right moment; to occur, to befall; to be a success; *— bene*, to turn out well; *tr.* to catch up with; to reach; (fig.) to touch, to compare with. **-ato** *part. adj. ben -ato!*, welcome!; *n.m.* successful man. **-iṣmo** *m.* unscrupulous ambition, arrivism. **-ista** *m.* arriviste.

**arrivedẹr-ci, -la,** *excl.* goodbye; see you again soon.

**arrivo** *m.* arrival; arrival platform; winning-post; (comm.) *gli ultimi arrivi di merci*, the latest supplies of goods.

**arroch-ire** [D2] *tr.* to make hoarse; *intr.* (*aux.* essere), *rfl.* to become hoarse. **-ito** *part. adj.* hoarse.

**arrog-ante** *adj.* arrogant, haughty, insolent. **-anza** *f.* arrogance.

**arrolare** [A1 d] *tr.* (mil.) to enrol, to recruit; *rfl.* (mil.) to enlist; to register.

**arrossare** [A1 c] *tr.* to redden; *intr.* (*aux.* essere), *rfl.* to grow red.

**arrossire** [D2] *intr.* (*aux.* essere) to blush; to flame; to turn red; to feel ashamed.

**arrostire** [D2] *tr.* to roast; to grill.

**arrosto** *adv.* roasted, roast; *cuocere —*, to roast; *castagne arrosto*, roast chestnuts; *n.m.* roast meat; grill; *— d'agnello*, roast lamb.

**arrotare** [A1 d] *tr.* to whet; to sharpen.

**arrotolare** [A1 s] *tr., rfl.* to roll up; to furl; to curl up.

**arrotondare** [A1 c] *tr.* to make round; to round off; *rfl.* to become round; (fig.) to put on weight, to fill out.

**arroventare** [A1] *tr.* to make red hot; *rfl., intr.* (*aux.* essere) to grow red hot.

**arrovesciare** [A3] *tr.* to overturn; to upset; to spill; to pour; to turn inside out; *— le maniche*, to

roll up one's sleeves; *rfl.* to be overturned; to fall.

**arruff-are** [A1] *tr.* to ruffle, to rumple; to entangle; *rfl.* to become ruffled; to become entangled. **-apo·poli** *m. indecl.* demagogue, political agitator. **-atọre** *m.* intriguer, mischief-maker, swindler. **-ọne** *m.* meddler; cheat; muddler.

**arrugginire** [D2] *tr.* to make rusty, to rust; — *i denti*, to set the teeth on edge; *rfl.*, *intr.* (*aux.* essere) to rust, to become rusty; to get out of practice.

**arruvidire** [D2] *tr.* to roughen; *intr.* (*aux.* essere), *rfl.* to become rough; to coarsen.

**arsenale** *m.* arsenal; dockyard; arms factory; workshop.

**arse·n-ico** *m.* arsenic. **-icale** *adj.* arsenical.

**ars-o** *part. adj.* burnt; parched; dry; thirsty. **-ic·cio** *adj.* singed; parched; *saper d'-iccio*, to smell of burning. **-ura** *f.* burning; raging thirst; feverish heat; dryness.

**art-e** *f.* art; *le belle -i*, the fine arts; profession; craft; artistry; *opera d'—*, work of art; the stage; *essere in —*, to be on the stage. **-efare** [B14] *tr.* to adulterate; to fake, to falsify. **-efatto** *part. adj.* artificial; falsified; *n.m.* artificial product; artefact.

**artẹfice** *m.* artificer; author; creator; artisan, craftsman.

**arte·ri-a** *f.* artery; arterial road; main line (of railway). **-ale** *adj.*, **-ọso** *adj.* arterial.

**ar·tico** *adj.* Arctic; northern; icy.

**articol-are** [A1 s] *tr.* to articulate; to pronounce distinctly; to link; *rfl.* to be articulate; *adj.* articular, jointed. **-azịone** *f.* articulation; clear pronunciation; (fig.) flexibility.

**arti·colo** *m.* article; matter, point; item; commodity; *pl.* goods; (gramm.) article; newspaper article; — *di fondo*, leader.

**artiere** *m.* artisan; craftsman; workman.

**artifi·ci-o** *m.* artifice; skill, art; artificiality; *fuochi d'—*, fireworks. **-ale** *adj.* artificial; unnatural. **-ọso** *adj.* artificial; contrived; artful.

**artigian-o** *m.* artisan; craftsman; workman, operative; (fig.) author, creator; *adj.* artisan. **-ato** *m.* class, etc., of artisans. **-ẹsco** *adj.* (*m.pl.* **-ẹschi**) pertaining to the artisan class.

**artigliere** *m.* artilleryman; gunner.

**artiglieri·a** *f.* artillery; *pezzo d'—*, cannon; ballistics.

**arti·gl-io** *m.* claw; talon; (fig.) *cadere negli -i di*, to fall into the clutches of.

**artista** *m.* artist; performer; — *di canto*, vocalist; — *drammatico*, actor.

**arti·stico** *adj.* artistic; tasteful; relating to art.

**arto**[1] *m.* (anat.) joint; limb.

**arto**[2] *adj.* narrow.

**artr-ite** *f.* arthritis. **-i·tico** *adj.* arthritic; *n.m.* sufferer from arthritis.

**arzillo** *adj.* sprightly; vigorous; brisk; pungent.

**ascell-a** *f.* armpit. **-are** *adj.* axillary.

**ascẹnd-ere** [C1 c] *intr.* (*aux.* essere, avere) to ascend; to climb, to mount; to rise; to amount; *tr.* to ascend, to climb up; to mount. **-entale** *adj.* ascendental; pertaining to ascent. **-ente** *part. adj.* ascending, mounting; *movimento -ente*, upward movement; outgoing; ascendant. *n.m.* ascendancy, influence; *pl.* ancestors, ascendants. **-enza** *f.* ascendants, ancestors; genealogical tree; origin.

**ascens-ịone** *f.* ascent; mounting; climb; (rel.) Ascension. **-ọre** *m.* lift, elevator.

**ascẹsa** *f.* ascent; climb.

**ascesso** *m.* abcess.

**asc-eta** *m.* ascetic. **-e·tico** *adj.*, *n.m.* ascetic. **-etịsmo** *m.* asceticism; self-discipline.

**a·scia** *f.* axe, hatchet, chopper; adze.

**asciol·vere** [C14] *intr.* (*aux.* avere) to breakfast; *tr.* — *il digiuno*, to break one's fast.

**asciug-are** [A2] *tr.* to dry; to dry up; to wipe; to drain (land); *rfl.* to dry oneself; *rfl.*, *intr.* (*aux.* essere) to get dry. **-amano** *m.* (*pl.* **-amani**) towel. **-ante** *part. adj.* drying; *carta -ante*, blotting-paper.

**asciutt-o** *adj.* dry; thirsty; *pasta -a*, macaroni, etc.; *risposta -a*, brusque reply; — *di quattrini*, penniless; *adv.* abruptly, tersely; drily; *n.m.* dry place; dryness. **-ẹzza** *f.* dryness, aridity; drought.

**ascolt-are** [A1 c] *tr.* to listen to; to heed; to overhear; — *un consiglio*, to follow advice; — *la messa*, to attend mass; *intr.* (*aux.* avere) to listen; to pay attention; *ascolta !*, listen!; — *dietro le porte*, to eavesdrop. **-atọre** *m.* listener; *pl.* audience; listeners, public.

**ascọlto** *m.* listening; hearing; *dare —*, to listen; *prestare — ai consigli di*, to follow the advice of.

**ascọndere** [C11 c] *tr.* to hide, to conceal; *rfl.* to hide oneself, to hide.

**ascọso** *part. adj.* hidden, secret.

**ascri·vere** [C12] *tr.* to enrol, to inscribe, to register; to attribute; *rfl.* (*dat.* of *prn.* si) to assume.

**ascrizịone** *f.* enrolment; attribution.

**a-sepsi** *f. indecl.* asepsis. **-set·tico** *adj.* aseptic.

**asfalt-o** *m.* asphalt; bitumen. **-are** [A1] *tr.* to asphalt.

**asfiss-i·a** *f.* asphyxia, suffocation; gassing. **-iante** *part. adj.* asphyxiating **-iare** [A4 *tr.* to asphyxiate, to suffocate.

**aṣilo** *m.* refuge, shelter; asylum; sanctuary; almshouse; — *infantile*, kindergarten.

**a·sin-o** *m.* ass, donkey; fool; *dare dell'— a*, to call (someone) an ass; *a schiena d'—*, hog-backed. **-eri·a** *f.* stupidity; *dire delle -erie*, to talk nonsense. **-ino** *adj.* asinine; *tosse -ina*, whooping cough.

**aṣm-a** *f.* asthma. **-a·tico** *adj.*, *n.m.* asthmatic(al).

**a·ṣola** *f.* buttonhole; eyelet; buttonholing.

**a·ṣolo** *m.* breath of air; light breeze; *dare — a*, to hang out to air.

**aspa·rago** *m.* (usu. *pl.*) asparagus.

**asper·gere** [C4] *tr.* to besprinkle; to strew.

**asperità** *f.* asperity, roughness; unevenness; harshness.

**asper·rimo** *adj. superl.* of **aspro**, q.v.

**aspers-o** *part. adj.* sprinkled; besprinkled; strewn. **-ịone** *f.* sprinkling.

**aspett-are** [A1] *tr.* to wait for, to await; to expect (someone); to look forward to; *intr.* (*aux.* avere) to wait; *far — qualcuno*, to keep someone waiting; *farsi —*, to be late; *rfl.* (*dat.* of *prn.*) to expect; *c'era da -arsela*, it was only to be expected. **-ativa** *f.* expectation; anticipation. **-azịone** *f.* expectation; expectancy; *rispondere all'-azione*, to come up to expectation.

**aspetto**[1] *m.* waiting; *stare in —*, to be waiting; *sala d'—*, waiting-room.

**aspetto**[2] *m.* look; mien; aspect; appearance; *a primo —*, at first sight; *sotto quest'—*, from this point of view.

**aspir-are** [A1] *tr.* to inhale, to breathe in; to suck up; *intr.* (*aux.* avere; *prep* a) to aspire (towards); to aim (at). **-ante** *part. adj.* aspiring; inhaling; *n.m.* applicant; aspirant. **-apọlvere** *m. indecl.* vacuum cleaner. **-azịone** *f.* inhalation; aspiration; ambition.

**aspirina** *f.* aspirin.

**asport-are** [A1] *tr.* to remove; to transport; *vino da —*, wine for sale (to be taken away). **-azịone** *f.* removal, carrying away.

**aspr-o** *adj.* harsh; sharp; rough; rugged; uncouth; sour, sharp. **-ẹzza** *f.* asperity; roughness; harshness; sourness, sharpness.

**assaggi-are** [A3] *tr.* to taste; to try; to sample; to test. **-atọre** *m.* taster. **-atura** *f.* assaying, assay.

**assag·gio** *m.* tasting; sampling; trial test; sample; assay.

**assa·i** *adv.* very; much; a great deal; quite; many; enough.

**assale** *m.* axle; *tappo di —*, axle cap.

**assal-ire** [D4, D2] *tr.* to assail; to attack; to seize. **-itọre** *m.* assailant; attacker.
**assalt-are** [A1] *tr.* (mil.) to attack, to assault, to invest; (fig.) to assault. **-atọre** *m.* assailant, aggressor.
**assalto** *m.* (mil.) attack, assault; onslaught, onset; *dare l'— (a)*, to attack; *prendere d'—*, to take by assault; (fig.) onslaught; *di primo —*, at first.
**assaporare** [A1 c] *tr.* to savour, to relish.
**assaporire** [D2] *tr.* to season, to flavour; to give a relish to; to spice.
**assassinare** [A1] *tr.* to assassinate; to murder; (fig.) to torment; to bore to death; to ruin.
**assassi·n-io** *m.* (*pl.* **-ii**) assassination; murder.
**assassin-o** *m.* assassin; murderer; villain; incompetent bungler; *adj.* murderous; *mano -a*, assassin's hand.
**asse**[1] *f.* board, plank; slab; *— da stirare*, ironing board.
**asse**[2] *m.* axis; centre line.
**asse**[3] *m.* (Rom. antiq.) as, copper coin; (leg.) *— patrimoniale*, estate.
**asseccare** [A1 c], **assecchire** [D2] *intr.* (*aux.* essere) to shrivel, to become thin.
**assecondare** [A1 c] *tr.* to support; to second; to comply with.
**assedi-are** [A4] *tr.* (mil.) to besiege, to lay siege to; (fig.) to beset; *— di domande*, to badger with questions. **-ante** *part. adj.* besieging; *n.m.* besieger.
**asse·dio** *m.* siege; *porre l'— (a)*, to lay siege (to); *levare l'—*, to raise siege.
**assegn-are** [A3 c] *tr.* to assign; to mete out; to award; to detail (a person to do a job); *— un termine*, to fix a term. **-ata·rio** *m.* assignee.
**assẹgno** *m.* allowance; payment; (comm.) *— bancario*, cheque; *libretto di assegni*, cheque-book; *emettere un —*, to draw a cheque.
**assemblag·gio** *m.* (industr.) assembly, assembling; *linea di —*, assembly line.
**assemble·a** *f.* assembly; congregation; *convocare un'—*, to call a meeting; *sciogliere un'—*, to adjourn a meeting.
**assembrare** [A1] *tr.*, *rfl.* to assemble, to collect, to muster.
**assennato** *adj.* wise, sensible, judicious; discreet.
**assenso** *m.* assent; approbation; consent.
**assentare** [A1] *rfl.* to absent oneself; to keep away; *tr.* to remove.
**assent-e** *adj.* absent; away; absent-minded; *n.m.* absentee; *quanti sono gli -i ?*, how many are absent ? **-eịsmo** *m.* absenteeism. **-eista** *m.* absentee landlord.
**assent-ire** [D1] *intr.* (*aux.* avere) to assent, to acquiesce; to approve. **-imẹnto** *m.* assent; consent.
**assenza** *f.* absence; *fare troppe assenze*, to be absent too often; *— senza licenza*, absence without leave; lack.
**assenziente** *adj.* assentient; willing.
**assen·zio** *m.* oil of wormwood, absinthe; (fig.) bitterness.
**asserella** *f.* small board, plank.
**asserire** [D2] *tr.* to assert; to affirm; to maintain.
**as·sero** *m.* shaft, axle.
**asserragliare** [A4] *tr.* to barricade.
**assert-o** *adj.* asserted; affirmed; *n.m.* assertion; affirmation. **-iva** *f.* assertion. **-ivo** *adj.* assertive. **-ọre** *m.* assertor; champion, defender; advocate. **-o·rio** *adj.* assertive.
**asservire** [D1] *tr.* to enslave; to enthral; to make subservient.
**asserziọne** *f.* assertion; statement; affirmation.
**assestare** [A1] *tr.* to adjust; to settle; to set in order; to aim true; *— un conto*, to balance an account; *— un colpo*, to deal a blow; *rfl.* to settle down; to put one's affairs in order.
**assesto** *m.* order, orderliness; *dar — a*, to put in order.
**asset-are** [A1 c] *tr.* to make thirsty; to deprive of water; (fig.) to fill with longing. **-ato** thirsty; deprived.
**assettare** [A1] *tr.* to arrange, to set in order; to adjust; *— i capelli*, to tidy one's hair; *rfl.* to become settled; to tidy oneself; (of a building) to settle.
**assetto** *m.* order; settled condition; arrangement; *mettere in —*, to set in order; *in bell'—*, in readiness.
**assever-are** [A1 s] *tr.* to assert; to affirm; to asseverate. **-ante** *part. adj.* assertive; dogmatic. **-anza** *f.* assertiveness; firmness; asservation; *con -anza*, firmly. **-ativo** *adj.* positive; assertive. **-aziọne** *f.* asseveration.
**assiale** *adj.* axial.
**assicur-are** [A1] *tr.* to secure; to fasten securely; to insure; to assure; to affirm; to ensure; *rfl.* to make sure; to assure oneself; to insure oneself; (*dat.* of *prn.*) to secure for oneself. **-ativo** *adj.* pertaining to insurance. **-atamente** *adv.* assuredly. **-atọre** *m.* insurer; underwriter. **-aziọne** *f.* assurance; guarantee; security, pledge; insurance.
**assider-are** [A1 s] *intr.* (*aux.* essere), *rfl.* to become frozen; to be numb with cold; *tr.* to freeze. **-amẹnto** *m.* freezing; *morire per -amento*, to freeze to death.
**assi·du-o** *adj.* assiduous; sedulous; regular in attendance; *n.m.* regular visitor. **-ità** *f.* assiduousness; regular attendance; constancy.
**assieme** *adv.* together; at the same time; jointly; *— a*, together with; *stare —*, to go well together; *n.m.* assembly; set.
**assiep-are** [A1 d] *tr.* to hedge; to encircle; to crowd round; *rfl.* to crowd together; to mass; *-arsi lungo i marciapiedi*, to line the streets.
**assillare**[1] [A1] *tr.* to goad, to spur on; *— di domande*, to pester with questions.
**assillare**[2] *adj.* axillary.
**assillo** *m.* robber fly; (fig.) torment; stimulus; *sotto l'— della fame*, goaded by hunger.
**assimil-are** [A1 s] *tr.* to assimilate; to absorb; to consider similar; *rfl.* to be assimilated. **-aziọne** *f.* assimilation; absorption.
**assiom-a** *m.* axiom; self-evident truth. **-a·tico** *adj.* axiomatic.
**assisa** *f.* uniform; livery.
**assịse** *f.pl.* (leg.) *Corte d'—*, Italian criminal court.
**assi·st-ere** [C24] *tr.* to assist, to aid; to attend, to treat (medically); *intr.* (*aux.* avere; *prep.* a) to attend, to be present (at). **-ente** *part. adj.* assisting; present; *n.m., f.* assistant, helper; bystander, onlooker. **-enza** *f.* assistance, help; *prestare -enza*, to assist; support; attendance, audience; treatment; *-enza pubblica*, public welfare services.
**assito** *m.* (archit.; bldg.) partition; hoarding, board fence; floor-board.
**assiuolo** *m.* (orn.) scops owl.
**asso**[1] *m.* ace, one (at cards, dice, dominoes); *— di briscola*, ace of trumps; (fig.) ace, champion.
**asso**[2] *adv. phr. lasciare in —*, to leave in the lurch; *rimanere in —*, to be left high and dry.
**associ-are** [A3] *tr.* to associate; to combine, to unite; to take into partnership; *rfl.* to associate oneself; to join; *recip. rfl.* to join with one another; to form a partnership. **-ato** *part. adj.* associated; *n.m.* associate; partner; member; subscriber. **-aziọne** *f.* association; partnership; society; guild; (leg.) *diritto d'-azione*, freedom of association.
**assodare** [A1] *tr.* to harden; to consolidate; to strengthen; to establish firmly; *intr.* (*aux.* essere) to become hard; *rfl.* to become solid; (fig.) to gain experience; *assodarsi di*, to ascertain.
**assoggettare** [A1] *tr.* to subject; to subdue; *rfl.* to subject oneself; to submit.
**assol-are** [A1] *tr.* to expose to the sun. **-ato** *part. adj.* sunny.
**assolati·o** *adj.* sunny.
**assolcare** [A2 c] *tr.* to furrow; to plough.

**assoldare** [A1] *tr.* (mil.) to enrol; *rfl.* to enlist.
**assolut-o**[1] *adj.* absolute; positive; utter, complete; *soprano* —, leading soprano; *prima donna -a*, leading lady; *n.m. l'*—, the absolute. **-amente** *adv.* absolutely; positively; at all costs; unconditionally. **-ezza** *f.* absoluteness; overstatement. **-ismo** *m.* absolutism. **-ista** *m., adj.* absolutist.
**assoluto**[2] *part. adj.* acquitted; absolved.
**assoluzione** *f.* (leg.) acquittal, absolution.
**assol·vere** [C14] *tr.* (leg.) to acquit, to absolve; (theol.) to absolve; to accomplish; — *bene la propria parte*, to acquit oneself well.
**assomigli-are** [A4] *tr.* (*prep.* a) to compare (with), to indicate resemblance (between); to make similar; *intr.* (*aux.* essere, avere) to be similar; *rfl. recip.* to resemble one another. **-ante** *part. adj.* resembling, like; *questo ritratto non è molto -ante*, this portrait is not a very good likeness. **-anza** *f.* resemblance, likeness.
**assommare**[1] [A1 c] *tr.* to add together; to combine; to conclude.
**assommare**[2] [A1] *tr.* (naut.) to surface (of a diver or submarine).
**asson-are** [A1 d] *intr.* (*aux.* essere, avere) to correspond in sound, to assonate. **-ante** *part. adj.* assonant. **-anza** *f.* assonance.
**assonn-are** [A1 c] *tr.* to send to sleep; *intr.* (*aux.* essere), *rfl.* to become sleepy; to fall asleep. **-acchiato** *adj.* drowsy. **-ato** *part. adj.* sleepy; asleep.
**assop-ire** [D2] *tr.* to send to sleep; to lull; to assuage; *rfl.* to nod off, to drowse; (of anger) to cool. **-ito** *part. adj.* drowsy, dozing.
**assorb-ire** [D1, D2] *tr.* to absorb; to imbibe; to soak up; to use up. **-ente** *part. adj.* absorbent; absorbing; *carta -ente*, blotting-paper; *n.m.* absorbent; *-ente acustico*, soundproofing.
**assord-are** [A1 c] *tr.* to deafen; to stun; *intr.* (*aux.* essere) to become deaf. **-ante** *part. adj.* deafening; stunning.
**assorgere** [C5] *intr.* (*aux.* essere) to rise; to soar; to attain (to).
**assort-ire** [D2] *tr.* to sort; to grade; to stock (a shop); to match. **-imento** *m.* sorting; assortment; selection, range, stock.
**assorto**[1] *adj.* (fig.) absorbed, preoccupied, distrait.
**assorto**[2] *part. adj.* risen.
**assottigliare** [A4] *tr.* to sharpen; to make pointed; to make thin; *rfl.* to become sharp, fine, pointed; to grow thin; (fig.) to sharpen one's wits.
**assuef-are** [B14] *tr.* to accustom; *rfl.* to become accustomed. **-atto** *part. adj.* used, accustomed; inured. **-azione** *f.* accustoming; custom, habit.
**assu·mere** [C8] *tr.* to assume; to incur; — *informazioni*, to make enquiries; *rfl.* (*dat.* of *prn.*) to take upon oneself.
**assunt-o** *part. adj.* assumed; raised; appointed; *n.m.* assumption; undertaking. **-a** *f.* (theol.) *l'Assunta*, Our Lady of the Assumption.
**assunzione** *f.* assumption; undertaking; (theol.) Assumption.
**assurd-o** *adj.* absurd, nonsensical; *n.m.* absurdity, nonsense. **-ità** *f.* absurdity; preposterousness.
**ast-a** *f.* lance, spear; shaft, handle; pole; *vendere all'*—, to sell by auction. **-atore** *m.* auctioneer.
**astant-e** *adj.* attending, in attendance; *n.m.* bystander; spectator; *gli -i*, those present. **-ori·a** *f.* reception ward of a hospital; first-aid post.
**aste·mio** *adj.* abstemious; *n.m.* abstainer, teetotaller.
**asten-ere** [B32] *rfl.* (*prep.* da) to abstain; to refrain; to forbear; *tr.* to restrain. **-ente** *part. adj.* abstaining; *n.m., f.* abstainer. **-imento** *m.* abstention.
**astension-e** *f.* abstention. **-ismo** *m.* abstentionism. **-ista** *m., f.* abstentionist.
**aster·gere** [C4] *tr.* to cleanse, to clean; to wipe; to dry.
**aster-isco** *m.* (*pl.* -ischi) asterisk; star; paragraph, brief note (in a newspaper). **-o·ide** *m.* asteroid.
**asters-ione** *f.* abstersion, cleansing. **-ivo** *adj.* cleansing, abrasive; abstersive.
**astinen-te** *adj.* abstinent, abstemious; abstaining. **-za** *f.* abstinence; moderation, restraint.
**a·sti-o** *m.* grudge; resentment; grievance. **-oso** *adj.* resentful; grudging.
**astrarre** [B33] *tr.* to abstract; *intr.* (*aux.* avere) to prescind; *rfl.* to abstract oneself, to withdraw.
**astratto** *part. adj.* abstracted, separated; abstract; absent-minded; *n.m. l'*—, the abstract; *in* —, in the abstract.
**astrazione** *f.* abstraction; abstract concept; *fatta* — *da*, apart from, setting aside; absentmindedness.
**astrin·g-ere** [C10] *tr.* to constrain; to coerce. **-ente** *part. adj., n.m.* astringent. **-enza** *f.* astringency.
**astro**[1] *m.* star, heavenly body; luminary; — *del cinema*, film star (man).
**astro**[2] *m.* (bot.) aster.
**astr-ologi·a** *f.* astrology. **-olo·gico** *adj.* astrological. **-o·logo** (*m.pl.* **-o·loghi, -o·logi**) *m.* astrologer. **-ona·utica** *f.* interplanetary travel, astronautics. **-onomi·a** *f.* astronomy. **-ono·mico** *adj.* astronomical; (fig.) extreme, excessive; *prezzi -onomici*, astronomical prices. **-o·nomo** *m.* astronomer.
**astrus-o** *adj.* abstruse; recondite; obscure; *n.m.* abstruseness. **-eri·a** *f.* abstruseness. **-ità** *f.* abstruseness.
**astuc·cio** *m.* case; box; sheath; holder.
**astut-o** *adj.* astute; sly; sagacious. **-ezza** *f.* astuteness; artfulness, slyness.
**astu·zia** *f.* astuteness; cunning; artfulness; guile; trick.
**a·t-avo** *m.* great-great-grandfather; ancestor. **-a·vico** *adj.*, **-avi·stico** *adj.* atavistic. **-avismo** *m.* atavism.
**atene·o** *m.* athenaeum; academy; university.
**a·te-o** *adj., n.m.* atheist. **-i·smo** *m.* atheism. **-i·sta** *m., f.* atheist. **-i·stico** *adj.* atheistic.
**ati·pico** *adj.* atypic(al), not conforming to type.
**atlante** *m.* atlas, book of maps; book of plates.
**at-leta** *m.* (*pl.* **-leti**) athlete; *f.* (*pl.* **-lete**) woman athlete. **-le·tica** *f.* athletics. **-le·tico** *adj.* athletic. **-letismo** *m.* athleticism.
**atmos-fera** *f.* atmosphere; mental or moral environment; background. **-fe·rico** *adj.* atmospheric.
**a·t-omo** *m.* (scient.) atom; (fig.) particle, jot. **-o·mico** *adj.* atomic; atomic-powered. **-omizzare** [A1] *tr.* to atomize, to vaporize. **-omizzatore** *m.* atomizer, vaporizer, spray.
**a·tono** *adj.* toneless; (gramm.) atonic, unstressed; (med.) poor in tone, weak.
**atos·sico** *adj.* non-toxic.
**a·trio** *m.* atrium; entrance hall; porch (of a church); lobby, vestibule.
**atroc-e** *adj.* atrocious; outrageous; ferocious; acute, severe. **-ità** *f.* atrociousness; actrocity.
**atr-ofi·a** *f.* (med.) atrophy. **-ofizzare** [A1 s] *tr., rfl.* to atrophy; to starve.
**attacc-are** [A2] *tr.* to attack, to assail; to combat; to broach, to begin; — *discorso*, to open a conversation; — *battaglia*, to join battle; — *un ballabile*, to strike up a dance number; to attach; to stitch on; to hang up; *intr.* (*aux.* essere; *prep.* a) to stick well, to adhere; to begin; *abs.* (fig.) to catch on, to find favour; to work, to be successful; *rfl.* to stick, to adhere; to cling. **-abottoni** *m., f. indecl.* bore, incessant talker. **-abrighe** *m., f. indecl.* quarrelsome person. **-a·gnolo** *m.* peg, hook; (fig.) pretext. **-alite** *m., f. indecl.* quarrelsome, conten-

tious person. **-apanni** *m. indecl.* peg, hatstand. **-atic·cio** *adj.* sticky; contagious; boring, importunate; *n.m.* sticky mess.

**attac-co** *m.* (*pl.* **-chi**) attack; assault; attachment; onset; cohesion; pretext.

**attanagliare** [A4] *tr.* to seize (with pincers); to claw.

**attardare** [A1] *rfl.* to dawdle, to dally, to tarry.

**attastare** [A1] *tr.* to touch, to feel; to handle.

**attecchire** [D2] *intr.* (*aux.* avere) to take root; to thrive; to sprout; to prosper.

**atteggi-are** [A3 c] *tr.* to pose; to compose, to arrange; to represent (by gesture or expression); *rfl.* (*prep.* a) to assume an attitude (of), to pose (as). **-amẹnto** *m.* attitude; pose; behaviour; air; characteristic movement. **-atura** *f.* pose; arrangement.

**attemp-are** [A1] *intr.* (*aux.* essere) to grow old. **-atello** *adj.* getting on in years. **-ato** *adj.* elderly; old, aged.

**attemperare** [A1 s] *tr.* (mus.) to tune, to temper.

**attend-are** [A1] *rfl.* to put up tents, to encamp; (mil.) to pitch camp. **-amẹnto** *m.* encampment. **-ato** *part. adj.* encamped; (mil.) under canvas.

**atten·d-ere** [C1] *tr.* to wait for; to await; to expect; to pay regard to; — *la promessa*, to keep one's promise; *intr.* (*aux.* avere; *prep.* a) to look after, to care for; to attend (to); *-eva ai fatti suoi*, he was minding his own business; *rfl.* (*dat.* of *prn.*) to expect; *non me lo -evo*, I didn't expect it. **-ente** *part. adj.* assisting; *donna -ente a casa*, domestic help; *n.m.* (mil.) batman; orderly. **-i·bile** *adj.* worthy of attention; authentic, well-founded; *una fonte -ibile*, a reliable source. **-ibilità** *f.* reliability, authenticity.

**atten-ẹre** [B32] *rfl.* (*prep.* a), *intr.* (*aux.* essere; *prep.* a) to concern; to be relevant (to); to be related (to); to belong to; to abide (by); *tr.* to keep, to maintain (faith, promise). **-enza** *f.* appurtenance; appendage.

**attent-are** [A1] *intr.* (*aux.* avere; *prep.* a) to commit an outrage (against); — *alla vita di*, to attempt to assassinate; *rfl.* (*prep.* a, di) to dare; *non si -ò di ripeterlo*, he hadn't the courage to repeat it. **-ato** *part. adj.*; *n.m.* outrage; attack; attempt on someone's life.

**attent-o** *adj.* attentive; alert; intent; careful; *stare* —, to pay attention; — *!*, look out!; — *a non scivolare*, mind you don't slip; (mil. command) *attenti !*, attention! **-ẹzza** *f.* attentiveness.

**attenu-are** [A5] *tr.* to attenuate; to minimize; *rfl.* to become weak; (radio) to fade. **-ante** *part. adj.* attenuating; extenuating; *n.f.* extenuating circumstance. **-aziọne** *f.* attenuation, diminution; extenuation; mitigation; *-azione di rumore*, noise abatement.

**attenziọne** *f.* attention; notice; heed, caution; *fare* —, to pay attention; *attenzione !*, look out!; attention, please!; *pl.* attentions, courtesies.

**attergare** [A2] *tr.* (comm.) to endorse (a document); to docket.

**atterr-are** [A1] *tr.* to knock down; to fell; to raze to the ground; *intr.* (*aux.* avere) (naut.) to make landfall; (aeron.) to land; (of birds) to alight. **-ag·gio** *m.* (aeron.) landing; *pista d'-aggio*, runway; *-aggio forzato*, forced landing. **-ata** *f.* (naut.) arrival; landing.

**atterr-ire** [D2] *tr.* to frighten, to terrify; *intr.* (*aux.* essere), *rfl.* to be terrified. **-imẹnto** *m.* terror, fright; frightening.

**attẹsa** *f.* waiting; expectation; delay; *sala d'*—, waiting-room; *ẹssere in — di*, to be waiting for.

**attẹso** *part. adj.* awaited; expected; attentive; considered; *attesa la sua buona condotta*, taking his good conduct into consideration; *conj.* — *che*, considering that.

**attest-are** [A1] *tr.* to attest; to testify; to certify; to bear witness to; *intr.* (*aux.* avere; *prep.* di) to attest, to witness. **-ato** *part. adj.*; *n.m.* testimonial; certificate; attestation; *pl.* *-ati di brevetto*, letters patent. **-atọre** *m.* testifier, witness. **-aziọne** *f.* attestation; testimony.

**at·tico** *adj.* Attic; *sale* —, Attic salt, wit; *n.m.* (archit.) attic storey.

**attiepid-ire** [D2 d] *rfl.*, *intr.* (*aux.* essere) to grow cool; (fig.) to cool off. **-ito** *part. adj.* cool, lukewarm.

**atti·gu-o** *adj.* adjacent; adjoining; *la stanza -a*, the next room. **-ità** *f.* adjacency; contiguity.

**attillare** [A1] *tr.* to dress up; to adorn, to deck; *rfl.* to dress (oneself) up, to deck oneself out.

**at·timo** *m.* instant, moment; *in un* —, in the twinkling of an eye.

**attinen-te** *adj.* belonging; pertaining; related, connected. **-za** *f.* connexion; *pl.* relations; dependants.

**attin·gere** [C5] *tr.* to derive, to draw; — *acqua*, to draw water; — *informazioni*, to derive information; to reach; to arrive at.

**attirare** [A1] *tr.* to attract; to draw; to entice; *rfl.* (*dat.* of *prn.*) to call down upon oneself.

**attitu·dine**[I] aptitude, disposition, propensity.

**attitu·din-e**[2] *f.* posture; attitude; pose. **-are** [A1 s] *intr.* (*aux.* avere) (paint.) to pose.

**attivare** [A1] *tr.* to bring into activity; to activate; to speed up; — *una macchina*, to start an engine.

**attiv-o** *adj.* active; working, effective; busy; (comm.) profitable; *n.m.* (comm.) assets, profits, *all'*—, on the credit side. **-ista** *m.*, *f.* voluntary helper; canvasser. **-ità** *f.* activity, energy; undertaking; *volcano in fase di -ità*, volcano in eruption; *pl.* (comm.) assets; credit entries.

**attizz-are** [A1] *tr.* to stir; — *il fuoco*, to poke the fire; (fig.) to stir up, to incite. **-atọio** *m.* poker. **-atọre** *m.* instigator, provoker. **-ino** *m.* trouble-maker.

**atto**[I] *m.* act, action, deed; *mettere in* —, to put into action; expression, gesture; movement; act (of a play); sign, token; *fare — di presenza*, to put in an appearance; *prendere — di*, to take note of; *dare — di*, to publish, to give notice of; — *di nascita*, birth certificate; *pl.* documents in a legal case.

**atto**[2] *adj.* apt, suitable, proper; fit, capable.

**atto·nito** *adj.* astonished, amazed; (fig.) spellbound, hushed.

**attor·cere** [C5] *tr.* to twist, to twine; to wring; *rfl.* to twist, to writhe.

**attorcigliare** [A4] *tr.*, *rfl.* to twist, to wind, to twine.

**attọre** *m.* actor; *attore comico*, comedian; *primo* —, leading man.

**attorniare** [A4 c] *tr.* to surround, to encompass; (fig.) to beset.

**attọrno** *adv.* about; around; round; *qui* —, hereabout; *levarsi uno d'*—, to get rid of someone; *darsi d'*—, to do one's utmost; *prep.* — *a*, round.

**attossic-are** [A2 s] *tr.* to poison; to infect; to pollute; to taint. **-ante** *part. adj.* poisonous.

**attraente** *part. adj.* attractive; charming; pleasing; interesting.

**attrappire** [D2] *rfl.* to shrink, to shrivel; to become stiff, to grow numb.

**attrarre** [B33] *tr.* to attract; to draw; to interest; *abs.* to be attractive.

**attratt-o** *part. adj.* attracted, drawn, allured. **-iva** *f.* attraction; charm, draw, appeal; *pl.* charms. **-ività** *f.* power of attraction. **-ivo** *adj.* attractive.

**attravers-are** [A1] *tr.* to cross, to traverse; to go through, to undergo; to pierce; to thwart; — *il passo a*, to get in the way of. **-a·bile** *adj.* passable, traversable. **-amẹnto** *m.* crossing; street-crossing.

**attraverso** *prep.* across; athwart; through; — *a*, across; (before *pers. prn.*) — *di*, through, through the agency of; *adv.* wrongly; obliquely; badly; crossly.

**attraziọne** *f.* attraction; spectacle, show.

**attrezz-are** [A1 c] *tr.* to equip; to fit out; to rig. **-atura** *f.* plant; equipment; *pl.* fittings. **-ista** *m.* (theatr.) property-man; scene-shifter.
**attrẹzzo** *m.* implement, instrument, tackle; tool; fixture; *pl.* equipment; apparatus.
**attribuire** [D2] *tr.* to attribute, to ascribe; to impute; — *importanza*, to attach importance; — *a lode*, to praise; *rfl.* (*dat.* of *prn.*) to take upon oneself.
**attribut-o** *m.* attribute, characteristic. **-ivo** *adj.* attributive.
**attribuziọne** *f.* attribution; function, responsibility; authority.
**attrice** *f.* actress; *prima* —, leading lady.
**attristare** [A1] *tr.* to sadden; to grieve; *rfl.* to grow sad; to mope; *intr.* (*aux.* essere) to pine away.
**attrito**[1] *m.* friction; abrasion; (on a rail) traction; (fig.) discord, attrition; *in* —, at variance.
**attrito**[2] *adj.* worn out.
**attriziọne** *f.* attrition, friction; difference of opinion.
**attual-e** *adj.* present, contemporary, current; (philos.; theol.) actual. **-ità** *f.* actuality; reality; (the) present; novelty; *cinema di -ità*, news theatre. **-mẹnte** *adv.* at present, nowadays; for the time being; effectively.
**attu-are** [A5] *tr.* to carry out, to put into effect; to actuate; *rfl.* to come into effect, to be realized; to come true. **-a·bile** *adj.* feasible, realizable.
**attua·ri-o** *m.* actuary. **-ale** *adj.* actuarial.
**attutire** [D2] *tr.* to deaden; to assuage, to mitigate; *rfl.* to grow calm; to be assuaged.
**aud-ace** *adj.* audacious, bold; *essere — di*, to dare to. **-a·cia** *f.* (*pl.* **-a·cie**) audacity, daring; act of boldness; act of rashness.
**audibilità** *f.* audibility.
**audi·fono** *m.* hearing aid.
**aud-itọre** *m.* listener, hearer. **-ito·rio** *m.* auditorium; (radio) studio; *adj.* auditory. **-iziọne** *f.* audition; hearing; *-izione radiofonica*, broadcast.
**a·uge** *m.* apogee; zenith; acme; *venire in* —, to find favour.
**augello** *m.* (poet.) bird.
**augnare** [A6] *tr.* to clutch, to seize; to claw.
**augurale** *adj.* augural; auspicious.
**augur-are** [A1 sa] *tr.* to wish; *vi -o un felice anno nuovo,* I wish you a Happy New Year; — *il malanno a*, to wish ill to; to augur; *rfl.* to wish, to hope; *mi -o di rivederti presto*, I hope to see you again soon. **-a·bile** *adj.* desirable; *è -abile che*, it is to be hoped that.
**a·ugur-e** *m.* augur. **-ọso** *adj.* of good omen; of ill omen; ominous; significant.
**augu·rio** *m.* wish; *gradite i miei sinceri auguri*, accept my sincere good wishes; *auguri !*, good luck!, happy birthday!, etc.; portent, sign; omen, augury.
**augusto** *adj.* august, venerable, sacred; majestic.
**a·ula** *f.* hall, reception-room; — *magna*, great-hall; auditorium.
**aulente** *adj.* (poet.) fragrant, scented.
**a·ulico** *adj.* courtly.
**aumentare** [A1 c] *tr.* to augment, to enlarge; to add to; *intr.* (*aux.* essere) to increase; to rise; — *di peso*, to put on weight.
**aumẹnto** *m.* increase; growth; enlargement; rise; advance (in price); *essere in* —, to be on the increase.
**a·ura** *f.* (poet.) breeze; light wind; air; (fig.) atmosphere; aura; — *popolare*, popular favour.
**aurato** *adj.* (poet.) golden.
**a·ureo** *adj.* gold; golden; resplendent; precious, excellent, noble.
**aure·ola** *f.* halo; glory; aureole, nimbus.
**auri·fero** *adj.* auriferous; gold, yielding gold.
**auror-a** *f.* sunrise, dawn; daybreak; (fig.) earliest beginnings, dawn. **-ale** *adj.* auroral, pertaining to the dawn.
**ausili-are** *adj.* auxiliary; helpful, giving support; ancillary; *n.m.* assistance, help. **-a·rio** *adj.*, *n.m.* auxiliary. **-arità** *f.* co-operation.
**ausi·lio** *m.* succour, help.
**auspic-are** [A2 s] *tr.*, *abs.* to prognosticate, to augur. **-a·bile** *adj.* hoped for, to be hoped. **-ato** *part. adj.* under good auspices; longed for.
**a·uspic-e** *m.* protector, supporter; — *il Re*, under the auspices of the King. **-ale** *adj.* auspicious; *pietra -ale*, foundation stone.
**ausp-i·cio, -i·zio** *m.* auspices, omen; favour, patronage.
**auster-o** *adj.* austere; strict; unadorned. **-ità** *f.* austerity.
**a·ustr-o** *m.* (poet.) south wind; south; auster. **-ale** *adj.* southern, austral.
**aut-archi·a** *f.* autarchy; self-sufficiency. **-ar·chico** *adj.* autarchic(al); self-sufficient.
**autenticare** [A2 s] *tr.* to authenticate, to give validity to.
**auten·tic-o** *adj.* authentic; genuine. **-a** *f.* authentication; authentic evidence. **-ità** *f.* authenticity; validity.
**autiere** *m.* (mil.) driver.
**autista** *m.* chauffeur, driver.
**a·uto**[1] *pref.* auto-, self-. **-avviatọre** *m.* (motor.) self-starter. **-biografi·a** *f.* autobiography. **-biogra·fico** *adj.* autobiographic. **-bio·grafo** *m.* autobiographer. **-didatta** *m.*, *f.* self-taught man, or woman. **-didat·tico** *adj.* pertaining to self-teaching. **-governo** *m.* self-government. **-intossicaziọne** *f.* auto-intoxication. **-ipno·ṣi** *f.* self-hypnosis. **-lesiọne** *f.* self-inflicted wound. **-pilota** *m.* automatic pilot. **-ritratto** *m.* self-portrait. **-sufficienza** *f.* conceit, self-satisfaction. **-suggestiọne** *f.* auto-suggestion; self-deception.
**a·uto-**[2] *pref.* auto-, motor-. **-ambulanza** *f.* motor ambulance. **-blinda** *f.*, **-blindata** *f.*, **-blindo** *m.* armoured car. **-bruco** *m.* tracked vehicle. **-carro** *m.* lorry; motor-van. **-furgọne** *m.* van; shooting brake. **-giro** *m.* autogiro, helicopter. **-gita** *f.* motor tour, excursion. **-mẹẓẓo** *m.* transport, vehicle. **-mo·bile** *f.* automobile, car. **-mobiliṣmo** *m.* motoring. **-mobilista** *m.*, *f.* motorist. **-mobili·stico** *adj.* motoring. **-nolẹggio** *m.* towing. **-parchẹggio** *m.*, **-parco** *m.* (*pl.* **-parchi**) car-park. **-ra·dio** *f.* car radio. **-rimẹssa** *f.* garage. **-staziọne** *f.* service station. **-strada** *f.* autobahn, trunk motor-road. **-tra·ino** *m.* haulage. **-trasporti** *m.pl.* road transport. **-treno** *m.* road train; trailer bus. **-vei·colo** *m.*, **-vettura** *f.* motor vehicle.
**a·uto**[3] *f.* car, auto, automobile.
**a·utobus** *m. indecl.* bus, motor-coach.
**auto·cr-ate, -ata** *m.* autocrat. **-a·tico** *adj.* autocratic. **-azi·a** *f.* autocracy.
**auto·ctono** *adj.* autochthonous; *n.m.*, *usu. pl.* aborigines, autochthones.
**auto·grafo** *adj.* in the author's handwriting, autograph; *n.m.* original MS.; autograph.
**autom-a** *m.* automaton. **-a·tico** *adj.* automatic; involuntary; mechanical; *n.m.pl.* press-studs. **-aziọne** *f.* automation.
**auto·nom-o** *adj.* autonomous; self-governing; independent; *ente* —, corporation. **-i·a** *f.* autonomy; independence.
**autopsi·a** *f.* autopsy, post mortem.
**autọr-e** *m.* creator, originator; author, writer; artist, painter; composer; *diritti d'*—, copyright royalties. **-ẹvole** *adj.* authoritative; imposing.
**autorit-à** *f.* authority; influence; persons in authority; authoritative source; *dare — a*, to empower; *fare* —, to be authoritative. **-a·rio** *adj.* autocratic; authoritative. **-ativo** *adj.* authoritative.
**autoriẓẓ-are** [A1] *tr.* to authorize; to entitle. **-aziọne** *f.* authorization; delegated power; *per -azione*, by authority.
**autrice** *f.* authoress, woman writer.
**autunn-o** *m.* autumn. **-ale** *adj.* autumnal.
**auziọn-e** *f.* auction. **-ista** *m.* auctioneer.

**avall-o** *m.* (comm.) guarantee. **-ante** *m.* (comm.) guarantor. **-are** [A1] *tr.* (comm.) to back (a bill); (fig.) to verify; to make valid; to legalize.

**avam-brac·cio** *m.* forearm. **-paese** *m.* frontier territory. **-porto** *m.* outer harbour. **-posto** *m.* advance post; outpost.

**avan-città** *f.* outskirts. **-guar·dia** *f.* advance guard; vanguard; (fig.) forefront, fore; *essere all'-guardia*, to hold advanced views; *letteratura d'-guardia*, avant-garde literature. **-spetta·colo** *m.* (theatr.) curtain-raiser.

**avani·a** *f.* tax, burden; insult, outrage.

**avanti** *prep.* before; — *Cristo* (abbrev. a.C.), B.C.; sooner than; — *a*, before, in the presence of; in front of; *adv.* before, in front; beforehand; ahead, forward; — *e indietro*, to and fro; *il mio orologio è* —, my watch is fast; *tirarsi — per una professione*, to go in for a profession; *d'ora in* —, from now on; *excl.* — *!*, come in!; go ahead!; (mil.) — *!*, forward!, advance!; (naut.) — *a tutto vapore !*, full steam ahead!; *n.m.* (football, rugby) forward.

**avantieri** *adv.* the day before yesterday.

**avanz-are** [A1] *tr.* to advance, to put forward; to promote; to surpass; to save; *intr.* (*aux.* essere, avere) to advance, to progress; to be in advance; to be left over, to remain; to be a survivor, to escape; *rfl.* to advance; to approach; to hang over, to stand out. **-amento** *m.* advance; progress; advancement.

**avanz-o** *m.* remains, remainder; remnant; (comm.) — *di cassa*, cash in hand; surplus; *mettere in* —, to save; *d'*—, more than enough, to spare; *pl.* ruins; leftovers. **-u·glio** *m.*, **-ume** *m.* residue; dregs.

**avar-i·a** *f.* damage; average. **-iare** [A4] *tr.* (comm.) to damage.

**avar-o** *adj.* mean, miserly; avaricious; covetous; (fig.) sparing; (poet.) desirous, eager; *n.m.* miser. **-i·zia** *f.* avarice; greed; miserliness.

**ave** *excl.* hail!; greetings!; *n.m.*, *f.* (rel.) Hail Mary; *in* (*men di*) *un* —, in the twinkling of an eye.

**avellano** *m.* nut-tree; hazel-nut tree.

**avello** *m.* (poet.) tomb, sepulchre.

**avemmari·a, avemari·a, ave mari·a** *f.* (the) Hail Mary; *ave* bead (of rosary); the Angelus (prayer or bell); sunset, curfew time.

**avena** *f.* oats; *farina d'*—, oatmeal; (mus.) oaten pipe.

**av-ere** [B3] *tr.* to have; to own; — *fame*, to be hungry; — *fretta*, to be in a hurry; — *paura*, to be afraid; — *moglie*, to be married; *quanti anni avete ?*, how old are you?; — *indosso*, to wear; (in *perf.*, *past def.* and *inf.*) to obtain, to get; to consider; — *a vile*, to consider cowardly; — *in onore*, to esteem; — *a mente*, to have in mind; — *per certo*, to know for certain; — *a* (foll. by *inf.*), to chance to; to have the misfortune to; — *da*, to have the wherewithal; to be obliged to; — *del buono*, to have good qualities; *avercela con*, to be angry with; *aversene a male*, to take offence at; to be; *non v'ha pace per me*, there is no peace for me; *n.m.* property; wealth; (comm.) credit; *pl.* possessions, substance.

**avia·rio** *m.* aviary.

**avi-atore** *m.* aviator; airman. **-ato·rio** *adj.* flying, aviation. **-azione** *f.* aviation, flying; air force. **-ere** *m.* aircraftman (Air Force rank).

**avicult-ore** *m.* bird fancier, aviculturist. **-ura** *f.* aviculture.

**a·vid-o** *adj.* avid; greedy; eager. **-ità** *f.* avidity; greed; eagerness.

**a·vio**[1] *pref.*, *adj. indecl.* air; — *benzina*, aviation petrol. **-getto** *m.* jet aircraft. **-lan·cio** *m.* parachute jump. **-li·nea** *f.* airline; airway. **-rimessa** *f.* hangar. **-trasporto** *m.* air travel.

**a·vio**[2] *adj.* (poet.) impervious; inaccessible, remote.

**av-o** *m.* grandfather; forefather, ancestor. **-ito** *adj.* ancestral; hereditary.

**avocare** [A2 s] *tr.* to arrogate.

**a·volo** *m.* grandfather; ancestor.

**avo·rio** *m.* ivory.

**avorn-iello, -io, -o** *m.* (bot.) laburnam; (poet.) ash.

**avvalere** [B34] *rfl.* (*prep.* di) to make use (of), to avail oneself (of).

**avvall-are** [A1] *tr.* to lower; to debase; *rfl.*, *intr.* (*aux.* essere) to subside; to slope. **-amento** *m.* (of earth, building) sinking; landslip; trough (of waves).

**avvalorare** [A1 c] *tr.* to make valuable; to improve; to strengthen; to test; *rfl.* to become stronger; to increase in value.

**avvamp-are** [A1] *tr.* to set ablaze; to inflame; *rfl.*, *intr.* (*aux.* essere) to blaze up; to shine; (fig.) — *di sdegno*, to burn with indignation. **-ante** *part. adj.* burning, blazing.

**avvantaggi-are** [A3] *tr.* to benefit, to favour; to endow; to ameliorate; *rfl.* (*prep.* di) to profit (by); to derive advantage (from); *-arsi in un lavoro*, to get ahead with one's work.

**avvantag·gio** *m.* advantage; *adv. d'*—, more.

**avved-ere** [B23] *rfl.* (*prep.* di) to become aware (of), to perceive; *senza -ersene*, without meaning to. **-imento** *m.* discernment; sagacity; *con -imento*, shrewdly, cautiously. **-uto** *part. adj.* aware; sagacious, discerning; shrewd, astute.

**avvelen-are** [A1c] *tr.* to poison; to make poisonous; (fig.) to embitter. **-atore** *m.* poisoner.

**avvenen-te** *adj.* handsome, comely; charming, pleasant. **-za** *f.* attractiveness; good looks; charm.

**avven-ire** [D17] *intr.* (*aux.* essere) to happen, to take place; *n.m.* future; prospects; *adj. indecl.* future, to come. **-imento** *m.* event, important occurrence. **-uto** *part.*, *n.m.* occurrence; *l'-uto*, what has occurred.

**avvent-are** [A1] *tr.* to hurl, to fling; to risk; *rfl.* to fling oneself; to rush. **-ata** *adv. phr. all'-ata*, precipitately. **-ato** *part. adj.* reckless, rash.

**avvent-o** *m.* coming, advent; arrival. **-iziato** *m.* (comm.) apprenticeship; temporary employment. **-i·zio** *adj.* adventitious; fortuitous; temporary; *operaio -izio*, casual labourer; *n.m.* temporary employee; apprentice. **-ore** *m.* customer, client.

**avventur-a** *f.* adventure; *per* —, by chance. **-are** [A1] *tr.* to risk; to adventure; *rfl.* to venture; to take a risk. **-ato** *part. adj.* ventured; fortunate; *male -ato*, unlucky. **-iere, -iero** *m.* adventurer. **-oso** *adj.* adventurous; venturesome; lucky.

**avverare** [A1 c] *tr.* to verify; to make valid; *rfl.* to be fulfilled, to come true; to occur.

**avver·bi-o** *m.* adverb. **-iale** *adj.* adverbial.

**avverdire** [D2] *tr.* to make green; to paint green; *intr.* (*aux.* essere) to grow green, to turn green.

**avvers-are** [A1] *tr.* to oppose; to thwart. **-ante** *part. adj.* opposing; hostile. **-atore** *m.* opponent, adversary.

**avversa·rio** *m.* adversary; opponent; *adj.* contrary; hostile.

**avvers-o** *adj.* adverse, unfavourable; opposite; averse; *per* —, on the contrary. **-ione** *f.* aversion; dislike; hatred. **-ità** *f.* adversity, misfortune.

**avvert-ire** [D1] *tr.* (*prep.* di) to warn, to caution (against); to point out; to inform; to remind; to feel, to notice; *intr.* (*aux.* avere) to pay attention; to be on the alert. **-enza** *f.* caution; care, attention; *usate -enza !*, be careful!; warning; instruction; notice; foreword. **-i·bile** *adj.* noticeable. **-imento** *m.* warning; caution; notice; prefatory note.

**avvezz-are** [A1 c] *tr.* to accustom; to train, to bring up; *rfl.* to accustom oneself. **-amento** *m.* training, habit.

**avvezzo** *adj.* accustomed; trained.

**avvi-are** [A4] *tr.* to set going, to start; to route; *rfl.* to set off; to start; *-arsi per una professione*, to begin training for a profession. **-amẹnto** *m.* starting, start; direction; introductory study; (mech.) starting; (comm.) goodwill. **-atọre** *m.* one who teaches the groundwork of a subject; (motor.) starter. **-atura** *f.* work begun; first stages.

**avvicinare** [A1] *tr.* to bring near; to compare; to approach; to frequent the company of; *rfl.* to approach; to draw near.

**avvil-ire** [D2] *tr.* to debase; to lower; to humiliate; to depreciate; *rfl.* to degrade oneself; to humiliate oneself; to lose heart. **-ente, -iente** *part. adj.* demoralizing; humiliating. **-imẹnto** *m.* dejection; degradation; depreciation.

**avviluppare** [A1] *tr.* to envelop; to wrap up; to entangle; to complicate.

**avvinare** [A1] *tr.* to soak in wine; to flavour with wine.

**avvin·c-ere** [C5] *tr.* to bind, to tie; to fascinate. **-ente** *adj.* fascinating, winning.

**avvincigliare** [A4] *tr.* to bind; to twist.

**avvincolare** [A1s] *tr.* to clasp.

**avvinghiare** [A4] *tr.* to seize, to grasp; *rfl. avvinghiarsi a*, to clasp; *recip. rfl.* to clasp one another.

**avvi·o** *m.* (*pl.* **avvi·i**) beginning; first steps; *prendre l'—*, to begin.

**avviṣa·glia** *f.* skirmish, brush with the enemy; conflict, set-to.

**avviṣ-are** [A1] *tr.* to inform; to advise, to warn; to instruct; to remind; *rfl.* to consider; to understand; *intr.* (*aux.* avere; *prep.* a) to think (about), to turn one's mind (to). **-atamẹnte** *adv.* cautiously; knowingly, intentionally. **-atọre** *m.* announcer; informant; (theatr.) call-boy; *-atore d'incendio*, fire-alarm.

**avviṣo** *m.* notice, announcement; advertisement; *contro —*, on notice; *— di consegna*, advice note; opinion, belief; *a mio —*, in my view.

**avvist-are** [A1] *tr.* to catch sight of; to tell at a glance; (naut.) to sight. **-ato** *part. adj.* alert, knowing; well-advised.

**avvit-are** [A1] *tr.* to screw; *rfl.* (aeron.) to go into a spin; (ski.) to swing the body round. **-atrice** *f.* wrench.

**avviticchiare** [A4] *tr.* to twine, to twist; *rfl.* (*prep.* a) to twine (round); to cling (to).

**avviv-are** [A1] *tr.* to enliven, to vivify; to bring to life; *rfl.* to revive, to grow animated. **-atọre** *m.* enlivener; animator; *adj.* animating.

**avvizzire** [D2] *intr.* (*aux.* essere) to wither, to fade.

**avvocat-o**[1] *m.* lawyer; (fig.) advocate, champion. **-ẹsco** *adj.* (*m.pl.* **-ẹschi**) captious. **-ura** *f.* lawyer's profession; *l'Avvocatura*, the Bar.

**avvocato**[2] *m.* (bot.) *pero —*, avocado pear.

**avvol·g-ere** [C5] *tr.* to wind; to roll up; to involve; to trick. **-i·bile** *adj.*; *n.m.* roller blind; roll shutter. **-imẹnto** *m.* winding up; trick, deceit; stratagem.

**avvoltọio** *m.* vulture.

**avvoltolare** [A1s] *tr., rfl.* to roll.

**aẓale·a** *f.* (bot.) azalea.

**aẓiend-a** *f.* business, firm, concern; direction, management. **-a·ria** *f.* business administration.

**aziọn-e** *f.* action; act, deed; movement; subject, theme; (comm.) share. **-are** [A1c] *tr.* to actuate; to set going; to power. **-a·bile** *adj.* actionable. **-ista** *m., f.* shareholder.

**aẓoto** *m.* nitrogen.

**azza** *f.* battle-axe.

**azzannare** [A1] *tr.* to seize with the teeth; to sink fangs into.

**aẓẓard-o** *m.* hazard, risk; *giuoco d'—*, game of chance. **-are** [A1] *tr.* to hazard; to risk; *intr.* (*aux.* avere) to take risks; *rfl.* to dare, to venture. **-ọso** *adj.* hazardous, risky; bold, daring.

**azzecc-are** [A2c] *tr.* to hit, to strike; *-arla*, to hit the mark. **-ato** *part. adj.* completely successful, just right.

**aẓẓimare** [A1s] *tr.* to dress ornately; *rfl.* to deck oneself out.

**az·zim-o** *adj.* unleavened; *n.m.* unleavened bread. **-a, -ella** *f.* unleavened bread.

**azzopp-are** [A1], **-ire** [D2] *tr.* to lame, to render lame; *intr.* (*aux.* essere), *rfl.* to fall lame.

**azzuff-are** [A1] *rfl.* (*prep.* con), *recip. rfl.* to come to blows; to scuffle. **-atọre** *m.* brawler, rioter.

**aẓẓurr-o** *adj.* azure; blue; sky-blue; *Principe —*, Prince Charming; *n.m.* the colour blue; the azure. **-ato** *adj.* coloured blue, painted blue.

**B, b** *f., m.* (pron. Bi) the letter B; the consonant B.

**baba·u** *m.* bogey, ogre; bugbear.

**babbe·o** *m.* fool, simpleton, blockhead.

**babbilano** *m.* man who is sexually impotent.

**babbo** *m.* daddy.

**babbuc·cia** *f.* bedroom slipper.

**babbuino** *m.* (zool.) baboon; (fig.) dolt, booby.

**Bab-ele** *pr.n.f.* (Bibl.) Babel; *torre di —*, tower of Babel; (fig.) place of confusion. **-e·lico** *adj.* uproarious, disorderly.

**Babilo·nia** *pr.n.f.* Babylon; (fig.) chaos, confusion.

**babọrdo** *m.* (naut.) port, larboard.

**bac-are** (A2) *intr.* (*aux.* essere), *rfl.* to become worm-eaten; to go bad. **-ato** *part. adj.* worm-eaten; gone bad; (fig.) sick; morally corrupt; (*fam.*) soft in the head.

**bacca** *f.* berry, fruit.

**baccalà** *m. indecl.* dried salt cod.

**baccalaureato** *m.* baccalaureate.

**baccanale** *m.* Bacchanalian orgy; noisy revel; *pl.* Bacchanalia; *adj.* Bacchic, Bacchanal.

**baccano** *m.* uproar, hubbub; *far —*, to kick up a shindy.

**baccante** *f.* Bacchante; *adj.* frenzied.

**baccarà** *m.* baccarat.

**baccellier-e** *m.* (Univ.) bachelor. **-ato** *m.* bachelor's degree.

**baccello** *m.* bean (*i.e.* pod with its beans).

**bacchẹtt-a** *f.* rod, staff; *commandare a —*, to be severe; mahlstick; *— magica*, wand. **-are** (A1c) *tr.* to thrash. **-ata** *f.* thrashing.

**bacchettọn-e** *m.*, **-a** *f.* devotee; pious humbug. **-eri·a** *f.* cant; humbug.

**bacchiare** [A4] *tr.* (agric.) to beat down with a pole.

**bac·chic-o** *adj.* Bacchic, Bacchanal; *canzone -a*, drinking song.

**bac·chio** *m.* pole; cudgel.

**Bacco** *pr.n.m.* (myth.) Bacchus.

**bacheca** *f.* jeweller's showcase; glass case; notice-board.

**bachelite** *f.* bakelite.

**bacher-ozzo, -oz·zolo** *m.* grub, maggot.

**bachicolt-ọre** *m.* breeder of silkworms; silk producer. **-ura** *f.* cultivation of silkworms; silk growing.

**baci-are** (A3) *tr.* to kiss; to touch lightly; (of water) to wash against; *recip. rfl.* to kiss one another, to kiss. **-amano** *m.* hand-kissing.

**bacile** *m.* basin; bowl.

**bacillo** *m.* bacillus; germ, microbe.

**bacino** *m.* basin; bowl; pan; (naut.) dock; (geog.) basin; (anat.) pelvis.

**ba·c-io** *m.* kiss; *adv. a —*, osculating; (colloq.) *al —*, perfect. **-ẹtto, -ino** *m. dim.* little kiss. **-iọne** *m. augm.* hearty kiss, smack.

**bacio** *adj.* shaded; having a

northerly aspect; *adv. a* —, in the shade; *n.m.* shady site, north outlook.

**bac-o** *m.* (*pl.* **bachi**) caterpillar, larva, grub; — *da seta*, silkworm; (fig.) defect, taint. **-olo·gi·a** *f.* science of silkworm breeding. **-olo·gico** *adj.* relating to silkworm breeding. **-o·logo** *m.* expert in silk-worm culture.

**bacucco** *adj.* stupid; *vecchio* —, dotard.

**bada** *f.* waiting; delay; *adv. phr. tenere a* —, to hold at bay; to ward off; to baffle.

**bad-are** (A1) *intr.* (*aux.* avere; *prep.* a) to pay attention (to); *senza — a*, regardless of; to look after; (*prep.* di) to be careful; *-a di non scivolare*, mind you don't slip; *abs. -a !*, look out!; *rfl.* to be careful; to be on one's guard; *tr.* to tend, to watch.

**badẹssa** *f.* abbess.

**bad-i·a** *f.* abbey; comfortable home. **-iale** *adj.* huge; comfortable.

**badil-e** *m.* shovel, spade. **-ata** *f.* shovelful.

**baff-o** *m.* (usu. *pl.*) moustache; whiskers; *farsene un* —, not to give a damn; *ridere sotto i -i*, to laugh up one's sleeve; *leccarsi i -i*, to lick one's lips; smudge, smear. **-uto** *adj.* moustached.

**baga·gli-o** *m.* luggage; *fare i bagagli*, to pack; *deposito bagagli*, left luggage office; baggage; equipment; (fig.) burden; (mil.) kit, pack. **-a·io** *m.* (motor.) boot; (rlwy.) luggage-van.

**bagarino** *m.* (econ.) person who makes a corner in a commodity; tout.

**baga·scia** *f.* prostitute.

**bagat(t)ella** *f.* bagatelle, trifle; trinket.

**bagg-e·o, -iano** *m.* booby, fool, dolt; *adj.* foolish.

**ba·glio** *m.* (naut.) beam.

**bagliọre** *m.* dazzling flash; glare; glow, ray.

**bagnai(u)olo** *m.* bath-attendant.

**bagn-are** (A5) *tr.* to wet; to soak; to bath; to bathe; (of waters) to wash; *rfl.* to get wet, to get caught in the rain; to bathe; to take a bath. **-ante** *part. adj.*; *n.m., f.* bather. **-asciuga** *m.* (naut.) motion of the ship placing the water line now under water, now above; water line; *al -asciuga*, 'twixt wind and water; (geog.) strip of land alternately dry and under water. **-ata** *f.* dip (bathing); wetting, soaking. **-ato** *part. adj.* wet; soaked; *se non è zuppa, è pan -ato*, it comes to the same thing.

**bagn-o** *m.* bath; bathroom; swimming bath; bathing resort; *mettere a* —, to put to soak; *fare il* —, to take a bath; to go bathing. **-ino** *m.*, **-ina** *f.* swimming-pool attendant. **-omari·a** *m. indecl.* (cul.) bain-marie, steam cooker. **-(u)olo** *m.* hot fomentation.

**bagọrd-o** *m.* (usu. *pl.*) revelry; meeting-place of revellers; *fare i -i*, to make merry. **-are** (A 1c) *intr.* (*aux.* avere) to revel.

**bai** (onom.) *senza dire nè ai nè* —, without a word; without warning.

**ba·ia**[1] *f.* bay, gulf; bight.

**ba·ia**[2] *f.* jest, joke; *dare la — a*, to chaff; *baie !*, nonsense!

**ba·io** *adj.* bay (colour of a horse); *n.m.* bay horse.

**baioc-co** *m.* (*pl.* **-chi**) (numis.) copper coin; *non vale un* —, it's not worth twopence.

**baionẹtt-a** *f.* bayonet; — *in canna*, with fixed bayonets; *innestare la* —, to fix bayonets. **-ata** *f.* bayonet thrust; bayonet wound.

**ba·ita** *f.* Alpine hut.

**balau·str-o** *m.* baluster; small balustrade. **-a** *f.* banisters. **-ata** *f.* balustrade; hand-rail.

**balbett-are** (A1 c) *intr.* (*aux.* avere) to stammer; to stutter; to lisp; to prattle; *tr.* to stammer out. **-ìo** *m.* stammering; prattle, babble. **-ọne** *m.* stammerer, stutterer.

**balbutire** (D2) *intr.* (*aux.* avere) to stammer; to stutter; to lisp, to prattle.

**balbu·zi-e** *f. indecl.* stammer; stutter; lisp. **-ente** *adj.* stammering; stuttering; lisping; *n.m., f.* stammerer; stutterer.

**Balc-ani** *pr.n.m.pl.* (geog.) Balkans. **-a·nico** *adj.* Balkan; *la Penisola -anica*, the Balkan Peninsula. **-ano** *adj., n.m.* Balkan.

**balcọn-e** *m.* balcony; **-ata** *f.* gallery; railed balcony.

**baldacchino** *m.* canopy; tester; (eccl.) baldacchino.

**bald-o** *adj.* bold, daring, fearless; in good spirits. **-amẹnte** *adv.* boldly; fearlessly. **-anza** *f.* boldness; self-assurance. **-anzọso** *adj.* bold; fearless; haughty.

**baldo·ria** *f.* gaiety; *fare* —, to make merry, to have a gay party.

**baldracca** *f.* slut, strumpet.

**Baleari** *pr.n.f.pl.* (Isole) Balearic Islands.

**balẹn-a** *f.* whale; *olio di* —, whale-oil. **-iera** *f.* (naut.) whaling-ship. **-ot·tera** *f.* blue whale. **-otto** *m.* young whale, calf.

**balen-are** (A1c) *intr.* (*aux.* essere), *impers.* to flash with lightning, to lighten; *mi -ò un'idea*, an idea came to me in a flash; to reel, to totter. **-amẹnto** *m.* flashing; lightning. **-ìo** *m.* continual flashing.

**balẹno** *m.* flash of lightning, thunderbolt; *in un* —, in a flash; *come un* —, as quick as lightning.

**balera** *f.* dance-hall.

**balestra** *f.* crossbow; catapult; (eng.) spring.

**balestruc·cio** *m.* (orn.) house-martin.

**bali·a**[1] *f.* power, authority; *in — di*, in the power of, at the mercy of.

**ba·li-a**[2] *f.* nurse; foster-mother; — *da latte*, wet-nurse; *mettere a* —, to put out to nurse. **-a·tico** *m.* suckling; wet-nurse's wages.

**bali·stic-a** *f.* ballistics. **-o** *adj.* ballistic.

**balla**[1] *f.* bale (of goods); package.

**balla**[2] *f.* ball; projectile; tall story.

**ball-are** (A1) *intr.* (*aux.* avere) to dance; *quando non c'è la gatta, i sorci -ano*, when the cat's away the mice will play; to bump up and down; to vibrate, to rattle. **-a·bile** *adj.* suitable for dancing; *n.m.* dance tune. **-ata** *f.* dance; ballade. **-erina** *f.* ballerina. **-erino** *m.* male ballet dancer; professional dancer.

**ballatọio** *m.* circular gallery round a building; platform; (theatr.) flies.

**ballerin-a** *f.* ballet dancer, ballerina. **-o** *m.* male ballet dancer.

**ballẹtto** *m.* ballet.

**ball-o** *m.* dancing; dance, ball; ballet; *corpo di* —, corps de ballet; — *in maschera*, masked ball; (fig.) *in* —, in play, in action; *tirare in* —, to drag in; *quando si è in — si deve ballare*, once you've begun you have to go on; (aeron.) bump. **-onzolare** (A2 sc) *intr.* (*aux.* avere) to trip along; to romp; to swing about in the breeze.

**ballotta** *f.* boiled chestnut.

**ballottare**[1] (A1) *tr.* to put to the vote; *intr.* (*aux.* avere) to cause a division; to vote. **-ag·gio** *m.* ballot.

**ballott-are**[2] (A1) *tr.* to bump about, to bounce. **-ata** *f.* (equit.) ballottade.

**balneare** *adj.* pertaining to bathing; *stazione* —, seaside resort.

**baloc-co** *m.* (*pl.* **-chi**) toy; plaything; trifle. **-care** (A2) *tr.* to amuse; *rfl.* to play; to idle away the time.

**balord-o** *adj.* dull; slow-witted; absurd; *un'idea -a*, a silly idea; *n.m.* dolt, simpleton. **-ag·gine** *f.* dullness; *dire delle -aggini*, to say stupid things.

**balsa** *f.* (bot.) balsa; *zattera di* —, raft of balsa wood.

**balsa·mico** *adj.* having healing properties; sweet-smelling; (of air) balmy.

**bal·samo** *m.* balsam; balm; fragrance; (fig.) comfort, solace.

**balta** *f.* overturning; collision, shock; *dare di* —, to overturn.

**Bal·tico** *pr.n.m.* (geog.) *il Mare* —, the Baltic Sea.

**baluardo** *m.* bulwark; rampart, bastion; (fig.) defence.

**balugin-are** (A1 s) *intr.* (*aux.* essere) to flash into view for a moment; to loom. **-ìo** *m.* (*pl.* **-ii**), winking, blinking.

**balza**[1] *f.* cliff, crag, precipice; rock.
**balza**[2] *f.* band of contrasting colour round a skirt; flounce.
**balzan-o** *adj.* strange, unusual; *un'idea -a*, a crack-brained idea.
**balz-are** (A1) (*aux.* essere, avere) to bounce; to bound; to leap; — *in piedi*, to leap to one's feet; *tr.* to bounce, to throw down. **-ellare** (A1) *intr.* (*aux.* essere, avere) to hop, to skip; *tr.* to leap out upon, to stalk; (fig.) to catch 'on the hop'. **-ellọne** *m.* hop, skip; *camminare a -elloni*, to skip along. **-ellọni** *adv.* hopping, skipping.
**balzello** *m.* heavy duty, crushing tax.
**balzo**[1] *m.* bound, bounce; rebound; *dare un —*, to start up; *di —*, bouncing; *d'un —*, in one bound; *prendere la palla al —*, to catch the ball on the bounce.
**balzo**[2] *m.* small precipice, promontory; terrace.
**bamba·gia** *f.* cotton, cotton wool; *tenere nella —*, to mollycoddle.
**bambin-o** *m.* baby; child; little boy; *fare un —*, to have a baby; *fare il —*, to behave childishly; *il Bambino Gesù*, the Christ Child. **-a** *f.* baby girl; little girl; young girl. **-ag·gine** *f.* childish action; childishness. **-a·ia** *f.* children's nurse. **-ata** *f.* babyish behaviour. **-ẹsco** *adj.* (*m.pl.* **-ẹschi**) of a child; childlike.
**bamboc·cio** *m.* bonny child; silly person, rag-doll.
**bam·bol-a** *f.* doll; (colloq.) pretty girl. **-eggiare** [A3c] *intr.* (*aux.* avere) to be babyish; to behave like a child; to simper. **-otto** *m.* baby doll.
**bambù** *m. indecl.* bamboo plant; bamboo cane.
**banal-e** *adj.* commonplace, banal; trite. **-ità** *f.* commonplace, banality.
**banan-a** *f.* banana; *pl.* (slang) cash, dibs. **-o** *m.* banana-tree.
**banc-a** *f.* table, bench; bank, banking house; *biglietto di —*, bank-note. **-arella** *f.* barrow, stall. **-a·rio** *adj.* banking, bank; *assegno -ario*, bank draft; *n.m.* bank clerk. **-arotta** *f.* bankruptcy.
**banchẹtt-o** *m.* banquet; stall. **-are** (A1c) *intr.* (*aux.* avere) to feast, to banquet; *tr.* to give a banquet in honour of, to feast.
**banchiere** *m.* banker.
**banchina** *f.* slab forming a seat; wharf, quay; (rlwy.) platform.
**banchịsa** *f.* ice-floe, pack-ice; — *polare*, shelf-ice.
**banc-o** *m.* (*pl.* **banchi**) slab; desk; bench; seat; settle; counter; — *di chiesa*, pew; bank; *tenere il —*, to be banker; *far saltare il —*, to break the bank; (geog.) bank, reef; shoal; floe; — *di nebbia*, fog bank. **-ogiro** *m.* (comm). clearing transaction. **-onota** *f.* banknote.
**banda**[1] *f.* side; sector; *mettere da —*, to set aside; band, border; leaf of a folding door or shutter; (radio; electr.) band; (cinem.) — *sonora*, sound-track; *pl.* flashes, stripes on uniform.
**band-a**[2] *f.* band; gang, group; company; (mus.) band; *maestro di —*, bandmaster; banner, ensign. **-ista** *m.* (mus.) bandsman.
**bander(u)ola** *f.* pennant, streamer; vane, weathercock; (fig.) fickle person.
**bandiera** *f.* flag, ensign, colours; *issare la —*, to hoist the flag; — *a mezz'asta*, flag at half-mast; *battere — italiana*, to fly the Italian flag.
**bandinella** *f.* roller-towel; blind.
**band-ire** (D2) *tr.* to publish; to proclaim; to notify; — *un concorso*, to hold a competition; to banish, to exile; to dispense with. **-ito** *part. adj.* proclaimed; banished; *n.m.* bandit; criminal outlaw. **-itọre** *m.* town crier; auctioneer.
**bandista** *m.* see under **banda**[2].
**bando** *m.* proclamation; edict; bann; banishment; *mettere al —*, to outlaw.
**bandoliera** *f.* shoulder belt; *a —*, slung across the shoulder.
**ban·dolo** *m.* head or end of a skein of wool or silk; (fig.) *trovare il — della matassa*, to discover the key to the problem.
**bandọne** *m.* sheet iron; plate; — *ondulato*, corrugated iron; corrugated iron rolling shutter.
**bar**[1] *m. indecl.* bar, coffee-house; cocktail cabinet.
**bar**[2] *m. indecl.* (phys.; meteor.) bar (unit of pressure), 1000 millibars.
**bara** *f.* bier; coffin; *fino alla —*, for ever; *avere un pie' nella —*, to have one foot in the grave.
**baraba·u** *m. indecl.* bogey-man.
**baracc-a** *f.* cabin, booth; hut; stall; (fig.) things in general; *aiutare la —*, to help things along; *piantare baracche e burattini*, to walk out and leave everything. **-ọne** *m. augm.* stall at a fair; *esibirsi nei -oni*, to be on show at a fair.
**barracchiere** *m.* stall keeper, stall attendant.
**baracchino** *m.* mess-tin; mountain hut.
**baraọnda** *f.* medley of persons; mass of papers; disorder, hubbub
**barare** (A1) *intr.* (*aux.* avere) to cheat.
**ba·ratro** *m.* gulf, chasm; the Abyss, Hell; den of iniquity.
**baratt-are** (A1) *tr.* to exchange; to barter. **-eri·a** *f.* corruption in public offices; barratry. **-iere** *m.* embezzler; barrator. **-o** *m.* exchange; barter; *in -o di*, in exchange for.
**barat·tolo** *m.* jar; jam-pot; tin, can; medicine bottle.
**barb-a** *f.* beard; *portare la —*, to have a beard; *farsi la —*, to shave oneself; *fare la — a*, to shave (someone); *in — a*, in defiance of; *notizia con tanto di —*, hoary old tale; *non c'è — d'uomo che possa farlo*, there's not a man alive who could do it; *che — !*, what a bore!; fibre tuft; deckle-edge; (bot.) root. **-ato** *adj.* bearded; barbed. **-ẹtta** *f. dim.* short beard; *-etta a punta*, goatee; small root; barb. **-icella** *f. dim.* small root. **-oncino** *m. dim.* poodle puppy. **-ọne** *m. augm.* long beard; bearded man, 'beaver'; poodle. **-uto** *adj.* bearded.
**barbabie·tola** *f.* beetroot; — *da zucchero*, sugar beet; — *da foraggio*, mangel wurzel.
**Barbablù** *pr.n.m.* Blue Beard.
**barbacane** *m.* buttress; barbican.
**barbagianni** *m. indecl.* barn owl; (fig.) blockhead.
**barba·glio** *m.* dazzle, glare; dizziness.
**Bar·bara** *pr.n.f.* Barbara.
**barbare** [A1] *intr.* (*aux.* avere) to take root; to put forth roots.
**barba·rico** *adj.* barbaric, barbarian; uncivilized.
**barba·rie** *f. indecl.* barbarity; brutality.
**bar·bar-o** *adj.* barbarous; cruel; crude; *n.m.* barbarian; savage. **-ịsmo** *m.* barbarism.
**barbazzale** *m.* curb-chain; (fig.) curb, check.
**barbic-are** (A2s) *intr.* (*aux.* avere) to take root. **-ato** *part. adj.* rooted; (fig.) deep seated, ingrained.
**barbiere** *m.* barber; barber's shop.
**barbiturato** *m.* barbiturate.
**barbitu·ric-o** *adj.* barbituric; *n.m.pl. i -i*, the barbiturates.
**barbo·gio** *adj.* senile, decrepit; *n.m.* dotard.
**barbọne** *m.* see under **barba**.
**barbottare** (A1c) *intr.* (*aux.* avere) to murmur; to grumble; to make a bubbling noise.
**barbugliare** (A4) *intr.* (*aux.* avere) to splutter; to falter; *tr.* to stammer out.
**barc-a**[1] *f.* boat; barge; launch; — *a remi*, rowing boat; — *a vela*, sailing boat; — *da pesca*, fishing boat. **-ac·cia** *f. pejor.* old boat, tub; (theatr.) stage box. **-ai(u)olo** *m.* boatman; ferryman. **-amenare** (A1c) *rfl.* to keep afloat; to steer a course between difficulties. **-arola** *f.* (mus.) barcarolle. **-ata** *f.* boatload.
**barca**[2] *f.* stack; heap of corn to be threshed; pile.
**Barcellọna** *pr.n.f.* (geog.) Barcelona.
**barchẹggio** *m.* boats; ship-to-shore traffic; boating.

**barchetta** *f. dim.* small boat; skiff, dinghy.
**barchino** *m. dim.* small motor boat; midget submarine.
**bar-co** *m.* (*pl.* **-chi**) large boat. **-cone** *m. augm.* barge; lighter.
**barcoll-are** (A1) *intr.* (*aux.* avere) to totter, to stagger; (fig.) to be precarious; to vacillate. **-amento** *m.* vacillation; reeling. **-ante** *part. adj.* tottering, insecure. **-oni** *adv.* staggering, tottering.
**bard-a** *f.* bard, a stuffed pack-saddle for ass or mule. **-amento** *m.* harnessing; trappings. **-are** (A1) *tr.* to harness. **-ato** *part. adj.* harnessed; (fig.) over-dressed. **-atura** *f.* trappings of a horse; harness; *-atura di guerra*, emergency measures taken during a war.
**bardella** *f.* pack-saddle.
**bardo** *m.* bard poet; *adj.* (poet.) bardic.
**barell-a** *f.* hand-barrow; stretcher; *portatore di —*, stretcher-bearer. **-are** (A1) *intr.* (*aux.* avere) to waver; to stagger; *tr.* to carry in a barrow; to carry on a stretcher.
**bargello** *m.* chief of police; (hist. Florence) police headquarters.
**bargi·gli-o, -one** *m.* wattles of a cock or turkey. **-uto** *adj.* wattled.
**bari-centro** *m.* centre of gravity. **-cen·trico** *adj.* barycentric; *asse -centrico*, axis of gravity.
**baril-e** *m.* barrel; cask. **-a·io** *m.* cooper.
**ba·rio** *m.* (chem.) barium.
**barisfera** *f.* the core of the earth, barysphere.
**barista** *m.* bartender; barman; *f.* barmaid.
**bari·ton-o** *adj.*, *n.m.* (mus.) baritone. **-ale** *adj.* (mus.) baritone.
**barlume** *m.* gleam, glimmer; (fig.) *— di speranza*, ray of hope.
**baro** *m.* cheat, swindler.
**baroc·ci-o** *m.* waggon; cart; tumbril; load; cart-load. **-a·io** *m.* waggoner; carter.
**baroc-co** *adj.* (*m.pl.* **-chi**) (archit.) baroque; (fig.) queer; grotesque; over-ornate; *n.m.* baroque style; baroque work. **-chismo** *m.* baroque; (fig.) oddness, queerness.
**baro·grafo** *m.* (meteor.) barograph, aneroid barometer.
**Barolo** *pr.n.m.* red wine of Piedmont.
**baro·m-etro** *m.* barometer, glass. **-e·trico** *adj.* barometric.
**baron-e**[1] *m.* baron; *— dell'industria*, tycoon. **-ale** *adj.* baronial. **-ato** *m.* barony. **-esco** *adj.* (*m.pl.* **-eschi**) baron-like. **-essa** *f.* baroness; dame. **-etto** *m.* baronet. **-i·a** *f.* barony, rank of baron.
**barone**[2] *m.* scoundrel; rogue; *baron cornuto*, an out-and-out rogue.
**barra** *f.* bar; rod; line; stroke; *tre — quattro*, three over four, $\frac{3}{4}$; dyke; dam; (motor.) *— di direzione*, steering-rod.
**barrare** (A1) *tr.* to bar; to block; to barricade.
**barricadiero** *adj.* revolutionary, extremist.
**barric-are** (A2s) *tr.* to barricade. **-ata** *f.* barricade; *fare le -ate*, to man the barricades.
**barriera** *f.* barrier; roadblock; breakwater; *— di razza*, colour-bar; *— scalabile*, stile.
**barro** *m.* bole; pottery.
**barroc·ci-o** *m.* cart. **-ata** *f.* cart-load.
**baruffa** *f.* squabble; scuffling; hurly-burly.
**barzellett-a** *f.* joke, funny story; *raccontare -e*, to tell funny stories; comic or gay song; cartoon; *prendere uno in —*, to pull someone's leg. **-are** [A1c] to joke, to tell funny stories.
**basale** *adj.* basal.
**bas-alto** *m.* basalt. **-al·tico** *adj.* basaltic.
**basare** (A1) *tr.* to base; to found; *rfl.* to be based; to be founded. **-amento** *m.* base; pedestal.
**Basco** *pr.n.m.* Basque; *n.m.* beret.
**base** *f.* base; basis; foundation; *senza —*, groundless; *a — di*, based on; *in — a*, on the basis of; *appos.* basic; *il salario base*, basic salary.
**basetta** *f.* (*usu. pl.*) side burns; (of an animal) whiskers.
**ba·sico** *adj.* (chem.) basic, fundamental.
**basilare** *adj.* basic, serving as a basis; *di importanza —*, of fundamental importance.
**Basile·a** *pr.n.f.* (geog.) Basle, Basel.
**basi·lic-a** *f.* basilica. **-ale** *adj.* basilican.
**basi·lico** *m.* (bot.) sweet basil.
**basilis-co** *m.* (*pl.* **-chi**) iguanid lizard; (myth.) basilisk.
**Basi·lio** *pr.n.m.* Basil.
**bas-ire** (D2) *intr.* (*aux.* essere) to swoon; to faint with hunger. **-imento** *m.* swoon.
**bassa** *f.* plain; low ground; shoal; south (of Italy, or of an Italian province).
**bassamente** *adv.* meanly; basely.
**bassetto**[1] *m.* the name of various Italian breeds of hound.
**bassetto**[2] *m.* a small bass viol; *corno —*, basset-horn.
**bassezza** *f.* lowness; baseness; vileness; low altitude; depth.
**bass-o** *adj.* low; low-lying; short (in stature); *a occhi -i*, with lowered gaze; *tenere —*, to keep under one's thumb; nether, lower; (of water) shallow; *essere in acque -e*, to be in difficulties; lowly; vulgar; *gente -a*, lower classes; shameful, vile; *di -a stagione*, out of season; (of currency) depreciated; *n.m.* the lower part, foot, base; depth; bottom, bed (of a river); *alti e -i*, ups and downs; (mus.) bass; *adv.* low down; *da —*, downstairs; downwards; *cadere in —*, to fall (morally or socially); below; *a — !*, down with!; *in —*, down; *guardare uno dall'alto in —*, to look a person up and down; **-ofondo** *m.* (*pl.* **-ifondi**) shoal, submarine sandbank; *pl.* (fig.) underworld; slums. **-opiano** *m.* (*pl.* **-ipiani**) low-lying plain, lowland. **-orilievo** *m.* bas-relief, low-relief.
**bassotto** *m.* basset-hound; dachshund; short man.
**bassoventre** *m.* lower abdomen.
**basta**[1] *f.* tuck; temporary hem.
**basta**[2] *excl.* (*3rd sing. pr. of* **bastare**, *q.v.*) that's enough!; be quiet!; shut up!
**bastard-o** *m.* bastard; foundling; mongrel; *adj.* bastard; illegitimate; spurious. **-ag·gine** *f.* illegitimacy; (fig.) spuriousness.
**bast-are** [A1] *intr.* (*aux.* essere) to suffice; *non -a*, it is not enough; to last; *-a che*, so long as, provided that. **-ante** *adj.* sufficient, enough. **-anza** *f.* sufficiency. **-evole** *adj.* sufficient.
**bastimento** *m.* ship; vessel; *— di guerra*, warship. *— a vela*, sailing ship.
**bastione** *m.* earthwork; bastion; rampart.
**basto** *m.* pack-saddle; *cinghie di —*, girths; *cavallo da —*, pack-horse; (fig.) heavy burden.
**baston-are** (A1c) *tr.* to beat, to cudgel; *— di santa ragione*, to beat soundly; *recip. rfl.* to fight; to come to blows. **-ata** *f.* blow with a stick.
**baston-e** *m.* stick; cane; golf-club; *— animato*, sword-stick; *— alpino*, alpenstock; *— della bandiera*, flag-staff; (fig.) support, prop; *mettere un — fra le ruote*, to put a spanner in the works. **-cino** *m. dim.* stick; rod; splint; *-cini di pesce*, fish fingers.
**batisfera** *f.* the ocean depths; bathysphere, deep diving bell.
**batista** *f.* (text.) cambric, lawn, batiste.
**batta·glia** *f.* battle; fight; disagreement; *campo di —*, battle-field; (fig., joc.) *cavallo di —*, hobby-horse.
**batta·glio** *m.* clapper (of a bell); door-knocker.
**battaglione** *m.* battalion; (fig.) multitude.
**battell-o** *m.* boat; *— a remi*, rowing-boat; *— di salvataggio*, lifeboat. **-iere** *m.* boatman, waterman.
**bat·t-ere** [B1] *tr.* **1.** to beat; *— le mani*, to clap one's hands; *un luogo -uto dal sole*, a sun-drenched spot. **2.** to defeat, to

vanquish; *ha -uto tutti*, he has come out top. **3.** to knock, to tap, to clatter; *— le ore*, to strike the hours; *— un chiodo*, to knock in a nail; *— a macchina*, to type. **4.** to tread, to traverse. **5.** to flutter, to bat; *in un batter d'occhio*, in the twinkling of an eye; *non — ciglio*, not to bat an eyelid. **6.** to insist upon, to emphasize; to drive home. **7.** *intr.* (*aux.* avere, essere) to pulsate, to palpitate; to twitch; to flap. **-ente** *m.* leaf of a folding door or shutter; clapper (of a bell); door-knocker; lid. **-itore** *m.* beater; scout; (sport) server; batsman. **-uta** *f.* blow; (tennis) service; quip, witty reply; beaten track.

**batteri·a** *f.* battery; outfit; set; (sport) heat.

**batt-e·rio** *m.* bacterium, bacillus. **-ericida** *m.* germicide. **-e·ridi** *m.pl.* microbes. **-eriologi·a** *f.* bacteriology. **-eriolo·gico** *adj.* bacteriological. **-erio·logo** *m.* bacteriologist.

**battesim-o** *m.* baptism, christening; blessing; *nome di —*, Christian name. **-ale** *adj.* baptismal; *tenere al fonte -ale*, to stand as a godparent to.

**battezz-are** [A1 c] *tr.* to baptize, to christen; to name; *rfl.* to be baptized; (fig.) to become initiated. **-amento** *m.* baptism; christening. **-ando** *m.* person to be baptized.

**batti-baleno** *adv. phr. in un —*, in an instant, in a flash. **-becco** *m.* (*pl.* **-becchi**) tiff, bickering, squabble; *venire a -becco*, to squabble. **-coda** *f.* (orn.) wagtail. **-cuore** *m.* heart-beat; (fig.) fear, fright, shock. **-mano**, **-mani** *m. indecl.* clapping; applause. **-palo** *m.* pile-driver. **-porta** *f.* double door; door-knocker. **-strada** *m. indecl.* outrider; pace-maker, tread (of a tyre).

**batti·gia** *f.* water-line on the shore.

**batti-o** *m.* (*pl.* **-ii**) prolonged clapping of hands.

**bat·tit-o** *m.* pulsation; heart-beat; throbbing; palpitation; knocking; (fig.) fear and trembling. **-ura** *f.* succession of blows; threshing.

**bat·tola** *f.* clack, clapper.

**batuf·folo** *m.* wad; pad.

**bau** *m. indecl.* dog's bark; bow-wow; ogre, bogey-man; *far — —*, to play peep-bo.

**bau·le** *m.* travelling-trunk; *far il —*, to pack; *disfare il —*, to unpack.

**bav-a** *f.* dribble, slaver, slobber; slime (of a snail); foam (at the mouth); *con la — alla bocca*, frothing at the mouth; (text.) floss-silk; *— di vento*, puff of wind, catspaw. **-etta** *f.* child's bib; *pl.* jabot. **-oso** *adj.* slobbering; foaming.

**bava·gl-io** *m.* bib; gag. **-ino** *m. dim.* baby's bib.

**ba·vero** *m.* collar of a coat; cape of a greatcoat.

**Baviera** *pr.n.f.* (geog.) Bavaria.

**bazza**[1] *f.* stroke of good luck; cheap purchase; bargain.

**bazz-a**[2] *f.* long, protruding chin. **-one** *m.*, **-ona** *f.* person with a protruding chin.

**bazze·cola** *f.* trifle, bagatelle.

**baz·zica**[1] *f.* (cards) bezique.

**baz·zic-a**[2] *f.* companion; company; conversation; **-are** [A1 s] *tr.* to frequent; to associate with; *intr.* (*aux.* avere) to be present, to be a frequenter.

**bazzotto** *adj.* (of an egg) lightly boiled; (of fruit) unripe; (fig.) ill-prepared; 'half-baked'.

**beare** [A6] *tr.* to make happy; *rfl.* to enjoy oneself; to rejoice; *bearsi di*, to delight in.

**beati·fic-o** *adj.* beatific. **-are** *tr.* [A2 s] to beatify. **-azione** *f.* beatification.

**beat-o** *adj.* happy, blessed; blissful; lucky; *— lui!*, lucky man!; *n.m.* blessed one; sanctimonious person. **-itu·dine** *f.* beatitude, blessedness, bliss; *Sua Beatitudine*, His Holiness.

**bebè** *m. indecl.* baby.

**becca** *f.* corner of a handkerchief; dog-ear.

**beccac·c-ia** *f.* (orn.) woodcock. **-ino** *m.* snipe.

**beccafi-co** *m.* (*pl.* **-chi**) (orn.) garden warbler.

**becca·io** *m.* butcher; (fig.) incompetent surgeon; murderer.

**becca-lite** *m. indecl.* wrangler; quarrelsome person. **-morti** *m. indecl.* gravedigger; undertaker.

**becc-are** [A2 c] to peck; to pick up in the beak; to nip; to earn; to learn, to pick up; *rfl.* (*dat.* of *prn.* si) to 'collar'; to catch; *recip. rfl.* to quarrel. **-atoio** *m.* bird's feeding trough; bird-table.

**becchime** *m.* bird-food.

**becchino** *m.* gravedigger; undertaker.

**becc-o**[1] *m.* (*pl.* **becchi**) beak, bill; *metterci il —*, to poke one's nose in; *ecco fatto il — all'oca*, that's the finishing touch; *dare di — in*, to begin to gobble up; prow (of a ship); spout; gas-ring. **-olare** [A1 s] *tr.* to peck at; to nibble. **-uc·cio** *m.* spout; lip of a jug; neck of a bottle. **-ume** *m.* bird food. **-uto** *adj.* beaked.

**bec-co**[2] *m.* (*pl.* **-chi**) buck, billy-goat; *— cornuto*, cuckold.

**becero** *m.* blackguard; cad; Florentine uneducated speech.

**Befana** *pr.n.f.* (pop.) Epiphany.

**beff-a** *f.* jest; practical joke; *farsi -e di*, to make fun of. **-ardo** *adj.* scoffing; scornful; scolding; *n.m.* scoffer, ridiculer. **-are** [A1] *tr.* to ridicule, to scoff; to rail at; *rfl.* (*prep.* di) to laugh (at); to make a fool (of); to trifle (with). **-eggiare** [A3 c] *tr.* to deride, to mock.

**bega** *f.* dispute; wrangle; *trovare delle beghe con*, to pick a quarrel with; distasteful task.

**bel-are** [A1] *intr.* (*aux.* avere) to bleat; (fig.) to whimper; to grizzle. **-ato** *m.* bleat; bleating.

**Bel-ga** *adj.*, *n.m.*, *f.* (*m.pl.* **-gi**; *f.pl.* **-ghe**) Belgian; *il Congo Belga*, the Belgian Congo.

**Bel·gio** *pr.n.m.* (geog.) Belgium.

**Belgrado** *pr.n.f.* (geog.) Belgrade.

**belladonna** *f.* (bot.) deadly nightshade.

**bellavita** *f.* life of idleness; *in —*, in one's shirtsleeves.

**bellett-a** *f.* slime; silt; dregs. **-oso** *adj.* muddy, alluvial.

**belletto** *m.* cosmetic, make-up; *darsi il —*, to make up; (fig.) affectation; *adj.* pretty.

**bellezza** *f.* beauty; good looks; *che — !*, how lovely!, how splendid!; large sum (of money).

**belli-co**[1] *m.* (*pl.* **-chi**) navel, umbilical. **-conchio** *m.* umbilical cord.

**bel·lic-o**[2] *adj.* relating to war; *periodo —*, war years. **-ismo** *m.* militarism. **-ista** *m.* militarist; warmonger. **-osità** *f.* pugnacity. **-oso** *adj.* bellicose; war-like.

**belli·ger-o** *adj.* warlike; belligerent. **-ante** *adj.*, *n.m.* belligerent. **-anza** *f.* belligerence.

**bell-o** *adj.* **1.** beautiful; lovely; handsome; good-looking; fine; *il bel sesso*, the fair sex; *le -e arti*, the fine arts. **2.** good; nice; pleasant; admirable; *un bell'ingegno*, a talented and able person; *bel tempo*, good weather; *che bei tempi!*, those were the days!; *un bel giorno*, one fine day, one of these days. **3.** good-sized, considerable; *un bel vento*, quite a strong wind; *avere una bell'età*, to be getting on in years. **4.** precise, very; *nel bel mezzo*, right in the very middle; *a -a posta*, on purpose; *vale un bel nulla*, it's worth precisely nothing. **5.** Ironical uses: *quest'è -a!*, that's a good one!; *ne ho viste delle -e*, I've seen a few things in my time. **6.** Intensification of *adj.* or *part.*: *bell'e finito*, quite finished; *bell'e morto*, dead as a doornail; *bell'e buono*, out and out; (of clothing) *bell'e fatto*, ready-made; *ho bell'e fatto, vengo subito*, I'm coming, I've just finished. **7.** *adv. phr. bel bello*, calmly, by degrees; *alla -a e meglio*, as best one can; *di bel nuovo*, all over again; *ho avuto un bel dire*, it was no use my saying. **8.** *n.m.* beau; handsome man; sweetheart, love; beauty; *ora viene il —*, the best of it is; *sul più —*, at the crucial point.

-**a** *f.* beautiful woman; belle; sweet-heart, girl-friend; *ricopiare in -a*, to make a fair copy of. -**ino** *adj.* pretty.

**bellọsguardo** *m.* viewpoint, belvedere; *stare a* —, to stand and stare.

**bellospi·rito** *m.* (*pl.* **beglispi·riti**) wit, wag.

**beltà** *f. indecl.* beauty; *che —!*, how lovely!

**belva** *f.* wild beast; big game; (fig.) brutal person; ferocious criminal.

**belvedẹre** *m.* look-out; terrace; place commanding a fine view; (rlwy.) *vettura* —, observation car.

**Belẓebù** *pr.n.m.* Beelzebub.

**bembè** *excl.* (iron.) well! well!

**bemolle** *m.* (mus.) flat; *doppio* —, double flat.

**ben-accetto** *adj.* acceptable; welcome. -**accon·cio** *adj.* suitable. -**affetto** *adj.* kindly disposed. -**allevato** *adj.* well brought up. -**alzato** *excl.* good morning! -**andare** *m. indecl.* the 'go-ahead', permission to proceed. -**arrivato** *excl.* welcome!; *n.m. dare il -arrivato a*, to welcome. -**augurato** *adj.* auspicious. -**avẹre** *m.* peace, tranquillity. -**avveduto** *adj.* prudent, circumspect. -**avventurato** *adj.* fortunate; successful. -**creato** *adj.* well-bred. -**educato** *adj.* well brought up; well-mannered. -**es·sere** *m.* comfort; well-being; prosperity; welfare. -**fare** *m.* good deeds, doing good. -**fatto** *adj.* well-made; handsome. -**guarito** *excl.* so glad you're better! -**intẹso** *adj.* understood; taken for granted; agreed. -**parlante** *adj.* well-spoken. -**parlare** *m.* correct use of language, good speech. -**pasciuto** *adj.* well-fed, sleek. -**pensante** *adj.* 'right-thinking'; orthodox. -**portante** *adj.* hale and hearty; well-preserved. -**servito** *m.* certificate of character. -**sì** *adv.* certainly; but, on the contrary. -**tornato** *excl.* welcome home!; *n.m. dare il -tornato a*, to welcome home. -**trovato** *excl.* well met! -**veduto** *adj.* well thought of. -**venuto** *adj.* welcome; *n.m.* person who is welcome. -**volẹre** [B3b] *tr.* to love; to be fond of; *n.m.* affection, goodwill. -**voluto** *adj.* much liked; beloved.

**benchẹ̀** *conj.* although; *il — minimo*, even the very least.

**bẹnd-a** *f.* band, bandage; (fig.) *gli cadde la — dagli occhi*, the scales fell from his eyes. -**ag·gio** *m.* bandage; bandaging. -**are** [A1c] *tr.* to bind up, to bandage; to blindfold; (naut.) to serve (a rope). -**atura** *f.* bandaging; bandages; blindfolding.

**bendidi·o** *m.* abundance; riches; fruits of the earth.

**ben-e** *adv.* **1.** well; *vedere — uno*, to think well of a person; *pensare* —, to be right-minded; *— o male*, by hook or by crook; *per* —, properly, gently. **2.** Uses with **stare**: *stare* —, to be well, to be in good health; *stare poco* —, to be poorly; *impers. non sta — parlare così*, it isn't right to talk like that; *ti sta —!*, serve you right!; *ti sta — quel vestito*, that dress is becoming to you; *stare — a quattrini*, to be well off. **3.** very, really, indeed; *ben bene*, really well, thoroughly. **4.** quite, at least; *ben due mila*, a good two thousand. **5.** *n.m.* good; happiness; blessing; love, darling; affection; *voler — a*, to love, to be fond of; *per* —, with good intentions; *gente per* —, honest people; *una signorina per* —, a respectable girl; *pl.* property, goods, wealth; *-i di consumo*, consumer goods. -**ino** *adv. dim.* fairly well; quite nicely; *per -ino*, nicely, properly; *adj. indecl.* prim and proper. -**is·simo** *adv. superl.* splendidly; excellently; perfectly well, quite well; *excl.* splendid!, excellent!, well done! -**ọne** *adv. augm.* (colloq.) very well indeed, splendidly; *excl.* fine!

**Benedettino** *adj.*, *n.m.* Benedictine.

**bene-dẹtto**[1] *adj.* blessed; holy; (colloq.) tiresome. -**dicente** *part. adj.* blessing, uttering praise. -**dicenza** *f.* praise. -**dire** [B10] *tr.* to bless; to consecrate. -**diziọne** *f.* benediction, blessing; Benediction (service). -**facente** *adj.* beneficent; beneficial. -**fattọre** *m.* benefactor. -**fattrice** *f.* benefactress. -**ficenza** *f.* charity; beneficence; donation; *serata di -ficenza*, benefit night. -**ficiare** [A3] *tr.* to benefit; *intr.* (*aux.* avere; *prep.* di) to benefit (by).

**Benedẹtto**[2] *pr.n.m.* Benedict.

**benefi·cio** *m.* benefit; kindness, courtesy; *chiedere a titolo di* —, to ask as a favour; advantage; benefice, living.

**bene·fic-o** *adj.* beneficial; kindly; charitable. -**are** [A2s] *tr.* to benefit; to help; to favour. -**ato** *part. adj.* benefited; *n.m.* beneficiary.

**benemeren-te** *adj.* meritorious, deserving; *— di*, that has deserved well of. -**za** *f.* merit; deserts; *in -za*, in recognition of good service.

**beneme·rit-o** *adj.* deserving; praiseworthy; *n.m.* merit. -**are** [A1s] *intr.* (*aux.* avere; *prep.* di) to be deserving (of).

**benepla·cito** *m.* permission, consent; *a — di*, at the disposal of.

**benestant-e** *adj.* comfortably off; *n.m.pl. i -i*, the well-to-do.

**benestare** *m.* comfort, prosperity; formal approval; consent.

**benevolen-te** *adj.* benevolent; favourable. -**za** *f.* benevolence; favour; goodwill.

**bene·volo** *adj.* benevolent, kindly; well-disposed.

**Bengal-a** *pr.n.m.* (geog.) Bengal. -**ẹse** *adj.*, *n.m.*, *f.* Bengali.

**Beniamino** *pr.n.m.* Benjamin; (fig.) benjamin; *il — della mamma*, mother's darling.

**benign-o** *adj.* kind; benign; *clima* —, mild climate; (med.) benign; light, mild. -**ità** *f.* mildness, clemency.

**ben·nola** *f.* weasel.

**benẓin-a** *f.* petrol; *serbatoio della* —, petrol-tank; *distributore della* —, petrol-pump; *far* —, to fill up. -**a·io** *m.*, -**aro** *m.* petrol-pump attendant.

**beọne** *m.* heavy drinker; wine-bibber.

**bequadro** *m.* (mus.) natural.

**berci-are** [A3] *intr.* (*aux.* avere) to screech. -**ata** *f.* screech.

**ber·cio** *m.* screech.

**bẹre** [B4] *tr.* to drink; to absorb; to suck up; (fig.) to believe; *— grosso*, to be credulous; *abs.* to drink; to have something to drink; *o — o affogare*, sink or swim.

**berillo** *m.* beryl.

**berleffe** *m.* (slang) face; chin.

**berlina**[1] *f.* pillory; stocks; *mettere alla* —, to pillory, to deride.

**berlina**[2] *f.* (motor.) saloon, coupé; state-coach.

**Berlin-o** *pr.n.f.* (geog.) Berlin. -**ẹse** *adj.* of Berlin; *n.m.*, *f.* Berliner.

**Bermude** *pr.n.f.pl.* (geog.) Bermudas.

**Berna** *pr.n.f.* (geog.) Berne.

**Bernardo** *pr.n.m.* Bernard.

**bernoc·col-o** *m.* bump, protuberance; swelling; (fig.) *aver il — di*, to have a flair for. -**uto** *adj.* bumpy; knotted, gnarled.

**berrẹtt-a** *f.* cap; *in* —, wearing a cap; biretta. -**o** *m.* cap with a peak or tassel; cardinal's hat; *-o a busta*, forage cap; *-o con visiera*, peaked cap; *-o basco*, beret.

**Bersaglier-e** *m.* sharpshooter, Bersagliere; *pl.* the name of an Italian army corps; *adv. phr. alla -a*, daringly, with dash; at full speed.

**bersa·gli-o** *m.* target; mark; shooting range; *tiro al* —, target practice; (fig.) laughing-stock. -**are** [A4] *tr.* to fire upon; to shell; (fig.) to make a target of.

**Berta**[1] *pr.n.f.* Bertha; (provb.) *il tempo che — filava*, the good old days.

**berta**[2] *f.* pile-driver; (pop.) jest; *fare la* —, to joke.

**bestẹm·mi-a** *f.* blasphemy; oath, curse. -**are** [A4c] *intr.* (*aux.* avere) to swear; *tr.* to curse; to blaspheme; to grumble at. -**atọre** *m.*, -**atrice** *f.* blasphemer.

**be·sti-a** *f.* beast, animal; creature; *pl.* cattle; animal kingdom; living creatures; fool, ignoramus. **-ale** *adj.* bestial, brutish; brutal; stupid. **-alità** *f.* bestiality; stupidity; *dire delle -alità*, to talk nonsense; animality. **-ame** *m.* cattle; livestock. **-a·rio** *m.* bestiary; herdsman. **-ola** *f.* little creature; fool; *povera -ola !*, poor creature!

**Betlemme** *pr.n.f.* Bethlehem.

**betọn-e** *m.* concrete. **-are** [A1 c] *tr.* to concrete; to cement. **-iera** *f.* cement-mixer.

**bẹttol-a** *f.* tavern; wine-shop; *parole da —*, vulgar language. **-iere** *m.* tavern-keeper.

**betto·nica** *f.* (bot.) betony; *conosciuto come la —*, very well known; *avere più virtù della —*, to be a cure-all.

**betulla** *f.* birch-tree.

**bẹv-a** *f.* beverage; *a buona —*, fit to drink. **-ace** *adj.* absorbent; porous.

**bevanda** *f.* drink; *i cibi e le bevande*, food and drink; *— alcoolica*, alcoholic beverage.

**bevazzare** [A1] *intr.* (*aux.* avere) to guzzle.

**beverag·gio** *m.* drink (esp. for cattle); tip, pourboire.

**bever-atọio** *m.* trough; horse-pond. **-ọne** *m.* bran mash; drenching, ducking.

**be·vero** *m.* (zool.) beaver.

**bev-i·bile** *adj.* drinkable; (fig.) credible. **-icchiare** [A4] *intr.* (*aux.* avere) to tipple; *tr.* to sip. **-itọre** *m.* hard drinker, tippler. **-uta** *f.* drink, beverage; draught; act of drinking.

**bezzicare** [A2 sc] *tr.* to peck at; to pick on; *recip.rfl.* to bicker; to nag at one another.

**bẹzzo** *m.* (Ven.) small coin.

**bi** *m., f. indecl.* the letter B.

**biacca** *f.* white lead.

**biac-co**[1] *m.* (*pl.* **-chi**) rattlesnake; *adj.* venomous; angry.

**biac-co**[2] *adj.* (*m.pl.* **-chi**) feeble, lacking in energy; *n.m.* coward.

**biad-a** *f.* corn; oats; fodder; *le —e*, the crops. **-ai(u)olo** *m.* corn-merchant. **-ume** *m.* corn; grain; cereal.

**biado** *adj.* sky-blue.

**Biancanẹve** *pr.n.f.* Snow White; *— e i sette nani*, Snow White and the Seven Dwarfs.

**biancheggi-are** [A3 c] *intr.* (*aux.* avere) to turn white; to shine with a white light; to blanch; (of hair), to turn white; *tr.* to bleach, to whiten. **-atọre** *m.* house-painter.

**biancheri·a** *f.* linen or cotton goods; laundry; *— dotale*, trousseau.

**bianch-ẹtto** *adj.* whitish; pale; *n.m.* whitewash; bleach. **-ẹzza** *f.* whiteness.

**bianchire** [D2] *tr., intr.* (*aux.* essere) to bleach; to blanch; to whiten.

**bian-co** (*m.pl.* **-chi**). **1.** white; *— come i gigli*, lily-white; *— come l'avorio*, ivory-white; *l'arte -ca*, the baking trade. **2.** pale, wan; *fare il viso —*, to turn pale; *voce -ca*, treble voice. **3.** fair, shining, bright; *vedere tutto —*, to look on the bright side; clear, evident. **4.** blank, empty; *carta -ca*, carte blanche; *tavola -ca*, dessert. **5.** *n.m.* (i) white; *mettere il nero sul —*, to put pen to paper; whitewash; white of egg, albumen; *pasta in —*, macaroni served with butter and without sauce; *pesce in —*, boiled fish; (ii) blank, blank space; *lasciare in —*, to leave blank; (fig.) *di punto in —*, like a bolt from the blue. **-ca** *f.* white woman; fair-haired woman; *la tratta delle -che*, white slave traffic. **-cọre** *m.* whiteness; pallor.

**biancosẹgno** *m.* (*comm.*) blank cheque.

**biancospino** *m.* (bot.) hawthorn, may-tree.

**bia·sci-a** *f.* slobber, slaver; foam, froth. **-are** [A3], **-icare** [A2 s] *tr.* to mix round in the mouth; to slobber over; to mumble, to mouth.

**bia·ṣim-o** *m.* blame, censure; ill repute; fault; *dare — a*, to blame, to censure; *avere —*, to be blamed. **-are** [A1 s] *tr.* to blame; to censure; to reprove; *rfl.* to complain. **-ẹvole** *adj.* culpable.

**bib·bia** *f.* Bible; (fig.) gospel-truth; *carta —*, India paper.

**bi·bita** *f.* soft drink; long drink; draught, potion.

**bi·blico** *adj.* biblical; solemn; prophetic.

**bibli-ofili·a** *f.* bibliophily. **-o·filo** *m.* booklover; bibliophile. **-ografi·a** *f.* bibliography. **-ogra·fico** *adj.* bibliographical. **-o·grafo** *m.* bibliographer. **-o·mane** *m.* bibliomaniac. **-omani·a** *f.* bibliomania.

**bibliotec-a** *f.* library; series (of books); *— pubblica di prestito*, public lending library. **-a·rio** *m.*, **-a·ria** *f.* librarian. **-ologi·a** *f.*, **-onomi·a** *f.* librarianship.

**bica** *f.* stook; heap of sheaves; rick.

**bicchier-e** *m.* drinking-glass; tumbler; cup; beaker; glassful. **-ata** *f.* glassful.

**bice·falo** *adj.* two-headed, bicephalous.

**bici** *f. indecl.* (slang) bike.

**bician·cole** *f.pl.* see-saw.

**bicicl-ẹtta** *f.* bicycle, cycle; *andare in —*, to cycle; *— a due posti*, tandem. **-ettare** [A1 c] *intr.* (*aux.* avere) to cycle. **-ista** *m., f.* cyclist.

**bici·pite**[1] *adj.* two-headed; *l'aquila —*, the two-headed eagle; (poet.) *il — monte*, Parnassus.

**bici·pite**[2] *m.* biceps.

**bicolọre** *adj.* two-coloured; variegated; *governo —*, two-party government.

**bicomando** *adj., indecl.* dual-control.

**bicorn-e** *m.* (zool.) black rhinoceros; *adj.* two-horned. **-uto** *adj.*, two-horned, twin-horned; *argomento -uto*, dilemma.

**bicromi·a** *f.* (typ.) two-colour illustration.

**bicu·spide** *adj.* two-pointed; double-pointed, bicuspid.

**bidello** *m.* beadle; usher.

**bidọn-e** *m.* can; drum; *— per benzina*, petrol tin; (slang) swindle. **-ista** *m.* (slang) swindler.

**biduano** *adj.* two-day-old.

**bie-co** *adj.* (*pl.* **-chi**) askew; slanting; evil; sullen; grim; *adv. guardar —*, to look askance at.

**bienn-e** *adj.* two-year; two-year-old; biennial. **-ale** *adj.* biennial, two-yearly; *n.m., f.* event occurring every two years.

**bien·nio** *m.* period of two years; two-year course of study.

**bie·tola** *f.* beet, beetroot; *— zuccherina*, sugar beet.

**biẹtta** *f.* wedge; (fig.) *mettere —*, to drive a wedge.

**bif-aṣe, -a·ṣico** *adj.* (electr.) two-phase.

**biff-a** *f.* (survey.) sighting-stake; white mark on a wall to be demolished. **-are** [A1] *tr.* to stake out; to cross out.

**bi·fido** *adj.* bifid; forked.

**bifocale** *adj.* (opt.) bifocal.

**bifol-co** *m.* (*pl.* **-chi**) ploughman; rough peasant.

**biforc-are** [A2 c] *tr.* to bifurcate; *rfl.* to branch off, to fork. **-aziọne** *f.* bifurcation; branch; branching off, forking.

**bifọrme** *adj.* having two shapes, biform.

**bi·foro** *adj.* (archit.) with two openings; with two lights.

**bifrọnte** *adj.* double-fronted; (fig.) two-faced.

**bi·gam-o** *adj.* bigamous; *n.m.* bigamist. **-i·a** *f.* bigamy.

**bigatt-o** *m.* silkworm. **-iere,** *m.*, **-ino** *m.* silkworm breeder.

**bighell-onare** [A1 c] *intr.* (*aux.* avere) to walk aimlessly, to idle. **-onag·gine** *f.*, **-onag·gio** *m.* idleness; vagrancy. **-ọne** *m.*, **-ọna** *f.* idler. **-ọni** *adv.* idly.

**bi·gher-o** *m.* lace. **-a.io** *m.* lace-maker; lace-seller.

**bi·g-io** *adj.* (*m.pl.* **-i**, *f.pl.* **-e**) grey; *pane —*, brown bread; dark; obscure; *giornata -ia*, dull day; (fig.) ill-disposed; irresolute. **-ero·gnolo, -io·gnolo** *adj.* greyish.

**bigiott-eri·a** *f.* costume jewellery; shop selling trinkets. **-iere** *m.* cheap jeweller.

**bi·gli-a** *f.* billiard-pocket; billiard-ball. **-ardo** *m.* billiards; billiard-table; billiard-room.

**bigliętt-o** *m.* ticket; note; invitation card; — *di abbonamento*, season ticket; — *di andata e ritorno*, return ticket; — *circolare*, tourist ticket; — *cumulativo*, group ticket; *fare un* —, to buy a ticket; — *di, da visita*, visiting-card. **-a·io, -a·rio** *m.* booking-office clerk; conductor (on bus or tram). **-eri·a** *f.* booking-office.

**bigodino** *m.* hair-curler; roller.

**bigǫnci-a** *f.* (*pl.* **bigǫnce**) bucket, tub; vat for pressing grapes; pulpit, rostrum. **-(u)olo** *m.* pail, bucket.

**bigott-o** *m.*, **-a** *f.* 'churchy' individual; pious humbug. **-eri·a** *f.*, **-ismo** *m.* sanctimoniousness; pious cant.

**bilan·ci-a** . pair of scales; balance; *dare il tracollo alla* —, to turn the scale; — *a ponte*, weighbridge; — *del commercio*, balance of trade. **-are** [A3] *tr.* to balance, to weigh; to counterpoise; to ponder; *intr.* (*aux.* avere), *recip. rfl.* to balance, to be in equilibrium. **-ere** *m.* balance; beam; pendulum.

**bilan·cio** *m.* budget; balance; balance-sheet; — *preventivo*, budget estimate; *mettere in* —, to estimate.

**bilateral-e** *adj.* bilateral; mutual; reciprocal. **-ità** *f.* bilateralism, reciprocity.

**bil-e** *f.* bile; anger; *muovere la* — *a*, to anger. **-iare** *adj.* pertaining to bile; *calcoli -iari*, gall-stones. **-iǫso** *adj.* bilious; bad-tempered peevish.

**bilic-are** [A2s] *tr.* to balance; to put or maintain in equilibrium; *rfl.* to swing; to see-saw. **-aziǫne** *f.* balancing; see-sawing; state of balance.

**bi·lico** *m.* equilibrium; balance; (fig.) doubt; *in* —, in the balance; (fig.) irresolute.

**bilingue** *adj.* bilingual; (fig.) insincere, two-faced.

**biliǫne** *m.* billion (1,000,000,000,000); *or* thousand million (1,000,000,000).

**bimb-o** *m.*, **-a** *f.* little child; baby.

**bimensile** *adj.* bi-monthly.

**bimestr-e** *m.* period of two months; *adj.* (agric.) ripening in two months. **-ale** *adj.* two-monthly.

**bimetal·l-ico** *adj.* (finan.) bimetallic. **-ismo** *m.* bimetallism.

**bina·rio** *adj.* binary; *n.m.* (rlwy.) line; track; *il treno parte dal* — 7, the train leaves from platform 7; (fig.) *stare in* —, to toe the line.

**binato** *adj.* double; coupled; twin.

**bino·colo** *m.* opera-glasses; field-glasses, binoculars.

**biobba** *f.* slush.

**biocca** *f.* broody hen.

**bioc·col-o** *m.* tuft of wool; flake (of snow); wisp, wreath. **-uto** *adj.* matted.

**biochi·mic-a** *f.* biochemistry. **-o** *m.* biochemist; *adj.* biochemical.

**bio-fili·a** *f.* instinct of self-preservation; love of life. **-fi·sica** *f.* biophysics. **-ge·nesi** *f.* biogenesis. **-gene·tico** *adj.* biogenetic. **-geni·a** *f.* biogeny.

**bio·gr-afo** *m.* biographer. **-afi·a** *f.* biography. **-a·fico** *adj.* biographical.

**bio·l-ogo** *m.* biologist. **-ogi·a** *f.* biology. **-o·gico** *adj.* biological.

**biǫnd-o** *adj.* blond, fair-haired; *n.m.* fair-haired man or boy. **-a** *f.* blonde, fair-haired woman. **-arę** [A1c] to bleach (the hair). **-eggiare** [A3c] *intr.* (*aux.* avere) to turn blonde; to start to ripen (of corn). **-ęzza** *f.* blondness; fairness.

**bio·scio** *adj.* flabby, inert.

**bios·sido** *m.* peroxide.

**bipartire** [D2] *tr.* to divide into two; to part; to halve; *rfl.* to split; to branch off, to diverge.

**bi·pede** *m.*, *adj.* biped; (joc.) — *implume*, featherless biped, man.

**bipǫsto** *m.*, *adj. indecl.* two-seater.

**birb-a** *f.* **-ante** *m.*, **-o** *m.*, **-ǫna** *f.*, **-ǫne** *m.* rascal, knave, rogue; scamp. **-oneri·a** *f.* roguery, knavery. **-onęsco** *adj.* (*m.pl.* **-onęschi**) roguish, rascally.

**bir·cio** *adj.* short-sighted; squinting; (fig.) equivocal.

**birichin-o** *m.* little rogue; cheeky youngster; *adj.* roguish; saucy. **-ata** *f.* prank; escapade. **-ęsco** *adj.* (*m.pl.* **-ęschi**) roguish, mischievous.

**birilla** *f.* marble (toy).

**birill-o** *m.* skittle; ninepin; *giuoco dei -i*, skittles; ninepins.

**Birm-a·nia** *pr.n.f.* (geog.) Burma. **-ano** *adj.*, *n.m.* Burmese.

**birr-a**[1] *f.* beer; ale; *fabbrica di* —, brewery. **-a·io** *m.* brewer. **-eri·a** *f.* beer-shop, ale-house. **-ifi·cio** *m.* brewery.

**birra**[2] *f.* (sport) vigour, energy.

**birr-o**[1] *m.* policeman; police agent; copper's nark, police spy. **-ęsco** *adj.* (*m.pl.* **-ęschi**) policeman-like; spying, snooping.

**birro**[2] *m.* (eccl.) mozzetta (cape with hood worn by Pope, etc.).

**bis** *excl.* encore!; *adj. indecl. treno* —, relief train; *n.m. indecl.* encore; *dare il* —, to encore.

**bisac·c-ia** *f.* (*pl.* **-e**) wallet; saddlebag; knapsack.

**bis-avo, -a·volo** *m.* great-grandfather; *pl.* ancestors. **-ava** *f.* great-grandmother.

**bisbe·tic-o** *adj.* crabbed; peevish; capricious. **-a** *f.* shrew; *La Bisbetica domata*, *The Taming of the Shrew*.

**bisbigli-are** [A4] *tr.*, *intr.* (*aux.* avere) to whisper. **-ato·rio** *m.* whispering gallery. **-ǫne** *m.* constant whisperer; tell-tale-tit.

**bisbi·gl-io** *m.* whisper. **-ìo** *m.* continual whispering.

**bisc-a** *f.* gambling house. **-ai(u)olo** *m.* gambler. **-azza** *f.* gambling den. **-azzare** [A1] *intr.* (*aux.* avere) to frequent gambling dens; *tr.* to gamble away.

**Bisca·glia** *pr.n.f.* (geog.) Biscay; *il golfo di* —, the Bay of Biscay.

**bi·scia** *f.* snake; *a* —, zig-zag.

**bi·sciolo** *adj.* lisping.

**biscott-o** *m.* biscuit; rusk; (naut.) hard tack; *adj.* baked twice. **-are** [A1] *tr.* to bake like a rusk; to anneal. **-eri·a** *f.*, **-ifi·cio** *m.* biscuit-shop; biscuit-bakery.

**bisec-are** [A2c] *tr.* to bisect. **-ante** *part. adj.* bisecting.

**bisessuale** *adj.* bisexual.

**bisest-o** *m.* the day added to February in leap year; space of four years. **-ile** *adj.* bissextile; *anno -ile*, leap year.

**bisettimanale** *adj.* twice weekly; *n.m.* journal published twice a week, bi-weekly.

**bisezione** *f.* bisection.

**bislac-co** *adj.* (*m.pl.* **-chi**) outlandish; eccentric; *una testa -ca*, an odd fish; *menti -che*, eccentrics. **-cheri·a** *f.* outlandishness; eccentricity.

**bislungo** *adj.* oblong; irregular in shape.

**bisnipote** *m.*, *f.* great-grandchild; great-nephew; great-niece; *pl.* descendants, posterity.

**bisnonn-o** *m.* great-grandparent; *pl.* ancestors, forefathers. **-a** *f.* great-grandmother.

**bisǫgna** *f.* business, work; affair; plight, need.

**bisogn-are** [A1c] *intr.* (*aux.* essere), *impers.* to be lacking; to be necessary; *-a*, one must, it is necessary; *-a bene*, one simply must; *non -a*, one must not; *più che non -a*, more than is necessary. **-anza** *f.* need, want; poverty. **-ęvole** *adj.* needful, necessary; poor, in need; *n.m. il -evole*, what is required.

**bisǫgn-o** *m.* need; requirement; *i -i della vita*, the necessities of life; want; poverty; *aver* — *di*, to need; *al* —, if necessary; *in caso di* —, in case of need; *trovarsi in* —, to be needy; *avere tutto il suo* —, to have all one requires; *non c'è* — *che venga*, there's no need for him to come. **-ǫso** *adj.* needy; poor; *n.m.* pauper.

**bissare** [A1] *tr.* to encore; to repeat; *intr.* (*aux.* avere) to call for an encore (*cf.* **bis**).

**bistęcca** *f.* beefsteak; steak; — *alla fiorentina*, grilled veal cutlets.

**bisticc-iare** [A3] *intr.* (*aux.* avere) to wrangle, to have words; *rfl.* (*prep.* con) to quarrel (with); *recip.rfl.* to quarrel, to wrangle. **-ìo** *m.* continual wrangling.

**bistic·cio** *m.* pun; play on words, jingle; quarrel, wrangle.
**bistorto** *adj.* crooked; twisted tortuous; evil.
**bistrattare** [A1] *tr.* to maltreat; to scold harshly; to snub.
**bistro**[1] *m.* bistro, inn, tavern.
**bistr-o**[2] *m.* bistre; eye-shadow. **-ato** *adj.* bistred.
**bisulco** *adj.* forked; cleft; cloven-hoofed.
**bisunto** *adj.* greasy; *unto e —*, too oily.
**bitorzol-o** *m.* wart; pimple, spot; small protuberance. **-oso, -uto** *adj.* warty; pimply, spotty.
**bitt-a** *f.* (naut.) bitt; *-e da rimorchio*, towing bollards. **-are** [A1] *tr.* to bitt (a cable). **-atura** *f.* turn of a cable round the bitts. **-oni** *m.pl.* bitts; cleats.
**bitum-e** *m.* bitumen. **-are** [A1], **-inare** [A1 s] *tr.* to tarmac. **-inoso** *adj.*, **-oso** *adj.* bituminous; *carbone -inoso*, soft coal.
**biut-a** *f.* greasy mixture; glazing for cakes and sweetmeats. **-are** [A1] *tr.* to glaze (confectionery). **-oso** *adj.* greasy.
**bivac-co** *m.* (*pl.* **-chi**) (mil.) bivouac. **-care** [A2] *intr.* (*aux.* avere) to bivouac.
**bi·vio** *m.* junction; road-fork; (fig.) parting of the ways; dilemma.
**bizantino** *adj.* (hist.) Byzantine; (fig.) academic, theoretical.
**bizz-a** *f.* caprice; waywardness; tantrum; *andare in —*, to fly into a rage. **-oso** *adj.* wayward; irritable.
**bizzarr-o** *adj.* bizarre; freakish; eccentric. **-i·a** *f.* oddity; eccentricity; whim, caprice.
**bizzeffe** *adv. phr. a —*, in large quantities, galore.
**bland-ire** [D2] *tr.* to blandish; to soothe; to entice. **-escente** *adj.*, **-iente** *part. adj.* blandishing; flattering; cajoling. **-itivo** *adj.* blandishing; soothing; winsome. **-i·zie** *f.pl.* caresses; blandishments, flattery.
**blando** *adj.* bland; mild; mellow; subdued.
**blasfem-are** [A1] *tr.*, *intr.* (*aux.* avere) to blaspheme. **-atore** *m.* blasphemer. **-o** *adj.* blasphemous; *n.m.* blasphemer.
**blason-e** *m.* heraldic drawing; heraldry; coat of arms; (fig.) nobility of birth; *— popolare*, popular saying. **-are** [A1 c] *tr.* to blazon (heraldic arms). **-ista** *m.* heraldic expert.
**blater-are** [A1 s] *intr.* (*aux.* avere) to chatter; to gossip; to blather. **-one** *m.*, **-ona** *f.* chatterbox.
**blatta** *f.* cockroach.
**bleso** *adj.* lisping; *n.m.* lisper.
**blind-a** *f.* reinforcement against gunfire. **-ag·gio, -amento** *m.* armour-plating. **-are** [A1] *tr.* to armour; to sheet (with metal); to lag. **-ato** *part. adj.* armoured; *camera -ata*, strongroom; (mil.) *carro -ato*, armoured car.
**blocc-are** [A2] *tr.* to block; *— al traffico*, to close to traffic; *— i freni*, to jam on the brakes; (mil.) to blockade; *intr.* (*aux.* avere) to join (with), to form a coalition (with); *rfl.* to jam, to stick. **-ag·gio** *m.* locking, blocking.
**bloc-co** *m.* (*pl.* **-chi**) block; lump; bulk; block of paper; blockade; lock, jam; (comm.) freeze; *il — degli affitti*, rent restriction.
**blu** *adj. indecl.* blue; dark blue; *avere una paura —*, to be in a blue funk.
**blus-a, -e** *f.* blouse; workman's blouse; smock. **-otto** *m. dim.* short-sleeved shirt.
**boa**[1] *m. indecl.* (zool.) boa constrictor; feather boa.
**boa**[2] *f.* buoy; *— d'ormeggio*, mooring-buoy; *— di salvataggio*, life-buoy.
**bo-a·rio** *adj.* pertaining to cattle; bovine; *mercato —*, cattle-market; *foro —*, cattle fair. **-aro** *m.* cowherd.
**boato** *m.* roar, bellow; lowing; rumbling.
**boatta** *f.* tin box .
**bobina** *f.* bobbin; spool, reel.
**bocc-a** *f.* **1.** mouth: (i) *stare a — aperta*, to gape; *torcere la —*, to make a wry mouth; *fare le bocche*, to sneer; *in — al lupo!*, good luck!; (ii) uses relating to taste and eating: *fare la — a*, to acquire a taste for; *avere la — amara*, to have a nasty taste in one's mouth (also fig.); *avere sei bocche da mantenere*, to have six to feed; *far venire l'acquolina in — a uno*, to make someone's mouth water; *fare a — e borsa*, to 'go Dutch'; *restare a — asciutta*, to be without food, (fig.) to come away empty-handed; *— scelta*, bonne bouche, titbit; (iii) uses relating to words, speech, utterance: *a —*, orally, by word of mouth; *dire a mezza —*, to hint at; *non gli si cava di — una parola*, you can't get a word out of him; *mi è scappato di —*, I let slip; *essere sulla — di tutti*, to be on everybody's lips. **2.** opening, orifice: plug-hole; muzzle (of a gun); *— da incendio*, hydrant, fire-plug; *— di accesso*, man-hole. **-ac·cia** *f. pej.* ugly mouth; grimace; *far -acce*, to pull faces. **-a·glio** *m.* nozzle. **-are** [A2 c] *tr.* to nibble, to mouth; to eat. **-ata** *f.* mouthful; *prendere una -ata d'aria*, to take a breather; *-ata di fumo*, puff of smoke.
**boccale** *m.* jug; tankard; pot.
**boccheggi-are** [A3 c] *intr.* to gasp; to open and shut one's mouth. **-ante** *adj.* gasping; dying, moribund; *n.m.*, *f.* dying person.
**bocchello** *m.* rivulet, weep.
**bocchetta** *f. dim.* of **bocca**, *q.v.*; small aperture; (mus.) mouthpiece.
**bocchino** *m. dim.* of **bocca**, *q.v.*; *fare il —*, to pout, to purse one's lips; cigarette holder; mouthpiece of pipe; *— di sughero*, cork-tip; (mus.) mouthpiece.
**boc·c-ia** *f.* (*pl.* **-e**) (bot.) bud; rose-hip; glass decanter; water-bottle; (techn.) flask; soap bubble; *fare le -e*, to be bubbly; *giuoco delle -e*, Italian game resembling bowls; boil, eruption on the skin. **-iare** [A3] *tr.* to blackball; to fail; *intr.* (*aux.* avere) *— a un esame*, to fail an exam; *— in una materia*, to fail in a subject; *essere -ato* to fail,
**boccicata** *f.* jot, iota; *non saperne una —*, not to know the first thing about it.
**boc·c-io** *m.* (*pl.* **-i**) (bot.) flower-bud, unopened calyx. **-i(u)ola** *f.* rosebud. **-i(u)olo** *m.* bud; cocoon.
**boccio·dromo** *m.* bowling-green; bowling-alley.
**boccio·filo** *adj. società bocciofila*, bowling club; *n.m.* bowls enthusiast.
**boccola** *f.* buckle; ear-ring; boss.
**boccolo** *m.* curl; ringlet.
**boccon-e** *m.* mouthful; *tutto in un —*, in one mouthful; snack, bite; morsel; (fig.) short spell; (cul.) *— del prete*, parson's nose; *buon —*, titbit; *un — amaro*, a bitter pill. **-ata** *f.* mouthful. **-cello** *m. dim.* little taste; pill. **-cino** *m. dim.* titbit; *un -cino*, just a little bit. **-i** *adv.*, *adj. indecl.* lying face downwards; prone; *cadere -i*, to fall flat on one's face.
**boc-iare** [A3 c] *intr.* to bawl; to brawl. **-io** *m.* (*pl.* **-ii**) continued bawling. **-ione** *m.*, **-iona** *f.* bawler; brawler.
**Bo-e·mia** *pr.n.f.* (geog.) Bohemia. **-emo, -emme** *m.* bohemian, artist; *vita di -emme*, vie de bohème; *adj.* bohemian.
**Boe·zio** *pr.n.m.* Boethius.
**bof·fic-e** *adj.* soft, puffy, spongy; plump; (cul.) puff; *pane —*, light bread. **-ione** *m.* plump person.
**bofonchi-o** *m.* grumbler; (pop.) bumble-bee. **-are** [A4 c] *intr.* (*aux.* avere) to grumble, to moan; to snort.
**bo·gia** *f.* speck, blemish, pimple.
**bo·i-a** *m. indecl.* executioner; hangman. **-ata** *f.* cruel or ruthless act.
**boicott-are** [A1] *tr.* to boycott. **-ag·gio** *m.* boycott(ing).
**boldron-e** *m.* fleece. **-a·io** *m.* fellmonger.
**boleto** *m.* (bot.) cap, cape (tuber-bearing fungus).
**bol·gia** *f.* bag; wallet; (Dante) bowge, pit.
**bo·lide** *m.* (astron.) bolide, meteor, shooting-star; fire-ball; *passare come un —*, to flash past.

**bọll-a**[1] *f.* bubble; *fare le -e*, to bubble; *livella a — d'aria*, spirit level; bleb, blister. **-ọso** *adj.* spotty.
**bọll-a**[2] *f.* seal; imprint; (eccl.) bull. **-are** [A1 c] *tr.* to seal, to stamp. **-ẹtta** *f. dim.* round-headed nail, stud; (comm.) bill; receipt. **-etta·rio** *m.* order book; receipt book. **-ettino** *m. dim.* bulletin; note; list.
**bollicare** [A2 sc) *intr.* (*aux.* avere) to boil gently, to simmer.
**boll-ire** [D1 c] *intr.* (*aux.* avere) to boil; to seethe; (fig.) *lasciar uno — nel suo brodo*, to let someone stew in his own juice; *tr.* to boil; to bring to the boil; — *adagio*, to simmer. **-ente** *part. adj.* boiling; hot-blooded; fiery. **-ita** *f.* boiling; boil; *dare una -ita a*, to bring to the boil. **-itọre** *m.* boiler; pressure cooker; *-itore elettrico*, electric kettle.
**bọll-o** *m.* seal; (admin.) stamp; — *postale*, postmark. **-ino** *m. dim.* stamp; coupon; token.
**bollọre** *m.* boiling; boiling point; *essere in* —, to be on the boil; (fig.) *a* —, at boiling point; fervour; tumult.
**bolsce·v-ico, bolscev-i·co** *adj.*, *n.m.* (*pl.* *-ichi*) bolshevik. **-iṣmo** *m.* bolshevism.
**boma** *f.* (naut.) boom.
**bọmb-a** *f.* bomb; bomb-shell; *a prova di* —, bomb-proof; — *all'idrogeno*, H bomb; tall story, fib; *che -e !*, what nonsense!; (cul.) pastry puff; top-hat. **-ire** [D2] *intr.* (*aux.* avere) to reverberate. **-o** *m.* reverberation.
**Bomba·i** *pr.n.f.* (geog.) Bombay.
**bombard-are** [A1] *tr.* to bombard; to bomb; to shell. **-amẹnto** *m.* bombardment, bombing; shelling. **-atọre** *m.* bomber. **-iere** *m.* artilleryman; bombardier; (aeron.) bomber-plane.
**bomba·stico** *adj.* bombastic, pompous.
**bombat-o** *adj.* rounded, arched, convex. **-ura** *f.* convexity; (roadm.) camber.
**bombẹtta** *f.* bowler hat.
**bom·bito** *m.* resonance, reverberation; buzzing.
**bom·bol-a** *f.* jug; cylinder. **-o** *m.* short, tubby person.
**bonac·c-ia** *f.* calm (at sea); (fig.) smooth-running, plain-sailing; prosperity. **-io** *adj.* well-disposed; favourably inclined. **-iọne** *adj.* kindly; easy-going; *n.m.* easy-going person; good-natured man. **-iọso** *adj.* calm; (fig.) well-disposed.
**bonagra·zia** *f.* benevolence; *pl.* (**bonegra·zie**) curtain-fixtures (rail and brackets).
**bonalana** *f.* (*pl.* **bonelane**) scoundrel.
**bona·nima** *f.* the dear departed; *mio padre*, —, my father, God rest him.
**bona·ri-o** *adj.* good-natured; benevolent; gentle; simple, credulous; *un — accordo*, an amicable agreement. **-età** *f.* good nature; kindliness; affability; good faith.
**boncuore** *m.* good-heartedness.
**boni·fica** *f.* reclamation (of land); drainage, irrigation.
**bonific-are** [A2 s] *tr.* to reclaim (land) by irrigation or drainage; to make good; (comm.) to grant a discount of. **-aziọne** *f.* (agric.) reclamation; (comm.) discount, reduction.
**bonifi·cio** *m.* (comm.) discount, allowance.
**bonimẹnto** *m.* showman's patter; pretentious speech; hanky-panky.
**bono** *adj.* and derivs. See **buono**; *n.m.* bonus; cheque; bill; coupon.
**bon-omi·a** *f.* goodness of heart, bonhomie. **-omo** *m.* easy-going person; simple fellow. **-peso** *m.* make-weight. **-prò** *m. indecl.* advantage; (iron.) *-prò vi faccia !*, much good may it do you! **-senso** *m.* common sense.
**bontà** *f. indecl.* goodness; virtue; kindness; *la — dell'aria di mare*, the good sea air.
**bontempọne** *m.* cheerful fellow, lively companion.
**bonuscita** *f.* key money; leaving or retirement gratuity.
**bor-ace** *m.*, *f.* borax. **-a·cico** *adj.* boracic, boric; *acido -acico*, boric acid.
**borbogliare** [A4] *intr.* (*aux.* avere) to mutter; to grumble; to rumble; to gurgle.
**borbog-ìo** *m.* (*pl.* *-ìi*) *m.* murmuring; grumbling; rumbling; gurgling.
**borbott-are** [A1] *tr.*, *intr.* (*aux.* avere) to mutter; to grumble; to rumble. **-ọne** *m.*, **-ọna** *f.* mutterer, mumbler; grumbler.
**bor·chi-a** *f.* metal disk; boss; horse brass. **-ettato** *adj.* ornamented with brasses; studded.
**borda·glia** *f.* mob, rabble.
**bordare**[1] [A1 c] *tr.* to cudgel; to beat; to slave-drive; *intr.* (*aux.* avere) to work like a slave.
**bord-are**[2] [A1 c] *tr.* to border, to edge; to bead. **-ato** *adj.* bordered, edged; *n.m.* striped cloth, ticking. **-atura** *f.* hemming; beading.
**bordello** *m.* brothel, disorderly house; (fig.) uproar.
**bordino** *m.* flange.
**bọrdo**[1] *m.* side of a ship; board; *a* —, on board; *fuori* —, overboard; *giornale di* —, log.
**bordo**[2] *m.* border, edge; rim, lip; verge; — *di marciapiede*, kerb.
**bordọne**[1] *m.* pilgrim's staff; *piantare il* —, to take up one's abode.
**bordọne**[2] *m.* feather on a fledgling; *pl.* down, fluff.
**bordọne**[3] *m.* (mus.) burden; drone; (fig.) *tenere — a*, to be the accomplice of.
**bordura** *f.* border, margin.
**bo·re-a** *n.m.* north wind; north. **-ale** *adj.* north, northern; *aurora -ale*, Northern Lights.
**borgata** *f.* village; scattered group of houses; township.
**borghẹṣ-e** *adj.* middle class, bourgeois; homely, plain; *n.m.*, *f.* middle-class person; commoner; *in* —, in civilian dress; *piccoli -i*, lower middle-class people. **-i·a** *f.* middle classes, professional and business people; bourgeoisie; (army slang) civvy street. **-iṣmo** *m.* middle-class way of life; middle-class outlook.
**bọr-go** *m.* (*pl.* **-ghi**) group of houses; village; small country town. **-ghigiano** *m.* villager. **-gomastro** *m.* burgomaster.
**Borgọgna** *pr.n.f.* (geog.) Burgundy; *vino di —, il—*, Burgundy (wine)
**bo·ri-a** *f.* arrogance, haughtiness; pride; *mettere su* —, to put on airs; *pieno di* —, conceited. **-are** [A1] *intr.* (*aux.* avere), *rfl.* to swagger; to be conceited; to be arrogant or haughty. **-ọne** *m.* swaggerer. **-ọso** *adj.* arrogant; conceited; ostentatious.
**boric-co** *m.* (*pl.* **-chi**) padding, stuffing.
**bọrlo** *m.* cylinder.
**bor·nia** *f.* tall story; false judgment.
**bor·nio** *m.* curbstone; projecting rock.
**borotalco** *m.* talcum powder.
**bọrra** *f.* clippings; shavings; packing; wad; (fig.) padding.
**borrac·cia** *f.* water-bottle; flask.
**borraccina** *f.* (bot.) moss.
**borra·cio** *m.* canvas.
**borra·gine** *f.* (bot.) borage.
**bọrro** *m.* deep ditch, drain; gully; watercourse.
**bọrs-a** *f.* purse; (fig.) money; — *di studio*, scholarship, grant; bag; handbag; briefcase; — *d'acqua calda*, hot water bottle; pouch; (econ.) stock exchange; market. **-ai(u)olo** *m.* pick-pocket; bag-snatcher. **-aro** *m.* profiteer; *-aro nero*, black marketeer. **-eggiare** [A3 c] *tr.* to pick pockets. **-ẹggio** *m.* pocket-picking, theft. **-ellino** *m. dim.* money purse (for coins); (eccl.) collection-bag (on stick). **-ẹtta** *f. dim.* woman's handbag. **-iere** *m.* bursar; treasurer. **-ista** *m.* (comm.) stockbroker, jobber; speculator; *m.*, *f.* holder of a scholarship, scholar.
**bos-co** *m.* (*pl.* **-chi**) wood, forest; — *ceduo*, copse. **-ca·glia** *f.* wooded country; thicket; under-growth. **-cai(u)olo** *m.* wood-man. **-cata** *f.* wooded tract. **-ato** *adj.* wooded. **-cherẹccio** *adj.* sylvan, woody. **-chẹtto** *m. dim.* grove, thicket; shrubbery.

-**chivo** *adj.* woody, wooded. -**coso** *adj.* wooded.
**Bo·sforo** *pr.n.m.* (geog.) Bosphorus.
**bosso**[1] *m.* (bot.) box-tree; boxwood; *siepe di* —, box-hedge; small wooden box.
**bosso**[2] *m.* boss, head, chief.
**bos·sol-a** *f.* horse-brush; lath or thin board. -**ato** *adj.* lathed; balustraded.
**bos·solo** *m.* small box; tin; cup for receiving alms; dice-box; — *della cartuccia*, cartridge case; ballot box; compass box.
**bota·nic-a** *f.* botany. -**o** *adj.* botanical; *giardino -o*, botanical gardens; *n.m.* botanist.
**bo·tola** *f.* cellar-flap; trapdoor; manhole.
**bo·tolo** *m.* small, snappish cur; bad-tempered dog; (fig.) bad-tempered individual.
**botro** *m.* deep ditch; stagnant watercourse; steep slope.
**botta**[1] *f.* toad; squat person; *camminare a* —, to hop; — *scudellaia*, tortoise.
**bott-a**[2] *f.* blow; bruise; slap; *dare le -e a*, to spank, jab; jibe; stroke of the pen; *pl.* cudgelling.
**bott-e** *f.* cask, barrel; culvert; *in una — di ferro*, secure, (fig.) impregnable, cast-iron. -**a·io** *m.* cooper.
**botteg-a** *f.* small shop; village store; workshop, studio; *tenere* —, to keep a shop; *chiudere* —, to close down; *ferro di* —, police spy. -**a·io** *m.* shopkeeper; small tradesman. -**ante** *m.* shopkeeper. -**are** [A2 c] *intr.* (*aux.* avere) to be in business, to keep a shop.
**bottell-o** *m.* label; title sheet. -**ame** *m.* posters, handbills.
**botti·gli-a** *f.* bottle; jar; *mettere vino in* —, to bottle wine; *verde* —, bottle green. -**eri·a** *f.* wine-cellar; wine-shop.
**bottin-o**[1] *m.* cesspool; sewage; water-tank. -**a·io** *m.* sewer-man.
**bottin-o**[2] *m.* booty; loot; *fare — di*, to plunder; *mettere a* —, to sack; (mil. slang) pack. -**atrice** *f.* worker bee.
**botto** *m.* blow; toll of a bell; *di* —, all at once, suddenly.
**botton-e** *m.* button; stud; pimple; boring speech; *attaccare un — a*, to bore, to buttonhole; — *da collo*, collar stud; *-i da polsino*, cuff links; — *automatico*, press-stud; rose-bud; *botton d'oro*, buttercup. -**iera** *f.* row of buttons; buttonhole; posy (as buttonhole). -**ifi·cio** *m.* button factory.
**bova**[1] *f.* serpent; worm.
**bova**[2] *f.* landslide, landslip.
**bov-e** *m.* (*pl.* **buoi**). See **bue**; *occhio di* —, bull's-eye window; *occhi di* —, big staring eyes, cow's eyes; (fig.) dullard. -**a·io**, -**aro** *m.* drover; cowherd, cowman. -**ile** *m.* cattle-stall, cowshed. -**ina** *f.* cow-dung. -**ino** *adj.* bovine.
**bozz-a**[1] *f.* rough-hewn stone; rough copy; proof-sheet; *-e in colonna*, galley-proofs. -**are** [A1] *tr.* to sketch; to rough out.
**bozza**[2] swelling, protuberance; (archit.) corbel; boss.
**bozza-go** *m.* (*pl.* -**ghi**) buzzard.
**bozz-o**[1] *m.* pond. -**ale** *m.* puddle.
**bozz-o**[2] *m.* rustic stone; rough sketch. -**etto** *m.* *dim.* plan, design; model; sketch, short article; *pl.* (theatr.) designs for scenery and costumes.
**boz·zolo**[1] *m.* cocoon.
**boz·zol-o**[2] *m.* boss; protuberance; lump. -**oso**, -**uto** *adj.* lumpy.
**bozzone** *m.* wether lamb.
**bra-ca** *f.* leg of a pair of breeches; baby's napkin; *pl.* trunks, shorts, pants, knickers, drawers. -**calone** *m.* slovenly individual; overalls. -**caloni** *adv.* in a slovenly way; *colle calze a -caloni*, with one's socks falling down. -**care** [A2] *intr.* (*aux.* avere) to pry; to gossip, to tattle. -**cheri·a** *f.* gossip, prattle.
**bracc-are** [A2] *tr.* to follow by scent; to pursue, to hunt; (fig.) to nose out. -**atore** *m.* (of a dog) hunter.
**braccetto** *m.* *dim.* of **braccio**; bracket; overarm stroke (swimming); *adv. phr.* *a* —, arm in arm; (fig.) *andare a — con*, to be great friends with.
**braccial-e** *m.* arm guard; armlet; arm-rest; *pl.* large wrought-iron rings; bracelet; wristlet. -**etto** *m.* *dim.* bracelet, wrist-band.
**bracci-ante** *m.* labourer, hand. -**ata** *f.* armful; *a -ate*, in abundance; (swimming) armstroke. -**atura** *f.* measurement; arm's length.
**brac·ci-o** *m.* (*pl. f.* -**a**. See also below for *pl. m.* -**i**) arm; *a -a aperte*, with open arms; *prendere in* —, to take up in one's arms; *prendere fra le -a*, to take in one's arms; workman, hand; power, authority; yard, ell; fathom; (*pl. m.* -**i**) support; bracket; branch; sector; ramification; wing (of a building); — *di scale*, flight of stairs. -**(u)olo** *m.* arm of an easy chair; *sedia a -uoli*, armchair; banister rail.
**brac-co** *m.* (*pl.* -**chi**) name of various Italian breeds of gundogs resembling pointers; (fig.) police spy, sleuth. -**chiere**, -**chiero** *m.* kennel-hand.
**braccon-ag·gio** *m.* poaching. -**iere** *m.* poacher.
**brace** *f.* embers; live coal; charred wood; *cadere dalla padella nella* —, to fall out of the frying pan into the fire.
**bracier-e**, -**o** *m.* brazier; charcoal burner; warming-pan.
**braciola** *f.* steak grilled on a low fire; cutlet; chump chop.
**brad-o** *adj.* wild; grazing; *pascolo* —, free pasture; *cavallo* —, unbroken horse; *adv.* *a* —, running wild. -**ume** *m.* herd of wild cattle.
**brago** *m.* mire; mud.
**bram-a** *f.* strong desire, yearning, longing; cupidity, lust. -**are** [A1] *tr.* to desire; to long for. -**osi·a** *f.* longing, eager desire; avidity, greed. -**oso** *adj.* longing, desirous; greedy; *-oso di*, desirous of.
**bramire** [D2] *intr.* (*aux.* avere) to roar, to bellow.
**bramito, bra·mito** *m.* roar, bellow.
**branc-a** *f.* branch; sector; claw, talon; tentacle; *pl.* pliers, pincers. -**are** [A2] *tr.* to seize with claws; (fig.) to clutch, to grasp. -**ata** *f.* clawful; handful; group, band, set.
**bran·chi-a** *f.* gill. -**ale** *adj.* branchial.
**brancicare** [A2 s] *tr.* to fumble over; to maul.
**bran-co** *m.* (*pl.* -**chi**) flock; drove, herd; troop; (fig.) *andare in* —, to go with the crowd; *a -chi*, in crowds.
**brancol-are** [A1 s] *intr.* (*aux.* avere) to grope; to falter; (fig.) to be uncertain, to waver. -**ante** *part. adj.* groping; (fig.) uncertain, hesitant. -**oni** *adv.* gropingly.
**branda** *f.* camp bed, folding bed; hammock.
**brandell-o** *m.* fragment, scrap; shred; *fare a -i*, to tear to shreds.
**brandire** [D2] *tr.* to seize in the hand; to brandish.
**brando** *m.* (poet.) sword; brand, firebrand.
**bran-o** *m.* shred, scrap; *fare a -i*, to tear to pieces; passage, extract.
**Brasil-e** *pr.n.m.* (geog.) Brazil; *nocciole del* —, Brazil nuts. -**iano** *adj., n.m.* Brazilian.
**bras·sica** *f.* (bot.) the cabbage genus or a plant belonging to it.
**bratt-are** [A1] *intr.* (*aux.* avere) (naut.) to scull. -**o** *m.* sculling oar.
**brav-are** [A1] *tr.* to challenge; to defy, to brave; *intr.* (*aux.* avere) to brag; to bluster. -**ata** *f.* menace, threat; act of bravado; bluff. -**atore** *m.* swaggerer. -**eggiare** [A3 c] *intr.* (*aux.* avere) to bluster, to swagger; (of a horse) to frisk; to rear.
**brav-o** *adj.* good, expert, capable; *non è — nemmeno a*, he can't even manage to; *è un brav'uomo*, he's a decent chap; *excl.* bravo!, well done!; *n.m.* good chap; *vieni, da* —, come along, like a good boy; *fare il* —, to show off; brigand; *adv.* *alla -a*, boldly. -**ura** *f.* ability, skill, expertise; courage.
**brecc-ia** (*pl.* -**ie**, -**e**) breach; gap; broken stone, gravel.
**Brema** *pr.n.f.* (geog.) Bremen.

**bren·doli** *m.pl.* (bot.) laburnum.
**bren·dol-o** *m.* tatter. **-are** [A1 s] *tr.* to tear into tatters. **-ọne** *m.* ragamuffin.
**brẹnna** *f.* 'screw'; nag, hack.
**brenta** *f.* milk-churn; wine-keg.
**bren·toli** *m.pl.* (bot.) heather, ling.
**Bretagna** *pr.n.f.* (geog.) Brittany; Britain; *la Gran —*, Great Britain.
**bretella** *f.* shoulder-strap; *pl.* braces.
**bre·tone** *adj.*, *n.m.*, *f.* Breton.
**brev-e** *adj.* short, brief; concise; unaccented; *n.m.* brief; (mus.) breve; *adv.* briefly; *adv. phr. fra —*, shortly; *per dirla in —*, to cut a long story short. **-ia·rio** *m.* summary; breviary. **-ità** *f.* conciseness; *per -ità*, for the sake of brevity.
**brevẹtta** *f.* trolley used by railway porters.
**brevẹtt-o** *m.* patent; brevet; warrant; diploma, certificate; licence. **-are** [A1 c] to patent; to license.
**brẹẓẓ-a** *f.* breeze. **-are** [A1] *tr.* to fan; *— il grano*, to winnow.
**bricchẹtta** *f.* brick.
**bric·cic-a** *f.* trifle. **-are** [A2 s] *intr.* (*aux.* avere) to waste time.
**bric-co**[1] *m.* (*pl.* **-chi**) jug; tankard; *— del latte*, milk jug; *— del caffè*, coffee-pot.
**bric-co**[2] *m.* (*pl.* **-chi**) donkey, ass.
**bric-co**[3] *m.* (*pl.* **-chi**) brick; squared stone for masonry.
**briccolato** *adj.* pock-marked.
**briccọn-e** *m.* **-a** *f.* rascal; scamp; *adj.* roguish; knavish. **-eggiare** [A3 c] *intr.* (*aux.* avere) to be up to tricks; to cheat. **-eri·a** *f.* rascality; roguery, knavery. **-ẹsco** *adj.* (*m.pl.* **-ẹschi**) roguish; knavish.
**bri·ciol-a** *f.* crumb; *non ne saper —*, to know nothing about it. **-are** [A1 s] *tr.* to crumble. **-o** *m.* tiny piece, morsel; *un -o !*, just a drop!; (fig.) *non ha un -o di giudizio*, he hasn't a grain of sense.
**bridgist-a** *m.*, *f.* (*pl.m.* **-i**, *f.* **-e**) bridge-player.
**brig-a** *f.* trouble; strife; difficulty; vexation; *darsi — di*, to go to the trouble of; *attaccare — con*, to quarrel with. **-are** [A2] *intr.* (*aux.* avere) to intrigue, to pull strings; *rfl.* to exert oneself. **-atọre** *m.* busybody; intriguer. **-ọso** *adj.* quarrelsome.
**brigadiere** *m.* (mil.) (Carabinieri) sergeant.
**brigant-e** *m.* bandit, brigand; (fig.) rogue. **-ag·gio** *m.* brigandage. **-ẹsco** *adj.* (*m.pl.* **-ẹschi**) brigand-like.
**brigantino** *m.* (naut.) brig.
**brigata** *f.* company, party of friends; *far —*, to get together; covey, flock of birds; (mil.) brigade; *generale di —*, brigadier.
**bri·glia** *f.* bridle; rein; *a — sciolta*, at full gallop; *tenere in —*, to rein in, (fig.) to restrain.
**brillant-e** *adj.* brilliant, shining; resplendent; lively, quick-witted; *uno spirito —*, a sparkling wit; *acqua —*, tonic water; *n.m.* brilliant, cut diamond. **-ina** *f.* brilliantine.
**brill-are**[1] [A1] *intr.* (*aux.* avere) to shine, to glitter, to sparkle; to glare; (fig.) to distinguish oneself; *— per l'assenza*, to be conspicuous by one's absence; to go off (of a mine); *tr.* to husk, to polish (cereals); to explode. **-io** *m.* glittering, glinting; sparkle.
**brillare**[2] [A1] *intr.* (*aux.* avere) to whirl round; to librate; (of a lark) to hover, to quiver; (of a ball) to spin, to twirl.
**brillo**[1] *adj.* tipsy, merry.
**brillo**[2] *m.* quivering, hovering; spinning, twirling.
**brillo**[3] *m.* (bot.) osier.
**brin-a** *f.* hoar-frost; rime; (fig.) whiteness, pallor. **-are** [A1] *impers.* to form hoar-frost; *è -ato*, there has been a fall of frost. **-ato** *part. adj.* hoary, frosty; (of hair) grizzled. **-ọso** *adj.* frost-covered, frosted.
**brindare** [A1] *intr.* (*aux.* avere; *prep.* a) to toast, to drink (to), to drink the health (of).
**brindell-o** *m.* tatter; rag; *a -i*, in tatters. **-ato** *adj.* in tatters. **-ọne** *m.* ragamuffin.
**brin·disi** *m. indecl.* toast to a person's health; music, etc., accompanying a toast; *fare un — a*, to drink a toast to.
**bri-o** *m.* vivacity, liveliness; sprightliness; *essere pieno di —*, to be in high spirits; (mus.) *con —*, with fire, with energy. **-ọso** *adj.* lively; sprightly; spirited.
**brio·nia** *f.* (bot.) bryony.
**bri·scola**[1] *f.* a card game; (fig.) *contare come il due di —*, to count for very little.
**bri·scol-a**[2] *f.* scolding; blow, beating; (fig.) *che — !*, what a blow! **-are** [A1 s] *tr.* to beat, to thrash.
**Brit-an·nia** *pr.n.f.* Britannia. **-an·nico** *adj.* British; Britannic; *n.m.pl. i -annici*, the British.
**bri·vid-o** *m.* shiver, trembling; shudder; thrill; *avere dei -i*, to shiver; *storie del —*, thrillers. **-ìo** *m.* (*pl.* **-ìi**) continual shivering or shuddering.
**brizzol-are** [A1 s] *tr.* to speckle; *rfl.* (of hair) to turn grey. **-ato** *part. adj.* speckled, mottled; (of hair) grizzled.
**brocca**[1] *f.* jug, pitcher; ewer.
**brocca**[2] *f.* shoot (of a plant); bull's-eye of a target.
**broccat-o**[1] *m.*, **-ello** *m.* brocade.
**brocatto**[2] *m.* stockade.
**broc-co** *m.* (*pl.* **-chi**) shoot, sprout; stalk, stick; stud, tack pin; *dare nel —*, to hit the nail on the head.
**broc·col-o** *m.* broccoli; (fig.) blockhead. **-ọso, -uto** *adj.* run to seed.
**broda** *f.* thin soup; weak coffee; dirty water; dish water; (fig.) insipid speech or writing; *andare in —*, to turn to liquid.
**brod-o** *m.* broth; clear soup; stock; (fig.) *lasciare cuocere uno nel suo —*, to let a person stew in his own juice; *tutto fa —*, it's all grist to one's mill. **-olọne** *m.* slovenly person. **-olọso** *adj.* greasy, soup-stained.
**bro·gli-o** *m.* intrigue, wangling; sharp practice; *— elettorale*, rigging of the election. **-are** [A4] *tr.* to embroil; *intr.* (*aux.* avere) to intrigue.
**brolo**[1] *m.* enclosure, garden; arbour; nursery garden.
**brolo**[2] *m.* ambition, desire for preferment; intrigue.
**brọn-chi** *m.pl.* (anat.) bronchi, bronchials. **-chiale** *adj.* bronchial. **-chite** *f.* bronchitis. **-copolmonite** *f.* bronchial pneumonia.
**brọnc-io** *m.* ill-temper; *fare il —*, to sulk, to pout; *tenere il — a*, to have a grudge against; *adj.* pouting; cross. **-ire** [D2] *intr.* (*aux.* avere) to sulk, to pout.
**brọn-co** *m.* (*pl.* **-chi**) trunk, stump, bough; *pl.* brushwood.
**brontol-are** [A1 sc] *intr.* (*aux.* avere) to grumble; to mutter; to rumble (of thunder); to gurgle. **-ìo** *m.* (*pl.* **-ìi**) continual grumbling, rumbling or gurgling. **-ọne** *m.*, **-ọna** *f.* grumbler, moaner. **-ọso** *adj.* grumbling.
**brontosa·uro** *m.* brontosaurus.
**brọnẓeo** *adj.* bronze-coloured; made of bronze.
**brọnẓ-o** *m.* bronze; *i sacri -i*, church bells; *cuore di —*, heart of stone; *avere una faccia di —*, to be brazen-faced. **-ino** *adj.* bronze-coloured; sun-tanned; *n.m. dim.* bell; bronze vessel.
**bro·scia** *f.* watery soup, slop.
**bruc-are** [A2] *tr.* to browse on; *intr.* (*aux.* avere) to browse. **-ato** *part. adj.* maggot-eaten.
**bruciacchiare** [A4] *tr.* to scorch; (of frost) to blacken.
**bruci-are** [A3] *tr.* to burn; to set fire to; to scorch; *— la scuola*, to play truant; *— le tappe*, to forge ahead; *-arsi le cervella*, to blow one's brains out; *intr.* (*aux.* avere) to burn; to be hot; to be scorching; to smart, to sting; *— della sete*, to be parched with thirst. **-acaffè** *m. indecl.* coffee roaster. **-ante** *part. adj.* burning; scorching; smarting. **-apeli, -apelo** *adv. phr. a -apelo*, at close range, point-blank. **-atic·cio** *m.* remains of something burnt; *sapere di -aticcio*, to taste burnt. **-atura**

*f.* burn; burning; scald, scorch. **-ọre** *m.* burning sensation; smart; (fig.) burning desire.

**bruciò** *m.* continual burning; constant itching.

**bru-co**[1] *m.* (*pl.* **-chi**) grub, caterpillar.

**bru-co**[2] *adj.* (*m.pl.* **-chi**) destitute; in dire need; *nudo —*, without a rag to one's back.

**bru·colo** *m.* boil, pustule.

**bruf·folo** *m.* pimple; spot; little boil.

**brughiera** *f.* moorland, heath; heather.

**bruli-care** [A2 s] *intr.* (*aux.* avere) to swarm; to crawl; to teem; (*prep.* di) to be crawling (with). **-came** *m.* swarm, multitude. **-cante** *part. adj.* swarming. **-chìo** *m.* (*pl.* **-chii**) swarming, seething; *-chìo di gente*, swarm of people; shiver, shudder; rustling.

**brullo** *adj.* bare, stripped (of foliage); barren, bleak, desolate.

**brum-a** *f.* cold damp weather; depth of winter; fog, mist. **-ale** *adj.* wintry; foggy. **-ọso** *adj.* foggy, misty.

**brun-ire** [D2] *tr.* to burnish; to polish. **-itọio** *m.* polishing stick; burnisher. **-itura** *f.* polish, shine, burnish.

**brun-o** *adj.* dark; brown; *— di capelli*, dark-haired; *— di carnagione*, swarthy; black; *n.m.* brown; dark colour; dark man; mourning. **-a** *f.* dark woman, brunette. **-eggiare** [A3 c] *intr.* (*aux.* avere) to be brownish; to turn brown. **-ẹzza** *f.* brownness; dark colouring (of a person); darkness.

**brus-ca** *f.* horse-brush; (bot.) horse-tail. **-care** [A2] *tr.* to prune, to trim; to brush (a horse). **-chinare** [A1] to brush, to groom.

**brus-co**[1] *adj.* (*m.pl.* **-chi**) sharp (in taste); brusque (in manner); harsh; *una -ca svolta*, a sharp bend (in the road); *-chi tempi*, difficult times; *aria -ca*, keen air; *n.m.* speck. **-chẹzza** *f.* brusqueness; sharpness, sourness.

**brusco**[2] *adv. phr. fra lusco e —*, at twilight; dimly.

**bru·scol-o** *m.* speck; splinter, shaving; *un — nell'occhio*, a smut in one's eye; (fig.) defect, fault; *pl.* first drops of a shower. **-ọso** *adj.* specked, blemished.

**bruṣ-ìo** *m.* (*pl.* **-ìi**) bustle, stir; hum; large quantity. **-ire** [D2] *intr.* (*aux.* avere) to make a noise, to rumble; to rustle.

**Brusselle** *pr.n.f.* (geog.) Brussels; *broccoletti di —*, Brussels sprouts.

**brut-o** *m.* brute, animal; *adj.* brutal; brutish; *forza -a*, brute force; *materia -a*, inert matter. **-ale** *adj.* brutal, savage; bestial. **-alità** *f.* brutality; bestiality; ferocity. **-alizzare** [A1] *tr.* to treat brutally; to brutalize; *intr.* (*aux.* avere) to behave in a brutish way.

**bruttare** [A1] *tr.* to soil, to tarnish; to defile.

**brutt-o** *adj.* ugly; nasty; repellent; filthy; foul; mean; bad; *-a copia*, rough copy; *— tiro*, dirty trick; stroke of bad luck; *alle -e*, at the worst; *fare una -a figura*, to cut a sorry figure; *avere dei -i modi*, to be ill-mannered; *rimanere —*, to sulk; *n.m.* ugly man; evil man; ugliness; *ora viene il — della faccenda*, the worst of it is. **-ẹzza** *f.* ugliness; filth; unpleasantness. **-ura** *f.* filth; ugliness; ugly thing; mean action.

**bruzza·glia** *f.* rabble; rubbish.

**bruz·zico** *m.*, **bruz·zolo** *m.* dawn, daybreak, morning twilight.

**bub·bol-a** *f.* incredible story; nonsense; *raccontare -e*, to tell fibs. **-are** [A1 s] *tr.* to swindle, to cheat; *intr.* (*aux.* avere) to rumble, to roar. **-ata** *f.* foolish nonsense, silly talk.

**bub·bola**[2] *f.* (orn.) hoopoe.

**bubbolare** [A1 s] *intr.* (*aux.* avere) to tremble with cold, to shiver, to shudder.

**bub·bolo** *m.* small bell (*e.g.* on a cat's collar).

**bubb-ọne** *m.* (med.) bubo. **-ọni** *m.pl.* (vet.) small pox. **-o·nico** *adj.* bubonic; *la peste -onica*, the Black Death.

**bub-o**[1] *m.* pigeon, dove. **-are** [A1] *intr.* (*aux.* avere) to coo.

**bubo**[2] *m.* pain; knock; bump.

**bubolare** [A1 s] *intr.* (*aux.* avere) to hoot (like an owl).

**buc-a** *f.* opening, hollow; large hole; *— delle lettere*, post-box; letter-box (in a door); pit; ditch; trench. **-are** [A2] *tr.* to make a hole in; to puncture; to punch (*e.g.* tickets); to tap; to lance; (fig.) to open (up); *— la palla*, to drop a catch; *intr.* (*aux.* avere) to get a puncture; *rfl.* to prick oneself (*cf.* **buco**).

**bucaneve** *m. indecl.* (bot.) snowdrop.

**bucanier-e, -o** *m.* buccaneer, pirate.

**bucato** *m.* washing, laundry; *mettere in —*, to send to the laundry; *di —*, freshly laundered.

**buc·ci-a** *f.* (*pl.* **bucce**) peel; crust; skin, rind; *togliere la — a*, to peel; bark; shell; *riveder le bucce a*, to find fault with. **-olina** *f.* cuticle. **-ọso** *adj.*, **-uto** *adj.* thick-skinned.

**buc·cin-a** *f.* trumpet. **-are** [A1 s] *intr.* (*aux.* avere) to sound the trumpet; *tr.* to noise abroad, to proclaim.

**buc·cino** *m.* (zool.) whelk.

**buc·col-a** *f.* curl; loop; drop ear-ring. **-o** *m.* curl; loop. **-otto** *m.* ringlet.

**bu·cero** *m.* (orn.) hornbill.

**bucher-are** [A1 s] *tr.* to pierce with holes; to riddle; *intr.* (*aux.* essere) to sneak in, to 'gate-crash'; to intrigue for votes, to lobby. **-ellare** [A1] *tr.* to puncture, to perforate. **-ello** *m. dim.* little hole.

**bucicare** [A2 s] *tr.*, *intr.* (*aux.* essere) to budge, to stir.

**bucin-are** [A1 s] *tr.* to whisper abroad, to spread a report of. **-ìo** *m.* rumours.

**bu-co** *m.* (*pl.* **-chi**) hole (usually smaller than **buca**); pit; pot-hole; dimple; hiding-place; lair, den; *— della chiave*, keyhole; *— degli orecchi*, ear-hole; (fig.) debt; *tappare un —*, to pay a debt; *a —*, exactly, precisely; in the nick of time.

**buco·lic-a** *f.* bucolic poem; pastoral poetry. **-o** *adj.* bucolic, idyllic, pastoral.

**budd-iṣmo** *n.* Buddhism. **-ista** *m.n.*, *f.*, *adj.* Buddhist; Buddhistic(al).

**budell-o** *m.* (*pl. f.* **-a**; in fig. uses, *m.* **-i**) bowel, gut, intestine; slummy street; blind alley; *pl.* bowels; entrails; padding, filling. **-ame** *m.* guts; entrails. **-ọne** *m.* guzzler.

**budino** *m.* pudding; black pudding; roly-poly.

**budriere** *m.* sword-belt, baldric.

**bu-e** *m.* (*pl.* **buoi**) ox, bullock, steer; *carne di —*, beef; *— salato*, corned beef; *occhio di —*, spotlight; *pl.* cattle; (fig.) blockhead; *mettere il carro innanzi ai buoi*, to put the cart before the horse. **-ina** *f.* cow-dung.

**bu·falo** *m.* buffalo; (fig.) numbskull.

**bufare** [A1] *impers.* (*aux.* essere) to snow with gusts of wind; to blow a blizzard.

**bufera** *f.* gale, wind-storm; squall; *— di neve*, snow-storm; (fig.) sudden disaster.

**buffa**[1] *f.* cap covering the ears and part of the face, balaclava helmet; (fig.) mask.

**buff-a**[2] *f.* gust of wind. **-are** [A1] *intr.* (*aux.* avere) to blow, to puff; to say silly things; *tr.* to huff (at draughts). **-ata** *f.* gust; (draughts) huff. **-atọre** *m.* glass-blower.

**buffett-are** [A1 c] *intr.* (*aux.* avere) to puff and blow. **-ata** *f.* buffeting.

**buff-o**[1] *m.* squall of wind, gust. **-ẹtto** *m.* snap of the fingers; buffet, blow; stroke of fortune. **-ettọne** *m.* box on the ear.

**buff-o**[2] *m.* buffoon; singer in opera with broad comedy part; *adj.* funny, comic, droll; queer, odd; *che —!*, how amusing! **-erì·a** *f.* trick, imposture.

**buffọn-e** *m.* buffoon; jester; *fare il —*, to play the fool. **-ata** *f.* buffoonery; slap-stick. **-erì·a**

*f.* tomfoolery, buffoonery. **-ęsco** *adj.* (*m.pl.* **-ęschi**) ridiculous, comical; jesting, facetious; clowning.
**bufọne** *m.* toad.
**bug·ger-a** *f.* trick, dodge, wangle; tall story. **-are** [A1 s] *tr.* to trick, to humbug; to bugger.
**bugi·a**[1] *f.* lie, falsehood; (provb.) *le -e hanno le gambe corte,* truth will out; *— pietosa,* white lie.
**bugi·a** *f.* candle-stick.
**bugiard-o** *adj.* untruthful, lying; deceitful, false; *n.m.* liar; story-teller; *fare — a,* to give the lie to. **-eri·a** *f.* pack of lies; untruthfulness, lying.
**bugigat·tolo** *m.* cubby-hole, dark recess; closet.
**bu·glia** *f.* concourse, crowd.
**bugliọne** *m.* bouillon; broth; mixture; bullion.
**bugli(u)olo** *m.* pimple, blister; wooden or canvas bucket; earth closet.
**bugn-a** *f.* boss, projection. **-ato** *adj.* studded with bosses.
**bugno** *m.* beehive.
**bugrane** *f.* buckram.
**bu·io** *adj.* dark; obscure; *n.m.* darkness, dark; *— pesto,* pitch darkness; *adv. a —,* at nightfall; *al —,* in the dark.
**bulb-o** *m.* bulb; root of hair; *— dell'occhio,* eyeball. **-ọso** *adj.* bulbous.
**Bulgari·a** *pr.n.f.* (geog.) Bulgaria.
**bul·gar-o** *adj., n.m.* Bulgarian; Russia leather. **-a** *f.* Bulgarian woman.
**bulic-are** [A2 s] *intr.* (*aux.* avere) to boil; to seethe; to bubble. **-ame** *m.* boiling spring; seething mass.
**bulin-o** *m.* graving tool, burin; (fig.) the engraver's art. **-are** [A1] *tr.* to engrave; to chisel. **-ista** *m.* engraver.
**bullętt-a** *f.* ticket; chit; delivery note; stud, hobnail; tack. **-a·rio** *m.* book of tickets with counterfoils. **-ina·io** *m.* booking clerk, box-office clerk. **-ino** *m.* bulletin; notice; summary of news; ticket.
**bullọn-e** *m.* bolt; rivet. **-are** [A1 c] *tr.* (eng.) to bolt.
**buongusta·io** *m.* gourmet, connoisseur.
**buon-o** *adj.* **1.** good; good-natured. kind; *di buon cuore,* good-hearted. **2.** virtuous, good-living; *squadra del buon costume,* vice squad. **3.** wholesome, enjoyable, palatable. **4.** proper, adequate, sufficient; *fare — per,* to credit with, to trust for. **5.** of good quality, genuine; *buon lavoro,* high-class work; *l'abito —,* Sunday-best; *oro —,* real gold; (finan.; comm.) valid. **6.** apt, propitious; *al momento —, in buon punto,* at the right moment. **7.** mild, gentle; *buono buono,* good as gold; *un clima —,* a mild climate; *essere — con,* to be gentle with. **8.** advantageous; *a buon mercato,* cheaply; *di buon'ora,* nice and early. **9.** good (in measure), goodish; *una buon'ora,* a good hour, at least an hour. **10.** iron. or emph. uses: *quel buon Toni che ci credeva!,* poor simple-minded Tony who fell for it!; *farla -a,* to drop a brick; *buon per te!,* lucky for you!; *alla buon'ora!,* finally! **11.** excl. uses: *buon giorno!,* good morning!; (fig.) *allora me ne vado e -a notte!,* in that case I'll walk out and that will be the end of that!; *-a, questa!,* that's a good one! **12.** with cosa, sorte, etc. understood: *averla avuta -a,* to get off lightly; *mettere in -a,* to make a fair copy of; *con le -e,* politely, nicely. **13.** adv. phrs. *alla -a,* simply, unpretentiously; *sono gente alla -a,* they're quite simple folk; *a —,* a lot, really, very; *di —,* seriously.
**buono** *m.* **1.** good, goodness; *ogni cosa ha il suo — e il suo cattivo,* there are two sides to every question; *sul —,* at the crucial moment. **2.** good man; *fare il —,* to be good; *i buoni,* good people, virtuous people; *un — a nulla,* a good-for-nothing. **3.** government bond; bonus; coupon; *— di consegna,* delivery note; voucher.
**burare** [A1] *tr., intr.* (*aux.* avere) to burn away slowly, to smoulder.
**burattin-o** *m.* puppet; marionette; *castello dei -i,* puppet stand. **-a·io** *m.* puppet-showman. **-ęsco** *adj.* (*m.pl.* **-ęschi**) puppet-like.
**buratt-o** *m.* bolting cloth. **-are** [A1] *tr.* to sift; (fig.) to discuss.
**burbanz-a** *f.* vanity, conceit; arrogance. **-ọso** *adj.* conceited; arrogant.
**bur·bera** *f.* windlass.
**bur·bero** *adj.* grumpy, crusty; gruff; *n.m.* grumpy person; *è un — benefico,* his bark is worse than his bite.
**bur·chi-o** *m.* (*pl.* **burchi**) barge. **-ello** *m. dim.* boat, wherry.
**bure** *m.* beam of a plough.
**buriana** *f.* tempest; gale.
**burl-a** *f.* practical joke; jest, prank; *mettere in —,* to treat as a joke; *per —,* in fun. **-are** [A1] *tr.* to play a joke on; to make a fool of; *intr.* (*aux.* avere) to joke; *rfl.* (*prep.* di) to make a joke (of), to make light (of). **-ęsco** *adj.* (*m.pl.* **-ęschi**) jesting; farcical; *n.m.* burlesque. **-ętta** *f. dim.* joke, farce; vaudeville; *fare -etta,* to put up a pretence.
**bur-o·crate** *m.* bureaucrat. **-ocra·tico** *adj.* bureaucratic. **-ocrazi·a** *f.* bureaucracy; red tape.
**burrasc-a** *f.* shower; squall; blizzard; (fig.) misfortune. **-ọso** *adj.* stormy; tempestuous.
**burr-o** *m.* butter; *al —,* cooked in butter; grease; (fig.) flattery, 'soft soap'; *dar del — a,* to 'butter up'. **-ato** *adj.* buttered. **-ọso** *adj.* buttery; creamy; (fig.) delicate, tender.
**burrọne** *m.* deep ravine.
**busc-a** *f.* quest, search; *andare in — di,* to go in search of; poaching. **-are** [A2] *tr.* to seek, to hunt after; to get, to catch (esp. blame or punishment); *-arne,* to 'catch it'; *-are la giornata,* to get one's living; (of a dog) to retrieve, to fetch; *rfl.* (*dat.* of *prn.* si) to obtain, to get.
**buscherare** [A1 s] *tr.* to waste, to squander; to cheat, to swindle.
**buss-a** *f.* smack, knock; (fig.) loss, damage. **-are** [A1] *tr.* to slap; to hit; *-are (alla porta),* to knock (at the door).
**bus·sola** *f.* compass; (fig.) *perdere la —,* to lose one's bearing; *della prima —,* first rate.
**bussolotto** *m.* wooden cup; dice shaker; jar; pot.
**bust-a** *f.* envelope; file-cover; *— degli occhiali,* spectacle case. **-apaga** *f. indecl.* pay-packet. **-arella** *f. dim.* tip; bribe.
**busto** *m.* bust; corset; bodice.
**butirr-o** *m.* butter or similar substance (*e.g.* cocoa-butter). **-o·metro** *m.* butter-fat tester. **-ọso** *adj.* buttery.
**butta-fuoco** *m. indecl.* flame-thrower. **-fuori** *m. indecl.* (theatr.) call-boy; (naut.) outrigger.
**buttalà** *m. indecl.* clothes-rack, clothes-horse.
**butt-are** [A1] *tr.* to throw, to cast; *— sangue,* to bleed; *— via,* to throw away; *— giù,* to gulp down; to jot down; *intr.* (*aux.* avere) to shoot (of plants); *rfl.* to throw oneself; *-arsi giù,* to lose heart, to become cast down. **-ata** *f.* throw; shoot (of a plant).
**but·ter-o** *m.* pock-mark, scar from smallpox. **-ato** *part. adj.* pock-marked; scarred; pitted.
**buz·zi-co** *m.* slight movement, rustle. **-care** [A2 s] *intr.* (*aux.* avere) to budge, to stir; to rustle. **— chìo** *m.* continued whispering or rustling.
**buzẓ-o** *m.* paunch, belly; guts; *di — buono,* with a right good will; *adj.* stormy (of weather); bad-tempered (of person). **-ame** *m.* guts, entrails.

**C** *f.*, *m.* (pron. **ci**) the letter C; the consonant C.

**Ca'** *f.* (Ven.) house (in names of Venetian palazzi or institutions, *e.g.* Ca' Pesaro, Ca' Foscari).

**cabal-a** *f.* Cabbala; Jewish clique, caucus; *la — del lotto*, the system of foretelling numbers in public lotteries; cabal, intrigue; *far —*, to conspire, to intrigue. **-are** [A1 s] *intr.* (*aux.* avere) to indulge in fantasies; to intrigue. **-ista** *m.* systematic player at lotteries; cabbalist. **-i·stico** *adj.* cabbalistic; (fig.) incomprehensible.

**cabestano** *m.* (naut.) capstan, winch.

**cabin-a** *f.* cabin; booth; *— telefonica*, call box; *— da bagno*, bathing hut; (eng.) cab; cage, car (funicular); (aeron.) cockpit. **-ista** *m.* (cinem.) projectionist.

**cabl-are** [A1], **-ografare** [A1 s] *tr.* to cable; *intr.* (*aux.* avere) to send a cable. **-ogramma** *m.* cable, cablegram.

**cabot(t)-ag·gio** *m.* (naut.) coasting; coasting trade; **-iere** *m.* captain of a coasting vessel. **-iero** *adj.* pertaining to coasting trade; *n.m.* coasting vessel.

**cacao** *m.* cocoa; (bot.) cacao.

**cac-are** [A2] *intr.* (*aux.* avere) (vulg.) to shit. **-asenno** *m.*, *f. indecl.* conceited individual, know-all. **-ata** *f.* motion (of the bowels). **-atura** *f.* excretion.

**cacatua** *m. indecl.* (orn.) cockatoo.

**cacca** *f.* excrement.

**cacchiọn-e** *m.* grub (of bee); maggot (of fly). **-ọso** *adj.* maggoty; fly-blown.

**cacci-a** *f.* chase; hunting; shooting; netting; trapping; *cane da —*, gun-dog; *leggi sulla —*, game laws; *— grossa*, big-game hunting; *dare la — a*, to chase, to hunt, (fig.) to hunt for; *— alle streghe*, witch hunt; *— del toro*, bull fight; game caught, 'bag'; *riserva di —*, game preserve; *m.* (aeron.) fighter air-craft.

**caccia-bombardiere** *m.* fighter-bomber. **-buoi** *m. indecl.* (rlwy.) cowcatcher. **-mosche** *m. indecl.* fly-flap, fly-whisk. **-passere** *m. indecl.* scarecrow. **-sommergibili** *m. indecl.* submarine chaser. **-torpediniere** *m. indecl.* torpedo-boat destroyer. **-vite** *m. indecl.* screwdriver.

**cacci-are** [A3] *intr.* (*aux.* avere) to go hunting; *— alla volpe*, to go fox hunting; to go shooting; *— alle gonnelle*, to run after women; *tr.* to pursue, to chase; *— una cosa di tasca*, to pull a thing from one's pocket; *— un grido*, to utter a cry; *rfl.* (*acc.* of *prn.* si) to hide oneself; to intrude oneself; to thrust oneself; to plunge; *-arsi nei guai*, to get into difficulties; (*dat.* of *prn.* si) *-arsi in testa una cosa*, to be obstinate about a thing. **-ata** *f.* hunting; expulsion; flush (of W.C.). **-atọio** *m.* extractor, marlin spike. **-atora** *f.* shooting-jacket. **-atọre** *m.* hunter, huntsman; (mil.) light infantryman; *-atori a cavallo*, light cavalry; (aeron.) fighter-plane; pilot of a fighter-plane.

**caccol-a** *f.* (vulg.) snot; rheum in the eye, *pl.* gossip, idle talk. **-ọso** *adj.* snotty; bleary-eyed.

**cachet** *m. indecl.* (pron. as Fr.) (med.) capsule; headache powder in a wafer container, cachet; colour-rinse at hairdresser's; professional fee; distinctive charm, unique fascination.

**cachi** *m. indecl.* (bot.) Japanese persimmon; *adj. indecl.* khaki (colour).

**cachinn-o** *m.* cackle. **-are** *intr.* (*aux.* avere) to cackle.

**cacino** *adj.* wretched; shabby.

**cac-io** *m.* cheese; (fig.) *il — sui maccheroni*, the finishing touch which makes something perfect; *esser pane e —*, to be hand in glove. **-iọso** *adj.* cheesy, cheese-like.

**caco-foni·a** *f.* cacophony; clashing sounds. **-fo·nico** *adj.* cacophonous, harsh-sounding. **-grafi·a** *f.* bad spelling; bad handwriting.

**cada·v-ere** *m.* corpse, dead body. **-e·rico** *adj.* corpse-like, cadaverous.

**cadenza** *f.* cadence; (mus.) cadence, close.

**cad-ẹre** [C3] *intr.* (*aux.* essere) to fall; to drop; to decline; to sink, to set; to droop; *mi cadde l'animo*, I became disheartened; *— dalle nuvole*, to be dumbfounded; *— a proposito*, to fall pat; *— dalla padella nella brace*, to jump from the frying-pan into the fire. **-ente** *part. adj.* falling, setting; decadent, failing; enfeebled, decrepit; limp, weak; *anno -ente*, year nearing the end. **-ẹvole** *adj.* falling; toppling; insecure; temporary, ephemeral.

**cadẹtto** *adj.* younger; *n.m.* younger son; younger brother, minor; junior; (mil.) cadet; (naut.) midshipman, cadet.

**Ca·dice** *pr.n.f.* (geog.) Cadiz.

**caduce·o** *m.* caduceus; herald's wand; emblem of peace.

**cadu-co** *adj.* (*pl.* **-chi**) short-lived, ephemeral; fleeting; windfallen (of fruit); deciduous; (med.) *mal —*, epilepsy. **-cità** *f.* frailty; perishableness; decay; transience.

**caduta** *f.* fall, drop; collapse; downfall; (fig.) fault, failure; (econ.) slump; *— dei prezzi*, fall in prices; drape, 'hang' (of a curtain, etc.)

**caff-è** *m. indecl.* coffee; *macchinetta da —*, coffee-machine, percolator; *macinino da —*, coffee-grinder; *di color —*, coffee-coloured; coffee-house; café. **-eina** *f.* (chem.) caffeine. **-eịsmo** *m.* (med.) caffeine poisoning. **-ellatte** *m.* white coffee; breakfast coffee.

**caffettier-e** *m.* coffee-house keeper; café proprietor. **-a** *f.* coffee-pot.

**caff-o** *adj.* odd, only, sole, unique; *n.m.* odd number; chance; *pari e —*, odd and even; *nè pari nè —*, neither one thing nor the other.

**cafọne** *m.* peasant; boor, oaf.

**cagiọn-e** *f.* cause; occasion; reason; motive. **-are** [A1 c] *tr.* to cause; to give rise to. **-ẹvole** *adj.* delicate, ailing.

**cagliare** [A4] *intr.* (*aux.* essere), *rfl.* to curdle; to clot.

**caglio** *m.* rennet; coagulant.

**cagn-a** *f.* bitch, she-dog; **-azzo** *m.* cur. **-ẹsco** *adj.* (*m.pl.* **-ẹschi**) dog-like; surly; *adv. phr. guardare in -esco*, to scowl at; *stare in -esco con*, to be cross with. **-olino** *m.* puppy.

**Caina** *pr.n.f.* Caina, the second division of the ninth circle of Dante's Hell.

**Cain-o** *pr.n.m.* Cain; murderer. **-iti** *m.pl.* (rel.) Cainites.

**Cairo** *pr.n.m.* (geog.) *il —*, Cairo.

**cala** *f.* inlet, bay; ship's hold.

**Cala·br-ia** *pr.n.f.* (geog.) Calabria. **-ẹse** *adj.*, *n.m.*, *f.* Calabrian.

**calabrọne** *m.* (ent.) hornet.

**calafat-are** [A1] *tr.* to caulk. **-o** *m.* caulker.

**calama·io** *m.* ink-well.

**calamar-o** *m.* (zool.) squid, *Loligo vulgaris.* **-ẹtto** *m. dim.* young squid, used as food.

**calamit-a** *f.* magnet; lodestone; (fig.) attraction. **-are** *tr.* [A1] to magnetize.

**calamit-à** *f. indecl.* calamity. **-ọso** *adj.* calamitous.

**ca·lam-o** *m.* reed; pen; arrow, dart. **-eggiare** [A3 c] *intr.* (*aux.* avere) to flute, to pipe.

**calanc-a** *f.* creek; gully, furrow. **-o** *m.* (geol.) series of falls of land. **-ọso** *adj.* friable.

**calandr-a** *f.* (orn.) calandra lark; (ent.) grain weevil; (motor. slang) radiator cowling. **-o** *m.* (orn.) tawny pipit.

**calapranzi** *m. indecl.* service-lift, dumb waiter.

**cal-are** [A1] *tr.* to lower, to drop; to let down; *intr.* (*aux.* essere) to drop, to get lower; to sink; *rfl.* to drop, to let oneself down. **-ando** (mus.) *gerund* becoming softer. **-ante** *part. adj.* waning; sinking; setting; falling. **-ata** *f.* fall; descent; *la -ata dei barbari*, the barbarian invasion; *a -ata di sole*, towards sunset; slope.

**calca** *f.* crowd, throng, press, crush.

**calcagn-o** *m.* (*pl.* **-i**; *fig. uses*: **-a** *f.*) heel; (vet.) point of the hock; *menare le -a*, to run away; *avere alle -a*, to be closely pur-

sued by. **-ata** *f.* kick with the heel.
**calcaneale** *adj.* relating to the heel; *tendine* —, Achilles tendon.
**calcara** *f.* lime kiln.
**calc-are**[1] [A2] *tr.* to trample upon, to tread; — *l'uva*, to tread grapes; to press down, to cram; to emphasize, to stress; — *la voce*, to speak with emphasis. **-afogli** *m. indecl.* paper-weight. **-alet·tere** *m. indecl.* letter-weight; clip, fastener (for papers).
**calcare**[2] [A2] *tr.* to trace, to outline; to calk; to make a carbon copy of; (fig.) to copy, to imitate.
**calcare**[3] *m.* (geol.) calcareous rock; limestone.
**calca·r-eo, -io** *adj.* calcareous.
**calce**[1] *m.* heel of a lance; foot, bottom, lower part; *in* —, at the foot of a page.
**calce**[2] *f.* lime; calcium oxide; — *viva*, quicklime; — *spenta*, slaked lime; *bianco di* —, whitewash.
**calcedo·ni-o** *m.*, **-a** *f.* chalcedony.
**calceola·ria** *f.* (bot.) — *dei fioristi*, calceolaria.
**calcestruzzo** *m.* concrete.
**calcẹtto** *m.* slipper, pump; plimsoll.
**calchino** *m.* engraving tool.
**calci-are** [A3] *intr.* (*aux.* avere) to kick; (sport) — *in porta*, to shoot at goal; *tr.* (sport) — *la palla*, to kick the ball. **-atọre** *m.* kicker; footballer (professional).
**cal·cico** *adj.* containing calcium.
**calcificare** [A2s] *tr.* to calcify.
**calcin-a** *f.* lime; limewash; mortar. **-a·io** *m.* pit for slaking lime; *fossa di -aio*, lime-pit; *adj.* lime-bearing, calcareous.
**calcin-are** [A1] *tr.* to burn, to calcine; to dress with lime. **-ọso** *adj.* lime-bearing, calcareous.
**cal·cio**[1] *m.* kick; *fare a calci*, to kick each other; butt of a gun; (naut.) foot of a mast; (sport) football (the game); kick.
**cal·cio**[2] *m.* calcium.
**calci·stic-o** *adj.* pertaining to football; *societa -a*, football club.
**calcitrare** [A1s] *intr.* (*aux.* avere) to be recalcitrant.
**cal-co** *m.* (*pl.* **-chi**) counter-drawing, calk; tracing; rubbing. **-cografi·a** *f.* copper engraving, steel engraving; engraving shop. **-co·grafo** *m.* engraver. **-coti·pi·a** *f.* copper engraving.
**cal·col-a** *f.* treadle (*e.g.* of a loom). **-ai(u)olo** *m.* weaver.
**calcol-are** [A1s] *tr.* to calculate; to reckon; to compute; to estimate. **-atọre** *m.* calculator; calculating person. **-atrice** *f.* calculator; calculating machine. **-aziọne** *f.* calculating; art of calculation; estimate.
**cal·colo**[1] *m.* calculation; reckoning; computation; estimation; *fare* — *su*, to count on; (math.) calculus.
**cal·col-o**[2] *m.* (med.) calculus, stone; — *alla vescica*, stone in the bladder. **-ọsi** *f.* (med.) calculous condition. **-ọso** *adj.* (med.) calculous.
**calda** *f.* (metall.) heating, forging; feverish cold.
**calda·i-a** *f.* boiler, copper; copper-full **-o** *m.* kettle; cauldron.
**caldalless-a** *f.* (*pl.* **-e**), **-o** *m. indecl.* boiled chestnut.
**caldana** *f.* heat; heat-wave; the hot time of the day; hot flush.
**caldan-o** *m.* brazier. **-ino** *m. dim.* foot-warmer.
**caldarrost-a** *f.* (*pl.* **-e**), **-o** *m. indecl.* roast chestnut. **-a·io, -aro** *m.* roast chestnut seller.
**caldeggiare** [A3c] *tr.* to favour; to support; to plead warmly for.
**calder-a·io** *m.* boiler-maker; tinker; coppersmith. **-ọne** *m.* cauldron; soup-kettle; melting-pot.
**cald-o** *adj.* hot; warm; (fig.) heated; impassioned; *n.m.* heat; (of weather) *che* —*!*, how hot it is!; *oggi fa* —, it's hot today; *c'è troppo* — *qui dentro*, it's too hot in here; (of a person) *aver* —, to be hot, to feel hot; *non mi fa nè* — *nè freddo*, I couldn't care less; (of animals) *essere in* —, to be on heat. **-ẹzza** *f.* hotness, heat; warmth; (fig.) vehemence. **-uc·cio** *adj.* warm and cosy; *n.m.* warmth. **-ura** *f.* great heat of summer.
**Caledo·nia** *pr.n.f.* (hist. geog.) Caledonia.
**caleido-sco·pio** *m.* kaleidoscope. **-sco·pico** *adj.* kaleidoscopic.
**calend-a·rio** *m.* calendar. **-e** *f.pl.* Kalends; *rimandare alle -e greche*, to put off until doom's day. **-imag·gio** *m.* May Day.
**calenz(u)ol-a** *f.* (bot.) spurge; **-o** *m.* (orn.) greenfinch.
**calere** (def.) *impers.* to matter; *poco mi cale*, it doesn't matter much to me; *adv. phr. avere in non cale*, not to care about.
**calẹtt-a** *f.* dovetail; mortice and tenon: slice. **-are** [A1c] *intr.* (*aux.* avere) to make a close joint; *tr.* to key; to dovetail; to fit flush.
**ca·libr-o** *m.* calipers; calibre, bore, gauge; *grossi -i*, heavy guns, (joc.) big shots. **-are** [A1s, A1] *tr.* to calibrate, to gauge.
**ca·lice** *m.* chalice, goblet; champagne glass; (liturg.) chalice; (fig.) *bere l'amaro* —, to taste a bitter cup; (bot.) calyx.
**califf-o** *m.* Caliph. **-ato** *m.* Caliphate.
**cali·gin-e** *f.* mist, fog; thick vapour. **-ọso** *adj.* misty; foggy.
**calla** *f.* (bot.) arum lily.
**call-e** *m.* country lane; way; (poet.) path; *f.* alley-way, lane. **-ẹtta** *f.* sluice.
**cal·lid-o** *adj.* crafty. **-ità** *f.* craftiness.
**calli·fu-go** *m.* (*pl.* **-ghi**) corn plaster.
**call-igrafi·a** *f.* handwriting; penmanship, calligraphy. **-igra·fico** *adj.* calligraphic; *arte -igrafica*, penmanship.
**callisteni·a** *f.* callisthenics.
**call-o** *m.* corn, hard skin; *fare il* — *a*, to become hardened to. **-ista** *m.* corn-curer, chiropodist. **-osità** *f.* horniness; corn; (fig.) callousness. **-ọso** *adj.* having corns; hardened; horny; (fig.) callous.
**callun-a** *f.* heather, ling. **-ẹto** *m.* heathland.
**calm-a** *f.* calm, tranquillity; *con* —, calmly; *zone delle -e*, doldrums; (econ.) — *negli affari*, stagnation. **-are** [A1] *tr.* to calm; to quieten; to soothe; *rfl.* to calm oneself; to abate. **-ante** *part. adj.* calming, soothing; *n.m.* (med.) sedative.
**calmier-e** *m.* controlled price list; *prezzo di* —, controlled price. **-are** [A1] *tr.* to subject to price control. **-i·stico** *adj.* price controlling.
**calmo**[1] *adj.* calm; tranquil, serene.
**calmo**[2] *m.* (hort.) graft.
**calo** *m.* drop, loss, waste.
**calomelano** *m.* calomel.
**calọr-e** *m.* heat; warmth; fervour; inflammation; (of animals) *in* —, on heat. **-i·a** *f.* (agric.) green manuring; (phys.) calorie. **-ifera·io** *m.* heating engineer. **-i·fero** *m.* central heating apparatus, radiator. **-ificaziọne** *f.* the production of heat. **-i·fico** *adj.* calorific, heat-producing. **-ọso** *adj.* heating; throwing out good heat; (fig.) heated; warm, cordial; *n.m.* hot-head; warm-hearted person.
**calorna** *f.* strong tackle, double pulley-block; grip, purchase.
**calo·scia** *f.* galosh, over-shoe.
**calotta** *f.* upper spherical section of any object; crown of a hat; *la* — *polare*, the ice cap at the poles; skull-cap; (archit.) spherical or spheroidal vault.
**calpest-are** [A1c] *tr.* to trample upon; (fig.) to ride rough-shod over. **-ato** *part. adj.* trampled upon; (fig.) crushed; downtrodden. **-ìo** *m.* noise of trampling.
**calta** *f.* (bot.) marigold; — *palustre*, kingcup, marsh marigold.
**calterire** [D2] *tr.* to scratch, to injure, to damage.
**calto** *m.* gully, ravine.
**calug·gine, calu·gine** *f.* down; fine hairs.
**calumare** [A1] *tr.* to pay out (a cable, a rope); *rfl.* to lower oneself, to let oneself down.
**calun·ni-a** *f.* calumny, slander. **-are** [A4] *tr.* to slander. **-ọso**

*adj.* slanderous, calumnious; *parole di lodi che sono -ose,* damning with faint praise.
**calura** *f.* (poet.) heat, warmth.
**calva·rio** *m.* calvary; *stazioni del —,* Stations of the Cross; (fig.) cross.
**Calvin-o** *pr.n.m.* (hist.) Calvin. **-ismo** *m.* Calvinism. **-ista** *m.* (*pl.* **-isti**) Calvinist; *adj.* calvinistic.
**calv-o** *adj.* bald, hairless; (fig.) bleak, bare. **-i·zie** *f. indecl.* baldness.
**calz-a** *f.* sock; stocking; hose; *infilarsi una —,* to pull on a sock; knitting; darning; *far la —,* to knit; to darn. **-ai(u)olo** *m.* hosier. **-etta** *f. dim.* sock; man's sock.
**calz-are**[1] [A1] *tr.* to wear (shoes, socks); to put on (shoes, socks, gloves); to provide shoes for; to fit closely; (fig.) to fit, to fall pat; *rfl.* to go shod. **-ante** *adj.* well-fitting; suitable. **-atura** *f.* footwear. **-aturifi·cio** *m.* boot and shoe factory.
**calzare**[2] *m.* boot; shoe; *pl.* footwear.
**calza-scarpe** *m. indecl.* shoehorn. **-stivali** *m. indecl.* riding-boot jacks.
**calzatoi-a** *f.* wedge, scotch; chock, chuck. **-o** *m.* shoehorn.
**calzerotto** *m.* short sock; legging, gaiter.
**calzino** *m. dim.* small sock.
**calzo** *m.* style of shoemaking; wedge, scotch.
**calzol-a·io** *m.* shoemaker; keeper of a shoeshop. **-eri·a** *f.* shoeshop.
**calzon-i** *m.pl.* trousers; *— a coscia,* tights; *sing.* trouser-leg. **-cini** *m.pl.* knickerbockers, shorts. **-etti** *m.pl.* pants, briefs.
**calzuolo** *m.* wedge, support, scotch.
**camaleont-e** *m.* chameleon; (fig.) fickle person; turncoat. **-e·o** *adj.* chameleon-like; fickle.
**camalingheri·a** *f.* treasury.
**camarling-o** *m.* bursar, public treasurer; officer of Papal court who deals with finance. **-ato** *m.* bursarship.
**cambiale** *f.* bill of exchange; promissory note.
**cambi-are** [A4] *tr.* to change; to exchange; to get change for; *cambiar casa,* to move house; *cambiar vita,* to mend one's ways; *abs.* (motor.) to change gear; *intr.* (*aux.* essere) to suffer change, to undergo alteration; *tutto -a,* everything is subject to change; *il tempo accenna a —,* the weather looks like changing; (*aux.* avere; *prep.* di) to change; *ho -ato di parere,* I have changed my mind; *voglio — di camera,* I'd like another room; *rfl.* (*acc.* of *prn.*) to undergo change, to alter; *ti sei molto -ato,* you've changed a lot; (*dat.* of *prn.*) *-arsi il vestito,* to change one's clothes; *recip. rfl.* to exchange with one another. **-adischi** *m. indecl.* record changer. **-avalute** *m. indecl.* bureau de change; money-changer.
**cam·bio** *m.* change, exchange; *in — di,* instead of; *corso del —,* rate of exchange; *agente di —,* stockbroker; *lettera di —,* bill of exchange; (eng.) gears; *albero del —,* gearshaft; *scatola —,* gearbox.
**camelopardo** *m.* giraffe.
**ca·mer-a** *f.* bedroom; *veste da —,* dressing-gown; room, chamber; *musica da —,* chamber music; debating chamber; legislative body; *— elettiva,* elective assembly; *— di commercio,* chamber of commerce; *— del lavoro,* trades union council; (techn.) chamber, space; *— d'aria,* air space, inner tube; cavity; camera (film, television). **-ata** *f.* dormitory; *m.* (*pl.* **-ati**) comrade. **-iera** *f.* maid; waitress; stewardess. **-iere** *m.* manservant; waiter; steward; Chamberlain. **-ino** *m.* (theatr.) dressing-room; box office; (naut.) cabin. **-otto** *m.* cabin boy.
**ca·mice** *m.* dentist's or surgeon's white coat; (liturg.) alb.
**cami·ci-a** *f.* (*pl.* **cami·cie**) shirt; *in maniche di —,* in shirtsleeves; *rimboccarsi la —,* to roll up one's sleeves; blouse; folder, file cover; (cul.) *uovo in —,* poached egg. **-etta** *f. dim.* blouse. **-(u)ola** *f.* vest. **-otto** *m.* workman's blouse; smock.
**camicino** *m.* false shirt-front.
**camin-o** *m.* fireplace; stove; chimney; funnel. **-etto** *m. dim.* fireplace; small stove; mantelpiece. **-iera** *f.* fireguard; mantelpiece mirror.
**ca·mion, camion** *m. indecl.* lorry, van; lorry-load. **-a·bile** *adj.* (of a road) suitable for lorries. **-cino** *m. dim.* small van. **-ista** *m.* lorry driver, vanman.
**camisac·cio** *m.* sailor's blouse.
**camma** *f.* cam; *albero a camme,* camshaft.
**cammell-o** *m.* camel; *pelo di —,* camel-hair; *color —,* buff, fawn. **-iere** *m.* camel driver.
**camm-e·o** *m.* cameo. **-eista** *m.* cutter of cameos.
**cammin-are** [A1] *intr.* (*aux.* avere) to walk; to proceed; *— al sicuro,* to go carefully; *il treno -a forte,* the train is going fast; *la faccenda -a,* the affair is progressing; *-a per i quaranta,* he's getting on for forty. **-a·bile** *adj.* (of a road) passable. **-ata** *f.* walk, stroll; gait; road. **-atura** *f.* gait.
**cammino** *m.* journey; walk; stretch of road; way; *mettersi in —,* to set out; *cammin facendo,* while walking along; (fig.) course; *far molto —,* to make good progress.
**camomilla** *f.* camomile; *decotto di —,* camomile tea.
**camorr-a** *f.* rogues' secret society; tribute exacted by members of the society; (fig.) hush-money; 'racket', swindle. **-ista** *m.* member of the 'camorra'; intriguer; racketeer.
**camo·sc-io** *m.* chamois; wash-leather. **-ino** *adj.* made of chamois leather; soft, pliant.
**camozza** *f.* chamois doe.
**campagn-a** *f.* country, open country; *in —,* in the country; *buttarsi alla —,* to turn brigand; campaign; *artiglieria di —,* field artillery. **-(u)olo** *adj.* rural, rustic; *topo -uolo,* field-vole; *n.m.* countryman; rustic, peasant, yokel.
**camp-a·io** *m.* country policeman; watchman. **-ai(u)olo** *adj.* pertaining to the fields.
**campale** *adj.* field; (mil.) *una giornata —.* a field day; *in tenuta —,* in battledress and fully armed.
**campan-a** *f.* bell; *a —,* bell-shaped; *dar nelle -e,* to start ringing the bells; *sordo come una —,* deaf as a post; any bell-shaped object. **-ac·cio** *m.* cow bell, sheep bell. **-a·io** *m.* bell-ringer; bell-founder. **-a·rio** *adj.* pertaining to bells; *torre -aria* bell tower. **-iforme** *adj.* bell-shaped.
**campanella** *f. dim. pl.* various bell-shaped flowers of the convolvulus family; ring-shaped object.
**campanello** *m.* door bell; harness bell; electric bell; *pl.* drops thrown up by heavy rain.
**campanil-e** *m.* bell tower; *amor di —,* love of one's native town or village. **-ismo** *m.* parochialism.
**campa·nula** *f.* (bot.) Canterbury bell; *— turchina selvatica,* harebell, bluebell.
**campare** [A1] *intr.* (*aux.* essere, avere) to get one's living; *— d'elemosina,* to live on charity; *tr.* to escape from; to save from danger; to provide for; *— la vita,* to make a livelihood.
**campeggi-are** [A3c] *intr.* (*aux.* avere) to camp, to be encamped; (fig.) to stand out (against a background); *tr.* (mil.) to deploy. **-amento** *m.* encampment; camping; deployment. **-ante** *m., f.* camper.
**campeggio** *m.* camping, camp; *fare un —,* to camp.
**campereccio** *adj.* thriving, flourishing.
**Campido·glio** *pr.n.m.* Capitol (Rome).
**campi·geno** *m.* physical training instructor.
**campion-e** *m.* (*f.* **-essa**) champion; record-holder; *farsi — di,*

to champion; standard, norm; sample, specimen; pattern. **-are** [A1 c] *tr.* to sample; to produce as a sample. **-a·rio** *m.* pattern book; *adj.* referring to samples; *fiera -aria*, sample fair. **-ato** *m.* championship. **-cino** *m.* cutting, pattern.

**campiọne-tipo** *m.* (comm.) standard.

**campire** [D2] *intr.* (*aux.* avere) (paint.) to paint the background.

**camp-o**[1] *m.* **1.** field; *la vita dei -i*, country life, rural existence; *fiori di —*, wild flowers; *torniamo ai -i*, back to the land. **2.** (mil.) field; *— di battaglia*, battlefield; *— di mine*, minefield; *sul —*, in the field; (fig.) on the spot; camp. **3.** ground; (sport) playing field; *— di tennis*, tennis court; *— di golf*, golf course; (football) pitch; (horse racing) *— pesante*, heavy going; *— d'aviazione*, airfield; *— di fortuna*, emergency landing ground. **4.** sphere, range, field; *— visivo*, field of vision; *— di visibilità*, range of visibility; (art) background. **5.** room, space, opportunity; *prendere — a*, to find occasion to. **6.** FIG. USES: *essere in —*, to be in question; *mettere in —*, to put forward, to advance; *perdere —*, to lose ground. **-erello** *m.* smallholding. **-estre** *adj.* rural; wild; *vita -estre*, country life. **-ic·cio** *m.* coppice.

**camp-o**[2] *m.* square, piazza. **-iello** *m.* small public square.

**camposanto** *m.* (*pl.* **camposanti**) cemetery, churchyard.

**camuff-are** [A1] *tr.* to muffle up; to deceive; to conceal; *intr.* (*aux.* avere) to pretend; *rfl.* to muffle oneself up; to disguise oneself. **-ato** *part. adj.* disguised, in disguise; pretended; *n.m.* impostor. **-atura** *f.* disguise; concealment.

**camuso** *adj.* snub-nosed.

**Ca·nad-a** *pr.n.m.* (geog.) Canada. **-ẹse** *adj.*, *n.m.*, *f.* Canadian.

**cana·gli-a** *f.* (*pl.* **-e**) rabble; scoundrel. **-ẹsco** *adj.* (*m.pl.* **-ẹschi**) blackguardly; belonging to the rabble; coarse. **-ume** *m.* mob, rabble.

**cana·io** *m.* dog-breeder, kennelman.

**canal-e** *m.* canal; *ponte —*, culvert; channel; groove; gulley, conduit; passage; (fig.) *-i gerarchici*, official channels; *mettere in —*, to set in motion.

**canalizẓare** [A1] *tr.* to canalize.

**ca·nap-a** *f.* hemp; marijuana. **-a·ia** *f.* hemp field; **-a·io** *m.* hemp worker; hemp field. **-ino** *adj.* hempen.

**canapè** *m. indecl.* sofa.

**canaperino** *m. dim.* footstool.

**ca·nap-o** *m.* hemp rope; cable-laid rope; hawser. **-ọne** *m. augm.* rope cable.

**Cana·rie** *pr.n.f.pl.* (Isole), Canary Islands, Canaries.

**canarino** *m.* canary; *adj.* canary coloured; *giallo —*, canary yellow.

**canata** *f.* scolding; rebuke.

**cancell-are** [A1] *tr.* to cancel; to annul; to rub out, to cross out. **-aẓione** *f.* cancellation, annulment.

**canceller-i·a** *f.* chancellery; chancellorship; stationer's shop; stationery; *spese di —*, clerical expenses. **-ẹsco** *adj.* (*m.pl.* **-ẹschi**) pertaining to a Chancellor or chancellery; *scrittura -esca*, chancery hand.

**cancellier-e** *m.* Chancellor; (leg.) Clerk of the Court, Registrar; *— dello Scacchiere*, Chancellor of the Exchequer. **-ato** *m.* office of Chancellorship.

**cancell-o** *m.* barred gate; iron railing. **-ata** *f.* railings. **-ato** *m.* large iron fence. **-ino** *m.* wicket (gate).

**cancerọso** *adj.* cancerous.

**can·cher-o** *m.* nuisance, pest; (pop.) cancer. **-ọso** *adj.* annoying; (pop.) cancerous.

**cancren-a** *f.* gangrene. **-are** [A1] *rfl.* to go gangrenous. **-ọso** *adj.* gangrenous.

**cancr-o** *m.* (med.) cancer, carcinoma; (zool.) crab; (astron.) Cancer; (geog.) *il Tropico del Cancro*, the Tropic of Cancer. **-ifọrme** *adj.* crab-like.

**candegg-iare** [A3 c] *tr.* to bleach. **-ina** *f.* bleach, bleaching powder.

**candẹggio** *m.* bleaching; *dare il — a*, to bleach.

**candẹl-a** *f.* candle; watt; sparking-plug. **-abro** *m.* table candlesticks; *-abro a muro*, bracket candle-holder; candelabrum. **-a·io** *m.* candle-maker. **-(l)iere** *m.* candlestick; *essere sul -iere*, to be very conspicuous; *reggere il -iere*, to aid and abet.

**Candel-a·ia, -ara, -ora** *pr.n.f.* Candlemas (2 Feb.).

**cand-ente** *adj.* lucent, shining, glowing. **-escente** *adj.* incandescent. **-ificare** [A2 s] *tr.* to cause to glow.

**candidat-o** *m.* candidate; aspirant. **-ura** *f.* candidature; *fare atto di -ura*, to stand for election; *presentare la -ura di*, to nominate.

**can·did-o** *adj.* white; shining; pure; candid. **-ẹzza** *f.* whiteness; brightness; purity.

**cand-ire** [D2] *tr.* to candy; (fig.) to hoard, to treasure. **-ito** *part. adj.* candied; *n.m.* candied fruit; candy.

**candọre** *m.* whiteness, brilliance; candour.

**can-e** *m.* dog; *razza di —*, breed of dog; *vita da —*, dog's life; *solo come un —*, all alone; *povero —*, poor devil; *drizzare le gambe ai -i*, to attempt the impossible; *faccia di —*, ugly mug; *fare il —*, to be cruel. **-e·a** *f.* noise of barking; (fig.) uproar. **-ettiere** *m.* kennelman. **-ile** *m.* kennel; (fig.) hovel; *adj.* doggy. **-ino** *adj.* canine; (fig.) tiresome; *dente -ino*, eye-tooth; *mosca -ina*, horse-fly. **-ita** *f.* act of brutality. **-izza** *f.* yelping of pack of hounds.

**canestr-a** *f.* wicker basket. **-a·io** *m.* basket-maker. **-ata** *f.* basketful.

**canestro** *m.* flower basket; shopping basket; *palla —*, game of basket-ball.

**can·fora** *f.* camphor.

**cangi-are** [A3] *tr.* (poet.) to change; *— consiglio*, to change one's mind, to think again. **-a·bile** *adj.* changeable, variable. **-ante** *part. adj.* changing; iridescent; *seta -ante*, shot silk.

**canguro** *m.* kangaroo.

**cani·c-ola** *f.* dog days; heat wave; hottest part of the day; *sotto la —*, in the midday sun. **-olare, -ulare** *adj.* pertaining to the dog days.

**canistro** *m.* can, petrol can.

**cani·zie** *f. indecl.* white hairs; old age.

**cann-a** *f.* cane; reed; (fig.) *— fessa*, broken reed; *povero in —*, poor as a church mouse; walking-stick, cross-bar of a bicycle; rod; small tube or pipe; *— del polmone*, windpipe, trachea; organ-pipe; barrel (of a gun). **-ai(u)ola** *f.* (orn.) reed warbler. **-uc·cia** *f.* drinking-straw; stem of a tobacco-pipe.

**cannabiṣmo** *m.* hashish poisoning.

**cannacoro** *m.* Indian hemp.

**cannẹggi-o** *m.* measurement, surveying. **-are** [A3 c] *tr.* to measure (land).

**cannella**[1] *f.* small tube; spout; tap; *lavarsi alla —*, to wash under a tap.

**cannell-a**[2] *f.* cinnamon. **-ato** *adj.* cinnamon-coloured; cinnamon-flavoured.

**cannell-o** *m.* internode, joint of a cane; spool; *— Bunsen*, Bunsen burner; *— ossidrico*, blowlamp, blowpipe. **-ọne** *m. augm.; pl.* (cul.) pasta for soup in shape of tubes.

**canni·bal-e** *m.* cannibal; (fig.) cruel man. **-ẹsco** *adj.* (*m.pl.* **-ẹschi**) cannibalistic. **-iṣmo** *m.* cannibalism.

**cannocchiale** *m.* telescope; field-glasses.

**cannoc·chio** *m.* root-stock of a cane; cob of maize.

**cannọn-e** *m.* cannon; *carne da —*, cannon fodder; water-pipe; conduit. **-ata** *f.* cannonade; (fig.) exaggeration; lie. **-iere** *m.* gunner.

**can-o·a** *f.* canoe. **-oiṣmo** *m.* canoeing. **-oista** *m.* canoeist. **-ottag·gio** *m.* rowing. **-ottiera** *f.* boater; sports vest; tee-shirt. **-ottiere** *m.* rower, oarsman; *società dei -ottieri*, rowing and sculling club. **-ottiero** *adj.*

pertaining to rowing. **-otto** *m.* skiff; speed-boat; *-otto di gomma*, rubber dinghy.
**ca·none** *m.* (eccl.) canon; (fig.) basic rule; *pl.* moral standards.
**cano·nic-a** *f.* (eccl.) priest's house, presbytery; canonry; canon law. **-ale** *adj.* (eccl.) of, suitable for, the canons of a chapter; *messa -ale*, capitular mass. **-o** *adj.* canonical; *diritto -o*, canon law; *n.m.* (eccl.) canon (of a chapter); *vita da -o*, easy life.
**canonizzare** [A1] *tr.* to regularize; to sanction; to authenticate; to canonize.
**canoro** *adj.* harmonious, melodious; singing; sweet; resonant.
**canotte** *f.* nightie (abbrev. of 'camicia da notte').
**canov-a** *f.* wine or provision shop; store, warehouse. **-a·io, -aro** *m.* storekeeper.
**canivac·cio** *m.* canvas.
**cans-are** [A1] *tr.* to remove; to discard; to escape, to avoid. **-atoia** *m.* place of refuge.
**cant-are** [A1] *tr.* to sing; to intone, to chant; to emphasize; *— la solfa*, to read the riot act; *intr.* (*aux.* avere) to sing, to chant; to talk, to be eloquent; *far — uno*, to make a person reveal what he knows; to squeak; to crackle; to chirp; to crow; to ring (of glass); *n.m.* singing. **-a·bile** *adj.* singable; *n.m.* (mus.) cantabile style. **-afa·vola** *f.* long narrative; (fig.) long, improbable story. **-ambanco** *m.* (*pl.* **-ambanchi**) strolling player, busker; charlatan. **-ando** *adj.* (mus.) in singing-style. **-ante** *adj.* singing; *n.m., f.* singer. **-asto·rie** *m. indecl.* (hist.) professional story-teller.
**can·taro** *m.* drinking-cup, goblet, chalice.
**canter-ale, -ano** *m.* chest of drawers.
**canterellare** [A1] *tr., intr.* (*aux.* avere) to hum, to sing to oneself.
**canterello** *m.* (bot.) chanterelle mushroom; tinsel.
**canterino** *adj.* singing; *uccello —*, decoy bird.
**can·tero** *m.* bed-pan; latrine.
**can·tica** *f.* poetic composition divided into cantos.
**canticchiare** [A4] *tr., intr.* (*aux.* avere) to sing softly, to hum.
**can·tico** *m.* canticle, hymn; *— di Natale*, Christmas carol.
**cantiere** *m.* yard, shed; shipyard; builder's works; work-site.
**cantilen-a** *f.* lullaby; old song, catch; long, dull poem or speech; sing-song intonation; (fig.) *è la solita —*, always the same old story. **-are** [A1] *tr., intr.* (*aux.* avere) to hum; to drawl.
**cantimplora** *f.* water-cooler; wine-cooler.
**cantin-a** *f.* cellar; *giù in —*, down in the cellar; wine-shop. **-ato** *m.* (bldg.) cellar, basement. **-etta** *f.* wine-cooler, ice-bucket. **-iere** *m.* head butler; cellarman.
**canto**[1] *m.* song; chant; poem; canto; *canti popolari*, folk-songs; crowing of a cock; chirping of an insect; (mus.) singing; art of singing.
**canto**[2] *m.* corner; side; *a —*, beside; *levarsi da —*, to get rid of; *dall'altro —*, on the other hand.
**canton-e** *m.* part, side; corner; *mettere in un —*, to put aside; slab of concrete. **-ata** *f.* exterior corner of a building; street corner. **-iere** *m.* road keeper; (rlwy.) permanent-way inspector.
**cantor-e** *m.* singer; (eccl.) cantor. **-ino** *m.* (mus.) choir-book, manual of plain-song.
**cantuc·cio** *m.* corner of a room; cubby hole; cosy corner; heel of a loaf; end bit of cheese.
**canuti·glia** *f.* tinsel; fringe or braid of gold or silver twist.
**canut-o** *adj.* hoary, white-haired; prudent, wary. **-ezza** *f.* hoariness; shock of white hair. **-ire** [D2] *intr.* (*aux.* essere) to go white-haired.
**canzon-are** [A1 c] *tr.* to make fun of; *intr.* (*aux.* avere) to joke. **-atura** *f.* joke, jest, leg-pull.
**canzon-e** *f.* song; a kind of lyric poem; *-i di gesta*, chansons de geste; *mettere in —*, to jeer at. **-etta** *f.* popular song. **-iere** *m.* poetry book; song book; all the lyric poems of an author. **-ettista** *m., f.* composer of popular songs. **-ista** *m.,f.* songwriter.
**caolino** *m.* kaolin, china clay.
**ca·os** *m. indecl.* chaos; (fig.) state of confusion; medley.
**cao·tico** *adj.* chaotic.
**capaccina** *f.* heaviness in the head; headache.
**capac-e** *adj.* capable, able; possible; *far —*, to persuade; capacious, capable of holding. **-ità** *f.* capacity; ability; skill.
**capacit-are** [A1 s] *tr.* to convince; to persuade; *rfl.* to understand, to grasp, to conceive; *non so -armi come sia successo*, I can't make out how it happened. **-a·bile** *adj.* comprehensible; reasonable, open to persuasion. **-ante** *part. adj.* persuasive; convincing.
**capann-a** *f.* shed, hut, barn; mountain hut; bathing hut; *a —*, lean-to, sloping (of a roof). **-o** *m.* hut; summer-house, arbour. **-one** *m.* barn; ox-stall; hangar; goods shed; (equit.) croupade.
**capar·bi-o** *adj.* self-willed, obstinate, determined. **-eri·a** *f.*, **-età** *f.* obstinacy.
**caparra** *f.* (comm.) deposit; earnest-money.
**capat-a** *f.* blow with the head; *dare una — in*, to butt against. **-ina** *f.* brief call; *fare una -ina a*, to drop in on.
**capecchio** *m.* tow; oakum.
**capeggiare** [A3 c] *tr.* to head, to be the head of.
**capell-o** *m.* hair (one single hair); *non torcere un —*, not to harm a hair (of a person's head); *a —*, exactly, precisely, to a 't'; *spaccare un — in quattro*, to split hairs; *pl.* hair, head of hair; *tirare per i -i*, to compel; *tirato per i -i*, far-fetched; *in -i*, bareheaded. **-ame** *m.*, **-iera** *f.* head of hair. **-uto** *adj.* hairy, hirsute; *cuoio -uto*, scalp.
**capelve·nere** *m.*(bot.) maidenhair fern.
**capestro** *m.* halter; (fig.) rein, check; rope; cord (of a religious).
**capezz-ale** *m.* bolster. **-iera** *f.* antimacassar, chair-back.
**capezzolo** *m.* nipple; teat, dug.
**capienza** *f.* capacity; *quant'è la — del serbatoio?*, how much does the reservoir hold?
**capi-fosso** *m.* main ditch, main drain. **-fuoco** *m.* (*pl.* **-fuochi**) andiron.
**capigliatura** *f.* head of hair; tresses.
**capilargo** *adj.* top-heavy; wider at the top than at the bottom.
**capillar-e** *adj.* capillary. **-ità** *f.* capillarity.
**capiner-a** *f.*, **-o** *m.* (orn.) blackcap.
**cap-ire** [D2] *tr.* to understand, to comprehend, to grasp; *si -isce*, naturally, of course; *non -isce nulla*, he's a fool; *-irai che*, of course you understand that; *intr.* (*aux.* essere) to be contained. **-evole** *adj.* capable; suitable, fit; intelligible; capacious; significant; *-evole di*, deserving of. **-ito** *part. adj.* understood; *-ito !*, right!, agreed!; *-ito che*, on the understanding that.
**capirosso** *m.* (orn.) any bird with a red head; *averla —*, woodchat.
**capital-e** *adj.* capital; supreme, main; cardinal; (leg.) *sentenza —*, death sentence; *n.f.* capital (city); capital (letter); *m.* (econ.; finan.) capital; (fig.) *fare — di*, to make capital out of. **-ismo** *m.* capitalism. **-ista** *m.* capitalist; (econ.) entrepreneur. **-i·stico** *adj.* capitalistic. **-izzare** [A1] *tr.* (finan.) to capitalize; (typ.) to write with a capital.
**capitan-o** *m.* captain. **-a** *f.* woman leader; (naut.) *nave -a*, flagship. **-anza** *f.* captaincy. **-are** [A1] *tr.* to command, to lead, to captain. **-ato** *part. adj.*; *n.m.* captaincy. **-eggiare** [A3 c] *tr.* to captain, to lead.
**capitare** [A1 s] *intr.* (*aux.* essere) to arrive; to turn up; to happen, to occur.
**ca·pite** *adj. phr. in —*, in chief; *parola in —*, headword; *pro —*, per head.
**capitello** *m.* (archit.) capital.
**capitol-are** [A1 s] *intr.* (*aux.*

avere) to capitulate; to make terms; to paragraph. **-azione** *f.* capitulation.

**capi·tolo** *m.* chapter; category; head; (eccl.) chapter.

**capitom·bol-o** *m.* headlong fall; tumble; (fig.) crash, collapse. **-are** [A1 s] *intr.* (*aux.* essere) to fall headlong; (fig.) to crash. **-oni** *adv.* headlong.

**capitozz-a** *f.* pollarded tree. **-are** [A1] *tr.* to pollard.

**capo** *m.* **1.** head; *mettersi in — il cappello,* to put on one's hat; *andare a — nudo,* to go bare-headed; *a — chino,* with bowed head; *da — ai piedi,* from head to foot; *giramenti di —,* attacks of dizziness; *pena del —,* capital punishment. **2.** mind, head; *mettersi in —,* to take (it) into one's head; *mi saltò in — un'idea,* I suddenly got an idea; *aver altro per il —,* to have something else to think about; *mettere il — a,* to put one's mind to. **3.** chief, head; *Capo dello Stato,* Head of State; *delegato —,* chief delegate; *lui è —,* he's the boss; *il — di casa,* the head of the house. **4.** end, extremity, head; *in — alla scala,* at the head of the stairs; *legare insieme i due capi di spago,* to tie the two ends of string together; *in — al mondo,* at the other side of the world; *fare — a,* to lead to, to come to; *le società che fanno — al gruppo,* the companies which go to make up the group; *in — a dieci anni,* at the end of ten years; (provb.) *cosa fatta — ha,* what's done is done. **5.** beginning; *Capo d'Anno,* New Year's Day; *da —,* again, from the beginning; (mus.) *da m,* go back to the beginning; *non ha nè — nè coda,* there's neither rhyme nor reason in it. **6.** item, head, chapter; *— per —,* one by one; *un — di vestiario,* an item of clothing. **7.** head, individual, person; *tanti capi di bestiame,* so many head of cattle; *dividere per —,* to share out per head; *un — ameno,* an amusing chap. **8.** knob, top, head; *— d'uno spillo,* head of a pin; *— d'un chiodo,* head of a nail; *— d'aglio,* clove of garlic; (bot.) bulb; vine sprout; shoot left on a plant when pruning. **9.** (naut.) cable; *— di fune,* standing end of a rope. **10.** (geog.) headland, ness, cape, end; *la Provincia del Capo,* Cape Province (S.A.); *il Capo di Buona Speranza,* the Cape of Good Hope; *la città del Capo,* Capetown.

**capo-banda** *m.* (*pl.* **capibanda**) ringleader; (mus.) bandmaster. **-bandito** *m.* brigand chief. **-barca** *m.* (*pl.* **capibarca**) master of a vessel. **-cervo** *m.* withers. **-cielo** *m.* (liturg.) baldachin. **-classe** *m.* (*pl.* **capiclasse**) (schol.) class-captain, 'form-captain'. **-co·mico** *m.* (theatr.) actor-manager. **-cordata** *m.* (*pl.* **capicordata**) climber at the head of a rope. **-cro·naca** *m.* (*pl.* **capicronaca**) leading article, leader. **-cronista** *m.* leader-writer. **-cuoco** *m.* (*pl.* **capicuochi**) head cook, chef. **-dilatte** *m.* top of the milk, cream. **-dipartimento** *m.* (*pl.* **capidipartimento**) head of a department, manager. **-fab·brica** *m.* (*pl.* **capifab·brica**) works manager; builder's foreman. **-fami·glia** *m.* (*pl.* **capifami·glia**) head of the family. **-fitto** *adj.* with head downwards; *adv. a -fitto,* head first, headlong; *n.m.* (sport) header (dive). **-giro** *m.* dizziness; (fig.) whim. **-lavoro** *m.* masterpiece. **-li·nea** *f.* (of tram or bus service) terminus. **-luogo** *m.* town which is administrative centre of a district. **-mu·sica** *m.* (*pl.* **capimu·sica**) (mus.) bandleader. **-parte** *m.* (*pl.* **capiparte**) leader of a political faction. **-po·polo** *m.* demagogue. **-riparto** *m.* (*pl.* **capiriparto**) head of a department. **-rove·scio** *adv.* head downwards. **-scala** *m.* (*pl.* **capiscala**) landing. **-scuola** *m.* (*pl.* **capiscuola**) founder of a school of thought or art. **-setta** *m.* (*pl.* **capisetta**) leader of a sect. **-sezione** *m.* (*pl.* **capisezione**) head of a department. **-stazione** *m.* (*pl.* **capistazione**) station master. **-sti·pite** *m.* head of a clan; founder of a family. **-torto** *m.* (orn.) wryneck. **-treno** *m.* (*pl.* **capitreno**) guard (of a train). **-verde** *m.* (*pl.* **capoverdi**) (orn.) mallard. **-verso** *m.* paragraph; beginning or end of a verse or paragraph. **-voga** *m.* (*pl.* **capivoga**) (naut.) stroke.

**capoc·chi-a** *f.* head of a pin or nail; knob of a club. **-eri·a** *f.* stubbornness, obstinacy. **-o** *m.* blockhead, dolt. **-uto** *adj.* knobbly.

**capoc·ci-a, -o** *m.* (*pl.* **capocci**) head of a peasant house; patriarch; foreman; (joc.) boss. **-uto** *adj.* obstinate.

**capolino** *m. dim.* of **capo,** q.v.; *far —,* to peep; (bot.) head, capitulum.

**ca·polo** *m.* hilt of a sword; handle of a plough.

**capon-e** *m. augm.* of **capo**; (fig.) blockhead, thickhead; large mask. **-ag·gine** *f.*, **-eri·a** *f.* stubbornness.

**caporal-e** *m.* (mil.) corporal; porter (in a hospital). **-ato** *m.* rank of corporal, 'stripe'. **-etto** *m. dim.* (hist.) *Il -etto,* the little Corporal, Napoleon.

**caporchestra** *m.* (*pl.* **capiorchestra**) (mus.) conductor.

**capotare** [A1] *intr.* (*aux.* avere) to capsize.

**capo-te** *m.*, **-tis** *m. indecl.* (motor.) hood.

**capovol·gere** [C5] *tr.* to turn upside down; *— la situazione,* to reverse the situation; *rfl.* to capsize.

**cappa**[1] *f.* cape, cloak, hood; *romanzo di — e spada,* cloak and dagger novel; (poet.) vault, canopy.

**cappa**[2] *f.* (zool.) bivalve mollusc.

**cappa**[3] *f.* name of the letter K.

**cappeggi-are** [A3 c] *intr.* (*aux.* essere) (naut.) to heave-to (in a storm). **-ato** *part. adj.* (naut.) lying-to.

**cappeggio** *m.* (naut.) lying-to.

**cappella**[1] *f.* (eccl.) chapel; *— della Madonna,* Lady chapel; *maestro di —,* choirmaster.

**cappella**[2] *f.* head of a nail; cap of a mushroom.

**cappellan-o** *m.* chaplain; curate. **-ato** *m.* chaplaincy.

**cappell-o** *m.* hat; head-gear, head covering; *far di — a,* to take off one's hat to; *amico di —,* bowing acquaintance; *tanto di — a,* hats off to; top part, head; lid; covering; preface, foreward. **-ac·cia** *f.* (orn.) crested lark. **-ac·cio** *m. pejor.* of **cappello**; (fig.) rebuke, reprimand; *pl.* (bot.) burdock. **-a·ia** *f.* milliner. **-a·io** *m.* hatter. **-ata** *f.* hatful; *quattrini a -ate,* bags of money. **-eri·a** *f.* hat shop (for men). **-iera** *f.* hat-box. **-uto** *adj.* crested, hooded (of bird, snake, etc.).

**cap·pero**[1] *m.* (bot.) caper.

**capper-o**[2], **-i** *excl.* good Lord!, good gracious!

**capperone** *m.* peasant's hood worn over the cap; jerkin.

**cap·pio** *m.* slip-knot; tassel; halter; loop, eye.

**cap·pita** *excl.* good gracious!; how amazing!

**cappon-e**[1] *m.* capon; *far venire la pelle di — a uno,* to make one go goose flesh. **-are** [A1 c] *tr.* to castrate (a fowl), to caponize.

**cappone**[2] *m.* (ichth.) gurnard.

**cappott-a** *f.* mantle; woollen hat, woman's hat; (motor.) hood. **-o** *m.* overcoat; cloak; evening jacket. **-ino** *m.* naval officer's uniform.

**cappuccin-a** *f.* (eccl.) Capuchin nun. **-o** *m.* (eccl.) Capuchin friar; coffee with whipped cream; (bot.) *fior -o,* nasturtium, *barba di -i,* salad plants, chicory or endive; *adj. insalata -a,* salad of small herbs; (orn.) *falco -o,* marsh harrier.

**cappuc·c-io** *m.* hood of a cloak; (bot.) *fior —,* garden delphinium, annual larkspur; *fior — scempio,* Venus's looking-glass. **-etto** *m. dim.* little hood; *Capuccetto Rosso,* Little Red Riding-Hood.

**capr-a** *f.* goat; nanny goat; *luoghi da -e,* mountainous places; trestle; sawing-horse. **-a·io** *m.* goatherd. **-ętto** *m.* kid; *guanti di -etto,* kid gloves. **-ino** *adj.* goat-like; *barba -ina,* goatee; *pelle -ina,* goatskin; *n.m.* smell of goats; goat manure. **-i·pede** *adj.* goat-footed.

**capric·c-io** *m.* caprice; whim; brief amour; passing fancy; vagary; (of a child) *fare i -i,* to have tantrums. **-ioso** *adj.* capricious; whimsical, fanciful; (of a child) spoilt; wilful.

**caprifi-co** *m.* (*pl.* **-chi**) (bot.) wild fig.

**caprifo·glio** *m.* (bot.) honeysuckle.

**caprimul-go** *m.* (*pl.* **-ghi**) goat-milker, goatherd; (orn.) night-jar.

**capri(u)ol-a** *f.* somersault, cart-wheel, caper; (of a horse) capriole; *fare la —,* to fall headlong; (fig.) volte-face; (zool.) doe of a roe deer. **-are** [A1] *intr.* (*aux.* avere) to somersault, to cut capers.

**capri(u)olo** *m.* roe buck.

**capr-o** *m.* goat; (fig.) *— emissario, — espiatorio,* scapegoat. **-one** *m.* billy goat, he-goat.

**cap·sico** *m.* (bot.) capsicum.

**captare** *tr.* (radio) to pick up; to capture.

**capzioso** *adj.* captious, fraudulent; insidious.

**cara**[1] *f.* dear one; *mia —,* my dear girl; *adj.f.* see **caro**[1].

**cara**[2] *f.* (bot.) stonewort.

**cara·bidi** *m.pl.* (ent.) carabids.

**carabin-a** *f.* carbine. **-ata** *f.* carbine-shot. **-iere** *m.* carabiniere, member of an Army corps which is also a police force.

**ca·rabo** *m.* (ent.) various species of carabid beetles.

**Caracci** *pr.n.f.* (geog.) Karachi.

**caracoll-are** [A1] *intr.* (*aux.* avere) (equit.) to caracol. **-o** *m.* caracol.

**caraffa** *f.* carafe, water jug, glass-jug.

**Car-a·ibi** *pr.n.m.pl.* (geog.) *Mar dei —,* Caribbean Sea. **-ai·bico** *adj.* (geog.) Caribbean.

**caram·bola** *f.* a game like snooker; cannon (at billiards); (fig.) collision, motor accident.

**caramele** *m.* caramel; crème brûlé; burnt sugar.

**caramell-a** *f.* sweet, candy; toffee; monocle. **-a·io** *m.* sweet-vendor.

**caran·col-a** *f.* cavil; pretext. **-are** [A1 s] *intr.* (*aux.* avere) to cavil; to seek pretexts.

**carapace** *m.* (zool.) carapace.

**carat-o** *m.* carat; (comm.) share in a commercial business. **-are** [A1] *tr.* to weigh in carats; to examine minutely. **-ista** *m.* (comm.) sharer.

**carat·ter-e** *m.* character; disposition; nature; property; style; literary portrait, sketch; print, type, handwriting; *scritto a -i di scatola,* written in large block capitals. **-ista** *m.* (theatr.) character actor. **-i·stica** *f.* characteristic, trait; feature; *pl.* (eng.) specification. **-i·stico** *adj.* characteristic, typical; distinctive; picturesque, quaint. **-izzare** [A1] *tr.* to characterize.

**caravanserra·glio** *m.* caravanserai.

**carboidrato** *m.* carbohydrate.

**carbon·chio** *m.* carbuncle; (vet.) *— maligno,* anthrax; (bot.) smut of wheat.

**carbon-e** *m.* charcoal; carbon; coal; *nero come il —,* black as soot. **-a·io** *m.* charcoal burner; coal merchant; (naut.) collier. **-are** [A1 c] *tr.* (naut.) to coal. **-arismo** *m.* (Ital. hist.) the policy of the Carbonari. **-aro** *m.* (Ital. hist.) member of the secret society of Carbonari formed in the nineteenth century for the liberation of Italy. **-cino** *m.* (art) charcoal stick; *disegno al -cino,* black chalk drawing. **-eri·a** *f.* (Ital. hist.) secret society of the Carbonari. **-iera** *f.* coal bunker; (naut.) collier. **-i·fero** *adj.* (geol.) carboniferous. **-izzare** [A1] *tr.* to carbonize; to char. **-oso** *adj.* (chem.) containing carbon.

**carbo·nico** *adj.* (chem.) carbonic; *anidride carbonica,* carbon dioxide.

**carbo·nio** *m.* (chem.) carbon; *idrato di —,* carbohydrate; *ossido di —,* carbon monoxide.

**carbur-o** *m.* (chem.) carbide. **-ante** *m.* motor fuel; vaporizing oil; *il consumo del -ante,* fuel consumption. **-atore** *m.* (eng.; motor.) carburettor; *annegamento del -atore,* flooding of the carburettor. **-azione** *f.* (motor.) carburation; *-azione ricca,* rich mixture; *-azione magra,* weak mixture.

**carcame** *m.* carcase; (naut.) wreckage of a hull.

**carcare** [A2] and derivs. (poet.). See **caricare,** under **carica.**

**carcassa** *f.* carcase; skeleton; *smagrito fino alla —,* reduced to skin and bone; (fig.) physical wreck; old crock; (naut.) hull.

**carcer-are** [A1 s] *tr.* to imprison. **-ato** *part. adj.*; *n.m.* prisoner. **-azione** *f.* incarceration.

**car·cer-e** *m., f.* (*pl.f.*) prison, gaol; imprisonment; *direttore delle -i,* prison governor. **-iere** *m.* prison warder; gaoler.

**carcino** *m.* (zool.) shore crab.

**carcin-oma** *m.* (med.) carcinoma. **-osi** *f.* (med.) carcinosis.

**carciofo** *m.* (bot.) globe artichoke; *— salvatico,* wild artichoke; *— grasso,* house leek.

**car-co** *adj.* (*m.pl.* **-chi**) (poet.) loaded; laden, burdened (*cf.* **carico**); *n.m.* (poet.) weight, load.

**carda** *f.* (text.) card, carding machine.

**card-a·io** *m.*, **-(u)olo** *m.* (text.) carder.

**card-are** [A1] *tr.* (text.) to card; (fig.) to backbite. **-ata** *f.* (text.) carding; *una -ata di lana,* quantity of wool carded. **-ato** *part. adj.* (text.) carded; (fig.) terse, precise, fine; *n.m.* (text.) type of woollen material (*e.g.* tweed, flannel). **-atore** *m.* carder. **-atrice** *f.* woman carder; carding machine.

**cardell-o** *m.*, **-ino** *m.* (orn.) goldfinch.

**cardi·aco** *adj.* (med.) cardiac.

**cardinal-e** *adj.* cardinal; principal; *numerali -i,* cardinal numbers; *virtù -i,* cardinal virtues; *n.m.* (eccl.) cardinal; (orn.) cardinal, pine grosbeak. **-ato** *m.* (eccl.) cardinalate. **-esco** *adj.* (*m.pl.* **-eschi**) cardinal-like; cardinal's.

**car·dine** *m.* pintle, hinge; (fig.) pivotal point; (astron.) cardinal point.

**car·dio** *m.* (zool.) cockle.

**cardio-gramma** *m.* (med.) cardiogram. **-palmo** *m.* palpitation of the heart.

**card-o** *m.* thistle; (text.) carding tool. **-uc·cio** *m.* thistle down.

**caren-a** *f.* (naut.) keel, (poet.) ship. **-ag·gio** *m.* (naut.) careening; *bacino di -aggio,* dry dock. **-are** [A1, A1 c] *tr.* (naut.) to careen; *-are a secco,* to dry dock; (industr.) to streamline, to fair. **-ato** *part. adj.* (naut.) careened; (industr.) *un profilo -ato,* streamline.

**carenza** *f.* privation; dearth; lack; *— di vitamine,* vitamin deficiency.

**carest-i·a** *f.* famine; dearth, shortage. **-oso** *adj.* of famine; barren; *anni -osi,* lean years; high-priced.

**carezza**[1] *f.* high price; shortage; dearth.

**carezza**[2] *f.* caress; act of kindness; affection.

**carezz-are** [A1 c] *tr.* to caress, to fondle; to stroke, to pat; *— un' idea,* to cherish an idea. **-ativo** *adj.* wooing, winning. **-evole** *adj.* caressing; wheedling; cuddly. **-oso** *adj.* loving, affectionate.

**cari** *m. indecl.* (cul.) curry.

**cari-are** [A4] *tr.* to cause to decay; *rfl.* to decay. **-ato** *part. adj.* decayed; very old, decrepit. **-azione** *f.* decaying; decay.

**caria·tide** *f.* (archit.) caryatid.

**ca·ric-a** *f.* charge; load; appointment, office; duties; *durata della —,* term of office; instructions; care, custody; (mil.)

*suonare la* —, to sound the charge; *a passo di* —, at the double; refill. **-are** [A2s] *tr.* (*prep.* di, con) to load; to heap (with), to pile up (with); to overload; to increase, to heighten, to deepen; *-are un orologio,* to wind up a clock; *-are la pipa,* to fill one's pipe; *-are una macchina fotografica,* to load a camera.

**caricatura** *f.* caricature.

**ca·rice** *f.* (bot.) sedge.

**ca·ri-co**[1] *m.* (*pl.* **-chi**) load; *fare il* —, to load up; burden; weight; *avere la famiglia a* —, to have a family to support; — *di coscienza,* load on one's conscience; heap, pile; blame, accusation; (leg.) accusation; charge; (naut.) cargo, freight; shipment; loading, lading.

**ca·ri-co**[2] *adj.* (*m.pl.* **-chi**) loaded, laden, burdened; charged; — *di onori,* heaped with honours; *tinte -che,* deep tones, warm colours; *caffè* —, strong coffee; *cielo* —, overcast sky; *il fucile è* —, the gun is loaded.

**Cariddi** *pr.n.f.* (myth.) Charybdis; *essere tra Scilla e* —, to be between Scylla and Charybdis.

**ca·ri-e** *f.* caries (in the bone, teeth); decay, dry rot. **-ọso** *adj.* carious, decayed.

**cariglịone** *f.* (mus.) carillon; musical box.

**Carin·zia** *pr.n.f.* (geog.) Carinthia.

**cariol-a** *f.* wheelbarrow. **-ata** *f.* wheelbarrow-load.

**carịsm-a** *m.* (*pl.* **carịsmi, cari·smati**) charisma. **-a·tico** *adj.* charismatic.

**carit-à** *f. indecl.* love; — *di patria,* love of country; charity; *ospizio di* —, almshouse; act of charity; kindness; gift; alms; *fatemi la* — *di star fermi!,* do please keep still!; *per* —*!* please!, for pity's sake!; most certainly not!; God forbid! **-atẹvole** *adj.* charitable; benevolent; compassionate.

**Carlo** *pr.n.m.* Charles.

**Carlomagno** *pr.n.m.* Charlemagne.

**carlọna** *adv. phr. alla* —, carelessly, in a slapdash manner.

**Carlotta** *pr.n.f.* Charlotte; (cul.) timbale of fruit.

**carme** *m.* (poet.) poem; hymn; *pl.* poetry.

**carmel-itano, -ita, -i·tico** *adj., pr.n.m.* (eccl.) Carmelite; *i Carmelitani scalzi,* the Discalced Carmelites.

**Carmelo** *pr.n.m.* (geog.) *Monte* —, Mount Carmel.

**carmi·n-(i)o** *m.* carmine. **-ato** *adj.* stained with carmine.

**carnagịone** *f.* complexion *cure della* —, care of the skin.

**carna·io** *m.* common burial ground; charnel hosue; (fig.) slaughter, massacre.

**carnale** *adj.* carnal; of the flesh, sensual; bodily, physical; worldly; blood (of relationship); *cugino* —, first cousin; affectionate, tender.

**carnascial-ẹsco** *adj.* (*m.pl.* **-ẹschi**) pertaining to carnival.

**carn-e** *f.* **1.** flesh; *in* — *e ossa,* incarnate, in the flesh; *color di* —, flesh-coloured; — *d'Adamo,* human frailty; *a* —, naked; (theol.) the flesh; *risurrezione della* —, resurrection of the body; *pl.* complexion, skin; *aver le -i morbide,* to have a tender skin. **2.** meat; — *di bue,* beef; — *di castrato,* mutton; — *di maiale,* pork; — *di vitello,* veal; — *col becco,* poultry; — *da cannone,* cannon fodder. **3.** pulp, flesh of fruit. **-acciọso** *adj.* meaty, fleshy. **-acciuto** *adj.* plump, well-covered. **-ame** *m.* carrion. **-icino** *adj.* flesh-coloured, pink.

**carnẹfic-e** *m.* executioner; butcher, torturer. **-ina** *f.* torture; (fig.) butchery.

**car·ne-o** *adj.* fleshy; of meat; *alimentazione -a,* meat diet.

**carneval-e** *m.* carnival; revelry; merrymaking; *far* —, to make merry. **-are** [A1] *intr.* (*aux.* avere) to keep carnival; to revel, to make merry. **-ata** *f.* carnival fun; prank; escapade. **-ẹsco** *adj.* (*m.pl.* **-ẹschi**) of carnival.

**carnier-a** *f.*, **-e** *m.* poacher's pocket; game bag; shooting jacket.

**carni·voro** *adj.* carnivorous; *n.m.* carnivore; meat eater.

**carnọs-o** *adj.* fleshy; meaty. **-ità** *f.* fleshiness; (paint.) softness.

**car-o**[1] *adj.* dear, beloved; precious; well-loved; *aver* —, *aver a* —, to prize; to esteem; *aver* — *di,* to long to; *tener* —, to take great care of; dear, expensive; costly; *adv.* dear, dearly; *n.m.* loved one; *i miei -i,* my loved ones; — *mio,* my dear man; expensiveness. **-ino** *adj.* pretty; lovely; nice.

**caro**[2] *m.* (bot.) caraway.

**car-o**[3] *m.* coma. **-ọsi** *f.* coma. **-o·tico** *adj.* carotid.

**carọgna** *f.* carrion; carcase; (vulg.) swine; slut.

**carol-a** *f.* dance accompanied by music and song; carol. **-are** [A1] *intr.* (*aux.* avere) to dance (round).

**Carolina** *pr.n.f.* Caroline.

**Carolin·gio** *adj., n.m.* (hist.) Carolingian, Carlovingian.

**Carolino** *adj.* (hist.) Carolingian; *scrittura carolina,* Carolingian minuscule.

**caron·cola** *f.* wattle (of birds).

**Carọnte** *pr.n.m.* (myth.) Charon.

**carọsello** *m.* merry-go-round, roundabout; pageant on horseback; tournament.

**carot-a** *f.* carrot; cock and bull story; hoax; (fig.) *piantar -e,* to tell cock and bull stories.

**caro·tide** *f.* (anat.) carotid artery.

**carovan-a** *f.* caravan; convoy; coachload. **-iera** *f.* caravan route. **-iere, -iero** *m.* caravan guide.

**carovita, carovi·veri** *m. indecl.* rise in the cost of living; *indennità di* —, cost-of-living bonus.

**carpa** *f.* (ichth.) carp.

**Carpazi** *pr.n.m.pl.* (geog.) Carpathians.

**carpent-eri·a** *f.* carpentry, joinery; joiner's shop. **-iere** *m.* joiner, carpenter; wheelwright.

**car·pin-e, -o** *m.* (bot.) hornbeam.

**carpire** [D2] *tr.* to snatch; to seize; to obtain by fraud.

**carpọn-i, -e** *adv.* on all fours, crawling.

**carra** *f.* stone, rock.

**carranco** *m.* ravine.

**carreggi-are** [A3c] *tr.* to cart; to travel (a road) by cart; *intr.* (*aux.* avere) to travel in a cart. **-a·bile** *adj. strada -abile,* cart-track. **-ata** *f.* cart-track; rut; *andare per la -ata,* to follow the beaten track.

**carrẹggio** *m.* constant cart traffic; carting, cartage.

**carrell-are** [A1] *tr.* (cinem.; telev.) to track. **-ata** *f.* tracking shot.

**carrello** *m.* (rlwy.) trolley; bogey; bogey-wheels; (aeron.) undercarriage; (cinem.; telev.) — *di camera,* camera dolly; (typewriter) carriage; — *portavivande,* tea-trolley.

**carrẹtt-a** *f.* cart; tramp steamer. **-a·io** *m.* carter. **-ata** *f.* cartload. van-load. **-iere** *m.*, **-iero** *m.* carter. **-o** *m.* hand-cart; stall.

**carrier-a** *f.* full gallop; *a tutta* —, at full speed; career; profession; *fare* —, to get on, to make a career for oneself; (mil.) *ufficiale di* —, regular officer. **-ịsmo** *m.* careerism, ambition. **-ista** *m., f.* careerist.

**carr-o** *m.* waggon; cart; lorry; (rlwy.) truck; (mil.) — *armato,* tank; *mettere il* — *avanti ai buoi,* to put the cart before the horse; chariot; cartload. **-a·io** *m.* waggoner.

**carrozz-a** *f.* carriage; coach; (rlwy.) carriage; *in* —*!,* all aboard!; — *letto,* sleeper. **-a·bile** *adj. strada -abile,* carriage road. **-eri·a** *f.* body of a car, coachwork; *-eria fuori serie,* coachwork to specification. **-iere** *m.* coachman; designer and maker of specially built bodies for cars. **-ina** *f. dim.* of **carozza;** perambulator; (motor.) sidecar.

**carru·col-a** *f.* pulley; (fig.) *ungere le -e,* to grease the palm. **-are** [A1s] *tr.* to hoist with a tackle; (fig.) to trick.

**carrug·gio** *m.* narrow alley-way.

**cart-a** *f.* **1.** paper; — *a righe,* ruled paper; — *a formato protocollo,* foolscap; — *asciugante,*

blotting paper; — *da imballo*, wrapping paper; — *velina*, tissue paper; *mettere in* —, to set down in black and white. **2.** paper document: *-e domestiche*, private papers; — *d'identità*, identity card; — *moneta*, paper money; menu; *mangiare alla* —, to choose a meal à la carte. **3.** page, sheet; *le Sacre Carte*, Holy Scripture. **4.** diploma; statute; charter; *la Carta Atlantica*, the Atlantic Charter. **5.** chart; — *topografica*, plan (of a town); — *celeste*, chart of the heavens. **6.** card; — *da visita*, visiting card; — *da gioco*, playing card; *cambiar le -e in tavola*, to shift one's ground; *scoprire la — più importante*, to play one's trump card. **-a·io** *m.* paper manufacturer; stationer.

**carta-bello** *m.* pamphlet. **-carbọne** *f.* carbon paper. **-pe·cora** *f.* parchment. **-pesta** *f.* papier-mâché.

**carta·ceo** *adj.* (made of) paper; paper-like.

**Carta·cin-e** *pr.n.f.* (geog.) Carthage. **-ẹse** *adj., n.m., f.* Carthaginian.

**cartẹggio** *m.* correspondence; collection of letters.

**cartella** *f.* portfolio; schoolbag, satchel; briefcase; file, folder; lottery ticket; notice-board; — *da scrittoio*, scribbling pad; (comm.) bond-certificate.

**cartell-o** *m.* large public notice; placard; poster, bill; inscription; name plate, name board (*e.g.* of a street); shop sign; book plate; — *indicatore*, road sign; *di* —, first class, famous; (theatr.) *tenere il* —, to run; (comm.) cartel, combine. **-a·rio** *m.* public archives. **-ino** *m.* label, ticket, tag; name-plate. **-ọne** *m.* poster; placard; (theatr.) list of plays or opera for a season.

**cartiera** *f.* papermill; (naut.) chart table.

**carti·gli-a** *f.* (in games) small cards. **-o** *m.* scroll.

**cartila·g-ine** *f.* (anat.) cartilage. **-i·neo, -inọso** *adj.* cartilaginous.

**cartina** *f.* *dim.* of **carta**; slip of paper; small inset map; (cards) a low card; — *di aghi*, packet of needles.

**cartoc·c-io** *m.* (*pl.* **-i**) paper bag; wrapper in form of a cone; (mil.) cartridge.

**cart-ografi·a** *f.* map-making, cartography; collection of maps or charts. **-ogra·fico** *adj.* cartographical. **-o·grafo** *m.* cartographer; geographer.

**cartol-a·io** *m.* stationer; bookseller. **-eri·a** *f.* stationer's. **-ina** *f.* postcard; *-ina illustrata*, picture postcard; *-ina vaglia*, postal order.

**cartolare**[1] [A1 s] *tr.* to number, to paginate.

**cartolare**[2] *m.* folder, file; paper cover; diary, memo book, notebook; (naut.) ship's log.

**cartoman-te** *m., f.* fortune-teller by cards. **-zi·a** *f.* fortune-telling by cards, cartomancy.

**cartọne** *m.* cardboard; *scatola di* —, cardboard box; (art) cartoon; (cinem.) — *animato*, cartoon.

**cartuc·ci-a** *f.* (*pl.* **cartucce**) cartridge; (typ.) insert or corrigenda slip. **-era** *f.* cartridge case; *cinghia reggi-cartucciere*, cartridge-belt.

**cartula·rio** (hist.) cartulary.

**cas-a** *f.* (for use as *m.* see under no. 2). **1.** house: *l'uscio di* —, the front door; — *di Dio*, house of God, church. **2.** home, household, residence: *è in — la signora?*, is the lady of the house at home?; *fatto in* —, home-made; *a* —, at home; *andiamo a* —, let's go home; *a — mia*, in my house, at home, where I live, (fig.) to my way of thinking; *fuori di* —, out, not at home; *dove sta di —, Lei?*, where do you live?; *mettere su* —, to set up house; *un — d. diavolo*, a shindy, a racket. **3.** family, line, stock, house, dynasty: *i miei di* —, my family; *amico di* —, family friend; *la Casa Reale*, the Royal Family. **4.** institution, home, firm; — *di cura*, nursing home; — *dello studente*, students' hostel; — *editrice*, publishing firm. **5.** (astron.) house, one of the zodiacal regions. **-u·pola** *f.* *dim.* hut; humble little house, cot.

**caṣacca** *f.* cloak; *voltare* —, to change sides; *pl.* jockey's colours.

**casale** *m.* hamlet.

**casalinga** *f.* housewife.

**casalingo** *adj.* domestic, household; home-made; home-loving; sedentary; *cucina casalinga*, plain home-cooking.

**casamatta** *f.* (mil.) casement; pill-box; (mil. slang) glasshouse.

**casamẹnto** *m.* apartment house.

**casat-a** *f.* family; clan. **-o** *m.* family name, surname; family.

**cascag·gine** *f.* muscular fatigue; nodding of the head through sleepiness.

**cascam-e** *m.* offal; waste; remnants; by-product; *-i di ferro*, scrap iron.

**ca·scara** *f.* (pharm.) cascara.

**casc-are** [A2] *intr.* (*aux.* essere) to fall; to drop; to droop, to sag; — *dalla fame*, to be faint with hunger; — *dalle nuvole*, to be dumbfounded. **-ante** *adj.* falling; drooping; round-shouldered; weak, fainting; *età -ante*, decrepitude.

**cascata** *f.* fall, drop; waterfall, cascade.

**Cascimir** *pr.n.m.* (geog.) Kashmir.

**cascina** *f.* cheese-press; dairy-farm.

**cas-co**[1] *m.* (*pl.* **-chi**) helmet, casque; crash-helmet; — *coloniale*, sun helmet.

**cas-co**[2] *m.* (*pl.* **-chi**) fall, drop; setback; *fare un* —, to suffer a setback; *un — di banane*, a bunch of bananas.

**caṣeario** *adj.* pertaining to cheese.

**caseggiato** *m.* block of houses and other buildings.

**casell-a** *f.* pigeon-hole, compartment; — *postale*, post-box; cell; square on ruled paper; (chess, draughts) square. **-a·rio** *m.* set of pigeon-holes; filing cabinet; *-ario aperto*, pigeon-hole; *-ario chiuso*, locker.

**ca·ṣe-o** *m.* milk curds. **-ifi·cio** *m.* cheese factory. **-ina** *f.* (chem.) casein.

**caserẹccio** *adj.* home-made; homely; domestic.

**caserma** *f.* (mil.) barracks; quarters; *consegnato in* —, confined to barracks.

**casier-e** *m.*, **-a** *f.* caretaker.

**caṣimi(r)r-a** *f.*, **-o** *m.* (text.) cashmere.

**casino** *m.* casino; gaming house.

**casi·pola** *f.* hut, hovel.

**caṣ-ista** *m.* (eccl.) casuist; (fig.) over-scrupulous person. **-i·stica** *f.* casuistry; (med.) case histories.

**caṣo** *m.* case; incident; chance; occasion; possibility; *non è il — di offendersi*, there's no need to get offended; *non c'è — di*, there's no possibility of; *al* —, should occasion arise; *fare al* —, to meet the case; *a* —, haphazardly, carelessly; *per* —, by chance; — *mai*, if need be; *non fa* —, it doesn't matter; *in ogni* —, in any case; *pl.* events, deeds; *i casi della vita*, the ups and downs of life; (gramm.) case.

**casolare** *m.* humble cottage; hovel; hut.

**casolineri·a** *f.* general stores.

**casott-o** *m.* sentry-box; hut; kiosk; bathing hut. **-a·io** *m.* bathing attendant.

**Ca·spio** *pr.n.m.* (geog.) *il Mar* —, the Caspian Sea.

**cassa** *f.* **1.** box, case; chest; bin; coffer; — *da morto*, coffin. **2.** container; tank; cavity, socket, chamber; (mus.) body, chest (of violin, etc.); *gran* —, bass drum. **3.** bank, fund, chest: — *di risparmio*, savings bank; — *infortuni*, accident fund. **4.** cash: cash-register; cash-desk; *libro di* —, day-book; *si paga alla* —, pay at the cash-desk; *denaro in* —, cash in hand; *tenere la* —, to be banker.

**cassa-forte** *f.* (*pl.* **casseforti**) safe, strong-box. **-panca** *f.* seat-locker; chest serving also as a seat.

**Cassandra** *pr.n. f.* (myth.) Cassandra.

**cass-are** [A1] *tr.* to nullify; to

abrogate; to annul; to cancel, to erase; to dismiss; to cashier. **-atọio** *m.* eraser. **-atura** *f.* erasure.
**cassata** *f.* ice-gâteau.
**casseruola** *f.* saucepan.
**cassẹtta** *f. dim.* of **cassa**; little box; drawer; collection box; — *delle lettere,* letter-box; cash-box; — *di sicurezza,* strong box; — *della spazzatura,* dust-pan; (theatr.) box-office.
**cassẹtt-o** *m.* drawer (of a cabinet, desk, etc.); (eng.) valve, chamber. **-ọne** *m.* chest of drawers.
**cassiere** *m.* cashier; treasurer.
**cassin-ense, -ese** *adj.* of Monte Cassino; Benedictine.
**Cassiope·a** *pr.n.f.* (myth.; astron.) Cassiopeia.
**cassọne** *m.* linen chest; caisson; coffin; water tank.
**casta** *f.* caste.
**castagn-a** *f.* chestnut; *-e secche,* roast, peeled chestnuts. **-a·io, -aro** *m.* chestnut-vendor. **-ẹto** *m.* chestnut copse. **-ẹtta** *f.* paper cracker; snap of the fingers; *pl.* (mus.) castanets. **-o** *m.* chestnut tree; *adj.* chestnut, of chestnut wood; chestnut-coloured.
**castaldo** *m.* steward in a nobleman's household.
**casta·neo, castano** *adj.* chestnut-coloured.
**castell-o** *m.* castle; mansion, palace; walled village or small town; (fig.) *-i in aria,* castles in Spain. **-ana** *f.* châtelaine. **-ano** *m.* commander of a castle; feudal lord; *adj.* pertaining to a castle; *le mura -ane,* the castle walls.
**castig-are** [A2] *tr.* to chastise, to punish; to correct; to chasten. **-ato** *part. adj.* punished; chastened; chaste; moderate; pure, pristine.
**casti-go** *m.* (*pl.* **-ghi**) punishment, chastisement; penalty; castigation; judgement.
**Casti·gli-a** *pr.n.f.* (geog.) Castille. **-ano** *adj., n.m.* Castilian.
**cast-o** *adj.* chaste; continent; pure; virgin; innocent. **-ità** *f.* chastity; continence; abstinence; purity.
**Castọre** *pr.n.m.* (myth.) Castor; — *e Polluce,* Castor and Pollux.
**castoro** *m.* (zool.) beaver; beaver-fur.
**castr-are** [A1] *tr.* to castrate, to emasculate. **-atello** *m.* lamb. **-ato** *part. adj.* castrated; *n.m.* eunuch; gelding mutton; (mus.) artificial male soprano or contralto.
**castrọne** *m.* castrated colt; castrated wether.
**caṣual-e** *adj.* casual, uncertain; unintentional; occasional; *un incontro* —, a chance encounter; (finan.) *guadagni -i,* casual earnings. **-mẹnte** *adv.* casually; by chance.
**casua·rio** *m.* (orn.) cassowary.
**cata-bo·lico** *adj.* descending; *curva -bolica,* downward trend. **-cliṣma** *m.* cataclysm; **-cọmba** *f.* catacomb, sepulchral tunnel.
**catadiottro** *m.* reflector, cat's eye.
**cata-falco** *m.* catafalque. **-fa·scio** *adv. phr. a -fascio,* higgledy-piggledy; *andare in -fascio,* to go to pieces.
**Cat-a·i, -a·ia** *pr.n. f.* (hist. geog.) Cathay.
**catalessi**[1] *f.* (med.) catalepsy.
**catalessi**[2] *f.* (prosod.) catalexis.
**cataletto** *m.* bier; portable bed, large stretcher.
**cat-a·lisi** *f.* (chem.) catalysis. **-ali·tico** *adj.* (chem.) catalytic. **-alizzare** [A1] *tr.* (chem.) to catalyse.
**Catalọgna** *pr.n.f.* (geog.) Catalonia.
**cata·lo-go** *m.* (*pl.* **-ghi**) catalogue; list. **-gare** [A2 s] *tr.* to catalogue. **-gatọre** *m.* cataloguer; archivist.
**Cata·n-ia** *pr.n.f.* (geog.) Catania. **-ẹse** *adj., n.m., f.* Catanian.
**catapẹcchia** *f.* tumble-down hovel.
**catapla**ṣ**ma** *m.* (med.) poultice, cataplasm; (fig.) tiresome person, bore.
**catapult-a** *f.* catapult. **-are** [A1] *tr.* to catapult.
**catarifrangente** *adj.* reflecting (back); *n.m.* red reflector on back of a vehicle; reflector on a road-sign; cat's eye.
**Catarina** *pr.n.f.* See **Caterina.**
**catarr-o** *m.* (med.) catarrh. **-ale, -ọso** *adj.* catarrhal.
**cat-arsi** *f.* (med.) catharsis, purging; (lit.) catharsis; (fig.) purification; expiation. **-ar·tico** *adj.* cathartic.
**catast-a** *f.* wood pile; pile of objects; funeral pyre. **-ale** *adj. imposta -ale,* land tax; *mappa -ale,* land survey map.
**cata·str-ofe** *f.* catastrophe. **-o·fico** *adj.* catastrophic; disastrous; (of a person) inclined to over-dramatize.
**catech-eṣi** *f.* (eccl.) catechesis, catechizing. **-iṣmo** *m.* catechism. **-iẓẓare** [A1] *tr.* (eccl.) to catechize; (fig.) to try to persuade, to argue into.
**categ-ori·a** *f.* category; group; class. **-o·rico** *adj.* categorical; absolute; precise.
**catẹn-a** *f.* chain; (fig.) *pazzo da* —, raving mad; (geog.) range of mountains. **-ella** *f. dim.* small chain; watch-chain.
**cateratta** *f.* cateract; sluice; portcullis; trap-door; shutter; (med.) cataract.
**Caterin-a** *pr.n.f.* Catherine, Catharine, Katharine; *Santa* —, St. Catherine (of Siena). **-ẹtta** *pr.n.f. dim.* Kate, Kitty.
**caterva** *f.* crowd, mob, herd.
**cate·tere, catetere** *m.* (surg.) catheter.
**catin-o** *m.* large basin; earthenware bowl; hollow; **-ella** *f.* small basin; *piovere a -elle,* to rain cats and dogs.
**ca·t-odo** *m.* (chem.; electr.) cathode, negative electrode. **-o·dico** *adj. raggi -odici,* cathode rays.
**Catọne** *pr.n.m.* (hist.) Cato (the Censor); Cato (of Utica).
**cator·cio, catorzo** *m.* bolt.
**cator·zol-o** *m.* stump left by pruning, snag; knot in wood. **-uto** *adj.* knotty, gnarled.
**catram-e** *m.* tar, pitch. **-ọso** *adj.* tarry.
**cat·tedr-a** *f.* professorial chair; teaching post; *sedere in* —, to hold a chair, to be a professor; (eccl.) bishop's throne; St. Peter's chair. **-ale** *adj.* professorial. **-a·tico** *adj.* professorial, academic; pedantic; pompous; *n.m.* professor.
**cattedrale** *f.* cathedral; *adj.* pertaining to a cathedral; *recinto* —, cathedral close.
**cattivare** [A1] *tr.* to captivate; *n.pl.* (*dat.* of *prn.*) to win for oneself.
**cattività** *f.* captivity.
**cattiv-o** *adj.* bad; naughty; evil; wrong; (of an animal) vicious, dangerous; *n.m.* bad person; naughty child. **-e·ria, -eri·a** *f.* naughtiness, mischievousness; maliciousness, spite; badness.
**catto·lic-o** *adj.* (rel.) Catholic; universal, catholic; *n.m.* Catholic. **-e·ṣimo, -iṣmo** *m.* Catholicism.
**cattur-a** *f.* capture; (leg.) arrest; seizure; *mandato di* —, warrant for arrest. **-are** [A1] *tr.* to capture; (leg.) to seize.
**Catullo** *pr.n.m.* Catullus.
**Ca·uc-aso** *pr.n.m.* (geog.) Caucasus. **-a·sico, -a·seo** *adj., n.m.* caucasian.
**caucciù** *m. indecl.* rubber.
**caud-ale** *adj.* caudal, tail-like. **-ato** *adj.* caudate, tailed.
**ca·us-a** *f.* cause, motive, reason; *a — di,* because of; (leg.) cause; action; suit. **-ale** *adj.* causal. **-are** [A1 s] *tr.* to cause; to bring about; to produce. **-aziọne** *f.* (philos.) causation.
**ca·ustic-o** *adj.* caustic, burning; *n.m.* caustic. **-ità** *f.* causticity.
**cautela** *f.* caution; cautiousness, circumspection; warning; caution money.
**cautelare**[1] [A1] *tr.* to secure; to protect by caution money.
**cautelare**[2] *adj.* (leg.) precautionary.
**caute·r-io** *m.* (surg.) cautery. **-iẓẓare** [A1] *tr.* to cauterize.
**ca·ut-o** *adj.* cautious; prudent;

wary; secured against loss; *mal —*, imprudent; *far —*, to warn. **-ęzza** *f.* cautiousness; prudence.
**cauziọn-e** *f.* (leg.) bail; security; guarantee; recognizance; *rilasciare dietro —*, to release on bail. **-are** [A1 c] *tr.* (comm.) to guarantee.
**cava** *f.* pit; quarry, mine.
**cava-chiodi** *m. indecl.* nail-extractor. **-fasciọni** *m. indecl.* (motor.) tyre-lever. **-tappi** *m. indecl.* corkscrew.
**cavagno** *m.* basket.
**cavalcare** [A2] *intr.* (*aux.* avere) to ride, to go riding; *tr.* to ride; to straddle, to mount; to overtop; to span.
**cavalcata** *f.* cavalcade; ride on horseback.
**cavalcavi·a** *f. indecl.* road bridge.
**cavalciọn-e, -i** *adv.* astride; *tenere le gambe a —*, to sit with one's knees crossed.
**cavalier-e** *m.* rider, horseman; knight; *fare —*, to knight; escort, male partner at a dance. **-ato** *m.* knighthood.
**cavalla** *f.* mare.
**cavaller-i·a** *f.* cavalry; chivalry; knighthood. **-ęsco** *adj.* (*m.pl.* **-ęschi**) knightly; *ordine -esco*, order of knighthood; chivalrous; gentlemanly; brave; loyal.
**cavallerizz-a** *f.* riding school; horsemanship. **-o** *m.* riding-master.
**cavallętto** *m. dim.* of **cavallo**; trestle, stand, tripod; easel.
**cavallin-a** *f. dim.* of **cavalla**; filly, young mare; (fig.) *correre la —*, to sow one's wild oats. **-o** *m. dim.* of **cavallo**; colt, foal; pony; *adj.* equine; *tosse -a*, whooping cough; *mosca -a*, horse-fly.
**cavallo** *m.* (sometimes **caval**, as in provbs.) horse; *— di razza*, thoroughbred; *— da caccia*, hunter; *— da corsa*, racehorse; *— da noleggio*, hack; *— di San Francesco*, shanks' pony; *salto al —*, vaulting; *a —*, on horseback; (provb.) *a caval donato non si guarda in bocca*, don't look a gift horse in the mouth; wave, breaker, white horse; (chess) knight.
**cav-are** [A1] *tr.* to excavate; to extract; to obtain; to take away; *-arsi la voglia*, to satisfy a desire; *-arsela*, to get out of a difficulty. **-atura** *f.* removal; hollow, cavity.
**cavern-a** *f.* cavern, cave; cavity. **-ọso** *adj.* cavernous; hollow; deep.
**caverni·cola** *m.* cave-dweller.
**cavęzza** *f.* halter; hangman's rope; *pagare sulla —*, to pay on the nail.
**ca·via** *f.* (zool.) guinea-pig.
**caviale** *m.* caviare.
**cavic·chi-a** *f.* bolt; large peg. **-o** *m.* wooden pin; peg for string of an instrument; rung of a ladder; (fig.) pretext.
**cavi·glia** *f.* peg; bolt; ankle; ankle-bone; shin.
**cavill-are** [A1] *intr.* (*aux.* avere) to quibble, to cavil; *tr.* to criticize, to pick faults in. **-o** *m.* quibble, petty argument; cavil. **-ọso** *adj.* quibbling.
**cavità** *f.* cavity; hollow, recess.
**cavo**[I] *adj.* hollow, concave; *n.m.* hollow, cavity; *— di barca*, interior of a boat; *— dell'onda*, trough of the wave.
**cavo**[2] *m.* cable; *— telefonico*, telephone line.
**ca·vol-o** *m.* cabbage; cauliflower; *— broccoluto*, broccoli; *starci come i -i a merenda*, to be like a fish out of water. **-a·ia** *f.* cabbage patch; (ent.) cabbage white butterfly. **-ino** *m. dim.* of **cavolo**; *-ini Bruxelles*, Brussels sprouts.
**cazz-a** *f.* crucible. **-ętta** *f.* ladle.
**cazzott-are** [A1] *tr.* to punch. **-ata** *f.* punch, thump. **-o** *m.* punch on the head; *fare a -i*, to come to fisticuffs.
**cazzuola** *f.* bricklayer's trowel; *maestro della —*, bricklayer; (zool.) tadpole.
**ce** *pers. prn.* form of **ci**, used before: lo, li, gli, la, le, ne.
**cecag·gine** *f.* blindness; drowsiness.
**cecca**[I] *f.* (orn.) magpie.
**Cecca**[2] *pr.n.f.* abbrev. of **Francesca,** Frances.
**Cecco** *pr.n.m.* abbrev. of **Francesco,** Francis.
**cęce** *m.* (bot.) chick-pea; *— di terra*, ground-nut plant; (cul.) *ceci maritati*, soup with pasta and lentils.
**Ceci·lia** *pr.n.f.* Cicely, Cecilia; (pop.) ladybird.
**cecità** *f.* blindness.
**ceco**[I] *adj.* See **cieco.**
**ceco**[2] *adj., n.m.* Czech.
**Cecoşlov-ac·chia** *pr.n.f.* (geog.) Czecho-Slovakia. **-acco** *adj., n.m.* Czecho-Slovak.
**cęd-ere** [B1] *intr.* (*aux.* avere) to yield; to surrender; to subside; *tr.* to give up; to hand over; to renounce; *— il passo a*, to make way for. **-ęvole** *adj.* yielding, pliant, supple; accommodating. **-imento** *m.* yielding; give, sag; *-imento del terreno*, subsidence.
**ce·dola** *f.* (comm.) coupon; voucher; *— di commissione libraria*, book-token.
**cedr-are** [A1 c] *tr.* to flavour with citron or lemon. **-ata** *f.* citron-flavoured drink; lemonade. **-ato** *adj.* lemon-flavoured; citron-flavoured; *n.m.* ice-cream soda with lemon flavouring; (bot.) citron-tree.
**cedro**[I] *m.* (bot.) genus of trees including orange, lemon, citron; fruit of citron tree.
**cedr-o**[2] *m.* (bot.) cedar; *— del Libano*, Cedar of Lebanon. **-ino** *adj.* (of) cedar.
**ce·duo** *adj.* (of a copse, etc.) suitable for cutting; *n.m.* coppice.
**cefa·lico** *adj.* cephalic.
**ce·falo** *m.* (ichth.) mullet.
**ceff-o** *m.* snout, muzzle; ugly mug; *guardare a — torto*, to make a wry face at. **-ata** *f.* slap in the face. **-ọne** *m.* cuff, slap, clout.
**Ce·ilan** *pr.n.m.* (geog.) Ceylon.
**cel-are** [A1] *tr.* to conceal; *rfl.* to hide (oneself). **-ato** *part. adj.* concealed; occult.
**celeber·rimo** *adj. superl.* of **celebre,** *q.v.*
**celebr-are** [A1 s] *tr.* to celebrate; to solemnize; to extol. **-ante** *m.* (liturg.) celebrant. **-ato** *part. adj.* celebrated; renowned. **-aziọne** *f.* celebration.
**ce·lebr-e** *adj.* celebrated, distinguished, renowned. **-ità** *f. indecl.* celebrity; renown; famous person.
**ce·ler-e** *adj.* rapid, swift; (of a train) fast. **-i·metro** *m.* speedometer. **-ità** *f.* celerity, rapidity.
**Celeste**[I] *pr.n.m., f.* Celeste.
**celest-e**[2] *adj.* celestial, heavenly; of the sky; divine; light blue, sky-blue; *n.m.* divinity; *i -i*, the gods. **-iale** *adj.* celestial, heavenly.
**ce·li-a**[I] *f.* jest, joke; *per —*, in fun; *reggere alla —*, to stand a joke. **-are** [A3] *intr.* (*aux.* avere) to joke.
**Ce·lia**[2] *pr.n.f.* Celia.
**ce·lib-e** *adj.* unmarried; celibate; *n.m.* bachelor. **-ata·rio** *m.* celibatarian, confirmed bachelor. **-ato** *m.* celibacy; bachelorhood.
**celido·nia** (bot.) greater celandine; *— minore*, lesser celandine.
**cell-a** *f.* cell, small room; *— frigorifera*, cold room. **-a·io** *m.* wine-cellar, store cupboard; buttery.
**cellofane, cellofa·bia** *f.* cellophane.
**cel·lul-a** *f.* cell. **-are** *adj.* cellular; (leg.) *segregazione -are*, solitary confinement; *n.m.* cluster of cells; prison. **-ato** *adj.* cellular. **-o·ide** *f.* celluloid; *adj.* cell-like, cellular. **-ọsa** *f.* (techn.) cellulose; wood pulp. **-ọso** *adj.* cellular, cell-like.
**Celta** *m.* Celt.
**ce·ltico** *adj.* Celtic.
**cemęnt-o** *m.* cement; concrete; *— armato*, reinforced concrete. **-are** [A1 c] *tr.* to cement, to concrete; (fig.) to reinforce, to strengthen, to cement. **-eri·a** *f.*, **-ifi·cio** *m.* cement works. **-ista** *m.* cement-worker, cement-layer.
**cęn-a** *f.* supper; (eccl.) *l'ultima —*, the Last Supper; *— eucaristica*, Holy Communion. **-a·colo** *m.* (archaeol.) cenaculum; (rel.) the

Upper Room; (art) *il Cenacolo di Leonardo*, Leonardo's 'Last Supper'; (fig.) clique. **-are** [A1 c] *intr.* (*aux.* avere) to have supper.

**cẹnc-io** *m.* (*pl.* **-i**) rag, cloth; duster; *bianco come un — lavato*, white as a sheet; *cadere come un —*, to collapse; person in a poor state of health. **-ia·io** *m.* rag picker, old-clothes man. **-iọso** *adj.* ragged. **-iume** *m.* bundle of rags.

**cẹner-e** *f.* ash; *pl.* ashes; ashes of a cremated corpse; *le Ceneri*, Ash Wednesday. **-a·io** *m.* ash-pit. **-a·rio** *adj.* cinerary. **-iera** *f.* ash-tray. **-ino, -o·gnolo** *adj.* ashen. **-ume** *m.* heap of ashes.

**Ceneren·tola** *pr.n.f.* Cinderella.

**Ceni·sio** *pr.n.m.* (geog.) Mont Cenis.

**cennamella** *f.* kind of bagpipe.

**cẹnno** *m.* sign; nod; hint; signal, command; *fare —*, to signal; to give an indication.

**ceno·b-io** *m.* monastery. **-ita** *m.* monk, cenobite.

**cenota·fio** *m.* cenotaph.

**cens-ire** [D2] *tr.* to take the census of; to assess; to tax. **-imẹnto** *m.* census-taking.

**censo** *m.* census; (finan.) *a —*, in return for an annual payment; (fig.) money, wealth; moneyed classes; big business.

**censọr-e** *m.* censor. **-ato** *m.* censorship.

**censo·rio** *adj.* censorial.

**censur-a** *f.* censorship; censor; censure; police station. **-are** [A1] *tr.* to censure; to criticize.

**centa·urea, centaure·a** *f.* (bot.) *— minore*, pink centaury; *— nera*, knapweed; *— maggiore*, great centaury.

**centa·uro** *m.* (myth.) centaur; (slang) racing motor-cyclist.

**centellin-are** [A1] *tr.* to sip. **-o** *m.* sip; *bere a -i*, to sip.

**centena·rio** *adj.* recurring every hundred years; *n.m.* centenary; centenarian.

**cent-ennale** *adj.* pertaining to a century. **-enne** *adj.* lasting a hundred years; centennial. **-en·nio** *m.* century.

**cente·ṣim-o** *adj.* hundredth; *n.m.* one-hundredth part; centime; cent; one-hundredth of a lira. **-ale** *adj.* centesimal, referring to hundredths.

**centifo·gli-o** *m.* (bot.) chickweed. **-a, -e** *f.* (bot.) cabbage rose.

**cent-i·grado** *adj.* centigrade; *il grado —*, the Centigrade measure of heat. **-igramma, -igrammo** *m.* centigramme. **-ilag·gio** *m.* intelligence quotient. **-i·metro** *m.* centimetre; tape-measure; ruler.

**centimbọcca** *m.pl.* (cul.) fish fry.

**centina·i-o** *m.* (*pl.f.* **-a**) a quantity of a hundred; *per -a*, in groups of a hundred.

**centi·pede** (zool.) centipede.

**centista** *m.* (sport) hundred-metre runner.

**cent-o** *num. adj. indecl.* one hundred; *per —*, per cent; *novantanove su —*, ninety-nine out of a hundred. **-ofo·glia, -ofo·glie** *f.* (bot.) yarrow, milfoil. **-omila** *card. num.* hundred thousand; *-omila volte*, time and time again. **-omille·ṣimo** *ord. num., adj., n.m.* hundred-thousandth.

**centọne** *m.* cento; miscellany; (fig.) hotchpotch.

**central-e** *adj.* central, centre, middle; *n.f.* main depot or works; main railway station. **-inista** *m., f.*, **-ino** *m.*, **-ista** *m., f.* telephone operator. **-ità** *f.* centrality.

**centraliẓẓ-are** [A1] *tr.* to centralize. **-aziọne** *f.* centralization.

**centrare** *tr.* [A1] (sport) to centre; *intr.* (*aux.* avere) to score a bull's eye; (fig.) to hit the nail on the head.

**centr-ifugare** [A1 s] *tr.* to centrifuge. **-i·fuga** *f.* centrifuge; spin drier; extractor. **-i·fugo** *adj.* (*m.pl.* **-i·fughi**) (phys.) centrifugal.

**centrista** *m., adj.* (pol.) adherent of a centre party.

**centr-o** *m.* centre, middle; town centre; hub, heart; core; centre, club; *fuori —*, out of position; *essere nel suo —*, to be in one's element; (football) *— mediano*, centre-half. **-oattacco** *m.* (*pl.* **-oattacchi**) (football, hockey) centre-forward. **-oavanti** *m. indecl.* (football) centre-forward. **-oe·urope·o** *adj.* Central European.

**centuno** *m.* (*f.* **centuna**) one hundred and one.

**centuplic-are** [A2 s] *tr.* to multiply a hundred-fold. **-ato** *part. adj.* multiplied many times. **-aziọne** *f.* centuplication.

**cen·tuplo** *adj.* one hundred times greater.

**cẹpp-a** *f.* tree-trunk. **-a·ia** *f.* stump of a tree just above the ground; *pl.* underwood. **-ata** *f.* quantity of stumps. **-ato** *adj.* rooted.

**cẹppo** *m.* stock; chopping block; support, base, rest; family; source, origin; (of a word) root; log; *Ceppo di Natale*, Christmas log; *pl.* fetters, shackles.

**cera**[1] *f.* air, mien, appearance; *fare cattiva —*, to look cross.

**cer-a**[2] *f.* wax; (fig.) *essere di —*, to be very delicate; candle. **-ai(u)olo** *m.* wax chandler; sculptor in wax. **-alacca** *f.* (*pl.* **ceralacche, cerelacche**) sealing wax. **-ame** *m.* quantity of wax.

**cera·m-ica** *f.* pottery; ceramics. **-ico** *adj.* ceramic.

**cer-are** [A1 c] *tr.* to wax. **-ato** *part. adj.* waxed; waterproofed; *tela -ata*, oilskin; *carta -ata*, greaseproof paper.

**Cer·bero** *pr.n.m.* (myth.; astron.) Cerberus.

**cerbiatto** *m.* (zool.) fawn.

**cerbottana** *f.* blowpipe; pea-shooter; speaking-tube; ear-trumpet.

**cẹrc-a** *f.* quest, search; *andare in — di*, to be in search of; *fare la —*, to go begging. **-apersone** *m. indecl.* staff-locating equipment.

**cerc-are** [A2 c] *tr.* to seek, to look for; to examine, to scrutinize; to fetch; (*prep.* di, followed by *infin.*) to try (to), to attempt (to). **-ata** *f.* search, scrutiny. **-ato** *part. adj.* looked-for; in demand.

**cẹrchia** *f.* circle (*e.g.* of the walls of a city); sphere of interest or influence; confines.

**cerchi-are** [A4 c] *tr.* to encircle; to ring; to hoop. **-atọre** *m.* cooper.

**cẹrchio** *m.* circle, ring; hoop; rim; halo; group of people; meeting; orbit, range.

**cẹrcine** *m.* round pad of cloth.

**cereal-e** *adj., n.m.* cereal. **-icoltura** *f.* (agric.) corn growing.

**cerebello** *m.* (anat.) cerebellum.

**cerebr-ale** *adj.* cerebral; (fig.) over-intellectual, sophisticated. **-aliṣmo** *m.* intellectualism. **-are** [A1 s] *intr.* (*aux.* avere) to cerebrate. **-aziọne** *f.* cerebration, brain action.

**ce·rebro** *m.* brain.

**ce·reo** *adj.* waxy, waxen; (fig.) pale, haggard; *n.m.* candle; candlestick.

**Ce·rere** *pr.n.f.* (myth.; astron.) Ceres.

**cerimo·ni-a** *f.* ceremony, rite; pomp; *stare sulle -e*, to stand on ceremony. **-ale** *adj.* ceremonial; *n.m.* protocol. **-ere** *m.* master of ceremonies.

**cerimoniọṣ-o** *adj.* ceremonious; formal; *n.m.* ceremonious person. **-ità** *f.* ceremoniousness.

**cerino** *m.* small wax match; wax taper.

**cer·n-ere** [C29] *tr.* to select; to discern; to sift; to sort. **-itura** *f.* separating; selection.

**cernier-a** *f.* hinged clasp; *lampo a —*, zip fastener (*e.g.* round a case). **-ato** *adj.* hinged.

**cer·nita** *f.* choice, selection; (techn.) grading, classification; *fare la — di*, to grade.

**cer-o** *m.* large wax candle (used in churches). **-ọne** *m. augm.* grease-paint. **-opla·stica** *f.* wax modelling. **-otto** *m.* (pharm.) wax plaster; *-otto adesino*, sticking plaster; *-otto plastico*, elastoplast.

**cerpelọne** *m.* blunder, gross error.

**cerretano** *m.* charlatan, quack, impostor.

**cerr-o**[1] *m.* (bot.) turkey oak. **-a** *f.* (bot.) acorn of the turkey oak.

**cerr-o**[2] *m.* mane, shock of hair. **-olino** *m.* fringe.
**certaldese** *adj.*, *n.m.* native of Certaldo; *il* —, Boccaccio.
**certame** *m.* (poet.) combat.
**certezza** *f.* certainty; proof.
**certific-are** [A2 s] *tr.* to certify, to prove; to certificate; to affirm; *rfl.* to satisfy oneself. **-ato** *part. adj.* certified; certificated; *n.m.* certificate, testimonial. **-azione** *f.* certification.
**cert-o** *adj.* certain, sure; persuaded; true; *avere per* —, to believe for certain; definite; any, some; *n.m.* certainty, *pl. prn.* some people; *adv.* certainly; doubtless; *certo!*, yes, indeed; *di* —, certainly. **-amente** *adv.* certainly; assuredly; with assurance.
**certos-a** *f.* (eccl.) charterhouse, Carthusian house; chartreuse. **-ina** *f.* Carthusian nun. **-ino** *adj.* (eccl.) Carthusian; *n.m.* Carthusian monk; chartreuse (drink).
**ceru·leo** *adj.* sky-blue, pale blue.
**cerussa** *f.* white lead.
**cervato** *adj.* dapple grey.
**cervell-o** *m.* (*pl.* **-a** *f.* when referring to human beings and animals; **-i** *m.* in other uses) brain, brains; *bruciarsi le -a*, to blow one's brains out; *lambiccarsi il* —, to rack one's brains; *essere in* —, to be all there; *mettere il — a partito*, to come to see reason. **-etto** *m.* (anat.) cerebellum; odd habit, whim, caprice. **-uto** *adj.* brainy.
**cervic-e** *f.* back of the neck, nape; (anat.) cervix; *di dura* —, stiffnecked. **-ale** *adj.* cervical.
**cervier-e** *m.* (zool.) lynx. **-o** *adj.* lynx-like.
**cervino**[1] *adj.* cervine, pertaining to deer; dapple-bay.
**Cervino**[2] *pr.n.m.* (geog.) Matterhorn.
**cerv-o** *m.* (zool.) stag, deer; (ent.) — *volante*, stag beetle; observation kite. **-a** *f.* hind.
**cervona** *f.* strong glue; *adj. colla* —, fish glue.
**Cesare, Ce·sare** (Rom.) *pr.n.m.* Caesar; emperor; *Giulio* —, Julius Caesar.
**cesa·r-eo** *adj.* (hist.) Caesarian; imperial; *taglio* —, Caesarian operation. **-iano** *adj.* (Rom. hist.) belonging to Julius Caesar's party. **-ismo** *m.* (pol.) Caesarism, absolute government.
**cesell-are** [A1] *tr.* to engrave; to chisel; (geog.) to erode. **-atura** *f.* engraving; chiselling.
**cesello** *m.* chisel, graving tool.
**cesoi-a** *f.* (eng.) shears. **-e** *pl.* shears, cutters; scissors. **-ata** *f.* snip.
**ce·spit-e** *m.* tuft; (leg.) capital asset. **-oso** *adj.* tufty, tufted.
**cespo** *m.* tuft.
**cespu·gli-o** *m.* bush; thicket; clump (of shrubs, etc.); mass (of hair). **-eto** *m.* (geog.) desert scrub, low bush. **-oso** *adj.* clumped, bushy. **-uto** *adj.* in clumps.
**cessa** *f.* cessation, respite; *senza* —, ceaselessly.
**cess-are** [A1] *intr.* (*aux.* avere) to cease, to stop, to come to an end; — *dal commercio*, to retire from business; *rfl.* to take refuge, to flee; *tr.* to stop; to hold off. **-ato** *part. adj.* ended; past; *-ato pericolo!*, all clear! **-azione** *f.* cessation; end.
**cession-e** *f.* (leg.) cession; transfer; assignment in bankruptcy. **-a·rio** *m.* (leg.) assignee; guarantee; transferee.
**cesso** *m.* earth closet, latrine.
**cest-a** *f.* hamper, basket; wicker cart. **-a·io** *m.* basket-maker; baker's boy.
**cestin-o** *m. dim.* small basket; — *da viaggio*, packed meal in a paper bag sold on railway platforms; waste-paper basket. **-are** [A1] *tr.* to put in the waste-paper basket; to scrap.
**cest-o**[1] *m.* tuft, clump; head (of plants). **-ire** [D2] *intr.* (*aux.* avere) to throw out shoots.
**cest-o**[2] *m.* basket, hamper; (sport) *palla al* —, basket-ball. **-ista** *m.* basket-ball player. **-i·stico** *adj.* pertaining to basket-ball.
**cesura** *f.* (prosod.) caesura.
**ceto** *m.* class; — *medio*, middle classes.
**cetra** *f.* (mus.) lyre; (fig.) poetry; *suonare la* —, to write poetry.
**cetriolo** *m.* cucumber; (colloq.) blockhead.
**che**[1] *rel. prn. indecl.* who; whom; which; that; what; *interr. prn. indecl.* what?; *adj. indecl.* — *uomo?*, what man?; *n.m. indecl.* something, a thing; *il* —, which, the which, which thing; (pron. **che,** not **che**) — *!, ma — !*, nonsense!
**che**[2] *conj.* than; as; *tanto* —, as soon as; *altro — !*, rather!, I should say so!
**che**[3] *conj.* that; *sia* —, whether; *sempre* —, provided that; *a* —, in order that; *se non* —, except that.
**che**[4] *conj.* because.
**checche** *prn. indecl.* whatever, no matter what.
**checchessi·a** *prn. indecl.* whatever it may be.
**chel-e, -i** *f.pl.* claws, nippers, pincers.
**che·lide** *f.* (zool.) tortoise.
**cheppia** *f.* (ichth.) shad.
**cher·m-es** *m. indecl.* kermes. **-is, -isi, -isi** *adj.*, *n.m. indecl.* **-isino** *adj.*, *n.m.* crimson.
**cheru·bico** *adj.* cherubic, cherub-like.
**cherubino** *m.* cherub; (theol.) *i Cherubini*, the Cherubim.
**chetare** [A1 c] *tr.* to quieten, to calm; *rfl.* to fall quiet; to be hushed.
**chetichella** *adv. phr. alla* —, quietly; secretly.
**cheto** *adj.* hushed, silent; tranquil, still; not divulged; *adv.* silently; *di* —, secretly.
**chi** *interr. prn. indecl.* who?; whom? — *sa?*, I wonder, who knows?; — *lo sa?*, who can tell?; — *è?*, who's there?, who is he?; *Chi è?*, Who's Who?; *indef. prn. indecl.* he who; they who; whoever; some people; *chi ... chi*, some ... others.
**chiac·chier-a** *f.* gossip, idle talk; *fare quattro -e*, to have a chat; *stare sulle -e*, to listen, to gossip. **-are** [A1 s] *intr.* (*aux.* avere) to chat, to talk; to chatter, to gossip; to backbite. **-ata** *f.* informal talk; chat. **-evole** *adj.* chattering, talkative. **-io** *m.* (*pl.* **-ii**) constant chattering; murmur, confused babble. **-one** *m.*, **-ona** *f.* chatterbox, gasbag; person who cannot keep a secret.
**chiama** *f.* call; roll-call; *fare la* —, to call the roll.
**chiam-are** [A1] *tr.* to call; to summon; to hail; to send for; to name; — *al telefono*, to ring up; — *in disparte*, to call aside; *rfl.* to be called; *come si -a, Lei?*, what is your name? **-ata** *f.* call; summons; *-ata telefonica*, telephone call.
**chiana** *f.* swamp, marsh.
**chianti** *m. indecl.* chianti, a red or white wine named after the district in Tuscany.
**chiappa**[1] *f.* seizing, catching catch.
**chiappa**[2] *f.* buttock.
**chiapp-are** [A1] *tr.* to catch; to seize by surprise; (colloq.) to get. **-arello, -atello, -erello** *m.* trap, catch.
**chiapp-o**[1] *m.* catch, object caught; trap. **-ino** *m. dim.* trap; catch; object caught; police spy.
**chiapp-o**[2] *m.* ring for attaching a rope. **-one** *m. augm.* ring bit.
**chiap·pol-a** *f.* bagatelle; frivolous person. **-are** [A1 s] *tr.* to catch (a person) out.
**Chiara**[1] *pr.n.f.* Clare; Clara.
**chiara**[2] *f.* raw white of egg; (paint.) light (in a picture).
**chiarezza** *f.* clearness, clarity; brightness; distinction.
**chiarific-are** [A2 s] *tr.* to clarify; to clear (up). **-azione** *f.* clarification.
**chiarire** [D2] *tr.* to clarify; to clear up; (paint.) to lighten; *rfl.* to become clear; to make oneself clear; to gain information; (of the sky) to clear up.
**chiarità** *f.* brightness, splendour; clarity.
**chiar-o** *adj.* clear, bright; *giorno* —, broad daylight; light (of a colour); *vestir di* —, to wear

light colours; transparent; pale; plain, intelligible; evident; famous, renowned; *n.m.* light; light colour, — *di luna*, moonlight; *mettere in* —, to make clear; *traduzione in* —, decoding; white of egg; (paint.) high light; *adv.* clearly, plainly; — *e tondo*, frankly. **-eggiare** [A3c] *tr.* to make clear; to represent clearly.

**chiarọre** *m.* light; glimmer, gleam; *il — dell'alba*, the first light of dawn; (paint.) brightness, light.

**chiaroscuro** *m.* (paint.) light and shade (in one colour), chiaroscuro.

**chiarosonante** *adj.* (poet.) resonant; clear-sounding.

**chiaroveggen-te** *adj.* clear-sighted; far-seeing; clairvoyant. **-za** *f.* clear-sightedness; clairvoyance.

**chiass-o**[1] *m.* shrill noise; babble of voices; rattle of plates, uproar; din. **-are** [A1] *intr.* (*aux.* avere) to make a noise. **-ata** *f.* noisy entertainment; disturbance; hubbub. **-ọso** *adj.* noisy; loud; garish.

**chiasso**[2] *m.* alley, narrow street.

**chiatt-a** *f.* flat-bottomed boat, lighter; *ponte di -e*, pontoon bridge; — *del passo*, ferry. **-ai(u)olo** *m.* lighterman, ferryman, bargee. **-o** *adj.* flat; flattened. **-ọne, -ọni** *adv.* quietly; *andare chiatton -oni*, to creep along quietly.

**chiavac·cio** *m.* large door-bolt; *con tanto di* —, bolted and barred.

**chiava·io** *m.* locksmith; keeper of the keys.

**chiavard-a** *f.* screw-bolt; horse-brass. **-are** [A1] *tr.* to bolt.

**chiav-e** *f.* key; *chiudere a* —, to lock; *sotto* —, under lock and key; *buco della* —, keyhole; (mus.) clef; key (tonality); *fuori* —, out of tune; in the wrong key; key (to a code, etc.); clue; (archit.) keystone; (fig.) *industrie-chiave*, key industries. **-ẹtta** *f. dim.* *-etta della luce*, electric-light switch; cock, tap; *-etta da orologio*, watch-key.

**chiavello** *m.* nail, peg.

**chia·vica** *f.* sewer; sluice-gate; transverse road drain.

**chiavistello** *m.* iron bolt; door-bolt; window-bolt; *tirare il* —, to draw the bolt, to unbolt; *mettere il* —, to shoot the bolt, to bolt; ratchet.

**chiazz-a** *f.* stain; large spot. **-are** [A1] *tr.* to stain, to cover with spots.

**chic·chera** *f.* small coffee cup; cup without handles; *pl.* (bot.) *chicchere e rampicanti*, climbers, cups-and-saucers.

**chicchessi·a** *prn. indecl.* anybody whatsoever, no matter who.

**chicchirichì** *m. indecl.* the crowing of a cock, cock-a-doodle-doo.

**chic-co** *m.* (*pl.* **-chi**) grain (of corn); bean (of coffee); berry (of a bunch); bead on a rosary; *un — d'uva*, a grape.

**chie·dere** [B6] *tr.* to ask; to ask for; — *perdono*, to beg pardon; — *scusa*, to apologize; — *in prestito*, to ask for the loan of.

**chiẹric-a** *f.* (eccl.) tonsure; (joc.) bald spot. **-uto** *adj.* (eccl.) tonsured; *n.m.* shaveling.

**chiẹri-co** *m.* (eccl.) cleric, ecclesiastic; sacristan. **-cato** *m.* clerical status; clergy. **-cheri·a** *f.* clerics, clergy.

**chiesa** *f.* church; *andare in* —, to go to church.

**chiesta** *f.* request, petition.

**chi·glia** *f.* (naut.) keel; *per* —, fore and aft.

**chilo**[1] *m.* (med.) chyle; *fare il* —, to let one's food settle, to rest after a meal.

**chil-o**[2] *m.* kilo, kilogramme. **-ogramma, -ogrammo** *m.* kilogramme. **-ometrag·gio** *m.* distance travelled in kilometres (equivalent to 'mileage'). **-o·metro** *m.* kilometre.

**chimera** *f.* (myth.) chimera; (fig.) foolish illusion.

**chime·rico** *adj.* imaginary, fanciful; chimerical.

**chi·mic-a** *f.* chemistry. **-o** *adj.* chemical; *n.m.* chemist, research chemist.

**chimono** *m.* kimono.

**china** *f.* downward slope; *alla* —, downhill; *a* —, sloping; (fig.) downward path; declining years.

**chin-are** [A1] *tr.* to incline; *rfl.* to bear; to bend; to stoop; to submit. **-ata** *f.* slope, descent. **-atura** *f.* curvature; bending; bow. **-ẹvole** *adj.* pliable.

**chinca·glie** *f.pl.* knick-knacks; trinkets.

**chinina** *f.* (pharm.) quinine.

**chino** *adj.* drooping, bent, bowed; *a capo* —, with bowed head.

**chioca** *f.* sewer.

**chioccare** [A2] *tr.* to crack (a whip); to snap (the fingers).

**chioc·ci-a** *f.* (*pl.* **chiocce**) brooding hen or other bird; mother hen; *far la* —, to crouch. **-are** [A3] *intr.* (*aux.* avere) to cluck; to give a cracked sound (of pottery); to crouch round the fire. **-ata** *f.* clutch (of eggs or chicks).

**chioc·c-io** *adj.* (*m.pl.* **-i**) hoarse, raucous.

**chioc·ciol-a** *f.* (zool.) snail, and any other gastropod with a snail-shaped shell; *scala a* —, spiral staircase. **-ino** *m.* bun shaped like spiral, twist.

**chio·ccol-o** *m.* bird whistle. **-are** [A1s] *intr.* (*aux.* avere) to whistle (of birds); to gurgle (of water). **-ìo** *m.* (*pl.* **-ìi**) whistling of birds.

**chiod-o** *m.* stud; — *a forcella*, staple; — *di garofono*, clove; — *a uncino*, wall hook; (in a road) *passaggio tracciato da -i*, studded crossing; *aver un — fisso*, to have a bee in one's bonnet; *roba da -i*, rubbish.

**chiom-a** *f.* head of hair, tresses; mane; tail (of a comet); (poet.) foliage. **-ato** *adj.* long-haired; with flowing hair; long-tailed (of a comet); (poet.) leafy. **-ọso** *adj.* long-haired.

**chiọsa** *f.* explanatory note; comment; gloss; dirty mark, stain.

**chiọs-are** [A1] *tr.* to annotate; to explain; to gloss. **-atọre** *m.* annotator; commentator.

**chios-co** *m.* (*pl.* **-chi**) kiosk; stall; bookstall; hut.

**chiostra** *f.* enclosed space; *la — dei monti*, the encircling hills.

**chiostro** *m.* cloister; cathedral close; (fig.) monastic life; (poet.) enclosed space.

**chiotto** *adj.* quiet as a mouse.

**chio·volo** *m.* peg; joint, articulation.

**chiozza** *f.* grassy turf.

**chi·rie, chi·riele·ison,** (pop.) **chirieleisonne** *m.* (liturg.; mus.) Kyrie (eleison).

**chirologi·a** *f.* deaf-and-dumb language.

**chirom-ante** *m., f.* palmist, fortune-teller. **-an·tico** *adj.* relating to palmistry, chiromantic. **-anzi·a** *f.* palmistry, fortune-telling, chiromancy.

**Chirọne** *pr.n.m.* (myth.) Chiron.

**chironomi·a** *f.* art of gesture; gesticulation.

**chirot·teri** *m.pl.* (zool.) chiroptera; bats.

**chir-urgi·a** *f.* surgery; — *estetica*, plastic surgery. **-ur·gico** *adj.* surgical. **-urgo** *m.* (*pl.* **-urghi**) surgeon.

**Chisciott-e** *pr.n.m.* *Don* —, Don Quixote. **-ẹsco** *adj.* (*m.pl.* **-ẹschi**) Quixotic (also **donchisciottẹsco**).

**chissà** *phr.* who knows?; Heaven knows.

**chissisi·a** *prn.* (*indecl.* or *pl.* **chissisi·ano**) whoever it is; whoever he may be; *pl.* whoever they are.

**chitarr-a** *f.* (mus.) guitar. **-ista** *m., f.* guitar-player.

**chiù** *m. indecl.* (orn.) scops owl.

**chiucchiupic·chio** *m.* (orn.) chaffinch.

**chiudenda** *f.* fence, partition; enclosure.

**chiu·dere** [B3] to shut, to close; — *a chiave*, to lock; — *bottega*, to shut up shop; — *in carcere*, to send to prison; — *il pugno*, to clench one's fist; — *la luce*, to switch off the light; *hanno chiuso l'acqua*, they've turned off the water; — *un buco*, to block up a hole; — *un discorso*, to conclude a speech; *intr.* (*aux.* avere) to

close, to shut; *chiudono la domenica*, they shut on Sundays; *Signori, si chiude!*, Time, gentlemen, please!; *rfl.* to shut oneself up; to close; to be closed; to come to an end; (of a wound) to heal, to close up; (of the sky) to become overcast.

**chiunque** *prn. indecl.* whoever; whomsoever; anyone, anybody; anyone who; anyone whom.

**chiurl-o** *m.* bird-catching with bird-lime and decoy owl or bird-call; (orn.) curlew. **-are** [A1] *intr.* (*aux.* avere) to hoot.

**chiusa** *f.* barrier, dam, lock-gate; water gate; smallholding, enclosure; ending, close.

**chiusino** *m.* stone lid; metal cover; secret drawer; partition.

**chiuso** *part.* of **chiudere**; *adj.* shut, closed; *a porte chiuse*, behind closed doors; off; enclosed; close; secret, taciturn, reserved; (of the sky) cloudy, overcast; *n.m.* enclosure; pen, fold.

**chiusura** *f.* closure; sluice-gate; fastening; — *lampo*, zip fastener; *discorso di* —, closing speech; (comm.) *data della* — *dei conti*, settling-day.

**ci**[1] *f., m.* name of the letter C.

**ci**[2] *pers. prn., 1st pl., acc., dat. conj.* (before lo, la, gli, li, le, ne: **ce**) us, to us; *eccoci*, here we are; *rfl. prn.* ourselves; *recip. rfl. prn.* each other, one another.

**ci**[3] *adv.* (before lo, la, gli, li, le, ne: **ce**). **1.** here; there; — *siamo*, here we are; there we are; *c'è*, there is; — *sono*, there are; *c'è chi dice*, there are some who say; *c'era una volta*, once upon a time there was; *qui — sono stato due anni*, I was here two years; *non c'è*, it's, he's, she's not here; *c'è Luigi?*, is Luigi there?; *non ce n'è*, there isn't any. **2.** Replacing a neuter prn.: to it, in it; by it; about it; it; — *credo*, I believe it; — *ho rimorso*, I regret it. **3.** Instead of pers. prn. 3rd sing., pl., dat. to him, with him; to her, with her; to them; — *parlo ora*, I'm talking to him (her, them) now; *con lui non — posso stare*, I can't bear him.

**cià**[1] *m.* (onomat.) the sound of water running softly; the sound of a slap.

**cià**[2] *m. indecl.* (bot.) tea-plant.

**ciab-a** *m.* chatterbox, jabberer. **-are** [A1] *intr.* (*aux.* avere) to jabber, to chatter. **-ọna** *f.*, **-ọne** *m.* chatterbox.

**ciabatt-a** *f.* slipper, worn-out shoe; (fig.) slut. **-are** [A1] *intr.* (*aux.* avere) to shuffle along; to walk with the flapping noise of backless slippers. **-ino** *m.* cobbler; bungler. **-ọna** *f.*, **ọne** *m.* slovenly person; bungler.

**ciac-co** *m.* (*pl.* **-chi**) hog; parasite; glutton; *adj.* hoggish.

**ciac·cola** *f.* slut, slattern.

**ciald-a** *f.* large wafer; waffle; cockade. **-ọne** *m.* thin curled-up wafer.

**ciambella** *f.* ring-shaped cake, air cushion.

**ciambellano** *m.* chamberlain, steward, court official.

**ciambolare** [A1 s] *intr.* (*aux.* avere) to prate, to prattle; to gossip.

**ciampicare** [A2 s] *intr.* (*aux.* avere) to shuffle along; to stumble; (fig.) to dawdle.

**cian-a** *f.* woman of the Florentine slums; slut. **-ẹsco** *adj.* (*m.pl.* **-ẹschi**) slatternly, sluttish. **-ìo** *m.* brawling. **-o** *m.* ruffian. **-ume** *m.* rabble, riff-raff.

**cianca** *f.* (joc.) leg; shank.

**cian·c-ia** *f.* (*pl.* **-e**) tittle-tattle, *dare -e*, to give promises (instead of payment); *uscire a -e*, to come to nothing. **-iare** [A3] *intr.* (*aux.* avere) to prate, to waste one's breath; to jest, to joke.

**ciancicare** [A2 s] *intr.* (*aux* avere) to mumble; to speak hesitantly.

**ciancịon-e** *m.*, **-a** *f.* chatterbox.

**cianfrugli-are** [A5] *tr.* to bungle; *intr.* (*aux.* avere) to idle; to bungle. **-ọna** *f.*, **-ọne** *m.* bungler.

**cianfrụsa·glia** *f.* rubbish, junk; *negozio di* —, junk shop.

**cian·gol-a** *f.* chatter; nonsense. **-are** [A1 s] *intr.* (*aux.* avere) to chatter.

**ciangott-are** [A1] *intr.* (*aux.* avere) to lisp; to twitter, to cheep. **-ìo** *m.* lisping; twittering, cheeping.

**cian-o**[1] *m.*, **-ume** *m.* see under **ciana.**

**ci·an-o**[2] *m.* blue colour; (bot.) — *minore*, cornflower; — *maggiore*, alpine cornflower. **-idrato** *m.* (chem.) cyanide. **-ografi·a** *f.* blueprint.

**cia·o** *excl.* (fam.) hello!; goodbye!

**ciappa** *f.* loop in a strap for a buckle.

**ciap·pol-a** *f.* graving tool, small chisel. **-are** [A1 s] *tr.* to grave, to carve.

**ciarl-a** *f.* gossip; hearsay; tittle-tattle. **-are** [A1] *intr.* (*aux.* avere) to gossip, to chatter. **-iera** *f.*, **-iere, -iero** *m.* gossip; chatterer. **-ìo** *m.* gossiping, gossip. **-ọna** *f.*, **-ọne** *m.* wind-bag, gossip.

**ciarlatan-o** *m.* charlatan, quack, impostor; mountebank; cheap-jack. **-eri·a** *f.*, **-ịsmo** *m.* charlatanism.

**ciarpa** *f.* scarf; neckerchief; sash.

**ciascheduno, ciascuno** *prn.* each one, every one; each person; everyone; *adj.* each, every.

**cib-are** [A1] *tr.* to feed; to nourish; *di che cosa -i il tuo cane?*, what do you feed your dog on?; *rfl.* to feed; *-arsi di*, to feed on; to eat; *i gufi si -ano di topi*, owls live on mice; *-arsi di speranza*, to live on hope. **-a·rio** *adj.* nutritive, alimentary.

**cibo** *m.* food.

**cibo·rio** *m.* (archit.) canopy above the High Altar; (liturg.) ciborium.

**cica** *f.* a mere nothing; *non saperne* —, to know nothing about it.

**cicad-a, cical-a** *f.* (ent.) cicada; *non valere una* —, to be not worth a button; chatterbox; (electr.; teleg.) buzzer.

**cicatr-ice** *f.* scar; scab; cicatrix. **-izzare** [A1] *tr.* to scar; to cicatrize; *rfl.* to form a scab; to heal.

**cicc-a** *f.* stub of a cigar; cigarette end; quid of tobacco. **-are** [A2] *intr.* (*aux.* avere) to chew tobacco; (fig.) to grumble.

**cic·chera** *f.* cup.

**cicchẹtt-o** *m.* glass of brandy; (colloq.) reproof, scolding. **-are** [A1 c] *intr.* (*aux.* avere) to drink spirits; to tipple.

**cic·ci-a** *f.* (pop.) meat; (fam.) flesh; *avere molta* —, to be plump; *di* —, in the flesh, real. **-ọna** *f.*, **-ọne** *m.* fat person, fatty. **-ọso** *adj.* plump. **-uto** *adj.* plump, fleshy.

**Cicerọn-e**[1] *pr.n.m.* Cicero. **-iano** *adj.* Ciceronian.

**cicerọne**[2] *m.* guide.

**cicịsbe·o** *m.* (hist.) recognized gallant of a married woman; (fig.) lady-killer.

**Ci·cladi** *pr.n.f.pl.* (geog.) Cyclades Islands.

**ciclamino** *m.* (bot.) cyclamen; (mil.) — *imboscato*, evader of military service, coward.

**ci·clico** *adj.* cyclic, cyclical.

**cicl-o** *m.* cycle; — *di una malattia*, course of a disease; (colloq.) bike. **-a·bile** *adj.* fit for cycling (of a road). **-ịsmo** *m.* cycling; cycle racing. **-ista** *m., f.* cyclist. **-i·stico** *adj.* pertaining to cycling or cycle racing. **-omotọre** *m.* autocycle, power-assisted cycle. **-opista** *f.* cycle track. **-oturịsmo** *m.* pleasure cycling. **-oturista** *m., f.* tourist cyclist.

**cicl-ọne** *m.* cyclone. **-o·nico** *adj.* cyclonic; *area -onica*, cyclonic depression.

**Cicl-ope** *pr.n.m.* (myth.) Cyclops; (fig.) monster, one-eyed creature. **-o·pico, -o·pio** *adj.* cyclopic.

**ciclostile** *m.* duplicator, cyclostyle; *carta per* —, stencil (for duplicator).

**cicọgna** *f.* (orn.) stork; (mech.) long lever.

**cico·ria** *f.* (bot.) endive; — *salvatica*, wild chicory; coffee-substitute.

**cicuta** *f.* (bot.) hemlock.

**cie-co** *adj.* (*pl.* **-chi**) blind;

sightless; — *da un occhio,* blind in one eye; (fig.) unquestioning; inconsiderate; unobservant; *alla -ca,* blindly, without looking; *vicolo —,* blind alley; *n.m.* blind person; ignorant person. **-ca** *f.* blind woman, blind girl.

**cielo** *m.* sky; heaven; *toccare il — con un dito,* to be overjoyed; *alzare al —,* to praise to the skies; climate; atmosphere; Heaven; *andare in —,* to go to Heaven; top, roof, ceiling; tester, canopy.

**cifr-a** *f.* cipher, figure, digit; code; secret writing; monogram, initials; (comm.) — *di affari,* turnover; — *globale,* aggregate amount. **-are** [A1] *tr.* to code; to embroider with a monogram. **-a·rio** *m.* code, cipher system.

**ci·gli-o** *m.* (*f.pl.* **-a**) eyelash; brow; (poet.) eye, face; *aggrottare le -a,* to frown; *in un batter di —,* in the twinkling of an eye; (*m.pl.* **cigli**) bank; brink; verge, rim. **-ọne** *m.* embankment; bank; border, edge; hill-brow, hill-side. **-uto** *adj.* with eyelashes, fringed.

**cigno** *m.* swan; (fig.) poet; musician; *canto del —,* swan-song; (astron.) Cygnus.

**cigol-are** [A1 s] *intr.* (*aux.* avere) to creak; to squeak; to hiss; to twitter. **-ìo** *m.* prolonged creaking, hissing.

**Cile** *pr.n.f.* (geog.) Chile.

**cilẹcca** *f.* broken promise; near-miss; misfire; *ho sparato e ho fatto —,* I shot and missed.

**cilestr-o** *adj.* (poet.) pale blue, sky-blue. **-ino** *adj.* pale blue.

**cili·cio** *m.* hairshirt; sackcloth; (fig.) penance, torment.

**cilie·g-ia** *f.* (*pl.* **-ie**) cherry; *ratafia di -ie,* cherry-brandy; (joc.) *l'amico —,* our friend (who shall be nameless). **-iẹto** *m.* cherry orchard. **-io** *m.* (*pl.* **-i**) (bot.) cherry-tree. **-i(u)olo** *adj.* cherry-coloured; *n.m.* cherry-brandy.

**cilin·drico** *adj.* cylindrical.

**cilindr-o** *m.* cylinder; *cappello a —,* top hat; roller; barrel; drum. **-are** [A1] *tr.* to roll; to put through a roller; to mangle (clothes); *-are una strada,* to roll a road.

**cima** *f.* top, summit; peak; *da — in fondo,* from top to bottom; *in — a,* on top of; highest point, highest degree; (fig.) eminent person; genius; tree-top; tip; end of rope.

**cim-are** [A1] *tr.* to shear (cloth), to clip to an even surface; to poll (a tree), to trim (a shrub); to decapitate. **-ata** *f.* clipping; trimming.

**cim·balo** *m.* (mus.) cymbal; harpsichord.

**cim·berli** *m.pl.* (mus.) cymbals.

**cime·lio** *m.* precious object, treasure; heirloom; relic; curio.

**ciment-are** [A1 c] *tr.* to purify (metals); to assay; to put to the test; to try, to prove; *rfl.* to take a risk; to put oneself to the test; *-arsi in,* to venture upon. **-atọre** *m.* tester; venturer.

**cimẹnt-o** *n.* hazardous trial; contest; testing, proving. **-ọso** *adj.* dangerous, hazardous; venturesome, rash.

**ci·mic-e** *f.* (ent.) bed bug; (colloq.) drawing-pin. **-iọso** *adj.* bug ridden.

**cimiero** *m.* crest of a helmet; (poet.) helmet.

**ciminiera** *f.* smokestack; factory chimney; funnel.

**cimiter-o** *m.* cemetery, graveyard; burial ground. **-iale** *adj.* pertaining to a cemetery.

**cimm-e·rico, -e·rio** *adj.* Cimmerian, gloomy.

**cimurro** *m.* (vet.) nasal catarrh; (joc.) a cold in the head.

**Cin-a** *pr.n.f.* (geog.) China; *inchiostro di —,* Indian ink. **-ẹse** *adj.* Chinese; *n.m.* Chinaman; the Chinese language, Chinese; *f.* Chinese woman. **-eseri·a** *f.* chinoiserie.

**cinabr-o** *m.* cinnabar; sulphide of mercury; red ink; (poet.) the red colour of the lips. **-ẹse** *m.* raddle, red ochre.

**cin·ci-a** *f.* (orn.) titmouse. **-allegra** *f.* (orn.) great tit. **-arella** *f.* (orn.) blue tit.

**cinci·glia** *f.* (zool.) chinchilla; chinchilla fur.

**cincinn-o** *m.* (poet.) curl, curly lock. **-are** [A1] *tr.* to curl (the hair).

**cin-e** *m.* *indecl.* (pop. abbrev.) cinema. **-easta** *m.* person professionally connected with films. **-egiornale** *m.* newsreel. **-ela·ndia** *f.* cinema land. **-epresa** *f.* cine-camera. **-eromanzo** *m.* film love story. **-eteca** *f.* film library. **-etec·nica** *f.* motion-picture technique.

**cinege·tic-a** *f.* sport, shooting, hunting (with dogs). **-o** *adj.* pertaining to hunting with dogs.

**cinnell-e** *f.pl.*, **-i** *m.pl.* (mus.) cymbals.

**ci·nem-a** *m.* *indecl.* cinema. **-a·tica** *f.* kinetics. **-atografare** [A1 s] *tr.* to make a film of, to screen. **-atografi·a** *f.* cinematography; film; cinema show. **-atogra·fico** *adj.* cinematographic, pertaining to the cinema. **-ato·grafo** *m.* cinematograph, projector; cinema. **-u·sica** *f.* film-music.

**cinera·rio** *adj.* cinerary.

**cine·r-eo** *adj.* ashy, ashen, grey; (astron.) *luce -ea,* earthshine. **-igno, -ino** *adj.* ashen, grey. **-i·zio** *adj.* ash-coloured, grey.

**cinẹse** *adj.*, *n.m.*, *f.* See under **Cina.**

**cin-e·tica** *f.* kinetics. **-e·tico** *adj.* kinetic. **-etosco·pio** *m.* kinetoscope.

**cingalẹse** *adj.* Cingalese; *n.m.* native of Ceylon; Cingalese language; *f.* Cingalese woman.

**cin·g-ere** [C5] *tr.* to gird; to girdle; to surround; to encompass; to wreathe; to border; *rfl.* to gird oneself; to put on a belt; *-ersi per i lombi,* to gird up one's loins.

**cin·ghi-a** *f.* strap; belt; *pl.* braces; guiding reins. **-are** [A4] *tr.* to lace up, to tie with a belt, to strap. **-atura** *f.* strapping up; girth of a saddle. **-ẹtta** *f.* *dim.* *-etta per l'orologio,* watch-strap.

**cinghial-e** *m.*, **-a** *f.* (zool.) wild pig; wild boar; pigskin. **-essa** *f.* wild sow.

**cingolato** *adj.* (eng.) tracked, caterpillar.

**cin·golo** *m.* belt, girdle; (eng.) track, caterpillar track; *suola di —,* track shoe.

**cinguett-are** [A1 c] *intr.* (*aux.* avere) to twitter, to chirp; to chatter, to prattle; to lisp, to speak indistinctly; *tr.* — *una lingua,* to speak a language badly. **-ìo** *m.* continual twittering, chirping; constant chattering. **-ọna** *f.*, **-ọne** *m.* chatterbox.

**ciniatri·a** *f.* veterinary care of dogs; canine medicine.

**ci·nico** *adj.* cynical; *n.m.* cynic.

**cini·gia** *f.* smouldering ashes.

**cinịsmo** *m.* cynicism.

**cinnamomo** *m.* (bot.) cinnamon-tree; bark of the same.

**cino** *adj.* *indecl.* (abbrev. of **cinese,** q.v. under **Cina**) *cino-giapponese,* Sino-Japanese.

**cinoce·falo** *m.* (zool.) baboon.

**cin-ofili·a** *f.* love of dogs. **-o·filo** *m.* dog-fancier. **-ofobi·a** *f.* fear of dogs. **-ọṣura** *f.* (astron.) Ursa Minor; (fig.) cynosure.

**cinquant-a** *card. num.* fifty. **-ena·rio** *m.* jubilee. **-enne** *adj.* fifty-year-old; *n.m.*, *f.* person of fifty. **-en·nio** *m.* period of fifty years, half-century. **-e·ṣimo** *ord. num.* fiftieth. **-ina** *f.* set, group or batch of (about) fifty; *essere sulla -ina,* to be getting on for fifty years of age.

**cinqu-e** *card. num.* five. **-ecente·ṣimo** *ord. num.* five-hundredth. **-ecento** *card. num.* five hundred; *n.m.* *il -ecento,* the sixteenth century. **-ecentẹsco** *adj.* (*m.pl.* **-ecentẹschi**) relating to the sixteenth century. **-ina** *f.* a set of five; about five. **-emila** *card. num.* five thousand. **-emille·ṣimo** *ord. num.* five-thousandth.

**cinque-fo·glie** *m.* (bot.) creeping cinquefoil. **-nervi, -nodi** *m.* (bot.) plantain.

**cinta** *f.* perimeter defences; circuit; bounds.

**cinto** *part.* of **cingere**; *adj.* girt; surrounded; fastened; *n.m.* belt; girdle; truss.
**cin·tol-a** *f.* waist; waistline; waistband. **-o** *m.* shoelace, bootlace; garter. **-ọne** *m.* strap; sling of a gun or rifle.
**cintur-a** *f.* belt, girdle; sash; waist; waistband; middle; — *porta-bretelle,* suspender-belt; safety-belt, seat-belt. **-ọne** *m.* belt; sling of a gun or rifle.
**Cin·zia** *pr.n.f.* Cynthia; (poet.) the moon.
**ciò** *prn. indecl.* that; this; *a — che,* so that, in order that; *con tutto —,* in spite of all that; *essere da —,* to be able for it; — *nonostante,* nevertheless.
**ciocca** *f.* lock of hair, tuft; cluster.
**ciocchẹ̀** *prn. indecl.* that which; whatever.
**cịocci-a**[1] *f.* (fam.) nipple. **-are** [A3 c] *intr.* (*aux.* avere) (of a baby) to suck.
**cioc·ci-a**[2] *f.* busybody, meddler. **-are** [A3] *intr.* (*aux.* avere) to meddle in other people's affairs. **-ọna** *f.*, **-ọne** *m.* busybody.
**cioc-co** *m.* (*pl.* **-chi**) log; block; (fig.) blockhead.
**cioccolat-a** *f.* drinking chocolate, cocoa. **-ino** *m.* a chocolate. **-o** *m.* chocolate.
**cioè** *adv.* that is, that is to say, namely.
**ciọn-co** *adj.* (*m.pl.* **-chi**) broken; downcast; drooping.
**ciondolare** [A1 sc] *intr.* (*aux.* avere) to dangle; to sway; to walk unsteadily; *tr.* to dangle; to swing.
**ciọndol-o** *m.* drop-earring; pendant; medal. **-ọni** *adv.* dangling; swinging from side to side.
**cio·tol-a** *f.* money-box; (anat.) socket of the hip-joint, acetabulum. **-ata** *f.* bowlful.
**ciott-a** *m.*, **-ọne** *m.* busybody, meddler; bore.
**ciotto** *adj.* lame; limping.
**ciot·tol-o** *m.* pebble; cobblestone. **-ato** *part. adj.* cobbled; *n.m.* cobbled road. **-ọso** *adj.* pebbly, pebbled.
**ciparisso** *m.* (bot.) cypress spurge.
**ci·pero** *m.* (bot.) sedge.
**cipi·gli-o** *m.* frown; *fare il —,* to frown. **-ọso** *adj.* frowning; touchy.
**cipoll-a** *f.* onion; *sottile come un velo di —,* paper-thin; bulb. **-ac·cio** *m.* (bot.) grape hyacinth. **-a·io** *m.* onion bed; onion seller. **-ẹtta** *f.*, **-ina** *f.* spring onion, young onion; *-ine sott'aceto,* pickled onions.
**cippo** *m.* cippus, sepulchral pillar.
**cipress-o** *m.* (bot.) cypress. **-a·ia** *f.*, **-ẹto** *m.* cypress grove. **-ino** *m.* tamarisk; Lombardy poplar.
**ci·pria** *f.* face powder; toilet powder.
**Ciprigna** *pr.n.f.* (myth.) Venus.
**ciprigno** *adj.* of Cyprus.
**Cipr-o** *pr.n.m.* (geog.) Cyprus; wine from Cyprus. **-iota, -iotto** *adj.*, *n.m.* Cypriot.
**circa** *adv.* about; approximately; nearly; *a un bel —,* more or less; *prep.* about, regarding, as to, concerning.
**Circas·s-ia** *pr.n.f.* (geog.) Circassia. **-o** *adj.*, *n.m.* Circassian.
**Circe** *pr.n.f.* (myth.) Circe.
**cir-co** *m.* (*pl.* **-chi**) circus; — *equestre,* circus (entertainment).
**circol-are**[1] [A1 s] *intr.* (*aux.* avere, essere) to circulate; to keep moving; to travel; (of money) to be current; *fare —,* to put into circulation; *tr.* to send round, to circulate. **-ante** *adj.* circulating; moving. **-azione** *f.* circulation, rotation, going round; traffic; *vietata la -azione,* no thoroughfare; *tassa di -azione,* road tax; (comm.) turnover, sales.
**circolar-e**[2] *adj.* circular; *biglietto —,* tourist ticket; (comm.) *assegno —,* bank draft. **-mẹnte** *adv.* round in a circle.
**circolare**[3] *f.* circular; *mandare una — a,* to circularize.
**cir·colo** *m.* circle; circuit, region, area; club, society, group.
**circon-ci·dere** [C3] *tr.* to circumcize. **-cisịone** *f.* circumcision.
**circondare** [A1 c] *tr.* to surround; to encircle; to accompany.
**circon-durre** [B2] *tr.* to lead round; to deceive. **-ferenza** *f.* circumference. **-flessịone** *f.* circumflexion. **-flesso** *adj.* circumflex; *n.m.* circumflex accent. **-fluenza** *f.* circumfluence. **-fluire** [D2] *intr.* (*aux.* avere) to flow round about. **-fọndere** [C2] *tr.* to fuse together, to blend; to diffuse. **-fuṣo** *part. adj.* fused, blended; diffused. **-locuzịone** *f.* circumlocution. **-vallare** [A1] *tr.* to circumvallate; to run a road round, to bypass. **-vallazịone** *f.* circumvallation; outer circle; ring road. **-venire** [D17] *tr.* to circumvent; to overreach; to outwit. **-venzịone** *f.* circumvention. **-vicino** *adj.* circumjacent, round about. **-volare** [A1 c] *intr.* (*aux.* avere) to fly round.
**circo-scri·vere** [C12] *tr.* to circumscribe, to restrict; to describe in minute detail. **-scritto** *part. adj.* circumscribed; (geom.) inscribed. **-scrizịone** *f.* circumscription; (admin.) district; *-scrizione elettorale,* electoral ward. **-spetto** *adj.* circumspect, wary, cautious, guarded. **-spezịone** *f.* circumspection.
**circostan-te** *adj.* nearby; surrounding; *n.m.*, *f.* bystander; person near. **-za** *f.* circumstance; *alla -za,* if the opportunity arises, according to circumstances. **-ziale** *adj.* circumstantial. **-ziare** [A4] *tr.* to circumstantiate.
**circu-ire** [D2] *tr.* to encircle. **-izịone** *f.* round-about speech, circumlocution.
**circu·ito** *m.* circuit; round; race; track.
**circum-cin·gere** [C5] *tr.* to surround, to circumscribe. **-circa** *adv.* about, more or less. **-navigazịone** *f.* circumnavigation.
**Cirena·ica** *pr.n.f.* (geog.) Cyrenaica.
**Cirene** *pr.n.f.* (geog.) Cyrene.
**cirr-o** *m.* curl; tendril; (meteor.) cirrus cloud. **-ato** *adj.* curly.
**ciṣalpino** *adj.* cisalpine, south of the Alps; *adv. alla cisalpina,* according to fashion current under the Cisalpine Republic; *n.f. La Cisalpina,* the Cisalpine Republic; *m.pl. Cisalpini,* soldiers of the Cisalpine Republic.
**ciscranna** *f.* armchair; (colloq.) piece of lumber.
**ciṣmarino** *adj.* on this side of the sea.
**ciṣmontano** *adj.* on this side of the mountain(s).
**ciṣolfaut, cisolfaut·te** *m. indecl.* (mus.) middle C.
**cisp-a** *f.* rheum in the eyes. **-ọso** *adj.* bleary; *l'età -osa,* old age.
**cispadano** *adj.* south of the river Po.
**Cisterc(i)ense** *adj.* Cistercian; *n.m.* Cistercian (monk).
**cisterna** *f.* cistern, tank, reservoir; *acqua di —,* rain-water.
**ci·tara** *f.* (mus.) cithara.
**cit-are** [A1] *tr.* to quote; to cite. **-ante** *part. adj.*, *n.m.*, *f.* (leg.) plaintiff. **-azịone** *f.* citation, quotation.
**Cite·r(e)a** *pr.n.f.* (myth.) Cytherea, Venus.
**citerịore** *adj.* (geog.) hither, on this side, nearer.
**citino** *m.* (bot.) pomegranate flower.
**ci·tiṣo** *m.* (bot.) laburnum.
**cito·fon-o** *m.* internal telephone. **-are** [A1 s] *tr.* to ring up on the internal telephone.
**citrato** *m.* (chem.) citrate.
**ci·trico** *adj.* (chem.) citric.
**citroniera** *f.* glasshouse, greenhouse; conservatory.
**citrull-o** *adj.* stupid; *n.m.* fool. **-ag·gine** *f.*, **-eri·a** *f.* foolishness.
**città** *f. indecl.* city, town; *luce —,* parking lights; — *di mare,* port; — *dei morti,* cemetery.
**cittadella** *f.* citadel; stronghold.
**cittadina**[1] *f. dim.* of **città,** *q.v.*
**cittadina**[2] *f.* citizen (woman).
**cittadin-o** *adj.* belonging to the city, civic, city; *n.m.* citizen; city-dweller. **-anza** *f.* body of citizens; citizenship. **-ẹsco** *adj.*

(*m.pl.* **-eschi**) civil; pertaining to city ways; citified.
**ciuci-are** [A3] *tr. intr.* (*aux.* avere) to hiss (in disapproval). **-ata** *f.* hiss, hissing. **-ato** *part. adj.* hissed off the stage.
**ciu-co** *m.* (*pl.* **-chi**) (pop.) donkey, ass; dunce. **-cag·gine** *f.*, **-cheri·a** *f.* stupidity; stubbornness. **-ca·io** *m.* donkey-driver.
**ciuff-o** *m.* tuft; forelock; quiff; tassel; cluster. **-etto** *m. dim.* child with a forelock; slap, smack. **-one** *m. augm.* person with long, untidy hair.
**ciuffolotto** *m.* (orn.) bullfinch.
**ciurl-are** [A1] *intr.* (*aux.* avere) to shift; — *nel manico*, to be shifty. **-o** *m.* twirl; *adj.* tipsy; infatuated.
**ciurm-a** *f.*, **-a·glia** *f.* rabble, crowd.
**ciurm-are** [A1] *tr.* to charm, to render secure by enchantment; to swindle. **-atore** *m.* charmer; swindler; charlatan.
**civanz-o** *m.* advantage, gain. **-are** *tr.* to provide; *rfl.* to secure, to obtain; *-arsi di*, to take advantage of.
**civare** [A1] *tr.* to prime (a gun).
**civett-a** *f.* (orn.) little owl; (naut.) *nave* —, decoy ship; (zool.) civet; (fig.) flirt. **-are** [A1 c] *intr.* (*aux.* avere) to shoot with little owl as a lure; to flirt. **-eri·a** *f.* coquettishness, flirting.
**ci·vico** *adj.* civic, municipal.
**civile** *adj.* civil; well-bred; civilized; (leg.) *diritto* —, civil law; *abito* —, civilian dress; *colore* —, quiet colour (of clothes); *coraggio* —, moral courage.
**civilizz-are** [A1] *tr.* to civilize. **-azione** *f.* civilization.
**civiltà** *f.* civility, good manners.
**civismo** *m.* good citizenship; civic spirit.
**clamor-e** *m.* clamour; outcry; din. **-oso** *adj.* clamorous; noisy; sensational.
**clandestin-o** *adj.* clandestine; secret; underground. **-amente** *adv.* clandestinely.
**clangore** *m.* sound of a trumpet; clang.
**claretto** *m.* claret.
**clarin-o** *m.* (mus.) clarino, high-pitched trumpet. **-ettista** *m.*, *f.* clarinettist. **-etto** *m.* (mus.) clarinet.
**Clarissa** *pr.n.f.* Clarissa; (eccl.) Poor Clare.
**clarone** *m.* (mus.) bass clarinet.
**class-e** *f.* class; *di* —, high-class; *fuori* —, unequalled. **-are** [A1] *tr.* to class. **-azione** *f.* classing, classification.
**clas·sic-o** *adj.* classic(al); *libro* —, standard work; (colloq.) *questa è -a !*, that's a good one!; *n.m.* classic. **-ista** *m.*, *f.* classicist. **-ismo** *m.* classicism. **-ità** *f. indecl.* quality of a classic.
**classi·fica** *f.* (sport) classified results; (schol.) mark; class-list; classification.
**classific-are** [A2 s] *tr.* to classify; to assess, to mark. **-a·bile** *adj.* classifiable. **-azione** *f.* classification; marking.
**Cla·udia** *pr.n.f.* Claudia; *f. adj. susina* —, greengage.
**claudic-are** [A2 s] *intr.* (*aux.* avere) to limp. **-azione** *f.* limping.
**cla·usola** *f.* clause; proviso; (mus.) cadence.
**claustr-o** *m.* (poet.) cloister, enclosure. **-ale** *adj.* claustral; monastic; *n.m.pl. i -ali*, monks and nuns (of enclosed orders). **-ofobi·a** *f.* claustrophobia.
**clav-a** *f.* club; truncheon. **-iforme** *adj.* club-shaped.
**clavi-cem·balo** *m.* (mus.) harpsichord. **-cor·dio, -cordo** *m.* (mus.) clavichord.
**clavi·col-a** *f.* (anat.) clavicle, collar-bone. **-are** *adj.* clavicular.
**clavi·gero**[1] *m.* key-bearer (*e.g.* St. Peter).
**clavi·gero**[2] *adj.* armed with a club; *n.m.* club-bearer (*e.g.* Hercules).
**clema·tide** *f.* (bot.) wild clematis, traveller's joy.
**Clemente**[1] *pr.n.m.* Clement.
**clemen-te**[2] *adj.* mild, clement; benign. **-za** *f.* clemency; mildness; leniency.
**clept-o·mane** *adj.*, *n.m.*, *f.* kleptomaniac. **-omani·a** *f.* kleptomania. **-osco·pio** *m.* periscope.
**clerical-e** *adj.* (eccl.; pol.) clerical; *n.m.* member of clerical party. **-ismo** *m.*(pol.) clericalism.
**clero** *m.* (eccl.) clergy.
**clessidra** *f.* clepsydra, water-clock; hour-glass.
**cliché** *m. indecl.* (pron. as Fr.) (typ.) block; illustration; cliché, commonplace.
**client-e** *m.*, *f.* client, customer. **-ela** *f.* customers, clientele; patronage.
**clima** *m.* climate; zone.
**climate·rico** *adj.* climacteric.
**clim-a·tico** *adj.* climatic; *stazione -atica*, health resort. **-atologi·a** *f.* climatology.
**cli·nic-a** *f.* clinic, practical teaching of medicine at the bedside; (in University or teaching hospitals) department, section; nursing-home. **-o** *adj.* clinical; *n.m.* doctor teaching at a University, clinical professor.
**cliste·re** *m.* (med.) enema.
**clivo** *m.* hill, rise, slope.
**cli·zia** *f.* (bot.) common sunflower.
**cloa·ca** *f.* sewer; — *massima*, main drain.
**clor-ale, -a·lio** *m.* (chem.) chloral. **-ite** *f.* (miner.) chlorite.
**clo·rico** *adj.* (chem.) chloric.
**clor-o** *m.* (chem.) chlorine. **-ato** *adj.* chlorinated; *n.m.* (chem.) chlorate. **-idrato** *m.* hydrochloride. **-i·drico** *adj.* hydrochloric. **-ofilla** *f.* chlorophyll. **-ofor·mio** *m.* chloroform. **-oformizzare** *tr.* to chloroform. **-osi** *f.* (med.) chlorosis. **-o·tico** *adj.* chlorotic. **-urare** [A1] *tr.* to chlorinate. **-uro** *m.* (chem.) chloride.
**club** *m. indecl.* (pron. **clœb**) club; society; — *nautico*, yacht club; — *alpino*, Alpine Club.
**coabit-are** [A1 s] *intr.* (*aux.* avere) to cohabit, to live together. **-azione** *f.* cohabitation.
**coaccade·mico** *m.* member of the same academy; colleague, fellow.
**coaccusato** *m.* (leg.) co-defendant (in criminal proceedings).
**coad-erire** [D2] *intr.* (*aux.* avere) to cohere. **-erente** *adj.* coherent. **-esione** *f.* cohesion; adhesion.
**coadiutore** *m.* assistant, coadjutor, fellow-helper; (eccl.) coadjutor; curate.
**coagul-are** [A1 s] *tr.*, *rfl.* to coagulate. **-azione** *f.* coagulation.
**coa·gulo** *m.* curds, coagulum; coagulation; rennet.
**coalescenza** *f.* coalescence.
**coal-ire** [D2] *intr.* (*aux.* avere) to join together, to unite. **-izione** *f.* (pol.) coalition.
**coallievo** *m.* fellow-pupil; fellow-disciple.
**coamministratore** *m.* joint-manager, co-director.
**coatt-o** *adj.* (leg.) compulsory; forced; *domicilio* —, internment. **-ivo** *adj.* coercive.
**coautore** *m.* co-author, joint author; joint perpetrator.
**cobalto** *m.* (chem.; miner.) cobalt.
**coboldo** *m.* kobold, brownie, pixie, gnome.
**cobra** *f.* (zool.) cobra.
**coc-ai·na** *f.* cocaine. **-ainismo** *m.*, **-ainomani·a** *f.* addiction to cocaine. **-aino·mane** *m.*, *f.* cocaine addict.
**cocca** *f.* notch in an arrow for the cord of the bow; flap; turned-up corner of a cloth; knot, kink; top, point; *far le cocche*, to snap one's fingers.
**coccarda** *f.* cockade; plait of ribbons of national colours; favour, ribbon or rosette worn as sign of support.
**coc·chia** *f.* (naut.) trawl net.
**coc·chi-o** *m.* coach; chariot. **-ere** *m.* coachman.
**cocchium-e** *m.* bung; bung-hole. **-are** [A1] *tr.* to plug, to close with a bung.
**coc·c-ia** *f.* (pl. **-e**) hilt, guard of a sword; sabre, foil, épée; protuberence; bowl of a pipe; shell of a tortoise or mollusc; (colloq.)

head, topknot. **-iare** [A3] *tr.* to butt, to bump into with one's head.
**coc·c-ige** *m.* (anat.) coccyx. **-i·geo** *adj.* (anat.) coccygeal.
**Coccincina** *pr.n.f.* (geog.) Cochin-China.
**coccinella** *f.* (ent.) ladybird beetle.
**coccinello** *m.* (naut.) toggle.
**coccini·glia** *f.* (ent.) cochineal insect; cochineal (dye.).
**coc·c-io** *m.* (*pl.* **-i**) potsherd; cracked pot; fragment of pottery. **-ia·ia** *f.* crockery cupboard. **-ia·io** *m.* crockery-seller; potter.
**cocciola** *f.* (zool.) cockle.
**cocciut-o** *adj.* pig-headed, stubborn; stiff-necked, proud. **-ag·gine** *f.* pig-headedness; pride.
**cocco**[1] *m.* kermes, cochineal; scarlet cloth.
**coc-co**[2] *m.* (*pl.* **-chi**) (infant.) egg, 'chucky egg'; — *di mamma*, mother's darling.
**coc-co**[3] *m.* (*pl.* **-chi**) (bot.) — *malefico*, poisonous fungus, fly agaric.
**coc-co**[4] *m.* (*pl.* **-chi**) (bot.) cocopalm; *noce di* —, coconut; (text.) coco; *fibra di* —, coir, coconut hair.
**coc-co**[5] *m.* (*pl.* **-chi**) (biol.) coccus.
**coccodrillo** *m.* (zool.) crocodile.
**coc·cola** *f.* (bot.) globular fruit of various plants; (joc.) head, knob; *pl.* berries and small cones of various plants; trinkets, odds and ends.
**coc·col-o** *m.* delicious treat; sort of pastry; cuddly baby. **-are** [A1 s] *tr.* to cuddle; *rfl.* to molly-coddle oneself.
**coc-ente** *adj.* scorching, searing, burning; ardent; pungent. **-imẹnto** *m.* roasting; cooking. **-iọre** *m.* burning; heat. **-itura** *f.* cooking.
**Cocincina** *pr.n.f.* (geog.) Cochin-China.
**co·clea** *f.* spiral staircase; screw.
**co·clide** *f.* (archit.) spiral column.
**cocò** *f.* (slang.) cocaine, 'snow'.
**cocolla** *f.* (eccl.) cowl; (bot.) an edible fungus.
**cocọmero** *m.* water-melon.
**cocoruzzo** *m.* (geog.) summit shaped like a pear.
**cocuzza** *f.* (fam.) pumpkin; head.
**cocuz·zolo** *m.* crown (of the head or of a hat); top of a mountain; topknot; very top, tip; heel of a loaf.
**cod-a** *f.* tail; queue; *fare la* —, to queue (up); (mus.) coda; tail (of a note); *pianoforte a* —, grand piano; pigtail; train (of a dress, etc.); corner (of the eye); *fanale di* —, rear light; — *del grappolo*, stalk of a bunch of grapes. **-ato** *adj.* tailed, having a tail. **-ino** *m.* pigtail; reactionary. **-uto** *adj.* tailed, having a tail; *n.m.* (orn.) pin-tail.
**codard-o** *adj.* cowardly; *n.m.* coward. **-i·a** *f.* cowardliness, cowardice.
**codiare** *tr.* [A4] to tail, to trail, to follow.
**codibu·gnolo** *m.* (orn.) long-tailed tit.
**co·dice** *m.* codex; manuscript; code.
**codicillo** *m.* (leg.) codicil.
**codific-are** [A2 s] *tr.* to codify. **-aziọne** *f.* codification.
**codi-mozzo** *adj.* short-tailed. **-rọsso** *m.* (orn.) redstart. **-rossọne** *m.* (orn.) rock thrush. **-tre·mola** *f.* (orn.) wagtail.
**codinzin·zola** (orn.) wagtail.
**codiọne** *m.* (orn.) rump.
**co·dolo** *m.* tang, the part of a knife that goes into the haft; (mus.) tail (of a violin).
**coefficien-te** *m.* (math.; scient.) coefficient; (fig.) factor, contributory cause. **-za** *f.* co-factor.
**coegual-e** *adj.* co-equal. **-ità** *f.* co-equality.
**coerc-i·bile** *adj.* coercible. **-itivo** *adj.* coercive. **-iziọne** *f.* restriction, compression.
**coered-e** *m.* (leg.) co-heir; *f.* co-heiress. **-ità** *f.* (leg.) co-inheritance.
**coeren-te** *adj.* coherent; consistent. **-za** *f.* coherence; consistence; integrity.
**coeserci·zio** *m.* (comm.) joint working.
**coeṣiọne** *f.* (phys.) cohesion; (fig.) oneness of mind or will.
**coeṣi·st-ere** [C24] *intr.* (*aux.* essere) to co-exist. **-ente** *adj.* co-existent. **-enza** *f.* co-existence.
**coeṣivo** *adj.* cohesive.
**coeta·neo** *adj.* contemporary; of the same age; of the same generation; *n.m.* contemporary.
**coetern-o** *adj.* (theol.) co-eternal. **-ità** *f. indecl.* (theol.) co-eternity.
**coevo** *adj.* coeval, contemporaneous, of the same epoch.
**co·fan-o** *m.* jewel-case; casket; ammunition box; (motor.; aeron.) bonnet. **-ẹtto** *m. dim.* trinket box; *-etto pic-nic*, picnic hamper.
**coffa** *f.* (naut.) crow's nest.
**cogit-are** [A1 s] *intr.* (*aux.* avere) to cogitate; *tr.* to cogitate upon; to think over. **-abọndo** *adj.* pondering, meditative. **-ativa** *f.* thinking faculty. **-ativo** *adj.* relative to thought. **-aziọne** *f.* thinking, reasoning, cogitation. **-ọso** *adj.* pensive.
**co·gliere** [B27] *tr.* to gather; to grasp, to seize; to collect; — *nel segno*, to hit the mark; — *nel fallo*, to catch in the act.
**cogn-ata** *f.* sister-in-law. **-ati·zio** *adj.* by marriage (of a relationship). **-ato** *m.* brother-in-law; *adj.* cognate. **-aziọne** *f.* relationship (by marriage).
**cogniziọne** *f.* knowledge; cognition; cognizance; notion; item of knowledge.
**cognọme** *m.* surname.
**coinci·d-ere** [B1] *intr.* (*aux.* avere) to coincide; to correspond. **-enza** *f.* coincidence; combining; point of intersection; clash (on a time-table); (of trains) connection.
**coinquilino** *m.* fellow-tenant.
**cointeress-are** [A1] *tr.* to implicate, to involve (esp. financially); to share. **-anza** *f.*, **-enza** *f.* participation, association.
**coinvol·gere** [C5] *tr.* to implicate, to drag in.
**co·ito** *m.* coitus, sexual intercourse; copulation; (astron.) conjunction.
**col** *contr.* See under **con.**
**cọla** *f.* sieve, filter, strainer.
**colà** *adv.* there, over there; yonder; *così* —, so so, middling.
**cola-brodo** *m. indecl.* broth-strainer, sieve. **-pasta** *m. indecl.* utensil for straining pasta.
**col-are** [A1 c] *tr.* to strain, to sift, to filter; to pour; *intr.* (*aux.* essere) to trickle, to leak; to drip; to flow; (naut.) — *a fondo*, to sink. **-atọio** *m.* sieve, filter; colander; crucible.
**colaziọne** *f.* breakfast; (N. Ital.) lunch; *prima* —, breakfast.
**col·chico** *m.* (bot.) meadow-saffron.
**colei** *pers. prn. f.* (*pl.* **coloro**) she her; that woman.
**coleot·tero** *m.* (ent.) coleopteron, beetle.
**col-era** *f.* (med.) cholera. **-e·rico** *adj.* choleric. **-erọso** *adj.* affected with cholera; dead as a result of cholera.
**co·lere** (def.) *tr.* (poet.) to revere; to venerate.
**colibrì, co·libri** *m. indecl.* (orn.) humming-bird.
**colimbo** *m.* (orn.) diver, grebe.
**cọlla**[1] *contr.* See under **con.**
**colla**[2] *f.* glue; gum; — *d'amido*, starch paste; (paperm.) size; *dare la* — *a*, to size; — *di pesce*, isinglass; (paint.) — *di rosso d'uovo*, tempera; *colori a* —, gouache.
**collabor-are** [A1 s] *intr.* (*aux.* avere) to collaborate, to co-operate. **-atọre** *m.*, **-atrice** *f.* collaborator, colleague. **-aziọne** *f.* collaboration, co-operation.
**collag·gio** *m.* (paperm.) size.
**collana** *f.* necklace; series, collection.
**collare**[1] *m.* collar for dog, horse or draught animal; neck-band; (eng.) collar; (eccl.) clerical stock or collar.
**collare**[2] [A1] *tr.* (paperm.) to size; *rfl.* (techn.) to cake together.
**collasso** *m.* (med.) collapse.
**collaterale** *adj.* collateral; *n.m.* a collateral kinsman.
**collat-o** *adj.* bestowed, given.

-**ore** *m.* (eccl.) patron of a benefice.
**collaud-are** [A1 s] *tr.* to approve officially; to test; to try; to inspect. -**atore** *m.* (industr.) tester; inspector; (aeron.) *pilota -atore*, test pilot. -**azione** *f.* official approval.
**colla·udo** *m.* approval (of work done or contract fulfilled); (eng.) test; testing; *banco di* —, test-bench.
**collazion-e** *f.* comparison of a copy with an original; textual criticism; collation. -**are** [A1 c] *tr.* to compare; to collate.
**colle** *m.* hill (not so high as a **collina**); (geog.) col, saddle.
**colle-ga** *m.*, *f.* (*m.pl.* -**ghi**, -**ghe**) colleague.
**colleg-are** [A2] *tr.* to unite, to put together; to act as liaison between, to link. -**amento** *m.* union; *comitato di -amento*, liaison committee; linking, uniting; (radio; telev.) relay, link-up; network.
**colle·gi-o** *m.* college; corporation; body (of like people); boarding-school. -**ale** *adj.* done in collaboration. -**ato** *adj.* collegiate.
**col·lera** *f.* anger, rage, ire; *andare in* —, to fly into a rage.
**colle·rico** *adj.* angry, enraged; choleric.
**collettiv-o** *adj.* collective; *firma -a*, joint signature. -**ismo** *m.* collectivism. -**ista** *m.* collectivist. -**ità** *f.* *indecl.* collectivity; the social community; all and sundry; *l'opinione della -ità pubblica*, public opinion; *nell'interesse della -ità*, in the general interest.
**colletto** *m.* collar.
**collezion-e** *f.* collection. -**are** [A1 c] *tr.* to collect, to be a collector of. -**ista** *m.*, *f.* collector.
**collidere** *intr.* to collide; (prosod.) to elide; *rfl.* to collide (with); (prosod.) to elide (with).
**colligiano** *adj.* dwelling in the hills; *n.m.* hill-dweller.
**collilungo** *adj.* long-necked.
**collim-are** [A1] *intr.* (*aux.* avere) to have a common aim, to harmonize, to agree; to match, to correspond; to concur; (eng.; opt.) to collimate, to centre. -**azione** *f.* collimation.
**collin-a** *f.* hill (higher than **colle**). -**oso** *adj.* hilly.
**collisione** *f.* collision; contrast; hiatus.
**collo**[1] *m.* neck; throat; — *del piede*, instep; opening in a garment for the neck; *avere il braccio al* —, to have one's arm in a sling; *tenere in* —, to hold in one's arms; (geog.) col; (mech.) — *d'oca*, crank-shaft.
**collo**[2] *m.* package, bundle; item of luggage. — *postale*, parcel.
**collo**[3] *contr.* See under **con**.
**colloc-are** [A2 s] *tr.* to place; to find employment for; — *a riposo*, to pension off; — *denari*, to invest money; *rfl.* to settle down. -**a·bile** *adj.* employable; marketable. -**amento** *f.* collocation, classification; placing; arrangement.
**collocutore** *m.* one who takes part in a discussion.
**collo·id-e** *adj.*, *n.m.* (chem.) colloid. -**ale** *adj.* (chem.) colloidal.
**collo·quio** *m.* interview; colloquium; discussion.
**collos-o** *adj.* sticky, glutinous. -**ità** *f.* stickiness.
**collotorto** *m.* (*pl.* **collitorti**) hypocrite; (orn.) wryneck.
**collot·tola** *f.* nape of the neck; thick neck.
**colloverde** *m.* (*pl.* **colliverdi**) (orn.) mallard.
**collu·dere** [C3] *intr.* (*aux.* avere) (leg.) to collude, to commit collusion.
**collus-ione** *f.* (leg.) collusion. -**ivo** *adj.* (leg.) collusive.
**collu·vie** *f.* *indecl.* cesspool; mass of filth.
**colma** *f.* (naut.) high water; high water spring.
**colmare** [A1 c] *tr.* to fill to the brim; — *di onori*, to load with honours; — *di gentilezze*, to overwhelm with kindness; — *un vuoto*, to supply a want.
**colmigno** *m.* ridge (of a roof).
**colmo**[1] *m.* top, summit; peak; crown; high tide; prime (of life); *è il* — *!*, it's the limit!.
**colmo**[2] *apocop. part.* of **colmare**, *q.v.*; *adj.* full to the brim; curved, arched.
**colo** *m.* sieve.
**colomb-a** *f.* (orn.) dove; — *migratrice*, passenger pigeon, — *sassarola*, rock dove. -**a·ia** *f.* dovecote. -**a·rio** *m.* pigeon-holes. -**ella** *f.* (orn.) stock dove. -**ina** *f.* *dim.* of **colomba**; Easter egg; Easter cake.
**Colombia** *pr.n.f.* (geog.) Columbia.
**Colombo**[1] *pr.n.m.* Columbus; *Cristoforo* —, Christopher Columbus.
**colombo**[2] *m.* (orn.) pigeon; — *messaggero*, carrier pigeon; — *torraiolo*, rock dove; — *viaggiatore*, homing pigeon.
**co·lon** *m.* *indecl.* (anat.) colon. -**ite** *f.* (med.) colitis.
**Colo·nia** *pr.n.f.* (geog.) Cologne; *acqua di* —, eau-de-Cologne.
**colo·ni-a** *f.* colony; school camp and similar institutions; — *penale*, penal settlement. -**ale** *adj.* colonial; *casa -ale*, farmhouse; *casco -ale*, sun-helmet.
**colo·nic-o** *adj.* relating to a tenant or farm under an agricultural lease on a profit-sharing basis; *casa -a*, farmhouse.
**colonizz-are** [A1] *tr.* to colonize. -**atore** *m.* colonizer. -**azione** *f.* colonization.
**colonn-a** *f.* column; pillar; — *di cifre*, column of figures; (typ.) galley; *bozze in* —, galley-proofs; — *vertebrale*, spinal column; (cinem.) — *sonora*, sound track. -**ato** *m.* colonnade; *adj.* having columns, pillared.
**colonnello** *m.* colonel.
**color-are** [A1 c] *tr.* to colour, to give colour to; to simulate; *rfl.* to paint one's face, to make-up. -**ante** *part. adj.* colouring; *materie -anti*, colouring matter, dyes; *n.m.* (chem.; techn.) dye, dyestuff, colouring material. -**azione** *f.* coloration, colouring; pigmentation.
**color-e** *m.* colour; tint; *di* —, coloured; *-i solidi*, fast colours; *scatola dei -i*, paint-box; *un* — *di verità*, a semblance of truth; *sotto* — *di timidezza*, with a show of timidity; *farne di tutti i -i*, to be up to all sorts of mischief; dye, stain; paint. -**ifi·cio** *m.* paint-factory.
**color-ire** [D2] *tr.* to colour, to paint. -**itura** *f.* colour wash.
**coloro** *pers. prn. pl.* they, those; them.
**Colosse·o** *pr.n.m.* Colosseum.
**coloss-o** *m.* colossus. -**ale** *adj.* colossal, enormous.
**colostro** *m.* (med.) colostrum; (agric.) beest, beestings, beastlings.
**colpa** *f.* guilt; fault; *essere in* —, to be in the wrong; *riconoscere la propria* —, to confess one's guilt; *far* — *ad uno di*, to charge someone with.
**colpabilità** *f.* culpability; imputability; (leg.) guilt; guiltiness.
**colpevol-e** *adj.* culpable; guilty; (leg.) *dichiararsi* —, to plead guilty; *n.m.*, *f.* culprit. -**ezza** *f.* guilt.
**colpire** [D2] *tr.* to hit, to strike; — *nel segno*, to get a bull's eye; — *nel vivo*, to hit the mark; (fig.) to make an impression on, to strike.
**colpo** *m.* blow, thrust, hit; (fig.) disappointment; — *del pennello*, brush-stroke; — *di telefono*, telephone call; — *d'occhio*, glance; *tutto d'un* —, all at once.
**colta** *f.* harvesting, gathering; pond, tank.
**coltell-o** *m.* knife; blade; cutting edge. -**ame** *m.* cutlery. -**ata** *f.* knife wound; (fig.) sorrow, anguish. -**iera** *f.* cutlery cabinet. -**ino** *m.* pocket-knife, penknife; (bot.) iris.
**coltiv-are** [A1 sc] *tr.* to cultivate, to till; to tend. -**atore** *m.* cultivator; grower. -**azione** *f.* cultivation.
**coltivo** *adj.* cultivated; arable.
**colto**[1] *m.* cultivated land; cultivation; religious rite, cult; *adj.* cultured; well-mannered; well-educated.

**colto**[2] *part.* of **cogliere,** *q.v.*
**cọltr-e** *f.* pall; bed-cover. **-ọne** *m. augm.* quilt.
**cọltrice** *f.* feather bed, mattress.
**cọltro** *m.* (agric.) coulter.
**coltur-a** *f.* cultivation; farming; raising; *la rotazione di -e,* rotation of crops.
**co·lubro, colubro** *m.* (zool.) — *liscio,* harmless snake resembling the grass-snake; — *lacertino,* a poisonous, but not dangerous snake; (poet.) snake.
**colu·i** *pers. prn.* he; that person; — *che,* he who, the one who.
**coma** *m.* coma; *in* —, in a coma.
**comand-are** [A1] *tr.* to command; to be in charge; to control; *-i !,* your order, sir ?; — *a distanza,* to remote control. **-ante** *m.* commandant; commander; (naut.) captain.
**comando** *m.* command; order; *al* —, in command; headquarters; *pl.*(eng.) control; drive; — *a mano,* hand drive; — *a distanza,* remote control.
**comare** *f.* godmother; (pop.) gossip, neighbour.
**comas-co** *adj.* (*m.pl.* **-chi**) (geog.) pertaining to Como in N. Italy.
**cọmba** *f.* (geog.) coomb.
**combaciare** [A3] *intr.* (*aux.* avere) to meet at a point; to fit together; to coincide.
**combat·t-ere** [C1] *intr.* (*aux.* avere) to fight; *tr.* to combat; to assail. **-ente** *adj.* fighting, combatant; *n.m.* combatant; service-man. **-imẹnto** *m.* combat, fight; struggle, travail. **-ivo** *adj.* bellicose, combative.
**combin-are** [A1] *tr.* to arrange; to combine; to settle; *intr.* (*aux.* avere) to match, to go with; to chance; *recip. rfl.* to come to an agreement; to coincide. **-azịone** *f.* combination; chance; *per pura -azione,* by sheer coincidence.
**combric·col-a** *f.* gang; merry party of friends; coterie, clique. **-are** [A1 s] *intr.* (*aux.* avere) to gang together. **-ọne** *m.* member of a gang.
**combu·glio** *m.* confusion; medley, hotch-potch.
**combust-i·bile** *adj.* combustible; *n.m.* fuel. **-iọne** *f.* combustion; (med.) burn. **-ivo** *adj.* burnable, suitable as fuel. **-o** *adj.* burned; set on fire; (astron.) *Via -a,* Milky Way.
**combutta** *f.* conspiratorial group; tangled mass, confusion; *in* —, in a gang, conspiring.
**cọme** *adv.* how; in what way; *come?,* — *dici?,* what did you say ?; *ma* — *!,* surely not!; as; like; in the same way as; to the same extent as; in the capacity of.
**come(c)chẹ** *conj.* in whatever way, no matter how, however; although.
**comẹta** *f.* (astron.) comet; (on a horse) blaze, star.
**co·mic-o** *adj.* comic, comical; funny; (theatr.) relating to comedy; dramatic; *n.m.* (theatr.) comedian; actor; *Capo* —, actor manager. **-ità** *f. indecl.* (theatr.) comic quality; burlesque.
**comi·gnolo** *m.* (bldg.) ridge of a roof; ridge-tile; top of a stack.
**cominci-are** [A3] *tr.*, *intr.* (*aux.* essere, avere) to begin, to commence, to start; *n.m.* beginning opening; *al* —, at the outset. **-amẹnto** *m.* beginning, start; *fin dal -amento,* right from the outset.
**comitale** *adj.* pertaining to a count or earl.
**comitato** *m.* committee; — *direttivo,* steering committee; — *per l'ospitalità,* reception committee; *sotto* —, sub-committee.
**comitiva** *f.* party, group of persons; band.
**co·mit-o, -e** *m.* boatswain; — *di fischietto,* boatswain's mate.
**comi·zio** *m.* meeting; reunion; rally; — *elettorale,* electoral meeting.
**comme·dia** *f.* (theatr.) comedy; play; — *a tesi,* problem play; (fig.) make-believe, deception; *mettere in* —, to make fun of.
**commedi-are** [A4] *tr.* to write a comedy about. **-ante** *m.*, *f.* comedian, comédienne; actor, actress; (fig.) hypocrite, one who feigns emotion. **-o·grafo** *m.* playwright.
**commemor-are** [A1 s] *tr.* to commemorate. **-ativo** *adj.* commemorative. **-azịone** *f.* commemoration.
**commenda** *f.* title, rights or stipend belonging to a member of an Order of Chivalry.
**commend-are** [A1] *tr.* to commend. **-ati·zia** *f.* letter of recommendation. **-ati·zio** *adj.* recommending. **-atọre** *m.* one who commends; Knight of an order of chivalry. **-azịone** *f.* commendation. **-ẹvole** *adj.* commendable, praise-worthy.
**commensale** *m.*, *f.* table-companion; messmate; fellow-guest.
**commensur-are** [A1 s] *tr.* to compare, to set beside, to measure (against). **-a·bile** *adj.* commensurate. **-azịone** *f.* commensuration.
**comment-are** [A1 c] *tr.* to comment upon, to remark upon; to annotate. **-atọre** *m.* commentator.
**commẹnt-o** *m.* comment, remark; commentary, exposition; *far -i,* to make remarks. **-a·rio** *m.* commentary, summary, digest.
**commerci-are** [A3] *tr.* (econ.) to market, to sell; *intr.* (*aux.* avere) to trade; to deal, to hold dealings. **-a·bile** *adj.* saleable; marketable; negotiable. **-ante** *part. adj.* trading; *n.m.* business man; merchant; dealer; tradesman.
**commer·ci-o** *m.* commerce business; trade; *Camera di* — Chamber of Commerce; *codice di* —, commercial law; *fuori di* —, not on the market; *in* —, on sale; commercial class; business people; *far* — *di,* to trade in. **-ale** *adj.* commercial.
**commescolare** [A1 sc] *tr.* to mix together, to blend.
**commẹssa** *f.* shop girl; female clerk; order; *a* —, bespoke; jobbing.
**commẹsso**[1] *part.* of **commẹttere**[1], *q.v.*; *adj.* committed; imposed; pledged; *n.m.* clerk; assistant; — *di negozio,* shop assistant; — *viaggiatore,* commercial traveller.
**commẹsso**[2] *part.* of **commẹttere**[2], *q.v.*; *adj.* put together; joined side by side; *n.m.* mosaic work; splicing.
**commesti·bile** *adj.* edible; *n.m.* food, comestible; *non commestibile,* inedible.
**commẹttere**[1] [C1] *tr.* to commit; to entrust; to commission; to devote; *rfl.* to commit oneself.
**commẹtt-ere**[2] [C1] *intr.* (*aux.* avere) to fit together; to meet properly; *tr.* to fit together, to join together. **-imale** *m.*, *f. indecl.* mischiefmaker. **-itura** *f.* union; fitting together; mosaic.
**commiato** *m.* leave-taking; dismissal; discharge; permission to withdraw.
**commisẹr-are** [A1 s] *tr.* to commiserate, to have compassion on. **-ativo** *adj.* sympathetic; commiserating. **-azịone** *f.* commiseration. **-ẹvole** *adj.* deserving of sympathy; wretched; pathetic.
**commissa·r-io** *m.* commissar; inspector; delegate. **-iato** *m.* commissariat; *-iato di polizia,* divisional police station.
**commissiọn-e** *f.* commission; order; errand; committee. **-are** [A1 c] *tr.* to order; to commission; to send on an errand. **-a·rio** *m.* (comm.) commission agent; selling agent.
**commisụr-are** [A1] *tr.* to compare in size; to measure together. **-azịone** *f.* proportion; proportioning.
**committente** *m.*, *f.* one who orders or commissions; purchaser, customer.
**commodoro** *m.* (naut.) commodore.
**commosso** *part.* of **commovere,** *q.v.*; *adj.* moved, touched; shaken.
**commo·v-ere** [C15] *tr.* to move, to effect, to touch; to excite; to shake; *rfl.* to be moved; to become agitated. **-ente** *part. adj.* moving, affecting, touching.

**commozione** *f.* perturbation; agitation; emotion; — *cerebrale*, concussion; upheaval; — *tellurica*, earthquake.
**commuo·vere** [C15] see **commovere.**
**commutare** [A1] *tr.* to change, to alter; (leg.) to commute.
**Como** *pr.n.f.* (geog.) Como; *il lago di* —, Lake Como.
**comod-are** [A1 s] *tr.* to lend, to accommodate; *intr.* (*aux.* avere) to suit. **-atamente** *adv.* easily, comfortably, conveniently.
**comodino** *m.* pedestal cupboard, bedside cupboard; (theatr.) drop-scene.
**comodità** *f. indecl.* convenience; comfort; opportunity.
**co·mod-o** *adj.* convenient, comfortable; *stia —!*, don't get up!, don't trouble!; *prendersela -a*, to take one's time, to be in no hurry; commodious; willing, amenable; *n.m.* convenience, comfort; *faccia il suo* —, do as you please. **-amente** *adv.* comfortably.
**com-padrone** *m.* co-proprietor, joint-owner. **-paesano** *m.* fellow-villager; person from the same district.
**compaginare**[1] [A1 s] *tr.* to put (parts) together, to assemble.
**compaginare**[2] [A1 s] *tr.* to make up into pages, to page.
**compa·gine** *f.* union, closely-fitting joint, connexion; internal structure; (fig.) structure, frame-work; (sport) team.
**compagna** *f.* (woman) companion, (woman) friend; partner in a game.
**compagni·a** *f.* company; *tener — a uno*, to keep someone company; (mil.) company; (eccl.) confraternity, guild; (finan.) company.
**compagn-o** *m.* companion; friend; mate; partner in a game; school-fellow; (pol.) comrade, fellow Communist; *adj.* alike, belonging to one another. **-esco** *adj.* (*m.pl.* **-eschi**) pertaining to companions; *guerra -esca*, civil war. **-evole** *adj.* sociable; friendly. **-is·simo** *adj. superl.* *-issimo di*, most friendly with, the great friend of. **-one** *m. augm.* boon companion; accomplice.
**compana·tico** *m.* food to be eaten with bread.
**compar-are** [A1 s, A1] *tr.* to compare. **-a·bile** *adj.* comparable. **-ativo** *adj.* comparative. **-ato** *part. adj.* compared, comparative; *grammatica -ata*, comparative grammar. **-azione** *f.* comparison; *a -azione*, in comparison; similarity.
**compar-e** *m.* godfather; witness at wedding, groomsman; friend, crony; accomplice, confederate. **-ino** *m.* godson.
**compar-ire** [D2] *intr.* (*aux.* essere) to appear; to make an appearance; to turn up; to seem; — *gran signore*, to put on airs; to be conspicuous. **-iscente** *part. adj.* showy; striking; apparent, obvious. **-ita** *f.* appearing, appearance.
**comparsa** *f.* appearance; *fare* —, to show up, to be noticeable; (mil.) review, parade; tourney; (theatr.) stage-set; stage-extra; film-extra; (fig.) *fare da* —, to be merely an onlooker; to put in an appearance.
**compartecip-are** [A1 sc] *intr.* (*aux.* avere; *prep.* a) to participate; to share (in). **-azione** *f.* participation; sharing.
**compartecipe** *adj.* participating.
**compart-ire** [D1, D2] *tr.* to divide, to share; to bestow. **-imento** *m.* compartment, division; *-imento stagno*, watertight compartment. **-izione** *f.* division into compartments; distribution; administrative division.
**compass-are** *tr.* to measure with compasses; (fig.) to measure. **-ato** *part.* measured; carefully thought out; dignified and formal.
**compassion-are** [A1 c] *tr.* to have compassion on. **-evole** *adj.* pitiful; compassionate, sympathetic.
**compassione** *f.* compassion; pity; sympathy.
**compasso** *m.* pair of compasses, dividers.
**compat-ire** [D2] *tr.* to pity; to sympathize with; to be indulgent towards; *farsi* —, to make a pitiful exhibition of oneself. **-i·bile** *adj.* deserving of pity; compatible. **-ibilità** *f.* compatibility. **-imento** *m.* sympathy; indulgence; tolerance.
**compatriota** *m., f.* compatriot; fellow-countryman.
**compatt-o** *adj.* compact; concise. **-ezza** *f.* compactness; concision.
**compaziente** *adj.* compassionate, sympathetic.
**compendiare** [A4] *tr.* to abridge, to make a précis of, to summarize.
**compen·di-o** *m.* compendium, abridgment, summary; *in* —, in brief. **-oso** *adj.* shortened, abridged, summarized.
**compenetr-are** [A1 s] *tr.* to interpenetrate, to permeate. **-azione** *f.* permeation, infiltration.
**compens-are** [A1] *tr.* to compensate, to make up for, to make good; to reward. **-ato** *part. adj.* compensated; *legno -ato*, ply-wood. **-azione** *f.* compensation; (leg.) satisfaction; (finan.) *stanza di -azione*, clearing house.
**compenso** *m.* compensation; making good; reward.
**competen-te** *adj.* suitable; apt; *mancia* — generous tip **-za** *f.* competence; qualifications; *pl.* fees; allowances.
**compe·t-ere** [C1 def.] *intr.* (*aux.* avere) to compete; to dispute. **-itore** *m.* competitor, rival.
**compiacen-te** *adj.* obliging; complaisant; willing. **-za** *f.* satisfaction; complaisance; courtesy; *abbia la -za di*, be good enough to.
**compiac-ere** [B20] *intr.* (*aux.* avere; *prep.* a) to please; to satisfy; to fall in with the whims (of); *rfl.* to feel satisfaction; *-ersi con*, to congratulate; *-ersi di*, to take pleasure in; to be pleased to; *tr.* to please, to satisfy. **-evole** *adj.* pleasing, satisfying; flattering. **-imento** *m.* pleasure, satisfaction; consent, approval.
**compian·gere** [C5] *tr.* to pity; to lament, to mourn; *rfl.* (*prep.* di, per) to complain (of); to lament, to mourn.
**compianto** *part.* of **compiangere**; *adj.* lamented, mourned, late; *n.m.* mourning, lament.
**compicciare** [A3] *tr.* (colloq.) to put together, to finish; — *bugie*, to tell lies; *non — nulla*, to be unable to achieve anything.
**compiegare** [A2] *tr.* to fold together; to enclose.
**compiere** [D11]. See **compire.**
**compieta** *f.* (liturg.) compline; (fig.) eventide (of life).
**compilare** [A1] *tr.* to compile; to compose, to write; — *un modulo*, to fill in a form.
**comp-ire** [D1] *tr.* to fulfil, to accomplish; to carry out; to complete; *oggi mia figlia -ie nove anni*, my daughter is nine years old today; *rfl.* to come to pass. **-itezza** *f.* politeness, good manners. **-ito** *part. adj.* fulfilled; accomplished; well-mannered.
**compitare** [A1 sc] *tr.* to spell out, to pronounce syllable by syllable.
**com·pito** *m.* task, duty, job; *pl.* (schol.) homework.
**compleanno** *m.* birthday; anniversary.
**complement-o** *m.* complement; supplement. **-are** *adj.* complementary; (finan.) *imposta -are*, direct tax on income.
**complessione** *f.* constitution, state of health; disposition.
**complessivo** *adj.* comprehensive; aggregate; *studio* —, survey; (finan.) gross; *n.m.* (eng.) assembly, unit; assembly drawing.
**complesso** *adj.* complex; robust, sturdy; *n.m.* complex; mass, aggregate; *in* —, on the whole; assembly, unit, set; (theatr.) opera company; ballet company; (mus.) ensemble; combination; (psych.) complex; (comm.) group, chain, combine; (industr.) large works.
**complet-are** [A1] *tr.* to complete. **-ato** *part. adj.* completed; *-ato*

*con*, furnished with, complete with.

**completo** *adj.* complete, entire; finished, done; full up; *al* —, entirely; *siamo al —?*, are we all here?; — *di*, complete with; *n.m.* suit (of jacket, waistcoat and trousers).

**complic-are** [A2s] *tr.* to complicate; *rfl.* to become complicated; **-ato** *part. adj.* complicated; complex; involved. **-azione** *f.* complication.

**com·plic-e** *m.* (leg.) accomplice; associate; accessory; *un — nella congiura*, a party in the conspiracy. **-ità** *f. indecl.* (leg.) complicity.

**complimentare** [A1c] *tr.* to compliment; to congratulate.

**compliment-o** *m.* compliment, wish, salutation; *non faccia -i*, don't stand on ceremony, make yourself at home; *senzi -i*, without flattery. **-oso** *adj.* full of compliments, obsequious; ceremonious.

**complott-o** *m.* plot, conspiracy. **-are** [A1] *tr.* to plot against; *intr.* (*aux.* avere) to plot.

**componente** *adj.* component, conciliatory; *n.m.* component, constituent; — *di una commissione*, member of a committee.

**componimento** *m.* composition; essay; literary work; conciliation; agreement.

**componitore** *m.* composer of differences, conciliator.

**comporre** [B21] *tr.* to compound; to make up; to compose; *rfl.* to be composed; to behave correctly.

**comport-are** [A1] *tr.* to tolerate, to put up with, to bear; to involve; *prezzi che non -ano riduzioni*, prices on which no reduction can be made; *rfl.* to behave; to contain oneself. **-amento** *m.* behaviour; actions.

**comporto** *m.* tolerance; grace; *tre giorni di* —, three days' grace.

**compositivo** *adj.* synthetic.

**compo·sito** *adj.* compound; (archit.) composite.

**compositore** *m.* composer; (typ.) compositor.

**composizione** *f.* composition.

**compost-a** *f.* compote; compost. **-iera** *f.* compote dish.

**compost-o** *part.* of **comporre,** *q.v.*; *adj.* compounded; combined; neat and tidy; *n.m.* compound. **-ezza** *f.* calmness; orderliness; modesty.

**com·pr-a** *f.* purchase; — *a pagamento rateale*, hire purchase; *fare le -e*, to shop.

**compr-are** [A1] *tr.* to buy, to purchase; (fig.) to buy over, to bribe. **-atore** *m.* purchaser; buyer.

**compren·dere** [C1] *tr.* to comprise; to embrace; to comprehend.

**comprens-i·bile** *adj.* understandable, comprehensible. **-ione** *f.* comprehension, understanding; sympathy. **-iva** *f.* faculty of understanding. **-ivo** *adj.* sympathetic; understanding; comprehensive.

**compreso** *part.* of **comprendere**; *adj.* comprised, included, embraced; contained; comprehended; occupied; — *di meraviglia*, filled with wonder; *n.m.* circuit, area, district.

**compress-a** *f.* compress; tablet. **-i·bile** *adj.* compressible. **-ione** *f.* compression; compress, dressing. **-ivo** *adj.* compressing.

**compress-o** *part.* of **comprimere,** *q.v.*; *adj.* compressed; concise; oppressed. **-ore** *adj.* compressing; *rullo -ore*, steam-roller; *n.m.* compressor; roller; *-ore stradale*, street-roller.

**comprima·rio** *adj.* (theatr.) pertaining to a secondary role; *n.m.* (theatr.) actor cast for a secondary role; *le parti di* —, supporting roles.

**compri·mere** [C18] *tr.* to compress; to restrain; to repress.

**compromesso** *part.* of **compromettere,** *q.v.*; *adj.* compromised; *n.m.* conditional contract.

**compromettere** [C20] *tr.* to compromise; *rfl.* to compromise oneself, to be compromised; to become committed.

**compromissione** *f.* compromise.

**compropriet-à** *f. indecl.* joint-ownership. **-a·rio** *m.* joint-owner, part-owner.

**comprov-are** [A1] *tr.* to prove, to confirm absolutely. **-azione** *f.* proof, confirmation; approval.

**compulsione** *f.* compulsion; restriction.

**compun·gere** [C5] *tr.* to sting, to cause pain to; to prick (of conscience), to cause remorse to; *rfl.* to feel remorse.

**compunto** *part.* of **compungere,** *q.v.*; *adj.* remorseful, grieved; demure; wearing an expression of sorrow; (rel.) contrite, remorseful.

**compunzione** *f.* compunction; demureness.

**comput-are** [A1] *tr.* to compute, to reckon, to count; to take into account. **-azione** *f.* computation, calculation, reckoning.

**comput-ista** *m.* accountant. **-isteri·a** *f.* accountancy; book-keeping; accountant's office. **-i·stico** *adj.* rel. to accountancy.

**com·puto** *m.* calculation, computation.

**comunale** *adj.* belonging to the commune; municipal, civic, public; communal; *palazzo* —, town hall; commonplace, ordinary.

**comunanza** *f.* community; society; fellowship; *in* —, in common; — *d'interessi*, interests in common.

**comune**[1] *adj.* **1.** common, ordinary, plain; *l'uomo* —, the man in the street; vulgar; (mil.) *soldato* —, private soldier; (naut.) *marinaio* —, ordinary seaman. **2.** common, shared, mutual; *diritto* —, common law; *il nostro — amico*, our mutual friend; *adv. phr. in* —, in common; *avere in* —, to share. **3.** common, usual, habitual, general; *senso* —, usual meaning.

**comun-e**[2] *m., f.* generality; the general run; *il — degli uomini*, most people; (usu. *m.*) civic centre, municipal offices or buildings; urban district; commune; local government; *Palazzo del Comune*, town hall; (mil.) private soldier. **-ella** *f. dim.* small party, group; *far -ella*, to band together; master-key.

**comunic-are** [A2s] *tr.* to communicate, to impart; (eccl.) to give Holy Communion to; *intr.* (*aux.* avere) to communicate; to be in touch; (eccl.) to make one's communion. **-ando** *m.*, **-anda** *f.* (eccl.) communicant. **-ante** *adj.* communicating; *n.m.* communicant. **-ativa** *f.* faculty of imparting knowledge; aptitude for teaching. **-ativo** *adj.* communicative; (med.) catching. **-ato** *part. adj.* communicated, imparted; *n.m.* communicant; communiqué, bulletin; *-ato stampa*, press release. **-azione** *f.* communication; means of communication; message; *-azione telefonica*, telephone call; *strada di grande -azione*, main road, trunk road.

**comunione** *f.* communion; community.

**comun-ismo** *m.* communism. **-ista** *m., f.* (*m.pl.* **-isti,** *f.pl.* **-iste**) communist.

**comunit-à** *f.* community; fellowship; association. **-ativo** *adj.* municipal.

**comunque** *adv., conj.* in whatever manner; although; however; anyhow, all the same.

**con** *prep.* (sometimes *contr.* with *def. art.*: col, coll', coi, cogli, colla, colle) with; accompanied by; by means of; — *l'alba*, at dawn; *gentile — tutti*, charming to everyone; — *tutto ciò*, nevertheless, all the same; in spite of, notwithstanding.

**conato** *m.* effort, attempt; — *di vomito*, retching.

**conc-a** *f.* large earthenware washing-pot; basin; hollow container; (geog.) large hollow surrounded by hills; conch, shell (of a vault). **-ata** *f.* tubful, basinful.

**concatenare** [A1c] *tr.* to link together; to connect, to join.

**conca·us-a** *f.* joint cause; contributary cause. **-are** [A1] *tr.*

to help to cause, to contribute towards.
**con·cav-o** *adj.* concave; *n.m.* hollow. **-ità** *f.* concavity, concaveness; cavity.
**conce·d-ere** [C19] *tr.* to grant, to concede; to admit; *rfl.* (*acc.* of *prep.* si) to yield; to give in; to give oneself up; (*dat.* of *prep.* si) to allow to oneself. **-i·bile** *adj.* admissible.
**concento** *m.* (mus.) harmony of voices and instruments; (poet.) *dolce* —, sweet harmony.
**concentr-are** [A1] *tr.* to concentrate, to gather in one place; *rfl.* to concentrate; *-arsi in un pensiero*, to fix one's mind on a thought. **-amẹnto** *m.* concentrating; *campo di -amento*, concentration camp. **-ato** *part. adj.* concentrated; condensed; *pomodoro -ato*, tomato purée. **-aziọne** *f.* concentration; (pol.) coalition.
**concen·trico** *adj.* concentric.
**concep-ire** [D2] *tr.* to conceive; to engender, to create; — *sospetti*, to entertain suspicions; *abs* to conceive, to become pregnant. **-i·bile** *adj.* conceivable.
**conceri·a** *f.* tannery; tanning, leather-dressing.
**concer·n-ere** (cdef.) *tr.* to concern, to relate to, to regard. **-ente** *part. prep.* concerning, about, relating to.
**concert-are** [A1] *tr.* to concert; to plan; to arrange; to agree; (mus.) to conduct; to rehearse; to orchestrate, to score. **-amẹnto** *m.* (mus.) ensemble; arrangement. **-ante** *n.m., f.* (mus.) performer in a concert; concerted part. **-aziọne** *f.* (mus.) arrangement; orchestration.
**concert-o** *m.* (mus.) concert; concerto; ensemble; *fare* —, to go well together; *di* —, in agreement. **-ina** *f.* (mus.) concertina. **-ista** *m., f.* concert-giver; recitalist. **-i·stico** *adj.* relating to a concert; *società -istiche*, concert societies.
**concess-iọne** *f.* concession; permission; permit; — *di pesca*, fishing licence. **-iona·rio** *m.* (leg.) concessionaire; agent. **-ivo** *adj.* (gramm.) concessive.
**concesso** *part.* of **concedere,** *q.v.*; *adj.* granted, conceded; allowed; admitted; *dato e non* —, granted for the sake of argument.
**concett-o** *m.* concept, notion, idea; *essere in buon* —, to have a good reputation; conceit (literary). **-uale** *adj.* conceptual.
**conceziọne** *f.* conception; axiom; principle.
**conchi·gl-ia** *f.* (zool.) shell (of a mollusc); (archit.) conch-shaped ornament. **-ifọrme** *adj.* shell-shaped.
**cọncia** *f.* (*pl.* **cọnce**) trade or science of tanning; tan, tanning material; tanyard; dye-bath.
**conci-are** [A3c] *tr.* to tidy up, to dress, to do (*e.g.* hair); to adorn; to tan; (fig.) to ill-use, to knock about; to disfigure. **-acalda·ie** *m. indecl.* tinker. **-apelli** *m. indecl.* leather-dresser. **-atọre** *m.* tanner, leather-dresser.
**concilia·bile** *adj.* reconcilable.
**concili-are** [A4] *tr.* to reconcile; to conciliate; — *il sonno*, to induce slumber; — *la fame*, to tempt appetite; — *l'allegria*, to excite merriment; to conclude (an arrangement); *rfl.* (*dat.* of *prn.* si) *-arsi uno*, to make friends with someone. **-ante** *part. adj.* conciliating, conciliatory. **-atọre** *m.* conciliator, peace-maker; *arbitro -atore*, referee. **-aziọne** *f.* conciliation; reconciliation.
**conci·lio** *m.* (eccl.) council, synod; (fig.) assembly, gathering.
**concim-e** *m.* manure, fertilizer. **-a·ia** *f.*, **-a·io** *m.* manure-heap. **-are** [A1] *tr.* to manure, to spread fertilizer upon. **-atura** *f.*, **-aziọne** *f.* manuring, fertilizing.
**cọnci-o** *apocop. part.* of **conciare;** *adj.* tanned, dressed; worked; *pietra -a*, hewn stone; the worse for wear; *mal* —, in a poor condition; *n.m.* manure; *in* —, in order, ready; decoration.
**concis-iọne** *f.* conciseness; concision. **-o** *adj.* concise, brief.
**concistor-o** *m.* (eccl.) consistory; (fig., joc.) group of people. **-iale** *adj.* (eccl.) consistorial.
**concit-are** [A1s] *tr.* to stir up, to arouse, to provoke. **-aziọne** *f.* excitement, agitation; emotion.
**concittadin-o** *adj., n.m.* fellow-citizen. **-anza** *f.* citizenship of the same place.
**conclam-are** [A1] *tr.* to call in a loud voice; to acclaim. **-aziọne** *f.* acclamation.
**conclave** *m.* (eccl.) conclave.
**concluden-te** *part.* of **concludere**; *adj.* conclusive, effective; purposeful. **-za** *f.* conclusiveness; effectiveness.
**conclu·d-ere** [C3] *tr.* to conclude; to bring to a conclusion; to clinch; to comprise; *intr.* (*aux.* avere) to be conclusive; to succeed; *non -e niente*, he never achieves anything.
**conclusiọne** *f.* conclusion; *senza* —, inconclusive.
**conclusivo** *adj.* conclusive.
**concomitan-te** *adj.* concomitant. **-za** *f.* concomitance.
**concord-are** [A1] *tr.* to reconcile, to make agree; to agree upon; to tune; *intr.* (*aux.* avere; *prep.* con) to agree (with); *recip. rfl.* to become reconciled to one another. **-a·bile** *adj.* reconcilable; compatible. **-ante** *part. adj.* agreeing, consenting. **-anza** *f.* agreement; concordance. **-ato** *part. adj.* agreed, in agreement; reconciled; *n.m.* pact, concordat.
**concord-e** *adj.* in accord; *plauso* —, unanimous applause; *siamo -i*, we are in agreement. **-ità** *f. indecl.* agreement, concord; conformity.
**concor·dia** *f.* agreement, concord; unanimity; good will.
**concọrr-ere** [C5] *intr.* (*aux.* avere) to assemble, to come together; to flow together; to converge; to contribute; to strive together; to participate; to concur; to compete. **-ente** *part. adj.* concurrent; competing; *n.m.* competitor; applicant, candidate. **-enza** *f.* concurrence; concourse; competition; rivalry.
**concọrso** *n.* competition; competitive examination; concourse.
**conc-otto** *adj.* digested, assimilated. **-oziọne** *f.* digestion, assimilation.
**concret-o** *adj.* concrete; substantial; factual; *in* —, in actual fact. **-ẹzza** *f.* concreteness. **-izzare** [A1] *tr.* to realize, to put into practice; *intr.* (*aux.* avere) to be factual.
**concubin-a** *f.* concubine. **-ato** *m.* concubinage.
**concupire** [D2] *tr.* to covet; to lust for.
**concupi·sc-ere** (def.) *tr.* to lust after. **-ente** *part. adj.* lustful. **-enza** *f.* lust; concupiscence.
**concuss-o** *adj.* shaken. **-ivo** *adj.* shaking; concussive.
**condann-a** *f.* condemnation; (leg.) verdict or judgement of guilty; sentence; penalty; — *a morte*, death sentence. **-are** [A1] *tr.* to condemn; to blame, to censure; (leg.) to sentence. **-ato** *part. adj.* condemned, blamed; *n.m.* convict; *la cella dei -ati*, the condemned cell. **-aziọne** *f.* condemnation.
**condẹgn-o** *adj.* suitable; worthy, deserved; adequate. **-ità** *f.* merit, worthiness.
**condens-are** [A1] *tr., rfl.* to condense. **-aziọne** *f.* condensation.
**condenso** *adj.* dense, opaque; obscure.
**condi·cere** [B10] *intr.* (*aux.* avere; *prep.* a) to be fitting; to be appropriate.
**cond-ire** [D2] *tr.* to flavour, to season; to dress (a salad). **-imẹnto** *m.* condiment; seasoning, flavouring.
**condirettọre** *m.*, co-director; co-editor.
**condiscẹpolo** *m.* fellow-disciple.
**condit-o** *part.* of **condire,** *q.v.*; *adj.* seasoned; dressed; flavoured; *n.m.* seasoning; condiment. **-ura** *f.* seasoning; dressing; flavouring.
**condivi·dere** [C3] *tr.* to divide, to share out.
**condizionale** *adj.* conditional.

**condizion-are** [A1 c] *tr.* to condition; to prepare; to season; *ho -ato la mia offerta alla sua venuta*, I made my offer on condition he came; *rfl.* to prepare oneself; to become conditioned. **-amẹnto** *m.* (techn.) conditioning; *-amento dell'aria*, air-conditioning. **-ato** *part. adj.* conditioned, prepared; packed; *aria -ata*, air-conditioning; conditional.

**condiziọne** *f.* condition; circumstance; *a —*, on condition; proviso; *pl.* terms.

**condoglianz-a** *f.* condolence; sympathy; *fare le -e a*, to offer condolences to.

**condol-ẹre** [B11] *rfl.* to sorrow, to grieve; *-ersi con*, to offer one's sympathy to. **-ọre** *m.* condolence, fellow-feeling.

**condomi·nio** *m.* (leg.) co-ownership; joint government; condominium.

**condo·mino** *m.* (leg.) co-owner, owner in common.

**condonare** [A1 c] *tr.* to condone, to excuse; to remit.

**condọre** *m.* (orn.) condor.

**condọtt-a** *f.* conduct; behaviour; good conduct; *senza —*, ill-mannered; command; leadership; organization; *linea di —*, policy; supply (of gas, electricity, etc.); convoy; escort. **-iere, -iero** *m.* (hist.) leader of a city militia; soldier of fortune commanding troops.

**condọtto** *part.* of **condurre,** *q.v.*; *n.m.* water main; pipe, tube; conduit.

**conduc-ente** *part.* of **condurre,** *q.v.*; *adj.* leading, guiding; *n.m.* chauffeur; driver. **-ẹvole** *adj.* conducive. **-i·bile** *adj.* suitable, amenable. **-imẹnto** *m.* leading, guiding; command.

**condurre** [B2] *tr.* to conduct, to lead; to direct; to carry out; to drive (a vehicle); *rfl.* to behave oneself.

**condutt-ọre** *m.* leader; guide; driver; landlord (of an inn); (phys.) conductor; **-ura** *f.* conduit, pipe; channel; main.

**conduziọne** *f.* farming by owner; transporting; driving (a vehicle); (phys.) conduction.

**conesta·bile** *m.* high constable.

**confabul-are** [A1 s] *intr.* (*aux.* avere) to gossip, to chat; to talk together. **-ato·rio** *adj.* chatty. **-aziọne** *f.* chat, gossip; conversation.

**confac-ente, -ẹvole** *adj.* suitable, fitting, appropriate. **-evolẹzza** *f.* suitability, appropriateness; adaptability.

**confare** [B14] *rfl.* (*prep.* a) to be fitting, to be appropriate.

**confeder-are** [A1 s] *tr.*, *rfl.* to federate. **-ativo** *adj.* federative. **-ato** *part. adj.* federated; federal. **-aziọne** *f.* federation; *la Confederazione Elvetica*, Switzerland; alliance; *-azione del lavoro*, trade union.

**conferenz-a** *f.* conference; *— stampa*, press conference; lecture, paper; parley, colloquy. **-iere** *m.* lecturer; speaker.

**conferire** [D2] *tr.* to confer, to bestow; (eccl.) to administer; *intr.* (*aux.* avere) to confer, to hold a conference; (*prep.* a) to help, to benefit.

**confẹrma** *f.* confirmation; renewal (*e.g.* of office).

**conferm-are** [A1 c] *tr.* to confirm; to retain in employment; to approve; *rfl.* to become firmer (in an opinion); (signing a letter) *mi -o*, I remain. **-ativo** *adj.* confirming, corroborative. **-ato·rio** *adj.* confirmatory. **-aziọne** *f.* confirmation; corroboration.

**confessare** [A1] *tr.* to admit, to confess; to declare, to profess; *rfl.* to make one's confession.

**confessionale** *adj.* (rel.) confessional; *n.m.* confessional box.

**confessiọne** *f.* admission, confession; creed, persuasion; religious body.

**confesso** *adj.* self-convicted.

**confessọre** *m.* confessor.

**confett-are** [A1] *tr.* to candy. **-ato** *part. adj.* candied.

**confetto**[1] *adj.* worked, prepared; worn out; (of soil) baked.

**confett-o**[2] *n.m.* sweetmeat, sugar plum; sugared almond. **-iere** *m.* confectioner. **-ura** *f.* confectionary; jam.

**confeziọn-e** *f.* tailoring, dressmaking; *pl.* clothing for sale; product; manufacture; packaging; packet. **-are** [A1 c] *tr.* to manufacture; to prepare; to pack up; *-are un pacco*, to do up a parcel; (industr.) to make. **-atọre** *m.* manufacturer; packer.

**conficcare** [A2] *tr.* to thrust in; to hammer in; to nail up; to spike (a gun).

**confidare** [A1] *tr.* to entrust; to confide; *intr.* (*aux.* avere; *prep.* in) to have faith (in); to trust (to); *rfl.* (*prep.* con) to confide in; (*prep.* a) to entrust oneself (to); to rely (on).

**confidente** *adj.* trusting; confident; trustworthy; *n.m.*, *f.* confidant; close friend; confidential agent.

**confidenz-a** *f.* confidential communication; familiarity, intimacy; confidence; *prendersi una —*, to take a liberty; (provb.) *— toglie riverenza*, familiarity breeds contempt. **-iale** *adj.* confidential; friendly, familiar.

**configur-are** [A1] *tr.* to form a likeness of; to outline. **-aziọne** *f.* likeness; outline; configuration.

**confin-are** [A1] *tr.* to confine, to restrict; to banish; *intr.* (*aux.* avere; *prep.* con) to border (upon); (leg.) to adjoin. **-ato** *part. adj.* confined, restricted; banished; *n.m.* person subjected to political confinement. **-aziọne** *f.* frontier demarcation.

**confine** *m.* boundary, frontier, confine; *mandare al —*, to exile; *a — con*, bordering upon.

**confiscare** [A2] *tr.* to confiscate; to seize.

**conflagr-are** [A1] *intr.* (*aux.* essere) to burn, to ignite. **-aziọne** *f.* conflagration.

**conflitto** *m.* conflict; clash; *venire a —*, to conflict.

**conflu-ire** [D2] *intr.* (*aux.* essere, avere) to flow together; to be confluent. **-ente** *adj.* confluent; *n.m.* meeting-place; affluent. **-enza** *f.* confluence.

**confọnd-ere** [C2] *tr.* to confuse; to confound; *rfl.* to be confused; to become blurred; to merge; *-ersi in lagrime*, to melt into tears. **-i·bile** *adj.* likely to be confused or mistaken.

**conform-are** [A1 c] *tr.* to conform (to). **-aziọne** *f.* conformation, structure; *di -azione*, constitutional; inborn.

**confọrm-e** *adj.* (*prep.* a, con) similar, in conformity (with), according (to); *adv.* conformably, accordingly; *prep.* in conformity with; *conj.* according as, as. **-ịsmo** *m.* (rel.; pol.) conformity. **-ista** *m.*, *f.* (*pl.* **-isti** *m.*, **-iste** *f.*) conformist. **-i·stico** *adj.* conformist. **-ità** *f. indecl.* conformity.

**confort-are** [A1] *tr.* to comfort; to console; to vote for, to support; to stimulate; to urge, to exhort; *rfl.* to take comfort; to find relief. **-ante** *adj.* comforting, encouraging; *n.m.* medicine to settle the stomach. **-ẹvole** *adj.* comforting; encouraging; comfortable, cosy.

**conforto** *m.* comfort, consolation, solace; exhortation, incitement; encouragement; comfort; ease.

**confratello** *m.* fellow-member; colleague.

**confrontare** [A1 c] *tr.* to compare; to confront; *intr.* (*aux.* avere) to agree in all respects.

**confrọnto** *m.* comparison; collation; *chiamare a —*, to confront; *in — con*, compared with.

**Confu·c-io** *pr.n.m.* Confucius. **-ianịsmo** *m.* Confucianism. **-iano** *m.*, *adj.* Confucian.

**confuṣiọn-e** *f.* confusion. **-ịsmo** *m.* to-do, bustle; confused state of mind.

**confuṣo** *part.* of **confọndere,** *q.v.*; *adj.* confused, disordered; embarrassed; *in —*, higgledy-piggledy.

**confut-are** (A1, A1 s) *tr.* to confute; to disprove. **-aziọne** *f.* confutation.

**congedare** [A1] *tr.* to give leave

to; to dismiss; to discharge; *rfl.* to take leave.

**congedo** *m.* leave of absence; *in* —, on leave; — *assoluto*, discharge.

**congegn-are** [A5c] *tr.* to put together; to contrive; to concoct. **-ato** *part. adj.* devised; *ben -ato*, cleverly thought out. **-atura** *f.* contrivance.

**congęgno** *m.* device; mechanism.

**congel-are** [A1] *tr.*, *intr.* (*aux.* essere), to freeze; to congeal; *rfl.* to become frost-bitten. **-atọre** *m.* refrigerator; deep-freeze.

**congeniale** *adj.* congenial; like-minded.

**conge·nito** *adj.* congenital, hereditary.

**conge·rie** *f. indecl.* mass of miscellaneous objects, congeries.

**congestiọn-e** *f.* congestion; accumulation; traffic jam. **-are** [A1c] *tr.* to congest. **-ato** *part. adj.* congested; crowded.

**congettur-a** *f.* conjecture; speculation. **-ale** *adj.* conjectural; speculative. **-are** [A1] *tr.* to conjecture; to speculate.

**congiun·gere** [C] *tr.* to join, to unite; — *una retta*, to draw a straight line; *rfl.* (*prep.* a, con) to join; to meet; *recip. rfl.* to join together.

**congiuntiv-a** *f.* (med.) conjunctiva. **-ite** *f.* (med.) conjunctivitis. **-o** *adj.* conjunctive; subjunctive; conjunctional.

**congiunt-o** *part.* of **congiungere**; *adj.* joined; related; *n.m.* relative, relation. **-ura** *f.* junction; join, seam; conjuncture, occasion.

**congiunziọne** *f.* junction, joint; conjunction.

**congiur-are** [A1] *intr.* (*aux.* avere) to conspire, **-a** *f.* conspiracy; plot. **-amẹnto** *m.* swearing; oath; conspiracy. **-ato** *part. adj.* conspired, agreed; *n.m.* conspirator.

**conglob-are** [A1] *tr.* (finan.) to make a lump sum of. **-amẹnto** *m.* consolidation (wages, salaries); amalgamation. **-ato** *part. adj.* lump, total; *n.m.* lump sum.

**conglomer-are** [A1s] *tr.* to conglomerate, to amass. **-ato** *part. adj.* conglomerated; *n.m.* (geol.) conglomerate, pudding stone; (bldg.) concrete. **-aziọne** *f.* conglomeration.

**conglutin-are** [A1s] *tr.* to glue together; to join. **-ativo** *adj.* adhesive.

**congratul-are** [A1s] *rfl.* (*prep.* con) to congratulate; *mi -o con Lei*, I congratulate you. **-ato·rio** *adj.* congratulatory. **-aziọne** *f.* congratulation.

**congrega** *f.* group; religious guild, confraternity.

**congreg-are** [A2] *tr.* to call together, to assemble; *rfl.* to congregate, to gather together. **-aziọne** *f.* assembly, gathering.

**congress-o** *m.* congress, conference; concourse, gathering. **-ista** *m.*, *f.* (*pl.* **-isti** *m.*, **-iste** *f.*) delegate to a congress; member of a congress.

**congro** *m.* (ichth.) conger-eel.

**congru-ire** [D2] *intr.* (*aux.* essere) to be congruent. **-ente** *adj.* congruent. **-enza** *f.* congruence, suitability.

**con·gru-o** *adj.* congruous; suitable, apposite; **-ità** *f. indecl.* congruity.

**conguagli-are** [A4] *tr.* to equalize, to balance (accounts). **-ato** *part. adj.* adjusted, squared up.

**congua·glio** *m.* balancing, squaring up; *in* —, to square the count.

**coni-are** [A1s] *tr.* to coin, to mint; to trick. **-atọre** *m.* coiner, investor; counterfeiter. **-atura** *f.* coining, minting.

**co·nico** *adj.* conic, conical; tapering.

**coni·fero** *m.* (bot.) conifer; *adj.* coniferous.

**coni·gli-o** *m.* (zool.) rabbit; (fig.) timid individual. **-a** *f.* (zool.) female rabbit, doe. **-cultura** *f.* rabbit-breeding. **-era** *f.* rabbit-hutch.

**co·nio** *m.* wedge; die for striking coins; seal, stamp; imprint.

**coniugale** *adj.* conjugal; married; matrimonial.

**coniug-are** [A2s] *tr.* (gramm.) to conjugate. **-aziọne** *f.* conjugation.

**co·niug-e** *m.* consort, partner in marriage; *pl.* married couple; *i -i Rossi*, Mr and Mrs Rossi.

**connato** *adj.* born together, cognate.

**connaturale** *adj.* innate; of the same nature.

**connazionale** *adj.* of the same country; *n.m.*, *f.* compatriot.

**conness-o** *part.* of **connettere**, *q.v.*; *adj.* connected; *n.m.* thing connected; *annessi e -i*, accessories.

**connet·tere** [C19] *tr.* to connect; *abs. non* — to be inconsequential.

**conniven-te** *adj.* conniving; *n.m.*, *f.* conniver. **-za** *f.* connivance.

**connotato** *m.* characteristic feature or peculiarity; *pl.* official description.

**connu·bi-o** *m.* marriage; (fig.) partnership; (pol.) deal. **-ale** *adj.* conjugal, connubial.

**connumer-are** [A1s] *tr.* to number in series. **-aziọne** *f.* numbering.

**cono** *m.* cone; *a* —, conical.

**conoc·chia** *f.* distaff; *trarre la* —, to spin.

**conoscenza** *f.* consciousness; acquaintanceship; acquaintance; knowledge; *venire a* — *di*, to get to know about; cognizance; intimation.

**conọsc-ere** [B9] *tr.* to know; to have knowledge of; to know for a fact; to experience; to know personally; — *di vista*, to know by sight; *vi farò* — *mio padre*, I will introduce you to my father; *darsi a* —, to prove to be; to recognize, to distinguish; *intr.* (*aux.* avere) to be conscious; *non -e più*, he has lost consciousness; to understand; *rfl.* to know oneself; *-ersi vinto*, to acknowledge defeat. **-ente** *part. adj.* knowing; *n.m.*, *f.* connoisseur; expert; acquaintance. **-i·bile** *adj.* recognizable; knowable; *n.m.* (philos.) cognoscible. **-itivo** *adj.* (philos.) capable of knowing; cognitive; (pop.) recognizable. **-itọre** *m.* connoisseur; art expert. **-iuto** *part. adj.* known; well known.

**conquassare** [A1] *tr.* to shake violently; to shatter.

**conquiṣitọre** *m.* investigator; spy.

**conquista** *f.* conquest; *paese di* —, conquered country; (fig.) *fare una* —, to make a conquest.

**conquist-are** [A1] *tr.* to conquer; to overcome; *rfl.* (*dat.* of *prn.* si) to win for oneself. **-atọre** *m.* conqueror; maker of conquests.

**consacr-are** [A1] *tr.* to hallow; to consecrate; to ordain; to annoint; to deify; to sanction; to devote. **-ando** *n.m.* ordinand. **-aziọne** *f.* (rel.) consecration.

**consangui·ne-o** *adj.* related by blood. **-ità** *f.* consanguinity, blood relationship.

**consapẹvol-e** *adj.* aware; conscious. **-ẹzza** *f.* awareness.

**con·scio** *adj.* conscious; aware.

**consecutiv-o** *adj.* consecutive; successive; *fenomeni -i*, after-effects.

**consẹgn-a** *f.* consignment, delivery; handing-over; (comm.) *pagare alla* —, to pay cash on delivery. **-are** [A5c] *tr.* to consign, to deliver, to hand over; to give in charge.

**conseguenz-a** *f.* consequence. **-iale** *adj.* consequent; consequential.

**consegu-ire** [D2] *tr.* to achieve; to win; *intr.* (*aux.* essere) to follow in succession, to result, to follow. **-ente** *adj.* consequent; logical; *-ente a se stesso*, consistent. **-imẹnto** *m.* attainment.

**consenso** *m.* consent; consensus; agreement.

**consenta·neo** *adj.* corresponding; agreeing; — *a*, in accordance with.

**consentire** [D1] *intr.* (*aux.* avere; *prep.* a) to agree (to); to consent; *tr.* to permit, to concede.

**consenziente** *adj.* consenting, willing.

**consertare** [A1] *tr.* to intertwine.

**conserto** *apocop. part. adj.* (poet.) intertwined; (of arms) folded; *di* —, concerted, in agreement.

**conserva** *f.* preserved food; *carne in* —, tinned meat; — *di prugne*, plum jam; — *di pomodoro*, tomato purée; store; *far* — *di*, to preserve, to lay by.

**conserv-are** [A1] *tr.* to preserve, to keep; *rfl.* to keep; (of a person) to be well preserved. **-ativo** *adj.* preservative, protective. **-atọre** *m.* preserver, preservative; curator; custodian; (pol.) *il partito -atore*, the Conservative party. **-ato·rio** *adj.* preserving, preservative; *n.m.* convent school; (mus.) conservatoire. **-aziọne** *f.* preservation; *diritto di -azione*, right of self-preservation; keeping; conservation.

**consesso** *m.* assembly, meeting.

**consider-are** [A1 s] *tr.* to consider; to deem, to estimate. **-ato** *part. adj.* considered, deliberate; *molto -ato*, highly thought of; *visto e -ato*, whereas; *conj. -ato che*, considering that. **-aziọne** *f.* consideration; esteem. **-ẹvole** *adj.* considerable.

**consigli-are**[1] [A4] *tr.* to advise, to counsel; to recommend; *rfl. -arsi con*, to seek advice from, to consult. **-atọre** *m.* adviser, counsellor.

**consigliare**[2] *adj.* relating to a council; *adunanza* —, board-meeting.

**consigliere** *m.* adviser, counsellor; councillor.

**consi·glio** *m.* advice, counsel; suggestion; council; board.

**consili-are** *adj.* conciliar. **-a·rio** *adj.* advisory.

**consi·st-ere** [B1] *intr.* (*aux.* essere) to consist; to persist; — *in*, to consist of. **-ente** *part.* consisting; *adj.* having consistence; persistent. **-enza** *f.* consistency; (comm.) *-enza di cassa*, cash in hand; consistence, density; resistance, substance.

**consoci-are** [A3] *tr.* to associate. **-ato** *part. adj.* associated; *n.m.* associate. **-aziọne** *f.* association, society.

**conso·cio** *m.* colleague; fellow-member; (comm.) co-partner.

**consol-are** [A1 c] *tr.* to console, to solace; to restore. **-ante** *part. adj.* consoling, comforting. **-ato** *part. adj.* consoled, comforted; peaceful; pleasant; *acqua -ata*, gentle rain. **-atọre** *m.*, **-atrice** *f.* consoler. **-ato·ria** *f.* letter of condolence. **-ato·rio** *adj.* consoling, soothing; *parole -atorie*, words of consolation. **-aziọne** *f.* consolation.

**con·sol-e** *m.* consul. **-are** *adj.* consular. **-ato** *m.* consulate.

**consolid-are** [A1 s] *tr.* to consolidate; to reinforce; to make solid. **-aziọne** *f.* consolidation.

**conson-are** [A1 d] *intr.* (*aux.* avere) to be consonant; to sound in agreement. **-ante** *part. adj.* consonant, in accord; *n.f.* consonant. **-anza** *f.* consonance, harmony, concord.

**con·sono** *adj.* consonant; suitable; — *a*, *con*, in conformity with.

**consort-e** *adj.* associated, related; *n.m.* consort, husband; *f.* wife. **-eri·a** *f.* political faction; clique. **-ile** *adj.* referring to a clique or party.

**consor·zio** *m.* partnership, association; society; union; syndicate; consortium.

**const-are** [A9] *intr.* (*aux.* essere; *prep.* di) to consist (of); *impers.* to be proved; *non -a che*, it does not appear that; *mi -a che*, it has come to my knowledge that.

**constat-are** [A1 s, A1] *tr.* to verify, to authenticate; to ascertain; to note. **-aziọne** *f.* proof; observation; *fare la -azione che*, to establish that; *faccio una semplice -azione*, I am merely stating a fact.

**consud·dito** *m.* fellow-subject.

**consue·to** *adj.* usual, accustomed; customary; *n.m.* usual custom.

**consuetu·din-e** *f.* custom, habit, usage; general practice; — *del paese*, local custom. **-a·rio** *adj.* habitual, customary; (leg.) *diritto -ario*, customary law.

**consulente** *adj.* consulting; *n.m.* consultant.

**consult-a** *f.* consultation; consulting room; Council of State; consultative body. **-are** [A1] *tr.* to consult; to refer to; *rfl.* (*prep.* con) to consult; to confer with; *recip. rfl.* to confer. **-ativo** *adj.* consultative. **-aziọne** *f.* consultation; advice; *libro di -azione*, reference book.

**consultivo** *adj.* consultative; *comitato* —, advisory committee.

**consult-o** *m.* professional consultation; counsel; legal advice. **-ọre** *adj.* consulting; *n.m.* consultant. **-o·rio** *adj.* advisory, consulting; *n.m.* consulting room.

**consum-a** *f.* consumption; destruction. **-are** [A1] *tr.* to consume; to consummate; to fulfil; *-are un delitto*, to commit a crime; (fig.) to complete, to perfect. **-ato** *part. adj.* worn out; consummate; *n.m.* (cul.) consommé. **-atọre** *m.* consumer; patron (of restaurant). **-aziọne** *f.* consumption. **-o** *m.* consumption; use; provisions; *per -o*, for everyday use; *-o interno*, home consumption.

**consuntivo** *adj.* consuming, using; *n.m.* (finan.) balance-sheet; account; budget; final balance.

**consunto** *adj.* worn out, used up; wasted; tubercular.

**consunziọne** *f.* consumption; waste.

**conta·bil-e** *m.* accountant; book-keeper. **-ità** *f.* book-keeping; accountancy.

**contadin-o** *adj.* country, rustic; *n.m.* peasant; countryman; farm-worker; boor. **-a** *f.* peasant woman; peasant girl; country dance. **-ẹsco** *adj.* (*m.pl.* **-ẹschi**) rustic; *alla -esca*, countrified.

**contado** *m.* countryside round a city; country district.

**conta·gi-o** *m.* contagion; (fig.) contact; contamination. **-are** [A3] *tr.* to spread by contagion; to contaminate. **-ọso** *adj.* contagious; catching.

**contamin-are** [A1 s] *tr.* to contaminate; to corrupt. **-aziọne** *f.* contamination; corruption. **-ọso** *adj.* contaminating; impure, unclean.

**contante** *n.m.* (finan.) cash; *pl.* ready money.

**cont-are** [A1 c] *tr.* to count; to reckon; to esteem; to indicate; to narrate; *intr.* (*aux.* avere) to count, to matter; *non -a*, it's of no consequence; — *su*, to count on. **-achilo·metri** *m. indecl.* distance gauge; (motor.) mileometer; speedometer. **-apassi** *m. indecl.* pedometer. **-asecọndi** *m. indecl.* stopwatch. **-ata** *f.* count; reckoning. **-ato** *part. adj.* counted, numbered, told; *denaro -ato*, exact amount; *pl.* few. **-atọre** *m.* counter, reckoner; meter.

**contatt-o** *m.* contact; *a* — *con*, in contact with; *in* —, in touch; (electr.) — *a spina*, two-(three-) pin plug. **-ọre** *m.* contacter.

**cọnt-e** *m.* count; earl. **-e·a** *f.* countship; earldom; county.

**contẹggio** *m.* accounting, keeping of accounts; check of voting.

**contẹgn-o** *m.* bearing; behaviour, conduct; appearance; dignity, reserve; *stare in* —, to stand on one's dignity. **-ọso** *adj.* staid, reserved, stiff.

**contemperare** [A1 s] *tr.* to temper, to moderate; to mitigate.

**contempl-are** [A1] *tr.* to contemplate; to meditate upon; to foresee. **-ativo** *adj.* contemplative; meditative; *n.m.* contemplative. **-aziọne** *f.* contemplation; *in -azione*, in consideration.

**contempo** *adv. phr. nel* —, at the same time, in the meanwhile.

**contempora·ne-o** *adj.* contemporary; contemporaneous, simultaneous; *n.m.* contemporary. **-ità** *f.* contemporaneousness.

**conten·d-ere** [C1] *tr.* to contend; to contest; to dispute; to prohibit. **-ente** *part. adj.* contending; *n.m.* rival, contestant. **-ẹvole** *adj.* contentious, quarrelsome.

**conten-ẹre** [B32] *tr.* to contain; to hold; to include; to repress; *rfl.* to contain oneself; to

restrain oneself; *non potè -ersi dal ridere*, he couldn't help laughing. **-ente** *part. adj.* containing; including; *n.m.* container, receptacle. **-enza** *f.* content, capacity; behaviour; reserve.

**conten·nere** [B1] *tr.* to despise; to contemn.

**content-are** [A1] *tr.* to satisfy; to gladden; *rfl.* to be satisfied, to content oneself; *bisogna -arsi*, we mustn't grumble; to allow; *si -a ?*, may I ?, will you allow me ? **-atura** *f.* contentedness; *di difficile -atura*, difficult to please.

**content-o**[1] *adj.* content, contented; satisfied; glad, pleased, happy; *mal —*, dissatisfied. **-ẹzza** *f.* contentment, satisfaction; joy, gladness; pleasure, delight. **-ino** *m.* make-weight, a bit extra; stop-gap.

**contento**[2] *m.* contentment, satisfaction; happiness, pleasure.

**contenuto** *part.* of **contenere,** *q.v.*; *adj.* contained; included; restrained, held back; *n.m.* contents, content; subject, matter.

**contenziọne** *f.* contention, dispute.

**contenziọs-o** *adj.* contentious; questionable. **-ità** *f. indecl.* contentiousness.

**conterello** *m. dim.* of **conto,** *q.v.*; little account, little bill; small sum owing; arithmetical exercise, sum.

**contẹsa** *f.* contest, opposition, disagreement; contention, strife; *venire a —*, to contend, to quarrel.

**contẹss-a** *f.* countess. **-ina** *f. dim.* courtesy title of a daughter of a count.

**contes·s-ere** [C29] *tr.* to interweave; to entwine; (fig.) to compose. **-imẹnto** *m.* interweaving; entwining; (fig.) composition.

**contest-are** *tr.* to contest; to dispute; to oppose; to challenge. **-aziọne** *f.* contestation; dispute; objection; (leg.) issue; dispute; lawsuit.

**contest-o**[1] *altern. part.* of **contessere,** *q.v.*; *adj.* interwoven; put together, composed. **-ura** *f.* interweaving, entwining.

**contest-o**[2] *m.* context; a text viewed as a whole; gist. **-uale** *adj.* relating to the whole of a document, contextual.

**contẹzza** *f.* cognisance, knowledge, awareness; *ne ebbi — da lui*, he informed me of it.

**conti·gu-o** *adj.* contiguous, adjoining, neighbouring. **-ità** *f. indecl.* contiguity, proximity; contiguousness.

**continent-e**[1] *m.* (geog.) continent; (in relation to Ital. islands) mainland; *l'antico —*, the Old World; *il nuovo —*, the New World; *il novissimo —*, Australia. **-ale** *adj.* continental; relating to the mainland of Italy.

**continen-te**[2] *adj.* continent, abstemious; chaste; continuous; constant. **-za** *f.* continence, abstinence, abstemiousness; temperance; chastity.

**contin·g-ere** [C def.] *intr.* to happen. **-ente** *adj.* contingent; incidental; due, expected; *n.m.* quota, allocation; coincidental occurrence. **-enza** *f.* contingency, eventuality.

**continu-are** [A6] *tr.* to continue; to proceed with; *intr.* (*aux.* essere, avere) to continue, to go on; to be in process; (*aux.* avere; *prep.* a, foll. by *infin.*) to continue, to go on; *-ava a parlare*, he went on speaking; to preserve, to keep on. **-aziọne** *f.* continuation; continuing, continuance.

**conti·nu-o** *adj.* continual; continuous; unbroken, uninterrupted; (math.) *frazione -a*, recurring fraction; (electr.) *corrente -a*, direct current; *adv. phr. di —*, continually; *n.m.* continuum. **-ità** *f. indecl.* continuity.

**cọnto**[1] *m.* **1.** addition, calculation, reckoning; *fare il —*, to add up; (boxing) count. **2.** bill, account; *fare i conti*, to do one's accounts; *saldare un —*, to settle an account. **3.** account, reckoning, notice; *tenere — di*, to take account of; *rendersi — di*, to realize, to become aware of; *far — su*, to count on. **4.** account, esteem, regard; *tenere di —*, to hold in esteem, to cherish; *dare ad alcuno il suo —*, to give a person his due; *tornare — a*, to be of value to; *non merita —*, it's not worth while; *non gli mette —*, it doesn't pay him; *di nessun —*, of no value, worthless. **5.** account, report; *render —*, to report; *non dover render — a nessuno*, to be accountable to no one; *dare — di sè*, to give an account of oneself. **6.** account, matter, concern; *è un altro —*, that's another matter; *sapere il suo —*, to know one's business; *a buon —*, with good reason; *per — mio*, for my part; *a nessun —*, on no account. **7.** opinion, intention; *fo — di partir subito*, I intend to leave immediately; *per — mio*, in my opinion; *fare — che*, to think that.

**conto**[2] *m.* narration, account.

**contor·cere** [C5] *tr.* to contort, to twist; *rfl.* to writhe, to twist (as in pain).

**contornare** [A1 c] *tr.* to surround; (cul.) to garnish; (paint.) to sketch in outline; to border, to edge; *rfl.* (*prep.* di) to surround oneself (with), to associate (with).

**contọrno** *m.* outline, contour; ornamental border; trimming, edging; rim; (cul.) the vegetables which go with a meat or fish dish; suite, entourage; *pl.* surroundings, environment.

**contorsiọne** *f.* contorsion, twisting.

**contorto** *part.* of **contorcere;** *adj.* contorted, twisted; distorted; warped.

**cọntra**[1] *prep.* (poet.). See **cọntro.**

**contra**[2] *m.* factor counting against; *il pro e il —*, the pros and cons.

**cọntra**[3] *pref.* contra-; counter-.

**contrabband-o** *m.* contraband, smuggling; *merce di —*, smuggled goods; *di —*, clandestinely, surreptitiously. **-iere** *m.*, **-ista** *m.* smuggler.

**contrab(b)ass-o** *m.* (mus.) double-bass; double diapason (organ stop). **-ista** *m.* double-bass player, contrabassist.

**contrac-cambiare** [A4] *tr.* to reciprocate, to return; *grazie per gli auguri di Natale, che -cambio*, thank you for your Christmas wishes, which I reciprocate; *— un favore*, to return a favour. **-cam·bio** *m.* recompense, return; exchange.

**contraccọlpo** *m.* counter-blow; repercussion; recoil; (motor.) back fire.

**contraccoperta** *f.* dust cover (of a book).

**contraccorente** *f.* counter-current; cross-current; *adj.* running counter, flowing in the opposite direction.

**contrada** *f.* street; village street; district; (poet.) country.

**contrad(d)anza** *f.* country dance; square dance; folk dance.

**contradd-ire** [B10] *tr.* to contradict; to gainsay; to be contradictory; *rfl.* to contradict oneself. **-icente** *part. adj.* contradicting; rebellious. **-ittọre** *m.* one who contradicts; heckler. **-itto·rio** *adj.* contradictory; opposing; heckling; *n.m.* (leg.) confrontation; cross-examination; (fig.) public discussion; *accettare il -ittorio*, to hear the other side. **-iziọne** *f.* contradiction; discrepancy; opposition; *spirito di -izione*, perversity. **-isti·nguere** [C6] *tr.* to distinguish; to mark, to label; to counter-check.

**contradivieto** *m.* contraband, illicit goods.

**contraente** *part.* of **contrarre,** *q.v.*; *adj.* contracting; *n.m.* (comm.) contractor.

**contrae·re-o** *adj.* anti-aircraft. **-a** *f.* anti-aircraft guns, ack-ack.

**contrafagott-o** *m.* (mus.) double-bassoon. **-ista** *m.*, *f.* double-bassoon player.

**contraffac-ente** *part. adj.* counterfeiting; simulating, aping. **-itọre** *m.* counterfeiter, forger.

**contraff-are** [B14] *tr.* to counter-

feit, to forge; to copy, to ape; to disguise. **-attọre** *m.* counterfeiter, forger; imitator. **-aziọne** *f.* counterfeiting; forgery; copy; imitation; piracy, plagiarism.

**contrafforte** *m.* buttress; heavy iron bar for securing a door; (geog.) buttress, spur.

**contrafforza** *f.* reaction, countering force.

**contragge·nio** *m.* disinclination; dislike; aversion; *a* —, unwillingly, against the grain.

**contralto** *m., f.* (mus.) contralto; alto; *chiave di* —, alto clef.

**contrappasso** *m.* fitting retribution, retaliation, an eye for an eye.

**contrappelo** *m.* the wrong way of the hair; *a* —, against the grain.

**contrappesare** [A1 c] *tr.* to counterbalance; to counterpoise; (fig.) to weigh the pros and cons of.

**contrappẹso** *m.* counterpoise.

**contrap-pọrre** [B21] *tr.* (*prep.* a) to oppose, to set against; to contrast (with); *rfl.* to oppose. **-poṣiziọne** *f.* contraposition; opposition; contrast; antithesis.

**contrappunt-o** *m.* (mus.) counterpoint. **-i·stico** *adj.* contrapuntal.

**contrariare** [A4] *tr.* to gainsay, to thwart; to disappoint.

**contra·ri-o** *adj.* contrary; adverse; opposite; reverse; *n.m.* contrary, opposite; *al* —, on the contrary. **-età** *f.* contrariness; opposition; disappointment; *-età del tempo,* unseasonable weather.

**contrarre** [B33] *tr.* to contract; — *debiti,* to incur debts; — *matrimonio,* to enter into matrimony; — *amicizia con,* to form a friendship with; *rfl.* to contract, to shrink.

**contras-segnare** [A5 c] *tr.* to place a mark upon; to label; to countersign. **-sẹgno** *m.* mark, distinctive sign; password; token; (comm.) *-segno per posta,* cash on delivery.

**contrast-are** [A1] *tr.* (*prep.* con) to set (against); to contrast (with); (*prep.* a) to dispute; to resist; *intr.* (*aux.* avere; *prep.* a) to struggle (against); to compete (with); to be in contrast (with); *recip. rfl.* to vie with each other. **-a·bile** *adj.* open to question; controversial.

**contrasto** *m.* conflict; opposition; discord; contrast; *non c'è* —, there's no comparison.

**contratt-are** [A1] *tr.* to bargain concerning, to haggle over; *intr.* (*aux.* avere) to talk business. **-aziọne** *f.* negotiation; business deal; bargaining.

**contrattempo** *m.* delay, short interval; untoward incident, hitch; disappointment; *a* —, at the wrong moment, inopportunely.

**contratto**[1] *part. adj.* contracted; shrunken.

**contratt-o**[2] *m* contract; *in* —, in negotiation. **-uale** *adj.* contractual.

**contravvelẹno** *m.* antidote.

**contravven-ire** [D17] *intr.* (*aux.* avere) to transgress, to trespass; — *a,* to contravene, to infringe. **-ziọne** *f.* breach, contravention; infringement; trespass; *pagare una -zione,* to pay a fine; (colloq.) *ho avuto una -zione,* I got fined.

**contravvite** *f.* nut (of a screwbolt).

**contraziọne** *f.* contraction; shrinking; reduction.

**contribu-ire** [D2] *intr.* (*aux.* avere; *prep.* a) to have a part (in); to contribute (to). **-ente** *part. adj.* contributing; *n.m., f.* contributor; taxpayer; ratepayer.

**contribu-to** *m.* contribution; *mettere a* —, to make use of; sum contributed; quota; share. **-tọre** *m.* contributor; colleague, fellow-worker. **-ziọne** *f.* contribution; participation; quota; levy, tax.

**contristare** [A1] *tr.* to sadden; to afflict; *rfl.* to become sad; to distress oneself.

**contrito** *adj.* contrite, penitent; afflicted.

**contriziọne** *f.* contrition; *far atto di* —, to make an act of contrition.

**cọntro**[1] *prep.* against; over against, opposite to; (comm.) — *pagamento,* against payment; — *assegno,* cash on delivery; *adv.* against, on the opposite side.

**cọntro**[2] *pref.* counter-; contra-.

**cọntro**[3] *m. il pro e il* —, the pros and cons.

**contro-avviso** *m.* contrary information. **-bat·tere** [B1] *tr.* to counter, to answer; to refute; *intr.* (*aux.* avere) to rebound, to recoil; to return blow for blow; to make a riposte. **-bilanciare** [A3] *tr* to counterbalance. **-corrente** *f.* countercurrent; *andare a -corrente,* to go against the current. **-figura** *f.* (cinem.) stand-in. **-firma** *f.* counter-signature. **-governo** *m.* (pol.) opposition. **-indicaziọne** *f.* contra-indication. **-luce** *m.* picture taken against the light; *adv.* in the wrong light; against the light. **-lume** *m.* wrong light; light in one's eyes. **-mandare** [A1] *tr.* to countermand. **-mano** *adv.* (motor.) on the wrong side of the road; *io tenevo la destra, invece lui m'è venuto -mano e così ci siamo scontrati,* I was keeping to the right, but he came towards me on the wrong side of the road and we collided. **-marca** *f.* countermark; sign; pass-out ticket. **-mar·cia** *f.* (mil.) about turn; (cinem.) flash-back; (eng.; motor.) reverse gear. **-palo** *m.* strut. **-parte** *f.* (leg.) opponent; (theatr.) supporting part, foil; (mus.) counterpart. **-porta** *f.* double door; screen-door. **-progetto** *m.* counter-plan; alternative scheme. **-propọsta** *f.* counter-proposal. **-prova** *f.* repetition of a test; recount of a vote. **-relaziọne** *f.* minority report. **-riforma** *f.* (hist.) Counter-Reformation. **-rispọsta** *f.* counter-reply. **-riva** *f.* opposite bank. **-rivoluziọne** *f.* counter-revolution. **-scarpa** *f.* overshoe, galosh. **-scena** *f.* (theatr.) business; by-play. **-senso** *m.* misconstruction; wrong sense; *a -senso,* in the wrong way. **-serratura** *f.* double-lock. **-spionag·gio** *m.* counter-espionage. **-stimolante** *adj.* tranquillizing. **-sto·maco** *n.m.* repugnance, nausea; *adv.* with repugnance. **-ver·sia** *f.* controversy; disagreement. **-verso** *adj.* controversial; disputed, debated. **-vi·ṣita** *f.* return visit. **-vọto** *m.* counter-vote.

**controllare** [A1] *tr.* to check; to examine; to verify; to control; *rfl.* to control oneself.

**controll-o** *m.* checking, verification, inspection; *giro di* —, tour of inspection; control; *il — di sè,* self-control; (sport) marking. **-ọre** *m.* inspector; reviser; ticket inspector.

**contrọrdin-e** *m.* counter-order; countermanding. **-are** [A1 sc] *tr.* to countermand.

**contumace** *adj.* (leg.) contumacious; (fig.) obstinate.

**contuma·cia** *f.* obstinacy, stubbornness; insubordination; (leg.) contumacy.

**contume·li-a** *f.* contumely; obloquy; disgrace; *fare — a,* to insult, to be offensive to. **-ọso** *adj.* contumelious; insolent.

**contun·d-ere** [C1] *tr.* to bruise; to blunt. **-ente** *part. adj.* bruising; liable to bruise easily; *corpo -ente,* blunt instrument.

**conturb-are** [A1] *tr.* to disturb; to perturb. **-aziọne** *f.* disturbance; perturbation.

**contuṣiọne** *f.* (med.) bruise, contusion.

**contutto-chẹ** *conj.* although, in spite of the fact. **-ciò** *adv.* nevertheless; in any case. **-quẹsto** *adv.* in spite of this, nevertheless.

**convalesc-ente** *adj., n.m. f.* convalescent. **-enza** *f.* convalescence.

**conva·lid-a** *f.* confirmation, proof. **-are** [A1 s] *tr.* (leg.) to confirm; to ratify; (fig.) to reinforce; to prove true.

**convalle** *f.* dale; meeting-place of two or more valleys;

(bot.) *giglio delle convalli,* lily-of-the-valley.

**convẹgno** *m.* meeting; meeting-place; conference.

**convenẹvole** *adj.* suitable; fitting; seemly; opportune; *n.m.* that which is suitable or seemly; *pl.* conventional expressions of good manners; *stare sui convenevoli,* to stand on ceremony.

**convenien-te** *adj.* fitting, appropriate; expedient; advantageous; requisite. **-za** *f.* suitability; aptness; advantage; expediency; propriety; *mancare di -za,* to behave improperly; *pl.* polite usage; formality; *sapere le -ze,* to know how to behave.

**conven-ire** [D17] *intr.* (*aux.* essere) to come together, to meet; to concur; to converge; (*aux.* avere) to agree; *ne -go,* I agree; *recip. rfl.* to agree; to suit each other; *impers.* to be suitable; to be proper; to be advisable; to be necessary. **-imẹnto** *m.* meeting; assembly.

**conventi·cola** *f.* secret meeting; gathering of people conspiring together.

**convento**[1] *m.* religious house; priory; convent (of friars or nuns).

**convento**[2] *m.* agreement; convention.

**convenuto** *part. adj.* come together; agreed, fixed; *n.m.* what has been agreed; accord, pact.

**convenziọn-e** *f.* convention; custom; agreement; covenant, pact; *esser di —,* to be in league. **-ale** *adj.* conventional; pertaining to a convention. **-alista** *m.* conventionalist. **-alità** *f.* conventionality.

**conver·g-ere** [C4] *intr.* (*aux.* essere) to converge. **-ente** *adj.* converging; *lente -ente,* convex lens. **-enza** *f.* convergence.

**conversa**[1] *f.* (bldg.) valley-tile.

**conversa**[2] *f.* lay sister in a convent.

**convers-are** [A1] *intr.* (*aux.* avere) to converse, to hold conversation; *n.m.* conversing; conversation. **-aziọne** *f.* conversation; talk. **-ẹvole** *adj.* sociable, friendly.

**conversiọne** *f.* conversion; converting, changing; turning; rotation.

**converso**[1] *part.* of **convergere,** *q.v.*

**converso**[2] *adj.* converted; transformed; *n.m.* converse; opposite, contrary; *per —,* conversely; lay brother.

**convert-ire** [D1] *tr.* to convert; to transmute; *rfl.* to be converted, to change; to be convinced. **-i·bile** *adj.* convertible; exchangeable. **-ibilità** *f.* convertibility. **-imẹnto** *m.* conversion; transformation. **-ito** *part. adj.* converted; transmuted; *-ito ad altro uso,* put to another use; *n.m.* convert.

**convess-o** *adj.* convex; *n.m.* convexity. **-ità** *f.* convexity.

**convin·c-ere** [C5] *tr.* to convince; to persuade; to convict; *intr.* (*aux.* avere) to be convincing; *rfl.* to be convinced. **-ente** *part. adj.* convincing; telling; conclusive.

**convinto** *part. adj.* convinced; won over, persuaded; convicted.

**convinziọne** *f.* conviction, persuasion, belief; convincing.

**convit-are** [A1] *tr.* to invite to dinner; to entertain; to convoke. **-ato** *part. adj.* invited; *n.m.* guest.

**convito** *m.* banquet.

**convitt-o** *m.* boarding-school. **-ọre** *m.* pupil at a boarding school; inmate.

**convi·v-ere** [C16] *intr.* (*aux.* essere) to live together, to cohabit. **-enza** *f.* living together, cohabitation; *l'umana -enza,* human society.

**convi·vi-o** *m.* banquet. **-ale** *adj.* convivial.

**convoc-are** [A2 sc] *tr.* to convoke, to convene; *— d'urgenza,* to call an emergency meeting. **-ato** *part. adj.* convoked; convened; *n.m.* guest; *i -ati,* those summoned to the meeting. **-aziọne** *f.* convocation; convening.

**convogli-are** [A4] *tr.* to convoy; to sweep away; *— a mezzo di tubazioni,* to pipe. **-atọre** *m.* (techn.) conveyor; *-atore a nastro,* conveyor belt.

**convo·glio** *m.* convoy, escort; train; *— funebre,* funeral cortège.

**convolare** [A1] *intr.* (*aux.* essere) to fly together; to hasten together.

**convol·volo** *m.* bindweed.

**convuls-iọne** *f.* convulsion; *soffre di -ioni,* he has fits. **-ivo** *adj.* convulsive.

**convulso** *adj.* convulsed; convulsive; shaken; (fig.) jerky; *n.m.* nervous trembling; twitch.

**cooper-are** [A1 s] *intr.* (*aux.* avere) to co-operate; to collaborate; *— a,* to work towards. **-ante** *part. adj.* co-operative; *n.m., f.* co-operator. **-ativa** *f.* co-operative society. **-ativo** *adj.* co-operative. **-aziọne** *f.* co-operation.

**coordin-are** [A1 sc] *tr.* to co-ordinate; to correlate; to arrange. **-atọre** *m.* co-ordinator. **-aziọne** *f.* co-ordination.

**coper·chi-o** *m.* lid, cover, hood; covering. **-are** [A4] *tr.* to cover with a lid.

**copert-a** *f.* blanket; rug; coverlet; (naut.) *sopra —,* on deck; *sotto —,* below deck; book-cover, jacket; envelope; pretext, excuse. **-ina** *f. dim.* coverlet; paper-cover, jacket, wrapper. **-ọne** *m. augm.* tarpaulin; outer cover of a tyre; thick bed-covering.

**copert-o** *part. adj.* covered; wearing a hat; closed in; sheltered; *cielo —,* overcast sky; *n.m.* cover; roof; shelter; *al —,* under cover; place laid at table; cover-charge. **-ura** *f.* covering, cover; tyre; *lettera di -ura,* covering letter; (comm.) cover, security; wrapping.

**co·pia**[1] *f.* plenty, abundance; *— di dire,* fluency.

**co·pia**[2] *f.* copy; transcription; *bella —,* fair copy; *brutta —,* rough copy; *— per conoscenza a,* copy for information.

**copiafatture** *f.pl.* bill-book; invoice-book.

**copi-are** [A4] *tr.* to copy; to imitate; to transcribe; (photog.) to print. **-atọre** *m.* copyist. **-atura** *f.* copying; transcribing.

**copilota** *m.* co-pilot.

**copiọne** *m.* actor's copy, script; prompt copy.

**copiọs-o** *adj.* copious, abundant. **-ità** *f.* copiousness, plenty.

**copist-a** *m., f.* copyist; copy-typist. **-eri·a** *f.* copying office; typing office.

**coppa** *f.* goblet; (sport) cup, trophy; pan of a pair of scales; cranium; ice-cream in a tub.

**coppell-a** *f. dim.* crucible; *argento di —,* purest silver; *reggere a —,* to stand the test. **-are** [A1] *tr.* (metall.) to assay; to refine. **-aziọne** *f.* assaying; cupellation.

**cop·pi-a** *f.* married couple; pair; *a -e,* in pairs.

**coppi-ere, -ero** *m.* cup-bearer.

**coppino** *m.* back of the head.

**cọpp-o** *m.* earthenware jar; oil-jar; tile gutter. **-oluto** *adj.* rounded, domed.

**copri-busto** *m.* bodice; under-vest. **-capo** *m.* headgear, hat. **-fuoco** *m.* curfew; lights-out. **-piatti** *m. indecl.* dish-cover; meat-cover. **-piedi** *m. indecl.* coverlet for the feet. **-vivande** *m. indecl.* dish cover; meat cover.

**copr-ire** [D1] *tr.* to cover; to hide; to muffle; to shield, to shelter; *— una vacanza,* to fill a vacancy; *rfl.* to cover oneself; to shield oneself; (of weather) to become overcast. **-itura** *f.* covering; cover; pretext.

**copto** *adj., n.m.* Coptic; *lingua copta,* Coptic (language).

**co·pul-a** *f.* connexion; copulation. **-are** [A1 s] *tr.* to join together, to couple; *intr.* (*aux.* avere) to copulate. **-aziọne** *f.* copulation; connexion; coupling.

**corag·gi-o** *m.* courage; boldness; *far — a,* to encourage; to comfort; impudence, 'cheek'; *ha un bel —,* he's got a nerve; *— civile,* public-spiritedness. **-ọso** *adj.*

courageous; fearless; *n.m.* courageous man.
**corale** *adj.* choral; *libro —*, choir-book; *n.m.* chorale; plain-chant; choirbook.
**corall-o** *m.* coral. **-i·fero** *adj.* coral-bearing; *atollo -ifero*, coral reef. **-ino** *adj.* coralline; red.
**corame** *m.* hides and skins; stamped leather.
**Corano** *pr.n.m.* Koran.
**corata** *f.* (anat.) pericardium; (cul.) lights; giblets; offal, pluck.
**corazz-a** *f.* cuirass; breast-plate; carapace. **-are** [A1] *tr.* to arm, to armour-plate. **-ata** *f.* battleship; dreadnought.
**corbell-are** [A1] *tr.* to make a fool of. **-ato·rio** *adj.* derisive, mocking. **-eri·a** *f.* nonsense, foolishness.
**corbello**[1] *m.* blockhead.
**corbello**[2] *m.* large basket; hamper.
**cord-a** *f.* cord; rope; hawser; string, wire; *-e della borsa*, purse-strings; *— d'arco*, bow-string; chord; note; *strumenti a —*, stringed instruments; sinew; *-e vocali*, vocal cords; physical tone, fitness; thread, cloth; *mostrare la —*, to be threadbare. **-ag·gio** *m.* rope; cordage; *-aggio nero*, tarred rope. **-a·io, -ai(u)olo** *m.* rope-maker. **-ame** *m.* cordage. **-ata** *f.* length of rope; two or more mountaineers roped together. **-eri·a** *f.* rope-making; rope-factory; rope-walk. **-ifi·cio** *m.* ropery, rope works.
**cordial-e** *adj.* cordial; genial; heart-felt; *n.m.* cordial. **-mente** *adv.* cordially; *-mente antipatico*, heartily disliked. **-ità** *f.* cordiality; warmth of manner.
**cordo·gli-o** *m.* affliction; anguish; lamentation. **-oso** *adj.* sorrowful; anguished.
**cor·dolo** *m.* kerbstone.
**cordonare** [A1 c] *tr.* to gird; to surround; to deceive.
**cordone** *m.* cord, rope; priest's girdle; kerb (of pavement); *— del campanello*, bell-pull; (electr.) flex, lead; cordon; edging, border.
**core·a**[1] *f.* (med.) chorea, St Vitus' dance.
**Core·a**[2] *pr.n.f.* (geog.) Korea.
**coreo·graf-o** *m.* choreographer. **-i·a** *f.* choreography.
**coricare** [A25] *tr.* to lay down; to put to bed; *rfl.* to lie down; to retire for the night; (of the sun) to set.
**co·ril-o** *m.* hazel. **-eto** *m.* hazel-copse.
**Cor-into** *pr.n.f.* (geog.) Corinth. **-in·tio, -in·zio** *adj.*, *n.m.* Corinthian.
**corista** *m.* member of choir; choirboy; tuning-fork; *f.* chorus-girl.
**cornac·chi-a** *f.* crow; (fig.) bird of ill omen. **-are** [A4] *intr.* (*aux.* avere) to caw; to chatter.
**cornamus-a** *f.* bagpipe. **-are** [A1] *intr.* (*aux.* avere) to pipe, to skirl.
**cornare** [A1] *intr.* (*aux.* avere) to sound the horn; to buzz; *tr.* to butt (with horns).
**cor·neo** *adj.* horn-like; made of horn.
**cornett-a** *f.* (mus.) cornet in B flat; *— segnale*, bugle; (naut.) pennant. **-ista** *m.* cornet-player.
**cornett-o** (*pl.m.* **-i**, or *f.* **-a**) horn (of an animal); (cul.) cornet; croissant; *— acustico*, ear trumpet; horn of an anvil.
**cor·nia** *f.* agate.
**cornic-e** *f.* picture-frame; *mettere in —*, to frame; (fig.) *fare — a*, to frame; setting; cornice. **-ia·io** *m.* frame-maker. **-iare** [A3] *tr.* to frame; to set in a frame. **-ione** *m.* projecting moulding; entablature; *-ione di gronda*, eaves.
**corn-o** *m.* (*pl.f.* **-a**) horn; antler; corn (on foot); *dire -a di*, to speak evil of; *portare le -a*, to be cuckold; horn (substance); *— da scarpe*, shoehorn; (*pl.m.* **-i**) projection; tip, point (of a flame); beak (of anvil); branch (of road); reach (of river); *i -i di un dilemma*, the horns of a dilemma (also, *le -a*); (mus.) horn; French horn; (vulg.) damn all; *un bel —*, nothing at all. **-i·fero** *adj.* horned. **-ista** *m.* (mus.) horn-player.
**Cornova·glia** *pr.n.f.* (geog.) Cornwall.
**cornuco·pia** *f.* cornucopia, horn of plenty.
**cornuto** *adj.* horned; cuckold; *argomento —*, dilemma.
**coro**[1] *m.* choir; chorus; *in —*, in chorus; (fig.) of one accord; *far —*, to chime in.
**coro**[2] *m.* north-west wind; north-westerly direction.
**corolla** *f.* (bot.) corolla.
**corolla·rio** *m.* corollary.
**coron-a** *f.* crown; garland, wreath; ring, circle; *far —*, to form a circle; series; *recitare la —*, to say the rosary. **-are** [A1 c] *tr.* to crown; to complete. **-a·rio** *adj.* (anat.) coronary.
**coro·nio** *m.* corona, halo.
**corpacc-iolo** *m.* fatty. **-iuto** *adj.* corpulent; pot-bellied.
**corp-o** *m.* body; physique; corpse, cadaver; belly; *mettersi in —*, to gulp down; *a — pieno*, on a full stomach; material, matter; *-i semplici*, elements; *-i composti*, compounds; *— contundente*, blunt instrument; thickness, body, bulk; *dare — a*, to give substance to; *vino che ha molto —*, full-bodied wine; section; collection; corpus of writings; corporation; corps; *in —*, in a body; *— insegnante*, teaching staff; (naut.) hull; *— dell'Armata*, main fleet; (leg.) *— della compagnia*, corporation; *— del delitto*, corpus delicti. OATHS: *— di Bacco!*, *— del diavolo!*, what the devil! **-uto** *adj.* stout; dense (of a gas or liquid).
**corporal-e**[1] *adj.* corporeal, bodily; corporal; *esercizi -i*, physical exercises, carnal. **-ità** *f.* corporality.
**corporale**[2] *n.* (mil.) corporal.
**corpor-ativo** *adj.* corporate, corporative. **-atura** *f.* figure, form, shape. **-azione** *f.* corporation.
**corp-o·reo** *adj.* corporeal; material. **-oruto** *adj.* large-bodies. **-ulento** *adj.* corpulent. **-ulenza** *f.* corpulence; thickness, consistency.
**corpu·scolo** *m.* corpuscle; small particle.
**Corpusdo·mini** *m. indecl.* (Feast of) Corpus Christi.
**corred-are** [A1] *tr.* (*prep.* di) to equip, to fit out, to rig out (with). **-ato** *part. adj.* equipped, furnished; accompanied, supported (by).
**corredo** *m.* outfit, equipment; *— della sposa*, trousseau; household goods; (fig.) wealth.
**correg·gere** [C12] *tr.* to correct; to rectify; to revise; to reform; to guide (animals); to lace with spirits.
**correggia** *f.* leather strap; thong; shoelace.
**corregionale** *adj.* belonging to the same region.
**correla-tivo** *adj.* correlative; reciprocal, mutual. **-zione** *f.* correlation; mutual relationship; *in -zione*, in proportion.
**correligiona·rio** *adj.* of the same persuasion (religion, politics, etc.); *n.m.* co-religionist; fellow-thinker, like-minded person.
**corrent-e**[1] *adj.* running, flowing; current; present-day; usual; due, payable; (comm.) *conto —*, current account; cursive; racy (of style); fluent; *adv. phr. al —*, up-to-date. **-ac·qua** *adj. indecl.* *camera -acqua*, bedroom with running water.
**corrente**[2] *f.* current, stream; *— d'aria*, draught; (fig. general current of opinion; trend.
**corrent-e**[3] *m.* joist, beam; rafter. **-ame** *m.* boarding, joisting.
**corr-e·o** *m.* accomplice; *— in un delitto*, accessory to a crime. **-eità** *f.* complicity.
**corr-ere** [C5] *intr.* (*aux.* avere, with ref. to action; essere, with ref. to destination); to run; *fare a —*, to run a race; *— dietro a*, to run after; to rush; to travel rapidly, to speed, to fly; to be current; to be valid; to circulate; *il mese che -e*, the current month; *-e la voce che*, it is

rumoured that; to flow, to run smoothly; *lasciar* –, to let things take their course; to do things quickly; *come -e scrivendo!*, how quickly he writes!; to intervene, to extend; *-e una bella differenza*, there's a world of difference; *ci -e*, that's different!; to pass, to go by; *è corso un secolo da quando*, it's a hundred years since; to fall due; *ogni settimana -e la pigione*, every week the rent is due; *mi -e l'obbligo di*, I am faced with the necessity of; *tr.* to run; – *un pericolo*, to run a risk; to sack, to plunder; to overrun.

**correspettiv-o** *adj.* corresponding; reciprocal; compensating; *n.m.* compensation; corresponding amount; equivalent. **-ità** *f.* proportion, relation.

**corrett-o** *part. adj.* corrected; accurate, exact; right; *caffè* –, coffee laced with grappa. **-ẹzza** *f.* correctness; accuracy; honesty, fairness. **-ivo** *adj., n.m.* corrective.

**correziọne** *f.* correction; improvement; revision; reform.

**corrida** *f.* bull-fight; cycle-race.

**corridọio** *m.* corridor; passageway; lobby; (naut.) main deck; (cinem.) – *del film*, film track.

**corridọre** *n.m.* runner; rider; racehorse.

**corrier-a** *f.* mail-coach; mail van; country bus; charabanc. **-e, -o** *m.* postman; carrier; courier; post, mail; newspaper; *a volta di -e*, by return of post.

**corrig-endo** *m.* corrigendum. **-i·bile** *adj.* corrigible; open to correction.

**corrimano** *m.* handrail.

**corrisponden-te** *adj.* corresponding; relating; proportionate; *n.m.* correspondent. **-za** *f.* correspondence; post, mail; reciprocated affection; agreement; proportion; *con guanti in -za*, with gloves to match; (rlwy.) connexion; *biglietto di -za*, through ticket.

**corrispọndere** [C11] *intr.* (*aux.* avere; *prep.* a) to correspond (to); to be in keeping (with); to respond (to); – *alla fiducia*, to justify confidence; (*prep.* con) to correspond (with); to be connected (with); (*prep.* su) to look out (over), to give on (to); *tr.* (comm.) to pay, to remit.

**corrivo** *adj.* easy-going; credulous; hasty, careless; banal; facile.

**corrobor-are** [A1 s] *tr.* to strengthen; to fortify; to support, to corroborate. **-ante** *part. adj.* strengthening; corroborating; *n.m.* tonic. **-ativo** *adj.* corroborative. **-aziọne** *f.* strengthening; support, corroboration.

**corrọd-ere** [C1] *tr.* to corrode; to wear away; *rfl.* to be consumed. **-ente** *part. adj.* corroding, corrosive.

**corrọmpere** [C26] *tr.* to corrupt; to contaminate; to seduce; *rfl.* to become corrupted; to rot; to decompose.

**corroṣ-iọne** *f.* corrosion, eating away. **-ivo** *adj.* corrosive; consuming; *n.m.* corrosive. **-o** *part. adj.* corroded, eaten away.

**corrọtto**[1] *part.* of **corrọmpere,** *q.v.*; *adj.* corrupt; contaminated, foul; decomposed; *n.m.* corrupt person.

**corrucciare** [A3] *tr.* to anger, to vex; to grieve; *rfl.* to be roused to anger; to fly into a passion.

**corruc·ci-o** *m.* rage; vexation; hostility; sorrow, regret; **-ọso** *adj.* angry, enraged.

**corrugare** [A2 s] *tr.* to wrinkle; to corrugate; – *le ciglia*, to frown; *rfl.* to knit one's brow.

**corrus-care** [A2] *intr.* (*aux.* avere) to sparkle, to coruscate, to flash. **-co** *adj.* (*m.pl.* **-chi**) sparkling, coruscating.

**corruttela** *f.* corruption; depravity.

**corrutt-i·bile** *adj.* corruptible; perishable; *n.m.* (poet.) the flesh. **-ibilità** *f.* corruptibility. **-ivo** *adj.* corrupting. **-ọre** *m.* corruptor.

**corruziọne** *f.* corruption; graft; depravity; contamination; deterioration; putrefaction.

**cọrsa** *f.* running; *pigliar la* –, to set off at a run; *fare una* –, to run an errand; *di* –, running, at speed; run, trip, course; *perdere la* –, to miss a train; *cavallo da* –, racehorse.

**corsar-o** *m.* pirate, corsair; privateer. **-ẹsco** *adj.* (*m.pl.* **-ẹschi**) piratical.

**corsi·a** *f.* gangway; passage; hospital ward; dormitory.

**Cor·sica** *pr.n.f.* (geog.) Corsica.

**corsier-e, -o** *m.* steed, charger.

**corsi·o** *adj.* running, flowing.

**corsivo** *adj.* flowing, running; cursive; italics; *n.m.* short leader article.

**cọrso**[1] *part.* of **cọrrere,** *q.v.*; *adj.* run; coursed; past, elapsed; undergone; raided, overrun.

**cọrso**[2] *m.* run, running; course, progress, development; *lavori in* –, work in progress; flow, stream; course, layer; street, road; series of lessons, course; *frequentare i corsi*, to attend lectures; – *di aggiornamento*, refresher course; *avere* – *legale*, to be legal tender; *in* –, current, valid, (fig.) in fashion.

**corso**[3] *adj., n.m.* Corsican.

**corsọio** *adj.* slipping, sliding; *nodo* –, slip-knot.

**cọrte** *f.* court; *uomo di* –, courtier; (fig.) *tenere* – *bandita*, to keep open house; *far la* – *a*, to court; courtyard; walled garden; small square.

**cortẹccia** *f.* bark (of trees); rind; crust; cortex; shell; surface.

**cortegg-iare** [A3 c] *tr.* to pay court to; to woo; to flatter. **-atọre** *m.* suitor; flatterer.

**cortẹggio** *m.* suite, retinue, cortège.

**corte·o** *m.* procession, train, cortège; – *nuziale*, wedding party.

**cortẹṣ-e** *adj.* kind; courteous; gracious; *di modi -i*, obliging; *poco* –, discourteous. **-i·a** *f.* courtesy; kindness; *usare -ia*, to be courteous; tip, gratuity; *per -ia*, as a favour, please.

**cor·tice** *m.* (anat.) cortex; bark (of trees).

**cortigian-o** *adj.* courtly, refined; *n.m.* courtier; flatterer. **-a** *f.* courtesan. **-ẹsco** *adj.* (*m.pl.* **-ẹschi**) subservient; obsequious.

**cortile** *m.* courtyard, court; farmyard.

**cortin-a** *f.* curtain (of a bed or door), hanging; (mil.) curtain; – *di fumo*, smoke screen; (pol., fig.) – *di ferro*, iron curtain; *adv. phr. oltre* –, behind the iron curtain. **-ag·gio** *m.* (bed)-curtains, (bed)-hangings; canopy. **-are** [A1] *tr.* to curtain.

**cọrt-o** *adj.* short, brief; (provb.) *le bugie hanno le gambe -e*, truth will out; – *di vista*, short-sighted; *per farla -a*, in short; *alle -e!*, get to the point!; limited, in short supply; *venir* –, to draw a blank. **-ẹzza** *f.* shortness, brevity; scarcity; *-ezza di mente*, dull-wittedness.

**corv-o** *m.* bird of the crow amily, (pop.) 'crow'; rook; (joc.) priest, parson. **-ẹtto** *m.* jackdaw.

**cosà** *adv. prn. così o* –, one way or another; *così o* –?, this way or that way?

**cos-a** *f.* thing; object; *qualche* –, something; *ogni* –, everything; *non è gran* –, it's nothing much; *avere qualche* – *con*, to have a grudge against; *tante* –*e!*, all the best!; matter, affair, fact; *la* – *pubblica*, public affairs; *la somma delle -e*, public authority; *le -e di casa*, household affairs; *è* – *mia*, it's my affair; *tutt'altra* –, quite another matter; event, deed, occurrence; *di* – *nasce* –, one thing leads to another; *a* – *fatta*, after the event; (*che*) – *volete?*, what do you want?; (*che*) – *hai?*, what's the matter with you?, what's wrong?; – ?, what?; *non so* – *dire*, I don't know what to say; *pl.* property, possessions; goods and chattels. **-are** [A1] *tr.* (pop.) to 'fix', to 'cause'; *vedere come l'hanno -ato*, look at the mess they've made of it.

**cosac-ca** *f.* Cossack dance; Cossack woman. **-co** *adj., n.m.* (*pl.* **-chi**) Cossack.

**coscętt-a** *f.* leg (of a fowl). **-o** *m.* leg (of lamb).
**co·scia** *f.* (*pl.* **cosce**) thigh; haunch; flank; *calzoli a* —, tights; leg of meat.
**coscen-te** *adj.* conscious; aware; — *di sè,* self-aware. **-za** *f.* consciousness; awareness; conscience; *direttore di -za,* spiritual director, confessor; *uomo di -za,* conscientious man; *senza -za,* unscrupulous; *in -za,* honestly. **-ziọso** *adj.* conscientious; scrupulous.
**co·sci-o** *m.* leg, joint (of meat). **-otto** *m.* leg (of lamb); *-otto di selvaggina,* haunch of venison.
**coscritto** *part.* of **coscrivere,** *q.v.*; *adj.* conscripted; *n.m.* conscript; recruit.
**coscri·vere** [C12] *tr.* to conscript; to levy.
**coscriziọne** *f.* conscription.
**così** *adv.* thus; so; — *detto,* so-called; *e — via,* and so on; *per — dire,* so to speak; — *sia,* so be it, amen; *così così,* so so, not too bad; likewise, similarly; as; *adj. indecl.* such, similar, of this kind; *conj.* would that; — *l'avesse saputo!,* would that he had known!
**cosicchę̀** *conj.* so that, with the result that.
**cosiddętto** *adj.* so-called; styled.
**cosiffatto** *adj.* such, similar, such-like.
**coṣmeṣi** *f.* the cosmetic art; beautifying.
**coṣme·tic-a** *f.* cosmetics; beauty culture; beauty treatment. **-o** *adj.*, *n.m.* cosmetics; *pl.* cosmetics.
**co·ṣmic-o** *adj.* cosmic; *raggi -i,* cosmic rays, radiation.
**coṣm-o** *m.* cosmos; universe; (fig.) order. **-ogoni·a** *f.* cosmogony. **-ografi·a** *f.* cosmography. **-ologi·a** *f.* cosmology. **-opolita** *m.* cosmopolitan.
**coso** *m.* (colloq.) thingummy, whatsit; nonentity.
**cospar·gere** [C4] *tr.* to sprinkle, to strew.
**cosparso** *part.* of **cospargere,** *q.v.*; *adj.* sprinkled, strewn; — *di rossore,* suffused with blushes.
**cospersiọne** *f.* sprinkling.
**cosperso** *adj.* sprinkled.
**cospetto** *m.* face, presence; view, sight; *nel — di,* in the presence of; *dinanzi al — di Dio,* in the sight of God.
**cospi·cu-o** *adj.* conspicuous, outstanding; considerable; remarkable. **-ità** *f.* conspicuousness.
**cospir-are** [A1] *intr.* (*aux.* avere) to conspire; to plot. **-atọre** *m.* conspirator; plotter; confederate. **-aziọne** *f.* conspiracy.
**cosso** *m.* pimple; *male del* —, ear-ache; (fig.) whim.
**cost-a** *f.* rib; *male di* —, pleurisy; *di* —, sideways; (butcher.) sirloin; slope, hillside; coast. **-ale** *adj.* coastal; (anat.) costal.
**cost-à** *adv.* over there. **-aggiù** *adv.* down there. **-assù** *adv.* up there.
**costante** *adj.* constant; steady, firm; unremitting; (of weather) settled; *n.f.* constant.
**Costantino·poli** *pr.n.f.* (hist.) Constantinople.
**costanza**[1] *f.* constancy; firmness; perseverance; steadfastness.
**Costanza**[2] *pr.n.f.* Constance; (geog.) *Lago di* —, Lake Constance.
**costare** [A1] *intr.* (*aux.* essere) to cost; to be expensive; *gli è costata cara,* he paid dearly for it; *tr.* to cost; (fam.) — *un occhio della testa,* to cost the earth.
**costeggiare** [A3c] *tr.* to coast, to skirt; to flank; *intr.* (*aux.* avere) to hug the shore, to coast.
**coste·i** *pers. prn*: *f. sing.* this woman.
**costell-are** [A1] *tr.* to strew with stars; to spangle. **-ato** *part. adj.* star-spangled; *-ato di,* studded with, strewn with. **-aziọne** *f.* constellation.
**costern-are** [A1] *tr.* to throw into consternation, to dismay; *rfl.* to be dismayed; to suffer consternation. **-ato** *part. adj.* dismayed. **-aziọne** *f.* consternation.
**cost-ì** *adv.* over there, not far off; over there by you. **-inci** *adv.* thence.
**costier-a** *f.* slope; stretch of coast. **-o** *adj.* coastal, littoral.
**costip-are** [A1s] *tr.* to constipate; to heap up; to pile together; *rfl.* to catch a bad cold; to become constipated. **-ato** *part. adj.* suffering from a bad cold; stuffed up, congested; constipated. **-aziọne** *f.* bad head cold; *-azione di ventre,* constipation.
**costitu-ire** [D2] *tr.* to constitute, to form; to create; *lo -irono capo,* they made him head; *rfl.* to come into being; *si è -ita una società,* a company has been formed. **-ente** *part. adj.* constituting; *n.f.* constituent assembly; *m.* member of same; *pl.* constituents.
**costituziọn-e** *f.* constitution. **-ale** *adj.* constitutional
**costo** *m.* cost; *a prezzo di* —, at cost price; *rifarsi del* —, to meet expenses; — *di esercizio,* running expenses; *a nessun* —, on no account.
**co·stol-a** *f.* rib; *stare alle -e di,* to importune; back, spine (of book). **-ame** *m.*, **-atura** *f.* ribs, ribbing; framework. **-ętta** *f.* cutlet.
**costọro** *pers. prn. pl.* these people.
**costọso** *adj.* costly dear.
**costrettivo** *adj* coercive; restrictive.
**costrętto** *part.* of **costringere,** *q.v.*; *adj.* compelled, constrained; confined.
**costrin·gere** [C10] *tr.* to compel, to constrain; to restrict; to constrict.
**costrittivo** *adj.* constrictive; restrictive.
**costriziọne** *f.* constriction; constraint.
**costruire** [D9] *tr.* to build, to erect; to construct; to construe.
**costrutt-o** *part. adj.* constructed; built, erected; construed; *n.m.* (gramm.) construction; (fig.) sense, interpretation; advantage, benefit. **-ọre** *m.* constructor, builder; *adj.* building; *società -rice,* civil engineering company. **-ura** *f.* construction, building.
**costruziọne** *f.* construction, building; *in* —, in course of construction; (gramm.) parsing; *far la — di,* to analyse, to parse.
**costu·i** *pers. prn. m. sing.* this man, this fellow.
**costum-are** [A1] *intr.* (*aux.* essere) to be customary; to be fashionable; (*prep.* di, followed by *infin.*) to be in the habit (of); *tr.* to bring up, to educate. **-anza** *f.* old custom; old-fashioned convention. **-atęzza** *f.* good moral behaviour; good manners. **-ato** *part. adj.* well-mannered, well-trained; *mal -ato,* badly brought-up.
**costum-e** *m.* usage; habit, custom; costume; fancy dress; manners; *essere di buoni -i,* to be good-living; *senza* —, mannerless, uncouth. **-ista** *m.*, *f.* costume designer; wardrobe man; wardrobe mistress.
**costura** *f.* seam.
**cotale** *adj.* such; *indef. prn.* such a one.
**cotanto** *adv.* so much.
**cote** *f.* hone, sharpener; whetstone.
**cotęnn-a** *f.* hide; pigskin; *di grossa* —, thick-skinned; crust, skin; (fig.) miser. **-ọso** *adj.* thick in the hide.
**cotęst-o** *adj.* that; such; *prn. m.* that of yours; that one. (**-a** *f.*).
**cotọgn-a** *f.* quince. **-ata** *f.*, **-ato** *m.* quince jam, quince jelly. **-o** *m.* quince tree.
**cotolętta** *f.* cutlet.
**cotọn-e** *m.* cotton; — *idrofilo,* cotton-wool; *refe di* —, sewing cotton; canvas; wad, pad, tampon; *pl.* cotton goods. **-ato** *adj.* lined with cotton. **-eri·e** *f.pl.* cotton goods. **-iere** *m.* cotton manufacturer; mill-hand. **-iero** *adj.* relating to cotton; *industria -iera,* cotton industry. **-ifi·cio** *m.* cotton-spinning mill. **-ọso** *adj.* cottony, downy, fluffy.
**cotta**[1] *f.* surplice, cotta; cloak.
**cotta**[2] *f.* cooking; baking; amount cooked or baked; (slang) infatuation; drunkenness; *pigliare*

*una* –, to fall in love; to get drunk.
**cot·tile** *adj.* brick.
**cot·tim-o** *m.* job, contract; *lavoro a* –, piece-work, jobbing. **-ante** *m.*, **-ista** *m.* jobbing workman; piece-worker.
**cotto** *part. adj.* cooked; done; – *al forno*, baked; fired; (fig.) *nè* – *nè crudo*, neither one thing nor the other; scorched; (slang) drunk, tight; lovesick; *n.m.* cooked food; earthenware; *l'industria del* –, ceramics.
**cottura** *f.* cookery; cooking; baking; *venire a* –, to be completely cooked; burn, scorch.
**coturnice** *f.* partridge; quail.
**coturno** *m.* buskin.
**cọv-a** *f.* brooding; sitting; *in* –, sitting; *fare la* – *di*, to hatch out; nesting-place; brood. **-ac·ciolo** *m.* nest of birds or small animals; lair, den.
**cov-are** [A1 c] *tr.* to hatch; to hatch out; (fig.) to brood over; to cherish secretly; *intr.* (*aux.* avere) to be broody; to smoulder; to lie in wait; *gatta ci -a*, there's more in this than meets the eye. **-ata** *f.* brood; hatching. **-atic·cio** *adj.* broody.
**covarello** *m.* woodlark.
**covile** *m.* lair, den; hovel.
**cọvo** *m.* lair; nest; form (of a hare); sett (of a badger); (fig.) haunt, hiding-place, den; (joc.) bed; (fig.) *farsi un* –, to feather one's nest.
**covọne** *m.* sheaf, shock (of corn); bundle (of hay).
**coziọne** *f.* cooking; digestion; decoction.
**cozzare** [A1] *tr.* to butt, to toss; to gore; to collide with; *intr.* (*aux.* avere) to be in conflict; – *insieme con*, to be at variance with; – *contro*, to crash against.
**cozzo** *m.* butt, toss; clash, shock; collision; impact; – *delle opinioni*, clash of opinion; *dar di* – *in*, to butt, to bump against; (fig.) to meet, to run into; *fare ai cozzi*, to collide.
**crac**[1] *m. indecl.* (onomat.) crack; rattle, crackle; (sport) crack, ace; favourite.
**crac**[2] *m. indecl.* crash; bankruptcy; downfall.
**Craco·via** *pr.n.f.* (geog.) Cracow.
**cra·ni-o** *m.* skull, cranium. **-ato** *adj.*, *n.m.* vertebrate. **-ologi·a** *f.* craniology; phrenology.
**cra·pul-a** *f.* debauchery; licentiousness. **-are** [A1 s] *intr.* (*aux.* avere) to gormandize, to guzzle. **-ọne** *m.* guzzler; debauchee.
**crass-o** *adj.* dense; crass. **-ẹzza** *f.* denseness; coarseness.
**cratere** *m.* crater; goblet, drinking bowl; small pot or beaker.
**cravatta** *f.* tie, necktie, cravat; *farsi la* –, to tie one's tie.
**creanz-a** *f.* good manners; breeding; *non sapete la* – ?, where are your manners? **-ato** *adj.* well-mannered; well-bred.
**cre-are** [A6] *tr.* to create; to establish, to institute; to appoint; to produce; *rfl.* (*acc.* of *prn.* 'si') to be formed; to be founded; to come into being; (*dat.* of *prn.* 'si') to gain for oneself. **-ativo** *adj.* creative. **-ato** *part. adj.* created; brought up, bred; *n.m.* creation, all created things. **-atọre** *m.* creator; author; *andare al Creatore*, to go to meet one's Maker. **-atura** *f.* creature; baby; child; favourite. **-aziọne** *f.* creation; foundation; thing created.
**credent-e** *m.*, *f.* (rel.) believer; *i -i*, the faithful.
**credenz-a** *f.* belief, opinion; trust; credence; *lettere di* –, credentials; (rel.) belief, faith, creed; (comm.) *a* –, on credit; sideboard, buffet, serving-table; food-cupboard; (liturg.) credence table. **-iale** *adj.* credential; *f.pl.* credentials. **-iera** *f.* food cupboard; housekeeper. **-iere** *m.* butler; steward.
**crẹd-ere** [B1 c] *tr.* to believe; to trust; to hold as an opinion; *fate quel che -ete*, do as you think best; *lo -o!*, I should think so!; to believe, to have faith; *non -o*, I don't think so; *intr.* (*aux.* avere; *prep.* in) to believe (in); (*prep.* a) to attach credence (to), to believe; *non ci -o*, I don't believe it; (*prep.* di) to have an opinion (about), to think (of); *n.m.* belief; *a mio* –, in my opinion. **-i·bile** *adj.* credible; reliable, trustworthy. **-ibilità** *f.* credibility.
**crẹdit-o** *m.* credit; trust; standing, repute; belief; *saldo a* –, credit balance; *istituto di* –, banking establishment. **-ọre** *m.* creditor; *-ore ipotecario*, mortgagee.
**credo** *m.* (rel.) Credo, Creed; (fig.) views, ideas.
**cre·dul-o** *adj.* credulous. **-ità** *f.* credulity, credulousness. **-ọna** *f.*, **-ọne** *m.* foolish, credulous person.
**crem-a** *f.* (cul.) dish made of eggs, sugar and milk; sweet liqueur; – *del latte*, top of the milk; – *per la barba*, shaving cream. **-ọso** *adj.* creamy.
**cremagliera** *f.* rack; *ferrovia a* –, rack railway.
**crem-are** [A1] *tr.* to cremate. **-atọio** *m.* crematorium. **-aziọne** *f.* cremation.
**cre·mis-i** *adj. indecl.* crimson; *n.m. indecl.* the colour crimson. **-ino** *adj.* crimson.
**Cremlino** *pr.n.m.* Kremlin.
**cremọre** *m.* (fig.) cream, best part.
**crenno** *m.* horseradish.
**creọṣoto** *m.* creosote.
**crep-a** *f.* crack, fissure, split. **-ac·cio** *m.* large crack, fissure; crevasse.
**crepa-corpo** *adv. phr. a* –, fit to burst. **-cuore** *m.* heartbreak. **-pan·cia**, **-pelle** *adv. phr. mangiare a -pancia, a -pelle*, to eat fit to burst; *ridere a -pelle*, to split one's sides with laughter.
**crepare** [A1] *intr.* (*aux.* essere) to burst, to split; – *di dolore*, to be racked with pain; (fam.) to die.
**crepit-are** [A1 s] *intr.* (*aux.* avere) to crackle; to clang. **-aziọne** *f.* noise of crackling; crackle; (med.) crepitation. **-ìo** *m.* prolonged crackling; *-ìo delle pallottole*, rattle of bullets.
**cre·pito** *m.* crepitation; crackling.
**crepol-are** [A1 s] *intr.* (*aux.* essere) to split; to trickle. **-ìo** *m.* noise of splitting; sound of trickling.
**crepu·scol-o** *m.* twilight, dusk, gloaming; (fig.) decline. **-are** *adj.* crepuscular, twilit; dim, shadowy.
**crẹsc-ere** [B9] *intr.* (*aux.* essere) to grow; to increase; to rise; to be left over; *tr.* to rear. **-ente** *part. adj.* growing, increasing; *luna -ente*, crescent moon; *n.m.* *-ente del mare*, tide. **-enza** *f.* growth; excrescence; rise. **-imẹnto** *m.* growth, increase. **-itọre** *m.* grower, breeder. **-iuta** *f.* growth; increase; flood-tide.
**cresciọne** *m.* – *d'acqua*, watercress.
**crẹscita** *f.* growth; period of growth; *malattie della* –, childhood illnesses; – *dei capelli*, growth of hair.
**cre·ṣim-a, crẹṣim-a** *f.* (liturg.) confirmation; *tenere uno a* –, to be someone's sponsor at confirmation. **-ando** *adj.*, *n.m.* confirmation candidate. **-are** [A1 s] *tr.* (liturg.) to confirm; *rfl.* to be confirmed.
**Creṣo** *pr.n.m.* (myth.) Croesus.
**crẹsp-a** *f.* wrinkle; curl; ripple; fold; tuck; pleat; *pl.* smocking. **-o** *adj.* curly; curled; wrinkled; puckered; crisp; rippled; *n.m.* (text.) crêpe; *-o di cina*, crêpe de chine. **-ọso, -uto** *adj.* wrinkled; curly.
**crẹst-a** *f.* crest, comb; plume; *alzare la* –, to show pride; ridge (of mountains); peak; *valore di* –, peak value. **-ato, -uto** *adj.* crested.
**crestomazi·a** *f.* anthology.
**cret-a**[1] *f.* chalk; clay; vessel, pot. **-a·ceo, -ọso** *adj.* chalky.
**Cret-a**[2] *pr.n.f.* (geog.) Crete. **-ẹse** *adj.*, *n.m.*, *f.* Cretan.
**cretin-o** *m.* idiot; fool; cretin; *adj.* imbecile. **-eri·a** *f.* stupidity; idiotic remark. **-iṣmo** *m.* (med.) cretinism; imbecility.
**crẹtt-o** *m.* crack; flaw.

-**are** [A1 c] *intr.* (*aux.* avere) to crack; to chap.
**cri·a**[1] *m.* youngest bird of a brood; the smallest and weakest of a litter, cad; runt.
**cri·a**[2] *f.* small eel, elver.
**cribr-are** [A1] *tr.* to sift, to sieve. -**o** *m.* sieve.
**cricchiare** [A4] *intr.* (*aux.* avere) to creak; to crackle.
**cric·chio** *m.* creak, crack.
**cric-co** *m.* (*pl.* -**chi**) hand-jack, *coltello a* —, clasp knife.
**cricẹto** *m.* hamster.
**Crime·a** *pr.n.f.* (geog.) Crimea.
**criminal-e** *adj.* criminal; *codice* —, criminal code; *n.m., f.* criminal. -**ista** *m.* criminal lawyer. -**ità** *f. indecl.* criminality; *la -ità è in aumento*, crime is on the increase.
**cri·min-e** *f.* crime, felony; *m.* accusation. -**osità** *f.* guiltiness; criminality. -**ọso** *adj.* criminal.
**crin-e** *m.* mane; horsehair; tresses, locks; tail of a comet. -**ale** *adj.* pertaining to hair; *n.m.* (geog.) ridge, watershed.
**criniera** *f.* mane; plume; tail of a comet; mountain ridge.
**crin-o** *m.* horsehair; — *vegetale*, vegetable fibre. -**uto** *adj.* with flowing mane.
**crinolina** *f.* crinoline; hoop-petticoat.
**cripta** *f.* crypt.
**criptocomunista** *m., f.* crypto-communist.
**crịsa·lide** *f.* chrysalis, pupa.
**crịsantemo, crisan·temo** *m.* chrysanthemum.
**crịsi** *f. indecl.* crisis; *in* —, in crisis; — *di pianto*, outburst of crying; attack, fit; — *nervosa*, nervous breakdown; slump; shortage; — *delle abitazioni*, housing shortage.
**crịsma** *m.* (liturg.) chrism; (fig.) sanction; — *ufficiale*, official approval.
**cristall-a·io, -aro** *m.* glass-blower; dealer in glassware. -**ame** *m.* glassware, crystal. -**eri·a** *f.* glassware factory; glassware shop; crystal ware. -**ino** *adj.* crystalline; crystal; crystal-clear.
**cristallịẓẓ-are** [A1] *tr.* to crystallize; *intr.* (*aux.* essere), *rfl.* to become crystallized. -**aziọne** *f.* crystallization.
**cristall-o** *m.* glass; pane; lens; wineglass; looking-glass; crystal; (motor.) headlamp. -**ografi·a** *f.* crystallography.
**cristian-o** *adj., n.m.* Christian; (colloq.) human being; *ora da -i*, reasonable hour; *cibo da -i*, food fit to eat. -**ẹsimo** *m.* Christianity. -**ità** *f.* Christendom; Christian status. -**iẓẓare** [A1] *tr.* to make Christian, to convert to Christianity.
**Cristo** *pr.n.m.* Christ; *Gesù* —, Jesus Christ; *un cristo*, a crucifix.
**crite·rio** *m.* norm; criterion.
**cri·tic-a** *f.* criticism; critical judgement; review; censure. -**ante** *part. adj.* criticizing; critical; *n.m., f.* grumbler. -**are** [A2 s] *tr.* to criticize; to censure; to examine critically. -**o** *adj.* critical; crucial; censorious; *n.m.* critic; reviewer.
**critta** *f.* crypt; grotto; cellar.
**critt-ografi·a** *f.* cryptography, cipher, code writing. -**ogra·fico** *adj.* cryptographical, in code. -**ogramma** *m.* cryptogram.
**crivell-are** [A1] *tr.* to sieve, to sift; to riddle with holes. -**atura** *f.* sifting; residue. -**aziọne** *f.* screening, sifting, riddling. -**o** *m.* sieve; screening machine.
**Cro-a·zia** *pr.n.f.* (geog.) Croatia. -**ato** *adj., n.m.* Croatian, Croat.
**crocca** *f.* crutch.
**crocc-are** [A2] *intr.* (*aux.* avere) to crack, to give a cracked sound. -**ante** *part. adj.* crisp, crackling; *n.m.* almond cake.
**croc·chia**[1] *f.* chignon, bun in the neck.
**croc·chia**[2] *f.* blow, stroke, hit.
**crocchiare** [A4] *intr.* (*aux.* avere) to sound cracked; to be in poor health; to creak; to cluck; to chatter; *tr.* to 'sound', to tap for sound.
**croc·chio**[1] *m.* cracked sound.
**croc·chi-o**[2] *m.* group, circle, knot of persons; *stare a* —, to sit chatting. -**ọna** *f.*, -**ọne** *m.* chatterbox; gossip.
**croc·cia** *f.* crutch.
**croccolare** [A1 s] *intr.* (*aux.* avere) to cackle; to gurgle.
**crọc-e** *f.* cross; *in* —, crosswise; *testa o* — ?, heads or tails?; *mettere in* —, to crucify; (fig.) to distress; trial, affliction; *a occhio e* —, approximately, roughly; *punto in* —, cross-stitch; *braccia in* —, arms folded; (typ.) dagger, obelus. -**ẹtta** *f. dim.* little cross; *pl.* (naut.) cross-trees. -**erossina** *f.* Red Cross nurse.
**cro·ceo** *adj.* saffron-coloured.
**crocevi·a** *m.* cross-roads.
**croci-are** [A3] *tr.* to mark with a cross; (biol.) to cross. -**amẹnto** *m.* crossing; (rlwy.) frog. -**ata** *f.* crusade; cross-roads. -**ato** *part. adj.* in form of a cross; wearing a cross; (biol.) crossed; *n.m.* crusader.
**crocic·chio** *m.* criss-cross of streets, cross-roads.
**crocidare** [A2 s] *intr.* (*aux.* avere) to croak, to caw.
**crocier-a** *f.* arrangement in the form of a cross; cross-bar; crossing-place; cruise; *andare in* —, to go on a cruise; (aeron.) long-distance flight; *velocità di* —, cruising speed. -**e** *m.* crossbill. -**ista** *m., f.* passenger on a cruise.
**croci·fero** *m.* cross-bearer, crucifer.
**crocifig·gere** [C17] *tr.* to crucify; (fig.) to harass, to vex.
**crocifiss-o** *part. adj.* crucified; *n.m. il* —, the Crucified; crucifix. -**iọne** *f.* crucifixion.
**crocifọrme** *adj.* cruciform, cross-shaped; *adv.* crosswise.
**cro-co** *m.* (*pl.* -**chi**) crocus; saffron.
**crod-a** *f.* rock face, crag. -**ai(u)olo** *m.* rock climber.
**cro·giol-o** *m.* cooking at a gentle heat; (fig.) *pigliare il* —, to toast oneself gently; annealing. -**are** [A1 s] *tr.* to roast gently; to anneal; *rfl.* to take one's ease; to savour to the full.
**crogi(u)olo** *m.* crucible.
**croll-are** [A1] *tr.* to shake; — *le spalle*, to shrug one's shoulders; — *il capo*, to toss one's head; *intr.* (*aux.* essere) to totter; to crumble. -**amẹnto** *m.* collapse, ruin; downfall. -**ante** *part. adj.* shaky. -**ata** *f.* shake; toss; shrug. -**o** *m.* shake; collapse; downfall; *dar il -o a*, to overthrow, to upset; *dare il -o alla bilancia*, to turn the scale.
**crom-a** *f.* (mus.) quaver. -**a·tico** *adj.* chromatic; *senso -atico*, colour sense.
**crom-are** [A1] *tr.* to chrome, to chromium plate. -**ato** *part. adj.* chromium plated. -**atura** *f.* chromium plating. -**o** *m.* chromium, chrome. -**ofotografi·a** *f.* colour photography. -**otipografi·a** *f.* colour printing.
**cro·na-ca** *f.* chronicle; current gossip; *notizia di* —, news item; commentary; (fig.) public opinion. -**chista** *m.* chronicler; newspaper diarist.
**cro·nic-o** *adj.* chronic; incurable; *n.m.* incurable patient. -**ità** *f.* chronic condition.
**cronista** *m.* chronicler; reporter; commentator.
**cron-ografi·a** *f.* chronography. -**ogra·fico** *adj.* chronographical. -**o·grafo** *m.* chronographer; chronicler. -**ologi·a** *f.* chronology. -**olo·gico** *adj.* chronological. -**ologista, -o·logo** *m.* chronologist. -**ometrag·gio** *m.* (sport) time-keeping; (industr.) time and motion study. -**ometri·a** *f.* chronometry, time-keeping. -**ometrista** *m.* (sport) time-keeper. -**o·metro** *m.* chronometer; (mus.) metronome; (sport) stopwatch.
**crosciare** [A3] *intr.* (*aux.* avere) to make a splashing noise; to gurgle; to roar (of water, applause); to splutter; to hiss; *impers.* (*aux.* essere) to rain hard, to pour.
**cro·scio** *m.* gurgling; rattling;

hiss; splash; — *di applausi*, roar of applause.
**crost-a** *f.* crust; rind; scab; superficial meaning; bad painting, daub. **-oso** *adj.*, **-uto** *adj.* crusty, scabby; incrusted.
**crosta·ceo** *m.* (zool.) crustacean.
**crost-are** [A1] *tr.* (cul.) to brown, to crust. **-ata** *f.* tart; *-ata di mele*, apple tart, apple pie.
**crucc-iare** [A3] *tr.* to vex, to torment; *rfl.* to be distressed; to fret. **-iamento** *m.* annoyance, vexation.
**cruc·ci-o** *m.* mental or bodily suffering; distress; vexation; resentment. **-oso** *adj.* angry, vexed.
**cruciale** *adj.* crucial.
**cruciare** [A3] *tr.* to torment; to torture.
**cruciforme** *adj.* cross-shaped, cruciform.
**cruciverba** *m. indecl.* crossword puzzle.
**crudel-e** *adj.* cruel; harsh; grievous; painful; *n.m.*, *f.* cruel person. **-tà** *f.* cruelty; harshness; grievousness.
**crud-o** *adj.* raw, uncooked; immature; unripe; harsh, cruel; crude; rough. **-ezza** *f.* rawness, roughness; harshness; crudity; immaturity. **-ità** *f.* rawness, roughness; crudity.
**cruento** *adj.* bloody, sanguinary; ferocious; blood-stained; dreadful.
**crumiro** *m.* blackleg, strikebreaker.
**cruna** *f.* eye (of a needle).
**crusca**[1] *f.* chaff, bran.
**Crusca**[2] *pr.n.f.* (hist.) *La* —, the Florentine Academy, founded 1583.
**Cub-a** *pr.n.f.* (geog.) Cuba. **-ano** *adj.*, *n.m.* Cuban.
**cubare** *tr.* (math.) to cube; to determine the cubic capacity of; to find the volume of.
**cubi·colo** *m.* cubicle, bed-chamber; solitary cell.
**cubiforme** *adj.* cube-shaped, cubic.
**cub-ismo** *m.* (paint.) Cubism. **-ista** *m.*, *f.* Cubist artist.
**cubitale** *adj.* a cubit long; (fig.) large; *lettere cubitali*, letters a foot high.
**cu·bito** *m.* (poet.) elbow; forearm; (anat.) ulna.
**cubo** *m.* (math.) cube; *elevare al* —, to cube; *adj.* cubic; *metro* —, cubic metre.
**cuccagna** *f.* abundance, plenty; *albero della* —, greasy pole; *paese di Cuccagna*, land of Cockaigne.
**cuccetta** *f.* berth, couchette; bunk.
**cucchia·i-a** *f.* ladle; scoop. **-ata** *f.* spoonful. **-o** *m.* spoon; spoonful. **-one** *m. augm.* tablespoon; soup-ladle.
**cucchiaino** *m. dim.* coffee-spoon; teaspoon; — *raso*, level teaspoon; — *abbondante*, heaped teaspoon.
**cuc·ci-a** *f.* resting-place, bed; dog's bed; cat's basket; lapdog. **-are** [A3] *intr.* (*aux.* avere) to curl up and lie down; (to a dog) *cuccia!*, down!
**cuc·ciolo** *m.* puppy; whelp.
**cucco** *m.* favourite, pet; *il — della mamma*, mother's darling; *vecchio* —, doddering old fool.
**cuccù** *m. indecl.* cuckoo; *orologio a* —, cuckoo clock; *fare* —, to play peek-a-boo.
**cuc·cuma** *f.* coffee-pot; (fam.) topknot.
**cucin-a** *f.* kitchen; (naut.) galley; cuisine, style of cooking; cookery; *fare* —, to cook; cooking-stove; — *a gas*, gas cooker. **-are** [A1] *tr.* to cook; to prepare; (slang) to 'cook up'. **-a·rio** *adj.* kitchen; culinary.
**cuc-ire** [D1] *tr.*, *intr.* (*aux.* avere) to sew; to stitch; (fig.) to cheat; to double-cross; *macchina da* —, sewing-machine; *ago da* —, sewing needle. **-ito** *part. adj.* sewn, stitched; darned; mended; (fig.) *bocca -ita*, sealed lips; constructed, put together; *n.m.* sewing; *lavoro di -ito*, needlework. **-itrice** *f.* seamstress, needlewoman; stapler; machine for stitching. **-itura** *f.* sewing; stitching; seam; *calze senza -itura*, seamless stockings.
**cucù** (onomat.) cuckoo (the sound); *excl.* expressing disbelief; *far* —, to play peep-bo.
**cuculo, cu·culo** *m.* (orn.) cuckoo.
**cucur·bita** *f.* (bot.) name applied to various gourd-like plants; retort; cucurbit.
**cuf·fia** *f.* bonnet; coif, woman's cap; — *da bagno*, bathing-cap; (radio; telegr.) headphones, earphones; (theatr.) — *del suggeritore*, prompter's box.
**cugin-o** *m.*, **-a** *f.* cousin; *nipote* —, first cousin once removed. **-anza** *f.* cousinship.
**cu·i** *pers. prn. dat.* whom; to whom; *di* —, whose; of whom; *l'uomo il — figliuolo*, the man whose son.
**culatta** *f.* hinder part, bottom; breech (of a gun); seat of a pair of trousers; spine of a book.
**culbianco** *m.* (orn.) wheatear.
**cu·lice** *m.* (ent.) gnat.
**culina·ri-a** *f.* cookery, the culinary art. **-o** *adj.* culinary; *scuola -a*, school of cookery.
**culisse** *f.pl.* runners, slides; *porta a* —, sliding door; (theatr.) wings; (fig.) intrigue.
**cull-a** *f.* cradle; cot; (fig.) hearth; birthplace; *dalla — alla tomba*, from the cradle to the grave. **-are** [A1] *tr.* to rock; to soothe; to dandle; *rfl.* (*prep.* di) to delude oneself, to cherish illusions (about).
**culmin-are** [A1 s] *intr.* (*aux.* essere) to culminate; to mount to a crisis. **-ante** *part. adj.* culminating; crowning. **-azione** *f.* culmination.
**cul·mine** *m.* top, highest point, apex; — *della gloria*, height of glory.
**culo** *m.* bottom, buttocks; backside; — *di una bottiglia*, bottom of a bottle; *culi di bicchieri*, false brilliants.
**culto**[1] *adj.* cultured, well-educated, erudite.
**culto**[2] *m.* (rel.) worship (of God), veneration (of saints); cultus; liturgy; cult; *libertà di* —, freedom of worship.
**cultore** *m.* cultivator; erudite person; — *delle lettere*, man of letters.
**cultur-a** *f.* culture; higher education; scholarliness; cultivation; farming; crop. **-ale** *adj.* cultural. **-are** [A1] *tr.* to cultivate.
**cumul-are** [A1 s] *tr.* to heap up, to amass, to accumulate; — *due cariche*, to combine two functions; — *due stipendi*, to draw two salaries. **-ativo** *adj.* cumulative; inclusive; (rlwy.) *biglietto -ativo*, group ticket. **-azione** *f.* accumulation, heaping up, amassing.
**cu·mulo** *m.* heap; accumulation; (meteor.) cumulus.
**cuna** *f.* (poet.) cradle; (archit.) *volta a* —, barrel vault.
**cu·ne-o**[1] *m.* wedge; punch, stamp. **-ale** *adj.* wedge-shaped.
**cuo·c-ere** [C15] *tr.* to cook; to roast; to bake; to stew; to boil; to burn, to heat; to ripen; to vex, to torment; (ceram.) — *a fuoco*, to fire; *intr.* (*aux.* avere) to cook; *lasciatelo — nel suo brodo*, let him stew in his own juice. **-itura** *f.* cooking; cookery.
**cuo-co** *m.* (*pl.* **-chi**) (male) cook; *primo* —, chef; *capo* —, head cook. **-ca** *f.* woman cook.
**cuo·i-o** *m.* (*pl.m.* **cuo·i**) leather; skin; — *scamosciato*, chamois leather; — *verniciato*, patent leather; (anat.) — *cappelluto*, scalp; (*pl.f.* **cuo·ia**) leg; *stendere le -a*, to lie stretched out. **-a·ceo** *adj.* leathery. **-a·io** *m.* tanner; leather-seller. **-ame** *m.* leather, leather goods.
**cuore** *m.* heart; love; *cuor mio!*, my love!; feelings; generosity; *di* —, heartily; *uomo di* —, kind-hearted man; *senza* —, heartless; *di tutto* —, with all one's heart; *a* —, heart-shaped; depth; height; middle, core, centre, heart; *nel cuor della notte*, at dead of night.
**cupidi·gia** *f.* cupidity, covetousness; greed.
**cu·pid-o** *adj.* covetous, desirous; greedy; — *di guadagni*, eager for gain. **-ità** *f.* cupidity, covetousness; greed.

**Cupido**[2] *pr.n.m.* (myth ) Cupid.
**cup-o** *adj.* gloomy; dejected; sullen; taciturn; sepulchral; *n.m.* depth, profundity; hollow. **-ẹzza** *f.* darkness, gloom; sombreness; depth.
**cu·pol-a** *f.* (archit.) dome, cupola; summer-house; the vault of heaven. **-are** *adj.* cupular, dome-shaped.
**cupọne** *m.* coupon; — *del dividendo*, dividend coupon.
**cu·pr-eo** *adj.* copper-coloured; (chem.) cuprous. **-i·fero** *adj.* copper-bearing.
**cupro** *m.* copper.
**cur-a** *f.* care, looking after, charge; *aver — di*, to take care of; *a — di*, looked after by, edited by; care; anxiety; cure, treatment; *casa di —*, nursing-home; *località di —*, spa, health-resort; care, attention; accuracy; diligence; *con —*, carefully, accurately; (eccl.) cure (of souls); parish. **-are** [A1] *tr.* to take care of; to care for; to pay regard to; to edit; (med.) to cure, to treat; to dress; (eccl.) — *le anime*, to have a cure of souls; *rfl.* (*acc.* of *prn.* 'si'; *prep.* di) to take care; to pay heed (to), to mind; (*dat.* of *prn.* 'si') *-arsi la salute*, to look after one's health. **-a·bile** *adj.* curable. **-ante** *part. adj.* careful, attentive; *non -ante del pericolo*, heedless of the danger; *medico -ante*, doctor in charge of case. **-atela** *f.* (leg.) guardianship; curatorship; trusteeship. **-ativo** *adj.* curative. **-ato** *part. adj.* cured; tended; taken care of; edited; *n.m.* (eccl.) parish priest; curate. **-atọre** *m.* guardian; curator; editor; (leg.) guardian; trustee.
**cu·ria** *f.* (Rom. antiq.; eccl.) curia; (leg.) court of justice; legal profession.
**curiọs-o** *adj.* curious, inquisitive; peculiar; attentive, diligent; *n.m.* inquisitive person; *pl.* onlookers. **-ità** *f. indecl.* curiosity; inquisitiveness; quaintness; curio.
**cursọre** *m.* runner; messenger; the sliding portion of a zip fastener; (mech.) slide-rule.
**curv-a** *f.* bend; curve; turn; — *a forcella*, hairpin bend; — *occulta*, concealed turning; (math.) curve, graph. **-are** [A1] *tr.* to bend; to curve; to arch; *-are la fronte*, to bow the head; *rfl.* to stoop, to bend; to obey. **-atura** *f.* bending, curving; camber; sweep (of curve); curvature, convexity. **-ità** *f.* curvature.
**curv-o** *adj.* bent; curved; hunched; *spalle -e*, round shoulders; *n.m.* roundedness; curvature. **-ẹzza** *f.* curvedness, curvature.
**cuscin-o** *m.* cushion; pillow; bolster; — *pneumatico*, air cushion. **-ẹtto** *m. dim.* small cushion; pin-cushion; *-etto a rulli*, roller-bearing; *-etto a sfere*, ball-bearing.
**cu·spid-e** *f.* point; apex, vertex; (archit.) spire, pinnacle. **-ale** *adj.* pointed.
**custode** *m., f.* guardian; curator; caretaker; attendant; doorkeeper; warder; *angelo —*, guardian angel.
**custo·dia** *f.* custody; care; protection; safe-keeping; *avere in —*, to have in one's care; *camera di —*, strong-room.
**custodire** [D2] *tr.* to take care of; to watch over; to protect; to preserve; to hold in custody; *rfl.* to look after oneself.
**cut-e** *f.* (anat.) skin (human), dermis. **-a·neo** *adj.* cutaneous, of the skin.
**cuticagna** *f.* nape of the neck; hair growing on the nape of the neck; hair of the head.
**cuti·cola** *f.* cuticle; epidermis; (bot.) cuticle.
**cutret·tola** *f.* (orn.) blue-headed or yellow wagtail.
**cz-.** See **z-,** for certain foreign words sometimes spelt with **cz-**; *e.g.* for **czar,** see **zar.**
**cze-co** *adj.* (*m.pl.* **-chi**) Czech, Czecho-Slovakian; *n.m.* Czech; the Czech language. **-ca** *f.* Czech woman.
**Czecọslovachi·a** *pr.n.f.* (geog.) Czecho-Slovakia.

**D** *f.* (pron. **di**) the letter **d**; the consonant D.
**d'** *contr.* of **di** before a vowel; *contr.* of **da** before the vowel 'a'.
**da** *prep.* (*contr.* with *def. art.*: dal, dallo, dai, dagli, dalla, dalle, dall'). **1.** from; — *Roma a Firenze*, from Rome to Florence; *salvato — morte*, saved from death; *lo seppi — lui*, I learnt it from him. **2.** by; *ucciso — briganti*, killed by brigands; *giudicare dai fatti*, to judge by events; *lo feci — me solo*, I did it all by myself. **3.** to; at; at the house of; in relation to; towards; *viene — me ogni sabato*, he comes to see me every Saturday; — *noi*, at our house; — *parte mia*, as far as I am concerned; *dalle parti di*, in the vicinity of; *passò — Perugia*, he travelled via Perugia; *farsi — parte*, to draw to one side. **4.** for; *uomo — nulla*, good-for-nothing; *biglietto — mille lire*, thousand-lire note; *casa — vendere*, house for sale; *macchina — scrivere*, typewriter; *stanza — bagno*, bathroom. **5.** as; — *bambino era biondo*, he was fair as a child; *vivere — re*, to live like a king; *fare — mamma a*, to be a mother to; *fare — cuoco*, to do the cooking. **6.** characterized by; *fanciulla dagli occhi neri*, girl with dark eyes; *giovanotto dalla giacca verde*, young man wearing a green jacket. **7.** WITH NUMERALS: upwards of, round about; *rubarono — cento mila lire*, they stole about a hundred thousand lire; *guadagno — mille sterline*, profits of upwards of £1000. **8.** IN TEMPORAL PHRASES: since, for; *sono qui — tre mesi*, I've been here for three months; *fin dall'infanzia*, ever since infancy; *fin — quando lo incontrai*, ever since I met him. **9.** WITH INFINITIVE CONSTR.: *molto — fare*, much to do; *qualcosa — mangiare*, something to eat.
**dabbasso** *adv.* below, down below; downstairs.
**dabbene** *adj. indecl.* well-behaved, decent; upright; honest; respectable.
**daccanto** *adv.* near, nearby; to one side; aside; *prep.* beside; by the side of; *adj. indecl.* near.
**daccapo** *adv.* once more, over again; *ricominciare —*, to begin all over again; *siamo —*, we're back where we started; at the top.
**dacchẹ** *conj.* since, since the time when; since, in as much as, seeing that, given that.
**dad-o** *m.* die; point in the game of dice; cube; *il — è tratto*, the die is cast; *tessuto a -i*, cloth with a check pattern; (cul.) beef-cube; (archit.) dado.
**daffare** *m.* work, business; duties; task; *un gran —*, a great deal to do; *avrà il suo —*, he'll have his work cut out.
**Dafne** *pr.n.f.* Daphne.
**da·in-o** *m.*, **-a** *f.* fallow deer; doeskin.
**da·lia**[1] *f.* (bot.) dahlia.
**Da·lia**[2] *pr.n.f.* Dahlia.
**dallato** *adv.* nearby; to one side; *prep.* — *a*, beside; *adj. indecl.* near.
**dal·mato** *adj., n.m.* Dalmatian.
**Dalma·zia** *pr.n.f.* (geog.) Dalmatia.
**daltrọnde, d'altrọnde** *adv.* on the other hand; in other respects; besides.
**dam-a** *f.* noble woman; dancing-partner; — *compagnia*, lady companion; — *della Regina*,

lady-in-waiting; *giuocare a* –, to play draughts; king (at draughts); queen (at cards, chess). **-are** *tr.* (draughts) to crown; (chess) to make a queen. **-iere** *m.* draughtboard. **-igella** *f.* damsel; bridesmaid; *-igella di compagnia*, lady companion. **-ista** *m., f.* draughts-player.

**Damasco**[1] *pr.n.m.* (geog.) Damascus.

**damasc-o**[2] *m.pl.* damask. **-are** [A2] *tr.* to damask. **-ato** *part. adj.* damasked; damask. **-eno** *adj.* damascene; (bot.) *m.* damson.

**damigiana** *f.* demijohn.

**damista** *m., f.* see under **dama**.

**danaro** *m.* small coin; *pl.* coins; money.

**danda** *f.* strip, string; *pl.* leading-strings; braces.

**danẹse** *adj.* Danish; *cane* –, Great Dane; *n.m.* Dane; Danish language, Danish; *f.* Danish woman, Dane.

**Daniele** *pr.n.m.* Daniel.

**Danimarca** *pr.n.f.* (geog.) Denmark.

**dann-are** [A1] *tr.* to damn; to condemn; to doom; to blame; *rfl.* (*acc.* of *prn.* 'si') to be damned; to condemn oneself; (*dat.* of *prn.* 'si') *-arsi l'anima*, to be driven distracted. **-ato** *part. adj.* damned; damnable; miserable, full of worries; appalling. **-aziọne** *f.* condemnation; damnation; pest, trial, curse.

**danneggi-are** [A3 c] *tr.* to damage; to impair; to injure, to harm. **-ato** *part. adj.* damaged; injured; *n.m.* victim; injured party.

**dann-o** *m.* loss; damage, harm; *accertare il* –, to assess the damage; *è un* –, it's a great pity; *tuo* –, so much the worse for you; *far – alla salute*, to impair one's health. **-ọso** *adj.* injurious; damaging.

**dannunziano** *adj.* in the style of D'Annunzio; *n.m.* follower, imitation of D'Annunzio.

**dante**[1] *m.* See **daino**; *pelle di* –, buckskin, doeskin, tanned skin of various deer.

**dante**[2] *part. adj.* of **dare**, *q.v.*; (leg.) *n.m. il – causa*, the person from whom one's legal title is derived; predecessor in title.

**Dant-e**[3] *pr.n.m.* (abbrev. of **Durante**) Dante; edition of Dante. **-ẹsco** *adj.* (*m.pl.* **-ẹschi**) Dantesque; *n.m.* Dantist.

**Danu·bio** *pr.n.m.* (geog.) Danube.

**danz-a** *f.* dance; (fig.) scheming, intrigue. **-are** [A1] *intr.* (*aux.* avere), *tr.* to dance.

**Dan·zica** *pr.n.f.* (geog.) Danzig.

**dappertutto** *adv.* everywhere; on all sides.

**dappiedi, dappiede, dappiè** *adv.* at the bottom, at the foot, below.

**dappiù** *adv.* more; *adj. indecl.* worth more, better.

**dappoc-o** *adj. indecl.* worthless; inefficient; *n.m., f. indecl.* useless individual, good-for-nothing. **-ag·gine** *f.* worthlessness; inefficiency; stupid action.

**dappoi** *adv.* afterwards, next, then. **-chẹ̀** *conj.* after, since; seeing that, since.

**dappresso** *adv.* near, close by, nearby; next; *adj. indecl.* near; next.

**dapprima** *adv.* at first; in the beginning.

**dapprinci·pio** *adv.* from the beginning; to start with.

**Dardanelli** *pr.n.m.pl.* (geog.) Dardanelles.

**dard-o** *m.* dart; (poet.) arrow; ardent glance; fiery ray. **-eggiare** [A3 c] *tr.* to dart; to flash; *intr.* (*aux.* avere) to shine; to quiver.

**dare** [A8] *tr.* **1.** to give; to give away; to give up; *non mi è dato di*, it's not in my power to. **2.** to administer, to deliver; *gli diedi un calcio*, I gave him a kick; – *un crollo a*, to shake; – *fuoco a*, to set fire to; – *una risposta*, to make a reply; – *il benvenuto a*, to welcome; – *del tu*, to use the intimate form of address. **3.** to credit with; to lay on; *quanti anni mi date?*, how old would you say I was?; *dò la colpa a voi*, I put the blame on you; *vorrebbe che tutto il merito si desse a lui*, he'd like to claim all the credit; – *ragione a*, to consider in the right; *ti dò torto*, I think you're wrong; *da' retta a me*, listen to me. **4.** to yield, to give forth; – *guadagni*, to yield profit; – *una lacrima*, to shed a tear; – *un sospiro*, to heave a sigh; – *un grido*, to let out a yell. **5.** to take, to make, to undertake; – *un passo*, to take a step; – *un gesto*, to make a gesture; – *una commedia*, to put on a comedy; *che cosa danno al cinema?*, what's on at the cinema?. **6.** to give out; to regard as; – *una cosa per fatta*, to declare something finished; – *ad intendere*, to give to understand. **7.** *intr.* (*aux.* avere) – *nell'occhio*, to catch the eye; – *in*, to bump into, (fig.) to meet unexpectedly; *diede in un sasso*, he tripped over a stone; – *addosso a*, to fall upon, to attack; – *ai nervi di*, to get on the nerves of; – *nel segno*, to hit the mark; – *a*, – *in*, to incline towards, to tend to; – *in lagrime*, to burst into tears; – *nelle risa*, to burst out laughing; *una casa che dà sul mare*, a house facing the sea; *dagli! dagli!*, hit him! hit him!; *dai! dai!*, come on! go it!; *dagli oggi, dagli domani*, by sheer persistence. **8.** *rfl.* (*acc.* of *prn.* 'si') to give oneself, to devote oneself; *darsi agli studi*, to devote oneself to one's studies; *darsi per vinto*, to give in, to surrender; *darsi per dotto*, to claim to be a learned man; *darsi a correre*, to break into a run; *si diede il caso che*, it happened that; *può darsi*, it may be, perhaps; (*dat.* of *prn.* 'si') to give to oneself, to take on, to assume; *darsi delle arie*, to put on airs; *darsi da fare per*, to busy oneself about; *darsela a gambe*, to take to one's heels; *recip. rfl.* to give to each other; *quei due ragazzi se la danno*, those two boys are just of an age. **9.** *n.m.* debt; debit; *il – e l'avere*, debit and credit.

**dar·sena** *f.* wet dock; dockyard; boat-house.

**dar-vinịsmo, -winịsmo** *m.* Darwinism.

**dat-a** *f.* date; *la vostra lettera in – 12 giugno*, your letter of 12th June; (sport) service; (cards) deal; trick; *avere la* –, to lead. **-are** [A1] *tr.* to date; to identify the date of; *intr.* (*aux.* avere) to date; *a -are da quel giorno*, dating from that day; to go out of date.

**dativo** *adj.* (gramm.) dative.

**dat-o** *part.* of **dare**; *adj.* given; addicted; inclined; fixed; – *che*, since, given that; – *e non concesso*, supposing, let us say for the sake of argument; *n.m.* datum; clue; item of evidence; *pl.* data. **-ọre** *m.* giver; (econ.) *-ore di lavoro*, employer; producer; (leg.) *-ore di leggi*, legislator, law-giver.

**dat·tero** *m.* date (fruit); date-palm.

**dattil-ografare** [A1 s] *tr.* to type. **-o·grafa** *f.* typist. **-ografi·a** *f.* typewriting, typing. **-ogra·fico** *adj.* typewriting, pertaining to typing; *ufficio -ografico*, typewriting office. **-oscopi·a** *f.* the science of fingerprints. **-osco·pico** *adj. rilievo -oscopico* fingerprints. **-oscritto** *m.* typescript.

**dattọrno** *adv.* around; round about; *levarsi uno* –, to get rid of someone; *qui* –, hereabouts.

**davanti** *adv.* before, in front; *levarsi* –, to be off, to remove oneself; *prep.* (foll. by 'a') in the presence of; *mettere – a*, to put in front of, to serve with; *adj. indecl. la parte* –, the fore part; *n.m. il* –, the front part.

**davanzale** *m.* window sill.

**Da·v-ide** *pr.n.m.* David; (bibl.) song of David; psalms of David; (art) Michelangelo's David. **-i·dico** *adj.* of David, relating to David; *canti -idici*, psalms of David.

**davvero** *adv.* really, seriously; indeed; *dire* –, to be in earnest; – *?*, really?

**da·zio** *m.* toll, excise; toll-house.

**de** *prep.* See **di.** *Note*: this form, now chiefly archaic, is used before titles of works beginning with a

definite article, *e.g. una nuova edizione de "I Promessi Sposi"*, a new edition of *I Promessi Sposi*; as part of a surname, *e.g.* De Sanctis, De Marchi.

**de'** *contr.* of **dei.** See under **di.**

**dea** *f.* goddess.

**debilit-are** [A1 s] *tr.* to debilitate. **-azione** *f.* debilitation; infirmity.

**debit-o** *adj.* due; owing; proper; *n.m.* duty; debt; *comprare a —*, to buy on account; *saldare un —*, to settle a debt; *— pubblico*, national debt. **-amente** *adv.* duly; properly; rightly.

**debol-e** *adj.* weak; feeble; faint; dim; *n.m.* weak point; *avere un — per*, to have a weakness for. **-ezza** *f.* weakness; foible; mistake.

**debraiare** [A4] *intr.* (*aux.* avere) (motor.) to declutch.

**debutt-o** *m.* début; beginning. **-ante** *m.* débutant; beginner; *f.* débutante. **-are** [A1] *intr.* (*aux.* avere) to make one's début.

**deca** *f.* series of ten books.

**de·cade** *f.* decade.

**decad-ere** [B5] *intr.* (*aux.* essere) to fall into decadence, to decay. **-ente** *adj.* decadent; *n.m., f.* decadent person. **-enza** *f.* decadence; decline. **-imento** *m.* decay, degeneration.

**dec-a·litro** *m.* decalitre. **-a·metro** *m.* decametre. **-asil·labo** *adj.* decasyllabic; *n.m.* decasyllabic. **-astero** *m.* decastere, ten cubic metres. **-a·stilo** *m.* (archit.) decastyle. **-atlon** *m. indecl.* (sport) decathlon, contest of ten events.

**Deca·logo** *pr.n.m.* Decalogue, Ten Commandments.

**Decameron(e)** *pr.n.m. Decameron*, the title of a collection of 100 short stories by Boccaccio.

**decan-o** *m.* doyen, senior member; dean. **-ato** *m.* deanship.

**decantare**[1] [A1] *tr.* to sing the praises of.

**decant-are**[2] *tr.* to decant. **-azione** *f.* decanting.

**decapit-are** [A1 s] *tr.* to behead, to decapitate. **-azione** *f.* beheading; decapitation.

**decarbur-are** [A1] *tr.* to decarbonize. **-azione** *f.* decarbonization.

**dece·dere** [C22 b] *intr.* (*aux.* essere) to decease.

**deceler-are** [A1 s] *intr.* (*aux.* avere) to decelerate; to throttle down. **-azione** *f.* deceleration.

**dec-enne** *adj.* ten years old; of ten years standing. **-ennale** *adj.* decennial; *n.m.* tenth anniversary. **-en·nio** *m.* decade.

**decen-te** *adj.* seemly, decent, respectable. **-za** *f.* decency, propriety; *gabinetti di -za*, toilets.

**decentrare** [A1] *tr.* (admin.) to decentralize.

**decesso** *m.* decease, death.

**deci·d-ere** [C3] *tr.* to decide, to settle, to resolve; to decide upon, to arrange for; *intr.* (*aux.* avere; *prep.* di) to decide (to); to be decisive; *questo non -e*, this is not conclusive; *questo decise della sua sorte*, this determined his fate; *rfl.* (*prep.* a) to make up one's mind, to resolve (to); (*prep.* per) to choose in favour of, to choose.

**deci·du-o** *adj.* (bot.) deciduous; (astron.) *stella -a*, falling star.

**decifr-are** [A1] *tr.* to decipher, to decode; to make out. **-ante** *part. adj. codici e tabelle -anti*, key to a cipher.

**de·cima** *f.* tenth part; tenth thing; tenth woman; tithe; (mus.) tenth (interval).

**De·cima** *pr.n.f.* Decima.

**decimale** *adj.* decimal; *sistema metrico —*, decimal system.

**decimare** [A1 a] *tr.* to decimate.

**dec-i·metro** *m.* decimetre (equiv. to 3·937 inches). **-imilli·-metro** *m.* tenth of a millimetre.

**de·cimo** *adj.* tenth; *n.m.* tenth part; tenth man.

**De·cimo** *pr.n.m.* Decimus.

**decimo-primo, -secondo, -terzo** *ord. num.* eleventh, twelfth, thirteenth.

**decisione** *f.* settlement, decision; resolution, determination; *— presidenziale*, ruling.

**decisivo** *adj.* decisive; conclusive; positive; critical; *voto —*, casting vote.

**decis-o** *part.* of **decidere,** *q.v.*; *adj.* decided, settled; determined, resolute. **-o·rio** *adj.* decisive; charged with making a decision.

**declam-are** [A1] *tr., intr.* (*aux.* avere) to declaim; to recite; to inveigh; *— biasimi*, to hurl abuse. **-ato·rio** *adj.* declamatory; ranting. **-azione** *f.* declamation; ranting.

**declin-are** [A1] *tr.* (gramm.) to decline; (fig.) *— le generalità*, to give particulars about oneself; to refuse, to turn down; *intr.* (*aux.* avere) to sink; *— da*, to diverge from. **-azione** *f.* decline; sinking, waning; slope; (gramm.) declension. **-o** *m.* decline, decadence; (fig.) wane.

**decl-ive** *adj.* sloping; *n.m.* slope. **-i·vio** *m.* slope. **-ività** *f. indecl.* slope, incline, declivity.

**decoll-are** [A1] *intr.* (*aux.* avere) (aeron.) to take off. **-ag·gio** *m.*, **-o** *m.* (aeron.) take-off.

**decomporre** [B21] *tr.* to decompose; to separate, to disintegrate; *rfl.* to decompose; to putrefy.

**decomposizione** *f.* decomposition; putrefaction.

**decompressione** *f.* decompression; *camera di —*, decompression chamber.

**decor-are** [A1] *tr.* to decorate; to adorn. **-ativo** *adj.* decorative. **-atore** *m.* decorator. **-azione** *f.* decoration, adornment; ornament; *-azione al valore*, decoration for valour.

**decor-o** *m.* decorum, propriety; dignity. **-oso** *adj.* decorous; seemly, respectable.

**decorr-ere** [C5] *intr.* (*aux.* essere) to run downwards; (fig.) to run on; to pass, to elapse; *a — dal 15 corrente*, from the 15th of this month. **-enza** *f.* anniversary; (comm.) *con -enza dal primo aprile*, starting from 1 April.

**decorso** *part.* of **decorrere,** *q.v.*; *adj.* past, elapsed, gone by; *n.m.* course (*e.g.* of illness).

**decotto** *adj.* (cul.) stewed.

**decremento** *m.* decrease; diminution; waning.

**decre·pit-o** *adj.* decrepit; worn out. **-ezza** *f.* decrepitude.

**decresc-ere** [B9] *intr.* (*aux.* essere) to decrease, to lessen; to abate, to wane; to diminish. **-endo** *m.* (mus.) decrescendo, becoming softer. **-enza** *f.* decrease; diminution; wane.

**decret-o** *m.* decree. **-are** [A1 c] *tr.* to decree; to ordain.

**de·cupl-o** *adj.* tenfold; ten times the amount. **-icare** [A2 s] *tr.* to multiply by ten, to increase tenfold.

**De·dalo** *pr.n.m.* (myth.) Daedalus; *m.* labyrinth, maze.

**de·dica** *f.* dedication; author's inscription.

**dedic-are** [A2] *tr.* to dedicate; to devote; to give, to offer up; to consecrate; to inscribe; *rfl.* (*prep.* a) to dedicate oneself (to). **-ante** *part. adj., n.m., f.* dedicator. **-ato·rio** *adj.* dedicatory.

**de·dito** *adj.* (*prep.* a) given over (to), devoted; *— agli studi*, engrossed in study; *— agli affari*, wholly taken up with business.

**dedizione** *f.* self-surrender; devotion, sacrifice.

**deduci·bile** *adj.* deducible; to be logically derived or inferred.

**dedurre** [B2] *tr.* to derive, to draw; to deduce, to infer; to conclude; *io ne deduco che*, my conclusion is that; to deduct, to subtract.

**deduttivo** *adj.* deductive.

**deduzione** *f.* deducing; deduction, inference.

**defec-are** [A2] *tr.* to free from impurities, to remove foreign matter from; *intr.* (*aux.* avere) to defecate, to stool. **-azione** *f.* defecation.

**defer-ire** [D2] *tr.* to submit (to a competent authority); *intr.* (*aux.* avere; *prep.* a), *rfl.* to defer, to bow, to conform (to). **-ente** *part. adj.* deferential, submissive. **-enza** *f.* deference, consideration. **-imento** *m.* deferring; submitting.

**defeziọn-e** *f.* defection; backsliding; (mil.) desertion. **-are** [A1 c] *intr.* (*aux.* avere) to desert; to defect.

**deficien-te** *adj.* deficient, insufficient; simple-minded, wanting; below examination standard; *n.m., f.* mental deficient. **-za** *f.* lack, insufficiency; mental deficiency; shortage.

**defin-ire** [D2] *tr.* to define; to determine; to settle. **-itiva** *f.* *in* **-itiva,** in point of fact. **-itivo** *adj.* definitive, decisive. **-ito** *part. adj.* defined; definite. **-iziọne** *f.* definition; settlement; description.

**deflet·tere** [C19] *intr.* (*aux.* avere) to deflect, to alter course, to deviate; to diverge; to give way; — *da,* to withdraw from.

**deflor-are** [A1] *tr.* to deflower; to ravish. **-aziọne** *f.* deflowering; ravishing; violation.

**deflu-ire** [D2] *intr.* (*aux.* essere) to flow down; to flow. **-ente** *part. adj.* defluent.

**deflusso** *m.* downward flow; backwash.

**deform-are** [A1 c] *tr.* to deform; to disfigure; to distort; *rfl.* to become distorted; to get out of shape; to warp; to buckle. **-a·bile** *adj.* collapsible.

**defọrm-e** *adj.* deformed, misshapen; mutilated. **-ità** *f. indecl.* deformity; disfigurement; malformation.

**defraudare** [A1 a] *tr.* (*prep.* di) to defraud; to cheat (of); to deprive (of).

**defunto** *adj., n.m.* deceased, defunct.

**degener-are** [A1 s] *intr.* (*aux.* avere, essere) to degenerate; to deteriorate. **-ato** *part. adj., n.m.* degenerate. **-aziọne** *f.* degeneration; degeneracy.

**dege·nere** *adj.* degenerate; deteriorated.

**degen-te** *adj., n.m., f.* patient in hospital; in-patient; inmate. **-za** *f.* stay in hospital; rest in bed.

**degn-are** [A5 c] *tr.* to regard as worthy; *non lo -ai d'una risposta,* I didn't deign to reply to him; *rfl., intr.* (*aux.* essere) to deign; to condescend. **-aziọne** *f.* condescension; amiability.

**dẹgno** *adj.* deserving; worthy; — *di lode,* praise-worthy; honourable; dignified-looking.

**degrad-are** [A1] *tr.* to degrade from rank or office; to disgrace, to dishonour; *rfl.* to degrade oneself; to be disgraced. **-ante** *part. adj.* degrading; lowering; sloping down in tiers. **-aziọne** *f.* degradation; disgrace.

**degust-are** [A1] *tr.* to taste; to sample. **-atọre** *m.* taster; *-atore di vino,* wine-taster. **-aziọne** *f.* tasting; sampling.

**deh** *excl.* (*pron.* **dè**) (poet.) ah, pray!; alas!

**deific-are** [A2 s] *tr.* to deify; to make a cult of. **-aziọne** *f.* deification, apotheosis.

**de-iṣmo** *m.* deism. **-ista** *m.* deist. **-ità** *f. indecl.* deity, godhead.

**del-atọre** *m.* police informer; (leg.) delator, accuser. **-aziọne** *f.* laying of information; denouncing.

**de·leg-a** *f.* proxy; agency; delegation of power; *per* —, by proxy. **-are** [A2 s] *tr.* to assign; to delegate; to appoint as representative. **-ato** *part. adj.* delegated; deputed; appointed; *n.m.* delegate. **-aziọne** *f.* delegation; commission.

**delete·rio** *adj.* deleterious; injurious.

**delfino**[1] *m.* dolphin.

**Delfin-o**[2] *m.* (hist.) Dauphin. **-ato** *pr.n.m.* (geog.) Dauphiné.

**deliber-are** [A1 s] *tr.* to resolve upon; to decide in favour of; *intr.* (*aux.* avere) to deliberate; to make up one's mind; (at an auction) *signori! si -a,* gentlemen, the bidding is open; *rfl.* to decide; to resolve. **-ato** *part. adj.* determined, resolute; *-ato di venire,* set on coming; *-ato a tutto,* ready for anything. **-aziọne** *f.* decision, deliberation.

**delicat-o** *adj.* delicate; weak; dainty; (of food) light, digestible; fastidious, refined. **-ẹzza** *f.* delicacy; daintiness; softness; refinement; tact; *agitare con -ezza,* to stir gently.

**delimit-are** [A1 s] *tr.* to delimit, to define. **-aziọne** *f.* delimitation.

**deline-are** [A6] *tr.* to delineate, to outline; to trace, to sketch. **-aziọne** *f.* delineation.

**delin·qu-ere** [def.] *intr.* to commit a crime or offence, to break the law. **-ente** *part. adj., n.m., f.* delinquent. **-enza** *f.* delinquency.

**delir-are** [A1] *intr.* (*aux.* avere) to rave, to talk wildly; to be delirious. **-ante** *part. adj.* raving, delirious; *n.m., f.* delirious person.

**deli·rio** *m.* delirium, frenzy; wild desire; excessive enthusiasm.

**delitto** *m.* crime; offence; felony; misdemeanour.

**deli·zi-a** *f.* delight; pleasure; joy. **-are** [A4] *tr.* to delight, to entrance; to charm; *rfl.* (*prep.* in, di, con) to take great pleasure (in); to go into ecstasies (over). **-ọso** *adj.* delightful; charming; delicious.

**delta** *m.* (the letter) delta; (geog.) delta.

**delu·dere** [C3] *tr.* to disappoint; to delude, to deceive.

**deluṣ-iọne** *f.* disappointment; delusion; deception; illusion. **-o** *part.* of **deludere,** *q.v.*; *adj.* deluded; deceived; disappointed. **-o·rio** *adj.* delusive, delusory.

**demag-ogi·a** *f.* demagogy; mob-rule. **-o·gico** *adj.* demagogic. **-ogo** *m.* (*pl.* **-oghi**) demagogue.

**demarc-are** [A2] *tr.* to demarcate. **-aziọne** *f.* demarcation.

**demen-te** *adj.* demented, insane. **-za** *f.* dementia, madness.

**deme·rit-o** *m.* demerit; bad mark. **-are** [A1 s] *tr.* to forfeit; to deserve to lose.

**democra·t-ico** *adj.* democratic; *n.m.* democrat. **-iẓẓare** [A1] *tr.* to democratize.

**democrazi·a** *f.* democracy.

**democristiano** *m., adj.* (pol.) Christian Democrat.

**demo-grafi·a** *f.* demography. **-gra·fico** *adj.* demographic.

**demo·grafo** *m.* demographer.

**demol-ire** [D2] *tr.* to demolish, to pull down. **-iziọne** *f.* demolition; bombed site.

**de·m-one** *m.* demon, devil; (fig.) ruling passion. **-o·nico** *adj.* demonic. **-oni·aco** *adj.* demoniacal.

**demo·n-io** *m.* demon, devil; *un — di donna,* a virago. **-ologi·a** *f.* demonology.

**demoraliẓẓ-are** [A1] *tr.* to demoralize; *rfl.* to become demoralized. **-aziọne** *f.* demoralization.

**Demo·stene** *pr.n.m.* Demosthenes.

**denaro** *m.* money; coin; *pl.* money; pence.

**denigr-are** [A1] *tr.* to denigrate; to belittle. **-ante** *part. adj.* disparaging; denigrating. **-aziọne** *f.* denigration; defaming; disparagement

**denomin-are** [A1 s] *tr.* to denominate; to designate. **-atọre** *m.* denominator. **-aziọne** *f.* denomination; title.

**denotare** [A1] *tr.* to denote; to signify; to imply, to show.

**dens-o** *adj.* dense, thick; close; *libro — d'idee,* book packed with ideas. **-ità** *f. indecl.* density; thickness; closeness.

**dentale** *adj.* dental; *n.f.* dental consonant.

**dentat-a** *f.* bite; tooth mark. **-o** *adj.* toothed, cogged; serrated. **-ura** *f.* dentition; set of teeth; dentures; teeth of a comb; serration.

**dente** *m.* tooth; — *del giudizio,* wisdom-tooth; — *canino,* eye-tooth; — *molare,* molar; — *incisivo,* incisor; — *di latte,* milk tooth; *otturare un* —, to stop a tooth; *cavare un* —, to take a tooth out; tusk; prong; notch; (eng.) tooth, cog.

**dentellare** [A1] *tr.* to notch; to indent.

**dentiera** *f.* denture; rack; *ferrovia a* —, cog railway.

**dentifri·cio** *m.* toothpaste.

**dentista** *m., f.* dentist; dental surgeon.

**dentizione** *f.* (med.) teething, dentition.

**dentro** *adv.* inside, within, in; inwardly; *darci* —, to fall into; *dare — a*, to attack, to fall upon; to make inroads upon; *dentrovi*, therein, in it; *prep.* inside; *esser — a qualcosa*, to be in on something; *dentr'oggi*, some time today; *n.m.* inside.

**denuclearizz-are** [A1] *tr.* (pol.) to render nuclear free. **-ato** *part. adj.* (pol.) nuclear free, free of atomic weapons.

**denudare** [A1] *tr.* to denude, to strip.

**denun·ci-a** *f.* declaration (*e.g.* of income); denunciation; bans of marriage. **-are** [A3] *tr.* to make known, to notify, to declare; to denounce, to inform against; to repudiate. **-azione** *f.* declaration, notification; denunciation.

**denutr-ito** *adj.* undernourished; *n.m.* person suffering from malnutrition. **-izione** *f.* malnutrition.

**deper-ire** [D2] *intr.* (*aux.* essere) to waste away; to decline; to perish; to go bad. **-i·bile** *adj.* perishable. **-imento** *m.* decline. **-izione** *f.* wasting, withering; perishing; decay.

**deplor-are** [A1] *tr.* to bewail, to lament, to deplore; to blame, to complain of; *rfl.* to be mourned; *non si -ano vittime*, there are no casualties. **-azione** *f.* lament, complaint. **-evole** *adj.* deplorable, lamentable.

**deponente** *part.* of **deporre**, *q.v.*; *adj.* (gramm.) deponent; (leg.) testifying; *n.m.* (gramm.) deponent; (leg.) deponent; (typ.) inferior figure.

**deporre** [B21] *tr.* to lay down; to put aside; to leave off; — *una carica*, to relinquish an office; to abandon; to lay to rest; to depose; (leg.) to testify; to declare upon oath; to depose; *intr.* (*aux.* avere; *prep.* a) to redound to; *depone a suo favore*, it speaks well for him.

**deport-are** [A1] *tr.* to deport; to exile. **-azione** *f.* deportation; transportation (of convicts).

**depositare** [A1 s] *tr.* to deposit; to hand in; to consign; *intr.* (*aux.* avere) (chem.) to deposit, to form a sediment.

**depo·sito** *m.* deposit; storehouse, depository; object deposited; (rlwy.) cloak-room, left-luggage office.

**deposizione** *f.* laying down, depositing; laying of eggs; deposition; dethroning; (rel.; art) Deposition; Descent from the Cross.

**deprav-are** [A1] *tr.* to deprave, to corrupt; to vitiate; to pervert. **-azione** *f.* depravation, depravity; perversion.

**depred-are** [A1] *tr.* to plunder, to devastate. **-azione** *f.* plunder, devastation; pillage.

**depress-ione** *f.* depression; dejection; lowering. **-ivo** *adj.* lowering, depressive.

**depresso** *part.* of **deprimere**, *q.v.*; *adj.* depressed; dispirited.

**deprezzare** [A1] *tr.* to depreciate; to lower the price of; to discredit.

**depri·m-ere** [C18] *tr.* to depress; to crush; to dishearten. **-ente** *part. adj.* depressing.

**depurare** [A1] *tr.* to purify; to purge.

**deput-are** [A1 s] *tr.* to depute; to appoint, to assign. **-ato** *part. adj.* deputed; assigned; *n.m.* representative, deputy; *Camera dei -ati*, Chamber of Deputies. **-azione** *f.* deputation, delegation; committee.

**derap-are** [A1] *intr.* (*aux.* avere) to skid. **-ata** *f.* skidding; skid.

**derelitto** *adj.* abandoned, forsaken; derelict; *n.m.* waif, foundling.

**deretano** *m.* behind, bottom; rear; *adj.* rear, hind.

**deri·dere** [C3] *tr.* to deride, to ridicule.

**deris-ione** *f.* derision, mockery. **-ivo** *adj.* derisive, mocking. **-o·rio** *adj.* derisive, derisory; *a un prezzo -orio*, absurdly cheap.

**deriva** *f.* (naut.) drift, set; *andare in* —, to drift; *alla* —, adrift; (fig.) *andare alla* —, to drift along aimlessly.

**deriv-are** [A1] *tr.* to divert; to draw off; to tap; *intr.* (*aux.* essere) to derive, to be derived; to ensue; to deviate; (*prep.* da) to have origin (in), to be the outcome (of), to be due (to). **-ativo** *adj.* derivative. **-azione** *f.* derivation; diverting; deviation.

**derog-are** [A2 s] *tr.* (leg.) to repeal, to revoke; (fig.) to derogate; *intr.* (*aux.* avere; *prep.* a) to detract (from), to derogate (from); — *alla regola*, to depart from the rule. **-ato·rio** *adj.* derogatory.

**derrata** *f.* commodity, merchandise; victuals, foodstuff; *giunta alla* —, make-weight.

**derub-are** [A1] *tr.* to rob. **-ato** *part. adj.* robbed; bereft; *n.m.* victim of a theft.

**descritt-o** *part.* of **descrivere**, *q.v.*; *adj.* described. **-ivo** *adj.* descriptive. **-ore** *m.* describer.

**descri·vere** [C12] *tr.* to describe; to give an account of; to trace.

**descrizione** *f.* description.

**deserto** *adj.* deserted; lonely, forlorn; *n.m.* desert, wilderness.

**desider-are** [A1 s] *tr.* to desire; to want; *lasciare a* —, to leave to be desired. **-a·bile** *adj.* desirable; alluring. **-ante** *part. adj.* desiring, desirous; *n.m.*, *f.* applicant. **-ata** *m.pl.* desiderata. **-ato** *part. adj.* desired; welcome; desirable; *n.m.* desideratum.

**deside·rio** *m.* desire, longing; wish; regret; *lasciò molto — di sè*, he was greatly missed.

**desideroso** *adj.* desirous; eager, full of longing; — *di venire*, anxious to come.

**design-are** [A6] *tr.* to designate; to appoint. **-ato** *part. adj.* designated; appointed; *console -ato*, consul designate. **-azione** *f.* designation; *comitato di -azione*, nominations committee.

**desinare** [A1 s] *intr.* (*aux.* avere) to dine; *n.m.* dinner.

**des-i·o** *m.* (*pl.* -ìi) (poet.) desire; loved one; delightful thing, joy. **-ioso** *adj.* (poet.) desirous.

**desi·stere** [C24] *intr.* (*aux.* avere) to desist; to forbear; to cease.

**desol-are** [A1 s] *tr.* to lay waste, to devastate; *rfl.* to become distressed; to grow disheartened. **-ato** *part. adj.* desolate; disconsolate. **-azione** *f.* desolation.

**de·spota** *m.* despot.

**destare** [A1 c] *tr.* to arouse, to awaken; to give rise to; *rfl.* to be aroused; to become alert.

**destin-are** [A1] *tr.* (*prep.* a) to destine; to intend (for); to allot. **-ata·rio** *m.* addressee; consignee. **-azione** *f.* destination; *con -azione per*, bound for.

**destino** *m.* destiny; fate.

**destitu-ire** [D2] *tr.* (*prep.* di) to deprive (of), to dismiss, to discharge. **-ito** *part.* **-to** *adj.* devoid; destitute; discharged. **-zione** *f.* destitution; deprivation.

**desto** *apocop. part.* of **destare**, *q.v.*; *adj.* awake; alert; agile, quick.

**destra** *f.* right hand; right side; *a* —, to the right; (motor.) *tenere la* —, to drive on the right; *tenere a* —, to keep to the right; *prendere a* —, to bear right; (pol.) right wing.

**destreggiare** [A3 c] *rfl.* to manoeuvre cleverly, to act adroitly; to manage.

**destrezza** *f.* adroitness, dexterity, skill.

**destrier-e, -o** *m.* (poet.) steed, charger, destrier.

**destro** *adj.* right; right-hand; dexterous, skilful; propitious, favourable.

**destrorso** *adj.* dextrorse; clockwise.

**desuet-o** *adj.* obsolete; antiquated, old-fashioned. **-u·dine** *f.* desuetude, disuse; *cadere in -udine*, to fall into disuse.

**desulto·rio** *adj.* desultory; random.

**des-u·mere** [C8] *tr.* to infer, to deduce; to extract (information). **-unto** *part. adj.* inferred, deduced.

**deten-ere** [B32] *tr.* to hold; — *un primato*, to hold a record;

to detain. **-tọre** *m.* title-holder. **-ziọne** *f.* detention; holding; imprisonment.

**deter·g-ere** [C4] to cleanse. **-ente** *adj., n.m.* detergent.

**deterior-are** [A1 c] *tr.* to spoil, to damage; *intr.* (*aux.* essere), *rfl.* to deteriorate. **-aziọne** *f.* deterioration; wear and tear.

**determin-are** [A1 s] *tr.* to determine; to ascertain; to decide, to settle; to bring about; *intr.* (*aux.* avere), *rfl.* to make up one's mind, to determine; *-ò di accettare,* he decided to accept. **-ato** *part. adj.* determined, decided; resolute. **-aziọne** *f.* determination; decision. **-ịsmo** *m.* determinism. **-ista** *m., f.* determinist.

**deters-iọne** *f.* cleansing. **-ivo** *adj., n.m.* detergent. **-o** *part.* of **detergere,** *q.v.*; *adj.* purged, cleansed, scoured.

**detest-are** [A1] *tr.* to detest. **-a·bile** *adj.* detestable. **-aziọne** *f.* detestation.

**deton-are** [A1 c] *tr.* to detonate; *intr.* (*aux.* avere) to blow up, to explode. **-ante** *part. adj.* detonating; *n.m.pl.* explosives. **-aziọne** *f.* detonation.

**detr-arre** [B33] *tr.* to take away, to remove; to belittle; *intr.* (*aux.* avere; *prep.* a) to detract (from). **-attọre** *m.* detractor; *adj.* slanderous. **-aziọne** *f.* subtraction; detraction.

**detrimẹnt-o** *m.* detriment; harm. **-ọso** *adj.* detrimental.

**detr-ito** *m.* detritus; *pl.* relics; flotsam and jetsam. **-i·tico** *adj.* (geog.) alluvial.

**dẹtta** *f.* statement, assertion; *a — sua,* according to what he says.

**detta·gli-o** *m.* detail; retail; *al —, in —,* by retail. **-are** [A4] *tr.* to detail, to relate in detail; to sell by retail.

**dettame** *m.* dictate, precept; saying.

**dett-are** [A1 c] *tr.* to dictate; *— legge,* to lay down the law; to compose. **-ato** *part. adj.* dictated; *n.m.* dictation; proverb, saying. **-atura** *f.* dictation.

**dẹtto** *part.* of **dire,** *q.v.*; *adj.* said; *— fatto,* no sooner said than done; named, known as, called; aforesaid; *n.m.* (the) aforesaid; saying; tale; narrative.

**Deuterono·mio** *pr.n.m.* (bibl.) Deuteronomy.

**devalutaziọne** *f.* (finan.) devaluation.

**devast-are** [A1] *tr.* to devastate, to ravage, to lay waste. **-aziọne** *f.* devastation, ruin.

**devi-are** [A4] *tr.* to divert, to deflect; to send astray; *intr.* (*aux.* avere) to deviate; to turn aside; to swerve. **-amẹnto** *m.* deviating; by-pass. **-aziọne** *f.* deviation, deflection; derailment; by-pass. **-azionista** *m., f.* (pol.) deviationist.

**devoluziọne** *f.* devolution; transference.

**devol·vere** [C14] *tr.* to devolve; *rfl.* (*prep.* a) to devolve (upon).

**devot-o** *adj.* devoted; dedicated; affectionate, attached; (rel.) devout; devotional; *n.m.* devout person. **-is·simo** *superl. adj.* (formally, at end of letters) *Suo -issimo,* yours sincerely.

**devoziọne** *f.* devotedness, devotion; (rel.) devoutness, piety.

**di** *prep.* (*contr.* with *def. art.*: del, dello, dei, degli, de', della, delle, dell' d' before a vowel). **1.** of (possession, relationship, authorship, origin, material, kind); *la casa — mio padre,* my father's house; *il ricordo — quel giorno,* the memory of that day; *il quadro non è — Giotto,* the painting is not by Giotto; *è — buona famiglia,* he comes of good family; *Domenico — Filippo,* Dominic, son of Philip; *Lorenzo de' Medici, i.e.* Lorenzo of the Medici family. **2.** from, out of, away from (movement, change, distance); *uscire — casa,* to go out of the house; *— serio diventò allegro,* from grave he became gay; *lontano — qui,* far from here. **3.** by, with (means, instrument, extent, degree, manner); *colpo — martello,* hammer-blow; *lavorare — cesello,* to work with a chisel; *campare d'elemosina,* to live on charity; *— buona voglia,* willingly; *— nascosto,* secretly; *— gran lunga,* by a long way, greatly; *— modo che,* in such a way that. **4.** at, in; during, lasting; *— mattina,* in the morning; *un congresso — una settimana,* a conference lasting a week. **5.** as regards, about, concerning, on; *stare male — salute,* to be in poor health; *pronto — lingua,* glib; *parlavo — te,* I was talking about you; *cambiare — colore,* to change colour. **6.** because of, as a result of; *morì — colera,* he died of cholera; *pazzo d'amore,* madly in love; *piangere d'ira,* to weep for vexation. **7.** than (with *nouns, prns.* and *numerals*); *più — dieci,* more than ten; *meglio — me,* better than I. **8.** FOLL. BY INFIN. CONSTR. (when the subject of the main verb and the infinitive are the same): *riconosco — aver torto,* I know I am in the wrong; *disse — esser venuto,* he said he had come. **9.** WITH ADJS. OR EPITHETS: *qualcosa — buono,* something good; *niente — male,* nothing bad; *dare dell'asino a uno,* to call someone an ass; *quello stupido — Carlo,* that idiot of a Charles. **10.** AS A PARTITIVE *con dei fiori,* with flowers; *delle penne, della carta, dell'inchiostro,* some pens, paper and ink; *fare — tutto,* to do all sorts of things. **11.** ADV. OR PREP. PHRS.: *verso — te,* towards you; *senza — lui,* without him; *per — qua,* through here, this way; *— giù,* downwards, down below; *— su,* upwards, up there. **12.** WITH 'ESSERE', OR 'STARE' AS PART OF THE PREDICATE: *essere — grande aiuto,* to be a great help; *che n'è stato — lui?,* what became of him? **13.** SYNTACTICAL USES: *circondare —,* to surround with; *riempire —,* to fill with; *ridere —,* to laugh at.

**dì** *m. indecl.* day; *a — 10 di luglio,* 10 July; *al — d'oggi,* nowadays.

**diab-ete** *m.* diabetes. **-e·tico** *adj.* diabetic.

**diabo·lico** *adj.* diabolical.

**diacon-ale** *adj.* (eccl.) diaconal; of or relating to a deacon. **-ato** *m.* (eccl.) diaconate. **-ẹssa** *f.* (eccl.) deaconess.

**dia·cono** *m.* deacon.

**diadema** *m.* diadem; nimbus, aureole; tiara.

**dia·fano** *adj.* diaphanous, transparent.

**diaframma** *m.* diaphragm; (fig.) interval, space, gap.

**diag·n-ọsi** *f.* diagnosis. **-osticare** [A2 s] *tr.* to diagnose. **-o·stico** *adj.* diagnostic; *n.m.* diagnostician.

**diagonale** *adj.* diagonal; on the cross; *n.m.* diagonal.

**diagramma** *m.* diagram; (math.) graph.

**dialet·tic-a** *f.* dialectic, dialectics. **-o** *adj.* dialectic; *n.m.* dialectician.

**dialett-o** *m.* dialect; regional speech; vernacular. **-ale** *adj.* dialectal.

**dia·lo-go** (*pl.* **-ghi**) *m.* dialogue; formal talk; (pol.) conference, meeting; *aprire il —,* to open negotiations.

**diamant-e** *m.* diamond; *a punta di —,* diamond-cut, faceted. **-ino** *adj.* diamond-like; adamantine.

**dia·metr-o** *m.* diameter. **-ale** *adj.* diametric(al).

**dia·mine, dia·mici** excl.; (euph. for 'diavolo') the deuce!; what the dickens!

**Diana**[1] *pr.n.f.* Diana.

**diana**[2] *f.* morning star; reveillé; *battere la —,* to sound the reveillé, (fam.) to tremble with cold.

**dianzi** *adv.* a short time ago, just now.

**dia·r-io** *m.* diary, journal. **-ista** *m., f.* diarist.

**diarre·a** *f.* diarrhoea.

**diaspro** *m.* (miner.) jasper.

**diatriba** *f.* diatribe, bitter dispute.

**dia·vol-o** *m.* devil, field; *fare il —,* to make a noise; *è un buon —,* he's not a bad sort; *è un — di problema,* it's the devil of a problem; *il — volle che,* as ill

luck would have it; *adv. phr. alla -a*, carelessly, any old how. **-eri·a** *f.* diabolical action; tangled affair; oddity, absurdity. **-ęsco** *adj.* (*m.pl.* **-ęschi**) devilish; attractive, smart. **-ęto** *m.* uproar, pandemonium.

**dibat·t-ere** [B1] *tr.* to beat; to beat up, to whisk; to flutter; to discuss, to debate; — *i denti*, to gnash one's teeth; *rfl.* to struggle; to writhe. **-imęnto** *m.* violent movement; struggling; debate, discussion.

**dibat·tito** *m.* debate, discussion, dispute.

**dicast-ero** *m.* government department or board; ministry. **-e·rico** *adj.* bureaucratic.

**dicembre** *m.* December.

**diceri·a** *f.* long rigmarole, boring speech; hearsay; rumour.

**dicęvol-e** *adj.* seemly; becoming; fitting, suitable. **-męnte** *adv.* becomingly, suitably. **-ęzza** *f.* seemliness, propriety.

**dichiar-are** [A1] *tr.* to declare; to state; to proclaim; *rfl.* to declare oneself, to make one's position clear. **-aziǫne** *f.* declaration; avowal; proposal of marriage; explanation; statement.

**diciannov-e** *card. num.* nineteen. **-enne** *adj., n.m., f.* nineteen-year-old. **-e·ṣimo** *ord. num.* nineteenth.

**diciassett-e** *card. num.* seventeen. **-enne** *adj., n.m., f.* seventeen-year-old. **-e·ṣimo** *ord. num.* seventeenth.

**diciott-o** *card. num.* eighteen. **-enne** *adj., n.m., f.* eighteen-year-old. **-e·ṣimo** *ord. num.* eighteenth.

**dicit-ǫre** *m.* speaker; reciter; elocutionist. **-ura** *f.* diction, phrasing, wording.

**dicotomi·a** *f.* dichotomy.

**didascali·a** *f.* instruction; information; stage-directions.

**didat·tic-a** *f.* didactics. **-o** *adj.* educational, instructive.

**didęntro** *adv.* inside; *n.m. il* —, the inside.

**didietro** *adv.* behind; *n.m.* back part, back, behind.

**Didǫne** *pr.n.f.* Dido.

**diec-i** *card. num.* ten. **-imila** *card. num.* ten thousand. **-ina** *f.* set of ten; about ten.

**die·reṣi** *f.* diareresis; umlaut.

**die·ta**[1] *f.* assembly, diet.

**die·t-a**[2] *f.* regimen, diet; *stare a* —, to be on a diet. **-are** [A1] *tr.* to diet, to put on a diet. **-e·tica** *f.* dietetics. **-e·tico** *adj.* dietetic.

**dietro** *adv.* **1.** behind; at the back; *lì* —, behind there; *lui stava seduto davanti ed io di* —, he sat in front and I behind; *tenere a* —, to hold back; *zampe di* —, hind legs; *il di* —, the back part. **2.** after, following; *andare* —, to tag along behind; *venire* —, to succeed, to follow on; *mi gridò — di fermarmi*, he shouted after me to stop.

**dietro** *prep.* **1.** behind; *uno — l'altro*, one behind the other; — *le quinte*, behind the scenes; *dire — a uno*, to talk behind a person's back. **2.** after; — *a me*, after me; *essere — a una cosa*, to be engaged on something; *correre — a*, to run after; *tenere — a uno*, to keep a close watch on someone. **3.** upon; as a result of, in consequence of; — *richiesta*, upon request.

**dietro-bottega** *f.* back of a shop; room behind a shop. **-ca·mera** *f.* back room. **-guar·dia** *f.* rearguard. **-scena** *f.* backstage.

**difatt-i, -o** *adv.* indeed; as a matter of fact.

**difend-ere** [C1] *tr.* to guard; to preserve; to prevent; *rfl.* to defend oneself. **-i·bile** *adj.* defensible.

**difens-iva** *f.* defensive; *stare sulla* —, to be on the defensive. **-ivo** *adj.* defensive; *n.m.* means of defence. **-ǫre** *m.* defender.

**difes-a** *f.* defence, protection; *-e dell'elefante*, elephant tusks; *legittima* —, self-defence.

**difett-are** [A1] *intr.* (*aux.* essere; *prep.* di) to be lacking; *-ano i viveri*, there is a shortage of provisions; to be defective (in); to be short (of). **-ivo** *adj.* defective; lacking.

**difett-o** *m.* defect; fault; lack; short-coming; weakness, failing; draw-back, snag; *essere in* —, to be at fault; *in — di*, failing; *riparare a un* —, to make good a lack; *la memoria gli fa* —, his memory is failing. **-ǫso** *adj.* defective.

**diffam-are** [A1] *tr.* to defame; to disparage. **-ativo** *adj.* slanderous. **-aziǫne** *f.* defamation; libel; slander.

**differente** *adj.* different; dissimilar; various; differing.

**differenz-a** *f.* difference; *tre è la — fra cinque e otto*, the difference between five and eight is three; *a — di*, unlike; disagreement; *accomodare le -e*, to settle one's differences. **-iale** *adj., n.m.* differential. **-iare** [A4] *tr.* to differentiate; to render distinct; *rfl.* to differ.

**differ-ire** [D2] *tr.* to defer, to put off; *intr.* (*aux.* avere) to differ; to dissent. **-imęnto** *m.* postponement.

**diffi·cil-e** *adj.* difficult; exacting, unreliable; unlikely; *è — che ti venga a trovare*, he's not likely to come and see you; *n.m.* difficulty. **-męnte** *adv.* with difficulty; improbably.

**difficoltà** *f. indecl.* difficulty; obstacle; handicap; objection; *non trovo nessuna* —, I don't find it difficult; ill-feeling, disagreement.

**diffidare** [A1] *intr.* (*aux.* avere) to be distrustful, to be suspicious; to be diffident; — *da*, to beware of; *tr.* to warn.

**diffiden-te** *adj.* diffident; distrustful. **-za** *f.* diffidence; distrustfulness.

**diffǫndere** [C2c] *tr.* to diffuse; to spread abroad, to give currency to; — *a mezzo radio*, to broadcast; *rfl.* to spread; to be poured out; to talk at length.

**difform-are** [A1c] *tr.* to spoil, to disfigure; *intr.* (*aux.* essere) to change, to lose one's former appearance. **-ato** *part. adj.* spoiled, disfigured; changed.

**diffǫrm-e** *adj.* unlike; diverse. **-ità** *f. indecl.* unlikeness; difference.

**diffr-an·gere** [C5] *rfl.* to be diffracted. **-aziǫne** *f.* diffraction.

**diffuṣ-o** *part.* of **diffǫndere**, *q.v.*; *adj.* diffused; diffuse; widespread; (radio) broadcast. **-iǫne** *f.* diffusion; scattering; circulation; diffuseness; (radio) broadcast.

**difil-are** [A1] *intr.* (*aux.* avere) to file past, to defile. **-ata** *f.* (mil.) march past, defile. **-ato** *part. adj.* direct, immediate; *adv.* forthwith, straightway.

**difuori** *adv.*. See **fuori.**

**diga** *f.* dike, dam; sea-wall, breakwater; embankment.

**diger-ire** [D2] *tr.* to digest; to assimilate; to make a digest of; (fig.) to put up with, to stomach. **-i·bile** *adj.* digestible; (joc.) credible; tolerable.

**digest-iǫne** *f.* digestion; assimilation. **-ivo** *adj.* digestive; *apparato -ivo*, digestive organs; *cibo -ivo*, food which aids digestion.

**digesto** *m.* digest.

**Digiǫne** *pr.n.f.* (geog.) Dijon.

**digital-e** *adj.* digital; *impronte -i*, finger-prints; *n.f.* foxglove.

**digitare** [A1s] *tr., intr.* (*aux.* avere) (mus.) to finger.

**digiun-are** [A1] *intr.* (*aux.* avere) to fast. **-o** *m.* fast, fasting; *a -o*, on an empty stomach; dearth, need; *adj.* fasting; *sono -o da tre giorni*, I haven't eaten for three days; lacking (in), devoid (of); *-o di notizie*, cut off from news.

**dignit-à** *f. indecl.* dignity; rank; dignitary. **-a·rio** *m.* dignitary. **-ǫso** *adj.* dignified; grave; decorous; seemly; suitable.

**digradare** [A1] *intr.* (*aux.* essere) to slope down; to lessen, to diminish gradually; *tr.* to lessen, to diminish; (paint.) to tone down.

**digrassare** [A1] *tr.* to remove fat from; to skim; to remove grease stains from.

**digress-iǫne** *f.* digression; digressing, meandering. **-ivo** *adj.* digressive.

**digrignare** [A5] *tr.* to grind; — *i denti*, to gnash one's teeth.
**digrossare** [A1] *tr.* to make smaller, to trim, to whittle; to rough-hew, to rough-plane.
**diguazzare** [A1] *tr.* to shake; to beat up, to whisk; *intr.* (*aux.* avere) to splash about; to wallow.
**dii** *m.pl.* (poet.) gods (see **dio**).
**dilagare** [A2] *tr.* to flood; *intr.* (*aux.* essere), *rfl.* to overflow; to come flooding in; to spread; *n.m.* spreading, spread.
**dilaniare** [A4] *tr.* to tear to pieces, to rend; to lacerate; (fig.) to denigrate; to torment.
**dilapid-are** [A1 s] *tr.* to squander, to dissipate. **-azione** *f.* dissipation; waste; squandering.
**dilat-are** [A1] *tr.* to dilate; to stretch; to widen; — *la mente*, to broaden the mind. **-azione** *f.* dilation.
**dilavare** [A1] *tr.* to wash away; to wash out, to wash the colour from.
**dilazion-e** *f.* delay; deferment, postponement; respite. **-are** [A1 c] *tr.* (comm.) to put off, to defer, to postpone.
**dileggi-o** *m.* mockery, derision; jeer, gibe; *mettere in* —, to jeer at. **-are** [A3 c] *tr.* to mock.
**dilegu-are** [A6] *tr.* to disperse, to dispel; to scatter; *intr.* (*aux.* essere), *rfl.* to vanish; to fade away; *il suono s'andava dileguando*, the sound grew gradually fainter and fainter.
**dilemma** *m.* dilemma; *i corni di un* —, the horns of a dilemma.
**dilett-are** [A1] *tr.* to please; to entrance; to amuse; *intr.* (*aux.* avere) to give pleasure; (provb.) *non a tutti -ano le stesse cose*, tastes differ; *rfl.* (*prep.* di) to take pleasure (in), to enjoy. **-ante** *part. adj.* pleasing, delighting; *n.m.*, *f.* amateur; *compagnia di -anti*, amateur theatrical company. **-azione** *f.* delight, pleasure. **-evole** *adj.* pleasing amusing; delectable.
**dilett-o** *m.* delight; beloved, darling; *adj.* favourite; dear to one's heart. **-oso** *adj.* delightful.
**diligen-te** *adj.* diligent; industrious; painstaking; careful; accurate. **-za** *f.* diligence; industriousness; conscientiousness; stage-coach.
**dilucidare** [A1 s] *tr.* to explain, to elucidate.
**dilu-ire** [D2] *tr.* to dilute, to water down; to weaken; to thin; *rfl.* to become diluted; to dissolve. **-ente** *adj.* diluting; *n.m.* diluent. **-izione** *f.* dilution.
**dilungare** [A2] *tr.* to prolong; to defer; to set at a distance; *rfl.* to move away; to expatiate; to meander.
**dilungo** *adj.* straight on, continuously, without pause or delay; *sonare a* —, to ring a full peal.
**diluviale** *adj.* torrential.
**diluvi-are** [A4] *tr.* to flood; *intr.* (*aux.* avere) to rain in torrents; (fig.) to flood; *la corrispondenza -ava*, there was a flood of correspondence.
**dilu·vio** *m.* flood; downpour; deluge; *il — universale*, the Flood; abundance; greed; *a* —, in great abundance.
**dimagr-are** [A1] *tr.* to make thin; to impoverish; *intr.* (*aux.* essere), *rfl.* to grow thin; to shrink. **-ante** *part. adj.* thinning, impoverishing; slimming.
**dimagrire** [D2] *intr.* (*aux.* essere) to grow thin; to lose weight.
**dimen-are** [A1] *tr.* to shake, to toss; to wag; *il cane -ava la coda*, the dog was wagging its tail; *rfl.* to fidget; to wave one's arms about. **-ìo** *m.* constant movement; fidgeting; agitation.
**dimension-e** *f.* dimension; size; (cinem.) *un film a tre -i*, a 3-D film.
**dimentic-are** [A2 sc] *tr.* to forget; to forget about; *rfl.* (*prep.* di) to forget; *si -a di tutto, quello lì*, that man forgets everything; *se ne -ò*, he dismissed it from his mind; to forget oneself. **-ag·gine** *f.* absent-mindedness. **-anza** *f.* forgetfulness; inadvertence; oversight. **-atoio** *m.* oblivion; *mettere nel -atoio*, to consign to oblivion.
**dimenti-co** *adj.* (*m.pl.* **-chi**) forgetful, oblivious; unmindful; *non — di*, not unmindful of, bearing in mind. **-chevole** *adj.* forgetful. **-cona** *f.*, **-cone** *m.* absent-minded person.
**dimesso** *part.* of **dimettere** *q.v.*; *adj.* laid aside; dismissed; passed over; humble, modest; (of voice) low; (of dress) plain.
**dimestich-evole** *adj.* tame; friendly, sociable. **-ezza** *f.* familiarity, intimacy; affectionate behaviour.
**dimett'ere** [C20] *tr.* to release; to discharge; *rfl.* to design.
**dimezzare** [A1] *tr.* to halve, to divide in two.
**diminuendo** *m.* (mus.) diminuendo, becoming softer.
**diminu-ire** [D2] *tr.* to diminish, to lessen; to decrease; to reduce; *intr.* (*aux.* essere) to grow less; to decrease; to abate; to drop, to lower. **-tivo** *adj.*, *n.m.* diminutive. **-zione** *f.* diminution; diminishing.
**dimission-e** *f.* resignation; *dare le -i*, to resign; dismissal. **-are** [A1 c] *tr.* to dismiss; *intr.* (*aux.* avere) to resign. **-a·rio** *adj.* out-going, who has resigned.
**dimor-a** *f.* stay, residence; dwelling; home; *senza fissa* —, of no fixed abode; delay; *senza* —, without more ado. **-are** [A1] *intr.* (*aux.* avere) to live, to dwell, to reside.
**dimostr-are** [A1 c] *tr.* to show; to prove; to demonstrate; (geom.) *come si voleva* —, q.e.d.; to explain; to display; — *più anni del vero*, to look older than one is; *intr.* (*aux.* avere) to demonstrate; *rfl.* to show oneself; to prove oneself; to turn out to be; to appear. **-a·bile** *adj.* demonstrable; verifiable. **-ante** *part. adj.* demonstrating; *n.m.*, *f.* political demonstrator. **-ativo** *adj.* demonstrative.
**dina·mic-a** *f.* (phys.) dynamics. **-o** *adj.* dynamic; endowed with vitality, energetic.
**dinamismo** *m.* dynamism.
**dinamite** *f.* dynamite.
**di·namo** *m.*, *f. indecl.* dynamo.
**dinanzi** *adv.* before, in front; — *a*, before; in the presence of; in comparison with; *n.m. il* —, the front, the forepart.
**din-asta** *m.* ruler, dynast. **-asti·a** *f.* dynasty. **-a·stico** *adj.* dynastic.
**dinoccolare** [A1 s] *tr.* to dislocate; to break the neck of; *rfl.* to become dislocated; to break one's neck.
**dintorno**[1] *adv.* around, about; *levarsi* —, to clear out; *prep.* — *a*, round, around.
**dintorno**[2] *m.* neighbourhood; *pl.* surroundings, environs.
**Dio** *m.* (*pl.* **dei, dii,** *f.* **dea**) God; god; *per l'amor di* —, for God's sake, in heaven's name; *mio —!*, my goodness, oh dear!; — *lo sa*, goodness knows; — *ce la mandi buona*, let's hope it turns out all right.
**dipan-are** [A1] *tr.* (text.) to unwind, to reel off; (fig.) to disentangle, to unravel. **-atoio** *m.* winder, reel.
**dipartimento** *m.* department; detachment.
**dipartire** [D1] *intr.* (*aux.* essere), *rfl.* to depart, to go away; to diverge; to branch off; to differ.
**dipen·d-ere** [C1] *intr.* (*aux.* essere; *prep.* da) to depend (on); to be due (to); to derive (from); *-e da te*, it's up to you; to be dependent (on); to be subordinate (to). **-ente** *adj.* depending; dependent; *n.m.*, *f.* dependant; subordinate; employee. **-enza** *f.* dependence; subordination; *alle -enze di*, employed by, in the service of; *in -enza di*, as a result of; derivation; dependency; annexe.
**dipin·gere** [C5] *tr.* to paint; to depict, to portray, to represent; *abs.* to paint; *rfl.* to represent oneself; to use make-up.
**dipinto** *part.* **dipingere**; *adj.* painted; coloured; portrayed; wearing cosmetics, painted.
**diplom-a** *m.* diploma; charter; certificate; degree. **-a·tico** *adj.* diplomatic; *n.m.* diplomat. **-ato** *adj.* certified; *n.m.* person

holding a diploma or degree; graduate. **-azi·a** *f.* diplomacy; diplomatic corps or service.

**diporto** *m.* amusement, pastime, pleasure; place of recreation; *andare a —*, to go for a walk.

**dipresso** *adv. phr. a un —*, approximately.

**diradare** [A1] *tr.* to thin out; to dispose; *— le visite*, to call less frequently; *intr.* (*aux.* essere), *rfl.* to become thinned out; to grow sparse; to clear (of clouds); to dissolve; to become less frequent.

**diram-are** [A1] *tr.* to clear (a tree) of boughs, to lop, to prune; to send out, to circulate; to distribute; to issue; *rfl.* to branch out, to divide, to ramify; to branch off; to spread. **-azione** *f.* lopping; branch (of river, railway line); branching out; sending out, circulation.

**dire** [B10] *tr.*, *intr.* (*aux.* avere) to say; *— addio*, to say farewell; *— di sì*, to say yes; *si dice*, people say, it is said; to speak, to tell; *— la verità*, to speak the truth; to talk; *lasciatelo —*, let him talk; *avete un bel —, non vi dà retta*, it's no use your talking, he won't listen to you; to mean, to signify, to express; *non vuol — nulla*, it doesn't mean a thing; *che cosa vuol — questo ?*, what does this mean ?; to recite, to utter; *— la lezione*, to recite one's lesson; to call, to name; *lo disse animoso*, he called him brave; *lo dicono un asino*, they call him a fool; to suit, to befall; *il giuoco mi dice*, my luck is in; to criticise; to speak adversely; *trovarci a —*, to find something to criticize; *rfl.* to think oneself, to consider oneself; *si dice gran uomo*, he thinks he's a great man; *n.m.* speech; talk; account; description; *l'arte del —*, rhetoric.

**direttiv-o** *adj.* directive, directing; *consiglio —*, managing board; *n.m.* steering committee. **-a** *f.* rule of conduct, directive; direction.

**dirett-o** *part.* of **dirigere**; *adj.* directed; addressed; (rlwy.) *vettura -a*, through carriage. **-amente** *adv.* directly; without intermediary; immediately, instantly. **-is·simo** *adj. superl*; *n.m.* (rlwy.) express.

**dirett-ore** *m.* director; manager; newspaper editor; principal, head; *— di scena*, stage-manager; *— d'orchestra*, conductor. **-rice** *f.* directress; manageress; principal; headmistress; guiding rule, principle.

**direzione** *f.* guidance, management, direction, control, administration; head office; *volante di —*, steering-wheel.

**diri·g-ere** [C13] *tr.* to manage; to control; to direct; to administer; to conduct; to send, to direct, to aim; to address; to dedicate; *rfl.* to head, to aim; to move (towards). **-ente** *part. adj.* directing, guiding; *classi -enti*, ruling classes; *n.m., f.* (admin.) manager. **-i·bile** *adj.* that can be directed.

**diri·mere** [B def] *tr.* to conclude; to solve.

**dirimpetto** *adv.* opposite; over yonder; *prep. phr. — a*, opposite; *— a me*, facing me.

**diritt-o**[1] *adj.* straight; erect, upright; honest; right-hand; *n.m.* right side; front; obverse; *adv.* straight ahead; *sempre —*, straight on. **-a** *f.* right hand; place of honour; direct road, straightest way. **-an·golo** *m.* rectangle.

**diritto**[2] *m.* law; *— civile*, civil law; due, duty; fee; perquisite; tax; *— di bollo*, stamp duty; right; *a buon —*, rightly, justifiably; *membro di —*, member as of right; *pl.* rights; *diritti di autore*, royalties; *diritti civili*, civil rights.

**diroccare** [A2] *tr.* to demolish, to raze; *intr.* (*aux.* essere) to crumble, to fall into ruins.

**dirompere** [C26] *tr.* to break; to soften, to make pliant; to break in; to inure; *intr.* (aux. essere) to burst, to break; *— in lagrime*, to burst into tears; *rfl.* to break oneself in, to become inured.

**dirotto** *part* of **dirompere**; *adj.* softened, broken; inured; *pianto —*, unrestrained weeping; *adv. phr. a —*, violently, in torrents; rapidly; headlong.

**dirozzare** [A1] *tr.* to rough-hew, to rough-dress; to rough out.

**dirugginire** [D2] *tr.* to clear of rust; *— i denti*, to grind one's teeth.

**dirup-are** [A1] *intr.* (*aux.* essere) to plunge down; (fig.) to fall, to sink. **-ato** *part. adj.* precipitous, abrupt.

**dirupo** *m.* rocky precipice; crag; ruin.

**disabellire** [D2] *tr.* to disfigure; to mar; *rfl.* to lose one's beauty.

**disabitato** *adj.* uninhabited.

**disabituare** [A6] to disaccustom; to break of a habit.

**disaccoppiare** [A4] *tr.* to uncouple, to disjoin.

**disadatto** *adj.* unfit; ill-suited, inappropriate; incapable; awkward.

**disadorno** *adj.* plain, bare, unpolished, unadorned; simple; austere.

**disaffezionare** [A1 c] *tr.* to alienate, to estrange; *intr.* (*aux.* essere), *rfl.* to become estranged.

**disaffezione** *f.* estrangement.

**disagevole** *adj.* uncomfortable, painful, distressing; difficult.

**disaggradare** [A1] *intr.* (*aux.* essere) to be displeasing.

**disaggreg-are** [A2] *tr.* to separate; *rfl.* to lose cohesion, to fall apart. **-azione** *f.* separation.

**disa·gio** *m.* (*pl.* **disagi**) discomfort; hardship; privation; uneasiness; *stare a —*, to be uncomfortable.

**disamare** [A1] *tr.* to cease to love; to hate; *intr.* (*aux.* avere) to be no longer in love.

**disameno** *adj.* unpleasant, disagreeable; (of landscape) barren.

**disa·min-a** *f.* careful scrutiny. **-are** [A1 s] *tr.* to consider carefully, to scrutinize.

**disamorare** [A1 c] *tr.* to estrange, to alienate; *rfl.* to cease to love; to become estranged.

**disamore** *m.* indifference; dislike; estrangement.

**disanimare** [A1s] *tr.* to dishearten, to deject, to depress.

**disappetenza** *f.* lack of appetite.

**disapplicazione** *f.* lack of application; neglect of duty.

**disapprov-are** [A1] *tr.* to disapprove of; to rebuke. **-azione** *f.* disapproval, disapprobation.

**disappunto** *m.* trouble, trial, vexation; disappointment; *con mio —*, to my disappointment.

**disarcionare** [A1 c] *tr.* to unhorse.

**disarm-are** [A1] *tr.* to disarm; to dismantle; (naut.) to lay up, to put into reserve; *— i remi*, to ship oars; *intr.* (*aux.* avere) to give up, to withdraw. **-ista** *m.* (neol.) person in favour of disarmament.

**disarmo** *m.* disarmament; dismantling.

**disassociare** [A3] *tr.* to dissociate; to disunite; *rfl.* to dissociate oneself, to dissent; to sever one's connection.

**disastr-o** *m.* disaster; calamity; (colloq.) total loss. **-ato** *adj.* visited by disaster; *n.m.* victim.

**disatten-to** *adj.* inattentive; heedless, careless, negligent. **-zione** *f.* inattention; carelessness, negligence; absent-mindedness.

**disavanzo** *m.* deficit.

**disavveduto** *adj.* heedless; inadvertent.

**disavvenente** *adj.* unattractive; unprepossessing.

**disavventur-a** *f.* mishap, mischance, misadventure. **-ato** *adj.* unfortunate; ill-omened.

**disavvertenza** *f.* inadvertence, inattention; oversight.

**disavvezz-o** *adj.* disaccustomed; out of practice. **-are** [A1 c] *tr.* to disaccustom; *rfl.* to break a habit.

**disbrigare** [A2] *tr.* to free from impediment; to disengage; *rfl.* to disentangle oneself, to get out of a difficulty.

**disbri·go** *m.* (*pl.* **-ghi**) clearing up, settlement; *il — della*

*corrispondenza*, dealing with correspondence.

**dişbrogliare** [A4] *tr.* to disentangle.

**discanto** *m.* (mus.) descant.

**disca·pito** *m.* loss; depreciation; detriment; loss of esteem.

**disca·rica** *f.* voucher; (naut.) unloading.

**discaricare** [A2s] *tr.* to release from a burden, to free; to unload.

**disca·rico** *adj.* freed, unburdened; unloaded; *n.m.* unloading; draining off; easing, alleviating; *a — di coscienza,* to ease one's conscience.

**discaro** *adj.* disagreeable, displeasing; unacceptable; *se non vi è —,* if you have no objection.

**discẹnd-ere** [C1] *intr.* (*aux.* essere, avere) to come down; to go down; to dismount, to get down; to slope, to descend; to be a descendant; *tr.* to go down, to descend; *— le scale,* to go down the stairs. **-ente** *part. adj.* descending; sloping; *n.m., f.* descendant. **-enza** *f.* descent; posterity; race.

**discentrare** [A1] *tr.* to remove from the centre; to decentralize; *rfl.* to become detached; to be decentralized.

**discẹpol-o** *m.* pupil, learner; disciple; follower. **-ato** *m.* discipleship.

**discer·n-ere** [Bdef.] *tr.* to discern, to distinguish; to judge between; to discriminate; to recognize, to descry. **-imẹnto** *m.* discernment; judgement; insight.

**discẹsa** *f.* descent; going down; *in —,* downhill; alighting; fall; slope; invasion, incursion.

**dischiu·dere** [C3] *tr.* to open slightly; to disclose.

**dischiuso** *part.* of **dischiudere**; *adj.* half open, ajar.

**discio·gliere** [B27] *tr.* to undo, to untie; to dissolve, to melt; to break up; to resolve (doubt).

**disciolto** *part.* of **disciogliere**; *adj.* dissolved; melted; loose; free, untrammelled.

**disciplina** *f.* teaching, instruction; intellectual training; branch of learning; discipline; control; *tenere la —,* to keep discipline.

**disciplinare**[1] *adj.* disciplinary.

**disciplin-are**[2] [A1] *tr.* to discipline; to instruct; to train; to chastise; *rfl.* to discipline oneself; to train oneself. **-ato** *part. adj.* disciplined, trained; orderly; law-abiding.

**dis-co** *m.* (*pl.* **-chi**) disk, disc; railway signal; *— combinatore,* telephone dial; (mus.) gramophone record; *— microsolco, — a lunga durata,* long-playing record.

**di·scolo** *adj.* disorderly; undisciplined; impertinent; idle; *n.m.* scamp; truant; idler; dissolute young man.

**discọlp-a** *f.* exculpation; proof of innocence; excuse; defence. **-are** [A1c] *tr.* (*prep.* di) to exculpate; to justify; to prove innocent; *rfl.* to defend oneself (against), to clear oneself (of a charge).

**discommẹttere** [C20] *tr.* to pull to pieces.

**discompagnare** [A5] *tr.* to separate; to part; to isolate; to break up (pair, set).

**disconosc-ere** [B9] *tr.* to refuse to recognize; to disallow; to disregard; to ignore; to slight. **-ente** *part. adj.* ungrateful. **-iuto** *part. adj.* misjudged; disregarded.

**discontinuità** *f.* lack of continuity; interruption.

**disconti·nuo** *adj.* discontinuous; erratic; uneven.

**discord-are** [A1] *intr.* (*aux.* avere; *prep.* da) to disagree, to be at variance, to clash (with); (mus.) to be out of tune (with). **-anza** *f.* variance; disagreement; clash.

**discorde** *adj.* discordant; clashing; differing; *— da,* not in agreement with, different from.

**discor·dia** *f.* discord; dissension, variance; disagreement.

**discọrr-ere** [C5c] *intr.* (*aux.* avere) to talk, to converse; *tr.* to discuss, to treat of; *-ersela con,* to be on good terms with.

**discọrsa** *f.* long rambling talk, rigmarole.

**discorsivo** *adj.* fluent; talkative; relating to discourse.

**discọrso**[1] *m.* speech; talk; conversation; gossip; commentary, treatise, oration, address; *cambiare il —,* to change the subject; (gramm.) *parti del —,* parts of speech.

**discọrso**[2] *part.* of **discọrrere**; *adj.* talked over, discussed, spoken of.

**discost-are** [A1] *tr.* to remove; to displace; *intr.* (*aux.* essere) to be separate, to be at a distance, to differ, to be at variance.

**discosto** *adj.* separated, distant; *adv.* away; afar; far off; *abitava —,* he lived some distance away.

**discoteca** *f.* collection of gramophone records, record library.

**discre·dere** [B1] *tr.* to cease to believe; to disavow; to lose faith in; *rfl.* (*prep.* di) to change one's mind (about).

**discrẹdit-o** *m.* discredit; disrepute; *cadere in —,* to fall into disrepute. **-are** [A1sc] *tr.* to discredit; *rfl.* to become discredited.

**discrepan-te** *adj.* discrepant; *opinioni -ti,* divergent views. **-za** *f.* discrepancy.

**discrẹt-o** *adj.* discreet; discerning; tactful; modest; moderate; *anni -i,* years of discretion; pretty good, not bad; decent, passable; *prezzo —,* moderate price. **-amẹnte** *adv.* passably; to a considerable extent; quite well. **-ẹzza** *f.* discretion, prudence; moderation.

**discreziọne** *f.* discretion; prudence; tact; moderation; good sense; judgement; will; disposal; choice; *a —,* optional, if desired.

**discrimin-are** [A1s] *tr.* to discriminate; to distinguish. **-aziọne** *f.* discrimination.

**discucire** [D1] *tr.* to unstitch, to undo.

**discussiọne** *f.* discussion; argument, debate; controversy.

**discusso** *part.* of **discutere**; *adj.* discussed; talked of; in the public eye; controversial.

**discu·t-ere** [C19] *tr.* to discuss; to consider; to debate. **-i·bile** *adj.* arguable; disputable.

**dişdẹgn-o** *m.* disdain; scorn; *avere a —,* to hold in disdain. **-are** [A5c] *tr.* to disdain. **-ọso** *adj.* disdainful.

**dişdẹtta** *f.* denial; cancellation; ill-fortune; persistent bad luck; *che —!,* what rotten luck!.

**dişdẹtto** *part.* of **disdire**; *adj.* forbidden; resolved; released.

**dişdire** [B10] to deny; to unsay; to refuse; to cancel; *rfl.* to go back on what one has said.

**dişdoro** *m.* disgrace, dishonour, shame.

**disegn-are** [A5c] *tr.* to draw, to sketch; to outline; to describe, to indicate; to design; to intend. **-atọre** *m.* designer; draughtsman.

**disẹgno** *m.* drawing, design; plan; (archit.) *— in pianta,* ground-plan; *- in altezza,* elevation; (fig.) project, intention.

**dişerb-are** [A1] *tr.* to weed. **-ante** *part., n.m.* weed-killer. **-atura** *f.* weeding.

**dişered-are** [A1] *tr.* to disinherit. **-ato** *part. adj.* disinherited; *n.m.* misfit; *pl.* have-nots.

**dişertare** [A1] *tr.* to desert; (mil.) to desert from; to lay waste, to ravage; *intr.* (*aux.* avere, essere) to be a deserter.

**dişertọre** *m.* (mil.) deserter.

**disfare** [B14] *tr.* to undo; to untie; to take to pieces, to pull apart; to destroy; to pull down; *rfl.* to collapse; to decay; to disintegrate; *disfarsi di,* to get rid of.

**disfatt-a** *f.* defeat; downfall; overthrow. **-işmo** *m.* defeatism. **-ista** *m., f.* defeatist.

**disfatt-o** *part.* of **disfare**; *adj.* undone; done away with; worn out; ruined; wretched; exhausted; *volto —,* haggard face. **-ọre** *m.* destroyer.

**disfavọre** *m.* disfavour; *a — di,* in opposition to; misfortune.

**disfigur-are** [A1] *tr.* to disfigure;

to mar. **-azione** *f.* disfigurement; grimace.
**disforme** *adj.* irregular; unharmonious.
**disfunzione** *f.* (med.) irregular functioning.
**disgel-are** [A1] *tr., intr., impers.* (*aux.* essere), *rfl.* to thaw; to defrost. **-ante** *part. adj.* thawing; *n.m.* de-icer.
**disgelo** *m.* thaw.
**disgiun·gere** [C5] *tr.* to separate, to part; to unyoke.
**disgiunt-o** *part.* of **disgiungere**; *adj.* separated, detached; (mus.) disjunct. **-ivo** *adj.* disjunctive. **-ore** *m.* (electr.) circuit-breaker.
**disgiunzione** *f.* separation; dissolution of a bond.
**disgradare** [A1] *tr.* to put to shame; to discredit; to outclass, to outdo.
**disgravare** [A1] *tr.* to disburden. to relieve, to lighten.
**disgra·zi-a** *f.* accident, mishap; ill-luck, misfortune; *per* —, unluckily; disfavour; *cadere in* —, to fall out of favour. **-ato** *adj.* unfortunate, unlucky; evil; unlovely; awkward; ungraceful; *n.m.* wretch.
**disgreg-are** [A2] *tr.* to break into pieces; to fragment; (mil.) — *le forze nemiche*, to scatter enemy forces; *rfl.* to break up; to disintegrate; to decompose. **-ativo** *adj.* disruptive. **-azione** *f.* breakdown; disintegration; decomposition.
**disguido** *m.* going astray (of letter, etc.); — *postale*, error in postal delivery.
**disgustare** [A1] *tr.* to offend; to disgust, to vex; to shock; *rfl.* to be offended; to be disgusted to fall out (with).
**disgust-o** *m.* distaste, dislike; disgust. **-oso** *adj.* disgusting, repugnant.
**disidrat-are** [A1] *tr.* to dehydrate. **-azione** *f.* dehydration.
**disil·l-abo** *adj.* disyllabic; *n.m.* disyllable. **-a·bico** *adj.* disyllabic.
**disill-u·dere** [C1] *tr.* to undeceive; to disillusion. **-usione** *f.* disenchantment, disillusion.
**disimballare** [A1] *tr.* to unpack.
**disimparare** [A1] *tr.* to unlearn; to forget.
**disimpegnare** [A5 c] *tr.* to release from an obligation; to redeem (pledge); to discharge, to perform; *rfl.* to release oneself from an obligation; to get free.
**disimpegno** *m.* disengagement, release, fulfilment.
**disincarnare** [A1] *tr.* to disembody.
**disinclinazione** *f.* disinclination; dislike, antipathy.
**disinfest-are** [A1] *tr.* to disinfest, to rid of pests or vermin. **-ante** *m.* insecticide. **-azione** *f.* disinfestation.
**disinfett-are** [A1] *tr.* to disinfect. **-ante** *adj., n.m.* disinfectant. **-azione** *f.* disinfecting. **-ore** *m.* disinfectant.
**disinfezione** *f.* disinfection.
**disingann-are** [A1] *tr.* to undeceive, to disabuse; *rfl.* to be disillusioned. **-o** *m.* disillusionment; disappointment; re-awakening to reality.
**disinnamorare** [A1 c] *tr.* to estrange; *rfl.* (*prep.* di) to lose one's affection (for), to fall out of love (with).
**disinnestare** [A1] *tr.* (eng.) to disconnect, to disengage; (motor.) — *la frizione*, to let out the clutch; *rfl.* to slip out of gear.
**disinser-ire** [D2] *tr.* (mech.) to throw out; (electr. eng.) to disconnect. **-ito** *part. adj.* disconnected; (of a switch) off.
**disintegr-are** [A1] *tr.* to disintegrate. **-azione** *f.* disintegration; *-azione dell'atomo*, splitting of the atom.
**disinteress-are** [A1] *tr.* to cause to lose interest; (comm.) to buy (a person) out; *rfl.* *-arsi di*, to lose interest in; to wash one's hands of. **-ato** *adj.* disinterested.
**disinteresse** *m.* disinterestedness; indifference, lack of interest.
**disintossicare** [A2] *tr.* to free from toxic substance.
**disinvol·gere** [C5] *tr.* to undo; to unwrap; to unwind; to unroll.
**disinvolt-o** *part.* of **disinvolgere**; *adj.* (fig.), unembarrassed, unconstrained; natural; uninhibited. **-ura** *f.* ease of manner; self-possession.
**disistim-a** *f.* lack of esteem; disrepute. **-are** [A1] *tr.* to despise; to have a low opinion of.
**dislivello** *m.* difference in level; disparity.
**disloc-are** [A2] *tr.* to displace; to remove; (med.) to dislocate. **-azione** *f.* displacement; dislocation.
**dismissione** *f.* cessation, abandonment.
**dismisura** *f.* excess, lack of restraint; *a* —, beyond measure.
**dismisurato** *adj.* excessive, immoderate; exorbitant.
**disnebbiare** [A4 c] *tr.* to clear of mist; (fig.) to clarify, to free from obscurity.
**disnodare** [A1] *tr.* to untie; to release.
**disobbligante** *adj.* disobliging; uncivil.
**disobbligare** [A2 s] *tr.* to release from an obligation.
**disoccup-ato** *adj.* unemployed; unoccupied. **-azione** *f.* unemployment; *sussidio di -azione*, unemployment benefit.
**disonest-o** *adj.* dishonest; dishonourable; shameless; immodest; corrupt; fraudulent. **-à** *f.* dishonourable behaviour; dishonesty; trickery, fraud; indecency.
**disonorare** [A1 c] *tr.* to dishonour; to spoil; to vituperate; *rfl.* to be dishonoured; to lose one's reputation; to behave dishonourably.
**disonore** *m.* dishonour; shame, ignominy; disgrace; *essere il — della famiglia*, to be the black sheep of the family.
**disopra** *adv.* above; upstairs; *per* —, into the bargain; *n.m. il* —, the upper part; *prendere il* —, to gain the upper hand.
**disordin-are** [A1 sc] *tr.* to throw into disorder; to disarrange; to confuse. **-ato** *part. adj.* disorderly; untidy; immoderate.
**disordine** *m.* disorder; confusion; untidiness; excess; intemperate habits; disease; *pl.* riot, rioting.
**disorga·nico** *adj.* incoherent; wanting in order; disjunct.
**disorganizz-are** [A1] *tr.* to disorganize; *rfl.* to become disorganized; to fall into disorder. **-azione** *f.* disorganization.
**disorientare** [A1] *tr.* to disorientate; to bewilder; *rfl.* to lose one's bearings; to be at a loss.
**disormeggiare** [A3 c] *tr.* (naut.) to cast off; to weigh; *rfl.* to weigh anchor.
**disossare** [A1] *tr.* to bone, to remove bones from.
**disotto** *adv.* below; underneath; downstairs; *prep. phr. al — di*, below, under, lower than; *n.m. il* —, the lower part.
**dispac·cio** *m.* despatch; telegram; communiqué; *pl.* (mil.) despatches.
**disparato** *adj.* not matching, unlike, disparate.
**disparere** *m.* difference of opinion, disagreement.
**di·spari** *adj. indecl.* uneven, odd; different; unequal; *è permesso il parcheggio nei giorni* —, parking on uneven dates.
**dispar-ire** [D2] *intr.* (*aux.* essere) to disappear, to vanish. **-iscente** *part. adj.* fading. **-izione** *f.* disappearance.
**disparità** *f.* disparity; inequality; difference.
**disparte** *adv.* apart; *adv. phr. in* —, apart, to one side.
**dispen·di-o** *m.* expense; expenditure; outlay. **-oso** *adj.* expensive, incurring expenditure; costly.
**dispens-a** *f.* distribution; pantry, storeroom; sideboard; instalment, section (of book published in parts); written text of University lecture; exemption; dispensation. **-are** [A1] *tr.* to distribute; to dispense; to exempt; *-are dal servizio*, to dispense with the services of; *rfl.* to be exempt; to abstain; *-arsi da*, to

get out of. -**a·rio** *m.* dispensary; clinic. -**atore** *m.* dispenser; bestower.
**dispensiere** *m.* steward; dispenser, bestower.
**dis-pepsi·a** *f.* indigestion, dyspepsia. -**pep·tico** *adj.* dyspeptic.
**disper-are** [A1] *tr.* (*prep.* di) to despair (of); *intr.* (*aux.* avere) to despair; *rfl.* to be in despair; to distress oneself. -**ato** *part. adj.* despaired of; given up (by doctors); *un caso -ato*, a hopeless case; *anima -ata*, lost soul; *n.m.* destitute man; desperado. -**azione** *f.* despair, desperation; despondency; trouble, worry.
**disper·dere** [C3] *tr.* to scatter, to disperse, to dispel, to destroy; to waste; *rfl.* to be scattered; to get lost; to disperse one's energies.
**disper·gere** [C3] *tr.* to scatter; to disperse; to dissipate; to put to flight; to diffuse; *rfl.* to scatter, to disperse.
**dispersione** *f.* dispersion; scattering; loss; waste.
**disperso**[1] *part.* of **disperdere**; *adj.* scattered, dispersed; lost, missing; *dato per —*, reported missing; *n.m.* missing person.
**disperso**[2] *part.* of **dispergere**; *adj.* scattered, dispersed; dissipated; put to flight; diffused, diffuse.
**dispett-o** *m.* annoying or spiteful action; act of mischief; *per —*, out of spite; vexation; *a — di*, in spite of, in defiance of; scorn; *avere in —*, to despise. -**oso** *adj.* spiteful; mischievous, teasing; scornful.
**dispiac-ere** [B20] *impers.* (*aux.* essere; *prep.* a) to displease, to cause sorrow (to); *mi -e*, I'm sorry; *intr.* (*aux.* essere) to be displeasing, to give offence. -**ente** *part. adj.* displeasing, unpleasant; regretful, sorry. -**iuto** *part. adj.* displeasing; sorry, displeased; *-iuto di*, sorry about.
**dispiacere** *m.* regret; sorrow, grief; displeasure; trouble; disappointment; misfortune.
**displu·vio** *m.* (geog.) rainfall divide.
**disponente** *part.* of **disporre**; *adj.* ordaining; *n.m.* (leg.) testator; *f.* testatrix.
**dispon-i·bile** *adj.* disposable; available, vacant; *n.f.* (leg.) disposable portion of an estate. -**ibilità** *f.* availability.
**disporre** [B21] *tr.* to arrange; to dispose; to set in order; *intr.* (*aux.* avere) to order things; *l'uomo propone e Dio dispone*, man proposes and God disposes; to decide, to resolve; *rfl.* to get ready, to prepare; to resolve.
**dispositivo** *adj.* dispositive; *n.m.* appliance, mechanism, device, gadget.
**disposizione** *f.* arrangement, disposition; distribution; *avere a —*, to have available; intention; inclination; *a — di*, at the disposal of.
**disposto** *part.* of **disporre**; *adj.* arranged, ordered; inclined; willing; *— a tutto*, ready for anything; *ben —*, well disposed.
**dispo·t-ico** *adj.* despotic; of a despot. -**ismo** *m.* despotism.
**dispregiare** [A4] *tr.* to think little of, to despise; to undervalue, to belittle.
**dispre·gio** *m.* disregard; disdain; disparagement.
**disprezz-are** [A1] *tr.* to despise, to scorn, to disdain; to undervalue, to disparage; *rfl.* not to take proper care of oneself. -**o** *m.* contempt, disdain, scorn; carelessness, neglect.
**di·sputa** *f.* dispute, debate; quarrel, altercation.
**disput-are** [A1] *intr.* (*aux.* avere) to debate, to argue, to dispute; to discuss; *recip. rfl.* to contend for. -**a·bile** *adj.* disputable. -**ante** *m., f.* disputant.
**disquili·brio** *m.* lack of balance.
**disquisizione** *f.* elaborate investigation; scholarly research; disquisition.
**dissalare** [A1] *tr.* to remove salt from.
**dissangu-are** [A6, A1] *tr.* to drain of blood, to bleed to exhaustion; (fig.) to bleed, to ruin. -**amento** *m.* bleeding; bloodletting; *morire per -amento*, to die of loss of blood.
**disseccare** [A2 c] *tr.* to dry up, to parch.
**dissellare** [A1] *tr.* to unsaddle; *intr.* (*aux.* avere) to be unhorsed.
**dissemin-are** [A1 sc] *tr.* to disseminate, to spread abroad, to sow. -**azione** *f.* (fig.) dissemination, diffusion.
**dissenn-are** [A1 c] *tr.* to deprive of sense, to drive mad. -**ato** *part. adj.* senseless, foolish.
**dissens-o** *m.* dissent, disagreement. -**ione** *f.* dissension.
**dissenteri·a** *f.* (med.) dysentery.
**dissentire** [D1] *intr.* (*aux.* avere; *prep.* da) to dissent (from), to disagree (with), to differ (from).
**disseppellire** [D2] *tr.* to disinter; to unearth; to bring to light again.
**dissert-are** [A1] *intr.* (*aux.* avere) to discourse, to dissert; to expatiate; to argue. -**azione** *f.* dissertation; thesis.
**disservi·zio** *m.* disservice.
**dissestare** [A1] *tr.* to disarrange; to upset; (fig.) to put in an embarrassing position.
**dissesto** *m.* confusion; disorder; financial embarrassment.
**dissetare** [A1 c] *tr.* to quench the thirst of.
**dissezione** *f.* dissection.
**dissid-ente** *adj.* dissident; *n.m., f.* dissenter. -**enza** *f.* dissension.
**dissi·dio** *m.* disagreement; point in dispute; quarrel.
**dissigillare** [A1] *tr.* to unseal, to break the seal of.
**dissi·mile** *adj.* unlike, different.
**dissimul-are** [A1 s] *tr.* to dissimulate, to dissemble, to disguise; *rfl.* to be concealed, to lie hidden. -**atore** *m.* dissembler. -**azione** *f.* dissimulation, feigning, concealment.
**dissip-are** [A1 s] *tr.* to dissipate; to squander; to dispel; *rfl.* to become dissipated, to be scattered; (of mist, clouds) to clear, to lift. -**azione** *f.* dispersion; squandering, waste; dissipation.
**dissoci-are** [A3] *tr.* to dissociate; to separate; to sever. -**azione** *f.* dissociation; separation.
**dissod-are** [A1] *tr.* to break up (ground), to clear for tillage. -**amento** *m.* tillage.
**dissolu·bil-e** *adj.* dissoluble; impermanent. -**ità** *f.* dissolubility; impermanence.
**dissolut-o** *part.* of **dissolvere**; *adj.* dissolved; dissolute, licentious, loose. -**ezza** *f.* dissoluteness, licentiousness, looseness.
**dissoluzione** *f.* dissolution; dissolving, solution; corruption.
**dissol·v-ere** [C14] *tr.* to dissolve; to separate, to disperse; to dispel; to break up; *rfl.* to be dissolved; to be dispersed, to scatter. -**ente** *n.m.* solvent. -**enza** *f.* (cinem.; telev.; radio) fading; *apertura in -enza*, fade in; *chiusura in -enza*, fade-out. -**imento** *m.* dissolving; dispersing; breaking up.
**dissomigli-are** [A4] *intr.* (*aux.* essere), *recip. rfl.* to be unlike, to differ. -**anza** *f.* unlikeness; difference.
**disson-are** [A1 d] *intr.* (*aux.* avere) to be out of tune, to sound discordant; to be out of keeping; to disagree. -**anza** *f.* dissonance; discord, discordance; divergence.
**dissotter-are** [A1] *tr.* to exhume, to disinter; to bring to light again. -**amento** *m.* exhumation, disinterment.
**dissuadere** [C3] *tr.* to dissuade, to deter, to discourage.
**dissuasione** *f.* dissuasion.
**dissuggellare** [A1] *tr.* to unseal, to open.
**distacc-are** [A2] *tr.* to detach, to separate; to unstick; to pull apart; (motor.) *— la frizione*, to declutch; *intr.* (*aux.* essere) (art) to be prominent, to stand out; *rfl.* to come apart; to be detached; to get separated; to part; *-arsi da uno*, to break with someone; *-arsi dal mondo*, to withdraw from the world. -**amento** *m.* detachment; separation.
**distac-co** *m.* (*pl.* -**chi**) detach-

ment, separation; parting; withdrawal; (aeron.) take-off.
**distante** *adj.* distant, remote; far off; *è — di qui,* it is a good way from here; diverse; *adv.* far off, afar.
**distanz-a** *f.* distance; length; range; length; *tenere uno a —,* to keep a person at arm's length. **-iare** [A4] *tr.* to leave behind, to outstrip; (sport) to outdistance.
**distare** [A9 s] *intr.* (*aux.* essere; *prep.* da) to be distant (from); *distano 300 metri l'uno dall'altro,* they are three hundred metres apart.
**disten·d-ere** [C1] *tr.* to spread, to extend; to lay; *— le ali,* to stretch one's wings; to hammer out; to roll out; to bring down heavily; *— un colpo,* to strike a heavy blow; to put down in writing, to record; *rfl.* to extend, to spread, to stretch; to expatiate. **-imẹnto** *m.* spreading, extending; stretching out.
**distensiọne** *f.* tension, stretching; *— di un muscolo,* straining of a muscle; relaxation; easing of tension.
**distẹsa** *f.* expanse, sweep; vast array; extent, stretch; *ridere alla —,* to laugh boisterously.
**distẹso** *part.* of **distendere**; *adj.* stretched, laid out; long, extended; *lungo —,* lying full length; *per —,* in full; ample, wide, spacious; extensive; *n.m.* report; memorandum.
**distill-are** [A1] *tr.* to distil; *intr.* (*aux.* essere) to fall drop by drop. **-ato** *part. adj.* distilled; *n.m.* extract, essence. **-atọre** *m.* still; distillation plant. **-aziọne** *f.* distillation. **-eri·a** *f.* distillery.
**distin·gu-ere** [C6] *tr.* to distinguish; to draw a distinction between; to perceive, to make out; *non -o senza gli occhiali,* I can't see properly without my glasses; to mark off, to divide, to differentiate; to lend distinction to; to make notable, to mark out; *farsi —,* to draw attention to oneself; *rfl.* to distinguish oneself. **-i·bile** *adj.* distinguishable.
**distinta** *f.* list; schedule; (comm.) price list; invoice.
**distintivo** *adj.* distinctive; *n.m.* badge; emblem; distinguishing mark; (naut.) flag.
**distinto** *part.* of **distinguere**; *adj.* distinct, separate; distinguished; eminent; refined; gentlemanly; ladylike; *con saluti distinti,* yours sincerely.
**distinziọne** *f.* distinction; difference; *fare —,* to distinguish; *senza —,* without distinction, indiscriminately.
**disto·gliere** [B2] *tr.* to dissuade, to deter; *— uno da un'idea,* to persuade someone to give up an idea; *rfl.* (*prep.* da) to think better (of).
**distorto** *adj.* crooked, twisted; deformed; distorted.
**distrarre** [B33] *tr.* to pull aside, to twist, to sprain; to detach; to distract, to divert; *rfl.* to be inattentive, to let one's mind wander; to be absent-minded; to divert oneself.
**distratto** *part.* of **distrarre**; *adj.* absent-minded; inattentive; *n.m.* absent-minded person.
**distraziọne** *f.* absent-mindedness; distraction, inattentiveness; amusement, recreation.
**distrẹtt-o** *m.* region, administrative district. **-uale** *adj.* relating to a district.
**distribuire** [D2] *tr.* to distribute; to hand out, to deal out; to share; to allot, to assign; to arrange; (cards) to deal.
**distributọre** *m.* distributor; *— di benzina,* petrol pump.
**distribuziọne** *f.* distribution; issue, assignment; (theatr.) casting; (cards) deal.
**districare** [A2] *tr.* to disentangle; to unravel; to extricate; *rfl.* to extricate oneself; *districarsi da,* to get out of.
**distrug·gere** [C12] *tr.* to destroy; to ruin; to lay waste; to demolish; to consume; *rfl.* to be destroyed; to wear oneself out; to waste away.
**distrutt-i·bile** *adj.* destructible; precarious. **-ivo** *adj.* destructive; disruptive. **-ọre** *m.* destroyer
**distruziọne** *f.* destruction; ruin; havoc.
**disturb-are** [A1] *tr.* to disturb; to trouble; to distress; to worry; to be a nuisance to; to vex, to annoy; *vi -o?,* am I in your way?; *rfl.* to distress oneself; to take trouble; to put oneself out, to bother; *non si -i,* please don't trouble. **-o** *m.* trouble; annoyance; distress; inconvenience, disturbance; (med.) complaint, disorder.
**dișubbid-ire** [D2] *intr.* (*aux.* avere; *prep.* a) to disobey; to disregard. **-ienza** *f.* disobedience.
**disuguaglianza** *f.* inequality; unevenness; discrepancy.
**dișugual-e** *adj.* unequal; uneven; irregular; disparate. **-ità** *f.* inequality; unevenness.
**dișuman-o** *adj.* inhuman, cruel, barbarous; bestial, subhuman. **-ità** *f.* inhumanity, cruelty, barbarity. **-iẓẓare** [A1] *tr.* to dehumanize.
**dișuniọne** *f.* disunion, separation.
**dișunire** [D2] *tr.* to disunite, to separate, to cause a rift between; *rfl.* to become disunited.
**dișuș-o** *m.* disuse; desuetude; *cadere in —,* to fall into disuse. **-are** [A1] *tr.* to cease using, to give up; to disaccustom, to break of a habit.
**dișu·tile** *adj.* useless; worthless; superfluous; harmful, injurious; good-for-nothing; *n.m.* uselessness; harm, disadvantage; good-for-nothing.
**dișv-i·o** *m.* (*pl.* -i·i) straying; deviating; leading astray; driving away (of customers); going astray (of post).
**ditale** *m.* finger of a glove; finger stall; thimble.
**ditata** *f.* tap with the finger; finger-mark; as much as will go on a finger.
**Dite** *pr.n.m.* (class. myth.) Dis.
**ditirambo** *m.* (lit. hist.) dithyramb.
**dito** *m.* (*pl. f.* **dita**) finger; digit; *— del piede,* toe; *— pollice, — grosso,* thumb; *— grosso del piede,* big toe; *— indice,* forefinger; *— medio,* middle finger; *— anulare,* fourth finger; *— mignolo,* little finger; (*pl. m.* **diti**) finger of a glove; *un — di vino,* a drop of wine.
**ditta** *f.* business firm; company; *Spettabile Ditta...,* Messrs...
**ditta·fono** *m.* dictaphone.
**dittat-ọre** *m.* dictator. **-oriale** *adj.* dictatorial. **-o·rio** *adj.* relating to a dictator. **-ura** *f.* dictatorship.
**ditton-go** *m.* (*pl.* **-ghi**) diphthong.
**diurn-o** *adj.* diurnal; *spettacolo —,* matinée; *albergo —,* establishment providing 24-hour service of 'wash and brush up', bath, shave, etc.
**diva** *f.* goddess; star of stage, screen or television.
**divag-are** [A2] *intr.* (*aux.* avere) to ramble, to roam; (fig.) to wander from the point, to divagate; *tr.* to entertain, to divert; to distract; *rfl.* to amuse oneself, to seek diversion. **-aziọne** *f.* straying, digression; diversion, recreation.
**divampare** [A1] *intr.* (*aux.* essere) to flare up, to burst into flame.
**divano** *m.* divan, settee.
**divaric-are** [A2 s] *tr.* to stretch apart. **-ato** *part. adj.* wide apart, opened wide; *a gambe -ate,* with legs apart.
**diva·rio** *m.* difference; variation; discrepancy.
**divedẹre** [B35] *tr. dare a —,* to reveal; to give to understand.
**divel·lere** [B31] *tr.* to uproot, to pull up; to eradicate.
**divenire** [D17] *intr.* (*aux.* essere) to become; to develop into, to grow into; *— rosso,* to turn red, to blush; *n.m.* becoming, developing.
**diventare** [A1] *intr.* (*aux.* essere) to become; to change into, to turn into; *— matto,* to go crazy.
**diver·bio** *m.* dispute, altercation.

**diver·g-ere** [C def.] *intr.* to diverge; to deviate. **-ente** *part. adj.* divergent. **-enza** *f.* divergence; *-enza di opinioni*, difference of opinion.
**diversific-are** [A2 s] *intr.* (*aux.* essere), *rfl.* to be different; to differ, to vary; *tr.* to make different. **-azione** *f.* difference, distinction.
**diversione** *f.* diversion; turning aside; deflection; pastime, recreation.
**diversità** *f.* diversity; variety; difference.
**diverso** *adj.* completely different; *pl.* various, several; *diversi giorni fa*, some days ago.
**divertente** *adj.* diverting, amusing; funny.
**divert-ire** [D1] *tr.* to divert; to distract; to amuse, to entertain; *rfl.* to amuse oneself, to enjoy oneself; to be amused. **-imento** *m.* amusement; pastime, recreation.
**diviato** *adj., adv.* straight (on).
**dividendo** *m.* (math.) divident; (finan.) *stabilire un —*, to declare a dividend.
**divi·dere** [C3] *tr.* to divide; to distribute; to share out; to separate, to part; *rfl.* to be divided; to split; to be separated; to part.
**divieto** *m.* prohibition; *— di sosta*, no parking; *— di transito*, no thoroughfare; *— d'affissione*, stick no bills; *giorni di —*, days of abstinence.
**divin-are** [A1] *tr.* to divine; to foresee; to predict. **-ato·rio** *adj.* divinatory; *verga -atoria*, divining rod. **-azione** *f.* divination; prophecy.
**divincolare** [A1 s] *rfl.* to twist, to wriggle free.
**divinità** *f. indecl.* divinity; god.
**diviniżż-are** [A1] *tr.* to deify. **-azione** *f.* deification; apotheosis.
**divino** *adj.* divine; godlike; sacred; sublime.
**divisa**[1] *f.* parting (in hair); division: sharing.
**divisa**[2] *f.* uniform; *in —*, wearing uniform; *— di gala*, full dress; *— di fatica*, fatigue dress; *— di professore*, academic dress; livery; heraldic arms, device.
**divis-are** [A1] *intr.* (*aux.* avere) to plan, to intend; to propose; *ho -ato di andare*, I have planned to go; *tr.* to conceive, to plan. **-amento** *m.* design; intention; project, plan.
**divisi·bile** *adj.* divisible.
**divisione** *f.* division; distinction; disagreement; partition; (admin.) department; *capo —*, head of a department.
**divis-o** *part.* of **dividere**; *adj.* distinct; split, separated, severed; at variance. **-ore** *m.* (math.) divisor. **-o·rio** *adj.* (*m.pl.*-**ori**) dividing, separating; divisive; *muro -orio*, party wall.
**divo** *adj.* divine; of a god; *n.m.* god, divinity; male celebrity of stage, screen or television.
**divorare** [A1, A1 c] *tr.* to devour; to eat up; *— con gli occhi*, to gaze intently at; to waste, to squander, to consume.
**divorzi-are** [A4] *intr.* (*aux.* avere; *prep.* da) to divorce from; *— dal marito*, to divorce one's husband; *rfl.* to get a divorce. **-ata** *f.* divorcée. **-ato** *part. adj.* divorced; *n.m.* divorced man.
**divor·zio** *m.* divorce; *fare — da*, to divorce; *Tribunale dei Divorzi*, Divorce Court; *causa di —*, divorce suit, divorce proceedings; (fig.) detachment, separation.
**divulg-are** [A2] *tr.* to publish; to make known; to spread; to divulge, to disclose. **-azione** *f.* publication; spreading; popularization; disclosure.
**diziona·rio** *m.* dictionary; *— geografico*, gazetteer.
**do** *m.* (mus.) doh; the note C; the key of C.
**docci-a** *f.* (*pl.* **docce**) douche; shower; shower-bath; (fig.) discouragement; (bldg.) gulley, gutter; spout; jet; (fig.) cold shower, check to enthusiasm. **-one** *m.* drainpipe; conduit; spout.
**docen-te** *adj.* teaching; *n.m., f.* teacher, instructor; *libero —*, lecturer; qualified tutor. **-za** *f.* teaching, instruction; *libera -za*, University teaching degree.
**do·cil-e** *adj.* docile; apt; manageable; tractable; amenable; *materia —*, workable material. **-ità** *f.* docility; submissiveness; tractableness.
**document-o** *m.* document; certificate; proof, evidence; voucher; deed; *pl.* documents; records; papers; instructions; writings, precepts; *provare con -i*, to prove by documentary evidence. **-ale** *adj.* (leg.) documentary; *prova -ale*, documentary evidence. **-are** [A1 c] *tr.* to document, to support with documentary evidence. **-a·rio** *adj.* documentary; (cinem.) *film -ario*, documentary film; also *n.m.* **-azione** *f.* documentation; documenting.
**dodec-a·dico** *adj.* (math.) duodecimal. **-ae·dro** *m.* (geom.) dodecahedron. **-afoni·a** (mus.) twelve-note system. **-afo·nico** adj. (mus.) *serie -afonica*, twelve note series, tone row. **-a·gono** *m.* (geom.) dodecagon. **-asil·labo** *adj.* (prosod.) dodecasyllabic; *n.m.* dodecasyllable; *-asillabo francese*, Alexandrine.
**Dodecane·so** *pr.n.m.* (the) Dodecanese.
**dodic-i** *card. num. indecl.* twelve; *n.m.* the number twelve. **-enne** *adj., n.m.* twelve-year-old. **-e·simo** *adj. ord. num., n.m.* twelfth.
**doga** *f.* stave (of cask, etc).); band, stripe.
**dogan-a** *f.* customs, customhouse; duty; bonded warehouse; *in —*, in bond. **-ale** *adj.* relating to the Customs. **-iere** *m.* custom-house officer.
**dog-e** *m.* doge (of Venice or Genoa). **-ale** *adj.* dogal; *n.m.* doge's dress. **-ato** *m.* dogate; a doge's period of office or territory.
**do·glia** *f.* pain; ache.
**dogm-a** *m.* dogma; creed **-a·tica** *f.* dogmatic theology;. dogmatics. **-a·tico** *adj.* dogmatic; opinionated. **-atismo** *m.* dogmatism. **-atiżżare** [A1] *intr.* (*aux.* avere) to dogmatize.
**dolc-e** *adj.* sweet; *acqua —*, fresh water, soft water; soft; smooth; gentle, easy; gradual; mild; tender; dear, sweet, amiable; *adv.* sweetly; softly; gently; *n.m.* sweetness; dessert, sweet. **-ezza** *f.* sweetness; softness; smoothness; gentleness; delicacy; good nature; tenderness.
**dolci-a·rio** *adj.* (comm.) relating to sweets; *industria -aria*, sweet-manufacturing industry. **-ere** *m.* confectioner.
**dolcificare** [A2 s] *tr.* to sweeten; to add sweetening to, to add sugar to.
**dolciume** *m.* sweetness; sickliness; *pl.* sweetmeats, sweets.
**dolere** [B11] (*aux.* for *pers.* use, essere, avere; for *impers.*, essere only); *intr.* to cause pain, to hurt; to ache; *impers. mi duole che sia morto*, I am sorry he is dead; *rfl.* to be sorry, to lament; to take offence.
**dol·laro** *m.* dollar.
**dol-o** *m.* fraud. **-oso** *adj.* fraudulent; *incendio -oso*, arson.
**dolor-e** *m.* pain, ache. **-oso** *adj.* painful, aching; sorrowful; grievous, doleful.
**domand-a** *f.* question; request; application. **-are** [A1] *tr.* to ask; to ask for; to request; to demand; *le -ò scusa*, he begged her pardon; *rfl.* to ask oneself, to wonder; *-arsi di*, to wonder about.
**domani** *adv.* tomorrow; in the future; *— sera*, tomorrow evening; *doman l'altro*, the day after tomorrow; *— a otto*, tomorrow week; *n.m. il —*, the next day.
**domare** [A1 c] *tr.* to tame; to break in; to subdue; to master, to curb; to check, to control; to 'break in'.
**domattina** *adv.* tomorrow morning.
**domenic-a** *f.* Sunday. **-ale** *adj.* (of) Sunday; *riposo -ale*, Sunday rest.
**domenican-a** *f.* (eccl.) Domini-

can nun. -o *adj.* (eccl.) Dominican; *n.m.* Dominican friar.

**dome·stica** *f.* maid, servant.

**domesticare** [A2 s] *tr.* to tame, to domesticate; to cultivate (plants).

**domestichęzza** *f.* intimacy, close association, friendly behaviour.

**domes·tic-o** *adj.* domestic; of the house; of the family or household; simple, homely; *prelato* —, domestic prelate; *n.m.* servant, manservant. **-ità** *f.* domesticity.

**domiciliare**[1] *adj.* (leg.) domiciliary; *perquisizione* —, police search of a house.

**domiciliare**[2] [A4] *tr.* (leg.) to domicile; *rfl.* to take up one's residence, to make one's home, to settle.

**domici·lio** *m.* domicile, place of residence; address; *d'ignoto* —, of no known address.

**domin-are** [A1 s] *intr.* (*aux.* avere) to hold sway, to be dominant; to rule; to prevail; to be domineering; *tr.* to dominate; to master; to overpower; to sway. **-ante** *part. adj.* dominant; *n.f.* (mus.) dominant. **-anza** *f.* dominance. **-azione** *f.* domination.

**domi·nio** *m.* rule, sway, power, command; mastery (of a language); territory ruled or held, dominion, domain.

**do·mino** *m. indecl.* domino; the game of dominoes.

**don, dọn** *m.* (title) Don; (of monks) Dom; — *Chisciotte*, Don Quixote.

**don-are** [A1 c] *tr.* to present, to bestow, to give, to donate; *intr.* (*aux.* avere) to suit, to go well with, to be becoming; *il vestito nero le -a*, she looks well in black. **-atọre** *m.* giver, bestower; *-atore di sangue*, blood-donor; (leg.) donor. **-aziọne** *f.* donation, gift, present.

**donchisciott-ęsco** *adj.* (*m. pl.* **-ęschi**) quixotic (from the name, **Don Chisciọtte,** Don Quixote); **-ișmo** *m.* quixotry.

**dọnde** *interr.*, *adv.* whence, from where; of which, from which, wherewith; wherefore, why.

**dọndol-a** *f.* rocking chair. **-are** [A1 sc] *tr.* to rock, to swing; to dangle; to keep waiting, to put off; *intr.* (*aux.* avere), *rfl.* to swing, to sway, to rock; to idle. **-o** *m.* swinging object; plaything; dangling ornament; *orologio a -o*, pendulum clock; *sedia a -o*, rocking chair; *cavallo a -o*, rocking-horse.

**donn-a** *f.* woman; married woman; lady; — *di casa*, housewife; (cards) queen; *Nostra Donna*, Our Lady; (title) Donna. **-ęsco** *adj.* (*m.pl.* **-ęschi**) womanly; feminine; relating to women; *lavori -eschi*, domestic tasks. **-ętta** *f. dim.* little woman; girl; *farsi -etta*, to be growing up. **-ina** *f. dim.* dear little woman; sensible little girl. **-ọna** *f. augm.* overgrown girl. **-ọne** *m. augm.* tall, big-boned woman.

**dọno** *m.* gift, present.

**donzell-a** *f.* (poet.) damsel, maiden, maid. **-o** *m.* (hist.) noble youth; page; squire.

**dọpo** *prep.* after; — *domani*, the day after tomorrow; — *tutto*, after all; — *di me*, after me; *adv.* afterwards, later; next; behind; *il giorno* —, the next day; *subito* —, immediately afterwards.

**dopo-barba** *adj. indecl.* after-shave. **-guerra** *m. indecl.* post-war. **-pranzo** *m.* afternoon.

**doppiare** [A4 c] *tr.* to double; (sport) to lap; (cinem.) to dub.

**dọppi-o** *adj.* double, twofold; dual; duplex; *fare il — gioco a*, to double-cross; two-faced, insincere; *a — petto*, double-breasted. **-ęzza** *f.* doubleness; double thickness; (fig.) duplicity, deceitfulness.

**dor-are** [A1] *tr.* to gild; (cul.) to glaze. **-atura** *f.* gilding; gilt decoration.

**do·rico** *adj.* Dorian; Doric.

**dormicciare** [A4] *intr.* (*aux.* avere) to doze, to drowse; (fig.) to nod, to be caught napping.

**dormigl-iare** [A4] *intr.* (*aux.* avere) to doze. **-iọna** *f.*, **-iọne** *m.* sleepy-head, late riser, lazy bones.

**dorm-ire** [D1] *intr.* (*aux.* avere) to sleep; to be asleep; to slumber; (fig.) to be at rest; *-irci sopra*, to sleep on it; *tr.* to sleep; to sleep through; — *il sonno dei giusti*, to sleep the sleep of the just; *rfl.* *-irsela*, to sleep peacefully. **-ito·rio** *m.* dormitory. **-ivęglia** *f.* state between sleeping and waking; drowsiness.

**dors-o** *m.* back; summit; ridge, crest; spine (of a book); (swimming) *nuoto sul* —, back-stroke. **-ale** *adj.* of the back, dorsal; *spina -ale*, spine, vertebral column, backbone.

**doș-e** *f.* dose. **-are** [A1] *tr.* to dose; to fix the dose of; to dole out; to meter. **-ag·gio** *m.* dosage. **-atura** *f.* dose.

**doss-o** *m.* back; *portare in* —, to carry on one's back; *levarsi di* —, to take off (garment). **-iere** *m.* back-rest.

**dot-e** *f.* dowry; endowment. **-are** [A1] *tr.* (*prep.* di) to endow (with), to bestow; *-are qualcuno di qualcosa*, to bestow something on someone; (fig.) to enrich; to furnish, to equip. **-aziọne** *f.* (leg.) endowment; dowry; settlement.

**dotto** *adj.* learned, scholarly; pedantic; expert; skilful, practised; *n.m.* scholar, learned man.

**dottọr-e** *m.*, *f.* doctor; — *in legge*, doctor of law; medical man; doctor of the Church; (in Italian Universities) holder of a first degree, graduate. **-ato** *m.* doctorate; doctor's degree. **-ęssa** *f.* woman graduate or woman holding a doctor's degree.

**dottrina** *f.* doctrine; learning, scholarship; teaching, theory.

**dọve** *interr.* where? — *mai?*, where on earth?; *per —?*, which way?; *adv.* where; *vado — dice lui*, I am going where he tells me; *da —, di —*, whence, from where; *conj.* (foll. by *indic.*) where; whereas; while; (foll. by *subj.*) if; — *mancasse qualcosa, scrivetemi*, if anything should be lacking, write to me; — *che*, wherever; *n.m.* place; *per ogni* —, everywhere.

**dovẹr-e** [B12] *tr.* to owe; (comm.) *deve avere*, due to, credit; *deve dare*, due from, debtor; *aux. vb.* foll. by *inf.* to have to, to be obliged to; *avrei dovuto scrivere*, I ought to have written; *dovè andare*, he was obliged to go (and he did); *doveva andare*, he was under an obligation to go; *come și deve*, properly; to be probable; *dev'essere vero*, it must be true; *n.m.* duty; propriety, fitness; *a* —, in the right way; *come di* —, as is right and proper; the right amount; *pagare più del* —, to be overcharged; what one deserves; *gli sta il* —, it serves him right; school task, homework; *pl.* respects. **-ọso** *adj.* due, dutiful, right and proper.

**dovi·zi-a** *f.* wealth, plenty; *a* —, in abundance. **-ọso** *adj.* wealthy, rich; abundant.

**dovunque** *adv.* (with *subj.*) wherever; *indef. adv.* no matter where, anywhere, everywhere.

**dovuto** *adj.* due, proper, fitting; due, owed, outstanding; deserved; *n.m.* debt; due.

**dozzin-a** *f.* dozen; *a -e*, in crowds; *mettere uno in* —, to put someone on the same level as everyone else; *di* —, cheap, commonplace; payment for board and lodging; *prendere a* —, to take boarders; *stare a* —, to be a boarder. **-ale** *adj.* second-rate, cheap, ordinary. **-ante** *m.*, *f.* boarder.

**drag-a** *f.* (naut.) dredger; sea anchor, drogue. **-ag·gio** *m.* (naut.) dredging; minesweeping. **-amine** *m. indecl.* minesweeper. **-are** [A2] *tr.* (naut.) to dredge.

**dra-go** *m.* (*pl.* **-ghi**) dragon; — *volante*, — *pallone*, boy's kite; (aeron.) kite balloon.

**dragọn-e** *m.* dragon; (mil.) dragoon. **-ęssa** *f.* dragoness, she-dragon.

**dramma**[1] *m.* play, drama; tragedy (also fig.); *fare un* —, to exaggerate.

**dramma**[2] *f.* (numis.) drachma; (weight) drachm, dram; tiny

quantity, *a — a —*, little by little, gradually.
**dramm-a·tica** *f.* art of drama, dramatics; dramatic poetry. **-a·tico** *adj.* dramatic; *scrittore -atico*, dramatist. **-atizzare** [A1] *tr.* to dramatize, to render dramatic; *abs.* to exaggerate; to be melodramatic. **-aturgo** *m.* (*pl.* **-aturghi**) playwright, dramatist.
**drapp-eggiare** [A3 c] *tr.* to drape; (fig.) to clothe; *rfl.* to drape oneself; to strike an attitude, to pose. **-eggio** *m.* draping; hangings.
**drappello** *m.* (mil.) squad, platoon; band, group of people.
**drapp-o** *m.* precious cloth; fine fabric; — *mortuario*, pall; — *inglese*, court sticking-plaster. **-eri·a** *f.* drapery; collection of fabrics; draper's shop. **-iere** *m.* draper.
**dra·stico** *adj.* drastic.
**drenag·gio** *m.* draining; drainage; drain; *tubo di —*, drain pipe; (fig.) drain; *il — sulla sterlina*, the drain on sterling.
**Dresda** *pr.n.f.* (geog.) Dresden.
**dri·ade** *f.* dryad.
**dritta** *f.* right, right-hand-side; (naut.) starboard.
**dritto** *adj.* straight; *a —*, vertical; upright; honest; favourable; proper, right; exact (of time); *n.m.* right side of material; upright (piece); (leg.) *il —*, that which law directs; the right; (fig.) *un —*, a straight man; *adv.* straight on; *sempre —*, keep straight on.
**drizza** *f.* (naut.) lift, halyard.
**drizzare** [A1] *tr.* to direct, to turn; to straighten, to correct; to set upright, to raise; — *le orecchie*, to prick up one's ears; (naut.) to hoist.
**dro-ga** *f.* article of grocery, esp. imported (*e.g.* pepper, coffee); spice; narcotic, drug. **-gare** [A2] *tr.* to spice, to flavour; to doctor, to adulterate; to drug. **-gheri·a** *f.* drysaltery; grocer's shop. **-ghiere** *m.* drysalter, grocer.
**dromeda·rio** *m.* (zool.) dromedary.
**dromo** *m.* (naut.) beacon; bollard.
**drud-a** *f.*, **-o** *m.* paramour.
**dru·id-a** *m.*, **-o** *m.* Druid. **-a**, **-essa** *f.* Druidess.
**dru-i·dico** *adj.* Druidic, Druidical. **-idismo** *m.* Druidism.
**drup-a** *f.*, **-o** *m.* (bot.) drupe, stone fruit. **-i·fero** *adj.* drupe-bearing.
**dual-e** *adj.* dual, twofold. **-ismo** *m.* (philos.; theol.) dualism; (neol.) rivalry, antagonism. **-ista** *m.* dualist. **-i·stico** *adj.* dualistic. **-ità** *f.* duality.
**dub·bi-o** *adj.* doubtful, uncertain; hesitant; ambiguous; dubious; *persona di -a fama*, person of dubious reputation; questionable; untrustworthy; *n.m.* doubt; hesitation; misgiving; suspicion; risk; *nel — sarà meglio fare così*, if there's any doubt it will be best to do this; *fare un —*, to raise a difficulty, to put forward an objection; *in —*, in danger; *mettere in —*, to throw doubt on, to endanger; *chiarire un —*, to clear, up a doubtful point. **-ezza** *f.* hesitation, doubtfulness. **-oso** *adj.* doubtful, doubting; irresolute; uncertain, dubious; questionable.
**dubit-are** [A1 s] *intr.* (*aux.* avere) to doubt; *c'è poco da —*, there's not much room for doubt; to suspect, to fear; *-o che sia tardi*, I'm afraid it's late; — *di*, to distrust; to hesitate, to waver. **-a·bile** *adj.* questionable; uncertain; *non è -abile*, it cannot be doubted. **-ante** *part. adj.* doubtful, hesitant; uncertain; groping. **-ativo** *adj.* dubitative, hesitant; expressing doubt. **-oso** *adj.* full of doubts; timid, shy; suspicious; uncertain.
**Dublino** *pr.n.f.* (geog.) Dublin.
**du-ca** *m.* (*pl.* **-chi**) duke. **-cale** *adj.* ducal; *palazzo -cale*, Doge's Palace. **-cato** *m.* duchy; dukedom; dukeship; (numis.) ducat. **-chessa** *f.* duchess.
**duce** *m.* guide; leader, captain, commander.
**ducentista** *m.* writer of the 13th century.
**duch-esco** *adj.* (*m.pl.* **-eschi**) ducal.
**due** *card. num.* two; *a — a —*, two by two; *lavorare per —*, to work twice as hard as anyone else; — *parole*, a word or two; *far — passi*, to go for a little stroll; *stare fra —*, to be in two minds; *adoperare — pesi e — misure*, to be unfair, to discriminate; *n.m. indecl.* the figure two; *un — posti*, a two-seater; *un — pezzi*, a two-piece.
**duecent-o** *card. num.*, *adj. indecl.*, *n.m. indecl.* two hundred; *il Duecento*, the thirteenth century. **-enne** *adj.* two hundred years old. **-esco** *adj.* (*m.pl.* **-eschi**) of the thirteenth century. **-e·simo** *card. num.* two hundredth. **-omila** *card. num.*, *n.m.* two hundred thousand.
**duell-o** *m.* duel; *battersi in —*, to fight a duel; *sfida a —*, challenge to a duel. **-ante** *part. adj.* duelling; *n.m.* party to a duel. **-are** [A1] *intr.* (*aux.* avere) to duel, to fight a duel. **-ista** *m.* habitual duellist, fighter of duels.
**duemila** *ord. num.*, *adj. indecl.*, *n.m. indecl.* two thousand.
**duennale** *adj.* biennial.
**duetto** *m.* (mus.) duet; (joc.) angry dialogue.
**dulcine·a** *f.* lady-love.
**duli·a** *f.* (theol.) dulia.
**duna** *f.* sand-dune.
**Duncherche** *pr.n.f.* (geog.) Dunkirk.
**dunque** *adv.* then; so; well then, well now; now then; therefore, accordingly; *n.m. venire al —*, to come to the point.
**duo** *m. indecl.* (mus.) duet, duo.
**duode·cimo** *ord. num.* twelfth.
**duoden-o** *m.* (anat.) duodenum. **-ale** *adj.* (med. anat.) duodenal.
**duolo** *m.* (poet.) grief, sorrow; mourning.
**duomo** *m.* cathedral; other principal church in a town.
**duplic-are** [A2 s] *tr.* to double; to duplicate. **-ato** *part. adj.* doubled; duplicated; *n.m.* duplicate; spare copy; counterpart; doubling of words or lines. **-atore** *m.* duplicator. **-azione** *f.* doubling; duplication.
**du·plic-e** *adj.* double, twofold. **-ità** *f.* doubleness, duplicity.
**duplo** *adj.* double; *n.m.* double quantity.
**dur-are** [A1] *intr.* (*aux.* essere, avere) to last, to continue, to go on; *finchè la -a!*, as long as it lasts!; to keep (of perishable goods); *-ò a lavorare*, he kept on working; (with *aux.* avere) to hold out, to persevere; *ha -ato poco in quell'ufficio*, he didn't stay in that office very long; *provb. chi la -a la vince*, dogged does it. **-a·bile** *adj.* lasting, likely to last. **-abilità** *f.* durability, lasting quality. **-ante** *part. adj.* lasting; *vita natural -ante*, throughout one's life; *prep.* during, in the course of. **-ata** *f.* duration, length of time; length of currency; *-ata della carica*, term of office; *di -ata*, lasting, permanent; hard-wearing; *colore di lunga -ata*, fast colour; *articoli di breve -ata*, perishable goods. **-aturo** *adj.* durable, permanent, likely to remain. **-azione** *f.* duration. **-evole** *adj.* lasting, enduring, abiding.
**dur-o** *adj.* hard; tough; firm; difficult; bitter; severe; *una vita -a*, a hard life; *patti -i*, harsh terms; *l'è -a!*, hard lines!; *pane —*, stale bread; *pietra -a*, precious stone; obstinate; slow witted; *osso —*, hard nut to crack; *testa -a*, dense or mulish person; — *d'orecchi*, hard of hearing; *avere la pelle -a*, to have a tough constitution; *n.m.* hard part; difficulty; *adv. tener —*, to hold out, to refuse to yield. **-ezza** *f.* hardness; (fig.) harshness, severity; insensibility.
**dut·til-e** *adj.* ductile; (fig.) pliable. **-ità** *f.* ductility; (fig.) pliability.
**dutto** *m.* (anat.) duct.

**Ẹ**[1] *f.sing., m.pl.* the letter E; the vowel E; *una E maiuscola,* a capital E; *una e minuscola,* a small e; *un'e stretta,* a close e (as in 'sera'); *un'e larga,* an open e (as in 'bello').

**ẹ**[2] *conj.* (**ed** is sometimes used before another vowel) and; also; and so; *e...e,* both...and; *tutti — due,* both; *tutte e tre le ragazze,* all three girls; *bell' — fatto,* ready-made; *se è riuscito lui — noi riusciremo,* if he succeeded we shall too; and yet, but; *doveva arrivare — non s'è visto,* he was due to arrive but there isn't a sign of him; *— che volete ?,* well, what do you want ?; *— commerciale,* ampersand.

**è** *3rd sing. pr. ind. of* **essere;** is.

**ebanite** *f.* ebonite.

**e·bano** *m.* (bot.) ebony-tree; *— falso,* laburnum.

**ebbene** *conj.* well; well then.

**e(b)br-o** *adj.* intoxicated, drunk; excited, elated; *— di gioia,* delirious with joy. **-ẹzza** *f.* intoxication; rapture, bliss; elation; exultation. **-ietà** *f.* see **ebrietà.**

**ebdo·mad-a** *f.* week. **-a·rio** *adj.* weekly, hebdomadal; *n.m.* weekly journal.

**Ebe** *pr.n.f.* (myth.) Hebe.

**e·bet-e** *adj.* stupid, dull, obtuse. **-u·dine** *f.* dullness, stupidity; hebetude.

**ebollizione** *f.* boiling; *punto di —,* boiling point.

**ebra·i-co** *adj.* (*pl.* **-ci**) Hebrew; Hebraic; Jewish; *ristorante —,* Kosher restaurant; *n.m.* Jew, Hebrew; Hebrew language.

**ebraismo** *m.* Judaism; (ling.) Hebraism.

**ebr-e·o** *m.* Jew; *l'Ebreo errante,* the wandering Jew; *confondere Ebrei e Samaritani,* to mix things that are incompatible; *adj.* Jewish, Hebrew. **-e·a** *f.* Jewess.

**E·bridi** *pr.n.f.* (geog.) Hebrides.

**ebrietà** *f.* intoxication, inebriety; drunkenness; (fig.) madness, blindness.

**ebulliente** *adj.* ebullient; boiling; (fig.) boisterous.

**ebur·neo** *adj.* of ivory; as white as ivory; ivory-like.

**Ẹcate** *pr.n.f.* (myth.) Hecate.

**ecatọmbe** *f.* hecatomb; mass slaughter.

**ecce·d-ere** [B1] *tr.* to exceed; *— la velocità permessa,* to exceed the speed limit; to go beyond; to surpass; *intr.* (*aux.* avere) to be excessive; *— nel mangiare,* to overeat; *ora voi -ete,* now you are going too far. **-ente** *part. adj.* exceeding; excessive; in excess; *-ente il peso,* overweight; *n.m.* excess, surplus. **-enza** *f.* excess; surplus; (comm.) surplus stock.

**eccellen-te** *adj.* excellent; exquisite; *ha un cuore —,* he has a good heart; good to eat. **-za** *f.* excellence; pre-eminence; *per -za,* par excellence, pre-eminently; (title) Excellency.

**eccel·lere** [B1] *intr.* (*aux.* essere) to excel, to be pre-eminent; (*prep.* su, tra) to surpass; *— sui contemporanei,* to be outstanding among one's contemporaries.

**eccelso** *adj.* lofty; high; (fig.) magnificent, best; *pr.n.m. l'Eccelso,* the Most High.

**eccen·tric-o** *adj.* eccentric; odd, strange; not symmetrical; far from the centre; *luogo —,* outlying spot; *n.m.* eccentric man; (eng.) eccentric; cam. **-ità** *f.* eccentricity; strangeness; distance from the centre.

**eccep-ire** [D2] *tr.* to except, to object; *non ho nulla da —,* I have no objection. **-i·bile** *adj.* exceptionable, reprehensible.

**eccessiv-o** *adj.* excessive; immoderate; extreme; *idee -e,* extremist ideas. **-ità** *f.* excessiveness.

**eccesso** *m.* excess; *all'—,* excessively; *è gentile fino all' —,* he is even too kind; *dare in eccessi,* to fly into a passion; *per —,* in excess; *da un — all'altro,* from one extreme to the other; *— di peso,* excess weight.

**ecce·tera** *adv.* (abbrev. **ecc.**) etcetera, etc., and so on; *n.m.pl. indecl.* etceteras.

**eccetto** *prep.* except, excepting; save, barring, but; *tutti — uno,* all but one; *conj. — che, — che non, — se,* unless.

**eccettu-are** [A6] *tr.* to except; *se ne -ano pochi,* with few exceptions. **-ato** *part. adj.* excluding, except.

**eccezion-e** *f.* exception; *a — di,* with the exception of; *fare -i,* to make exceptions; *d'—,* exceptional; *opporre — a,* to take exception to; reproach, reproof, criticism. **-ale** *adj.* exceptional; extraordinary.

**ecci·dio** *m.* slaughter, massacre.

**eccit-are** [A1 s] *tr.* to excite; to incite; to rouse; to stimulate; *— il riso,* to provoke laughter; *— l'invidia,* to arouse envy; *rfl.* to get excited; to grow angry. **-a·bile** *adj.* excitable. **-ante** *part. adj.* exciting, stimulating; *n.m.* stimulant. **-ato** *m.* excited; agitated; angry.

**Ecclesiaste** *pr.n.m.* (bibl.) Ecclesiastes.

**ecclesia·stico** *adj.* ecclesiastical; *l'abito —,* clerical dress; *storia ecclesiastica,* Church history; *n.m.* ecclesiastic, churchman, priest.

**ecco** *adv.* here; there; *eccomi,* here I am; *— fatto il becco all'oca,* that's the finishing touch; *— servito l'amico,* that's cooked his goose; *— tutto,* that's all; *excl.* behold!; look!.

**eccọme** *excl.* rather!; and how!

**echeggi-are** [A3 c] *intr.* (*aux.* avere, essere) to echo; to resound; *tr.* to echo, to re-echo. **-ante** *part. adj.* echoing; resounding; resonant.

**echino** *m.* (zool.) sea urchin.

**eclet·tic-o** *adj.* eclectic. **-ismo** *m.* eclecticism.

**eclissare** [A1] *tr.* to eclipse; (fig.) to outshine, to throw into the shade; *rfl.* to be eclipsed; (fig.) to be outshone.

**ecliss-e** *m., f.,* **-i** *m. indecl.* eclipse.

**eclit·tic-a** *f.* (astron.; geog.) ecliptic. **-o** *adj.* relating to the ecliptic; relating to eclipses.

**ec-o** *m., f.* (*pl.* **echi** *m.* or *indecl.*) echo; *fare — di,* to repeat; *farsi — di una diceria,* to repeat a rumour; repercussion.

**ecologi·a** *f.* (zool.; bot.) ecology.

**eco·metro** *m.* echo sounder.

**economi·a** *f.* economy; thrift; *fare —,* to save, to be economical; economics; *— domestica,* domestic economy; *— politica,* political economy; *— pubblica,* national economy.

**econo·mico** *adj.* economical; cheap; thrifty; economic.

**economista** *m., f.* economist.

**economizzare** [A1] *tr.* to save; *intr.* (*aux.* avere) to economize.

**eco·nom-o** *m.* steward; bursar; almoner; custodian; *adj.* economical; thrifty; sparing. **-ato** *m.* stewardship; bursarship; bursar's office.

**E·cuba** *pr.n.f.* (myth.) Hecuba.

**ecume·nic-o** *adj.* (eccl.) oecumenical. **-ità** *f.* ecumenicity.

**eczem-a** *m.* (med.) eczema. **-atọso** *adj.* (med.) eczematous.

**edac-e** *adj.* devouring; destructive. **-ità** *f.* voracity, edacity.

**edema** *m.* (med.) oedema. **-a·tico, -atọso** *adj.* (med.) oedematous.

**Ẹden** *pr.n.m.* Eden; *l'—,* the Garden of Eden.

**ẹdera** *f.* (bot.) ivy; *— terrestre,* ground ivy.

**edi·cola** *f.* small chapel or shrine; newspaper stall, kiosk.

**edific-are** [A2 s] *tr.* to build; to erect; to raise; to edify. **-ativo** *adj.* edifying. **-ato·rio** *adj.* relating to building; *arte -atoria,* architecture; *suolo -atorio,* building land. **-azione** *f.* building, constructing; edification.

**edifi·c-io** *m.* (*pl.* **-i**) building; structure; block of buildings; fabric; *l'— sociale,* the social order.

**edil-e, e·dil-e** *adj.* relating to building. **-i·zia** *f.* building trade; *materiale per -izia,* building material. **-i·zio** *adj.* relating to building; *regolamento -izio,* building regulations.

**Edimburgo** *pr.n.f.* (geog.) Edinburgh.

**Ẹdipo** *pr.n.m.* (myth.) Oedipus.

**e·dit-o** *adj.* published; edited.

**-ore** *m.* publisher, editor; *adj.* publishing; *casa -rice*, publishing firm. **-ori·a** *f.* editing; publishing industry. **-oriale** *adj.* editorial; relating to publishing. **-orialista** *m.* leader-writer.
**editto** *m.* edict; (fig.) decree, law.
**edizione** *f.* publication; publishing; edition; — *tascabile*, pocket edition.
**edon-ismo** *m.* hedonism. **-ista** *m., f.* hedonist. **-i·stico** *adj.* hedonistic.
**edotto,** *adj.* informed; — *di*, informed about; *rendere qualcuno —*, to inform someone, to put someone in the picture.
**edredone** *m.* (orn.) Eider duck; eiderdown quilt.
**educand-a** *f.* girl pupil (in convent or boarding-school); *divisa da —*, school uniform for girls. **-ato** *m.* boarding-school for girls (*e.g.* in a convent).
**educ-are** [A2 s] *tr.* to bring up; to educate, to train. **-ativo** *adj.* educative; educational. **-atamente** *adv.* politely. **-ato** *part. adj.* well-bred, polite; educated, trained; *mal -ato*, rude. **-atore** *m.*, **-atrice** *f.* educator, teacher. **-ato·rio** *m.* (*pl.* **-atori**) (hist.) girls' school; charity school.
**educazione** *f.* good breeding, good manners; *quel giovanotto è senza —*, that young man is really ill-bred; education; — *fisica*, physical training; *Ministero dell'— nazionale*, Ministry of Education; culture, rearing (of plants, silk worms).
**efe·lide** *f.* freckle.
**Efeso** *pr.n.m.* (geog.) Ephesus.
**effe** *m., f. indecl.* name of the letter F; *la città dell'—*, Florence.
**effeme·ride** *f.* almanac; journal; periodical publication; *effemeridi nautiche*, nautical almanac.
**effe(m)min-are** [A1 sc] *tr.* to make effeminate; to corrupt; *rfl.* to become effeminate. **-atezza** *f.* effeminacy. **-ato** *part. adj.* effeminate.
**efferat-o** *adj.* brutal; ferocious, savage; cruel. **-ag·gine** *f.*, **-ezza** *f.* brutality; savagery; atrocity.
**effervescen-te** *adj.* sparkling, effervescent. **-za** *f.* effervescence; excitement.
**effettiv-o** *adj.* real; actual; *costo —*, actual cost; *moneta -a*, cash; effective; *socio —*, working partner; *n.m.* total; net amount; total personnel. **-ità** *f.* effectiveness; actuality, reality.
**effetto** *m.* effect; consequence, result; *in —*, in effect, in actual fact; *fare —*, to have effect; to be effective; *il giallo col bruno non fa —*, yellow and brown are not a very striking combination; *mi fece — vederlo così*, it gave me quite a turn to see him like that; *mandare ad —*, to put into effect; aspect; *fare l'— di uno sciocco*, to look like a fool; (finan.) bill, note of hand; — *cambiario*, bill of exchange; (leg.) *per — di legge*, by law; *pl.* effects, belongings.
**effettual-e** *adj.* real, effectual, actual. **-ità** *f.* reality.
**effettu-are** [A1 s] *tr.* to effect, to execute, to carry out; to bring about; *rfl.* to be accomplished, to take place. **-a·bile** *adj.* feasible. **-azione** *f.* execution, fulfilment.
**efficace** *adj.* efficacious; effectual; adequate.
**effica·cia** *f.* efficacy; potency; (mech.) efficiency; (leg.) *avere — giuridica*, to have legal effect.
**efficien-te** *adj.* efficient; serviceable; *causa —*, effective cause. **-za** *f.* efficiency; *in -za*, in working order.
**effigiare** [A3] *tr.* to portray; to represent in art.
**effi·gie** *f. indecl.* effigy, image; bust, statue.
**effi·mero** *adj.* ephemeral; lasting a day; transient.
**efflorescen-te** *adj.* (chem.) efflorescent. **-za** *f.* (chem.) efflorescence; (techn.) bloom.
**efflu-ire** [D2] *intr.* (*aux.* essere) to flow out, to run out. **-ente** *adj.* effluent, outflowing; *n.m.* effluent, outflow, outfall.
**efflusso** *m.* effusion, discharge; outflow; — *di sangue*, flow of blood.
**efflu·vio** *m.* effluvium; exhalation.
**effondere** [C2] *tr.* to pour out, to pour forth; to be generous with; to effuse; to give vent to.
**effosso·rio** *adj.* designed for excavating; *arnesi effossori*, digging tools.
**effrazione** *f.* (leg.) house-breaking; *furto con —*, larceny and house-breaking.
**effrenato** *adj.* immoderate, unbridled.
**effusione** *f.* effusion; — *di lagrime*, shedding of tears.
**efi·mera** *f.* (ent.) mayfly.
**ege·mon-e** *m.* leader. **-i·a** *f.* hegemony.
**Ege·o** *pr.n.m.* (geog.) Aegean (Sea).
**e·gida** *f.* (myth.) aegis; shield; (fig.) protection; *sotto l'— di*, under the ægis of.
**Egi·dio** *pr.n.m.* Giles.
**Egina** *pr.n.f.* (geog.) Aegina.
**e·gira** *f.* (hist.) hegira, the flight of Mahomet from Mecca in A.D. 622.
**Egitt-o** *pr.n.m.* (geog.) Egypt. **-ologi·a** *f.* Egyptology. **-o·logo** *m.* Egyptologist.
**egiziano** *adj., n.m.* Egyptian.
**egi·zio** *adj.* ancient Egyptian.
**eglantina** *f.* (bot.) eglantine; sweet briar.
**egli** *m.prn. 3rd pers. sing.* (formal usage) he (*cf.* **lui**); (pleon.) it; *che vi pare —?*, what do you think of it?
**eglino** *m. prn. 3rd pers. pl.* (formal usage), they (*cf.* **loro**).
**e·gloga** *f.* eclogue.
**egocen·tric-o** *adj.* self-centred, egocentric. **-ità** *f.* egocentricity, self-centredness.
**ego-ismo** *m.* selfishness; (philos.) egoism. **-ista** *m., f.* selfish person; egoist. **-i·stico** *adj.* selfish; egotistical. **-tismo** *m.* egotism.
**egre·gio** *adj.* remarkable, distinguished; noble; excellent; worthy; — *signore*, Dear Sir.
**egresso** *m.* egress, exit; going out.
**egretta** *f.* (orn.) egret.
**egro** *adj.* (poet.) sick, weak, infirm; languishing.
**eguale** *adj.* equal; even; *n.m.* equal; *non ha l'—*, he has no equal.
**eh** *excl.* ah! (expressing disapproval, doubt, wonder); eh! (expressing surprise, impatience).
**ehi** *excl.* hello!; I say!; hoy!
**ehm** *excl.* ahem!
**eia, e·ia, alalà** *excl.* hip, hip, hooray.
**Eidelberga** *pr.n.f.* (geog.) Heidelberg.
**elabor-are** [A1 s] *tr.* to elaborate; to work out; to devise. **-atezza** *f.* elaborateness. **-ato** *part. adj.* elaborated; elaborate. **-azione** *f.* elaboration.
**elabro** *m.* (bot.) hellebore.
**elarg-ire** [D2] *tr.* to give liberally; to grant. **-izione** *f.* donation, gift.
**ela·stic-o** *adj.* elastic; springy; resilient; *coscienza -a*, accommodating conscience; *intelligenza -a*, nimble wits; *n.m.* elastic; spring mattress; rubber band. **-ità** *f.* elasticity; flexibility; resilience; springiness.
**Elba** *pr.n.f.* (geog.) *l'Isola d'—*, Elba.
**elefant-e** *m.* (zool.) elephant; — *di mare*, lobster. **-esco** *adj.* (*m.pl.* **-eschi**) elephantine. **-essa** *f.* female elephant. **-i·asi** *f.* (med.) elephantiasis.
**elegan-te** *adj.* elegant; stylish, fashionable, smart; graceful; polished. **-za** *f.* elegance; distinction; style; grace.
**eleg·g-ere** [C12] *tr.* to elect, to appoint; to select, to choose; to prefer. **-i·bile** *adj.* eligible. **-ibilità** *f.* eligibility.
**eleg-i·a** *f.* elegy. **-i·aco** *adj.* elegiac.
**element-o** *m.* element; unit; member; part (of a machine), section; *trovarsi nel suo —*, to be in one's element; *lottare contro gli -i*, to battle with the elements. **-are** *adj.* elementary; *scuola -are*, primary school; simple, easy; basic, rudimentary.
**elemo·sin-a** *f.* alms; charity; *campare d'—*, to live on charity; *fare l'—*, to give alms. **-are** [A1 s]

*intr.* (*aux.* avere) to beg. **-iere** *m.* almoner.
**E·lena** *pr.n.f.* Helen; Helena; (geog.) *Sant'—*, St. Helena.
**elen-co** *m.* (*pl.* **-chi**) list; catalogue; inventory; — *telefonico*, telephone directory. **-care** [A2] *tr.* to make a list of, to list; to enumerate.
**elett-a** *f.* choice; élite. **-ivo** *adj.* elective; chosen.
**elett-o** *adj.* elect; chosen; (bibl.) *il Popolo —*, the Chosen People; choice; distinguished; *n.m.* elect, chosen; successful candidate. **-amẹnte** *adv.* with distinction.
**elettọr-e** *m.* elector; constituent; (hist.) Elector. **-ale** *adj.* electoral; *scheda -ale*, ballot-paper; *urna -ale*, ballot-box. **-ato** *m.* franchise; (hist.) Electorate.
**Elettra** *pr.n.f.* (myth.) Electra.
**elettra·uto** (motor.) *m.* workshop for electrical repairs.
**elettric-o** *adj.* electric(al). **-ista** *m.* electrician. **-ità** *f.* electricity.
**elettrific-are** [A2 s] *tr.* to electrify. **-ato** *part. adj. ferrovia -ata*, electric railway. **-aziọne** *f.* electrification.
**elettrizẓ-are** [A1] *tr.* to charge with electricity; (fig.) to thrill, to excite; to electrify. **-ante** *part. adj.* (fig.) thrilling, exciting.
**elettro-acu·stica** *f.* electro-acoustics. **-acu·stico** *adj.* electro-acoustic. **-ana·lisi** *f. indecl.* (chem.) electro-analysis. **-biologi·a** *f.* electro-biology. **-calamita** *f.* electromagnet. **-cardiogramma** *m.* (med.) electrocardiogram, E.C.G. **-chi·mica** *f.* electrochemistry. **-chi·mico** *adj.* electrochemical; *n.m.* electrochemist. **-choc** *m. indecl.* (*prn.* as in French) (med.) electric shock treatment. **-cuziọne** *f.* electrocution. **-deposiziọne** *f.* electroplating. **-dina·mica** *f.* electrodynamics. **-dina·mico** *adj.* electrodynamic. **-dome·stici** *m.pl.* household electric appliances. **-dọtto** *m.* electric main, power line. **-magne·tico** *adj.* electro-magnetic. **-metal-lurgi·a** *f.* electrometallurgy. **-mecca·nico** *adj.* electro-mechanical. **-motọre** *m.* electric motor; *adj.* electromotive. **-motrice** *f.* (rlwy.) electric rail car. **-sco·pio** *m.* electroscope. **-sta·tico** *adj.* electrostatic. **-tec·nica** *f.* electrical engineering. **-tec·nico** *adj.* relating to electrical engineering; *n.m.* electrical engineer. **-terapi·a** *f.* (med.) electro-therapy. **-treno** *m.* (rlwy.) express luxury train.
**elettrodo** *m.* electrode.
**elettr-o·fono** *m.* (mus.) electric organ. **-o·grafo** *m.* electrograph. **-o·lisi** *f. indecl.* electrolysis. **-o·metro** *m.* (electr.) electrometer. **-o·nico** *adj.* electronic. **-o·tipo** *m.* (typ.) electrotype.

**Ele·uṣ-i** *pr.n.f.* Eleusis. **-ino** *adj.* Eleusinian.
**elev-are** [A1 s] *tr.* to raise; to erect; to elevate; to promote; to extol; — *ai sette cieli*, to laud to the skies; *rfl.* to rise; to raise oneself; to get to one's feet. **-ato** *part. adj.* raised; erected; elevated; high; noble; high-minded; *a prezzo -ato*, expensive. **-aziọne** *f.* elevation; raising; rise; height.
**eleziọne** *f.* election; appointment; choice; (pol.) election; — *parziale*, by-election.
**elfo** *m.* elf, sprite.
**e·lica** *f.* helix, spiral; propeller, screw; (zool.) snail.
**Elicọna** *pr.n.m.* (geog.) Mt. Helicon.
**elicot·tero** *m.* helicopter.
**eli·dere** [C3] *tr.* (gramm.) to elide; to neutralize, to annul, to cancel; to suppress; *recip. rfl.* to cancel each other out.
**eligibilità** *f.* eligibility.
**elimin-are** [A1 s] *tr.* to eliminate; to weed out; (euphem.) to kill. **-ato·rio** *adj.* serving to eliminate; (sport) *gara -atoria*, eliminating race, bout, trial. **-aziọne** *f.* elimination; expulsion.
**e·li-o** *m.* (chem.) helium. **-ogra-fi·a** *f.* heliography; (typ.) process engraving; heliogravure. **-o·grafo** *m.* heliograph. **-osco·pio** *m.* helioscope, solar prism.
**eliotro·pio** *m.* (bot.) heliotrope.
**eliporto** *m.* (aeron.) helicopter landing-ground, heliport.
**Eliṣabẹtt-a** *pr.n.f.* Elizabeth. **-iano** *adj.*, *n.m.* Elizabethan.
**eli·ṣio** *adj.* (myth.) Elysian; *i Campi Elisi*, the Elysian fields.
**eliṣiọne** *f.* (gramm.) elision.
**eliṣi·r** *m. indecl.*, **eliṣire** *m.* elixir.
**ella** *prn.f.* (*pl.* **esse**) she; *prn.m.*, *f.* you (in formal usage).
**elle** *m.*, *f.* name of the letter L.
**elle·n-ico** *adj.* Hellenic, Greek. **-iṣmo** *m.* Hellenism. **-ista** *m.*, *f.* Hellenist. **-i·stico** *adj.* Hellenistic.
**Ellesponto** *pr.n.m.* (geog.) Hellespont.
**ellisse** *f.* (geom.) ellipse.
**ellissi** *f. indecl.* (gramm.) ellipsis.
**ellit·tico** *adj.* (geom.; gramm.) elliptical.
**ẹlm-o, -ẹtto** *m.* helm, helmet.
**elocuziọne** *f.* elocution; diction; expression, propriety of style.
**elogi-are** [A3] *tr.* to commend; to praise; to eulogize. **-atọre** *m.* eulogist; *adj.* laudatory.
**elo·g-io** *m.* eulogy, praise. **-ista** *m.*, *f.* eulogist.
**eloquen-te** *adj.* eloquent; moving; significant. **-za** *f.* eloquence; power of expression; oratory; significance.
**elo·quio** *m.* speech, language; mode of expression.
**ẹlsa** *f.* hilt.
**Elsinore** *pr.n.f.* (geog.) Elsinore.

**elucidare** [A1 s] *tr.* to elucidate, to explain.
**elucubr-are** [A1 s] *tr.* to compose with painstaking effort, to lucubrate. **-aziọne** *f.* lucubration, painstaking cerebral effort.
**elu·dere** [C3] *tr.* to elude, to avoid; to evade.
**eluṣ-iọne** *f.* evasion, eluding. **-ivo** *adj.* elusive, evasive.
**elve·tico** *adj.* Swiss; *la Confederazione elvetica*, the Swiss Confederation, Switzerland.
**elẓevir-iano, -o** *adj.* (typ.) Elzevir, from the press of the Elzevirs. **-ista** *m.*, *f.* (journ.) feature-writer. **-o** *adj.* (typ.) Elzevir; *carattere -o*, old style, old face; *n.m.* book printed by the Elzevir press; book printed in Elzevir type; (journ.) short story or literary article.
**emaci-are** [A3] *tr.* to emaciate; *rfl.* to become emaciated. **-aziọne** *f.* emaciation.
**eman-are** [A1] *intr.* (*aux.* essere) to emanate, to issue; to derive; *tr.* to issue, to promulgate. **-aziọne** *f.* emanation; issuing, promulgation.
**emancip-are** [A1 s] *tr.* (leg.) to emancipate. **-ato** *part. adj.* emancipated. **-aziọne** *f.* emancipation.
**Emanuele** *pr.n.m.* Emmanuel.
**embar-go** *m.* (*pl.* **-ghi**) embargo, a suspension of commerce.
**emblem-a** *m.* emblem, symbol; badge; attribute, sign, mark. **-a·tico** *adj.* emblematic.
**em·bol-o** *m.* (med.) embolus, clot or foreign body occluding an artery. **-i·a** *f.* (med.) embolism, occlusion of a blood-vessel. **-iṣmo** *m.* (astron.) embolism, a year coinciding with thirteen lunar months.
**embri-ologi·a** *f.* embryology. **-o·logo** *m.* embryologist. **-ọne** *m.* embryo. **-onale** *adj.*, **-o·nico** *adj.* pertaining to an embryo; embryonic; *un progetto ancora allo stato -onale*, a project still in its early stages.
**emend-are** [A1] *tr.* to emend; to correct; to improve; *rfl.* to correct one's faults; *se non ti -i, finirai male*, if you don't mend your ways, you will come to a bad end. **-a** *f.* amends, act of reparation. **-aziọne** *f.* emendation, correction; improvement.
**emer·g-ere** [C4] *intr.* (*aux.* essere) to emerge, to issue, to come into view; to achieve distinction; *-erà dalla turba*, he will make a name for himself. **-ente** *part. adj.* emergent. **-enza** *f.* emergence; emergency.
**eme·rito** *adj.* emeritus; retired; *professore —*, Professor Emeritus.
**emersiọne** *f.* emersion; emerging; emergence, reappearance; (of a submarine) *in —*, on the surface of the water.

**eme·tico** *adj., n.m.* (med.) emetic.
**emętt-ere** [C20] *tr.* to emit; to give out; to utter; to express; — *un giudizio,* to deliver a judgement; to issue; to put in circulation. **-itǫre** *m.* (teleph.; radio) sender, transmitter.
**emi-** *pref.* hemi-, semi-, half-.
**emiciclo** *m.* (archit.) hemicycle; body of a hall.
**emicra·nia** *f.* (med.) migraine; headache.
**emigr-are** [A1] *intr.* (*aux.* avere, essere) to emigrate; to migrate; **-ante** *part. adj.* emigrating; migrating; *n.m., f.* emigrant. **-ato** *m.* refugee; political exile. **-aziǫne** *f.* emigration; migration.
**eminen-te** *adj.* eminent; distinguished; prominent; lofty. **-za** *f.* eminence; distinction; prominence; high place; Eminence (title given esp. to Cardinals).
**emi-ple·gia** *f.* (med.) hemiplegia, paralysis of one side of the body. **-ple·gico** *adj., n.m.* hemiplegic.
**emisf-ero** *m.* hemisphere. **-e·rico** *adj.* hemispherical.
**emissa·rio** *m.* outlet, effluent; emissary; spy; *capro* —, scapegoat.
**emissiǫne** *f.* emission, issuing, issue; (finan.) *banca d'*—, issuing bank; (radio) broadcast.
**emisti·ch-io** *m.* (*pl.* **-i**) (prosod.) hemistich.
**emittente** *adj.* emitting, issuing; *n.m.* issuer; *f.* (radio) transmitting station.
**emme** *f., m.* name of the letter M.
**emofili·a** *f.* (med.) haemophilia.
**emoglobina** *f.* haemoglobin.
**emolliente** *adj.* soothing; (industr.) softening, plasticizing; *n.m.* emollient.
**emolumęnto** *m.* emolument, salary; *percepire gli emolumenti,* to draw one's salary.
**emorragi·a** *f.* (med.) haemorrhage.
**emorro·idi** *f.pl.* (med.) haemorrhoids, piles.
**emosta·tico** *adj.* haemostatic, styptic; *n.m.* styptic pencil.
**emoteca** *f.* blood-bank.
**emotiv-o** *adj.* emotive; easily moved; emotional. **-ità** *f.* emotiveness; excitability.
**emoziǫn-e** *f.* emotion; tender sentiment, compassion; lively interest; excitement, thrill; fright. **-ante** *part. adj.* thrilling, exciting; upsetting. **-are** [A1 c] *tr.* to excite, to thrill; to touch, to move; to upset, to frighten.
**Empe·docle** *pr.n.m.* Empedocles.
**ęmpi-o** *adj.* (*m.pl.* **ęmpi,** *f.pl.* **ęmpie**) impious; irreligious; pitiless; wicked; *n.m.* wicked man; *pl. gli empi,* the wicked. **-età** *f.* impiety; impiousness.
**empire** [D11] *tr.* to fill; to satisfy; to stuff; to crowd; *rfl.* to stuff oneself; to be filled; to get crowded.
**empi·reo** *adj.* relating to the Empyrean; *il cielo* —, the Empyrean, the highest heaven.
**empi·r-ico** *adj.* (philos.) empirical; (fig.) that works by rule of thumb. **-iṣmo** *m.* (philos.) empiricism.
**empore·tico** *adj.* (of paper) coarse, absorbent.
**empo·rio** *m.* emporium, market; trade centre; warehouse, store.
**emul-are** [A1 s] *tr.* to emulate, to seek to rival. **-aziǫne** *f.* emulation, rivalry.
**e·mulo** *adj.* emulous, emulating; *n.m.* emulator, imitator.
**emulsiǫn-e** *f.* emulsion. **-are** [A1 c] *tr.* to emulsify.
**emun·gere** [C5] *tr.* to mulct; to extract moisture from.
**emunto** *adj.* dry, dried up; emaciated.
**enca·ust-o** *m.* encaustic painting. **-ica** *f.* art of encaustic painting. **-ico** *adj.* encaustic.
**ence·f-alo** *m.* (anat.) encephalon; brain. **-a·lico** *adj.* encephalic, pertaining to the brain. **-alite** *f.* encephalitis.
**enci·clic-a** *f.* encyclical letter, Papal letter. **-o** *adj.* circular.
**enciclop-edi·a** *f.* encyclopædia. **-e·dico** *adj* encyclopædic. **-edista** *m.* encyclopædist.
**encomi-are** [A4] *tr.* to commend, to praise highly; to award official recognition to. **-a·bile** *adj.* worthy of encomium, praiseworthy. **-aste** *m.* encomiast. **-a·stico** *adj.* laudatory.
**enco·mio** *m.* encomium; official honour or recognition.
**end-emi·a** *f.* endemic disease. **-e·mico** *adj.* endemic.
**en·dice** *m.* nest-egg; china egg; decoy.
**endo-** *pref.* inner, inside. **-cardite** *f.* (med.) endocarditis. **-carpo** *m.* inner skin of fruit. **-crinologi·a** *f.* endocrinology. **-venǫso** *adj.* (med.) intravenous.
**endo·geno** *adj.* endogenous, growing from within.
**En-e·a** *pr.n.m.* (myth.) Aeneas. **-e·ide** *pr.n.f.* Aeneid.
**energe·tic-a** *f.* (scient.) energetics. **-o** *adj.* relating to energy or power.
**energi·a** *f.* energy; vigour; resolution; power; — *idraulica,* water power; — *atomica,* atomic energy; — *nucleare,* nuclear power.
**ener·gico** *adj.* energetic; vigorous; powerful.
**energizẓare** [A1] *tr.* (electr.) to energize.
**energu·meno** *adj.* possessed by a devil; quick-tempered; active; *n.m.* one possessed; termagant; *è un* —, there's no holding him.
**en·fasi** *f. indecl.* bombast, pomposity; exaggeration.
**enfa·tico** *adj.* bombastic, pompous; exaggerated.
**enfi-are** [A4 c] *tr.* to swell; to inflate; *intr.* (*aux.* essere), *rfl.* to become swollen. **-agiǫne** *f.* swelling. **-ato** *part. adj.* swollen, puffed up; (fig.) conceited, proud. **-atura** *f.* swelling.
**ęnfi-o** *adj.* swollen. **-ǫre** *m.* swelling, tumour.
**enfiṣema** *m.* (med.) emphysema.
**enigm-a** *m.* enigma; riddle; puzzle involving words. **-a·tico** *adj.* enigmatic. **-i·stica** *f.* puzzle-games involving words.
**enn-e** *f., m. indecl.* name of the letter N. **-e·ṣimo** *adj.* (math.) *n*th; *all'-esimo grado,* to the *n*th degree; *per l'-esima volta,* for the *n*th time.
**ennè** *m. indecl.* henna.
**en-o·filo** *adj.* concerned with the production of wine; fond of wine; *circolo -ofilo,* wine-growers' society; *n.m.* wine-grower; wine-bibber. **-ologi·a** *f.* wine making. **-olo·gico** *adj.* relating to wine making; *industria -ologica,* wine industry. **-o·logo** *m.* œnologist.
**enǫrm-e** *adj.* enormous, huge; extraordinary; monstrous, outrageous; absurd. **-ità** *f.* hugeness; enormity, outrageousness; absurdity.
**Enrico** *pr.n.m.* Henry.
**ente** *m.* being; — *supremo,* God; society; corporation; body; object, thing; — *nazionale italiano turistico* (ENIT), Italian tourist information bureau; (leg.) legal entity; institution.
**entelechi·a** *f.* (philos.) entelechy.
**enteralgi·a** *f.* (med.) intestinal pain.
**ente·r-ico** *adj.* intestinal, enteric. **-ite** *f.* (med.) enteritis.
**entità** *f.* entity; importance; amount; — *degli affari,* extent of business.
**entom-ologi·a** *f.* entomology. **-o·logo** *m.* entomologist.
**entramb-i** *prn.m.pl.* (*f.* **-e**) both.
**entr-are** [A1 c] *intr.* (*aux.* essere; *prep.* in, a) to enter; to go in; to come in; *non c'-o più nel mio soprabito,* I have grown too big for my overcoat; — *in vigore,* to come into force; *che c'-o io?,* what is that to do with me?; *che c'-a?,* what's that got to do with it?; *il due nell'otto c'-a quattro volte,* two into eight goes four. **-ante** *part. adj.* entering; in-coming; *la settimana -ante,* at the beginning of next week.
**entrat-a** *f.* entrance, going in, entry; way in; access, admittance; admission fee; (theatr.) *le -e di favore,* complimentary seats; (comm.) entry; revenue; income; — *ed uscita,* income and expenditure. **-ura** *f.* entrance

entry; entrance fee; *diritto d'-ura*, right of entry.
**ẹntro** *prep.* in; within; in the course of; *adv.* inside.
**ẹntro-bordo** *m.* in-board motorboat; *adj. indecl.* in-board. **-terra** *f.* (geog.) inland, inland region, interior.
**entropi·a** *f.* (phys.) entropy.
**entuşiaşm-o** *m.* enthusiasm; rapture. **-are** [A1] *tr.* to arouse enthusiasm in; to enrapture; to enthuse; *rfl. -arsi per*, to go into raptures over.
**entuşi-asta** *m., f.* enthusiast; *adj.* enthusiastic; **-a·stico** *adj.* enthusiastic; rapturous.
**enumer-are** [A1 s] *tr.* to enumerate; to specify. **-azịone** *f.* enumeration; specification.
**enunci-are** [A3] *tr.* to express clearly; to state; to enunciate. **-azịone** *f.* enunciation; pronouncement; expression.
**enuresi** *f.* (med.) enuresis; bed-wetting.
**enzima** *m.* (biol.; chem.) enzyme.
**eo·l-ico** *adj.* (hist. geog.) Aeolian; (scient.) aeolian, wind-formed. **-io** *adj.* (mus.) *arpa -ia*, Aeolian harp.
**eo·ne** *m.* aeon.
**epat-algi·a** *f.* (med.) hepatalgia. **-ite** *f.* (med.) hepatitis.
**epa·tic-a** *f.* (bot.) hepatica, liverwort. **-o** *adj.* (med.) hepatic; relating to the liver.
**e·pica** *f.* epic; epic poetry.
**epice·dio** *m.* (mus.) epicedium, threnody, funeral ode.
**epiceno** *adj.* epicene, of either gender.
**epiciclo** *m.* (astron.) epicycle.
**e·pico** *adj.* epic; *poema* —, epic poem; *n.m.* epic poet.
**epicur-e·o** *adj.* (philos.) Epicurean; epicurean, voluptuary; also *n.m.* **-eişmo** *m.* (philos.) Epicurism; pursuit of pleasure.
**Epicuro** *pr.n.m.* Epicurus.
**epid-emi·a** *f.* epidemic. **-e·mico** *adj.* epidemic(al).
**epider·mide** *f.* (biol.) epidermis.
**epidiasco·pio** *m.* epidiascope.
**epifani·a** *f.* (liturg.) Epiphany; *la notte dell'*—, Twelfth Night.
**epiglot·t-a, -ide** *f.* (anat.) epiglottis.
**epi·gono** *m.* imitator, successor or follower of a genius.
**epi·graf-e** *f.* epigraph; title, quotation, motto. **-i·a** *f.* epigraphy. **-ista** *m.* epigraphist.
**epigramm-a** *m.* epigram. **-a·tico** *adj.* epigrammatic. **-atista, -ista** *m.* writer of epigrams.
**epil-ato·rio** *adj.* depilatory. **-azịone** *f.* depilation.
**epil-essi·a** *f.* epilepsy. **-et·tico** *adj., n.m.* (*pl.* **-et·tici**) epileptic.
**epilo·bio** *m.* (bot.) willow-herb.
**epilogare** [A2 s] *tr.* to sum up.
**epi·lo-go** *m.* (*pl.* **-ghi**) epilogue.
**Epiro** *pr.n.m.* (geog.) Epirus.
**episcop-ale** *adj.* (eccl.) episcopal; Episcopalian. **-ato** *m.* episcopate.
**epiş-o·dio** *m.* episode, incident, event; instalment of a serial. **-o·dico** *adj.* episodic; fragmentary.
**epistemologi·a** *f.* (philos.) epistemology.
**episti·lio** *m.* (archit.) epistyle, architrave.
**epi·stol-a** *f.* epistle. **-are** *adj.* epistolary. **-a·rio** *m.* collection of letters.
**episto·mio** *m.* stopcock.
**epitaf·fio** *m.* epitaph.
**epitala·mio** *m.* epithalamium, nuptial ode.
**epi·teto** *m.* epithet.
**epi·tom-e** *f.* epitome, abridgement. **-are** [A1 s] *tr.* to epitomize; to summarize.
**epiz-oo·tico** *adj.* (vet.) *afta -ootica*, foot-and-mouth disease. **-oozi·a** *f.* (vet.) cattle disease.
**e·poca** *f.* epoch; age; era; time, period; (comm.) — *della consegna*, fixed delivery date.
**epo·nimo** *adj.* eponymous; *n.m.* surname.
**epope·a** *f.* epic (also fig.); epic poem.
**epos** *m. indecl.* epic poem.
**eppure** *adv.* nevertheless, all the same; *eppur si muove*, nevertheless it moves (Galileo); *conj.* yet; and yet.
**epulọn-e** *m.* one who lives in luxury; (bibl.) *il ricco* —, Dives (*Luke* 16). **-işmo** *m.* gluttony.
**epurare** [A1] *tr.* to purify; to refine; to purge; (fig.) to make clear; — *un dubbio*, to clear up a doubtful point; to disentangle; (finan.) to pay, to settle; (pol.) to purge.
**equa·bil-e** *adj.* equable. **-ità** *f. indecl.* equability.
**equa·nim-e** *adj.* even-tempered; serene; just, equable. **-ità** *f.* equanimity; serenity; composure; equability.
**equare** [A6] *tr.* (math.) to equate.
**equatọr-e** *m.* equator; — *celeste*, celestial equator, equinoctial; — *terrestre*, terrestrial equator; *passaggio dell'*—, crossing the line; (geog.) *la Repubblica dell'Equatore*, Ecuador. **-iale** *adj.* equatorial; *regione delle calme -iali*, doldrums.
**equazịone** *f.* (math.) equation.
**equestre** *adj.* equestrian; *circo* —, circus; knightly; *ordine* —, order of chivalry.
**equi-an·golo** *adj.* (geom.) equiangular. **-distante** *adj.* equidistant. **-distanza** *f.* equidistance. **-la·tero, -laterale** *adj., n.m.* (geom.) equilateral.
**equilibr-are** [A1] *tr.* to balance; to poise; to counter-balance; (aeron.) to trim; *rfl.* to be balanced; *recip. rfl.* to counterbalance. **-ato** *part. adj.* balanced, in equipoise; (fig.) well-balanced. **-atọre** *m.* equalizer; balancer; (aeron.) elevator. **-atrice** *f.* (eng.) balancing machine; balancing. **-azịone** *f.* balancing; balance.
**equili·br-io** *m.* equilibrium, balance, poise. **-işmo** *m.* (philos.) theory of free-will as presupposing an equilibrium of determinants; (pol.) political acrobatics. **-ista** *m.* equilibrist, rope-dancer, tightrope-walker.
**equino** *adj.* equine; *n.m.pl.* horses and closely related animals (mules, asses, etc.).
**equino·zi-o** *m.* equinox; — *di primavera*, vernal equinox. **-ale** *adj.* equinoctial; *n.m.* celestial equator, equinoctial.
**equipag·gio** *m.* (naut.) crew; (mil.) baggage train, supplies; luggage; equipage; carriage.
**equit-à** *f.* (leg.) equity; natural justice; fairness; impartiality. **-ativo** *adj.* equitable.
**equitazịone** *f.* equitation, riding; *scuola d'*—, riding-school.
**equival-ẹre** [B34] *intr.* (*aux.* avere, essere; *prep.* a) to be worth as much, to be equivalent (to). **-ente** *adj.* equivalent; tantamount; *n.m.* equivalent. **-enza** *f.* equivalence.
**equivoc-are** [A2 s] *intr.* (*aux.* avere) to misunderstand; to mistake; to equivocate. **-azịone** *f.* equivocation; misunderstanding, mistake.
**equi·voco** *adj.* equivocal, ambiguous; dubious, doubtful, questionable; *n.m.* misunderstanding, mistake; *a scanso di equivoci*, to avoid any misunderstanding; equivocation, play on words, pun.
**equo** *adj.* just, equitable, fair; even.
**era** *f.* epoch, era.
**Era·clito** *pr.n.m.* Heraclitus.
**era·ri-o** *m.* Exchequer, Treasury; state finances. **-ale** *adj.* fiscal; *imposte -ali*, public taxation; *Ufficio Tecnico Erariale*, Inland Revenue Surveyor's Office.
**Eraşmo** *pr.n.m.* Erasmus.
**erb-a** *f.* herb; grass; *in* —, green, immature. **-ac·cia** *f. pejor.* weed. **-a·ceo** *adj.* herbaceous. **-ag·gio** *m.* pot-herbs, green vegetables, salad. **-a·rio** *m.* herbarium; *adj.* relating to herbs or botany. **-ato** *adj.* grassy, grass-covered; *n.m.* grass; grassy plain.
**erbicida** *m.* (agric.) weed-killer.
**erbiven·dolo** *m.* greengrocer.
**erbi·voro** *adj.* herbivorous, vegetable-feeding.
**erbola·io** *m.* herbalist.
**erbolina** *f.* fine grass; young moss; *andare con l'— in mano*,

to be anxious to make a good impression.
**erbor-are** [A1] *intr.* (*aux.* avere) to collect plants, to herborize. **-ista** *m.* collector of herbs; herbalist. **-i·stico** *adj.* pertaining to the knowledge of herbs and plants; *la medicina -istica,* herbalist remedies.
**erbọso** *adj.* greasy; grass-grown.
**Ercolano** *pr.n.f.* Herculaneum.
**Er·col-e** *pr.n.m.* (myth.) Hercules; *Colonne d'—,* Pillars of Hercules (*i.e.* Straits of Gibraltar).
**ercu·leo** *adj.* Herculean.
**E·rebo** *pr.n.m.* (myth.) Erebus.
**ered-e** *m., f.* heir; heiress; (leg.) heir; residuary legatee; — *legittimo,* lawful heir, statutory next-of-kin. **-ità** *f. indecl.* inheritance; *fare un'-ità,* to come into an inheritance; *lasciare in -ità,* to bequeath, to devise; (biol.) heredity. **-itare** [A1 s] *tr.* to inherit, to come into; *intr.* (*aux.* avere) to be heir. **-ita·rio** *adj.* hereditary; *Principe -itario,* heir to the throne.
**eremit-a** *m.* hermit; (zool.) hermit crab. **-ag·gio, -o·rio** *m.* hermitage.
**eremi·tico** *adj.* pertaining to a hermit.
**e·remo** *m.* hermitage; solitary place, retreat.
**ereṣ-i·a** *f.* heresy; (pop.) blasphemous, shocking, or nonsensical language. **-iarca** *m.* (*pl.* **-iarchi**) heresiarch.
**ere·tico** *adj.* (theol.) heretical; *n.m.* heretic.
**erett-o** *adj.* erect, upright; standing; erected, founded. **-ọre** *m.* erector, founder.
**erezịone** *f.* erection; building; foundation; establishment.
**erga·stol-o** *m.* convict-prison; *condannato all'—,* sentenced to penal servitude. **-ano** *m.* convict.
**er·gere** [C4] *tr.* to raise, to erect; to elevate; to puff up with pride; *rfl.* to rise.
**ergo** *adv.* (joc.) therefore; *n.m. venire all'—,* to conclude, to come to the point.
**e·rica** *f.* (bot.) heather; rustic broom (made from heather).
**eri·gere** [C13] *tr.* to erect; to raise; to build; to found, to institute; *rfl.* (*prep.* a) to set oneself up (as), to assume the authority (of).
**Erinni** *pr.n.f.pl.* (myth.) Erinyes, Furies.
**eriṣipela** *f.* (med.) erysipelas.
**eritema** *m.* (med.) erythema; rash.
**Eritr-e·a** *pr.n.f.* (geog.) Eritrea. **-e·o** *adj., n.m.* Eritrean; *il Mare -eo,* the Red Sea.
**ermafrod-iṣmo** *m.* hermaphroditism. **-ito** *m.* hermaphrodite.
**ermellino** *m.* (zool.) ermine; stoat.
**ermene·utic-a** *f.* hermeneutics, interpretation, esp. of the Scriptures. **-o** *adj.* hermeneutic, interpretative.
**Er·mes, Ermete** *pr.n.m.* (myth.) Hermes.
**erme·tic-o** *adj.* hermetic; airtight; gas-proof; secret; (lit. hist.) *poesia -a,* verse of esoteric appeal, esp. modern. **-ità** *f. indecl.* (eng.) tightness, airtightness.
**ermetiṣmo** *m.* (philos.) hermeticism, hermetic doctrine; (fig.) obscure or esoteric character.
**ẹrmo** *adj.* (poet.) solitary; *n.m.* (poet.) solitary place; retreat.
**er·ni-a** *f.* hernia, rupture. **-a·rio** *adj.* hernial; *cinto -ario,* truss. **-ọso** *adj.* ruptured.
**Ero** *pr.n.f.* (myth.) Hero; — *e Leandro,* Hero and Leander.
**Erode** *pr.n.m.* Herod.
**erọdere** [C3] *tr.* to erode.
**Ero·doto** *pr.n.m.* Herodotus.
**ero·e** *m.* hero.
**erog-are** [A2 s] *tr.* to supply; to devote (money) to a purpose, usually of public utility; to distribute (*e.g.* water supply). **-azịone** *f.* supply; erogation, expenditure; public distribution; (techn.) yield, output.
**ero·ic-o** *adj.* heroic; *verso —,* hexameter. **-iẓẓare** [A1] *tr.* to hero-worship; *intr.* (*aux.* avere) to indulge in heroics.
**eroico·mico** *adj.* (lit.) mock-heroic.
**eroina**[1] *f.* heroine.
**eroina**[2] *f.* (pharm.) heroin.
**eroiṣmo** *m.* heroism.
**erọmpere** [C26] *intr.* (*aux.* avere) to burst forth; to rush out.
**eroṣ-iọne** *f.* erosion. **-ivo** *adj.* erosive.
**erọṣo** *part.* of **erọdere**; *adj.* eroded; bronze (of coins).
**ero·t-ico** *adj.* erotic; amatory. **-omani·a** *f.* erotomania.
**er·pete** *m.* (med.) herpes.
**er·pic-e** *m.* (agric.) harrow. **-are** [A2 s] *tr.* (agric.) to harrow.
**err-are** [A1] *intr.* (*aux.* avere) to wander; to roam, to rove; to stray from the right way; to err. **-abọndo** *adj.* wandering, rambling. **-ante** *part. adj.* wandering; errant. **-ato** *part. adj.* mistaken; *locuzione -ata,* wrong usage, ungrammatical expression; *andare -ato,* to be mistaken.
**errata-cor·rige** *m., f.* (typ.) table of misprints or errata; corrigendum, corrigenda.
**erra·tico** *adj.* wandering; straying.
**err-e** *f., m. indecl.* name of the letter R; *gli manca l'—,* he can't pronounce R. **-ato** *adj.* spelt with an R.; (provb.) *nei mesi -ati non seder sopra gli erbati,* don't sit on the grass when there's an R in the month.
**erro·ne-o** *adj.* erroneous, false, mistaken; wrong; illogical. **-ità** *f. indecl.* erroneousness; error; falsity.
**errọre** *m.* mistake; fallacy; — *di stampa,* misprint; *salvo —,* if I am not mistaken; — *materiale,* clerical error; — *d'ortografia,* spelling mistake; — *di calcolo,* miscalculation.
**erso** *adj.* Erse; *n.m.* Erse language.
**ẹrt-a**[1] *f.* steep ascent, hill; steep path or street. **-o** *adj.* steep; erect.
**erta**[2] *adv. phr. all'erta!,* look out!; *stare all'erta,* to be on the alert.
**erud-ito** *part. adj.* erudite, learned; scholarly; *n.m.* learned man, scholar. **-izịone** *f.* erudition, scholarship.
**erutt-are** [A1] *intr.* (*aux.* avere) to belch; to eruct; *tr.* to throw out, to eject. **-ivo** *adj.* eruptive.
**eruzịone** *f.* (med.) eruption, rash; (geol.) eruption; (mil.) sortie.
**erv-o** *m.* (bot.) lentil. **-alenta** *f.* lentil-flour.
**eṣacerb-are** [A1] *tr.* to exacerbate, to aggravate; to embitter; to exasperate. **-azịone** *f.* exacerbation.
**eṣager-are** [A1 s] *tr.* to exaggerate; to overstate; *intr.* (*aux.* avere) to go too far; to overdo things. **-ato** *part. adj.* exaggerated; not in good taste; excessive. **-azịone** *f.* exaggeration; excess.
**eṣa·gono** *m.* (math.) hexagon; *adj.* hexagonal.
**eṣal-are** [A1] *tr.* to exhale; — *l'anima,* to die; *intr.* (*aux.* essere) to be exhaled; to issue. **-azịone** *f.* exhalation; fume, vapour.
**eṣalt-are** [A1] *tr.* to exalt, to raise; to extol; — *il sapore,* to heighten the flavour; *rfl.* to become excited; to become elated; to become enthusiastic. **-ato** *part. adj.* exalted; excited; beside oneself; *testa -ata,* excitable person; *n.m.* hot-head; eccentric enthusiast. **-azịone** *f.* exalting; excitement; fervour.
**eṣame** *m.* examination, exam; *dare un —,* to take an examination; *bocciare, essere bocciato, a un —,* to fail an exam; investigation, inspection; scrutiny; (comm.) *inviare in —,* to send on approval.
**eṣa·mina** *f.* examination; survey, appraisal of evidence.
**esamin-are** [A1 s] *tr.* to examine; to investigate; to scrutinize. **-a·bile** *adj.* examinable; open to investigation. **-ando** *n.m.* candidate. **-ante** *part. adj.* examining; *n.m.* examiner. **-atọre** *m.* examiner; inspector. **-azịone** *f.* examining.
**eṣangue** *adj.* bloodless; pale dead.
**eṣa·nim-e** *adj.* lifeless; dead **-are** [A1 s] *tr.* to discourage, to dishearten.

**eṣapodi** *m.pl.* (zool.) hexapods, insects.
**eṣasper-are** [A1 s] *tr.* to treat harshly; to exasperate, to infuriate; *rfl.* to become exasperated. **-ante** *part. adj.* exasperating, maddening. **-azione** *f.* exasperation.
**eṣatt-o¹** *adj.* exact; correct; punctual; *adv.* precisely, exactly, just so. **-ẹzza** *f.* exactness; precision; punctuality.
**eṣatt-o²** *part.* of **esigere**; *adj.* exacted, demanded, insisted upon. **-ọre** *m.* collector; *-ore delle imposte*, tax collector. **-ori·a** *f.* collector's office.
**eṣaud-ire** [D2] *tr.* to grant, to concede; to assent to; — *un desiderio*, to comply with a wish. **-i·bile** *adj.* that may be complied with. **-imẹnto** *m.* assent; fulfilment.
**eṣaur-ire** [D2] *tr.* to exhaust; to use up; to wear out; *rfl.* to become used up; (comm.) to sell out. **-i·bile** *adj.* exhaustible; limited. **-iente** *part. adj.* exhausting; exhaustive; thorough; definitive. **-imẹnto** *m.* exhausting; depleting; exhaustion; *-imento nervoso*, nervous breakdown. **-ito** *part. adj.* exhausted; used up; worn out; out of stock; out of print.
**eṣa·usto** *adj.* exhausted; *erario* —, empty treasury.
**eṣazione** *f.* exacting; collection of taxes; taxes collected.
**eṣbọrso** *m.* payment, disbursement; outlay.
**ẹsca** *f.* bait; lure; (fig.) allurement; tinder; fuse.
**escandescen-te** *adj.* white-hot; (fig.) hot-headed, irascible. **-za** *f.* outburst of rage; *dare in -ze*, to flare up.
**escatol-ogi·a** *f.* (theol.) eschatology. **-o·gico** *adj.* eschatological.
**escav-are** [A1] *tr.* excavate. **-atọre** *m.* excavator; digger. **-azione** *f.* excavation; dig.
**E·schil-o** *pr.n.m.* Aeschylus. **-e·o** *adj.* Aeschylean.
**eschimese** *adj.*, *n.m.*, *f.* Eskimo.
**esclam-are** [A1] *tr.*, *intr.* (*aux.* avere) to exclaim; to cry out; to lament. **-ativo** *adj.* exclamatory; *punto -ativo*, exclamation mark. **-azione** *f.* exclamation; (gramm.) interjection.
**esclu·d-ere** [C3] *tr.* to exclude, to leave out; to shut out; to debar. **-ente** *part. adj.* excluding, debarring. **-itọre** *adj.* excluding.
**escluṣ-ione** *f.* exclusion; *sono tutti ladri senza* —, they are all thieves without exception. **-iva** *f.* exclusion; (leg.) patent right; exclusive rights, sole agency; copyright; *in -iva mondiale*, with world copyright. **-ività** *f.* exclusiveness; monopoly; sole right; patent right. **-ivo** *adj.* exclusive; sole.
**escluso** *adj.* excluded; *esclusi i rischi di guerra*, exclusive of war-risks; deprived; *prep.* except.
**escogit-are** [A1 s] *tr.* to think out; to contrive; to excogitate. **-ativo** *adj.* cogitative; *facoltà -ativa*, inventive faculty. **-azione** *f.* excogitation.
**escori-are** [A4] *tr.* to flay, to excoriate; *rfl.* to flog oneself; (fig.) to drive oneself. **-azione** *f.* flaying, excoriation; abrasion.
**escremẹnto** *m.* excrement; refuse; lees.
**escrẹsc-ere** *intr.* (*aux.* essere) to grow upon the surface, to be an excrescence. **-ente** *adj.* excrescent. **-enza** *f.* excrescence.
**escre-tivo** *adj.* excretive, excretory. **-to·rio** *adj.* excretory. **-zione** *f.* excretion.
**Escula·pio** *pr.n.m.* Aesculapius.
**esculento** *adj.* esculent, edible.
**escursiọn-e** *f.* excursion; outing; — *a piedi*, walking-tour; (mil.) raid. **-ista** *m.*, *f.* excursionist; tripper.
**escu·tere** [C19] *tr.* (leg.) to examine; to question; — *testimoni*, to examine witnesses.
**eṣecr-are** [A1] *tr.* to detest, to abhor; to execrate; to curse. **-a·bile, -ando** *adj.* abhorrent, execrable.
**eṣecutare** [A1] *tr.* (leg.) to enforce; to distrain.
**eṣecutivo** *adj.* executive; *potere* —, executive power; *n.m.* executive power; executive committee.
**eṣecut-ọre** *m.* executor; executive officer; minister; performer; (mus.) executant; (leg.) — *testamentario*, executor; — *di giustizia*, executioner. **-rice** *f.* (leg.) executrix.
**eṣecuzione** *f.* execution; carrying out; performance; *buono il concetto, cattiva l'*—, the idea is good but badly carried out; (leg.) execution; enforcement; *dare* — *a*, to enforce.
**eṣe·g-eṣi** *f. indecl.* exegesis. **-eta** *m.* exegete, expounder. **-e·tica** *f.* (theol.) exegetics. **-e·tico** *adj.* exegetic.
**eṣegu-ire** [D2, D1] *tr.* to execute; to perform; to fulfil. **-i·bile** *adj.* executable, that can be performed; (leg.) enforceable. **-imẹnto** *m.* executing; performance, fulfilment.
**eṣempigra·zia** *adv.* for example, for instance, e.g.
**eṣempio** *m.* example; *per* —, *ad* —, for instance; pattern; sample; precedent; *senza* —, unexampled; *dare l'*—, to set an example.
**eṣemplar-e** *adj.* exemplary, model; *n.m.* model, example; (philos.) exemplar; copy, specimen. **-ità** *f.* exemplariness.
**eṣemplific-are** [A2 s] *tr.* to exemplify, to show by examples. **-ativo** *adj.* serving to exemplify.
**eṣent-e** *adj.* exempt; free; — *di spese*, free of charge; — *d'imposte*, free of tax; — *dal servizio militare*, exempt from military service; immune. **-are** [A1] *tr.* to exempt; to free, to discharge; to relieve.
**esenziọn-e** *f.* exemption. **-are** [A1 c] *tr.* to exempt.
**eṣe·quie** *f.pl.* funeral; obsequies, funeral rites; *a — avvenute*, after the funeral.
**eṣerc-ire** [D2] *tr.* to practise; to ply. **-ente** *part. adj.* practising; plying; *n.m.*, *f.* practitioner; proprietor of hotel, restaurant, shop; retail dealer; *gli -enti*, the trade.
**eṣercit-are** [A1 s] *tr.* to exercise, to train by exercise; to drill; — *la mano*, to get one's hand in; to practise, to perform; (leg.) to practise; to enforce; — *un diritto*, to exercise a right; *rfl.* (*prep.* a) to exercise oneself; to exert oneself. **-azione** *f.* exercise; drill; practise; training; exertion.
**eṣer·cito** *m.* army; (mil.) division; *l'*— *dei credenti*, the church militant; host; (fig.) vast collection, array; (poet.) flock.
**eṣerci·zio** *m.* exercise; practice; drill; *essere fuori d'*—, to be out of practice; (provb.) *l'*— *è buon maestro*, practice makes perfect; activity, management; *essere in* —, to be in working order, to function; (leg.) assertion; *licenza d'*—, licence to carry on a business; business, concern, shop; — *finanziario*, financial year.
**eṣibire** [D2] *tr.* to exhibit; to produce; to offer; *rfl.* to offer one's services; to make an exhibition of oneself.
**esibiziọn-e** *f.* offer (esp. of one's services); exhibition; (leg.) production (of a document or thing) as evidence or for inspection. **-iṣmo** *m.* (med.; psychol.) exhibitionism; self-advertisement. **-ista** *m.*, *f.* exhibitionist.
**eṣi·g-ere** [D1] *tr.* to exact, to require; to necessitate; (leg.) to collect; to recover. **-ente** *pres. part.* exacting; exigent; fastidious. **-enza** *f.* exigency, necessity, urgent need; *corrispondere alle -enze di*, to meet the requirements of.
**eṣi·gu-o** *adj.* (lit.) exiguous; scanty; slender; small. **-ità** *f.* exiguousness; scantiness.
**eṣilar-are** [A1 s] *tr.* to exhilarate, to cheer. **-ante** *part. adj.* exhilarating; cheering; (colloq.) amusing, ridiculous; *gas -ante*, laughing gas.
**e·ṣile** *adj.* thin, slender, slim; (of a voice) weak; faint.
**eṣi·li-o** *m.* exile, banishment; place of exile. **-are** [A4] *tr.* to banish; to exile; *rfl.* to go into exile. **-ato** *part. adj.* exiled, banished.

**eṣi·mere** [C9] *tr.* to exempt; to free from an obligation; *rfl.* to gain exemption.
**eṣi·mio** *adj.* eminent, distinguished; outstanding.
**eṣist-ere** [C24] *intr.* (*aux.* essere) to exist; to be; to be extant. **-ente** *part. adj.* existing; in existence. **-enza** *f.* existence; life; (comm.) stock in hand; *in -enza*, in stock. **-enziale** *adj.* (philos.) existential. **-enzialiṣmo** *m.* (philos.) existentialism.
**eṣit-are**[1] [A1 s] *intr.* (*aux.* avere) to hesitate; to waver; to falter. **-ante** *part. adj.* hesitating, hesitant; doubtful; irresolute. **-anza, -azione** *f.* hesitancy, hesitation.
**eṣit-are**[2] [A1 s] *tr.* to sell; to dispose of. **-a·bile** *adj.* rateable, easy to sell.
**e·ṣito** *m.* issue; result, outcome; dénouement; catastrophe; (comm.) sale; issue; outgoings.
**eṣi·zi-o** *m.* ruin, slaughter. **-ale** *adj.* ruinous, fatal; pernicious; *malattia -ale*, fatal illness. **-oso** *adj.* pernicious.
**e·ṣodo**[1] *m.* exodus; flight.
**E·ṣodo**[2] *pr.n.m.* Exodus; *l'—*, the Book of Exodus.
**eṣo·fa-go** *m.* (*pl.* **-ghi, -gi**) (anat.) oesophagus, gullet.
**eṣonerare** [A1 s] *tr.* to exonerate; to release; to exempt; *— dall'ufficio*, to relieve of office, to dismiss.
**eṣo·nero** *m.* (leg.) release; *clausola di — da responsabilità*, clause providing for release from liability.
**Eṣopo** *pr.n.m.* Aesop.
**eṣorbit-are** [A1 s] *intr.* (*aux.* avere) to be exorbitant; to go beyond just limits; *— dai poteri di uno*, to lie outside a person's sphere or department. **-ante** *part. adj.* exorbitant; excessive. **-anza** *f.* exorbitancy; excessiveness.
**eṣorc-iṣmo** *m.* exorcism. **-ista** *m.* exorcist. **-izzare** [A1] *tr.* (eccl.) to exorcize; to exhort, to urge.
**eṣor·d-io** *m.* (*pl.* **-i**) beginning, opening remarks, exordium; *— d'una carriera*, entrance upon a career, début.
**eṣord-ire** [D2] *intr.* (*aux.* avere) to begin a discourse; to enter a profession; to make one's début; to begin. **-iente** *m., f.* débutant, débutante; (sport) beginner.
**eṣort-are** [A1] *tr.* to exhort, to urge. **-ativo, -ato·rio** *adj.* exhortatory; admonishing. **-azione** *f.* exhortation; admonishment.
**eṣoṣo** *adj.* odious, hateful; greedy, avid; mean.
**eṣote·r-ico**[1] *adj.* esoteric; meant only for the initiated. **-iṣmo** *m.* esotericism.
**esote·r-ico**[2] *adj.* exoteric; intelligible to outsiders. **-iṣmo** *m.* exotericism.
**eṣo·tic-o** *adj.* exotic; strange; foreign. **-iṣmo** *m.* exoticism; predilection for what is foreign.
**espan·dere** [C25] *tr., rfl.* to expand, to spread, to extend; *rfl.* to talk freely, to air one's opinions.
**espansion-e** *f.* expansion; spreading; settling, colonizing; *pl.* (fig.) effusiveness; enthusiasm. **-iṣmo** *m.* (pol.) expansionism. **-ista** *m.* expansionist.
**espansivo** *adj.* expansive; effusive, demonstrative; exuberant; talkative.
**espatriare** [A3] *intr.* (*aux.* avere, essere) to emigrate, to settle abroad; *tr.* to expatriate, to banish.
**espa·trio** *m.* (leg.) expatriation.
**espediente** *adj.* expedient, opportune; *n.m.* expedient, device, resource; *pl.* ways and means.
**esped-ire** [D2] *tr.* to expedite, to dispatch; *rfl.* to make haste, to carry out a task quickly. **-ito** *part. adj.* quick; ready; unimpeded.
**espedizione** *f.* expedition; undertaking, enterprise.
**espel·lere** [C23] *tr.* to expel; to eject; to drive out; (sport) to order off the field.
**Espe·ridi** *pr.n.f.pl.* Hesperides.
**esperienza** *f.* experiment; experience; *avere — di*, to experience.
**esperimentale** *adj.* experimental.
**esperiment-are** [A1 c] *tr.* to test, to make trial of; to experiment with; to experience. **-ato** *part. adj.* tried, proved; tested; experienced, expert. **-atore** *m.* tester; experimenter; *adj.* experimental.
**esperiment-o** *m.* experiment, proof, trial, examination; test. **-ista** *m.* (techn.) tester.
**esper-ire** [D2] (leg.) to prove; to bring; to start; *— indagini*, to carry out investigations. **-iente** *part. adj.* experienced, expert; *n.m.* experimenter.
**E·spero** *pr.n.m.* Hesperus; evening star.
**esperto** *adj.* experienced; expert; skilled; *n.m.* expert.
**espettor-are** [A1 s] *tr.* to expectorate. **-azione** *f.* expectoration.
**espi-are** [A4] *tr.* to expiate; to make amends for; to suffer, to undergo. **-ato·rio** *adj.* expiatory; *capro -atorio*, scapegoat. **-azione** *f.* expiation.
**espil-are** [A1] *tr.* (leg.) to defraud; to embezzle. **-atore** *m.* embezzler. **-azione** *f.* embezzlement.
**espir-are** [A1] *tr.* to breathe out, to exhale. **-azione** *f.* exhalation, breathing out.
**espletare** [A1] *tr.* (admin.) to fulfil, to carry out, to despatch; to see through.
**espletivo** *adj., n.m.* expletive.
**esplic-are** [A2 s] *tr.* to explain, to expound; to develop; *— un'attività*, to carry on an activity; *rfl.* to explain, to make oneself clear. **-a·bile** *adj.* explicable. **-azione** *f.* explanation, declaration; development.
**espli·cito** *adj.* explicit; clear; definite.
**esplo·d-ere** [C3] *tr.* to explode; to blow up; *intr.* (*aux.* avere, essere) to go off, to fire (of firearms); (fig.) to burst; *fare —*, to fire, to set off. **-ente** *part. adj., n.m.* explosive. **-itore** *m.* (eng.) detonator.
**esplor-are** [A1] *tr.* to investigate, to explore; *— una ferita*, to probe a wound; (mil.) to reconnoitre. **-atore** *m.* explorer; (mil.) scout, reconnaissance patrol; *giovane -atore*, boy scout. **-atrice** *f.* woman explorer; *giovane -atrice*, girl guide; *nave -atrice*, patrol-boat. **-ato·rio** *adj.*, (*m.pl.* **-ato·rii**) exploratory. **-azione** *f.* exploration; (mil.) reconnaissance.
**esploṣ-ione** *f.* explosion, report; outbreak of anger; outburst; (med.) outbreak. **-ivo** *adj., n.m.* explosive.
**esploṣo** *part.* of **esplodere**; *adj.* exploded; fired.
**espon-ente** *n.m.* exponent; petitioner; member of a political party; (comm.) representative; heading. **-i·bile** *adj.* that can be expounded or exhibited.
**esporre** [B21] *tr.* to expose; to set forth; to exhibit; to expound; *rfl.* to expose oneself; to submit oneself.
**esport-are** [A1] *tr., abs.* to export. **-atore** *m.* exporter. **-azione** *f.* exportation; export; *tassa di -azione*, export duty.
**espoṣit-ivo** *adj.* explanatory, expository. **-ore** *m.* exhibitor; exposer; expounder, interpreter.
**espoṣizione** *f.* exhibition; show, fair; display; aspect (of a house); exposition, explanation; *— dei fatti*, factual report; lying in state; (photog.) exposure.
**esposto** *part.* of **esporre**; *adj.* exposed; exhibited, displayed; *bambino —*, foundling; *— a soffrire danni*, liable to break, fragile; *n.m.* foundling; *ospizio degli esposti*, foundling hospital; statement, petition.
**espression-e** *f.* expression; *non trovo -i per*, I have no words to express . . .; *senza —*, expressionless; phrase, saying. **-iṣmo** *m.* (lit.; art) expressionism.
**espressiv-o** *adj.* expressive. **-ità** *f.* expressiveness.
**espress-o** *adj.* pressed out; extracted; extorted; expressed; express; *caffè —*, coffee made with pressure and filter machine; *n.m.* express parcel or letter; cup of black coffee made with pressure

and filter machine; *adv. lettera espresso*, express letter. **-ọre** *m.* squeezer.

**espri·m-ere** [C18] *tr.* to express; to voice; to declare; to explain; *rfl.* to express oneself. **-i·bile** *adj.* expressible.

**espropri-are** [A4] *tr.* (leg.) to expropriate; to dispossess. **-aziọne** *f.* (leg.) expropriation; dispossession.

**espro·prio** *m.* (leg.) expropriation; selling up; — *forzato*, eviction; *causa di* —, action for eviction.

**espugnare** [A5] *tr.* (mil.) to take by storm, to seize; to defeat.

**espuls-iọne** *f.* expulsion; (leg.) deportation. **-ivo** *adj.* expulsive; *calza -iva*, elastic stocking. **-o** *adj.* expelled; ejected. **-ọre** *m.* expellent; (mil.) ejector.

**espun·gere** [C5] *tr.* to expunge, to cancel, to delete.

**espunziọne** *f.* expunging, deletion.

**espurg-are** [A2] *tr.* to clean out; to disinfect; to cleanse; to expurgate, to bowdlerize. **-aziọne** *f.* cleansing; expurgation.

**esquimẹse** *adj.*, *n.m.*, *f.* Eskimo.

**ẹssa** *prn.f.* she; her; it.

**ẹsse**[1] *prn.f.pl.* they; them.

**esse**[2] *m.*, *f. indecl.* name of the letter S; *a* —, S-shaped.

**essendochè** *conj.* since, seeing that, inasmuch as.

**essenz-a** *f.* essence; *somma* —, God; inmost character; — *di rose*, attar of roses; petrol, motor spirit. **-iale** *adj.* essential; real; *n.m.* important thing; essential.

**es·s-ere** [B13] *intr.* (*aux.* essere) **1.** to exist, to be; — *o non* —, to be or not to be; *Dio disse 'Sia fatta la luce' e la luce fu*, God said 'Let there be light' and there was light; *c'era una volta*, once upon a time there was . . .; *chi siete ?*, who are you ?; *per* —, in actual fact, to tell the truth. **2.** to come to be, to happen, to become; *così sia*, so be it, amen; *sia pure*, so be it, very well; *e sia !*, very well then !; *sarà*, it may be; *sia . . . sia*, whether it be . . ., either . . . or; *che sarà di me ?*, what will become of me ?; *cos'è stato ?*, what has happened ?; *che c'è ?*, what is it ?, what's up ? **3.** to cost, to amount to, to weigh; *quant'è questo libro ?*, how much is this book ?; *quant'è quel pollo ?*, how much does that chicken weigh ?; *quanto c'è da Roma a Milano ?*, how far is it from Rome to Milan ? **4.** *essere in*, to be in the shoes of; *s'io fossi in te*, if I were you; to amount to, to number; *siamo in tre*, there are three of us. **5.** *essere di*, to belong to, to be concerned with or engaged in, to come from, to be made of; *di chi è ?*, whose is it ?; *è di mio fratello*, it's my brother's; *è di settimana*, he's on duty this week; *sarò di ritorno di qui a tre giorni*, I shall return three days from now; *sono di Roma*, I come from Rome; *è di legno*, it's made of wood. **6.** *essere da*, to be up to, to be capable of; — *da tanto di camminare*, to be strong enough to walk; *non credevo che fosse da tanto*, I didn't think he had it in him. **7.** *essere per*, to be about to; *sono per partire*, they're just about to leave. **8.** *esserci*, to understand, to follow; *ci sono*, I understand, I'm with you. **9.** IN PAST DEF.; to go, to reach; *quando furono al ponte*, when they reached the bridge; to go at once; *furono nella stanza*, before you could say Jack Robinson they were in the room; (poet.) to be no more; *ei fu*, he is no more, his life is ended. **10.** *che è* (with repeated noun and usually with neg.) even; *un soldo che è un soldo non ce l'ho*, I haven't (even) a penny; *che è che non è*, from one moment to the next. **11.** IN EXPRESSIONS of time, season, duration; *che ore sono ?*, what time is it ?; *è un mese che l'aspetto*, I've been waiting for it for a month; *l'ho visto tre giorni sono*, I saw him three days ago; *era d'autunno*, it was autumn. **12.** *n.m.* being, existence; *dare l'— a*, to bring into being; identity, status, condition; *gli domandai dell'— suo*, I asked him who he was; *trovarsi in (buon)* —, to be in good condition; being, creature, person; *sono un — disgraziato*, I am a poor wretch.

**ẹssi** *prn.m.pl.* they.

**essicc-are** [A2] *tr.* to dry up, to dry; (industr.) to desiccate. **-aziọne** *f.* desiccation; drying, drying process.

**ẹsso** *prn.m.* he; it; the aforesaid, this, such.

**essudare** [A1] *tr.*, *intr.* (*aux.* avere) to exude.

**est** *m. indecl.* east; *verso* —, eastwards; *all'*—, in the east.

**e·stas-i** *f. indecl.* ecstasy, rapture; (med.) swoon, trance. **-iare** [A4] *tr.* to send into ecstasy; *rfl.* to go into ecstasy.

**estate** *f.* summer; — *di san Martino*, Indian summer.

**esta·tico** *adj.* ecstatic, enraptured.

**estempora·ne-o** *adj.* extemporary, improvised. **-ità** *f.* extemporaneousness, improvisation.

**esten·dere** [C1] *tr* to extend; to spread; to enlarge; to increase; to prolong; — *un documento*, to draw up a document; *rfl.* to extend; to spread.

**estense** *adj.* (geog.) of Este; *pr.n.m.pl.* (hist.) *gli Estensi*, ducal family of Ferrara.

**estensi·bile** *adj.* extensible.

**estensiọne** *f.* extension; amplification; extent, length; compass, range; *in tutta l'— della parola*, in every sense of the word.

**estensivo** *adj.* extensive; (agric.) *coltura estensiva*, extensive cultivation.

**estens-o** *adv. phr. per* —, in full. **-ọre** *m.* expander, enlarging or stretching device; chest-expander.

**estenuare** [A6] *tr.* to extenuate, to enfeeble; to impoverish; to exhaust.

**esteriọr-e** *adj.* exterior, outer, external; *aspetto* —, outward appearance; *doti -i*, physical gifts; *il mondo* —, the world about us; *n.m.* outside, exterior. **-ità** *f. indecl.* appearance(s).

**esterminare** [A1 s] *tr.* to exterminate.

**estermi·nio** *m.* extermination; destruction.

**estern-o** *adj.* outside, external; *pregi -i*, physical qualities; *atti -i*, outward and visible acts; *maglieria -a*, knitted outer garments; *allievo* —, day-boy (in a boarding-school); (med.) *per uso* —, not to be taken internally; *n.m.* outside; exterior; *all'*—, on the outside; day-boy; (sport) 'away' game. **-are** [A1] *tr.* to express, to manifest; to show openly; *rfl.* to open one's heart.

**e·stero** *adj.* foreign; *affari esteri*, foreign affairs; *politica estera*, foreign policy; *n.m.* countries abroad; *all'*—, abroad; *pl.* foreign affairs; *ministero degli esteri*, ministry of foreign affairs.

**esterrefatto** *adj.* appalled, terrified; in a state of consternation.

**estẹso** *adj.* extended; extensive; ample; large; wide; *per estesa*, in full.

**est-eta** *m.* aesthete. **-e·tica** *f.* aesthetics; beauty. **-e·tico** *adj.* aesthetic; *n.m.* aesthete. **-etịsmo** *m.* aestheticism.

**estim-are** [A1] *tr.* to value, to esteem, to appreciate. **-a·bile** *adj.* estimable. **-aziọne** *f.* estimation, judgement, esteem; appraisal.

**e·stimo** *m.* estimate; valuation; land valuation office or register.

**estin·guere** [C6] *tr.* to extinguish, to put out; to quench; — *un debito*, to pay off a debt; (chem.) to slake (lime); *rfl.* to become extinct to fade away, to die off; (leg.) to be dissolved.

**estint-o** *adj.* extinguished; deceased; dead; *debito* —, debt paid or settled; extinct. **-ọre** *m.* fire-extinguisher.

**estinziọne** *f.* extinction; putting out; paying; (leg.) discharge; — *di ipoteca*, redemption of a mortgage.

**estirp-are** [A1] *tr.* to extirpate; to eradicate; to uproot. **-aziọne** *f.* extirpation; uprooting; extraction; (surg.) removal.

**estivo** *adj.* summer; summery;

*vacanze estive*, summer holidays; *ora estiva*, summer time; *stazione estiva*, summer resort.
**estol·lere** (def.) *tr.* (poet.) to raise; to exalt; to extol; *rfl.* (poet.) to rise.
**Esto·nia** *pr.n.f.* (geog.) Estonia.
**estor·cere** [C5] *tr.* to extort, to gain by extortion.
**estorsione** *f.* extortion.
**estrad-are** [A1] *tr.* (leg.) to extradite. **-izione** *f.* (leg.) extradition.
**estra-giudiziale** *adj.* (leg.) extrajudicial. **-legale** *adj.* (leg.) outside the law. **-soggettivo** *adj.* irrelevant, not relating to the subject. **-territoriale** *adj.* (leg.) extraterritorial.
**estra·neo** *adj.* (*prep.* a) foreign, extraneous; *rimanere — a*, not to take part in; *n.m.* stranger; outsider.
**estrarre** [B33] *tr.* to extract; to take out; to draw; to draw by lot; to quarry, to mine.
**estrattivo** *adj.* extractive; *industrie estrattive*, mining industries.
**estratto** *part.* of **estrarre**; *adj.* extracted; drawn out; *n.m.* extract; summary; excerpt; offprint; — *conto*, statement of account; — *di carne*, meat extract.
**estravagante** *adj.* erratic.
**estrazione** *f.* extraction; drawing at lotteries; digging; quarrying; removal.
**estrem-o** *adj.* extreme; utmost; last; greatest; (geog.) *l'— Oriente*, the Far East; *n.m.* extremity, end; tip; extreme; (rugger) full-back. **-ismo** *m.* extremism. **-ista** *m., f.* extremist. **-ità** *f. indecl.* end; tip; edge; extremity.
**estrinsecare** [A2 s] *tr.* to manifest; to express; *rfl.* to appear, to become visible; to express one's thoughts.
**estrin·seco** *adj.* extrinsic; beside the point.
**estr-o**[1] *m.* caprice, fancy; *mancare di —*, to be uninspired; *gli saltò l'— di partir subito*, he took it into his head to go away at once; — *poetico*, poetic inspiration. **-oso** *adj.* capricious; whimsical; animated; original, talented.
**estro**[2] *m.* (ent.) horse-fly.
**estua·rio** *m.* estuary; firth.
**esuberan-te** *adj.* exuberant; superabundant; lively; loud. **-za** *f.* exuberance.
**esulare** [A1 s] *intr.* (*aux.* avere, essere) to go into (voluntary) exile; to go abroad; (*prep.* da) to be outside, to go beyond; *questo -a dalla questione*, this is beside the point.
**esulcerare** [A1 s] *tr.* to ulcerate; (fig.) to exasperate.
**e·sule** *m., f.* exile; *adj.* exiled.
**esult-are** [A1] *intr.* (*aux.* avere) to exult, to rejoice. **-ante** *part. adj.* exultant, rejoicing. **-azione** *f.* exultation, rejoicing.
**esum-are** [A1] *tr.* to exhume, to disinter; (fig.) to unearth, to discover. **-azione** *f.* exhumation, disinterment.
**et** *Lat.* in telegraphese used for **e**, and.
**età** *f. indecl.* age; *di — maggiore*, of age; *di minore —*, under age; *il decano d'—*, the oldest member, the doyen; *l'— dell'oro*, the golden age; *l'— di mezzo*, the Middle Ages; *di mezza —*, middle-aged; *avere una bella —*, to be quite old.
**e·t-ere** *m.* ether; aether; (poet.) sky. **-e·reo** *adj.* ethereal; heavenly.
**etern-o** *adj.* eternal; everlasting; never-ending; (theol.) *il Padre —*, God the Father; *n.m. l'Eterno*, God. **-are** [A1] *tr.* to immortalize, to make eternal; to perpetuate; *rfl.* to win immortal fame. **-ità** *f. indecl.* eternity; eternal life; long time, an age; *ho aspettato un'-ità*, I waited for ages.
**eter-odossi·a** *f.* heterodoxy. **-odosso** *adj.* heterodox. **-ogeneità** *f.* heterogeneity. **-oge·neo** *adj.* heterogeneous. **-osessuale** *adj.* heterosexual.
**e·tica** *f.* ethics; ethic.
**etichetta** *f.* label; ticket; docket; tally; etiquette.
**e·tico**[1] *adj.* ethical.
**e·tico**[2] *adj.* (med.) hectic; consumptive; *n.m.* consumptive.
**e·tim-ologi·a** *f.* etymology. **-olo·gico** *adj.* etymological. **-o·logo** *m.* etymologist; philologist.
**Et-io·pia** *pr.n.f.* (geog.) Ethiopia. **-i·ope, -io·pico** *adj., n.m.* Ethiopian.
**etni·a** *f.* ethnic group.
**et·nico**[1] *adj.* Gentile, pagan, heathen.
**et·nico**[2] *adj.* ethnological, ethnic.
**etn-ografi·a** *f.* ethnography. **-ogra·fico** *adj.* ethnographic. **-o·grafo** *m.* ethnographer. **-ologi·a** *f.* ethnology. **-olo·gico** *adj.* ethnological. **-o·logo** *m.* ethnologist.
**etra** *f.* (poet.) air; sky.
**etrus-co** *adj., n.m.* (*pl.* **-chi**) Etruscan. **-cologi·a** *f.* Etruscology. **-co·logo** *m.* Etruscologist.
**etta·gon-o** *m.* heptagon. **-ale** *adj.* heptagonal.
**et·taro** *m.* hectare, 10,000 sq. metres (about 2½ acres).
**ette** *m.* jot, particle, tittle, iota.
**etto** *m. abbrev.* of **ettogrammo**.
**ettogrammo** *m.* hectogram, 100 grams (3.527 oz.).
**etto·litro** *m.* hectolitre, 100 litres (22.01 imperial gallons).
**etto·metro** *m.* hectometre, 100 metres (328.089 feet).
**Et·tore** *pr.n.m.* Hector.
**eucal-ipto, -itto** *m.* eucalyptus.
**eucar-isti·a** *f.* (theol.) Eucharist. **-i·stico** *adj.* (theol.) Eucharistic.
**Euclide** *pr.n.m.* Euclid.
**euf-emi·a** *f.* euphemy. **-emismo** *m.* euphemism. **-emi·stico** *adj.* euphemistic.
**euf-oni·a** *f.* euphony. **-o·nico** *adj.* euphonic, euphonious.
**euf-ori·a** *f.* (med.) euphory, sense of well-being; (fig.) buoyant spirits; euphoria. **-o·rico** *adj.* (med.) in a state of euphory.
**Eufrate** *pr.n.m.* Euphrates.
**eufu-ismo** *m.* (lit. hist.) euphuism. **-i·stico** *adj.* euphuistic.
**euga·neo** *adj.* (geog.) Euganean; *i colli euganei*, the Euganean Hills.
**eug-ene·tica, -e·nica** *f.* eugenics. **-ene·tico** *adj.* eugenic.
**Eume·nidi** *pr.n.f.pl.* (myth.) Eumenides, Furies.
**eunu-co** *m.* (*pl.* **-chi**) eunuch; *adj.* feeble, servile.
**Euri·dice** *pr.n.f.* (myth.) Eurydice.
**Euri·pide** *pr.n.m.* Euripides.
**eur-itmi·a** *f.* harmonious proportions; eurhythmics. **-it·mico** *adj.* eurhythmic; (med.) *polso -itmico*, regular pulse.
**Europ-a** *pr.n.f.* Europe. **-e·o** *adj., n.m.* European.
**eutana·sia** *f.* euthanasia.
**Eva** *pr.n.f.* Eva; Eve.
**evacu-are** [A6] *tr.* to evacuate; to void; to clear out; *fare — l'aula*, to order the hall to be cleared; *intr.* (*aux.* avere) to move out (from); to evacuate the bowels. **-ante** *part. adv., n.m.* purgative, laxative. **-azione** *f.* evacuation; motion of the bowels.
**eva·dere** [C3] *intr.* (*aux.* essere; *prep.* a) to escape (from); *tr.* to carry out, to perform; (admin.) — *una domanda*, to meet a request, to reply to a question; — *una lettera*, to reply to a letter.
**evanescen-te** *adj.* evanescent, fading away. **-za** *f.* evanescence; (radio; telev.) fading.
**evang-e·lico** *adj.* evangelic; Protestant; *n.m.* Protestant. **-elista** *m.* Evangelist. **-elizzare** [A1] *tr., intr.* (*aux.* avere) to evangelize.
**evapor-are** [A1 s, A1 c] *intr.* (*aux.* essere) to evaporate; (*aux.* avere) to give off vapour. **-azione** *f.* evaporation; vaporization; exhalation, vapour.
**evasione** *f.* (leg.) evasion; escape; (admin.) business reply; dealing with or handling of a matter; — *fiscale*, tax evasion; (fig.) escapism; *letteratura di —*, escapist literature.
**evasivo** *adj.* evasive.
**evaso** *m.* fugitive.
**evel·lere** [B31] *tr.* to uproot, to eradicate.
**evenien-te** *adj.* occurring, liable to happen. **-za** *f.* occurrence, event; *pronto ad ogni -za*, ready for any eventuality.
**evento** *m.* event; outcome; issue,

result; *in ogni* —, in any case, at all events; (sport) fixture.
**eventual-e** *adj.* possible; casual. **-ità** *f. indecl.* possibility; possible event; eventuality. **-mẹnte** *adv.* possibly; *conj.* *-mente capitasse che,* if it should happen that.
**eviden-te** *adj.* evident, obvious, plain; convincing; conclusive. **-za** *f.* obviousness; *provare all'-za,* to give incontrovertible proof; (leg.) evidence.
**evin·cere** [C5] *tr.* (leg.) to recover possession of, to repossess.
**evirare** [A1] *tr.* to castrate, to emasculate.
**evit-are** [A1 s] *tr.* to avoid; to shun; to evade; to steer clear of. **-a·bile** *adj.* avoidable.
**evizịone** *f.* (leg.) dispossession; recovery of possession.
**evo** *m.* age, period, epoch; *Medio* —, Middle Ages.
**evoc-are** [A2 s] *tr.* to evoke, to conjure, to recall, to awaken. **-azịone** *f.* evocation.
**evoluto** *adj.* evolved, fully developed; adult; holding advanced views.
**evoluzịon-e** *f.* evolution; development; (mil.) — *campale,* field exercise; *pl.* manœuvres. **-ịsmo** *m.* evolutionism. **-ista** *m.* evolutionist.
**evol·v-ere** *tr.* to evolve; *rfl.* to be evolved, to develop. **-ente** *part. adj.* evolving; developing.
**evulso** *adj.* uprooted, eradicated.
**evviva** *excl.* (abbrev. vv) long life!; hurrah! (iron.) — *la modestia!,* how modest!; *n.m. indecl.* shout, cheer; *gli evviva,* the shouts of applause.
**ex**[1] *pref.* ex- (generally used without a hyphen): *l'ex combattente,* the ex-serviceman; *ex libris,* book-plate; *ex voto,* votive offering.
**ex**[2] *m., f. indecl.* (colloq.) ex-husband; ex-wife.
**extra-** *pref.* extra; super; *extrafino,* top grade; *adj. indecl.* top grade, prime quality; *burro* —, finest quality butter. **-coniugale** *adj.* extra-conjugal.
**ex voto** *m. indecl.* see under **ex**[1].
**Ezechi·a** *pr.n.m.* (bibl.) Hezekiah.
**Ezechiello** *pr.n.m.* (bibl.) Ezekiel.
**eziandi·o** *adv.* even; also.

**F** *f., m.* (pron. **effe**) the letter F; the consonant F; *una F maiuscola,* a capital F; *la città del F (dell'effe),* Florence; (mus.) *f.* and *ff.,* abbrev. of forte and fortissimo.
**fa**[1] *m.* (mus.) fa (*i.e.* the fourth degree of the scale; the note F; the key of F.
**fa**[2] *3rd pers. sing. pr. indic.* of **fare.**
**fabbisọgno** *m.* requisites, requirements, what is needed; (theatr.) prop.
**fab·brica** *f.* building; *in* —, in course of construction; *nuovo di* —, brand new; fabric (of a building); (fig.) *una — d'inganni,* a tissue of lies; factory, works; *marchio di* —, trade-mark.
**fabbric-are** [A2 s] *tr.* to manufacture, to make; to construct, to build; to forge; (fig.) to fabricate, to invent; to falsify. **-ativo** *adj.* for building upon; *terreno -ativo,* building land. **-ato** *part. adj.* manufactured, made, made up; built, built on; (fig.) fabricated; *n.m.* building; fabric of a building; (rlwy.) *-ato viaggiatori,* station building, public rooms. **-atọre** *m.* maker; builder; constructor. **-azịone** *f.* manufacture; construction; make; *-azione italiana,* made in Italy.
**fabbro** *m.* smith; wright; — *ferraio,* blacksmith; (fig.) maker, creator; shaper, moulder; (poet.) craftsman; builder.
**faccend-a** *f.* affair; business; job; work; matter; thing; *regolare una* —, to settle a matter; *-e domestiche,* housework, household chores; *mettere in -e,* to keep busy. **-eri·a** *f.* troubles, difficulties; curiosity about other people's affairs, interference. **-iera** *f.*, **-iere** *m.* busybody.
**faccẹtt-a** *f.* facet; *a -e,* cut in facets. **-are** [A1 c] *tr.* to cut (a gem).
**facchin-o** *m.* porter; *vita da* —, dog's life. **-eggiare** [A3 c] *intr.* (*aux.* avere) to fag; to lug weights about; to act as porter. **-eri·a** *f.* porter's job; heavy task; low behaviour; 'Billingsgate language'.
**fac·ci-a** *f.* (*pl.* **facce**) face; — *tosta,* brazen face, 'cheek', effrontery; *a doppia* —, two-faced, insincere; *perdere la* —, to lose face; *in — al mondo,* in the eyes of the world; *voltar* —, to change sides; *senza* —, shameless; *a — a* —, face-to-face; *di* —, opposite; *alla prima* —, at first sight, prima facie; (of a book, etc.) page; (mus.) side (of gramophone record). **-ale** *adj.* facial; *valore -ale,* face value.
**facciata** *f.* (archit.) façade; front, frontage; elevation; page; side (of gramophone record).
**face** *f.* (poet.) torch; light; splendour; fire; heavenly orb.
**facendo** *ger.* of **fare**; *strada* —, *cammin* —, walking along, on the way.
**faceto** *adj.* facetious, humorous.
**face·zia** *f.* jest, witticism.
**faci-bene** *m., f. indecl.* welldoer. **-danno** *m., f.* **-male** *m., f. indecl.* evildoer; despoiler; mischief-maker.
**fa·cil-e** *adj.* easy; simple; — *a farsi,* easy to do; *di — smercio,* saleable; facile; light; likely, probable; *è — che piova,* it will probably rain; accommodating, easy-going; inclined, prone. **-ità** *f.* ease; aptitude; facility; fluency. **-ọne** *adj.* lax; superficial; amateurish; slick, glib.
**facilit-are** [A1 s] *tr.* to facilitate; — *un compito,* to make a task less difficult. **-azịone** *f.* facilitation; pulling of strings; letter of introduction.
**facinorọso** *adj.* lawless; violent; ruffianly; *n.m.* ruffian; desperado; malefactor.
**facit-ọre** *m.* maker, creator; (leg.) official administrator; agent, steward; man of business. **-ura** *f.* work; constructing, building.
**fa·cola** *f.* (poet.) torch.
**facolt-à** *f. indecl.* faculty, power; *in possesso delle proprie* —, in full possession of one's faculties; authority; University faculty; (leg.) right; authority, permission; option; *ciò non rientra nelle sue* —, he has not the authority to do that; *pl.* property; wealth, riches. **-ativo** *adj.* optional; *fermata -ativa,* request stop; (leg.) permissive. **-ọso** *adj.* wealthy; well-off.
**facọnd-ia** *f.* readiness of speech; eloquence; fluency. **-o** *adj.* fluent; eloquent; glib, garrulous.
**fag·gio** *m.* beech tree, beech-wood.
**fagiano** *m.* pheasant.
**fagiol-o** *m.* (bot.) name of various kidney beans; *pl.* (cul.) haricot beans; broad beans; (fig.) *questo mi va a* —, this is just what I wanted; *a forma di* —, kidney-shaped. **-ini** *m.pl.* runner beans; French beans.
**fa·gli-a** *f.* (geol.) fault. **-are** [A4] *intr.* (*aux.* avere) to lack (a card of a given suit); *tr.* to discard (cards).
**fagott-o** *m.* bundle; *far* —, to pack up and go away; (mus.) bassoon. **-ista** *m., f.* (mus.) bassoonist.
**fa·ida** *f.* (hist.) feud; right of revenge.
**falang-e** *f.* (mil. hist.) phalanx; solid mass of people; (anat.) phalanx, finger-bone. **-ịsmo** *m.* (pol.) Falangism. **-ista** *m., f.* (pol.) Falangist.
**falbo** *adj.* tawny.

**falc-are** [A2] *tr.* (mil. hist.) to arm (a chariot) with scythes; *intr.* (*aux.* essere) (equit.) to falcade; (fig.) to run and leap at great speed. **-ata** *f.* (equit.) falcade; (sport) stride, step. **-ato** *part. adj.* sickle-shaped; crescent; armed with scythes.
**falce** *f.* sickle; scythe; bill-hook for pruning; (poet.) crescent; *— di luna*, crescent moon.
**falci-are** [A3] *tr.* to mow; to scythe; (fig.) to mow down. **-atore** *m.* mower, reaper; hay-cutter. **-atrice** *f.* lawn-mower; reaping machine.
**falciglione** *m.* (orn.) snipe.
**falco** *m.* (*pl.* **falchi**) (orn.) falcon, hawk.
**falconare** [A1 c] *intr.* (*aux.* avere) to go hawking.
**falcon-e** *m.* (orn.) falcon, esp. the peregrine falcon. **-eri·a** *f.* falconry. **-iere** *m.* falconer.
**falda** *f.* flake; layer of snow; drift of snow; slice, hunk, slab; pleat; flounce, hem; brim of a hat; lower slope of a mountain; (geol.) layer, stratum; (bldg.) pitch of a roof; *attaccarsi alle falde di*, to cling to the coat-tails of.
**faldisto·r(i)o** *m.* (liturg.) fald-stool.
**faldoso** *adj.* streaky, striated; (of a mountain) many-sloped.
**falegnam-e** *m.* joiner, carpenter; *nodo da —*, timber hitch. **-eri·a** *f.* journey; carpentery.
**falena** *f.* moth; ash of burnt paper.
**fa·lera** *f.* horse brass.
**Falerno** *pr.n.m.* Falernian (wine).
**fale·sia** *f.* cliff, steep bank.
**falla** *f.* leak; *formazione d'una —*, springing of a leak; outlet, out-flow; *tamponare una —*, to stop a leak.
**fallac-e** *adj.* fallacious; false; misleading; deceitful; fleeting, quickly fading (of colour); likely to go bad (of fruit). **-ia** *f.* fal-laciousness; deception; fallacy; failure (of a crop which has promised well). **-ità** *f.* falla-ciousness; falseness, treachery.
**fall-are** [A1] *intr.* (*aux.* avere) to err, to be mistaken; to make mistakes; (naut.) to make water. **-a·bile** *adj.* fallible; fallacious. **-ato** *part. adj.* mistaken, in error; failed.
**falli·bil-e** *adj.* fallible; fallacious. **-ità** *f.* fallibility.
**fal·lico** *adj.* phallic.
**falliment-o** *m.* falling short, failing, failure; (leg.) bankruptcy. **-are** *adj.* relating to bankruptcy; (fig.) bankrupt.
**fall-ire** [D2] *intr.* (*aux.* avere) to fail; to be unsuccessful; to fall short; to make a mistake; to misfire; *— alla promessa*, to break one's word; (comm.) to go bank-rupt; *tr.* to miss; *— il colpo*, to miss one's aim. **-ito** *part. adj.* failed; unsuccessful; unfulfilled; *-ito di mente*, out of one's mind; bankrupt; *n.m.* bankrupt.
**fall-o**[1] *m.* failing, slight fault; slip; *cogliere in —*, to catch out; *senza —*, without fail; (geol.) fault; (sport) foul, fault. **-oso** *adj.* (sport) *gioco -oso*, foul play.
**fallo**[2] *m.* phallus.
**falò** *m. indecl.* bonfire; beacon.
**falsa** *f.* (mus.) discord; (dressm.) insertion.
**falsa-monete** *m. indecl.* coiner, counterfeiter. **-riga** *f.* (*pl.* **falsarighe**) guide rule.
**fals-are** [A1] *tr.* to falsify; to dis-tort; to misrepresent; (dressm.; tailor.) to pad. **-atore** *m.* falsifier.
**falsa·rio** *m.* forger; falsifier; counterfeiter; liar; perjurer.
**falseggiare** [A3 c] *intr.* (*aux.* avere) (mus.) to sing falsetto; to sing out of tune.
**falsetto** *m.* (mus.) falsetto voice.
**falsific-are** [A2 s] *tr.* to falsify; to distort; to adulterate; *— una firma*, to forge a signature. **-ato** *part. adj.* falsified; *moneta -ata*, counterfeit money. **-atore** *m.* falsifier, counterfeiter. **-azione** *f.* falsifying; (leg.) forgery.
**falsilo·quio** *m.* lie, falsehood.
**falsi·loquo** *m.* liar.
**falsità** *f.* falsity; lie, falsehood; duplicity; (leg.) deceit; forgery.
**fals-o** *adj.* false; deceitful; hypo-critical; counterfeit, forged; not genuine, sham; dummy; erron-eous; *essere sopra una -a strada*, to be on a wrong track; (mus.) out of tune; discordant; *adv.* falsely; *parole che suonano —*, words which do not ring true; *n.m.* falsehood, lies; perjury, fraud, forgery; *giurare il —*, to forswear; fake, fraud; *impugnare di —*, to challenge the truth of; *mettere un piede in —*, to stumble, (fig.) to make a false step; (fencing) feint.
**fam-a** *f.* fame; reputation; repute, renown; notoriety; report; *godere —*, to be famous; *di dubbia —*, of doubtful reputation; *essere in —*, to be in vogue; *è — che*, it is rumoured that; *conoscere per —*, to know by reputation. **-ato** *adj.* famed; *mal -ato*, ill-famed.
**fame** *f.* hunger, appetite; famine, lack of food; *aver —*, to be hungry; *avere una — da lupo*, to be as hungry as a hunter; *cavarsi la —*, to satisfy one's hunger; desire; craving.
**fame·lico** *adj.* famishing; starv-ing, ravenous; *— d'onore*, eager for honour.
**famigerato** *adj.* notorious; ill-famed; (joc.) famous.
**fami·glia** *f.* family; lineage, race, stock; related group, section; body, association; religious order; *mettere su —*, to raise a family; *di —*, domestic, domes-ticated.
**fami·glio** *m.* servant; attendant; member of a household.
**familiar-e** *adj.* family, domestic; familiar; homelike; easy-going; forward, outspoken; private, intimate; *lettere -i* private cor-respondence; *gli è più — il francese dell'italiano*, he knows French better than Italian; *avere — una cosa*, to know a thing well; *stile —*, simple style; *alla —*, in private, in confidence; *n.m.* friend; servant; member of a household. **-ità** *f.* familiarity; intimacy, confidence; *non ci ho -ità*, I don't know him well; simplicity, spontaneity; *prendersi troppa -ità*, to take liberties. **-izzare** [A1] *rfl.* (*prep.* con) to familiarize onself (with); to become the close friend (of); (of animals) to grow tame.
**famoso** *adj.* famous, celebrated, renowned; notorious; infamous; libellous; memorable.
**famulato** *m.* servitude; deference, respect.
**fanal-e** *m.* light, lamp, lantern; carriage lamp; lighthouse; navi-gation light; (rlwy.) *-i di treno*, signal lights; (motor.) *-i anteriori*, head-lamps; *— di coda*, rear-light. **-ino** *m. dim.* little lamp; *-ino della bicicletta*, bicycle lamp; (motor.) *-ino di targa*, tail-lamp. **-ista** *m.* lamplighter; (naut.) lighthouse-keeper.
**fana·tico** *adj.* fanatic(al); bigoted; *zelo —*, fanaticism; *— per la musica*, mad about music; *n.m.* fanatic, enthusiast, bigot; parti-san, supporter, 'fan'; *dare nel —*, to become fanatical.
**fanatismo** *m.* fanaticism; frenzy; bigotry.
**fanciull-a** *f.* girl, young girl; maid, virgin; unmarried woman. **-eri·a** *f.* childishness. **-esco** *adj.* (*m.pl.* **-eschi**) childish; puerile; child-like. **-ezza** *f.* childhood; early youth; boyhood; girlhood; infancy. **-o** *m.* child; boy; simpleton; immature, youthful.
**fando·nia** *f.* idle story, wild tale; lie; fib; malicious rumour.
**fanello** *m.* (orn.) linnet.
**fanfaluca** *f.* ash blown about in the air; idle story; triviality; bauble.
**fan·fano** *m.* chatter-box; med-dler; (ichth.) pilot fish.
**fanfara** *f.* (mus.; mil.) fanfare.
**fanfaron-e** *m.* braggart, boaster. **-ata** *f.* fanfaronade; boastful behaviour.
**fang-a** *f.* deep mud. **-atura** *f.* mud-bath.
**fanghi·glia** *f.* mire; soft mud; muddy water; (geog.) fine clay; slurry, sludge.
**fang-o** *m.* (*pl.* **fanghi**) mud; mire; sludge; *fare i fanghi*, to have

mud baths; (fig.) *cadere nel —*, to become morally degraded; *gettare — addosso a*, to fling mud at. **-oso** *adj.* muddy; filthy; low, base, corrupt.

**fannullone** *m.* lazybones, idler.

**fano** *m.* temple; sanctuary.

**fantascienza** *f.* science fiction, 'scientifiction'.

**fantas-i·a** *f.* fancy; imagination; fantasy; vision; whim, thought, mind; *articoli di —*, fancy goods; (mus.) fantasia; *suonare a —*, to improvise; *adj. indecl.* fancy, patterned. **-iare** [A4] *intr.* (*aux.* avere) to daydream. **-ioso** *adj.* strange, fanciful.

**fantasm-a** *m.* ghost, spectre, apparition; phantasm, phantom; fantasy, fancy; illusion; *-i di dominio*, delusions of grandeur. **-agori·a** *f.* phantasmagoria; hallucinations; *-agoria di cifre*, jumble of figures. **-ago·rico** *adj.* phantasmagoric; spectacular.

**fantasticag·gine** *f.* fantasy; reverie.

**fantastic-are** [A2s] *intr.* (*aux.* avere) to indulge in fancies, to daydream; *tr.* to dream about; to imagine; *che cosa mai vai -ando?*, whatever are you dreaming of? **-atore** *m.* dreamer, visionary.

**fantasticheri·a** *f.* reverie, daydream; fantasy, fancy.

**fanta·stico** *adj.* fantastic, fanciful; imaginary, imaginative; *facoltà fantastica*, power of imagination; marvellous, wonderful; *n.m.* whimsical person; eccentric.

**fant-e** *m.* (mil.) foot soldier; (naut.) officer's servant; (cards) knave, jack. **-eri·a** *f.* (mil.) infantry; *-eria di marina*, marines. **-ino** *m. dim.* young boy, child; jockey. **-oc·cia** *f.* doll; lay-figure, tailor's dummy; silly woman. **-oc·cio** *m.* ragdoll; lay figure, tailor's dummy; scarecrow; boy; (theatr. and fig.) puppet; *governo -occio*, puppet government.

**fantoma·tico** *adj.* phantom-like; spooky, eerie.

**farabutto** *m.* rascal; swindler, impostor; blackguard.

**faraglione** *m.* tall rock resembling a column; lighthouse.

**faraona** *f.* (orn.) guinea-fowl.

**Faraone** *pr.n.m.* (hist.) Pharaoh; Faro, game of chance played with cards.

**farc-ire** [D2] *tr.* (cul.) to stuff; (fig.) to cram. **-ito** *part. adj.* (cul.) stuffed.

**fard-a** *f.* filth; filthy thing. **-are** [A1] *tr.* to paint; *rfl.* to make up (one's face).

**fardello** *m.* bundle, package; (fig.) burden; *fare —*, to pack up and go away; *— di noie*, weight of cares.

**fardo** *m.* large bundle, bale; paint, rouge.

**fare** [B14] **1.** *tr.* to make, to create, to produce; *— figli*, to have children; to bear children; to beget children; *— le uova*, to lay eggs; *— frutti*, to bear fruit; *tutto fa brodo*, everything comes in useful; *— da mangiare*, to cook a meal; *due più due fa quattro*, two and two make four; (naut.) *— acqua*, to spring a leak. **2.** to do; *— il proprio dovere*, to do one's duty; *ne ha fatto d'ogni sorte*, he has been up to all sorts of tricks; *l'hai fatta bella!*, now you've done it!; *farla finita*, to put an end to it. **3.** to perform, to conduct, to carry out; to wage; *— un duetto*, to perform a duet; *— una guerra*, to wage war; *— una scoperta*, to make a discovery. **4.** to arouse, to excite, to inspire, to cause; *— orrore*, to inspire horror; *— compassione a*, to arouse pity in; *— paura a*, to frighten. **5.** to say, to remark; *fece lui*, said he; *non ne fate parola*, don't breathe a word about it; *— un urlo*, to let out a yell. **6.** to give; to give off; *fammi un bacio*, give me a kiss; *— un gesto*, to make a gesture; *— un sospiro*, to give a sigh; *— fumo*, to give forth smoke; *faceva il sangue dalla bocca*, he was bleeding from the mouth. **7.** to experience, to have, to entertain; *— un sogno*, to have a dream; *— un sospetto*, to harbour a suspicion. **8.** to signify, to convey, to suggest, to give the impression of; *non fa niente*, it doesn't matter; *fa lo stesso*, it is all the same; (colloq.) *non mi fa nè caldo nè freddo*, I couldn't care less; *un vestito che fa molto distinto*, a dress which makes a very elegant impression. **9.** to number, to contain; to fix the price of, to sell at, to amount to; *la città fa 800 mila abitanti*, the city has a population of 800,000; *dieci anni fa*, ten years ago; *quanto fa in tutto?*, what is the total?; *a — assai*, at the most; *il mio orologio fa le due*, it's two o'clock by my watch. **10.** to acquire, to come by, to take, to get, to develop; *— eredità*, to come into a legacy; *— debiti*, to get into debt; *— un bagno*, to take a bath; *— un passo*, to take a step; (motor.) *— benzina*, to fill up with petrol; *— scuola*, to acquire a following, (of a fashion) to spread; *— la bocca a*, to acquire a taste for. **11.** to suppose, to believe; *lo facemmo morto*, we thought he was dead. **12.** OF THE WEATHER, SEASONS: to be, to turn out; *fa caldo*, it is hot; *fa freddo*, it is cold; *domani fa la luna*, tomorrow there will be a new moon. **13.** to work as, to exercise the trade or profession of, to lead the life of, to be, to pretend to be, to play the part of; *— l'avvocato*, to practise as a lawyer; *— l'Otello*, to play Othello; *— il signore*, to lead a life of leisure; *— le veci di*, to act as, to represent; *— il sordo*, to pretend to be deaf. **14.** to do in, to 'fix'; *— un vitello*, to kill a calf; (joc.) *— la pelle a*, to kill; *— a pezzi*, to tear to pieces; *— a metà*, to divide into two; *— la testa a*, to cut off the head of; *— l'ora*, to kill time. **15.** FOLL. BY INFIN.: to make, to compel (to), to cause (to); *lo feci andare*, I made him go; *mi fece aspettare*, he kept me waiting; *devo farmi tagliare i capelli*, I must get my hair cut. **16.** FOLL. BY SUBJUNCT.: *— che*, to contrive that, to give orders that; *fece sì che l'altro non partisse*, he saw to it that the other person did not leave. **17.** *intr.* (*aux.* avere) to do; *faccia pure!*, please do!; *— per tre*, to do the work of three; *— bene*, to do well; *— male*, to do wrong; *avere da —*, to have a lot to do; *farne a meno*, to do without (it); *— da capo*, to begin again; *non avrò niente a che — con lui*, I won't have anything to do with him; *il saper —*, know-how. **18.** to behave, to act; *— a tempo*, to act in time; *lasciar —*, to leave alone; *il lasciar —*, laissez-faire. **19.** to compete, to fight, to play; *— a pugni*, to come to blows; *— a chi arriva prima*, to race; *— a gara a*, to compete with; *— a mosca cieca*, to play hide-and-seek. **20.** to grow, to thrive; *l'ulivo non fa nelle regioni alte*, the olive does not thrive at high altitudes. **21.** to be suitable, to work, to be useful; *ciò non fa per me*, that is no use to me. **22.** *fare da*, to play the part of, to act as; *gli fece da mamma*, she was a mother to him; *— da podestà*, to represent the mayor. **23.** *fare del*, to pretend to be; *— dello scemo*, to pretend to be stupid. **24.** *rfl.* (*acc.* of *prn.* 'si') to become; *farsi prete*, to become a priest; *farsi sposa*, to get married; *farsi avanti*, to get ahead; (*dat.* of *prn.* 'si') *farsi coraggio*, to take courage; *farsi strada*, to make headway; *farsi largo*, to clear a space before one. **25.** *n.m.* doing; making; *il da —*, business, things to be done; *ha il suo da — anche lei*, she too has her hands full.

**faretra** *f.* quiver.

**farfalla** *f.* (ent.) butterfly; moth; (fig.) scatterbrain; bow-tie (swimming) butterfly stroke; (motor.) *aprire la —*, to open the throttle; *pl.* (cul.) a kind of pasta.

**farin-a** *f.* flour, meal, powder; *fior di —*, fine flour; *— d'avena*, oatmeal; *— di riso*, ground rice; *— lattea*, dried milk powder.

**-a·ceo** *adj.* farinaceous. **-ai(u)-olo** *m.* flour-merchant, miller. **-ata** *f.* pap; *-ata d'avena*, oatmeal porridge. **-ọso** *adj.* farinaceous; floury, powdery.
**faring-e** *f.* (anat.) pharynx. **-ite** *f.* (med.) pharyngitis.
**fariṣ-a·ico** *adj.* pharisaic(al); hypocritical. **-e·o** *m.* Pharisee; hypocrite; *adj.* pharisaic; hypocritical.
**farmace·ut-ica** *f.* pharmaceutics; pharmaceutical department. **-ico** *adj.* pharmaceutical.
**farmac-i·a** *f.* chemist's shop; chemist's dispensary; pharmacy; pharmaceutical preparation. **-ista** *m.* pharmacist, chemist.
**far·ma-co** *m.* (*pl.* **-chi, -ci**) drug; medicine; remedy; poison. **-cologi·a** *f.* pharmacology. **-cope·a** *f.* pharmacopoeia.
**farneticare** [A2s] *intr.* (*aux.* avere) to rave, to be delirious; to talk wildly.
**faro** *m.* lighthouse, beacon; strait (of the sea); (motor.) headlamp; — *anti-nebbia*, foglamp; — *anti-abbagliante*, anti-dazzle lamp.
**farra·gin-e** *f.* mixed fodder; (fig.) farrago, medley. **-ọso** *adj.* muddled, jumbled.
**fars-a** *f.* (theatr.) farce; (fig.) mockery, buffoonery. **-ẹsco** *adj.* (*m.pl.* **-ẹschi**) farcical.
**farsẹtto** *m.* doublet.
**fascẹtt-a** *f.* small band; corset; paper band round a book. **-a·ia** *f.* corset-maker.
**fa·scia** *f.* band; bandage; *pl.* swaddling clothes; *un bambino in fasce*, an infant in arms; wrapper; *spedire sotto* —, to send under cover.
**fasciame** *m.* (naut.) hull plating.
**fasci-are** *tr.* [A3] to bandage; to swathe; — *una ferita*, to bind up a wound; to surround, to fortify. **-atura** *f.* bandaging; bandage; belt.
**fasci·colo** *m.* part, number, issue (of a publication); booklet; folder, file.
**fascin-a** *f.* bundle of sticks, faggot; bonfire; **-a·ia** *f.* woodpile. **-ame** *m.* firewood.
**fascin-are** [A1s] *tr.* to fascinate, to charm. **-atọre** *m.* fascinator, charmer; *adj.* fascinating, charming. **-aziọne** *f.* fascination; charm; sorcery.
**fa·scino** *m.* fascination; charm; spell.
**fa·scio** *m.* bundle; burden, weight; group; *mettere in* —, to muddle, to fail to distinguish; *fare d'ogni erba* —, to treat everything alike, (phys.; opt.) — *di luce*, beam of light; (radio) beam.
**fasc-iṣmo** *m.* Fascism. **-ista** *m., f., adj.* Fascist.
**faṣe** *f.* phase, period; stage; cycle.
**fastello** *m.* bundle; faggot.
**fasti·di-o** *m.* trouble, annoyance, worry; affliction; repugnance, disgust; *dare* — *a*, to annoy; *smetti, mi dai* — *!*, do stop, you're getting on my nerves!; *pigliare uno in* —, to take a dislike to someone. **-ọso** *adj.* troublesome, annoying, trying; fastidious.
**fasti·gio** *m.* pinnacle, coping; (fig.) crowning feature.
**fasto**[1] *adj.* propitious, favourable.
**fast-o**[2] *m.* pomp, splendour; magnificence; display, ostentation. **-osità** *f.* pomp, splendour; pageantry; luxury. **-ọso** *adj.* sumptuous, splendid; gorgeous; luxurious; ostentatious.
**faṣullo** *adj.* fake, bogus.
**fata** *f.* fairy; *paese delle fate*, fairyland; *racconti delle fate*, fairytales.
**fatal-e** *adj.* fatal; fated; destined; disastrous; *colpo* —, mortal blow; *è* — *che*, it is inevitable that. **-iṣmo** *m.* fatalism. **-ista** *m., f.* fatalist; *adj.* fatalistic. **-ità** *f. indecl.* fatality; fate, destiny; fatal event; mischance.
**fat-are** [A1] *tr.* to bewitch, to enchant; to cast a spell on; to charm. **-atura** *f.* enchantment; witchcraft, sorcery.
**fatica** *f.* toil, labour, effort; *vivere col frutto della* —, to live by the sweat of one's brow; trouble, hardship; travail; *ingrata* —, drudgery; fatigue, weariness; *le fatiche d'Ercole*, the labours of Hercules; *buttar via la* —, to labour in vain; *avere* — *a intendere*, to have difficulty in understanding.
**faticare** [A2] *intr.* (*aux.* avere) to work hard; to strive; to have difficulty; *rfl.* to work hard; to get tired; to strive.
**faticọso** *adj.* hard, difficult, laborious; troublesome, trying; tiring; weary.
**fati·dico** *adj.* prophetic; destined, fateful.
**fatiga** *f.* (metall.) fatigue.
**fatiscenza** *f.* disintegration.
**fato** *m.* fate, destiny, lot; death, doom.
**fatt-a**[1] *f.* sort, kind; action; *gente d'ogni* —, people of every sort; *male -e*, wicked deeds. **-amẹnte** *adv. sì -amente*, in this way.
**fatta**[2] *f.* droppings, spoor, trail of dung.
**fattapposta** *adj. indecl.* purpose-made, made to customer's own design.
**fattẹzze** *f.pl.* features; figure; appearance; charms.
**fatti·bile** *adj.* practicable; possible, feasible; realizable; *n.m.* possibility; what can be done.
**fatticchiare** [A4] *tr.* to do half-heartedly; to do incompletely.
**fattispe·cie** *f. indecl.* case, instance; (leg.) case in issue, present case.
**fattitivo** *adj.* (gramm.) factitive.
**fatt-ivo** *adj.* effective; efficacious; active, busy, energetic; *una persona -iva*, a person with drive. **-i·zio** *adj.* artificial, factitious; insincere.
**fatt-o**[1] *adj.* done; *è presto* —, it is soon done; made; — *a mano*, handmade; — *a macchina*, machine-made; *abiti -i*, ready-made clothes; *bell'e* —, ready-made; constructed; produced; formed; composed; ripe, mature; ready, done; exhausted; suitable; *nato* —, born to it; *uomo* —, grown man; *tanto* —, as big as this; *a notte -a*, when it is quite dark; *a conti -i*, when the account is settled; *detto* —, no sooner said than done; *non è* — *per te*, it doesn't suit you; *se ti vien* — *di*, if you happen to.
**fatto**[2] *m.* fact; action, act, deed; event, occurrence; *mettere uno al corrente del* —, to acquaint someone with the facts; — *di cronaca*, news item; affair, business; story, tale; plot; *il* — *si svolge a*, the story is laid in; *raccontami il* —, tell me what happened; *fatti, non parole*, deeds, not words; *dopo il* —, after the event; *badare ai fatti suoi*, to mind one's own business; *dire il* — *suo*, to speak one's mind; *venire al* —, to come to the point; *in* — *di*, in the matter of; — *sta che*, the fact is that; *di* —, in fact.
**fattọio** *m.* oil-press.
**fattọr-e** *m.* maker, creator; farm-bailiff, steward; (math.) factor; (fig.) factor, element. **-i·a** *f.* farm, country estate; farmhouse. **-iale** *adj.* (math.) factorial. **-ino** *m.* office-boy; telegraph-boy.
**fattrice** *f.* brood-mare; mother cat; brood-bitch.
**fattucchier-a** *f.* witch, sorceress. **-e** *m.* wizard, sorcerer. **-i·a** *f.* witchcraft, sorcery; intrigue, fraud.
**fattur-a** *f.* make; making; work, workmanship, craftsmanship; creation; witchcraft, sorcery, enchantment; *lavorante a* —, piece-worker; (comm.) invoice. **-are** [A1] *tr.* to adulterate; to concoct; to cast a spell on; (comm.) to invoice; to charge for. **-ato** *part. adj.* (comm.) invoiced; *n.m.* (comm.) proceeds of sales; turnover. **-ista** *m., f.* (comm.) invoice clerk.
**fa·tu-o** *adj.* fatuous; conceited; *fuoco* —, will o' the wisp. **-ità** *f.* fatuousness; stupidity.
**fatutto** *m., f. indecl.* busybody.
**fa·uci** *f. pl.* throat, gullet; mouth, opening; *le* — *del leone*, the lion's maw.
**fa·un-a** *f.* (zool.) fauna. **-i·stico** *adj.* relating to fauna.
**fa·un-o** *pr.n.m.* faun; satyr. **-ẹsco** *adj.* (*m.pl.* **-ẹschi**) faun-like.
**Fa·usto**[1] *pr.n.m.* Faust; Faustus.

**fa·usto**[2] *adj.* propitious; lucky, fortunate; happy.
**fautọre** *m.* favourer, supporter, follower, adherent.
**fav-a** *f.* (bot.) broad bean; trifle. **-ata** *f.* dish of beans; bean soup. **-azzo** *m.* (orn.) wood-pigeon.
**favell-a** *f.* speech; language, tongue, dialect, idiom; *il dono della —*, the gift of tongues. **-are** [A1] *tr.* to speak, to tell; *intr.* (*aux.* avere) to converse, to talk; *n.m.* speech, discourse.
**favilla** *f.* spark; glimmer; light, gleam; glow.
**fav-o** *m.* honeycomb; (motor.) radiator. **-ọso** *adj.* like a honeycomb.
**fa·vola** *f.* fable; fiction, myth; plot, story; idle tale; *essere la — di*, to be the laughing-stock of.
**favol-are** [A1 s] *intr.* (*aux.* avere) to tell stories. **-atọre** *m.* fabulist; story-teller.
**favoleggiare** [A3 c] *intr.* (*aux.* avere) to tell fables or tales; to chat.
**favolẹs-co** *adj.* (*m.pl.* **-chi**) fantastic, improbable; like a fairy-tale.
**favolọso** *adj.* fabulous, mythical; fictitious, legendary; wonderful; *prezzi favolosi*, exorbitant prices.
**favọre** *m.* favour, kindness; aid, assistance; goodwill, approval; sympathy, affection; partiality, bias; *per —*, please; *a — di*, on behalf of; *biglietto di —*, complimentary ticket; (comm.) *assegno bancario a — del portatore*, a bearer cheque; *prezzo di —*, special price.
**favoregg-iare** [A3 c] *tr.* to aid and abet; to harbour, to protect; to support. **-iatọre** *m.* favourer, supporter, accomplice; (leg.) abettor; accessory.
**favor-ire** [D2] *tr.* to favour; to encourage, to assist, to protect, to promote; *— il commercio*, to promote trade; to approve, to support. **-ẹvole** *adj.* favourable; propitious. **-ita** *f.* favourite; royal mistress. **-itịsmo** *m.* favouritism. **-ito** *part. adj.* favoured; favourite; *n.m.* favourite; pet.
**favule** *m.* haulm, dried beanstalks; bean-field.
**faziọne** *f.* faction, party, sect.
**faziọso** *adj.* factious, turbulent, seditious, subversive; *n.m.* agitator, rebel.
**fazzolẹtto** *m.* handkerchief; kerchief, head-scarf.
**febbra·io** *pr.n.m.* February.
**febbr-e** *f.* fever; excitement; burning desire; *avere la —*, to have a temperature; *la — del fieno*, hay-fever. **-icità** *f.* feverishness. **-icitante** *part. adj.* feverish. **-icitare** [A1 s] *intr.* (*aux.* avere) to have a fever, to be feverish. **-ifu·gio** *m.* febrifuge. **-ile** *adj.* febrile.
**Febo** *pr.n.m.* (myth.) Phoebus.
**fec·ci-a** *f.* dregs, lees, grounds, sediment; rabble, scum; (bot.) fumitory. **-a·ia** *f.* spigot-hole (in a cask), vent. **-ọso** *adj.* full of dregs; foul, base; impure. **-ume** *m.* dregs, lees; refuse; (fig.) scum, rabble.
**fec-i** *f.pl.* faeces, excrement, stools. **-ale** *adj.* faecal.
**feciale** *adj.* fetial.
**fecond-are** [A1 c] *tr.* to fertilize; to make fruitful; to make productive. **-ativo** *adj.* fecundative. **-atọre** *m.* fertilizer; *adj.* fertilizing. **-aziọne** *f.* fertilization; *-azione artificiale*, artificial insemination.
**fecondità** *f.* fecundity; fertility; productiveness; (fig.) richness, wealth.
**fecọndo** *adj.* fertile; fruitful; prolific; rich in yield.
**fẹde** *f.* faith, trust, confidence; belief, credence; creed; religion; *aver — in una persona*, to believe in someone; *serbare — a*, to keep faith with; *prestare — a*, to give credit to; *in — mia*, on my honour; *far —*, to bear witness; fidelity, honour, word of honour; safe-conduct; wedding-ring; honesty, integrity; document, certificate; *— di nascita*, birth-certificate; (leg.) faith; witness; *in buona —*, in good faith.
**fedẹle** *adj.* faithful, constant, true; loyal; *copia —*, exact copy; authentic, genuine; devout, orthodox; *ogni — minchione*, every Tom, Dick or Harry; *n.m.* loyal subject, believer, Christian; *i fedeli*, the faithful.
**fedeltà** *f. indecl.* fidelity, faithfulness, constancy; truth, accuracy; loyalty; (radio) definition; *alta —*, high fidelity.
**fe·dera** *f.* pillowcase; mattress cover.
**feder-ale** *adj.* federal; *la Germania —*, West Germany. **-alịsmo** *m.* federalism. **-alista** *m.*, *f.*, *adj.* federalist. **-ativo** *adj.* federative, confederal. **-ato** *part. adj.*, *n.m.* federate, confederate. **-aziọne** *f.* federation; confederation.
**fedi·fra-go** *adj.* (*pl.* **-ghi**) faithless; unfaithful; *n.m.* faithless person.
**fedina** *f.* (leg.) certificate; record.
**fedine** *f.pl.* side-whiskers.
**Fedra** *pr.n.f.* (myth.) Phaedra.
**fegatella** *f.* (bot.) common liverwort.
**fẹgat-o** *m.* (anat.) liver; *mal di —*, liver complaint; *olio di — di merluzzo*, cod-liver oil; (fig.) courage, guts. **-ọso** *adj.* liverish, bilious; peevish.
**fẹlc-e** *f.* (bot.) fern; *— aquilina*, bracken. **-ẹta** *f.*, **-ẹto** *m.*, **-iata** *f.* bed of ferns; grove of bracken.
**felice** *adj.* happy; contented; glad; delighted; fortunate, lucky; felicitous; *vento —*, favourable wind.
**felicità** *f.* happiness; felicity; bliss; success; *vi auguro ogni —*, I wish you every happiness; *felicità!*, God bless you!
**felicit-are** *tr.* [A1 s] to make happy, to bless; to call happy; *che Dio vi -i!*, may God bless you!; to congratulate; *rfl.* to congratulate; *mi -o con Lei per il suo successo*, I congratulate you on your success. **-aziọne** *f.* felicity; congratulation; *-azioni!*, congratulations!
**felino** *adj.*, *n.m.* (zool.) feline; *n.m. pl.* cats and other Felidae.
**fell-o** *adj.* fell, sinister, evil, impious; dire. **-ọne** *adj.* wicked; cruel; ferocious; (of a horse) vicious; (of a river) swollen and angry; *n.m.* villain. **-onẹsco** *adj.* (*m.pl.* **-onẹschi**) villainous. **-oni·a** *f.* felony; rebellion; treason, defection; wickedness.
**felp-a** *f.* plush. **-ato** *adj.* plush-covered; *passi -ati*, stealthy tread.
**feltr-are** [A1c] *tr.* (text.) to felt; to cover with felt; *rfl.* to become felted. **-atura** *f.* felting.
**fẹltr-o** *m.* felt garment of felt; under-blanket; saddle-cloth; filter, sieve. **-ino** *adj.* felt-like.
**fẹlza** *f.* (mil.) strong point; (Ven.) cabin of a gondola.
**fẹmmin-a** *f.* female; woman; girl; *scuola di maschi e -e*, co-educational school; *mala —*, loose woman; *vite —*, female screw; (carpen.) *— dell'incastro*, mortise. **-ẹzza** *f.* womanhood. **-ile** *adj.* feminine, womanly; female; *n.m.* feminine gender. **-inità** *f.* femininity, womanliness. **-ino** *adj.* feminine; *n.m.* femininity. **-ịsmo** *m.* feminism. **-ista** *m.*, *f. adj.* feminist.
**femmi·neo** *adj.* feminine; female; effeminate.
**fe·mor-e** *m.* (anat.) femur, thigh-bone. **-ale** *adj.* femoral.
**fend-ere** [B1] *tr.* to split, to break, to crack; to cleave; *rfl.* to crack, to split. **-ente** *part. adj.* splitting, cleaving; slashing; *n.m.* downward stroke. **-i·bile** *adj.* which can be split; liable to split or break. **-ineb·bia** *m. indecl.* (motor.) fog lamp. **-itọre** *m.* cutter, cleaver. **-itura** *f.* split, crack, cleft; slit; fissure, crevice.
**fenice** *f.* phoenix; (fig.) great rarity; *volere l'araba —*, to yearn for something unattainable.
**Feni·ci-a** *pr.n.f.* (hist.) Phoenicia. **-o** *adj.*, *n.m.* Phoenician.
**fe·nic-o** *adj.* (chem. pop.) carbolic; *acido —*, carbolic acid, phenol. **-ato** *adj.* soaked in phenol; *carta -ata*, carbolic paper.
**fenicot·tero** (orn.) flamingo.
**fenolo** *m.* (chem.) phenol, carbolic acid.

**fenomenale** *adj.* (philos.) phenomenal; (colloq.) extraordinary; amazing.
**feno·meno** *m.* phenomenon; (colloq.) marvel.
**fenomenologi·a** *f.* phenomenology.
**ferac-e** *adj.* fertile, fruitful; rich, productive. **-ità** *f.* fertility, productiveness.
**ferale** *adj.* deathly; gloomy; sinister.
**fe·retro** *m.* bier; coffin; *seguire il* —, to walk in a funeral procession.
**fe·ri-a** *f.* holiday, day of rest; *pl.* holidays; (leg.) vacation; *periodo annuale di -e retribuito,* annual holiday with pay. **-ale** *adj.* ordinary, not festive; *giorno -ale,* working-day; business day. **-almẹnte** *adv.* in an ordinary way, without ceremony. **-are** [A4] *intr.* (*aux.* avere) to keep holiday, to be on holiday. **-ato** *adj.* pertaining to holiday; *giorno -ato,* holiday; *n.m.* holiday.
**ferigno** *adj.* feral; bestial; wild.
**ferino** *adj.* ferine, feral; bestial.
**fer-ire** [D2] *tr.* to wound, to injure; (fig.) to strike, to touch; — *la vista,* to catch the eye. **-i·bile** *adj.* vulnerable. **-ito** *part. adj.* wounded; hit, struck; *rimanere -ito,* to be wounded, to be hit; *n.m.* wounded man; (mil.) casualty; *i -iti di guerra,* the war wounded. **-itọia** *f.* arrowslit-view; louvre, air hole.
**ferita**[1] *f.* wound; — *mortale,* fatal wound; — *che sanguina,* bleeding wound; — *rimarginata,* wound that has closed up.
**ferita**[2] *f.* wounded woman.
**ferità** *f.* wildness, savageness; cruelty.
**ferma-bu·e** *m. indecl.* (bot.) rest-harrow. **-carte** *m. indecl.* paper-weight. **-cravatta** *m. indecl.* tie-pin. **-porta** *m. indecl.* doorstop.
**ferma·glio** *m.* clasp, clip; fastening; buckle, brooch; paperclip.
**ferm-are** [A1] *tr.* to stop, to halt; to detain, to arrest; to parcook; to fix, to make firm; — *l'animo su,* to fix one's mind on; — *l'accampamento,* to set up camp; — *la successione,* to ensure the succession; — *un accordo,* to conclude an agreement; — *un punto,* to decide a matter; *rfl.* to stop, to halt; to stay; *il treno si -a,* the train is stopping; *il mio orologio s'è -ato,* my watch has stopped. **-ata** *f.* stop, pause; stopping-place; *-ata facoltativa,* request stop; (mus.) pause. **-atura** *f.* fastening; clasp.
**ferment-are** [A1 c] *intr.* (*aux.* essere) to ferment; *tr.* to cause to ferment. **-aziọne** *f.* fermentation.
**fermẹnto** *m.* ferment; yeast, leaven, barm; (biol.) enzyme; (fig.) ferment, excitement.
**fẹrm-o** *adj.* firm, steady, stable; *salute mal -a,* poor health; certain, sure, firm; *tenere per* —, to be convinced of; motionless, still, stationary; *acqua -a,* stagnant water; — *come un piolo,* stock still; — *in posta,* poste restante; (mil.) — *là!,* halt!; *punto* —, full stop; (mus.) *canto* —, plainchant; *n.m.* arrest, detention; seizure, distraint; firmness, stability; catch, hook; *dare il* — *a,* to put a stop to; *cane da* —, pointer, setter. **-ẹzza** *f.* firmness; stability, steadiness.
**ferọce** *adj.* ferocious, fierce; wild, savage, harsh; proud.
**fero·c-ia** *f.* (*pl.* **-ie**) ferocity, brutality; *pl.* acts of ferocity. **-ità** *f.* wildness, savageness; ferocity; boldness.
**Fero·e** *pr.n.f.pl.* (geog.) Faroes, Faroe Islands.
**ferracavallo** *m. indecl.* farrier, shoeing-smith.
**ferrac·cia** *f.* (ichth.) ray; — *pastinaca,* sting ray.
**ferra·glia** *f.* scrap-iron; (mil.) grapeshot.
**ferragọsto** *pr.n.m.* August State holiday (15 August).
**ferra·io, ferraro** *m.* blacksmith.
**ferram-e** *m.* quantity of iron, iron goods; *negozio di -i,* ironmongery. **-ẹnto** *m.* (*pl.* **-i** *m.*, **-a** *f.*) iron tool; *pl.* ironware, hardware; *negozio di -enta,* ironmonger's shop.
**ferrana** *f.* (agric.) forage crop.
**ferr-are** [A1] *tr.* to bind with iron; to shackle; — *un cavallo,* to shoe a horse. **-ante** *part. adj.* *maniscalco -ante,* farrier. **-ato** *part. adj.* shod; fitted with iron; *stivali -ati,* hobnailed boots; *strada -ata,* railway.
**ferrata** *f.* iron grating; railway.
**ferravec·chio** *m.* dealer in old iron.
**fer·reo** *adj.* iron; (fig.) severe; harsh.
**ferreri·a** *f.* iron implements, ironmongery.
**ferri-bot** *m. indecl.*, **-botto** *m.* ferry-boat; train ferry.
**fer·rico** *adj.* (chem.) ferric.
**ferriera** *f.* iron-mine; iron-foundry; tool-bag.
**ferri·fero** *adj.* ferriferous; iron-yielding.
**ferrigno** *adj.* ferruginous; like iron; robust.
**ferr-o** *m.* iron; — *in verghe,* bar iron; *minerale di* —, iron ore; *tocca* —*!,* an Ital. equivalent to Eng. 'touch wood!'; iron implement; *i -i del mestiere,* the tools of the trade; *-i da calza,* knitting needles; — *da stiro,* flat-iron; — *da cavallo,* horseshoe; *pl.* chains, shackles, irons; *mettere ai -i,* to clap in irons; *mettere i -i a,* to put the handcuffs on; (cul.) *ai -i,* grilled; (poet.) sword. **-ọso** *adj.* (chem.; metall.) ferrous.
**ferrov-i·a** *f.* railway, railroad; railway station; **-ia·rio** *adj.* railway; *materiale -iario,* rolling-stock. **-iere** *m.* railway employee.
**ferrug-igno, -i·neo, -inọso** *adj.* ferruginous; rust-coloured.
**ferruminare** [A1 s] *tr.* to weld.
**fer·til-e** *adj.* fertile, fruitful; productive; prolific. **-ità** *f.* fertility; richness; productivity.
**fertilizz-are** [A1] *tr.* to fertilize. **-ante** *part. adj.* fertilizing; *n.m.* fertilizer. **-aziọne** *f.* fertilization; (agric.) *-azione a spandimento,* top dressing.
**fe·rula** *f.* (bot.) rod, stick, cane; splint.
**fer·v-ere** [B1] *intr.* (*aux.* avere) to be fervent; to be ardent; to blaze; to seethe; *-e la disputa,* the dispute is at its height. **-ẹnte** *part. adj.* fervent; blazing, hot; seething; zealous.
**fer·vid-o** *adj.* fervid, ardent; impassioned; *-i auguri,* warmest wishes. **-ẹzza** *f.* fervour; warmth, heat.
**fervọr-e** *m.* fervour; vehemence; *nel* — *della battaglia,* in the heat of battle. **-ino** *m.* (eccl.) exhortation; (colloq.) a 'talking-to'; *fare un -ino a,* to scold. **-ọso** *adj.* fervent; ardent; zealous, impassioned.
**fẹss-o** *adj.* split, cracked, broken; cloven; (colloq.) 'cracked'; *animali dall'unghia -a,* cloven-footed animals; *n.m.* crack, chink, opening. **-ura** *f.* fissure, split; chink; crevice.
**festa** *f.* feast; festivity; party; fête, entertainment; — *da ballo,* ball; feast-day, holiday; Saint's day; name-day; *feste di Natale,* Christmas holidays; *mezza* —, half-holiday; *far* —, to be on holiday; *abiti da* —, 'Sunday best'; *fare* — *a uno,* to welcome someone.
**festante** *adj.* rejoicing, joyful, jubilant.
**festeggi-are** [A3 c] *tr.* to celebrate; to keep as a holiday. **-ante** *part. adj.* feasting, rejoicing, merry; *n.m., f.* merry-maker. **-ato** *part. adj.* fêted, celebrated; *n.m.* guest of honour.
**festẹvole** *adj.* festive; merry; joyous; gay, cheerful.
**festiv-o** *adj.* festive, festal; *i giorni -i,* official holidays; *abiti -i,* Sunday clothes. **-ità** *f. indecl.* festivity; conviviality; gaiety.
**festọne** *m.* festoon, garland.
**festọs-o** *adj.* gay; joyful, cheerful; merry; jovial, hearty. **-ità** *f.* merriment, gaiety; festiveness.
**festu-ca** *f.* piece of straw, a straw; *vedere la* — *nell'occhio altrui e non la trave nel proprio,* to see the mote in another's eye,

and not the beam in one's own. -**co** *m.* (*pl.* -**chi**) piece of straw; stalk; tendril.

**feten-te** *adj.* stinking, fetid; (fig.) foul, disgusting. -**za** *f.* stench.

**fetic·c-io** *m.* fetish; idol. -**ismo** *m.* fetishism; idolatry.

**fe·tid-o** *adj.* fetid, stinking; foul, filthy. -**ezza,** -**ità** *f.* baseness, foulness; stench. -**oso** *adj.* filthy; foul. -**ume** *m.* stench, fetor; foulness; stinking things.

**fet-o** *m.* foetus; egg of insect. -**ale** *adj.* foetal.

**Fetonte** *pr.n.m.* (myth.) Phaeton.

**fetore** *m.* fetor, stench.

**fett-a** *f.* slice; clod of earth; ribbon, band; (cul.) fillet; *tagliare a -e*, to slice. -**uccine** *f.pl.* kind of pasta cut in strips.

**fe·ud-o** *m.* feud, fee, fief; feudal domain; feudal tribute. -**ale** *adj.* feudal. -**alismo** *m.* feudalism. -**ata·rio** *adj.*; *n.m.* feudatory; lord of manor; landed proprietor.

**fia** *3rd pers. sing.* future of **essere**, *q.v.*; (poet.) will be; shall be; may be.

**fiab-a** *f.* fairy-tale; fib, taradiddle. -**esco** *adj.* (*m.pl.* -**eschi**) fabulous; like a fairy-tale.

**fiacca** *f.* listlessness; slackness; lassitude.

**fiaccacollo** *m. indecl.* scatterbrain; harum-scarum.

**fiacc-are** [A2] *tr.* to tire, to weary, to exhaust; to weaken; *rfl.* (*acc.* of *prn.* 'si') to grow weary, to tire; *rfl.* (*dat.* of *prn.* 'si') *-arsi il collo*, to break one's neck.

**fiac-co** *adj.* (*pl.* -**chi**) weary, fatigued; exhausted; feeble; slack, lazy. -**chezza** *f.* weariness; exhaustion; lassitude; weakness; slackness, laziness.

**fiac·col-a** *f.* torch, flame; (eng.) blowlamp; *portatore di —*, torchbearer, link-boy. -**are** [A1 s] *intr.* (*aux.* avere) to flare. -**ata** *f.* torchlight procession.

**fiaccon-a** *f.* exhaustion, languor; lazy woman. -**e** *m.* idler; lazybones; *adj.* lazy, idle.

**fiala** *f.* phial.

**fiamm-a** *f.* flame; flare, blaze; *dare alle -e*, to burn; *andare in -e*, to go up in flames; (fig.) passion, love; sweetheart; *gli vennero le -e al viso*, he grew red in the face; (motor.) *ritorno di —*, backfire.

**fiamm-are** [A1] *intr.* (*aux.* avere) to flame; to flare; to blaze. -**ante** *part. adj.* flaming; blazing; flashing; *nuovo -ante*, brand new; *n.m.* (orn.) flamingo. -**ata** *f.* blaze, flare.

**fiammeggi-are** [A3 c] *intr.* (*aux.* avere) to flame, to blaze; to shine, to sparkle, to flash. -**ante** *part. adj.* flaming, blazing; shining.

**fiammi·fer-o** *n.m.* match; *— di sicurezza*, safety match; *scatola di -i*, box of matches; *mi favorisca un —?*, may I trouble you for a match?; *adj.* flame-bearing.

**fiammin-go** *adj.* (*m.pl.* -**ghi**) Flemish; *la lingua -ga*, the Flemish language; *n.m.* Fleming; Flemish; (orn.) flamingo.

**fianc-are** [A2] *tr.* to flank. -**ata** *f.* side, flank; broadside; (motor.) side panel; *-ata del parafango*, mudguard apron.

**fiancheggiare** [A3 c] *tr.* to flank, to border; to line; to help, to support; (mil.) to cover the flank of.

**fian-co** *m.* (*pl.* -**chi**) flank, side; *avere una punta nel —*, to have a stitch in one's side; *stare a — di qualcuno*, to be at someone's side; (theatr.) *parte di —*, supporting role; (mil.) wing; flank; *girare il —*, to turn a flank; (naut.) ship's side; *adv. phr. di —*, sideways, obliquely.

**Fiandr-a,** -**e** *pr.n.f., pl.* (geog.) Flanders.

**fiasca** *f.* flask; jar; hip-flask; (mil.) water-bottle.

**fias-co** *m.* (*pl.* -**chi**) glass bottle (with straw covering); (fig.) failure, fiasco; *far —*, to fail. -**cheggiare** [A3 c] *intr.* (*aux.* essere) to fail, to be unsuccessful; (theatr.) to be a flop. -**cheri·a** *f.* quantity of bottles. -**chetteri·a** *f.* retail wine-shop.

**fiatare** [A1] *intr.* (*aux.* avere) to breathe; to whisper.

**fiato** *m.* breath; breathing; *tirar —*, to draw breath; *— grosso*, panting; *sin che c'è —, c'è speranza*, while there's life, there's hope; (mus.) *strumenti a —*, wind instruments.

**fib·bia** *f.* buckle.

**fibr-a** *f.* fibre; (fig.) stamina. -**oso** *adj.* fibrous.

**fi·bula** *f.* (Rom. antiq.) fibula, buckle; (anat.) fibula.

**fica** *f.* (vulg.) female genitals.

**ficcanas-o,** -**i** *m. indecl.* Paul Pry; Nosey Parker.

**ficc-are** [A2] *tr.* to thrust; to drive in, to poke; to plant; *rfl.* (*acc.* of *prn.* 'si') to thrust oneself, to intrude; to hide; (*dat.* of *prn.* 'si') *-arsi in capo una cosa*, to get a thing into one's head. -**atoia** *f.*, -**atoio** *m.* quagmire. -**atura** *f.* thrusting, driving; pushing.

**fichereto, ficheto** *m.* fig-orchard.

**fico** *m.* (*pl.* **fichi**) (bot.) fig-tree, fig; *— d'India*, prickly pear; *— della gomma*, India rubber tree; (fig.) *— secco*, dried fig; *non vale un — secco*, it's not worth a fig.

**fidanza** *f.* confidence, trust; security, guarantee.

**fidanz-are** [A1] *tr.* to betroth; to promise in marriage; *rfl.* (*prep.* con) to become engaged (to); *recip. rfl.* to become engaged to each other. -**amento** *m.* engagement of marriage. -**ato** *part. adj.* betrothed, engaged; about to be married; *n.m.* fiancé; (fig.) boy-friend. -**ata** *f.* fiancée; (fig.) girl-friend.

**fid-are** [A1] *tr.* to entrust, to confide; *intr.* (*aux.* avere; *prep.* in) to trust; to confide, to have confidence; *— in Dio*, to trust in God; *rfl.* (*prep.* di) to trust, to rely upon; *non ti — !*, beware! -**ato** *part. adj.* trustworthy.

**fidecommiss-o** *adj.* (leg.) entrusted; *n.m.* fideicommissum. -**a·rio** *adj.* (leg.) entrusted; fiduciary; *n.m.* beneficiary, trustee.

**fidecom-mit·tere,** -**mettere** [C20] *tr.* (leg.) to entrust; to leave (by will) in trust.

**fidente** *adj.* trusting, confident.

**Fi·dia** *pr.n.m.* Phidias.

**fido**[1] *adj.* trusty, faithful; devoted.

**fido**[2] *m.* (comm.) credit; *a —*, on credit; *far —*, to give credit.

**fidu·ci-a** *f.* confidence; trust; *— in sè*, self-confidence; *riporre — in*, to place trust in; *voto di —*, vote of confidence; *di —*, confidential; (leg.) trust. -**a·rio** *adj.* (leg.) fiduciary; *n.m.* trustee. -**oso** *adj.* confident; trustful.

**fiele** *m.* (anat.) bile; (med.) jaundice; (fig.) gall, rancour.

**fien-o** *m.* hay; *pagliaio di —*, haystack; *febbre da —*, hay-fever. -**ale** *adj.* relating to hay; *forca -ale*, hay-fork. -**ile** *m.* hay-loft; barn.

**fiera**[1] *f.* fair, market; bazaar; show; exhibition; *— di bestiame*, cattle-market; *— di beneficenza*, charity-bazaar.

**fiera**[2] *f.* wild animal, wild beast; (fig.) beast, brute.

**fier-o** *adj.* proud; bold; undaunted; harsh, severe; cruel, savage; fierce, wild. -**ezza** *f.* pride; boldness; fierceness.

**fievol-e** *adj.* weak, feeble. -**ezza** *f.* weakness, feebleness; debility.

**fifa**[1] (orn.) peewit.

**fif-a**[2] *f.* (mil. slang; colloq.) fear, 'blue funk'. -**one** *m.* coward. -**oso** *adj.* cowardly; afraid.

**fig·gere** [C12] *tr.* to fix; to drive in; to stick; *— gli occhi su*, to fix one's gaze on; *rfl.* (*dat.* of *prn.* 'si') *figgersi in capo*, to get into one's head.

**fi·glia** *f.* daughter; girl; (comm.) counterfoil; *bollettario a madre e —*, block of tickets with counterfoils.

**figli-are** [A4] *tr.* to bring forth young, to give birth to; to produce; *abs.* to calve; to lamb; to foal. -**ata** *f.* litter.

**figliastr-a** *f.* stepdaughter. -**i** *m.pl.* stepchildren. -**o** *m.* stepson.

**fi·glio** *m.* son; *mio —*, my son; *il mio — maggiore*, my eldest son; *pl.* sons; children; descendants; offspring; young (of an animal); suckers (of a plant); *tra maschi e femmine, ebbe sei figli*, he had six children, male and female.

**figlioc·ci-a** *f.* goddaughter. **-o** *m.* godson.

**figli(u)ol-a** *f.* daughter; girl; *una bella —*, a good-looking girl. **-o** *m.* son; boy; young (of an animal); (bot.) sucker. **-ame** *m.* a lot of children; brats, kids. **-anza** *f.* children, progeny.

**fi·gnol-o, fignol-o** *m.* boil. **-ọso** *adj.* suffering from boils.

**fi·gulo** *m.* potter.

**figur-a** *f.* figure; form, shape; appearance, aspect; (cards) court-card; symbol; *in — umana*, in human shape; *far bella —*, to cut a fine figure, to look very impressive; *che — !*, what a fool he made of himself!; apparition, spectre; (art) *scuola di —*, life class; (naut.) figurehead. **-ale** *adj.* figurative.

**figur-are** [A1] *tr.* to figure, to shape, to form; to represent, to symbolize; *intr.* (*aux.* avere) to act, to behave; *— bene*, to behave decently; to appear; to be clearly visible; to cut a fine figure; to pretend; *rfl.* (*acc.* of *prn.* 'si') to imagine oneself, to suppose oneself; *rfl.* (*dat.* of *prn.* 'si') to picture to oneself; to think; *-arsi!*, just fancy!; *figùrati*, of course. **-a·bile** *adj.* imaginable. **-ativo** *adj.* figurative, symbolic; *arte -ativa*, representational art. **-ato** *part. adj.* figured; *libro -ato*, illustrated book; *linguaggio -ato*, figurative language.

**figurin-o** *m.* fashion-model; sketch of model; fashion-magazine; rascal; *pl.* (theatr.; cinem.; telev.) sketches for costumes. **-ista** *m.* (motor.) body design stylist; *f.* (*pl.f.* **-iste**) dress-designer.

**figurista** *m.* (paint.) figure painter; sculptor of human figures.

**figuro** *m.* scoundrel, cad.

**fila** *f.* row, line; *mettere in —*, to place in a row; *far —*, to queue; *tre giorni di —*, three days running; (mil.) file; *serrare le file*, to close the ranks.

**filac·ci-a** *f.* ravelling, shred of cloth; rope yarn; lint. **-o** *m.* (naut.) old rope; rope yard. **-ọso** *adj.* threadbare, frayed; (of meat) stringy.

**filamẹnt-o** *m.* (*pl.* **-i** *m.*, **-a** *f.*) filament, thread; fibre.

**filand-a** *f.* (silkb.) silk factory; spinning-mill. **-a·ia** *f.* silk-spinner.

**filandra** *f.* (zool.) thread worm.

**filantr-opi·a** *f.* philanthropy. **-o·pico** *adj.* philanthropic. **-opiṣmo** *m.* philanthropism.

**filan·tropo** *m.* philanthropist.

**fil-are**[1] *tr.* [A1] to spin; to exude; *— sangue*, to ooze blood; (naut.) *— dodici miglia all'ora*, to steam (at) twelve knots; *intr.* (*aux.* avere) (colloq.) to clear out, to make off; *-a!*, clear off!; *— all'inglese*, to take French leave; to go stringy; *la candela -a*, the candle is smoking; to purr; to proceed, to follow logically; *intr.* (*aux.* essere) to file past. **-ante** *part. adj.* spinning; viscous; *stella -ante*, shooting-star. **-ata** *f.* long line, row. **-atera** *f.* succession; string; rigmarole. **-atic·cio** *m.* floss-silk.

**filare**[2] *m.* row, line; vein of minerals; (colloq.) line of writing; *n.m.* (naut.) stanchion; *pl.* battens of a hatch.

**filarmo·nic-o** *adj.* (mus.) philharmonic; *n.m.* music lover; *società dei -i*, philharmonic society. **-a** *f.* music society.

**filastr-occa, -oc·cola** *f.* rigmarole; nonsense-poetry; ballad; rhymed charm.

**filat-eli·a, -e·lica** *f.* philately. **-e·lico** *adj.* philatelic; *n.m.* philatelist.

**filẹtto** *m.* filament; fine thread; fillet.

**filiale** *adj.* filial; *n.f.* (comm.) branch.

**filiaziọne** *f.* filiation; derivation; (leg.) issue, offspring.

**filifọrme** *adj.* filiform, thread-like.

**filigran-a** *f.* filigree; (paperm.) watermark. **-ato** *adj.* filigreed; *carta -ata*, watermarked paper.

**Filippi** *pr.n.f.* (geog.) Philippi.

**filip·pic-a** *f.* Philippic, invective. **-o** *adj.* Philippic.

**Filippine** *pr.n.f.pl.* (geog.) Philippines.

**filippin-o** *m.* (eccl.) Oratorian, Father of the Oratory.

**filist-e·o** *adj.*, *n.m.* Philistine. **-eiṣmo** *m.* philistinism.

**film** *m. indecl.* (cinem.) film; *— muto*, silent film; *— sonoro*, film with sound track; *— parlato*, talkie. **-ina** *f. dim.* film strip. **-i·stico** *adj.* pertaining to films; *l'industria -istica*, the film industry. **-oteca** *f.* library of films.

**film-are** [A1] *tr.* (cinem.) to film, to shoot. **-a·bile** *adj.* suitable for filming; photogenic.

**fil-o** *m.* (*pl.* **-i** *m.*, **-a** *f.*) thread; twine; string; clothes line; *— per cucire*, sewing thread; *— di perle*, string of pearls; *— di ferro*, wire; *— spinato*, barbed wire; *telegrafo senza -i*, wireless telegraphy; *— d'erba*, blade of grass; cutting-edge; *un — d'acqua*, a tiny stream of water; *non c'è — di speranza*, there is not the slightest hope; *rispondere con un — di voce*, to reply faintly; the grain (of wood); *— di trama*, woof; *— di ordito*, warp; clue; thread of an argument; *manovrare le -a*, to pull the strings; *per - e per segno*, exactly; *di —*, consecutively; *far le -a*, to be viscous (of a liquid). **-ọso** *adj.* stringy; thread-like.

**fi·lobus** *m. indecl.* trolley-bus.

**filocarro** *m.* trolley-truck.

**filodramma·tico** *adj.* philodramatic; *n.m.* amateur actor; *società dei filodrammatici*, amateur dramatic society.

**filologi·a** *f.* literary study; scholarship; philology.

**filolo·gico** *adj.* scholarly; literary; *circolo —*, literary club, modern language club.

**filo·logo** *m.* literary expert; classical scholar; linguist.

**Filom-ela, -ena** *pr.n.f.* (myth.) Philomel; (poet.) nightingale.

**filọne** *m.* coarse thread; rogue; *un — di pane*, a long French loaf; flow; *il — della marea*, the race of the tide; (miner.) vein, seam; inclination, bent; *prendere il — di*, to develop a tendency to.

**filoṣofare** [A1 s] *tr.*, *intr.* (*aux.* avere) to philosophize.

**filoṣofi·a** *f.* philosophy; philosophical system; (fig.) resignation; *con —*, philosophically.

**filoṣo·fico** *adj.* philosophical; resigned; absent-minded.

**filo·ṣof-o** *m.* philosopher; student of philosophy; (fig.) resigned person; *fare il —*, to talk ponderously. **-ale** *adj.* philosophic; *pietra -ale*, philosopher's stone.

**filov-i·a** *f.* trolley-bus route; aerial railway. **-ia·rio** *adj.* relating to a trolley-bus; *linea -iaria*, trolley-bus line.

**filtr-are** [A1] *tr.* to filter; to strain, to percolate; (fig.) to analyse, to clarify; *intr.* (*aux.* essere) to ooze, to filter through. **-ato** *part. adj.* filtered; *n.m.* filtrate.

**filtro** *m.* filter; strainer; philtre; love-potion; cup of coffee (percolated); *sigarette con —*, cork-tipped cigarettes.

**filza** *f.* string; series; *— di perle*, string of pearls; *— di bugie*, string of lies.

**fim·bri-a** *f.* fringe, border, hem. **-ato** *adj.* fringed, hemmed.

**fimo** *m.* dung, manure.

**final-e** *adj.* final; last; ultimate; conclusive; definitive; (theol.) *giudizio —*, Last Judgement; *n.m.* (mus.) finale; *f.* (sport) final. **-mẹnte** *adv.* finally, at last; eventually; in the end. **-ista** *m.*, *f.* (sport) finalist. **-ità** *f. indecl.* finality; purpose, aim.

**finanza** *f.* finance; *pl.* financial situation; cash, money; Treasury; *il Ministro delle Finanze*, Chancellor of the Exchequer.

**finanz-iare** [A4] *tr.* to finance. **-ia·rio** *adj.* financial. **-iatọre** *m.*

backer, financer; sleeping partner. **-iere** *m.* financier.

**finca** *f.* column in a register book; *registro ad una sola —*, single-cash account book; *registro a doppia —*, double-cash account book.

**fine**[1] **1.** *f.* (sometimes *m.*) end, close, conclusion, ending; termination, completion; result; *a — mese*, at the end of the month; *alla —, in —*, in the end, at last, finally; *in fin dei conti*, when all is said and done; *buona — e buon principio!*, happy New Year!; *in fin di vita*, on the point of death. **2.** *m.* (never *f.*) aim, purpose, intention, end; *un secondo —*, an ulterior aim; *a che — ?*, to what end?; *a — di*, in order to; *a fin di bene*, with good intentions; *il — giustifica i mezzi*, the end justifies the means.

**fine**[2] *adj.* fine, refined, pure; subtle, cunning; thin, slender; *n.m.* thin part; delicate thing.

**finestr-a** *f.* window; *— a ghigliottina*, sash-window; *porta —*, French window; *affacciarsi alla —*, to appear at the window; *la — dà sulla piazza*, the window looks onto the square; opening. **-ata** *f.* slamming of a window; *una -ata di sole*, a gleam of sunshine. **-ato** *adj.* glazed; *n.m.* row of windows. **-ino** *m. dim.* window of a rlwy. compartment; booking-office window.

**finẹzza** *f.* fineness, refinement, delicacy; subtlety, sharpness; favour, courtesy.

**fin·g-ere** [C5] *tr., intr.* (*aux.* avere) to feign, to pretend; to imagine, to invent; to suppose; to simulate, to counterfeit; to represent, to figure; *-iamo pure che sia così*, just suppose that it is so; to be insincere; *rfl.* (*acc.* of *prn.* 'si') to feign oneself, to pretend to be; (*dat.* of *prn.* 'si') to imagine to oneself. **-itọre** *m.* pretender, deceiver.

**finimẹnto** *m.* finishing, completion; finishing touches; complete set; *un — da tavola*, a set of table-linen; *pl.* harness, trappings; horse brasses.

**finimọndo** *m.* end of the world; disaster; chaos.

**fin-ire** [D2] *tr.* to finish, to terminate, to end; to conclude; *-iscila!*, stop it!; *— uno*, to kill someone; *intr.* (*aux.* avere, essere) to end, to finish, to come to an end; to die; *ha -ito di penare*, his sufferings are ended; *dove va a — questa strada ?*, where does this road end up?; *dove è andato a — ?*, what became of him? **-iente** *part. adj.* finishing, ending; *tutte le parole -ienti in a*, all words ending in a. **-itẹzza** *f.* finish, perfection. **-itivo** *adj.* final; *modo -itivo*, indicative mood. **-ito** *part. adj.* finished, ended; settled; exhausted; *farla -ita*, to have done with it; perfect, accomplished; finite. **-itura** *f.* finish; finishing touches. **-iziọne** *f.* end, termination; (industr.) fittings, trimmings.

**fini·timo** *adj.* neighbouring, bordering, adjacent.

**Finlan·d-ia** *pr.n.f.* (geog.) Finland. **-ẹse** *adj., n.m., f.* Finnish; Finn.

**fino**[1] *adj.* fine, pure, noble; refined; sharp, acute, shrewd, subtle; delicate, thin.

**fin-o**[2] *prep.* until, till; as far as, up to; *— a quando ?*, how long?; *fin da ieri*, since yesterday; *— a che, fin tanto che*, until; *— in chiesa*, even in church. **-allora** *adv.* up to that time. **-anche, -anco** *adv.* even. **-chẹ̀** *conj.* until, till; as long as, while; *aspettami -chè io venga*, wait for me until I come. **-ọra** *adv.* until now. **-tanto, -tantochẹ̀** *conj.* until, till; while.

**finoc·chio** *m.* (bot.) fennel.

**finodicitọre** *m.* compère; patter-comedian.

**finta** *f.* feint; pretence; *fare — di*, to pretend to.

**finto** *adj.* feigned, counterfeit, simulated; insincere; *denti finti*, false teeth; *fiori finti*, artificial flowers.

**finziọne** *f.* feigning, deceiving; fiction, invention; falsehood, sham; figment; (leg.) *— giuridica*, legal fiction.

**fio** *m. indecl.* penalty; *ne pagherà il —*, he will pay for it.

**fiocc-are** [A2] *intr.* (*aux.* essere) to fall thickly, to drift down in flakes; *la neve -a*, it is snowing; (fig.) to be numerous; to come thick and fast; *-arle a*, to insult, to abuse. **-ante** *part. adj.* falling in flakes; abounding. **-ato** *part. adj.* snow-clad; hoary, flecked with white.

**fioc-co** *m.* (*pl.* **-chi**) knot, bow; lock; flock (of wool); powder-puff; flake of snow; tassel; tuft; *il — delle scarpe*, shoelaces tied in a bow; *il — della cravatta*, the knot in a tie; *un berretto col —*, a cap with a tassel; *fare il —*, to do the trick. **-chẹtto** *m.* (mil.) tassel, badge, tab.

**fioc·colo** *m.* snow-flake.

**fio·cin-a, fiocin-a** *f.* harpoon; trident. **-are** [A1S, A1] *tr.* to harpoon.

**fio·cine** *m.* pip, stone (*e.g.* of grapes).

**fio-co** *adj.* (*m.pl.* **-chi**) weak, feeble, faint; dim; hoarse. **-chẹzza** *f.* hoarseness; faintness; feebleness, weakness.

**fionco** *m.* halyard.

**fiọnda** *m.* sling; catapult.

**fiora·i-a** *f.*, **-o** *m.* flower-seller; florist.

**fior-ale** *adj.* floral. **-ame** *m.* flowering branch; floral design.

**fiorato** *adj.* flowered.

**fiordaliṣo** *m.* (bot.) fleur-de-lis; (pop.) corn-flower.

**fiordo** *m.* (geog.) fiord, fjord.

**fiọr-e** *m.* flower; blossom; bloom; *-i di campo*, wild flowers; *-i di serra*, hot-house flowers; *la città del Fiore*, Florence; *— a mandorla*, clock (on a sock or stocking); the flower, the best, the pick; *fior di latte*, top of the milk; surface; *a fior d'acqua*, on the surface of the water; *a fior di pelle*, just grazing the skin; abundance; *fior di quattrini*, lots of money; *pl.* (cards) clubs.

**fiorentin-o** *adj.* Florentine; *n.m.* Florentine, the Florentine tongue; a Florentine. **-iṣmo** *m.* Florentine expression.

**Fiorenz-a** *pr.n.f.* Florence. **-o** *pr.n.m.* Florentius.

**fiorẹtt-o** *m.* little flower; flowerlet; (fig.) selection; selected passage, the 'cream' or highest quality; (fencing) foil; good deed. **-atura** *f.* flourish; embellishment.

**fiori·fero** *adj.* floriferous, flower-bearing.

**fiorino** *m.* little flower; (numis.) Florentine coin; florin.

**fior-ire** [D2] *intr.* (*aux.* essere) to flower, to bloom, to blossom; (fig.) to flourish, to prosper, to thrive; to be covered with mould; to peel (of plaster); to cause to flower; to strew with flowers; to embellish. **-ente** *part. adj.* flourishing, prospering, thriving; flowering, blooming. **-ita** *f.* flowering; *-ita di neve*, sprinkling of snow; *-ita di canti*, collection of songs. **-ito** *part. adj.* flowering; flowery; florid; flourishing; *vino -ito*, wine on which mould is beginning to form. **-itura** *f.* flowering; flourishing; time of flowering; efflorescence; embellishment.

**fiorista** *m., f.* (art) flower-painter.

**fiorọne** *m.* (archit.) rose-window.

**fiorran·cio** *m.* (bot.) marigold.

**fiott-are** [A1] *intr.* (*aux.* avere) to gurgle, to gush, to murmur (of waters); to wave, to sway, to undulate; to grumble, to whimper. **-ìo** *m.* gurgling, murmuring; whimpering.

**fiotto** *m.* stream; wave; murmur; whimper; lamentation; surge; lapping of water; ebb; flow; *— di luce*, flood of light.

**Firenze** *pr.n.f.* (geog.) Florence.

**firma** *f.* signature; name, celebrity; *falsificare una —*, to forge a signature.

**firmamẹnto** *m.* firmament.

**firmano** *m.* firman, decree, edict.

**firm-are** [A1] *tr.* to sign; to ratify; *— in bianco un assegno*, to sign a blank cheque; *— per procura*, to sign per pro. **-ante** *m., f.* signatory.

**fiṣa·lia** *f.* (zool.) Portuguese man-o'-war.
**fiṣarmo·nica** *f.* (mus.) accordion; piano-accordion.
**fiscale** *adj.* fiscal; relating to inland revenue; *anno* –, financial year; (leg.) *avvocato* –, Judge Advocate General; (fig.) rigorous; inquisitorial; *n.m.* (leg.) inspector of public revenue.
**fischi-are** [A4] *intr.* (*aux.* avere) to whistle; to hiss; to boo; to hoot; *-ano gli uccelli*, the birds are singing; to be ragged, to be worn out (of clothes); *tr.* to whistle; to hiss, to boo. **-ante** *part. adj.* whistling; hissing; *lettere -anti*, sibilants. **-ata** *f.* whistle, whistling; hissing; *mi è costata una -ata*, I got it for a song. **-erellare** [A1] *intr.* (*aux.* avere) to whistle softly.
**fi·schio** *m.* whistle; hiss; *accogliere con fischi*, to greet with hisses; *non me ne importa un* –, I don't care a hoot; (naut.) ship's siren; *un colpo di* –, one blast on the siren; – *del nostromo*, boatswain's pipe.
**fis-co** *m.* (*pl.* **-chi**) public treasury; Treasury; inland revenue.
**fisetere, fisetro** *m.* (zool.) sperm whale.
**fi·ṣica** *f.* physics.
**fi·ṣico** *adj.* physical; *n.m.* physicist; physique; figure, appearance.
**fi·ṣima** *f.* (usu. *pl.*) whim, caprice, fancy.
**fiṣi-ochi·mica** *f.* physio-chemistry. **-ochi·mico** *adj.* physio-chemical; *n.m.* physio-chemist. **-ognomi·a** *f.*, **-ogno·mica** *f.* physiognomy.
**fiṣi-ologi·a** *f.* physiology. **-olo·gico** *adj.* physiological. **-o·logo** *m.* physiologist.
**fiṣionomi·a** *f.* physiognomy; features, countenance; external appearance.
**fiṣioter-api·a** *f.* physiotherapy. **-a·pico** *adj.* physiotherapeutic.
**fiṣo** *adj.* (poet.) fixed, intent; *adv.* fixedly; *guardare* –, to stare at.
**fiss-are** [A1] *tr.* to fix; to make fast; to establish, to set up; to establish, to set up; to arrange; to book, to engage; to stare at; *rfl.* to become fixed; to settle. **-ag·gio** *m.* fastening; clamp, fastener; (photog.) fixing; **-ativo** *adj.*, *n.m.* fixative. **-atọre** *m.* fixer; fixative. **-aziọne** *f.* fixation, fixing; fixed idea.
**fis·sile** *adj.* tending to split; (atom. phys.) fissile.
**fissiọne** *f.* (atom. phys.) fission; *la – dell'atomo*, the splitting of the atom.
**fissità** *f.* fixity; *guardare con* –, to stare at; *la – delle specie*, the immutability of species; (cinem.) steadiness (of picture).
**fisso** *adj.* fixed; fast, firm, steady; fixed, arranged; *prezzo* –, price on which there can be no discount; (mil.) *fissi!*, eyes front!, *stare – in una città*, to reside in a city; *adv.* fixedly, intently; *n.m.* fixed salary.
**fi·stola** *f.* (med.) fistula; (mus.) Pan-pipes, syrinx.
**fitta** *f.* sharp pain, stitch; pang; crowd, mass; soft ground; hole in the ground; pit; dent, impression.
**fittai(u)olo** *m.* tenant-farmer; (leg.) lessee of rural property.
**fit·tile** *adj.* fictile, made of clay.
**fittìo** *m.* thickness; density; closeness.
**fittivo** *adj.* fictitious, imaginary.
**fitti·zio** *adj.* false, unreal; imaginary; fictitious.
**fitto**[1] *m.* rent; *prendere in* –, to hire; – *bloccato*, restricted rent.
**fitt-o**[2] *adj.* thrust in, stuck in; driven in; *a capo* –, head first; fixed, firmly placed; thick, dense; *tessuti -i*, closely woven cloth; *pettine* –, fine tooth comb; *buio* –, pitch dark; *nel più – inverno*, in the depths of winter; *n.m.* thickest part; *nel – della mischia*, in the thick of the fight; *adv.* thickly; frequently; *nevicare* –, to snow heavily. **-ẹzza** *f.* thickness, density.
**fittọne** *m.* (bot.) tap-root.
**fiumalbo** *m.* (orn.) moorhen.
**fium-e** *m.* river; stream, current; *contro* –, against the current; *il – reale*, the main river (as compared with tributaries); (fig.) stream, flood; *romanzo* –, long novel, 'saga'. **-ana** *f.* flood; swollen river; (fig.) flood, crowd. **-icello** *m. dim.* small river; stream.
**fiut-are** [A1] *tr.* to scent, to catch the scent of; to sniff, to smell; to suspect; – *tabacco*, to take snuff. **-ata** *f.* sniff; search.
**fiuto** *m.* scent, smell; sense of smell; flair; *tabacco da* –, snuff.
**flac·cido** *adj.* flaccid; flabby.
**flacọne** *m.* flask; phial.
**flagell-are** [A1] *tr.* to flagellate, to scourge; to lash. **-ante** *part. adj.* flagellant; scourging; *n.m.* (eccl. hist.) Flagellant. **-aziọne** *f.* flagellation; scourging.
**flagello** *m.* scourge, whip; scourging; punishment, visitation; (fig.) torment; *adv. phr. studiare a* –, to overwork.
**flagiolẹtto** *m.* (mus.) flageolet.
**flagran-te** *adj.* flagrant; *in* –, in the act. **-za** *f.* flagrancy.
**flanella** *f.* flannel.
**flan·gia** *f.* flange.
**flash** *m. indecl.* (photog.) flash; (pop.) electric torch.
**flat-o** *m.* flatus, wind. **-ulento** *adj.* flatulent. **-ulenza** *f.* flatulence.
**fla·ut-o** *m.* (mus.) flute; – *a becco*, recorder. **-ista** *m.*, *f.* flautist.
**flavo** *adj.* (poet.) fair, blonde, golden; tawny.
**flẹ·bile** *adj.* mournful, plaintive; pitiful, weak.
**flebite** *f.* phlebitis.
**Flegetọnte** *pr.n.m.* (myth.) Phlegethon.
**flemm-a** *f.* phlegm; indifference, sang-froid, slowness. **-a·tico** *adj.* phlegmatic; (fig.) self-possessed.
**fless-i·bile** *adj.* flexible; pliable; pliant; (bookb.) *rilegatura* –, limp cover; *n.m.* flexible tube; flex. **-ibilità** *f.* flexibility; pliability. **-iọne** *f.* flexion; (gymn.) bend; (gramm.) inflection. **-uọso** *adj.* graceful, supple; rippling; (fig.) yielding. **-ura** *f.* bending, flexing.
**Flessinga** *pr.n.f.* (geog.) Flushing.
**flet·tere** [C19] *tr.* to bend, to flex; (gramm.) to inflect, to decline; (gymn.) – *il busto*, to bend from the waist; *intr.* (*aux.* essere) to weaken.
**flirt** *m. indecl.* (pron. as Eng.) flirtation. **-are** [A1] *intr.* (*aux.* avere) to flirt.
**flogo** *m.* (bot.) phlox.
**flor-a** *f.* flora. **-ale** *adj.* floral.
**florescenza** *f.* florescence.
**floricultura** *f.* flower-growing, floriculture.
**flo·rid-o** *adj.* prosperous, thriving; flourishing; florid; *gli anni -i*, youth; bright, vivid, colourful. **-ẹzza** *f.* floridness; prosperity; glow, bloom.
**florile·gio** *m.* florilegium; anthology.
**flo·scio** *adj.* soft; flabby; limp; floppy; *cappello* –, soft hat.
**flott-a** *f.* (naut.) fleet; convoy; – *aerea*, fleet air-arm. **-i·glia** *f.* (naut.) flotilla; fishing-fleet.
**flottante** *adj.* (comm.) floating; *vendita di merce* –, sale afloat.
**flu·id-o** *adj.* fluid; fluent; *n.m.* fluid. **-ità** *f.* fluidity, fluency.
**flu-ire** [D2] *intr.* (*aux.* essere) to flow; to be fluent; to be fluid; to be abundant. **-ente** *part. adj.* fluent; flowing; variable.
**fluor-e** *m.* (med.) discharge; (miner.) fluor; *spato* –, fluorspar. **-escente** *adj.* fluorescent. **-escenza** *f.* fluorescence. **-ina** *f.*, **-ite** *f.* (miner.) fluorite, fluorspar.
**fluoro** *m.* (chem.) fluorine.
**flussiọne** *f.* (med.) inflammation; flux, discharge.
**flusso** *m.* (med.) flux, discharge, flow; dysentery; – *e riflusso*, ebb and flow; (naut.) flood tide; (cards) flush.
**flutt-o** *m.* wave; billow, surge, swell; – *del fondo*, ground swell; – *corrente*, drift. **-uọso** *adj.* surging, swelling; tempestuous, stormy; (fig.) irresolute, vacillating.
**fluttu-are** [A6] *intr.* (*aux.* avere) to fluctuate; to toss in the waves; to vacillate; to rise and fall. **-ante** *part. adj.* fluctuating;

vacillating; (finan.) *debito -ante*, floating debt; *n.m.* temporary resident.

**fluviale** *adj.* fluvial; *per via —*, by river; *navigazione —*, river navigation.

**fobi·a** *f.* (med.) phobia; dread; fear; strong aversion.

**foca** *f.* (zool.) seal.

**focac·cia** *f.* cake, bun.

**foca·ia** *adj.* flint; of flint; *pietra —*, flint.

**focal-e** *adj.* (opt.) focal; *distanza —*, focal length; *profondità —*, depth of focus. **-iẓẓaziọne** *f.* (phys.) focusing.

**focara** *f.* brazier.

**fọco** *f.* (geog.) mouth, outlet; outfall.

**focena** *f.* (zool.) porpoise.

**focheggiatura** *f.* (photog.) focusing.

**fochista** *m.* maker or seller of fireworks; fireman; stoker.

**focile** *m.* steel (used with flint); (fig.) incitement.

**focola·io** *m.* (med.) centre of infection; (fig.) hotbed.

**focolare** *m.* hearth, fireplace; fireside; (fig.) home.

**focọso** *adj.* fiery; blazing, hot; (fig.) fiery; mettlesome.

**fo·dera** *f.* lining; sheath, casing.

**foder-are** [A1 s] *tr.* to line; to sheathe, to encase. **-atura** *f.* lining; sheathing; casing.

**fo·dero** *m.* sheath, scabbard.

**fog-a** *f.* impetus; ardour; impetuosity. **-ata** *f.* flight, fleeing.

**fog·gi-a** *f.* fashion, style; way, manner; shape; *alla — di*, in the style of; *a — di*, shaped like. **-are** [A3] *tr.* to form, to shape; to fashion, to mould.

**fo·gli-a** *f.* leaf; *mettere le -e*, to put forth leaves; *la pagina inferiore di una —*, the underside of a leaf; (techn.) foil; lamina; *— di stagno*, tinfoil. **-a·ceo** *adj.* foliaceous; leaf-like. **-ame** *m.* foliage; leaf pattern. **-ọso, -uto** *adj.* leafy; in leaf.

**fogliẹtto** *m.* slip of paper; (typ.) octavo; *— volante*, handbill.

**fo·glio** *m.* sheet of paper folded in two; *un libro in —*, a book in folio; *quaderno a fogli sciolti*, loose-leaf notebook; newspaper; pamphlet; page; note (of paper-money); permit, licence; receipt.

**fogn-a** *f.* drain, sewer; culvert; hole in the bottom of a flower-pot. **-atura** *f.* sewerage. **-ọne** *m. augm.* main sewer.

**fo·i-a** *f.* lust, desire; craze. **-ọso** *adj.* lustful, libidinous.

**fola**[1] *f.* fable; taradiddle; old wives' tale.

**fola**[2] *f.* (cards) pool, stack.

**fo·laga** *f.* (orn.) coot.

**folata** *f.* gust, puff; *lavorare a folate*, to work by fits and starts; gush, spurt; swarm; crowd; *una — di uccelli*, a flight of birds; burst (of cheering, *etc.*).

**folgor-are** [A1 sc] *intr.* (*aux.* avere) to flash; to lighten; to shine; to gleam; *tr.* to strike with lightning. **-ante** *part. adj.* flashing, shining; gleaming; *dolore -ante*, piercing pain.

**fọlgore** *f.* flash of lightning; thunderbolt.

**folclor-e, folklor-e** *m.* folk-lore, folk customs. **-iṣmo** *m.* study of folk-lore. **-ista** *m., f.* student of folk-lore. **-i·stico** *adj.* connected with folk-lore; *concerto di canti -istici*, folk-song recital.

**fo·lio** *m.* folio.

**fọlla** *f.* crowd, throng, multitude; mob; crush; *far —*, to throng, to crowd together.

**foll-are** [A1 c] *tr.* to press (grapes); (text.) to full, to mill. **-ata** *f.* pressing; fulling. **-atọio, -atọre** *m.* grape-press.

**foll-e** *adj.* crazy, foolish, mad; senseless; *cambio in —*, gear in neutral. **-eggiare** [A3 c] *intr.* (*aux.* avere) to act like a madman; to play the fool; to frolic. **-ẹtto** *adj. dim.* silly; *n.m.* goblin, elf, sprite; imp. **-i·a** *f.* folly; madness; extravagance; *amare alla -ia*, to be madly in love with.

**folli·col-o** *m.* (med.; biol.) follicle. **-are** *adj.* follicular.

**fọlta** *f.* crush, press, throng.

**fọlt-o** *adj.* thick; dense; close-set; teeming; abundant; *n.m.* press; thickness; *nel — della mischia*, in the thick of the fight; thicket; overgrown area. **-ẹzza** *f.* thickness; abundance.

**foment-are** [A1 c] *tr.* to foment, to incite; to cause; to excite. **-atọre** *m.* fomenter; instigator. **-aziọne** *f.* fomentation; excitement, stimulation.

**fomẹnto** *m.* (med.) fomentation; (fig.) fuel; stimulus, encouragement.

**fo·mite** *m.* tinder; (fig.) origin, cause; incitement, incentive; *— del contagio*, source of contagion.

**fọnd-a** *f.* holster; (naut.) anchorage. **-ina** *f.* small holster, pistol-case.

**fọndaco** *m.* draper's shop; warehouse, store.

**fondale** *adj.* bottom, lowest; *n.m.* depth of water; (theatr.) backcloth; (naut.) ocean depth.

**fondamẹnta** *f.* (Ven.) paved street running along a canal.

**fondamẹnt-o** *m.* (*pl.* *-i m.*; *-a* ., of buildings) foundation; *porre le -a*, to lay the foundations; (fig.) support, ground, basis; *far — sopra*, to place reliance upon. **-ale** *adj.* fundamental; *pietra -ale*, foundation stone; *colore -ale*, primary colour.

**fond-are** [A1 c] *tr.* to found; to lay the foundations of; to build; to establish; *rfl.* (*prep.* su) to rely (upon), to base oneself (upon); to be founded (upon). **-ato** *part. adj.* founded; built; (fig.) established, based; well-founded; well-versed. **-aziọne** *f.* founding, building; foundation, establishment, institution; bequest.

**fọnd-ere** [C2] *tr.* to melt; to smelt; to cast; (fig.) to fuse; to blend; to dissipate; *rfl., intr.* (*aux.* essere) to melt, to dissolve; *recip. rfl.* to merge, to amalgamate. **-eri·a** *f.* foundry. **-itura** *f.* melting, fusing.

**fondia·rio** *adj.* landed, land; *imposta fondiaria*, land-tax; *proprietà fondiaria*, landed property.

**fondi·glio** *m.* deposit, dregs; sediment.

**fọnd-o** *m.* bottom; lowest part, base; ground-floor; basement; *a —*, thoroughly; *da cima a —*, from top to bottom; bed of the sea; *andare a —*, to founder; *— stradale*, road surface; *strato di —*, undercoat, priming; *-i del caffè*, coffee dregs; *bassi -i*, shallow water, (fig.) slums; *in — alla stanza*, at the far end of the room; *in — alla pagina*, at the foot of the page; *in — al discorso*, at the end of the speech; *in —*, fundamentally; *articolo di —*, editorial; character, disposition; background; fund; capital; bequest; farm, estate; holding; *adj.* deep.

**fone·t-ica** *f.* phonetics. **-ico** *adj.* phonetic. **-iṣmo** *m.* phoneticism.

**fo·nic-a** *f.* phonics, acoustics; tone, sound-quality. **-o** *adj.* phonic; phonetic; *mezzi -i*, acoustic resources; *n.m.* (cinem.; telev.) sound-recordist.

**fon-ofobi·a** *f.* horror of noise. **-ografi·a** *f.* phonography. **-gra·fico** *adj.* (mus.) *disco -grafico*, gramophone record. **-o·grafo** *m.* (mus.) gramophone; *-ografo a tastiera*, juke-box. **-ologi·a** *f.* phonology; phonetics. **-o·logo** *m.* phonologist. **-oregistratọre** *m.* tape-recorder and record-player combined.

**fontale** *adj.* original, primal.

**fontan-a** *f.* fountain; source, spring; fount; origin. **-ile** *m.* source of a stream; spring.

**fọnte** *f.* fountain; source, spring; (fig.) source, origin; *sapere da buona —*, to know on good authority; *m.* font; *— battesimale*, baptismal font.

**fora** *3rd pers. sing.* conditional of **essere**, *q.v.*; (poet.) would be.

**foracchi-are** [A4] *tr.* to make holes in, to riddle. **-ato** *part. adj.* perforated. **-atura** *f.* perforation; holes.

**foraggi-are** [A3] *intr.* (*aux.*

avere) to forage; to pillage. **-iere** *m.* (mil.) forager.

**forag·gio** *m.* forage; fodder.

**foramac·chie** *m. indecl.* (orn.) wren.

**forame** *m.* hole, aperture; slit; (anat.) foramen, opening.

**fora·min-e** *m.* hole, aperture. **-ọso** *adj.* perforated, porous.

**for-are** [A1 c] *tr.* to make a hole in; to perforate, to drill, to bore; to pierce, to prick. **-anẹve** *f. indecl.* (bot.) snowdrop. **-atọio** *m.* auger, gimlet. **-atrice** *f.* machine for punching holes. **-atura** *f.* hole, perforation; boring; piercing; puncture.

**for·bici** *f.pl.* scissors; shears; — *da unghie*, nail-scissors; claws; pincers, nippers; (surg.) forceps.

**forb-ire** [D2] *tr.* to furbish, to polish; to wipe, to clean. **-ito** *part. adj.* polished, studied; elegant; *oro -ito*, pure gold. **-itura** *f.* polishing, furbishing, cleaning; polish, elegance.

**fọrc-a** *f.* hayfork, pitchfork; fork in a road; gallows, gibbet; *far* —, to play truant. **-ato** *adj.* forked, fork-shaped. **-atura** *f.* forkful; bifurcation.

**forcell-a** *f.* forked stick; mountain-pass. **-uto** *adj.* forked, fork-shaped.

**forchẹtt-a** *f.* fork, table-fork; fork luncheon. **-ata** *f.* forkful. **-ato** *adj.* fork-shaped. **-ọne** *m. augm.* carving-fork.

**forcina** *f.* small fork; hairpin; harpoon.

**for·cipe** *m.* (surg.) obstetric forceps; *parto di* —, forceps delivery.

**forcọn-e** *m.* pitchfork. **-atura** *f.* fork of a tree.

**forcuto** *adj.* forked; split; fork-shaped.

**forense** *adj.* (leg.) forensic; juridical; *n.m.pl. i forensi*, lawyers.

**forest-a** *f.* forest; (fig.) *una — di capelli*, a mop of hair. **-ale** *adj.* forest, forestal; consisting of forest; *guardia -ale*, forester.

**forest-eri·a** *f.* guest-quarters. **-iera** *f.* hostel. **-iere, -iero** *m.* foreigner; stranger; visitor, guest; *adj.* foreign.

**forfẹcchia** *f.* (ent.) earwig.

**forfet(t)a·rio** *adj.* relating to a flat rate; *abbonamento* —, flat-rate subscription; *somma forfettaria*, lump sum; *prezzo* —, all-in price.

**fọrfor-a** *f.* scurf, dandruff. **-ọso** *adj.* scurfy.

**for·gi-a** *f.* forge, smithy. **-are** [A3] *tr.* to forge; (fig.) to shape.

**forgọne** *m.* van, wagon; (mil.) ration wagon.

**forier-e, -o** *adj.* preceding, forerunning; *n.m.* forerunner; precursor; (fig.) portent.

**fọrma** *f.* form, shape, appearance; *una — di formaggio*, a whole cheese; *a — di*, in the shape of; format; figure; style; *in — scritta*, in writing; *per la* —, for form's sake; *gli mancano le -e*, he has no manners; formality, convention; order, procedure; *calza a* —, fashioned stocking; (techn.) mould; (shoem.) last; (hatm.) hat-block: (typ.) forme; (sculpt.; paint.) mould, model; (archit.) order, style.

**formag·g-io** *m.* cheese; — *grattugiato*, grated cheese; — *dolce*, mild cheese. **-ia·io** *m.* cheese-monger. **-iera** *f.* cheese-dish.

**forma·io** *m.* last-maker.

**formal-e** *adj.* formal; explicit; exact. **-ità** *f.* formality. **-izzare** [A1] *tr.* to shock, to scandalize; to outrage.

**formalina** *f.* (chem.) formalin.

**form-are** [A1 c] *tr.* to form, to shape, to fashion, to model; to give form to; to constitute, to create; (teleph.) — *un numero*, to dial a number; — *un'idea*, to conceive an idea; to educate; to train; *rfl.* (*acc.* of *prn.* 'si') to be formed; to develop, to grow; to improve; (*dat.* of *prn.* 'si') *-arsi un'idea*, to get an idea; *-arsi una clientela*, to build up a clientèle. **-ativo** *adj.* formative. **-ato** *part. adj.* formed; *n.m.* shape, size, form; format. **-azịone** *f.* formation; creation, conception; constitution.

**formella** *f.* small form; (archit.) brick, tile used in patterned pavement; (archit.) panel.

**formene** *m.* (chem.) methane.

**formi-ca**[1] *f.* (ent.) ant. **-ca·io** *m.* (ent.) ants' nest. **-chiere** *m.* (zool.) anteater.

**for·mica**[2] *f.* (industr.) formica.

**formicol-are** [A1 s] *intr.* (*aux.* essere, avere; *prep.* di) to swarm; to be crowded (with); (of the pulse) to beat fast; to tingle, to have pins and needles. **-ante** *part. adj.* swarming, crowded; *piazza -ante di gente*, square crowded with people. **-azịone** *f.* tingling, pricking sensation. **-ìo** *m.* swarm; crowding; tingling, 'pins and needles'.

**formida·bile** *adj.* formidable; awe-inspiring; stupendous; frightful, awful, fearful.

**formọs-o** *adj.* beautiful; shapely; rounded. **-ità** *f.* beauty; shapeliness.

**for·mul-a** *f.* formula; form. **-are** [A1 s] *tr.* to formulate, to express; to draw up. **-a·rio** *m.* formulary; form; collection of precedents; standard form. **-azịone** *f.* formulation.

**fornace** *f.* furnace; kiln; foundry; brickyard.

**forna·io** *m.* baker; baker's shop.

**fornello** *m.* gas-ring; *cucina a gas con quattro fornelli*, gas cooker with four rings; — *a gas*, gas-ring; — *di una pipa*, bowl of a tobacco-pipe; hot-plate.

**fornic-are** [A2 s] *intr.* (*aux.* avere) to fornicate. **-atọre** *m.* fornicator. **-azịone** *f.* fornication.

**for·nice** *m.* (archit.) supporting arch, vault.

**forn-ire** [D2] *tr.* to furnish; to give, to supply, to provide, to equip; — *un'impresa*, to carry out an undertaking; *rfl.* (*dat.* of *prn.* 'si'; *prep.* di) to equip oneself; *-irsi di informazioni*, to get information; (*acc.* of *prn.* 'si') *-irsi da*, to buy from, to deal with. **-imẹnto** *m.* furnishing, supplying; supplies, equipment; requisites; *pl.* (eccles.) vestments. **-itọre** *m.* purveyor, supplier; retailer; *-itori della Real Casa*, by appointment to H.M...; *-itore navale*, ship's chandler; *pl.* wholesalers. **-itura** *f.* supplies; shipment; equipment.

**fọrno** *m.* oven; bakery, baker's shop; furnace, kiln; incinerator; *alto* —, blast furnace; *cuocere al* —, to bake; (theatr.) empty house; *fare* —, to play to an empty house.

**foro**[1] *m.* forum; market-place; square; — *boario*, cattle fair; (leg.) court; bench and bar; legal profession; *il — romano*, the Roman Forum.

**fọro**[2] *m.* hole; aperture; tunnel; bore; — *della serratura*, key-hole.

**forra** *f.* (geog.) ravine.

**fọrse** *adv.* perhaps; maybe; possibly; — *che sì*, — *che no*, it may be so, it may not; *n.m.* doubt; *stare in — della vita*, to be dangerously ill; *mettere in* —, to question, to doubt.

**forsennato** *adj.* frantic; beside oneself; mad, insane; delirious.

**fort-e** *adj.* strong, powerful, robust; *il sesso* —, the stronger sex; *star* —, to stand firm; *dar man — a*, to help, to defend; large; *-i spese*, heavy costs; *vento* —, high wind; *con — voce*, in a loud voice; bad, serious, severe; *è troppo* —, it is too much, that is too bad; *caffè* —, strong coffee; *latte* —, sour milk; *un — problema*, a difficult problem; *luoghi -i*, stronghold; (mus.) loud; *n.m.* strong point, forte; strong man, brave man; (mil.) fort, fortress; strong point; *adv.* strongly, powerfully; steadily; a great deal; heavily; aloud, loudly. **-is·simo** *adj. superl. adv.* (mus.) very loud.

**fortẹzza** *f.* fortitude, courage, strength; resistance; (mil.) fortress, stronghold; (theol.) fortitude.

**fortic·cio** *adj.* rather sharp (of tastes), sourish; (of game) high.

**fortific-are** [A2 s] *tr.* (mil.) to fortify, to protect with defensive works; to strengthen; *intr.* (*aux*

avere) to build defence works; *rfl.* (mil.) to become fortified; (fig.) to fortify oneself. **-ante** *part. adj.* fortifying, strengthening; invigorating; *n.m.* stimulant, tonic. **-ato** *part. adj.* (mil.) fortified; strengthened; armed; *n.m.* (mil.) defensive work, fort. **-azione** *f.* (mil.) fortification; defensive work or position; *-azione campale*, field works.

**fortili·zio** *m.* (mil.) redoubt; stronghold.

**fortino** *m.* (mil.) pill-box.

**fortire** [D2] *tr.* (mil.) to strengthen, to fortify.

**fort-ore** *m.* sourness, sharpness (of flavour or smell). **-ume** *m.* sourness; sour or sharp-flavoured food.

**fortu·ito** *adj.* fortuitous, accidental, casual, chance; (leg.) *atto* —, act of God.

**fortun-a** *f.* fortune, luck, chance; *per* —, luckily; — *volle che*, as luck would have it; *un colpo di* —, a stroke of luck; destiny; state, condition; inheritance, patrimony; (aeron.) *campo di* —, emergency landing ground; (poet.) storm, tempest; *in* —, storm-tossed. **-ale** *m.* (meteor.) storm, tempest at sea. **-ato** *adj.* fortunate, lucky; successful; happy, pleased. **-oso** *adj.* eventful, chequered; stormy; fraught with danger; chancy, risky.

**forun·colo** *m.* (med.) boil, furuncle.

**forviare** [A4] *intr.* (*aux.* essere) to go astray; *tr.* to lead astray; to send the wrong way.

**forza** *f.* force, strength, might; — *motrice*, motive power; *far* —, to make an effort; *far* — *a*, to encourage; *su*, — *!*, come on, try hard!, (sport) play up!, come on!; violence; (mil.) military power, regiment, army; (naut.) *mezza* —, half speed; *tutta* —, full speed; *casa di* —, prison; power, efficacy; *camicia di* —, strait-jacket; — *motrice idraulica*, water power; significance; *in* — *di avverbio*, in an adverbial sense; *le forze di Ercole*, the labours of Hercules; *è* —, it is inevitable; *per amore o per* —, willy-nilly; *a* — *di*, by dint of.

**forz-are** [A1] *tr.* to force, to oblige, to compel; to break open; to violate; to strain. **-ato** *part. adj.* forced, compelled; compulsory; strained; *lavori -ati*, hard labour.

**forziere** *m.* safe, strong-box, coffer.

**forzista** *m.* wrestler; participant in trials of strength.

**forz-oso** *adj.* forced, compulsory; strong, forceful. **-uto** *adj.* physically strong, robust; muscular.

**fos-co** *adj.* (*m.pl.* **-chi**) dark, dull, obscure; gloomy, murky; *n.m.* darkness; gloom; sadness. **-cag·gine** *f.* darkness, dullness; dull weather. **-chezza** *f.* darkness; dullness, gloominess. **-chi·a** *f.* (naut.) haze, mistiness; visibility; fog.

**fosf-a·tico** *adj.* (chem.) phosphate. **-ato** *m.* (chem.) phosphate.

**fosforescen-te** *adj.* phosphorescent. **-za** *f.* phosphorescence; *pl.* gleams, flashes.

**fosfo·rico** *adj.* (chem.) phosphoric.

**fo·sforo** *m.* (chem.) phosphorus; (fig.) brains, wits; *gli manca il* —, he hasn't any brains.

**foss-a** *f.* ditch; trench; pit; long narrow hole; grave; *avere un piede nella* —, to have one foot in the grave; *-e nasali*, nasal cavities; *Daniele nella* — *dei leoni*, Daniel in the lions' den; (mil.) moat. **-etta** *f.* dimple.

**fossato** *m.* (mil.) entrenchment; dug-out; ditch; *adj.* excavated.

**fos·sil-e** *adj.*, *n.m.* fossil. **-i·fero** *adj.* (geol.) fossiliferous. **-izzare** [A1] *tr.* to fossilize; *rfl.* (fig.) to be unprogressive. **-izzazione** *f.* fossilization.

**fosso** *m.* ditch, channel; — *di scolo*, gutter; — *d'irrigazione*, irrigation channel; (fig.) *stare a cavallo del* —, to sit on the fence.

**fot-o** *f. indecl.* photo. **-ocro·naca** *f.* illustrated magazine. **-oge·nico** *adj.* (photog.) photogenic. **-ografare** [A1 s] *tr.* to photograph. **-ografi·a** *f.* photograph; photography **-ogra·fico** *adj.* photographic; *apparecchio -ografico*, camera. **-o·grafo** *m.* photographer. **-o·metro** *m.* exposure meter. **-ostato** *m.* photostat. **-oteca** *f.* photographic library.

**fra**[1] *prep.* between, among, amid; through; *dire* — *sè*, to say to oneself; — *me e me*, to myself; within, in; — *due giorni*, in two days' time; — *poco*, shortly, soon.

**fra**[2] *m.* (eccl.) Brother (before religious name).

**frac** *m. indecl.* dress-coat; dinner-jacket; evening-dress.

**fracassare** [A1] *tr.* to smash, to shatter, to break; to rout, to defeat; *intr.* (*aux.* essere), *rfl.* to crash; (fig.) to go to pieces.

**fracasso** *m.* noise, crash; din, uproar; clashing, clatter; destruction, damage; *cadere con* —, to fall with a crash; *il libro fece* —, the book caused an uproar; *un* — *di gente*, a crowd of people.

**fracosta** *f.* (butcher.) ribs, rib (of beef).

**fra·dicio** *adj.* rotten, bad, putrid; corrupt; wet; *bagnato* —, soaking wet; *ubriaco* —, blind drunk

**fra·gil-e** *adj.* fragile, brittle; weak, frail. **-ità** *f.* fragility; weakness; frailty.

**fra·gol-a** *f.* (bot.) strawberry; strawberry mark. **-eto** *m.* strawberry-bed.

**fragor-e** *m.* crash; din, row, roar; clang, clash. **-io** *m.* crashing, roaring; clashing. **-oso** *adj.* noisy, loud; resounding; *applausi -osi*, thunderous applause.

**fragran-te** *adj.* fragrant, sweet-smelling; perfumed, scented. **-za** *f.* fragrance, sweet smell, scent, perfume.

**fraina** *f.* (bot.) buckwheat.

**frainten·d-ere** [C1] *tr.* to misunderstand; to misinterpret; not to hear properly. **-imento** *m.* misunderstanding; misinterpretation.

**frainteso** *adj.* misunderstood; misinterpreted.

**frale** *adj.* (poet.) frail, weak; delicate; *n.m.* the frail body; the mortal part of us.

**frammasson-e** *m.* freemason, mason. **-eri·a** *f.* freemasonry.

**framment-o** *m.* fragment, piece; extract. **-a·rio** *adj.* fragmentary. **-azione** *f.* (phys.) *-azione atomica*, atomic fission.

**frammesso** *adj.* inserted; interposed; *n.m.* insertion; interpolation.

**frammettere** [C20] *tr.* to interpose, to insert; to intermingle; *rfl.* to interpose, to intervene; to interfere, to intrude.

**frammezzare** [A1] *tr.* to intermingle; to interpose.

**framezzo** *adv.* in the midst; *prep. phr.* — *a*, between, among.

**frammischi-are** [A4] *tr.* to mix, to intermingle; to confuse; *rfl.* *-arsi con*, to intervene in, to interfere with; to mix with. **-amento** *m.* mingling; mixture; blend.

**fran-a** *f.* landslip; landslide. **-are** [A1] *intr.* (*aux.* essere) to slip, to fall (of rocks, etc.); to cave in. **-oso** *adj.* (geog.) unstable, subject to landslides.

**franc-are** [A2] *tr.* to free; to liberate; to set free; to compensate for; to frank; — *una lettera*, to stamp a letter. **-atura** *f.* franking, stamping; stamps, postage.

**Francesc-a** *pr.n.f.* Frances; Francesca. **-o** *pr.n.m.* Francis.

**francescan-o** *adj.* (eccl.) Franciscan; (fig.) evangelical; simple, humble; *n.m.* Franciscan (friar). **-a** *n.f.* (eccl.) Franciscan Sister.

**francese** *adj.* French; *andarsene alla* —, to take French leave; *alla* —, in the French style; *n.m.* the French language, French; *parlare* —, to speak French; Frenchman; *f.* Frenchwoman; French girl; *i Francesi*, the French.

**francheggiare** [A3 c] *tr.* to free; to assure, to encourage.
**franchęzza** *f.* assurance, freedom; frankness, openness, sincerity; boldness.
**franchi·gia** *f.* liberty; freedom; privilege, exemption, immunity; *in — postale,* postage free; *pl.* franchise.
**Fran·cia** *pr.n.f.* (geog.) France.
**franco**[1] *adj.* (hist.) Frank, Frankish; French; *guerra franco-germanica,* Franco-Prussian war; *n.m.* (hist.) Frank; franc (coin).
**fran-co**[2] *adj.* (*m.pl.* **-chi**) frank, open, sincere; free, clear; free, exempt; *porto —,* free port; *— di porto,* post-free; sure, skilled; bold, brave; *adv.* frankly; *n.m.* free man; freedman; *pl.* (naut.) libertymen.
**Franco**[3] *pr.n.m.* Frank.
**francobǫllo** *m.* postage-stamp; *unire un — per la risposta,* to enclose a stamp for the reply.
**Francoforte** *pr.n.f.* (geog.) Frankfurt.
**fran·g-ere** [C5] *tr.* to break; to smash; to crush; *rfl., intr.* (*aux.* essere) to break in pieces. **-ente** *part. adj.* breaking; *n.m.* crisis; danger; *trovarsi in un brutto -ente,* to be in a critical situation; (naut.) breaker, reef, shoal.
**fran·g-ia** *f.* fringe; fringe of hair, bang; *senza -e,* without frills.
**frangi-capo** *m. indecl.* cudgel; truncheon; club. **-ǫnda** *m.* breakwater, detached mole. **-zolle** *m. indecl.* (agric.) sod-breaker.
**frant-o** *adj.* broken, shattered; crushed, pressed. **-ǫio** *m.* oil-press.
**frantum-are** [A1] *tr.* to break into small pieces, to shatter. **-ato** *part. adj.* broken, shattered; *n.m.* (bldg.) crushed stone. **-azione** *f.* crushing; (geol.) detrition.
**frantume** *m.* fragment, piece, splinter.
**frapp-a** *f.* fringe; (paint.) representation of foliage. **-are** [A1] *tr.* to fringe. **-eggiare** [A3 c] *tr.* (paint.) to decorate with foliage.
**frappè** *m. indecl.* milk-shake; *caffè —,* coffee-shake.
**frappǫrre** [B21] *tr.* to interpose; *rfl.* to intervene; to interfere, to intrude.
**frapposiziǫne** *f.* interposition, insertion; intrusion, interference.
**fraş-a·io, -aiuolo** *m.* phrase-monger. **-a·rio** *m.* collection of phrases; phraseology; terminology.
**frasc-a** *f.* bough, branch; (fig.) scatter-brained person; *pl.* bean-sticks, peasticks; (fig.) trifles; idle tales. **-ame** *m.* brushwood. **-ato** *m.* bower, arbour, pergola; booth.
**fraschegg-iare** [A3 c] *intr.* (*aux.* avere) to rustle. **-ìo** *m.* rustling.
**fraschętta** *f.* small branch, twig; decoy for birds; (fig.) giddy woman; flirt.
**fraş-e** *f.* phrase; sentence; idiom, locution; style, diction; *— fatta,* commonplace, platitude; *pl.* empty talk, idle words; *è un uomo tutto -i,* he is all talk. **-eggiare** [A3 c] *intr.* (*aux.* avere) to construct sentences, to form phrases; (mus.) *tr., intr.* to phrase. **-ęggio** *m.* (mus.) phrasing. **-eologi·a** *f.* phraseology.
**frassi·neo** *adj.* made of ash-wood.
**fras·sin-o** *m.* (bot.) ash. **-ęto** *m.* ash-grove.
**frastagliare** [A4] *tr.* to cut across, to slash; to intersect; to indent.
**frasta·glio** *m.* slash (in a garment); fringe, ornament; indentation.
**frastornare** [A1 c] *tr.* to disturb; to distract; to impede.
**frastuono** *m.* uproar, din; *— di voci,* hubbub; *— di armi,* clash of arms.
**frat-e** *m.* friar; monk, religious; *— laico,* lay brother; *farsi —,* to become a monk; (before religious name) Brother; *i -i minori,* the Franciscans; *i -i predicatori,* the Dominicans. **-ęsco** *adj.* (*m.pl.* **-ęschi**) monkish.
**fratell-o** *m.* brother; *Adriano e Cristina sono -i,* Adrian and Christine are brother and sister; companion, comrade; colleague. **-anza** *f.* brotherhood; fraternity; brotherliness; (rel.) brotherhood. **-astro** *m.* half-brother, step-brother. **-ęvole** *adj.* brotherly, fraternal.
**fraternità** *f.* fraternity, brotherhood; brotherliness; (eccl.) fraternity.
**fraternizzare** [A1] *intr.* (*aux.* avere) to fraternize.
**fraterno** *adj.* fraternal, brotherly.
**fratricida** *m., f.* fratricide (person); *adj.* fratricidal; *guerra —,* civil war.
**fratrici·dio** *m.* fratricide (action).
**fratta** *f.* thicket; tangled undergrowth; hedge; (fig.) *essere per le fratte,* to be on the rocks.
**fratta·gli-a** *f.* (usu. *pl.*) entrails, internals; offal; tripe, giblets, chitterlings; liver and lights. **-a·io** *m.* seller of tripe.
**frattanto** *adv.* meanwhile, in the meantime.
**frattempo** *m.* meantime, meanwhile; interval; *nel —,* in the meantime.
**frattur-a** *f.* (med.; miner.) fracture; break. **-are** [A1] *tr.* (med.) to fracture.
**fraud-are** [A1 sa] *tr.* to defraud, to cheat; to deprive. **-atǫre** *m.* impostor; deceiver. **-ato·rio** *adj.* (*m.pl.* **-atorii**) fraudulent.
**fra·ude** *f.* (poet.) fraud, deceit.
**fraudolen-to** *adj.* fraudulent. **-za** *f.* fraudulence.
**fraziǫn-e** *f.* breaking, rupture; (math.) fraction; *— comune,* vulgar fraction; *— periodica,* recurring decimal; portion, fragment; group of houses, village. **-are** [A1 c] *tr.* to divide, to split. **-a·rio** *adj.* fractional.
**fręccia** *f.* arrow; *scagliare una —,* to shoot an arrow; *— del Parto,* Parthian shot; (agric.) shaft (of plough); (archit.) spire, pinnacle; dart; indicator, sign; (of a clock) hand; *— della bussola,* compass-needle; (of an arch) height, rise.
**frecci-are** [A3 c] *tr.* to shoot arrows at. **-ata** *f.* arrow-shot; (fig.) gibe.
**freddare** [A1 c] *tr.* to chill, to cool; (fig.) to damp; to curb; *intr.* (*aux.* essere), *rfl.* to cool.
**freddęzza** *f.* coldness, coolness; (fig.) chilliness; frigidity; indifference.
**frędd-o** *adj.* cold; coolness; (fig.) frigid; chilly; lifeless; *una -a accoglienza,* a cool reception; *ci lasciò -i,* it left us cold; *colori -i,* cold tones; *n.m.* cold; *oggi fa —,* it is cold today; *ho —,* I am cold; *prendere —,* to catch cold. **-olǫso, -ǫso** *adj.* susceptible to the cold.
**freddura** *f.* cold, cold weather; coolness; trifle, triviality; pun, play on words.
**frega** *f.* desire, craving; whim, caprice; (of animals) *in —,* on heat.
**fregac·cio** *m.* rough stroke (of a pen or pencil), scrawl, scribble.
**fregagiǫne** *f.* (med.) friction, massage.
**fregare** [A2 c] *tr.* to rub; to polish; to brush; (med.) to massage; to apply friction to; to cheat, to dupe; to get the better of; *li ha fregati in pieno,* he wiped the floor with them; (vulg.) to 'swipe', to 'pinch'; *rfl.* (vulg.) *me ne frego,* I don't care a damn.
**fregata** *f.* (naut.) frigate.
**fregi-are** [A3] *tr.* to decorate, to adorn, to embellish. **-atura** *f.* decoration, embellishment; (archit.) frieze, ornamentation.
**fre·gio** *m.* decoration, adornment; ornament; badge; frieze.
**frę‐go** *m.* (*pl.* **-ghi**) line, stroke, mark; *tirar un —,* to draw a line; *dar di — a,* to cross out; scrawl, scribble.
**fręgol-a** *f.* (vulg.) desire, craving; mania, craze; *ha la — di scrivere,* he has the itch to write; (ichth.) *andare in —,* to spawn. **-o** *m.* (ichth.) fish eggs, spawn.
**fremebǫndo** *adj.* frenzied, quivering; passionate.
**fre·mere** [B1] *intr.* (*aux.* avere) to quiver, to tremble; to shake; to thrill, to shudder; to rage; *n.m.* roaring; raging.
**fre·mito** *m.* roar; howl; murmur; quiver, tremor; *un — di gioia,* a thrill of joy.

**frenalgi·a** *f.* (med.) diaphragmatic pain; a stitch in one's side.
**fren-are** [A1 c] *tr.* to curb, to bridle, to check; to apply the brakes to; (fig.) to restrain, to moderate; *intr.* (*aux.* avere) to brake, to slow down; *rfl.* to restrain oneself, to refrain. **-ata** *f.* application of the brake(s). **-ato** *part. adj.* curbed; checked, restrained.
**fren-eşi·a** *f.* (med.) brain fever; fury, madness; frenzy; craze, rage. **-e·tico** *adj.* frenzied, raving; frantic; *pazzo -etico*, raving mad; *n.m.* frenzied person; delirium.
**fręn-o** *m.* bit; bridle; (fig.) check, restraint, control; *tenere a —*, to hold in check; *mordere il —*, to champ at the bit; brake; *— a mano*, hand-brake; *— a pedale*, foot-brake; *bloccare i -i*, to jam the brakes.
**fren-ologi·a** *f.* phrenology. **-o·logo** *m.* phrenologist.
**frequent-are** [A1 c] *tr.* to frequent; to visit often; to associate with; to attend. **-ato** *part. adj.* frequented; populated, crowded. **-atọre** *m.* frequenter, frequent visitor, associate.
**frequen-te** *adj.* frequent; numerous; *di —*, frequently; (med.) *polso —*, rapid pulse. **-za** *f.* frequency; frequence; oncourse; (techn.) frequency; repetition rate; (radio) *altissima -za*, V.H.F.; *pl.* attendance; *libretto delle -ze*, attendance register.
**frescheggiare** [A3 c] *intr.* (*aux.* avere) to enjoy the coolness, to enjoy the open air.
**freschętto** *adj.* rather cool, chilly.
**freschęzza** *f.* coolness; freshness; bloom, purity; *— della carnagione*, freshness of complexion.
**freschino** *adj.* coolish, rather fresh; *fa —*, there's a nip in the air; (naut.) *vento —*, light breeze.
**freschis·simo** *adj. superl.* of **fresco**; (naut.) *vento —*, strong wind.
**fręsc-o** *adj.* (*pl.* **fręschi**) cool, moderately cold; *acqua -a*, cold water; *tempo —*, cool weather; fresh, new; *uova fresche*, newlaid eggs; (naut.) *vento —*, fresh wind (steady); fresh, new; *— di malattia*. recently ill; *fiori freschi*, fresh flowers; rested, refreshed; *pittura -a*, wet paint; (colloq.) *star —*, to be in a mess; *adv. phr. di —*, recently, newly; *n.m.* coolness, freshness; open air; *fa —*, it is cool; (art) fresco; *dipingere a —*, to paint frescoes. **-ata** *f.* chill. **-ura** *f.* shady coolness.
**fre·şia** *f.* (bot.) freesia.
**frętta** *f.* haste, hurry; *avere —*, to be in a hurry; *in — e furia*, in a great hurry.
**frettolọso** *adj.* hasty, hurried.
**freudişmo** *m.* Freudism.
**fri-are** [A6] *tr.*, *intr.* (*aux.* essere) to crumble. **-a·bile** *adj.* friable, crumbly.
**Friburgo** *pr.n.f.* (geog.) Freiburg.
**fricasse·a** *f.* (cul.) fricassée; (fig.) jumble, medley.
**frig·g-ere** [C12] *tr.* to fry; *padella per —*, frying-pan; *intr.* (*aux.* avere) to fry, to hiss, to splutter; (fig.) to seethe. **-ìo** *m.* frying; hissing. **-itọre** *m.* vendor of fried food. **-itori·a** *f.* shop where fried food is sold.
**frigida·rio** *m.* (archit. hist.) frigidarium; refrigerator.
**fri·gid-o** *adj.* frigid, cold; (fig.) indifferent. **-ęzza, -ità** *f.* frigidity; coldness.
**frign-are** [A5] *intr.* (*aux.* avere) to whimper, to wail, to whine. **-ìo** *m.* whining.
**frigor-i·fero** *adj.* frigorific; *miscela -ifera*, freezing mixture; *n.m.* refrigerator; cold storage. **-i·fico** *adj.* frigorific.
**Frine** *pr.n.f.* Phryne.
**fringuello** *m.* (orn.) chaffinch.
**frinire** [D2] *intr.* (*aux.* avere) to chirp (of cicadas); *n.m.* stridulation, chirping.
**frinzello** *m.* botch; gash, sear.
**Fri·sia** *pr.n.f.* (geog.) Friesland.
**frişọne** *adj.*, *n.m.*, *f.* Frisian, Frieslander.
**fritilla·ria** *f.* (bot.) fritillary.
**frittata** *f.* omelette; fried dish; *una — di pesce*, a dish of fried fish; (fig.) blunder.
**frittella** *f.* pancake; fritter; grease-stain.
**fritt-o** *adj.* fried; (fig.; colloq.) *sono — !*, I'm done for!; *n.m.* (cul.) fried food, fry; *— misto di pesce*, a dish of various small fried fish. **-ura** *f.* frying; food for frying, fry; (fig.) small children, fry.
**fri·vol-o** *adj.* frivolous, trifling, empty, inane; futile. **-ęzza** *f.* frivolity; trifle.
**frizionare** [A1 c] *tr.* to massage, to apply a friction to; *intr.* (*aux.* avere) (motor. slang) to work the clutch.
**friziọne** *f.* friction; rubbing; dry shampoo; (motor.) clutch; *premere la — prima d'ingranare la marcia*, to press down the clutch before engaging gear.
**frizẓ-are** [A1] *tr.* to prick, to sting; *intr.* (*aux.* avere) to smart, to sting; *gli occhi mi -ano*, my eyes smart; to sparkle, to fizz. **-ante** *part. adj.* stinging, smarting; pungent; bracing; sparkling; *n.m.* sharp flavour. **-o** *m.* prick, smart, sting; witticism; gibe. **-ọre** *m.* sting, smart.
**frod-are** [A1] *tr.* to defraud, to cheat; to swindle; to extort. **-atọre** *m.* defrauder, cheat; swindler.
**frode** *f.* fraud; deception; extortion; swindle.
**frodo** *m.* smuggling, customs-evasion, contraband; *merce di —*, contraband goods; *pescatore di —*, *cacciatore di —*, poacher.
**froge** *f.pl.* (*sing.* **frogia**) (vet.) nostrils (of horses and cattle).
**froll-are** [A1] *tr.* to make tender, to soften, to hang (meat) until it is high; *intr.* (*aux.* essere) to become tender; *rfl.* to be tormented, to be consumed. **-amẹnto** *m.*, **-atura** *f.* tenderizing.
**frollo** *adj.* (of meat) tender; high; (of pastry) short; (fig.) soft, effeminate.
**frọmbol-a** *f.* sling, catapult. **-atọre** *m.*, **-iere** *m.* slinger, slingman.
**frọnd-a**[1] *f.* frond, branch; leaf; foliage; **-eggiante** *part. adj.* leafy, verdant. **-i·fero** *adj.* bearing leaves, leafy.
**Frọnd-a**[2] *pr.n.f.* (hist.) Fronde; (fig.) minor rebellion, opposition. **-ista** *m.* (hist.) member of the Fronde; (fig.) rebel; opponent; objector.
**frond-ire** [D2] *intr.* (*aux.* avere) to produce leaves, to leaf. **-ito** *part. adj.* leafy.
**frondọso** *adj.* leafy, covered in leaves; (fig.) ornate.
**frontale** *adj.* frontal; *n.m.* frontal; frontlet; mantel-shelf.
**frọnt-e** *f.* forehead, brow; *a — alta*, with head held high; face, head; *— a —*, face to face; (archit.) front, façade; *m.*, *f.* (fig.) front; *far — a un pericolo*, to face a danger; (mil.) front; *tener —*, to hold a line; *prima —*, front line; *di*, *a —*, facing, opposite; in front; *vento di —*, head wind. **-eggiare** [A3 c] *tr.* (mil.) to face; to resist, to oppose; (fig.) to meet, to confront; *-eggiare le spese*, to meet expenses; to be opposite, to face.
**frontespi·zio** *m.* title-page (not 'frontispiece'); (archit.) frontispiece, cornice.
**frontiera** *f.* frontier, border.
**frontọne** *m.* (archit.) pediment.
**frọnzolo** *m.* ribbon; frill; *pl.* finery.
**fronzuto** *adj.* leafy; in leaf.
**frotta** *f.* gathering, company, collection; band; mass, flock.
**frot·tola** *f.* popular song; invention, fib; tall story; *son frottole!*, it's a pack of lies!
**frugacchiare** [A4] *tr.* to rummage.
**frugal-e** *adj.* frugal, careful, sparing; moderate. **-ità** *f.* frugality, economy; moderation.
**frugare** [A2] *tr.* to search, to rummage; to ransack; to nudge; to poke.
**frugo** *m.* (comm.) *uso e —*, wear and tear.
**frugolare** [A1 s] *tr.*, *abs.* to search, to rummage; to ransack; to grub, to root, to rootle.
**fru·golo** *m.* fidgety child; smart, enterprising man; (colloq.) 'bright spark'.

**fru-ire** [D2] *tr.* to enjoy, to have the use of; to avail oneself of; — *una pensione*, to draw a pension; *intr.* (*aux.* avere; *prep.* di) to enjoy; — *di un diritto*, to have a right. **-izione** *f.* fruition; use, enjoyment.

**frull-are** [A1] *tr.* to beat, to whisk; to mill; — *uova*, to beat up eggs; *intr.* (*aux.* avere) to spin round; (fig.) to whirl; to flutter, to whirr; (fig.) *far — una faccenda*, to start things humming. **-ato** *part. adj.* beaten up, whisked, whipped; *n.m.* milk-shake. **-atore** *m.* shredder (in electric mixer); whisk, whisking machine. **-ino** *m.* whisk, beater. **-ìo** *m.* whirring, fluttering.

**frullo** *m.* spinning; whirring; buzzing; whisk; a baby's rattle; snap of the fingers; trifle, bagatelle.

**frument-a·rio** *adj.* grain-producing. **-azione** *f.* grain harvest. **-i·fero** *adj.* grain-producing.

**frument-o** *m.* (bot.) wheat. **-one** *m.* (bot.) maize.

**frusc-iare** [A3] *intr.* (*aux.* avere) to rustle. **-ìo** *m.* (*pl.* **-ìi**) rustling; murmuring; babbling; (radio; gramoph.) ground noise, needle noise.

**frusso** *m.* (cards) see **flusso**.

**frust-a** *f.* whip; lash; whisk; (fig.) severe criticism. **-ino** *m. dim.* (mil.) swagger cane; gallant, dandy, beau.

**frust-are** [A1] *tr.* to whip, to lash; to scourge; to criticize severely, to castigate; (mil.) — *con la mitraglia*, to sweep with machine-gun fire. **-ata** *f.* lash, blow with a whip; cutting remark. **-atore** *m.* lasher, scourger; castigator. **-atura** *f.* whipping, lashing; castigation.

**frusto**[1] *adj.* worn out, exhausted; shabby, worn, outworn.

**frusto**[2] *m.* piece, bit; morsel, scrap.

**frustr-are** [A1] *tr.* to frustrate; to thwart; to make useless, to nullify. **-ato·rio** *adj.* frustrative; vain, inefficacious.

**fru·tic-e** *m.* shrub, bush. **-eto** *m.* undergrowth, shrubbery.

**frutt-a** *f.* (*pl.* **-a**, **-e**) fruit (collectively); *pl.* fruit; *-e dolci*, dessert. **-a·io** *m.* fruit-cellar, fruit-store; *adj.* fruit-bearing. **-ai(u)olo** *m.* fruit-vendor. **-ame** *m.* fruit of various kinds. **-eto** *m.* orchard. **-iera** *f.* fruit-dish.

**frutt-are** [A1] *intr.* (*aux.* avere) to bear fruit; to yield, to bear; to pay; *tr.* to produce, to yield. **-ante** *part. adj.* yielding, bearing, producing. **-ata** *f.* open fruit tart. **-evole** *adj.* fruitful; profitable; fertile.

**frutticult-ore** *m.* fruit-grower. **-ura** *f.* fruit-growing.

**frutti·fero** *adj.* fruit-bearing; (fig.) useful, fruitful; *lavoro* —, work that pays well; (finan.) interest-bearing.

**fruttificare** [A2s] *intr.* (*aux.* avere) to fructify, to fruit.

**frutt-iven·dolo** *m.* fruiterer, fruit-seller. **-i·voro** *adj.* (zool.) fructivorous.

**frutt-o** *m.* (*pl.* **-i**, **-a** *f.*) a fruit; one single fruit; *alberi da* —, fruit trees; *essere alle -a*, to be at the fruit course; *-i di mare*, edible sea molluscs; (fig.) offspring, progeny; produce; use, profit, advantage, gain, reward; *con* —, successfully; *non ricavarne nessun* —, to get nothing out of it; *pl.* fruit, fruits; *i -i della terra*, the fruits of the earth; (finan.) yield.

**fruttuos-o** *adj.* fruitful; useful, profitable. **-ità** *f.* fruitfulness, fertility.

**fu**[1] *3rd pers. sing.* past definite of **essere**, *q.v.*; was.

**fu**[2] *adj. indecl.* late, deceased; *il — signor Rossi*, the late Mr. Rossi; *Carlo — Pietro Bruni*, Charles, son of the late Peter Brown.

**fucato** *adj.* painted; — *ad arte*, artificial.

**fucil-are** [A1] *tr.* to shoot (with a rifle); to execute. **-ata** *f.* shot; (mil.) volley; single shot; *fare alle -ate*, to exchange shots. **-atore** *m.* shooter; 'shot'; member of a firing squad. **-azione** *f.* shooting, execution.

**fucil-e** *m.* rifle; *ricaricare il* —, to reload; *inastare la baionetta al* —, to fix bayonets; *a un tiro di* —, at rifle range. **-eri·a** *f.* rifle fire; marksmanship. **-iere** *m.* (mil.) rifleman, fusilier.

**fucin-a** *f.* (metall.) forge; smithy; (fig.) factory. **-are** [A1] *tr.* (metall.) to forge.

**fuco**[1] *m.* (*pl.* **fuchi**) (ent.) drone (bee).

**fuco**[2] *m.* (bot.) wrack and other seaweeds.

**fuc·sia** *f.* (bot.) fuchsia.

**fuga** *f.* flight; *mettere in* —, to put to flight; *di* —, hurriedly; leak, escape; suite, succession; — *di scale*, flight of stairs; *la — dei cervelli*, the brain drain; (leg.) running away; (motor.) racing (of engine); spurt, sprint; (mus.) fugue.

**fugac-e** *adj.* fleeting, transitory, transient, brief. **-ità** *f.* fleetingness, transitoriness; instability.

**fug-are** [A2] *tr.* to put to flight, to chase away; to dispel; to drive away; (mil.) to rout. **-azione** *f.* flight, exodus.

**fuggias-co** *adj.* (*m.pl.* **-chi**) fugitive, runaway; *n.m.* fugitive; exile; (mil.) deserter; (naut.) man abandoning ship.

**fuggi-fatica** *m. indecl.* slacker. lazybones, sluggard. **-fuggi** *m. indecl.* headlong flight, confusion; stampede of a crowd.

**fugg-ire** [D1] *intr.* (*aux.* essere) to flee; to escape; to run away; *a scappa e -i*, in one moment, out the next; to pass rapidly, to fly; *come -e il tempo!*, how time flies!; *tr.* to shun, to avoid; to flee from; — *un pericolo*, to avoid a danger; (naut.) — *il vento*, to run before the wind; (art) to foreshorten. **-ente** *part. adj.* (poet.) fleeing, flying; fleeting, rapid; *mento -ente*, receding chin; *n.m.* fugitive. **-evole** *adj.* fleeting, brief, transitory. **-itivo** *adj.* fugitive, fleeing; fleeting, transitory; *n.m.* fugitive; deserter.

**fulcro** *m.* (eng.) fulcrum; pivot; (fig.) centre, heart, central point.

**ful·g-ere** (def.) *intr.* (poet.) to shine; to be resplendent; to flash, to gleam, to sparkle. **-ente** *part. adj.* shining, refulgent, resplendent.

**ful·gido** *adj.* resplendent, shining, bright; brilliant; untarnished.

**fulgore** *m.* splendour, brightness, radiance, brilliance.

**fulig·gin-e** *f.* soot; smuts; (paint.) lamp-black. **-oso** *adj.* sooty; black as soot; fuliginous.

**fullon-e** *m.* fuller. **-i·a** *f.* fulling.

**fulmin-are** [A1s] *tr.* to strike by lightning, to fulminate; to hurl; *intr.* (*aux.* avere) to emit flashes of lightning; to fulminate; to flash. **-ante** *part. adj.* fulminating; explosive; *un colpo -ante*, a violent blow; *cotone -ante*, guncotton; *n.m.* percussion cap, primer, detonator. **-azione** *f.* fulmination.

**ful·mine** *m.* lightning, flash of lightning; thunderclap, thunderbolt; *corse via come un* —, he ran off like a flash of lightning; *un — a ciel sereno*, a bolt from the blue; *colpito dal* —, struck by lightning.

**fulmi·neo** *adj.* rapid, flashing; quick as lightning; *uno sguardo* —, a threatening look.

**fulminìo** *m.* frequent lightning.

**fulvo** *adj.* reddish-yellow, tawny.

**fum-ac·chio** *m.* piece of smoky charcoal; jet of smoke; vapour; thermal spring giving off vapour; fumigation. **-ai(u)olo** *m.* chimney-pot, chimney; (naut.) funnel; smoke-stack.

**fum-are** [A1] *tr.* to smoke; *intr.* (*aux.* avere) to give off smoke; to steam; to fume (in anger). **-ata** *f.* cloud of smoke; puff of smoke; smoke-signal. **-ato** *part. adj.* smoked; (paint.) toned down, shaded. **-atore** *m.* smoker; (rlwy.) *compartimento per -atori*, smoking-compartment, smoker.

**fumasi·gari** *m. indecl.* cigar-holder.

**fumeggi-are** [A3c] *intr.* (*aux.* avere) to smoke, to emit smoke; *tr.* (art) to shade off, to gradate. **-ato** *part. adj.* (art) shaded, gradated, toned down.

**fumẹtto** *m.* anisette; balloon encircling words issuing from a figure's mouth; comic-strip.
**fumicare** [A2s] *intr.* (*aux.* avere) to smoke; to steam; to fume.
**fumicọso** *adj.* smoky; steamy.
**fu·mido, fumi·fero** *adj.* smoking; steamy.
**fumig-are** [A2s] *intr.* (*aux.* avere) to smoke, to steam, to give off vapour; to carry out fumigation. **-aziọne** *f.* fumigation; steam; vapour.
**fumo** *m.* smoke; *dove c'è —, c'è fuoco,* where there's smoke, there's fire; smoking; *il — è un gran vizio,* smoking is a bad habit; *tabacco da —,* pipe-tobacco; steam, vapour; fume, mist; vanity, pride, haughtiness; *è tutto —,* it's all emptiness; *vendere —,* to mystify, to deceive; *andare in —,* to go up in smoke, to come to nothing.
**fumọs-o** *adj.* smoking, steaming; proud, arrogant. **-ità** *f.* smokiness; steaminess; (fig.) vanity, pride.
**fun-a·io** *m.* rope-maker; ropeseller. **-am·bolo** *m.* tight-rope walker.
**fune** *f.* rope; *tiro alla —,* tug-of-war.
**fu·nebr-e** *adj.* funeral; *uffizio —, rito —,* funeral service; *impresario di pompe -i,* undertaker; funereal, gloomy.
**funerale** *adj.* funeral; funerary; *n.m.* funeral; obsequies.
**fu·nere** *m.* (poet.) massacre; death.
**fune·reo** *adj.* funereal; mournful.
**funestare** [A1] *tr.* to afflict; to oppress; to devastate; to vex, to distress; to desecrate, to profane.
**funesto** *adj.* fatal; grievous, ruinous; tragic.
**fung-a** *f.* mould. **-are** [A2] *intr.* (*aux.* essere) to become mouldy.
**funga·ia** *f.* mushroom-bed; (fig.) swarm, profusion.
**fun·g-ere** *tr.* [C5] to carry out, to fulfil; *intr.* (*aux.* avere) to function; *— da sindaco,* to act as mayor; *— da intermedio,* to act as go-between. **-ente** *part.* acting, functioning.
**funghẹto** *m.* mushroom-bed.
**funghire** [D2] *intr.* (*aux.* essere) to become mouldy.
**fungifọrme** *adj.* fungiform.
**fun-go** *m.* (*pl.* **-ghi**) (bot.) fungus; (cul.) mushroom or other edible fungus; *— velenoso,* toadstool. **-gọso** *adj.* fungous.
**funicolare** *adj.* (rlwy.) funicular; *n.f.* funicular; (naut.) chain ferry.
**funi·colo** *m.* cord; strand of cable.
**funivi·a** *f.* aerial ropeway, cableway; ski-lift.
**funzion-are** [A1c] *intr.* (*aux.* avere) to act; to work; to function; *— da sindaco,* to fill the office of mayor; *l'ascensore non -a,* the lift is out of order; *far —,* to operate, to work. **-amẹnto** *m.* functioning, working; *-amento a molla,* clockwork action.
**funziọn-e** *f.* function; *in —,* operative, working; (math.) *in — di,* in terms of; *— intellettuale,* intellectual faculty; significance, meaning; office, post; duties; *la Funzione Pubblica,* the Civil Service; (rel.) service. **-ale** *adj.* functional. **-a·rio** *m.* official, functionary; civil servant.
**fuochista** *m.* (eng.) stoker, fireman.
**fuo-co** *m.* (*pl.* **-chi**) fire; *accendere il —,* to light the fire; *al —!,* fire!; *prender —,* to catch fire; *dar — a,* to set on fire; *resistente al —,* fire-proof; *-chi d'artifizio,* fireworks; fireside, hearth; (fig.) heat, ardour; (mil.) shot; *far —,* to open fire; *arma da —,* firearm; focus; (opt.) *a —,* in focus. **-cato** *adj.* flame-coloured, scarlet.
**fuor-i** *adv.* outside; *fuori!,* get out!; *dar di —,* to overflow; *sporgersi in —,* to jut out; *da questo in —,* apart from this; *lasciar —,* to leave out; *il di —,* the outside; *prep., prep. phr. — di,* out of, outside; beyond; *— (di) commercio,* not for sale; *— (di) mano,* out of the way, remote; *— stagione,* out of season; *— scena,* off-stage. **-chẹ** *conj.* except, unless; excepting that; *prep.* except. **-ibọrdo** *m. indecl.* (naut.) ship's side; outboard motor boat. **-iclasse** *adj. indecl.* unequalled. **-ilegge** *m. indecl.* outlaw; bandit. **-ise·rie** *adj. indecl.* purpose-made, model. **-ivo·glia** *adv.* against one's will. **-misura** *adv.* excessively. **-uscito** *part. adj.* gone out; banished; exiled; *n.m.* exile; bandit.
**furb-eri·a** *f.* cunning, slyness; shrewdness; artfulness. **-ẹsco** *adj.* (*m.pl.* **-ẹschi**) cunning, sly; *linguaggio -esco,* thieves' lingo. **-i·zia** *f.* cunning, malice, artfulness.
**furbo** *adj.* shrewd, clever; artful; cunning, sly; malicious; *n.m.* cunning man, sly person.
**furente** *adj.* furious; raging, frenzied, mad; (rel.) inspired, possessed by a deity.
**fureri·a** *f.* (mil.) company office.
**furẹtto** *m.* (zool.) ferret.
**furfant-e** *adj.* rascal, rogue, scamp; scoundrel, knave. **-eri·a** *f.* roguery, knavery. **-ẹsco** *adj.* (*m.pl.* **-ẹschi**) roguish, knavish, scoundrelly.
**furgọn-e** *m.* van; *— per mobilia,* removal van. **-cino** *m. dim.* delivery van.
**fu·ri-a** *f.* fury, rage; temper; *montare in —,* to fly into a temper; *montò su tutte le -e,* he stormed and raged; violence, force, impetus; frenzy, passion; *in fretta e —,* in a tearing hurry; *a — di,* by dint of, by means of; craze; lust; furious person; *pl.* (myth.) Furies;
**furiare** [A4] *intr.* (*aux.* avere) to rage; *rfl.* to fly into a temper.
**furibọndo** *adj.* furious, violent, raging, wild.
**furier-e, -o** *m.* (mil.) quartermaster; (naut.) paymaster.
**furiọso** *adj.* furious, wild; violent, impetuous, vehement; insane.
**furọre** *m.* fury; *montò in —,* he became furious; furore, craze; *far —,* to be all the rage; force, vehemence; desire.
**furtivo** *adj.* furtive; clandestine, surreptitious; (leg.) *oggetti furtivi,* stolen goods.
**furto** *m.* stealing; theft; *— letterario,* plagiarism; *di —,* secretly; (leg.) larceny, stealing; *— parziale,* pilfering; *— con scasso,* housebreaking.
**fuscello** *m.* twig, small stick; piece of straw; *notare il — nell'occhio altrui e non veder la trave nel proprio,* to see the mote in one's neighbour's eye, but not the beam in one's own.
**fusciacca** *f.* sash (on a uniform); sash of office.
**fusellat-o** *adj.* (archit.) tapered, tapering. **-ura** *f.* tapering.
**fusello** *m.* small spindle; (eng.) spindle; stub axle.
**fuṣi·bile** *adj.* (phys.) fusible, meltable; (electr.) *tappo —,* fuse plug; *n.m.* (electr.) fuse, cut-out.
**fuṣifọrme** *adj.* spindle-shaped, tapering.
**fuṣiọne** *f.* fusion; (metall.) fusing, melting; casting; (leg.) amalgamation; (paint.) *— del colorito,* blending of colours.
**fuṣọ**[1] *part.* of **fọndere**; *adj.* fused; melted; cast; *ferro —,* cast iron; *formaggio —,* processed cheese.
**fuṣ-o**[2] *m.* (*pl.* **-i** *m.*, **-a** *f.*) (text.) spindle; (archit.) shaft (of a column); *— orario,* time zone; *far le -a,* to purr; *dritto come un —,* straight as a die.
**fuṣoliera** *f.* (aeron.) fuselage.
**fustagno** *m.* (text.) corduroy; fustian.
**fustame** *m.* cask, barrel.
**fusticello** *m.* twig.
**fustigare** [A2s] *tr.* to beat, to whip, to lash; to scourge.
**fusto** *m.* (bot.) stalk, stem; trunk; barrel, keg, cask; drum; (archit.) shaft (of a column); *— del letto,* bedstead.
**fu·til-e** *adj.* trifling, paltry; worthless, frivolous; futile, vain; useless. **-ità** *f.* futility; trifling matter; uselessness.
**futur-o** *adj.* future; coming; *n.m.* future; (gramm.) future tense; *il — anteriore,* the future-perfect; *pl. i -i,* posterity, future generations. **-iṣmo** *m.* futurism. **-ista** *m., f.* futurist.

**G** *f.*, *m.* (pron. **gi**) the letter G; the consonant G; *una G maiuscola*, a capital G; *una g minuscola*, a small g; *g raddoppiato*, double g.
**gabarr-a** *f.* (naut.) barge. **-iere** *m.* bargee.
**gabba-compagni** *m. indecl.* cheat, humbug. **-cristiani** *m. indecl.* rogue, impostor. **-deo** *m. indecl.* hypocrite. **-mọndo** *m. indecl.* charlatan; rogue. **-pensieri** *m. indecl.* distraction, diversion. **-santi** *m. indecl.* hypocrite.
**gabbanella** *f.* hospital-gown, white coat; overall.
**gabbano** *m.* sleeveless cloak; house-coat.
**gabb-are** [A1] *tr.* to cheat, to delude; to deceive; to mock; *rfl.* to amuse oneself; *-arsi di*, to make fun of. **-atọre** *m.* impostor; mocker; practical joker.
**gab·bi-a** *f.* cage; pen; bird-cage; hen-coop; *una — di matti*, a crowd of noisy people, (fam.) prison; (comm.) crate; — *dell'ascensore*, lift-cage; (leg.) — *degli accusati*, dock. **-ata** *f.* cageful.
**gabbiano** *m.* (orn.) gull.
**gabbo** *m.* joke, game; jest, mockery, derision; *prendere a* —, to make a joke of, to make fun of.
**gabell-a** *f.* (comm.) excise; tax on moveables; duty; toll. **-are** [A1] *tr.* to levy excise duty on; to impose local toll on; (fig.) *-are per*, to pass off as. **-iere** *m.* excise officer; toll-collector. **-ino** *m.* excise officer; toll-house.
**gabinẹtto** *m.* study; consulting room; laboratory; water-closet, lavatory; (leg.) cabinet; private secretariat.
**gaffa** *f.* (naut.) boat-hook.
**ga·gate** *m.* (miner.) jet.
**gaggi·a** *f.* (bot.) acacia flowers; mimosa flowers.
**gagliard-o** *adj.* strong, hardy, robust; vigorous; *vino* —, full-bodied wine; hale and hearty. **-i·a** *f.* boldness, bravery; strength, vigour.
**gagno** *m.* hiding place, lair; intrigue.
**gagnolare** [A5 s] *intr.* (*aux.* avere) to whine, to howl; to yelp.
**ga·i-o** *adj.* gay, joyful; joyous; vivacious; vivid; bright; gaudy. **-ẹzza** *f.* gaiety; happiness, joy; vivacity; brightness, vividness.
**gala**[1] *f.* piece of finery; frill; (naut.) *gran* —, ship dressed overall with flags.
**gala**[2] *f.* festivity, gala; pomp, luxury; *serata di* —, gala evening.
**galano** *m.* tassel; bow.
**galant-e** *adj.* polite; courteous; attentive; gallant; *donna* —, woman of easy virtue; elegant; showy; *n.m.* gallant, lover. **-eri·a** *f.* politeness; courtesy; gallantry; foppishness.
**galantina** *f.* (cul.) galantine.
**galanto** *m.* snowdrop.
**galantomịsmo** *m.* honourable or gentlemanly behaviour.
**galant-uomo** *m.* (*pl.* **-uo·mini**) man of integrity and honour; good man; *ve lo dico da* —, I tell you on my honour; (hist.) *il re* —, Vittorio Emanuele II.
**galas·sia** *f.* (astron.) galaxy, Milky Way.
**galate·o** *m.* book of etiquette; code of good manners; good breeding.
**Galati** *pr.n.m.pl.* (bibl.) Galatians.
**galat·t-ico** *adj.* (astron.) galactic. **-o·fago** *adj.* milk-fed. **-o·metro** *m.* lactometer. **-opoie·si** *f. indecl.* (med.) lactation.
**Gala·zia** *pr.n.f.* (geog.) Galatia.
**ga·le-a**[1] *f.* helmet. **-ato** *adj.* helmeted.
**gal-e·a**[2] *f.* (naut. history.) galley. **-eazza** *f.* galleass, large galley.
**galena** *f.* (miner.) galena; (radio) *apparecchio a* —, crystal set.
**galeọne** *m.* (naut. hist.) galleon.
**galeott-a** *f.* (naut.) galliot, small galley. **-o** *m.* galley-slave.
**galera** *f.* galley; convict prison.
**galestro** *m.* (geol.) marl.
**Galile·a** *pr.n.f.* (geog.) Galilee.
**galile·o**[1] *adj.*, *n.m.* Galilean.
**Galile·o**[2] *pr.n.m.* Galileo.
**Gali·zia** *pr.n.f.* (geog.) Galicia.
**galla**[1] *f.* (bot.) gall; — *della quercia*, oak-apple; — *del cipresso*, cone of cypress tree; — *moscata*, nutmeg; gall in the skin; air-bubble.
**galla**[2] *adv. a* —, afloat; *stare a* —, to keep one's head above water (also fig.).
**gallare** [A1] *tr.* to fertilize (an egg); *intr.* (*aux.* essere) to become fertilized (of an egg).
**galleggi-are** [A3 c] *intr.* (*aux* avere) to float; to keep afloat; to hover; to lie lightly on the top. **-abilità** *f.* buoyancy. **-amẹnto** *m.* floating; (naut.) *linea di -amento*, waterline. **-ante** *part. adj.* floating; *ghiaccio -ante*, iceberg; *n.m.* float; raft.
**galleri·a** *f.* gallery; arcade; art gallery; (rlwy.) tunnel; subway; — *aerodinamica*, wind tunnel.
**Galles** *pr.n.m.* (geog.) Wales; (also) *il paese di* —, Wales; *il Principe di* —, the Prince of Wales.
**gallẹse** *adj.* Welsh; *n.m.* Welshman; Welsh language; *f.* Welsh woman.
**Gal·lia** *pr.n.f.* (hist.) Gaul.
**gal·lic-o** *adj.* Gallic, French; *n.m.* Gaul. **-ịsmo** *m.* Gallicism.
**gallin-a** *f.* domestic fowl, hen; (cul.) *carne di* —, chicken; *latte di* —, egg-flip; *pelle di* —, goose-flesh; *meglio l'uovo oggi che la — domani*, a bird in the hand is worth two in the bush. **-a·io** *m.* poultry keeper. **-ame** *m.* poultry. **-ẹtta** *f.* (ent.) *-etta della Vergine*, ladybird.
**galliẓẓ-ante** *adj.* Frenchified. **-ato** *adj.* Gallicized.
**Gall-o**[1] *m.* Gaul; *adj.* Gallic. **-ẹsco** *adj.* (*m.pl.* **-ẹschi**) Frenchified. **-o·filo** *m.* Francophile. **-o·fobo** *m.* Francophobe.
**gall-o**[1] *m.* (orn.) cock; weather-cock; *il canto del* —, cockcrow; *camminare a* —, to strut; — *d'India*, turkey; (boxing) *peso* —, bantam-weight. **-ẹtto** *m. dim.* cockerel, bantam; *fare il -etto*, to be cocky.
**gallọn-e**[1] *m.* (text.) galloon, lace, braid; chevron; *pl.* (mil.) stripes. **-are** [A1 c] *tr.* to trim with lace or braid.
**gallọne**[2] *m.* gallon (=4.5459631 litres).
**gallo·ria** *f.* mirth; revelry, noisy merrymaking.
**galloz·zola** *f.* oak-apple; bubble; blister; pimple.
**galluzzare** [A1] *intr.* (*aux.* avere) to make merry.
**galoppare** [A1] *intr.* (*aux.* avere) (equit.) to canter; — *a tutta forza*, to gallop.
**galoppo** *m.* (equit.) canter; *gran* —, gallop; (fig.) *al* —, at the gallop, very fast; (mus.) galop.
**galo·scia** *f.* galosh, rubber over-shoe.
**galva·n-ico** *adj.* galvanic. **-ịsmo** *m.* galvanism. **-iẓẓare** [A1] *tr.* to galvanize; (fig.) to electrify.
**galvan-o** *m.* (typ.) galvanograph. **-o·metro** *m.* galvanometer. **-opla·stica** *f.* electro-plating. **-opla·stico** *adj.* electro-plated. **-oterapi·a** *f.* electro-therapy.
**gamb-a** *f.* leg; shank; *fare il passo secondo la* —, to cut one's coat according to one's cloth; *sgranchirsi le -e*, to stretch one's legs; *mettersi tra le -e di alcuno*, to get under someone's feet; *darsela a -e*, to run away; *una persona in* —, a competent person; *essere in* —, to be in good form; stem of a letter, number or note; *viola da* —, bass viol. **-ale** *m.* leg of a boot; legging; boot tree; splint.
**gam·ber-o** *m.* (pop.) lobster; (zool.) — *di fiume*, crayfish; — *marino*, lobster; — *delle rocce*, prawn; (fig.) *far il viaggio del* —, to go backwards. **-ello** *m. dim.* shrimp.
**gambẹtta** *f.* (orn.) ruff, reeve.
**gambettare** [A1 c] *intr.* (*aux.* avere) to gambol, to frolic.
**gambẹtto** *m.* little stem, slender stalk; *dare il — a*, to trip up; (zool.) — *di sabbia*, common shrimp.
**gambitto** *m.* (chess) gambit.
**gambo** *m.* stalk, stem; shaft, haft; shank; stroke of a letter.
**gambuto** *adj.* long-legged, spindle-shanked.
**game·lio** *adj.* bridal, nuptial.
**gamell-a** *f.* mess-tin. **-ino** *m.* billy-can.

**gamete** *m.* (biol.) gamete, sex cells.
**gamma** *m.* the Greek letter γ; *m.*, *f.* (photog.) gamma; (mus.) scale, (paint.) grades of colour, range of tints; (fig.) gamut, range.
**gammato** *adj.* shaped like a gamma; *croce gammata*, swastika.
**gana·scia** *f.* jaw; jowl; *carico di* —, heavy-jowled; (rlwy.) fish-plate.
**gan·c-io** *m.* hook; scribble; grabbing person. **-iata** *f.* act of hooking; load on a hook.
**Gand** *pr.n.f.* (geog.) Ghent.
**Gange** *pr.n.m.* (geog.) Ganges.
**gangheggiare** [A3 c] *intr.* (*aux.* avere) to chafe at the bit.
**gangherare** [A1 s] *tr.* to set on hinges; to provide with hooks.
**gan·gher-o** *m.* hook for an eye; — *e gangherella*, hook and eye; hinge; *essere fuori dei -i*, to be beside oneself with rage; (fig.) elusive movement, dodge; *dare* —, to turn about. **-ella** *f.* eye for a hook. **-ello** *m.* quick swerve.
**ganghire** [D2] *intr.* (*aux.* avere) to fret; to long.
**gan·glio** *m.* (anat.) ganglion; (fig.) nerve-centre.
**gan·gola** *f.* (pop.) swollen gland in the neck; swollen tonsil; scar on the neck; canker.
**Ganimede** *pr.n.m.* (myth.) Ganymede.
**gannire** [D2] *intr.* (*aux.* avere) to whimper, to whine.
**gara** *f.* rivalry; match; competition; race; *a* —, for a wager; *fare a* —, to compete, to vie; — *libera*, open event; — *avantaggi*, handicap event; — *eliminatoria*, heat; (comm.) tender.
**garante** *m.* (leg.) guarantor; *rendersi* —, to act as guarantor; *me ne rendo* —, I'll answer for it; *adj.* vouching, guaranteeing, warranting.
**garantire** [D2] *tr.* (leg.) to guarantee; to stand as surety on behalf of; to warrant.
**garanza** *f.* (bot.) madder.
**garanzi·a** *f.* guarantee; security; — *reale*, security on property; *atto di* —, security bond; — *ipotecaria*, mortgage security.
**garb-are** [A1] *intr.* (*aux.* essere, avere; *prep.* a) to suit, to be becoming to; to please; *tr.* to give form to, to shape. **-atẹzza** *f.* politeness; geniality; urbanity; polish. **-ato** *part. adj.* formed, shaped; well-mannered, polite, civil; graceful; in good taste. **-eggiare** [A3 c] *intr.* (*aux.* avere; *prep.* a) to please; *tr.* to beautify.
**garbo**[1] *m.* good manners, courtesy; charm; *con* —, politely, graciously; *di* —, honest, loyal; good cut of clothes; *prendere il* —, to take shape; gesture, sign.
**garbo**[2] *adj.* sour; harsh; bitter.
**garbu·glio** *m.* tangle, confusion; mix-up, disorder; turmoil; agitation.
**gareggiare** [A3 c] *intr.* (*aux.* avere) to vie, to compete; to race; to contend.
**garẹggio** *m.* long drawn-out competition; long-standing rivalry.
**garenna** *f.* rabbit-warren.
**garganella** *f.* gurgling-sound; *bere a* —, to gulp down.
**gargantuẹs-co** *adj.* (*m.pl.* **-chi**) gargantuan; voracious.
**gargar-ịsmo** *m.* gargle; gargling; (derog.) trilling, warbling. **-ịzzare** [A1] *intr.* (*aux.* avere) to gargle; to warble.
**gar·gia** *f.* (zool.) gill.
**gargotta** *f.* eating-house, chop-house.
**garibaldino** *adj.* (hist.) pertaining to Garibaldi; *n.m.* follower of Garibaldi.
**garitta** *f.* look-out tower or post; sentry-box; workman's hut.
**garo·fano** *m.* (bot.) clove pink, carnation; (cul.) *chiodi di* —, cloves; (pharm.) *essenza di* —, oil of cloves; (zool.) — *di mare*, sea anemone.
**garrẹse** *m.* withers.
**garrẹtto** *m.* back of the heel; (of a horse) pastern, hock, fetlock; (fig.) calf, strength of leg.
**garrire** [D2] *intr.* (*aux.* avere) to shriek; to squabble; to cackle; to chirp; *tr.* to chide, to scold.
**garrul-ante** *adj.* talkative; garrulous; chattering. **-ità** *f.* garrulousness.
**gar·rulo** *adj.* garrulous; talkative.
**garza**[1] *f.* jaw-bone of a horse.
**garz-a**[2] *f.* gauze; (naut.) eye splice. **-are** [A1] *tr.* (text.) to card. **-o** *m.* (bot.) thistle-head; (text.) *dare il -o a*, to card.
**garz-a**[3] *f.* (orn.) heron. **-ẹtta** *f.* (orn.) egret.
**garzọn-e** *m.* boy in service; farm-boy; shop-boy; errand-boy; apprentice. **-ato** *m.* apprenticeship.
**gas** *m. indecl.* gas; *becco del* —, gas-burner; *contatore del* —, gas-meter; *fornello a* —, gas-cooker; *radiatore a* —, gas-fire; (motor.) petrol; *pedale del* —, accelerator; *a tutto* —, at full speed.
**gasare** [A1] *tr.* to aerate, to charge with gas.
**gaschẹtto** *m.* gasket.
**gasdọtto** *m.* gas-pipe.
**gaso·lio** *m.*, **gasolina** *f.* gasoline, petrol.
**gass-are** [A1] *tr.* to gas. **-ista** *m.* gas-man, gas-fitter. **-o·metro** *m.* gasometer. **-ọso** *adj.* gaseous, aerated.
**gastr-algi·a** *f.* (med.) pain in the stomach. **-enterite** *f.* (med.) gastro-enteritis. **-i·loquo** *m.* ventriloquist. **-ite** *f.* gastritis. **-onomi·a** *f.* gastronomy. **-ono·mico** *adj.* gastronomic(al). **-o·nomo** *m.* gastronome, gourmet.
**ga·stric-a** *f.* (med.) gastric fever. **-o** *adj.* gastric.
**gatt-a** *f.* (zool.) female cat; puss, pussy; (provb.) *quando la* — *non c'è, i topi ballano*, when the cat's away the mice do play; *comprare la* — *nel sacco*, to buy a pig in a poke; — *cieca*, blind man's buff; (bot.) *erba* —, cat-mint.
**gatta-bu·ia** *f.* (joc.) prison, 'clink'. **-morta** *f. indecl.* (fam.) sly, wily person; *fare la -morta*, to lie low.
**gatteggiare** [A3 c] *intr.* (*aux.* avere) to glisten, to glint.
**gattẹs-co** *adj.* (*m.pl.* **-chi**) feline, cat-like.
**gatt-o** *m.* cat; — *maschio*, male cat, tom-cat; — *castrato*, neuter cat; *essere come cani e -i*, to fight like cat and dog; (bot.) catkin; (motor.) *occhi di* —, cat's-eye reflectors. **-ino** *m.* kitten; *far -ini*, to have kittens; (bot.) catkin. **-ọni** *m.pl.* mumps; *adv. gatton -oni*, quietly on all fours; stealthily.
**gaudente** *adj.* self-indulgent, pleasure-loving; jolly, cheerful, merry.
**ga·udi-o** *m.* bliss; happiness, joy. **-ọso** *adj.* joyful, joyous.
**gavazz-a** *f.* merry-making; revelry. **-iere** *m.* reveller, merry-maker.
**gavello** *m.* felloe.
**gavẹtta** *f.* mess-tin; mess-bowl; *venir dalla* —, to rise from the ranks.
**gavotta** *f.* (mus.) gavotte.
**gazz-a** *f.* (orn.) magpie; — *ghiandaia*, jay; (fig.) chattering woman.
**gazzarra** *f.* uproar, din.
**gazzella** *f.* (zool.) gazelle.
**gaz·zera** *f.* (orn.) magpie.
**gazzett-a** *f.* gazette, newspaper; journal. **-ino** *m.* news-sheet; announcements column of a newspaper.
**gazzo** *adj.* bluish green.
**Geen·na** *f.* (bibl.) Gehenna, hell.
**gel-are** [A1] *tr.* to freeze; to chill; *rfl.*, *intr.* (*aux.* essere) to freeze; *gli si -ò il sangue nelle vene*, his blood ran cold. **-atamẹnte** *adv.* in a cold manner; freezingly; chillingly. **-ateri·a** *f.* ice-cream shop. **-atiera** *f.* ice-cream machine. **-atiere** *m.* ice-cream vendor. **-atina** *f.* gelatine; jelly; isinglass; freezing mixture; *-atina esplosiva*, dynamite; (photog.) emulsion. **-atinọso** *adj.* gelatinous. **-ato** *part. adj.* frozen, chilled; iced; cold, frigid; (fig.) dead; *n.m.* ice-cream.
**ge·lido** *adj.* cold, chilly; icy; frigid.
**gel-o** *m.* frost; cold; freezing-point; *corroso dal* —, frost-bitten; (fig.) numbness, lack of feeling. **-ọne** *m.* chilblain.
**gelosi·a** *f.* jealousy; window-shutter.
**gelọso** *adj.* jealous; envious; zealous; touchy; easily put out of order; (of a boat) easily capsized; *negozio* —, ticklish business.

**gelso** *m.* (bot.) mulberry-tree; (ent.) *farfalla del* —, mulberry silk moth.
**gelsomino** *m.* (bot.) jasmine, jessamine.
**gemebọndo** *adj.* moaning; groaning; lamenting.
**gemella** *f.* twin sister.
**gemelli·para** *f.* mother of twins.
**gemello** *adj.* twin; one of a pair; *muscoli gemelli*, biceps; *anima gemella*, twin soul; *nave gemella*, sister ship; *n.m.* twin brother; double; *pl.* cuff-links; *pr.n.m.pl.* (astron.) *i Gemelli*, Gemini.
**ge·mere** [B1] *intr.* (*aux.* avere) to moan; to groan; (of a vessel) to leak; (of doves) to coo; (*aux.* essere) to leak, to drip; to ooze; to trickle.
**geminare** [A1 s] *tr.* to double; to couple, to duplicate; to repeat; *intr.* (*aux.* avere) (bot.) to germinate.
**gemire** [D2] *intr.* (*aux.* avere) to moan; to coo (of a dove); to ooze.
**ge·mito** *m.* groan; cooing.
**gemma** *f.* gem; jewel; pimple; (bot.) bud; *mettere le gemme*, to put forth buds.
**gemm-are** [A1] *intr.* (*aux.* avere) to produce buds, to bud; *rfl.* to put on gems. **-ato** *part. adj.* laden with buds; bejewelled; *la coda -ata*, the peacock's tail.
**gemm-a·rio** *adj.* pertaining to jewellery; *l'arte -aria*, the jeweller's art. **-i·fero** *adj.* producing buds. **-ọso** *adj.* rich in buds.
**gemme·o** *adj.* gem-like.
**gemmini** *m.pl.* (bot.) garden nasturtium.
**gendarm-e** *m.* policeman; (eccl.) *-i pontifici*, papal gendarmes. **-eri·a** *f.* police, gendarmerie.
**gene** *m.* (biol.) gene.
**geneal-ogi·a** *f.* genealogy; pedigree. **-o·gico** *adj.* genealogical; *albero -ogico*, family tree. **-ogista** *m.* genealogist.
**genearca** *m.* (leg.) genearch, head of a family; (fig.) founder of a race.
**general-e**[1] *adj.* general; *con parole -i*, in general terms; *in* —, generally speaking, as a rule; usual, commonly accepted; common; widespread; (comm.) *spese -i*, overhead expenses; *n.m.* general point of view; *f.pl. le -i*, general statements and ideas; *star sulle -i*, to keep to generalities; *sonar la* —, to beat to quarters; (naut.) — *!*, general quarters! **-mẹnte** *adv.* generally; *-mente parlando*, generally speaking; usually; commonly.
**general-e**[2] *m.* general; (mil.) — *di brigata*, brigadier; — *di divisione, tenente* —, major-general; — *di corpo d'armata*, lieutenant-general; — *d'armata*, general; (eccl.) superior-general. **-is·simo** *m.* (mil.) commander-in-chief.
**generalità** *f. indecl.* generality; the general run of things; majority; *pl.* general remarks; (leg.) personal particulars, name and address.
**generaliẓẓ-are** [A1] *tr.* to make general; to publish abroad, to broadcast, to spread; *intr.* (*aux.* avere) to generalize. **-aziọne** *f.* generalization; making generally known.
**gener-are** [A1 s] *tr.* to generate; to create, to produce; to breed; to beget. **-atọre** *m.* producer; creator; (eng.; electr.) generator. **-aziọne** *f.* generation; begetting; race; descendants; genus.
**ge·nere** *m.* kind, sort, type; genus; species; *il — umano*, mankind, the human race; *in* —, generally; (art; lit.) genre; (comm.) — *d'affari*, line of business; *pl.* (comm.) goods; commodities; articles; *generi alimentari*, foodstuffs.
**gene·rico** *adj.* generic; general; vague, indeterminate; (theatr.) *attore* —, 'character actor'.
**ge·nero** *m.* son-in-law.
**generọs-o** *adj.* generous; bountiful, lavish; unstinting; *vino* —, full-bodied wine. **-ità** *f.* generosity; liberality; productivity.
**ge·nẹsi** *f. indecl.* genesis; origin; formation; *pr.n.f.* (bibl.) *la Genesi*, Genesis.
**gene·tic-a** *f.* genetics. **-o** *adj.* genetic; relating to origins.
**genetista** *m.*, . geneticist.
**genetli·aco** *adj.* relating to a birthday; relating to a horoscope; *n.m.* birthday.
**gengiv-a** *f.* (anat.) gum. **-ite** *f.* (med.) gingivitis.
**geni·a** *f.* evil brood, disreputable crowd, low set.
**genial-e** *adj.* clever; ingenious; talented, inventive; brilliant; congenial; genial. **-ità** *f.* cleverness; brilliance; geniality; likeableness. **-o·ide** *adj.* gifted.
**ge·ni-o** *m.* genius; a person of genius; guardian spirit; talent; inclination, taste; *andare a — a*, to be to the liking of; character; (mil.) corps of engineers; *compagnia del* —, sappers; (naut.) — *navale*, corps of naval constructors. **-ere** *m.* (mil.) sapper.
**genitale** *adj.* genital; *n.m.pl.* genital organs.
**genitivo** *adj., n.m.* (gramm.) genitive.
**ge·nito** *adj.* born; begotten; *n.m.* offspring; *primo* —, first-born; *ultimo* —, youngest son.
**genit-ọre** *m.* parent; father; *i miei -ori*, my parents; creator. **-rice** *f.* mother; genetrix. **-ura** *f.* engendering; bringing forth; birth.
**genna·io** *pr.n.m.* January; *sudar di* —, to have great anxieties.
**genoci·dio** *m.* genocide.
**Ge·nov-a** *pr.n.f.* (geog.) Genoa. **-ẹse** *adj.* Genoese; *n.m.* Genoese; Genoese dialect; district round Genoa; *f.* Genoese woman. **-esịsmo** *m.* Genoese idiom; Genoese custom.
**gent-e** *f.* clan, tribe; people, nation; *diritto delle -i*, law of nations; people, persons; folk; *cosa dirà la — ?*, what will people say ?; crowd; company; visitors; *far* —, to draw a crowd. **-a·glia** *f.* mob, rabble.
**gentildonna** *f.* gentlewoman, noblewoman.
**gentil-e**[1] *adj.* noble, gentle; *Gentile Signore*, Dear Sir; kind, kindly; courteous polite; tender, delicate, soft; *carne* —, tender meat; *terra* —, ground that is easily worked; *pianta* —, cultivated plant. **-ẹsco** *adj.* (*m.pl.* **-ẹschi**) gentlemanly; lady-like. **-ẹzza** *f.* gentleness; nobility; courtesy, politeness; kind action; *fammi una -ezza*, do me a favour; delicacy, softness, tenderness. **-i·gia** *f.* nobility. **-i·zio** *adj.* noble, ancestral; (herald.) *stemma -izio*, heraldic bearings.
**gentil-e**[2] *adj.* Gentile: non-Jewish; pagan; non-Christian; *n.m., f.* Gentile. **-ẹsco** *adj.* (*m.pl.* **-ẹschi**) heathen, pagan.
**gentil-uomo** *m.* (*pl.* **-u·omini**) gentleman; nobleman.
**genufless-iọne** *f.* genuflection; — *profonda*, kneeling on both knees. **-o** *adj.* kneeling. **-o·rio** *m.* prie-Dieu.
**genuflet·tere** [C19] *rfl.* to genuflect; to kneel down.
**genuin-o** *adj.* genuine; authentic; real; characteristic. **-ità** *f.* genuineness.
**genziana** *f.* (bot.) gentian.
**geocen·trico** *adj.* geocentric.
**geod-eṣi·a** *f.* geodesy; topography. **-eṣi·metro** *m.* protractor. **-eta** *m., f.* geodesist. **-e·tico** *adj.* geodetic. **-ina·mica** *f.* geodynamics. **-ina·mico** *adj.* geodynamic.
**geofi·ṣic-a** *f.* geophysics. **-o** *adj.* geophysical.
**geogr-afi·a** *f.* geography. **-a·fico** *adj.* geographical.
**geo·grafo** *m.* geographer; *ingegnere* —, cartographer.
**geol-ogi·a** *f.* geology. **-o·gico** *adj.* geological.
**geo·lo-go** *m.* (*pl.* **-ghi**) geologist.
**geom-ante** *m.* geomancer. **-an·tico** *adj.* geomantic. **-anzi·a** geomancy.
**geo·metr-a** *m.* geometer; geometrician; land-surveyor. **-i·a** *f.* geometry.
**geome·trico** *adj.* geometric(al): (fig.) exact, real.
**geo-morfologi·a** *f.* geomorphology. **-pla·stica** *f.* relief model; relief map. **-poli·tica** *f.* political geography.

**Geor·gia** *pr.n.f.* Georgia (U.S.A., U.S.S.R.).
**geor·gic-a** *f.* georgic; *le Georgiche,* the *Georgics.* **-o** *adj.* agricultural; *poema -o,* georgic.
**Ge·ova** *pr.n.m.* Jehovah.
**gera·nio** *m.* (bot.) geranium.
**gerar-ca** *m.* (*pl.* **-chi**) hierarch; *il sommo —,* the Pope; high official. **-cato** *m.* office of hierarch. **-chi·a** *f.* hierarchy.
**gerar·chico** *adj.* hierarchic(al); *trasmettere una domanda per via gerarchica,* to forward a request through the proper channels.
**Gerem-i·a** *pr.n.m.* (bibl.) Jeremiah. **-i·ade** *f.* jeremiad.
**ger-ente** *m.* director; manager; *socio —,* managing partner; (journ.) managing editor. **-enza** *f.* management; agency. **-ire** [D2] *tr., intr.* (*aux.* avere) (admin.) to manage; to be a director or manager.
**ger-go** (*pl.* **-ghi**) slang; cant; jargon. **-gale** *adj.* pertaining to jargon or slang.
**geri-atri·a** *f.*, **-a·trica** *f.* geriatrics. **-a·trico** *adj.* geriatric.
**Ge·rico** *pr.n.f.* (geog.) Jericho.
**gerla** *f.* basket; *a gerle,* in basketfuls, (fig.) in abundance.
**Germa·nia** *pr.n.f.* (geog.) Germany.
**germ-ano**[1] *m.* Teuton. **-a·nico** *adj.* Germanic, Teutonic. **-anẹṣimo, -aniṣmo** *m.* Germanism. **-ano·filo** *m.* Germanophile. **-ano·fobo** *m.* Germanophobe.
**german-o**[2] *adj.* natural, blood, full (of brother or sister). **-ità** *f.* blood-relationship of true brothers.
**germano**[3] *m.* (orn.) mallard.
**germ-e** *m.* germ, seed; embryo; (fig.) first cause. **-icida** *adj., n.m.* germicide. **-inale** *adj.* germinal. **-inello** *m.* *dim.* seedling.
**germin-are** [A1 s] *intr.* (*aux.* essere, avere) to germinate, to shoot; *tr.* to produce. **-azịone** *f.* germination.
**germogli-are** [A4 c] *intr.* (*aux.* essere, avere) to shoot, to sprout; to bud; *tr.* to bring forth, to bear; to yield. **-azịone** *f.* shooting, sprouting.
**germọglio** *m.* shoot, sprout; bud.
**geroco·mio** *m.* home for aged.
**gerof-ante** *m.* high-priest. **-anti·a, -anzi·a** *f.* high-priesthood. **-an·tico** *adj.* hierophantic. **-an·tide** *f.* high priestess.
**gerogli·fico** *adj., n.m.* hieroglyphic; hieroglyph.
**Gero·lamo** *pr.n.m.* Jerome.
**gerontologi·a** *f.* (med.) gerontology.
**Geroṣo·lima** *pr.n.f.* (poet.) Jerusalem.
**Geroṣolimitani** *pr.n.m.pl.* Knights of St. John.
**gerun·d-io** *m.* (gramm.) gerund; (joc.) *dare nei -i,* to go mad. **-ivo** *adj.* (gramm.) gerundive.
**Gerusalemme** *pr.n.f.* (geog.) Jerusalem.
**gessa·i-a** *f.* gypsum quarry; chalk-pit. **-o** *m.* plaster-cast maker or seller. **-(u)olo** *m.* gypsum quarryman; plasterer; plaster-cast maker.
**gessare** [A1 c] *tr.* to clarify wine with gypsum; to plaster.
**gẹss-o** *m.* (miner.) gypsum; chalk; piece of chalk; plaster; plaster of Paris; *pipa di —,* clay pipe; (sculpt.) plaster-cast. **-ọso** *adj.* rich in gypsum; chalky.
**gest-a** *f.* (*indecl.* or *pl.* **-e**) enterprise, feat, deed; race, family; *canzoni di —,* chansons de geste.
**gest-are** [A1 c] *tr.* to gestate; *intr.* (*aux.* avere) to be pregnant. **-ante** *adj.* pregnant, expectant; *n.f.* expectant mother; *corredi per -anti,* maternity wear. **-azịone** *f.* (med.) gestation; (fig.) time of preparation.
**gesticol-are** [A1 s] *intr.* (*aux.* avere) to gesticulate. **-ante** *part. adj.* gesticulating; *n.m., f.* person gesticulating. **-azịone** *f.* gesticulation.
**gestịone** *f.* administration; conduct of affairs; tenure of office; *spese di —,* overheads; *capo —,* chief manager.
**gestire**[1] [D2] *intr.* (*aux.* avere) to accompany speech with appropriate actions; to make gestures.
**gestire**[2] [D2] *tr.* to administer, to direct, to manage; to run.
**gesto**[1] *m.* gesture; movement; gesticulation; act, action.
**gesto**[2] *m.* deed; geste, exploit.
**gestọre** *m.* administrator, director; supervisor; manager.
**gestr-o** *m.* grimace. **-ọso** *adj.* grimacing.
**Gesù** *pr.n.m.* Jesus; *— Cristo,* Jesus Christ.
**geṣu-ita** *m.* Jesuit. **-i·tico** *adj.* Jesuitical.
**gett-are** [A1] *tr.* to throw, to fling, to hurl; *— via,* to throw away; *— a mare,* to throw overboard; *— l'ancora,* to drop anchor; *— le basi di,* to lay the foundations of; (metall.) to cast; *intr.* (*aux.* avere) to throw, to give off; (of a fountain) to play; (bot.) to sprout; (econ.) to yield; *rfl.* to throw oneself; to jump; to rush. **-ata** *f.* throw, cast; (bot.) shoot; (naut.) jetty. **-atọio** *m.* rubbish tip; chute. **-atọre** *m.* thrower; iron-founder; one possessed of the evil eye.
**get·tito** *m.* (naut.) jettison, jetsam; (comm.) output, yield.
**getto** *m.* throw, cast; (leg.) tipping; *far — di,* to jettison; (metall.) casting; (med.) vomit; flux; jet, spurt, gush; chute; (bot.) shoot; (fig.) draft; *di primo —,* in the first version; (sport) *— del peso,* putting the weight.
**gettọn-e** *m.* counter, token; (gambling) chip; disc used in public telephones; *macchina a -i,* slot machine. **-are** [A1 c] *tr.* (slang) to ring up.
**ghepardo** *m.* (zool.) cheetah.
**ghẹppio** *m.* (orn.) kestrel.
**gheri·glio** *m.* kernel.
**gherminella** *f.* trick; sleight of hand; peccadillo.
**ghermire** [D2] *tr.* to seize; to snatch; to clutch; to claw.
**gherọne** *m.* gusset; gore; piece of cloth.
**ghẹtt-a** *f.* gaiter. **-ina** *f.* spat. **-ọne** *m.* legging.
**ghẹtto** *m.* ghetto; slum district; (fig.) confusion, chaos.
**ghiacci-are** [A3] *rfl., intr.* (*aux.* essere) to freeze; to turn to ice; (aeron.) to ice up. **-ato** *part. adj.* frozen; iced; ice-cold; *vetro -ato,* frosted glass.
**ghiac·ci-o** *m.* ice; *— galleggiante,* iceberg; *nave trattenuta dai ghiacci,* ice-bound ship; *adj.* icy, frozen; freezing cold. **-a·io** *m.* glacier. **-uolo** *m.* icicle; ice-bucket; hailstone.
**ghia·i-a** *f.* gravel; shingle. **-ata** *f.* fine gravel; gravel path. **-ọne** *m.* gravel, scree. **-ọso** *adj.* gravelly; shingly.
**ghiand-a** *f.* acorn; lump, swelling; (anat.) gland. **-i·fero** *adj.* acorn-bearing.
**ghianda·ia** *f.* (orn.) jay.
**ghiandale** *m.* (zool.) barnacle.
**ghian·dol-a** *f.* gland. **-ato** *m.* (vet.) strangles. **-ọso** *adj.* glandular.
**ghiarẹto** *m.* bank of shingle; gravelly river-bed.
**ghiattire** [D2] *intr.* (*aux.* avere) (of hounds) to bay; to yelp.
**Ghibellino** *adj., pr.n.m.* (hist.) Ghibelline.
**ghiera** *f.* ferrule; metal ring or cap.
**ghigle** *f.pl.* braid.
**ghigliottin-a** *f.* guillotine; *finestra a —,* sash window. **-are** [A1] *tr.* to guillotine.
**ghign-a** *f.* sinister, leering face; [A5] *intr.* (*aux.* avere) to sneer; to smile sarcastically. **-ata** *f.* sneer; sarcastic smile; derisive laugh. **-azzare** [A1] *intr.* (*aux.* avere) to sneer; to laugh derisively. **-o** *m.* leer; sneer; grin; derisive laugh. **-ọso** *adj.* leering; sneering.
**ghind-a** *f.* (naut.) a lift used for hoisting. **-ag·gio** *m.* hoisting. **-ale** *m.* hoisting rope. **-ame** *m.* rigging. **-are** [A1] *tr.* to hoist. **-azzo** *m.* windlass.
**ghine·a** *f.* guinea.
**ghin·gheri** *m.pl.* gewgaws.
**ghiọtt-o** *adj.* greedy; gluttonous; eager; fond of; delicious, appetizing; *boccone —,* tasty morsel;

*n.m.* greedy man, glutton. **-eri·a** *f.* gluttony; greed. **-orni·a** *f.* gluttony, greed; covetousness; tasty food.
**ghiottọn-e** *m.* greedy person; glutton; gourmand; *adj.* greedy. **-eri·a** *f.*, **-i·a** *f.* greediness; avidity; covetousness; tit-bit; dainty morsel.
**ghiova** *f.* sod, clod.
**ghiọẓẓo** *m.* drop; drip; tiny bit.
**ghirba** *f.* leather water bucket; *salvare la* —, to save one's skin.
**ghiribiẓẓ-o** *m.* whim, caprice, fancy; *gli è saltato il — di*, he has suddenly taken it into his head to; fantasy. **-are** [A1] *intr.* (*aux.* avere) to indulge in fantasy; to have caprices; to be whimsical; to romance. **-ante** *part. adj.*, **-ọso** *adj.* fanciful; whimsical; capricious.
**ghirigoro** *m.* scroll; flourish (in writing); rigmarole; doodle, squiggle; scribble.
**ghirland-a** *f.* garland, wreath; *far — d'ogni fiore*, to be indiscriminate; tiara, coronet; (lit.) anthology, miscellany. **-are** [A1] *tr.* to garland, to wreathe.
**ghiro** *m.* (zool.) dormouse; *dormire come un* —, to sleep like a top.
**ghironda** *f.* hurdy-gurdy, barrel-organ.
**ghiṣa** *f.* cast-iron; — *di prima fusione*, pig-iron.
**già** *adv.* already; *abiti — fatti*, ready-made clothes; formerly; once; yes, assuredly; indeed; *non* —, not at all, certainly not; *non — che*, not that.
**giacca** *f.* jacket; short coat; cardigan; — *a vento*, windcheater.
**giacchẹ̀** *conj.* since, inasmuch as, as, now that.
**giacchẹtta** *f.* jacket.
**giac·chio** *m.* casting-net.
**giac·ci-o** *m.* (naut.) tiller. **-are** [A3] *tr.* (naut.) to steer; *intr.* (*aux.* avere) to work the tiller.
**giac-ẹre** [B1] *intr.* (*aux.* essere) to lie; to be situated; to lie idle; to be inert, to stagnate; to be in abeyance; to lie low; (provb.) *non toccare il can che -e*, let sleeping dogs lie. **-ente** *part. adj.* lying; situated; in abeyance; (finan.) *capitale -ente*, idle capital; (of goods) unsold; inert, stagnant; (leg.) vacant; *n.m., f.* (sculpt.) recumbent figure. **-enza** *f.* lying; stay; (comm.) demurrage; stock unsold; (finan.) capital lying idle. **-i·glio** *m.* bed; lair; hammock, bunk. **-imẹnto** *m.* lying; coitus; layer; (geol.) stratum, seam, deposit. **-itọio** *m.* a place to lie down; couch; lair. **-itura** *f.* way of lying, position.
**Giacinto**[1] *pr.n.m.* Jacinth; Hyacinth.
**giacinto**[2] *m.* (bot.) hyacinth; (miner.) jacinth.
**Giacọbbe** *pr.n.m.* Jacob.
**giacob-ino** *m., adj.* (hist.) Jacobin. **-ita** *m., adj.* (hist.) Jacobite.
**Gia·como** *pr.n.m.* James.
**giad-a** *f.*, **-o** *m.* (miner.) jade.
**Giaffa** *pr.n.f.* (geog.) Jaffa.
**giaggi(u)olo** (bot.) gladiolus, iris.
**giaguaro** *m.* (zool.) jaguar.
**giaiẹtto** *m.* (miner.) jet.
**giallamina** *f.* (miner.) calamine.
**giall-o** *adj.* yellow; *farina -a*, maize meal; *romanzo* —, thriller; *n.m.* the colour yellow; yolk; thriller. **-astro, -ic·cio, -o·gnolo** *adj.* yellowish. **-ẹzza** *f.*, **-ọre** *m.* yellowness.
**Giama·ica** *pr.n.f.* (geog.) Jamaica.
**giam·b-ico** *adj.* (prosod.) iambic. **-o** *m.* iambic foot or verse, iamb.
**giamma·i** *adv.* (poet.) never, not ever.
**Giani·colo** *pr.n.m.* (hist.) Janiculum.
**Gianni** *pr.n.m.* (abbrev. of **Giovanni**) Johnnie; Ian.
**Giano** *pr.n.m.* (myth.) Janus.
**Giapeto** *pr.n.m.* (bibl.) Japheth.
**Giappọn-e** *pr.n.m.* (geog.) Japan. **-ẹse** *n.m., f., adj.* Japanese.
**giara** *f.* earthenware jar.
**giardin-ag·gio** *m.* gardening. **-a·io** *adj.* pertaining to gardens. **-iere** *m.* gardener; nurseryman.
**giardin-o** *m.* garden, flower-garden; — *zoologico*, zoo; *-i pubblici*, public park; — *d'infanzia*, kindergarten. **-ẹtta** *f.* shooting brake, estate car.
**gia·rolo, giaroncello** *m.* (orn.) sandpiper.
**giarrettiera** *f.* garter; *l'Ordine della Giarettiera*, the Order of the Garter.
**Giasọne** *pr.n.m.* Jason.
**Giava** *pr.n.f.* (geog.) Java.
**giavazzo** *m.* (miner.) jet.
**giavellotto** *m.* javelin.
**gibbọne** *m.* (zool.) gibbon.
**gibbọs-o** *adj.* gibbous; humped; hunch-backed. **-ità** *f.* hump, convexity.
**giberna** *f.* cartridge-box, cartridge-pouch.
**gibẹtto** *m.* gibbet, gallows.
**Gibilterra** *pr.n.f.* (geog.) Gibraltar.
**giga** *f.* (mus.) jig.
**gigant-e** *m.* giant; (fig.) *fare passi da* —, to progress by leaps and bounds. **-eggiare** [A3c] *intr.* (*aux.* avere) to tower, to loom. **-ẹsco** *adj.* (*m.pl.* **-ẹschi**) gigantic; pertaining to a giant. **-ẹssa** *f.* giantess.
**gi·gli-o** *m.* (bot.) lily; fleur-de-lis; — *di Sant'Antonio*, Madonna lily; — *tigrato*, tiger-lily; — *delle convalli*, lily-of-the-valley; *la città del* —, Florence. **-a·ceo** *adj.* liliaceous.
**gilda** *f.* guild.
**gilè** *m. indecl.* waistcoat.
**gin** *m. indecl.* gin (the liquor).
**ginan·tropo** *m.* hermaphrodite.
**gincana** *f.* gymkhana.
**ginec-ologi·a** *f.* gynaecology. **-o·logo** *m.* gynaecologist.
**ginẹpr-a** *f.* (bot.) juniper berry. **-a·io** *m.* juniper thicket; (fig.) thorny situation; dilemma; labyrinth. **-o** *m.* (bot.) juniper.
**ginestra** *f.* (bot.) broom.
**Ginevr-a** *pr.n.f.* Guinivere; (geog.) Geneva. **-ino** *m., adj.* Genevan.
**gingill-o** *m.* toy; nick-nack. **-are** [A1] *intr.* (*aux.* avere), *rfl.* to fritter time away; to trifle.
**ginna·ṣi-o** *m.* grammar-school. **-ale** *adj.* pertaining to grammar-school education; *licenza -ale*, school-leaving certificate.
**ginn-asta** *m.* gymnast; athlete. **-aste·rio** *m.* gymnasium. **-a·stica** *f.* gymnastics. **-a·stico** *adj.* gymnastic.
**ginoc·chi-o** *m.* (*pl.* **-a** *f.*) knee; *rotella del* —, knee-cap; *a* —, kneeling; (*pl.* **ginocchi** *m.*) movable joint; *a* —, jointed. **-ata** *f.* thrust with the knee. **-ello** *m.* knee-cap. **-ọne, -ọni** *adv.* on one's knees.
**Giobbe** *pr.n.m.* (bibl.) Job.
**gioc-are** [A2d] *intr.* (*aux.* avere) to play; — *a carte*, to play cards; to joke; *tr.* to play, to gamble; *quanto -a ?*, how much are you putting on?; *rfl.* *-arsi di*, to make game of; *rfl.* (*dat.* of *prn.* 'si') *-arsi l'anima*, to gamble away one's soul. **-ata** *f.* play; stake, bet; turn to play; *è la mia -ata*, it's my go; (cards) deal. **-atọre** *m.*, **-atrice** *f.* player; gambler; *-atore di borsa*, stock-jobber; *-atore di rialzo*, bull; *-atore al ribasso*, bear.
**giocat·tol-o** *m.* toy, plaything. **-a·io** *m.* toy-manufacturer.
**giocherell-are** [A1] *intr.* (*aux.* avere) to play; to amuse oneself; to fidget; to trifle; to waste time. **-o** *m. dim.* plaything; pastime.
**giochẹtto** *m. dim.* of **gioco**; joke; — *di parole*, play upon words, pun.
**giochẹvole** *adj.* playful; facetious.
**gio-co** *m.* (*pl.* **-chi**) game; play; — *di destrezza*, game of skill; *a* —, at will, freely, in fun; *fare al — di*, to play into the hands of; *dare — di sè*, to make a laughing stock of oneself; trick, deceit; (sport) game; ground; (theatr.) plot, action.
**giocoforza** *f.* necessity; *mi fu* —, my hand was forced.
**giocol-are** [A1s] *intr.* (*aux.* avere) to juggle; to perform. **-atọre, -iere** *m.* juggler.
**gio·colo** *m.* joke, trick.
**Giocọnda** *pr.n.f.* *la* —, the Mona Lisa.
**giocọnd-o** *adj.* joyful; blithe. **-ità** *f.* joyfulness.
**giocọs-o** *adj.* jocose, merry;

facetious; playful. **-ità** *f.* facetiousness; mirth.
**gioˌgo** *m.* (*pl.* **-ghi**) yoke; pair of oxen; (fig.) oppression; (geog.) mountain ridge; summit, peak. **-ga·ia** *f.* (geog.) mountain range; dewlap (of oxen).
**gio·ia**[1] *f.* joy, pleasure; sweetheart; delight; *fuochi di* —, fireworks, bonfires.
**gio·ia**[2] *f.* precious stone; jewel.
**Gio·ia**[3] *pr.n.f.* Joy.
**gioiell-o** *m.* jewel, piece of jewellery; (fig.) beloved, treasure. **-eri·a** *f.* jeweller's craft; jeweller's shop. **-iere** *m.* jeweller.
**gio-ire** [D2] *intr.* (*aux.* avere) to rejoice; — *di*, to rejoice in, to be glad of. **-ito** *part. adj.* cheery, happy.
**Giona** *pr.n.m.* (bibl.) Jonah.
**Gio·nata** *pr.n.m.* Jonathan.
**Giordano** *pr.n.m.* (geog.) Jordan; river Jordan.
**Giorgina**[1] *pr.n.f.* Georgina.
**giorgina**[2] *f.* (bot.) dahlia.
**Gio·rgio** *pr.n.m.* George.
**giornal-e** *adj.* daily, everyday; *n.m.* diary, journal; daily newspaper; — *radio*, news on the wireless; *stile da* —, journalese. **-a·io** *m.* newsagent. **-iero** *adj.* daily; everyday; *orario -iero*, twenty-four hours' time-table; *n.m.* day-labourer. **-iṣmo** *m.* journalism. **-ista** *m.*, *f.* (*pl.* **-isti** *m.*, **-iste** *f.*) journalist. **-i·stico** *adj.* journalistic. **-mẹnte** *adv.* daily, every day.
**giornante** *f.* daily help; charwoman.
**giornata** *f.* day; day's work; day's pay; day's journey, day's march; *in* —, before the day is over; *vivere alla* —, to live from hand to mouth; *lavorare a* —, to work by the day; *durata normale della — di lavoro*, normal working day.
**giorne·a** *f.* mantle, cloak.
**giọrn-o** *m.* day, daytime; *in pieno* —, in broad daylight; *di — o di notte*, by day or night; *a* —, at daybreak; *buon —!*, good morning!; — *artificiale*, artificial light; *fra otto -i*, in a week's time; *fra quindici -i*, in a fortnight's time; *mai dei miei -i*, never in my life; *a -i*, by fits and starts; *verrà a -i*, he will be here any day now; *di — in* —, day after day; *del* —, current; *al — di oggi*, nowadays; *mettere a* —, to bring up to date; — *feriale*, working day.
**Gio·safat** *pr.n.m.* (bibl.) Jehoshaphat.
**Giosi·a** *pr.n.m.* (bibl.) Josiah.
**giostr-a** *f.* joust; merry-go-round; joke, jest. **-are** [A1] *intr.* (*aux.* avere) to joust; to tilt; to jostle; to wrestle; *tr.* to trick.
**Gioṣuè** *pr.n.m.* Joshua.
**giovamẹnto** *m.* See under **giovare.**
**giọvan-e, giọvin-e** *adj.* young; younger, junior; youthful, immature; new, unpractised; early; *n.m.*, *f.* youth, young man, young woman; *da* —, as a young man; learner, apprentice; shop assistant. **-evec·chio** *m.* elderly bachelor. **-ẹzza** *f.* youth; youthful action; *tornare in -ezza*, to enter one's second childhood. **(an)-ile** *adj.* juvenile, youthful. **-otto** *m.* lad; bachelor; apprentice.
**Giovanna** *pr.n.f.* Joan, Jane, Joanna.
**Giovanni** *pr.n.m.* John.
**giov-are** [A1 c] *tr.*, *intr.* (*aux.* avere, essere) to be useful, to help, to avail; *impers. non -a*, it's no use; *rfl.* (*prep.* di) to profit (from); to make use (of). **-amẹnto** *m.* advantage, benefit; avail; relief. **-ẹvole** *adj.* useful, serviceable.
**Giove** *pr.n.m.* (myth.) Jove.
**giovedì** *pr.n.m.* Thursday.
**Giovenale** *pr.n.m.* Juvenal.
**giovenca** *f.* heifer.
**gioventù** *f. indecl.* youth, youthfulness, prime of life; young people.
**gioverẹccio** *adj.* helpful; pleasant; agreeable.
**giovẹvole** *adj.* see under **giovare.**
**giovial-e** *adj.* cordial, jovial; affable. **-ità** *f.* cordiality, joviality; jolliness; affability.
**giovine** *adj.* and *derivs.* See under **giovane.**
**gipsoteca** *f.* gallery of plaster casts.
**gira·bile** *adj.* See under **girare.**
**gira-capo** *m.* dizziness. **-dischi** *m. indecl.* turntable (of gramophone, radio); disc jockey; record-player.
**giraffa** *f.* (zool.) giraffe.
**giramọndo** *m.* globe-trotter.
**giran·dol-a** *f.* Catherine wheel; (fig.) *la — ha preso fuoco*, 'the balloon has gone up'; artifice; whim. **-are** [A1 s] *intr.* (*aux.* avere) to roam; (fig.) to romance. **-ino** *m.* weather-cock. **-ọne** *m.* loiterer, lounger. **-ọni** *adv.* wandering; *andar -oni*, to roam about.
**gir-are** [A1] *tr.* to turn round; to make to revolve; to rotate; to spin; to travel round; — *il discorso*, to change the subject; (comm.) to endorse; (mil.) — *la posizione*, to outflank; (cinem.) to shoot, to film; *intr.* (*aux.* avere) to revolve; to go round; to rotate; *che ti -a ?*, what have you got in your head now ?; *se mi -a*, if the fancy takes me; — *largo*, to keep one's distance; to wander round; *è tutt'oggi che -o senza trovarlo*, I've been trying to find him all day; to circulate; to be on the turn, to go bad. **-a·bile** *adj.* (comm.) negotiable. **-ante** *part. adj.* turning, returning; *n.m.* (leg.; comm.) endorser. **-ata** *f.* turn, twist; tour; (leg.) endorsement; (cards) deal. **-ato** *part. adj.* turned; *n.m.* roast; (cinem.) shot; location. **-ẹvole** *adj.* revolving; twisting; whirling; swivelling; (fig.) fickle.
**giravolt-a** *f.* right-about face; twist and turn; change of front; shift. **-are** [A1] *intr.* (*aux.* avere) to turn about; to twist and turn; to shift; to change one's ground.
**gire** (def.) *intr.* (*aux.* essere) (poet.) to go; *girsene*, to depart.
**girell-a** *f.* yo-yo; (eng.) pulley; (draughts, backgammon) piece, man; *pl.* (fig.) tricks, wiles; foibles; *m. indecl.* turncoat, political weathercock. **-are** [A1] *intr.* (*aux.* avere) to stroll; *andare -ando*, to stroll about; *fare -are*, to twirl. **-o** *m.* little ring; washer; (cul.) steak from back of thigh. **-ọne** *m.* saunterer; wanderer.
**girẹtto** *m.* see under **giro.**
**girigo·gol-o** *m.* scrawl; spiral. **-are** [A1 s] *intr.* (*aux.* avere) to scrawl, to draw flourishes.
**girino** *m.* (zool.) tadpole.
**girlo** *m.* die.
**gir-o** *m.* circle, ring; circuit; circumference; rim; — *della manica*, arm-hole; tour; *prendere in* —, to make fun of; turn; rotation; (fig.) *dare un — di vite a*, to put pressure on; *a — di posta*, by return of post; circulation; sphere, compass; (econ.) — *d'affari*, turnover. **-ẹtto** *m. dim.* stroll, short walk.
**girobus·sola** *f.* gyrocompass.
**girocọnto** *m.* (finan.) clearance account.
**Giro·lamo** *pr.n.m.* Jerome.
**girondino** *m.*, *adj.* (hist.) Girondist.
**gir-ọne** *m. augm.* of **giro**; encircling wall; — *di ritorno*, second half of a season; (sport) series, round, heat; — *finale*, cup final. **-ọni** *adv.* wandering, loitering; *andare -oni*, to loiter.
**gironẓ-are** [A1 c], **-olare** [A1 sc] *intr.* (*aux.* avere) to saunter; to ramble, to snoop.
**giropilota** *m.* (naut.; aeron.) automatic pilot, 'George'.
**girosco·pio** *m.* gyroscope.
**girotọndo** *m.* round, dance.
**girovag-are** [A2 s] *intr.* (*aux.* avere) to roam about. **-ante** *part. adj.* roaming, vagrant; *mercante -ante*, hawker.
**giro·va-go** *adj.* (*m.pl.* **-ghi**) wandering; rambling; *attore* —, strolling player; *n.m.* wanderer; hawker; tramp.
**gita** *f.* excursion; tour; jaunt; ramble; tradesman's round.
**gitan-a** *f.* Spanish gipsy woman. **-o** *m.* Spanish gipsy; *adj.* gipsy-like, gipsy-style.
**gitante** *m.*, *f.* tripper; — *a piedi*, hiker.
**gittare** [A1] *tr.* (poet.) to throw; to cast.

**giù** *adv.* down; below; downstairs; *in* —, down below; *guardare uno di — in su*, to look a person up and down; — —, a long way down; — *di qua*, down here; *mandare* —, to gulp down; *non lo posso mandare* —, I can't and won't put up with it; *su e* —, up and down; *su per* —, more or less; *buttare* —, to fling down, to jot down; (fig.) to cast down; *dare* —, to fall.
**giubb-a**[1] *f.* mane. **-ato** *adj.* maned, having a mane.
**giubb-a**[2] *f.* evening tail coat; *farsi tirar la* —, to run up bills; *rivoltar* —, to change sides; — *rivoltata*, turncoat. **-otto** *m.* jerkin; *-otto di salvataggio*, life jacket.
**giubil-are** [A1 s] *intr.* (*aux.* avere) to rejoice; to exult; *tr.* to pension off. **-ante** *part. adj.* jubilant. **-ato** *part. adj.* retired, pensioned off. **-azione** *f.* jubilation; superannuation; retirement.
**giubile·o** *m.* jubilee.
**giu·bilo** *m.* joy, jubilation.
**giuc-co** *adj.* (*m.pl.* **-chi**) foolish; — *per vino*, drunk; *n.m.* silly ass.
**Giuda** *pr.n.m.* (bibl.) Judah; Judas; (fig.) *un* —, a Judas.
**giuda·ico** *adj.* Judaic.
**Giudaismo** *n.* Judaism.
**Giud-e·a** *pr.n.f.* (geog.) Judea. **-e·o** *adj.* Jewish; *n.m.* Jew.
**giudic-are** [A2 s] *tr.* to judge; to think, to deem, to consider. **-a·bile** *adj.* that may be judged; *n.m., f.* (leg.) defendant. **-ante** *part. adj.* (leg.) judging judicial; *n.m.* judge. **-ato** *part. adj.* judged; *passare in cosa -ata*, to become final; decisive; *n.m.* judgement; *-ati passati*, precedents. **-atore** *m.* judge, critic. **-ato·rio** *adj.* (*m.pl.* **-ato·rii**) judiciary. **-atura** *f.* judicature. **-azione** *f.* judgement.
**giu·dice** *m.* judge; justice; magistrate; — *conciliatore*, justice of the peace; — *delegato*, official receiver; — *istruttore*, coroner; — *popolare*, juryman; (sport) — *di partenza*, starter; — *di arrivo*, judge at the finish; (fig.) *lasciar — alcuno*, to leave the decision to someone else.
**giudiciale** *adj.* judicial.
**giudici-a·rio, -oso** *adj.* judicious.
**Giuditta** *pr.n.f.* Judith.
**giudiziale** *adj.* judicial; court; *procedere per via* —, to take legal proceedings.
**giudizia·rio** *adj.* judiciary; *ufficiale* —, bailiff; *potere* —, judicial power.
**giudi·z-io** *m.* (leg.) judgement; decision; proceedings; trial; suit; *essere chiamato in* —, to be sued; *assistenza in* —, legal aid; *sotto* —, sub judice; *citare in* —, to cite; to summons; to sue; *rappresentare in* —, to represent legally; *comparire in* —, to appear in court; *spese di* —, legal costs; *deporre in* —, to give evidence; — *dei giurati*, verdict; (fig.) *avere* —, to be sensible, to be prudent; *abbi* —!, take care!, don't be hasty!; *a suo* —, in his opinion; *fare* —, to act fairly. **-ioso** *adj.* judicious, prudent.
**giug·giola** *f.* jujube sweet; (fig.) *andare in brodo di giuggiole*, to be gushing.
**giugno** *pr.n.m.* June.
**giu·gnolo** *adj.* pertaining to June.
**giugolare**[1] *adj.* (anat.) jugular.
**giugolare**[2] [A1 s] *tr.* to cut the throat of; to throttle, to strangle.
**giulebb-e** *m.* julep; (fig.) too sweet a thing; sweet illusion. **-are** [A1] *tr.* to coat with sugar; (fig.) to mollycoddle.
**Giulia** *pr.n.f.* Julia.
**Giuliano** *pr.n.m.* Julian.
**Giulie (Alpi)** *pr.n.f.pl.* (geog.) Julian Alps.
**Giulietta** *pr.n.f.* Juliet; — *e Romeo*, Romeo and Juliet.
**Giulio** *pr.n.m.* Julius; — *Cesare*, Julius Caesar.
**giuliv-o** *adj.* merry, festive, joyous. **-ità** *f.* joyfulness, festivity.
**giullare** *m.* strolling player; minstrel; jester.
**giumella** *f.* double-handful; *a giumelle*, in great quantity.
**giument-a** *f.* female donkey, mule, or horse used as a pack animal. **-o** *m.* donkey, mule or horse.
**giunca** *f.* (naut.) junk.
**giunchi·gli-a** *f.*, **-o** *m.* (bot.) jonquil.
**giunchina** *f.* junket.
**giun-co** *m.* (*pl.* **-chi**) (bot.) rush; reed; (naut.) halyard. **-ca·ia** *f.*, **-cheto** *m.* bed of rushes.
**giun·g-ere** [B5] *intr.* (*aux.* essere) to arrive; *mi -e nuovo*, that's news to me; — *a*, to succeed in, to manage to; to reach; *tr.* to unite; to combine; — *le mani*, to clasp hands; to hit, to reach. **-imento** *m.* joining, joint; arrival.
**giungla** *f.* jungle.
**Giunone** *pr.n.f.* (myth.) Juno.
**giunta**[1] *f.* addition; appendix; increase; surplus; make-weight; *per* —, in addition, into the bargain; *di prima* —, at once, at first sight; (sport) handicap, start; *pl.* addenda.
**giunta**[2] *f.* board of management; examination board; (pol.) junta.
**giunt-are** [A1] *tr.* to join together; to sew together; to trick. **-ag·gio** *m.* (techn.) jointing, splicing. **-atore** *m.* cheat. **-eri·a** *f.* trickery; swindle.
**giunt-o** *part.* of **giungere**; *adj.* arrived; joined; reached; added; tricked. **-amente** *adv.* jointly. **-ura** *f.* connexion, joint; *-ura a caldo*, welding; (anat.) joint.
**giunzione** *f.* (techn.) jointing; joint; *linea di* —, seam.
**Giura** *pr.n.f.* (geog.) Jura.
**giur-are** [A1] *tr., intr.* (*aux.* avere) (leg.) to swear; to take an oath; — *in falso*, to commit perjury; (colloq.) *-arci*, to be sure. **-amento** *m.* oath; swearing; *prendere -amento*, to take an oath; *-amento falso*, perjury. **-ato** *part. adj.* sworn; *n.m.* (leg.) juror.
**giuras·sico** *adj.* (geol.) jurassic.
**giur-e** *m.* (leg.) jurisprudence; law. **-i·a** *f.* jury; selection committee. **-i·dico** *adj.* juridical; *persona -idica*, corporation. **-isdizione** *f.* jurisdiction. **-isprudenza** *f.* jur sprudence. **-ista** *m.* jurist.
**giureconsulto** *m.* jurisconsult; lawyer.
**giuro** *m.* (poet.) oath.
**gius** *m. indecl.* (leg.) law; authority; equity; rule; right.
**giusdicente** *m.* (leg.) judge.
**Giuseppe** *pr.n.m.* Joseph.
**giuspatronato** *m.* (eccl.) patronage.
**giusta** *prep.* according to; in conformity with.
**giustap-porre** [B21] *tr.* to juxtapose. **-posizione** *f.* juxtaposition.
**giustappunto** *adv.* precisely; exactly, just.
**giustezza** *f.* exactness; correctness, rectitude; nicety.
**giustific-are** [A2 s] *tr.* to justify; to vindicate, to make good; (typ.) to justify; *rfl.* to justify oneself. **-a·bile** *adj.* justifiable. **-atamente** *adv.* justifiably, with good reason. **-ativo** *adj.* justifying; *n.m.* (comm.) voucher. **-ato** *part. adj.* justified. **-azione** *f.* justification; excuse.
**Giustiniano** *pr.n.m.* Justinian.
**giusti·zi-a** *f.* justice. **-are** [A4] *tr.* to execute, to put to death; *rfl.* to torment oneself. **-ato** *part. adj.* executed; *n.m.* man executed. **-erato** *adj.* justiciary.
**giust-o** *adj.* just, righteous; deserved; legitimate; *prezzo* —, fair price; *fare le cose -e*, to be fair; suitable, reasonable; *a passo* —, at an ordinary walking pace; *il — mezzo*, the happy mean; correct for size; *troppo* —, too tight a fit, (fig.) too true; proper, right; *n.m.* righteous man; rights, what is fair; *adv.* just; — *ora*, just now.
**glabro** *adj.* smooth, hairless.
**glaciale** *adj.* icy, frigid; glacial.
**gladiatore** *m.* gladiator.
**glan·dol-a** *f.* (anat.) gland; — *tiroide*, thyroid gland. **-are** *adj.* glandular.
**glassare** [A1] *tr.* (cul.) to glaze.
**gla·u-co** *adj.* (*m.pl.* **-chi**) sea-green.
**gli**[1] *def. art. m.pl.* (before vowel, s impure, z or gn) the.
**gli**[2] *pers. prn. m. sing. dat.* to him; to it; *f. sing. dat.* (combined with

lo, la, ne: gliele, gliela, gliene) to her; (colloq.) *m.pl.* to them.
**glob-o** *m.* globe; sphere; *in —*, all together, all-over; *— dell'occhio*, eyeball. **-ale** *adj.* inclusive; universal.
**glo·bulo** *m.* globule.
**glo·ria** *f.* glory; fame; honour; splendour; pride; *andare in —*, to be delighted; *farsi — di*, to exult in.
**glori-are** [A4] *intr.* (*aux.* avere), *rfl.* (*prep.* di) to be proud (of), to show off; *tr.* to exalt. **-ato** *part. adj.* glorified; held in high esteem.
**glorificare** [A2 s] *tr.* to glorify.
**glorioso** *adj.* glorious, illustrious.
**gloss-a**[1] *f.* explanatory note; (fig.) *far la — a*, to criticize adversely. **-are** [A1] *tr.* to annotate. **-a·rio** *m.* glossary. **-atore** *m.* commentator. **-ografi·a** *f.* lexicology. **-o·grafo** *m.* lexicographer. **-ologi·a** *f.* philology, linguistics.
**glossa**[2] *f.* (anat.) tongue.
**glott-a** *f.* tongue; glottis. **-ologi·a** *f.* linguistics. **-olo·gico** *adj.* philological. **-o·logo** *m.* philologist.
**glu·tin-e** *m.* glue. **-are** [A1 s] *tr.* to glue. **-oso** *adj.* glutinous.
**gnaffa** *f.* despicable person.
**gnaffo** *m.* flattened nose, ugly snout.
**gna·gnera** *f.* desire; caprice; lassitude.
**gna-o, -u** *m.* (onomat.) miaow. **-ulare** [A1 s] *intr.* (*aux.* avere) to mew (of a cat); to cry, to whine (of a child). **-ulata** *f.* mewing; whining.
**gne·gnera** *f.* monotonous whining, sing-song voice.
**gne·gnero** *m.* (fam.) brain, ideas, nous.
**gnoc-co** *m.* (*pl.* **-chi**) (cul.) a kind of dumpling.
**gnome** *f.* dictum; aphorism.
**gno·mico** *adj.* didactic.
**gnomo** *m.* elf, gnome.
**gnorri** *m. indecl. fare lo —*, to feign ignorance.
**gnucca** *f.* (vulg.) neck, nape; brains, sense, nous.
**gobb-a** *f.* hump. **-o** *adj.* hunchbacked; *n.m.* hump.
**gocc-ia** *f.* drop; drip; *rassomigliarsi come due -e d'acqua*, to be as like as two peas; *— a —*, drop by drop. **-iare** [A3 c] *intr.* (*aux.* avere) to drip.
**gocciol-a** *f.* drop; drop-earring; *pl.* lead shot. **-are** [A1 sc] *intr.* (*aux.* avere), *tr.* to drip, to drop; to leak, to ooze. **-atura** *f.* dripping; leakage; stain from drips. **-io** *m.* (*pl.* **-ìi**) constant dripping. **-o** *m.* (*pl.* **-e** *f.*) drop, very small dose or portion. **-oso** *adj.* dripping, guttering, running.
**god-ere** [B1] *intr.* (*aux.* avere) to rejoice; to be glad; to thrive; to benefit; (*prep.* a, di) to rejoice (in); to be glad (of); to possess, to enjoy; *— di una buona salute*, to enjoy good health; *tr.* to enjoy; to have pleasure in; to possess; to profit from; *rfl.* (*acc.* of *prn.* 'si', *prep.* di) to enjoy oneself; to content oneself (with); (*dat.* of *prn.* 'si') *-ersela*, to enjoy oneself, to enjoy life. **-ereccio** *adj.* merry; delightful, enjoyable. **-imento** *m.* pleasure, delight; enjoyment; exploitation, use.
**goff-o** *adj.* clumsy, awkward; stupid; embarrassed; *n.m.* clumsy person, dolt. **-ag·gine** *f.*, **-ezza** *f.* clumsiness; awkwardness; stupidity.
**Goffredo** *pr.n.m.* Godfrey; Geoffrey.
**gol** *m. indecl.* (sport) goal (scored).
**gol-a** *f.* throat; gullet; gorge; *mal di —*, sore throat; *a —*, up to the neck; *faccende a —*, a great deal to do; *a piena —*, hungrily, greedily; (of speech) vociferously; appetite, hunger; *mortificare la —*, to fast; greed, gluttony; (geog.) narrow valley, strait(s); neck (of vase or cup). **-eri·a** *f.*, **-osità** *f.* gluttony; greed. **-oso** *adj.* greedy; tasty; succulent.
**golf** *m. indecl.* golf; *una partita a —*, a game of golf; cardigan.
**golfist-a** *m.*, *f.* (*pl.m.* **-i**, *pl.f.* **-e**) golfer.
**golfo** *m.* gulf; *la Corrente del Golfo*, the Gulf Stream.
**Gol·gota** *pr.n.m.* (bibl.) Golgotha.
**Goli·a** *pr.n.m.* (bibl.) Goliath.
**golpe** *f.* (bot.) blight; mildew.
**gomena** *f.* cable; *— da rimorchio*, tow rope.
**gomit-o** *m.* elbow; (fig.) *riuscire a forza di -i*, to be ruthless; *olio di —*, elbow-grease; bend. **-ata** *f.* blow or shove with the elbow; *fare alle -ate*, to elbow one's way.
**gomi·tolo** *m.* ball or skein of wool; (fig.) swarm, knot.
**gomm-a** *f.* gum; resin; rubber; *— da masticare*, chewing-gum; *— elastica*, indiarubber. **-apiuma** *f.* foam rubber.
**gondol-a** *f.* gondola. **-are** [A1 sc] *intr.* (*aux.* avere) to go in a gondola. **-iere, -iero** *m.* gondolier.
**gonfalon-e** *m.* banner. **-iere** *m.* standard-bearer.
**gonfi-are** [A4 c] *tr.* to inflate; (fig.) to flatter; *rfl.*, *intr.* (*aux.* essere) to swell; to rise. **-ag·gio** *m.*, **-agione** *f.* inflation; swelling. **-atoio** *m.* tyre-pump. **-atura** *f.* inflation; swelling; flattery; exaggeration.
**gonfi-o** *m.* swelling; *adj.* swollen; (fig.) puffed up; (naut.) *a -e vele*, with a favourable wind. **-ezza** *f.* swelling; (fig.) pride. **-ore** *m.* swelling, lump.
**gongolare** [A1 sc] *intr.* (*aux.* avere) to chuckle; to be delighted; *rfl.* to hug oneself for joy; to preen oneself.
**gonn-a** *f.* skirt; petticoat; gown; *— calzoni*, divided skirt. **-ella** *f. dim.* petticoat; *star attaccato alla -ella di*, to be tied to the apron strings of.
**gonzo** *m.* simpleton.
**gor-a** *f.* irrigation canal; channel; millpond; marsh, stagnant water; (fig.) stream (*e.g.* of blood); tear-stain.
**gorbia** *f.* gouge.
**gordiano** *adj.* (hist.) Gordian; *tagliare il nodo —*, to cut the Gordian knot.
**gorgata** *f.* draught, gulp.
**gorgheggiare** [A3 c] *intr.* (*aux.* avere) to warble, to trill.
**gorgheggio** *m.* trill.
**gor·gi-a** *f.* burr. **-are** [A4] *intr.* (*aux.* avere) to speak with a burr.
**gorgiera** *f.* ruff; chain of office.
**gor-go** *m.* (*pl.* **-ghi**) whirlpool; abyss.
**gorgogliare** [A4 c] *tr.*, *intr.* (*aux.* avere) to gurgle, to bubble.
**gorgoglio** *m.* gurgle; bubbling.
**gota** *f.* jowl.
**Goti** *pr.n.m.pl.* (hist.) Goths.
**go·tico** *adj.* Gothic.
**gott-a** *f.* gout. **-oso** *adj.* gouty.
**gotto** *m.* goblet.
**govern-are** [A1] *tr.* to steer; to regulate; to govern; to look after; *intr.* (*aux.* avere) to steer; *rfl.* to control oneself. **-ativo** *adj.* official, state. **-atura** *f.* husbandry.
**governo** *m.* government; rule; management; steering.
**gozzo** *m.* crop (of a bird); goitre; double chin.
**gozzovi·gli-a** *f.* revelling; orgy. **-are** [A4] *intr.* (*aux.* avere) to revel; to banquet. **-ata** *f.* revelry.
**gracchiare** [A4] *intr.* (*aux.* avere) to croak (of a raven or frog); to chirp (of a grasshopper).
**grac·chio** *m.* (orn.) chough.
**Gracco** *pr.n.m.* (hist.) Gracchus.
**gracidare** [A1 s] *intr.* (*aux.* avere) to cackle; to croak.
**gra·cil-e** *adj.* delicate; graceful; slender; thin. **-ente** *adj.* sickly, delicate.
**grad-are** [A1] *tr.* to gradate. **-atamente** *adv.* step by step. **-ato** *part. adj.* made in steps; graded. **-azione** *f.* gradation.
**gradiente** *m.* gradient, slope.
**gradin-o** *m.* step; rung of a ladder. **-ata** *f.* (archit.) flight of steps.
**grad-ire** [D2] *tr.* to be pleased to accept; to appreciate; *intr.* (*aux.* essere) to please. **-evole** *adj.* pleasing. **-evolezza** *f.* agreeableness. **-imento** *m.* pleasure; approval. **-ito** *part. adj.* pleasing; approved.
**grado**[1] *m.* goodwill; *a —*, as desired; *andare a —*, to be pleasing; *avere a —*, to find agreeable; *di buon —*, willingly; *mal —*, displeasure; *a suo mal —*, against

his will; *saper — di*, to be grateful for; *render* —, to give thanks.

**grado**[2] *m.* step; *a — a* —, by degrees; rank, standing; *tenere al suo* —, to stand on one's dignity; shade (of a colour); state, condition; *in — di*, in a position to.

**gradual-e** *adj.* gradual; *erta* —, gentle slope. **-mẹnte** *adv.* gradually.

**gradu-are** [A6] *tr.* to grade; to confer a degree, rank or title upon. **-atamẹnte** *adv.* by degrees. **-ato** *adj.* graded; holding rank. **-aziọne** *f.* graduation; advancement.

**graffa** *f.* clip, fastener; parenthesis.

**graffi-are** [A4] *tr.* to scratch; (fig.) to wound; *rfl.* to scratch oneself; *recip. rfl.* (fig.) to scratch each other's eyes out. **-atura** *f.* scratch.

**graf·fio** *m.* scratch.

**graffito** *m.* graffito; (art) scratched or incised drawing.

**grafi·a** *f.* spelling; handwriting.

**gra·fic-a** *f.* graphic art, drawing. **-o** *adj.* graphic; *arti grafiche*, illustration; *stabilimento -o*, printing house; typographical; orthographical; *n.m.* graph, diagram, chart.

**grafite** *f.* (miner.) graphite, plumbago.

**graf-ologi·a** *f.* study of handwriting. **-ospaṣmo** *m.* writer's cramp.

**gragnol-are** [A1 s] *impers.* to hail. **-ata** *f.* hail-storm.

**gragn(u)ola** *f.* fine hail.

**grama·glia** *f.* (usu. *pl.*) mourning (clothes).

**gramigna** *f.* (bot.) grass; weed; (fig.) *attaccarsi come la* —, to cling like a limpet.

**gramma·tica** *f.* grammar.

**grammo** *m.* gram, gramme.

**grammo·fono** *m.* gramophone.

**gramo** *adj.* wretched, sad; meagre.

**gran**[1] *adj.* abbrev. of **grande,** *q.v.*

**gran**[2] *m.* abbrev. of **grano,** *q.v.*

**Gran Brettagna** *pr.n.f.* (geog.) Great Britain.

**grana** *f.* cochineal; grain in wood; particle; *di — fine*, fine-grained.

**grana·glie** *f.pl.* cereal; corn, grain.

**gran-are** [A1] *tr.* to granulate; to grain; *intr.* (*aux.* essere) to seed, to run to seed. **-ato** *part. adj.* granulated; grained; ripe, formed (of corn).

**Granata**[1] *pr.n.f.* (geog.) Granada.

**granat-a**[2] *f.* broom, brush; (provb.) — *nuova spazza ben tre giorni*, a new broom sweeps clean; (mil.) grenade; — *a pallottole*, shrapnel; shell. **-iere** *m.* (mil.) grenadier.

**ranato**[1] *part.* of **granare,** *q.v.*

**granato**[2] *m.* garnet.

**granbe·stia** *f.* (zool.) elk; (fig.) the mob, the many-headed.

**grancassa** *f.* big-drum, bass-drum.

**gran·chio** *m.* (zool.) crab; (fig.) muscular cramp; *avere il — alle mani*, to be tight-fisted.

**gran·cio** *m.* grappling-iron; (fig.) blunder; *pigliare un — porro*, to drop a brick.

**grancire** [D2] *tr.* to seize, to grab.

**grandangolare** *adj.* (photog.) wide-angle; *obiettivo* —, wide-angle lens.

**grand-e** *adj.* (before a noun beginning with a consonant other than **z** or impure **s, gran,** unless emphasis is desired) big; wide; great; *non è un gran che*, it's not up to much; tall; high; loud; heavy; chief; grand; numerous, many; *adv.* greatly, much; *n.m.* grown-up; a great man; greatness. **-eggiare** [A3 c] *intr.* (*aux.* avere) to loom up; to excel; to soar; to be ostentatious. **-ẹzża** *f.* size; greatness; grandness; grandeur, display. **-i·gia** *f.* ostentation; pride, arrogance. **-iọso** *adj.* grand; grandiose. **-ire** [D2] *intr.* (*aux.* avere) to grow bigger.

**gran·din-e** *f.* hail; *chicco di* —, hailstone; stye on the eyelid. **-are** [A1 s] *impers.* (*aux.* essere) to hail; *tr.* to hail down upon. **-ata** *f.* hail-storm.

**granell-o** *m.* (*pl.* **-i** *m.*, **-a** *f.*) grain (*e.g.* of corn, or sand); stone, pip (of fruit); seed; kernel; *le -a*, cereals. **-ọso** *adj.* granular; (of soil) sandy.

**granfatto** *adv.* much; very; a great deal, a lot.

**gran·fi-a** *f.* (zool.) claw; talon; *pl.* (fig.) clutches. **-are** [A4] *tr.* to seize; to claw; to clutch.

**grani·fero** *adj.* grain-producing; corn-carrying.

**gran-ire** [D2] *intr.* (*aux.* essere) (bot.) to seed; **-igiọne** *f.* (bot.) ripening of seed. **-ito** *part. adj.* (bot.) gone to seed. **-itura** *f.* seeding; milling, milled edge (of a coin).

**gran-ito** *m.* granite. **-i·tico** *adj.* granitic; (fig.) hard as granite.

**grani·voro** *adj.* granivorous.

**grano** *m.* (bot.) grain; wheat; pip; bead of a rosary.

**granoc·chi-a** *f.* (zool.) frog. **-a·ia** *f.* (orn.) heron, egret. **-a·io** *m.* swampy ground.

**granturco** *m.* (bot.) Indian corn, maize.

**granulare**[1] *adj.* granular.

**granul-are**[2] [A1 s] *tr.*, *intr.* (*aux.* essere) to granulate. **-atọio** *m.* powder-mill; sieve, riddle. **-aziọne** *f.* granulation.

**gra·nul-o** *m.* granule. **-ọso** *adj.* granular.

**grapp-a**[1] *f.* clamp. **-are** [A1] *tr.* to seize. **-ino** *m.* hook; grappling-iron.

**grappa**[2] *f.* strong, rough brandy.

**grap·polo** *m.* (bot.) raceme; *un — d'uva*, a bunch of grapes; *a grappoli*, in bunches, (fig.) thickly, in large quantities.

**gra·sc-ia** *f.pl.* victuals. **-ino** *m.* food inspector; weights inspector.

**grassatọre** *m.* (leg.) highway robber; bully.

**grass-o** *adj.* fat, stout; (of food) greasy, rich; *giovedì* —, the last Thursday before Lent; *martedì* —, Shrove Tuesday; *terreno* —, manured land; (typ.) *caratteri -i*, heavy type; coarse; lewd; *n.m.* grease; — *vegetale*, vegetable fat; — *di balena*, blubber. **-ẹzza** *f.* greasiness; stoutness; abundance. **-ime** *m.*, **-ina** *f.* manure. **-ume** *m.* fatty matter.

**grat-a** *f.* grating. **-ella** *f.* gridiron, grill; grid on a map. **-ina** *f.* grating; mesh.

**gratic·cio** *m.* hurdle; duckboard; trellis.

**grati·col-a** *f.* small grating; grate; gridiron, grill. **-are** [A1 s] *tr.* to draw lines across; to divide by a grid; to close with a grating. **-ato** *part. adj.* shut with a grating; *n.m.* railing; grating; trellis; espalier.

**grati·fica** *f.* gratuity, bonus.

**gratific-are** [A2 s] *tr.* to give a gratuity to; to give a bonus to; to reward; *intr.* (*aux.* avere; *prep.* a) to be gratifying (to); *rfl.* (*prep.* a) to win the favour (of); to ingratiate oneself (with). **-aziọne** *f.* gratuity; bonus; special fee; gratification.

**gratis** *adv.* free of charge, gratis.

**gratitu·dine** *f.* gratitude; thankfulness.

**grato** *adj.* pleasing; kind; grateful, welcome; *ci è — informarvi*, we are pleased to inform you; *n.m.* satisfaction, pleasure; *a mio* —, to my satisfaction; *di buon* —, gladly.

**gratta-ca·cio** *m. indecl.* cheese-grater. **-capo** *m.* worry, anxiety; problem. **-cielo** *m.* skyscraper.

**gratt-are** [A1] *tr.* to scratch; (fig.) — *gli orecchi a*, to flatter; to grate; to scrape; to scratch out. **-atic·cio** *m.* erasure.

**grattu·gi-a** *f.* grater. **-are** [A4] *tr.* to grate. **-ato** *part. adj.* grated.

**gratu·it-o** *adj.* gratuitous; free of charge; unearned; unprovoked. **-à** *f.* gratuitousness.

**gratulato·rio** *adj.* congratulatory

**grav-ame, -a·mine** *m.* accusation; grievance; tax.

**grav-are** [A1] *intr.* (*aux.* avere) to weigh heavy; to be displeasing; *tr.* to load; to weigh down; to afflict; to oppress; (leg.) to mortgage; to levy. **-amẹnto** *m.* weighing; burden; (leg.) charge; mortgage.

**grav-e** *adj.* heavy; serious;

difficult; stern; *suono* —, deep sound; *n.m.* seriousness; weight; *adv.* seriously. **-ẹzza** *f.* heaviness; weightiness; seriousness; hardship.

**gra·vid-o** *adj.* pregnant; (fig.) loaded; fraught; stuffed. **-anza** *f.* pregnancy.

**gravina** *f.* pickaxe.

**gravit-à** *f.* gravity; dignity; (phys.) density. **-aziọne** *f.* gravitation.

**gravọs-o** *adj.* grievous; onerous; troublesome. **-ità** *f.* seriousness.

**gra·zia** *f.* grace, favour; boon; *avere in* —, to be fond of; *con vostra buona* —, by your leave; *in — di*, on account of, thanks to; *per — d'esempio*, by way of example; *di* —, graciously; comeliness, elegance; (theol.) grace; mercy; *colpo di* —, coup de grâce, finishing stroke; (leg.) pardon; *pl.* thanks, thank you; *grazie al cielo*, thank Heavens.

**graziare** [A4] *tr.* to pardon; to grant a favour to.

**graziọs-o** *adj.* gracious; charming; apt; witty. **-ità** *f.* graciousness; graces; prettiness.

**Gre·cia** *pr.n.f.* (geog.) Greece; *la — antica*, ancient Greece.

**grec-o** *adj.* Greek; Grecian. *n.m.* Greek; Greek language. **-ista** *m., f.* Hellenist.

**greg-ale** *adj.* gregarious; lacking in individuality; mass-produced. **-a·rio** *adj.* ordinary; following the crowd.

**grẹgge** *m.* (*pl.* **grẹggi** *f.*) flock; herd, drove; *cane da* —, sheep-dog.

**greg·gio** *adj.* raw, crude; unbleached; unprocessed; *materia greggia*, raw material; *zucchero* —, brown sugar.

**Grego·ri-o** *pr.n.m.* Gregory. **-ano** *adj.* Gregorian.

**grembiale** *m.* apron.

**grembo** *m.* lap; (fig.) bosom; womb; centre; *in — alla famiglia*, in the bosom of one's family.

**gremire** [D2] *tr.* to stuff; to crowd; to load.

**grẹppia** *f.* manger; crib; rack.

**greppina** *f.* lounging-chair.

**grẹppo** *m.* steep, rocky bank; cliff, crag.

**grẹt-o** *m.* pebbly shore. **-ọso** *adj.* gritty, gravelly; pebbly.

**grẹtt-o** *adj.* mean; niggardly; petty; narrow-minded. **-ẹzza** *f.* meanness.

**greve** *adj.* heavy; grievous.

**gric·ciolo** *m.* shudder shiver; whim.

**grida** *f.* proclamation; edict; ban.

**grid-are** [A1] *intr.* (*aux.* avere) to shout; to clamour; to scream; *tr.* to shout for; to proclaim. **-atọre** *m.* town-crier.

**grid-o** *m.* (*pl.* **-a** *f.*) cry; shout; scream; outcry, tumult; — *di guerra*, war-cry; repute; rumour; *di* —, famous, celebrated; *a — di popolo*, by popular acclamation; (*pl.* **-i** *m.*) quiet utterances; *i -i della coscienza*, the still, small voice of conscience.

**grifagno** *adj.* rapacious, ravenous; fierce; frightening; hawk-like; (of eyes) piercing.

**grifare** [A1] *tr.* to devour, to eat greedily.

**grifo** *m.* snout; muzzle, nose; *torcere il* —, to turn up one's nose.

**grifọne** *m.* griffin.

**gri·gio** *adj.* grey.

**Grigiọni** *pr.n.m.pl.* (geog.) *i* —, the Grisons.

**gri·glia** *f.* iron grating, grill; (cul.) *alla* —, grilled; (radio) grid.

**grillare** [A1] *intr.* (*aux.* avere) to sizzle; to simmer; to seethe; (of wine) to ferment.

**grillo** *m.* (ent.) cricket; — *di mare*, lobster; fancy, whim, caprice; *gli saltò il* —, he took a fancy; *avere qualche — per la testa*, to have a bee in one's bonnet.

**grimo** *adj.* miserable, wretched; wrinkled; rugged.

**grin·fia** *f.* claw, talon; (fig.) *nelle grinfie di*, in the clutches of.

**grinta** *f.* sinister-looking face; sulky expression; insolence; *a — dura*, severely.

**grinza** *f.* wrinkle; crease; fold; (fig.) *non fa una* —, it is going on smoothly.

**grip·pe** *m.* (pron. as Fr.) influenza, 'flu.

**Groenlan·dia** *pr.n.f.* (geog.) Greenland.

**grogo** *m.* (bot.) crocus.

**grọmm-a** *f.* damp incrustation; crust; tartar (in a wine-cask); fur (in a water-pipe). **-are** [A1 c] *intr.* (*aux.* essere) to fur up.

**grọnchio** *adj.* numbed with the cold; *n.m.* slow-witted person.

**grọnd-a** *f.* eaves. **-a·ia** *f.* gutter (on a roof); rain-pipe.

**grond-are** [A1 c] *intr.* (*aux.* avere) to run off, to pour away; to trickle; to gush; to stream; to ooze; *tr.* to shed, to drip with. **-atura** *f.* drip, dripping.

**gropp-a** *f.* crupper; rump; *in* —, pillion; shoulder of a hill; mountain ridge. **-ọne** *m.* back; (fig.) *piegare il -one*, to put one's back into it.

**grọppo** *m.* knot; tangle; small group.

**gross-o** *adj.* big; *caccia -a*, big-game; *dito* —, thumb, big toe; *pesce* —, important person; *dirle -e*, to lie, to exaggerate; (of a river) swollen; (of the sea) heavy, rough; thick; coarse; gross; harsh; wholesale; *n.m.* greater part, majority; tumour, lump; *adv. phr. di* —, in great number; *in* —, roughly speaking; — *modo*, roughly; *a un di* —, more or less. **-a** *f.* gross, twelve dozen; *dormir della* —, to be sound asleep; rough life; *vivere alla* —, to rough it. **-ag·gine** *f.* grossness; coarseness. **-agrana** *f.* (text.) grosgrain. **-ẹzza** *f.* thickness; size; swelling; density; volume. **-ista** *m.* wholesaler; *adj. casa -ista*, wholesale firm. **-ura** *f.* coarseness, rudeness; roughness, ignorance.

**grossolano** *adj.* coarse; rough; crude; gross; *adv. phr. alla grossolana*, coarsely, roughly.

**grott-a** *f.* cave, grotto, cavern; cellar. **-o** *m.* grotto; steep, rocky place.

**grottẹs-co** *adj.* (*m.pl* **-chi**), *n.m.* grotesque; (theatr.) medley, fantasy.

**grov-i·glio** *m.* kink in a twisted string; tangle; (fig.) entanglement, confusion. **-i·gliola** *f.* kink.

**gru** *f. indecl.* (orn.) crane; (eng.) crane. **-ista** *m.* (eng.) crane driver.

**gru gru** (onomat.) coo (of doves).

**gruc·cia** *f.* crutch; *tenere alcuno sulla* —, to keep someone on tenterhooks.

**grufolare** [A1 s] *intr.* (*aux.* avere) to root; to poke about; to nose; *rfl.* to wallow.

**grugare** [A2] *intr.* (*aux.* avere) to coo.

**grugn-ire** [D2] *intr.* (*aux.* avere) to grunt; to snort. **-ito** *m.* grunt; snort.

**grugno** *m.* snout.

**grum-a** *f.* incrustation; clot. **-ọso** *adj.* encrusted, furred; stickily coated.

**grumerẹccio** *m.* aftermath.

**grum-o** *m.* clot; lump in a liquid. **-ọso** *adj.* clotted.

**gru·molo** *m.* heart of a cabbage, lettuce, etc.; core.

**gruppo** *m.* group; batch; set; — *di lavoro*, working party; — *di studi*, study group.

**gruz·zolo** *m.* savings, hoard, nest-egg.

**guadagn-are** [A5] *tr.* to gain; to earn; *-arsi la vita*, to earn one's living; to win; to acquire; to make up for; *intr.* (*aux.* avere) to improve; to gain in quality.

**guadagno** *m.* gain; profit; — *lordo*, gross profit; — *netto*, net profit; wages, earnings; winnings; advantage.

**guadare** [A1] *tr.* to ford; to wade across.

**guad-o** *m.* ford; *passare a* —, to ford. **-ọso** *adj.* shallow in parts; fordable.

**guai** *excl.* woe!

**guai·me** *m.* (agric.) aftermath.

**guaina** *f.* (zool.) tube; sheath; scabbard; corset or tight-fitting dress; slot (for ribbon or cord).

**gua·io** *m.* woe; mishap; calamity; accident; failure; trouble; *è un* —, it's a pity; *il — è che*, the trouble is that.

**guai·re** [D2] *intr.* (*aux.* avere) to squeal; to howl; to yelp; to whine.

**guai·to** *m.* yelp; whining; howl.
**gualcire** [D2] *tr.* to crease; to crush; to wrinkle.
**guan·ci-a** *f.* cheek; *porgere l'altra* —, to turn the other cheek. **-ata** *f.* slap in the face.
**guancial-e** *m.* pillow; cushion. **-ino** *m. dim.* *-ino da cucire*, pin-cushion; (surg.) pad, tampon.
**guant-o** *m.* glove; *-i monchini*, mittens; gauntlet; (swimming) *-i palmati*, flippers. **-one** *m.* gauntlet; boxing-glove.
**guarda-barriere** *m., f. indecl.* (rlwy.) level-crossing keeper. **-boschi** *m. indecl.* woodman. **-cac·cia** *m. indecl.* gamekeeper. **-casa** *m., f. indecl.* caretaker. **-coste** *m. indecl.* coastguard. **-li·nee** *m. indecl.* (sport) linesman. **-magazzino** *m. indecl.* storekeeper. **-man·drie** *m. indecl.* herdsman. **-mano** *m. indecl.* leather gauntlet; handrail. **-porto** *m. indecl.* port superintendent; coastguard cutter. **-portone** *m. indecl.* commissionaire. **-roba** *f. indecl.* linen-cupboard; wardrobe; cloakroom; *m.* clothing; contents of wardrobe. **-robiera** *f.*, **-robiere** *m.* cloakroom attendant. **-spalle** *m. indecl.* bodyguard.
**guard-are** [A1] *intr.* (*aux.* avere) to look; — *a*, to pay attention to, to look after; — *di* (foll. by *neg. infin.*) to take care not to; *tr.* to look at; to observe; *-a chi si vede!*, look who's here!; to examine; to attend to; to keep; to watch; to protect; *Dio ne -i*, God forbid; *rfl.* to look at oneself; *-arsi allo specchio*, to look at oneself in the looking-glass; to keep oneself; *-arsi da*, to be on one's guard against; *recip. rfl.* to look at one another. **-ata** *f.* look; glance. **-atina** *f. dim.* peep, glimpse.
**guar·dia** *f.* guard; *di* —, on duty; *stare in* —, to be on guard; *cane da* —, watch-dog; *fare la* — *a*, to watch over; (naut.) watch; — *morta*, scarecrow; — *notturna* night watchman.
**guardian-o** *m.* guardian; custodian; curator; warden; (sport) goalkeeper. **-ato** *m.* guardianship.
**guardin-go** *adj.* (*m.pl.* **-ghi**) cautious; wary; circumspect.
**guar·di-o** *m.* (naut.) guard rail. **-(u)ola** *f.* guard-house.
**guardo** *m.* (poet.) glance, look.
**guarent-i·gia** *f.* (leg.) mortgage; guarantee; security; bond. **-igiare** [A4] *tr.* (leg.) to guarantee; *intr.* (*aux.* avere) to act as security. **-i·gio** *m.* (leg.) guarantee; security.
**guarentire** [D2] *tr.* (leg.) to vouch for; to guarantee.
**guari** *adv.* (used only with neg.) much; very; a long time; *non ha* —, not long ago.
**guar-ire** [D2] *tr.* to cure, to heal; *intr.* (*aux.* essere) to be cured, to recover. **-i·bile** *adj.* curable. **-igione** *f.* cure; recovery.
**guarn-ire** [D2] *tr.* to fit out, to provide; to equip; to adorn. **-igione** *f.* (mil.) garrison; (naut.) crew. **-itore** *m.* supplier. **-itura** *f.* provision; fitting out; garnishing; (naut.) stores; rigging. **-izione** *f.* supply, provision; (cul.) dressing of a dish.
**Guascogna** *pr.n.f.* (geog.) Gascony; *golfo di* —, Bay of Biscay.
**guascon-e** *m., adj.* Gascon. **-ata** *f.* gasconade.
**guast-are** [A1] *tr.* to spoil, to ruin; (mil.) to lay waste; *rfl.* to spoil, to go bad; *-arsi con*, to quarrel with; *soggetto a -arsi*, perishable; (of weather) to cloud over. **-afeste** *m. indecl.* spoil-sport. **-amento** *m.* havoc; devastation. **-atore** *m.* spoiler; (mil.) pioneer, sapper. **-atura** *f.* spoiling, laying waste.
**guasto** *apocop. part.* of **guastare**; *adj.* spoilt; devastated; tainted; decayed; corrupt, depraved; *n.m.* laying waste, ruin; damage, something needing repairs; *c'è un* — *al motore*, there is something wrong with the engine.
**guatare** [A1] *tr.* to gaze at in fear or suspicion; to pry into; to eye; to look askance at.
**guattire** [D2] *intr.* (*aux.* avere) to give tongue (of hounds); to yelp.
**guazza** *f.* morning mist; heavy dew.
**guazzabu·gli-o** *m.* muddle; medley; mass of contradictions; mixture of foods, concoction. **-are** [A4] *tr.* to muddle, to confuse. **-one** *m.* muddler.
**guazz-are** [A1] *tr.* to ford; to shake (a liquid) in a container; *intr.* (*aux.* avere) to splash when shaken (*e.g.* of a bad egg); to splash about; to wallow. **-atoio** *m.* watering-place for horses and cattle.
**guazz-o** *m.* pool; flood; ford; *passare a* —, to ford; slush; wetness; *adj.* rotten, gone bad. **-oso** *adj.* wet; soft; rotten; slushy.
**Guelfo** *adj., pr.n.m.* (hist.) Guelf, Guelph.
**guer·cio** *adj.* squinting, cross-eyed; *è* — *dall'occhio destro*, he has a squint in his right eye.
**guerr-a** *f.* war; strife; feud; *dichiarare* —, to declare war; — *di logoramento*, war of attrition; — *lampo*, blitzkrieg; *danni di* —, war damage. **-ai(u)olo** *m.* war-monger. **-i·glia** *f.* guerrilla warfare. **-igliero** *m.* guerrilla fighter.
**guerreggiare** [A3 c] *intr.* (*aux.* avere) to wage war; *tr.* to make war on.
**guerr-esco** *adj.* (*m.pl.* **-eschi**) warlike; martial. **-iere, -iero** *n.m.* warrior; *adj.* warlike; wartime.
**guf-o** *m.* (orn.) owl. **-are** [A1] *intr.* (*aux.* avere) to hoot; *tr.* to mock.
**gu·gli-a** *f.* spire; obelisk. **-ata** *f.* threaded needle. **-etta** *f.* pinnacle.
**Guglielmo** *pr.n.m.* William.
**guida** *f.* guide; guidance; guide-book; instruction book; rail; *volante di* —, steering-wheel; *scuola* —, school of motoring.
**guidales-co** *m.* (*pl.* **-chi**) sore, gall (on a draught animal); (fig.) trouble, sore point.
**guid-are** [A1] *tr.* to guide; to steer; to lead; to conduct; — *un'automobile*, to drive a car. **-atore** *m.*, **-atrice** *f.* driver.
**guiderdon-e** *m.* recompense; reward; incentive; merit; esteem. **-are** [A1 c] *tr.* to recompense; to reward.
**guidoslitta** *f.* bob-sleigh.
**guig·gia** *f.* sandal-strap; shoe-strap.
**guinz-a·glio** *m.* dog's lead; leash; (fig.) check, restraint. **-agliare** [A4] *tr.* to put on the lead.
**guisa** *f.* wise, mode, manner; guise; *a* — *di*, after the manner of; *di* — *che*, so that.
**guizz-are** [A1] *intr.* (*aux.* avere) to dart (esp. of fish); to quiver; to squirm; to flicker; — *via*, to flash past; *tr.* to brandish, to wave. **-o** *m.* flick; flip; dart; (radar) blip, pip.
**guntero** *m.* (math.) slide-rule.
**gu·scio** *m.* shell; husk; pod; hull; cover; *gusci della bilancia*, scales.
**gust-are** [A1] *tr.* to taste; to try; to enjoy; to relish; to like; *impers.* (*aux.* avere) to be pleasing; *rfl.* (*prep.* di) to enjoy. **-evole** *adj.* pleasing; tasty, palatable, appetizing.
**gust-o** *m.* taste; flavour; relish; gusto, zest; pleasure; liking; *prendere* — *a*, to acquire a taste for; *cavarsi il* — *di*, to satisfy a long felt wish to; *avere* — *a*, to be glad of (often vindictively); *ma che* — *c'è . . . ?*, what's the point of . . . ? **-osità** *f.* tastiness; delicacy of flavour. **-oso** *adj.* tasty, savoury; amusing; pleasant, enjoyable.
**gutturale** *adj., n.m.* guttural.

**H** *f.* (pron. **'acca'**; always mute at the beginning of a word; c and g followed by h are hard); the letter h; *un'— minuscola*, a small h; *un'— maiuscola*, a capital H.
**ha** *excl.* ha!
**handicap** *m. indecl.* (pron. as Eng.) handicap; **-pato** *adj.* (sport and fig.) handicapped.
**hara** *f.* pigsty.
**hegelian-o** *adj.* (philos.) Hegelian; (fig.) abstruse, obscure. **-ișmo** *m.* (philos.) Hegelianism.
**hiho·n** *excl.* (onomat.) hee-haw (a donkey's bray).
**hockey** *m. indecl.* (pron. as Fr.) — *su ghiaccio*, ice-hockey; — *su prato*, hockey; — *a rotelle*, hockey on roller-skates. **-eista** *m., f.* hockey-player.
**hostess** *f. indecl.* (pron. as Eng.) air-hostess.
**humu·s** *f. indecl.* humus; (fig.) ground suitable for the growth of a certain feeling or opinion.
**hurrà** *excl.* hurrah!

**I**[1] *m., f.* the letter i; the vowel i; *i lungo*, the letter j; *i greco*, the letter y; (fig.) *mettere i punti sugli i*, to speak plainly.
**I**[2] *def. art. m.pl.* (except before s impure, z, x, gn, ps), the.
**iacint-e·o, -ino** *adj.* hyacinthine.
**I·adi** *pr.n.f.pl.* (myth.) Hyades.
**Iafet** *pr.n.m.* (bibl.) Japheth.
**ialino** *adj.* hyaline, translucent.
**iarda** *f.* yard (0.914399 metre).
**iato** *m.* hiatus; gap.
**ịatt-anza** *f.* arrogance, boasting. **-ura** *f.* misfortune, ruin, wreck; *per nostra somma -ura*, to crown our misfortunes.
**Ib-eri** *pr.n.m.pl.* (geog.) Iberians. *adj.* Iberian.
**ibern-ante** *adj.* hibernating. **-aziọne** *f.* hibernation.
**i·brid-o** *adj.* (biol.) hybrid; cross-bred, mongrel; (fig.) spurious; *n.m.* hybrid. **-aziọne** *f.* cross-breeding.
**ic·chese** *f.* see **ics.**
**icnografi·a** *f.* ground plan; horizontal section of a building.
**icọn-a** *f.* (eccl.) icon. **-oclasta** *m.* iconoclast. **-oclasti·a** *f.* iconoclasm. **-ografi·a** *f.* iconography.
**ics** *f.* name of the letter **x**; *i raggi* —, X-rays.
**idd-i·o** *m.* (*pl.* **-i·i**) God; god.
**ide·a** *f.* idea; thought; conception, notion; impression; *da non averne* —, inconceivably; *farsi un'— di*, to get a rough idea of; *nemmeno per* —, by no means; opinion, belief; *cambiare* —, to change one's mind; plan, intention; *questa sarebbe la mia* —, here is what I suggest; *ho una mezza — di*, I am half inclined to; caprice, whim; *l'ho fatto di mia* —, it was all my own idea; aim, purpose; likeness, style; *appena un'— di*, the merest hint of.
**ideal-e** *adj.* ideal; perfect; imaginary; fictitious; relating to ideas; *n.m.* ideal. **-mẹnte** *adv.* ideally; in imagination. **-ișmo** *m.* idealism. **-ista** *m., f.* idealist; dreamer. **-i·stico** *adj.* idealistic. **-iẓẓare** [A1] *tr.* to idealize.
**ide-are** [A6] *tr.* to conceive; to imagine; to devise; to plan; to think of. **-a·bile** *adj.* thinkable, conceivable.
**iden·tico** *adj.* identical.
**identific-are** [A2 s] *tr.* to identify; to make identical; *rfl.* to identify oneself; to be identical with. **-aziọne** *f.* identification; identifying.
**identità** *f.* identity; individuality.
**ideo-logi·a** *f.* ideology. **-lo·gico** *adj.* ideological.
**ideo·logo** *m.* ideologist; (fig.) visionary.
**idil·lico** *adj.* idyllic; romantic.
**idil·l-io** *m.* idyll; **-i·aco** *adj.* relating to an idyll.
**idiom-a** *m.* idiom; turn of phrase; language; *l'— materno*, one's native tongue. **-a·tico** *adj.* idiomatic.
**idi-ota** *m., f.* idiot. **-o·tico** *adj.* idiotic, stupid and uneducated. **-otișmo** *m.* idiom; (med.) idiocy, imbecility. **-ozi·a** *f.* (med.) idiocy; (fig.) stupidity.
**idolatr-a** *m., f.* idolater; *adj.* idolatrous. **-are** [A1] *tr.* to idolize. **-i·a** *f.* idolatry.
**idola·trico** *adj.* idolatrous.
**i·dol-o** *m.* idol. **-eggiare** [A3 c] *tr.* to make an idol of; (fig.) to idolize.
**ido·ne-o** *adj.* fitting; proper; suitable; serviceable; able. **-ità** *f.* fitness, suitability.
**idra** *f.* (myth.) hydra.
**idrante** *m.* (hydraul.) hydrant; — *da incendio*, fire-hose.
**idrato** *adj.* hydrated; *n.m.* — *di carbonio*, carbohydrate.
**idra·ulic-a** *f.* hydraulics. **-o** *adj.* hydraulic; *energia -a*, water power; *n.m.* hydraulic engineer; plumber.
**i·drico** *adj.* watery; for water; *approvvigionamento* —, water supply; *impianto* —, waterworks.
**idr-oaeroplano** *m.* seaplane. **-ocarbonato** *m.* carbohydrate. **-oelet·trico** *adj.* hydro-electric. **-oestrattọre** *m.* spin-dryer. **-o·filo** *adj.* absorbent; *cotone -ofilo*, cotton wool. **-ofobi·a** *f.* (med.) hydrophobia, rabies. **-o·foro** *adj.* bearing water. **-o·geno** *m.* hydrogen. **-ometri·a** *f.* hydrodynamics. **-o·metro** *m.* hydrodynamometer; rain-gauge. **-oscalo** *m.* seaplane base. **-o·scopo** *m.* water-diviner. **-ovolante** *m.* seaplane.
**Iefte** *pr.n.m.* (bibl.) Jephtha.
**ịella** *f.* bad luck, misfortune; evil eye.
**Ịemen** *pr.n.m.* (geog.) Yemen.
**Ịena**[1] *pr.n.f.* (geog.) Jena.
**iena**[2] *f.* (zool.) hyaena; (fig.) cruel person.
**Ịe·ova** *pr.n.m.* Jehovah.
**iera·tico** *adj.* hieratic; (fig.) solemn; stylized; enigmatic.
**ieri** *adv.* yesterday; *l'altro* —, the day before yesterday; — *mattina*, yesterday morning; *n.m.* yesterday; *tutto* —, the whole of yesterday.
**ịett-are** [A1] *tr.* to bewitch. **-atọre** *m.* one who has the evil eye. **-atura** *f.* the evil eye; bad luck.
**Ifigeni·a** *pr.n.f.* (myth.) Iphigenia.
**igi-ene** *f.* hygiene; health; sanitation; public health. **-e·nico** *adj.* hygienic; healthful; salubrious.
**ignaro** *adj.* unaware; inexperienced.
**ign-a·via** *f.* laziness; cowardice. **-avo** *adj.* slothful; cowardly.
**i·gn-eo** *adj.* fiery; flaming; (geol.) igneous. **-i·fugo** *adj.* (*m.pl.* **-i·fughi**) fire-proof, fire-resistant. **-iziọne** *f.* ignition; igniting.
**igno·bile** *adj.* vulgar; ignoble; *metallo* —, base metal.
**ignomi·ni-a** *f.* ignominy; shameful action; disgrace. **-ọso** *adj.* ignominious; disgraceful; shameful.
**ignoran-te** *adj.* ignorant; uneducated; illiterate; ill-mannered; *n.m., f.* ignoramus; illiterate person; ill-mannered person. **-za** *f.* ignorance.
**ignor-are** [A5] *tr.* to be ignorant of, to be unaware of. **-ato** *part. adj.* unknown; neglected; to take no notice of; to ignore.
**ignoto** *adj.* unknown; *n.m.* unknown person; the unknown.
**ignudo** *adj.* naked, bare; in the nude; destitute; *n.m.* destitute person.
**il**[1] *def. art. m. sing.* (except before s impure, z, x, gn, ps) the; — *che*, which, a thing which; *cento lire — mese*, a hundred lire a month.
**il**[2] *prn.m. sing. acc.* (poet.) him; it.
**i·lar-e** *adj.* cheerful, merry; hilarious. **-ità** *f.* hilarity, good humour, cheerfulness.

**Ildebrando** *pr.n.m.* Hildebrand.
**Ili·ade** *pr.n.f.* Iliad.
**i·lice** *f.* (bot.) ilex.
**I·lio, I·lion** *pr.n.m.* (myth.), Ilium, Troy.
**illagazione** *f.* inundation.
**illanguidire** [D2] *tr.* to weaken; to enfeeble; *intr.* (*aux.* essere), *rfl.* to become languid; to grow feeble; to droop.
**illazione** *f.* deduction; (leg.) inference; conclusion; consequence.
**illecito** *adj.* illicit.
**illegal-e** *adj.* illegal, unlawful. **-ità** *f.* illegality.
**illeggi·bil-e** *adj.* illegible; unreadable. **-ità** illegibility.
**illegit·tim-o** *adj.* illegitimate; unfounded, baseless. **-ità** *f.* illegitimacy.
**illeso** *adj.* unhurt; safe and sound; intact.
**illetterato** *adj.* illiterate.
**illibat-o** *adj.* unsullied; chaste; above reproach. **-ezza** *f.* purity; integrity.
**illiberal-e** *adj.* illiberal; *le arti -i*, manual skills, technology. **-ità** *f.* illiberality; lack of tolerance.
**illimitat-o** *adj.* unlimited; indefinite. **-azione** *f.* boundlessness.
**Illinese** *pr.n.m.* (geog.) Illinois.
**Illi·ria** *pr.n.f.* Illyria.
**illi·rico** *adj.* Illyrian.
**illo·gico** *adj.* illogical; absurd.
**illu·dere** [C3] *tr.* to delude; to deceive; *intr.* (*aux.* essere), *rfl.* to delude onself; to hope; to believe.
**illumin-are** [A1 s] *tr.* to illuminate; (fig.) to enlighten; *rfl.* to grow bright; (fig.) to become radiant; to educate oneself, to acquire knowledge. **-ante** *part. adj.* illuminating. **-ato** *part. adj.* illuminated; lit up, lighted; (fig.) informed, enlightened. **-azione** *f.* lighting; illuminations; *-azione a fluorescenza*, fluorescent lighting; (fig.) enlightenment.
**illusion-e** *f.* illusion; — *ottica*, optical illusion; phantasm; dream; *una pia* —, a pious illusion. **-ismo** *m.* conjuring. **-ista** *m.* conjurer.
**illus-o** *part.* of **illu·dere**; *adj.* deluded; deceived. **-o·rio** *adj.* illusory; deceptive.
**illustr-are** [A1] *tr.* to illuminate; (fig.) to illustrate, to explain; to reflect glory upon; *rfl.* to achieve fame, to become illustrious. **-ativo** *adj.* illustrative, explanatory. **-azione** *f.* illustration; plate, picture; explanation, annotation.
**illustre** *adj.* illustrious; renowned.
**illuvione** *f.* inundation; flood; (fig.) invasion, incursion.
**Imala·ia** *pr.n.m.* (geog.) Himalaya.
**imbacucc-are** [A2] *tr.* to muffle up, to wrap up; *rfl.* to muffle oneself up. **-ato** *part. adj.* muffled up; wrapped up; hooded.
**imbaldanz-ire** [D2] *intr.* (*aux.* essere), *rfl.* to grow bold; to be defiant; *tr.* to embolden. **-ito** *part. adj.* emboldened; perky, cocky.
**imball-are** [A1] *tr.* to wrap up; to pack into crates; *rfl.* (motor.) to race (of an engine). **-ag·gio** *m.* packing; wrapping; *carta d'-aggio*, wrapping paper.
**imbalsam-are** [A1 s] *tr.* to embalm; to stuff. **-atore** *m.* embalmer; taxidermist. **-azione** *f.* embalming; taxidermy.
**imbambol-ato** *adj.* (of eyes) half-closed, heavy with sleep or illness. **-ire** [D2] *intr.* (*aux.* essere) to grow childish.
**imbandierare** [A1] *tr.* to deck with flags; (naut.) to dress.
**imbandire** [D2] *tr.* to prepare for a banquet; (iron.) to make sumptuous arrangements for.
**imbarazz-are** [A1] *tr.* to embarrass; to obstruct; to perplex; *rfl.* to become entangled. **-ante** *part. adj.* embarrassing; perplexing. **-o** *m.* embarrassment; obstacle; perplexity; *esser d'-o a*, to cause embarrassment to.
**imbarc-are** [A2] *tr.* (naut.) to put on board, to embark; *rfl.* to embark; (also fig.) **-atoio** *m.* landing-stage. **-azione** *f.* embarkation; taking on board.
**imbar-co** *m.* (*pl.* **-chi**) *m.* embarkation; landing-stage; boat.
**imbardare** [A1] *tr.* to caparison; to harness.
**imbastardire** [D2] *intr.* (*aux.* essere), *rfl.* to degenerate; *tr.* to debase, to corrupt.
**imbastire** [D2] *tr.* (dressm.) to baste, to tack; (fig.) to sketch, to outline.
**imbat·tere** [B1] *rfl.* to happen; (*prep.* in) to meet by chance; *n.m.* merest chance; *è un imbattersi*, it's all a matter of luck.
**imbatti·bile** *adj.* unbeatable; indefatigable.
**imbaulare** [A1] *tr.* to pack in a trunk.
**imbavagliare** [A4] *tr.* to gag; (fig.) to muzzle, to silence.
**imbecc-are** [A2 c] *tr.* (of birds) to feed; (fig.) to prompt; to cram. **-atoio** *m.* seed-box or food-tray for birds.
**imbecherare** [A1] *tr.* to wheedle; to suborn; to win over; *lasciarsi* —, to give way to persuasion.
**imbecill-e** *adj.* foolish; *n.m.*, *f.* imbecile. **-ag·gine** *f.* folly; imbecility. **-ità** *f.* imbecility.
**imbelle** *adj.* timid, cowardly.
**imbellettare** [A1 c] *tr.* to make up (the face); to embellish; *rfl.* to make oneself up.
**imbell-ire** [D2] *intr.* (*aux.* essere) to become prettier; *tr.* to adorn. **-ito** *part. adj.* improved in looks.
**imberbe** *adj.* beardless.
**imbestialire** [D2] *intr.* (*aux.* essere), *rfl.* to become like a wild animal; to fly into a rage; to be very obstinate; *tr.* to brutalize.
**imbev-ere** [B4] *tr.* to soak up; to imbibe; *rfl.* (*prep.* di) to be impregnated (with); to be soaked (in, with); (fig.) to become imbued (with). **-uto** *part. adj.* saturated; (fig.) imbued (with).
**imbiancare** [A2] *tr.* to whiten; to whitewash; to wash white; to bleach; *rfl.*, *intr.* (*aux.* essere) to grow white, to turn white.
**imbianchino** *m.* house-painter; whitewasher.
**imbianchire** [D2] *tr.* to bleach; to whiten; *intr.* (*aux.* essere) to be bleached; to grow white; to turn pale.
**imbibire** [D2] *tr.* (techn.) to absorb, to soak up; to imbibe.
**imbiettare** [A1 c] *tr.* to wedge.
**imbiond-are** [A1 c] *tr.* to dye yellow; to cause to turn yellow. **-ire** [D2] *tr.* to dye yellow; *intr.* (*aux.* essere), *rfl.* to become blonde; to dye one's hair blonde; (of wheat) to ripen.
**imbitum(in)are** [A1] *tr.* to asphalt; to tar.
**imbizzarrire** [D2] *tr.* to excite; *intr.* (*aux.* essere), *rfl.* to get excited or angry; (of a horse) to get out of control.
**imbizzire** [D2] *intr.* (*aux.* essere), *rfl.* to fly into a rage, to get upset; to become angry or unmanageable.
**imbocc-are** [A2 c] *tr.* to feed, to spoon-feed; to cram; to put to one's mouth; to prompt; to enter; — *la scala*, to go upstairs; to fit, to insert; *intr.* (*aux.* essere; *prep.* in) to fit into; to flow into; to open into; *recip. rfl.* to fit together. **-atura** *f.* feeding; (fig.) opening, mouth, entrance.
**imbocci-are** [A3] *intr.* (*aux.* essere) to come into bud. **-ato** *part. adj.* in bud, budding.
**imboc-co** *m.* (*pl.* **-chi**) opening, entrance; mouthpiece.
**imbonire** [D2] *tr.* to pacify; to cajole; *rfl.* to grow calm, to die down (of wind or waves).
**imbosc-are** [A2] *tr.* to hide in a wood; to place in ambush; *intr.* (*aux.* essere), *rfl.* to go into the bush; to lie in ambush; to lie low. **-ata** *f.* (mil.) ambush. **-ato** *part. adj.* thickly wooded; lying in ambush; hidden.
**imbosch-ire** [D2] *tr.* to afforest; *intr.* (*aux.* essere) to become covered with trees. **-ito** *part. adj.* afforested; wooded; overgrown.
**imbottare** [A1 c] *tr.* to put (wine) into casks.
**imbottigliare** [A4] *tr.* to bottle; (naut.) to blockade.

**imbott-ire** [D2] *tr.* to stuff, to pad; to upholster. **-ita** *f.* quilt. **-ito** *part. adj.* padded, filled; (cul.) stuffed. **-itura** *f.* stuffing; padding, quilting.

**imbozzacchire** [D2] *intr.* (*aux.* essere) to be stunted; to shrivel; to wither away.

**imbrac-a** *f.* (harness) breeching; (fig.) *buttarsi sull'—*, to hang back, to go slow. **-are** [A2] *tr.* to tie up in a sling. **-atura** *f.* sling; strapping; harness (of parachute).

**imbrancare** [A2] *tr.* to herd together; (fig.) to gather together, to assemble.

**imbrandire** [D2] *tr.* to seize, to grasp the handle of; to brandish.

**imbratt-are** [A1] *tr.* to dirty, to soil, to stain. **-acarte, -afogli** *m. indecl.* scribbler, hack. **-amondo** *m. indecl.* troublemaker. **-amuri** *m. indecl.* dauber. **-o** *m.* pig-swill; badly-cooked food; daub; scribble.

**imbrecci-are** [A3 c] *tr.* to gravel; to ballast. **-ata** *f.* layer of gravel; foundation of a road.

**imbri·fero** *adj.* catchment; *bacino —*, catchment area.

**imbrigli-are** [A4] *tr.* to bridle, to harness; to curb, to restrain. **-ato** *part. adj.* bridled; harnessed; curbed, restrained.

**imbroccare** [A2] *tr.* to hit (the mark); (fig.) to guess correctly; to meet (by good luck); to find.

**imbrod-are** [A1] *tr.* to soil; **-olare** [A1 s] *tr.* to stain, to spot; *rfl.* to splash oneself in eating. **-olìo** *m.* soiling; slovenly eating.

**imbrogli-are** [A4] *tr.* to tangle, to confuse; to swindle; to get in the way of; *rfl.* to get confused; to meddle (with), to get mixed up (in). **-ante** *part. adj.* entangling; *n.m.* swindler. **-atore** *m.* cheat, fraud.

**imbro·glio** *m.* confusion; obstacle; misunderstanding; fraud.

**imbronci-are** [A3 c] *intr.* (*aux.* essere) to be sulky; to take offence. **-ato** *part. adj.* sulky; surly.

**imbrumare** [A1] *intr.* (*aux.* essere) (naut.) to run into fog, to be held up in fog.

**imbrunire** [A1] *intr.* (*aux.* essere) (poet.) to grow dark; *tr.* to make dark, to blacken; to tan; *n.m. sull'—*, at dusk, at nightfall.

**imbruttare** [A1] *tr.* to dirty; to defile.

**imbruttire** [D2] *tr.* to make ugly; to deform; to disfigure; to mar; *intr.* (*aux.* essere) to grow ugly.

**imbucare** [A2] *tr.* to put in a hole; to post; *rfl.* to creep into a hole; (fig.) to hide.

**imburrare** [A1] *tr.* to butter; (fig.) to flatter, to soft-soap.

**imbusto** *m.* bust; thorax; upper part of the body.

**imbuto** *m.* funnel.

**imbuzzire** [D2] *intr.* (*aux.* essere), *rfl.* to sulk; to grow surly.

**Imen-e, -e·o** *pr.n.m.* Hymen.

**imine·o** *adj.* nuptial; *n.m.pl.* (poet.) *iminei*, wedding.

**imit-are** [A1 s, A1] *tr.* to imitate; to be similar to, to look like. **-ativo** *adj.* imitative. **-azione** *f.* imitation; mimicry.

**immacchiare** [A4] *rfl.* to take to the woods, to hide in the 'macchia'; to live as an outlaw.

**immacolat-o** *adj.* immaculate. **-a** *n.f.*; *L'Immacolata*, the Virgin Mary.

**immagazzin-are** [A1] *tr.* to store; (fig.) to store up; to accumulate. **-ag·gio** *m.* storage, storing; *piazzale per -aggio*, storage yard.

**immagin-are** [A1 s] *tr.* to imagine; to conjecture; to invent; to think up; *rfl.* (*dat.* of prn. 'si') to imagine; *me l'-o*, I can just imagine it. **-a·bile** *adj.* credible; conceivable. **-azione** *f.* fancy, fantasy; imagination; concept; supposition.

**immagina·rio** *adj.* imaginary; imagined; fanciful; unreal; ideal; *ammalato —*, hypochondriac.

**immaginativ-a** *f.* faculty of imagination; fancy. **-o** *adj.* imaginative; *potenza -a*, power of imagination.

**imma·gin-e** *f.* image; likeness; figure; picture; portrait. **-oso** *adj.* imaginative; fantastic, fanciful.

**immanca·bil-e** *adj.* certain; unfailing. **-mente** *adv.* unfailingly; without fail.

**imman-e** *adj.* monstrous; huge; horrible; cruel; immeasurable. **-ità** *f.* bestiality; savagery, cruelty; ferocity.

**immaneggia·bile** *adj.* intractable, unmanageable.

**immanen-te** *adj.* inherent. **-za** *f.* inherence.

**immangia·bile** *adj.* uneatable.

**immansueto** *adj.* untamed, fierce; intractable.

**immantinente** *adv.* immediately.

**immateriale** *adj.* non-material; incorporeal; spiritual.

**immatricol-are** [A1 s] *rfl.* to matriculate; *tr.* to register; to admit to a University. **-azione** *f.* matriculation; registration.

**immatur-o** *adj.* immature; premature, precocious. **-ità** *f.* immaturity.

**immedesimare** [A1 sc] *tr.* to combine, to unite; *rfl.* (*prep.* con) to identify oneself (with); to sympathize (with).

**immediat-o** *adj.* immediate; direct; first-hand. **-ezza** *f.* immediacy.

**immedica·bile** *adj.* incurable; irremediable.

**immelensire** [D2] *tr.* to make dull or stupid; to stun; to stupefy; *intr.* (*aux.* essere) to become dull or stupid.

**immellettare** [A1] *tr.* to muddy, to begrime; *rfl.* to become smeared, to become filthy.

**immelmare** [A1] *rfl.* to sink in mud; (fig.) to become corrupt, to touch pitch.

**immemora·bile** *adj.* immemorial.

**imme·more** *adj.* (*prep.* di) unmindful, forgetful (of); forgetting; (poet.) bringing forgetfulness; lifeless, senseless.

**immens-o** *adj.* immense; enormous. **-ità** *f.* immensity; infiniteness.

**immensura·bil-e** *adj.* measureless. **-ità** *f.* immensity.

**immer·gere** [C4] *tr.* to dip, to immerse; to soak; *rfl.* to immerse oneself; to merge.

**immerit-ato** *adj.* unmerited, undeserved. **-evole** *adj.* undeserving, unworthy.

**immersione** *f.* immersion; plunge; *in — a*, under water, submerged; (naut.) *linea d'—*, Plimsoll line.

**immerso** *part.* of **immergere** *q.v*; *adj.* immersed.

**immettere** [C20] *tr.* to put in; to introduce; to induct.

**immigr-are** [A1 s] *intr.* (*aux.* essere) to immigrate. **-ante** *part. adj.* immigrating; *n.m., f.* immigrant. **-azione** *f.* immigration.

**imminen-te** *adj.* imminent, impending; *un libro d'— pubblicazione*, forthcoming publication. **-za** *f.* imminence.

**immischiare** [A4] *tr.* (*prep.* in) to thrust; *rfl.* (*prep.* a, con) to thrust oneself; to interfere (with, in).

**immiserire** [D2] *tr.* to impoverish; to make wretched; to wither; *intr.* (*aux.* essere) to become poor; to wither.

**immissa·rio** *m.* affluent; intake, sluice.

**immissione** *f.* induction; letting in; inlet.

**immisto** *adj.* unmixed; unadulterated.

**immite** *adj.* harsh, pitiless.

**immo·bil-e** *adj.* motionless; still; immobile; fixed; *beni -i*, real estate. **-ismo** *m.* (pol.) ultra-conservatism. **-ità** *f.* immobility. **-izzare** [A1] *tr.* to immobilize.

**immoderat-o** *adj.* immoderate; unrestrained. **-ezza** *f.* immoderation; excess.

**immode·st-ia** *f.* immodesty; brazenness. **-o** *adj.* immodest; brazen.

**immol-are** [A1] *tr.* (rel.) to immolate, to sacrifice; *rfl.* (fig.) to sacrifice oneself. **-azione** *f.* (rel.) immolation, sacrifice.

**immollare** [A1] *tr.* to wet; to drench.

**immond-o** *adj.* unclean; foul;

evil-living. **-ẹẓẓa·io** *m.* rubbish dump. **-i·zia** *f.* filth; (fig.) filthiness, obscenity; *pl.* refuse; trash, rubbish.
**immoral-e** *adj.* immoral. **-ità** *f.* immorality.
**immortal-e** *adj.* immortal; *n.m.* immortal being. **-ità** *f.* immortality; enduring fame. **-iẓẓare** [A1] *tr.* to immortalize.
**immoto** *adj.* motionless; unmoved.
**immun-e** *adj.* immune, exempt; uninjured. **-ità** *f.* immunity, exemption. **-iẓẓare** [A1] *tr.* to immunize.
**immuta·bil-e** *adj.* immutable; unchanging. **-ità** *f.* immutability.
**imo** *adj.* lowest, low; degraded; *n.m.* deepest part; bottom.
**impac-care** [A2] *tr.* to pack; to wrap up. **-catura** *f.* packing; cost of packing. **-chettare** [A1 c] *tr.* to pack, to package.
**impacci-are** [A3] *tr.* to hinder; to impede; *rfl.* (*prep.* con) to meddle (in). **-ato** *part. adj.* impeded; clumsy. **-o** *m.* hindrance; *dare -o a*, to encumber; *cavarsi d'-o*, to get out of an awkward situation. **-ọne** *m.* meddler, trouble-maker. **-ọso** *adj.* meddling.
**impadronire** [D2] *rfl.* (*prep.* di) to master; to appropriate; to take charge (of); to seize hold (of).
**impagliare** [A4] *tr.* to pack in straw; to stuff with straw.
**impalancato** *m.* palisade, fence of boards.
**impal-are** [A1] *tr.* to impale; to stake (plants or trees); *rfl.* to stand stiff like a stake. **-atura** *f.* impaling.
**impalc-are** [A2] *tr.* (bldg.) to floor. **-atura** *f.* flooring; scaffolding; (fig.) framework.
**impal-co** *m.* (*pl.* **-chi**) scaffolding; trellis.
**impallid-ire** [D2] *intr.* (*aux.* essere) to turn pale; to fade. **-ito** *part. adj.* pale; dim.
**imparagona·bile** *adj.* incomparable.
**imparare** [A1] *tr.* to learn; to get to hear; *— a mente, — a memoria*, to learn by heart.
**impareggia·bile** *adj.* incomparable; unrivalled.
**imparent-are** [A1] *tr.* to ally by marriage; *rfl.* (*prep.* a) to become related (to); (*prep.* con) to marry (into). **-ato** *part. adj.* related by marriage.
**im·par-i** *adj. indecl.* unequal; uneven. **-ità** *f.* disparity; *essere in condizioni d'-ità*, to be on an unequal footing.
**impartire** [D2] *tr.* to impart; to assign.
**imparzial-e** *adj.* impartial; equitable. **-ità** *f.* impartiality.
**impassi·bil-e** *adj.* impassive, unemotional. **-ità** *f.* imperturbability.
**impast-are** [A1] *tr.* to knead; to paste; *intr.* (*aux.* avere) (paint.) to mix colours. **-o** *m.* kneading; paste; (fig.) medley.
**impasticciare** [A3] *tr.* to make a mixture of; to botch.
**impastoiare** [A4 c] *tr.* to fetter; to tether; (fig.) to cramp.
**impatto** *m.* impact.
**impaurire** [D2] *tr.* to frighten; *intr.* (*aux.* essere), *rfl.* to become afraid; *impaurirsi di tutto*, to take fright at everything.
**impa·vido** *adj.* fearless, undaunted.
**impazi-ente** *adj.* impatient, eager; *— di*, intolerant of. **-entire** [D2] *rfl.*, *intr.* (*aux.* essere) to lose patience. **-enza** *f.* impatience; intolerance.
**impazzire** [D2] *intr.* (*aux.* essere) to go mad; to lose one's head; *far —*, to drive mad; *— per*, to be crazy about.
**impecca·bile** *adj.* impeccable, faultless.
**imped-ire** [D2] *tr.* to hinder; to impede; *— un delitto*, to prevent a crime; *un macigno -iva il passo*, a boulder blocked the way. **-imẹnto** *m.* hindrance; impediment. **-itivo** *adj.* obstructive.
**impegn-are** [A5 c] *tr.* to pledge; to pawn; to engage; to reserve; *rfl.* to pledge oneself; to make a social or business engagement. **-ativo** *adj.* binding; *offerta -ativa*, firm offer; (fig.) exacting. **-ato** *part. adj.* pledged; engaged; committed; *sono già -ato*, I have a previous engagement.
**impẹgn-o** *m.* pledge; obligation; commitment; social or business engagement; diligence, zeal; *assumersi un —*, to undertake a responsibility; (finan.) liability. **-ọso** *adj.* troublesome; requiring care; quarrelsome.
**impel·l-ere** [C23] *tr.* to impel; to thrust. **-ente** *part. adj.* impelling, compelling.
**impenetra·bil-e** *adj.* impenetrable; impervious; *— all'aria*, airtight; (fig.) inscrutable. **-ità** *f.* impenetrability.
**impeniten-te** *adj.* impenitent, unrepentant; incorrigible. **-za** *f.* impenitence; obduracy.
**impennare** [A1 c] *tr.* to feather; to give wings to, to wing; *rfl.* to become fledged; (fig.) to become ruffled.
**impens-a·bile** *adj.* unthinkable. **-ata** *adv.phr. all'-ata*, unexpectedly; *cogliere all'-ata*, to take unawares. **-ato** *adj.* unforeseen, unexpected.
**impensierire** [D2] *tr.* to make anxious, to worry; *rfl.* to become anxious, to be worried.
**imper-are** [A1] *intr.* (*aux.* avere) to be emperor; to reign; (fig.) to prevail. **-ante** *part. adj.* reigning; dominant. **-ativo** *adj.* imperative.
**imperat-ọre** *m.* emperor. **-rice** *f.* empress.
**impercetti·bil-e** *adj.* imperceptible. **-ità** *f.* imperceptibility.
**imperdona·bile** *adj.* unforgivable, unpardonable.
**imperfetto** *adj.* imperfect; defective; unfinished.
**imperfezịone** *f.* imperfection; flaw; *nessuno è senza imperfezioni*, nobody is perfect.
**imperial-e** *adj.* imperial. **-ịsmo** *m.* imperialism. **-ista** *m.*, *f.* imperialist.
**impe·rio** *m.* (poet.) dominion, command, empire.
**imperiọs-o** *adj.* imperious, peremptory; imperative. **-ità** *f.* imperiousness.
**imper-ito** *adj.* unskilled, inexperienced; awkward. **-i·zia** *f.* inexperience; lack of skill; awkwardness.
**imperituro** *adj.* imperishable, immortal.
**imperl-are** [A1] *tr.* to pearl; to adorn with pearls. **-ato** *part. adj.* pearled; pearly.
**impermal-ire** [D2] *tr.* to offend; to vex; *rfl.*, *intr.* (*aux.* essere) to take umbrage; to be touchy. **-ito** *part. adj.* vexed; offended.
**impermea·bile** *adj.* weatherproof; airtight; impermeable, impervious; *n.m.* raincoat.
**imperniare** [A4] *tr.* to pivot; to hinge; *rfl.* to be pivoted; (fig.) *imperniarsi su*, to be founded on.
**impero** *m.* empire; imperial rule; command; *l'— della legge*, the authority of the law.
**imperò** *conj.* for the reason that, inasmuch as.
**imperscruta·bile** *adj.* inscrutable.
**impersonal-e** *adj.* impersonal; impartial. **-ità** *f.* impartiality.
**impersonare** [A1 c] *tr.* to personify; to impersonate; to act the part of; *rfl.* to be personified.
**imperter·rito** *adj.* intrepid, undaunted.
**impertinen-te** *adj.* not pertinent, irrelevant; impertinent, insolent. **-za** *f.* impertinence; *dire delle -ze*, to make insolent remarks.
**imperturba·bil-e** *adj.* imperturbable, calm. **-ità** *f.* imperturbability.
**imperturbato** *adv.* unperturbed.
**impervers-are** [A1] *intr.* (*aux.* avere) to rage, to storm; to be furious. **-ato** *part. adj.* raging; cruel.
**imper·vi-o** *adj.* inaccessible; impervious. **-età** *f.* inaccessibility; imperviousness.
**im·peto** *m.* impetus; vehemence; onset; *in un — di gioia*, in a transport of joy; *di primo —*, at the first onset.
**impetr-are**[I] [A1] *tr.* to obtain (by asking); to ask for. **-ante** *part.*

*adj.* beseeching; *n.m.*, *f.* suppliant.

**impetrare**[2] *intr.* (*aux.* essere) to turn to stone.

**impettito** *adj.* with chest thrown out; (fig.) conceited; *camminare —*, to strut.

**impetuọs-o** *adj.* impetuous; violent. **-ità** *f.* impetuosity.

**impianell-are** [A1] *tr.* to tile. **-ato** *part. adj.* tiled; *n.m.* tiling; paving.

**impiantare** [A1] *tr.* to fit; to install; to establish.

**impianto** *m.* establishment, foundation; installation; *— di riscaldamento*, heating-plant; *spese d'—*, installation charges.

**impiastr-are** [A1] *tr.* to plaster; to daub; to scribble. **-o** *m.* plaster, poultice; (fig.) daub; botched work.

**impicc-are** [A2] *tr.* to hang, to execute by hanging; *rfl.* to hang oneself; (fig.) to put one's head in a noose. **-agiọne** *f.* hanging, execution.

**impicci-are** [A3] *tr.* to encumber; to hinder; *intr.* (*aux.* avere) to be a nuisance; to be in the way. **-o** *m.* hindrance; nuisance; troublesome affair or task; intrigue. **-ọne** *m.* meddler. **-ọso** *adj.* inconvenient; cumbersome; annoying.

**impiccolire** [D2] *tr.* to reduce in size; to lessen; *rfl.* to grow smaller; to humble oneself.

**impieg-are** [A2] *tr.* to employ; to make use of; to spend; to invest; *-ai tre ore per arrivare a casa*, it took me three hours to get home; *rfl.* to be employed; to employ oneself; to obtain employment. **-ato** *part. adj.* employed; *n.m.* employee; clerk; *-ato di Stato*, Civil Servant.

**impie-go** *m.* (*pl.* **-ghi**) employment; job; *offerte d'—*, situations vacant; investment.

**impietosire** [D2] *tr.* to move to pity, to touch; *rfl.* (*prep.* di) to be touched, to pity.

**impietrire** [D2] *tr.* to petrify; to harden the heart of; *rfl.* to be turned into stone; to harden one's heart.

**impigliare** [A4] *tr.* to entangle; to entrap; *rfl.* to be entangled; to get caught.

**impi·glio** *m.* entanglement, hindrance.

**impigrire** [D2] *tr.* to make lazy; *intr.* (*aux.* essere), *rfl.* to grow lazy.

**impinguare** [A6] *tr.* to fatten; (fig.) to enrich; to pad, to fill out; *rfl.* to grow fat; (fig.) to get rich.

**impiombare** [A1 c] *tr.* to seal with lead; to line with lead; *— un dente*, to stop a tooth.

**impiumare** [A1] *tr.* to adorn with plumes or feathers; to feather; to give wings to; *rfl.* to become fledged.

**implaca·bil-e** *adj.* implacable, unrelenting. **-ità** *f.* implacableness.

**implacato** *adj.* unrelenting; inveterate.

**implic-are** [A2] *tr.* to implicate; to involve; to imply. **-aziọne** *f.* implication.

**impli·cit-o** *adj.* implied, implicit. **-ẹzza** *f.* implicitness.

**implor-are** [A1] *tr.* to implore; to pray for. **-ante** *part. adj.* imploring; *n.m.*, *f.* suppliant.

**implume** *adj.* unfledged; beardless.

**impoe·tico** *adj.* unpoetical.

**impoli·tico** *adj.* impolitic; imprudent.

**impolpare** [A1] *tr.* to fatten; to stuff; (fig.) to pad; *intr.* (*aux.* essere), *rfl.* to grow fat.

**impoltronire** [D2] *tr.* to make lazy; to make cowardly; *intr.* (*aux.* essere), *rfl.* to grow lazy; to become cowardly.

**impolverare** [A1 sc] *tr.* to cover with dust; *rfl.* to get dusty.

**impondera·bile** *adj.* imponderable; that cannot be weighed.

**imponen-te** *part. adj.* imposing; majestic; solemn. **-za** *f.* grandeur; solemnity.

**imponi·bil-e** *adj.* taxable; rateable; *n.m.* taxable amount or value. **-ità** *f.* taxability.

**impopolar-e** *adj.* unpopular. **-ità** *f.* unpopularity.

**imporporare** [A1 sc] *tr.* to dye purple; *rfl.* to grow purple; to redden.

**impọrre** [B21] *tr.* to impose; to inflict; *— una colpa a*, to lay blame on; *— un nome a*, to give a name to; to command; *intr.* (*aux.* avere) to be imposing; *rfl.* to assume authority; to take command; to be necessary.

**importan-te** *adj.* important; significant; *n.m.* *l'—*, the important thing. **-za** *f.* importance; *darsi aria d'-za*, to give oneself airs.

**import-are** [A1] *tr.* to import; to signify; to imply; to amount to; *intr.* (*aux.* avere) to matter, to be important; to be of interest; *impers.* (*aux.* essere) *non -a*, it does not matter. **-atọre** *m.* importer; *adj.* importing. **-aziọne** *f.* importation; import. **-o** *m.* (comm.) value; total cost.

**importun-are** [A1] *tr.* to pester, to importune. **-ante** *part. adj.* pestering; importunate.

**importun-o** *adj.* importunate; pestering; *n.m.* person who is a nuisance, pest. **-ità** *f.* importunity; tiresome persistence.

**imposiziọne** *f.* imposition; impost, tax.

**impossente** *adj.* powerless.

**impossessare** [A1] *rfl.* (*prep.* di) to take possession (of), to appropriate; to master.

**impossi·bil-e** *adj.* impossible; improbable; unacceptable; *pare —!*, it can't be true!; *n.m.* what is impossible. **-ità** *f.* impossibility.

**impọsta**[1] *f.* imposition, tax, impost; income-tax.

**imposta**[2] *f.* shutter; leaf of a folding door.

**impost-are**[1] [A1 c] *tr.* to put in position, to erect (*e.g.* a dome or arch); *— un problema*, to state a problem; to make a plan of, to do the preliminary work for; (comm.) *— un conto*, to open an account; to enter (in a ledger), to post. **-atura** *f.* seating, bearing (of an arch or vault); (fig.) pose, attitude.

**impost-are**[2] [A1 c] *tr.* to post (letters, etc.). **-aziọne** *f.* posting; postage.

**impost-ọre** *m.* impostor; fraud. **-ura** *f.* imposture; deception fake.

**impota·bile** *adj.* unfit for drinking.

**impoten-te** *adj.* impotent; powerless; *essere — al lavoro*, to be unable to work; *n.m.* weakling; man who is sexually impotent. **-za** *f.* feebleness; *ridurre all'-za*, to render powerless; impotence.

**impoverire** [D2] *tr.* to impoverish; *intr.* (*aux.* essere), *rfl.* to be reduced to poverty.

**impratica·bil-e** *adj.* impracticable; impassable. **-ità** *f.* impracticability; *l'-ità delle strade*, the bad state of the roads.

**impratichire** [D2] *tr.* to train; to drill; to make expert; *rfl.* (*prep.* di, a) to practise; to exercise oneself (in); to become expert.

**imprec-are** [A2] *tr.* to curse; *intr.* (*aux.* avere; *prep.* a, contro) to curse, to wish ill (to). **-atọre** *m.* curser; ill-wisher. **-ato·rio** *adj.* (*m.pl.* **-atorii**) imprecatory; *giuramento -atorio*, curse. **-aziọne** *f.* imprecation, curse.

**imprecis-iọne** *f.* inexactness, inaccuracy. **-o** *adj.* inaccurate, incorrect; inexact, not precise.

**impregn-are** [A5 c] *tr.* to impregnate, to fecundate; (fig.) to imbue. **-aziọne** *f.* fecundation; impregnation.

**impremeditato** *adj.* unpremeditated, spontaneous; *adv.* extempore.

**impren·d-ere** [C1] *tr.* to undertake; to initiate. **-i·bile** *adj.* well-defended, impregnable. **-itọre** *m.* contractor; entrepreneur.

**imprepar-ato** *adj.* unprepared. **-aziọne** *f.* unpreparedness.

**imprẹs-a** *f.* undertaking, enterprise; deed; feat; contract; business, firm; management. **-a·rio** *m.* (*m.pl.* **-ari**) (theatr.; mus.) manager, impresario; *-ario di pompe funebri*, undertaker.

**imprescienza** *f.* lack of prescience.

**imprescindi·bile** *adj.* necessary, indispensable.
**imprescritto** *adj.* not prescribed; unforfeited.
**impreso** *part. adj.* undertaken; begun.
**impression-are** [A1 c] *tr.* to impress; to shock; *rfl.* to be deeply moved; *-arsi facilmente,* to be impressionable. **-a·bile** *adj.* impressionable, easily moved. **-ante** *part. adj.* impressive; striking.
**impressione-e** *f.* impression; *fare — a,* to affect deeply, to surprise; sensation; imprint; issue. **-ismo** *m.* (art) impressionism. **-ista** *m., f.* (art) impressionist. **-i·stico** *adj.* (art) impressionistic.
**impress-o** *part.* of **impri·mere** *q.v.*; *adj.* impressed; imprinted, stamped. **-ore** *m.* printer.
**impreteri·bile** *adj.* indispensable; inescapable.
**imprevedi·bile** *adj.* unforeseeable; unforeseen.
**impreveduto** *adj.* unforeseen.
**impreviden-te** *adj.* without foresight; heedless. **-za** *f.* lack of foresight.
**imprevisto** *adj.* unforeseen; unexpected; *n.m.* unexpected occurrence.
**imprigion-are** [A1 c] *tr.* to imprison; to shut in. **-amento** *m.* imprisonment.
**imprima** *adv.* in the first place; *all'—,* at once.
**impri·m-ere** [C18] *tr.* to impress; to imprint; to stamp; *rfl.* to be imprinted; *-ersi nella mente,* to be impressed upon the mind. **-i·bile** *adj.* printable. **-itura** *f.* priming, preparatory coat.
**improba·bil-e** *adj.* improbable. **-ità** *f.* improbability, unlikelihood.
**im·prob-o** *adj.* wicked; dishonest; unendurable; *fatica -a,* laborious toil. **-ità** *f.* wickedness; dishonesty.
**improduttivo** *adj.* unproductive; *terreno —,* barren soil.
**impronta** *f.* imprint, mark; *— del piede,* footprint; *impronte digitali,* fingerprints.
**improntare**[1] [A1 c] *tr.* to imprint, to mark.
**improntare**[2] [A1 c] *tr.* to lend; to borrow; (comm.) to advance (a loan).
**impront-o**[1] *adj.* importunate; impudent. **-itu·dine** *f.* importunity; effrontery.
**impronto**[2] *adv. phr. all'—,* at sight, at first sight; without rehearsal; (mus.) *lettura all'—,* sight-reading.
**impronunzia·bile** *adj.* unpronounceable; not to be uttered.
**improperi·r-io** *m.* abuse; insult. **-iare** [A4] *tr.* to abuse, to insult.
**improporzion-ale** *adj.* badly proportioned. **-ato** *adj.* disproportionate.
**impro·pr-io** *adj.* improper; inappropriate; unsuitable, unfit. **-ietà** *f.* impropriety.
**improvveduto** *adj.* unprovided.
**improv·vid-o** *adj.* imprudent, improvident. **-enza** *f.* imprudence; improvidence.
**improvvis-are** [A1] *tr., intr.* (*aux.* avere) to improvise; to speak extempore. **-ata** *f.* pleasant surprise. **-atore** *m.* improviser; improvisator. **-azione** *f.* improvisation.
**improvvis-o** *adj.* sudden; improvised; *n.m.* improvisation; *adv.* unexpectedly; extempore; *adv. phr. d'—, all'—,* unexpectedly.
**improvvist-o** *adj.* unprovided; *adv. phr. all'-a,* unexpectedly.
**impruden-te** *adj.* imprudent; rash. **-za** *f.* imprudence; heedlessness; *commettere un'-za,* to commit an indiscretion.
**impuden-te** *adj.* impudent; immodest; *un'— menzogna,* a barefaced lie. **-za** *f.* impudence; shamelessness.
**impudi-co** *adj.* (*m.pl.* **-chi**) immodest; indecent; obscene. **-ci·zia** *f.* immodesty; indecency; obscenity.
**impugn-are**[1] [A5] *tr.* to grasp, to hold; (mil.) to attack; *intr.* (*aux.* avere) to clench one's fist. **-atura** *f.* hilt (of sword); handle (of knife, etc.); grip.
**impugn-are**[2] [A5] *tr.* to contest; to impugn. **-ativo** *adj.* contesting, tending to impugn. **-atore** *m.* contestant, opponent. **-azione** *f.* contradiction, opposition; (leg.) appeal.
**impulit-o** *adj.* rough; unpolished; crude. **-ezza** *f.* roughness; crudity.
**impuls-atore** *m.* propeller, propellant. **-ione** *f.* impulsion, propulsion. **-ore** *m.* instigator.
**impuls-o** *m.* impulse, impetus; urge; *dare — a,* to encourage, to stimulate. **-ivo** *adj.* impelling; impulsive.
**impun-e** *adj.* unpunished; not liable to punishment. **-emente** *adv.* with impunity. **-ità** *f.* impunity. **-ito** *adj.* unpunished.
**impuntare** [A1] *intr.* (*aux.* avere) to stumble; (*prep.* in) to strike one's foot (against); (fig.) to falter; *rfl.* to jib, to be obstinate.
**impuntigliare** [A4] *rfl.* to be obstinate; to be pernickety.
**impunt-ire** [D2] *tr.* to sew, to stitch; to quilt. **-itura** *f.* quilting. **-ura** *f.* back-stitching.
**impuntual-e** *adj.* unpunctual. **-ità** *f.* unpunctuality.
**impur-o** *adj.* impure; adulterated; unchaste. **-ità** *f.* impurity.
**imput-are** [A1 s, A1] *tr.* to impute; to ascribe; (leg.) to charge. **-ante** *part. adj.* imputing; *n.m., f.* accuser. **-ato** *part. adj.* imputed; (leg.) charged; *n.m.* accused, defendant. **-azione** *f.* imputation; (leg.) charge.
**imputridire** [D2] *intr.* (*aux.* essere) to putrefy, to decay; *tr.* to cause to putrefy, to rot.
**in** *prep.* (*contr.* with *def. art.*: nel, nello, nei, negli, nella, nelle) **1.** in, at, (of place); *— Italia,* in Italy; *— casa,* in the house; *— mano,* in one's hand; *— fondo a,* at the bottom of. **2.** (condition, feeling) *— moto,* in movement; *— buona salute,* in good health; *avere — odio,* to hate; *— guerra,* at war. **3.** by, on, by means of (transport); *andare — macchina,* to go by car; *— bicicletta,* on a bicycle, by bicycle; *viaggiare — treno,* to travel by train; *— viaggio,* on the journey. **4.** into; *cadere nel pozzo,* to fall into the well; *intoppare — un muro,* to bump into a wall; *dividere — due,* to divide into two; *andare — collera,* to get angry. **5.** to (motion towards, sequence); *andare — America,* to go to America; *portare — tavola,* to bring to the table; *venire — mente a,* to come to (one's) mind; *di giorno — giorno,* from day to day; *di male — peggio,* from bad to worse; *d'ora — avanti,* henceforward. **6.** on, on to, on top of; *— capo,* on one's head; *— tavola,* on the table; *— piedi,* standing; *— terra,* on the ground. **7.** during (of time); in, at; *si spicciò — poco tempo,* he got through his work in a short time; *nel frattempo,* in the meantime; *nell'Ottocento,* in the nineteenth century; *— punto di morte,* at the point of death; *— capo a un anno,* at the end of a year. **8.** wearing; *— cappello,* wearing a hat; *— borghese,* in civilian dress. **9.** regarding; *dottore — medicina,* doctor of medicine; *bravo — latino,* good at Latin. **10.** (of form, material) *statua — gesso,* plaster cast; *fatto — velluto,* made of velvet. **11.** in the place of; *vorrei essere — lui,* I'd like to be in his shoes. **12.** as, in the form of; *avere — dono,* to receive as a gift; *chiedere — cortesia,* to ask as a favour. **13.** towards, for, against; *con gli occhi — terra,* with eyes cast down; *volto — altra parte,* facing the other way; *farla — barba a uno,* to defy someone. **14.** (cul.) *pesce — bianco,* boiled fish; *carne — umido,* meat in casserole.
**ina·bil-e** *adj.* unable, disabled; unqualified, ineligible; *— al servizio militare,* unfit for military service. **-ità** *f.* disablement; inability. **-itazione** *f.* disablement; incapacity.
**inabissare** [A1] *tr.* to plunge into an abyss, to engulf; *rfl.* to sink.
**inabita·bile** *adj.* uninhabitable, unfit for habitation.

**inabitato** *adj.* uninhabited.
**inaccessi·bil-e** *adj.* inaccessible; impenetrable. **-ità** *f.* inaccessibility; impenetrability.
**inaccesso** *adj.* inaccessible, beyond reach.
**inaccetta·bile** *adj.* unacceptable; *dichiarare* —, to declare out of order.
**inaccorto** *adj.* unwary, improvident.
**inacerbire** [D2] *tr.* to embitter; to exacerbate; *rfl.* to become embittered.
**inacutire** [D2] *tr.* to sharpen; to make pointed; *rfl.* to become more acute.
**inadatta·bil-e** *adj.* unadaptable. **-ità** *f.* unadaptability; unsuitableness.
**inadatto** *adj.* unsuited.
**inadeguat-o** *adj.* inadequate; unsuitable. **-ęzza** *f.* inadequacy; unsuitableness.
**inadop(e)ra·bile** *adj.* unserviceable, not usable.
**inafferra·bile** *adj.* that cannot be grasped; incomprehensible; elusive.
**inal-are** [A1] *tr.* to inhale. **-ante** *part. adj., n.m.* inhalant.
**inalberare** [A1 s] *tr.* to hoist, to fly, to run up (a flag); to brandish (a spear); to raise, to proclaim.
**inaliena·bile** *adj.* inalienable; not transferable.
**inalter-a·bile** *adj.* unalterable; *colore* —, permanent colour; *affetto* —, constancy. **-ato** *adj.* unaltered; unvarying.
**inama·bil-e** *adj.* unamiable; disagreeable. **-ità** *f.* unamiability; disagreeableness.
**inamarire** [D2] *tr.* to embitter, to make bitter; to afflict; *intr.* (*aux.* essere) to become embittered; to be troubled.
**inamen-o** *adj.* unpleasant; desolate. **-ità** *f.* displeasing aspect.
**inamid-are** [A1 s] *tr.* to starch. **-ato** *part. adj.* starched; (fig.) (of a person) stiff, standing on his dignity.
**inammissi·bil-e** *adj.* inadmissible; unacceptable. **-ità** *f.* inadmissibility, unacceptableness.
**inan-e** *adj.* empty, vain, useless; inane; *vanto* —, empty boast. **-ità** *f.* emptiness; uselessness.
**inanimato** *adj.* inanimate; lifeless; cold, indifferent.
**inappag-a·bile** *adj.* insatiable; unquenchable. **-ato** *adj.* unsatisfied.
**inappeten-te** *adj.* lacking appetite. **-za** *f.* loss of appetite.
**inapplica·bil-e** *adj.* inapplicable. **-ità** *f.* inapplicability.
**inapplicazįone** *f.* lack of application.
**inapprezza·bile** *adj.* priceless, invaluable.
**inappunta·bile** *adj.* irreproachable, faultless.
**inarcare** [A2] *tr.* to arch, to curve; — *la schiena*, to bend one's back; — *le ciglia*, to raise one's eyebrows.
**inargentare** [A1] *tr.* to silver.
**inaridire** [D2] *tr.* to dry, to make arid; *intr.* (*aux.* essere), *rfl.* to dry up; to wither.
**inarriva·bile** *adj.* unattainable, unreachable; (fig.) incomparable.
**inarticolato** *adj.* not articulated; slurred.
**inascoltato** *adj.* unheard; unheeded.
**inaspetta·bile** *adj.* unforeseeable, not to be expected.
**inaspettato** *adj.* unexpected, unforeseen; *adv. phr. all'inaspettata*, unexpectedly.
**inasprire** [D2] *tr.* to embitter; to make harsher; to aggravate; to stunt, to wither; *intr.* (*aux.* essere), *rfl.* to become rough; to wither.
**inastare** [A1] *tr.* (naut.) to hoist on a mast; — *la bandiera*, to fly the flag; (mil.) — *la baionetta*, to fix bayonets.
**inattacca·bile** *adj.* unassailable; — *dalle tarme*, moth-proof; (fig.) unimpeachable.
**inattendi·bile** *adj.* unfounded; unreliable.
**inatten-to** *adj.* inattentive. **-zįone** *f.* inattention.
**inattęso** *adj.* unexpected.
**inattingi·bile** *adj.* unreachable.
**inattiv-o** *adj.* inactive; inert; sluggish. **-ità** *f.* inactivity; inertness.
**inatt-o** *adj.* inapt; unskilful. **-itu·dine** *f.* inaptitude; lack of skill.
**inaud-i·bile** *adj.* inaudible. **-ito** *adj.* unheard of; incredible.
**inaugurale** *adj.* inaugural.
**inaugur-are** [A1] *tr.* to inaugurate; to unveil. **-azįone** *f.* inauguration; ceremonial opening; unveiling.
**inauspicato** *adj.* inauspicious, ill-omened.
**inavvedut-o** *adj.* inadvertent; imprudent, unwise. **-ęzza** *f.* inadvertence; carelessness; unwisdom.
**inavvertenza** *f.* inadvertence; heedlessness; *per* —, inadvertently.
**inavvertito** *adj.* overlooked; uninformed; heedless.
**inazįone** *f.* inaction; inactivity.
**incagion-ire** [D2] *intr.* (*aux.* essere) to become infirm, to fall into poor health. **-ito** *part. adj.* infirm, sickly.
**incagliare**[1] [A4] *intr.* (*aux.* essere) (naut.) to run aground; (fig.) to come to a standstill; *rfl.* to encounter obstacles; *tr.* to hinder.
**incagliare**[2] [A4] *intr.* (*aux.* essere) to coagulate, to clot; to curdle; *tr.* to cause to coagulate; to cause to curdle.
**inca·glio** *m.* (naut.) grounding, running aground; (fig.) obstruction, impediment; *c'è un* —, there's something in the way.
**incalcin-are** [A1] *tr.* to plaster; to mix with lime. **-atura** *f.* plastering; lime-washing.
**incalcola·bile** *adj.* incalculable.
**incaligin-are** [A1 s] *tr.* to obscure with fog or mist; to cloud (the vision). **-ire** [D2] *intr.* (*aux.* essere) to become obscured; to grow misty; to cloud over.
**incall-ire** [D2] *intr.* (*aux.* essere), *rfl.* to form corns, to become hardened; (fig.) to grow callous; *tr.* to harden. **-ito** *part. adj.* hardened; horny; *dalle mani -ite*, horny-handed; (fig.) callous.
**incalorire** [D2] *tr.* to warm; *rfl.* to grow warm; to become hot.
**incalz-are** [A1] *tr.* to pursue closely, to follow on the heels of; *il tempo -a*, time presses. **-ante** *adj.* pressing, urgent. **-o** *m.* chase, pursuit; urging on.
**incammin-are** [A1] *tr.* to put on the road; to initiate, to show the way to; *rfl.* (*prep.* per) to set out (for); to embark on a career; *-arsi per ingegnere*, to be going in for engineering.
**incanal-are** [A1] *tr.* to canalize; to direct. **-atura** *f.* canalizing; channel; groove; directing.
**incancella·bile** *adj.* indelible; irremovable; unforgettable.
**incandescen-te** *adj.* incandescent, white-hot. **-za** *f.* incandescence; *lampada a -za*, electric-light bulb.
**incant-are**[1] [A1] *tr.* to bewitch, to enchant; to delight; *rfl.* to stand as if spellbound; to be enchanted; *-arsi a guardare*, to gaze spellbound. **-ademǫni** *m. indecl.*, **-adia·voli** *m. indecl.* wizard, sorcerer. **-ato** *part. adj.* under a spell, bewitched, enchanted; *stare lì -ato*, to stand staring; charmed, delighted. **-atǫre** *m.* sorcerer, wizard; enchanter; *adj.* enchanting, fascinating. **-atrice** *f.* sorceress; enchantress; charmer. **-ęsimo** *m.* magic art, sorcery, witchcraft; *rompere l'-esimo*, to break the spell. **-ęvole** *adj.* bewitching, (fig.) enchanting, delightful.
**incantare**[2] [A1] *tr.* to auction; to sell by auction.
**incanto**[1] *m.* spell, enchantment, magic; (fig.) charm; delight; *d'*—, charmingly.
**incanto**[2] *m.* auction; public sale; *vendere all'*—, to sell by auction; *mettere all'*—, to put up for auction.
**incanutire** [D2] *intr.* (*aux.* essere) to become white-haired; to go grey; *tr.* to cause to turn grey or white.
**incapac-e** *adj.* (*prep.* di) unable (to); incapable (of); unfit (for); unable to contain; *n.m.* disabled or incapacitated person. **-ità** *f.*

incapacity, inability; unsuitability.

**incaparb-ire** [D2] *intr.* (*aux.* essere), *rfl.* to become obstinate; to persist obstinately. **-ito** *part. adj.* stubborn.

**incapestrare** [A1] *tr.* to put a halter on; — *i piedi a*, to tether, to hobble; *rfl.* (fig.) to get into trouble, to become entangled.

**incappare**[1] [A1] *tr.*, *rfl.* to put a cape on; to put on a cloak or gown.

**incappare**[2] [A1] *intr.* (*aux.* essere; *prep.* in) to fall in (with); to encounter; to run (into); — *col piede*, to stumble; *recip. rfl.* to bump into one another.

**incappellare** [A1] *tr.* to put a hat on; *rfl.* to put on one's hat; (eccl.) to become cardinal.

**incappottato** *adj.* wearing a thick overcoat; well wrapped up.

**incappucciare** [A3] *tr.* to muffle up; *rfl.* to put on a hood; to muffle oneself up.

**incapriccire** [D2] *rfl.* (*prep.* di) to take a fancy (to); to get a bee in one's bonnet.

**incarbonire** [D2] *tr.* to carbonize, to char.

**incarcer-are** [A1 s] *tr.* to imprison, to incarcerate. **-azione** *f.* imprisonment, incarceration.

**incaric-are** [A2 s] *tr.* (*prep.* di) to charge (with); to charge, to instruct; *vorrei -arvi di un favore*, I should like to ask you a favour; *rfl.* to take upon oneself (to); to assume responsibility (for); *me ne -o io*, I will see to it. **-ato** *part. adj.* (*prep.* di) entrusted (with), responsible (for); holding office; *n.m.* official; employee; *-ato di un ufficio*, holder of an office; business agent.

**inca·ri-co** *m.* (*pl.* -chi) responsibility, charge; office; commission; *assumere l'— di*, to undertake.

**incaritatevole** *adj.* uncharitable.

**incarn-are** [A1] *tr.* (theol.) to incarnate; (fig.) to express in corporeal form; to embody; *rfl.* (theol.) to become incarnate; (fig.) to be realized; to be joined, to be united. **-ato** *part. adj.* (theol.) incarnate; (fig.) embodied; fused; *n.m.* flesh-colour. **-azione** *f.* (theol.) incarnation; (fig.) embodiment; (paint.) rosy flesh-colour.

**incarogn-ire** [D2] *intr.* (*aux.* essere), *rfl.* to putrefy, to become carrion; (fig.) to become good-for-nothing. **-ito** *part. adj.* putrefied; *-ito nell'ozio*, sunk in sloth.

**incart-are** [A1] *tr.* to wrap in paper; *intr.* (*aux.* avere) to become hard and stiff. **-amento** *m.* wrapping up; documentation; dossier.

**incarto** *m.* carton.

**incartocciare** [A3] *tr.* to put into a paper bag; to wrap in paper.

**incaschito** *adj.* old and weak.

**incasellare** [A1] *tr.* to pigeon-hole; (fig.) to shelve, to put on one side.

**incass-are** [A1] *tr.* to pack in a case; — *una gemma*, to set, to mount a jewel; (comm.) to collect; to cash; *intr.* (*aux.* avere) to fit (*e.g.* into a slot); to tally. **-ato** *part. adj.* packed; fitted; cased; *strada -ata*, sunken road; *occhi -ati*, deep-set eyes; (comm.) cashed. **-o** *m.* amount collected; takings.

**incastellare** [A1] *tr.* to fortify with castles.

**incaston-are** [A1 c] *tr.* to set (jewellery), to mount; to insert. **-atura** *f.* (of jewels) setting; mount.

**incastr-are** [A1] *tr.* to fit in, to fix in; to enmesh; (fig.) to insert, to introduce; *intr.* (*aux.* essere) to fit, to fit in; *recip. rfl.* to fit together. **-o** *m.* fitting; fit; (carp.) mortise joint.

**incatenare** [A1] *tr.* to secure with chains; to fetter; (fig.) to captivate, to enthral; *recip. rfl.* to be chained together; (fig.) to be connected.

**incatramare** [A1] *tr.* to tar.

**incattivire** [D2] *tr.* to make hostile; to make ill-tempered; *intr.* (*aux.* essere) to become ill-tempered; (of fruit, etc.) to go bad; (fig.) to become depraved; *rfl.* to lose one's temper; to turn ugly.

**inca·uto** *adj.* imprudent, heedless, rash.

**incavalcare** [A2] *tr.* to put on horseback, to set astride; to superimpose; to stagger, to space.

**incav-are** [A1] *tr.* to hollow out, to carve deeply; to pierce, to perforate. **-ato** *part. adj.* hollowed out; *occhi -ati*, deep-set eyes. **-o** *m.* hollow, depression; *lavoro d'-o*, incised carving.

**incen·d-ere** [C1] *tr.* to burn; (surg.) to cauterize; *rfl.* to catch fire. **-imento** *m.* burning; fire, conflagration; burning pain.

**incendi-are** [A4] *tr.* to set on fire; to burn down; *rfl.* to catch fire, to burn. **-a·rio** *adj.* incendiary; (fig.) inflammatory; *occhi -ari*, blazing eyes; *n.m.* incendiary.

**incen·dio** *m.* fire; house on fire; *bocca d'—*, fire hydrant; (fig.) ardour; fire, passion.

**incenerare** [A1 sc] *tr.* to strew with ashes, to cover with cinders.

**incenerire** [D2] *tr.* to reduce to ashes; to cremate; to incinerate; *rfl.* to be reduced to ashes; to be annihilated.

**incens-are** [A1] *tr.* (rel.) to incense; (fig., joc.) to flatter, to eulogize. **-amento** *m.* (rel.) censing; (fig.) exaggerated praise; *società di mutuo -amento*, mutual admiration society. **-atura** *f.* flattery, adulation, fulsome praise. **-iere** *m.* thurible, censer. **-o** *m.* incense. **-omanna** *m.* frankincense.

**incensur-a·bile** *adj.* irreproachable, faultless. **-ato** *adj.* free from blame; *n.m.* first offender.

**incentivo** *m.* incentive; stimulus; incitement.

**incentrare** [A1] *tr.* to place in the centre, to make central; *rfl.* (*prep.* in) to centre (in); (fig.) to be comprised (in).

**inceppare** [A1 c] *tr.* to impede, to hinder; *rfl.* to jam, to stick.

**incer-are** [A1] *tr.* to wax; to put wax polish on. **-ata** *f.* waterproof material; tarpaulin.

**incerchiare** [A4] *tr.* to curve into a circle; to hoop (a cask).

**incert-o** *adj.* uncertain; variable; irresolute; dubious; *tempo —*, unsettled weather; *n.m.* uncertainty; *pl.* occasional earnings. **-ezza** *f.* uncertainty; unreliability; irresoluteness.

**incespicare** [A2 sc] *intr.* (*aux.* avere) to stumble, to trip; — *in una pietra*, to trip over a stone; — *nel parlare*, to stammer.

**incessante** *adj.* incessant, perpetual.

**incest-o** *m.* incest; incestuousness. **-uoso** *adj.* incestuous.

**incett-a** *f.* buying up; cornering. **-are** [A1] *tr.* to buy up; to corner; to monopolize.

**inchiedere** [B6] *tr.* to investigate minutely.

**inchiesta** *f.* inquiry, investigation; inquiry; survey; inquest.

**inchin-are** [A1] *tr.* to incline, to bow down; *rfl.* to bow; *-arsi a uno*, to bow to someone; *intr.* (*aux.* essere; *prep.* a) to be inclined (to, towards). **-evole** *adj.* inclined; (fig.) prone, having a propensity.

**inchino** *m.* bow; curtsey; *accennare un —*, to make a bow, to drop a curtsey; nod.

**inchiod-are** [A1] *tr.* to nail; — *alla croce*, to crucify. **-ato** *part. adj.* nailed down, nailed; (joc.) *è -ata in cucina tutto il giorno*, she is stuck in the kitchen all day.

**inchiostrare** [A1] *tr.* to ink; to blot, to smudge with ink.

**inchiostro** *m.* ink.

**inciamp-are** [A1] *intr.* (*aux.* avere, essere) to stumble, to trip; — *in uno*, to bump into someone. **-o** *m.* obstacle, hindrance; *pietra d'-o*, stumbling-block; *sei d'-o*, you are in the way.

**inciden-te** *part. adj.* coming to pass; incidental; *n.m.* incident; accident; — *stradale*, road accident; — *avviatorio*, air crash. **-tale** *adj.* incidental, secondary. **-za** *f.* incidence; *fare -za*, to digress; *per -za*, incidentally; accidentally.

**inci·dere**[1] [B1] *intr.* (*aux.* avere)

to come to pass, to fall out; — *sulla spesa*, to add to expense.
**inci·dere**[2] [C3] *tr.*, *intr.* (*aux.* avere) to cut into, to incise; to engrave, to carve, to do intaglio work; to make a recording (of).
**incinera~tọre** *m.* incinerator. **~zịone** *f.* (agric.) dressing of land with ashes; cremation.
**incinta** *part. adj. f.* pregnant, with child; — *di*, pregnant with; — *di tre mesi*, three months pregnant; *n.f.* expectant mother.
**incipiente** *adj.* incipient; in its early stages.
**incipriare** [A4] *tr.* to powder; *rfl.* to powder one's face.
**incirca** *adv.* about, approximately; round about; nearby; *all'—*, *a un —*, nearly (also **in circa**).
**incirconciṣo** *adj.*, *n.m.* uncircumcised.
**incircoscritto** *adj.* unlimited.
**inciṣ~ịone** *f.* incision; engraving; etching; incision; recording. **~ivo** *adj.* incisive, penetrating. **~o** *part. adj.* incised, engraved; *riproduttore di musica ~a*, record-player. **~ọre** *m.* engraver; recording machine.
**incit~are** [A1 s] *tr.* to incite; to instigate. **~amẹnto** *m.* incitement; stimulus. **~atọre** *m.* instigator. **~azịone** *f.* inciting; instigation.
**incivil~e** *adj.* rude, discourteous; uncivilized, barbarous. **~tà** *f.* rudeness, discourtesy; barbarity.
**incivilire** [D2] *tr.* to civilize; *rfl.* to become civilized.
**inclemen~te** *adj.* severe; intemperate. **~za** *f.* severity.
**inclin~are** [A1] *tr.* to incline; to bow; to tilt; (fig.) to influence; *intr.* (*aux.* avere) to incline, to be inclined; to lean, to slope; (naut.) to list; *rfl.* to bow down; to slope, to tilt; (aeron.) *~arsi in curva*, to bank. **~ante** *part. adj.* inclining; tending. **~ato** *part. adj.* bowed down, slanting; tilted; lop-sided; inclined. **~atura** *f* bend. **~azịone** *f.* tilt; inclination; slope; slant.
**incline** *adj.* inclined, disposed; bent; bowed.
**in·clito** *adj.* glorious, illustrious, famous.
**inclu·dere** [C3] *tr.* to enclose; to include; to imply.
**incluṣ~ịone** *f.* including; inclusion. **~ivo** *adj.* inclusive; to be included; implied.
**incocciare** [A3] *intr.* (*aux.* essere), *rfl.* to persist obstinately.
**incoeren~te** *adj.* incoherent; disconnected; inconsistent. **~za** *f.* incoherence; inconsistency.
**inco·gliere** [B7] *tr.* to catch in the act; *intr.* (*aux.* essere) to befall, to happen unexpectedly; *c'incolse una disgrazia*, we had a misfortune.
**inco·gnito** *adj.* unknown; *n.m.* unknown factor; unknown person.
**incollare**[1] [A1] *tr.* to gum; to glue; to paste; to stick; *rfl.* to get stuck.
**incoll~are**[2] [A1] *tr.* to put (a load) on the shoulders of; *rfl.* to sling over one's shoulder. **~atura** *f.* the set of the head; (of a horse) the head and neck; (racing) *vincere di un'~atura*, to win by a neck.
**incolma·bile** *adj.* that cannot be filled up; *un abisso —*, a bottomless abyss.
**incolore** *adj.* colourless; (fig.) insipid, faded.
**incolp~are** [A1 c] *tr.* to blame. **~azịone** *f.* blame, inculpation, incrimination, censure.
**incolpẹvol~e** *adj.* blameless, guiltless, innocent. **~ẹzza** *f.* guiltlessness.
**incọlt~o** *adj.* uncultivated, wild, waste; (fig.) unkempt, untidy, uncultured. **~ẹzza** *f.* boorishness; lack of culture; ignorance.
**inco·lum~e** *adj.* safe and sound; intact; unhurt. **~ità** *f.* safety.
**incombatti·bile** *adj.* unassailable.
**incọmb~ere** [B1 def.] *intr.* (*prep.* a) to weigh (upon), to be incumbent (on). **~ente** *part. adj.* incumbent; impending; *n.m.pl.* duties. **~ẹnza** *f.* job, errand, task, commission.
**incombusti·bil~e** *adj.* not combustible, fire-proof. **~ità** *f.* resistance to fire.
**incominciare** [A3] *intr.* (*aux.* essere) to begin; (of an illness) to set in.
**incommensura·bil~e** *adj.* immeasurable; immense. **~ità** *f.* incommensurability.
**incommercia·bile** *adj.* unsaleable; not having a price; that cannot be bought and sold.
**incomod~are** [A1 s] *tr.* to cause inconvenience to; to disturb, to trouble; *scusi se l'~o*, forgive me for troubling you. **~ato** *part. adj.* inconvenienced; indisposed, slightly unwell.
**inco·mod~o** *adj.* uncomfortable; inconvenient; annoying; *n.m.* inconvenience, trouble, annoyance; *posso farlo senz'—*, it will be no trouble, I can quite easily do that; indisposition, infirmity, ailment. **~ità** *f.* inconvenience; indisposition.
**incompara·bil~e** *adj.* incomparable, matchless, peerless; beyond compare. **~ità** *f.* incomparableness.
**incompati·bil~e** *adj.* incompatible; irreconcilable; intolerable. **~ità** *f.* incompatibility.
**incompeten~te** *adj.* incompetent, unqualified; *n.m.* incompetent person. **~za** *f.* incompetence; lack of qualifications.
**incompiut~o** *adj.* incomplete; **~ẹzza** *f.* unfinished state.
**incompleto** *adj.* incomplete; imperfect; defective.
**incomport~a·bile, ~ẹvole** *adj.* intolerable, unbearable, insufferable; inadmissible. **~abilità** *f.* intolerableness.
**incompọsto** *adj.* disordered; ill-arranged.
**incomprensi·bil~e** *adj.* incomprehensible. **~ità** *f.* incomprehensibility.
**incomprẹso** *adj.* not included; not understood.
**incomputa·bile** *adj.* incalculable; insignificant, not worth counting.
**incomunica·bile** *adj.* incommunicable.
**inconcepi·bile** *adj.* inconceivable; incredible.
**inconcilia·bile** *adj.* irreconcilable; incompatible.
**inconcludente** *adj.* inconclusive, indecisive; undecided, irresolute.
**incondizionato** *adj.* (leg.) unconditional; (philos.) absolute.
**inconfessa·bile** *adj.* unspeakable, shameful.
**inconfesso** *adj.* not owning to a charge; (rel.) unconfessed, unshriven.
**inconfondi·bile** *adj.* unmistakable.
**inconforta·bile** *adj.* inconsolable.
**inconfuta·bile** *adj.* irrefutable, inconfutable.
**incongruen~te** *adj.* inconsistent; not in conformity. **~za** *f.* inconsistency; inconsistent statements; things not in conformity.
**incon·gru~o** *adj.* incongruous. **~ità** *f.* incongruity; incongruousness.
**inconosci·bile** *adj.* unknowable, unfathomable.
**inconsapẹvol~e** *adj.* unaware. **~mẹnte** *adv.* unawares; unwittingly. **~ẹzza** *f.* ignorance; unconsciousness.
**incon·scio** *adj.* unconscious; *n.m.* (psych.) *l'—*, the unconscious.
**inconseguen~te** *adj.* inconsequent; falsely inferred; inconsistent. **~za** *f.* inconsequence; inconsistency.
**inconsidera·bile** *adj.* inconsiderable, insignificant.
**inconsiderat~o** *adj.* unconsidered; inconsiderate; impetuous. **~ẹzza** *f.* lack of consideration; thoughtlessness.
**inconsisten~te** *adj.* unsubstantial; unreal; unfounded; inconsistent. **~za** *f.* lack of foundation; inconsistency.
**inconsola·bile** *adj.* inconsolable.
**inconsueto** *adj.* unusual, strange, extraordinary; unaccustomed.
**inconsulto** *adj.* ill-advised, injudicious; imprudent.
**inconsuma·bile** *adj.* not consumable.

**incontaminat-o** *adj.* uncontaminated, pure. **-ęzza** *f.* purity, hygienic property.
**incontenta·bil-e** *adj.* insatiable; hard to please. **-ità** *f.* insatiability; exacting standards.
**incontesta·bil-e** *adj.* unquestionable; incontrovertible; (leg.) incontestable; undisputed. **-ità** *f.* incontrovertibility.
**incontinen-te**[1] *adj.* incontinent, intemperate, unrestrained. **-za** *f.* incontinence, lack of restraint, intemperance.
**incontinente**[2] *adv.* immediately, straightway, forthwith.
**incontrare** [A1 c] *tr.* to meet, to encounter; — *il favore di,* to find favour with; to face; to stand up to; *intr.* (*aux.* essere) to occur, to happen; *recip. rfl.* to meet each other; to agree, to fit; *i geni s'incontrano,* great minds think alike; to clash, to come into conflict.
**incontrast-a·bile** *adj.* invincible. **-ato** *adj.* undisputed; uncontested.
**incontro**[1] *m.* meeting, encounter; favourable reception; joining; occasion; duel; (sport) match.
**incontro**[2] *adv.* opposite, over there, across the way; *adv. phr. all'—,* on the other hand; *prep.* (foll. by 'a') towards; opposite; against; *andare — a,* to go to the help of, to meet, to view, to face.
**incontrover-so** *adj.* undisputed; unquestioned. **-ti·bile** *adj.* incontrovertible, indisputable.
**inconvenien-te** *adj.* unsuitable; unbecoming; improper; inconvenient; *n.m.* disadvantage; snag, catch; defect; trouble. **-za** *f.* unsuitableness; impropriety; inconvenience.
**inconverti·bil-e** *adj.* immutable; not interchangeable; not exchangeable. **-ità** *f.* inconvertibility; immutability.
**inconvinci·bile** *adj.* difficult to convince; impossible to convince.
**incoraggi-are** [A3] *tr.* to encourage; to incite; *rfl.* to take heart. **-ante** *part. adj.* encouraging; heartening.
**incordare** [A1] *tr.* to string; to cord; *rfl.* to become stiff, to become knotted.
**incornare** [A1] *tr.* to gore; to cuckold.
**incornici-are** [A3] *tr.* to frame. **-atura** *f.* framing; frame.
**incoron-are** [A1 c] *tr.* to crown; to award a prize to. **-azione** *f.* coronation.
**incorpor-are** [A1 s] *tr.* to incorporate; to assimilate; *rfl.* (*acc.* of *prn.* si) to be incorporated; to be united; (*dat.* of *prn.* si) to annex. **-azione** *f.* incorporation; annexation; assimilation.
**incorpo·re-o** *adj.* incorporeal; disembodied. **-ità** *f.* incorporeality.
**incorreggi·bil-e** *adj.* incorrigible; incurable. **-ità** *f.* incorrigibleness.
**incorrere** [C5] *intr.* (*aux.* essere; *prep.* in) to run (into); — *in difficoltà,* to come up against difficulties; *tr.* to incur.
**incorrett-o** *adj.* incorrect; improper. **-ęzza** *f.* incorrectness; impropriety.
**incorrotto** *adj.* uncorrupted; not decomposed.
**incorrutti·bil-e** *adj.* not liable to decay; incorruptible; eternal. **-ità** *f.* incorruptibleness.
**incoscien-te** *adj.* unconscious; unaware; irresponsible; *n.m.* irresponsible person. **-za** *f.* unconsciousness; irresponsibility.
**incospi·cuo** *adj.* inconspicuous.
**incostan-te** *adj* changeable, fickle; unsettled. **-za** *f.* fickleness, inconstancy, mutability.
**incostituzional-e** *adj.* unconstitutional. **-ità** *f.* unconstitutionality; unconstitutional act.
**increanza** *f.* bad manners; incivility; impolite action.
**incredi·bil-e** *adj.* unbelievable, incredible. **-ità** *f.* incredibility.
**incre·dul-o** *adj.* incredulous, sceptical; (rel.) unbelieving; *n.m.* unbeliever. **-ità** *f.* incredulity, scepticism.
**incremęnt-o** *m.* increase, increment. **-are** [A1 c] *tr.* to increase, to increment; *intr.* (*aux.* avere) to grant an increment.
**incręsc-ere** [B9 c] *impers.* (*aux.* essere; *prep.* a) to be displeasing (to), to occasion displeasure or regret; *m'-e,* I regret, I'm sorry. **-ioso** *adj.* annoying; unpleasant; regrettable.
**incresp-are** [A1 c] *tr.* to wrinkle; to curl; to pleat; *rfl.* to grow wrinkled; to become creased; to ripple. **-atura** *f.* wrinkle; ripple; curl; pleat.
**incretinire** [D2] *tr.* to make stupid; to dull the mind of; *intr.* (*aux.* essere) to become a dullard; to grow stupid.
**incrimin-are** [A1 s] to incriminate. **-azione** *f.* incrimination.
**incrin-are** [A1] *tr., intr.* (*aux.* avere), *rfl.* to crack. **-atura** *f.* crack; flaw.
**incroci-are** [A3 c] *tr.* to cross; — *le braccia,* to fold one's arms, (fig.) to stand idle; *recip. rfl.* to cross (of persons, letters, etc. travelling in opposite directions); to intersect. **-ato** *part. adj.* crossed; *punto -ato,* cross-stitch; *parole -ate,* crossword puzzle; (mil.; fig.) *fuochi -ati,* cross-fire. **-atore** *m.* (naut.) cruiser. **-atura** *f.* crossing; cross; point of intersection.
**incrocicchiare** [A4] *tr.* to interlace; *rfl.* to form a network.
**incrocio** *m.* crossing, intersection; cross-roads; hybrid; crossing (of letters in the post); passing (of trains).
**incrolla·bile** *adj.* unshakable; steadfast.
**incrost-are** [A1] *tr.* to cover with a crust; to form a deposit on. **-ato** *part. adj.* (*prep.* di) encrusted (with). **-azione** *f.* incrustation; deposit.
**incrudelire** [D2] *tr.* to make cruel; *intr.* (*aux.* essere) to become cruel; to be pitiless; (*aux.* avere) to perform acts of cruelty; — *contro,* to treat cruelly; *rfl.* to become pitiless or cruel.
**incrudire** [D2] *intr.* (*aux.* essere) (of weather) to become inclement; (of persons) to become harsh or cruel; *tr.* to make harsh; to aggravate; to embitter.
**incruento** *adj.* bloodless.
**incrunare** [A1] *tr.* to fill or thread (a needle); (fig.) — *l'ago,* to put a piece of work in hand.
**incub-atrice** *f.* incubator. **-azione** *f.* incubation; hatching.
**in·cubo** *m.* nightmare, incubus; weight on one's mind; burden.
**incu·dine** *f.* anvil; (fig.) *esser fra l'— e il martello,* to be between the devil and the deep sea.
**inculcare** [A2] *tr.* to inculcate; — *buone abitudini a,* to train in good habits; to impress upon.
**incult-o** *adj.* uncultivated. **-ura** *f.* lack of culture.
**incuneare** [A6] *tr.* to wedge; to fix in; *rfl.* to be wedged; to penetrate like a wedge.
**incupire** [D2] *tr., intr.* to darken; to deepen; (*aux.* essere), *rfl.* to become hollowed out, to deepen; to become surly or melancholy.
**incura·bile** *adj.* incurable; incorrigible; *n.m., f.* chronic invalid, incurable.
**incuran-te** *adj.* careless, unheeding; indifferent. **-za** *f.* carelessness, heedlessness; indifference; negligence.
**incu·ria** *f.* negligence, carelessness, indifference.
**incuriosire** [D2] *tr.* to excite the curiosity of; to arouse the interest of; *rfl., intr.* (*aux.* essere) to become curious.
**incursione** *f.* raid; — *aerea,* air-raid; incursion; inroad.
**incurv-are** [A1] *tr.* to bend, to curve; *rfl.* to bend, to become bent; to bulge. **-ire** [D2] *intr.* (*aux.* essere) to grow bent, to become bowed.
**incustodito** *adj.* unguarded, untended; without a keeper.
**incu·tere** [B1 def.] *tr.* to arouse, to excite; — *rispetto,* to command respect; — *timore a,* to strike terror into; — *coraggio,* to instil courage.
**indag-are** [A2] *tr.* to investigate; to conduct research into; *intr.* (*aux.* avere) to make inquiries.

~**atọre** *m.* investigator, researcher; *adj.* inquiring, searching.
**inda·gine** *f.* investigation; research; *far delle indagini su,* to conduct research into, to inquire into.
**indebit~are** [A1 sc] *tr.* to burden with debts, to cause to run into debt; *rfl.* to contract liabilities; *~arsi con,* to get into debt with.
**indẹbit~o** *adj.* not owing; undeserved; undue, improper; *appropriazione ~a,* misappropriation. ~**amẹnte** *adv.* unduly; wrongfully; undeservedly.
**indebolire** [D2] *tr.* to weaken, to enfeeble; *rfl.* to grow weak, to grow feeble; to become faint; to grow faded.
**indecen~te** *adj.* indecent, improper; untidy, in one's working clothes; *vestito —,* shabby, dirty garment. ~**za** *f.* indecency, obscenity; act of indecency; untidiness, untidy appearance.
**indecifra·bile** *adj.* illegible; enigmatic.
**indeciṣ~iọne** *f.* indecision, hesitation. ~**o** *adj.* undecided, irresolute, doubtful, hesitant.
**indeclina·bile** *adj.* (gramm.) indeclinable; invariable.
**indecoroso** *adj.* indecorous; undignified; unseemly.
**indefesso** *adj.* indefatigable; unrelenting; unceasing.
**indefini·bile** *adj.* indefinable; enigmatic.
**indefinit~o** *adj.* indefinite; *persona ~a,* unspecified person, anyone; (gramm.) indefinite.
**indeforma·bile** *adj.* that will not lose its shape.
**indẹgn~o** *adj.* unworthy; base; undeserving; unworthy. ~**ità** *f.* unworthiness; baseness; worthlessness; indignity.
**indele·bile** *adj.* indelible; ineffaceable; enduring.
**indeliber~ato** *adj.* unpremeditated. ~**atamẹnte** *adv.* without forethought, on the spur of the moment. ~**aziọne** *f.* lack of forethought, hastiness.
**indelicat~o** *adj.* wanting in delicacy, indiscreet; unscrupulous. ~**ẹzza** *f.* want of discretion; lack of scruple; act of indiscretion; unscrupulous action.
**indemaglia·bile** *adj.* (of a stocking) non-run.
**indemoniare** [A4] *intr.* (*aux.* essere), *rfl.* to become possessed by a devil; to become furious.
**indenn~e** *adj.* unhurt, undamaged; (leg.) harmless; not to be held liable. ~**ità** *f.* compensation, damages, indemnity; expenses allowance; *~ità carovita,* cost of living bonus; *richiedere un'~ità,* to demand compensation. ~**izzare** [A1] *tr.* to compensate, to reimburse. ~**izzo** *m.* compensation, indemnity.
**indent~are** [A1] *intr.* (*aux.* avere) to cut teeth, to teethe. ~**atura** *f.* teething.
**indẹntr~o** *adv.* inside, within; *all'—,* inwards. ~**are** [A1 c] *rfl.* (*prep.* a) to penetrate (into).
**inderoga·bile** *adj.* (leg.) that cannot be derogated from.
**indescrivi·bile** *adj.* indescribable.
**indesidera·bil~e** *adj.* undesirable; *ospite —,* unwelcome guest. ~**ità** *f.* undesirability.
**indetermin~a·bile** *adj.* indeterminable. ~**atẹzza** *f.* indefiniteness, indeterminateness. ~**ativo** *adj.* (gramm.) indefinite. ~**ato** *adj.* indefinite, undecided, vague, undetermined; unspecified. ~**aziọne** *f.* indefiniteness; irresolution, uncertainty. ~**iṣmo** *m.* (philos.) theory of free-will.
**indettare** [A1 c] *tr.* to coach, to prime; *lo hanno indettato,* they put him up to it; *recip. rfl.* to agree beforehand.
**indi** *adv.* thence; thereafter.
**In·di~a** *pr.n.f.* (geog.) India; *le ~e Orientali,* the East Indies; *le ~e Occidentali,* the West Indies; *canna d'—,* bamboo cane; *castagno d'—,* horse-chestnut; *fico d'—,* prickly pear; *pollo d'—,* turkey; *porcellino d'—,* guinea-pig.
**indian~o** *adj.* Indian; Red Indian; *n.m.* Indian; Red Indian, redskin; *far l'—,* to feign ignorance. ~**a** *f.* Indian woman. ~**iṣmo** *m.* Indian studies.
**indiavol~are** [A1 s] *tr.* to bedevil; *rfl.* to fly into a rage. ~**ato** *part. adj.* bedevilled; furious; naughty; lively.
**indic~are** [A2 s] *tr.* to point out; to point to, at; to indicate; to advise. ~**a·bile** *adj.* advisable. ~**ato** *part. adj.* pointed out; pointed at; indicated; obvious; suitable; *è l'uomo ~ato,* he is the right man; *n.m.* the obvious thing; the person indicated. ~**atọre** *m.* indicator, gauge; directory; *cartello ~atore,* road sign; *adj.* indicative. ~**aziọne** *f.* indication; information, directions.
**in·dice** *adj.* (*prep.* di) indicative (of); *n.m.* forefinger, index-finger; index (of a book); indication, sign; pointer, hand, needle.
**indici·bile** *adj.* unspeakable, inexpressible.
**indietr~o** *adv.* behind; back; backwards; *voltarsi —,* to turn round; *andare avanti e —,* to go to and fro; *essere —,* to be behind the times; (of a clock) to be slow; (motor.) *dare macchina —,* to reverse; *marcia —,* reversing, backing. ~**eggiare** [A3 c] *intr.* (*aux.* avere, essere) to draw back; to retreat; to withdraw; to give way.
**indifendi·bile** *adj.* indefensible.
**indifẹso** *adj.* undefended; unprotected; unarmed.
**indifferen~te** *adj.* indifferent; *mi è —,* it's all the same to me; unimportant; uninterested; apathetic; *per me è persona —,* I neither like nor dislike him. ~**temẹnte** *adv.* indiscriminately. ~**za** *f.* indifference, apathy.
**indifferi·bile** *adj.* that cannot be delayed; urgent.
**indi·geno** *adj.* native, indigenous; home-grown; *n.m.* native.
**indigen~te** *adj.* extremely poor, indigent, destitute; *n.m.* pauper; *pl. gli ~ti,* the poor. ~**za** *f.* poverty, indigence, penury, destitution.
**indigeri·bile** *adj.* indigestible; (fig.) insufferable.
**indigest~i·bile** *adj.* indigestible. ~**iọne** *f.* indigestion; *prendere un'~ione,* to get indigestion; (fig.) more than enough, plethora, surfeit. ~**o** *adj.* indigestible; undigested; (joc.) sickening, boring; crude; (fig.) confused, uncoordinated.
**indign~are** [A5] *tr.* to make indignant; *rfl.* to be indignant; to be roused to anger; to rage. ~**ato** *part. adj.* indignant; angry; shocked, disgusted. ~**aziọne** *f.* indignation, wrath.
**indimentica·bile** *adj.* unforgettable, memorable.
**indimostr~a·bile** *adj.* not susceptible of proof. ~**ato** *adj.* unproved.
**indipenden~te** *adj.* independent; *— da,* independent of, free from; underivative; self-reliant; unrelated. ~**za** *f.* independence.
**indire** [B10] *tr.* to announce, to arrange; to appoint; to establish; to summon; *— un'adunanza,* to call a meeting.
**indiretto** *adj.* indirect; oblique; *adv. phr. per —,* indirectly.
**indirizz~are** [A1] *tr.* to direct; to dedicate; to send, to refer; *rfl.* (*prep.* a) to make one's way (towards); to set out (for); to apply (to); to go to see; to refer to. ~**atrice** *f.* addressing machine.
**indirizzo** *m.* direction, course, turn; *gl'indirizzi seguiti,* the lines followed; guiding rule; address; domicile; discourse, speech, address; petition; dedication.
**indiscerni·bile** *adj.* imperceptible; indiscernible.
**indisciplin~a** *f.* lack of discipline. ~**a·bile** *adj.* intractable. ~**atẹzza** *f.* unruliness, disorderly conduct. ~**ato** *adj.* undisciplined, ill-trained; disorderly, unruly.
**indiscrẹt~o** *adj.* indiscreet; inquisitive. ~**ẹzza** *f.* indiscretion.
**indiscreziọne** *f.* act of indiscretion.
**indiscusso** *adj.* indisputable; self-evident.
**indiscuti·bile** *adj.* unquestionable, indisputable.
**indispensa·bil~e** *adj.* indispens-

able; basic; unavoidable; *n.m.* what is necessary; *l'— per l'accampamento,* basic camping equipment. **-ità** *f.* indispensableness.
**indispett-ire** [D2] *tr.* to make angry, to vex, to annoy; *rfl., intr.* (*aux.* essere) to become angry, to be vexed. **-ito** *part. adj.* angry; vexed, annoyed; piqued.
**indisporre** [B21] *tr.* to annoy, to impress unfavourably; to cause to become indisposed.
**indisposizione** *f.* indisposition, slight malaise.
**indisposto** *part. adj.* indisposed; unwell; annoyed.
**indisputa·bile** *adj.* unquestionable; indisputable.
**indisputato** *adj.* undisputed.
**indissolu·bile** *adj.* indissoluble.
**indistacca·bile** *adj.* undetachable; inseparable.
**indistingui·bile** *adj.* indistinguishable; imperceptible.
**indistint-o** *adj.* indistinct; blurred; indeterminate; faint. **-amente** *adv.* indistinctly; *tutti -amente,* every single one without exception.
**indistinzione** *f.* indistinctness; confusion.
**indistrutti·bile** *adj.* indestructible.
**indisturbato** *adj.* undisturbed.
**individual-e** *adj.* individual; particular, personal. **-ismo** *m.* individualism; egoism. **-ista** *m., f.* individualist; egoist. **-ità** *f. indecl.* individuality; important person. **-izzare** [A1] *tr.* to specify, to individualize.
**individu-are** [A6] *tr.* to characterize; to specify exactly; to locate; to single out; to pinpoint. **-a·bile** *adj.* easily identifiable, recognizable. **-azione** *f.* location, locating; identification; *sigla di -azione,* identification mark.
**indivi·duo** *adj.* individual; single and indivisible; *n.m.* individual; person, fellow.
**indivisi·bil-e** *adj.* indivisible, inseparable; joint. **-ità** *f.* indivisibility.
**indivis-o** *adj.* undivided; *proprietà -a,* owned in common. **-amente** *adv.* without distinction; jointly.
**indi·zi-o** *m.* sign; indication; symptom; clue; *— di prova,* circumstantial evidence. **-are** [A3] *tr.* to point to; to throw suspicion on. **-ato** *part. adj.* suspect.
**Indo** *pr.n.m.* (geog.) Indus (river).
**indo·cil-e** *adj.* undisciplined, recalcitrant; not amenable. **-ità** *f.* unruliness, lack of discipline.
**Indocina** *pr.n.f.* (geog.) Indo-China.
**indolcire** [D2] *tr.* to sweeten; (fig.) to mitigate, to sweeten, to soften; to make tractable; *intr.* (*aux.* essere) to become sweeter, to sweeten; to grow milder.
**in·dole** *f.* character; disposition, nature; *l'— umana,* human nature; temperament; *lo fa per —,* it is his nature to do it; *l'— di una malattia,* the nature of an illness.
**indol-ente** *adj.* indolent, inert; listless; insensible; (med.) painless. **-enza** *f.* indolence; apathy.
**indolenz-ire** [D2] *tr.* to make numb; *intr.* (*aux.* essere) to become numb or torpid. **-imento** *m.* numbness; stiffness; soreness.
**indolire** [D2] *tr.* to cause to ache, to give pain; *rfl.* (*aux.* essere) to ache; to feel pain or discomfort.
**indolore** *adj.* painless; (med.) *parto —,* natural childbirth.
**indoma·bile** *adj.* untameable, indomitable.
**indomani** *m. l'—,* the next day, the day after.
**indomato** *adj.* untamed, refractory.
**indo·mito** *adj.* untamed, unsubdued; indomitable.
**indorare** [A1] *tr.* to gild; (fig.) *— la pillola,* to sugar the pill.
**indoss-are** [A1] *tr.* to put on (clothes); to wear, to be dressed in. **-ata** *f.* trying on, fitting. **-atrice** *f.* mannequin, model girl. **-o** *adv.* on; *avere -o,* to wear, to be wearing.
**Indost-an** *pr.n.m.* (geog.) Hindustan. **-a·nico, -ano** *adj., n.m.* Hindustani.
**indotto** *part.* of **indurre**; *adj.* induced, persuaded, led.
**indovin-are** [A1] *tr.* to guess; to divine; to surmise; *-arla,* to guess right, to hit it; *non ne -a una,* he is never right; *intr.* (*aux.* avere) to hit the mark, to succeed. **-a·bile** *adj.* open to conjecture. **-a·glia** *f.* matter for conjecture, riddle. **-atore** *m.* guesser, diviner, soothsayer. **-azione** *f.* divination, soothsaying. **-ello** *m.* riddle; enigma; puzzle, guessing-game. **-o** *m.* soothsayer, fortune-teller.
**indub·bio** *adj.* undoubted, unquestioned.
**indubita·bile** *adj.* indubitable.
**indubitato** *adj.* not doubted.
**inducimento** *m.* instigation; temptation; inducement.
**indugiare** [A3] *tr.* to delay, to postpone; to defer; *intr.* (*aux.* avere), *rfl.* to linger.
**indu·gio** *m.* delay.
**indul·g-ere** [C5] *tr.* to grant, to allow; *intr.* (*aux.* avere) to be indulgent. **-ente** *part. adj.* indulgent; lenient. **-enza** *f.* indulgence.
**indumento** *m.* garment; *pl.* clothing; (eccl.) *sacri indumenti,* vestments.
**indurire** [D2] *tr.* to harden; to make resistant; *intr.* (*aux.* essere; *prep.* a), *rfl.* to harden, to set; to become inured (to).
**indurre** [B2] *tr.* to induce; to impel; to infer; *— in errore,* to mislead; *rfl.* to resolve.
**industre** *adj.* busy, industrious.
**indu·stri-a** *f.* industry; manufacture; factory, works. **-ale** *adj.* industrial; *n.m.* industrialist; manufacturer. **-alismo** *m.* industrialism. **-alizzare** [A1] *tr.* to industrialize. **-are** [A4] *rfl.* to try, to do one's best. **-oso** *adj.* industrious; diligent.
**induttivo** *adj.* inductive.
**induzione** *f.* inducement; induction; conjecture.
**ine(b)briare** [A4] *tr.* to make drunk; (fig.) to intoxicate; *rfl.* to get drunk, to become intoxicated; (fig.) to go into raptures.
**ineccepi·bile** *adj.* above criticism; *informazione —,* reliable information.
**ine·dia** *f.* abstention from food; starvation; tedium; *è un'—,* it bores me to death.
**ine·dito** *adj.* unpublished; inedited; *n.m.* unpublished work.
**ineffa·bile** *adj.* ineffable, unutterable.
**ineffettua·bile** *adj.* unrealizable; unfeasible.
**ineffic-ace** *adj.* ineffectual. **-a·cia** *f.* inefficacy.
**inefficien-te** *adj.* not effective; inefficient. **-za** *f.* inefficiency.
**ineguagli-a·bile** *adj.* unbeatable. **-anza** *f.* inequality, unevenness; dissimilarity. **-ato** *adj.* unequalled, unparalleled.
**inegual-e** *adj.* unequal; uneven; changeable. **-ità** *f.* inequality; unevenness.
**inelegan-te** *adj.* inelegant. **-za** *f.* lack of elegance.
**ineleggi·bil-e** *adj.* ineligible. **-ità** *f.* ineligibility.
**inelutta·bil-e** *adj.* unavoidable, inevitable. **-ità** *f.* unavoidability, inevitability.
**inenarra·bile** *adj.* unspeakable, indescribable.
**inequivoca·bile** *adj.* unequivocal.
**iner-ire** [D2 def.] *intr.* (no *past part.* or *comp.* tenses; *prep.* a) to inhere; to be inherent (in). **-ente** *part. adj.* (*prep.* a) inherent (in), attached (to); concerning. **-enza** *f.* inherence.
**inerme** *adj.* unarmed; disarmed.
**inerpicare** [A2 sc] *rfl., intr.* (*aux.* essere; *prep.* su) to climb, to clamber (up).
**inerte** *adj.* inert, idle, motionless.
**iner·zia** *f.* idleness, inertness; inertia.
**inesatt-o** *adj.* inaccurate; unpunctual; (of debts) unpaid. **-ezza** *f.* inaccuracy; mistake.
**inesauri·bile** *adj.* inexhaustible.
**inescare** [A2 c] *tr.* to bait (a hook); (fig.) to entice.
**inescusa·bile** *adj.* inexcusable.

**ineṣegui·bile** *adj.* impossible to carry out.

**ineṣigi·bile** *adj.* irrecoverable; *debito* —, bad debt.

**ineṣora·bile** *adj.* inexorable; implacable.

**inesperienza** *f.* inexperience.

**inesperto** *adj.* inexperienced; inexpert, unskilled.

**inespi-a·bile** *adj.* inexpiable. **-ato** *adj.* unexpiated.

**inesplica·bile** *adj.* inexplicable, unaccountable.

**inesplor-a·bile** *adj.* that cannot be explored. **-ato** *adj.* unexplored.

**inesploso** *adj.* unexploded.

**inesprimi·bile** *adj.* inexpressible, unutterable.

**inespugna·bile** *adj.* impregnable; (fig.) incorruptible.

**inespurgato** *adj.* unexpurgated.

**inestima·bile** *adj.* inestimable, invaluable.

**inestingui·bile** *adj.* unquenchable.

**inestrica·bile** *adj.* inextricable.

**inett-o** *adj.* inept; unsuitable; foolish. **-itu·dine** *f.* ineptitude.

**inevaṣo** *adj.* unanswered; unattended to.

**inevita·bile** *adj.* inevitable; inescapable.

**ine·zia** *f.* trifle, bagatelle; foolish remark.

**infagottare** [A1] *tr.* to wrap up; to make into a bundle.

**infalli·bil-e** *adj.* infallible; unfailing. **-ità** *f.* infallibility.

**infam-are** [A1] *tr.* to slander; to disgrace; *rfl.* to bring shame upon oneself; to be dishonoured. **-ante** *part. adj.* libellous. **-ato·rio** *adj.* slanderous, defamatory; disgraceful.

**infame** *adj.* infamous; scandalous; *n.m.* infamous person, scoundrel.

**infa·mia** *f.* slander; defamation; (fig.) infamous behaviour; insult.

**infangare** [A2] *tr.* to bespatter with mud; (fig.) to smirch; *rfl.* to get spattered with mud; (fig.) to become degraded.

**infant-e** *m., f.* infant. **-icida** *m., f.* one guilty of infanticide. **-ici·dio** *m.* infanticide. **-ile** *adj.* infantile, childish; *asilo -ile*, nursery, kindergarten.

**infan·zia** *f.* infancy; infants.

**infarc-ire** [D2] *tr.* (cul.) to stuff; (fig.) to fill out, to pad. **-imẹnto** *m.* stuffing; padding.

**infarin-are** [A1] *tr.* (cul.) to dip in flour; (fig.) — *alcuno d'una scienza*, to teach someone a smattering of a science; *rfl.* to get covered with flour. **-atura** *f.* dusting with flour; powdering; (fig.) smattering.

**infastidire** [D2] *tr.* to annoy; to disturb; to molest; to bore; to disgust; *rfl.* to feel annoyed; to be impatient; to be bored; to become disgusted.

**infatica·bile** *adj.* indefatigable, unwearying.

**infatti** *adv.* in fact; indeed; really.

**infatu-are** [A6] *tr.* to infatuate; *rfl.* (*prep.* di) to have one's head turned (by), to become infatuated with. **-ato** *part. adj.* fond, foolish; infatuated. **-aziọne** *f.* infatuation.

**infa·usto** *adj.* unlucky; ill-omened.

**infecọnd-o** *adj.* barren; (fig.) fruitless. **-ità** *f.* barrenness.

**infedẹl-e** *adj.* unfaithful; inaccurate; dishonest; *n.m.* infidel. **-tà** *f.* infidelity, unfaithfulness.

**infelic-e** *adj.* unhappy; unfortunate; unpropitious; wretched; mad, imbecile; *n.m., f.* wretch; imbecile. **-ità** *f.* unhappiness; misfortune; wretchedness; affliction, calamity.

**inferenza** *f.* inference; deduction.

**inferiọr-e** *adj.* lower; less tall; inferior; southern; nether; under, bottom; *n.m.* inferior, underling, subordinate. **-ità** *f.* inferiority; *complesso di -ità*, inferiority complex.

**inferire** [D2] *tr.* to cause, to occasion; to infer, to deduce.

**inferm-o** *adj.* ill, sick, ailing, infirm; weak, cowardly; — *di mente*, of unsound mind; *n.m.* sick person, patient. **-eri·a** *f.* sickroom, sanatorium. **-iera** *f.* nurse. **-iere** *m.* hospital orderly, stretcher-bearer; male nurse. **-ità** *f.* sickness, infirmity, illness; weakness; *-ità mentale*, insanity.

**Infern-o** *pr.n.m.* Hell, the Underworld; (fig.) *un tizzone d'*—, a fire-brand; *all'*—*!*, go to hell!; (industr.) reservoir, depository. **-ale** *adj.* infernal, hellish; *n.m.pl.* gods of the Underworld; demons.

**inferoc-ire** [D2] *tr.* to make fierce; to make cruel; *intr.* (*aux.* essere), *rfl.* to become fierce, to turn ferocious; to become cruel; (*aux.* avere) to act ferociously, to commit atrocities. **-ito** *part. adj.* fierce; ferocious; cruel.

**infer·tile** *adj.* sterile; infertile.

**infervorare** [A1 c] *tr.* to excite, to fill with fervour; *rfl.* to be filled with fervour; to become overheated or excited.

**infest-are** [A1] *tr.* to infest; to importune. **-aziọne** *f.* infestation; harassing.

**infesto** *adj.* (lit.) harmful; noxious.

**infett-are** [A1] *tr.* to infect; (fig.) to taint, to corrupt; *rfl.* to become infected; (fig.) to become tainted; *recip. rfl.* to infect each other. **-ivo** *adj.* (med.) infectious; contagious. **-o** *adj.* (med.) infected; septic; (fig.) contaminated, corrupt.

**infeziọne** *f.* (med.) infection; contagion; (fig.) contamination.

**infiacchire** [D2] *tr.* to enfeeble; *intr.* (*aux.* essere), *rfl.* to grow weak; (of the wind) to die down, to drop.

**infiamm-are** [A1] *tr.* to set fire to, to kindle; (fig.) to inflame, to excite; *rfl.* to catch fire; (fig.) to get excited; to be inflamed **-a·bile** *adj.* inflammable; (fig., excitable; passionate. **-aziọne** *f.* inflaming; excitement, irritation; instigation; (med.) inflammation.

**infiasc-are** [A2] *tr.* to bottle. **-ato** *part. adj.* bottled. **-atura** *f.* bottling; cost of bottling.

**infido** *adj.* untrustworthy.

**infier-ire** [D2] *intr.* (*aux.* avere) to behave with ferocity; to act cruelly; (*aux.* essere) to rage. **-ito** *part. adj.* ferocious; cruel; increased in severity.

**infig·gere** [C17] *tr* to drive in; *rfl.* to penetrate; to be driven in; to go deep.

**infil-are** [A1] *tr.* to thread (a needle, beads, etc.); to insert; to slip (in, on); — *il soprabito*, to slip on one's overcoat; *non ne -a mai una*, he never succeeds in anything; to transfix; *intr.* (*aux.* essere) to follow on, to come in succession; — *per una via*, to go down a street; *rfl.* to be threaded; to slip (in), to squeeze (through); *recip. rfl.* to follow each other, to come one after the other. **-acappi** *m. indecl.* bodkin. **-ata** *f.* series, suite; row, file. **-ato** *part. adj.* threaded, strung together.

**infiltr-are** [A1] *rfl.* (*prep.* in) to filter (into, through), to seep; to infiltrate; *tr.* to insinuate, to introduce stealthily. **-aziọne** *f.* infiltration; penetration; seepage.

**infilz-are** [A1] *tr.* to run through, to pierce; to skewer; to string together; (fig.) to bring forth a string of. **-ata** *f.* string (*e.g.* of pearls); series; yarn; (sewing) tacking.

**in·fimo** *adj.* (*superl.* of **inferiọre**) lowest; extremely low; last; base; *n.m.* lowest place; worst person or thing.

**infine** *adv.* at last, after all, finally; in short.

**infinestr-are** [A1] *tr.* to mend or patch up (a torn page). **-atura** *f.* transparent gummed strip mending a torn page.

**infingard-o** *adj.* lazy, slothful, slack, lax. **-ag·gine** *f.* laziness, slackness; sloth.

**infinità** *f.* infinity; vast number, great quantity; *un'*— *di gente*, a great concourse of people.

**infinit-o** *adj.* infinite; unending; innumerable; immense; *n.m.* infinite; *all'*—, without end. **-e·ṣimo** *adj., n.m.* infinitesimal.

**infino** *prep.* (*foll.* by *prep.* 'a') till, until; up to; as far as.

**infiocc-are** [A2] *tr.* to adorn with tassels. **-ato** *part. adj.* tasselled; decked out.

**infior-are** [A1 c] *tr.* to strew with flowers; *rfl.* to deck oneself with flowers; to blossom. **-ata** *f.* flower arrangement. **-ato** *part. adj.* decked with flowers; flowery, in bloom.

**infischiare** [A4] *rfl.* (*prep.* di) (colloq.) not to care (for, about), not to mind; to laugh (at); *me ne infischio,* I don't give a hoot.

**infittire** [D2] *rfl., intr.* (*aux.* essere) to grow thicker, to become more dense; (of darkness) to deepen; *tr.* to thicken, to make denser.

**inflaziọn-e** *f.* (econ.) inflation. **-ista** *m.* (econ.) inflationist.

**inflessi·bil-e** *adj.* inflexible; inexorable; unyielding. **-ità** *f.* inflexibility.

**inflessiọne** *f.* flexion, bending; (gramm.) inflection.

**inflesso** *part.* of **inflet·tere**; *adj.* bent, flexed; (gramm.) inflected.

**inflet·tere** [C19] *tr.* to bend, to flex; (gramm.) to inflect.

**inflig·g-ere** [C12] *tr.* to inflict; to impose. **-imẹnto** *m.* infliction.

**influenz-a**[1] *f.* influence; power; **-are** [A1] *tr.* to influence; to sway; *intr.* (*aux.* avere; *prep.* su). to have an influence (upon) **-ato** *part. adj.* influenced, swayed.

**influenz-a**[2] *f.* influenza. **-ato** *adj.* suffering from influenza.

**influ-ire** [D2] *intr.* (*aux.* avere; *prep.* su) to have an influence (upon); (*prep.* a) to contribute (to); (*prep.* in) (of rivers) — *in,* to flow into. **-ente** *part. adj.* influential; *-ente in,* flowing into; *n.m.* influential person; tributary.

**influsso** *m.* influence; effect; influx.

**infoc-are** [A2 d] *tr.* to make red-hot; (fig.) to excite; *rfl.* to become red-hot; (fig.) to get over-excited, to be inflamed. **-ato** *part. adj.* red-hot, burning; aflame.

**infoderare** [A1 s] *tr.* to sheathe; to line.

**infoltire** [D2] *intr.* (*aux.* essere) to thicken, to grow thick.

**infondat-o** *adj.* unfounded, baseless, false. **-ẹzza** *f.* baselessness, falseness.

**infọnd-ere** [C2 c] *tr.* to pour in; to infuse, to instil. **-imẹnto** *m.* infusing.

**inforcare** [A2 c] *tr.* to take up on a pitchfork; to bestride; — *gli occhiali,* to put on one's spectacles; *intr.* (*aux.* avere) to play truant; *rfl.* to fork, to bifurcate.

**inform-are** [A1 c] *tr.* to shape, to form; to spread through, to permeate; to inform, to instruct, to notify; — *di,* to notify concerning, to acquaint with; *rfl.* to make enquiries; to collect information; to take shape. **-ativa** *f.* instruction, letter of information. **-ativo** *adj.* formative; informative. **-atọre** *m.* informer, spy; (mil.) scout. **-aziọne** *f.* information; *assumere -azioni,* to make inquiries; *ufficio -azioni,* inquiry office; (mil.) intelligence.

**infọrme** *adj.* shapeless; formless.

**infornaci-are** [A3] *tr.* to put into a furnace, to put into a kiln. **-ata** *f.* firing (bricks, etc.) **-ato** *part. adj.* fired.

**inforn-are** [A1 c] *tr.* to put in the oven. **-ata** *f.* batch (of loaves, etc.).

**infortire** [D2] *intr.* (*aux.* essere) to turn sour; to taste more acid; *tr.* to fortify; to make more acid.

**infortunabilità** *f.* (industr.) accident-proneness.

**infortunato** *adj.* injured in an accident; *n.m.* person injured, casualty.

**infortu·n-io** *m.* accident; misfortune; (naut.) shipwreck, collision. **-i·stico** *adj.* relating to accidents.

**infoscare** [A2 c] *tr.* to darken; *intr.* (*aux.* essere), *rfl.* to grow dark; to grow sad.

**infoss-are** [A1] *tr.* to bury, to inter; *rfl.* to sink; to become emaciated. **-ato** *part. adj.* hollow; *occhi -ati,* sunken eyes.

**infra** *prep.* among, between; within.

**infradici-are** [A3 s] *tr.* to drench, to soak; *rfl.* to get drenched; to go bad. **-ata** *f.* (a) drenching. **-ato** *part. adj.* drenched, soaking wet.

**infran·g-ere** [C5] *tr.* to crush; to shatter; (fig.) to violate; to break; *rfl.* to be crushed; to be shattered. **-i·bile** *adj.* unbreakable; (fig.) inviolable. **-imẹnto** *m.* breaking.

**infrant-o** *part.* of **infran·gere**; *adj.* crushed; broken; (fig.) exhausted.

**infra(r)rọsso** *adj.* infra-red; *n.m.* infra-red ray.

**infrascare** [A2] *tr.* to cover with branches; to stake, to tie (plants); (fig.) to overload with ornament; *rfl.* to hide among branches; (fig.) to be over-elaborate in style.

**infras-co** *m.* (*pl.* **-chi**) branch used to support a climbing plant.

**infrastruttura** *f.* infrastructure; (aeron.) ground organization.

**infraziọne** *f.* infringement; breach; violation.

**infredd-are** [A1 c] *tr.* to chill; to cool; *intr.* (*aux.* essere), *rfl.* to catch a cold, to get a chill. **-ato** *part. adj.* suffering from a cold. **-atura** *f.* cold, chill. **-olire** [D2] *intr.* (*aux.* essere), *rfl.* to feel very cold, to shiver with cold. **-olito** *part. adj.* chilled to the bone.

**'nfren-are** [A1 c] *tr.* to check, to restrain, to moderate. **-a·bile** *adj.* unrestrainable.

**infrequen-te** *adj.* infrequent; rare. **-za** *f.* infrequency; rarity.

**infrollire** [D2] *intr.* (*aux.* essere), *rfl.,* to become feeble, to grow limp; (of meat) to become tender.

**infrutt-i·fero** *adj.* unfruitful. **-uọso** *adj.* fruitless.

**infuori** *adv.* outwards; out; *all'—di,* with the exception of.

**infurbire** [D2] *intr.* (*aux.* essere), *rfl.* to grow cunning; to become shrewd.

**infuri-are** [A4] *intr.* (*aux.* essere), *rfl.* to rage, to become furious; to fly into a temper; (*aux.* avere) to act furiously, to rage. **-ato** *part. adj.* infuriated, enraged; in a rage.

**infusiọne** *f.* infusion.

**infuso** *part.* of **infọndere**; *adj.* infused; *n.m.* infusion.

**infustire** [D2] *intr.* (*aux.* essere) to grow stiff, to stiffen; *tr.* to make stiff, to stiffen.

**ingabbiare** [A4] *tr.* to cage.

**ingaggiare** [A3] *tr.* to engage; to join (battle); *intr.* (*aux.* avere) (of a rope) to foul.

**ingag·gio** *m.* pledge; engagement; (sport) *premio di —,* transfer fee.

**ingagliardire** [D2] *tr.* to strengthen, to invigorate, to harden; *intr.* (*aux.* essere), *rfl.* to grow strong; to take courage.

**ingann-are** [A1] *tr.* to deceive, to cheat, to swindle; — *il tempo,* to kill time; to defraud; *rfl.* to be mistaken; *se non m'-o,* if I am not mistaken; *-arsi di grosso,* to be greatly mistaken. **-a·bile** *adj.* credulous, gullible. **-atọre** *m.* deceiver; cheat; swindler. **-ẹvole** *adj.* deceptive, false, misleading.

**inganno** *m.* deceit; deception; trick; fraud; stratagem.

**ingegn-are** [A5 c] *rfl.* to strive, to endeavour; to resort to expedients; *-arsi alla meglio,* to do the best one can.

**ingegner-e** *m.* engineer; architect; technologist. **-i·a** *f.* engineering; profession of engineering.

**ingẹgn-o** *m.* talent, intelligence, liveliness of mind; *uomo d'—,* gifted man; *avere —,* to be talented, to have a certain flair; *un — vivace,* a lively, quick-witted mind; ingenuity; *ci mise —,* he used his ingenuity; *a forza d'—,* by using one's ingenuity; mind, intellect; *alzata d'—,* brainwave; *è un —,* he has a good brain; expedient, contrivance, mechanism; genius, special talent; *l'— inventivo,* inventive genius. **-ọso** *adj.* ingenious; witty; resourceful; *il bisogno fa l'uomo -oso,* necessity is the mother of invention.

**ingelosire** [D2] *tr.* to make jealous; *rfl., intr.* (*aux.* essere; *prep.* di) to become jealous (of); to be jealous.

**ingemmare** [A1] *tr.* to adorn with jewels; to embellish; *intr.* (*aux.*

avere) (bot.) to bud; *rfl.* to bedeck oneself with jewels.
**ingenerare** [A1 s] *tr.* to generate, to engender; to give rise to; *rfl.* (*prep.* da) to originate, to arise (from).
**ingeneroṣ-o** *adj.* ungenerous; grudging. **-ità** *f.* lack of generosity; meanness.
**inge·nito** *adj.* innate, congenital, inborn.
**ingente** *adj.* enormous, vast; outside.
**ingentilire** [D2] *tr.* to refine, to civilize; to cultivate; *rfl.*, *intr.* (*aux.* essere) to become civilized; to acquire polish.
**inge·nu-o** *adj.* natural, simple, ingenuous; *n.m.* ingenuous person. **-a** *f.* (theatr.) ingénue. **-ità** *f.* ingenuousness; ingenuous action or remark.
**inger-ire** [D2] *tr.* to ingest, to absorb; (fig.) to take in; *rfl.*, *intr.* (*aux.* essere) to interfere, to meddle. **-enza** *f.* interference; participation. **-imẹnto** *m.* ingestion, absorption.
**ingessare** [A1] *tr.* to plaster; to whitewash; (surg.) to set in plaster.
**ingestiọne** *f.* ingestion, absorption.
**inghiai-are** [A4] *tr.* to cover with gravel. **-ata** *f.* ballast; load of gravel.
**Inghilterra** *pr.n.f.* England.
**inghiott-ire** [D2] *tr.* to swallow, to engulf. **-itọio** *m.* drain, sewer; intake.
**inghirlandare** [A1] *tr.* to garland, to wreathe; (fig.) to encircle, to form a wreath round; to fill to the brim.
**ingiall-are** [A1], **-ire** [D2] *tr.* (poet.) to cause to turn yellow; *rfl.*, *intr.* (*aux.* essere) to turn yellow.
**ingigantire** [D2] *tr.* to magnify; to exaggerate; *rfl.*, *intr.* (*aux.* essere) to appear gigantic; to be magnified; to be exaggerated.
**inginocchi-are** [A4] *rfl.* to kneel down. **-amẹnto** *m.* kneeling down, falling on one's knees; genuflexion; show of humility or subservience.
**ingioiell-are** [A1] *tr.* to adorn with jewels; *rfl.* to put on jewellery. **-ato** *part. adj.* wearing jewels.
**ingiovanire** [D2] *intr.* (*aux.* essere), *rfl.* to be rejuvenated.
**ingiù** *adv.* down, downwards; (of running water) downstream; *all'—*, down below; (fig.) *lasciar correre l'acqua all'—*, to let things take their course.
**ingiun·gere** [C5] *tr.* to enjoin; to prescribe, to command, to order.
**ingiunziọne** *f.* injunction, order, command.
**ingiu·ri-a** *f.* insult; injury, wrong; outrage; offensive remark; *pl.* abuse; damage; *le -e del tempo*, the ravages of time. **-are** [A4] *tr.* to insult; to wrong. **-ọso** *adj.* insulting; harmful, damaging; wrongful.
**ingiustific-a·bile** *adj.* unjustifiable; unwarrantable. **-ato** *adj.* unjustified, unwarranted.
**ingiust-o** *adj.* unjust; unfair; unlawful, wrongful; *n.m.* unjust (man); unfair thing. **-i·zia** *f.* injustice; unfairness; wrong, injury.
**inglẹse** *adj.* English; *n.m.* English language; Englishman; *gli Inglesi*, the English; *f. la Inglese*, the English woman.
**ingloriọso** *adj.* inglorious; obscure.
**ingobbire** [D2] *rfl.*, *intr.* (*aux.* essere) to become hunchbacked; *— sul lavoro*, to sit hunched over one's work, to swot.
**ingoffire** [D2] *tr.* to make look clumsy; *intr.* (*aux.* essere), *rfl.* to become ungainly; to behave clumsily.
**ingoiare** [A4 c] *tr.* to swallow, to gulp down; to read through at speed.
**ingolf-are** [A1 c] *rfl.* (of the sea) to form a gulf; (fig.) *-arsi in*, to plunge into, to become immersed in; *tr.* to engulf, to implicate, to involve; to flood.
**ingollare** [A1] *tr.* to gulp down; to guzzle.
**ingolosire** [D2] *tr.* to whet the appetite of; to excite the greed of; *rfl.*, *intr.* (*aux.* essere) to become greedy.
**ingombr-are** [A1 c] *tr.* to encumber; to obstruct; to crowd; to load; *troppi dettagli -ano la mente*, too many details confuse the mind. **-ante** *part. adj.* encumbering; cumbersome.
**ingọmbro**[1] *m.* encumbrance; obstruction, obstacle; impediment; *fare —*, to be an obstruction, to get in the way.
**ingọmbro**[2] *adj.* (*prep.* di) encumbered with, impeded by, laden with.
**ingomm-are** [A1 c] *tr.* to gum. **-ato** *part. adj.* gummed; sticky.
**ingọrd-o** *adj.* voracious; gluttonous; covetous; exorbitant; *n.m.* glutton. **-i·gia** *f.* voracity; covetousness; exorbitance.
**ingorgare** [A2 c] *tr.* to block, to choke; to check; *rfl.* to become choked; to be blocked; to get stopped up; (of traffic) to be held up.
**ingor-go** *m.* (*pl.* **-ghi**) blocking; obstruction, blockage; *— stradale*, traffic jam.
**ingoverna·bile** *adj.* ungovernable; unruly.
**ingozz-are** [A1] *tr.* to gulp down; to swallow quickly; (fig.) *non posso -arla*, it sticks in my throat; *— un'ingiuria*, to swallow an insult.
**ingran-are** [A1] *tr.* (eng.) to engage, to put into gear; *intr* (*aux.* essere) to engage, to mesh; *recip. rfl.* to engage; to seize up; (colloq.) to understand each other. **-ag·gio** *m.* (eng.) gears; cog-wheels; gear system; engaging; (fig.) wheels within wheels.
**ingranch-ire** [D2] *tr.* to make numb, to benumb; *intr.* (*aux.* essere) to grow numb. **-ito** *part. adj.* numbed, numb.
**ingrand-ire** [D2] *tr.* to enlarge; to magnify; to increase; to augment; *intr.* (*aux.* essere), *rfl.* to grow taller; to increase in size; (fig.) to become more important. **-imẹnto** *m.* enlargement, increase; *lente d'-imento*, magnifying-glass. **-itọre** *m.* enlarger; magnifier.
**ingrass-are** [A1] *tr.* to fatten; to enrich; to manure; to grease; *abs. il burro -a*, butter is fattening; *intr.* (*aux.* essere), *rfl.* to grow fat, to get stout. **-ag·gio** *m.* greasing; oiling, lubricating. **-o** *m.* fattening substance; manure, fertilizer.
**ingratitu·dine** *f.* ingratitude; ungrateful action.
**ingrato** *adj.* unpleasant; unrewarding; thankless; *n.m.* ungrateful person, ingrate.
**ingraziare** [A4] *rfl.* (*acc.* of *prn.* si; *prep.* con) to ingratiate oneself, to curry favour (with); (*dat.* of *prn.* si) *ingraziarsi uno*, to gain someone's favour.
**ingrediente** *m.* ingredient; (fig.) element, component part.
**ingresso** *m.* entrance; way in; admittance; entering.
**ingrossare** [A1] *tr.* to enlarge; to swell; to coarsen; *intr.* (*aux.* essere), *rfl.* to grow bigger; to swell; to grow stout; (of the sea) to get rough; (fig.) to grow insensitive; to become gross.
**ingrosso** *adv. phr. all'—*, wholesale.
**ingualci·bil-e** *adj.* crease-proof, uncrushable. **-ità** *f.* crease-resistance.
**inguant-are** [A1] *rfl.* to put on one's gloves. **-ato** *part. adj.* gloved.
**inguari·bile** *adj.*, *n.m.*, *f.* incurable.
**in·guin-e** *m.* (anat.) groin. **-ale** *adj.* of the groin.
**ingurgitare** [A1 s] *tr.* to devour; to gobble.
**inib-ire** [D2] *tr.* (leg.) to prohibit; (psych.) to inhibit. **-iziọne** *f.* (leg.) prohibition; (psych.) inhibition.
**inido·ne-o** *adj.* unfit, unsuitable. **-ità** *f.* unfitness, unsuitability.
**iniett-are** [A1] *tr.* to inject; *— con*, to impregnate with. **-ato** *part. adj.* injected; *occhi -ati di sangue*, bloodshot eyes. **-ọre** *m.* injector, syringe.
**iniezịone** *f.* injection

**inimicare** [A2] *tr.* to alienate; to estrange; *rfl.* (*acc.* of *prn.* si; *prep.* con) to fall out (with); (*dat.* of *prn.* si) to make an enemy of; *recip. rfl.* to become enemies.
**inimici·zia** *f.* hostility; enmity.
**inimita·bile** *adj.* inimitable; unrivalled.
**ini·qu-o** *adj.* wicked, iniquitous; unjust; (colloq.) frightful. **-ità** *f.* iniquity; *-ità della stagione*, inclement weather.
**iniziale** *adj.* initial; opening, beginning; *stipendio* —, commencing salary; *n.f.* initial letter, initial.
**inizi-are** [A4] *tr.* to initiate; to begin; *rfl.* to have its beginning, to originate; to be initiated. **-ativa** *f.* initiative; enterprise; undertaking; *a -ativa di*, on the initiative of. **-atore** *m.* initiator; promoter. **-azione** *f.* beginning; initiation.
**ini·zio** *m.* beginning, start; *fin dall'*—, from the very beginning; *avere — da*, to originate in; to begin with; *pl.* elements, rudiments; first steps; initiation.
**innalzare** [A1] *tr.* to raise; to set up; to promote; to exalt; *rfl.* to rise.
**innamor-are** [A1 c] *tr.* (*prep.* di) to inspire with love; to enchant, to delight; *abs.* to be delightful; *rfl.* (*prep.* di) to fall in love (with); to conceive a passion (for); *recip. rfl.* to fall in love with each other. **-amento** *m.* enamourment; courtship. **-ata** *f.* mistress. **-ato** *adj.* (*prep.* di) in love (with); enamoured (of); *n.m.* lover.
**innanzi** *prep.* before; — *tempo*, before the proper time; (*foll.* by 'a') before, in the presence of; in preference to; (*foll.* by 'di') — *di fare così*, before doing so; *adv.* before, in the past; in front, ahead, first; further; *tirare* —, to go ahead, to keep on; *tirarsi — per una professione*, to study for a profession; *d'ora* —, henceforth; *farsi* —, to come forward; *procedere troppo* —, to go too far; *n.m.* future; *per l'*—, henceforth.
**inna·rio** *m.* hymn book, hymnal.
**innato** *adj.* innate, inborn; congenital.
**innaturale** *adj.* unnatural.
**innaviga·bile** *adj.* unnavigable.
**innega·bile** *adj.* undeniable, unquestionable.
**inneggiare** [A3] *tr* to hymn; to praise, to laud; *intr.* (*aux.* avere; *prep.* a) to sing hymns (to); (fig.) to sing the praises (of).
**innestare** [A1] *tr.* to graft; to vaccinate, to inoculate.
**innesto** *m.* graft, scion, grafting; — *del vaiolo*, inoculation against smallpox.
**inno** *m.* hymn, song of praise; — *nazionale*, national anthem.
**innocen-te** *adj.* innocent; innocuous, harmless. **-za** *f.* innocence.
**inno·cu-o** *adj.* innocuous; without venom; (fig.) harmless. **-ità** *f.* innocuousness; harmlessness.
**innomina·bile** *adj.* unspeakable, unmentionable.
**innominato** *adj.* unnamed; nameless; of unknown name.
**inoccupato** *adj.* unoccupied, vacant, untenanted; uninhabited; not yet employed.
**inocul-are** [A1 s] *tr.* to graft by budding; to inoculate. **-azione** *f.* grafting; inoculation.
**inodore** *adj.* odourless; unscented.
**inoliare** [A4] *tr.* to oil; to season with oil.
**inoltr-are** [A1 c] *rfl.* to go further, to proceed; *l'inverno s'-a*, the winter is far advanced; *tr.* (admin.) to forward, to transmit. **-ato** *part. adj.* advanced; *a notte -ata*, late at night.
**inoltre** *adv.* besides, furthermore.
**inond-are** [A1 c] *tr.* to flood, to inundate. **-azione** *f.* flood, inundation.
**ino·pia** *f.* poverty, indigence; lack, want.
**inoperoso** *adj.* idle, inactive, inert; unemployed.
**inopportun-o** *adj.* untimely, inopportune; inconvenient. **-ità** *f.* untimeliness; unsuitability.
**inorga·nico** *adj.* inorganic; without organic unity.
**inorgoglire** [D2] *tr.* to make proud; to turn (a person's) head; *intr.* (*aux.* essere), *rfl.* to grow proud; to be elated; to have one's head turned.
**inorrid-ire** [D2] *tr.* to strike with horror; *intr.* (*aux.* essere) to be terrified; *-ii a vederlo*, I was horrified to see him. **-ito** *part. adj.* horrified; *fuggirono -iti* they fled in terror.
**inospitale** *adj.* inhospitable, unwelcoming.
**ino·spite** *adj.* (of territory) wild, uninhabitable.
**inossida·bile** *adj.* inoxidizable; *acciaio* —, stainless steel.
**inquadr-are** [A1] *tr.* to frame; — *in un sistema*, to incorporate in a system; *rfl.* to fit (into), to take its place (in); *questa iniziativa s'-a nella politica del governo*, this undertaking forms part of government policy. **-atura** *f.* framing; (cinem.; telev.) shot.
**inqualifica·bile** *adj.* indescribable; unspeakable.
**inquiet-are** [A1] *tr.* to make uneasy, to worry; *rfl.* to become worried; *intr.* (*infin.* after 'fare') *fare — uno*, to cause someone to worry. **-ante** *adj.* disquieting; worrying.
**inquiet-o** *adj.* restless; uneasy; *sonno* —, disturbed sleep. **-u·dine** *f.* uneasiness, uncertainty; worry, cause for anxiety.
**inquilino** *m.* lodger, paying guest; tenant.
**inquinare** [A1] *tr.* to make filthy; to pollute; to infect; to foul.
**inquiṣ-ire** [D2] *tr.* to investigate; to pry into; to be inquisitive about. **-itore** *m.* investigator; snooper; inquisitor. **-izione** *f.* investigation; inquiry; inquest; (hist.) Inquisition.
**insacc-are** [A2] *tr.* to put into sacks; (fig.) to pocket; to gulp; *rfl.*, *intr.* (*aux.* essere) to squeeze, to crowd (into a small space). **-ato** *part. adj.* in sacks; *carne -ata*, sausages, salami.
**insal-are** [A1] *tr.* to salt, to pickle; to season with salt; *rfl. intr.* (*aux.* essere), to become salt. **-ata** *f.* salad; (fig.) muddle, hotch-potch. **-atiera** *f.* salad-bowl. **-ato** *part. adj.* salted; salt.
**insaldare** [A1] *tr.* to starch.
**insalu·br-e** *adj.* unhealthy, insalubrious. **-ità** *f.* unhealthiness.
**insana·bile** *adj.* incurable; irremediable.
**insanguinare** [A1] *tr.* to make bloody, to stain with blood.
**insa·nia** *f.* insanity, madness; folly.
**insano** *adj.* insane, demented; mad; foolish.
**insapon-are** [A1 c] *tr.* to soap, to lather; (fig.) to flatter, to 'soft-soap'. **-atura** *f.* lather; flattery.
**insapor-ire** [D2] *tr.* to flavour; to make appetizing. **-ito** *part. adj.* flavoured; tasty; appetizing.
**insaporo** *m.* tasteless, insipid.
**insaputa** *adv. phr. a mia* —, unbeknown to me; *all'— di*, without the knowledge of, behind the back of.
**insazia·bil-e** *adj.* insatiable. **-ità** *f.* insatiableness.
**insaziato** *adj.* unsatiated, unsatisfied; voracious; never satisfied.
**inscatol-are** [A1 s] *tr.* to tin, to can. **-ato** *part. adj.* tinned, canned; in tins. **-atrice** *f.* canning machine.
**inscen-are** [A1] *tr.* (theatr.) to produce, to put on, to stage. **-atore** *m.* scenographer.
**inscritto** *part. adj.* inscribed, registered; *n.m.* inscribed member; *gli inscritti al partito*, party members.
**inscruta·bile** *adj.* inscrutable.
**inscurire** [D2] *tr.* to darken; *rfl.*, *intr.* (*aux.* essere) to grow darker.
**insecchire** [D2] *intr.* (*aux.* essere) to become dry; to wither; *tr.* to dry up, to wither.
**insediare** [A4] *tr.* to install; to induct; *rfl.* to enter upon office, to be installed; to establish oneself; to settle.

**insęgna** *f.* insignia; badge; decoration; coat of arms; signboard; board; standard, ensign; (fig.) attribute, sign.
**insegn-are** [A5 c] *tr.* to teach; to indicate, to point out; *abs.* to be a teacher; *intr.* (*aux.* avere) *-ò a leggere al bambino,* he taught the child to read. **-amęnto** *m.* teaching; education; lesson, precept; *quadri per l'-amento oggettivo,* visual aids. **-ante** *part. adj.* teaching; *n.m., f.* teacher, schoolmaster, schoolmistress; instructor; *-ante universitario,* university lecturer. **-ativo** *adj.* relating to teaching; *metodo -ativo,* teaching method.
**insegu-ire** [D1] *tr.* to follow, to pursue. **-ente** *part. adj.* pursuing; *n.m.* pursuer. **-imęnto** *m.* pursuit, chase.
**insensato** *adj.* senseless, foolish; lifeless.
**insensi·bil-e** *adj.* imperceptible, very slight; insensible, insensitive; apathetic, indifferent. **-ità** *f.* insensibility; insensitiveness.
**insepara·bile** *adj.* inseparable; indivisible.
**insepolto** *adj.* unburied.
**inserire** [D2] *tr.* to insert; to interpolate; *rfl.* to be inserted; to fit in; to get included.
**inserto** *adj.* inserted; included; enclosed; *n.m.* enclosure; dossier.
**inservi·bile** *adj.* useless; unserviceable; *rendere* —, to put out of action.
**inserzione** *f.* insertion; advertisement; announcement.
**insett-o** *m.* insect. **-icida** *m.* insecticide.
**insi·di-a** *f.* snare, trap; ambush; (fig.) deception, deceit; danger. **-are** [A4] *tr.* to lay a trap for; to ensnare, to lie in wait for; *intr.* (*aux.* avere; *prep.* a) to behave treacherously; *-are alla vita di,* to make an attempt on the life of. **-ọso** *adj.* insidious; treacherous; underhand.
**insieme** *adv.* together; at the same time; — *a,* in addition to; — *con,* in company with; *levare d'—,* to separate; *n.m.* whole; *nell'—,* on the whole.
**insign-e** *adj.* notable; remarkable; signal; famous. **-ire** [D2] *tr.* (*prep.* di) to honour; to decorate, to invest (with).
**insignificante** *adj.* meaningless; insignificant, trivial.
**insincer-o** *adj.* insincere, false. **-ità** *f.* lack of sincerity; duplicity.
**insino** *prep.* till; until, as far as; — *a,* even, including.
**insinu-are** [A6] *tr.* to insinuate, to insert gradually; (fig.) to suggest; *rfl.* (*prep.* in) to find one's way (into), to creep (into); (fig.) to curry favour (with). **-ante** *part. adj.* insinuating. **-aziọne** *f.* insinuation.
**insi·pid-o** *adj.* tasteless; insipid; *diventare* —, to lose flavour; **-ęzza** *f.* tastelessness; insipidity.
**insi·st-ere** [C24] *intr.* (*aux.* avere; *prep.* in, sopra, su; before an *infin.* a) to persist, to persevere; to persist (in); to insist (on). **-ente** *part. adj.* insistent; persistent; persevering. **-enza** *f.* insistence; persistence, perseverance; *cedere all -enze,* to yield to pressure.
**in·sito** *adj.* innate, congenital; inherent.
**insociẹvole** *adj.* unsociable.
**inso(d)disfatto** *adj.* unsatisfied; dissatisfied.
**insofferen-te** *adj.* intolerant; impatient, irritable; — *di,* unable to bear. **-za** *f.* intolerance; impatience.
**insoffri·bile** *adj.* unbearable; insufferable.
**insolazione** *f.* exposure to sunshine; sunstroke.
**insolent-e** *adj.* insolent; arrogant; *n.m., f.* insolent person. **-ire** [D2] *intr.* (*aux.* essere) to be insolent; (*aux.* avere; *prep.* contro) to be insolent (to); *tr.* to treat insolently.
**insolenza** *f.* insolence; insolent remark.
**inso·lito** *adj.* unusual; unaccustomed; extraordinary.
**insolu·bil-e** *adj.* insoluble; unsolvable. **-ità** *f.* insolubility.
**insoluto** *adj.* undissolved; unsolved; unpaid; *cambiale insoluta,* dishonoured bill.
**insolven-te** *adj.* insolvent; bankrupt. **-za** *f.* insolvency; bankruptcy.
**insolventi·bile** *adj.* insolvent.
**insọmma** *adv.* in conclusion; in short; in other words; on the whole; *excl.* well!
**insommergi·bile** *adj.* unsinkable; not submersible.
**insonne** *adj.* sleepless; wakeful; vigilant.
**inson·nia** *f.* insomnia; sleeplessness.
**insonnolito** *adj.* sleepy, drowsy.
**insopporta·bile** *adj.* unbearable; intolerable.
**insordire** [D2] *intr.* (*aux.* essere) to grow deaf.
**insọrg-ere** [C5] *intr.* (*aux* essere; *prep.* contro) to rise in revolt; to rebel. **-ente** *part. adj.* insurgent; arising. **-enza** *f.* insurgence, uprising.
**insormonta·bile** *adj.* insurmountable.
**insọrto** *part. adj.* risen, in revolt; *la provincia insorta,* the rebel province; *n.m.* insurgent, rebel.
**insospett-a·bile** *adj.* above suspicion. **-ato** *adj.* unsuspected.
**insospett-ire** [D2] *tr.* to make suspicious; to arouse suspicion in; *rfl., intr.* (*aux.* essere) to become suspicious; *s'-ì della cosa,* he got wind of the matter. **-ito** *part. adj.* suspicious.
**insosteni·bile** *adj.* untenable; unendurable.
**insostitui·bile** *adj.* irreplaceable.
**insozzare** [A1 c] *tr.* to soil, to stain; to sully; to corrupt.
**inspera·bile** *adj.* not to be hoped for; *fortuna* —, unlooked-for good fortune.
**insperato** *adj.* unhoped for; unexpected.
**inspir-are** [A1] *tr.* to breathe in; to inhale; to breathe into. **-atọre** *m.* one who inhales; *adj.* inspiratory. **-aziọne** *f.* inhaling, breathing in.
**insta·bil-e** *adj.* unstable; insecure; variable; inconstant. **-ità** *f.* instability; inconstance.
**install-are** [A1] *tr.* to install; *rfl.* to take a seat; to become installed. **-aziọne** *f.* installation.
**instanca·bile** *adj.* tireless; indefatigable; unwearying.
**instaur-are** [A1 a] *tr.* to restore; to institute; to set up. **-aziọne** *f.* restoration; instituting.
**instill-are** [A1] *tr.* (*prep.* in) to instil (into); to infuse; to inculcate; *rfl.* to become instilled; to penetrate; to permeate. **-aziọne** *f.* instilling; inculcation.
**insù** *adv.* upwards; up; *gli uomini dai venti anni* —, men of twenty and over; *col naso all'* —, with one's nose in the air.
**insubordinat-o** *adj.* insubordinate; refractory; undisciplined. **-ęzza** *f.* rebelliousness.
**insubordinaziọne** *f.* insubordination.
**insuccesso** *m.* failure; (theatr.) flop, frost.
**insudiciare** [A3 s] *tr.* to dirty; to soil; *rfl.* to become soiled; (fig.) to touch pitch.
**insufficien-te** *adj.* insufficient; inadequate; deficient. **-za** *f.* insufficiency; deficiency; incapacity.
**insular-e** *adj.* relating to an island; characteristic of an island; insular. **-ità** *f.* insularity.
**insuls-o** *adj.* tasteless, insipid; witless; dull. **-ag·gine** *f.* silliness; foolish remark; boring conversation.
**insult-are** [A1] *tr.* to insult; to abuse; to attack; to assault. **-ante** *part. adj.* insulting; insolent; offensive.
**insulto** *m.* insult; attack, assault; fit, access, paroxysm.
**insupera·bile** *adj.* insuperable; unsurmountable.
**insuperato** *adj.* unsurpassed; matchless.
**insuperb-ire** [D2] *tr.* to make proud; to turn the head of; *intr.* (*aux.* essere), *rfl.* to be proud; to give oneself airs; *-irsi di,* to take pride in. **-ito** *part. adj.* proud; puffed up.
**insurreziọn-e** *f.* insurrection; rising; revolt. **-ale** *adj.* insurrectionary, insurrectional.

**insussisten-te** *adj.* baseless; non-existent; unreal. **-za** *f.* baselessness; unreality.
**intacc-are** [A2] *tr.* to notch; to cut into; to corrode; to etch; to attack; to impugn; *intr.* (*aux.* avere) to stammer; to hesitate in speech. **-atura** *f.* notch; indentation; damage; injury.
**intac-co** *m.* (*pl.* **-chi**) incision; notch; defect; slur.
**intagliare** [A4] *tr.* to carve; — *all'acqua forte*, to etch; to engrave; to incise.
**inta·glio** *m.* carving; engraving.
**intanare** [A1] *rfl.* to hide; to go to earth.
**intangi·bil-e** *adj.* intangible; untouchable. **-ità** *f.* intangibleness; inviolability.
**intanto** *adv.* meanwhile; in the meantime; but, yet; *conj.* — *che*, while.
**intarl-are** [A1] *intr.* (*aux.* essere) to become worm-eaten. **-ato** *part. adj.* worm-eaten; *dente -ato*, decayed tooth.
**intarmare** [A1] *intr.* (*aux.* essere) to become moth-eaten.
**intarsiare** [A4] *tr.* to inlay; (fig.) to decorate.
**intar·sio** *m.* inlay; *lavoro d'—*, inlaid work.
**intaṣare** [A1] *tr.* to stop up, to choke; to obstruct; to clog; *intr.* (*aux.* essere), *rfl.* to be stopped up; to become stuffed up.
**intascare** [A2] *tr.* to pocket; to receive (payment).
**intatto** *adj.* intact; untouched; unbroken; unimpaired; *puro e* —, unsullied.
**intavol-are** [A1 s] *tr.* to put on the table; to surround with planks; to board up; (fig.) to broach; — *le trattative*, to open negotiations. **-ato** *part. adj.* put on the table; surrounded by planks; broached, begun; *n.m.* wooden partition; wood floor (planks); roof-boarding.
**integer·rimo** *adj.* (superl. of **integro**) strictly honest; of the utmost integrity.
**integral-e** *adj.* entire; complete; unexpurgated; *pane* —, wholemeal bread; *n.m.* (math.) integral. **-mẹnte** *adv.* fully; completely; *pagato -mente*, paid in full.
**integr-are** [A1 s] *tr.* to complete; to make up into a whole; (math.) to integrate; *rfl.* to be completed; to become integrated. **-ativo** *adj.* tending to integrate; *esame -ativo*, entrance examination. **-aziọne** *f.* integration; *corsi d'-azione*, supplementary classes.
**in·tegr-o** *adj.* entire; honest; upright; showing integrity. **-ità** *f.* completeness; wholeness; (fig.) uprightness; integrity.
**intelai-are** [A4] *tr.* to put on a loom; to set up. **-atura** *f.* setting up; framework; trestle; (motor.) chassis.
**intellett-o** *m.* intellect; understanding; intelligence; brain; mind. **-uale** *adj.*, *n.m.* intellectual.
**intelligen-te** *adj.* intelligent; clever; bright. **-za** *f.* intelligence; understanding; ability; mind, intellect.
**intelligi·bile** *adj.* intelligible, comprehensible.
**intemerato** *adj.* unblemished; irreproachable.
**intemperan-te** *adj.* intemperate; excessive. **-za** *f.* intemperance; excess; violence.
**intempe·rie** *f. indecl.* bad weather; inclemency; *pl.* storms.
**intempestivo** *adj.* untimely; unseasonable; inopportune; unexpected.
**intenden-te**[1] *m.* superintendent; bailiff; steward; manager; administrator; inspector. **-za** *f.* superintendence; bailiffship; stewardship; manager's office.
**intendente**[2] *part. adj.* understanding; competent; well-informed; *n.m.,f.* connoisseur; expert.
**inten·d-ere** [C1] *tr.* to intend; to mean; to understand; to grasp mentally, to take in; to hear; to listen to; to see, to conceive, to regard; *intr.* (*aux.* avere; *prep.* a) to be intent (on); to pay heed (to); *rfl.* (*prep.* di) to have a good knowledge (of), to be a good judge (of), to be a connoisseur (in, of); *recip. rfl.* to be in agreement; to come to terms; *-ersela*, to have an understanding; *impers. s'-e che*, it is understood that, it is agreed that; *s'-e!*, of course!, naturally! **-imẹnto** *m.* understanding; intelligence; meaning; purpose; intention; idea; opinion.
**intenerire** [D2] *tr.* to soften; to make tender; (fig.) to move to pity; *rfl.* to grow soft; to become tender; to be moved.
**intens-o** *adj.* intense; vehement; violent; *colore* —, vivid colour. **-ificare** [A2 s] *tr.* to intensify; to make more frequent. **-ità** *f.* intensity; accentuation. **-ivo** *adj.* intensive.
**intentato** *adj.* untried; unattempted; unexplored.
**intento**[1] *adj.* intent; tense; bent (on); attentive.
**intento**[2] *m.* intent; intention; aim; purpose; object.
**intenziọn-e** *f.* intention; purpose; wish. **-ale** *adj.* intentional; premeditated. **-ato** *adj.* intentioned; inclined; disposed; willing.
**inter-** *prep.* inter-; between.
**intercalare**[1] *adj.* inserted; interpolated; *giorno* —, 29 February, Leap-year day.
**intercalare**[2] [A1] *tr.* to insert; to interpolate; to intercalate.
**intercambiale** *adj.* interchangeable.
**interce·dere** [B1] *intr.* (*aux.* avere) to intercede; (of time) to be; to lie between; *tr.* to obtain by intercession.
**intercess-iọne** *f.* intercession; intervention. **-ọre** *m.* intercessor.
**intercettare** [A1] *tr.* to intercept; to seize; to carry off; to cut off; to interrupt.
**intercetto** *adj.* intercepted; stopped; cut.
**intercọrrere** [C5] *intr.* (*aux.* essere) to elapse; to intervene; to come to pass; to exist between.
**interdẹtto** *part.* of **interdire**; *adj.* prohibited; forbidden; *n.m.* interdict.
**interdire** [B10] *tr.* to forbid; to prohibit; to ban.
**interdiziọne** *f.* prohibition; interdiction.
**interess-are** [A1] *tr.* to interest; to concern; to touch; to affect; to apply to; *abs.* to be interesting; *intr.* (*aux.* avere; *prep.* a) to be of importance or relevance (to); *rfl.* (*prep.* a) to take an interest (in); (*prep.* di, per) to interest oneself (on behalf of); (*prep.* di) to care (about), to care (for). **-ante** *part. adj.* interesting; exciting. **-ato** *part. adj.* interested; concerned; selfish; calculating; amused; *n.m.* interested party.
**interesse** *m.* interest; advantage; affair, concern; (finan.) interest.
**interẹzza** *f.* wholeness; entirety.
**interfer-enza** *f.* interference; overlapping. **-ire** [D2] *intr.* (*aux.* avere; *prep.* a) to interfere (in, with).
**interieziọne** *f.* (gramm.) interjection.
**interin-o** *adj.* temporary; *n.m.* locum (tenens). **-ale** *adj.* temporary.
**interiọr-e** *adj.* interior; inner; inside; mental; spiritual; *n.m.* interior, inside; the inner man; mind; heart. **-a** *f.pl.* innards, entrails.
**interli·ne-a** *f.* space between lines. **-are** *adj.* between the lines; interlinear. **-are** [A6] *tr.* to interline; to space.
**interlocutọre** *m.* interlocutor; speaker.
**interloquire** [D2] *intr.* (*aux.* avere) to put in a word; to join in a conversation; (colloq.) to butt in.
**interlu·dio** *m.* interlude, entr'acte.
**interl-unare** *adj.* interlunar. **-u·nio** *m.* interlunar period.
**interme·di-o** *adj.* intermediate, middle; *persona -a*, go-between,

intermediary. -**a·rio** *adj.* intermediary, intermediate; *n.m.* go-between, middle-man; intermediary, mediator

**intermẹttere** [C20c] *tr.* to interrupt, to intermit; to omit; *intr.* (*aux.* essere) (med.) to be intermittent, to become irregular; *rfl.* to intervene; to interfere.

**intermẹẓẓo** *m.* interval; interlude; intermezzo.

**intermina·bile** *adj.* endless, interminable.

**intermissiọne** *f.* cessation, intermission, respite.

**intermitten-te** *adj.* intermittent, fitful. -**za** *f.* intermittence.

**intern-are** [A1] *tr.* to thrust in; to plant; to bury; to imprison; to intern; *rfl.* (*prep.* in) to penetrate, to enter; to dive; (fig.) to become absorbed, to bury oneself. -**amẹnto** *m.* internment; imprisonment; penetration; burying.

**internato** *m.* boarding-school; boarding system; interned person.

**internazionale** *adj.* international; *pr.n.f.* International.

**intern-o** *adj.* internal; interior; indoor; inside, inner; inland; *foro* —, conscience; *nemici -i*, fifth column; *alunno* —, boarder; *medico* —, house physician; *n.m.* inside, interior; soul, mind; *Ministro dell'Interno*, Minister for Home Affairs.

**intẹro** *adj.* whole, entire; intact, unabridged; undamaged; complete, perfect; *n.m.* whole, entirety; total.

**interpellare** [A1] *tr.* to interrupt; to question; to call in, to consult.

**interpol-are** [A1 s] *tr.* to interpolate; to insert. -**aziọne** *f.* interpolation; insertion.

**interpọrre** [B21] *tr.* to interpose, to insert; *rfl.* (*prep.* tra) to intervene (in); to mediate, to cause delay.

**interpret-are** [A1 s] *tr.* to interpret; to explain; to translate. -**aziọne** *f.* interpretation, exposition; (theatr.) performance.

**inter·prete** *m.*, *f.* interpreter; translator; commentor; spokesmen; (mus.) performer; (theatr.) actor.

**interpunziọne** *f.* punctuation.

**interrare** [A1] *tr.* to bury, to inter; to cover with earth; to silt up.

**interrog-are** [A2 s] *tr.* to question, to interrogate; to consult. -**ativo** *adj.* interrogative; *n.m.* problem, mystery. -**aziọne** *f.* questioning, interrogation; question.

**interrọmpere** [C26] *tr.* to interrupt; to discontinue, to suspend; *rfl.* to break off, to stop.

**interrọtto** *part.* of **interrọmpere**; *adj.* interrupted; broken off; discontinued; cut.

**interruttọre** *m.* interrupter; (electr.) switch.

**interruziọne** *f.* interruption; breaking off; (electr.) cut.

**intersecare** [A2] *tr.* to intersect; to cut across.

**interspaziale** *adj.* space; *viaggi interspaziali*, space travel.

**intersti·zio** *m.* interstice; momentary pause.

**intervallo** *m.* interval; space; gap.

**interven-ire** [D17] *intr.* (*aux.* essere) to happen, to come about, to come to pass; (*prep.* a) to be present (at), to attend; to interfere; (*prep.* in) to take part (in). -**uto** *part. adj.* present; attending; *n.m.pl. gl'-uti*, the audience, those present.

**intervento** *m.* presence, attendance; intervention, interference.

**intervist-a** *f.* interview. -**are** [A1] *tr.* to interview.

**intẹsa** *f.* understanding, agreement.

**intẹso** *part.* of **inten·dere**; *adj.* intended; understood; heard, agreed.

**intes·sere** [B1] *tr.* to weave, to entwine.

**intest-are** [A1] *tr.* to head; to inscribe; to assign; *rfl.* to take into one's head; to be obstinate. -**ato** *part. adj.* headed, entitled; obstinate; (leg.) intestate.

**intestino** *adj.* intestine, internal; *n.m.* intestine, gut.

**intiepidire** [D2] *tr.* to cool, to make tepid; to warm; to take the chill off; to abate, to mitigate; *intr.* (*aux.* essere), *rfl.* to cool off.

**intignare** [A5] *intr.* (*aux.* essere), *rfl.* to become moth-eaten; to grow bald.

**intim-are** [A1] *tr.* to order; to enjoin; to notify, to intimate; — *la guerra*, to declare war. -**aziọne** *f.* order; injunction, summons; notification.

**intimidire** [D2] *tr.* to intimidate; to make shy; to frighten.

**in·timo** *adj.* innermost; deepest; intimate; very friendly; *n.m.* close friend.

**intimorire** [D2] *tr.* to frighten; *intr.* (*aux.* essere), *rfl.* to be frightened; to become afraid.

**intin·gere** [C5] *tr.* to dip (into a liquid); to moisten; to soak; *intr.* (*aux.* avere) to have a share in.

**intin·golo** *m.* (cul.) gravy, sauce; ragout; — *di lepre*, jugged hare.

**intinto** *part.* of **intin·gere**; *adj.* soaked, wet; moistened; tainted; *n.m.* gravy, sauce.

**intiriẓẓire** [D2] *tr.* to numb, to benumb; to stiffen; *intr.* (*aux.* essere), *rfl.* to become stiff or numb.

**intisịchire** [D2] *tr.* to make consumptive; to weaken; to impoverish; *intr.* (*aux.* essere), *rfl.* to become consumptive; to grow weak and thin; to pine away.

**intitolare** [A1 s] *tr.* to entitle; to name, to call; to confer a title upon; *rfl.* to be called; to bear the title of.

**intoller-a·bile** *adj.* unbearable; intolerable; insufferable. -**ante** *adj.* intolerant; prejudiced; impatient.

**intonacare** [A2 s] *tr.* to plaster; to smooth; to whitewash; *rfl.* to plaster oneself; to get spattered.

**into·naco** *m.* plaster.

**inton-are** [A1 d] *tr.* to start to sing; to intone; to tune; to match (colours); to tone down; *rfl.* (*prep.* con) to be in tune (with); to be in harmony (with). -**aziọne** *f.* intoning; intonation; tuning; prelude, beginning.

**intontire** [D2] *tr.* to stun; to amaze; *rfl.*, *intr.* (*aux.* essere) to be stunned; to be astonished.

**intoppare** [A1] *tr.* to bump into; to stumble upon; *intr.* (*aux.* essere, avere), *rfl.* (*prep.* in) to bump (into, against); to stumble.

**intoppo** *m.* obstacle, stumbling-block; hindrance; stumble.

**intorbidare** [A1 s] *tr.* to trouble; to make turbid, to make muddy; to confuse; *intr.* (*aux.* essere), *rfl.* to become turbid; to become muddy; to cloud over.

**intormentire** [D2] *tr.* to benumb.

**intorniare** [A4 c] *tr.* to surround; to walk or travel round.

**intọrno** *adv.* around; on every side; *prep.* (*foll.* by 'a') around; round; about.

**intorpidire** [D2] *tr.* to enervate; to make inert; *rfl.*, *intr.* (*aux.* essere) to become inert; to grow sluggish.

**intossicare** [A2 s] *tr.* to poison; *rfl.* to take poison; to poison oneself.

**intra**[1] *prep.* among; between.

**intra-**[2] *pref.* among; inside; intra-.

**intraduci·bile** *adj.* untranslatable.

**intralasciare** [A4] *tr.* to leave undone; to omit, to neglect.

**intralciare** [A4] *tr.* to entangle; to impede; to hamper; *rfl.* to become entangled, involved.

**intral·cio** *m.* entanglement, hindrance, impediment; obstacle.

**intrallazzo** *m.* racket, black-marketeering.

**intramẹttere** [C20 c] *tr.* to interpose; to interrupt; *rfl.* to intervene; to interfere.

**intrameẓẓare** [A1] *tr.* to interpose; to alternate.

**intransigen-te** *adj.* intransigent; obstinate; intolerant; strict; severe. -**za** *f.* intransigence.

**intrappolare** [A1 s] *tr.* to entrap, to ensnare.

**intrapren·d-ere** [C1] *tr.* to undertake; to enter upon; to

engage in. **-ente** *part. adj.* enterprising; amorous, gallant; risky. **-enza** *f.* enterprise; boldness; initiative. **-itọre** *m.* contractor; impresario; undertaker.

**intratta·bile** *adj.* unreasonable; rude; intractable.

**intrattenẹre** [B32] *tr.* to entertain; to amuse; to hold in conversation; *rfl.* to stay (talking), to linger, to dwell; *recip. rfl.* to converse.

**intravedẹre** [B35] *tr.* to catch a glimpse of; to see indistinctly; to foresee.

**intraversare** [A1] *tr.* to cross; to cross-plough; (dressm.) to cut on the bias.

**intravvenire** [D17] *intr.* (*aux.* essere) to be present; to take part; to happen.

**intrecciare** [A3c] *tr.* to plait, to braid; to twist; to weave; to entwine; to interlace; — *le gambe*, to cross one's legs; *rfl.* to be twisted, plaited together; to intermingle.

**intrẹccio** *m.* plait; knot; interlacing; (fig.) plot.

**intre·pid-o** *adj.* intrepid, fearless; bold, brazen. **-ẹzza** *f.*

**intricare** [A2] *tr.* to entangle; *rfl.* to get entangled, to become involved.

**intri·dere** [C3] *tr.* to soak; to make into a paste; to knead; to stain.

**intrig-are** [A2] *tr.* to entangle, to tangle; *intr.* (*aux.* avere) to intrigue, to scheme. **-ante** *part. adj.* intriguing, meddling; *n.m.* intriguer, meddler.

**intri-go** *m.* (*pl.* **-ghi**) intrigue, plot; plotting; entanglement; difficult position, fix.

**intrin·seco** *adj.* intrinsic, internal; intimate; essential; *adv. phr. nell'*—, essentially.

**intrịso** *part.* of **intri·dere**; *adj.* soaked, moistened; mixed; *n.m.* paste; mixture, mash; mortar; plaster.

**intristire** [D2] *intr.* (*aux.* essere) to languish; to droop; to decay; (of plants) not to thrive; to be stunted.

**introdurre** [B2] *tr.* to introduce; to put in, to insert; to show in; to let in; *rfl.* (*prep.* in) to get (into); to penetrate (into).

**introdutt-ivo** *adj.* introductory. **-ọre** *m.* introducer; footman announcing guests.

**introduziọne** *f.* introduction; commencement; preamble.

**introitare** [A10] *tr.* (admin.) to encash; to enter.

**intro·ito** *m.* entrance; introit; (admin.) cash received; entry; takings.

**intromettere** [C20c] *tr.* to insert; to introduce; *rfl.* (*prep.* in) to intervene; to interfere (in).

**intromissiọne** *f.* intervention; interference.

**intron-are** [A1] *tr.* to stun with noise; to deafen. **-amẹnto** *m.* thunderous noise; deafening.

**intronizzare** [A1] *tr.* to enthrone.

**introspeziọne** *f.* introspection.

**introva·bile** *adj.* not to be found; out of currency; off the market.

**intru·dere** [C3] *tr.* to insert; *rfl.* to intrude.

**intru·glio** *m.*(fig.) shady business; intrigue.

**intruppare** [A1] *rfl.* (*prep.* con) to join company (with); *recip. rfl.* to flock together.

**intrusiọne** *f.* intrusion.

**intrụso** *part.* of **intru·dere**; *adj.* inserted; *n.m.* intruder; interloper.

**intu-ire** [D2] *tr.* to perceive by intuition; to guess. **-itivo** *adj.* intuitive; *facolta -itiva*, intuition. **-iziọne** *f.* intuition; perception.

**intu·ito** *m.* intuition.

**inturgidire** [D2s] *intr.* (*aux.* essere) to swell up; to become turgid.

**inuman-o** *adj.* inhuman, brutal; inhumane; barbarous. **-ità** *f.* inhumanity.

**inumare** [A1] *tr.* to inter, to bury.

**inumidire** [D2] *tr.* to damp; to moisten.

**inu·til-e** *adj.* useless; idle; unnecessary. **-izzare** [A1] *tr.* to render useless; to put out of action.

**inva·dere** [C3] *tr.* to invade; to encroach upon.

**invaghire** [D2] *tr.* to charm, to attract; *rfl.* (*prep.* di) to become fond (of); to fall in love (with).

**invalẹre** [B34] *intr.* (*aux.* essere) to be established, to be introduced, to prevail, to come into force.

**inva·lido** *adj.* infirm, invalid, disabled; (leg.) invalid.

**invalso** *part.* of **invalẹre**; *adj.* established, prevailing.

**invanire** (D2) tr. to make vain, to turn the head of; *intr.* (*aux.* essere), *rfl.* to become vain; to melt away.

**invano** *adv.* in vain, to no purpose; uselessly.

**invaria·bile** *adj.* invariable; constant.

**invariato** *adj.* unchanged, constant.

**invasare**[1] [A1] *tr.* to obsess; (of a devil) to possess; *rfl.* to be obsessed, to be possessed.

**invasare**[2] [A1] *tr.* to pot, to put into pots or jars.

**invas-iọne** *f.* invasion; flooding. **-ọre** *m.* invader; *adj.* invading; (of water) flooding.

**invecchi-are** [A4] *intr.* (*aux.* essere) to grow old; to age; *tr.* to make old, to age; to make (one) look old. **-ato** *part. adj.* grown old (or older), obsolete.

**invẹce** *adv.* on the other hand; on the contrary; but; *prep. phr.* — *di*, instead of.

**inveire** [D2] *intr.* (*aux.* avere; *prep.* contro) to inveigh (against), to rail (at).

**invelenire** [D2] *tr.* to poison, to envenom, to embitter; *intr.* (*aux.* avere), *rfl.* to become embittered; to grow venomous.

**invendi·bile** *adj.* unsaleable.

**invendicato** *adj.* unavenged; unpunished.

**invenduto** *adj.* unsold; *roba invenduta*, remnants.

**inventare** [A1] *tr.* to invent; to find out; to imagine; to fabricate; to make up.

**inventa·rio** *m.* inventory; catalogue; (fig.) monotonous account.

**inventiv-a** *f.* inventiveness; imagination; originality **-o** *adj.* inventive; fictitious

**inventọre** *m.* inventor; discoverer; romancer; story-teller.

**invenziọne** *f.* invention; contrivance, fabrication, lie; fiction.

**inverdire** [D2] *intr.* (*aux.* essere) to turn green, to become green; *tr.* to make green.

**inverecọnd-ia** *f.* immodesty; impudence. **-o** *adj.* immodest; bold; impudent.

**inverniciare** [A3] *tr.* to varnish; to paint; to polish.

**invern-o** *m.* winter. **-ale** *adj.* wintry; occurring in the winter; *vestiti -ali*, winter clothes.

**invero** *adv.* indeed, in fact.

**inverosimiglianza** *f.* unlikelihood, improbability.

**inverosi·mile** *adj.* unlikely, improbable; strange.

**inversiọne** *f.* inversion; reversal.

**inverso** *adj.* inverse; contrary; opposite; *adv. phr. all'inversa*, badly, wrong; *prep.* towards.

**invertire** [D1] *tr.* to invert; to reverse; to transpose.

**invescare** [A2] *tr.* to spread with bird-lime; to lure.

**investig-are** [A2s] *tr.* to investigate; to inquire into. **-atọre** *m.* investigator, detective.

**invest-ire** [D1] *tr.* to collide with, to come into collision with; to run down; to beset; to lay siege to; (finan.) to invest. **-imẹnto** *m.* collision, accident; (finan.) investment; (mil.) sudden attack; besieging. **-itura** *f.* investiture.

**invetr-iare** [A4] *tr.* to glaze; to make like glass. **-iata** *f.* window-pane; glass-partition.

**invettiv-a** *f.* invective. **-o** *adj.* invective, abusive.

**invi-are** [A4] *tr.* to send, to dispatch; to put on the right road. **-ato** *part. adj.* sent; *n.m.* envoy; delegate.

**invi·di-a** *f.* envy; *da fare* —, enviable. **-a·bile** *adj.* enviable, desirable. **-are** [A4] *tr.* to envy;

to take away, to deprive of. **-ọso** *adj.* envious; invidious.

**invigilare** [A1 s] *intr.* (*aux.* avere; *prep.* a) to watch (over); to be attentive (to); *tr.* to supervise, to invigilate.

**invigliacchire** [D2] *intr.* (*aux.* essere), *rfl.* to become inert; to grow cowardly.

**invigorire** [D2] *tr.* to strengthen, to invigorate; *intr.* (*aux.* essere), *rfl.* to gain strength; to take heart.

**invilire** [D2] *tr.* to debase; to degrade; to lower; to make cowardly; *intr.* (*aux.* essere), *rfl.* to be debased; to grow cowardly; to become contemptible; to lose value.

**invilupp-are** [A1] *tr.* to wrap up; to envelop; to surround; *rfl.* to wrap oneself up; to become entangled. **-o** *m.* tangle; confusion; covering, wrapping.

**invinci·bile** *adj.* invincible, unconquerable.

**inv-i·o** *m.* (*pl.* **-i·i**) dispatch, forwarding; shipment; sending; posting.

**inviolato** *adj.* inviolate; intact.

**invischiare** [A4] *tr.* to snare with bird-lime; to entangle, to entice; *rfl.* to be ensnared.

**invisi·bile** *adj.* invisible; unseen; imperceptible.

**invit-are**[1] [A1] *tr.* to invite; to ask; to call, to convoke; to provoke, to challenge. **-ato** *part. adj.* invited; called, convoked; *n.m.* guest; beneficiary.

**invitare**[2] [A1] *tr.* to screw in; to screw up; to screw on.

**invito** *m.* invitation; exhortation; hint.

**invitto** *adj.* unconquered; invincible, indomitable.

**invoc-are** [A2] *tr.* to invoke; to call upon; to call to witness; to appeal to. **-aziọne** *f.* invocation.

**invogliare** [A4] *tr.* to induce; to lure; to arouse a wish or desire in; *rfl.* (*prep.* di) to develop a desire (for).

**invo·glio** *m.* package, parcel; bundle; wrapping.

**involare**[1] [A1] *tr.* (poet.) to steal away; to ravish; *rfl.* to disappear; to flee.

**involare**[2] [A1] *intr.* (*aux.* essere) to take off (of aircraft).

**invol·gere** [C5] *tr.* to wrap up, to pack; to envelop; (fig.) to involve, to implicate.

**involonta·rio** *adj.* involuntary.

**involtare** [A1] *tr.* to wrap up; to pack up.

**involto** *part.* of **invol·gere**; *adj.* twisted; enveloped; involved; *n.m.* package, parcel; bundle; cover; wrapping-paper.

**invo·lucro** *m.* covering; pod; sheath; casing.

**involuto** *adj.* involved, intricate.

**involuziọne** *f.* involution; complication.

**invulnera·bile** *adj.* invulnerable, beyond reproach.

**inzaccherare** [A1 s] *tr.* to splash with mud; to bespatter.

**inzeppare** [A1] *tr.* to fix with a wedge; to cram.

**inzolfare** [A1 c] *tr.* to spray, to fumigate with sulphur.

**inzuccherare** [A1 s] *tr.* to sugar; to add sugar to; (fig.) to sweeten, to flatter.

**inzuppare** [A1] *tr.* to soak; to drench; to dip; to immerse; *rfl.* to get wet, soaked, drenched.

**i·o** *pers. prn. 1st sing. nom.* I; *sono* —, it is I, it's me; *da quel giorno non sono stato più* —, since that day I have not been myself; *n.m.* ego; the self.

**io·dio** *m.* iodine.

**iota** *m. indecl.* iota, jot.

**iper-** *prefix.* hyper-.

**iper·bole** *f.* hyperbole; exaggeration.

**iperbo·lico** *adj.* hyperbolical; exaggerated; excessive.

**ipn-ọsi** *f. indecl.* hypnosis. **-o·tico** *adj.* somniferous; hypnotic; *n.m.* sedative; tranquillizer. **-otiẓẓare** [A1] *tr.* to hypnotize.

**ipocondr-i·a** *f.* hypochondria. **-i·aco** *adj. n.m.* hypochondriac.

**ipocriṣi·a** *f.* hypocrisy; insincerity.

**ipo·crit-a** *m., f.* hypocrite. **-o** *adj.* hypocritical.

**ipotec-a** *f.* mortgage; *mettere in* —, to pawn. **-are** [A2] *tr.* to mortgage.

**ipo·teṣi** *f. indecl.* hypothesis; supposition.

**ipote·tico** *adj.* hypothetical; conditional.

**ip·pic-a** *f.* horsemastership; horse-racing. **-o** *adj.* of or concerning horses; *concorso -o*, horse-show.

**ippocastano** *m.* horse-chestnut.

**Ippo·crate** *pr.n.m.* Hippocrates.

**Ippocrene** *pr.n.f.* (myth.) Hippocrene.

**ippo·dromo** *m.* hippodrome; race-course.

**Ippo·lit-a** *pr.n.f.* Hippolyta. **-o** *pr.n.m.* Hippolytus.

**ippopo·tamo** *m.* hippopotamus.

**ip·silon** *m. indecl.* the letter y.

**ira** *f.* anger, wrath, rage, fury.

**iracọnd-ia** *f.* wrath, anger; wrathful deed or word. **-o** *adj.* wrathful, choleric, quick to anger.

**irasci·bil-e** *adj.* irascible; irritable; hot-tempered. **-ità** *f.* irascibility.

**irato** *adj.* irate.

**ire** (*def.*) *intr.* (*aux.* essere) (poet.) to go.

**i·rid-e** *f.* iris; rainbow. **-ato** *adj.* iridescent; coloured like the rainbow.

**I·ride** *pr.n.f.* Iris.

**Irlanda** *pr.n.f.* (geog.) Ireland; (hist.) *Stato Libero d'*—, Irish Free State.

**irlandẹse** *adj.* Irish; *n.m.* Irishman; Irish language; *f.* Irish woman; *la Repubblica irlandese*, The Republic of Ireland.

**ir-oni·a** *f.* irony. **-o·nico** *adj.* ironic(al).

**irọso** *adj.* wrathful, prone to anger.

**irradiare** [A4] *tr.* to light (up), to shed light upon, to irradiate; to illumine; *intr.* (*aux.* avere) to radiate (light), to shine out.

**irraggiare** [A3] *tr.* (fig.) to irradiate, to illumine, to shine upon.

**irraggiungi·bile** *adj.* unattainable, out of reach.

**irragionẹvol-e** *adj.* irrational; unreasonable; absurd. **-ẹzza** *f.* irrationality; unreasonableness.

**irrazionale** *adj.* irrational; illogical; absurd; *numero* —, irrational number, surd.

**irreal-e** *adj.* unreal. **-tà** *f.* unreality.

**irrecupera·bile** *adj.* irrecoverable; irretrievable; lost.

**irrecuṣa·bile** *adj.* undeniable; irrefutable.

**irredent-o** *adj.* unredeemed; not liberated. **-iṣmo** *m.* (pol.) Irredentism.

**irredimi·bile** *adj.* irredeemable.

**irrefraga·bile** *adj.* irrefutable, indisputable.

**irrefuta·bile** *adj.* irrefutable, incontrovertible, incontestable.

**irregolar-e** *adj.* irregular; unusual; against the rule; abnormal. **-ità** *f.* irregularity; abnormality.

**irremovi·bile** *adj.* irremovable; immovable; unshakeable.

**irrepara·bile** *adj.* irreparable; without remedy.

**irreperi·bile** *adj.* not to be found.

**irreprensi·bile** *adj.* irreproachable, blameless.

**irrepugna·bile** *adj.* irrefutable, incontestable.

**irrequiet-o** *adj.* restless. **-ẹzza** *f.* restlessness.

**irresisti·bile** *adj.* irresistible.

**irresolut-o** *adj.* irresolute, undecided, uncertain; unsolved. **-ẹzza** *f.* uncertainty, indecision; perplexity.

**irresponsa·bil-e** *adj.* irresponsible; immune. **-ità** *f.* immunity.

**irrestringi·bile** *adj.* unshrinkable.

**irretire** [D2] *tr.* to net, to catch in a net; (fig.) to beguile; to entangle.

**irriconosci·bile** *adj.* unrecognizable.

**irriduci·bile** *adj.* irreducible; *volontà* —, unshakeable will.

**irrifless-iọne** *f.* thoughtlessness. **-ivo** *adj.* thoughtless, inconsiderate.

**irrig-are** [A2] *tr.* to irrigate; to water; (fig.) to flood, to bathe. **-ato** *part. adj.* irrigated; lined; furrowed. **-aziọne** *f.* irrigation.

**irrigid-ire** [D2] *intr.* (*aux.* essere)

to grow stiff, numb or rigid; to stiffen; to become hard-hearted. **-ito** *part. adj.* stiff; hardened; hard-hearted.
**irriguardoso** *adj.* disrespectful; irreverent.
**irri·guo** *adj.* well-watered.
**irrilevante** *adj.* unimportant.
**irremedia·bile** *adj.* irremediable, irreparable; incurable.
**irriṣ-ione** *f.* derision, mockery. **-o·rio** *adj.* (*m.pl.* **-o·rii**) derisory; paltry, laughable.
**irrit-are** [A1] *tr.* to irritate; to provoke, to inflame; to excite. **-azione** *f.* irritation; provocation; anger.
**irriveren-te** *adj.* irreverent; disrespectful. **-za** *f.* irreverence; insolence; disrespect.
**irrompere** [C26] *intr.* (*aux.* essere; *prep.* in) to break (into); to rush (into); to flood (into, over); *abs.* to break all bounds; to flood, to surge.
**irrorare** [A1] *tr.* to bedew, to sprinkle; (agric.) to spray.
**irruente** *adj.* impetuous; rash; violent; surging.
**irrugginire** [D2] *intr.* (*aux.* essere), *rfl.* to rust; (fig.) to get rusty; *tr.* to rust, to make rusty.
**irruvidire** [D2] *tr.* to roughen; *intr.* (*aux.* essere), *rfl.* to become rough.
**irruzione** *f.* breaking in, irruption; invasion.
**irsuto** *adj.* shaggy, hairy, hirsute; rough.
**irto** *adj.* bristling; shaggy; thorny.
**Isabella** *pr.n.f.* Isabel; Isabella.
**Isacco** *pr.n.m.* Isaac.
**Isa·ia** *pr.n.m.* Isaiah.
**Isara** *pr.n.f.* (geog.) Isère.
**Iscri·vere** [C12] *tr.* to register; to inscribe; to enter, to record; *rfl.* to register, to enter, to put one's name down.
**iscrizione** *f.* inscription; entry; *chiedere l'—*, to apply for membership.
**Iside** *pr.n.f.* (myth.) Isis.
**Iṣlam** *pr.n.m.* Islam. **-ita** *m.* Muslim; *adj.* Islamic.
**Iṣlanda** *pr.n.f.* (geog.) Iceland.
**iṣlandese** *adj.* Icelandic; *n.m.* Icelander; Icelandic language.
**Iṣmaele** *pr.n.m.* (bibl.) Ishmael.
**iṣo-** prefix, used in many scientific terms, signifying equality.
**isobara** *f.* (meteor.; geog.) isobar.
**i·ṣol-a** *f.* island, isle; *le -e britanniche*, the British Isles. **-ano** *adj.* inhabiting an island; insular; *n.m.* islander.
**iṣol-are** [A1 s] *tr.* to isolate; to separate; to insulate; *rfl.* to live apart, to shun society. **-ato** *part adj.* isolated; *n.m.* block of flats. **-atore** *m.* isolator; (electr.) insulator.
**isome·trico** *adj.* (geom.) isometric.
**iṣo·scele** *adj.* (geom.) isosceles.
**isoterma** *f.* (phys.; meteor.) isotherm.
**isotopo** *m.* isotope.
**isp-a·nico** *adj.* Spanish; of Spain. **-ano** *adj.* Hispanic; *-ano americano*, Spanish American.
**ispet-tore** *m.* inspector. **-trice** *f.* inspectress.
**ispezion-e** *f.* inspection; examination. **-are** [A1 c] *tr.* to inspect.
**i·spido** *adj.* bristling; hairy; shaggy; (fig.) rude.
**ispir-are** [A1] *tr.* (*prep.* a) to inspire (with); to breathe into; (fig.) to inspire, to arouse, to instil, to suggest. **-ato** *part. adj.* inspired; *non bene -ato*, ill-advised. **-azione** *f.* inspiration; breathing; inspired idea.
**Iṣrael-e** *pr.n.m.* Israel, Jacob, Hebrews. **-ita** *adj.* Israelite, Hebrew, Jewish; *n.m.* Israelite, Jew.
**issare** [A1] *tr.* to hoist.
**istanta·ne-o** *adj.* instantaneous. **-a** *f.* snapshot.
**istante** *adj.* imminent; pressing; urgent; insistent; *n.m.* instant, moment.
**istanza** *f.* importunity; entreaty; application, petition, request.
**iste·rico** *adj.* hysterical.
**isterilire** [D2] *tr.* to make barren; to dry up, to check.
**isteriṣmo** *m.* hysteria.
**istigare** [A2] *tr.* to instigate.
**istinto** *m.* instinct; *per —*, instinctively; inspiration, genius.
**istituire** [D2] *tr.* to institute, to found, to establish; to initiate; to nominate.
**istitut-o** *m.* institute; *— di magistero superiore*, teachers' training college; institution; constitution. **-ore** *m.* founder; author; schoolmaster; tutor; instructor. **-rice** *f.* schoolmistress; governess.
**istituzion-e** *f.* institution; teaching, education. **-ale** *adj.* institutional.
**i·stmo** *m.* isthmus.
**istoriografi·a** *f.* historiography.
**istradare** [A1] *tr.* to put on the road, to put in the way; to direct.
**i·strice** *m., f.* porcupine.
**istrione** *m.* (derog.) actor; clown, buffoon.
**istru-ire** [D2] *tr.* to teach, to instruct; to educate; to advise. **-ito** *part. adj.* well educated; well informed; trained; broken in.
**istrument-o** *m.* instrument; tool; (leg.) deed. **-are** [A1 c] *tr.* (mus.) to orchestrate.
**istrutt-o** *adj.* well-informed. **-ore** *m.* teacher, instructor.
**istruzione** *f.* education; teaching, instruction; *pl.* instructions; detailed orders.
**istupidire** [D2] *tr.* to make stupid; to stupefy; to stun; *intr.* (*aux.* essere), *rfl.* to grow stupid, to become dull.
**I·taca** *pr.n.f.* (geog.) Ithaca.
**Ita·lia** *pr.n.f.* (geog.) Italy.
**italian-o** *adj.* Italian; *n.m. un Italiano*, an Italian; Italian language, Italian. **-a** *f.* Italian woman. **-ità** *f.* Italian character; Italian sentiments; Italian nationality.
**ita·lico** *adj.* Italic; (typ.) italic.
**i·talo** *adj.* (poet.) Italian; (in compounds) *italo-greco*, Graeco-Italian; *italo-britannico*, British Italian.
**iter-are** [A1 s] *tr.* to repeat. **-azione** *f.* iteration; repetition.
**itinera·rio** *m.* itinerary, route.
**ito** *part.* See **ire.**
**it·tico** *adj.* relating to or concerning fish.
**itti-ocolla** *f.* fish-glue, isinglass. **-ologi·a** *f.* ichthyology.
**Iugoṣla·via** *pr.n.f.* (geog.) Jugo-Slavia.
**Iugoṣlavo** *adj., n.m.* Jugo-Slav.
**iuta** *f.* jute.
**Iutland** *pr.n.m.* (geog.) Jutland.
**ivi** *adv.* there; (of time) then; *— a poco tempo*, shortly afterwards.

**J** *m., f. i lungo, i lunga,* the letter J.; used only in words of foreign origin.
**Ja·copo** *pr.n.m.* James.
**jazz** *m. indecl.* jazz.
**jolly** *m. indecl.* (cards) joker.
**judò** *m. indecl.* judo.
**juta** *f.* (text.) jute.
**Juven·tus** *pr.n.f.* name of a Turin football club.

**K** *m., f.* (pron. 'cappa') the letter K.
**kantiano** *adj.* (philos.) Kantian.
**kapoc** *m. indecl.* kapok.
**karakiri** *m. indecl.* hara-kiri.
**kepleriano** *adj.* (hist.) of Kepler.
**kimono** *m. indecl.* kimono.
**kla·xon** *m. indecl.* (motor.) horn.
**knut** *m. indecl.* knout.
**kodak** *m. indecl.* Kodak; camera.
**kopeck** *m. indecl.* copeck.
**kummel** *m. indecl.* kummel.

**L** *m.*, *f.* (pron. '**elle**') the letter L, the consonant L.

**la**[1] *def. art. f. sing.* (*pl.* **le**) the; *contr.* with *preps.* **di, a, da, in, su** to form **della, alla, dalla, nella, sulla**; with *prep.* **con** it does not usually form a compound in modern Italian; used untranslatably with proper nouns, e.g. *la Maria*, Mary; *la Bianchi*, Mrs Bianchi, Miss Bianchi (*cf.* **il**)

**la**[2] *pers. prn. f. 3rd sing. acc.* her; — *conosco*, I know her; it; *ho qui la lettera, — leggerò*, I have the letter here, I'll read it.

**La**[3] *pers. prn. acc.* (polite form of address) you; *La vedremo domani*, we shall see you tomorrow.

**la**[4] *impers. prn.* it; things in general; — *va male*, things are bad.

**la**[5] *impers. conj. prn.* it; *smettila!*, stop it; *darsela a gambe*, to take to one's heels; *prendersela*, to take offence, to take it to heart.

**la**[6] *m.* (mus.) lah, the note A; the key of A; *dare il* —, to give the A; (fig.) to set the tone.

**là** *adv.* there; *chi va —?*, who goes there?; about; *di* —, over there; *di — delle Alpi*, beyond the Alps; *più in* —, further on; *in — con gli anni*, well on in years; *excl. alto là!*, halt!; *va —!*, get on with you!

**labbr-o** *m.* (*pl. f.* **-a**) lip; *leccarsi le -a*, to lick one's lips; mouth; — *leporino*, hare-lip; (*pl. m.* **-i**) rim; brim; border; edge.

**labiale** *adj.* labial; (mus.) *canna* —, flue-pipe (of organ).

**la·bile** *adj.* fleeting, ephemeral; transient, unsteady.

**labirinto** *m.* labyrinth; maze.

**laborato·rio** *m.* laboratory; workshop; workroom.

**laborioso** *adj.* laborious; hard-working; industrious; *pasto* —, heavy, indigestible meal.

**labur-ismo** *m.* (pol.) Labour, Labour politics; Labour policy. **-ista** *adj.* (pol.) Labour; *n.m., f.* member of the Labour Party.

**lacc-a** *f.* lacquer; lac; shellac; — *nera*, black japan. **-are** [A2] *tr.* to lacquer; to japan.

**lac·c-io** *m.* noose; slip knot; thong, lace; snare, gin, trap; ambush; *-i delle scarpe*, shoelaces. **-ia·ia** *f.* lassoo.

**lacer-are** [A1s] *tr.* to tear; to rend; to lacerate, to wound; to pierce; to waste, to squander; to slander. **-atore** *m.* lacerator; *adj.* wounding; (of sound) piercing. **-azione** *f.* rending, tearing; (fig.) distress, hurt.

**la·cero** *adj.* torn; rent; in rags and tatters.

**la·crim-a** *f.* tear; drop, drip. **-a·bile** *adj.* pitiful, pathetic. **-ante** *part. adj.* weeping; *n.m., f.* weeping person. **-are** [A1s] *intr.* (*aux.* avere) to shed tears, to weep; *tr.* to mourn. **-evole** *adj.* pitiful, pathetic; tearful. **-o·geno** *adj.* lachrimatory; *gas -ogeno*, tear gas. **-oso** *adj.* tearful; lachrymose; weeping; pitiful.

**lacuna** *f.* gap; hiatus; blank; lacuna.

**lacustre** *adj.* lake-side; lake-dwelling; lacustrine.

**laddove** *conj.* while; whilst; whereas; *rel. adv.* there where, in circumstances which.

**ladino** *adj.* (philol.) Ladin; *n.m.* Ladin.

**ladr-o** *m.* thief; robber; — *di strada*, pickpocket, bag-snatcher; — *di casa*, burglar; *adj.* thieving, thievish; dishonest. **-esco** *adj.* (*m.pl.* **-eschi**) thieving; typical of a thief. **-one** *m.* thief; assassin; highwayman. **-onesco** (*m.pl.* **-oneschi**) *adj.* thieving, thievish.

**laggiù** *adv.* down there; there below; down yonder; yonder.

**lagn-are** [A5] *rfl.* (*prep.* di) to complain; to grumble (about). **-anza** *f.* complaint; lament. **-o** *m.* lament, plaint. **-oso** *adj.* complaining.

**la-go** *m.* (*pl.* **-ghi**) lake; mere; flood. **-ghetto** *m. dim.* pond. **-ghista** *m.* lake-dweller; (liter.) Lake poet, painter; (lit. hist.) lake poet.

**lagun-a** *f.* lagoon. **-are** *adj.* pertaining to lagoon.

**la·i** *m. indecl.* (prosod.) lay; (poet.) lamentations.

**la·ic-o** *adj.* lay; *frate* —, lay brother; secular. **-ato** *m.* laity.

**la·id-o** *adj.* foul; loathsome, repugnant; filthy; obscene. **-ezza** *f.* foulness; filth, obscenity.

**lama** *f.* blade; steel; cutting edge.

**lambicc-are** [A2] *tr.* to distil; *rfl.* (*dat.* of *prn.* 'si') *-arsi il cervello*, to rack one's brains. **-ato** *part. adj.* distilled; (fig.) strained, far-fetched; affected.

**lambic-co** *m.* (*pl.* **-chi**) (chem.) retort; alembic.

**lamb-ire** [D2] *tr.* to lap; to lap up; to lick, to graze lightly; to skim over. **-ente** *part. adj.* lapping; grazing, glancing; *fuoco -ente*, lambent fire, will o' the wisp.

**lament-are** [A1c] *rfl.* to lament, to complain; to moan; *-arsi con*, to reproach; *tr.* to bewail, to mourn; to deplore, to regret. **-azione** *f.* lamentation; reproach. **-evole** *adj.* lamenting; complaining; lamentable.

**lament-o** *m.* lament; complaint; plaint; cry of pain; reproof, reproach, remonstrance. **-oso** *adj.* complaining; doleful, mournful.

**lamiera** *f.* sheet metal; — *ondulata*, corrugated sheet-iron.

**la·min-a** *f.* thin plate; lamina; thin sheet, thin layer. **-are** [A1s] *tr.* to roll (metal); to laminate. **-atoio** *m.* rolling-mill.

**lam·pad-a** *f.* lamp; oil-lamp; (fig.) light; — *ad arco*, arc-lamp; — *di sicurezza*, safety-lamp; — *chiusa*, hurricane lamp. **-a·rio** *m.* chandelier; lamp stand.

**lampante** *adj.* shining, brilliant; clear; evident; lucid; limpid, transparent; *n.m.* new coin.

**lampeggiare** [A3c] *intr.* (*aux.* avere) to flash; to gleam; to glisten; *impers.* to flash lightning, to lighten.

**lampeggi-o** *m.* lightning; sheet lightning; flash of lightning. **-are** [A3c] *intr.* (*aux.* avere) to flash; to gleam; to glisten; *impers.* to flash lightning, to lighten.

**lampegg-ìo** *m.* (*pl.* **-ìi**) continual flashing; flashes; coruscation.

**lampion-e** *m.* street lamp; lamp-post. **-cino** *m. dim.* dairy lamp; paper lantern.

**lampo** *m.* flash; lightning; gleam; *un — di genio*, a stroke of genius; *chiusura* —, zip fastener; *guerra* —, blitzkrieg.

**lampone** *m.* (bot.) raspberry.

**lana** *f.* wool; — *pettinata*, worsted; (joc.) rascal, scamp.

**lancetta** *f.* lancet; hand, pointer, needle.

**lan·ci-a**[1] *f.* lance; spear; javelin; dart; nozzle of a hosepipe. **-ere** *m.* lancer.

**lan·cia**[2] *f.* ship's boat; launch (sail or oars); — *a motore*, motorboat; — *di salvataggio*, lifeboat.

**lanci-are** [A3] *tr.* to throw; to fling; to hurl; to shy; to toss; to pitch; to drop (bombs); to launch; to initiate; *rfl.* to hurl oneself; to fling oneself. **-asiluri** *m. indecl.* torpedo tube.

**lancinante** *adj.* (of pain) stabbing, piercing, shooting; lancinating.

**lan·cio** *m.* fling; throw; launching.

**landa** *f.* sandy waste; heath, moor; prairie.

**lan·guido** *adj.* languid; languishing; weak, drooping.

**langu-ire** [D2] *intr.* (*aux.* avere) to languish. **-ente** *part. adj.* languishing; weak, faint; (of business) slow, quiet.

**languore** *m.* languor; listlessness; weakness, faintness.

**lan-iero** *adj.* pertaining to wool. **-ifi·cio** *m.* wool mill; wool manufacture. **-olina** *f.* lanoline, wool grease. **-oso** *adj.* woolly; similar to wool.

**lanterna** *f.* lantern, lamp; hurricane lamp.

**lan-u·gine** *f.* down; downy beard. **-uginoso** *adj.* downy. **-uto** *adj.* woolly, covered with wool; *n.m.* woolly animal.

**lanzo** *m.* (mil. hist.) pikeman.

**Laocoọnte** *pr.n.m.* (myth.) Laocoon.
**laọnde** *adv.* therefore; wherefore; there, thence; where, whence.
**lapicida** *m.* stone-mason.
**la·pid-e** *f.* headstone, memorial stone, memorial tablet **-are** [A1 s] to stone. **-a·rio** *adj.* lapidary.
**la·pis** *m. indecl.* pencil; — *di gomma*, ink eraser.
**lappare** [A1] *tr.* to lap, to lap up.
**lard-o** *m.* bacon; lard; pork dripping. **-are** [A1] *tr.* to lard, to grease. **-ellare** [A1] *tr.* to lard, to stuff with bacon; to interlard. **-ọso** *adj.* fat, greasy.
**largheggi-are** [A3 c] *intr.* (*aux.* avere) to be profuse; to be generous, to be liberal. **-amẹnto** *m.* pouring forth, profusion.
**larghẹzza** *f.* width, breadth; diameter; largeness; size; (fig.) open-handedness, generosity, liberality.
**largire** [D2] *tr.* to grant, to bestow.
**lar-go** *adj.* (*pl.* **-ghi**) wide, broad, large, vast, extensive; liberal, generous; abundant; (naut.) out at sea, offshore; *n.m.* width, breadth; wide space; square; open sea; *adv.* widely, broadly; generously, amply; *excl.* make way!, mind your backs!; *adv. phr. alla -ga*, at a distance.
**laring-e** *f.* larynx. **-ite** *f.* laryngitis.
**larva** *f.* spectre, shade, ghost; phantom; (zool.) larva.
**laṣagne** *f. pl.* (cul.) broad strips of macaroni.
**lasciapassare** *m. indecl.* pass, permit.
**lasci-are** [A3] *tr.* to leave, to quit, to go away from; to abandon, to desert, to foresake, to leave; to leave untouched; to leave on one side, to save; to leave behind; to forget; to leave off, to give up, to interrupt; to bequeathe; to leave alone, to let be; to entrust, to leave, to give; to lose; *-arci la vita*, to lose one's life; to permit, to allow; *vivere e — vivere*, live and let live; to cease, to stop; *rfl.* to permit oneself; *-arsi vedere*, to put in an appearance.
**la·scito** *m.* legacy, bequest.
**lasci·via** *f.* lasciviousness; sensuousness; licentiousness.
**lascivo** *adj.* lascivious; dissolute; wanton; lustful.
**lassativo** *adj.*, *n.m.* laxative.
**lasso**[1] *adj.* tired, weary; slack; unhappy, wretched; *excl. ahi, —!*, alas! alack!
**lasso**[2] *m.* lapse.
**lassù** *adv.* up there, above.
**lastr-a** *f.* slab, sheet, plate; paving-stone, flagstone. **-ọne** *m. augm.* slab; sheer face of rock.
**lastric-are** [A2 s] *tr.* to pave; to pave with stones, to flag; to slate, to tile. **-atura** *f.* paving; tiling.
**la·stri-co** *m.* (*pl.* **-chi**) pavement, paving.
**latente** *adj.* latent; dormant; potential; hidden, obscure.
**laterale** *adj.* side; lateral; *carrozzino —*, side-car.
**lateri·zio** *adj.* made of terracotta, earthenware, brick; *n.m.pl.* earthenware, bricks, tiles; *fabbrica di laterizi*, brick-kiln.
**lati·bolo** *m.* hiding-place; lair, den.
**lati-fo·lio** *adj.* (bot.) broad-leaved. **-fondista** *m.* large landowner. **-fọndo** *m.* extensive landed estate.
**latin-o** *adj.* Latin; Roman; (naut.) lateen; *n.m.* Latin. **-iṣmo** *m.* Latinism. **-ista** *m.*, *f.* Latinist, Latin scholar; humanist. **-ità** *f.* Latinity.
**latit-are** [A1] *intr.* (*aux.* avere) (leg.) to abscond, to hide from justice. **-ante** *part. adj.* absconding, hiding from justice; *n.m.* fugitive from justice.
**latitu·din-e** *f.* width; latitude; breadth. **-a·rio** *adj.*, *n.m.* (rel.) latitudinarian.
**lato**[1] *m.* side; part; faction; flank; *al — di*, beside.
**lat-o**[2] *adj.* broad, wide. **-ẹzza** *f.* breadth, width, broadness.
**latọre** *m.* bearer (of a document).
**latr-are** [A1] *intr.* (*aux.* avere) to bark; to howl. **-ato** *m.* bark; howl.
**latrina** *f.* public lavatory, latrine.
**latroci·nio** *m.* theft, larceny.
**latt-a** *f.* tinplate, tinned sheet iron; tin, can. **-oniere** *m.* tinsmith; brass worker.
**latta·io** *adj.* milk-producing; *n.m.* milkman, dairyman.
**latt-are** [A1] *tr.* to suckle, to breast-feed; *intr.* (*aux.* avere), *tr.* to suck. **-atrice** *f.* nursing mother; wet nurse. **-aziọne** *f.* lactation; breast feeding.
**latt-e** *m.* milk; — *acido*, sour milk; *figliuolo di —*, foster child; *denti di —*, milk teeth; — *in polvere*, powdered milk; *fiore del —*, cream; — *scremato*, — *spannato*, skimmed milk, separated milk; (bot.) latex, milky juice. **-eggiante** *adj.* milky. **-ici·nio** *m.* dairy product. **-iera** *f.* milk-jug; dairy, buttery. **-ivẹndolo** *m.* milkman.
**lat·te-o** *adj.* milky; *dieta -a*, milk diet; (astron.) *Via Lattea*, Milky Way.
**lat·tico** *adj.* (chem.) lactic.
**lattuga** *f.* lettuce.
**la·ud-a** (*pl.* **-e**), **la·ud-e** (*pl.* **-i**) *f.* (lit. hist.) spiritual poem (in ballad-like form); *pl.* (liturg.) *le -i*, lauds; (mus.) *-e, -i spirituali*, hymns of praise; (schol.) *dieci con -e*, full marks and commended.
**la·udano** *m.* laudanum.
**La.ura** *pr.n.f.* Laura.
**la·ure-a** *f.* University degree; diploma; laurel wreath. **-ando** *m.* candidate for the 'laurea'. **-are** [A6] *tr.* to crown with laurels; to confer a degree on; *rfl.* to graduate, to take a University degree. **-ato** *part. adj.* possessing a University degree; *n.m.* graduate. **-aziọne** *f.* degree ceremony; crowning with laurel.
**Laurenziana** *pr.n.f.* Laurentian Library in Florence.
**la·ur-o** (bot.) laurel. **-ẹto** *m.* laurel grove.
**la·ut-o** *adj.* sumptuous, splendid; lavish; bountiful; handsome; *una -a mancia*, a generous tip. **-ẹzza** *f.* sumptuousness; lavishness; generosity.
**lava** *f.* lava.
**lavabo** *m. indecl.* wash-hand basin; washing place.
**lavacro** *m.* bath; water for irrigation.
**lavag·gio** *m.* washing (earth for gold, etc.); cleansing; cleaning; — *a secco*, dry cleaning.
**lavagna** *f.* (miner.) slate; blackboard; school slate.
**lavanda** *f.* (bot.) lavender.
**lav-are** [A1] *tr.* to wash; to clean; to wash down; *intr.* (*aux.* avere) to do the washing; *rfl.* (*acc.* of *prn.* 'si') to wash (oneself); (*dat.* of *prn.* 'si') *-arsi le mani*, to wash one's hands. **-anda·ia** *f.* washerwoman, laundress. **-anda·io** *m.* laundryman. **-anderi·a** *f.* laundry; washhouse. **-ata** *f.* wash; wash down; *-ata di capo*, shampoo, (colloq.) scolding. **-atọio** *m.* public washhouse; wash tub; sheep-dip. **-atrice** *f.* washing-machine.
**lavor-are** [A1 c] *tr.*, *intr.* (*aux.* avere) to work; — *a giornata*, to work by the day; — *a cottimo*, to do piece-work; to labour; to toil; to be employed. **-ante** *part. adj.* working; *n.m.* workman, worker, hand. **-atọre** *m.* worker; labourer. **-ato·rio** *m.* workshop. **-atura** *f.* processing, working. **-aziọne** *f.* processing, treatment, manufacture; *in -azione*, in the course of manufacture. **-ìo** *m.* (*pl.* **-ìi**) constant work; intense toil; intrigue.
**lavọro** *m.* work; — *di mano*, manual work; — *straordinario*, overtime; *stanza da —*, study; *bestia da —*, draught animal; task; workmanship; business.
**La·zio** *pr.n.m.* (geog.) Latium.
**Laz·zaro**[1] *pr.n.m.* Lazarus.
**laẓ·ẓar-o**[2] *n.m.* leper; beggar. **-ẹtto** *m.* fever hospital; quarantine station.
**laẓẓo**[1] *m.* quip, jest, gibe; drollery; buffoonery.
**lazzo**[2] *adj.* sour, tart, sharp; bitter.
**le**[1] *def. art. f. pl.* the.

**le**[2] *pers. prn. f. pl. conj. acc.* them.

**le**[3] *pers. prn. f. sing. conj. dat.* to her, her; to you.

**leal-e** *adj.* true, sincere, honest, trustworthy. **-ismo** *m.* loyalty to the crown. **-tà** *f.* loyalty, faithfulness; dependability.

**leardo** *adj.* dapple grey.

**lebbr-a** *f.* leprosy; (fig.) scourge, plague, evil. **-oso** *adj.* leprous; *n.m.* leper.

**lecc-are** [A2c] *tr.* to lick; to lap; to skim; (fig.) to flatter; *rfl.* (*acc.* of *prn.* 'si') *-arsi le labbra,* to lick one's lips. **-a** *m.* slight slap, brush, flip. **-ata** *f.* lick; skimming. **-atura** *f.* licking; lick; graze, brush, flick; flattery; affection; (paint.) light touch (of the brush). **-azampe** *m., f. indecl.* cringing flatterer, toady, lick-spittle.

**lecc-io** *m.* (bot.) ilex oak, holm oak. **-eto** *m.* grove of ilex.

**lec-co** *m.* (*pl.* **-chi**) titbit; bait, incentive; profit. **-cone** *m.* glutton; parasite, sponger; lecher; flatterer. **-oneri·a** *f.*, **-orni·a, -or·nia** *f.* gluttony; titbit.

**lecito** *adj.* permissible; permitted; sanctioned by law.

**le·dere** [def.] *tr.* to injure, to harm.

**lega**[1] *f.* league, alliance; union; alloy; the base metal part of an alloy; quality, class.

**lega**[2] *f.* league (measure of distance).

**legac·cio** *m.* band, fastening; garter; bootlace; ribbon.

**legal-e** *adj.* legal; lawful; *corso —,* legal tender; *medicina —,* forensic medicine; *n.m.* lawyer, legal adviser. **-ità** *f.* legality; lawfulness. **-izzare** [A1] *tr.* to certify; to authenticate; to legalize.

**legame** *m.* bond, connection, tie, link; union.

**leg-are**[1] [A2c] *tr.* to tie, to bind; to alloy; to amalgamate; to connect, to link together; to set, to mount (of jewels, etc.); *intr.* (*aux.* avere; *prep.* con) to mix (with), to go well (with); *rfl.* to be bound, to be linked; (mus.) to be slurred; to be tied. **-amento** *m.* bond, link; connection; joint, fastening; ligament; sinew. **-ato** *part. adj.* tied, bound up; tied together, bound together, united; smooth, easy; (of script) cursive; (mus.) legato, played (or sung) smoothly. **-atori·a** *f.* bookbinder's workshop. **-atura** *f.* tying, binding; connecting stroke, ligature; jewel setting; bookbinding; (mus.) tie; suspension.

**leg-are**[2] [A2c] *tr.* (leg.) to bequeath; to leave by will. **-ante** *m., f.* testator. **-ata·rio** *m.* legatee.

**legato**[1] *part. adj.* bequeathed; *n.m.* bequest.

**legato**[2] *m.* ambassador; legate.

**legazione** *f.* legation.

**legge** *f.* (leg.) law; act; rule; *offendere la —,* to break the law; *ledere la —,* to violate the law; *ricorrere alla —,* to go to law; *un fuori —,* an outlaw; Act (of Parliament); *progetto di —,* (parliamentary) Bill; *abrogare una —,* to repeal an Act.

**leggend-a** *f.* legend; fable; old wives' tale; caption; explanatory note. **-a·rio** *adj.* legendary; *n.m.* collection of legends.

**leg·g-ere** [C12] *tr.* to read; to peruse; — *sul giornale,* to read in the paper; to interpret, to read, to understand; *abs., intr.* (*aux.* avere) to read, to be a reader. **-i·bile** *adj.* legible; readable. **-itore** *m.* (techn.) reader.

**leggerezza** *f.* lightness, agility.

**leggiadr-o** *adj.* pretty, graceful; comely; charming. **-i·a** *f.* prettiness, elegance; pretty thing.

**leggiero** *adj.* light; agile, nimble; *tinta leggiera,* pale colour; slight; frivolous; *adv. camminare —,* to walk with light steps.

**legg-ìo** *m.* (*pl.* **-ii**) reading-desk; (eccl.) lectern; pulpit; (mus.) music stand, desk.

**legion-e** *f.* legion; great multitude. **-a·rio** *adj., n.m.* legionary.

**legisl-ativo** *adj.* legislative. **-atura** *f.* legislature. **-azione** *f.* legislation.

**legit·tim-o** *adj.* legitimate; *moneta -a,* legal coin. **-are** [A1s] *tr.* to legitimize. **-ità** *f.* legitimacy.

**legn-a** *f.* firewood; fuel. **-a·ia** *f.* wood-store. **-ai(u)olo** *m.* cabinet-maker. **-ame** *m.* timber; woodwork. **-ata** *f.* blow; beating.

**legn-o** *m.* (*pl.* **-i**) wood; (mus.) *col —,* with the stick of the bow; *i -i,* the woodwind; stick; log; club; (naut.) vessel; carriage, coach; (*pl.* **-a, -e,** *f.*) firewood. **-a·ceo** *adj.* woody. **-oso** *adj.* woody.

**lei**[1] *pers. prn. 3rd sing. f. disj.* she; her.

**Lei**[2] *pers. prn. 3rd sing. m., f. disj.* you (formal); *dare del Lei,* to use the formal mode of address.

**Le·ida** *pr.n.f.* (geog.) Leyden.

**Lemano** *pr.n.m.* (geog.) *Lago —,* Lake Leman, Lake of Geneva.

**lembo** *m.* border, edge; margin; side; strip; hem; flap.

**lemme** *adv. phr.* slowly, *lemme, lemme,* bit by bit; gently.

**Lemosi** *pr.n.f.* (geog.) Limoges.

**lena** *f.* courage, will to carry on; vigour, effort, staying power; breath, wind.

**lene** *adj.* (poet.) light, soft, gentle; mellow, sweet.

**leniente** *adj.* (med.) soothing, calming.

**Leningrado** *pr.n.f.* (geog.) Leningrad.

**len-ire** [D2] *tr.* to soothe, to mitigate, to placate. **-itivo** *adj.* calming, soothing; *n.m.* lenitive, demulcent.

**Lenno** *pr.n.m.* (geog.) Lemnos.

**len-oci·nio** *m.* (leg.) panderism; (fig.) blandishment. **-ona** *f.* procuress. **-one** *m.* (leg.) pander; pimp.

**lentare** [A1] *tr.* to loosen, to slacken.

**lente**[1] *f.* (bot.) lentil.

**lente**[2] *f.* lens; bob (of a pendulum); *pl.* pince-nez.

**lenteggiare** [A3c] *intr.* (*aux.* essere) to be loose; to work loose.

**lentezza** *f.* slowness; laziness; looseness; slackness.

**lent-ic·chia** *f.* (bot.) lentil; *un piatto di -icchie,* a mess of pottage. **-icolare** *adj.* lenticular; *riflettore -icolare,* spotlight. **-ig·gine** *f.* freckle. **-igginoso** *adj.* freckled.

**lent-o** *adj.* slow; tardy; long; drawn out; lazy, inert; loose, slack; *adv.* slowly, ponderously. **-ezza** *f.* slowness; laziness; slackness.

**lenza** *f.* fishing-line.

**lenzuol-o** *m.* (*pl.* **-a** *f.,* **-i** *m.*) sheet (of a bed).

**leon-e**[1] *m.* (zool.) lion. **-ato** *adj.* tawny; *n.m.* tawny colour. **-cino** *m.* (zool.) lion cub. **-esco** *adj.* (*m.pl.* **-eschi**) lion-like. **-essa** *f.* lioness. **-ino** *adj.* lion-like, leonine.

**Leone**[2] *pr.n.m.* Leo.

**leopardo** *m.* leopard.

**le·pid-o** *adj.* sprightly; smart, facetious; jaunty. **-ezza** *f.* sprightliness; facetiousness; witticism.

**lepidot·teri** *m. pl.* (ent.) butterflies and moths, lepidoptera.

**lepora·rio** *m.* game preserve.

**lepore** *m.* sprightliness, gaiety; facetiousness.

**leporino** *adj.* relating to a hare; *labbro —,* hare-lip.

**lepr-e** *f., m.* (zool.) hare. **-a·io** *m.* game preserve; gamekeeper. **-atto** *m.,* **-otto** *m.* leveret.

**ler·ci-o** *adj.* filthy; foul. **-oso** *adj.* dirty. **-ume** *m.* filth.

**le·sb-ico** *adj.* Lesbian. **-ismo** *m.* Lesbianism.

**lesin-a** *f.* awl; (fig.) stinginess; miserliness; thrift. **-a·io** *m.* miser, curmudgeon. **-are** [A1sc] *intr.* (*aux.* avere) to be thrifty, to be stingy, to haggle; *tr.* to grudge. **-eri·a** *f.* economy; stinginess, meanness.

**lesion-e** *f.* (med.) lesion; break, interruption; (archit.) crack; (leg.) damage to property or rights. **-are** [A1c] *tr.* to cause cracking in, to crack.

**lesivo** *adj.* wounding; injuring.

**lessare** [A1 c] *tr.* to boil, to stew; to cook in water.
**les·sic-o** *m.* lexicon, dictionary; vocabulary. **-ale** *adj.* lexic, pertaining to vocabulary. **-ografi·a** *f.* lexicography. **-ogra·fico** *adj.* lexicographical. **-o·grafo** *m.* lexicographer. **-ologi·a** *f.* lexicology. **-olo·gico** *adj.* lexicological.
**lesso** *adj.* boiled; stewed; tasteless, insipid; *n.m.* boiling; boiled beef; — *di vitello*, stewed veal.
**lest-o** *adj.* agile, nimble; quick, swift, rapid; early, speedy; *adv.* quickly, speedily. **-ezza** *f.* nimbleness, agility; swiftness. **-ofante** *m.* rogue, twister, swindler; cheap-jack.
**lesura** *f.* lesion; damage; offence.
**letale** *adj.* deadly, lethal, mortal, vital, fatal.
**letam-e** *m.* stable manure, dung. **-a·io** *m.* dung-heap. **-are** [A1] *tr.* to manure.
**letargi·a** *f.* (path.) lethargy.
**letar·gico** *adj.* lethargic.
**letargo** *m.* lethargy; torpor; inertia; hibernation.
**Lete** *pr.n.f.* (myth.) Lethe.
**letificare** [A2 s] *tr.* to gladden.
**leti·zia** *f.* joy; gladness; happiness; object of delight.
**letta** *f.* hasty reading; *dare una* — *a*, to skim.
**let·ter-a** *f.* letter; epistle; note; — *per via aerea*, airmail letter; — *raccomandata*, registered letter; *carta da* —, writing paper; — *di cambio*, bill of exchange; character; type; — *maiuscola*, capital letter; — *minuscola*, lower case letter; *-e di scatola*, block capitals; *alla* —, literally, word for word; *pl.* letters, literature; knowledge; *uomo di -e*, man of letters; tails (when tossing a coin). **-ale** *adj.* literal. **-a·rio** *adj.* literary; *proprietà -aria*, copyright.
**letterato** *m.* well-read man, man of letters; author; scholar; *adj.* literary.
**letteratura** *f.* literature; writing, literary culture.
**lettico** *adj., n.m.* Latvian.
**lettiera** *f.* bedding for animals; bedstead.
**letti-ga** *f.* litter; stretcher on wheels. **-ghiere** *m.* litter-bearer.
**lettime** *m.* bedding for animals.
**lett-o** *m.* bed; bedstead; *camera da* —, bedroom; — *a una piazza*, single bed; — *matrimoniale*, double bed; *-i gemelli*, *-i inglesi*, twin beds; — *a canapè*, divan bed; *rifare il* —, to make the bed; *figli del primo* —, children of the first marriage; couch; bedding for animals. **-icino** *m. dim.* cot; doll's bed. **-uc·cio** *m.* litter; couch.
**lettor-e** *m.* reader; lector. **-ato** *m.* readership; lectorship.
**lettura** *f.* reading; perusal; *sala di* —, reading room; interpretation; *libro di* —, reading book, primer; lecture.
**leucemi·a** *f.* (med.) leukaemia.
**leva** *f.* lever; fulcrum; swell (of the sea); *onda di* —, ground swell; (mil.) conscription, levy, call-up.
**Levante** *pr.n.m.* Levant; East; East wind.
**lev-are** [A1] *tr.* to raise, to lift; to bring up; to elevate; to take off, to take away, to remove; to take out; — *le tende*, to strike camp; — *una sete*, to quench a thirst; to deduct, to subtract; (naut.) — *l'ancora*, to weigh anchor; *rfl.* (*acc.* of *prn.* 'si') to rise, to get up; *-arsi in piedi*, to rise to one's feet; *al -arsi del sole*, at sunrise; to remove oneself, to get out of the way; (*dat.* of *prn.* 'si') to remove from oneself; *lèvati la giacca*, take off your coat. **-ante** *part. adj.* rising. **-ata** *f.* raising; removal, taking away; collection (of letters from a posting box); rising; getting up (from bed); *-ata del sole*, sunrise. **-atoio** *adj. ponte -atoio*, drawbridge. **-atore** *m.* lifter, raiser; riser; *buon -atore*, early riser. **-atrice** *f.* midwife; riser. **-atura** *f.* lifting, raising, rise; removal; standard, level; talent; degree of intelligence; moment, importance.
**levigare** [A2 s] *tr.* to polish; to smooth.
**levit-à** *f. indecl.* lightness. **-are** [A1 sd] to levitate. **-azione** *f.* levitation.
**Lev-ita** *m.* (*pl.* **-iti**) *m.* (bibl.) Levite. **-i·tico** *adj.* Levitical; *il Levitico*, Leviticus.
**levrier-e, -o** *m.* greyhound.
**le·zio** *m.* affection, smirking; *pl.* mincing ways.
**lezione** *f.* lesson; class; reprimand; reading; variant; interpretation.
**lezios-o** *adj.* affected; mincing. **-ag·gine** *f.* affected habit. **-ità** *f.* affectedness.
**lezzo** *m.* stink, stench; filth; *adj.* stinking, filthy.
**li**[1] *pers prn. 3rd pl. m. conj.* them.
**li**[2] *def. art. m. pl.* the (in certain uses only, otherwise **i** or **gli**); — *17 dicembre*, the 17th of December.
**lì** *adv.* there; over there; *quello* —, that man over there; *di* — *a un mese*, in a month from then; — *per* —, then and there; *essere* — — *per*, to be on the verge of; *excl.* there!
**Li·bano** *pr.n.m.* (geog.) Lebanon.
**lib-are** [A1] *tr.* to make libations to; to touch lightly with the lips; to sip, to taste. **-azione** *f.* libation.
**libbra** *f.* pound weight.
**libeccio** *m.* south-west wind.
**libell-o** *m.* polemical pamphlet; libel. **-ista** *m.* pamphleteer; (leg.) libeller; defamer.
**libel·lula** *f.* (ent.) dragonfly.
**liberal-e** *adj.* liberal; open-handed; *le arti -i*, the liberal arts; *n.m., f.* (pol.) liberal. **-ismo** *m.* (pol.) liberalism. **-ità** *f.* liberality; generosity; munificence.
**liber-are** [A1 s] *tr.* to liberate, to relieve; to set free, to release; to deliver; *Dio ci -i!*, Heaven forbid!; *rfl.* to free oneself. **-atore** *m.* liberator; deliverer. **-azione** *f.* liberation, release; redemption.
**liber-ismo** *m.* theory of free market, free economy. **-ista** *m.* free-trader.
**li·ber-o** *adj.* free; independent; freed; released; untrammelled; frank, uninhibited; free and easy; unoccupied; coarse, loose; available; *occhio* —, naked eye; *disegno a mano -a*, freehand drawing.
**libertà** *f. indecl.* liberty, freedom; free time.
**libertin-o** *m.* libertine, profligate; *adj.* rakish, libertine. **-ag·gio** *m.* libertinism, libertinage; licentiousness.
**Li·bia** *pr.n.f.* (geog.) Libya.
**li·bico** *adj., n.m.* Libyan.
**libi·din-e** *f.* lust; lechery. **-oso** *adj.* lustful, lascivious, libidinous.
**librare** [A1] *tr.* to balance, to poise; *rfl.* to balance; (aeron.) to hover.
**libr-o** *m.* book; volume; — *di consultazione*, reference book; — *giallo*, thriller, 'whodunnit'; — *maestro*, ledger; — *di bordo*, log. **-a·io** *m.* bookseller; bookshop. **-a·rio** *adj.* pertaining to books. **-eri·a** *f.* bookshop; bookcase. **-ettista** *m.* (mus.) librettist. **-etto** *m.* note-book; booklet; *-etto di assegni*, cheque book; (mus.) libretto.
**licenza** *f.* licence; leave, permit; diploma; school-leaving certificate; notice, dismissal.
**licenzi-are** [A4] *tr.* to give leave to, to release; to discharge, to fire, to sack; to dismiss; to allow; to license; *rfl.* to take one's leave. **-ata·rio** *m.* licensee. **-oso** *adj.* licentious, dissolute.
**lic-e·o** *m.* Lyceum; high school, grammar school; (mus.) — *musicale*, college or academy of music; conservatoire. **-eale** *adj.* pertaining to a 'liceo'; *n.m., f.* pupil at a 'liceo'.
**Lido**[1] *pr.n.m.* (geog.) *il* —, the Lido (Venice).
**lido**[2] *m.* shore; lido; bathing beach; (geog.) sand-bar; (fig., poet.) native shores.
**Liegi** *pr.n.f.* (geog.) Liège.

**liet-o** *adj.* glad; joyous, joyful; (poet.) fertile; thriving. **-ęzza** *f.* gladness, joyousness.
**liev-e** *adj.* light, slight; easy; trifling; soft; *adv.* lightly. **-ità** *f.* lightness; inconstancy, levity; frivolousness.
**lie·vit-o** *m.* yeast; ferment; *pane senza —*, unleavened bread. **-are** [A1] *intr.* (*aux.* essere) to ferment; to be leavened; to rise; to be slaked (of lime); *tr.* to leaven; to slake (lime).
**li·gio** *m.* sworn vassal; liege; *adj.* loyal, true.
**lignag·gio** *m.* lineage, pedigree.
**li·gneo** *adj.* woody, ligneous.
**Li·g-ure** *adj.*, *n.m.*, *f.* Ligurian. **-u·ria** *pr.n.f.* (geog.) Liguria.
**lili-a·ceo** *adj.* (bot.) liliaceous. **-ale** *adj.* lily-white, pure as a lily.
**Lilla** *pr.n.f.* (geog.) Lille.
**lim-a** *f.* file, rasp; (fig.) nagging thought. **-are** [A1] *tr.* to file; to sharpen.
**Limbo** *m.* (theol.) Limbo.
**li·mine** *m.* threshold; border, limit.
**limitare**[1] *m.* threshold; (fig.) beginning, outset.
**limit-are**[2] [A1 s] *tr.* to limit; to restrict; to restrain; to curtail; *rfl.* to be limited, to be bounded, to restrict oneself. **-ativo** *adj.* restrictive. **-azione** *f.* limitation; limit; restraint.
**li·mite** *m.* limit; boundary; restraint; extent.
**limi·trofo** *adj.* bordering, border; marginal.
**limo** *m.* mud, slime; mire.
**limon-e** *m.* (bot.) lemon-tree; lemon; citron; *spremuta di —*, fresh lemon juice. **-ata** *f.* lemonade.
**limoso** *adj.* muddy; slimy.
**lim·pid-o** *adj.* clear, limpid. **-ęzza** *f.*, **-ità** *f.* clarity; limpidity; purity; transparency.
**linc-e** *m.* (zool.) lynx. **-e·o** *adj.* lynx-like; *occhi -ei*, lynx eyes.
**linci-are** [A3] *tr.* to lynch. **-ag·gio** *m.* lynching, lynch-law.
**lind-o** *adj.* neat, trim; tidy. **-ęzza** *f.* neatness, trimness. **-ura** *f.* neatness; elegance.
**li·ne-a** *f.* line; *in — d'aria*, as the crow flies; cable; route, line. **-ale** *adj.* linear; in a straight line. **-amęnto** *m.* outline; feature; (art) outline. **-are** [A6] *tr.* to delineate, to outline; to line, to rule with lines; *adj.* linear; in outline. **-ętta** *f.* hyphen; dash; (math.) minus sign; *due -ette*, equals sign.
**linf-a** *f.* lymph; (bot.) sap. **-a·tico** *adj.* lymphatic; anaemic.
**lingotto** *m.* ingot, nugget.
**lingu-a** *f.* tongue; *tenere la — a freno*, to hold one's tongue; strip of land; language; idiom, speech; *— materna*, mother tongue. **-ag·gio** *m.* language; style; parlance; diction. **-ale** *adj.* lingual, of the tongue. **-ętta** *f.* wagging tongue; wick; tongue (of a shoe); flap; catch. **-ifǫrme** *adj.* tongued; tongue-shaped. **-ista** *m.*, *f.* linguist. **-i·stica** *f.* linguistics. **-i·stico** *adj.* linguistic.
**Linguadoca** *f.* (geog.) Languedoc.
**linifi·cio** *m.* linen mill; flax mill.
**linimęnto** *m.* liniment.
**lin-o** *m.* (bot.) flax; linen; *olio di —*, linseed oil; *adj.* linen. **-eri·a** *f.* linen goods. **-ęto** *m.* flax plantation. **-sęme** *m.* linseed.
**lino-tipi·a** *f.* linotype. **-ti·pico** *adj.* linotype. **-tipista** *m.* linotype operator.
**Lione** *pr.n.f.* (geog.) Lyons.
**Li·psia** *pr.n.f.* (geog.) Leipzig.
**liqu-efare** [B14] *tr.* to liquefy. **-efazione** *f.* liquefaction.
**liquid-are** [A1 s] *tr.* (comm.; leg.) to wind up; to liquidate; (euphem.) to 'liquidate', to 'eliminate'. **-azione** *f.* liquidation; winding up.
**li·quid-o** *adj.* liquid; fluid; *n.m.* liquid; fluid. **-ęzza** *f.*, **-ità** *f.* fluidity; the liquid state.
**liquiri·zia** *f.* liquorice.
**liquore** *m.* liquor; liqueur.
**lira**[1] *f.* (finan.) lira, the monetary unit in Italy.
**lira**[2] *f.* (mus.) lyre.
**li·ric-a** *f.* lyric. **-o** *adj.* lyric, lyrical; (mus.) *artista -o*, opera singer; *opera -a, dramma -o*, opera; *teatro -o*, opera theatre, opera (as art-form); *stagione -a*, opera season; *n.m.* lyric poet.
**lirismo** *m.* lyricism; lyrical form.
**Lisbona** *pr.n.f.* (geog.) Lisbon.
**lisca** *f.* fish bone; *ogni pesce ha la sua —*, no rose without a thorn.
**lisciare** [A3] *tr.* to smooth, to stroke; to caress; to preen; to flatter.
**li·scio** *adj.* smooth, soft; plain, simple; (of a drink) neat; *adv.* smoothly; *tutto è andato —*, everything went beautifully.
**liso** *adj.* worn; worn out; threadbare.
**list-a** *f.* strip; line; streak; stripe; band; (archit.) fillet; list; *— delle viande*, menu; *— elettorale*, electoral roll. **-are** [A1] *tr.* to border, to edge. **-ino** *m.* list; *-ino di borsa*, stock exchange price-list.
**litani·a** *f.* (liturg.) litany; (fig.) rigmarole.
**litantrace** *m.* anthracite.
**lite** *f.* brawl; quarrel; row; controversy; lawsuit; (leg.) case; suit; *muovere una — a*, to bring an action against.
**litig-are** [A2 s] *intr.* (*aux.* avere) to quarrel; to fall out; (leg.) to litigate; *tr.* (leg.) to contest; to sue. **-ante** *part. adj.* litigating; quarrelling; *n.m.* contending party; litigant.
**litigh-ino** *m.* mischief maker, quarrel-seeker. **-ìo** *m.* continual quarrelling.
**liti·gi-o** *m.* altercation; dispute; quarrel. **-oso** *adj.* quarrelsome.
**lit-ocromi·a** *f.* chromo-lithography, chromo-lithograph. **-ofotografi·a** *f.* lithophotograph(y). **-ofotogra·fico** *adj.* lithophotographic. **-ografare** [A1] *tr.* to lithograph. **-ografi·a** *f.* lithography. **-o·grafo** *m.* lithographer.
**litor-ale** *adj.* littoral, coastal. **-a·neo** *adj.* relating to a shore.
**litorina** *f.* (zool.) winkle.
**litro** *m.* litre.
**littorina** *f.* diesel-powered rail-car.
**Litu-a·nia** *pr.n.f.* (geog.) Lithuania. **-ano** *adj.*, *n.m.* Lithuanian.
**lit-urgi·a** *f.* liturgy. **-ur·gico** *adj.* liturgical.
**liut-o** *m.* lute. **-ista** *m.* (mus.) lutanist.
**livella** *f.* mason's level; plummet.
**livellare**[1] *adj.* level; on the level.
**livell-are**[2] [A1] *tr.* to level; to take the levels of; *intr.* (*aux.* essere; *prep.* con) to be on a level (with); *rfl.* to find one's level. **-atore** *m.* leveller; surveyor. **-azione** *f.* levelling; surveying.
**livell-are**[3] [A1] *tr.* (leg.) to lease for a term of years. **-azione** *f.* deed of lease.
**livello**[1] *m.* level; *passaggio a —*, level crossing; mason's level; *— a bolla d'aria*, spirit level.
**livell-o**[2] *m.* (leg.) property held on a long lease; deed of lease. **-a·rio** *m.* long lease holder; *adj.* (leg.) leasable.
**li·vid-o** *adj.* livid; grey; ashen; bruised; envious; *n.m.* bruise. **-astro** *adj.* bluish, greyish. **-ęzza** *f.* greyness, lividness; bruiseds tate, bruising. **-ore** *m.* livid colour; bruise. **-ume** *m.* mass of bruises; bruised patch. **-ura** *f.* bruise.
**livore** *m.* lividness; envy.
**Livorno** *pr.n.f.* (geog.) Leghorn.
**livre·a** *f.* livery; uniform.
**lizza** *f.* lists, arena.
**lo**[1] *def. art. m. sing.* (*pl.* **gli**; used before impure **s, z, gn, ps, x, bd, cn**) the.
**lo**[2] *pers. prn. m. sing. acc.* him; it; *— so*, I know.
**lobo** *m.* lobe.
**local-e** *adj.* local; *n.m.* room; place; house. **-ità** *f.* locality; place; position; whereabouts. **-izzare** [A1] *tr.* to localize; to circumscribe; to prevent from spreading.
**locand-a** *f.* inn. **-iera** *f.* inn-keeper's wife; landlady; hostess of an inn. **-iere** *m.* inn-keeper, landlord, host.
**loc-are** [A2] *tr.* (leg.) to let on hire; to let on lease; to rent. **-ata·rio** *m.* (leg.) lessee; tenant

hirer. **-ativo** *adj.* locative; pertaining to location; (leg.) for letting. **-atọre** *m.* lessor. **-aziọne** *f.* (leg.) lease; letting on hire; letting at a rent; tenancy.

**loco-mo·bile** *f.* traction-engine. **-motiva** *f.* locomotive, engine. **-motivo** *adj.* locomotive. **-motọre** *adj.* (med.; phys.) locomotor; *n.m.* electric locomotive. **-motrice** *f.* locomotive. **-moziọne** *f.* locomotion.

**locusta** *f.* (ent.) locust.

**locuziọne** *f.* locution; expression; phrase; idiom; saying.

**lod-are** [A1] *tr.* to praise, to laud, to extol; *rfl.* to praise oneself; (*prep.* di) to be satisfied (with); to be fond (of). **-ativo** *adj.* praising, complimentary. **-atọre** *m.* praiser; commender. **-ẹvole** *adj.* praiseworthy, laudable, commendable. **-evolẹzza** *f.* praiseworthiness.

**lode** *f.* praise; approval; (in an examination) mark of distinction.

**Lod-i** *pr.n.f.* (geog.) Lodi; **-igiano** *adj.*, *n.m.* (native, inhabitant) of Lodi.

**lodo** *m.* award; approval of work done.

**lo·dola** *f.* skylark.

**loga-ritmo** *m.* logarithm. **-ri·tmico** *adj.* logarithmic.

**log·g-ia** *f.* balcony; (archit.) loggia, gallery; masonic lodge. **-iato** *m.* long portico, gallery. **-iọne** *m.* (theatr.) gallery.

**lo·gic-a** *f.* logic. **-o** *adj.* logical; rational; reasoned; reasonable, what one would expect; *n.m.* logician.

**log-ista** *m.* accountant. **-i·stica** *f.* accountancy; logistics. **-i·stico** *adj.* logistic(al).

**lo·glio** *m.* (bot.) darnel; (fig.) tare.

**logor-are** [A1sc] *tr.* to wear out; to waste; to use up, to consume; *rfl.* to wear oneself out; to worry; to become worn out. **-amẹnto** *m.* wearing out; wear; wear and tear. **-ìo** *m.* constant wear.

**lọgoro** *adj.* worn, worn out; consumed; threadbare; in tatters; *n.m.* wear.

**lo·ia** *f.* dirt, layer of grease and dirt.

**lolla** *f.* husk.

**lombag·gine** *f.* lumbago.

**Lombard-i·a** *pr.n.f.* (geog.) Lombardy. **-o** *adj.*, *n.m.* Lombard.

**lọmb-o** (anat.) loin; (butcher.) rump. **-ale, -are** *adj.* (anat.) lumbar. **-ata** *f.* loin (of meat).

**lombri-co** *m.* (*pl.* **-chi**) (zool.) earthworm.

**Lọn-dra** *pr.n.f.* (geog.) London. **-dinẹse** *adj.* London; *n.m.*, *f.* Londoner.

**longa·nim-e** *adj.* patient; forbearing; long-suffering; indulgent. **-ità** *f.* patience, forbearance; long-suffering.

**longev-o** *adj.* long-lived. **-ità** *f.* longevity.

**longitu·din-e** *f.* longitude. **-ale** *adj.* longitudinal.

**lontra** *f.* (zool.) otter.

**lonza**[1] *f.* jaguar; (poet.) leopard, panther.

**lọnza**[2] *f.* loin (of meat); side, flank.

**loquac-e** *adj.* talkative, loquacious; eloquent. **-ità** *f.* talkativeness; loquacity; eloquence.

**loquela** *f.* talking, power of speech; way of talking; *dono della —*, gift of the gab.

**lordare** (A1 c) *tr.* to soil; to sully, to make filthy; *intr.* (*aux.* avere) to commit a nuisance; *rfl.* to dirty oneself; to get dirty.

**lọrd-o** *adj.* dirty, filthy; vicious; (comm.) gross; *stipendio —*, gross salary; (of a metal) crude; *ancora -a*, foul anchor. **-ẹzza** *f.* filth; ordure. **-ura** *f.* filth; excrement; evil behaviour; evil people, scum.

**Loren-a** *pr.n.f.* (geog.) Lorraine. **-ẹse** *adj.* of Lorraine; *n.m.*, *f.* Lorrainer.

**lo·rica** *f.* cuirass; (bot.) pod.

**lọro** *pers. prn. 3rd pl. m., f. disj.* they; them; *poss. adj., prn. indecl.* their; theirs.

**losanga** *f.* (geom.) rhombus; (herald.) lozenge.

**Losanna** *pr.n.f.* (geog.) Lausanne.

**lọs-co** *adj.* (*m.pl.* **-chi**) short-sighted; squint-eyed; one-eyed; furtive, underhand, suspect; *affari -chi*, shady business, sharp practice.

**lọto**[1] *m.* mud, filth; clay.

**lot-o**[2] *m.* (bot.) lotus. **-o·fago** *adj.* lotus-eating; *n.m.* lotus-eater.

**lott-a** *f.* wrestling; *— giapponese*, jujitsu; *— americana*, all-in wrestling; struggle; fight; contest; strife; *— di classe*, class warfare; (mil.) combat, battle. **-are** [A1] *intr.* (*aux.* avere) to wrestle; to struggle, to fight. **-atọre** *m.* wrestler; fighter.

**lott-o** *m.* lottery; lot; share; allotment. **-eri·a** *f.* lottery.

**Lova·nio** *pr.n.f.* (geog.) Louvain, Leuven.

**loziọne** *f.* lotion.

**lu·bric-o** *adj.* lewd, indecent. **-ità** *f.* indecency, lubricity; regularity of bowel-movement.

**lubrific-are** [A2 s] *tr.* to lubricate, to oil, to grease. **-ante** *adj.*, *n.m.* lubricant. **-atọre** *m.* lubricator, oiler, greaser. **-aziọne** *f.* lubrication, oiling, greasing.

**Luca** *pr.n.m.* Luke.

**lucchẹse** *adj.* of Lucca; *n.m.*, *f.* Luccan; *il —*, region round Lucca.

**lucchẹtto** *m.* padlock; *— a cifra*, combination lock.

**lucci-care** [A2 s] *intr.* (*aux.* avere) to sparkle, to shine; to glister. **-chio** *m.* sparkle, glisten, glitter.

**luc·cico** *m.* first light of day.

**luc·cio** *m.* (ichth.) pike.

**luc·ciol-a** *f.* (ent.) firefly. **-o** *m.* (ent.) glow-worm.

**luc-e** *f.* light; *accendere la —*, to put on the light; *spegnere la —*, to put out the light; brightness; splendour; *anno —*, light year; aperture; port-hole; (motor.) *— città*, parking lights; (naut.) *-i di posizione*, navigation lights.

**lu·c-ere** (C def.) *intr.* to shine, to glitter; *non è tutto oro quel che -e*, all is not gold that glitters. **-ente** *adj.* shining, bright.

**Lucerna**[1] *pr.n.f.* (geog.) Lucerne.

**lucern-a**[2] *f.* oil-lamp; three-cornered hat. **-a·io** *m.* skylight.

**lucer·tola** *f.* lizard.

**Luci·a** *pr.n.f.* Lucy, Lucia.

**lucid-are** [A1s] *tr.* to polish; to burnish. **-atọre** *m.* polisher. **-atrice** *f.* polishing machine; burnishing machine; floor polisher. **-aziọne** *f.* polishing.

**lu·cid-o** *adj.* shining; bright; clear, lucid; (art) *carta -a*, tracing paper; *n.m.* brightness; shine; polish; starch for linen. **-ẹzza** *f.* brightness; shine. **-ità** *f.* lucidity.

**Luci·fero** *pr.n.m.* Lucifer; morning star.

**luci·gnolo** *m.* wick.

**luci·metro** *m.* photometer.

**lucr-are** [A1] *tr.* to earn, to win, to gain. **-ativo** *adj.* lucrative.

**Lucre·zia** *pr.n.f.* Lucrece.

**Lucre·zio** *pr.n.m.* Lucretius.

**lucr-o** *m.* lucre, revenue; (leg.) gain; profit. **-ọso** *adj.* lucrative, profitable.

**ludi·brio** *m.* ridicule, scorn; mockery; (fig.) plaything.

**ludo** *m.* public games, spectacle.

**lu-e** *f.* pestilence, plague, contagious disease; (fig.) scourge. **-e·tico** *adj.* pestilent.

**lu·glio** *m.* July.

**lu·gubre** *adj.* lugubrious, dismal.

**lu·i** *pers. prn. m. sing. disj.* him; he.

**Luigi** *pr.n.m.* Lewis, Louis.

**Lui·gia** *pr.n.f.* Louise

**Luigiana** *pr.n.f.* (geog.) Louisiana.

**lumaca** *f.* slug; snail; spiral; *scala a —*, winding staircase; (eng.) worm; coil; (fig.) slow-coach.

**lum-e** *m.* light; portable light, lantern; (theatr.) *batteria di -i*, footlights; intelligence, wisdom; enlightenment. **-eggiare** [A3 c] *tr.* to light up; to illustrate, to throw light on.

**lumiera** *f.* lamp-stand; chandelier; touch-hole of a gun.

**luminare** *m.* luminary.

**luminello** *m.* float for a night light; socket of a candlestick.

**lumini·stica** *f.* lighting technique.
**luminọs-o** *adj.* luminous; shining. **-ità** *f.* luminousness; brightness.
**lun-a** *f.* moon; satellite; *chiaro di —*, moonlight; month; *— di miele*, honeymoon; temper, humour, whim. **-are** *adj.* lunar. **-a·ria** *f.* (bot.) honesty; (miner.) moonstone. **-a·tico** *adj.* moony; *n.m.* moody person who changes with the phases of the moon. **-ato** *adj.* crescent-shaped. **-azịone** *f.* lunar month.
**lunedì** *pr.n.m.* Monday.
**lung-ac·cio** *adj. pejor.* tediously long; endless; boring. **-ag·gine** *f.* slow, tedious procedure; dallying, dawdling. **-agnata** *f.* long tedious speech; rigmarole; drawling pronunciation.
**Lungarno** *pr.n.m.* street alongside the Arno (Pisa, Florence).
**lungheri·a** *f.* delays, dawdling; long-windedness.
**lunghẹzza** *f.* length: extent; duration; height; *— d'onda*, wavelength.
**lung-i** *adv.* far away; a long way off. **-imiranza** *f.* farsightedness.
**lun-go**[I] *adj.* (*m.pl.* **-ghi**) long; tall; elongated; thin, diluted, weak; lasting a long time; *a — andare*, in the long run; slow, tedious, long-drawn out; *adv. phr. a —*, at length, for a long time; *alla -ga*, in the long run, eventually; *di gran -ga*, by far, by a long chalk; *alla più -ga*, at the latest, at the most; *n.m.* length; distance; *tre metri di —*, three metres long. **-gometrag·gio** *m.* (cinem.) full-length film. **-gọne** *m.augm.* very tall person; person who delays or rambles on.
**lun-go**[2] *prep.* along, by the side of, beside, by. **-golago** *m.* lakeside promenade. **-gomare** *m.* seaside promenade.
**Lungote·vere** *pr.n.m.* street alongside the Tiber.
**lu·nula** *f.* meniscus; crescent; half-moon (of fingernail).
**luog-o** (*pl.* **luoghi**) *m.* place; spot; site; region; extract, passage (in a text); *in — di*, instead of; occasion, cause; *fuor di —*, out of place, inappropriate; *aver —*, to occur; to take place, to happen. **-otenente** *m.* replacement, stand-in; (mil.) lieutenant.
**lupa** *f.* she-wolf; (agric.) mildew, rot.
**lupino**[I] *m.* (bot.) lupin.
**lupino**[2] *adj.* pertaining to a wolf, lupine.
**lup-o** *m.* (zool.) wolf; (naut.) *— di mare*, old sea dog. **-a·ia** *f.* wolf's den. **-a·io** *m.* wolf hunter. **-atto** *m.* (Boy Scouts) wolf cub. **-ẹsco** *adj.* (*m.pl.* **-ẹschi**) wolfish, wolf-like.
**lup·pol-o** *m.* (bot.) hop. **-iera** *f.* hop-field.
**lur-co** *adj.* (*m.pl.* **-chi**) gluttonous; *n.m.* glutton.
**lu·rid-o** *adj.* lurid; foul, filthy, squalid; loathsome. **-ẹzza** *f.* filthiness; squalor.
**lușing-a** *f.* flattery; *pl.* pleasures; caresses; false declarations of love. **-are** [A2] *tr.* to flatter; to delight; *rfl.* to flatter oneself; to delude oneself.
**lușingh-eri·a** *f.* flattery. **-ẹvole** *adj.* flattering; tempting, alluring. **-iero** *adj.* flattering, caressing; alluring; promising; sympathetic; favourable.
**lussare** *tr.* (med.) to dislocate.
**Lussemburgo** *pr.n.m.* (geog.) Luxembourg.
**luss-o** *m.* luxury; pomp; magnificence; lavishness; *di —*, luxury, de luxe. **-uọso** *adj.* luxurious; luxuriant; magnificent.
**lussureggiare** [A3 c] *intr.* (*aux.* avere) to luxuriate; to live luxuriously.
**lussu·ri-a** *f.* wantonness, lasciviousness; luxuriance. **-are** [A4] *intr.* (*aux.* avere) to live in luxury; to luxuriate; to be lustful; to commit acts of lewdness. **-ọso** *adj.* luxurious; lascivious, dissolute.
**lustr-o**[I] *adj.* shiny, polished; lustrous; glittering; *n.m.* lustre, sheen, polish; polishing; brilliance. **-are** [A1] *tr.* to polish, to shine; to burnish; to furbish. **-ascarpe** *m. indecl.*, **-astivali** *m. indecl.* boot-black. **-ata** *f.* polishing. **-atọre** *m.* polisher. **-ino** *m.* boot-black, 'boots'; shine, brightness; false ornament, tinsel; affectation.
**lustro**[2] *m.* lustre, period of five years.
**lu·teo** *adj.* intense yellow; saffron.
**Luter-o** *pr.n.m.* Luther. **-anẹșimo, -anișmo** *m.* Lutheranism. **-ano** *adj., n.m.* Lutheran.
**luto** *m.* mud; clay.
**lutt-o** *m.* mourning; grief; *abito di —*, mourning clothes; *carta da —*, black-edged writing-paper. **-uọso** *adj.* mournful, doleful.
**lutulento** *adj.* muddy; miry.

**M** *f., m.* (pron. **emme**) the letter M; the consonant M.
**ma** *conj.* but; notwithstanding, yet, still; *excl.* heaven knows!; well!; *— che errore hai fatto!*, why, what a mistake you've made!; *— che!*, not at all!, please don't mention it!, what nonsense! (*or* affirm.) yes, indeed!; (*or* iron.) you don't say!; *n.m. indecl.* but, objection.
**ma·cabro** *adj.* macabre; grim, gruesome; ghastly.
**macada·m** *m. indecl.* (civ. eng.) macadam. **-iẓẓare** [A1] *tr.* to macadamize.
**maca·o** *m.* (orn.) macaw.
**macca** *f.* (colloq.) plenty; *a —*, in abundance.
**Maccab-e·o** *pr.n.m.* (bibl.) Maccabeus; *i -i*, the Maccabees; *adj.* maccabean.
**maccarello** *m.* (ichth.) mackerel.
**maccherọni** *m.pl.* (cul.) macaroni.
**maccher-one·a** *f.* macaronic poem. **-o·nico** *adj.* macaronic.
**mac·chi-a**[I] *f.* spot; stain; speck; blotch; smudge; shame, disgrace. **-are** [A4] *tr.* to spot; to stain; to dirty; (fig.) to tarnish. **-ato** *part. adj.* spotted; dirtied; stained; dappled; *latte -ato*, milk with a spot of coffee in it. **-ettare** [A1 c] *tr.* to speckle. **-ẹtto** *m. dim.* speck; dot.
**mac·chia**[2] *f.* copse, thicket; bush, scrub.
**mac·chin-a** *f.* machine; engine; machinery; motor car; *— da cucire*, sewing-machine; *— tipografica*, printing-machine; *foglio di —*, final proof; *— da scrivere*, type-writer; *— fotografica*, camera; machination, plot. **-ale** *adj.* mechanical; automatic. **-are** [A1 s] *tr.* to plot, to contrive, to machinate. **-azịone** *f.* plot, machination. **-ista** *m.* machinist; (rlwy.) engine-driver; (naut.) ship's engineer.
**mace** *f.* (cul.) mace.
**mace·done** *adj., n.m.* macedonian.
**Macedo·nia**[I] *pr.n.f.* (geog.) Macedonia.
**macedo·nia**[2] *f.* (cul.) macédoine; *— di frutti*, fruit salad; *— di legumi*, vegetable hotch-potch.
**macell-are** [A1] *tr.* to slaughter, to butcher; (fig.) to kill. **-a·io** *m.* butcher. **-eri·a** *f.* butcher's shop.
**macello** *m.* slaughter-house; (fig.) slaughter.
**macerare** [A1 s] *tr.* to macerate, to steep; (techn.) *— la calcina*, to slake lime; (fig.) to mortify; to abuse, to vilify; *rfl.* (fig.) to do penance; to be afflicted, to waste away.
**mace·ria** *f.* dry wall; *pl.* ruins; (bldg.) rubble.
**ma·cero**[I] *m.* macerating-vat; tank for slaking lime.
**ma·cero**[2] *adj.* macerated,

steeped; (fig.) exhausted, worn out; mortified.
**ma·chia** *f.* cunning.
**machiavel·l-ico** *adj.* Machiavellian; crafty. **-ismo** *m.* Machiavellism.
**maci·a** *f.* heap of stones.
**macigno** *m.* hard blue-grey sandstone; large stone; (fig.) blockhead.
**macilen-to** *adj.* emaciated. **-za** *f.* emaciation.
**ma·cin-a** *f.* millstone. **-are** [A1 s] *tr.* to grind; to mill; to crush; to pound; (fig.) to consume. **-ata** *f.* grinding; milling. **-atoio** *m.* press, mill. **-atore** *m.* grinder. **-atura** *f.*, **-azione** *f.* grinding. **-ello** *m.* miller. **-ino** *m. dim.* *-ino da caffè*, coffee-grinder; *-ino da pepe*, pepper-mill. **-ìo** *m.* (*pl.* **ìi**) continuous or frequent grinding.
**maciull-a** *f.* brake (for flax). **-are** [A1] *tr.* to brake (flax), to scutch; to masticate.
**macolare** [A1 s] *tr.* to bruise.
**macro-** *pref.* (scient.) macro-; long. **-cosmo** *m.* macrocosm. **-sco·pico** *adj.* macroscopic, visible to the naked eye.
**ma·cul-a** *f.* spot, blemish, stain; damage, injury. **-are** [A1 s] *tr.* to spot, to stain, to blemish; to corrupt.
**Maddalena** *pr.n.f.* Magdalen; Madeleine; (hist.) bell of the Bargello tower in Florence rung at executions.
**Madera** *pr.n.f.* (geog.) Madeira; *m.* madeira (wine).
**ma·dia** *f.* chest; household recipient for bread.
**ma·d-ido** *adj.* moist, damp; wet through, moistened, wetted. **-ore** *m.* dampness, moisture; slight sweat.
**Madonna** *pr.n.f.* Our Lady, the Virgin Mary; madonna.
**madre** *f.* mother; female parent; dam; bitch; — *di latte*, foster mother; — *lingua*, mother tongue; mould; counterfoil; female screw; socket; cause, source; (comm.) *ufficio* —, head office. **-pa·tria** *f.* mother-country. **-perla** *f.* (zool.) pearl-oyster; mother of pearl. **-pora** *f.* (zool.) madrepore; (pop.) corals. **-selva** *f.* (bot.) honeysuckle. **-vite** *f.* (eng.) female screw.
**Madrid** *pr.n.f.* (geog.) Madrid.
**madrigal-e** *m.* (mus.) madrigal. **-ista** *m.* (mus.) madrigal composer.
**madrigna** *f.* see **matrigna.**
**madrina** *f.* godmother.
**maestà** *f.* majesty; *Sua maestà*, His, Her Majesty; image of God or of the Madonna; wayside shrine; grandeur, majestic aspect.
**maestos-o** *adj.* majestic; stately; grand, imposing. **-ità** *f.* stateliness, majesty.
**mae·str-a** *f.* schoolmistress; teacher; (ent.) queen-bee; (naut.) *vela di* —, mainsail. **-ina** *f. dim.* young woman teacher; nursery governess.
**maestrale** *adj.* north-west; *n.m.* north-west wind.
**maestranza** *f.* the masters of a trade; mastery of a trade; freedom of a company, right to membership of a guild; staff, hands; *pl.* guilds.
**maestrevole** *adj.* masterly; skilful.
**maestri·a** *f.* mastery; skill; proficiency; control; trick, stratagem.
**mae·stro** *m.* master; teacher; tutor, instructor; — *di campo*, field-marshal; foreman; (mus.) conductor; teacher of music; composer; *adj.* chief; main; *colpo* —, master-stroke; *libro* —, ledger; (naut.) *albero* —, mainmast.
**Ma·fi-a** *f.* mafia, secret criminal society originating from Sicily. **-oso** *m.* member of the Mafia.
**maga** *f.* witch; sorceress; enchantress.
**magagn-a** *f.* flow, blemish, defect; vice. **-are** [A5] *tr* to spoil, to damage; to corrupt.
**magari** *excl.* would that it were so!, I wish it were true; *adv.* even, maybe, perhaps.
**magazzin-o** *m.* warehouse; storehouse. **-ag·gio** *m.* storage; cost of storage; warehousing; *-aggio refrigerato*, cold storage. **-iere** *m.* warehouseman.
**Magellano** *pr.n.m.* Magellan.
**magenta** *f.* magenta (colour).
**magges-e** *m.* (agric.) fallow; fallow-land; *adj.* of May. **-are** [A1 c] *tr.* to lay fallow.
**mag·gi-o** *m.* May; festival of May; May song. **-olata** *f.* May song. **-olino** *m.* cockchafer, may bug.
**maggiorana** *f.* marjoram.
**maggioranza** *f.* majority; *in* —, for the most part, mostly; — *di voti*, majority vote.
**maggiorare** [A1 c] *tr.* (comm.) to increase; — *i prezzi*, to raise prices.
**maggiordomo** *m.* major-domo; steward; butler.
**maggior-e** *adj.* greater; larger, bigger; older; major; *età* — full age, majority; (mil.) *Stato* — general staff; *n.m.* major; (mus.) major; *pl.* ancestors, forefathers. **-enne** *adj.* of full age. **-ità** *f.* (mil.) majority. **-mente** *adv.* more; to a greater extent; more fully.
**Magi** *pr.n.m.pl.* Magi (*cf.* **magio**).
**magi·a** *f.* magic.
**magiaro** *m., adj.* Magyar.
**ma·gic-o** *adj.* magic; magical; *bacchetta -a*, wand.
**ma·gio** *m.* wise man, magician; *i tre Magi*, the three Magi.
**magistero** *m.* mastery; teaching profession; doctor's degree; *scuola di* —, College of education; department of education.
**magistrale** *adj.* magistral; magisterial; professorial; masterly; haughty.
**magistrat-o** *m.* magistrate. **-ura** *f.* magistracy; judiciary.
**ma·gli-a** *f.* stitch; mesh; link; mail; *lavoro di* —, knitting; *lavorare a* —, to knit; *a* —, knitted; tights; pullover. **-eri·a** *f.* hosiery. **-etta** *f.* light knitted garment.
**Magliabechiana** *pr.n.f.* library in Florence founded by A. Magliabechi, now the National Library of Florence.
**ma·glio** *m.* mallet; hammer.
**magli(v)olo** *m.* (agric.) cutting; shoot; sucker.
**maglione** *m.* thick pullover.
**magna·nim-o** *adj.* magnanimous; generous. **-ità** *f.* magnanimity.
**magnano** *m.* locksmith; coppersmith.
**magnat-e** *m.* magnate. **-i·zio** *adj.* noble; rich.
**magne·si-a** *f.* magnesia. **-o** *m.* magnesium.
**magnet-e** *m.* magnet; magneto. **-ismo** *m.* magnetism. **-ite** *f.* lodestone. **-izzare** [A1] *tr.* to magnetize.
**magne·tico** *adj.* magnetic.
**magnific-are** [A2 s] *tr.* to magnify; to exalt. **-at** *m. indecl.* Magnificat.
**magni·fico** *adj.* magnificent; splendid; fine; title of honour now reserved for Vice-Chancellor of a University: *il Magnifico Rettore.*
**magniloquen-te** *adj.* grandiloquent. **-za** *f.* grandiloquence.
**magnitu·dine** *f.* magnitude.
**magn-o** *adj.* great; *Carlo* —, Charlemagne; *Gregorio* —, Gregory the Great; *aula -a*, great hall; *la -a Carta inglese*, the Magna Carta.
**magno·lia** *f.* magnolia.
**mago** *m.* magician; wizard; sorcerer.
**Magon-za** *pr.n.f.* (geog.) Mainz. **-tino** *adj., n.m.* (inhabitant) of Mainz.
**magra** *f.* thin woman; (geog.) low water.
**magrezza** *f.* thinness; leanness; meagreness; scantiness.
**magro** *adj.* thin; meagre; lean; poor; scanty; *n.m.* thin part; lean of meat; *mangiare di* —, to abstain from meat.
**mai** *adv.* ever; *più che* —, more than ever; *se* —, if ever; *caso* —, if anything, if by any chance; never (with neg., expressed or implied); *non lo vidi* —, I never saw him; — *e poi* — *!*, never,

never!; — *più*, never more, never again; *ora o* —, now or never; *meglio tardi che* —, better late than never; *non si sa* —, you never can tell.

**maial-e** *m.* pig, swine; pork. **-ẹsco** *adj.* (*m.pl.* **-ẹschi**) filthy, dirty. **-ino** *m. dim.* piglet. **-ọne** *m. augm.* large pig; (fig.) filthy pig.

**maiest-à** *f.* majesty. **-a·tico** *adj.* pertaining to majesty; *il 'Noi' -atico*, the royal 'We'.

**maio·lica** *f.* majolica.

**maionẹse** *f.* (cul.) mayonnaise.

**Maiorca** *pr.n.f.* (geog.) Majorca.

**mais** *m. indecl.* maize.

**maiu·scolo** *adj.* capital (of letter); (fig.) big, gross.

**mal-** *pref.* evil-, ill-. **-accẹtto** *adj.* unacceptable. **-accọlto** *adj.* ill-received; undesired, unwelcome. **-accọncio** *adj.* unfit, unsuitable. **-accorto** *adj.* incautious; imprudent; rash; awkward. **-affare** *m.* base life; evil living; *donna di -affare*, prostitute. **-affetto** *adj.* ill-disposed. **-agiato** *adj.* badly-off; hard-up. **-andare** [A7] *intr.* (*aux.* essere) to go to ruin; to take a bad turn; to fall into a poor condition. **-anno** *m.* grave misfortune, calamity; illness, disease; (fig.) blackguard. **-a·ria** *f.* bad air; malaria. **-a·rico** *adj.* malarial; *n.m.* person suffering from malaria. **-augurato** *adj.* unlucky, unfortunate; inauspicious. **-augu·rio** *m.* bad omen. **-augurọso** *adj.* of ill omen, inauspicious. **-avveduto** *adj.* imprudent, unwise. **-avventura** *f.* mischance; misfortune. **-avventurato** *adj.* unlucky, unfortunate. **-avviṣato** *adj.* ill-advised; unwise. **-capitato** *adj.* unfortunate, unlucky. **-ca·uto** *adj.* incautious, imprudent. **-cominciato** *adj.* badly begun. **-compọsto** *adj.* awkward; disorderly. **-concepito** *adj.* ill-conceived. **-cọncio** *adj.* damaged; in a sorry state. **-considerato** *adj.* ill-considered. **-consigliato** *adj.* ill-advised; incautious. **-contento** *adj.* discontented, dissatisfied; *n.m.* discontent; dissatisfaction; malcontent. **-curante** *adj.* careless, negligent. **-curato** *adj.* badly cared for. **-destro** *adj.* awkward, clumsy. **-dicente** *adj.* slanderous; evil-speaking; *n.m.* slanderer. **-dicenza** *f.* slander; scandal; backbiting. **-difẹso** *adj.* ill-defended. **-dispọsto** *adj.* ill-disposed. **-educato** *adj.* ill-bred; ill-mannered; *n.m.* ill-bred person. **-e·fico** *adj.* evil; baleful; malignant. **-erba** *f.* weed. **-es·sere** *m.* indisposition; malaise: uneasiness; bad financial condition. **-estro** *m.* mischief. **-famato** *adj.* of bad reputation. **-fare** [B14] *intr.* (*aux.* avere) to do evil; *n.m.* evil-doing. **-fatto** *adj.* ill-done; ill-shaped; *n.m.* misdeed. **-fattọre** *m.* evil-doer; malefactor. **-fẹrmo** *adj.* unsafe, insecure; shaky; feeble. **-fidato** *adj.* distrustful; diffident. **-fidente** *adj.* distrustful. **-fido** *adj.* unreliable, untrustworthy. **-fondato** *adj.* ill-founded; (of an argument) weak, feeble. **-formato** *adj.* ill-formed. **-formazione** *f.* malformation. **-garbo** *m.* clumsiness; boorishness; *con -garbo*, with a bad grace. **-giudicare** [A2 s] *tr.* to misjudge. **-governo** *m.* misgovernment, maladministration, mismanagement; maltreatment. **-gradito** *adj.* unwelcome. **-grado** *prep.* in spite of; *adv.* willy nilly; *suo -grado*, against his will. **-graziọso** *adj.* ungracious; unattractive; uncouth. **-intenzionato** *adj.* with evil intentions; evil-minded. **-intẹso** *adj.* misconceived, wrong; *n.m.* misunderstanding. **-menare** [A1] *tr.* to ill-treat; to treat roughly. **-mẹsso** *adj.* poorly dressed; in a poor condition; badly off. **-nato** *adj.* ill-born; unlucky; *n.m.* unfortunate individual. **-oc·chio** *m.* the 'evil-eye'. **-ọra** *f.* ruin, perdition; *andare in -ora*, to go to the devil. **-ọre** *m.* illness. **-pensante** *adj.* wrong-thinking. **-pensato** *adj.* badly thought out; ill-contrived. **-pi·glio** *m.* act of disdain, or anger; scorn; frown. **-pra·tico** *adj.* inexperienced; unskilful. **-preparato** *adj.* ill-prepared. **-provveduto** *adj.* ill-provided. **-sano** *adj.* unwholesome; unsound. **-sicuro** *adj.* uncertain, unsafe; unsteady. **-soddisfatto** *adj.* dissatisfied. **-sofferente** *adj.* (*prep* di) intolerant (of); putting up (with) unwillingly; impatient (of). **-talento** *m.* evil disposition; bad frame of mind; ill-will. **-tempo** *m.* bad weather. **-tenuto** *adj.* badly kept. **-tolto** *adj.* ill-gotten; *n.m.* ill-gotten gain. **-trattare** [A1] *tr.* to ill-treat; to ill-use. **-umọre** *m.* bad humour; bad temper; spleen. **-va·gio** *adj.* wicked. **-vedẹre** [B5] *tr.* to treat with ill-will; to hate. **-veduto** *part. adj.* disliked, hated. **-versaziọne** *f.* (leg.) embezzlement; fraudulent conversion. **-vestito** *adj.* badly dressed. **-visto** *part. adj.* disliked, hated. **-vivente** *adj.* dissolute, ill-living; *n.m.* rogue, scamp; criminal. **-vivenza** *f.* dissoluteness. **-volente** *part. adj.* malevolent; *n.m., f.* malevolent person. **-volentieri** *adv.* unwillingly. **-volẹre** [B36] *tr.* to dislike, to hate; *n.m.* ill-will.

**mala-** *pref.* evil; inferior. **-bẹs·tia** *f.* monster. **-creanza** *f.* (*pl.* **malecreanze**) bad manners; ill-breeding; rudeness. **-fatta** *f.* fault, slip; *pl.* (**malefatte**) evil deeds. **-fẹde** *f.* bad faith. **-fitta** *f.* quagmire, bog. **-gra·zia** *f.* uncouthness; rudeness; bad grace; ungraciousness. **-lingua** *f.* (*pl.* **malelingue**) slanderer, backbiter. **-pena** *adv. phr.* *a -pena*, scarcely, hardly; with difficulty. **-vita** *f.* low life; rogues, ruffians. **-vo·glia** *f.* ill-will; reluctance; sloth.

**Malacca** *pr.n.f.* (geog.) Malacca; *stretto di* —, Straits of Malacca; *penisola di* —, Malay Peninsula.

**Malachi·a** *pr.n.m.* (bibl.) Malachi.

**malachite** *f.* (miner.) malachite.

**malat-o** *adj.* ill; sick; sore; *n.m.* sick person, patient. **-ic·cio** *adj. dim.* sickly, ailing.

**malatti·a** *f.* illness; disease, malady; ailment, complaint; — *cardiaca*, heart disease; (fig.) evil; trouble; ill.

**mal-e** *m.* (usu. abbreviated to **mal** before *prep.* 'di'); evil; *la scienza del bene e del* —, knowledge of good and evil; pain; ache, illness; *mal di testa*, headache; *mal di cuore*, heart disease; *mal di denti*, toothache; *mal di gola*, sore throat; *mal di mare*, sea-sickness; *far — a*, to hurt; sorrow; *la notizia mi fece molto* —, the news caused me much pain; harm; *niente di* —, no harm done; bad; *di — in peggio*, from bad to worse; misunderstanding; trouble; discord; *metter — fra due persone*, to make trouble between two people; *adv.* badly, ill; *sentirsi* —, to feel ill; unsuitably; *questo cappello vi sta* —, this hat doesn't suit you; to one's disadvantage, in bad condition; *cavarsela* —, to come off badly; with malice, harmfully; *parla — di voi*, he speaks ill of you; *manco — !*, fortunately!; *meno — che sei venuto*, I'm very glad you've come. **-edẹtto** *adj.* cursed; abominable; *sia -edetto*, cursed be; *excl.* curse it! **-edire** [B10] *tr.* to curse. **-ediziọne** *f.* curse, malediction. **-efi·cio** *m.* wicked action; misdeed; witchcraft. **-e·fico** *adj.* harmful; pernicious.

**Mal-e·ṣia** *pr.n.f.* (geog.) Malaya, Malaysia. **-ẹse** *adj., n.m., f.* Malay; *Stati Federati -esi*, Federated Malay States.

**malestro** *m.* damage, mischief.

**male·vol-o** *adj.* malevolent; hostile, malignant. **-enza** *f.* malevolence.

**mal-i·a** *f.* charm, enchantment. **-iardo** *m.* sorcerer, wizard; *adj.* enchanting; bewitching.

**-ọso** *adj.* casting a spell upon; enchanting; charming.

**malign-are** [A5] *intr.* (*aux.* avere) to think or speak malignantly; *tr.* to malign. **-ità** *f.* malignancy; wickedness. **-o** *adj.* malignant, evil; malicious; mischievous; *n.m.* evil person.

**malin-coni·a** *f.* melancholy. **-co·nico** *adj.* melancholy; gloomy; sad. **-coniọso** *adj.* melancholy.

**malincorpo** *adv. phr. a —,* unwillingly; resentfully.

**malincuore** *adv. phr.* against one's will; reluctantly.

**mali·zi-a** *f.* malice; knowledge of evil; cunning. **-ọso** *adj.* malicious, cunning; mischievous.

**mallea·bile** *adj.* malleable; (fig.) adaptable.

**mallev-adọre** *m.* guarantor; (leg.) surety; *essere —,* to go bail. **-ador·ia** *f.* (leg.) recognizance(s); *prestare -adoria,* to put up bail. **-eri·a** *f.* guarantee; suretyship.

**mallo** *m.* husk.

**malloppo** *m.* parcel.

**malo** *adj.* bad, wicked; *in — modo,* badly, rudely; *mala lingua,* spiteful tongue.

**malta**[I] *f.* mortar; *riempimento con —,* grouting.

**Malt-a** *pr.n.f.* (geog.) Malta. **-ẹse** *adj., n.m., f.* Maltese.

**malt-o** *m.* malt. **-eri·a** *f.* malthouse

**malva** *f.* (bot.) mallow.

**malvọne** *m.* (bot.) hollyhock.

**mamma** *f.* mother; mamma; mummy; *— mia!,* goodness gracious!

**mammella** *f.* breast; udder; teat.

**mammellọne** *m.* (geog.) hummock, rounded peak.

**mammi·fero** *adj.* (zool.) mammalian; *n.m.* (zool.) mammal.

**mammillare** *adj.* (anat.) mamillary.

**mam·mola** *f.* (bot.) violet.

**mammu·t** *m. indecl.* (zool.) mammoth.

**manata** *f.* handful; blow with the hand, cuff; slap.

**manca** *f.* left, left-hand side.

**manc-are** [A2] *intr.* (*aux.* avere, essere) to be lacking; to be missing; to fail; to give way; *sentirsi —,* to turn faint; *-a un quarto alle sette,* it's a quarter to seven; *— di parola,* to break one's word. **-ante** *adj.* lacking; wanting; missing; *-ante di,* in need of. **-anza** *f.* want, lack; absence; breach; defect; default.

**manchẹvol-e** *adj.* lacking; wanting; defective, deficient; faulty. **-ẹzza** *f.* defect, deficiency, imperfection.

**man·cia** *f.* tip, gratuity, gift; *una lauta —,* a lavish tip.

**manciata** *f.* handful; a good handful.

**mancina** *f.* left; left hand.

**mancin-o** *adj.* left; left-handed; treacherous; underhand; *n.m.* left-handed man. **-a** *f.* left hand; left-handed woman.

**Man·ci-ù** *pr.n.m., adj.* Manchu. **-u·ria** *pr.n.f.* (geog.) Manchuria.

**manco** *m.* want, lack; defect, fault; *verrò senza —,* I'll come without fail; *adj.* defective, weak; left; *a mano manca,* to the left; *adv.* less; *nè —,* not even; *— male,* all the better.

**mancorrente** *m.* handrail.

**mandamẹnt-o** *m.* command; commission; area of jurisdiction of local authority; borough; district. **-ale** *adj.* of the borough, of the district; *consiglio -ale,* district council.

**mandare** [A1] *tr.* to send; to forward; to put into circulation; to drive; *— via,* to send away, to dismiss; *— giù,* to swallow; *— ad effetto,* to carry out, to put into practice; *— a male,* to spoil, to ruin; (leg.) to discharge; (naut.) *— a fondo,* to sink.

**mandarino** *m.* mandarin; mandarine orange.

**mandata** *f.* quantity sent; batch, lot; series; turn of the key.

**mandata·rio** *m.* (leg.) agent; (comm.) *— commerciale,* mercantile agent; *— generale,* general agent.

**mandato** *m.* order, command; mandate; warrant; *— di pagamento,* money order; *— di cattura,* warrant of arrest.

**mandi·bola** *f.* mandible; jaw.

**mandolino** *m.* (mus.) mandoline.

**man·dorl-a** *f.* almond; kernel of any stone fruit. **-ato** *m.* almond-cake; nougat; lattice-work; *adj.* almond-shaped. **-o** *m.* (bot.) almond tree.

**mandra** *f.* herd, flock; cattle-shed.

**man-dra·gola, -dra·gora** *f.* mandrake; mandragora.

**mandriano** *m.* herdsman, shepherd.

**mandritta** *f.* right hand; *voltare a —,* to turn to the right.

**mane** *f.* (poet.) morning; *da — a sera,* from morn till eve.

**maneggẹvol-e** *adj.* manageable, easily handled, handy. **-ẹzza** *f.* (eng.) manoevrability.

**maneggiare** [A3c] *tr.* to handle; to finger; to manage; to use; *rfl.* to manage skilfully; to behave with cunning.

**manẹggio** *m.* handling; management; cunning; plot; riding-school; horsemanship.

**manẹs-co** *adj.* (*pl.* **-chi**) ready with one's hands, ready to strike a blow; aggressive; manageable, portable.

**manẹtta** *f.* handcuff; grip, handle.

**manganello** *m.* cudgel, club.

**man·gano** *m.* mangle; pressing-machine.

**mangerẹccio** *adj.* edible; nice to eat, tasty.

**mangeri·a** *f.* illegitimate gains; swindle.

**mangi-are** [A3] to eat; to devour; *ci si -a bene,* the food is good there; to corrode; to take bribes; *— il patrimonio,* to squander one's inheritance; *— la strada,* to devour the road; *n.m.* eating; food, victuals. **-a·bile** *adj.* edible; eatable. **-aformiche** *m. indecl.* (zool.) anteater. **-apreti** *m. indecl.* priest-hater, anticlerical. **-ata** *f.* plentiful meal. **-atọia** *f.* crib, manger. **-atọre** *m.* eater; hearty eater. **-ato·ria** *f.* eating; (fig.) swindling. **-atura** *f.* bite, sting.

**mangime** *m.* food for animals or birds; fodder.

**mangiọne** *m.* great eater, glutton.

**mangiucchiare** [A4] *tr.* to eat slowly, to eat without appetite; to nibble.

**mang-ọsta, -usta** *f.* (zool.) mongoose.

**man-i·a** *f.* mania; madness; (fig.) craze; fad; hobby. **-i·aco** *m.* maniac; *adj.* maniacal; (fig.) eccentric, odd.

**ma·ni-ca**[I] *f.* sleeve; *essere in -che di camicia,* to be in one's shirt sleeves; *quello è un altro paio di -che,* that's another kettle of fish; wing (of a house); armlet; handle; hilt; troop of soldiers; *— a vento,* wind sock.

**ma·nica**[2] *f.* (geog.) inlet; *pr.n.f. la Manica,* English Channel.

**maniche·o** *adj.* Manichaean; *n.m.* Manichee.

**manichẹtta** *f.* ruffle; cuff; hosepipe.

**manichẹtto** *m.* small handle; cuff.

**manichino** *m.* manikin; mannequin; cuff; handcuff; ruffle.

**ma·nico** *m.* handle; *— di scopa,* broomstick; helve; (mus.) neck of a stringed instrument.

**manico·mio** *m.* lunatic asylum.

**manicotto** *m.* muff; (eng.) clutch; socket; pipe lining.

**manier-a** *f.* manner, way, style; *in nessuna —,* not at all; *di — che,* so that. **-ato** *adj.* affected, mannered; *pittore -ato,* mannerist. **-ịsmo** *m.* mannerism. **-ista** *m., f.* mannerist. **-ọso** *adj.* well-mannered; polite.

**maniero** *m.* manor house.

**manifattọre** *m.* workman; manufacturer; *adj.* manufacturing.

**manifattur-a** *f.* manufacture; manufactory, works; cost of manufacture. **-iere** *m.* manufacturer. **-iero** *adj.* manufacturing; industrial.

**manifest-are** [A1] *tr.* to manifest; to show; to declare; to reveal; to exhibit; *rfl.* to show oneself; to reveal oneself; to appear. **-azịone** *f.* manifesta-

tion; event; (pol.) demonstration.

**manifesto** *m.* public announcement, poster; manifesto.

**mani·gli-a** *f.* handle; shackle; bracelet; strap; *pl.* handcuffs. **-are** [A4] *tr.* to shackle; to handcuff.

**manigoldo** *m.* rascal, ruffian; scoundrel.

**manimettere** [C20] *tr.* to begin using; to broach.

**manina** *f. dim.* of **mano**; little hand; (typ.) fist, pointer.

**manipolare**[1] *m.* Roman soldier; *adj.* pertaining to a maniple or band of soldiers.

**manipol-are**[2] [A1 s] *tr.* to manipulate, to work; to handle; to treat, to deal with; — *con cura*, handle with care; to adulterate; to falsify. **-atore** *m.* manipulator; plotter.

**mani·polo** *m.* handful, bundle; handle.

**maniscal-co** *m.* (*pl.* **-chi**) farrier; smith.

**manna**[1] *f.* manna; blessing; *è stata una* —, it's been a godsend.

**manna**[2] *f.* sheaf, bundle.

**mannag·gia** *excl.* damn!; devil take it!

**manna·i-a** *f.* axe, chopper; (fig.) tyranny, despotism. **-ola** *f.* axe; bill-hook. **-uolo** *m. dim.* hatchet.

**mannaro** *adj.* bogey; *lupo* —, werewolf; (pop.) epileptic.

**mannello** *m.* sheaf, bundle.

**man-o** *f.* (*pl.* **-i**; abbrev. to **man** in some phrases) hand; *stringere la — a*, to shake hands with; *una stretta di* —, a handshake; *battere le -i*, to clap, to applaud; *fatto a* —, hand-made; *giuoco di* —, sleight of hand, trick, artifice; power; possession; influence, control; agency; custody; *cadere in — a*, to fall into the hands of; *riconosco la tua — in questo*, I can see you have had a hand in this; help, assistance, a helping hand; *prestare — a*, to lend a hand to; — *d'opera*, labour, workmen, hands; handful; small quantity; handwriting; *scrive una bella* —, he writes a good hand; touch; style; (cards) deal; hand; (the) lead; range, reach; *sotto* —, at hand, handy; *a portata di* —, within reach; side, direction, source; *a man destra*, to, on the right; *di prima* —, at first hand; *da ogni* —, on all sides; coat, covering; *due -i di vernice*, two coats of varnish; — *del fondo*, undercoat; *ultima* —, top coat, (fig.) finishing touch; *adv. phr. a — a* —, gradually; *man — che*, as soon as, just as.

**manodo·pera** *f.* manual labour; cost of labour; hands employed in manual labour (also *mano d'opera*).

**mano·metro** *m.* (eng.) pressure gauge.

**manomettere** [C20] *tr.* to begin the use of; to open; to lay hands upon; to tamper with; to handle roughly; to violate; to plunder; to lay waste; to search illegally.

**manomissione** *f.* violation; *segni di* —, signs of having been tampered with.

**mano·pola** *f.* gauntlet; iron glove; fencing glove; sling for the wrist; elbow-rest; handle, hand grip; (radio, etc.) knob.

**manoscritto** *m.* manuscript; *adj.* handwritten; in manuscript.

**manovale** *m.* labourer, unskilled worker; day-labourer.

**manovella** *f.* handle, lever; hand-spike; (eng.) crank; *albero a* —, crankshaft; — *alza-cristalli*, window-winder.

**manovr-a** *f.* move; manœuvre; (rlwy.) shunting; *camera di* —, control room. **-abilità** *f.* manœuvrability. **-are** [A1] *tr.* to manœuvre. **-atore** *m.* (eng.) driver; (rlwy.) *-atore di scambi*, shunter, pointsman.

**manrove·scio** *m.* back-handed blow; back-stroke; (tennis) back hand.

**mansalva** *adv. phr. a* —, with impunity.

**mansarda** *f.* (archit.) mansard.

**mansione** *f.* stay, sojourn; halt; abode; address; office, duty, function; permanent post.

**mansuefare** [B14] *tr.* to tame; to subdue; to domesticate; to pacify, to soothe, to quiet.

**mansuet-o** *adj.* gentle; docile; tame; meek. **-u·dine** *f.* gentleness; docility; tameness; meekness.

**manteca** *f.* pomade.

**mantella** *f.* woman's long cloak or mantle.

**mantell-o** *m.* cloak, cape, mantle; *mutare il* —, to be a turncoat; (of animals) coat. **-are** [A1] *tr.* to cloak, to cover with a mantle.

**manten-ere** [B32] *tr.* to keep; to maintain; to support; *rfl.* to keep oneself; *-ersi in buona salute*, to keep in good health. **-imento** *m.* maintenance, keeping; preservation.

**man·tic-e** *m.* bellows; hood of a carriage; (rlwy.) vestibule (corridor connecting two coaches); (mus.) organ-bellows. **-ia·io** *m.* bellows-maker.

**man·tide** *f.* (ent.) praying mantis.

**manti·glia** *f.* mantilla.

**manto** *m.* cloak, mantle; (fig.) protection, defence.

**Man·tov-a** *pr.n.f.* Mantua. **-ano** *adj.*, *n.m.* Mantuan.

**manuale**[1] *adj.* manual; *lavoro* —, manual labour.

**manual-e**[2] *m.* handbook, manual. **-ista** *m.* writer of a handbook.

**manuale**[3] *m.* (mus.) manual.

**manu·brio** *m.* haft; handle, grip; dumb-bell; (of cycle) handle bar; (of organ) stop-handle.

**manufatto** *adj.* manufactured; *n.m.* manufactured article.

**manuten·golo** *m.* receiver of stolen goods; accomplice.

**manutenzione** *f.* maintenance, upkeep; (eng.) servicing.

**manz-o** *m.* steer; bullock; beef; — *lesso*, boiled beef; (fig.) fat man, clumsy person. **-a** *f.* heifer.

**mao** *onom.* miaow.

**Maomett-o** *pr.n.m.* Mohammed. **-ano** *adj.*, *n.m.* Mohammedan. **-ismo** *m.* Mohammedanism.

**mapp-a** *f.* map; plan; — *celeste*, map of the heavens. **-amondo** *m.* map of the world; map shown in hemispheres; globe. **-atore** *m.* cartographer.

**marame** *m.* rubbish; refuse.

**maras-ca** *f.* (bot.) morello cherry. **-chino** *m.* maraschino liqueur.

**marasma** *f.* (med.) wasting disease; (fig.) decay, atrophy.

**Maratona** *pr.n.f.* (geog.) Marathon; (fig.) marathon (race).

**marca** *f.* mark; token; counter; — *di fabbrica*, trade mark; — *depositata*, registered trade mark; — *a fuoco*, brand; border; district, region; (geog.) *le Marche*, the Marches.

**Marcanto·nio** *pr.n.m.* Mark Antony

**marc-are** [A2] *tr.* to mark; to note, to make a note of; — *i punti*, to keep the score; — *dei punti*, to score, to score points; — *a fuoco*, to brand; *intr.* (*aux.* avere) to march, to be bordering. **-apiano** *m. indecl.* (building) string course. **-atore** *m.* marker; scorer.

**Marc'aure·lio** *pr.n.m.* Marcus Aurelius.

**marches-a** *f.* marchioness. **-ato** *m.* marquisate. **-e** *m.* marquis.

**Marchesi** *pr.n.f.pl.* (geog.) Marquesas (Islands).

**marchiano** *adj.* huge, enormous; gross.

**marchigiano** *adj.* (geog.) of the Marches; *n.m.* native or inhabitant of the Marches.

**mar·ch-io** *m.* (*pl.* **-ii**) (leg.; comm.) brand, mark; — *di impresa*, trade mark.

**mar·cia**[1] *f.* (*pl.* **mar·cie**) march; *a marcie forzate*, by forced marches; (motor.) gear; *cambiare* —, to change gear; *a tre marcie*, three-speed; (mus.) *alla* —, with the style and rhythm of a march; — *funebre*, dead march; — *nuziale*, wedding march; (fig.) progress, advance.

**mar·cia**[2] *f.* pus, festering matter.

**Marciana** *pr.n.f.* St. Mark's Library (Venice).

**marciapiede** *m.* pavement; footpath; (rlwy.) platform.
**marciare** [A3] *intr.* (*aux.* avere) to march; to go; to advance, to progress; to function.
**mar·cido** *adj.* rotting; going bad; withered; tainted; (colloq.) drunk, tight.
**marcime** *m.* (agric.) stable manure.
**mar·cio** *adj.* rotten, bad; spoiled; tainted; *uova marce*, rotten eggs; *carne marcia*, bad meat; (of a wall) crumbling; *avere torto —*, to be totally in the wrong; *n.m.* rottenness, rotten part; *rompere il —*, to stop the rot.
**marc-ire** [D2] *intr.* (*aux.* essere) to decay, to go bad, to fester, to rot; (of a wall) to crumble; to waste away; to become morally corrupt. **-itura** *f.* rotting; maceration. **-iume** *m.* rottenness, rot; festering sore; pus; (fig.) corruption.
**Marco**[1] *pr.n.m.* Mark; Marcus.
**mar-co**[2] *m.* (*pl.* **-chi**) (finan.) mark; (rugby) mark.
**mare** *m.* sea; *in alto —*, on the high sea, (fig.) at sea; *— grosso*, heavy sea; *braccio di —*, inlet; *mal di —*, sea-sickness; *gettare in —*, to throw overboard, to jettison; (fig.) crowd, vast quantity.
**mare·a** *f.* tide; ebb and flow; *alta —*, high tide; *bassa —*, low tide; *— stanca*, slack tide; *— quadraturale*, neap tide; *— sigiziale*, spring tide.
**mareggi-are** [A3 c] *intr.* (*aux.* avere) to rise and fall in waves; to undulate; to surge; to swell; to float; *n.m.* swell, surge. **-ata** *f.* heavy sea; surge, swell.
**marẹggio** *m.* undulation; surge, swell.
**marẹmm-a** *f.* (geog.) maremma; fen, marsh, swampy coast. **-ano** *adj.* relating to a marsh or to fenland; relating to the Tuscan Maremma; *n.m.* inhabitant of the Maremma.
**maremoto** *m.* sea-quake, submarine earthquake; *onda di —*, tidal wave.
**marenga** *f.* (cul.) meringue.
**mareo·grafo** *m.* tide-gauge.
**maresciallo** *m.* (mil.) marshal; highest grade of non-commissioned officer (equiv. to R.S.M.); police inspector; (naut.) Chief Petty Officer.
**marẹtta** *f.* choppy sea; slight swell.
**marezẓare** [A1 c] *tr.* to water (silk); to give a veining to (wood); to marble.
**marga** *f.* (agric.) marl, loam.
**Margherita**[1] *pr.n.f.* Margaret; Marguerite.
**margherita**[2] *f.* pearl; (bot.) ox-eye daisy.
**margin-ale** *adj.* marginal. **-a·lia** *m.pl.* marginalia. **-are** [A1 s] *tr.* (typ.) to margin; *intr.* (*aux.* avere) to leave a margin. **-atura** *f.* (typ.) margining; (fig.) edging, border. **-ọso** *adj.* having a wide margin.
**mar·gine** *m.* border, margin, edge; scar; *in — a*, on the subject of, talking of; (typ.) *— di taglio*, fore-edge.
**Mari·a** *pr.n.f.* Mary, Maria.
**mariano** *adj.* of Mary; consecrated to the Virgin; *il mese —*, the month of May.
**marina** *f.* sea, ocean; sea-coast; sea-side resort; esplanade; navy; *fanteria di —*, marines; (paint.) sea-piece.
**marina·io** *m.* sailor; *mastro —*, captain of a ship; *adj.* maritime.
**marinare** [A1] *tr.* (cul.) to marinate; (fig.) to keep laid by; *— la scuola*, to play truant.
**marinar-o** *adj.* (pop.) sea-faring; seamanlike; *nazione -a*, seafaring nation; *adv. phr. alla -a*, in sailor fashion; *colletta alla -a*, middy collar. **-a** *f.* child's sailor suit; sailor's hat; sou'-wester. **-ẹsco** *adj.* (*m.pl.* **-ẹschi**) nautical.
**marineri·a** *f.* naval strength; seamanship.
**marino** *adj.* of the sea, marine; *acqua marina*, sea-water; (zool.) *vitello —*, seal; (naut.) water-spout.
**mariol-eri·a** *f.* trick, fraud, swindling; roguery; prank. **-ẹsco** *adj.* (*m.pl.* **-ẹschi**) fraudulent, swindling. **-o** *m.* rogue, cheat, swindler.
**marionẹtt-a** *f.* marionette; puppet. **-ista** *m.* marionettist; puppet-master, puppet-showman.
**marit-ale** *adj.* marital. **-are** [A1] *tr.* to marry; to give in marriage; *rfl.* to marry, to get married. **-ata** *f. adj.* married; *n.f.* married woman.
**marito** *m.* husband; *una figlia in età da —*, a daughter of marriageable age.
**marit·timo** *adj.* marine, maritime; *n.m.pl.* seafaring folk.
**marma·glia** *f.* rabble.
**marmellata** *f.* jam; marmalade; preserve.
**marmitta** *f.* saucepan; pot; kettle.
**marm-o** *m.* marble; marble bust; marble statue; *cava di —*, marble quarry; *pallina di —*, marble (child's toy); *pl.* kinds of marble; statues. **-i·fero** *adj.* marble-bearing. **-ista** *m.* worker in marble. **-o·reo** *adj.* of marble; in marble; marmoreal.
**marmoc·ch-io** *m.* (*pl.* **-i**) brat; urchin.
**marmor-a·rio** *m.* marble-cutter, worker in marble. **-izẓare** [A1] *tr.* to marble.
**marmotta** *f.* (zool.) marmot; (fig.) idler, lazy-bones; recluse.
**marna** *f.* (geol.) marl.
**marocchino** *m.*, *adj.* morocco (leather).
**Marocco** *pr.n.m.* Morocco.
**marr-a** *f.* hoe; mattock; (naut.) fluke. **-aiuolo** *m.* sapper; delver, pioneer. **-eggiare** [A3 c] *tr.*, *intr.* (*aux.* avere) to hoe.
**marrano** *m.* traitor, miscreant; bully.
**marrọn-e** *m.* (bot.) Spanish chestnut; *— candito*, marron glacé; gross error, blunder; *adj.* chestnut-coloured. **-ẹto** *m.* chestnut plantation.
**Marsala** *pr.n.f.* (geog.) Marsala; *m.* marsala (wine).
**Marsi·gl-ia** *pr.n.f.* (geog.) Marseilles. **-ẹse** *adj.* of Marseilles; *n.m.*, *f.* inhabitant of Marseilles; *la Marsigliese*, the Marseillaise.
**marsina** *f.* evening dress (men's), tails; tail-coat.
**marsovino** *m.* (zool.) porpoise.
**marsu·pi-o** *m.* (zool.) pouch. **-ale** *adj.* (zool.) marsupial. **-ali** *n.m.pl.* (zool.) marsupials.
**Marta** *pr.n.f.* Martha.
**Marte** *pr.n.m.* (myth.) Mars.
**martedì** *pr.n.m.* Tuesday; *— grasso*, Shrove Tuesday.
**martellare** [A1] *tr.* to hammer; to torture; *intr.* (*aux.* avere) to throb, to pulsate.
**martello** *m.* hammer; *— da fabbro*, sledge hammer; *campana —*, alarm-bell; door-knocker; gavel, auctioneer's hammer; (sport) *lancio del —*, hammer throwing.
**martinello** *m.* (mech.) lifting-jack; (orn.) plover.
**Martinica** *pr.n.f.* (geog.) *Isola —*, Martinique.
**Martino**[1] *pr.n.m.* Martin; *estate di San —*, St. Martin's summer, Indian summer; *fare il San —*, to move house.
**martino**[2] *m.* (orn.) *martin pescatore*, kingfisher.
**mar·tire** *m.*, *f.* martyr.
**marti·r-io** *m.* (*pl.* **-ii**) martyrdom; torment; torture.
**martir-izẓare** [A1] *tr.* to martyr; to martyrize. **-izẓato** *part. adj.* martyred; *n.m.* martyr. **-olo·gio** *m.* martyrology; book of martyrs.
**mar·tora** *f.* (zool.) marten.
**martoriare** [A4] *tr.* to torture; to torment.
**marx-iṣmo** *m.* (pol.) Marxism. **-ista** *m.*, *f.*, *adj.* Marxist.
**marzapane** *m.* (cul.) marzipan.
**marziale** *adj.* martial, bellicose; warlike; soldierly.
**marziano** *adj.*, *n.m.* Martian.
**mar·zio** *adj.* relating to Mars; martial; *campo —*, parade ground.
**marz-o** *pr.n.m.* March; *gl'idi di —*, the Ides of March. **-uolo** *adj.* of March; *galletto -uolo*, spring chicken.
**Marzocco** *pr.n.m.* Marzocco, the heraldic lion of Florence.

**mascalci·a** *f.* farriery; horse-shoeing.
**mascalzone** *m.* rascal, rogue; scoundrel, blackguard.
**mascell-a** *f.* jaw; jaw-bone. **-are** *adj.* maxillary; *osso -are*, jaw-bone; *dente -are*, molar.
**ma·scher-a** *f.* mask; disguise; face, expression, features; *una — interessante*, an interesting head; *ballo in —*, fancy-dress ball; masque; masker; make-up; (archit.) gargoyle. **-are** [A1 s] *tr.* to mask; to disguise; to camouflage; *rfl.* to put on a mask; to masquerade; to be camouflaged. **-ata** *f.* masque; masquerade.
**maschile** *adj.* male; virile, manly; *scuola —*, boys' school; (gramm.) masculine.
**ma·schio** *adj.* male; *un figlio —*, a son; manly, masculine; vigorous, manful, virile; *n.m.* male, boy, son; keep (of a castle), fortress; (techn.) piston-shaft.
**mascolin-o** *adj.* masculine; manly. **-ità** *f.* masculinity; manliness.
**masnad-a** *f.* set, gang. **-iere** *m.* highway robber; brigand; bandit.
**masoch-ismo** *m.* masochism. **-ista** *m.*, *f.* masochist.
**massa** *f.* mass, bulk; heap, pile; lump; large crowd; *adunata in —*, mass-meeting; *la — della gente*, the majority of people; *le masse*, the masses; (comm.) *vendere in —*, to sell by bulk.
**massacr-o** *m.* massacre; slaughter. **-are** [A1] *tr.* to massacre; to slaughter; (fig.) to ruin.
**massag·gi-o** *m.* massage. **-are** [A3] *tr.* to massage. **-atore** *m.* masseur. **-atrice** *f.* masseuse.
**mass-a·ia** *f.* housewife. **-a·io** *m.* householder; steward.
**massell-are** [A1] *tr.* to hammer, to beat out, to strike (hot iron). **-o** *m.* lump of red hot or beaten iron; block, mass; *oro in -o*, gold ingot.
**masseri·a** *f.* large farm; collection of farms under one management; herds of cattle, stock.
**masseri·zia** *f.* furniture; household goods or effects; thrift; good husbandry; *pl.* utensils; implements; fittings.
**massicci-are** [A3] *tr.* to lay down foundation for (a road); to ballast. **-ata** *f.* foundation; ballast.
**massic·cio**[1] *adj.* massive, bulky; solid; stout; *oro —*, solid gold; *n.m.* bulk; main body.
**massic·cio**[2] *m.* massif, group of mountain peaks.
**mas·sima** *f.* maxim, principle; rule; *in —*, as a rule, as a matter of principle; *in linea di —*, generally speaking.
**massimamente,** *adv.* see under **massimo.**
**massime** *adv.* especially, chiefly, above all; particularly; most.
**massimizzare** [A1] (neol.) to maximize.
**mas·sim-o** *adj.* greatest; most; maximum; *n.m.* maximum; utmost; highest. **-amente** *adv.* especially; most of all.
**masso** *m.* boulder; block (of stone); rock.
**mass-one** *m.* freemason; mason. **-oneri·a** *f.* freemasonry. **-o·nico** *adj.* masonic; *loggia -onica*, masonic lodge.
**mastello** *m.* tub, bucket; *— per bucato*, wash-tub.
**mastic-are** [A2] *tr.* to chew, to masticate; to mutter; to chew over; to ponder. **-azione** *f.* mastication.
**ma·stice** *m.* gum mastic; cement; *— di vetraio*, putty.
**mastino** *m.* mastiff.
**mastodonte** *m.* (zool.) mastodon.
**mastro**[1] *m.* see **maestro.**
**mastro**[2] *m.* (comm.) ledger; *riportare a —*, to post (in a ledger), *— a fogli sciolti*, loose leaf ledger; *adj. libro —*, ledger.
**masturb-are** [A1] *tr.*, *rfl.* to masturbate. **-azione** *f.* masturbation.
**matassa** *f.* (text.) hank, skein; (fig.) tangle; *trovare il bandolo della —*, to disentangle a complicated matter.
**matema·tic-a** *f.* mathematics. **-o** *m.* mathematician; *adj.* mathematical.
**materassa** *f.* mattress; *— a molle*, spring mattress.
**mate·ria** *f.* matter; substance, material; subject; *indice delle materie*, table of contents; (econ.) *— prima*, raw material.
**material-e** *adj.* material; physical; manual; gross, coarse; sensual; actual, effectual; *possesso —*, vacant possession; *un errore —*, a clerical error; *n.m.* material; *consumo del —*, wear and tear. **-ismo** materialism. **-ista** *m.*, *f.* materialist. **-i·stico** *adj.* materialistic. **-izzare** [A1] *tr.* to render material.
**matern-o** *adj.* maternal; motherly; *lingua -a*, mother tongue. **-ità** *f.* maternity, motherhood.
**matit-a** *f.* black lead, graphite; pencil, lead-pencil; crayon, chalk; *— sfera*, ball-pointed pen. **-atoio** *m.* pencil-box, pencil-case.
**matriarc-ale** *adj.* matriarchal. **-ato** *m.* matriarchy.
**matric-e** *f.* (anat.) womb, matrix; (fig.) mould; (comm.) counterfoil; (typ.) matrix. **-ale** *adj.* (anat.) uterine.
**matric-ida** *m.*, *f.* (*pl.m.*, *f.* **-idi**) (leg.) (person guilty of matricide. **-i·dio** *m.* (*pl.* **-i·dii**) crime of matricide; case of matricide.
**matri·col-a** *f.* register, roll; (Univ.) matriculation; freshman, first year man (or woman) student. **-are** [A1 s] *tr.* to register; (Univ.) to enter on the matriculation roll; *rfl.* to matriculate; to enter a University. **-azione** *f.* registration; (Univ.) matriculation.
**matrigna** *f.* stepmother; (fig.) cruel mother.
**matrimo·ni-o** *m.* wedlock; matrimony; *chiedere in —*, to ask in marriage; wedding; match; *— legittimo*, lawful wedlock; marriage lines. **-ale** *adj.* matrimonial; conjugal; nuptial; *letto -ale*, double-bed.
**matrizzare** [A1] *intr.* (*aux.* avere) to take after one's mother.
**matron-a** *f.* matron, married woman. **-ale** *adj.* matronly.
**mattacino** *m.* strolling dancer; acrobat; jester; mimic.
**mattadore** *m.* matador.
**mattana** *f.* fit of depression, bad temper; spleen; whim.
**Matte·o** *pr.n.m.* Matthew.
**matterello** *m.* rolling-pin; roller (for a towel).
**mattin-a** *f.* morning; dawn; forenoon; *domani —*, tomorrow morning; *ier —*, yesterday morning. **-ale** *adj.* matutinal; *lezioni -ali*, morning lessons. **-ata** *f.* duration of the morning; forenoon; (mus.) aubade, dawn-song; (theatr.) matinée, afternoon performance. **-iero** *adj.* early morning; good at getting up in the morning. **-o** *m.* early morning; dawn; *di buon -o*, early in the morning.
**matt-o**[1] *adj.* mad, insane, deranged; crazy, eccentric, foolish; extreme; *— di*, wild about; *n.m.* madman, lunatic; crazy fool; (cards) joker. **-a** *f.* mad woman; foolish woman.
**matto**[2] *adj.* (chess) mate; *scacco —*, checkmate; *dare scacco — a*, to checkmate; (fig.) to defeat.
**matto**[3] *adj.* mat; dull, lustreless.
**matton-e** *m.* brick; tile; *-i lustri*, glazed bricks; (cards) diamonds. **-a·ia** *f.* brick-yard, brickfield. **-a·io** *m.* brick-maker, brick-manufacturer. **-ame** *m.* quantity of bricks (usu. rubble); brick-work. **-are** [A1 c] *tr.* to pave with bricks; to cover (floor) with tiles.
**mattutino** *adj.* of the morning; matutinal; early; *stella mattutina*, the morning star; *n.m.* (liturg.) Matins.
**matur-are** [A1] *intr.* (*aux.* essere) to ripen, to mature; to become due; *tr.* to cause to mature, to ripen; *rfl.* to become ripe; (fig.) to come to a head. **-azione** *f.* ripening; maturation; (comm.) maturity; *precoce -azione*, early ripening.
**matur-o** *adj.* ripe, mature; fully developed; sound, experienced. **-ità** *f.* ripeness; maturity; completion; *esame di -ità*,

entrance examination to a University.

**Matuṣalemme** *pr.n.m.* Methuselah.

**Mauri·zio** *pr.n.m.* Maurice; (geog.) *l'Isola* –, Mauritius.

**mauṣole·o** *m.* mausoleum.

**mazz-a** *f.* cudgel, club; walking-stick; hammer; staff; mallet; mace; (sport) bat; (mus.) drumstick; (paint.) mahlstick. **-iere** *m.* mace-bearer.

**mazz-o** *m.* bunch; group; bundle; club, stick; (cards) the pack; *fare il* –, to deal; *mischiare il* –, to shuffle. **-olino** *m. dim.* little bunch; (of flowers) nosegay. **-otto** *m.* mallet.

**me** *1st pers. prn. disjunct.* me; *secondo* –, in my opinion; *dissi tra* –, I said to myself; *l'ho fatto da* –, I did it by myself.

**meandro** *m.* curve, bend; meandering, winding; maze.

**mecc-a·nica** *f.* mechanics. **-a·nico** *adv.* mechanical; machine-like; automatic; *n.m.* mechanic; mechanician; engineer; driver. **-aniṣmo** *m.* mechanism; gear; works; machinery. **-aniẓẓare** [A1] *tr.* to mechanize.

**Mecenate** *pr.n.m.* Maecenas; (fig.) patron.

**mẹco** *pers. prn.* and *prep.* (poet.) with me.

**meda·gl-ia** *f.* medal; ancient coin; horse brass; *il rovescio della* –, the reverse of the medal; *il diritto della* –, the obverse of the medal. **-iọne** *m.* medallion. **-ista** *m.* numismatist; maker of medals, engraver.

**medẹsimo** *adj.* same, self-same; *prn.* self: *lo vidi io* –, I saw it myself.

**me·dia** *f.* average, mean; *in* –, on an average.

**mediana** *f.* centre line; (soccer) half-back line.

**mediano** *adj.* middle; medium; (naut.) *albero* –, mizzen mast; *n.m.* (soccer) half-back; *pl.* (rugger) backs.

**mediante** *prep.* by means of; through.

**medi-are** [A4] *intr.* (*aux.* essere) to be interposed; to mediate; *tr.* to strike an average between. **-atọre** *m.* mediator; intermediary, middle-man, broker, agent; *-atore di borsa*, stockbroker. **-aziọne** *f.* mediation; brokerage, commission.

**medic-are** [A2s] *tr.* to doctor, to treat; to heal; to medicate; *rfl.* to doctor oneself; to dose oneself. **-a·bile** *adj.* curable. **-amẹnto** *m.* medicament, remedy; treatment. **-amentọso** *adj.* medicinal. **-atọre** *m.* medicator; healer; *adj.* healing, curative. **-aziọne** *f.* medication, treatment; *posto di -azione*, first-aid post.

**medi·ceo** *adj.* (Ital. hist.) Medicean.

**mediche ri·a** *f.* out-patient department.

**medicin-a** *f.* medicine; *studente in* –, medical student; – *legale*, forensic medicine; physic, medicine; remedy; (fig.) cure. **-ale** *adj.* medicinal; *n.m.* drug, medicine; remedy.

**me·dic-o** *m.* doctor; physician; medical officer; (fig.) healer; – *condotto*, panel doctor; – *chirurgo*, surgeon, (or) general practitioner; *adj.* medicinal; medical; *cura -a*, medical treatment. **-astro** *m. pejor.* quack doctor.

**me·dio** *adj.* intermediate; middle; middling; average; mean, medium; *il* – *Evo*, the Middle Ages; *età media*, middle age; *scuole medie*, secondary schools (in Italy); *n.m.* mean; mean term; middle finger

**mediocr-e** *adj.* mediocre; middling; common-place, ordinary; indifferent, second-rate. **-ità** *f.* mediocrity; *l'aurea -ità*, the golden mean.

**medioev-ale** *adj.* medieval. **-alista** *m.* medievalist. **-o** *m.* Middle Ages.

**medit-are** [A1s] *tr.* to meditate upon, to ponder; to plan, to design, to think out; to plot; *intr.* (*aux.* avere) to meditate, to muse. **-abọndo** *m.* meditative; sunk in meditation. **-ativo** *adj.* meditative. **-aziọne** *f.* meditation; thoughtfulness, pensiveness; musing.

**Meduṣa**[1] *pr.n.f.* (myth.) Medusa.

**meduṣa**[2] *f.* medusa, jelly-fish.

**Mefisto·f-ele** *pr.n.m.* Mephistopheles. **-e·lico** *adj.* Mephistophelian.

**mef-ite** *f.* fetid air; (zool.) skunk. **-i·tico** *adj.* fetid, mephitic.

**megaciclo** *m.* (phys.) megacycle.

**mega·fono** *m.* megaphone; loud-speaker.

**megal-ito** *m.* megalith. **-i·tico** *adj.* megalithic.

**megal-o·mane** *m.* megalomaniac. **-omani·a** *f.* megalomania.

**me·glio** *adv. comp.* of **bene**; better; *mi sento* –, I feel better; *tanto* –*!*, so much the better!

**mẹl-a** *f.* apple; – *cotogna*, quince. **-ẹto** *m.* apple-orchard. **-o** *m.* apple-tree.

**melagran-a** *f.* (bot.) pomegranate. **-o** *m.* pomegranate tree.

**melanzana** *f.* (bot.) aubergine, egg-plant.

**melassa** *f.* molasses.

**melato** *adj.* sweet, honeyed.

**Meleagro** *pr.n.m.* (myth.) Meleager.

**melens-o** *adj.* dull, stupid, silly. **-ag·gine** *f.* stupidity; silliness.

**melli·fero** *adj.* honey-bearing; honey-producing.

**mellific-are** [A2s] *intr.* (*aux.* avere) to make honey. **-aziọne** *f.* honey-making.

**melli·flu-o** *adj.* mellifluous. **-ità** *f.* mellifluence.

**mẹlm-a** *f.* mire, mud, slime. **-oṣo** *adj.* muddy.

**mel-odi·a** *f.* melody; – *popolare*, folk song. **-o·dico** *adj.* melodic. **-odiọso** *adj.* melodious. **-odramma** *m.* a form of Italian opera. **-o·mane** *adj.* music-mad; *n.m.*, *f.* person who is mad about music. **-otrage·dia** *f.* tragic opera.

**melọne** *m.* (bot.) melon; – *d'acqua*, water melon.

**melopopọne** *m.* (bot.) squash, pumpkin.

**melopsit·taco** *m.* (orn.) budgerigar.

**Melpo·mene** *pr.n.f.* (myth.) Melpomene.

**membrana** *f.* (anat.; bot.) membrane; (fig.) thin tissue, film.

**membratura** *f.* frame, structure; framework.

**membr-o** (*pl.* -**a** *f.*) limb, member; (fig.) part, section; (*pl.* -**i** *m.*) member; – *a vita*, life-member.

**memor-a·bile** *adj.* memorable; worthy of commemoration; *n.m.pl.* memorabilia. **-ando** *adj.* memorable; not to be forgotten. **-andum** *m. indecl.* memorandum; reminder; engagement-book, diary.

**me·more** *adj.* mindful; full of memories.

**memo·ria** *f.* memory; *di buona* –, of blessed memory; *imparare a* –, to learn by heart; note of reminder; remembrance; short dissertation; memorial; record; souvenir; *pl.* memoirs; transactions, records.

**memorial-e** *m.* book of memorials; memoir; catalogue; memorandum. **-ista** *m.* memorialist.

**mẹna** *f.* underhand dealing; intrigue.

**me·nade** *f.* maenad, Bacchante.

**menadito** *adv. phr. a* –, perfectly, with complete accuracy; *sapere a* –, to know inside out, to have at one's finger tips.

**Menandro** *pr.n.m.* Menander.

**men-are** [A1] *tr.* to lead, to conduct; to take, to pull, to carry along; – *a fine*, to finish; – *un colpo*, to deliver a blow; – *calci a*, to kick; – *la frusta*, to wield the whip; – *la coda*, to wag its tail; – *il capo*, to shake one's head.

**mẹncio** *adj.* flabby, soft.

**menda** *f.* fault, defect.

**mend-ace** *adj.* mendacious, lying; false. **-a·cia** *f.* mendacity.
**mendic-are** [A2s] *tr.* to beg; to beg for; *intr.* (*aux.* avere) to go begging, to be a beggar. **-ante** *adj.* begging; *n.m.* beggar; mendicant; *pl.* (eccl.) mendicant friars. **-ità** *f.* beggary; mendicity; beggars; street begging.
**men·dico** *adj.* begging, mendicant; *n.m.* beggar.
**meneghino** *m.* the Milanese dialect; inhabitant or native of Milan; *adj.* relating to Milanese dialect or local customs.
**Menela·o** *pr.n.m.* (myth.) Menelaus.
**Menfi** *pr.n.f.* (geog.) Memphis.
**meningite** *f.* (med.) meningitis.
**mẹno**[1] *adj. indecl., adv.* (often abbrev. to **men**) less; *venir —*, to faint; to fail; *a —*, unless; *fare a — di*, to abstain from; *— male!*, that's lucky!; (math.) minus; *sette — cinque fa due*, five from seven leaves two; *n.m. indecl.* the less, the lesser; *ragionare del più e del —*, to talk of this and that; *per lo —, al —*, at least; *pl. i —*, the minority.
**Meno**[2] *pr.n.f.* (geog.) Main (river).
**menomare** [A1s] *tr.* to diminish, to lessen.
**me·nomo** *adj.* least; smallest.
**menopa·usa** *f.* (med.) menopause.
**mensa** *f.* table; (fig.) meal; *apparecchiare la —*, to lay the table; (mil.) *— degli ufficiali*, officers' mess; (industr.) canteen.
**mensile** *adj.* monthly; *n.m.* monthly pay or salary.
**men·sola** *f.* (archit.) corbel, bracket, console; shelf.
**mẹnta** *f.* (bot.) mint; *— peperina*, peppermint.
**mental-e** *adj.* mental; *calcolo —*, mental arithmetic. **-ità** *f.* mentality; intelligence. **-mẹnte** *adv.* mentally; silently.
**mẹnte** *f.* mind; intellect; intelligence, understanding; *imparare a —*, to learn by heart; *avere in — di*, to intend to.
**mentecatto** *adj.* imbecile, half-witted; *n.m.* idiot.
**mentire** [D2] *intr.* (*aux.* avere) to be misleading; to lie; to be a liar.
**mẹnto** *m.* chin.
**mentolo** *m.* (chem.) menthol.
**men·tore** *m.* mentor, adviser.
**mẹntre** *conj.* while, whilst; whereas; *n.m. in quel —*, in the meantime; just at that moment.
**menziọn-e** *f.* mention; record. **-are** [A1c] *tr.* to mention.
**menzọgn-a** *f.* lie, untruth; falsehood. **-ero** *adj.* lying, false; deceitful: illusory.
**meravi·gli-a** *f.* marvel, wonder; amazement, astonishment; *adv. phr. a —*, marvellously. **-are** [A4] *tr.* to surprise, to astonish; *rfl.* to marvel, to be amazed. **-ọso** *adj.* wonderful, marvellous; wondrous.
**mercant-e** *m.* merchant; dealer; *— all'ingrosso*, wholesale dealer; *fare l'orecchio di —*, to pretend not to hear. **-ẹsco** *adj.* (*m.pl.* **-ẹschi**) mercantile; relating to merchants. **-ile** *adj.* mercantile; *Marina — ile*, Merchant Navy.
**mercanzi·a** *f.* merchandise, goods; *— reale*, real property.
**mercato** *m.* market; mart, money-market; bargain; *sopra —*, into the bargain; *a buon —*, cheaply; *cattivo —*, disadvantageous deal.
**merce** *f.* goods, wares, merchandise; (rlwy.) *un treno merci*, a goods train; *stazione merci*, goods station; *deposito di merci*, warehouse.
**mercè** *f.* grace, help, pity; mercy; *alla — di*, at the mercy of; *fu gran — che*, it was a great mercy that...
**mercẹde** *f.* reward, recompense; wages, payment; (comm.) salary, wage.
**mercena·rio** *adj.* mercenary; grasping; corrupt; (hist.) *soldati mercenari*, mercenary troops; *n.m.* mercenary soldier.
**merceri·a** *f.* haberdasher's shop; *pl.* haberdashery.
**merci-a·io, -aiolo** *m.* haberdasher; pedlar.
**merco** *m.* branded mark on cattle.
**mercoledì** *pr.n.m.* Wednesday; *il — delle Ceneri*, Ash-Wednesday.
**merc-u·rio**[1] *m.* mercury, quicksilver. **-uriale** *adj.* mercurial.
**Mercu·rio**[2] *pr.n.m.* (myth.) Mercury.
**merd-a** *f.* shit; dung. **-a·io** *m.* dunghill; cess-pool.
**merenda** *f.* light meal; afternoon tea; snack.
**meretr-ice** *f.* prostitute; whore; harlot. **-i·cio** *adj.* meretricious.
**meridian-a** *f.* sun-dial; (astron.) meridian line. **-o** *m.* (astron.) meridian line; *adj.* meridian, midday.
**meridionale** *adj.* southern, south, southerly; meridional; *l'Italia —*, Southern Italy; *n.m., f.* person from the South of Italy; southerner.
**merig·gio** *m.* noon, midday; midday-sun; (geog.) south; south wind.
**merit-are** [A1s] *tr.* to deserve; to earn; to merit; to reward; to win; *intr.* (*aux.* avere) to be worth while; *non -a*, it's not worth the trouble; *rfl.* (*dat.* of *prn.* 'si') to earn; to be entitled to; *se l'è -ato*, he has earned it, *or* serve him right.
**me·rit-o** *m.* merit; reward; *in — a*, as to, about. **-ẹvole, -o·rio** *adj.* deserving, meritorious; worthy.
**merlẹtt-o** *m.* (usu. *pl.*) lace; *— all'ago*, point-lace; *— a fuselli*, pillow-lace. **-are** [A1c] *tr.* to trim with lace.
**Merlino**[1] *pr.n.m.* Merlin.
**merlino**[2] *m.* (naut.) marline.
**merl-o**[1] *m.* (orn.) blackbird; (fig.) sly person; simpleton. **-otto** *m.* young blackbird; (fig.) simpleton.
**merlo**[2] *m.* (usu. *pl.*) (archit.) battlements.
**merluzzo** *m.* (ichth.) cod; hake.
**mero** *adj.* pure, mere; *per — caso*, by pure chance; simple; undiluted.
**Merovin·gio** *adj., pr.n.m.* (hist.) Merovingian.
**mẹscere** [B1] *tr.* to pour out; to pour forth; to shed; to mingle, to mix.
**meschino** *adj.* poor, miserable wretched; mean; shabby; petty; paltry; *n.m.* wretched person; stingy man.
**mẹscit-a** *f.* pouring; tap-room; wine-shop. **-ọre** *m.* pourer; bar-tender; barman.
**mescol-are** [A1sc) *tr.* to mix; to mingle; to blend; to confound, to confuse; *— le carte*, to shuffle the cards; *-ate prima dell'uso*, (of medicine) to be shaken before use; (cul.) to stir; to whip; *rfl.* to mix (with). **-anza** *f.* mixture; combination; blend. **-ata** *f.* mixing; shuffling. **-atọre** *m.* mixer; cocktail shaker **-ìo** *m.* continual mixing; thorough mixing; mix-up; muddle.
**mẹs-e** *m.* month; *il — corrente*, the present month; *il — scorso, passato*, last month; *il — prossimo*, next month; month's salary; *quanti ne abbiamo del — ?*, what day of the month is it?; *pl.* menses, menstruation. **-ata** *f.* a month's wages.
**mesm-e·rico** *adj.* mesmeric. **-erịsmo** *m.* mesmerism.
**mẹssa**[1] *f.* (liturg.; mus.) mass; *— solenne*, high mass; *— cantata*, sung mass; *libro da —*, missal; (mus.) Mass.
**mẹssa**[2] *f.* putting; putting-up; setting-up; laying; placing; *— in scena*, mise en scène; *— in piega*, set, wave (of hair); putting forth of buds; (cards) stake; (motor.) *— in marcia*, starting.
**messaggeri·a** *f.* goods department, parcels office; forwarding agency; mail-service.
**messaggero** *m.* messenger; harbinger; envoy.
**messag·gio** *m.* message; communication, note; news.
**messale** *m.* missal.
**messe** *f.* harvest; crop.
**messere** *m.* (now joc.) Sir; Mr.; Master; gentleman.

**Mess-i·a** *pr.n.m.* Messiah. **-ia·nico** *adj.* Messianic.
**Mes·sic-o** *pr.n.m.* (geog.) Mexico. **-ano** *adj., n.m.* Mexican.
**messinscena** *f.* (theatr.) production, mise-en-scène.
**mẹsso** *adj.* put; situated; placed; set; *mal* —, badly arranged; badly dressed; *n.m.* messenger; public crier.
**mest-are** [A1 c] *tr.* to stir; *abs.* to interfere, to stir up trouble. **-atọre** *m.* stirrer; (fig.) one who interferes or stirs up trouble.
**me·sti-ca** *f.* (paint.) priming; mixed colours; paints on a palette. **-care** [A2 s] *tr.* to mix, to prepare (paints, colours); to prime. **-cheri·a** *f.* oil and paint shop, colour stores. **-chino** *m.* palette knife.
**mestier-e** *m.* trade, occupation. **-ante** *m.* jobber; clock-watcher; opportunist.
**mest-o** *adj.* sad, sorrowful, mournful; dejected. **-i·zia** *f.* sadness.
**mẹstol-a** *f.* ladle; trowel; *pl.* (pejor.) hands; paws; *adoperar le -e*, to fight. **-o** *m.* ladle; skimmer; wooden spoon for cooking.
**mestru-ale** *adj.* menstrual. **-are** [A6] *intr.* (*aux.* avere) to menstruate. **-aziọne** *f.* menstruation.
**meta** *f.* goal, aim, end, object; conical mass, heap; haycock; boundary; (archit.) spire; pinnacle.
**metà** *f.* half; moiety; *tagliare a* —, to cut in half; *fare le cose a* —, to do things by halves; (colloq.) *la mia* —, my better half.
**metaboliṣmo** *m.* (biol.) metabolism.
**metafi·sic-a** *f.* metaphysics. **-o** *adj.* metaphysical; *n.m.* metaphysician.
**meta·f-ora** *f.* metaphor; figurative speech. **-o·rico** *adj.* metaphorical.
**metal·lico** *adj.* metallic; metal, made of metal; *spazzola metallica*, wire brush.
**metall-o** *m.* metal; tone, timbre (of voice). **-i·fero** *adj.* metalliferous. **-urgi·a** *f.* metallurgy. **-urgo** *m.* (*pl.* **-urghi**) metallurgist.
**meta-mor·fico** *ad.* metamorphic. **-morfiṣmo** *m.* (geol.) metamorphism. **-mor·fosi** *f.* metamorphosis.
**met-e·ora** *f.* any atmospheric phenomenon; *la — fallace dei deserti*, mirage; meteor. **-eo·rico** *adj.* meteoric. **-eorite** *f.* meteorite. **-eorologi·a** *f.* meteorology. **-eorolo·gico** *adj.* meteorological; *bollettino -eorologico*, weather forecast. **-eorologista, -eoro·logo** *m.* meteorologist.
**metic·cio** *adj., n.m.* half-breed, half-caste.
**meticolọs-o** *adj.* meticulous; fastidious. **-ità** *f.* meticulousness; fastidiousness.
**me·t-odo** *m.* method, system, way; rule; order; custom. **-o·dico** *adj.* methodical; orderly. **-odologi·a** *f.* methodology. **-odolo·gico** *adj.* methodological.
**me·topa, me·tope** *f.* (archit.) metope.
**metrag·gio** *m.* measurement (in metres); length (in metres); (cinem.) footage.
**me·trica** *f.* prosody, metrics; metre; versification.
**me·trico** *adj.* metric; metrical; *sistema — decimale*, metric system, decimal system.
**metr-o** *m.* metre; — *quadrato*, square metre; — *cubo*, cubic metre; (prosod.) metre. **-o·nomo** *m.* (mus.) metronome
**metr-o·poli** *f. indecl.* metropolis. **-opolita** *m.* inhabitant of a metropolis; metropolitan bishop. **-opolitana** *f.* underground railway, tube; metropolitan church **-opolitano** *adj.* metropolitan; *n.m.* (eccl.) metropolitan; policeman (in large town).
**mẹtt-ere** [C20] *tr.* to put; to place; — *in italiano*, to translate into Italian; — *all'asta*, to put up for auction; — *in scena*, to stage; — *in musica*, to set to music; — *piede in*, to set foot in; to put on; to apply; to attach; — *un vestito nuovo*, to put on a new dress; to put, to add, to say, to write; *ora -i il nome e la data*, now put your name and the date; to admit, to grant, to suppose; *-iamo che*, let us suppose that; to contribute, to invest; to stake, to risk; *ci ho messo molto lavoro*, I have put a lot of work into it; to give rise to, to cause, to inspire; — *discordia fra*, to cause disharmony between; to install, to lay on, to lay in; — *la luce elettrica*, to install electric light; to lay down, to put down, to lay; to set up, to institute; — *le basi*, to lay the foundations; to rate, to put at, to ask for, to require; *quanto -e queste pere ?*, how much are you asking for these pears ?; *le -o venti lire*, I'm asking twenty lire for them; *quanto -e il treno di qui a Firenze ?*, how long does the train take between here and Florence ?; to put forth, to emit; to exhibit; *l'albero -e le foglie*, the tree is putting forth leaves; — *a soqquadro*, to turn topsy-turvy; to thrust, to stick, to intrude; — *le mani in*, to interfere in; *intr.* (*aux.* avere) to flow, to discharge; *l'uscio -e in salotto*, the door leads to the sitting-room; to proceed; *la cosa -e bene*, the affair is going on well; *rfl.* (*acc.* of *prn.* 'si') to put oneself, to set oneself; *-ersi al lavoro*, to set to work; to dress; *si -e bene*, he is well turned out; (*dat.* of *prn.* 'si') *si mise il cappello ed uscì*, he put on his hat and went out; *recip. rfl. -ersi d'accordo*, to come to an agreement; *impers.* (of weather) *s'è messo a piovere*, it has begun to rain. **-itura** *f.* putting; laying.
**metti-bọcca** *m., f. indecl.* interferer, meddler. **-male** *m., f. indecl.* mischief-maker.
**meẓẓ-a** *f.* half-portion; half share; one half; half-hour; *sonata la* —, it has struck the half-hour. **-abotta** *f. indecl.* (archit.) barrel vault. **-aluna** *f. indecl.* half-moon, crescent. **-anotte** *f.* midnight. **-atinta** *f.* (paint.) half-tone, medium tint; shading.
**mezz-adri·a** *f.* (leg.) métayage; métayer system; a form of agricultural holding under which landlord and tenant go shares in produce. **-adro** *m.* métayer.
**meẓẓana** *f.* go-between, procuress; (naut.) mainsail; *albero di* —, mizzen mast.
**meẓẓano** *adj.* mean, middle, medium; middle-sized; intermediate.
**meẓẓeri·a** *f.* métayage; (geom.) centre line.
**mẹzzo**[1] *adj.* (of fruit) overripe; (of pears) sleepy; (of persons) sickly; flabby; *n.m.* the soft part of a fruit.
**meẓẓo**[2] *adj.* half; part; semi-; incomplete; *una mezz'ora*, half an hour; *bandiera a mezz'asta*, flag at half-mast; (mus.) *un — soprano*, a mezzo-soprano (voice or singer); — *tono*, semi-tone; *i vestiti di mezza stagione*, mid-season clothing; slight; *una mezza speranza*, a faint hope; close, near, approximate; *adv.* half; partly; almost, nearly; — *morto*, half-dead; *n.m.* half; *due -i fanno un intero*, two halves make a whole; centre, middle; middle part; mid-position; *nel bel* —, right in the middle; means, expedient; *per — di*, by means of; — *di trasporto*, means of transport; *non avere mezzi*, to have no means, to be destitute; medium, mean; *il giusto* —, the happy medium.
**mezzo-**[3] *pref.* semi-, half-. **-cer·chio** *m.* semicircle. **-dì** *m. indecl.* noon, midday. **-fọndo** *m.* middle-distance. **-giọrno** *m.* midday, noon; south; *il Mezzogiorno d'Italia*, Southern Italy. **-rilievo** *m.* (sculp.) high-relief.
**meẓẓọmbra** *f.* (paint.) shading, shadow, half-shadow.
**mi**[1] *pers. prn. conjunct. 1st sing.* me; to me; *rfl. prn.* — *diverto*, I am having an amusing time; — *lavo le mani*, I am washing my hands.

**mi**[2] *m. indecl.* (mus.) mi; the note E; the key of E.
**miagol-are** [A1 s] *intr.* (*aux.* avere) to mew, to miaow; (fig.) to whine. **-io** *m.* (*pl.* -ii) continued mewing; caterwauling.
**mia·golo** *m.* mew, miaow
**mia·o** *onom.* miaow.
**mica**[1] *f.* crumb; *adv.* not at all, not in the least.
**mica**[2] *f.* (miner.) mica.
**mic·cia** *f.* fuse, slow-match; powder train.
**miccino** *m.* tiny crumb; scrap; *adv. phr. a* —, stingily, meanly; sparingly.
**Micene** *pr.n.f.* (geog.) Mycenae.
**Michelan·gel-o** *pr.n.m.* Michael Angelo. **-ẹsco** *adj.* (*m.pl.* **-ẹschi**) in the style of Michael Angelo; (fig.) grandiose, majestic.
**Michele** *pr.n.m.* Michael; *giorno di San* —, Michaelmas.
**micidiale** *adj.* deadly; killing; murderous; homicidal; mortal.
**mi·cio** *m.* cat; (pop.) pussycat.
**micr-o·bio** *m.* (biol.) microbe. **-obiologi·a** *f.* microbiology. **-ocosmo** *m.* microcosm. **-o·fono** *m.* microphone; *parlare al -ofono,* to broadcast; mouthpiece (of a telephone). **-organismo** *m.* micro-organism. **-oscopi·a** *f.* microscopy. **-osco·pio** *m.* microscope. **-osolco** *adj. indecl.* (gramoph.) long-playing; *dischi -osolco,* long-playing records; *n.m.* (*pl.* **-osolchi**) long-playing record. **-otele·fono** *m.* (teleph.) receiver.
**Mida** *pr.n.m.* (myth.) Midas.
**midọll-a** *f.* pulp of orange or other fruit; crumb (of a loaf). **-o** *m.* marrow, pith; (anat.) medulla; (zool.) *-o spinale,* spinal cord. **-ọso** *adj.* full of marrow; pithy.
**miei** *poss. adj., prn.m.pl.* mine, my; *i* —, my family, my people.
**miele** *m.* honey; *luna di* —, honeymoon.
**mie·t-ere** [B1] *tr.* to reap, to mow; (fig.) to gather. **-itọre** *m.* reaper, harvester; mower. **-itrice** *f.* woman reaper; harvesting machine. **-itura** *f.* reaping, harvesting; mowing.
**miglia·i-o** *m.* (*pl.* **-a** *f.*) thousand; *a -a,* in thousands, by the thousand.
**mi·gli-o**[1] *m.* (*pl.* **-a** *f.*) mile; — *inglese,* English mile (1·524 km.); — *terrestre,* statute mile; — *marino,* nautical mile.
**mi·glio**[2] *m.* (bot.) millet; birdseed.
**miglior-are** [A1 c] *tr.* to improve, to make better; *intr.* (*aux.* essere) to improve, to get better; to recover, to mend; *rfl.* to improve, to mend one's ways; to improve oneself. **-a·bile** *adj.* capable of improvement. **-amẹnto** *m.* improvement, amelioration; betterment; recovery (of health). **-ativo** *adj.* ameliorative.
**migliọr-e** *adj. comp.* of **buono**; better; superior; *n.m., f. il!* (*la*) —, the best. **-i·a** *f.* improvement, amelioration.
**mignatta** *f.* (zool.) leech; (fig.) usurer, blood-sucker; importunate person.
**mi·gnola** *f.* olive-blossom.
**mi·gnolo** *m.* little finger; little toe; olive bud; *adj.* little; *il dito* —, the little finger.
**migr-are** [A1] *intr.* (*aux.* avere, essere) to migrate. **-atọre** *m., adj.* migrant. **-ato·rio** *adj.* migratory. **-aziọne** *f.* migration.
**mila** *pl.* of **mille,** when conjoined with another numeral; *diecimila,* ten thousand.
**miliardo** *m.* milliard (in Italy a thousand million).
**miliare** *adj.* marking miles; *pietra* —, milestone; *n.m.* milestone; (fig.) landmark.
**miliọn-e** *m.* million. **-a·rio** *m.* millionaire. **-e·ṣimo** *adj.* millionth; *la -esima parte,* the millionth part.
**militante** *adj.* militant; combative.
**militar-e**[1] *adj.* military; *n.m.* soldier. **-ẹsco** *adj.* (*m.pl.* **-ẹschi**) soldierly; overbearing. **-iṣmo** *m.* militarism.
**militare**[2] [A1 s] *intr.* (*aux.* avere) to serve; to militate.
**mi·lite** *m.* soldier, militiaman; *il — Ignoto,* the Unknown Soldier.
**mili·zia** *f.* the profession of arms; warfare; soldiering; a body of soldiers, militia; — *territoriale,* Territorial Army.
**millant-are** [A1] *tr.* to boast of; to exaggerate; *rfl.* to boast, to brag. **-atọre** *m.* boaster, braggart. **-eri·a** *f.* boasting, bragging.
**mille** *card. num.* (*pl.* **mila**) thousand; *il Mille,* the eleventh century; — *grazie,* very many thanks.
**millena·rio** *adj.* millenary; millenarian.
**millen·nio** *m.* millennium.
**milleṣimo** *ord. num.* thousandth; (fig.) *per la millesima volta,* for the nth time; *n.m.* thousandth part; figure indicating thousands.
**mill-igrammo** *m.* milligram, milligramme. **-i·metro** *m.* millimetre.
**milza** *f.* (anat.) spleen; (butcher.) milt; (fig.) *avere male alla* —, to have a stitch in one's side.
**mim-a** *f.* mime; dancer in mime. **-are** [A1] (*aux.* avere) to mime. **-ẹsco** *adj.* (*m.pl.* **-ẹschi**) pertaining to mime. **-eṣi** *f. indecl.* mimesis, imitation. **-e·tico** *adj.* mimetic. **-etiṣmo** *m.* mimicry. **-o** *m.* mime; clown; mimic.
**mimetiẓẓ-are** [A1] *tr.* to camouflage. **-aziọne** *f.* camouflage.
**mi·mic-a** *f.* mimicry; gesticulation. **-o** *adj.* relating to mime; *l'arte -a,* mime.
**mimọsa** *f.* (bot.) sensitive plant; *erba* —, mimosa.
**mina** *f.* mine (to be exploded).
**minac·c-ia** *f.* threat, menace. **-ẹvole** *adj.* menacing, threatening. **-iare** [A3] *tr.* to threaten; *lo -iò di morte,* he threatened to kill him. **-iọso** *adj.* threatening; menacing.
**min-are** [A1] *tr.* to mine (with an explosive mine); to undermine; to sap. **-atọre** *m.* sapper; miner, collier.
**minarẹto** *m.* minaret.
**minato·rio** *adj.* minatory; menacing.
**minchiọn-e** *m.* fool, simpleton; *adj.* silly, stupid. **-ag·gine** *f.* foolishness, silliness. **-are** [A1 c] *tr.* to mock, to ridicule; to make a fool of; *farsi -are,* to make a fool of oneself.
**mineral-e** *adj.* mineral; *n.m.* mineral, ore; — *di ferro,* iron ore. **-ista** *m.* mineralogist. **-ogi·a** *f.* mineralogy.
**minera·rio** *adj.* (pertaining to) mining; *industria mineraria,* mining industry.
**minestr-a** *f.* soup; (fig.) mixture. **-ọne** *m.* soup with vegetables, pasta and various forms of protein.
**min·gere** [C5] *intr.* (*aux.* avere) to urinate.
**mingherlino** *adj.* slim, lean; slender.
**mini-are** [A4] *tr.* (paint.) to miniate, to paint with red-lead; to illuminate; (fig.) to describe in detail; to embellish; *intr.* (*aux.* avere) to paint miniatures. **-atọre** *m.* illuminator of MSS. **-atura** *f.* miniature; illumination. **-aturista** *m., f.* miniaturist.
**miniera** *f.* mine; quarry.
**mi·nima** *f.* (mus.) minim.
**mi·nimo** *adj.* least; smallest lowest; slightest; very small; *n.m.* the least; the least important; minimum; the least little thing.
**mi·nio** *m.* (chem.) red-lead.
**minist-ero** *m.* office, function, ministry; board, department; — *degli Affari Esteri,* Foreign Office; — *dell'Interno,* Home Office; (eccl.) ministry. **-eriale** *adj.* ministerial.
**ministrare** [A1] *tr.* to administer; to minister, to govern; *intr.* (*aux.* avere; *prep.* a) to minister (to).
**ministro** *m.* minister; *Primo* —, Prime Minister; — *degli Affari Esteri,* Foreign Secretary; — *di Stato,* cabinet minister; (Protestant clergy) minister.

**minọr-e** *adj.* less, minor; lesser; younger; (mus.), minor; *n.m. il* —, the lesser, the smaller; (leg.) minor. **-anza** *f.* minority; *i diritti della -anza,* minority rights. **-enne** *adj.* under age; *n.m., f.* person under age; *Tribunale per i -enni,* Juvenile Court.

**Minosse** *pr.n.m.* (myth.) Minos.

**minuẹtto** *m.* (mus.) minuet.

**minu·gia** *f.* (mus.) gut, catgut; string.

**minu·scol-o** *adj.* small; little, tiny; *lettere -e,* lower-case letters; (fig.) paltry; trivial. **-a** *f.* small letter; minuscule (handwriting). **-i** *m.pl.* (typ.) lower-case letters.

**minuta** *f.* draft; rough copy; bill of fare; menu.

**minut-o**[1] *adj.* minute, tiny; fine; *pioggia -a,* fine rain; detailed; precise; (comm.) *commercio* —, retail trade; *al* —, retail; *popolo* —, common people. **-a·glia** *f.* small things; minutiae; small fry. **-ante** *m., f.* one who draws up documents; minutes-secretary. **-are** [A1] *tr.* to draw up, to draft; to minute. **-ẹzza** *f.* minuteness; fine detail; pettiness; *pl.* trifles; minutiae.

**minuto**[2] *m.* minute (of time); instant; — *primo,* minute; — *secondo,* second; *lancetta dei minuti,* minute hand.

**minu·zi-a** *f.* small detail. **-ọso** *adj.* paying attention to details; pedantic; fastidious.

**minuz·zolo** *m.* bit; shred; morsel, scrap; little shrimp (of a child).

**minziọne** *f.* urination.

**mi·o** *poss. adj.* (*m. pl.* **miei**) my; mine; *la mia casa,* my house; — *padre,* my father; *un — cugino,* a cousin of mine; *questo è* —, this is mine; *poss. prn. il* —, mine; *vivo del* —, I have independent means; *i miei,* my relatives.

**mi·op-e** *adj.* short-sighted, myopic; *n.m., f.* short-sighted person. **-i·a** *f.* myopia, short-sightedness.

**mira** *f.* aim; *prendere, pigliare la* —, to take aim; direction; purpose, object.

**mira·bile** *adj.* admirable; wonderful, marvellous.

**mira·col-o** *m.* miracle; wonder; prodigy; marvel; *operare -i,* to work wonders. **-ọso** *adj.* miraculous; marvellous, wonderful; prodigious.

**mirag·gio** *m.* mirage; (fig.) illusion.

**mirare** [A1] *tr.* to look at, to stare at; to gaze on; to admire; to aim at; to tend towards; *intr.* (*aux.* avere; *prep.* a) to take aim; — *intorno,* to look round.

**miri·ade** *f.* myriad.

**mirica** *f.* (bot.) tamarisk.

**mirino** *m.* sight (of gun); (photog.) viewfinder.

**mirra** *f.* (bot.) myrrh.

**mirtillo** *m.* (bot.) bilberry.

**mirto** *m.* (bot.) myrtle.

**miṣan·tr-opo** *m.* misanthropist. **-opi·a** *f.* misanthropy. **-o·pico** *adj.* misanthropic.

**miṣavventura** *f.* misadventure; misfortune.

**miscela** *f.* mixture; medley; blend.

**miscella·ne-a** *f.* miscellany; anthology. **-o** *adj.* miscellaneous.

**mi·schi-a** *f.* fight; scuffle, hand-to-hand fight; fray, affray; mêlée. **-are** [A4] *tr.* to mix; to mingle; to blend; to jumble; (cards) to shuffle; *recip. rfl.* to mix, to intermingle; to become jumbled. **-atura** *f.* mixture; jumble.

**mi·schio** *m.* mixture; medley; jumble.

**misconọscere** [B9] *tr.* to refuse to recognize; to repudiate, to disown; to disregard.

**miscreden-te** *adj.* unbelieving; *n.m.* unbeliever. **-za** *f.* unbelief.

**miscu·glio** *m.* mixture; sorry mixture; medley.

**miṣer-a·bile** *adj.* wretched; mean; needy, poor; miserable; *n.m.* wretch. **-ando** *adj.* pitiable, pitiful. **-ere** *m.* miserere; *ridotto al -ere,* at the last extremity; *excl.* mercy! **-ẹvole** *adj.* miserable; lamentable; piteous.

**miṣe·ria** *f.* poverty; scarcity; want; lack; misery; bad piece of work; something of no account; weakness; meanness.

**miṣericorde** *adj.* merciful; kind.

**miṣerico·rd-ia** *f.* mercy; *sentir — di,* to feel pity for. **-iọso** *adj.* merciful.

**mi·ṣero** *adj.* poor, indigent; pitiable; wretched; paltry; mean; miserly, niggardly.

**misfatto** *m.* misdeed; crime; wrong-doing; *pl.* misbehaviour.

**miṣo·gin-o** *m.* misogynist. **-i·a** *f.* misogynism.

**mis·sil-e** *m., adj.* missile. **-i·stico** *adj.* relating to missiles, missile.

**missino** *m.* (pol.) member of the Movimento Sociale Italiano (M.S.I.), the neo-Fascist party.

**missiọn-e** *f.* mission; expedition. **-a·rio** *m.* missionary.

**missiva** *f.* missive; message.

**mistago-go** *m.* (*pl.* **-ghi**) mystagogue.

**mist-ero** *m.* mystery; mystery-play; problem; secret. **-e·rico** *adj.* pertaining to a religious mystery. **-eriọso** *adj.* mysterious.

**mi·sti-co** *adj.* (rel.) mystic(al); occult, esoteric; *n.m.* **-ca** *f.* mystical theology; mysticism; (fig.) mystique. **-ciṣmo** *m.* mysticism.

**mistific-are** [A2s] *tr.* to mystify; to hoax. **-atọre** *m.* mystifier; hoaxer. **-aziọne** *f.* mystification; hoax.

**mist-o** *adj.* mixed; combined; compounded; variegated; *matrimonio* —, mixed marriage; *scuola -a,* co-educational school; (cul.) *fritto* —, mixed grill; *n.m.* mixture; combination.

**mistur-a** *f.* mixture; blend; medley; combination; compound. **-are** [A1] *tr.* to mix; to mingle; to blend.

**miṣura** *f.* measure; — *a nastro,* tape-measure; measurement, size; extent; *a — che,* in measure as; (prosod.) metre, scansion; (mus.) time measure, bar; expedient; precaution.

**miṣur-are** [A1] *tr.* to measure, to gauge, to pace; to survey (land); *rfl.* to try one's strength. **-apiog·gia** *m.* rain-gauge. **-ato** *part. adj.* measured; moderate. **-atọre** *m.* instrument for measuring; meter. **-aziọne** *f.* measuring; gauging; surveying.

**mit-e** *adj.* mild, gentle; docile; moderate. **-ẹzza** *f.* mildness; gentleness.

**mi·tico** *adj.* mythical.

**mitig-are** [A2s] *tr.* to mitigate; to alleviate, to ally, to assuage; to appease, to placate. **-aziọne** *f.* mitigating; alleviation.

**mit-o** *m.* myth; legend; parable. **-ologi·a** *f.* mythology. **-olo·gico** *adj.* mythological. **-o·logo** *m.* mythologist.

**mitr-a**[1] *f.* (eccl.) mitre; turban. **-ale** *adj.* mitre-shaped. **-are** [A1] *tr.* to mitre. **-ato** *part. adj.* (eccl.) mitred; *i -ati,* prelates.

**mitra**[2] *m., f. indecl.* small automatic weapon; sub-machine gun.

**mitra·gli-a** *f.* (mil.) grapeshot. **-are** [A4] *tr.* (mil.) to sweep with machine-gun fire. **-atọre** *m.,* **-ere** *m.* (mil.) machine-gunner. **-atrice** *f.,* **-era** *f.* (mil.) machine-gun; *nastro di -atrice,* machine-gun belt.

**mittente** *m.* sender; *da rispedire al* —, to be returned to the sender; *adj.* forwarding, sending.

**mnemo·nic-a** *f.* mnemonic. **-o** *adj., n.m.* mnemonic.

**Mnemo·ṣine** *pr.n.f.* (myth.) Mnemosyne.

**mo'** *m.* (abbrev. of '**modo**') *a mo' d'esempio,* by way of example.

**mo** *adv.* (poet.) now.

**mo·bil-e** *adj.* movable; *festa* —, movable feast; mobile; (fig.) fickle, capricious, inconstant; *libro a fogli -i,* loose-leaf book; (leg.) *beni -i,* personal estate; *sabbie -i,* quicksands; *n.m.* piece of furniture; *i -i,* the furniture. **-i·lia** *f.,* **-i·lio** *m.* furniture; suite of furniture. **-iare** [A4] *tr.* to furnish; *adj. proprietà -iare,* personal property, personality. **-iere** *m.*

furniture-maker. **-ità** *f.* mobility; fickleness, changeableness. **-itare** [A1 s] *tr.* (mil.) to mobilize.

**mọcc-io** *m.* mucus; catarrh. **-icare** [A2 s] *intr.* (*aux.* avere) (of nose) to run; to cry, to snivel. **-ico** *m.* mucus, snot. **-icone** *m.* person with dirty nose. **-icọso** *adj.* snivelling; snotty.

**moc·colo** *m.* wax taper; candle-end.

**moda** *f.* fashion; *essere di* —, to be in fashion.

**modal-e** *adj.* modal. **-ità** *f. indecl.* modality; particular; way; mode of procedure; *pl.* terms.

**mo·dan-o** *m.* mould, model, design; crocket-needle; (archit.) module. **-atura** *f.* (archit.) moulding.

**modell-o** *m.* model, pattern; (paint.) model; lay-figure. **-a** *f.* artist's (female) model; model-girl, mannequin. **-are** [A1] *tr.* to model; to mould, to shape, to fashion; *rfl.* to model oneself. **-atọre** *m.* modeller. **-atura** *f.* modelling.

**Mo·den-a** *pr.n.f.* (geog.) Modena. **-ẹse** *adj., n.m., f.* (native) of Modena.

**moder-are** [A1 s] *tr.* to moderate; to check, to curb; to restrain; *rfl.* to check oneself; to restrain oneself; to become moderate. **-atẹzza** *f.* moderateness; restraint; temperance. **-ato** *part. adj.* moderated; moderate; restrained, temperate. **-atọre** *m.* moderator; *adj.* moderating. **-aziọne** *f.* moderation, restraint; discretion; temperance.

**modern-o** *adj.* modern; recent; new; up-to-date; *n.m.* modern. **-ità** *f.* modernity. **-iẓẓare** [A1] *tr.* to modernize; to bring up to date; to renovate.

**mode·stia** *f.* modesty; humility; simplicity.

**modesto** *adj.* modest; humble; simple; moderate.

**mo·dic-o** *adj.* moderate; modest; cheap; *prezzi -i*, moderate prices. **-ità** *f.* moderation; cheapness.

**modi·fica** *f.* modification, alteration, change.

**modific-are** [A2] *tr.* to modify, to alter, to change. **-atọre** *m.* modifier; *adj.* modifying. **-aziọne** *f.* modification, change.

**modigliọne** *m.* (archit.) modillion, bracket.

**modist-a** *f.* milliner; dressmaker; modiste. **-eri·a** *f.* art of millinery or dressmaking; milliner's shop; dressmaker's shop.

**mod-o** *m.* mode, way, manner; condition; *in ogni* —, in any case; *ad ogni* —, at any rate; *di — che*, in such a way that, so that; style, shape; *a — degli Inglesi*, in the English style; moderation; *oltre* —, extremely, excessively; *pl.* means; manners; (gram.) mood; (mus.) mode.

**modul-are** [A1 s] *tr.* to modulate. **-aziọne** *f.* modulation.

**mo·dulo** *m.* form; *riempire un* —, to fill in a form; draft; model; (archit.) module.

**mo·gano** *m.* (bot.) mahogany.

**mog·g-io** *m.* (*pl.* **-ia** *f.*) measure of capacity generally equal to eight bushels; *mettere la lucerna sotto il* —, to hide one's light under a bushel.

**mo·gio** *adj.* crestfallen, low-spirited, dejected; quiet.

**mọglie** *f.* (*pl.* **mọgli**) wife; *dar in* —, to give in marriage; *prender* —, to take a wife.

**moi·n-a** *f.* simper, smirk; *pl.* blandishments; cajolery; mincing ways. **-eri·a** *f.* affected blandishments.

**mola** *f.* grindstone, millstone.

**molare**[1] *adj. pietra* —, millstone; (anat.) *dente* —, molar.

**mol-are**[2] [A1] *tr.* (techn.) to grind. **-ato** *part. adj.* (techn.) ground; *vetro -ato*, ground glass.

**mole** *f.* mass, pile; massive building; size, bulk.

**mole·col-a** *f.* (chem.) molecule. **-are** *adj.* molecular.

**molend-a** *f.* multure. **-are** [A1] *tr.* to exact multure; to grind.

**molestare** [A1] *tr.* to molest; to annoy, to trouble; to disturb; to vex; to tease.

**mole·stia** *f.* molestation; trouble; nuisance.

**molesto** *adj.* troublesome; annoying; vexatious; grievous.

**moll-a** *f.* spring; *serratura a* —, spring lock; *funzionamento a* —, clockwork action; (watchm.) — *del bariletto*, mainspring; *pl.* tongs. **-ẹtte** *f.pl.dim.* *-ette per lo zucchero*, sugar-tongs. **-ẹtto** *m.* hair-grip.

**mollare** [A1] *tr.* (naut.) to let go, to ease; to slacken; — *l'ancora*, to cast anchor.

**moll-e** *adj.* soft; wet; (fig.) effeminate; luxurious; flabby; lax; *n.m.* wet, liquid; *mettere in* —, to put to soak; (of wine) weak. **-ẹzza** *f.* softness; pliability; effeminacy; laxness.

**molleggiare** [A3 c] *intr.* (*aux.* avere) to be elastic, to be springy.

**mollẹggio** *m.* (eng.) springing, suspension.

**mollica** *f.* crumb, soft part of bread.

**mollificare** [A2 s] *tr.* to mollify; to soften.

**mollus-co** *m.* (*pl.* **-chi**) (zool.) mollusc.

**molo** *m.* breakwater, mole; pier; quay, wharf; (comm.) *diritti di* —, wharfage.

**moltẹplic-e** *adj.* manifold; numerous; complex. **-ità** *f.* multiplicity.

**moltiplic-are** [A1 s] *tr.* to multiply; to increase; (math.) to multiply; *rfl., intr.* (*aux.* essere) to multiply. **-aziọne** *f.* multiplication; increase.

**moltitu·dine** *f.* multitude.

**mọlto** *adj.* much; *pl.* many; *prn.* much; *a dir* —, at most; *adv.* very; very much, a great deal; — *bene*, very well.

**momẹnt-o** *m.* moment; *a -i arriverà*, he will be here any moment now; importance, moment. **-a·neo** *adj.* momentary.

**mo·na-co**[1] *m.* (*pl.* **-ci**) (eccl.) monk; (bldg.) post; — *unico*, king-post. **-ca** *f.* (eccl.) nun; *farsi -ca*, to take the veil. **-cale** *adj.* monastic; monkish; nun-like. **-care** [A2 s] *rfl.* to become a nun. **-cato** *m.* monastic or convent life; monasticism.

**Mo·naco**[2] *pr.n.f.* (geog.) Monaco; — *di Baviera*, Munich.

**monar-ca** *m.* (*pl.* **-chi**) monarch. **-chi·a** *f.* monarchy; sovereignty, rule. **-chịsmo** *m.* monarchism.

**monar·chico** *adj.* monarchic; *n.m.* monarchist, royalist.

**monastero** *m.* (eccl.) monastery; convent, nunnery.

**mona·stico** *adj.* monastic.

**Monceni·sio** *pr.n.m.* (geog.) Mont Cenis.

**mọn-co** *adj.* (*pl.* **-chi**) maimed; (fig.) deficient, incomplete, stunted; *n.m.* person who has lost one, or both of his hands; cripple. **-ca** *f.* woman with one or no arm. **-cherino** *m.* handless arm; stump. **-cọne** *m.* stump; stump of limb.

**mondan-o** *adj.* of this world, terrestrial; worldly. **-ità** *f. indecl.* worldliness; frivolity; *pl.* vanities.

**mond-are** [A1 c] *tr.* to peel; to clean; to weed; — *il grano*, to winnow the corn; — *le uova sode*, to shell hard-boiled eggs; (fig.) to cleanse. **-atura** *f.* peeling; winnowing; weeding; peel taken off in peeling; chaff; dirt; siftings. **-aziọne** *f.* peeling; cleaning, winnowing.

**mọnd-o**[1] *adj.* clean, spotless, pure; clear; peeled; winnowed. **-ẹzza** *f.* cleanliness, purity. **-ezza·io** *m.* rubbish-heap; dung-heap. **-i·glia** *f.* siftings; chaff; refuse; dross; rubbish; alloy.

**mọnd-o**[2] *m.* world; *mettere al — un bambino*, to bring a child into the world; *andare all'altro* —, to die; *uomo di* —, man of the world; *il bel* —, high society; a great deal, an infinite amount. **-iale** *adj.* world-like; universal; *lingua -iale*, world language.

**monell-o** *m.* urchin; rascal, rogue. **-eri·a** *f.* trick, prank. **-ẹsco** *adj.* (*m.pl.* **-ẹschi**) rascally.

**monẹt-a** *f.* coin; change; *non ho — spicciola*, I have no small change; *battere* —, to strike coins; *carta* —, paper money. **-are**

[A1 c] *tr.* to mint, to coin. **-a·rio** *adj.* monetary. **-azịone** *f.* minting, coining. **-iere** *m.* coiner.

**Mongo·lia** *pr.n.f.* (geog.) Mongolia.

**mon·golo** *adj.*, *n.m.* mongol.

**mo·nit-o** *m.* warning, admonition. **-ọre** *m.* admonisher, adviser; monitor.

**monna** *f.* abbreviation of Madonna; (form of address) lady.

**mon-o·colo** *adj.* one-eyed; *m.* monocle. **-ocolọre** *adj.* monochrome; (pol.) one-party. **-ocordo** *m.* single-stringed instrument. **-ogami·a** *f.* monogamy. **-o·gamo** *adj.* monogamous; *n.m.* monogamist. **-ografi·a** *f.* monograph. **-ogramma** *m.* monogram. **-oli·tico** *adj.* monolithic. **-olito** *m.* monolith. **-o·logo** *m.* (*pl.* **-o·loghi**) monologue. **-omani·a** *f.* monomania. **-omani·aco** *adj.* monomaniac. **-opat·tino** *m.* scooter. **-opo·lio** *m.* monopoly. **-opolista** *m.* monopolist. **-opolịzzare** [A1] *tr.* to monopolize. **-opọsto** *adj.* single-seater. **-orota·ia** *f.* monorail. **-osilla·bico** *adj.* monosyllabic. **-osil·labo** *m.* monosyllable. **-os·sido** *m.* (chem.) monoxide. **-oteịsmo** *m.* monotheism. **-otipi·a** *f.* monotype. **-otoni·a** *f.* monotony. **-o·tono** *adj.* monotonous.

**Monreale** *pr.n.f.* (geog.) Montreal; (Sicily) Monreale.

**monsignọr-e** *m.* (eccl.) monsignore. **-ato** *m.* status of monsignore.

**monsọne** *m.* monsoon.

**mọnta** *f.* mating (of animals); *menare una cavalla alla —*, to take a mare to stud; (equit.) seat, way of riding.

**montaca·richi** *m. indecl.* hoist; goods-lift.

**montag·gio** *m.* mounting; (eng.) assembly; (cinem.) editing.

**montagn-a** *f.* mountain; hill; *mal di —*, mountain sickness; *il sermone della —*, the Sermon on the Mount. **-ọso** *adj.* mountainous. **-(u)olo** *m.* mountaineer; *adj.* of the mountains.

**montan-aro** *m.*, *adj.* mountaineer; highlander; of the mountains. **-ino** *adj.* of the mountains. **-o** *adj.* of or on the mountains; *strada -a*, mountain road.

**montante** *adj.* ascending; *n.m.* amount; stand, support.

**mont-are** [A1 c] *intr.* (*aux.* essere) to mount, to climb; to rise; to increase; *— a cavallo*, to mount a horse, to ride; *— in carrozza*, to get into a carriage; *il vino gli -ò alla testa*, the wine went to his head; to amount; to be of consequence; *non -a*, it does not matter; *tr.* to mount, to set up, to set; *— un cavallo*, to ride a horse; to mount, to organize; (cul.) *— la panna*, to whip the cream; (mil.) *— la guardia*, to mount guard; (fig.) to stir, to rouse, to excite; *rfl.* (*dat.* of *prn.* 'si') *-arsi la testa*, to get excited, to get a swollen head. **-ata** *f.* ascent; rise, hill. **-atọio** *m.* step; footboard; mounting-block. **-atọre** *m.* fitter; assembler; (cinem.) editor. **-atura** *f.* assembling; puffing, boosting; stunt.

**mọnt-e** *m.* mount, hill; mountain; *a —*, upstream; heap, mass, pile; *salire sul —*, to climb the hill; *— di pietà*, pawnshop; *portare l'orologio al —*, to pawn one's watch; *andare a —*, to come to nothing. **-icello** *m.dim.* hillock, mound.

**montọne** *m.* ram; sheepskin; *carne di —*, mutton.

**montuọs-o** *adj.* mountainous. **-ità** *f.* mountainousness.

**montura** *f.* harness; (mil.) cavalry equipment.

**monumẹnt-o** *m.* monument; tomb; important building; statue. **-ale** *adj.* monumental; huge.

**mora**[1] *f.* delay, interval; (leg.) default; period of grace.

**mora**[2] *f.* (bot.) blackberry.

**mora** *f.* mora, morra, a game in which one player guesses the number of fingers held up by another.

**moral-e** *adj.* moral; *filosofia —*, moral philosophy, ethics; virtuous; *n.f.* morals, morality; *la — della favola*, the moral of the fable; *n.m.* morale, moral condition. **-eggiare** [A3 c] *intr.* (*aux.* avere) to moralize. **-ista** *m.* moralist. **-ità** *f.* morality. **-ịzzare** [A1] *tr.* to moralize; to expound in a moral sense.

**morato·ria** *f.* moratorium; deferment; postponement.

**mor·bid-o** *adj.* soft; *cappello —*, felt hat; tender (of meat); easily worked (of ground); mellow; effeminate; delicate. **-ẹzza** *f.* softness.

**morb-o** *m.* disease; plague; illness; vice. **-illo** *m.* (med.) German measles. **-osità** *f.* morbidity, unhealthiness. **-ọso** *adj.* morbid.

**mọrchia** *f.* dregs of pressed olives.

**mordac-e** *adj.* biting; pungent, stinging; given to biting. **-ità** *f.* pungency; mordacity.

**mor·d-ere** [B1] *tr.* to bite; to gnaw; to sting; *-ersi le labbra*, to bite one's lips; (fig.) to profit; (fig.) *— il freno*, to champ at the bit. **-ente** *part. adj.* biting, pungent; caustic. **-icchiare** [A3] *tr.* to nibble. **-itọre** *m.* biter; backbiter.

**morello** *adj.* nearly black; *n.m.* horse of that colour.

**morena** *f.* (geol.) moraine.

**morẹs-co** *adj.* (*m.pl.* **-chi**) Moorish. **-ca** *f.* (mus.) Morisca, Morris dance.

**morẹtto** *m.* Moorish boy; negro boy; black servant.

**Morfe·o** *pr.n.m.* (myth.) Morpheus.

**morfin-a** *f.* (chem.; pharm.) morphine. **-omani·a** *f.* (med.) morphine addiction. **-o·mane** *m.* (med.) morphine addict.

**morfol-ogi·a** *f.* morphology. **-o·gico** *adj.* morphological.

**mori·a** *f.* high mortality; pestilence.

**moribọndo** *adj.* moribund.

**morigerato** *adj.* of good morals; of good manners.

**mor-ire** [D3] *intr.* (*aux.* essere) to die; *— impiccato*, to be hanged; *— di crepacuore*, to die of a broken heart; *— dalle risa*, to die of laughter; *— di fame*, to starve; (fig.) to go out, to die away; *lasciar — il fuoco*, to let the fire go out; *n.m.* death. **-endo** *ger.* (mus.) dying away, becoming softer. **-ente** *part. adj.* dying; moribund; fading away; faint.

**mormor-are** [A1 sc] *intr.* (*aux.* avere) to murmur, to mutter; to speak in an undertone; *— di*, to complain about; *tr.* to murmur, to mutter. **-ante** *part. adj.* murmuring; complaining. **-azịone** *f.* murmuring; complaining. **-ìo** *m.* (*pl.* **-ii**) murmuring; muttering; grumbling.

**moro**[1] *m.* Moor, negro; *adj.* black, dark-complexioned.

**moro**[2] *m.* (bot.) mulberry-tree.

**morọso** *adj.* tardy; (leg.) behindhand, in arrear; *debitore —*, defaulting debtor.

**mors-o** *adj.* bitten; *n.m.* bite; morsel, bit; bit (for horse). **-a** *f.* vice; *-a da banco*, bench vice. **-ẹtto** *m.dim.* morsel; *m.* (electr.) terminal; (eng.) clamp; clip. **-icare** [A2 s] *tr.* to bite; to sting; to nibble. **-icchiare** [A3] *tr.* to nibble.

**mortadella** *f.* *m.* (cul.) mortadella, spiced pork sausage.

**morta·io** *m.* mortar; (mil.) mortar, heavy calibre, high-trajectory gun.

**mortal-e** *adj.* mortal; deadly; *peccato —*, mortal sin; *salto —*, somersault; *n.m.* mortal. **-ità** *f.* mortality; loss-of-life; death-rate.

**mort-e** *f.* death; *essere in punto di —*, to be at death's door; *darsi la —*, to commit suicide; (leg.) *l'atto di —*, registration of death; *certificato di —*, death certificate; (fig.) cause of death; end, cessation; destruction.

**mortella** *f.* (bot.) myrtle.

**morti·fero** *adj.* death-dealing; *veleno —*, deadly poison.

**mortific-are** [A2 s] *tr.* to mortify; to grieve, to vex; to humiliate; to repress; (med.) to anaesthetize locally; *rfl.* to mortify oneself; to be humiliated. **-azione** *f.* mortification; humiliation; grave rebuke; shame.
**mort-o** *adj.* dead; *acqua -a,* stagnant water; *nato —,* still-born; (comm.) *capitale —,* unemployed capital; spent, extinguished; lost; ruined; fruitless, sterile; *n.m.* dead man, deceased; (at cards) dummy; hoard of money, treasure; (naut.) mooring bollard. **-a** *f.* dead woman. **-icino** *m. dim.* dead child. **-o·rio** *m.* funeral, burial; (fig.) boring occasion. **-ua·rio** *adj.* mortuary; *carro -uario,* hearse; *letto -uario,* bier; *registro -uario,* register of deaths; *fede -uaria,* death certificate.
**morva** *f.* (vet.) glanders.
**Mosa** *pr.n.f.* (geog.) Meuse.
**moṣa·ic-o** *m.* (art) mosaic; (fig.) patchwork. **-ista** *m.* mosaicist.
**mọsc-a** *f.* (ent.) fly; house fly; *— cieca,* blind man's buff. **-a·io** *m.* swarm of flies.
**moscat-o** *m.* muscat; muscatel; *adj.* marked with dark spots; having a flavour of musk; muscat; *vino —,* muscat wine; *noce -a,* nutmeg. **-ello** *m., adj.* muscadine; muscatel.
**moscerino** *m.* (ent.) any small fly.
**mosche·a** *f.* mosque.
**moschẹtt-o** *m.* musket. **-are** [A1 c] *tr.* to shoot with a musket. **-eri·a** *f.* musketry. **-iere** *m.* musketeer.
**mọsc-io** *adj.* flabby, soft; muffled; *cappello —,* soft hat; (of a person) dull; (of pockets) empty. **-ịone** *adj. augm.* flabby; inert.
**moscọne** *m.* (ent.) large fly; *— azzurro,* bluebottle.
**Mosè** *pr.n.m.* Moses.
**Mosella** *pr.n.f.* (geog.) Moselle; moselle wine.
**moss-a** *f.* movement, move; gesture; (mil.) movement of troops; (med.) *— di corpo,* motion of the bowels; *pl.* start, starting-place; *dar le -e,* to give the signal to start. **-iere** *m.* starter. **-o** *adj.* moved, agitated; *capelli -i,* wavy hair; *mare -o,* rough sea; (mus.) *più -o,* faster; *meno -o,* slower.
**mostard-a** *f.* mustard. **-iera** *f.* mustard-pot.
**mọst-o** *m.* (of wine) must. **-ọso** *adj.* full of must.
**mọstra** *f.* show, display, exhibition; *sala di —,* show-room; *— di panno,* sample of cloth; dial (of watch); (naut.) regatta; naval review; (mil.) tattoo; (fig.) ostentation; *far — di,* to pretend to.
**mostrare** [A1 c] *tr.* to show, to point out, to exhibit, to display; *— a dito,* to point to; to demonstrate, to prove; to seem, to look; *rfl.* to show oneself; to be seen; to come out.
**mọstr-o** *m.* monster; prodigy; (paint.) grotesque. **-uọso** *adj.* monstrous; enormous.
**mot-a** *f.* mud, mire. **-ọso** *adj.* muddy.
**motiv-are** [A1] *tr.* to state the reasons for; to justify; to motivate, to cause. **-azịone** *f.* motivation; statement of the reasons (for).
**motivo** *m.* motive; reason, cause; ground; motif.
**moto** *m.* motion; *— perpetuo,* perpetual motion; *mettere in —,* to set in motion, (eng.) to start up; emotion; commotion; movement, exercise, exertion.
**moto-ciclẹtta** *f.,* **-ciclo** *m.* motor-cycle. **-ciclịsmo** *m.* motor-cycling. **-ciclista** *m.* motor-cyclist. **-livellatọre** *m.* bulldozer. **-na·utica** *f.* speed-boat racing. **-scafo** *m.* motor-boat.
**mot-ọre** *m.* motor; mover; engine; *— a benzina,* petrol engine; *avviare il —,* to start the engine; *spegnere il —,* to shut off the engine; (naut.) *— fuori bordo,* outboard motor; *adj.* driving, impelling; *forza -rice,* motive power; (anat.) *nervi -ori,* motor nerves. **-o·rio** *adj.* (*m.pl.* **-orii**), **-ori·stico** *adj.* motor; *gare -oristiche,* motor races. **-orista** *m.* (eng.) mechanic. **-orịẓẓato** *adj.* motorized.
**mott-o** *m.* saying, word; pleasantry, witticism; motto. **-eggiare** [A3 c] *intr.* (*aux.* avere) to jest, to joke; *tr.* to mock, to make fun of. **-ẹggio** *m.* jest, joke. **-eggìo** *m.* frequent jesting, banter.
**mottẹtto** *m.* (mus.) motet.
**moven-te** *adj.* moving; *n.m.* motive, cause. **-za** *f.* movement; gesture; bearing.
**movimẹnt-o** *m.* movement; stir; gesture; motion; slight emotion. **-are** [A1c] *tr.* to make busy; to fill with movement. **-ato** *part. adj.* busy; *una strada -ata,* a busy street; eventful; agitated; lively.
**Mozambico** *pr.n.m.* (geog.) Mozambique.
**mozịone** *f.* motion; resolution; *la — è respinta,* the motion is rejected; *la — è approvata,* the resolution is carried.
**mozz-are** [A1] *tr.* to cut off, to lop off; to dock; *— il fiato a,* to take one's breath away. **-icọne** *m.* stump; *-icone di sigaretta,* cigarette-end, stub.
**mọẓẓo**[1] *m.* hub, wheel-hub.
**mọzzo**[2] *adj.* cut off, docked; *guanto —,* mitten; *n.m.* boy stable-boy; *— di stalla,* groom.
**mucca** *f.* dairy cow.
**muc·chio** *m.* heap; pile; crowd; flock; *a mucchi,* in plenty.
**mu·cido** *adj.* musty; rotten; mouldy; bad; *n.m.* mould; dampness.
**muc-o** *m.* mucus. **-ọsa** *f.* (anat.) mucous membrane. **-ọso** *adj.* mucous.
**muffa** *f.* (bot.) mould; must; *sentir di —,* to smell mouldy.
**mugghiare** [A4] *intr.* (*aux.* avere) to bellow, to low; (of sea) to roar; (of wind) to howl.
**mug·ghio** *m.* lowing; bellow; roar; howling.
**mugg-ire** [D1] *intr.* (*aux.* avere) to bellow; to low; (of sea) to roar. **-ito** *m.* bellowing; lowing; roar.
**mughẹtto** *m.* (bot.) lily of the valley.
**mugna·io** *m.* miller; (orn.) gull.
**mugol-are** [A1 s] *intr.* (*aux.* avere) to yelp; to whine; to howl; to moan; to mumble. **-ìo** *m.* yelping; moaning; mumbling.
**mu·gol-o** *m.* moaning; whining. **-ọne** *m.* yelping; whining dog.
**mulac·chia** *f.* (orn.) hooded crow, jackdaw.
**muliebre** *adj.* feminine, womanly; womanish.
**mulin-o** *m.* mill; *— ad acqua,* water-mill; *— a vento,* windmill; *— da olio,* olive press. **-aio** *m.* miller. **-are** [A1] *tr.* to whirl round; *intr.* (*aux.* avere) (fig.) to indulge in idle fancies; to muse. **-ello** *m.dim.* whirl; swivel; reel; fan driven by wind; whirlwind; whirlpool; (fig.) intrigue; (meteor.) eddy.
**mul-o** *m.* mule. **-ag·gine** *m.* obstinacy, mulishness. **-attiera** *f.* mule-track. **-attiere** *adj.* pertaining to mule; *sentiero -attiere,* mule-path; *n.m.* muleteer.
**mult-a** *f.* (leg.) fine; mulct; *liquidare una —,* to pay a fine. **-are** [A1] *tr.* (leg.) to fine; to mulct; to surcharge.
**mult-icolọre** *adj. indecl.* many-coloured. **-ifọrme** *adj.* multiform. **-ilaterale** *adj.* multilateral. **-ilingue** *adj.* multilingual. **-imiliona·rio** *adj., n.m.* multi-millionaire.
**mul·tiplo** *adj., n.m.* multiple.
**mum·mi-a** *f.* mummy. **-ficare** [A2 s] *tr.* to mummify; *intr.* (*aux.* essere) to become mummified. **-ficazịone** *f.* mummification.
**mun·g-ere** *tr.* to milk; (fig.) to exploit; to sponge on. **-itọio** *m.* milking-pail. **-itrice** *f.* (pop.). **-itọre** *f.* milkmaid. **-itura** *f.* milking; (fig.) exploitation.
**municipal-e** *adj.* municipal; *palazzo —,* town-hall; *impiegati -i,* local government officers. **-ità** *f. indecl.* municipality.

**munici·pio** *m.* municipality; town-hall.
**muni·fic-o** *adj.* munificent; bountiful; generous. **-enza** *f.* munificence; generosity.
**mun-ire** [D2] *tr.* to fortify; to furnish, to provide, to supply. **-ito** *part. adj.* (*prep.* di) supplied (with), furnished (with). **-izione** *f.* munition; stores; equipment.
**munto** *part.* of **mun·gere**; *adj.* milked; (fig.) exploited; exhausted; pale.
**muo·v-ere** [C15] *tr.* to move; (fig.) to make a move, to act; to work, to drive; to stir; (fig.) — *i primi passi*, to take the first steps; — *le gambe*, to 'stretch one's legs'; — *causa*, to start proceedings; *intr.* (*aux.* essere) to go; to come; to begin; to start (from); to advance; *rfl.* to move, to stir; to bestir oneself; to set off.
**mura**[1] *f.* (naut.) tack; *cambiare le mure*, to change tack, *i.e.* to go about.
**mura**[2] *f.pl.* of **muro**, *q.v.*
**mura·gli-a** *f.* wall; high wall; *la Gran — della Cina*, the Great Wall of China; rampart, (fig.) barrier. **-one** *m.augm.* barrier; great wall; dike.
**murale** *adj.* mural; *carta* —, wall map.
**mur-are** [A1] *tr.*, *intr.* (*aux* avere) to wall; to build; — *a secco*, to build a dry wall; to wall up; to build in; to immure; to build a wall around; *rfl.* to immure oneself. **-a·rio** *adj.* of a mason, of building; *arte -aria*, the art of building. **-atore** *m.* bricklayer; mason; *franco -atore*, freemason. **-atura** *f.* construction; masonry; brickwork.
**mu·rice** *m.* marine gastropod.
**mur-o** *m.* wall; (*pl.* **-i** *m.*, **-a** *f.*, the latter in the sense of peripheral walls); (aeron.) — *del suono*, sound barrier. **-azzo** *m.* dike, sea-wall. **-icci(u)olo** *m.* *dim.* low wall; parapet wall; *andare a finire sui -icciuoli*, (of books) to find their way to the secondhand bookstalls.
**musa** *f.* muse.
**mu·schi-o** *m.* musk, moss. **-ato** *adj.* musky; (bot.) *rosa -ata*, musk rose.
**mus-co** *m.* (bot.) moss. **-chini** *m.pl.* grape hyacinth. **-oso** *adj.* mossy.
**mu·scol-o**[1] *m.* muscle; sinew. **-are** *adj.* muscular; sinewy. **-atura** *f.* musculature. **-osità** *f.* muscularity. **-oso** *adj.* muscular, brawny; sinewy.
**muscolo**[2] *m.* (zool.) edible mussel.
**muse·o** *m.* museum.
**museruola** *f.* muzzle; noseband.
**mu·sic-a** *f.* music; musical work; military band; *porre in* —, to set to music; *carta da* —, music paper; — *da camera*, chamber music; orchestra, band; — *del reggimento*, regimental band. **-a·bile** *adj.* suitable to be set to music. **-ale** *adj.* musical; *fondo -ale*, background music. **-alità** *f.* musicianship. **-ante** *m.* itinerant musician. **-are** [A2s] *tr.* to set to music. **-ista** *m.*, *f.* musician. **-o·logo** *m.* musicologist.
**musivo** *adj.* mosaic, tessellated.
**mus-o** *m.* snout, muzzle; (derog.) *che brutto —!*, what an ugly mug! **-iera** *f.* nose-bag. **-one** *m.augm.* large face; sulky fellow; slap, blow. **-oneri·a** *f.* pouting, sulkiness, sullenness; haughty behaviour.
**mussare** [A1] *intr.* (*aux.* avere) to foam, to froth, to hiss.
**mussolina** *f.* (text.) muslin.
**mustacchi** *m.pl.* (joc.) moustache(s).
**musulmano** *m.*, *adj.* Mussulman; Mohammedan.
**muta**[1] *f.* pack of hounds; team of horses.
**muta**[2] *f.* moult; change.
**mut-are** [A1] *tr.* to change, to alter; — *nome*, to change one's name; — *idea*, to change one's mind; (of animals) — *la pelle*, to shed the skin; (of birds) — *le penne*, to moult; (of wine) to decant; *intr.* (*aux.* essere) to change; to alter; *rfl.* to change, to alter; *-arsi di scarpe*, to change one's shoes; to move; (of a boy's voice) to break. **-a·bile** *adj.* mutable, inconstant. **-abilità** *f.* mutability, inconstancy. **-ande** *f.pl.* drawers; *-ande da bagno*, bathing-trunks. **-andine** *f.pl.* shorts; knickers. **-azione** *f.* change, alteration; mutation. **-evole** *adj.* mutable; variable, changeable; inconstant.
**mutil-are** [A1s] *tr.* to mutilate, to maim. **-ato** *part. adj.* maimed; crippled; mutilated; incomplete; *n.m.* disabled man; *i -ati di guerra*, the war-disabled. **-azione** *f.* mutilation.
**mu·tilo** *adj.* mutilated; incomplete.
**mut-o** *adj.* mute; dumb; speechless; (cinem.) *film* —, silent film; (theatr.) *scena -a*, dumb show; *n.m.* deaf man; *sordo* —, deaf mute. **-a** *f.* dumb woman. **-ezza** *f.* dumbness; muteness. **-ismo** *m.* obstinate silence, taciturnity; dumbness.
**mu·tolo** *adj.* dumb; taciturn.
**mu·tria** *f.* haughtiness; pouting, sulkiness; pout.
**mu·tua** *f.* mutual benefit society.
**mutual-e** *adj.* mutual. **-ità** *f.* mutuality.
**mutu-are** [A6] *tr.* to lend; to borrow; to mortgage. **-ante** *part. adj.* lending; *n.m.*, *f.* lender. **-ata·rio** *m.* borrower. **-azione** *f.* mutual exchange.
**mu·tuo** *adj.* mutual, reciprocal; *società di — soccorso*, benefit-society, friendly society; *n.m.* loan; — *ipotecario*, mortgaged loan; — *garantito*, secured loan.

**N** *f.*, *m.* (pron. **enne**) the letter N; the consonant N.
**Nabucodo·nosor** *pr.n.m.* (bibl.) Nebuchadnezzar.
**nac·chera** *f.* (mus.) kettledrum, naker; *pl.* castanets.
**nafta** *f.* naphtha.
**na·iade** *f.* naiad, water-nymph; (bot.) water lily.
**na·ilon** *m. indecl.* nylon.
**Nanchino** *pr.n.f.* (geog.) Nankin(g); *m.* (text.) nankeen.
**nanna** *f.* (fam.) bye-byes; *fare la* —, to go to bye-byes; hush-a-bye.
**nano** *m.* dwarf; *adj.* dwarfish, stunted.
**Nante** *pr.n.f.* (geog.) Nantes.
**Napole-one** *pr.n.m.* Napoleon; (numism.) napoleon, gold coin of twenty francs. **-o·nico** *adj.* Napoleonic; *il codice -onico*, the Napoleonic Code.
**Na·pol-i** *pr.n.f.* (geog.) Naples. **-etano** *adj.*, *n.m.* Neapolitan.
**nappa** *f.* tassel; tuft; sprinkler, rose.
**nappo** *m.* goblet; receptacle for oil.
**Narcis-o**[1] *pr.n.m.* (myth.) Narcissus. **-ismo** *m.* (psychol.) narcissism.
**narciso**[2] *m.* (bot.) narcissus; daffodil.
**nardo** *m.* (bot.) lavender.
**narice** *f.* (anat.) nostril.
**narr-are** [A1] *tr.* to narrate; to recount; to relate. **-ativa** *f.* fiction; narration. **-ativo** *adj.* narrative. **-atore** *m.* narrator. **-azione** *f.* narration; narrative; tale; account.
**na·scere** [B18] *intr.* (*aux.* essere) to be born; to come into the world; to sprout; to come up; to grow; to hatch out; to begin; to arise; to rise; to dawn; (of a train) to start (from); to issue; to emanate; *far* —, to give rise to, to originate, to occasion; *n.m.* birth; beginning; outset.

**na·sc-ita** *f.* birth; *fede di -ita,* birth certificate; *essere inglese di —,* to be English by birth; (leg.) *atto di —,* record of birth. **-ituro** *adj.* about to be born; future; *n.m.* unborn child.
**nascọnd-ere** [C11] *tr.* to hide; to conceal; to keep secret; to dissimulate; to disguise; *rfl.* to hide, to be hidden; to keep out of sight, to go into hiding. **-i·glio** *m.* hiding-place; lair; den.
**nascọsto** *part. adj.* hidden; concealed; disguised; covered; *adv. phr. di —,* secretly; stealthily.
**nasello** *m.* (ichth.) hake.
**nas-o** *m.* nose; *tabacco da —,* snuff; *fazzoletto da —,* pocket handkerchief; *aver buon — per,* to have a flair for; *— a —,* face to face; snout; nozzle. **-ale** *adj.* (anat.) nasal; *n.f.* nasal consonant.
**nastro** *m.* ribbon; band; tape; strip; border; decoration; medal-ribbon; *registratore a —,* tape-recorder; *— trasportatore,* conveyor belt.
**nastur·zio** *m.* (bot.) watercress; (garden) nasturtium.
**natal-e**[1] *adj.* native; natal; *giorno —,* birthday; *n.m.* birthday; birthplace; (fig.) beginnings; origin. **-ità** *f.* birth-rate. **-i·zio** *adj.* natal; *vacanze -izie,* Christmas holidays; *n.m.* birthday; birthday celebrations.
**Natale**[2] *pr.n.m.* Christmas; *il giorno di —* Christmas Day; *la Vigilia di —,* Christmas Eve; *cantico di —,* Christmas carol.
**nat-ante** *part. adj.* floating; swimming; *n.m.* craft; boat. **-atọia** *f.* (zool.) fin; webbed foot; swimming-bladder. **-ato·rio** *adj.* rel. to swimming; *piscina -atoria,* swimming-pool.
**na·tica** *f.* (anat.) buttock.
**nat-ìo** *adj.* (*m.pl.* **-ii**) native; *essere — di,* to be a native of; indigenous; innate, natural. **-ività** *f.* birth, nativity; (of a city) foundation. **-ivo** *adj.* native; local; indigenous; innate; natural; *n.m.* native.
**nato** *part. adj.* born; hatched out; sprouted; launched, begun; *Maria Gigli nata Bosi,* Maria Gigli née Bosi; *n.m.* son, child; little one; *pl.* young (of animals).
**na·tola** *f.* (naut.) rowlock.
**natrice** *f.* (zool.) grass-snake.
**natta** *f.* (med.) wen, cyst.
**natur-a** *f.* nature; natural world; *— madre,* Mother Nature; *le scienze della —,* the natural sciences; countryside, scenery; natural order; property, natural characteristic; character, temperament; constitution; *la — umana,* human nature; kind, sort, class; natural species, form of life; (paint.) *— morta,* still life. **-ale** *adj.* natural; *storia -ale,* Natural History; in a natural state; normal; innate, inborn; simple, uncouth, unlettered; easy, unselfconscious; illegitimate; *figlio -ale,* natural son; real, genuine; ordinary, obvious; *n.m.* state of nature; life-size; life, living model; *disegnare dal -ale,* to draw from life; constitution; nature, disposition, temperament. **-alẹzza** *f.* naturalness, unselfconsciousness. **-alịsmo** *m.* naturalism; realism. **-alista** *m.* naturalist; realist. **-ali·stico** *adj.* naturalistic. **-alità** *f.* political status; citizenship; *ottenere la -alità italiana,* to become a naturalized Italian. **-alịẓẓare** [A1] *tr.* (leg.) to naturalize; *rfl.* to become naturalized. **-ịsmo** *m.* 'back-to-nature' movement.
**nauclero** *m.* (orn.) kite.
**naufragare** [A2s] *intr.* (*aux. essere, avere*) to shipwreck; to be wrecked; (fig.) to come to grief, to founder; to fail.
**naufra·gio** *m.* shipwreck; (fig.) wreck, ruin; failure.
**na·ufrag-o** *m.* (*pl.* **-ghi**) shipwrecked person; wreck; drowning man; castaway; (fig.) failure in life, a down-and-out.
**na·uṣe-a** *f.* nausea; queasiness; loathing, disgust, repulsion. **-abọndo** *adj.* nauseous; loathsome. **-are** [A1] *tr.* to nauseate; to disgust, to make sick.
**na·utico** *adj.* nautical; *architettura nautica,* ship designing.
**Navarr-a** *pr.n.f.* (geog.) Navarre. **-ẹse** *adj.* of Navarre; *n.m., f.* native of Navarre.
**navata**[1] (archit.) nave.
**navata**[2] *f.* ship-load, cargo.
**nav-e** *f.* ship; vessel; boat; craft; liner; (archit.) nave. **-ale** *adj.* naval. **-ẹtta** *f.* shuttle.
**navig-are** [A2s] *intr.* (*aux.* avere) to cruise, sail or row; *— sui bordi,* to tack; *tr. — i mari,* to sail the seas; to transport. **-a·bile** *adj.* navigable; seaworthy. **-ante** *part. adj.* navigating; *n.m.* navigator. **-atọre** *m.* navigator; *adj.* seafaring. **-aziọne** *f.* navigation; art of navigating; *società di -azione,* steamship company.
**navi·glio** *m.* (naut.) fleet; squadron; flotilla; craft; convoy.
**navọne** *m.* (bot.) rape, colza; swede.
**naziọn-e** *f.* nation; people, country; nationality. **-ale** *adj.* national; *prodotti -ali,* home products; *n.f. la -ale,* trunk road. **-alịsmo** *m.* nationalism. **-alista** *m., f., adj.* nationalist. **-alità** *f.* nationality; nation. **-alịẓẓare** [A1] *tr.* to nationalize. **-alịẓẓaziọne** *f.* nationalization.
**naz-ịsmo** *m.* (hist.) Nazism. **-ista** *m., f.* Nazi.
**Naẓ(ẓ)ar-et** *pr.n.f.* (geog.) Nazareth. **-eno** *adj., n.m.* Nazarene.
**nẹ** *prn. conj.* of him; of her; of it; of them; his; her; its; their; *— sentii i passi,* I heard his (her, its, their) footsteps; with it; *che — fai ?,* what do you do with it ?; about it; *non — parlare,* don't talk about it; thence, from thence; *— veniamo proprio adesso,* we've just this minute come from there; *partit.* some of it, any; *dammene,* give me some.
**nè** *conj.* neither; nor; *nè...nè,* neither...nor.
**nean·che** *conj.* not even; *— per sogno,* I wouldn't dream of it; your life; neither, nor.
**nẹbbi-a** *f.* fog; mist; haze; indistinctness, obscurity. **-olina** *f. dim.* drifting mist. **-ọne** *m. augm.* dense fog; smog. **-ọso** *adj.* misty; foggy; hazy; (fig.) nebulous; abstruse.
**nebulịẓẓ-are** [A1] *tr.* to atomize. **-atọre** *m.* spray, atomizer.
**nebulọs-a** *f.* (astron.) nebula. **-o** *adj.* nebulous; misty, hazy; vague; obscure.
**necessa·ri-o** *adj.* necessary; indispensable; requisite; essential; evident, obvious; *n.m.* necessity; the necessary. **-amẹnte** *adv.* necessarily; of necessity.
**necessit-à** *f. indecl.* necessity; want, indigence; destiny. **-are** [A1s] *intr.* (*aux.* avere; *prep.* di) to be in want (of); *impers.* to be necessary; *tr.* to lead to, to involve.
**necr-ofili·a** *f.* necrophilism. **-ofobi·a** *f.* necrophobia. **-ologi·a** *f.* necrology; funeral oration. **-olo·gio** *m.* announcement of death, obituary notice. **-omanzi·a** *f.* necromancy. **-o·poli** *f. indecl.*; necropolis.
**nefando** *adj.* infamous, execrable; abominable.
**nefasto** *adj.* fateful, ill-omened, unpropitious; unlucky.
**nefrite** *f.* (med.) nephritis.
**neg-are** [A2] *tr.* to deny; to disavow; to refuse; to disown, to repudiate; to contradict. **-a·bile** *adj.* deniable. **-ativa** *f.* denial; negative; negative reply; *n.f.* (photog.) negative. **-ativo** *adj.* negative; *voto -ativo,* adverse vote; *risposta -ativa,* refusal; denial; (fig.) inactive; negative. **-aziọne** *f.* negation; disavowal; negative.
**neghittọso** *adj.* slothful, indolent; listless; careless.
**negletto** *adj.* uncared for, untidy, dishevelled; negligent; inaccurate.
**negli·g-ere** [C13] *tr.* to neglect; to slight; to disregard; to leave out; to omit.
**-ente** *part. adj.* negligent; neglectful; inattentive, careless, lazy, slothful. **-enza** *f.* negligence;

carelessness, heedlessness, inattention.
**negozi-are** [A4] *intr.* (*aux.* avere) to negotiate; (comm.) to trade; to transact business; to bargain; *tr.* to negotiate; (comm.) to sell, to deal in. **-a·bile** *adj.* negotiable; marketable. **-ante** *part. adj.* negotiating; *n.m.* tradesman; dealer. **-ato** *part. adj.* negotiated; *n.m.* business deal; negotiation; transaction; *pl.* negotiations. **-atọre** *m.* negotiator. **-aziọne** *f.* negotiation; transaction; business dealing.
**nego·zio** *m.* business; bargain; transaction; (fig.) concern, affair; shop, store, business; *commesso di —*, shop-assistant.
**nẹgr-o** *adj.* negro, black; *n.m.* negro. **-a** *f.* negress. **-iere** *m.* slave-dealer; (fig.) slave-driver. **-o·ide** *adj.*, *n.m.* negroid.
**negro-mante** *m.* necromancer, sorcerer. **-manzi·a** *f.* necromancy.
**neh** *excl.* eh; *è bello, —?,* it's lovely, isn't it ?.
**nẹmbo** *m.* cloud; rain-cloud, nimbus; cloud-burst, squall; dense mass, large cluster.
**Nembrotte** *pr.n.m.* (bibl.) Nimrod.
**ne·mesi** *f.* fate, nemesis; retributive justice, vengeance.
**nemico** *adj.* hostile, inimical; contrary, adverse; opposed, averse; harmful; *n.m.* enemy; opponent.
**nemmẹno** *conj.* not even; neither.
**ne·nia** *f.* dirge; children's song; rigmarole; lamentation; tedious speech.
**nenu·fero** *m.* (bot.) yellow waterlily.
**neo** *m.* mole (on the skin); slight imperfection; patch, beauty-spot.
**neo-catto·lico** *m.* (recent) Catholic convert. **-classicịsmo** *m.* neo-classicism. **-classicista** *m., f.* neo-classicist. **-clas·sico** *adj.* neo-classical; *n.m.* neo-classicist. **-greco** *adj., n.m.* modern Greek. **-li·tico** *adj.* neolithic. **-logịsmo** *m.* neologism. **-nato** *adj.* newborn; *n.m.* new-born child. **-plato·nico** *adj.* Neoplatonic; *n.m.* Neoplatonist. **-platonịsmo** *m.* Neoplatonism.
**neo·fito** *m.* neophyte; new convert.
**nepot-ịsmo** *m.* nepotism; favouritism. **-ista** *m.* nepotist.
**neppure** *conj.* not even.
**nerb-o** *m.* scourge, lash, thong; sinew, muscle; stamina, force; best part, core. **-are** [A1] *tr.* to scourge. **-ata** *f.* stroke of the whip; flogging. **-atura** *f.* scourging. **-oruto** *adj.*, **-uto** *adj.* muscular, sinewy; sturdy; vigorous.
**nere·ide** *f.* (myth.) nereid, seanymph.
**nẹr-o** *adj.* black; (fig.) sad, gloomy, sombre; dark; dirty; evil, atrocious; livid with envy; *borsa -a*, black market; *n.m.* black, the colour black. **-ẹzza** *f.* blackness; darkness. **-igno, -ọgnolo** *adj.* blackish, on the dark side. **-ume** *m.* blackness; smut; soot; black stuff; black stains.
**Nerọne** *pr.n.m.* (hist.) Nero.
**nerv-o** *m.* (anat.) sinew; muscle; nerve; *pl.* nerves; *il caffè dà ai -i*, coffee stimulates the nervous system; *attacco di -i*, fit of nerves; courage, strength, vigour. **-atura** *f.* (med.) constitution. **-osịsmo** *m.* nervousness, excitability; nervous disorder. **-osità** *f.* nervous excitability, restlessness; (of style) vigour. **-ọso** *adj.* sinewy; muscular; nervous; excitable, temperamental; vigorous, muscular, robust.
**nesc-i** *m. fare il —*, to feign ignorance; to turn a deaf ear. **-iente** *adj.* unaware; ignorant. **-ienza** *f.* ignorance.
**ne·spol-a** (bot.) medlar. **-o** *m.* (bot.) medlar tree.
**nesso**[I] *m.* connexion, link; nexus; (mus.) tie.
**Nesso**[2] *pr.n.m.* (myth.) Nessus.
**nessuno** *adj.* no; none; any; *prn.* no one, nobody.
**Nestọre** *pr.n.m.* (myth.) Nestor.
**nettare**[I] [A1 c] *tr.* to clean; to wash; to cleanse; to clear. **-atọio** *m.* cleaning equipment; cleaning material. **-atọre** *m.* cleaner. **-atura** *f.* cleaning; washing; cleansing; clearing.
**net·tare**[2] *m.* nectar.
**nẹtt-o** *adj.* clean; neat; whole; exact, precise; clean, sharp; free, unencumbered; honest, upright; pure, unadulterated; *adj.* (comm.) net; *rendita -a*, net income; *n.m.* clear part; *mettere al —*, to make a fair copy of. **-ẹzza** *f.* cleanness, cleanliness; *la -ezza urbana*, municipal department concerned with the removal of rubbish; precision; clarity; neatness; purity; brightness.
**Nettuno** *pr.n.m.* (myth.) Neptune.
**neur-ite** *f.* neuritis. **-ologi·a** *f.* neurology.
**ne·utr-o** *adj.* neuter; neutral; indeterminate; *n.m.* (gramm.) *il —*, the neuter gender; (biol.) neuter. **-ale** *adj.* neutral; *n.m.* neutral State; neutral person. **-alịsmo** *m.* policy of nonintervention. **-alista** *m., f.* partisan of neutrality. **-alità** *f.* neutrality. **-alịẓẓare** [A1] *tr.* to neutralize; to counterbalance. **-alịẓẓaziọne** *f.* neutralization. **-ọne** *m.* (phys.) neutron.
**nẹv-e** *f.* snow; *fiocco di —*, snowflake; *bufera di —*, snowstorm; (fig.) bitter cold; snowy whiteness. **-ata** *f.* snowfall. **-ato** *adj.* snow-white; snow-covered; *n.m.* snowdrift; glacier. **-icare** [A2 sc] *impers.* (*aux.* essere, avere) to snow. **-icata** *f.* snowstorm; snowfall. **-i·schio** *m.* sleet; very fine wind-driven snow. **-ọso** *adj.* snowy; snow-capped; snow-covered; snow-white.
**nevr-algi·a** *f.* (med.) neuralgia. **-ọsi** *f. indecl.* neurosis. **-o·tico** *adj.* neurotic.
**nevvẹro** *excl.* isn't that so?; isn't it?
**nib·bio** *m.* (orn.) kite.
**nic·chi-a** *f.* (zool.) shell; (archit.) niche; corner, hole, recess; (fig.) niche, job. **-are** [A4] *intr.* (*aux.* avere) to hesitate, to waver; *rfl.* to retire into one's shell.
**nic·chio** *m.* (zool.) shell of a snail.
**nich-el, -e·lio** *m.* nickel. **-el(l)are** [A1, A1 s] *tr.* to nickelplate. **-el(l)atura** *f.* nickelplating.
**nichil-ịsmo** *m.* (philos.) nihilism. **-ista** *m., f.* nihilist.
**nicotin-a** *f.* nicotine. **-ịsmo** *m.* (med.) nicotine poisoning.
**nid-o** *m.* nest; roost; brood; swarm; den, lair; (fig.) home, shelter. **-iace** *adj.* unfledged; *n.m.* fledgling, nestling. **-iata** *f.* brood of nestlings; hatch; (fig.) swarm, crew, set. **-ificare** [A2 s] *intr.* (*aux.* avere) to build a nest. **-ificaziọne** *f.* nest-building.
**nient-e** *prn. indef.* nothing; *un —*, a trifle, a mere nothing; nothingness, nullity; unimportance; (in interrog., conditional or quasi-neg. phrases) anything; *se ti occorre —*, if you want anything; *adv.* in no way, certainly not, by no means; *adj. indecl.* no; *— scuse*, no apologies. **-edimẹno** *adv.* none the less, nevertheless, notwithstanding.
**Nil-o** *pr.n.m.* (geog.) Nile. **-o·tico** *adj.* relating to the river Nile.
**nimbo** *m.* flash of light; bright light; halo, aureole.
**ninf-a** *f.* nymph. **-ale** *adj.* nymph-like. **-e·a** *f.* (bot.) white water lily. **-omani·a** *f.* (med.) nymphomania.
**Ninive** *pr.n.f.* (geog.) Nineveh.
**ninn-a** *f.* (fam.) bye-byes. **-ananna** *f.* lullaby.
**nin·nolo** *m.* toy, plaything; trifle; trinket; knick-knack.
**nipọte** *m., f.* nephew; niece; grandson; granddaughter; grandchild; *pl.* descendants; progeny; issue; (leg.) nephews and nieces.
**ni·tid-o** *adj.* bright, shining; clear, translucent; lucid; distinct, precise; sharp. **-ẹzza** *f.* brightness; clearness, translucence; lucidity; distinctness, precision; definition; sharpness.

**ni·trico** *adj.* (chem.) nitric.
**nitr-ire** [D2] *intr.* (*aux.* avere) to neigh; to whinny. **-ito** *m.* neigh; neighing; whinny; whinnying.
**nitr-o** *m.* (miner.) nitre, saltpetre. **-ato** *m.* (chem.) nitrate. **-ǫso** *adj.* (chem.) nitrous.
**Nizz-a** *pr.n.f.* (geog.) Nice. **-ardo** *adj.* of Nice; *n.m.* native of Nice; *il gran -ardo,* Garibaldi.
**no** *neg. particle* no; *come —?,* of course, most certainly; *rispondere di —,* to say 'no'; *credo di —,* I don't think so, I think not; not; *perchè —?, come —?,* why not?; *se —,* if not, otherwise; *n.m. indecl.* the answer no; denial; refusal; *pl. i —,* the noes.
**no·bil-e** *adj.* noble; elevated; illustrious; magnanimous; excellent; worthy, dignified; of noble birth; stately, imposing; (archit.) *piano —,* first floor; *n.m.* nobleman. **-iare** *adj.* of the nobility. **-itare** [A1 s] *tr.* to ennoble, to confer nobility upon; *rfl.* to be ennobled; to distinguish oneself. **-tà** *f.* nobility; excellence, distinction; magnanimity, generosity; splendour, lordliness; noble rank; *la -tà,* the nobility, the aristocracy.
**noc-ca** *f.* (anat.) joint connecting fingers to the hand and toes to the foot; knuckle. **-coluto** *adj.* having large knuckles, bony.
**nocchier-e** *m.* (poet.) boatman, pilot. **-o** *m.* (naut.) coxswain.
**noc·chi-o** *m.* knot (in wood). **-erǫso** *adj.* (of wood) knotty. **-eruto** *adj.* knotted.
**nocci(u)ol-a** *f.* (bot.) hazel nut, cob nut. **-o** *m.* (bot.) hazel-nut tree.
**noc·ciolo** *m.* (bot.) stone (of fruit).
**nǫc-e** *m.* (bot.) walnut tree; *f.* walnut; nut; walnut wood; (cul.) *una — di burro,* a knob of butter.
**nocivo** *adj.* harmful; injurious; noxious.
**nǫd-o** *m.* knot; noose; knot (measure of speed); *avere un — alla gola,* to have a lump in one's throat; problem, difficulty, puzzle; knotty situation; bond, tie; (astron.) node. **-erǫso** *adj.* knotty, full of knots.
**nodǫso** *adj.* nodose; knotty, knotted; gnarled.
**no·dulo** *m.* nodule.
**Noè** *pr.n.m.* Noah.
**nǫi** *pers. prn.* we; us; *— stessi,* ourselves.
**no·i-a** *f.* tedium; boredom; ennui; aversion; trouble, annoyance; bore. **-ǫso** *adj.* boring, tedious; annoying, irritating; troublesome.
**noialtri** *pers. prn.* we ourselves.
**nol-o** *m.* hire; cost of hire. **-eggiare** [A3 c] *tr.* to hire; to let on hire; (naut.) to charter. **-ęggio** *m.* hire; price of hire; shop which hires out cars, bicycles, etc.; (naut.) *freightage;* charter.
**no·mad-e** *adj.* nomadic; *n.m.* nomad. **-ịṣmo** *m.* nomadism.
**nǫm-e** *m.* name; first name, Christian name; *— e cognome,* name and surname; word, term; title; *— di ragazza,* maiden name; reputation; meaning; noun; substantive; name-day; signature. **-e·a** *f.* renown, reputation; notoriety. **-i·gnolo** *m.* nickname; pet-name.
**nomenclatura** *f.* nomenclature.
**no·min-a** *f.* appointment, nomination; right of nominating for appointment. **-a·bile** *adj.* mentionable. **-ale** *adj.* nominal; *appello -ale,* roll-call. **-are** [A1 s] *tr.* to name; to appoint; to nominate; to call; to term; *rfl.* to be called; to be named; to appoint oneself. **-aziǫne** *f.* nomination; naming; mention; election, appointment.
**nominativo** *adj.* nominative; nominal; *n.m.* (gramm.) nominative case.
**nǫn** *adv.* not; *— so,* I do not know; *tuo figlio lo fece, — io,* your son did it, not I; *— sporgersi,* do not lean out; *il — intervento,* non-intervention; *può essere e può — essere,* it may be and it may not be; *— appena lo vidi,* as soon as I saw him; *finché — venne,* until he came; *— ho visto nessuno,* I have seen no one; *dubito che — venga,* I doubt whether he will come; *pregava — fossero uccisi,* he prayed that they might not be killed; *se —,* except, apart from; *se — che,* but, moreover; *— che,* not only, not just; *un — so che,* a certain something; *— affatto,* not at all; *— ancora,* not yet. **-curante** *adj.* careless, heedless; indifferent. **-curanza** *f.* carelessness, heedlessness; indifference, nonchalance; disdain. **-dimęno** *adv.* nevertheless. **-nulla** *m.* a nothing, a mere nothing, trifle. **-ostante** *prep.* notwithstanding, in spite of; *-ostante che,* in spite of the fact that. **-ti-scordar-di-me** *m. indecl.* (bot.) forget-me-not.
**nonn-o** *m.* grandfather; grandpa. **-a** *f.* grandmother, grandma, granny.
**non-o** *ord. num.* ninth. **-agena·rio** *m.* nonagenarian. **-age·ṣimo** *adj.* ninetieth. **-e** *f.pl.* (Rom. antiq.) Nones. **-ode·cimo** *ord. num.* nineteenth.
**nord** *m.indecl.* north.
**nor·dico** *adj.* northern; Nordic; *n.m.* northerner.
**Norimberga** *pr.n.f.* (geog.) Nuremberg.
**norm-a** *f.* guide, standard, measure, norm; rule, regulation; *secondo le -e ora vigenti,* according to the present regulations. **-ale** *adj.* normal, conforming to standard, regular, usual; guiding, setting the standard; *n.f.* (math.) perpendicular; *m.* normality; standard pattern; normal state. **-alità** *f.* normality. **-aliẓẓare** [A1] *tr.* to normalize, to make normal; to standardize. **-ativo** *adj.* normative, setting up a norm or standard.
**Norm-andi·a** *pr.n.f.* (geog.) Normandy. **-anno** *adj., n.m.* Norman.
**Norvęg-ia** *pr.n.f.* (geog.) Norway. **-ęse** *adj., n.m., f.* Norwegian.
**nost-algi·a** *f.* nostalgia. **-al·gico** *adj.* nostalgic.
**nostr-o** *poss. adj.* our. **-ale** *adj.* home-grown, national, domestic. **-(u)omo** *m.* (naut.) coxswain; boatswain.
**nota** *f.* sign; mark; distinguishing feature; token; characteristic; note; comment; *— a pie' di pagina,* footnote; (mus.) note; *pl.* music; *mettere in note,* to set to music; distinction; notice, attention; *degno di —,* worthy of note; list; *— del bucato,* laundry list; account; report; (finan.) *— di banca,* banknote.
**nota·io** *m.* notary.
**not-are** [A1] *tr.* to mark; to indicate; to make a note of; to register, to record; to observe; to notice; *farsi —,* to call attention to oneself, to distinguish oneself. **-abene** *m. indecl.* note, annotation. **-a·bile** *adj.* notable, remarkable; eminent; considerable; memorable; *n.m.* important personage, notability. **-aziǫne** *f.* marking; annotation; (mus.) notation. **-ęvole** *adj.* notable, eminent; remarkable; considerable.
**notarile** *adj.* relating to a notary; attested, done or made by a notary.
**notes** *m. indecl.* note-book; writing-pad.
**noti·fic-a** *f.* notice, notification; communication. **-are** [A2 s] *tr.* to notify; to announce, to make known; to report. **-aziǫne** *f.* notification.
**noti·zi-a** *f.* knowledge, notice; notion, concept; (philos.) *prime -e,* first principles; *le -e di un'arte,* the rudiments of an art; item of news; rumour, report; information; account; *pl.* news. **-a·rio** *m.* (radio) news, news bulletin; (journ.) news column.
**noto** *adj.* known; *rendere —,* to make known; well-known; noted, famous; *n.m.* the known.
**noto·ri-o** *adj.* well-known, commonly known; notorious. **-età** *f.* notoriety, fame.
**nott-e** *f.* night; *di —,* by night; *camicia da —,* night-gown; night-

shirt; (fig.) darkness, obscurity. **-ata** *f.* night, duration of a night; *passare una buona -ata,* to have a good night. **-etempo** *adv.* by night, at night time.

**notturno** *adj.* nocturnal; nightly, of the night; *guardiano —,* night-watchman; *n.m.* (mus.) nocturne.

**novant-a** *card. num.* ninety; *n.m. il —,* the number ninety. **-acinque** *card. num.* ninety-five. **-enne** *adj.* ninety years old; *n.m.* nonagenarian. **-en·nio** *m.* space of ninety years. **-e·ṣimo** *ord. num.* ninetieth; *-esimo primo,* ninety-first; *n.m.* ninetieth part. **-ina** *f.* about ninety.

**nov-e** *card. num.* nine; *— volte su dieci,* nine times out of ten. **-ecento** *card. num.* nine hundred; *n.m. il -ecento,* the twentieth century; *adj. indecl.* characteristic of the twentieth century. **-ecente·ṣimo** *ord. num.* nine hundredth; *-ecentesimo primo,* nine hundred and first. **-ecentiṣmo** *m.* twentieth-century school of thought or artistic fashion. **-ecentista** *m., f.* person living in the twentieth century; follower of a twentieth-century school of thought or artistic fashion. **-emila** *card. num.* nine thousand. **-e·ṣimo** *ord. num.* ninth.

**novell-a** *f.* short story; tale; chatter, gossip. **-a·io** *m.* short-story writer; story-teller. **-iere** *m.* story-teller; short-story writer. **-ista** *m., f.* short-story writer; story-teller. **-i·stica** *f.* writing of short stories; art of short-story writing; *la -istica italiana,* Italian short stories

**novell-o** *adj.* new; fresh; (of plants) early; inexpert, untrained; *n.m.pl. i -i,* the new shoots of a plant. **-ino** *adj. dim.* new; young; tender; early; inexperienced; *n.m. essere un -ino,* to be a novice.

**novembr-e** *pr.n.m.* November. **-ino** *adj.* of November.

**noven-a** *f.* (rel.) novena. **-nale** *adj.* recurring every nine years; of nine years' duration. **-ne** *adj.* nine-year-old, lasting nine years.

**noven·nio** *m.* space of nine years.

**no·vero** *m.* class, category; group; *includere nel — degli amici,* to count among one's friends.

**novilu·nio** *m.* time of the new moon.

**novis·simo** *adj. superl.* newest, very new; last.

**novità** *f.* newness; originality; novelty; innovation; new book, new play, etc.; news.

**novi·zi-o** *m.* novice; beginner; **-ato** *m.* novitiate; training; apprenticeship.

**nozịone** *f.* notion, idea; knowledge; element, rudiment; meaning, sense; (philos.) concept.

**nozze** *f.pl.* marriage, wedding; nuptials; *viaggio di —,* honeymoon; *passare a seconde —,* to marry a second time.

**nub-e** *f.* cloud; haze, mist. **-ifra·gio** *m.* cloudburst.

**nu·bile** *adj.* (of a woman) unmarried; marriageable, nubile.

**nuca** *f.* nape of the neck.

**nu·cl-eo** *m.* nucleus; core. **-eare** *adj.* nuclear; *energia -eare,* nuclear power.

**nuda** *f.* naked woman; nude model.

**nud-o** *adj.* naked; *— nato,* stark naked; undressed; plain, unadorned; uncovered, bare; (of ground) barren, waste; *n.m.* naked person; nude. **-iṣmo** *m.* nudism. **-ista** *m., f.* nudist. **-ità** *f.* nakedness; bareness, plainness.

**null-a** *neg. part., n.m. indecl.* nothing; nonentity; worthlessness, nullity; anything; *c'è — per me?,* is there anything for me?; *adv.* not at all, by no means. **-ag·gine** *f.* nothingness; insignificance. **-atenente** *m., f.* one who owns nothing; *adj.* owning nothing. **-ità** *f.* nullity; something or someone of no worth. **-o** *adj.* null, invalid; void.

**nume** *m.* divinity, god.

**numer-are** [A1 s] *tr.* to count; to pay; to number. **-azịone** *f.* numbering; system of numbering.

**nume·rico** *adj.* numerical.

**nu·mer-o** *m.* number, figure; cipher; *— del telefono,* telephone number; *formazione del —,* dialling; group, class, category; quality, gift; *avere tutti i -i,* to have all the good points. **-ale** *adj.* numeral. **-ọso** *adj.* numerous; plentiful.

**numism-a** *m.* coin; medallion; medal. **-a·tica** *f.* numismatics; **-a·tico** *adj.* numismatic; *n.m.* numismatist.

**Nunziata** *pr.n.f.* abbrev. of **Annunziata.**

**nun·zio** *m.* (theol.) *— celeste,* heavenly messenger, angel; (eccl.; leg.) nuncio.

**nuo·cere** [B15] *intr.* (*aux.* avere; *prep.* a) to be harmful, to be injurious, to be hurtful.

**nuora** *f.* daughter-in-law.

**nuot-are** [A1 d] *intr.* (*aux.* avere) to swim; to float; to wallow. **-ata** *f.* swim; swimming; swimming-stroke. **-atọre** *m.* swimmer. **-o** *m.* swimming; *gara di -o,* swimming competition.

**nuov-o** *adj.* new; *un uomo —,* an upstart; recent; modern; unused; *— di zecca,* brand-new, newly minted; *di —,* again; young, early; other, further; strange, unaccustomed; extraordinary; unexampled, rare; *n.m.* newness, originality, novelty; *che c'è di —?,* what's the news? **-a** *f.* news.

**nutrice** *f.* wet-nurse; foster-mother.

**nutr-ire** [D1, D2] *tr.* to nourish; to feed; to nurture; to foster; to suckle; to harbour, to entertain (feelings); *rfl.* (*prep.* di), to feed (on); to delight (in). **-iente** *adj.* nutritious. **-imẹnto** *m.* nourishment; nutriment; food; feeding. **-itivo** *adj.* nutritious, nourishing. **-itọre** *m.* provider; feeder. **-izịone** *f.* nourishment; nutrition.

**nu·vol-a** *f.* cloud; cloudiness. **-a·glia** *f.* mass of clouds. **-ata** *f.* cloud-burst, sharp shower; mass of clouds. **-ato** *m.* cloudiness, bank of clouds; *adj.* overcast; cloudy.

**nu·vol-o** *m.* threatening cloud; cloudy weather; (fig.) mass, swarm; *adj.* cloudy. **-ọso** *adj.* cloudy, clouded; overcast; turbid.

**nuzial-e** *adj.* nuptial; bridal. **-ità** *f.* marrying; *anno di elevata -ità,* year with a high marriage rate.

**O**[1] *f.* the letter O; the vowel O; *un'— stretta,* a close O; *un'— larga,* an open O; *m.* the shape of an O.

**O**[2] *excl.* O; (introducing vocative) *— Dio,* O Lord; (emphatic) Oh; *— sì!,* Oh yes!

**ọ**[3] (before a vowel, **ọd**) *conj.* or; *o...o,* either...or; *o che...o che,* whether...or.

**o·aṣi** *f. indecl.* (geog.) oasis.

**obbedien-te** *adj.* obedient, docile; submissive. **-za** *f.* obedience.

**obbedire** [D2] *intr.* (*aux.* avere; *prep.* a) to be obedient (to); to obey, to submit (to); to respond (to); *tr.* to obey.

**obblig-are** [A2 s] *tr.* to compel, to oblige; to be kind or helpful to; to constrain; *rfl.* to enter into an obligation; to bind oneself. **-ato** *part. adj.* obliged, grateful; forced, constrained; (leg.) legally bound; liable; *n.m.* (mus.) obbligato. **-ato·rio** *adj.* obligatory, compulsory; *fermata -atoria,* (bus, etc.) stop (as distinct from 'fermata facoltativa', request stop). **-azịone**

*f.* obligation; bond; debt; duty; liability.

**ob·bli-go** *m.* (*pl.* **-ghi**) obligation; compulsion; duty; (mil.) — *di leva*, military service.

**obbro·bri-o** *m.* disgrace; infamy; opprobrium. **-ọso** *adj.* shameful; infamous; disgraceful.

**obelis-co** *m.* (*pl.* **-chi**) obelisk.

**o·belo** *m.* obelus.

**oberare** [A1 s] *tr.* to overwhelm, to overload.

**obeṣ-o** *adj.* corpulent; (med.) obese. **-ità** *f.* corpulence; (med.) obesity.

**o·bice** *m.* (mil.) mortar; shell.

**obiettare** *tr.* [A1 c] to adduce, to bring forward (argument, difficulty); to allege; to object to; *intr.* (*aux.* avere; *prep.* su) to raise objections (concerning).

**obiettiv-o** *adj.* objective; detached, impartial; *n.m.* objective, purpose, aim; (opt.) object glass, lens. **-ità** *f.* objectivity.

**obietto** *m.* object; aim, purpose.

**obiezịone** *f.* objection.

**o·bit-o** *m.* death. **-o·rio** *m.* mortuary. **-ua·rio** *m.* register of deaths.

**oblazịone** *f.* offering, gift; oblation, offertory.

**obl-iare** [A4 i] *tr.* (poet.) to forget. **-io** *m.* (poet.) oblivion; forgetfulness.

**obliqu-o** *adj.* oblique; slanting; sideways; devious. **-ità** *f.* obliquity; deviousness.

**obliter-are** [A1 s] *tr.* to obliterate; to efface. **-azịone** *f.* obliteration.

**oblun-go** *adj.*, *n.m.* (*pl.* **-ghi**) oblong.

**o·bo-e** *m.* *indecl.* (mus.) oboe. **-ista** *m.*, *f.* oboist.

**o·bolo** *m.* obol, obolus; small coin, mite.

**obsole-scenza** *f.* obsolescence. **-to** *adj.* obsolete, outworn.

**oca** *f.* goose; *pelle d'—*, gooseflesh; *parere un'—*, to look a fool; *appos.* foolish; stupid.

**occaṣịon-e** *f.* occasion; juncture; opportunity; chance; bargain; *d'* —, second-hand; *all'—*, on occasion. **-ale** *adj.* fortuitous. **-are** [A1 c] *tr.* to occasion, to cause.

**occhi-a·ia** *f.* eye-socket; *pl.* dark rings under the eyes. **-ali** *m.pl.* glasses, spectacles goggles; *-ali a stringinaso*, pince-nez; *-ali da sole*, sun-glasses. **-aluto** *adj.* bespectacled. **-are** [A4] *tr.* to eye; to set eyes on; to espy. **-ata** look, glance; glimpse; *scambiarsi un' -ata*, to exchange looks. **-eggiare** [A3 c] *tr.* to ogle; to cast glances at; *intr.* (*aux.* avere) to gleam, to glint.

**oc·ch-io** *m.* eye; *orbita dell'* —, eye-socket; *in un batter d'—*, in the twinkling of an eye; *strizzare l'—*, to wink; *a quattr'-i*, privately, tête-à-tête; eye-sight, vision; glance, look; *a — nudo*, with the naked eye; *a perdita d'* —, as far as the eye can reach; attention, observation; *tenere d'* —, to keep an eye on; *quel colore dà nell'* —, that colour is too startling; regard, way of looking; view; *vedere di buon* —, to have a high regard for; *agli -i miei*, in my view; round hole; eye-hole; — *di bue*, bull's eye window; (bot.) bud; eye of potato. **-ello** *m.* *dim.* small hole; buttonhole. **-iolino** *m.* *dim.* little eye; *far l' -iolino a*, to make eyes at. **-iuto** *adj.* sharp-eyed; shrewd; cautious; (bot.) well furnished with buds.

**occident-e** *m.* west; occident. **-ale** *adj.* western, occidental; westerly.

**occlu·dere** [C3] *tr.* to occlude; to close; to obstruct; to stop up.

**occluṣịone** *f.* occlusion; (med.) stoppage.

**occọrr-ere** [C5 c] *intr.* (*aux.* essere) to be necessary; to be required; to be lacking; *mi -ono mille lire*, I need a thousand lire; *impers.* *-e farlo*, it must be done. **-ente** *part. adj.* necessary, needful; *n.m.* what is needed. **-enza** *f.* circumstance, occasion; need; *all' -enza*, if need be, when required.

**occult-are** [A1] *tr.* to conceal, to hide; to keep secret. **-azịone** *f.* concealment; (astron.) occultation.

**occult-o** *adj.* hidden, secret; occult. **-iṣmo** *m.* occultism.

**occup-are** [A1 s] *tr.* to occupy; to employ; to use; to take possession of; *rfl.* (*prep.* di) to busy oneself (with, in); to be interested (in), to be concerned (with); to find work. **-ante** *part. adj.* occupying; *n.m.*, *f.* occupier; possessor; holder. **-ato** *part. adj.* occupied; working, busy, engaged. **-azịone** *f.* occupation, work, business; pursuit; employment.

**Ocea·nia** *pr.n.f.* Oceania.

**oce-a·nico** *adj.* oceanic; oceangoing; deep-sea. **-anografi·a** *f.* oceanography. **-anogra·fico** *adj.* oceanographical.

**oce·ano** *m.* ocean, esp. the Atlantic; (fig.) vast amount, unending quantity.

**ocra** *f.* (miner.) ochre.

**ocul-are** *adj.* ocular, optical; *nervo* —, optic nerve; *testimonio* —, eyewitness; *lente* —, eyepiece. **-ato** *adj.* sharp-sighted; wary. **-ista** *m.* oculist; eye specialist, ophthalmologist.

**ode** *f.* ode; (fig.) panegyric.

**odiare** [A3] *tr.* to hate, to detest, to loathe, to dislike; to shun.

**odierno** *adj.* of today; contemporary, modern.

**o·di-o** *m.* hatred, hate; loathing; *avere in* —, to abhor; odium. **-ọso** *adj.* hateful; odious.

**Odisse·a** *pr.n.f.* Odyssey.

**odont-iatri·a** *f.* dentistry. **-ia·trico** *adj.* dental; pertaining to dentistry. **-oiatra** *m.* dentist. **-ologi·a** *f.* odontology. **-otec·nica** *f.* dental mechanics.

**odor-are** [A1 c] *tr.* to smell; to perfume, to scent; *intr.* (*aux.* avere) to have a smell; — *di buono*, to smell nice, to smell good; *n.m.* sense of smell. **-ato** *m.* sense of smell; scent (of hound).

**odọr-e** *m.* smell, odour, fragrance; stench; scent; perfume; flavour. **-ọso** *adj.* sweet-smelling, fragrant; odorous.

**Ofe·lia** *pr.n.f.* Ophelia.

**offen·d-ere** [C3] *tr.* to hurt, to damage; (mil.) to attack, to bombard; to insult, to outrage; *intr.* (*aux.* avere) to be offensive, to give offence; *rfl.* (*prep.* di, per) to take offence, to take umbrage (at).

**offens-iva** *f.* (mil.) offensive, attack; *prendere l'* —, to take the offensive. **-ivo** *adj.* offensive. **-ọre** *m.* offender; attacker.

**offert-a** *f.* offer; offering; proposal; (comm.) bid; tender; (econ.) — *e domanda*, supply and demand. **-o·rio** *m.* (liturg.) offertory.

**offẹsa** *f.* harm, damage, injury; offence; affront; insult, outrage; (mil.) *stare sull'* —, to be on the offensive.

**officina** *f.* workshop; works; workroom; factory; *capo* —, foreman.

**offi·ci-o** *m.* good office, service; task. **-ọso** *adj.* obliging, helpful.

**offrire** [D8] *tr.* to offer; to give; to present; to afford; to offer up; (comm.) to bid; — *all'asta*, to bid at an auction; *rfl.* to offer oneself; to present oneself; to stand forth, to come forward; to volunteer.

**offuscare** [A2] *tr.* to darken; to dim; to obscure, to blur; *rfl.* to grow dark; to grow dim; to become clouded.

**oggett-o** *m.* object; subject; theme; thing, article; aim, purpose; object. **-ività** *f.* objectivity. **-ivo** *adj.* objective; *n.m.* goal, objective.

**oggi** *adv.* today; *da — in poi*, from today on; — *a otto*, today week; nowadays; *n.m.* the present time. **-dì, -giọrno** *adv.* nowadays.

**ogiv-a** *f.* (archit.) ogive; pointed arch. **-ale** *adj.* (archit.) ogival.

**ọgn-i** *adj.* every, each; — *due giorni*, every other day; — *tanto*, every so often; — *qual volta*, whenever; *in — caso*, in any case. **-issanti** *pr.n.m.* All Saints' Day. **-ọra** *adv.* always; *-ora che*, whenever, every time that. **-uno** *prn.* everyone; each.

**ohi** *excl.* oh!, ah! (esp. of pain).

**ohimè** *excl.* alas!; oh dear!
**olà** *excl.* hallo!; hi there!; look!
**Oland-a** *pr.n.f.* Holland. **-ẹse** *adj.* Dutch; *n.m., f.* Dutchman; Dutchwoman.
**ole-a·ceo** *adj.* oily. **-aginọso** *adj.* oleaginous.
**oleandro** *m.* (bot.) oleander.
**ole-odọtto** *m.* (oil) pipeline. **-ografi·a** *f.* oleography; oleograph. **-o·metro** *m.* (motor.) oil gauge. **-ọso** *adj.* oily; containing oil.
**olezẓ-are** [A1] *intr.* (*aux.* avere) to smell sweet. **-ante** *part. adj.* sweet-smelling, fragrant. **-o** *m.* fragrance, scent.
**olfatt-ivo** *adj.* relating to the sense of smell, olfactory. **-o** *m.* sense of smell. **-o·rio** *adj.* olfactory.
**oli-are** [A4] *tr.* to oil. **-ata** *f.* oiling; yield of oil (for one year). **-ato** *adj.* dressed with oil, oiled; *carta -ata*, greaseproof paper. **-atọre** *m.* oil-can.
**oliera** *f.* cruet-stand; oil-bottle.
**olig-arca** *m.* oligarch. **-archi·a** *f.* oligarchy. **-ar·chico** *adj.* oligarchic.
**Olim·pia** *pr.n.f.* Olympia.
**olimp-i·aco** *adj.* Olympic; *periodo —*, Olympiad. **-i·ade** *f.* Olympiad; *pl.* modern 'Olympic games'; *adj.* Olympian.
**ol-im·pico** *adj.* Olympic; Olympian. **-impio·nico** *m.* victor at the Olympic games (ancient or modern); *adj.* Olympic.
**o·lio** *m.* olive-oil; oil; *— combustibile*, fuel oil; *— lubrificante*, lubricating oil; *— da tavola*, salad oil; *— di ricino*, castor oil; *— di merluzzo*, cod-liver oil; (cul.) *sott' —*, in oil; *dipingere a —*, to paint in oils; (rel.; fig.) *— santo*, holy oil.
**oliv-a** *f.* olive; *verde —*, olive-green. **-ello** *m.* (bot.) common privet. **-ẹto** *m.* olive grove. **-icultọre** *m.* olive-grower. **-icoltura** *f.* olive-growing. **-o** *m.* olive tree.
**olla** *f.* earthenware pot; *— podrida*, pot-pourri.
**ọlm-o** *m.* (bot.) elm. **-ẹto** *m.* elm wood, plantation of elms.
**oloca·usto** *m.* (burnt-) offering; sacrifice; (fig.) slaughter, holocaust.
**Oloferne** *pr.n.m.* (bibl.) Holophernes.
**oltracciò** *adv.* moreover, furthermore.
**oltrag·gi-o** *m.* outrage, insult; offence; (leg.) *— alla Corte*, contempt of Court. **-are** [A3] *tr.* to outrage, to insult, to offend. **-ọso** *adj.* outrageous; offensive, insulting.
**oltr-alpe** *adv.* beyond the Alps. **-amontano** *adj., n.m.* (rel. hist.) ultramontane. **-anza** *adv. phr. a -anza*, to the bitter end, to the death.
**ọltre** *prep.* beyond; *per — un mese*, for more than a month; *— a ciò*, as well as this; *— misura*, beyond measure; *adv.* beyond, further; *vedremo più —*, we shall see later on; *qui —*, hereabouts, somewhere here; *passare — a*, to overrule **-mare** *adv.* overseas; *n.m.* lapis lazuli; ultramarine blue. **-marino** *adj.* overseas, from beyond the seas; ultramarine. **-miṣura** *adv.* extremely, immeasurably. **-modo** *adv.* exceedingly. **-passare** [A1] *tr.* to pass; to surpass; to go beyond; to outstrip. **-tọmba** *adv.* beyond the grave; *n.m.* the life beyond, the next world.
**omac·cio** *m.* unpleasant man; ill-bred man.
**omag·gio** *m.* homage; *rendere — a*, to do homage to; *copia in —*, presentation copy; *omaggi dell'autore*, with the author's compliments; gift.
**oma·i** *adv.* (poet.) now; henceforth, from now on; at last.
**o·maro** *m.* lobster.
**ombe·li-co** *m.* (*pl.* **-chi**) navel. **-cale** *adj.* umbilical; *cordone -cale*, umbilical cord.
**ọmbr-a** *f.* shadow; shade; *stare all'—*, to be in the shade; (fig.) *un' — di sospetto*, a shade of suspicion; *latte con un' — di caffè*, milk with a dash of coffee; ghost, shade; umbrage; pretence; *sotto l' — dell'amicizia*, under the guise of friendship; protection; *all' — della legge*, under shelter of the law. **-eggiare** [A3c] *tr.* to shade; (fig.) to sketch, to adumbrate. **-ọso** *adj.* shady; touchy; skittish.
**ombrell-o** *m.* umbrella; *— da sole*, parasol. **-a·io** *m.* umbrella-maker; umbrella-seller. **-ino** *m. dim.* parasol, sunshade.
**Omburgo** *pr.n.f.* (geog.) Homburg.
**omeo-pati·a** *f.* (med.) homoeopathy. **-pa·tico** *adj.* homoeopathic.
**Om-ero**[1] *pr.n.m.* Homer. **-e·rico** *adj.* Homeric.
**o·mero**[2] *m.* shoulder; (anat.) humerus.
**omertà** *f.* (Sicil.) conspiracy of silence (in criminal underworld).
**omẹttere** [C20] *tr.* to omit, to leave out.
**omicida** *m., f.* murderer, slayer; *adj.* murderous, homicidal.
**omici·dio** *m.* homicide; murder.
**omissiọne** *f.* omission; oversight; neglect.
**om·nibus** *m. indecl.* horse-bus, omnibus; slow train, stopping train; *adj. indecl. treno —*, slow train.
**omoge·ne-o** *adj.* homogeneous. **-ità** *f.* homogeneity.
**omo·nimo** *adj.* homonymous; *n.m.* homonym; namesake.
**omosessual-e** *adj., n.m., f.* homosexual. **-ità** *f.* homosexuality.
**ọncia** *f.* ounce; inch.
**ọnd-a** *f.* wave, billow; surge; *lunghezza d' —,* wave-length; *— corta*, short wave; (poet.) sea, main. **-ata** *f.* wave, undulating movement; surge; breaker; *-ata di caldo*, heat-wave. **-aziọne** *f.* undulation; billowy motion; (phys.) wave motion; oscillation. **-eggiare** [A3c] *intr.* (*aux.* avere) to wave, to undulate; to surge; to waver. **-ọso** *adj.* wavy; billowy. **-ulare** [A1s] *tr.* to wave (hair), to make wavy; *intr.* (*aux.* essere) to undulate.
**ondatra** *f.* (zool.) beaver.
**ọnde** *interr. adv.* whence?, from where?; *rel. adv.* whence, from where, from which, with which, wherewith; *final conj.* (with *subj.*) *— egli impari*, so that he may learn.
**o·ner-e** *m.* burden, task, load; onus. **-ọso** *adj.* burdensome, onerous, oppressive.
**onestà** *f.* probity, uprightness; integrity; honour; honesty; propriety.
**onesto** *adj.* honourable, upright, fair, honest; decent, respectable.
**o·nice** *f.* onyx.
**onni-potente** *adj.* omnipotent; *n.m.* Almighty. **-potenza** *f.* omnipotence; Almighty. **-presenza** *f.* omnipresence. **-scienza** *f.* omniscience.
**onni·voro** *adj.* omnivorous.
**onom-a·stico** *adj.* onomastic, of a name or names; *giorno -astico*, name-day; *n.m.* name-day, feast of one's patron saint. **-atope·a** *f.* onomatopoeia. **-atope·ico** *adj.* onomatopoeic.
**onor-are** [A1c] *tr.* to honour; *rfl.* to be honoured. **-a·bile** *adj.* honourable; respected. **-anza** *f.* mark of honour; sign of esteem; *pl.* public tribute to a great man. **-ẹvole** *adj.* honourable, respectable; (as title of member of Italian Parliament) Honourable; *n.m. l'Onorevole*, the M.P., the Honourable Member.
**onọr-e** *m.* honour; distinction; rank; glory; *fare — a*, to honour; *dama d' —*, lady-in-waiting. **-a·rio** *adj.* honorific; honorary; *n.m.* honorarium. **-ificenza** *f.* (mark of) honour. **-i·fico** *adj.* honourable, distinguished; honorary.
**ọnta** *f.* shame, disgrace; insult; affront; *ad — di*, in defiance of, in spite of.
**ontano** *m.* (bot.) alder.
**opa-co** *adj.* (*pl.* **-chi**) opaque; dull; (paint.) matt; *vetro —*, ground glass. **-cità** *f.* opacity; dullness.
**opal-e** *m.* opal. **-escente** *adj.* opalescent. **-ino** *adj.* opaline.

**o·per-a** *f.* work; *mano d' —*, labour, man-power; workmanship; *capo d' —*, masterpiece; *per — di*, through the action of, thanks to; (mus.) opera; composition, work; *— buffa*, an Italian form of comic opera; *— lirica*, opera. **-a·io** *m.* workman; worker, hand; *ora di -aio*, man-hour; *adj.* working, working-class; *Società -aia*, trade union. **-ẹtta** *f.* (mus.) operetta, light opera. **-i·stico** *adj.* operatic.

**oper-are** [A1 s] *intr.* (*aux.* avere) to act; to operate; to behave; to work, to function; (med.) to operate; *tr.* to do, to work. **-a·bile** *adj.* practicable, feasible. **-ante** *part. adj.* operating, working, functioning; *n.m., f.* operator. **-ativo** *adj.* operative; effective. **-ato** *part. adj.* operated; worked on; operated on; *n.m.* action, deed, behaviour; patient operated on. **-atọre** *m.* operating surgeon; (cinem.) camera-man; (finan.) *-atore di borsa*, stockbroker. **-aziọne** *f.* operation; functioning; working; *-azione di borsa*, stock-exchange transaction.

**operọs-o** *adj.* industrious, active, busy. **-ità** *f.* industry, activity.

**opifi·cio** *m.* factory, works.

**opiniọne** *f.* opinion; matter of opinion; belief, view.

**op·pi-o** *m.* opium. **-a·ceo** *adj. n.m.* opiate, narcotic. **-are** [A14] *tr.* to mix with opium; to drug with opium. **-o·mane** *m., f.* opium-addict; drug-fiend. **-omani·a** *f.* opium addiction.

**opponente** *adj.* opposing; *n.m., f.* opponent, adversary.

**oppọrre** [B21] to oppose; to set against; to contrast, to refute; *rfl.* (*prep.* a) to be opposed (to), to object (to); to thwart; to set oneself (against).

**opportun-o** *adj.* opportune; seasonable, timely; advisable, expedient; well-chosen. **-ịsmo** *m.* opportunism. **-ista** *m., f.* opportunist. **-ità** *f.* expediency, appropriateness; opportunity, favourable occasion.

**opposi-tọre** *m.* opponent; opposer. **-ziọne** *f.* opposition, objection, argument.

**oppọsto** *part.* opposed; *adj.* opposite; opposing, contrary; *n.m.* opposite, reverse; *all' —*, on the contrary.

**oppress-o** *part.* of **oppri·mere**; *adj.* oppressed; downtrodden. **-iọne** *f.* oppression; affliction; annoyance. **-ivo** *adj.* oppressive; over-bearing. **-ọre** *m.* oppressor; tyrant.

**oppri·mere** [C18] to oppress, to burden; to overwhelm; to lie heavy on.

**oppugn-are** [A5] *tr.* to oppose, to assail, to attack; to impugn, to refute. **-a·bile** *adj.* assailable.

**oppure** *conj.*; *adv.* or; else, or else.

**optare** [A1] *intr.* (*aux.* avere; *prep.* per) to opt (for); to decide (in favour of).

**opulen-to** *adj.* opulent; rich; fertile. **-za** *f.* opulence, wealth; fertility.

**opu·scolo** *m.* pamphlet; brochure; short study.

**opziọne** *f.* option.

**ọr-a**[1] *f.* hour; *-e straordinarie*, overtime; *che — fate voi?*, what time do you make it?; *sarebbe — di andare*, it is time to go; *di buon' —*, early; *non veder l' — di partire*, to long to go; *l' — d'accendere le luci*, lighting-up time; *l' — di chiusura*, closing-time. **-ẹtta** *f. dim.* about an hour, under an hour.

**ọra**[2] *adv.* now; *or —*, just now, a moment ago; *d' — in poi*, henceforward; *— è un anno*, a year ago.

**ora·colo** *m.* oracle.

**orale** *adj.* oral; *n.m.* oral (examination), 'viva'.

**orama·i** *adv.* now, by now, henceforward.

**orare** [A1] *intr.* (*aux.* avere) to pray.

**ora·rio** *adj.* of hours, by the hour; *velocità oraria*, speed per hour; *tavola oraria*, time-table; *segnale —*, time signal; *n.m.* time-table; *in —*, punctual; *partire in —*, to leave on time.

**orat-ọre** *m.* orator; speaker. **-o·ria** *f.* the art of speaking, oratory. **-o·rio** *adj.* oratorical, rhetorical; *n.m.* oratory, chapel; (mus.) oratorio.

**Ora·zi-o** *pr.n.m.* Horace. **-ano** *adj.* Horatian.

**oraziọne** *f.* oration, speech; (rel.) prayer; *— domenicale*, the Lord's Prayer.

**orbare** [A1] *tr.* to bereave; to deprive.

**orbe** *m.* orb, sphere.

**orbene** *adv.* well; well now; well then.

**or·bita** *f.* orbit; limit; (anat.) eye-socket.

**orbo** *adj.* bereft; widowed, orphaned; blind; *n.m.* blind man.

**orca** *f.* (zool.) killer whale; (myth.) sea monster, orc.

**Or·cadi** *pr.n.f.pl.* (geog.) Orkney Islands; Orkney.

**orchestr-a** *f.* orchestra. **-ale** *adj.* orchestral ; *n.m., f.* player in an orchestra. **-are** [A1] *tr.* (mus.) to orchestrate, to score; (fig.) to organize. **-aziọne** *f.* (mus.) orchestration.

**orchide·a** *f.* (bot.) orchid.

**or-co** *m.* (*pl.* **-chi**) ogre, bogey.

**orda** *f.* horde.

**ordigno** *m.* implement; gear, device; (fig.) tool.

**ordinale** *adj.* (math.) ordinal; *n.m.* (eccl.) ordinal.

**ordin-are** [A1 sc] *tr.* to put in order, to arrange; to regulate; to tidy; to decree, to command, to order; *— il pranzo*, to order dinner; (eccl.) to ordain. **-amẹnto** *m.* ordering; order; ordinance. **-ando** *m.* ordinand. **-anza** *f.* ordinance; law, rule, precept. **-ata·rio** *m.* (comm.) payee. **-ativo** *adj.* directive; ordinal (of numerals); *n.m.* (comm.) order; note. **-aziọne** *f.* order, ordering; (eccl.) ordination.

**ordina·rio** *adj.* ordinary, usual; normal; common, rough, coarse; *n.m.* custom, usual way; professor; (eccl.) ordinary.

**or·dine** *m.* order; position in a series; *in ~ alfabetico*, in alphabetical order; rank; class, category; *— cavalleresco*, order of knighthood; order, orderliness; control; disposition, arrangements; order, command; regulation, writ; religious order; (archit.) order.

**ord-ire** [D2] *tr.* (text.) to wrap; to mount on the loom; (fig.) to weave (plots), to scheme. **-ito** *part. adj.* warped; (fig.) schemed; *n.m.* web; plot.

**orecchi-are** [A4 c] *intr.* (*aux.* avere) to listen, to eavesdrop; to pick up by ear. **-a·bile** *adj.* easily remembered; (of a tune) catchy. **-ante** *m.* one who sings or plays by ear; amateur, dabbler; eavesdropper.

**orecchino** *m.* ear-ring.

**orẹcchi-o** *m.* ear; *a portata d' —*, within ear-shot; *dolore all' —*, ear-ache; *aver — per la musica*, to have an ear for music *duro d' —*, hard of hearing; (naut.) fluke (of anchor). **-a** *f.* ear; hearing.

**orẹfic-e** *m.* goldsmith; jeweller. **-eri·a** *f.* goldsmith's or jeweller's workshop; jeweller's shop; gold, silver, platinum ware; jewellery.

**oreri·a** *f.* goldsmith's work; gold things; gold plate.

**or·fan-o** *m.* orphan; *adj.* orphan, orphaned; *è — del padre*, his father is dead. **-otro·fio** *m.* orphanage, children's home.

**Orfe·o** *pr.n.m.* (myth.) Orpheus.

**or·fico** *adj.* Orphic.

**orga·nic-o** *adj.* organic; *regno —*, animal kingdom; structural; (fig.) fundamental; inherent; (mus.) pertaining to organs; *l'arte -a*, organ-building; *n.m.* (mus.) combination, ensemble; (admin.) body, staff, personnel.

**organiẓẓ-are** [A1] *tr.* to organize; to arrange; to set up. **-atọre** *m.* organizer. **-aziọne** *f.* organization, method, arrangement; structure; body, organizing body.

**or·gan-o** *m.* organ; *gli -i vocali*, the vocal organs; (admin.)

— *direttivo*, governing body; newspaper, organ; (mus.) organ; — *a bocca*, mouth-organ; — *di Barberia*, barrel-organ. **-aro** *m.* (mus.) organ-builder. **-ismo** *m.* organism; living structure; system. **-ista** *m., f.* (*pl.m., f.* **-isti**) organist.

**orgasmo** *m.* great agitation; violent excitement; anxiety; orgasm.

**or·g-ia** *f.* (*pl.* **-e, -ie**) (Gk. antiq.) orgy. **-iasta** *m.* Bacchante. **-ia·stico** *adj.* orgiastic.

**orgogli-o** *m.* pride; ostentation; boasting. **-oso** *adj.* proud, haughty, boastful, conceited; (of an animal) lively, spirited; (of wine) vigorous, generous.

**orient-are** [A1] *tr.* to orientate; to direct; to point, to set; *rfl.* to get one's bearings, to orientate oneself. **-amento** *m.* orientating; orientation; *senso d'-amento*, sense of direction. **-azione** *f.* orientation, direction; bearings.

**orient-e** *m.* (geog.) east, orient; (astron.) east. **-ale** *adj.* oriental, eastern; *n.m., f.* Oriental.

**orifi·zio** *m.* orifice; hole, aperture; mouth, opening.

**Origene** *pr.n.m.* (hist. theol.) Origen.

**ori·gin-e** *f.* origin, beginning; source, starting-point; cause; (theol.) *peccato d'* —, original sin. **-ale** *adj.* original; first; new; inventive; eccentric, queer, odd; *n.m.* original; manuscript; queer person, odd individual. **-alità** *f.* originality; novelty; inventiveness, eccentricity. **-are** [A1 s] *tr.* to originate, to give rise to, to set going; *intr.* (*aux.* essere; *prep.* da) to originate; to spring (from); to take rise, to start. **-a·rio** *adj.* original, first, pristine; originating; native. **-atore** *m.* originator, inventor.

**origliare** [A4] *intr.* (*aux.* avere) to eavesdrop; to pry, to spy.

**Orione** *pr.n.m.* (myth.; astron.) Orion.

**orin-a** *f.* urine; *fare l'* —, to urinate, to make water. **-ale** *m.* chamber-pot; urinal. **-are** [A1] *intr.* (*aux.* avere) to urinate, to make water. **-a·rio** *adj.* (anat.) urinary. **-atoio** *m.* public urinal. **-ato·rio** *adj.* urinary. **-azione** *f.* urinating, urination.

**oriundo** *adj.* (*prep.* di) native (of).

**orizzont-e** *m.* horizon. **-ale** *adj.* pertaining to the horizon; horizontal; level, flat; *n.m.pl.* (in crossword puzzles) 'across'.

**Orlando** *pr.n.m.* Roland; Orlando.

**orlare** [A1 c] *tr.* to hem, to edge, to border.

**orlo** *m.* border, edge; — *vivo*, sharp edge; hem; — *a giorno*, openwork hem; rim, brim; brink.

**orma** *f.* footmark, footprint; trace, track, imprint; mark, sign; slot; (of a tyre) tread.

**ormeggi-o** *m.* (naut.) securing a ship or making fast; anchorage or ships' berths; *banchina d'* —, quay; *boa d'* —, mooring buoy; *piloni d'* —, bollards, mooring posts; *posto d'* —, berth. **-are** [A3 c] *tr.* (naut.) to secure a ship or boat, to moor.

**ormone** *m.* (biol.) hormone.

**ornament-o** *m.* ornament; decoration; embellishment, adornment; grace. **-ale** *adj.* ornamental.

**orn-are** [A1 c] *tr.* (*prep.* di) to adorn, to ornament; to embellish; *rfl.* to adorn oneself; to deck oneself (in). **-ato** *part. adj.* adorned; elegant; ornate; rich; flowery (of style); *n.m.* ornamental design; decoration.

**ornit-ologi·a** *f.* ornithology. **-olo·gico** *adj.* ornithological. **-o·logo** *m.* ornithologist.

**oro** *m.* gold; — *di zecchino*, fine gold; — *laminato*, rolled gold; *placcato in* —, gold-plated; (finan.) — *di lega*, pure gold; *pesce d'* —, goldfish; *d'* —, made of gold, golden.

**orolo·g-io** *m.* watch; clock; — *da polso*, wrist-watch. **-eri·a** *f.* watchmaking, clockmaking; clockmaker's, watchmaker's shop; clockwork. **-ia·io** clockmaker, watchmaker.

**oro·scopo** *m.* horoscope.

**orpell-o** *m.* tinsel. **-are** [A1] *tr.* to cover with tinsel; (fig.) to gild.

**orrendo** *adj.* horrible, terrifying; hideous; dreadful, awful; repellent.

**orri·bil-e** *adj.* horrible, frightful, awful; dreadful. **-ità** *f.* dreadfulness; atrociousness.

**or·rid-o** *adj.* fearful; horrid; grim, awesome, wild. **-ezza** *f.* frightfulness; awesomeness.

**orripilante** *adj.* hair-raising; *film* —, horror film.

**orrore** *m* horror, terror; awe; dread; loathing.

**ors-o** *m.* bear; — *bruno*, brown bear; — *bianco*, polar bear; — *grigio*, grizzly bear; (fig.) bear-like, uncouth person. **-ac·chio** *m.* bear cub. **-ino** *adj.* ursine; bear-like.

**Or·sol-a** *pr.n.f.* Ursula. **-ina** *adj., n.f.* (rel.) Ursuline.

**orsù** *excl.* come now!; forward!; on!

**ort-aggi** *m.pl.* vegetables; greens; pot-herbs; market gardens. **-a·glia** *f.* kitchen garden, vegetable garden; market garden; *pl.* garden produce.

**ortense** *adj.* (bot.) cultivated in gardens, garden; pertaining to gardens.

**orten·sia** *f.* (bot.) hydrangea.

**ortic-a** *f.* (bot.) stinging nettle. **-a·io** *m.* nettle-bed. **-a·ria** *f.* (med.) urticaria, nettle-rash.

**orticolt-ore** *m.* horticulture. **-ura** *f.* horticulture.

**ort-o** *m.* garden; — *botanico*, botanical garden; — *secco*, herbarium. **-ivo** *adj.* relating to a garden. **-olano** *m.* greengrocer; (orn.) ortolan.

**ort-odossi·a** *f.* orthodoxy; (eccl.) Orthodoxy, the Orthodox Church. **-odosso** *adj.* orthodox, Orthodox. **-ografi·a** *f.* orthography, spelling; (archit.) elevation (drawing). **-ogra·fico** *adj.* orthographic; *errori -ografici*, spelling mistakes. **-opedi·a** *f.* (med.) orthopaedics.

**Orvieto** *pr.n.f.* (geog.) Orvieto; *m.* white wine of Orvieto.

**orza** *f.* (naut.) windward or weather side; *andare ad* —, to sail close to the wind.

**orzo** *m.* (bot.) barley.

**osann-a** *excl., n.m. indecl.* (rel.) hosanna; (fig.) shout of praise, acclamation. **-are** [A1] *intr.* (*aux.* avere) to sing hosanna, to cry hosanna; to sing hymns of praise.

**osare** [A1] *intr.* (*aux.* avere) to dare; *tr.* to risk, to venture.

**oscen-o** *adj.* obscene, lewd, indecent; ill-omened. **-ità** *f.* obscenity; indecency; disgusting behaviour.

**oscill-are** [A1] *intr.* (*aux.* avere) to oscillate; to swing; to vibrate; to fluctuate. **-azione** *f.* oscillation; (comm.) fluctuation; swing.

**oscur-are** [A1] *tr.* to obscure, to darken; to dim, to cloud; to eclipse; to tarnish; to besmirch; *rfl.* to grow dark; to become tarnished or dim; (of the sky) to become overcast. **-antismo** *m.* obscurantism. **-antista** *m.* obscurantist. **-azione** *f.* obscuration.

**oscur-o** *adj.* dark; overcast; clouded; dim; obscure; little known, humble; (fig.) *n.m.* darkness; *essere all'* —, to be in the dark. **-ità** *f.* obscurity; dimness; darkness.

**Osi·ride** *pr.n.m.* (myth.) Osiris.

**ospedal-e** *m.* hospital; infirmary. **-iero** *adj.* of a hospital.

**ospital-e** *adj.* hospitable; welcoming. **-ità** *f.* hospitality.

**o·spit-e** *m., f.* host, hostess; guest. **-are** [A1 s] *tr.* to offer hospitality to; to entertain; to put up for the night; to house, to contain.

**ospi·zio** *m.* asylum, almshouse, hospice; hostel.

**ossame** *m.* heap of bones.

**ossa·rio** *m.* charnel-house, ossuary.

**ossatura** *f.* frame, framework; skeleton; hull.

**os·seo** *adj.* (med.; anat.) osseous, bony.

**ossequ-ente** *adj.* deferential, respectful; submissive. **-iare**

[A4] *tr.* to pay one's respects to, to do homage to, to wait upon.
**osse·qui-o** *m.* homage; respect, deference; obedience; *i migliori ossequi*, kindest regards. **-oso** *adj.* respectful, polite; obsequious.
**osserv-are** [A1] *tr.* to observe; to notice; to watch; to look at; to comply with; to remark, to point out. **-anza** *f.* observance. **-atore** *m.* onlooker, spectator; observer. **-ato·rio** *m.* (*pl.* **-atorii**) observatory. **-azione** *f.* observation; reflection; remark, comment; observance, fulfilment.
**ossession-e** *f.* obsession; fixation. **-are** [A1 c] *tr.* to obsess, to haunt, to worry. **-ato** *part. adj.* obsessed; *n.m.* person obsessed.
**ossesso** *adj.* obsessed; maniacal; *n.m.* one possessed; person suffering from obsessions.
**ossi·a** *conj.* or; that is, in other words, or rather.
**Os·si-an** *pr.n.m.* Ossian. **-a·nico** *adj.* Ossianic.
**ossid-are** [A1 s] *tr.*, *rfl.* (chem.) to oxidize. **-azione** *f.* oxidation, oxidizing.
**os·sido** *m.* (chem.) oxide.
**ossi·f-ero** *adj.* ossiferous; containing fossilized bones. **-icare** [A2 s] *tr.* to ossify; *rfl.* to become ossified. **-icazione** *f.* ossification.
**ossi·gen-o** *m.* (chem.) oxygen. **-are** [A1 s] *tr.* to oxygenate.
**oss-o** *m.* (*pl.* **-a** *f.*, **-i** *m.*) bone; fruit-stone. **-obuco** *m.* (*pl.* **-ossibuchi**) (cul.) marrow-bone. **-oso** *adj.* osseous, bony. **-ua·rio** *m.* ossuary; charnel-house. **-uto** *adj.* bony, big-boned.
**osta·col-o** *m.* obstacle; obstruction; handicap; hurdle. **-are** [A1 s] *tr.* to hinder, to impede; to handicap; to obstruct.
**ostag·gio** *m.* hostage.
**oste**[1] *m.* innkeeper, host; landlord.
**oste**[2] *f.* army, host.
**osteggiare** [A3 c] *tr.* to oppose, to show hostility to; to obstruct.
**ostello** *m.* abode; refuge.
**ostensi·bile** *adj.* ostensible; professed.
**ostent-are** [A1], *tr.* to display, to show off; to parade, to make a show of; to boast. **-azione** *f.* ostentation, show; pomp, affectation; pretence.
**oste-oartrite** *f.* (med.) osteoarthritis. **-opati·a** *f.* (med.) osteopathy.
**osteri·a** *f.* inn, tavern; wine-shop; eating-house.
**os-te·trica** *f.* midwife. **-tetri·cia** *f.* obstetrics. **-te·trico** *adj.* obstetric; *n.m.* obstetrician.
**o·stia** *f.* (rel.) sacrificial victim; (rel.) offering, sacrifice; (liturg.) host; wafer.
**ostil-e** *adj.* hostile, inimical, unfriendly; sullen; adverse. **-ità** *f. indecl.* hostility; hostile action; opposition; *pl.* (mil.) hostilities.
**ostin-are** [A1] *rfl.* to show obstinacy; to grow obstinate; *-arsi nell'errore*, to persist in error. **-atezza** *f.* obstinacy; persistence. **-ato** *adj.* obstinate, stubborn; pig-headed, persistent; (mus.) *basso -ato*, ground bass; *n.m.* (mus.) ostinato, ground. **-azione** *f.* obstinacy, stubbornness; doggedness, persistence.
**ostrac-ismo** *m.* ostracism. **-izzare** [A1] *tr.* to ostracize.
**o·strica** *f.* (zool.) oyster.
**ostro**[1] *m.* purple dye; purple garment.
**ostro**[2] *m.* (poet.) south; south wind.
**ostruire** [D2] *tr.* to obstruct, to hinder, to bar; to stop up, to block.
**ostruttivo** *adj.* obstructive.
**ostruzion-e** *f.* obstruction; hindrance; impediment; stoppage. **-ismo** *m.* (pol.) obstructionism. **-ista** *adj.*, *n.m.* (pol.) obstructionist.
**Otello** *pr.n.m.* Othello.
**otite** *f.* (med.) otitis, inflammation of the ear.
**otre** *m.* leather bottle.
**ott-a·gono** *m.* octagon. **-an·golo** *adj.* (geom.) octagonal; *n.m.* octagon.
**ottano** *m.* (motor.; aeron.) *numero di* —, octane number, octane rating.
**ottant-a** *card. num.* eighty. **-enne** *adj.* eighty years old; *n.m.*, *f.* octogenarian. **-e·simo** *ord. num.* eightieth. **-ina** *f.* four score; *aver passato l'-ina*, to be over eighty.
**ottativo** *adj.* (gramm.) optative.
**ottava** *f.* octave.
**ottavo** *ord. num.* eighth; *volume in* —, octavo volume.
**otten-ere** [B32] *tr.* to obtain; to get; to win; to reach; to achieve.
**Ottentotto** *m.* Hottentot.
**ot·tic-a** *f.* optics; lens. **-o** *adj.* optical; optic; *n.m.* optician.
**ot·tim-o** *adj.* excellent, admirable, very good; first-rate; *n.m. l'* —, the best. **-ismo** *m.* optimism. **-ista** *m.*, *f.* optimist. **-i·stico** *adj.* optimistic.
**ott-o** *card. num.* eight; *oggi a* —, today week; *n.m.* (figure) eight. **-enne** *adj.* eight years old. **-en·nio** *m.* period of eight years. **-ocento** *card. num.* eight hundred; *pr.n.m. l'Ottocento*, the nineteenth century. **-ocentesco** *adj.* (*m.pl.* **-ocenteschi**) nineteenth-century. **-omila** *card. num.* eight thousand. **-osil·labo** *adj.* (prosod.) octosyllabic; *n.m.* octosyllabic line.
**ottobr-e** *pr. n.m.* October. **-ino** *adj.* (of) October; ripening in October.
**ottoman-o** *m.* Ottoman; Turk; *adj.* Turkish. **-a** *f.* Turkish woman; ottoman, settee.
**ottona·rio** *adj.* (prosod.) octosyllabic; *n.m.* octosyllabic line.
**otton-e** *m.* brass; *pl.* (mus.) *gli -i*, the brass (instruments).
**ottuagena·rio** *adj.*, *n.m.* octogenarian.
**ottun·dere** [C1] *tr.* to blunt; to deaden; to dull.
**ot·tuplo** *adj.* eight-fold.
**otturare** [A1] *tr.* to block up, to stop up; to plug; to stop (a tooth).
**ottus-o** *part. adj.* blunt, dull; obtuse; *suono* —, muffled sound. **-ione** *f.* dullness, dazed condition. **-ità** *f.* obtuseness.
**ovale** *adj.*, *n.m.* oval.
**ova·rio** *m.* ovary.
**ovato** *adj.* ovate; oval.
**ovatt-a** *f.* wadding; cotton wool. **-are** [A1] *tr.* to line with wadding.
**ovazione** *f.* ovation.
**ov-e** *conj.* (poet.) where; — *che* (with *subj.*) wherever; when; if, provided that. **-unque** *conj.* wherever; *adv.* anywhere, everywhere.
**o·vest** *m. indecl.* west.
**Ovi·dio** *pr.n.m.* Ovid.
**ov-ile** *m.* sheepfold. **-ino** *adj.* ovine, of sheep.
**ov-o** *m.* (*pl.* **-a** *f.*) see **uovo.**
**ovvero** *conj.* or, or else.
**ovviare** [A4] *tr.* to obviate, to avoid; *intr.* (*aux.* avere; *prep.* a) to provide a remedy (for).
**ov·vio** *adj.* obvious, plain, ordinary, everyday.
**oziare** [A4] *intr.* (*aux.* avere) to idle, to lounge, to loaf.
**o·zi-o** *m.* idleness, laziness; sloth; leisure, spare time; *in* —, free. **-osag·gine** *f.* sloth. **-osità** *f.* sloth; idleness, laziness. **-oso** *adj.* idle; leisurely; fruitless, otiose; *n.m.* idler.

**P** *m., f.* (pron. **pi**) the letter P; the consonant P.
**pa·bolo** *m.* pasture; (fig.) pabulum.
**pac-are** [A2] *tr.* to quieten; to placate; to pacify. **-atamente** *adv.* peacefully. **-atezza** *f.* calm. **-ato** *part. adj.* calmed; pacified.
**pacca** *f.* slap, smack; flick with a whip.
**pacchetto** *m.dim.* see under **pacco.**
**pac·chia** *f.* life of eating, drinking and being merry.
**pacciame** *m.* litter of dead leaves, and twigs; rotten fruit.
**pac-co** *m.* (*pl.* **-chi**) parcel; packet, package; bundle. **-chetto** *m.dim.* small parcel; small packet; packet-boat, mail-boat. **-cotti·glia** *f.* trumpery goods, trash; job-lot.
**pac-e** *f.* peace; pax; *darsi* —, to resign oneself; *siamo* —, we are quits. **-iere** *m.* peace-maker. **-ificare** [A2 s] *tr.* to pacify, to appease, to placate; to reconcile; *rfl.* to become reconciled. **-i·fico** *adj.* peaceful, pacific, peace-loving; obvious, indubitable, undisputed; *l'Oceano -ifico*, the Pacific Ocean. **-ifismo** *m.* pacifism. **-ifista** *m., f.* pacifist. **-iona** *f.*, **-ione** *m.* easy-going person. **-ioso** *adj.* indolent.
**pachiderma** *m.* pachyderm; (fig.) thick-skinned person.
**padella** *f.* frying-pan; *cascar dalla — nella brace*, to jump out of the frying-pan into the fire; warming-pan; bed-pan.
**padiglione** *m.* pavilion, tent; canopy; festal hangings; ward of a hospital.
**Pa·dov-a** *pr.n.f.* Padua. **-ano** *adj., n.m.* Paduan.
**padr-e** *m.* father; *i nostri -i*, our ancestors; (fig.) mentor, guide; sire. **-igno** *m.* see **patrigno.** **-ino** *m.* godfather; second (in a duel).
**padron-a** *f.* woman owner; mistress; landlady; proprietress. **-cina** *f.* young mistress.
**padron-e** *m.* master; owner, proprietor, head of a firm, 'boss'; skipper, captain; patron; landlord. **-ale** *adj.* belonging to the owner. **-anza** *f.* ownership, proprietorship; mastery; domineering manner. **-cino** *m. dim.* young master. **-eggiare** [A3 c] *tr.* to master, to be master of, to rule; *rfl.* to control oneself.
**paes-e** *m.* country; land; — *natìo*, native village; country, rural area; landscape, countryside. **-ag·gio** *m.* landscape, countryside; view. **-ano** *adj.* native, indigenous, local; *n.m.* native, local inhabitant; fellow-countryman; peasant. **-ista** *m., f.* landscape painter.
**paf, paffe, paf·fete** *excl. onomat.* smack!; bang!; wallop!
**paffut-o** *adj.* plump; fat; stuffed, full; blown out. **-ezza** *f.* plumpness.
**Pafo** *pr.n.f.* (geog.) Paphos.
**paga** *f.* payment; wages; salary.
**paga·bile** *adj.* payable.
**paga·i-a** *f.* paddle (of canoe). **-are** [A4] *intr.* (*aux.* avere) to paddle.
**pagamento** *m.* payment; *giorno di* —, pay-day; reward; punishment, deserts.
**pagan-o** *adj., n.m.* pagan; heathen. **-esimo,** paganism, heathendom. **-izzare** [A1] *tr.* to paganize.
**pag-are** [A2] *tr.* to pay; to settle; to pay for; *rfl.* to insist on one's due, to enforce payment. **-ante** *part. adj.* paying; *carica -ante*, payload; *n.m., f.* payer. **-ato** *part. adj.* paid; settled.
**pagella** *f.* account for a professional fee; school report or certificate.
**pag·g-io** *m.* (*pl.* **-i**) page-boy.
**pagherò** *m. indecl.* (comm.) I.O.U.
**pa·gin-a** *f.* page. **-atura, -azione** *f.* paging, numbering of pages, pagination.
**pa·gli-a** *f.* straw; filter tip (of cigarette); straw colour. **-ac·cio** *m.* straw chopped fine; mattress; clown. **-a·io** *m.* straw stack. **-eric·cio** *m.* palliasse. **-etto** *m.* straw mat; chair seat made of plaited straw; netting. **-uzza** *f.* bit of straw; speck.
**pagnotta** *f.* small loaf; (fig.) wages, living.
**pa-go** *adj.* (*m.pl.* **-ghi**) contented.
**pa·i-o** *m.* (*pl.* **-a** *f.*) pair, couple, brace; *un altro — di maniche*, another matter altogether.
**pal-a** *f.* shovel; — *da fornaio*, baker's peel; blade of an oar or propeller; pall. **-ata** *f.* shovelful, stroke of an oar.
**paladino** *m.* paladin; knight-errant; champion.
**palafitt-a** *f.* pile; prehistoric lake village built on piles. **-i·colo** *adj.* lake-dwelling.
**palafren-o** *m.* palfrey; saddle-horse. **-iere** *m.* groom; footman.
**palan-ca** *f.* pole, large stake beam; plank-bridge; stockade. **-cato** *m.* stockade, palisade; enclosure. **-chino** *m.* palanquin; crowbar. **-co** *m.* (*pl.* **-chi**) tackle; roller for moving heavy weights.
**palan·cola** *f.* plank-bridge; gang-way.
**palata** *f.* see under **pala.**
**palatin-o** *adj.* (hist.) Palatine; *guardie -e*, papal guards; *n.m.* (Elector) Palatine; Palatine (hill, in Rome).
**palat-o** *m.* palate; taste. **-ale** *adj.* palatal.
**palazz-o** *m.* palace; mansion; block of flats; — *municipale*, Town Hall. **-etto** *m. dim.* small palace; annexe to a main building. **-ina** *f. dim.* small palace; country house, villa.
**pal-co** *m.* (*pl.* **-chi**) platform; flooring; stand; scaffold; top-floor, attic, lumber-room; (theatr.) box; stall; — *di platea*, pit-stall.
**palcosce·nico** *m.* stage.
**pale·o** *m.* spinning-top, peg-top.
**pale-ografi·a** *f.* palaeography. **-o·grafo** *m.* palaeographer. **-oli·tico** *adj.* palaeolithic.
**pales-e** *adj.* clear, manifest; well-known; obvious. **-amento** *m.* disclosure. **-are** [A1 c] *tr.* to disclose, to reveal; to make known; *rfl.* to reveal oneself; to become evident.
**Palestina** *pr.n.f.* (geog.) Palestine.
**palestra** *f.* gymnasium.
**palett-a** *f. dim.* of **pala**; palette; knee-cap. **-ata** *f.* shovelful. **-o** *m.* bolt; wedge; stake; pole; crow-bar.
**palinodi·a** *f.* palinode, recantation, retraction.
**palinsesto** *m.* palimpsest.
**pa·l-io** *m.* (*pl.* **-ii**) cloak; canopy; cloth given as prize; *la festa del* —, horse-race in Siena.
**palischermo** *m.* boat, launch.
**palissandro** *m.* rosewood.
**palizzata** *f.* palisade; stockade; railing.
**pall-a** *f.* ball; — *di neve*, snow-ball; globe; bullet; shot; *pl.* the arms of the Medici. **-acanestro** *f. indecl.* netball; basket-ball. **-a·io** *m.* ball-boy; maker or seller of balls; billiard marker; bowling-alley; bowling-green. **-anuoto** *m.* water-polo. **-ata** *f.* blow from a ball; *fare a -ate di neve*, to snowball. **-eggiare** [A3 c] *intr.* (*aux.* avere) to play ball; (football) to dribble, to pass; *tr.* to toss; to bandy; *recip. rfl.* *-eggiarsi la responsabilità*, to shift the responsibility on to one another. **-etta** *f. dim.* little ball; (mil.) grape-shot. **-ina** *f. dim.* little ball; marble; *pl.* small shot; lead pellets. **-ino** *m.* little ball; (bowls) jack; small shot, pellet; knob.
**Pal·lade** *pr.n.f.* (myth.) Pallas.
**palladiano** *adj.* (archit.) Palladian.
**palla·dio** *m.* palladium, talisman; safeguard, shield.
**palles-co** *adj.* (*m.pl.* **-chi**) (hist.) follower of the Medici.
**palli-are** [A4] *tr.* (fig.) to cloak, to cover up. **-ativo** *adj.* palliative. **-azione** *f.* palliation; dissimulation.
**pal·lid-o** *adj.* pale, pallid; (of light) faint. **-ezza** *f.* paleness, pallor.

**pallọn-e** *m. augm.* of **palla**; football; name of an Italian game; balloon. **-cino** *m. dim.* Chinese lantern; toy balloon.
**pallọre** *m.* pallor; paleness.
**pallot·tol-a** *f.* little ball; pellet; bullet; bowl (for playing bowls); pill. **-iere** *m.* abacus.
**palm-a**[1] *f.* (bot.) palm; (fig.) victory, victor's crown. **-ẹto** *m.* palm-grove.
**palm-a**[2] *f.* (anat.) palm; *battere le -e*, to clap one's hands; webbed foot. **-are** *adj.* (anat.) palmar; (fig.) evident, clear. **-a·rio** *m.* lawyer's fee; remuneration; hush-money. **-ata** *f.* clap; blow with, or on, the palm of the hand; bribe, tip. **-ato** *adj.* webbed. **-i·pede** *adj.* web-footed.
**palmo** *m.* span; hand's breadth; hand (unit of height for measuring horses).
**palo** *m.* pole; post; stake; pile; *— della porta*, goal-post; *— indicatore*, signpost.
**palp-are** [A1] *tr.* to pat; to feel, to touch; to handle. **-a·bile** *adj.* palpable, that can be felt; tangible, manifest.
**pal·pebra** *f.* eyelid; *battere le palpebre*, to blink.
**palpeggiare** [A3 c] *tr.* to handle, to feel, to touch; to finger.
**palpit-are** [A1 c] *intr.* (*aux.* avere) to throb, to pulsate; to palpitate; to tremble. **-ante** *part. adj.* palpitating; throbbing.
**pal·pito** *m.* throb, beat; flutter; *— di gioia*, thrill of pleasure.
**paltò** *m. indecl.* overcoat.
**palud-e** *f.* marsh, fen. **-ale** *adj.* *terreno -ale*, marsh land.
**palustre** *adj.* marshy; of the marshes.
**pam·pino** *m.* vine-leaf, vine-tendril, vine-branch.
**panace·a** *f.* panacea; universal remedy; hogweed.
**pan-ca** *f.* bench, form. **-chẹtta** *f. dim.* footstool; plank-bridge. **-chẹtto** *m.* stool; footstool; *-chetto piegatore*, camp-stool. **-china** *f.* garden-seat, stone bench; railway station platform.
**pan·c-ia** *f.* belly, paunch; bulge. **-iotto** *m.* waistcoat. **-iuto** *adj.* paunchy, corpulent; bulging.
**pancọne** *m. augm.* of **panca**; bench; workbench; *— di sabbia*, sandbank.
**pandemo·nio** *m.* pandemonium; confusion, uproar.
**pan-e**[1] *m.* bread; loaf; lump; ingot; living, livelihood; *rendere — per focaccia*, to give tit for tat. **-ello** *m. dim.* cake; loaf; oilcake. **-ettiere** *m.* baker. **-ettọne** *m.* a kind of Milanese cake. **-ino** *m. dim.* roll; bun.
**Pane**[2] *pr.n.m.* (myth.) Pan.
**panegi·rico** *adj.* panegyric(al); *n.m.* panegyric, eulogy.
**panfilo** *m.* yacht, galley.
**pa·nia** *f.* bird-lime; pitch, sticky substance; (fig.) trap, snare.
**panico**[1] *m.* millet.
**pa·ni-co**[2] *adj.* (*m.pl.* **-chi**) panic; *n.m.* panic.
**panier-e** *m.* basket. **-a** *f.* pannier.
**panificare** [A2 s] *intr.* (*aux.* avere) to make bread, to bake; *tr.* to make into bread.
**panifi·cio** *m.* bread-making, baking; bakehouse, bakery.
**panna**[1] *f.* cream; *— montata*, whipped cream.
**panna**[2] *f.* puncture; breakdown; *rimanere in —*, to have a breakdown.
**panna**[3] *f.* (naut.) boom, sea defence.
**pannello** *m.* panel.
**pann-o** *m.* cloth; film, skin, layer; *pl.* clothes; **-eg·gio** *m.* drapery; draping.
**panorama** *m.* panorama; view.
**Pantalọne**[1] *pr.n.m.* (theatr.) Pantaloon; (provb.) *paga —*, the taxpayer pays.
**pantalọne**[2] *m.* pantaloon; *pl.* trousers.
**pantan-o** *m.* bog, swamp; *adj.* boggy, swampy. **-ọso** *adj.* boggy, swampy.
**pante-iṣmo** *m.* pantheism. **-ista** *m., f.* pantheist. **-i·stico** *adj.* pantheistic.
**Pan·teon** *pr.n.m.* Pantheon (in Rome); *n.m.* pantheon.
**pantera** *f.* panther.
**panto·fola** *f.* slipper.
**panto-mima** *f.* pantomime; (iron.) play-acting. **-mimo** *m.* mimic actor; mime.
**Pa·ol-a** *pr.n.f.* Paula. **-o** *pr.n.m.* Paul.
**paolotto** *adj.* pious; bigoted.
**paonazzo** *adj., n.m.* violet; purple; peacock-blue.
**papà** *m. indecl.* daddy, papa; *figlio di —*, idle and wealthy young man.
**Pap-a** *m.* pope. **-ale** *adj.* papal, of the pope. **-alina** *f.* skull-cap; smoking-cap. **-ato** *m.* papacy. **-iṣmo** *m.* Popery. **-ista** *m.* papist.
**papa·vero** *m.* poppy.
**pa·per-o** *m.* gosling; (fig.) silly goose. **-a** *f.* (fig.) silly woman; blunder; gaffe.
**papiro** *m.* papyrus; (joc.) paper, document.
**pappa** *f.* pap; bread poultice; paste.
**pappafi-co** *m.* (*pl.* **-chi**) hood; cowl; diver's helmet.
**pappagall-o** *m.* parrot. **-ẹsco** (*m.pl.* **-ẹschi**) parrot-like. **-iṣmo** *m.* parrot-like imitation.
**pappagor·gia** *f.* wattles; (fig.) double-chin.
**papp-are** [A1] *tr.* to eat up, to gobble up; to gulp down; *intr.* (*aux.* avere), *rfl.* to eat one's fill. **-ata** *f.* feast, hearty meal.
**pappolata** *f.* thin soup; sloppy food; *la — dei porci*, pig-swill.
**pa·pula** *f.* boil, pustule.
**para-** *pref.* para near.
**para·bola**[1] *f.* parable; fable, invention.
**para·bola**[2] *f.* parabola, curve.
**Paracleto** *pr.n. m.* Paraclete, Holy Ghost; (fig.) consoler.
**paradigm-a** *m.* (*pl.* **-i**) paradigm.
**paradiṣ-o** *m.* paradise; perfect bliss. **-i·aco** *adj.* heavenly, celestial.
**paradoss-o** *m.* paradox. **-ale** *adj.* paradoxical.
**paraffina** *f.* paraffin, paraffin wax.
**parafraṣare** [A1] *tr.* to paraphrase.
**para·fraṣi** *f. indecl.* paraphrase.
**parag·gio** *m.* (usu. *pl.*) part, quarter, neighbourhood.
**paragọn-e** *m.* comparison; *senza —*, unequalled; paragon, model; test, trial. **-are** [A1 c] *tr.* (*prep* con, a) to compare.
**para·grafo** *m.* paragraph sign; paragraph; sub-section.
**para·l-iṣi** *f. indecl.* paralysis. **-iẓẓare** [A1] *tr.* to paralyse; (fig.) to slow down.
**parallel-a** *f.* parallel line, parallel. **-o** *adj.* (geom.) parallel; *n.m.* parallel.
**paran-co** *m.* (*pl.* **-chi**) (naut.) purchase, tackle; pulley block.
**paranza** *f.* sailing trawler; fishing trawler.
**par-are** [A1] *tr.* to adorn, to deck, to decorate; to prepare; to parry, to ward off; to prevent, to hinder; to drive away; to hold out, to offer; *rfl.* to adorn oneself; to protect oneself, to take shelter. **-abrezza** *m. indecl.* windscreen. **-acadute** *m. indecl.* parachute. **-acarro** *m.* kerbstone. **-acẹnere** *m.* fireguard; fender. **-acọlpi** *m. indecl.* bumper, buffer. **-afango** *m.* mudguard. **-aful·mine** *m.* lightning conductor. **-afuoco** *m.* firescreen; fireguard. **-alume** *m.* lampshade. **-amẹnto** *m.* decoration, furnishing; hanging(s), curtains. **-amọsche** *m. indecl.* fly-net; wire gauze dish-cover. **-aoc·chi** *m. indecl.* goggles; eye-shield; blinkers (for a horse). **-apetto** *m.* parapet; balustrade; bulwark; taffrail; gunwale. **-asọle** *m.* sunshade, parasol; awning. **-ata** *f.* parry; (fig.) *star sulle -ate*, to be on one's guard; parade, display. **-ato** *part. adj.* decorated, decked; hung with curtains; prepared, ready; parried; *n.m.* hangings, curtains; ornament. **-aurti** *m. indecl.* shock-absorber; bumper, buffer. **-avento** *m.* screen; windscreen.
**parass-ita** *m.* (*pl.* **-iti**) parasite; hanger-on; sponger. **-i·tico** *adj.* parasitic. **-iṣmo** *m.* parasitism.
**Parca** *pr.n.f.* (myth.) Fate.

**parcella** *f.* honorarium, fee; (agric.) parcel of land.
**par-co**[1] *m.* (*pl.* **-chi**) park; enclosure; paddock; yard. **-care** [A2] *tr.* to park. **-cheggio** *m.* parking; parking-place, car park.
**par-co**[2] *adj.* (*m.pl.* **-chi**) sparing, frugal, parsimonious.
**parecchio** *adj.* some, many; a good deal; a good many; a lot of; *pl.* several; several people.
**pareggi-are** [A3c] *tr.* to equal; to equalize, to make equal; to level; to balance; *intr.* (*aux.* avere) to equalize, to draw (in a game). **-a·bile** *adj.* comparable; that can be equalled.
**pareggio** *m.* equalization; balance; draw.
**parent-e** *m.*, *f.* relation, relative, kinsman; *pl.* parents. **-ado** *m.* relationship, kinship; kindred, kin, stock; lineage, parentage. **-ela** *f.* relationship, kinship; affinity; relatives, relations.
**paren·tesi** *f. indecl.* parenthesis; (fig.) lull, interval, pause; bracket(s); *fra* —, incidentally, by the way.
**parere** [B19] *intr.* (*aux.* essere) to seem, to appear; to look like; *n.m.* opinion, judgement; advice.
**parete** *f.* wall, inner wall; shelter; obstacle.
**par·gol-o** *m.* little child; baby. **-etto** *m.* little child; baby; *adj.* tiny, small, little.
**par-i** *adj. indecl.* equal, like, same; (of numbers) even; *alla* —, at par; (of a surface) even, level; *n.m.* peer; equal; *il — e l'impari*, odd and even; *n.f. portarsi alla* —, to catch up, to get up to date. **-imenti** *adv.* likewise, similarly; also.
**pa·ria**[1] *m. indecl.* pariah, outcast, untouchable.
**pari·a**[2] *f.* peerage.
**parificare** [A2s] *tr.* to equalize.
**Parig-i** *pr.n.f.* Paris. **-ina** *f.* Parisienne; (circus) woman tight-rope walker. **-ino** *adj.* Parisian, Paris; *n.m.* Parisian.
**pari·glia** *f.* pair; couple; brace; *render la* —, to give tit for tat
**parità** *f.* parity, equality.
**parlamentare**[1] [A1] *intr.* (*aux.* avere) to discuss, to parley, to arrange terms.
**parlamentare**[2] *adj.* parliamentary; *n.m.* parliamentarian.
**Parlamento** *p.n.m.* Parliament.
**parl-are** [A1] *intr.* (*aux.* avere) to talk, to speak; to make a speech; *tr.* to speak; *qui si -a inglese*, English spoken here; *n.m.* talk; way of speaking; speech; dialect; words; language. **-ante** *part. adj.* speaking, talking; *ben -ante*, eloquent. **-atore** *m.* (colloq.) good talker. **-ottare** [A1] *intr.* (*aux.* avere) to whisper, to murmur.
**parmigiano** *adj.* Parmesan; *n.m.* native or inhabitant of Parma; Parmesan cheese.
**Parnas(s)-o** *pr.n.m.* (myth.) Parnassus. **-iano** *adj.* (lit. hist.) Parnassian.
**parod-i·a** *f.* parody. **-iare** [A4] *tr.* to parody.
**parol-a** *f.* word; term; speech; doctrine; maxim; promise; *venire a -e*, to have words, to quarrel. **-ac·cia** *f. pejor.* bad word, swear word. **-a·io** *m.* talkative person; wordy speaker; *adj.* wordy, long-winded; loquacious.
**parossismo** *m.* paroxysm.
**parri-cida** *m.* parricide; traitor, regicide; *adj.* parricidal. **-ci·dio** *m.* parricide (action, crime).
**parrochetto** *m.* parakeet.
**parroc·chi-a** *f.* parish; parish church. **-ale** *adj.* parochial. **-ano** *m.* parishioner.
**par·roco** *m.* parish priest.
**parruc-ca** *f.* wig; periwig; long hair; (fig.) scolding, wigging; intoxication. **-chiere** *m.* hairdresser, barber; wig-maker.
**parsimo·ni-a** *f.* frugality; parsimony. **-oso** *adj.* parsimonious.
**parte** *f.* part; *parti di ricambio*, spare parts; portion, share; *la — del leone*, the lion's share; side, quarter; *egli stette dalla nostra* —, he sided with us; *mettere da* —, to lay aside; *d'altra* —, on the other side, on the other hand; *da — a* —, right through; district; *in qualche altra* —, somewhere else; (mus.) part, voice; (theatr.) part; role; actor; (pol.; leg.) party; *prese la cosa in buona* —, he took it in good part; *mettere uno a — di*, to inform someone of; *ditegli da — mia che*, tell him from me that; *per — mia*, as far as I am concerned.
**partecip-are** [A1sc] *intr.* (*aux.* avere; *prep.* a) to participate, to take part; to share; to attend, to be present (at); (*prep.* di) — *di una cosa*, to have something (of the nature) of a thing; *tr.* to announce; to communicate, to impart. **-ante** *part. adj.* present, attending; partaking; *n.m.* participant, person present. **-azione** *f.* participation.
**partecipe** *adj.* participating; acquainted, informed.
**parteggiare** [A3c] *intr.* (*aux.* avere) to take sides; — *per*, to side with.
**Partenone** *pr.n.m.* Parthenon.
**Parte·nop-e** *pr.n.f.* Parthenope. **-e·o** *adj.* (poet.; pol.) Parthenopean, Neapolitan.
**partenza** *f.* departure; leaving; setting out; *in — per*, leaving for; passing away, death.
**particella** *f. dim.* of **parte**; particle; suffix; conjunction.
**partici·pio** *m.* participle.
**particolar-e** *adj.* particular; peculiar; special; private; *n.m.* particular; detail; private individual, person. **-eggiare** [A3c] *intr.* (*aux.* avere) to particularize; *rfl.* to stand out, to be distinguished. **-ità** *f. indecl.* particular, detail; partiality.
**partigian-o** *adj.* partisan, partial; factious; *spirito* —, party spirit; *n.m.* partisan, follower, supporter. **-eri·a** *f.* partisanship, partiality; factious action.
**part-ire**[1] [D1] *tr.* to divide; to separate; to share out; to part with. **-ita** *f.* panel; shutter; game (of cards, etc.), round, rubber; *-ita d'onore*, duel; *-ita di piacere*, excursion, outing. **-itivo** *adj.* partitive. **-ito** *part. adj.* divided, separated; parted (of hair, etc.); *n.m.* choice, alternative; *prendere -ito*, to take sides; *per -ito preso*, having made up one's mind; (pol.) party; marriage partner; advantage, profit, benefit; purpose, resolve; situation, condition; *mal -ito*, sorry plight, predicament. **-itura** *f.* (mus.) score.
**part-ire**[2] [D2] *intr.* (*aux.* essere) to go away; to set out; to start; (of a ship) to sail; *a — da domani*, from tomorrow. **-ita** *f.* departure; parting.
**part-o**[1] *m.* birth, childbirth; delivery; new-born baby; (fig.) parturition; output. **-oriente** *adj.* parturient, in labour; *n.f.* woman in labour. **-orire** [D] *tr.* to bear, to bring forth, to give birth to; to be delivered of; (of animals) to drop, to foal, to litter; *intr.* (*aux.* avere) to be delivered; to be in foal.
**parto**[2] *adj.*, *n.m.* Parthian; *la freccia del* —, the Parthian shot.
**parven-te** *adj.* seeming, apparent; visible. **-za** *f.* appearance, aspect; apparition; show, pretence.
**parzial-e** *adj.* partial; incomplete; unfair, biased. **-ità** *f.* partiality; favouritism.
**pa·sc-ere** [B17] *intr.* (*aux.* avere) to graze; to pasture; *tr.* (of animals) to browse on, to feed on; (fig.) to eat; to feed; to lead to pasture, to put out to grass; — *di promesse*, to put off with promises; *rfl.* (*prep.* di) to feed (on); (fig.) *-ersi d'illusioni*, to cherish illusions. **-iuto** *part. adj.* *ben -iuto*, well-fed, plump.
**pa·scol-o** *m* pasture, meadow, grass; (fig.) food, nourishment. **-are** [A1s] *intr.* (*aux.* avere) to graze; to pasture; (fig.) *-are di speranze*, to feed on hope.
**Pasqu-a** *pr.n.f.* Easter; — *degli Ebrei*, Passover; — *di rose*, Whitsunday, Pentecost; (fig.) *far* —, to make merry. **-ale** *adj.* pertaining to Easter, Easter; Paschal.

**passa·bile** *adj.* passable, tolerable; fair.

**passag·gio** *m.* passing; passage; crossing; transit; transition; extract, quotation; way; corridor; — *pedonale*, pedestrian crossing; *chiedere un* —, to ask for a lift; *vietato il* —, no thoroughfare; — *interdetto*, no entry; voyage; (schol.) promotion.

**passamano** *m.* passing from hand to hand; lace trimming; braid.

**passaporto** *m.* see under **passare.**

**pass-are** [A1] *intr.* (*aux.* essere) to pass; to pass by; to pass along; to die; to occur, to happen, to come to pass; to elapse; — *a un esame*, to pass (in) an examination; (schol.) — *ad un'altra classe*, to be promoted; — *in seconde nozze*, to marry again; to exist, to pass for; to pass off, to subside; *tr.* to pass; to surpass; to overtake; to spend (time); to hand; to transfer; to put; *-arla male*, to have a bad time; *la -ai liscia*, I got off scot free; to exceed, to overstep, to go beyond; to pierce, to transfix; to pass into; to filter, to sift, to strain; *rfl.* (*prep.* di) to do without, to abstain (from), to dispense (with); (*dat.* of *prn.* 'si') *-arsela bene*, to get on well. **-ante** *part. adj.* passing; *n.m., f.* passer-by; pedestrian. **-aporto** *m.* passport. **-ata** *f.* passage, action of passing; look, glance; (bldg.) doorway; (cul.) mash, purée. **-atina** *f.* slight application, touch; brief glance; slight shower.

**passatempo** *m.* pastime, amusement; game; hobby.

**passato** *part.* of **passare**; *adj.* past, gone by; faded; over; *n.m.* past; time gone by.

**passatọia** *f.* strip of carpet, runner; stair-carpet.

**passatọio** *m.* foot-bridge; stepping-stone; stile.

**passatura** *f.* darn; darning.

**passavi·a** *m.* flying bridge.

**passavivande** *m. indecl.* service-hatch.

**passegger-o** *adj.* transient, passing, fleeting; *n.m.* passenger; traveller. **-a** *f.* female passenger; passenger ship.

**passeggi-are** [A3 c] *intr.* (*aux.* avere) to take a walk, to go for a walk; — *a cavallo*, to ride. **-ata** *f.* walk; drive, ride; excursion; promenade.

**passẹggio** *m.* walk; drive; walking; promenade, public walk.

**pas·ser-a** *f.*, **-o** *m.* sparrow. *-o solitario*, blue rockthrush.

**passerella** *f.* gangplank; footbridge.

**passi·bile** *adj.* liable, susceptible.

**passiọn-e** *f.* passion, suffering; love; keen desire; sorrow; anxiety. **-ale** *adj.* relating to suffering; relating to passion; impassioned.

**passiv-o** *adj.* passive; unprofitable; *n.m.* liability; debit. **-ità** *f. indecl.* passivity; insensibility; liabilities.

**passo**[I] *m.* step, pace; stride; walk, gait; march; *fare due passi*, to go for a short walk; *andar di pari — con*, to keep pace with; footfall, tread; footprint; *un — falso*, a false step, a mistake; procedure, precedence; (geog.) pass; inlet; straits, passage; extract (from a book); *uccello di* —, bird of passage.

**passo**[2] *adj.* dried; withered, shrivelled; *uva passa*, raisins.

**pasta** *f.* (cul.) 'pasta'; dough; pastry; cake; — *sfoglia*, puff pastry; sweet; pulp, paste; wet plaster, clay; (fig.) nature, temperament; constitution.

**pasteggiare** [A3 c] *intr.* (*aux.* avere) to eat at table; to have one's meals.

**pastello** *m.* pastel; pastel drawing.

**pasticca** *f.* pastille, lozenge, tablet.

**pasticceri·a** *f.* pastrycook's shop, confectioner's; pastry; confectionery.

**pasticciare** [A3] *tr.* to make a mess of; to bungle.

**pastic·c-io** *m.* pie; mess, muddle; embarrassment; imitation, copy; bad picture. **-iere** *m.* pastrycook, confectioner.

**pasti·glia** *f.* pastille; paste imitation of precious stones.

**past-o** *m.* meal; food; repast; *vino da* —, table wine. **-oc·chia** *f.* idle talk, fib, nonsense; humbug.

**pastọia** *f.* pastern; hobble; fetters.

**pastọr-e** *m.* shepherd; *bastone da* —, shepherd's crook; leader, ruler; minister, pastor. **-ale** *adj.* pastoral; bucolic; *n.m.* (eccl.) pastoral, bishop's letter. **-i·zia** *f.* sheep-rearing.

**pastoriẓẓare** [A1] *tr.* to pasteurize.

**pastọso** *adj.* soft; sticky; mellow; (of wine) rather sweet.

**pastrano** *m.* overcoat, greatcoat; cloak with sleeves.

**pastur-a** *f.* pasture, pasturage. **-are** [A1] *tr.* to pasture, to put out to graze; *rfl.* to feed, to graze.

**patata** *f.* potato; *patate fritte*, fried potatoes, chips.

**patella** *f.* (anat.) knee-cap; (zool.) limpet.

**patema** *m.* trouble, anxiety; suffering; chagrin.

**patent-e** *adj.* wide open; self-evident, manifest; patent; *n.f.* licence, certificate, diploma; — *di circolazione*, car licence; — *di guida*, driving licence. **-ato** *adj.* patented; certificated; licensed.

**patern-o** *adj.* paternal; father's; fatherly. **-ale** *adj.* paternal; *n.f.* scolding, rebuke. **-ità** *f.* paternity; fatherhood.

**paternostro** *m.* Paternoster, Lord's Prayer; *il — della scimmia*, a string of oaths.

**pate·tic-o** *adj.* pathetic; touching; moving; mawkish; melancholy. **-ume** *m.* sentimentality; sob-stuff.

**pati·bolo** *m.* gallows, scaffold; gibbet.

**pa·tina** *f.* varnish; glazing; patina; coating.

**pat-ire** [D2] *tr.* to suffer; to bear, to stand, to endure; to experience; to undergo; *intr.* (*aux.* avere) to suffer; to grieve; (*prep.* di) to suffer (from). **-ito** *part. adj.* suffering; sickly; *n.m.* admirer; fan.

**patos, pathos** *m. indecl.* pathos.

**Patrasso** *pr.n.f.* (geog.) Patras.

**pa·tria** *f.* native land, country; home; *in — e fuori*, at home and abroad.

**patriar-ca** *m.* (*pl.* **-chi**) patriarch; founder of a family.

**patri-cida** *m.* parricide (person); *adj.* parricidal. **-ci·dio** *m.* (*pl.* **-ci·dii**) parricide (act).

**patrigno** *m.* step-father.

**patrimo·ni-o** *m.* patrimony; heritage; estate; total assets. **-ale** *adj.* inherited, hereditary.

**pa·tri-o** *adj.* paternal; native; domestic; *amor* —, patriotism. **-ota, -otta** *m.* patriot; compatriot, fellow-countryman.

**patrocinare** [A1] *tr.* to defend, to support, to protect; to champion.

**patroci·nio** *m.* protection, support; defence; legal representation.

**patroni·mico** *adj.* named after one's father; *n.m.* patronymic; family name.

**patron-o** *m.* patron; patron saint; patron of a living. **-ato** *m.* patronage; charitable institution.

**patt-a** *f.* draw, quits. **-are** [A1] *intr.* (*aux.* avere) to be quits, to be all square.

**pat·tin-o** *m.* skate; — *a rotelle*, roller-skate; shoe; runner; pad. **-ag·gio** *m.* skating. **-are** *intr.* (*aux.* avere) to skate.

**patt-o** *m.* agreement; pact; covenant; condition; treaty; *pl.* terms; understanding. **-eggiare** [A3 c] *intr.* (*aux.* avere) to bargain, to negotiate; to come to terms; *tr.* to negotiate; to arrange the terms of.

**pattu·gli-a** *f.* patrol; *essere di* —, to be on patrol. **-are** [A4] *intr.* (*aux.* avere) to go on patrol; *tr.* to patrol.

**pattuire** [D2] *tr.* to negotiate; to agree (upon); to arrange, to settle; *abs.* to bargain.

**pattum-e** *m.* refuse, litter; dust-heap. **-iera** *f.* dust-bin.

**pau·r-a** *f.* fear, dread; fright;

*aver — di*, to be afraid of, to fear; anxiety, concern; *da far* —, awful, terrible; *da far* —, terribly. **-ọso** *adj.* timorous, timid; shy; fearful; alarming, dreadful.

**pa·uṣ-a** *f.* pause, stop; rest. **-are** [A1 a] *intr.* (*aux.* avere) to pause; *tr.* to interrupt, to introduce pauses in.

**Pavi·a** *pr.n.f.* (geog.) Pavia.

**pavent-are** [A1] *intr.* (*aux.* avere) to be afraid; (of animals) to be timid. **-ọso** *adj.* afraid, fearful; frightful, dreadful.

**paveṣare** [A1 c] *tr.* to reveal, to make obvious; (naut.) to dress (ships); *rfl.* to be revealed; to be evident.

**pavẹse** *adj.*, *n.m.*, *f.* (native) of Pavia.

**pa·vido** *adj.* timid, fearful; frightened; cowardly; shy.

**pavimẹnt-o** *m.* pavement; floor; — *intavolato*, parquet floor. **-are** [A1 c] *tr.* to pave; to floor; to macadamize, to metal (a road).

**pavọn-e** *m.*, **-a**, **-ẹssa** *f.* peacock, peahen. **-azzo** *adj.*, *n.m.* peacock-blue; violet; purple. **-eggiare** [A3 c] *rfl.* to strut; to show off; to be as proud as a peacock.

**pazient-e** *adj.* patient, forbearing; suffering; *n.m.* patient, sick person; sufferer. **-are** [A1] *intr.* (*aux.* avere) to be patient. **pazienza** *f.* patience. forbearance; endurance; game of patience; —*!*, never mind!

**pazz-o** *adj.* mad, insane, lunatic; wild; foolish; *n.m.* madman, lunatic. **-erello** *m.* fool; silly person; madcap. **-ẹsco** *adj.* (*m.pl.* **-ẹschi**) mad; foolish; crazy. **-i·a** *f.* madness, lunacy, insanity; frenzy; folly.

**pecca** *f.* fault; blemish; defect, flaw.

**peccaminọso** *adj.* sinful.

**pecc-are** [A2] *intr.* (*aux.* avere) to sin; to transgress; to err; to be at fault; to be wrong. **-ato** *m.* sin; fault; error; *che -ato!*, what a pity! **-atọre** *m.*, **-atrice** *f.* sinner; *adj.* sinful; sinning.

**pẹcchi-a** *f.* bee. **-ọne** *m.* drone; bumble-bee.

**pẹce** *f.* pitch; — *liquida*, tar.

**Pechin-o** *pr.n.f.* (geog.) Peking. **-ẹse** *adj.* of Peking; *n.m.*, *f.* native of Peking; (dog) Pekingese.

**pe·cor-a** *f.* sheep; ewe; mutton. **-ag·gine** *f.* servility; stupidity, silliness. **-a·io** *m.* shepherd. **-ella** *f. dim.* little sheep; *-ella smarrita*, lost sheep; *pl.* sea-foam, 'white horses'; fleecy clouds. **-ẹsco** *adj.* (*m.pl.* **-ẹschi**) stupid, foolish, sheepish. **-ile** *adj.* of sheep; *n.m.* sheepfold; sheep's dung. **-ino** *m.* sheep's milk cheese. **-ọne** *m. augm.* ram; big sheep; (fig.) blockhead; poor-spirited creature.

**peculiare** *adj.* peculiar, special, particular.

**pecu·lio** *m.* savings, nest-egg; gratuity.

**pecu·ni-a** *f.* money. **-a·rio** *adj.* (of) money; pecuniary.

**pedag·gio** *m.* toll; canal tax.

**pedagn-a** *f.* foot-rest used in rowing. **-uolo** *m.* stock of a young tree; plank-bridge.

**pedago·gic-a** *f.* pedagogics. **-o** *adj.* pedagogic(al).

**pedago-go** *m.* (*pl.* **-ghi**) pedagogue; teacher. **-gi·a** *f.* pedagogy, education.

**pedal-e** *m.* stock (of a vine), trunk (of a tree); stem; foot (of a stocking); pedal, treadle; — *della frizione*, clutch pedal. **-are** [A1] *intr.* (*aux.* avere) to pedal; to work a treadle; to cycle. **-eggiare** [A3 c] *tr.*, *intr.* (*aux.* avere) (mus.) to pedal. **-ista** *m.*, *f.* pedaller; cyclist.

**pedana** *f.* foot-rest; fender; beside rug; running-board; platform; springboard.

**pedano** *m.* trunk of a tree.

**pedant-e** *m.* pedant. **-eggiare** [A3 c] *intr.* (*aux.* avere) to be pedantic. **-eri·a** *f.* pedantry.

**pedata** *f.* footprint; footstep; stair, step; (bldg.) tread.

**pederasta** *m.* paederast.

**pedestre** *adj.* pedestrian; (fig.) dull, uninspired.

**pedicure** *m.*, *f.* chiropodist.

**pedilu·vio** *m.* foot-bath; paddling.

**pedin-a** *f.* (chess) pawn; (draughts) man, piece. **-are** [A1] *tr.* to follow, to shadow, to trail, to stalk.

**pedis·sequo** *adj.* servile, fawning; clumsy; literal-minded; *n.m.* lick-spittle.

**pedo·metro** *m.* pedometer.

**pedọn-e** *m.* pedestrian; *adj.* foot-passenger; *adj. strada -a*, foot-path. **-ale** *adj.* (reserved) for foot-passengers, pedestrian.

**pedule**[1] *m.* stocking foot.

**pedule**[2] *f.pl.* boots for rock-climbing.

**Pe·gaso** *pr.n.m.* (myth.) Pegasus.

**peg·gi-o** *adv.*, *adj. indecl.* worse; *n.m.* the worst; *f.* worsening; defeat. **-orare** [A1 c] *intr.* (*aux.* essere) to get worse, to become worse; *tr.* to make worse. **-orativo** *adj.* pejorative, depreciative. **-ọre** *adj.* worse; *n.m.*, *f.* the worst.

**pẹgno** *m.* pledge; token; pawn; *agenzia di* —, pawnshop; *polizza di* —, pawn-ticket.

**pẹgola** *f.* pitch.

**pela·gico** *adj.* marine.

**pe·la-go** *m.* (*pl.* **-ghi**) sea, ocean.

**pelare** [A1 c] *tr.* to strip (the hair) from; to peel; to skin; to pluck (fowls); (fig.) to fleece; *rfl.* to lose one's hair, to go bald; to moult; (of trees) to lose their leaves.

**pell-e** *f.* skin; *una ferita a fior di* —, a graze; hide; leather, skin; (fam.) life; *amici per la* —, friends for life; peel; rind; crust; coat (of plaster, etc.). **-a·io** *m.* leather dresser; tanner; leather merchant. **-ame** *m.* hide, leather; skins. **-etteri·a** *f.* hides, leather; leather goods.

**pellegrin-o** *adj.* vagrant; exotic, foreign; strange; *i Padri -i*, the Pilgrim Fathers; *n.m.* pilgrim; traveller. **-ag·gio** *m.* pilgrimage. **-are** [A1] *intr.* (*aux.* avere) to go on a pilgrimage; to travel; to wander.

**pellicano** *m.* pelican.

**pellic·c-ia** *f.* fur; fur coat. **-eri·a** *f.* furs; furrier's shop; fur-trade. **-ia·io** *m.* furrier.

**pelli·cola** *f.* thin skin, membrane; (photog.) film.

**pellirọsse** *f.pl.* Red Indians; *un pellirossa*, a Redskin; *una pellirossa*, a squaw.

**pellu·cido** *adj.* pellucid; transparent.

**pẹl-o** *m.* hair; (of animals) fur, coat; *un — di ciglio*, an eye-lash; thin crack; vein (in marble); surface (of a liquid); hairsbreadth, very little; *contro* —, the wrong way, against the grain. **-ame** *m.* the skin or coat of an animal. **-ọso** *adj.* hairy, hirsute; shaggy.

**pẹltro** *m.* pewter; metal; wealth.

**pelu·ria** *f.* downy covering; soft hair; floss silk; fluff.

**peluto** *adj.* hairy.

**pelvi** *f.* pelvis.

**pẹn-a** *f.* penalty; punishment; pain, suffering, trouble, distress; sorrow; pity; difficulty; *non ne vale la* —, it is not worth while; *mi fate* —, I pity you; *a* —, hardly, scarcely. **-ale** *adj.* criminal; penal; *n.f.* penalty. **-alità** *f.* (leg.; sport) penalty. **-aliẓẓare** [A1] *tr.* to penalize. **-are** [A1 c] *intr.* (*aux.* avere; *prep.* a) to suffer; to find it difficult, to be hardly able; to wait (for); to take pains.

**pencolare** [A1 s] *intr.* (*aux.* avere) to dangle; to be unsteady, to totter.

**pen·d-ere** [B1] *intr.* (*aux.* avere) to hang, to hang down; to dangle; to overhang; to lean; to be inclined; to slope; to be pending; to depend. **-ente** *part. adj.* hanging; dangling; drooping; leaning; *torre -ente*, leaning tower; inclined, sloping; *n.m.* slope; pendant; ear-drop. **-enza** *f.* slope, gradient, declivity; (fig.) affair pending; outstanding balance. **-ice** *f.* slope, declivity; hill-side. **-ìo** *m.* (*pl.* **-ìi**) slope, declivity; gradient.

**pen·dola** *f.* pendulum clock.

**pendolare**[1] *adj.* pendulous, oscillating, swinging.
**pendol-are**[2] [A1 s] *intr.* (*aux.* avere) to swing; to be pendulous; to slope. **-one, oni** *adv.* dangling.
**pen·dolo** *m.* pendulum; plumb-line.
**pen·dulo** *adj.* pendulous.
**pene** *m.* penis.
**penetr-are** [A1 s] *intr.* (*aux.* essere; *prep.* in) to penetrate, to enter; to sink in; *tr.* to pierce, to break into; to pervade; to sink into; to fathom, to see through; *rfl.* to enter thoroughly (into a part); to identify oneself (with). **-ante** *part. adj.* penetrating; piercing; acute, searching. **-azione** *f.* penetration; (fig.) insight; intuition; *-azione pacifica*, peaceful penetration.
**peninsulare** *adj.* peninsular.
**peni·sola** *f.* peninsula.
**peniten-te** *adj.*, *n.m.*, *f.* penitent. **-za** *f.* penitence; penance; pain, trouble. **-zia·rio** (leg.) *n.m.* penitentiary; reformatory; convict prison.
**penn-a** *f.* feather; quill; plume; *metter le -e*, to be fledged; pen; *— stilografica*, fountain pen; *— a sfera*, ball-point pen; (poet.) wing. **-ac·chio** *m.* plume; cloud of smoke. **-ato** *adj.* feathered; *n.m.* bill-hook; *pl.* the feathered tribe, birds.
**pennell-o** *m.* paint-brush, brush; (fig.) painter; triangular flag, pennant; windvane. **-are** [A1] *intr.* (*aux.* avere) to paint, to work with a brush. **-ata** *f.* brush-stroke; brush-work. **-eggiare** [A3 c] *tr.* to paint, to colour; *intr.* (*aux.* avere) to use the brush, to paint.
**pennon-e** *m. augm.* of **penna**; pennant; regimental flag (cavalry). **-cello** *m. dim.* small flag; streamer; plume.
**pennuto** *adj.* feathered; fledged.
**penombra** *f.* penumbra; shadow, half-light.
**penoso** *adj.* painful; troublesome; distressing; difficult.
**pens-are** [A1] *intr.* (*aux.* avere) to think, to reflect, to meditate; *— a*, to think of; *ci -erò*, I'll think it over; *— di*, to think of, to hold a certain opinion of; *che ne -i ?*, what do you think of it ?; to believe; to consider; to mean, to resolve, to intend; *tr.* to think out, to think over; to imagine; to meditate upon; to contrive; to plan; *n.m.* thinking, thought. **-a·bile** *adj.* conceivable, imaginable, thinkable. **-ante** *part. adj.* thinking; *n.m.*, *f.* thinker. **-atore** *m.* thinker; *libero -atore*, free-thinker.
**pensier-o** *m.* thought; idea; mind, way of thinking; intention; anxiety, solicitude; care; attention. **-oso** *adj.* thoughtful, pensive; serious.
**pen·sile** *adj.* hanging; suspended.
**pension-e** *f.* pension; board; boarding-house; boarding-school. **-are** [A1 c] *tr.* to pension (off). **-a·rio** *m.* pensioner; boarder, paying-guest. **-ato** *part. adj.* pensioned (off); on a pension; *n.m.* pensioner; holder of a bursary; boarding-school.
**pensoso** *adj.* pensive, thoughtful; grave; anxious.
**pent-a·colo** *m.* five-pointed star, pentacle. **-a·gono** *m.* pentagon. **-a·metro** *m.* pentameter.
**Pentate·uco** *pr.n.m.* (bibl.) Pentateuch.
**Pentecoste** *pr.n.f.* Pentecost; Whitsuntide.
**pent-ire** [D1] *rfl.* (*prep.* di) to repent, to be sorry; to regret. **-imento** *m.* repentance, regret; *pl.* corrections; second thoughts. **-ito** *part. adj.* sorry, penitent, repentant; *n.m.* penitent.
**pentola** *f.* pot; saucepan; saucepanful, panful.
**penul·timo** *adj.* last but one, penultimate.
**penu·ria** *f.* scarcity, lack, penury.
**penzolare** [A1 s] *intr.* (*aux.* avere) to dangle, to hang down, to be suspended.
**penzolon-i, -e** *adv.* dangling; drooping.
**pep-e** *m.* pepper. **-aiuola** *f.* pepper-pot. **-erone** *m.* chilli.
**per** *prep.* (sometimes *contr.* with *def. art.*: pel, pello, pei, pegli, pella, pelle) through, by way of; during; *una volta — sempre*, once for all; *— Natale*, by Christmas; *— tempo*, early; *— anno*, yearly; *— ferrovia*, by rail; for; *regali — Natale*, Christmas presents; as for, in relation to; *— me non ci vado*, as for me, I am not going; on account of, owing to; for the price of; *— che cosa mi prendete ?*, what do you take me for ?; to, in order to, for the purpose of; *sto — fare . . .* I am just going to . . .; *essere — partire*, to be on the point of leaving; *— così dire*, so to speak, as it were; *— di fuori*, outside, on the outside; *— lo meno*, at least; *— lo più*, for the most; *— poco*, almost; *— di più*, in addition; *una signorina — bene*, a respectable girl; *— Bacco !*, by Jove!; *— l'appunto !*, exactly!; *— Dio !*, by God!; times, by; *4 — 3*, 4 times 3; *uno — uno*, one by one; *— uno*, *— due*, by ones, by twos; *— quanto ricco*, however rich.
**pera** *f.* pear; (fig., fam.) head; pear-switch; bell-pull.
**percentuale** *f.* percentage; *adj.* proportional per cent.
**percep-ire** [D2] *tr.* to perceive, to notice, to collect; (finan.) to draw. **-i·bile** *adj.* perceptible, discernible, noticeable.
**percett-i·bile** *adj.* perceptible. **-iva** *f.* perceptive faculty, intelligence. **-ivo** *adj.* perceptive.
**percezione** *f.* perception; discernment; (finan.) drawing, cashing, realizing.
**perchè** why ?; *n.m. indecl.* the reason why; (*follow.* by *indic.*) because, since; *— sì !*, because I say so!; (*follow.* by *subjunc.*) so that, in order that.
**per-ciò** *conj.* therefore, so; for that reason. **-ciocchè** *conj.* since, as; for.
**percome** *m. indecl.* the wherefore; *il perchè e il —*, the why and the wherefore.
**percorr-ere** [C5] *tr.* to run through; to cross, to traverse, to travel through, or over; to cover (distance); to scour. **-enza** *f.* run; way; time taken by a journey.
**percorso** *part.* of **percorrere**; *adj.* traversed, completed; *n.m.* run, stretch, distance; way, course; journey.
**percossa** *f.* blow; stroke; crash.
**percuo·tere** [C15] *tr.* to strike, to beat, to hit; to knock; to bump.
**percussione** *f.* percussion; blow, striking; *pl.* (mus.) percussion.
**per·d-ere** [B1, C3] *tr.* to lose; to miss; to ruin; to waste; *— tempo*, to waste time; *abs.* to waste (away); to leak; *intr.* (*aux.* avere) to be the loser, to lose; *rfl.* to lose oneself, to get lost; to disappear, to go astray, to be spoilt, to be ruined. **-ente** *part. adj.* losing; *n.m.* loser. **-ifiato** *adv. phr.* *a -ifiato*, at the top of one's voice. **-igiorno** *m. indecl.* idler. **-itempo** *m.* waste of time; useless work. **-izione** *f.* perdition; loss; ruin.
**per·dita** *f.* loss; leak; *— di tempo*, waste of time; *a — d'occhio*, as far as the eye can see.
**perdon-are** [A1 c] *tr.* to forgive, to pardon; to excuse; to spare. **-a·bile** *adj.* pardonable; excusable.
**perdono** *m.* pardon; forgiveness.
**perdurare** [A1] *intr.* (*aux.* avere, essere) to last, to endure; to persist; to persevere.
**perduto** *part.* of **per·dere**; *adj.* lost; missing; ruined, destroyed.
**peregrin-o** *adj.* strange, foreign; rare, precious. **-are** [A1] *intr.* (*aux.* avere) to wander abroad, to travel; to roam.
**perenne** *adj.* everlasting; perennial; perpetual; inexhaustible.
**perento·rio** *adj.* peremptory.
**perfett-o** *adj.* perfect; complete; thorough; full; *n.m.* perfection; (gramm.) perfect tense. **-amente** *adv.* perfectly; completely; fully; quite; *excl.* exactly!.
**perfezione** *f.* perfection; com-

pletion; faultlessness; excellence; finish.
**perfezion-are** [A1 c] *tr.* to perfect; to improve, to complete. **-a·bile** *adj.* perfectible; capable of improvement. **-atọre** *m.* perfectionist. **-atrice** *f.*; *adj.* *educazione -atrice*, specialized education.
**perfi·dia** *f.* perfidy, perfidiousness; treachery; wickedness.
**per·fido** *adj.* perfidious; treacherous; (colloq.) horrible.
**perfino** *adv.* even; as far as.
**perfor-are** [A1 c] *tr.* to perforate, to pierce, to drill; to punch; to bore. **-atọre** *m.* piercer, borer, drill.
**pergamẹna** *f.* parchment; greaseproof paper.
**per·gola** *f.* pergola; arbour; vine-trellis.
**Pe·ricle** *pr.n.m.* Pericles.
**pericol-are** [A1 s] *intr.* (*aux.* avere) to be in danger, to be unsafe. **-ante** *part. adj.* in danger; unsafe; tottering.
**peri·col-o** *m.* danger, peril; (fam.) *non c'è —!*, no fear! **-ọso** *adj.* dangerous; perilous; risky.
**periferi·a** *f.* periphery; boundary; outskirts.
**peri·frași** *f. indecl.* periphrasis, circumlocution.
**peri·metro** *m.* perimeter; circuit.
**perio·dico** *adj.* periodic, recurrent; periodical; *n.m.* periodical, magazine, review.
**peri·odo** *m.* period; stage; phase.
**peripate·tico** *adj.*, *n m.* peripatetic.
**peripezi·a** *f.* vicissitude; change of fortune; (theatr.) dénouement; *pl.* ups and downs.
**per-ire** [D2] *intr.* (*aux.* essere) to perish; to be destroyed; to languish. **-ituro** *adj.* perishable; transient.
**perisco·pio** *m.* periscope.
**peristi·lio** *m.* peristyle; colonnade.
**perito** *adj.* expert; skilled.
**peri·zi-a** *f.* skill; dexterity; expert's opinion, report; examination; valuation. **-are** [A4] *tr.* to appraise; to value.
**perl-a** *f.* pearl. **-a·ceo** *adj.* pearly. **-ato** *adj.* pearly; nacreous; adorned with pearls; *orzo -ato*, pearl barley.
**perlomẹno** *adv.* at least, at the very least.
**perlustrare** [A1] *tr.* to search, to look through; to scout; to patrol.
**permalọso** *adj.* irritable, touchy; peevish.
**perman-ẹre** [B25] *intr.* (*aux.* essere) to remain, to stay; to last, to persist. **-ente** *part. adj.* permanent, lasting; standing; *n.m.* (rlwy.) permanent way; *n.f.* permanent wave. **-enza** *f.* permanence, permanency; stay; residence.
**perme-are** [A5] *tr.* to permeate. **-a·bile** *adj.* permeable.
**permẹss-o** *part.* of **permẹttere**; *adj.* allowed, permitted; *permesso ?*, may I come in?; *n.m.* permission, leave; leave of absence; licence; permit.
**permẹtt-ere** [C20] *tr.* to allow, to permit; *rfl.* (*acc.* of *prn.* 'si') to allow oneself; (*dat.* of *prn.* 'si') to take the liberty (of).
**permissiọne** *f.* permission, leave, licence.
**pernice** *f.* partridge.
**pernicioso** *adj.* pernicious; malignant.
**perno** *m.* pivot; hinge; stud; support; axis.
**pernottare** [A1] *intr.* (*aux.* avere) to stay overnight, to spend the night.
**però** *conj.* however; but, yet; still, nevertheless; therefore, on that account.
**peror-are** [A1] *tr.*, *intr.* (*aux.* avere; *prep.* presso) to plead; to defend; to perorate; to harangue. **-aziọne** *f.* peroration.
**perpendi·col-o** *m.* plumb-line, plummet. **-are** *adj.* perpendicular; vertical; *n.f.* perpendicular.
**perpetrare** [A1s] *tr.* to perpetrate; to commit.
**perpe·tu-o** *adj.* perpetual; continuous; permanent; constant; for life; eternal. **-are** [A6] *tr.* to perpetuate; *rfl.* to last, to persist, to continue. **-ità** *f.* perpetuity; persistence.
**perpless-o** *adj.* perplexed; baffled. **-ità** *f.* perplexity; irresolution.
**perquiș-ire** [D2] *tr.* to search; to rummage. **-itọre** *m.* investigator; detective. **-iziọne** *f.* perquisition, search; *mandato di -izione*, search warrant.
**per·sea** *f.* avocado pear.
**persecu-tọre** *m.* persecutor. **-ziọne** *f.* persecution; pestering, importunity.
**persegu-ire** [D1] *tr.* to pursue; to follow; to continue. **-itare** [A1 s] *tr.* to persecute.
**persever-are** [A1s] *intr.* (*aux.* avere) to persevere; to persist; to insist. **-anza** *f.* perseverance.
**persiana** *f.* window-shutter; — *avvolgibile*, Venetian blind.
**persino** *adv.* even.
**persi·st-ere** [C24] *intr.* (*aux.* avere) to persist; to persevere, to insist; to continue. **-ente** *part. adj.* persistent; persevering; obstinate.
**perso**[1] *part.* of **per·dere**; *adj.* lost; wasted.
**perso**[2] *adj.* deep purple; dark.
**persọn-a** *f.* person; self; man; woman; *pl.* people; *di —*, personally; figure; body; *piccolo di —*, short in stature; (with *neg.*) nobody, no one; *non c'è —*, there is nobody there. **-ag·gio** *m.* personage; figure; character. **-ale** *adj.* personal; *n.m.* staff, personnel; figure, body **-alità** *f. indecl.* personality; personage; *pl.* well-known people. **-eggiare** [A3 c] to impersonate.
**perspic-ace** *adj.* perspicacious, discerning; shrewd. **-a·cia** *f.* perspicacity; shrewdness.
**perspi·cu-o** *adj.* clear; perspicuous. **-ità** *f.* perspicuity; clearness; lucidity.
**persuad-ẹre** [C3] *tr.* to persuade, to convince; to influence; *rfl.* to be convinced; to persuade oneself; *si -a!*, you must admit it!
**persuaș-o** *part.* of **persuadẹre**; *adj.* persuaded; convinced. **-iọne** *f.* persuasion; conviction; belief.
**pertanto** *conj.* on that account, therefore, consequently.
**per·tic-a** *f.* pole, rod, perch; (fig.) tall, thin person. **-aziọne** *f.* field measurement, surveying.
**pertinace** *adj.* pertinaceous, persevering; *battaglia —*, hard-fought battle.
**pertinente** *adj.* pertinent, pertaining; belonging.
**pertọsse** *f.* whooping-cough.
**pertu·gio** *m.* hole, aperture, opening, orifice.
**perturb-are** [A1] *tr.* to perturb, to agitate; to disturb, to trouble. **-atọre** *m.* agitator.
**Perù** *pr.n.m.* (geog.) Peru. **-viano** *adj.*, *n.m.* Peruvian.
**Peru·g-ia** *pr.n.f.* (geog.) Perugia. **-ino** *adj.* of Perugia; *n.m.* native of Perugia.
**perva·dere** [C3] *tr.* to pervade; to permeate; to penetrate.
**pervenire** [D17] *intr.* (*aux.* essere; *prep.* a) to arrive; to reach, to attain.
**pervers-o** *adj.* perverse; wicked; depraved. **-iọne** *f.* perversion. **-ità** *f.* perversity; depravity.
**pervertire** [D1] *tr.* to pervert; to lead astray; to corrupt.
**pervinca** *f.* (bot.) periwinkle.
**per·vio** *adj.* open, accessible.
**peș-are** [A1 c] *tr.* to weigh; (fig.) to ponder; to weigh up; *intr.* (*aux.* avere, essere) to weigh (more or less heavy); to be heavy; (fig.) to carry weight; to be a burden. **-a** *f.* weighing; weighing-in; weighing-machine; weighbridge. **-ante** *adj.* heavy; weighty; ponderous; tiresome; boring. **-antẹzza** *f.* heaviness; weight; dullness; tiresomeness.
**pesca**[1] *f.* peach.
**pẹsca**[2] *f.* fishing.
**pesc-are** [A2 c] *tr.* to fish (for), to catch; to fish out; (fig.) to pick up; *abs.* to go fishing; *— con la lenza*, to angle; (rowing) *— un granchio*, to catch a crab. **-a·ia** *f.* dam, weir. **-ata** *f.* catch. **-atọre** *m.* fisherman, angler; *martin -atore*, kingfisher.
**pẹsc-e** *m.* fish; *colla di —*, fish·

glue, isinglass. **~ecane** *m.* shark; dog-fish; (fig.) profiteer. **~ivẹndolo** *m.* fishmonger.

**pescher-ẹccio** *adj.* (pertaining to) fishing; *industria ~eccia*, fisheries; well-stocked with fish; *n.m.* fishing-boat trawler. **~i·a** *f.* fish-market.

**peschiera** *f.* fish-pond; fishing-ground, fishery; weir.

**pes-co** *m.* (*pl.* **~chi**) peach-tree.

**pẹso** *m.* weight; burden; load; *levare di —*, to lift up, to carry away bodily; (fig.) weight, importance; authority; burden.

**pe·ssim-o** *adj.* very bad; worst; awful. **~ịsmo** *m.* pessimism. **~ista** *m.*, *f.* pessimist.

**pẹsta** *f.* beaten track; trail; footprint.

**pest-are** [A1 c] *tr.* to pound, to crush; to tread upon; to trample on; (fig.) to harp on, to keep repeating. **~ello** *m.* pestle; rammer; tamper. **~o** *apocop. part. adj.* crushed, pounded; trampled; *carta ~a*, papier maché.

**pest-e** *f.* plague; pestilence; stench; (fig.) pest. **~i·fero** *adj.* pestiferous, pestilential; noxious. **~ilenza** *f.* pestilence, plague; stench.

**pe·talo** *m.* petal.

**petardo** *m.* mortar; grenade; Chinese cracker; fog-signal.

**petiziọne** *f.* petition; formal request; supplication.

**Petrar-ca** *pr.n.m.* Petrarch. **~cheggiare** [A3] *intr.* (*aux.* avere) to imitate Petrarch's style. **~chẹsco** *adj.* (*m.pl.* **~chẹschi**) Petrarcan.

**petrol-iera** *f.* oil-tanker. **~i·fero** *adj.* oil-bearing, rich in petroleum; *pozzo ~ifero*, oil-well.

**petro·lio** *m.* paraffin (oil), kerosene; *— grezzo*, petroleum, crude oil.

**petrọso** *adj.* stony.

**pettẹgol-a** *f.* gossip. **~are** [A1 sc] *intr.* (*aux.* avere) to gossip. **~ẹzzo** *m.* tittle-tattle.

**pe·ttin-e** *m.* comb. **~are** [A1 s] *tr.* to comb; to card (wool); *rfl.* to comb one's hair. **~atọre** *m.* hairdresser. **~atura** *f.* combing; comb-out; hair style.

**pett-o** *m.* breast; *tenere al —*, to suckle; chest; *— di camicia*, shirt-front; (fig.) heart; *stare a — con*, to stand comparison with. **~irọsso** *m.* robin. **~orale** *adj.* pectoral; *n.m.* breast-plate; pectoral. **~oruto** *adj.* proud, haughty; *andar ~oruto*, to strut.

**petulan-te** *adj.* brash, arrogant; bad-tempered; nagging. **~za** *f.* arrogance; impertinence.

**pezz-a** *f.* piece of cloth; rag; patch; length of time; *gran —*, long while. **~ato** *adj.* dappled; speckled.

**pezzent-e** *m.* beggar; ragamuffin. **~eri·a** *f.* beggary; meanness; crowd of beggars.

**pezzo** *m.* piece; portion, fragment; *fare a pezzi* to break to pieces; *tutto d'un —*, solid, rigid, unyielding; *un — grosso*, a person of importance; article.

**pezz(u)ola** *f.* handkerchief; kerchief; rag.

**piac-ẹre** [B20] *intr.* (*aux.* essere; *prep.* a) to please, to be pleasing (to); *mi ~e*, I like it; *n.m.* pleasure; delight; satisfaction, enjoyment; amusement; favour; kindness; *per —*, please. **~ente** *part. adj.* pleasing, pleasant; agreeable. **~ẹvole** *adj.* pleasant; agreeable. **~evolẹzza** *f.* charm; courtesy; agreeableness; jest, pleasantry.

**piag-a** *f.* wound; sore; scar; blow; calamity, plague; (fig.) bore, nuisance. **~are** [A2] *tr.* to ulcerate, to produce a sore in; to wound.

**pia·ggia** *f.* slope, declivity; (poet.) seashore; coast.

**piaggiare** [A3] *tr.* to flatter, to coax.

**piagn-iste·o** *m.* whining; wailing; keening; lament. **~ucolare** [A1 s] *intr.* (*aux.* avere) to whimper, to whine, to cry. **~ucolọso** *adj.* tearful; whining; mournful.

**piall-a** *f.* plane; planing machine. **~are** [A1] *tr.* to plane.

**pian-a** *f.* level ground; plain; shoal. **~are** [A1] *tr.* to smooth; to flatten; to level. **~eggiare** [A3 c] *intr.* (*aux.* avere) to be almost flat; *tr.* to level.

**pianẹta**[1] *m.* planet.

**pianẹta**[2] *f.* chasuble.

**pia·ng-ere** [C5] *intr.* (*aux.* avere) to weep, to cry, to mourn; (fig.) to drip, to ooze; *tr.* to weep over, to mourn for; to bewail; to regret; *rfl.* to grieve, to complain; *n.m.* weeping, tears, lament. **~ente** *part. adj.* weeping, in tears, tearful.

**pian-o** *adj.* level, flat; smooth; even; simple, plain; easy; *adv.* softly, gently, quietly; in a low voice; slowly; *pian piano*, very gently or slowly; *n.m.* level ground, plain; plane; *fuori —*, not in the same plane; *— prospettivo*, perspective plane; *in —*, horizontally; *in primo —*, in the foreground; (archit.) staircase-landing; floor, storey; *al primo —*, on the first floor; plan; large-scale map; design, drawing; project. **~ero·ttolo** *m.* landing (above stairs); **~ificaziọne** *f.* planning. **~ino** *adv. dim.* quite slowly; softly. **~oforte** *m.* piano; *~oforte a coda*, grand piano. **~terrẹno** *m.* ground-floor.

**piant-a** *f.* plant; shrub; *male ~e*, weeds; sole (of the foot); (archit.) ground plan; map; *— stradale*, road map; design, project. **~a·ggine** *f.* plantain. **~agiọne** *f.* (work of) planting; plantation. **~are** [A1] *tr.* to plant; *~are carote*, to tell cock and bull stories; to place, to put; to plunge; to thrust; to set up; *~are una tenda*, to pitch a tent; (colloq.) to quit, to leave in the lurch; *rfl.* to stop dead. **~atọre** *m.* planter.

**pianto**[1] *m.* tears; weeping; lamentation.

**pia·nto**[2] *part.* of **pia·ngere**; *adj.* wept, mourned; regretted.

**piantọne** *m.* cutting, shoot (for planting); (mil.) orderly; watchman; *stare di —*, to be on the alert; (archit.) mullion; (motor.) *— di guida*, steering column.

**pianura** *f.* open plain.

**piastr-a** *f.* metal-plate; thin slab; armour plate, shield. **~ella** *f.* floor tile. **~ellare** [A1] *tr.* to tile. **~ọne** *m. augm.* large metal plate; breastplate; shirt-front; plastron; flagstone.

**piatt-o** *adj.* flat; even; plain; (fig.) dull, uninspired; plate; dish, course; turntable of a record-player. **~afọrma** *f.* platform. **~a·ia** *f.* plate-rack; flat (of a sword, *etc.*).

**piazz-a** *f.* square; market-place; business; *prezzo di —*, market price; *far — pulita*, to make a clean sweep; *far —*, to make room. **~aforte** *f.* fortress, fortified town. **~ale** *m.* large square; open space in front of a building. **~are** [A1] *tr.* to place; to plant; *rfl.* to plant oneself, to be placed. **~ista** *m.* commercial traveller; canvasser.

**pic-ca** *f.* pike; regiment of pikemen; (fig.) obstinacy, pig-headedness; pique; (cards) *le ~che*, spades. **~cante** *part. adj.* sharp, pungent, piquant. **~care** [A2] *rfl.* to be offended, to be piqued; to plume oneself.

**picchẹtto** *m.* picket.

**picchi-are** [A4] *tr.* to knock; to strike, to hit; to tap; *intr.* (*aux.* avere) to knock; to persevere; *recip. rfl.* to come to blows. **~ata** *f.* knock; blow; *~ata verticale*, nose dive. **~erellare** [A1] *tr.* to tap, to drum, to rattle. **~ettare** [A1 c] *tr.* to tap repeatedly, to drum; to spot, to speckle.

**pi·cchi-o**[1] *m.* knock, blow; knocking; *adv. phr. di —*, all of a sudden. **~otto** *m.* door-knocker.

**pi·cchio**[2] *m.* woodpecker.

**piccino** *adj.* little, tiny; mean; humble; *n.m.* little one, child.

**picciọn-e** *m.* pigeon. **~a·ia** *f.* pigeon house, dove-cot; (theatr.) gallery.

**picco** *m.* peak; *a —*, vertically; *calare a —*, to sink.

**pi·ccol-o** *adj.* little, small; short; diminutive; trifling, unimportant; narrow-minded, petty; *~a cassa*, petty cash; *— borghese*,

lower middle-class; *n.m.* little boy, child; *pl.* children, little ones. **-ẹzza** *f.* smallness; pettiness; meanness, mean act; trifle.

**piccọne** *m.* pick, mattock.

**piccọso** *adj.* touchy; peevish, irritable.

**piccozza** *f.* hatchet; chopper; ice-axe.

**pi·cea** *f.* spruce.

**pido·cchi-o** *m.* louse; (fig.) upstart. **-eri·a** *f.* stinginess, meanness. **-ọso** *adj.* lousy; (fig.) miserly.

**piè** *m. indecl.* See **piede.**

**pied-e** *m.* foot; *corsa a -i,* footrace; *lungo dieci -i,* ten feet long; footing; foothold; stand; *prendere —,* to gain ground; base, pedestal; leg, foot; stalk, stem; trestle; small easel; (prosod.) metrical foot. **-istallo** *m.* pedestal.

**pieg-are** [A2] *tr.* to fold; to bend, to flex; to subdue; *intr.* (*aux.* avere) to turn, to lean; to give way; to submit; *rfl.* to become folded, creased or bent; to bow, to yield. **-a** *f.* fold, crease, pleat, wrinkle; tuck; turn; (of hair) wave; *messa in pieghe,* set. **-a·bile** *adj.* flexible, pliable, folding; collapsible. **-ata** *f.* bend, turn; fold(ing).

**pieghettare** [A1 c] *tr.* to pleat; to ruche; to smock.

**pieghẹvole** *adj.* pliant; folding; flexible; yielding, submissive; *n.m.* folder, brochure, leaflet.

**pie-go** *m.* (*pl.* **-ghi**) cover, envelope; wrapper; folder.

**Piemọnt-e** *pr.n.m.* Piedmont. **-ẹse** *adj., n.m., f.* Piedmontese.

**pien-o** *adj.* full; entire; complete; full-bodied; (fig., fam.) sick, tired, 'fed-up'; *n.m.* fullness; perfection; height; depth; full part. **-a** *f.* flood, spate; overflow; crowd; stream. **-ẹzza** *f.* fullness; abundance.

**pietà** *f.* pity, mercy; compassion; piety; *senza —,* pitiless, pitilessly; *monte di —,* pawnbroker's.

**pietanza** *f.* dish; portion, helping, plate(ful).

**pietọso** *adj.* compassionate, merciful; piteous, pitiable; pitiful, wretched; loving; pious.

**pietr-a** *f.* stone; *— preziosa,* precious stone, gem; *— per affilare,* whetstone, grindstone; *— sepolcrale,* tombstone; *— di paragone,* touchstone. **-a·ia** *f.* quarry. **-ame** *m.* dressed stone(s), for building; heap of stones.

**pietrino** *m. dim.* small stone; doorstop; *adj.* made of stone.

**pietrisco** *m.* rubble, ballast, gravel.

**Pietro** *pr.n.m.* Peter.

**pietrọso** *adj.* stony; made of stone; flinty.

**piev-e** *f.* parish church; parish. **-ano** *m.* parish priest.

**pi·ffer-o** *m.* pipe, fife, flageolet, shepherd's pipe, rustic bag-pipe; piper. **-are** [A1 s] *tr., intr.* (*aux.* avere) (mus.) to pipe. **-aro** *m.* piper.

**pigiama** *m.* pyjama suit, pyjamas.

**pigiare** [A3] *tr.* to press, to crush, to squeeze; *rfl.* to crowd, to crush.

**pigino** *m.* push-button.

**pi·gio** *m.* crushing, squeezing; crowd; crusher, rammer.

**pigiọn-e** *f.* rent. **-ale** *m., f.* lessee, tenant; lodger.

**pigli-are** [A4] *tr.* to take; to seize; to catch; to hit, to 'get'; *intr.* (*aux.* avere) to take; to set; to catch on; *rfl.* (*dat.* of *prn.* 'si') to take on oneself; *-arsela con uno,* to get angry with someone. **-amọsche** *m. indecl.* flycatcher.

**pi·glio**[1] *m.* hold; catch; *dar di — a,* to get hold of, to seize.

**pi·glio**[2] *m.* look, aspect, bearing; action.

**Pigmaliọne** *pr.n.m.* (myth.) Pygmalion.

**pigmento** *m.* colouring matter, pigment.

**pigme·o** *m.* pigmy; (fig.) nonentity.

**pigna** *f.* (bot.) cone; (archit.) cone-shaped ornament, gable.

**pignatta** *f.* pot, cooking-pot.

**pignọne** *m.* cut-water; dyke, embankment; pinion.

**pignorare** [A1] *tr.* to distrain; to pledge; to pawn.

**pigol-are** [A1 s] *intr.* (*aux.* avere) to chirp, to chirrup; to cry out; (fig.) to complain, to grumble. **-ìo** *m.* (*pl.* **-ìi**) constant chirping.

**pigr-o** *adj.* lazy, indolent; slothful; slow; dull. **-i·zia** *f.* laziness, idleness; indolence.

**pil-a** *f.* pier (of a bridge), buttress; heap, pile; basin; font. **-astro** *m.* pillar, pier, post, column. **-ọne** *m. augm.* large basin; ditch; (electr.) *-one a traliccio,* pylon.

**Pilato** *pr.n.m.* Pilate; *Ponzio —,* Pontius Pilate; (fig.) *mandare da Erode a —,* to send from pillar to post.

**pill-are** [A1] *tr.* to pound; to tread, to ram down. **-o** *m.* tamper, rammer.

**pi·llola** *f.* pill.

**pillottare** [A1] *tr.* to baste (meat).

**pilot-a** *m.* pilot. **-are** [A1] *tr.* to pilot; to drive; to ride.

**piluccare** [A2] *tr.* to pluck, to pick; to tear to bits; (fig.) to fleece, to rob.

**pimento** *m.* red pepper.

**pimpinella** *f.* pimpernel.

**pina** *f.* fir cone; pine cone.

**pinac·cia** *f.* pinnace.

**pinacoteca** *f.* picture-gallery.

**Pind-aro** *pr.n.m.* Pindar. **-a·rico** *adj.* Pindaric.

**pinẹt-a** *f.*, **-o** *m.* pine forest, pine wood.

**pi·ngere** [C5] see **dipi·ngere.**

**pingu-e** *adj.* fat; corpulent; rich (in). **-e·dine** *f.* obesity, corpulence, fatness; fertility, richness.

**pinguino** *m.* penguin.

**pinna·colo** *m.* pinnacle, battlement.

**pin-o** *m.* fir; pine. **-ẹto** *m.* pine forest.

**pino·cchio** *m.* pine-seed.

**pinz-a** *f.* pliers; pincers; *— per fili,* wire nippers. **-are** [A1] *tr.* to sting; to prick. **-ẹtte** *f.pl.* tweezers.

**pìo**[1] *m.* (*pl.* **pìi**) chirping.

**pi·o**[2] *adj.* (*m.pl.* **pii**) dutiful, obedient; pious; compassionate.

**pio·gg-ia** *f.* rain; *una — leggera,* drizzle; *scroscio di —,* shower; *— di lagrime,* flood of tears. **-erella** *f. dim.* fine rain, drizzle; light shower.

**piolo** *m.* stick; paling; stump.

**piọmb-o** *m.* lead; shot, bullet; plummet; *fuori di —,* out of perpendicular; (dressm.) hang, fall; *cadere di —,* to fall violently. **-a·ggine** *f.* (miner.) graphite, black lead. **-are** [A1 c] *tr.* to plumb; to affix a leaden seal to; *-are un dente,* to stop a tooth; *intr.* (*aux.* essere) to fall heavily; to plunge; to pounce; to sink like lead. **-ato** *part. adj.* leaded; leaden; *mazza -ata,* cosh. **-atura** *f.* soldering. **-ino** *m.* plummet, plumb-line; *adj.* lead-coloured.

**pioniere** *m.* pioneer; sapper.

**piọpp-o** *m.* poplar; *dormire come un —,* to sleep like a log. **-a·ia** *f.* poplar grove.

**piot-a** *f.* sole of the foot; sod, turf; clump of earth. **-are** [A1] *tr.* to turf.

**piovano** *adj.* relating to rain; *acqua piovana,* rain-water.

**pio·v-ere** [C27] *impers.* (*aux.* essere, avere) to rain; to drip; *— a dirotto,* to pour with rain; *— a catinelle,* to rain cats and dogs; (of a roof) to slope; *tr.* to rain, to pour down; to let fall; to shed. **-igginare** [A1 s] *intr.* (*aux.* essere, avere) to drizzle. **-igginọso** *adj.* rainy, drizzling. **-ọso** *adj.* rainy, wet.

**pio·vra** *f.* octopus.

**pip-a** *f.* pipe; tobacco-pipe. **-are** [A1] *intr.* (*aux.* avere) to smoke a pipe.

**pipistrello** *m.* bat.

**pi·ppolo** *m.* pip, grain, stone; pimple, small excrescence.

**pira** *f.* pyre, funeral pile.

**pira·mide** *f.* pyramid.

**pirata** *m.* pirate; *— della strada* road-hog.

**pira·tico** *adj.* piratic(al).

**Pirene·i** *pr.n.m.pl.* (geog.) Pyrenees.

**Pire·o** *pr.n.m.* (geog.) Piraeus.

**piro-mani·aco** *adj., n.m.* pyromaniac. **-manzi·a** *f.* pyromancy, divination by fire. **-te·cnica** *f.* pyrotechnics.

**piroẹtta** *f.* pirouette.

**pirọne** *m.* peg; plug; cleat, belaying pin.
**piro·scafo** *m.* steamship, steamer.
**piscato·rio** *adj.* relating to fishing and fishermen; piscatory.
**pi·sci-a** *f.* piss, urine. **-are** [A3] *intr.* (*aux.* avere) to pee, to pass water; (fig.) to spout, to spurt. **-acane** *m.* dandelion.
**piscicoltura** *f.* fish-breeding.
**piscina** *f.* fish-pond; swimming-pool; watering-trough.
**pisell-o** *m.* pea; *verde —*, pea-green. **-ata** *f.* dish of peas; pease-pudding.
**pi·ṣol-o** *m.* doze, nap, snooze. **-are** [A1 s] *intr.* (*aux.* avere) to nod, to doze, to snooze. **-ino** *m. dim.* little nap, 'forty winks'.
**pisp-igliare** [A4] *intr.* (*aux.* avere) to whisper. **-i·glio** *m.* whisper.
**pi·sside** *f.* ciborium; pyx.
**pista** *f.* race-track, ice-rink, (toboggan) run; (aeron.) runway, strip; foot-prints; trail.
**pistagna** *f.* coat-collar; facings; flounce.
**pistola**[1] *f.* pistol; *— a spruzzo*, spray gun.
**pistola**[2] *f.* pistole.
**pistọne** *m.* piston; ram, plunger.
**Pita·gora** *pr.n.m.* Pythagoras.
**pitago·rico,** Pythagorean; *tavola pitagorica*, multiplication table.
**pitoc-co** *m.* (*pl.* **-chi**) beggar; stingy person, miser. **-cheri·a** *f.* beggary; meanness.
**pit-ọne** *m.* python. **-onẹssa** *f.* pythoness; fortune-teller, clairvoyante.
**pitt-ọre** *m.* painter; artist. **-orẹsco** *adj.* (*m.pl.* **-orẹschi**) relating to painting, picturesque, painterly. **-o·rico** *adj.* pictorial; graphic. **-ura** *f.* painting; picture.
**più** *adv.* more; *— bello*, finer, more beautiful; *il — costoso*, the most expensive; *sempre —*, more and more; *non —*, no longer, no more; *mai —*, never again; (math.) plus; *dieci volte —*, ten times as much; *adj. indecl.* more; larger, greater; *n.m. indecl.* the greater part; *per lo —*, for the most part; *pl. i —*, the majority, most people.
**pium-a** *f.* feather; plumage; down pillow; *pl.* (poet.) pinions, wings. **-a·ccio** *m.* feather pillow; cushion. **-a·ggio** *m.* plumage. **-are** [A1] *tr.* to pluck. **-ino** *m.* down; eiderdown quilt. **-ọso** *adj.* downy, feathery.
**pi(u)olo** *m.* peg, post; rung of a ladder; paling.
**piuttosto** *adv.* sooner; rather; instead.
**piva** *f.* pipe, bagpipe.
**piviale** *m.* (liturg.) cope, pluvial.
**piviere** *m.* plover.
**pizza** *f.* savoury dish made of pastry, tomato purée, anchovies and olives.
**pizzare** [A1] *tr., intr.* (*aux.* avere) to sting.
**pizzi-ca·gnolo** *m.* pork-butcher. **-cheri·a** *f.* pork-butcher's shop; delicatessen.
**pizzic-are** [A2 s] *tr.* to pinch, to nip; to sting, to bite, to peck; to prick, to stimulate; *intr.* (*aux.* avere) to itch; to tingle; to smart. **-ata** *f.* sting; prick; pinch. **-ato** *part. adj.* (mus.) pizzicato, plucked.
**pi·zzi-co** *m.* pinching, pinch; (fig.) tingling; small amount, smattering. **-cọre** *m.* sting; tingling; itch; smart; keen desire. **-cotto** *m.* pinch; nip; flick (with a whip).
**pizzo** *m.* mountain peak; imperial, goatee (beard); lace.
**placare** [A2] *tr.* to appease, to soothe, to placate; to calm; *rfl.* to be appeased; to grow calm.
**placca** *f.* metal plate, plaque; metal badge.
**pla·cido** *adj.* calm, peaceful, tranquil; serene; mild, gentle.
**pla·cito** *m.* judgement, decree; approval.
**plaga**[1] *f.* expanse of sky, region, district.
**plaga**[2] *f.* affliction, plague.
**pla·gi-o** *m.* plagiarism; plagiary. **-a·rio** *adj.* plagiaristic; *n.m.* plagiarist.
**planare** [A1] *intr.* (*aux.* avere) (aeron.) to glide.
**planeta·rio** *adj.* planetary; *n.m.* planetarium, orrery.
**plaṣm-a** *m.* mould; terracotta figure; plasma. **-are** [A1] *tr.* to mould, to shape; to model.
**pla·stic-a** *f.* plastic art, modelling; casting; plastic material. **-o** *adj.* plastic; *n.m.* modeller; model; plastic, synthetic material.
**plastro·n** *m. indecl.* large made-up necktie; plastron, shirt front.
**pla·tano** *m.* plane-tree.
**plat-e·a** *f.* foundations; platform supported by piles; bed of concrete; (theatr.) pit, spectators in the pit. **-eale** *adj.* low, vulgar; commonplace.
**pla·tino** *m.* platinum.
**Plat-one** *pr.n.m.* Plato. **-o·nico** *adj.* of Plato; Platonic; *n.m.* Platonist.
**plauṣi·bile** *adj.* plausible.
**pla·uṣo** *m.* approbation; praise.
**Pla·ut-o** *pr.n.m.* Plautus. **-ino** *adj.* Plautine.
**pleb-e** *f.* common people; lower classes. **-a·glia** *f.* mob, rabble. **-eiṣmo** *m.* vulgarism; vulgar action. **-e·o** *adj.* vulgar, plebeian; coarse; *n.m.* plebeian. **-iscito** *m.* plebiscite.
**ple·iade** *f.* pleiad; (astron.) *le Pleiadi*, the Pleiades.
**plena·rio** *adj.* plenary.
**plenil-unare** *adj.* of the full moon. **-u·nio** *f.* full moon.
**plenipotenz-a** *f.* plenary power(s). **-ia·rio** *adj.*, *n.m.* plenipotentiary.
**plenitu·dine** *f.* plenitude.
**ple·tora** *f.* plethora, superabundance.
**pli-co** *m.* (*pl.* **-chi**) cover, envelope; folder; (postal) packet.
**Pli·nio** *pr.n.m.* Pliny.
**plinto** *m.* plinth.
**plotọne** *m.* (mil.) platoon.
**plu·mbeo** *adj.* lead-coloured; livid; (fig.) heavy, dull; boring.
**plural-e** *adj.* plural. **-ità** *f.* plurality; majority.
**plu·rimo** *adj.* multiple; *voto —*, plural vote.
**Plutarco** *pr.n.m.* Plutarch.
**Pluto** *pr.n.m.* (myth.) Pluto; Plutus.
**pluto·cr-ate** *m.* plutocrat. **-azi·a** *f.* plutocracy.
**pluviale** *adj.* (of) rain; pluvial; *acqua —*, rainwater; *n.m.* (bldg.) drainpipe.
**pneuma·tic-o** *adj.* pneumatic; *macchina -a*, air-pump; *trapano —*, pneumatic drill; *n.m.* (pneumatic) tyre.
**Po** *pr.n.m.* (geog.) Po.
**po-co** *adj.* (*m.pl.* **-chi**) little, small; *pl.* few; scarce, insufficient; *indef. prn.* little; *contentarsi del —*, to be satisfied with little; *un —*, a little, a certain amount, some; *non —*, not a little; *adv.* little; not much; a little while; *a — a —*, little by little; *fra —*, before long, shortly; *ad ogni —*, every now and then; *— manca che* (*non*), almost, nearly, all but; *per — che* (foll. by *subj.*), however little; *adv. phr. assaggia un po' questo caffè!*, just try this coffee! **-chẹzza** *f.* smallness; narrowness; scantiness, scarcity; lack, insufficiency.
**podagra** *f.* gout.
**podẹr-e** *m.* farm; agricultural holding. **-ale** *adj.* relating to a farm; *casa -ale*, farmhouse.
**poderọso** *adj.* powerful, mighty.
**podest-à** *m. indecl.* head of a commune; mayor. **-eri·a** *f.* town-hall; office of podestà.
**poem-a** *m.* (*pl.* **-i**) epic poem.
**poeṣi·a** *f.* poetry; poem.
**poet-a** *m.* poet; (fig.) dreamer. **-are** [A1] *intr.* (*aux.* avere) to write poetry, to be a poet.
**poe·tic-a** *f.* poetics; poetic theory; art of poetry. **-o** *adj.* poetic(al); suitable for treatment in poetry.
**poggi-are** [A3] *tr.* to rest, to lean, to place; *rfl.* to lean. **-acapo** *m. indecl.* head-rest, antimacassar.
**po·ggio** *m.* hill, hillock, knoll; eminence; parapet; balcony.
**poi** *adv.* then, next; subsequently, later; afterwards; *da ora in —*, from now on; *o prima o —*, sooner or later; *n.m.* the future; the time to come; *il senno di —*, hindsight.
**poichẹ̀** *conj.* since, as, for; when, after.

**polac-co** *adj.* (*m.pl.* **-chi**) Polish; *n.m.* Pole; Polish.

**polare** *adj.* polar, pole; *circolo —*, Arctic Circle.

**pole·mic-a** *f.* polemics; controversy. **-o** *adj.* polemic(al), controversial; *n.m.* controversialist.

**polenta** *f.* (cul.) a kind of pudding made chiefly of maize flour.

**policroma·tico** *adj.* polychromatic.

**poli·gam-o** *adj.* polygamous; *n.m.* polygamist. **-i·a** *f.* polygamy.

**poliglotto** *adj., n.m.* polyglot.

**poli·gono** *m.* polygon.

**poli·graf-o** *m.* polygraph; hectograph; copying machine. **-are** [A1 s] *tr.* to copy, to duplicate.

**polisil·labo** *adj.* polysyllabic; *n.m.* polysyllable.

**politec·nico** *adj.* polytechnic; *n.m.* polytechnic, technical school.

**polite-iṣmo** *m.* polytheism. **-ista** *m.* polytheist.

**politẹzza** *f.* high finish, polish; refinement.

**poli·tic-a** *f.* politics; policy; political theory. **-ante** *m.* (derog.) politician. **-o** *adj.* political; politic; cautious; crafty; *n.m.* politician; politic person; schemer.

**polit·tico** *m.* (art.) polyptych.

**polizi-a** *f.* police; *Commissariato di —*, Police Station; policing, public order; *agente di —*, policeman. **-ẹsco** *adj.* (*m.pl.* **-ẹschi**) relating to the police; *romanzo -esco*, detective novel. **-otto** *m.* policeman; detective.

**po·lizza** *f.* voucher; card, ticket; voting-paper; receipt form; note, bill; lottery ticket; *— di assicurazione*, insurance policy.

**pọlla** *f.* spring (of water).

**poll-a·io** *m.* fowl-house, hencoop; poultry-yard; poultry. **-ame** *m.* poultry. **-anca** *f.* young turkey-hen; pullet. **-astra** *f.* pullet. **-astro** *m.* cockerel.

**poll-eri·a** *f.* poultry market; poulterer's shop; poultry. **-icoltura** *f.* poultry-farming.

**pol·lice** *m.* thumb; big toe; inch.

**pol·line** *m.* pollen.

**pollino** *m.* swamp; bog; quicksand; floating island.

**pollivẹndolo** *m.* poulterer.

**pọllo** *m.* chicken, barndoor fowl; *allevamento di -i*, poultry-farm; *— d'India*, turkey.

**pollọne** *m.* (bot.) sucker.

**Polluce** *pr.n.m.* (myth.) Pollux; *Castore e —*, Castor and Pollux.

**polmọn-e** *m.* lung. **-ite** *f.* pneumonia.

**polo**[1] *m.* pole; *— nord, — artico*, North Pole; *— sud, — antartico*, South Pole.

**polo**[2] *m.* (sport) polo.

**Polo·nia** *pr.n.f.* Poland.

**pọlp-a** *f.* pulp; flesh; pith. **-ac·cio** *m.* calf (of the leg); base of the thumb. **-ẹtta** *f.* rissole, meat-ball. **-uto** *adj.* fleshy, plump; *gambe -ute*, fat legs; *terreno -uto*, rich land.

**pọlpo** *m.* octopus.

**pọlso** *m.* pulse; *tastare il — a uno*, to feel someone's pulse; (fig.) strength, nerve, energy; skill. **-ino** *m. dim.* cuff; wristband

**polti·glia** *f.* gruel, mush; slush.

**poltrire** [D2] *intr.* (*aux.* avere) to be lazy; to live in idleness; to wallow.

**poltrọn-a** *f.* lazy woman; armchair, easy-chair; *— a sdraio*, chaise-longue; (theatr.) stall. **-ag·gine** *f.* laziness. **-e** *m.* slacker; poltroon; *adj.* lazy, cowardly. **-eri·a** *f.* laziness, indolence; cowardice.

**pọlver-e** *f.* dust; powder; *— da fucile*, gun-powder; **-iera** *f.* powder magazine. **-ina** *f. dim.* (medicinal) powder; pollen; dusting.

**poma·rio** *m.* orchard; nursery for fruit trees.

**pomata** *f.* pomade; ointment salve.

**pomer-idiano** *adj.* (of the) afternoon; *alle 5 -idiane*, at 5 p.m. **-ig·gio** *m.* afternoon.

**pọmice** *f.* pumice.

**pom-o** *m.* apple; *vino di —*, cider; knob; orb; rose (of watering-can). **-ẹto** *m.* (apple-) orchard; fruit-garden. **-odoro** *m.* tomato.

**pọmpa**[1] *f.* pomp; ostentation, display; *pompe funebri*, funerals.

**pọmp-a**[2] *f.* pump; *— da incendio*, fire-engine. **-are** [A1 c] *tr.* to pump (up).

**pompeggiare** [A3 c] *intr.* (*aux.* avere) to make a display; to strike the eye; *rfl.* to deck oneself out; to show off.

**Pomp-e·i** *pr.n.f.* (geog.) Pompeii. **-eiano** *adj., n.m.* Pompeian.

**Pompe·o** *pr.n.m.* Pompey.

**pompelmo** *m.* grape-fruit.

**pompiẹre** *m.* fireman; *i pompieri*, the fire-brigade.

**pompọs-o** *adj.* stately, ostentatious, magnificent; pompous. **-ità** *f.* pomp; magnificence; pomposity.

**pọnce** *m.* punch (drink).

**ponder-are** [A1 c] *tr.* to ponder, to think over, to weigh; to meditate upon; *intr.* (*aux.* avere) to meditate; to muse. **-ọso** *adj.* ponderous; laborious.

**ponente** *m.* west; west wind.

**pọnt-e** *m.* bridge; scaffolding; (naut.) deck; *— di comando*, bridge; (cards) *giuoco del —*, bridge. **-ecanale** *m.* aqueduct. **-ẹggio** *m.* scaffolding. **-icello** *m. dim.* small bridge, footbridge.

**ponte·fice** *m.* pontifex; the Supreme Pontiff, the Pope.

**pontific-ale** *adj.* pontifical. **-are** [A2 s] *intr.* (*aux.* avere) (eccl.; fig.) to pontificate.

**pontile** *m.* landing-stage, boatwharf.

**Pontine** *pr.n.f.pl.* Pontine (marshes).

**pontọne** *m.* lighter, pontoon; hulk.

**ponzare** [A1 c] *intr.* (*aux.* avere) to strain, to make an effort.

**Po·nzio** *pr.n.m.* Pontius; *— Pilato*, Pontius Pilate.

**popolar-e**[1] *adj.* popular; common, prevalent; of the people; *n.m., f.* man, or woman, of the people. **-ẹsco** *adj.* (*m.pl.* **-ẹschi**) common, vulgar, plebeian.

**popolare**[2] [A1 s] *tr.* to populate; to people; to colonize; to crowd; *rfl.* to become populated; to become crowded.

**popolaziọne** *f.* population; populace, people; race.

**po·pol-o** *m.* people; nation; tribe; crowd, multitude, populace. **-ano** *adj.* of the people, democratic; *n.m.* man of the people; workman, artisan; commoner. **-ọso** *adj.* populous; abundant, numerous.

**popọne** *m.* melon.

**pọpp-a**[1] breast; *dare la — a*, to suckle. **-aiola** *f.* feeding bottle. **-ante** *part., n.m., f.* suckling. **-are** [A1c] *intr.* (*aux.* avere) to suck. **-ata** *f.* feed. **-atọio** *m.* rubber teat; dummy; feeding-bottle.

**pọpp-a**[2] *f.* stern; poop. **-iero** *adj.* aft, astern.

**porcellana** *f.* porcelain; china.

**por-co** *m.* pig, swine; pork; boar; *-spino*, porcupine; *adj.* (fam.) filthy, disgusting; *-a miseria!*, hell! **-cheri·a** *f.* dirt, filth; dirty trick; obscenity, indecency. **-cile** *m.* pigsty; wild boar's den. **-cino** *adj.* porcine.

**po·rfido** *m.* porphyry.

**po·rgere** [C4] *tr.* to hold out, to offer; to proffer; to hand; *— orecchio*, to lend ear.

**pornogr-afi·a** *f.* pornography. **-a·fico** *adj.* pornographic.

**por-o** *m.* pore. **-ọso** *adj.* porous.

**po·rpor-a** *f.* purple; crimson; (fig.) cardinalship. **-ato** *adj.* wearing purple *n.m.* (eccl.) cardinal. **-ino** *adj. dim.* (of lips, etc.) rosy; reddish; red.

**pọrre** [B21] *tr.* to put, to set, to place; to lay; *— ad effetto*, to make effective, to carry out; *rfl.* to place oneself, to set oneself; *mi pongo a sedere*, I'll take a seat.

**porr-o** *m.* leek; wart. **-ọso** *adj.* warty.

**port-a**[1] *f.* door; doorway; gate; gateway; main gate of a city; exit; *— di soccorso*, emergency exit.

**porta**[2]- *pref.* carrier; holder.

**port-ae·rei** *m. indecl.* aircraft-carrier. **-baga·gli** *m. indecl.* luggage-rack; porter. **-cẹnere**

*m. indecl.* ash-tray. **-feriti** *m. indecl.* stretcher-bearer. **-fo·glio** *m. indecl.* note-case, wallet; portfolio. **-le·ttere** *m. indecl.* postman; *f.* postwoman. **-monete** *m. indecl.* purse. **-ritratti** *m. indecl.* photograph frame. **-riviste** *m. indecl.* newspaper rack. **-sapone** *m. indecl.* soap-dish. **-sigarette** *m. indecl.* cigarette-case; cigarette-holder. **-si·gari** *m. indecl.* cigar-case. **-(u)ovo** *m.* (*pl.* **-uova**) egg-cup. **-voce** *m. indecl.* speaking-tube; megaphone; (fig.) mouthpiece, spokesman.

**porta-finestra** *f.* French window.

**port-are** [A1] *tr.* to take; to bring; to carry; to wear; to have on; to bear; to suffer, to feel; — *amore a*, to love; to cause, to bring about; to produce; to bring forward, to bring to light, to adduce; to lead, to conduct; — *bene*, to bring good luck; *rfl.* (*acc.* of *prn.* 'si') to go, to betake oneself; to behave; to put oneself forward; (*dat.* of *prn.* 'si') *-arsi le mani al volto*, to put one's hands to one's face. **-amento** *m.* carriage, bearing; gait; conduct, deportment. **-ata** *f.* reach, range, compass, scope, span; capacity; importance, significance; purport; *di prima -ata*, of the first importance. **-a·tile** *adj.* portable. **-ato** *part. adj.* carried, borne; (of clothes) worn, second-hand; *-ato a*, inclined to; nominated, put forward; *n.m.* outcome, result, issue.

**portent-o** *m.* prodigy, miracle. **-oso** *adj.* prodigious, marvellous.

**po·rtico** *m.* portico porch; *pl.* colonnade, arcade.

**port-iera** *f.* door-curtain; (motor.) door; portress; concierge. **-iere, -ina·io** *m.* porter, doorkeeper.

**porto**[1] *m.* carriage, transport; carrying, wearing.

**porto**[2] *part.* of **po·rgere.**

**porto**[3] *m.* harbour; port; dockyard; anchorage.

**porto**[4] *m.* port, port wine.

**Porto-gallo** *pr.n.m.* (geog.) Portugal. **-ghese** *adj.*, *n.m.*, *f.* Portuguese.

**portone** *m. augm.* main door; main gateway.

**portuale** *adj.* of a port, appertaining to a harbour.

**porzione** *f.* portion; part, share; helping; ration.

**pos-a** *f.* laying, placing; pause, rest; (gramm.) accent, stress; attitude, posture, pose. **-are** [A1] *tr.* to place, to put; to lay; to set; to lay aside; *intr.* (*aux.* avere) to rest, to stand; to settle (down); to pose, to sit (for a portrait); to lie, to repose; *rfl.* to alight, to settle; to rest; to sit; to perch; *adv. phr. piglia e -a*, with frequent interruptions. **-ata** *f.* cover (knife, fork and spoon); sediment. **-ato** *part. adj.* resting; at rest; seated; sedate; staid. **-atoio** *m.* perch.

**po·scia** *adv.* (poet.) then, afterwards.

**poscritto** *m.* postscript.

**positiv-o** *adj.* positive; real, certain; practical, matter of fact; **-ista** *m.*, *f.*, *adj.* positivist; realist.

**positura** *f.* position, place, site; attitude, posture, pose.

**posizione** *f.* situation, position.

**pos-porre** [B21] *tr.* to place after; to postpone, to defer. **-posizione** *f.* deferment; postponement, adjournment; placing after; (gramm.) postposition.

**poss-a** *f.* (poet.) power, strength, vigour. **-anza** *f.* (poet.) might, dominion, puissance; strength.

**possed-ere** [B28] *tr.* to possess, to own, to have; to hold; to obsess; *abs.* to have property. **-imento** *m.* possession; estate, property.

**possente** *adj.* vigorous; powerful, mighty; potent.

**possess-ione** *f.* possession; ownership; property, estate. **-ivo** *adj.* possessive.

**possess-o** *m.* (leg.) possession; occupation. — *di una lingua*, mastery of a language; *pl.* property, estate. **-ore** *m.* possessor; owner; proprietor.

**possi·bil-e** *adj.* possible; feasible. **-mente** *adv.* possibly; if possible.

**possidente** *adj.* owning (property); wealthy; *n.m.*, *f.* landowner; person of property.

**post-a** *f.* post, post-office; mail; *spese di* —, postage; place; spot; rendezvous, meeting-place; placing, putting; (cards) stake; *a bella* —, on purpose, deliberately. **-ale** *adj.* postal; *ufficio -ale*, post-office; *cassetta -ale*, letter-box. **-are** [A1] *tr.* to place, to post; to station; *rfl.* to place onself, to take up one's position.

**postbe·llico** *adj.* post-war.

**posteggio** *m.* stand; cab-rank; parking-place.

**postelegra·f-ico** *adj.* postal and telegraphic. **-o·nico** *adj.* postal, telegraphic and telephonic.

**po·ster-i** *m.pl.* descendants, posterity. **-iore** *adj.* hind(er), back; posterior; subsequent. **-ità** *f.* posterity, descendants, issue; later times.

**posti·ccio** *adj.* artificial; false, sham.

**posticipare** [A1 s] *tr.* to postpone, to defer.

**postill-a** *f.* marginal note; gloss. **-are** [A1] *tr.* to annotate.

**postino** *m.* postman.

**posto**[1] *part.* of **porre**; *adj.* placed, put; set; supposed.

**posto**[2] *m.* place; spot; position, site; seat; place; room; space; post, appointment; situation; station; — *di primo soccorso*, first-aid post.

**postul-are** [A1 s] *tr.* to demand, to claim; to postulate. **-ante** *m.* petitioner. **-ato** *part. adj.*; *n.m.* postulate; principle.

**po·stumo** *adj.* posthumous; *il libro fu pubblicato* —, the book was published posthumously.

**postura** *f.* place; position; situation; posture.

**pota·bile** *adj.* fit for drinking; drinkable; *acqua* —, drinking-water.

**pota·ggio** *m.* soup, pottage.

**potare** [A1] *tr.* to prune; to lop.

**poten-te** *adj.* powerful, forcible, mighty; influential. **-tato** *m.* potentate, power. **-za** *f.* power; might; strength, force. **-ziale** *adj.* potential. **-zialità** *f.* potentiality; power; capacity.

**pot-ere** [B22] *intr.* (*aux.* avere; essere). to be able; *non posso alzarlo*, I can't lift it; *non potè parlare*, he was not allowed to speak; *si può ?*, may I come in ?; *può darsi*, it may be; *l'esempio può più delle parole*, actions speak louder than words.

**potere** *m.* power; authority; sway, influence; ability.

**potestà** *f.* power; authority.

**po·ver-o** *adj.* poor; needy; humble; scanty; *stile* —, plain style; *n.m.* poor man; pauper; beggar. **-ello** *m.* poor man; *il -ello d'Assisi*, St. Francis. **-etto** *m.* poor fellow; *-etto !*, poor thing! **-tà** *f.* poverty; want; scarcity; meanness.

**pozione** *f.* potion, decoction.

**pozz-a** *f.* pool, puddle. **-a·nghera** *f.* muddy pool; puddle; duck-pond.

**pozzo** *m.* well; shaft; (fig.) fount, fountain.

**Praga** *pr.n.f.* (geog.) Prague.

**pramma·tica** *f.* custom; customary manner; prescribed method.

**pranz-o** *m.* (N.Ital.) dinner; (Tusc. and S.Ital.) lunch; midday dinner. **-are** [A1] *intr.* (*aux.* avere) to dine; to have dinner; to have lunch.

**prassi** *f. indecl.* practice; routine procedure.

**Prassi·tele** *pr.n.m.* Praxiteles.

**prataiuolo** *adj.* of the fields or meadows, field.

**pra·tica** *f.* practice; experience; practical knowledge; familiarity; intercourse, intrigue; business; matter; affair; *pl.* practical arrangements, means or steps.

**pratic-are** [A2 s] *tr.* to practise, to put into practice; to carry out; to exercise; to frequent, to associate with; to make, to open, to execute; — *un buco*, to bore a hole. **-a·bile** *adj.* practicable; feasible; possible; practical; convenient; accessible. **-ante** *part. adj.* practising; *n.m.*, *f.*

apprentice; church-goer, practising Christian.
**pra·tic-o** *adj.* practical; experienced; efficient; *n.m.* practitioner; expert. **-ità** *f.* practicality; convenience.
**prat-o** *m.* meadow; *regina dei —i,* meadow-sweet. **-eri·a** *f.* grassland; prairie. **-olina** *f.* daisy. **-olino** *m.* mushroom.
**preaccennato** *adj.* aforesaid.
**prea·mbolo** *m.* preface, preamble.
**preannu·nzi-o** *m.* announcement; prediction. **-are** [A4] *tr.* to forecast; to give notice of; to announce beforehand.
**preavvișare** [A1] *tr.* to inform in advance; to give early notice to.
**preca·rio** *adj.* precarious; uncertain.
**precauzione** *f.* precaution; care, caution.
**prece·d-ere** [B1] *tr.* to precede; to come before; to go before; to lead; *intr.* (*aux.* essere) to come first. **-ente** *part. adj.* preceding; former, previous; *n.m.* precedent. **-enza** *f.* precedence.
**precessione** *f.* precession; advance, lead.
**precett-o** *m.* precept; maxim; order; — *di polizia,* police warning. **-are** [A1] *tr.* to enjoin, to order; to summon. **-ivo** *adj.* preceptive, didactic.
**preci·dere** [C1] *tr.* to cut short, to cut off.
**precipit-are** [A1 s] *tr.* to cast down headlong; to throw down; to hasten; to precipitate; *intr.* (*aux.* essere) to fall headlong, to crash; to drop, to fall; to hurry; to come to a head; (fig.) to be ruined; *rfl.* to rush, to run precipitately; to throw oneself down. **-ato** *part. adj.* rash, hasty, precipitate. **-azione** *f.* precipitation. **-oso** *adj.* hasty, precipitate, hurried; precipitous.
**precipi·zio** *m.* precipice; headlong fall; ruin; *parlare a —,* to speak hastily.
**precis-o** *adj.* precise, exact; punctual; accurate; strict; absolute. **-are** [A1] *tr.* to state precisely; to specify; to tell exactly.
**preclu·dere** *tr.* [C3] to preclude; to block, to bar.
**precoc-e** *adj.* precocious; early; premature. **-ità** *f.* precocity.
**precognizione** *f.* foreknowledge.
**preconcetto** *adj.* preconceived; *n.m.* preconception, prejudice.
**preconizzare** [A1] *tr.* to announce solemnly; to predict.
**preconosc-ere** [B9] *tr.* to have foreknowledge of; to foresee. **-enza** *f.* foreknowledge; prescience.
**precorrere** [C5] *tr.* to anticipate; to forestall; to outrun; *intr.* (*aux.* essere) to hasten in advance.
**precursore** *m.* forerunner, harbinger; *adj.* precursory, premonitory.
**pred-a** *f.* quarry; prey; booty. **-are** [A1] *tr.* to plunder, to pillage, to sack; to prey upon. **-ato·rio** *adj.* predatory.
**predella** *f.* foot-rest, footboard; carriage-step; platform, dais.
**predestin-are** [A1] *tr.* to predestine; to destine. **-azione** *f.* predestination.
**predetto** *part.* of **predire**; *adj.* aforesaid; foretold.
**pre·dic-a** *f.* sermon; (fam.) lecture. **-are** [A2 s] *tr., intr.* (*aux.* avere) to preach, to proclaim; to praise. **-ato** *part.* proclaimed; praised; *n.m.* (gramm.) predicate. **-atore** *m.* preacher; eulogist. **-azione** *f.* preaching; sermon.
**predil-etto** *part.* of **predili·gere**; *adj.* favourite, dearest; *n.m.* favourite, darling; pet. **-i·gere** [C13] *tr.* to prefer, to have a special liking for.
**predire** [B10] *tr.* to foretell, to predict, to forecast.
**predis-porre** [B21] *tr.* to arrange in advance; to predispose; — *a,* to induce; *rfl.* to prepare oneself. **-posizione** *f.* predisposition; partiality.
**predizione** *f.* prediction, prophecy.
**predominare** [A1 s] *intr.* (*aux.* avere) to predominate, to prevail; to be dominant.
**predomi·nio** *m.* predominance, supremacy; prevalence.
**predone** *m.* robber; plunderer; — *del mare,* pirate.
**prefabbricare** [A2 s] *tr.* to prefabricate.
**prefa·z-io** *m.* Preface (in the Mass). **-ione** *f.* preface, introduction.
**prefer-ire** [D2] *tr.* to prefer, to like better. **-enza** *f.* preference; favouritism. **-enziale** *adj.* preferential. **-i·bile** *adj.* preferable.
**prefett-o** *m.* prefect; — *di polizia,* police superintendent. **-i·zio** *adj.* prefect's, prefectoral. **-ura** *f.* prefecture.
**prefi·ggere** [C12] *tr.* to fix beforehand; to prefix; *rfl.* (*dat.* of *prn.* 'si') to intend, to set before oneself.
**prefisso** *part.* of **prefi·ggere**; *adj.* prefixed; *n.m.* (gramm.) prefix.
**preg-are** [A2] *tr.* to ask, to pray, to beg, to request; to invite; *farsi —,* to stand on ceremony, to wait to be asked; *-o,* please, don't mention it. — *malanno su,* to curse.
**pregevol-e** *adj.* valuable, good; precious. **-ezza** *f.* value, goodness, worth.
**preghiera** *f.* prayer; request, entreaty.
**pregi-are** [A3 c] *tr.* to esteem, to value, to appreciate; to esteem, to praise. **-ato** *part. adj.* esteemed.
**pre·gio** *m.* esteem; value, merit, excellence.
**pregiud-icare** [A2 s] *tr.* to prejudge; to prejudice; to harm; *rfl.* to harm oneself; to compromise oneself. **-icato** *part. adj.* prejudged, settled. **-i·zio** *m.* prejudice; superstition; harm, detriment.
**pregnante** *adj.* pregnant; *n.f.* pregnant woman, expectant mother.
**pregn-o** *adj.* pregnant; full, filled, saturated; impregnated; rich (in), teeming (with).
**pregustare** [A1] *tr.* to have a foretaste of; to look forward to.
**preisto·ria** *f.* prehistory.
**prelato** *m.* prelate.
**prelevare** [A1] *tr.* to withdraw; to take out; to deduct; to take, to capture; to call for.
**prelibato** *adj.* choice, exquisite.
**preliminare** *adj.* preliminary; introductory; *progetto —,* first draft; *n.m.* element, principle.
**prelu·dere** [C3] *intr.* (*aux.* avere; *prep.* a) to be a prelude (to), to lead (to).
**prelu·dio** *m.* prelude; (fig.) introduction, portent.
**prematuro** *adj.* premature.
**premeditare** [A1 s] *tr.* to premeditate; to design, to plan.
**pre·mere** [B1] *tr.* to press; to weigh upon; to bear heavily upon; to crush; (fig.) to repress; to restrain; *intr.* (*aux.* avere) to exert pressure; *impers. mi -e di sapere,* I want to know.
**premessa** *f.* premiss; previous statement.
**premettere** [C20] *tr.* to say first, to state in advance.
**premi-are** [A4] *tr.* to reward; to give a prize to. **-ando** *adj.* deserving a prize; *n.m.* prizewinner. **-ato** *part. adj. numeri -ati,* (lottery) winning numbers.
**preminen-te** *adj.* pre-eminent. **-za** *f.* pre-eminence, superiority.
**pre·mio** *m.* prize; reward; award; premium; bonus.
**premoni-tore** *adj.* premonitory; *n.m.* one who forewarns. **-zione** *f.* premonition; warning.
**premorire** [D12] *intr.* (*aux.* essere) to die previously; — *alla moglie,* to predecease one's wife.
**premunire** [D2] *tr.* to fortify beforehand; to forearm; *rfl.* to be forearmed, to protect oneself.
**premur-a** *f.* urgency; solicitude; care, attention; courtesy; kindness; eagerness. **-oso** *adj.* attentive, kind, thoughtful; careful; solicitous; eager; urgent.
**prena·scere** [B18] *intr.* (*aux.* essere; *prep.* a) to be born previously; — *a,* to be older than.

**pre·nd~ere** [C1] *tr.* to take; to lay hold of; to pick up; to capture, to seize; to take possession of; to surprise, to attack; *~erle* (*busse, percosse*) to be hit, to take a beating; to take away; to steal; to remove; to occupy; to take on; to engage; to assume; to use; to need, to take; — *tempo*, to take one's time; to move towards, to make for; — *la destra*, to turn to the right; — *le mosse*, to start moving; to begin; *prese a dire*, he began to say; to take over, to adopt, to borrow; to partake of; to have; to catch (a disease); to acquire (a vice); — *fuoco*, to catch fire; to receive, to get; to charge; to cost; — *le misure di*, to measure; — *con le buone*, to treat well; — *meraviglia*, to be amazed; — *stanza*, to establish oneself; — *mano*, to get one's hand in; — *di mire*, to aim at; *intr.* (*aux.* avere) to set, to congeal, to curdle; to take root; — *a sinistra*, to turn to the left; to come upon, to happen (to); *rfl.* (*acc.* of *prn.* 'si') to be taken; to be understood; (*dat.* of *prn.* 'si') to take for oneself, to allow oneself; *~ersela comoda*, to take it easy; *recip. rfl. ~ersi a pugni*, to come to blows. **~itọre** *m.* receiver; payee.

**prenọme** *m.* Christian name, first name.

**prenot~are** [A1] *tr.* to book, to engage; to bespeak; *rfl.* (*dat.* of *prn.* 'si') to put one's name down for. **~ato** *part. adj.* reserved; engaged.

**prenoziọne** *f.* foreknowledge, prescience.

**pre·nsile** *adj.* prehensile.

**preoccup~are** [A1 s] *tr.* to preoccupy, to make anxious, to trouble; *rfl.* to be preoccupied; to be anxious. **~ato** *part. adj.* preoccupied; worried, anxious. **~aziọne** *f.* preoccupation; worry, anxiety.

**preordin~are** [A1 sc] *tr.* to order, to establish beforehand; to prearrange; to predetermine. **~aziọne** *f.* predetermination; predestination.

**prepar~are** [A1] *tr.* to prepare; to make ready; — *la tavola*, to lay the table; *rfl.* to prepare, to get ready. **~ativo** *m.* preparation; *pl.* arrangements.

**preponder~are** [A1 sc] *intr.* (*aux.* avere) to weigh more heavily; (fig.) to preponderate, to prevail. **~anza** *f.* preponderance; predominance; superiority.

**pre~pọrre** [B21] *tr.* to place in front; to prefix; to prefer, to put at the head of. **~posiziọne** *f.* placing before, prefixing; (gramm.) preposition.

**prepoten~te** *adj.* overbearing, arrogant; tyrannical; insolent; *n.m.* overbearing person, bully. **~za** *f.* arrogance; insolence.

**prerogativa** *f.* prerogative, privilege.

**prẹs~a** *f.* capture, seizure, taking; catching; grasp, grip, hold; pinch; *venire alle ~e con*, to come to grips with; pretext, occasion; knob, handle; — *d'acqua*, fire-hydrant, water-cock; (of cement, etc.) setting; (electr.) point; pinch (of salt, snuff, etc.), mouthful, bite, bit, tot; dose.

**preṣa·g~io** *m.* presage; presentiment; foreboding; omen. **~ire** [D2] *tr.*, *intr.* (*aux.* avere) to predict, to foretell, to presage.

**preṣa~go** *adj.* (*m.pl.* **~ghi**) foreboding, presaging; *essere — di*, to have a presentiment of.

**preṣbit~erato** *m.* priesthood. **~e·rio** *m.* priest's house, presbytery.

**preṣbitiṣmo** *m.* long-sightedness, presbyopia.

**prescẹgliere** [B27] *tr.* to select, to choose, to prefer.

**prescienza** *f.* prescience; presentiment.

**presci·ndere** [C21] *intr.* (*aux.* avere; *prep.* da) to leave out of consideration, to put aside.

**prescr~i·vere** [C12] *tr.* to prescribe; to establish, to ordain; to fix. **~itto** *part. adj.* prescribed; fixed; obligatory.

**preṣent~are** [A1] *tr.* to present, to offer; to introduce; to produce, to show; *rfl.* to introduce oneself; to present oneself; to appear; to occur, to arise; to offer (itself, oneself). **~atọre** *m.* presenter, introducer; compère. **~aziọne** *f.* presentation; introduction.

**preṣent~e** *adj.* present; *nel — mese*, in the current month; *n.m.* present, present time; *al —*, now; (gramm.) present tense; person present; *i ~i*, those present. **~emẹnte** *adv.* at present, now.

**presentire** [D1] *tr.* to have a presentiment of, to anticipate; to foresee; to presage.

**preṣenz~a** *f.* presence; appearance, aspect; *di —*, personally; attendance; — *di spirito*, presence of mind. **~iare** [A4] *intr.* (*aux.* avere; *prep.* a) to attend, to be present (at).

**prese·pio** *m.* manger, crib.

**preserv~are** [A1] *tr.* to preserve, to keep; to guard against. **~aziọne** *f.* preservation.

**pre·side** *m.* principal, headmaster, dean.

**presiden~te** *m.* president, chairman; — *del consiglio*, prime minister. **~za** *f.* presidency; chairmanship.

**presi·dio** *m.* garrison.

**presie·d~ere** [B28] *intr.* (*aux.* avere; *prep.* a) to preside (over); to be chairman; to be at the head, to be in charge; *tr.* — *un'assemblea*, to preside at a meeting.

**prẹso** *part.* of **pre·ndere**; *adj.* taken, caught, captured; occupied; imprisoned; *partito —*, prejudice.

**pressa** *f.* press; pressure; crowd, crowding, throng.

**press~are** [A1] *tr.* (techn.) to press; (fig.) to press, to urge. **~acarte** *m. indecl.* paper-weight.

**pressiọne** *f.* pressure.

**press~o** *adj.* near; *essere — a*, to be about to; *prep.* (*usu. follow.* by 'a') near, by, beside, with; in company with; in business with; among, in the opinion of; *adv.* near, near-by, near at hand; *adv. phr.* — *che*, almost; *press'a poco*, very nearly; *a un di —*, nearly, about; *n.m.pl.* neighbourhood, vicinity.

**prestabil~ire** [D2] *tr.* to lay down, to establish in advance. **~ito** *part. adj.* pre-arranged; appointed; fixed.

**prest~are** [A1] *tr.* to lend; to give, to render; to attribute; *rfl.* (*prep.* a) to lend oneself to; to countenance; to give way (to); to lay oneself open (to). **~ante** *part. adj.* excellent, eminent; outstanding; of noble presence. **~anza** *f.* excellence, eminence; dignity. **~aziọne** *f.* lending; service; tax; performance; bearing.

**presti·gi~o** *m.* sleight of hand, conjuring, trick; prestige; influence; authority. **~are** [A4] *tr.* to deceive by conjuring; to delude. **~atọre** *m.* conjurer, juggler; impostor.

**pre·stito** *m.* loan; *dare a —*, to lend.

**presto** *adj.* ready, prompt, quick; *adv.* early; soon; quickly; *più —*, earlier, sooner; *si fa — a dire!*, that's easily said!

**pre~ṣu·mere** [C8] *intr.* (*aux.* avere) to presume; to think, to believe. **~ṣuntivo** *adj.* presumptive; foreseeable, calculable. **~ṣunto** *part. adj.* presumed, estimated; supposed; apparent; presumptive. **~ṣuntuoso** *adj.* presumptuous, arrogant. **~ṣunziọne** *f.* presumption, arrogance; conjecture.

**presup~pọrre** [B21] to presuppose, to take for granted. **~pọsto** *part. adj.* supposed, conjectured; *n.m.* presupposition.

**pret~e** *m.* priest; clergyman; **~ẹsco** *adj.* (*m.pl.* **~ẹschi**) (derog.) priestly.

**prete·nd~ere** [C1] *tr.* to claim; to profess; to pretend; to assert; to contend; to want, to exact; *intr.* (*aux.* avere; *prep.* a) to lay claim (to), to pretend (to).

**-ente** *part. adj., n.m.* claimant; applicant; suitor.
**preterito** *adj.* past, gone-by; *n.m.* (gramm.) preterite.
**preternaturale** *adj.* preternatural.
**pretẹsa** *f.* pretension, claim; pretence; pretentiousness.
**pretesto** *m.* pretext, excuse; pretence; plea.
**pretto** *adj.* mere; pure, real; good, correct.
**preval-ẹre** [B34] *intr.* (*aux.* avere, essere) to prevail; *rfl.* (*prep.* di) to avail oneself, to take advantage (of). **-ente** *part. adj.* prevalent. **-enza** *f.* prevalence; preponderance supremacy; majority.
**prevaric-are** [A2s] *intr.* (*aux.* avere) to betray one's trust; to act dishonourably. **-aziọne** *f.* breach of trust; embezzlement.
**prevedẹre** [B35] *tr.* to foresee; to expect; to forecast, to allow for.
**preven-ire** [D17] *tr.* to precede; to forestall, to anticipate; to meet; to provide against; to forewarn; to inform; to prevent; *recip. rfl. cercar di -irsi*, to see who can do something first. **-ziọne** *f.* prevention; prejudice; bias; suspicion; precautionary measure; warning.
**preventiv-o** *adj.* preventive; anticipated, estimated; *n.m.* estimate; budget. **-are** [A1] *tr.* to estimate; to budget.
**providen-te** *adj.* foreseeing, provident; prudent. **-za** *f.* foresight; prudence.
**pre·vio** *adj.* previous.
**previṣiọne** *f.* prevision, expectation; forecast.
**preziọs-o** *adj.* precious; costly, valuable; affected. **-ità** *f.* preciousness, costliness; preciosity.
**prezzare** [A1] *tr.* to value, to assess.
**prezzẹmolo** *m.* parsley.
**prezzo** *m.* price; cost; fare; terms; fee; rate; charge; value, worth.
**pri·a** *adv.* (poet.) before.
**Pri·amo** *pr.n.m.* Priam.
**prigiọn-e** *f.* prison; gaol, jail; imprisonment, detention. **-i·a** *f.* imprisonment; detention; captivity. **-iero** *m.* prisoner.
**prima**[1] *adv.* previously, before, beforehand, first; further back; rather, preferably, sooner; *prep. phr. — di*, before; *conj. — che*, before.
**prima**[2] *f.* the first one; the first thing; the first time; first-class; first form; (theatr.) first night; *adv. phr. alla —*, at once; *sulle prime*, in the beginning.
**prima·rio** *adj.* primary; principal; paramount.
**primati·ccio** *adj.* early; premature.
**primat-o** *m.* pre-eminence, primacy; supremacy; *tenere il —*, to be supreme. **-ista** *m., f.* record-holder.
**primaver-a** *f.* spring, springtime; *equinozio di —*, vernal equinox. **-ile** *adj.* vernal, spring.
**primeggiare** [A3c] *intr.* (*aux.* avere) to excel, to be pre-eminent; to take the lead.
**primitiv-o** *adj.* primitive, primal, original; primeval; early; simple, credulous; *n.m.* primitive man. **-ità** *f.* primitiveness.
**primi·zia** *f.* (*usu. pl.*) first fruits, early fruit or vegetables; first shoot; latest news; novelty.
**primo** *adj.* first; chief, foremost, principal; old, ancient; prime; former; staple; prime; *materie prime*, staple commodities, or raw materials; *prn.* first, former; *adv.* first of all, firstly.
**primoge·nit-o** *adj.* firstborn, eldest; *n.m.* firstborn, eldest son. **-ura** *f.* primogeniture; birthright.
**primo·rdi-o** *m.* beginning, origin; outset. **-ale** *adj.* primordial, primeval; original.
**pri·mula** *f.* primrose, primula.
**principale** *adj.* principal; chief; *n.m.* manager; master, chief, 'boss'; main point.
**pri·ncip-e** *m.* prince; *adj.* chief, principal, first. **-ato** *m.* principality; sovereignty; princedom. **-ẹsco** *adj.* (*m.pl.* **-ẹschi**) princely. **-essa** *f.* princess. **-otto** *m.* princeling.
**principi-are** [A4] *tr., intr.* (*aux.* essere, avere) to begin, to commence, to start. **-ante** *part. adj.* beginning; inexpert; *n.m., f.* beginner.
**princi·p-io** *m.* (*pl.* **-ii**) beginning; *da —*, from the beginning; *dare — a*, to begin; origin; principle.
**priọra** *f.* prioress.
**priọr-e** *m.* prior; parish priest. **-ato** *m.* priorship; magistracy.
**priorità** *f.* priority, precedence.
**priṣm-a** *m.* (*pl.* **-i**) prism. **-a·tico** *adj.* prismatic.
**pri·stino** *adj.* former; ancient; *n.m.* former state.
**priv-are** [A1] *tr.* (*prep.* di) to deprive (of); to relieve (of); *rfl.* to deny oneself. **-aziọne** *f.* privation; suffering; loss, deprivation.
**privativa** *f.* monopoly, patent; sole right.
**privato** *adj.* private; personal; particular; *n.m.* individual; private person; *adv. vivere —*, to live in retirement.
**privile·gi-o** *m.* privilege; monopoly; lien. **-are** [A4] *tr.* to privilege, to bestow a privilege on. **-ato** *part. adj.* privileged, favoured; gifted.
**privo**[1] *adj.* (*prep.* di) devoid (of); destitute (of); lacking (in).
**privo**[2] *apocop. part.* of **privare**; deprived; bereft.
**pro**[1] *m.* advantage; benefit; profit; *a — nostro*, to our advantage; *buon — !*, good health!
**pro**[2] *prep.* for, on behalf of; *n.m. il — e il contro*, the pros and cons.
**proba·bil-e** *adj.* probable; likely; *n.m.* probability. **-ità** *f.* probability, likelihood.
**probativo** *adj.* proving; tending to prove; testing.
**probaziọne** *f.* probation.
**problem-a** *m.* (*pl.* **-i**) problem; question. **-a·tico** *adj.* problematic(al); uncertain.
**prob-o** *adj.* upright; honest; just. **-ità** *f.* probity; uprightness, honesty.
**procacciare** [A3] *tr.* to procure; to get by effort; to seek, to try; *rfl.* (*dat.* of *prn* 'si') to get, to procure; *procacciarsi noie*, to get into trouble.
**procaccino** *m.* factotum; messenger.
**procace** *adj.* impudent; provoking.
**proce·d-ere** [B1] *intr.* (*aux.* essere) to proceed; to go on; to act; (*aux.* avere) to begin, to undertake, to start proceedings; *n.m.* conduct, behaviour. **-imẹnto** *m.* proceeding(s); course; conduct; process.
**procella** *f.* storm, tempest; (fig.) calamity.
**processiọne** *f.* procession; succession.
**process-o** *m.* process; course; (leg.) action; suit; trial. **-are** [A1] *tr.* to prosecute.
**procinto** *adv. phr. in — di*, on the point of, about to.
**proclam-a** *m.* announcement; proclamation; ban. **-aziọne** *f.* proclamation; declaration.
**procliv-e** *adj.* inclined, disposed; prone. **-ità** *f.* proclivity.
**procrastinare** [A1] *tr.* to postpone, to put off; to defer; *intr.* (*aux.* avere) to procrastinate; to temporize.
**procre-are** [A6] *tr.* to procreate, to generate; to beget; to give birth to. **-aziọne** *f.* procreation.
**procur-are** [A1] *tr.* to procure, to get; to cause; *intr.* (*aux.* avere; *prep.* 'di') to endeavour (to); to succeed (in); *rfl.* (*dat.* of *prn.* 'si') to procure, to get. **-a** *f.* power of attorney; office of attorney; proxy. **-atọre** *m.* attorney; holder of Power of Attorney.
**proda** *f.* foreshore; edge, border, side.
**prod-e**[1] *adj.* brave, valiant; bold; *n.m.* brave man; hero. **-ẹzza** *f.* gallantry, bravery, deed of valour.
**prode**[2] *m.* (poet.) good, benefit.
**prodig-alità** *f.* prodigality; lavishness. **-are** [A2s] *tr.* to

lavish; to squander; to pour out; *rfl.* to devote oneself; to do one's very best.

**prodi·gi-o** *m.* prodigy; marvel; miracle. **-ọso** *adj.* prodigious, miraculous; wonderful.

**pro·di-go** *adj.* (*m.pl.* **-ghi**) prodigal, lavish; liberal.

**prodito·rio** *adj.* treacherous.

**prodọtto**[1] *part.* of **produrre**; *adj.* produced; created.

**prodọtto**[2] *m.* product; produce.

**pro-durre** [B2] *tr.* to produce, to bring forth, to bear; to yield; to show; to cause; *rfl.* to be produced; to happen; to occur; **-duttività** *f.* productivity. **-duttivo** *adj.* productive; yielding; to appear. **-duttọre** *m.* producer; manufacturer. **-duzi-ọne** *f.* production; manufacture; output; yield.

**proe·mi-o** *m.* foreword, preface, introduction. **-ale** *adj.* introductory.

**profan-are** [A1] *tr.* to profane, to desecrate; to pollute. **-atọre** *m.* profaner. **-aziọne** *f.* profanation.

**profan-o** *adj.* profane, secular; irreverent; ignorant, unskilled. **-ità** *f.* profanity; sacrilege; profane word or action; ignorance.

**pro(f)ferire** [D2] *tr.* to utter, to pronounce; to proffer; to offer; *rfl.* to offer.

**professare** [A1] *tr.* to profess; to show; to practise; to teach; *abs.* to teach, to be a professor; *rfl.* to profess (to be), to declare oneself.

**professiọn-e** *f.* profession; declaration; calling. **-ista** *m., f.* professional.

**professo** *adj.* professed; *n.m.* professed monk.

**professọr-e** *m.* professor; schoolmaster; teacher. **-ale** *adj.* professional; pedantic.

**profet-a** *m., f.* prophet. **-are** [A1] *tr., intr.* (*aux.* avere) to prophesy, to predict. **-ẹssa** *f.* prophetess; sibyl.

**profe·tico** *adj.* prophetic.

**profetiẓẓare** [A1] *tr., intr.* (*aux.* avere) to predict, to prophesy, to foretell.

**profezi·a** *f.* prophecy, prediction.

**proficiente** *adj.* making progress, advancing.

**profi·cuo** *adj.* profitable; useful; of benefit.

**profil-o** *m.* profile; outline, contour; section; (fig.) sketch, short study. **-are** [A1] *tr.* to draw in profile (outline); to edge, to frame, to outline; *rfl.* to appear in profile; to stand out. **-atura** *f.* outlining, outline, profile; edging, border, hem.

**profitt-o** *m.* profit; *far — negli studi*, to make progress in one's studies; proceeds, income. **-are** [A1] *intr.* (*aux.* avere) to profit, to gain an advantage; to make good progress; to be useful. **-atọre** *m.* profiteer. **-ẹvole** *adj.* profitable.

**proflu·vio** *m.* flow; flood, torrent; plenty.

**profondare** [A1 c] *intr.* (*aux.* essere) to sink, to go down; *rfl.* to sink; *tr.* to sink; to deepen; to plant or sink deeply.

**profọndere** [C2] *tr.* to lavish, to pour out freely; to squander *rfl.* to be lavish, to be profuse.

**profọnd-o** *adj.* deep; profound; *poco —*, shallow; *n.m.* depth(s); deep; *adv.* deeply, deep. **-ità** *f.* depth; profundity.

**pro·fu-go** *adj., n.m.* (*pl.* **-ghi**) refugee; fugitive.

**profum-o** *m.* scent, fragrance; perfume. **-are** [A1] *tr.* to scent, to perfume; *rfl.* to use scent. **-ato** *part. adj.* sweet-smelling, fragrant; scented. **-eri·a** *f.* perfumery. **-iere** *m.* perfumer.

**profuṣ-o** *part.* of **profọndere**; *adj.* profuse; lavish. **-iọne** *f.* profusion; abundance; squandering.

**proge·n-ie** *f.* progeny, offspring, issue, descendants; race, stock. **-itọre** *m.* ancestor, progenitor.

**progett-o** *m.* plan, project; scheme; proposal; intention. **-are** [A1] *tr.* to plan, to design; to project.

**programm-a** *m.* (*pl.* **-i**) programme; syllabus; prospectus; (pol.) platform, policy; manifesto. **-are** [A1] *tr.* to put in a programme; (theatr.) to put on, to stage; (techn.) to programme (a computor). **-azione** *f.* (techn.) 'programme'.

**progredire** [D2] *intr.* (*aux.* avere, essere) to progress, to advance; to develop; to proceed, to go forward; *n.m.* progress, advance.

**progress-iọne** *f.* progression, advance, progress. **-ivo** *adj.* progressive; *tassa -iva*, graduated tax.

**progress-o** *m.* progress; *fare dei -i*, to progress; advance.

**proib-ire** [D2] *tr.* to forbid, to prohibit; to hinder, to bar, to impede. **-iziọne** *f.* prohibition. **-iziọniṣmo** *m.* prohibitionism.

**proiettare** [A1] *tr.* to project; to cast, to throw; *rfl.* to project, to protrude; to fall; *intr.* (*aux.* avere) to project, to jut out.

**proie·ttile** *m.* projectile, missile, bullet.

**proiett-o** *adj.* projected, thrown; *n.m.* (mil.) projectile; (archit.) projection. **-ọre** *m.* projector; searchlight; head-lamp; floodlight.

**proiezịọne** *f.* projection; casting, falling (of a shadow).

**prole** *f.* issue, offspring, progeny.

**proleta·r-io** *adj., n.m.* proletarian. **-iato** *m.* proletariat.

**proli·f-ero** *adj.* prolific. **-erare** [A1 s] *intr.* (*aux.* avere) to proliferate. **-eraziọne** *f.* proliferation.

**proli·fic-o** *adj.* prolific, fertile. **-are** [A2 s] *intr.* (*aux.* avere) to proliferate.

**prolisso** *adj.* prolix; long-winded.

**pro·lo-go** *m.* (*pl.* **-ghi**) prologue, foreword; hors d'oeuvres.

**prolung-are** [A2] *tr.* to prolong, to extend, to lengthen; to defer, to postpone; to delay; *rfl.* to continue, to extend. **-a** *f.* extension, extension-piece; transport vehicle. **-amẹnto** *m.* prolongation, extension, continuation.

**proluṣiọne** *f.* inaugural lecture.

**promemo·ria** *f. indecl.* memorandum, note.

**promẹssa** *f.* promise; undertaking; promising pupil, person who shows talent.

**promẹss-o** *part.* of **promẹttere**; *adj.* promised; betrothed; *n.m.* fiancé. **-a** *f.* fiancée.

**Prome·teo** *pr.n.m.* (myth.) Prometheus.

**promẹttere** [C20] *tr., abs.* to promise; to show promise; to give hope; *rfl.* (*acc.* of *prn.* 'si') to pledge oneself, to become engaged; (*dat.* of *prn.* 'si') to promise oneself (something).

**prominen-te** *adj.* prominent, jutting out. **-za** *f.* prominence, protuberance; knoll, rise, embankment.

**promi·scu-o** *adj.* mixed; *matrimonio —*, mixed marriage; promiscuous; *attore —*, versatile actor, character actor. **-ità** *f.* promiscuity; promiscuousness.

**promisso·rio** *adj.* promissory.

**promonto·rio** *m.* promontory, headland; cape.

**promosso** *part.* of **promuo·vere**; *adj.* promoted; moved up (in school), successful (in an examination).

**promo-tọre** *m.* promoter, organizer. **-ziọne** *f.* promotion; furtherance; advancement.

**promulg-are** *tr.* to promulgate, to publish. **-aziọne** *f.* promulgation.

**promuo·vere** [C15] *tr.* to promote; to induce; to stimulate, to encourage, to favour.

**pronipọte** *m.* grand-nephew; *f.* grand-niece; great-grandchild; *m.pl.* descendants.

**prono** *adj.* prone; prostrate; bowed down; (fig.) prone, inclined, disposed.

**prono·stic-o** *m.* prediction, forecast; (med.) prognosis. **-are** [A2s] *tr.* to prognosticate; to predict, to foretell, to forecast.

**prọnt-o** *adj.* ready; quick, alert; prompt; immediate. **-ẹzza** *f.* readiness; quickness; ease; animation; promptitude.

**prontua·rio** *m.* handbook, reference book.
**pronu·nzi-a** *f.* pronunciation; accent, way of speaking; voice; pronouncement. **-are** [A4] *tr.* to pronounce; to utter; *rfl.* to pronounce oneself, to give one's opinion.
**propagand-a** *f.* propaganda; advertising. **-are** [A1] *tr.* to advertise; to publicize. **-ista** *m., f.* propagandist; agent.
**propag-are** [A2] *tr.* to propagate; to spread; *rfl.* to spread. **-azione** *f.* propagation.
**propagginare** [A1 s] *tr.* (bot.) to propagate by layering; (fig.) to disseminate.
**propa·ggine** *f.* layer (shoot or twig of a plant); (fig.) offshoot; issue, offspring.
**propalare** [A1] *tr.* to publish abroad; to divulge, to spread.
**propellente** *adj., n.m.* propellent.
**prope·ndere** [B1] *intr.* (*aux.* avere; *prep.* a) to incline (towards); to lean.
**propensione** *f.* propensity, tendency; inclination, liking.
**propenso** *adj.* inclined; disposed.
**Prope·rzio** *pr.n.m.* Propertius.
**propinare** [A1] *tr.* to give (to drink), to administer.
**propinquo** *adj.* neighbouring, near; related, akin.
**propi·zi-o** *adj.* propitious; favourable. **-are** [A4] *tr.* to propitiate, to placate. **-azione** *f.* propitiation.
**propon-ente** *part. adj.* propounding; intending; *n.m.* proposer. **-imento** *m.* purpose; resolution; intention.
**proporre** [B21] *tr.* to propose; to propound; to put forward; — *un premio*, to offer a prize; *rfl.* (*dat.* of *prn.* 'si') to purpose, to intend; to resolve.
**proporzion-e** *f.* proportion. **-ale** *adj.* proportional. **-are** [A1 c] *tr.* to proportion; to make to fit; to put into proper relation.
**propo·sito** *m.* purpose, intention; aim, object; design; subject; *a* —, to the point, suitably, appropriately; by the way; *di — a*, on purpose; *uomo di* —, reliable man.
**proposizione** *f.* proposition; sentence, clause; argument.
**proposta** *f.* proposal; offer; — *di legge*, bill.
**propriet-à** *f. indecl.* property; — *fondiaria* landed property; ownership; propriety; characteristic. **-a·rio** *m.* proprietor, owner.
**pro·prio** *adj.* proper; (one's) own; peculiar, characteristic; appropriate; right, exact; neat, clean; *n.m.* quality, property, characteristic; one's own; *rispondere in* —, to reply personally; *adv.* quite, just; exactly; really, indeed.
**propugn-are** [A5] *tr.* to fight for, to support; to plead for, to advocate. **-atore** *m.* champion, supporter, defender.
**prora** *f.* (naut.) bows, stem, forecastle.
**prorog-are** [A2 s] *tr.* (leg.) to adjourn; to extend; to put off; to delay. **-ativo** *adj.* dilatory. **-azione** *f.* extension, deferment; prorogation.
**prorompere** [C26] *intr.* (*aux.* avere) to break out, to burst out.
**pros-a** *f.* prose; (theatr.) drama, legitimate theatre. **-a·ico** *adj.* prosaic; commonplace, matter-of-fact. **-a·stico** *adj.* written in prose; prosaic. **-atore** *m.* prose-writer.
**proscio·gliere** [B26] *tr.* to release.
**prosciugare** [A2] *tr.* to drain; to render arid; *intr.* (*aux.* essere), *rfl.* to dry, to become dry.
**prosciutto** *m.* ham; bacon.
**proscr-i·vere** [C26] *tr.* to proscribe; to outlaw; to banish. **-itto** *part. adj.* banished; *n.m.* exile; outlaw.
**proseguire** [D1] *tr.* to continue, to go on with; to pursue; *intr.* (*aux.* avere) to continue, to proceed; (on letters) *far* —, to forward.
**prose·lito** *m.* proselyte, convert.
**prosodi·a** *f.* prosody; scansion.
**prosopope·a** *f.* prosopopoeia; (fig.) affectation; affected gravity.
**pro·sper-o** *adj.* favourable, propitious, lucky; prosperous, flourishing. **-are** [A1 s] *intr.* (*aux.* avere) to thrive, to flourish; to be prosperous. **-ità** *f.* prosperity; wealth. **-oso** *adj.* healthy, vigorous, lusty; thriving, flourishing.
**prospe·ttico** *adj.* perspective.
**prospettiva** *f.* perspective; (fig.) prospect; view.
**prospett-o** *m.* front elevation, façade; prospect, view; *di prospetto*, facing; prospectus; table, summary. **-are** [A1] *tr.* to put before (one), to present; *rfl.* to present an appearance; to look, to seem.
**prospiciente** *adj.* looking out, commanding a view (over), facing.
**pro·ssim-o** *adj.* very near, at hand; nearest, next; *n.m.* neighbour; fellow creature; people. **-amente** *adv.* very soon, presently. **-ità** *f.* proximity, nearness, vicinity.
**prostitu-ire** [D2] *tr.* to prostitute; *rfl.* to prostitute oneself; to sell oneself. **-ta** *f.* prostitute; whore.
**prostr-are** [A1] *tr.* to prostrate; to dispirit, to cast down; to exhaust; *abs.* to fatigue, to be fatiguing; *rfl.* to prostrate oneself. **-azione** *f.* prostration; depression; exhaustion.
**protagonist-a** *m., f.* (*m.pl.* **-i**, *f.pl.* **-e**) protagonist; (theatr., cinem.) leading role, leading actor.
**prote·gg-ere** [C12] *tr.* to protect, to shelter; to defend, to support. **-itore** *m.* protector, patron.
**prote·ndere** [C1] *tr.* to stretch (out), to extend, to hold out; *rfl.* to stretch oneself; to lean out.
**Pro·te-o** *pr.n.m.* (myth.) Proteus; (fig.) ever-changing person. **-ismo** *m.* variability, versatility.
**prote·rv-ia** *f.* arrogance; stubbornness. **-o** *adj.* arrogant; stubborn.
**protest-a** *f.* protest; remonstrance; protestation, declaration. **-ante** *part. adj.* protesting; *n.m., f.* Protestant. **-are** [A1] *intr.* (*aux.* avere) to protest; *tr.* to make a protestation of; *-are la guerra*, to declare war.
**protett-o** *part.* of **prote·ggere**; *adj.* protected, sheltered; defended; patronized; *n.m.* favourite, protégé. **-ore** *m.* protector, patron.
**protezion-e** *f.* protection; patronage, favour. **-ismo** *m.* protectionism. **-ista** *m.* protectionist.
**proto**[1] *pref.* proto-.
**proto**[2] *m.* foreman in a printing-press; overseer; printer.
**protocoll-o** *m.* protocol; register; file; *essere a* —, to be on record. **-are** [A1] *tr.* to file; to register; to record; *adj.* relating to protocol.
**protoplasma** *m.* protoplasm.
**proto·tipo** *m.* prototype; model.
**protrarre** [B33] *tr.* to protract, to prolong; to draw out, to postpone.
**protuber-are** [A1 s] *intr.* (*aux.* essere) to bulge, to swell; to be protuberant. **-ante** *part. adj.* protuberant. **-anza** *f.* protuberance; prominence; swelling.
**prova** *f.* proof; test; trying-on; examination; ordeal; evidence; token, pledge; *a — di fuoco*, fire-proof; (theatr.) rehearsal.
**prov-are** [A1] *tr.* to prove, to demonstrate; to test; to rehearse; to try; to taste; to feel; to experience; *intr.* (*aux.* avere) (agric.; bot.) — *bene*, to take root, to become established; *rfl.* (*acc.* of *prn.* 'si') to try, to endeavour; (*dat.* of *prn.* 'si') to try, to try on. **-a·bile** *adj.* demonstrable, capable of proof.
**proven-ire** [D17] *intr.* (*aux.* essere; *prep.* da) to derive, to come (from); to originate (in). **-ienza** *f.* origin, place of origin; provenance; source.
**provento** *m.* proceeds; income; *proventi illeciti*, ill-gotten gains.
**Provenz-a** *pr.n.f.* Provence. **-ale** *adj.* Provençal; *n.m., f.* Provençal

(person); *m.* Provençal (language).

**prove·rbi-o** *m.* proverb; saying. **-ale** *adj.* proverbial; notorious.

**provętto** *adj.* advanced; experienced; skilful.

**provi·nci-a** *f.* province; district. **-ale** *adj.* provincial; *strada -ale*, secondary road.

**provoc-are** [A2 s] *tr.* to provoke; to rouse; to excite; to inspire. **-ante** *part. adj.* provoking; seductive. **-ato·rio** *adj.* (*m.pl.* **-atorii**) provocative; challenging. **-azịone** *f.* provocation; challenge.

**provved-ęre** [B35] *tr.* to provide, to supply; to furnish; to lay in a stock of; to furnish (with); *intr.* (*aux.* avere; *prep.* a) to make provision, to provide. **-imęnto** *m.* provision; precaution; *pl.* measures. **-itọre** *m.* superintendent, supervisor; steward; manager; *-itore agli studi*, Director of Education.

**provviden-te** *adj.* provident; far-seeing, prudent. **-za** *f.* providence; prudence; *la -za divina*, Divine Providence.

**pro·vvido** *adj.* provident; thrifty; beneficent.

**provvigiọne** *f.* commission; *pl.* supplies.

**provviṣiọn-e** *f.* provision; victuals. **-are** [A1 c] *tr.* to provide, to furnish (with salary, food, etc.); to pay.

**provviṣo·rio** *adj.* provisional; temporary.

**provvist-a** *f.* supply. **-o** *part.* of **provvedęre**; *adj.* (*prep.* di) provided (for, with); supplied; prepared in mind, informed.

**pro-zi·o** *m.* great-uncle. **-zi·a** *f.* great-aunt.

**prua** *f.* bows; *da poppa a —*, from stem to stern.

**pruden-te** *adj.* prudent, cautious; wise; timid. **-za** *f.* prudence; common-sense; caution.

**pru·dere** [B1 def.] *intr.* (no compound tenses) to itch, to prick.

**prugn-o** *m.* plum-tree. **-a** *f.* plum.

**pru·gnolo** *m.* sloe, blackthorn.

**prun-a·io** *m.*, **-a·ia** *f.* thornbush; thicket; (fig.) trouble, difficulties, mess. **-ęto** *m.* blackthorn thicket; (fig.) difficulties. **-o** *m.* plum; *-o selvatico*, sloe, blackthorn; bramble; thorn. **-ọso** *adj.* thorny; prickly.

**pruri·gin-e** *f.* itching; tickling; (fig.) itch; excitement. **-ọso** *adj.* itchy; titillating.

**prurito** *m.* itch, itching; (fig.) bug, itch.

**Pru·ssi-a** *pr.n.f.* Prussia; *blù di —*, prussian blue. **-ano** *adj.*, *n.m.* Prussian.

**pse·ud-o** *pref.* pseudo-. **-o·nimo** *m.* pseudonym; pen-name.

**psican-a·liṣi** *f.* psychoanalysis. **-alista** *m.*, *f.* psychoanalysis. **-ali·tico** *adj.* psychoanalytical.

**Psiche** *pr.n.f.* Psyche; psyche.

**psi·chico** *adj.* psychic(al).

**psic-ologi·a** *f.* psychology. **-ọlogo** *m.* psychologist.

**pte·ride** *f.* fern.

**pubblic-are** [A2 s] *tr.* to publish, to make public, to divulge; to issue, to edit; to make public property; to confiscate. **-azịone** *f.* publication; issue; banns; pronouncement; manifesto; published matter.

**pu·bbli-co** *adj.* public; national, state, government(al); *scuola -ca*, state school; *agente di -ca sicurezza*, policeman; *— ufficiale*, civil servant; *n.m.* public; people; audience. **-cista** *m.* student of international law; freelance writer; publicist. **-cita·rio** *adj.* advertising; *n.m.* publicity agent.

**pud-ibọndo, -ico** *adj.* modest, bashful; chaste. **-ọre** *m.* modesty; shame.

**puer-ile** *adj.* childish, puerile; boyish. **-ilità** *f.* puerility. **-i·zia** *f.* childhood; boyhood, girlhood.

**pue·rp-era** *f.* woman in childbed. **-e·rio** *m.* confinement, lying-in.

**pu·gil-e** *m.* boxer. **-ato** *m.* boxing. **-atọre** *m.* boxer.

**Pu·gli-a** *pr.n.f.* (geog.) Apulia. **-ęse** *adj.*, *n.m.*, *f.* (native) of Apulia.

**pugn-a** *f.* (poet.) fight, battle. **-ace** *adj.* pugnacious, warlike, aggressive.

**pugnal-e** *m.* dagger; (fig.) blow. **-are** [A1] *tr.* to stab with a dagger.

**pugn-o** *m.* (*pl.* **-i** *m.*, **-a** *f.*) fist; punch, blow; *fare a -i*, to box, to fight, (fig.) to clash, to disagree; (fig.) *un — d'uomini*, a handful of men. **-ata** *f.* handful; punch.

**pulce** *f.* flea; *color —*, puce.

**pulcella** *f.* maiden, damsel.

**Pulcinell-a** *pr.n.m.* Punch, Punchinello; *il segreto di —*, an open secret. **-ata** *f.* piece of buffoonery, silly behaviour; Punch and Judy show.

**pulcino** *m.* newly hatched chick.

**puledr-o** *m.* unbroken colt. **-a** *f.* filly.

**pulęggia** *f.* pulley.

**pul-ire** [D2] *tr.* to clean, to polish; to wash; *— dalla polvere*, to dust; *rfl.* (*acc.* of *prn.* 'si') to wash (oneself), to tidy oneself up; (*dat.* of *prn.* 'si') *-irsi le scarpe*, to clean one's shoes. **-imęnto** *m.* cleaning; final polish, finishing touch. **-itęzza** *f.* cleanliness; polish; neatness; propriety; politeness. **-ito** *part. adj.* clean; neat; well-kept, tidy; *fare piazza -ita*, to make a clean sweep; polished; smooth; elegant; *adv. scrivere -ito*, to write neatly. **-itrice** *f.* (eng.) polishing machine, buffer. **-izi·a** *f.* cleaning; cleanliness; tidiness; sweeping, dusting, scrubbing; *fare la -izia*, to do the housework.

**pullmann** *f. indecl.* motor-coach; (rlwy.) pullman car.

**pullover** *m. indecl.* pullover; sweater; cardigan.

**pullulare** [A1 s] *intr.* (*aux.* avere) to spring up, to shoot (of plants); to spread; to swarm, to pullulate; *n.m. un gran — d'insetti*, swarms of insects.

**pu·lpito** *m.* pulpit; (iron.) *montare in —*, to preach, to sermonize.

**puls-are** [A1] *intr.* (*aux.* avere) to throb, to beat; to pulsate; *tr.* to knock at (a door). **-azịone** *f.* beat, throbbing, pulsation.

**pulvi·scolo** *m.* fine dust; fine spray; pollen.

**pu·ng-ere** [C5] *tr.* to prick; to sting; to pierce; *rfl.* to prick oneself; to get stung; **-ente** *part. adj.* prickly; stinging; pungent; piquant. **-iglịone** *m.* sting; thorn; (fig.) spur, stimulus.

**pu·ngolo** *m.* goad; (fig.) spur, prick; incentive.

**pun-ire** [D2] *tr* to punish; to chastise, to correct. **-izịone** *f.* punishment, chastisement; penalty.

**punt-a** *f.* point; tip; corner; end; top, peak; headland, promontory; stitch (in the side), sharp pain; small amount, pinch, touch, trace; *ore di —*, rush hour, peak hour. **-ale** *m.* metal tip; ferrule; tag of a shoelace); tongue (of a buckle).

**punt-are** [A1] *tr.* to point, to aim; to fix, to direct; to lay; *— i piedi a terra*, to dig one's heels in; to bet, to wager; *intr.* (*aux.* avere) to hoist sail, to set course; to make an objection. **-ata** *f.* thrust; part, number, instalment; stake, bet. **-azịone** *f.* punctuation.

**punteggi-are** [A3 c] *tr.*, *intr.* (*aux.* avere) to punctuate; to dot, to draw dotted lines; (needlew.) to prick out a design; to stitch. **-atura** *f.* punctuation; dotting; speckling.

**puntęggio** *m.* dotting; pricking; marking; score.

**puntell-o** *m.* prop, support; stay. **-amęnto** *m.* shoring. **-are** [A1] *tr.* to prop, to shore up, to support, to buttress.

**punteruolo**[1] *m.* punch; awl; bodkin; stiletto.

**punteruolo**[2] *m.* *— del grano*, grain weevil.

**punti·gli-o** *m.* obstinacy; spite; *star sul —*, to stick at trifles, to be awkward. **-are** [A1] *intr.* (*aux.* avere), *rfl.* to jib; to refuse

to budge. **-oso** *adj.* obstinate about trifles, difficult.
**punto**[1] *part.* of **pu·ngere**; *adj.* pricked, stabbed, punctured; (fig.) goaded.
**punt-o**[2] *m.* dot, spot, point, mark; — *fermo*, full stop; (needlew.) stitch; *pl.* blackheads; (fig.) blemishes; *di — in bianco*, point blank; *in —*, *a —*, in order; state, condition; *far —*, to leave off, to stop payment; detail, item, particular; particle. **-ato** *adj.* dotted; speckled. **-ino** *m. dim. mettere i -ini sugl'i*, to dot the i's; *adv. phr. a -ino*, exactly, precisely. **-olino** *m. dim.* little spot, dót; *pl.* dots (marking a break in a sentence).
**punto**[3] *neg.* not at all; no, not any.
**puntual-e** *adj.* punctual; exact. **-ità** *f.* punctuality; exactitude.
**puntura** *f.* prick; sting, (insect) bite; puncture; stabwound, stabbing pain; stitch in one's side.
**puntuto** *adj.* pointed, sharp.
**punzecchi-are** [A4] *tr.* to prick, to sting, to bite; (fig.) to goad, to tease.
**pup-a** *f.* baby; little girl; doll; (ent.) pupa. **-a·ttola** *f.* doll; little child; doll-like woman. **-azzo** *m.* puppet.
**pupilla** *f.* pupil of the eye.
**pupill-o** *m.* ward; (fig.) simpleton. **-are** *adj.* relating to a ward or minor.
**pupo** *m.* marionette, puppet.
**pur-e** *adv.*, *conj.* also, too; yet, still, even; however; somehow, anyhow; really, indeed; only; hardly; not even; *entri —*, please come in; *faccia —!*, please do! **-chè** *conj.* provided that; if only.
**purè** *m. indecl.* (cul.) purée; — *di patate*, mashed potatoes.
**purezza** *f.* purity; transparency, limpidity; sincerity; chastity.
**purg-are** [A2] *tr.* to purify; to purge; to cleanse, to clean, to clear, to expiate; to expurgate; *rfl.* to take an aperient; to purify oneself. **-a** *f.* aperient; (pol.) purge. **-ante** *part. adj.* cleansing; *n.m.* laxative, aperient. **-ata** *f.* purge, purging.
**Purgato·rio** *pr.n.m.* Purgatory; (fig.) torture, torment.
**purific-are** [A2s] *tr.* to purify, to cleanse; *rfl.* to purify oneself; to become purified. **-azione** *f.* purification.
**purit-à** *f.* purity; clearness; innocence; chastity. **-anismo** *m.* puritanism. **-ano** *m.* Puritan; *adj.* puritanical.
**puro** *adj.* pure; unadulterated, unalloyed; neat (not diluted); mere, sheer, plain.
**purosangue** *adj.*, *n. m. indecl.* thoroughbred.
**purpu·reo** *adj.* red; crimson; purple.
**purulento** *adj.* purulent.
**pus** *m. indecl.* pus, matter.
**pusilla·nime** *adj.* pusillanimous, faint-hearted, cowardly; *n.m.* coward.
**pu·stol-a** *f.* pustule, carbuncle; blister. **-oso** *adj.* pimply.
**putacaso** *adv. phr.* suppose, supposing.
**Putifarre** *pr.n.m.* Potiphar.
**putife·rio** *m.* uproar; row; mess; stink.
**putr-e·dine** *f.* rottenness, rot; putrefaction; (fig.) moral corruption. **-efare** [B14] *intr.* (*aux.* essere), *rfl.* to rot, to putrefy, to go bad.
**putrella** *f.* beam; girder.
**pu·trid-o** *adj.* putrid, rotten; *n.m.* (fig.) corruption. **-ume** *m.* rottenness, rot; filth.
**puttana** *f.* whore, strumpet; prostitute.
**putto** *m.* child, little boy; (art) cupid, amorino.
**puzz-a** *f.* pus; festering matter; stink, stench. **-are** [A1] *intr.* (*aux.* avere) to stink. **-o** *m.* stench, stink; bad smell, festering matter; (fig.) fuss, row.
**pu·zzola** *f.* polecat.
**puzzolente** *adj.* stinking, fetid; (fig.) foul.

**Q** *f.* (pron. **cu**) the letter Q; the consonant Q.
**qua** *adv.* here; in this place; *di — e di là*, on this side and on that; hither; *per di —*, this way, along here; *di — da*, on this side of; *più qua*, later.
**qua qua qua** (onomat.) quack quack.
**qua·ccher-o** *m.* Quaker, 'Friend'; *adj.* Quaker. **-ismo** *m.* Quakerism.
**quaderna** *f.* see **quaterna.**
**quadern-o** *m.* notebook, exercise book; part (of a book published in parts); quire. **-a·rio** *adj.* quaternary; *n.m.* set of four. **-etto** *m. dim.* small note book.
**quadragen·ario** *adj.* forty-year-old; *n.m.* a forty-year-old man.
**Quadrage·sima** *pr.n.f.* Lent.
**quadra·ngol-o** *adj.* four-cornered; *n.m.* quadrilateral. **-are** *adj.* quadrangular.
**quadr-are** [A1] *tr.* to square; to adjust; to balance; *intr.* (*aux.* essere, avere) to fit in. **-ante** *part. adj.* fitting; in place; *n.m.* quadrant; quarter of a day; dial, face (of a clock). **-a·tico** *adj.* quadratic. **-ato** *part. adj.* squared; square; stocky, robust; (fig.) sound, sensible; *n.m.* square; (boxing) ring. **-atura** *f.* quarter of the moon; squaring; caisson, square panel.
**quadrie·nn-io** *m.* space of four years. **-ale** *adj.* four-yearly; *n.f.* exhibition held every four years. **-ifo·glio** *m.* quatrefoil; four-leaved shamrock, clover.
**quadri·glia** *f.* quadrille.
**quadr-ila·tero** *adj.* four-sided; *n.m.* quadrilateral. **-ilungo** *adj.* oblong. **-imotore** *adj.* (aeron.) four-engined; *n.m.* four-engined aircraft. **-isi·llabo** *adj.* quadrisyllabic. **-i·vio** *m.* meeting of four roads; (hist.) quadrivium.
**quadro**[1] *adj.* square; robust, stocky; strong.
**quadr-o**[2] *m.* painting; picture; (fig.) description; outline; caisson, square compartment in a ceiling; *pl.* (cards) diamonds. **-ello** *adj.* four-edged, four-sided (*e.g.* of a tool); *n.m.* (hist.) quarrel, square-headed arrow; square flooring-tile; gusset. **-ettato** *adj.* squared, chequered, check. **-etto** *m. dim.* small tile; square of a chess-board. **-otta** *f.* square-ruled paper. **-u·pede** *m.* quadruped; *adj.* four-footed. **-uplicare** [A2s] *tr.* to quadruplicate; to multiply by four. **-u·plice** *adj.* quadruple.
**qua·druplo** *adj.* four times as much; four times the size; *n.m.* quadruple.
**quaggiù** *adv.* down here; here below; (fig.) in this world, in this life.
**qua·glia** *f.* quail.
**qual-che** *adj. indecl.* some, several; a few; some sort of; — *libro*, some books; — *volta*, sometimes. **-cheduno** *indef. prn.* somebody, someone. **-cosa** *indef. prn.* something. **-cuno** *indef. prn. m.* anybody, someone, somebody; one or two.
**qual-e** *adj.*, *prn. interr.* what?; which?; *indef adj.* what, what a; as; *tale —*, such as; *tale e —*, just the same; *rel. prn. il —* (*f.* la —, *m.pl.* i -i, *f.pl.* le -i) who; which; *excl. — catastrofe!*, what a catastrophe! **-ora** *adv*,. *conj.* when, whenever; if; in case. **-si·a, -si·asi, si·ansi, -sisi·a, -sisi·ano, -sivo·glia** *indef. adj.* whichever, whatever; any. **-unque** *indef. adj. indecl.* any, any whatever; whatever. **-volta** *adv.*, *conj.* whenever.
**quali·fica** *f.* qualification; title; attribute; name, designation.

**qualific-are** [A2s] *tr.* to qualify, to define, to call, to describe; *rfl.* to describe oneself. **-ato** *part. adj.* qualified; named, entitled; endowed; distinguished, excellent. **-azione** *f.* qualification; attribute, title; definition.

**qualità** *f. indecl.* quality; merit, capacity; condition; kind, species; — *di membro*, membership.

**quando** *adv.* when; at the time that; *da — la vidi*, ever since I saw her; *di — in —*, now and then, from time to time; *n.m.* the time when, the moment; *il dove e il —*, the where and when.

**quantità** *f. indecl.* quantity; number; amount; abundance.

**quant-o** *adj. interr.* how much, how many; how long; *indef. prn., adj.* as much; *tutto —*, the whole; *tutti -i*, the whole lot of them, all and sundry; *indef. rel. prn.* all that which; *n.m.* amount; (phys.) quantum; *adv.* how, how much; *in — a*, in regard to; *per —*, as far as; *per — si possa tentare*, however much one tries. **-unque** *conj.* although; though.

**quarant-a** *card. num. indecl.* forty. **-amila** *card. num. indecl.* forty thousand. **-ena** *f.* quarantine. **-enne** *adj.* forty-year-old. **-e·nnio** *m.* period of forty years. **-e·şimo** *ord. num. adj., n.m.* fortieth. **-ina** *f.* set of forty; *sulla -ina*; about forty.

**quareşim-a** *f.* Lent; *fare la —*, to observe Lent; (fig., joc.) interminable period. **-ale** *adj.* relating to Lent.

**quarta** *f.* quadrant (of a circle); point of the compass; quarter of the moon; fourth in a series (of feminine nouns).

**quartiere** *m.* quarter, region, district of a city; quarters, lodgings; barracks; paddock, enclosure.

**quart-o** *ord. num.* fourth; *n.m.* fourth; quarter; quarters, apartment; segment of a wheel. **-ina** *f.* quatrain; quarto. **-u·ltimo** *adj., n.m.* last but three; fourth (syllable) from the end.

**quarzo** *m.* quartz.

**quaş-i** *adv.* almost, nearly; approximately. **-ichè** *conj.* as if. **-imodo** *m.* Low Sunday, First Sunday after Easter.

**quassù** *adv.* up here; here above.

**quatern-a** *f.* set of four numbers. **-a·rio** *adj.* quaternary; *n.m.* (prosod.) quatrain of four syllables.

**quatt-o** *adj.* crouched, huddled up; squatting; cowering; *adv. quatto quatto*, quietly, softly.

**quatto·rdic-i** *card. num.* fourteen. **-enne** *adj., n.m., f.* fourteen-year-old. **-e·şimo** *ord. num.* fourteenth.

**quattrino** *m.* (fig.) very small sum, farthing; *pl.* (colloq.) cash, dibs.

**quattr-o** *card. num.* four; *farsi in — per*, to do one's utmost to (for); *a — occhi*, face to face; *fare — passi*, to take a stroll. **-ocentesco** *adj.* (*m.pl.* **-ocenteschi**) (of the) fifteenth-century. **-ocento** *card. num.* four hundred; *n.m.* fifteenth century. **-omila** *card. num.* four thousand.

**quell-o** *demons. adj.* (*m.pl.* **quei, quegli**; *m. sing.* **quel** before an ordinary consonant) that; *indef. prn. m.* that man, that person; that thing; — *che ti dissi*, what I told you. **-a** *indef. prn. f.* that woman; that thing; *me ne dice di -e!*, he says such things!; that hour, that moment.

**que·rc-ia** *f.* oak. **-eto** *m.* grove of oaks.

**querel-a** *f.* complaint, lament; criminal charge; summons. **-ante** *m., f.* (leg.) plaintiff; informant. **-are** [A1] *tr.* to summons; *rfl.* to complain; to lament; (leg.) to institute criminal proceedings.

**que·rulo** *adj.* querulous; complaining; peevish.

**queşito** *m.* inquiry; problem.

**questi** *pers. prn. m. sing.* he; this person, this man; the latter (*cf.* **questo**).

**question-e** *f.* question; the main issue. **-are** [A1c] *intr.* (*aux.* avere) to argue; to discuss; to dispute.

**quest-o** *demons. adj.* this; *l'ho visto con -i occhi*, I saw it with my own eyes; *demons. prn. m.* this man, this person; the latter; *pl.* these; these ones. **-a** *f. indef. prn.* this woman; this girl; this thing; this hour, this moment.

**quest-ore** *m.* police-superintendent, the Chief of Police in a province. **-ura** *f.* police-station; police headquarters.

**que·st-ua** *f.* house-to-house collection; begging for alms. **-uare** [A6] *intr.* (*aux.* avere) to collect for a charity; to beg for alms.

**qui** *adv.* here; these parts, this region; — *intorno*, hereabouts; — *presso*, close by; *di —*, hence; *di — a poco*, in a short while from now; *da —*, from here, from now.

**quia** *m. indecl.* the reason why; *venire al —*, to come to the point.

**quid** *prn. indecl.* what; *un certo —*, a certain something.

**quidam** *prn. indecl.* a certain; *un —*, some person.

**quiddità** *f.* essence, basic nature, quiddity.

**quiescen-te** *adj.* quiescent. **-za** *f.* quiescence.

**quiet-are** [A1] *tr.* to still, to hush; to quieten; to soothe; *rfl.* to be quietened; to calm down. **-anza** *f.* receipt; discharge; release; quittance. **-e** *f.* quiet; rest, repose; quietude; calm. **-o** *adj.* quiet, still, calm, peaceful.

**quina·rio** *adj.* quinary; *n.m.* set of five; (prosod.) line of five syllables.

**quinci** *adv.* hence; from here; on this side.

**quindi** *adv.* hence; thence; on that side; therefore; afterwards; — *innanzi*, henceforth.

**qui·ndic-i** *card. num.* fifteen; *oggi a —*, in a fortnight's time; — *giorni*, fortnight. **-enne** *adj., n.m., f.* fifteen-year-old. **-e·şimo** *ord. num.* fifteenth.

**quinquag-ena·rio** *n.m.* fifty-year-old. **-e·şima** *f.* (eccl.) Quinquagesima (Sunday); **-e·şimo** *ord. num.* fiftieth.

**quinqu-ennale** *adj.* five-yearly; quinquennial; *piano -ennale*, five-year plan. **-enne** *adj., n.m., f.* five-year-old. **-e·nnio** *m.* quinquennial; five-year period; lustre. **-ereme** *adj., m., f.* (hist.) quinquereme.

**quintale** *m.* quintal, a hundred kilogrammes.

**quint-o** *ord. num.* fifth. **-a** *f.* (mus.) fifth; *pl.* (theatr.) flies; wings; (fig.) *dietro le -e*, behind the scenes. **-erno** *m.* quire. **-essenza** *f.* quintessence. **-etto** *m.* (mus.) quintet.

**qui·nt-uplo, -u·plice** *adj.* fivefold; *n.m.* quintuple.

**Quirinale** *pr.n.m.* Quirinal.

**quivi** *adv.* there; here; then.

**quot-a** *f.* quota; portion; altitude; height above sea-level. **-are** [A1] *tr.* (comm.) to quote; to estimate. **-azione** *f.* (comm.; finan.) quotation; *-azione di borsa*, Stock Exchange price.

**quotidiano** *adj.* daily; everyday; *n.m.* daily (newspaper).

**quoto, quoziente** *m.* (math.) quotient.

**R** *m., f.* (pron. **erre**) the letter R; the consonant R; *gli manca l' —*, he has a lisp.
**raba·rbaro** *m.* rhubarb.
**rabballinare** [A1] *tr.* to roll up, to make into a bundle; to wrap up.
**rabbaruffare** [A1] *tr.* to ruffle; *rfl.* to become dishevelled; *recip. rfl.* to scuffle.
**rabbassare** [A1] *tr.* to lower again.
**rabba·ttere** [B1] *tr.* to pull to; to half-close.
**rabbellire** [D2] *tr.* to beautify; to embellish anew; *rfl.* to adorn oneself; to gain in beauty.
**rabberciare** [A3] *tr.* to patch; to mend; to botch.
**rabbi** *m. indecl.* rabbi.
**ra·bbi-a** *f.* (vet.) rabies, hydrophobia; (fig.) rage, anger; fury. **-ọso** *adj.* (vet.) rabid; (fig.) raging; furious.
**rabbi·nico** *adj.* rabbinical.
**rabbino** *m.* master of Hebrew law, rabbi; il Gran Rabbino, the Chief Rabbi.
**rabbiọs-o** *adj.* (vet.) rabid; (fig.) furious; choleric. **-amẹnte** *adv.* furiously; madly.
**rabboccare** [A2 c] *tr.* to fill up, to fill to the brim; to refill.
**rabbon-acciare** [A3] *tr.* to calm; *rfl.* to quieten down. **-ire** [D2] *tr.* to pacify, to appease; to calm; *intr.* (*aux.* essere), *rfl.* to be pacified.
**rabbottonare** [A1 c] *tr.* to button up again.
**rabbracciare** [A3] *tr., recip. rfl.* to re-embrace.
**rabbriccicare** [A2]' *tr.* to patch up.
**rabbrividire** [D2] *intr.* (*aux.* essere, avere) to shiver; (fig.) to shudder.
**rabbruscare** [A2] *intr.* (*aux.* essere), *rfl.* (of sky) to become overcast; (fig.) to become gloomy.
**rabbruscolare** [A1 s] *tr.* to save up little by little; to put by.
**rabbuffare** [A1] *tr.* to rumple, to disorder; *rfl.* to roughen; to become rumpled; *recip. rfl.* to come to blows.
**rabbuffo** *m.* rebuff; rebuke.
**rabbuiare** [A4] *rfl., intr.* (*aux.* essere) to grow dark; to become cloudy; to become overcast; (fig.) to become gloomy.
**rabdoman-te** *m.* dowser, water-diviner. **-zi·a** *f.* water-divining.
**rabelesiano** *adj.* Rabelaisian.
**rabẹs-co** *m.* (*pl.* **-chi**) arabesque. **-came** *m.* arabesques. **-care** [A2] *tr.* to adorn with arabesques.
**ra·bico** *adj.* (med.) rabid.
**ra·bido** *adj.* furious, angry.
**raccapezzare** [A1] *tr.* to find; to collect; to gather; to earn; *intr.* (*aux.* avere, with *adv.* ci) (fig.) *non ci raccapezzo proprio nulla*, I don't understand it at all; *rfl.* (fig.) to find one's way; *non mi ci -o raccapezzo*, I can't make head or tail of it.
**raccapri·cci-o** *m.* horror, terror; disgust. **-ante** *adj.* horrifying. **-are** [A4] *intr.* (*aux.* essere, avere), *rfl.* to be horrified; to be shocked; to shudder.
**raccatt-are** [A1] *tr.* to pick up; to gather; to scratch together; (fig.) *l'ho -ato per via*, I met him in the street. **-ace·nere** *m. indecl.* ash-pan. **-apalle** *m. indecl.* (sport) ball-boy. **-ati·ccio** *m. pejor.* rubbish, odds and ends. **-atọre** *m.* picker up, collector of rubbish.
**raccenciare** [A3] *tr.* to mend; to patch; to darn.
**racce·ndere** [C1] see **riacce·ndere.**
**raccertare** [A1] *tr.* to ascertain; to confirm; *rfl.* to make sure; to reassure oneself.
**racchetare** [A1] *tr.* to pacify; to console; to soothe; *rfl.* to be consoled.
**racchẹtta** *f.* racquet; **—** *da neve*, snow-shoe.
**racchiocciolare** [A1 sc] *rfl.* to huddle, to crouch, to cower.
**racchiu·dere** [C3] *tr.* to enclose; to contain; to keep shut up, to guard.
**racciabattare** [A1] *tr.* to patch up, to cobble.
**racco·gli-ere** [B7] *tr.* to collect, to gather; to pick up; to harvest; to reap; to receive, to shelter; to perceive; (naut.) — *le vele*, to take in sail; — *le reti*, to haul nets; *rfl.* to assemble; to collect ones thoughts; to concentrate; to settle; to retire. **-mẹnto** *m.* concentrated attention; absorption; retirement. **-ti·ccio** *adj.* picked up here and there, gathered haphazard; *n.m.* haphazard collection. **-tọre** *m.* gatherer; collector; card-index; file cover; filing cabinet.
**raccolta** *f.* gathering; collection; harvest, crop; *chiamare a —*, to rally; (mil.) *sonare a —*, to sound the retreat.
**raccolto** *part.* of **racco·gliere**; *adj.* collected, harvested; absorbed; compact; slender, slim; *n.m.* harvest, crop.
**raccomand-are** [A1] *tr.* to recommend; to entrust, to hand over for safe keeping; to secure; to fasten up; — *una lettera*, to register a letter; *rfl.* to commend oneself; to implore favour; *mi -o*, please, I beg you. **-ata** *f.* registered letter. **-ata·rio** *m.* person to whom one is recommended; (naut.) shipping agent. **-ati·zio** *adj. lettera -atizia*, letter of recommendation. **-aziọne** *f.* recommendation; advice; (post) registration; *tassa di -azione*, registration fee.
**raccomodare** [A1] *tr.* to repair, to mend; to adjust.
**racconci-are** [A3 c] *tr.* to repair, to mend; to amend; to improve; *rfl.* to tidy oneself, to make oneself presentable; to recover (health); (of weather) to change for the better. **-atura** *f.* mending, repair; *-atura del Ministero*, Cabinet reshuffle; clearing up (of weather).
**raccọncio** *apocop. part.* of **racconciare**; *adj.* repaired; adjusted; *n.m.* repair; adjustment.
**raccont-are** [A1 c] *tr.* to tell, to relate; to narrate. **-afa·vole** *m. indecl.* (joc.) romancer, storyteller. **-atọre** *m.*, **-atrice** *f.* narrator.
**raccọnto** *m.* tale, story; account; narrative; — *di fate*, fairy-tale.
**raccoppiare** [A4 c] *tr.* to couple, to pair; to reunite.
**raccorciare** [A3 c] *tr.* to shorten; *rfl.* to become shorter; (of days) to draw in.
**raccord-o** *m.* connexion; joint; (rlwy.) junction; branch line; *binario di —*, siding. **-are** [A1] *tr.* to join, to link; *rfl., intr.* (*aux.* avere) to unite; to be brought together. **-ato** *part. adj.* joined, linked; *ad angoli -ati*, with rounded corners.
**raccostare** [A1] *tr.* to bring near; to bring together; to put side by side; to compare; *rfl.* to draw near, to come close together.
**raccozzare** [A1] *tr.* to put together; to scrape together; *recip. rfl.* to meet; to be in agreement.
**racemo** *m.* bunch, cluster.
**rachi·tico** *adj.* suffering from rickets; stunted; blighted; *n.m.* person suffering from rickets.
**rachi·tide** *f.* rickets.
**raci·mol-o** *m.* small cluster in a bunch of grapes; (fig.) small group, knot (*e.g.* of people). **-are** [A1 s] *intr.* (*aux.* avere) to glean in vineyards; *tr.* (fig.) to glean, to gather; to collect together.
**racquist-are** [A1] *tr.* to regain; to recover; *intr.* (*aux.* avere), *rfl.* to regain the initiative. **-o** *m.* regaining; recovery; reconquest.
**rada** *f.* (naut.) anchorage; roads.
**radamẹnte** *adv.* see under **rado.**
**radar** *m. indecl.* radar. **-ista** *m.* radar operator.
**radazz-a** *f.* (naut.) mop. **-are** [A1] *tr.* (naut.) to swab.
**raddensare** [A1] *tr.* to thicken; *intr.* (*aux.* essere), *rfl.* to become thicker.
**raddobb-o** *m.* (naut.) hull repairs; *bacino di —*, refitting basin. **-are** [A1] *tr.* (naut.) to refit.
**raddolcire** [D2] *tr.* to sweeten; (fig.) to soften, to soothe; to assuage; *intr.* (*aux.* essere), *rfl.* to become milder.
**raddọppi-o** *m.* double; doubling,

redoubling. **-are** [A4c] *tr.* to double, to redouble; *intr.* (*aux.* avere, essere), *rfl.* to double, to redouble; to become more intense.

**raddrizzare** [A4] *tr.* to straighten; to erect; (fig.) to put right; *rfl.* to draw oneself up; to stand up straight.

**ra·dere** [C3] *tr.* to shave; to file down; to scrape; to raze; to erase; to graze; to brush against; *rfl.* to shave oneself.

**radẹzza** *f.* see under **rado.**

**radiale** *adj.* radial.

**radiante** *adj.* radiant; beaming.

**radi-are** [A4] *intr.* (*aux.* avere, essere) to radiate; *tr.* (admin.) to strike out (from a list); to remove, to erase; (leg.) to cancel. **-atọre** *m.* radiator. **-aziọne** *f.* radiation; cancellation; erasure.

**ra·dica** *f.* (pop.) root; root of a tooth; *pipa di —*, briar-pipe; *— gialla*, carrot; *— rossa*, beetroot.

**radical-e** *adj.* radical; *n.m.* (pol.) Radical. **-iṣmo** *m.* (pol.) Radicalism.

**radicare** [A2s] *intr.* (*aux.* essere), *rfl.* to take root.

**radi·cchio** *m.* (bot.) chicory.

**radice** *f.* root; (fig.) origin; source; *la — di ogni male*, the root of all evil; (math.) root; *— quadrata*, square root.

**ra·di-o**[1] *m.* radium. **-oattività** *f.* radio-activity. **-oattivo** *adj.* radio-active. **-ologi·a** *f.* (med.) radiology. **-o·logo** *m.* (med.) radiologist. **-oterapi·a** *f.* (med.) radiotherapy.

**ra·di-o**[2] *f.* wireless, radio; *trasmettere per —*, to broadcast; *giornale —*, news; *Radio Audizione Italiana* (R.A.I.), Italian Broadcasting Corporation. **-ale** *adj.* radial. **-oascoltatọre** *m.* listener. **-oaudiziọne** *f.* broadcast; wireless programme. **-diffọndere** [C3] *tr.* to broadcast. **-odiffusiọne** *f.* broadcasting; broadcast. **-odisturbi** *m.pl.* atmospherics, statics. **-ografi·a** *f.* radiography; X-ray, radiograph. **-ogrammo·fono** *m.* radiogram. **-oọnda** *f.* radio wave. **-ote·cnico** *m.* wireless engineer. **-otraṣmẹttere** [C20] *tr.* to broadcast. **-otraṣmissiọne** *f.* broadcasting; broadcast.

**radiọs-o** *adj.* radiant; beaming. **-ità** *f.* radiance; brilliance; luminosity.

**raditura** *f.* erasure; scratching out.

**rad-o** *adj.* sparse, rare; *capelli -i*, thin hair; infrequent; *di —*, rarely. **-amẹnte** *adv.* sparsely, scarcily, thinly. **-ẹzza** *f.* rareness; scantiness; thinness. **-ume** *m.* bare patch (in cultivation). **-ura** *f.* clearing (in woods); thin, worn part of cloth.

**radun-are** [A1] *tr.* to assemble; to gather together; *rfl.* to assemble, to congregate. **-anza** *f.*, **-ata** *f.* assembly; gathering. **-o** *m.* rally.

**ra·fano** *m.* (bot.) horse radish.

**raffa** *f.* robbery with violence; rapine; *fare a ruffa —*, snatch as snatch can.

**Raffaello** *pr.n.m.* Raphael.

**raffazzonare** [A1] *tr.* to do up; to repair; to patch.

**rafferm-a** *f.* confirmation; renewal. **-are** [A1] *tr.* to renew (contract); to confirm; to strengthen; to solidify. **-o** *apocop. part.*, *adj.* firm, hard; *pane -o*, stale bread.

**raf·fica** *f.* squall; shower of hail; *— di neve*, sudden snowstorm.

**raffigurare** [A1] *tr.* to recognize; to represent, to portray; *rfl.* (*dat.* of *prn.* 'si') to imagine.

**raffil-are** [A1] *tr.* to sharpen, to whet; to pare, to trim; *intr.* (*aux.* avere) *— sulle spese*, to cut down expenses. **-atọio** *m.* whetstone, strop. **-atura** *f.* sharpening, trimming; *pl.* trimmings, shavings, clippings.

**raffin-are** [A1] *tr.* to refine; to purify; *rfl.* to become refined. **-atẹzza** *f.* refinement; subtlety. **-ato** *part. adj.* refined; *gusto -ato*, cultivated taste; subtle; artful; *n.m.* epicure; dandy. **-atọio** (metall.) refining furnace. **-eri·a** *f.* refinery.

**ra·ffio** *m.* grappling hook; grapnel; *di riffi o di raffi*, by hook or by crook.

**raffittire** [D2] *tr.* to thicken; to make more frequent; *intr.* (*aux.* essere), *rfl.* to grow thicker.

**rafforzare** [A1] *tr.* to strengthen, to reinforce; *rfl.* to grow stronger; (fig.) to fortify oneself.

**raffredd-are** [A1c] *tr.* to cool; to chill; *intr.* (*aux.* essere), *rfl.* to get cold; to cool down; *la minestra si -a*, the soup is getting cold; to catch cold, to take a chill. **-atọre** *m.* cooler; (motor.) radiator. **-atura** *f.* cooling; catching cold.

**raffreddọre** *m.* common cold; chill.

**raffren-are** [A1] *tr.* to restrain, to check; to repress; *rfl.* to restrain oneself. **-ato** *part. adj.* restrained; temperate.

**raffresc-are** [A2] *intr.* (*aux.* essere) to cool off; to grow cold; *impers.* (of temperature) to get cooler. **-ata** *f.* cooling; fall in temperature.

**raffrọnt-o** *m.* comparison; collation. **-are** [A1c] *tr.* to bring face to face; to compare; to collate.

**ra·fia** *f.* (bot.) raffia.

**raganella** *f.* (zool.) tree-frog; clapper; rattle.

**ragazz-o** *m.* boy, lad; child; boy-friend, young man; *avanti, -i!*, come on, boys! **-a** . girl; young woman; *nome di -a*, maiden name; maidservant; shop-girl; waitress; barmaid; girl-friend. **-ata** *f.* boyish trick. **-otto** *m.* big boy; young man, youth.

**raggentilire** [D2] *tr.* to refine; to educate; to civilize; *rfl.* to become more refined.

**raggiante** *adj.* radiant; beaming, joyful.

**raggiare** [A3] *intr.* (*aux.* avere, essere) to shine; to beam; *tr.* to radiate.

**ra·ggio** *m.* ray, beam; gleam; spoke; (poet.) fame, glory; *pl.* (poet.) eyes; (geom.) radius; (scient.) *raggi X*, X-rays; *raggi ultra-violetti*, ultraviolet rays.

**raggiornare** [A1c] *intr.* (*aux.* essere), *impers.* to be daylight again; to dawn again; *tr.* to adjourn.

**raggir-are** [A1] *tr.* to swindle, to cheat; to get the better of; *rfl.* to go round and round; to prowl. **-amẹnto** *m.* swindle; cheating; trick. **-atọre** *m.* swindler, trickster. **-o** *m.* trick; subterfuge.

**raggiu·ng-ere** [C5] *tr.* to reach, to get to, to arrive at; to catch up with; to overtake; *rfl.* to be joined; *recip. rfl.* to meet, to join; to unite. **-i·bile** *adj.* attainable.

**raggiuntare** [A1] *tr.* to stitch up; to piece together.

**raggiustare** [A1] *tr.* to mend, to repair; to put in order; to settle; *rfl.* to become adjusted; *recip. rfl.* to become reconciled; to come to an agreement.

**raggomitolare** [A1s] *tr.* to rewind; to wind into a ball; to coil; to roll up; *rfl.* to curl oneself up.

**raggranchito** *adj.* benumbed; numb.

**raggranellare** [A1] *tr.* to gather, to scrape together; to glean.

**raggrinz-are** [A1], **-ire** [D2] *tr.* to wrinkle, to crease; *intr.* (*aux.* essere), *rfl.* to become wrinkled; to become creased. **-ato, -ito** *part. adj.* wrinkled; creased; shrivelled; withered.

**raggrumare** [A1] *tr.*, *rfl.* to clot.

**raggruppare** [A1] *tr.* to arrange in groups; to gather together; to regroup; *rfl.* to form a group; to cluster.

**raggruzzolare** [A1s] *tr.* to scrape together, to save up.

**ragguagliare** [A4] *tr.* to equalize; to level; to compare; to inform.

**raggua·glio** *m.* comparison; (math.) *tavole di —*, comparative tables; conversion; rate; report, detailed information; *pl.* news, notification.

**ragguardẹvol-e** *adj.* considerable; notable; important;

worthy of regard. **-ęzza** *f.* importance.

**ra·gia** *f.* resin, rosin; *acqua di —*, turpentine.

**ragion-are** [A1 c] *intr.* (*aux.* avere) to reason; to argue; to think; to discourse; to talk; *tr.* to support with reasons; to argue (a case). **-amęnto** *m.* reasoning; argument; *-amento a priori*, a priori reasoning. **-atọre** *m.*, **-atrice** *f.* reasoner, speaker; *adj.* reasonable; reasoning.

**ragiọn-e** *f.* reason; reasonableness; discourse, argument, proof; *aver —*, to be right; *di —*, properly; of right; *a —*, rightly; *con —*, with good reason; nature, quality, kind; ratio, proportion, measure; (leg.) justice; (comm.) account; firm; *rendere —*, to render account. **-eri·a** *f.* accountancy; book-keeping. **-ęvole** *adj.* reasonable; moderate. **-evolęzza** . reasonableness; judiciousness. **-evolmęnte** *adv.* reasonably. **-iere** *m.* accountant; book-keeper; *perito -iere*, chartered accountant.

**ragliare** [A4] *intr.* (*aux.* avere) to bray; (fig.) to talk like an ass; *tr.* (derog.) to bray forth.

**ra·glio** *m.* bray; braying.

**ragn-a** *f.* cobweb, spider's web; threadbare patch; thin, light cloud. **-are** [A5] (*aux.* avere, essere), *rfl.* to grow threadbare; (of sky) to form thin fleecy clouds. **-atela** *f.*, **-atelo** *m.* spider's web; cobweb. **-ato** *part. adj.* threadbare; *cielo -ato*, mackerel sky. **-atura** *f.* threadbare condition; thin patch; thin, light clouds.

**ragno** *m.* (zool.) spider.

**ragù** *m. indecl.* ragout; rich meat sauce served with pasta.

**rai** *m.pl.* (poet.) eyes, beams.

**ra·ia**[1] *f.* (ichth.) ray.

**ra·ia**[2] *m.* rajah.

**ra·id** *m. indecl.* (mil.) raid.

**ra·in-a** *f.*, **-otto** *m.* (ichth.) carp.

**ra·ion** *m. indecl.* (text.) rayon.

**rallargare** [A2] *tr.* to widen, to enlarge; *intr.* (*aux.* essere), *rfl.* to grow wider.

**rallegrare** [A1] *tr.* to gladden, to cheer; *rfl.* to rejoice; to be glad.

**rallent-are** [A1] *tr.* to relax, to slacken; to ease; to slow down; *intr.* (*aux.* essere), *rfl.* to become slower; to become less active; to become slack; to become relaxed. **-ando** *ger.* (mus.) slowing down.

**rallignare** [A5] *intr.* (*aux.* essere) to take root again; *rfl.* (of plants) to spring up again.

**ram-a** *f.* branch, spray, twig. **-a·glia** *f.* dead branches; clippings; prunings, loppings of trees.

**ramanẓina** *f.* scolding, talking to.

**ram-are** [A1] *tr.* to copper-plate. **-atura** *f.* copper-plating.

**ramarro** *m.* (zool.) green lizard.

**rame** *m.* (metall.; chem.) copper; copper coin; copper engraving; *età del —*, Bronze Age; *pl.* copper cooking vessels.

**ramific-are** [A2 s] *intr.* (*aux.* avere) to branch out, to grow branches; *rfl.* to ramify. **-aziọne** *f.* ramification.

**ramin-go** *adj.* (*m.pl.* **-ghi**) (fig.) wandering, roving; fugitive; *n.m.* wanderer; refugee; fledgling. **-gare** [A2] *intr.* (*aux.* avere) to wander, to rove, to roam.

**ramino** *m.* copper pot or vessel.

**rammagliare** [A4] *tr.* (knitting) to graft; to repair ladders in.

**rammaricare** [A2 s] *tr.* to grieve; to vex; *rfl.* to regret, to be sorry; to complain.

**ramma·ri-co** *m.* (*pl.* **-chi**) regret; sorrow, grief; vexation.

**rammend-are** [A1] *tr.* to darn; to mend. **-o** *m.* darning.

**rammentare** [A1] *tr.* to recall; to call to mind; to remember; *intr.* (*aux.* avere) (theatr.) to prompt; *rfl.* (*dat.* of *prn.* 'si') to remember, to recollect, to recall.

**rammoll-ire** [D2] *tr.* to soften; to soak; to melt; (fig.) to mollify; to make effeminate; *rfl.* to become soft; to melt; *intr.* (*aux.* essere) to become childish; (fig.) to become effeminate or soft. **-ito** *part. adj.* softened; effeminate; feeble-minded; *un vecchio -ito*, an old man grown childish.

**rammorbidire** [D2] *tr.* to soften; to mitigate; to make gentler; *intr.* (*aux.* essere), *rfl.* to grow soft; to become gentler.

**ram-o** *m.* branch; antler. **-oscello** *m.* twig, small branch. **-ọso** *adj.* branching; full of branches.

**ramp-a** *f.* paw with claws; steep ascent; steps; flight of stairs; ramp. **-ante** *part. adj.* climbing; (herald.) rampant; *n.m.* flight of stairs. **-icante** *part. adj.* climbing; creeping. **-icare** [A2 s] *intr.* (*aux.* avere, essere) to climb. **-ichino** *m.* (bot.) climber; (orn.) tree-climber; *adj.* climbing. **-ino** *m.* hook; staple; prong of a fork; paw with claws. **-ọne** *m.* harpoon; hob-nail.

**rampoll-are** [A1 c] *intr.* (*aux.* essere) (of a spring) to rise; (of water) to spring forth, to gush; (of a plant) to shoot. **-o** *m.* spring (of water); jet; (of trees) shoot; (fig.) son, scion.

**ran-a** *f.* (zool.) frog; *uomini-rana*, frog-men; *nuoto a —*, breaststroke. **-ista** *m.*, *f.* (sport) breaststroke swimmer.

**ra·ncid-o** *adj.* rancid. **-ume** *m.* something rancid; rancid smell or taste.

**ra·ncio**[1] *adj.* orange (-coloured); *n.m.* (bot.) marigold.

**ra·ncio**[2] *m.* (mil.; naut.) mess; ration.

**rancọre** *m.* grudge; rancour.

**randa·gio** *adj.* stray; wandering.

**randello** *m.* cudgel, truncheon, club.

**ran-go** *m.* (*pl.* **-ghi**) rank, status; (mil.) file, line.

**rannicchiare** [A4] *rfl.* to crouch, to huddle; to cower.

**rannodare** [A1] *tr.* to tie; to join together again; (fig.) to reunite.

**rannuvol-are** [A1 s] *intr.* (*aux.* essere), *rfl.* to become cloudy, to cloud over; to become gloomy, to grow dark; (fig.) *si -ò in viso*, his face darkened.

**rano·cchi-o** *m.*, **-a** *f.* (zool.) frog, esp. the edible frog.

**ra·ntol-o** *m.* (med.) death-rattle; loud, hoarse cry. **-are** [A1 s] *intr.* (*aux.* avere) to breathe stertorously; to cry hoarsely. **-ìo** *m.* (*pl.* **-ìi**) frequent rattling in the throat. **-ọso** *adj.* stertorous, rough (of breathing).

**rap-a** *f.* (bot.) turnip. **-a·io** *m.* turnip-field.

**rapac-e** *adj.* rapacious; greedy; predatory. **-ità** *f.* rapacity.

**rapare** [A1] *tr.* to crop the hair; to clip close.

**ra·pida** *f.* rapid (in a river).

**ra·pid-o** *adj.* swift; rapid; quick; *treno —*, express train; *n.m.* express train. **-ità** *f.* speed; rapidity; quickness; swiftness.

**rapin-a** *f.* robbery; pillage; rapine; abduction; *uccello di —*, bird of prey; plunder. **-are** [A1] *tr.* to rob, to plunder, to pillage; to abduct, to kidnap.

**rap-ire** [D2] *tr.* to carry off; to steal; to snatch; to abduct, to kidnap; to rape; (fig.) to ravish, to entrance. **-imęnto** *m.* carrying off; abduction; rape.

**rappaciare** [A3] *tr.* to reconcile.

**rappacificare** [A2 s] to pacify.

**rappattumare** *tr.* to reconcile; *recip. rfl.* to be reconciled.

**rappezz-are** [A1] *tr.* to patch; to piece together. **-o** *m.* patching; patch.

**rapport-are** [A1] *tr.* to report; to relate; to tell; to transfer; *rfl.* (*prep.* a) to refer (to); to relate (to). **-o** *m.* report; denunciation; information; connexion, relation.

**rappre·ndere** [C1] *tr.*, *rfl.* to curdle; to coagulate; to set.

**rappresa·glia** *f.* reprisal; retaliation.

**rapprẹsent-are** [A1] *tr.* to present; to represent; to deputize for; (theatr.) to perform; to symbolize; *rfl.* (*acc.* of *prn.* 'si') to be represented; (*dat.* of *prn.* 'si') to imagine, to picture to oneself. **-anza** *f.* representation; agency; assembly. **-ativo**

*adj.* representative. **-azione** *f.* representation; (theatr.) performance; *-azione diurna*, matinée.

**rap-sodi·a** *f.* rhapsody; recitation or composition of epic. **-so·dico** *adj.* rhapsodic.

**rar-o** *adj.* rare; uncommon; exceptional; scanty, thinly scattered; *adv. phr. di* —, seldom, rarely. **-efare** [B14] *tr.* to rarefy. **-efatto** *part. adj.* rarefied; (fig.) subtle, refined. **-ità** *f.* rarity; unusualness; scarcity; curiosity.

**ras-are** [A1c] *tr.* to level; to smooth; to shave. **-ato** *part. adj.* smooth; clean shaven.

**raschiare** [A4] *tr.* to scrape; *intr.* (*aux.* avere) to clear one's throat; to cough.

**raschino** *m.* eraser; foot-scraper.

**ra·schio** *m.* clearing one's throat; sore throat.

**rasciugare** [A2] *tr.* to dry; *rfl.* to dry oneself; to become dry.

**rasent-e** *prep.* along by; close to; — *al muro*, close to the wall. **-are** [A1c] to pass close to; (fig.) to come close to.

**raso** *part.* of **ra·dere**; *adj.* shaven; smooth; *terreno* —, levelled ground; *pieno* —, full to the brim; cancelled; *n.m.* satin.

**rasoi-o** *m.* razor; — *di sicurezza*, safety razor; — *elettrico*, electric razor. **-ata** *f.* razor-cut.

**rasp-a** *f.* scraper; rasp. **-are** [A1] *tr.* to rasp, to scrape, to file down; to scrawl; to rummage.

**rassegare** [A2c] *intr.* (*aux.* essere), *rfl.* to form a layer of cold fat; to congeal.

**rassegna** *f.* (mil.) display; review; criticism; report; periodical; recapitulation.

**rassegn-are** [A5c] *tr.* to resign; to review, to enumerate; (mil.) to inspect; to take a census of; *rfl.* to resign oneself. **-azione** *f.* resignation; submission.

**rasserenare** [A1c] *tr.* to clear; (fig.) to cheer up; *rfl.* to become bright again; (fig.) to recover one's serenity.

**rassettare** [A1] *tr.* to arrange; to rearrange; to tidy up; to set in order; to adjust; *rfl.* to make oneself tidy, to tidy oneself up.

**rassicur-are** [A1] *tr.* to reassure; *rfl.* to assure oneself; to be reassured; to make certain. **-azione** *f.* assurance, reassurance.

**rassodare** [A1] *tr.* to harden; to make firm; to dry; to consolidate; *intr.* (*aux.* essere), *rfl.* to harden; to set; to dry; to become stronger; to be consolidated.

**rassomigli-are** [A4] *intr.* (*aux.* essere), *rfl.* to be like, to resemble; to appear like; *tr.* *-a lo zio*, he looks like his uncle; to compare; *recip. rfl.* to resemble each other. **-ante** *part. adj.* like, alike; bearing a resemblance. **-anza** *f.* likeness; resemblance; comparison.

**rastrell-are** [A1] *tr.* to rake; to ransack; to gather up, to collect. **-iera** *f.* rake; hay-rack; gun-rack; plate-rack. **-o** *m.* rake.

**rat-a** *f.* instalment; *comprare, vendere, a* —, to buy, to sell, by instalments on hire-purchase; proportion; *a, per, pro* —, proportionately; rate, share. **-eale** *adj.* relating to instalments; *sistema -eale di rendita*, hire-purchase.

**rati·fic-a** *f.* ratification; sanction, approval **-are** [A2s] *tr.* to ratify; to confirm; *rfl.* to declare; to confirm one's statement. **-azione** *f.* ratification; confirmation; approval.

**rato** *adj.* (leg.) decided; confirmed; ratified; agreed.

**rattacconare** [A1c] *tr.* to heel (boots and shoes).

**rattemp(e)rare** [A1, A1s] *tr.* to moderate; *rfl.* to restrain oneself, to keep calm.

**rattenere** [B32] *tr.* to hold back; to retain; *rfl.* to hold oneself in, to exercise restraint.

**ratto**[1] *m.* rapine; theft; abduction; rape; *il — delle Sabine*, the rape of the Sabines.

**ratto**[2] *adj.* (poet.) swift.

**ratto**[3] *m.* (zool.) rat.

**rattopp-are** [A1] *tr.* to patch, to mend; to cobble; (fig.) to revise. **-o** *m.* patch; mend.

**rattrappire** [D2] *tr.* to cause to contract; to paralyse; to benumb; *intr.* (*aux.* essere), *rfl.* to become stiff, numb or paralysed; to shrink, to contract.

**rat-trarre** [B33] *tr.* to cause to contract; to paralyse; *intr.* (*aux.* essere), *rfl.* to become stiff. **-tratto** *part. adj.* drawn together; stiff, paralysed.

**rattristare** [A1] *tr.* to grieve, to sadden; to afflict; *rfl.* to grow sad, to grieve; to droop.

**ra·u-co** *adj.* (*m.pl.* **-chi**) hoarse; harsh (of voice). **-camente** *adv.* hoarsely. **-ce·dine** *f.* hoarseness.

**ravanello** *m.* (bot.) radish.

**ravennate** *adj.* of Ravenna; *n.m., f.* inhabitant of Ravenna.

**ravizzone** *m.* (bot.) rape, cole.

**ravvalorare** [A1c] *tr.* to strengthen, to reinforce; to enhance the value of.

**ravvedere** [B1] *rfl.* to acknowledge one's faults; to mend one's ways; to reform.

**ravviare** [A1] *tr.* to set going again, to start again; to put on the right road again; to put right; *rfl.* (*acc.* of *prn.* 'si') to tidy oneself.

**ravvicinare** [A1] *tr.* to bring closer; to bring together again; to compare; *recip. rfl.* to draw closer; to be reconciled.

**ravviluppare** [A1] *tr.* to entangle; to confuse; to complicate; *rfl.* to become entangled, entwined.

**ravvisare** [A1] *tr.* to recognize; to perceive.

**ravvivare** [A1] *tr.* to revive; to give new life to; to restore to life; to enliven; *rfl.* to revive; to cheer up.

**ravvolg-ere** [C5] *tr.* to wrap up; to wrap round and round; *rfl.* to wrap oneself up; to go round and round; to twist and turn. **-imento** *m.* wrapping up; turning, twisting; (fig.) tortuousness; deviousness.

**ravvoltolare** [A1s] *tr.* to wrap up; *rfl.* to wrap oneself up; *ravvoltolarsi nel fango*, to wallow in the mire.

**raziocinare** [A1] *intr.* (*aux.* avere) to reason, to argue logically.

**razioci·nio** *m.* reasoning; ratiocination.

**razional-e** *adj.* rational; endowed with reason; rationalist(ic). **-ismo** *m.* rationalism. **-ista** *m., f.* rationalist. **-i·stico** *adj.* rationalistic. **-ità** *f.* rationality; reason. **-izzare** [A1] *tr.* to rationalize, to render efficient.

**razion-e** *f.* ration. **-are** [A1c] *tr.* to ration.

**razz-a**[1] *f.* race; breed; *la — umana*, the human race, mankind; *di ogni* —, of all kinds; *che — d'uomo è?*, what sort of a man is he? **-ismo** *m.* racialism. **-ista** *m., f.* racialist.

**razza**[2] *f.* (ichth.) ray, skate.

**razzi·a** *f.* raid; plunder.

**razzo** *m.* rocket; spoke of a wheel.

**razzolare** [A1s] *intr.* (*aux.* avere) to scratch about (of fowls); *tr.* to rummage for.

**re**[1] *m. indecl.* king; *i — Magi*, the Magi, the Three Kings; (cards, chess) king.

**re**[2] *m.* (mus.) re; the note D; the key of D.

**re**[3] *f.* (leg.) matter; *prep.* in the matter of, re.

**reag-ire** [D2] *intr.* (*aux.* avere) to react; to show opposition. **-ente** *n.m.* (chem.) reagent.

**real-e**[1] *adj.* real; actual. **-mente** *adv.* really; in reality; in fact, indeed. **-ismo** *m.* (philos.) realism; (arts and literature) realism. **-ista** *m., f.* realist. **-i·stico** *adj.* realistic. **-izzare** [A1] *tr.* to make real; to implement; (comm.) to realize, to convert into cash; *rfl.* to come true; to come to pass. **-tà** *f. indecl.* reality; true state of affairs; *in -tà*, in reality, in fact.

**real-e**[2] *adj.* royal; *n.f.* (mil.) guard of a royal residence; *n.m.* (numism.) real, a Spanish coin; *n.m.pl. i Reali*, the King

and Queen; the Royal House. **-ista** *m., f.* royalist.
**reame** *m.* realm, kingdom.
**reato** *m.* crime; offence; (leg.) criminal offence.
**reatt-ivo** *adj.* reacting; (chem.) reactive; *n.m.* (psych.) test. **-ore** *m.* nuclear reactor; jet aircraft; jet engine.
**reazion-e** *f.* reaction; response; opposition; (pol.) reactionary tendencies; (chem.; med.) reaction; *aeroplano a —*, jet plane; *motore a —*, jet engine. **-a·rio** *m. adj.* (pol.) reactionary.
**rebbi-o** *m.* prong. **-are** [A4] *tr.* to thresh.
**rebus** *m. indecl.* riddle, conundrum; picture-puzzle.
**recapitare** [A1 s] *tr.* to deliver; to hand; *intr.* (*aux.* avere; *prep.* a) to attend; to refer (to).
**reca·pito** *m.* address, office; *pronto —*, prompt delivery; (comm.) acknowledgement; delivery; *pl.* effects; securities.
**recare** [A2] *tr.* to bring, to carry, to take; to translate; *rfl.* (*acc.* of *prn.* 'si') to go, to come, to betake oneself; (*dat.* of *prn.* 'si') *recarsi addosso*, to take upon oneself; *recarsi a mente*, to bear in mind, to remember.
**recens-ione** *f.* review; *fare la — di un libro*, to review a book; critical examination. **-ire** [D2] *tr.* to review. **-ore** *m.* reviewer.
**recent-e** *adj.* recent; late; new; *di —*, recently, lately. **-emente** *adv.* recently, not long ago. **-is·sime** *f.pl.* latest news; stop press.
**recere** [B1] *tr.* to retch, to vomit.
**recessione** *f.* recession; receding.
**recettiv-o** *adj.* receptive. **-ità** *f.* receptivity.
**reci·dere** [C3] *tr.* to cut off; to curtail; *rfl.* to split, to tear; (of the skin) to crack.
**recidiv-o** *adj.* relapsing; recidivous; *n.m.* backslider; old offender, recidivist. **-a** *f.* relapse; backsliding; recidivism; woman recidivist. **-are** [A1] *intr.* (*aux.* essere) to relapse. **-ità** *f.* recidivism.
**reci·n-gere** [C5] to enclose; to fence in. **-to** *part. adj.* enclosed, fenced in, railed off; *n.m.* enclosure; surrounding wall; *pl.* precincts. **-zione** *f.* fence; (bldg.) enclosure.
**recipiente** *m.* recipient; container; vessel.
**reci·proc-o** *adj.* reciprocal, mutual; *n.m.* (math.) reciprocal. **-amente** *adv.* reciprocally; alternately. **-ità** *f.* reciprocity.
**recis-o** *part.* of **reci·dere**; *adj.* cut off; cut away; *fiori -i*, cut flowers; (fig.) resolute; sharp. **-ura** *f.* crack (in the skin), chap.
**re·cit-a** *f.* performance; *prima —*, first performance, first night; recitation; recital. **-are** [A1 s] *tr.* to recite; (theatr.) to perform, to act, to play; to declaim. **-ativo** *adj.* (mus.) *stile -ativo*, recitative style; *n.m.* (mus.) recitative. **-atore** *m.* actor; elocutionist, reciter. **-azione** *f.* recitation; recital; reading; acting; elocution.
**recitic·cio** *m.* vomit.
**reclam-are** [A1] *intr.* (*aux.* avere) to complain, to protest; *tr.* to claim, to demand; to complain of. **-o** *m.* formal complaint.
**reclame** *f. indecl.* (pron. as Fr.) publication; publicity.
**reclus-ione** *f.* seclusion; (eccl.) *suore di —*, enclosed nuns; (leg.) imprisonment with hard labour. **-o** *m.* recluse; prisoner.
**re·clut-a** *f.* recruit; notice. **-are** [A1 s, A1] *tr.* to recruit, to enrol; to call up; to engage.
**recon·dito** *adj.* hidden; concealed; secret; recondite.
**recrimin-are** [A1 s] *tr.* to recriminate; (leg.) to bring a counter-charge against; (fig.) to reproach; *intr.* (*aux.* avere) to make recriminations. **-azione** *f.* (leg.) counter-charge; (fig.) recrimination.
**recrudescenza** *f.* recrudescence.
**recto** *m. indecl.* (of page) face, recto.
**redarguire** [D2] *tr.* to reproach, to scold; to find fault with.
**red-atto** *part.* of **redi·gere**; *adj.* drawn up; compiled; edited. **-attore** *m.* compiler, writer; editor; journalist. **-azione** *f.* drawing up; compilation; editing; editorial staff; editor's office; version; drafting.
**red·dit-o** *m.* income; revenue; annuity; net profit; *imposta sul —*, income-tax. **-i·zio** *adj.* profitable; lucrative; yielding an income.
**reden-to** *part.* of **redi·mere**; *adj.* redeemed; ransomed; liberated. **-tore** *m.* (theol.) Redeemer; *adj.* redeeming; liberating; *guerra -trice*, war of liberation. **-zione** *f.* ransom; redemption; liberation; (theol.) Redemption.
**redi·gere** [C32] *tr.* to draw up (a document); to compile; to edit; (leg.) to draft.
**redi·mere** [C9] *tr.* to redeem, to ransom; to set free, to liberate; *rfl.* to redeem oneself; to free oneself.
**re·dine** *f.* rein.
**redivivo** *adj.* alive again, returned to life.
**re·duce** *adj.* returned (from war, exile, expedition); *n.m.* ex-serviceman, veteran; survivor.
**reduplicare** [A2 s] *tr.* to redouble; to reduplicate.
**refe** *m.* thread (hemp, flax).
**referenza** *f.* testimonial, reference.
**referto** *m.* official report.
**refert-oriere** *m.* kitchen-manager. **-o·rio** *m.* refectory, dining-hall; canteen.
**refezione** *f.* light repast.
**refratta·rio** *adj.* refractory; resistant; fireproof; *n.m.* (mil.) unwilling conscript; conscientious objector; (techn.) refractory, fireproof; *mattone —*, firebrick.
**refrattore** *m.* (astron.) refractor, refraction telescope.
**refriger-are** [A1 s] *tr.* to cool; to refresh; to refrigerate; *rfl.* to cool down; to feel refreshed. **-azione** *f.* cooling; refrigeration.
**refrige·rio** *m.* (feeling of) coolness; refreshment, relief.
**refurtiva** *f.* (leg.) stolen property.
**regalare** [A1] *tr.* to give (as a present); *rfl.* (*dat.* of *prn* 'si') to make oneself a present of.
**regal-e** *adj.* regal, kingly; royal. **-i·a** *f.* regalia; gratuity.
**regalo** *m.* present, gift; donation; *dare in —*, to give as a present.
**regata** *f.* boat-race; regatta.
**reg·g-ere** [C12] *tr.* to hold (up, upright); to bear, to support, to carry; to guide, to rule, to govern; to hold in, to restrain; (gramm.) to govern; *rfl.* to stand; (of business) to keep going; *intr.* (*aux.* avere) to bear; to stand, to resist. **-ente** *part. adj.* supporting; ruling; *n.m.* regent; rector; governor. **-enza** *f.* regency.
**reg·g-ia** *f.* (*pl.* **-ie**) royal palace.
**reggi-calze** *m. indecl.* suspender-belt. **-lume** *m. indecl.* lamp-stand. **-moc·colo** *m.* candle-holder; (fig.) gooseberry. **-pan·cia** *m. indecl.* girdle. **-petto** *m. indecl.* brassière, bra.
**reggimento** *m.* government, rule; control; (mil.) regiment.
**reggitore** *m.* ruler; governor; manager.
**regi·a** *f.* board of excise; shop for sale of excisable goods; tobacco-shop; (theatr.; cinem.) production.
**regic-ida** *m., f.* (*pl.* **-idi**) regicide (person); *adj.* regicidal. **-i·dio** *m.* (*pl.* **-idii**) regicide (act).
**regime** *m.* régime, government; diet.
**regina** *f.* queen; *— madre*, Queen Mother; *— vedova*, Dowager Queen; (chess, cards) queen.
**re·gio** *adj.* royal.
**region-e** *f.* region, district; realm, domain. **-ale** *adj.* regional; district. **-alismo** *m.* provincialism, regionalism.
**regista** *m.* (theatr.; telev.) producer; (cinem.) director.
**registr-are** [A1] *tr.* to register; to record; to enter. **-atore** *m.* register; *-atore di cassa*, cash register; *-atore di velocità*,

speedometer; *-atore a nastro*, tape-recorder; (person) registrar; recorder. **-azione** *f.* registration; recording; *-azione a nastro*, tape-recording.

**registro** *m.* register; registry; (naut.) log, ship's book.

**regn-are** [A5 c] *intr.* (*aux.* avere) to reign; to prevail; to flourish; *tr.* to rule, to dominate. **-ante** *part. adj.* reigning; prevailing; *venti -anti*, prevailing winds; *n.m.* sovereign, monarch, ruler; *pl.* king and queen.

**regno** *m.* kingdom.

**re·gola** *f.* rule; *di —*, usually, as a rule; example, model; order; moderation; custom.

**regolamentare**[1] *adj.* relating to regulations; prescribed; (admin.) *è — questa mozione?*, is this motion in order?

**regolamentare**[2] [A1] *intr.* (*aux.* avere) to lay down regulations; *tr.* to control by regulations.

**regolamento** *m.* regulation; rule.

**regol-are**[1] [A1 s] *tr.* to regulate; to settle; to control; *rfl.* to behave, to act. **-atore** *m.* regulator; (eng.) governor; *adj.* regulating; *piano -atore*, redevelopment plan. **-azione** *f.* regulation; control; (eng.) adjustment.

**regolar-e**[2] *adj.* regular. **-ità** *f.* regularity; punctuality. **-izzare** [A1] *tr.* to regularize.

**re·golo** *m.* ruler, rule; (set-) square; *— calcolatore*, slide-rule; (chess) file.

**regredire** [D2] *intr.* (*aux.* avere, essere) to go back, to turn; to recede.

**regress-ione** *f.* regression, recession, decadence. **-ivo** *adj.* regressive; retrograde. **-o** *m.* regress, retrogression; decadence; exit, way out; way back.

**reincarnazione** *f.* reincarnation.

**reintegr-are** [A1 a] *tr.* to reinstate; to indemnify; to restore; *rfl.* to be restored; to regain one's position. **-azione** *f.* reinstatement; restoration; compensation, indemnification.

**reità** *f.* guilt.

**reiter-are** [A1 s] to reiterate, to repeat. **-azione** *f.* reiteration.

**relativ-o** *adj.* relative; respective; proportionate; pertinent. **-amente** *adv.* relatively; comparatively; *-amente a*, with regard to. **-ismo** *m.* relativism. **-ità** *f.* (phys.) relativity.

**relatore** *m.* reporter.

**relazione** *f.* report; *— ufficiale*, official report; *pl.* relations, connexions; contacts; acquaintances; relationship; kinship.

**releg-are** [A2 s] *tr.* to relegate; to confine; to banish, to exile. **-azione** *f.* relegation; confinement; exile, banishment.

**religione** *f.* religion; religious life; cult; *con —*, devoutly; scrupulously.

**religios-o** *adj.* religious; devout; monastic; scrupulous; *n.m.* religious, monk. **-a** *f.* nun. **-amente** *adv.* religiously; with scrupulous care. **-ità** *f.* piety; devoutness; conscientiousness.

**reli·qui-a** *f.* relic. **-a·rio** *m.* (eccl.) reliquary.

**relitto** *part.* of **relin·quere**; *adj.* left, relinquished; abandoned; *n.m.* dereliction; derelict land; *pl.* waifs and strays; jetsam.

**rem-are** [A1] *intr.* (*aux.* avere) to row; to paddle. **-ata** *f.* rowing; row; stroke (of the oar). **-atore** *m.* oarsman; rower.

**remig-are** [A2 s] *intr.* (*aux.* avere) to row; (of birds) to fly, to beat their wings. **-ante** *part. adj.* rowing; beating; *n.m.* rower, oarsman. **-ata** *f.* (in rowing) stroke; rowing.

**reminiscenza** *f.* remembrance; recollection; reminiscence.

**remiss-i·bile** *adj.* pardonable. **-ione** *f.* remission; forgiveness; liberation; submission; giving up; remedy, way out. **-ivo** *adj.* submissive, meek; humble; gentle.

**remo**[1] *m.* oar; sweep; *pala del —*, blade; *un colpo di —*, a stroke.

**Remo**[2] *pr.n.m.* Remus.

**re·mol-o** *m.* tornado, hurricane; vortex; (naut.) squall. **-ino** *m.* eddy; gust.

**re·mora** *f.* delay, impediment; (ichth.) pilot fish.

**remoto** *adj.* remote, distant; far-off; secluded.

**ren-a** *f.* sand; sands. **-a·io** *m.* sand-bank; sand-pit; sandy ground. **-are** [A1 c] *tr.* to clean with sand, to sprinkle with sand.

**renano** *adj.* of the Rhine; Rhenish (*cf.* **Reno**).

**ren·d-ere** [C1] *tr.* to give back; to restore, to pay back; to give in exchange; to bring in, to yield; to express; to translate; to render, to make; *abs.* to pay; *rfl.* to render oneself, to make oneself; to become; to surrender; to yield; *-ersi conto di*, to realize. **-evole** *adj.* pliant, yielding; productive. **-iconto** *m.* statement of accounts, account; report; *pl.* minutes. **-imento** *m.* rendering, giving up, yielding; productive capacity.

**ren·dita** *f.* income; interest; revenue; *imposta sulla —*, income-tax; *— vitalizia*, life annuity; *pl.* rents and profits; (finan.) government or public stock.

**ren-e** *m.* (*m.pl.* *-i*) (anat.) kidney; *f.pl.* loins; the small of the back; *voltare le -i*, to turn one's back. **-ella** *f.* (med.) gravel.

**reniten-te** *adj.* unwilling, reluctant; recalcitrant; stubborn; *essere — alla leva*, to fail to register for military service; *n.m.pl.* shirkers. **-za** *f.* unwillingness, reluctance; stubbornness.

**renna** *f.* (zool.) reindeer.

**Reno** *pr.n.m.* (geog.) Rhine; Reno.

**renoso** *adj.* sandy.

**reo** *adj.* accused; guilty; wicked; evil, cruel; fell; *n.m.* accused; delinquent.

**reparto** *m.* distribution; department; (mil.) detachment.

**repel·l-ere** [C23] *tr.* to repel, to repulse. **-ente** *part. adj.* repellent, repulsive.

**repenta·glio** *m.* peril, danger; *mettere a —*, to jeopardize.

**repent-e** *adj.* sudden; unexpected; sheer, steep; *adv. phr.* *di —*, suddenly, all of a sudden. **-ino** *adj.* sudden, unexpected.

**reper-ire** [D2] *tr.* (admin.) to find, to trace. **-i·bile** *adj.* available; to be found.

**reperto·rio** *m.* collection; index; directory; inventory; (theatr.) repertory.

**re·pli-ca** *f.* reply; repartee, retort; objection; (theatr.) run; *molte -che*, a long run; repetition; (paint.) copy, replica; (comm.) *in — a*, in reply to. **-care** [A2 s] *tr.* to repeat; to retort; to object. **-cativo** *adj.* replying; repetitive.

**reprens-i·bile** *adj.* blameworthy, reprehensible. **-ione** *f.* reproach.

**repressione** *f.* repression; putting down, quelling.

**repri·m-ere** [C18] *tr.* to suppress; to put down; to check, to restrain, to repress; *rfl.* to exercise restraint, to restrain, to check oneself. **-enda** *f.* reprimand.

**re·probo** *adj., n.m.* reprobate.

**repub·(b)lic-a** *f.* republic; State; commonwealth. **-ano** *adj., n.m.* republican.

**repulisti** *phr.* *fare (un) —*, to make a clean sweep.

**repulsore** *m.* (rlwy.) buffer.

**reput-are** [A1 s] *tr.* to deem; to judge, to consider; *rfl.* to consider oneself. **-ato** *part. adj.* esteemed. **-azione** *f.* reputation.

**re·quie** *f.* rest, peace; *m., f.* (rel.) requiem (mass); (liturg.; mus.) *messa di —*, requiem (mass).

**re·quiem** *m., f. indecl.* (liturg.) requiem (mass).

**requis-ire** [D2] *tr.* to requisition, to commandeer. **-ito** *part. adj.* requisitioned; *n.m.* requisite, requirement; *pl.* particulars, documents required. **-izione** *f.* requisition; demand.

**resa** *f.* surrender; yield; delivery; return; (comm.) *alla — dei conti*, on the rendering of accounts.

**rescin·dere** [C21] *tr.* to cut into pieces; (leg.) to rescind; to annul, to cancel.

**rescritto** *m.* rescript.

**reseda** *f.* (bot.) mignonette.

**residen-te** *adj.* resident; *n.m., f.* resident. **-za** *f.* residence; residency; domicile. **-ziale** *adj.* residential.

**reṣi·du-o** *adj.* left over, remaining; *n.m.* rest, residue, remainder; surplus. **-ale** *adj.* remaining, residual; *n.m.* remainder, residue. **-are** [A6] *tr.* to reduce by instalments; *intr.* (*aux.* essere) to be left over, to remain.

**reṣilien-te** *adj.* (eng.; bldg.) resilient. **-za** *f.* resilience.

**re·ṣin-a** *f.* resin; rosin; amber. **-ọso** *adj.* resinous.

**resipiscenza** *f.* recognition of error.

**resi·st-ere** [C1] *intr.* (*aux.* avere) to hold out; to bear up; to stay; with *prep.* 'a'; to resist, to withstand, to endure. **-ente** *adj.* resistant; strong; hard-wearing; (of colour) fast. **-enza** *f.* resistance; endurance; durability.

**rẹso** *part.* of **ren·dere.**

**resocọnt-o** *m.* report; account; (bank) return. **-ista** *m.* reporter.

**respi·ng-ere** [C5] *tr.* to repel, to drive back; to repulse; to reject; to return, to send back. **-ente** *adj.* repellent; *n.m.* embankment; (rlwy.) buffer. **-imẹnto** *m.* repelling; rejecting; rejection.

**respinto** *part.* of **respi·ngere;** *fu respinto agli esami*, he failed his examination.

**respir-are** [A1] *intr.* (*aux.* avere) to breathe; to respire; *tr.* to exhale; to breathe; *— l'aria fresca*, to breathe fresh air. **-atọre** *m.* respirator. **-ato·rio** *adj.* (*m.pl.* **-ato·rii**) respiratory. **-aziọne** *f.* breathing; respiration.

**respiro** *m.* breath; *esalare l'ultimo —*, to breathe one's last; rest, pause, breathing space; delay, respite; (fig.) small instalment.

**responsa·bil-e** *adj.* responsible; answerable. **-ità** *f.* responsibility; (leg.; comm.) liability.

**responsivo** *adj.* answering; responsive.

**responso** *m.* answer (*e.g.* of an oracle); reply; decision.

**ressa** *f.* crowd, throng; (fig.) insistence, pressure.

**resta**[1] *f.* beard of corn; fish-bone.

**resta**[2] *f.* string (of onions).

**resta**[3] *f.* rest (for a lance).

**rest-are** [A1] *intr.* (*aux.* essere) to stay, to remain; to be left, to be left over; to cease, to leave off; to be situated, to stand, to lie; to stop; *— di stucco*, to be amazed. **-ante** *part. adj.* remaining; *n.m.* remainder, rest.

**restaur-are** [A1a] *tr.* to restore; to renovate; to repair; to re-establish; *rfl.* to be restored; to recover. **-ativo** *adj.* restorative. **-atọre** *m.*, **-atrice** *f.* restorer. **-aziọne** *f.* restoration; re-establishment; recovery.

**resta·uro** *m.* restoration work; repair.

**rest-i·o** *adj.* (*m.pl.* **-i·i**) reluctant, unmanageable, restive; stubborn; loath, disinclined; *n.m.* restiveness; reluctance; impediment (in speech); hesitation.

**restitu-ire** [D2] *tr.* to return, to give back; to restore. **-ziọne** *f.* restitution; return; restoration; repayment.

**resto** *m.* remainder, rest, residue; (money) change; *pl.* remains; *adv. phr. del —*, moreover, besides, for the rest.

**restri·ng-ere** [C5] *tr.* to tighten, to bind tighter; to squeeze; to narrow; to restrict; to reduce; to lessen; to take in (clothes); *rfl.* to tighten; to contract; to shrink; to restrain oneself; *recip. rfl.* to draw closer together. **-imẹnto** *m.* narrowing, contracting; tightening; shrinking. **-itivo** *adj.* restrictive.

**restrittivo** *adj.* restrictive.

**restriziọne** *f.* restriction; limitation.

**retag·gio** *m.* heritage, inheritance; property.

**rẹt-e** *f.* net; netting; network; wire-netting; string-bag; (fig.) trap; (sport) net of goal; actual goal scored; (rlwy.) luggage-rack. **-are** [A1c] *tr.* (naut.) to net. **-ata** *f.* cast of a net; catch; network. **-icella** *f.* little net; hair-net; (rlwy.) *-icella per le valige*, luggage-rack.

**reticen-te** *adj.* reticent; reluctant or refusing to speak. **-za** *f.* reticence.

**reticol-are**[1] [A1s] *tr.* to reticulate; *intr.* (*aux.* avere) (paint.) to draw squares on a surface for copying or spacing a design. **-amẹnto** *m.* reticulating. **-ato** *adj.* reticulate, reticulated; *n.m.* barbed wire fence. **-aziọne** *f.* reticulation.

**reticolare**[2] *adj.* reticular; reticulated.

**re·tina**[1] *f.* (anat.) retina.

**retina**[2] *f. dim.* of **rẹte.**

**retinenza** *f.* retentive force.

**re·tore** *m.* rhetor; rhetorician.

**reto·ric-a** *f.* rhetoric; oratory, eloquence. **-are** [A2s] *intr.* (*aux.* avere) to teach rhetoric; (derog.) to speak with affected elegance. **-o** *adj.* rhetorical; *figure retoriche*, figures of speech; *n.m.* teacher of rhetoric.

**retrat·tile** *adj.* retractable.

**retribu-ire** [D2] *tr.* to pay, to repay; to recompense, to reward. **-ziọne** *f.* reward, recompense; pay; retribution.

**retrivo** *adj.* backward, reactionary; *n.m.* reactionary.

**retro**[1] *adv.* behind; *vedi —*, see back; *segue —*, continued on back; *n.m.* back; back-room; (of a coin) reverse; *negozio con —*, shop with a room at the back.

**retro-**[2] *pref.* rear; back. **-andare** [A7] *intr.* (*aux.* essere) to retrace one's steps. **-bottẹga** *f.* back-room (behind a shop). **-ca·mera** *f.* back-room (leading from a bedroom). **-ca·rica** *f.* (mil.) breech-loading. **-ce·dere** [B1] *intr.* (*aux.* avere, essere) to go back, to withdraw, to retreat; to recede. **-cessiọne** *f.* withdrawal; retrocession, retrogression. **-gradare** [A1] *intr.* (*aux.* avere) to withdraw, to recede; (astron.) to retrograde. **-grado** *adj.* retrograde; backward; reactionary. **-gressiọne** *f.* retrogression. **-gua·rdia** *f.* (mil.) rearguard. **-ma·rcia** *f.* (motor.) *in -marcia*, in reverse. **-scena** *f.* (theatr.) back-stage. **-scritto** *adj., n.m.* (something) written on the back, on the next page(s); 'see over'. **-spettivo** *adj.* retrospective; *n.m.* (cinem.) flashback. **-stanza** *f.* back-room. **-terra** *m.* hinterland. **-versiọne** *f.* retranslation. **-vi·e** *f.pl.* (mil.) supply lines. **-viṣọre** *m.* (motor.) driving mirror.

**retta**[1] *f.* (geom.) straight line; (racing) *— d'arrivo*, home stretch.

**retta**[2] *f. dar — a*, to pay attention to, to listen to; *date — a me*, mark my words.

**retta**[3] *f.* charge, terms (for board and lodging).

**retta**[4] *f.* resistance; durability.

**rettamẹnte** *adv.* rightly; honestly; uprightly.

**rettan·gol-o** *m.* (geom.) rectangle; oblong; court (*e.g.* for tennis); *adj.* (geom.) right-angled. **-are** *adj.* rectangular; oblong.

**retti·fic-a** *f.* correction, rectification; adjustment. **-are** [A2s] *tr.* to rectify, to correct; to straighten; to adjust. **-aziọne** *f.* rectification; correction; adjustment.

**rettifilo** *m.* straight road.

**ret·tile** *m.* (zool.) reptile.

**rett-o** *adj.* straight; upright; correct; *n.m.* (anat.) rectum; (geom.) right angle; recto. **-ẹzza** *f.* rectitude. **-ili·neo** *adj.* straight; rectilinear; *n.m.* straight road; (racing) the straight. **-itu·dine** *f.* rectitude, honesty.

**rettọr-e** *m.* ruler; governor; rector; president; *Rettore Magnifico*, Vice-Chancellor; *preside —*, headmaster. **-ato** *m.* rectorship, rectorate.

**re·um-a** *m.* (med.) rheumatism; cold, catarrh. **-a·tico** *adj.* (med.) rheumatic. **-atiṣmo** *m.* (med.) rheumatism. **-atiẓẓare** [A1] *tr.* to give rheumatism to; *rfl.* to get rheumatism. **-atiẓẓato** *part. adj.* afflicted with rheumatism.

**reveren-do** *adj.* reverend; *n.m.* Reverend; *buon giorno, —!*, good

morning, Father! **-dis·simo** *adj.* (eccl.) Right Reverend.

**reveren-te** reverent, respectful. **-za** *f.* reverence. **-ziale** *adj.* reverential.

**reviş-ione** *f.* revision; rehearing. **-ionare** [A1 c] *tr.* (eng.) to overhaul; to recondition. **-ore** *m.* reviser; (typ.) *-ore di bozze*, proof-reader.

**revoc-are** [A2 s] *tr.* to recall; to revoke, to repeal. **-azione** *f.* revocation.

**revo·lver** *m. indecl.* revolver. **-ata** *f.* revolver-shot.

**rezzo** *m.* shade; coolness; cool breeze.

**riabbassare** [A1] *tr.* to lower again; to lower still more.

**riabbracciare** [A3] *tr.*, *recip. rfl.* to embrace again; to meet again after a long time.

**riabilit-are** [A1 s] *tr.* to rehabilitate; to redeem; *rfl.* to recover one's reputation. **-azione** *f.* rehabilitation.

**riaccen·dere** [C1] *tr.* to rekindle; to relight.

**riaccomodare** [A1 s] *tr.* to mend (again); *recip. rfl.* to make up a quarrel, to become friends again.

**riaccostare** [A1] *tr.* to approach again; *recip. rfl.* to become reconciled.

**riacquist-are** [A1] *tr.* to recover; to buy back, to regain by purchase; *rfl.* to recover (oneself); to recover one's senses. **-o** *m.* recovery; repurchase.

**riaddormentare** [A1] *tr.* to put to sleep again; *rfl.* to fall asleep again.

**riagganciare** [A4] *tr.*, *abs.* to replace (telephone receiver); to hang up.

**rialto**[1] *m.* height, eminence, rise; knoll; raised embroidery.

**Rialto**[2] *pr.n.m.* Rialto; *il Ponte di* —, Rialto Bridge (in Venice).

**rialz-are** [A1] *tr.* to raise, to lift up (again); to heighten; *intr.* (*aux.* essere), *rfl.* (of barometer) to rise; to raise oneself, to go up. **-amento** *m.* lifting up, raising; heightening; rise. **-ista** *m.* (finan.) bull. **-o** *m.* rise; raising; lifting; hump; prominence.

**riamare** [A1] *tr.* to love in return.

**riammalare** [A1] *intr.* (*aux.* essere), *rfl.* to fall ill again, to have a relapse.

**riammettere** [C20] *tr.* to readmit (to membership); to admit again.

**riandare** [A7] *intr.* (*aux.* essere) to go again; to go back; *tr.* to recall, to call to mind; to go over again in one's mind.

**rianimare** [A1 s] *tr.* to revive, to restore to life; *rfl.* to recover (oneself), to regain consciousness, to revive.

**riapertura** *f.* reopening.

**riaprire** [D3] *tr.*, *rfl.* to reopen.

**riarm-are** [A1] *tr.*, *rfl.* to rearm, to refit; to equip; (archit.) to reinforce. **-o** *m.* rearmament.

**riarso** *adj.* dry; parched.

**riassett-are** [A1] *tr.* to rearrange; to set in order; *rfl.* to settle down. **-o** *m.* rearrangement; order; balance.

**riassu·mere** [C8] *tr.* to resume, to take up again; to re-employ; to summarize; to sum up.

**riassunt-o** *part.* of **riassu·mere**; *adj.* resumed; summed up, summarized; *n.m.* summary, recapitulation; abstract; **-ivo** *adj.* recapitulatory.

**riassunzione** *f.* resumption; re-employment.

**riattare** [A1] *tr.* to repair, to recondition.

**riattivare** [A1] *tr.* to bring into use again.

**riav-ere** [B3] *tr.* to get back, to recover; to restore; *rfl.* to recover (oneself, one's strength); *si è -uto*, he is better (in health). **-uta** *f.* recovery; (sport) return match; revenge.

**riavvicinare** [A1] *tr.* to approach again; to resume friendly relations with; to reconcile; *recip. rfl.* to be reconciled; to become friendly.

**ribad-ire** [D2] *tr.* to clinch, to rivet, to fix; (fig.) to confirm; to support (a statement) with additional reasons; *rfl.* (*acc.* of *prn.* 'si') to be clinched. **-itore** *m.* riveter (person); *adj.* clinching. **-itura** *f.* riveting.

**ribald-o** *m.* scoundrel, rascal; *adj.* rascally. **-a·glia** *f.* pack of scoundrels, gang of ruffians. **-eri·a** *f.* dirty trick.

**ribalta** *f.* flap; trap-door; (theatr.) foot-lights; front of the stage; *presentarsi alla* —, to take a (curtain) call.

**ribaltare** [A1] *tr.* to overturn, to upset; to tip; *intr.* (*aux.* essere, avere), *rfl.* to overturn, to roll over; to be upset.

**ribass-are** [A1] *tr.* to reduce (a price); to lower; *intr.* (*aux.* essere) (of prices) to fall, to drop, to be reduced. **-ista** *m.* (finan.) bear. **-o** *m.* fall (in price); reduction; sale; *-i fenomenali*, prices slashed.

**ribat·t-ere** [B1] *tr.* to beat again; to knock again (at a door); — *la palla*, to return the ball; to whet, to sharpen; to reflect; (of light) to strike, to fall upon; to confute; *intr.* (*aux.* avere) to insist; to reply, to retort; (mil.) to fall back, to retreat. **-imento** *m.* beating; echo; retort; confutation. **-itura** *f.* clinching; riveting; (of sound) reverberation; seam. **-uta** *f.* reply, retort; (sport) return of service.

**ribellare** [A1] *tr.* to rouse, to cause to rebel; to stir to rebellion; *rfl.* (*prep.* contro) to rebel, to rise (against); to protest (against).

**ribelle** *m.* rebel; *adj.* rebellious, rebel; disobedient.

**ribellione** *f.* rebellion, revolt, insurrection, sedition.

**ribes** *m. indecl.* (bot.) currant (black, white or red).

**riboc-co** *m.* (*pl.* **-chi**) overflow. **-care** [A2 c] *intr.* (*aux.* essere) to overflow.

**riboll-ire** [D1] *intr.* (*aux.* avere) to boil (again); to get hot by fermentation; *tr.* to boil up again; to boil for a long time. **-io** *m.* bubbling; sound of boiling. **-itura** *f.* reboiling; something boiled up again.

**ribotta** *f.* spree; revelry; debauch.

**ribrezzo** *m.* disgust; horror; shudder; shivering.

**ributt-are** [A1] *tr.* to throw again; to hurl back; to bring up, to vomit; to repel; to disgust; to rebut, to confute; *intr.* (*aux.* avere) (of a wound) to bleed again. **-ante** *part. adj.* disgusting; shocking. **-o** *m.* repulsion; refusal; vomit.

**ricacciare** [A3] *tr.* to drive (away or back); to repel.

**ricad-ere** [B5] *intr.* (*aux.* essere) to fall down (again); to relapse. **-imento** *m.* relapse; fall. **-uta** *f.* relapse; (atom. phys.) fall-out.

**ricalc-are** [A2] *tr.* to press down, to tread down; to retrace (steps); to follow; to transfer. **-ata** *f.* pressing down; transfer, copy. **-atoio** *m.* apparatus for making transfers. **-atura** *f.* transfer; copy made from a tracing.

**ricalcitr-are** [A1 s] *intr.* (*aux.* avere) to kick (of horses); to resist; to be recalcitrant. **-ante** *part. adj.* recalcitrant. **-azione** *f.* recalcitrance; resistance.

**rical-co** *m.* (*pl.* **-chi**) transfer (drawing); cast.

**ricam-are** [A1] *tr.* to embroider. **-atura** *f.* embroidering, embroidery work. **-o** *m.* embroidery.

**ricambiare** [A4] *tr.* to reciprocate, to return, to repay (greeting, act of courtesy, injury); to exchange; to replace.

**ricam·bio** *m.* exchange (of greetings, presents); reciprocation, return (of affection); requital; replacement; *pezzo di* —, spare part.

**ricant-are** [A1] *tr.*, *intr.* (*aux.* avere) to sing again; to repeat; to recant. **-azione** *f.* recantation.

**ricapitol-are** [A1 s] *tr.* to sum up, to summarize; to recapitulate. **-azione** *f.* recapitulation, summing up; summary.

**rica·ric-a** *f.* (watchm.) rewinding; *a — automatica*, self-winding. **-are** [A2 s] *tr.* to reload, to recharge; (of clock, watch) to rewind.

**ricasc-are** [A2] *intr.* (*aux.* essere) to fall again; to relapse. **-ata** *f.* relapse; fall. **-atẹzza** *f.* flabbiness, limpness.
**ricas-co** *m.* (*pl.* **-chi**) flounce.
**ricatt-are** [A1] *tr.* to recover expenses; to blackmail; *rfl.* to take one's revenge. **-amẹnto** *m.* recovery, revenge. **-atọre** *m.*, **-atrice** *f.* blackmailer. **-o** *m.* ransom; blackmail; revenge.
**ricav-are** [A1] *tr.* to draw, to extract; to obtain, to get. **-ato**, **-o** *m.* proceeds, yield, return.
**riccamẹnte** *adv.* richly.
**ricchẹzza** *f.* wealth, riches; earnings; income; *imposta di — mobile*, income-tax; (fig.) richness.
**ric·cio**[1] *m.* (zool.) hedgehog; sea urchin; prickly husk of chestnut.
**ricci-o**[2] *m.* curl, curly lock; (mus.) scroll (of a violin); *adj.* curly. **-uto** *adj.* curly.
**ric·ciol-o** *m.* curl (of hair). **-ina** *f.* curly endive; curly-headed girl. **-ino** *m.* little curl; curly-headed boy. **-uto** *adj.* curly.
**ric-co** *adj.* (*m.pl.* **-chi**) rich, wealthy; magnificent; — *di*, rich in, abounding in; *n.m.* rich man. **-cọne** *m. augm.* very wealthy man.
**ricerca** *f.* search; *la — dell'assassino continua*, the search for the murderer continues; investigation; research; (comm.) demand; *viva —*, brisk demand; (leg.) investigation; inquiry.
**ricerc-are** [A2] *tr.* to search for, to seek; to investigate; to inquire into; *rfl.* to examine oneself; to search one's conscience. **-ata** *f.* search; investigation; research. **-atẹzza** *f.* extreme care; elegance; affectation. **-ato** *part. adj.* affected; far-fetched; studied; in demand. **-atọre** *m.*, **-atrice** *f.* researcher; searcher.
**ricett-a** *f.* (chem.) formula; (pharm.; med.) prescription; (cul.) recipe; (comm.) *-e lorde*, gross receipts. **-a·rio** *m.* book of prescriptions, pharmacopoeia; cookery-book.
**ricetta·colo** *m.* refuge, shelter; receptacle.
**ricett-are** [A1] *tr.* to shelter, to hide; (leg.) to receive (stolen property); *rfl.* to take shelter, to hide. **-atọre** *m.* receiver, one who receives; receiver of stolen goods. **-aziọne** *f.* sheltering, receiving; (leg.) receiving (stolen property). **-ività** *f.* receptivity, sensitivity. **-ivo** *adj.* receptive, sensitive.
**ricetto** *m.* refuge, harbour, shelter.
**ricẹv-ere** [B1] *tr.* to receive; to accept; to take in; to be at home (to visitors); to take; to get; to experience, to feel. **-imẹnto** *m.* receiving; receipt; reception. **-itọre** *m.* receiver; customs and excise officer; (teleph.) receiver. **-itori·a** *f.* receiving office (for collection of taxes, lottery money). **-uta** *f.* receipt; quittance; *accusare -uta di*, to acknowledge receipt of.
**richiam-are** [A1] *tr.* to call again; to call back; to refer to; (mil.) to call up; to recall (from exile, or office abroad); to rebuke, to scold; *rfl.* to appeal; to lodge a complaint. **-ata** *f.* call; recall.
**richiamo** *m.* decoy; allurement; call; signal; order to retire; admonition, warning; reproof; appeal; reference, reference mark; catch-word.
**richie·d-ere** [C19] *tr.* to ask again (for); to request; to demand; to require; to necessitate; *impers.* to be necessary. **-ente** *m.*, *f.* applicant; petitioner.
**richiesta** *f.* request; demand.
**richiesto** *part.* of **richi·edere**; *adj.* sought after; in demand.
**richiu·d-ere** [C3] *tr.* to shut again; to shut up (in); to close again; to receive; to shelter; *abs.* to lock the doors; *rfl.* to close, to shut again; *la ferita si richiuse*, the wound closed up.
**richiuso** *part.* of **richiu·dere.**
**ri·cino** *m.* (bot.) castor-oil plant; *olio di —*, castor oil.
**rico·gl-iere** [B7] *tr.* to gather, to pick; to harvest; to catch again; *rfl.* to take shelter; to compose oneself; *recip. rfl.* to gather together again. **-imẹnto** *m.* gathering, collecting. **-itọre** *m.* gatherer; collector; *-itrice del parto*, midwife.
**ricognizione** *f.* recognition; reward; reconnaissance.
**ricollegare** [A2] *tr.* to join again, to connect again.
**ricolloc-are** [A2] *tr.* to replace; to place again. **-amẹnto** *m.* replacement.
**ricọlm-o** *adj.* brimful; overloaded. **-are** [A1 c] *tr.* to fill to the brim.
**ricolta** *f.* (mil.) retreat; fatigue party.
**ricominci-are** [A3] *tr.* to begin again, to start again; to recommence. **-amẹnto** *m.* beginning again, fresh start.
**ricompar-ire** [D1] *intr.* (*aux.* essere) to reappear. **-sa** *f.* reappearance.
**ricompens-a** *f.* reward; recompense; compensation. **-are** [A1] *tr.* to reward; to recompense; to requite.
**ricompọrre** [B21] *tr.* to put together again; to reassemble; to recompose; to reconstruct; (typ.) to reset; *rfl.* to be put together again; to be reconstructed; (fig.) to recover oneself, to regain one's composure.
**ricomprare** [A1 c] *tr.* to buy back; to buy another; to regain; to pay for twice over.
**riconcili-are** [A4] *tr.* to reconcile; *rfl.* to be reconciled; (eccl.) to make one's peace (with God); to be reconciled (with the Church); *recip. rfl.* to be reconciled one with another. **-aziọne** *f.* reconciliation.
**ricondurre** [B2] *tr.* to bring back, to take back; to lead back; (mil.) to recall; *rfl.* to go (to a place) again; to go back.
**riconfẹrma** *f.* confirmation; fresh confirmation.
**riconfermare** [A1 c] *tr.* to confirm (again), to reconfirm; *rfl.* to show, to prove oneself once more.
**ricongiun·gere** [C5] *tr.* to join again, to reunite; *rfl.* (*prep.* a) to be reunited (with); *recip. rfl.* to meet again; to be joined together again.
**riconọsc-ere** [B9] *tr.* to recognize, to acknowledge; to identify; (mil.) to reconnoitre; *rfl.* to acknowledge oneself; to confess; to be grateful. **-enza** *f.* gratitude; financial reward. **-i·bile** *adj.* recognizable. **-imẹnto** *m.* recognition, acknowledgement; confession; identification; mark serving for recognition or identification; (motor.) *targa di -imento*, number plate. **-itọre** *m.* one who recognizes; one who makes a reconnaissance; *adj.* grateful; rewarding.
**riconquist-a** *f.* recovery, reconquest. **-are** [A1] *tr.* to recover, to regain; to reconquer.
**riconsẹgn-a** *f.* redelivery; handing back. **-are** [A1 sc] *tr.* to redeliver; to hand back, to give back; to restore.
**riconver-tire** [D1] *tr.* to reconvert; to turn; *rfl.* to reform; to mend one's ways again. **-siọne** *f.* reconversion.
**rico·pi-a** *f.* fresh copy. **-are** [A4] *tr.* to copy again; to make a fair copy of. **-atura** *f.* copying; copying out; cost of copying; reproduction.
**ricopr-ire** [D1] *tr.* (*prep.* di, con) to re-cover; to cover up; to mask; *rfl.* to cover oneself (again); *-irsi di gloria*, to win great glory. **-itura** *f.* covering up; re-covering.
**ricordare**[1] *tr.* (mus.) to restring; (sport) *far — una racchetta*, to have a racket restrung.
**ricord-are**[2] [A1] *tr.* to recall; to remember; to remind of; to mention, to record; to commemorate; *rfl.* (*prep.* di) to remember; *non vi -ate di me ?*, don't you remember me ? **-a·bile** *adj.* memorable. **-anza** *f.* remembrance; memory. **-ativo** *adj.* aiding memory; relating to memory; memorable; commemorative. **-ẹvole** *adj.* mindful; memorable.
**ricordo** *m.* memory, recollection; remembrance; keepsake, souvenir; note; memorandum;

reminder; record; monument, memorial; *pl.* memoirs.

**ricọrr-ere** [C5] *intr.* (*aux.* avere, essere) to recur; (of anniversary, festival) to come round again, to fall; to have recourse (to), to apply (to); *tr.* to traverse again, to pass through again. **-enza** *f.* recurrence; occasion; anniversary; *-enze festive*, bank holidays. **-imẹnto** *m.* recurrence; frequent return; recourse, appeal.

**ricọrsa** *f.* running back; running again; (of pendulum) return, oscillation.

**ricọrso** *part.* of **ricọrrere**; *adj.* returned; recurrent; *n.m.* return, recurrence; appeal, complaint; application; *far — a*, to have recourse to; petition.

**ricostitu-ire** [D2] *tr.* to reconstitute, to re-form; to re-establish; *rfl.* to be reconstituted; to re-form; to recover. **-ente** *n.m.* tonic. **-ziọne** *f.* reconstitution; re-establishment; restoration.

**ricostru-ire** [D2] *tr.* to rebuild; to reconstruct. **-ziọne** *f.* rebuilding; reconstruction.

**ricotta** *f.* buttermilk curd; kind of cottage cheese; (fig.) *uomo di —*, weakling, spiritless person.

**ricotto** *part.* of **ricuo·cere**; *adj.* (techn.) annealed.

**ricover-are** [A1 s] *tr.* to give shelter to; to receive; to admit (to hospital); *rfl.* to take shelter; to find refuge. **-ato** *part. adj.*; *n.m.* inmate (of hospital, refugee-camp, etc.); refugee.

**rico·vero** *m.* refuge, shelter; dug-out.

**ricre-are** [A6] *tr.* to re-create, to re-elect; to restore; to refresh; *rfl.* to take recreation; to amuse oneself. **-ativo** *adj.* recreational; recreative; light, amusing. **-atọre** *adj.* refreshing, restorative. **-ato·rio** *adj.* (*m.pl.* **-atorii**) recreational; *n.m.* kindergarten; recreation-room. **-aziọne** *f.* recreation; pastime, amusement; play.

**ricrẹdere** [B1] *rfl.* to change one's mind; to recant; to be undeceived.

**ricrẹsc-ere** [B9] *intr.* (*aux.* essere) to grow, to increase again; to rise. **-enza** *f.* swelling, growth, excrescence. **-imẹnto** *m.* new growth, increase, rise.

**ricrẹscita** *f.* increase; swelling; new growth.

**ricuc-ire** [D1] *tr.* to sew up (again); (fig.) to string together. **-itura** *f.* sewing up, mending; seam; (fig.) stringing together.

**ricuo·c-ere** [C1] *tr.* to cook again; to boil up again; to rebake; to reheat; (techn.) to anneal. **-itura** *f.* second cooking.

**ricuper-are** [A1 s] *tr.* to recover, to regain; to recuperate; to rescue; to salvage; *rfl.* to be recovered; to take shelter. **-aziọne** *f.* recovery; regaining; getting back.

**ricu·pero** *m.* salvage; recovery; rescue.

**ricuṣ-a** *f.* refusal; rejection. **-are** [A1] *tr.* to refuse; to deny, to reject; (leg.) to challenge (a judge, juror) upon any suspicion of partiality; *rfl.* to refuse. **-aziọne** *f.* (leg.) challenge; exception.

**ridacchiare** [A4] *intr.* (*aux.* avere) to giggle; to snigger; to sneer.

**ridare** [A8] *tr.* to give back, to return; *intr.* (*aux.* avere, essere) *— giù*, to fall ill again, to have a relapse; *rfl.* to give oneself again.

**ridd-a** *f.* round dance, reel; wild dance; whirl. **-are** [A1] *intr.* (*aux.* avere) to dance a round; to dance in a ring. **-ọni** *adv.* in a round; whirling.

**ri·d-ere** [C3] *intr* (*aux.* avere) to laugh; (fig.) to shine brightly, to seem gay; to smile; *rfl.* (*dat.* of *prn.* 'si') to laugh at, to deride; *-ersela*, to laugh it off. **-ente** *part. adj.* laughing; (fig.) bright; smiling. **-ẹvole** *adj.* laughable, funny; ridiculous.

**ridestare** [A1] *tr.* to reawaken, to revive; to stir up; *rfl.* to wake up; to be revived.

**ridi·col-o** *adj.* ridiculous; funny; *n.m.* ridicule; absurdity; ridiculousness. **-ag·gine** *f.* absurdity. **-ẹzza** *f.* ridiculousness, absurdity; foolishness.

**ridipi·ngere** [C5] *tr.* (paint.) to repaint, to retouch.

**ridond-are** [A1 c] *intr.* (*aux.* essere, avere) to be superabundant; to overflow; to redound. **-amẹnto** *m.* redundancy, overflowing. **-ante** *part. adj.* redundant. **-anza** *f.* redundance; superabundance, superfluity; redundancy.

**ridọppio** *m.* more than double; *pagare a —*, to pay more than double.

**ridosso** *m.* shelter; (naut.) lee; *a —*, behind; in shelter; (fig.) close by; at one's back.

**ridọtto** *part.* of **ridurre**; *adj.* reduced; adjusted; corrected; compelled; *n.m.* private room; card-room; *mal —*, in a bad way; club-house; resort; retreat; *— del teatro*, foyer; (mil.) redoubt.

**ridurre** [B2] *tr.* to reduce; to bring back; to blight; to depress, to drive (to despair); to restrict; to convert, to change; to adjust, to adapt; (mus.) to arrange; *rfl.* to repair (to); to retire, to go; to take refuge; to be reduced.

**riduziọne** *f.* reduction; bringing back; discount; (theatr.) adaptation; (mus.) arrangement.

**riecco** *excl.* here (it) is again!; *rieccoli!*, here they are again!

**riecheggiare** [A3 c] *tr.*, *intr.* (*aux.* avere) to re-echo.

**rie·dere** *intr.* (poet.) to return.

**riedificare** [A2 se] *tr.* to rebuild.

**rieduc-are** [A2 s] *tr.* to re-educate; to rehabilitate. **-aziọne** *f.* re-education; rehabilitation.

**ri-eleg·gere** [C12] *tr.* to re-elect. **-eleziọne** *f.* re-election.

**riem·p-iere, riemp-ire** [D6] *tr.* to fill, to fill up, to fill in; *— di nuovo*, to refill; (cul.) to stuff; *rfl.* to be filled; to eat too much; to become pregnant. **-imẹnto** *m.* filling up; stuffing. **-ita** *f.* fill. **-itivo** *adj.* filling; superfluous; pleonastic; *n.m.* pleonasm; expletive; filling, stuffing; stop-gap. **-itura** *f.* filling; stuffing.

**rientr-are** [A1] *intr.* (*aux.* essere) to go in again, to come in again; to re-enter; to go home; to recede; to withdraw; *— in sè*, to come to oneself, (of wood, cloth) to shrink; (typ.) *far —*, to indent. **-ante** *part. adj.* receding. **-anza** *f.* (typ.) indent, indentation. **-ata** *f.* re-entry; re-entrance; reappearance; return, retreat; withdrawal. **-o** *m.* shrinkage.

**riepilog-are** [A2 s] *tr.* to recapitulate, to summarize. **-aziọne** *f.* recapitulation, summarizing, summing-up.

**riepi·lo-go** *m.* (*pl.* **-ghi**) summary, recapitulation; résumé; epitome.

**rieṣame** *m.* (leg.) re-examination.

**riesposiziọne** *f.* (mus.) recapitulation.

**rievoc-are** [A2 s] *tr.* to call up (again), to conjure up (again); to recall. **-aziọne** *f.* recalling; tribute (obituary).

**rifabbricare** [A2 s] *tr.* to rebuild.

**rifacimẹnto** *m.* remaking; remodelling; restoration; rewriting; adaptation; compensation.

**rifare** [B14] *tr.* to do again; to remake; to make again; to rebuild; to renew; to do up; to repair; to make good; to imitate; to retrace; *rfl.* (*acc.* of *prn.* 'si') to begin again; to recover one's strength; to cover one's losses; to make good; to be revenged; (of weather) to clear up.

**rifasci-are** [A4] *tr.* to bind, to bind round and round; to swaddle. **-ata** *f.* binding. **-atura** *f.* binding.

**rifa·scio** *adv. phr. a —*, in disorder; pell-mell.

**rifatt-o** *part.* of **rifare**; *adj.* restored, rebuilt; *villano —*, upstart; (cul.) rechauffé. **-ura** *f.* restoration; repair; rebuilding.

**rifaziọne** *f.* restoration; rebuilding.

**rifer-ire** [D2] *tr.* to report, to relate, to tell; to ascribe, to attribute; to return (thanks); *rfl.* to refer; to relate. **-imento** *m.* reference; relation; returning;

giving. **-itọre** *m.* reporter; tale-bearer.

**rifermare** [A1] *tr.* to refasten; to stop again; to confirm; to strengthen; *rfl.* to renew an engagement (of service).

**riffa**[1] *f.* raffle; lottery.

**riff-a**[2] *f.* violence. **-ọso** *adj.* rowdy; violent.

**rifiat-are** [A1] *intr.* (*aux.* avere) to breathe again; to breathe freely; to have time to breathe; *non —,* don't breathe a word. **-ata** *f.* breath; sigh of relief; pause.

**rifil-are** [A1] *tr.* to spin again; to trim; to trim to size; (fig.) to report (words spoken). **-atọre** *m.* reporter, tale-bearer, spy.

**rifin-ire** [D2] *tr.* to finish, to put the finishing touch to; to exhaust, to wear down, to wear out; *intr.* (*aux.* avere; *prep.* a) to be satisfactory (to); *rfl.* to wear oneself out. **-itẹzza** *f.* exhaustion; weariness. **-ito** *part. adj.* exhausted; worn out; *-ito morto,* dead tired; hard up. **-itura** *f.* finishing off. **-iziọne** *f.* finishing off; finish.

**rifior-ire** [D2] *intr.* (*aux.* avere, essere) to bloom again; to flourish again; to be renewed; to regain strength; *tr.* to embellish; to re-touch; to make up (a road), to dress with gravel; (paint.) to touch up, to brighten. **-imẹnto** *m.* revival; (paint.) ornament; embellishment; (roads, paths) making up with gravel. **-ita** *f.* bloom, reflorescence. **-itura** *f.* reflorescence; embellishment; dressing of gravel; reappearance of spots or stains of mould or grease.

**rifiut-are** [A1] *tr.* to refuse; to decline; to reject; *rfl.* to refuse oneself; to decline. **-o** *m.* refusal; rejection; renunciation; reject, person or thing rejected; *pl.* refuse, waste matter; scum; *-i di carta,* waste paper.

**rifless-o** *n.m.* reflexion; reflex (action); *di —,* by reflex action. **-amẹnte** *adv.* indirectly by reflection. **-i·bile** *adj.* worth thinking about; important. **-iọne** *f.* reflexion; meditation; deliberation. **-ivo** *adj.* reflecting; (fig.) thoughtful, reflective; (gramm.) reflexive. **-ọre** *m.* reflector.

**riflet·t-ere** [C19] *tr.* to reflect, to throw back; *intr.* (*aux.* avere) to reflect, to ponder; *ci -erò,* I will think it over; *rfl.* to be reflected. **-ọre** *m.* reflector; spotlight, searchlight; floodlight.

**rifluire** [D2] *intr.* (*aux.* avere, essere) to flow again, to flow back; to ebb.

**riflusso** *m.* reflux; refluence; ebb; *il flusso e il — del mare,* the ebb and flow of the sea.

**rifocill-are** [A1] *tr.* to revive; to refresh; to comfort; *rfl.* to take refreshment. **-amẹnto** *m.* taking of refreshment.

**rifoderare** [A1 s] *tr.* to reline, to put new lining in.

**rifondare** [A1 c] *tr.* to found again; to rebuild; (archit.) to repair the foundations.

**rifọnd-ere** [C2] *tr.* (metall.) to recast; (comm.) to refund, to reimburse; (fig.) to recast. **-i·bile** *adj.* reimbursable, to be refunded.

**riforbire** [D2] *tr.* to refurbish.

**rifọrma** *f.* reform; correction; emendation; (hist.) *la Riforma,* the Reformation; *la — cattolica,* the Counter-Reformation.

**riform-are** [A1 c] *tr.* to re-form, to form anew; to reform, to amend; to correct; (mil.) to discharge; to put on half-pay; *rfl.* to be restored to its former shape; to be reformed, amended. **-ativo** *adj.* reformative, reforming. **-ato** *part. adj.* re-formed; modified; reformed; (mil.) discharged; retired; *n.m.* man unfit for service; *pl.* (eccl.) members of a reformed religious order. **-atọre** *m.*, **-atrice** *f.* reformer. **-ato·rio** *adj.* (*m.pl.* **-atorii**) (leg.) reformatory. **-aziọne** *f.* reformation; new formation. **-ịsmo** *m.* reformism. **-ista** *m.*, *f.* reformist.

**riforn-ire** [D2] *tr.* (*prep.* di) to supply, to provide (with); *rfl.* to provide oneself (with); to take in a fresh supply (of). **-imẹnto** *m.* supply, provision(s); (motor.) *stazione di -imento,* filling station. **-itọre** *m.* (rlwy.) water tank.

**rifra·ng-ere** [C5] *tr.* (phys.) to refract; to break up, to throw back; *rfl.* (phys.) to be refracted; (of sound) to be echoed. **-ente** *part. adj.* (opt.) refracting. **-imẹnto** *m.* refraction.

**rifrattiv-o** *adj.* (phys.) refractive; refracting. **-ità** *f.* (phys.) refractivity.

**rifrattọre** *m.* refractor.

**rifraziọne** *f.* (phys.; opt.) refraction.

**rifreddare** [A1 c] *tr.* to cool (after cooking); to chill; *intr.* (*aux.* essere), *rfl.* to get cold.

**rifrẹddo** *adj.* cold; *n.m.pl.* cold meats.

**rifrig·gere** [C12] *tr.* to fry again; (fig.) to serve up again.

**rifritt-o** *part.* of **rifrig·gere**; *adj.* fried up again; (fig.) repeated many times; *n.m.* smell of frying fat; seasoning of fried herbs. **-ume** *m.* food dried up again; (fig.) rehash. **-ura** *f.* food fried again; (fig.) rehash; tedious repetition.

**rifrutt-are** [A1], **-ificare** [A2 s] *intr.* (*aux.* avere) to bear, to fructify (again). **-o** *m.* (comm.) compound interest.

**rifuggire** [D1] *intr.* (*aux.* essere) to flee again, to run away again; to take refuge; (*aux.* avere) to shrink, to be averse (from); *tr.* to shun.

**rifugi-are** [A3] *rfl.* to take refuge, to seek shelter. **-ato** *part. adj.* sheltered; *n.m.* refugee.

**rifu·gio** *m.* refuge, retreat, shelter, asylum; *— sotterraneo,* dug-out; *— contraereo,* air-raid shelter.

**rifu·lg-ere** [C30] *intr.* (*aux.* essere, avere) to shine, to be resplendent; to be refulgent; to be clear. **-ente** *part. adj.* refulgent.

**rifuṣ-o** *adj.* remelted; *adv. phr.* (fig.) *a —,* in abundance; refunded. **-iọne** *f.* remelting; (fig.) recasting (of written composition); reimbursement.

**rifuta-tivo** *adj.* refutative. **-ziọne** *f.* refutation.

**riga** *f.* line; row, stripe, streak; *la — dei capelli,* the parting in one's hair; (mil.) file; *in —!,* fall in!; *rompere le righe!,* fall out!; ruler; *— a forma di T,* T-square; (mus.) line (of stave).

**riga·glie** *f. pl.* giblets.

**riga·gnolo** *m.* rivulet; trickle, thin stream; gutter.

**rig-are** [A2] *tr.* to rule (lines); to score; to irrigate, to furrow; (mil.) to rifle; (fig.) *— diritto,* to act straightforwardly. **-ame** *m.* ruling, lines; stripes; (archit.) fluting; (mil.) rifling. **-ata** *f.* ruling, line; (mus.) stave. **-atino** *m.* striped material. **-ato** *part. adj.* irrigated, watered; lined, ruled; striped; (mil.) rifled; *n.m.* print, design. **-atọni** *m.pl.* (cul.) a kind of 'pasta' marked with flutings.

**rigatt-eri·a** *f.* old clothes; junk. **-iere** *m.* second-hand dealer.

**rigener-are** [A1 s] *tr.* to regenerate; *rfl.* to reproduce oneself; to grow again. **-amẹnto** *m.* reproduction. **-atọre** *m.*, **-atrice** *f.* regenerator; *-atore dei capelli,* hair restorer; *adj.* regenerating. **-aziọne** *f.* regeneration; reproduction.

**rigermogliare** [A4 c] *intr.* (*aux.* essere, avere) to bud again, to sprout again; (fig.) to flourish again.

**rigett-are** [A1] *tr.* to throw again; to throw back; to throw away; to reject; to postpone; *abs.* to throw back; to throw away; to reject; to postpone; *abs.* to sprout again; to vomit. **-amẹnto** *m.* rejection, throwing back; vomit; fresh sprouting. **-o** *m.* rejection; throw-out; *pl.* *-i del mare,* jetsam.

**righẹtt-a** *f.* (archit.) string course; cornice. **-are** [A1 c] *tr.* to rule, to line; to stripe.

**ri·gid-o** *adj.* stiff (with cold); rigorous (of climate); rigid; strict; austere; *n.m.* rigour,

extreme cold. **~ęzza** *f.* strictness, rigour, severity; rigidity; stiffness. **~ità** *f.* rigidity; severity.

**rigiocare** [A2] *tr.*, *intr.* (*aux.* avere) (sport) to replay.

**rigir~are** [A1] *intr.* (*aux.* essere, avere) to go round about; to walk again; *tr.* to twist (again); to turn; to stir; to surround; — *denari*, to invest money, to employ money in trade; to deceive; *rfl.* to turn round; to walk about. **~amęnto** *m.* turning round. **~ata** *f.* turn. **~atǫre** *m.* one who turns or twists; manager, leader; swindler, 'twister'. **~o** *m.* turning; winding; going to and fro; traffic; movement (of money), buying and selling; trick; intrigue.

**ri~go** *m.* (*pl.* **~ghi**) line, boundary; watercourse; line (of writing); (mus.) *~ghi finti*, leger lines. **~ghello** *m.* ruler, straight edge, set square. **~golino** *m. dim.* groove.

**rigǫgli~o** *m.* exuberance; rankness; luxuriance. **~ǫso** *adj.* luxuriant; in full bloom; full of vigour; rank.

**rigǫnfi~o** *adj.* swollen, distended; blown up; *n.m.* swelling, tumour. **~are** [A4c] *tr.* to blow up (again); *intr.* (*aux.* essere), *rfl.* to swell; (of the sea) to become rough.

**rigǫr~e** *m.* extreme cold, rigour; stiffness; (fig.) severity, strictness; *è di — l'abito nero*, evening dress is obligatory. **~įsmo** *m.* rigour; strictness; austerity. **~ista** *adj.* strict, rigorous; scrupulous; austere; *m.*, *f.* rigorist; stickler for discipline. **~ǫso** *adj.* rigorous; strict; severe.

**rigovernare** [A1] *tr.* to clean up, to set in order; — *i piatti*, to wash up; to groom, to curry; *abs.* to wash up.

**riguadagnare** [A5] *tr.* to regain; to win back, to recover.

**riguard~are** [A1] *tr.* to look again at, to look over; to look at closely; to examine carefully, to revise; to concern; to care for, to hold in regard; *intr.* (*aux.* avere; *prep.* a) to consider, to have regard (to); to look out (upon), to have a view (over); *rfl.* (*prep.* da) to look out (for), to guard (against); to beware (of); to abstain; *~arsi dal bere*, to abstain from drinking. **~ata** *f.* look, glance; look over. **~ato** *part. adj.* circumspect, prudent, wary. **~ęvole** *adj.* respectable, worthy of respect; considerable, remarkable.

**riguard~o** *m.* regard; respect, consideration; care; *fare —*, to be careful; *in — a*, with regard to; look; outlook; concerning, as regards. **~ǫso** *adj.* careful; respectful; considerate.

**riguarnire** [D2] *tr.* (eng.) to reline.

**rigurgit~are** [A1s] *intr.* (*aux.* avere) to overflow; to regurgitate; to gush out; (fig.) to swarm. **~ante** *part. adj.* overflowing; swarming.

**rigu·rgito** *m.* backwash, regurgitation; overflowing.

**rila·ncio** *m.* another throw; (at an auction) higher bid.

**rilasci~are** [A4] *tr.* to leave again; to let go again; to release; to relinquish; to issue; — *un passaporto*, to issue a passport; (comm.) to deliver, to consign; to ease; *rfl.* to relax, to become slack; to weaken; to go limp; *recip. rfl.* to part, to separate. **~amęnto** *m.* slackening, relaxation; weakening.

**rila·scio** *m.* release; concession; surrender; weakening; delivery.

**rilass~are** [A1] *tr.* to slacken, to loosen; to relax; to weaken; *rfl.* to slacken; to ease up; to become loose. **~amęnto** *m.* slackening; relaxation; weakening; weariness. **~ante** *part. adj.* slackening; loosening. **~atęzza** *f.* laxity, looseness; lack of enthusiasm. **~ativo** *adj.* laxative.

**rilecc~are** [A2] *tr.* to lick again; (fig.) to put the finishing touches to, to polish up. **~ata** *f.* lick; (fig.) finishing touch.

**rileg~are** [A2] *tr.* to bind again; to tie again; (of books) to bind; (of gems) to set. **~ato** *part. adj.* bound again; (of books) bound. **~atǫre** *m.* bookbinder. **~atura** *f.* binding; bookbinding.

**rileg·gere** [C12] *tr.* to re-read, to read again; to revise.

**rilento** *adv. phr. a —*, slowly; cautiously.

**rilev~are** [A1] *tr.* to take up again; to take away; to point out, to draw attention to; to notice; to understand, to realize; to learn; to take over; to raise again; to relieve; (art) to throw into relief; *intr.* (*aux.* avere) to rise (with yeast); to work (of liquid in fermentation); to amount to something, to be of consequence; (art) to stand out, to be in relief; *rfl.* to get up again; to rise again; (fig.) to get on one's feet again, to make good; (art) to stand out, to be in relief. **~ante** *part. adj.* considerable, important; weighty. **~ato** *part. adj.* raised (again); prominent, elevated; considerable; in relief; (comm.) taken over; *n.m.* height, elevation; high bank; embankment; (raised) pavement; figure in relief.

**rilievo** *m.* relief, prominence; projection; survey; (needlw.) *ricamo in —*, raised embroidery; *alto —*, high relief; *basso —*, low relief; (mil.) *dare — alla sentinella*, to change the sentry; relief map, elevation, high ground; *pl.* leavings.

**rilu·c~ere** [C def.] *intr.* to shine; to glisten; to gleam, to glitter. **~ente** *part. adj.* shining, glittering; (fig.) illustrious; brilliant.

**rilutt~are** [A1] *intr.* (*aux.* avere) to resist, to be reluctant; to object. **~ante** *part. adj.* reluctant. **~anza** *f.* reluctance.

**rima**[1] *f.* rhyme; poetry; — *piana*, feminine rhyme; — *tronca*, masculine rhyme; *terza —*, a three-line system of rhyming used by Dante in the *Divina Commedia; ottava —*, heroic stanzas of eight lines (as used by Ariosto in *Orlando Furioso*); *pl.* lyrical poems.

**rima**[2] *f.* crack, fissure; opening, slit.

**rimand~are** [A1] *tr.* to send again; to send back; to send away, to dismiss; to postpone, to put off, to defer; to refer. **~o** *m.* sending back; postponement; (in ball games) return; *di ~o*, in reply.

**rimaneggi~are** [A3c] *tr.* to change, to alter; to rehandle; to remodel; to rearrange; to re-adjust. **~amęnto** *m.* rehandling; remodelling; rearrangement; revision, revised edition.

**riman~ęre** [B2s] *intr.* (*aux.* essere) to stay, to remain; to be left over; (following 'ci') to die; to remain speechless; — *male*, to be in trouble; *sono rimasto molto male*, I was very upset; *sono rimasto senza benzina*, I have run out of petrol; to be situated; to agree; *foll. by prep.* 'a': to be attributed to, to be owned by; *impers.* to depend upon. **~ente** *part. adj.* remaining; left over; *n.m.* rest, remainder; residue; successor; *pl. i ~enti*, those remaining; *adv. phr. nel ~ente*, for the rest, moreover. **~enza** *f.* (comm.) residue; remainder.

**rimar~care** [A2] *tr.* to mark again; to note, to notice. **~chęvole** *adj.* remarkable. **~co** *m.* remark; note; reproof, censure.

**rim~are** [A1] *tr.* to compose in rhyme, to write in verse; to rhyme; *intr.* (*aux.* avere) to write poetry; to rhyme, to be in rhyme. **~a·rio** *m.* rhyming dictionary. **~atǫre** *m.* rhymster, versifier.

**rimarginare** [A1s] *tr.* to draw together the edges of; to heal; *rfl.*, *intr.* (*aux.* essere) to heal.

**rimaritare** [A1] *tr.*, *rfl.* to remarry.

**rimasticare** [A2s] *tr.* to masticate again, to chew thoroughly; to ruminate, to chew the cud of; (fig.) to ponder.

**rimasto** *part.* of **rimanęre**.

**rimaşu·glio** *m.* remainder, residue; *pl.* scraps, left-overs.

**rimatǫre** *m.* see under **rimare**.

**rimbacuccare** [A2] *rfl.* to muffle oneself up.

**rimballare**[1] [A1] *tr.* to pack up again.

**rimballare**[2] [A1] *intr.* (*aux.* avere) to bounce; to jog.

**rimbalz-are** [A1] *intr.* (*aux.* essere, avere) to rebound; to bounce; (mil.) to ricochet; *tr.* to send back, to return (*e.g.* a ball); to reflect. **-atura** *f.* rebounding, rebound. **-ello** *m.* game of ducks and drakes. **-o** *m.* rebound; bounce; (mil.) *colpo di -o*, ricochet; (telev.) relay television.

**rimbamb-inire, -ire** [D2] *intr.* (*aux.* essere) to enter one's second childhood; to grow childish in old age.

**rimbarc-are** [A2] *tr.* to put on board ship again; *rfl.*, *intr.* (*aux.* essere) to re-embark. **-o** *m.* re-embarkation.

**rimbẹc-co** *m.* (*pl.* **-chi**) retort, smart reply; pecking at one another; bickering. **-care** [A2 c] *tr.* to answer back; to retort; *-care la palla*, to return the ball; *recip. rfl.* to peck one another; (fig.) to bicker.

**rimbellire** [D2] *tr.* to embellish; to make more beautiful; *intr.* (*aux.* essere), *rfl.* to grow more beautiful.

**rimbọc-co** *m.* (*pl.* **-chi**) turn-up; tuck, wide hem. **-care** [A2 c] *tr.* to turn up (*e.g.* one's sleeves); to fold in (*e.g.* the top of a sack); *-care il lenzuolo*, to turn down the sheet; to fill up. **-catura** *f.* tuck; turn-up.

**rimbọmb-o** *m.* roar; thundering; reverberation. **-are** [A1 c] *intr.* (*aux.* avere) to thunder, to roar; to reverberate, to re-echo; to resound. **-ìo** *m.* (*pl.* **-ìi**) continued roaring; rumbling.

**rimbọrs-o** *m.* repayment; reimbursement; refund. **-are** [A1 c] *tr.* to repay; to refund, to pay back, to reimburse; *rfl.* to reimburse oneself; to obtain repayment.

**rimbos-care** [A2 c], **-chire** [D2] *tr.* to replant with trees; to carry out reafforestation in; *rfl.* to take to the woods, to hide in a forest.

**rimbrott-are** [A1] *tr.* to scold, to reproach, to rebuke; to taunt; *recip. rfl.* to reproach one another, to indulge in mutual recriminations. **-o** *m.* reproach, rebuke; *pl.* fault-finding.

**rimbrun-are** [A1], **-ire** [D2] *intr.* (*aux.* essere), *rfl.* to get darker; (fig.) to become gloomy.

**rimbucare** [A2] *tr.* to put in a hole; to hide; to put to the wash again.

**rimedi-are** [A4] *intr.* (*aux.* avere; *prep.* a) to provide a remedy (for); *tr.* to remedy, to cure, to put right; to mend; to put together, to make up. **-a·bile** *adj.* remediable.

**rime·dio** *m.* remedy; cure; medicine; *non c'è —*, it can't be helped.

**rimembr-are** [A1] *tr.* (poet.) to recall, to remember; *impers. mi -a*, I remember; *rfl.* (*acc.* of *prn* 'si'; *prep.* di) to remember, to recall. **-anza** *f.* remembrance, memory; recollection.

**rimen-are** [A1] *tr.* to bring again; to bring back; to handle; *rfl.* to be bustling and stirring; *n.m. un gran -arsi*, a great stir. **-ata** *f.* handling; mixing, kneading. **-ìo** *m.* (*pl.* **-ìi**) continued stirring; shaking up.

**rime·rit-o** *m.* recompense; reward. **-are** [A1 s] *tr.* to recompense, to reward; to requite; to pay back.

**rimescol-are** [A1 sc] *tr.* to mix up; to stir; to rummage among; (cards) to shuffle; *rfl.* to interfere (in); to be upset; (of the sea) to get rough; (of emotion) to be aroused. **-amẹnto** *m.* mixing up; stirring up; (cards) shuffling. **-anza** *f.* mixture, blend. **-ata** *f.* mixing; stir. **-ìo** *m.* (*pl.* **-ìi**) continued, frequent mixing, stirring, shaking up; bustling.

**rimẹssa** *f.* remission; sending back; (sport) return; remittance; store; shed; provision; coachhouse; *— di automobili*, garage; *vendere a —*, to sell at a loss; (of a plant) shoot; sprout.

**rimessiọne** *f.* remission.

**rimẹss-o** *part. adj.* of **rimẹttere**; restored; recovered; remitted; placid; submissive, meek; *n.m.* (paint.) retouching; (techn.) *lavoro di —*, marquetry, inlaid work. **-amẹnte** *adv.* submissively.

**rimest-are** [A1] *tr.* to stir (up) again; to shake up. **-atọre** *m.*, **-atrice** *f.* agitator; troublemaker.

**rimẹtt-ere** [C20] *tr.* to put back; to put on again; to refer, to submit; to remit, to forgive; to entrust; to lose; to correct; to postpone, to defer; to abate, to diminish; to lower; (comm.) to remit, to consign; *intr.* (*aux.* avere) (of plants) to sprout, to shoot again; to do inlaid work; *rfl.* (*acc.* of *prn.* 'si') to set to again; to be restored; *-ersi in salute*, to get well again; to resign oneself, to refer (to), to submit (to); (*dat.* of *prn.* 'si') *-ersi i guanti*, to put on one's gloves again. **-itura** *f.* putting back; setting (a fracture).

**rimirare** [A1] *tr.* to stare at, to gaze at; to behold; to look with admiration at.

**rimodern-are** [A1] *tr.* to modernize; *rfl.* to undergo modernization; to move with the times. **-atọre** *m.*, **-atrice** *f.* modernizer; *adj.* modernizing. **-atura** *f.* modernization.

**rimọnd-o** *adj.* clean; cleared; (hort.) lopped. **-are** [A1 c] *tr.* to clean; to clear out (drains, ditches); to clean again; (hort.) to lop.

**rimọnta** *f.* (mil.) remounting; (shoem.) resoling.

**rimont-are** [A1 c] *intr.* (*aux.* avere) to remount, to get on horseback again; (*aux.* essere) to go up again; to go back; *tr.* to remount; to go up again; to reassemble (watch, machine); *— cavalieri*, to remount a cavalry unit. **-atura** *f.* reassembling.

**rimo·rchi-o** *m.* (naut.) tow; vessel or object towed; cable used for towing; *banchina da —*, towpath; *a —*, in tow; (motor.) trailer; *cavo di —*, towrope. **-amẹnto** *m.* towing. **-are** [A4] *tr.* (naut.) to tow; (fig.) to lug. **-atọre** *m.* (naut.) tug, towing vessel. **-atrice** *adj. f.* (naut.) *una nave -atrice*, a towing vessel.

**rimo·rdere** [C3] *tr.* to bite again; (fig.) to torment, to prick; to rebuke; to reprove; *intr.* (*aux.* avere) to prick (of conscience).

**rimorso** *part.* of **rimo·rdere**; *n.m.* remorse.

**rimostr-are** [A1] *tr.* to show again; to remonstrate. **-anza** *f.* remonstrance; complaint; representation; protest.

**rimoto** *adj.* remote; secluded.

**rimo·v-ere** [C15] see **rimuovere**. **-i·bile** *adj.* removable. **-imẹnto** *m.* removal; dismissal. **-itọre** *m.* remover.

**rimoziọne** *f.* removal; (school) expulsion.

**rimpagliare** [A4] *tr.* to pack in straw again; to re-seat (a straw-seated chair).

**rimpall-are** [A1] *intr.* (*aux.* avere) (billiards) to cannon. **-o** *m.* (billiards) cannon.

**rimpast-are** [A1] *tr.* to knead again; to mix up again; (fig.) to recompose; to rearrange, to reconstitute; to recast; to revise. **-o** *m.* recomposition; reshuffle.

**rimpa·tri-o** *m.* repatriation. **-are** [A4] *intr.* (*aux.* avere, essere), *rfl.* to return home; *tr.* to repatriate.

**rimpettire** [D2] *intr.* (*aux.* essere), *rfl.* to swell with pride.

**rimpetto** *adv.* opposite; face to face; *prep. phr. di — a*, opposite, facing.

**rimpia·ngere** [C5] *tr.* to regret; to lament.

**rimpianto** *part.* of **rimpia·ngere**; *adj.* lamented; *il — Signor Bruni*, the late Mr. Brown; *n.m.* regret.

**rimpiatt-are** [A1] *tr.* to hide; to conceal; *rfl.* to creep away and hide. **-ino** *m.* hide-and-seek.

**rimpiazz-are** [A1] *tr.* to replace,

to substitute. **-o** *m.* substitute, replacement.

**rimpiccinire** [D2] *tr.* to dwarf; *intr.* (*aux.* essere) to become smaller.

**rimpicc(i)olire** [D2] *tr.* to make smaller; *rfl.* to lessen, to decrease.

**rimpieg-are** [A2] *tr.* to re-employ; (finan.) to reinvest. **-o** *m.* re-employment; (finan.) reinvestment.

**rimpinzare** [A1] *tr.* to stuff, to cram; *rfl.* to stuff oneself; to overeat.

**rimpolpare** [A1 c] *intr.* (*aux.* essere), *rfl.* to put on flesh, to grow fat; to become rich; *tr.* to fatten; (fig.) to enrich, to adorn.

**rimpolpettare** [A1 c] *tr.* to cover up (*e.g.* an indiscreet remark); to recast, to adapt.

**rimpro·ver-o** *m.* reproof, reproach; reprimand. **-are** [A1 s] *tr.* to reprove, to rebuke, to reproach; (*prep.* a) to grudge (to); *rfl.* (*prep.* di) to reproach oneself (with); to repent (of).

**rimuginare** [A1 s] *tr.* to turn over and over; to stir; *abs.* to rummage, to turn things upside down.

**rimuner-are** [A1 s] *tr.* to reward, to recompense, to remunerate. **-amẹnto** *m.* rewarding; remunerating. **-ativo** *adj.* rewarding, remunerative, profitable. **-ato·rio** *adj.* (*m.pl.* **-atorii**) remunerative. **-aziọne** *f.* recompense, remuneration; reward.

**rimunire** [D2] *tr.* to refurnish.

**rimuo·vere** [C15] *tr.* to remove; to clear away; to put away; to keep away; to deter; *rfl.* to withdraw.

**rimutare** [A1] *tr.* to change again; *rfl.* to change one's mind (again).

**rina·sc-ere** [B18] *intr.* (*aux.* essere) to be born again; to spring up again; to revive; to return. **-ente** *part. adj.* renascent; reviving. **-enza** *f.* renascence.

**rinascimẹnt-o** *m.* revival; rebirth; *pr.n.m.* (hist.) Renaissance. **-ale** *adj.* relating to the Renaissance.

**rina·scit-a** *f.* revival, renaissance; rebirth. **-uro** *adj.* about to be born again.

**rincacciare** [A4] *tr.* to drive back; to repel.

**rincagn-are** [A5] *rfl.* to scowl; to flatten one's nose. **-ato** *part. adj. naso -ato,* snub-nose.

**rincalcare** [A2] *tr.* to pull down.

**rincalorire** [D2] *tr.* to warm up (again); *intr.* (*aux.* avere) to produce heat; to cause intestinal irritation; *rfl.* to warm up, to get heated.

**rincalz-are** [A1] *tr.* to press upon; to follow closely; (agric.) to plant firmly; to earth up; — *un letto,* to tuck up the sides of a bed; to prop, to fix. **-amẹnto** *m.* support. **-ata** *f.* an act of reinforcement, support, earthing up, etc. **-atọre** *m.* (agric.) ridger, ridging plough. **-atura** *f,* earthing up. **-o** *m.* reinforcement, support; *a -o di,* in support of; (sport) reserve.

**rincantucciare** [A3] *tr.* to drive into a corner; to corner; *rfl.* to hide in a corner.

**rincar-are** [A1] *tr.* to raise the price of; to increase (quantity, dose); *intr.* (*aux.* essere) to become dearer; (of prices) to rise. **-o** *m.* rise in prices; *il -o dei viveri,* the rising cost of living.

**rincarn-are** [A1], **-ire** [D2] *tr.*, *intr.* (*aux.* essere) to make (to become) fatter; to put on flesh; *rfl.* to put on flesh; (of toe-nails) to grow in. **-ato, -ito** *part. adj.* fatter; *unghia -ita,* ingrowing toe-nail.

**rincaro** *m.* see under **rincarare.**

**rincasare** [A1] *tr.* to take home; *intr.* (*aux.* essere), *rfl.* to return home.

**rinchi-u·dere** [C3] *tr.* to shut up; to lock up; to shut in; *rfl.* to shut oneself in; to lock oneself in. **-uso** *part. adj.* shut up; locked in; (rel.) enclosed; *n.m.* enclosure; enclosed space; *saper di -uso,* to smell close, to smell fusty; (rel.) member of an enclosed order.

**rincọntr-o** *m.* encounter; meeting; *adv. gli veniva* —, he came towards him; *adv. phr. a, di* —, opposite. **-are** [A1 c] *tr.* to meet (again); to encounter; *intr.* (*aux.* essere) to come about, to happen; *recip. rfl.* to meet each other (again).

**rincorare** [A1] *tr.* to encourage; to cheer; *rfl.* to be encouraged; to take heart again.

**rincorniciare** [A3] *tr.* to reframe.

**rincorpor-are** [A1 s] *tr.* to reincorporate; (mil.) to re-form; *rfl.* to be reincorporated. **-amẹnto** *m.* reincorporation; (mil.) re-formation of troops.

**rincọrrere** [C5] *tr.* to chase, to pursue; to run after; *recip. rfl.* to chase each other; *fare a rincorrersi,* to play 'tig'.

**rincọrsa** *f.* run, sprint.

**rincrẹsc-ere** [B9] *intr.* (*aux.* essere; *prep.* a) to cause regret or displeasure (to); to cause sorrow (to); to be a matter of regret (to); *impers. mi -e di non potervi aiutare,* I am sorry I cannot help you. **-ẹvole** *adj.* regrettable; unpleasant; annoying. **-imẹnto** *m.* regret. **-iọso** *adj.* regrettable; disagreeable; unwilling.

**rincrud-ire** [D2] *tr.* to aggravate; to increase the pain of; to embitter; *intr.* (*aux.* essere), *rfl.* to become sharper, to become colder, to grow more severe. **-imẹnto** *m.* aggravation.

**rincul-are** [A1] *intr.* (*aux.* essere, avere) to draw back, to shrink back, to recoil; to back away. **-o** *m.* recoil.

**rinfacciare** [A3] *tr.* (*prep.* a) to throw (in the face of), to cast (in the teeth of); to taunt with.

**rinfanciullire** [D2] *intr.* (*aux.* essere) to become childish, to enter one's second childhood.

**rinfervorare** [A1 s] *tr.* to rouse to fresh enthusiasm; *rfl.* to become more enthusiastic.

**rinfian-care** [A2] *tr.* (archit.) to support at the sides; to prop. **-camẹnto** *m.* support, reinforcement. **-cheggiare** [A3c] *tr.* to support. **-co** *m.* (*pl.* **-chi**) support.

**rinfocare** [A2 d] *tr.* to rekindle; to inflame.

**rinfocolare** [A1 s] *tr.* to rekindle; to stir up; to revive; *rfl.* to burst into flame again.

**rinfoderare** [A1 s] *tr.* to re-sheathe; to reline.

**rinforz-are** [A1] *tr.* to strengthen; to reinforce; to confirm to clinch (an argument). **-amẹnto** *m.* strengthening, reinforcement. **-o** *m.* strengthening; reinforcement; prop, support.

**rinfrancare** [A2] *tr.* to hearten, to reassure; to encourage; *rfl.* to be reassured, to take heart again, to pluck up courage; to make good one's losses.

**rinfranchire** [D2] *rfl.* to be reassured; to improve, to become more skilful.

**rinfra·ngere** [C5] *tr.* to break up, to break to pieces; *rfl.* to break into pieces, to break up; to be broken up.

**rinfresc-are** [A2] *tr.* to cool, to make cooler; to refresh; to replenish; to renew; to restore; *intr.* (*aux.* essere) to become cool; to be cooling, to be refreshing; *rfl.* to become cooler, to cool down; to refresh oneself; to take refreshment; (of the wind) to freshen. **-amẹnto** *m.* cooling; freshening; rest; refreshment; provisions, restocking; fresh troops. **-ante** *part. adj.* cooling; refreshing; *n.m.* freshener; mild laxative. **-ata** *f.* cooling; sprinkling or dashing with water; aperient. **-ativo** *adj.* refreshing; cooling. **-atọio** *m.* ventilator; water-cooler. **-atura** *f.* cooling (down); cooler weather; (paint.; sculp.) restoration, touching up.

**rinfrẹs-co** *m.* (*pl.* **-chi**) light refreshments; liqueur; rest; aid.

**rinfrign-are** [A5] *tr.* to cobble up, to sew badly, to pucker. **-o** *m.* pucker; scar. **-olito** *adj.* badly sewn up; puckered.

**rinfrinzellare** [A1] *tr.* to sew up badly, to pucker.

**rinfronẓ-ire** [D2] *intr.* (*aux.* essere, avere) to grow fresh leaves; *rfl.* to deck oneself out. **-olare** [A1 s], **-olire** [D2] *intr.* (*aux.* essere), *rfl.* to titivate oneself.

**rinfuṣ-o** *adj.* confused, mixed up; *adv. phr. alla -a,* higgledy-piggledy, in great confusion; (comm.) sold loose, not packed.

**ringalluzzire** [D2] *intr.* (*aux.* essere), *rfl.* to be elated, to be proud, to be 'cocky'; *tr.* to make proud.

**ringangherare** [A1 s] *tr.* to replace on hinges; to put together again; (fig.) to piece together.

**ringhiare** [A4] *intr.* (*aux.* avere) to snarl; to growl.

**ringhiera** *f.* rostrum, platform; balcony; rail, railing; banisters.

**ri·nghi-o** *m.* snarl; growl. **-ọso** *adj.* snarling; bad-tempered; *n.m.* bad-tempered man.

**ringiallire** [D2] *tr., intr.* (*aux.* essere) to turn yellow; to turn yellow again.

**ringiovan-ire** [D2] *tr.* to make younger, to rejuvenate; *intr.* (*aux.* essere) to grow young again; to look younger. **-imẹnto** *m.* (med.) rejuvenescence.

**ringrazi-are** [A4] *tr.* to thank. **-amẹnto** *m.* thanks; *gradisca i miei -amenti,* accept my thanks; (rel.) thanksgiving.

**rinneg-are** [A2 c] *tr.* to deny; to disown. **-ato** *part. adj.* disowned; denied; *n.m.* renegade. **-aziọne** *f.* denial; disowning.

**rinnov-are** [A1 d] *tr.* to renew; — *le lenzuola,* to change the sheets; — *una cambiale,* to renew a bill; (paint.) to restore; *rfl.* to be renewed; to begin again; to be renovated; to be restored or repaired. **-amẹnto** *m.* renewal; return; revival, reawakening; renovating. **-ativo** *adj.* tending to renew. **-aziọne** *f.* renewal; restoration; (comm.) *-azione di cambiale,* renewal of a bill.

**rinnovellare** [A1] *tr.* to renew; to repeat; to refresh; to revive; to call to mind; *intr.* (*aux.* essere), *rfl.* to be renewed; to change.

**rinnovo** *m.* renewal; renovation.

**rinocerọnte** *m.* (zool.) rhinoceros.

**rino·log-o** *m.* (med.) rhinologist, nose specialist. **-i·a** *f.* (med.) rhinology.

**rinom-are** [A1] *tr.* to celebrate; to praise. **-anza** *f.* renown, fame. **-ato** *part. adj.* renowned; famous.

**rinominare** [A1 s] *tr.* to name again to renominate; to re-appoint.

**rinsaldare** [A1] *tr.* to stiffen; to strengthen.

**rinsangu-are** [A6] *tr.* to put fresh blood into; (fig.) to give new strength to ; *rfl.* to get fresh strength; to recover. **-inare** [A1] *tr.* to stain with blood again; *rfl.* to get fresh blood; to recover; (fig.) to make good one's losses.

**rinsanire**[1] [D2] *intr.* (*aux.* essere) to recover one's health; to recover one's sanity.

**rinsanire**[2] [D2] *intr.* (*aux.* essere) to return to reason; to recover one's wits; to become sensible again.

**rinserr-are** [A1] *tr.* to shut up again; to conceal, to hide; *rfl.* to shut oneself up; to hide. **-ato** *part. adj.* shut up; hidden; *n.m.* house, room, etc. which is shut up; *odore di -ato,* close, musty smell.

**rinsonare** [A1 d] *intr.* (*aux.* essere, avere) to resound; to roar.

**rintanare** [A1] *rfl.* to shut oneself up; to re-enter a den; (fig.) to hide; *tr.* to chase into a den.

**rintegolare** [A1 sc] *tr.* to repair the roof of; to retile.

**rintegr-are** [A1] *tr.* to make good, to restore to proper condition; (comm.) to renew, to restore; *rfl.* to recover; to be restored. **-aziọne** *f.* restoration; recovery.

**rintọc-co** *m.* (*pl.* **-chi**) tolling; knell; chime of a bell; blast of a horn. **-care** [A2 c] *intr.* (*aux.* essere, avere) to toll; (of a clock) to strike; to ring.

**rintopp-o** *m.* meeting, encounter; obstacle; *adv. phr. di* —, by way of contrast; in return. **-are** [A1] *tr.* to stumble against, to run into; to patch; to mend; *recip. rfl.* to meet each other, to run into each other; to come across each other.

**rintracci-are** [A3] *tr.* to trace; to track down; to follow up. **-a·bile** *adj.* traceable. **-amẹnto** *m.* tracking, tracing; investigation.

**rintron-are** [A1] *tr.* to shake; to deafen, to stun; *intr.* (*aux.* essere, avere) to thunder, to boom; to resound. **-amẹnto** *m.* deafening, stunning; booming, thundering. **-o** *m.* deafening noise.

**rintuono** *m.* thundering; booming; reverberation.

**rintuzzare** [A1] *tr.* to blunt; to dull; to check; *rfl.* to shrink, to cower.

**rinu·nci-a, rinu·nzi-a** *f.* renunciation; surrender. **-are** [A4] *tr.* to renounce; to give up; to disclaim; *intr.* (*aux.* avere) *prep.* a) to renounce; to resign; *-are al trono,* to abdicate; to abstain (from); to waive.

**rinven-ire** [D17] *tr.* to discover, to find (out); to bring round (from a faint); *intr.* (*aux.* essere) to recover one's senses; to come to oneself; to revive, to recover; *rfl.* to remember; to find one's way. **-imẹnto** *m.* discovery; recovery.

**rinverd-ire** [D2] *tr.* to make green again; to revive; *intr.* (*aux.* essere) to grow green again; to revive. **-imẹnto** *m.* growing green again; revival.

**rinvest-ire** [D1] *tr.* to reinvest; to install again; to strengthen; to reinstate; (mil.) to lay siege to again. **-imẹnto** *m.* reinvesting; reinstallation (in a position of authority); (mil.) *-imento di fortezza,* investment, besieging of a fortress. **-itura** *f.* reinvestiture.

**rinviare** [A4] *tr.* to send back; to put off, to postpone, to adjourn.

**rinvigor-ire** [D2] *tr.* to invigorate, to strengthen; *intr.* (*aux.* essere), *rfl.* to revive; to gain new strength, to grow strong again. **-imẹnto** *m.* strengthening; invigoration.

**rinvi·lio** *m.* reduction; cheapening; depreciation, fall in price.

**rinvilire** [D2] *tr.* to cheapen; to lower the price of; *intr.* (*aux.* essere) to become cheaper; to be reduced in price.

**rinv-i·o** *m.* (*pl.* **-i·i**) sending back; cross reference; adjournment; postponement; (eng.) transmission, gear.

**rio**[1] *m.* stream, brook; (Venice) canal; — *terrà,* canal earthed over.

**rio**[2] *adj.* wicked; evil.

**rioccup-are** [A1 s] *tr.* to re-occupy; *rfl.* to occupy oneself again. **-aziọne** *f.* reoccupation.

**riọn-e** *m.* quarter (of a city); ward, district. **-ale** *adj.* relating to a quarter, ward, etc. not of the city-centre; *un teatro -ale,* a theatre in an outlying district; (fig.) cheap, shoddy.

**riordin-are** [A1 s] *tr.* to re-arrange; to reorganize; (mil.) to re-form; *rfl.* to get into order again. **-amẹnto** *m.* rearrangement; reordering; re-forming. **-atọre** *m.*, **-atrice** *f.* reorganizer; *adj.* reorganizing. **-aziọne** *f.* rearrangement; reorganization; (eccl.) reordination.

**riorganiẓẓ-are** [A1] *tr.* to re-organize, to rearrange. **-aziọne** *f.* reordering; reconstruction, reorganization.

**riottọs-o** *adj.* litigious; quarrelsome; refractory; sulky. **-ità** *f.* quarrelsomeness; sulkiness.

**ripa** *f.* bank; shore; precipice.

**ripagare** [A2] *tr.* to pay again; to repay; to pay back; to recompense.

**ripar-are**[1] [A1] *tr.* to repair, to mend; to make good; (naut.) to re-fit; to shield, to shelter; to parry; *intr.* (*aux.* avere; *prep.* a) to provide (for), to remedy, to make good; to see (to), to make arrangements (for); *rfl.* to take shelter. **-amento** *m.* repair; remedy; restoration; defence. **-ata** *f.* hurried repair(s). **-azione** *f.* repair(s); reparation; satisfaction; restoration.

**riparare**[2] [A1] *intr.* (*aux.* essere) to repair, to make away; to escape.

**ripa·rio** *adj.* riparian, living on river banks.

**riparlare** [A1] *intr.* (*aux.* avere) to speak again; *recip. rfl.* to talk things over.

**riparo** *m.* shelter, protection, cover, defence; *al* —, in safety; *mettersi al* —, to get under cover; remedy; *senza* —, beyond repair; *non c'é* — there is nothing to be done about it; fence, embankment; fender.

**ripartire**[1] [D1] *intr.* (*aux.* essere) to leave again.

**ripart-ire**[2] [D1] *tr.* to share; to divide; to distribute; to separate, to part. **-imento** *m.* division, distribution; compartment. **-izione** *f.* division; distribution; sharing out; (comm.) allotment; assessment. **-o** *m.* distribution; compartment, department; share; (mil.) unit.

**ripass-are** [A1] *tr.* to cross again; to look over again, to revise; to iron (with a smoothing-iron); — *un rasoio*, to strop a razor; to sieve, to sift, to strain; to beat, to hit; (paint.; sculp.) to touch up, to retouch; to overhaul; *intr.* (*aux.* essere) to pass again; to call again. **-ata** *f.* passing again; repassing; look over; rub; *-ata col ferro*, pressing, ironing. **-atura** *f.* (eng.) overhauling. **-o** *m.* returning; repetition; revision.

**ripens-are** [A1] *intr.* (*aux.* avere) to think again; to reconsider; *tr.* to recall; *rfl.* (*acc.* of *prn.* 'si') to change one's mind; (*dat.* of *prn* 'si') to recall to mind. **-amento** *m.* thinking things over; change of mind.

**ripent-ire** [D1] *rfl.* to repent (again); to regret; to change one's mind. **-imento** *m.* repentance; regret.

**ripercossa** *f.* see **ripercussione.**

**riperc(u)o·t-ere** [C15] *tr.* to strike again, to beat; to send back, to throw back; to reflect; *rfl.*, *intr.* (*aux.* essere) to echo; to be reflected, to reverberate.

**ripercussione** *f.* repercussion; reflection; echo, reverberation.

**ripescare** [A2 c] *tr.* to fish out again; to pick up; to get hold of; to find again.

**ripe·t-ere** [B1] *tr.* to repeat; to recite; to tell again; (theatr.) to rehearse; to derive; *rfl.* to repeat oneself; to recur. **-ente** *part. adj.* repeating; *n.m.*, *f.* pupil remaining in the same class for a second year. **-itore** *m.* repeater; coach. **-izione** *f.* repetition; revision; private lesson; recitation; rehearsal; (mil.) *fucile a -izione*, repeating gun; *orologio a -izione*, repeater; (mus.) repetition; rehearsal. **-utamente** *adv.* repeatedly. **-uto** *part. adj.* repeated; reiterated.

**ripianare** [A1] *tr.* to level; (accounts) to balance; to settle; (agric.) to level (ground) after ploughing.

**ripiano** *m.* landing (of a staircase); level space; terrace; shelf.

**ripicco** *m.* pique; resentment; *per* —, out of pique.

**ri·pid-o** *adj.* steep; precipitous. **-ezza** *f.* steepness.

**ripieg-are** [A2] *tr.* to fold again; to fold up; to bend again; (naut.) to furl; *intr.* (*aux.* avere) (mil.) to retreat; to make shift; *rfl.* to fold; to bend; to withdraw into oneself; (of light) to be reflected; (mil.) *-arsi a sinistra*, to incline to the left. **-amento** *m.* folding, folding again; bending; reflection (in thought); (mil.) retreat. **-ata** *f.* folding, fold; bend. **-atura** *f.* double fold; folding; lap.

**ripie-go** *m.* (*pl.* **-ghi**) expedient; makeshift; remedy; pretext, excuse.

**ripien-o** *adj.* (*prep.* di) full up, quite full; replete, stuffed (with); (fig.) filled; *n.m.* filling; padding; feeling of repletion; (cul.) stuffing; (text.) weft, woof; (mus.) full sound; filling up, ripieno; *violino da* —, second violin. **-ezza** *f.* repletion; surfeit; (of river) fullness, flood. **-ista** *m.*, *f.* (mus.) rank-and-file player.

**ripigliare** [A4] *tr.* to take again, to catch again; to recover, to regain; to curl up; to darn (a hole); to resume, to begin again; to repeat; to reply; *intr.* (*aux.* avere) to recover, to revive; *rfl.* to resume; to begin again; to correct oneself; resumption.

**ripiglino** *m.* game of cat's cradle.

**ripi·glio** *m.* reproof.

**ripiombare** [A1 c] *intr.* (*aux.* essere) to fall down again; to sink down again; to fall sheer; *tr.* to plunge back.

**riporre** [B21] *tr.* to replace; to put back; to place (again); to put away; to hide; to deposit; to repair, to restore; *rfl.* to place oneself again.

**riport-are** [A1] *tr.* to bring back; to take back; to carry back; to relate; (math.) to carry; (accountancy) to carry forward; *rfl.* (*prep.* a) to go back; to be traceable (to); to refer (to); to appeal (to). **-atore** *m.*, **-atrice** *f.* reporter. **-atura** *f.* transfer.

**riporto** *m.* relationship; *neve di* —, drift snow; (comm.) amount carried or brought forward; (finan.) contango.

**ripos-are** [A1] *tr.* to put back, to put down again; to lay down again; to rest; *intr.* (*aux.* avere) to rest; to sleep; to die; to be buried; *rfl.* to rest; to cease work; to take time off. **-ante** *part. adj.* restful; soothing; relaxing. **-ata** *f.* rest; pause, stop. **-atamente** *adv.* restfully; peacefully. **-ato** *part. adj.* rested; quiet, peaceful; tranquil. **-atoio** *m.* landing (of a staircase); resting place.

**riposizione** *f.* putting on one side; reservation; deposition.

**riposo** *m.* rest, repose; resting place; *buon* —*!*, sleep well!; *giorno di* —, day off; (theatr.) no performance; (mil.) — *!*, stand easy!; *a* —, in retirement.

**ripost-o, ripost-o** *part.* of **riporre**; *adj.* put back, put away; hidden, secret; *n.m.* (mil.) store. **-amente** *adv.* secretly. **-i·glio** *m.* repository; locker; nook, hiding place; lumber-room.

**ripren·dere** [C1] *tr.* to take back; to take up again; to retake, to recapture; to resume; — *una maglia*, to pick up a stitch; to strike, to attack again; to criticize, to blame; to reply, to retort; (cinem.) to film; *rfl.* to correct oneself; to recover; to resume (the thread of one's speech); *intr.* (*aux.* avere) to recover strength.

**riprens-i·bile** *adj.* reprehensible; blameworthy. **-ione** *f.* reproof; blame. **-ivo** *adj.* critical, reproving.

**ripresa** *f.* resumption, recommencement, renewal; retaking; recapture; *a più riprese*, several times over; (photog.) shot, exposure; (cinem.) take; *macchina da* —, ciné camera; (telev.) — *diretta*, live television; (sport) second half; (boxing) round; bout; (prosod.) refrain; (mus.) repeat; repeat-mark; refrain; recapitulation; (theatr.) revival.

**ripreso** *part.* of **ripre·ndere.**

**ripri·stin-o** *m.* restoration; renewal; *lavori di* —, work of restoration. **-are** [A1 s] *tr.* to restore; to renew; to reinstate.

**riproduci·bile** *adj.* reproducible.

**ripro-durre** [B2] *tr.* to reproduce; to produce again; *rfl.* to reproduce one's kind; to breed; to be reproduced; to recur. **-duttivo** *adj.* reproductive. **-duttore** *adj.*, **-duttrice** *f.* reproducing; *organi -duttori*, organs of reproduction; *n.m.*

reproducer; *-duttore fonografico,* record player; (of animals) sire. **-duzione** *f.* reproduction; copy; replica.

**ripromett-ere** [C20] *tr.* to promise again; *rfl.* (*dat.* of *prn.* 'si') to hope (for); *-ersi da,* to expect of, from. **-itore** *m.* surety, guarantor.

**ripromissione** *f.* guarantee; promise; (bibl.) *terra della —,* the promised land.

**riprova** *f.* new proof; new evidence; confirmation; (leg.) *stare alla —,* to undergo cross-examination; (math.) proof.

**riprov-are** [A1] *tr.* to try again, to test again; to obtain confirmation; to disprove; to reject; to disapprove, to blame. **-amento** *m.* reprobation; reproof; blame. **-atore** *m.*, **-atrice** *f.* reprover, blamer; rejector. **-azione** *f.* reprobation; rejection; (theol.) reprobation. **-evole** *adj.* blameworthy; despicable; shameful.

**ripu·di-o** *m.* disowning; repudiation; rejection; (hist.) *fare il —,* to divorce a wife. **-are** [A4] *tr.* (leg.) to disavow; to disclaim; to disown; to reject; to repudiate.

**ripugn-are** [A5] *intr.* (*aux.* avere; *prep.* a) to be contrary (to); to be repugnant to. **-ante** *part. adj.* repugnant; contrary. **-anza** *f.* repugnance; aversion; reluctance; incompatibility.

**ripul-ire** [D2] *tr.* to clean again; to tidy: to clear away; to clean up; to purge; to polish, to revise; to eat up; to make a clean sweep of; (in a game) to sweep the board; *rfl.* to tidy oneself; to smarten oneself up. **-ita** *f.* cleaning up; clearing away; revising, polishing; touching up. **-itura** *f.* cleaning; clearing; waste, refuse.

**ripulisti** *m.* (pop.) see **repulisti.**

**ripuls-a** *f.* refusal, rejection, repulse. **-are** [A1] *tr.* to repulse, to refuse; to reject; to deny. **-azione** *f.* rejection; confutation. **-ione** *f.* repulsion; aversion; repugnance. **-ivo** *adj.* repulsive; repellent.

**ripurg-are** [A2] *tr.* to purify; to revise, to correct. **-amento** *m.* purging; purifying. **-ativo** *adj.* purgative.

**riquadr-are** [A1] *tr.* to square; to dress (stone); to true up; to measure (surface); *— le stanze,* to redecorate walls with a cornice or border; *intr.* (*aux.* avere) to be square; to be true; to measure. **-ato** *part. adj.* squared; true, quite square; marked, or arranged in squares; (math.) squared; *n.m.* square. **-atura** *f.* squaring; square. **-o** *m.* square; rectangular panel; inset.

**risa·i-a** *f.* paddy-field, rice-field; building for threshing and polishing rice. **-uola** *f.*, **-uolo** *m.* worker in paddy-fields.

**risald-are** [A1] *tr.* to resolder; to mend; to solder. **-amento** *m.* soldering; mending; healing (of wound). **-atura** *f.* resoldering; soldering; mending; solder.

**risal-ire** [D13] *intr.* (*aux.* essere) to go up again; to go back; to travel upstream; to go back (to), to date back (to); *tr.* to ascend (again); *— la corrente,* to stem the current. **-ita** *f.* projection, prominence; fresh ascent.

**risalt-are** [A1] *tr.* to jump over, across, again; *intr.* (*aux.* avere, essere) to spring up again; to stand out, to be prominent; to be conspicuous; (of truth) to be self-evident; *fare —,* to enhance, to emphasize, to make conspicuous. **-o** *m.* prominence; relief; vividness; projection; *porre in -o,* to emphasize.

**risan-are** [A1] *tr.* to heal, to cure; to restore to health; to reclaim; *intr.* (*aux.* essere), *rfl.* to recover; to be restored to health. **-a·bile** *adj.* curable; capable of reformation; (of land) reclaimable. **-amento** *m.* cure; recovery; reformation; improvement; slum clearance; (of land) reclamation. **-atore** *m.*, **-atrice** *f.* healer; *adj.* healing; curative; reforming.

**risap-ere** [B26] *tr.* to get to know; to hear about; to find out; *intr.* (*aux.* avere) to smell, to taste. **-uto** *part. adj.* very well known.

**risarc-ire** [D2] *tr.* to repair; to mend; to restore; to indemnify, to make good; *— il danno,* to make good the damage; *— i danni,* to pay damages. **-i·bile** *adj.* reparable. **-imento** *m.* repair; restoration; compensation; damages; indemnity; reparation.

**risarella** *f.* (colloq.) giggles.

**risat-a** *f.* laugh; burst of laughter. **-ina** *f. dim.* sly laugh, laugh up one's sleeve; snigger.

**risa·zio** *adj.* sated.

**riscald-are** [A1] *tr.* to warm; to heat; to heat again; (fig.) to excite; *intr.* (*aux.* essere) (of weather) to become milder; to generate heat; *rfl.* to warm oneself; to get warm; (fig.) to get excited; to get heated. **-amento** *m.* heating; *-amento centrale,* central heating; excitement, irritation; (med.) feverishness; heat spots. **-ata** *f.* warm; warming up. **-atore** *m.* heater; *-atore ad immersione,* immersion heater. **-o** *m.* heat; sudden access of passion; irritation; inflammation.

**riscatt-are** [A1] *tr.* to ransom; to redeem; to liberate; *rfl.* to redeem oneself; to free oneself, to vindicate oneself. **-o** *m.* ransom; redemption; liberation; recovery.

**rischiar-are** [A1] *tr.* to light up; to illumine, to illuminate; to make lighter, to lighten; to elucidate, to explain; *rfl.*, *intr.* (*aux.* essere) (of the sky, weather) to clear; to clear up. **-amento** *m.* lighting up; illumination; clearing up; brightening; clarification; elucidation.

**rischiarire** [D2] *intr.* (*aux.* essere), *rfl.* (of sound, voice, etc.) to clear; to become clear.

**ri·schi-o** *m.* risk, hazard; *correre il —,* to run the risk. **-are** [A4] *tr.* to risk, to expose to risk; to venture; to hazard; *intr.* (*aux.* avere) to run a risk; to run risks. **-oso** *adj.* risky; dangerous; hazardous; rash.

**risciacqu-are** [A1] *tr.* to rinse again; to rinse well; *rfl.* (*acc.* of *prn.* 'si') to rinse oneself; (*dat.* of *prn.* 'si'). *-arsi la bocca di,* to speak ill of. **-ata** *f.* rinse; (fig.) reproach, scolding. **-atura** *f.* rinsing; rinse; rinsing-water; dish-water.

**risciò** *m. indecl.* rickshaw.

**riscont-o** *m.* (leg.) rediscount. **-are** [A1 c] *tr.* (leg.) to rediscount.

**riscontr-are** [A1 c] *tr.* to meet; to go to meet; to find, to notice; to verify, to check; to compare; to rediscount; *recip. rfl.* to meet; *le nostre lettere si -arono,* our letters crossed. **-a·bile** *adj.* verifiable. **-ata** *f.* check; verification. **-atore** *m.*, **-atrice** *f.* checker; *-atore di conti,* auditor; inspector.

**riscontro** *m.* checking; control; *ufficio del —,* controller's office; collation; comparison; *far —,* to tally; *mettere a —,* to compare; meeting; reply; *in — alla vostra lettera,* in reply to your letter; (mus.) clash.

**riscoppiare** [A4 c] *intr.* (*aux.* essere) to burst out again.

**riscoprire** [D8] *tr.* to rediscover.

**riscoss-a** *f.* recovery; redemption; redress; liberation; insurrection; shocking; shock; (mil.) recovery. **-ione** *f.* collection (of payment); encashment; *pl.* takings.

**riscosso** *part.* of **riscuo·tere**; *n.m.* cash collected.

**riscot-i·bile** *adj.* (finan.) recoverable. **-imento** *m.* (finan.) recovery; collection; shock, start.

**riscuo·tere** [C15] *tr.* to rouse; to awaken; to receive payment of; to cash (a cheque), to redeem, to take out of pawn; to get back; *rfl.* to give a start, to start; to come to, to rouse oneself; to take revenge, to get one's own back; to free oneself.

**risecare** [A2] *tr.* to cut away; to prune; to cut down; — *le spese,* to reduce expenses.
**risec-co** *adj.* (*m.pl.* -**chi**) dry; dried up; withered. -**care** [A2c] *tr.* to dry up again; *intr.* (*aux.* essere), *rfl.* to dry up; to wither.
**risedere** [B28] *intr.* (*aux.* avere) to sit again.
**risent-ire** [D1] *tr.* to hear again; to feel again; to feel acutely; to feel the effect of; to suffer, to experience; *intr.* (*aux.* avere; *prep.* di) to show traces; to resound, to echo (with); *rfl.* to wake up; to recover one's senses, to come to; *-irsi di,* to feel the effects of; to be offended by; (of plants) to recover. -**imento** *m.* resentment; (med.) after-effect. -**ito** *part. adj.* resentful; angry.
**riserb-are** [A1] *tr.* to keep, to reserve; to save. -**atezza** *f.* reserve, reservedness. -**ato** *part. adj.* reserved; reticent. -**o** *m.* reserve, reservedness; reticence, circumspection; discretion; restraint; custody.
**riseri·a** *f.* rice mill.
**riserrare** [A1] *tr.* to shut again; to close, to compress; to keep safe; *rfl.* to shut oneself up.
**riserv-a** *f.* exception; restriction; stock; (mil.) reserve force; reserve; rest; spares, spare parts; store (also as place); (fishing or shooting) preserve. -**are** [A1] *tr.* to keep, to reserve, to set aside; to put off; to book (a seat); *rfl.* to reserve oneself; to delay; (*dat.* of *prn.* 'si') to reserve for oneself. -**atamente** *adv.* with reservations; conditionally; with reserve. -**atezza** *f.* circumspection, caution. -**ato** *part. adj.* reserved; confidential; circumspect. -**ista** *m.* (mil.) reservist.
**risi·bil-e** *adj.* ridiculous; laughable. -**ità** *f.* ridiculousness.
**risicoltura** *f.* rice-growing, rice-cultivation.
**risie·dere** [B28] *intr.* (*aux.* avere) to reside; to be resident; to be situated, to lie; (of a liquid) to settle.
**risi·pola** *f.* (med.) erysipelas.
**risma** *f.* (of paper) ream; quality, sort, kind.
**ris-o**[1] *m.* (*pl.* -**a** *f.*) laugh, laughter; gaiety; brightness, splendour.
**ris-o**[2] *m.* (bot.) rice. -**otto** *m.* (cul.) dish of rice cooked with gravy, mushrooms, scampi; *-otto alla milanese,* risotto flavoured with saffron.
**risol-are** [A1] *tr.* (shoem.) to resole. -**atura** *f.* (shoem.) resoling.
**risolino** *m. dim.* of **riso**[1]; little laugh; smile.
**risollevare** [A1] *tr.* to raise again, to lift up again; to comfort; to rouse again; *rfl.* to be cheered, comforted (again), to take fresh courage.
**risolto** *part.* of **riso·lvere**.
**risolu·bile** *adj.* soluble; solvable; resolvable.
**risolut-o** *part. adj.* dissolved; melted; faded away; resolved; decided. -**amente** *adv.* resolutely. -**ezza** *f.* resolution. -**ivo** *adj.* resolutive; (med.) laxative.
**risoluzione** *f.* resolution; decision; solution; (med.) clearing up; (fig.) freedom of touch, fluency.
**riso·lv-ere** [C14] *tr.* to solve; to dissolve; to resolve; (leg.) to annul; to determine; to make void; to determine, to decide; *intr.* (*aux.* avere) (med.) to clear up; (of weather) to change; *rfl.* to dissolve, to melt; to disintegrate; to resolve, to decide, to make up one's mind; to be reduced, to end. -**i·bile** *adj.* soluble.
**rison-are** [A1d] *intr.* (*aux.* essere, avere) to resound; to ring; to echo; *tr.* to ring again; to play (music) again. -**ante** *part. adj.* resonant. -**anza** *f.* resonance; echo; sound; sonority. -**atore** *m.* resonator.
**risone** *m.* (agric.) paddy; unpolished rice.
**risorgere** [C5] *intr.* (*aux.* essere) to rise again; to be resurrected; to be restored; to flourish again.
**risorgimento**[1] *m.* revival; resurgence; renaissance; (theol.) — *della carne,* resurrection of the body.
**Risorgimento**[2] *pr.n.m.* (hist.) Risorgimento, the movement in the nineteenth century by which Italy acquired independence and unity.
**risorsa** *f.* resource; expedient; shift.
**risorto** *part.* of **risorgere**.
**risotto** *m.* see under **riso**[2].
**risovvenire** [D16] *impers.* to be remembered; *intr.* (*aux.* essere; *prep.* a) to come again to the help (of); *rfl.* to remember; to recollect.
**risparmi-are** [A4] *tr.* to save; to spare; *abs.* to economize; *rfl.* (*acc.* of *prn.* 'si') to spare oneself; (*dat.* of *prn.* 'si') *-arsi la fatica di,* to save oneself the effort of. -**atore** *m.*, -**atrice** *f.* saver; *adj.* saving, thrifty. -**o** *m.* saving; *fare risparmi,* to economize; *Cassa nazionale di -o,* Post Office Savings Bank.
**rispecchiare** [A4] *tr.* to reflect; to mirror; *rfl.* to be mirrored.
**risped-ire** [D2] *tr.* to send again; to send back; to forward. -**izione** *f.* sending back; reshipping; forwarding.
**rispetta·bil-e** *adj.* respectable; worthy; estimable. -**ità** *f.* respectability.
**rispett-are** [A1] *tr.* to respect; to have regard for; to honour; to concern, to regard; *rfl.* to have self-respect. -**ato** *part. adj.* respected; esteemed; held in regard.
**rispettiv-o** *adj.* respective; own; particular. -**amente** *adv.* respectively; relatively; *-amente a,* in comparison with.
**rispett-o** *m.* respect; regard; — *a,* in respect of, as regards; *per ogni* —, in every respect; *di* —, in reserve; (comm.) account; (liter. hist.) folk-lyric. -**oso** *adj.* respectful.
**risple·nd-ere** [B1] *intr.* (*aux.* essere, avere) to shine; to glitter; to be brilliant; to be famous. -**ente** *adj.* resplendent; aglow; glittering.
**rispond-ere** [C11] *intr.* (*aux.* avere; *prep.* a) to answer, to reply (to); to acknowledge (a salute); to respond, to comply; to pay what is due; — *a mezzogiorno,* to have a southern aspect; *recip. rfl.* to correspond. -**ente** *part. adj.* answering; corresponding; in harmony. -**enza** *f.* correspondence; relation, agreement, harmony; repercussion; reply.
**risposare** [A1] *intr.* (*aux.* avere), *rfl.* to marry again, to remarry.
**rispost-a, rispost-a** *f.* answer, reply; response; counter-measure; *con — pagata,* reply paid. -**ac·cia** *f. pejor.* rude answer.
**riss-a** *f.* brawl; fray; polemic. -**are** [A1] *intr.* (*aux.* avere), *recip. rfl.* to brawl, to quarrel; to fight. -**oso** *adj.* quarrelsome.
**ristabil-ire** [D2] *tr.* to re-establish; to restore; *rfl.* to be re-established; to be restored. -**imento** *m.* restoration; re-establishment; recovery.
**ristagn-are**[1] [A5] *intr.* (*aux.* avere) to stagnate, to become stagnant, to revert to marsh; (of blood) to congeal, to cease flowing; *tr.* to make stagnant; to stanch. -**ativo** *adj.* styptic; which restricts or stops the flow. -**o** *m.* ceasing to flow; stagnation; marsh; stagnant pool; (comm.) slack period.
**ristagnare**[2] [A5] *tr.* (techn.) to re-tin; to solder.
**ristamp-a** *f.* reprint; reprinting; new impression. -**are** [A1] *tr.* to reprint.
**ristare** [A9] *intr.* (*aux.* essere) to stay again; to stay; to stop, to cease, to leave off; to hesitate; *rfl.* to stop; to refrain; *non ristarsene,* to keep at it.
**ristorante** *m.* see under **ristorare.**
**ristor-are** [A1] *tr.* to restore; to refresh; to replenish; to make amends for; *rfl.* to refresh one-

self; to eat something; to rest. **-ante** *part. adj.* refreshing, restorative; *n.m.* restaurant; (rlwy.) *vagone -ante*, dining car. **-ativo** *adj.* refreshing; *n.m.* restorative. **-atọre** *m.* restorative, cordial; restaurant-keeper; (rlwy.) refreshment-room; *adj.* refreshing. **-aziọne** *f.* restoration, repair; compensation, refreshment.

**ristọrn-o** *m.* rebound. **-are** [A1 c] *intr.* (*aux.* essere) to bounce back, to rebound.

**ristoro** *m.* refreshment; relief; rest; compensation.

**ristrẹtt-o** *part.* of **ristri·ngere**; *adj.* narrow; limited; restricted; confined; reduced; (cul.) *brodo —*, clear soup, consommé; *n.m.* summary; epitome; reduced price. **-amẹnte** *adv.* narrowly; in a limited way. **-ẹzza** *f.* narrowness; poverty; dearth; lack.

**ristri·ngere** [C5] *tr.* to grasp, to clasp again; to draw close again; to restrict; (eng.) to re-tighten; *recip. rfl.* to sit closer together, to squeeze up.

**ristuc-care** [A2] *tr.* (bldg.) to re-plaster; (fig.) to cloy, to disgust; to tire, to weary. **-co** *adj.* (*m.pl.* **-chi**) tired, weary; bored; 'fed up'.

**risuc·chi-o** *m.* eddy, suction. **-are** [A4] *tr.* to suck back; to absorb again; (fig.) to listen to with boredom.

**risult-are** [A1] *intr.* (*aux.* essere) to result; to spring; to follow; to emerge; to come out; *impers. mi -a che sta per partire*, I hear he is just going away. **-ante** *part. adj.* resultant, resulting. **-anza** *f.* result; outcome, issue. **-ato** *part. adj.* resulted, resulting; *n.m.* result; issue; outcome.

**risuonare** [A1] see **risonare**.

**risurreziọne** *f.* resurrection; revival.

**risuscit-are** [A1 s] *tr.* to resuscitate; to revive; *intr.* (*aux.* essere) to revive; to rise; (theol.) to rise again, to rise from the dead. **-aziọne** *f.* resuscitation.

**riṣvẹgli-o** *m.* awakening; revival. **-are** [A4 c] *tr.* to wake up; to rouse; to waken; to revive; *rfl.* to wake up again; to revive. **-amẹnto** *m.* awakening; rousing; coming of life. **-atọre** *m.*, **-atrice** *f.* awakener; knocker-up; *adj.* awakening, rousing.

**riṣvolt-a** *f.* turn back; lapel (of coat); cuff. **-are** [A1] *intr.* (*aux.* avere) to turn back; to reverse. **-o** *m.* lapel, facing, cuff; flap (of book cover).

**ritagli-are** [A4] *tr.* to cut again; to cut away; to cut out; to clip off. **-o** *m.* cutting, clipping, piece cut out; snippet; *-o di giornale*, newspaper cutting; (of cloth) remnant; lapel; *nei -i del tempo*, at odd moments.

**ritard-are** [A1] *tr.* to delay; to defer, to put off, to postpone; to retard; *intr.* (*aux.* avere, essere) to be late; (of a clock) to be slow; to delay. **-amẹnto** *m.* delaying; deferment; postponement; delay; slowing down. **-ata·rio** *m.* late-comer; unpunctual person; defaulter (in payment). **-atọre** *m.*, **-atrice** *f.* laggard; person who delays.

**ritardo** *m.* delay; lateness; slowness; lag; *in —*, late.

**ritẹgno** *m.* reserve; reservedness; restraint; impediment.

**ritemp(e)rare** [A1, A1 s] *tr.* to retemper; to strengthen; to resharpen; *rfl.* to recover one's strength.

**ritenẹre** [B32] *tr.* to detain; to withhold; to stop, to hold back; to regard, to consider; to think; to maintain; to remember; to possess; to keep; to accept; *rfl.* to restrain oneself; to stop, to stay; to consider oneself.

**ritentare** [A1, A1 c] *tr.*, *intr.* (*aux.* avere) to try again; to tempt again.

**ritentiv-a** *f.* memory, retentive faculty. **-o** *adj.* retentive.

**ritenut-a** *f.* deduction; stoppage; retention. **-amẹnte** *adv.* reservedly; moderately. **-ẹzza** *f.* reserve; moderation. **-o** *part.* of **ritenẹre**; *adj.* reserved; restrained; self-possessed.

**ritenziọne** *f.* reserve; restraint; retention; arrest, detention; possession.

**riti·ngere** [C5] *tr.* to re-dye; to re-paint.

**ritinto** *part.* of **riti·ngere**; *adj.* dyed; re-dyed; painted.

**ritir-are** [A1] *tr.* to withdraw; to retract; to take back, to revoke; to shorten, to import; to draw; to accept delivery of; to collect, to fetch; *rfl.* to retire, to withdraw, to retreat; to go away, to depart; to go home; to shrink; *intr.* (*aux.* avere) to shrink; to take after, to resemble. **-ata** *f.* withdrawal; retirement; (mil.) retreat, departure; latrine, closet; lavatory; pretext; excuse for withdrawal; place of retirement, refuge. **-atẹzza** *f.* retirement; seclusion; reserve. **-ato** *part. adj.* retired; secluded; *vivere -ato*, to lead a secluded life.

**ritiro** *m.* retirement; withdrawal; retreat; convent; penitentiary; shrinkage, contraction; confiscation; (mil.) *in —*, on the retired list.

**ri·tmic-o** *adj.* rhythmical, rhythmic. **-a** *f.* rhythmics. **-amẹnte** *adv.* rhythmically.

**ritm-o** *m.* rhythm; measure; verse; rate, pace. **-ato** *adj.* rhythmic; of marked beat.

**rito** *m.* rite, ceremony; usage; custom.

**ritocc-are** [A2 c] *tr.* to retouch; to touch up; *intr.* (*aux.* avere) to insist; *rfl.* to tidy oneself. **-ata** *f.* touch; retouching, touching up; finishing touch; correction.

**ritọc-co** *m.* (*pl.* **-chi**) retouch; finishing touch; correction; adjustment; revision. **-chino** *m. dim.* (colloq.) little snack; little drop more; another little bit to eat.

**ritọgliere** [B27] *tr.* to take back, to take again; to take away, to take off; *rfl.* to take oneself off.

**rito·rcere** [C5] *tr.* to twist again; to retort, to rebut; *rfl.* to twist backwards, to get twisted.

**ritornare** [A1 c] *intr.* (*aux.* essere) to return; to come back; to go back; to become once more; to recur; *rfl.* to turn back, to go back; *tr.* to give back, to bring back, to return.

**ritornello** *m.* (verse) refrain; (mus.) ritornello; repeat.

**ritọrno** *m.* return; *biglietto di andata e —*, return ticket; *partita di —*, return match; *— di fiamma*, backfire; recurrence, repetition.

**ritorsiọne** *f.* retort; retaliation.

**ritorta** *f.* withy; chain; bond.

**ritorto** *part.* of **rito·rcere**; *adj.* twisted, contorted; *via ritorta*, tortuous path; *n.m.* (text.) yarn.

**ritraente** *adj.* representing; reproducing; portraying.

**ritrarre** [B33] *tr.* to draw back; to draw again; to withdraw; to turn away; to obtain; to reproduce, to represent; (paint.) to portray; to reproduce (a drawing, etc.); to depict; *intr.* (*aux.* avere) to approach; to resemble; *— da*, to take after; *rfl.* to draw back; to withdraw; to portray oneself.

**ritratt-are**[1] [A1] *tr.* to treat again; to retract, to recant, to recall; to withdraw; to report; *rfl.* to retract what one has said; to recant. **-aziọne** *f.* retraction; recantation; withdrawal; re-handling.

**ritrattare**[2] [A1] *tr.* to make a portrait of; to photograph; *rfl.* to portray oneself; to have one's portrait made; to have one's photograph taken.

**ritrat·tile** *adj.* retractile; (aeron.) *carro —*, retractable undercarriage.

**ritratt-o** *part.* of **ritrarre**; *adj.* drawn back; reported; represented, portrayed; *n.m.* portrait; picture; image. **-ista** *m.*, *f.* (paint.) portrait-painter; *adj.* relating to portrait-painting.

**ritraziọne** *f.* retraction, diminution; contraction.

**ritrito** *adj.* hashed, minced; (fig.) trite.

**ritrọsa** *f.* bag-net; net for birds; tuft of hair.

**ritrọs-o** *adj.* moving backwards; averse; reluctant; shy; stubborn; *adv. phr. a —*, backwards; against the grain; *n.m.* eddy, backwash; slow or shy person. **-a·ggine** *f.* shyness; reluctance; stubbornness. **-i·a** *f.* shyness; aversion; reluctance; stubbornness.

**ritrov-are** [A1] *tr.* to find again, to recover; to retrace (a path), to follow (footsteps); to discover; to meet, to visit; to recognize; *rfl.* to find oneself to be; to come to one's senses, to awake; to feel at home; *recip. rfl.* to meet. **-amẹnto** *m.* finding; meeting; discovery. **-ata** *f.* finding; discovery; invention. **-ato** *part. adj.* found (again); met; *n.m.* invention; contrivance; device; lie; meeting; meeting-place. **-atọre** *m.*, **-atrice** *f.* discoverer; inventor, deviser.

**ritrovo** *m.* meeting, gathering; meeting-place, resort, haunt; rendezvous; sentry post.

**ritto** *adj.* straight; standing; upright; right; *n.m.* right side; (coin or medal) obverse, 'heads'; straight line; vertical line; upright; *adv.* straight; quite.

**ritual-e** *adj.* ritual; customary; *n.m.* ritual. **-işmo** *m.* (rel.) ritualism. **-ista** *m., f.* (rel.) expert on ritual; liturgiologist. **-mẹnte** *adv.* ritually; according to custom.

**riuniọne** *f.* reunion; meeting; gathering.

**riun-ire** [D2] *tr.* to reunite, to bring together again; to unite; to reconcile; *rfl.* to be reunited; to join; to meet; to be joined, to combine. **-ito** *part. adj.* reunited; combined.

**riusc-ire** [D16] *intr.* (*aux.* essere) to go out again; to go out; to come out; to reach; to succeed; to become, to turn out to be; to be able; *impers. non mi riesce di farlo*, I can't manage it. **-i·bile** *adj.* feasible. **-ita** *f.* result, event; success; issue, exit. **-ito** *part. adj.* successful.

**riva** *f.* bank; shore; *andare in — al mare*, to go to the seaside; street running alongside a river or canal.

**rival-e** *m.* rival; competitor; *adj.* rival. **-eggiare** [A3 c] *intr.* (*aux.* avere; *prep.* di) to be the rival (of); to emulate; to compete (with), to vie (with). **-ità** *f.* rivalry.

**rivalẹre** [B34] *rfl.* (*prep.* su) to recover; to make good (one's losses).

**rivalsa** *f.* (comm.) redraft.

**rivalut-are** [A1] *tr.* to revalue. **-aziọne** *f.* revaluation.

**rivangare** [A2] *tr.* to dig up again; (fig.) to rake up, to revive.

**rived-ẹre** [B35] *tr.* to see again; *a rivederla* (*arrivederla*), goodbye, see you again soon; to revisit; to look over, to examine (again), to revise, to correct; to edit (a text); *recip. rfl.* to meet again; *a rivederci* (*arrivederci*), goodbye, see you again soon. **-itọre** *m.* reviser; proof-reader. **-itura** *f.* (techn.) inspection. **-uta** *f.* second glance; revision. **-uto** *part. adj.* revised.

**rivel-are** [A1] *tr.* to reveal, to disclose; to display; *rfl.* to reveal oneself; to show oneself to be; to be revealed. **-atọre** *m.*, **-atrice** *f.* revealer; (radio) detector; *adj.* revealing. **-aziọne** *f.* revelation, disclosure; manifestation.

**rivẹnd-ere** [B1] *tr.* to re-sell; to retail; to repeat; to surpass. **-itọre** *m.* seller, retailer; shopkeeper. **-u·gliolo** *m.* hawker; costermonger.

**rivendic-are** [A2 s] *tr.* to vindicate; to claim successfully; to recover; to avenge again; *rfl.* to vindicate oneself; to take revenge again. **-atọre** *m.*, **-atrice** *f.* vindicator. **-aziọne** *f.* vindication.

**riven·dita** *f.* resale; retail selling; small retail shop.

**rivenire** [D18] *intr.* (*aux.* essere) to come back; to come again.

**riverber-are** [A1 s] *tr.* to reflect; to echo; to throw back, to reverberate; *intr.* (*aux.* essere), *rfl.* to be reflected; to reverberate. **-ante** *part. adj.* reverberating. **-aziọne** *f.* reverberation; radiation; reflection.

**rive·rbero** *m.* reverberation; reflection; glint; reflector.

**river-ire** [D2] *tr.* to respect; to revere, to venerate; to pay one's respects to. **-ente** *part. adj.* reverent; respectful. **-enza** *f.* act of reverence; bow; respectful salutation.

**riverniciare** [A3] *tr.* to repaint.

**rivers-are** [A1] *tr.* to pour (out, in); to pour out again; to upset, to overturn; to defeat; (cinem.) to dub; *intr.* (*aux.* essere) to boil over; *rfl.* to pour, to flow; to overflow. **-amẹnto** *m.* outpouring; overflow.

**riversiọne** *f.* reversion; return.

**riverso** *adj.* turned back; reversed; supine; *n.m.* reverse; overturning; wrong side, back; contrary; blow with the back of the hand; disaster.

**rivest-ire** [D1] *tr.* to dress (again); to fit out (with clothes), to provide with an outfit; to line (a garment); *rfl.* to dress oneself again; to change one's clothes. **-imẹnto** *m.* dressing again; reclothing, recovering; facing; covering, upholstery. **-itura** *f.* covering; lining.

**rivẹtto** rivet.

**rivier-a** *f.* coast; *la Riviera*, the Riviera (French and Italian). **-asco** *adj.* (*m.pl.* **-aschi**) of the Riviera; *n.m.* inhabitant of the Riviera.

**rivi·ncere** [C5] *tr.* to win again; to win back.

**rivi·ncita** *f.* revenge; recovery; return match.

**rivista** *f.* review; magazine; revision; (mil.) march-past; (theatr.) revue.

**rivi·v-ere** [C16] *intr.* (*aux.* avere, essere) to live again; to return to life; to be revived; *tr.* to live over again; to experience again. **-ificare** [A2 s] *tr.* to revivify; to reinvigorate.

**rivo** *m.* stream; little stream; brook; flow; flood.

**rivo·lg-ere** [C5] *tr.* to turn; to turn back; to turn over; to turn over in one's mind; to convert, to distract; *rfl.* to turn round; to apply; *a chi devo -ermi per informazione?*, to whom should I apply for information?; to turn sour; to revolve. **-imẹnto** *m.* change, aversion, upheaval.

**ri·volo** *m.* rivulet.

**rivolta** *f.* turn; turning; turnback (of cuff, glove, *etc.*); revolt, rebellion; aversion.

**rivoltare** [A1] *tr.* to turn (again); to turn over, to turn inside out, upside down; (mus.) to invert (chords, intervals or counterpoint); *rfl.* to turn round and round, over and over; to revolt, to rebel; (of wine, *etc.*) to turn, to go bad; to turn for help; *intr.* (*aux.* essere) to turn back.

**rivoltell-a** *f.* revolver. **-ata** *f.* revolver shot.

**rivolto** *part.* of **rivo·lgere**; *adj.* turned; disposed (towards); inclined (to); *n.m.* (mus.) inversion; reverse side (of material).

**rivoltol-are** [A1 s] *tr.* to turn over; *rfl.* to toss and turn; to roll about; to wallow. **-ọne** *m.* sudden turn; lurch; (fig.) somersault. **-ọni** *adv.* tossing and turning.

**rivoltọso** *adj.* rebellious; *n.m.* rebel; revolutionary.

**rivoluziọn-e** *f.* revolution; cycle. **-are** [A1 c] *tr.* to revolutionize. **-a·rio** *adj., n.m.* revolutionary. **-arişmo** *m.* revolutionary ideas or tendencies.

**rizz-are** [A1] *tr.* to erect; to set up; *rfl.* to spring erect; (of hair) to bristle. **-amẹnto** *m.* erection; straightening; bristling.

**roano**[1] *adj., n.m.* roan (horse).

**Roano**[2] *pr.n.f.* (geog.) Rouen.

**rob-a** *f.* things; goods; furniture; cloth, material; clothes, belongings, 'things'. **-a·ccia** *f. pejor.* worthless stuff, rubbish. **-ẹtta** *f. dim.* (derog.) stuff, things of little value.

**rọbbia** *f.* (bot.) madder.

**robinẹtto** *m.* see **rubinetto.**

**ro·bot** *m. indecl.* robot, automaton.
**robust-o** *adj.* strong; robust, sturdy. **-ęzza** *f.* strength; sturdiness; vigour.
**roc-ca**[1] *f.* (mil.) citadel; fort; (fig.) rock. **-caforte** *f.* stronghold.
**rọcca**[2] *f.* distaff.
**rocchętto**[1] *m.* reel; spool; (text.) bobbin; (electr.) coil.
**ro·cci-a** *f.* rock; cliff, crust, incrustation. **-ọso** *adj.* rocky; encrusted, grimed with dirt.
**roc-co** *m.* (*pl.* **-chi**) (chess) rook, castle.
**ro-co** *adj.* (*m.pl.* **-chi**) hoarse; *n.m. mal del* —, croup. **-camęnte** *adv.* hoarsely. **-chęzza** *f.* hoarseness.
**rococò** *adj. indecl.*, *n.m.* rococo.
**Ro·dano** *pr.n.m.* (geog.) Rhône.
**rod-are** [A1] *tr.* (motor.) to run in. **-a·ggio** *m.* (motor.) *in -aggio*, running in.
**rode·o** *m.* rodeo.
**ro·d-ere** [C3] *tr.* to gnaw; to nibble; to corrode; to erode; *rfl.* to chafe; to be worried; *recip. rfl. -ersi l'un l'altro*, to hate one another. **-imęnto** *m.* gnawing, nibbling; (fig.) anxiety, worry; (archit.) erosion, corrosion. **-ìo** *m.* continual gnawing, nibbling; sound of nibbling. **-itọre** *m.* one who gnaws; *pl.* (zool.) rodents; *adj.* gnawing.
**Rodęsi-a** *pr.n.f.* (geog.) Rhodesia. **-ano** *adj.*, *n.m.* Rhodesian.
**Rodi** *pr.n.f.* (geog.) Rhodes.
**rodomọnt-e** *m.* braggart (after Rodomonte in Ariosto's *Orlando Furioso*). **-ata** *f.* rodomontade; boastful talk.
**rog-are** [A2] *tr.* to draw up; to attest; — *un atto*, to draw up a deed; *rfl.* to be attested, verified or witnessed. **-aziọne** *f.* rogation.
**rọggio** *adj.* russet, reddish; *n.m.* rust colour, russet.
**ro·gito** *m.* (leg.) the drawing-up and attestation by Notary Public of execution of deed.
**rọgn-a** *f.* (med.) itch, scabies; (vet.) itch; mange; sheep scab; worry; trouble. **-ọso** *adj.* (vet.) scabby; (fig.) dirty, diseased; *n.m.* one who has the itch.
**rognọne** *m.* (cul.) kidney.
**rogo** *m.* pyre; stake.
**Rolando** *pr.n.m.* Roland.
**roll-are** [A1] *intr.* (*aux.* avere) (naut.) to roll; *tr.* to roll, to roll up. **-ata** *f.* (naut.) roll; rolling. **-ìo** *m.* (naut.) roll.
**Rọma** *pr.n.f.* (geog.) Rome.
**Romagn-a** *pr.n.f.* (geog.) Romagna. **-uolo** *adj.*, *n.m.* of the Romagna.
**roma·ico** *adj.*, *n.m.* Romaic.
**Roma·nia** *pr.n.f.* (geog.) Romania.
**roman-o** *adj.* Roman; *numeri -i*, Roman numerals; *lattuga -a*, cos lettuce; *n.m.* Roman. **-a** *f.* Roman woman, Roman girl; cos lettuce. **-ęsco** *adj.* (*m.pl.* **-ęschi**) modern Roman; of Rome; *n.m.* Roman dialect. **-ịsmo** *m.* idiom of the Roman dialect. **-ità** *f.* Romanity, Roman character. **-ịzzare** [A1] *tr.* to Romanize.
**roma·nti-co** *adj.*, *n.m.* romantic. **-cheri·a** *f.* romantic attitude, notions. **-cịsmo** *m.* romanticism; romance; *pr.n.m.* (lit. hist.) *il Romanticismo*, the Romantic movement.
**romanza** *f.* ballad; romance.
**romanz-o** *adj.* romance, neo-Latin; *n.m.* novel. **-atọre** *m.*, **-atrice** *f.* romancer. **-ęsco** *adj.* (*m.pl.* **-ęschi**) romantic; adventurous. **-iera** *f.*, **-iere** *m.* novelist.
**rombare** [A1 c] *intr.* (*aux.* avere) to roar; to rumble.
**rọmb-ico** *adj.* (geom.) rhombic. **-ododecaedro** *m.* (cryst.) rhombo-dodecahedron. **-oe·drico** *adj.* rhombohedral. **-oedro** *m.* rhombohedron. **-oidale** *adj.* (geom.) rhomboid(al). **-o·ide** *m.*, *adj.* rhomboid.
**rọmbo**[1] *m.* buzzing (of bees or sim.); (sound of) fluttering, beating of wings.
**rọmbo**[2] *m.* turbot.
**rombo**[3] *m.* (naut.) point of the compass; (math.) rhombus.
**romeno** *adj.*, *n.m.* Romanian.
**rome·o**[1] *adj.* pilgrim.
**Rome·o**[2] *pr.n.m.* Romeo; *Giulietta e* —, Romeo and Juliet.
**romit-o** *m.* hermit; *adj.* solitary. **-a·ggio** *m.* hermitage; hermit's life. **-o·rio** *m.* hermitage; lonely place.
**Ro·molo** *pr.n.m.* (hist.) Romulus.
**rọmp-ere** [C26] *tr.* to break; to interrupt; (phys.) — *l'atomo*, to split the atom; (mil.) — *il nemico*, to defeat the enemy; *intr.* (*aux.* avere) to break; (phys.) to be refracted; to be shipwrecked; *rfl.* (*acc.* of *prn.* 'si') to break, to be broken; (*dat.* of *prn.* 'si') *-ersi la testa*, to rack one's brains. **-icapo** *m. indecl.* trouble; troublesome person; puzzle. **-icollo** *adj.* breakneck; ruinous; *n.m.* ruinous bargain, business; dare-devil; thoughtless person. **-ighia·ccio** *m. indecl.* ice-breaker. **-imęnto** *m.* breaking; break; rupture; shipwreck; breach. **-isca·tole, -istivali, -itasche** *m. indecl.* (colloq.) bore, troublesome person. **-itọre** *m.* breaker.
**ronchi-ọne** *m.* rock, crag; block of stone. **-ọso** *adj.* rugged; gnarled.
**ronci·glio** *m.* hook.
**rọncol-a** *f.* (agric.) pruning-hook, billhook. **-o** *m.* large knife with a blade like a billhook.
**roncọne** *m.* reaping-hook.
**rọnda** *f.* (mil.) rounds, night rounds; patrol; *far la* —, to do the rounds.
**rondello** *m.* (mus.) roundelay.
**rọndin-e** *f.* (orn.) swallow. **-ella** *f.* house-martin.
**rondò** *m. indecl.* (mus.) rondo; (prosod.) rondeau.
**rondọne** *m.* (orn.) swift.
**ronz-are** [A1 c] *intr.* (*aux.* avere) to buzz; to hum; (of arrows) to whirr, to whistle; (of bullets) to whistle; to whine. **-atọre** *m.* (orn.) humming-bird. **-ìo** *m.* (**-ii** *pl.*) continued buzzing, hum, murmur.
**ronzino** *m.* nag, jade; packhorse.
**rọnz-o** *m.* (poet.) buzz, hum, murmur. **-ọne** *m.* (ent.) cockchafer, May bug; (fig.) admirer.
**ro·rido** *adj.* dewy; bedewed.
**rọs-a**[1] *f.* (bot.) rose; (archit.) rose-window; — *della bussola*, compass rose; *acqua di -e*, rosewater; *vino* —, vin rosé; *adj. indecl.* pink, rosy; *n.m.* the colour pink. **-a·ceo** *adj.* rosy, rose-coloured. **-a·io** *m.* (bot.) rose-plant, rose-bush. **-ali·a** *f.* (pop.) see **rọsoli·a**. **-arino** *m.* little wreath. **-a·rio** *m.* rosary.
**Rọsa**[2] *pr.n.f.* Rose.
**rọsbif(fe)** *m. indecl.* roast beef.
**ro·sęo** *adj.* rosy; rose-coloured; crimson.
**rosęto** *m.* rose-garden; rose-bed.
**rosętta** *f. dim.* of **rosa**; little rose; rosette.
**rosic-are** [A2 sc] *tr.* to gnaw, to nibble. **-ante** *part. adj.* gnawing; *n.m.pl.* (zool.) rodents.
**rosicchi-are** [A4] *tr.* to nibble, to gnaw. **-amęnto** *m.* nibbling. **-ato** *part. adj.* nibbled; gnawed; (fig.) half-consumed.
**rosi·cchio** *m.* dry crust of bread.
**rosmarino** *m.* (bot.) rosemary.
**rosola·ccio** *m.* (bot.) field poppy.
**rosolare** [A1 s] *tr.* (cul.) to brown.
**rosoli·a** *f.* (med.) German measles, rubella.
**rosọne** *m.* (archit.) rose window; (typ.) tail-piece; (electr.) rosette.
**rospo** *m.* (zool.) toad; (fig.) boor.
**rọss-o** *adj.* red; *pesce* —, goldfish; (paint.) *terra -a*, red ochre; *il Mare Rosso*, the Red Sea; *n.m.* red, the colour red; — *d'uovo*, yolk of egg; — *di piombo*, (miner.) red lead. **-ac·cio** *adj. pejor.*; *n.m.* red-haired person, 'carrots'; (pol.) red. **-astro** *adj.* reddish, dark red. **-eggiante** *part. adj.* reddish; turning red. **-eggiare** [A3 c] *intr.* (*aux.* avere) to be reddish; to appear red. **-ętto** *adj.* bright red; *n.m.* rouge; *-etto per le labbra*, lipstick. **-ęzza** *f.* redness; flush. **-i·ccio** *adj.* reddish; *n.m.* russet, rust colour. **-ọre** *m.* red, redness; flush, blush; shame; modesty; *pl.* blushes.
**rosta** *f.* fly whisk; fanlight.
**rosti·ccio** *m.* clinker.

**rosticceri·a** *f.* cook-shop; snack-bar.
**rostr-o**[1] *m.* beak, bill; muzzle; snout. **-ato** *adj.* beaked.
**rostro**[2] *m.* rostrum.
**rot-a** *f.* see **ruota. -a·ia** *f.* rut, wheel-track; rail.
**rot-are** [A1] *tr.* to rotate, to whirl round; *intr.* (*aux.* avere) to revolve, to wheel, to rotate; to run on wheels; to roll. **-a·bile** *adj.* fit for carriages; *strada -abile,* carriage road; (rlwy.) permanent way; *n.f.* carriage road. **-ata** *f.* blow from a wheel. **-ativa** *f.* rotary printing press. **-ativo** *adj.* (eng.) rotary, rotating. **-ato·rio** *adj.* (*m.pl.* **-atorii**) rotatory; circular; (traffic sign) *circolazione -atoria,* roundabout. **-azione** *f.* rotation; (agric.) *-azione agraria,* rotation of crops.
**rote-are** [A6] *intr.* (*aux.* avere) to rotate, to wheel; to whirl; *tr.* to roll; to whirl; *n.m.* the sound of wheels. **-azione** *f.* rotation; wheeling.
**rotella** *f. dim.* small wheel; roller; castor; rowel; *pattino a rotelle,* roller-skate; (anat.) knee-cap.
**roto-calco** *m.* (typ.) rotogravure press. **-calcografi·a** *f.* (typ.) rotogravure. **-grafi·a** *f.* (typ.) rotogravure.
**ro·tol-o** *m.* roll. **-amento** *m.* rolling. **-are** [A1 s] *tr.* to bowl, to roll; *intr.* (*aux.* essere) to roll down; *rfl.* to roll, to wallow. **-oni** *adv.* rolling, head first; *a -oni,* to rack and ruin.
**rotonda** *f.* (archit.) rotunda, round building.
**rotond-are** [A1 c] *tr.* to make round; to round off. **-eggiare** [A3 c] *intr.* (*aux.* essere) to fill out, to become round; *tr.* to round, to make round.
**rotond-o** *adj.* round; rotund; plump; spherical; cylindrical; circular; *n.m.* round. **-ità** *f.* roundness; rotundity.
**rotore** *m.* (eng.) rotor.
**rott-a**[1] *f.* break; breach; break in the weather; rain; thunderstorm. **-ame** *m.* fragment(s); scrap(s); *pl.* wreckage; lumber; *-ami di ferro,* scrap-iron.
**rotta**[2] *f.* route; course.
**rott-o** *part.* of **rompere**; *adj.* broken; *n.m.* break, fracture. **-amente** *adv.* brokenly; jerkily. **-ura** *f.* breakage, break; breaking off; rupture, fraction, split; (phys.) *-ura dei raggi,* refraction of rays; (of river) breaking its banks, overflowing; (eng.) failure, breakdown; (leg.) *-ura di un contratto,* breach of a contract; (mil.) breach; (surg.) fracture; breaking off of diplomatic relations); outbreak (of war).
**ro·tula** *f.* rowel; (anat.) patella.
**rova·io** *m.* north wind.
**rovente** *adj.* red-hot; scorching.
**rover-e** *f.* (bot.) common oak. **-eto** *m.* oak wood, plantation.
**rove·scia** *f.* wrong side; reverse, lapel; facing; cuff (turned back).
**rovesci-are** [A3] *tr.* to overturn; to upset; to turn inside out; *rfl.* to throw oneself (down); (of a boat) to capsize. **-amento** *m.* overthrow, overturning; upsetting; reversal; (of a boat) capsizing.
**rove·sci-o** *adj.* turned upside down, inside out; *adv. phr. alla -a,* inversely, upside down; *n.m.* wrong side; *adv. phr. a —,* upside down, back to front, backwards; *rovesci di fortuna,* reverses of fortune, bad luck; (mus.) contrary motion; fall; ruin; downpour; slap; (tennis) backhand stroke. **-one** *m. augm.* heavy reversal; heavy blow with back of the hand; blow with the flat of a sword; (tennis) backhand stroke. **-one, -oni** *adv.* on one's back.
**roveto** *m.* bramble thicket; briar patch.
**rovin-a** *f.* fall; collapse; ruin; landslide; death; slaughter; *pl.* ruins. **-are** [A1] *intr.* (*aux.* essere) to fall crashing, to crash down; to crumble; to rush; to dash; *tr.* to ruin; to bring down; to demolish; to harm, to injure; *rfl.* (*acc.* of *prn.* 'si') to ruin oneself; to be ruined; (*dat.* of *prn.* 'si') *-arsi la salute,* to ruin one's health. **-ati·ccio** *adj.* falling into decay; shaky. **-ato** *part. adj.* ruined; in ruins. **-ìo** *m.* (*pl.* **-ìi**) downfall; crumbling; crashing; noise of falling. **-oso** *adj.* violent; furious; ruinous.
**rovistare** [A1] *tr.* to rummage; to ransack; *abs.* to make a noise of rummaging.
**rovo** *m.* (bot.) blackberry, bramble.
**rozza** *f.* jade, broken-down horse.
**rozz-o** *adj.* rough, rude; crude; clumsy; rustic. **-amente** *adv.* roughly; crudely. **-ezza** *f.* roughness; clumsiness; boorishness. **-ume** *m.* rough things; roughness; rough appearance.
**ruba** *f.* sack, pillage, plunder; *andare a —,* to sell like hot cakes.
**rubacchiare** [A4] *tr.* to pilfer.
**rub-are** [A1] *tr.* to steal. **-acuori** *adj., n.m., f. indecl.* lady-killer, heart-breaker; attractive woman. **-apaga, -apaghe** *m. indecl.* an employee not worth his pay.
**ruberi·a** *f.* theft, robbery; fraud; booty.
**rubicondo** *adj.* ruddy, rubicund; rosy-red.
**Rubicone** *pr.n.m.* (geog.) Rubicon.
**rubinetto** *m.* tap; *aprire il —,* to turn on the tap.
**rubino** *m.* (miner.) ruby.
**rubizzo** *adj.* hale; florid; healthy-looking.
**rublo** *m.* (finan.) rouble.
**rubric-a** *f.* rubric, title, chapter heading in red ink; subsection, subheading; (journ.) page, feature, column. **-are** [A2] *tr.* to mark in red; to mark in an index.
**rud-e** *adj.* rough; coarse; rude; *materia —,* raw material. **-ezza** *f.* coarseness; rudeness.
**ru·der-e, -o** *m.* ruin; *pl.* remains.
**rudiment-o** *m.* rudiment. **-ale** *adj.* rudimentary.
**ruffa** *f.* scramble; *fare a — raffa,* to snatch as snatch can.
**ruffian-o** *m.* pander, pimp; procurer; go-between. **-a** *f.* procuress. **-eggiare** [A3 c] *intr.* (*aux.* avere) to pander. **-eri·a** *f.* procuring.
**ruga** *f.* wrinkle; crease.
**rugbista** *m.* (sport) rugby-player.
**rug·gin-e** *f.* rust; filth, pollution; (on the teeth) tartar; stain; (on corn) rust, blight, mildew; (fig.) bad blood; rancour. **-ire** [D2] *intr.* (*aux.* essere), *rfl.* to rust. **-oso** *adj.* rusty; rust-coloured.
**rugg-ire** [D1] *intr.* (*aux.* avere) to roar; to howl; to boil, to bubble; (of intestines) to rumble; *tr.* to shout, to roar. **-ito** *part. adj.* roared, shouted; *n.m.* roar; howl; rumbling.
**rugiad-a** *f.* dew; (fig.) balm. **-oso** *adj.* dewy; bedewed.
**rugliare** [A4] *intr.* (*aux.* avere) to growl; to rumble; to roar; (of pigeons) to coo.
**rugos-o** *adj.* wrinkled; lined; crinkled. **-ità** *f.* roughness, unevenness.
**ruina** *f.* see **rovina.**
**ruletta** *f.* roulette.
**rull-are** [A1] *intr.* (*aux.* avere) (of drums) to roll; (aeron.) to taxi; *tr.* to roll (with a roller). **-a·ggio** *m.* taxi-ing. **-amento** *m.* roll; rolling. **-ìo** *m.* roll, rolling.
**rullo** *m.* roll, beating (of drums); skittle, ninepin.
**rum** *m. indecl.* rum.
**Rum-a·nia** *pr.n.f.* (geog.) Romania. **-eno** *adj., n.m.* Romanian.
**rumin-ante** *part. adj.* ruminant, ruminating; (fig.) ruminating, meditating; *n.m.pl.* (zool.) ruminants. **-are** [A1 s] *intr.* (*aux.* avere) to ruminate, to chew the cud; *tr.* (fig.) to think over, to ponder, to meditate upon. **-azione** *f.* rumination; chewing the cud.
**rumor-e** *m.* noise; din; uproar; fame; rumour. **-eggiante** *part. adj.* rumbling; muttering; noisy. **-eggiare** [A3 c] *intr.* (*aux.* avere) to make a noise; to rumble; to talk loudly; to murmur; to put about a rumour; *tr.* to incite; to stir up; to murmur against;

to shout down. **-ìo** *m.* (*pl.* **-ìi**) noise; continued sound of talking; murmur. **-ista** *m.* (cinem.) sound effects man. **-ọsità** *f.* noise, noisiness. **-ọso** *adj.* noisy; loud.
**run-a** *f.* (*pl.* **-e, -i** *m.*) rune.
**ru·nico** *adj.* runic.
**ruolo** *m.* roll; nominal list; class-list; *di* —, on the regular staff.
**ruota** *f.* wheel; — *dentata*, cog-wheel; — *di ricambio*, spare-wheel; — *d'ingranaggio*, gear wheel.
**rup-e** *f.* rock; cliff. **-estre** *adj.* rocky; *flora -estre*, rock plants.
**rupi·a** *f.* (finan.) rupee.
**rurale** *adj.* country; rural; *n.m.* countryman.
**ruscell-o** *m.* brook, stream. **-ẹtto** *m. dim.* brooklet.
**ruspare** [A1] *intr.* (*aux.* avere) to scratch about; to rummage; to glean.
**russ-are** [A1] *intr.* (*aux.* avere) to snore. **-amẹnto** *m.* snoring.
**Ru·ss-ia** *pr.n.f.* (geog.) Russia. **-o** *adj., n.m.* Russian. **-o·filo** *adj., n.m.* Russophil. **-o·fobo** *adj., n.m.* Russophobe.
**ru·sti-co** *adj.* rustic; *adv. phr. alla -ca*, simply, roughly, with simplicity; *n.m.* countryman; rustic; cottage. **-ca·ggine** *f.* rudeness; roughness; simplicity (in manners). **-cale** *adj.* rustic; rural. **-cano** *adj.* (of the) country; rustic. **-chẹtto** *adj. dim.* simple rather rough. **-chẹzza** *f.* rudeness; shyness. **-cità** *f.* rusticity; shyness, bashfulness; simplicity; ignorance.
**ruta** *f.* (bot.) rue.
**ruteno** *adj., n.m.* Ruthenian.
**rutilante** *adj.* (poet.) shining; sparkling.
**rutt-o** *m.* belch **-are** [A1] *intr.* (*aux.* avere) to belch; *tr.* to belch forth.
**ru·vid-o** *adj.* rough to the touch; harsh; coarse; (fig.) rough, coarse. **-ẹzza** *f.* roughness; harshness; rudeness.
**ruzz-are** [A1] *intr.* (*aux.* avere) to romp, to gambol. **-o** *m.* romping; noise of romping; horse-play; playfulness; caprice; quarrel, tiff.
**ru·zzol-a** *f.* spinning; disk. **-are** [A1 s] *intr.* (*aux.* essere, avere) to tumble; to roll down, to roll; *far -are un cerchio*, to trundle a hoop; *tr.* to roll. **-ata** *f.* tumble. **ìo** *m.* (*pl.* **-ìi**) continued rolling, tumbling. **-ọne** *m.* heavy fall, tumble. **-ọni** *adv.* tumbling down, headlong.

**S** *f., m.* (pron. **esse**) the letter S; the consonant S.
**Saba** *pr.n.f.* Sheba.
**saba·tico** *adj.* sabbatical; *anno* —, sabbatical year.
**sa·bat-o** *m.* Saturday; — *inglese*, Saturday afternoon off; (eccl.) — *santo*, Holy Saturday. **-ino** *adj.* born on a Saturday; *n.m.* Saturday's child.
**saba·udo** *adj.* of Savoy; of the house of Savoy.
**sa·bb-ia** *f.* sand; *-ie mobili*, quicksand. **-ia·ia** *f.* sandpit. **-iare** [A4] *tr.* (eng.) to sandblast. **-iatrice** *f.* sandblasting machine. **-iatura** *f.* (eng.) sandblasting. **-iọne** *m.* gravel; sandy soil. **-iọso** *adj.* sandy.
**sabot-are** [A1] *tr.* to sabotage. **-a·ggio** *m.* sabotage. **-atọre** *m.* saboteur.
**sac-ca** *f.* bag; satchel; wallet; kitbag. **-capane** *m.* haversack. **-cata** *f.* sackful. **-cheri·a** *f.* sacking-works; supply of sacks. **-chẹtta** *f. dim.* nosebag. **-chettare** [A1 c] *tr.* to sandbag; to hit with a sandbag.
**saccarin-a** *f.* (chem.) saccharin. **-o** *adj.* saccharine, sugary.
**saccent-e** *adj.* presumptuous; pretentious; *n.m.* wiseacre, know-all; pedant; *f.* blue-stocking. **-eri·a** *f.* presumption; smattering of knowledge; pedantry. **-ọna** *f.*, **-ọne** *m.* wiseacre; pedant.
**sacchẹggi-o** *m.* sacking, sack, plunder. **-are** [A3 c] *tr.* to sack; to pillage; to plunder. **-amẹnto** *m.* sacking; plundering. **-atọre** *m.* pillager; plunderer; *adj.* pillaging, plundering.
**sac-co** *m.* (*pl.* **-chi**) sack; bag; pouch; — *postale*, mail bag; — *di carbone*, sack of coal; — *di montagna*, rucksack; — *a terra*, sandbag; — *a pelo*, sleeping bag. **—rchẹtto** *m.dim.* of **sacco**; (naut.) housewife (pron. 'husif'). **-co·ccia** *f.* pocket; wallet. **-cocciata** *f.* pocketful. **-cọne** *m.* palliasse, straw mattress; *-cone a molla*, sprung mattress.
**sacello** *m.* (eccl.) chapel, shrine.
**sacerdot-e** *m.* (rel.) priest (Christian or non-Christian); *sommo* —, the Pope. **-ale** *adj.* priestly, sacerdotal. **-ẹssa** *f.* priestess.
**sacerdo·zio** *m.* (eccl.) priesthood; clergy.
**sacramẹnt-o** *m.* oath; (theol.) sacrament; *il Santo* —, *il Divino* —, the Blessed Sacrament. **-ale** *adj.* (theol.) sacramental; solemn; binding; *n.m.pl.* sacramentals. **-are** [A1c] *tr.* (eccl.) to administer a sacrament to; *intr.* (*aux.* avere) to swear; *rfl.* to receive a sacrament, esp. the Viaticum.
**sacr-are** [A1] *tr.* to consecrate, to hallow, to dedicate; to ordain. **-a·rio** *m.* (antiq.) shrine; small chapel. **-ato** *part. adj.* consecrated; *n.m.* consecrated ground; churchyard; oath.
**sacresti·a** *f.* see **sagrestia.**
**sacrificare** [A2 s] *tr.* to offer (to God); to sacrifice; (fig.) to sacrifice, to forego; to give up; *rfl.* to sacrifice oneself; to make sacrifices; to be unselfish; to make a martyr of oneself.
**sacrifi·cio** *m.* sacrifice; offering; (theol.) *il* — *divino*, the holy sacrifice, the Mass; privation; act of self-denial.
**sacrile·gio** *m.* (rel.) sacrilege; larceny from a church.
**sacri·le-go** *adj.* (*m.pl.* **-ghi**) sacrilegious, profane; *n.m.* sacrilegious person.
**sacripante** *m.* blusterer; bully.
**sacr-o** *m.* sacred; holy; inviolate. **-osanto** *adj.* sacrosanct.
**saẹtt-a** *f.* arrow; dart; thunderbolt, flash; hand (watch); (colloq.) restless child. **-amẹnto** *m.* shooting with arrows; archery. **-are** [A1 c] *tr.* to shoot with an arrow; to fling, to lance, to dart. **-ata** *f.* shot (with an arrow); bow-shot. **-atọre** *m.* archer; *adj. arco -atore*, bow. **-atrice** *f.* huntress; *adj. caccia -atrice*, hunting with bow and arrows.
**saf·fico** *adj.* sapphic.
**Saffo** *pr.n.f.* Sappho.
**saga** *f.* saga.
**sagac-e** *adj.* sagacious; shrewd; clever, smart. **-ità** *f.* sagacity; shrewdness.
**saggẹzza** *f.* wisdom; prudence; experience.
**saggiamẹnte** *adv.* wisely; prudently; sensibly.
**saggi-are** [A3] *tr.* to test, to sample; to try, to taste. **-atọre** *m.* tester; assayer; taster. **-atura** *f.* testing; sampling; test. **-avino** *m. indecl.* wine-taster.
**sa·ggio**[1] *adj.* wise; prudent; judicious; experienced; sage; (of a child) good, well behaved; *n.m.* wise man; sensible person; sage.
**sa·gg-io**[2] *m.* test; trial; sample; taste; essay; exam-paper, script. **-ista** *m., f.* essayist, essay-writer.
**saggitta·rio**[1] *m.* archer.
**Saggitta·rio**[2] *pr.n.m.* (astron.) Sagittarius.
**sa·gom-a** *f.* (archit.) profile, section of design; moulding; (techn.) outline, shape; (fig.) shape, outline, figure. **-are**

[A1 s] *intr.* (*aux.* avere) (archit.) to make a moulding; *tr.* to draw in profile or section; to mould or shape; to carve.

**sagra** *f.* festival; commemoration; consecration; *la — dell'uva*, the grape festival.

**sagrestan-o** *m.* (eccl.) sacristan; sexton. **-a** *f.* (eccl.) sextoness; sister sacristan (in convent).

**sagresti·a** *f.* sacristy.

**sagù** *m. indecl.* (bot.) sago.

**sa·ia** *f.* twill.

**sa·io** *m.* (*pl.* **sai**) monastic gown; religious habit.

**sal-a**[1] *f.* hall; lounge; room; *— da pranzo*, dining-room; *— d'aspetto*, *— d'attesa*, waiting room; *— da ballo*, ballroom, dance-hall; *— da concerto*, concert hall; (hosp.) *— operatoria*, operating theatre; (theatr.) auditorium.

**sala**[2] *f.* (eng.) axle, axletree.

**salacca** *f.* pilchard.

**salac-e** *adj.* salacious; risqué; pungent; lascivious. **-ità** *f.* salaciousness; lasciviousness; pungency.

**salamandra** *f.* salamander.

**salame** *m.* sausage, salami.

**salamlec-co** (*pl.* **-chi**) deep bow; obsequious salutation; salaam.

**salamo·i-a** *f.* brine; pickle. **-are** [A4] *tr.* to put in brine; to pickle, to marinate.

**sal-are** [A1] *tr.* to salt; to sprinkle salt on. **-ata** *f.* salting, adding of salt. **-ato** *part. adj.* salted; *n.m.* salami, salted meat; salt pork; *adv. costare -ato*, to be very expensive. **-atọre** *m.*, **-atrice** *f.* (industr.) salter. **-atura** *f.* salting; curing.

**sala·ri-o** *m.* wages, pay; salary. **-ale** *adj.* relating to salaries; *aumento -ale*, salary rise. **-are** [A4] *tr.* to pay, to pay wages to; to remunerate.

**salass-are** [A1] *tr.* (med.) to bleed; to let blood from; (fig.) to overcharge; *rfl.* to open one's veins. **-o** *m.* bloodletting.

**salc-e, sa·lc-io** *m.* (bot.) willow. **-ẹto** *m.* willow grove. **-igno** *adj.* of willow; tough; knotty; (fig.) cross-grained.

**salcra·ut, salcra·uti, salcra·utte** *m. indecl.* sauerkraut.

**salda** *f.* solution of starch.

**saldamẹnte** *adv.* firmly; soundly; solidly.

**sald-are** [A1] *tr.* to consolidate; to strengthen; (comm.) to balance; to settle; (med.) to heal; to cicatrize; (eng.) to weld. **-amẹnto** *m.* consolidating; strengthening; (med.) healing; cicatrization; (eng.) welding; soldering; blazing. **-atọio** *m.* (eng.) soldering iron. **-atọre** *m.* solderer. **-atura** *f.* strengthening; (fig.) healing; (med.) healing; (eng.) welding.

**saldẹzza** *f.* firmness; stability; solidity; soundness.

**saldo** *adj.* firm, sound; solid; robust; steady; rigid; (fig.) staunch, steadfast; constant; (comm.) balanced; *n.m.* (comm.) balance; remainder; settlement.

**sale** *m.* salt; *un pizzico di —*, a pinch of salt; (fig.) mother-wit; good judgement.

**salgemma** *m.* rock salt, common salt.

**sa·lic-e** *m.* willow. **-ẹto** *m.* willow-grove.

**saliente** *adj.* rising, mounting; salient; projecting; (fig.) important; conspicuous; *n.m.* (mil.) salient.

**sal-iera** *f.* salt cellar (for the table.) **-i·fero** *adj.* containing salt. **-igno** *adj.* salt, salty; saline. **-ina** *f.* salt-works; salt pan; crude salt. **-ino** *adj.* containing salt; (chem.) saline.

**sal-ire** [D1] *intr.* (*aux.* essere) to ascend; to rise; to go up; *— (su) per le scale*, to go upstairs; (of prices) to rise, to mount; *tr.* to mount. **-iscendi** *m. indecl.* going up and down, ups and downs. **-ita** *f.* ascent; upward slope.

**saliv-a** *f.* saliva. **-ale** *adj.* salivary. **-are** [A1] *intr.* (*aux.* avere) to salivate. **-aziọne** *f.* salivation.

**salma** *f.* corpse; dead body; remains; (fig.) heavy burden.

**salmastro** *adj.* brackish.

**salmeggi-are** [A3 c] *intr.* (*aux.* avere) (mus.) to sing psalms; to chant **-amẹnto** *m.* psalm-singing. **-atọre** *m.*, **-atrice** *f.* (mus.) psalm-singer.

**salmeria** *f.* (mil.) baggage train.

**salmì** *m. indecl.* (cul.) stew, salmi.

**salm-o** *m.* psalm. **-ista** *m.* psalmist. **-odi·a** *f.* (mus.) psalmody. **-odiare** [A4] *intr.* (*aux.* avere) to sing psalms; (fig.) to speak in a monotonous way, to intone.

**salmọne** *m.* (ichth.) salmon.

**salnitro** *m.* saltpetre; mitre.

**Salomọne** *pr.n.m.* Solomon.

**salọne** *m.* hall; large hall; saloon; reception room.

**Salonicco** *pr.n.f.* (geog.) Salonika.

**salott-o** *m.* drawing-room, sitting room, parlour; reception room; *— letterario*, salon. **-iere** *m.* person who frequents salons habitually. **-iero** *adj.* relating to salons; frivolous and fashionable. **-ino** *m. dim.* parlour.

**salpare** [A1] *intr.* (*aux.* avere) (naut.) *— l'ancora*, *— il ferro*, to weigh anchor.

**sals-a** *f.* sauce, gravy; *— di pomodoro*, tomato sauce. **-iera** *f.* sauce-boat; gravy boat.

**salsapari·glia** *f.* (bot.) sarsaparilla.

**salsapietra** *f.* (chem.) saltpetre, nitre.

**salse·dine** *f.* saltiness.

**salsi·cci-a** *f.* pork sausage; sausage meat; force meat. **-a·io** *m.* sausage-maker.

**sals-o** *adj.* salt, salty; salted; *n.m.* saltiness, salt. **-ume** *m.* salt, pungent smell; saltiness.

**salt-are** [A1] *intr.* (*aux.* avere) to jump, to spring; to vault; to skip; to leap; (*aux.* essere) to jump; *— giù dal letto*, to leap out of bed; *— in aria*, to blow up, to explode; *tr.* to jump, to jump over; to clear; to leave out. **-abẹcca, -acavalla** *f.* grasshopper. **-ato** *part. adj.* jumped; cleared; skipped; omitted; (cul.) *patate -ate*, sauté potatoes; (mus.) sautillé, jeté, ricochet (bowing). **-atọio** *m.* perch (in a bird cage). **-atọre** *m.* jumper, leaper; tumbler, acrobat; hurdler; dancer; *pl.* (ent.) grasshoppers, locusts, crickets.

**saltell-are** [A1] *intr.* (*aux.* avere) to hop; to skip along; to dart in and out, to peep; (of the thoughts) to flit; (of the pulse) to palpitate; (of the heart) to beat rapidly. **-ọne, -ọni** *adv.* skipping along.

**salterell-are** [A1] *intr.* (*aux.* avere) to hop on the tips of the toes. **-o** *m.* little hop; jumping cracker; (pop.) grasshopper; (mus.) jack (of harpsichord).

**salte·rio** *m.* (mus.) psaltery; (bibl.) Psalter.

**salticchiare** [A4] *intr.* (*aux.* avere) to jump lightly on tiptoe.

**saltimban-co** (*pl.* **-chi**) mountebank; tumbler; acrobat.

**saltimbọcca** *m. indecl.* (cul.) a thin slice of veal and a thin slice of ham wrapped together and first braised, and then stewed in anchovy sauce.

**salt-o** *m.* jump, leap; *di —*, rapidly; *in quattro -i*, no sooner said than done; *— mortale*, somersault; *— con l'asta*, pole vault; *pl.* rapids, falls, cateracts. **-ua·rio** *adj.* without continuity; desultory; intermittent.

**saluber·rimo** *adj. superl.* of **salubre**; most salubrious.

**salubr-e** *adj.* healthy, wholesome, salubrious. **-ità** *f.* healthiness; healthfulness; salubrity.

**salum-e** *m.* salt meat; salt provisions; preserved foods. **-a·io** *m.* pork-butcher; dealer in salt provisions. **-eri·a** *f.* pork-butcher's shop; salt provision shop.

**salutare**[1] *adj.* salutary, beneficial, wholesome.

**salut-are**[2] [A1] *tr.* to salute; to greet; to bow to; to acknowledge; to welcome; to send regards to; *recip. rfl.* to greet one another. **-aziọne** *f.* salutation; greeting; message.

**salut-e** *f.* health; well-being, *bere alla — di*, to drink to the health of, to drink a toast to; *casa di —*, sanatorium, nursing home; (excl.) —!, good health!; welfare, safety, refuge; (rel.) salvation. **-ista** *m.* health crank; (rel.) member of the Salvation army.

**saluto** *m.* greeting; bow; salutation; *tanti saluti a*, kindest regards to; (comm.) *distinti saluti*, yours truly; (mil.) salute.

**salva** *f.* gun salute; salvo; volley.

**salv-acondọtto** *m.* safe-conduct; permit. **-adana·io, -adanaro** *m.* money box. **-agente** *m. indecl.* life-belt; lifebuoy; traffic island; *-agente a sacco*, breeches-buoy. **-aguardare** [A1] *tr.* to safeguard; to protect; *rfl.* to safeguard one-self. **-agua·rdia** *f.* safeguard; protection.

**salv-are** [A1] *tr.* to save; to rescue; to deliver; to preserve; *rfl.* to save oneself; to escape. **-amẹnto** *m.* saving; rescue. **-ando** *ger.*, *prep.* saving, except for. **-ata·ggio** *m.* rescue; salvage; *battello di -ataggio*, lifeboat; (naut.) *apparecchio di -ataggio*, lifesaving apparatus; *cintura di -aggio*, lifebelt. **-atọre** *m.* (theol.) Saviour; rescuer; deliverer. **-aziọne** *f.* salvation.

**salva·tico** see **selvatico.**

**salv-e** *excl.* hail!; (colloq.) so long!; cheerio! **-ete** *excl.* (Latin *2nd pl. imp.*) hail!

**salvẹzza** *f.* safety; salvation; *ancora di —*, sheet anchor.

**sa·lvia** *f.* (bot.) garden sage.

**salviẹtta** *f.* (table) napkin, serviette; paper napkin.

**salvo**[1] *adj.* safe; secure; *sano e —*, safe and sound; *n.m.* safety; safe place; *porre in —*, to save.

**salvo**[2] *prep.* save, except; barring; apart from; *conj. —che*, (*foll.* by *subj.*) unless.

**sambu-co** *m.* (*pl.* **-chi**) (bot.) elder.

**Samo** *pr.n.f.* (geog.) Samos.

**sampier-o, sampietr-o** *m.* (ichth.) John Dory. **-ino** *adj.* of St. Peter's, Rome; *n.m. pl.* workmen permanently employed on the fabric of St. Peter's.

**San** (abbrev. of **Santo**) Saint.

**sana·bile** *adj.* curable.

**san-are** [A1] *tr.* to heal; to cure; to rectify; to make good; *rfl.* to get better; to recover; (of a wound) to heal. **-ativo** *adj.* healing; curative. **-atọre** *m.*, **-atrice** *f.* healer; *adj.* healing, curative. **-ato·rio** *adj.* (*m.pl.* **-atorii**) remedial; *n.m.* sanatorium.

**sancire** [D2] *tr.* to sanction; to enforce; to ratify; to decree.

**sanculotti** *pr.n.m.pl.* (hist.) Sansculottes.

**sa·ndalo** *m.* sandal; sandalwood; (naut.) lighter.

**sanẹse** *adj.*, *n.m.*, *f.* Sienese.

**sangu-e** *m.* blood; *fare —*, to bleed; (fig.) *cattivo —*, bad blood, rancour; *a — freddo*, in cold blood; lineage, family; *cavallo di —*, thoroughbred horse; relationship, relations. **-idọtto** (anat.) blood vessel. **-igna** *f.* blood-stone; (paint.) red crayon drawing. **-igno** *adj.* sanguine; full blooded; *arancia -igna*, blood orange; *n.m.* blood red colour. **-ina·ccio** *m.* black pudding, blood sausage. **-inante** *part. adj.* bleeding. **-inare** [A1 s] *intr.* (*aux.* avere) to bleed; *tr.* to stain with blood. **-ina·rio** *adj.* bloody; sanguinary; blood-thirsty; *n.m.* killer; homicidal maniac. **-i·neo** *adj.* blood stained; *n.m.* (med.) plethoric subject. **-inità** *f.* (leg.) consanguinity; blood relationship. **-inoso** *adj.* blood-thirsty, bloody; profusely bleeding. **-isuga** *f.* (zool.) leech; (fig.) blood-sucker.

**sanit-à** *f.* soundness; good health; sanity; *Ministero della — Pubblica*, Ministry of Health; (leg.) sanity; soundness of mind. **-a·rio** *adj.* sanitary; concerning public health; *ufficiale -ario*, health officer; (mil.) *corpo -ario*, medical corps.

**sano** *adj.* sound; healthy; well; wholesome; *— e salvo*, safe and sound; entire, whole.

**sa·nscrito** *m.* Sanskrit.

**Sansọne** *pr.n.m.* Samson.

**santaba·rbara** *f.* (naut.) magazine, hold for gunpowder.

**santarell-a** *f.*, **-o** *m.* young devotee; prig.

**santelmo** *m.* Saint Elmo's fire.

**santific-are** [A2 s] *tr.* to sanctify, to hallow; to keep holy; to consecrate; to canonize; to offer to God. **-aziọne** *f.* sanctification; hallowing; consecration; observance (of Holy Days).

**santimo·nia** *f.* holiness; sanctimoniousness.

**santino** *m. dim.* of **santo**; young saint; small image of saint.

**Santippe** *pr.n.f.* Xantippe; (fig.) scold.

**santità** *f.* sanctity, holiness; saintliness; *Sua Santità*, His Holiness.

**sant-o** *adj.* (rel.) holy, blessed, sacred; sainted; *lo Spirito —*, the Holy Spirit; *il — Padre*, the Holy Father; *la -a sede*, the Holy See; *vino —*, communion wine; *giovedì —*, Maundy Thursday; *Venerdì —*, Good Friday; *anno —*, Jubilee year; *la terra -a*, the Holy Land; *tutto il — giorno*, the whole blessed day; *n.m.* saint; holy one; holy thing.

**sa·ntolo** *m.* godfather.

**santua·rio** *m.* sanctuary; holy place; shrine.

**sanziọn-e** *f.* sanction; approval; penalty. **-are** [A1 c] *tr.* to sanction; to approve; to apply sanctions against.

**sap-ẹre** [B26] *tr.* to know; *— l'italiano*, to know Italian; *abs.* to know; (foll. by *inf.*) to know how (to), to be able (to); *— ballare*, to know how to dance; *intr.* (*aux.* avere; *prep.* di) to smell (of); to taste (of); *non — di nulla*, to be insipid; *n.m.* knowledge; learning. **-uta** *f.* knowledge; *a mia -uta*, as far as I know.

**sa·pid-o** *adj.* tasty, pleasing to the taste. **-ità** *f.* sapidity.

**sapien-te** *adj.* wise; learned; sapient; *n.m.* wise man, sage; scholar; savant; well-informed person. **-za** *f.* wisdom; learning; knowledge.

**sapon-a·ceo** *adj.* soapy. **-a·io** *m.* soap-maker.

**sapọn-e** *m.* soap; *— per barba*, shaving-soap, shaving-stick; empty promises; *dare il — a*, to flatter, to 'soft soap'. **-ata** *f.* soap suds; lather. **-ẹtta** *f.* (cake of) soap; flat pocket watch, hunter. **-iera** *f.* soap-dish. **-ifi·cio** *m.* soap-works. **-ọso** *adj.* soapy; slippery.

**sapọr-e** *m.* flavour; taste; relish; (fig.) savour, pungency. **-ino** *m. dim.* delicate flavour. **-itamẹnte** *adv.* deliciously; with relish; *dormire -itamente*, to sleep soundly. **-ito** *adj.* savoury; tasty; delicious; piquant; lively; witty; (of prices) high. **-ọso** *adj.* tasty; (fig.) witty; pungent.

**sarabanda** *f.* (mus.) saraband, sarabande.

**saraceno** *adj.*, *n.m.* Saracen.

**saracin-o** *m.*, *adj.* quintain; (fig.) butt, object ridicule. **-ẹsca** *f.* rolling shutter; (hist.) portcullis.

**Saragọzza** *pr.n.f.* (geog.) Saragossa.

**sarc-aṣmo** sarcasm; sarcastic remark. **-a·stico** *adj.* sarcastic.

**sa·rchi-o** *m.* (agric.) light hoe. **-are** [A4] *tr.* (agric.) to hoe, to weed with a hoe. **-atọre** *m.* (agric.) hoer. **-atrice** *f.* (agric.) mechanical hoe. **-atura** *f.* hoeing.

**sarco·fa-go** *m.* (*pl.* **-ghi**) sarcophagus.

**sard-a** *f.* pilchard. **-ella** *f.* sardine. **-ellina** *f.* sprat. **-ina** *f.* sardine.

**Sard-ẹgna** *pr.n.f.* (geog.) Sardinia. **-o** *adj.*, *n.m.* Sardinian.

**sardo·nice** *m.* (miner.) sardonyx.

**sardo·nico** *adj.* sardonic.

**sargasso** *m.* (bot.) sargasso; (geog.) *Mare dei Sargassi*, Sargasso Sea.

**sa·rgia** *f.* cretonne; bedspread.

**sa·riga** *f.* (zool.) opossum.

**sarmẹnto** *m.* (bot.) vine branch; tendril.

**sarta** *f.* dressmaker; tailoress.

**sa·rtia** *f.* (naut.) stay, stroud.

**sart-o** *m.* tailor. **-ori·a** *f.* tailoring; dressmaking; tailor's shop.
**sass-a·ia** *f.* dam; barrier of stones; stony ground. **-ai(u)ola** *f.* volley of stones. **-ata** *f.* blow from a stone.
**sassi·fraga** *f.* (bot.) saxifrage.
**sass-o** *m.* stone, rock pebble; *tirare -i,* to throw stones; *il Gran Sasso d'Italia,* Monte Corno. **-ẹtto** *m. dim.* pebble. **-olino** *m.* pebble; *pl.* gravel.
**sasso·fono** *m.* (mus.) saxophone.
**sa·ssola** *f.* baler, baling pan.
**sassọne**[1] *m. augm.* of **sasso**; large stone.
**sassọne**[2] *adj., n.m., f.* Saxon.
**Sasso·nia** *pr.n.f.* (geog.) Saxony.
**sassọso** *adj.* stony.
**Sa·t-ana** *pr.n.m.* Satan. **-a·nico** *adj.* Satanic.
**satel·lite** *f.* satellite; (fig.) follower; hired ruffian, assassin.
**satin** *m. indecl.* (pron. as French) satin **-are** [A1] *tr.* to satin, to give a glossy surface to.
**sa·tir-a** *f.* satire. **-eggiante** *part. adj.* satirizing; satirical. **-eggiare** [A3 c] *tr.* to satirize.
**sati·rico**[1] *adj.* satirical; *n.m.* satirical writing, satire; satirist.
**sati·rico**[2] *adj.* satyr-like; (Gk. lit.) *dramma —,* satyr play.
**sa·tir-o** *m.* satyr; (fig.) lascivious person. **-ẹsco** *adj.* (*m.pl.* **-ẹschi**) satyr-like; lascivious. **-ista** *m.* (theatr. hist.) actor who danced the role of satyr.
**sativo** *adj.* (agric.) cultivated.
**satọll-a** *f.* filling meal; bellyful. **-amẹnto** *m.* satiating; full meal, 'blow out'; (agric.) manuring. **-are** [A1 c] *tr.* to satiate, to stuff with food; (agric.) to manure. **-o** *adj.* satiated, sated; full.
**sa·trapo** *m.* (Persian hist.) satrap; (fig.) bigwig.
**satur-are** [A1 s] *tr.* to saturate; to glut; *rfl.* to become saturated. **-aziọne** *f.* saturation.
**Saturno** *pr.n.m.* (myth.; astron.) Saturn.
**sa·turo** *adj.* saturated; full.
**sa·uri** *m.pl.* (zool.) lizards.
**sa·uro** *adj.* (vet.) bay, roan; *n.m.* bay or roan horse; sorrel.
**sa·vi-o** *adj.* wise; judicious; skilled; sage; (of a child) good; *n.m.* sage. **-ẹzza** *f.* wisdom; prudence.
**Savo·i-a** *pr.n.f.* (geog.) Savoy. **-ardo** *adj., n.m.* Savoyard.
**sax** *m. indecl.* (mus.) saxhorn.
**sazi-are** [A4] *tr.* to satisfy; to satiate; to content; *rfl.* to be satiated; to have one's fill. **-amẹnto** *m.* satisfaction; contenting, satisfying.
**sa·zi-o** *adj.* satiated; sated; full (up); (fig.) tired, wearied. **-età** *f.* satiety; fullness. **-ẹvole** *adj.* cloying.
**ṣbaccellare** [A1] *tr.* to shell (peas).
**ṣbacchettare** [A1 c] *tr.* to beat (rugs).
**ṣba·cchi-o** *m.* bang; slam. **-are** [A4] *tr., intr.* (*aux.* avere) to bang; to slam. **-ata** *f.* bang, slam.
**sbada·cchio** *m.* (bldg.) horizontal strut.
**ṣbadat-o** *adj.* careless; heedless; inattentive; *n.m.* careless person. **-ag·gine** *f.* carelessness. **-amẹnte** *adv.* carelessly; heedlessly. **ọna** *f.*, **-ọne** *m.* careless, heedless individual.
**ṣbadi·gli-o** *m.* yawn; yawning. **-amẹnto** *m.* yawn; yawning. **-are** [A4] *intr.* (*aux.* avere) to yawn, to gape; to be wide open.
**ṣbaf-are** [A1] *intr.* (*aux.* avere; *prep.* da) to scrounge (from); to sponge (on). **-atọre** *m.* scrounger. **-o** *m.* scrounging; *mangiare a -o,* to eat without paying, to scrounge a meal.
**ṣbagli-are** [A4] *tr.* to mistake; to miscalculate; — *strada,* to miss one's way; *intr.* (*aux.* avere) to make a mistake; *rfl.* to be mistaken; to be confused; to be wrong; to blunder. **-ato** *part. adj.* mistaken; wrong; erroneous; incorrect.
**ṣba·glio** *m.* mistake; blunder; error; fault; *fare degli sbagli,* to make mistakes.
**ṣbalestr-are** [A1] *intr.* (*aux.* avere) (fig.) to miss the target; to be wide of the mark; to wander from the point; *tr.* to fling, to hurl; to drive; to thrust; to send away; to get rid of; *rfl.* to be ruined, to crash. **-amẹnto** *m.* missing the mark; erratic movement. **-ato** *part. adj.* flung at random; wide of the mark; wild; unbalanced.
**ṣball-are** [A1] *tr.* to unpack; to unbale; *intr.* (*aux.* avere) to overshoot. **-onata** *f.* tall story. **-ọna** *f.*, **-ọne** *m.* exaggerator; teller of tall stories.
**ṣballott-are** [A1] *tr.* to toss up and down in one's arms; to toss about; to push around. **-amẹnto** *m.*, **-ìo** *m.* tossing up and down; jerking; jolting.
**ṣbalord-ire** [D2] *tr.* to stun; to bewilder; to amaze; to dumbfound; *intr.* (*aux.* avere) to be dumbfounded. **-imẹnto** *m.* amazement astonishment; stupefaction; bewilderment. **-ita·ggine** *m.* bewilderment; embarrassment. **-itivo** *adj.* bewildering; astonishing. **-ito** *part. adj.* amazed; astonished; dumbfounded.
**ṣbalz-are** [A1] *tr.* to fling; to hurl; to throw down; to cast out; *intr.* (*aux.* essere) to bounce; to spring (down); to dart; to leap. **-amẹnto** *m.* hurling down; flinging away; overthrow; dismissal.
**ṣbalzell-are** [A1] *intr.* (*aux.* avere) to bounce up and down; *tr.* to jolt. **-ìo** *m.* continual jolting. **-ọne** *m.* violent jerk. **-ọni** *adv.* bouncing up and down.
**ṣbalzo** *m.* bound; spring; leap; bounce; sudden dash; start.
**ṣbancare**[1] [A2] *tr.* (bldg.) to remove earth from.
**ṣbancare**[2] [A2] *intr.* (*aux.* avere) (in gambling) to win the bank.
**ṣband-are** [A1] *tr.* to disband; to disperse; *intr.* (*aux.* avere) (naut.) to be listing; *rfl.* to disperse; (motor.) to skid. **-amẹnto** *m.* disbanding; dispersal; (motor.) skid; (naut.) list, listing. **-ata** *f.* (motor.) skid.
**ṣbandeggi-are** [A3 c] *tr.* to banish. **-amẹnto** *m.* banishment.
**ṣbandellare** [A1] *tr.* to unhinge.
**ṣbandier-are** [A1] *intr.* (*aux.* avere) to wave flags; to hang out flags; *tr.* to display (flag.); (fig.) to show off. **-amẹnto** *m.* (iron.) flag-waving. **-ata** *f.* waving of flags; wave with a flag.
**ṣband-ire** [D2] *tr.* to banish, to exile; to send away; to dismiss. **-imẹnto** *m.* banishment; exile; renunciation; dismissal.
**ṣbara·gli-o** *m.* rout; confusion; turmoil; risk; jeopardy. **-amẹnto** *m.* routing; dispersal. **-are** [A4] *tr.* to throw into confusion; to rout; to disperse; *rfl.* to disperse, to disband, to scatter.
**ṣbarazzare** [A1] *tr.* (*prep.* di) to free (from), to clear (of); *rfl.* to free oneself; to rid oneself (of).
**ṣbarazzin-o** *m.* scamp; street urchin. **-ata** *f.* prank.
**ṣbarb-are** [A1] *tr.* to uproot; to weed. **-atello** *m.* young lad, beardless youth.
**ṣbarbicare** [A2 s] *tr.* to uproot; (fig.) to eradicate.
**ṣbarc-are** [A2] *tr.* to put ashore; to unload (grain) — *il pilota,* to drop the pilot; to pass; to spend; to get through; *intr.* (*aux.* essere) to disembark; to go ashore; to land; *rfl.* *-arsela,* to get through as best one can, to manage. **-atọio** *m.* landing place; quay; wharf.
**ṣbar-co** *m.* (*pl.* **-chi**) disembarkation; landing, unloading; *ponticello di —,* gangplank.
**ṣbarello** *m.* tipping lorry (used for carrying earth).
**ṣbarr-a** *f.* bar; barrier; (rlwy.) bar, road barrier; (naut.) — *del timone,* tiller; (mil.) barricade; (leg.) *presentarsi alla —,* to appear in the dock; (of a typewriter) — *spaziatrice,* space bar; (mus.) bar line; double bar; (herald.) bend sinister. **-amẹnto** *m.* barricading; blocking; (hydraul.) weir; (naut.) minefield; boom; river or harbour defence; (mil.) *tiro di -amento,* barrage fire. **-are** [A1] *tr.* to bar; to block, to barricade; (comm.) *-are un*

*assegno,* to cross a cheque; to unbar; to open wide. **-ata** *f.* (mil.) trench. **-ętta** *f.* (typ.) solidus, oblique stroke.

**ṣbatacchi-are** [A4] *tr.* to flap; to bang; to throw about; to slam; *intr.* (*aux.* avere), *rfl.* to toss about, to fling oneself about; to rattle; to flap about. **-amęnto** *m.* banging, bang; slamming, slam; swinging to and fro; clattering, clashing. **-ata** *f.* bang; slam; clash.

**ṣbatacchìo** *m.* continual banging; clatter.

**ṣba·tt-ere** [B1] *tr.* to shake; to toss; to fling; to flap; to bang; to fend off; to resist; *rfl.* to toss (oneself) about, to fling (oneself) about; to be restless; *intr.* (*aux.* avere) to bang; to slam. **-imęnto** *m.* banging; slamming; battering; clattering. **-itura** *f.* banging; bang; crashing; crash; flapping; shaking; shake. **-itutto** *m. indecl.* (cul.) whisk. **-uta** *f.* bang; slam.

**ṣba·ttito** *m.* banging; battering; slamming.

**ṣbaulare** [A1 a] *tr., abs.* to unpack.

**ṣbav-are** [A1] *intr.* (*aux.* avere) to slobber, to slaver; to dribble; *rfl.* to slobber down one's chin. **-amęnto** *m.* slobbering, slavering; dribbling. **-atura** *f.* slobber; dribble; slimy track (of a snail); (paperm.) deckle-edge. **-ọna** *f.*, **-ọne** *m.* slobberer.

**ṣbeff-are** [A1] *tr.* to mock cruelly; to deride. **-amęnto** *m.* deriding. **-atura** *f.* cruel mockery.

**ṣbeffeggi-are** [A3 c] *tr.* to poke fun at maliciously, to 'get at'. **-amęnto** *m.* mocking, making game of.

**ṣbellicare** [A2] *tr.* to split open; to disembowel; *rfl.* to split oneself; *sbellicarsi dalle risa,* to split one's sides with laughter.

**ṣbendare** [A1] *tr.* to unbandage.

**ṣberciare**[1] [A3] *intr.* (*aux.* avere) to shoot wide of the mark; *tr.* to mock, to satirize, to lampoon.

**ṣberciare**[2] [A3] *intr.* (*aux.* avere) to shriek, to yell.

**ṣberleffo** *m.* grimace.

**ṣberrettare** [A1 c] *rfl.* to take off one's cap; to lift one's cap (in greeting).

**ṣbertucciare** [A3] *tr.* to crush, to crumple; to rumple.

**ṣbevazz-are** [A1] *intr.* (*aux.* avere) to tipple. **-amęnto** *m.* drinking bout. **-atọre** *m.*, **-atrice** *f.* toper.

**ṣbiad-ire** [D2] *intr.* (*aux.* essere) to fade, to grow pale; *tr.* to cause to fade; to take the colour out of. **-ito** *part. adj.* pale; faded.

**ṣbianc-are** [A2] *intr.* (*aux.* essere), *rfl.* to turn white; to fade; to grow pale; *tr.* to whiten; to whitewash; (text.) to bleach. **-atrice** *f.* bleaching agent.

**ṣbiasci-are** [A3] *tr., intr.* (*aux.* avere) to mumble. **-atura** *f.* mumbling.

**ṣbie-co** *adj.* (*m.pl.* **-chi**) oblique; awry; *di —,* edgeways; *presa di —,* angle shot. **-camęnte** *adv.* obliquely. **-care** [A2] *tr.* to distort; to look askance at; to straighten; *intr.* (*aux.* avere, essere), *rfl.* to be crooked.

**ṣbigott-ire** [D2] *tr.* to terrify; to dismay; *intr.* (*aux.* essere), *rfl.* to be dismayed; to lose heart; to be discouraged. **-imęnto** *m.* dismay; consternation; terror; discouragement. **-ito** *part. adj.* dismayed; dejected.

**ṣbilanci-are** [A3] *tr.* to throw off balance; to unsettle; to derange; *intr.* (*aux.* avere) to overbalance; to be weighed down on one side; to lose one's balance; *rfl.* (fig.) to take on too many commitments; to spend beyond one's means. **-amęnto** *m.* loss of balance; derangement.

**ṣbila·ncio** *m.* lack of balance; disproportion; (finan.) deficiency; deficit.

**ṣbilen-co** *adj.* (*m.pl.* **-chi**) crooked; bowlegged.

**ṣbirci-are** [A3] *tr.* to eye; to watch closely; to cast sidelong glances at; to watch out of the corner of one's eye; *intr.* (*aux.* avere) to give sidelong glances. **-ata** *f.* sidelong glance, scrutiny.

**ṣbirichinare** [A1] *intr.* (*aux.* avere) to play childish tricks, to get up to pranks.

**ṣbirr-o** *m.* (derog., of a policeman) bogey. **-a·glia** *f.* (derog.) gang of police.

**ṣbiẓẓ-arire, -ire** [D2] *tr.* to satisfy the whim of; *rfl.* to give way to one's caprices; to indulge in a show of temper.

**ṣbloccare** [A2] *tr.* (mil.) to lift the siege, to lift the blockade of.

**ṣbocc-are** [A2 c] *intr.* (*aux.* essere; *prep.* in) (of water) to flow (into); to have its outlet (in); to fall (into); (of a street) to open (into), to lead (to); to debouch; to come out (onto); to emerge; to overflow; *tr.* to break the rim of. **-amęnto** *m.* outflow; outfall; outlet; mouth (of river). **-atọio** *m.* outlet.

**ṣbocciare**[1] [A3] *tr.* (bowls) to knock away (the bowl of).

**ṣbocciare**[2] [A3] *intr.* (*aux.* essere) to bud, to blossom; to open (of flowers); (fig.) to blossom.

**ṣbo·ccio** *m.* bud; blossom; bloom.

**ṣbọc-co** *m.* (*pl.* **-chi**) outlet; opening; river mouth.

**ṣbocconcell-are** [A1] *tr.* to nibble; to bite little pieces off; to cut in small pieces; to chip. **-atura** *f.* nibbling; chip; fragmentation.

**ṣbollare** [A1 c] *tr.* to unseal, to break the seal of.

**ṣbollire** [D2] *intr.* (*aux.* essere, avere) to go off the boil; (fig.) to die down.

**ṣbomb-are** [A1 c] *tr.* to reveal, to let out; to disclose indiscreetly; *intr.* (*aux.* avere) to exaggerate. **-ọne** *m.* exaggerator.

**ṣbo·rni-a** *f.* (colloq.) drunkenness; binge; (fig.) infatuation. **-are** [A4] *rfl.* (colloq.) to get drunk, to go on a binge. **-ọna** *f.*, **-ọne** *m.* tippler, toper; drunkard.

**ṣbọrs-o** [A1 c] *tr.* disbursement; outlay; payment. **-are** [A1 c] *tr.* to disburse, to pay out.

**ṣbotton-are** [A1 c] *tr.* to unbutton; to undo; *rfl.* to unbutton one's clothing; (fig.) to unbutton oneself; to let oneself go; to unbosom oneself. **-atura** *f.* unbuttoning; (fig.) confiding.

**ṣbozz-o** *m.* rough outline; (paint.) sketch. **-are** [A1 c] *tr.* to sketch out; to outline; (paint.) to make a rough sketch of.

**ṣbozzolare** [A1 s] *intr.* (*aux.* essere) (silkb.) to come out of the cocoon; to remove the cocoons from the mulberry leaves.

**ṣbracalato** *adj.* slovenly; sloppily dressed; with trousers slipping down.

**ṣbracare** [A2] to unbreech; *rfl.* to take one's trousers off.

**ṣbracciare** [A3] *rfl.* to roll up one's sleeves; (fig.) to work hard; to strive.

**ṣbraci-are** [A3] *tr.* to poke, to stir (fire); *intr.* (*aux.* avere) (of sparks) to leap from the living coals. **-ata** *f.* stir, poke. **-atọio** *m.* poker.

**ṣbrait-are** [A1] *intr.* (*aux.* avere) to shout loudly, angrily. **-amęnto** *m.* loud shouting; bawling. **-ìo** *m.* (*pl.* **-ìi**) continual loud shouting; bawling; uproar. **-ọna** *f.*, **-ọne** *m.* bawler, shouter.

**ṣbran-are** [A1] *tr.* to tear to pieces; to rend; to lacerate; to destroy; *rfl.* to destroy oneself; *recip. rfl.* to rend one another. **-amęnto** *m.* tearing, rending; lacerating.

**ṣbranc-are** [A2] *tr.* to take from the flock; to separate; to detach; *rfl.* to scatter; to stray. **-amęnto** *m.* separating from a flock; straying. **-ata** *f.* part of a flock that has strayed.

**ṣbrattare** [A1] *tr.* to clean; to clear; to tidy, to put in order; *intr.* (*aux.* essere) to clear out; to be off.

**ṣbravazz-are** [A1] *intr.* (*aux.* avere) to swagger; to brag, to boast. **-ata** *f.* bragging, boasting; swaggering. **-ọna** *f.*, **-ọne** *m.* swaggerer.

**ṣbręndol-o** *m.* shred; rag; tatter. **-are** [A1 sc] *intr.* (*aux.* avere, essere) to fall to rags; to hang in tatters. **-ọna** *f.*, **-ọne** *m.* ragamuffin.

**ṣbriciol-are** [A1 s] *tr.* to crumble; (fig.) to crush; to annihilate; to shatter; *rfl.* to crumble; to fall to pieces. **-amẹnto** *m.* crumbling; crushing. **-atura** *f.* crumbling; crumbled pieces.

**ṣbrig-are** [A2] *tr.* to dispatch; to finish off; to expedite; *rfl.* to hurry; to make haste; (*prep.* di) to get rid (of). **-amẹnto** *m.* dispatch; haste; expedition; hurry. **-ativo** *adj.* quick; expeditious.

**ṣbrigli-are** [A4] *tr.* to unbridle; (fig.) to relieve; to loosen; to set free, to liberate. **-amẹnto** *m.* unbridling; loosening; releasing, release. **-atẹzza** *f.* unruliness; unbridled behaviour. **-ato** *part. adj.* unbridled; sprightly; spirited.

**ṣbrin-are** [A1] *tr.* to defrost. **-amẹnto** *m.* defrosting (of a refrigerator).

**ṣbroccolare** [A1 s] *tr.* to nibble the tender branches of, to browse on.

**ṣbrogliare** [A4] to disentangle; to extricate; *rfl.* to get clear of; to release oneself; to get free; (*dat.* of *prn.* 'si') *sbrogliarsela*, to get out of a difficult situation.

**ṣbruff-are** [A1] *tr.* to bespatter, to besprinkle; to spurt. **-ata** *f.* sprinkling; spurt, squirt. **-o** *m.* squirt, spurt; gush; (fig.) bribe.

**ṣbucare** [A2] *intr.* (*aux.* essere; *prep.* da) to emerge; to come forth; to issue; *tr.* to draw out; to pull out; to dislodge; to start (*e.g.* a fox).

**ṣbucci-are** [A3] *tr.* to skin, to peel; to pare; to shell; to husk; (fig.) to have a smattering of; *rfl.* (*acc.* of *prn.* si) to take the skin off oneself; (ent.) to moult; (*dat.* of *prn.* 'si') *-arsi il ginocchio*, to graze one's knee. **-afatiche** *m. indecl.* idler. **-amẹnto** *m.* peeling, shelling. **-apatate** *m. indecl.* potato-peeler. **-atura** *f.* peeling; shelling; abrasion, graze, scratch.

**ṣbudellare** [A1] *tr.* to disembowel; to gut; to stab; *rfl.* to be disembowelled; to receive injuries to the abdomen; *recip. rfl.* to knife each other.

**ṣbuff-are** [A1] *intr.* (*aux.* avere) to snort; to puff; to pant; (of wind) to rage, to bluster; *tr.* to belch forth; to puff. **-ata** *f.* puff; snort. **-o** *m.* puff; snort; gust.

**ṣbugiardare** [A1] *tr.* to convict of lying; to give the lie to.

**sca·bbi-a** *f.* (med.) scabies. **-ọsa** *f.* (bot.) field scabious. **-ọso** *adj.* rough; (med.) scabious, affected with scabies.

**scabr-o** *adj.* rough; rugged; harsh. **-ẹzza** *f.* roughness; ruggedness; harshness.

**scabrọs-o** *adj.* rugged; unequal; knotty; uneven; (fig.) scabrous. **-ità** *f.* roughness; ruggedness; unevenness; inequality; (fig.) scabrousness.

**scaccato, scacheggiato** *adj.* chequered.

**scacch-i** *m.pl.* chess (see also **scacco**) **-iera** *f.* chessboard; draughtboard. **-iere** *m.* Exchequer; *Cancelliere dello -iere*, Chancellor of the Exchequer. **-ista** *m., f.* chess-player. **-i·stico** *adj.* pertaining to chess; *un torneo -istico*, a chess tournament.

**sca·ccia** *m. indecl.* (sport.) beater.

**scacci-are** [A3] *tr.* to drive out; to chase away; to expel; to dispel; to dismiss. **-amẹnto** *m.* chasing away; expulsion; dismissal; exile, banishment; rebuff. **-amọsche** *m. indecl.* flyswatter. **-pensieri** *m. indecl.* pastime; distraction.

**scaccino** *m.* verger, sexton.

**scac-co** *m.* (*pl.* **-chi**) square; check; *a -chi*, chequered; *pl.* (*chess*). — *!*, check! **-comatto** *m.* checkmate.

**scad-ẹre** [B1] *intr.* (*aux.* essere) to decline; to decay; to sink; to fall off; to decrease; to devolve; (leg.; comm.) to fall due; to expire; to mature. **-ente** *part. adj.* declining; falling; (leg.; comm.) falling due; expiring. **-enza** *f.* (leg.; comm.) maturity; expiration. **-enza·rio** *m.* (comm.) bill book. **-imẹnto** *m.* decline; falling off; decadence. **-uto** *part. adj.* due; expired; declined; decayed.

**scafandro** *m.* (naut.) diving apparatus.

**scaffal-e** *m.* bookcase; set of bookshelves; (typ.) composing frame. **-are** [A1] *tr.* to shelve (books); to fit (a room) with shelves. **-ata** *f.* bookshelf full of books, bookshelf. **-atura** *f.* shelving.

**scafo** *m.* (naut.) hull; boat, yacht; (aeron.) body.

**scagionare** [A1 c] *tr.* to excuse; to exculpate; to acquit; to justify; *rfl.* to justify oneself.

**sca·gli-a** *f.* (zool.) scale (of reptile); (sculp.) chip, flake; fragment. **-amẹnto** *m.* scaling; flaking; hurling. **-are** [A4] *tr.* to scale; to flake; (sculp.) *-are il marmo*, to chip the marble; to fling; to hurl; to throw; *rfl.* to fling oneself, to hurl oneself.

**scagliọn-e** *m.* large step; mountain terrace; (archit.) step, tread (of a staircase); *a —*, in echelon. **-are** [A1 c] *tr.* (mil.) to draw up (troops) in echelon formation.

**scagliọso** *adj.* scaly.

**scagnare** [A5] *intr.* (*aux.* avere) to yelp; to bay.

**scagnozzo** *m.* impoverished broken-down artist.

**scala**[1] *f.* staircase; stairs; *salire le scale*, to go upstairs; step; *— mobile*, escalator; *— a chiocciola*, spiral staircase; *pozzo della —*, well of stairs; *— a piuoli*, ladder.

**scala**[2] *f.* scale; proportion; order, sequence, series; (mus.) scale.

**Scal-a**[3] *pr.n.m.* (hist.) Scala (family ruling Verona); *gli —*, the Scalas. **-i·gero** *adj., n.m.* Scaliger; *le Tombe -igere*, the tombs of the Scaligers (Verona).

**Scala**[4] *pr.n.f. La —, il Teatro della —*, the Scala opera-house in Milan.

**scal-are**[1] [A1] *tr.* to scale, to climb; to graduate, to reduce by degrees. **-amẹnto** *m.* scaling, climbing; graduating; scaling down. **-ata** *f.* scaling, climbing; escalade. **-atọre** *m.*, **-atrice** *f.* climber, mountain climber; rock climber.

**scalare**[2] *adj.* pertaining to stairs, staircase or ladder.

**scalare**[3] *adj.* graduated; proportional.

**scalcagnato** *adj.* down-at-heel; shabby.

**scalciare** [A3] *intr.* (*aux.* avere) to kick, to be a kicker (*e.g.* of a mule).

**scalcin-are** [A1] *tr.* (bldg.) to strip the plaster off. **-ato** *part. adj.* stripped of plaster; (fig.) shabby. **-atura** *f.* (bldg.) removal of plaster; bare patch where plaster has broken away. **-aziọne** *f.* (bldg.) removal of plaster.

**scal-co** *m.* (*pl.* **chi**) (hist.) steward; carver; *coltello da —*, carving knife.

**scald-are** [A1] *tr.* to heat, to warm up, to heat up; to scald; to excite; *rfl.* (*acc.* of *prn.* 'si') to warm oneself; to get warm; to become excited; to excite oneself; (*dat.* of *prn.* 'si') *-arsi le mani*, to warm one's hands. **-abagno** *m. indecl.* heater, geyser; *-abagno ad immersione*, immersion heater. **-acolla** *m. indecl.* (carpent.) glue pot. **-aletto** *m. indecl.* warming pan. **-amẹnto** *m.* heating, warming. **-apiatti** *m. indecl.* plate warmer. **-apiedi** *m. indecl.* foot warmer; hot water bottle. **-ata** *f.* heating; warming. **-avivandi** *m. indecl.* chafing dish. **-ino** *m.* foot warmer; brazier.

**scale·a** *f.* (archit.) flight of steps.

**scaleno** *adj.* (geom.) scalene.

**scalẹtta** *f. dim.* of **scala**[1]; short ladder; narrow stairway.

**scalf-ire** [D2] *tr.* to scratch; to graze. **-itura** *f.* scratch; graze.

**scali·gero** *adj.* see under **Scala**[3].

**scalin-o** *m.* step; stair; rung. **-ata** flight of steps.

**scalman-a** *f.* chill, cold; (fig.) craze, enthusiasm. **-are** [A1] *rfl.* to catch a chill; (fig.) to fluster; to worry; to fuss. **-ata** *f.* hurry; pother, fuss, to-do. **-ato** *part. adj.* flustered. **-atura** *f.*

cold; chill; (fig.) fussing, hurrying; pother.
**scalmo** *m.* (naut.) rowlock; thole pin.
**scal-o** *m.* wharf; landing-stage; port of call; *fare — a*, to call at; *volo senza* —, non-stop flight; (rlwy.) — *passaggeri*, passenger quay; — *merci*, goods station.
**scalǫgna** *f.* bad luck; evil eye.
**scalǫgno** *m.* (bot.) shallot.
**scalopp-a, -ina** *f.* (cul.) escalope; — *di vitello*, escalope de veau.
**scalpell-o** *m.* chisel; scalpel; — *pneumatico*, rock drill, pneumatic drill. **-are** [A1] *tr.* to chisel; (sculp.) to cancel, to cut away (with the chisel). **-atura** *f.* chiselling. **-ino** (sculp.) stone-mason; stone cutter.
**scalpicc-are** [A3] *intr.* (*aux.* avere) to shuffle one's feet; to tramp; *tr.* to frequent, to tread. **-ìo** *m.* continual shuffling of feet; sound of footsteps; tramping.
**scalpit-are** [A1 s] *intr.* (*aux.* avere) to paw the ground. **-ìo** *m.* continual trampling; thud of feet.
**scalpǫre** *m.* altercation; squabble; row.
**scaltr-ire** [D2] *tr.* to sharpen the wits of; to smarten; *rfl.* to become shrewd; to learn from experience. **-imęnto** *m.* development in sagacity; smartening of wits; shrewd action. **-ito** *part. adj.* sharp-witted; cunning; experienced; shrewd; artful.
**scaltr-o** *adj.* smart, sharp; alert; astute, shrewd; cunning; crafty. **-ęzza** *f.* astuteness, shrewdness; expertness; cunning; craftiness.
**scalz-are** [A1] *tr.* to remove shoes and stockings from; to remove the shoes of; to make barefoot; *rfl.* to take off one's shoes and socks; to go about barefoot; (eccl.) to become a discalced religious. **-acane, -acani** *m. indecl.* a down and out; impoverished, shabby person; quack. **-atura** *f.* divesting of shoes and socks.
**scalzo** *adj.* barefoot, barefooted; *a piedi scalzi*, in bare feet; poor, ragged; impoverished; (eccl.) *adj.*, *n.m.* discalced; religious who goes barefoot or wears sandals.
**scambi-are** [A4] *tr.* to exchange; to change; to mistake; *rfl.* to be exchanged; *recip. rfl.* to exchange with each other; to be confused, mistaken for one another. **-amęnto** *m.* exchanging, exchange; confusion. **-ęvole** *adj.* reciprocal; mutual. **-evolęzza** *f.* reciprocity; mutuality.
**sca·mb-io** *m.* exchange; barter; (comm.) trade; *libero* —, free trade; error, mistake; confusion; substitute; replacement; (rlwy.) points; switch. **-ista** *m.* (comm.) trader; *libero -ista*, free trader; (rlwy.) pointsman.
**scamici-are** [A3] *rfl.* to take one's jacket off; to be in one's shirt sleeves. **-ato** *part. adj.* in shirt sleeves; (fig.) plebeian; *n.m.* vulgarian.
**scamo·scio** *m.* (zool.) chamois; *adj. pelle scamoscia*, chamois leather.
**scampafǫrca** *m. indecl.* gallows-bird.
**scampagn-are** [A5] *intr.* (*aux.* avere) to go for a trip to the country; to spend a holiday in the country. **-ata** *f.* trip to the country; day in the country; picnic.
**scampan-are** [A1] *intr.* (*aux.* avere) to ring the bells; to chime; to peal; *n.m.* ringing of bells; peal. **-amęnto** *m.* (motor.) piston-slap. **-ata** *f.* peal of bells. **-ìo** *m.* (*pl.* -ìi) continual ringing of bells; incessant chiming.
**scampanell-are** [A1] *intr.* (*aux.* avere) to ring a bell. **-ata** *f.* ringing of a bell; ring at a door bell. **-ìo** *m.* (*pl.* -ìi) continual loud ringing of bells.
**scamp-are** [A1] *tr.* to save; to rescue; to liberate, to free. *intr.* (*aux.* essere) to come through, to survive. **-amęnto** *m.* rescuing; escaping; survival.
**scampo** *m.* rescue; liberation; escape; survival; safety; (zool.) Dublin Bay prawn; *pl.* scampi.
**sca·mpolo** *m.* remnant, piece of cloth left over from a roll.
**scanal-are** [A1] *tr.* to groove; to channel. **-atura** *f.* grooving; groove; (archit.) fluting.
**scancellare** [A1] *tr.* to erase; to scratch out.
**scancio** *m.* oblique line; *adv. phr. di* —, askew, awry, obliquely; *tagliare a* —, to cut on the bias.
**scanda·gli-o** *m.* (naut.) sounding machine, lead line; sounding; depth of water; *compiere lo* —, to sound; *lanciare lo* —, to heave the lead line; (fig.) probe test. **-are** [A4] (naut.) to sound. **-atǫre** *m.* (naut.) leadsman. **-atrice** *f.* (naut.) *macchina -atrice*, sounding machine.
**sca·ndal-o** *m.* scandal; calumny; gossip; disgrace, shame; bad example. **-iẓẓare** [A1] *tr.* to scandalize; to outrage; to shock; to try to corrupt; *rfl.* to be scandalized; to be shocked. **-ǫso** *adj.* scandalous; shocking; outrageous.
**Scandina·via** *pr.n.f.* Scandinavia.
**scandi·navo** *adj.*, *n.m.* Scandinavian.
**scandire** [D2] *tr.* to scan (verse); to pronounce carefully, to articulate.
**scann-are** [A1] *tr.* to cut the throat of; to butcher; (fig.) to bleed, to extort money from; (text.) to unwind, to unreel. **-abęcco** (bot.) *m.* butcher's broom. **-afosso** *m.* open culvert. **-amęnto** *m.* throat-cutting, butchery. **-atǫre** *m.* cut-throat; assassin; moneylender. **-atura** *f.* throat cutting; butchering, slaughtering. **-auo·mini** *m. indecl.* money lender; usurer.
**scannell-are** [A1] *tr.* to groove; (archit.) to flute; (text.) to unwind, to unreel. **-amęnto** *m.* (art.) flute; fluting; (text.) unreeling. **-atura** *f.* grooving; (archit.) fluting.
**scannello** *m.* portable writing-desk; small bench; stool.
**scanno** *m.* bench; seat; dune, sand-bank.
**scans-are** [A1] *tr.* to avoid; to shun; to escape, to escape from; *rfl.* to move aside; to get out of the way; to move to one side. **-afatiche** *m. indecl.* slacker, shirker. **-amęnto** *m.* avoidance; withdrawing, moving aside. **-arote** *m. indecl.* bollard by a doorway to prevent damage by cartwheels.
**scansi·a** *f.* bookcase; set of shelves; cupboard.
**scansiǫne** *f.* scansion, scanning; articulation, distinct utterance.
**scanso** *m.* avoidance; *a — di*, in order to avoid.
**scantinato** *m.* cellar, basement.
**scanton-are** [A1 c] *tr.* to round the corners of; to cut off the corners of; to dog's-ear; (fig.) to avoid, to give the slip to; *intr.* (*aux.* avere) to turn a corner; (fig.) to take a wrong turning; *rfl.* to break off at the corners. **-amęnto** *m.* trimming off corners; dog's-earing; avoiding.
**scantucciare** [A3] *tr.* to cut the edges off.
**scanzonat-o** *adj.* free and easy; easy-going; informal. **-ura** *f.* informality; ease of manners.
**scapacciǫne** *m.* clout on the head; slap, smack.
**scapare** [A1] *tr.* to decapitate, to behead; to cut off the head of; *rfl.* (fig.) to lose one's head.
**scap-ato** *part.* of **scapare**; *adj.* reckless; thoughtless. **-ata·ggine** *f.* heedlessness; recklessness. **-atǫna** *f.*, **atǫne** *m.* thoughtless person; flighty person.
**scapestrat-o** *adj.* wild; dissolute; licentious; *n.m.* libertine; scapegrace. **-a·ggine** *f.* dissolute life; wild behaviour; recklessness.
**scapezzare** [A1 c] *tr.* to prune; to lop; to pollard.
**scapigli-are** [A4] *tr.* to ruffle, to rumple; *rfl.* to become dishevelled; to rumple one's hair; (fig.) to lead a dissolute life. **-ato** *part. adj.* dishevelled; dissolute. **-atura** *f.* dissoluteness; loose living; free and easy

manners; bohemianism. (liter. hist.) *Scapighatura*, late-19th-century school of N. Italian writers.

**scapitare** [A1 s] *intr.* (*aux.* avere) to suffer loss, to lose.

**sca·pito** *m.* loss. loss; detriment; damage; *a — di*, to the detriment of.

**scapo** *m.* shaft of a column.

**sca·pola** *f.* (anat.) scapula.

**scapolare**[1] *adj.*, *n.m.* (rel.) scapular.

**scapolare**[2] [A1 s] *intr.* (*aux.* avere; *prep.* a) to escape; to flee; *tr.* to get out of, to avoid; to escape.

**sca·polo** *adj.* single, unmarried (of a man); *n.m.* bachelor.

**scapp-are** [A1] *intr.* (*aux.* essere) to escape; to flee; to run away; to hurry away. **-amẹnto** *m.* escaping, escape; (watchm.) escapement; (motor.) exhaust; *tubo di -amento*, exhaust pipe; escape (of gas). **-ata** *f.* escape; flight; escapade; excursion; outburst. **-atina** *f.* minor escapade; short excursion. **-atọia** *f.* subterfuge; evasion; pretext. **-atọre** *m.* fugitive; *adj.* fleet, fast. **-avi·a** *m. indecl.* hurry, rush.

**scappell-are** [A1] *tr.* to remove the hat from; *rfl.* to take off one's hat (in greeting). **-ata** *f.* raising of one's hat, salutation.

**scappellott-o** *m.* cuff, slap on the head, box on the ears; (colloq.) *a -i*, without paying; *passare a -i*, to get through (an exam) by hook or by crook. **-are** [A1] *tr.* to cuff.

**scappucciare**[1] [A3] *tr.* to lift the hood off; *rfl.* to remove one's hood.

**scappucci-are**[2] [A3] *intr.* (*aux.* avere) to trip; (fig.) to blunder. **-ata** *f.* stumble; (fig.) to blunder.

**scapu·ccio** *m.* stumble; (fig.) blunder; mistake.

**scarabe·o** *m.* (ent.) scarab.

**scarabo·cchi-o** *m.* scribble; scrawl; blot. **-are** [A4] *tr.* to scribble on, to scrawl over, to jot down; *intr.* (*aux.* avere) to scribble. **-atọre** *m.*, **-atrice** *f.* scribbler. **-atura** *f.* scribbling, scribble; scrawl.

**scarafa·ggio** *m.* beetle; cockchafer; *— delle cucine*, cockroach; *— della patata*, Colorado beetle.

**scaramu·cci-a** *f.* (mil.) skirmish; (fig.) brush; controversy. **-are** [A3] *intr.* (*aux.* avere) to skirmish. **-atọre** *m.* (mil.) skirmisher.

**scaraventare** [A1] *tr.* to hurl, to fling; *rfl.* to hurl oneself, to hurtle.

**scarcer-are** [A1 s] *tr.* to release from prison; to set free. **-amẹnto** *m.* setting free, freeing from prison. **-aziọne** *f.* release from prison, liberation.

**scarco** *adj.* see **scarico.**

**scardare** [A1] *tr.* to husk (chestnuts).

**scardass-are** [A1] *tr.* (text.) to card. **-atọre** *m.* (text.) carder. **-atura** *f.* (text.) carding. **-o** *m.* (text.) card.

**scardinare** [A1 s] *tr.* to take (a door) off its hinges; to unhinge.

**sca·rica** *f.* unloading; valley; discharge; motion (of the bowels).

**scaric-are** [A2 s] *tr.* to unload; to discharge; *— di*, to relieve of; to shoot; to let fly; *rfl.* to get wound down, to run down; to relieve oneself; to deliver oneself; to flow. **-amẹnto** *m.* unloading; discharging. **-atọio** *m.* unloading place, dump; tip; depot; (archit.) gutter. **-atọre** *m.* unloader, docker; lighterman.

**sca·ri-co** *adj.* (*m.pl.* **-chi**) unloaded; empty; not wound up, run down; discharged; (fig.) serene, untroubled; *cielo —*, clear sky; *n.m.* unloading; rubbish dump, refuse tip; *baroccio di —*, dustcart; evacuation, motion; demurrage, unloading time; (motor.) exhaust; *tubo di —*, exhaust pipe.

**scarificare** [A2 s] *tr.* to scarify.

**scarlatt-o** *adj.* scarlet; *n.m.* scarlet, the colour scarlet; scarlet cloth; doctor's gown. **-ina** *f.* (med.) scarlet-fever. **-ino** *adj.* scarlet; (med.) *febbre -ina*, scarlet fever.

**scarmigliare** [A4] *tr.* to ruffle, to rumple; *rfl.* to tear one's hair.

**scarn-are** [A1] *tr.* to strip the flesh from; (tanning) to flesh; *rfl.* to grow thin, to lose flesh. **-amẹnto** *m.* stripping of flesh; (tanning) fleshing. **-atọio** *m.* (tanning) fleshing knife. **-atrice** *f.* (tanning) fleshing machine. **-atura** *f.* (tanning) fleshing.

**scarnificare** [A2 s] *tr.* to tear the flesh from; to lacerate.

**scarn-ire** [D2] *tr.* to strip the flesh from; to make lean. **-ito** *part. adj.* emaciated, lean; (fig.) meagre; scanty.

**scarno** *adj.* emaciated.

**scarp-a** *f.* shoe; drag (on a carriage wheel); skid (on a car wheel). **-ata** *f.* slap with a slipper; (bldg.) escarpment; scarp; embankment. **-ẹtta** *f. dim.* baby's shoe; *-ette da ballo*, dancing shoes, pumps, ballet-shoes. **-ina** *f. dim.* baby's shoe.

**scarrozz-are** [A1] *tr.* to take for a drive in a carriage; *intr.* (*aux.* avere) to go for a drive in a carriage. **-ata** *f.* drive in a carriage.

**scarsamẹnte** *adv.* barely; scarcely.

**scarsella** *f.* purse, wallet; (pilgrim's) scrip.

**scars-o** *adj.* scarce; scanty; slight, trifling; inadequate; poor; rare; short; *n.m.* scarcity, famine. **-eggiare** [A3 c] *intr.* (*aux.* essere) to be scarce; to be in short supply. **-ẹzza** *f.* scarcity; shortage; lack; insufficiency. **-ità** *f.* scarcity.

**scartabellare** [A1] *tr.* to turn over (the pages of); to skim.

**scartafa·ccio** *m.* scribbling block; rough paper.

**scart-are** [A1] to unwrap; to discard; to reject; to put on one side; *intr.* (*aux.* avere) (of a car) to skid; (football) to dribble; *rfl.* to be set laterally off one's course. **-amẹnto** *m.* discarding; swerving; skid; (rlwy.) gauge. **-ata** *f.* discarding, rejection; (of a car) to skid. **-o** *m.* discarding; putting aside; *pl.* refuse, scrap, waste; swerve, skid; (post office) sorting; (football) dribbling. **-occiare** [A3] *tr.* to unwrap, to take the wrappings off; to strip.

**scasare** [A1] *tr.* to turn out, to evict; *intr.* (*aux.* avere) to move house; to change lodgings.

**scassare**[1] [A1] *tr.* to unpack; to remove from boxes or bales.

**scassare**[2] [A1] *tr.* to break up (ground); (fig.) to smash, to destroy; to exhaust, to fatigue.

**scassin-are** [A1] *tr.* to pick the lock of; to force the lock of. **-atọre** *m.* picklock.

**scasso** *m.* breaking up of earth; forcing; breaking into; burglary.

**scatenacciare** [A3] *intr.* (*aux.* avere) to unbolt a door; to rattle chains.

**scaten-are** [A1] *tr.* to unchain; (fig.) to let loose; to unleash; *rfl.* to free oneself from chains; to be set free; (fig.) to be unleashed; to break loose. **-amẹnto** *m.* unchaining; freeing; unleashing. **-ìo** *m.* rattling of chains.

**sca·tol-a** *f.* box; *— di fiammiferi*, box of matches; match-box; tin, can; *carne in -e*, tinned meat; *lettere di —*, block capitals; *— armonica*, musical box. **-a·io** box-maker. **-ame** *m.* tinned food. **-ino** *m. dim.* little box; case; *-ino per gli occhiali*, spectacle case.

**scatt-o** release; spurt; sudden movement; jerk; click; spring-catch; (fig.) outburst; fit; impulse; convulsive movement; *avere degli -i*, to have sudden inspirations. **-are** [A1] *intr.* (*aux.* essere, avere) to spring up; *-are in piedi*, to spring to one's feet; (of a gun) to go off; to burst out; to differ, to diverge; *abs.* (cinem.) to shoot; *tr.* to mistake; to miss out; *senza -are una nota*, without playing a wrong note; (photog.) to take, to snap.

**scaturi·gine** *f.* spring, source, fount.

**scatur-ire** [D2] *intr.* (*aux.* essere) to spring, to gush; to spout; to

rise; (fig.) to arise, to ensue; to originate.
**scavalc-are** [A2] *intr.* (*aux.* essere) to dismount; *tr.* to unhorse; to surmount, to clamber over; to oust; to be promoted over. **-amẹnto** *m.* dismounting; unhorsing; straddling.
**scavallare** [A1] *intr.* (*aux.* avere) to run free, to run wild; to gallop about.
**scav-are** [A1] *tr.* to excavate; to dig out; to hollow out; (fig.) to discover; to nose out; to come upon; to hunt out. **-afossi** *m. indecl.* ditch digger. **-amẹnto** *m.* excavating; digging; hollowing; excavation; hole. **-apozzi** *m. indecl.* well-sinker. **-atọre** *m.* excavator; digger; miner. **-atura** *f.* hole; cavity; earth dug up.
**scavezz-are** [A1 c] *tr.* to take the halter off; to break, to fracture; *-arsi il collo,* to break one's neck. **-acollo** *m.* headlong fall; rash undertaking; (fig.) reckless individual; daredevil; madcap; *adv. phr. a -acollo,* at breakneck pace; headlong; *precipizio a -acollo,* sheer drop.
**scavo** *m.* excavation; digging; hole; cavity; hollow; *— di galleria,* piercing of a tunnel; *pl.* (archaeol.) excavation, dig.
**scẹgl-iere** [B7] *tr.* to choose; to select; to pick. **-iti·ccio** *m.* residue, remains; left-overs. **-itọre** *m.*, **-itrice** *f.* selector; chooser.
**sceic-co** *m.* (*pl.* **-chi**) sheik.
**sceller-a·ggine** *f.* **-ata·ggine, -atẹzza** *f.* wickedness; evil; villainy; cruelty. **-ato** *adj.* wicked, evil; cruel; villainous; *n.m.* villain; wretch; scoundrel.
**scellino** *m.* shilling.
**scẹlta** *f.* choice; pick; option; quality.
**scẹlt-o** *part* of **scẹgliere**; *adj.* choice; select; distinguished; exquisite. **-ẹzza** *f.* choiceness; distinction; exquisiteness.
**scem-are** [A1 c] *tr.* to diminish; to lessen; to reduce; *intr.* (*aux.* essere) to diminish; to lessen; to be reduced; (of the moon) to be on the wane; (of the tide) to be going out. **-amẹnto** *m.* reduction; diminution; abatement; *-amento della luna,* waning of the moon.
**scẹm-o** *adj.* diminished; reduced; lacking; half-full; half empty; half-witted; *n.m.* reduction; diminution; half-wit; *che — !,* what a fool! **-enza** *f.* stupidity; idiocy.
**scẹmpi-o**[1] *adj.* simple; single; *fiore —,* single flower; silly; simple; *n.m.* simpleton. **-a·ggine** *f.* foolishness, stupidity. **-are** [A4 c] *tr.* to use single; to divide, to split. **-ọne** *m.* blockhead.
**scẹmpio**[2] *m.* slaughter; havoc.
**scen-a** *f.* scene; (theatr.) stage; theatre; scene; set; *dietro le -e,* behind the scenes, backstage; *calcare le -e,* to tread the boards; *fare —,* to play a part; *colpo di —,* sensational turn in the action of a play; (mus.) scena; (fig.) scene, row; *fare delle -e,* to make scenes. **-a·rio** *m.* (theatr.) stage; scenery, set, backcloth, flats; scenario. **-arista** *m.* (cinem.) scenarist, script writer. **-ata** *f.* scene, row; quarrel.
**scẹnd-ere** [C1] *intr.* (*aux.* essere, avere) to descend; to go down; to come down; to flow down; to sink; to slope; *— a,* to put up at, to stay the night at; to be descended (from); *tr. — le scale,* to descend the stairs. **-iletto** *m. indecl.* bedside mat or carpet.
**sceneggi-are** [A3 c] *tr.* (theatr.) to adapt for the stage. **-amẹnto** *m.* (theatr.) arrangement (of a play); adaptation. **-atọre** *m.* (theatr.) adapter (of other work) for the stage; (cinem.) script-writer. **-atura** *f.* (theatr.) adaptation, arrangement; (cinem.) scenario.
**sce·n-ico** *adj.* scenic; theatrical; *palco —,* stage; *n.m.* (theatr.) actor; (hist.) gladiator. **-ografi·a** *f.* scene painting; stage decoration; (cinem.) art direction. **-o·grafo** *m.* scene painter; (cinem.) art director. **-ote·cnica** *f.* stage management.
**sceriffo** *m.* sheriff.
**sce·rn-ere** [C29] *tr.* to discern; to distinguish; to select; to separate. **-imẹnto** *m.* discerning; discernment.
**scervell-are** [A1] *tr.* to drive to distraction; *rfl.* to rack one's brains. **-ato** *part. adj.* distracted; hare-brained.
**scẹsa** *f.* descent; slope, declivity; downward path.
**scẹso** *part.* of **scẹndere**.
**sce·tt-ico** *adj.* Sceptic; sceptical (person); *n.m.* Sceptic; sceptic. **-icịsmo** *m.* Scepticism; scepticism.
**scettr-o** *m.* sceptre; royal authority. **-ato** *adj.* sceptred.
**scever-are** [A1 sc] *tr.* to sever; to divide; to part, to separate; to distinguish; *rfl.* to be separated; to disperse. **-amẹnto** *m.* separating; separation.
**scẹvro** *adj.* free (from); exempt.
**sched-a** *f.* slip of paper; index card; form; application form; counterfoil; *— per votazione,* voting-paper, ballot-paper; *urna per le -e,* ballot-box. **-are** [A1] *tr.* to annotate (on cards); to index. **-a·rio** *m.* card-index. **-atura** *f.* indexing; filing. **-ina** *f.* slip; coupon; *-ina del Totocalcio,* football pools coupon.
**schẹggi-a** *f.* splinter; flake; chip. **-amẹnto** *m.* splintering. **-are** [A3 c] *tr.*, *rfl.* to splinter; to flake.
**schele·trico** *adj.* skeleton-like.
**sche·letr-o** *m.* skeleton; frame; carcass. **-ire** [D2] *tr.* to reduce to a skeleton; *rfl.* to grow as thin as a skeleton. **-ito** *part. adj.* reduced to a skeleton.
**schem-a** *m.* (*pl.* **-i**) scheme; plan; outline; project.
**schẹrma** *f.* fencing; swordsmanship; *fare la —,* to fence; (fig.) polemic.
**scherma·glia** *f.* skirmish; duel; controversy; debate.
**schermi-dọre** *m.* fencer. **-dọra, -tọra, -trice** *f.* woman fencer.
**scherm-ire** [D2c] *intr.* (*aux.* avere) to fence; *rfl.* to defend oneself; *-irsi da,* to parry, to ward off. **-itọre** *m.* see **schermidore**.
**schẹrmo** *m.* screen; protection; shield; *diva dello —,* film star.
**schẹrn-o** *m.* scorn; derision; mockery; sneer; taunt. **-ẹvole** *adj.* scornful; derisory, sneering. **-ire** [D2] to scorn; to deride; to sneer at. **-itọre** *m.*, **-itrice** *f.* scoffer; sneerer; derider; *adj.* sneering.
**scherz-o** *m.* joke; jest; whim, caprice; trifle; game; (mus.) scherzo. **-are** [A1] *intr.* (*aux.* avere) to joke; to jest; to frolic. **-ẹtto** *m. dim.* trick; prank. **-ẹvole, -ọso** *adj.* playful; whimsical; joking, jesting; frolicsome.
**sche·ttin-o** *m.* roller-skate. **-a·ggio** *m.* roller-skating. **-are** [A1 s] *intr.* (*aux.* avere) to roller-skate.
**schia·ccia** *f.* weighted trap.
**schiacci-are** [A3] *tr.* to crush; to squash; to flatten; to smash; to trample on; to run over. **-amẹnto** *m.* crushing; squashing; flattening. **-ante** *part. adj.* crushing; overwhelming; decisive. **-anoci** *m. indecl.* nutcracker; nutcrackers. **-ata** *f.* crushing; squashing; flattening; squeezing.
**schiaffare** [A1] *tr.* to fling; to chuck; to throw carelessly; *rfl.* to fling oneself.
**schiaff-o** *m.* slap in the face; smack; box on the ears. **-eggiare** [A3 c] *tr.* to slap; to smack; to box the ears of; *recip. rfl.* to slap each other's face.
**schiamazz-are** [A1] *intr.* (*aux.* avere) to cackle; to squawk; to cluck; to raise a din; to shout; to clamour. **-o** *m.* din; uproar; shouting; cackle; squawk; clucking.
**schiant-are** [A1] *tr.* to break; to split; to shatter; to wrench away; to snap off; to tear; *intr.* (*aux.* essere) to burst; to split; *rfl.* to burst, to split. **-o** *m.* crash; burst; wrench; ripping, tearing;

*adv. phr. di* ~*o*, suddenly; violently.
**schiappa** *f.* kindling wood; stake; (fam.) duffer, booby; rabbit (at games).
**schiar-ire** [D2] *tr.* to lighten; to illumine; to clarify; to explain; to clear up; *intr.* (*aux.* essere) to grow brighter; (of the weather) to clear up, to lighten; *rfl.* to become clear; to brighten; to grow lighter. **~imẹnto** *m.* clarifying; elucidating; clearing up, brightening. **~ita** *f.* turn for the better (in weather), bright interval.
**schiatta** *f.* race, line, stock; family.
**schiattire** [D2] *intr.* (*aux.* avere) to bay, to give tongue; to yelp.
**schiav-o** *m.* slave; (fig.) devoted admirer; *adj.* enslaved; subject. **~a** *f.* woman slave. **~ẹsco** *adj.* (*m.pl.* **~ẹschi**) pertaining to a slave; slave-like. **~ista** *m.* slaver; slave owner. **~itù** *m.* slavery.
**schiavọne** *m.*, *adj.* Sclavonian.
**schiccher-are**[1] [A1 s] *tr.* to bedaub; to scribble over; to blurt out; to rattle off. **~acarte, ~afogli** *m. indecl.* scribbler, dauber. **~atura** *f.* scribbling; daubing. **~ìo** *m.* (*pl.* **~ii**) continual scribbling; frequent daubing.
**schiccherare**[2] [A1 s] *tr.* to guzzle; to gulp down; *intr.* (*aux.* avere) to tipple.
**schidiọn-e** *m.* (roasting) spit; (eng.) spindle. **~are** [A1 c] *tr.* to roast on a spit; to spit. **~ata** *f.* row of poultry on a spit.
**schien-a** *f.* spine; backbone; back. **~ale** *m.* back (of a chair); (cul.) 'marrow' from bones of spine.
**schier-a** *f.* band; troop; group; company; herd; flock (of birds); *una — di formiche*, a swarm of ants. **~amẹnto** *m.* marshalling. **~are** [A1 d] *tr.* to line up; (mil.) to draw up; *rfl.* to deploy one's forces; to take sides.
**schiett-o** *adj.* frank; sincere; open-hearted; downright; plain, unadorned; simple; pure; genuine. **~amẹnte** *adv.* frankly; plainly. **~ẹzza** *f.* frankness; openness; sincerity; genuineness; plainness.
**schif-are** [A1] *tr.* to loathe; *intr.* (*aux.* avere) — *da*, to shun, to avoid; — *di*, to be loth to, to be reluctant to; *rfl.* (*prep.* di) to feel repugnance (for), to be disgusted (by). **~ano·ia** *m.pl.* pleasure palace.
**schif-o** *m.* disgust, loathing; nausea; *avere a* —, to loathe; *fare — a*, to disgust, to inspire with loathing; *adj.* revolting, disgusting; loathsome; revolted, disgusted; fastidious; queasy. **~ẹzza** *f.* disgust; loathing; object of loathing. **~iltà** *f.* repugnance; nausea, queasiness, reluctance. **~iltọso** *adj.* faddy; fussy; fastidious. **~osità** *f.* loathsomeness. **~ọso** *adj.* disgusting, revolting; nauseating; loathsome.
**schiocc-are** [A2] *tr.* to crack; to snap; to smack; — *le labbra*, to smack one's lips; — *un bacio*, to give a loud, smacking kiss; *intr.* (*aux.* avere) to make a cracking noise, to crack; to crackle; to hiss; to snap. **~ata** *f.* crack; crack of a whip; snap; smacking noise; smack.
**schioc-co** *m.* (*pl.* **~chi**) crack; snap; smacking noise; smack.
**schiodare** [A1] *tr.* to draw out a nail from; to unfasten; to prise open; to unlock.
**schiopp-o** *m.* (mil. hist.) carbine; (colloq.) gun. **~ettata** *f.* shot, gunshot; gunshot wound.
**schiribizzo** *m.* whim, caprice.
**Schiro** *pr.n.f.* (geog.) Scyros.
**schisto** *m.* (geol.) schist, shale.
**schiu·dere** [C3] *tr.* to open; to unclose; to reveal; *rfl.* to open.
**schium-a** *f.* foam; froth; lather; scum; (fig.) dregs. **~ai(u)ola** *f.* skimming spoon. **~are** [A1] *tr.* to skim; to remove the scum from; *intr.* (*aux.* avere) to foam; to froth; to lather. **~ọso** *adj.* frothy; foamy; in a lather.
**schiusa** *f.* opening; unfolding; (zool.) hatching (of an egg).
**schiuso** *part.* of **schiu·dere.**
**schiv-are** [A1] *tr.* to avoid; to shun. **~a·bile** *adj.* avoidable. **~afatiche** *m. indecl.* shirker; slacker.
**schivo** *adj.* shy; bashful; retiring; averse.
**schizo-freni·a** *f.* (med.) schizophrenia, split mind. **~fre·nico** *adj.*, *n.m.* schizophrenic.
**schizz-are** [A1] *intr.* (*aux.* essere) to squirt, to spurt, to gush; to leap; to dart; *tr.* to spurt; to shoot; (art) to sketch. **~ata** *f.* spurt, gush; splash; (art) sketching; sketch. **~atọio** *m.* syringe.
**schizzinọso** *adj.* squeamish; fastidious; hard to please; fussy.
**schizzo** *m.* squirt, spurt; dart, dash; leap; jet; splash; (art) sketch.
**sci** *m. indecl.* ski; ski-ing; *fare lo* —, to ski.
**sci·a** *f.* (naut.) wake; (fig.) track.
**scià** *m. indecl.* Shah.
**scia·bol-a** *f.* sabre. **~are** [A1 s] *tr.* to slash with a sabre. **~ata** *f.* sabre cut; (fig.) slashing, savage criticism. **~atọre** *m.* swordsman.
**sciacallo** *m.* (zool.) jackal.
**sciaqu-are** [A6] *tr.* to rinse; — *i piatti*, to wash up; *rfl.* to be rinsed; to rinse oneself. **~abọcca** *m. indecl.* throat-spray. **~adenti** *m. indecl.* mouth-wash. **~adita** *m. indecl.* finger bowl. **~amẹnto** *m.* rinsing; sluicing. **~ata** *f.* rinse. **~atọio** *m.* mill-race. **~atura** *f.* rinsing, sluicing; rinsing water; slops. **~ìo** *m.* (*pl.* **~ii**) continual rinsing.
**scia·cqu-o** *m.* rinsing of the mouth; mouth-wash. **~ọne** *m.* (bldg.) W.C. cistern.
**sciagur-a** *f.* calamity; misfortune; disaster; mishap. **~ato** *part. adj.* ill-starred; wretched; calamitous; *n.m.* wretch; spiteful person.
**scialacqu-are** [A6] *tr.* to lavish, to waste; to dissipate; *rfl.* to spend money lavishly; to live riotously. **~amẹnto** *m.* waste, extravagance. **~atọre** *m.*, **~atrice** *f.* waster; spendthrift; prodigal.
**scial-are** [A1] *intr.* (*aux.* avere) to spend money extravagantly; to waste one's substance; to lead a dissipated life. **~o** *m.* waste; profusion. **~ọna** *f.*, **~ọne** *m.* spendthrift.
**scialb-o** *adj.* pale; faint, dim; wan; faded. **~ọre** *m.* drabness.
**scialle** *m.* shawl; scarf.
**scialo** *m.* see under **scialare.**
**scialuppa** *f.* sloop, longboat.
**sciamann-are** [A1] *tr.* to handle carelessly; to crumple; *rfl.* to be untidy; to be slovenly. **~ato** *part. adj.* slovenly; clumsy. **~ọna** *f.*, **~ọne** *m.* untidy, slovenly person.
**sciam-e** *m.* swarm; (fig.) crowd, host. **~are** [A1] *intr.* (*aux.* avere, essere) to swarm; (fig.) to emigrate. **~atura** *f.* swarming.
**sciampagna** *m.* champagne.
**sciampo** *m. indecl.* shampoo.
**scianc-are** [A2] *tr.* to dislocate the hip of; *rfl.* to dislocate oneself. **~ato** *part. adj.* lame; (fig.) lop-sided; *n.m.* cripple.
**sciarada** *f.* charade.
**sci-are** [A4] *intr.* (*aux.* avere) to ski. **~atọre** *m.*, **~atrice** *f.* skier.
**Sciari** *pr.n.f.* (geog.) Shari, Cleari.
**sciarpa** *f.* scarf; sash.
**scia·tica** *f.* (med.) sciatica.
**sciatọre** *m.* see under **sciare.**
**sciatt-o** *adj.* slovenly, untidy, careless; clumsy. **~a·ggine** *f.* slovenliness, untidiness; awkwardness. **~are** [A1] *tr.* to crumple; to spoil. **~eri·a** *f.* slovenliness; silliness. **~ọna** *f.*, **~ọne** *m.* slovenly person.
**sci·bile** *adj.* knowable; *n.m.* knowledge.
**sci(b)bole·t** *m. indecl.* shibboleth.
**scient-e** *adj.* aware; conscious; learned; knowing. **~emẹnte** *adv.* knowingly; wittingly.
**scienti·fico** *adj.* scientific.
**scienz-a** *f.* knowledge; science; *la pura* —, pure science; *la — applicata*, applied science; learning; lore. **~iato** *adj.* learned; *n.m.* scientist; learned man.
**scilacc-a** *f.* slap; tap; blow with the flat of a sword. **~are** [A2] *tr.*

to hit with the flat of a sword. **-ata** *f.* slap; rap.

**scilingu-a·gnolo** *m.* (anat.) tongue-string; (fig.) tongue, speech; *avere lo — sciolto,* to have a ready tongue. **-are** [A6] *intr.* (*aux.* avere) to stutter, to stammer; to lisp. **-atura** *f.* stuttering; stammer; impediment in one's speech.

**Scilla** *pr.n.f.* (geog.; myth.) Scylla; — *e Cariddi,* Scylla and Charybdis.

**scimitarr-a** *f.* scimitar. **-ata** *f.* blow with a scimitar.

**sci(m)·mi-a** *f.* (zool.) monkey; ape. **-ata** *f.* mimicry; monkey-trick. **-eggiare** [A3 c] *tr.* to ape, to mimic. **-eggiatura** *f.* mimicry, aping. **-ẹsco** *adj.* (*m.pl.* **-ẹschi**) simian; monkey-like. **-ottare** [A1] *tr.* to ape, to mimic. **-ottata** *f.* mimicry. **-otto** *m.* young monkey.

**scimpanzẹ̀** *m. indecl.* chimpanzee.

**scimunit-o** *adj.* silly, foolish, stupid; *n.m.* fool, blockhead. **-a·ggine** *f.* silliness, foolishness; stupid action.

**sci·ndere** [C21] *tr.* to sever; to separate; to split; to tear.

**scintill-a** *f.* spark; sparkle. **-are** [A1] *intr.* (*aux.* avere) to give off sparks; to sparkle; to scintillate; to twinkle. **-azịone** *f.* scintillation; twinkling. **-ìo** *m.* (*pl.* **-ìi**) sparkling; twinkling; flashing.

**scioc-co** *adj.* (*m.pl.* **-chi**) insipid, tasteless; (fig.) silly, stupid, foolish; inane; *n.m.* fool. **-ca·ggine** [A3 c] *f.* foolishness, silliness. **-cheri·a** *f.* foolish action or remark. **-chẹzza** *f.* foolishness, silliness; stupidity; inanity; foolish action; stupid remark. **-cọne** *m. augm.* utter fool; idiot.

**scio·gl-iere** [B27] *tr.* to undo, to untie; to loose, to loosen; to let loose, to release; to set free; to solve; to dissolve; to melt; to resolve (doubt); to fulfil (vow); to raise (song); *rfl.* to free oneself, to release oneself; to melt, to dissolve. **-ilingua** *m. indecl.* tongue-twister. **-imẹnto** *m.* solution, dissolving; disbanding; dissolution; melting; (theatr.) dénouement.

**sciolta** *f.* (colloq.) diarrhoea; looseness of the bowels.

**scioltamẹnte** *adv.* loosely; freely; easily.

**sciolt-o** *part.* of **scio·gliere**; *adj.* untied, unbound, loose; *quaderno a fogli -i,* looseleaf notebook; free; easy; *a briglia -a,* at full speed; *burro —,* melted butter; *versi -i,* blank verse; solved; (comm.) loose, not packed, wrapped or bottled; *vini -i,* wines from the wood. **-ẹzza** *f.* ease; fluency; agility.

**scioper-are** [A1 s] *intr.* (*aux.* avere) to strike; to go on strike. **-a·ggine** *f.* idleness, laziness. **-ante** *part. adj.* striking; on strike; *n.m.* striker. **-ata·ggine** *f.* idleness (due to a strike); strike mentality. **-atẹzza** *f.* unemployment. **-ato** *part. adj.* out of work; on strike.

**scio·pero** *m.* strike; — *bianco,* sit-down strike; — *della fame,* hunger strike.

**sciorin-are** [A1] *tr.* to hang out to dry; to air (clothes); *intr.* (*aux.* essere) (of liquid) to run away, to pour out. **-amẹnto** *m.* airing; disclosure; display.

**sciovi·a** *f.* ski-lift.

**sciovin-ịsmo** *m.* chauvinism. **-ista** *m.* (*pl.* **-isti**) chauvinist; *adj.* chauvinistic.

**scipit-o** *adj.* insipid, tasteless; dull. **-a·ggine** *f.* fatuity; dullness; insipidity. **-ẹzza** *f.* insipidity; dullness; fatuity.

**sciroc-o** *m.* (geog.) Sirocco; a hot, moist wind. **-ale** *adj.* sirocco; hot and blighting.

**sciropp-o** syrup. **-are** [A1] *m.* to candy with syrup; to sweeten. **-ọso** *adj.* syrupy.

**scịsm-a** *m.* (eccl.; fig.) schism. **-a·tico** *adj., n.m.* schismatic.

**sci·ss-ile** *adj.* fissile. **-ịone** *f.* splitting, split; division; (biol.) fission; *-ione nucleare,* nuclear fission.

**sciss-o** *part.* of **sci·ndere**. **-ura** *f.* cleft, split; furrow; disagreement.

**scita** *adj., n.m.* Scythian.

**sciup-are** [A1] *tr.* to spoil, to damage, to mar; to injure; to ruin; to waste, to squander; *rfl.* to be spoiled, to spoil; to be ruined. **-acarte** *adj., n.m. indecl.* scribbler. **-acchiare** [A4] *tr.* to spoil bit by bit; to damage slightly. **-atọre** *m.*, **-atrice** *f.* waster, squanderer. **-ìo** *m.* (*pl.* **-ìi**) constant waste; wastage. **-o** *m.* waste. **-ọna** *f.*, **-ọne** *m.* waster, squanderer; spendthrift.

**scivol-are** [A1 s] *intr.* (*aux.* essere, avere) to slip; to slide; to glide. **-ata** *f.* slide; sliding. **-atọio** *m.* slipway.

**sci·vol-o** *m.* slip, slide; (aeron.) runway. **-ọne** *m. augm.* bad fall.

**sclerọsi** *f.* (med.) sclerosis.

**scoccare** [A2 c], [A2] *intr.* (*aux.* essere) to shoot out; to go off; to dart, to fly; (of a catch) to spring; (of the hours) to strike; *tr.* to shoot; to shoot off, to let fly; to throw, to fling; to dart; (of clock) to strike; *n.m.* beginning, start.

**scocci-are** [A4] *tr.* to break; (fig.) to bore; to harass. **-amẹnto** *m.* breaking; (fig.) harassing. **-ante** *part. adj.* boring. **-atura** *f.* breakage.

**scoc-co** *m.* (*pl.* **-chi**) shooting off; letting fly; twang; (of a kiss) smack; (of a clock) stroke, striking.

**scodare** [A1] *tr.* to dock the tail of.

**scodell-a** *f.* soup-plate; bowl. *pl.* scales of a balance. **-a·io** *m.* maker or vendor of crockery. **-are** [A1] *tr.* to dish out, to serve up. **-ata** *f.* plateful; helping. **-ino** *m. dim.* small bowl.

**scodinzol-are** [A1 s] *intr.* (*aux.* avere) to wag the tail. **-ìo** *m.* tail-wagging.

**sco·gli-o** *m.* rock; cliff; reef; (fig.) difficulty; stumbling block. **-era** *f.* reef of rocks; rocky cliff. **-ọso** *adj.* rocky; (fig.) difficult; dangerous.

**scoia·ttolo** *m.* (zool.) squirrel.

**scol-are** [A1] *tr.* to drain; to leave to drip; to pass through a strainer; *intr.* (*aux.* essere) to drip, to drain off, to run off. **-afritto** *m. indecl.* frying basket. **-amẹnto** *m.* draining, dripping. **-andino** *m.* colander. **-atọio** *m.* drain; drain pipe; sink; strainer; drip pan; *adj.* serving to drain. **-atura** *f.* draining; dripping; drains, drips, dregs. **-ìo** *m.* (*pl.* **-ìi**) constant dripping; draining away.

**scolar-o** *m.* schoolboy; pupil; scholar; student. **-a** *f.* girl pupil; schoolgirl. **-ẹsca** *f.* the pupils in a class or in school; students, student body. **-ẹsco** *adj.* (*m.pl.* **-ẹschi**) relating to schools and schoolchildren.

**scola·stic-o** *adj.* scholastic; relating to school; *anno —,* school year; *aula -a,* schoolroom; (philos.) scholastic; *n.m.* schoolman, scholastic philosopher; schoolmaster. **-a** *f.* scholastic philosophy and theology, scholasticism. **-ịsmo** *m.* scholasticism.

**scoliaste** *m.* scholiast.

**sco·lio** *m.* (textual criticism) gloss.

**scollacci-are** [A3] *rfl.* to wear a dress that is décolleté. **-ato** *part. adj.* décolleté. **-atura** *f.* décolletage.

**scoll-are**[1] [A1] to unglue; *rfl.* to come off, to come unstuck. **-atura** *f.* ungluing; coming unstuck.

**scoll-are**[2] [A1] *tr.* to cut the neck hole (in a garment); *rfl.* to wear a low-necked dress. **-ato** *part. adj.* low-necked, cut low in the neck; wearing a low-necked garment; *scarpa -ata,* court show, shoe leaving the instep uncovered; *n.m.* neck opening; cutting out the neck of a garment.

**scolleg-are** [A2] *tr.* to disconnect, to separate; *rfl.* to come undone. **-amẹnto** *m.* disconnection, untying, uncoupling; lack of continuity.

**scoll-o** *m.* neck-opening (of a

garment). **-ino** *m.* neckerchief, square.
**scọlo** *m.* drain; drain pipe; drainage; liquid that drains away; (med.) discharge; (naut.) *canale di —*, scupper.
**scolor-are** [A1 c] *tr.* to cause to fade; to discolour; to remove colour from; *rfl.* to fade; to become discoloured; to grow pale. **-amẹnto** *m.* fading discoloration.
**scolor-ire** [D2] *tr.*, *intr.* (*aux.* essere) to lose colour; to grow pale. **-ina** *f.* ink eradicator; stain-remover. **-ito** *part. adj.* colourless; pale; faded.
**scolpare** [A1 c] *tr.* to excuse; to exculpate; to justify; *rfl.* to make excuses, to defend oneself; to justify oneself.
**scolp-ire** [D2] *tr.* (sculp.) to carve; to sculpt, to sculpture; to cut, to chisel; to engrave. **-itamẹnte** *adv.* clearly; distinctly. **-ito** *part. adj.* carved; chiselled; engraved. **-itura** *f.* groove (*e.g.* in a tyre tread).
**scọlta** *f.* (mil.) sentry, nightwatchman; *fare la —*, to be on sentry go; patrol, round.
**scombaciare** [A3] *tr.* to prise asunder, to part.
**scombiccherare** [A1 s] *tr.*, *intr.* (*aux.* avere) to scribble.
**scombinare** [A1] *tr.* to disarrange; to upset; (typ.) to distribute.
**scọmbro** *m.* (ichth.) mackerel.
**scombu·glio** *m.* disorder, confusion.
**scombussolare** [A1 s] *tr.* to confuse (with regard to direction); to upset; to disturb; to derange.
**scommẹssa** *f.* bet, wager; stake.
**scommẹtt-ere¹** [C20] *tr.* to bet, to wager, to stake; (fig.) *-o che*, I am quite certain that; *intr.* (*aux.* avere) to bet, to gamble. **-itọre** *m.* gambler; one who bets.
**scommẹtt-ere²** [C2] *tr.* to undo, to untie; to disconnect; *rfl.* to come apart; to separate. **-imẹnto** *m.* undoing; disconnecting. **-itura** *f.* lack of cohesion, state of being disconnected.
**scomodare** [A1 s] *tr.* to trouble, to inconvenience, to disturb; *rfl.* to put oneself out, to trouble oneself.
**sco·mod-o** *adj.* inconvenient; uncomfortable, troublesome; *n.m.* discomfort; inconvenience. **-ità** *f.* discomfort; inconvenience.
**scompagin-are** [A1 s] *tr.* to disarrange; to upset, to throw into disorder; (typ.) to distribute. **-amẹnto** *m.* disarrangement, upsetting. **-atura** *f.* disarrangement; disorder, confusion. **-aziọne** *f.* action of disarranging, upsetting.
**scompa·gine** *f.* lack of order.
**scompagn-are** [A5] *tr.* to part, to separate (a pair); *rfl.* (*prep.* da) to part (from); *recip. rfl.* to separate, to part. **-ato** *part. adj.* parted; not matching; odd. **-atura** *f.* parting, separating.
**scomparire** [D2] *intr.* (*aux.* essere) to disappear, to vanish; to fade away; to retire; to cut a poor figure.
**scomparsa** *f.* disappearance.
**scomparso** *part.* of **scomparire**; *adj.* disappeared; vanished; extinct; *n.m.* deceased person.
**scompart-ire** [D1] *tr.* to divide up; to share out; to allot. **-imẹnto** *m.* division; dividing up; sharing out; (rlwy.) compartment; (archit.) partition. **-o** *m.* compartment, section.
**scompiac-ẹre** [B15] *intr.* (*aux.* essere; *prep.* a) to be disobliging; to be unaccommodating. **-enza** *f.* disobligingness; lack of cooperation.
**scompigli-are** [A4] *tr.* to disarrange, to upset, to throw into disorder; to ruffle; *rfl.* to become upset. **-amẹnto** *m.* disorder; confusion; upsetting.
**scompi·gl-io** *m.* confusion, disorder; fuss; discord; **-ìo** *m.* continual fuss, confusion; continual dissension.
**scompleto** *adj.* incomplete, broken.
**scompọrre** [B21] *tr.* to break up; to take to pieces; to analyse; to discompose; to worry; to resolve; (math.) *— in fattori*, to factorize; (typ.) to distribute; *rfl.* to decompose; to be worried, to worry; to lose one's temper.
**scomposiziọne** *f.* breaking up, breaking down, analysis; disorder; (mech.) resolution (of a force).
**scompọst-o,** *part.* of **scompọrre**; broken up; discomposed, disordered; untidy; troubled; confused. **-ẹzza** *f.* disorderliness.
**sco·mput-o** *m.* deduction, subtraction; amount to be deducted. **-are** [A1 s] *tr.* to deduct; to subtract.
**scomu·nic-a** *f.* (eccl.; fig.) excommunication. **-are** [A2 s] *tr.* to excommunicate. **-aziọne** *f.* sentence of excommunication, anathema.
**sconcaten-are** [A1] *tr.* to disconnect; to unchain, to loose. **-amẹnto** *m.* disconnecting; unchaining.
**sconcert-are** [A1] *tr.* to disconcert; to baffle; to trouble. **-ante** *part. adj.* disconcerting. **-ato** *part. adj.* disconcerted; disorderly; (mus.) out of tune.
**sconcerto** *m.* disturbance (esp. of stomach), sickness; (mus.) false intonation.
**sconci-are** [A3 c] *tr.* to spoil, to mar; to deform; *rfl.* to be marred; to strain; to miscarry. **-atura** *f.* marring; miscarriage.
**scọnc-io** *adj.* indecent; obscene; filthy, nasty; deformed; *n.m.* indecent, obscene thing; shame. **-ẹzza** *f.* indecency; obscenity; filth.
**sconclusionato** *adj.* inconclusive; inconsequent; rambling.
**sconfacente** *adj.* unsuitable; unbecoming.
**sconfess-are** [A1] *tr.* to disavow; to disown; to repudiate. **-iọne** *f.* disavowal; repudiation.
**sconficc-are** [A2] *tr.* to pull out, to extract; to unfasten; to take to pieces. **-atura** *f.* pulling out, extraction; mark left after extraction; removal.
**sconfi·gg-ere** [C12] *tr.* to defeat; to discomfit. **-imẹnto** *m.* defeat; discomfiture.
**sconfin-are** [A1] *intr.* (*aux.* avere, essere) to break bounds; to trespass; to cross the frontier; (fig.) to exceed the limits (of); to digress widely. **-amẹnto** *m.* breaking of bounds; trespass; escape. **-atamẹnte** *adv.* endlessly; infinitely. **-ato** *part. adj.* boundless; unlimited.
**sconfitta** *f.* defeat; discomfiture; rout.
**sconfort-o** *m.* discouragement; depression; distress; dejection. **-ante** *part. adj.* disheartening; discouraging. **-are** [A1] *tr.* to dishearten, to discourage; to distress; *rfl.* to become disheartened; to lose courage; to distress oneself.
**scongiur-are** [A1] *tr.* to entreat, to implore, to beseech; to exorcize. **-amẹnto** *m.* entreaty, invocation; exorcism; incantation, charm. **-o** *m.* exorcism; entreaty.
**sconness-o** *part.* of **sconne·ttere**; *adj.* disconnected; desultory. **-iọne** *f.* disconnectedness; desultoriness.
**sconne·ttere** [C19] *tr.* to disconnect.
**sconọsc-ere** [B9] *tr.* to fail to recognize; to refuse to recognize; to slight; to be ignorant of; to underrate; *intr.* (*aux.* avere) to be ungrateful. **-ente** *part. adj.* ignorant; ungrateful, thankless; *n.m. gli -enti*, ungrateful people. **-enza** *f.* ingratitude, ungratefulness. **-imẹnto** *m.* refusal to recognize (a claim, right). **-iuto** *part. adj.* unknown; disregarded; unappreciated; *n.m.* unknown person; stranger.
**sconquass-are** [A1] *tr.* to smash; to crash; to shatter. **-o** *m.* destruction; smashing; ruin; crash.
**sconsacrare** [A1] *tr.* (rel.) to profane; to desecrate; to unfrock (priest); to turn to a secular purpose.
**sconsiderat-o** *adj.* thoughtless; heedless; rash. **-amẹnte** *adv.* thoughtlessly; rashly. **-ẹzza** *f.*

thoughtlessness; lack of consideration; rashness.

**sconsigli-are** [A4] *tr.* (*prep.* da) to dissuade (from); to deter, to discourage; *lasciarsi* —, to let oneself be persuaded not to. **-atẹzza** *f.* rashness; inconsiderateness; thoughtlessness. **-ato** *part. adj.* dissuaded; ill-advised; not recommended; rash, foolish.

**sconsol-are** [A1] *tr.* to dishearten; to depress; to sadden. **-ante** *part. adj.* disheartening; depressing. **-atẹzza** *f.* disconsolateness; sadness. **-ato** *part. adj.* disconsolate.

**scontare** [A1 c] *tr.* to discount; to deduct; to expiate, to atone for; (comm.) — *una cambiale*, to discount a bill.

**scontent-o** *adj.* discontented, dissatisfied; disappointed; *n.m.* discontent; dissatisfaction. **-are** [A1] *tr.* to dissatisfy; to displease; to disappoint; *rfl.* to be dissatisfied, disappointed. **-ẹzza** *f.* discontent; dissatisfaction; disappointment.

**scọnt-o** *m.* deduction; rebate; discount; *tasso di* —, bank-rate. **-ista** *m.* (*pl.* **-isti**) (comm.) discounter.

**sconto·r-cere** [C5] *tr.* to contort, to twist; *rfl.* to twist oneself up; to perform contortions; to writhe. **-cimẹnto** *m.* contortion; writhing.

**scontrare** [A1 c] *tr.* to meet, to encounter; to collate; to compare; *recip. rfl.* to encounter one another; to meet in battle; to collide.

**scọntr-o** *m.* encounter; collision; crash; (mil.) action, engagement. **-ino** *m.* check; ticket; receipt; voucher. **-ọso** *adj.* cantankerous; peevish; irritable; sulky; reluctant, coy; *n.m.* peevish person; *fare lo -oso*, to be peevish.

**sconven-ire** [D17] *intr.* (*aux.* essere) to be unsuitable; to be improper. **-ẹvole** *adj.* unseemly; indecorous; improper; indecent. **-evolẹzza** *f.* unseemliness; breach of good manners. **-ienza** *f.* unsuitableness; impropriety; unseemliness; indecency; breach of good manners.

**sconvo·lg-ere** [C14] *tr.* to upset; to overturn; to convulse; to trouble; to throw into confusion. **-imẹnto** *m.* upset; overturning; confusion.

**sconvolto** *part.* of **sconvo·lgere**; *adj.* perturbed; convulsed; troubled.

**scooter** *m.* (motor.) scooter. **-ista** *m., f.* scooter rider.

**scọpa**[1] *f.* (bot.) besom heath.

**scọpa**[2] *f.* broom; besom; birch; stiff, bushy hair.

**scọp-a**[3] *f.* popular Italian card game; *fare* —, to sweep the board. **-ista** *m., f.* player of the game of 'scopa'.

**scop-are** [A1 c] *tr.* to sweep. **-ata** *f.* sweep; sweeping. **-atọio** *m.* besom. **-atọre** *m.* sweeper; road sweeper. **-atrice** *f.* woman sweeper. **-atura** *f.* sweeping.

**scoperchi-are** [A4] *tr.* to uncover; to remove the lid from. **-atura** *f.* uncovering.

**scoperta** *f.* discovery; disclosure; revelation; invention; (naut.) exploration; (mil.) reconnaissance.

**scopert-o** *part.* of **scoprire**; *adj.* uncovered; exposed; bare; *a capo* —, bareheaded; *adv.* openly; *n.m.* open space; open air; *allo* —, in the open; overdraft. **-amẹnte** *adv.* openly. **-ura** *f.* openness; bareness; revelation.

**scopẹto** *m.* heath.

**scopẹtta** *f. dim.* of **scopa**[2] small broom or brush.

**scopo** *m.* purpose; object; aim; end; target; design; *a — di*, with the aim of.

**scoppi-are**[1] [A4] *intr.* (*aux.* essere) to burst, to explode; to break out; to erupt; — *in lagrime*, to burst into tears. **-amẹnto** *m.* exploding; bursting. **-ata** *f.* explosion; burst. **-atura** *f.* bursting; breaking out; crack (in the skin).

**scoppiare**[2] [A4 c] *tr.* to uncouple; *rfl.* (of a pair) to separate.

**sco·ppio** *m.* burst; explosion; bang; crack (of a whip); blow, affliction; (eng.) *motore a* —, internal combustion engine; — *del carro*, traditional firework display outside the Cathedral of Florence on Easter Eve.

**scopiett-are** [A1 c] *intr.* (*aux.* avere) to crackle; to flicker; to crack, to snap. **-amẹnto** *m.* crackling, crackle; snapping. **-iere** *m.* (mil. hist.) fusilier. **-io** *m.* (*pl.* **-ii**) continual crackling.

**scoppiẹtto** *m. dim.* of **sco·ppio**; shot; (fig.) quip.

**scopr-ire** [D8] *tr.* to uncover, to lay bare; to disclose; to unveil; to discover, to find out; to descry; to sight (land); to reveal; *rfl.* to uncover oneself; to undress; to raise one's hat; to expose oneself; to betray oneself. **-imẹnto** *m.* uncovering; exposure, discovery; revelation. **-itọre** *m.* discoverer; inventor. **-itura** *f.* uncovering; discovery.

**scoragg-iare** [A3], **-ire** [D2] *tr.* to discourage, to dishearten; *rfl.* to lose heart, to become disheartened. **-iamẹnto** *m.*, **-imẹnto** *m.* discouragement; depression.

**scor-are** [A1] *tr.* to cause acute depression in. **-amẹnto** *m.* profound dejection.

**sco·rb-uto** *m.* (med.) scurvy. **-u·tico** *adj.* scorbutic, affected with scurvy.

**scorc-iare** [A3 c], **-ire** [D2] *tr.* to shorten; to curtail; to abbreviate; (art) to foreshorten; *intr.* (*aux.* essere) (art) to be foreshortened; *rfl., intr.* (*aux.* essere) to shorten, to grow shorter. **-iamẹnto** *m.* shortening. **-iatọia** *f.* short cut.

**scọrcio** *m.* foreshortening; grimace; end, close.

**scordare**[1] [A1] *tr., rfl.* (*prep.* di) to forget; (bot.) *non-ti-scordar-di-me*, forget-me-not.

**scord-are**[2] [A1] *tr.* (mus.) to mistune; to untune; *intr.* (*aux.* avere) (mus.) to be out of tune; *rfl.* (mus.) to go out of tune. **-anza** *f.* false intonation. **-atamẹnte** *adv.* discordantly. **-ato** *part. adj.* out of tune. **-atura** *f.* (mus.) intentional mistuning of a string for the purpose of an unusual effect.

**sco·rg-ere** [C5] *tr.* to perceive; to discern; to descry. **-imẹnto** *m.* perception, notice; discernment.

**sco·ri-a** *f.* dross; skimmings; (metall.) slag, dross; scum; scale; clinker. **-ficare** [A2 s] *tr.* to scorify, to slag. **-ficaziọne** *f.* scorification.

**scorn-are** [A1] *tr.* to dishorn; (of a bull) to gore; to toss; (fig.) to put to shame; to hold up to ridicule. **-ata** *f.* butt, toss, blow (with horns).

**scornici-are** [A3] *tr.* to remove from a frame; *intr.* (*aux.* avere) to construct frames. **-amẹnto** *m.* framing; unframing. **-atura** *f.* frame, framing; cornice.

**scorno** *m.* shame, ignominy; disgrace; *avere a* —, to hold in scorn; *avere — di*, to be disgraced by.

**scoronare** [A1 c] *tr.* to uncrown; to dethrone; to poll (a tree).

**scorpacciata** *f.* bellyful.

**scorpiọne** *m.* (zool.) scorpion.

**scorpor-are** [A1 s] *tr.* (leg.) to disembody; to disincorporate; to separate from the mass; to spend from capital. **-aziọne** *f.* (leg.) drawing off, separation (of money) from capital; distribution of an interest or share under a will.

**sco·rporo** *m.* outlay; heavy expense.

**scorrazz-are** [A1] *intr.* (*aux.* avere) to run hither and thither; to rove; (mil.) to raid; to overrun. **-amẹnto** *m.* roving; (mil.) raiding.

**scọrrer-e** [C5] *intr.* (*aux.* essere) to flow; to glide; (of time) to pass quickly, to fly; to elapse; to overflow; *tr.* to travel through; to run over; to scour; to raid; to run one's eye over, to glance over. **-i·a** *f.* raid, incursion.

**scorrett-o** *adj.* incorrect; im-

proper; unbecoming; indecent. **-amẹnte** *adv.* incorrectly; improperly. **-ẹzza** *f.* incorrectness; error; impropriety; incorrect behaviour.

**scorrẹvol-e** *adj.* fluent; flowing; gliding; grooved. **-ẹzza** *f.* fluency; (eng.) smoothness (of running).

**scorreziọne** *f.* incorrectness; error; mistake; slip.

**scorribanda** *f.* incursion, raid; (fig.) excursion, digression.

**scorridọre** *m.* (mil. hist.) outrider, forerunner.

**scọrsa** *f.* excursion, trip; (fig.) glance, rapid examination; hurried skimming through a book.

**scọrs-o** *part.* of **scọrrere**; *adj.* past; gone by; *la settimana -a*, last week; *n.m.* slip; error; oversight. **-ọio** *adj.* sliding; running; *nodo -oio*, slipknot; also *n.m.*

**scort-a** *f.* escort; guide; convoy; provision. **-are** [A1] *tr.* to escort, to convoy.

**scortecchiare** [A3 c] *tr.* to peel, to strip, to bark; *rfl.* to be stripped; to be peeled.

**scortẹṣ-e** *adj.* rude, impolite; uncivil; discourteous; unkind. **-i·a** *f.* rudeness; incivility; discourtesy; unkindness; discourteous action.

**scortic-are** [A2 s] *tr.* to skin, to flay; to graze (*e.g.* skin); to shell (peas, etc.). **-amẹnto** *m.* skinning, flaying; (fig.) fleecing. **-ata** *f.* (butcher.) action of cutting up carcasses; tearing; tear, rent. **-atọio** *adj.* serving for the process of skinning; *n.m.* flaying knife; knacker's yard. **-atọre** *m.* skinner; (fig.) skin-flint; usurer. **-atura** *f.* abrasion, scratch; skinning; (fig.) extortion.

**scor-ẓa** *f.* bark; rind, peel, skin; crust. **-ẓare** [A1] *tr.* to peel; to strip, to bark; *rfl.* to be stripped; to be peeled; to shed skin, to peel. **-ẓatura** *f.* peeling, stripping; barked part (of a tree). **-ẓọna** *f.*, **-ẓọne** *m.* boor; thick-skinned person; stubborn person. **-ẓoneri·a** *f.* rudeness, boorishness. **-ẓọso** *adj.* with thick bark; thick-skinned.

**scoscend-ere** [C1] *tr.* to break; to split; to cleave; *intr.* (*aux.* essere), *rfl.* to fall; to crash down; to collapse; to split. **-imẹnto** *m.* collapse; fall (of rock) landslide; crag.

**scoscẹso** *part.* of **scoscẹndere**; *adj.* rugged; precipitous.

**sco·scio** *m.* 'splits' (as done by dancers); (tailor.) fork, crutch.

**scoss-a** *f.* shock; shake; shaking; jerk; — *elettrica*, electric shock; — *di terremoto*, earthquake. **-ọne** *m. augm.* severe shock; violent shaking; heavy shower.

**scosso** *part.* of **scuo·tere**; *adj.* shaken; jolted; *cavallo* —, riderless horse.

**scost-are** [A1] *tr.* (*prep.* da) to remove; to put aside; to detach; *rfl.* to stand aside; to get out of the way; to withdraw; to leave; to swerve; *intr.* (*aux.* essere) to stand some distance away; to stand out (from). **-amẹnto** *m.* removal, separation; distance apart.

**scostumat-o** *adj.* dissolute, licentious; low; ill-mannered. **-ẹzza** *f.* coarse manners; evil living; dissoluteness; licentiousness.

**scotenn-are** [A1] *tr.* to scalp; to skin; to flay. **-atọio** *m.* scalping knife; flaying-knife.

**scotimẹnto** *m.* shaking; jolting; tossing.

**scott-a**[1] *f.* sheet. **-ame** *m.* (naut.) set of sheets. **-are** [A1] *intr.* (*aux.* avere) (naut.) to trim the sheets, to take in the sheets. **-ina** *f.* (naut.) topsail.

**scotta**[2] *f.* whey.

**scott-are** [A1] *tr.* to scorch; to burn; to scald; (fig.) to sting; to nettle; to offend, to hurt, to irritate; *intr.* (*aux.* avere) to scorch, to burn; to be burning hot. **-amẹnto** *m.* scorching, burning, scalding. **-ante** *part. adj.* scorching; burning; stinging. **-ata** *f.* scalding; light cooking; heating up; burn; scald. **-atura** *f.* burn; scald; burning; parboiling; sunburn; (surg.) cauterizing.

**scotto**[1] *m.* bill, score, reckoning; share (of a bill), scot.

**scotto**[2] *adj.* over-cooked.

**scov-are** [A1] *tr.* to drive out, to dislodge; to rouse (game); to find, to discover. **-amẹnto** *m.* driving out; rousing; discovering; discovery, find.

**Sco·zia** *pr.n.f.* (geog.) Scotland.

**scozz-are** [A1] *tr.* to shuffle (cards). **-ata** *f.* shuffle, shuffling.

**scozzẹse** *adj.* Scotch; Scottish; *stoffa* —, tartan, plaid; *n.m.* Scot, Scotsman; *f.* Scotswoman.

**scozzọn-e** *m.* horsebreaker, trainer. **-are** [A1 c] *tr.* to break in, to train (horses); to initiate. **-atura** *f.* breaking in, training; initiation.

**scranna** *f.* high-backed chair.

**screanzato** *adj.* unmannerly; ill-bred; discourteous; uncouth; coarse; *n.m.* unmannerly person; boor.

**scrẹdit-o** *m.* discredit; disrepute. **-are** [A1 sc] *tr.* to discredit; to bring into disrepute; *rfl.* to be discredited; to incur disgrace.

**screm-are** [A1] *tr.* to skim; to separate (cream from milk). **-atrice** *f.* milk separator, skimming machine. **-atura** *f.* milk separation, skimming.

**screpol-are** [A1 s] *rfl.*, *intr.* (*aux.* essere) to crack; to chap; *tr.* to cause to crack or chap. **-ato** *part. adj.* cracked; chapped. **-atura** *f.* crack; chap; fissure.

**scre·zi-o** *m.* variegation; speckling; (fig.) variance, difference; friction; disagreement. **-are** [A4] *tr.* to variegate; to speckle. **-ato** *part. adj.* variegated; speckled. **-atura** *f.* variegation; speckling.

**scrib-a** *m.* (*pl.* **-i**) scribe; copyist; (bibl.) Scribe, interpreter of the Law. **-acchiare** [A4] *tr.*, *intr.* (*aux.* avere) to scribble.

**scricciol-are** [A1 s] *intr.* (*aux.* avere) to creak; to grate; to squeak; (of ice) to crack, to crackle. **-amẹnto** *m.* creaking; grating; squeaking; scrunching, scrunch. **-ata** *f.* creak; squeak. **-ìo** *m.* (*pl.* **-ìi**) continued creaking; grating.

**scri·cciolo** *m.* (orn.) wren.

**scrigno** *m.* strong-box; jewel-case, money-box; casket.

**scriminatura** *f.* parting (of the hair).

**scri·molo** *m.* edge, rim.

**scristianiẓẓare** [A1] *tr.* to de-christianize.

**scritta** *f.* written contract, legal document; marriage lines; inscription; notice, placard, poster.

**scritt-o** *part.* of **scri·vere**; *adj.* written; inscribed; (fig.) fated, bound to happen; *n.m.* script; writing; written document; hand-writing; *pl.* literary works, writing; essays. **-ọio** *m.* study, office; writing-desk; *-oio a saracinesca*, roll-top desk. **-ọre** *m.* writer; author. **-rice** *f.* authoress; woman writer. **-o·rio** *adj.* (*m.pl.* **-orii**) relating to writing.

**scrittur-a** *f.* writing; handwriting; — *a macchina*, type-writing; (leg.) document; agreement; contract; (comm.) posting; entry; text, reading; (theatr.) engagement, contract; (bibl.) la (Sacra) —, (Holy) Scripture. **-a·bile** *adj.* (book-keeping) suitable for entry. **-ale** *adj.* scriptural; *n.m.* clerk; book-keeper; copyist, scribe. **-are** [A1] *tr.* (book-keeping) to enter; (theatr.) to engage; to sign on; (comm.) to post.

**scrivani·a** writing desk; bureau; writing cabinet.

**scrivano** *m.* clerk; copyist, scribe; amanuensis.

**scri·v-ere** [C12] *tr.*, *abs.* to write; *come si -e questa parola?*, how do you spell this word?; to be an author; *lui -e, lei dipinge*, he writes, she paints; — *sui giornali*, to write for the papers; to ascribe; to describe, to tell, to relate; to inscribe; *n.m.* writing; *macchina da* —, type-writer.

**scrocc-are** [A2] *tr.* to scrounge; to sponge, to cadge. **-atọre** *m.* scrounger, sponger.

**scrocchiare**[1] [A4] *intr.* (*aux.* avere) to creak; to crackle.

**scrocchiare**[2] [A4] *tr.* to lend out on interest; to pawn.

**scro·cchio**[1] *m.* creak; crackling, cracking.

**scro·cchi-o**[2] *m.* pawnbroking; *dare a —*, to pawn. **-ọne** *m.* moneylender, usurer.

**scrocc-o**[1] *m.* sponging, scrounging; *vivere a —*, to live on one's wits by scrounging. **-ọna** *f.*, **-ọne** *m.* sponger, scrounger; swindler, sharper.

**scrocco**[2] *m.* spring; *coltello a —*, clasp-knife.

**scrocco**[3] *m.* crackle; crunch, scrunch.

**scrofa** *f.* sow; (slang) loose woman.

**scro·fol-a** *f.* (med.) scrofula. **-are** *adj.* scrofulous; *n.m.*, *f.* sufferer from scrofula.

**scroll-are** [A1] *tr.* to shake, to toss; to shrug. **-amẹnto** *m.* shaking; tossing. **-ata** *f.* shake; toss of the head; shrug of the shoulders. **-o** *m.* shake, shaking; vibration.

**scro·sci-o** *m.* heavy shower; thunderclap; bubbling; crackling; creaking; roar; storm; outburst. **-ante** *part. adj. pioggia -ante*, pelting rain; *applausi -anti*, thunderous applause. **-are** [A4] *intr.* (*aux.* avere, essere) to hiss; to bubble; to splash; to crash; to pelt; to crackle; to creak; to rumble; to roar.

**scrost-are** [A1] *tr.* to remove the crust from, to peel; (techn.) to descale, to scrape, to strip; *rfl.* to lose the crust; to flake. **-amẹnto** *m.* peeling, stripping; removing of plaster. **-atura** *f.* stripping; peeling; cleaning (of pictures); wall that has been stripped.

**scru·pol-o** *m.* scruple; qualm; scruple (weight). **-eggiare** [A3c] *intr.* (*aux.* avere) to be scrupulous, to have scruples; to hesitate. **-osità** *f.* scrupulousness. **-ọso** *adj.* scrupulous, meticulous; full of scruples; exact.

**scrut-are** [A1] *tr.* to investigate; to inquire into; to search; to pry into; to scrutinize. **-amẹnto** *m.* scrutiny; search; investigation. **-atọre** *m.* investigator; teller (of votes); *adj.* inquisitive; searching; scrutinizing.

**scrut-inare** *tr.* to investigate; to scrutinize; to hold a ballot. **-inamẹnto** *m.* scrutiny. **-i·nio** *m.* counting of votes; addition of marks.

**scuc-ire** [D1] *tr.* to unpick; to unstitch; *rfl.* to come unstitched. **-ito** *part. adj.* unstitched; (fig.) incoherent, disconnected. **-itura** *f.* seam that has come unstitched; unpicking.

**scuderi·a** *f.* stable; stables (collectively; *garzone di —*, groom; *ragazzo di —*, stable-boy; coach house; tram-depot; (sport) racing car organization.

**scudiero** *m.* squire; groom; *adj. phr. calzoni alla scudiera*, riding breeches; *stivali alla scudiera*, top-boots, riding boots.

**scudi·sci-o** *m.* riding-whip; lash, thong. **-are** [A3] *tr.* to lash; to whip. **-ata** *f.* whipping; thrashing.

**scud-o** *m.* shield; gun-shield; (fig.) defence; defender; (herald.) escutcheon; (coin) scudo. **-ẹtto** *m. dim.* small shield; keyhole guard.

**scu·ffia** *f.* cap; coif; caul.

**scugnizzo** *m.* street urchin.

**sculacci-are** [A3] *tr.* to smack (on the bottom), to spank. **-ata** *f.* spanking.

**scult-ọre** *m.* sculptor. **-rice** *f.* woman sculptor. **-o·rio** *adj.* (*m.pl.* **-orii**) statuesque; *stile -orio*, vivid, descriptive style. **-ura** *f.* sculpture, carving; (piece of) sculpture.

**sc(u)oiare** [A4] *tr.* to skin, to flay.

**scuola** *f.* school; schoolhouse; schoolroom; class; *— elementare*, primary school; *— media*, secondary school; (motor.) *— guida*, driving school; *— di belle arti*, art school; (naut.) *nave —*, training ship; (paint.) school (of painting).

**scuo·t-ere** [C19d] *tr.* to shake; to shake off; *— le spalle*, to shrug one's shoulders; to stir; to move; to startle; to rouse; to disregard; to weaken, to impair; *rfl.* to rouse oneself; to wake up; to stir; to be startled; (fig.) to be moved. **-imẹnto** *m.* see **scotimento**.

**scure** *f.* axe; hatchet.

**scur-o** *adj.* dark; dim; *rosso —*, dark red, deep red; obscure; gloomy; *n.m.* dark, darkness; deep colour; (art) shaded part; shading; (window) shutter. **-ire** [D2] *tr.* to darken; to obscure; to tone down; *rfl.*, *intr.* (*aux.* essere) to darken, to grow dark.

**scurril-e** *adj.* scurrilous. **-ità** *f.* scurrility.

**scuṣ-a** *f.* apology; excuse; pretext. **-are** [A1] *tr.* to excuse; to pardon, to forgive; to justify; *-i !*, excuse me, I beg your pardon; *rfl.* to excuse oneself; to decline an invitation; to justify oneself; *-arsi con*, to apologize to. **-a·bile** *adj.* pardonable, excusable. **-ante** *part. adj.* (leg.) *circostanza -ante*, extenuating circumstance.

**scusso** *adj.* bare; plain; *pane —*, dry bread.

**scuter** *m. indecl.* scooter.

**scute·rzola** *f.* (zool.) polecat.

**ṣdazi-are** [A4] *tr.* (comm.) to clear through the toll-gates. **-a·bile** *adj.* ready for clearance. **-amẹnto** *m.* clearing of goods through the toll-gates, clearance.

**ṣdebitare** [A1s] *rfl.* to get out of debt, to pay a debt; to discharge one's obligations; *tr.* to clear from debt; to release from an obligation.

**ṣdẹgn-o** *m.* indignation; anger; scorn, disdain; contempt. **-are** [A sc] *tr.* to disdain; to scorn; to loathe; to refuse; (of the stomach) to refuse to digest; to enrage; *rfl.* (*prep.* di) to get angry (at); to be offended (by); (of the stomach) to refuse (food). **-ọso** *adj.* scornful; disdainful; haughty; irascible.

**ṣdent-are** [A1] *tr.* to pull out the teeth of; to break the teeth of; *rfl.* to lose one's teeth; to break one's teeth. **-ato** *part. adj.* toothless. **-atura** *f.* breaking or pulling out of teeth; loss of teeth.

**ṣdiacciare** [A3] *tr.*, *intr.* (*aux.* avere, essere) to thaw.

**ṣdigiun-are** [A1] *tr.* to put onto food again after a fast; *rfl.* to break one's fast. **-o** *m.* breakfast.

**ṣdilinqu-ire** [D2] *tr.* to weaken; *rfl.*, *intr.* (*aux.* essere) to swoon; to droop. **-imẹnto** *m.* swoon; drooping.

**sdogan-are** [A1] *tr.* to clear through the customs. **-amẹnto** *m.* clearing through the customs, clearance. **-aziọne** *f.* clearance.

**ṣdolcinato** *adj.* sickly; too sweet; (fig.) mawkish; maudlin; affected; *n.m.* maudlin person; affected person.

**ṣdoppi-are** [A4c] *tr.* to uncouple; to divide; to use one instead of two. **-amẹnto** *m.* uncoupling.

**sdra·ia** *f.* chaise-longue; couch.

**ṣdrai-are** [A4] *rfl.* to lie down, to stretch oneself at ease; *tr.* to stretch out at full length. **-ata** *f.* lying down, *fare una -ata*, to lie down for a while.

**sdra·i-o** *adv.* lying down; *a —*, full length; *sedia a —*, deck chair; chaise-longue; *poltrona a —*, easy chair; *mettersi a —*, to lie down, to stretch out; *n.m.* cradle (for working underneath a car). **-ọne, -ọni** *adv.* reclining, lolling.

**ṣdrucciol-are** [A1s] *intr.* (*aux.* avere, essere) to slip, to slide; (of water) to flow down; (of time) to fly. **-ẹvole** *adj.* slippery.

**ṣdru·cciol-o** *adj.* slippery; *parola -a*, word accented on the third last syllable; *n.m.* slippery place; slip; slide; slippery slope, steep path; *scala a —*, ramp. **-ọni** *adv.* sliding, slipping.

**ṣdru·cio** *m.* tear; cut; rip.

**sdruc-ire** [D2] *tr.* to tear; to rend, to rip; to unstitch; to cut. **-ito** *part. adj.* rent; threadbare; unstitched. **-itura** *f.* unstitching; rent; rip.

**sẹ**[1] *conj.* **1.** if; *anche —*, even if; *come —*, as if; *— vuoi*, if you wish; *— non è vero è ben trovato*, if it isn't true it's a good tale anyway; *— fossi in te*, if I were you; *come — non lo sapesse*, as if he didn't know. **2.** Used emphatically, with suppression of main verb: *— lo so!*, of course I know! **3.** Used in conjunction with other parts of speech: *— no*, if not, otherwise, or else; *— non che*, unless; *— bene*, though, although; *— non altro*, at least. **4.** *n.m. indecl.* if; *va bene ma qui c'è un gran —*, all right but there's a serious condition attached to it.

**se**[2] *prn. rfl. conjunct.* (form of **si** used before lo, la, li, le, ne) oneself; itself; himself; herself; themselves.

**sè**[3] *prn. rfl. disjunct.* oneself; itself; himself; herself; themselves; *fare da —*, to act alone; *diceva fra —*, he said to himself; *n.m.* self; *il — di una volta*, one's former self.

**sebbẹne** *conj.* although, though.

**secare** [A2] *tr.* to cut; (fig.) to glide; to intersect.

**sẹcc-a** *f.* shoal, sandbank; reef. **-a·ggine** *f.* dryness; (fig.) weariness; annoyance.

**secc-are** [A2 c] *tr.* to dry; to dry up; to wither; to weary, to bore, to annoy; *intr.* (*aux.* essere), *rfl.* to dry (up); to wither; to get bored; to be weary. **-amẹnto** *m.* drying (up); desiccation; (fig.) annoyance. **-ante** *part. adj.* tiresome, boring; *colore -ante*, quick-drying paint. **-ati·ccio** *adj.* partly dried; *legna -aticcia*, dry wood (for kindling); (of a person) very thin; *n.m.* thin, wiry person. **-atọio** *m.* drying room; oast house. **-atọre** *m.* bore. **-atura** *f.* drying; nuisance; trouble.

**sẹcchi-a** *f.* bucket, pail. **-ata** *f.* bucketful.

**sẹcchio** *m.* bucket; large milk-pail; *— per carbone*, coal-scuttle.

**sẹcci-a** *f.* stubble. **-a·io** *m.* stubble field.

**sec-co** *adj.* (*pl.* **-chi**) dry; dried up; withered; parched; spare, lean; stingy; distinct; harsh; bald (of style); (cul.) *carne -ca*, dried and salted meat; *n.m.* dryness; dry place; dry ground; dry weather; drought; thin, gaunt or wizened person; *adv.* curtly; stiffly. **-cume** *m.* dry things (branches, leaves); dried fruits.

**secent-ẹṣimo** *ord. num.* six-hundredth. **-iṣmo** *m.* seventeenth-century mannerism of style; baroque. **-ista** *m., f.* writer or artist of the seventeenth century; scholar specializing in seventeenth-century history or culture.

**sece·rnere** [def.] *tr.* to secrete.

**secessiọn-e** *f.* secession. **-ista** *m.* (*pl.* **-isti**) secessionist.

**sẹco** *prn.* (poet.) with him; with her; with them.

**se·col-o** *m.* century; time; age; this world; secular life; *l'altro —*, the world (life) to come. **-are** *adj.* age-old; (rel.) secular; *n.m.* secular; layman; *pl.* laity. **-arẹsco** *adj.* (*m.pl.* **-arẹschi**) secular, lay; worldly. **-ariẓẓare** [A1] *tr.* to secularize.

**secọnda** *f.* see under **secọndo.**

**secọnd-o**[1] *ord. num., adj.* second; *la -a volta*, the second time; *al — piano*, on the second floor; *minuto —*, second; *mobili di -a mano*, second-hand furniture; subsequent; (cul.) *piatto —*, main dish on a menu; (theatr.) *-a parte*, supporting role; *-a galleria*, upper circle; *n.m.* second; the one following the first; (duelling, boxing) second; (of time) second; (watchm.) *lancetta dei -i*, second-hand. **-a** *f.* (person, woman, girl, thing); second; (rlwy.) second class; *viaggiare in -a*, to travel second; (med.) afterbirth; (mus.) second (interval). **-amẹnto** *m.* seconding; support. **-are** [A1 c] *tr.* to second; to support; to back up; to favour, to be propitious to. **-a·rio** *adj.* secondary; (rlwy.) *linea -aria*, branch line. **-atọre** *m.* secondary. **-oge·nito** *adj.* second-born, younger; *n.m.* second son.

**secọndo**[2] *prep.* according to; in accordance with; *— me*, in my opinion; *conj. — che*, according as.

**Secọndo**[3] *pr.n.m.* Secundus.

**secrẹto** *part.* of **sece·rnere**; *adj.* secreted; *n.m.* (physiol.) secretion.

**secreziọne** *f.* (physiol.) secretion.

**se·dano** *m.* celery.

**sed-are** [A1] *tr.* to assuage; to ally; to appease, to calm; to quell; to sedate. **-ativo** *adj., n.m.* sedative.

**sede** *f.* seat; residence; office; *— centrale*, head-office; (eccl.) see; *la Santa —*, the Holy See; (mil.) headquarters; session; sitting; (fig.) *in — tecnica*, from the technical point of view.

**sed-ẹre** [B28] *intr.* (*aux.* avere) to be seated; to be sitting; (leg.) to sit; *rfl.* to sit down, to take a seat; *n.m.* sitting; backside, posterior; seat (of a chair). **-enta·rio** *adj.* sedentary; *n.m.* person of sedentary habits.

**se·d-ia** *f.* chair, seat; *— a braccioli*, armchair; *— a dondolo*, rocking chair; *— a sdraio*, deck chair; *— pieghevole*, camp stool, folding chair.

**sedicenne** *adj.* see under **sedici.**

**sedicente** *adj.* self-styled, would-be.

**se·dic-i** *card. num.* sixteen. **-enne** *adj.* sixteen years old; *n.m., f.* sixteen-year-old. **-ẹṣimo** *ord. num.* sixteenth; (paperm.; bookb.) *in -esimo*, sixteenmo, 16mo.

**sedile** *m.* seat, chair; bench.

**sedimẹnto** *m.* sediment, deposit; dregs, lees; (geol.) deposit, sediment.

**sedizi-ọne** *f.* sedition; disagreement. **-ọso** *adj.* seditious; turbulent; *n.m.* rebel; rioter.

**seducente** *part. adj.* seductive; charming, fascinating; tempting.

**sedurre** [B2] *tr.* to seduce; to lure; to corrupt; to tempt; to fascinate; to please; to allure.

**seduta** *f.* sitting; meeting; session.

**sedut-tọre** *m.* seducer; tempter; enticer; *adj.* seductive; corrupting. **-trice** *f.* temptress; also *adj.*

**seduziọne** *f.* seduction; temptation; allurement, charm.

**seenne** *adj.* six years old; of six years duration; *n.m., f.* six-year-old.

**sẹga** *f.* saw; saw-shaped object; toothed edge of a wall.

**sẹgal-e** *f.* rye. **-a·io** *m.* rye-field.

**segantino** *m.* sawyer.

**seg-are** [A2] *tr.* to saw, to saw off; to mow, to reap; to cut; (geom.) to intersect. **-amẹnto** *m.* sawing; cutting. **-ata** *f.* sawing. **-atọre** *m.* mower. sawyer. **-atrice** *f.* sawing-machine. **-atura** *f.* sawing; mowing; sawdust.

**se·ggi-o** *m.* seat; chair (official); throne; (fig.) place, office; seat (in Parliament or on municipal council); *— elettorale*, polling station; (leg.) seat; bench. **-ovi·a** *f.* chair-lift.

**se·ggiol-a** *f.* chair. **-a·io** *m.* chair-maker; seller or mender of chairs. **-ino** *m.* baby's chair; (aeron.) pilot's seat. **-ọne** *m. augm.* arm-chair; easy chair; baby's high-chair.

**segheri·a** *f.* saw-mill.

**seghẹtta** *f. dim.* of **sega**; fret-saw.

**seghettato** *adj.* serrated (of leaves); notched like a saw, having a saw edge.

**seghẹtto** *m. dim.* handsaw; small hacksaw.

**segmẹnto** *m.* (geom.) segment; (motor.) piston ring; *— per freni*, brake lining.

**segna·colo** *m.* mark; sign; emblem.

**segnal-e** *m.* signal; sign; token; omen; *— di traffico*, traffic signal; *brutto —*, bad omen; (naut.) beacon; (rlwy.) *— d'allarme*, communication cord.

**-are** [A1] *tr.* to signalize; to point out; to notify; to signal; to mark; to mention; *rfl.* to distinguish oneself. **-atọre** *m.* signaller; (rlwy.) signalman. **-aziọne** *f.* signalling; *cabina di -azione,* signal-box; *-azioni stradali,* road-traffic signals; notification. **-e·tica** *f.* system of signs. **-e·tico** *adj.* relating to signs; *dati -etici,* identification marks.

**segn-are** [A5 c] *tr.* to mark; to note down, to enter (in a register); to indicate; to mark out, to trace; to sign; to seal; (sport) to score; *rfl.* to cross oneself. **-acarte** *m indecl.* book-marker, book-mark. **-achilo·metri** *m. indecl.* taxi-meter. **-ata·rio** *m., adj.* signatory. **-atọre** *m.,* **-atrice** *f.* marker (person); indicator; scorer; signatory; *adj. freccia -atrice,* weather vane. **-atura** *f.* marking, stamp(ing); signing. **-avento** *m. indecl.* (aeron.) wind cone.

**sẹgn-o** *m.* mark; sign; trace; target; *cogliere, dare nel —,* to hit the bull's eye; limit; token; trace, track, vestige; symbol; scratch, scar; spot; degree, measure; *per filo e per —,* in all details, in full; nod, wave, gesture; *un — di mano,* a wave of the hand; *i -i dello zodiaco,* the signs of the Zodiac; *-i d'interpunzione,* punctuation marks; (math.) *— di addizione,* plus sign; *— di eguaglianza,* equals sign; *— meno,* minus sign.

**sẹg-o** *m.* tallow; suet. **-ọso** *adj.* tallowy, greasy; (cul.) rich.

**sẹgolo** *m.* pruning-hook.

**segọne** *m. augm.* of **sega**; two-handed saw.

**segreg-are** [A2 s] *tr.* to segregate; to isolate; to secrete; *rfl.* to withdraw, to retire in isolation. **-aziọne** *f.* segregation; seclusion; isolation; *-azione cellulare,* solitary confinement.

**segret-a·rio** *m.* secretary; *— particolare,* private secretary; *— comunale,* town-clerk; (orn.) secretary bird. **-a·ria** *f.* woman secretary. **-ariato** *m.* secretariat(e); secretaryship. **-eri·a** *f.* secretary's office; secretarial staff; writing-desk.

**segrẹt-o** *adj.* secret; hidden; private; *Consiglio —,* Privy Council; *n.m.* secret; secret drawer; secrecy; (mus.) wind-chest (of organ); privacy. **-ẹzza** *f.* secrecy.

**seguace** *m., f.* follower; adherent; disciple.

**seguen-te** *part.* of **seguire**; *adj.* following; next; ensuing. **-za** *f.* sequence.

**segu·gio** *m.* bloodhound; (police) sleuth.

**seguire** [D1] *tr.* to follow; to accompany; to imitate; to obey; *abs.* to follow; to ensue; to happen; to result; to continue; to follow as a consequence; *non segue,* it doesn't follow, not necessarily.

**seguit-are** [A1 sc] *tr.* to continue; to follow up, to pursue; *intr.* (*aux.* avere; *prep.* a) to go on, to keep on, to continue; to persevere; *impers.* (*aux.* essere) *è -ato a piovere,* it has continued to rain; to follow as a consequence.

**sẹguito** *m.* suite, train, attendants, retinue; set; sequence, series; consequence; *il — al prossimo numero,* 'to be continued in our next'.

**sei** *card. num.* six; *ha — anni,* he is six years old; *n.m., indecl.* the number six; *il — del mese,* the sixth of the month. **-centeṣimo** *m. ord. num.* six hundredth. **-centiṣimo** *m.* seventeenth-century style and mannerisms. **-centista** *m.* seventeenth-century writer; specialist in seventeenth-century history, art, literature. **-cento** *card. num.* six hundred; *n.m. indecl. il -cento,* the seventeenth century. **-mila** *card. num.* six thousand.

**sẹlc-e** *f.* shingle; pebble; flint. **-ia·io** *m.* pavior. **-iare** [A3] *tr.* to pave. **-iata** *f.* pavement; flagstones. **-iato** *part. adj.* paved; *n.m.* pavement; paved street. **-iatọre** *m.* paver; pavior. **-iatura** *f.* paving. **-iọso** *adj.* flinty.

**sele·n-io** *m.* (chem.) selenium. **-ite** *f.* (miner.) selenite, gypsum.

**selettiv-o** *adj.* selective, having the faculty to select. **-amẹnte** *adv.* selectively. **-ità** *f.* selectivity.

**selettọre** *m.* (electr.) selector.

**selezịọn-e** *f.* selection; choice. **-are** [A1 c] *tr.* to select; to pick out; to sort, to grade. **-atọre** *m.* selector.

**sell-a** *f.* saddle. **-a·io** *m.* saddler. **-are** [A1] *tr.* to saddle. **-ato** *part. adj.* saddled; saddle-backed. **-atura** *f.* saddling; saddlery; (motor.) upholstery. **-eri·a** *f.* saddler's shop; harness room. **-ino** *m. dim.* saddle (of bicycle or motorcycle).

**seltz** *m. indecl.* (*acqua di*) *—,* soda-water.

**selv-a** *f.* wood; forest; anthology, 'treasury'. **-aggina** *f.* (sport) game. **-a·ggio** *adj.* wild; savage; uncivilized; extremely shy; *n.m.* savage.

**selva·ti-co** *adj.* wild; uncultivated; untamed; uncouth; lonely, uninhabited; *n.m.* woodland, forest. **-chẹzza** *f.* wildness; rudeness; rough, untutored behaviour.

**selvọso** *adj.* wooded, woody.

**sema·for-o** *m.* instrument used for signalling, semaphore; (rlwy.) signal; (road) traffic light(s). **-ista** *m.* signaller.

**sema·ntic-a** *f.* (ling.) semantics. **-o** *adj.* semantic.

**sembian-te** *m.* semblance; appearance, aspect, mien; countenance. **-za** *f.* look; appearance; aspect; features.

**sembr-are** [A1 c] *intr.* (*aux.* essere) to seem, to appear; to appear to be; to look like; to resemble; *impers. -a che voglia piovere,* it looks like rain.

**sẹm-e** *m.* seed; *-i duri,* peas, beans, lentils; pip; (cards) suit; semen; (fig.) race, breed; origin; cause; source. **-a·io** *m.* seedsman.

**semẹnt-a** *f.* sowing; seed time. **-are** [A1 c] *tr.* to sow. **-ato** *part. adj.* sown; *n.m.* sown field. **-atọre** *m.* sower. **-e** *f.* seed; seed-corn.

**semenz-a** *f.* seed; (fig.) origin; descent; race, progeny. **-a·io** *m.* seedbed; seed-merchant.

**semestr-e** *m.* half year, six months; semester; *adj.* half-yearly. **-almẹnte** *adv.* every six months.

**semi** *pref.* half-, semi, demi-. **-breve** *f.* (mus.) semibreve. **-cadenza** *f.* (mus.) half close, imperfect cadence. **-ce·rchio** *m.* (geom.) semicircle. **-circolare** *adj.* semicircular. **-ci·rcolo** *m.* semicircle; protractor. **-croma** *f.* (mus.) semiquaver. **-di·o** *m.* (*pl.* **-de·i**) demigod. **-finale** *adj., n.f.* (sport) semi-final. **-finalista** *m., f.* (sport) semi-finalist. **-fusa** *f.* (mus.) semiquaver. **-luna** *f.* half-moon. **-lunare** *adj.* half-moon shaped. **-mi·nima** *f.* (mus.) crotchet. **-sfera** *f.* hemisphere. **-tono** *m.* (mus.) semitone. **-vivo** *adj.* half-alive; half-dead. **-volata** *f.,* **-vọlo** *m.* (tennis) half-volley.

**sẹmin-a** *f.* seed; sowing; seed-time. **-agiọne** *f.* sowing. **-ale** *adj.* seed; relating to seed. **-are** [A1 c] *tr.* to sow; (fig.) to scatter, to spread; to disseminate. **-ata** *f.* seed sown; sowing. **-ato** *part. adj.* sown; *n.m.* ground under seed. **-atọio** *m.* seed-drill. **-atọre** *m.* sower. **-atrice** *f.* woman sower; sowing machine, drill. **-atura** *f.* sowing.

**semina·r-io** *m.* (eccl.) seminary; seminar. **-ista** *m.* seminarist.

**sem-ita** *m., f.* (*m.pl.* **-iti,** *f.pl.* **-ite**) Semite. **-i·tico** *adj.* Semitic. **-itista** *m., f.* Hebrew scholar; student of Semitic languages.

**sẹmol-a** *f.* bran; *pl.* freckles. **-ata** *f.* bran-mash. **-ino** *m.* semolina.

**semovente** *adj.* self-moving; (motor.) self-propelled.

**Sempiọne** *pr.n.m.* (geog.) Simplon (pass, tunnel).

**sempiterno** *adj.* everlasting, eternal, perpetual.
**sẹmplic-e** *adj.* simple, ordinary; *soldato —*, private soldier; unpretentious; inexperienced; natural; mere; easy; *n.m.pl.* simples **-iọna** *f.*, **-iọne** *m.* simpleton. **-ioneri·a** *f.* ingenuousness. **-iotto** *m.* simpleton (also *adj.*) **-iṣmo** *m.* oversimplification. **-ista** *m.* herbalist; one who oversimplifies. **-ità** *f.* simplicity; plainness; naturalness.
**semplific-are** [A2 s] *tr.* to simplify. **-aziọne** *f.* simplification.
**sempr-e** *adv.* always; on all occasions; still; yet. **-evẹrde** *adj.*, *n.m.* evergreen. **-eviva** *f.* everlasting (plant).
**sena** *f.* (bot.) senna.
**se·nap-e** *f.* mustard. **-iere** *f.* mustard-pot.
**sena·rio** *m.* line of six syllables.
**senata** *f.* (naut.) seine net.
**senat-o** *m.* senate. **-ọre** *m.* senator. **-orẹssa** *f.* senator's wife. **-oriale** *adj.*, **-o·rio** *adj.* senatorial. **-rice** *f.* woman senator.
**senescen-te** *adj.* senescent. **-za** *f.* senescence.
**senẹse** *adj.*, *n.m.*, *f.* Sienese.
**senil-e** *adj.* senile. **-ità** *f.* senility.
**seniọre** *adj.*, *n.m.* elder; senior.
**Senna** *pr.n.f.* (geog.) Seine.
**sẹnno** *m.* (good) sense, judgment; wisdom; *— di poi*, hindsight.
**sẹno** bosom; breast; (fig.) heart, centre; depth; (geog.) inlet, bay; cove; (anat.) sinus.
**senof-obi·a** *f.* xenophobia. **-o·fobo** *m.* xenophobe.
**Senofọnte** *pr.n.m.* Xenophon.
**sensale** *m.* (comm.) broker; middleman; *— marittimo*, shipping agent; insurance broker.
**sensat-o** *adj.* sensible; prudent; judicious. **-amẹnte** *adv.* sensibly; judiciously. **-ẹzza** *f.* sound sense; judgment; discretion.
**sensaziọn-e** *f.* sensation; feeling; excitement. **-ale** *adj.* sensational; thrilling; exciting. **-aliṣmo** *m.* sensationalism.
**senseri·a** *f.* brokerage; agency.
**sensi·bil-e** *adj.* sensitive; susceptible; sentient; sensible, aware; tender-hearted; appreciable; palpable; perceptible; *n.f.* (mus.) leading note. **-ità** *f.* sensitiveness; feeling, sensibility; touchiness. **-izẓare** [A1] *tr* (photog.) to sensitize. **-izẓaziọne** *f.* (photog.) sensitization.
**sensitiv-a** *f.* sensitiveness, sensibility; (bot.) sensitive plant. **-ità** *f.* sensitivity, sensitiveness. **-o** *adj.* sensitive; sensory; of the senses; sensual.

**sens-o** *m.* sense: *i cinque -i*, the five senses; meaning, import; sensation; feeling; sentiment; judgement; direction; way; *una strada a — unico*, a one-way street; *— vietato*, no entry; *— orario*, clockwise direction; *— antiorario*, anti-clockwise direction. **-o·rio** *m.* organ of sense; *adj.* sensory. **-uale** *adj.* sensual; sensuous. **-ualiṣmo** *m.* hedonism; sensuality. **-ualità** *f.* sensuality; voluptuousness; (art) sensuousness.
**sentenz-a** *f.* opinion; judgement; aphorism; pronouncement; (leg.) judgement. **-iare** [A4] *tr.* to judge, to criticize; (leg.) to pronounce judgement (on); *intr.* (*aux.* avere) to decide; to talk sententiously. **-iọso** *adj.* sententious; aphoristic; epigrammatic; critical.
**sentiero** *m.* footpath, pathway; track; way.
**sentimẹnt-o** *m.* feeling, sentiment; sense; opinion; meaning; good sense; judgement; intelligence. **-ale** *adj.* sentimental; mawkish; *n.m.*, *f.* sentimentalist. **-aliṣmo** *m.* sentimentality. **-alità** *f.* sentimentality.
**sentina** *f.* (naut.) bilge.
**sentinella** *f.* sentry; sentinel; guard; *posto di —*, sentry box.
**sent-ire** [D1] *tr.* to feel; to hear; to listen to; to learn; to be conscious of; to smell; to scent; to taste; *— dolore*, to feel pain; *— un concerto*, to listen to a concert; *abs.* to listen; *intr.* (*aux.* avere) to taste; to smell of, to be redolent of; *rfl.* to feel; *-irsi male*, to feel ill; *n.m.* feeling. **-itamẹnte** *adv.* cordially, heartily; sincerely; deeply, warmly. **-ito** *part. adj.* felt; heard; heart-felt; warm; sincere; *per -ito dire*, by hearsay. **-ọre** *m.* sense, feeling, inkling; sign; rumour; scent, smell.
**senza** *prep.* without; *— di me*, without me; *senz'altro*, without fail; *senz'altro!*, of course!; *n.m.* (bridge) *tre —*, three no trumps.
**senziente** *adj.* sentient.
**separ-are** [A1 s] *tr.* to separate, to sever; to divide; *rfl.* to become separated; to be severed; to part. **-atamẹnte** *adv.* separately. **-ato** *part. adj.* separate; divided. **-aziọne** *f.* separation; parting.
**sepọlcr-o** *m.* sepulchre; grave. **-ale** *adj.* sepulchral.
**sepoltura** *f.* burial; burial-place; tomb.
**seppell-ire** [D2] *tr.* to bury, to inter; *rfl.* (fig.) to bury oneself, to hide. **-imẹnto** *m.* burial. **-itọre** *m.* grave digger, sexton.
**sẹppia** *f.* (zool.) cuttlefish.
**seppure** *conj.* even though, even if.
**sepsi** *f.* (med.) sepsis.

**sequela** *f.* succession, sequence.
**sequenza** *f.* succession, sequence.
**sequestr-o** *m.* (leg.) attachment; distraint; distress; seizure; sequestration. **-amẹnto** *m.* distraining; seizing; attaching; sequestration. **-are** [A1] *tr.* (leg.) to distrain; to attach; to seize; to sequestrate. **-ata·rio** *m.* bailiff. **-aziọne** *f.* sequestration.
**sẹra** *f.* evening; night; *di —*, in the evening; *abito da —*, evening dress.
**sera·fico** *adj.* (theol.) seraphic.
**serafino** *m.* (theol.) seraph.
**seral-e** *adj.* evening; *scuola —*, night school. **-mẹnte** *adv.* in the evening; every evening.
**serata** *f.* evening; evening-party; (theatr.) evening performance.
**serb-are** [A1] *tr.* to keep; to put aside, to reserve; to save up; to preserve; *rfl.* to be saved up; to be reserved; to hold oneself ready. **-atọio** *m.* reservoir; tank; magazine (of a rifle); barrel (of fountain-pen).
**serbo** *m.* keeping; custody; reserve; *mettere in —*, to put by.
**serẹnata** *f.* serenade; alfresco concert.
**seren-o** *adj.* serene, cloudless, clear; calm; *n.m.* clear sky. **-i·ssima** *f.* (hist.) *la Serenissima* (*Repubblica*), Venice. **-ità** *f.* serenity; cloudlessness; tranquillity.
**sergente** *m.* (mil.) sergeant; *allievo —*, lance-sergeant.
**se·ri-co** *adj.* (of) silk; silky; silken. **-coltọre, -cultọre** *m.* silk-producer. **-coltura, -cultura** *f.* sericulture, silk culture.
**se·rie** *f. indecl.* series, succession; range; *macchina fuori —*, special model (car).
**seri·fero** *adj.* silk-producing.
**se·ri-o** *adj.* serious, earnest, steady; thoughtful; reliable; virtuous; genuine; (mus.) *opera -a*, grand opera. **-età** *f.* seriousness; gravity, trustworthiness.
**sermọn-e** *m.* speech; discourse; talk; sermon; (fig.) admonition, reproof. **-cino** *m. dim.* short sermon; (fig.) little lecture; rebuke. **-eggiare** [A3 c] *intr.* (*aux.* avere) to sermonize, to preach.
**sero·tino** *adj.* (agric.) ripening late; tardy.
**serp-e** *m.* snake; serpent. **-a·io** *m.* snake-pit. **-aro** *m.* snake-charmer.
**serpeggi-are** [A3 c] *intr.* (*aux.* avere) to wind; to meander. **-amẹnto** *m.* winding; meandering; (rlwy.) shunting. **-ante** *part. adj.* winding; twisting.
**serpent-e** *m.* (zool.) snake, serpent; *— a sonagli*, rattlesnake; (mus.) serpent. **-i·fero** *adj.* snake-infested. **-ifọrme**

*adj.* snake-like; in the form of a serpent. **-ino** *adj.* serpentine; tortuous.
**serpi·gine** *f.* (med.) ringworm.
**sẹrqua** *f.* dozen; large amount.
**serra** *f.* dyke, embankment; narrow gorge; waistband, belt; crowd, greenhouse; *fiore di —*, hothouse flower; *— per viti*, vinery; *— per palme*, palm house.
**serra·glio** *m.* enclosure; cage for wild beasts; menagerie; harem, seraglio; (archit.) keystone.
**serrame** *m.* lock; fastening.
**serr-are** [A1] *tr.* to lock; to lock up; to shut, to close; to squeeze; to bind, to harden (of snow); to conclude; to hide; *intr.* (*aux.* avere) to fit tight; to close properly (of window); *rfl.* (*prep.* a) to stand close (to). **-acarte** *m. indecl.* filing-cabinet. **-amẹnto** *m.* locking; tightening. **-ata** *f.* fence; dam; (industr.) lock-out. **-ato** *part. adj.* locked; closed; close; compact; concise; serried; swift; tight. **-atura** *f.* lock; *buco della -atura*, keyhole; (archit.) keystone.
**Serse** *pr.n.m.* Xerxes.
**serto** *m.* garland; wreath.
**serva** *f.* domestic servant.
**serva·ggio** *m.* servitude, slavery; bondage; serfdom.
**servente** *adj.* see under **servire**.
**servil-e** *adj.* servile; slavish; menial. **-ità** *f.* servility.
**serv-ire** [D1] *tr.* to serve; to assist; to wait on; to attend to; *intr.* (*aux.* avere, essere) to be of use; to serve; *rfl.* (*prep.* di) to make use (of), to use; to help oneself (at table). **-ente** *adj.* serving; (hist.) *cavaliere -ente*, cavalier in attendance; *n.m.* servant; *f.* maid, servant. **-itọre** *m.* servant; civil servant; hall-stand; *-itore muto*, dumb-waiter. **-itù** *f.* servitude, slavery; bondage; serfdom; servants, domestic staff.
**servi·zi-o** *m.* service; favour; kindness; (tennis) serve, service; *— da tavola*, dinner-service; (rlwy.) *— diretto*, through service. **-ẹvole** *adj.* helpful; serviceable; obliging.
**servo** *adj.* servile; base; *n.m.* servant; manservant; slave.
**se·samo** (bot.) sesame; *apriti — !*, open sesame!
**sessagena·rio** *adj.* sixty years old; *n.m.* sexagenarian.
**sessagẹsim-a** *f.* Sexagesima Sunday. **-o** *ord. num.* sixtieth.
**sess-anta** *card. num.* sixty. **-antamila** *card. num.* sixty thousand. **-antenne** *adj.* sixty years old; *n.m.* sexagenarian. **-antẹsimo** *ord. num., adj.* sixtieth. **-antina** *f.* three score; *essere sulla -antina*, to be about sixty.
**sess-ennale** *adj.* six-yearly; recurring every six years. **-enne** *adj.* six years old. **-e·nnio** *m.* period of six years.
**sessiọne** *f.* session.
**sessitura** *f.* tuck (in clothes); hem.
**sesso** *m.* sex.
**sessual-e** *adj.* sexual. **-ità** *f.* sexuality.
**sesta** *f.* (liturg.) sext; (mus.) sixth (interval); leg of a compass; *pl.* pair of compasses.
**sest-ẹtto** *m.* (mus.) sextet. **-ina** *f.* (prosod.) sestina, six-line stanza.
**sest-o**[1] *ord. num.* sixth. **-angolare** *adj.* hexagonal. **-a·ngolo** *m.* hexagon. **-ante** *m.* sextant. **-ode·cimo** *ord. num.* sixteenth.
**sesto**[2] *m.* order, orderliness, good order; format; (archit.) curvature of anarch; rib of a vault.
**se·stuplo** *adj.* sixfold, sextuple.
**sẹt-a** *f.* silk; *— greggia*, raw silk; *— vegetale*, artificial silk; *commercio della —*, silk trade. **-a·ceo** *adj.* silky. **-aiolo** *m.* silk merchant, mercer; silk manufacturer. **-eri·a** *f.* silk goods; silk factory. silk farmer. **-icoltọre** *m.*, **-icoltura** *f.* silk production. **-ifi·cio** *m.* silk farm; silk factory.
**sẹt-e** *f.* thirst; *aver —*, to be thirsty; (fig.) longing, eager desire; greed.
**sẹtol-a** *f.* bristle; coarse hair; chap, crack in the skin. **-ino** *m.* clothes-brush; hat-brush. **-ọso** *adj.* bristling; cracked, chapped.
**setta** *f.* sect; faction; secret society.
**sett-a·gono** *m.* (geom.) heptagon. **-angolare** *adj.* heptagonal.
**settant-a** *card. num.* seventy. **-enne** *adj.* seventy years old; seventy-year-long; *n.m.* septuagenarian. **-ẹsimo** *ord. num.* seventieth. **-ina** *f.* age of seventy or thereabouts; the seventies; *essere sulla -ina*, to be about seventy.
**setta·rio** *adj.* sectarian; parochial; *spirito —*, party spirit; *n.m.* member (of a sect or party).
**sett-e** *card. num.* seven. **-ecentẹsco** *adj.* (*m.pl.* **-ecentẹschi**) relating to the eighteenth century. **-ecentẹsimo** *ord. num.* seven hundredth. **-ecentista** *m., f.* eighteenth-century writer, artist; specialist in eighteenth-century studies. **-ecento** *card. num.* seven hundred; *n.m.* the number 700; *il -ecento*, the eighteenth century. **-emila** *card. num.* seven thousand. **-ino** *m.* (mus.) septet.
**settembr-e** *m.* September **-ino** *adj.* of, relating to September.
**sette·mplice** *adj.* sevenfold; septuple.
**settena·rio** *m.* period of seven days or seven years; line of seven syllables; *adj.* septenary; (mus.) *misura settenaria*, septuple time.
**settenn-ale** *adj.* septennial, recurring every seven years. **-e** *adj.* seven years old; seven-year-long.
**sette·nnio** *m.* period of seven years.
**settentriọn-e** *m.* north. **-ale** *adj.* north, northern; northerly; *n.m.* northerner.
**se·ttic-o** *adj.* (med.) septic. **-emi·a** *f.* (med.) septicaemia.
**settiman-a** *f.* week; *fine di —*, week-end. **-ale** *adj.* weekly; *giornale -ale*, weekly journal; *n.m.* weekly; week's pay. **-almẹnte** *adv.* weekly; every week; by the week.
**se·ttim-o** *ord. num.* seventh; *n.m.* seventh. **-a** *f.* (mus.) seventh (interval). **-ino** *m.* (mus.) septet.
**setto** *m.* (anat.) septum.
**settọre** *m.* sector; quadrant; area.
**settu-agena·rio** *adj., n.m.* septuagenarian. **-agẹsima** *f.* Septuagesima. **-agẹsimo** *ord. num.* seventieth; *n.m.* (the) seventieth.
**se·ttuplo** *adj.* sevenfold, septuple.
**sever-o** *adj.* severe; strict; austere; stern; harsh; rigorous. **-ità** *f.* severity, strictness; sternness.
**sevi·zi-a** *f.* (usu. *pl.*) cruelty. **-are** [A4] *tr.* to ill-treat; to torture.
**sezion-are** [A1 c] *tr.* (microscopy) to section. **-amẹnto** *m.* sectioning.
**seziọne** *f.* section; part; sectional drawing; team; (surg.) dissection; (geom.) *— conica*, conic section; intersection; division; department; group; *— elettorale*, electoral division
**sfaccend-are** [A1] *intr.* (*aux.* avere) to be busy; to bustle. **-ato** *adj.* idle, unoccupied; *n.m.* idler, loafer.
**sfaccett-are** [A1 c] *tr.* (jewel.) to facet. **-atura** *f.* (jewel.) cutting; facet.
**sfacchin-are** [A1] *intr.* (*aux.* avere), *rfl.* to toil, to drudge. **-ata** *f.* heavy work, back-breaking labour; tough job.
**sfacciat-o** *adj.* impudent; shameless; bold; loud. **-a·ggine** *f.* boldness; impudence; effrontery. **-ẹzza** *f.* loudness (of colours), showiness.
**sfacelo** *m.* collapse, ruin, breakdown; disaster.
**sfacimẹnto** *m.* decay; weakening; ruin; undoing.
**sfa·gli-o** *m.* discarding; cards discarded. **-are** [A4] *tr.* (cards) to discard; *rfl.* (*prep.* di) to get rid of.
**sfald-are** [A1] *tr.* to cut into slices; to cause to flake or scale. **-atura** *f.* flaking; scaling.
**sfamare** [A1] *tr.* to feed; to

appease the hunger of; *rfl.* to appease one's hunger.

**sfang-are** [A2] *intr.* (*aux.* avere) to splash through mud; (fig.) to drudge, to toil; *tr.* to clean mud from. **-atrice** *f.* mud-clearing machine. **-atura** *f.* street-cleaning, removing of mud.

**sfare** [B14] *tr.* to undo; to dissolve; to melt; to take apart; *rfl.* to decompose; to melt; (of bubble) to burst; *sfarsi di*, to get rid of.

**sfarfall-are** [A1] *intr.* (*aux.* avere) to come out of the cocoon; to flutter about, to flit; (of flowers) to shed their petals. **-amẹnto** *m.* fluttering, flitting. **-ìo** *m.* fluttering; (motor.) wobble (of wheels); (cinem.) flicker. **-atura** *f.* emerging from the cocoon; fluttering, flitting.

**sfarin-are** [A1] *tr.* to grind to flour; to pulverize; *rfl.* to be reduced to powder; to crumble. **-amẹnto** *m.* crumbling. **-ato** *part. adj.* ground; pulverized; (of pears) sleepy; (of potatoes) overcooked.

**sfarz-o** *m.* pomp; magnificence; splendour; brilliance. **-ọso** *adj.* magnificent; sumptuous; luxurious; ostentatious.

**sfasci-are** [A3] *tr.* to unbind; to undo; to dismantle; to demolish; *rfl.* to break down, to collapse; to come undone. **-amẹnto** *m.* unwrapping, unbinding; collapse, ruin. **-atura** *f.* unbinding; removing of bandages, splints etc. **-ume** *m.* ruins; rubbish, litter; (fig., of person) wreck.

**sfat-are** [A1] *tr.* to discredit, to unmask, to expose. **-amẹnto** *m.* discrediting; unmasking; exposure.

**sfatto** *part.* of **sfare**; *adj.* undone; ruined; flabby.

**sfavill-are** [A1] *intr.* (*aux.* avere) to sparkle; to shine; to glitter. **-amẹnto** *m.* sparkle; glitter; brilliance. **-ìo** *m.* (*pl.* **-ìi**) continual sparkling, glittering, flashing.

**sfavọr-e** *m.* disfavour; disapproval; disgrace. **-ẹvole** *adj.* unfavourable; adverse. **-ire** [D2] *tr.* to place in an unfavourable position; to oppose; to disapprove.

**sfebbrare** [A1] *tr.* to reduce the temperature of; *rfl.*, *intr.* (*aux.* essere) to be cured of a fever.

**sfegat-are** [A1 s] *rfl.* to exert oneself to the utmost; to wear oneself out; to work oneself into a passion; to bawl and yell. **-ato** *part. adj.* passionate; overheated; *n.m.* hothead.

**sfer-a** *f.* sphere; globe, orb; circle; *cuscinetto a -e*, ball bearing; *penna a —*, ball pen; (watchm.) hand.

**sfe·r-ico** *adj.* spherical. **-oidale** *adj.* (geom.) spheroidal. **-o·ide** *m.* (geom.) spheroid.

**sferr-a** *f.* piece of old iron; worn horseshoe; clout; *pl.* cast-off clothing. **-are** [A1] *tr.* (vet.) to remove the shoes from (a horse), to unshoe; to free (a prisoner) from irons, from chains; to deliver (kick, attack); *rfl.* (vet.) to cast a shoe; to break loose (from chains).

**sferz-a** *f.* whip; lash; scourge; rebuke; whiplash. **-are** [A1] *tr.* to whip; to lash; to flog, to scourge; to rebuke. **-ata** *f.* cut with a whip; thrashing; (fig.) sharp rebuke. **-atọre** *m.*, **-atrice** *f.* flogger; flagellant.

**sfiammare** [A1] *intr.* (*aux.* avere) to blaze; to burn away.

**sfiancare** [A2] *tr.* to destroy; to break through the sides of; (fig.) to exhaust by overwork; *intr.* (*aux.* essere) to give way; to cave in; to burst; *rfl.* to overwork.

**sfiat-are** [A1] *intr.* (*aux.* avere) to exhale; (*aux.* essere) (of gas, air) to escape, to leak; *rfl.* to talk oneself breathless. **-ato** *part. adj.* breathless. **-atọio** *m.* vent; ventilation shaft. **-atura** *f.* exhalation; escape (of gas, etc.); hole (allowing escape or leak).

**sfibbiare** [A4] *tr.* to unbuckle; to unfasten, to unclasp; to unbutton; (fig.) to let fly (insults, oaths); *rfl.* to let oneself go, to speak without reserve; to unbutton oneself.

**sfibrare** [A1] *tr.* to weaken, to enervate; to unnerve.

**sfid-a** *f.* challenge; defiance. **-ante** *part. adj.* challenging; *n.m.*, *f.* challenger. **-are** [A1] *tr.* to challenge; (fig.) to defy; *abs.* to be certain, to be sure; to be confident; *-o io!*, I bet!; *recip. rfl.* to challenge each other. **-atọre** *m.*, **-atrice** *f.* challenger; *adj.* challenging.

**sfidu·ci-a** *f.* mistrust, distrust; lack of confidence. **-are** [A3] *tr.* to discourage; to dishearten; *rfl.* to lose confidence, to lose heart; to grow discouraged.

**sfigur-are** [A1] *tr.* to disfigure; to deform; *intr.* (*aux.* avere) to cut a poor figure; to look out of place. **-ato** *part. adj.* disfigured; deformed.

**sfila·cci-a** *f.* loose threads. **-are** [A3] *tr.* to fray out; (text.) to unravel; *rfl.* to become frayed. **-atura** *f.* unravelling; fraying out.

**sfil-are** [A1] *tr.* to unthread (a needle); to unstring; to unhitch; *intr.* (*aux.* avere) (mil.) to defile (on a narrow front); to march past (on parade); *rfl.* to come unthreaded; to come unstrung. **-amẹnto** *m.* unthreading; unstringing; (mil.) march past; (naut.) long line of ships. **-ata** *f.* file; row; procession, march past. **-atura** *f.* unthreading; unstringing; (in a stocking) ladder.

**sfilzare** [A1] *tr.* to detach from a string, series, file; *rfl.* to become detached.

**sfinge** *f.* sphinx; (ent.) hawk moth.

**sfin-ire** [D2] *tr.* to exhaust; to wear out; *intr.* (*aux.* essere) to faint, to swoon; *rfl.* to become exhausted; to tire oneself out; to faint; to swoon. **-imẹnto** *m.* exhaustion, extreme weakness, faint, swoon. **-itẹzza** *f.* exhaustion; weakness. **-ito** *part. adj.* exhausted; worn out.

**sfintere** *m.* (anat.) sphincter.

**sfiocc-are** [A2] *tr.* to unravel so as to form a tassel; *rfl.* to become unravelled. **-amẹnto** *m.* loosening into tassels, tufts or flakes.

**sfior-are** [A1 c] *tr.* to touch lightly; to graze, to brush, to skim over; to caress. **-amẹnto** *m.* touching, grazing, caressing. **-atọre** *m.* overflow (-pipe).

**sfior-ire** [D2] *intr.* (*aux.* essere) to fade; (of a flower) to drop its petals; to wither. **-itura** *f.* fading; decay.

**sfissare** [A1] *tr.* to cancel (*e.g.* an arrangement).

**sfocat-o** *adj.* out of focus; astigmatic; dull, dim. **-ura** *f.* (photog.) fuzziness.

**sfoci-are** [A3] *tr.* to widen the mouth of (river or stream); *intr.* (*aux.* essere; *prep.* in) to flow out (into); to debouch. **-amẹnto** *m.* clearing, widening (of a river's mouth). **-atura** *f.* work or cost of clearing a river's mouth.

**sfoderare** [A1 s] *tr.* to unsheath; to display.

**sfog-are** [A2 c] *tr.* to give vent to, to let out; to give free play to; to disclose; *rfl.* to give vent to one's feelings; *intr.* (*aux.* essere) (of smoke, water) to escape, to flow away. **-atọio** *m.* outlet; air-hole, ventilation shaft; vent.

**sfoggi-are** [A3] *intr.* (*aux.* avere) to show off; to be ostentatious; to dress smartly; *tr.* to flaunt, to display, to show off.

**sfo·ggio** *m.* display; ostentation, show, parade; luxury; abundance.

**sfo·glia** *f.* foil; metal flake; (cul.) *pasta —*, puff-pastry.

**sfogli-are** [A4] *tr.* to strip off (leaves, petals); to cut into thin flakes; *— un libro*, to turn over the pages of a book, to open uncut pages of a book; *rfl.* to shed leaves; to drop petals; to flake off. **-ata** *f.* rapid glance (through a book); (cul.) flaky pastry. **-atura** *f.* falling of leaves in autumn.

**sfọ-go** *m.* (*pl.* **-ghi**) vent, outlet; relief; free play; *dare — a*, to give vent to; outburst; (fig.) *fare i suoi -ghi con uno*, to unbosom oneself to someone.

**sfolgor-are** [A1 sc] *intr.* (*aux.* essere, avere) to flash; to blaze; to move like lightning; *tr.* to blaze forth; to flash forth. **-ante** *part. adj.* resplendent; flashing; *ingegno -ante*, brilliant mind. **-ìo** *m.* (*pl.* **-ìi**) continual flashing; blazing; glitter.

**sfoll-are** [A1] *intr.* (*aux.* essere, avere), *rfl.* (of a crowd) to disperse; to become less crowded; *tr.* to clear (a crowd); to evacuate. **-amẹnto** *m.* dispersal; reduction; (mil.) evacuation. **-ato** *part. adj.* dispersed; *n.m.* evacuee.

**sfond-are** [A1 c] *tr.* to wear a hole in; to knock the bottom out of; to demolish; to break open; to go deeply into; *— poco*, to be shallow-minded; *intr.* (*aux.* avere) to make headway; (mil.) to break through. **-amẹnto** *m.* breaking open. **-ato** *part. adj.* broken; burst; worn out, in ruins; bottomless, boundless; (fig.) *ricco -ato*, rolling in money.

**sfọndo** *m.* background; view; backcloth; recess for a painting.

**sforbici-are** [A3 s] *tr.* to cut (with scissors); to snip. **-atura** *f.* press-cutting.

**sform-are** [A1 c] *tr.* to deform; to disfigure; to pull out of shape; *abs.*, *rfl.* to lose shape; (fig., fam.) to lose patience, to be rude. **-ato** *part. adj.* shapeless; disfigured. **-atura** *f.* casting (in a mould).

**sfornare** [A1 c] *tr.* to take out of the oven; to dish up, to serve out.

**sforn-ire** [D2] *tr.* (*prep.* di) to strip (of); to deprive (of); to dispossess; *rfl.* to run short (of). **-ito** *part. adj.* stripped; deprived; destitute.

**sfortun-a** *f.* bad luck; misfortune. **-ato** *part. adj.* unlucky; unfortunate.

**sforz-are** [A1] *tr.* to force; to compel; *rfl.* (*prep.* di) to strive (to); to strain oneself. **-ato** *part. adj.* forced; coerced; excessive; unnatural; under pressure. **-o** *m.* effort; endeavour; exertion.

**sfọttere** [B1] *tr.* (pop.) to tease.

**sfracassare** [A1] *tr.* to shatter; to smash.

**sfracellare** [A1] *tr.* to shatter; to smash; *rfl.* to smash oneself up, to get badly hurt.

**sfranchire** [D2] *tr.* to free; to give free play to; *rfl.* to acquire facility; to gain confidence.

**sfrangiare** [A3] *tr.* to fray out, to make into a fringe.

**sfrantumare** [A1] *tr.* to shatter, to break to pieces.

**sfrascare** [A2] *tr.* to cut out boughs and foliage from; *intr.* (*aux.* avere) (of foliage) to rustle.

**sfratare** [A1] *tr.* to unfrock (friar or monk).

**sfratt-are** [A1] *tr.* to expel, to turn out; to dismiss; to evict. **-o** *m.* expulsion; dismissal; eviction; notice to quit.

**sfrecciare** [A3 c] *intr.* (*aux.* essere) to flash past.

**sfregare** [A2] *tr.* to rub; to rub lightly; to graze; to scrawl on.

**sfrẹgi-o** *m.* disfigurement; gash, cut, scar; (fig.) slur, affront; disgrace. **-are** [A3 c] *tr.* to disfigure; to deface; (fig.) to disgrace; to sully.

**sfren-are** [A1 c] *tr.* to let loose; to give rein to; to let fly; *rfl.* to let oneself go. **-atamẹnte** *adv.* uncontrolledly; immoderately. **-atẹzza** *f.* looseness, wildness; profligacy. **-ato** *part. adj.* uncontrolled; unbridled; unrestrained; dissolute.

**sfrido** *m.* (industr.) wastage; scrap.

**sfri·ggere** [C5] *intr.* (*aux.* essere).

**sfri(g)golare** [A1 s] *intr.* (*aux.* avere) to hiss, to splutter, to sizzle.

**sfritellare** [A1] *intr.* (*aux.* avere) to cook fritters; *tr.* to spatter with grease; *rfl.* to spatter oneself with grease.

**sfrondare** [A1 c] *tr.* to strip of leaves; (fig.) to remove superfluities from; to curtail; to diminish the reputation of; *rfl.* (of a plant) to lose its leaves.

**sfrontat-o** *adj.* shameless; impudent; cheeky. **-ẹzza** *f.* effrontery; impudence; shamelessness.

**sfrutt-are** [A1] *tr.* to overwork; *— il suolo*, to exhaust the soil; to exploit; to make the most of; to misuse; to sweat. **-amẹnto** *m.* exploitation; exhausting. **-atọre** *m.* explorer; profiteer.

**sfuggẹvole** *adj.* fleeting; transitory; ephemeral.

**sfugg-ire** [D1] *tr.* to escape; to avoid; to shun; *intr.* (*aux.* essere; *prep.* a) to escape; to slip out; to pass unnoticed; to recede, to be foreshortened, to diminish in perspective; *— a una promessa*, to break a promise. **-ita** *f.* short visit; little jaunt; trip; *adv. phr. alla -ita, di -ita*, hastily, stealthily, in passing.

**sfum-are** [A1] *intr.* (*aux.* essere) to smoke, to evaporate; to vanish; (fig.) to end in smoke, to come to nothing; *tr.* to evaporate; to shade off, to soften; to diminish gradually, to fade. **-atura** *f.* (paint.) shading, gradation of colours; light wash of colour; shade, nuance; hint, trace.

**sfuri-are** [A4] *intr.* (*aux.* avere), *rfl.* to fly into a passion; *tr.* to give vent to. **-ata** *f.* outburst (of passion, anger); scolding; burst of energy.

**ṣgabello** *m.* stool; bench (with no back).

**ṣgabuẓẓino** *m.* small room; lumber room; recess.

**ṣgamb-are** [A1] *intr.* (*aux.* avere) to stride along; to walk fast. **-ettare** [A1 c] *intr.* (*aux.* avere) to walk with short, quick steps; to trip along; (of a child) to toddle; to frolic; to caper.

**ṣganasci-are** [A3] *tr.* to dislocate the jaw of; *rfl.* to break one's jaw; *-arsi dalle risa*, to split one's sides with laughter.

**ṣganciare** [A3] *tr.* to uncouple; to unhook; to release; *rfl.* (mil.) to disengage.

**ṣgangher-are** [A1 s] *tr.* to unhinge; to dislocate; to pull to pieces. **-ato** *part. adv.* unhinged; disjointed; awkward; loose; ramshackle; coarse, immoderate.

**ṣgarb-o** *m.* discourtesy; rudeness, incivility. **-atẹzza** *f.* rudeness. **-ato** *adj.* rude; unmannerly; rough; awkward, clumsy.

**ṣgargi-are** [A3] *intr.* (*aux.* avere) to show off, to cut a dash. **-ante** *part. adj.* showy; gaudy; (of colour) loud, violent.

**ṣgarrare** [A1] *intr.* (*aux.* avere) to err, to be mistaken; *tr.* to mistake.

**ṣgattaiolare** [A1] *intr.* (*aux.* essere) to wriggle out; to slip away; *rfl. phr.* (colloq.) *sgattaiolarsela*, to get away with it.

**ṣgel-are** [A1] *intr.* (*aux.* essere, avere), *tr.* to melt; to thaw. **-o** *m.* thaw.

**ṣghẹmb-o** *adj.* crooked; oblique, slanting; (fig.) odd, queer, comical; *adv. phr. a —*, aslant, obliquely, crookedly.

**ṣgheronato** *adj.* cut aslant; *sottana sgheronata*, gored skirt.

**ṣgherro** *m.* hired ruffian, assassin.

**ṣghignazz-are** [A1] *intr.* (*aux.* avere) to laugh scornfully; to guffaw. **-ata** *f.* guffaw.

**ṣghimbe·scio** *m.* oblique line.

**ṣgobb-o** *m.* hard work, grind; *lavoro di —*, drudgery. **-are** [A1] *intr.* (*aux.* avere) to work hard; to slave; (slang) to swot. **-ọna** *f.*, **-ọne** *m.* hard worker; drudge; (slang) swot.

**ṣgocciol-are** [A1 sc] *tr.* to pour out in drops; to drain; *intr.* (*aux.* avere, essere) to drip, to trickle; (of a secret) to leak out. **-atọio** *m.* eaves; cornice over a window; drip-stone. **-atura** *f.* dripping. **-io** *m.* constant dripping.

**ṣgocciolo** *m.* dripping; last drop; (fig.) very end; last little bit, fag-end.

**ṣgolare** [A1 c] *rfl.* to shout oneself hoarse.

**ṣgọmbero, ṣgọmbro** *apocop.*

*part.* of **sgomb(e)rare**; *adj.* clear; free; empty; untenanted; *n.m.* clearing away; removal.

**sgomb(e)r-are** [A1 sc] *tr.* to clear; to remove; to sweep away; *intr.* (*aux.* avere) to go away; to move house; to clear out. **-atore** *m.* furniture remover.

**sgomentare** [A1 c] *tr.* to terrify; to dismay; to alarm.

**sgomento** *apocop. part. adj.* frightened, alarmed, dismayed; discouraged; *n.m.* dismay; alarm, fright; discouragement.

**sgominare** [A1] *tr.* to throw into disorder; to rout.

**sgomitolare** [A1 s] *tr.* to unwind (*e.g.* a bale of wool); *rfl.* (of ball of wool) to come unwound, to unwind.

**sgonfi-are** [A1 sc] *tr.* to deflate; to reduce; (fig.) to annoy, to vex; to bore; *rfl.* to be deflated; (of a swelling) to go down; to flatten out. **-amento** *m.* deflation; going flat; collapse.

**sgonfio** *apocop. part.* of **sgonfiare**; deflated; flattened; gone soft and flabby; punctured; emptied.

**sgonnell-are** [A1] *intr.* (*aux.* avere) (of a woman) to gad about, to be flighty. **-ona** *f.* gad-about; flighty woman.

**sgorbia** *f.* gouge; chisel.

**sgo·rbi-o** *m.* blot; scrawl; crossing out; daub; (of a person) a 'fright'. **-are** [A4] *tr.* to blot; to scrawl upon; to daub.

**sgor-go** *m.* (*pl.* **-ghi**) pouring; gush; *adv. phr. a —*, abundantly, freely. **-gare** [A2 c] *intr.* (*aux.* essere) to gush; to spout; to spring; to well up; to flow; *tr.* to disgorge; to pour out.

**sgovern-o** *m.* misgovernment; mismanagement. **-are** [A1] *tr.* to misgovern; to mismanage.

**sgozz-are** [A1 c] *tr.* to cut the throat of; (fig.) to bleed (by usury). **-atore** *m.* cut-throat. **-ino** *m.* usurer.

**sgradevole** *adj.* unpleasant; disagreeable.

**sgrad-ire** [D2] *tr.* to be displeased with; not to welcome; not to return or respond to; *intr.* (*aux.* essere; *prep.* a) to be displeasing or unwelcome (to). **-ito** *part. adj.* displeasing; unwelcome.

**sgraffiare** [A4] *tr.* to scratch; to steal; (colloq.) to 'pinch'.

**sgra·ffio** *m.* scratch.

**sgrammatic-are** [A2 s] *intr.* (*aux.* avere) to make mistakes in grammar. **-atura** *f.* mistake in grammar.

**sgranare** [A1] *tr.* to shell; to hull; to husk; *— il rosario*, to say one's rosary; to devour, to eat with great relish; *— gli occhi*, to open one's eyes wide; *rfl.* to crumble.

**sgranchire** [D2] *tr.* to stretch; *rfl.* to stretch oneself; to wake oneself up.

**sgranellare** [A1] *tr.* to pick (grains) from the ear; to pick (grapes) from the bunch.

**sgranocchiare** [A4] *tr.* to munch; to crunch; to eat with enjoyment.

**sgrassare** [A1] *tr.* to remove grease from, to skim the fat off.

**sgrav-are** [A1] *tr.* to unload; to lighten; *rfl.* to unburden oneself; *-arsi la coscienza*, to ease one's conscience. **-amento** *m.* lightening; alleviation; relief.

**sgra·vio** *m.* relief; alleviation; reduction; lightening; evacuation; justification.

**sgraziato** *part. adj.* awkward; clumsy; ungainly.

**sgretolare** [A1 sc] *tr.* to grind; to pound; *rfl.* to fall to pieces; to crumble.

**sgrid-are** [A1] *tr.* to scold; to rebuke; to reprimand; to rail at. **-ata** *f.* scolding; rebuke.

**sgrond-o** *m.* dripping; *terreno a —*, sloping, well-drained ground. **-are** [A1 c] *intr.* (*aux.* essere) to drip; to trickle; *tr.* to put to drip; to leave to drain.

**sgroppare**[1] [A1] *tr.* to unknot; to untie; to disentangle.

**sgroppare**[2] [A1] *intr.* (*aux.* avere) (of a horse) to kick out with both hind legs.

**sgrossare** [A1] *tr.* to whittle down; to shape; (sculp.) to rough out, to rough cast.

**sgrovigli-are** [A4], **-olare** [A1 s] *tr.* to disentangle; to untie.

**sgrugnata** *f.* (colloq.) blow in the face.

**sguaiat-o** *adj.* ill mannered; awkward; rude; shameless; unpleasant; *n.m.* lout. **-a·ggine** *f.* awkwardness; clumsiness.

**sguainare** [A1] *tr.* to unsheath.

**sgualcire** [D2] *tr.* to rumple.

**sgualdrina** *f.* strumpet; trollop.

**sguardo** *m.* look; glance; *bello —*, beautiful view.

**sguarnire** [D2] *tr.* to strip; to dismantle.

**sgua·tter-o** *m.* scullion; scullery-boy. **-a** *f.* scullery-maid.

**sguazzare** [A1] *intr.* (*aux.* avere) to splash about; to shake (of liquid in a vessel); to wallow; (fig.) *— nell'oro*, to be rolling in money; *tr.* to ford; to fritter away.

**sguinzagliare** [A4] *tr.* to let off the lead; to unleash.

**sgusci-are** [A3] *tr.* to shell; to hull; to husk; *intr.* (*aux.* essere) to slip away, to steal away; to slough, to shed (a skin). **-ato** *part. adj.* (of peas, beans, etc.) shelled; hollowed out.

**si**[1] *rfl. prn. conjunct.* himself; herself; itself; oneself; themselves; *recip.* each other; one another; *indef. prn.* one; people; we; they; *— dice*, they say, it is said; *— parla inglese*, English spoken.

**sì**[2] *affirm. part.* yes; *forse che —, forse che no*, maybe or maybe not; *mi par di —*, I think so; *adv. phr. — e no*, about, more or less; *n.m.* yes, affirmative answer.

**sì**[3] *adv.* so; thus; *— fatto* (or **siffatto**) such.

**si**[4] *m.* (mus.) the key of B.

**sia...sia** *conj.* both...and; either...or; whether...or.

**Siam** *pr.n.m.* (geog.) Siam. **-ese** *adj.* Siamese; *fratelli -esi*, Siamese twins; *n.m., f.* Siamese.

**sibarit-a** *m.* (*pl.* **-i**) sybarite.

**Sibe·ri-a** *pr.n.f.* (geog.) Siberia. **-ano** *adj., n.m.* Siberian.

**sibil-are** [A1 s] *intr.* (*aux.* avere) to whistle; to hiss; to whizz; to wheeze. **-ante** *part. adj.* whistling; *n.f.* sibilant.

**sibill-a** *f.* sibyl. **-ino** *adj.* sibylline.

**si·bilo** *m.* hiss; whistle; singing in the ears; wheezing.

**sica·rio** *m.* assassin, hired ruffian, cut-throat.

**sicché** *conj.* so that; so; then.

**siccità** *f.* drought, dryness; aridity; (fig.) dryness; (of style) flatness.

**siccome** *adv., conj.* as; since; for the reason that.

**Sici·li-a** *pr.n.f.* (geog.) Sicily. **-ano** *adj., n.m.* Sicilian.

**sicofante** *m.* spy, informer; sycophant.

**sicomoro** *m.* sycamore.

**sicumera** *f.* pomposity; complacency; self-satisfied air.

**sicura** *f.* safety-catch.

**sicur-o** *adj.* safe; secure; sure, confident, assured; reliable, trustworthy; bold; skilful; *adv.* undoubtedly, certainly; of course; *n.m.* safety; shelter, certainty. **-ezza** *f.* safety, security; certainty; *lampada di -ezza*, safety lamp; *rasoio di -ezza*, safety razor; *uscita di -ezza*, emergency exit; *agente di Pubblica Sicurezza*, policeman. **-tà** *f.* guarantee; security.

**side·r-eo** *adj.* of or pertaining to the stars. **-ale** *adj.* sidereal.

**siderite** *f.* loadstone.

**sider-urgi·a** *f.* iron-working. **-u·rgico** *adj.* iron-working; *stabilimento -urgico*, iron-works.

**sidro** *m.* cider.

**siepe** *f.* hedge; *— viva, — naturale*, quickset hedge; barrier, hurdle; obstacle; wall; *corsa su siepi*, hurdle-race; steeple-chase.

**siero** *m.* serum; whey. **-terapi·a** *f.* serum therapy.

**siesta** *f.* siesta; afternoon nap.

**siffatto** *adj.* such, of such a nature.

**sifi·lide** *f.* (med.) syphilis.

**sifone** *m.* syphon; waterspout; drain trap; U-bend.

**si·gar-o** *m.* cigar; **-a·io** *m.* cigar-maker. **-ẹtta** *f.* cigarette.
**sigill-o** *m.* seal; signet; stamp; mark. **-are** [A1] *tr.* to seal; to close; (colloq.) to round off; to stop up; to mark, to stamp.
**sigl-a** *f.* initials, monogram; abbreviation; signet. **-are** [A1] *tr.* to initial.
**signi·fero** *m.* (hist.) standard-bearer.
**signific-are** [A2 s] *tr.* to mean, to signify; to symbolize; to denote; to imply; to notify, to make known. **-ante** *part. adj.* expressive; signifying; significant. **-ativo** *adj.* significant; expressive; meaningful. **-ato** *part. adj.* signified; implied; made known; *n.m.* meaning, sense, purport.
**signọra** *f.* lady; *la Signora Rossi*, Mrs. Rossi; *Nostra Signora*, Our Lady; wife; woman; Madam.
**signọr-e** *m.* gentleman; *il signor Rossi è qui*, Mr. Rossi is here; *vivere da —*, to live like a lord; *Nostro Signore*, Our Lord. **-eggiare** [A3 c] *tr.* to rule; to master; to dominate; to govern; *intr.* (*aux.* avere) to rule; to be domineering.
**signori·a** *f.* Lordship; Ladyship; lordship, dominion, rule.
**signoril-e** *adj.* gentlemanlike; lordly; courtly; (fig.) distinguished; aristocratic. **-ità** *f.* refined manners; distinction.
**signorina** *f.* young lady; (as a title, equiv. to Miss); spinster; girl.
**signor-ino** *m.* young gentleman. **-otto** *m.* country squire.
**Sileno** *pr.n.m.* (myth.) Silenus.
**sile·nzi-o** *m.* silence. **-atọre** *m.* (techn.) silencer. **-ọso** *adj.* silent; quiet; noiseless.
**silente** *adj.* (poet.) silent.
**si·lfide** *f.* sylph; ballet dancer.
**si·lice** *f.* silex; flint.
**si·llab-a** *f.* syllable; *non dir —*, not to say a word. **-are** [A1 s] *tr.* to spell out; to pronounce by syllables. **-a·rio** *m.* spelling-book, elementary reading-book.
**silla·bico** *adj.* syllabic.
**si·llabo** *m.* syllabus; index.
**si·llog-e** *f.* collection. **-ịsmo** *m.* syllogism.
**silo** *m.* granary; silo.
**silo·fono** *m.* xylophone.
**silogli·ttica** *f.* fine wood-carving.
**sil-ografi·a** *f.* wood-engraving. **-o·grafo** *m.* wood-engraver.
**siloteca** *f.* museum containing specimens of wood.
**siluẹtta** *f.* silhouette.
**silur-o** *m.* torpedo. **-ante** *part. adj., n.f.* torpedo-boat. **-are** [A1] *tr.* to torpedo; (fig.) to cashier; (colloq.) to sack.
**silv-ano** *adj.* sylvan; rural. **-estre** *adj.* wild; rustic; of the woods.
**si·lvia**[1] *f.* wood anemone.
**Si·lvia** *pr.n.f.* Sylvia.
**silvicult-ọre** *m.* forester. **-ura** *f.* forestry, sylviculture.
**simbol-eggiare** [A3 c], **-iẓẓare** [A1] *tr.* to symbolize; to stand for, to represent.
**simbo·lico** *adj.* symbolic(al).
**si·mbol-o** *m.* symbol; emblem; type. **-ịsmo** *m.* symbolism.
**si·mil-e** *adj.* like; alike; such; similar; *n.m.* like; fellow; *i nostri -i*, our fellow-creatures. **-itu·dine** *f.* likeness; similarity; simile.
**simmetri·a** *f.* symmetry.
**simme·trico** *adj.* symmetric(al).
**Simọne** *pr.n.m.* Simon.
**simon-i·a** *f.* simony. **-eggiare** [A3 c] *intr.* (*aux.* avere) to practise simony.
**simpati·a** *f.* liking; sympathy.
**simpaticiẓẓare** [A1] *intr.* (*aux.* avere) to take a liking (to); *recip. rfl.* to take a liking to each other.
**simpa·tico** *adj.* nice; pleasant; agreeable; congenial; likeable.
**simpo·sio** *m.* banquet; symposium.
**simulacro** *m.* simulacrum; image; semblance; mere pretence, sham.
**simul-are** [A1 s] *tr.* to feign, to simulate, to sham. **-ato** *part. adj.* feigned; false; sham; counterfeit; faked; *asta -ata*, mock auction. **-aziọne** *f.* simulation.
**simulta·ne-o** *adj.* simultaneous; *n.m.* simultaneous interpreter. **-amẹnte** *adv.* simultaneously. **-ità** *f.* simultaneousness.
**sinagoga** *f.* synagogue.
**sincer-o** *adj.* pure; genuine, true; sincere, candid, unfeigned. **-amẹnte** *adv.* sincerely; truly; candidly. **-are** [A1] *tr.* to convince; to assure; to absolve; *rfl.* (*prep.* di) to make sure (of). **-ità** *f.* sincerity; truth; candour.
**sinchẹ̀** *conj.* see **finchẹ̀**.
**si·ncop-e** *f.* syncope. **-are** [A1 s] *tr.* to syncopate. **-ato** *part. adj.* syncopated. **-atura** *f.* syncopation.
**sincron-i·a** *f.* (phys.) synchrony. **-ịsmo** *m.* synchronization, synchronizing. **-iẓẓare** [A1] *tr., intr.* (*aux.* avere) to synchronize.
**si·ncrono** *adj.* synchronous; contemporary, contemporaneous.
**si·ndac-o** *m.* mayor, Lord Mayor; syndic; auditor. **-a·bile** *adj.* subject to inspection, censure or audit; verifiable. **-ale** *adj.* syndical. **-alịsmo** *m.* syndicalism; trade-unionism. **-amẹnto** *m.* inspection, audit. **-are** [A2 s] *tr.* to audit, to inspect. to censure. **-ato** *m.* syndicate; trade union; association; inspection, audit; mayor's (term of).
**si·ndone** *f.* shroud, winding sheet.
**sinecura** *f.* sinecure.
**sine·drio** *m.* sanhedrin.
**sinfoni·a** *f.* symphony.
**sinfo·nico** *adj.* symphonic.
**singalẹse** *adj.* of or pertaining to Ceylon (Sri Lanka); *n.m., f.* Sinhalese.
**singhiozz-o** *m.* sob; hiccup; *avere il —*, to have hiccups. **-are** [A1] *intr.* (*aux.* avere) to sob; to hiccup.
**singolar-e** *adj.* singular; peculiar; quaint; single; *n.m.* (gramm.) singular; (tennis) singles. **-ità** *f.* singularity. **-mẹnte** *adv.* singularly; singly.
**si·ngolo** *adj.* single, individual; *pl.* individuals.
**singulto** *m.* hiccup; sob.
**siniscal-co** (*pl.* **-chi**) seneschal.
**sinistra** *f.* see under **sinistro**.
**sinistr-o** *adj.* left, left-hand; crooked; sinister, ominous; lurid; contrary, unfavourable; *n.m.* accident, disaster. **-a** *f.* left hand; left side; (pol.) left; *a -a*, to the left; left wing; (naut.) port. **-amẹnte** *adv.* ominously, unfavourably. **-are** [A1] *intr.* (*aux.* avere) (of a horse) to jib, to shy; *rfl.* to put oneself out. **-ato** *part. adj.* injured; *n.m.* victim of accident, disaster, bombing; *i -ati*, the injured.
**sino** *adv.* even; *prep.* *— qui*, up to here; (*foll. by prep.* 'a') till, until; up to, as far as (*cf.* **fino**).
**sinodo** *m.* synod.
**sino·logo** *m.* Chinese scholar; sinologue.
**sino·nimo** *adj.* synonymous; *n.m.* synonym.
**sino·pia** *f.* sinopite; red ochre, rubric; (art) sinopia.
**sin-ossi** *f.* synopsis. **-o·ttico** *adj.* synoptic.
**sin-tassi** *f.* syntax. **-ta·ttico** *adj.* syntactic.
**si·ntesị** *f.* synthesis; résumé, summary.
**sinte·tico** *adj.* synthetic; (art) generalized, using only outlines.
**si·ntom-o** *m.* symptom; sign, token. **-a·tico** *adj.* symptomatic.
**sinuọs-o** *adj.* sinuous, winding; concave. **-ità** *f.* bend; curl; curving (of the lips).
**sipa·rio** *m.* curtain; (theatr.) *cala il —*, the curtain falls; (fig.) veil; covering.
**Siracusa** *pr.n.f.* (geog.) Syracuse.
**Sire** *m.* Sire (form of address to a King).
**sirena** *f.* (myth.) siren; mermaid; siren, hooter.
**Si·ria** *pr.n.f.* (geog.) Syria.
**sir-i·aco** *adj., n.m.* Syriac. **-iano** *adj., n.m.* Syrian.
**siring-a** *f.* panpipes, syrinx; (med.) syringe; (eng.) grease gun; (bot.) lilac.
**Si·rio** *pr.n.m.* (astron.) Sirius, Dog-Star.

**Si·sifo** *pr.n.m.* (myth.) Sisyphus.
**si·ṣmico** *adj.* seismic.
**siṣm-o** *m.* earthquake, earth tremor. **-ografi·a** *f.* seismography. **-o·grafo** *m.* seismograph. **-o·logo** *m.* seismologist.
**sissignọr-a** yes, madam. **-e** yes, sir.
**sissitura** *f.* tuck (to shorten a garment).
**sistem-a** *m.* (*pl.* **-i**) system; method; rule; arrangement. **-are** [A1 s] *tr.* to arrange; to regulate; to settle; to put up (for the night); to kill; *rfl.* to settle down; (fig.) to marry. **-a·tico** *adj.* systematic. **-aziọne** *f.* regularization; arrangement; settlement; lay-out; set-up.
**sistino** *adj.* Sistine; Sixtine.
**sitibọndo** *adj.* thirsty; (fig.) eager, thirsting.
**sito**[1] *m.* place, site, spot; position; *adj.* situated; placed; sited.
**sito**[2] *m.* bad, musty smell.
**situ-are** [A6] *tr.* to place, to site; to set. **-aziọne** *f.* situation; position; list, schedule.
**Sivi·glia** *pr.n.f.* (geog.) Seville.
**siẓẓa** *f.* cold blast of wind, esp. the tramontana.
**ski** *m.pl.* see **sci.**
**ṣlabbrare** [A1] *tr.* to damage the edge, brim or mouth of; to enlarge, to open out; *intr.* (*aux.* essere) to overflow, to spill over.
**ṣlacciare** [A3] *tr.* to unlace, to untie; (fig.) to set free.
**ṣlamare** [A1] *intr.* (*aux.* essere) (of ground) to fall; to collapse (in a landslide).
**sla·nc-io** *m.* rush; dash; bound; onset; jump; start; impulse. **-are** [A3] *tr.* to hurl, to fling; to throw; *rfl.* to rush; (fig.) to be bold. **-ato** *part. adj.* slim; slender; graceful; well-built.
**ṣlargare** [A2] *tr.* to enlarge; to widen; — *la folla*, to disperse the crowd.
**ṣlattare** [A1] *tr.* to wean.
**ṣlavato** *adj.* pale, colourless; washed out; wan.
**ṣlavina** *f.* avalanche; landslide.
**ṣlav-o** *adj.*, *n.m.* Slav. **-iṣmo** *m.* (pan)slavism.
**ṣleal-e** *adj.* unfaithful; disloyal; unfair, dishonest. **-tà** *f.* disloyalty.
**ṣleg-are** [A2] *tr.* to unbind; to untie; to undo; to loosen; (fig.) to release. **-ato** *part. adj.* loose; unbound.
**Ṣlesia** *pr.n.f.* (geog.) Silesia.
**ṣlitt-a** *f.* sledge, sleigh; slide. **-are** [A1] *intr.* (*aux.* avere, essere) to sledge; to slide; (motor.) to skid. **-ata** *f.* (motor.) skid.
**ṣlog-are** [A2] *tr.* to dislocate, to displace. **-amẹnto** *m.*, **-atura** *f.* dislocation.
**ṣloggiare** [A3] *tr.* to dislodge; *intr.* (*aux.* avere) to decamp, to clear out.
**ṣlo·ggio** *m.* (leg.) eviction; *diffida di* —, notice to quit.
**ṣlombare** [A1 c] *tr.* to break the back of; to wear out; to exhaust; *intr.* (*aux.* essere), *rfl.* to hurt one's back; to exhaust oneself.
**Slov-a·cchia** *pr.n.f.* (geog.) Slovakia. **-acco** *adj.*, *n.m.* (*pl.* **-acchi**) Slovak. **-ẹno** *adj.*, *n.m.* Slovene.
**ṣlungare** [A2] *tr.* to prolong; to lengthen; *rfl.* to stretch.
**ṣmaccato** *adj.* excessive; nauseous.
**ṣmacchi-are**[1] [A3] *tr.* to remove stains from; to clean, to scour. **-atọre** *m.* (dry-)cleaner; scourer; detergent; cleanser.
**ṣmacchiare**[2] [A4] *tr.* to clear of brushwood, trees, etc.
**ṣmac-co** *m.* (*pl.* **-chi**) affront; insult; shame; disgrace.
**ṣmagli-are** [A4] *tr.* to undo (knitting); to undo the meshes of; to break the links of; to take (fishes) out of a net; to ladder (a stocking); *rfl.* to come unravelled; to ladder (of a stocking); *intr.* (*aux.* avere) to shine brightly; to sparkle. **-ante** *part. adj.* shining, brilliant; dazzling; gaudy.
**ṣmagnetiẓẓare** [A1] *tr.* to demagnetize.
**ṣmagr-ire** [D2] *intr.* (*aux.* essere) to grow thin, to lose weight; *tr.* to make thin. **-imẹnto** *m.* emaciation; loss of weight; exhaustion.
**ṣmaltare** [A1] *tr.* to enamel; — *a vetrino*, to glaze.
**ṣmaltire** [D2] *tr.* to sell off; to get rid of; to digest.
**ṣmalto** *m.* enamel, enamel-work; glaze; pavement; (paint.) colour, paint.
**ṣmancer-i·a** *f.* affectation; simpering; mawkishness. **-ọso** *adj.* affected; mincing.
**ṣmangiare** [A3] *tr.* to eat away; to corrode; to wear down.
**ṣma·ni-a** *f.* craze; rage; frenzy; eager desire; restlessness. **-are** [A4] *intr.* (*aux.* avere) to rave; to be delirious; to be restless; to desire ardently.
**ṣmaniọso** *adj.* filled with eager longing; frenzied.
**ṣmantellare** [A1] *tr.* (industr.) to dismantle.
**ṣmargiass-o** *m.* bully; blusterer; braggart. **-ata** *f.* bullying action. **-eri·a** *f.* boasting; swagger, bravado.
**ṣmargin-are** [A1 s] *tr.* (bookb.) to trim the margins of.
**ṣmarra** *f.* (pop.) see **marra.**
**ṣmarr-ire** [D2] to mislay; to lose; to mislead; to bewilder; — *la vista a*, to dazzle; *rfl.* to lose one's way; to become confused. **-ito** *part. adj.* lost; bewildered; strayed; *ufficio di oggetti -iti*, lost property office.
**ṣmascellare** [A1] *rfl.* to dislocate one's jaw; (fig.) *smascellarsi dalle risa*, to split one's sides with laughter.
**ṣmascherare** [A1 s] *tr.* to unmask.
**ṣmatton-are** [A1 c] *tr.* to demolish. **-ato** *part. adj.* demolished; *pavimento -ato*, broken pavement.
**ṣmembrare** [A1] *tr.* to dismember; to partition, to split up.
**ṣmemor-are** [A1 s] *intr.* (*aux.* avere) to lose one's memory. **-ata·ggine** *f.* forgetfulness; loss of memory; bewilderment. **-ato** *part. adj.* forgetful; absent-minded; scatterbrained; silly.
**ṣment-ire** [D2] *tr.* to deny; to contradict; to give the lie to; *rfl.* to contradict oneself; to be unworthy of oneself; to break one's word. **-ita** *f.* denial; contradiction.
**ṣmerald-o** *m.* emerald. **-ino** *adj.* emerald green.
**ṣmerciare** [A3] *tr.* (comm.) to sell off; to deal in.
**ṣme·rcio** *m.* (comm.) sale; selling off.
**ṣmeri·gli-o** *m.* emery; *tela* —, emery cloth. **-are** [A4] *tr.* to rub with emery; to grind (glass); to polish. **-ato** *part. adj.* polished; ground; (glassm.) frosted; *carta -ata*, emery paper.
**ṣmerl-o** *m.* (needlew.) purl; picot edging; scallop; indented edge. **-are** *tr.*; *intr.* (*aux.* avere) (needlew.) to trim with purl, buttonhole or picot edging. **-ato** *part. adj. fazzoletto -ato*, lace-edged handkerchief; *torre -ata*, embattled (crenellated) tower.
**ṣmẹsso** *part.* of **smẹttere**; *adj.* (of clothes) cast-off, left-off; out of practice.
**ṣmẹttere** [C20] *tr.* to leave off; to give up; (colloq.) to 'drop'; to stop; *smèttila !*, stop it!
**ṣmeẓẓare** [A1] *tr.* to halve; to divide.
**ṣmidollare** [A1] *tr.* to remove the marrow from; to remove the crumb from (a loaf); *rfl.* to lose strength.
**ṣmilitariẓẓare** [A1] *tr.* to demilitarize.
**ṣmilzo** *adj.* thin, slim; slender; spare.
**ṣminare** [A1] *tr.* to clear of mines.
**ṣminu-ire** [D2] *tr.* to diminish, to lessen. **-ito** *part. adj.* diminished; enfeebled.
**ṣminuzz-are** [A1] *tr.* to mince; to hash; to break into little pieces; (fig.) to chew over, to discuss in minute detail; *rfl.* to break into tiny fragments; to turn to spray. **-atọre** *m.* mincer, mincing machine. **-olare** [A1 s] *tr.* to crush, to grind; to pulverize.
**Ṣmirne** *pr.n.f.* (geog.) Smyrna.
**ṣmist-are** [A1] *tr.* to sort out; to sort (letters); *tr.* (rlwy.) to

shunt. **-amęnto** *m.* sorting; (rlwy.) shunting; (mil.) *posto di -amento*, clearing-station.
**şmişurato** *adj.* immense, boundless; enormous.
**şmobili-are** [A4] *tr.* to empty of furniture. **-ato** *part. adj.* empty, unfurnished.
**şmobilitare** [A1 s] *tr.* (mil.) to demobilize.
**şmoccol-are** [A1 s] *tr.* to snuff; *intr.* (*aux.* avere) (fam.) to swear, to curse. **-atǫio** *m.* suffers.
**şmodato** *adj.* immoderate.
**şmoderat-o** *adj.* excessive; intemperate; immoderate. **-ęzza** *f.* excess; lack of moderation; exaggeration.
**şmoking** *m. indecl.* dinner jacket.
**şmonta·ggio** *m.* dismounting; disassembling.
**şmontare** [A1 c] *tr.* to take down; to bring down; — *le scale*, to go downstairs; to take to pieces, to dismantle; (fig.) to discharge; to deflate; *intr.* (*aux.* essere) to dismount; to get out; to alight; to go down; (of colours) to fade; (of prices) to drop.
**şmo·rfi-a** *f.* grimace; affected smile or gesture; languishing look; pose. **-ǫso** *adj.* affected; mincing; skittish; wheedling; *n.m.* wheedler.
**şmorto** *adj.* pale; wan; listless, lifeless; dull; dim; (of colour) mat.
**şmorz-are** [A1] *tr.* to extinguish; to dim; to shade; to appease, to quench; to slake; to tone down; *rfl.* to grow fainter; to die away; to be extinguished. **-atǫ·re** *m.* damper; *-atore di scosse*, shock absorber.
**şmosso** *part.* of **smuo·vere**; *adj.* displaced, removed, shifted; agitated; dislocated; sprained.
**şmozzare** [A1] *tr.* to lop off; to chip off; to chop off.
**şmozzicare** [A2 sc] *tr.* to cut to pieces; to mutilate; to maim; to clip.
**smu·ngere** [C5] *tr.* to drain; to suck dry; to milk dry; (fig.) to exhaust; to fleece.
**şmunto** *part.* of **smu·ngere**; *adj.* pale, emaciated; haggard; exhausted; lean, scraggy; impoverished.
**şmuo·vere** [C15] *tr.* to shift; to displace; to move, to stir; to set in motion; to affect, to excite; to deter; *rfl.* to be moved; to shift.
**şmuss-are** [A1] *tr.* to blunt; (fig.) to smooth, to soften. **-atura** *f.* bevelling; chamfered edge. **-o** *apocop. part.*, *adj.* bevelled, chamfered; blunted at the corners; broken; (fig.) softened.
**şnatur-are** [A1] *tr.* to alter the nature of; to change; to distort; *intr.* (*aux.* essere) to degenerate. **-amęnto** *m.* change of nature; perversion. **-ato** *part. adj.* unnatural; cruel; monstrous.
**şnebbiare** [A4c] *tr.* to clear fog from; to dispel the mist from; (fig.) — *la mente*, to clear the mind; *rfl.* to become clear.
**şnell-o** *adj.* nimble; brisk; active; quick, agile; slim; slender. **-ęzza** *f.* nimbleness; agility; slenderness.
**şnerv-are** [A1] *tr.* to exhaust; to enfeeble; to enervate; (colloq.) to get on the nerves of; to cut the tendons of. **-ante** *part. adj.* enervating; enfeebling. **-atęzza** *f.* debility, weakness; prostration.
**şnidare** [A1] *tr.* to dislodge; to drive from the nest; to drive from shelter; – *una lepre*, to start a hare; *intr.* (*aux.* essere), *rfl.* to come out (from a shelter).
**şnob** *m. indecl.* snob; member of the 'smart set'; *adj. indecl.* smart, fashionable. **-işmo** *m.* snobbery.
**şnocciolare** [A3 s] *tr.* to remove the kernel from, to stone; (fig.) to talk glibly about; to pay out readily.
**şnod-are** [A1] *tr.* to untie; to loosen; to unravel; to loosen up; *rfl.* to come loose; to become supple; to wriggle. **-ato** *part. adj.* loosened; flexible; supple. **-atura** *f.* loosening; suppleness; articulation.
**şnudare** [A1] *tr.* to lay bare; to unsheath.
**soav-e**[1] *adj.* sweet, soft; mild; gentle. **-ità** *f.* softness; sweetness.
**Soave**[2] *pr.n.m.* white wine of the region of that name.
**sobbalz-are** [A1] *intr.* (*aux.* avere) to jolt; to jerk; to bounce; to leap; to give a start. **-o** *m.* start, jump; jolt; jerk.
**sobbarcare** [A2] *tr.* to impose a burden on; *rfl.* to take on responsibility.
**sobbǫr-go** *m.* (*pl.* **-ghi**) suburb.
**sobillare** [A1] *tr.* to instigate; to incite (to rebellion).
**so·bri-o** *adj.* temperate, sober. **-età** *f.* temperance, moderation, sobriety.
**socchiu·dere** [C3] *tr.* to half-close; to leave ajar; to draw to.
**socchiuso** *part.* of **socchiu·dere**; *adj.* half-closed; half-open; ajar.
**soccǫmbere** [B1] *intr.* (*aux.* essere; *prep.* a) to succumb; to give way (to); to be overcome; to die.
**soccǫrr-ere** [C5] *tr.* to help; to assist; to relieve; to succour; *intr.* (*aux.* avere, essere) to come to mind; *recip. rfl.* to help one another. **-ęvole** *adj.* helpful; charitable.
**soccǫrso** *part.* of **soccǫrrere**; *adj.* helped, relieved; succoured; *n.m.* help, aid; relief; *uscita di* —, emergency exit; *primo* —, first-aid; *società di mutuo* —, benefit society.
**so·cer-a** *f.*, **-o** *m.* see **suocer-a -o.**
**social-e** *adj.* social; corporate; gregarious; *assistente* —, welfare officer; *attivo* —, partnership assets; *capitale* —, capital of company; *statuto* —, articles of association. **-işmo** *m.* socialism. **-ista** *adj.*; *n.m.*, *f.* socialist.
**socializzare** [A1] *tr.* to socialize; to collectivize; to nationalize.
**societ-à** *f. indecl.* society; community; companionship; club; party; company, firm; — *anonima*, joint stock company; — *di mutuo soccorso*, Friendly Society; *Società delle Nazioni*, League of Nations; — *edilizia*, building society.
**sociẹvole** *adj.* sociable; companionable.
**so·c-io** *m.* (*pl.* **-i**) member; associate; fellow; partner.
**sociol-ogi·a** *f.* sociology. **-o·gico** *adj.* sociological.
**socio·logo** *m.* sociologist.
**So·cr-ate** *pr.n.m.* Socrates. **-a·tico** *adj.* Socratic.
**soda** *f.* soda; sodium carbonate; soda-water.
**soda·glia** *f.* untilled land.
**sodal-e** *m.* fellow, companion, colleague. **-i·zio** *m.* association; brotherhood; guild.
**sodamęnte** *adv.* firmly; solidly; compactly.
**sodare** [A1] *tr.* to consolidate; to strengthen, to make firm.
**so(d)dis-fare** [B14] *tr.* to satisfy; to gratify; to fulfil; to comply with; *intr.* (*aux.* avere; *prep.* a) to satisfy; — *al proprio dovere*, to do one's duty. **-facente** *part. adj.* satisfactory; satisfying. **-facimęnto** *m.* satisfaction; fulfilment; discharge (of debt or obligation). **-faziǫne** *f.* satisfaction; gratification; consolation, pleasure; reparation.
**so·dio** *m.* sodium.
**sod-o** *adj.* solid, firm, substantial; strong; hard; heavy; *uovo* —, hard-boiled egg; *adv. parlar* —, to speak clearly and firmly; *lavorare* —, to work hard; *n.m.* firm ground; foundation; (fig.) *sul* —, seriously. **-ęzza** *f.* solidity, firmness; compactness; steadiness.
**sofà** *f. indecl.* sofa; settee; couch.
**sofferen-te** *adj.* suffering; ailing, unwell, sickly; enduring. **-za** *f.* suffering, pain; patience; endurance.
**sofferm-are** [A1] *tr.* to detain; *rfl.* to stay a while; to pause for a moment; to linger. **-ata** *f.* short stay; pause; stop.
**sofferto** *part.* of **soffrire**; *adj.* suffered; endured.
**soffi-are** [A4] *intr.* (*aux.* avere) to blow; to breathe; to puff, to pant; *tr.* to blow out; to

blow; (of a cat) to spit; to fan (flames); to whisper, to prompt; *rfl.* (*dat.* of *prn.* 'si') to prime; *-arsi il naso,* to blow one's nose. **-amẹnto** *m.* blowing; *-amento di maldicenza,* breath of scandal. **-ata** *f.* puff; breath (of wind). **-atọre** *m.* blower; (theatr.) prompter.

**so·ffice** *adj.* soft; gentle; light; tender; yielding; *n.m.* softness; *dormire nel —,* to sleep soft.

**soffieri·a** *f.* bellows.

**soffiẹtto** *m.* see under **sọffio.**

**sọffi-o** *m.* puff; breath; breathing; blowing; breath of wind; breath of air; whiff; (fig.) *in un —,* in an instant. **-ẹtto** *m.* bellows; (journalistic) 'puff'. **-ọne** *m.* bellows-pipe; forge-blower; (geol.) jet of steam or gas; (fig.) spy; (bot.) dandelion.

**soffitt-a** *f.* garret, attic; lumber-room. **-o** *m.* ceiling; false ceiling.

**soffoc-are** [A2 s] *tr.* to suffocate; to strangle; to stifle; to choke; to suppress; to quell; to hush up; *intr.* (*aux.* avere) to feel suffocated. **-amẹnto** *m.* choking; suffocating. **-ante** *part. adj.* suffocating; stifling; stuffy, sultry. **-atọre** *m.* strangler; suffocator. **-aziọne** *f.* suffocation.

**soffọndere** [C5] *tr.* to suffuse.

**soffreddare** [A1 c] *tr., rfl., intr.* (*aux.* essere) to cool; to cool down.

**soffregare** [A2] *tr.* to rub gently.

**soffri·bile** *adj.* endurable; bearable.

**soffri·ggere** [C12] *tr., intr.* (*aux.* avere) to fry lightly; (joc.) to grumble, to complain.

**soffrire** [D1] *tr.* to suffer; to endure, to bear, to stand; *intr.* (*aux.* avere) to suffer; to grieve; to take harm, to deteriorate.

**soffritto** *part.* of **soffri·ggere;** *adj.* lightly fried.

**soffuṣo** *part.* of **soffọndere;** *adj.* suffused; sprinkled.

**sof-i·a**[1] *f.* wisdom. **-iṣma, -iṣmo** *m.* sophism. **-i·stica** *f.* sophistry; dialectic. **-isticare** [A2 s] *intr.* (*aux.* avere) to cavil; *tr.* to adulterate; to sophisticate.

**Sofi·a**[2] *pr.n.f.* Sophia.

**So·focle** *pr.n.m.* Sophocles.

**soggettivo** *adj.* subjective.

**soggett-o** *adj.* subject, subjected; subordinate; liable; amenable; *n.m.* subject; subject matter, topic; (derog.) individual. **-are** [A1] *tr.* to subject; to subdue.

**soggeziọne** *f.* subjection; awe; timidity; shyness; uneasiness; embarrassment; *mi fa —,* he makes me feel shy.

**sogghign-are** [A5] *intr.* (*aux.* avere) to smile contemptuously; to grin maliciously; to laugh up one's sleeve; to sneer; to jeer. **-o** *m.* grin; grimace; sneer.

**soggiac-ẹre** [B15] *intr.* (*aux.* essere; *prep.* a) to be subject (to); to be liable; to succumb; to yield; to put up (with). **-imẹnto** *m.* subjection.

**soggiog-are** [A2] *tr.* to subjugate; (fig.) to subdue. **-amẹnto** *m.* subjugation; subjection.

**soggiọrn-o** *m.* stay, sojourn; resort; residence; *stanza di —,* living room; bed-sitting room. **-are** [A1 c] *intr.* (*aux.* avere) to stay, to sojourn; to reside.

**soggiu·ngere** [C5] *tr.* to say in addition, to add; to subjoin.

**soggiunt-o** *part.* of **soggiu·ngere;** *adj.* added; subjoined. **-ivo** *adj., n.m.* (gramm.) subjunctive.

**sogguardare** [A1] *tr.* to eye shyly; to eye slyly; to peer up at.

**sogguatare** [A1] *tr.* to eye with suspicion, scorn, fear.

**so·glia** *f.* threshold; doorstep; window-sill.

**so·glio** *m.* throne; (poet.) palace; court.

**so·gliola** *f.* sole (fish).

**sognare** [A5 c] *tr., intr.* (*aux.* avere) to dream; to dream of; to dream up; to muse; to long for; *rfl.* (*dat.* of *prn.* 'si') to imagine, to fancy (to oneself).

**sọgno** *m.* dream; vision; reverie; fancy; illusion; fable; vision, fantasy; *neppure per — !,* by no means!

**sol** *m.* (mus.) sol (the key of G).

**sola** *f.* See under **solo.**

**sola·io** *m.* (bldg.) loft; garret; attic; frame of a ceiling; *su in —,* up in the attic.

**solamẹnte** *adv.* only; merely; solely.

**solare** *adj.* relating to the sun, solar; *orologio —,* sundial.

**sola·rio** *m.* sun parlour; sun terrace.

**solat-a** *f.* long spell in hot sunshine; sunstroke. **-i·o** *m.* sunny spot; *adj.* sunny, facing south.

**solc-are** [A2 c] *tr.* to plough; to dig; (fig.) to furrow, to line. **-ata** *f.* furrow; wake; track. **-ato** *part. adj.* furrowed; lined; wrinkled.

**sọl-co** *m.* (*pl.* **-chi**) furrow; track; (fig.) *uscir dal —,* to leave the beaten track; streak; wrinkle. **-co·metro** *m.* (naut.) log.

**soldat-o** *m.* soldier; *pl.* troops, army. **-ẹsca** *f.* soldiery; troops; undisciplined soldiers. **-escamẹnte** *adv.* in soldierly fashion. **-ẹsco** (*m.pl.* **-ẹschi**) soldierly; soldier-like.

**soldo** *m.* coin of small value; (fig.) penny, copper; pay; *essere al — di,* to be in the pay of; *prendere il — di,* to enlist; *pl.* money; wages.

**sọl-e** *m.* sun; *orologio al —,* sundial; sunshine, sunlight. **-ẹcchio** *m.* shield from the sun's rays; canopy.

**soleciṣmo** *m.* solecism.

**soleggi-are** [A3 c] *tr.* to sun, to spread in the sun; *intr.* (*aux.* avere) to bask in the sun. **-ato** *part. adj.* sunny.

**solenn-e** *adj.* solemn; grave; formal; *abito —,* ceremonial dress; (colloq.) thorough; terrific. **-emẹnte** *adv.* solemnly. **-ità** *f.* solemnity; celebration. **-iẓẓare** [A1] *tr.* to solemnize.

**solẹre** [B30] *intr.* (*aux.* essere) to be in the habit of; to be wont to; *impers. come suole accadere,* as usually happens.

**solerte** *adj.* diligent, industrious; enterprising; ingenious; careful.

**sole·rzia** *f.* diligence; industriousness; attention to detail.

**solẹtt-a**[1] *f.* sole of a stocking; (shoem.) insole. **-are** [A1 c] *tr.* to furnish (a shoe) with a sock.

**solẹtta**[2] *f.* woman all alone.

**solẹtto** *adj.* see under **solo.**

**solfa** *m. indecl.* gamut; sol-fa; musical scale.

**solf-ara** *f.* sulphur deposit. **-atara** *f.* (geog.) fumerole.

**solfẹggi-o** *m.* sol-fa; solfeggio. **-are** [A3 c] *intr.* (*aux.* avere) to sing sol-fa.

**solfito** *m.* sulphite.

**sọlf-o** *m.* sulphur. **-erino** *m.* sulphur match. **-o·rico** *adj.* sulphuric. **-orọso** *adj.* sulphurous. **-uro** *m.* sulphide.

**so·lid-o** *adj.* solid; firm; compact; substantial; strong; safe; sound; *colori -i* fast colours; *n.m.* solid; *in —,* jointly. **-ale** *adj.* (leg.) joint and several. **-are** [A1 s] *tr.* to solidify; to make firm, to strengthen. **-arietà** *f.* solidarity; loyalty; (leg.) joint and several liability. **-a·rio** *adj.* (leg.) joint and several. **-ẹzza, -ità** *f.* solidity; firmness; strength; steadiness. **-ificare** [A2 s] *tr., rfl.* to solidify.

**solilo·quio** *m.* soliloquy.

**solin-go** *adj.* (*m.pl.* **-ghi**) lonely; solitary; alone.

**solino** *m.* starched, detachable collar or cuff.

**solista** *m., f.* See under **solo.**

**solita·rio** *adj.* solitary; lonely; alone; secluded; deserted; *n.m.* hermit; solitary; recluse; (cards) solitaire, patience.

**so·lito** *part.* of **solere**; *adj. era — venire ogni mattina,* he used to come every morning; usual, habitual; *n.m.* the usual thing; custom, habit; *adv. phr. al —, di —,* as a rule, usually.

**solitu·dine** *f.* solitude, loneliness; solitary place; seclusion; wilderness, wild.

**sollazz-o** *m.* pleasure; amusement, recreation, pastime; sport. **-are** [A1] *tr.* to amuse, to divert, to entertain. **-ẹvole** *adj.* amusing, entertaining; pleasant; merry, jolly.

**sollẹcit-o** *adj.* prompt, speedy; ready; eager; solicitous; having

the habit of early rising. **-amẹnte** *adv.* readily; promptly; eagerly. **-are** [A1 sc] *tr.* to hasten; to urge; to request, to entreat. **-aziọne** *f.* entreaty; solicitation. **-u·dine** *f.* speed, readiness, promptness; diligence; despatch; solicitude, care; eagerness.

**solleọne** *m.* dog-days.

**sollẹtic-o** *m.* tickling; stimulus; *fare il —*, to tickle. **-amẹnto** *m.* tickling, excitement. **-ante** *part. adj.* appetising; exciting. **-are** [A2 sc] *tr.* to tickle; (fig.) to excite; to flatter; to tempt.

**sollev-are** [A1] *tr.* to lift; to raise; to heave up; to relieve, to comfort; *rfl.* to rise; to rebel; to get up. **-ato** *part. adj.* raised; exalted, eminent; rebellious; in high spirits; *n.m.pl.* insurgents. **-atọre** *m.* agitator; leader of revolt. **-aziọne** *f.* rising, revolt, insurrection, rise, rising; elevation.

**sollievo** *m.* relief; alleviation; comfort.

**sollu·cher-o** *m.* thrill; emotional excitement; *andare in —*, to go into raptures. **-are** [A1 s] *tr.* to move, to touch emotionally.

**sọl-o** *adj.* alone; only; unique, sole; *una -a volta*, once only; single, one; *n.m.* (the) only man; *adv.* only; *— che*, provided that. **-a** *f.* (the) only woman; (the) only thing. **-amẹnte** *adv.* only; merely; solely. **-ẹtto** *adj. dim.* all alone; *solo soletto*, all on one's own. **-ista** *m., f.* (*pl.* **-isti, -iste**) soloist. **-i·stico** *adj.* (mus.) for soloist.

**Solọne** *pr.n.m.* Solon.

**solsti·zio** *m.* solstice.

**soltanto** *adv.* only; merely; solely.

**solu·bile** *adj.* soluble.

**solutivo** *adj., n.m.* laxative.

**so·luto** *part.* of **so·lvere**; *adj.* loose; (fig.) solved; *digiuno —*, broken fast.

**soluziọne** *f.* solution; *— madre*, stock solution; substance dissolved; break in continuity; decision, resolve.

**so·lv-ere** [C14] *tr.* to dissolve; to solve; to settle (debt); to liquefy; *— il digiuno*, to break one's fast. **-ente** *part. adj.* dissolving; *n.m.* solvent. **-enza, -ibilità** *f.* solvency.

**som-a** *f.* burden; load; weight. **-aro** *m.* ass, donkey; (fig.) ass, fool.

**Soma·lia** *pr.n.f.* (geog.) Somaliland.

**somigli-are** [A4] *tr.* to resemble, to be like; *intr.* (*aux.* avere; *prep.* a) to resemble, to be similar (to). **-ante** *part. adj.* (*prep.* a) similar, like; resembling; *adv.* similarly; *n.m.* the same. **-anza** *f.* resemblance, likeness.

**sọmm-a** *f.* addition; sum; *segno di —* plus sign; total; amount; conclusion; gist; comprehensive treatise; *adv. phr. in —*, in short, after all. **-amẹnte** *adv.* in the highest degree, highly; extremely. **-are** [A1 c] *tr.* to add up; to sum up; to reckon; *intr.* (*aux.* essere; *prep.* a) to amount (to). **-ato** *part. adj.* added up; *tutto -ato*, all in all.

**somma·ri-o** *adj.* summary, compendious; brief; scant; *n.m.* summary, synopsis; epitome; précis; table of contents. **-amẹnte** *adv.* in short; summarily.

**somme·rg-ere** [C4] *tr.* to submerge; to sink; to flood, to swamp; (fig.) to overwhelm; *rfl.* to be submerged; to sink. **-i·bile** *adj.* submersible; *n.m.* submarine.

**somme·rs-o** *part.* **somme·rgere**; *adj.* submerged, sunk; (fig.) overwhelmed. **-iọne** *f.* submersion; submergence.

**sommẹss-o** *adj.* subdued; soft, low; humble; submissive. **-amẹnte** *adv.* humbly; softly; in a subdued tone.

**somministr-are** [A1] *tr.* to provide, to supply; to administer. **-aziọne** *f.* supply; provision.

**sommissiọne** *f.* submission; compliance.

**sọmm-o** *adj.* highest; very great; sublime; *n.m.* summit, top. **-ità** *f. indecl.* summit, top; sublime height(s).

**sommoss-a** *f.* uprising; riot; sedition. **-o** *part.* of **sommuovere**; *adj.* troubled, excited.

**sommovimẹnto** *m.* agitation; stirring up; revolt.

**sommozzatọre** *m.* skin diver; underwater swimmer; frogman; deep-sea diver.

**somm(u)o·vere** [C15] *tr.* to stir up, to agitate; to disturb, to trouble; to rouse.

**sonacchiare** [A4] *tr., intr.* (*aux.* avere) to strum.

**sona·gl-io** *m.* bell; sheep-bell; rattle; (fig.) fool; *serpente a -i*, rattlesnake; bubble, splash of rainwater; little drop of oil. **-iare** [A4] *intr.* (*aux.* avere) to shake (of bells), to tinkle. **-iera** *f.* collar or string of bells; jingling.

**son-are** [A1 d] *tr.* to ring; to play; to blow; to sound; to mean, to signify; (fam.) *gliel'ho -ata*, I told him straight; *intr.* (*aux.* avere) to ring; to strike; to sound; to resound. **-ante** *part. adj.* ringing; sounding; sonorous; *denaro -ante*, ready cash. **-ata** *f.* (mus.) sonata. **-atọre** *m.*, **-atrice** *f.* player; performer; executant(e).

**sọnd-o** *f.* sounding line, probe; drill. **-are** [A1 c] *tr.* to sound; to probe; to gauge; to feel.

**soneri·a** striking mechanism (of a clock); alarm.

**sonẹtt-o** *m.* sonnet. **-ista** *m., f.* sonnet-writer.

**sonicchiare** [A4] *tr., intr.* (*aux.* avere) to strum.

**so·nico** *adj.* sonic; *barriera sonica*, sound barrier.

**sonnacchiọso** *adj.* sleepy, drowsy; (fig.) sluggish, dull.

**sonna·mbul-o** *m.*, **-a** *f.* sleepwalker, somnambulist. **-ịsmo** *m.* somnambulism.

**sonnecchi-are** [A4 c] *intr.* (*aux.* avere) to doze, to slumber, to nod.

**sọnn-o** *m.* sleep; slumber; *aver —*, to feel sleepy; *prender —*, to go to sleep; *nel —*, in one's sleep; *a pensarci perdo i miei -i*, thinking about it keeps me awake at night. **-ellino** *m. dim.* nap; doze. **-i·fero** *adj.* somniferous; narcotic; soporific; *n.m.* narcotic. **-ilo·quio** *m* talking in one's sleep. **-olento** *adj.* somnolent; drowsy; sleepy. **-olenza** *f.* somnolence; drowsiness; sleepiness.

**sọno** *1st pers. sing., 3rd pers. pl. pres. indic.* of **essere**, q.v.

**sonor-o** *adj.* sonorous; resonant; high-sounding; *onda -a*, sound-wave; (cinem.) *colonna -a*, sound-track; *film —*, sound-film. **-ità** *f.* sonority; sonorousness.

**sontuọs-o** *adj.* sumptuous; luxurious; lavish. **-amẹnte** *adv.* sumptuously.

**sop-ire** [D2] *tr.* to calm; to appease; to soothe. **-imẹnto** *m.* lulling to sleep; soothing; drowsiness. **-ọre** *m.* drowsiness; light sleep; gentle sleep; torpor; lethargy.

**soppal-co** *m.* (*pl.* **-chi**) garret, attic; lumber room.

**sopperire** [D2] *intr.* (*aux.* avere; *prep.* a) to provide (for); to cope (with); to make up (for).

**soppesare** [A1 c] *tr.* to weigh in one's hand; (fig.) to ponder, to think over.

**soppiantare** [A1] *tr.* to supplant; to oust; to dispossess.

**soppiatto** *adj.* concealed; *adv. phr. di —*, secretly; stealthily.

**sopport-are** [A1] *tr.* to bear; to endure, to tolerate; to support; to hold up; to substantiate, to bear out; to second. **-a·bile** *adj.* bearable, endurable; tolerable. **-o** *m.* support; stand, mounting; *-o a rulli*, roller bearings; (fig.) toleration; grace, patience.

**soppress-o** *part.* of **soppri·mere**; *adj.* suppressed; abolished. **-iọne** *f.* suppression; abolition.

**soppri·mere** [C18] *tr.* to suppress; to abolish; to do away with; (euphem.) to kill.

**sọpra**[1] *prep.* over; above; *— ogni cosa*, above anything; beyond; on, upon; *prep. phr. — a*, on, on top of; *— di* (follow. by *pers. prn.*) on, upon; after;

next to; on the surface of; on the subject of; above; on the top; on the outside; *adv. phr. di* —, upstairs, up above; *prep. phr. al di — di*, above; *n.m.* the upper side; the top.

**sọpra-**[2] *pref.* (for words in which the stress falls on the second syllable, *e.g.* **sopra·bito,** see separate entries) super-; sur-; extra; above; upper. **-ccarta** *f.* envelope, cover; address, superscription. **-cci·glio** *m.* (*pl.f.* **-cci·glia**) eyebrow. **-ccitato** *adj.* above-quoted. **-ccoperta** *f.* counterpane; coverlet. **-ddẹtto** *adj.* aforesaid; above-mentioned. **-ffare** [B14] *tr.* to overcome; to overpower. **-ffaziọne** *f.* oppression. **-ffino** *adj.* superfine. **-ggiu·ngere** [C5] *intr.* (*aux.* essere) to arrive; to turn up; to occur; *tr.* to overtake. **-ggiunta** *f.* unexpected arrival; *per -ggiunta*, in addition; into the bargain. **-intendente** *m.* superintendent. **-intendenza** *f.* superintendence. **-inte·ndere** [C1] *intr.* (*aux.* avere; *prep.* a) to superintend. **-(l)luogo** *adv.* on the spot; *n.m.* on-the-spot investigation. **-mmercato** *m.* surplus; *per -mmercato*, into the bargain. **-mmodo** *adv.* exceedingly. **-mmontare** [A1c] *intr.* (*aux.* essere) to superabound. **-nnaturale** *adj.* supernatural. **-nnọme** *m.* nickname. **-nnominare** [A1s] *tr.* to nickname. **-nnumera·rio** *adj., n.m.* supernumerary. **-ppassa·ggio** *m.* fly-over bridge; railway bridge. **-ppensiero** *adv.* absent-mindedly; *quasi adj.* lost in thought. **-ppẹso** *m.* overweight; *per -ppeso*, for good measure. **-ppiù** *m. indecl.* extra; addition. **-rrivare** [A1] *intr.* (*aux.* essere) to supervene; to occur, to happen. **-scarpa** *f.* overshoe; galosh. **-scritta** *f.* superscription. **-scritto** *adj.* aforesaid, said; above-mentioned. **-sensi·bile** *adj.* super-sensible. **-ssalto** *m.* sudden start. **-ssedẹre** [B28] *intr.* (*aux.* avere) to delay, to suspend action; to wait. **-stante** *adj.* overhanging; impending; *n.m.* watchman; overseer; superintendent. **-stare** [A9] *intr.* (*aux.* avere; *prep.* a) to be at the head, to superintend; to be superior (to); *tr.* to dominate; to overcome; to put off. **-ttassa** *f.* surtax. **-ttutto** *adv.* above all; especially; principally; *n.m.* overcoat; overall. **-vanzare** [A1] *tr.* to surpass; *intr.* (*aux.* essere) to project; to be left over. **-vanzo** *m.* surplus, remainder, balance. **-vvedẹre** [B35] *tr.* to examine, to observe closely. **-vveduto** *part. adj.* circumspect, wary. **-vveglianza** *f.* surveillance. **-vvegliare** [A4] *tr.* to watch over, to watch carefully; to superintend. **-vvenire** [D17] *intr.* (*aux.* essere) to arrive, to come on the scene; to happen; *tr.* to overtake, to come upon suddenly, to surprise. **-vveste** *f.* overall; cape, outer garment; surcoat. **-vvi·a** *f.* upper road; fly-over road. **-vvi·ncere** [C5] *tr., intr.* (*aux.* avere) to overcome; to be victorious. **-vvi·vere** [C16] *intr.* (*aux.* essere) to survive. **-vvissuto** *adj.* surviving; *n.m.* survivor.

**sopra·bito** *m.* light overcoat.

**soprano** *m.* soprano voice; soprano part; *adj.* (poet.) highest.

**soprinte·ndere** [C1] *intr.* (*aux.* avere; *prep.* a) to be superintendent (of); to be responsible (for), to have charge (of); to superintend.

**sopruṣo** *m.* abuse of power, act of tyranny; insult, injury, outrage.

**soqquadr-o** *m.* disorder, confusion; ruin. **-are** [A1] *tr.* to turn upside-down; to throw into confusion.

**sor-** *pref. abbrev.* of **sopra**[2].

**sorba** *f.* sorb, sorb-apple.

**sorbẹtto** *m.* sorbet; water-ice; iced drink.

**sorbire** [D2] *tr.* to sip; to suck; to absorb; (fig.) to swallow.

**Sorbọna** *pr.n.f.* Sorbonne (University of Paris).

**sọrc-io** *m.* (*pl.* -i) mouse. **-ino, -igno** *adj.* mouse-coloured, mousey. **-ẹtto, -ino** *m. dim.* little mouse, young mouse.

**sorda·ggine** *f.* see under **sordo**.

**so·rdid-o** *adj.* dirty; sordid; mean, niggardly; ignoble. **-ẹzza** *f.* dirt; meanness.

**sord-o**[1] *adj.* deaf; (fig.) unresponsive; inexorable; inarticulate; toneless, dull; (of sound) rumbling, low; underhand, secret; *n.m.* deaf person; *i -i*, the deaf. **-a·ggine** *f.* deafness. **-ina** *f.* subdued sound; (mus.) a kind of clavichord; mute; damper; *adv. phr. alla -ina*, noiselessly; stealthily. **-ino** *m.* (mus.) mute; damper. **-ità** *f.* deafness. **-omuto** (*pl.* **-omuti**) *adj.* deaf and dumb; *n.m.* deaf-mute.

**sọrdo**[2] *m.* (math.) surd.

**sorell-a** *f.* sister. **-astra** *f.* stepsister; half-sister.

**sọrg-ere** [C5] *intr.* (*aux.* essere) to rise; to stand up; to arise; to emerge; *n.m.* rise, rising. **-ente** *part. adj.* rising; *n.f.* spring; fountain; source; origin, cause.

**sorgiv-o** *adj.* (of a) spring; *acqua -a*, spring water. **-a** *f.* spring (of water).

**soriano** *adj., n.m.* Syrian; *gatto* —, cypress cat.

**sormontare** [A1c] *tr.* to surmount; to surpass; to overcome; to overflow.

**sorniọne** *adj.* sly, crafty, artful; surly; *n.m.* slyboots, sneak.

**sorpass-are** [A4] *tr.* to surpass, to outdo, to excel; (motor.) to pass, to overtake. **-ato** *part. adj.* surpassed; overtaken; old-fashioned.

**sorpre·nd-ere** [C1] *tr.* to deceive; to take advantage of; to swindle; to take by surprise; to surprise; *rfl.* (*prep.* di) to be surprised (at, by). **-ente** *part. adj.* surprising, astonishing; strange.

**sorprẹṣ-a** *f.* surprise; astonishment; sudden trick; stratagem; police raid; *con mia* —, to my surprise; *adv. phr. di* —, unexpectedly. **-o** *part.* of **sorpre·ndere**; *adj.* surprised.

**sorre·ggere** [C12] *tr.* to hold up, to support, to sustain; to prop up; (fig.) to sustain; to encourage; *rfl.* to stand upright; to be able to stand.

**sorretto** *part.* of **sorre·ggere**; *adj.* supported; propped up; sustained.

**sorri·d-ere** [C3] *intr.* (*aux.* avere; *prep.* a) to smile (at, on); to be favourable (to); to appeal to, to be pleasing to. **-ente** *part. adj.* smiling; propitious; favourable.

**sorriso**[1] *part.* of **sorri·dere**; *adj.* smiled upon, gladdened.

**sorris-o**[2] *m.* smile; *fare un* —, to give a smile. **-ẹtto, -ino** *m. dim.* little smile.

**sọrs-o** *m.* draught, drink, drop. **-ata** *f.* gulp; draught. **-eggiare** [A3c] *tr., intr.* (*aux.* avere) to sip; to savour.

**sorta** *f.* kind, sort; (colloq.) *farne di ogni* —, to make all kinds of mistakes; quality.

**sort-e** *f.* lot, fate, destiny; chance, luck; augury; *pl.* augury, fortune (foretold); oracle; *tirar le -i*, to tell fortunes; destiny. **-eggiare** [A3c] *tr.* to draw by lot; to assign by lot. **-ẹggio** *m.* drawing (of lots), draw. **-ile·gio** *m.* witchcraft; sorcery; spell. **-ire** [D2] *tr.* to draw (in a lottery); to allot, to assign; to have, to get; to be endowed with; [D1] *intr.* (*aux.* essere) to be drawn (in a lottery), to come out; to fall to one's lot. **-ita** *f.* (theatr.) sortie; entrance; (fig.) sally; witty remark.

**sọrto** *part.* of **sọrgere**; *adj.* risen, raised; sprung.

**sorvegli-are** [A4] *tr.* to watch over; to superintend; to keep an eye on. **-ante** *part. adj., n.m.* watchman, caretaker; keeper; overseer; superintendent. **-anza** *f.* superintendence; supervision.

**sorvolare** [A1] *tr.* to fly over; to fly higher than; to rise above; (fig.) to touch lightly upon; *intr.*

(*aux.* essere) to fly higher; to pass over.

**so·sia** *m. indecl.* double (of a person).

**sospe·ndere** [C1] *tr.* to hang up; to suspend; (fig.) to stop, to put a stop to; to suspend; to adjourn, to defer; — *un assegno,* to stop a cheque.

**sospens-iọne** *f.* suspension; temporary adjournment; *lume a* —, hanging lamp; *molla di* —, suspension spring; uncertainty; interruption; stoppage. **-iva** *f.* delay; adjournment.

**sospẹso** *part.* of **sospe·ndere**; *adj.* hanging; hanging up; *ponte* —, suspension bridge; (fig.) uncertain, in suspense; irresolute; suspended; deferred, adjourned; *n.m.* suspense; *in* —, in suspense; in abeyance.

**sospett-are** [A1] *tr.* to suspect; to distrust; to doubt; to surmise; *intr.* (*aux.* avere; *prep.* di) to be suspicious of. **-a·bile** *adj.* arousing suspicion, suspect; dubious.

**sospett-o** *adj.* suspect, suspicious; doubtful, risky; *n.m.* suspicion; fear; mistrust; difference; suspect. **-ọso** *adj.* full of suspicion; wary; diffident.

**sospi·ngere** [C5] *tr.* to push; to push on; to impel; to goad; to urge.

**sospint-a** *f.* push. **-o** *part.* of **sospi·ngere**; *adj.* pushed, driven, urged.

**sospir-o** *m.* sigh; gasp; long-drawn breath; lament; desire; *pl.* air-holes, vents. **-are** [A1] *intr.* (*aux.* avere) to sigh; to breathe out; *tr.* to sigh for; to long for; to hanker after; to lament. **-ato** *part. adj.* longed for; lamented. **-ọso** *adj.* full of sighs.

**sossọpra** *adv.* upside-down, topsy-turvy.

**sosta** *f.* rest, halt, pause; stay; respite; *divieto di* —, no parking.

**sostantivo** *adj.* substantive; substantial; *n.m.* noun, substantive.

**sostanz-a** *f.* substance; essence; matter; property; patrimony; — *alimentare,* foodstuff. **-iale** *adj.* substantial; well-founded. **-iare** [A4] *tr.* to substantiate; to make substantial. **-iọso** *adj.* substantial; nourishing; (of wine) full-bodied.

**sostare** [A9] *intr.* (*aux.* avere), *rfl.* to stop, to halt; to rest; to pause.

**sostẹgno** *m.* support, prop; bracket; column; weir, lock.

**sostenẹre** [B32] *tr.* to sustain; to support; to uphold; to maintain; to bear; to afford; (theatr.) to act, to perform.

**sostent-are** [A1] *tr.* to support. **-amẹnto** *m.* support.

**sostenut-o** *part.* of **sostenẹre**; *adj.* sustained; (fig.) reserved; stiff; distant in manner. **-ẹzza** *f.* gravity; stiffness; reserve.

**sostitu-ire** [D2] *tr.* to replace; to deputize for; to take the place of. **-to** *m.* substitute; deputy. **-ziọne** *f.* substitution; replacement; change; *in -zione di,* in place of.

**sostrato** *m.* substratum.

**sottacẹti** *m.pl.* pickles.

**sottacqua** *adv.* underwater.

**sottana** *f.* petticoat; (eccl.) cassock.

**sottẹcchi** *adv.* by stealth.

**sottentrare** [A1] *intr.* (*aux.* essere) to creep in, to slip in.

**sotterfu·gio** *m.* subterfuge.

**sotterr-a** *adv.* underground. **-a·neo** *adj.* subterranean; *n.m.* cave; vault; dungeon. **-are** [A1] *tr.* to bury; to hide.

**sottigliẹzza** *f.* fineness; thinness; (of air) lightness, purity; (of vision) sharpness, keenness; (of mind) intelligence; (arguments) subtlety, acuteness, ingenuity; sophistry.

**sottil-e** *adj.* thin, fine, slender; *spiaggia* —, narrow beach; *fiume* —, shallow river; *orecchio* —, sharp ear; subtle, sharp, sly. **-ità** *f.* fineness, delicacy; thinness; daintiness; subtlety, ingenuity. **-izzare** [A1] *intr.* (*aux.* avere) to split hairs; *tr.* to introduce subtleties into; to examine minutely.

**sottinsù** *adv. phr. di* —, from beneath, upwards.

**sottinte·nd-ere** [C1] *tr.* to understand (what is not expressed); to leave unexpressed; to imply; to guess. **-ente** *part. adj.* understanding; implying; *n.m.* sub-manager; assistant-superintendent. **-enza** *f.* assistant managership. **-imẹnto** *m.* understanding; implicit meaning.

**sottintẹso** *part.* of **sottinte·ndere**; *adj.* understood, not expressed; *n.m.* implication; *parlare sottintesi,* to hint.

**sọtto**[1] *prep.* **1.** under, underneath; beneath, below; *restare — un'automobile,* to be run over by a car; — *a noi,* — *di noi,* below us. **2.** this side of; — *il Natale,* this side of, before Christmas. **3.** less than, below, short of; — *zero,* below zero. **4.** serving, under; subject to. **5.** concealed under, in the guise of. **6.** under the stress or influence of; — *l'impulso dell'ira,* impelled (driven) by anger; — *pena di morte,* on pain of death. **7.** from; — *un certo punto di vista,* from a certain point of view. **8.** *adv.* down; (of the sun) *andar* —, to set; *restar* —, to lose, to be inferior; (fam.) *dargli* —, to attack him, to set about him.

**sọtt-o**[2] *pref.* sub-, under-. (Before a vowel the final *o* is often elided, *e.g.* **sottispettọre**; for words in which the accent falls on the second syllable, *e.g.* **sotto·rdine,** see separate entries.) **-alimentaziọne** *f.* under-nourishment. **-archivista** *m., f.* assistant keeper of archives. **-arco** *m.* (archit.) underside of an arch or vault. **-ascelle** *m. indecl.* dress-shield. **-obicchiere** *m.* glass-stand, mat, saucer. **-ocapo** *m.* assistant chief. **-o·cchio** *adv.* under one's eye. **-ocommissiọne** *f.*, **-ocomitato** *m.* sub-committee. **-ocoperta** *f.* coverlet; undercover; (naut.) lower deck. **-ocoppa** *f.* saucer. **-ocuta·neo** *adj.* subcutaneous. **-ofa·scia** *m. indecl.* (postal) under a wrapper. **-ogambe** *adv.* in one's stride. **-olineare** [A6] *tr.* to underline; (fig.) to emphasize. **-olunare** *adj.* sublunary. **-omarino** *adj., n.m.* submarine. **-omẹsso** *adj.* submissive; obedient; respectful. **-omẹttere** [C2] *tr.* to subdue; to subject; to vanquish; to reduce to obedience; *rfl.* to submit, to acquiesce. **-opa·ncia** *m. indecl.* girth-strap; belly-band. **-opassa·ggio** *m.* subway; underpass. **-opọrre** [B21] *tr.* to submit, to subject; to expose; *rfl.* to submit. **-oposiziọne** *f.* subjection. **-oprefetto** *m.* sub-prefect. **-oscri·vere** [C12] to sign; to subscribe; to underwrite; *intr.* (*aux.* avere; *prep.* a) to assent; to agree; to subscribe; *rfl.* (*prep.* a) to subscribe; to sign, to append one's signature. **-oscritto** *part. adj., n.m.* undersigned. **-oscrittọre** *m.* signatory. **-oscriziọne** *f.* signature; subscription; subscription list; inscription. **-osọpra** *adv.* upside down; topsy-turvy; *adj. indecl.* in a turmoil, confused; *n.m. indecl.* utter chaos, total confusion. **-ospe·cie** *f. indecl.* sub-species. **-ostare** [A9] *intr.* (*aux.* essere; *prep.* a) to lie below; to be subordinate; to give in; to experience; to endure. **-osuolo** *m.* subsoil. **-otenente** *m.* second-lieutenant. **-oti·tolo** *m.* subtitle. **-ovento** *m.* (naut.) lee. **-oveste** *f.* waistcoat; undergarment. **-ovọce** *adv.* in a low voice; in an undertone.

**sottrarre** [B33] *tr.* to subtract; to withdraw; to embezzle; to conceal; *rfl.* (*prep.* a) to get out (of), to escape (from); to evade.

**sottratto** *part.* of **sottrarre**; *adj.* subtracted; deducted; stolen.

**sottraziọne** *f.* subtraction; deduction; removal; withdrawal.

**sottufficiale** *m.* (mil.) warrant officer; (naut.) petty officer.

**sovente** *adv.* often, frequently.

**sove·rchi-o** *adj.* excessive, superfluous; immoderate; *n.m.* excess, (fig.) overbearing conduct, insolence; *adv.* excessively, too much. **-amẹnte** *adv.* excessively

-ante *adj.* overwhelming. -are [A4] *tr.* to surpass, to overcome; to overflow; to overwhelm, to browbeat; *intr.* (*aux.* avere) to be in excess; to be superfluous; to rise in flood; to protrude.

**sovra-** *pref.* (*cf.* **sopra**[2]). **-bbondante** *part. adj.* superabundant; superfluous, excessive. **-ccaricare** [A2s] *tr.* to overload; *intr.* (*aux.* avere) to exaggerate. **-ccennato** *adj.* above-mentioned. **-ppọrre** [B21] *tr.* (*prep.* a, su) to place upon; to lay on top (of); to superimpose (on); *rfl.* to be superimposed. **-produzịone** *f.* over-production. **-stare** [A9] *intr.* (*aux.* avere; *prep.* a) to hang (over); to threaten; to overhang; to dominate; to be superior (to).

**sovrana** *f.* sovereign (coin); female ruler.

**sovrano** *adj.* sovereign; supreme; *n.m.* sovereign; reigning prince; king.

**sovrastare** [A9] *intr.* (*aux.* avere; *prep.* a) to overhang; to impend; to threaten.

**sovr-impọrre** [B21] *tr.* to superimpose; to lay (an additional burden) upon. **-impọsta** *f.* additional tax.

**sovrumano** *adj.* superhuman.

**sovvenire** [D17] *tr.* to help, to assist; to subsidize, to support; *intr.* (*aux.* essere; *prep.* a) to supply, to find a remedy (for); *impers.* to come to mind; to occur (to); *rfl.* (*prep.* di) to remember; *n.m.* memory, recollection, remembrance.

**sovvenzịone** *f.* subvention; subsidy.

**sovvers-ịone** *f.* overthrow; destruction; subversion. **-ivo** *adj.* subversive; tending to subversion; revolutionary; extremist.

**sovvert-ire** [D1] *tr.* to subvert; to overturn, to overthrow; to upset; to undermine the loyalty of. **-imẹnto** *m.* overturning; upsetting; revolt.

**sọẓẓ-o** *adj.* filthy, dirty; nasty; foul; loathsome. **-amẹnte** *adv.* filthily; foully. **-ume** *m.*, **-ura** *f.* filth; pollution.

**spacc-are** [A2] *tr.* to split; to crack; to break open; to chop, to cleave; *rfl.* (*acc.* of *prn.* 'si') to split, to crack; to burst; (*dat.* of *prn.* 'si') *-arsi la testa, cadendo,* to fall and cut one's head open. **-alẹgna** *m. indecl.* woodcutter. **-amẹnto** *m.* splitting; cleaving. **-amontagne, -amọnti** *m. indecl.* braggart. **-apietre** *m. indecl.* stone-breaker. **-atura** *f.* cleft; split; crack.

**spacchettare** [A1c] *tr.* to undo, to unwrap (a parcel).

**spacci-are** [A3] *tr.* to sell; to sell out; to sell off; to get rid of; to kill; *rfl.* *-arsi per,* to give oneself out to be; to hurry; to make haste; *spàcciati!,* be quick! **-a·bile** *adj.* saleable. **-amẹnto** *m.* sale; dispatch. **-ativo** *adj.* quick, expeditious, efficient. **-ato** *part. adj.* done for. **-atọre** *m.* seller; distributor.

**spa·ccio** *m.* sale; selling; *avere pronto —,* to sell readily; shop; dispatch.

**spac-co** *m.* (*pl.* **-chi**) split, crack, cleft; tear, rent. **-conata** *f.* bragging, braggadocio. **-cọne** *m.* braggart, boaster; bully.

**spad-a** *f.* sword; *— corta,* dagger. **-accino** *m.* swordsman. **-a·io** *m.* sword-maker. **-ino** *m. dim.* dirk. **-ọne** *m. augm.* broadsword.

**spadroneggiare** [A3c] *intr.* (*aux.* avere) to lord it; to domineer; to be arrogant.

**spaeṣato** *adj.* out of one's own country or region; (fig.) out of one's depth; lost, bewildered.

**spaghẹtti** *m.pl.* spaghetti, thin strips of macaroni.

**spagliare**[1] [A4] *tr.* to remove straw from; to unpack; *intr.* (*aux.* avere) (of animals) to scatter straw.

**spagliare**[2] [A4] *intr.* (*aux.* avere) (of water) to flood, to overflow.

**spa·glio** *m.* flood; *seminare a —,* to sow broadcast.

**Spagn-a** *pr.n.f.* Spain. **-ola·ggine** *f.*, **-olata** *f.* bravado, braggadocio. **-olẹtta** *f.* window-bolt; spool, reel. **-(u)ola** *f.* Spanish woman, Spanish girl; Spanish influenza. **-(u)olo** *adj.* Spanish; *n.m.* Spaniard; Spanish; (dog.) spaniel.

**spa-go** *m.* (*pl.* **-ghi**) string, twine; packthread. **-ghẹtto** *m. dim.* thin string; (fig., colloq.) fear, 'wind up'; *pl.* (cul.) spaghetti.

**spai-are** [A4] *tr.* to separate (a pair); to unmatch. **-ato** *part. adj.* (of a pair) separated; *scarpe -ate,* odd shoes.

**spalanc-are** [A2] *tr.* to open wide, to throw open. **-ato** *part. adj.* wide open.

**spal-are** [A1] *tr.* to shovel away. **-ata, -atura** *f.* shovelling; sweeping away. **-atọre** *m.* sweeper; snow-shoveller.

**spaldo** *m.* projection, balcony; battlements.

**spall-a** *f.* **1.** shoulder; *dare di — a,* to help, give a helping hand to, to support; *stringere nelle -e,* to shrug one's shoulders. **2.** *pl.* back; *cogliere alle -e,* to fall upon suddenly. **3.** (of a garment) shoulder. **4.** (fig.) strength; courage. **-are** [A1] *tr.* to sprain or dislocate the shoulder of. **-ata** *f.* push, heave; shrug of the shoulders. **-ato** *part.* having a dislocated shoulder; *adj.* finished, done for. **-eggiare** [A3c] *tr.* to support, to back. **-ẹtta** *f. dim.* parapet, embankment; retaining wall; splay of a window. **-iera** *f.* back (of a chair, bench, sofa); head or foot (of a bed); espalier; grassy bank. **-ina** *f.* épaulette; shoulder strap of an apron. **-uc·cia** *f.* narrow shoulder; *fare -ucce,* to shrug ones shoulders.

**spall'armi** *excl.* (mil.) shoulder arms!

**spalmare** [A1] *tr.* to smear.

**spalto** *m.* glacis; bastion; embankment.

**spampan-are** [A1] *tr.* (agric.) to strip (a vine) of its leaves; *rfl., intr.* (*aux.* essere) to shed petals. **-ato** *part. adj.* overblown.

**spa·nd-ere** [C5] *tr.* to shed; to scatter, to spread; to spill; to slop; *intr.* (*aux.* avere) to leak, to drip. **-imẹnto** *m.* spreading; scattering.

**spanna** *f.* span (of the hand).

**spann-are** [A1] *tr.* to skim (milk) to cream. **-atọia** *f.* skimmer.

**spanno·cchi-a** *f.* corn-cob. **-are** [A4] *tr.* to strip, to husk (corn-cobs). **-atura** *f.* maize harvest, gathering of the cobs.

**spanto** *part.* of **spa·ndere**; *adj.* spread; scattered; spilt; poured forth.

**spappagallare** [A1] *intr.* (*aux.* avere), *rfl.* to chatter like a parrot; to jabber.

**spappolare** [A1s] *tr.* to pulp; *rfl.* to go to a pulp, to become mushy.

**sparadrappo** *m.* sticking plaster, strapping.

**spa·rag-io** *m.* (*pl.* **-i**) garden asparagus.

**spar-are**[1] [A1] *tr.* to shoot (a firearm), to discharge, to fire; *-arle grosse,* to 'shoot a line'; *intr.* (*aux.* avere) to fire, to shoot. **-ata** *f.* discharge; volley. **-atọre** *m.* shooter; boaster, swaggerer. **-ato·ria** *f.* shooting; exchange of shots.

**spar-are**[2] [A1] *tr.* to rip open; to gut; to cut lengthwise. **-ato** *part. adj.* ripped open; gutted; *n.m.* front opening of a coat.

**sparecchiare** [A4c] *tr.* to clear away; *— la tavola,* to clear the table; *abs.* to clear away after a meal.

**sparẹggio** *m.* inequality; unevenness; disparity.

**spa·rg-ere** [C4] *tr.* to spread, to scatter, to strew; to disseminate; to issue; to sow; to spill; to shed. **-imẹnto** *m.* shedding; spilling; *-imento di sangue,* bloodshed.

**sparigliare** [A4] *tr.* to break up (a pair), to separate, to unmatch.

**spar-ire** [D2] *intr.* (*aux.* essere) to disappear; to vanish; to fade away; to perish. **-izịone** *f.* disappearance; vanishing; death.

**sparl-are** [A1] *intr.* (*aux.* avere; *prep.* di) to speak ill (of); to

slander. **-atọre** *m.*, **-atrice** *f.* slanderer.

**sparo** *m.* shot, discharge; detonation, explosion; report.

**sparpagliare** [A4] *tr.* to scatter, to disperse; to disseminate; to spread about; to squander.

**spars-o** *part.* of **spa·rgere**; *adj.* scattered; loose; (of hair) loose, ruffled; (of blood) shed; *rime -e*, collected poems. **-amẹnte** *adv.* sparsely, here and there; thinly.

**spart-ire** [D2] *tr.* to divide, to separate; to partition. **-iacque** *m. indecl.* watershed. **-i·bile** *adj.* divisible. **-itamẹnte** *adv.* separately; one by one. **-ito** *part. adj.* separated; *adv. phr. alla -ita*, disconnectedly. **-iziọne** *f.* division; partition; distribution.

**sparto** *m.* esparto grass.

**sparuto** *adj.* lean, thin, spare; emaciated.

**sparvier-e** *m.*, **-o** *m.* sparrow-hawk; (bldg.) mortar-board, hawk.

**spa·ṣim-o** *m.* spasm, convulsion; pang. **-ante** *part.*; *n.m.* ardent lover; (iron.) suitor. **-are** [A1 s] *intr.* (*aux.* avere) to suffer agonies; to be racked with pain; to long ardently; *-are per*, to be in love with, to long for passionately.

**spaṣmo·dico** *adj.* spasmodic.

**spass-are** [A1] *tr.* to amuse; to divert; to provide amusement for; *rfl.* (*acc.* of *prn.* 'si') to amuse oneself; (*dat.* of *prn.* 'si') *-arsela*, to enjoy oneself.

**spasseggiare** [A3 c] *intr.* (*aux.* avere) (pop.) to go out for a walk.

**spassion-are** [A1 c] *rfl.* to give vent to one's feelings; to calm oneself. **-atamẹnte** *adv.* dispassionately. **-atẹzza** *f.* impartiality; tranquillity.

**spasso** *m.* pastime, amusement, recreation; *andare a —*, to go for a walk; *menare a —*, to make fun of, to 'lead up the garden path'.

**spastoiare** [A4 c] *tr.* to unshackle, to set free; *rfl.* (*prep.* di) to get rid of.

**spa·tola** *f.* spatula; ladle; flat trowel; *— d'Arlecchino*, slapstick.

**spaura·cchio** *m.* scarecrow; bogey; bugbear.

**spaurire** [D2] *tr.* to frighten, to terrify, to alarm.

**spavald-o** *adj.* arrogant; defiant, insolent. **-amẹnte** *adv.* arrogantly; defiantly, insolently; aggressively. **-eri·a** *f.* effrontery; defiance; boastfulness.

**spavent-are** [A1] *tr.* to frighten, to terrify; to scare off; *intr.* (*aux.* avere; *prep.* di), *rfl.* to take fright (at); to be terrified (by). **-atamẹnte** *adv.* timorously; in terror. **-ato** *part. adj.* frightened; fearful.

**spavent-o** *m.* terror; fright; fear. **-ẹvole** *adj.* terrifying, frightening; appalling; awful; enormous; horrible.

**spaziale** *adj.* spatial; *tenuta —*, space-suit.

**spaziare** [A4] *intr.* (*aux.* avere) to range, to roam freely, to rove; (fig.) to expatiate.

**spazieggi-are** [A3 c] *tr.* to space. **-atura** *f.* spacing.

**spazient-ire** [D2] *rfl.* to lose patience. **-ito** *part. adj.* out of patience.

**spa·zi-o** *m.* space; room; distance; space of time, interval; *pl.* space (beyond the earth's atmosphere). **-ọsità** *f.* spaciousness. **-ọso** *adj.* spacious; wide; broad; ample; large.

**spazz-are** [A1] *tr.* to sweep, to clean; to sweep away. **-amẹnto** *m.* sweeping. **-amine** *m. indecl.* mine-sweeper. **-anẹve** *m. indecl.* snow-plough. **-ata** *f.* sweeping, sweep. **-acamino** *m.* chimney sweep. **-atura** *f.* sweeping; sweepings, refuse, dirt; metal filings. **-atura·io** *m.* sweeper; dustman; scavenger. **-ino** *m.* road-sweeper.

**spazzo** *m.* level ground; flat open space.

**spa·zzol-a** *f.* brush; frond (of a palm tree); horse-hair. **-are** [A1 s] *tr.* to brush. **-ata** *f.* brushing. **-ino** *m. dim.* small brush; *-ino per i denti*, tooth-brush; *-ino per le unghie*, nail-brush.

**speaker** *m. indecl.* (pron. as English) (radio) announcer.

**specchi-are** [A4] *rfl.* (*prep.* in) to be reflected; to look at one's reflection. **-ato** *part. adj.* reflected, mirrored; (fig.) flawless, spotless, blameless.

**spe·cchi-o** *m.* mirror, looking glass; *— d'acqua*, sheet of water; model, pattern; *farsi — di*, to model oneself on; list, register; handbook, brief description, schedule; (motor.) *— retrovisore*, driving mirror. **-era** *f.* large mirror; dressing-table. **-ẹtto** *m. dim.* hand-mirror; (fig.) synopsis, conspectus.

**spe·ci-e**[1] *f. indecl.* species; sort, kind; variety; *in ispecie*, especially; *sotto — di*, with the pretext of; appearance, form, shape; ornament; beauty; spice, aroma; *pl.* simples. **-ale** *adj.* special, particular; peculiar. **-alità** *f. indecl.* speciality; peculiarity. **-alizzare** [A1] *tr.* to specify, to particularize; *rfl.* (*prep.* in) to specialize (in).

**spe·cie**[2] *adv.* especially.

**speci·fic-a** *f.* detailed list; bill; note; specification. **-amẹnto** *m.*, **-are** [A2 s] *tr.* to specify. **-aziọne** *f.* specification.

**specimen** *m. indecl.* (typ.) specimen page; specimen binding.

**speciọs-o** *adj.* specious; singular. **-ità** *f.* speciousness.

**spe-co** *m.* (*pl.* **-chi**) cave, den; cavern; grotto.

**spẹcola** *f.* observatory.

**speculare**[1] *adj.* mirror-like.

**specul-are**[2] [A1 s] *tr.* (surg.) to examine; (fig.) to speculate upon, to investigate; *intr.* (*aux.* avere) to speculate, to mediate; to observe; (finan.) *— in, su*, to speculate in. **-amẹnto** *m.* observation; speculation. **-ativa** *f.* speculative faculty. **-ativo** *adj.* speculative. **-atọre** *m.*, **-atrice** *f.* speculator. **-aziọne** *f.* speculation; inquiry; meditation; (finan.) speculation; venture.

**spedal-e** *m.* hospital. **-ino** *m.* medical student; house surgeon, houseman; *adj.* of, relating to, a hospital. **-ità** *f.* hospital treatment.

**spediente** *m.* expedient; make-shift; contrivance.

**sped-ire** [D2] *tr.* to perform, to execute, to carry out with dispatch; to send; to post; to forward; to ship; to settle, to arrange finally; *rfl.* to hurry, to make haste, to be quick. **-ita-mẹnte** *adv.* expeditiously; readily. **-itẹzza** *f.* quickness; readiness; expedition; dispatch. **-itivo** *adj.* prompt. **-ito** *part. adj.* sent; quick, prompt, easy, fluent; beyond hope, done for; *adv.* quickly, promptly; fluently. **-itọre** *m.*, **-itrice** *f.* sender; consignor, shipper; forwarding agent. **-iziọne** *f.* sending; dispatch; forwarding; consignment; shipping; shipment. **-izioniere** *m.* forwarding-agent.

**spẹgn-ere,** [C7] *tr.* to extinguish, to put out; to blow out; to turn out; to switch off; *— il motore*, to turn off the engine; to quench; to allay; *— la polvere*, to lay the dust; to check; to destroy; to kill; *— la calce*, to slake lime. **-imo·ccolo** *m.* candle-snuffers. **-itọio** *m.* extinguisher.

**spelacchiare** [A4] *tr.* to pull out the hair of; (fig.) to fleece; *rfl.* to lose one's hair; to go bald.

**spelare** [A1] *tr.* to strip of hair; to shear; *intr.* (*aux.* essere) to lose one's hair, to moult.

**speleologi·a** *f.* speleology.

**spellare** [A1] *tr.* to skin, to flay, (fig.) to fleece.

**spelọnca** *f.* cave; den; cavern; (fig.) large, gloomy house.

**speme** *f.* (poet.) hope.

**spendacciọn-a** *f.*, **-e** *m.* spendthrift.

**spe·nd-ere** [C1] *tr.* to spend; to

expend; to lay out; to consume; to use up; to make use of; *abs., intr.* (*aux.* avere) to make purchases, to go shopping; *rfl.* to give one's services; to take trouble. **-erẹccio** *adj.* lavish, prodigal; extravagant. **-itọre** *m.*, **-itrice** *f.* spender; spendthrift.

**spe·ndita** *f.* spending; putting into circulation.

**spennacchi-are, spenn-are** [A1] *tr.* to pluck, to strip of feathers; (fig.) to fleece; *rfl.* (of birds) to moult.

**spensierat-o** *adj.* thoughtless; careless. **-amẹnte** *adv.* thoughtlessly. **-a·ggine, -ẹzza** *f.* thoughtlessness; carelessness.

**spẹnto** *part.* of **spẹgnere**; *adj.* extinguished, put out; extinct; lifeless, dead; spent; cancelled; finished.

**spenzol-are** [A1 s] *intr.* (*aux.* avere) to dangle, to hang down; to overhang. **-ọne, -ọni** *adv.* dangling; hanging down.

**sper-a** *f.* (poet.) sphere; globe; sky; small, round mirror.

**sper-are**[1] [A1] *intr.* (*aux.* avere) to hope; — *in*, to rely on; to trust in; *tr.* to hope for; to expect. **-a·bile** *adj.* to be hoped (for). **-anza** *f.* hope; expectation; confidence; trust. **-anzọso** *adj.* hopeful. **-ato** *part. adj.* expected, hoped for.

**sperare**[2] [A1] *tr.* to look through against the light; — *uova*, to candle eggs.

**spe·rd-ere** [C3] *tr.* to disperse, to scatter; to drive away; to lose; to nullify; *rfl.* to disperse, to go astray; to disappear. **-uto** *part. adj.* lost; dispersed; bewildered; *luogo -uto*, wild place.

**spergiura** *f.* woman perjurer.

**spergiur-are** [A1] *intr.* (*aux.* avere) to perjure oneself; *tr.* — *il vero*, to lie on oath. **-aziọne** *f.* perjury. **-o** *adj.* perjured; *n.m.* perjury; perjurer.

**spericol-are** [A1 s] *rfl.* to take fright. **-ato** *part. adj.* daring.

**sperimẹnt-o** *m.* experiment. **-ale** *adj.* experimental. **-are** [A1 c] *tr.* to test; to try; to experiment with; to make trial of. **-ato** *part. adj.* experienced, expert; skilful; well-tried. **-atọre** *m.*, **-atrice** *f.* experimenter.

**sperma** *m.* sperm.

**sperma-ceti** *m.* spermaceti. **-tozo·o** *m.* spermatozoon.

**sperọn-e** *m.* spur; (archit.) abutment. **-are** [A1 c] *tr.* to ram (a ship).

**spe·rper-o** *m.* waste; squandering. **-are** [A1 s] *tr.* to squander, to waste; to spoil. **-atọre** *m.*, **-atrice** *f.* waster; squanderer.

**sperso** *part.* of **spe·rdere**; *adj.* scattered; bewildered; lost.

**spertic-are** [A2 s] *rfl.* (of a tree) to shoot up, to grow too tall; (fig.) to exaggerate. **-ato** *part. adj.* overgrown; (fig.) exaggerated; *lodi -ate*, fulsome flattery.

**spẹs-a** *f.* expense; cost; *pl.* expenses; *fare le -e*, to do the shopping. **-are** [A1] *tr.* to pay the expenses of; to pay the keep of. **-ato** *part. adj.* with all expenses paid.

**spẹso** *part.* of **spe·ndere**; *adj.* spent; expended.

**spẹss-o** *adj.* thick; dense; compact; occurring frequently; *-e volte*, often; *adv.* often, frequently. **-eggiare** [A3 c] *tr.* to repeat; to reiterate; *intr.* (*aux.* avere, essere) to happen often. **-ẹzza** *f.* thickness; density. **-ire** [D2] *intr.* (*aux.* essere) to thicken, to become thick or thicker. **-ọre** *m.* thickness.

**spetezẓare** [A1 c] *intr.* (*aux.* avere) to fart.

**spetta·bil-e** *adj.* worthy of respect; (on an envelope) *Alla Spett. Ditta*..., Messrs... **-ità** *f.* importance; eminence.

**spetta·col-o** *m.* spectacle; sight; scene; entertainment, play; show. **-are** *adj.* spectacular; theatrical; (fig.) amazing. **-ọso** *adj.* spectacular; showy; sensational.

**spett-are** [A1] *intr.* (*aux.* essere; *prep.* a) to belong (to); to be the duty, concern (of); to be the turn (of). **-ante** *part. adj.* belonging; due. **-anza** *f.* concern, business; competence; property; *pl.* fees.

**spettat-ọre** *m.*, **-rice** *f.* spectator; onlooker, bystander; *m.pl.* (theatr.) audience.

**spetteggolare** [A1 sc] *intr.* (*aux.* avere) to gossip.

**spettin-are** [A1 s] *tr.* to ruffle the hair of; *rfl.* to become dishevelled. **-ato** *part. adj.* dishevelled; uncombed; unkempt.

**spettr-o** *m.* spectre, ghost, apparition. **-ale** *adj.* spectral, ghostly.

**spettrosco·pio** *m.* spectroscope.

**spe·zi-e** *f. indecl.* (usu. *pl.*) spice, spices. **-ale** *m.* druggist, chemist; chemist's shop; grocer; grocer's shop; *pl.* spices. **-eri·a** *f.* spices; druggist's shop; grocer's shop.

**spezz-are** [A1] *tr.* to break into pieces; to shatter; to chop up; to split; *rfl.* to break, to be broken; to be shattered. **-a·bile** *adj.* breakable; fragile. **-atamẹnte** *adv.* brokenly; bit by bit; spasmodically. **-atino** *m.* (cul.) meat cut up small and stewed or braised. **-ato** *part. adj.* broken; interrupted; *legna -ata*, chopped wood; *adv. phr. alla -ata*, bit by bit, with interruptions; *n.m.pl.* small change. **-atura** *f.* breakage.

**spezzettare** [A1 c] *tr.* to cut into small pieces; to mince; to hash.

**spezzọne** *m.* bomb-stick; incendiary bomb.

**spia** *f.* spy; informer; tell-tale; sneak; indication, clue; (in a door) judas.

**spiacente** *adj.* displeasing, unpleasant.

**spiac-ẹre** [B20] *intr.* (*aux.* essere; *prep.* a) to displease; to cause displeasure (to); *mi -e che non sia venuto*, I am sorry he did not come. **-ẹvole** *adj.* unpleasant; disagreeable; unfortunate. **-evolẹzza** *f.* disagreeableness; unpleasantness.

**spia·gg-ia** *f.* (*pl.* -e) beach; shore; seaside resort. **-ẹtta** *f. dim.* little beach; small portable writing-desk.

**spian-are** [A1] *tr.* to level, to smooth; to plane (wood); to bulldoze; to roll out (pastry); to iron, to press; *intr.* (*aux.* essere; *prep.* su) to rest evenly (upon). *rfl.* to stretch out; to lie down. **-ata** *f.* levelling; level ground; esplanade; (mil.) parade ground. **-ato** *part. adj.* levelled; ironed; explained; *n.m.* level space (smaller than **spianata**). **-atọia** *f.* pastry board. **-atọio** *m.* rolling pin. **-atrice** *f.* (bldg.) bulldozer.

**spiano** *m.* levelling; smoothing; *adv. phr. a tutto* —, abundantly, profusely, lavishly.

**spiantare** [A1] *tr.* to uproot; to dig out; to demolish; to destroy; *rfl.* to go to rack and ruin.

**spianto** *m.* ruin; destruction.

**spi-are** [A4] *tr.* to spy upon; to pry into; to watch; to enquire into. **-arola** *f.* spy-hole, peephole.

**spiattell-are** [A1] *tr.* to declare openly; to tell flatly; to blab. **-atamẹnte** *adv.*, *adv. phr. alla -ata*, flatly, openly, plainly.

**spiazzo** *m.* open space; clearing.

**spiccante** *adj.* see under **spiccare**.

**spicc-are** [A2] *tr.* to detach, to cut off; to pluck; to articulate, to pronounce distinctly; — *un salto*, to take a leap; — *il volo*, to rise, to take off in flight; *intr.* (*aux.* avere) to be striking, to be conspicuous; to stand out, to excel; *rfl.* to come to the boil; to drop off; to become detached. **-ante** *adj.* striking, conspicuous; (of colours) bright. **-atamẹnte** *adv.* strikingly; distinctly; conspicuously. **-ato** *part. adj.* distinct; clear; remarkable, notable; prominent; conspicuous.

**spi·cchi-o** *m.* section. segment; gore. **-are** [A4] *tr.* to divide into sections; to slice.

**spicci-are** [A3] *intr.* (*aux.* essere) to spurt out, to gush forth; to dash away; *tr.* to detach; to tear off; to dispatch; (of money)

to give small change for; *rfl.* *acc.* of *prn.* si) to make haste; (*dat.* of *prn.* si) to get rid (of). **-ativo** *adj.* expeditious, quick; (of a person) energetic.

**spiccicare** [A2 s] *tr.* to detach, to tear off; to unstick; to articulate; *rfl.* to come unstuck; to be torn off; to tear oneself away.

**spi·ccio** *adj.* expeditious, quick, prompt; *avere le mani spicce*, to have one's hands free; *n.m.pl.* *gli spicci*, loose change, small change.

**spi·cciol-o** *adj.* broken up small; *moneta -a*, small change; *n.m.* small coin; *pl.* small change. **-are** [A1 s] *tr.* to pluck; to change into small money; *adv. phr. alla -ata*, little by little.

**spicco** *m.* relief; vividness; *fare —*, to stand out, to catch the eye.

**spicile·gio** *m.* scrap book, miscellany.

**spidocchiare** [A4] *tr.* to delouse, to rid of lice; (fig.) to lift from poverty.

**spiedo** *m.* (kitchen) spit; spear, boar spear; spike for keeping papers on.

**spieg-are** [A2] *tr.* to spread out; to unfold; to lay out; to display; to explain; to justify; to interpret; (mil.) to reply; *rfl.* to be unfolded; to spread; (of a flower) to open; to explain oneself, to make oneself understood. **-a·bile** *adj.* explicable. **-amẹnto** *m.* explaining; explanation; unfolding; spreading out; (mil.) deployment. **-atamẹnte** *adv.* openly. **-ativo** *adj.* explanatory. **-atura** *f.* unfolding. **-aziọne** *f.* explanation.

**spiegazzare** [A1] *tr.* to crease, to crumple.

**spietato** *adj.* pitiless, ruthless; cruel; implacable.

**spiffer-are** [A1 s] *intr.* (*aux.* avere) to pipe, to play the pipe (or other wind instrument); to whistle; *tr.* to report, to tell. **-ata** *f.* playing of pipes.

**spi·ffer-o** *m.* (colloq.) piercing draught. **-ọne** *m.* tell-tale.

**spig-a** *f.* ear (of corn, etc.); *punto a —*, herring-bone stitch. **-are** [A2] *intr.* (*aux.* essere, avere) (of corn) to come into ear.

**spighẹtta** *f.* braid; trimming.

**spigliat-o** *adj.* easy; free and easy; nimble; self-possessed. **-amẹnte** *adv.* freely; easily; nimbly. **-ẹzza** *f.* ease; agility; self-possession.

**spigo** *m.* lavender.

**spi·gola** *f.* (ichth.) bass.

**spigol-are** [A1 s] *tr.* to glean. **-atọre** *m.*, **-atrice** *f.* gleaner. **-atura** *f.* gleaning.

**spi·golo** *m.* sharp corner; corner of a field; edge (of a step).

**spigrire** [D2] *tr.* to rouse to action; *intr.* (*aux.* essere), *rfl.* to shake off laziness.

**spilla** *f.* brooch; tie-pin.

**spillaccherare** [A1 s] *tr.* to brush mud from.

**spill-o** pin; hair-pin; *— di sicurezza*, safety-pin; *tacchi a —*, stiletto heels; thin jet of wine, water or other liquid; piercer, gimlet. **-a·io** *m.* pin-maker. **-are** [A1] *tr.* to pierce; to broach; to tap (cask); to draw (wine, blood); *intr.* (*aux.* avere) to pour, to spill. **-a·tico** *m.* pin-money. **-atura** *f.* tapping; broaching; piercing. **-ọne** *m.* hat-pin; brooch; tie-pin.

**spilọrc-io** *adj.* stingy, mean, niggardly; miserly, close-fisted; sordid; *n.m.* niggardly or miserly man. **-eri·a** *f.* niggardliness, stinginess, meanness.

**spiluccare** [A2] *tr.* to pluck off.

**spilungọn-e** *adj.* tall and lanky; *n.m.* lanky man. **-a** *f.* tall girl.

**spina** *f.* (bot.) spine; thorn; prick (of fortune), annoyance, trouble; *— dorsale*, backbone; (electr.) plug.

**spin-ace** *m.*, **-a·cio** *m.* spinach; (cul.) *gli -aci*, spinach.

**spinapẹsce** *m.* (archit.) herringbone brick-work.

**spinato** *adj.* thorny; *filo di ferro —*, barbed wire; (of cloth) twilled; boned, filleted.

**spinẹto** *m.* thicket (of thorn bushes.)

**spinẹtta** *f. dim.* of **spina**; (mus.) spinet; virginal.

**spi·ngere** [C5] *tr.* to push; to thrust; to shove; to drive; to propel; to incite, to induce; (on a door) push; *rfl.* to push forward; to venture.

**spin-o** *m.* thorn-tree; *— bianco*, hawthorn, may; *— nero*, blackthorn, sloe; (zool.) spine (of a hedgehog); *adj.* prickly; (bot.) *uva -a*, gooseberry; (zool.) *porco —*, porcupine; hedgehog. **-osità** *f.* prickliness; thorniness; (fig.) awkwardness, ticklishness. **-ọso** *adj.* prickly; thorny; (fig.) difficult; awkward; *n.m.* hedgehog.

**spint-a** *f.* push, shove; thrust; (fig.) stimulus, inducement. **-arella, -erella** *f. dim.* little push. **-ọne** *m. augm.* violent shove.

**spinte o sponte** *adv. phr.* by hook or by crook.

**spinto** *part.* of **spi·ngere**; *adj.* pushed; carried forward; led on; driven; inclined.

**spiombare** [A1 c] *tr.* to remove lead from; to bring tottering down; to unseal; *intr.* (*aux.* avere, essere) to bulge; to lean from the vertical; to weigh as heavy as lead.

**spiọn-e** *m.* master-spy; secret agent. **-a·ggio** *m.* espionage; secret service. **-cino** *m.* peep-hole.

**spio·v-ere** [C27] *impers.* (*aux.* essere) to stop raining; *intr.* (*aux.* essere) to flow, to run away. **-ente** *part. adj.* flowing; draining; *baffi -enti*, drooping moustache; *n.m.* watershed.

**spippolare** [A1 s] *tr.* to pick, to pluck; (fig.) to rattle off.

**spira** *f.* coil; spiral; loop; curl (of smoke); *— ornamentale*, scroll.

**spira·bile** *adj.* See under **spirare.**

**spira·glio** *m.* air-hole, vent; breath of air; small skylight; peep, glimmer.

**spirale** *adj.*, *n.f.* spiral.

**spir-are** [A1] *intr.* (*aux.* avere) to breathe, to exhale; (of wind, breeze, etc.) to blow; (*aux.* essere) to breathe one's last, to expire; *tr.* to breathe out; to give off; to inspire; *n.m.* expiry, expiration, end. **-a·bile** *adj.* (of air) fit to breathe, breathable. **-ame** *m.* air-hole; vent; crack. **-aziọne** *f.* inspiration.

**spiri·t-ico** *adj.* spiritualistic. **-ịsmo** *m.* spiritualism. **-ista** *m.*, *f.* (*pl.* **-isti, -iste**) spiritualist.

**spi·rit-o** *m.* breath of life; spirit; ghost; mind; soul; wit; courage; temper; boldness; leader, inspiration; opinion, feeling; alcohol. **-ale** *adj.* spiritual; holy, divine; inspired. **-ato** *part. adj.* possessed (by an evil spirit); crazy, mad; terrified. **-ello** *m. dim.* sprite, elf, goblin; (of a child) imp.

**spiritọs-o** *adj.* alcoholic, spirituous; (of wine) strong; witty; vivacious; ingenious; *fare lo —*, to be facetious. **-a·ggine** *f.* forced wit; witticism. **-ịsmo** *m.* (philos.) spiritualism. **-ità** *f.* wit; wittiness; vivacity.

**spiritual-e** *adj.* spiritual; intellectual. **-ịsmo** *m.* (philos.) spiritualism. **-ista** *m.*, *f.* anti-materialist.

**spiro** *m.* (poet.) breath; spirit; soul.

**spir-oidale, -o·ide** *adj.* spiral.

**spium-are** [A1] *tr.* to pluck, to strip of feathers; (fig.) to fleece; *rfl.* to moult. **-acciare** [A3] *tr.* to shake up (bed, pillows, cushions).

**spi·zzi-co** *m.* (*pl.* **-chi**) pinch; *adv. phr. a —*, little by little, in driblets. **-care** [A2 s] *tr.* to pinch; to nibble; to take a little of.

**sple·nd-ere** [B1] *intr.* (*aux.* essere, avere) to shine; to be resplendent; to sparkle; to glitter; to be illustrious. **-ente** *part. adj.* bright; shining; resplendent.

**sple·ndid-o** *adj.* bright, brilliant, dazzling; splendid, gorgeous, magnificent; glistening; *n.m.*

munificent and lavish person. **~ęzza** *f.* magnificence.

**splendǫre** *m.* brightness, brilliance; splendour; magnificence.

**splene·tico** *adj.* splenetic.

**Spluga** *pr.n.m.* (geog.) *Passo dello —*, Splügen Pass.

**spodestare** [A1] *tr.* to dispossess; to dethrone; to depose; to deprive of power.

**spoet-are** [A1] *tr.* to deprive of the title of poet. **~iẓẓare** [A1] *tr.* to disillusion; to disenchant; *rfl.* to lose one's ideals.

**spo·gli-a** *f.* (of a snake) slough; (of a wild beast) skin; (of a human being) mortal remains; spoil, booty; (of an onion) skin or layer; (of pastry) case, shell. **~are** [A4] *tr.* (*prep.* di) to divest (of); to despoil, to plunder; *rfl.* to undress (oneself), to strip (oneself); to divest oneself (of); to give up; to shed. **~arellista** *f.* strip-tease dancer, stripper. **~arello** *m.* strip-tease act or show. **~atǫio** *m.* dressing-room; locker-room; cloak-room. **~atǫre** *m.* despoiler. **~aziǫne** *f.* spoliation; plundering.

**spo·glio** *adj.* bare, stripped, naked, undressed; *n.m.* cast off clothing; undressing; (of a snake) slough; culling; scrutiny; *procedere allo —*, to count the votes.

**spol-a** *f.* shuttle; spool; (fig.) *far la — fra*, to go to and fro between. **~ętta** *f.* fuse.

**spolmonare** [A1 c] *rfl.* to get out of breath (with talking); to shout or talk oneself hoarse.

**spolpare** [A1 c] *tr.* to strip flesh from; (fig.) to fleece.

**spoltr-ire** [D2] *tr.*, **~onire** [D2] *tr.* to cure of laziness; to rouse; *rfl.* to rouse oneself.

**spolver-are** [A1 sc] *tr.* to dust; to brush; (fig.) to make a clean sweep of; to eat up everything; to steal, to sprinkle; *rfl.* to dust oneself; to be pulverized. **~atǫre** *m.* duster; *~atore elettrico*, vacuum cleaner. **~atura** *f.* dust-coat; overall. **~ino** *m.* duster; powder; fine sand. **~ìo** *m.* (*pl.* ~ìi) cloud of dust. **~iẓẓare** (A1) *tr.* to powder, to dust; to pulverize.

**spǫlvero** *m.* dusting; dust raised by dusting; (fig.) mere show, superficiality; smattering.

**spǫnda** *f.* bank; edge, border; side; coast; parapet; quay, embankment.

**spongi-fǫrme** *adj.* spongy. **~ǫso** *adj.* spongiose, spongy.

**sponsale** *adj.* relating to a wedding; matrimonial, nuptial; *n.m.pl.* nuptials, wedding; betrothal.

**sponta·ne-o** *adj.* spontaneous; natural, sincere; voluntary. **~ità** *f.* spontaneity; spontaneousness.

**sponte** *adv. phr.* — *o spinte*, willy-nilly.

**spopolare** [A1 s] *tr.* to depopulate; to empty (of people); *abs.* to draw crowds (i.e. leaving all other places empty).

**spoppare** [A1] *tr.* to wean.

**spora** *f.* (bot.) spore.

**spora·dico** *adj.* sporadic; scattered, rare.

**sporc-acciare, ~are** see under **sporco.**

**sporcheri·a** *f.* See **porcheria.**

**sporchęzza** *f.* dirtiness, filth(iness).

**sporchi·zia** *f.* See **sporcizia.**

**sporci·zia** *f.* dirt, filth; filthiness; disgraceful conduct, indecency.

**spor-co** *adj.* (*m.pl.* ~**chi**) dirty; foul; filthy; soiled; *patente ~ca*, endorsed licence; (fig.) *parole ~che*, dirty talk, obscene language. **~cacciare** [A3] *tr.* to make filthy. **~cacciǫne** *m.* filthy person. **~care** [A2] *tr.* to dirty, to soil; to foul; to make a mess on; to besmirch; *rfl.* (*acc.* of *prn.* 'si') to get dirty, to dirty oneself; (*dat.* of *prn.* 'si') *~carsi le mani*, to soil one's hands.

**spo·rg-ere** [C5] *intr.* (*aux.* essere) to jut out, to project; *tr.* to stretch out; to put out; to put forward; to present; to hand out; to institute; to start; *rfl.* to lean out; (rlwy.) *è pericoloso ~ersi*, it is dangerous to lean out; to jut out; to stand out, to protrude; to reach. **~ente** *part. adj.* projecting; protruding; overhanging; prominent. **~enza** *f.* protrusion; projection.

**sport** *m. indecl.* (pron. as Fr.) sport. **~ivo** *adj.* sporting; good at sport; *n.m.* one who is good at sport; spectator, patron of sport.

**sporta** *f.* hamper; basket; shopping-basket; *cappello a —*, wide-brimmed straw hat.

**sportare** [A1] *tr.*, *intr.* (*aux.* essere) (archit.) to project.

**sportell-o** *m.* wicket gate; shutter; hatch; small door (in a large door or gate); door of a coach, railway carriage or motor car; counter, cash desk; ticket-window; counter; booking-office.

**sporto** *part.* of **spo·rgere**; *adj.* stretched out; *n.m.* projection; balcony; penthouse; shutter; stall for display of goods outside a shop.

**spoș-a** *f.* betrothed, bride-to-be. **~ali·zio** *m.* wedding. **~amęnto** *m.* marriage. **~are** [A1] *tr.* to marry; to wed; to give in marriage; (fig.) to embrace, to espouse; *rfl.* (*acc.* of *prn.* 'si'; *prep.* a, con) to get married (to), to marry; (*dat.* of *prn.* 'si') *se la ~a domani*, he's marrying her tomorrow. **~ina** *f. dim.* young bride. **~ino** *m. dim.* young bridegroom; young husband. **~o** *m.* bridegroom, husband-to-be; *novelli ~i*, newly married couple; *I Promessi Sposi*, *The Betrothed* (title of a novel by Alessandro Manzoni).

**sposs-are** [A1] *tr.* to exhaust; to fatigue; to tire out; to weaken. **~amęnto** *m.*, **~atęzza** *f.* exhaustion; weakness. **~atamęnte** *adv.* wearily. **~ato** *part. adj.* exhausted.

**spost-are** [A1] *tr.* to displace; to move, to shift; to change, to unsettle; *rfl.* to move, to shift. **~amęnto** *m.* displacement; shift. **~ato** *part. adj.* displaced, moved; unsettled; mentally deranged; *n.m.* mentally deranged person.

**sprang-a** *f.* bar; cross-bar; bolt; arm of a balance; rail; rivet. **~are** [A2] *tr.* to bar; to bolt. **~ato** *part. adj.* riveted; tied (with metal); barred, bolted.

**spranghętta** *f. dim.* of **spranga**; (mus.) bar-line.

**sprazzo** *m.* splash; spray; flash, gleam, beam.

**sprec-are** [A2] *tr.* to waste; to squander. **~amęnto** *m.* waste; squandering. **~atǫre** *m.* wastrel.

**spre-co** *m.* (*pl.* ~**chi**) waste, squandering. **~cǫna** *f.*, **~cǫne** *m.* squanderer, waster; wastrel.

**spregi-are** [A3] *tr.* to despise; to disdain; *rfl.* to despise oneself; to neglect oneself. **~ativo** *adj.* disdainful; derogatory; disparaging. **~atǫre** *m.*, **~atrice** *f.* scorner; despiser.

**spre·g-io** *m.* contempt, scorn, disdain. **~ęvole** *adj.* contemptible; despicable; mean.

**spregiudic-are** [A2 s] *rfl.* to rid oneself of prejudice; *tr.* to rid of prejudice. **~atęzza** *f.* open-mindedness. **~ato** *part. adj.* unprejudiced; open-minded; *n.m.* fair-minded man; free-thinker.

**spre·m-ere** [B1] to squeeze; to press; to wring. **~ilimǫni** *m. indecl.* lemonsqueezer. **~uta** *f.* squeeze; squash; *~uta di limone*, lemon-squash. **~uto** *part. adj.* pressed; squeezed; wrung out.

**spretare** [A1] *tr.* to unfrock (a priest).

**sprezz-are** [A1] *tr.* to despise, to disdain, to scorn. **~a·bile** *adj.* despicable. **~ante** *part. adj.* contemptuous; haughty; *n.m.*, *f.* haughty, disdainful person. **~atǫre** *m.*, **~atrice** *f.* scorner; despiser. **~atura** *f.* nonchalance; ease; natural skill.

**sprezzo** *m.* disdain; contempt; scornful manner.

**sprigionare** [A1 c] *tr.* to release (from prison); to set free; to exhale, to emit.

**sprill-are** [A1] *intr.* (*aux.* essere) to spurt, to spout. **~o** *m.* jet, spout, spurt.

**sprimacciare** [A3] *tr.* to shake up (cushion, pillow).
**sprizzare** [A1] *intr.* (*aux.* essere) to spray; *tr.* to sprinkle, to spray; — *scintille*, to send forth a shower of sparks.
**sproc-co** *m.* (*pl.* **-chi**) shoot, sprout; twig.
**sprofond-are** [A1 c] *intr.* (*aux.* essere) to sink; to founder, to go to the bottom; to collapse; *rfl.* to sink; to give way; *tr.* to sink. **-amęnto** *m.* sinking; foundering. **-ato** *part. adj.* sunk, deep; (fig.) immersed, absorbed; collapsed; ruined; *adv.* out and out, extremely; *buio -ato*, pitch dark.
**sprolo·quio** *m.* long, tedious speech.
**spron-e** *m.* spur; (fig.) stimulus, incentive; footing (of a wall); cutwater (of a bridge); groyne. **-are** [A1 c] *tr.* to set spurs to; (fig.) to incite, to goad. **-ata** *f.* spurring. **-ella** *f.* rowel.
**sproporzion-e** *f.* disproportion. **-ale, -ato** *adj.* disproportionate.
**spropo·ṣit-o** *m.* mistake, blunder; *costa uno* —, it costs an excessive amount; *adv. phr. a* —, inopportunely. **-are** [A1 s] *intr.* (*aux.* avere) to blunder, to make mistakes; to talk nonsense. **-ato** *part. adj.* mistaken, absurd; excessive.
**spropriare** [A4] *tr.* (*prep.* di) to dispossess; to despoil; *rfl.* to sell ones property.
**sprovved-ęre** [B35] *tr.* (*prep.* di) to deprive (of); to leave unprovided (with). **-utęzza** *f.* unpreparedness. **-uto** *part. adj.* destitute; unprovided; *adv. phr. alla -uta*, unexpectedly.
**sprovvist-o** *part.* of **sprovvedęre**; *alla -a*, unexpectedly.
**spruzz-are** [A1] *tr.* (*prep.* di) to spray, to sprinkle (with); to splash (with); *impers.* (of rain) to drizzle. **-a·glia** *f.* fine spray; drizzle. **-ata** *f.* sprinkling; light shower. **-atọio** *m.* sprinkler.
**spruzz-o** spray; sprinkling; *doccia a* —, shower-bath; jet, spurt. **-olare** [A1 s] *tr.* to sprinkle; *impers.* (of rain) to drizzle.
**spudorato** *adj.* shameless, impudent.
**spugn-a** *f.* sponge; tell-tale; gossip; Turkish towelling. **-ata, -atura** *f.* sponging; sponge-down. **-ọso** *adj.* spongy.
**spulare** [A1] *tr.* to winnow; to hull; to fan.
**spulci-are** [A3] *tr* to rid of fleas; (fig.) to scrutinize; to examine minutely; to go through with a fine comb. **-atura** *f.* scrutiny; close inspection.
**spum-a** *f.* foam; froth. **-ante** *part. adj.* foaming; (of wine) sparkling; *n.m.* sparkling wine. **-are** [A1], **-eggiare** [A3 c] *intr.* (*aux.* avere) to foam; to froth; to sparkle. **-ọso** *adj.* frothy; foam-like.
**spuntare** [A1] *tr.* to blunt; to break the point of; to trim; to undo, to unpin; (fig.) to overcome; to remove, to erase, to strike out; to tick; *intr.* (*aux.* essere) to appear, to poke out, to come into view, to peep out; (of the sun) to rise; *n.m.* appearance; *allo spuntar del giorno*, at daybreak.
**spuntellare** [A1] *tr.* to unprop.
**spuntino** *m.* snack; light refreshment; snack bar.
**spunt-o** *m.* starting point; rise, origin, impulse, start; (theatr.) cure; spurt. **-ọne** *m. augm.* large spike; pike; halberd.
**spur-go** *m.* (*pl.* **-ghi**) mucus; expectoration; — *sanguigno*, discharge of blood; cleaning; drain, drainage; *pl.* rubbish, matter cleared away. **-gare** [A2] *tr.* to clear out; to purge.
**spu·rio** *adj.* spurious; illegitimate.
**sputacchiare** [A4] *intr.* to spit repeatedly.
**sputacchiera** *f.* spittoon.
**sput-o** *m.* spit, spittle; spitting. **-are** [A1] *intr.* (*aux.* avere) to spit; *vietato -are*, no spitting; *tr.* to spit out.; *-are tondo*, to speak solemnly. **-asentenze** *m., f. indecl.* wiseacre. **-ato** *part. adj.* spat out; (pop.) real, evident; *una bugia -ata*, a downright lie.
**squadernare** [A1] *tr.* to turn over the leaves of (a book); to display; *rfl.* to be dispersed, to be scattered.
**squadra**[1] *f.* square; *doppia* —, T-square; *essere a* —, to be at right-angles.
**squadr-a**[2] *f.* team; group; squad. **-i·glia** *f.* squadron; squad; flotilla.
**squadrare** [A1] *tr.* to square; to look at squarely; *intr.* (*aux.* avere; *prep.* a) to square (with); (fig.) to suit, to go well with.
**squadro** *m.* squaring; (eng.) square.
**squadrọne**[1] *m. augm.* of **squadro**; large set square used in shipbuilding.
**squadrọne**[2] *m.* squadron.
**squagliare** [A4] *tr.* to melt, to melt down, to liquefy; *rfl.* to melt.
**squali·fica** *f.* (sport) foul, disqualification; suspension.
**squa·llido** *adj.* squalid; dismal, dreary, wretched; gloomy; unkempt; wan.
**squallọre** *m.* pallor; wretched appearance; dreariness; gloom; squalor.
**squam-a** *f.* scale (of fish); flake of metal. **-are** [A1] *tr.* to scale, to remove scales from. **-ọso** *adj.* scaly; flaky.
**squarci-are** [A3] *tr.* to rend, to tear, to rip; *rfl.* to be torn asunder; to part. **-agola** *adv. phr. a -agola*, at the top of one's voice. **-ato** *part. adj.* torn, rent; loud.
**squa·rcio** *m.* tear, rent; gash; hole; leak; excerpt, extract.
**squart-are** [A1] *tr.* to quarter; to tear to pieces; to cut up; — *i minuti*, not to waste a minute. **-amęnto** *m.* quartering. **-atọio** *m.* chopper, butcher's cleaver.
**squass-are** [A1] *tr.* to shake violently; to rock; — *le spalle*, to shrug one's shoulders. **-amęnto** *m.* violent shaking. **-o** *m.* violent shaking, shock.
**squattrin-are**[1] [A1] *tr.* to leave penniless; to count out penny by penny; *rfl.* to be left penniless; *intr.* (*aux.* avere) to spend lavishly. **-ato** *part. adj.* penniless.
**squattrinare**[2] [A1] *tr.* to scrutinize; to peer at.
**squilibr-are** [A1] *tr.* to unbalance; to unsettle; to embarrass; *rfl.* to lose one's balance. **-ato** *part. adj.* unbalanced; deranged, insane.
**squili·brio** *m.* lack of balance; — *mentale*, mental derangement; difference; inequality.
**squill-a** *f.* bell; small bell; harness-bell; cow-bell; angelus (-bell). **-ante** *part. adj.* shrill; pealing; (of trumpets) blaring. **-are** [A1] *intr.* (*aux.* avere) to ring; to peal; to blare.
**squillo** *m.* ring, ringing; sound, note; blast; *ragazza* —, 'call girl'.
**squina·nzia** *f.* quinsy.
**squinternare** [A1] *tr.* to unbind; (fig.) to ruffle; to disarrange.
**squiṣit-o** *adj.* delicious, delicate; exquisite. **-ęzza** *f.* delicacy; perfection.
**squitti·nio** *m.* balloting; scrutiny of votes.
**squittire** [D2] *intr.* (*aux.* avere) to yelp; to squeal; to squeak.
**ṣradicare** [A2 s] *tr.* to uproot; (fig.) to eradicate, to extirpate.
**ṣragion-are** [A1 c] *intr.* (*aux.* avere) to reason falsely; to talk nonsense. **-amęnto** *m.* irrational talk. **-ęvole** *adj.* unreasonable; irrational; senseless.
**ṣregol-are** [A1 s] *tr.* to throw into disorder; to upset. **-atęzza** *f.* disorder; intemperance, excess; dissipation. **-ato** *part. adj.* disordered; dissolute.
**sta'** *abbrev.* of **stai**, *imp. 2nd pers. sing.* of **stare.**
**sta·bbi-o** *m.* (agric.) manure, dung; compost; fold, pen. **-are** [A4] *intr.* (*aux.* essere) to be in a stall, fold or pen; *tr.* to stable; to pen, to fold; to manure.

**-(u)olo** *m.* sty, pig-sty; small fold.

**sta·bile** *adj.* stable, steady, firm; durable; permanent; *beni stabili*, real estate; *n.m.* landed property; building; house.

**stabil-ire** [D2] *tr.* to establish; to ascertain; to fix; to settle; to assign; to state; to decree; *rfl.* to establish oneself; to settle. **-imẹnto** *m.* establishment; stabilization; factory, works.

**stabilità** *f.* stability; steadiness; firmness.

**stabiliẓẓare** [A1] *tr.* to stabilize.

**stacca·bile** *adj.* detachable.

**stacc-are** [A2] *tr.* (*prep.* da) to take off; to detach; to pull off; to unhook; to separate, to sever; to pronounce distinctly; — *il bollore*, to come to the boil; *rfl.* to come off, to come loose; to leave; to come unstuck; *intr.* (*aux.* avere) to come off; to stand out. **-ato** *part. adj.* detached, separate; distinct; interrupted, broken up.

**sta·cci-o** *m.* sieve; hair-sieve. **-are** [A3] *tr.* to sift, to sieve; to bolt; to riddle; to screen; (fig.) to sift. **-atura** *f.* siftings; bran.

**stac-co** *m.* (*pl.* **-chi**) separation, detachment; gap; detached; ticket; *fare* —, to stand out, to be prominent; (fig.) *fare* — *con*, to be in contrast with.

**stadera** *f.* steelyard (balance); — *a ponte*, weighbridge.

**sta·dio** *m.* stadium; sports ground; (fig.) stage.

**staff-a** *f.* stirrup; (fig.) *perdere le -e*, to lose one's temper; foot-board. **-ẹtta** *f. dim.* small bolt or bar; clamp; latch-holder; courier, dispatch-rider. **-iere** *m.* groom, footman.

**staffil-e** *m.* stirrup-leather; whip; strap. **-are** [A1] *tr.* to beat with a leather thong; to thrash.

**sta·ggi-o** *m.* prop; stay, stay-rod; one of the two stringers of a ladder; upright bar of cage; measuring rod. **-are** [A3] *tr.* to prop; to stay.

**stagiọn-e** *f.* season; high season; *fuori* —, off season; *cattiva* —, bad weather; *adv. phr. alla* —, as occasion offers. **-are** [A1c] *tr.* to season; to mature; *intr.* (*aux.* essere), *rfl.* to mature, to ripen; to be seasoned. **-ato** *part. adj.* seasoned; mature; ripe; (fig.) elderly.

**sta·gli-o** *m.* rough reckoning. **-are** [A4] *tr.* to hack; to cut unevenly; to lop; to keep a tally of.

**stagn-are**[1] [A5] *intr.* (*aux.* avere) to be stagnant; to lie, to collect; *tr.* to stanch, to stop the flow of. **-ante** *part. adj.* stagnant.

**stagn-are**[2] [A5] *tr.* to tin, to solder. **-ata** *f.* tin, can; packet wrapped in tin foil; soldering.

**stagno**[1] *m.* stagnant water; pond, pool.

**stagn-o**[2] *m.* tin; tin-ware; — *battuto*, tin-foil. **-a·io** *m.* tin-smith; tinker.

**stagno**[3] *adj.* proof; waterproof, watertight; airtight.

**sta·i-o** *m.* (*pl.* **sta·i** *m.*, **sta·ia** *f.*) bushel; *cappello a* —, top hat.

**stal-agmite** *f.* stalagmite. **-attite** *f.* stalactite.

**stall-a** *f.* stable; horsebox; cowshed; pigsty; sheepfold. **-a·ggio** *m.* stabling. **-are** [A1] *intr.* (*aux.* essere) to be stabled, to be in a stall; (of sheep) to be folded. **-iere** *m.* stableman, stable-boy, groom. **-ọne** *m.* stallion.

**stallo** *m.* choir stall; (fig.) seat of honour; residence; (chess) stalemate.

**sta-mane, -mani, -mattina** *adv.* this morning.

**stambẹc-co** *m.* (*pl.* **-chi**) wild goat.

**stamberga** *f.* dog-hole; hovel; garret.

**stambu·gio** *m.* dark little room.

**stambur-are** [A1] *intr.* (*aux.* avere) to beat the drum; to drum; *tr.* to proclaim. **-ata** *f.* drumming.

**stame** *m.* thread; (bot.) stamen.

**stamp-a** *f.* **1.** print; printing; presswork; *dare alle -e*, to print, to publish; engraving; print; *pl.* (on an envelope), printed matter. **2.** press; *addetto* —, press attaché. **3.** sort, class; type, character. **4.** mould, form; pastry-cutter.

**stamp-are** [A1] *tr.* to stamp, to press; to impress; to print; to publish; to mould; to punch; (fig.) to coin, to invent, to improvise. **-atello** *m.* block capital(s); heavy type.

**stampella** *f.* crutch; hurdy-gurdy.

**stamp-eri·a** *f.* printing-works, printing-house. **-ẹtta** *f.* stamping-die. **-i·glia** *f.* rubber or metal stamp; placard; (printed) form.

**stamp-ina** *f.* printer's proof. **-inare** [A1] *tr.* to stencil. **-ino** *m.* stencil; stencil plate; punch (for punching holes).

**stampo** *m.* stamp; mould; (fig.) kind, sort, type, class.

**stanare** [A1] *tr.* to drive (an animal) from its den; (fig.) to dislodge, to drive out.

**stan-co** *adj.* (*m.pl.* **-chi**; *prep.* di) tired; weary; fatigued; exhausted; worn out. **-care** [A2] *tr.* to tire, to fatigue; to weary; to bore; *rfl.* (*prep.* di, a) to get tired. **-cheggiare** [A3c] *tr.* to irritate; to bore; to annoy. **-chẹvole** *adj.* tiring. **-chẹzza** *f.* weariness, fatigue.

**standard** *adj.*, *n.m. indecl.* model. **-iẓẓare** [A1] *tr.* to standardize.

**stan-ga** *f.* bar, barrier; cross-bar. **-gare** [A2] *tr.* to bar, to prop; (fig.) to ill-treat. **-ghẹtta** *f.* small bar; bolt of a lock; curved ear-piece of spectacles; (equit.) bit.

**stanotte** *adv.* tonight; last night.

**stante** *part.* of **stare**; existing; current; present; this; *seduta* —, during the sitting; *n.m.* column, prop, support; bracket; *prep.* in view of, considering; *conj.* — *che*, as, since, seeing that.

**stanti·o** *adj.* stale; not fresh; stuffy.

**stantuffo** *m.* piston; plunger.

**stanz-a** *f.* (place of) residence; room; apartment; (prosod.) stanza; verse. **-iale** *adj.* permanent; stable. **-iamẹnto** *m.* deliberation; decree; appropriation, allocation. **-iare** [A4] *tr.* to appropriate, to allocate; to assign; *intr.* (*aux.* avere) to deliberate, to decree. **-ino** *m.* little room; dressing-room; privy, closet; lumber-room; (theatr.) box.

**stappare** [A1] *tr.* to uncork; *abs.* to open a bottle; to have a drink.

**stare** [A9] *intr.* (*aux.* essere). **1.** STATE, CONDITION: to be; *come sta?*, how are you?; — *seduto*, to be sitting down; to remain, to keep; to stay; — *in casa*, to stay at home. **2.** to live, to reside; to be situated. **3.** to stand; — *in piedi*, to stand up, to stand on one's feet. **4.** IN COMPOUND TENSES FOLLOWED BY 'DA': to have gone to see; *sono stato dal dentista*, I have been to the dentist; *sua moglie era stata dalla sarta*, his wife had gone to see her dressmaker. **5.** to delay; to wait; *stette un po', poi scrisse la lettera*, he waited a little, then wrote the letter. **6.** FOLLOWED BY PREPOSITION 'A': — *ai patti*, to stand by an agreement, to keep a bargain; — *a uno*, to fall to the lot of, to be the duty of; to suit. **7.** FOLLOWED BY PREPOSITION 'A' AND INFINITIVE: — *a vedere*, to wait and see; — *ad ascoltare*, to listen. **8.** FOLLOWED BY PREPOSITION 'PER' AND INFINITIVE: — *per partire*, to be on the point of going. **9.** FOLLOWED BY OTHER PREPOSITIONS. **su**: — *sulle generali*, to keep to generalities. in: *non* — *in sè dalla gioia*, to be beside oneself with joy. **10.** FOLLOWED BY 'BENE': *sta bene!*, all right!, very well!; *ti sta bene*, it serves you right; *il vestito ti sta bene*, the dress suits you. **11.** FOLLOWED BY GERUND: to be in the act of; *stavamo parlando*, we were just talking. **12.** WITH PLEONASTIC RFL. PRONOUN AND ENCLITIC 'NE': *starsene con le mani in mano*, to be idle; *starsene di mangiare*, to stop eating. **13.** *n.m.* standing; stay.

**starn-a** *f.* partridge. **-azzare** [A1] *intr.* (*aux.* avere) (of birds) to flutter; *tr.* *-azzare le ali*, to flap their wings.

**starnutare** [A1] and derivs. See **starnutire.**

**starnut-ire** [D2] *intr.* (*aux.* avere) to sneeze. **-o** *m.* sneeze; sneezing.

**stasare** [A1] *tr.* to unstop, to clear.

**stasẹra** *adv.* this evening; to-night.

**stạsi** *f. indecl.* inactivity, stoppage; standstill.

**statale** *adj.* See under **stato**[2].

**stata·rio** *adj.* steady; static; stable; fixed.

**sta·tica** *f.* statics.

**sta·tico** *adj.* static; immobile; steady.

**stati·stica** *f.* statistics.

**stativo** *m.* stand; tripod.

**stato**[1] *part.* of **stare** or **essere.**

**stat-o**[2] *m.* **1.** state, condition; situation; repair, order, trim; position, posture; status; occupation; record; — *di servizio*, record of service; account, return, list. **2.** (leg.) — *civile*, legal status; *registri dello — civile*, records of births, marriages and deaths. **3.** (pol.) state; government; *Chiesa e —*, Church and State; *il terzo —*, the third estate. **4.** (mil.) — *di guerra*, state of war; — *maggiore generale*, General Staff. **5.** (geog.) *gli -i balcanici*, the Balkan States; *lo Stato Libero d'Irlanda*, the Irish Free State; *gli Stati Uniti*, the United States of America. **-ale** *adj.* (of the) State, government; *impiegati -ali*, civil servants; *n.m., f.* civil servant. **-ista** *m.* statesman. **-ịẓẓare** [A1] *tr.* to nationalize. **-ịẓẓaziọne** *f.* nationalization.

**sta·tu-a** *f.* statue; — *a bassorilievo*, figure in low relief. **-a·ria** *f.* statuary; sculpture. **-a·rio** *adj.* statuesque; *n.m.* sculptor. **-ẹtta** *f. dim.* statuette.

**statuire** [D2] *tr.*, *intr.* (*aux.* avere) to decree; to ordain.

**statunitense** *adj.* relating to, belonging to the United States of America; *n.m., f.* American (of the U.S.A.).

**statura** *f.* stature, height, size; (fig.) grandeur, eminence.

**statut-o** *m.f.* statute; constitution; articles of association; *pl.* rules (of a club). **-ale, -a·rio** *adj.* statutory.

**stavolta** *adv.* this time.

**staziọn-e** *f.* station; — *balneare*, watering-place; — *climatica*, health resort. **-are** [A1 c] *intr.* (*aux.* avere) to stand, to stay; (of vehicles) to park, to be parked.

**stazzare** [A1] to measure, to gauge; (naut.) — *la nave*, to measure or calculate the ship's tonnage.

**stazzo** *m.* station, stand; post; roadstead; fold (standing) for sheep.

**stẹc-ca** *f.* small stick; slat; rib (of fan, umbrella); splint; paper-knife; (billiards) cue; (rlwy.) fish-plate. **-care** [A2] to fence, to rail off; to put in splints; to cut with a paper-knife. **-cata** *f.* palisade, fence, stockade; wall. **-china** *f.*, **-chino** *m. dim.* toothpick; little stick. **-chire** [D2] *tr.* to kill outright; *intr.* (*aux.* essere), *rfl.* to grow thin, to dry up; to go stiff (with cold). **-chito** *part. adj.* extremely thin; *morto -chito*, stone dead. **-co** *m.* (*pl.* **-chi**) stick; dry twig; wooden peg, pin; thorn; toothpick. **-conare** [A1 c] *tr.* to fence in. **-conato** *part. adj.* fenced in; *n.m.* enclosure; stockade.

**Ste·fano** *pr.n.m.* Stephen; (fam.) stomach, belly, 'little Mary'.

**stẹgola** *f.* handle of a plough.

**stel-a, -e** *f.* pillar.

**stẹll-a** *f.* star; (fig.) paper streamer; rowel; asterisk; film star. **-are** [A1 c] *tr.*, *rfl.* to shine like a star; to spangle; *adj.* stellar; star-shaped. **-eggiare** [A3 c] *tr.* to embroider in cross-stitch; to star; *intr.* (*aux.* avere) to scintillate. **-ẹtta** *f. dim.* asterisk; small star. **-ina** *f. dim.* asterisk.

**stẹlo** *m.* stalk, stem, bole; axis; support.

**stemm-a** *m.* (*pl.* **-i**) coat of arms, armorial bearings, shield.

**stemper-are** [A1 s], **stemprare** [A1] *tr.* to dilute; to dissolve; to mix; — *la calcina*, to slake lime; (fig.) to water down; *rfl.* to melt; to grow blunt. **-atamẹnte** *adv.* immoderately, excessively.

**stempiare** [A4] *rfl.* to go bald.

**stendardo** *m.* standard, banner.

**ste·nd-ere** [C1] *tr.* to extend, to stretch; to spread out; to hang out (washing); — *l'arco*, to release the bowstring; (admin.) — *il processo verbale*, to draw up the minutes.

**stenebrare** [A1 s] *tr.* to illuminate, to light up; (fig.) to enlighten.

**stenodattilo·graf-o** *m.*, **-a** *f.* shorthand-typist. **-i·a** *f.* shorthand-typing.

**stenografare** [A1 s] *tr.* to write in shorthand.

**steno·grafo** *m.* shorthand writer, stenographer.

**stent-are** [A1] *intr.* (*aux.* avere) to be in need; to find it hard; to be hardly able; *rfl.* to strive, to exert oneself; to endeavour. **-atẹzza** *f.* difficulty; poverty; straitened circumstances. **-ato** *part. adj.* difficult, hard; straitened; stunted; *n.m.* difficulty, awkwardness; effort.

**stent-o** *m.* hardship; suffering; privation; difficulty; effort; *adv. phr.* *a —*, hardly, with difficulty; *adj.* stunted. **-ino** *adj.*, *n.m.* stunted (child).

**ster-co** *m.* (*pl.* **-chi**) excrement; dung.

**stere-ofoni·a** *f.* stereophone. **-ofo·nico** *adj.* stereophonic. **-ometri·a** *f.* solid geometry. **-otipare** [A1] *tr.* to stereotype. **-osco·pico** *adj.* stereoscopic. **-otipato** *part. adj.* stereotyped; stereotype.

**ste·ril-e** *adj.* sterile, barren, unfruitful, useless; vain. **-ità** *f.* sterility; barrenness; unproductiveness. **-ire** [D2] *intr.* (*aux.* essere), *rfl.* to become sterile, barren, unproductive; *tr.* to make barren, to exhaust the fertility (of). **-ịẓẓare** [A1] *tr.* to sterilize.

**sterlina** *f.* pound (sterling); *due sterline*, £2.

**stermin-are** [A1 s] *tr.* to ravage, to destroy; to exterminate; to root out. **-amẹnto** *m.* extermination; destruction. **-atẹzza** *f.* boundlessness; immensity. **-ato** *part. adj.* exterminated; boundless; immense. **-atọre** *m.*, **-atrice** *f.* exterminator; destroyer; *adj.* destroying.

**stermi·nio** *m.* extermination, massacre; destruction; enormous quantity.

**sterno** *m.* breastbone.

**sternuto** *m.* see **starnuto,** under **starnutire.**

**sterp-o** *m.* shoot from an old stump; stump; thorn-bush. **-a·glia** *f.* thicket. **-a·io** *m.* thicket, brake. **-ame** *m.* heap of brushwood. **-amẹnto** *m.* rooting out.

**sterr-are** [A1] *tr.*, *abs.* to dig out, to dig trenches for foundations; to level down. **-ato** *part. adj.* dug out; levelled; *n.m.* unmetalled road; dust road.

**sterro** *m.* muck-shifting; ditch.

**stertọre** *m.* stertorous breathing.

**sterzare**[1] [A1] *tr.* to divide into three parts; — *un bosco*, to thin out a wood; — *tabacchi*, to blend tobaccos; *rfl.* to work in shifts.

**sterzare**[2] [A1] *intr.* (*aux.* avere) to swerve; *tr.* (motor.) to steer.

**sterzo** *m.* steering; steering-wheel; *adv. phr.* *di sotto —*, secretly, indirectly.

**stẹsa** *f.* spread; display; smear(ing); *una — di vernice*, a coat of varnish.

**stẹso** *part.* of **ste·ndere**; *adj.* stretched out; extended; spread; smeared; written down.

**stes·sere** [B1] *tr.* to unravel; (fig.) to unweave.

**stẹsso** *adj.* same; very; *è la gentilezza stessa*, he is kindness itself; *n.m.* the same (thing);

*adv. phr. lo stesso*, notwithstanding.
**stesura** *f.* drawing up, drafting; version; draft.
**stetosco·pio** *m.* stethoscope.
**sti·a**[1] *f.* hen-coop.
**sti·a**[2] *1st, 2nd, 3rd pers. pres. subj.* of **stare**; *imp.* — *seduto*, don't get up.
**Stige** *pr.n.m.* (myth.) Styx.
**stigm-a** *m.* (*pl.* **-ate** *f.*) stigma; stamp, brand.
**stil-e**[1] *m.* writing-style, stylus; engraving tool; beam (of a balance); probe; pit-prop. **-ẹtto** *m.* small dagger, stiletto. **-ogra·fica** *f.* fountain-pen.
**stil-e**[2] *m.* style; (calendar) style of reckoning; (sport) form, style. **-ista** *m., f.* stylist. **-i·stica** *f.* rhetoric; stylistics. **-i·stico** *adj.* stylistic.
**still-a** *f.* drop. **-are** [A1] *tr.* to drip, to ooze, to exude; to distil; to instil, to infuse; *intr.* (*aux.* avere) to drizzle, to spot with rain, to drip. **-ato** *part. adj.* oozed; drawn up (in writing); dictated.
**stilo**[1] *m.* (for sound recordings) stylus.
**stilo**[2] *m.* (archit.) rustic column, term, terminus; shaft (of a column).
**stilogra·fica** *f.* see under **stile**[1].
**stim-a** *f.* esteem; estimation; respect, consideration, valuation. **-are** [A1] *tr.* to value; to reckon; to esteem, to appreciate; to consider, to deem; to estimate.
**sti·mmate** *f.pl.* the Five Wounds of Christ, the stigmata; brand (on a convict); scar.
**sti·mol-o** *m.* goad; spur; stimulus, incentive; annoyance. **-are** [A1 s] *tr.* to goad, to urge on; to whet; to excite; to stimulate; to encourage.
**stin-co** *m.* (*pl.* **-chi**) shin-bone, tibia.
**sti·ngere** [C5] *tr.* to fade, to discolour; (fig.) to obscure; to deface; *intr.* (*aux.* essere), *rfl.* to fade; to lose colour.
**stinto** *part.* of **sti·ngere**; *adj.* faded.
**stip-a**[1] *f.* brushwood, firewood; stubble. **-are** [A1] *tr.* to clear of undergrowth.
**stip-a**[2] *f.* heap; crowd, throng. **-are** [A1] *tr.* to crowd, to pack closely.
**stipe·ndi-o** *m.* salary; pay. **-are** [A4] *tr.* to pay a salary to; to engage; to employ, to hire. **-ato** *part. adj.* salaried, engaged; *n.m.* employee; clerk.
**stipẹtt-o** *m.* small cabinet. **-a·io** *m.* cabinet-maker; *cf.* **stipo.**
**sti·pite** *m.* post; upright of a cross; shaft (of a column); jamb; doorpost; stem; stock, family.
**stipo** *m.* cabinet; chiffonier; casket, jewel-case.
**stipsi** *f.* (med.) constipation; stypsis.
**stipul-are** [A1 s] *tr.* to stipulate; to lay down; to draw up, to arrange. **-aziọne** *f.* stipulation.
**stiracchi-are** [A4] *tr.* to stretch, to pull, to tug; (fig.) to distort, to twist; *abs.* to haggle, to bargain. **-atẹzza** *f.* sophistry; quibbling. **-ato** *part. adj.* stretched; forced.
**stir-are** [A1] *tr.* to stretch (out); to iron; to press; *rfl.* to stretch oneself. **-acalzọni** *m. indecl.* trouser-press. **-amẹnto** *m.* stretching; pulling. **-atọio** *m.* ironing-board. **-atọra, -atrice** *f.* laundress. **-atura** *f.* ironing.
**stiro** *m.* ironing; *ferro da* —, iron.
**stirpe** *f.* race, stock; extraction, birth; offspring, issue; descent.
**sti·tico** *adj.* styptic; constipated; astringent; (fig.) sour-tempered, surly; strict; miserly.
**stiva**[1] *f.* plough-handle.
**stiv-a**[2] *f.* (naut.) hold; — *del vino*, wine store. **-ag·gio** *m.* (naut.) stowage; loading plan.
**stival-e** *m.* boot, riding-boot. **-ẹtto** *m. dim.* half-boot. **-ọne** *m.* top-boot; jack-boot.
**stiv-are** [A1] *tr.* to stow (away); to cram, to pack. **-atọre** *m.* stevedore; trimmer.
**stizz-a**[1] *f.* anger; vexation; ill-humour. **-ire** [D2] *intr.* (*aux.* essere), *rfl.* to get angry; to fly into a passion; *tr.* to make angry, to vex. **-ito** *part. adj.* angry. **-ọso** *adj.* irascible; irritable.
**sto** *adj., prn.* (colloq.) see **questo.**
**stoccafisso** *m.* dried cod, stockfish.
**Stoccarda** *pr.n.f.* (geog.) Stuttgart.
**stoc-co**[1] *m.* (*pl.* **-chi**) dagger; rapier; swordstick. **-cata** *f.* stab, dagger-thrust; (fig.) sudden demand for money.
**stoc-co**[2] *m.* (*pl.* **-chi**) pole of a strawstack; stalk of maize.
**Stoccọlma** *pr.n.f.* (geog.) Stockholm.
**stoffa** *f.* cloth, material; stuff; (fig.) character, nature, quality.
**sto·ia** *f.* hassock; mat; sun-blind.
**sto·ic-o** *n.m.* Stoic; *adj.* stoical. **-iṣmo** *m.* Stoicism; courage.
**stola** *f.* stole.
**sto·lido** *adj.* dull, stupid.
**stọlt-o** *adj.* foolish, silly; stupid; *n.m.* fool. **-ẹzza** *f.* stupidity.
**sto·ma-co** *m.* (*pl.* **-chi**) stomach; *un'arcata di* —, *sforzi di* —, retching, vomiting; (cul.) tripe; (fig.) cheek, impudence; courage. **-cale** *adj.* good for the stomach, digestible. **-care** [A2 s] *tr.* to sicken; to disgust; *intr.* (*aux.* avere; *prep.* a) to sicken; to disgust; *rfl.* (*prep.* di) to be sickened. **-chẹvole** *adj.* disgusting, loathsome, revolting.
**stoma·tico** *adj., n.m.* stomachic, tonic.
**ston-are** [A1] *intr.* (*aux.* avere) (mus.) to sing (or play) out of tune; (of colours) to clash; to disagree, to be out of place. **-ato** *part. adj.* out of tune; out of place. **-atura** *f.* dissonance; false note.
**stọpp-a** *f.* (text.) tow. **-abuchi** *m. indecl.* wad; (fig.) stop-gap. **-a·ccio** *m.* wadding. **-are** [A1] *tr.* to plug, to stop up with tow.
**sto·ppia** *f.* (agric.) stubble; stubble field.
**stoppino** *m.* wick; taper.
**sto·rcere** [B1] *tr.* to twist; to wrench; to dislocate; to sprain; to unravel (fig.), to alter, to misrepresent; *rfl.* to twist; to writhe.
**stord-ire** [D2] *tr.* to stun; to daze, to bewilder; to make dizzy; *rfl.* to be dazed, to be bewildered; *intr.* (*aux.* essere) to be amazed. **-imẹnto** *m.* dizziness; dullness; bewilderment. **-ita·ggine** *f.* mistake, stupid action, folly. **-itẹzza** *f.* silliness. **-ito** *part. adj.* amazed, bewildered; stunned; giddy; thoughtless; foolish; scatter-brained; *n.m.* fool, scatterbrain.
**sto·ri-a** *f.* story, tale; history. **-ella** *f. dim.* short story; fable, fanciful story; fib, lie. **-ografi·a** *f.* historiography. **-o·grafo** *m.* historiographer.
**sto·rico** *adj.* historical; *n.m.* historian.
**storiọne** *m.* sturgeon.
**stormire** [D2] *intr.* (*aux.* avere) to rustle.
**stọrmo** *m.* host, crowd; flock, swarm; pack.
**stornare** [A1 c] *tr.* to avert; to divert; to turn aside, to ward off; *intr.* (*aux.* essere) to turn back, to be diverted.
**stornello**[1] *m.* (orn.) see **storno**; grey horse.
**stornello**[2] *m.* ditty of three lines.
**storno** *m.* (orn.) starling; *adj.* grey, dappled grey.
**storpi-are** [A4] *tr.* to cripple; to maim; to spoil; to bungle. **-amẹnto** *m.*, **-atura** *f.* crippling; maiming. **-ato** *part. adj.* crippled; badly pronounced; *n.m.* cripple.
**sto·rpio** *adj.* crippled; maimed; *n.m.* cripple; maiming.
**storta** *f.* wrenching; twisting; bend; twist; sprain; wrick.
**stort-o** *part.* of **sto·rcere**; *adj.* crooked, twisted, deformed; bent; (of eyes) squinting. **-ẹzza** *f.* crookedness; (fig.) falseness. **-ura** *f.* deformity; (fig.) false idea.
**stovi·gli-e** *f.pl.* crockery, pottery, earthenware; kitchen utensils; pots and pans. **-a·io** *m.* dealer in earthenware and crockery.

**stozz-o** *m.* gouge. **-are** [A1] *tr.* (eng.) to slot. **-atrice** *f.* (eng.) slotting machine.

**stra-** *pref.* (equiv. to Latin *extra*) indicating: **1.** INTENSITY, superiority or excess. **2.** MISCALCULATION, disproportion, error, distortion. **-balzare** [A1] *intr.* (*aux.* essere, avere) to jump about, to toss (about); *tr.* to jolt, to toss (about). **-balzo** *m.* jolt. **-bastare** [A1] *intr.* (*aux.* essere) to be more than enough. **-bẹre** [B4] *intr.* (*aux.* avere) to drink too much. **-biliare** [A4] *intr.* (*aux.* avere), *rfl.* to be astonished. **-boccare** [A2 c] *intr.* (*aux.* essere, avere) to overflow, to be superabundant. **-canare** [A1] *rfl.* to work like a navvy; to lead a dog's life. **-ca·rico** *adj.* (*m.pl.* **-ca·richi**) overloaded. **-collare** [A1] *intr.* (*aux.* essere) to fall over; to topple. **-contento** *adj.* (pop.) overjoyed. **-cuo·cere** [C15 d] *tr.* to overcook. **-fare** [B14] *intr.* (*aux.* avere) to overdo things, to do too much. **-fatto** *part. adj.* over-done. **-gọnfio** *adj.* extremely swollen. **-grande** *adj.* outsize; exceptionally large. **-lodare** [A1] *tr.* to overpraise. **-lunare** [A1] *tr.* to open one's eyes wide; to roll. **-lunato** *part. adj.* (of the eyes) staring wildly; rolling. **-pagare** [A2] *tr.* to overpay. **-pieno** *adj.* overfull; overflowing. **-piombare** [A1 c] *intr.* (*aux.* essere, avere) to be out of the perpendicular; to be out of true. **-piọmbo** *m.* overhang. **-potente** *adj.* overpowering; excessively powerful. **-potenza** *f.* excessive power. **-ripare** [A1] *intr.* (*aux.* essere, avere) (of a river) to overflow. **-sibilare** [A1 s] *rfl.* to be indifferent, not to care. **-vaṣare** [A1] *intr.* (*aux.* essere), *rfl.* to overflow (from a vessel). **-ve·cchio** *adj.* very old; (of food) mature, ripe. **-vedẹre** [B35] *tr.*, *intr.* (*aux.* avere) to see very clearly; to view mistakenly; to take a biased view (of). **-vi·ncere** [C5] *intr.* (*aux.* avere) to win easily, to achieve complete victory; to abuse one's victory. **-vi·zio** *m.* intemperance; excess. **-vo·lgere** [C5] *tr.* to roll; to twist; to upset. **-volto** *part.* of **stravo·lgere**; *adj.* twisted; contorted; distorted; convulsed; agitated; upset.

**stra·b-ico** *adj.* cross-eyed; *n.m.* person with a squint. **-iṣmo** *m.* squinting; squint.

**strac-ca** *f.* fatigue; *adv. phr.* *alla —*, wearily, indifferently, lazily. **-care** [A2] *tr.* to tire out; to weary, to wear out.

**stracceri·a** *f.* rags, rag.

**stracci-are** [A3] *tr.* to tear; to rend. **-a·io** *m.*, **-aiolo** *m.* rag-and-bone merchant, old-clothes man.

**stra·ccio** *adj.* torn, in rags; (paperm.) *carta straccia*, waste; *n.m.* rag, tatter; rent, tear; (text.) *lana da stracci*, shoddy.

**strac-co** *adj.* (*m.pl.* **-chi**) tired out; worn out; (fig.) poor; weak.

**strad-a** *f.* street; road; way; *— maestra*, main road; *— di circonvallazione*, by-pass (road). **-ale** *adj.* of the road(s), road; *incidenti -ali*, road accidents; *codice -ale*, highway code. **-are** [A1] *tr.* to direct, to put on the right road. **-iere** *m.* customs officer (for local customs).

**strafọro** *m.* piercing; perforation; small hole; *lavoro di —*, filigree work; *adv. phr. di —*, stealthily, secretly.

**strage** *f.* slaughter, massacre; havoc; (fam.) abundance.

**stra·lci-o** *m.* pruning, etc.; excerpt; clearance, clearance sale. **-are** [A3] *tr.* to prune; to lop off; (comm.) to clear (stock).

**strale** *m.* (poet.) arrow, dart; wound.

**stramazzo**[1] *m.* weir, overfall.

**stramazz-o**[2] *m.* heavy fall. **-are** [A1] *tr.* to fell; to knock senseless; *intr.* (*aux.* essere) to fall heavily.

**stramb-o** *adj.* crooked; odd, queer. **-eri·a** *f.* oddity, eccentricity.

**strame** *m.* straw, hay; litter; fodder.

**strampal-ato** *adj.* odd, queer; bold; illogical. **-eri·a** *f.* odd behaviour.

**stranẹzza** *f.* see under **strano.**

**strangol-are** [A1 s] *tr.* to strangle, to throttle; to suffocate; *rfl.* to shout or scream one's head off; to choke; to hang oneself. **-amẹnto** *m.* strangling; choking; strangulation.

**straniare** [A4] *tr.* (*prep.* da) to alienate, to estrange (from); *rfl.* to become estranged; to drift.

**straniero** *adj.* foreign; *n.m.* foreigner.

**stran-o** *adj.* strange, queer; odd, unusual. **-ẹzza** *f.* strangeness, oddity; queerness.

**straordina·ri-o** *adj.* extraordinary, uncommon, exceptional; special, extra; *lavoro —*, overtime; *n.m.* temporary clerk, teacher, lecturer. **-amẹnte** *adv.* extraordinarily; uncommonly; immensely.

**strapazz-are** [A1] *tr.* to ill-use, to ill-treat; to overwork; to scold, to bungle, to botch; *rfl.* to overwork, to wear oneself out. **-ata** *f.* scolding. **-o** *m.* rough usage; common use; fatigue; excess; *lingua da -o*, coarse language; rebuke, reprimand; *adj.* stark, staring mad.

**strapp-are** [A1] *tr.* (*prep.* a) to snatch, to tear; to pluck (from); to wrench; to extort. **-ata** *f.* sharp tug; pull.

**strapunt-o** *m.* quilt. **-ino** *m.* folding seat.

**stra·sci-co** *m.* (*pl.* **-chi**) trailing, dragging; trail; following; escort; train. **-care** [A2 s] *tr.* to drag, to trail; to shuffle; *rfl.* to drag oneself along. **-cọna** *f.*, **-cọne** *m.* person who drags his feet or shuffles along; loafer, idler.

**strascinare** [A1 s] *tr.* to drag.

**stra·scino** *m.* dragging; drag-net; sledge; truck, trailer.

**strasecolare** [A1 s] *intr.* (*aux.* essere, avere) to be amazed.

**stratagemm-a** *m.* (*pl.* **-i**) stratagem; trick.

**strat-ega** *m.* (*pl.* **-eghi**) strategist. **-egi·a** *f.* strategy. **-e·gico** *adj.* strategic, strategical.

**strat-o** *m.* (geol.) stratum, layer; (of paint, etc.) coat. **-ificare** [A2 s] *tr.* to stratify. **-ificaziọne** *f.* stratification. **-osfera** *f.* stratosphere.

**stratt-a** *f.* pull, tug, jerk. **-ọne** *m. augm.* violent jerk.

**stravagan-te** *adj.* queer, odd; eccentric; fantastic; whimsical; extravagant; excessive. **-za** *f.* oddness; eccentricity; freak of nature; extravagance; whimsicality.

**strazi-are** [A4] *tr.* to torture; to tear to pieces; to hurt, to spoil; to ruin. **-amẹnto** *m.* torture; havoc, destruction. **-ante** *part. adj.* heart-rending.

**stra·zio** *m.* havoc, destruction; laceration; torture.

**strẹ-ga** *f.* witch. **-gare** [A2 c] *tr.* to bewitch; to charm.

**strẹg-o** *m.* wizard; miser. **-ọne** *m.* wizard; witchdoctor. **-oneri·a** *f.* witchcraft, sorcery; spell.

**strẹgua** *f.* rate; standard; measure

**strem-are** [A1] *tr.* (*prep.* di) to exhaust, to drain (of); to reduce. **-ato** *part. adj.* exhausted.

**strenna** *f.* New Year's gift; *— di Natale*, Christmas present.

**stre·nu-o** *adj.* strenuous; vigorous. **-amẹnte** *adv.* strenuously; vigorously.

**stre·pit-o** *m.* din, noise; uproar, shouting, clamour. **-are** [A1 s] *intr.* (*aux.* avere) to shout and yell; to complain loudly. **-ọso** *adj.* noisy, loud.

**strẹtta** *f.* grasp; grip; pressure; *— di mano*, hand-clasp.

**strẹtt-o** *part.* of **stri·ngere**; *adj.* tight; narrow; pinched; near, close; restricted; strict; intimate; (mus.) *tempo —*, quickening time; *adv.* strictly, tight(ly); narrowly; closely; meanly; *n.m.* (geog.) strait(s), narrows. **-amẹnte** *adv.* strictly. **-ẹzza** *f.* narrowness; tightness; closeness;

scarcity; *pl.* straits; straitened circumstances. **-ọio** *m.* press.

**stri-a** *f.* stripe, thin streak; furrow. **-are** [A4] *tr.* to streak, to stripe.

**stricnina** *f.* strychnine.

**stri·d-ere** [B1] *intr.* (*aux.* avere) to creak; to screech, to shriek; to chirp; to hiss; (of colours) to clash, to jar. **-ente** *part. adj.* shrill, strident; creaking; rasping.

**strid-o** *m.* (*pl.* **-a** *f.* of the human voice, otherwise, **-i** *m.*) shrill cry; shriek, screech. **-ọre** *m.* creaking, shrieking; (of teeth) gnashing, grating; scraping (sound); piercing cold, biting wind. **-ìo** *m.* (*pl.* **-ìi**) continuous creaking, screeching. **-ọre** *m.* creaking; screeching; gnashing.

**stri·dulo** *adj.* shrill, piercing; strident.

**strigare** [A2] *tr.* to unravel; to disentangle.

**strige** *f.* screech-owl.

**stri·gli-a** *f.* currycomb. **-are** [A4] *tr.* to currycomb; (fig.) to scold.

**stri·golo** *m.* scream, shrill cry.

**strill-are** [A1] *intr.* (*aux.* avere) to shriek, to scream; to complain loudly. **-o** *m.* scream, shriek; loud protest. **-ọne** *m.* newspaper seller.

**strimpell-are** [A1] *tr.* to strum; to scrape. **-amẹnto** *m.* strumming; scraping.

**strinare** [A1] *tr.* to singe; to scorch.

**string-a** *f.* lace, shoelace. **-are** [A2] *tr.* to lace tightly. **-atẹzza** *f.* tightness; neatness; (fig.) conciseness.

**stri·ng-ere** [C5] *tr.* to draw tight, to tighten; to press, to squeeze, to grasp, to clasp; to clench; to bind together; to constrain, to compel; *impers. stringi stringi*, after all, when all's said and done; *intr.* (*aux.* avere) to be tight, to fit tightly. **-ente** *part. adj.* pressing; cogent; compelling; urgent.

**stri·sci-a** *f.* (*pl.* **striscie**) strip; stripe; streak; streamer. **-amẹnto** *m.* stroking; grazing, skimming; trailing, dragging; shuffling; creeping; (fig.) flattery, fawning. **-are** [A4] *tr.* to graze, to skim; to creep along by; to drag; to trail; to slur; to cut or tear into strips; *intr.* (*aux.* avere) to creep, to crawl; to glide, to bow and scrape; to cringe; *rfl.* to crawl, to creep; *-arsi a*, to fawn upon, to suck up to.

**stri·sci-o** *m.* dragging; shuffling; gliding. **-ọne** *m. augm.* large streak or strip; flatterer. **-ọni** *adv.* shuffling along.

**stritolare** [A1 s] *tr.* to crush; to grind down; to smash.

**strizz-are** [A1] *tr.* to squeeze; to wring (out); to press; — *l'occhio*, to wink. **-alimọni** *m. indecl.* lemonsqueezer. **-ata** *f.* squeeze; *-ata d'occhio*, wink.

**strof-a, -e** *f.* stanza, strophe; verse.

**strofin-are** [A1] *tr.* to rub; to polish, to wipe; *rfl. -arsi a*, to rub oneself against. **-a·ccio** *m.* kitchen teacloth; rag, duster; floorcloth.

**strologare** [A2] *tr.* to predict, to foretell; *intr.* (*aux.* avere) to tell fortunes; to rack one's brains.

**strombazzare** [A1] *tr.* to trumpet, to noise abroad; to boast about.

**strombett-are** [A1 c] *tr.*, *abs.* to play (badly) on the trumpet; (fig.) to boast, to blow one's own trumpet. **-iere** *m.* trumpeter, bugler.

**stronc-are** [A2 c] *tr.* to break off; to maim; to criticize harshly; *-arsi la gamba*, to break one's leg. **-atura** *f.* breaking off; maiming; (fig.) destructive criticism, savage review.

**strọn-co** *adj.* broken; maimed; *n.m.* cripple. **-cọne** *m.* stump.

**stropicciare** [A3] *tr.* to rub; to scrub; to scrape; to drag; to shuffle.

**strozz-a** *f.* throttle, gullet, throat; windpipe. **-are** [A1] *tr.* to strangle, to throttle; to choke; (fig.) to fleece, to rob; to stifle.

**stru·gg-ere** [C12] *tr.* to destroy; to consume; to melt; to waste; to afflict; *rfl.* to be destroyed; to be consumed. **-icuore** *m.* heartache; heartbreak; (cards) beggar-my-neighbour. **-imẹnto** *m.* melting; liquefaction; tender emotion; longing; boredom; destruction. **-itọre** *m.*, **-itrice** *f.* destroyer; *adj.* destructive.

**strullo** *m.* silly, stupid; *n.m.* simpleton.

**strumẹnt-o** *m.* tool; implement; instrument. **-ale** *adj.* instrumental. **-are** [A1 c] *tr.* to instrument; (leg.) to draw up.

**strusci-are** [A3] *tr.* to rub; to chafe; to wear out; *rfl.* to cringe; *-arsi a, contro*, to rub oneself against, (fig.) to fawn upon, to flatter.

**strutto** *part.* of **stru·ggere**; *adj.* melted (down); liquefied; consumed; wasted away, destroyed; *n.m.* lard.

**struttura** *f.* structure; construction; form, shape.

**struzzo** *m.* (orn.) ostrich.

**Stuard-o** *pr.n.m.*, **-a** *f.* Stuart.

**stuc-co**[1] *m.* (*pl.* **-chi**) plaster, stucco; stucco-work; plaster figure; plaster-cast. **-care** [A2] *tr.* (bldg.) to stucco; (eng.) to putty; (fig.) to surfeit, to bore. **-catọre** *m.* plasterer. **-catura** *f.* plastering.

**stuc-co**[2] *apocop. part.* of **stuccare**; *adj.* (*m.pl.* **-chi**) disgusted, sick (of). **-chẹvole, -cọso** *adj.* boring, tiresome.

**student-e** *m.* student; undergraduate; pupil. **-ẹsca** *f.* student-body. **-ẹsco** *adj.* (*m.pl.* **-ẹschi**) student-like; pertaining to students. **-ẹssa** *f.* woman student.

**studiacchiare** [A4] *tr.*, *abs.* to study listlessly; to be unable to concentrate on study.

**studi-are** [A4] *tr.* to study; to observe; to watch closely; to read, to examine; to survey; *intr.* (*aux.* avere) to study, to work; *rfl.* (*prep.* a, di) to try; to endeavour.

**stu·di-o** *m.* study, subject of study; reparation; office; study; studio; (fig.) inclination, affection; vocation; *a bello* —, on purpose. **-ọso** *adj.* studious; desirous; *n.m.* scholar; student.

**stuf-a** *f.* stove; oven. **-ai(u)ola** *f.* casserole, stew-pan. **-are** [A1] *tr.* to stew; (fig.) to bore, to weary; *rfl.* (fig.) to grow weary, to get bored. **-ato** *part. adj.* stewed; *n.m.* stewed meat; stew. **-o** *apocop. part. adj.* tired, sick, fed up, bored.

**stuo·i-a** *f.* mat, matting; lath. **-are** [A4] *tr.* (bldg.) to lath.

**stuolo** *m.* troop; group; band; host; crowd; flock.

**stupe-facente** *adj.* stupefying, narcotic; astonishing; *n.m.* narcotic; drug. **-fare** [B14] *tr.* to stupefy; to surprise, to astonish. **-faziọne** *f.* stupefaction.

**stupendo** *adj.* marvellous, stupendous; magnificent.

**stu·pid-o** *adj.* idiotic; utterly stupid; *n.m.* dolt, blockhead, idiot. **-a·ggine** *f.* act of stupidity; nonsense. **-amẹnte** *adv.* stupidly; foolishly.

**stup-ire** [D2] *rfl.*, *intr.* (*aux.* essere) to be amazed, astonished; *tr.* to amaze, to astonish. **-ọre** *m.* amazement; astonishment.

**stupr-o** *m.* rape. **-are** [A1] *tr.* to rape.

**stur-a** *f.* opening (of a bottle), uncorking; (fig.) beginning, opening. **-are** [A1] *tr.* to uncork; to open. **-abotti·glie** *m. indecl.* corkscrew; bottle-opener.

**sturb-are** [A1] *tr.* to disturb. **-amẹnto** *m.* disturbance; upset.

**stuzzi-care** [A2 s] *tr.* to stir; to poke; to stir up; to prod; to excite, to provoke. **-cadenti** *m. indecl.* toothpick. **-cante** *part. adj.* stimulating; irritating. **-chino** *m.* poker; (fig.) annoying person.

**su** *prep.* (*contr.* with *def. art.* sul, sulla, sui, sugli, sull'). **1.** above, over; on, upon. **2.** on, towards; in the direction of. **3.** about, towards, near, close to.

**4.** *adv.* up, upwards; *adv. phr.* — *per giù*, approximately, by and large. **-accennato** *adj.* beforementioned, aforesaid.

**subaccoll-are** [A1] *tr.* to delegate; to subcontract. **-ata·rio** *m.* subcontractor.

**suba·cqueo** *adj.*, *n.m.* submarine.

**subaffitt-are** [A1] *tr.* to sublet. **-o** *m.* sublease; subletting.

**subalpino** *adj.* (geog.) subalpine; Piedmontese.

**subalterno** *adj.* subordinate, subaltern; inferior; dependant; *n.m.* (mil.) subaltern (officer).

**subappalt-are** [A1] *tr.* to subcontract. **-atore** *m.* subcontractor. **-o** *m.* sub-contract.

**subasta** *f.* auction; forced sale.

**su·bbi-a** *f.* stone mason's chisel; chisel. **-are** [A4] to chisel; (fam.) to beat, knock about.

**subbu·glio** *m.* hubbub; turmoil; confusion; upheaval.

**subcosciente** *adj.*, *n.m.* subconscious.

**su·bdolo** *adj.* cunning, crafty; deceitful.

**subentrare** [A1] *intr.* (*aux.* essere; *prep.* a) to replace; to succeed.

**subire** [D2] *tr.* to undergo; to suffer, to ensure.

**subiss-are** [A1] *tr.* to overthrow, to ruin, to raze to the ground. **-o** *m.* ruin, confusion; heap; (fig.) outburst.

**subitamente** *adv.* immediately.

**subita·ne-o** *adj.* sudden; *uomo* —, hasty man. **-amente** *adv.* suddenly. **-ità** *f.* suddenness.

**su·bito**[1] *adj.* sudden, prompt, ready; hasty; *adv.* immediately; quickly; at once; soon; *conj.* — *che*, no sooner than, as soon as; *n.m.* moment, instant.

**subito**[2] *part.* of **subire.**

**sublimare** [A1] *tr.* to raise up, to exalt; to sublimate.

**sublim-e** *adj.* sublime, exalted; excellent; high; *n.m.* (the) sublime; supreme excellence. **-ità** *f.* sublimity; supreme excellence; loftiness.

**subloc-are** [A2] *tr.* to sublet. **-ata·rio** *m.* (leg.) sub-lessee; subtenant.

**sublunare** *adj.* sublunary.

**subocea·nico** *adj.* underwater, submarine.

**subodorare** [A1 c] *tr.* to get wind of, to suspect.

**subordin-are** [A1 s] *tr.* to subordinate. **-ato** *part. adj.* subordinate; *n.m.* subordinate; underling.

**subornare** [A1] *tr.* to suborn.

**suburbano** *adj.* suburban.

**subu·rbio** *m.* see **sobborgo.**

**succeda·neo** *adj.* substituted, substituting; surrogate, deputy; *n.m.* substitute.

**succe·dere** [C22] *intr.* (*aux.* essere; *prep.* a) to succeed, to follow; to occur, to happen, to befall; *recip. rfl.* to occur in succession; *n.m.* succession.

**success-o** *part.* of **succe·dere;** *adj.* following, substitute(d); occurred; *n.m.* result, success; event, occurrence. **-ione** *f.* succession, inheritance; course of time; offspring, descendants. **-ivo** *adj.* subsequent; next; following.

**succhi-are** [A4] *tr.* to suck; to sip; *rfl.* (*dat.* of *prn* 'si') to 'swallow', to put up with. **-amento** *m.* sucking; suction. **-ata** *f.* suck.

**succhiell-o** *m.* gimlet, auger. **-are** [A1] *tr.* to bore.

**su·cchio**[1] *m.* gimlet, auger, drill; (mil.) screwhead on a ramrod.

**su·cchi-o**[2] *m.* (bot.) sap; juice. **-one** *m.* (bot.) sucker; (fig.) bloodsucker; parasite.

**succinto** *adj.* succinct, brief; *n.m.* précis, summary.

**succitato** *adj.* quoted above, aforesaid.

**suc-co** *m.* (*pl.* **-chi**) juice; sap; (fig.) substance, essence.

**succos-o** *adj.* juicy. **-amente** *adv.* pithily; juicily. **-ità** *f.* juiciness.

**succulento** *adj.* succulent, juicy; substantial; pithy.

**succursale** *m.* branch office, branch.

**sud** *m.*, *adj. indecl.* south; *verso* —, southward(s).

**sud-are** [A1] *intr.* (*aux.* avere) to perspire, to sweat; to exude (moisture); (fig.) to toil, to drudge; *tr.* to sweat. **-a·rio** *m.* shroud. **-ata** *f.* sweat; sweating. **-ato** *part. adj.* wet with sweat.

**suddetto** *adj.* aforesaid; above-mentioned.

**su·ddit-o** *adj.*, *n.m.* subject (person). **-anza** *f.* subjection; citizenship.

**suddivi·dere** [C3] *tr.* to subdivide; to split up.

**suddivisione** *f.* subdivision.

**sud-est** *adj.*, *n.m. indecl.* south-east.

**su·dic-io** *adj.* dirty, filthy; foul, indecent; *guadagni -i*, filthy lucre; *n.m.* dirt, filth. **-eri·a** *f.* dirtiness, filthiness; indecency; dirty trick; miserliness. **-iume** *m.* dirt; filth.

**sudore** *m.* sweat; perspiration.

**sud-ovest** *adj.*, *m. indecl.* south-west; (naut.) sou'wester (wind).

**suesposto** *adj.* above-stated.

**sufficien-te** *adj.* sufficient, enough; adequate; capacious; *n.m.* sufficiency; enough. **-za** *f.* sufficiency; complacency; pass-mark.

**suffisso** *m.* suffix.

**suffrag-are** [A2] *tr.* to support, to assist. **-ante** *part.*, *n.m.* supporter, voter (in favour).

**suffra·g-io** *m.* vote, suffrage; approval, support. **-ista** *m.*, *f.* suffragist. **-etta** *f.* suffragette.

**suffumicare** [A2 s] *tr.* to fumigate.

**suffumi·gio** *m.* fumigation.

**suffusione** *f.* (med.) suffusion.

**suga** *adj.* (pup.) *carta* —, blotting-paper.

**suggell-o** *m.* seal; pledge. **-are** [A1] *tr.* to seal; to stamp; *intr.* (*aux.* avere) to fit closely, to close.

**sugger-ire** [D2] *tr.* to suggest; to prompt; to advise. **-imento** *m.* suggestion. **-itore** *m.* (theatr.) prompter.

**suggest-ione** *f.* (hypnotic) suggestion; instigation; temptation. **-iona·bile** *adj.* suggestible. **-ionato** *part. adj.* hypnotized; unduly influenced. **-ivo** *adj.* stimulating; interesting; picturesque.

**su·ghero** *m.* cork oak; cork (stopper); cork float.

**sugn-a** *f.* lard; (lubricating) grease. **-oso** *adj.* containing lard; greasy.

**su-go** *m.* (*pl.* **-ghi**) juice; sap; gravy; sauce; (fig.) essence, substance; interest.

**suicid-a** *adj.* (*m.pl.* **-i**) suicidal; *n.m.* suicide (person). **-are** [A1] *rfl.* to commit suicide; to kill oneself.

**suici·dio** *m.* suicide, self-murder.

**suindicato** *adj.* above-mentioned.

**suino** *adj.* of, pertaining to, swine; *carne suina*, pork; *n.m.pl.* swine.

**sulfu·reo** *adj.* sulphureous; sulphurous.

**sultan-o** *m.* Sultan; (colour) deep red. **-a** *f.* Sultana; divan. **-ina** *f.* sultana, raisin.

**summentovato** *adj.* above-mentioned.

**sunt-o** *m.* summary, précis, recapitulation. **-eggiare** [A3 c] *tr.* to summarize.

**suntu-a·rio** *adj.* sumptuary. **-oso** *adj.* sumptuous, lavish, magnificent.

**suo** *poss. adj.* (*m.pl.* **suoi,** *f.* **sua,** *pl.* **sue**) his, her, its; one's own; *poss. prn.* his, hers, its; *vuole dir la sua*, he will have his say; *star sul suo*, to stand, insist, on one's rights.

**suo·cer-o** *m.* father-in-law. **-a** *f.* mother-in-law.

**suola** *f.* sole (of boot or shoe).

**suolo** *m.* ground, soil.

**suonare** [A1 d] see **sonare.**

**suoneri·a** *f.* (watchm.) alarm; striking mechanism (of a clock).

**suono** *m.* sound; note, ringing; buzzing, singing, in the ears.

**suora** *f.* (eccl.) nun; sister.

**super-are** [A1 s] *tr.* to surpass, to excel; to overcome; to get through, to get over; to exceed; to climb over; *intr.* (*aux.* essere) to be too big; to be too

many; to be excessive. **-a·bile** *adj.* surmountable; surpassable.

**supe·rbia** *f.* pride, arrogance.

**superbo** *adj.* proud; arrogant, haughty; superb, splendid; extremely high; *n.m.* proud man.

**superfi·c-ie** *f. indecl.* (or *pl.* -i) surface; area; outside. **-iale** *adj.* superficial; hasty; shallow. **-ialità** *f.* superficiality; surface; smattering.

**supe·rflu-o** *adj.* superfluous; redundant; gratuitous; *n.m.* surplus. **-ità** *f.* superfluity.

**superior-e** *adj.* superior; upper, higher; *n.m.* person of higher rank, superior. **-ità** *f.* superiority. **-mẹnte** *adv.* in a higher degree.

**superlativo** *adj., n.m.* superlative.

**superno** *adj.* (poet.) celestial; divine; supernal.

**su·pero** *adj.* (poet.) upper, superior; *n.m.pl.* the powers above, the gods.

**superpoṣiziọne** *f.* supremacy, overlordship.

**supe·rstite** *adj.* surviving; *n.m., f.* survivor.

**superstizi-ọne** *f.* superstition. **-ọso** *adj.* superstitious.

**super-uomo** *m.* (*pl.* **-uo·mini**) superman.

**supin-o** *adj.* lying on one's back; supine; indolent; servile. **-amẹnte** *adv.* supinely; carelessly; indolently; servilely.

**suppelle·ttile** *f.* furniture; equipment; fittings.

**suppergiù** *adv.* approximately, nearly; roughly speaking.

**supplemẹnt-o** *m.* supplement; addition; extra; (comm.) — *di dichiarazione doganale*, post entry. **-are** *adj.* supplementary; additional; *ore -ari*, overtime.

**supplen-te** *m., f.* substitute; deputy; supply-teacher; locum tenens. **-za** *f.* substitution; temporary post.

**suppletivo** *adj.* supplementary.

**su·pplica** *f.* petition; supplication, entreaty.

**supplic-are** [A2s] *tr.* to beg, to implore, to entreat. **-ante** *part. adj.* suppliant; *n.m., f.* petitioner, suppliant.

**su·pplice** *adj., n.m., f.* suppliant.

**supplichẹvole** *adj.* suppliant, imploring, entreating.

**supplire** [D2] *intr.* (*aux.* avere; *prep.* a) to take the place (of); to make up (for); *tr.* to take the place of; to make up for.

**suppli·zio** *m.* punishment; torture; extreme penalty.

**supponi·bile** *adj.* feasible, possible; imaginable.

**suppọrre** [B12] *tr.* to suppose, to assume; to imagine.

**suppoṣizione** *f.* supposition.

**suppọsta** *f.* (med.) suppository.

**suppọsto** *part.* of **suppọrre**; *adj.* supposed, conjectured; substituted; *n.m.* supposition; *conj.* — *che*, supposing.

**suppur-are** [A1] *intr.* (*aux.* avere) (med.) to suppurate; to come to a head. **-amẹnto** *m.*, **-aziọne** *f.* suppuration.

**suprem-o** *adj.* highest; supreme; greatest; *il — addio*, the last goodbye. **-azi·a** *f.* supremacy.

**surreal-iṣmo** *m.* surrealism. **-ista** *m., f.* surrealist.

**surretti·zio** *adj.* surreptitious.

**su·rroga** *f.* substitution.

**surrog-are** [A2] *tr.* (*prep.* a) to replace; to substitute (for). **-ante** *part. adj.* replacing; *n.m., f.* supply, substitute. **-ato** *part. adj., n.m.* subrogate; substitute.

**suscett-i·bile** *adj.* (*prep.* di) susceptible, capable (of); touchy, easily offended. **-ivo** *adj.* receptive; susceptible.

**suscitare** [A1s] *tr.* to arouse, to stir up; to give rise to.

**susin-a** *f.* plum. **-o** *m.* plum-tree.

**suso** *adv.* (poet.) up.

**sussegu-ire** [D1] *intr.* (*aux.* essere; *prep.* a) to be subsequent (to), to follow. **-ente** *part. adj.* subsequent, following; next; successive. **-enza** *f.* succession.

**sussi·di-o** *m.* help, aid, reinforcement(s); subsidy; grant. **-are** [A4] *tr.* to subsidize; to aid. **-a·rio** *adj.* subsidiary.

**sussie-go** *m.* (*pl.* **-ghi**) imposing air, hauteur.

**sussi·st-ere** [C] *intr.* (*aux.* essere, avere) to exist; to subsist. **-enza** *f.* subsistence; existence; victualling.

**sussult-are** [A1] *intr.* (*aux.* avere) to start; to tremble. **-o** *m.* start, jump.

**sussurr-are** [A1] *tr.* to whisper; to murmur; *intr.* (*aux.* avere) to whisper; to murmur; to buzz; (poet.) to rustle. **-o** *m.* whisper; murmur; hum; rustle.

**sutura** *f.* suture.

**ṣvag-are** [A2] *tr.* to amuse, to divert; *rfl.* to amuse oneself. **-atẹzza** *f.* absent-mindedness. **-ato** *part. adj.* absent-minded; heedless; relaxed.

**sva-go** *m.* (*pl.* **-ghi**) amusement, diversion, relaxation, recreation.

**ṣvaligi-are** [A4] *tr.* (usu. joc.) to ransack, to rifle, to plunder; (slang) to clean out. **-amẹnto** *m.* robbery; burglary.

**ṣvalut-are** [A1] *tr.* to undervalue; to depreciate; to devalue. **-aziọne** *f.* depreciation; devaluation.

**ṣvampare**[1] [A1] *intr.* (*aux.* essere, avere) to blaze forth; to burst out; to escape; to go up in smoke.

**ṣvampare**[2] [A1] *intr.* (*aux.* essere) to die down; to diminish; to cool.

**ṣvan-ire** [D2] *intr.* (*aux.* essere) to vanish; to disappear; to evaporate; to lose strength. **-imẹnto** *m.* fading away; enfeebling.

**ṣvano** *m.* door or window-opening; recess, cavity.

**ṣvanta·ggi-o** *m.* disadvantage, drawback; detriment. **-ọso** *adj.* unfavourable; detrimental.

**svapor-are** [A1c] *intr.* (*aux.* essere) to evaporate; (fig.) to vanish, to fade away; to die down; *tr.* to (make) evaporate. **-ata** *f.* (joc.) trip in a steamboat.

**svari-are** [A4] *tr.* to change; to divert; *intr.* (*aux.* avere, essere) to vary, to change; to waver. **-amẹnto** *m.* variation. **-ante** *part. adj.* various, varied. **-ato** *part. adj.* varied; various.

**sva·ri-o** *m.* difference; recreation. **-ọne** *m.* blunder.

**ṣvaṣare** [A1] *tr.* (hort.) to plant out; to re-pot.

**ṣva·stica, sva·stika** *f.* swastika.

**ṣvecchi-are** [A4c] *tr.* to renew, to freshen up; to modernize. **-amẹnto** *m.* modernizing. **-atura** *f.* renewal.

**ṣvedese** *adj.* Swedish; *n.m.*, Swedish language; Swede; *f.* Swedish woman.

**ṣvẹgli-a** *f.* waking; reveille; alarm clock. **-are** [A4c] *tr.* to awaken, to wake; (fig.) to rouse, to excite; *rfl.* to wake, to wake up. **-ata** *f.* awakening. **-atẹzza** *f.* wakefulness, liveliness; vivacity.

**ṣvẹglio** *adj.* awake; wide awake; vigilant; quick-witted.

**ṣvel-are** [A1] *tr.* to unveil, to reveal, to disclose. **-atamẹnte** *adv.* openly; undisguisedly.

**ṣvelenare** [A1c] *tr.* to remove poison from; *rfl.* to give vent to one's anger or malice.

**sve·llere** [B31] *tr.* to uproot; to pluck out; (fig.) to extirpate, to eradicate.

**svelto**[1] *part.* of **sve·llere.**

**svelt-o**[2] *adj.* slender, svelte; lively, brisk; quick-witted, smart; *adv.* rapidly. **-ire** [D2] *tr.* to make slender; to liven up, to smarten up; to make supple; *rfl.* to become slender, quick.

**sven-are** [A1] *tr.* to bleed to death. **-ato** *part. adj.* bled; (fig.) impoverished.

**ṣvẹndita** *f.* selling off; underselling.

**ṣvenẹvole** *adj.* see under **svenire.**

**ṣve·nia** *f.* sentimental affection; wheedling.

**ṣven-ire** [D17] *intr.* (*aux.* essere), *rfl.* to faint, to swoon. **-ẹvole** *adj.* languishing; sentimental; simpering, affected. **-evolẹzza** *f.* mawkishness.

**ṣventagliare** [A4] *tr.* to wave, to flap; to scatter; *rfl.* to fan (oneself).

**svent-are** [A1] *tr.* to foil; to baffle; — *una mina*, to frustrate a mine by countermining; *intr.*

(*aux.* essere) (of gas, air) to escape; *rfl.* to fan oneself. **-ata·ggine** *f.*, **-atẹzza** *f.* thoughtlessness, carelessness.

**sve·ntol-a** *f.* fan; (pop.) slap; *pl.* big ears, flapping ears. **-are** [A1 s] *tr.* to unfurl, to fly (flag); to wave, to flap, to flutter; *rfl.* to fan oneself.

**sventrare** [A1] *tr.* disembowel, to rip open; (of fish) to gut; to clear (slums); *intr.* (*aux.* avere) to eat too much.

**ṣventur-a** *f.* misfortune; bad luck. **-ato** *adj.* unfortunate.

**ṣvenuto** *part.* of **ṣvenire**; unconscious; in a faint

**ṣvergogn-are** [A1 c] *tr.* to disgrace, to humiliate; to put to shame. **-a·ggine** *f.* shamelessness; impudence. **-atẹzza** *f.* impudence, shamelessness. **-ato** *part. adj.* shameless; impudent; put to shame.

**ṣvernare** [A1] *intr.* (*aux.* avere) to spend the winter.

**sverniciatọre** *m.* paint-remover; 'stripper'.

**ṣverza** *f.* stick; splinter.

**svesci-are** [A3 c] *tr.* to blurt out; to blab. **-atọre** *m.*, **-ọne** *m.* windy gas-bag, person who blabs.

**ṣvestire** [D1] *tr.* to undress; to take off; to strip; to divest; to lay aside; *rfl.* to undress; *svestirsi nudo*, to strip naked.

**ṣvettare** [A1] *tr.* to poll, to trim the tops of; — *un bastoncino*, to whittle a stick.

**Sve·zia** *pr.n.f.* Sweden.

**ṣvezzare** [A1 c] *tr.* to wean; — *da un vizio*, to rid of a habit.

**ṣvi-are** [A4] *tr.* to turn aside; to lead astray; *rfl.* to go astray. **-amẹnto** *m.* deviation. **-ato** *part. adj.* misguided. **-atọre** *m.* (rlwy.) pointsman.

**ṣvicolare** [A1 s] *intr.* (*aux.* essere, avere) to turn into an alley; to dodge; *rfl.* (*dat.* of *prn.* 'si') *svicolarsela*, to 'skip'.

**svignare** [A5] *intr.* (*aux.* essere) (fam.) to sneak away; to slip away; to make off.

**svigor-ire** [D2] *tr.* to weaken; to attenuate. **-imẹnto** *m.* enfeeblement.

**ṣvil-ire** [D2] *tr.* to debase; to depreciate; to reduce (prices). **-imẹnto** *m.* debasing; depreciation.

**ṣvillaneggiare** [A3 c] *tr.* to abuse, to revile; to insult.

**ṣvilupp-are** [A1] *tr.* to loose, to untie; to extricate; to develop, to amplify; *rfl.*, *intr.* (*aux.* essere, avere) to develop, to grow; *rfl.* to free oneself, to break away. **-amẹnto** *m.* development. **-ato** *part. adj.* untied; developed. **-o** *m.* development; spread; growth; expansion.

**ṣvinare** [A1] *intr.* (*aux.* essere) to draw the wine from the vat.

**ṣvi·ncol-o** *m.* release, clearance. **-are** [A1 s] *tr.* to release, to free; to redeem; *rfl.* to be released; to get free.

**ṣviṣ-are** [A1] *tr.* (joc.) to smash the face of; (fig.) to misrepresent; to distort. **-amẹnto** *m.* disfigurement; misrepresentation.

**ṣviscer-are** [A1 s] *tr.* to disembowel; (fig.) to exhaust; to examine thoroughly. **-amẹnto** *m.* disembowelling; exhaustive research. **-ata-mẹnte** *adv.* ardently; passionately. **-atẹzza** *f.* ardent love; deep affection. **-ato** *part. adj.* eviscerated, gutted; (fig.) passionate, ardent; deep; tender; sincere; *amico -ato*, bosom friend.

**ṣvista** *f.* oversight; mistake.

**ṣvit-are** [A1] *tr.* to unscrew. **-atura** *f.* unscrewing.

**ṣviticchiare** [A4] *tr.* to disentangle.

**Ṣvi·zzer-a** *pr.n.f.* (geog.) Switzerland. **-o** *adj.*, *n.m.* Swiss.

**ṣvogli-are** [A4 c] *tr.* (*prep.* di) to make disinclined (for); to make indifferent (to); *rfl.* to take a dislike (to). **-ato** *part. adj.* listless; lazy; unwilling; loath; disinclined; without appetite; *n.m.* lazy person.

**ṣvolare** [A1] *intr.* (*aux.* avere) to fly; to flit; to flutter.

**ṣvolazzare** [A1] *intr.* (*aux.* avere) to fly, to flutter; to flit; to hover.

**ṣvolazzo** *m.* flutter; flourish.

**svo·lg-ere** [C14] *tr.* to unroll, to unwind; to display; to develop; to work out; *rfl.* to turn back; to develop, to take shape; to take place. **-imẹnto** *m.* development; unfolding; expansion.

**ṣvolt-a** *f.* turn; turning point; corner; winding; (fig.) crossroads. **-are** [A1] *tr.* to unroll; to turn, to twist; to dissuade; *intr.* (*aux.* avere) to turn, to change direction. **-ata** *f.* turn; turning.

**svolto** *part.* of **svo·lgere**; *adj.* unfolded; unwrapped; developed; frank; dislocated.

**svoltolare** [A1 s] *tr.* to roll; *rfl.* to roll about, to tumble, to wallow.

**ṣvotare** [A1 d] *tr.* (*prep.* di) to empty out completely; to clear out.

**T** *f.*, *m.* (pron. **ti**) the letter T; the consonant T; *fatto a* T, T-shaped.

**ta** *onomat.* pom; ta ta ta, pompty-pom.

**tabac-co** *m.* (*pl.* **-chi**) (bot.) tobacco plant; tobacco; — *da fiuto*, — *da naso*, snuff. **-ca·io** *m.* tobacconist. **-chiera** *f.* snuff-box. **-cọso** *adj.* snuffy; tobacco-stained.

**tabarro** *m.* cloak; loose overcoat.

**tabe** *f.* (med.) tabes.

**tabella** *f.* schedule, table; board carried by sandwich-man; list; tablet.

**taberna·colo** *m.* tabernacle; shrine.

**tablò** *m. indecl.* (pron. as Fr. 'tableau') tableau.

**tablo·ide** *m.* tablet, tabloid.

**tabù, tabu** *m.*, *adj. indecl.* taboo.

**tac** *onom.* sound of a little sharp blow; the ticking of a clock; *tic* —, tick-tock.

**tacca** *f.* notch; nick; scratch; mark; blemish; dent; (fig.) size; height.

**taccagn-o** *adj.* stingy, niggardly; miserly; *n.m.* miser, skinflint. **-eri·a** *f.* miserliness; stinginess.

**taccheggi-are** [A3 c] *tr.* to shoplift. **-atọre** *m.*, **-atrice** *f.* shoplifter.

**taccherella** *f.* slight fault; blemish.

**tacchett-are** [A1 c] *intr.* (*aux.* avere) to clatter noisily with one's heels. **-ìo** *m.* (*pl.* **-ii**) clicking; clacking.

**tacchino** *m.* turkey.

**ta·cci-a** *f.* blemish; stain; patch; imputation; charge. **-a·bile** *adj.* (*prep.* di) chargeable (with). **-are** [A3] *tr.* (*prep.* di) to accuse (of), to tax (with), to charge (with).

**tacco** *m.* heel (of a shoe).

**ta·ccola**[1] *f.* (orn.) jackdaw.

**ta·ccola**[2] *f.* slight fault; flaw; trifle.

**taccọne** *m. augm.* of **tacco**; big heel; (shoem.) patch.

**taccuino** *m.* note-book; pocket-diary.

**tacẹre** [B20] *intr.* (*aux.* avere) to be silent; to hold one's tongue; *far* —, to silence; *tr.* to be silent about, to pass over in silence; to leave unsaid; to omit.

**ta·cit-o**[1] *adj.* silent; tacit; implied; secret; *socio* —, sleeping partner. **-amẹnte** *adv.* tacitly; silently; noiselessly. **-are** [A1 s] *tr.* to pay off, to satisfy (creditor); *rfl.* to come to terms (with).

**Ta·cito**[2] *pr.n.m.* Tacitus.

**taciturn-o** *adj.* taciturn; withdrawn; sulky. **-ità** *f.* taciturnity.

**tafano** *m.* (pop.) horsefly; (fig.) nuisance; bloodsucker.

**tafferi·a** *f.* wooden dish; bowl.

**tafferu·glio** *m.* brawl; scuffle; scrimmage.

**ta·ffete** *onom. excl.* bump!; bang!; clatter.

**taffettà** *m.* taffeta; — *inglese*, court-plaster.

**ta·glia** *f.* (agric.) cutting (esp. of olive-trees); act of cutting; ransom; price on a person's head; indemnity; tally; tackle; figure, build, height.

**tagli-are** [A4] *tr.* to cut; to cut off; to cut up; to cut out; to hew; to lop; to clip; *intr.* (*aux.* avere) (of knife, scissors) to cut; *vento che -a*, biting wind. **-acarta** *m. indecl.* paper-cutting machine. **-acarte** *m. indecl.* paper-knife; letter-opener. **-a·cqua** *m. indecl.* (bldg.) cut-water, nosing (of a bridge or pier). **-afili** *m. indecl.* wire-cutters. **-alęgna** *m. indecl.* woodcutter. **-ando** *m.* detachable coupon; warrant; slip. **-apęsce** *m. indecl.* fish-slice; fish-knife. **-apietre** *m. indecl.* stonecutter, stonemason. **-ata** *f.* cut; cutting; mowing, reaping, gathering; felling. **-atelle** *f. pl.*, **-atelli** *m. pl.* (cul.) thin strips of 'pasta'. **-atọio** *m.* (techn.) cutter. **-atrice** *f.* (dressm.) cutter (woman); (eng.) cutting machine. **-atura** *f.* cutting; felling, pruning; *pl.* clippings. **-ente** *adj.* cutting; sharp; keen; *poco -ente*, blunt; *n.m.* cutting edge.

**ta·gli-o** *m.* cutting; felling; mowing; cut; stature, height, build; edge; *adv. phr. di* —, edge-wise; *per* —, aslant; *venire, cadere, in* —, to occur opportunely. **-olini** *m.pl.* (cul.) thin strips of 'pasta' served in soup. **-uzzare** [A1] *tr.* to cut into little bits; to cut into shreds, to shred; to mince; to hash.

**tagliọne**[1] *m.* talion; *legge del* —, law of retaliation.

**tagliọne**[2] *m. augm.* of **taglio**.

**Tago** *pr.n.m.* (geog.) Tagus.

**tailleur** *m. indecl.* (pron. as Fr.) tailor-made coat and skirt.

**ta·it** *m. indecl.* (also written **tight**) tight-fitting coat; morning coat.

**tal** *adj.* see **tale**.

**ta·lamo** *m.* (poet.) bridal bed; bride-chamber.

**talare** *adj.* ankle-length; *abito* —, cassock.

**talchę̀** *conj.* so that; such that.

**tal-e** *adj.* (*m.pl.* -**i**). **1.** such; — *il padre*, — *il figlio*, like father, like son; (with correlative 'quale') *è ancora* — *quale*, it is still as it was. **2.** *demonstr. prn.* such a one; *un* —, a certain person; *il signor Tal dei Tali*, Mr. So and So. **3.** *adv.* so; so great; so big; — *che* (*talchè*), so that, to such an extent that. **-męnte** *adv.* so; *-mente che*, so much that. **-ọra** *adv.* sometimes. **-uno** *demonstr. prn.* someone; *pl. adj.* certain. **-volta** *adv.* sometimes; at times.

**talent-o**[1] *m.* talent; aptitude; gift; genius; will; *a suo* —, at his pleasure; *di suo* —, of his own accord; *mal* —, ill-will, grudge, hatred. **-are** [A1] *intr.* (*aux.* essere; *prep.* a) to please, to be to one's liking.

**talento**[2] *m.* (antiq.) talent.

**Talete** *pr.n.m.* Thales.

**talişmano** *m.* talisman; amulet.

**tallo** *m.* (bot.) thallus; sprout; cutting; graft; grass running to seed (planted with cuttings).

**tallọn-e** *m.* heel; footing of a wall; (comm.) counterfoil, stub. **-cino** *m. dim.* receipt-form; detachable slip; voucher; cut-out coupon.

**tal-męnte, -ọra** see under **tale**.

**talpa** *f.* (zool.) mole.

**tal-uno** *prn.*, **-volta** *adv.* see under **tale**.

**tamarindo** *m.* (bot.) tamarind.

**tamaris-co** *m.* (*pl.* **-chi**) (bot.) tamarisk.

**tamburell-o** *m. dim.* of **tamburo**; small drum; tambourine; timbrel. **-are** [A1] *intr.* (*aux.* avere) to drum; to beat; to thud.

**tamburin-o** *m. dim.* of **tamburo**; little drum; toy drum; tambourine; drummer-boy. **-are** [A1] *intr.* (*aux.* avere) to drum with the fingers.

**tambur-o** *m.* drum; drummer; *capo* —, drum-major; cylinder; barrel (of a clock); chamber, drum, magazine (of revolver); pill-box. **-are** [A1] *tr.* to beat (a drum or drums); (joc.) to beat, to thrash. **-eggiare** [A3 c] *intr.* (*aux.* avere) to drum. **-lano** *m.* clothes-dryer.

**Tamigi** *pr.n.m.* (geog.) Thames.

**tampọn-e** *m.* (surg.) tampon; (eng.) pad, buffer, shock-absorber; (rlwy.) buffer; pad; ink-pad; plug, stopper bung. **-are** [A1 c] *tr.* to plug, to stop, to bung; to bump.

**tana** *f.* den; hole, lair; hole (in wall).

**tana·gli-e** *f.pl.* pincers; nippers; pliers; tongs. **-are** [A4] *tr.* to torture with pincers; to pinch; to nip.

**tandem** *m. indecl.* tandem bicycle.

**tanf-o** *m.* stench; musty smell. **-ata** *f.* whiff of foul air.

**tangente** *adj.* tangential; *n.f.* tangent.

**ta·ngere** [C def.] *tr.* (poet.) to touch.

**Ta·ngeri** *pr.n.f.* (geog.) Tangier.

**ta·nghero** *m.* boor, bumpkin.

**tangi·ble** *adj.* tangible.

**tan-go** *m.* (*pl.* **-ghi**) tango.

**tannino** *m.* tannin; tannic acid.

**tantafer-a, -ata** *f.* rigmarole; twaddle.

**Ta·ntalo** *pr.n.m.* (myth.) Tantalus; *m.* tantalus; (miner.) tantalum.

**tantino** *adv. dim.* see under **tanto**.

**tant-o** *adj.* **1.** so much; *pl.* so many; *-e grazie!*, many thanks! **2.** *adv.* so; so much; — *meglio*, so much the better; *una volta* —, once in a way, just this once; (with correlative 'quanto') as; — *quanto*, as much as. **3.** *indecl. prn.* so much, such a lot; *un* — *ogni mese*, so much every month; *ogni* —, every now and then; *di* — *in* —, from time to time; *emphatic uses*: *gli costò* —, it cost him a good deal; *lo guardò con* — *d'occhio*, he stared at him so hard; *aveva* — *di barba*, he had a great long beard. **4.** *pers. prn. pl.* *-i dicono*, a lot of people say; *-i quanti*, as many as; ELLIPTICAL USES: *ne ha fatte -e*, he has got up to a few tricks in his time; *-i ne guadagna e -i ne spende*, he spends as much as he earns. **5.** *conj.* — *che*, so that, whilst; — *più che*, all the more (so) that; anyhow. **-ino** *m.* a little; *a ogni -ino*, every little while.

**tapin-o** *adj.* wretched, miserable; humble. **-are** [A1] *intr.* (*aux.* avere) to lead a wretched life; *rfl.* to be afflicted.

**tappa** *f.* stop, halting-place; stage; lap.

**tapp-are** [A1] *tr.* to stop up, to stop, to cork; to plug; to bung; *rfl.* to shut oneself up; to muffle oneself up. **-abuchi** *m. indecl.* stop-gap. **-ato** *part. adj.* stopped-up; shut-up; muffled-up.

**tappęt-o** *m.* carpet, rug; mat; — *verde*, green baize table, gaming-table; (fig.) *mettere sul* —, to table; — *erboso*, lawn, grass plot. **-ino** *m. dim.* rug; small carpet.

**tappezz-are** [A1] *tr.* (*prep.* di) to hang with tapestry; to upholster; (fig.) to cover, to plaster (with). **-eri·a** *f.* tapestry; arras; hangings, soft furnishings; wall-paper; upholstery; upholsterer's shop. **-iere** *m.* upholsterer; decorator; paper-hanger; house-furnisher; tapestry-maker.

**tappo** *m.* stopper, plug, bung; cork; — *di assale*, axle cap; — *di valvola*, valve cap.

**tara** *f.* defect; weakness; taint; (finan.) tare.

**tarabuşo** *m.* (orn.) bittern.

**tarantella** *f.* (zool.) see **tara·ntola**; tarantella (dance).

**tara·ntola** *f.* (zool.) tarantula spider.

**tarato** *adj.* tainted; sickly; degenerate.
**tarchiato** *adj.* thickset; sturdy; strongly-built.
**tard-o** *adj.* slow; lazy; tardy, late; slow-witted. **-are** [A1] *intr.* (*aux.* avere) to delay; to be late; (*aux.* essere) to be late; to seem late, to seem to take a long time; to loiter; *tr.* to delay; to retard; to hold back. **-ẹzza** *f.* slowness; tardiness. **-i** *adv.* late; too late; *si fa -i*, it is getting late; slowly. **-ità** *f.* slowness; delay; laziness; dullness. **-ivo** *adj.* slow, late; sluggish; backward.
**targ-a** *f.* targe, shield; coat of arms; name-plate, door-plate; (motor.) number-plate. **-are** [A2] *tr.* (motor.) to affix a number-plate to. **-ato** *part. adj.* bearing a number-plate; *una macchina -ata Verona*, a car with a Verona number-plate.
**targhẹtta** *f. dim.* of **targa**; name-plate; tag.
**tariffa** *f.* charge; duty; fee; rate; scale; table of charges, tariff, price-list.
**tarl-o** *m.* clothes-moth, wood-worm; dust left by woodworm; (fig.) gnawing of conscience, remorse; consuming anxiety. **-are** [A1] *intr.* (*aux.* essere), *rfl.* to get worm-eaten. **-atura** *f.* worm-hole; dust from worm-holes.
**tarm-a** *f.* grub of the clothes moth. **-are** [A1] *intr.* (*aux.* essere), *rfl.* to get moth-eaten.
**taroc-co** *m.* (*pl.* **-chi**) tarot; tarot-card. **-care** [A2] *intr.* (*aux.* avere) to play a trump-card; (fig.) to be offensive; to grumble. **-cọne** *m.* grumbler.
**tarpano** *adj.* boorish; rustic; uncouth; *n.m.* boor; rough, uncouth person.
**tarpare** [A1] *tr.* to clip; to pare; to trim.
**tarsi·a, ta·rsia** *f.* inlaid wood-work, tarsia; marquetry; — *di metallo*, inlaid metalwork.
**tarso**[1] *m.* tarsus (of the foot); tarsus (of the eyelids).
**Tarso**[2] *pr.n.f.* (geog.) Tarsus.
**tartagli-are** [A4] *intr.* (*aux.* avere) to stutter; to stammer; *tr.* to stammer out; to mumble. **-ọna** *f.*, **-ọne** *m.* stammerer; stutterer.
**tarta·rico** *adj.* tartaric.
**ta·rtaro**[1] *m.* (chem.) tartar.
**ta·rtaro**[2] *adj.*, *n.m.* (hist.) Tartar.
**Ta·rtaro**[3] *pr.n.m.* (myth.) Tartarus.
**tartaruga** *f.* tortoise; turtle; *pettine di —*, tortoise-shell comb; (fig.) sluggard, slow-coach.
**tartassare** [A1] *tr.* to vex; to bully; to treat badly.
**tartina** *f.* slice of bread with butter.
**tartufo**[1] *m.* truffle; Jerusalem artichoke.
**Tartufo**[2] *pr.n.m.* Tartuffe; (fig.) hypocrite.
**tas-ca** *f.* pocket; case; satchel; (fig.) *averne piene le -che*, to have had enough of. **-ca·bile** *adj.* suitable for the pocket; *vocabolario -cabile*, pocket dictionary. **-capane** *m. indecl.* haversack. **-cata** *f.* pocketful. **-chino** *m. dim.* waistcoat pocket; fob.
**tass-a** *f.* tax; fee; — *d'ingresso*; entrance fee; — *di soggiorno*, visitors' tax; — *sullo spettacolo*, entertainment tax; — *di bollo*, stamp duty. **-a·bile** *adj.* taxable; assessable; subject to duty. **-a·metro** *m.* taximeter. **-are** [A1] *tr.* to tax; to charge. **-ato** *part. adj.* taxed; assessed; (of letters) surcharged; accused, charged (with); definite. **-azịone** *f.* taxation; rating; assessment; charges.
**tassell-o** *m.* peg; wedge; dowel. **-are** [A1] *tr.* to put in plugs; (cheese) to sample.
**tass-ì** *m. indecl.* taxi-cab, taxi. **-ista** *m.* taxi-driver.
**tassidermi·a** *f.* taxidermy.
**tasso**[1] *m.* yew.
**tasso**[2] *m.* (zool.) badger.
**tasso**[3] *m.* rate; — *di sconto*, discount.
**tast-are** [A1] *tr.* to feel; to touch; to try; to prove; to sound. **-ata** *f.* touch; probing; feeling; sounding. **-iera** *f.* finger-board; keyboard, manual. **-o** *m.* touch; feel; key; tapper; (teleg.) touch; trial shaft; (fig.) subject. **-ọne, -ọni** *adv.* by groping, gropingly; *andar -oni*, to feel one's way.
**ta·ttic-a** *f.* tactics. **-o** *adj.* (mil.) tactical; *n.m.* tactician.
**ta·ttile** *adj.* tactile.
**tatto** *m.* touch; the sense of touch; (fig.) tact.
**tatu-are** [A6] *tr.* to tattoo. **-a·ggio** *m.* tattooing; tattoo.
**ta·umat-urgi·a** *f.* thaumaturgy, miracle-working; magic. **-urgo** *m.* (*pl.* **-urghi**) wonder-worker.
**ta·ur-o** *m.* (poet.) bull. **-ino** *adj.* taurine. **-omachi·a** *f.* bull-fight.
**tautol-ogi·a** *f.* tautology. **-o·gico** *adj.* tautological.
**tavern-a** *f.* public-house; tavern. **-iere** *m.* innkeeper, landlord.
**ta·vol-a** *f.* **1.** board; plank; — *da stirare*, ironing-board; slab, tablet; (of gems) facet. **2.** table; — *da pranzo*, dining-table; *in —*, on the table, served; meals; *biancheria da —*, table linen; — *allungabile*, draw-leaf table; — *da giuoco*, gaming table; *la Tavola Rotonda*, the Round Table. **3.** table, list; index; — *pitagorica*, multiplication table; illustration (in book); *indice delle -e*, list of plates; *-e geografiche*, maps. **4.** (art) panel; painting (on board). **-ẹtta** *f. dim.* small board, small plank; slab; small table; dressing-table; writing-tablet. **-iere** *m.* chess-board; draught-board; card-table.
**ta·vol-o** *m.* table; small table; writing-table. **-a·ccio** *m. pejor.* plank bed; bare board. **-ino** *m. dim.* little table; desk; *-ino da notte*, bed-side table.
**taxì** *m. indecl.* see **tassì**.
**tazza** *f.* cup; mug; — *di fontana*, basin of a fountain.
**tẹ**[1] *pers. prn. disjunct.* thee; you; *a — !*, over to you!, it's your turn!; — *stesso*, yourself.
**tẹ**[2] *pers. prn. conjunct.* form of **ti**[1], before lo, la, li, le or ne.
**tè** *m. indecl.* tea plant; tea.
**te'** *abbrev.* of **tene** (**tieni**) take!
**teatr-o** *m.* theatre; — *di varietà*, music-hall; audience, 'house'; dramatic works, plays; (fig.) scene; seat; centre; stage. **-ale** *adj.* theatrical; dramatic. **-ante** *m.*, *f.* actor, actress; theatrical person. **-ino** *m. dim.* puppet-show; *il -ino di Pulcinella*, Punch and Judy show.
**Tebe** *pr.n.f.* (geog.) Thebes.
**teca** *f.* case; casket.
**teck** *m. indecl.* teak.
**te·cnic-a** *f.* technique. **-o** *adj.* technical; *direttore -o*, production manager; *n.m.* technician.
**tecnicolọre** *m.* technicolour.
**tecnol-ogi·a** *f.* technology. **-o·gico** *adj.* technological.
**tecno·logo** *m.* technologist.
**tẹco** (contr. of **te** and **con**) with thee; with you.
**tedẹs-co** *adj.*, *n.m.* (*m.pl.* **-chi**) German; German-speaking. **-cheggiare** [A3 c] *intr.* (*aux.* avere) to fraternize with Germans, to be pro-German. **-cheri·a** *f.* German ways; hordes of Germans.
**te·di-o** *m.* tedium, tediousness; weariness. **-are** [A4] *tr.* to weary; to bore. **-ọso** *adj.* tedious; tiresome; wearisome.
**tegame** *m.* pan; frying-pan; *uova al —*, fried eggs.
**tẹglia** *f.* baking-pan; pie-dish.
**tẹgol-a** *f.*, **-o** *m.* curved roofing-tile; *cotto come un -o*, 'pickled', very drunk; madly in love.
**teiera** *f.* tea-pot.
**te-ịsmo** *m.* theism. **-ista** *m.*, *f.* theist.
**tẹl-a** *f.* cloth; linen; — *di cotone*, calico; — *incerata*, — *impermeabile*, oilcloth, waterproof canvas; (theatr.) curtain; (art) canvas; (fig.) web; plot, intrigue. **-a·ggio** *m.* quality of cloth; weave, web. **-a·io** *m.* loom; frame.
**tele-** *pref.* equiv. to Eng. 'tele-'. (For derivatives in which the

stress falls on the second syllable, *e.g.* **tele·fono,** see separate entries.) **-abbonato** *m.* television licence-holder. **-comando** *m.* remote control. **-cronista** *m.* television announcer. **-diffọndere** [C2 c] *tr.* to televise, to telecast. **-fonare** [A1 s] *tr.*, *intr.* (*aux.* avere) to telephone, to ring up. **-giornale** *m.* television newsreel. **-grafare** [A1 s] *tr.* to telegraph; to wire; to cable. **-grafi·a** *f.* telegraphy. **-gra·fico** *adj.* telegraphic. **-grafista** *m.* telegraphist. **-gramma** *m.* telegram; wire. **-pati·a** *f.* telepathy; presentiment; thought-reading. **-sco·pio** *m.* telescope. **-vedẹre** [B35] *tr.* to look in, to view (on television). **-visiọne** *f.* television. **-visọre** *m.* television set.

**tele·fon-o** *m.* telephone, phone; *chiamare al* —, to ring up. **-ata** *f.* telephone call. **-ista** *m.*, *f.* telephonist.

**tele·grafo** *m.* telegraph (apparatus); telegraph office; — *senza fili*, wireless.

**tele·metro** *m.* range-finder.

**teleri·a** *f.* linen cloth; soft goods, drapery.

**tẹlo**[I] *m.* length of material.

**telo**[2] *m.* (poet.) arrow; dart; javelin; lance.

**tẹma**[I] *f.* (poet.) fear.

**tem-a**[2] *m.* (*pl.* -i) theme; subject; topic; (school) exercise, composition. **-a·tico** *adj.* thematic.

**temenza** *f.* see under **temẹre.**

**temera·ri-o** *adj.* rash; foolhardy; reckless. **-età** *f.* temerity, rashness; recklessness.

**tem-ẹre** [B1] *tr.* to fear; to be afraid (of), to dread; to shrink from; to hesitate; *intr.* (*aux.* avere; *prep.* di) to be anxious (about); to be in doubt (concerning). **-enza** *f.* fear; dread; awe; anxiety; shyness. **-erità** *f.* temerity, rashness, foolhardiness. **-i·bile** *adj.* to be feared. **-uto** *part. adj.* feared; dreaded.

**Temi, Te·mide** *pr.n.f.* (myth.) Themis.

**te·mpera** *f.* tempera; distemper; timbre; (fig.) temper, temperament.

**temper-are** [A1 s] *tr.* to temper; to mitigate; to moderate; (paint.) to mix (colours) for tempera painting; to blend; *rfl.* to be temperate; to exercise self-control. **-alapis, -amatite** *m. indecl.* pencil-sharpener. **-amẹnto** *m.* tempering; temper; disposition; temperament; just proportion; compromise; expedient; mitigation; air-conditioning. **-ante** *part. adj.* temperate; moderate; soothing. **-anza** *f.* temperance. **-ato** *part. adj.* tempered; temperate. **-atura** *f.* temperature; tempering.

**tempe·rie** *f.pl.* mild, seasonable weather.

**temperino** *m.* pen-knife; pocket-knife.

**tempest-a** *f.* storm; bad weather; tempest; thunderstorm; squall; (fig.) shower. **-are** [A1] *intr.* (*aux.* avere) to rage; to storm; *tr.* (*prep.* di) to vex, to annoy, to importune; to shake; to pull about; to knock furiously; to pelt (with); to shower (with). **-ato** *part. adj.* beaten; shaken; decked; spangled. **-ìo** *m.* (fig.) flood; outburst. **-ività** *f.* timeliness, seasonableness. **-ivo** *adj.* timely; opportune; seasonable. **-ọso** *adj.* stormy; tempestuous; violent; vehement; boisterous.

**te·mpia** *f.* temple; *pl.* head; hair at the temples.

**te·mpio** *m.* (*pl.* **templi**) temple; church; pagan temple; Jewish synagogue; Protestant church; fane.

**tempi·ssimo** *adv. phr. a* —, in the nick of time; *per* —, very early.

**Templare** *m.* Templar; Knight Templar.

**temp-o** *m.* time; times, days; delay; term; period; *da molto* —, long since, for a long time (in the past); *per* —, early, betimes; period, age; (mus.) beat, tempo; phase; (gramm.) tense; season; weather; *bel* —, fine weather. **-a·ccio** *m. pejor.* bad weather. **-ọne** *m. augm.* gaiety; a good time.

**te·mpora** *f.pl.* (eccl.) Ember Days.

**temporale**[I] *adj.* temporal; secular, worldly; lay; relating to time; *n.m.* (eccl.) the temporal power.

**temporal-e**[2] *m.* thunderstorm. **-ẹsco** *adj.* (*m.pl.* **-ẹschi**) stormy.

**tempora·ne-o** *adj.* temporaneous, temporary; transitory; seasonal; temporal. **-ità** *f.* temporary character; transitoriness.

**temporeggi-are** [A3 c] *intr.* (*aux.* avere) to temporize; to gain time; to procrastinate; *tr.* to postpone. **-atọre** *m.* temporizer.

**temuto** *part.* of **temẹre.**

**tenace** *adj.* tenacious; adhesive; tough; retentive; persevering; stubborn.

**tena·c-ia** *f.* tenacity; perseverance. **-ità** *f.* cohesiveness; toughness; stickiness.

**tena·glie** *f.pl.* see **tana·glie.**

**tend-a** *f.* tent; awning; curtain; hanging; *grande* —, marquee. **-ato** *part. adj.* tented; furnished with tents; pitched, erected; stretched. **-ina** *f.* curtain; blind; shutter; eye-shade.

**te·ndenza** *f.* see under **te·ndere.**

**te·nd-ere** [C1] *tr.* to stretch, to hold out; to strain; to draw tight; to tighten, to pull tight; to lay; to spread; — *una trappola*, to set a snare; — *il cammino verso*, to direct one's steps towards; *intr.* (*aux.* avere; *prep.* a) to tend (towards), to aim (at); to lead (to). **-enza** *f.* tendency; trend; bent; inclination; propensity; liking; love. **-enziọso** *f.* tendentious, partial, biased. **-itọio** *m.* drying-room; drying-place, shed; clothes-horse; clothes-line post.

**te·ndine** *m.* tendon; sinew.

**te·nebr-e** *f.pl.* darkness; gloom; obscurity; *al cader delle* —, at nightfall; (liturg.) (*ufficio delle*) —, (office of) Tenebrae; (fig.) ignorance; confusion and clamour. **-ọne** *m.* one who speaks obscurely; gloomy person; obscurantist. **-ọso** *adj.* gloomy; dark; sombre; obscure; secret; confused; disturbing.

**ten-ẹre** [B32] *tr.* to hold; to hold on to; to hold back; to restrain; to keep; to keep back; to have; to gain, to win; to obtain; (fig.) to hold, to consider, to regard: to think; to contain, to hold, to take, to occupy; *abs. tieni!*, take that!, *or* here, take it!; *intr.* (*aux.* avere) to be lasting; (of colours) to be fast, to be fadeless; to care (about); *-go a dirvi*, I must tell you; — *da*, to take after, to resemble; *rfl.* to hold oneself; to consider oneself; to keep (oneself). **-ente** *part. adj.* holding; keeping; lasting; *n.m.* lieutenant; *-ente colonnello*, lieutenant-colonel.

**te·ner-o** *adj.* tender; soft; pliable; fresh, new; early; sensitive; affectionate; *n.m.* tender part; (fig.) weak or soft side (of character, etc.). **-ẹzza** *f.* tenderness; softness; fondness, love, affection; *pl.* caresses; loving words; (iron.) affectation; cajolery. **-ume** *m.* soft part; soft things; mawkishness.

**te·nia** *f.* tape-worm.

**ten-i·bile** *adj.* tenable. **-imento** *m.* holding. **-itọre** *m.* holder, keeper; *-itore dell'asta*, auctioneer.

**tenọr-e** *m.* tenor, proceeding; — *di vita*, standard of living; tenour; contents; bearing; manner; system; grade; standard; (mus.) tenor voice; tenor part; tenor singer. **-eggiare** [A3 c] *intr.* (*aux.* avere) to sing tenor. **-ile** *adj.* tenor.

**te·nsile** *adj.* tensile, ductile; (mus.) *strumenti tensili*, stringed instruments.

**tensiọne** *f.* tension; strain; pressure; tightness.

**tenta** *f.* (surg.) probe.

**tenta·colo** *m.* tentacle.

**tent-are** [A1, A1 c] *tr.* to try, to attempt; to tempt; trying, attempting; *il — non nuoce*, there's no harm in trying. **-a·bile** *adj.* open to trial; open to temptation. **-ativo** *m.* attempt, try; endeav-

our, trial; *adj.* tentative. **-atọre** *m.* tempter; *adj.* tempting. **-atrice** *f.* temptress. **-aziọne** *f.* temptation.

**Tentẹnna** *pr.n.m.* name for a waverer, indecisive person.

**tentenn-are** [A1 c] *tr.* to shake; *intr.* (*aux.* avere) to oscillate; to waver; to hesitate; to stagger; to be unsteady; to waggle. **-amẹnto** *m.* uncertainty; havering; waggling. **-ata** *f.* shake, knock; a moment of hesitation. **-ọna** *f.*, **-ọne** *m.* waverer.

**tentọn-e, -i** *adv.* gropingly, feeling one's way; hesitatingly.

**te·nue** *adj.* thin, fine, tenuous; small; slight; slender; (of fluid) watery.

**tenut-a** *f.* estate, farm; holding (of land); capacity; possession; — *dei libri*, book-keeping; (mil.) fort; dress, uniform, kit; — *di fatica*, working clothes. **-a·rio** *m.* (leg.) holder; owner.

**tenuto** *part.* of **tenẹre**; *adj.* kept; owned; held; considered; obliged, bound.

**tenzọn-e** *f.* combat; poetic contest. **-are** [A1 c] *intr.* (*aux.* avere) to contend; to dispute.

**teocr-a·tico** *adj.* theocratic. **-azi·a** *f.* theocracy.

**Teo·crito** *pr.n.m.* Theocritus.

**teo·l-ogo** *m.* theologian. **-ogi·a** *f.* theology. **-o·gico** *adj.* theological.

**teorem-a** *m.* (*pl.* -i) theorem.

**te-ore·tico, -o·rico** *adj.* theoretic(al); *n.m.* theorist.

**teori·a** *f.* theory; hypothesis; speculation; doctrine; (Gk. antiq.) procession, cortège; file, series.

**teo·sof-o** *m.* theosophist. **-i·a** *f.* theosophy. **-ista** *m.*, *f.* theosophist.

**tepidẹzza** *f.* pleasant warmth; coolness; tepidity.

**te·pido** *adj.* see **tiepido**.

**tepọre** *m.* pleasant warmth; lukewarmness; mildness.

**tẹpp-a** *f.* mob, gang. **-ịsmo** *m.* hooliganism. **-ista** *m.* hooligan.

**terap-e·utica** *f.* therapeutics. **-e·utico** *adj.* therapeutic.

**terapi·a** *f.* therapy.

**Tere·nzio** *pr.n.m.* Terence.

**tergale** *m.* see under **tergo.**

**te·rg-ere** [C def.] *tr.* to wipe; to wipe off; to wipe away; to scour; to polish. **-icristallo** *m. indecl.* (motor.) windscreen-wiper.

**tergiversare** [A1] *intr.* (*aux.* avere) to answer evasively; to hesitate; to tergiversate.

**terg-o** *m.* (*pl.* **-a** *f.*) back; *stare a — a*, to stand behind; *a —*, on one's back; (*pl.* **terghi** *m.*) reverse side, back; *vedi a —*, please turn over. **-ale** *m.* ornamental chair-back.

**term-e** *f.pl.* hot springs; hot baths; spa, mineral springs. **-ale** *adj.* thermal; *stazione -ale*, spa.

**terminale** *adj.*, *n.m.* see under **termine.**

**termin-are** [A1 s] *tr.* to finish; to terminate; to wind up; to mark the boundary of; *intr.* (*aux.* essere) to end, to finish, to cease. **-ato** *part. adj.* ended; finished; defined. **-aziọne** *f.* end; close; conclusion; termination; ending.

**te·rmin-e** *m.* term; limit; boundary; bound; space; end; time; date; aim; object; (logic) term; — *medio*, middle term; *mezzo —*, compromise; *pl.* terms, conditions (of an agreement); state, condition. **-ale** *adj.* terminal; final; *n.m.* boundary.

**terminol-ogi·a** *f.* terminology. **-o·gico** *adj.* terminological.

**termio·nico** *adj.* thermionic; *valvola termionica*, thermionic valve.

**te·rmite** *m.* termite.

**termo-dina·mica** *f.* thermodynamics. **-ele·ttrico** *adj.* thermo-electric.

**termo·metro** *m.* thermometer.

**termo-nucleare** *adj.* thermonuclear. **-terapi·a** *f.* heat treatment.

**termo·st-ato** *m.* thermostat. **-a·tico** *adj.* thermostatic.

**tern-o** *adj.* relating to the number three; threefold; *n.m.* group of three; triplet; tercet; (fig.) stroke of luck; winning number. **-a·rio** *adj.* ternary; triple; threefold.

**terr-a** *f.* **1.** earth; world. **2.** land; shore; coast; *scendere a —*, to land. **3.** ground; floor; *per —*, on the ground; on the floor; *a —*, down, low. **4.** soil, earth; — *vegetale*, loam. **5.** clay; — *bianca*, china clay; — *di porcellana*, kaolin; ware, pottery. **6.** land, estate, property. **7.** country; village; locality. **8.** (electr.) earth; *mettere a —*, to earth. **9.** *adj. indecl. terra terra*, terre à terre, ordinary; *adv. terra terra*, close to the ground. **10.** (geog.) land; *Terra di Baffin*, Baffinland. **-acotta** (*pl.* **-ecotte**) terracotta (figure); *vasi di -acotta*, earthenware. **-aferma** *f.* land, dry land; continent. **-a·glia** *f.* (*pl.* **-a·glie**) pottery; earthenware; *-aglia durissima*, crockery. **-ame** *m.* heaps of earth; rubble. **-apieno** *m.* (mil.) glacis; platform; terrace; embankment; bank; level surface; open space. **-a·tico** *m.* rent (which may be paid in kind); lease, contract of a tenant-farmer. **-ato** *m.* embankment; terrace; attic; flat roof.

**Terra-nova** *pr.n.f.* (geog.) Newfoundland; (dog) Newfoundland. **-santa** *pr.n.f.* Holy Land.

**terrazz-a** *f.* flat roof with parapet; balcony; terrace. **-iere** *m.* navvy; labourer. **-o** *m.* loggia; balcony; terraced roof; 'terrazzo' flooring.

**terremoto** *m.* earthquake.

**terreno** *adj.* earthly, worldly; *pian —*, ground floor; *n.m.* ground; soil; land; field; site.

**te·rreo** *adj.* earthy; earth-coloured; yellowish; wan.

**terrestre** *adj.* of the earth; terrestrial; land.

**terri·bil-e** *adj.* terrible; dreadful; awful; formidable; frightful. **-ità** *f.* awfulness; formidableness.

**terri·ccio** *m.* mould, loam, humus.

**terriero** *adj.* land-owning; landed; *proprietario —*, landowner.

**terri·fic-o** *adj.* terrific. **-ante** *part. adj.* terrifying; frightful; appalling. **-are** [A2 s] *tr.* to terrify; to frighten; to appal.

**terrigno** *adj.* earthy; earth-coloured; (of animals) living underground.

**terrina** *f.* earthenware dish; pie-dish; soup-tureen; bowl; (cul.) terrine.

**territo·ri-o** *m.* territory; district. **-ale** *adj.* territorial; *imposta -ale*, land-tax.

**terrọr-e** *m.* terror; dread; fright. **-ista** *m.* terrorist.

**Tersi·core** *pr.n.f.* (myth.) Terpsichore.

**terso** *part.* of **te·rgere**; *adj.* terse; clear; polished.

**terz-a** *f.* (eccl.) tierce; (rlwy.) third class. **-ana** *f.* tertian fever.

**terz-o** *ord. num.* third; *la Terza Italia*, Modern Italy; *decimo —*, thirteenth; *vigesimo —*, twenty-third; *-a rima*, triple rhyme; *n.m.* the third (in a series); a third (fraction); third party; *adv.* thirdly, in the third place. **-avo, -a·volo** *m.* great-great-grandfather. **-ẹtto** *m.* trio. **-ina** *f.* (mus.) triplet; (prosod.) tercet. **-ọne** *m.* packing canvas; wrapper. **-u·ltimo** *adj.*, *n.m.* last-but-two, antepenultimate.

**tẹsa** *f.* tension, stretching; spreading, laying; visor; brim (of a hat).

**tẹsa·uro** *m.* (poet.) see **tesoro.**

**te·schio** *m.* skull; cranium.

**tẹsi** *f.* thesis; proposition.

**tẹso** *part.* of **te·ndere**; *adj.* taut; tight; tense; overstrung; stretched out; (fig.) alert, attentive; *rapporti tesi*, strained relations.

**tẹsor-o** *m.* treasure; treasury; (as term of affection) darling. **-eggiare** [A3 c] *tr.* to hoard; to treasure up. **-eri·a** *f.* treasury. **-iere** *m.* treasurer.

**Tespi** *pr.n.f.* Thespis; *il carro di —*, travelling theatre.

**Tessa·lia** *pr.n.f.* (geog.) Thessaly.

**tessella** *f.* a small tessera.

**te·sser-a** *f.* tessera (used in mosaic); card, ticket; pass; tally; — *annonaria*, ration-card; — *di riconoscimento*, identification card. **-are** [A1 s] *tr.* to ration (a commodity); to provide with a membership card. **-ato** *part. adj.* rationed; holding a card; *n.m.* member (of a party).

**te·ss-ere** [B1] *tr.* to weave; (fig.) to compose; to plot. **-itọre** *m.*, **-itrice** *f.* weaver. **-itura** *f.* weaving; *-itura a maglia*, hosiery knitting; texture; composition. **-uto** *part. adj.* woven; composed; *n.m.* cloth, fabric; (fig.) tissue, web.

**testa** *f.* **1.** head; *in* —, on one's head; *dar di — in*, to bump one's head against; *lavata di* —, reprimand; brains, wits. **2.** face; person; — *quadra*, sensible person; clever man; — *di Turco*, Aunt Sally. **3.** head, leading position; *marciare in* —, to march at the head. **4.** top, chief part; — *carica*, war-head (torpedo); — *di ponte*, bridge-head; — *di sbarco*, beach-head.

**testamẹnt-o** *m.* will; testament; *il Vecchio, il Nuovo Testamento*, the Old, the New Testament. **-a·rio** *adj.* testamentary.

**testard-o** *adj.* obstinate, stubborn; headstrong; *n.m.* stubborn person. **-a·ggine** *f.* obstinacy; stubbornness.

**test-are** [A1] *intr.* (*aux.* avere) to make a will; *tr.* to bequeath. **-ante** *m.*, *f.* testator.

**testata** *f.* head; top; heading; blow, butt with the head.

**testa·tico** *m.* poll-tax.

**testè** *adv.* lately; just now.

**testi·colo** *m.* testicle.

**testificare** [A1 s] *tr.* (leg.) to testify; to bear witness to; to declare, to attest.

**testimon-e** *m.*, *f.* witness. **-iale** *adj.* given in evidence. **-ianza** *f.* deposition; testimony; evidence given; mark; token. **-iare** [A4] *intr.* (*aux.* avere) to bear witness; to give evidence.

**testimo·nio** *m.* evidence; witness; *firmare come* —, to sign as a witness.

**testo**[1] *m.* flower-pot; earthenware pot-lid.

**testo**[2] *m.* text; *libri di* —, text-books.

**testual-e** *adj.* textual; precise. **-mẹnte** *adv.* exactly, precisely; textually.

**testu·ggine** *f.* tortoise; turtle; tortoise-shell; (archit.) vault, ceiling.

**te·tano** *m.* (med.) tetanus, lock-jaw.

**tetra·gono** *adj.* four-sided; (fig.) four-square; unflinching.

**tetr-o** *adj.* gloomy; dismal. **-a·ggine** *f.* gloom; sadness.

**tẹtta** *f.* teat, nipple; breast.

**tẹtt-o** *m.* roof; house-top; — *mobile*, sliding roof; (fig.) house, home. **-ọia** *f.* shed, penthouse; roof of station or market; open building; roofing.

**Te·ut-ọne** *m.* Teuton. **-o·nico** *adj.* Teutonic.

**Tẹvere** *pr.n.m.* (geog.) Tiber.

**thè** *m. indecl.* see **tè**.

**ti**[1] *pers. prn. conjunct. 2nd sing. acc., dat.* thee, to thee; you, to you.

**ti**[2] *m.* T, name of 18th letter of the Italian alphabet.

**tiberino** *adj.* of the Tiber.

**ti·bia** *f.* tibia, shin-bone; ancient flute.

**Tibullo** *pr.n.m.* Tibullus.

**tic**[1], **tic-che** *m. indecl.* tick, ticking, beat. **-chettare** [A1 c] *intr.* (*aux.* avere) to tick; to click.

**tic**[2] *m. indecl.* tic, facial spasm.

**ti·cchio** *m.* see **tic**[2]; (fig.) caprice, whim, fancy; mannerism.

**tie·pid-o** *adj.* lukewarm; warm. **-amẹnte** *adv.* coolly; without enthusiasm; lazily.

**tif-o** *m.* typhus. **-o·ide** *f.* typhoid fever. **-ọso** *adj.* typhous; *n.m.* (colloq.) fan; fanatic; (sport) supporter.

**tifọne** *m.* typhoon; hurricane.

**tight** *m. indecl.* see **tait**.

**ti·glio**[1] *m.* (bot.) lime; lime-wood.

**ti·gli-o**[2] fibre; bast; vein (in stone). **-ọso** *adj.* fibrous; (of meat) tough, stringy.

**tign-a** *f.* ringworm. **-ọso** *adj.* scabby; suffering from ringworm; (Tusc., pop.) miserly.

**tign(u)ola** *f.* clothes-moth.

**tigr-e** *f.*, *m.* tiger; (fig.) fierce, cruel person. **-ato** *adj.* striped; dappled; *gatto -ato*, tabby cat. **-atura** *f.* striping. **-ẹsco** *adj.* (*m.pl.* **-ẹschi**) tigerish.

**Tigri** *pr.n.m.* (geog.) Tigris.

**tilde** *m.* (typ.) tilde.

**timballo** *m.* kettledrum; (cul.) timbale.

**timbr-o**[1] *m.* official stamp; — *in gomma*, rubber stamp; — *postale*, postmark. **-are** [A1] *tr.* to stamp. **-atura** *f.* stamping.

**timbro**[2] *m.* timbre.

**ti·mid-o** *adj.* timid; nervous; shy, bashful. **-ẹzza** *f.* timidity; shyness, bashfulness.

**timo** *m.* (bot.) thyme.

**timọn-e** *m.* rudder; shaft, pole; (of bicycle) handle-bar(s); (fig.) helm; direction. **-eggiare** [A3 c] *tr.* to steer; (fig.) to govern. **-iera** *f.* wheel-house. **-iere** *m.* helmsman; steersman.

**timọr-e** *m.* fear; awe; — *panico*, panic. **-ato** *adj.* respectful; scrupulous. **-ọso** *adj.* timorous, fearful; cowardly.

**ti·mpano** *m.* kettledrum; (anat.) tympanum; (archit.) spandrel.

**tin-a** *f.* small vat; tub. **-a·ia** *f.* vat-room, cellar. **-ello** *m. dim.* small cask for carrying grapes; (fig.) board; *avere il -ello*, to have free board; *a tutto -ello*, all found; (archit.) dining recess.

**ti·ngere** [C5] *tr.* to dye; to paint; to stain; to tint; to blot, to spot.

**ti·nnulo** *adj.* jangling, twanging.

**tin-o** *m.* vat; tub. **-ozza** *f.* tub; wash-tub; bath-tub.

**tint-a** *f.* dye; hue, colour; tint; tinge; shade; *ce n'è di tutte le -e*, there are some of all sorts; (fig.) tincture, veneer. **-arella** *f.* sun-tan. **-eggiare** [A3 c] *tr.* to tint; to tinge.

**tintìn** *m. indecl.* (onom.) ding-dong; tinkling.

**tintinn-are** [A1], **-ire** [D2] *intr.* (*aux.* essere, avere) to tinkle; to ring; to jingle; to clink. **-a·bolo, -a·bulo** *m.* bell. **-o** *m.* bell; ringing; sound, resonance.

**tint-o** *part.* of **ti·ngere**; *adj.* dyed; stained; tinged; tinted. **-ọre** *m.* dyer. **-ori·a** *f.* dyeing; dye-house, dye-works. **-ura** *f.* dyeing; dye; tint; colour; (fig.) tincture, smattering.

**ti·pic-o** *adj.* typical; perfect of its kind. **-amẹnte** *adv.* typically.

**tipo** *m.* type; specimen; model; standard; (derog.) fellow, chap.

**tip-ografi·a** *f.* typography; printing; printing-house; printing-works. **-ogra·fico** *adj.* typographical; letterpress. **-o·grafo** *m.* printer, typographer.

**tip tap, ti·ppete, ta·ppete** *onom.* tap, tap.

**tira** *adv. phrs.* see under **tirare.**

**tira·nnico** *adj.* tyrannical; arbitrary; high-handed.

**tira·nnide** *f.* despotism; absolute rule.

**tirann-o** *m.* tyrant, absolute ruler; *adj.* tyrannous. **-eggiare** [A3 c] *tr.* to tyrannize over; to oppress; *intr.* (*aux.* avere) to play the tyrant; to rule with a rod of iron. **-ẹsco** *adj.* (*m.pl.* **-ẹschi**) tyrannous, despotic. **-i·a** *f.* tyranny; despotism; oppression. **-icida** *m.* (*pl.* **-icidi**) tyrannicide (person). **-ici·dio** *m.* (*pl.* **-icidii**) tyrannicide (act).

**tir-are** [A1] *tr.* **1.** to pull; to draw; to drag; to attract; — *su*, to pull up, (fig.) to bring up, to rear; — *una linea*, to draw, to trace, a line; (typ.) to print, to print off. **2.** to stretch, to lengthen, to draw out. **3.** to win, to get; to draw. **4.** to attract, to absorb. **5.** to throw; to fling, to chuck; — *calci*, to kick; — *pugni a*, to punch; — *giù*, to throw down, to jot down. **6.** *intr.* (*aux.* avere; *prep.* a) to tend, to be inclined (to); to aim (at); — *via*, to go on, to proceed; — *avanti*, to get on fairly well; (of wind) to blow. **7.** *rfl.* (*acc.* of *prn.* 'si') to draw; *-arsi più vicino*, to draw nearer; (*dat.* of *prn.* 'si') *-arsi dietro*, to drag after one. **-a** *adv. phr.*

*fare a tira tira,* to wrangle; to dispute; *n.m.* pull, hold, attraction; *un tira tira,* wrangling. **-a·ggio** *m.* draught, drawing. **-ama·ntici** *m. indecl.* organ-blower. **-ante** *part. adj.* drawing; carrying; attractive; *n.m* connecting-rod; tie-rod; (naut.) *-ante d'acqua,* draught; *-ante d'aria,* draught. **-astivali** *m. indecl.* boot-jack, shoe-horn. **-ata** *f.* pull; draw; *-ata di campana,* ring; length, (run) of buildings; tirade; long speech; scolding; blow; hit. **-atappi** *m. indecl.* corkscrew. **-atura** *f.* drawing; pulling; pull (book paper print); printing; impression, edition; circulation.

**ti·rchi-o** *adj.* stingy, niggardly, mean; miserly; *n.m.* miser, skin-flint. **-eri·a** *f.* miserliness.

**tirella** *f.* (equestr.) trace.

**tiremmolla** *m. indecl.* something alternately tight and slack; (fig.) indecision, hesitation; wavering; waverer.

**tirẹtto** *m.* drawer.

**tiritera** *f.* rigmarole; long-winded yarn.

**tiro** *m.* draught; *cavallo da —,* draught-horse; throw, cast; shooting; shot; firing; fire; range; (billiards) stroke; *— con l'arco,* archery; *a —,* within range; (cul.) *essere a —,* to be done to a turn; trick; *un brutto —,* a dirty trick.

**tiroci·n-io** *m.* apprenticeship; novitiate. **-ante** *m.* apprentice; beginner; tyro.

**tiro·id-e** *f.* thyroid. **-e·o** *adj.* thyroid.

**Tirol-o** *pr.n.m.* (geog.) Tyrol. **-ẹse** *adj., n.m., f.* Tyrolese.

**tirrẹno** *adj.* Tyrrhenian.

**tiṣana** *f.* infusion, decoction; herb.

**tiṣi** *f.* tuberculosis, phthisis.

**ti·ṣico** *adj.* tubercular; wretched, puny; feeble, stunted.

**tita·nico** *adj.* titanic.

**Titano** *pr.n.m.* (myth.) Titan.

**titillare** [A1] *tr.* to titillate.

**ti·tol-o** *m.* title; title-page, heading; name; qualification, evidence; right; *pl.* bonds; stock; securities; certificate; claim; fineness (coins); precious metal in alloy; inscription, votive tablet. **-are** [A1 s] *adj.* titular; regular; rightful; nominal; *n.m.* occupant; holder; incumbent.

**Titọne** *pr.n.m.* (myth.) Tithonus.

**titub-are** [A1 s] *intr.* (*aux.* avere) to hesitate, to falter; to waver. **-ante** *part. adj.* hesitant, irresolute; perplexed. **-aziọne** *f.* hesitation; perplexity.

**Tiziano** *pr.n.m.* Titian.

**tizz-o** *m.* brand, firebrand; smoking coal. **-ọne** *m. augm.* large firebrand.

**to'!, toh!** *excl.* I say! (surprise); look here!; hallo!; here!

**toboga** *m. indecl.* toboggan, sledge.

**toca·i** *m.* Tokai.

**tocc-are** [A2 c] *tr.* to touch; to feel; to finger; to tap; to hit, to strike; to press; to play; to call at; (fig.) to move, to affect, to touch; to please, to impress; to concern; to injure; to offend; to touch on, to allude to; to meddle with; to adjoin; *intr.* (*aux.* essere; *prep.* a) to befall; to fall to the lot (of); to be the duty (of); to be the turn (of); (*aux.* avere; *prep.* su) to hint at, to touch upon; *recip. rfl.* to meet, to touch; *gli estremi si -ano,* extremes meet. **-ata** *f.* touch; (fig.) *dare una -ata a,* to touch upon, to allude to; (mus.) toccata.

**toccheggiare** [A3 c] *intr.* (*aux.* avere) (of bells) to toll, to ring.

**toc-co**[1] *m.* (*pl.* **-chi**) toque; cap or hat without brim.

**toc-co**[2] *m.* (*pl.* **-chi**) lump; piece; hunk; figure. **-chẹtto** *m. dim.* bit, morsel; tit-bit.

**tọc-co**[3] *m.* (*pl.* **-chi**) touch; blow, stroke; toll (of bell); *al —,* at one o'clock. **-chẹtto** *m. dim.* accidental blow, tap, touch. **-cọne** *m.* meddlesome person.

**tọc-co**[4] *apocop. part.* of **toccare**; *adj.* (*m.pl.* **-chi**) touched; moved; struck; received; hinted at; (colloq.) *— nel cervello,* 'touched'.

**toelẹtta** *f.* dressing-table; mirror; toilet; toilet-table; dressing-room; *gabinetto di —,* lavatory, W.C.; *sala di —,* hairdresser's; costume, style of dress, 'toilette'.

**tog-a** *f.* toga; (academic) gown. **-ato** gowned.

**to·gli-ere** [C] *tr.* (*prep.* a, da) to take; to take (off), to take away (from); *— di mezzo a,* to take out of the way, to get rid of; to carry away, to carry off; to seize, to steal; to prevent; to hinder; *tolga Dio!,* God forbid!; to accept; to elect, to appoint (to an office); to buy; to get; *rfl.* to remove oneself; to get away.

**toh** *excl.* see **to'**.

**tolẹtta** *f.* see **toeletta.**

**toller-are** [A1 s] *tr.* to tolerate; to bear; to suffer; to endure; to allow. **-a·bile** *adj.* tolerable, bearable; passable, fairly good. **-ante** *part. adj.* tolerant. **-anza** *f.* tolerance; toleration; endurance.

**Tolome·o** *pr.n.m.* Ptolemy.

**Tolọsa** *pr.n.f.* (geog.) Toulouse.

**tolto** *part.* of **to·gliere**; *adj.* taken away, removed; stolen.

**tọma** *f.* (in the phrase) *promettere Roma e —,* to make boundless promises.

**toma·io** *m.* (shoem.) upper; vamp.

**tọmb-a** *f.* tomb; grave; vault; (fig.) death. **-ale** *adj.* relating to tombs or graves; *pietra -ale,* grave-stone.

**tọmbola**[1] *f.* tombola; lotto; housey-housey, bingo.

**tọmbol-a**[2] *f.,* **-o** *m.* tumble; headlong fall. **-are** [A1 sc] *intr.* (*aux.* essere) to fall headlong; to tumble.

**tom-iṣmo** *m.* (theol.; philos.) Thomism. **-ista** *m., f.* Thomist.

**tomo** *m.* volume; tome; part of a book; (colloq.) *un bel —,* a 'queer fish', a 'card'.

**to·naca** *f.* tunic; habit; cassock.

**ton-are** [A1 d] *intr.* (*impers., aux.* essere; *pers., aux.* avere) to thunder; to boom; (fig., of person) to thunder; to roar; to rail. **-ante** *part. adj.* thundering.

**tondare** [A1 c] *tr.* to round, to turn on a lathe; to trim.

**tondeggiare** [A3 c] *intr.* (*aux.* essere) to be roundish; *tr.* to round off; to make round; *n.m.* (paint.) roundness.

**tọnd-o** *adj.* round; *arco —,* round arch, semicircular arch; full; complete; *adv.* roundly; *chiaro e —,* clearly, frankly, plainly; *n.m.* ring, circle; (art) tondo, round picture; plate, saucer; round tray; globe, sphere. **-ino** *m. dim.* small plate; saucer; (archit.) astragal; (metall.) roa; (paint.) tondo.

**tọnfo** *m.* thud; bang; noise; splash; plunge.

**to·nic-a** *f.* (mus.) tonic; keynote. **-o** *adj., n.m.* tonic.

**tonificare** [A2 s] *tr.* to tone up; to invigorate.

**tonnell-a·ggio** *m.* (naut.) tonnage. **-ata** *f.* ton.

**tọnn-o** *m.* tunny fish. **-ara** *f.* tunny fishing; tunny nets.

**tono**[1] *m.* tone; tune; accent; stress; style; manner.

**tono**[2] *m.* see **tuono.**

**tonsill-a** *f.* tonsil. **-ite** *f.* tonsillitis.

**tonsur-a** *f.* tonsure. **-are** [A1] *tr.* to tonsure. **-ato** *part. adj.* tonsured; *n.m.* cleric.

**tọnto** *adj., n.m.* stupid, dull.

**topa·ia** *f.* see under **topo.**

**to·pico** *adj.* topical; to the point; local.

**top-o** *m.* rat; *— d'acqua,* water rat; (fig.) *— di biblioteca,* 'book-worm'. **-a·io** *m.* rat's nest; place infested with rats; hovel. **-olino** *m.* mouse; *pr.n.m.* Mickey Mouse; *pr.n.f.* name of a small Fiat car.

**topogr-afi·a** *f.* topography. **-a·fico** *adj.* topographical.

**topo·grafo** *m.* topographer.

**toponoma·stica** *f.* toponymy, study of place-names.

**toporagno** *m.* (zool.) shrew.

**toppa** *f.* lock; keyhole; patch; piece let in.

**toppo** *m.* stump; block of wood; log.

**torace** *m.* thorax.
**tọrba** *f.* peat.
**tọrbido** *adj.* turbid; muddy; troubled; gloomy; cloudy; confused; angry; (fig.) dirty, nasty, obscene; *n.m.* gloom; trouble, disorder, disturbance.
**torbiera** *f.* peat-bog.
**to·rc-ere** [C5] *tr.* to twist; to wring; to turn; — *il naso*, to turn up one's nose; to distort; to wrench; *intr.* (*aux.* avere) to wind, to turn, to twist; *rfl.* to turn, to revolve; to bend; to twist; to writhe. **-icollo** *m.* stiff neck, torticollis; (orn.) wryneck; (fig.) hypocrite, pious humbug.
**to·rchi-o** *m.* hand-press; (fig.) printing press; *essere sotto i torchi*, to be in the press, i.e. printing. **-are** [A4] *tr.* to press.
**to·rcia** *f.* candle; torch; taper.
**torcicollo** *m.* see under **to·rcere.**
**tọrdo** *m.* thrush; (fig.) simpleton.
**torello** *m.* young bull.
**tor-e·o** *m.* bull-fight. **-ero** *m.* bull-fighter.
**Torin-o** *pr.n..f.* (geog.) Turin. **-ẹse** *adj.* of Turin; *n., m., f.* native of Turin.
**tor-iṣmo** *m.* (pol.) Toryism. **-ista** *m., f.* (pol.) Tory.
**torlo** *m.* yolk (of egg).
**tọrma** *f.* crowd; swarm; herd.
**tormẹnta** *f.* snowstorm; blizzard.
**tormẹnt-o** *m.* torment; torture; (fig.) pain, agony; annoyance. **-are** [A1 c] *tr.* to torture, to torment; to rack, to plague, to worry, to vex; to tease; to hurt; *rfl.* to torment oneself; to worry; *intr.* (*aux.* essere) to torment oneself; to worry. **-ọso** *adj.* tormenting; troublesome; vexatious.
**tornado** *m. indecl.* tornado, whirlwind.
**torn-are** [A1 c] *intr.* (*aux.* essere); **1.** to return; to go back; to come back; — *a dire*, to say again; to recur. **2.** to turn out, to prove to be; — *bene*, to turn out well. **3.** to turn (into), to become. **4.** to be worth while; to be correct. **5.** *tr.* to turn, to turn round; to bring back; to change. **-acọnto** *m.* profit; benefit; utility. **-ante** *adj.* turning; curving; *n.m.* zig-zag, winding road. **-asọle** *m.* (chem.) litmus; (bot.) sunflower. **-ata** *f.* return.
**torn-e·o** *m.* tournament; tourney; tournament; jousting. **-eare** *intr.* (*aux.* avere) to joust, to tilt; to wheel round.
**tornichẹtto** *m.* turnstile.
**tọrnio** *m.* lathe.
**torn-ire** [D2] *tr.* to turn (on a lathe); (fig.) to shape, to polish. **-ito** *part. adj.* turned; shaped; (fig.) shapely, polished. **-itọre** *m.* turner. **-itura** *f.* turning; (fig.) shaping; polishing; shavings; filings.

**tọrno**[1] *m.* period; *in quel* —, thereabouts.
**tọrno**[2] *prep.* round, about; *adv. torno torno*, all round.
**tor-o** *m.* bull. **-ọso** *adj.* bull-like; thick-set.
**torpe·din-e** *f.* torpedo, mine; depth-charge. **-iera** *f.* torpedo-boat.
**torped-o** *f. indecl.* sports-car, racing-car. **-ọne** *m.* motor-coach.
**to·rpido** *adj.* torpid; sluggish; dull.
**torpọre** *m.* torpor, numbness; (fig.) sluggishness; lethargy; dullness, stupidity.
**tọrr-e** *f.* tower; — *d'avorio*, ivory tower; (radio) — *di antenna*, aerial mast; (chess) rook. **-eggiare** [A3 c] *intr.* (*aux.* avere) to tower; to loom. **-ẹtta** *f. dim.* turret, small tower. **-iọne** *m.* strong, embattled tower.
**torren-te** *m.* torrent, stream; *un — di luce*, a flood of light; **-ziale** *adj.* torrential.
**to·rrido** *adj.* torrid; burning; scorching.
**torrọne** *m.* nougat.
**torsiọne** *f.* torsion; twist; contortion; (fig.) mental anguish; *pl.* gripes, colic.
**tọrso** *m.* torso, trunk; core of an apple or pear; stalk of a cabbage or other plant.
**tọrsolo** *m.* stump; core.
**tọrta**[1] *f.* cake; pie; tart.
**torta**[2] *f.* twist, twisting; (colloq.) *fare la* —, to pull wires, to form a clique.
**torto**[1] *part.* of **to·rcere**; *adj.* twisted; crooked; twisty; tortuous.
**torto**[2] *m.* wrong; *avere* —, to be wrong, to be mistaken; injury; injustice; *dare — a*, to put the blame on, to prove in the wrong.
**tor·tora** *f.* turtle-dove.
**tortoreggiare** [A3 c] *intr.* (*aux.* avere) to coo (like a dove); (fig.) to bill and coo.
**tortuọso** *adj.* tortuous, crooked; twisting; curving; winding.
**tortur-a** *f.* torture; (fig.) torment; agony; vexation. **-are** [A1] *tr.* to torture.
**tọrvo** *adj.* surly; grim; threatening.
**toṣ-are** [A1] *tr.* to clip; to shear. **-amẹnto** *m.* shearing. **-ato** *part. adj.* clipped, shorn. **-atọre** *m.* shearer. **-atrice** *f.* clipper, hair-clippers; sheep-shearing machine. **-atura** *f.* clipping; shearing; *-atura delle pecore*, sheep-shearing.
**Toscan-a** *pr.n.f.* (geog.) Tuscany. **-eggiare** [A3 c] *intr.* (*aux.* avere) to affect a Tuscan style of writing and speaking. **-o** *adj.*, *n.m.* Tuscan; a kind of cigar.
**tọsco**[1] *adj.*, *n.m.* (poet.) Tuscan.
**tosco**[2] *m.* (poet.) poison (*cf.* **to·ssico**).

**tosọne** *m.* fleece; *Il Toson d'Oro*, the Golden Fleece.
**tọsse** *f.* cough; *colpo di* —, fit of coughing; — *canina*, whooping-cough.
**to·ssic-o** *adj.* toxic; poisonous; *n.m.* poison; distasteful food; gall. **-ologi·a** *f.* toxicology.
**tossire** [D1 c] *intr.* (*aux.* avere) to cough.
**tost-are** [A1] *tr.* to roast (coffee, almonds, etc.); to toast. **-apane** *m. indecl.* (electric) toaster. **-ino** *m.* coffee-roaster (machine).
**tosto**[1] *adj.* hard; toasted; *pan* —, hard bread; *faccia -a*, cheek, impudence; *n.m.* toast.
**tosto**[2] *adv.* quickly; hurriedly; soon; — *che*, as soon as; *o — o tardi*, sooner or later.
**total-e** *adj.* total; whole, entire; absolute; gross; *n.m.* total. **-ità** *f.* totality; entirety; whole body. **-ita·rio** *adj.* complete; absolute; (pol.) totalitarian. **-iẓẓatọre** *m.* totalisor. **-mẹnte** *adv.* totally; entirely; wholly; utterly.
**totoca·lcio** *m.* football pool(s).
**tova·gli-a** *f.* table-cloth. **-olino** *m.* bib; small napkin. **-(u)olo** *m.* napkin; tray-cloth.
**tozzo**[1] *m.* piece, morsel, bit.
**tozzo**[2] *adj.* stocky; thick-set; stumpy; squat.
**tra**[1] *prep.* between, among; *volersi bene — loro*, to be fond of each other; — *me*, to myself.
**tra-**[2] *pref.* beyond, across, over.
**traball-are** [A1] *intr.* (*aux.* avere) to stagger; to totter; to sway; to lurch; to reel; to toddle. **-io** *m.* reeling; staggering. **-ọne** *m.* stagger; lurch; jolt.
**trabalz-are** [A1] *tr.* to shift; to remove; *intr.* (*aux.* essere) to jolt; to jerk; to rebound. **-ọne** *m.* jolt; *adv. phr. a -oni*, jerkily.
**trabi·ccolo** *m.* kind of clothes-horse or drying frame; rickety vehicle; rickety piece of furniture.
**trabocc-are** [A2 c] *intr.* (*aux.* avere, essere) to brim over, to overflow; *far — la nave*, to capsize the boat; *tr.* to hurl to the ground; to cast down; to destroy. **-ante** *part. adj.* overflowing, superabundant; *adv.* like a flood; in excess.
**trabocchẹtto** *m.* pitfall, snare, trap.
**trabọc-co** *m.* (*pl.* **-chi**) overflowing; overflow; flood; downfall, ruin. **-chẹvole** *adj.* overflowing, superabundant; excessive.
**tracannare** [A1] *tr.* to gulp down; to drink at one draught; *abs.* to swill.
**traccagnotto** *adj.* stocky; squat; dumpy.
**traccheggiare** [A3 c] *intr.* (*aux.* avere) to dally; to delay; *tr.* to delay; to hold up.

**tra·cci-a** *f.* trace; trail; track; spoor; footprint; mark; vestige; (fig.) outline, general plan. **-are** [A3] *tr.* to trace, to lay out, to mark out; to map out; to sketch; to outline. **-ato** *part. adj.* traced, drawn; *n.m.* trace; tracing; line; outline. **-atore** *m.* (techn.) tracer.
**trach-e·a** *f.* windpipe, trachea. **-eite** *f.* (med.) tracheitis. **-eotomi·a** *f.* tracheotomy.
**Tra·cia** *pr.n.f.* (geog.) Thrace.
**tracoll-a** *f.* shoulder-belt; (mil.) bandolier; *adv. phr. a —*, slung over the shoulder. **-are** [A1] *intr.* (*aux.* essere) to stagger; to fall; to overbalance; to collapse; *far -are la bilancia*, to turn the scale. **-o** *m.* collapse; breakdown; downfall; ruin.
**tracoma** *m.* (med.) trachoma.
**tracotan-te** *adj.* overbearing, overweening, arrogant. **-za** *f.* arrogance, haughtiness.
**trad-ire** [D2] *tr.* to betray; to deceive; to be unfaithful to; to reveal; *rfl.* to betray oneself, to give oneself away. **-imento** *m.* betrayal; treason, treachery. **-itore** *m.*, **-itrice** *f.* betrayer; deceiver; traitor, traitress; *adj.* treacherous; deceitful.
**tradizion-e** *f.* tradition; handing-down. **-ale** *adj.* traditional.
**tradotta** *f.* (mil.) troop train; leave train.
**tradotto** *part.* of **tradurre**; *adj.* translated; turned; expressed.
**traduci·bile** *adj.* translatable; expressible.
**tra-durre** [B2] *tr.* to translate; to interpret; to summon, to take; to transfer. **-duttore** *m.* translator; *-duttore traditore*, translation is a tricky business. **-duzione** *f.* translation.
**traente** *m.*, *f.* (finan.) drawer (of a bill).
**trafel-are** [A1] *intr.* (*aux.* avere) to breathe heavily; to be out of breath; to pant. **-ato** *adj.* panting; breathless.
**traffic-are** [A2 s] *tr.*, *intr.* (*aux.* avere) to deal, to trade, to traffic; to do business (in); (fig.) to be busy. **-a·bile** *adj.* negotiable. **-ante** *part. adj.* dealing; *n.m.* dealer, trader.
**tra·ffico** *m.* trade; dealing, trading; traffic; commerce.
**trafi·ggere** [C12] *tr.* to transfix, to pierce through; to wound; (fig.) to grieve; to give pain to.
**trafil-a** *f.* draw-plate; wire-gauge; (fig.) series. **-are** [A1] *tr.* to draw (wire).
**trafiletto** *m.* (journ.) paragraph, short notice; lampoon.
**trafitt-a** *f.* stab wound; (fig.) pang; stabbing pain; cutting remark. **-o** *part.* of **trafi·ggere**; *adj.* transfixed; pierced through; wounded. **-ura** *f.* pang; stabbing pain.
**trafor-o** *m.* piercing; boring through; tunnel(ling); perforation; *arte del —*, *lavoro di —*, fretwork, (jewell.) filigree work, (needlew.) openwork. **-are** [A1 c] *tr.* to bore through; to pierce; to embroider with openwork.
**trafug-are** [A2] *tr.* to steal; to carry off secretly; to kidnap; *rfl.* to steal away, to slip away. **-atamente** *adv.* stealthily.
**trage·d-ia** *f.* tragedy; (fig.) disaster; (iron., etc.) *che —!*, what a pity! **-iante** *m.*, *f.* tragedian, playwright; tragic actor, actress.
**traghett-o** *m.* passage, crossing (esp. by ferry); cross-Channel steamer; ferryboat; car-ferry. **-are** [A1 c] *tr.* to ferry across.
**tra·gi-co** *adj.* tragic, tragical; *n.m.* tragedian. **-comme·dia** *f.* tragicomedy. **-co·mico** *adj.* tragicomic.
**tragitt-o** *m.* ferry; crossing. **-are** [A1] *tr.* to ferry across.
**traguard-are** [A1] *tr.* to sight (with a sight-vane); to glance at; to glimpse; (fig.) to foresee. **-o** *m.* sight-vane; winning-post.
**Traiano** *pr.n.m.* Trajan.
**tra·in-o** *m.* drawing, dragging, haulage; truck; sledge; waggon-load; luggage; baggage train; towing; tow. **-are** [A1 s] *tr.* to drag, to draw, to haul; to tow.
**tralasciare** [A3] *tr.* to leave out, to omit; to leave off; to give up; to neglect.
**tra·lcio** *m.* vine-shoot; vine-branch; shoot (of any climbing plant).
**trali·ccio** *m.* trellis; trellis-work; sacking; ticking; *— metallico*, wire netting.
**tralice** *adv. phr. in —*, obliquely.
**tralignare** [A5] *intr.* (*aux.* avere, essere) to degenerate.
**tralu·c-ere** [B1 def.] *intr.* (not used in compound tenses) to shine; to shine through. **-ente** *part. adj.* translucent; transparent.
**tram** *m. indecl.* tram; tramway (*cf.* **tranvai, tranvia**).
**trama** *f.* weft, woof; (fig.) design; scheme; plot; intrigue; *pl.* tissues.
**trama·glio** *m.* drag-net; trammel.
**tramandare** [A1] *tr.* to hand down; to hand on; to transmit.
**tramare** [A1] *tr.*, *intr.* (*aux.* avere) to plot, to scheme; to weave.
**trambusto** *m.* turmoil; confusion; bustle; *— di stomaco*, upset stomach.
**trameni·o** *m.* stir, bustle, fuss.
**tramescolare** [A1 s], **tramestare** [A1] *tr.* to turn topsy-turvy; to untidy; to jumble; *intr.* (*aux.* avere) to make a muddle.
**tramettere** [C20] *tr.* to insert; to interrupt; *rfl.* to intervene; to interfere, to meddle.
**tramezz-are** [A1] *tr.* to partition off; to separate; to intersperse; *rfl.* to intervene. **-atura** *f.* partitioning. **-ino** *m.* sandwich; sandwich-man.
**tramezzo** *m.* partition; (naut.) bulkhead; (eccl.) *— tra navata e coro*, rood screen; *prep.* between; among.
**tra·mite** *m.* path; way; course; means; medium.
**tramo·ggia** *f.* hopper; feed-box; seed-box.
**tramontan-a** *f.* north wind; north; (fig.) *perdere la —*, to lose one's way. **-o** *adj.* northerly; (hist.) ultramontane.
**tramont-o** *m.* setting; sunset; (fig.) end; decline. **-are** [A1 c] *intr.* (*aux.* essere) (of sun, moon) to set; to go down; (fig.) to decline, to fade; to pass away.
**tramort-ire** [D1] *intr.* (*aux.* essere) to faint, to swoon. **-ito** *part. adj.* in a swoon; unconscious; stunned.
**tra·mpol-i** *m.pl.* stilts. **-ino** *m.* spring-board; diving-board.
**tramutare** [A1] *tr.* to transmute; to transfer; to transplant; to rebottle (wine).
**tramva·i** *m. indecl.* see **tranvai.**
**tra·nci-a** *f.* slice; rasher; shears. **-are** [A3] *tr.* to shear. **-atrice** *f.* slicing-machine.
**tranello** *m.* trap; snare; plot; catch.
**trangugiare** [A3] *tr.* to gulp down, to bolt; to swallow.
**tranne** *prep.* except, save, but.
**tranquill-are** [A1] *tr.* to calm, to soothe; to quiet; to tranquillize; *rfl.* to calm oneself. **-ante** *part. adj.* soothing; *n.m.* tranquillizer, sedative.
**tranquill-o** *adj.* quiet, peaceful; calm; still; tranquil; serene; untroubled; *lascialo —*, leave him alone. **-ità** *f.* calm, peace, peacefulness.
**trans-** *pref.* beyond, across.
**trans-alpino** *adj.* transalpine. **-atla·ntico** *adj.* transatlantic; *n.m.* Atlantic liner.
**transatto** *part.* of **transi·gere**; *adj.* transacted, settled.
**transazione** *f.* compromise; settlement; transaction.
**transetto** *m.* (archit.) transept.
**transi·gere** [B1] *tr.* to compromise; to come to an agreement concerning; to compound; to settle amicably; *intr.* (*aux.* avere) to come to terms; to yield; to compromise.
**tra·nsit-o** *m.* transit; *vietato il —*, no thoroughfare. **-are** [A1 s] *intr.* (*aux.* essere) to pass (across, through, over). **-o·rio** *adj.* transitory, transient; temporary.
**transizione** *f.* transition; *di —*, temporary.

**transpadano** *adj.* relating to the left bank of the Po.
**transunto** *m.* summary; extract.
**transustazione** *f.* (rel.) transubstantiation.
**tran tran** *m. indecl.* routine, daily round.
**tran-va·i** *m.*, **-vi·a** *f.* tram, tramcar; tramway, tramline. **-via·rio** *adj.* relating to the tramway. **-viere** *m.* tram-driver; tram-conductor.
**tra·pan-o** *m.* drill; auger; drilling machine. **-are** [A1 s] *tr.* to drill; to trepan.
**trapass-are** [A1] *tr.* to pierce, to pass through, to transfix; to overstep; to pass over, to pass by; to neglect; *intr.* (*aux.* essere) to pass, to pass on; to pass away; to die. **-ante** *part. adj.* passing; transient; perishable; transparent. **-ato** *part. adj.* dead, deceased; passed; changed. **-o** *m.* passage, pass(ing); death, decease; (leg.) transfer.
**trapelare** [A1 c] *intr.* (*aux.* essere) to trickle forth; to ooze out, to leak out; *tr.* to hear of, to get to know.
**trapelo** *m.* spare horse; (theatr.) understudy; walking-on part, extra.
**trape·z-io** *m.* circus trapeze; (geom.) trapezium. **-ista** *m.*, *f.* trapeze-artist.
**trapiantare** [A1] *tr.* to transplant; *rfl.* to be transplanted.
**trappist-a** *adj.*, *n.m.* (*pl.* **-i**) (rel.) Trappist.
**trappoco** *adv.* in a short time, shortly.
**tra·ppol-a** *f.* trap, snare; pitfall. **-are** [A1 s] *tr.* to trap. **-atore** *m.* trickster. **-eri·a** *f.* trickery. **-one** *m.* swindler.
**trappolino** *m.* springboard.
**trapunt-a** *f.* quilt; quilted doublet. **-are** [A1] *tr.* to quilt. **-o** *n.m.* embroidery, quilting; quilt.
**trarre** [B33] *tr.* to draw, to pull, to drag; to attract; to derive, to obtain; to throw; to fling; — *un sospiro*, to heave a sigh; *intr.* (*aux.* essere) to betake oneself; — *da*, to take after, to resemble; *rfl.* to drag.
**trasalire** [D1] *intr.* (*aux.* avere, essere) to leap, to give a start; *far* —, to startle.
**trasand-are** [A7] *tr.* to neglect. **-ato** *part. adj.* neglected; uncared for; slovenly.
**trasbord-are** [A1 c) *tr.* to tranship; to transfer. **-o** *m.* transhipment.
**tra-scegliere** [B27] *tr.* to pick out; to choose carefully, to select. **-scelto** *part. adj.* picked out, selected; choice.
**trascend-ere** [C1] *tr.* to transcend; to surpass; to rise above; *intr.* (*aux.* essere) to go too far; to descend, to stoop. **-ente** *part. adj.* transcendent, surpassing; infinite. **-enza** *f.* transcendence.
**trascinare** [A1 s] *tr.* to drag; to pull; to trail; to carry; (fig.) to carry away, to fascinate.
**trascolor-are** [A1 c] *intr.* (*aux.* essere), *rfl.* to change colour; to grow pale; to blush. **-amento** *m.* discoloration; change of colour.
**trascorr-ere** [C5] *tr.* to spend, to pass (time); to run over, to run through; to skim (book, pages, etc.); to travel through; to roam (country); to pass over, to omit to mention; *intr.* (*aux.* essere) to pass (of time), to elapse; (*aux.* avere) to go too far, to run to excess. **-evole** *adj.* transient.
**trascorso** *part.* of **trascorrere**; *adj.* past; passed over; elapsed; *n.m.* fault, oversight, mistake.
**trascrit-to** *part.* of **trascri·vere**; *adj.* transcribed, copied. **-tore** *m.*, **-trice** *f.* transcriber; copyist.
**trascri·vere** [C12] to transcribe; to copy; to record; to register.
**trascrizione** *f.* transcript(ion), copy; registration.
**trascur-are** [A1] *tr.* to neglect; to disregard; to ignore; to be careless about. **-a·bile** *adj.* negligible. **-a·ggine** *f.* neglect; carelessness. **-anza** *f.* carelessness; thoughtlessness; neglect. **-ato** *part. adj.* neglected; careless, negligent, slovenly.
**trasecolare** [A1 s] *intr.* (*aux.* essere, avere) to be amazed, astonished; to be startled; to be shocked; to show surprise.
**trasentire** [D1] *tr.* to hear vaguely; to learn by hearsay; to get wind of; to mis-hear.
**trasfer-ire** [D2] *tr.* to move, to remove; to transfer; to shift; to translate (bishop). **-i·bile** *adj.* transferable; *non -ibile*, not negotiable. **-imento** *m.* removal; change; transfer. **-ta** *f.* transfer.
**trasfigur-are** [A1] *tr.* to transfigure; to transform; *rfl.* to be transformed. **-azione** *f.* transfiguration.
**trasfondere** [C2] *tr.* to transfuse; (fig.) to instil.
**trasform-are** [A1 c] *tr.* to change; to transform. **-ista** *m.* (*pl.* **-isti**) transformist; quick-change artist; trimmer, political weathercock.
**trasfusione** *f.* transfusion; decanting.
**trasgredire** [D2] *tr.* to transgress; to infringe, to violate; *intr.* (*aux.* avere; *prep.* a) to transgress.
**trasgressione** *f.* transgression; infringement; disobedience; trespass.
**traslat-o** *adj.* transferred; figurative, metaphorical; *n.m.* metaphor; trope. **-are** [A1] *tr.* to transfer; to remove.
**traslazione** *f.* removal; transfer; conveyance.
**trasloc-are** [A2] *tr.* to move, to transfer; *intr.* (*aux.* avere) to move, to remove, to change one's address. **-amento** *m.* removing.
**traslo-co** *m.* (*pl.* **-chi**) removal; *fare* —, to move house.
**trasmesso** *part.* of **trasmettere** *adj.* handed on; handed down; transmitted; conveyed; broadcast.
**trasmettere** [C20] *tr.* to pass on, to hand on; to transmit; to convey; to send; to broadcast; to transfer.
**trasmiss-i·bile** *adj.* transmissible, transferable; negotiable. **-ione** *f.* transmission; broadcasting; *cinghia -ione*, conveyor belt. **-ore** *m.* transmitter.
**trasmod-are** [A1] *intr.* (*aux.* avere) to go to excess; to overstep proper bounds; to exaggerate. **-ato** *adj.* immoderate; excessive.
**trasmutare** [A1] *tr.* to transmute; to transform; to change over, to transfer.
**trasogn-are** [A5 c] *intr.* (*aux.* avere) to daydream; to be lost in reverie. **-ato** *part. adj.* dreamy, daydreaming; half-asleep; lost in reverie; amazed.
**traspadano** *adj.* north of the Po.
**traspar-ire** [D3] *intr.* (essere) to shine through, to appear (through); to be transparent; to be obvious. **-ente** *part. adj.* apparent, clear; transparent, diaphanous; *n.m.* illuminated screen; transparency (picture). **-enza** *f.* transparence, transparency.
**traspir-are** [A1] *intr.* (*aux.* essere) to perspire; (bot.) to transpire; (fig.) (*aux.* essere) to leak out, to become known. **-azione** *f.* perspiration; (bot.) transpiration.
**trasporre** [B21] *tr.* to transpose; to transfer, to move; to transplant.
**trasport-are** [A1] *tr.* to transport; to convey; to carry; to transfer; *rfl.* to go, to betake oneself; to be transported; *lasciarsi — dall'ira*, to fly into a rage. **-o** *m.* transport; conveyance; carriage; transfer; (fig.) rapture; joy; *un -o d'ira*, a transport of rage; zeal.
**trasposto** *part.* of **trasporre.**
**Trastevere** *pr.n.m.* quarter o Rome across the river.
**trastull-are** [A1] *tr.* to amuse; to beguile; *rfl.* (*prep.* di) to amuse oneself; to trifle (with). **-o** *m.* play; toy; game; amusement; sport; fun.
**trasudare** [A1] *intr.* (*aux.* avere)

to sweat, to perspire; to transude; (*aux.* essere) to ooze out.

**trasumanare** [A1] *intr.* (*aux.* essere), *rfl.* to become more than human, to be transfigured.

**trasvers-o** *adj.*, *n.m.* transverse; oblique. **-ale** *adj.* transversal.

**trasvol-are** [A1] *tr.* to fly across. **-ata** *f.* flight; *-ata atlantica*, flight acrcss the Atlantic.

**tratta** *f.* pull, tug; drawing of lots, etc., draw; distance, stretch; (rlwy.) section; (comm.) draft; bill; period; train; throng; export permit; — *dei negri*, slave trade.

**tratt-are** [A1] *tr.* to treat; to handle; to employ; to work, to play; to deal with; to deal in; to discuss; to provide food; *intr.* (*aux.* avere; *prep.* di) to deal (with); to negotiate; to treat (of); *rfl.* to eat, to live; *impers.* to be a question of, to have to do with; *di che si -a?*, what is the question? **-a·bile** *adj.* tractable; manageable; easy to work. **-amento** *m.* treatment, usage; reception; entertainment; salary, emoluments; allowance of food, table; dinner; supper; treating. **-ative** *f.pl.* negotiations; arrangements. **-ato** *part. adj.* negotiated; dealt with; *n.m.* treatise; tract; treaty; agreement. **-azione** *f.* treatment, handling; negotiation; management.

**tratteggi-o** *m.* outlining; sketching; marks, short strokes. **-are** [A3 c] *tr.* to draw, to sketch, to delineate; (fig.) to describe.

**tratten-ere** [B32] *tr.* to keep; to hold; to hold back; to restrain; to keep waiting; to entertain; to amuse; *rfl.* to stay, to remain, to restrain oneself. **-imento** *m.* detaining; stay; sojourn; party entertainment. **-uta** *f.* (finan.) deduction; docking.

**trattino** *m.* hyphen; dash.

**tratto** *part.* of **trarre**; *adj.* led, pulled, drawn; *n.m.* stroke; line, dash; trait, feature; gesture; pull, tug; touch; distance, stretch; space; period of time; moment; reference; passage (in a book); — *d'unione*, hyphen; *adv. phrs. tratto tratto, di — in —*, now and then, from time to time; *tutto d'un —*, all at once.

**trattore**[1] *m.* tractor; — *a cingoli*, caterpillar tractor.

**tratt-ore**[2] *m.* innkeeper; restaurant-keeper. **-ori·a** *f.* inn; restaurant.

**trava·gli-o** *m.* toil, labour; trouble; pain; travail; distress. **-are** [A4] *tr.* to trouble, to torment, to harass; to disturb; to overwork (a horse, etc.); *intr.* (*aux.* avere) to toil; to labour; *rfl.* to be troubled, tormented, upset; to take trouble.

**travalicare** [A2 s] to traverse; to disregard.

**travas-o** *m.* pouring off, decanting; transferring; instilling. **-are** [A1] *tr.* to pour off; to decant; (cinem.) to dub.

**trav-e** *f.* beam; rafter; girder. **-ata** *f.* beams; framework.

**travedere** [B1] *tr.* to catch a glimpse of; to see dimly; *intr.* (*aux.* avere) to be mistaken (in seeing).

**traveggole** *f.pl.* illusion; distorted vision.

**travers-a** *f.* cross-bar; cross-piece; (rlwy.) sleeper; barrier; cross-street, side-turning; draw-sheet. **-are** [A1] *tr.* to cross; to place across; *-are la via* (*a uno*), to bar the way. **-ata** *f.* crossing, sea-crossing, passage. **-ina** *f. dim.* small cross-bar; (rlwy.) sleeper. **-o** *adj.* transverse, cross; oblique; (fig.) *per vie -e*, by underhand methods; adverse; *adv. phrs. di -o*, askew, awry; amiss; askance; *n.m.* breadth; (naut.) beam.

**travertino** *m.* (geol.) travertine.

**travest-ire** [D1] *tr.* (*prep.* da) to disguise; (fig.) to travesty, burlesque; to misrepresent; *rfl.* to disguise oneself (as); (of actors) to make up (as). **-imento** *m.* disguise; fancy dress. **-ito** *part. adj.* disguised; dressed up; burlesqued; made a mock of.

**travestismo** *m.* transvestism.

**travi-are** [A4] *tr.* to mislead, to lead astray; to pervert; *intr.* (*aux.* avere) to stray. **-amento** *m.* deviation; aberration; leading astray. **-ata** *f.* courtesan.

**travicello** *m.* joist, small beam; rafter; *Il Re Travicello*, King Log.

**travisare** [A1] *tr.* to distort, to misrepresent; to alter; to falsify; to disguise.

**travo·lg-ere** [C5] *tr.* to sweep away, to carry away; to overwhelm; to overcome; to upset; to throw into confusion. **-imento** *m.* overturning; overthrow; confusion.

**travolto** *part.* of **travo·lgere**; *adj.* overturned; overwhelmed; upside-down; knocked down.

**trazione** *f.* traction.

**tre** *card. num.* three; *n.m. il —*, the third (of the month); *regola del —*, rule of three; *le —*, three o'clock. **-a·lberi** *m. indecl.* (naut.) three-master.

**trebbi-a** *f.* threshing-flail; (poet.) threshing. **-are** [A4 c] *tr.* to thresh. **-atore** *m.* thresher. **-atrice** *f.* threshing-machine. **-atura** *f.* threshing.

**Trebbiano** *pr.n.m.* white wine of Romagna.

**treccia**[1] *f.* tress; plait, pigtail; — *di cipolle*, string of onions.

**treccia**[2] *f.* team of horses or oxen used to tread corn on the threshing-floor.

**trecent-o** *card. num.* three hundred; *n.m. il — a.C.*, the fourth century B.C.; *il — d.C.*, the fourth century A.D.; *il —*, the fourteenth century. **-e·simo** *ord. num., adj.* three-hundredth; *n.m.* three-hundredth (part). **-ista** *m.* fourteenth-century writer or artist; scholar specializing in fourteenth-century studies. **-ocinque** *m. indecl.* (mil.) 305-millimetre gun.

**tredic-i** *card. num.* thirteen; *n.f.pl. le —*, one o'clock (in the afternoon). **-enne** *adj.* thirteen years old; *n.m., f.* boy, girl, of thirteen. **-e·simo** *adj.* thirteenth; *n.m.* a thirteenth (part.) **-ina** *f.* a 'baker's dozen'

**trefolo** *m.* strand of rope; strand of steel cable.

**tregenda** *f.* horde (of witches, demons); coven; crowd, host.

**treggi·a** *f.* sledge; drag.

**tregua** *f.* truce; respite; rest.

**trem-are** [A1] *intr.* (*aux.* avere) to tremble; to shake; to quake; to shiver. **-acuore** *m.* palpitation; trepidation; anxiety, agitation. **-arella** *f.* nervous anxiety; trembling; (slang) blue funk.

**tremebondo** *adj.* trembling; full of trepidation.

**tremendo** *adj.* awful, fearful, terrible; dreadful.

**trementina** *f.* turpentine.

**tremila** *card. num.* three thousand.

**tremille·simo** *ord. num.* three-thousandth.

**tre·mito** *m.* trembling; shake; quiver.

**tremol-are** [A1 s] *intr.* (*aux.* avere) to tremble; to quiver; to quaver; *n.m.* trembling; shimmering, rippling. **-io** *m.* (*pl.* -ii) constant trembling, quivering; quaking.

**tre·mol-o** *adj.* quivering; trembling; tremulous; *n.m.* (mus.) tremolo. **-ino** *m.* aspen.

**tremore** *m.* trembling; shivering; tremor; vibration.

**tre·mula** *f.* (bot.) aspen tree.

**trem(u)oto** *m.* (pop. for **terremoto**) earthquake; (fig.) whirlwind; commotion.

**treno**[1] *f.* (rlwy.) train; — *accelerato*, stopping train; — *merci*, goods train; retinue, train; manner, way (of life); pace rate; routine.

**tren-o**[2] *m.*, **-odi·a** *f.* lamentation; threnody.

**trent-a** *card. num., adj. indecl., n.m.* thirty. **-enne** *adj.* thirty years old. **-e·nnio** *m.* period of thirty years. **-e·simo** *ord. num.* thirtieth. **-ina** *f.* period of about thirty years; *ha passato la -ina*, he is in his thirties.

**Trento** *pr.n.f.* (geog.) Trento; (hist.) *il Concilio di —*, the Council of Trent.

**trentun-o** *card. num.* thirty-one. **-e·ṣimo** *ord. num.* thirty-first.
**tre·pid-o** *adj.* trembling; anxious; timorous; fluttering. **-anza** *f.* trepidation; flurry, flutter; anxiety. **-are** [A1 s] *intr.* (*aux.* avere) to be anxious; to tremble; *tr.* to fear.
**trep-piede, -piedi, -piè** *m. indecl.* tripod; trivet; three-legged stool.
**trequarti** *m. sing. indecl.* (rugby) three-quarters, back.
**trẹsc-a** *f.* intrigue; liaison; country dance. **-are** [A2 c] *intr.* (*aux.* avere; *prep.* con) to have dealings (with); to dance, to prance.
**trẹspolo** *m.* trestle; support; modelling table.
**trevigiano** *adj.* of Treviso; *n.m.* native of Treviso.
**Tre·viri** *pr.n.f.* (geog.) Treves.
**tri-** *pref.* triple, threefold.
**tr·iade** *f.* triad; three inseparable companions.
**tria·ngol-o** *m.* triangle; *cappello a —*, tricorn, cocked-hat. **-ato** *adj.* triangular, three-cornered.
**tri·bol-o** *m.* trouble, trial, suffering, tribulation. **-are** [A1 s] *tr.* to trouble; to torment; to afflict; to vex, to worry; *intr.* (*aux.* avere) to toil, to labour; to suffer. **-aziọne** *f.* tribulation, trouble; suffering; torment.
**tribù** *f. indecl.* tribe.
**tribuna** *f.* apse; dome; vault; tribune; rostrum, platform; — *centrale*, grandstand.
**tribunale** *m.* tribunal; court; *chiamare in —*, to summon; — *di penitenza*, confessional.
**tribuno** *m.* tribune; demagogue.
**tribut-o** *m.* tribute; tax; (fig.) debt. **-are** [A1] *tr.* to render (homage), to pay (tribute), to give, to offer, to bestow. **-a·rio** *adj.* tributary; *fiume -ario*, tributary (river); relating to taxation.
**triciclo** *m.* tricycle.
**trici·pite** *adj.* three-headed.
**tri-colọre** *adj.*. of three colours; *n.m.* tricolour. **-corde** *adj.* three-stringed. **-corno** *m.* three-cornered hat, tricorn. **-croma** *f.* (mus.) demisemiquaver. **-cromi·a** *f.* three-colour printing.
**tric trac** *onom.* tap, tap; tapping; clatter; backgammon.
**tricu·spide** *adj.* tricuspid, three-pointed.
**tridente** *m.* trident; hayfork.
**tridentino** *adj.* (geog.) of Trent; (hist.) *il Concilio —*, The Council of Trent.
**trienn-e** *adj.* three years old; of three years' duration. **-ale** *adj.* triennial; of three years.
**trie·nnio** *m.* period of three years.
**trifo·glio** *m.* trefoil; clover; shamrock.
**tri·fora** *n.f.* (archit.) window with three lights.
**trifo·rio** *m.* (archit.) triforium.
**tri·gamo** *adj.* trigamous, thrice-married; *n.m.* trigamist.
**trige·mino** *adj.* triple; *parto —*, birth of triplets; *n.m.* triplet.
**trige·ṣimo** *ord. num.*, *adj.* thirtieth.
**tri·glia** *f.* red mullet.
**triglifo** *m.* (archit.) triglyph.
**tri·gone** *m.* (ichth.) sting ray.
**tri·gon-o** *adj.* trigonal. **-ometri·a** *f.* (math.) trigonometry.
**trilingue** *adj.* trilingual.
**triliọne** *m.* trillion, a million millions.
**trill-o** *m.* trill; ringing. **-are** [A1] *intr.* (*aux.* avere) to trill; to vibrate, to shake.
**tri·lobo** *m.* (archit.) trefoil; *adj.* (biol.) three-lobed.
**trilogi·a** *f.* trilogy.
**trilustre** *adj.* fifteen years old.
**trimestre** *m.* quarter, three months; (school) term; quarter's rent; quarter's salary.
**trimpellare** [A1] *intr.* (*aux.* avere) to stagger; to strum hesitatingly (on guitar, etc.); to dally.
**trina** *f.* lace.
**trincare**[1] [A2] *tr.* to lash, to secure, to haul taut.
**trinc-are**[2] [A2] *tr.* to drink greedily; to toss off; to swill. **-ata** *f.* swill; draught. **-ato** *part. adj.* drunk; (fig.) deep, crafty.
**trince·a** *f.* trench.
**trincer-are** [A1] *tr.* to entrench; *rfl.* to entrench oneself. **-amẹnto** *m.* entrenching; entrenchment.
**trinci-are** [A3] *tr.* to cut up, to carve; to mince, to hash; to slash; to cut; — *l'aria*, to saw the air. **-ante** *part. adj.* cutting, sharp; *n.m.* carving-knife; carver. **-apa·glia** *m. indecl.* reaping-hook; hay-cutter. **-ata** *f.* cut; slice. **-ato** *part. adj.* carved; cut; *n.m.* cut tobacco.
**tri·ncio** *m.* cut; tear; slash.
**trinità**[1] *f.* Trinity; (Florence) *il Ponte della Trinità*, (pronoun. **tri·nita**) Trinity Bridge.
**Trinità**[2] *pr.n.f.* (geog.) Trinidad.
**triọnf-o** *m.* triumph; victory; glory; (cards) trump. **-ale** *adj.* triumphal. **-almẹnte** *adv.* triumphally; in triumph. **-are** [A1 c] *intr.* (*aux.* avere) to triumph; to be victorious; to be triumphant; to be blessed (in heaven); to exult; to enjoy oneself (*e.g.* at table); to be striking; (of countryside) to be fertile and prosperous; (of food-stuffs) to soar in price; *tr.* to overcome; to dominate.
**Triọni** *pr.n.m.pl.* (astron.) Great and Little Bear.
**tripart-ire** [D1] *tr.* to divide into three. **-ito** *part. adj.* tripartite.
**tri·plic-e** *adj.* threefold, treble, triple; triplicate. **-are** [A2 s] *tr.* to treble; to triplicate.
**triplo** *adj.* triple; *n.m.* three times as much.
**tri·pode** *m.* tripod.
**Tri·poli**[1] *pr.n.f.* (geog.) Tripoli.
**tri·poli**[2] *m. indecl.* (miner.) infusional earth, kieselguhr.
**tripp-a** *f.* tripe; paunch, fat belly. **-eri·a** *f.* tripe-shop. **-ọne** *f.*, *-ọne m.* pot-bellied person.
**tripu·di-o** *m.* exaltation; jumping for joy; jubilation. **-are** [A4] *intr.* (*aux.* avere) to exult; to rejoice.
**trirẹgno** *m.* papal tiara.
**trireme** *f.* trireme.
**tris** *m. indecl.* (cards) three of a kind (at poker).
**triṣ-arca·volo** *m.* great-great-great-grandfather; remote ancestor. **-a·volo** *m.* great-great-grandfather; ancestor. **-illa·bico** *adj.* trisyllabic. **-i·llabo** *m.* trisyllable.
**tristamẹnte** *adv.* evilly.
**Tristano** *pr.n.m.* Tristram, Tristan.
**trist-e** *adj.* sad, sorrowful, woeful; dreary, dismal. **-ẹzza** *f.* sadness, sorrow; gloominess.
**trist-o** *adj.* bad; wicked, sorry, wretched; mean; *n.m.* wicked fellow; rogue, wickedness; roguery. **-i·zia** *f.* wickedness; evil deed.
**trit-are** [A1] *tr.* to mince, to hash. to pound. **-acarne** *m. indecl.* mincer. **-amẹnte** *adv.* finely; minutely. **-o** *adj.* minced, hashed; pounded; beaten; (fig.) trite, commonplace; mincing, finikin.
**Tritọne** *pr.n.m.* Triton.
**tri·ttico** *m.* (paint.) triptych.
**tritumi** *m.pl.* bits, scraps; crumbs.
**trivell-a** *f.* auger; borer; drill. **-are** [A1] *tr.* to bore; *intr.* (*aux.* avere) (of water) to swirl, to eddy. **-o** *m.* brace and bit; gimlet.
**tri·vi-o** *m.* place where three roads meet; low quarter. **-ale** *adj.* low, vulgar, coarse; commonplace. **-alità** *f.* vulgarity, coarseness; coarse expression.
**trofe·o** *m.* trophy.
**troglodit-a** *m.* (*pl.* **-i**) troglodyte, cave-dweller; (fig.) uncouth, primitive persons.
**tro·golo** *m.* trough, water-trough, feeding-trough.
**tro·ia**[1] *f.* sow; whore, prostitute.
**Tro·i-a**[2] *pr.n.f.* Troy. **-ano** *adj. n.m.* Trojan.
**Tro·ilo** *pr.n.m.* Troilus.
**trọmb-a** *f.* (mus.) trumpet; trump; bugle; horn; tube-water-spout; tornado, cloudburst; — *d'incendio*, firepump; well (of staircase); siphon (for drawing off wine). **-are** [A1 c] *tr.* to draw off (wine, with a siphon). **-ẹtta** *f.* (mus.) small trumpet; bugle; toy trumpet; *m. indecl.* bugler, trumpeter. **-ettare** [A1 c] *tr.* to trumpet. **-ettiere** *m.* trumpeter. **-ọne** *m.* (mus.) trombone; blunderbuss; *pl.* large riding-boots.
**trombọṣi** *f.* (med.) thrombosis.

**troncare** [A2 c] *tr.* to cut off; to truncate; to break in two; to interrupt; to clip (end of word).
**tronco** *adj.* (*m.pl.* **-chi**) maimed; mutilated; truncated; *n.m.* trunk; (fig.) unfinished condition. **-cone** *m. augm.* stump; trunk (of the body).
**troneggiare** [A3 c] *intr.* (*aux.* avere) to sit (as) on a throne; to reign supreme.
**tronfiare** [A4 c] *intr.* (*aux.* avere) (of peacock) to spread its feathers; to strut; (of pigeons) to pout; to puff.
**tronfio** *adj.* puffed out; pompous.
**trono** *m.* throne; *salire al* —, to ascend to the throne.
**tro·pic-o** *m.* (geog.) tropic; — *del Cancro*, tropic of Cancer; — *del Capricorno*, tropic of Capricorn. **-ale** *adj.* tropical.
**tropo** *m.* trope.
**troppo** *adv.* too; too much; much too much; *pur* —, unfortunately; *adj.*, *prn.* too much; *pl.* too many.
**trota** *f.* trout.
**trott-are** [A1] *intr.* (*aux.* avere) to trot; (fig.) to trot along, to walk fast. **-ata** *f.* trot; run.
**trotterell-are** [A1] *intr.* (*aux.* avere) to trot along; to toddle. **-o** *m.* jog-trot.
**trotto** *m.* trot.
**tro·ttol-a** *f.* top, spinning top. **-are** [A1 s] *intr.* (*aux.* avere) to spin, to whirl round; to toddle about. **-ino** *m.* toddler.
**trov-are** [A1] *tr.* to find; to discover; to catch; to think, to consider; to encounter, to meet; *rfl.* to be found; to be; to happen to be; to be situated. **-a·bile** *adj.* discoverable. **-adore** *m.* troubadour. **-arobe** *m. indecl.* (theatr.) property man. **-ata** *f.* discovery; invention, contrivance; trick, expedient. **-atello** *m.* foundling. **-ato** *part. adj.* found, discovered; (provb.) *se non è vero è ben -ato*, it's a good story; *n.m.* invention; discovery; fiction; trick. **-atore** *m.* finder; inventor; troubadour.
**trucc-are** [A2] *tr.* to cheat; to make up; *rfl.* to make up one's face. **-atura** *f.* (theatr.) make-up; making up.
**truc-co** *m.* (*pl.* **-chi**) trick; make-up.
**truc-e** *adj.* fierce; threatening; grim; cruel; savage. **-emente** *adv.* fiercely; cruelly.
**trucidare** [A1 s] *tr.* to slay, to slaughter.
**tru·cio** *adj.* ragged; shabby; poverty-stricken.
**tru·ciolo** *m.* (wood-) shaving; curl; chip.
**truculento** *adj.* threatening, grim, truculent; (of sea) stormy.
**truff-a** *f.* swindle, swindling; fraud. **-are** [A1] *tr.* to get by swindling; to cheat. **-atore** *m.*, **-atrice** *f.* swindler; cheat; *-atore di carte*, card-sharper. **-eri·a** *f.* cheating; swindling.
**trull-o** *adj.* silly; *n.m.* simpleton, nincompoop. **-a·ggine** *f.* silliness.
**truppa** *f.* troop; band; gang; troupe; flock; (mil.) *uomini di* —, other ranks.
**tu** *prn. 2nd pers. sing.* thou; you; *dare del* —, to use the familiar form of address.
**tuba** *f.* (mus.) tuba, bass tuba; top hat, silk hat.
**tubare** [A1] *intr.* (*aux.* avere) (of pigeons, doves) to coo; (of owls) to hoot; (fig.) to bill and coo.
**tub-atura, -azione** *f.* piping; system of tubes, pipes.
**tube·rcol-o** *m.* tubercle. **-are** *adj.* tubercular. **-osi** *f.* tuberculosis. **-oso** *adj.* tuberculosis; *n.m.* tubercular patient.
**tu·ber-o** *m.*, *f.* bulb, corm; tuber. **-osa** *f.* tuberose.
**tub-o** *m.* pipe; tube; — *di scarico*, exhaust pipe. **-olare** *adj.* tubular.
**Tuci·dide** *pr.n.m.* Thucydides.
**tufato** *adj.* stuffy.
**tuff** *onom.* puff; bump; splash.
**tuff-are** [A1] *tr.* to plunge; to dip; to dive; *rfl.* to plunge; to dive; to sink. **-o** *m.* dip, plunge; dive; plump; sudden, heavy shower; throb.
**tufo** *m.* (geol.) tufa, tuffa.
**tugu·rio** *m.* hovel; hut; dog-kennel.
**tulipano** *m.* tulip; young fop; bell-mouth.
**tulle** *m.* tulle.
**tume-fare** [B14] *rfl.* to tumefy; to swell. **-fatto** *part. adj.* swollen.
**tu·mid-o** *adj.* swollen, tumid, inflated; turgid. **-ezza** *f.* tumidity.
**tu·mul-o** *m.* tumulus; grave; barrow; cairn; catafalque; sand-hill. **-are** [A1 s] *tr.* to bury, to inter; *adj.* tumular.
**tumult-o** *m.* tumult, uproar; riot. **-uante** *part. adj.* riotous. **-uare** [A6] *intr.* (*aux.* avere) to riot; to be in uproar. **-ua·rio** *adj.* tumultuary. **-uoso** *adj.* tumultuous.
**tungsteno** *m.* (chem.) tungsten.
**tu·nica** *f.* long tunic; (fig.) binding of a book.
**Tunis-i** *pr.n.f.* (geog.) Tunis. **-i·a** *pr.n.f.* (geog.) Tunisia. **-ino** *adj.*, *n.m.* Tunisian.
**tu-o** *poss. adj. m. sing.* thy; your; *poss. prn.* thine; yours; *n.m. il* —, your property; *pl. i tuoi*, your people.
**tuonare** [A1] see **tonare**.
**tuono** *m.* thunder; roar.
**tuorlo** *m.* see **torlo**.
**tu·ppete** *onom.* bump; bang.
**tur-a** *f.* bung; shopper. **-are** [A1] *tr.* to stop, to stop up; to plug; to cork; *rfl.* (*acc. of prn.* 'si') *-arsi in casa*, to stay at home. **-abuchi** *m. indecl.* stop-gap. **-a·cciolo** *m.* cork; stopper.
**turba** *f.* crowd; mob, rabble.
**turbante** *m.* turban.
**turb-are** [A1] *tr.* to trouble; to disturb; to upset; to agitate. **-a·bile** *adj.* easily disturbed. **-amento** *m.* disturbance; uneasiness; excitement. **-ato** *part. adj.* troubled; uneasy; disturbed; overcast, gloomy. **-atore** *m.*, **-atrice** *f.* disturber.
**turbina** *f.* turbine.
**tu·rbin-e** *m.* whirlwind; gale; hurricane. **-are** [A1 s] *intr.* (*aux.* avere) to whirl; to eddy. **-ìo** *m.* (*pl.* **-ìi**) continual whirling, eddying. **-oso** *adj.* stormy; eddying; whirling.
**turbolen-to** *adj.* turbulent, unruly; restless; stormy. **-za** *f.* turbulence, disorder; rioting.
**turcasso** *m.* quiver (for arrows).
**turch-ese** *f.* (miner.) turquoise. **-inetto** *adj. dim.* bluish; *n.m.* (laundress's) blue; indigo; prussian blue. **-ino** *adj.*, *n.m.* dark blue.
**Turchi·a** *pr.n.f.* (geog.) Turkey.
**turcimanno** *m.* (derog.) interpreter; go-between.
**turc-o** *adj.* (*m.pl.* **turchi**) Turkish; wicked, cruel; *grano* —, maize; *n.m.* Turk. **-omanno** *m.* Turkoman.
**Turena** *pr.n.f.* (geog.) Touraine.
**tu·rgid-o** *adj.* swollen; (fig.) turgid; pompous; bombastic. **-ezza** *f.* turgidity; pompousness; bombast.
**turi·bolo** *m.* censer, thurible.
**tur-ismo** *m.* tourism, touring. **-ista** *m.*, *f.* tourist. **-i·stico** *adj.* relating to tourism; touring; tourist.
**turlupinare** [A1] *tr.* to fool, to swindle, to cheat.
**turno** *m.* turn; rotation; shift.
**turo** *m.* stopper; cover.
**turp-e** *adj.* abject, base; mean; filthy; indecent. **-ilo·quio** *m.* coarse language; filthy conversation. **-itu·dine** *f.* turpitude; baseness.
**turrito** *adj.* turreted; many-towered.
**tuta** *f.* overalls; boiler-suit.
**tutel-a** *f.* tutelage; guardianship; wardship; protection. **-are** [A1] *tr.* to protect; to defend; *adj.* tutelar(y).
**tut-ore** *m.*, **-rice** *f.* (leg.) guardian. **-o·rio** *adj.* tutelar; tutorial.
**tuttavi·a** *adj.* nevertheless; still, yet; all the same.
**tutt-o** *prn. sing.* all, the whole; everything; anything; — *quanto*, the whole lot; *pl.* all, everybody; *adj.* all, the whole (of); every; any; full; only; *adv.* all, entirely, wholly; very; fully; quite. **-oché** *conj.* though, although. **-odì** *adv.* continually; always. **-ora** *adv.* yet, still; continually.
**tzigan-o** *adj.*, *n.m.* gipsy, esp. of Hungary. **-a** *f.* gipsy.

**U** *f.*, *m.* (pronoun. **oo**) the letter U; the vowel U.
**uà** (*onom.*) wa! wa! (sound of a baby crying).
**uadì** *m. indecl.* (geog.) wadi, North African watercourse.
**ubbi·a** *f.* superstition; delusion; fad, timidity.
**ubbidien-te** *adj.* obedient; docile. **-za** *f.* obedience; submission.
**ubbidire** [D2] *intr.* (*aux.* avere; *prep.* a) to obey; to show respect; to respond; *tr.* to obey; to carry out, to fulfil.
**ubbioso** *adj.* superstitious; full of fads.
**ube·rrimo** *adj. superl.* abundant, copious.
**ubert-à** *f.* fertility; abundance; prosperity. **-oso** *adj.* fertile; fruitful; abundant.
**Uberto** *pr.n.m.* Hubert.
**ubic-are** [A2 s] *tr.* to place, to position; to site. **-ato** *part. adj.* located, situated. **-azione** *f.* whereabouts; situation.
**ubiquità** *f.* ubiquity.
**ubria-co** *adj.* (*m.pl.* **-chi**) drunk, intoxicated; tipsy; — *fradicio*, — *marcio*, dead drunk; *n.m.* drunken man, drunk; drunkard. **-care** [A2] *rfl.* to get drunk; to become intoxicated. **-catura** *f.* intoxication. **-chezza** *f.* drunkenness. **-cona** *f.*, **-cone** *m.* drunkard.
**uccell-o** *m.* bird; fowl; *veduta a volo d'*— bird's eye view; (fig.) fool, simpleton. **-agione** *f.* feathered game. **-are** [A1] *intr.* (*aux* avere) to catch birds; (fig.) to make fun of. **-atore** *m.* bird catcher; (fig.) deceiver. **-atura** *f.* fowling; (fig.) trickery. **-iera** *f.* aviary.
**ucci·d-ere** [C3] *tr.* to kill; to slay; to slaughter; to murder. **-ente** *part. adj.* killing; *n.m.* killer.
**u·ccio** *adj.* (pop.) bad, poor, rotten.
**uccis-ione** *f.* killing; slaying; murder. **-o** *part.* of **ucci·dere**; *adj.* killed, dead; slain; *n.m.* dead man; victim. **-ore** *m.* killer; slayer.
**Ucrai·na** *pr.n.f.* (geog.) Ukraine.
**ud-ire** [D15] *tr.* to hear; to listen to; to pay heed to; to understand; *n.m.* hearing. **-i·bile** *adj.* audible. **-ienza** *f.* audience; interview. **-ita** *f.* hearing; *per -ita*, on hearsay. **-ito** *part. adj.* heard; *n.m.* hearing, sense of hearing. **-itore** *m.*, **-itrice** *f.* hearer; listener; auditor. **-ito·rio** *m.* audience, listeners; *adj.* auditory.
**uff** *excl.* what a bore!; what a nuisance!
**uffi·ci-o** *m.* office; place of business; study, work-room; department; post, position, office; *d'* —, official(ly). **-ale** *adj.* official; formal; authorized; *n.m.* official; officer; representative; functionary. **-are** [A3] *intr.* (*aux.* avere) to officiate. **-oso** *adj.* courteous; obliging; officious; semi-official.
**uffi·zio** *m.* and derivs. see **ufficio.**
**ufo** *adv. phr. a* —, free, gratis.
**u·ggi-a** *f.* gloom; deep shade; shadow; (fig.) ennui, boredom; dislike. **-oso** *adj.* tiresome; boring; troublesome; gloomy.
**uggiol-are** [A1 s] *intr.* (*aux.* avere) to howl; to whine. **-io** *m.* (*pl.* **-ii**) constant whining.
**ugna** *f.* see **u·nghia.**
**u·gola** *f.* uvula.
**Ugonotto** *pr.n.m.* (hist.) Huguenot.
**uguagli-are** [A4] *tr.* to equalize; to make even; to even up; to balance; to compare; *rfl.* (*prep.* a) to be equal (to). **-amento** *m.* equalizing. **-anza** *f.* equality; similarity.
**ugual-e** *adj.* equal; identical; same; similar; even, regular; smooth; even-tempered; *n.m.* equal. **-mente** *adv.* equally; likewise; all the same.
**uh, uhi** *excl.* alas!; alack!; woe is me!; ah!; oh!
**Ulano** *m.* (mil. hist.) Uhlan.
**u·lcer-a** *f.* ulcer. **-amento** *m.*, **-azione** *f.* ulceration. **-are** [A1 s] *tr.* to ulcerate; *rfl.* to become ulcerated. **-oso** *adj.* ulcerated; ulcerous.
**uli·gin-e** *f.* moisture, dampness. **-oso** *adj.* moist, damp.
**Ulisse** *pr.n.m.* Ulysses.
**uliva** *f.* see **oliva.**
**Ulma** *pr.n.f.* (geog.) Ulm.
**ulterior-e** *adj.* further; subsequent. **-mente** *adv.* further on; later on.
**u·ltim-o** *adj.* last; final; newest, latest; utmost; ultimate; *l'— piano*, the top floor; *adv. phr. all'*— in the end; *in* — at the end, in the end, eventually. **-amente** *adv.* lately, in recent times; at last. **-are** [A1 s] *tr.* to terminate, to complete, to finish. **-a·tum** *m. indecl.* ultimatum. **-azione** *f.* completion; termination. **-oge·nito** *m.* last-born child.
**ultra-** *pref.* ultra; super. **-corto** *adj.* (radio) *onda -corta* ultra-short wave, V.H.F. wave. **-potente** *adj.* supercharged. **-rosso** *adj.* infra-red. **-violetto** *adj.* ultra-violet.
**u·lula** *f.* hawk owl.
**u·lul-o** *m.* howl, howling. **-are** [A1 s] *intr.* (*aux.* avere) to howl; to hoot. **-ato** *m.* howling.
**uman-o** *adj.* human; natural; humane; mundane; courteous; genial; *n.m.* human being; humaneness. **-amente** *adv.* humanly; humanely; courteously. **-are** [A1] *tr.* to make human; to humanize. **-esimo** *m.* humanism. **-ista** *m.*, *f.* humanist; classicist; arts student. **-ità** *f.* humanity; mankind; human nature; humaneness; humane studies; culture. **-ita·rio** *adj.*, *n.m.* humanitarian. **-izzare** [A1] *tr.* to humanize; to civilize.
**umbilico** *m.* see **ombelico.**
**umbra·tile** *adj.* (poet.) shady; dark, illusory.
**U·mbr-ia** *pr.n.f.* (geog.) Umbria. **-o** *adj.*, *n.m.* Umbrian.
**umettare** [A1 c] *tr.* to moisten, to damp.
**u·mid-o** *adj.* damp; wet; moist; watery; *n.m.* damp, humidity; (cul.) stew, stewed meat. **-ezza** *f.* dampness. **-ità** *f.* humidity; moisture.
**u·mil-e** *adj.* humble; lowly; meek; modest; simple. **-mente** *adv.* humbly; meekly.
**umili-are** [A4] *tr.* to humiliate; to humble; *rfl.* to humble oneself; to ask pardon. **-ante** *part. adj.* humiliating; mortifying. **-azione** *f.* humiliation; mortification.
**umiltà** *f.* humility; simplicity; modesty; submission.
**umor-e** *m.* moisture; liquid; sap; secretion; humour; temperament; mode, fashion; vivacity, wit. **-ismo** *m.* humour; sense of humour. **-ista** *m.*, *f.* humorist. **-i·stico** *adj.* humorous; funny, comic; facetious.
**un, una** *indef. art. m.*, *f.* see under **uno.**
**una·nim-e** *adj.* unanimous. **-ità** *f.* unanimity; consensus; *all'-ità*, unanimously.
**uncin-o** *m.* hook; (fig.) pretext, excuse. **-are** [A1] *tr.* to hook; to grapple; (fig.) to steal; *recip. rfl.* to grapple with each other. **-ato** *part. adj.* hooked; *croce -ata*, swastika. **-etto** *m. dim.* crochet needle; *lavoro all'-etto*, crochet work. **-ino** *m.* hook.
**u·ndic-i** *card. num. indecl.* eleven. **-e·nne** *adj.* eleven years old; *n.m.*, *f.* eleven-year-old. **-e·simo** *ord. num.* eleventh (also **unde·cimo**).
**u·ngere** [C5] *tr.* to grease; to smear; to oil; to anoint; (fig.) to flatter.
**Ungher-i·a** *pr.n.f.* (geog.) Hungary. **-ese** *adj.*, *n.m.*, *f.* Hungarian.
**u·nghi-a** *f.* nail; *le -e delle mani*, finger-nails; *le -e dei piedi*, toe nails; claw; (fig.) strip, slither. **-ata** *f.* scratch; graze; claw-mark. **-ato** *adj.* furnished with claws; clawed.
**unguento** *m.* unguent, ointment; (fig.) balm; remedy.
**ungulato** *adj.* hoofed; *n.m.* ungulate.
**unicameralismo** *m.* (pol.) single chamber system.

**u·nic-o** *adj.* only; sole; single; one, unique. **-amente** *adv.* solely; uniquely; only. **-ità** *f.* uniqueness.
**unicolore** *adj.* of one colour.
**unicorno** *m.* unicorn.
**unific-are** [A2 s] *tr.* to unify; to unite; to consolidate; to standardize. **-azione** *f.* unification.
**uniform-e** *adj.* uniform; even; regular; monotonous, same; *n.f.* uniform; regimentals. **-are** [A1 c] *tr.* to render uniform; to level; to bring into line; *rfl.* to adapt oneself. **-azione** *f.* standardization; equalizing. **-emente** *adv.* uniformly; evenly.
**unige·nito** *adj.* (theol.) only-begotten; *m.* only son.
**unilaterale** *adj.* one-sided; unilateral.
**uninominale** *adj.* (pol.) single-member; *collegio —*, single-member constituency.
**union-e** *f.* union; unity; society; league, association; group; agreement; *Unione Sud-africana*, Union of South Africa; *Unione delle Repubbliche Socialiste Sovietiche*, U.S.S.R.
**un-ire** [D2] *tr.* to unite; to join together; *— a*, to add to; to enclose (in a letter); to harmonize. **-itamente** *adv.* unitedly; conjointly; *-itamente a*, in company with. **-ito** *part. adj.* united; uniform; joined; in harmony.
**uni·sono** *adj.* in unison; *n.m.* unison.
**unit-à** *f. indecl.* unity; unit; union; oneness; concord. **-a·rio** *adj.* unitarian; (rel.) Unitarian.
**universal-e** *adj.* universal; common; widespread; all-round; *erede —*, sole heir; *giudizio —*, last judgement; *n.m.* totality. **-ità** *f.* universality; entirety. **-izzare** [A1] *tr.* to make universal, or general; *rfl.* to become universal, or general; to spread.
**universit-à** *f. indecl.* university. **-a·rio** *adj.* of a university; *n.m.* university teacher, academic.
**universo** *m.* universe; whole world; all mankind; creation, cosmos; *adj.* universal; whole.
**Unni** *pr.n.m.pl.* (hist.) Huns.
**uni·voco** *adj.* not equivocal, unambiguous.
**un-o** **1.** *indef. art. m.*; **-a** *f.* (contracted to **un** before a masculine noun beginning with a vowel or before a consonant other than **z** or **s** impure) a, an; one; *un cento*, about a hundred. **2.** *card. num.* one; one single; the number one; the figure one; unity; totality. **3.** *indef. prn.* one; someone; *l'un l'altro*, each other. **4.** *adj.* united, one.
**unt-o** *part.* of **u·ngere**; *adj.* greasy; oily; dirty; anointed; *n.m.* grease; lard; (fig.) flattery. **-ume** *m.* dripping; lard; grease; fat; dirt, filth. **-uoso** *adj.* greasy; oily; (fig.) unctuous; sanctimonious.
**unzione** *f.* greasing; anointing, unction.
**uo·m-o** *m.* (*pl.* **uo·mini**) man; grown man, adult; human being; *un — da nulla*, a nonentity; *— qualunque, — inedio*, ordinary man, man in the street.
**uopo** *m.* need; necessity; benefit, advantage; *essere d'—*, to be necessary.
**uosa** *f.* legging; *pl.* hose, leggings; tights; thigh boots.
**uov-o** *m.* (*pl.f.* **-a**) egg.
**u·pupa** *f.* (orn.) hoopoe.
**uragano** *m.* hurricane; (fig.) storm.
**Urali** *pr.n.m.pl.* (geog.) Urals.
**uran-go** *m.* (*pl.* **-ghi**) (zool.) orang-utan.
**ura·nio** *m.* (miner.) uranium.
**urban-o** *adj.* urban, city; urbane, polite; civilized. **-esimo** *m.* growth of towns; movement of population into cities. **-i·stica** *f.* town planning. **-ità** *f.* urbanity; civility, courtesy.
**Urbe** *f.* the City (Rome), the Eternal City.
**uremi·a** *f.* (med.) urœmia.
**uretere** *m.* (anat.) ureter.
**u·retra** *f.* (anat.) urethra.
**urgen-te** *adj.* urgent; pressing; immediate; *n.m.* express telegram. **-za** *f.* urgency; emergency; *d'-za*, urgent, urgently; in an emergency.
**u·rgere** [def.] *tr.* to urge; to press; *intr.* (no compound tenses) to be urgent; to be pressing; *urgono aiuti*, help is needed urgently.
**uri** *f. indecl.* houri, huri.
**u·rico** *adj.* uric.
**urina·rio** *adj.* urinary.
**url-o** *m.* (*pl.* **-i** *m.*) howl; howling; (*pl.* **-a** *f.*) shout (of a human), shriek. **-are** [A1] *intr.* (*aux.* avere) to howl; to shriek; to bawl; to shout. **-ata** *f.* howl; yell; hoot(s) of derision.
**urna** *f.* urn; ballot-box; (poet.) tomb.
**urrà, urrah** *exl.* hurrah!; hooray!; *n.m. indecl. un triplice —*, three cheers.
**urt-are** [A1] *tr.* to jolt; to shove; to collide with; to stumble against; to jar upon; *intr.* (*aux.* avere; *prep.* in) to run up against; *recip. rfl.* to jostle one another; to collide; to quarrel. **-ante** *part. adj.* jostling; (fig.) brusque; irritating. **-ata** *f.* shove; push. **-o** *m.* push; shove; knock; clash; collision; (rlwy.) crash; (fig.) *-o di nervi*, irritation; *-o d'idee*, clash of ideas. **-one** *m. augm.* violent shove.
**us-are** [A1] *tr.* to use; to make use of; to employ; to wear out; to use up; *intr.* (*aux.* avere) to be accustomed to; to keep company (with); (*prep.* di) to avail oneself of, to make use of; *impers.* to be customary. **-a·bile** *adj.* usable; fit for use; current. **-anza** *f.* usage; custom. **-ato** *part. adj.* used; employed; worn out; second hand; usual, customary; trained, accustomed; *n.m.* custom.
**usbergo** *m.* hauberk, coat of mail; (fig.) defence, protection.
**u·sci-o** *m.* door; *stare sull'—*, to stand in the doorway. **-ere** *m.* usher; doorkeeper. **-olino, -olo** *m. dim.* small door; wicket.
**usc-ire** [D16] *intr.* (*aux.* essere) to go out; to come out; *fare —*, to let out; to come through; *— di sè*, to be beside oneself; to originate; to issue; to end, to terminate; to burst out, to act precipitately; *rfl.* *-irsene*, to get out of it, to get rid of it, to get through somehow. **-ita** *f.* exit; way out; *giornata di -ita*, day off; *all'-ita di*, on leaving; outcome; departure; withdrawal; end; remark; outlet. **-ito** *part. adj.* issued; out; descended, sprung, born.
**usign(u)olo** *m.* nightingale.
**usitato** *adj.* in common use; frequented; usual; *poco —*, little used.
**uso** *adj.* accustomed; in the habit; used (to); *n.m.* use, *fare — di*, to use; custom, usage, habit; fashion; *pl.* conventions.
**u·ssaro, u·ssero** *m.* hussar.
**Ussiti** *pr.n.m.pl.* (hist.) Hussites.
**usta** *f.* scent (of hounds).
**ustion-e** *f.* burn. **-are** [A1 c] *tr.* to burn; to scorch.
**ust-o** *adj.* (poet.) burnt. **-o·rio** *adj.* burning; *specchio -orio*, burning glass.
**ustolare** [A1 s] *intr.* (*aux.* avere) to whine, to beg.
**usuale** *adj.* usual; customary; ordinary.
**usufruire** [D2] *intr.* (*aux.* avere; *prep.* di) to benefit (by, from); to take advantage (of).
**usur-a**[1] *f.* usury; high interest; excessive profit. **-a·io** *m.* usurer; miser, skinflint.
**usura**[2] *f.* wear; wear and tear.
**usurp-are** [A1] *tr.* to usurp; to supplant. **-atore** *m.*, **-atrice** *f.* usurper. **-azione** *f.* usurpation.
**ute·nsile** *m.* utensil; implement; tool.
**uten-te** *m.*, *f.* user. **-za** *f.* use; users.
**u·ter-o** *m.* womb; (fig.) bosom; heart. **-ino** *adj.* uterine.
**u·til-e** *adj.* useful; serviceable; effective; usable; profitable; *carico —*, payload; *n.m.* profit;

usefulness; benefit. ~ità *f. indecl.* utility; profit; advantage; usefulness. ~ita·rio *adj.* utilitarian. ~itarịsmo *m.* utilitarianism. ~iẓẓa·bile *adj.* utilizable. ~iẓẓare [A1] to utilize.

**uva** *f.* grapes; *un chicco d'—*, a grape; — *passa*, — *secca*, raisins; — *spina*, gooseberry.

**u·vula** *f.* see **ugola**.

**uẓẓa** *f.* sharpness in the air.

**u·ẓẓolo** *m.* whim; urge.

**utop~i·a** *f.* utopia. **~ista** *m.* utopian. **~i·stico** *adj.* utopian.

**V** *m.*, *f.* (pron. **vu**) the letter V; the consonant V.

**va'**[1] *excl.* see!; look!

**va'**[2] *imp.* of **andare**.

**va bene!** *excl.* all right! (*cf.* **andare**).

**vac~are** [A2] *intr.* (*aux.* essere) to be vacant; to be unoccupied; (of a person) to be free, to have nothing to do. **~ante** *adj.* vacant; unoccupied. **~anza** *f.* vacancy; emptiness; vacation, holiday; *pl.* holidays; parliamentary recess.

**vacc~a** *f.* cow; — *da latte*, milch cow; (colloq.) slacker; (vulg.) slut. **~a·io** *m.* cowherd.

**vaccher~ella** *f.* heifer. **~i·a** *f.* cowshed; byre; dairy (farm).

**vacchẹtta** *f.* cow-hide.

**vaccin~a** *f.* cattle; cow flesh; cow dung. **~are** [A1] *tr.* to vaccinate. **~aziọne** *f.* vaccination. **~o** *adj.* bovine; relating to cattle; *n.m.* vaccine, lymph.

**vacill~are** [A1] *intr.* (*aux.* avere) to reel; to totter, to wobble; (of a flame or light) to flicker; (fig.) to vacillate, to hesitate; to be unstable. **~amẹnto** *m.* unsteadiness. **~aziọne** *f.* vacillation; perplexity; hesitation.

**va·cu~o** *adj.* (fig.) vacuous; empty, vacant; free. **~ità** *f.* vacuity; emptiness.

**va-e-vieni** *m. indecl.* coming and going.

**vagabọnd~o** *adj.* vagabond, wandering, vagrant, casual; (fig.) errant; *n.m.* vagabond, tramp; loafer. **~a·ggio** *m.* vagrancy; *n.m.* wandering. **~are** [A1c] *intr.* (*aux.* avere) to wander, to stray, to ramble; to be a tramp; (fig.) to wander; to be lazy.

**vagamẹnte** *adv.* vaguely; gracefully; prettily.

**vagare** [A2] *intr.* (*aux.* avere) to wander, to ramble; to rove; to digress; (of clouds) to drift.

**vagellare** [A1] *intr.* (*aux.* avere) to rave; to be delirious; (fig.) to talk wildly.

**vaghegg~iare** [A3 c] *tr.* to gaze upon fondly; to woo, to court; to desire; to covet; to cherish. **~ino** *m.* ladies' man, flirt; fop, dandy.

**vaghẹzza** *f.* vagueness, indetermination; beauty, charm, grace; adornment; delight; wish, desire.

**vagina** *f.* (anat.) vagina; sheath.

**vag~ire** [D2] *intr.* (*aux.* avere) (of a baby) to whimper; to bleat. **~ito** *m.* infant's cry; whimper; bleat.

**va·glia**[1] *f.* merit, worth, ability.

**va·glia**[2] *m. indecl.* money order; postal order; — *bancario*, bank draft.

**va·gli~o** *m.* sieve; riddle; examination, scrutiny. **~are** [A4] *tr.* to sift; to winnow; (fig.) to scrutinize.

**va~go** *adj.* (*m.pl.* **~ghi**) wandering, straying; drifting; vague; wanton, fickle; — *di*, desirous of, fond of; (poet.) charming, lovely, pleasing; *n.m.* lover; favourite; charm, beauty.

**vagọne** *m.* (rlwy.) truck; carriage; coach, car; — *letti*, sleeping-car.

**va·io** *m.* (zool.) squirrel, and its fur; *adj.* piebald.

**vai(u)ol~o** *m.* (med.) smallpox. **~ọso** *adj.* suffering from smallpox; *n.m.* smallpox patient.

**Valachi·a** *pr.n.f.* (geog.) Walachia.

**valanga** *f.* avalanche; landslide.

**Valchiusa** *pr.n.f.* (geog.) Vaucluse.

**Valdarno** *pr.n.m.* (geog.) Valley of the Arno.

**valdẹse** *adj.*, *n.m.*, *f.* (rel.) Waldensian.

**vale** *excl.* farewell; *n.m.* farewell greeting.

**valente** *adj.* see under **valẹre**.

**Valenza** *pr.n.f.* (geog.) Valencia.

**val~ẹre** [B34] *intr.* (*aux.* essere, avere) to be worth; to yield, to afford a profit of; — *nel dipingere*, to be good at painting; to mean; to be equal to; to deserve; to suffice; *~e*, it is meet; *rfl.* (*prep.* di) to make use (of); to avail oneself (of). **~ente** *adj.* able, clever. **~entuomo** *m.* (*pl.* **~entuo·mini**) man of merit; good man, honest man.

**valeriana** *f.* (bot.) valerian.

**Valẹsia** *pr.n.f.* (geog.) Valois.

**valete** *excl.* fare ye well (*cf.* **vale**).

**valetudina·rio** *m.* valetudinarian.

**valẹvole** *adj.* valid; efficacious.

**va·li~co** *m.* (*pl.* **~chi**) ford, way, passage, crossing-place; mountain pass; railway tunnel. **~ca·bile** *adj.* that may be forded; surmountable. **~care** [A2 s] *tr.* to cross; to ford; to surmount.

**va·lid~o** *adj.* valid; sound; *ragioni ~e*, good reasons; effectual; able. **~amẹnte** *adv.* validly; effectually. **~ità** *f.* validity; ability.

**vali·g~ia** *f.* (*pl.* **~ie**, **~e**) suitcase; small portmanteau; attaché case. **~ia·io** *m.* trunk-maker. **~eri·a** *f.* saddler's shop; factory where trunks and suitcases are made.

**vallata** *f.* wide valley; dale.

**vall~e** *f.* valley; *a —*, downstream; *pl.* marshes, marshland. **~e·a** *f.* (poet.) valley. **~ẹtta** *f. dim.* dale. **~ivo** *adj.* (of ground) low-lying; marshy; relating to a valley or marsh.

**Valle·sia** *pr.n.f.* (geog.) Vaud.

**vallẹtto** *m.* valet; page; groom.

**valligiano** *adj.* relating to a valley; *n.m.* dalesman.

**vallo** *m.* (hist.) rampart, vallum; — *d'Adriano*, Hadrian's Wall.

**vallọn~e**[1] *m. augm.* of **valle**; deep valley. **~ata** *f.* wide valley.

**Vallọne**[2] *pr.n.m.*, *adj.* (hist.) Walloon.

**valọr~e** *m.* worth, value; validity; merit; virtue; courage, bravery; *pl.* valuables; values; stock; shares, bonds, securities. **~iẓẓare** [A1] *tr.* to utilize, to put to use, to improve; to make valuable. **~ọso** *adj.* talented, skilful, clever; brave, valiant.

**Valpolicella** *pr.n.f.* (geog.) region in province of Verona; red wine from that area.

**valsente** *m.* cash value; price.

**valut~a** *f.* value, price; money, currency. **~are** [A1] *tr.* to value, to appraise, to estimate the value of; to estimate, to judge; to esteem highly. **~aziọne** *f.* valuation.

**valva** *f.* (zool.) valve.

**va·lvola** *f.* (techn.) valve; — *di sicurezza*, safety valve.

**valzer** *m. indecl.* waltz; *ballare il —*, to waltz.

**vamp~a** *f.* blaze, heat, fiery glow; flush. **~ata** *f.* flush; flame. **~eggiare** [A3 c] *intr.* (*aux.* avere) to blaze, to flame; to glow. **~o** *m.* sudden blaze, flame.

**vampiro** *m.* vampire.

**vanaglo·ri~a** *f.* vainglory; self-love; arrogance. **~are** [A4] *rfl.* to boast; to be conceited. **~ọso** *adj.* vainglorious; boastful; conceited.

**vaneggi~are** [A3 c] *intr.* (*aux.* avere) to rave; to be wandering; to be delirious. **~amẹnto** *m.* raving.

**vanerello** *adj.* rather vain.

**vanescente** *adj.* fading, evanescent.

**vane·ṣio** *adj.* fatuous and con-

ceited, foppish; *n.m.* fop; conceited fool.

**vang-a** *f.* spade. **-are** [A2] *tr.* to dig, to turn up the ground. **-ata** *f.* dig; turn with the spade. **-atọre** *m.* digger. **-atura** *f.* digging.

**vang-elo** *m.* gospel. **-e·lico** *adj.*, **-elista** *m.* see **evang-e·lico, -elista.**

**vani·glia** *f.* vanilla.

**vanilo·quio** *m.* idle talk; twaddle; raving.

**vanità** *f. indecl.* vanity, emptiness, fruitlessness, futility; frivolousness; conceit.

**vanno** *m.* feather; *pl.* (poet.) pinions.

**vano** *adj.* empty, hollow; groundless, deceptive; useless, ineffectual; *n.m.* empty space, void; (archit.) embrasure; opening.

**vanta·ggi-o** *m.* advantage; gain; superiority; extra, something thrown in; *adv.* more, extra; *per* —, in addition, extra. **-are** [A3] *tr.* to surpass, to exceed, to overcome; to benefit, to favour. **-ọso** *adj.* advantageous; profitable; favourable.

**vant-are** [A1] *tr.* to vaunt; to boast of; to praise; *rfl.* to boast; to brag. **-atọre** *m.*, **-atrice** *f.* boaster, braggart. **-eri·a** *f.* boasting, bragging; boastfulness. **-o** *m.* boast; vaunt; *darsi -o di*, to pride oneself on; honour, reputation.

**va·nvera** *adv. phr. a* —, at random.

**vapọr-e** *m.* steam, vapour; steam-boat, steamer. **-are** [A1 c] *intr.* (*aux.* avere) (poet.) to dissolve into mist; to appear mistily. **-iera** *f.* steam engine. **-iẓẓare** [A1] *tr.* to vaporize; to spray. **-iẓẓatọre** *m.* spray; atomizer. **-ọso** *adj.* vaporous; misty; flimsy; gauzy; (fig.) vague.

**varare** [A1] *tr.* to launch.

**var-co** *m.* (*pl.* **-chi**) narrow way, passage, opening; ford; mountain pass. **-ca·bile** *adj.* passable. **-care** [A2] *tr.* to cross, to pass; to surmount.

**vari-are** [A4] *tr.* to change; to vary, to alter; *intr.* (*aux.* avere, essere) to vary, to have a change. **-a·bile** *adj.* (of wind, weather, etc.) variable, changeable; temperamental, moody. **-ante** *adj.* varying; *n.m.* variant. **-aziọne** *f.* variation; change.

**varicella** *f.* chicken-pox.

**variegat-o** *adj.* variegated. **-ura** *f.* variegation.

**va·ri-o** *adj.* various; *lo vidi -e volte*, I saw him several times; varied; of different colours; *chioma -a*, greying hair; *n.m.* variety. **-amẹnte** *adv.* variously, in various ways. **-età** *f. indecl.* variety; diversity; miscellaneous news; *spettacolo di -età*, variety show. **-olato** *adj.* pockmarked. **-opinto** *adj.* many-coloured; speckled.

**varo** *m.* launching.

**Varsa·via** *pr.n.f.* (geog.) Warsaw.

**vaṣ-a·io** *m.* potter. **-ame** *m.* pottery.

**vasca** *f.* basin; pond; — *da bagno*, bath, bath-tub.

**vascello** *m.* (naut.) ship; full-rigged ship.

**vaṣelina** *f.* vaseline; petroleum jelly.

**vaṣellame** *m.* crockery, china, dishes; plate.

**vaṣello** *m. dim.* of **vaso**; (theol.) — *dello Spirito Santo*, vessel of the Holy Ghost.

**vaṣọ** *m.* vase, vessel; jar, pot; — *da notte*, chamber-pot; — *da fiori*, flower-pot.

**vassallo** *m.* vassal, feudal tenant.

**vassọio** *m.* tray; pen-tray; — *da tè*, tea-tray.

**vast-o** *adj.* large; spacious; wide; ample; vast. **-ità** *f.* great extent; spaciousness.

**vate** *m.* prophet, soothsayer, seer; poet, bard.

**Vaticano** *pr.n.m.* Vatican.

**vati-cinare** [A1] *tr.* to prophesy, to foretell, to predict. **-cinaziọne** *f.* vaticination, prophecy. **-ci·nio** *m.* prophecy, prediction.

**vattelappẹsca** *excl.* who knows?; my guess is as good as yours.

**ve**[1] *pers. prn.* you, to you; form of *pers. prn.* **vi** used before oblique cases of pronouns.

**ve**[2] *adv.* there; form of *adv.* **ivi,** or **vi** used before oblique cases of pronouns; — *n'erano venti*, there were twenty of them.

**ve', veh** *excl.* look!; see!; *attenti*, — *!*, look out!

**ve·cchi-o** *adj.* old; aged; former, previous; mellow; *i vecchi tempi*, the old days; *n.m.* old man; *il* —, old things; *i vecchi*, old people; the ancients. **-a** *f.* old woman. **-a·ia** *f.* old age; old things, old customs; out-of-date things. **-arello, -erello, -erellino** *adj.* poor old; *n.m.* poor old man. **-ẹtto** *adj. dim.* ageing, elderly; *n.m.* brisk, lively old man. **-ẹzza** *f.* (of people) old age; (of things) the quality and appearance of age. **-ọne** *m. augm.* old gentleman; venerable old man. **-otto** *adj.* ageing, approaching old age; *n.m.* flourishing old man.

**vẹccia** *f.* (bot.) vetch.

**vẹc-e** *f.* place, stead; *fare le -i di direttore*, to act as manager; *in sua* —, in his stead.

**ved-ẹre** [B35] *tr.* to see; *far* —, to show; to try; — *di*, to see if one can; — *bene*, to think well of; — *male*, to dislike; *non* — *l'ora di*, to long for the time (when); *non -o l'ora di rivederti*, I am longing to see you again; *aver che (da)* —, (with *prep.* 'con' or 'in') to have something to do with; to resemble; *in questo non ci ho che* —, I have nothing to do with this; *intr.* (*aux.* avere) to see; — *doppio*, to see double; *-erci*, to be able to see; *non ci si -e più*, it has grown too dark to see; *n.m.* sight; *perdere il* —, to lose one's sight; *fare un bellissimo* —, to make a wonderful sight.

**vedẹtta** *f.* (mil.) look-out post; look out; sentry; — *del cinema*, film-star; — *del teatro*, famous actor, star.

**vẹdov-o** *m.* widower; relict; *adj.* bereaved; (fig.) bereft. **-a** *f.* widow. **-anza** *f.* widowhood; bereavement; deprivation. **-ella** *f. dim.* poor widow, little widow. **-ile** *adj.* of or pertaining to a widow or widower; *n.m.* widow's pension; widow's weeds, mourning.

**veduta** *f.* view; sight.

**veduto** *part.* of **vedẹre**; *adj.* seen; regarded; — *di buon occhio*, well like, favourably regarded; — *di mal occhio*, disliked.

**veemen-te** *adj.* vehement; intense. **-temẹnte** *adv.* vehemently; intensely. **-za** *f.* vehemence; impetus; ardour.

**ve·get-o** *adj.* vigorous, strong, thriving, flourishing, luxuriant. **-ale** *adj.* vegetal, vegetable; *regno -ale*, vegetable kingdom; *n.m.* vegetable life; vegetable. **-are** [A1 s] *intr.* (*aux.* avere) to vegetate. **-arianiṣmo** *m.* vegetarianism. **-ariano** *adj.*, *n.m.* vegetarian. **-aziọne** *f.* vegetation.

**veggente** *adj.* seeing; *n.m.* seer, prophet, soothsayer; *f.* clairvoyante.

**vẹglia** *f.* wakefulness; watchfulness; vigil; evening; gathering; wake; watch(man).

**vegliardo** *m.* old man.

**vegli-are** [A4 c] *intr.* (*aux.* avere) to be awake; to be wakeful; to watch; to stay up late; to take care; — *su*, to watch over; *tr.* — *un ammalato*, to watch by an invalid's bed during the night.

**ve·glio** *m.* (poet.) old man.

**vegliọne** *m.* ball, evening party.

**veh** *excl.* look!; see!

**vei·colo** *m.* vehicle; conveyance; medium, conveyer.

**vela** *f.* (naut.) sail; canvas; ship.

**velame** *m.* veil; covering.

**vel-are** [A1] *tr.* to veil, to cover with a veil; (fig.) to cover, to hide; *rfl.* to veil oneself; to grow misty. **-amẹnto** *m.* veiling; pretext, excuse; appearance; guise.

**velatura**[1] *f.* veiling; *una* — *d'argento*, a thin coating of silver; mistiness.

**velatura**[2] *f.* (naut.) construction and furnishing with sails; quan-

tity of sails; trim of the sails; rig.
**veleggiare** [A3 c] *intr* (*aux.* avere) to sail; *tr.* to sail (the seas); to provide with sails.
**veleni·fero** *adj.* see under **veleno.**
**velen-o** *m.* poison; venom; love-potion, love-philtre. **-i·fero** *adj.* poisonous, venomous. **-oso** *adj.* poisonous; poisoned, venomous; malicious, malevolent.
**veliero** *m.* (naut.) sailing-ship; sailing-boat; windjammer; *adj. barca veliera*, sailing-boat.
**velin-o** *adj.* vellum; *carta -a*, tissue-paper.
**velleità** *f. indecl.* velleity; empty wish, foolish aspiration.
**vellic-are** [A2 s] *tr.* to pinch; to string; to tickle; to titillate, to stimulate. **-amento** *m.*, **-azione** *f.* tickling; tingling.
**vell-o** *m.* furry or woolly skin of animal; coat; (of sheep) fleece. **-oso** *adj.* fleecy, shaggy; hairy.
**vellut-o** *m.* velvet; — *di cotone*, velveteen; — *a grosse coste*, corduroy; *adj.* hairy, shaggy. **-ato** *adj.* velvety.
**velo** *m.* veil; mourning-veil; velum; tissue; muslin; gauze; voile; mist; fog; mask, blind.
**veloc-e** *adj.* swift, fast, rapid, quick, speedy. **-emente** *adv.* swiftly, fast, rapidly, quickly, speedily. **-i·pede** *adj.* swift-footed; *n.m.* bicycle, velocipede. **-ista** *m., f.* (sport) sprinter. **-ità** *f. indecl.* velocity, speed.
**velo·dromo** *m.* cycling stadium; cycle-track.
**veltro** *m.* wolf-hound; grey-hound.
**vena** *f.* vein; (fig.) trickle; streak; *acqua di* —, spring water; mood; luck.
**venal-e** *adj.* venal; marketable; *prezzo* —, sale price. **-ità** *f.* venality.
**ven-are** [A1] *tr.* to vein, to cover as with veins; *rfl.* to be veined. **-ato** *part. adj.* veined. **-atura** *f.* veining.
**vendemmi-a** *f.* grape-harvest; grape-gathering; vintage time, vintage. **-are** [A4 c] *tr.* to reap, to gather, to harvest; to plunder; *intr.* (*aux.* avere) to gather grapes, to profit handsomely. **-atore** *m.*, **-atrice** *f.* vintager, grape-gatherer.
**vend-ere** [B1] *tr.* to sell; to sell up; — *all'asta*, to sell by auction; *rfl.* to hire oneself out; to prostitute oneself, to sell oneself; *intr.* (*aux.* avere) to be a shop-keeper, to have a business. **-ereccio** *adj.* saleable; venal; corruptible. **-i·bile** *adj.* saleable; for sale, on sale; (of person) corruptible.
**vendetta** *f.* feud, vendetta.
**vendic-are** [A2 s] *tr.* to avenge; to vindicate. **-ativo** *adj.* vengeful, revengeful; vindictive. **-atore** *m.*, **-atrice** *f.* avenger; vindicator; *adj.* vindicating.
**vendit-a** *f.* sale; *in* —, on sale, for sale; — *a rate*, hire purchase; shop; — *di pane*, baker's shop. **-ore** *m.* seller, vendor; *-ore ambulante*, pedlar.
**venduto** *part.* of **vendere.**
**venefi·cio** *m.* poisoning.
**vene·fico** poisonous; venomous; *clima* —, unhealthy climate.
**vener-are** [A1 s] to venerate, to revere; to worship. **-a·bile** *adj.* venerable. **-ando** *adj.* venerable, worthy of reverence. **-azione** *f.* veneration, reverence.
**venerdì** *pr.n.m.* Friday; *il Venerdì Santo*, Good Friday.
**Ve·nere** *pr.n.f.* Venus.
**vene·reo** *adj.* pertaining to Venus; sensual, lascivious, lustful; (med.) venereal.
**Ve·neto** *pr.n.m.* (geog.) Veneto, Venetia.
**Vene·zi-a** *pr.n.f.* (geog.) Venice. **-ano** *n.m.* Venetian; Venetian dialect; *adj.* Venetian.
**ve·ni-a** *f.* indulgence, pardon. **-ale** *adj.* venial; pardonable.
**veniente** *part. adj.* coming; next.
**ven-ire** [D17] *intr.* (*aux.* essere) **1.** to come; *far — uno*, to send for someone. **2.** to move, to pass, to proceed. **3.** to arrive, to get; — *alla verità*, to arrive at the truth. **4.** to derive, to originate. **5.** to happen, to arise, to befall; to occur; (of a date) to fall; *il Natale scorso -ne di domenica*, last year Christmas fell on a Sunday. **6.** to grow, to progress. **7.** to develop, to form. **8.** to become, to turn. **9.** to result, to add up to, to come out; *il problema non gli viene*, he cannot solve the problem. **10.** to be about to come; *viene l'inverno*, winter is coming. **11.** to be sent, to be directed, to be addressed. **12.** to appear; — *fuori*, to emerge. **13.** SYNTACTICAL USES: (i) as an *aux.* in a Passive Construction: *per questo viene ammirata*, she is admired for this; — *fatto*, to happen. (ii) with a gerund expressing gradual fulfilment of an action: *si viene accorgendo*, he gradually begins to notice. **-uto** *part. adj.* come; arrived; returned; grown; happened; appeared; resolved.
**venoso** *adj.* venous.
**venta·gli-o** *m.* fan; *coda a* —, fan-tail. **-a·io** *m.* fan-maker. **-are** [A4] *rfl.* to fan oneself.
**vent-are** [A1] *intr.* (*aux.* avere) to blow, to blow hard. **-ai(u)ola** *f.* weather-cock. **-ata** *f.* gust of wind.
**vent-i** *card. num.* twenty; *arriverò il* —, I shall arrive on the twentieth. **-enne** *adj., n.m.f.* twenty-year-old. **-e·nnio** *m.* period of twenty years. **-e·simo** *ord. num.* twentieth part. **-icinque** *card. num.* twenty-five. **-icinque·nnio** *m.* period of twenty-five years; twenty-fifth anniversary. **-idue** *card. num.* twenty-two. **-imila** *card. num.* twenty thousand. **-ina** *f.* set, group or batch of (about) twenty; score. **-inove** *card. num.* twenty-nine. **-inovennale** *adj.* of twenty-nine years' duration. **-iquattro** *card. num.* twenty-four. **-isei** -twenty-six. **une·simo** twenty-first. **-uno** twenty-one.
**venticello** *m. dim.* of **vento**; light wind; breeze.
**ventilabro** *m.* winnowing-fan.
**ventil-are** [A1 s] *tr.* to winnow; to air, to ventilate; *intr.* (*aux.* avere) to blow, to be windy; to flap, to flutter. **-atore** *m.* ventilator; electric fan. **-azione** *f.* ventilation; airing; blowing; winnowing; sifting.
**vento** *m.* wind; air; puff.
**ve·ntol-a** *f.* fire-fan; winnowing-fan. **-are** [A1] *tr.* to ventilate, to air; to wave in the wind; to winnow; *intr.* (*aux.* avere) to be windy; to flutter.
**ventos-o** *adj.* windy; puffed up. **-ità** *f.* windiness; (fig.) emptiness, vanity.
**ventr-e** *m.* belly, abdomen; paunch; womb; — *a terra*, at full gallop. **-ale** *adj.* ventral. **-i·colo** *m.* ventricle. **-iera** *f.* body-belt. **-ilo·quio** *m.* ventriloquy, ventriloquism. **-i·loquo** *m.* ventriloquist.
**vent-uno** *card. num.*, **-une·simo** *ord. num.* see under **venti.**
**ventur-a** *f.* fortune, future; *far la* —, to tell fortunes. **-iere, -iero** *m.* adventurer. **-o** *adj.* next, coming, future; *il mese -o*, next month. **-oso** *adj.* fortunate, lucky; happy.
**venust-à** *f.* beauty, grace, loveliness. **-o** *adj.* beautiful, graceful.
**venuta** *f.* arrival; coming.
**verac-e** *adj.* true, real; truthful. **-ità** *f.* veracity; truthfulness.
**veramente** *adv.* see under **vero.**
**veranda** *f.* veranda(h).
**verbal-e** *adj.* verbal, oral; *processo* —, minute(s); *mettere a* —, to minute. **-mente** *adv.* verbally; literally; aloud.
**verbena** *f.* (bot.) vervain.
**verbigra·zia** *adv.* for instance.
**verb-o** *m.* verb; word. **-osità** *f.* verbosity. **-oso** *adj.* verbose.
**verd-e** *adj.* green; fresh, young; full of sap; *i -i anni*, youth; *n.m.* green; greenness; (colloq.) *essere al* —, to be broke. **-astro** *adj.* greenish. **-azzurro** *adj., n.m.* bluish green. **-echiaro** *adj., n.m.* light green. **-ebruno, -ecupo, -escuro** *adj., n.m.* dark green. **-egiallo** *adj., n.m.* apple-green. **-emare** *adj., n.m.*

sea-green. **-ẹzza** *f.* greenness. **-i·ccio, -o·gnolo** *adj.* greenish.
**verdeggi-are** [A3c] *intr.* (*aux.* avere) to turn green; to appear green; to flourish. **-ante** *part. adj.* verdant.
**verderame** *m.* verdigris.
**verdẹtto** *m.* verdict.
**verdọne** *m.* (orn.) greenfinch.
**verdura** *f.* verdure; greenery; greenness; green vegetables, greens; *minestra con —*, vegetable soup.
**verecọnd-ia** *f.* bashfulness; modesty. **-o** *adj.* bashful; modest; chaste.
**vẹrg-a** *f.* small branch; twig; rod; wand. **-are** [A2c] *tr.* to flog; to cane; to mark with streaks or stripes; to draw lines on; to jot down; *rfl.* to become streaky. **-ata** *f.* stroke with a cane. **-ato** *part. adj.* striped; streaky; *carta -ata*, ruled paper. **-atura** *f.* stripes; striped pattern.
**vẹrgin-e** *f.* virgin; maiden, girl; *m.* virgin, male virgin; *la Beata Vergine*, the Virgin Mary; *adj.* virgin; pure, chaste. **-ità** *f.* virginity; maidenhood.
**vergọgn-a** *f.* shame; modesty, diffidence; infamy; disgrace. **-are** [A1] *rfl.*, *intr.* (*aux.* essere) to be ashamed; *vergògnati!*, you ought to be ashamed of yourself!; to be shy. **-ato** *part. adj.* shamed, put to shame; disgraced. **-ọso** *adj.* ashamed; shameful; inglorious.
**veri·dic-o** *adj.* veracious. **-ità** *f.* veracity.
**veri·fic-a** *f.* inspection; verification. **-are** [A2s] *tr.* to verify, to ascertain, to check, to prove; to audit; *rfl.* to happen, to come to pass; to come true. **-atọre** *m.* examiner, inspector. **-aziọne** *f.* verification; realization; inspection; auditing.
**verisi·mi-le** *adj.*, **-glianza** *f.* see **verosi·mile,** *etc.* under **vẹro.**
**ver-iṣmo** *m.* Italian realist movement (19th century). **-ista** *m.*, *f.* Italian realist writer or artist.
**verit-à** *f. indecl.* truth; verity; truthfulness; justice, right. **-iero** *adj.* truthful, veracious, trustworthy; true; *n.m.* truthful man; trustworthy, loyal person.
**verm-e** *m.* (zool.) worm; (pop.) grub; maggot; weevil; chrysalis. **-icelli** *m.pl.* vermicelli. **-icolare** vermicular, wormlike. **-ifọrme** *adj.* vermiform. **-i·fugo** (*pl.* **-i·fughi**) *m.* vermifuga.
**vermena** *f.* young branch or shoot; twig.
**vermi·glio** *adj.* brilliant red, carmine, vermilion; *n.m.* vermilion colour.
**verminọso** *adj.* verminous.
**vermut, vermutte** *m.* vermouth.
**verna·ccia** *f.* strong white wine.
**verna·colo** *m.* vernacular; dialect; *adj.* vernacular; dialectal.
**vern-ale** *adj.* (poet.) wintry, vernal. **-are** [A1] *intr.* (*aux.* avere) to (pass the) winter.
**vernic-e** *f.* varnish; polish; glaze; paint; (fig.) veneer. **-iare** [A3] *tr.* to varnish; to paint; to glaze; to polish. **-iato** *part. adj.* *cuoio -iato*, patent leather; varnished. **-iatọre** *m.* varnisher; polisher. **-iatura** *f.* varnishing; glazing.
**verno**[1] *m.* (poet.) winter.
**verno**[2] *adj.* (poet.) vernal, of spring.
**vẹr-o** *adj.* true; real; genuine; right; thorough; out-and-out; *n.m.* truth; *dire il —*, to be accurate; reality; life; nature. **-amẹnte** *adv.* truly; truthfully; really; indeed. **-osi·mile** *adj.*, **-osimigliante** *adj.* probable, likely; lifelike; *n.m.* likelihood. **-osimiglianza** *f.* likelihood; verisimilitude.
**Verọn-a** *pr.n.f.* (geog.) Verona. **-ẹse** *adj.*, *n.m.*, *f.* Veronese.
**verọne** *m.* balcony; loggia.
**verro** *m.* boar.
**verruc-a** *f.* verruca; wart. **-ọso** *adj.* warty.
**Versa·glia** *pr.n.f.* (geog.) Versailles.
**vers-are** [A1] to pour; to pour out; to ladle; to spill, to upset; to shed (tears, blood); to spend, to dissipate; *intr.* (*aux.* avere) to spill, to leak, to overflow; *rfl.* to spill, to be split, to leak, to flow. **-amẹnto** *m.* outpouring; (finan.) remittance; *distinta di -amento*, pay-in-slip; *-amento parziale*, part-payment. **-ante** *m.* side; slope; drainage area; watershed; prayer; depositor. **-a·tile** *adj.* versatile; changeable, unstable; reversible. **-atilità** *f.* versatility. **-ato** *part. adj.* versed; skilled; proficient (in).
**verseggi-are** [A3c] *intr.* (*aux.* avere) to versify, to write verse; *tr.* to turn into verse. **-atọre** *m.*, **-atrice** *f.* versifier.
**versẹtto** *m.* verse; versicle; short line.
**versicolọre** *adj.* of changing hue, iridescent.
**versiera** *f.* the wife of the devil; she-devil, hobgoblin, evil spirit; (fig.) ugly old woman, old witch.
**versific-are** [A2s] *tr.* to versify, to put into verse. **-atọre** *m.* versifier.
**versiọne** *f.* translation; version; unseen.
**versipelle** *adj.* cunning, crafty, two-faced; *n.m.* rogue, crafty fellow.
**vers-o**[1] *m.* line (of writing); verse; line (of verse); (bibl.) verse; sound, noise, note; song (of birds) intonation, cadence; peculiar sound; direction; inclination, aptitude; *andare a — a*, to get on well with; *mutar —*, to change one's tone; manner, way, possibility; *non c'è — di*, there is no way of.
**verso**[2] *m.* reverse (of coin); verso (of book leaf); *adj.* turned, changed; *vice versa*, on the other hand, on the contrary.
**verso**[3] *prep.* towards; *guardare — il mare*, to face the sea; *— est*, eastwards; (usu. with *prep.* 'di' before *pers. prn.*) *— di me*, towards me; (also) *— di*, in comparison with; (fig.) *poco pietoso — i debitori*, not very lenient to his debtors; about.
**ve·rtebr-a** *f.* vertebra. **-ale** *adj.* vertebral; spinal. **-ato** *adj.*, *n.m.* vertebrate.
**ve·rt-ere** [B1 def.] *intr.* (only found in *3rd pers. sing.* of indicative tenses) to regard, to concern, to be about; *— su*, to turn on, to regard. **-ente** *part. adj.* (leg.) pending; undecided. **-enza** *f.* difference, dispute.
**vertical-e** *adj.* vertical; upright; *n.f.* vertical. **-mẹnte** *adv.* vertically.
**ve·rtice** *m.* vertex.
**verti·gin-e** *f.* (med.) vertigo; dizziness, giddiness. **-ọso** *adj.* vertiginous; dizzy; giddy.
**veruno** *adj.* (in *neg.* context) not any; *prn.* anyone; nobody.
**verẓicare** [A2s] *intr.* (*aux.* avere) (poet.) to turn green; to flourish, to thrive.
**verẓiere** *m.* orchard; kitchen-garden; fruit and vegetable market.
**vẹscia** *f.* puff-ball (fungus).
**vesci-ca** *f.* bladder; (anat.) vesica. **-cante** *m.* blistering ointment. **-chẹtta** *f. dim.* vesicle; blister.
**vẹscov-o** *m.* bishop. **-ado** *m.* bishop's palace. **-ato** *m.* episcopate; bishop's see; episcopal revenue. **-ile** *adj.* episcopal.
**vesp-a** *f.* (ent.) wasp; a make of motor scooter, Vespa. **-a·io** *m.* wasp's nest; (fig.) hornets' nest.
**Vespaṣiano** *pr.n.m.* Vespasian; *m.* street urinal.
**Ve·spero** *pr.n.m.* Hesperus, Vesper; *m.* (poet.) evening.
**vesperti·lio** *m.* (zool.) bat.
**vespertino** *adj.* evening.
**vespro** *m.* vespers, evensong; evening.
**vess-are** [A1] *tr.* to vex, to molest, to harass. **-atọre** *m.*, **-atrice** *f.* oppressor; *adj.* oppressive. **-ato·rio** *adj.* oppressive; vexatious. **-aziọne** *f.* vexation.
**vessillo** *m.* flag; standard; ensign.
**vesta·glia** *f.* dressing-gown; house-coat.
**veste** *f.* dress; clothing; garment; (fig.) guise; pretext; appearance;

right, authority; *pl.* clothing; attire.

**Vestfa·lia** *pr.n.f.* (geog.) Westphalia.

**vestia·r-io** *m.* clothing, clothes; (theatr.) wardrobe. **-ista** *m.* (theatr.) costumier.

**vesti·bolo** *m.* vestibule, entrance-hall; foyer (of a theatre).

**vesti·g-io** *m.* (*pl.* **-i** *m.*, **-ia** *f.*) trace, vestige; footprint; track; *pl.* footprints; remains.

**vest-ire** [D1] *tr.* to dress; to put on (clothing); *rfl.*, *intr.* (*aux.* avere) to dress; to dress oneself; to be dressed; *n.m.* dress. **-imẹnto** *m.* (*pl.* **-imenti** *m.*, **-imenta** *f.*) clothing, clothes; garment; vestment. **-ito** *part. adj.* clothed; *n.m.* outfit; suit, outfit; *pl.* clothes. **-iziọne** *f.* (rel.) clothing.

**Vesu·vio** *pr.n.m.* Vesuvius.

**veterano** *adj. m.* (mil.) veteran; ex-serviceman.

**veterina·ri-a** *f.* veterinary science. **-o** *adj.* veterinary; *n.m.* veterinary surgeon.

**veto** *m. indecl.* veto.

**vetri(u)olo** *m.* vitriol.

**vetr-o** *m.* glass; pane of glass; lens; article of glassware; tumbler, glass. **-a·io** *m.* glass-maker; glass-blower; glass-manufacturer; glazier. **-ame** *m.* glassware. **-ata** *f.* glass window; glass door. **-eri·a** *f.* glass-works. **-ificare** [A2s] *tr.* to vitrify. **-ino** *f.* glass-case, show-case; shop window. **-inọ** *adj.* of glass; glassy; brittle; *n.m.* microscopic slide.

**vẹtta** *f.* top, peak, summit; *in — a*, on the top of.

**vettọre** *m.* (math.) vector.

**vettova·gli-a** *f.* (usu. *pl.*) provisions, food, victuals. **-amẹnto** *m.* provisioning; victualling. **-are** [A4] *tr.* to provision; to victual.

**vettur-a** *f.* conveyance, transport; hire of transport; vehicle; carriage; (rlwy.) coach; *signori, in —!*, take your seats please! **-ino** *m.* driver; coachman; cab-man.

**vetust-o** *adj.* ancient. **-à** *f.* antiquity; old age.

**vezzeggi-are** [A3c] *tr.* to fondle; to cherish; to pet; to coax; to pamper; *intr.* (*aux.* avere) to flirt. **-ativo** *adj.* coaxing; (gramm.) denoting endearment; *n.m.* pet-name.

**vẹzz-o** *m.* habit; pet trick; affectation; caress; endearment; necklace; toy, plaything. **-ọso** *adj.* pretty, graceful, charming.

**vi**[1] *pers. prn., acc., dat.* (before **lo, la, li, le, ne,** becomes **ve**) you; to you.

**vi**[2] *adv.* there (before **lo, la, li, le, ne** becomes **ve**).

**via** *f.* road; street; (railway) line; way, path; *adv.* away; *e così —*, and so on; *excl.* go away!, be off!; *conj. — che*, as, as soon as. **-bilità** *f.* condition of the roads; viability. **-dọtto** *m.* viaduct.

**viaggi-are** [A4] *intr.* (*aux.* avere) to travel; to journey; to voyage; (of goods) to be carried. **-atọre** *m.*, **-atrice** *f.* traveller; passenger.

**via·ggio** *m.* journey; *in —*, on the journey; *buon —!*, good journey!; trip; tour; *pl.* travels.

**viale** *m.* avenue; shady path.

**viandante** *m.* traveller, wayfarer; passer-by; tramp.

**via·tico** *m.* provisions for a journey.

**viava·i** *m. indecl.* bustling; coming and going.

**vibr-are** [A1] *tr.* to vibrate; to quiver; to shake, to brandish; to hurl; to deal, to strike (a blow); *intr.* (*aux.* avere) to resound; (of a bell) to ring; to vibrate; to thrill. **-ante** *part. adj.* vibrating; quivering; vibrant. **-a·tile** *adj.* vibrating; pulsating. **-ato** *part. adj.* forceful; flung; (mus.) tremolo. **-aziọne** *f.* vibration; quivering; (fig.) thrill.

**vica·ri-o** *adj.* vicarious; substituted; *n.m.* vicar; curate; deputy, representative. **-ato** *m.* vicariate; curacy; living.

**vice**[1] *f.* stead, place; *— versa*, on the other hand, on the contrary.

**vice**[2] *pref.* vice-; deputy, assistant. **-direttọre** *m.* assistant manager. **-presidente** *m.* vice-president. **-rè** *m. indecl.* viceroy. **-reale** *adj.* viceregal. **-regina** *f.* vice-reine.

**vicend-a** *f.* vicissitude; event; affair; alternation; *a —*, in turn; by turns; reciprocally, mutally. **-ẹvole** *adj.* alternate; mutual, reciprocal. **-evolẹzza** *f.* reciprocity. **-evolmẹnte** *adv.* mutually; reciprocally; in turn; by turns.

**vice·nn-io** *m.* period of twenty years. **-ale** *adj.* recurring, renewable every twenty years.

**viceversa** *adv.* see 'vice versa', under **vice**[1].

**vicin-o** *adj.* near, close; neighbouring; *n.m.* neighbour; *adv.* near, nearby; *prep. phr. — a*, near; close to; beside. **-ale** *adj.* local; *strada -ale*, by-road, by-way. **-anza** *f.* nearness; neighbourhood. **-ato** *m.* vicinity, neighbourhood; people of the neighbourhood.

**vicissitu·dine** *f.* vicissitude; *pl.* events; circumstances; changes.

**vi·colo** *m.* lane, alley.

**vidimare** [A1] *tr.* to stamp as correct; to endorse; to authenticate.

**Vienn-a** *pr.n.f.* (geog.) Vienna. **-ẹse** *adj.*, *n.m.*, *f.* Viennese.

**viepiù, vieppiù** *adv.* much more.

**viet-are** [A1] *tr.* to forbid, to prohibit; (fig.) to prevent. **-ato** *part. adj.* forbidden; prohibited; *-ata l'affissione*, stick no bills; *-ato fumare*, no smoking.

**vieto** *adj.* stale, rancid; old-fashioned; *n.m.* rancid taste.

**vi·g-ere** [B1 def.] *intr.* (no *past. part.*) to flourish, to thrive; (of laws) to be in force. **-ente** *part. adj.* in force; having effect.

**vige·ṣimo** *card. num.* twentieth.

**vigil-are** [A1s] *tr.* to watch over, keep an eye on; *intr.* (*aux.* avere) to be awake, to be wakeful; to be on the alert. **-ante** *part. adj.* watchful; wakeful; *n.m.pl.* watchmen, guards. **-anza** *f.* care, supervision; vigilance; inspection.

**vi·gile** *adj.* wakeful, watchful; alert; *n.m.* watchman; policeman; fireman.

**vigi·lia** *f.* vigil; watch; eve, day before; *la Vigilia di Natale*, Christmas Eve.

**vigliac-co** *adj.* (*m.pl.* **-chi**) vile, ignoble, low, mean; cowardly; *n.m.* bully; coward. **-cheri·a** *f.* meanness; cowardice.

**vign-a** *f.* vineyard. **-ai(u)olo** *m.* vine-dresser. **-ẹto** *m.* vineyard.

**vigọr-e** *m.* vigour, strength; efficacy, validity. **-i·a** *f.* vigour, strength, force. **-ọso** *adj.* vigorous, strong; brave.

**vile** *adj.* (abbrev. to **vil** before certain nouns) cheap; mean, modest; insignificant; cowardly; contemptible, mean, despicable, ignoble.

**vilificare** [A2s] *tr.* to debase; to lower; to humiliate; to disgrace; to scorn.

**vili-pe·ndere** [C1] *tr.* to despise, to scorn; to humiliate, to defame. **-pe·ndio** *m.* contempt, scorn; humiliation; disparagement. **-pẹso** *part. adj.* despised; scorned.

**vill-a** *f.* country-house; country-seat; country villa. **-eggiare** [A3c] *intr.* (*aux.* avere) to pass the summer at a country villa. **-eggiatura** *f.* life at a villa; country holiday; holiday place; *in -eggiatura*, on holiday.

**villa·ggio** *m.* village; *vita di —*, village life.

**villan-o** *m.* countryman, peasant; boor; *villan rifatto*, upstart; *adj.* rustic; low born; loutish; insulting; cruel. **-ella** *f.*, **-ello** *m.* young country lass, lad. **-ẹsco** *adj.* (*m.pl.* **-ẹschi**) rustic; boorish. **-i·a** *f.* boorish manners; injury; abuse; offence; *pl.* insults.

**vi·llico** *m.* villager, countryman.

**villino** *m.* small country dwelling; country cottage.

**villọso** *adj.* hairy; shaggy.

**viltà** *f.* cheapness; meanness; cowardice.

**viluppo** *m.* entanglement, tangle; (fig.) bundle; muddle, confusion.

**vi·min-e** *m.* osier; withy. **-ata** *f.* wicker-work.
**vin-a·ccia** *f.* dregs of pressed grapes. **-a·ccio** *m. pejor.* inferior wine. **-a·io** *m.* wine merchant, vintner. **-a·rio** *adj.* relating to wine.
**vinca** *f.* (bot.) periwinkle.
**vincastro** *m.* staff; shepherd's crook.
**vi·nc-ere** [C5] *tr.* to conquer, to vanquish, to overcome; to win; to excel, to surpass; *intr.* (*aux.* avere) to win; *rfl.* to master oneself; to control oneself. **-i·bile** *adj.* conquerable. **-ibosco** *m.* (bot.) honeysuckle. **-itore** *m.*, **-itrice** *f.* winner; victor; conqueror.
**vinci·glio** *m.* (bot.) withy.
**vi·ncita** *f.* winnings; gain.
**vin-co**[1] *m.* (*pl.* **-chi**) (bot.) osier. **-cheto** *m.* osier-bed.
**vin-co**[2] *adj.* (*m.pl.* **-chi**) soft, flexible; (of bread) doughy.
**vi·ncol-o** *m.* tie; bond; *pl.* chains, bonds, fetters. **-are** [A1 s] *tr.* (fig.) to tie, to bind.
**vi·ndice** *adj.* avenging, vengeful; *n.m.* avenger.
**vin-o** *m.* wine. **-ello** *m.* wine made from grape skins and water. **-i·colo** *adj.* wine-producing. **-icoltura** *f.* vine cultivation. **-i·fero** *adj.* wine-producing. **-ificazione** *f.* wine-making. **-oso** *adj.* vinous.
**vinto** *part.* of **vi·ncere**; *adj.* beaten, conquered; *n.m.* loser.
**viola**[1] *f.* (mus.) viola; viol.
**viola**[2] *f.* (bot.) violet; — *del pensiero*, pansy.
**Viola**[3] *pr.n.f.* Viola.
**viola·ceo** *adj.* violet (colour).
**viol-are** [A1 s] to violate; to pollute; to profane; to break. **-atore** *m.*, **-atrice** *f.* violator. **-azione** *f.* violation.
**violent-o** *adj.* violent. **-amento** *m.* use of violence, forcing. **-are** [A1] *tr.* to do violence to; to force, to compel.
**violenza** *f.* violence; force, duress.
**violett-a**[1] *f.* (bot.) violet. **-o** *adj.*, *n.m.* violet (colour).
**Violetta**[2] *pr.n.f.* Violet.
**violin-o** *m.* violin, fiddle. **-a·io** *m.* violin-maker. **-ista** *m.*, *f.* violinist.
**violoncell-o** *m.* violoncello, 'cello. **-ista** *m.*, *f.* cellist.
**vio·ttol-a** *f.* country lane; footpath. **-o** *m.* footpath, track; narrow street.
**vi·per-a** *f.* (zool.) viper, adder. **-ino** *adj.* viperous.
**vira·ggio** *m.* (naut.) turning; tacking; (photog.) toning.
**vir-ago** *f.* (*pl.* **-a·gini**) virago; amazon.
**virare** [A1] *intr.* (*aux.* avere) (naut.) to go about; (aeron.) to bank; *tr.* (photog.) to tone.
**Virgi·li-o** *pr.n.m.* Virgil. **-ano** *adj.*, *n.m.* Virgilian.
**virginale** *adj.* maidenly; virgin; virginal; *n.m.* (mus.) virginal.
**vi·rgol-a** *f.* comma; *punto e* —, semicolon. **-are** [A1 s] *tr.* to put in inverted commas. **-ette** *f.pl.* inverted commas, quotation marks.
**virgulto** *m.* young shoot; shrub.
**viril-e** *adj.* virile; male; strong, brave. **-ità** *f.* manhood; virility; manliness.
**virt-ù** *f. indecl.* virtue; potency; strength; valour, courage; merit; talent; means. **-uale** *adj.* virtual, potential. **-ualità** *f.* potentiality. **-uosità** *f.* virtuosity. **-uoso** *adj.* virtuous; skilled; *n.m.* virtuoso.
**virulen-to** *adj.* virulent. **-za** *f.* virulence.
**vi·rus** *m. indecl.* (biol.) virus.
**visaggista** *m.*, *f.* beauty-specialist.
**vi·scer-e** *m.* internal organ. **-i** *pl.* viscera. **-e** *f.pl.* bowels; (fig.) compassion; heart. **-ale** *adj.* visceral.
**vi·schio** *m.* bird-lime; (bot.) mistletoe.
**vi·scido** *adj.* viscous, glutinous.
**visconte** *m.* viscount.
**viscos-o** *adj.* viscous; sticky. **-ità** *f.* viscosity.
**vis-i·bile** *adj.* visible; perceptible; evident; available. **-ibi·lio** *m.* great number; *andare in -ibilio*, to go into ecstasies. **-ibilità** *f.* visibility.
**visiera** *f.* visor; fencing-mask; peak (cap).
**vision-e** *f.* vision, sight, eyesight; fantasy; hallucination. **-a·rio** *adj.*, *n.m.* visionary.
**visir** *m. indecl.* vizi(e)r.
**vi·sit-a** *f.* visit; call; examination, inspection; *biglietto di* —, visiting card; — *doganale*, customs' examination. **-are** [A1 s] *tr.* to visit, to call upon, to frequent; to look at; to examine medically; to inspect; *intr.* (*aux.* avere) to visit, to call on one's neighbours. **-atore** *m.*, **-atrice** *f.* visitor. **-azione** *f.* (eccl.) visitation.
**visivo** *adj.* visual; of sight; *campo* —, field of vision.
**viso** *m.* face; *l'aria del* —, the expression; *a — aperto*, openly; *far buon — a*, to look favourably on; to put a good face on.
**visone** *m.* mink.
**visore** *m.* (microfilm) reader.
**visp-o** *adj.* brisk, lively, sprightly. **-ezza** *f.* liveliness.
**vissuto** *part.* of **vi·vere.**
**vista** *f.* faculty of seeing, sight, view, act of looking; *a — d'occhio*, visibly; spectacle, view, prospect; appearance, likeness; window, opening.
**vistare** [A1] *tr.* to visé (passport).
**vist-o** *part.* of **vedere**; *adj.* seen; *n.m.* visa; authorizing signature. **-osità** *f.* showiness; ostentation. **-oso** *adj.* striking; conspicuous; gaudy, showy; magnificent.
**Vi·stola** *pr.n.f.* (geog.) Vistula.
**visual-e** *adj.* visual; *n.f.* view, prospect. **-izzare** [A1] *tr.* to visualize. **-izzazione** *f.* visualization.
**vit-a** *f.* life; liveliness, animation; lifetime; *condannato a* —, condemned for life; biography; living, livelihood; waist; stature, figure. **-a·ccia** *f. pejor.* wretched life. **-ina** *f. dim.* slender waist.
**vitalba** *f.* (bot.) clematis, traveller's joy.
**vital-e** *adj.* vital, life-giving; essential; important; living, alive. **-ismo** *m.* (philos.; biol.) vitalism. **-ità** *f.* vitality. **-i·zio** *adj.* life-long; *n.m.* life annuity.
**vitamina** *f.* vitamin.
**vit-e**[1] *f.* grapevine. **-ato** *adj.* planted with vines. **-i·ccio** *m.* vine-tendril. **-icoltore** *m.* wine grower. **-icoltura** *f.* vine growing.
**vit-e**[2] *f.* screw; screw thread. **-ino** *m. dim.* small screw.
**vitello** *m.* calf; calf leather; veal.
**viti·colo** *adj.* (of district) vine-growing; viticultural.
**vi·treo** *adj.* vitreous, glassy.
**vi·ttima** *f.* victim; sacrifice.
**vitto** *m.* food; nutrient; — *e alloggio*, board and lodging.
**Vittore** *pr.n.m.* Victor.
**vitto·ri-a**[1] *f.* victory. **-oso** *adj.* victorious; triumphal.
**Vitto·ria**[2] *pr.n.f.* Victoria.
**Vitto·rio** *pr.n.m.* Victor.
**vittrice** *adj.*, *f.* (poet.) victorious.
**vituper-are** [A1 s] *tr.* to vituperate; to execrate; to shame, to disgrace, to blame; *rfl.* to disgrace oneself. **-ando** *adj.* contemptible; worthy of obloquy. **-ativo** *adj.* vituperative. **-azione** *f.* vituperation; shame; disgrace. **-evole** *adj.* blameworthy.
**vitupe·r-io** *m.* vituperation; abuse; reproach; disgrace; *pl.* insults. **-oso** *adj.* vituperous.
**viuzza** *f. dim.* of **via**; lane; alley; narrow street.
**viva** *excl.* hurrah!; hurray!; bravo!; (abbrev. on walls, *etc.*) W, long live...!
**vivacchiare** [A4] *intr.* (*aux.* avere) to be hard up; to live from hand to mouth.
**vivac-e** *adj.* flourishing, thriving, full of life; vivid; (of colour) bright. **-ità** *f.* vitality; intensity; brightness; vivacity, liveliness; keenness; quietness.
**vivaddi·o** *excl.* good heavens, yes!; good lord, no!
**vivagno** *m.* selvedge, selvage; edge, border.
**viva·io** *m.* game-preserve; fish pond; (bot.) nursery.

**vivamẹnte** *adv.* keenly; sharply; deeply; heartily; in a lively manner.

**vivand-a** *f.* food; dish; *pl.* viands. **-iere** *m.* sutler; canteen-keeper. **-iera** *f.* sutler's wife; vivandière.

**viven-te** *adj.* living. **-za** *f.* (admin.) *-za a carico*, dependent relatives.

**vi·vere** [C16] *intr.* (*aux.* essere, vivere) to live; to dwell; to feed, to sustain oneself; to be in existence; to endure; to thrive, to flourish; (typ.) *vive*, stet; *tr.* to lead, to live (a life); *n.m.* life; way of life; living; *pl.* foodstuffs, victuals, provisions.

**vivẹzza** *f.* liveliness; brightness; splendour.

**vi·vido** *adj.* lively, vigorous; thriving; bright, vivid.

**vivificare** [A2 s] *tr.* to vivify; to quicken; to enliven.

**vivi·paro** *adj.* viviparous.

**vivisezịone** *f.* vivisection; *fare la — di*, to vivisect.

**viv-o** *adj.* alive; living; live; thriving, strong; brisk, vigorous; excitable; keen; intense; acute; fresh, bright, pure; *aria -a*, fresh air; *acqua -a*, fresh spring water; *n.m.* living person; living flesh; (fig.) heart, centre; (art) life; *i -i*, the living; *al —*, to the life. **-ucchiare** [A4] see **vivacchiare.**

**vi·zi-o** *m.* bad habit; fault, defect; vice. **-are** [A4] *tr.* to spoil, to over-indulge; to vitiate. **-ato** *part. adj.* spoilt; *bambino -ato*, spoilt child. **-ọso** *adj.* vicious; defective; tainted.

**vizzo** *adj.* faded, withered; flabby.

**voca·bol-o** *m.* word; term. **-a·rio** *m.* dictionary; vocabulary.

**vocal-e** *adj.* vocal; *n.f.* vowel. **-iẓẓare** [A1] *intr.* (*aux.* avere) to vocalize.

**vocativo** *adj.* (gramm.) vocative.

**vocazịone** *f.* vocation, calling; (rel.) call.

**vọc-e** *f.* voice; register; speech; cry (of an animal); noise, sound; tone; vote; rumour; word, term; heading; voice (of verb). **-ẹtta** *f. dim.* little voice. **-iare** [A3] *intr.* (*aux.* avere) to shout, to bawl; to gossip. **-iferare** [A1 s] *intr.* (*aux.* avere) to vociferate. **-ina** *f. dim.* little voice. **-ìo** *m.* (*pl.* **-ii**) constant bawling; shouting. **-iọna** *f.*, **-iọne** *m.* bawler; loud talker.

**voga**[1] *f.* fashion, vogue; mood, disposition; *non sono in — di farlo*, I don't feel in the mood to do it.

**vog-a**[2] *f.* (naut.) rowing; stroke; (fig.) alacrity; *mettersi con — al lavoro*, to set to work with a will. **-are** [A2] *intr.* (*aux.* avere) (naut.) to row. **-ata** *f.* row, rowing. **-atọre** *m.* rower, oarsman.

**vo·gli-a** *f.* (*pl.* **voglie**) wish; craving, longing, desire; will. **-ọso** *adj.* desirous; capricious. **-uzza** *f.* caprice.

**vọi** *pers. pron.* (*2nd pers. pl.*) you.

**volano** *m.* shuttlecock.

**vol-are** [A1 c] *intr.* (*aux.* essere, avere) to fly; to travel by air; to hurry, to move fast. **-ante** *part. adj.* flying; *cervo -ante*, kite; *squadra -ante*, flying squad; *foglio -ante*, fly-sheet; paper kite; *n.m.* (motor.) steering-wheel; flounce, frill. **-ata** *f.* flight. **-a·tile** *adj.* able to fly; winged; volatile, flighty; *n.m.pl.* winged creatures. **-ativo** *adj.* suitable for flying. **-atọre** *m.*, **-atrice** *f.* flyer.

**volatiliẓẓare** [A1] *tr.* to volatilize; *rfl.* to evaporate.

**volent-e** *part.* of **volẹre**; *adj.* willing. **-erọso** *adj.* willing, keen, eager. **-ieri** *adv.* willingly, gladly; with pleasure; *mangio -ieri la carne*, I like meat.

**vol-ẹre** [B36] *tr.* to want; to long for; to will; to like, to wish; to permit; to deserve; to intend; to mean; to wish to see; to require, to need; *-erci*, to be needed, necessary; *-ercene*, to take some doing; *— bene a*, to love; *— dire*, to matter, to mean; *-erla con uno*, to have a grudge against someone; *non —*, to refuse; (as an *aux.* followed by an *infin.*) to be about to; to try to; *vuol piovere*, it looks like rain; *intr.* (*aux.* avere) to will; *n.m.* *il —*, the will.

**volgar-e** *adj.* vulgar; coarse; uneducated; common; low; popular; vernacular; *n.m.* vulgar tongue, vernacular. **-ità** *f.* vulgarity; coarseness. **-iẓẓare** [A1] *tr.* to translate into the vernacular; to popularize.

**vo·lg-ere** [C5] *tr.* to turn; to change; to revolve; to surround, to enwrap; to wind round; to direct; *intr.* (*aux.* essere, avere) (of a road, wheel) to turn; (of time) to roll on, to pass; *— a*, to tend towards, to verge on, to approach; *rfl.* to turn; to revolve; to turn round; to change. **-imẹnto** *m.* turning; change of direction.

**vọl-go** *m.* (*pl.* **-ghi**) crowd, multitude; herd; common people.

**volitare** [A1 s] *intr.* (*aux.* avere) to flit.

**volitivo** *adj.* volitive, volitional; headstrong.

**volizịone** *f.* volition.

**vọlo** *m.* flight; (fig.) speed; *a —*, immediately; in passing.

**volont-à** *f. indecl.* will; willingness; *pl.* wishes. **-a·rio** *adj.* spontaneous; self-willed; intentional; voluntary; *n.m.* (mil.) volunteer; voluntary worker. **-erọso** *adj.* willing, full of good will; eager.

**vọlp-e** *f.* (zool.) fox; fox-fur. **-acchiotto** *m.* young fox. **-a·ia** *f.* fox's den; fox-hole. **-ino** *adj.* vulpine, fox-like; *n.m.* fox-cub. **-ọne** *m.* old fox.

**volt-a**[1] *f.* turn, twist; turning round, flight; turning (of path or road); turning upside-down; *pl.* twistings, turnings; trip, spin; direction; change; alteration; time, occasion; *quante -e ?*, how many times ?; *c'era una —*, once upon a time there was; turn; *a sua —*, in his turn.

**volta**[2] *f.* (archit.) vault.

**volt-a**[3] *m.* (electr.) volt. **-a·ggio** *m.* voltage. **-a·ico** *adj.* voltaic. **-a·metro** *m.* voltameter. **-i·metro** *m.* voltmeter.

**volt-are** [A1] *tr.* to turn; to turn over; to revolve; to roll over; to transfer; to translate; to turn round, to reverse; to turn aside; to change (in character and ideas); *intr.* (*aux.* avere) to turn; to go back; to take a turning; *rfl.* to turn; to turn round; to turn back; to roll; to change; to change one's mind; *-arsi a*, to apply oneself, to turn to. **-ata** *f.* turn; turning, bend; curve; corner; change of direction.

**volteggiare** [A3 c] *intr.* (*aux.* avere) to turn about, to twist about; to shuffle, to wriggle; to wind, to meander; to flit, to flutter; to flap; to hesitate; to vault; *tr.* to navigate; to go round.

**voltẹggio** *m.* turning; vaulting; trick-riding.

**volterrano** *adj.*, *n.m.* (inhabitant) of Volterra.

**volterriano** *adj.* (liter. hist.) Voltairian (also **volteriano**).

**vọlto**[1] *m.* face, countenance; look, expression.

**volto**[2] *part.* of **vo·lgere**; turned; given (to); devoted; *naso — all'insù*, tip-tilted nose; *n.m.* arch, vault.

**voltol-are** [A1 s] *tr.* to roll, to turn over, to roll along; *rfl.* to roll; to roll over; to turn over; to wallow. **-ọni** *adv.* rolling; tumbling.

**volu·bil-e** *adj.* inconstant; unstable; variable; fickle; glib, voluble; rotating, revolving; twisting; (bot.) twining. **-ità** *f.* inconstancy; instability; volubility, rapidity of speech.

**volum-e** *m.* volume; tome; bulk; measurement. **-inọso** *adj.* voluminous, bulky.

**voluta** *f.* (archit.) volute; spiral curve.

**voluto** *part.* of **volẹre**; *adj.* desired; wanted; intentional.

**volutt-à** *f. indecl.* delight; pleasure; voluptuousness; sensual enjoyment. **-ua·rio** *adj.* voluptuary. **-uǫso** *adj.* voluptuous; pleasure-loving.

**vo·mere** *m.* ploughshare.

**vo·mico** *adj.* emetic; vomitory.

**vomit-are** [A1 s] *tr., intr.* (*aux.* avere) to vomit. **-ativo** *adj.* emetic.

**vo·mito** *m.* vomit; vomiting.

**vorac-e** *adj.* voracious; greedy; insatiable; ravenous; devastating. **-ità** *f.* voracity; greed.

**vora·gine** *f.* whirlpool; gulf; abyss; chasm; gorge; hollow.

**vo·rtic-e** *m.* vortex; whirlpool; whirlwind; whirl, whirling. **-ǫso** *adj.* whirling; swirling.

**Vosgi** *pr.n.m.pl.* (geog.) Vosges.

**Vossignori·a** *f.* Your Lordship; Your Ladyship.

**vostr-o** *poss. adj. 2nd pers. pl.* your; *poss. prn.* yours; your property; *i -i*, your people.

**votare**[1] [A1] and derivs. see **vuotare.**

**vot-are**[2] [A1] *tr.* to vote; to pass, to carry; to offer up; to consecrate; *intr.* (*aux.* avere) to vote; *rfl.* to offer oneself, to devote oneself. **-ante** *part. adj.* voting; *n.m., f.* voter. **-aziǫne** *f.* voting; vote.

**votazza** *f.* scoop; ladle; baler.

**votivo** *adj.* votive.

**voto**[1] *m.* vow; prayer, solemn wish, desire.

**voto**[2] *m.* vote; mark; *con pieni voti*, with full marks; (rel.) *ex voto*, votive offering, ex-voto.

**voto**[3] *adj.* (poet.) see **vuoto.**

**vulc-ano**[1] *m.* volcano. **-a·nico** *adj.* volcanic; (fig.) fiery, impetuous.

**Vulcano**[2] *pr.n.m.* (myth.) Vulcan.

**Vulgata** *pr.n.f.* (bibl.) Vulgate.

**vulgo**[1] *m.* see **volgo.**

**vulgo**[2] *Lat. adv.* (joc.) commonly, vulgarly, in vulgar language.

**vulner-are** [A1 s] *tr.* to wound; to hurt; to violate; to offend. **-a·bile** *adj.* vulnerable.

**vuota·ggine** *f.* emptiness.

**vuot-are** [A1] *tr.* to empty; to turn out, to clear out; to evacuate; to rifle; *rfl.* to empty; to empty oneself; to be emptied. **-ata** *f.* emptying; clearing. **-atura** *f.* clearance; evacuation.

**vuotẹzza** *f.* emptiness.

**vuoto** *adj.* empty; hollow; vacant, unoccupied; free; deserted; empty, vain; meaningless; silly, empty-headed, unthinking; *n.m.* empty space; void; vacuum; *lasciare un* —, to leave a gap; empty container.

**W** *m.* (pron. **doppio vu**) the letter W; (written W) monogram for **viva**!; used only in a few foreign words (*e.g.* **watt, chilowatt**).

**X** *m., f.* (pron. **ics**) the letter **X**; *raggi X*, X-rays; used at beginning of a few foreign words.

**xen-ofobi·a** *f.* hatred of foreigners, xenophobia. **-o·fobo** *m.* xenophobe (see also **senofobi·a**).

**xeres** *m.* sherry.

**xilo·fon-o** *m.* (mus.) xylophone. **-ista** *m.* xylophone-player (see also **silofono**).

**xil-ografi·a** *f.* (art of) wood-engraving. **-ogra·fico** *adj.* of wood-engraving. **-o·grafo** *m.* wood-engraver (see also **silografia**).

**xilolite** *f.* wood chipboard, hardboard.

**Y** *f., m.* (pron. **ipsilon** but generally called 'i greco') the letter Y; found in a few foreign words; used also as a mathematical symbol.

**yacht** *m. indecl.* (pron. as English) yacht.

**yoga** *m. indecl. lo* —, yoga.

**yoghurt** *m. indecl. lo* —, yoghurt.

**Z** *f.* (pron. **ẓeta**) the letter Ẓ; the consonant Z.

**ẓabagliọne, ẓabaiọne** *m.* a dessert of egg beaten with sugar and Marsala wine; (fig.) medley.

**za·ccher-a** *f.* splash of mud. **-ọna** *f.*, **-ọne** *m.* slovenly person, slattern; mud-bespattered individual. **-ọso** *adj.* spattered with mud.

**ẓaf, ẓaffe, za·ffete** *excl.* (onom.) swish!

**zaff-are** [A1] *tr.* to plug, to bung, to stop up. **-ata** *f.* whiff (of foul air), stench; angry words; recriminations.

**ẓafferano** *m.* (bot.) saffron.

**ẓaffiro** *m.* sapphire.

**zaffo** *m.* wooden plug, bung; (joc.) little runt.

**ẓaga·glia** *f.* assegai.

**ẓa·ino** *m.* (mil.) knapsack, kit-bag; pack.

**zamp-a** *f.* paw; claw; leg (of an animal, bird, insect); foot (of animal); *-e di maiale*, pigs' trotters; *-e di gallina*, crow's-feet; claw-foot (of a table); (joc.) hand, 'paw'. **-ata** *f.* blow with a paw; kick; hoof-mark, claw-mark, footprint. **-ettare** [A1c] *intr.* (*aux.* avere) to toddle, to trot, to patter.

**zampill-are** [A1] *intr.* (*aux.* essere, avere) to gush forth, to spurt, to squirt; to spring; *tr.* to cause to spurt. **-o** *m.* jet, spurt, gush; fountain.

**zampino** *m. dim.* of **zampa**; (fig.) *mettere lo — in*, to interfere in, to have a finger in.

**zampọgn-a** *f.* (mus.) rustic bagpipe. **-aro** *m.* piper.

**zana** *f.* basket; wicker cradle.

**za·ngol-a** *f.* churn. **-are** [A1 s] *tr., intr.* (*aux.* avere) to churn.

**zann-a** *f.* fang; tusk. **-ata** *f.* bite, savaging; scar from fangs; blow with a tusk.

**ẓanni** *m. indecl.* clown, zany.

**ẓanẓar-a** *f.* (ent.) gnat, mosquito. **-iera** *f.* mosquito-net.

**zapp-a** *f.* mattock; hoe. **-are** [A1] *tr., intr.* (*aux.* avere) to hoe; to dig. **-atọre** *m.* digger; hoer; (mil.) sapper; *Genio degli -atori*, Corps of Sappers.

**zar** *m.* Czar. **-ina** *f.* Czarina.

**ẓara** *f.* hazard, chance.

**za·ttera** *f.* (naut.) raft; lighter.

**ẓavorr-a** *f.* ballast. **-are** [A1] *tr.* to ballast.

**za·zzer-a** *f.* long hair, hair worn shoulder-length. **-uto** *adj.* long-haired.

**ẓeb-ra** *f.* (zool.) zebra. **-ata** *f.* (motor.) zebra-crossing. **-ato** *adj.* striped.

**zẹcca** *f.* mint (for money); *nuovo di* —, brand-new.

**zecchino** *m.* small coin, sequin.

**ẓe·f(f)iro** *m.* zephyr.

**Zeland-a, -ia** *pr.n.f.* (geog.) Zealand; *la Nuova Zelanda*, New Zealand.

**ẓel-o** *m.* zeal; fervour; ardour. **-ante** *adj.* zealous; ardent; conscientious; *n.m.* zealot.

**ẓendado** *m.* (poet.) sendal, light veil.

**ẓenit** *m. indecl.* zenith.

**ẓẹnẓero** *m.* (bot.) ginger.

**ẓeppa** *f.* wedge; bung; (fig.) padding.

**zẹppo** *adj.* full; crammed; packed; *pien* —, bung full.

**ẓerbino**[1] *m.* door-mat.

**ẓerbino**[2] *m.* dandy, coxcomb.

**ẓero** *m.* zero; nought; (fig.) nothing; *uno* —, a mere nothing.

**ẓeta** *m., f.* (*pl. indecl.* or **ẓete**) the letter **z**; *dall'A alla* —, from A to Z.

**Zeus** *pr.n.m.* (myth.) Zeus.

**zi·a** *f.* aunt.

**ẓibaldọne** *m.* medley, miscellany; notebook; commonplace book.

**ẓibellino** *m.* (zool.) sable.

**ẓibẹtto** *m.* (zool.) civet.

**zigano** *m., adj.* Hungarian gipsy, tzigane.
**ẓi·gomo** *m.* cheek-bone.
**ẓigrino** *m.* shagreen.
**ẓigẓag** *m. indecl.* zigzag.
**ẓimarra** *f.* robe; dressing-gown; priest's cassock.
**zi·mbalon** *m. indecl.* (mus.) cimbalon, dulcimer.
**zimbell-o** *m.* bird used as a decoy; (fig.) attraction; lure, bribe; laughing-stock. **-are** [A1] *tr.* to decoy; to lure; *intr.* (*aux.* avere) to flirt; to be alluring.
**zinale** *m.* apron.
**zinc-o** *m.* (chem.; metall.) zinc. **-are** [A2] *tr.* to galvanize. **-ografi·a** *f.* zincography. **-o·grafo** *m.* zincographer; (typ.) block-maker; process engraver. **-otipi·a** *f.* zincotype.
**zi·ngar-o** *m.*, **-a** *f.* gipsy. **-ẹsco** *adj.* (*m.pl.* **-ẹschi**) gipsy; gipsy-like.
**zinna** *f.* nipple.
**zi·nnia** *f.* (bot.) zinnia.
**zinzino** *m.* little bit; pinch; drop, drip; sip; crumb; speck.
**zi·o** *m.* uncle.
**zi·polo** *m.* spigot.
**zirl-are** [A1] *intr.* (*aux.* avere) to trill, to whistle. **-o** *m.* trill, trilling; whistle (of a thrush).
**ẓiro** *m.* pitcher, jar.
**zitell-a** *f.* spinster; unmarried woman. **-ọna** *f.* old maid. **-ọne** *m.* old bachelor.
**zittire** [D2] *intr.* (*aux.* avere) to hiss; to whisper.
**zitto** *adj.* quiet; silent; *star* —, to keep silent; *—!*, hold your tongue; *n.m.* whisper, murmur.
**ẓiẓẓa·nia** *f.* (bot.) darnel; (fig.) discord; dissension.
**zoc·col-o** *m.* clog; sabot, wooden shoe; hoof; clod; sod; turf; (archit.) plinth, socle; skirting-board. **-a·io** *m.* clog-maker. **-ante** *m.* Franciscan friar. **-are** [A1 s] *intr.* (*aux.* avere) to clip-clop, to tramp about in clogs.
**ẓodi·ac-o** *m.* zodiac. *adj.* **-ale** zodiacal.
**ẓọlf-o** *m.* sulphur. **-anello** *m.* lucifer, sulphur-match. **-ara, -atara** *f.* sulphur mine. **-ino** *adj.* sulphurous; sulphur-coloured; *n.m.* sulphur-match; (fig.) spitfire. **-orato** *adj.* sulphurated.
**zoll-a** *f.* clod; sod; turf; glebe. **-ẹtta** *f. dim.* lump of sugar.
**ẓombare** [A1] *tr.* to thump.
**ẓona** *f.* zone; area; belt; girdle; — *delle calme,* doldrums.
**ẓọnẓo** *adv. phr. a* —, here and there; *andare a* —, to wander about, to saunter, to stroll; to loaf, to loiter.
**ẓo·o** *m. indecl.* zoo, zoological gardens.
**ẓo-ologi·a** *f.* zoology. **-olo·gico** *adj.* zoological. **-ologista** *m.* dealer in exotic animals. **-o·logo** *m.* zoologist.
**zoppeggiare** [A3 c] see under **zoppo.**
**zoppic-are** [A2 s] *intr.* (*aux.* avere) to limp; to be lame; to wobble, to be unsteady, to be shaky; (fig.) to vacillate. **-ante** *part. adj.* limping; lame; unsteady; wobbly; hesitant.
**zopp-o** *adj.* lame; limping; unsteady; wobbling, tottering; (of speech) halting, hesitant; weak, ineffectual; *n.m.* cripple. **-a·ggine** *f.* lameness. **-eggiare** [A3 c] *intr.* (*aux.* avere) to limp a bit, to have a slight limp; (fig.) to be rather underhand.
**ẓo·ti-co** *adj.* boorish; rough; loutish. **-ca·ggine, -chẹzza** *f.* boorishness; rusticity; **-cọne** *m.* boor, lout, oaf.
**ẓuavo** *m.* (mil. hist.) zouave.
**zucc-a** *f.* gourd; pumpkin; (slang) head, top-knot, pate. **-ata** *f.* blow on the head; (fig.) *fare alle -ate,* to bang one's head against the wall.
**zu·ccher-o** *m.* sugar. **-are** [A1 s] *tr.* to sugar, to sweeten. **-ato** *part. adj.* sugared; sugary; (fig.) honeyed. **-iera** *f.* sugar-basin. **-iere** *m.* manufacturer of sugar. **-ifi·cio** *m.* sugar-refinery. **-ino** *m.* sweetie; bonbon; (fig.) sweetener; *adj.* sugary. **-ọso** *adj.* full of sugar; sugary.
**zucchino** *m. dim.* of **zucca**; courgette.
**zuccọne** *m. augm.* of **zucca**; large pumpkin; (fig.) stupid person, blockhead.
**zuffa** *f.* scuffle, scrimmage; tussle.
**zu·fol-o** *m.* tin whistle; flageolet; (fig.) spy. **-amẹnto** *m.* whistling; hissing; buzzing. **-are** [A1 s] *intr.* (*aux.* avere) to whistle; to hiss; to whisper; to carry tales. **-ìo** *m.* (*pl.* **-ìi**) incessant whistling, buzzing; tittle-tattle.
**Ẓulù** *m. indecl.* Zulu; *il paese degli* —, Zululand.
**zupp-a** *f.* soup; sop; pap; — *inglese,* tipsy cake, trifle; (fig.) confusion, mess, mix-up. **-are** [A1] *tr.* to dip, to soak; to plunge. **-iera** *f.* soup-tureen. **-o** *adj.* drenched; soaked; wet.
**Zurigo** *pr.n.f.* (geog.) Zürich.
**ẓuẓẓurull-ọna** *f.* romping girl, tomboy. **-ọne** *m.* rollicking fellow.

# ENGLISH-ITALIAN

**A,** a *n.* (first letter of the alphabet) a *f.*; *from A to Z,* dall'a alla zeta; (teleph.) — *for Andrew,* a come Ancona; (mus.) la *m.*

**a,**[1] **an,**[1] *indef. art.* un, uno, *m.*; una, un' *f.*; — *great many,* molti; — *little,* poco, un poco; — *few,* alcuni; *half-an-hour,* una mezz'ora; *to set an example,* dare l'esempio; *to have — big mouth,* aver la bocca grande; *he is — barrister,* è avvocato; *what — pity!,* che peccato!

**a,**[2] **an,**[2] *prep.* ogni, a, al, il; *once — year,* una volta all'anno; *twice an hour,* due volte all'ora.

**aback** *adv.* (naut.) a collo di vele; *to take —,* accollare; (fig.) *to be taken —,* essere colto di sorpresa.

**abacus** *n.* abaco.

**abaft** *adv.* (naut.) a poppa.

**abandon** *n.* abbandono; disinvoltura; trasporto, gioia.

**abandon** *tr.* abbandonare, lasciare; rinunziare a; *rfl. to — oneself to,* darsi a. **-ed** *adj.* abbandonato; *-ed woman,* donna dissoluta. **-ment** *n.* abbandono; rinuncia.

**abase,** *tr.* abbassare, umiliare.

**abash** *tr.* confondere, sconcertare, imbarazzare.

**abate** *tr.* diminuire, ridurre a meno; alleviare; *intr.* diminuire; abbassarsi; abbonacciarsi. **-ment** *n.* diminuzione, riduzione, soppressione; ribasso; *noise -ment,* eliminazione di rumore.

**abattoir** *n.* mattatoio, macello.

**abbess** *n.* badessa.

**abbey** *n.* badia, abbazia.

**abbot** *n.* abate.

**abbreviat-e** *tr.* abbreviare, accorciare. **-ion** *n.* abbreviazione; accorciamento; contrazione.

**ABC** *n.* abbiccì *m.*

**abdicat-e** *intr.* abdicare, rinunziare (al trono); *tr. to — one's rights,* rinunziare ai propri diritti. **-ion** *n.* abdicazione; rinunzia.

**abdom-en** *n.* addome, ventre *m.*; *lower part of the —,* basso ventre. **-inal** *adj.* addominale; *-inal belt,* ventriera.

**abduct** *tr.* rapire; trafugare. **-ion** *n.* ratto, rapimento.

**abeam** *adv.* (naut.) al traverso.

**abed** *adv.* a letto; coricato.

**aberration** *n.* aberrazione; sviamento.

**abet** *tr.* istigare, incitare, incoraggiare; *to aid and —,* farsi complice di.

**abeyance** *n.* sospensione; *in —,* non più in vigore, in sospeso; (leg.) giacente.

**abhor** *tr.* aborrire, detestare. **-rence** *n.* aborrimento; detestazione; ripugnanza; *to hold in -rence,* avere in orrore. **-rent** *adj.* ripugnante, odioso.

**abid-e** *tr.* aspettare; *to — one's time,* aspettare l'occasione; soffrire, sopportare, tolerare; *intr.* dimorare, abitare; *to — by,* mantenere (una promessa), conformarsi (ad una decisione). **-ing** *adj.* durevole, costante; perenne; *law -ing,* ubbidiente alla legge.

**ability** *n.* abilità, capacità; ingegno, talento; *to the best of my —,* come meglio potrò.

**abject** *adj.* abietto, vile; *he made an — apology,* si scusò umilmente; — *poverty,* miseria degradante. **-ness** *n.* abiettezza, viltà.

**abjur-e** *tr.* abiurare; rinnegare, ritrattare; rinunziare a. **-ation** *n.* (eccl.) abiura.

**ablative** *n., adj.* (gramm.) ablativo; — *absolute,* ablativo assoluto.

**ablaze** *adj., adv.* in fiamme; (fig.) — *with anger,* rosso di collera; — *with lights,* che risplende di luci.

**able** *adj.* capace, efficace, abile; *to be — to,* potere; sapere; essere in grado di.

**able-bodied** *adj.* robusto, sano; — *seaman,* marinaio scelto.

**ablution** *n.* abluzione; *to perform one's -s,* fare abluzione.

**abnegation** *n.* abnegazione; sacrificio; (eccl.) abiura.

**abnormal** *adj.* anormale; irregolare. **-ity** *n.* anormalità.

**aboard** *adv.* a bordo; *to go —,* imbarcarsi.

**abode** *n.* abitazione, dimora; domicilio; *to take up one's —,* stabilirsi.

**abolish** *tr.* abolire, sopprimere; annullare.

**abolition** *n.* abolizione, soppressione; annullamento.

**abomin-able** *adj.* abominevole, detestabile; infame. **-ate** *tr.* abominare, detestare. **-ation** *n.* abominazione; infamia; sacrilegio.

**aborigin-al** *n., adj.* aborigeno. **-es** *n.pl.* aborigeni *m.pl.*

**abort** *intr.* abortire; (fig.) fallire. **-ion** *n.* aborto; (fig.) mostro; orrore *m.* **-ive** *adj.* abortivo; (fig.) vano, fallito.

**abound** *intr.* abbondare; *to — in,* abbondare di; *to — with,* essere pieno di, avere in abbondanza. **-ing** *adj.* abbondante, abbondevole; *-ing in,* ricco di.

**about** *adv.* attorno, vicino, circa, pressappoco; *there is no one —,* qui non c'e nessuno; *mind wha you are —!,* fate attenzione!; *turn and turn —,* a vicenda; — *as big as,* grande quasi come; *to be — to,* essere in procinto di; (mil.) — *turn!,* dietro front!; (naut.) *to go —,* virare di bordo.

**about** *prep.* circa, all'incirca, intorno a, riguardo a; *what is it all —?,* di che cosa si tratta?; *a book — history,* un libro sulla storia; *I know nothing — this,* non so niente di questo; — *five o'clock,* verso le cinque; *there's not much to be cheerful —,* c'è poco da stare allegri; *I have no money — me,* non ho denaro con me; *much ado — nothing,* molto rumore per nulla.

**above** *adv.* in alto, in cielo, lassù, di sopra; *from —,* dall'alto; *as —,* come sopra; *the powers —,* le potestà celesti; (iron.) i pezzi grossi; *n. the —,* quanto si è detto sopra.

**above** *prep.* sopra, al di sopra di, soprastante a; — *twenty,* più di venti; — *sea level,* sopra il mare; — *the average,* oltre la mèdia; — *all,* soprattutto, anzitutto; *over and —,* oltre . . . e più; — *reproach,* al di sopra di ogni critica; *to fly —,* sorvolare.

**above-mentioned** *adj.* suddetto, predetto, succitato.

**aboveboard** *adv.* apertamente; *adj.* leale, aperto.

**abrade** *tr.* abradere, scorticare; corrodere, logorare.

**abras-ion** *n.* abrasione; logorìo. **-ive** *n., adj.* abrasivo.

**abreast** *adv.* di fianco; *to come — of,* affiancarsi a; *two —,* a due a due; *to keep — of,* tenersi al corrente di.

**abridg-e** *tr.* abbreviare, accorciare; *-ed edition,* edizione ridotta; **-(e)ment** *n.* sunto, sommario, compendio.

**abroad** *adv.* all'estero; *to live —,* vivere all'estero; *at home and —,* in patria e all'estero; fuori casa; *to venture —,* uscire da casa; *the news got —,* la notizia si diffuse; *there is a rumour —,* corre voce.

**abrog-ate** *tr.* abrogare, revocare. **-ation** *n.* abrogazione, revoca.

**abrupt** *adj.* brusco; *an — answer,* unarisposta recisa; ripido, a picco.

**abscess** *n.* ascesso.

**abscond** *intr.* scappare; rendersi latitante.

**absence** *n.* assenza; — *of taste,* mancanza di gusto; — *of mind,* distrazione; *leave of —,* permesso; — *makes the heart grow fonder,* la lontananza avvicina i cuori; *to be conspicuous by one's —,* farsi desiderare.

**absent** *adj.* assente, lontano; *those —,* gli assenti. **-ee** *n.* assente *m., f.* **-eeism** *n.* assenteismo. **-er** *n.* chi si assenta. **-ly** *adv.* distrattamente.

**abse·nt** *rfl.* assentarsi, allontarsi (da); mancare (a).

**absent-minded** *adj.* distratto; *to be —,* distrarsi. **-ly** *adv.* distrattamente. **-ness** *n.* distrazione.

**absinth(e)** *n.* assenzio.

**absolute** *adj.* assoluto; autoritario; — *government,* governo assolutista; puro; — *nonsense,* niente che sciocchezze; *n.* (*philos.*) *the —,* l'assoluto. **-ly** *adv.* assolutamente; in senso assoluto; *you are -ly right,* hai perfettamente ragione; addirittura; senz'altro.

**absolution** *n.* assoluzione.

**absolut-ism** *n.* assolutismo; dis-

dispotismo. **-ist** *n.*, *adj.* assolutista *m.*, *f.*
**absolve** *tr.* assolvere; liberare da un'imputazione; (theol.; leg.) assolvere.
**absorb** *tr.* assorbire; impegnare; tenere occupato o assorto. **-ed** *part. adj.* assorbito, assorto; *-ed in work*, immerso nel lavoro. **-ent** *adj.* assorbente; *-ent cotton wool*, cotone idrofilo; *n.* assorbente *m.* **-ing** *adj.* interessantissimo, affascinante.
**absorption** *n.* assorbimento.
**abstain** *intr.* astenersi (da); fare a meno (di); non prendere parte alla votazione. **-er** *n.* astemio; chi si astiene, astinente *m.*, *f.*
**abstemious** *adj.* astemio; sobrio; frugale. **-ness** *n.* frugalità; temperanza; sobrietà.
**abstention** *n.* astensione; atto di rinuncia.
**abstinence** *n.* astinenza; rinuncia continuata; (rel.) digiuno.
**ab'stract** *adj.* astratto; non concreto; ottenuto per astrazione; *too —*, che pecca per astrattezza. *n.* astratto; *in the —*, in astratto; estratto, sunto; compendio.
**abstract** *tr.* astrarre; *to — from*, fare astrazione da; staccare; sottrarre, rubare; riassumere. **-ed** *adj.* astratto; distratto. **-ion** *n.* astrazione; idea astratta; sottrazione; furto.
**abstruse** *adj.* astruso; difficilmente comprensibile.
**absurd** *adj.* assurdo; ridicolo; sciocco; *n.* l'assurdo. **-ity** *n.* assurdità; contraddittorietà annullatrice; *the height of -ity*, il colmo dell'assurdità. **-ly** *adv.* in modo assurdo.
**abund-ance** *n.* abbondanza; copia; ricchezza; dovizia. **-ant** *adj.* abbondante; copioso. **-antly** *adv.* abbondantemente; con larghezza; *-antly clear*, chiarissimo, ovvio.
**abus-e** *n.* abuso; eccesso; ingiurie *f.pl.*; linguaggio offensivo, oltraggio. **-ive** *adj.* abusivo; ingiurioso; offensivo.
**abuse** *tr.* abusare; ingiuriare, oltraggiare, insultare; sparlare di; ingannare; malmenare, maltrattare.
**abut** *intr.* confinare (con), sboccare (in); (archit.) appoggiarsi. **-ment** *n.* (archit.) spalla; appoggio; rinfianco.
**abysmal** *adj.* abissale; profondo, insondabile; *— ignorance*, ignoranza abissale.
**abyss** *n.* abisso; voragine *f.*; baratro.
**Abyssinia** *pr. n.* (geog.) Abyssinia. **-n** *adj.*, *n.* abissino.
**acacia** *n.* (bot.) acacia.
**academic(al)** *adj.* accademico; universitario; *n.* accademico; *accademicals*, veste accademica, toga.
**academician** *n.* membro di un'accademia.
**academy** *n.* accademia; scuola; liceo; collegio; *— of music*, conservatorio.
**acanthus** *n.* (bot.) acanto.
**accede** *intr.* accedere; *to — to the throne*, salire al trono; *to — to a request*, aderire ad una richiesta; acconsentire; *to — to a position*, accedere ad una carica.
**acceler-ate** *tr.* accelerare; *intr.* (motor.) aumentare di velocità. **-ation** *n.* accelerazione, acceleramento. **-ator** *m.* acceleratore.
**ac'cent** *n.* accento; tono.
**accent** *tr.* accentuare; mettere in evidenza; (gramm.) accentare.
**accentu-ate** *tr.* (gramm.) accentare. **-ation** *n.* accentuazione; (gramm.) accentatura.
**accept** *tr.* accettare, accogliere, gradire; acconsentire a, approvare; ammettere; riconoscere valido; *to — the inevitable*, inchinarsi davanti all'inevitabile; *-ed term*, frase consacrata. **-able** *adj.* accettabile; gradevole. **-ance** *n.* accettazione; consenso; accoglienza; *to meet with general -ance*, essere approvato da tutti. **-ation** *n.* accettazione. **-or** *n.* accettante *m.*, *f.*; (comm.) *-or for honour*, accettante per intervento.
**access** *n.* accesso; ammissione; abbordo; adito; entrata; *to have free —*, avere l'entrata libera; attacco, accesso, parossismo. **-ible** *adj.* accessibile; abbordabile. **-ibility** *n.* accessibilità.
**accession** *n.* accessione; *— to the throne*, assunzione al trono; aggiunta; *-s to a library*, nuovi acquisti in una biblioteca; *list of -s*, registro d'ingresso.
**accessory** *adj.* accessorio; complementare; *n.* accessorio; *toilet accessories*, articoli da toeletta; (leg.) complice *m.*, *f.*
**accidence** *n.* (gramm.) morfologia.
**accident** *n.* incidente *m.*; infortunio; disastro; disgrazia; *a chapter of -s*, una serie di disgrazie; *street —*, incidente stradale; caso; *quite by —*, per puro caso; *-s will happen*, sono gli incerti della vita. **-al** *adj.* accidentale, fortuito, casuale; accessorio; *n.* (mus.) accidente *m.*, segno accidentale. **-ally** *adv.* per caso; fortuitamente; accidentalmente.
**accident-prone** *adj.* *to be —*, avere una disposizione alle disgrazie.
**acclaim** *tr.* acclamare; applaudire; *n.* applauso; approvazione.
**acclamation** *n.* acclamazione; applauso.
**acclimatiz-e** *tr.* acclimatare, acclimare; *to become -d*, acclimatarsi, acclimarsi. **-ation** *n.* acclimatazione, acclimazione.
**acclivity** *n.* erta; salita.
**accolade** *n.* accollata; (fig.) abbraccio.
**accommodat-e** *tr.* accomodare; adattare; conciliare; agevolare; ospitare; alloggiare; *to — a client*, favorire un cliente; *to — with*, provvedere di. **-ing** *adj.* accomodante; compiacente; servizievole; soccorrevole. **-ion** *n.* accomodamento; accordo; facilitazione, agevolazione; adattamento; compromesso; alloggio, dimora; *the hotel has -ion for a hundred guests*, l'albergo può ospitare cento persone; (comm.) *-ion bill*, cambiale *f.* di comodo.
**accompan-iment** *n.* accompagnamento; (fig.) *to the — of*, fra. **-ist** *n.* (mus.) accompagnatore *m.*, accompagnatrice *f.*
**accompany** *tr.* accompagnare; (fig.) associarsi a; *sickness accompanied by a high temperature*, nausea unita a febbre. **-ing** *adj.* (in letter) accompagnatorio, accluso.
**accomplice** *n.* complice, *m.*, *f.*; (leg.) correo.
**accomplish** *tr.* compiere, adempiere, effettuare, realizzare; eseguire; *to — one's end*, raggiungere lo scopo. **-ed** *adj.* compito, compiuto; finito; *-ed fact*, fatto compiuto; istruito, colto. **-ment** *n.* compimento, adempimento; realizzazione; talento; qualità; compitezza; *of many -ments*, da molte doti.
**accord** *n.* accordo; consenso; *with one —*, di comune accordo; *of one's own —*, spontaneamente, di sua propria volontà; *tr.* accordare; concedere; dare; *intr.* accordarsi, confarsi (con).
**accordance** *n.* conformità; accordo; *in — with*, conforme a, d'accordo con; (comm.) *in — with your instructions*, in base alle Vostre istruzioni.
**according** *adv.*, *compd. prep.* *— to*, secondo, a seconda di; conformemente a; in base a; *— to what he says*, a quanto dice, a detta sua; *— to the newspapers*, i giornali dicono che . . .; *compd. conj.* *— as*, *— to whether*, secondo che a misura che, come. **-ly** *adv.* conformemente, in conformità; *conj.* e perciò, dunque, quindi, in conseguenza, pertanto.
**accordion** *n.* (mus.) accordion *m. indecl.*; fisarmonica.
**accost** *tr.* abbordare per strada; rivolgersi, accostarsi a.
**account** *n.* (finan.) conto; *to have an — at the bank*, avere un conto in banco; *statement of —*, estratto conto; *overdrawn —*, partita scoperta; *on —*, in acconto; *— of expenses*, nota delle spese; *as per — rendered*, come da conto reso; *to balance -s*, sistemare i conti; *keeping of -s*, conteggio; resoconto, relazione, rapporto; *to*

*give an — of oneself*, dare chiarimenti su se stesso, (fig.) dare buona prova di se stesso; *by all -s*, a quanto si dice; *to call someone to —*, chiedere spiegazioni a qualcuno; *on — of*, a causa di; *on one's own —*, per propria iniziativa; *on no —*, nemmeno per sogno; *I did it on your —*, l'ho fatto per te; *to turn to —*, volgere a vantaggio; *people of no —*, gente da poco; *to hold of little —*, tener poco conto di.

**account** *tr.* stimare, considerare; *to — oneself lucky*, considerarsi fortunato; *intr. to — for*, rendere conto di; *to — for certain expenditure*, giustificare certe spese; *I can't — for it*, non so spiegarmelo; *that -s for a great deal*, ciò spiega tante cose; *there is no -ing for tastes*, sui gusti non ci si disputa. **-ability** *n.* responsabilità. **-able** *adj.* responsabile; da attribuirsi.

**account-ancy** *n.* contabilità, ragioneria; computisteria. **-ant** *n.* contabile, ragioniere *m.*; *chartered -ant*, ragioniere diplomato.

**accoutre** *tr.* vestire; arredare; guarnire; equipaggiare. **-ment(s)** *n.* equipaggiamento, guarnimento; (of horse), finimenti *m.pl.*; bardatura.

**accredit** *tr.* accreditare; fornire di credenziali. **-ed** *part. adj.* accreditato, autorizzato, riconosciuto.

**accretion** *n.* accrescimento, aumento; aggiunta.

**accrue** *intr.* accrescere, maturarsi, accumularsi; provenire, derivare; *-d interest*, interessi maturati; ed aggiunti al capitale.

**accumulat-e** *tr.* accumulare; ammassare; *intr.* accumularsi. **-ion** *n.* accumulazione; ammasso, monte *m.*, mucchio; *-ion of capital*, aumento di capitale. **-or** *n.* accumulatore.

**accur-acy** *n.* esattezza, precisione; giustezza. **-ate** *adj.* esatto, preciso; giusto; fedele.

**accursed, accurst** *adj.* maledetto; infame, esecrando.

**accusation** *n.* accusa; incolpazione; incriminazione.

**accusative** *adj.*, *n.* (gramm.) accusativo.

**accus-e** *tr.* accusare; *to — of a crime*, incolpare di un reato. **-ed** *part. adj.* accusato, incolpato; *n. the -ed*, l'accusato, l'imputato, l'incolpato. **-er** *n.* accusatore, accusatrice. **-ing** *adj.* accusante.

**accustom** *tr.* abituare, assuefare, avvezzare; *rfl.* abituarsi. **-ed** *part. adj.* abituato, assuefatto, avvezzo; *to get -ed to*, abituarsi a; *to be -ed*, solere; *the -ed journey*, il solito viaggio.

**ace** *n.* asso; *within an — of*, vicinissimo a, a un pelo da; *he was within an — of being killed*, mancò pochissimo che non fosse ucciso; campione *m*; esperto; *— of trumps*, asso di briscola; *an — up one's sleeve*, un asso nella manica.

**acerbity** *n.* acerbità, acredine *f.*, asprezza.

**acet-ate** *n.* acetato. **-ic** *adj.* acetico.

**acetylene** *n.* acetilene *m.*; *— lamp*, lampada ad acetilene.

**ache** *n.* dolore *m.*, male *m.*; sofferenza; *intr.* dolere; *my head -s*, mi duole la testa, la testa mi fa male; (fig.) *it makes my heart —*, mi fa male al cuore; *to — for*, desiderare ardentemente; bramare.

**achiev-e** *tr.* compiere, ultimare; ottenere, raggiungere; *he will never — anything*, non concluderà mai niente; *to — success*, riuscire, arrivarci, emergere. **-able** *adj.* raggiungibile; fattibile. **-ement** *n.* compimento, raggiungimento, conseguimento; impresa; trionfo; successo; fatto; *pl.* gesta *f.pl.*

**aching** *adj.* doloroso; palpitante; afflitto, accorato; *n.* pena, sofferenza; dolore *m.*

**achromatic** *adj.* acromatico.

**acid** *adj.* acido; (fig.) acerbo, aspro, agro; *n.* acido. **-ity** *n.* acidità, agrezza. **-ulate** *tr.* acidulare.

**acknowledg-e** *tr.* riconoscere; ammettere; accettare; confessare; *to — defeat*, ammettere di essere stato vinto; rispondere a; *to — receipt of*, accusare ricevuta di. **-(e)ment** *n.* riconoscimento; ammissione; (of letter) cenno di ricevuta; ringraziamenti *m.pl.*

**acme** *n.* acme *f.*; colmo, apogeo; *the — of perfection*, il massimo della perfezione.

**acne** *n.* (med.) acne *m.*

**acolyte** *n.* (eccl.) accolito.

**aconite** *n.* (bot.) aconito.

**acorn** *n.* ghianda.

**acoustic** *adj.* acustico; *n. science of -s*, acustica; proprietà acustiche.

**acquaint** *tr.* avvertire, avvisare, informare; *to be -ed with*, conoscere; *to become -ed with*, fare la conoscenza di; *to make oneself -ed with*, mettersi al corrente di, informarsi di. **-ance** *n.* conoscenza; conoscente *m.*, *f.*; *friends and -ances*, amici e conoscenti; *he is an -ance of mine*, è persona di mia conoscenza; *to make the -ance of*, fare la conoscenza di; *I made his -ance in Florence*, l'ho conosciuto a Firenze. **-anceship** *n.* conoscenze *f.pl.*

**acquiesc-e** *intr.* aderire, consentire (a); dichiararsi soddisfatto; sottomettersi. **-ence** *n.* consentimento; acquiescenza, sommissione.

**acquire** *tr.* acquistare, ottenere; conseguire; acquisire; *to — a taste for*, prendere gusto a; *an -d taste*, un gusto acquisito; *to — a language*, imparare una lingua. **-ment** *n.* acquisto; cognizione.

**acquisition** *n.* acquisto; acquisizione; vantaggio, beneficio.

**acquisitive** *adj.* acquisitivo, avido di guadagno. **-ness** *n.* attitudine *f.* ad acquisire; avarizia.

**acquit** *tr.* assolvere, esonerare; (comm.) saldare (debiti); *rfl. to — oneself well*, comportarsi bene, dare buona prova di se stesso. **-tal** *n.* assoluzione; sgravio.

**acre** *n.* acro (= 40.46 are *f.pl.*); *God's —*, campo santo, cimitero. **-age** *n.* quantità di acri.

**acrid** *adj.* acre, pungente; (fig.) mordace, aspro. **-ity** *n.* agrezza; mordacità.

**acrimon-y** *n.* acrimonia; astio. **-ious** *adj.* acrimonioso, astioso.

**acrobat** *n.* saltimbanco, acrobata *m.*, funambolo. **-ic** *adj.* acrobatico; *n.pl.* acrobazie *f.pl.*, acrobatismo.

**across** *adv.* attraverso; di, per traverso; *the distance —*, la distanza in larghezza; *to go —*, traversare; *where did you come — him?*, dove l'hai incontrato?; *to put something —*, riuscire a spuntarla; (crosswords) orizzontali, orizzontalmente.

**across** *prep.* attraverso, dall'altra parte di; al di là di; *— the Channel*, oltre la Manica.

**acrostic** *n.* acrostico.

**act** *n.* atto; decreto; legge *f.*, *— of parliament*, legge del parlamento; azione; gesto; (theatr.) atto; *by — of God*, per causa di forza maggiore; *to catch in the —*, cogliere sul fatto, in flagrante; *in the — of*, sul punto di, nel momento di.

**act** *intr.* agire, fare; comportarsi; *it is time to —*, è ora di agire; *the policeman refused to —*, il poliziotto rifiutò di intervenire; *to — for*, agire per conto di; *to — as*, fare le veci di, fare da, fungere da; *to — upon advice*, seguire un consiglio; *to — up to one's principles*, conformarsi ai propri principi; funzionare, operare; *medicine which -s on the heart*, una medicina che agisce sul cuore; (theatr.) recitare; (fig.) *he is only -ing*, non fa che fingere; *tr.* (theatr.) rappresentare, impersonare; recitare la parte di; *to — the fool*, comportarsi da sciocco; *stop -ing!*, smetti di fare la commedia!

**acting** *part. adj.* facente funzione di, supplente; *— manager*, direttore interinale; *gerund.*, *n.* recitazione; *to go in for —*, essere in arte, fare del teatro.

**action** *n.* azione *f.*; *to take —*, agire; *in my sphere of —*, nel mio ambiente; *to put in —*, far funzionare, iniziare; *out of —*, fuori uso, fuori servizio; *in full —*, in

pieno funzionamento; gesto; gesticolazione; *to suit the — to the word*, adattare il gesto alla parola; (of athlete, horse) movimenti *m.pl.*; (mil.) combattimento, battaglia; *killed in —*, ucciso in combattimento; (theatr.) *the — takes place in . . .*, la scena si volge a . . .; (leg.) processo. **-able** *adj.* (leg.) processabile.

**activate** *tr.* attivare, rendere attivo.

**activ-e** *adj.* attivo, agile, fattivo, operoso, lesto; *to be still —*, essere ancora in piene forze; (gramm.) attivo; (mil.) *on — service*, in servizio attivo. **-ity** *n.* attività, operosità; moto, movimento; agilità.

**actor** *n.* attore, commediante *m.*; comico; *actor-manager*, capocomico.

**actress** *n.* attrice, commediante *f.*

**actual** *adj.* effettivo, reale, vero; *in — fact*, effettivamente. **-ity** *n.* verità, realtà; condizioni reali *f.pl.* **-ly** *adv.* in verità, effettivamente; di fatto; realmente; *do you -ly mean it ?*, lo dite sul serio ?

**actuary** *n.* attuario.

**actuate** *tr.* mettere in moto, attuare, effettuare; spingere; *-d by jealousy*, spinto dalla gelosia.

**acumen** *n.* acume *m.*

**acute** *adj.* acuto, aguzzo; penetrante; perspicace; sottile; vivo, intenso, pungente; *acute-angled*, acutangolo. **-ly** *adv.* acutamente; sottilmente. **-ness** *n.* acutezza; sagacità, perspicacia; penetrazione.

**adage** *n.* adagio, proverbio; massima.

**Adam** *pr.n.* Adamo; *—'s ale*, acqua; *—'s apple*, pomo d'Adamo.

**adamant** *adj.* duro, inflessibile; adamantino. **-ine** *adj.* adamantino; (fig.) inflessibile.

**adapt** *tr.* adattare, accomodare; aggiustare, acconciare; modificare; *rfl.* adattarsi. **-ability** *n.* adattabilità. **-able** *adj.* adattabile. **-ation** *n.* adattamento; (theatr.) riduzione. **-ed** *part. adj.* adattato; adatto, confacente; ridotto. **-er** *n.* riduttore (di opere); (phot.) adattore; (electr.) pezzo di raccordo.

**add** *tr.* aggiungere; addizionare; sommare; unire; *to — up*, far la somma di; *to — to*, aumentare, aggiungere a; *to — two to four*, sommare due a quattro; *to — X to Y*, addizionare Y di X; *-ed to which*, e per giunta; (fig.) *to — two and two together*, capire di che cosa si tratta; *'I'm coming later', he -ed*, 'Vengo più tardi', soggiunse.

**addendum** *n.* aggiunta.

**adder** *n.* vipera.

**ad·dict** *m.* tossicomane *m., f.*; *opium —*, oppiomane *m., f.*

**addict** *tr.* abituare; *to become -ed to*, abituarsi, darsi, abbandonarsi a; *-ed to gambling*, dedito al gioco. **-ion** *n.* dedizione; inclinazione; abitudine *f.*

**addition** *n.* aggiunta; addizione; somma; *in — to*, in aggiunta a, oltre. **-al** *adj.* supplementare; aggiunto; *-al duty*, sopratassa.

**additive** *adj., n.* additivo.

**addle** *intr.* (of eggs) marcire, imputridire; *tr. to — one's brains*, scervellarsi. **-headed, -pated** *adj.* sventato, confuso, confusionario.

**address** *n.* indirizzo; recapito; (leg.) domicilio elettivo; *what is your — ?*, dove abita ?; *sender's —*, l'indirizzo del mittente; *of no fixed —*, senza fissa dimora; discorso; prontezza, speditezza; *to act with —*, agire con destrezza; *to pay one's -es to*, fare la corte a.

**address** *tr.* indirizzare; rivolgere; fare un discorso a; *rfl. to — oneself to*, parlare a; dedicarsi a. **-ee** *n.* destinatario. **-er** *n.* mittente *m., f.*

**adduce** *tr.* addurre, allegare; arrecare, fornire.

**adenoids** *n. pl.* adenoidi *f.pl.*

**adept** *adj.* esperto, abile; *n.* esperto, perito.

**adequ-acy** *n.* adeguatezza. **-ate** *adj.* adeguato; sufficiente; *an -ate result*, un risultato discreto; ragionevole; atto; efficace; **-ately** *adv.* bastevolmente, a sufficienza; adeguatamente.

**adher-e** *intr.* aderire; attaccarsi; attenersi; *to — to a promise*, mantenere una promessa. **-ence** *n.* aderenza. **-ent** *adj.* aderente; *n.* fautore, seguace *m., f.*

**adhes-ion** *n.* adesione. **-ive** *adj.* adesivo; tenace; *-ive paper*, carta gommata; viscoso; *-ive plaster*, cerotto. **-iveness** *n.* tenacità, viscosità.

**adieu** *excl., n.* addio.

**adipos-e** *adj.* adiposo, grasso. **-ity** *n.* adiposità.

**adit** *n.* adito, accesso; entrata.

**adjacent** *adj.* adiacente; contiguo; vicino; limitrofo.

**adjectiv-e** *n.* (gramm.) aggettivo. **-al** *adj.* (gramm.) aggettivale.

**adjoin** *intr.* aggiungere; essere contiguo; *tr.* essere contiguo a, confinare con. **-ing** *adj.* adiacente, contiguo; attiguo; *in the -ing room*, nella camera appresso.

**adjourn** *tr.* aggiornare, rinviare; rimandare; *intr.* aggiornarsi; *to — to the drawing-room*, passare nel salotto. **-ment** *n.* aggiornamento; rinvio.

**adjudge, adjudicat-e** *tr.* aggiudicare. **-ion** *n.* sentenza; giudizio. **-or** *n.* arbitro; membro di giuria.

**adjunct** *n.* aggiunta; (gramm.) complemento.

**adjur-e** *tr.* scongiurare, supplicare. **-ation** *n.* scongiuro; supplica.

**adjust** *tr.* mettere a punto; aggiustare, accomodare, adattare; *to — accounts*, pareggiare i conti; *rfl. to — oneself*, adattarsi. **-able** *adj.* aggiustabile, regolabile; abbassabile; *-able spanner*, chiave *f.* inglese. **-ment** *n.* aggiustamento, adattamento; rettifica.

**adjutant** *n.* (mil.) aiutante *m.* maggiore; (orn.) marabù *m. indecl.*

**administ-er** *tr.* amministrare, governare; fornire; *to — medicine*, somministrare una medicina; *— an oath*, far prestare giuramento. **-ration** *n.* amministrazione; gestione, gerenza; somministrazione. **-rative** *adj.* amministrativo. **-rator** *n.* amministratore; gerente *m., f.*

**admirable** *adj.* ammirabile, ammirevole; mirabile.

**admiral** *n.* ammiraglio; *— of the fleet*, commandante *m.* di squadra; *vice-admiral*, vice-ammiraglio; *rear-admiral*, contrammiraglio. **-ty** *n.* ammiragliato; Ministero della Marina; *First Lord of the -ty*, Ministro della Marina.

**admir-e** *tr.* ammirare. **-ation** *n.* ammirazione; stupore *m.* **-er** *n.* ammiratore, ammiratrice; *to be a great -er of*, essere entusiasta per. **-ing** *adj.* ammirativo. **-ingly** *adv.* con ammirazione, con meraviglia.

**admiss-ible** *adj.* ammissibile; accettabile. **-ion** *n.* ammissione; ricevimento; accesso, entrata, ingresso; confessione; riconoscimento; *ticket of -ion*, biglietto d'ingresso; *-ion free*, entrata libera.

**admit** *tr.* ammettere; lasciar entrare; riconoscere; confessare; concedere; permettere; ricevere; *— bearer*, lasciar entrare; *intr. it -s of no doubt*, è fuori dubbio. **-tance** *n.* entrata; ingresso; *no -tance*, vietato l'ingresso. **-tedly** *adv.* ammesso; *-tedly but . . .*, d'accordo, ma . . ., ammesso e non concesso.

**admixture** *n.* miscela, mescolanza, commistione.

**admon-ish** *tr.* ammonire; riprendere; avvertire; esortare. **-ition** *n.* ammonimento; rimprovero; consiglio; avvertimento; riprensione. **-itory** *adj.* ammonitorio.

**ado** *n.* rumore *m.*; confusione; affaccendamento; *without more —*, senza tante chiacchiere, senz'altro; *much — about nothing*, molto rumore per nulla.

**adolesc-ence** *n.* adolescenza. **-ent** *adj., n.* adolescente *m., f.*

**Adonis** *pr.n.* (myth.) Adone; (fig.) *an —*, un Adone.

**adopt** *tr.* adottare; scegliere; prendere. **-ed** *part. adj.* adottato; *-ed son*, figlio adottivo; *-ed country*, patria adottiva, seconda

patria. -**ion** *n.* adozione; scelta, elezione. -**ive** *adj.* adottivo.
**ador-e** *tr.* adorare; amare appassionatamente; (colloq.) *I — your new hat,* mi piace immensamente il tuo cappello nuovo. -**able** *adj.* adorabile. -**ation** *n.* adorazione. -**er** *n.* adoratore; adorante *m., f.*
**adorn** *tr.* adornare, ornare, abbellire; decorare; guarnire. -**ment** *n.* adornamento, ornamento, abellimento; fregio.
**adrenalin** *n.* (pharm.) adrenalina.
**Adrian** *pr.n.* Adriano.
**Adriatic** *pr.n., adj.* Adriatico.
**Adrienne** *pr.n.* Adriana.
**adrift** *adj., adv.* alla deriva; all'abbandono; *to cut oneself — from,* isolarsi da, staccarsi da; *to be all —,* divagare.
**adroit** *adj.* destro; abile; sagace; svelto. -**ness** *n.* destrezza; sveltezza; accordezza.
**adulat-e** *tr.* adulare. -**ion** *n.* adulazione. -**ory** *adj.* adulatorio.
**adult** *n.* adulto *m.*; adulta *f.*; una persona matura; *adj.* adulto; maturo.
**adulterat-e** *tr.* adulterare; alterare, sofisticare; falsificare; corrompere. -**ion** *n.* adulterazione; sofisticazione; falsificazione; corruzione.
**adulterate** *adj.* adulterato.
**adulter-er** *n.* adultero. -**ess** *n.* adultera. -**ous** *adj.* adultero; colpevole di adulterio. -**y** *n.* adulterio.
**adulterine** *adj.* adulterino; falso.
**adumbrate** *tr.* adombrare; abbozzare; far presagire.
**advance** *n.* avanzamento; movimento in avanti; cammino; progresso; (comm.) aumento; rialzo; *in —,* in anticipo, anticipatamente; *to book in —,* prenotare; *to make the first —,* fare il primo passo; (mil.) avanzata; *— guard,* avanguardia.
**advance** *tr.* avanzare; promuovere; portar innanzi; suggerire; sostenere; (finan.) aumentare; anticipare, prestare; *intr.* avanzarsi; farsi avanti; progredire. -**d** *part. adj.* avanzato; *-d in years,* alquanto attempato; *-d ideas,* idee d'avanguardia. -**ment** *n.* avanzamento; progresso; promozione.
**advantage** *n.* vantaggio; profitto; beneficio; convenienza; *mutual —,* vantaggio reciproco; *to take — of,* trarre profitto di, abusare della bontà di; *to have the — over,* avere la meglio su; *to turn out to the — of,* tornare a vantaggio di; *to turn to —,* trarre vantaggio da; *to show off to —,* far bella figura; (tennis) vantaggio; *— in,* vantaggio alla battuta; *— out,* vantaggio alla rimessa. -**ous** *adj.* vantaggioso; favorevole.
**advantage** *tr.* avvantaggiare; favorire, servire.
**advent** *n.* avvento; apparizione; venuta; (rel.) Avvento.
**adventitious** *adj.* avventizio; fortuito; casuale.
**adventure** *n.* avventura; impresa rischiosa; caso.
**adventur-e** *tr.* avventurare, rischiare; mettere alla ventura; *intr.* avventurarsi; arrischiare di. -**er** *n.* avventurier-o, -e. -**ess** *n.* avventuriera. -**ous** *adj.* avventuroso, ardito; intraprendente; audace.
**adverb** *n.* (gramm.) avverbio; *— of number,* avverbio di quantità. -**ial** *adj.* avverbiale.
**adversary** *n.* avversario; nemico.
**advers-e** *adj.* avverso; contrario; ostile; *— criticism,* critica sfavorevole. -**ity** *n.* avversità; opposizione; *companions in -ity,* compagni di sventura.
**advert** *intr.* alludere, accennare, riferirsi; volgere l'attenzione. -**ence** *n.* avvertenza; riguardo.
**advertis-e** *tr.* annunziare; avvisare; fare della pubblicità a; *to — in a newspaper,* fare un'inserzione sul giornale; (fig.) far conoscere, scoprire; *to — for,* cercare per mezzo della pubblicità. -**ement** *n.* avviso; inserzione; reclame *m.*; affisso; cartellone pubblicitario; *classified -ements,* piccola pubblicità, annunzi economici. -**er** *n.* inserzionista *m., f.*; annunziatore. -**ing** *n.* pubblicità; *-ing agency,* agenzia di pubblicità; *-ing agent,* consulente *m.* per la pubblicità.
**advice** *n.* consiglio; avviso; *to take medical —,* consultare un medico; notizie, comunicazioni *f.pl.*
**advis-e** *tr.* consigliare; raccomandare; suggerire; avvisare; avvertire; (comm.) notificare. -**ability** *n.* opportunità. -**able** *adj.* consigliabile; opportuno. -**edly** *adv.* deliberatamente; prudentemente. -**edness** *n.* saggezza. -**er** *n.* consigliere *m.*; *legal —,* consulente legale *m., f.* -**ory** *adj.* consultivo.
**advoc-ate** *n.* avvocato; difensore, patrocinatore; (fig.) sostenitore. -**acy** *n.* avvocatura; difesa; patrocinio.
**advocate** *tr.* patrocinare, difendere; (fig.) sostenere; suggerire; consigliare.
**advowson** *n.* (leg.; eccl.) collazione di beneficio; patronato; diritto di nomina.
**adze** *n.* ascia.
**Aegean** *adj.* (geog.) egeo; *the — sea,* il Mare Egeo, l'Egeo.
**aegis** *n.* egida.
**Aeolian** *adj.* eolio.
**Aeolic** *adj.* eolico.
**aeon** *n.* ciclo cosmico; (fig.) eternità, epoca di un'immensa durata.
**aerate** *tr.* aerare, arieggiare, ventilare; (chem.) aggiungere acido carbonico a; *-d water,* acqua gassosa; *-d bread,* pane piuma.
**aerial** *adj.* aereo; etereo; *— ropeway,* teleferica.
**aerial** *n.* (radio) antenna; *transmitting —,* antenna di emissione.
**aerie, aery** *n.* nido d'aquila.
**aerodrome** *n.* aerodromo; campo d'aviazione.
**aerodynamic** *adj.* aerodinamico; *n.pl.* aerodinamica.
**aerolite** *n.* aerolito, meteorite *f.*
**aeronaut** *n.* aeronauta *m.* -**ic(al)** *adj.* aeronautico. -**ics** *n.pl.* aeronautica.
**aeroplane** *n.* aeroplano; aereo; velivolo; apparecchio.
**Aesop** *pr.n.* Esopo.
**aesthet-e** *n.* esteta *m.* -**ic(al)** *adj.* estetico. -**icism** *n.* estetismo. -**ics** *n.pl.* estetica; filosofia della bellezza.
**aether** *n.* etere *m.*
**afar** *adv.* (poet.) lontano; lungi; *from —,* da lontano.
**affab-le** *adj.* affabile; cortese. -**ility** *n.* affabilità; cortesia; condiscendenza.
**affair** *n.* affare *m.*; faccenda; impresa; *love —,* relazione amorosa; *that is my —,* è cosa che riguarda soltanto me stesso, è affar mio.
**affect** *tr.* affettare, simulare; fingere; ostentare; darsi arie di. -**ation** *n.* affettazione; simulazione; ricercatezza. -**ed** *part. adj.* affettato; ricercato; insincero.
**affect** *tr.* toccare, riguardare; commuovere; far impressione a; far soffrire; *-ed by a disease,* affetto da una malattia; *that does not — the result,* ciò non cambia il risultato; *he is easily -ed,* è facilmente impressionabile; *those most directly -ed,* quelli maggiormente colpiti. -**ing** *adj.* commovente, emozionante; patetico.
**affection**[1] *n.* affetto; affezione; amore *m.* -**ate** *adj.* affettuoso; affezionato; amorevole.
**affection**[2] *n.* (med.) affezione, malattia.
**affianced** *adj.* fidanzato.
**affidavit** *n.* (leg.) dichiarazione; *to take an —,* deporre con giuramento.
**affiliat-e** *tr.* affiliare, associare; *-d firm,* filiale *f.*; *-d company,* società collegata; *to become -d,* affiliarsi; associarsi. -**ion** *n.* affiliazione; adozione.
**affinity** *n.* affinità; parentela; somiglianza.
**affirm** *tr.* affermare, confermare; dichiarare positivamente; (leg.) ratificare; deporre. -**ation** *n.* affermazione; conferma; dichiarazione solenne; ratifica.
**affirmative** *adj.* affermativo; (math.) positivo; *n.* affermativa; *to answer in the —,* rispondere affermativamente.
**affix** *tr.* apporre, attaccare; affiggere.

**af·fix** *n.* (gramm.) affisso; particella.
**afflict** *tr.* affliggere, tormentare; angosciare. **-ed** *part. adj.* afflitto; sofferente; ammalato. **-ion** *n.* afflizione; calamità; *the -ions of old age,* gli acciacchi della vecchiaia; (fig.) disperazione.
**affluence** *n.* affluenza, ricchezza; opulenza; abbondanza.
**affluent** *adj.* ricco, opulento; *— society,* società ad alto tenore di vita; *to be in — circumstances,* stare nell'opulenza.
**affluent** *n.* (geog.) affluente *m.*
**afford** *tr.* offrire, fornire, dare; provvedere; *it will — me an opportunity,* mi darà un'occasione; *I can — to wait,* posso permettermi di aspettare; *to — to buy,* avere i mezzi per comprare.
**afforest** *tr.* imboschire. **-ation** *n.* rimboschimento.
**affranchise** *tr.* liberare; affrancare.
**affray** *n.* rissa; tafferuglio; mischia; avvisaglia.
**affreightment** *n.* trasporto per mare.
**affront** *n.* affronto, insulto; offesa; *to take — at,* offendersi per; *tr.* insultare, offendere; affrontare.
**Afghan** *adj., n.* (geog.) afghano. **-istan** *pr.n.* (geog.) Afghanistan.
**afield** *adv.* nei campi; *far —,* molto lontano.
**afire** *adv.* in fiamme; (fig.) *to be — with the desire to,* bruciare dal desiderio di.
**aflame** *adv.* in fiamme; *adj.* infiammato; (fig.) *to be — with colour,* brillare di vivi colori.
**afloat** *adj., adv.* a galla, galleggiante, in mare; *to keep —,* stare a galla; (fig.) in corso, in circolazione; in piedi.
**afoot** *adv.* a piedi; (fig.) in atto; in moto; *something is —,* qualche progetto sta combinandosi; *what's — ?,* che cosa accade?
**afore-mentioned** *adj.* soprannominato.
**afore-said** *adj.* suddetto, predetto.
**afraid** *adj.* spaventato, impaurito; timoroso; *to be —,* aver paura, temere; *I am — I cannot help you,* sono spiacente di non potervi aiutare; *don't be —,* non abbia paura.
**afresh** *adv.* di nuovo; da capo; nuovamente; *to start —,* ricominciare.
**Africa** *pr.n.* (geog.) Africa. **-n** *adj., n.* africano.
**aft** *adv.* (naut.) a poppa; *fore and —,* da prora a poppa.
**after** *adj.* seguente, successivo; *— years,* anni successivi; (naut.) poppiero, di poppa; *— hold,* stiva di poppa; *adv.* dopo, poi, in seguito; *the day —,* il giorno dopo; *prep.* dopo, in seguito a; *— that,* poi; *— all,* dopo tutto, insomma; *the day — tomorrow,* dopo domani; *day — day,* di giorno in giorno; *— you, sir,* prego, dopo di Lei; *what is he —* q., che cosa sta cercando?; *to go —,* andar dietro; *— the French manner,* alla francese; *to call a child — its mother* dare a una bambina il nome della mamma; *to take —,* ritrarre da, rassomigliare; *to look —,* attendere a; *conj.* dopo che, poichè.
**afterbirth** *n.* placenta.
**after-effect** *n.* seguito; conseguenza.
**afterglow** *n.* bagliore dopo il tramonto; (fig.) gioia che perdura.
**after-life** *n.* vita futura; *in —,* più tardi nella vita.
**aftermath** *n.* (agric.) secondo taglio; (fig.) ripercussioni, conseguenze *f.pl.*; seguito.
**aftermost** *adj* ultimo, in coda.
**afternoon** *n.* pomeriggio, dopopranzo; *good — !,* buon giorno!, buona sera!; (fig.) meriggio; *attrib.* pomeridiano, del pomeriggio; (theatr.) *— performance,* spettacolo diurno.
**after-taste** *n.* sapore *m.* che ritorna a gola. **-thought** *n.* secondo pensiero, ripensamento.
**afterwards** *adv.* dopo, poi, in seguito; più tardi.
**again** *adv.* di nuovo, ancora, in più; un'altra volta; *— and —,* molte volte, ripetutamente; *once —,* ancora una volta; *never —,* mai più; *now and —,* ogni tanto; *as much —,* due volte tanto; *as many —,* altrettanti; (fam.) *what, — ?,* o che si ricomincia?
**against** *prep.* contro; contrario a; vicino, presso; *over —,* di fronte a; *to run up —,* imbattersi in; *to go — the grain,* non andare a genio; *— one's will,* a malincuore; *— the light,* controluce; *to lean —,* appoggiarsi a.
**agape** *adv.* a bocca aperta; *with eyes —,* cogli occhi spalancati.
**a·gape** *n.* (rel. hist.) agape *f.*
**agate** *n.* agata.
**age** *n.* età; *what is your — ?,* che età avete?, quanti anni avete?; *under —,* minorenne; *to come of —,* diventar maggiorenne; *old —,* vecchiaia; *middle —,* mezza età; *he does not look his —,* non dimostra i suoi anni; *he is of the same — as I am,* è un mio coetaneo; periodo, epoca; *in our —,* ai tempi nostri; (colloq.) *it's -s since I saw you,* è un secolo che non ti vedo; *the Middle Ages,* il Medio Evo. **-d** *adj.* della età di; *a little girl -d six,* una bambina che ha sei anni. **-less** *adj.* sempre giovane; di età indefinibile; eterno. **-long** *adj.* perenne, sempiterno.
**age** *intr.* invecchiare. **-d** *adj.* vecchio; attempato; *n.pl. the -d,* i vecchi.
**agency** *n.* azione, effetto; influenza; mediazione; *by the — of,* per intervento di; (comm.) agenzia; rappresentanza; *sole —,* rappresentanza esclusiva; *government —,* organizzazione parastatale; *employment —,* ufficio di collocamento; *news —,* agenzia d'informazioni.
**agenda** *n.* ordine *m.* del giorno.
**agent** *n.* agente *m.*; fiduciario; *to be a free —,* agire secondo la propria volontà; (comm.) agente, rappresentante *m.*; *forwarding —,* spedizioniere *m.*; *estate —,* mediatore.
**agglomerat-e** *intr.* agglomerarsi; raccogliersi. **-ion** *n.* agglomerazione.
**aggrandize** *tr.* ingrandire; ampliare; esagerare.
**aggravat-e** *tr.* aggravare, accrescere; irritare; seccare; esasperare. **-ing** *adj.* aggravante; irritante; *-ing child,* bambino insopportabile. **-ion** *n.* aggravamento; esasperazione, irritazione.
**aggregate** *n.* aggregato; *in the —,* collettivamente, in massa, nell'insieme; *adj.* aggregato; globale.
**aggregate** *tr.* aggregare, unire; *intr.* ammontare, elevarsi.
**aggress-ion** *n.* aggressione. **-ive** *adj.* aggressivo, offensivo; *-ive spirit,* aggressività; *to take the -ive,* prendere l'offensiva. **-iveness** *n.* aggressività. **-or** *n.* aggressore; *the -or nation,* la nazione aggreditrice.
**aggrieve** *tr.* affliggere, addolorare; *-d party,* parte lesa.
**aghast** *adj.* atterrito; stupefatto; sbigottito; esterrefatto.
**agil-e** *adj.* agile, svelto; snello; destro. **-ity** *n.* agilità, sveltezza; destrezza; elasticità.
**agitat-e** *tr.* agitare, scuotere; turbare; *to — for,* promuovere una campagna in favore di. **-ed** *part. adj.* agitato, turbato; commosso, emozionato. **-ing** *adj.* turbante; commovente, emozionante. **-ion** *n.* agitazione; turbamento; commozione; campagna. **-or** *n.* agitatore.
**aglow** *adj.* ardente, risplendente, raggiante.
**agnate** *adj.* (leg.) agnatico; *n.* agnato.
**Agnes** *pr.n.* Agnese.
**agnostic** *adj., n.* agnostico. **-ism** *n.* agnosticismo.
**ago** *adv.* fa, or sono; *three days —,* tre giorni or sono; *how long — ?,* quanto tempo fa?; *long —,* molto tempo fa.
**agog** *adj.* smanioso; in ansiosa attesa; *to be all — to,* bramare di.
**agoniz-e** *tr.* tormentare, cruciare; far soffrire; *intr.* tormentarsi, soffrire. **-ing** *adj.* straziante; angoscioso.
**agony** *n.* angoscia, strazio; *to be in —,* soffrire dolori atroci; *death —,* agonia.
**agrarian** *adj.* agrario, agricolo.
**agree** *intr.* accordarsi, andare d'accordo, convenire; *to — to a*

*proposal*, acconsentire a una proposta; *unless otherwise -d*, salvo caso contrario; *to — to differ*, rimanere di comune accordo ciascuno della propria opinione; *wine does not — with me*, il vino mi fa male; *tr.* concordare. **-able** *adj.* gradevole, favorevole, piacevole; simpatico; *I am -able*, per me va bene; conforme, compatibile. **-ableness** *n.* piacevolezza; amabilità. **-ably** *adv.* piacevolmente; gradevolmente; *-ably to*, conformemente a. **-d** *adj.*, *adv.* d'accordo; inteso, convenuto. **-ment** *n.* accordo, patto; intesa; convenzione; contratto; *as per -ment*, come convenuto; *by mutual -ment*, di comune accordo; *to come to an -ment*, venire ad un accordo; *gentleman's -ment*, patto d'onore.

**agricultur-e** *n.* agricoltura, agraria. **-al** *adj.* agricolo; *-al engineer*, agronomo.

**agronom-ist** *n.* agronomo. **-y** *n.* agronomia.

**aground** *adj.* arenato, incagliato; *adv.* in secco; *to run —*, arenarsi, incagliarsi.

**ague** *n.* febbre malarica.

**ah** *excl.* ah!; deh!; ahimè!; ahì!

**ahead** *adv.* avanti, in avanti; in testa; *to get —*, farsi avanti; *full speed —*, avanti a tutta forza; *go —!*, faccia pure!; avanti!; *— of*, più avanti di; *to get — of*, superare; *to go straight —*, tirare diritto.

**aid** *n.* aiuto, soccorso, sussidio; *first —*, pronto soccorso; *in — of*, a favore di; *tr.* aiutare, soccorrere, assistere; contribuire a.

**aide-de-camp** *n.* (mil.) aiutante *m.* di campo.

**ail** *tr.* affliggere, far soffrire; *what -s you?*, che cosa hai?; *intr.* sentirsi male. **-ing** *adj.* sofferente; (poet.) egro. **-ment** *n.* indisposizione, disturbo; malattia.

**aim** *n.* mira; *to take —*, mirare; (fig.) scopo; intento; *with the — of*, allo scopo di. **-less** *adj.* senza scopo; inutile. **-lessness** *n.* mancanza di scopo.

**aim** *tr.* puntare; *to — a stone at*, lanciare una pietra contro; *intr.* mirare, prendere la mira; *to — at*, prendere di mira; (fig.) aspirare.

**air** *n.* aria; atmosfera; brezza, venticello; *in the open —*, all'aria aperta; *to live on —*, campare d'aria; *to walk on —*, essere pazzo di gioia; *to be on the —*, parlare per radio; *to vanish into thin —*, scomparire, volatilizzarsi; *Air Force*, aviazione militare; *Air Ministry*, Ministero dell'Aeronautica; *attrib.* aereo; (fig.) aspetto, apparenza, contegno; sembianza; *to give oneself -s*, darsi delle arie; (mus.) aria, melodia; *tr.* arieggiare, ventilare; mettere all'aria. **-borne** *adj.* aerotrasportato; *to become -borne*, decollare. **-craft** *n.* aereo; velivolo; *-craft carrier*, portaerei *m. indecl.*; *jet -craft*, aviogetto. **-craftsman** *n.* aviere *m.* **-field** *n.* campo d'aviazione. **-less** *adj.* senz'aria, senza vento. **-mail** *n.* posta aerea. **-man** *n.* aviatore; (rank) aviere *m.* **-port** *n.* aeroporto. **-tight** *adj.* ermetico. **-woman** *n.* aviatrice.

**air-conditioning** *n.* condizionamento d'aria; aria condizionata. **-gun** *n.* fucile ad aria compressa. **-hole** *n.* spiraglio. **-lift** *n.* ponte aereo. **-line** *n.* aviolinea. **-lock** *n.* inceppamento d'aria. **-pocket** *n.* vuoto d'aria. **-raid** *n.* incursione aerea; *-raid shelter*, rifugio contraereo. **-shaft** *n.* pozzo di ventilazione. **-sickness** *n.* mal d'aria.

**air-y** *adj.* arioso, arieggiato; elevato; (fig.) gaio, gioioso; noncurante, disinvolto. **-ily** *adv.* agilmente; con disinvoltura. **-iness** *n.* aerazione; (fig.) disinvoltura.

**aisle** *n.* navata; corridoio; *side —*, laterale *f.*

**aitch** *n.* acca; *to drop one's -es*, non aspirare l'acca.

**ajar** *adj.* socchiuso; *the door is —*, la porta sta socchiusa.

**akimbo** *adv.* *with arms —*, con le mani ai fianchi e i gomiti fuori, con le mani alle anche.

**akin** *adj.* consanguineo, parente; (fig.) simile, affine.

**alabaster** *n.* alabastro; *adj.* alabastrino.

**alacrity** *n.* alacrità.

**alarm** *n.* allarme *m.*; avvertimento; *to give the —*, dare l'allarme; spavento, paura; *to take —*, allarmarsi; *— bell*, campana martello, campanello d'allarme; *tr.* allarmare; spaventare. **-ing** *adj.* allarmante; impressionante; spaventevole. **-ist** *n.* allarmista *m., f.*

**alarm-clock** *n.*, **alarum** *n.* sveglia.

**alas** *excl.* purtroppo!; ahimè!

**alb** *n.* (liturg.) camice *m.*

**albatross** *n.* albatro.

**albeit** *conj.* quantunque.

**albin-o** *n.*, *adj.* albino. **-ism** *n.* albinismo.

**album** *n.* album, albo.

**album-en** *n.* albume *f.* **-in** *n.* albumina.

**alchem-y** *n.* alchimia. **-ist** *n.* alchimista *m.*

**alcohol** *n.* alcool *m.* **-ic** *adj.* alcoolico; *n.* alcoolizzato. **-ism** *n.* alcoolismo. **-ize** *tr.* alcoolizzare.

**alcove** *n.* alcova; nicchia.

**alder** *n.* (bot.) ontano.

**alderman** *n.* consigliere *m.* municipale, anziano.

**ale** *n.* birra; *brown —*, birra scura; *pale, light —*, birra chiara, bionda.

**alert** *adj.* vigilante, attento, svelto; *n.* allarme *m.*; *to be on the —*, stare all'erta; *tr.* avvertire. **-ness** *n.* vigilanza; sveltezza.

**Alexandr-ia** *pr.n.* (geog.) Alessandria d'Egitto. **-ian, -ine** *adj.*, *n.* alessandrino.

**alfresco** *adj.*, *adv.* all'aria aperta, al fresco; arioso.

**algebr-a** *n.* algebra. **-aic(al)** *adj.* algebrico.

**Algeria** *pr.n.* (geog.) Algeria. **-n** *adj.*, *n.* Algerino.

**Algiers** *pr.n.* (geog.) Algeri *m.*

**alias** *adv.* altrimenti detto; *n.* pseudonimo, falso nome.

**alibi** *n.* alibi *m. indecl.*

**alien** *adj.* estraneo; straniero; forestiero; alieno, contrario; *n.* straniero, forestiere *m.*

**alienable** *adj.* alienabile.

**alienat-e** *tr.* alienare; (fig.) allontanare, estraniare; distaccare. **-ion** *n.* alienazione.

**alienist** *n.* alienista *m., f.*

**alight**[1] *adj.* acceso, illuminato; *to get the fire —*, accendere il fuoco.

**alight**[2] *intr.* scendere; (of birds) posarsi; (of aeroplanes) atterrare, (on water) ammarare.

**align** *tr.* allineare. **-ment** *n.* allineamento.

**alike** *adj.* simile, somigliante; pari, uguale; *to be —*, assomigliarsi; *no two are —*, non vi sono due uguali; *adv.* del pari, allo stesso modo.

**aliment** *n.* alimento, cibo. **-ary** *adj.* alimentario; nutritivo. **-ation** *n.* alimentazione; nutrizione.

**alimony** *n.* alimonia, pensione alimentaria, assegnamento alimentario.

**alive** *adj.* vivo, vivente, in vita; vitale; al mondo; *any man —*, chiunque; *no man —*, nessuno al mondo; vivace, sveglio, attivo; *look —*, muòviti; *to be — with*, brulicare di; (fig.) *— to*, sensibile a.

**alkal-i** *m.* (chem.) alcali *m. indecl.*; prodotto alcalino. **-ine** *adj.* (chem.) alcalino. **-oid** *n.* alcaloide *m.*

**all** *adj.* tutto; *— the time*, tutto il tempo; *— the way*, per tutta la strada, fino in fondo; *for — his faults*, malgrado i suoi difetti; *on — fours*, a carponi; *not at —*, affatto, non c'è di che; *nothing at —*, niente; *once and for —*, una volta per sempre; *All Saints*, Ognissanti; *All Souls' Day*, il giorno dei morti.

**all** *adv.* completamente, interamente; *it's — over*, è finito; *— over the place*, dappertutto; *— right*, va bene, benissimo; *to be all right*, star bene; *once for —*, una volta per sempre; *— at once*, tutto a un tratto; *he is not — there*, gli manca una rotella; *— the better*, tanto meglio; *— the same*, con tutto ciò.

**all** *n.* *one's —*, tutto il proprio avere; *pl.* tutti; *— who*, tutti quelli

che, quanti; — *but one*, tutti meno uno.
**allay** *tr.* calmare, lenire; (fig.) dissipare.
**alleg-e** *tr.* asserire, dichiarare; *-d*. cosìddetto, sedicente. **-ation** *n.* asserzione, allegazione.
**allegiance** *n.* fedeltà, ubbidienza (al sovrano); lealtà; *oath of* —, giuramento di fedeltà.
**allegor-y** *n.* allegoria. **-ic(al)** *adj.* allegorico.
**allerg-y** *n.* allergia. **-ic** *adj.* allergico.
**alleviat-e** *tr.* alleviare, lenire; attenuare. **-ion** *n.* alleviamento, lenimento.
**alley** *n.* vicolo, vicoletto; piccolo viale; *blind* —, vicolo cieco.
**alliance** *n.* alleanza; *to enter into an — with*, allearsi con; unione; matrimonio.
**alligator** *n.* (zool.) alligatore *m.*
**alliteration** *n.* allitterazione.
**allocat-e** *tr.* assegnare, distribuire; collocare. **-ion** *n.* assegnazione, distribuzione; assegnamento; stanziamento; collocamento.
**allocution** *n.* allocuzione.
**allot** *tr.* assegnare; distribuire, spartire; devolvere. **-ment** *n.* assegnazione; parte assegnata; pezzo di terreno, lotto.
**allow** *tr.* permettere; autorizzare; concedere, ammettere; lasciare; *no smoking -ed*, vietato fumare; — *me*, permetta; *to — for*, tener conto di. **-able** *adj.* permesso, lecito, ammissibile. **-ance** *n.* indennità; assegno; supplemento; *family -ance*, assegni familiari; *free -ance of luggage*, franchigia di bagaglio; *monthly -ance*, mesata, tanto al mese; *to make -ance for*, tenere in debito conto; *to be put on -ance*, essere messo a razione.
**al·loy** *n.* lega.
**alloy** *tr.* legare, amalgamare; (fig.) alterare.
**all-powerful** *adj.* onnipotente. **-round** *adj.* compiuto, perfetto; con molte doti.
**allspice** *n.* pimento.
**allude** *intr.* alludere, riferirsi (a).
**allur-e** *n.* attrattiva; fascino; *tr.* allettare; adescare; sedurre; attrarre. **-ement** *n.* allettamento; fascino; richiamo. **-ing** *adj.* allettante; affascinante; seducente.
**allus-ion** *n.* allusione, riferimento. **-ive** *adj.* allusivo.
**alluv-ion, -ium** *n.* alluvione *f.* **-ial** *adj.* alluvionale; *-ial soil*, ricolmo.
**al·ly** *n.* alleato; *to become allies*, allearsi.
**ally** *tr.* alleare; collegare; congiungere; unire; imparentare; *intr.* allearsi.
**almanac** *n.* almanacco; lunario; calendario.
**almight-y** *adj.*, *n.* onnipotente; *the Almighty*, l'Onnipotente. **-iness** *n.* onnipotenza.
**almond** *n.* mandorla; — *eyes*, occhi a mandorla; *almond-tree*, mandorlo.
**almoner** *n.* elemosiniere *m.*; *woman* —, elemosiniera.
**almost** *adv.* quasi; pressochè, press'a poco; poco meno che; circa; vicino a.
**alms** *n.* elemosina, limosina; carità; *to give* —, fare la carità.
**alms-house** *n.* ospizio di carità, ospizio dei poveri.
**aloe** *n.* (bot.) aloe *m.*; *American* —, agave *m.*; *pl.* succo d'aloe.
**aloft** *adv.* in alto; lassù; (naut.) sopra.
**alone** *adj.* solo, solitario, solingo; *all* —, solo soletto; *to let* —, lasciar tranquillo; non toccare; *adv.* solo, da solo; soltanto, solamente.
**along** *prep.* lungo; — *the shore*, lungo la spiaggia; *all — the road*, per tutta la strada; — *with*, in compagnia di, assieme a; *adv.* *come* —, andiamo; *move* —*!*, avanti!, movetevi!; *I knew that all* —, l'ho sempre saputo; *to get* —, fare progressi; *they get — well*, vanno molto d'accordo; *he will be — soon*, verrà fra poco. **-side** *prep.* accanto a; (naut.) a fianco di; *adv.* sottobordo; *to come -side*, accostarsi.
**aloof** *adj.* freddo, riservato; indifferente; *adv.* in disparte (da); *to keep* —, stare a distanza; *to stand* —, starsene da banda. **-ness** *n.* freddezza; indifferenza.
**aloud** *adv.* ad alta voce; forte.
**alpaca** *n.* alpaca *m.*
**alpha** *n.* alfa *m.*
**alphabet** *n.* alfabeto; abbiccì *m.* **-ic(al)** *adj.* alfabetico.
**alpin-e** *adj.* alpino, alpestre; — *climbing*, alpinismo; — *troops*, Alpini *m.pl.* **-ist** *n.* alpinista *m.*, *f.*
**Alps** *pr.n.pl.* (geog.) *the* —, le Alpi.
**already** *adv.* già, di già; — *done*, bell'e fatto.
**Alsace** *pr.n.* (geog.) Alsazia.
**Alsatian** *adj.*, *n.* (geog.) alsaziano; (dog) cane-lupo.
**also** *adv.* anche, pure; inoltre; altresì; parimenti.
**altar** *n.* altare *m.*; *high* —, altare maggiore; — *cloth*, paliotto, tovaglia da altare; — *piece*, pala d'altare.
**alter** *tr.* alterare, cambiare, mutare; correggere, ritoccare; *to — one's mind*, cambiare idea; *to — the date of*, trasferire, rimandare; *intr.* alterarsi, cambiarsi, mutarsi. **-ation** *n.* alterazione; cambio, cambiamento; modifica; ritocco.
**altercat-e** *intr.* altercare, litigare. **-ion** *n.* alterco; battibecco; diverbio; contesa.
**alter·nate** *adj.* alterno, alternativo; *on — days*, ogni due giorni. **-ly** *adv.* alternativamente; a turno.
**alternat-e** *tr.* alternare; *intr.* alternarsi; succedersi. **-ing** *adj.* alternante; alternato. **-ion** *n.* alternazione; successione reciproca; avvicendamento; vicissitudine *f.*
**alternative** *n.* alternativa; *adj.* alternativo; scambievole; vicendevole.
**although** *conj.* benchè, sebbene; quantunque; ancorchè; malgrado che.
**altimeter** *n.* (aeron.) altimetro.
**altitude** *n.* altezza; altitudine *f.*; (aeron.) quota.
**alto** *n.* (mus.) alto *m.*; — *clef*, chiave *f.* di do.
**altogether** *adv.* interamente, complessivamente, in tutto, nell'insieme; tutt'insieme; *he is — right*, egli ha perfettamente ragione.
**altru-ism** *n.* altruismo. **-ist** *n.* altruista *m.*, *f.* **-istic** *adj.* altruistico.
**alum** *n.* allume *m.*
**aluminium** *n.* alluminio.
**always** *adv.* sempre; continuamente; *for* —, per sempre.
**amalgam** *n.* amalgama *m.* **-ate** *tr.* amalgamare, unire; *intr.* amalgamarsi, fondersi, unirsi. **-ation** *n.* amalgamazione, fusione *f.*
**amanuensis** *n.* amanuense *m.*, copista *m.*; segretario.
**amass** *tr.* ammassare, accumulare; adunare.
**amateur** *n.* dilettante *m.*, *f.*; *attrib.* — *dramatic society*, filodrammatica; — *status*, qualità di dilettante. **-ish** *adj.* da dilettante, dilettantesco. **-ism** *n.* dilettantismo.
**amatory** *adj.* d'amore, amoroso, erotico.
**amaz-e** *tr.* stupire, sbalordire; *to stand -d*, stupirsi, rimanere di stucco. **-ing** *adj.* sorprendente; meraviglioso. **-ement** *n.* stupore *m.*; meraviglia.
**Amazon** *n.* amazzone *f.*; (geog.) *the — (river)*, il fiume delle Amazzoni.
**ambassad-or** *n.* ambasciatore. **-ress** *n.* (wife of ambassador) ambasciatrice.
**amber** *n.* ambra. **-gris** *n.* ambra grigia.
**ambidext(e)rous** *adj.* ambidestro.
**ambigu-ous** *adj.* ambiguo, equivoco. **-ity** *n.* ambiguità.
**ambit** *n.* ambito; limiti *m.pl.*
**ambit-ion** *n.* ambizione. **-ious** *adj.* ambizioso; pretenzioso.
**amble** *n.* ambio, ambiatura; *intr.* ambiare, andare all'ambio; (fig.) andare adagio.
**ambrosi-a** *n.* ambrosia. **-al** *adj.* ambrosiale.
**ambulance** *n.* ambulanza; lettiga.
**ambulatory** *adj.*, *n.* ambulatorio.

**ambuscade** *n.* imboscata.
**ambush** *n.* imboscata; agguato; tranello; *to lie in —*, stare in agguato; *tr.* tendere un agguato per.
**ameer** *n.* emiro.
**ameliorat-e** *tr.* migliorare. **-ion** *n.* miglioramento.
**amen** *excl.* così sia; *n.* amen.
**amenable** *adj.* suscettibile, docile; soggetto; sottomesso; *— to reason*, ragionevole; *— to a fine*, possibile di multa.
**amend** *tr.* emendare, correggere, rettificare; *intr.* emendarsi; riformarsi. **-ment** *n.* emendamento, rettifica. **-s** *n.pl.* ammenda; riparazione; compenso; *to make -s (for)*, fare riparazione, risarcire.
**amenity** *n.* amenità; *pl.* bellezze, comodità.
**America** *pr.n.* (geog.) America. **-n** *adj., n.* americano; *-n cloth*, tela cerata.
**amethyst** *n.* ametista; *adj.* ametistino.
**amiab-le** *adj.* amabile, gentile. **-ly** *adv.* gentilmente. **-ility** *n.* amabilità, gentilezza.
**amicable** *adj.* amichevole.
**amid, amidst** *prep.* in mezzo a; fra, tra; entro; dentro.
**amidships** *adv.* a mezza nave.
**amiss** *adv.* a male; *to do —*, fare di male; *to come —*, fare male; *to take something —*, aversene a male; a sproposito, fuori posto; di traverso; *what's — ?*, che cosa è andata male ?
**amity** *n.* amicizia; buoni rapporti; *to live in peace and —*, vivere in pace ed amicizia.
**ammonia** *n.* (chem.) ammoniaca.
**ammunition** *n.* munizioni *f.pl.*; *— wagon*, vettura-cassone, carro di munizioni.
**amnesty** *n.* amnistia.
**among, amongst** *prep.* fra, tra; in mezzo a; nel numero di; presso; *— strangers*, spaesato.
**amoral** *adj.* amorale.
**amorous** *adj.* amoroso; affettuoso; innamorato. **-ness** *n.* affetto; amorosità.
**amorphous** *adj.* amorfo, informe.
**amortiz-e** *tr.* ammortizzare. **-ation** *n.* ammortizzazione.
**amount** *n.* ammontare *m.*, importo, totale *m.*, montante *m.*, quantità, somma; *intr.* ammontare; ascendere; sommare, (fig.) equivalere; (fig.) *it -s to nothing*, non ha nessuna importanza; *-ing to*, ammontante a.
**ampere** *n.* (electr.) ampere *m. indecl.*
**ampersand** *n.* (typ.) il segno et, et commerciale.
**amphib-ian** *n.* anfibio. **-ious** *adj.* anfibio.
**amphitheatre** *n.* anfiteatro.
**ample** *adj.* ampio; largo; spazioso; abbondante, sufficiente. **-ness** *n.* ampiezza; abbondanza.
**amplif-y** *tr.* amplificare, ampliare; esagerare. **-ication** *n.* amplificazione. **-ier** *n.* (electr.) amplificatore.
**amplitude** *n.* ampiezza; estensione.
**amputat-e** *tr.* amputare; recidere. **-ion** *n.* amputazione.
**amulet** *n.* amuleto.
**amus-e** *tr.* divertire, dilettare; distrarre, svagare; *rfl.* divertirsi, distrarsi; *to be -ed at*, divertirsi di; *I was -ed at him*, egli m'ha fatto ridere. **-ement** *n.* divertimento; passatempo; svago, distrazione; *place of -ement*, luogo di divertimento. **-ing** *adj.* divertente; piacevole.
**an**[1] *indef. art.* see under **a**[1]
**an**[2] *prep.* see under **a**[2]
**Anacreon** *pr.n.* Anacreonte
**anachron-ism** *n.* anacronismo. **-istic** *adj.* anacronistico.
**anaem-ia** *n.* anemia. **-ic** *adj.* anemico.
**anaesth-esia** *n.* anestesia. **-etic** *adj. n.* anestetico. **-etist** *n.* anestesista *m., f.* **-etize** *tr.* anestetizzare.
**anagram** *n.* anagramma *m.*
**analog-y** *n.* analogia; *on the — of*, per analogia con. **-ous** *adj.* analogo.
**anal-yse** *tr.* analizzare, fare l'analisi di. **-ysis** *n.* analisi *f. indecl.* **-yst** *n.* analista *m., f.* **-ytic(al)** *adj.* analitico.
**anarch-y** *n.* anarchia. **-ic(al)** *adj.* anarchico. **-ism** *n.* anarchismo. **-ist** *n.* anarchico.
**anathema** *n.* anatema *m.*
**anatom-y** *n.* anatomia. **-ical** *adj.* anatomico.
**ancest-or** *n.* antenato, avo. **-ral** *adj.* avito; degli avi, degli antenati. **-ress** *n.* antenata, ava. **-ry** *n.* schiatta, razza, stirpe *f.*, nascita.
**anchor** *n.* ancora; *to weigh —*, levare l'ancora; salpare; *to cast —*, gettare l'ancora; *safety —*, ancora di salvezza; *tr.* ancorare. **-age** *n.* ancoraggio.
**anchorite** *n.* anacoreta *m.*
**anchovy** *n.* acciuga.
**ancient** *adj.* antico; vecchio; *the ancients*, gli antichi.
**ancillary** *adj.* sussidiario, ausiliario; subordinato.
**and** *conj.* e; (before vowel) ed; (in telegrams) et; *both you and I*, e tu ed io; *— even, — yet*, eppure; *— so on*, e così via; *now — then*, di quando in quando, ogni tanto; *more — more*, sempre più; *better — better*, di bene in meglio; *worse — worse*, di male in peggio; *by — by*, fra poco; *two — two*, a due a due; *go — see*, andate a vedere.
**anecdot-e** *n.* aneddoto; storiella; barzelletta. **-al** *adj.* aneddotico.
**anemone** *n.* (bot.) anemone *m.*; *wood —*, silvia; (zool.) *sea —*, attinia.
**aneurism** *n.* (med.) aneurisma *m.*
**anew** *adv.* di nuovo; da capo; *to begin —*, ricominciare.
**angel** *n.* angelo; *guardian —*, angelo custode. **-ic(al)** *adj.* angelico; (fig.) buono come il pane.
**angelus** *n.* avemmaria.
**anger** *n.* ira, rabbia, collera; stizza; *in a fit of —*, in un accesso di rabbia; *tr.* irritare; far arrabbiare; *he is easily -ed*, si arrabbia facilmente.
**angl-e**[1] *n.* angolo; canto; cantonata; (fig.) punto di vista. **-ed** *adj.* angolato, angolare; ad angoli. **-ing** *n.* (mech.) angolazione.
**angl-e**[2] *intr.* pescare con l'amo; (fig.) *to — for*, adescare. **-er** *n.* pescatore con l'amo. **-ing** *n.* pesca con l'amo.
**Angle**[3] *pr.n.* (hist.) anglo.
**Anglican** *adj., n.* (rel.) anglicano; *— Church*, la chiesa anglicana. **-ism** *n.* anglicanismo.
**anglic-ism** *n.* anglicismo. **-ize** *tr.* anglicizzare.
**anglo-mania** *n.* anglomania. **-phil(e)** *adj., n.* anglofilo. **-phobe** *adj., n.* anglofobo. **-phobia** *n.* anglofobia.
**Anglo-Saxon** *adj., n.* anglosassone *m., f.*
**angr-y** *adj.* arrabbiato, incollerito, stizzito, irato; *to get —*, arrabbiarsi; *to make someone —*, far arrabbiare qualcuno. **-ily** *adv.* rabbiosamente, stizzosamente, con ira.
**anguish** *n.* angoscia, tormento; *tr.* angosciare, tormentare.
**angular** *adj.* angolare; ad angoli. **-ity** *n.* angolarità, forma angolare.
**animadversion** *n.* animadversione; biasimo, censura.
**animal** *n.* animale *m.*; bestia; (pejor.) bruto; *adj.* animale; *the — kingdom*, il regno animale. **-ity** *n.* animalità. **-ism** *n.* sensualità; animalismo.
**animate** *adj.* vivo, vivente, animato.
**animat-e** *tr.* animare, stimolare; rianimare. **-ed** *part. adj.* vivace, animato, vivo; *to become -ed*, animarsi; *-ed cartoon*, cartone animato. **-ion** *n.* animazione.
**animosity** *n.* animosità, ostilità.
**animus** *n.* malanimo; animosità.
**aniseed** *n.* seme d'anice *m.*
**ankl-e** *n.* caviglia; *— bone*, astragalo; *— deep*, sino alla caviglia; *to sprain one's —*, slogarsi la caviglia; *— sock*, calzino. **-et** *n.* anello da caviglia, cavigliera.
**annal-s** *n.pl.* annali *m.pl.* **-ist** *n.* annalista *m.*
**anneal** *tr.* temperare; ricuocere.
**annex** *tr.* annettere; aggiungere; unire; allegare. **-ation** *n.* annessione.
**an·nex(e)** *n.* annesso; dipendenza; (of document) allegato.
**annihilat-e** *tr.* annientare, anni-

chilire. **-ion** *n.* annientamento, annichilamento.
**anniversary** *adj.* anniversario; *n.* anniversario; ricorrenza.
**annotat-e** *tr.* annotare, postillare, chiosare, commentare. **-ion** *n.* annotazione, chiosa, postilla, commento. **-or** *n.* annotatore, chiosatore, commentatore.
**announc-e** *tr.* annunziare; rivelare; far sapere, comunicare. **-ement** *n.* annuncio; dichiarazione; comunicazione. **-er** *n.* presentatore; banditore; (radio) annunziatore; *woman -er*, annunziatrice.
**annoy** *tr.* seccare, infastidire; importunare; dar noia a. **-ance** *n.* seccatura, fastidio; noia. **-ing** *adj.* seccante, fastidioso; noioso; *how -ing !*, che fastidio!
**annual** *adj.* annuo, annuale; *n.* annuario; (bot.) pianta annuale. **-ly** *adv.* annualmente, ogni anno.
**annuity** *n.* annualità; *life —*, vitalizio.
**annul** *tr.* annullare; cancellare, elidere. **-ment** *n.* annullamento; cancellazione; (leg.) rescissione.
**Annunciation** *n.* Annunziazione; *Our Lady of the —*, l'Annunziata; *angel of the —*, angelo annunziatore.
**anode** *n.* (electr.) anodo.
**anodyne** *adj.*, *n.* anodino.
**anoint** *tr.* ungere; (rel.) dare il crisma a, sacrare. **-ing** *n.* unzione.
**anomal-y** *n.* anomalia; irregolarità. **-ous** *adj.* anomalo; irregolare.
**anon** *adv.* fra poco; *ever and —*, ogni tanto.
**anonym** *n.* anonimo, pseudonimo. **-ity** *n.* anonimato, anonimia. **-ous** *adj.* anonimo; *to remain -ous*, conservare l'anonimo.
**another** *prn.* un altro; altrui *m.*, *f.*; *one —*, l'un l'altro; *adj.* altro; *in — way*, diversamente; *that is quite — thing*, è tutt'altra cosa; *in one way or —*, in un modo o nell'altro.
**answer** *n.* risposta, replica; riscontro; *to give an —*, rispondere; soluzione; *tr.* rispondere a; riscontrare; *to — the door*, andare ad aprire; *this -s the purpose*, questo serve allo scopo; *intr.* rispondere; *to — back*, ribattere, rimbeccare; *to — for*, essere responsabile di. **-able** *adj.* responsabile; confutabile.
**ant** *n.* formica; *— heap*, *— hill*, formicaio.
**antagon-ism** *n.* antagonismo, ostilità. **-ist** *n.* antagonista *m.*, *f.* avversario. **-istic(al)** *adj.* antagonistico. **-ize** *tr.* rendere ostile, provocare l'ostilità di.
**ante-** *pref.* anti-.
**ant-eater** *n.* (zool.) formichiere *m.*
**anteced-ence** *n.* anteriorità, precedenza. **-ent** *adj.* antecedente; *-ent to*, anteriore a; *n.* precursore; (gramm.) antecedente *m.*; *pl.* (of a person) il passato.
**ante-chamber** *n.* anticamera. **-date** *tr.* antidatare, anticipare. **-diluvian** *adj.* antidiluviano. **-natal** *adj.* prenatale. **-penultimate** *adj.*, *n.* antipenultimo. **-room** *n.* anticamera.
**antelope** *n.* antilope *m.*
**antenna** *n.* antenna.
**anterior** *adj.* anteriore, precedente.
**anthem** *n.* antifona; inno; *national —*, inno nazionale.
**antholog-y** *n.* antologia, florilegio, crestomazia. **-ist** *n.* antologista *m.*
**Anthony** *pr.n.* Antonio.
**anthropoid** *adj.*, *n.* antropoide *m.*
**anthropolog-y** *n.* antropologia. **-ical** *adj.* antropologico. **-ist** *n.* antropologo.
**anti-** *pref.* anti-, contro-.
**anti-aircraft** *adj.* controaereo.
**antibiotic** *adj.*, *n.* antibiotico.
**antibody** *n.* anticorpo.
**antic** *n.* buffoneria, stramberia; *to indulge in -s*, fare il buffone.
**anticipat-e** *tr.* anticipare; prevedere; pregustare. **-ion** *n.* anticipazione, anticipo; *thanking you in -ion*, ringraziandovi in anticipo.
**anti-clerical** *adj.* anticlericale; also *n.m.*, *f.* **-clericalism** *n.* anticlericalismo. **-climax** *n.* gradazione discendente; brusco passaggio nel banale. **-clockwise** *adj.*, *adv.* in senso antiorario. **-cyclone** *n.* anticiclone *m.*
**anti-dazzle** *adj.* (motor.) antiabbagliante.
**antidote** *n.* antidoto.
**anti-freeze** *n.* antigelo, anticongelante *m.* **-friction** *n.* antiattrito, antifrizione. **-knock** *n.* (motor.) antidetonante *m.*
**antipathy** *n.* antipatia, avversione.
**anti-patriotic** *adj.* antipatriottico.
**antiquar-y** *n.* antiquario. **-ian** *adj.*, *n.* antiquario; archeologo.
**antiquated** *adj.* antiquato, vecchio.
**antiqu-e** *adj.* antico; antiquato; all'antica; *n.* antichità; oggetto d'arte antica; *— dealer*, antiquario. **-ity** *n.* antichità; l'antico; *in -ity*, in antico.
**antisemitism** *n.* antisemitismo.
**antiseptic** *adj.*, *n.* antisettico.
**anti-skid** *adj.* antisdrucciolevole. **-social** *adj.* antisociale.
**antistrophe** *n.* antistrofe *f.*
**anti-tank** *n.* anticarro.
**antith-esis** *n.* antitesi *f. indecl.* **-etic(al)** *adj.* antitetico.
**antler** *n.* palco; corno di cervo.
**Antony** *pr.n.* Antonio.
**Antwerp** *pr.n.* (geog.) Anversa.
**anus** *n.* (anat.) ano.
**anvil** *n.* incudine, ancudine *f.*
**anxiety** *n.* ansietà, inquietudine *f.*; preoccupazione; affanno; sollecitudine *f.*
**anxious** *adj.* ansioso, inquieto; preoccupato.
**any** *adj.* qualche, alcuno; qualunque, qualsiasi; *not —*, nessuno; *have you — wine ?*, avete del vino ?; *do you know — Italians ?*, conoscete degli Italiani ?; *prn.* alcuno; nessuno; *hasn't he read — of these books ?*, non ha letto alcuno di questi libri ?; (when not followed by noun) ne; *have we — ?*, ne abbiamo ?; *I haven't — more*, non ne ho più; *is he — better ?*, sta meglio ?; *it isn't — good*, non serve a nulla.
**anybody, anyone** *prn.* qualcuno, alcuno, taluno; (after negative) nessuno; *if — speaks*, se parla qualcuno; *I can't see —*, non vedo nessuno; chiunque, chichessia, qualsiasi persona; *— can do that*, chiunque può farlo; *is he — ?*, è qualcuno ?
**anyhow** *adv.* ad ogni modo, in ogni caso; in qualsiasi modo; alla buona; *do it —*, fatelo come potete.
**anything** *prn.* qualchecosa, qualcosa; qualunque cosa; *he eats —*, mangia di tutto; *— but*, tutt'altro che; (after negative) niente, nulla; *without doing —*, senza far nulla; *adv. phr. to work like —*, lavorare con ardore; *to run like —*, correre a precipizio.
**anyway** *adv.* ad ogni modo, in ogni caso; *— you like*, nel modo che ti piace.
**anywhere** *adv.* dovunque, dove che sia, in qualunque luogo; (after negative) in nessun luogo.
**apace** *adv.* presto, velocemente; *to grow —*, crescere a vista d'occhio.
**apart** *adv.* a parte; in disparte; da parte; lontano, distante; *these lines are two inches —*, queste linee distano due pollici l'una dall'altra; *to stand with legs wide —*, stare a gambe divaricate; *can you tell them — ?*, li riconoscete l'uno dall'altro ?
**apartheid** *n.* discriminazione razziale. (dell'Unione Sudafricana).
**apartment** *n.* appartamento; *pl.* alloggio.
**apath-y** *n.* apatia. **-etic** *adj.* apatico, indifferente.
**ape** *n.* scimmia; *tr.* scimmiottare; contraffare, imitare.
**aperient** *adj.*, *n.* lassativo.
**apéritif** *n.* aperitivo.
**aperture** *n.* apertura; pertugio.
**apex** *n.* apice, vertice *m.*; (fig.) apogeo, colmo.
**aphor-ism** *n.* aforismo. **-istic** *adj.* aforistico.
**aphrodisiac** *adj.*, *n.* afrodisiaco.
**apiary** *n.* apiario, alveare *m.*
**apiece** *adv.* a testa, per uno, ciascuno; *how much — ?*, quanto costa l'uno ?

**aplomb** *n.* disinvoltura; padronanza di sè; tatto.
**apocalyp-se** *n.* apocalisse *f.* **-tic** *adj.* apocalittico.
**apocryph-a** *n.* libri apocrifi *m.pl.* **-al** *adj.* apocrifo.
**apogee** *n.* apogeo.
**apolog-y** *n.* scusa; giustificazione; *with apologies for troubling you*, chiedendo scusa per il disturbo; (fig.) *an — for*, un esemplare meschino di, solo un'apparenza di. **-etic(al)** *adj.* apologetico. **-ist** *n.* apologista *m.* **-ize** *intr.* scusarsi, chiedere scusa.
**apopl-exy** *n.* apoplessia. **-ectic** *adj.* apoplettico; *-ectic fit*, colpo apoplettico, accidente *m.*
**apost-asy** *n.* apostasia. **-ate** *n.* apostata *m.* **-atize** *intr.* apostatare.
**apost-le** *n.* apostolo; *Acts of the -s*, Atti degli Apostoli. **-leship, -olate** *n.* apostolato. **-olic(al)** *adj.* apostolico.
**apostrophe** *n.* (gramm.) apostrofo.
**apostrophize** *tr.* apostrofare.
**apothecary** *n.* farmacista *m.*
**apotheosis** *n.* apoteosi *f. indecl.*
**appal** *tr.* spaventare, atterrire, sgomentare, sbigottire. **-ling** *adj.* spaventoso, terribile.
**appannage** *n.* appannaggio.
**apparatus** *n.* apparato; apparecchio, congegno; dispositivo.
**apparel** *n.* abbigliamento; vestiti *m.pl.*; vestiario; *tr.* vestire; arredare; ornare.
**apparent** *adj.* evidente; manifesto; visibile, chiaro; *to become —*, emergere; *heir —*, erede legittimo. **-ly** *adv.* evidentemente; a quanto pare.
**apparition** *n.* apparizione; spettro; fantasma *m.*
**appeal** *n.* appello; ricorso; *to make an — to*, appellarsi a; preghiera, supplica; *intr.* appellarsi, ricorrere; pregare; (leg.) ricorrere in appello. **-ing** *adj.* commovente; attraente; supplichevole.
**appear** *intr.* apparire; presentarsi; mostrarsi, affacciarsi; sembrare, parere; *so it -s*, così pare; *it -s not*, non pare, sembra di no; *there -s to be a mistake*, sembra che vi sia un errore.
**appearance** *n.* apparenza, sembianza; aspetto; aria; presenza; *for the sake of -s*, per salvare le apparenze; *to all -s*, a quanto sembra; comparsa, apparizione; *first —*, debutto; *to put in an —*, far atto di presenza; *of good —*, prestante.
**appease** *tr.* calmare, placare, pacificare, appagare. **-ment** *n.* pacificazione; appagamento; *policy of -ment*, pacificazione a prezzo di concessioni.
**appellation** *n.* denominazione; appellativo; nome; titolo.
**append** *tr.* appendere; apporre; aggiungere. **-age** *n.* aggiunta, annesso; complemento.
**append-ix** *n.* appendice *f.* **-icitis** *n.* appendicite *f.*
**appertain** *intr.* appartenere, spettare; riferirsi.
**appet-ite** *n.* appetito, gusto; (fig.) brama. **-izer** *n.* cibo, bevanda stuzzicante. **-izing** *adj.* appetitoso, gustoso; che stuzzica.
**applaud** *tr.* applaudire; approvare, acclamare.
**applause** *n.* applauso; acclamazione; ovazione.
**apple** *n.* mela, pomo; (tree) melo; *— core*, torsolo di mela; *Adam's —*, pomo di Adamo; *— of discord*, pomo della discordia; *— of the eye*, pupilla dell'occhio.
**apple-cart** *n.* carretto a mano; (fig.) *to upset the —*, sconvolgere i piani, mettere un bastone fra le ruote. **-orchard** *n.* meleto, pomaio. **-pie** *n.* torta di mele; *in -pie order*, in perfetto ordine. **-tart** *n.* torta di mele.
**appliance** *n.* dispositivo, congegno; apparecchio; arnese *m.*; accessori *m.pl.*; forniture *f.pl.*
**applicab-le** *adj.* applicabile, adatto, idoneo. **-ility** *n.* applicabilità.
**applicant** *n.* candidato; aspirante, postulante, richiedente *m., f.*
**application** *n.* applicazione; diligenza, cura; uso; ricorso; *— for a job*, domanda d'impiego; *— form*, modulo di richiesta; *samples are sent on —*, si spediscono campioni dietro richiesta; *on — to*, rivolgendosi a.
**apply** *tr., intr.* applicare; dedicare, consacrare; ricorrere, rivolgersi; *this does not — to him*, questo non si riferisce a lui; *— within*, rivolgersi qui; *to — for*, chiedere; *to — the brake*, frenare; *rfl.* applicarsi; dedicarsi.
**appoint** *tr.* nominare; fissare, designare; stabilire; assegnare. **-ed** *part. adj.* nominato; stabilito; fissato; *a well-appointed house*, una casa ben ordinata; *newly -ed*, di nuova nomina. **-ment** *n.* appuntamento; *to keep an -ment*, mantenere un appuntamento; *to break an -ment*, mancare a un appuntamento; nomina; impiego, posto.
**apportion** *tr.* distribuire, ripartire; assegnare.
**apposit-e** *adj.* apposito, opportuno. **-ion** *n.* apposizione.
**apprais-e** *tr.* valutare; stimare. **-able** *adj.* valutabile; stimabile. **-al** *n.* valutazione; stima; perizia.
**appreciable** *adj.* apprezzabile; sensibile.
**appreciat-e** *tr.* apprezzare, stimare, pregiare; rendersi conto che; *intr.* aumentare. **-ion** *n.* apprezzamento; stima; aumento di valore; riconoscenza. **-ive** *adj.* sensibile; elogiativo.
**apprehend** *tr.* comprendere, capire; temere; arrestare, fermare.
**apprehens-ible** *adj.* apprensibile, comprensibile. **-ion** *n.* comprensione; timore *m.*; apprensione; arresto. **-ive** *adj.* apprensivo, timoroso; preoccupato. **-iveness** *n.* apprensione, preoccupazione.
**apprentice** *n.* apprendista *m., f.*; novizio; *tr.* mettere in tirocinio; *to be -d*, fare l'apprendista. **-ship** *n.* tirocinio, apprendistato.
**apprise** *tr.* informare; avvertire.
**approach** *n.* avvicinamento, accostamento; *at the — of*, all'avvicinarsi di; (fig.) approccio; accesso; *tr.* avvicinare, accostare, mettersi in contatto con; *intr.* avvicinarsi, accostarsi. **-ing** *adj.* prossimo, imminente; che si avvicina.
**approachab-le** *adj.* accessibile, di facile accesso; affabile. **-ility** *n.* accessibilità.
**approbation** *n.* approbazione; consenso.
**appropriate** *adj.* appropriato, adatto, opportuno; conveniente; *at the — moment*, al momento opportuno. **-ly** *adv.* propriamente; giustamente; a proposito. **-ness** *n.* proprietà; convenienza.
**appropriat-e** *tr.* appropriarsi, impadronirsi di; (finan.) stanziare. **-ion** *n.* appropriazione; applicazione; (finan.) stanziamento.
**approval** *n.* approvazione; benestare *m.*; (comm.) *on —*, in prova, in visione, in esame.
**approv-e** *tr.* approvare; assentire a; convalidare; dare il benestare a; lodare. **-ed** *adj.* approvato; convalidato; riconosciuto; *-ed school*, riformatorio. **-ing** *adj.* approvativo.
**approximate** *tr.* avvicinarsi a; *adj.* approssimativo. **-ly** *adv.* approssimativamente; all'incirca, circa; su per giù.
**approximative** *adj.* approssimativo.
**approximation** *n.* approssimazione.
**appurtenance** *n.* appartenenza, pertinenza; *pl.* accessori *m.pl.*
**apricot** *n.* (fruit) albicocca; (tree) albicocco.
**April** *n.* aprile *m.*; *— shower*, acquazzone d'aprile; *— fool*, vittima di un pesce d'aprile; *to make an — fool of*, giocare un pesce d'aprile a.
**apron** *n.* grembiale, grembiule *m.*; (aeron.) area di stazionamento; (theatr.) proscenio.
**apron-string** *n.* laccio di grembiule; *to be tied to one's mother's apron strings*, essere attaccato alle gonnelle della mamma.
**apropos** *adv.* a proposito.

**apse** *n.* (archit.) abside *f.*
**apt** *adj.* atto; adatto, idoneo; giusto; propenso; sveglio, intelligente. **~ly** *adv.* giustamente, bene a proposito. **~ness** *n.* proprietà; convenienza; idoneità.
**aptitude** *n.* attitudine *f.*; idoneità; intelligenza, perspicacia.
**aqualung** *n.* autorespiratore *m.*
**aquarium** *n.* acquario.
**aquatic** *adj.* acquatico.
**aquatint** *n.* acquatinta.
**aqueduct** *n.* acquedotto.
**aqueous** *adj.* acqueo, acquoso.
**aquiline** *adj.* aquilino.
**Arab** *pr.n.*, *adj.* (ethn.; geog.) arabo.
**arabesque** *n.* arabesco.
**Arabian** *adj.*, *n.* arabo; *the — Nights*, Le Mille e una Notte.
**arabic** *adj.* arabico; *— numerals*, numeri arabici; *n.* la lingua araba, l'arabo.
**arable** *adj.* arabile.
**arbiter** *n.* arbitro; *— of taste*, arbitro dell'eleganza.
**arbitrar~y** *adj.* arbitrario. **~iness** *n.* modi arbitrari *m.pl.*
**arbitrat~e** *intr.* arbitrare. **~ion** *n.* arbitraggio; *by ~ion*, arbitrariamente. **~or** *n.* arbitro.
**arbour** *n.* pergola; pergolato, frascato.
**arbutus** *n.* (bot.) albatro, arbuto, corbezzolo.
**arc** *n.* arco.
**arc-lamp** *n.* lampada ad arco.
**arcade** *n.* (archit.) porticato, portico; (with shops) galleria.
**arcadian** *adj.* arcadico, pastorale.
**arch**[1] *adj.* birichino, furbetto, malizioso. **~ness** *n.* malizia, birichineria; affettazione.
**arch**[2] *n.* arco; arcata; volta; *triumphal —*, arco trionfale; *tr.* inarcare, curvare; *intr.* inarcarsi, curvarsi. **~ed** *part. adj.* ad arco, arcato, inarcato, arcuato.
**arch-**[3] *pref.* arci-.
**archaeolog~y** *n.* archeologia. **~ical** *adj.* archeologico. **~ist** *n.* archeologo.
**archa~ic** *adj.* arcaico, antiquato. **~ism** *n.* arcaismo.
**archangel** *n.* arcangelo.
**archbishop** *n.* arcivescovo; *archbishop's palace*, arcivescovado. **~ric** *n.* arcivescovato; arcidiocesi *f. indecl.*
**archdeacon** *n.* arcidiacono.
**arch~duke** *n.* arciduca *m.* **~ducal** *adj.* arciducale. **~duchess** *n.* arciduchessa. **~duchy** *n.* arciducato.
**arch-enemy** *n.* arcinemico, nemico mortale.
**archer** *n.* arciere *m.*; (astron.) *the Archer*, il Sagittario. **~y** *n.* tiro all'arco.
**archetype** *n.* archetipo, prototipo.
**arch-fiend** *n.* arcidiavolo; Satana *m.*, il grande avversario.
**archi~episcopal** *adj.* arcivescovile. **~mandrite** *n.* archimandrita *m.* **~pelago** *n.* arcipelago.
**Archimed~es** *pr.n.* Archimede. **~ean** *adj.* *~ean screw*, vite *f.* d'Archimede.
**architect** *n.* architetto; (fig.) artefice *m.* **~onic(al)** *adj.* architettonico.
**architectur~e** *n.* architettura. **~al** *adj.* architetturale.
**architrave** *n.* architrave *m.*
**archiv~es** *n.pl.* archivio; documenti di archivio. **~ist** *n.* archivista *m.*, *f.*
**archpriest** *n.* arciprete *m.*
**archway** *n.* (archit.) arco; (over street) arcivolto; volta.
**arctic** *adj.* artico.
**ardent** *adj.* ardente, focoso; appassionato.
**ardour** *m.* ardore *m.*; fervore *m.*; zelo.
**arduous** *adj.* arduo, difficile; strenuo.
**area** *n.* area; superficie *f.*; zona; *basement —*, cortile *m.* del seminterrato; *postal —*, distretto postale.
**arena** *n.* arena.
**argent** *adj.* (poet.) argenteo; (herald.) argento.
**Argentin~e** *pr.n.* (geog.) Argentina. **~ian** *adj.*, *n.* argentino.
**argue** *intr.* argomentare. discutere; ragionare; *tr.* contendere; dimostrare.
**argument** *n.* argomento; discussione; ragionamento. **~ative** *adj.* argomentativo, polemico.
**aria** *n.* (mus.) aria.
**arid** *adj.* arido; secco. **~ity**, **~ness** *n.* aridità; siccità.
**aright** *adv.* bene, giustamente.
**arise** *intr.* levarsi, alzarsi, sorgere; (fig.) nascere; risultare; presentarsi.
**aristocr~acy** *n.* aristocrazia. **~at** *n.* aristocratico. **~atic** *adj.* aristocratico.
**arithmetic** *n.* aritmetica. **~al** *adj.* aritmetico. **~ian** *n.* aritmetico.
**ark** *n.* arca; *Noah's —*, l'arca di Noè.
**arm**[1] *n.* (anat.) braccio; *to fold one's ~s*, incrociare le braccia; *to keep someone at ~'s length*, tenere qualcuno a distanza; *— in —*, a braccetto; *within ~'s reach*, a portata di mano. **~ful** *n.* bracciata. **~hole** *n.* giro della manica. **~less** *n.* senza braccia. **~let** *n.* bracciale *m.* **~pit** *n.* ascella.
**arm**[2] *n.* arma, arme *f.*; *to bear ~s*, essere sotto le armi; *to lay down ~s*, deporre le armi; *to take up ~s*, prendere le armi; *to be up in ~s against*, essere in rivolta contro; *to ~s!*, all'armi!; *pl.* (herald.) *~s*, stemma *m.*; *tr.* armare; *intr.* armarsi; *~ed to the teeth*, armato fino ai denti.
**armada** *n.* armata.
**armament** *n.* armamento.
**armature** *n.* armatura.
**armchair** *n.* poltrona.
**Armenia** *pr.n.* (geog.) Armenia. **~n** *adj.*, *n.* armeno.
**armistice** *n.* armistizio; tregua.
**armorial** *adj.* araldico; *— bearings*, stemma gentilizio.
**armour** *n.* armatura; corazzatura; corazza. **~ed** *adj.* armato; corazzato, blindato; *~ed car*, autoblindo. **~er** *n.* armaiuolo; (mil.) armiere *m.* **~y** *n.* arsenale *m.*; armeria; sala d'armi.
**armour-plated** *adj.* corazzato, blindato.
**arms-permit** *n.* porto-d'armi *m.*
**army** *n.* esercito; armata; *standing —*, esercito permanente; *to be in the —*, essere sotto le armi; *to join the —*, andare (a fare il) soldato; *— corps*, corpo d'armata; *Army Service Corps*, Intendenza; *Salvation Army*, Esercito della Salute.
**arom~a** *n.* aroma *m.*; fragranza. **~atic** *adj.* aromatico.
**around** *prep.* attorno a, intorno a; *adv.* intorno, all'intorno; *all —*, tutt'intorno, da tutte le parti.
**arouse** *tr.* destare, svegliare, ridestare; (fig.) eccitare, stimolare, suscitare.
**arraign** *tr.* accusare, citare in giudizio; (fig.) biasimare. **~ment** *n.* accusa; imputazione; (fig.) biasimo.
**arrange** *tr.* ordinare, disporre, assettare; combinare. **~ment** *n.* ordinamento, assestamento; distribuzione; combinazione; congegno; dispositivo; (comm.) concordato; *to make an ~ment with*, intendersi con.
**array** *n.* apparato; abbigliamento; (mil.) ordine *m.*, schieramento; *tr.* abbigliare, ornare; (mil.) schierare, spiegare.
**arrears** *n.* arretrati *m.pl.*
**arrest** *n.* arresto; *under —*, in stato d'arresto, (mil.) agli arresti; *tr.* arrestare; fermare; frenare; far cessare; *to — attention*, richiamare l'attenzione.
**arrival** *n.* arrivo; venuta; (person) arrivato; *a new —*, un nuovo venuto; un neonato; (comm.) *the latest ~s*, gli ultimi arrivi.
**arrive** *intr.* arrivare, giungere; capitare; succedere.
**arrog~ant** *adj.* arrogante; altero. **~ance** *n.* arroganza; alterigia.
**arrogate** *tr.* arrogarsi; pretendere a.
**arrow** *n.* freccia, saetta; *broad —*, freccia ottusa.
**arse** *n.* culo.
**arsenal** *n.* arsenale *m.*
**arsenic** *n.* arsenico.
**arson** *n.* incendio doloso.
**art** *n.* arte *f.*; *work of —*, opera d'arte; abilità tecnica; *— for ~'s sake*, l'arte per l'arte; *the black —*, magia; *fine —*, belle arti; *pl.* belle lettere; *Bachelor of Arts*, laureato in lettere; *Faculty of Arts* facoltà di lettere.
**arter~y** *n.* arteria. **~ial** *adj.* arteriale, arterioso; *~ial road*, strada nazionale.

**artesian** *adj.* artesiano; — *well,* pozzo artesiano.
**artful** *adj.* astuto, furbo, scaltro; artificioso. **-ness** *n.* astuzia; scaltrezza; artificio.
**arthritis** *n.* (med.) artrite *f.*
**artichoke** *n.* carciofo; *Jerusalem* —, topinamburo, carciofo bianco.
**article** *n.* articolo; oggetto; *leading* —, articolo di fondo; statuto; *pl. ship's -s,* contratto di arruolamento; *-s of war,* codice penale militare *m.*
**article** *tr.* collocare come apprendista; *-d clerk,* apprendista *m.*
**articulate** *adj.* articolato; chiaro, distinto; capace di parlare.
**articulat-e** *tr., intr.* articolare, parlare distintamente; *to — the syllables,* scandire le sillabe. **-ion** *n.* articolazione.
**artifact** *n.* artefatto; prodotto lavorato.
**artific-e** *n.* artificio, artifizio; astuzia; stratagemma *m.*; abilità. **-er** *n.* artefice *m.*; artigiano.
**artificial** *adj.* artificiale, finto; posticcio. **-ity** *n.* artificiosità.
**artillery** *n.* artiglieria. **-man** *n.* artigliere *m.*
**artisan** *n.* artigiano.
**artist** *n.* artista *m., f.* **-ic(al)** *adj.* artistico. **-ry** *n.* abilità artistica; arte *f.*
**artless** *adj.* senz'arte; naturale; ingenuo, semplice. **-ness** *n.* naturalezza; semplicità, ingenuità.
**Aryan** *pr.n., adj.* (hist.) ariano.
**as** *adv.* così, come, tanto, quanto; *so* —, in modo da; *conj.* come; siccome, poichè, giacchè, quando; — *far* —, fino a; — *far — I am concerned,* per quanto mi riguarda; — *far — I can see,* per quanto io ci vedo; — *for,* quanto a; — *from,* da; — *if,* come se; — *long* —, finchè, purchè; — *much* —, tanto quanto; — *soon* —, (non) appena; — *well,* anche, pure; — *well* —, come pure.
**asbestos** *n.* amianto, asbesto.
**ascend** *intr.* salire, ascendere; innalzarsi; risalire; *to — the throne,* salire al trono; *to — into heaven,* salire nel cielo.
**ascend-ancy** *n.* ascendente *m.*; influenza; superiorità; autorità morale. **-ant** *adj., n.* ascendente *m.*; *to gain the -ant,* impadronirsi dell'autorità.
**ascension** *n.* ascensione; salita; *Ascension Day,* festa dell'Ascensione.
**ascent** *n.* salita; ascensione; ascesa; pendìo.
**ascertain** *tr.* accertarsi di, informarsi di, assicurarsi di; constatare, verificare; venire a sapere. **-able** *adj.* accertabile, verificabile. **-ment** *n.* accertamento; constatazione.
**ascetic** *adj.* ascetico; *n.* asceta *m.* **-ism** *n.* ascetismo; ascesi *f.*
**ascrib-e** *tr.* ascrivere, attribuire. imputare. **-able** *adj.* attribuibile, ascrivibile, imputabile.
**asep-sis** *n.* (med.) asepsi *f.* **-tic** *adj.* asettico.
**asexual** *adj.* asessuale.
**ash**[1] *n.* (bot.) frassino.
**ash**[2] *n.* cenere *f.*; *Ash Wednesday,* Mercoledì delle Ceneri; *to turn to -es,* ridursi in cenere; (fig.) andare in fiele. **-en, -y** *adj.* di color cenerino, cenerognolo.
**ashamed** *adj.* vergognoso, confuso; *to be — of,* aver vergogna di, vergognarsi di.
**ashbin** *n.* bidone delle spazzature.
**ash-blond** *adj., n.* biondo cenerino.
**ash-heap** *n.* catasta di ceneri; immondezzaio.
**ashlar** *n.* (archit.) concio; bugna.
**ashore** *adv.* a terra, sulla riva; *to go* —, sbarcare, prendere terra.
**ashtray** *n.* portacenere *m.*
**Asia** *pr.n.* (geog.) Asia; — *Minor,* Asia minore.
**Asian, Asiatic** *adj., n.* asiatico.
**aside** *adv.* da parte; a parte, in disparte; *to turn* —, voltarsi altrove; sviare.
**asinine** *adj.* asinino; sciocco.
**ask** *tr.* chiedere, domandare; invitare; interpellare, informarsi; *to — someone for something,* chiedere qualcosa a qualcuno; *to — about,* informarsi di; *to — after,* chiedere notizie di; domandare di; *to — for trouble,* cercare fastidi.
**askance** *adv.* di traverso; *to look — at,* guardare di sbieco.
**askew** *adv.* obliquamente; a sghembo.
**aslant** *adv.* di traverso, obliquamente.
**asleep** *adj.* addormentato, che dorme; *to be* —, dormire; *to fall* —, addormentarsi; *to be fast* —, dormire della grossa; *to be half* —, essere in un dormiveglia.
**asp** *n.* (zool.) aspide *m.*
**asparagus** *n.* asparagi *m.pl.*
**aspect** *n.* aspetto; apparenza; veduta; *to have a southern* —, guardare verso sud, dare a mezzogiorno.
**aspen** *n.* (bot.) pioppo tremolo.
**asperity** *n.* asperità; asprezza; (of climate) rigore *m.*
**aspers-e** *tr.* aspergere. **-ion** *n.* aspersione; *to cast -ions on,* diffamare.
**asphalt** *n.* asfalto; *tr.* asfaltare.
**asphodel** *n.* (bot.) asfodelo.
**asphyxi-a, -ate** *tr.* asfissiare; *-ating gas,* asfissiante *m.* **-ation** *n.* asfissia.
**aspic** *n.* (bot.) spigo; (cul.) gelatina.
**aspidistra** *n.* (bot.) aspidistra.
**aspirant** *n.* aspirante *m., f.*; candidato.
**aspirate** *adj.* (gramm.) aspirato; *n.* (consonante) aspirata; il suono dell'acca; *tr.* (gramm.) aspirare.
**aspir-e** *intr.* aspirare; ambire; *to — towards,* agognare. **-ation** *n.* aspirazione; ambizione; *to have -ations,* essere ambizioso. **-ing** *adj.* ambizioso.
**aspirin** *n.* aspirina.
**ass** *n.* asino, ciuco; somaro; *she* —, asina; *wild* —, onagro; (fig.) *conceited* —, asino presuntuoso; *silly* —, pezzo d'asino.
**assail** *tr.* assalire, attaccare, aggredire; invadere; (fig.) investire. **-ant** *n.* assalitore, aggressore.
**assassin** *n.* assassino; sicario; *-'s hand,* mano assassina. **-ate** *tr.* assassinare. **-ation** *n.* assassinio.
**assault** *n.* assalto, attacco; (leg.) aggressione, violenza; (mil.) — *troops,* reparti *m.pl.* di assalto; *tr.* assalire, attaccare; aggredire; (leg.) passare a vie di fatto contro; *to be -ed,* essere vittima di un'aggressione.
**assay** *n.* (metall.) assaggio; analisi *f. indecl.*; *tr.* assaggiare.
**assembl-e** *tr.* riunire, adunare; (mech.) montare; (intr.) riunirsi, adunarsi. **-age** *n.* assembramento; adunata; (mech.) montaggio. **-ing** *n.* assembramento; (mech.) montaggio.
**assembly** *n.* assemblea; riunione, adunanza; — *room,* sala da ballo, da riunioni; (mech.) — *line,* catena di montaggio.
**assent** *n.* assenso, assentimento; consenso; *intr.* assentire, acconsentire, dare l'assenso; approvare.
**assert** *tr.* asserire, affermare, sostenere; *to — a right,* rivendicare un diritto; *rfl. to — oneself,* farsi valere. **-ion** *n.* asserzione, assertimento; assertiva; affermazione; (of right) rivendicazione. **-ive** *adj.* assertivo; positivo; dogmatico. **-iveness** *n.* presunzione; imperiosità.
**assess** *tr.* valutare, stimare; accertare; tassare. **-able** *adj.* valutabile; imponibile, tassabile. **-ment** *n.* valutazione; imposta, tassa. **-or** *n.* assessore; agente *m.* del fisco.
**asset** *n.* bene; vantaggio; *pl.* (comm.) attivo, attività, disponibilità; *-s and liabilities,* attivo e passivo.
**asseverat-e** *tr.* asseverare. **-ion** *n.* asseverazione.
**assidu-ity** *n.* assiduità. **-ous** *adj.* assiduo; diligente.
**assign** *tr.* assegnare; cedere, trasferire; (leg.) delegare. **-ee** *n.* assegnatario, mandatario; (of bankruptcy) curatore. **-ment** *n.* assegnazione; stanziamento; cessione; compito, incarico.
**assignation** *n.* assegnazione; appuntamento galante; (leg.) cessione.
**assimilat-e** *tr.* assimilare; assorbire, digerire. **-ion** *n.* assimilazione.
**assist** *tr.* assistere; aiutare; collaborare con; soccorrere. **-ance**

*n.* assistenza; aiuto, soccorso; *to render ~ance,* prestare assistenza. **~ant** *n.* assistente *m., f.*; aiuto, collaboratore; *~ant lecturer,* professore aggiunto; *~ant manager,* vicedirettore; *shop ~ant,* commesso di negozio.
**assize(s)** *n.* assise *f.pl.*
**associate** *adj.* associato; socio; collega *m., f.* collaboratore; *tr.* associare; *intr.* associarsi; *to — with,* frequentare, praticare.
**association** *n.* associazione, società; consorzio; (sport) federazione; *— football* (giuoco del) calcio.
**asson~ance** *n.* assonanza. **~ant** *adj.* assonante.
**assort** *tr.* assortire; *an ill-assorted couple,* una coppia male assortita; *intr. to — with,* frequentare, praticare. **~ment** *n.* assortimento; scelta.
**assuage** *tr.* calmare, placare, sedare; mitigare; lenire, addolcire; *to be ~d,* calmarsi, placarsi; mitigarsi. **~ment** *n.* lenimento; sollievo; mitigazione.
**assume** *tr.* assumere; prendere, appropriarsi; fingere; *an ~d name,* un nome falso; presumere, supporre; *assuming that,* supposto che.
**assumption** *n.* assunzione; supposizione; finzione; (eccl.) *Feast of the —,* l'Assunzione, Ferragosto.
**assurance** *n.* assicurazione; promessa formale; fiducia, confidenza, sicurezza.
**assur~e** *tr.* assicurare; *to rest ~ed,* essere sicuro. **~ed** *part. adj.* assicurato; fiducioso; baldanzoso. **~edly** *adv.* sicuramente, certo. **~edness** *n.* sicurezza, certezza; fiducia.
**Assyria** *pr.n.* (hist. geog.) Assiria. **~n** *adj., n.* assiro.
**aster** *n.* (bot.) astro; *wild —,* amello.
**asterisk** *n.* asterisco.
**astern** *adv.* (naut.) a poppa, indietro; *full speed —,* indietro a tutta velocità; *to have the wind —,* avere il vento in poppa.
**asteroid** *n.* (astron.) asteroide *f.*
**asthm~a** *n.* asma *f., m.* **~atic(al)** *adj.* asmatico.
**astigmatism** *n.* (med.) astigmatismo.
**astir** *adv.* in piedi, fuori dal letto; *to be — early,* essere alzato per tempo; in agitazione, in moto.
**astonish** *tr.* stupire, sbalordire, sorprendere. **~ing** *adj.* sbalorditivo, sorprendente. **~ment** *n.* stupore *m.*; sorpresa, meraviglia.
**astound** *tr.* stupire, sbalordire, sorprendere. **~ing** *adj.* stupefacente, sbalorditivo.
**astragal** *n.* (archit.) astragalo.
**astral** *adj.* astrale.
**astray** *adv.* fuori strada, fuori via; *to go —,* smarrirsi; *to lead —,* fuorviare, traviare; *the letter must have gone — in the post,* ci dev'essere stato un disguido postale.
**astride** *adv. phr.* a cavalcioni.
**astring~ency** *n.* astringenza; (fig.) severità. **~ent** *adj.* astringente; (fig.) severo, austero.
**astrolog~y** *n.* astrologia. **~er** *n.* astrologo. **~ical** *adj.* astrologico.
**astronaut** *n.* astronauta *m.* **~ics** *n.* astronautica.
**astronom~y** *n.* astronomia. **~er** *n.* astronomo. **~ic(al)** *adj.* astronomico; (fig.) *~ical prices,* prezzi astronomici.
**astute** *adj.* astuto; scaltro, furbo. **~ness** *n.* astuzia; scaltrezza, furberia.
**asunder** *adv.* separatamente, in pezzi; *to fall —,* rompersi; *to tear —,* sbranare.
**asylum** *n.* asilo, rifugio, ricovero; *lunatic —,* manicomio.
**asymmetr~y** *n.* assimetria. **~ic(al)** *adj.* asimmetrico.
**at** *prep.* a, ad, in, da; con; *— home,* a casa; *— church,* in chiesa; *we'll meet — John's house,* ci vedremo da Giovanni; *— five o'clock,* alle cinque; *— one blow,* con un solo colpo.
**atav~ism** *n.* atavismo. **~istic** *adj.* atavistico.
**Athanasian** *adj.* di Sant'Anastasio.
**athe~ism** *n.* ateismo. **~ist** *n.* ateo, ateista *m.* **~istic(al)** *adj.* ateo, ateistico.
**Athen~s** *pr.n.* (geog.) Atene *f.* **~ian** *adj., n.* ateniese.
**athirst** *adj.* assetato, sitibondo; (fig.) avido, desideroso.
**athlet~e** *n.* atleta *m., f.* **~ic** *adj.* atletico. **~ics** *n.* atletica.
**at-home** *n.* ricevimento in casa.
**athwart** *adv.* per traverso, obliquamente.
**Atlantic** *pr.n.* (geog.) Atlantico; (attrib.) atlantico; *— liner,* transatlantico; (hist.) *— Charter,* Carta atlantica; *North — Treaty,* Patto atlantico.
**Atlas**[1] *pr.n.* (myth.) Atlante *m.*
**atlas**[2] *n.* atlante *m.*
**atmospher~e** *m.* atmosfera; (fig.) ambiente *m.* **~ic(al)** *adj.* atmosferico; (paint.) *~ical perspective,* prospettiva aerea; (radio) *atmospherics,* scariche *f.pl.,* disturbi atmosferici *m.pl.*
**atom** *n.* atomo; *— bomb,* bomba atomica; *to split the —,* frantumare l'atomo; *to crush to ~s,* sbriciolare. **~ic(al)** *adj.* atomico. **~ize** *tr.* atomizzare; polverizzare; nebulizzare. **~izer** *n.* polverizzatore; nebulizzatore; spruzzatore.
**atone** *tr.* espiare, purgare; *intr. to — for one's sins,* espiare i peccati. **~ment** *n.* espiazione; riparazione; (rel.) *Day of Atonement,* giorno della propiziazione.
**atroc~ious** *adj.* atroce; (colloq.) pestifero. **~ity, ~iousness** *n.* atrocità; efferatezza.
**atrophy** *n.* atrofia; *tr.* atrofizzare; *intr.* atrofizzarsi.
**attach** *tr.* attaccare; unire; (fig.) *to — importance to,* attribuire importanza a; *to become ~ed to,* affezionarsi a; (leg.) sequestrare; (mil.) aggregare; *intr.* attaccarsi. **~ment** *n.* attaccamento; affezione; (leg.) sequestro; (mech.) accessorio.
**attaché** *n.* addetto; *Press —,* Addetto Stampa.
**attack** *n.* attacco; assalto; offensiva; aggressione; *to make an — on,* attaccare; (med.) accesso; *— of nerves,* crisi nervosa; *tr.* attaccare; assalire; aggredire; (med.) attaccarsi a; (mus.) prendere con slancio; (chem.) *not ~ed by,* inattaccabile da. **~er** *n.* assalitore, aggressore.
**attain** *tr.* ottenere; raggiungere, giungere a; conseguire. **~able** *adj.* raggiungibile; conseguibile. **~ment** *n.* raggiungimento; successo; conseguimento; *pl.* cognizioni *f.pl.,* cultura.
**attempt** *n.* tentativo; sforzo; prova; *an — on the life of,* un attentato alla vita di; *tr.* tentare; cercare, provare.
**attend** *tr.* servire, accompagnare; frequentare; assistere a, intervenire a; (med.) assistere, curare; *intr.* prestare attenzione; *to — to,* badare a. **~ance** *n.* servizio; *to be in ~ance on,* essere al servizio di; intervento; *good ~ance,* pubblico numeroso; *~ance register,* registro delle presenze; *to dance ~ance,* far anticamera; (med.) assistenza, cura. **~ant** *n.* custode, sorvegliante *m.*; *medical ~ant,* medico; frequentatore; *adj.* che accompagna; conseguente.
**attention** *n.* attenzione, interessamento; cura; *to call — to,* richiamare l'attenzione a; *to pay — to,* stare attento a; *to be all —,* essere tutt'orecchi; (mil.) *—!,* attenti!; *to stand at —,* stare sull'attenti.
**attentive** *adj.* attento; sollecito, riguardoso, premuroso. **~ness** *n.* attenzione; cura; premura.
**attenuat~e** *tr.* attenuare; assottigliare; moderare; *intr.* attenuarsi; dimagrire. **~ion** *n.* attenuazione; assottigliamento.
**attest** *tr.* attestare; testimoniare, certificare; affermare; (leg.) far giurare; *to — a signature,* vidimare una firma. **~ation** *n.* attestazione; testimonianza.
**Attic**[1] *adj.* attico, ateniese; *— salt,* arguzia attica.
**attic**[2] *n.* (archit.) attico; mansarda; soffitta.
**attire** *n.* abbigliamento; vestiti, abiti *m.pl.*; *tr.* abbigliare, vestire; parare.
**attitud~e** *n.* atteggiamento; posa, posizione; *to strike an —,* assumere un atteggiamento; *— of mind,* modo di pensare. **~inize** *intr.* posare, atteggiarsi.
**attorney** *n.* avvocato; *Attorney-*

*General*, Procuratore Generale; *power of* —, (mandato di) procura.
**attract** *tr.* attrarre, attirare; cattivarsi, allettare. **-ion** *n.* attrazione, attrattiva; fascino; vezzi *m.pl.* **-ive** *adj.* (of magnet) attrattivo; (of persons, things) attraente, affascinante; seducente. **-iveness** *n.* attrattiva, fascino.
**at'tribute** *n.* attributo; qualità.
**attribut-e** *tr.* attribuire, ascrivere, imputare. **-able** *adj.* attribuibile, imputabile. **-ion** *n.* attribuzione.
**attrition** *n.* attrito; logoramento.
**attune** *tr.* accordare, intonare, armonizzare.
**aubergine** *n.* melanzana.
**auburn** *adj.* tizianesco.
**auction** *n.* incanto, asta; *to sell by* —, vendere all'incanto, all'asta. **-eer** *n.* venditore all'asta; banditore.
**audac-ious** *adj.* audace; intrepido, ardito. **-ity** *n.* audacia; temerità.
**audib-le** *adj.* udibile, intelligibile. **-ility** *n.* udibilità; intelligibilità.
**audience** *n.* pubblico, uditorio; spettatori; *to grant an* —, concedere un'udienza.
**audit** *tr.* rivedere, verificare; *n.* revisione, verifica dei conti.
**auditing** *n.* verifica.
**audition** *n.* audizione; (phys.) udito.
**auditor** *n.* revisore (di conti); (of company accounts) sindaco; *board of -s*, collegio dei sindaci; (eccl.) uditore.
**auditorium** *n.* sala, auditorio; (eccl.) parlatorio
**auger** *n.* trivella, trapano, succhiello.
**aught** *n.* ogni cosa, qualcosa; *for — I know*, per quanto io sappia.
**augment** *tr.* aumentare, accrescere; *intr.* aumentarsi, crescere. **-ation** *n.* aumento, accrescimento. **-ative** *adj.* aumentativo; (gramm.) accrescitivo.
**augur** *n.* (hist.) augure *m.*; *tr.* predire, pronosticare; *intr. it -s well*, promette bene. **-y** *n.* presagio, pronostico.
**augu'st** *adj.* augusto, maestoso.
**August** *pr.n.* agosto; — *Bank Holiday*, ferragosto inglese.
**Augustan** *adj.* augusteo, di Augusto.
**auk** *n.* (orn.) alca.
**aunt** *n.* zia; *great-aunt*, prozia.
**aura** *n.* aura.
**aureole** *n.* aureola; nimbo; alone *m.*
**Aurora** *pr.n.* Aurora; — *borealis*, aurora boreale.
**auspices** *n.pl.* auspici, auspizi *m.pl.*; (fig.) patronato, protezione.
**auspicious** *adj.* propizio, fausto. **-ly** *adv.* sotto felici auspici.
**auster-e** *adj.* austero; ascetico, severo. **-eness, -ity** *n.* austerità; severità.
**austral** *adj.* australe, meridionale.
**Australasia** *pr.n.* (geog.) Australasia.
**Australia** *pr.n.* (geog.) Australia. **-n** *adj.*, *n.* australiano.
**Austria** *pr.n.* (geog.) Austria. **-n** *adj.*, *n.* austriaco.
**autarchy** *n.* autarchia.
**authentic** *adj.* autentico. **-ate** *tr.* autenticare; convalidare, legalizzare. **-ity** *n.* autenticità.
**author** *n.* autore, autrice; creatore; scrittore, scrittrice. **-ship** *n.* paternità; professione di scrittore.
**authoritarian** *adj.* autoritario.
**authoritative** *adj.* autorevole; autoritario; imperativo. **-ness** *n.* autorevolezza.
**authority** *n.* autorità; influenza; ascendente *m.*; *by* —, per autorizzazione; (fig.) fonte *f.*
**authoriz-e** *tr.* autorizzare; permettere. **-ation** *n.* autorizzazione. **-ed** *part. adj.* autorizzato; competente.
**auto** *n.* macchina, auto *f.*
**autobiograph-y** *n.* autobiografia. **-er** *n.* autobiografo. **-ic(al)** *adj.* autobiografico.
**autocr-acy** *n.* autocrazia. **-at** *n.* autocrata *m.*, autocrate *m.* **-atic(al)** *adj.* autocratico.
**autodrome** *n.* autodromo.
**autogenous** *adj.* autogeno.
**autograph** *adj.* autografo; *n.* autografo; firma; *tr.* autografare, firmare.
**automatic** *adj.* automatico; — *machine*, distributore automatico. **-ally** *adv.* automaticamente; (fig.) macchinalmente.
**automation** *n.* automazione.
**automaton** *n.* automa *m.*
**automobile** *n.* automacchina; automobile *f.*; *Italian — Club*, Automobile Club d'Italia.
**autonom-y** *n.* autonomia. **-ous** *adj.* autonomo.
**autopsy** *n.* autopsia.
**auto-suggestion** *n.* autosuggestione.
**autumn** *n.* autunno; *attrib.* autunnale. **-al** *adj.* autunnale, di autunno.
**auxiliary** *adj.*, *n.* ausiliare; — *verb*, verbo ausiliare; (mil.) ausiliario; *Auxiliary Territorial Service*, Servizio femminile dell'esercito.
**avail** *n.* vantaggio; utilità; *of what — ?*, a che serve ?; *to be of no* —, non servir a nulla; *tr.*, *intr.* servire, giovare a; *to — oneself of*, servirsi di, approfittare di.
**availab-le** *adj.* disponibile; libero; accessibile, sotto mano. **-ility** *n.* disponibilità.
**avalanche** *n.* valanga.
**avaric-e** *n.* avarizia, cupidigia. **-ious** *adj.* avaro, cupido. **-iousness** *n.* avarizia, cupidigia.
**aveng-e** *tr.* vendicare; *to — oneself*, vendicarsi; *to — an insult*, vendicarsi di un'ingiuria. **-er** *n.* vendicatore.
**avenue** *n.* viale alberato; (fig.) via di accesso.
**average** *adj.* medio, normale, ordinario; *the — Englishman*, l'inglese comune; *n.* media; *on an* —, in media; (comm.) avaria; *tr.* raggiungere la media di, avere in media; lavorare una media di; calcolare la media.
**avers-e** *adj.* avverso; contrario; alieno; riluttante; *I am not — to it*, non ho nulla in contrario. **-ion** *n.* avversione, antipatia.
**avert** *tr.* sviare, allontanare, distogliere; *to — suspicion*, allontanare i sospetti; *to — one's gaze*, distogliere gli occhi.
**aviary** *n.* uccelliera.
**aviat-ion** *n.* aviazione; *adj.* aviatorio. **-or** *n.* aviatore.
**avid** *adj.* avido. **-ity** *n.* avidità; *-ity for money*, l'avidità del denaro.
**avocation** *n.* occupazione; mestiere *m.*; (leg.) avocazione.
**avoid** *tr.* evitare, scansare; schivare; sfuggire. **-able** *adj.* evitabile; scansabile. **-ance** *n.* fuga, scampo; l'evitare.
**avow** *tr.* ammettere, confessare, dichiarare. **-al** *n.* ammissione, confessione, dichiarazione. **-ed** *part. adj.* ammesso; aperto, manifesto.
**avulsion** *n.* avulsione; separazione forzata.
**avuncular** *adj.* di zio; *in an — manner*, da zio.
**await** *tr.* aspettare, attendere; *-ing*, in attesa di.
**awake** *adj.* sveglio, desto; *wide* —, ben sveglio; (fig.) conscio, sensibile; *tr.* svegliare, risvegliare; *intr.* svegliarsi, risvegliarsi; (fig.) *to — to*, diventare conscio di, rendersi conto di.
**awaken** *tr.* risvegliare; (fig.) *to — someone*, far aprire gli occhi a qualcuno. **-ing** *adj.* che si risveglia; *n.* risveglio; (fig.) *a rude -ing*, un amaro disinganno.
**award** *n.* sentenza, aggiudicazione; giudizio arbitrale; ricompensa; onorificenza; premio; borsa di studio; (mil.) ricompensa al valore; *tr.* aggiudicare, assegnare; accordare; *to — damages*, ordinare il risarcimento dei danni.
**aware** *adj.* consapevole, cosciente, conscio; prevenuto, informato; *to be — of*, sapere, accorgersi di. **-ness** *n.* consapevolezza; sensibilità; prontezza di spirito.
**awash** *adv.* a galla, a fior d'acqua; *adj.* inondato.
**away** *adv.* via, fuori; lontano, assente; — *with you!*, via!, vattene!; *to be five miles* —, distare cinque miglia.
**awe** *n.* timore *m.* reverenziale; *to stand in — of*, avere timore di; *to strike with* —, ispirare timore a; *to keep in* —, tenere in soggezione; *tr.* incutere timore a; far tremare. **-some** *adj.* tremendo, che incute

timore. **-strúck** *adj.* in preda a timore.
**awe-inspiring** *adj.* imponente; che incute rispetto; impressionante.
**awful** *adj.* terribile; spaventevole; (fam.) orribile; pestifero; *you're an — fool,* sei un gran cretino. **-ly** *adv.* terribilmente; (fam.) molto, tanto; *thanks -ly,* grazie mille; *she's -ly nice,* è simpaticissima. **-ness** *n.* terribilità; (fam.) mostruosità.
**awhile** *adv.* un momento, un po'; *wait —,* aspetta un po'; *not yet —,* non ancora.
**awkward** *adj.* goffo, sgraziato; scomodo, imbarazzante, delicato; *to feel —,* sentirsi imbarazzato; *an — corner,* una svolta pericolosa. **-ly** *adv.* goffamente; in modo imbarazzante; *to be -ly placed,* trovarsi in una situazione difficile. **-ness** *n.* goffaggine *f.*; difficoltà; imbarazzo.
**awl** *n.* lesina, punteruolo.
**awning** *n.* tenda di riparo.
**awry** *adj.* storto; *adv.* a sghembo, a sbieco, di traverso.
**axe** *n.* scure *f.*, ascia, accetta; *executioner's —,* mannaia del boia; *tr.* tagliare con la scure; (fig.) cancellare.
**axial** *adj.* assiale.
**axill-a** *n.* (anat.) ascella. **-ary** *adj.* ascellare.
**axiom** *n.* assioma *m.* **-atic(al)** *adj.* assiomatico.
**axis** *n.* asse *m.*; (hist. pol.) *the Rome-Berlin —,* l'asse Roma-Berlino.
**axle** *n.* asse, assale *m.*; perno; *axle-box,* boccola.
**axle-tree** *n.* asse *m.* della ruota.
**ay(e)** *excl.* sì; *n.* voto affermativo; (naut.) *aye, aye, Sir!,* Signorrsì!
**azalea** *n.* (bot.) azalea.
**azimuth** *n.* (astron.) azimut *m.*
**Azores** *pr.n.pl.* (geog.) *the —,* le Azzorre.
**azure** *adj., n.* azzurro; (fig.) cielo.

**B** *n.* bi *m., f.* (teleph.) *— for Benjamin,* bi come Bologna; (mus.) si *m.*
**baa** *n.* (onom.) belato; *intr.* belare.
**baa-lamb** *n.* agnellino.
**babble** *n.* balbettamento; ciarla; mormorìo; *tr., intr.* balbettare, ciarlare; mormorare.
**babe** *n.* bambino; *-s and sucklings,* gli innocenti; *— in arms,* bambino in braccia.
**Babel** *pr.n.* (bibl.) Babele *f.*; *the tower of —,* la torre di Babele; (fig.) babele; confusione.
**baboon** *n.* babbuino.
**baby** *n.* bimbo, neonato, piccino; *— boy,* bambino, maschietto; *— girl,* bambina, femminuccia; *— brother,* fratellino; *— sister,* sorellina; *the — of the family,* il beniamino; *to have a —,* fare un bambino; (mus.) *a — grand,* un pianoforte a mezza coda; *— clothes,* pannolini *m.pl.*, corredino. **-hood** *n.* prima infanzia. **-ish** *adj.* bambinesco, infantile.
**Babylon** *pr.n.* (hist. geog.) Babilonia. **-ian** *adj., n.* babilonese.
**bacchanal** *adj.* bacchico; *n.* baccanale *m.*; **-ia** *n.* baccanali *m.pl.*; (fig.) orgia, baldoria.
**bacchant(e)** *n.* baccante *m., f.*
**Bacch-us** *pr.n.* (myth.) Bacco. **-ic** *adj.* bacchico.
**bachelor** *n.* scapolo, celibe *m.*; *— of Arts* (B.A.), dottore, laureato in lettere. **-hood** *n.* celibato.
**bacillus** *n.* bacillo.
**back** *adv.* dietro; indietro; di ritorno; *to make one's way —,* rifare il cammino; *there and —,* andata e ritorno; *keep —!,* indietro!; *to be —,* essere di ritorno; *to get —,* ritornare; *— and forth,* avanti e indietro.
**back** *n.* dorso; schiena; reni *f.pl.*; posteriore *m.*; *behind my —,* dietro di me, alle mie spalle; *to turn one's — on,* volgere le spalle a; *to laugh behind someone's —,* ridere alle spalle di qualcuno; *to lie on one's —,* giacere supino; *to fall on one's —,* cadere a rovescio; *to put one's — into something,* darci sotto; *he gets my — up,* mi fa arrabbiare; *— to —,* addossati; *— to front,* a rovescio; *the — of the hand,* il dorso della mano; (of chair) schienale, dossale *m.*; (of cloth, medal) rovescio; (of page) verso; (of house) retro; *at the — of,* a tergo di, in fondo a; *the — of the shop,* la retrobottega; (football) *full —,* terzino. **-ache** *n.* mal di schiena. **-bone** *n.* spina dorsale; (fig.) forza, fermezza; *English to the -bone,* inglese fino al midollo.
**back** *tr.* appoggiare, sostenere; spalleggiare; (with lining) foderare; far indietreggiare; *to — a car,* far marcia indietro; (comm.) controfirmare, avallare; (betting) scommettere su, puntare su; *intr.* indietreggiare, rinculare; *to — out,* ritirarsi indietreggiando; (fig.) abbandonare un'impresa. **-er** *n.* sostenitore, finanziatore; (betting) scommettitore. **-ing** *n.* appoggio; (of material) fodera; (motor.) marcia indietro.
**back** *adj.* retro; *— door,* porta di servizio; (fig.) mezzo segreto. *— garden,* giardino interno; *— room,* camera interna; *— seat,* posto dietro; posto inferiore; *to take a — seat,* relegarsi ad una posizione inferiore; *— street,* via secondaria; *— yard,* cortiletto.
**backbit-e** *tr., intr.* sparlare (di), calunniare, denigrare. **-er** *n.* denigratore, calunniatore. **-ing** *n.* maldicenza.
**back-breaking** *adj.* massacrante, estenuante. **-chat** *n.* rimbecco; impertinenza. **-cloth** *n.* (theatr.) sfondo; retroscena *m., f.* **-dated** *adj.* retrodatato.
**back-door** *adj.* segreto; clandestino. **-fire** *n.* (motor.) ritorno di fiamma; *intr.* far ritorno di fiamma; (fig.) fallire.
**backgammon** *n.* tavola reale, trictrac *m.*
**background** *n.* fondo, sfondo, retroscena *m., f.*; (fig.) ambiente *m.*; *to keep in the —,* tenersi in disparte; *to fade into the —,* eclissarsi.
**backhand** *n.* (sport) rovescio. **-ed** *adj.* *-ed blow,* manrovescio; (of writing) inclinato verso sinistra; (fig.) equivoco, dubbio. **-er** *n.* (sport) rovescio.
**backing** *n.* see under **back** *tr.*
**backlash** *n.* contraccolpo; giuoco inutile; (fig.) ripercussione.
**backless** *adj.* (of chair) senza schienale; (of dress) che lascia nuda la schiena.
**backlog** *n.* arretrati *m.pl.*; redditi non riscossi.
**backmost** *adj.* il più indietro.
**back-number** *n.* numero arretrato; (fig.) persona antiquata, persona che non conta più. **-pay** *n.* arretrati di paga. **-pedal** *intr.* contropedalare; (fig.) ritirarsi, far marcia indietro. **-room** *adj.* *-room boys,* esperti sconosciuti al pubblico. **-seat** *adj.* (colloq.) *-seat driver,* uno che dà consigli a chi guida una macchina.
**backside** *n.* deretano, sedere *m.*
**backslid-e** *intr.* apostatare; ricadere nell'errore. **-er** *n.* apostata *m.* (also fig.). **-ing** *n.* ricaduta.
**backstage** *n.* (theatr.) retroscena *m., f.*; *adv.* dietro la scena, dietro le quinte.
**backstairs** *n.* scala di servizio; (fig.) *— influence,* influenza segreta, appoggio nascosto.
**backstay** *n.* (naut.) paterasso.
**backstitch** *n.* (needlew.) punto indietro, impuntura *f.*
**back-stroke** *n.* (sport) rovescio; rovesciata; (swimming) nuoto sul dorso.
**backward** *adj.* tardivo, retrogrado, arretrato; *to be — in doing something,* esitare a fare qualcosa. **-ness** *n.* tardità.
**backward(s)** *adv.* indietro, addietro, a rovescio, a ritroso;

*-s and forwards*, avanti e indietro; *to know something -s*, conoscere perfettamente qualcosa.

**backwash** *n.* risacca; riflusso; risucchio.

**backwater** *n.* acqua stagnante; (of river) braccio; (fig.) *this place is a —*, qui non succede mai niente.

**backwoods** *n.* foreste *f.pl.* vergini. **-man** *n.* uomo delle foreste; (fig.) uomo rozzo.

**bacon** *n.* lardo affumicato, pancetta; (fig.) *to save one's —*, salvarsi la pelle.

**bacteri-a** *n.* batteri *m.pl.* **-al** *adj.* batterico. **-ological** *adj.* batteriologico. **-ology** *n.* batteriologia.

**bad** *adj.* non buono; cattivo, malvagio, tristo; brutto; malsano, insalubre, nocivo; forte; marcio, guasto; falso; *— weather*, brutto tempo; *— climate*, clima insalubre; *— feeling*, cattivo sangue; *— language*, turpiloquio; *to feel —*, sentirsi male; *to go —*, andare a male, marcire; *to go to the —*, andare in malora; *a — habit*, una brutta abitudine; *a — job*, un brutto affare; *to make the best of a — job*, far buon viso a cattivo giuoco; *that's too — !*, che peccato!; *not so —*, non c'è male; *to be — at doing something*, non essere bravo a far qualcosa. **-ly** *adv.* male, malamente; *-ly off*, povero, squattrinato; *to behave -ly*, comportarsi male; *to need something -ly*, avere urgente bisogno di qualcosa; *to treat someone -ly*, trattar male qualcuno. **-ness** *n.* cattiveria; malvagità; cattivo stato.

**badge** *n.* distintivo; medaglia; (fig.) simbolo; (mil.) gallone *m.*; stelletta.

**badger**[1] *n.* (zool.) tasso.

**badger**[2] *tr.* tormentare, molestare, importunare.

**bad-tempered** *adj.* irascibile; irato; di cattivo umore.

**baffle** *n.* (mech.) deflettore, schermo.

**baffl-e** *tr.* eludere, confondere, sconcertare. **-ing** *adj.* sconcertante; insolubile; (of wind) contrario.

**bag** *n.* sacco; *to let the cat out of the —*, lasciarsi sfuggire un segreto, (fam.) cantare; borsa, borsetta; *— and baggage*, armi *f.pl.* e bagaglio; *pl.* (fam.) calzoni *m.pl.* **-ful** *n.* sacco pieno, saccata.

**bag** *tr.* impadronirsi di, insaccare; (hunt.) prendere, ammazzare.

**bagatelle** *n.* bagatella, inezia.

**baggage** *n.* bagaglio; (mil.) salmeria; (fam.) *a saucy —*, una ragazza sfrontata.

**baggy** *adj.* rigonfio; senza pieghe.

**bagman** *n.* (lit.) commesso viaggiatore.

**bagpipe** *n.* cornamusa.

**bag-snatch-er** *n.* (fam.) scippatore, scippista *m.* **-ing** *n.* (fam.) scippo.

**bail** *n.* (leg.) cauzione, garanzia; *to grant —*, concedere la libertà provvisoria su cauzione; *to go — for someone*, rendersi garante di qualcuno; (cricket) sbarretta.

**bail** *tr.* (leg.) dar garanzia per; *to — someone out*, ottenere per qualcuno la libertà provvisoria versando una cauzione; (naut.) *to — out a boat*, aggottare una barca; *intr.* (aeron.) *to — out*, lanciarsi col paracadute.

**bailiff** *n.* fattore, amministratore di una tenuta; funzionario incaricato di fare sequestri; usciere addetto a un tribunale.

**bairn** *n.* (Scot.) bambino.

**bait** *n.* esca; (fig.) lusinga; allettamento; *tr.* fornire d'esca, inescare; (fig.) adescare, allettare; aizzare cani contro; (fig.) tormentare.

**baize** *n.* panno pesante di lana; *green —*, tappeto verde, panno verde.

**bake** *tr.* cuocere al forno, infornare; *intr.* (fam.) cuocersi; soffrire il caldo. **-house** *n.* panificio; forno.

**bakelite** *n.* bachelite *f.*

**bak-er** *n.* fornaio, panettiere *m.* **-ery** *n.* panificio, forno.

**baking** *adj.* che si sta cuocendo; (fig.) scottante, caldissimo; *— hot*, torrido, rovente.

**baking** *n.* cottura al forno; (of bread) infornata; (of bricks) cotta; *— tin*, teglia.

**balance** *n.* bilancia; equilibrio; contrappeso; (comm.) bilancio, saldo; *credit —*, saldo a favore; *debit —*, saldo a debito; *— of trade*, bilancio esportazioni-importazioni; *— of payments*, bilancio dei pagamenti.

**balance** *tr.* bilanciare; equilibrare; *intr.* bilanciarsi; mantenere l'equilibrio; (comm.) fare il bilancio di.

**balance-sheet** *n.* bilancio.

**balcony** *n.* balcone *m.*; terrazza; loggia; (theatr.) balconata.

**bald** *adj.* calvo, spelacchiato; (of landscape) senza vegetazione; (of style) monotono, disadorno. **-ly** *adv.* recisamente; schiettamente; *to put it -ly*, per dirla in parole povere. **-ness** *n.* calvizie *f.pl.*; (med.) alopecia; (fig.) povertà.

**balderdash** *n.* ciance, frottole *f.pl.*

**bald-faced** *adj.* sfacciato. **-headed** *adj.* calvo; *adv.* (colloq.) *to go -headed at*, precipitarsi su.

**Bâle** *pr.n.* (geog.) Basilea.

**bale** *n.* balla di merce; *tr.* imballare.

**Balearic Islands** *pr.n.* (geog.) Baleari *f.pl.*, le Isole Baleariche.

**baleful** *adj.* funesto; maligno; sinistro; ostile.

**balk**[1] *n.* trave *f.*

**balk**[2] *tr.* frustrare, impedire; *to — someone of his prey*, privare qualcuno della preda; *intr.* impennarsi.

**Balkan** *adj.* (geog.) balcanico.

**Balkans** *pr.n.* (geog.) la Balcania, i Balcani.

**ball**[1] *n.* ballo, festa da ballo; *fancy-dress —*, ballo in costume; *masked —*, ballo in maschera.

**ball**[2] *n.* palla; pallone *m.*; (mil.) palla, pallottola; *— of string*, gomitolo di spago; sfera; globo; (anat.) *— of the eye*, globo oculare; *— of the foot*, avampiede *m.*; *— of the thumb*, polpastrello del pollice; *— and chain*, palla e catena; (fig.) *to keep the — rolling*, mandare avanti la baracca; *to set the — rolling*, avviare (una discussione); *to catch the — on the rebound*, cogliere la palla al balzo; *on the —*, in gamba; (mech.) *— and socket*, articolazione sferica; *pl. -s !*, balle!; *that's all -s*, è tutto corbellerie; *tr.* appallottolare, aggomitolare; *intr.* appallottolarsi, aggomitolarsi.

**ballad(e)** *n.* ballata; canzone popolare *f.*

**ballast** *n.* (naut.; fig.) zavorra; (eng.) massicciata; *tr.* (naut.) zavorrare; (eng.) massicciare.

**ball-bearing** *n.* cuscinetto a sfera. **-boy** *n.* (tennis) raccattapalle *m.* **-cock, ball-tap** *n.* rubinetto a galleggiante.

**ballerina** *n.* ballerina.

**ballet** *n.* balletto; corpo di balletto.

**ballet-dancer** *n.* ballerino; ballerina.

**balletomane** *n.* tifoso del balletto.

**ballistic** *adj.* balistico. **-s** *n.* balistica.

**balloon** *n.* pallone *m.*; aerostato; *captive —*, pallone frenato; *toy —*, palloncino; *intr.* gonfiarsi come un pallone. **-ist** *n.* aeronauta *m.* di pallone.

**ballot** *n.* ballottaggio; scrutinio; votazione; *by —*, dietro scrutinio; pallina per votare; *intr.* votare a scrutinio segreto.

**ballot-box** *n.* urna. **-paper** *n.* scheda di votazione, scheda elettorale.

**ball-pen** *n.* penna a sfera; biro *f.*

**ballroom** *n.* sala da ballo.

**balls** *tr.* (slang) *to — up*, imbrogliare, pasticciare.

**ball-shaped** *adj.* sferico.

**bally** *adj.* (slang) maledetto, porco; *what a — nuisance !*, che scalogna!

**ballyhoo** *n.* (slang) strombazzata.

**ballyrag** *tr.* see **bullyrag.**

**balm** *n.* balsamo; (bot.) melissa; (fig.) conforto. **-iness** *n.* dolcezza, fragranza, mitezza. **-y** *adj.* (of air) dolce, fragrante, mite, soave; (slang) matto.

**balsam** *n.* balsamo; (bot.) balsamina.

**Balthasar, Balthazar** *pr.n.* Baldassare.

**Baltic** *adj.*, *n.* (geog.) baltico; *Baltic Sea*, Mar Baltico.
**baluster** *n.* balaustro, balaustrino.
**balustrade** *n.* balaustrata *f.*
**bamboo** *n.* bambù *m.*
**bamboozle** *tr.* (slang) corbellare; mistificare.
**ban**[1] *n.* bando; annunzio pubblico; (eccl.) *to publish the -s*, (*or* banns), fare le pubblicazioni matrimoniali.
**ban**[2] *n.* proibizione; interdizione; censura; *tr.* proibire, interdire; censurare; mettere all'indice.
**banal** *adj.* banale, trito, comune. **-ity** *n.* banalità; luogo comune.
**banana** *n.* (fruit) banana; (tree) banano.
**band**[1] *n.* legame *m.*; vincolo; fascia; nastro; striscia; lista; *elastic* —, elastico; cerchio; (mech.) cintura; *tr.* riunire, associare; *intr.* riunirsi, associarsi.
**band**[2] *n.* banda; schiera; comitiva; (mus.) banda, orchestrina, musica; *brass* —, fanfara; (radio) banda.
**bandag-e** *n.* benda; fascia; fasciatura; *tr.* bendare, fasciare. **-ing** *n.* fasciatura.
**bandit** *n.* bandito, brigante *m.* **-ry** *n.* brigantaggio.
**bandmaster** *n.* capobanda *m.*; maestro di banda.
**bandolier** *n.* bandoliera.
**bandsman** *n.* bandista *m.*; musicante *m.*
**bandstand** *n.* palco per banda.
**band-wag(g)on** *n.* carro della banda musicale che precede un corteo; (fig.) *on the* —, dalla parte del vincitore.
**bandy**[1] *adj.* storto, curvo.
**bandy**[2] *tr.* scambiare, palleggiare.
**bandy-legged** *adj.* dalle gambe storte.
**bane** *n.* veleno; (fig.) flagello; sventura. **-ful** *adj.* velenoso.
**bang** *n.* rumore improvviso; colpo; botta; scoppio; detonazione; *excl.* pam!; pum!; *adv.* improvvisamente, di colpo; (fam.) — *went all my money*, ho perduto di colpo tutto il mio denaro; *to go* —, scoppiare; (slang) *the whole — lot*, tutto quanto.
**bang** *tr.* battere, sbattere, sbatacchiare; *to — the door*, sbattere la porta; *to — the piano*, strimpellare; *intr.* sbattere; (fam.) *to — into someone*, imbattersi in qualcuno; *to — at the door*, battere alla porta.
**bangle** *n.* braccialetto.
**banish** *tr.* bandire; esiliare; relegare; cacciare; mandare al confino. **-ment** *n.* bando; esilio.
**banister(s)** *n.* ringhiera.
**bank**[1] *n.* riva, sponda; — *of clouds*, banco di nuvoli; — *of earth*, terrapieno; (naut.) secca.
**bank**[2] *n.* (finan.) banca; banco; — *of issue*, banca di emissione; *discount* —, banco di sconto; *savings* —, cassa di risparmio; *Bank Holiday*, festa legale; (gambling) banco; *to break the* —, far saltare il banco; (seat) banco; sedile *m.*
**bank**[1] *tr.* arginare, sopraelevare; (naut.) *to — fires*, mettere i fuochi indietro; *intr.* accumularsi; (aeron.) inclinarsi in virata; *to — up*, accastarsi.
**bank**[2] *tr.*, *intr.* depositare in una banca; *whom do you — with?*, in quale banca hai il conto?; (fam.) *to — on*, contare su.
**bank-account** *n.* conto in banca, conto corrente. **-clerk** *n.* impiegato di banco.
**banker** *n.* banchiere *m.*
**bank-manager** *n.* direttore di banca. **-messenger** *n.* fattorino di una banca.
**banking** *adj.* bancario, di banca; *n.* le banche, professione di banchiere.
**bank-note** *n.* banconota; biglietto.
**bankrupt** *adj.* fallito; (fig.) carico di debiti, senza soldi; *to go* —, fallire; *n.* fallito; *discharged* —, fallito riabilitato; *tr.* far fallire; (fig.) rovinare.
**bankruptcy** *n.* fallimento; bancarotta; *fraudulent* —, fallimento doloso.
**banner** *n.* vessillo; bandiera; stendardo; gonfalone *m.*; (journ.) — *headline*, titolo a caratteri cubitali.
**banns** See **ban**[1].
**banquet** *n.* banchetto; convito; *tr.* offrire un banchetto a; *intr.* banchettare.
**banqueting-hall** *n.* sala da banchetti.
**banshee** *n.* (Ireland) spirito di donna proannunciante la morte; (fig.) fantasma *m.* che urla.
**bantam** *n.* pollo piccolissimo; (boxing) — *weight*, peso gallo.
**banter** *n.* motteggio; canzonatura; *tr.*, *intr.* motteggiare; canzonare. **-ing** *adj.* canzonatorio.
**baptism** *n.* battesimo. **-al** *adj.* battesimale; *-al font*, fonte *f.* di battesimo.
**baptist** *n.* chi battezza; *St. John the* —, San Giovanni Battista; membro della setta protestante dei 'Baptists'.
**baptist(e)ry** *n.* battistero.
**baptize** *tr.* battezzare; (fig.) soprannominare, dare un nomignolo a.
**bar** *n.* sbarra; stanga; spranga; barriera; stecca; striscia; riga; — *of soap*, saponetta; (gold) lingotto; (herald.) see **bend**; (leg.) barra; *prisoner at the* —, imputato; *the Bar*, l'Ordine degli avvocati; *to be called to the* —, essere iscritto all'albo degli avvocati; (mus.) battuta, sbarretta; (for drinks) bar *m. indecl.*; banco; (naut.) entrata di un porto.
**bar** *tr.* sprangare, sbarrare; (fig.) ostacolare; proibire, escludere; *to — oneself in*, barricarsi.
**bar** *prep.* eccetto, tranne.
**barb** *n.* punta; spina; aculeo; uncino; *tr.* munire di punta. **-ed** *adj.* spinato, uncinato; *-ed wire*, filo di ferro spinato; *-ed wire entanglement*, reticolato; (fig.) pungente, acuto; (bot.) barbato.
**Barbado(e)s** *m.pl.* (geog.) Barbados *f.*
**Barbara** *pr.n.* Barbara.
**barbarian** *adj.*, *n.* barbaro; pelvaggio.
**barbar-ic** *adj.* barbarico; primitivo. **-ism** *n.* barbarie *f. indecl.*; (gramm.) barbarismo. **-ity** *n.* barbarie *f. indecl.*
**barbarous** *adj.* barbaro; crudele; disumano.
**Barbary** *pr.n.* (geog.) Barberia.
**barber** *n.* barbiere, parrucchiere *m.*
**barbican** (archit.) antemurale *m.*
**barbiturate** *n.* (pharm.) barbiturato.
**barcarolle** *n.* (mus.) barcarola.
**Barcelona** *pr.n.* (geog.) Barcelona.
**bard** *n.* (hist.) rapsodo; aedo; (fam.) bardo; poeta *m.*
**bare** *adj.* nudo; spoglio; scoperto; *to lay* —, mettere a nudo; (fig.) vuoto; semplice; — *necessities*, strette necessità; (naut.) *under — poles*, a secco di vele; *tr.* mettere a nudo; denudare; (fig.) revelare; esporre. **-faced** *adj.* imberbe; (fig.) sfacciato, sfrontato. **-foot** scalzo, a piedi scalzi.
**bare-headed** *adj.* a capo scoperto. **-legged** *adj.* con le gambe nude.
**barely** *adv.* appena; scarsamente.
**bareness** *n.* nudità; scarsezza; povertà.
**bargain** *n.* affare *m.*; (fig.) patto; occasione; *a good* —, un buon affare; *a capital* —, un affarone; *into the* —, per giunta, in più; *it's a —!*, è un'occasione!; *to strike a* —, concludere un affare, (fig.) concludere un patto; *to make the best of a bad* —, trarre il meglio da un cattivo affare.
**bargain** *intr.* contrattare, pattuire, mercanteggiare; (fig.) *we didn't — for that*, questo non ce lo aspettavamo.
**barge** *n.* chiatta; barcone *m.*; (in Navy) lancia; *tr.* trasportare su chiatta; *intr.* (fam.) *to — into*, urtare contro; *to — about*, avanzare traballando; *to — in*, intervenire a sproposito.
**bargee** *n.* chiattaiuolo *m.*; barcaiuolo; battelliere *m.*
**barge-pole** *n.* asta da chiatta; (fam.) *I wouldn't touch it with a* —, lo allontanerei ad ogni costo.
**baric** *adj.* (chem.) barico.
**baritone** *n.* baritono; *adj.* baritonale, da baritono.
**barium** *n.* (chem.) bario.
**bark**[1] *n.* scorza; corteccia; *tr.* scortecciare, scorzare; *to — one's knuckles*, sbucciarsi le nocche.

**bark**[2] *n.* latrato; *his — is worse than his bite*, è can che abbaia ma non morde; *intr.* abbaiare, latrare; (fig.) *to — up the wrong tree*, prendersela con chi non c'entra.
**bark**[3] *n.* (poet.) barca, nave *f.*; (naut.) brigantino a palo.
**bar-keeper** *n.* proprietario di un bar.
**barley** *n.* orzo. **-corn** *n.* grano d'orzo; (fig.) whisky *m. indecl.*
**barley-sugar** *n.* zucchero d'orzo.
**barmaid** *n.* cameriera al banco.
**barman** *n.* barista *m. indecl.*
**barmy** *adj.* che contiene lievito; (fig.) matto.
**barn** *n.* granaio; (derog.) baracca. **-yard** *n.* cortile di una fattoria.
**barnacle** *n.* cirripede; (fig.) attaccabottoni *m. indecl.*
**barn-dance** *n.* danza campestre. **-owl** *n.* civetta.
**barograph** *n.* barografo.
**baromet-er** *n.* barometro. **-ric(al)** *adj.* barometrico.
**baron** *n.* barone *m.*; (fig.) grande industriale *m.*; (cul.) *— of beef*, lombata di manzo. **-ess** *n.* baronessa. **-et** *n.* baronetto. **-ial** *adj.* baronale.
**baroque** *adj.*, *n.* barocco.
**barque** *n.* (naut.) brigantino a palo.
**barquentine** *n.* (naut.) goletta.
**barrack(s)** *n.* (mil.) caserma; (fig.) baracca; *tr.* accasermare; (sport) fischiare. **-ing** *n.* (sport) il fischiare.
**barrage** *n.* sbarramento.
**barratry** *n.* baratteria; corruzione.
**barrel** *n.* barile *m.*; botte *f.*; fusto; (of gun) canna; (archit.) *— vault*, volta a botte.
**barrel-organ** *n.* organetto di Barberia.
**barren** *adj.* sterile; arido. **-ness** *n.* sterilità; infecondità; aridità.
**barricade** *n.* barricata; *tr.* barricare.
**barrier** *n.* barriera; barricata; recinto; cancello.
**barring** *prep.* eccetto, tranne; *— accidents*, salvo incidenti.
**barrister** *n.* avvocato.
**barrow**[1] *n.* carriuola, carretta; carrettino.
**barrow**[2] *n.* (archaeol.) tumulo.
**bartender** *n.* barista *m.*
**barter** *n.* baratto; scambio; *tr.*, *intr.* barattare, scambiare, praticare il baratto; (fig.) *to — away*, vendere.
**Bartholomew** *pr.n.* Bartolomeo.
**basalt** *n.* basalto.
**base**[1] *adj.* basso, vile; *— metals*, metalli vili. **-ness** *n.* bassezza; viltà.
**base**[2] *n.* base *f.*; fondamento; piedistallo; zoccolo; (mil.) base; *tr.* basare; fondare. **-less** *adj.* infondato; senza base. **-lessness** *n.* infondatezza.
**baseball** *n.* palla a basi.
**basement** *n.* fondamento; *— flat*, appartamento al seminterrato.
**bash** *n.* colpo violento; *tr.* colpire violentamente; fracassare.
**bashful** *adj.* timido; vergognoso. **-ness** *n.* timidezza.
**basic** *adj.* fondamentale; (chem.) basico.
**Basil**[1] *pr.n.m.* Basilio.
**basil**[2] *n.* (bot.) basilico.
**basilica** *n.* (archit.) basilica.
**basilisk** *n.* (myth.) basilisco.
**basin** *n.* bacino; catino; scodella; *wash-hand —*, lavabo *m. indecl.*; (naut.) bacino, darsena; (geol.) bacino; (of fountain) vasca.
**basis** *n.* base *f.*; fondamento.
**bask** *intr.* sdraiarsi; *to — in the sun*, prendere il sole; (fig.) *to — in someone's favour*, godere il favore di qualcuno.
**basket** *n.* cesto; canestro; sporta; *waste-paper —*, cestino; (fig.) *the pick of the —*, il migliore fra tutti. **-ful** *n.* panierata.
**basket-ball** *n.* pallacanestro. **-chair** *n.* sedia di vimini. **-maker** *n.* cestaio, panieraio, canestraio.
**Basle** *pr.n.* (geog.) Basilea.
**Basque** *adj.*, *n.* (ethn.; geog.) basco; *the — language*, il basco.
**bas-relief** *n.* (art) bassorilievo.
**bass**[1] *n.* (mus.) basso; *— drum*, gran cassa.
**bass**[2], **bast** *n.* (bot.) tiglio americano; (gardening) stuoia, fibra di tiglio.
**bass**[3] *n.* (ichth.) addotto, cerniola, branzino.
**basset** *n.* cane bassotto.
**basset-horn** *n.* (mus.) corno di bassetto.
**bassoon** *n.* (mus.) fagotto, bassone *m.*
**bast** *n.* see **bass**[2].
**bastard** *adj.* bastardo, illegittimo; (fig.) spurio; *n.* bastardo.
**baste** *tr.* (needlew.) imbastire; (cul.) spruzzare con lardo; (slang) bastonare.
**bastion** *n.* bastione *m.*
**bat**[1] *n.* (zool.) pipistrello; (fig.) *as blind as a —*, cieco come una talpa; (fam.) *to have -s in the belfry*, essere un po' matto.
**bat**[2] *n.* (sport) mazza; racchetta; *tr.* battere; *he didn't — an eyelid*, non battè ciglio; *intr.* (sport) maneggiare la mazza, battere (la palla) con la mazza.
**batch** *n.* (of goods) lotto; (of persons) gruppo; (of bread) infornata; (fig.) *I have received a — of letters*, ho ricevuto un mucchio di lettere.
**bate** *tr.* abbassare, ridurre; (fig.) *with -d breath*, con un fil di voce.
**bath** *n.* bagno; vasca da bagno; *to take a —*, fare un bagno (in vasca); *swimming —*, piscina; *pl.* stazione termale.
**bath** *tr.* fare il bagno a; *intr.* fare un bagno.
**Bath chair** *n.* carrozzella per invalidi.
**bath-e** *n.* bagno; *to go for a —*, andare a fare il bagno; *tr.* bagnare; *intr.* fare il bagno. **-er** *n.* bagnante *m.*, *f.* **-ing** *n.* il bagnarsi; i bagni *m.pl.*
**bathing-cap** *n.* cuffia da bagno. **-costume** *n.* costume *m.* da bagno. **-establishment** *n.* stabilimento di bagni; bagni pubblici. **-hut** *n.* cabina da bagno. **-place** *n.* stazione balneare; luogo dove è permesso di fare il bagno. **-pool** *n.* piscina. **-season** *n.* stagione dei bagni.
**bath-mat** *n.* stuoia da bagno. **-robe** *n.* accappatoio. **-salts** *n.* sali *m.pl.* da bagni. **-towel** *n.* tovaglia da bagno. **-tub** *n.* vasca da bagno, tinozza.
**bathos** *n.* discesa dal sublime al ridicolo.
**bathroom** *n.* stanza da bagno.
**bathysphere** *n.* batiscafo.
**batman** *n.* (mil.) ordinanza; attendente *m.*
**baton** *n.* (field-marshal) bastone *m.*; (policeman) manganello; (mus.) bacchetta.
**batsman** *n.* (cricket) battitore.
**battalion** *n.* battaglione *m.*
**batten** *n.* assicella, piccola traversa; (naut.) serretta; *tr.* (naut.) *to — down*, chiudere i boccaporti con rinforzi di legno; *intr. to — on*, sfruttare.
**batter**[1] *n.* (cul.) pastella.
**batter**[2] *tr.*, *intr.* battere; colpire ripetutamente; percuotere; fracassare; (cul.) sbattere; *to — down*, abbattere. **-ing** *n.* il battere; (fam.) bastonatura.
**battering-ram** *n.* (mil. hist.) ariete *m.*
**battery** *n.* batteria; (mil.) reggimento di artiglieria; (leg.) *assault and —*, vie *f.pl.* di fatto; (electr.) batteria, accumulatore; (mus.) batteria.
**battle**[1] *n.* battaglia; combattimento; (fig.) lotta; *to join — with*, entrare in lotta con; (fam.) *that's half the —*, ecco un gran vantaggio; *intr.* combattere, battersi, lottare. **-field** *n.* campo di battaglia. **-ment** *n.* merlo, merlatura; bastione *m.* **-mented** *adj.* merlato. **-ship** *n.* corazzata.
**battle-axe** *n.* azza; (fig.) donna bisbetica. **-cruiser** *n.* incrociatore da battaglia. **-cry** *n.* grido di battaglia. **-dress** *n.* uniforme *m.* da campo.
**batty** *adj.* (slang) tocco, atto.
**bauble** *n.* bagattella, bazzecola; giuocattolo.
**baulk.** See **balk**[2].
**Bavari-a** *pr.n.* (geog.) Baviera. **-an** *adj.*, *n.* bavarese *m.*, *f.*
**bawd** *n.* mezzana; ruffiana. **-iness** *n.* oscenità. **-y** *adj.* osceno, lurido; *— story*, barzelletta spinta; *-y house*, bordello.

**bawl** *tr.*, *intr.* vociare, urlare, gridare a squarciagola. **-ing** *n.* vociò, grido; schiamazzo.

**bay**[1] *n.* (bot.) lauro, alloro.

**bay**[2] *n.* (geog.) baia, golfo, insenatura; (archit.) recesso.

**bay**[3] *n.* latrato; *to be at —*, essere agli estremi, trovarsi in scacco; *to bring to —*, ridurre agli estremi; *to hold at —*, tenere a bada; *intr.* latrare; *to — at the moon*, abbaiare alla luna.

**bay**[4] *adj.*, *n.* (of horse) baio.

**bayonet** *n.* baionetta; *with fixed -s*, con le baionette innastate; *— thrust*, baionettata; *tr.* colpire con la baionetta.

**bay-window** *n.* bovindo.

**bay-wreath** *n.* corona d'alloro.

**bazaar** *n.* bazar *m. indecl.*; *charity —*, vendita di beneficenza; emporio.

**be** *intr.* essere; *to — or not to —*, essere o non essere; *Thy will — done*, sia fatta la Tua volontà; esistere; stare; trovarsi; *how are you?*, come stai?; *he is in Italy now*, ora si trova in Italia; aver luogo; *when is the wedding to be?*, quando avrà luogo il matrimonio?; *he is writing a letter*, sta scrivendo una lettera; *I was to have gone to London yesterday*, ieri dovevo andare a Londra; avere, fare; *I am cold*, ho freddo; *it is cold*, fa freddo; *it is to — hoped*, è da sperare; *to — off*, andarsene; *to — about to*, stare per, essere sul punto di.

**beach** *n.* spiaggia; riva; lido; ghiaia marina; *tr.* tirare a spiaggia; arenare. **-comber** *n.* uomo che vive di ciò che il mare rigetta sulla spiaggia; (fig.) buono a nulla, vagabondo.

**beacon** *n.* falò che si accende per segnalare un pericolo; (fig.) faro; *radio —*, radiofaro.

**bead** *n.* grano; perlina; goccia; (on gun) mirino; (fig.) *to draw a — on*, prendere di mira; *pl.* vezzo di perline; *to tell one's -s*, dire il rosario; *tr.*, *intr.* imperlare, imperlarsi; infilare perline. **-work** *n.* guarnizione con perline. **-y** *adj.* piccolo e lucente.

**beadle** *n.* bidello; sagrestano; scaccino.

**beagle** *n.* cane *m.* da caccia alla lepre.

**beak** *n.* becco; rostro; (naut.) sperone *m.*; (fam.) naso; (slang) *to be up before the —*, trovarsi davanti al pretore.

**beaker** *n.* coppa; calice *m.*

**beam** *n.* trave *f.*; (of light) raggio; (radio) fascio, segnale *m.* unidirezionale; (of scales) giogo; (naut.) fianco di nave, traverso; *tr.*, *intr.* irradiare, brillare, raggiare, sfavillare; (radio) individuare a mezzo radar; (fig.) *to — upon*, guardare con viso raggiante. **-ing** *adj.* raggiante.

**beam-ends** *n.* (naut., of ship) *to be on her —*, essere coricato sul fianco; (fig.) trovarsi in cattive acque, essere senza soldi.

**bean** *n.* fava; fagiolo; (of coffee) chicco; *French -s*, fagiolini *m.pl.*; *haricot -s*, fagioli *m.pl.*; (fam.) *old —*, caro amico, amico mio; *I haven't a —*, non ho neppure un soldo, sono al verde; *to be full of -s*, essere pieno di energia; *it isn't worth a —*, non vale un fico; *to spill the -s*, rivelare un segreto, cantare. **-feast** *n.* pranzo annuale offerto dal padrone ai dipendenti; (fig.) festa allegra. **-stalk** *n.* gambo di pianta di fagiolo.

**beano** *n.* (slang) baldoria.

**bear**[1] *n.* (zool.) orso; (astron.) *the Great Bear*, l'Orsa Maggiore; *the Little Bear*, l'Orsa Minore; (finan.) speculatore al ribasso; (fig.) *to be like a — with a sore head*, essere immusonito. **-skin** *n.* pelle *f.* d'orso; (mil.) colbacco.

**bear**[2] *tr.* portare, reggere; *to — arms*, portare le armi; *to — in mind*, tenere a mente; *to — witness*, far testimonianza; *to — comparison with*, reggere il paragone con; soffrire, sopportare; *I cannot — him*, non lo posso soffrire; *to — pain*, sopportare dolore; generare, dare alla luce; *she bore three sons*, ha avuto tre figli; *to — fruit*, dare frutti; *to — the consequences*, subire le conseguenze; *intr.* girare, svoltare; (naut.) poggiare; *— right!*, svoltare a destra!; *to bring influence to — on*, far pesare la propria autorità su; *to — with*, aver pazienza con; *to — up*, resistere; *— up!*, coraggio!; *to — down upon*, piombare su; *rfl.* *to — oneself*, comportarsi. **-able** *adj.* sopportabile. **-er** *n.* portatore, latore; (mil.) *-er of a flag of truce*, parlamentario.

**bear-baiting** *n.* (hist.) combattimento di cani contro un orso. **-garden** *n.* recinto degli orsi; (fig.) baraonda. **-pit** *n.* fossa degli orsi.

**beard** *n.* barba; *to grow a —*, lasciarsi crescere la barba; (astron.) chioma; (bot.) resta. **-ed** *adj.* barbuto. **-less** *adj.* imberbe, senza barba.

**beard** *tr.* sfidare; *to — the lion in his den*, sfidare il leone nel suo covo, (fig.) affrontare l'ira di qualcuno.

**bearing** *adj.* portante, che porta; *n.* il portare, il sopportare; *beyond all —*, insopportabile; contegno, condotta; piglio; (herald.) stemma *m.*; (naut.; aeron.) rilevamento; *to take a — on*, rilevare; *pl.* (fig.) senso di direzione; *to lose one's -s*, disorientarsi, non sapere dove si è; (mech.) cuscinetto.

**beast** *n.* bestia; animale *m.*; bruto; *— of burden*, bestia da soma; *pl.* bestiame *m.*; *wild —*, fiera, belva, (fig., of human being) animale *m.*, bruto, sporcaccione *m.*; *to make a — of oneself*, fare una porcheria. **-liness** *n.* bestialità, brutalità; (fig.) oscenità. **-ly** *adj.* bestiale; brutale; sporco; schifoso; *-ly weather*, tempaccio, tempo da cane.

**beat** *tr.* battere, percuotere, picchiare; bastonare; (mus.) battere; (eggs, wings) sbattere; (mil.) *to — a retreat*, battere in ritirata; (sport) battere, vincere, superare; *to — a record*, battere il primato; (fam.) *to — about the bush*, menare il can per l'aia; (slang) *to — it*, darsela a gambe; *to — down*, abbattere, abbacchiare; (prices) far ribassare; *to — off*, respingere; (slang) *to — up*, picchiare a santa ragione; *intr.* battere, palpitare; *part. adj.* (slang) vinto; *dead —*, stanco morto; *— generation*, generazione bruciata. **-en** *part. adj.* battuto, picchiato, vinto, sconfitto; *-en earth*, terra battuta; *-en track*, strada battuta, via seguita da tutti; *off the -en track*, (luogo) poco frequentato. **-er** *n.* (hunt.) battitore, scaccione *m.*; (industr.) agitatore, battitore.

**beat** *n.* il battere; colpo; battito, palpito; (policeman's) ronda, zona; (mus.) battuta; ritmo.

**beatif-y** *tr.* (eccl.) beatificare; (fig.) rendere felice. **-ic** *adj.* beatifico; (fig.) beato. **-ication** *n.* beatificazione.

**beating** *adj.* palpitante; *n.* bastonata; sconfitta; *to take a —*, essere sconfitto; battito; palpitazione; (of drums) rullo.

**beatitude** *n.* beatitudine *f.*, felicità.

**beatnik** *n.* (slang) esponente *m.*, *f.* della generazione bruciata; tifoso della musica popolare.

**Beatrice, Beatrix** *pr.n.* Beatrice.

**beau** *n.* damerino, zerbinotto; cicisbeo; (fam.) pretendente, spasimante *m.*

**beaut-iful** *adj.* bello, bellissimo; stupendo. **-eous** *adj.* vago; leggiadro. **-ician** *n.* estetista *m.*, *f.* **-ify** *tr.* abbellire; ornare.

**beauty** *n.* bellezza; beltà; vaghezza; bella donna, bella ragazza; *the Sleeping Beauty*, la Bella Addormentata; (fig.) il bello; *the — of it is that*, il bello si è che; (iron.) *you're a —!*, sei un bel tipo!

**beauty-parlour** *n.* istituto di bellezza. **-sleep** *n.* primo sonno. **-spot** *n.* luogo pittoresco; (on face) neo.

**beaver** *n.* castoro; (slang) uomo barbuto.

**becalm** *tr.* (naut.) abbonacciare; *to be -ed*, restare in bonaccia.

**because** *conj.* perchè; poichè; *compd. prep.* *— of*, a causa di, a cagione di, per.

**beck**[1] *n.* cenno; segno; *to be at someone's — and call,* essere sempre agli ordini di qualcuno.
**beck** [2] *n.* ruscello.
**beckon** *tr., intr.* chiamare con un cenno, far segnali (a).
**becom-e** *tr., intr.* diventare, divenire; farsi; tornare; *to — acquainted with,* fare la conoscenza di; *to — old,* invecchiare; *to — bankrupt,* fallire; *what has — of him?,* che ne è di lui?, com'è andato a finire?; addirsi a, stare bene a, convenire, donare a. **-ing** *adj.* adatto; conveniente; che si addice; che sta bene. **-ingness** *n.* convenienza; eleganza.
**bed** *n.* letto; *single —,* letto semplice; *double —,* letto matrimoniale; *twin -s,* letti gemelli; *in —,* a letto; *to go to —,* andare a letto; *to make a —,* rifare un letto; *to keep to one's —,* essere costretto al letto; *— and board,* vitto e alloggio; (fig.) *you have made your —, now you must lie on it,* ti sei messo nei guai, ora arrangiati; (river) greto, alveo; (sea) fondo; (geol.) giacimento; (machine) basamento; base *f.*; *tr.* mettere a letto; piantare; (mech.) fissare, assestare. **-chamber** *n.* camera; *gentleman of the -chamber,* gentiluomo di camera. **-clothes** *n.* coperte *f.pl.* da letto; *to get under the -clothes,* ficcarsi sotto le lenzuola. **-fellow** *n.* compagno di letto. **-post** *n.* colonna del letto. **-ridden** *n.* costretto a letto. **-room** *n.* camera da letto; *spare -room,* camera degli ospiti; *-room slippers,* pantofole *f.pl.* **-side** *n.* fianco del letto, capezzale *m.* *-side manner,* modi rassicuranti (di medico); *-side table,* tavolino da notte, comodino. **-sore** *n.* piaga da decubito. **-spread** *n.* copriletto. **-stead** *n.* telaio del letto. **-time** *n.* l'ora di andare a letto.
**bedaub** *tr.* imbrattare di colore.
**bed-bug** *n.* cimice *m.*
**bedding** *n.* biancheria da letto; tutto quanto occorre per fare il letto.
**bedeck** *tr.* ornare, abbellire, decorare, addobbare.
**bedevil** *tr.* ammaliare; (fig.) vessare, tormentare.
**bedew** *tr.* irrorare.
**bedlam** *pr.n.* manicomio; (fig.) confusione, baraonda.
**bed-linen** *n.* biancheria da letto. **-pan** *n.* padella per ammalati. **-warmer** *n.* scaldaletto.
**bedouin** *adj., n.* beduino.
**bedraggled** *adj.* inzaccherato, fradicio.
**bedrock** *n.* fondo.
**bed-sitting-room, bed-sitter** *n.* camera con letto.
**bee** *n.* ape *f.*; pecchia; *a swarm of -s,* uno sciame di api; (fam.) *to have a — in one's bonnet,* avere un'idea fissa, avere una zanzara nella testa.
**beech** *n.* (bot.) faggio.
**beef**[1] *n.* manzo, bue *m.*; *boiled —,* manzo lesso; *roast —,* arrosto di manzo, rosbif *m.*; *tinned —,* manzo in scatola; (fig.) muscolo, nerbo; *to have plenty of —,* essere robusto. **-eater** *n.* guardiano alla Torre di Londra. **-steak** *n.* bistecca.
**beef**[2] *intr.* (slang) brontolare.
**beef-tea** *n.* brodo fatto con estratto di carne di manzo.
**beef-y** *adj.* (fam.) robusto; gagliardo. **-iness** *n.* muscolosità; robustezza.
**beehive** *n.* alveare *m.*, arnia.
**bee-keep-er** *n.* apicoltore. **-ing** *n.* apicoltura.
**bee-line** *n.* linea d'aria, linea retta; *to make a — for something,* dirigersi con decisione verso qualcosa.
**Beelzebub** *pr.n.* Belzebù.
**beer** *n.* birra; *bottled —,* birra in bottiglia; *draught —,* birra alla spina; (fig.) *small —,* poca roba, cosa di nessuna importanza; *life is not all — and skittles,* la vita non è tutta rose e fiori. **-house** *n.* birreria. **-y** *adj.* di birra; alticcio.
**beer-barrel** *n.* barile *m* da birra. **-garden** *n.* birreria, caffè *m. indecl.* all'aperto.
**beeswax** *n.* cera vergine.
**beet** *n.* barbabietola; *— sugar,* zucchero di barbabietola.
**beetle**[1] *n.* (ent.) coleottero; scarabeo; *black —,* scarafaggio.
**beetle**[2] *intr.* (of eyebrows) sporgere; (of rocks) strapiombare.
**beetle-crusher** *n.* (fam.) scarpone *m.*; (slang) poliziotto.
**beetroot** *n.* barbabietola.
**befall** *intr.* accadere, succedere.
**befit** *tr.* convenire a, addirsi a. **-ting** *adj.* conveniente, che si addice.
**befog** *tr.* annebbiare; offuscare.
**before** *adv.* prima, già, innanzi, in precedenza; *as —,* come prima; *prep.* prima di; *— long,* fra non molto; davanti a, dinanzi a; *— Christ* (B.C.), avanti Cristo (a.C.); *conj.* prima che; piuttosto che. **-hand** *adv.* anticipatamente, in anticipo.
**befoul** *tr.* insudiciare, sporcare.
**befriend** *tr.* aiutare, favorire, trattare da amico.
**beg** *tr.* chiedere, domandare; *to — a favour,* chiedere un favore; *to — pardon,* chiedere scusa; *I — your pardon,* mi scusi!; pregare; *I — you,* ti prego, mi raccomando; *to — and implore,* pregare e ripregare; *to — someone off,* chiedere grazia per qualcuno; (fig.) *to — the question,* prendere una cosa per certa, schivare una domanda; *intr. to — for,* chiedere insistentemente; *to — (for alms),* mendicare, chiedere l'elemosina; (comm.) pregiarsi; *we — to inform you,* ci pregiamo di informarvi; (to dog) *—!,* tò!
**beget** *tr.* procreare, generare; (rel.) *the only Begotten,* il Figlio unigenito. **-ter** *n.* generatore, padre.
**beggar** *n.* mendicante, accattone, pezzente *m.*; (fig.) poverino, poveraccio; (fam.) *lucky —!,* beato te!; (pej.) villano, insolente *m.*; (provb.) *-s can't be choosers,* o mangiar questa minestra o saltar dalla finestra; *tr.* ridurre alla miseria, rovinare; (fig.) *it -s description,* è impossibile descriverlo. **-ly** *adj.* meschino, gretto, misero. **-y** *n.* miseria; povertà.
**beggar-my-neighbour** *n.* (cards) rubamazzetto.
**begging** *n.* accattonaggio; questua; *adj.* che chiede l'elemosina; *— friar,* frate *m.* mendicante; (fig.) *a — letter,* una lettera con la quale si chiede dei soldi.
**begin** *tr., intr.* cominciare, incominciare, esordire; iniziare, dare inizio a, principiare; *to — afresh,* ricominciare, riprendere; *to — business,* esordire negli affari; *to — from the -ning,* cominciare dal principio; *to — with,* in primo luogo, anzitutto; *to — by doing something,* cominciare col fare qualcosa. **-ner** *n.* principiante *m., f.*; esordiente *m., f.*; novizio. **-ning** *n.* principio; inizio.
**begone** *excl.* vattene!
**begrime** *tr.* annerire, insudiciare.
**begrudge** *tr.* invidiare; lesinare, dare malvolentieri.
**beguile** *tr.* ingannare, incantare, sedurre; persuadere; *to — the time,* far passare il tempo.
**behalf** *n.* vantaggio; *on — of,* a nome di, nell'interesse di, a favore di; *on my —,* per conto mio, a nome mio.
**behave** *intr.* comportarsi, agire; *to — like a hero,* comportarsi da eroe; funzionare; *rfl. — yourself!,* sta buono!, comportati bene.
**behaviour** *n.* condotta; comportamento; contegno; *to be on one's best —,* comportarsi bene, fare del proprio meglio; funzionamento.
**behead** *tr.* decapitare, decollare; mozzare il capo a. **-ing** *n.* decapitazione, decollazione.
**behest** *n.* comando; richiesta.
**behind** *adv.* dietro, di dietro, indietro, in ritardo; *to be — with,* essere in arretrato con; *to stay —* restare indietro; *to leave —,* dimenticare; *prep.* dietro (di), dopo; *— the scenes,* dietro le quinte; *— someone's back,* dietro le spalle di qualcuno, all'insaputa di qualcuno; *to put — one,* volgere le spalle a; *— time,* in ritardo; *— the times,* antiquato. **-hand** *adv.* indietro, in ritardo, in arretrato.

**behind** *n.* (fam.) deretano, sedere *m.*
**behold** *tr.* guardare, vedere, scorgere; contemplare.
**beholden** *adj. to be — to,* essere obbligato verso.
**behoof** *n.* vantaggio; interesse *m.*
**behove** *tr.* convenire a, essere necessario a.
**beige** *adj.* bigio; *n.* bigello.
**being** *part.* of **be**; *for the time —,* per il momento.
**being** *n.* essere *m.*; *human —,* essere umano; esistenza; l'essere; *in —,* esistente; ancora vigente; *to call into —,* dar vita a; *to come into —,* nascere.
**bejewel** *tr.* ornare con gioielli.
**belabour** *tr.* bastonare, picchiare; (fig.) assalire con parole.
**belated** *adj.* tardivo, in ritardo.
**belay** *tr.* (naut.) legare, attaccare, dar volta; *— there!,* ferma!, basta!; (mountaineering) assicurare una corda.
**belaying-pin** *n.* (naut.) caviglia.
**belch** *n.* rutto; (of smoke) zaffata; (fig.) eruzione; scoppio; *tr., intr.* ruttare, eruttare; (fig.) vomitare.
**beleaguer** *tr.* assediare, investire.
**belfry** *n.* campanile *m.*; cella campanaria.
**Belg-ium** *pr.n.* (geog.) Belgio *m.* **-ian** *adj., n.* belga *m., f.*
**Belgrade** *pr.n.* (geog.) Belgrado *f.*
**belie** *tr.* smentire; mancare a; deludere.
**belief** *n.* credenza; credo; fede *f.*; *beyond —,* incredibile; *to the best of my —,* per quanto io ne sappia, in fede mia.
**believ-e** *tr., intr.* credere, prestare fede a, aver fiducia in; *to make —,* far finta, fingere. **-able** *adj.* credibile; attendibile. **-er** *n.* credente *m., f.*
**belittle** *tr.* rimpicciolire; (fig.) deprezzare, denigrare.
**bell** *n.* campanello; *to ring the —,* suonare il campanello; campana; (on animal's neck) sonaglio; (bot.) campanula, corolla; (naut.) turno di mezz'ora di guardia; *ship's —,* campana di bordo; (fig.) *as sound as a —,* sano come un pesce in acqua; *tr.* attaccare un sonaglio a. **-ringer** campanaro. **-wether** *n.* montone *m.* guida.
**bell-boy** *n.* (hotel) piccolo. **-buoy** *n.* (naut.) boa a campana. **-clapper** *n.* batacchio. **-cord** *n.* cordone *m.* del campanello. **-metal** *n.* bronzo di campana. **-push** *n.* pulsante *m.* del campanello. **-rope** *n.* fune *f.* di campana. **-shaped** *adj.* a forma di campana. **-tent** *n.* tenda conica. **-tower** *n.* campanile *m.*
**belle** *n.* bella figliuola; (joc.) fidanzata; *the — of the ball,* la reginetta del ballo.
**bellicos-e** *adj.* bellicoso. **-ity** *n.* bellicosità.
**bellied** *adj.* panciuto, corpulento.
**belliger-ent** *adj., n.* belligerante *m., f.* **-ency** *n.* belligerenza.
**bellow** *tr., intr.* muggire, mugghiare; urlare rabbiosamente; *to — out a song,* urlare una canzone; *m.* muggito; urlo rabbioso. **-ing** *n.* muggito.
**bellows** *n.* soffietto, mantice *m.*; *a pair of —,* i mantici.
**bell-y** *n.* ventre *m.*; addome *m.*; pancia; *tr., intr.* gonfiare, gonfiarsi. **-ied** *adj.* panciuto, corpulento. **-yache** *n.* mal *m.* di pancia, mal di ventre; *intr.* (slang) brontolare. **-yful** *n.* scorpacciata; (slang) *to have had a -yful of,* essere stufo di.
**belly-band** *n.* (of horse) sottopancia *m.* **-belt** *n.* ventriera. **-landing** *n.* (aeron.) atterragio sulla pancia. **-laugh** *n.* risata grassa.
**belong** *intr.* appartenere (a), spettare (a); essere (di), provenire (da); *that -s to me,* appartiene a me, è mio; *it -s to me to decide,* spetta a me decidere; *they — to London,* sono di Londra; *things that — together,* cose che vanno accompagnate; *to — to a club,* essere socio di un club. **-ings** *n.* roba; *personal -ings,* effetti *m.pl.* personali.
**beloved** *adj.* amato, caro; diletto, prediletto.
**below** *adv.* sotto, di sotto, al di sotto; laggiù; sottostante; *here —,* quaggiù; *the names mentioned —,* i nomi sottoelencati; (naut.) sottocoperta; *prep.* sotto, al di sotto di, inferiore a; *— sea level,* sotto il livello del mare; *a sum — a hundred pounds,* una somma inferiore a cento sterline; *— zero,* sotto zero; (comm.) *— par,* sotto la pari; (fig.) *to be — par,* stare poco bene.
**Belshazzar** *pr.n.* (bibl.) Baldassarre.
**belt** *n.* cintura; cinghia; fascia; (boxing; fig.) *to hit below the —,* dare un colpo basso; *to tighten one's —,* tirar la cinghia, saltare il pasto; zona; striscia; *green —,* zona verde.
**belt** *tr.* cingere con una cintura; (fig.) circondare; (slang) picchiare; (joc.) *-ed earl,* signore di alto lignaggio.
**bemoan** *tr.* lamentare; rimpiangere; *intr.* lamentarsi.
**bemuse** *tr.* confondere, stupefare.
**bench** *n.* panca; banco; seggio; scanno; (leg.) seggio di giudice; *the Bench,* la magistratura; (industr.) banco; *test —,* banco di prova.
**bend** *n.* piega; piegatura; curva; svolta; (of river) gomito; *hairpin —,* curva a forcella; (herald.) banda; *— sinister,* sbarra; (naut.) nodo, gruppo.
**bend** *tr.* piegare; chinare; *to — someone to one's will,* piegare qualcuno ai propri voleri; (naut.) annodare, grillare, assicurare con nodo; *intr.* piegarsi; chinarsi; fare una curva, svoltare.
**beneath** *adv.* giù, abbasso; *prep.* sotto, al di sotto di, più in basso di; *— contempt,* indegno, ignobile; *to marry — one,* sposarsi con qualcuno di condizione inferiore.
**Benedict** *pr.n.* Benedetto, Benito.
**Benedictine** *pr.n., adj.* Benedettino; (liqueur) benedettino.
**benediction** *n.* benedizione.
**benefact-ion** *n.* beneficenza; donazione a un'opera di beneficenza. **-or** *n.* benefattore. **-ress** *n.* benefattrice.
**benefice** *n.* (eccl.) beneficio; prebenda.
**benefic-ent** *adj.* benefico, generoso; salubre. **-ence** *n.* beneficenza, opera di carità; liberalità.
**beneficial** *adj.* utile; vantaggioso; che fa bene.
**benefit** *n.* vantaggio; utilità; bene *m.*; *the public —,* il bene pubblico; *for the — of,* a vantaggio di; (iron.) *for your —,* per tua norma; (theatr.) serata di beneficenza; indennità; *unemployment —,* indennità di disoccupazione; (leg.) *— of the doubt,* beneficio di dubbio.
**benefit** *tr.* giovare a, far bene a, beneficare; *intr.* approfittare, giovarsi.
**benevol-ent** *adj.* benevolo; caritatevole. **-ence** *n.* benevolenza; bontà.
**Bengal** *pr.n.* (geog.) Bengala *m.*; *— light,* bengala *m.*, fuoco del Bengala. **-i, -lee** *adj., n.* bengalese.
**benighted** *adj.* sorpreso dalla notte; (fig.) ottenebrato.
**benign** *adj.* benevolo, favorevole; (med.) benigno. **-ant** *n.* benevolo; gentile. **-ancy, -ity** *n.* benevolenza; benignità.
**benison** *n.* benedizione.
**Benjamin** *pr.n.* Beniamino.
**bent** *part.* of **bend**; piegato; *to be — on doing something,* essere deciso a far qualcosa; *homeward —,* avviato verso casa; (slang) corrotto.
**bent** *n.* disposizione; inclinazione; *to have a natural — for music,* avere disposizione per la musica; *to follow one's own —,* seguire la propria inclinazione.
**benumb** *tr.* intorpidire, intirizzire; (fig.) paralizzare.
**bequeath** *n.* legare, lasciare per testamento; (fig.) trasmettere.
**bequest** *n.* lascito; disposizione testamentaria.
**berate** *tr.* sgridare, rimproverare.
**bereave** *tr.* privare, spogliare; *to be -d,* perdere un congiunto; *bereft of sight,* privo della vista. **-ment** *n.* lutto.
**beret** *n.* beretto; basco.

**Berlin** *pr.n.* (geog.) Berlino *f.*; (vehicle) berlina.
**Bermudas** (the) *pr.n.* (geog.) le Bermude.
**Bernard** *pr.n.* Bernardo.
**Bernardine** *pr.n.* Bernardina; (eccl.) cistercense *m.*
**Berne** *pr.n.* (geog.) Berna.
**berry** *n.* bacca, coccola, chicco; (bot.) acino; *as brown as a —*, nero come un tizzo; *to go -ing*, raccogliere bacche.
**berserk** *adv. to go —*, essere preso da pazzia sanguinaria, (fig.) montare su tutte le furie.
**berth** *n.* cuccetta; (at quay) posto d'ormeggio; ancoraggio; (fig.) posto; *to have a good —*, avere un buon impiego; *to give a wide — to*, scansare, evitare; *intr.* (naut.) attraccare, amarrare; ancorare.
**Bertha** *pr.n.* Berta.
**Bertram, Bertrand** *pr.n.* Bertrando.
**beryl** *n.* (miner.) berillo, pietra acquamarina.
**beseech** *tr.* supplicare; implorare; impetrare.
**beset** *tr.* circondare; (fig.) assediare, assalire; *to be — by doubts*, essere assalito da dubbi. **-ting** *adj.* abituale; *-ting sin*, peccato inveterato.
**beside** *prep.* accanto a, vicino a, presso, allato di, di fianco a; *— the seaside*, sulla riva del mare; fuori di; *to be — oneself*, essere fuori di sè; *that's — the question*, questo non c'entra.
**besides** *adv.* inoltre, per di più, del resto, d'altronde, altrimenti; *many more —*, molti altri ancora; *prep.* oltre a.
**besieg-e** *tr.* assediare, investire, assalire. **-er** *n.* assediante *m.*
**besmear, besmirch** *tr.* imbrattare; sporcare; macchiare.
**besom** *n.* scopa.
**besot** *tr.* istupidire; abbrutire.
**bespeak** *tr.* ordinare, prenotare; (fig.) rivelare.
**bespoke** *adj. — tailor*, sarto che fornisce abiti solo su misura.
**Bess** *pr.n.* (*dimin.* of **Elizabeth**) Bettina; (hist.) *Good Queen —*, la buona regina Elisabetta; (fig.) *in the days of Good Queen —*, al tempo che Berta filava.
**best** *adj.* migliore; meglio; ottimo; *the — people*, gente per bene; *— man* (at wedding), testimone *m.* dello sposo; *n.m.* il migliore; il meglio; *to the — of my judgement*, secondo il mio modesto parere; *to make the — of a bad job*, cavarsela alla meno peggio, far di necessità virtù; *to do the — one can*, fare del proprio meglio; *to dress up in one's —*, farsi bello; *the — of it is that*, il bello è che; *we must make the — of it*, bisogna adattarci, pazienza!; *to have the — of both worlds*, salvar capra e cavoli.
**best** *adv.* nel modo migliore, meglio; *I work — in the morning*, lavoro meglio di mattina; *as — I can*, come meglio posso, quanto posso; *do as you think —*, fate come meglio vi pare; *to like —*, preferire; *adv. phr. at —*, tutt'al più.
**best** *tr.* vincere, superare.
**bestial** *adj.* bestiale, brutale, animalesco. **-ity** *n.* bestialità, brutalità.
**bestiary** *n.* bestiario.
**bestir** *tr.* muovere, agitare; *to — oneself*, muoversi, spicciarsi.
**best-looking** *adj.* il più attraente.
**bestow** *tr.* conferire; concedere; *to — a favour on someone*, accordare un favore a qualcuno; *to — in marriage*, dare in matrimonio; *to — grace*, dispensare grazia. **-al** *n.* concessione; conferimento.
**bestrew** *tr.* disseminare, cospargere.
**bestride** *tr.* cavalcare, stare a cavalcioni su, inforcare.
**best-seller** *n.* ultimo successo.
**bet** *n.* scommessa; *to have a — on*, fare una scommessa su.
**bet** *tr.*, *intr.* scommettere; *to — ten to one that*, scommettere dieci contro uno che; (fig.) essere sicurissimo; *you can — on it*, è cosa certa, puoi starne sicuro; *you can — your boots*, puoi scommetterci la testa; *you —!*, sfido io!
**betake** *rfl. to — oneself*, recarsi a, dirigersi verso.
**bethink** *rfl. to — oneself*, riflettere, considerare, ricordare.
**Bethlehem** *pr.n.* (geog.) Betlemme *f.*
**betide** *tr.*, *intr.* accadere, avvenire; *woe — you!*, guai a voi!
**betimes** *adv.* per tempo, presto.
**betoken** *tr.* presagire, significare, suggerire.
**betray** *tr.* tradire; (fig.) denunciare, accusare, palesare; *to — someone's trust*, abusare della fiducia di qualcuno. **-al** *n.* tradimento. **-er** *n.* traditore; (of secret) delatore.
**betroth** *tr.* fidanzare, promettere in matrimonio. **-al** *n.* fidanzamento *m.* **-ed** *adj.*, *n.* fidanzato, fidanzata; (Manzoni's novel) *The Betrothed*, 'I Promessi Sposi'.
**better**[1] *adj.* migliore, meglio; *to be —* (in health), sentirsi, stare meglio; *to get —*, migliorare; *to look —*, aver miglior cera; (fig.) *it would look — if I accepted the invitation*, farebbe miglior impressione se io accettassi l'invito; più bravo; *he's a — man than you are*, vale più di te; *the — classes*, le classi superiori; (joc.) *my — half*, la mia dolce metà; *the — part of*, la maggior parte di; *for — or for worse*, nella buona e nell'avversa fortuna; *all the —*, tanto meglio; *the sooner the —*, più presto è, meglio è, *he is no — than a fool*, non è altro che uno sciocco; *— off*, più ricco, più fortunato.
**better**[1] *adv.* meglio, in modo migliore; *— and —*, di bene in meglio; *— late than never*, meglio tardi che mai; *to like —*, preferire; *he had — go*, sarebbe bene che andasse; *you had — mind your own business*, ti conviene badare ai fatti tuoi; *to think — of something*, cambiar idea; *— known*, più conosciuto; *n.* il meglio; *all for the —*, tutto per il meglio; *our -s*, i nostri superiori; *to get the — of*, superare, raggirare.
**better**[1] *tr.* migliorare; *rfl. to — oneself*, migliorare la propria situazione economica; superare, battere. **-ment** *n.* miglioramento, miglioria.
**better**[2], **bettor** *n.* scommettitore *m.*
**betting** *n.* lo scommettere; *the -'s three to one against*, si scommette tre contro uno.
**Betty** *pr.n.* Bettina; *cf.* **Bess.**
**between** *adv.* in mezzo; *few and far —*, a lunghi intervalli; *to get —*, mettersi di mezzo; *prep.* fra, tra, in mezzo a; *— the two wars*, tra le due guerre; *— you and me*, fra noi due, a quattr'occhi; detto fra noi; *we bought the house — us*, abbiamo comperato la casa in società; *— the devil and the deep blue sea*, tra l'incudine e il martello. **-while** *adv.* nel frattempo, negli intervalli.
**betwixt** *prep.* (poet.) fra, tra.
**bevel** *n.* sghembo; angolo obliquo; (mech.) smusso; *tr.* tagliare a sghembo, smussare; *a -led looking-glass*, uno specchio molato.
**bevel-edged** *adj.* dall'angolo smussato.
**beverage** *n.* bevanda, bibita.
**bevy** *n.* frotta; (of birds) stormo; (of girls) gruppo di belle ragazze.
**bewail** *tr.* lamentare, deplorare; *intr.* lamentarsi; *to — one's lot*, lamentarsi della propria sorte.
**beware** *intr.* guardarsi (da), stare attento (a); *I will —*, mi guarderò, starò attento; *— of the dog!*, attenti al cane!; *— of pickpockets!*, attenti ai borsaiuoli!
**bewilder** *tr.* sconcertare, rendere perplesso, disorientare; *to be -ed*, essere perplesso. **-ing** *adj.* sconcertante, che rende perplesso, sbalorditivo. **-ment** *n.* confusione; smarrimento; disorientamento.
**bewitch** *tr.* stregare; (fig.) affascinare. **-ing** *adj.* affascinante, seducente.
**beyond** *adv.* oltre, più in là; *prep.* oltre, di là di, più in là di; *— the seas*, oltremare; *— the Alps*, oltr'Alpi; *to be — the pale*, essere escluso dalla società; *this is — me*, non sono in grado di capire ciò;

*it's got — a joke*, questo è di troppo.
**beyond** *n.* l'aldilà *m.*; la vita futura; *the back of* —, l'angolo più remoto della terra.
**bezique** *n.* (cards) bazzica.
**biannual** *adj.* semestrale. **-ly** *adv.* ogni sei mesi, due volte l'anno.
**bias** *n.* pregiudizio; prevenzione; preconcetto; predisposizione; *free from* —, senza pregiudizi; *without* —, senza preconcetti; (needlew.) cucitura diagonale, sbieco; (bowls) peso eccedente su un lato di una boccia; inclinazione di una boccia causata da peso eccedente.
**bias** *tr.* fare inclinare, influenzare; *he's -ed*, ha una prevenzione, è prevenuto.
**bib** *n.* bavaglino; pettino; (joc.) *to put on one's best — and tucker*, mettersi gli abiti migliori, farsi bello.
**bibber** *n.* bevitore.
**bible** *n.* bibbia.
**bible-oath** *n.* giuramento sulla bibbia.
**biblical** *adj.* biblico; — *scholar*, biblista *m., f.*
**bibliograph-er** *n.* bibliografo. **-ic(al)** *adj.* bibliografico. **-y** *n.* bibliografia.
**biblio-mania** *n.* bibliomania. **-phile** *n.* bibliofilo.
**bibulous** *adj.* bibulo; assorbente.
**bicarbonate** *n.* (chem.) bicarbonato.
**bicentenary** *n.* bicentenario.
**biceps** *n.* (anat.) bicipite *m.*
**bicker** *intr.* altercare, disputare, litigare, bisticciare, rimbeccarsi. **-ing** *adj.* che litiga, litigioso; *n.* bisticcio; altercazione; *I can't stand their endless -ing*, non posso soffrire il loro continuo bisticciarsi.
**bicoloured** *adj.* bicolore.
**bicycl-e** *n.* bicicletta; *to ride a* —, andare in bicicletta; *to jump on one's* —, inforcare la bicicletta; *racing* —, bicicletta da corsa; *intr.* andare in bicicletta. **-ing** *n.* ciclismo. **-ist** *n.* ciclista *m., f.*
**bid** *n.* (at auctions) offerta; *higher* —, rilancio; *to make a higher* —, rilanciare; (fig.) *to make a — for*, fare un tentativo per ottenere; (comm.) offerta di appalto; (finan.) *take-over* —, offerta di acquisto; (cards) dichiarazione, apertura.
**bid** *tr.* comandare, ordinare; *to — someone to dinner*, invitare qualcuno a pranzo; *to — welcome*, dare il benvenuto a; *to — good-bye*, accomiatarsi (da), salutare, dire addio (a); *to — good morning*, augurare il buon giorno; (at auctions) offrire; *to — higher*, rilanciare; (comm.) fare offerta di appalto; (cards) dichiarare; *intr.* promettere; *to — fair*, promettere bene.
**bidd-able** *adj.* obbediente, docile, arrendevole. **-er** *n.* offerente *m., f.*; *highest* —, miglior offerente; (at auction) aggiudicatario; (comm.) appaltatore. **-ing** *n.* ordine *m.*; comando; *to be at someone's* —, essere agli ordini di qualcuno; *to do someone's -ing*, ubbidire a un ordine di qualcuno; *I did his -ing*, ho fatto quel che mi ha detto; invito; (at auctions) offerte *f.pl.*; *the -ing is open!*, si delibera!; *the -ing was brisk*, c'era una rapida successione di offerte; (cards) dichiarazione.
**bide** *intr.* aspettare; (Scots) dimorare; *tr. to — one's time*, aspettare il momento propizio.
**biennial** *adj.* biennale, bienne. **-ly** *adv.* biennalmente, ogni due anni.
**biennium** *n.* biennio.
**bier** *n.* bara, feretro cataletto.
**biff** *n.* (slang) scapaccione *m.*, schiaffo; *tr.* dare uno scapaccione a, schiaffeggiare.
**bifurcat-e** *adj.* biforcuto, biforcato; *tr.* biforcare; *intr.* biforcarsi. **-ion** *n.* biforcazione; bivio.
**big** *adj.* grande, grosso; importante, notevole; *a — man*, un uomo grande, grosso; (great) un grand'uomo, un uomo importante; *to grow* —, crescere, ingrandire; *to do things in a — way*, fare le cose in grande; *to have — ideas*, avere delle idee grandiose, essere ambizioso; — *rise*, forte aumento; — *game*, caccia grossa; — *toe*, alluce *m.*; (mech.) — *end*, testa; (fam.) *a — noise*, un pezzo grosso; *to be a — eater*, mangiare molto; *to earn — money*, guadagnare molto; *to be too — for one's shoes*, darsi arie, pavoneggiarsi; gonfio, pieno; — *with child*, incinta; — *with young*, gravida; *adv. to talk* —, dire smargiassate, millantarsi. **-gish** *adj.* piuttosto grosso, piuttosto grande. **-ness** *n.* grandezza; grossezza.
**bigam-ist** *n.* bigamo, bigama. **-ous** *adj.* bigamo. **-y** *n.* bigamia.
**big-bellied** *adj.* panciuto.
**bight** *n.* golfo; baia; (in river) ansa *f.*; (naut., of rope) doppino.
**bigot** *n.* bigotto; bacchettone *m.*; fanatico; settario. **-ed** *adj.* bigotto; fanatico; settario. **-ry** *n.* bigotteria, bigottismo; fanatismo; settarismo.
**bigwig** *n.* (fam.) pezzo grosso.
**bike** *n.* (slang) bici *f.indecl.*
**bikini** *n.* bikini, due-pezzi *m. indecl.*
**bilateral** *adj.* bilaterale.
**bilberry** *n.* (bot.) mirtillo.
**bile** *n.* bile *f.*; (fig.) rabbia; ira; *to rouse someone's* —, far rodere qualcuno dalla bile.
**bile-stone** *n.* (med.) calcolo biliare.
**bilge** *n.* (naut.) sentina; (fam.) *to talk* —, raccontare delle balle.
**bilge-keel** *n.* (naut.) chiglia di rollio; alettone *m.* **-water** *n.* (naut.) acqua di sentina.
**bilingual** *adj.* bilingue.
**bilious** *adj.* (med.) biliare; — *attack*, travaso di bile; *to feel* —, avere la nausea; (of temperament) collerico, irritabile, stizzoso. **-ness** *n.* nausea; travaso di bile; crisi epatica.
**bilk** *tr.* ingannare, defraudare; (fam.) fregare.
**bill**[1] *n.* (orn.) becco, rostro; (geog.) capo, promontorio; (naut., of anchor) unghia; *intr.* beccuzzarsi; *to — and coo*, tubare, tortoreggiare; (agric.) falcetto; roncola.
**bill**[2] *n.* conto; fattura; nota; *to make out the* —, fare il conto; *my —, please*, mi favorisca il conto; *put it on my* —, me lo metta sul conto; *to pay the* —, saldare il conto; (poster) affisso; *stick no -s*, divieto d'affissione; (theatr.) cartellone *m.*; locandina; — *of fare*, lista delle vivande; menù *m. indecl.*; (comm.) effetto; — *of exchange*, cambiale *f.*; certificato; patente *f.*; — *of health*, patente sanitaria, certificato medico; (banknote) biglietto, banconota; (leg.) atto; (pol.) progetto di legge.
**bill**[2] *tr.* fatturare; mettere in conto; affiggere; (theatr.) mettere in programma.
**Bill**[3] *pr.n. dimin.* of **William**; Guglielmino.
**bill-book** *n.* scadenzario, scadenziere *m.* **-broker** *n.* (comm.) sensale *m.*
**billet**[1] *n.* (mil.) alloggio; accantonamento; (fam.) *to find a good* —, trovare un buon posto, sistemarsi; *tr.* alloggiare; accantonare.
**billet**[2] *n.* — *doux*, lettera amorosa.
**bill-hook** *n.* falcastro, falcino.
**billiard-cue** *n.* stecca da biliardo.
**billiards** *n.* biliardo.
**billion** *n.* (British) trilione *m.*; (USA) bilione, miliardo. **-aire** *n.* (USA) miliardario; (fig.) arcimilionario.
**billow** *n.* onda; flutto; *pl.* (poet.) *the -s*, il mare, l'onda; *intr.* ondeggiare; fluttuare. **-y** *adj.* ondoso, fluttuante.
**bill-sticker** *n.* attacchino. **-sticking** *n.* affissione.
**billygoat** *n.* capro, becco.
**bimetallism** *n.* (econ.) bimetallismo.
**bimonthly** *adj.* bimensile, bimestrale; *adv.* due volte al mese, ogni due mesi.
**bin** *n.* bidone *m.*; recipiente *m.*; (for wine) ripostiglio; (min.) silo.
**binary** *adj.* binario.

**bind** *tr.* legare; fasciare; allacciare; attaccare; bendare; *to — hand and foot*, legare mani e piedi; (bookb.) rilegare; (fig.) legare, impegnare, vincolare, costringere; *to be bound by affection*, sentirsi legato da affetto; (fam.) *to be bound* (*to*), essere certo (che), dovere; *he is bound to win*, vincerà certamente; *I am bound to admit*, debbo per forza ammettere; *to — down*, impegnare, costringere; (leg.) *to — over*, (leg.) obbligare sotto pena di multa; *intr.* legarsi, agglomerarsi; indurirsi; (fam.) brontolare. **-er** *n.* rilegatore; (for holding papers) rilegatura mobile; (agric.) macchina per legare, legatrice; (chem.) legante, agglutinante *m.* **-ery** *n.* legatoria. **-ing** *adj.* impegnativo, che lega, obbligatorio; (chem.) legante, agglutinante; *n.* legatura; (of books) rilegatura; copertina; il rilegare; (needlew.) bordura; (fam.) brontolamento.

**bindweed** *n.* (bot.) convolvolo, vilucchio.

**binge** *n.* (slang) baldoria, festa rumorosa; *to go on a —*, far baldoria.

**bingo** *n.* (game) lotto.

**binnacle** *n.* (naut.) chiesuola; abitacolo.

**binocular** *adj.* binoculare; *n.pl.* binocolo.

**binomial** *adj.* (math.) appartenente a un binomio; *— theorem*, binomio.

**bio-** *pref.* bio-.

**biochem-ical** *adj.* biochimico. **-ist** *n.* biochimico. **-istry** *n.* biochimica.

**biograph-y** *n.* biografia, vita. **-er** *n.* biografo. **-ic(al)** *adj.* biografico.

**biolog-y** *n.* biologia. **-ic(al)** *adj.* biologico. **-ist** *n.* biologo.

**bipartite** *adj.* bipartito.

**biped** *n.* bipede *m.*

**biplane** *n.* biplano.

**birch** *n.* (bot.) betulla *f.*; (rod) verga, sferza; *tr.* sferzare.

**birch-rod** *n.* verga.

**bird** *n.* uccello; volatile *m.*, (poet.) augello; *— of passage*, uccello migratore; *— of prey*, uccello rapace; *— of ill omen*, uccello di malaugurio; (fig.) *the — is flown*, il prigioniero è scappato, è uccel di bosco; *-s of a feather*, gente *f.* dello stesso stampo; (provb.) *-s of a feather flock together*, dimmi con chi vai e ti dirò chi sei; *a — in the hand is worth two in the bush*, meglio un uovo oggi che una gallina domani; *the early — catches the worm*, chi dorme non piglia pesci; *to kill two -s with one stone*, prendere due piccioni con una fava; (fam.) tipo, individuo; *a cunning old —*, una vecchia volpe, un furbone; (slang) ragazza, tosa; (theatr.) abbaiata; *to get the —*, essere fischiato. **-like** *adj.* da uccello; simile ad uccello, (fig.) di volo.

**bird-cage** *n.* gabbia per uccelli, uccelliera. **-catcher** *n.* uccellatore. **-catching** *n.* uccellagione *f.* **-fancier** *n.* allevatore di uccelli, avicoltore; commerciante *m.* di uccelli. **-fancying** *n.* avicoltura. **-lime** *n.* vischio; pania. **-lore** *n.* ornitologia. **-of-paradise** *n.* uccello del paradiso. **-seed** *n.* miglio, panico.

**bird's-eye** *n.* (bot.) veronica *f.*; (fig.) *— view*, vista a volo d'uccello. **-nest** *n.* nido di uccello. **-nesting** *n.* caccia ai nidi.

**biretta** *n.* berretta da prete.

**birth** *n.* nascita; parto; *Italian by —*, italiano di nascita; *to give — to*, partorire, mettere al mondo, dare alla luce, (of animals) figliare; stirpe *f.*, lignaggio, discendenza, parentado; (fig.) nascere *m.*, origine *f.*, genesi *f.*; *the — of an idea*, la genesi di un'idea; *to see the — of*, vedere nascere. **-day** *n.* giorno natalizio, compleanno; *-day present*, regalo di compleanno; *tomorrow is my —*, domani ricorre il mio compleanno; (joc.) *-day suit*, costume adamitico. **-place** *n.* luogo di nascita, luogo natio; paese *m.* **-right** *n.* diritto di primogenitura; patrimonio, retaggio.

**birth-certificate** *n.* certificato, fede *f.* di nascita. **-control** *n.* limitazione, controllo delle nascite. **-rate** *n.* natalità, media delle nascite; indice *m.* demografico; *fall in -rate*, denatalità; *campaign for higher -rate*, campagna demografica.

**Biscay** *pr.n.* (geog.) Biscaglia; *the Bay of —*, il golfo di Biscaglia, il golfo di Guascogna.

**biscuit** *n.* biscotto; *ship's —*, galletta; *— factory*, biscottificio; (fam.) *that takes the —!*, questo è il colmo; *adj.*, *n.* marrone *m.* chiaro.

**bisect** *tr.* dividere in due parti; (geom.) bisecare; *intr.* biforcarsi. **-ion** *n.* divisione in due parti; (geom.) bisezione.

**bisexual** *adj.* bisessuale; anfigonico.

**bishop** *n.* (eccl.) vescovo; *-'s palace*, vescovado; *-'s tenure of office*, vescovato; *-'s ring*, anello vescovile; *-'s letter*, pastorale *m.*; (chess) alfiere *m.* **-ric** *n.* vescovato.

**bismuth** *n.* (chem.) bismuto.

**bison** *n.* bisonte *m.*

**bit**[1] *n.* (of horse) morso; *to champ the —*, mordere il freno; *to take the — between one's teeth*, ribellarsi; (mech.) punta, morsa; (of key) ingegno; *tr.* imbrigliare, ammorsare, mettere il morso a.

**bit**[2] *n.* pezzo, pezzetto, pezzettino; *in -s*, a pezzi; *twopenny —*, moneta da due penny; *to break to -s*, *tr.* fare a pezzi, spezzare, *intr.* spezzarsi; *to take to -s*, smontare, disfare; *to tear to -s*, stracciare, lacerare; (fig.) *to tear an argument to -s*, demolire una tesi; *to do one's —*, fare il proprio dovere; un poco, un pochino; *— by —*, a poco a poco; *wait a —*, aspetta un po'; *a — older*, un po' più vecchio; *a good — older*, molto più vecchio; *a — of a coward*, alquanto vile; *to be not a — wiser*, sapere meno di prima; *a — of advice*, un consiglio; *a — of luck*, una vera fortuna; *not a — of use*, perfettamente inutile; *every — as*, tanto quanto; *not a — of it!*, tutt'altro, niente affatto!; *I don't care a —*, non mi importa un bel niente.

**bit**[3] *p.def.* of **bite**

**bitch**[1] *n.* (dog) cagna; (wolf) lupa; (other animals) femmina; (slang, of woman) cagna; *what a —!*, che vipera!; *son of a —*, figlio di puttana. **-iness** *n.* (slang) puttaneria; (fig.) cattiveria, malvagità. **-y** *adj.* (slang) puttanesco; (fig.) cattivo, malvagio.

**bitch**[2] *tr.* (slang) sciupare, rovinare, fregare.

**bite** *n.* (of man, animal) morso; (of insect) morsicatura, puntura; (of fish) l'abboccare *m.*, abboccatura; (of food) boccone *m.*; (fig.) morso; *to be lacking in —*, mancare di mordente; (provb.) *his bark is worse than his —*, can che abbaia non morde.

**bit-e** *tr.* mordere, morsicare, addentare; morsicchiare; (fig.) pungere, tagliare; *to — one's lips*, mordersi le labbra; *to — the dust*, mordere la polvere; (fam.) *to get bitten*, farsi imbrogliare; *once bitten twice shy*, il gatto scottato teme l'acqua fredda; *to — into*, addentare, (chem.) corrodere; *to — off*, portare via con un morso; (fig.) *to — off more than one can chew*, fare il passo più lungo della gamba; *intr.* (of fish) abboccare; (naut., of anchor) far presa, agguantare. **-er** *n.* chi morde; morditore, morsicatore; animale che morde; *the — bit*, il truffatore truffato. **-ing** *adj.* mordente, pungente, tagliente; *-ing cold*, freddo mordente; (fig.) mordace, caustico, pungente; *-ing irony*, ironia amara; *n.* il mordere, morso, morsicatura.

**bitt** *n.* (naut.) bitta; bittone *m.*; *tr.* abbittare.

**bitter** *adj.* amaro; acerbo; acre; (fig.) aspro, agro; rigido, pungente; *a — experience*, una esperienza penosa; *a — pill*, un boccone amaro; *— words*, parole

*f.pl.* aspre; *to the — end*, a oltranza; *to feel — towards*, avere dell'amaro contro; *to have a — taste in one's mouth*, avere la bocca amara; *to make —*, amareggiare; *— resistance*, resistenza accanita; *— enemies*, nemici mortali; *n.* amaro; (beer) birra amara; *pl.* angostura. **-ness** *n.* amarezza; acerbità, agrezza; rigidità; (fig.) asprezza, acredine *f.*; acrimonia; rancore *m.*

**bittern** *n.* (orn.) tarabuso.

**bitter-sweet** *adj.* agrodolce; *n.* (bot.) dulcamara, vite *f.* di Giudea.

**bitumen** *n.* bitume *m.*; asfalto.

**bivalve** *adj.*, *n.* bivalve *m.*; ostrica.

**bivouac** *n.* bivacco; *intr.* bivaccare.

**bi-weekly** *adj.* (twice a week) bisettimanale; (every fortnight) quindicinale; *adv.* due volte la settimana; ogni quindici giorni.

**bizarre** *adj.* bizzarro, strano; strambo.

**blab** *intr.* (slang) cianciare, chiacchierare; *tr. to — out*, spiattellare, spifferare. **-ber** *n.* ciarlone, chiacchierone, spifferone *m.*

**black** *adj.* nero; *— as coal*, nero come il carbone; *— as jet*, nero lucente; *— as pitch*, nero come la pece, buio pesto; *— as soot*, nero come la fuliggine; buio, oscuro; sporco, annerito; funesto, minaccioso, tetro, torvo; *things are looking —*, le cose prendono una brutta piega; *to give someone a — look*, lanciare una occhiataccia a qualcuno; (fig.) *a — deed*, un delitto atroce; *— and white*, bianco e nero; *to put something down in — and white*, mettere qualcosa per iscritto; *to be — and blue all over*, essere pieno di lividi; *to turn —*, diventare nero, annerirsi, (fig.) oscurarsi; *— art*, *— magic*, magia nera, negromanzia; *— currant*, ribes *m. indecl.*; *— death*, peste *f.*; *— eye*, occhio nero, occhio pesto; *— friar*, frate domenicano; *— frost*, freddo intenso senza brina; *— lead*, grafite *f.*; *— list*, lista nera; *— Maria*, furgone *m.* cellulare; *— market*, mercato nero, borsa nera; *— marketeer*, borsanerista *m.*; *— pudding*, sanguinaccio; *the — Sea*, il Mar Nero; *— sheep*, pecora nera; *— tidings*, brutte notizie *f.pl.*; *n.* nero; *ivory —*, nero di avorio; *to wear —*, vestirsi di nero, (mourning) mettere il lutto; (person) negro; (agric.) golpe *f.* **-ish** *adj.* nerastro. **-ness** *n.* nerezza; oscurità.

**black** *tr.* annerire, tingere di nero; lucidare, verniciare, pulire; *to — out*, cancellare; oscurare. **-ing** *n.* lucido nero per scarpe.

**blackball** *tr.* votare contro, bocciare.

**black-beetle** *n.* (ent.) scarafaggio, blatta *f.*

**black-berry** *n.* (bot.) mora selvatica; *— bush*, rovo. **-bird** *n.* (orn.) merlo.

**blackboard** *n.* lavagna.

**black-bordered** *adj.* orlato di nero; *— writing-paper*, carta listata a lutto.

**blackcap** *n.* (orn.) capinero.

**black-coated** *adj.* vestito di nero; *the — workers*, la classe impiegatizia, gli impiegati.

**blacken** *tr.* annerire, tingere di nero; lucidare, verniciare di nero; affumicare; imbrattare, insudiciare; (fig.) calunniare, denigrare, *to — someone's character*, diffamare qualcuno; *intr.* diventare nero; annerirsi; *the sky -ed*, il cielo si oscurò. **-ing** *n.* annerimento; (fig.) diffamazione; denigrazione.

**blackguard** *n.* birbone, furfante, mascalzone *m.* **-ly** *adj.* da furfante, da mascalzone; disonesto, malvagio; *a -ly trick*, un brutto tiro.

**black-hearted** *adj.* malvagio, maligno.

**blackleg** *n.* crumiro.

**blackmail** *n.* ricatto; estorsione; *tr.* ricattare; *intr.* fare il ricattatore. **-er** *n.* ricattatore, ricattatrice.

**blackout** *n.* oscuramento; annebbiamento; svenimento; (cinem.; radio) mascheramento; *tr.* oscurare, schermare; mascherare, obliterare; *intr.* perdere temporaneamente coscienza, svenire.

**blackshirt** *n.* (hist.) camicia nera.

**blacksmith** *n.* fabbro, ferraio, mariscalco; *-'s shop*, fucina.

**blackthorn** *n.* (bot.) prugnolo.

**bladder** *n.* (anat.) vescica; (of football) anima, camera d'aria; (balloon) pallone gonfiato.

**blad-e** *n.* lama; (safety-razor) lametta; (fig., of person) spadaccino, tipo ameno; (of grass) filo; stelo; (of leaf) lamina; (of oar) pala; (anat.) scapola. **-ed** *adj.* munito di lame; (bot.) munito di stelo; che comincia a spuntare.

**blaeberry** *n.* (bot.) mirtillo.

**blah** *n.* (fam.) chiacchiere, balle *f.pl.*; *to talk a lot of —*, blaterare.

**blain** *n.* pustola, vescicola cutanea.

**blame** *n.* biasimo; colpa; responsabilità; *the — was mine*, fu per colpa mia; *free from —*, irreprensibile; *to bear the —*, accollarsi il biasimo; *to deserve —*, essere biasimevole; *to lay the — on*, addossare la colpa a. **-ful** *adj.* biasimevole. **-less** *adj.* innocente, senza colpa; irreprensibile. **-lessness** *n.* innocenza; irrepresensibilità. **-worthy** *adj.* biasimevole; responsabile.

**blam-e** *tr.* biasimare, incolpare, rimproverare, addossare la copla a; *I have nothing to — myself for*, non ho nulla da rimproverarmi; *you have only yourselves to —*, la colpa è vostra; attribuire, imputare; *to — fate*, accusare il destino; *to be to —*, essere colpevole; *who is to — ?*, di chi è la colpa?; *to declare one is not to —*, discolparsi; *I am in no way to —*, non si può dare la colpa a me; *don't — me!*, non è colpa mia!; (fam.) *I am not blaming you*, non è con te che me la prendo. **-able** *adj.* biasimevole.

**blanch** *tr.* imbiancare, sbiancare; mondare; *intr.* impallidire; imbiancarsi.

**bland** *adj.* blando; dolce; mite; placido; soave; affabile, simpatico; (iron.) mellifluo, dolciastro. **-ness** *n.* dolcezza; soavità; affabilità.

**blandish** *tr.* blandire, lusingare. **-ment** *n.* blandizie *f.pl.*; lusinghe *f.pl.*; fascino.

**blank** *adj.* in bianco; *— cheque*, assegno in bianco; *to leave —*, lasciare in bianco; vuoto, nudo; *— space*, spazio vuoto; *— wall*, parete nuda; *— window*, finestra cieca; *— cartridge*, cartuccia a salve; *point —*, a bruciapelo; (fig.) vacuo; (prosod.) *— verse*, versi *m.pl.* sciolti; *n.* vuoto; lacuna; *to draw a —*, sortire un biglietto in bianco, (fig.) non riuscire a combinare niente, non trovare nulla. **-ly** *adv.* senza espressione; con aria sconcertata; recisamente. **-ness** *n.* vacuità; espressione vacua; vuoto.

**blanket** *n.* coperta di lana; coltre *f.*; (fig.) *— of snow*, coltre di neve; *to be covered with a — of*, essere avvolto in; *to be born on the wrong side of the —*, essere illegittimo; *wet —*, guastafeste *m.*; *tr.* coprire con una coltre; (fig.) avvolgere; (fam.) soffocare.

**blare** *n.* squillo; *intr.* squillare, suonare; *tr. to — forth the news*, proclamare la notizia a squarciagola.

**blasphem-e** *intr.* bestemmiare, rinnegare Dio. **-er** *n.* bestemmiatore, blasfemo. **-ous** *adj.* blasfemo; empio; profano. **-y** *n.* bestemmia; empietà *f. indecl.*

**blast** *n.* raffica; colpo di vento; soffio; corrente *f.* d'aria; squillo; scoppio; esplosione; spostamento d'aria; *at full —*, a tutta velocità, in piena attività.

**blast** *tr.* far brillare, fare esplodere, fare saltare; rovinare, distruggere; fare inaridire; spazzare via; fulminare; (fam.) maledire; *that -ed noise*, quel maledetto rumore; *— you!*, che il diavolo ti porti!

**blast-furnace** *n.* altoforno.

**blat-ancy** *n.* schiamazzo, strepito, clamore *m.*; sfoggio, ostentazione. **-ant** *adj.* assordante, strepitoso, chiassoso; appariscente, vistoso; *-ant injustice*, ingiustizia flagrante.

**blather** *n.* chiacchiere sciocche

*f.pl.*; *intr.* chiacchierare scioccamente, blaterare.

**blaze**[1] *n.* fiamma; fuoco; vampa; fiammata; (fig.) — *of anger*, vampa di passione, scatto d'ira; splendore *m.*; — *of light*, bagliore *m.* di luce; (fam.) *go to -s!*, va all'inferno!; *what the -s?*, che diavolo?; *like -s*, come una furia; *to run like -s*, correre a gambe levate.

**blaz-e**[1] *intr.* ardere; avvampare, divampare; splendere, sfavillare; (fig.) *his eyes -ed with anger*, gli fiammeggiavano gli occhi per l'ira; *to — away*, ardere a lungo, imperversare, sparare alla cieca; *to — down*, splendere dall'alto, dardeggiare; *to — forth*, divampare; *tr.* divulgare, diffondere; *to — news abroad*, diffondere notizie. **-ing** *adj.* in fiamme, ardente, fiammeggiante; splendente, caldissimo.

**blaze**[2] *n.* macchia bianca (sulla fronte); (on tree) segnavia *m.*; *tr.* indicare con incisioni su alberi; *to — a trail*, segnare una pista.

**blazer** *n.* giacca sportiva.

**blazon** *n.* blasone, stemma *m.*; *tr.* blasonare; (fig.) proclamare, divulgare; esaltare, celebrare, dare lustro a.

**bleach** *n.* scolorimento, imbianchimento, candeggio; (chem.) decolorante *m.*; *tr.* scolorire, imbiancare, candeggiare, decolorare; *intr.* scolorirsi, imbiancarsi.

**bleak** *n.* brullo; nudo; squallido; (fig.) triste, brutto, lugubre; pallido, incolore. **-ness** *n.* freddezza; squallore *m.*; tristezza; desolazione.

**blear** *adj.* cisposo, velato; ottuso; oscuro, indistinto, confuso; *tr.* rendere cisposo; offuscare, annebbiare; ottenebrare; rendere indistinto.

**bleat** *n.* belato; (fig.) piagnucolìo; *intr.* belare; (fig.) piagnucolare; *tr. to — out*, spiattellare; *to — out a protest*, protestare con voce piagnucolosa. **-ing** *adj.* pignucoloso; *n.* belato.

**bleed** *tr.* cavar sangue a, salassare; estorcere denaro a; *intr.* sanguinare, perdere sangue, dissanguarsi; *his nose is -ing*, perde sangue dal naso; *to — to death*, morire dissanguato; (fig.) *my heart is -ing*, mi duole il cuore; (bot.) piangere, perdere linfa. **-er** *n.* salassatore *m.*; (med.) paziente *m.*, *f.* malato di emofilia. **-ing** *adj.* sanguinante, sanguinolente; *n.* (med.) emoraggia; (surg.) salasso; fuga; perdita; (bot.) pianto.

**blemish** *n.* difetto; imperfezione; macchia; *tr.* sfigurare; macchiare; offuscare.

**blench** *tr.* chiudere gli occhi su; *intr.* ritrarsi; impallidire; *without -ing*, senza battere ciglio.

**blend** *n.* miscela, mistura; (mus.) impasto; *tr.* mescolare, mischiare; armonizzare, temperare; (fig.) fondere, combinare; (mus.) impastare; *intr.* mescolarsi, armonizzare, fondersi, confluire, unirsi. **-ing** *n.* mescolamento, mescolanza; fusione; unione.

**bless** *tr.* benedire; *God — you!*, Dio ti benedica!; *— my soul!*, Dio mio!; consacrare, invocare il favore divino su; (fig.) *to be -ed with*, essere dotato di, godere di. **-ed** *part.* benedetto. **-èd** *adj.* beato; *the -èd Trinity*, la Santissima Trinità; (fam.) *every -èd day*, ogni santo giorno; *the whole -èd lot*, tutti quanti. **-edness** *n.* beatitudine *f.*; (iron.) *single -edness*, il beato celibato. **-ing** *n.* benedizione; *he gave us his -ing*, c'impartì la benedizione; (fig.) *what a -ing!*, che fortuna!; *it's a -ing in disguise*, è un beneficio inaspettato.

**blest** *adj.* see **blessed.**

**blight** *n.* (bot.) golpe *f.*; carbonchio; *endemic —*, enfizia; (fig.) influenza maligna; peste *f.*; *to be a — upon*, avvelenare; *tr.* far appassire per golpe; *to be -ed*, annebbiare; (fig.) aduggiare, rovinare, frustrare; *his hopes were -ed*, le sue speranze svanirono. **-ing** *adj.* che fa appassire; (fig.) *-ing influence*, influenza malefica; *n.* appassimento; sfioritura; (fig.) *the -ing of his hopes*, il crollo delle sue speranze.

**blighter** *n.* (pop.) tizio, tipo; *you lucky — !*, beato te!

**Blighty** *n.* (mil. slang) l'Inghilterra.

**blimey** *excl.* (pop.) accidenti!, porco!

**blind**[1] *adj.* cieco; *a — man*, un cieco; *— from birth*, cieco nato; *— in one eye*, cieco da un occhio; *to be struck —*, essere colpito da cecità; *to go —*, diventare cieco; *— as a bat*, cieco come una talpa; (fig.) *to be — to*, essere cieco a, essere incapace di vedere; *— to beauty*, insensibile alla bellezza; *to be — with rage*, non vederci più dalla rabbia; *to turn a — eye to*, chiudere gli occhi di fronte a; *to be — to one's own interests*, non vedere dove stanno i propri interessi; *— alley*, vicolo cieco; *— corner*, svolta pericolosa; *— side*, lato debole; *— window*, finestra murata; *adv.* alla cieca; *to fly —*, volare cieco; *— drunk*, ubriaco fradicio; *n.* cieco; *the —*, i ciechi. **-ness** *n.* cecità; (fig.) ignoranza; incoscienza; inconsapevolezza.

**blind**[1] *tr.* accecare, rendere cieco, colpire di cecità; *-ed ex-servicemen*, i ciechi di guerra; (fig.) abbagliare; *-ed by passion*, accecato dalla passione; ingannare; (mil.) blindare; (radio) schermare. **-ing** *adj.* accecante; abbagliante; (fig.) abbacinante.

**blind**[2] *n.* tendina, cortina; *Venetian —*, persiana alla veneziana; *roller —*, bandinella; (fig.) pretesto; finzione.

**blindfold** *adj.* con gli occhi bendati, alla cieca; (fig.) irriflessivo; *tr.* bendare gli occhi a.

**blindman** *n. to play -'s buff*, giuocare a mosca cieca.

**blindworm** *n.* (zool.) angue *m.*

**blink** *n.* ammicco; occhiata; *— of light*, guizzo di luce; *intr.* ammiccare; lampeggiare; *tr. to — one's eyes*, battere le palpebre; (fig.) schivare, eludere; *to — the facts*, chiudere gli occhi ai fatti. **-er** *n.* (motor.) lampeggiatore *m.*; *pl.* paraocchi *m. indecl.*; occhiali ortottici *m.pl.* **-ing** *adj.* ammiccante, che batte le palpebre; lampeggiante, luccicante, intermittente; (slang) *you — fool!*, scemo che sei!; *n.* ammicco; luccichìo.

**bliss** *n.* beatitudine *f.*; felicità; gaudio. **-ful** *adj.* beato, felice; (fam.) delizioso. **-fulness** *n.* beatitudine; felicità.

**blister** *n.* pustola, vescica, bolla; (pharm.) vescicante *m.*; *tr.* produrre vesciche su, produrre bolle su; (pharm.) applicare un vescicante a; *intr.* coprirsi di vesciche.

**blithe** *adj.* gaio, gioioso, allegro, giocondo; *— as a lark*, felice come una Pasqua. **-ness** *n.* allegria; gioia. **-some** *adj.* gaio, gioioso, allegro.

**blitz** *n.* guerra lampo; attacco improvviso; (hist.) *the —*, gli attacchi aerei del 1940–1; *tr.* distruggere con attacco aereo; *-ed areas*, quartieri distrutti da bombardamenti intensivi.

**blizzard** *n.* bufera di neve; burrasca; tormenta.

**bloat** *tr.* gonfiare; (cul.) affumicare. **-ed** *adj.* gonfio, gonfiato; *-ed aristocrat*, nobiluomo tronfio; *-ed face*, viso congestionato. **-er** *n.* (cul.) aringa affumicata (specialmente di Yarmouth).

**blob** *n.* macchia; chiazza; goccia; fiocco; (cricket) zero.

**bloc** *n.* (pol.) blocco; *en —*, in blocco.

**block** *n.* ceppo; forma di legno; blocco; massa; masso; pane *m.*; tavoletta; cubo; *— of buildings*, isolato, edificio; ingombro, ostacolo; *road —*, posto di blocco; *traffic —*, ingombro stradale; (mech.) carrucola; (naut.) bozzello; (typ.) cliché *m. indecl.*, zincotipia; *— letters*, stampatelli *m.pl.*; (hist., place of execution) patibolo; (fig.) *a chip off the old —*, un figlio che rassomiglia al padre, il ritratto di suo padre.

**block** *tr.* bloccare; ostruire; chiudere; sbarrare; *road -ed*, strada sbarrata; (fig.) opporsi a,

intralciare; *intr.* bloccarsi; *to — in*, schizzare, progettare, (sculpt.) sbozzare; *to — up*, chiudere, ostruire, murare.

**blockade** *n.* blocco; assedio; *to raise the —*, togliere il blocco; *to run the —*, forzare il blocco; *tr.* bloccare, assediare; (fig.) ostruire.

**blockade-runner** *n.* nave *f.* che forza il blocco, corsaro.

**blockhead** *n.* (fam.) zucca vuota, testa di cavolo.

**blockhouse** *n.* (mil.) casamatta; fortino.

**block-maker** *n.* (typ.) zincografo.

**bloke** *n.* (fam.) tizio, tipo, individuo.

**blond** *adj.* biondo, biondino.

**blond(e)** *n.* bionda, biondina; *platinum —*, bionda ossigenata.

**blood** *n.* sangue *m.*; razza; stirpe *f.*; prole *f.*; *the — rushed to his face*, il sangue gli montò al viso; *in cold —*, a sangue freddo; *bad —*, cattivo sangue; *— is thicker than water*, il sangue non è acqua; *— will tell*, il sangue non stinge; *to draw — from a stone*, cavar sangue da una rapa; *to infuse new — into*, infondere nuovo vigore in; *it makes my — boil*, mi guasta il sangue; *to make one's — run cold*, far rimescolare il sangue; *his — is up*, è in collera; zerbinotto, elegantone *m.* **-curdling** *adj.* raccapricciante; agghiacciante; a forti tinte.

**blood** *tr.* (med.) see **bleed**; (hunt.) far odorare il sangue a.

**blood-and-thunder** *attrib. adj.* sensazionale, drammatico; (pop.) giallo.

**blood-bank** *n.* banca del sangue; emoteca. **-brother** *n.* fratello carnale; fratello consanguineo; fratello uterino. **-coloured** *adj.* rosso sangue, sanguineo, sanguigno. **-donor** *n.* donatore di sangue. **-feud** *n.* faida, vendetta. **-group** *n.* gruppo sanguigno. **-heat** *n.* temperatura normale del sangue. **-letting** *n.* (med.) salasso, flebotomia; spargimento di sangue. **-money** *n.* prezzo del sangue. **-orange** *n.* arancia sanguigna. **-poisoning** *n.* (med.) setticemia. **-pudding** *n.* sanguinaccio. **-red** *adj.* rosso sangue. **-relation** *n.* consanguineo. **-stream** *n.* flusso del sangue. **-test** *n.* analisi *f. indecl.* del sangue. **-transfusion** *n.* trasfusione di sangue. **-vessel** *n.* vaso sanguigno.

**bloodhound** *n.* segugio.

**bloodily** *adv.* sanguinosamente, efferatamente.

**bloodiness** *n.* l'essere *m.* insanguinato; istinto sanguinario; efferatezza.

**bloodless** *adj.* esangue, anemico; incruento, senza spargimento di sangue; (fig.) freddo, insensibile.

**bloodshed** *n.* spargimento di sangue; strage *f.*; carneficina.

**bloodshot** *adj.* iniettato di sangue; *— eyes*, occhi arrossati.

**bloodstain** *n.* macchia di sangue. **-ed** *adj.* macchiato di sangue; (fig.) colpevole di omicidio, omicida *m.*, *f.*

**bloodstone** *n.* diaspro sanguigno.

**bloodsucker** *n.* sanguisuga; mignatta; (fig.) vampiro; usuraio; *to be a —*, bere del sangue.

**bloodthirst-y** *adj.* assetato di sangue, sanguinario, sanguinoso. **-iness** *n.* sete *f.* di sangue.

**bloody** *adj.* insanguinato, macchiato di sangue; sanguinoso, cruento; sanguinario; (hist.) *— Mary*, Maria la Sanguinaria; *a bloody-Mary*, un cocktail con vodka e sugo di pomodoro; (slang) maledetto; *— fool*, maledetto idiota, scemo; *adv.* molto, maledettamente; *— fine*, maledettamente bello; *not — likely!*, non c'è pericolo!; *tr.* macchiare di sangue, insanguinare.

**bloody-minded** *adj.* sanguinario, crudele; (fig.) perverso, ostinato. **-ness** *n.* perversità, malvagità.

**bloom** *n.* fiore *m.*; fioritura; *to burst into —*, sbocciare, schiudersi; *a flower in full —*, un fiore pienamente sbocciato; *these flowers will be in — again in a month*, fra un mese questi fiori rifioriranno; lanugine *f.*, pruina, patina; profumo, aroma *m.*; (telev.) bagliore *m.*, sopraluminosità; (fig.) fiore *m.*, rigoglio, freschezza; *in the — of youth*, nel rigoglio della giovinezza; *beauty that has lost its —*, bellezza appassita. **-ing** *adj.* fiorente, florido, in fiore, rigoglioso; *to look -ing*, apparire fiori e baccelli; (slang) *a -ing fool*, un perfetto imbecille; *a -ing nuisance*, una vera seccatura; *n.* fioritura; rigoglio.

**bloom** *intr.* fiorire, essere in fiore; sbocciare; arrossire; risplendere; (fam.) *to — into*, diventare.

**bloomer** *n.* (fam.) sbaglio madornale; *to make a —*, fare una gaffe, prendere un granchio.

**blossom** *n.* fiore *m.* d'albero; *in full —*, in piena fioritura; *spray of —*, ramoscello fiorito; *intr.* fiorire, sbocciare; (fig.) *to — out into*, diventare.

**blot** *n.* macchia d'inchiostro; sgorbio; scarabocchio; (fig.) disdoro; *a — on one's escutcheon*, una macchia sulla propria reputazione; *tr.* macchiare, sgorbiare; (fig.) infamare; *to — one's reputation*, macchiarsi la reputazione; asciugare (con carta assorbente); *to — out*, cancellare; nascondere, offuscare; annientare.

**blotch** *n.* macchia; chiazza; sgorbio; bolla, pustola; *tr.* coprire di macchie, chiazzare, screziare. **-y** *adj.* macchiato, screziato, chiazzato; (of face) bitorzoluto.

**blotter, blotting-pad** *n.* tampone *m.* di carta assorbente.

**blotting-paper** *n.* carta assorbente.

**blotto** *adj.* (fam.) ubriaco marcio.

**blouse** *n.* blusa; camicetta.

**blow**[1] *n.* colpo; pugno; colpo di bastone, bastonata; *slight —*, buffetto; *-s fell thick and fast*, piovevano i colpi; *to come to -s*, venire alle mani, venire alle prese; *to deal a —*, assestare un pugno, vibrare un colpo; *without striking a —*, senza colpo ferire; (fig.) *to strike a — for*, intervenire a favore di.

**blow**[2] *n.* soffio; raffica; colpo di vento; soffiatura; *give your nose a good —*, soffiati bene il naso.

**blow**[2] *tr.* soffiare; *to — one's nose*, soffiarsi il naso; *to — the dust off*, spolverare soffiando; *to — a kiss*, lanciare un bacio; *to — air into*, insufflare; *to — bubbles*, fare bolle di sapone; *to — a trumpet*, suonare la tromba; *to — one's own trumpet*, cantare le proprie lodi; *the wind blew the door open*, un colpo di vento spalancò la porta; *the ship was -n ashore*, il vento spinse la nave verso la spiaggia; *it's an ill wind that -s nobody any good*, non tutto il male viene per nuocere; *to — a safe*, far saltare la serratura di una cassaforte; (fam.) *well I'm -ed!*, porco cane!; *— the expense*, me ne frego della spesa; *I'll be -ed if I will*, neanche per sogno; (slang) *to — the gaff*, cantare; *intr.* soffiare, spirare; *it is -ing hard*, tira vento forte; ansare, ansimare, sbuffare; (electr.) *the fuse has -n*, è saltata la valvola; (fig.) *to — hot and cold*, vacillare, tentennare; *to — about*, *tr.* agitare, far volare di qua e di là, sballottare, *intr.* volare di qua e di là; *to — away*, *tr.* spazzar via, portare via, *intr.* essere portato via dal vento; *to — down*, *tr.* abbattere, rovesciare, *intr.* essere rovesciato dal vento; *to — in*, *tr.* far saltare, rompere, *intr.* entrare, (fam.) fare una visitina, entrare come un ciclone; *to — off*, *tr.* spazzare via, portare via, *intr.* volare via, essere portato via; *to — off steam*, sfogarsi; *to — out*, *tr.* spegnere, *intr.* spegnersi; *to — out one's brains*, bruciarsi le cervella; *to — over*, *intr.* essere rovesciato dal vento, (of storm) placarsi, calmarsi, (fig.) svanire, essere dimenticato; *to — up*, *tr.* far saltare, far brillare, (tyre) gonfiare, (fam.) dare una lavata di capo a, *intr.* scoppiare, saltare; (of wind) alzarsi; *it is -ing up for a storm*, spira aria di tempesta.

**blow**[3] *intr.* fiorire, sbocciare, schiudersi.

**blower** *n.* soffiatore; (mus.) suonatore; (of organ) tiramantici *m. indecl.*
**blowfly** *n.* (ent.) tafano.
**blow-hole** *n.* sfiatatoio.
**blowpipe** *n.* cerbottana; (mus.) soffiatoio *m.*; (mech.) cannello per soffiare.
**blown**[1] *part.* of **blow**; *adj.* sfiatato, ansimante, senza fiato.
**blown**[2] *part.adj.* sfiorito, appassito.
**blow-out** *n.* (of tyre) scoppio; (electr.) fusione; (slang) scorpacciata.
**blowy** *adj.* ventoso, tempestoso, burrascoso.
**blowz-y** *adj.* sciatto, trasandato, spettinato, discinto; rosso in viso. **-iness** *n.* sciatteria, sciattaggine *f.*
**blubber**[1] *n.* grasso di balena; (pop.) medusa.
**blubber**[2] *intr.* singhiozzare, piangere dirottamente. **-er** *n.* piagnucolone *m.*
**bludgeon** *n.* randello; *tr.* colpire con un randello.
**blue** *adj.* azzurro, celeste, blu; — *blood*, sangue blu; *once in a — moon*, molto raramente; livido; triste, nervoso, depresso; (colloq.) indecente, osceno; *n.* azzurro, celeste, blu *m.*; mare *m.*; cielo; *bolt from the —*, fulmine *m.* a ciel sereno; *pl.* tristezza, depressione; *to have the blues*, essere depresso; *tr.* tingere in blu; (colloq.) spendere pazzamente, scialacquare. **-ness** *n.* azzurrità; livido.
**Bluebeard** *pr.n.* Barbablù.
**bluebell** *n.* campanula; giacinto di bosco.
**bluebird** *n.* (orn.) cutrettola.
**blue-black** *adj.* blu nero. **-eyed** *adj.* dagli occhi azzurri; (slang) *-eyed boy*, beniamino.
**bluebottle** *n.* (bot.) fiordaliso; (ent.) tafano.
**blueprint** *n.* cianografia; (fig.) progetto; programma *m.*
**bluff**[1] *adj.* ripido; franco, cordiale; brusco, sgarbato; *n.* ripida scogliera. **-ness** *n.* franchezza.
**bluff**[2] *tr.* bluffare (al poker); ingannare; *rfl.* vantarsi; fare lo smargiasso; *n.* inganno; millanteria. **-er** *n.* ingannatore; millantatore.
**blunder** *n.* errore grossolano; fallo; sbaglio; equivoco; *to make a —*, prendere un granchio; *intr.* muoversi goffamente; inciampare; commettere un errore grossolano; agire stupidamente.
**blunt** *adj.* smussato, spuntato; senza spigoli; *— pencil*, matita senza punta; *this knife is —*, questo coltello non taglia; ottuso; schietto, brusco; *tr.* smussare; attutire; ottundere. **-ness** *n.* schiettezza; ottusità.
**blur** *n.* offuscamento; apparenza confusa; *tr.* rendere confuso; oscurare.
**blurb** *n.* soffietto editoriale.
**blurt** *tr.* dire inconsideratamente; *to — a secret*, svelare un segreto senza riflettere.
**blush** *n.* rossore *m.*; color roseo; *intr.* arrossire; *to — for shame*, vergognarsi. **-ing** *adj.* vergognoso. **-ingly** *adv.* con rossore, arrossendo.
**bluster** *n.* temporale *m.*; raffica; baccano; turbolenza; scoppio d'ira; *intr.* infuriare, rumoreggiare; parlare violentemente. **-er** *n.* chiassone, fanfarone *m.* **-ing** *adj.* chiassoso; da spaccone.
**boar** *n.* (zool.) verro; *wild —*, cinghiale *m.*
**board** *n.* asse *m.*; assito; pancone *m.*; tavola; *pl.* (theatr.) palcoscenico; *to tread the -s*, calcares le scene; desco; mensa; vitto; pensione; *— and lodging*, vitto e alloggio; *full —*, pensione completa; *— of directors*, consiglio d'amministrazione; *to serve on the —*, far parte del consiglio; (naut.) bordo, ponte *m.*; *to go on —*, imbarcarsi, andare a bordo. **-er** *m.* pensionante *m.*, *f.*; convittore; educanda; *to take in -ers*, tenere dei pensionanti.
**board** *tr.* fornire di assi; intavolare; essere, prendere a pensione; (naut.) abbordare; attaccare; imbarcarsi; *to — out*, mettere a pensione; *to — up*, chiudere con assi.
**boast** *n.* vanto; vanteria; *tr.* vantare; (sculpt.) sbozzare; *intr.* vantarsi. **-er** *n.* spaccone, fanfarone *m.*, millantatore, vantatore. **-ful** *adj.* vanaglorioso. **-fulness** *n.* millanteria; vanagloria; lattanza.
**boat** *n.* barca; battello; scafo; *to burn one's -s*, tagliarsi i ponti alle spalle. **-er** *n.* canottiera, paglietta. **-house** *n.* riparo coperto per barche. **-ing** *n.* canottaggio; *to go -ing*, andare in barca, fare del canottaggio. **-load** *n.* il contenuto di una barca. **-man** *n.* barcaiolo. **-race** *n.* gara di canottaggio.
**boatswain** (naut., pronounced **bosun**) *n.* (naut.) nostromo.
**boat-hook** *n.* gaffa.
**bob**[1] *tr.* tagliare (capelli) a zazzera; moncare.
**bob**[2] *intr.* muoversi in avanti o indietro; inchinarsi; fare un inchino; *to — up*, venire improvvisamente a galla; *n.* movimento in avanti e indietro; inchino.
**bob**[3] *n.* (fam.) scellino; *two —*, due scellini.
**bob**[4] *n.* (sport) bob *m.*; guidoslitta.
**Bob**[5] *pr.n.* (*dim.* of **Robert**) Bertino.
**bobbin** *n.* bobina; rocchetto; spola.
**Bobby** *pr.n.* (*dim.* of **Robert**) Bertino; (fam.) vigile *m.*
**bod-e** *intr.* presagire; *to — well, ill*, essere di buono, di cattivo augurio. **-ing** *adj.* presago; *n.* presagio.
**bodice** *n.* corsetto; busto.
**bodily** *adj.* corporeo; corporale; *adv.* corporalmente; di persona; in massa; tutt'insieme; interamente.
**bodkin** *n.* punteruolo; spillone *m.*; passanastro.
**body** *n.* corpo; struttura fisica; tronco, torso; cadavere *m.*; carogna; gruppo di persone; sodalizio; corporazione; società; *a public —*, un ente pubblico; *the public —*, lo Stato; massa; quantità; sostanza, consistenza; (geom.) solido; *the heavenly bodies*, i corpi celesti; (fam.) persona. **-guard** *n.* guardia del corpo.
**Boer** *pr.n.* (hist.) Boero; *the — War*, la guerra dei Boeri.
**bog** *n.* palude *f.*; pantano; acquitrino; (slang) toeletta; *tr.* impantanare; *intr.* impantanarsi, affondare in un pantano.
**boggle** *intr.* trasalire; esitare.
**bogus** *adj.* falso, finto; simulato.
**bogy** *n.* spettro; spauracchio; babau *m. indecl.*; *— man*, orco (dei bambini).
**Bohemia** *pr.n.* (geog.) Boemia; (fig.) vita zingaresca, scapigliatura. **-n** *adj.*, *n.* boemo; (fig.) zingaresco, scapigliato.
**boil**[1] *n.* punto d'ebollizione, bollitura; *the water is on the —*, l'acqua è in ebollizione; *intr.* bollire; (fig.) ribollire; *to — with rage*, ribollire di rabbia; (fam.) *to keep the pot -ing*, far andare avanti la baracca, guadagnarsi la vita; *tr.* far bollire; lessare. **-ed** *adj.* bollito; lesso; *-ed egg*, uovo da bere; *hard -ed egg*, uovo sodo. **-er** *n.* caldaia; bollitore; *-er works*, fabbrica di caldaie, *-er suit*, tuta. **-ing** *adj.* bollente; *n.* ebollizione; bollitura; *-ing point*, punto di ebollizione.
**boil**[2] *n.* foruncolo; vescichetta.
**boisterous** *adj.* chiassoso, rumoroso; tempestoso; violento. **-ness** *n.* fracasso; tumulto.
**bold** *adj.* audace; coraggioso; sfacciato, sfrontato; *to make — to*, prender la libertà di; vigoroso; chiaro; ben delineato; *— handwriting*, calligrafia chiara. **-ly** *adv.* arditamente, coraggiosamente, sfacciatamente. **-ness** *n.* audacia, coraggio, sfacciataggine *f.*, impudenza.
**bold-faced** *adj.* sfrontato.
**bole** *n.* tronco d'albero.
**Bolivia** *pr.n.* (geog.) Bolivia. **-n** *adj.*, *n.* boliviano.
**bollard** *n.* (naut.) bitta, palo d'ormeggio.
**Bologna** *pr.n.* (geog.) Bologna; *inhabitant of —*, bolognese *m.*, *f.*
**bolshev-ik** *adj.*, *n.* bolscevico. **-ism** *n.* bolscevismo. **-ist** *adj.*, *n.* boscevico.
**bolster** *n.* capezzale *m.*; cuscinetto; supporto; *tr.* sostenere; dare

appoggio a. **-ing** *n.* sostegno; appoggio.

**bolt**[1] *n.* catenaccio; chiavistello; stagna; spranga; bullone *m.*; *nuts and -s*, bulloneria; freccia, dardo; *a — from the blue*, un fulmine a ciel sereno; salto, balzo; scappata; *tr.* chiudere con catenaccio; sprangare; imbullonare; inghiottire senza masticare; *intr.* svignarsela.

**bolt**[2] *adv.* come una freccia; — *upright*, diritto come un fuso.

**bolt**[3] *n.* setaccio, buratto; *tr.* setacciare abburattare.

**bolter**[1] *n.* cavallo in fuga; chi fugge.

**bolter**[2] *n.* setaccio, buratto.

**bomb** *n.* bomba; *atomic* —, bomba atomica; *H* —, bomba all'idrogeno; *fire* —, bomba incendiaria; *smoke* —, bomba fumogena; *tr.* bombardare; lanciare bombe (a). **-er** *n.* bombardiere *m.*; apparecchio da bombardamento. **-ing** *n.* bombardamento. **-proof** *adj.* a prova di bomba. **-shell** *n.* obice *m.*; granata; (fig.) notizia sconvolgente.

**bombard** *n.* bombarda; *tr.* bombardare. **-ier** *n.* bombardiere *m.* **-ment** *n.* bombardamento.

**bombast** *n.* magniloquenza; ampollosità; enfasi *f.* **-ic** *adj.* ampolloso; enfatico.

**bombed-out** *adj.* sinistrato.

**bond** *adj.* schiavo; *n.* vincolo; legame *m.*; *the — of wedlock*, il legame matrimoniale; *to be in -s*, essere in prigionia; *to break one's -s asunder*, spezzare le catene; patto; impegno; *to enter into a* —, impegnarsi; obbligazione; (finan.) polizza, buono; titolo; (leg.) cauzione; *goods in* —, merci in attesa di sdoganamento; (chem.) legame; sostanza agglutinante, cemento; *tr.* (comm.) mettere in deposito doganale; (bldg.) allineare. **-age** *n.* schiavitù, servitù *f.* **-ed** *adj.* legato; vincolato; *-ed warehouse*, magazzino doganale. **-maiden** *n.* schiava. **-slave, -sman** *n.* schiavo; *to be -sman for*, rendersi garante per.

**bon-e** *n.* osso; *skin and* —, pelle ed ossa; *to pick a* —, rosicchiare un osso; — *of contention*, pomo della discordia; *he was chilled to the* —, era gelato fino alle ossa; *pl.* (fig.) resti *m.pl.* mortali; *to make no -s*, non esitare, non farsi scrupolo; — *idle*, pigrone; *tr.* disossare; mettere le stecche a. **-ed** *adj.* ossuto; disossato; fornito di stecche. **-eless** *adj.* senz'ossa; disossato. **-eshaker** *n.* (fam.) veicolo traballante.

**bone-dry** *adj.* secco come un chiodo.

**bonfire** *n.* falò *m. indecl.*

**bonkers** *adj.* (fam.) matto.

**bonnet** *n.* berretto scozzese da uomo; cuffia da donna; (fig.) *to have a bee in one's* —, essere fissato; (motor.) cofano. **-ed** *adj.* che porta il berretto.

**bonny** *adj.* grazioso; fiorente.

**bonus** *n.* compenso, premio; indennità; gratifica; *cost of living* —, carovita *m. indecl.*; *long service* —, premio di anzianità.

**bony** *adj.* osseo; ossuto; scarno.

**boo** *intr.* fischiare; *excl.* oibò.

**booby** *n.* sciocco; balordo; — *prize*, premio scherzoso dato al peggiore dei concorrenti; (fam.) seno; — *trap*, trappola; (mil.) ordigno esplosivo.

**boohoo** *n.* pianto; rumore *m.* di pianto; *intr.* (colloq.) piangere a dirotto.

**book** *tr.* prendere nota di; registrare; *we are heavily -ed*, abbiamo molti ordini da eseguire; prenotare, fissare; *I'm -ed up for the whole day*, sono impegnato per l'intera giornata. **-ing** *n.* registrazione; prenotazione.

**book** *n.* libro; — *of reference*, libro di consultazione; *pocket-size* —, libro tascabile; *to talk like a* —, parlare come un libro stampato; (comm.) registro; *to keep the -s of a firm*, tenere la contabilità di una ditta; *the good Book*, la Bibbia; *to swear on the Book*, giurare sulla Bibbia; libretto d'opera; *telephone* —, guida telefonica; *exercise* —, quaderno dei compiti. **-binder** *n.* rilegatore di libri. **-binding** *n.* rilegatura di libri. **-case** *n.* libreria; scaffale *m.* **-ish** *adj.* studioso; pedante. **-let** *n.* opuscolo; libricino. **-mark** *n.* segnalibro. **-seller** *n.* libraio. **-shelf** *n.* scaffale *m.* **-shop** *n.* libreria. **-stall** *n.* edicola, chiosco; bancarella. **-worm** *n.* tignuola; (fig.) topo di biblioteca.

**bookie** *n.* see **book-maker.**

**booking-clerk** *n.* impiegato della biglietteria. **-office** *n.* biglietteria, ufficio prenotazioni.

**book-keeper** *n.* contabile *m.* **-keeping** *n.* contabilità. **-maker** *n.* allibratore. **-rest** *n.* leggìo.

**boom**[1] *n.* (naut.) boma; asta; palo.

**boom**[2] *n.* rombo, rimbombo; tuono; *intr.* rimbombare; tuonare.

**boom**[3] *n.* (econ.) aumento improvviso di attività; rapido fiorire; improvvisa popolarità raggiunta con mezzi reclamistici; *intr.* (econ.) essere in periodo di voga; *his books are -ing*, i suoi libri sono in gran voga; *tr.* (comm.) fare il lancio pubblicitario di.

**boon** *n.* favore *m.*; dono; grazia; *to ask a — of*, chiedere una grazia a.

**boon** *adj.* (poet.) generoso, benigno; allegro; — *companion*, compagno di bagordi.

**boor** *n.* persona rozza. **-ish** *adj.* rustico; maleducato. **-ishness** *n.* rozzezza; zoticaggine *f.*

**boost** *n.* lancio pubblicitario; (electr.) aumento della tensione; spinta; pressione; (mech.) sovralimentazione; *tr.* lanciare con pubblicità; (electr.) elevare la tensione di; spingere.

**boot** *n.* stivale *m.*; (motor.) portabagagli *m. indecl.*; (fig.) *to lick someone's -s*, lustrare gli stivali ad uno; *tr.* calciare; mandare via a pedate. **-black** *n.* lustrascarpe *m. indecl.* **-ee** *n.* scarpetta di lana per bambini; stivaletto per donna. **-ed** *adj.* che calza stivali.

**booth** *n.* baracca; capanna; *telephone* —, cabina telefonica.

**boot-lace** *n.* stringa.

**bootless** *adj.* vano, inutile.

**booty** *n.* preda; bottino.

**booz-e** *n.* (colloq.) sbornia; bevanda alcoolica; *intr.* (colloq.) ubriacarsi. **-er** *n.* (fam.) beone, ubriacone *m.* **-y** *adj.* (fam.) ubriaco.

**bor-ax** *n.* (chem.) borace *m.* **-acic** *adj.* (chem.) boracico.

**border** *n.* orlo; bordo; limite *m.*; frontiera; *intr.* orlare; *to — upon*, confinare con; esser situato sul confine di. **-line** *n.* linea di demarcazione.

**border-land** *n.* terra di confine; confine *m.*

**bor-e**[1] *n.* buco, foro; calibro; scandaglio; *intr.* forare, bucare, perforare; trapanare; scandagliare, sondare. **-ing** *n.* (mech.) alesatura; sondaggio.

**bor-e**[2] *n.* seccatura, noia; seccatore; *tr.* annoiare; infastidire; (fam.) seccare; *I was -ed to death*, mi sono seccato a morte. **-edom** *n.* noia; fastidio. **-ing** *adj.* noioso.

**boreal** *adj.* boreale.

**boric** *adj.* (chem.) borico.

**born** *adj.* nato; generato; *he is a — poet*, è un poeta nato; — *and bred*, nato e cresciuto; *in all my — days*, da quando sono al mondo; *London* —, nativo di Londra.

**borough** *n.* borgo; cittadina; municipio; circoscrizione elettorale.

**borrow** *tr.* prendere a prestito; farsi prestare; *the book I -ed last week*, il libro che mi prestarono la settimana scorsa; *they will — money from him*, si faranno prestare del denaro da lui; *-ed plumes*, penne di pavone; adottare; derivare. **-er** *n.* chi prende a prestito, accattatore. **-ing** *n.* il prendere a prestito; adozione.

**bosh** *n.* (slang) chiacchiera; sciocchezza; follia.

**bosom** *n.* petto, seno; *in the — of one's family*, in seno alla famiglia; *to keep in one's* —, tenere segreto; *to nurse a viper in one's* —, scaldar la serpe in seno; (fig.) affetto; cuore *m.*; *my — friend*, il mio più intimo amico.

**Bosphorus** *pr.n.* (geog.) *the —*, il Bosforo.
**boss**[1] *n.* (slang) capo, direttore, padrone *m.*; *tr.* spadroneggiare; comandare. **-y** *adj.* prepotente; autoritario.
**boss**[2] *n.* protuberanza; (archit.) bugna; borchia; risalto; aggetto.
**bosun** *n.* see **boatswain.**
**botan-y** *n.* botanica. **-ic(al)** *adj.* botanico; *-ical gardens*, orto botanico. **-ist** *n.* botanico; botanista *m., f.* **-ize** *intr.* erborare, erborizzare; raccogliere piante. **-izer** *n.* erborista *m., f.* **-izing** *n.* erborizzazione.
**botch** *n.* bitorzolo; lavoro male eseguito; rattoppo mal fatto; *intr.* abborracciare, rappezzare, rattoppare malamente; raffazzonare. **-er** *n.* rappezzatore; pasticcione *m.* **-y** *adj.* pieno di bitorzoli; rappezzato; fatto malamente.
**both** *adj.* ambedue, entrambi, tutti e due; *on — sides*, d'ambo le parti; *prn.* ambedue, entrambi, tutti e due; *— of us*, noi due; *— are poets*, sono entrambi poeti; *— of them saw you*, ti videro tutti e due; *they are — alike*, sono tutti e due uguali; *adv.* nel medesimo tempo, ad un tempo, insieme; *— . . . and*, e . . . e, sia . . . sia, tanto . . . quanto; *he is — a poet and a painter*, egli è ad un tempo poeta e pittore; *she is — beautiful and clever*, è tanto bella quanto intelligente; *he — sings and acts well*, egli è valente sia come cantante che come attore.
**bother** *n.* seccatura, noia; *what a —!*, che seccatura!; *intr.* infastidire; seccare; *— it!*, all'inferno!; *don't — me!*, lasciami stare!; preoccuparsi; *don't — about me*, non disturbatevi per me. **-ation** *n.* seccatura; *excl.* diamine! **-some** *adj.* seccante, noioso.
**bottl-e** *n.* bottiglia; fiasco; boccetta; *to crack a —*, sturare una bottiglia; *tr.* imbottigliare; infiascare; mettere in bottiglia; *-ed wine*, vino in bottiglia; *to — up*, imbottigliare, bloccare; (fig.) reprimere, nascondere dentro di sè.
**bottle-fed** *adj.* allevato artificialmente. **-green** *adj.* verde bottiglia. **-neck** *n.* collo di bottiglia; (fig.) ingorgo; congestione.
**bottom** *adj.* inferiore; ultimo; basilare; fondamentale; essenziale; *n.* fondo; estremità; letto di fiume; *from top to —*, dall'alto al basso; *to go to the —*, colare a picco; *to send a ship to the —*, affondare una nave; *to touch —*, toccare il fondo; (fig.) fondamento; essenza; causa, origine *f.*; *at —*, in fondo; *to be at the — of*, avere la parte principale in; *to get to the — of*, andare a fondo in; sedere *m.*, deretano; fondamenta *f.pl.*; (naut.) chiglia, carena. **-less** *adj.* insondabile; senza fondo; (fig.) senza fine; smisurato; *the -less pit*, l'inferno.
**bottomry** *n.* (comm.) cambio marittimo.
**botulism** *n.* (med.) botulismo.
**boudoir** *n.* salottino.
**bough** *n.* ramo d'albero; ramoscello.
**boulder** *n.* macigno; (geol.) masso erratico.
**boulevard** *n.* viale *m.*; corso.
**bounc-e** *n.* balzo; rimbalzo; *to catch the ball on the —*, cogliere la palla al balzo; (fam.) vanteria, millanteria; *intr.* rimbalzare; *to — out of a room*, balzar fuori da una stanza; vantarsi, fare il fanfarone; *tr.* far rimbalzare. **-ing** *adj.* vigoroso; vivace; *a -ing baby*, un bambino pieno di salute.
**bound**[1] *n.* confine, limite *m.*; restrizione; *to go beyond the -s of reason*, uscire dai limiti della ragione; *to keep within -s*, non uscire dai limiti; *tr.* confinare; porre limiti a; restringere.
**bound**[2] *n.* salto; balzo; rimbalzo; *at a —*, con un balzo; *to advance by leaps and -s*, far passi da gigante; *intr.* balzare; rimbalzare; saltare.
**bound**[3] *adj.* diretto, incamminato; (naut.) *— for*, in partenza per, con destinazione per; *where are you — for?*, dove siete diretto?; *homeward —*, diretto verso la patria.
**bound**[4] *part.* of **bind**, *q.v.*; *adj.* rilegato; *— in leather*, rilegato di pelle; obbligato, costretto; impegnato; certo; destinato; *the best horse is — to win*, vincerà certamente il cavallo migliore; *he is — to come*, è certo che verrà. **-en** *adj.* *-en duty*, sacro dovere.
**boundary** *n.* limite, termine *m.*; frontiera.
**bounder** *n.* (fam.) mascalzone *m.*
**boundless** *adj.* illimitato; sconfinato. **-ness** *n.* infinità; vastità.
**bount-y** *n.* generosità; bontà; munificenza; premio. **-eous, -iful** *adj.* abbondante; liberale; generoso; benefico.
**bouquet** *n.* mazzo; profumo, fragranza; aroma *m.*
**bourgeois** *adj., n.* borghese *m., f.* **-ie** *n.* borghesia.
**bourn** *n.* ruscello; corso d'acqua.
**bourn(e)** *n.* confine *m.*; meta *m.*; limite *m.*
**bourse** *n.* (comm.) borsa valori.
**bout** *n.* periodo di attività; attacco (di malattia); lotta; partita; turno; ripresa.
**bovine** *adj.* bovino; (fig.) ottuso, stupido.
**bow**[1] *n.* (pron. **bo**) arco; curvo; fiocco; (mus.) archetto; (equit.) arcione *m.*; *tr.* suonare (uno strumento) con l'archetto.
**bow**[2] *n.* saluto, inchino; *to make one's —*, salutare; *intr.* piegarsi; curvarsi; chinarsi, inchinarsi; *to — and scrape*, prosternarsi; *to — low*, inchinarsi profondamente; *to — to*, salutare, (fig.) sottomettersi (a); *tr.* piegare; curvare; *to — one's head*, chinare il capo; *to — out*, accompagnare fuori; *rfl. to — oneself out*, prender congedo.
**bow**[3], **bows** *n.* (naut.) prua, prora.
**bowdlerize** *tr.* espurgare.
**bowel(s)** *n.* (anat.) viscere *f.pl.*; budella *f.pl.*; *to have a motion of the -s*, andare di corpo; *the -s of the earth*, le viscere della terra; (fig.) sentimenti di compassione; (attrib.) intestinale.
**bower** *n.* pergolato, luogo ombreggiato; (poet.) dimora, ritiro campestre; appartamento femminile.
**bowl**[1] *n.* scodella, tazza; vaso; bacino. **-ful** *n.* scodellata.
**bowl**[2] *n.* boccia; *game of -s*, giuoco delle bocce; *to play -s*, giuocare alle bocce. **-ing** *n.* giuoco alle bocce; *-ing alley*, pallottolaio; *-ing green*, campo di bocce.
**bowl**[3] *intr.* rotolare; *tr.* far rotolare; (cricket) servire (la palla).
**bow-legged** *adj.* dalle gambe arcuate.
**bowler**[1] *n.* bombetta, cappello duro.
**bowler**[2] *n.* (cricket) giocatore che serve la palla.
**bowline** *n.* (naut.) bolina.
**bow-man** *n.* arciere *m.* **-shot** *n.* tiro d'arco. **-string** *n.* corda d'arco; laccio.
**bowsprit** *n.* (naut.) bompresso.
**bow-tie** *n.* cravatta a farfalla. **-window** *n.* bovindo; finestra ad arco.
**box**[1] *adj.* (bot.) di bosso; *n.* bosso.
**box**[2] *n.* scatola, cassa, cassetta; bossolo; cabina; stanzetta; cubicolo; scompartimento; (horse) stallo; (theatr.) palco; *— number*, casella postale; *Christmas —*, strenna, gratifica natalizia; *tr.* porre in scatola; incassare; (fig.) *-ed up*, ristretto, soffocato.
**box**[3] *n.* pugno; schiaffo, ceffone *m.*; *intr.* lottare a pugni, fare del pugilato; *to — someone's ears*, schiaffeggiare qualcuno. **-er** pugile *m.* **-ing** *n.* pugilato.
**box-calf** *n.* cuoio di vitello cromato.
**Boxing-day** *n.* giorno delle strenne (S. Stefano).
**boxing-glove** *n.* guanto da pugilato. **-match** *n.* partita di pugilato.
**box-office** *n.* botteghino del teatro.
**boxwood** *n.* bosso.
**boy** *n.* ragazzo; adolescente *m.*; *little —*, bambino; *my dear —*, mio caro; *old —!*, vecchio mio!; fanciullo; garzone *m.*, fattorino; *cabin —*, mozzo; servo indigeno; *Boy Scout*, giovane esploratore; —

*friend*, compagno, amante. **-hood** *n.* fanciullezza; puerizia; *late -hood*, adolescenza. **-ish** *adj.* fanciullesco; puerile. **-ishness** *n.* fanciullaggine *f.*; aspetto puerile. **-like** *adj.* fanciullesco; da ragazzo.
**boycott** *n.* boicottaggio; *tr.* boicottare.
**bra** *n.* (*abbr.* of **brassière**) reggipetto.
**brace**[1] *n.* (techn.) sostegno; collegamento; (carp.) trapano; *— and bit*, trapano a manubrio; (mus.) legatura; paio; *three — of partridges*, tre coppie di pernici; *pl.* bretelle *f. pl.*
**brac-e**[2] *tr.* fortificare; (fig.) rinvigorire; (naut.) bracciare; accoppiare; *rfl.* farsi coraggio. **-ing** *adj.* invigorante; salubre, tonificante.
**bracelet** *n.* braccialetto.
**brachial** *adj.* (anat.) brachiale.
**bracken** *n.* (bot.) felce *f.*
**bracket** *n.* mensola; braccio; (techn.) tassello di sostegno; parentesi *f. indecl.*; *between -s*, fra parentesi; *tr.* mettere fra parentesi; accoppiare; pareggiare.
**brackish** *adj.* salmastro, salato. **-ness** *n.* salsedine *f.*; sapore salmastro.
**bract** *n.* (bot.) brattea.
**brad** *n.* chiodo con testa piccola. **-awl** *n.* punteruolo; lesina.
**brag** *n.* vanto, millanteria; fanfaronata; *intr.* vantare; vantarsi (di). **-gart** *adj.*, *n.* fanfarone, spaccone *m.*; millantatore.
**brahmin** *n.* bramino.
**braid** *n.* treccia; gallone *m.*; spighetta; *tr.* intrecciare (capelli, nastri); guarnire di treccia, di gallone.
**brain** *n.* (anat.) cervello; *pl.* (*usu.* -a, *f. pl.*) capacità intellettiva; *he has no -s at all*, è senza cervello; *to cudgel one's -s*, lambiccarsi il cervello; *— washing*, lavaggio del cervello; *— work*, lavoro intellettuale; *tr.* far saltar le cervella a, romper la testa a. **-less** *adj.* senza cervello; stupido. **-pan** *n.* (anat.) cranio. **-storm** *n.* attacco di pazzia. **-wave** *n.* (fam.) idea luminosa, lampo di genio. **-y** *adj.* intelligente; geniale; abile; *how -y of you!*, che geniale idea!
**braise** *tr.* brasare, cuocere a stufato.
**brake**[1] *n.* felce *f.*; macchia; cespuglio.
**brake**[2] *n.* (agric.) gramola, maciulla; *tr.* gramolare, maciullare.
**brake**[3] *n.* freno; *to put on the —*, serrare il freno; *— drum*, tamburo di freno; *air —*, freno ad aria compressa; *emergency —*, freno di sicurezza; *foot —*, freno a pedale; *hand —*, freno a mano; *parking —*, freno di blocco; *tr.*, *intr.* frenare. **-sman** *n.* frenatore.
**bramble** *n.* rovo, pruno. **-berry** *n.* mora. **-bush** *n.* roveto.
**bran** *n.* crusca; *— mash*, pastone *m.*
**branch** *n.* ramo; ramificazione; frasca; braccio; diramazione; reparto; succursale, filiale *f.*; *— line*, ferrovia di diramazione; *— office*, agenzia filiale; *adj.* (fig.) *root and —*, radicale, completo; *intr.* metter rami; ramificarsi; *to — off*, biforcarsi, diramarsi; *to — out*, estendersi. **-ed, -ing** *adj.* ramoso; diramato.
**brand** *n.* tizzone *m.*; marcio a fuoco; marchio d'infamia, stigma *m.*; *— of Cain*, marchio di Caino; marchio di fabbrica; marca, qualità (di merce); *a famous —*, una marca famosa; (poet.) spada, brando; *tr.* marchiare con ferro rovente; (fig.) stigmatizzare; *to — on one's memory*, imprimere indelebilmente nella memoria.
**branding-iron** *n.* ferro da marchio.
**brandish** *tr.* brandire.
**brand-new** *adj.* nuovo fiammante, nuovo di zecca.
**brandy** *n.* acquavite *f.*, cognac *m.*
**brash** *adj.* crudo; zotico; immaturo.
**brass** *n.* ottone *m.*; (poet.) bronzo; (fam.) impudenza, sfrontatezza; *pl.* (mus.) *the —*, gli ottoni; *— band*, fanfara; *— plate*, targa d'ottone; (fam.) *— hat*, ufficiale superiore, pezzo grosso; *I don't care a — farthing*, non me ne importa un bel niente; *let's get down to — tacks*, veniamo al sodo. **-ie** *n.* (golf) mazza con paletta d'ottone. **-iness** *n.* sfrontatezza. **-ware** *n.* ottoname *m.* **-y** *adj.* d'ottone; che somiglia all'ottone; (fig.) sfacciato.
**brassière** *n.* reggipetto.
**brat** *n.* marmocchio, monello, birichino.
**bravado** *n.* bravata; smargiassata.
**brave** *adj.* coraggioso; ardito; audace; prode; vistoso; *a — show*, un bell'effetto; *n.* prode *m.*; guerriero pellirossa; bravo; *tr.* sfidare; affrontare; resistere a. **-ry** *n.* coraggio; audacia; splendore *m.*, magnificenza; bravura.
**brawl** *n.* rissa; schiamazzo; *intr.* rissare, azzuffarsi, schiamazzare. **-er** *n.* sbraitore *m.*; attaccabrighe *m. indecl.* **-ing** *n.* rissa; schiamazzo.
**brawn** *n.* muscolo; forza muscolare; (cul.) carne *f.* di testa di maiale. **-iness** *n.* muscolosità; robustezza. **-y** *adj.* muscoloso; robusto.
**bray** *intr.* echeggiare; ragliare. **-(ing)** *n.* raglio.
**brazen** *adj.* di ottone; ottonato; sfrontato, sfacciato; *tr.* rendere sfacciato; *to — it out*, comportarsi con sfacciataggine, fare lo sfacciato. **-ly** *adv.* sfacciatamente. **-ness** *n.* sfacciataggine *f.*
**brazier** *n.* (man) ottonaio; calderaio; (pan) braciere *m.*
**Brazil** *pr.n.* (geog.) Brasile *m.* **-ian** *adj.*, *n.* brasiliano.
**breach** *n.* frattura; (naut.) rottura; (mil.) breccia; *to stand in the —*, sostenere l'assalto; (fig.) stare sulla breccia; (fig.) violazione; *— of contract*, rottura di contratto; *— of duty*, infrazione al dovere; *— of the peace*, violazione dell'ordine pubblico; *— of promise*, rottura di promessa di matrimonio; *— of trust*, abuso di fiducia, infedeltà; *tr.* aprire una breccia in.
**bread** *n.* pane *m.*; *a loaf of —*, una pagnotta; *new —*, pane fresco; *a roll of —*, un panino; *stale —*, pane raffermo; *unleavened —*, pane azzimo; (fig.) vitto, sostentamento, cibo; *daily —*, cibo quotidiano; *brown —*, pane scuro.
**bread-basket** *m.* cestino per il pane; (slang) stomaco. **-crumb** *n.* mollica; *pl.* briciole *f.pl.*; pan grattato; *tr.* impanare. **-fruit** *n.* frutto dell'albero del pane. **-winner** *n.* sostegno della famiglia, chi guadagna il pane.
**breadth** *n.* larghezza, ampiezza; (of material) altezza; *ten feet in —*, largo dieci piedi; *— of wings*, apertura d'ali; *to a hair's —*, a pennello, esattamente; (fig.) liberalità; larghezza di vedute.
**break** *n.* rottura, frattura; *a — in the voice*, un'incrinatura nella voce; *— of day*, lo spuntar del giorno; interruzione; intervallo; pausa; infrazione, violazione, irregolarità; (fam.) opportunità, occasione.
**break** *tr.* rompere; spezzare; frantumare; *this -s my heart*, questo mi spezza il cuore; *the waves — against the rocks*, le onde si infrangono contro gli scogli; *to — the ice*, rompere il ghiaccio; *to — one's neck*, rompersi l'osso del collo; *to — the news*, comunicare per primo la notizia; *to — a record*, battere un primato; interrompere; soggiogare, domare; *to — faith*, venir meno alla parola; *to — down*, demolire, abbattere; (comm.) analizzare; *to — off*, cessare bruscamente; *the marriage was broken off*, il matrimonio andò a monte; *to — off an appointment*, mandare a monte un appuntamento; *to — open*, aprire con violenza, scassinare; *to — up*, rompere, fare in pezzi; disperdere; *intr.* spezzarsi; andare in frantumi; *to — away, loose*, spezzare i legami, scappare; *to — into*, irrompere in; *he broke into laughter*, scoppiò in una risata; *to — down*, deprimersi, rovinarsi; *to — out*, scoppiare; scappare, fuggire; *to — up*, sciogliersi, disperdersi; (schol.) iniziare le

vacanze. **-able** *adj.* fragile; (notice) posa piano. **-age** *n.* rottura, spezzatura, frattura; *to pay for the -ages*, pagare i danni. **-away** *n.* separazione; defezione; fuga; *adj.* di ultima moda. **-er** *n.* rompitore; ammaestratore; (naut.) frangente *n.*

**break-down** *n.* collasso; insuccesso; rottura; dissesto; sfacelo; crollo; sospensione di servizio; (admin.) analisi *f. indecl.*; (motor.) panna, guasto, danno; — *service*, servizio riparazioni; *nervous* —, esaurimento nervoso. **-neck** *n.* rompicollo; *adj.* pericoloso; *-neck speed*, a rompicollo, a rotta di collo. **-off** *n.* rottura; interruzione. **-through** *n.* (geol.) affioramento; (mil.) penetrazione nelle linee nemiche; (fig.) scoperta. **-up** *n.* collasso; demolizione; dispersione; smembramento.

**breakwater** *n.* frangiflutti *m. indecl.*; argine *m.*; diga.

**breast** *n.* petto; mammella, poppa; (fig.) sorgente *f.* di nutrimento; cuore; coscienza; affetto; *to make a clean — of*, farne una completa confessione; (archit.) parapetto; *tr.* affrontare; resistere a. **-bone** *n.* (anat.) sterno. **-work** *n.* (archit.) parapetto, muro basso di difesa.

**breast-high** *adj.* all'altezza del petto. **-plate** *n.* corazza. **-stroke** *n.* (sport) nuoto a rana.

**breath** *n.* respiro, alito, fiato; *the — of life*, il soffio della vita; *bad* —, alito cattivo; *last* —, l'ultimo respiro; *out of* —, senza fiato; *to be short of* —, avere il respiro corto; *to draw* —, respirare, vivere; *to hold one's* —, trattenere il respiro; *to recover* —, riprendere fiato; *to take* —, riposare; *to take someone's — away*, togliere il fiato a qualcuno; *to waste one's* —, sprecare il fiato; *below one's* —, sottovoce; venticello, brezza; *a — of wind*, un soffio di vento; mormoriò, sussurro. **-less** *adj.* senza fiato; ansante; esanime, senza vita. **-lessly** *adv.* con il fiato sospeso; con viva attesa. **-lessness** *n.* mancanza di respiro, affanno.

**breath-e** *intr.* respirare, prender fiato; soffiare; *to — new life into*, rianimare; *to — one's last*, esalare l'ultimo respiro; *to — a sigh*, sospirare; sussurrare; *to — a prayer*, mormorare una preghiera; *to — forth perfume*, esalare profumo; *to — in*, inspirare; *to — out*, espirare. **-able** *adj.* respirabile. **-er** *n.* chi respira; (fam.) piccola pausa; sfiatatoio. **-ing** *adj.* respirante, vivente, esalante; *n.* respiro, respirazione; (Gk. gramm.) spirito.

**breathing-hole** *n.* spiraglio. **-space** *n.* intervallo di riposo.

**breath-taking** *adj.* sorprendente, che toglie il fiato.

**breathy** *adj.* accompagnato da emissione di respiro.

**breech** *n.* parte posteriore *f.*; culatta di fucile; deretano; (mil.) — *loading*, retrocarica; *tr.* mettere in calzoncini (un bimbo, per la prima volta). **-es** *n.pl.* calzoni *m.pl.*; brache *f.pl.*

**breed** *n.* razza; famiglia; stirpe *f.*; progenie *f.*; *intr.* generare, procreare; nascere, originare; (fig.) produrre, causare; allevare; educare. **-er** *n.* chi genera; allevatore. **-ing** *n.* generazione, procreazione; allevamento; educazione; buone maniere; finezza.

**breez-e** *n.* brezza, venticello, soffio d'aria; (colloq.) litigio. **-ily** *adv.* con vento; (colloq.) cordialmente, con giovialità; con disinvoltura. **-iness** *n.* cordialità, giovialità; disinvoltura; brio. **-y** *adj.* ventoso, ventilato; arieggiato; (colloq.) gioviale; allegro, brioso.

**Bremen** *pr.n.* (geog.) Brema.

**Breslau** *pr.n.* (geog.) Breslavia.

**Breton** (geog.) *adj.*, *n.* bretone.

**breviary** *n.* (eccl.) breviario.

**brevity** *n.* brevità; concisione.

**brew** *n.* mescolanza, mistura; infuso, tisana; fermentazione; *tr.* mescolare; fare un infuso di; (fig.) macchinare; tramare; *intr.* essere in fermentazione; (fig.) *to know what is -ing*, sapere cosa bolle in pentola. **-er** *n.* birraio. **-ery** *n.* fabbrica di birra. **-ing** *n.* fabbricazione della birra; quantità di birra fatta in una volta.

**briar** *n.* see **brier**.

**brib-e** *n.* dono offerto a scopo di corruzione; esca; allettamento; *tr.* corrompere; sedurre; *to — to silence*, comprare il silenzio di. **-able** *adj.* corruttibile. **-ery** *n.* corruzione; *open to -ery*, corruttibile.

**bric-a-brac** *n.* anticaglie, cianfrusaglie *f.pl.*

**brick** *n.* mattone *m.*; laterizio; (colloq.) *to drop a* —, fare una gaffe; persona buona e fidata; *he was a real — to me*, fu un vero amico per me; *tr.* murare; costruire in mattoni; *adj.* di mattoni. **-bat** *n.* pezzo di mattone; (fig.) insulto. **-layer** *n.* muratore. **-maker** *n.* mattonaio. **-making** *n.* fabbricazione dei mattoni. **-work** *n.* muratura in mattoni. **-yard** *n.* mattonaia.

**brick-dust** *n.* polvere *f.* di mattone. **-field** *n.* mattonaia. **-flooring** *n.* ammattonato. **-kiln** *n.* fornace *f.* per mattoni. **-red** *adj.* rosso mattone.

**brid-e** *n.* sposa, sposa novella; *to become a* —, maritarsi; *the — and bridegroom*, gli sposi. **-al** *adj.* nuziale. **-egroom** *n.* sposo. **-esmaid** *n.* damigella d'onore di una sposa.

**bridg-e**[1] *n.* ponte *m.*; ponte di comando, plancia; (mus.) ponticello di strumento ad arco; (anat.) dorso del naso; *tr.* costruire un ponte sopra; attraversare come un ponte; (fig.) *to — a gap*, colmare una lacuna; (electr.) collegare. **-eless** *adj.* senza ponte; (fig.) insormontabile, insuperabile. **-ing** *adj.* che attraversa; rche sostituisce; provvisorio.

**bridge**[2] *n.* (cards) bridge, ponte *m.*

**bridle** *n.* briglia; ostacolo; ritegno; freno; *intr.* imbrigliare; frenare; alzare il capo in atteggiamento sdegnoso; fare l'offeso, risentirsi, stizzirsi.

**bridle-path** *n.* strada percorribile a cavallo.

**brief**[1] *adj.* breve; conciso; *to be* —, essere breve nel discorso; *n.pl.* calzonetti *m.pl.*, mutandine *f.pl.*; *in* —, a farla breve, in sunto; **-ly** *adv.* brevemente, in breve. **-ness** *n.* brevità; concisione.

**brief**[2] *n.* riassunto; breve *f.*; lettera papale; *tr.* riassumere per sommi capi; *to — a case*, fare il riassunto di una causa; *to — a barrister*, affidare una causa ad un avvocato; impartire istruzioni a.

**brief-case** *n.* borsa (da avvocato).

**brier**[1] *n.* (bot.) rovo; rosa selvatica; *sweet* —, rosa selvatica profumata; — *rose*, rosa canina.

**brier**[2] *n.* (bot.) erica bianca; pipa di erica bianca.

**brig** *n.* (naut.) brigantino.

**brigade** *n.* (mil.) brigata; (colloq.) associazione; corpo; *one of the old* —, uno della vecchia guardia.

**brigadier-general** *n.* (mil.) comandante *m.* di brigata.

**brigand** *n.* brigante *m.* **-age** *n.* brigantaggio.

**brigantine** *n.* brigantino.

**bright** *adj.* lucido, risplendente; vivido; — *red*, rosso vivo; — *and early*, di prima mattina; gioioso; vivace; intelligente; *a — girl*, una ragazza sveglia; *the — side of things*, il lato buono delle cose; *to look on the — side*, vedere tutto rosa, essere ottimista; *adv.* luminosamente; allegramente. **-en** *intr.* brillare; *things are brightening up*, l'avvenire si annuncia più sereno; *tr.* far brillare; ravvivare; (fig.) animare; rallegrare. **-ly** *adv.* luminosamente; allegramente; vivacemente. **-ness** *n.* splendore *m.*; luminosità; gaiezza; vivacità.

**Bright's disease** *n.* nefrite cronica.

**brilli-ance, -ancy** *n.* lucentezza, brillantezza; splendore *m.*; vivezza d'ingegno; (opt.) luminosità. **-ant** *adj.* brillante, lucente, vivace; pieno di talento;

*n.* brillante *m.*; diamante sfaccettato; taglio a brillante. **-antly** *adv.* brillantemente, con lucentezza; vivacemente; con talento.

**brim** *n.* orlo; bordo; margine *m.*; sponda; *full to the —*, pieno fino all'orlo, colmo; (hat) tesa, ala. **-ful** *adj.* colmo, ricolmo; pieno. **-less** *adj.* senza orlo; senza tesa. **-med** *adj.* con orlo; *broad-brimmed hat*, cappello a larga tesa.

**brim** *intr.* essere pieno fino all'orlo; *to — over*, traboccare; *-ming over with life*, traboccante di vita; *eyes -ming over with tears*, occhi pieni di lagrime; *tr.* colmare. **-med** *part. adj.* colmo sino all'orlo.

**brimstone** *n.* zolfo; (fig.) zolfo infernale; *— yellow*, giallo zolfo.

**brindle(d)** *adj.* macchiato, chiazzato; pezzato.

**brin-e** *n.* acqua salmastra; acqua salata per salamoia; (poet.) mare *m.* **-ish** *adj.* salmastro. **-y** *adj.* salato; marino; *n.* (slang) *the -y*, il mare; *tr.* mettere in salamoia.

**bring** *tr.* portare; condurre; recare; *to — into question*, fare entrare in discussione; *to — to pass*, causare, far succedere; *to — home to*, aprire gli occhi a; far capire; *to — influence to bear on*, esercitare influenza su; indurre, persuadere; (fig.) *you have brought it on yourself*, te lo sei tirato addosso da solo; (leg.) addurre; presentare; *to — an action against*, intentare un processo contro; *to — a charge against*, presentare un'accusa contro; *to — about*, causare, far accadere; ottenere; effettuare; conseguire; *to — about a change*, operare un cambiamento; *to — about a war*, provocare una guerra; *to — back*, restituire; riportare; richiamare alla memoria; *to — down*, far scendere; abbattere; atterrare; *to — down the house*, far crollare il teatro dagli applausi; *to — forth*, dare alla luce; esibire; *to — in*, introdurre; presentare; far entrare; (leg.) *to — in a verdict*, emettere un verdetto; *to — off*, portar via, liberare, salvare; portare felicemente a compimento; *to — on*, produrre; cagionare; far fare dei progressi; (theatr.) portare in scena; *to — out*, far uscire; mettere in evidenza, dar valore a; pubblicare; esporre; lanciare; presentare in società; *to — over*, trasportare; persuadere, convincere; convertire; *to — round*, far rinvenire; *to — through*, far passare, far attraversare; salvare; *to — together*, riunire; mettere in contatto; *I brought them together again*, li feci riconciliare; *to — up*, far salire; vomitare; avvicinare; allevare, educare; richiamare l'attenzione su. **-er** *n.* portatore, latore.

**brink** *n.* orlo; bordo; margine *m.*; *on the — of despair*, sull'orlo della disperazione; *he was on the — of*, era sul punto di. **-manship** *n.* lo spingersi, nell'azione politica, sino all'estremo rischio di guerra.

**briony** *n.* (bot.) brionia; (pop.) vite bianca.

**brisk** *adj.* vivace, vispo; svelto; *— manners*, modi spicci; *at a — pace*, a passo svelto; *— air*, aria fresca, frizzante; (comm.) *— market*, mercato attivo; *tr.* animare; rianimare; *intr. to — up*, rianimarsi. **-ly** *adv.* attivamente; vivacemente; in modo spicciativo. **-ness** *n.* vivacità; sveltezza.

**brisket** *n.* (cul.) punta di petto.

**bristl-e** *n.* setola; pelo ruvido; *intr.* rizzarsi (di peli, capelli); (fig.) andare in collera. **-y** *adj.* setoloso; ruvido; irto; spinoso.

**Bristol Channel** *pr.n.* (geog.) il canale di Bristol.

**Britain** *pr.n.* (geog.) Gran Bretagna.

**Britannia** *pr.n.* Britannia; *— metal*, metallo inglese.

**Britannic** *adj.* britannico; *Her — Majesty*, Sua Maestà britannica.

**British** *adj.* britannico; inglese; *the — Isles*, le Isole britanniche; *the —*, i britannici; gli inglesi.

**Briton** *n.* britanno.

**Brittany** *pr.n.* (geog.) Bretagna.

**brittle** *adj.* fragile; friabile. **-ness** *n.* fragilità; friabilità.

**broach** *n.* spiedo; punteruolo, spina; (archit.) guglia; *tr.* spillare; intavolare, avviare un discorso su; accennare.

**broad** *adj.* largo; ampio; esteso; *a — outlook*, ampie vedute; *in — daylight*, in pieno giorno; *a road thirty feet —*, una strada larga trenta piedi; *to have a — back*, avere le spalle robuste; marcato; rustico; volgare; salace; tollerante, liberale; generale; *in — outline*, a grandi linee; *adv.* ampiamente; completamente; *— awake*, completamente sveglio. **-en** *tr.* allargare; estendere; *intr.* allargarsi; spandersi. **-ly** *adv.* largamente; ampiamente; *-ly speaking*, in termini generali. **-ness** *n.* larghezza, ampiezza; volgarità, grossolanità.

**broad-arrow** *n.* marchio che denota le proprietà dello Stato. **-backed** *adj.* dal dorso largo. **-brimmed** *adj.* dalle tese larghe. **-minded** *adj.* di larghe vedute. **-mindedness** *n.* larghezza di vedute, tolleranza. **-shouldered** *adj.* dalle spalle larghe.

**broadcast** *adj.* radiodiffuso; *n.* radiodiffusione; radiocomunicazione; (agric.) seminato; (fig.) sparso; *— announcement*, comunicazione radiofonica; *tr.* radiodiffondere, trasmettere per radio; (agric.) seminare; (fig.) disseminare, divulgare; *adv.* in modo sparso; largamente. **-er** *n.* apparecchio trasmittente, trasmettitore; chi parla alla radio. **-ing** *n.* radiodiffusione; *British Broadcasting Corporation* (abbr. B.B.C.), Ente Radiofonico Britannico; *-ing station*, stazione radiotrasmittente.

**broad-sheet** *n.* manifesto; (lit. hist.) pasquinato. **-side** *n.* (naut.) bordata; murata; (lit. hist.) see **broadsheet.** **-sword** *n.* sciabola. **-ways, -wise** *adv.* nel senso della larghezza.

**brocad-e** *n.* broccato; *tr.* broccare. **-ed** *adj.* di broccato.

**brochure** *n.* opuscolo.

**brogue** *n.* rozza scarpa di cuoio grezzo; scarpa chiodata per il golf; cadenza dialettale irlandese.

**broil** *n.* rissa; tumulto; *tr.* cuocere prima alla griglia poi al lesso; *intr.* essere esposto a grande calore. **-er** *n.* pollastro da cuocere al lesso.

**broke** *adj.* (slang) squattrinato; rovinato; *to go —*, fallire, far bancarotta.

**broken** *adj.* rotto, spezzato, interrotto; *a — promise*, una promessa mancata; *in — tones*, con voce rotta; *— sleep*, sonno agitato; incerto, variabile; ineguale, accidentato; increspato; *— health*, salute *f.* debole; accorato, avvilito, scoraggiato; *a — man*, un uomo finito; *— English*, inglese parlato male da uno straniero; *— meats*, avanzi *m.pl.* **-ly** *adv.* a scatti; irregolarmente; singhiozzando.

**broken-backed** *adj.* dalla schiena rotta. **-down** *adj.* avvilito; finito, rovinato. **-hearted** *adj.* dal cuore spezzato.

**broker** *n.* (comm.) sensale *m.*, mediatore; agente *m.*, commissionario. **-age** *n.* senseria, mediazione.

**brolly** *n.* (slang) ombrello.

**brom-ate** *n.* (chem.) bromato. **-ide** *n.* (chem.) bromuro.

**bronch-ial** *adj.* bronchiale. **-itic** *adj.* di bronchite; affetto da bronchite. **-itis** *n.* (med.) bronchite *f.*

**broncho-pneumonia** *n.* (med.) broncopolmonite *f.*

**bronze** *n.* bronzo; oggetto, opera in bronzo; *the — age*, l'età del bronzo; color bronzo; *tr.* bronzare; brunire; *intr.* abbronzarsi.

**brooch** *n.* fermaglio; spilla.

**brood** *n.* covata, nidiata; (joc.) prole *f.*; figliolanza; (fig.) sciame *m.*; turba; *intr.* covare; (fig.) rimuginare, meditare. **-er** *n.* (hen) chioccia; (fig.) chi medita. **-iness** *n.* (of hens) tendenza a covare; (fig.) malinconia. **-y** *adj.* (of hens) che

vuole covare; (fig.) meditabondo; che rimugina.
**brood-mare** *n.* cavalla di razza.
**brook**[1] *n.* ruscello.
**brook**[2] *tr.* tollerare, soffrire, sopportare; ammettere.
**broom** *n.* (bot.) ginestra; scopa; *a new — sweeps clean*, scopa nuova scopa bene; (bot.) *butcher's —*, pungitopo; *prickly —*, ginestrone *m.*; *tr.* scopare. **-stick** *n.* manico di scopa.
**broth** *n.* brodo; *thin —*, brodo leggero.
**brothel** *n.* casa di malaffare, bordello.
**brother** *n.* fratello; *elder —*, fratello maggiore; *younger —*, fratello minore; collega *m.*; camerata *m.*; confratello; *lay —*, frate laico, converso. **-hood** *n.* fratellanza; cameratismo; amor fraterno, confraternità. **-less** *adj.* senza fratelli. **-liness** *n.* fratellanza. **-ly** *adj.* fraterno.
**brother-in-law** *n.* cognato.
**brow** *n.* fronte *f.*; *pl.* sopracciglia *f.pl.*; *to knit one's -s*, aggrottare le sopracciglia; orlo; cima; sommità di rampa stradale. **-beat** *tr.* guardare con cipiglio; intimidire con parole.
**brown** *adj.* bruno, marrone; castano; scuro; abbronzato; *— eyes*, occhi castani; *— shoes*, scarpe gialle; *— study*, meditazione, fantasticheria; *— bread*, pane integrale; *— paper*, carta d'imballaggio; *— sugar*, zucchero grezzo; *n.* color bruno, marrone *m.*; *tr.* render bruno; abbronzare; (cul.) rosolare; *intr.* diventare bruno; (slang) *-ed off*, annoiato seccato.
**brownie** *n.* folletto; giovane esploratrice.
**brows-e** *intr.*, *tr.* pascolare; brucare; (fig.) scorrere libri, leggere per diletto; *to — among books*, curiosare fra i libri. **-ing** *adj.* pascolante; *n.* il brucare; (fig.) il leggere a spizzico.
**bruis-e** *n.* ammaccatura; contusione; intaccatura; *tr.* ammaccare; contundere; schiacciare, stritolare; *intr.* mostrare ammaccature. **-ed** *adj.* ammaccato; contuso; *-ed all over*, tutto ammaccato. **-er** *n.* pugile *m.*; (fig.) persona prepotente; uomo combattivo; (techn.) macinatrice; frantoio, frantumatrice. **-ing** *n.* ammaccatura; contusione.
**bruit** *tr.* spargere, divulgare rumore, diceria; *it was -ed that . . .*, correva voce che . . . .
**brunette** *adj.*, *n.* bruna, brunetta.
**brunt** *n.* urto, scontro; forza.
**brush** *n.* spazzola; spazzolino; spazzolata, colpo di spazzola; pennello; (fig.) pittore; *from the same —*, dello stesso pennello; (fig.) rissa, scontro, schermaglia; (fox) coda; *tr.* spazzolare; *to — one's hair*, spazzolarsi i capelli; *to — against*, rasentare, sfiorare; *to — aside*, scostare; (fig.) passar sopra a, ignorare; *to — away*, spazzar via; *to — away a tear*, asciugarsi una lagrima; *to — up*, spazzolare accuratamente; (fig.) rinfrescare la memoria; rivedere, rileggere, ripassare.
**brush-up** *n.* spazzolata; ripasso (di studio).
**brushwood** *n.* macchia; sottobosco.
**brusque** *adj.* brusco; rude. **-ness** *n.* rudezza; asprezza.
**Brussels** *pr.n.* (geog.) Brusselle *f.*; *— sprouts*, cavoli *m.pl.* di Brusselle.
**brutal** *adj.* brutale. **-ity** *n.* brutalità. **-ize** *intr.* imbestialire, abbrutire, brutalizzare. **-ly** *adv.* brutalmente, da bruto.
**brut-e** *adj.* brutale, selvaggio, animale; *n.* bruto. **-ish** *adj.* brutale, bestiale; abbrutito; rozzo; ignorante. **-ishness** *n.* abbrutimento; brutalità.
**bryony** *n.* (bot.) brionia; (pop.) vite bianca.
**bubbl-e** *n.* bolla; cavità visibile; gorgoglio; (fig.) sogno; chimera; impostura, frode *f.*; *intr.* far bolle; gorgogliare; ribollire; spumeggiare; *to — over*, traboccare; *to — up*, scaturire. **-ly** *adj.* pieno di bolle; che emette bolle; *n.* (colloq.) champagne.
**bubble-car** *n.* piccola automobile utilitaria.
**bubonic** *adj.* bubbonico; *— plague*, peste bubbonica.
**buccaneer** *n.* bucaniere, filibustiere *m.*; pirata *m.*; *intr.* pirateggiare. **-ing** *n.* pirateria.
**buck**[1] *n.* daino, cervo; caprone *m.*; coniglio; (fig.) zerbinotto. **-skin** *n.* pelle *f.* di daino.
**buck**[2] *intr.* (horse) saltare col dorso arcuato, impennarsi.
**buck**[3] *n.* (slang, poker) gettone *m.*; *to pass the — to someone*, scaricare su di un altro la propria responsabilità.
**buck**[4] *n.* (slang) dollaro.
**buck**[5] *tr.* rincuorare, rallegrare; *intr. to — (up)*, rallegrarsi; rinvigorirsi; *— up !*, sbrigati!; *I was frightfully -ed*, mi sentii molto rallegrato.
**bucket** *n.* secchio, secchia; (slang) *to kick the —*, crepare. **-ful** *n.* secchiata.
**bucket-shop** *n.* (comm.) agenzia di cambio clandestina.
**buckle** *n.* fibbia; fermaglio; *tr.* affibbiare; allacciare con fibbia; *to — on one's sword*, cingersi la spada; curvarsi; piegarsi; deformarsi; *to — down to work*, mettersi al lavoro.
**buckler** *n.* scudo; (fig.) protezione.
**buckram** *n.* tela da fusto; garza rigida.
**buckwheat** *n.* grano saraceno.
**bucolic** *adj.* bucolico, agreste, pastorale; *n.* (poet.) bucolica; *Virgil's Bucolics*, le Bucoliche del Virgilio.
**bud** *n.* gemma; germoglio; bottone *m.*; boccio, bocciuolo; *in the —*, in boccio; (fig.) *poet in the —*, poeta in erba; *to nip in the —*, troncare sul nascere; *intr.* germogliare; spuntare; sbocciare; (fig.) nascere, svilupparsi. **-ding** *n.* riproduzione per innesto; *adj.* in boccio; (fig.) in erba.
**buddh-ism** *n.* buddismo. **-ist** *adj.* buddistico; *n.* buddista *m.*, *f.*
**budge** *intr.* scostarsi; *he refused to —*, si rifiutò di muoversi; *tr.* smuovere, scostare; *I can't — him*, non riesco a smuoverlo.
**budget** *n.* bilancio preventivo; *to introduce the —*, presentare il bilancio; *household —*, entrate ed uscite, contabilità di casa; *intr.* fare un bilancio preventivo; *to — for an expenditure*, stanziare una spesa nel bilancio.
**buff**[1] *adj.* scamosciato; marrone; *n.* pelle scamosciata di bufalo, di bovino; color camoscio; *tr.* lucidare (un metallo) con pelle scamosciata; brillantare; scamosciare.
**buff**[2] *n.* buffetto, colpetto; *blindman's —*, mosca cieca.
**buffalo** *n.* bufalo.
**buffer**[1] *n.* (techn.) pulitrice.
**buffer**[2] *n.* (mech.) respingente, paracolpi; *— State*, Stato cuscinetto.
**buffer**[3] *n.* (slang) individuo inetto, imbecille *m.*; *old —*, vecchio imbecille.
**buffet**[1] *n.* schiaffo; (fig.) colpo avverso; *tr.* schiaffeggiare; *intr. to — with the waves*, lottare con le onde.
**buffet**[2] *n.* (pron. as Fr.) credenza; tavola di rinfreschi; *cold —*, cibi freddi.
**buffoon** *n.* buffone *m.* **-ery** *n.* buffoneria; buffonata.
**bug** *n.* cimice *f.*; piccolo insetto; (slang) *a big —*, un pezzo grosso, un big; idea pazza.
**bugaboo, bugbear** *n.* spauracchio; babau *m. indecl.*
**bugger** *n.* (vulg.) sodomita *m.*; (excl.) accidenti! **-y** *n.* sodomia.
**bugl-e**[1] *n.* tromba. **-er** *n.* trombettiere *m.*
**bugle**[2] *n.* (bot.) bugola.
**buhl** *adj.* intarsiato in ottone o tartaruga.
**build** *tr.* costruire; fabbricare; edificare; nidificare; *to — castles in the air*, fare castelli in aria; fondare; (colloq.) *he's built that way*, è fatto così; *to — up*, erigere, stabilire; *n.* costruzione; struttura; corporatura. **-er** *n.* costruttore; capomastro; fabbricante; muratore. **-ing** *n.* edificio; costruzione; casa; stabile *m.*; fabbricato; monumento; il costruire, il fabbricare; *adj.* edile, edilizio; *-ing materials*, materiali *m.pl.* di costruzione.

**building-society** *n.* società immobiliare, credito edilizio.
**build-up** *n.* (slang) campagna pubblicitaria.
**built-up area** *n.* agglomerato urbano.
**bulb** *n.* (bot.) bulbo; globo; ampolla; vaschetta; lampadina elettrica. **-ous** *adj.* bulboso.
**Bulgaria** *pr.n.* (geog.) Bulgaria. **-n** *adj.*, *n.* bulgaro.
**bulg-e** *n.* convessità; gonfiore *m.*; protuberanza; pancia; (slang) *to have the — on*, avere vantaggio su; *intr.* gonfiare, gonfiarsi; sporgere. **-ing** *adj.* gonfio; protuberante; *-ing eyes*, occhi sporgenti.
**bulk** *n.* (naut.) carico; grande massa, volume *m.*; *of vast —*, di notevole grossezza; *to buy*, *to sell in —*, comprare, vendere all'ingrosso; la maggior parte; il grosso; *intr.* essere grande; *to — large*, essere d'importanza, sembrare ingombrante. **-head** *n.* (naut.) paratia, compartimento; *water-tight -head*, paratia stagna. **-ily** *adv.* voluminosamente. **-iness** *n.* voluminosità; l'essere ingombrante. **-y** *adj.* massiccio; voluminoso; ingombrante.
**bull**[1] *n.* toro; *to take the — by the horns*, affrontare una situazione con decisione; (comm.) rialzista *m.*; *-'s eye*, centro del bersaglio; (window) occhio di bue; lente sporgente; *— elephant*, elefante maschio.
**bull**[2] *n.* bolla (pontificia).
**bull-dog** *n.* mastino. **-fight** *n.* corrida. **-fighter** *n.* toreadore, torero. **-fighting** *n.* tauromachia. **-headed** *adj.* ostinato. **-ring** *n.* arena.
**bulldozer** *n.* (mech.) apripista *m. indecl.*
**bullet** *n.* pallottola.
**bullet-proof** *adj.* blindato.
**bulletin** *n.* bollettino; avviso; *news —*, giornale radio; *war —*, comunicato di guerra.
**bullfinch** *n.* (orn.) ciuffolotto.
**bullfrog** *n.* rana gigante.
**bullion** *n.* oro, argento in verghe.
**bullock** *n.* manzo.
**bully**[1] *n.* spaccone *m.*, bravaccio, bullo; persona prepotente e crudele; *intr.* fare lo spaccone; *tr.* comandare, tiraneggiare; costringere.
**bully**[2] *n.* manzo lesso in scatola.
**bulrush** *n.* giunco.
**bulwark** *n.* bastione *m.*; spalto; baluardo; (naut.) parapetto.
**bum**[1] *n.* (vulg.) deretano.
**bum**[2] *n.* (fam.) fannullone *m.*; *intr.* mendicare.
**bumble-bee** *n.* calabrone *m.*
**bump** *n.* urto; colpo; enfiagione *f.*; protuberanza; bernoccolo; *tr.* urtare; battere, colpire; (slang) *to — off*, assassinare; *intr.* cozzare; scontrarsi; *to — against*, andare a sbattere contro.
**bumper** *n.* bicchiere pieno; (motor.) paraurti *m. indecl.*; *adj.* abbondante.
**bumpkin** *n.* zoticone *m.*
**bumptious** *adj.* presuntuoso. **-ness** *n.* presunzione.
**bump-y** *adj.* ineguale; con protuberanze. **-iness** *n.* irregolarità (di strada).
**bun** *n.* focaccia, ciambella dolce; 'chignon', crocchia.
**bunch** *n.* fascio, mazzo; *a — of grapes*, un grappolo d'uva; (colloq.) gruppo (di persone); *the best of the —*, il migliore fra tutti; *intr.* riunire in fascio; *to — together*, serrarsi, ammucchiarsi, raggrupparsi; *tr.* raggruppare.
**bundle** *n.* fagotto; involto; rotolo; *— of wood*, fascina di legna; (fig.) *he is a — of nerves*, è tutto nervi; *tr.* legare a fasci; riunire in mazzo; affastellare; impacchettare, fare un involto di; (fig.) *to — off*, mandare via senza complimenti.
**bung** *n.* tappo, turacciolo; zipolo; *tr.* tappare; *-ed up*, chiuso, otturato.
**bung-hole** *n.* cocchiume *m.*
**bungl-e** *n.* lavoro mal fatto, pasticcio, abborracciatura; *tr.* abborracciare; guastare, sciupare; *intr.* lavorare alla peggio; tirar via. **-er** *n.* confusionario; guastamestieri *m. indecl.* **-ing** *adj.* mal fatto; sciupato, malaccorto, goffo, balordo; *n.* goffaggine, balordaggine *f.*
**bunion** *n.* callo ai piedi.
**bunk**[1] *n.* cuccetta; *intr.* dormire in cuccetta; *the crew — forward*, l'equipaggio ha le cuccette a prua.
**bunk**[2] *n.* (slang) fuga; *to do a —*, darsela a gambe, fuggire.
**bunk**[3], **bunkum** *n.* (colloq.) chiacchiere, parole vuote *f.pl.*; *that's all — !*, sono tutte sciocchezze!
**bunker** *n.* carbonile *m.*; deposito di combustibile; (golf) ostacolo.
**bunny** *n.* (fam.) coniglietto.
**bunting**[1] *n.* (orn.) zigolo.
**bunting**[2] *n.* stamigna, tessuto per far bandiere; bandiere *f.pl.*; pavese *m.*
**buoy** *n.* (naut.) gavitello; boa; *mooring —*, boa d'ormeggio; *tr.* far galleggiare; tenere a galla; riportare a galla; (fig.) sostenere, appoggiare; *-ed up*, animato, sostenuto; (naut.) segnare con boe; disporre le boe. **-ancy** *n.* galleggiabilità; (naut.) spinta di galleggiamento; (aeron.) spinta statica, forza ascensionale; (fig.) elasticità di mente; ottimismo; *full of -ancy*, pieno di risorse, che non si lascia scoraggiare; (comm.) tendenza al rialzo dei prezzi. **-ant** *adj.* galleggiante; galleggiabile; che sostiene bene; (fig.) ottimista, allegro; *to be of a -ant disposition*, tendere all'ottimismo; (finan.) *the market is -ant*, il mercato è alto.
**bur** *n.* (bot.) lappola, bardana; riccio di castagna.
**burble** *intr.*, *tr.* gorgoliare; parlottare.
**burden** *n.* peso, fardello, carico; obbligo; *beast of —*, bestia da soma; (naut.) tonnellaggio; ritornello di canzone; tema *m.*; *tr.* caricare, gravare; (fig.) opprimere. **-some** *adj.* gravoso; pesante.
**burdock** *n.* (bot.) lappa, bardana.
**bureau** *n.* studio, ufficio; ufficio statale; scrittoio con cassetti. **-cracy** *n.* burocrazia. **-crat** *n.* burocrate *m.* **-cratic** *adj.* burocratico.
**burgeon** *n.* (poet.) germoglio, gemma; *intr.* (poet.) germogliare.
**burgess** *n.* cittadino; elettore.
**burgher** *n.* cittadino.
**burglar** *n.* scassinatore notturno; svaligiatore; *— alarm* campanello antifurto. **-y** *n.* furto notturno con scasso.
**burgl-e** *tr.* svaligiare una casa; *intr.* commettere un furto con scasso. **-ing** *n.* furto con scasso, svaligiamento.
**burgomaster** *n.* borgomastro.
**Burgundy** *pr.n.* (geog.) Borgogna; (wine) vino di Borgogna.
**burial** *n.* sepoltura; esequie *f.pl.*; inumazione.
**burial-ground** *n.* cimitero. **-place** *n.* luogo di sepoltura. **-service** *n.* ufficio funebre.
**burlesque** *adj.* burlesco; *n.* farsa; parodia; poema eroicomico; *tr.* mettere in ridicolo, parodiare.
**burl-y** *adj.* grande e grosso; robusto; corpacciuto. **-iness** *n.* corpulenza.
**Burm-a** *pr.n.* (geog.) Birmania. **-ese** *adj.*, *n.* birmano.
**burn** *tr.* bruciare; ardere; *to — to ashes*, incenerire; *to — the midnight oil*, lavorare fino a notte alta; *to — one's boats*, precludersi ogni via di ritirata; *to — one's fingers*, rimanere scottato; *to be burnt to death*, morire carbonizzato; *to — down*, radere al suolo con un incendio; *to — up*, consumare; adirarsi; *intr.* ardere; scottare; illuminare, divampare; mandar luce, risplendere; *to — dim*, far poca luce. **-er** *n.* chi, che brucia; becco a gas; bruciatore. **-ing** *adj.* bruciante; ardente; scottante; cocente; *-ing question*, problema scottante; *-ing shame*, cocente vergogna; *n.* incendio; combustione; bruciatura; bruciore *m.*; *a smell of -ing*, un odore di bruciato.
**burnish** *n.* brunitura; *tr.* lustrare, brunire. **-ing** *n.* brunitura.
**burnt** *adj.* bruciato; tostato. *— offering*, olocausto.
**burr** *n.* pronunzia arrotata della r; (metall.) superficie rozza, pietra da macina.
**burrow** *n.* tana, covo; *intr.* farsi una tana; rintanarsi; nascondersi; (fig.) *to — into the archives*, fare

delle ricerche negli archivi; *tr.* scavare; traforare.

**bursar** *n.* economo. **-y** *n.* ufficio dell'economato; borsa di studio.

**burst** *n.* scoppio; esplosione; scroscio; — *of gunfire,* raffica di fucileria; squarcio; fenditura; (sport) volata finale; *intr.* scoppiare; prorompere; esplodere; zampillare; sgorgare; *to — into laughter,* scoppiare a ridere; *to — in,* comparire improvvisamente; *the truth — upon me,* improvvisamente mi apparve la verità; *to — with envy,* crepare di invidia; irrompere; *tr.* fare esplodere; spalancare; forzare, sfondare; *the river — its banks,* il fiume ruppe gli argini; *to — open,* aprire violentemente. **-ing** *adj.* che scoppia; *-ing heart,* cuore gonfio, che sta per scoppiare; *n.* esplosione; scoppio.

**bury** *tr.* seppellire; sotterrare, interrare; *to — the hatchet,* fare la pace; immergere, affondare; *to — one's head in one's hands,* nascondere la testa tra le mani. **-ing** *n.* sepoltura.

**bus** *n.* autobus *m. indecl.*; *to miss the —,* perdere l'autobus, (colloq.) lasciarsi sfuggire l'occasione. **-man** *n.* conducente di autobus; *-man's holiday,* vacanza passata facendo un lavoro simile a quello abituale.

**bush**[1] *n.* cespuglio; macchia; fratta; (fig.) *to beat about the —,* menare il can per l'aia; frasca; *good wine needs no —,* il buon vino non ha bisogno d'insegna.

**bush**[2] *n.* (mech.) boccola, bussola; (electr.) rivestimento, guaina isolante.

**bushel** *n.* staio; (colloq.) grande quantità. **-ful** *n.* staiata.

**bush-y** *adj.* folto, spesso; cespuglioso; — *eyebrows,* sopracciglia folte. **-iness** *n.* cespugliosità.

**business** *n.* affare *m.*; occupazione; mestiere *m.*; *he means —,* intende fare le cose sul serio; *it is not my —,* non mi riguarda; *mind your own —,* bada ai fatti tuoi; *you had no — to do so,* non toccava a te farlo; affari *m.pl.*; commercio; *to be in —,* essere nel commercio; *to have — with,* avere rapporti di affari con; *to talk —,* parlare d'affari; *man of —,* agente *m.* legale; ditta, azienda, casa di commercio; scopo; *to make it one's — to,* farsi un dovere di; *— hours,* orario d'ufficio.

**business-like** *adj.* metodico, sistematico; pratico, intendente; perito. **-man** *n.* uomo d'affari.

**busker** *n.* (theatr. hist.) cantante od attore vagabondo, cantambanchi *m. indecl.*; chi canta per la strada, per l'elemosina.

**buskin** *n.* (theatr.) coturno; (fig.) tragedia; vena tragica.

**bust**[1] *n.* busto; petto.

**bust**[2] *tr.* (colloq.) rompere; *intr.* rompersi; *part. adj.* rotto.

**bustard** *n.* (orn.) otarda.

**bustl-e** *n.* trambusto; scompiglio; agitazione; *intr.* muoversi, agitarsi, essere in agitazione; *to — in and out,* entrare e uscire con aria affaccendata; *to — about,* darsi da fare, affaccendarsi; *tr.* incalzare; sollecitare. **-ing** *adj.* affaccendato.

**bustle**[2] *n.* puf *m. indecl.*

**bus-y** *adj.* affaccendato, occupato; attivo; *tr.* occupare, affaccendare; *to — oneself with,* occuparsi di. **-ily** *adv.* attivamente; alacremente. **-ybody** *n.* ficcanaso; intrigante *m., f.* **-yness** *n.* attività; l'essere affaccendato.

**but** *conj.* ma; *adv.* solo, soltanto; *had I — known it!,* se solo l'avessi saputo!; *he can — refuse,* può solo rifiutare; *I have — two friends,* non ho che due amici; *— a little,* soltanto un poco; *— for,* se non fosse per, senza; *— that,* se non; *— then,* ma d'altra parte; *nothing —,* null'altro che; *he is anything — intelligent,* è tutt'altro che intelligente; *to do nothing —,* non far altro che; *prep.* eccetto, tranne, fuorchè; *the last — one,* il penultimo; *neg. rel. prn.* che non, se non, a meno che; *n.* ma *m. indecl.*; obiezione; *there is a —,* c'è un ma.

**but** *tr. — me no buts,* non dirmi dei 'ma', non sollevare obiezioni.

**butcher** *n.* macellaio; *-'s shop,* macelleria; *-'s meat,* carne macellata; *-'s broom* (bot.), pungitopo; *tr.* macellare; massacrare. **-y** *n.* macelleria; (fig.) macello, strage *f.*

**butler** *n.* maggiordomo; cantiniere *m.*; cameriere addetto all'argenteria, ai vini.

**butt**[1] *n.* botte *f.*; barile *m.*

**butt**[2] *n.* calcio (di arma da fuoco); impugnatura; ceppo; mozzicone *m.*; matrice *f.* di assegno.

**butt**[3] *n.* monticello di terra dietro al bersaglio; riparo per la caccia alla starna; *pl.* poligono di tiro; mira, scopo; zimbello.

**butt**[4] *n.* cozzo; cornata; *tr.* urtare con la testa, con le corna; cozzare; *intr.* (fig.) *to — into a discussion,* gettarsi a capofitto in una discussione; *to — in,* intrammettersi; capitare d'improvviso; *let me — in,* lasciatemi dire la mia.

**butter** *n.* burro; *melted —,* burro fuso; *she looks as though — wouldn't melt in her mouth,* fa la santerellina; *tr.* imburrare; *-ed bread,* pane imburrato; (fig.) *his bread is -ed on both sides,* vive nell'abbondanza; (slang) *to — up,* adulare, lusingare. **-y** *adj.* burroso; *n.* dispensa.

**buttercup** *n.* (bot.) botton d'oro ranuncolo.

**butterfly** *n.* farfalla; (fig.) persona frivola.

**butterfly-net** *n.* rete *f.* per acchiappare le farfalle. **-nut** *n.* (mech.) dado ad alette, galletto. **-stroke** *n.* nuoto a farfalla.

**buttock** *n.* natica.

**button**[1] *n.* bottone *m.*; *to sew a — on,* attaccare un bottone; *I don't care a —,* non me ne importa un fico; *tr.* abbottonare; *he -ed up his coat,* si abbottonò il cappotto. **-ed** *part. adj.* abbottonato; (fig.) *-ed up,* di poche parole.

**button-hook** *n.* allaciabottoni *m. indecl.* **-hole** *n.* occhiello; asola; fiore *m.* da mettere all'occhiello; *tr.* (fig.) trattenere colle ciance; attaccare un bottone a; *he -holed me,* mi attaccò un bottone.

**buttress** *n.* sostegno, appoggio; contrafforte, sperone *m.*; *tr.* sostenere con pilastro.

**buxom** *adj.* paffuto, grassoccio; avvenente. **-ness** *n.* avvenenza; formosità.

**buy** *tr.* comprare; acquistare; *to — for cash,* comprare a contanti; *to — back,* ricomprare; riscattare; *to — over,* corrompere, comprare; *to — up,* comprare in quantità, accaparrare; *n.* (colloq.) acquisto; compera. **-er** *n.* compratore; acquirente *m., f.*; addetto all'ufficio acquisti.

**buzz** *n.* ronzìo; bruslo; *intr.* ronzare; mormorare, bisbigliare; *to — about,* affannarsi; (slang) *to — off,* tagliare la corda. **-er** *n.* insetto che ronza; persona che bisbiglia; segnale acustico; cicala; sirena; (motor.) clacson *m. indecl.* **-ing** *adj.* ronzante; *n.* ronzìo; brusìo.

**buzzard** *n.* (orn.) poiana.

**by** *adv.* vicino; *close —,* molto vicino; *when no-one was —,* quando non c'era nessuno; accanto; *to go —,* passare; *to hurry —,* passare in fretta; *to run —,* passare correndo; in disparte; *to put —,* mettere da parte, tenere in riserva; *to stand —,* stare in attesa; *tr.* appoggiare, sostenere, aiutare; *— and —,* fra breve; *— and large,* generalmente parlando.

**by** *prep.* per, da, con, a, di; *— paying,* mediante pagamento; *he lives — writing novels,* vive scrivendo romanzi; *I took her — the hand,* la presi per mano; *it was done — him,* fu fatto da lui; *the letter came — post,* la lettera arrivò per posta; *they make things — machinery,* lavorano a macchina; *to be known — the name of,* essere conosciuto sotto, con, il nome di; *to begin —,* cominciare con; *to end —,* finire con; *to learn — heart,* imparare a memoria; *to*

*travel — rail*, viaggiare per ferrovia; *to swear — God*, giurare nel nome di Dio; *— chance*, per caso; *— oneself*, da solo; *— sight*, di vista; *— your leave*, con il vostro permesso; durante, di, entro, per; *— day*, di giorno; *day — day*, di giorno in giorno; *he ought to be here — now*, a quest'ora dovrebbe già essere qui; *the work will be finished — tomorrow*, il lavoro sarà finito per domani; vicino a, al lato di, presso (di, a), davanti, via, attraverso; *— the side of*, a lato di; *a house — the sea*, una casa sul mare; *side — side*, lato a lato; *I have no money — me*, non ho denaro con me; *I shall do my duty — you*, farò il mio dovere verso di te; per, a, di; *— degrees*, per gradi; *— hundreds*, a centinaia; *younger — ten years*, più giovane di dieci anni; *one — one*, ad uno ad uno; *he is — far the best*, egli è di gran lunga il migliore; *to sell — the pound*, vendere a libbre; da, secondo; *to judge — appearances*, giudicare dalle apparenze; *— all means*, certamente, senz'altro; *— the way*, cammin facendo, incidentalmente; tra parentesi; *this is — no means true*, questo non è affatto vero.

**by, bye** (in compounds) secondario; indiretto; **-blow** *n.* colpo traverso; (fig.) figlio illegittimo. **-effect** *n.* effetto secondario. **-election** elezione straordinaria. **-law** legge *f.* locale; **-name** *n.* soprannome *m.*, nomignolo; *-passer n.* passante *m., f.*; **-pass** *n.* circonvallazione; *tr.* girare intorno a, evitare; fornire di circonvallazione. **-path** *n.* sentiero appartato. **-play** *n.* controscena, azione secondaria. **-product** *n.* **-road** *n.* strada secondaria. prodotto secondario. **-stander** *n.* astante *m., f.* **-street** *n.* via appartata, viuzza. **-way** *n.* scorciatoia; via traversa; (fig.) *-ways of history*, meandri della storia. **-word** *n.* proverbio, detto; (derog.) zimbello.

**bye-bye** (*abbr.* of **'good-bye'**) addio, arrivederci; **(-s)** *n.* (colloq.) nanna; *to go to -s*, andare a nanna.

**bygone** *adj.* passato, del passato; *in — days*, nei tempi che furono; *n.pl.* passato; *let -s be -s*, metti una pietra sul passato, acqua passata non macina più.

**byre** *n.* vaccheria.

**Byzant-ium** *pr.n.* Bizanzio. **-ian, -ine** *adj., n.* bizantino.

**C** *n.* ci *m., f.*; (mus.) ut, do *m.*; (Rom. num.) cento; (teleph.) *— for Charlie*, ci come Como.

**cab** *n.* vettura di piazza, carrozza; tassì *m. indecl.*; (of lorry) cabina.

**cabal** *n.* congiura; intrigo; cricca, combriccola.

**cabaret** *n.* spettacolo di varietà, caffè concerto; cabaret *m. indecl.*

**cabbage** *n.* cavolo; *Savoy —*, verza, cavolo cappuccio; *— butterfly*, cavolaia; — (fig.) *to live like a —*, vegetare.

**cabbage-lettuce** *n.* cespo di lattuga. **-patch** *n.* cavolaio. **-rose** *n.* rosa centifoglia. **-tree** *n.* palmisto.

**cab(b)al-a** *n.* cabala *f.* **-istic** *adj.* cabalistico.

**caber** *n.* tronco di pino; (Scot.) *tossing the —*, gara di lancio di un tronco di pino.

**cabin** *n.* capanna; (naut.) cabina; (class on board ship) classe unica.

**cabin-boy** *n.* mozzo; addetto ai servizi di cabina.

**cabinet** *m.* stanzino, gabinetto; armadietto, scrigno, stipo; vetrina; *cocktail —*, bar *m. indecl.*; (pol.) gabinetto; consiglio dei ministri; *— minister*, membro del gabinetto.

**cabinet-maker** *n.* ebanista *m.* **-making** *n.* ebanisteria.

**cable** *n.* cavo; cablogramma, telegramma *m.*; (naut.) fune *f.*; gomena; ormeggio; *— railway*, funicolare *f.*; (measurement) catena. **-gram** *n.* cablogramma, telegramma.

**cable** *tr.* legare con cavo; *intr.*, *tr.* spedire un cablogramma, telegrafare (a).

**cable-laying** *n.* posa di cavi.

**caboose** *n.* (naut.) cambusa, cucina.

**cab-rank, -stand** *n.* posteggio di vetture pubbliche *or* di tassì.

**cache** *n.* nascondiglio; provviste *f. pl.* nascoste.

**cachet** *n.* marca; sigillo; (pharm.) capsula.

**cackle** *n.* schiamazzo; (fig.) chiacchierìo; riso da gallina, *intr.* schiamazzare, chiocciare; (fig.) chiacchierare; ridere come una gallina.

**cacophon-ous** *adj.* cacofonico. **-y** *n.* cacofonia.

**cactus** *n.* (bot.) cacto; fico d'India.

**cad** *n.* mascalzone *m.* **-dish** *adj.* villano, maleducato. **-dishness** *n.* villania.

**cadaver** *n.* cadavere *m.* **-ous** *adj.* cadaverico; (fig.) esangue, pallidissimo, allampanato.

**caddie** *n.* portabastoni *m. indecl.*

**caddy** *n.* scatola da tè.

**cadence** *n.* cadenza; ritmo; intonazione. **-d** *adj.* cadenzato; ritmico.

**cadet** *n.* cadetto; (mil.; naval) aspirante *m.* ufficiale, allievo.

**cadge** *tr.*, *intr.* accattare, mendicare; (fam.) scroccare. **-r** *n.* (fam.) scroccone *m.*

**Cadiz** *pr.n.* (geog.) Cadice *f.*

**cadmium** *n.* (chem.) cadmio.

**cadre** *n.* (mil.) quadro.

**caducity** *n.* caducità; fugacità.

**caecum** *n.* (anat.) intestino cieco.

**Caesar** *pr.n.* Cesare; *Julius —*, Giulio Cesare; *render unto — the things that are -'s*, dare a Cesare quello che è di Cesare; *like -'s wife*, al di sopra di ogni sospetto; *to appeal to —*, appellarsi alle autorità superiori.

**Caesarean** *adj.* di Cesare; (surg.) *— section*, parto cesareo.

**caesura** *n.* (prosod.) cesura.

**café** *n.* caffè, bar *m. indecl.*

**caffeine** *n.* caffeina.

**cage** *n.* gabbia; *tr.* mettere in gabbia; rinchiudere. **-bird** *n.* uccello da gabbia.

**cagey** *adj.* (slang) furbo; di poche parole.

**Cain** *pr.n.* Caino; *the brand of —*, il marchio di Caino; (fam.) *to raise —*, far bordello, fare una scenata.

**Caiphas** *pr.n.* (bibl.) Caifasso.

**cairn** *n.* tumulo commemorativo.

**Cairo** *pr.n.* (geog.) il Cairo.

**caisson** *n.* (archit.) cassettone *m.*; formella; (naut.) cassone *m.*; (mil.) cassonetto.

**cajol-e** *tr.* blandire, allettare, fare moine a. **-ery** *n.* adulazione; lusinghe, moine *f.pl.*

**cake** *n.* torta; focaccia; pasticcino; *— of soap*, saponetta; (techn.) focaccia; (of blood, *etc.*) grumo, crosta; (fig.) *-s and ale*, le buone cose della vita; *it's a piece of —!*, è facilissimo!; *to take the —*, riportare la palma; (iron.) *that takes the —*, è il colmo; *to go like hot -s*, andare a ruba; *you can't have your — and eat it*, non si può avere la botte piena e la moglie ubriaca.

**cake** *intr.* incrostarsi, rapprendersi, coagularsi, agglutinarsi; *tr.* comprimere, agglutinare; *-d with blood*, incrostato di sangue; *-d with mud*, impiastrato di fango.

**cake-shop** *n.* pasticceria. **-stand** *n.* servitore muto.

**calabash** *n.* caravazza.

**Calabrian** *adj.*, *n.* (geog.) calabrese *m., f.*

**calamit-y** *n.* calamità *f. indecl.*; disastro; disgrazia. **-ous** *adj.* calamitoso; funesto; disastroso.

**calcareous** *adj.* (geol.) calcareo.

**calcif-y** *tr.* calcificare; *intr.* calcificarsi. **-ication** *n.* calcificazione.

**calcium** *n.* calcio; — *carbonate,* carbonato di calcio.
**calculable** *adj.* calcolabile.
**calculat-e** *tr.* calcolare, stimare, valutare, misurare; *intr. to — on,* contare su; *to — on doing something,* contare di fare qualcosa. **-ed** *adj.* calcolato; premeditato; *-ed to,* tale da, idoneo a. **-ing** *adj.* calcolatore; *n.* see **calculation**; *-ing machine,* macchina calcolatrice. **-ion** *n.* calcolo; (fig.) previsione; *to be out in one's -s,* sbagliare il calcolo; *to leave something out of one's -s,* non tenere conto di qualcosa; *to upset someone's -s,* rovinare i piani di qualcuno. **-or** *n.* calcolatore; macchina calcolatrice.
**calculus** *n.* (math.; med.) calcolo.
**Caledonian** *adj., pr.n.* caledone, scozzese *m., f.*; (geol.) caledoniano.
**calendar** *n.* calendario; almanacco; elenco; — *year,* anno solare.
**calender** *n.* (mech.) calandra; *tr.* calandrare, cilindrare.
**Calends** *pr.n.* (Rom. hist.) calende *f.pl.*
**calf**[1] *n.* (zool.) vitello; *cow with —,* mucca gravida; (of other animals) piccolo; *to kill the fatted —,* uccidere il vitello grasso, (fig.) far festa (a chi ritorna); *the golden —,* il vitello d'oro; (cul.) *-'s head,* testa di vitello; (bookb.) pelle *f.* di vitello; (fig.) — *love,* amore *m.* adolescente.
**calf**[2] *n.* (anat.) polpaccio.
**calibrate** *tr.* calibrare, misurare il calibro di; (techn.) tarare.
**calibre** *n.* calibro; (fig.) qualità.
**calico** *n.* (text.) calico, cotone stampato; (attrib.) di calico.
**California** *pr.n.* (geog.) California. **-n** *adj., n.* californiano.
**Caliph** *n.* califfo.
**call** *n.* chiamata; richiamo; appello; grido; voce *f.*; squillo; vocazione; *a — for help,* un grido d'aiuto; *within —,* a portata di voce; — *to arms,* chiamata alle armi; *the — of the wild,* il richiamo della foresta; *to answer the —,* rispondere all'appello; (teleph.) chiamata; *long-distance —,* chiamata interurbana; (cards) dichiarazione; *it's your —,* tocca a te; *to pay someone a —,* fare una breve visita a qualcuno; *formal —,* visita di dovere; *to return a —,* restituire una visita; (naut.) *port of —,* scalo; (fig.) diritto; autorità; *the — of the blood,* il vincolo del sangue; *to have many -s on one's time,* avere molti impegni; *to be on —,* essere disponibile; *to be at someone's beck and —,* essere sempre agli ordini di qualcuno.
**call** *tr.* chiamare; richiamare; gridare; proclamare; nominare; *to — by name,* chiamare per nome; *what do you — it in Italian?,* come si dice in italiano?; *to be -ed,* chiamarsi; *to be -ed after,* portare il nome di; *to — (someone) a liar,* dare del bugiardo a; (cards) dichiarare; (fam.) — *it ten pounds,* diciamo dieci sterline; *to — to account,* chiamare alla resa dei conti; *to — aside,* chiamare in disparte; *to — a meeting,* convocare un'assemblea; *to — to order,* richiamare all'ordine; *to — in question,* mettere in dubbio; *to — the roll,* fare l'appello; *to — a spade a spade,* dire pane al pane; *to — as a witness,* citare come testimonio; *to — back,* richiamare, (fig.) revocare, ritrattare; *to — down,* far scendere, chiamare giù, (fig.) invocare; *to — forth,* far nascere, causare, suscitare; *to — in,* far entrare, invitare a entrare; far venire, rivolgersi a; *to — into play,* fare appello a; *to — off,* far desistere, richiamare; rimandare, rinviare; annullare, revocare; *let's — it off!,* allora rinunciamo!; *to — out,* far uscire, sfidare (a duello); (police, troops) chiamare in aiuto; *to — together,* riunire, radunare; *to — up,* (mil.) richiamare (sotto le armi); (teleph.) chiamare al telefono; (fig.) evocare, ricordare; *intr.* gridare, chiamare; (radio) *this is London -ing,* qui parla Londra; (visit) fare una breve visita, passare; *to — again,* ripassare; *I have -ed to see you,* sono venuto a trovarti; *to — at,* passare da, (of ship), far scalo a, (of train) fermarsi a; *to — for,* chiedere, esigere; passare a prendere; *to — for help,* gridare all'aiuto; *to — for volunteers,* chiedere volontari; (of parcel) *to be -ed for,* si prega di trattenere fino al ritiro, da ritirarsi; *I feel -ed upon to,* mi sento in dovere di. **-ed** *part. adj.* chiamato, nominato di nome; detto, soprannominato. **-er** *n.* chiamatore, chi chiama; visitatore; (teleph.) richiedente *m., f.*
**call-box** *n.* (teleph.) cabina telefonica. **-boy** *n.* (theatr.) buttafuori *m. indecl.,* avvisatore; (hotel) piccolo *m.* **-girl** *n.* ragazza squillo.
**calligraph-er** *n.* calligrafo. **-ic** *adj.* calligrafico. **-y** *n.* calligrafia, scrittura; mano *f.*
**calling** *n.* chiamata; appello; professione, vocazione; (trade) mestiere *m.*, occupazione; visita. — **up** *n.* (mil.) chiamata sotto le armi; — *up papers,* cartolina precetto.
**calliper(s)** *n.* calibro, compasso a grossezze.
**callisthenics** *n.* ginnastica ritmica, callistenia.
**callosity** *n.* callo, callosità, indurimento.
**callous** *adj.* calloso; (fig.) duro, insensibile, incallito. **-ly** *adv.* senza pietà. **-ness** *n.* insensibilità, durezza di cuore, indifferenza.
**callow** *adj.* implume; (fig.) imberbe, inesperto.
**callus** *n.* callo, callosità *f. indecl.*
**calm** *adj.* calmo, quieto; tranquillo; sereno; *to grow —,* calmarsi; *to keep —,* star tranquillo; — *as a millpond,* liscio come uno specchio; *n.* calma; serenità; tranquillità; (of sea) bonaccia; *dead —,* bonaccia piatta; — *before a storm,* bonaccia prima della tempesta; *after a storm comes a —,* dopo la tempesta viene il sereno. **-ly** *adv.* con calma; tranquillamente.
**calm** *tr.* calmare, sedare, placare, acquietare, abbonire; *to — someone down,* rabbonire qualcuno; *intr. to — down,* placarsi, rasserenarsi, calmarsi, rabbonacciarsi. **-ing** *adj.* calmante. **-ness** *n.* calma; tranquillità; serenità; (fam.) sfacciataggine *f.*
**calomel** *n.* calomelano.
**calor-ic** *adj.* calorico. **-ific** *adj.* calorifico. **-imeter** *n.* calorimetro.
**calory, calorie** *n.* caloria.
**calumniat-e** *tr.* calunniare. **-or** *n.* calunniatore, calunniatrice.
**calumny** *n.* calunnia.
**Calvary** *pr.n.* Calvario.
**calve** *tr.* partorire, figliare.
**Calvin** *pr.n.* Calvino. **-ism** *n.* calvinismo. **-ist** *adj., n.* calvinista *m., f.*
**Calypso** *pr.n.* (myth.) Calipso.
**calypso** *n.* canzonetta popolare delle Indie Occidentali.
**calyx** *n.* (bot.) calice *m.*
**cam** *n.* (mech.) camma; eccentrico.
**camaraderie** *n.* cameratismo.
**camber** *n.* curvatura, convessità, bombatura; (naut.) allunamento. **-ed** *adj.* curvato ad arco, bombè, convesso; (naut.) allunato.
**cambrian** *adj.* (hist. geog.) gallese; (geol.) cambriano, cambrico.
**cambric** *n.* (text.) cambrì *m.,* batista.
**came** *p. def.* of **come,** *q.v.*
**camel** *n.* cammello; *female —,* cammella; *-'s hump,* gobba del cammello; (mil.) — *corps,* corpo di meharisti; (provb.) *it's the last straw that breaks the -'s back,* è l'ultima goccia che fa traboccare il vaso.
**camel-driver** *n.* cammelliere *m.* **-hair** *m., adj.* (di) pelo di cammello.
**camellia** *n.* (bot.) camelia.
**cameo** *n.* cammeo.
**camera** *n.* (photog.) macchina fotografica, apparecchio fotografico; *ciné-camera,* macchina da presa; *television —,* telecamera; (leg.) *in —,* a porte chiuse. — **man** *n.* (journ.) giornalista fotografo; paparazzo; (cinem.) operatore cinematografico.
**Cameroons** *pr.n.* (geog.) *the —,* il Camerun.

**camomile** *n.* camomilla; — *tea*, tisana di camomilla.

**camouflage** *n.* (mil.) mimetizzazione; (fig.) mascheramento; travestimento; dissimulazione; *tr.* (mil.) mimetizzare; (fig.) mascherare; nascondere; dissimulare.

**camp**[I] *n.* (mil.) campo; accampamento; *concentration* —, campo di concentramento; *holiday* —, campeggio; *to be in* —, essere accampato; *to pitch* —, attendarsi, accamparsi, impiantare un accampamento; *to have a foot in both -s*, tenere il piede in due staffe.

**camp**[I] *intr.* accamparsi, attendarsi, essere accampato; *to — out*, dormire all'addiaccio, bivaccare; *to go -ing*, fare il campeggio. **-er** *n.* campeggiatore *m.*, campeggiante *m.*, *f.* **-ing** *n.* (mil.) accampamento; (holiday) campeggio; *-ing site*, camping *m. indecl.*

**camp**[2] *adj.* affettato; esagerato; omosessuale; da omosessuale; *n.* modi affettati; *tr.* esagerare; *intr.* *to — it up*, comportarsi in modo esagerato o da omosessuale.

**campaign** *n.* campagna; *advertising* —, pubblicità; *intr.* fare una campagna; *to — against*, scendere in lizza contro, polemizzare contro. **-er** *n.* militare *m.* in campagna; *old -er*, veterano, reduce *m.* **-ing** *n.* vita militare; (pol.) *-ing for a candidate*, il fare propaganda per un candidato.

**campanology** *n.* campanologia.

**camp-bed** *n.* brandina, letto da campo. **-chair** *n.* sedia pieghevole. **-fire** *n.* fuoco di bivacco. **-follower** *n.* civile *m.*, *f.* al seguito di un esercito. **-stool** *n.* seggiolino pieghevole.

**camphor** *n.* canfora.

**camper, camping** see under **camp**[I], *intr.*

**campus** *n.* terreno su cui sorge un'università.

**camshaft** *n.* (mech.) albero dell'eccentrico.

**can**[I] *n.* recipiente *m.*; scatola; barattolo; bidone *m.*; latta; *tr.* mettere in scatola, inscatolare; (slang) smettere, finirla.

**can**[2] *defect. aux. vb.* (be able) potere; sapere; — *you drive a car?*, sai guidare una macchina?; *it can't be done*, non si può, non è possibile; *as soon as — be*, appena possibile; *as sure as — be*, indubbiamente; *I -not help thinking that*, non posso fare a meno di pensare che; *it can't be helped*, è inevitabile!; (non c'è) niente da fare!; *I — but . . .*, non posso che . . ., non mi resta che . . .; *he could not come yesterday*, ieri non potè venire; (conditional) *I could not say*, non potrei (*or* non saprei) dire; *I could have written to him*, avrei potuto scrivergli; (if following verb normally takes *aux.* 'essere', then *aux.* of 'potere' is 'essere', though many Italians use 'avere' in such cases); *he could have come*, sarebbe (*or* avrebbe) potuto venire; (often not translated) — *you see him?*, lo vedi?; *-'t you understand?*, non capisci?; *one -'t very well . . .*, è difficile . . .

**Canada** *pr.n.* (geog.) il Canadà.

**Canadian** *adj.*, *n.* canadese *m.*, *f.*

**canaille** *n.* canaglia.

**canal** *n.* canale *m.* **-ize** *tr.* canalizzare; (fig.) convogliare.

**canard** *n.* panzana, frottola.

**canary** *n.* (orn.) canarino; (wine) vino delle Canarie; (colour) canarino; *the — Islands, the Canaries*, le isole Canarie.

**cancel** *tr.* cancellare, annullare, disdire, revocare; (contract) rescindere; (math.) elidere; *intr.* *to — out*, cancellarsi, annullarsi; elidersi.

**cancellation** *n.* annullamento; soppressione; cancellatura; disdetta.

**cancer** *n.* (med.) cancro, carcinoma *m.*; (geog.) *the Tropic of Cancer*, il tropico di Cancro. **-ed, -ous** *adj.* canceroso.

**candelabrum** *n.* candelabro; lampadario.

**candesc-ence** *n.* candescenza. **-ent** *adj.* candescente.

**candid** *adj.* franco, sincero, schietto, candido; imparziale, disinteressato. **-ness** *n.* schiettezza; sincerità; buona fede.

**candid-ate** *n.* candidato; aspirante *m.*, *f.*; concorrente *m.*, *f.*; *to offer oneself as* —, presentarsi come candidato. **-acy, -ature** *n.* candidatura.

**candied** *adj.* candito.

**candle** *n.* candela; cero; *wax* —, candela di cera; *Roman* —, candela romana, bengala *m.*; — *end*, moccolo; *to be not fit to hold a — to*, non reggere al confronto con; *the game is not worth the* —, il giuoco non vale la candela; *to burn the — at both ends*, strapazzarsi, sgobbare; (phys.) candela; *tr.* mirare (uova) in trasparenza.

**candlelight** *n.* lume *m.* di candela.

**Candlemas** *pr.n.* (eccl.) Candelora.

**candle-power** *n.* intensità luminosa in candele.

**candlestick** *n.* candeliere *m.*; candelabro; bugia.

**candour** *n.* sincerità; franchezza; candore *m.*; imparzialità.

**candy** *n.* zucchero cristallizzato; (sweets) dolci *m.pl.*; *tr.* candire.

**candy-floss** *n.* zucchero filato.

**candytuft** *n.* (bot.) iberide *f.*, iberia.

**cane** *n.* (bot.) canna; giunco; (rod) verga, bacchetta; bastoncino; *Malacca* —, bastone di Malacca; *rattan* —, canna d'India; — *sugar*, zucchero di canna; — *chair*, sedia con sedile di canna; *tr.* bastonare con una verga; (chair) inserire cannucce a, impagliare.

**cane-brake, cane-plantation** *n.* canneto.

**canful** *n.* bidone pieno.

**canicular** *adj.* canicolare.

**canine** *adj.* canino; — *tooth*, dente canino.

**caning** *n.* bastonata.

**canister** *n.* scatola di latta; — *shot*, proietto a mitraglia.

**canker** *n.* cancro; ulcera; (med.; vet.) stomatite aftosa; (fig.) influenza maligna.

**canned** *adj.* conservato in scatola, inscatolato; — *goods*, conserve in scatola, scatolame *m.*; (pop.) — *music*, musica riprodotta; (slang) sbronzo.

**cannery** *n.* fabbrica di conserve alimentari.

**cannibal** *n.* cannibale *m.*, antropofago. **-ism** *n.* cannibalismo, antropofagia. **-istic** *adj.* cannibalesco. **-ize** *tr.* (mech.) cannibalizzare, smontare (una macchina) per utilizzarne i pezzi.

**canniness** *n.* astuzia; circospezione; furberia.

**canning** *n.* inscatolamento; conservazione in scatola; — *factory*, fabbrica di conserve alimentari.

**cannon** *n.* (mil.) cannone *m.*; (collect.) artiglieria; (billiards) carambola; *tr.* cannoneggiare; *intr.* (billiards) fare carambola; (fig.) *to — into*, scontrarsi con, urtare violentemente. **-ade** *n.* cannonata; cannoneggiamento; sparatoria; *tr.* cannoneggiare; bombardare.

**cannon-ball** *n.* palla da cannone. **-fodder** *n.* carne *f.* da cannone. **-shot** *n.* colpo di cannone; cannonata; *within -shot*, a gittata cannone.

**canny** *adj.* scaltro, furbo, astuto; prudente, circospetto.

**canoe** *n.* canoa; (Indian) piroga; (fig.) *to paddle one's own* —, viaggiare in canoa. **-ing** *n.* l'andare in canoa.

**canon**[1] *n.* (eccl.) canonico.

**canon**[2] *n.* (eccl.; mus.) canone *m.*; regola; disciplina; criterio; — *law*, diritto canonico.

**canoness** *n.* (eccl.) canonichessa.

**canonical** *adj.* canonico; *n.pl.* abiti sacerdotali.

**canoniz-e** *tr.* (eccl.) canonizzare. **-ation** *n.* (eccl.) canonizzazione.

**canonry** (eccl.) canonicato.

**canoodle** *intr.* (fam.) baciucchiarsi.

**can-opener** *n.* apriscatole *m. indecl.*

**canop-y** *n.* baldacchino; padiglione *m.*; (over bed) cielo; calotta; *the — of Heaven*, la volta del cielo; (archit.) pensilina; (fig.) ombrella; (aeron.) calotta; (of parachute) cupola. **-ied** *adj.* coperto con baldacchino; (archit.) a volta.

**cant**[1] *n.* gergo; — *phrase*, luogo comune; bacchettoneria, parlata piena di unzione.
**cant**[2] *n.* inclinazione, pendenza; (archit.) angolo smussato; (rlwy.) sopraelevazione; *tr.* inclinare, far pendere, chinare; (archit.) smussare; *intr.* inclinarsi, pendere; *to — over*, sbandare.
**cantaloup** *n.* cantalupo, melone *m.*
**cantankerous** *adj.* stizzoso, scontroso; litigioso; arcigno; burbero, cattivo. **-ness** *n.* carattere scontroso; cattiveria.
**cantata** *n.* (mus.) cantata.
**canteen** *n.* cantina; dispensa; circolo ricreativo, dopolavoro; (mil.) *dry* —, cantina per provvigioni; *wet* —, cantina per liquori.
**canter** *n.* piccolo galoppo; (fig.) *to win in a* —, vincere facilmente; *intr.* andare al piccolo galoppo.
**Canterbury bell** *n.* (bot.) campanula.
**cantharid** *n.* (ent.) — *beetle*, vescicante *m.* **-es** *n.pl.* (pharm.) cantaridi *f.pl.*
**canticle** *n.* cantico; (bibl.) *the -s*, il Cantico dei Cantici.
**cantilever** *n.* (archit.) trave *f.* a sbalzo, mensola; — *bridge*, ponte *m.* a mensola.
**canting** *adj.* pieno di unzione; *a — hypocrite*, un bacchettone, un collotorto.
**canto** *n.* (lit.; mus.) canto.
**canton** *n.* (geog.) cantone *m.*
**cantonment** *n.* (mil.) accantonamento; acquartieramento.
**cantor** *n.* (rel.) cantore *m.*
**canvas** *n.* canovaccio; tela di canapa; (art) tela; pittura su tela; (naut.) velatura; *under* —, (mil.) sotto la tenda, attendato, (naut.) sotto vela, a vele spiegate, veleggiando.
**canvass** *tr.*, *intr.* vagliare, discutere; (comm.) sollecitare ordini; (pol.) sollecitare voti. **-er** *n.* (comm.) piazzista *m.*; (pol.) sollecitatore di voti. **-ing** *n.* esame *m.*; (pol.) sollecitazione di voti.
**canyon** *n.* (geog.) vallone, burrone *m.*
**cap**[1] *n.* berretto; copricapo; (cardinal's) berretta; (academic) tocco; (woman's) cuffia; (housemaid's) cuffietta; cresta; *peaked* —, berretto con visiera; *dunce's* —, berrettocco; (med.) *Dutch* —, diaframma *m.*; (mil.) *forage* —, berretto a busta; *skull* —, papalina, calotta; (chem.; mech.) tappo, capsula, coperchio, cappello; (of cartridge) capsula, cappellotto; — *in hand*, umilmente, col cappello in mano; — *and bells*, berretto a sonagli; — *of liberty*, berretto frigio; *in — and gown*, in tocco e toga; (fig.) *the — fits*, torna a proposito; *a feather in one's* —, un motivo d'orgoglio; *to put on one's thinking* —, pensarci sopra; *to set one's — at*, cercare di cattivarsi le simpatie di; (archit.) capitello, coronamento; (naut.) berretto da marinaio; (of mast) testa di moro; (sport) *to get one's* —, giuocare nella squadra nazionale.
**cap**[1] *tr.* coprire con un berretto, mettere un berretto su; (fig.) sorpassare; *and to — it all*, e sul più bello; *that -s everything!*, è il colmo!; *to — an anecdote*, far seguito ad un aneddoto con un altro; (sport) scegliere per la squadra nazionale.
**cap**[2] *n.* (*abbrev.* of **capital**) maiuscola.
**capability** *n.* capacità, abilità, facoltà *f. indecl.*
**capable** *adj.* capace; abile; competente; (fig.) suscettibile, che ammette.
**capacious** *adj.* capace, ampio, vasto, spazioso. **-ness** *n.* ampiezza, capacità, vastità, spaziosità *f. indecl.*
**capacitate** *tr.* rendere capace; dare il potere a.
**capacity** *n.* capacità, abilità, facoltà, *f. indecl.*; (leg.) competenza; capienza; potenza; *in the — of*, nella qualità di; *in an administrative* —, con mansioni amministrative; *in one's official* —, nell'esercizio delle proprie funzioni; *business* —, attitudine agli affari; *carrying* —, portata; *seating* —, numero di posti a sedere.
**caparison** *tr.* bardare, ingualdrappare; (fig.) drappeggiare.
**cape**[1] *n.* (geog.) capo; promontorio; *Cape Colony*, la Colonia del Capo; *Cape of Good Hope*, Capo di Buona Speranza; *Cape Horn*, Capo Hoorn; *Cape Town*, la Città del Capo.
**cape**[2] *n.* mantello; mantellina; cappa; — *and sword novel*, romanzo di cappa e spada.
**caper**[1] *n.* (bot.; cul.) cappero.
**caper**[2] *n.* capriola; salto; *to cut -s*, far capriole, (fig.) far stramberie; *intr.* saltellare.
**capercailzie** *n.* (orn.) gallo cedrone.
**capillary** *adj.* capillare; *n.* (anat.) vaso capillare.
**capital** *adj.* capitale; importante; eccellente; *of — importance*, della massima importanza, di importanza capitale; — *punishment*, pena capitale; *a — fellow*, un bravo ragazzo; (excl.) —*!*, benone!, magnifico!; (naut.) — *ship*, corazzata; (typ.) maiuscolo.
**capital** *n.* capitale *f.*; metropoli *f. indecl.*; capoluogo; (finan.) capitale *m.*; *paid-up* —, capitale versato; — *levy*, imposta sul capitale; *registered, authorized* —, capitale sociale nominale; *working* —, capitale circolante; (fig.) *to make — out of*, trarre vantaggio da, sfruttare; (archit.) capitello; (typ.) maiuscola; *small* —, maiuscoletto.
**capital-ism** *n.* capitalismo **-ist** *n.* capitalista *m.*, *f.* **-istic** *adj.* capitalistico.
**capitaliz-e** *tr.* capitalizzare; (typ.) scrivere con maiuscola. **-ation** *n.* capitalizzazione; (typ.) uso delle maiuscole.
**capitally** *adv.* benissimo, benone; a meraviglia.
**capitation** *n.* testatico.
**Capitol** *pr.n.* Campidoglio.
**capitoline** *adj.* capitolino.
**capitular** *adj.* (eccl.) capitolare.
**capitulat-e** *intr.* capitolare, arrendersi. **-ion** *n.* capitolazione; resa; patti *m.pl.* della resa.
**capless** *adj.* a capo scoperto, senza berretto.
**capon** *n.* cappone *m.*
**capric-e** *n.* capriccio; fantasia. **-ious** *adj.* capriccioso. **-iousness** *n.* capricciosità.
**Capricorn** *pr.n.* (astron.) Capricorno; *Tropic of* —, tropico del Capricorno.
**capriole** *n.* capriola; salto; (of horse) impennata.
**capsicum** *n.* (bot.) capsico; (cul.) pimento.
**capsiz-e** *tr.* capovolgere, rovesciare; *intr.* capovolgersi, rovesciarsi, far cappotto, ribaltarsi. **-able** *adj.* ribaltabile, rovesciabile.
**capstan** *n.* (naut.) argano; verricello *m.*; (lathe) revolver *m. indecl.*
**capsule** *n.* capsula; (bot.) pericarpo.
**captain** *n.* (army) capitano; (navy) capitano di vascello; *flag* —, comandante *m.* di bandiera; (merchant marine) capitano; — *of industry*, magnate *m.* industriale; (sport) capitano; *tr.* capitanare; comandare. **-cy** *n.* grado di capitano; *to obtain one's -cy*, essere promosso capitano; (fig.) *under the -cy of*, sotto la guida di.
**caption** *n.* (typ.) didascalia; (leg.) arresto, mandato di cattura.
**captious** *adj.* capzioso; insidioso; ipercritico, sofistico.
**captivat-e** *tr.* cattivare, affascinare, incantare, ammaliare. **-ing** *adj.* cattivante, affascinante, seducente. **-ion** *n.* seduzione, fascino, incanto.
**captiv-e** *n.* prigioniero; schiavo; *to hold* —, tenere prigioniero; *to take* —, far prigioniero; — *balloon*, pallone frenato. **-ity** *n.* cattività; prigionia.
**captor** *n.* catturatore.
**capture** *n.* cattura; presa; preda; *tr.* catturare; far prigioniero; arrestare; prendere; (fig.) *to — someone's attention*, cattivarsi l'attenzione di qualcuno; *to — the market*, accaparrare il mercato.
**capuchin** *n.* (eccl.) cappuccino; (zool.) — *monkey*, cebo.
**car** *n.* carro; carretta; *triumphal* —, carro trionfale; (motor.) auto-

mobile *f.*; (fam.) macchina; *to go by —*, andare in macchina; (rlwy.) vagone *m.*, carrozza, vettura; *pullman —*, vettura salone; (mil.) *armoured —*, autoblinda.
**carabineer** *n.* carabiniere *m.*
**carafe** *n.* caraffa.
**caramel** *n.* caramello, zucchero bruciato; *a —*, una caramella.
**carapace** *n.* carapace *m.*
**carat** *n.* carato.
**caravan** *n.* carovana; (motor.) roulotte *f.*
**caravanserai** *n.* caravanserraglio.
**caraway** *n.* comino, caro.
**caraway-seeds** *n.* semi *m.pl.* di comino.
**carbide** *n.* (chem.) carburo.
**carbine** *n.* carabina.
**carbohydrate** *n.* carboidrato.
**carbolic** *n.*, *adj.* fenico.
**carbon** *n.* (chem.) carbonio; *— dioxide*, anidride carbonica; (electr.) carbone *m.* *— black*, nerofumo; (comm.) *— copy*, copia (su carta) carbone; *— paper*, carta carbone. **-ate** *n.* (chem.) carbonato. **-ic** *adj.* (chem.) carbonico.
**carboniz-e** *tr.* carbonizzare; *intr.* carbonizzarsi. **-ation** *n.* carbonizzazione.
**carboy** *n.* damigiana.
**carbuncle** *n.* (miner.) carbonchio; (med.) pustola; carbonchio, foruncolo maligno.
**carburate** *tr.* carburare.
**carburettor** *n.* (motor.) carburatore *m.*
**carcase, carcass** *n.* carcame *m.*; carcassa; (of ship) ossatura.
**carcinoma** *n.* carcinoma *m.*
**card** *n.* cartoncino; carta; *a game of -s*, una partita a carte; *court —*, figura; *a house of -s*, un castello di carte; *pack of -s*, mazzo di carte; *to deal the -s*, distribuire le carte; *to play one's -s well*, giuocar bene le proprie carte; *to put one's -s on the table*, mettere le carte in tavola; *to shuffle the -s*, mescolare le carte; *to have a — up one's sleeve*, avere un asso nella manica; *it's on the -s*, è molto probabile; *he's a queer —*, è un tipo strano; *it's a sure —*, è una cosa certa; scheda, schedina; cartolina; *visiting —*, biglietto da visita; *business —*, biglietto da visita della ditta; *invitation —*, biglietto d'invito; *admission —*, biglietto d'entrata; *identity —*, carta d'identità; *membership —*, tessera; *ration —*, tessera di razionamento; (naut.) *compass —*, rosa della bussola.
**card** *tr.* schedare, annotare su cartoncini; (text.) cardare.
**cardamom** *n.* (bot.) cardamomo.
**cardboard** *n.* cartone *m.*; cartoncino.
**card-case** *n.* portabiglietti *m. indecl.* da visita.
**carder** *n.* cardatore; (machine) cardatrice.
**cardiac** *adj.* (med.) cardiaco.
**cardigan** *n.* giacca di lana; golf *m. indecl.*
**cardinal**[1] *adj.* cardinale; principale; sommo; *— numbers*, numeri cardinali; *the — points*, i punti cardinali; *the — virtues*, le virtù cardinali; *of — importance*, di somma importanza.
**cardinal**[2] *n.* cardinale *m.*; *-'s hat*, cappello cardinalizio. **-ate** *n.* cardinalato.
**card-index** *n.* schedario; *tr.* schedare. **-ing** *n.* schedatura.
**carding** *n.* (text.) cardatura.
**carding-machine** *n.* cardatrice.
**cardsharper** *n.* baro.
**care** *n.* cura; diligenza; attenzione; accuratezza; sollecitudine *f.*; premura; preoccupazione; affanno; responsabilità; *lack of —*, incuria, negligenza, trascuratezza; *— of*, presso; *in the — of*, sotto la cura di; *handle with —!*, fragile!; *take —!*, sta attento!, attenzione!; *to take — in doing something*, aver cura nel fare qualcosa; *to take — of*, curare, aver cura di, occuparsi di; *to take — to*, badare di.
**care** *intr.* curarsi; interessarsi; preoccuparsi; *to — for*, curare; occuparsi di; assistere; provvedere a; *well -d for*, ben curato; *I don't — for games*, non mi piace lo sport; *if you — to*, se ti piace, se vuoi; *I don't —*, non me ne importa, per me è lo stesso; *for all I —*, per quanto mi riguarda, per conto mio; *who -s?*, chi ci bada?, (vulg.) chi se ne frega?; *I couldn't — less*, non me ne importa un bel niente, (vulg.) me ne strafrego.
**careen** *tr.* (naut.) carenare, abbattere in carena; *intr.* (fig.) sbandare. **-ing** *n.* carenaggio.
**career** *n.* carriera; *to make a — for oneself*, far carriera; *to take up a —*, abbracciare una carriera, dedicarsi a una professione; corsa, andatura, carriera; *in full —*, a tutta carriera; *intr.* correre; galoppare. **-ist** *n.* arrivista *m.*, *f.*; ambizioso.
**carefree** *adj.* senza pensieri, spensierato.
**careful** *adj.* attento; sollecito; diligente; accurato; curato; cauto; prudente; guardingo; *be —!*, sta attento!, attenzione! **-ly** *adv.* con cura; sollecitamente; cautamente; adagio. **-ness** *n.* cura; cautela; attenzione; sollecitudine *f.*; accuratezza.
**care-laden** *adj.* pieno di preoccupazioni.
**careless** *adj.* noncurante, incurante; negligente; trascurato; disattento; distratto; spensierato; *to be — of*, non badare a. **-ness** *n.* noncuranza; trascuratezza; negligenza; spensieratezza; disattenzione; distrazione.
**caress** *n.* carezza; *tr.* accarezzare. **-ing** *adj.* accarezzevole; affettuoso.
**caretaker** *n.* custode *m.*, *f.*; guardiano; *— government*, governo interinale.
**care-worn** *adj.* preoccupato, pieno di ansietà.
**car-ferry** *n.* traghetto per automobili.
**cargo** *n.* carico; merce imbarcata; *deck —*, carico di coperta; *tr.* caricare.
**cargo-boat, cargo-steamer** *n.* nave *f.* da carico; vapore *m.* merci.
**carib** *adj.* caraibico; *n.* caraibo.
**Caribbean** *adj.* (geog.) caraibico; *— Sea*, Mare dei Caraibi.
**caribou** *n.* (zool.) caribù *m. indecl.*
**caricatur-e** *n.* caricatura; macchietta; *tr.* mettere in caricatura, fare la caricatura di. **-able** *adj.* che si presta alla caricatura. **-ist** *n.* caricaturista *m.*
**caries** *n.* (med.) carie *f.*
**carillon** *n.* scampanio; cariglione *m.*
**Carinthia** *pr.n.* (geog.) Carinzia.
**car-licence** *n.* patente *f.* di circolazione. **-load** *n.* carico di una vettura.
**carman** *n.* carrettiere *m.*
**Carmel** *pr.n.* (geog.) *Mount —*, Monte Carmelo.
**Carmelite** *n.* (eccl.) Carmelita *m.*, *f.*; carmelitano; *Discalced -s*, carmelitani scalzi.
**carminative** *adj.*, *n.* (pharm.) carminativo.
**carmine** *n.* carminio.
**carnage** *n.* strage *f.*; carneficina; macello.
**carnal** *adj.* carnale; sensuale.
**carnation** *n.* (bot.) garofano.
**carnelian** *n.* corniola, cornalina.
**carnival** *n.* carnevale *m.*
**carnivor-e** *n.* carnivoro. **-ous** *adj.* carnivoro.
**carob** *n.* carruba.
**carol** *n.* cantico, canto, inno; *Christmas —*, cantico di Natale; *tr.*, *intr.* cantare, inneggiare; gorgheggiare, trillare.
**Caroline** *adj.* (hist.) del tempo di Carlomagno, di Carlo I o di Carlo II d'Inghilterra.
**Caroline** *pr.n.* Carolina.
**Carolingian** *adj.* (hist.) carolingio.
**carotid** *n.* (anat.) carotide *f.*; *attrib.* carotico, carotideo.
**carous-e** *intr.* gozzovigliare, far baccano. **-al** *n.* gozzoviglia; orgia; bevuta.
**car(r)ousel** *n.* carosello.
**carp**[1] *n.* (ichth.) carpa.
**carp**[2] *intr.* cavillare, trovare da ridire.
**car-park** *n.* parcheggio, posteggio.
**Carpathians** *pr.n.* (geog.) Carpazi *m.pl.*

**carpent-er** *n.* falegname *m.*; carpentiere *m.*; *ship's* —, carpentiere di bordo; *stage* —, macchinista *m.* **-ering, -ry** *n.* carpenteria; falegnameria.
**carpet** *n.* tappeto; *bedside* —, scendiletto; *pile* —, tappeto vellutato; *tr.* tappezzare, coprire con tappeto; *-ed with flowers*, ammantato di fiori; (colloq.) *to be -ed*, essere sgridato.
**carpet-bag** *n.* sacco da viaggio. **-bagger** *n.* avventuriero politico. **-beater** *n.* battipanni *m. indecl.* **-slippers** *n.* pantofole *f.pl.* in tessuto da tappeto. **-sweeper** *n.* spazzola per tappeti.
**carping** *adj.* cavilloso, pignolo, capzioso.
**carriage** *n.* carrozza; vettura; — *and pair*, tiro a due; — *entrance*, porta carraia; *hackney* —, vettura pubblica; *railway* —, carrozza, vettura ferroviaria; (mil.) affusto; (mech.; aeron.) carrello; porto, trasporto; spese di trasporto; — *forward*, porto assegnato; — *free*, franco di porto, franco a domicilio; — *paid*, porto affrancato; portamento; contegno. **-way** *n.* carreggiata, strada carrozzabile.
**carriage-window** *n.* sportello.
**carrier** *n.* portatore; (comm.) spedizioniere, vettore, corriere *m.*, agente *m.* di trasporti; portapacchi *m. indecl.*; (mech.) trasportatore *m.*, piastra portante; (radio) — *wave*, onda portante.
**carrier-bag** *n.* sacchetto di carta (per contenere gli acquisti). **-pigeon** *n.* piccione *m.* viaggiatore.
**carrion** *n.* carogna; carne putrefatta; — *crow*, corvo nero.
**carrot** *n.* carota. **-y** *adj.* di colore carota; dai capelli rossi.
**carry** *n.* portata; (golf) traiettoria; (mil.) *sword at the* —, spada alla mano.
**carry** *tr.* portare; trasportare; sostenere; trasmettere; condurre; (math.) portare; prendere d'assalto, espugnare; (pol.) far approvare; *carried unanimously*, approvato all'unanimità; *to — all before one*, essere irresistibile, vincere; *to — authority*, avere autorità, avere peso; *to — the blame*, accollarsi il biasimo; *to — coals to Newcastle*, portare acqua al mare; *to — to a conclusion*, portare a conclusione, chiudere; *to — conviction*, essere convincente; *to — the day*, riportare la vittoria, vincere; *to — into effect*, effettuare; *to — to excess*, esagerare, portare all'estremo; *to — something in one's hand*, portare qualcosa in mano; *to — one's head high*, andare a testa alta; *to — one's hearers with one*, trascinare il proprio uditorio; (finan.) *to — interest*, fruttare interesse; *to — a joke too far*, spingere uno scherzo troppo lontano; *to — one's life in one's hands*, rischiare la propria vita; *to — one's liquor well*, sopportare bene gli alcoolici; (colloq.) *he's had as much as he can* —, ha bevuto più del dovuto; *to — oneself well*, avere un bel portamento; *to — one's point*, imporre il proprio modo di vedere; *intr.* portare; raggiungere; *his voice does not* —, la sua voce si perde. Followed by adv. or prep.: *to — about*, portarsi dietro, portare in giro; portare addosso; *to — across*, trasportare dall'altra parte; *to — along*, portare con sè, trascinare; *to — away*, portare via, portare altrove, asportare; (fig.) *to be carried away*, lasciarsi trasportare, essere rapito; *to — back*, riportare, portare indietro; *to — down*, far scendere, portare giù; (comm.) *to — forward*, riportare; *to — off*, portare via, (fig.) ottenere, riportare, vincere; *to — off a prize*, riportare un premio; *to be carried off by a disease*, morire di malattia; (fam.) *to — it off*, cavarsela, riuscire nel colpo; *to — on*, esercitare, gestire; continuare, persistere in, mandare avanti, proseguire; — *on!*, avanti!, proseguite!; (fam.) comportarsi male; fare una scenata; *to — out*, portare fuori; dare effetto a, eseguire, realizzare; mantenere; adempire a; *to — over*, trasportare; (comm.) riportare; trasportare attraverso; (fig.) portare a termine; *to — up*, portare su.
**carry-cot** *n.* culla portabile. **-forward** *n.* (comm.) riporto.
**carrying** *adj.* portante; *n.* il portare; trasporto; (pol.) approvazione; — *capacity*, portata; — *trade*, trasporto merci; — *away*, asportazione; — *off*, il portare via, rapimento, ratto; — *on*, proseguimento; esercizio; gestione; (fam.) *such -s on!*, che scandalo!, che vergogna!; — *out*, esecuzione, realizzazione, effettuazione; mantenimento; adempimento.
**carry-over** *n.* (finan.) riporto.
**cart** *n.* carro; carretta; (fig.) *to put the — before the horse*, mettere il carro innanzi ai buoi; (fam.) *to be in the* —, trovarsi nei guai; *tr.* trasportare con carro; (fig.) *to — about*, portare in giro; *to — away*, portar via.
**carte** *n.* — *blanche*, carta bianca, mano libera; *à la* —, alla carta.
**cartel** *n.* (comm.) consorzio, cartello; (hist.) cartello di sfida.
**carter** *n.* carrettiere *m.*
**Carthag-e** *pr.n.* (geog.) Cartagine *f.* **-inian** *adj.*, *n.* cartaginese *m.*, *f.*
**carthorse** *n.* cavallo da traino.
**Carthusian** *adj.*, *n.* certosino; — *monsastery*, certosa.
**cartilage** *n.* (anat.) cartilagine *f.*
**cartload** *n.* carrettata.
**cartograph-er** *n.* cartografo. **-y** *n.* cartografia.
**carton** *n.* scatola di cartone.
**cartoon** *n.* caricatura; vignetta; (art; cinem.) cartone *m.* **-ist** *n.* caricaturista *m.*
**cartouche** *n.* cartoccio.
**cartridge** *n.* cartuccia; (photog.) rotolo; *blank* —, cartuccia a salve.
**cartridge-belt** *n.* cartucciera, caricatore *m.* a nastro. **-case** *n.* bossolo. **-paper** *n.* carta da disegno. **-pouch** *n.* giberna.
**cartulary** *n.* cartolaro.
**cart-wheel** *n.* ruota da carro; (gymn.) *to turn -s.* far la ruota.
**cartwright** *n.* carradore *m.*
**carv-e** *tr.* scolpire; intagliare, incidere; tagliare, trinciare; (fig.) incidere; *to — out a career*, far carriera; *to — up*, spartire, dividere. **-er** *n.* scultore; intagliatore; incisore; trinciante *m.* **-ing** *n.* scultura; intaglio; incisione; il trinciare.
**carving-knife** *n.* trinciante *m.*
**caryatid** *n.* (archit.) cariatide *f.*
**cascade** *n.* cascata; *intr.* scendere come una cascata, cascare.
**case**[1] *n.* caso; fatto; avvenimento; *a — of conscience*, un caso di coscienza; questione; problema *m.*; *a — in point*, un esempio a proposito; *the — in point*, il problema di cui si tratta; *it is a very hard* —, è un caso pietosissimo; *it is a — for the doctor*, qui ci vuol un medico; *it's a — of life and death*, è questione di vita o di morte; *it was a — of love at first sight*, è stato un colpo di fulmine; *should the — occur*, al caso, magari, semmai; *if that be the* —, se è cosí; *that is often the* —, succede spesso; *but this is not the* —, ma non è cosí; *that alters the* —, la cosa cambia aspetto, questo è un altro paio di maniche; *that has nothing to do with the* —, questo non ci entra affatto; *as the — may be*, a secondo, secondo il caso; *as the — stands*, come stanno le cose; *as in the — of*, come nel caso di; *in — of*, in caso di; *in — of need*, al bisogno; *in* —, (as conj.) qualora, se, nel caso che; *just in* —, comunque; *in any* —, in ogni caso, ad ogni modo, comunque; *in either* —, in un modo o nell'altro; *in most -s*, in genere; *in nine -s out of ten*, nove volte su dieci; *in no* —, in nessun caso; *in such a* —, in tal caso; *in that* —, allora; *to meet the* —, fare al caso; *to state the* —, esporre i fatti; (leg.) causa; processo; *the — of the Crown is*, l'accusa sostiene che; *the — for the defence*, la difesa; *there's a woman in the* —, c'è di mezzo una donna; (gramm.) caso; affetto; (med.) caso.
**case**[2] *n.* astuccio; cassetta; scatola; custodia; fodero; (*packing-*) —, cassa; scrigno; valigia; (typ.)

*lower* —, bassa cassa, (lettere) minuscole; *upper* —, alta cassa, (lettere) maiuscole; (violin, *etc.*) cassa; *tr.* rinchiudere in astuccio; imballare; rivestire, ricoprire.
**case-book** *n.* raccolta di documenti.
**case-ending** *n.* (gramm.) desinenza.
**case-harden** *tr.* (metall.) indurire, temperare, cementare. **-hardened** *adj.* (metall.) cementato; (fig.) duro.
**case-history** *n.* (med.) cartella clinica.
**casein** *n.* (chem.) caseina.
**case-law** *n.* (leg.) giurisprudenza.
**casemate** *n.* (mil.) casamatta.
**casement** *n.* (of window) telaio; finestra a due battenti.
**cash** *n.* denaro; moneta; contanti *m.pl.*; *hard* —, denaro sonante; *petty* —, spese varie, piccola cassa *f.*; — *down,* in contanti, a pronta cassa; — *payment,* pagamento in contanti; — *price,* prezzo per contanti; — *in hand,* fondo di cassa; — *on delivery,* pagamento contro assegno; *to be in* —, avere soldi; *to be out of* —, essere senza soldi; *to sell for* —, vendere a contanti.
**cash** *tr.* incassare; riscuotere; convertire in denaro; *to — a cheque,* incassare un assegno; (fam.) *to — in on something,* approfittare di qualcosa.
**cash-book** *n.* libro cassa. **-box** *n.* cassetta dei contanti. **-desk** *n.* cassa.
**cashew-nut** *n.* (bot.) acagiù *m. indecl.*, anacardo.
**cashier**[1] *n.* cassiere *m.*; *-'s desk,* cassa.
**cashier**[2] *tr.* (mil.) destituire.
**cashmere** *n.* (text.) cascemir *m.*
**cash-register** *n.* registratore *m.* di cassa.
**casing** *n.* copertura; rivestimento; telaio.
**casino** *n.* casinò *m. indecl.*; casa da giuoco.
**cask** *n.* botte *f.*; barile *m.*; *to taste of the* —, sapere di botte.
**casket** *n.* scrigno; cofanetto; cassa da morto; urna per ceneri.
**Caspar** *pr.n.* Gaspare.
**Caspian** *adj.* (geog.) *the — Sea,* il Mar Caspio.
**casque** *n.* casco, elmo.
**cassation** *n.* (leg.) cassazione.
**casserole** *n.* casseruola; teglia; *en* —, in umido.
**Cassius** *pr.n.* Cassio.
**cassock** *n.* (eccl.) veste *f.* talare; abito lungo; sottana.
**cassowary** (orn.) casuario.
**cast** *n.* getto; lancio; tiro; colpo; (art) calco; abbozzo; (theatre) complesso; (math.) addizione; (fig.) forma; *plaster* —, calco in gesso; (metall.) getto, gettata, fusione; — *iron,* ghisa; *at a single* —, di getto; *to have a — in one's eye,* essere strabico; — *of features,* tratti, fisionomia; — *of mind,* mentalità; *a man of his* —, un uomo della sua tempra; *thoughts of a melancholy* —, pensieri tinti di malinconia.
**cast** *tr.* gettare; lanciare; buttare; (metall.) fondere, gettare; (sculp.) plasticare; *the die is* —, il dado è tratto; — *in the same mould,* di carattere identico, della stessa risma; *to — anchor,* gettare l'ancora, dar fondo all'ancora; *to — aspersions on someone,* denigrare qualcuno; *to — the blame on someone,* dare la colpa a qualcuno; (of bird) *to — its feathers,* mutare le penne; (provb.) — *not a clout till May be out,* aprile non ti scoprire, maggio va adagio; *to — a glance,* gettare uno sguardo; *to — a horoscope,* trarre un'oroscopo; (naut.) *to — the lead,* gettare lo scandaglio; *to — light on something,* mettere in luce qualcosa; (fishing) *to — the line,* gettare la lenza; *to — lots,* trarre a sorte, sorteggiare; *to — one's mind over something,* riflettere su qualcosa; *to — pearls before swine,* gettare le perle ai porci; (theatr.) *to — a play,* distribuire le parti; *I am — for Hamlet,* ho la parte di Amleto; *to — into prison,* gettare in prigione; *to — a shadow,* gettare l'ombra; (of horse) *to — a shoe,* perdere un ferro; (of reptile) *to — its skin,* buttare la spoglia; *to — a slur on someone's name,* macchiare la reputazione di qualcuno; *to — a spell on,* ammaliare, incantare; *to — in someone's teeth,* rinfacciare a qualcuno; (pol.) *to — one's vote,* dare il proprio voto, votare; *number of votes* —, numero di voti; (foll. by *adv.* or *prep.*) *tr. to — about,* gettare qua e là; *intr. to — about for an excuse,* cercare un prete; *to — adrift,* lasciar andare alla deriva, abbandonare, mollare; *to — aside,* gettare da parte, buttare via, smettere, disfarsi di; *to — away,* gettare via, (fig.) abbandonare; *to — back,* gettare indietro; *to — one's mind back,* ritornare col pensiero; *to — down,* gettare giù; (eyes) abbassare; (fig.) *to be — down,* essere abbattuto; *to — in one's lot with,* dividere la propria sorte con; *to — loose, tr., intr.* (naut.) mollare, disormeggiare; *to — off, tr.* buttare via, spogliarsi; (fig.) scuotere; *intr.* (naut.) mollare, salpare; (knitting) buttare giù i punti; *to — on* mettere su i punti; *to — out,* cacciare, scacciare, mettere fuori; (demons) esorcizzare; *to — up,* buttare su; (math.) calcolare, computare; (vomit) vomitare.
**castanets** *n.* (pair of) nacchere, castagnette *f.pl.*
**castaway** *n.* naufrago; (fig.) reprobo.
**caste** *n.* casta; *to lose* —, scendere di grado; (fig.) perdere la reputazione.
**castellated** *adj.* merlato, turrito.
**caster**[1] *n.* lanciatore; (metall.) fonditore; (machine) fondatrice.
**caster**[2] *n.* see **castor**[2].
**castigat-e** *tr.* castigare; punire. **-ion** *n.* castigo; punizione.
**Castile** *pr.n.* (geog.) Castiglia.
**Castilian** *adj.*, *n.* castigliano.
**casting** *n.* getto; lancio; (sculpt.) sformatura; (theatr.) distribuzione; (metall.) fusione; *adj.* — *vote,* voto preponderante.
**cast-iron** *n.* ghisa; *adj.* di ghisa; (fig.) duro, rigido, di ferro; — *constitution,* salute di ferro.
**castle** *n.* castello; (chess) torre rocca; (fig.) *-s in Spain,* castelli in aria; *tr., intr.* (chess) *to — (the King),* arroccare.
**cast-off** *adj.* vecchio; usato; (fig.) abbandonato; *n.* abito smesso.
**Castor**[1] *pr.n.* (myth.) Castore.
**castor**[2] *n.* spargizucchero; pepaiuola; saliera; *set of -s,* ampolliera; — *sugar,* zucchero raffinato; rotella, girella.
**castor**[3] *n.* (pharm.) ricino. **-oil** *n.* olio di ricino.
**castrat-e** *tr.* castrare. **-ion** *n.* castrazione, castratura.
**casual** *adj.* casuale, fortuito, accidentale; trascurato, sbadato; disinvolto; *to engage in — conversation,* discutere del più e del meno, parlare di cose banali; *he tried to sound* —, egli voleva parere indifferente; — *labourer,* avventizio, giornaliero. **-ism** *n.* (philos.) casualismo. **-ly** *adv.* con disinvoltura, come se nulla fosse. **-ness** *n.* noncuranza; mancanza di metodo; indifferenza; disinvoltura.
**casualty** *n.* incidente *m.*; infortunio; disgrazia; vittima; *there were no casualties,* non si deplorano vittime; — *ward,* pronto soccorso; (mil.) *casualties,* perdite, morti, feriti e dispersi.
**casuist** *n.* casista *m., f.* **-ry** *n.* casistica.
**cat**[1] *n.* gatto; gatta; felino; (fam.) micio; (fig.) *to be like — and dog,* essere come il diavolo e l'acqua santa; *to be like a — on hot bricks,* stare sui carboni ardenti; *to be the -'s whiskers,* essere un cannone; *to fight like Kilkenny -s,* combattere come cane e gatto; *to grin like a Cheshire* —, ridacchiare come un scemo; *to have as many lives as a* —, avere la pelle dura; *to let the — out of the bag,* rivelare un segreto, (fam.) cantare; *the — is out of the bag,* è scoppiata la bomba; *it would make a — laugh,* farebbe ridere i polli; *to play — and mouse with,* fare a tira e molla con; *to rain -s and dogs,* piovere a catinelle; *to wait*

*and see which way the — jumps*, star a vedere da che parte tira il vento; *to set the — among the pigeons*, suscitare un putiferio; *there's no room to swing a —*, non c'è spazio per girarsi; *to play —'s cradle*, fare la sega; (provb.) *a — may look at a king*, anche il più umile ha dei diritti; *when the —s away, the mice will play*, via la gatta i topi ballano; *curiosity killed the —*, tanto va il gatto al lardo che ci lascia lo zampino; (fam.) *she's a —*, è invidiosa; frusta; *to give someone a taste of the —*, far saggiare la frusta a qualcuno.

**cat**[2] *n.* (naut.) capone *m.*; *tr.* caponare (l'ancora); *intr.* (fam.) vomitare, recere.

**catabolism** *n.* catabolismo.

**cataclysm** *n.* cataclisma *m.*; disastro; catastrofe *f.*

**catacomb** *n.* catacomba; (archit.) ipogeo.

**catafalque** *n.* catafalco.

**Catalan** *adj.*, *n.* catalano.

**catalep-sy** *n.* catalessi *f. indecl.* **-tic** *adj.* catalettico.

**catalogue** *n.* catalogo; elenco; *tr.* catalogare; elencare.

**cataly-sis** *n.* (chem.) catalisi *f.* **-tic** *adj.* catalitico. **-zer** *n.* (chem.) catalizzatore.

**catamaran** *n.* (naut.) zattera; (fig.) donna litigiosa, megera.

**catapult** *n.* catapulta; (boy's) frombola; fionda *m.*; *tr.* catapultare; (fig.) scagliare.

**cataract** *n.* cascata; (med.) cateratta.

**catarrh** *n.* catarro.

**catastroph-e** *n.* catastrofe *f.*; calamità *f. indecl.* **-ic** *adj.* catastrofico.

**cat-burglar** *n.* ladro acrobata.

**catch** *n.* presa; cattura; preda; (of fish) pesca, retata; tranello, inganno; (on door) paletto, saliscendi *m.*, arresto di sicurezza; (of window) gancio; (mus.) ritornello; *a — of the breath*, sussulto; *there must be a — in it*, ci dev'essere un inganno; (fam.) *he's no great —*, non è un buon partito; (cricket) presa.

**catch** *tr.* cogliere; pigliare; prendere; agguantare; afferrare; acchiappare; pescare; *catch!*, to'!; (fam.) *— me! (doing such a thing)*, fossi matto!; (wrestling) *— as — can*, lotta libera; *to — in the act*, cogliere sul fallo; *to — one's breath*, trattenere il respiro; *to — cold*, prendere un raffreddore; (rowing) *to — a crab*, farsi mangiare il remo; *to — the drift (of the argument)*, capire dove si vuol arrivare; *to — the eye*, incontrare lo sguardo (di), (fig.) colpire; *to — someone's eye*, attirare l'attenzione di qualcuno; *to — fire*, prendere fuoco, incendiarsi; *to — one's foot in*, inciampare in; *to — a glimpse of*, intravvedere, vedere di sfuggita; *to — hold of*, afferrare; *to — the imagination*, accendere l'immaginazione; *to — sight of*, scorgere, avvistare; *to — someone doing something*, cogliere qualcuno sul fatto; *to — someone napping*, prendere qualcuno alla sprovvista; *to — a train*, prendere un treno; (fam.) *to — it*, prendersela; *intr.* attaccarsi, appiccarsi; (of fire) accendersi; (foll. by *adv.* or *prep.*) *to — at*, cercare di afferrare; (fig.) *to — at a straw*, attaccarsi a un filo; *to — on*, capire, afferrare a volo; diventare popolare, incontrare il gusto; *to — someone out*, pigliare qualcuno sul fatto; *to — up*, afferrare in fretta, raccogliere; (fig.) riprendersi, riguadagnare il tempo perduto; *to — up with someone*, raggiungere qualcuno.

**catching** *adj.* attraente; contagioso, attaccaticcio, infettivo.

**catchment** *n.* captazione; *— basin*, bacino idrico.

**catch-phrase** *n.* frase fatta; cliché *m.*

**catchword** *n.* parola d'ordine; slogan *m.*; (typ.) esponente *m.*

**catchy** *adj.* orecchiabile.

**catech-ism** *n.* (eccl.) catechismo; dottrina. **-ize** *tr.* catechizzare; interrogare.

**categoric(al)** *adj.* categorico.

**category** *n.* categoria; classe *f.*

**cater** *intr.* provvedere cibo, provvedere al nutrimento di; *to — for all tastes*, provvedere a soddisfare tutti i gusti. **-er** *n.* provveditore; fornitore; negoziante *m.* (di generi alimentari). **-ing** *n.* approvvigionamento; rifornimento; vitto.

**caterpillar** *n.* (ent.) bruco; (mech.) cingolo; *attrib.* a cingoli.

**caterwaul** *intr.* miagolare. **-ing** *n.* il miagolare, miagolio.

**catfish** *n.* (ichth.) lupo di mare.

**catgut** *n.* minugia.

**catharsis** *n.* catarsi *f.*; (med.) evacuazione.

**Cathay** *pr.n.* (geog.) Catai *m.*

**cathedral** *n.* cattedrale *f.*; duomo; *— city*, città sede episcopale.

**Catherine** *pr.n.* Caterina.

**catherine-wheel** *n.* girandola; (archit.) rosone *m.*

**catheter** *n.* (med.) catetere *m.*

**cathode** *n.* (electr.) catodo.

**catholic** *adj.* universale, eclettico; *adj.*, *n.* (rel.) cattolico; *Roman —*, cattolico (romano). **-ism** *n.* cattolicesimo. **-ity** *n.* universalità; eclettismo.

**catkin** *n.* (bot.) amento.

**catlike** *adj.* felino.

**catmint** *n.* (bot.) erba gatta, gattaria.

**Cato** *pr.n.* Catone, *— the Elder*, Catone il Censore; *— of Utica*, l'Uticense.

**cat's-eye** occhio di gatto; catarifrangente *m.* **-meat** *n.* corata; (fam.) *to make -meat of*, ridurre a pezzi. **-paw** *n.* occhio di vento; nodo di gancio doppio; (fig.) *to use as a -paw*, cavar la castagna con lo zampino del gatto.

**catsup** *n.* see **ketchup.**

**cattle** *n.* bestiame *m.*; buoi *m.pl.*; bestie *f.pl.*; armenti *m.pl.*; *200 head of —*, duecento capi di bestiame.

**cattle-market** *n.* mercato boario. **-stealing** *n.* abigeato. **-thief** abigeo. **-truck** *n.* vagone *m.* per bestiame.

**catty** *adj.* invidioso; dispettoso; sornione.

**Catullus** *pr.n.* Catullo.

**catwalk** *n.* passaggio stretto; camminamento; passerella.

**Caucasian** *adj.*, *n.* (geog.) caucasico; (ethn.) indoeuropeo.

**Caucasus** *pr.n.* (geog.) Caucaso.

**caucus** *n.* comitato; cricca.

**caudal** *adj.* caudale.

**caught** *p.def.*, *part.* of **catch**, *q.v.*

**caul** *n.* (anat.) amnio; (fig.) *born with a —*, nato con la camicia.

**cauldron** *n.* caldaia; calderone *m.*

**cauliflower** *n.* cavolfiore *m.*

**caulk** *tr.* (naut.) calafatare; (mech.) presellare. **-ing** *n.* (naut.) calafataggio; (mech.) presellatura.

**caus-al** *adj.* causale. **-ality**, **-ation** *n.* causalità; rapporto fra causa ed effetto. **-ative** *adj.* causativo.

**cause** *n.* causa; cagione; ragione; motivo; (leg.) causa, processo; *— and effect*, causa ed effetto; *and with good —*, e con ragione; *in a good —*, a fin di bene; *there is — to believe*, c'è motivo di credere; *to have good — for*, aver buone ragioni di; *to make common — with*, fare causa comune con, sposare la causa di; *to plead a —*, perorare una causa.

**cause** *tr.* causare; cagionare; provocare; eccitare; far nascere; suscitare; *to — much comment*, suscitare molte dicerie; *to — a thing to be done*, far fare una cosa; *to — someone to do something*, far sì che qualcuno faccia qualcosa.

**causeway** *n.* argine *m.*; strada rialzata.

**caustic** caustico; (fig.) mordace; aspro; acerbo; sarcastico; pungente. **-ity** *n.* causticità; (fig.) mordacità.

**cauteriz-e** *tr.* cauterizzare. **-ation** *n.* cauterizzazione.

**cautery** *n.* cauterio.

**caution** *n.* cautela; accortezza; prudenza; circospezione; *—! dangerous bend!*, attenzione! svolta pericolosa!; *to proceed with —*, andare a rilento; *to do a thing with great —*, fare qualcosa con grande circospezione; (leg.) *let off with a —*, assolto con diffida; *— money*, garanzia, cauzione; (fam.) *he's a —*, è un vero originale.

**caution** *tr.* ammonire, avvertire; premunire, mettere in guardia; (leg.) ammonire, diffidare.
**cautionary** *adj.* di sicurezza, di precauzione; (fig.) ammonitorio, moralistico.
**cautious** *adj.* prudente; cauto; guardingo; accorto; circospetto. **-ness** *n.* prudenza; cautela; circospezione.
**cavalcade** *n.* cavalcata.
**cavalier**[1] *n.* cavaliere *m.*; (hist.) realista *m.*, seguace *m.* di Carlo I.
**cavalier**[2] *adj.* brusco, disinvolto, superbo, altezzoso, prepotente.
**cavalry** *n.* (mil.) cavalleria. **-man** *n.* soldato di cavalleria.
**cave** *n.* grotta; caverna; antro; spelonca.
**cave** *tr.* scavare; *intr. to — in*, cedere, franare, (fig.) cedere, abbandonare la lotta, arrendersi.
**cave-dweller** *n.* troglodita *m.*, *f.*
**caveat** *n.* (leg.) opposizione legale, sospensiva.
**cavern** *n.* grotta; caverna. **-ous** *adj.* cavernoso.
**caviar(e)** *n.* caviale *m.*; *— to the general*, perle *f.pl.* per i maiali.
**cavil** *n.* cavillo; arzigogolo; ammennicolo; *intr.* cavillare; sottilizzare. **-ler** *n.* cavillatore.
**caving-in** *n.* franamento; crollo.
**cavity** *n.* cavità *f. indecl.*; buco; (anat.) antro; (archit.) intercapedine *f.*
**cavort** *intr.* (of horse) impennarsi; (of person) saltare goffamente.
**caw** *intr.* gracchiare; *n.* gracchiamento. **-ing** *n.* gracchiamento.
**Cayenne** *pr.n.* (geog.) La Caienna; *— pepper*, pepe di Caienna, pepe rosso.
**cease** *tr.* cessare; smettere; lasciare; abbandonare; sospendere; finire; *to — working*, smettere di lavorare, abbandonare il lavoro; (mil.) *to — fire*, cessare il fuoco; *intr.* cessare; desistere; smettere; *to — from*, smettere di; *without ceasing*, senza tregua, continuamente.
**ceasefire** *n.* tregua.
**ceaseless** *adj.* incessante; continuo; persistente. **-ness** *n.* continuità; persistenza.
**ceasing** *n.* cessazione; interruzione; fine *f.*
**Cecil** *pr.n.* Cecilio.
**Cecilia** *pr.n.* Cecilia.
**cedar** *n.* (bot.) cedro.
**cede** *tr.* cedere; rinunciare a.
**cedilla** *n.* (phon.) cediglia.
**ceil** *tr.* soffittare, fare il soffitto di; *intr.* (aeron.) volare alla quota di tangenza.
**ceiling** *n.* soffitto; (aeron.) quota di tangenza; (comm.) *— price*, limite massimo; (fam.) *to hit the —*, andare su tutte le furie.
**celandine** *n.* (bot.) celidonia.
**celebrant** *n.* (liturg.) celebrante, consacrante *m.*
**celebr-ate** *tr.* celebrare; commemorare; festeggiare; *intr.* far festa. **-ated** *adj.* celebre; rinomato; famoso; illustre. **-ation** *n.* celebrazione; commemorazione; festa. **-ity** *n.* celebrità; fama; rinomanza; pezzo grosso.
**celerity** *n.* celerità; velocità.
**celery** *n.* (bot.) sedano, apio.
**celestial** *adj.* celeste; celestiale; (fig.) divino; *— object*, astro.
**celibacy** *n.* celibato.
**celibate** *n.*, *adj.* celibe *m.*; (woman) nubile *f.*
**cell** *n.* cellula; cella; (of honeycomb) alveolo; (electr.) pila, elemento.
**cellar** *n.* cantina; scantinato; sottosuolo; seminterrato; (eccl.) celleraria. **-er** *n.* cantiniere *m.*; (eccl.) dispensiere *m.*; cellerario.
**'cellist, 'cello** see **violoncellist, violoncello.**
**cellophane** *n.* cellofane *m.*
**cellular** *adj.* cellulare; alveolare.
**celluloid** *n.* celluloide *f.*; *attrib.* di celluloide.
**cellulose** *n.* (chem.) cellulosa.
**Celsius** *pr.n.* Celsio; *— thermometer*, termometro centigrado.
**Celt** *n.* (hist.) celta *m.*; *the -s*, i Celti. **-ic** *adj.* celtico.
**cement** *n.* cemento; mastice *m.*; *tr.* cementare; (fig.) consolidare, rinsaldare.
**cement-mixer** *n.* betoniera.
**cemetery** *n.* cimitero, camposanto.
**Cenis** *pr.n.* (geog.) *Mont —*, Moncenisio; *Mont — tunnel*, galleria del Fréjus.
**cenobite** *n.* (eccl.) cenobita *m.*
**cenotaph** *n.* cenotafio.
**cense** *tr.* (liturg.) incensare.
**censer** *n.* (eccl.) turibolo. **-bearer** *n.* (eccl.) turiferario.
**censor** *n.* censore *m.*; *to pass the —*, essere approvato dalla censura; *tr.* censurare. **-ial** *adj.* censorio. **-ious** *adj.* ipercritico, severo. **-ship** *n.* censura; (hist.) censorato.
**censure** *n.* censura; biasimo; *vote of —*, censura; *to pass — on*, censurare; *to incur general —*, incorrere nel biasimo generale; *tr.* censurare; riprendere; biasimare; criticare.
**census** *n.* censimento; censo; *to take a — of*, censire, fare il censimento di.
**census-paper** *n.* scheda di censimento.
**cent** *n.* centesimo; (comm.) *per —*, percento; *a ten per — commission*, una provvigione del dieci per cento; *ninety-nine per — of people*, il novantanove per cento della gente; (fam.) soldo, quattrino.
**centaur** *n.* centauro.
**centen-arian** *adj.*, *n.* centenario. **-ary** *n.* centenario. **-nial** *adj.* secolare, centennale.
**centering** *n.* (archit.) centina.
**centi-grade** *adj.* centigrado. **-gram(me)** *n.* centigrammo. **-litre** *n.* centilitro. **-metre** *n.* centimetro. **-pede** *n.* (ent.) millepiedi *m. indecl.*
**central** *adj.* centrale; principale; fondamentale; *— heating*, termosifone *m.*, riscaldamento centrale.
**centraliz-e** *tr.*, *intr.* accentrare, concentrare; *to become -d*, accentrarsi. **-ation** *n.* accentramento; concentrazione.
**centre** *n.* centro; punta centrale; (fig.) centro; sede *f.*; (attrib.) centrale, del centro, di mezzo; *in the —*, nel mezzo, nel centro; *— of attraction*, centro d'attenzione; *— of gravity*, centro di gravità, baricentro; *— of learning*, centro culturale; (soccer) *— forward*, centro avanti; *— half*, centro mediano; *tr.* accentrare, concentrare; *intr.* accentrarsi, concentrarsi; (soccer) centrare.
**centreboard** *n.* (naut.) centrochiglia *m.*
**centre-piece** *n.* trionfo da tavola.
**centrifugal** *adj.* centrifugo.
**centupl-e** *adj.*, *n.* centuplo. **-icate** *adj.*, *n.* centuplicato; *tr.* centuplicare.
**centurion** *n.* centurione *m.*
**century** *n.* secolo; cento anni; *the twentieth —*, il novecento, il ventesimo secolo; *of the 15th —*, quattrocentesco, del secolo quindicesimo; cento; (Rom. hist.) centuria.
**century-old** *adj.* secolare.
**cephalic** *adj.* cefalico.
**ceramic** *adj.* ceramico; di terracotta. **-s** *n.* ceramica.
**Cerberus** *n.* (myth.) Cerbero.
**cereal** *adj.*, *n.* cereale *m.*; *— crops*, cereali *m.pl.*
**cere-bellum** *n.* (anat.) cervelletto. **-bral** *adj.* cerebrale. **-brum** *n.* (anat.) cervello.
**ceremonial** *adj.* da cerimonia; solenne; *n.* cerimonia; funzione; cerimoniale *m.*; (eccl.) rituale *m.*; *court —*, etichetta di corte; protocollo.
**ceremonious** *adj.* cerimonioso; pomposo; solenne. **-ness** *n.* modi cerimoniosi; pomposità.
**ceremony** *n.* cerimonia; funzione; solennità; rito; *without —*, senza complimenti, alla buona; *to stand on —*, far complimenti; *master of ceremonies*, cerimoniere *m.*
**Ceres** *pr.n.* (myth.) Cerere.
**cerise** *adj.* rosso ciliegia.
**certain** *adj.* certo; sicuro; vero; indubitabile; *for —*, di sicuro, certamente; *he is — to come*, è certo che verrà; *to be — of*, essere certo di; *to know for —*, avere per certo, sapere di sicuro; *to make — of*, assicurarsi di; *a — man*, un tale; *of a — age*, di una certa età;

*a — something*, un certo non so che; *a — way of*, un certo determinato modo di; *it happened on a — day that*, accadde un giorno che. **-ly** *adv.* certo, certamente; senza dubbio; sicuro, sicuramente; naturalmente; già. **-ty** *n.* certezza; sicurezza; cosa certa.

**certifiable** *adj.* che si può certificare; attestabile; *— lunatic*, classificabile come pazzo.

**certificate** *n.* certificato; atto; nullaosta *m. indecl.*; diploma *m.*; (finan.) titolo; *birth —*, atto di nascita, (pop.) fede di nascita; *doctor's —*, certificato medico; *— of health*, certificato di sana costituzione; *— of good character*, certificato di buona condotta; (naut.) *master's —*, brevetto di capitano marittimo.

**certification** *n.* certificazione.

**certified** *adj.* certificato; autenticato; documentato; diplomato; *— lunatic*, classificato come pazzo, dichiarato pericoloso a se stesso e agli altri.

**certify** *tr.* certificare; attestare; affermare; constatare; autenticare; legalizzare; vidimare; *I — this a true copy*, per copia conforme; *to — a death*, constatare una morte.

**certitude** *n.* certezza; sicurezza.

**cerulean** *adj.* ceruleo.

**cervical** *adj.* (anat.) cervicale.

**cessation** *n.* cessazione; sospensione.

**cession** (leg.) cessione; rinuncia.

**cess-pit** *n.* cesso; latrina. **-pool** *n.* pozzo nero; (fig.) cloaca.

**Ceylon** *pr.n.* (geog.) Ceylon (Sri Lanka) *m.*

**chafe** *tr.* frogare; strofinare; stropicciare; massaggiare; (fig.) irritare, rendere di cattivo umore; *intr.* irritarsi, infiammarsi; logorarsi, consumarsi; *to — under restraint*, mordere il freno.

**chaff**[1] *n.* beffa; motteggio; *tr.* beffare, canzonare; dare la baia a; prendere in giro.

**chaff**[2] *n.* pula; loppa; paglia; *to separate the wheat from the —*, fare la cernita.

**chaff-cutter** *n.* trinciapaglia *m.*

**chaffer** *intr.* mercanteggiare, tirare sul prezzo.

**chaffinch** *n.* fringuello.

**chafing** *n.* irritazione; infiammazione; frizione.

**chafing-dish, -pan** *n.* scaldavivande *m. indecl.*

**chagrin** *n.* dispiacere *m.*; dispetto; fastidio; amarezza; *tr.* dar fastidio a; indispettire; amareggiare; contrariare.

**chain** *n.* catena; ceppo; *in -s*, incatenato; *to burst one's -s*, spezzare le catene; *to put a dog on the —*, mettere un cane alla catena; (motor.) catena antineve; (fig.) *— of events*, serie di avvenimenti; *— of ideas*, concatenamento di idee; *tr.* incatenare; mettere alla catena; assicurare con una catena.

**chain-armour** *n.* (hist.) corazza a maglia. **-drive** *n.* (mech.) trasmissione a catena. **-shot** *n.* (mil.) palle incatenate. **-smoker** *n.* fumatore accanito. **-stitch** *n.* punto catenella. **-stores** *n.* negozi *m.pl.* a catena.

**chair** *n.* sedia; seggio; seggiola; (University) cattedra; presidenza; *to be in the —*, presiedere; *to take a —*, sedersi; *to take the —*, assumere la presidenza; *electric —*, sedia elettrica; (rlwy.) ganascia; *tr.* portare in trionfo; *to — the meeting*, presiedere l'assemblea.

**chair-back** *n.* schienale *m.* **-lift** *n.* seggiovia. **-maker** *n.* seggiolaio.

**chairman** *n.* presidente; *Mr. —*, Signor Presidente; *to act as —*, presiedere. **-ship** *n.* presidenza.

**chaise** *n.* calesse *m.*

**chalcedony** *n.* calcedonia.

**Chaldean** *adj.*, *n.* caldeo.

**chalet** *n.* villino; casetta.

**chalice** *n.* calice *m.*; coppa.

**chalk** *n.* gesso; calcare *m.*; (art) pastello; *— cliffs*, scogli bianchi; (fam.) *he doesn't know — from cheese*, non sa niente di niente, prende lucciole per lanterne; *they are as different as — and cheese*, sono del tutto dissimili; *not by a long —*, neanche per sogno; *tr.* scrivere, segnare col gesso.

**chalk-pit** *n.* cava di calcare.

**chalky** *adj.* gessoso; calcareo; (fig.) pallido, terreo.

**challenge** *n.* sfida; (mil.) intimazione; il chi va là; (leg.) opposizione; *to accept the —*, raccogliere la sfida; (sport) *to issue a —*, sfidare, lanciare una sfida.

**challenge** *tr.* sfidare; (mil.) intimare l'alt; (leg.) opporsi a; *to — to a duel*, sfidare a duello; (fig.) *to — a statement*, mettere in dubbio un'affermazione.

**challenge-cup** *n.* trofeo; coppa.

**challeng-er** *n.* sfidatore; provocatore; (sport) sfidante *m.*, *f.* **-ing** *adj.* provocatore, sfidante.

**chamber** *n.* camera; sala; gabinetto; *— of commerce*, Camera di Commercio; (pol.) *— of Deputies*, Camera dei Deputati; *— music*, musica da camera; *pl.* studio, ufficio; appartamento.

**chambered** *adj.* diviso in compartimenti; *six-chambered revolver*, rivoltella a sei colpi.

**chamberlain** *n.* ciambellano, camerlengo.

**chambermaid** *n.* cameriera.

**chamber-pot** *n.* vaso da notte.

**chameleon** *n.* (zool.) camaleonte *m.*

**chamois** *n.* (zool.) camoscio; *— leather*, pelle *f.* di camoscio.

**champ** *tr.* mordere, masticare; *to — the bit*, mordere il freno. **-ing** *n.* masticazione.

**Champagne** *pr.n.* (geog.) Sciampagna; *n.* (vino di) sciampagna *m.*

**champion** *n.* campione *m.*; *woman —*, campionessa; *world —*, campione mondiale; (fig.) fautore, difensore; *tr.* difendere; sostenere, propugnare; perorare. **-ship** *n.* campionato.

**chance** *adj.* fortuito; casuale; accidentale; *n.* caso; fortuna; sorte *f.*; ventura; occasione; opportunità; probabilità; possibilità; rischio; azzardo; *games of —*, giuochi d'azzardo; *as — would have it*, come volle la fortuna; *by —*, per caso, per avventura, fortuitamente; *on the off — that*, nell'eventualità che, nel caso che; *I shall come and visit you, the first — I get*, verrò a trovarti alla prima occasione; *the — is that*, è probabile che; *the -s are against it*, è molto improbabile; *it's the last —*, è l'ultima speranza; *to give someone a —*, dare a qualcuno l'occasione, assumere qualcuno in prova; *to leave things to —*, andare alla ventura; *to leave nothing to —*, non arrischiarsi, andare piano; *to seize one's —*, cogliere il destro; *to stand a —*, aver una buona possibilità di riuscita; *to take no -s*, non rischiare niente, non arrischiarsi; *to trust to —*, affidarsi alla ventura.

**chance** *tr.* arrischiare; *to — it*, tentare; *to — one's luck*, tentare la fortuna; *intr.* accadere per caso; avvenire; succedere; *to — to meet*, incontrare per caso; *to — upon*, imbattersi in, incontrare per caso.

**chancel** *n.* coro; presbiterio.

**chancellery** *n.* cancelleria.

**chancellor** *n.* cancelliere *m.*; *Lord —*, Gran Cancelliere; *— of the Exchequer*, Cancelliere dello Scacchiere, (Ital. equiv.) Ministro delle Finanze; (University) Rettore titolare. **-ship** *n.* cancellierato.

**chancery** *n.* cancelleria; *a ward in —*, un minorenne sotto tutela legale.

**chancy** *adj.* incerto; rischioso; arrischiato.

**chandelier** *n.* candelabro; lampadario.

**chandler** *n.* droghiere *m.*; fornitore *m.*; *ship's —*, fornitore navale.

**change** *n.* cambio; cambiamento; mutamento; variazione; (money) spiccioli *m.pl.*; resto; *fivepence —*, cinque penny di resto; *— for a pound*, il resto di una sterlina; *for a —*, tanto per cambiare; *a — for the better*, un cambiamento in meglio; *a — of abode*, cambiamento di domicilio; *a — of linen*, un cambio di biancheria; *to ring the -s*, scampanare con varia-

zioni, (fig.) cantarla in tutti i toni; *to undergo a —*, subire un cambiamento, cambiarsi; (Stock Exchange) Borsa; (motor.) *— of gear*, cambio di velocità; (naut.) *— round*, salto di vento; (med.) *— of life*, menopausa.

**change** *tr.* cambiare; mutare; variare; cambiare, dare il resto di; (mech.) sostituire; *to — one's clothes*, cambiarsi d'abito; (motor.) *to — gear*, cambiare velocità; *to — hands*, cambiare di proprietario; *to — one's mind*, cambiare idea, ripensarci; *to — places with*, cambiare di posto con; *to — the sheets*, rinnovare le lenzuola; *to — sides*, fare voltafaccia; *to — step*, cambiare il passo; *to — the subject*, cambiare argomento, parlare d'altro; *to — one's tune*, cambiare tattica, cambiare tono; *the leopard cannot — his spots*, il lupo cambia il pelo ma non il vizio; *intr.* cambiarsi; variare; cambiare; diventare altro; *he -d completely*, diventò un altro; *to — for the better, for the worse*, cambiare in meglio, in peggio; *to chop and —*, volere e disvolere; *all change!*, si cambia!; *— here for Como!*, per Como si cambia!; (foll. by *adv.* or *prep.*) *to — about*, fare voltafaccia; variare, cambiare continuamente; (motor.) *to — down*, passare a una velocità inferiore; *to — over from one system to another*, passare da un sistema a un altro; (of sentries) darsi il cambio.

**changeab-le** *adj.* variabile; mutabile; mutevole; incostante; capriccioso. **-ility, -leness** *n.* mutevolezza; variabilità; incostanza; volubilità *f.*

**changeless** *adj.* immutevole; costante; inalterabile.

**changeling** *n.* bambino sostituito.

**change-over** *n.* cambio; cambiamento; passaggio.

**changer** *n.* cambiatore; (of money) cambiavalute *m.*; (electr.) variatore.

**changing** *adj.* cangiante; mutevole; incostante; *n.* cambio; cambiamento; *— of the guard*, cambio della guardia.

**changing-down** *n.* (motor.) passaggio a velocità inferiore. **-room** *n.* spogliatoio.

**channel** *n.* canale *m.*; stretto; (of river) alveo; (fig.) via; mezzo; (archit.) scanalatura; (telev.; aeron.) canale; (mech.) canale, condotto; *entrance —*, canale d'accesso; *-s of communication*, vie di comunicazione; *the English Channel*, la Manica; *on the other side of the Channel*, oltremanica; *the Channel Islands*, le Isole Normanne; *to forward a request through the proper -s*, trasmettere una domanda per via gerarchica; *to go through official -s*, seguire la trafila burocratica; *to open up new -s for trade*, aprire nuovi sbocchi commerciali; *tr.* scavare un canale in; (archit.) scanalare; (fig.) incanalare.

**chant** *n.* canto; salmodia; *plain —*, canto fermo; *Gregorian —*, canto gregoriano; *tr.*, *intr.* cantare; salmodiare; *to — someone's praises*, cantare le lodi di qualcuno. **-er** *n.* cantore *m.*

**chanterelle** *n.* (bot.) gallinaccio.

**chantry** *n.* cappella.

**chaos** *n.* caos *m.*; (fam.) anarchia.

**chaotic** *adj.* caotico.

**chap**[1] *n.* tipo; individuo; tizio; *young —*, ragazzo; *my dear old —*, caro mio, vecchio mio; *a — can't work all the time*, non si può lavorare tutto il tempo.

**chap**[2] *tr.* screpolare; *intr.* screpolarsi. **-ped** *part. adj.* screpolato.

**chapman** *n.* venditore ambulante.

**chapter** *n.* capitolo; (fig.) *a — of accidents*, un susseguirsi di guai; *to give — and verse*, citare capitolo e verso.

**char**[1] *n.* see **charwoman.**

**char**[2] *tr.* carbonizzare; bruciacchiare; *intr.* carbonizzarsi.

**charabanc** *n.* torpedone *m.*, pullman *m. indecl.*

**character** *n.* carattere *m.*; indole *f.*; temperamento; genere *m.*; specie *f.*; qualità; reputazione; fama; (typ.) carattere; (lit.; theatr.) personaggio; *in —*, caratteristico, vero; *to be out of — with*, non essere in carattere con; *man of no —*, uomo senza personalità; *certificate of —*, benservito, certificato di buona condotta; *to give someone a good —*, parlare bene di qualcuno; (fam.) *he's (quite) a —*, è un tipo curioso, è un originale.

**character-building** *n.* formazione del carattere. **-drawing** *n.* caratterizzazione dei personaggi.

**characteristic** *adj.* tipico; proprio; *n.* caratteristica.

**characteriz-e** *tr.* caratterizzare; definire; essere tipico di. **-ation** *n.* caratterizzazione.

**characterless** *adj.* senza carattere.

**character-part** (theatr.) macchietta.

**charade** *n.* sciarada.

**charcoal** *n.* carbone *m.* di legna, carbonella *f.*; (art) carboncino.

**charcoal-burner** *n.* carbonaio.

**charge** *n.* prezzo, costo; spesa; *at a — of*, al prezzo di; *— for admittance*, ingresso; *no — for entry*, entrata libera; *no — for packing*, imballo compreso; *free of —*, gratuito, gratis, (comm.) esente da spese; *list of -s*, tariffa; *to make a — for something*, far pagare qualcosa; conteggiare qualcosa (al prezzo di); (fig.) *to be a — on*, essere a carico di; incarico, carica; custodia, cura, sorveglianza; *person in —*, incaricato, addetto; *the duties of his —*, le sue mansioni; (mil.) *the officer in —*, il comandante; *to be in — of*, essere responsabile di, avere la sorveglianza di, dirigere, comandare; *to take — of*, prendere cura di incaricarsi di, assumere la direzione di; *child in — of a nurse*, bambino sotto la sorveglianza di una bambinaia; (leg.) accusa; *on a — of*, sotto l'accusa di; *to bring a — against*, portare un'accusa contro; *to deny a —*, discolparsi; *to give in —*, consegnare alla polizia; *to take in —*, fermare; (of gun) carica; (attack) carica, assalto; (fig.) *to return to the —*, tornare alla carica.

**charge** *tr.* far pagare; addebitare, conteggiare, mettere in conto; *to — five pounds for something*, far pagare qualcosa (al prezzo di) cinque sterline; incaricare, affidare; *to — with a commission*, incaricare di una commissione; *he was -d with the task of*, gli fu affidato il compito di; *to — someone to do something*, incaricare qualcuno di fare qualcosa; *to — oneself with*, incaricarsi di, assumersi l'incarico di; (electr.; weapons) caricare; (fig.) *to be -d with*, essere saturo di; (leg.) *to — with*, accusare di; *to — the jury*, fare l'allocuzione ai giurati; (mil.) *to — the enemy*, caricare il nemico; *intr.* (mil.) caricare (il nemico), andare all'assalto; (fam.) lanciarsi; *to — into*, imbattersi in, urtare violentemente contro.

**chargé** *n.* *— d'affaires*, incaricato d'affari.

**chargeable** *adj.* a carico di; da addebitarsi a; *damage — to you*, danni a vostro carico; *interest is — from*, gli interessi decorrono da; *— income*, reddito imponibile; (leg.) accusabile, imputabile.

**charge-account** *n.* conto corrente.

**charger**[1] *n.* vassoio.

**charger**[2] *n.* destriero.

**charger**[3] *n.* caricatore, calcatoio.

**chariness** *n.* cautela; prudenza; parsimonia.

**chariot** *n.* carro; (hist.) biga. **-eer** *n.* auriga *m.*

**charitable** *adj.* caritatevole; di carità; pietoso; benevolo; *— institution*, istituto di beneficenza, opera pia.

**charity** *n.* carità; pietà; benevolenza; *out of —*, per carità; *— organization*, istituto di beneficenza, opera pia; *— performance*, rappresentazione di beneficenza; elemosina; *to ask for —*, chiedere l'elemosina; *to live on —*, campare d'elemosina; (provb.) *— begins at home*, la carità comincia in casa propria.

**charlatan** *n.* ciarlatano; vendi-

tore di fumo. **-ism, -ry** *n.* ciarlataneria.

**Charlemagne** *pr.n.* Carlomagno.

**Charles** *pr.n.* Carlo.

**Charlotte** *pr.n.* Carlotta.

**charm** *n.* incanto; fascino; allettamento; attrattiva; *devoid of —*, privo di attrattiva; incantesimo; *pl.* vezzi *m.pl.*; talismano, amuleto, portafortuna *m. indecl.*

**charm** *tr.* incantare; affascinare; allettare; ammaliare; deliziare; *I shall be -ed*, mi farà tanto piacere, sarò felicissimo; *to — away*, scongiurare; *he has a -ed life*, ha la pelle dura. **-er** *n.* incantatore, incantatrice. **-ing** *adj.* incantevole; dilettevole; delizioso; attraente; affascinante; *Prince Charming*, il Principe Azzurro.

**charnel-house** *n.* ossario.

**Charon** *pr.n.* (myth.) Caronte.

**chart** *n.* carta; marina, carta idrografica; diagramma *m.*; grafico; *tr.* (naut.) fare la carta idrografica di, rilevare (i mari); tracciare un grafico, un diagramma, di.

**charter** *n.* statuto; carta; documento; (comm.) contratto; (naut.; aeron.) noleggio; *attrib.* a nolo, noleggiato; *tr.* concedere statuto a, istituire; (comm.; naut.; aeron.) noleggiare; *-ed accountant*, ragioniere diplomato; *-ed company*, società privilegiata.

**charter-house** *n.* (eccl.) certosa.

**chartering** *n.* noleggio.

**chart-house, chart-room** *n.* (naut.) camera delle carte, casotto di navigazione.

**chartist** *n.* (hist.) cartista *m.*

**charwoman** *n.* donna ad ore.

**chary** *adj.* prudente; cauto; circospetto; *— of doing*, poco disposto a fare; *— of praise*, avaro di lodi; *— of words*, parco di parole.

**Charybdis** *pr.n.* (myth.) Cariddi *f.*; (fig.) *to be between Scylla and —*, essere tra Scilla e Cariddi.

**chase**[1] *n.* caccia; inseguimento; *to give — to*, dare la caccia a; *wild goose —*, inseguimento vano, impresa sbagliata; *tr.* cacciare; inseguire; rincorrere; *to — away*, scacciare; *intr. to go chasing after girls*, correre dietro alle ragazze.

**chase**[2] *n.* (typ.) telaio; (jewel.) castone *m.*; *tr.* (metall.) cesellare; incidere; sbalzare; (jewel.) incastonare.

**chaser**[1] *n.* cacciatore; *woman —*, donnaiolo; (slang) bibita presa subito dopo un'altra.

**chas-er**[2] *n.* (metall.) cesellatore; incisore. **-ing** *n.* (metall.) cesellatura; (jewel.) incastonatura.

**chasm** *n.* abisso; baratro; voragine *f.*; (fig.) vuoto.

**chassis** *n.* telaio; intelaiatura.

**chaste** *adj.* casto; puro; pudico; *to pretend to be —*, (of woman) fare la casta Susanna, (of man) fare il casto Giuseppe; decente, decoroso, conveniente; austero, severo, castigato.

**chasten** *tr.* castigare; punire; correggere; (fig.) purificare; raffinare. **-ed** *adj.* abbattuto; mortificato. **-ing** *n.* castigo; punizione; mortificazione; *adj.* che mortifica.

**chastise** *tr.* castigare; correggere; punire; disciplinare. **-ment** *n.* castigo; punizione.

**chastity** *n.* (of woman) verginità; (of man) castità; celibato; (fig.) castigatezza; austerità.

**chasuble** *n.* (liturg.) pianeta.

**chat** *n.* chiacchiera, chiacchierata; *to have a —*, fare due chiacchiere; *to drop in for a —*, capitare per una breve visita; *intr.* chiacchierare; ciarlare; *tr. to — up*, piaggiare.

**château** *n.* castello; villa.

**chatelaine** *n.* castellana; padrona di casa; catenella.

**chattel** *n.* (leg.) bene, mobile *m.*; (fam.) *with all one's goods and -s*, armi e bagagli.

**chatter** *n.* ciarla; chiacchiera; diceria; (bird) cinguettio; *intr.* ciarlare; chiacchierare; cicalare; (bird) cinguettare; (teeth) battere. **-box** *n.* chiacchierone *m.*, chiacchierona *f.*; (of a child) chiacchierino.

**chatt-y** *adj.* ciarliero; loquace; garrulo. **-iness** *n.* loquacità; garrulità.

**chauffeur** *n.* autista *m.*

**chauvin-ism** *n.* sciovinismo. **-ist** *n.* sciovinista *m.* **-istic** *adj.* sciovinista.

**cheap** *adj.*, *adv.* a buon mercato, a buon prezzo, economico, poco caro; di poco valore, mediocre, scadente; (fig.) superficiale, insincero; *to be —*, costare poco; *to be -er*, costare meno; *— and nasty*, di poco valore, scadente; *dirt —*, a prezzo bassissimo; *done on the —*, fatto in economia; *— seats*, posti *m.pl.* popolari; *— tickets*, biglietti *m.pl.* a tariffa ridotta; *— trip*, gita economica, treno popolare; *to feel —*, vergognarsi; *to get off —(ly)*, cavarsela a buon mercato; *to hold —*, far poco caso di, tenere in poco conto, disprezzare; *to make oneself —*, mancare alla propria dignità.

**cheapen** *tr.* abbassare il prezzo di; (fig.) screditare; deprezzare; sottovalutare; *intr.* calare di prezzo; diminuire di valore; diventare meno caro.

**cheapness** *n.* buon mercato; basso prezzo; scarso valore; mediocrità.

**cheat** *n.* imbroglione *m.*; truffatore; (at cards) baro; *tr.*, *intr.* imbrogliare; truffare; defraudare; ingannare; (at cards) barare; *to — someone out of something*, defraudare qualcuno di qualcosa; *to — the gallows*, sfuggire alla forca. **-ing** *n.* imbroglio; truffa; frode *f.*

**check** *n.* (chess) scacco; *to give — to the King*, dare scacco al re; (pattern) scacco, qudrettino; *attrib.* a scacchi, a quadretti, a dadi; controllo; verifica; fermata; pausa; impedimento; ostacolo; gettone *m.*; *pass-out —*, contromarca; *to hold in —*, tenere in scacco; *to keep a — on*, controllare, verificare; *to keep one's feelings in —*, raffrenarsi; *to meet with a —*, subire uno scacco, incontrare un ostacolo.

**check** *tr.* (chess) dare scacco a; fermare; arrestare; contenere; domare; moderare; verificare; controllare; riscontrare; *to — the books*, verificare la contabilità; *to — one's speed*, rallentare; *to — (off) names on a list*, verificare un elenco di nomi; *to — up*, *tr.* controllare, verificare, *intr.* fare il controllo; *to — up on*, assumere informazioni su, informarsi sul conto di; *intr.* fermarsi, rallentare; *to — in* (at hotel), registrare all'arrivo.

**checked** *part. adj.* controllato, verificato; ostacolato, impedito; *adj.* quadrettato, a scacchi, a dadi.

**checker** *n.* controllore; (sport) cronometrista *m.*

**check-in** *n.* (aeron.) accettazione. **-up** *n.* verifica; controllo; (med.) *to have a -up*, farsi visitare.

**checkmate** *n.* scacco matto; *tr.* dare scacco matto a.

**cheek** *n.* guancia; gota; (mech.) ganascia; *— by jowl with*, molto vicino a, intimo di; *tongue in —*, ironicamente; sfacciataggine *f.*, faccia, tosta; *I like your —!*, sei proprio sfacciato!; (naut., of block) alone *m.*; *tr.* (fam.) insolentire, fare l'insolente con.

**cheekbone** *n.* zigomo, pomello.

**cheeky** *adj.* sfrontato, sfacciato.

**cheep** *n.* pigolìo; *intr.* pigolare.

**cheer** *n.* allegria; buon umore; *to be of good —*, stare allegro; *-s!*, salute!; (fam.) *what —?*, come vai?; cibo; trattamento; vivande *f.pl.*; *plenty of good —*, una tavola bene imbandita; applauso, acclamazione *f.*; *to give a —*, gridare evviva; *three -s!*, evviva!, un triplice urrà!

**cheer** *tr.* rallegrare; incoraggiare; animare; confortare; acclamare; applaudire; *intr.* applaudire; *tr. to — on*, incitare; *to — up*, *tr.* confortare, incoraggiare, *intr.* rallegrarsi, riprendere coraggio; *— up!*, su, allegro!

**cheerful** *adj.* allegro; lieto; gaio; di buon umore; *there's not much to be — about*, c'è poco da stare allegri; *to keep —*, stare sempre allegro; *to look —*, avere l'aria

allegra. **-ness** *n.* allegrezza, allegria; buon umore; coraggio.
**cheeriness** *n.* buon umore; allegria; espansività.
**cheering** *adj.* consolante; incoraggiante; *n.* applausi *m.pl.*; evviva *m.pl.*; acclamazioni *f.pl.*
**cheerio** (fam.) ciao; arrivederci.
**cheer-leader** *n.* direttore della claque.
**cheerless** *adj.* triste; malinconico; tetro; squallido. **-ness** *n.* tristezza.
**cheers** *excl.* salute!
**cheery** *adj.* gaio; allegro; di buon umore.
**cheese**[1] *n.* formaggio; cacio; *a* —, una forma di formaggio; *cream* —, formaggino, formaggio di crema; *Dutch* —, formaggio olandese; *grated* —, formaggio grattugiato; *toasted* —, tosto al formaggio; (fig.) *to believe the moon is made of green* —, prendere lucciole per lanterne.
**cheese**[2] *tr.* (fam.) — *it!*, smettila!
**cheese-biscuit** *n.* salatino. **-cake** *n.* pasta regina, torta di formaggio. **-cloth** *n.* garza.
**cheesed** *adj.* (fam.) — *off*, stufo.
**cheese-dairy** *n.* caseificio. **-hopper** *n.* verme del formaggio. **-monger** *n.* formaggiaio. **-paring** *adj.* spilorcio, tirchio; *n.* crosta di formaggio; (fig.) parsimonia, lesineria.
**cheetah** *n.* (zool.) ghepardo.
**chef** *n.* capocuoco.
**chef-d'œuvre** *n.* capolavoro.
**chemical** *adj.* chimico; *n.* prodotto chimico.
**chemist** *n.* chimico; (druggist) farmacista *m.*; *dispensing* —, farmacista diplomato; *-'s shop*, farmacia.
**chemistry** *n.* chimica.
**chenille** *n.* ciniglia.
**cheque** *n.* assegno (bancario); — *to order*, assegno all'ordine; — *to bearer*, assegno al portatore; *blank* —, assegno in bianco; *crossed* —, assegno sbarrato; *dud* —, assegno a vuoto; *traveller's* —, assegno per viaggiatori; *to cash a* —, cambiare un assegno; *to pay by* —, pagare a mezzo assegno.
**cheque-book** *n.* libretto d'assegni.
**chequer** *n.* scacco, quadretto. **-ed** *adj.* quadrettato, a scacchi; (fig.) movimentato; vario.
**cherish** *tr.* nutrire; serbare; accarezzare; amare, aver caro, curare teneramente; *to* — *a grudge against*, nutrire risentimento contro; *to* — *the memory of*, serbare il ricordo di.
**cheroot** *n.* sigaro spuntato.
**cherry** *n.* ciliegia; — (*tree*), ciliego.
**cherry-brandy** *n.* cerasella.
**cherub** *n.* cherubino; (fam.) angioletto; (art) putto. **-ic** *adj.* di cherubino.
**chervil** *n.* (bot.) cerfoglio.
**chess** *n.* scacchi *m.pl.*; *a game of* —, una partita a scacchi; *to play* —, giuocare a scacchi; (bldg.) asse *f.* **-board** *n.* scacchiera. **-man** *n.* pezzo degli scacchi; *a set of -men*, un giuoco di scacchi.
**chest** *n.* cassa; cofano; forziere *m.*; cassapanca; cassone *m.*; *small* —, cassetta; (anat.) petto; torace *m.*; (fam.) *to get something off one's* —, sfogarsi; *to throw out one's* —, camminare impettito.
**chestnut** *adj.* di castagno; (colour) castagno; (of horse) sauro; *n.* castagna; marrone *m.*; (tree) castagno; (fig.) *an old* —, una storiella risaputa.
**chestnut-grove** *n.* castagneto.
**chest-of-drawers** *n.* cassettone *m.*
**chesty** *adj.* delicato di bronchi.
**cheval-glass** *n.* psiche *f.*
**chevron** *n.* (mil.) gallone *m.*; (archit.) puntone *m.*; (herald.) scaglione *m.*; capriolo.
**chew** *tr.* masticare; *to* — *the cud*, ruminare; (fig.) *to* — *over*, meditare; *to bite off more than one can* —, fare il passo più lungo della gamba; *n.* masticazione; — *of tobacco*, cicca. **-ing** *n.* masticazione.
**chewing-gum** *n.* gomma da masticare; chewing-gum *m.*
**chic** *adj.* elegante; alla moda; snob; *n.* eleganza; distinzione.
**chicane** *n.* artificio; inganno; cavillo.
**chicken** *n.* pollo; pollastro; pulcino; (cul.) *roast* —, pollo arrosto; *spring* —, pollo novello; (fig.) *she's no* —, non è più tanto giovane; *don't count your -s before they are hatched*, non dire quattro finchè non l'hai nel sacco; (orn.) *Mother Carey's* —, procellaria; *adj.* (slang) timido; *intr.* (slang) *to* — *out*, ritirarsi pauroso.
**chicken-coop** *n.* pollaio. **-farming** *n.* allevamento di polli. **-feed** *n.* cibo per polli; (fig.) bagatella; una miseria. **-hearted** *adj.* timido, pauroso. **-pox** *n.* varicella; vaiuolo spurio, morbiglione *m.*
**chick-pea** *n.* cece *m.*
**chickweed** *n.* (bot.) centonchio, alsina.
**chicory** *n.* (bot.) cicoria.
**chide** *tr.* sgridare; rampognare; rimproverare; *intr.* brontolare.
**chief** *adj.* capo; principale; primo; primario; il più importante; supremo; sommo; *the* — *thing is*, la cosa più importante è; *n.* capo; principale *m.*; superiore *m.*; (mil.) comandante *m.*; (fam.) padrone *m.*; capo; *in* —, in capo; — *clerk*, capo ufficio; — *constable*, questore *m.*; — *rabbi*, gran rabbino; — *surgeon*, primario; — *town*, capoluogo. **-ly** *adv.* soprattutto; principalmente.
**chieftain** *n.* capo.
**chiffonier** *n.* stipo a cassettini.
**chilblain** *n.* gelone *m.*
**child** *n.* bambino; ragazzo; fanciullo; figlio; figlia; *male* —, maschio; *female* —, femmina; *adopted* —, figlio adottivo; *firstborn* —, figlio primogenito; *foster* —, figlio di latte; *illegitimate* —, figlio naturale, illegittimo; *only* —, figlio unico; *problem* —, bambino difficile; *from a* —, fin da bambino; *be a good* —*!*, sta' buono!, su, da bravo!; *to be with* —, essere incinta; *to treat like a* —, trattare da bambino; *pl.* bambini, ragazzi; figli, figliuolanza; prole *f.*; *they have four -ren, two boys and two girls*, hanno quattro figli, due maschi e due femmine.
**child-bearing** *n.* gravidanza. **-birth** *n.* parto; *woman in -birth*, puerpera.
**childhood** *n.* infanzia; fanciullezza; — *friend*, amico d'infanzia; *second* —, seconda infanzia, senilità; *an old man in his second* —, un vecchio rimbambito.
**childish** *adj.* bambinesco; puerile; infantile; fanciullesco; senile, rimbambito; *don't be so* —*!*, non fare il bambino!; *to grow* —, rimbambire. **-ly** *adv.* da bambino. **-ness** *n.* puerilità; fanciullaggine *f.*; senilità *f.*
**childless** *adj.* senza figli, senza prole. **-ness** *n.* il non aver figli; sterilità.
**childlike** *adj.* infantile, da bambino; semplice, innocente.
**child-murder** *n.* infanticidio.
**child's-play** *n.* giuoco da bambini; compito facile; *it is mere* — *for him*, per lui è un giuoco.
**child-welfare** *n.* puericultura.
**Chil-e** *pr.n.* (geog.) Il Cile. **-ean, -ian** *adj.* cileno, del Cile; *n.* cileno, cilena.
**chill** *adj.* freddo; gelido; *the wind blows* —, soffia un vento gelido; *to run* —, agghiacciarsi; *n.* freddo; brivido; *a* — *came over me*, mi sono sentito rabbrividire; *to catch a* —, buscarsi un raffreddore; *to take the* — *off*, intiepidire, riscaldare; *tr.* raffreddare: gelare; agghiacciare; mettere freddo a; *to be -ed to the bone*, essere gelato fino alla midolla; congelare; (metall.) temprare.
**chilli** *n.* (bot.) peperone rosso; — *pepper*, pepe *m.* di Caienna.
**chill-y** *adj.* freddo; fresco; freddoloso; *it's* —, fa fresco; *to feel* —, aver freddo, rabbrividire; *a* — *reception*, un'accoglienza glaciale. **-iness** *n.* freddo; (fig.) freddezza. **-ing** *adj.* glaciale; gelido; agghiacciato.
**chime** *n.* scampanìo; cariglione *m.*; suoneria di campane; rintocchi *m.pl.*; *to ring the -s*, scampanare, suonare a festa; *tr.* scampanare; suonare; *to* — *the hour*, suonare le ore; *intr.* suonare; rintoccare; (fig.) *to* — *in*,

intervenire nella discussione; *to — in with*, associarsi a.
**chimer-a** *n.* (myth.) chimera; (fig.) illusione. **-ical** *adj.* chimerico; illusorio.
**chimney** *n.* camino; focolare *m.*; ciminiera; fumaiuolo; tubo; (fig.) *to smoke like a —*, fumare come un turco; (mountaineering) camino, diedro.
**chimney-corner** *n.* angolo del focolare. **-flue** *n.* gola del camino. **-piece** *n.* mensola del camino. **-pot** *n.* comignolo. **-stack** *n.* fumaiuolo, ciminiera. **-sweep** *n.* spazzacamino.
**chimpanzee** *n.* (zool.) scimpanzè *m. indecl.*
**chin** *n.* mento; *receding —*, mento sfuggente; *up to the —*, fino alla gola; *keep your — up!*, coraggio!
**China**[1] *pr.n.* (geog.) Cina.
**china**[2] *n.* porcellana; ceramica.
**china-clay** *n.* caolino.
**china-man** *n.* cinese *m.* **-town** *n.* quartiere cinese. **-ware** *n.* porcellana.
**chinchilla** *n.* cincilla, cinciglia.
**chine**[1] *n.* (anat.) spina dorsale; (cul.) lombata.
**chine**[2] *n.* (geog.) burrone *m.*; gola.
**Chinese** *adj.*, *n.* cinese *m.*, *f.*; *— lantern*, lampioncino alla veneziana; *— puzzle*, rompicapo cinese.
**chink**[1] *n.* fessura; crepa; apertura; interstizio.
**chink**[2] *n.* tintinnìo; *tr.* far tintinnare; *intr.* tintinnare.
**chinless** *adj.* dal mento sfuggente.
**chin-rest** *n.* (mus.) mentoniera *f.*
**chinstrap** *n.* sottogola *m. indecl.*, soggolo.
**chintz** *n.* indiana; tela di cotone stampata.
**chip** *n.* scheggia; truciolo; scaglia; (gambling) gettone *m.*; *he is a — off the old block*, è proprio figlio di suo padre; (cul.) *— potatoes*, patatine fritte; *fish and -s*, pesce fritto con patatine; (finan.) *blue -s*, titoli *m.pl.* sicuri.
**chip** *tr.* scheggiare; truciolare; scagliare; (fig.) canzonare; *to — a piece off*, staccare un pezzetto da; *to — off*, martellare via; *intr.* scheggiarsi; *to — in on*, intervenire in, intrufolarsi in, mettere il becco in.
**chipmunk** *n.* (zool.) tamiasciuro.
**chiromancy** *n.* chiromanzia.
**chiropodist** *n.* pedicure, callista *m.*
**chirp** *n.* cinguettìo, pigolìo; cicalìo, stridìo; *intr.* cinguettare; pigolare; cantare; frinire, stridere; (fig.) *to — up*, cominciare a parlare; rallegrarsi.
**chirp-y** *adj.* gaio; allegro. **-iness** *n.* umore gaio; allegria.
**chisel** *n.* cesello; scalpello; bulino; subbia; *tr.* cesellare; scalpellare; bulinare; (fig.) imbrogliare.
**chit**[1] *n.* biglietto; nota.
**chit**[2] *n.* marmocchio; donnetta.
**chit-chat** *n.* chiacchiera; cicaleccio.
**chitterlings** *n.* (cul.) frattaglia; rigaglie *f.pl.*
**chivalr-ous** *adj.* cavalleresco; cortese; galante. **-ry** *n.* condotta cavalleresca; cortesia; galanteria; (hist.) cavalleria.
**chive** *n.* (bot.) erba cipollina, cipolla porraia.
**chiv(v)y** *tr.* cacciare, inseguire, aizzare.
**chlor-ate** *n.* (chem.) clorato. **-hydrate** *n.* cloridrato. **-ic** *adj.* clorico. **-ide** *n.* cloruro. **-ine** *n.* cloruro. **-ite** *n.* clorito. **-odyne** *n.* clorodina.
**chloroform** *n.* cloroformio; *tr.* cloroformizzare.
**chlorophyll** *n.* (bot.) clorofilla.
**chlor-osis** *n.* (med.) clorosi *f.* **-otic** *adj.* clorotico.
**chock** *n.* cuneo; zeppa; tassello di legno; (naut.) passacavi *m. indecl.*; (of boat) morsa.
**chock-a-block, chock-full** *adj.* pieno zeppo, ricolmo.
**chocolate** *adj.* di cioccolato; color cioccolato; *n.* cioccolato, cioccolatino; *a bar of —*, una tavoletta di cioccolato; *a box of -s*, una scatola di cioccolatini.
**chocolate-maker** *n.* cioccolattiere *m.*
**choice** *adj.* scelto; squisito; di prima qualità; *n.* scelta; elezione; (comm.) assortimento; *Hobson's —*, scelta forzata; *the country of my —*, la mia patria d'elezione; *for —*, di preferenza; *without —*, senza alternativa; *there is no —*, non c'è alternativa; *from —* volentieri; *to have no — but to . . .*, non poter che . . .; *to take one's —*, scegliere, fare la scelta. **-ness** *n.* squisitezza, finezza.
**choir** *n.* coro.
**choir-book** *n.* corale *m.*
**choir-boy** *n.* corista *m.*; cantorino. **-master** *n.* maestro di cappella.
**choir-screen** *n.* chiudenda del coro. **-stalls** *n.* scanni *m.pl.*
**choke** *n.* soffocamento; accesso di soffocazione; strozzatura; *with a — in one's voice*, con voce strozzata; (mech.) strozzamento; ingorgo.
**choke** *tr.* togliere il respiro a; strozzare; soffocare; ostruire; ingombrare; ingorgare; *to — back*, trattenere; reprimere; *to — down*, trattenere, frenare, ingoiare; *to — off*, sbarazzarsi di, allontanare; *to — up*, ingombrare, ostruire completamente; *intr.* soffocarsi; strozzarsi.
**choky** *adj.* soffocante; *in a — voice*, con voce soffocata.
**choler** *n.* collera; bile *f.* **-ic** *adj.* collerico; irascibile.
**cholera** *n.* (med.) colera *m.*
**choose** *tr.* scegliere; eleggere; fare la scelta di; optare per; decidersi per; volere, preferire; *many are called but few are chosen*, molti sono i chiamati, ma pochi gli eletti; *to — from*, scegliere fra; *there is nothing to — between them*, l'uno vale l'altro; *I cannot but — to do so*, non ho altra alternativa; *he cannot — but obey*, non ha altra scelta che ubbidire; *he didn't — to go*, non ha voluto andare; *as you —*, come vuoi; *— for yourself*, lascio a te la scelta; *whether you — or not*, volente o nolente; *to pick and —*, scegliere meticolosamente, fare il pignolo.
**choos-er** *n.* chi sceglie; sceglitore; (provb.) *beggars can't be -ers*, o mangiar questa minestra o saltar quella finestra. **-ing** *n.* scelta; atto di scegliere; *the difficulty of -ing*, l'imbarazzo della scelta; *it was none of my -ing*, non l'ho mica voluto io. **-y** *adj.* pignolo.
**chop**[1] *n.* colpo di accetta; (cul.) braciola; (sport) taglio; *tr.* tagliare; tagliuzzare; spaccare; tritare; *to — away*, tagliar via, troncare; *to — down*, abbattere; *to — off*, recidere; *to — up*, sminuzzare; *to — logic*, cavillare; *intr.* *to — and change*, fare e disfare, volere e disvolere.
**chop**[2] (jaw) mascella; *to lick one's -s*, leccarsi i baffi. **-house** *n.* taverna.
**chopper** *n.* accetta; (butcher's) mannaia.
**chopping-block** *n.* tagliere *m.*
**choppy** *adj.* increspato; (naut.) *— sea*, maretta, mare corto.
**chopsticks** *n.* bastoncini *m.pl.*, bacchette *f.pl.* (per mangiare alla cinese); (fam.) scherzo da bambini da suonare al pianoforte.
**choral** *adj.* corale.
**chorale** *n.* corale *m.*
**chord** *n.* (mus.) accordo; (of instrument) corda; (anat., geom.) corda; (fig.) *to touch the right —*, toccare il tasto giusto.
**chore** *n.* lavoro; *pl.* (fam.) faccende domestiche.
**chorea** *n.* (med.) corea, ballo di San Vito.
**choreograph-er** *n.* coreografo. **-ic** *adj.* coreografico. **-y** *n.* coreografia.
**chorister** *n.* corista *m.*, *f.*
**chortle** *n.* riso represso; *intr.* ridacchiare.
**chorus** *n.* coro; (of song) ritornello; *to sing in —*, cantare in coro; *to join in the —*, cantare il ritornello in coro, (fig.) fare coro, fare eco; *intr.* fare coro, cantare in coro.
**chorus-girl** *n.* corista *f.*; ballerina di fila.
**chose** *p. def.* of **choose**, *q.v.*
**chosen** *part.* of **choose**, *q.v.*; *adj.* scelto; eletto; *the — people*, il

popolo eletto; *the — few*, gli eletti.
**chough** *n.* (orn.) gracchio.
**chow** *n.* (dog) chow(-chow) *m. indecl.*; (cul.) conserva di zenzero.
**chrestomathy** *n.* crestomazia.
**chrism** *n.* (liturg.) crisma *m.*
**Christ** *pr.n.* Cristo; *the Infant —*, Gesù bambino.
**Christabel** *pr.n.* Cristabella.
**christen** *tr.* battezzare; (joc.) soprannominare. **-ing** *n.* battesimo.
**Christendom** *n.* cristianità.
**Christian** *adj.*, *n.* cristiano; credente *m.*, *f.*; *to become a —*, farsi cristiano, cristianizzarsi; *— name*, nome *m.* di battesimo; (pol.) *— democrat*, democristiano. **-ity** *n.* cristianesimo. **-ize** *tr.* cristianizzare.
**Christine** *pr.n.* Cristina.
**Christlike** rassomigliante a Cristo; (fig.) evangelico.
**Christmas** *n.* Natale *m.*; *happy —!*, buon Natale!; *— Day*, giorno di Natale; *— Eve*, vigilia di natale; *— card*, cartoncino natalizio; *— present*, strenna natalizia, regalo di Natale; *— carol*, canto natalizio; *— pudding*, budino natalizio, budino all'inglese; *— tree*, albero di Natale.
**Christmas-box** *n.* gratifica natalizia.
**Christopher** *pr.n.* Cristoforo.
**chromatic** *adj.* cromatico.
**chrome, chromium** *n.* (chem.) cromo; *attrib.* cromato, al cromo.
**chromium-plated** *adj.* al cromo, cromato. **-plating** *n.* cromatura.
**chromosome** *n.* (biol.) cromosoma *m.*
**chronic** *adj.* cronico. **-ity** *n.* cronicità.
**chronicle** *n.* cronaca; (bibl.) *Chronicles*, I Paralipomeni; *tr.* registrare; raccontare; fare la cronaca di. **-r** *n.* cronista *m.*
**chronological** *adj.* cronologico.
**chronology** *n.* cronologia.
**chronomet-er** *n.* cronometro. **-ric(al)** *adj.* cronometrico.
**chrysal-id, -is** *n.* crisalide *f.*
**chrysanthemum** *n.* (bot.) crisantemo.
**chryso-lite** *n.* (miner.) crisolito. **-prase** *n.* (miner.) crisoprazio.
**chub** *n.* (ichth.) leucisco.
**chubb-y** *adj.* paffuto; grassoccio. **-iness** *n.* paffutezza.
**chuck**[1] *n.* (lathe) mandrino.
**chuck**[2] *tr.* buttare; gettare; lanciare; tirare; (fam.) *— it!*, finiscila!, basta!; *to — under the chin*, dare un buffetto sotto il mento a; *to — one's hand in*, rinunciare, darsi per vinto, gettare la spugna; *to — away*, sperperare, buttar via; *to — out*, mettere alla porta, buttar fuori; *to — up*, rinunciare a, (fam.) piantare; lanciare in aria.
**chuckle** *n.* riso basso; *intr.* ridacchiare, ridere sotto i baffi.
**chug** *intr.* (of locomotive) sbuffare; (fig.) *to — along*, tirare avanti.
**chum** *n.* compagno; amico; camerata *m.*; *intr. to — up with*, fare amicizia con.
**chump** *n.* ceppo; ciocco; (fig.) stupido, testa di legno; *to be off one's —*, essere un po' matto; (cul.) *— chop*, braciola di montone.
**chunk** *n.* fetta; grosso pezzo.
**church** *n.* chiesa; (Protestant) tempio; clero; *attrib.* ecclesiastico, religioso; *Established Church*, chiesa di stato, religione ufficiale; *the Church of England*, la chiesa anglicana; *the Church of Scotland*, la chiesa presbiteriana scozzese; *the Roman Catholic Church*, la Chiesa Cattolica Romana, *— history*, storia ecclesiastica; *— service*, ufficio divino; *to go to —*, andare in chiesa; *poor as a — mouse*, povero in canna.
**church-goer** *n.* praticante *m.*, *f.*; fedele *m.*, *f.*; devoto. **-going** *n.* pratica religiosa. **-ing** *n.* purificazione. **-man** *n.* uomo di chiesa; ecclesiastico. **-warden** *n.* fabbriciere *m.*; *-warden pipe*, lunga pipa di argilla. **-yard** *n.* cimitero; camposanto; sagrato.
**churl** *n.* villano; zoticone *m.* **-ish** *adj.* burbero; aspro; rozzo. **-ishness** *n.* asprezza; rustichezza; zotichezza.
**churn** *n.* zangola; *tr.* zangolare, fare nella zangola; (fig.) agitare, sbattere; *intr.* ribollire.
**chute** *n.* cascata; tela a scivolo; (mech.) scivolo.
**ciborium** *n.* (liturg.) ciborio.
**cicada, cicala** *n.* (ent.) cicala.
**cicatr-ix** *n.* (med.) cicatrice *f.* **-ize** *tr.* cicatrizzare; *intr.* cicatrizzarsi.
**Cicer-o** *pr.n.* Cicerone. **-onian** *adj.* ciceroniano.
**cider** *n.* sidro.
**cigar** *n.* sigaro.
**cigar-case** *n.* portasigari *m. indecl.* **-cutter** *n.* tagliasigari *m. indecl.*
**cigarette** *n.* sigaretta. **-case** *n.* portasigarette *m. indecl.* **-end** *n.* mozzicone *m.* **-holder** *n.* bocchino. **-lighter** *n.* accendisigaro *m.*, accenditore automatico.
**cigar-shaped** *adj.* a forma di sigaro.
**cinder** *n.* brace *f.*; cenere *f.*; (metall.) scoria; *burnt to a —*, carbonizzato; *— track*, pista di cenere.
**Cinderella** *pr.n.* Cenerentola.
**cine-camera** *n.* macchina da presa.
**cinema** *n.* cinema *m.*
**cinematograph** *n.* cinematografo. **-ic** *adj.* cinematografico. **-er** *n.* operatore cinematografico.
**cinerary** *adj.* cinerario, cenerario.
**Cingalese** *adj.*, *n.* singalese, cingalese *m.*, *f.*
**cinnabar** *n.* (chem.) cinabro; (paint.) cinabrese *m.*
**cinnamon** *n.* (bot.) cannella; cinnamomo.
**cinquefoil** *n.* (archit.) pentalobo; (bot.) cinquefoglie *m.*
**cipher, cypher** *n.* (math.) zero; (fig.) nullità, uomo di paglia; cifra; crittografia, cifrario, scrittura convenzionale; *tr.* cifrare, trasmettere in cifra; calcolare, conteggiare.
**Circassian** *adj.*, *n.* circasso.
**Circe** *pr.n.* (myth.) Circe.
**circle** *n.* cerchio; circolo; anello; alone *m.*; *vicious —*, circolo vizioso; *to come full —*, ritornare al punto di partenza; ambiente *m.*, sfera; ambito; cerchia; *family —*, ambito familiare; (theatr.) *dress —*, prima galleria; *upper —*, seconda galleria.
**circle** *tr.* accerchiare, cingere; girare intorno a; (aeron.) *to — an airfield*, volteggiare sopra un campo di aviazione; *intr.* girare; (aeron.) volteggiare.
**circlet** *n.* cerchietto; anello.
**circuit** *n.* circuito; giro; (leg.) circoscrizione; (electr.) *short —*, corto circuito. **-ous** *adj.* tortuoso; indiretto.
**circular** *adj.* circolare; *n.* circolare *f.*; volantino. **-ity** *n.* forma circolare.
**circularize** *tr.* inviare circolari a.
**circulat-e** *tr.* far circolare; mettere in circolazione; *intr.* circolare; girare. **-ing** *adj.* circolante; (math.) *-ing decimal*, decimale periodica. **-ion** *n.* circolazione; diffusione; tiratura; *to put in -ion*, emettere.
**circumcis-e** *tr.* circoncidere. **-ion** *n.* circoncisione.
**circumference** *n.* circonferenza; ambito.
**circumflex** *adj.*, *n.* circonflesso.
**circumlocu-tion** *n.* circonlocuzione; ambagi *f.pl.*; perifrasi *f.* **-tory** *adj.* perifrastico; involuto.
**circum-navigate** *tr.* circumnavigare. **-scribe** *tr.* circoscrivere. **-spect** *adj.* circospetto; cauto; riguardoso; guardingo. **-spection** *n.* circospezione; cautela.
**circumstance** *n.* circostanza; particolare *m.*; dettaglio; fatto, circostanza; condizioni *f.pl.*; situazione; *pomp and —*, pompa e cerimonia; (leg.) *extenuating -s*, circostanze *f.pl.* attenuanti.
**circumstantial** *adj.* accidentale; circostanziato, dettagliato, particolareggiato; (leg.) *— evidence*, prove indiziarie indirette.
**circumvallation** *n.* circonvallazione.
**circumvent** *tr.* circonvenire; aggirare; prevenire; ingannare.

-**ion** *n.* circonvenzione; aggiramento; raggiro.
**circumvolution** *n.* circonvoluzione.
**circus** *n.* circo; agone *m.*; arena; crocicchio; largo.
**cirrhosis** *n.* (med.) cirrosi *f.*; — *of the liver*, cirrosi epatica.
**cirrus** *n.* cirro.
**Cisalpine** *adj.* cisalpino.
**Cistercian** *adj.*, *n.* (eccl.) cisterc(i)ense *m.*
**cistern** *n.* cisterna; serbatoio; vasca.
**citadel** *n.* cittadella; rocca; (fig.) roccaforte *f.*
**citation** *n.* citazione.
**cite** *tr.* citare; addurre.
**citizen** *n.* cittadino, cittadina; *pl.* cittadinanza. **-ship** *n.* cittadinanza; nazionalità; *good -ship*, civismo.
**citr-ate** *n.* (chem.) citrato. **-ic** *adj.* citrico.
**citron** *n.* (bot.) cedro; (colour) color limone.
**citrus** *n.* (bot.) agrume *m.*
**city** *n.* città *f. indecl.* centro; *the Vatican* —, la Città del Vaticano; — *man*, uomo d'affari; — *editor*, redattore finanziario; — *hall*, municipio.
**civet** *n.* (zool.) zibetto.
**civic** *adj.* civico; municipale.
**civil** *adj.* civile; — *war*, guerra civile; — *servant*, funzionario statale, impiegato governativo, (pop.) statale *m.*,*f.*; *the — Service*, l'amministrazione statale; — *engineering*, ingegneria civile; cortese, gentile, educato, civile; (fam.) *to keep a — tongue in one's head*, parlare come si deve. **-ity** *n.* cortesia; civiltà; gentilezza; educazione.
**civilian** *n.* civile *m.*, *f.*; borghese *m.*, *f.*; *in — clothes*, in borghese.
**civiliz-e** *tr.* civilizzare; incivilire. **-ation** *n.* civiltà; civilizzazione; incivilimento. **-ed** *adj.* civilizzato; civile; (fam.) da cristiani; *to become -ed*, incivilirsi. **-ing** *adj.* civilizzatore.
**clack** *n.* schiocco; suono secco; (mech.) — *valve*, valvola ad animella; *tr.* far schioccare; *intr.* schioccare; (fig.) ciarlare.
**clad** *adj.* vestito.
**claim** *n.* diritto; titolo; rivendicazione; reclamo; pretesa; *to have a — on*, avere dei diritti da esigere da; *to have a — to*, avere diritto a; *to lay — to*, reclamare, pretendere; *to lodge a* —, inoltrare un reclamo; *to put forward a* —, accampare un diritto.
**claim** *tr.* chiedere; esigere; rivendicare; pretendere; attribuirsi; arrogarsi; *to — acquaintance with*, pretendere di conoscere; *to — damages*, chiedere il risarcimento dei danni; *to — one's due*, rivendicare i propri diritti; *to — back*, chiedere la restituzione di.
**claimant** *n.* richiedente *m.*, *f.*; rivendicatore; *rightful* —, l'avente *m.*, *f.* diritto.
**clairvoy-ance** *n.* chiaroveggenza. **-ant** *n.* chiaroveggente *m.*, *f.*
**clam** *n.* mollusco, mitilo, cozza.
**clamant** *adj.* insistente, pressante; rumoroso.
**clamber** *n.* arrampicata; *intr.* arrampicarsi (su), abbriccarsi; *to — over*, scavalcare.
**clamm-y** *n.* viscido, umidiccio, molliccio. **-iness** *n.* viscosità; mollore *m.*; umidità.
**clamorous** *adj.* clamoroso; strepitoso; rumoroso.
**clamour** *n.* clamore *m.*; strepito; vocio; schiamazzo; *intr.* gridare; strepitare; vociferare; *to — for*, chiedere a gran voce.
**clamp** *n.* morsa; morsetto; grappa; ganascia; graffa; *tr.* rinforzare con morsetti; assicurare con graffe; (fam.) *to — down*, smettere; *to — down on*, far cessare.
**clan** *n.* 'clan' *m. indecl.*; (fig.) cricca.
**clandestine** *adj.* clandestino.
**clang** *n.* clangore *m.*; fragore *m.*; *intr.* strepitare; produrre un suono metallico.
**clank** *n.* clangore *m.*; suono metallico; *tr.* far risuonare; *intr.* suonare; produrre un suono metallico.
**clap**[1] *n.* colpo; colpetto; *a — of thunder*, un colpo di tuono; *a — on the shoulder*, un colpetto sulla spalla; battimano, applauso; *tr.* battere; *to — one's hands*, battere le mani; *to — on the back*, dare una manata sulla spalla a; *to — on one's hat*, ficcarsi il cappello in testa; *to — into prison*, sbattere in prigione; applaudire.
**clap**[2] *n.* (slang) gonorrea.
**clapboard** *n.* (bldg.) assicella.
**clapper** *n.* battaglio, batacchio, batocchio, battola; raganella; (theatr.) applauditore, membro della claque.
**clapping** *n.* applausi *m.pl.*; battimano.
**claptrap** *n.* discorso demagogico; sproloquio.
**Clara, Clare** *pr.n.* Clara, Chiara.
**claret** *n.* (wine) bordò *m.*; chiaretto; (colour) rosso-violetto.
**clarif-y** *tr.* chiarificare, chiarire; raffinare, depurare; (leg.) acclarare. **-ication** *n.* chiarificazione; schiarimento.
**clarinet** *n.* clarinetto. **-tist** *n.* clarinettista *m.*, *f.*
**clarion** *n.* chiarina; trombetta; *attrib.* sonoro.
**clarity** *n.* chiarezza; chiarità.
**clash** *n.* cozzo; urto; collisione; strepito; rumore *m.*; (fig.) scontro; contrasto; *intr.* cozzarsi; urtarsi; scontrarsi; *tr.* percuotere. **-ing** *adj.* stridente; strepitoso; (fig.) contrastante, opposto; *n.* percossa.
**clasp** *n.* fermaglio; gancio; fibbia; abbraccio; amplesso; stretta; *tr.* agganciare; affibbiare; abbracciare; stringere; *with -ed hands*, a mani giunte.
**clasp-knife** *n.* coltello a serramanico.
**class** *n.* classe *f.*; categoria; ceto; corso; *the upper -es*, l'aristocrazia, i benestanti *m.pl.*; *the middle* —, il ceto medio, la borghesia; *upper middle* —, alta borghesia; *lower middle* —, piccola borghesia; *the lower -es*, il popolo, la plebe; — *war*, lotta di classe; (fig.) qualità; distinzione; (fam.) *no* —, piuttosto volgare; *he's in a — on his own*, è un fuori classe; *tr.* classificare; annoverare.
**class-conscious** *adj.* borioso, altero.
**classic** *n.* classico; *pl.* studi *m.pl.* classici; umanità *f.pl.*; *adj.* classico. **-al** *adj.* classico. **-ism** *n.* classicismo. **-ist** *n.* classicista *m.*, *f.*
**classif-y** *tr.* classificare; annoverare. **-iable** *adj.* classificabile. **-ied** *adj.* classificato; annoverato; confidenziale; *-ied document*, documento segreto.
**classing** *n.* classificazione.
**class-list** *n.* elenco di laureati. **-mate** *n.* compagno di classe.
**classroom** *n.* aula.
**classy** *adj.* distinto; di classe.
**clatter** *n.* acciottolio; (fig.) fracasso; chiasso; *tr.* acciottolare; far risuonare; *intr.* far fracasso, camminare rumorosamente.
**Claud(ius)** *pr.n.* Claudio.
**clause** *n.* (gramm.) clausola; proposizione; articolo; comma *m.*; paragrafo; *escape* —, clausola scappatoia; *restrictive* —, vincolo obbligatorio.
**claustral** *adj.* (eccl.) claustrale.
**claustrophobia** *n.* claustrofobia.
**clavate** *adj.* (bot.) claviforme.
**clavichord** *n.* (mus.) clavicordio.
**clavicle** *n.* (anat.) clavicola.
**claw** *n.* artiglio; unghia; chela; branca; (mech.) uncino, graffa; (fig.) *to get one's -s into*, attanagliare; *tr.* artigliare; aggraffare; adunghiare; attanagliare; dilaniare con gli artigli; (fig.) agguantare; (sculp.) gradinare; *intr. to — at*, cercare di agguantare.
**clay** *n.* argilla; creta; terra. **-ey** *adj.* argilloso.
**clay-pigeon** *n.* piattello.
**clean** *adj.* pulito; nitido; netto; (fig.) puro; mondo; — *hands*, mani pulite; — *linen*, biancheria di bucato; — *bill of health*, certificato sanitario netto; *to make a — breast*, confessare tutto, fare una completa confessione; *to make a — sweep of*, fare piazza pulita di; *to show a — pair of heels*, darsela a gambe; (sport) — *player*, giocatore impeccabile; *adv.* completamente, assolutamente; *I* —

*forgot,* mi sono completamente dimenticato; — *through,* da parte a parte (di); *n.* pulitura, pulita.
**clean** *tr.* pulire; nettare; mondare, smacchiare; *to — out,* vuotare e pulire; *to — someone out,* vuotare le tasche a qualcuno; *to — up,* pulire; purgare; *intr.* fare pulizia.
**clean-cut** *adj.* ben delineato.
**cleaner** *adj. comp.* of **clean,** *q.v.*; *n.* pulitore; donna ad ore; tintoria; (machine) pulitrice.
**cleaning** *n.* (ri)pulitura; pulizia; *dry —,* lavaggio a secco, smacchiatura; *spring —,* pulizia di Pasqua.
**cleanliness** *n.* pulizia; nettezza; lindura; nitidezza.
**clean-minded** *adj.* puro d'animo.
**cleans-e** *tr.* pulire; (rel.) purificare, lavare; (med.) depurare. **-ing** *adj.* purificante; purgativo; *n.* purificazione; purgazione; (med.) depurazione.
**clean-shaven** *adj.* sbarbato.
**clean-up** *n.* pulizia a fondo; (pol.) epurazione.
**clear** *adj.* chiaro, limpido, puro, nitido, terso; chiaro, manifesto, evidente, ovvio; certo, sicuro; netto; libero; (fig.) *the coast is —,* il campo è libero, non c'è pericolo; *— as daylight,* chiaro come il sole; *— majority,* maggioranza assoluta, netta maggioranza; *— profit,* utile netto; *— sky,* cielo terso; *— soup,* consommè *m.*, brodo; *all —,* cessato allarme, pericolo passato; *to be — of,* essere libero da; *to be — about,* essere sicuro di; *to get — of,* liberarsi da; *to jump — over,* saltare al di sopra di; *to keep — of,* tenersi lontano da, stare al largo di; *to make —,* mettere in chiaro; *to make one's position —,* dichiararsi; *to obtain a — lead over,* distaccarsi nettamente da; *to stand —,* stare lontano.
**clear** *tr.* chiarire, chiarificare; vuotare, sgombrare; dissodare; disboscare; superare; discolpare, assolvere, dichiarare innocente; sdoganare, svincolare; (comm.) fare un utile netto di; liquidare; *to — the air,* rinfrescare l'aria, (fig.) mettere a punto una questione; *the doctor recommended him to take something to — his blood,* il medico gli consigliò un depurativo del sangue; *to — oneself,* discolparsi; *to — someone of a charge,* dichiarare innocente un accusato; *to — goods through the customs,* svincolare merci in dogana; *to — a letter-box,* fare una levata di posta; *to — the table,* sparecchiare la tavola; *to — one's throat,* schiarirsi la gola; *to — the way for,* aprire la strada a; *intr.* (of weather) rasserenarsi; dissiparsi; *to — away, tr.* portare via, *intr.* (table) sparecchiare; (of fog) dissiparsi; *to — off,* andarsene, squagliarsi; *to — out, tr.* vuotare, pulire, *intr.* squagliarsi, levarsi di torno; *to — up,* risolvere, rassettare; chiarire, dilucidare, mettere in chiaro; *intr.* (of weather) rasserenarsi, rischiarirsi.
**clearance** *n.* sdoganamento; (comm.) *— sale,* liquidazione di merce; permesso; (mech.) giuoco; *ground —,* distanza dal suolo al mozzo delle ruote; (on typewriter) liberacarrello.
**clear-cut** *adj.* stagliato nettamente; tagliente; nitido.
**clearing** *n.* sgombro; (of letterbox) levata; radura; (comm.) *— house,* stanza di compensazione, clearing *m.*; *— transaction,* bancogiro; (mech.) *— lever,* annullatore.
**clear-sighted** *adj.* dalla vista buona; (fig.) perspicace. **-ness** *n.* buona vista; (fig.) perspicacità.
**clearway** *n.* strada in cui è vietata la sosta delle vetture.
**cleat** *n.* tassello; linguetta; (naut.) tacchetto; galloccia; castagnolo.
**cleav-e** *tr.* fendere; spaccare; *intr.* fendersi; spaccarsi; *intr.* attaccarsi; aderire; (fig.) essere fedele (a). **-age** *n.* fessura; spaccatura; (geol.) sfaldamento. **-er** *n.* mannaia.
**clef** *n.* (mus.) chiave *f.*
**cleft** *part.* of **cleave,** *q.v.*; *adj. — palate,* gola lupina; (fig.) *to be in a — stick,* essere tra due fuochi; *n.* fenditura; fessura; spaccatura; apertura.
**clematis** *n.* (bot.) clematide *f.*
**clem-ent**[1] *adj.* clemente; dolce; mite. **-ency** *n.* clemenza; indulgenza; mitezza.
**Clement**[2] *pr.n.* Clemente.
**Clementine** *pr.n.* Clementina.
**clench** *tr.* stringere; serrare; chiudere; *with -ed fists,* a pugni stretti; (naut.) arrestare e assicurare.
**clepsydra** *n.* idrologio; clessidra.
**clerestory** *n.* parete munita di finestre.
**clergy** *n.* clero; chiericato. **-man** *n.* ministro; ecclesiastico; *Protestant -man,* pastore evangelico.
**cleric** *n.* ecclesiastico; membro del clero; tonsurato. **-al** *adj.* (eccl.) clericale; del clero; ecclesiastico; *-al collar,* collare *m.*, collarino; *-al work,* lavoro d'ufficio; *-al error,* errore *m.* di trascrizione. **-alism** *n.* clericalismo.
**clerk** *n.* impiegato; scrivano; commesso; *chief —,* capo ufficio; *town —,* segretario comunale; (leg.) cancelliere del tribunale.
**clever** *adj.* abile; intelligente; ingegnoso; forte; bravo; sveglio; *to be — at,* essere abile in; *a — boy,* un ragazzo intelligente; *a — device,* un dispositivo ingegnoso. **-ness** *n.* abilità; intelligenza; ingegnosità.
**clew** *n.* (naut.) bugna; (of hammock) cordicella; *tr.* (naut.) *to — up,* imbrogliare.
**cliché** *n.* (typ.) cliché *m. indecl.*; zincotipia; (fig.) frase stereotipata, frase fatta.
**click** *n.* scatto; clic-clac *m. indecl.*; ticchettìo; *tr.* far scattare; *to — one's tongue,* schioccare la lingua; *to — one's heels,* battere i tacchi; *intr.* scattere; far clic-clac; ticchettare; (slang) aver fortuna, dare nel segno; andare d'accordo; prendere una cotta, innamorarsi.
**clickety-click** *adv.* clic-clac.
**client** *n.* cliente *m.*, *f.*; frequentatore.
**clientèle** *n.* clientela.
**cliff** *n.* scoglio; scogliera; dirupo; *the white -s of Dover,* le bianche scogliere di Dover.
**climacteric** *adj.* climaterico; *n.* climaterio, età critica.
**climat-e** *n.* clima *m.* **-ic** *adj.* climatico.
**climax** *n.* apogeo; apice *m.*; colmo.
**climb** *n.* erta; salita; arrampicata; scalata; (aeron.) ascensione; ascesa; *tr.* salire; scalare; arrampicarsi su; *intr.* salire; ascendere; innalzarsi; (plants) abbarbicarsi, aggraticciarsi; (aeron.) prendere quota, sollevarsi; *to — down,* scendere, (fig.) abbassar bandiera, tirarsi indietro; *to — into,* salire su; *to — out of,* uscire arrampicandosi da; *to — over,* scavalcare, scalare; *to — to the top of,* arrampicarsi in cima a.
**climber** *n.* scalatore; alpinista *m.*, *f.*; (fig.) arrampicatore; arrivista *m.*, *f.*
**climb-indicator** *n.* (aeron.) variometro.
**climbing** *adj.* che sale, in salita; (bot.) rampicante; *n.* salita; scalata; ascesa; (aeron.) *— angle,* inclinazione di ascesa; *— speed,* velocità di ascensione.
**clime** *n.* clima *m.*
**clinch** *tr.* annodare; combinare; ribadire; *n.* (boxing) stretta.
**cling** *intr.* aderire strettamente; afferrarsi; aggrapparsi; stringersi (a); (bot.) abbarbicarsi; *to — together,* stringersi l'uno all'altro.
**clinic** *n.* clinica; ambulatorio. **-al** *adj.* clinico. **-ian** *n.* clinico.
**clink** *n.* tintinnìo; (slang) *in the —,* in gattabuia; *tr.* far tintinnare; *intr.* tintinnare. **-ing** *adj.* tintinnante; (fam.) ottimo.
**clinker** *n.* scoria.
**clip**[1] *n.* taglio; tosatura; (fam.) *a — on the ear,* uno scappellotto; *tr.* tagliare; rasare; tosare; *to — the wings of,* tarpare le ali a; *to — someone on the ear,* scappellottare qualcuno.
**clip**[2] *n.* fermaglio; pinza; gancio; *tr.* unire con fermaglio; attaccare; bucare.
**clipper** *n.* tosatore; (machine)

tosatrice; *pl.* macchinetta per tosare; (naut.) goletta, clipper *m.*

**clipping** *n.* taglio; ritaglio; tosatura.

**clique** *n.* cricca; combriccola; cenacolo.

**clitoris** *n.* (anat.) clitoride *f.*

**cloak** *n.* mantello; cappa; gabbano; (fig.) manto; velo; maschera; (fig.) pretesto; scusa; *tr.* coprire con un mantello; (fig.) ammantare; coprire, velare; mascherare.

**cloak-and-dagger** *attrib.* — *novel,* romanzo di cappa e spada; *the — boys,* quelli del servizio segreto.

**cloakroom** *n.* guardaroba; toletta, gabinetto; (rlwy.) deposito bagagli.

**clock**[1] *n.* orologio; (in factory) orologio di controllo; *grandfather —,* grande orologio a pendolo; *to sleep round the —,* dormire dodici ore filate; *tr.* cronometrare; *intr. to — in (out),* far scattare l'orologio di controllo all'entrata (all'uscita), firmare il registro.

**clock**[2] *n.* (on stocking) fiore *m.* di mandorla, freccia, baghetta.

**clock-maker** *n.* orologiaio. **-wise** *adv.* in senso orario, da sinistra a destra. **-work** *n.* meccanismo d'orologio; *-work train,* trenino meccanico; *like -work,* con la regolarità di un orologio, (fam.) liscio liscio.

**clod** *n.* zolla; piota; (person) zoticone *m.* **-hopper** *n.* zoticone *m.*; villano; terrone *m.*

**clog** *n.* zoccolo; (fig.) intoppo, impaccio; *tr.* ingombrare; ostruire; intasare; inceppare.

**cloist-er** *n.* chiostro; *tr.* rinchiudere in un chiostro, inclaustrare. **-ral** *adj.* claustrale, di chiostro.

**close**[1] *adj.* vicino; contiguo; serrato; stretto; intimo; (of weather) afoso, opprimente; spilorcio, avaro; *to give one's — attention to,* ascoltare attentamente; *— contest,* lotta serrata; *after — examination* dopo un esame accurato, a vagliarlo bene; *— finish,* arrivo serrato; *— friend,* amico intimo; *at — quarters,* vicinissimo, da vicino; *to come to — quarters,* venire alle mani; *— resemblance,* rassomiglianza stretta; *— season,* stagione in cui è vietata la caccia; *— shave,* rasatura accurata; (fig.) *to have a — shave,* scamparla bella; *— texture,* tessuto fitto; *in — touch with,* in intimo contatto con; (mil.) *— arrest,* arresto di rigore; *— combat,* combattimento a corpo a corpo; *in — order,* in file serrate; *adv.* vicino; da vicino; dappresso; *— by, — at hand,* vicino, dappresso; *from — up,* da vicino; *— up against,* addosso a; *to be — behind,* seguire da presso; *to bring — together,* accostare; *to keep — to,* tenersi vicino a; *to sit — together,* sedersi vicino l'uno all'altro.

**close**[2] *n.* recinto; *cathedral —,* area circondante una cattedrale, sagrato.

**close**[3] *tr.* chiudere; serrare; *intr.* chiudersi; *to — the door,* chiudere la porta; *the door -d,* la porta si chiuse; terminare; finire; porre fine a; concludere; *to — with an offer,* accettare un'offerta; (mil.) *to — the enemy,* avvicinarsi al nemico; *to — the ranks,* serrare le fila; *to — down, tr.* chiudere, *intr.* chiudere bottega; *to — in, tr.* rinchiudere, *intr.* avvicinarsi; accorciarsi; *to — in upon,* circondare, accerchiare; *to — up, tr.* serrare, sbarrare, otturare, *intr.* (mil.) serrare le fila; *n.* fine *f.*; termine *m.*; chiusura; *to draw to a —,* volgere alla fine.

**close-cropped** *adj.* tagliato raso.

**closed** *p.def., part.* of **close,** *q.v.*; *adj.* chiuso; *— shop,* azienda che assume unicamente personale iscritto ai sindacati.

**close-down** *n.* chiusura.

**close-fisted** *adj.* spilorcio; avaro. **-fitting** *adj.* aderente.

**closely** *adv.* strettamente; da vicino; attentamente; con attenzione.

**closeness** *n.* prossimità; vicinanza; accuratezza; esattezza; precisione; strettezza; intimità; (of weather) afa.

**closet** *n.* gabinetto; studio; armadio; credenza; (w.c.) gabinetto.

**close-up** *n.* (cinema) primo piano.

**closing** *adj.* ultimo; di chiusura; *n.* chiusura; *— time,* ora di chiusura; *— time!,* si chiude!; *early —,* chiusura pomeridiana; *— price,* prezzo di chiusura.

**closure** *n.* chiusura; termine *m.*; fine *f.*; (pol.) *to move the —,* proporre la mozione di chiusura.

**clot** *n.* grumo; (med.) embolo; (slang) scemo; *intr.* raggrumarsi; coagularsi; *-ted cream,* panna; rappresa; *-ted hair,* capelli *m.pl.* appiccicati.

**cloth** *n.* panno; stoffa; tela; tessuto; *bound in —,* rilegato in tela; *woollen —,* tessuto di lana; tovaglia; *to lay the —,* stendere la tovalia; strofinaccio, cencio; (naut.) ferzo; (eccl.) abito; (fig.) *the —,* il clero.

**clothe** *tr.* (ri)vestire; abbigliare; coprire; (fig.) ammantare. **-d** *part.* vestito; (eccl.) *to be -d as a monk,* vestire l'abito religioso.

**clothes** *n.* abiti *m.pl.*; indumenti *m.pl.*; vestiti *m.pl.*; vestiario; abbigliamento; panni *m.pl.*; *a suit of —,* un completo; *cast-off —,* abiti smessi; *ready-made —,* abiti fatti; *in plain —,* in borghese; *to put on one's —,* vestirsi; *to take off one's —,* svestirsi, spogliarsi; *to spend a lot on —,* spendere molto per il vestiario.

**clothes-basket** *n.* cesta per il bucato. **-brush** *n.* spazzola per vestiti. **-horse** *n.* cavalletto per stendere il bucato.

**clothier** *n.* fabbricante *m.* di tessuti.

**clothing** *n.* see **clothes.** *the — trade,* l'industria dell'abbigliamento.

**clotting** *n.* coagulazione.

**cloud** *n.* nuvola; nube *f.*; (of insects) nugolo; (fig.) *to be under a —,* essere in discredito; (provb.) *every — has a silver lining.* dopo il brutto viene il bello; *tr.* annuvolare; oscurare; offuscare; *intr. to — over,* annuvolarsi; abbuiarsi.

**cloudburst** *n.* acquazzone *m.*

**cloud-ceiling** *n.* (aeron.) cappa di nubi.

**clouded** *adj.* annuvolato; coperto; *to become —,* annuvolarsi; coprirsi; (fig.) rannuvolato; (of liquid) torbido.

**cloudiness** *n.* nuvolosità; annuvolamento; (of liquid) torbidezza.

**cloudless** *adj.* senza nubi; sereno.

**cloudy** *adj.* see **clouded.**

**clout** *n.* schiaffo; *to give someone a — over the ear,* schiaffeggiare qualcuno; indumento; (provb.) *cast ne'er a — till May be out,* aprile non ti scoprire, maggio va adagio; *tr.* schiaffeggiare.

**clove**[1] *n.* spicchio.

**clove**[2] *n.* (bot.) garofano; (cul.) chiodo di garofano; (pharm.) *oil of -s,* essenza di garofano.

**clove-hitch** *n.* (naut.) nodo parlato.

**cloven** *part.* of **cleave,** *q.v.*; *adj. — hoof,* piede fesso, piede biforcuto.

**clover** *n.* (bot.) trifoglio; (fig.) *to be in —,* stare come un padre abate.

**clown** *n.* pagliaccio; buffone *m.*; zanni *m. indecl.*; (pejor.) tanghero, villano; *intr.* fare il pagliaccio. **-ery, -ing** *n.* pagliacciata; buffoneria. **-ish** *adj.* pagliaccesco; buffonesco; zotico; rozzo.

**cloy** *tr.* satollare; rimpinzare; stuccare.

**club** *n.* mazza; randello; bastone *m.*; *Indian —,* clave *f.*; (golf) mazza; (cards) fiori, bastoni *m.pl.*; *ace of -s,* asso di fiori; circolo, associazione, società, club *m.*; *country —,* circolo di campagna; *to become a member of a —,* farsi eleggere socio di un circolo.

**club** *tr.* colpire con una mazza; bastonare; picchiare; *to — to death,* uccidere a colpi di bastone; ammazzare; *intr. to — together,* associarsi; unirsi.

**club-foot** *n.* piede deforme, piede equino.

**clubhouse** *n.* sede *f.* del circolo; casino.

**cluck** *n.* chioccio; *intr.* chiocciare.

**clucking** *n.* see **cluck.**

**clue** *n.* indizio; indicazione;

chiave *f.*; *to find the — to*, scoprire la chiave di; (fam.) *not to have a —*, non saperne una boccata.

**clump** *n.* gruppo; zolla; massa; blocco; (fam.) *to give someone a — on the head*, dare una botta in testa a; *tr.* ammucchiare.

**clums-y** *adj.* maldestro; malaccorto; goffo; sgraziato. **-iness** *n.* imperizia; goffaggine *f.*; malaccortezza.

**clung** *p.def.* and *part.* of **cling**, *q.v.*

**cluster** *n.* gruppo; capannello; sciame *m.*; grappolo; mazzo; *intr.* crescere a grappoli, aggrapparsi; *to — round*, fare cerchio intorno a.

**clutch** *n.* stressa; presa; (of eggs) covata; *to make a — at*, cercare di afferrare; *to fall into the -es of*, cadere nelle grinfie di; (motor.) frizione; innesto; *to engage the —*, innestare la frizione; *to let out the —*, disinnestare la frizione; *tr.* afferrare; agguantare; impugnare; *intr. to — at, to — hold of*, aggrapparsi a.

**clutch-pedal** *n.* (motor.) pedale *m.* della frizione, d'innesto.

**clutter** *tr.* accumulare; ingombrare; *to be -ed up with*, essere pieno di; *n.* ingombro; robaccia.

**coach** *n.* carrozza; cocchio; vettura; diligenza; (motor.) pullman *m. indecl.*, torpedone *m.*; vettura, carrozza; vagone *m.*; (tutor) ripetitore; (sport) allenatore; *tr.* dare lezioni private a; (sport) allenare; *intr.* andare in carrozza.

**coachbuilder** *n.* carrozziere *m.*

**coaching** *n.* l'andare in carrozza; *in the old — days*, al tempo delle diligenze; *private —*, ripetizioni private; (sport) allenamento.

**coach-man** *n.* cocchiere *m.*, vetturino. **-work** *n.* carrozzeria.

**coadjutor** *n.* collaboratore; (eccl.) coadiutore.

**coagul-ate** *tr.* coagulare; *intr.* coagularsi; rappigliarsi; aggrumarsi; accagliarsi. **-ant** *n.* (sostanza) coagulante *m.* **-ation** *n.* coagulazione.

**coal** *n.* carbone *m.*; *— fire*, fuoco al carbone; *— tar*, catrame *m.* minerale; *to carry -s to Newcastle*, portare acqua al mare; *to call someone over the -s*, dare una lavata di testa a qualcuno; *to heap -s of fire on someone's head*, suscitar rimorso restituendo bene per male; *intr.* (of ship) rifornirsi di carbone.

**coal-bearing** *adj.* carbonifero. **-black** *adj.* nero come il carbone. **-bunker** *n.* (naut.) carbonile *m.* **-cellar** *n.* carboniera.

**coalesc-e** *intr.* unirsi; fondersi; confluire. **-ence** *n.* unione; fusione; (chem.) combinazione; (anat.) coalescenza.

**coalfield** *n.* bacino carbonifero.

**coal-gas** *n.* gas *m. indecl.* illuminante. **-heaver** *n.* scaricatore di carbone.

**coaling** *n.* (naut.) rifornimento di carbone.

**coalition** *n.* (pol.) coalizione; blocco.

**coal-merchant** *n.* negoziante *m.* di carbone. **-mine, -pit** *n.* miniera di carbone. **-miner** *n.* minatore. **-mining** *n.* sfruttamento delle miniere di carbone; l'industria del carbone. **-scuttle** *n.* secchio per il carbone.

**coarse** *adj.* grossolano; ordinario; volgare; rozzo; ruvido; greggio; emporetico; *— grain*, grana grossa.

**coarse-cut** *adj. — tobacco*, trinciato grosso.

**coarsen** *tr.* rendere grossolano; abbrutire; *intr.* diventare grossolano; abbrutirsi.

**coarseness** *n.* grossolanità; volgarità; rozzezza; ruvidezza.

**coast** *n.* (geog.) costa; litorale *m.*; riviera; (attrib.) da costa, costiero; *intr.* (naut.) costeggiare; navigare lungo la costa; (cycling) scendere a ruota libera; (motor.) discendere a folle.

**coast-al** *adj.* costiero. **-er** *n.* (naut.) nave costiera, cabotiera. **-ing** (naut.) *adj.* cabotiero; *n.* cabotaggio; (cycling) discesa a ruota libera; (motor.) discesa in folle.

**coat**[1] *n.* giacca; giubba; soprabito; *— and skirt*, tailleur *m.*; *to cut one's — according to one's cloth*, far la veste secondo il panno; *— of arms*, stemma *m.*, blasone *m.*; *— of mail*, cotta di maglia; (of animal) manto, pelame *m.*, pelliccia; (of paint) mano *f.*, strato; (of plaster) pelle *f.*; (anat.) parete *f.*, tunica.

**coat**[2] *tr.* rivestire; coprire; spalmare; *to — with paint*, verniciare; *to — a pill*, zuccherare una pillola. **-ed** *adj.* rivestito; coperto; vestito di giacca.

**coatee** *n.* giacchetta corta.

**coating** *n.* rivestimento; (of paint) mano *f.*, strato; *thin —*, velatura.

**coax** *tr.* blandire; persuadere con moine; *to — a child to sleep*, far addormentare un bambino; *to — into doing something*, persuadere a fare qualcosa. **-ing** *adj.* persuasivo; accarezzante; *n.* moine *f.pl.*; blandizie *f.pl.*

**co-axial** *adj.* coassiale.

**cob** *n.* cavallotto; cigno maschio; (of coal) ovulo; (of maize) pannocchia; (bldg.) stucco. **-loaf** *n.* pagnotta. **-nut** *n.* avellana.

**cobalt** *n.* (miner.) cobalto.

**cobble**[1] *n.* ciottolo; *paved with —*, acciottolato; (of coal) ovulo; pavimentare con ciottoli, acciottolare; *-d pavement*, acciottolatura.

**cobble**[2] *tr.* rattoppare; acciabattare.

**cobbler** *n.* ciabattino; calzolaio; *-'s last*, forma di scarpa; *-'s wax*, pece *f.* da calzolaio; *let the — stick to his last*, ciabattino parla sol del suo mestiere.

**cobblestone** *n.* ciottolo.

**cobra** *n.* (zool.) cobra.

**cobweb** *n.* ragnatela; *to blow away the -s*, prendere una boccata d'aria, rinfrescarsi le idee.

**cocaine** *n.* cocaina; *— addict*, cocainomane *m.*, *f.*

**coccyx** *n.* (anat.) coccige *m.*

**Cochin-china** *pr.n.* (geog.) Cocincina.

**cochineal** *n.* cocciniglia.

**cochlea** *n.* (anat.) coclea.

**cock**[1] *n.* gallo; *— bird*, uccello maschio; (fam.) *old —*, vecchio mio; (fig.) *— and bull story*, panzana; (joc.) *— of the walk*, padrone *m.* del baccellaio; *to live like a fighting —*, vivere come un papa; (tap) rubinetto; valvola; (of gun) cane *m.*, percussore; *at full —*, armato; *at half —*, in posizione di sicurezza; (fold) piega all'insù; *to give one's hat a —*, mettere il cappello sulle ventitrè.

**cock**[2] *n.* (of hay) covone *m.*, bica.

**cock**[3] *tr.* alzare, drizzare; *to — one's ears*, drizzare le orecchie; *to — one's eye at*, lanciare un'occhiata a; *to — a gun*, armare un fucile, alzare il cane di un fucile; (vulg.) *to — a snook*, far marameo.

**cockade** *n.* coccarda.

**cock-a-doodle-doo** *n.* chicchirichì *m.* **-a-hoop** *adj.* esultante; prepotente.

**cockatoo** *n.* (orn.) cacatoa, cacatua *m.*

**Cockayne** *pr.n.* Paese della Cuccagna.

**cockchafer** *n.* (ent.) maggiolino.

**cockcrow** *n.* canto del gallo, gallicinio.

**cocked** *part. adj.* drizzato; (of gun) armato; *— hat*, bicorno, tricorno.

**cockerel** *n.* galletto.

**cock-eyed** *adj.* strabico; (fig.) sghembo; assurdo. **-horse** *n.* cavallo a dondolo.

**cockiness** *n.* sfrontatezza; prepotenza.

**cockle**[1] *n.* (zool.) cardio; (bot.) loglio.

**cockle**[2] *n.* grinza; increspatura; (fig.) *to warm the -s of the heart*, infondere calore al cuore.

**cockleshell** *n.* conchiglia; (boat) guscio di noce.

**cockpit** *n.* arena per combattimento di galli; (fig.) campo di battaglia; arena; (aeron.) carlinga, abitacolo; (naut.) cassero, pozzetto.

**cockroach** *n.* (ent.) blatta; scarafaggio.

**cocksure** *adj.* sicurissimo, sicuro di sè; prepotente; presuntuoso.

-ness *n.* fiducia in se stesso; prepotenza; presunzione.
**cocktail** *n.* cocktail *m.*; bicchierino; — *cabinet*, bar *m. indecl.*
**cocky** *adj.* ringalluzzito; impertinente; *to be* —, ringalluzzirsi.
**cocoa** *n.* cacao; cioccolata.
**coconut** *n.* noce *f.* di cocco; — *palm*, cocco; (slang) testone *m.*
**cocoon** *n.* bozzolo.
**cod** *n.* (ichth.) merluzzo.
**coddle** *tr.* vezzeggiare; coccolare; viziare; tenere nel cotone.
**code** *n.* (leg.) codice *m.*; cifrario; *Morse* —, alfabeto Morse; (fig.) modo di comportarsi; *tr.* (leg.) codificare; cifrare, tradurre in cifra.
**codex** *n.* codice *m.*; manoscritto.
**codfish** *n.* merluzzo.
**codicil** *n.* (leg.) codicillo.
**codify** *tr.* codificare.
**co-director** *n.* condirettore *m.*
**cod-liver-oil** *n.* olio di fegato di merluzzo.
**co-educational** *adj.* misto.
**coefficient** *n.* coefficiente *m.*
**coequal** *adj.*, *n.* coeguale *m.*, *f.*
**coerc-e** *tr.* costringere; forzare; coartare. **-ive** *adj.* coercitivo; coatto. **-ion** *n.* coercizione; forza.
**coeval** *adj.* coevo, contemporaneo.
**coexist** *intr.* coesistere. **-ence** *n.* coesistenza.
**coffee** *n.* caffè *m.*; *black* —, caffè espresso; *strong black* —, caffè ristretto; *breakfast* —, caffelatte *m.*; *white* —, cappuccino; — *laced with spirits*, caffè corretto.
**coffee-bean** *n.* chicco di caffè. **-pot** *n.* caffettiera.
**coffer** *n.* cofano; cassa; forziere *m.*; (archit.) cassettone *m.*; formella; riquadro. **-ed** *adj.* (of ceiling) formellato, a cassettoni.
**coffin** *n.* cassa da morto; bara.
**cog** *n.* dente *m.*; (fig.) *a — in a wheel*, l'ultima ruota del carro; *tr.* (eng.) addentellare.
**cog-ent** *adj.* convincente; persuasivo; potente. **-ency** *n.* forza; urgenza.
**cogitat-e** *tr.* escogitare; *intr.* meditare; riflettere. **-ion** *n.* meditazione; riflessione. **-ive** *adj.* meditabondo; riflessivo; cogitabondo.
**cognac** *n.* (French) cognac *m.*; (Italian) acquavite *f.*, arzente *m.*, brandy *m.*
**cognate** *adj.* (leg.) cognato; (fig.) affine; analogo; che ha la stessa origine; *n.* cognato.
**cognition** *n.* cognizione; percezione.
**cognitive** *adj.* conoscitivo.
**cogniz-ance** *n.* conoscenza; percezione; *to take — of*, prendere conoscenza di. **-ant** *adj.* avente conoscenza; informato.
**cognomen** *n.* soprannome *m.*; (Rom. hist.) cognome *m.*
**cognoscib-le** *adj.* (philos.) conoscibile. **-ility** *n.* (philos.) conoscibilità.
**cogwheel** *n.* ruota dentata.
**cohabit** *intr.* coabitare. **-ation** *n.* coabitazione.
**coheir(ess)** *n.* coerede *m.*, *f.*
**cohere** *intr.* aderire; (fig.) essere coerente.
**coher-ence, -ency** *n.* coesione; aderenza; coerenza. **-ent** *adj.* aderente; coerente.
**cohes-ion** *n.* aderenza; coesione; appoggio; (scient.) adesione. **-ive** *adj.* aderente; coesivo; attaccaticcio; aggregativo.
**cohort** *n.* (Rom. hist.) coorte *f.*; (fig.) schiera.
**coif** *n.* cappuccio.
**coiffure** *n.* acconciatura.
**coign** *n.* (archit.) canto; angolo; — *of vantage*, posizione vantaggiosa.
**coil** *n.* rotolo; spirale *f.*; spira; (electr.) bobina; (of rope) accollo; (naut.) aduglia; (mech.) serpentina; — *spring*, molla ad elica; *tr.* avvolgere a spirale; attorcigliare; acciambellare; acchiocciolare; (naut.) adugliare; cogliere a ruota; *to — down*, abbisciare; (fig.) *to — oneself up*, rannicchiarsi; *intr.* avvolgersi; acchiocciolarsi; (fig.) serpeggiare. **-ed** *adj.* ravvolto; attorcigliato.
**coil**[2] *n.* tumulto; *to shuffle off this mortal* —, fuggire a questa vita di tumulto.
**coin** *n.* moneta; — *of the realm*, moneta sonante; (teleph.) — *box*, apparecchio a gettone; — *slot*, fessura per moneta, per gettone; (fig.) *to pay someone back in his own* —, rendere pan per focaccia.
**coin** *tr.* coniare; battere; (fam.) *to be -ing money*, far denari a palate; (fig.) inventare; fabbricare.
**coinage** *n.* coniatura; conio; sistema monetario; monete *f.pl.*; (fig.) invenzione; fabbricazione.
**coincide** *intr.* coincidere.
**coincid-ence** *n.* combinazione; *what an extraordinary* —, ma guarda un po', che combinazione! **-ental** *adj.* coincidente, di coincidenza.
**coiner** *n.* coniatore; falsario; (fig.) inventore.
**coir** *n.* fibra di cocco; (naut.) — *rope*, borasso.
**coition, coitus** *n.* coito.
**coke**[1] *n.* carbone fossile distillato.
**coke**[2] *n.* (slang) cocaina.
**coke**[3] (slang) cocacola.
**col** *n.* (geog.) collo; valico.
**colander** *n.* colabrodo, colatoio.
**cold** *adj.* freddo; gelido; rigido; (poet.) algido; (mech.) a freddo; *to be* —, *to feel* —, aver freddo, (of weather) far freddo; *my hands are* —, ho le mani fredde; *to feel* —, avere (*or* sentire) freddo; *to get* —, diventar freddo, raffreddarsi; *in — blood*, a sangue freddo; *a — snap*, un colpo di freddo; — *steel*, arma bianca; *in — storage*, in frigorifero; — *war*, guerra fredda; (fig.) *to have — feet*, aver la fifa; *to give someone the — shoulder*, trattare qualcuno freddamente; *to throw — water on*, dare una doccia fredda a, spegnere l'entusiasmo di; *it leaves me* —, non mi dice niente.
**cold** *n.* freddo; *in the* —, al freddo; *to feel the* —, soffrire per il freddo, essere molto freddoloso; *to be left out in the* —, restare a bocca asciutta; (med.) raffreddore *m.*; *a — in the head*, un raffreddore di testa; *to catch a* —, prendere un raffreddore, raffreddarsi; *to catch one's death of* —, morire di freddo; *to have a* —, essere raffreddato.
**cold-blooded** *adj.* freddo; insensibile, flemmatico; premeditato; a sangue freddo. **-cream** *n.* crema emolliente.
**coldness** *n.* freddezza.
**coleopter** *n.* (ent.) coleottero.
**colic** *n.* colica.
**Coliseum** *n.* Colosseo.
**colitis** *n.* (med.) colite *f.*
**collabor-ate** *intr.* collaborare, cooperare, lavorare insieme. **-ation** *n.* collaborazione; cooperazione; connubio; (pol.) collaborazionismo. **-ationist** *n.* (pol.) collaborazionista *m.*, *f.* **-ator** *n.* collaboratore.
**collapse** *n.* crollo; sprofondamento; (fig.) caduta; sfacelo; sgonfiamento; (med.) collasso; *intr.* crollare; rovinare; cadere; sprofondare; sgonfiarsi; afflosciarsi; (fig.) accasciarsi.
**collapsible** *adj.* pieghevole; smontabile; (motor.) — *hood*, capotta apribile, soffietto.
**collar** *n.* colletto; (of coat) bavero; (dog, horse) collare *m.*; (sailor's) solino; (mech.) anello, collare, fascetta; *tr.* afferrare per il colletto; (fam.) appropriarsi di, fare man bassa di.
**collate** *tr.* collazionare; confrontare; controllare; riscontrare.
**collateral** *adj.* collaterale; (fig.) accessorio; sussidiario; (comm.) — *security*, garanzia addizionale.
**collation** *n.* collazione; riscontro, confronto; (meal) merenda, spuntino.
**colleague** *n.* collega; *m.*, *f.* consocio; compagno di ufficio.
**col·lect**[1] *n.* (liturg.) orazione; colletta.
**collect**[2] *tr.* raccogliere; riunire; radunare; mettere insieme; prendere in consegna; ricuperare; riscuotere; *to — stamps*, fare una raccolta di francobolli; (fig.) *to — one's thoughts*, concentrarsi; *intr.* riunirsi, radunarsi; fare una colletta (per). **-ed** *adj.* riunito; raccolto; (fig.) calmo, tranquillo, padrone di sè. **-edness** *n.* calma; padronanza di sè. **-ing** *n.* il raccogliere; raccolta; *-ing station*, centro di raccolta.

**collection** *n.* riunione; raccolta; adunata; (pejor.) accozzaglia; (art) raccolta, collezione; *postal* —, levata; riscossione, esazione; — *for charity*, colletta, questua.
**collection-bag** *n.* borsellino. **-box** *n.* cassetta.
**collectiv-e** *adj.* collettivo; — *shipment*, collettame *m.* **-ity** *n.* collettività; comunità sociale.
**collector** *n.* raccoglitore; collezionista *m., f.*; (of taxes) esattore, ricevitore; (of alms) questuante *m., f.*; *ticket* —, bigliettario, controllore.
**colleen** *n.* ragazza irlandese.
**college** *n.* collegio; casa dello studente; istituto; accademia; università; liceo; convitto; (eccl.) collegio.
**collegiate** *adj.* di collegio; (eccl.) collegiato.
**collide** *intr.* scontrarsi; urtarsi; *to — with*, urtare, investire, scontrarsi con, cozzare contro.
**collie** *n.* cane da pastore scozzese.
**collier** *n.* minatore di carbone; (ship) nave carboniera. **-y** *n.* miniera di carbone fossile.
**collim-ate** *tr.* far collimare. **-ation** *n.* collimazione. **-ator** *n.* collimatore.
**collision** *n.* collisione; contro; investimento; conflitto; (naut.) abbordaggio; *to come into — with*, scontrarsi con, urtare contro.
**colloc-ate** *tr.* collocare; sistemare. **-ation** *n.* collocazione; sistemazione.
**collodion** *n.* (chem.) collodio.
**colloid** *adj., n.* (chem.) colloide *m.*
**colloquial** *adj.* familiare; d'uso corrente.
**colloquy** *n.* colloquio; conversazione; dialogo.
**collusion** *n.* collusione.
**Cologne** *pr.n.* (geog.) Colonia; (fam.) acqua di Colonia.
**colon**[1] *n.* (anat.) colon *m.*
**colon**[2] *n.* (gramm.) due punti *m.pl.*
**colonel** *n.* colonnello.
**colonial** *adj.* coloniale; *n.* colono, colonizzatore. **-ism** *n.* colonialismo; sistema coloniale. **-ist** *n.* colonialista *m., f.*
**colonist** *n.* colono, colonizzatore.
**coloniz-e** *tr.* colonizzare. **-ation** *n.* colonizzazione.
**colonnade** *n.* colonnato; portici *m.pl.*
**colophon** *n.* (typ.) colofon(e) *m.*
**Colorado** *pr.n.* (geog.) Colorado *m.*; (ent.) — *beetle*, dorifora.
**coloration** *n.* colorazione.
**colorimeter** *n.* colorimetro.
**colossal** *adj.* colossale; enorme.
**Colosseum** *n.* (archaeol.) Colosseo.
**colossus** *n.* colosso; *the — of Rhodes*, il Colosso di Rodi.
**colour** *n.* colore *m.*; tinta; *in* —, a colori; colorito, carnagione; *off* —, ammalazzato, (fam.) giù di corda; (fig.) aspetto; apparenza; *under — of*, sotto pretesto di, sotto l'apparenza di; *to change* —, cambiar colore; *to turn all the -s of the rainbow*, diventare di mille colori; *to wear light -s*, vestire di chiaro; bandiera; *regimental -s*, bandiera del reggimento; (mil.) *with the -s*, sotto le armi; *to call to the -s*, chiamare sotto le armi; *to sail under false -s*, navigare sotto bandiera falsa; *to strike the -s*, ammainare la bandiera; (fig.) *to come off with flying -s*, riuscire vittorioso; *to nail one's -s to the mast*, irrigidirsi sulle proprie posizioni.
**colour** *tr.* colorare, colorire; tingere; *intr.* colorirsi; arrossire. **-able** *adj.* plausibile; specioso; verosimile.
**colour-bar** *n.* barriera fra bianchi e uomini di colore; pregiudizi razziali; razzismo. **-bearer** *n.* (mil.) portabandiera *m.* **-blind** *adj.* daltonico. **-blindness** *n.* daltonismo; acromatopsia.
**coloured** *adj.* di colore, a colori, colorato, colorito; *highly* —, a tinte vivaci; *n.* uomo di colore; *the -s*, la gente di colore.
**colourful** *adj.* pieno di colore; a tinte vivaci; pittoresco; vivido.
**colouring** *n.* carnagione; colorito; colore *m.*; coloratura; colorazione.
**colourist** *n.* (paint.) colorista *m., f.*; coloritore.
**colourless** *adj.* senza colore, incolore; pallido; (fig.) insipido, scialbo. **-ness** *n.* assenza di colore; acromatismo; (fig.) insipidezza.
**colour-sergeant** *n.* (mil.) maresciallo.
**colporteur** *n.* distributore di libri religiosi.
**colt**[1] *n.* puledro; (sport) principiante *m., f.*
**colt**[2] *n.* pistola colt.
**coltsfoot** *n.* (bot.) farfara, tussilaggine *f.*
**columbine** *n.* (bot.) aquilegia; (pop.) amore nascosto; *pr.n.* (theatr.) Colombina.
**Columbus** *pr.n. Christopher* —, Cristoforo Colombo.
**column** *n.* colonna; (pol.) *fifth* —, quinta colonna; (anat.) *spinal* —, colonna vertebrale; (journ.) rubrica; (typ.) colonna; *to draw up in -s*, incolonnare; (mech.) *steering* —, albero dello sterzo, piantone *m.* di guida; (naut.) colonna di manovra.
**columnar** *adj.* a forma di colonna.
**columnist** *n.* (journ.) giornalista che cura una rubrica, elzevirista, cronista *m.*
**colza** *n.* (bot.) navone *m.*; colza.
**coma** *n.* (med.) coma *m.*; (astron.) chioma. **-tose** *adj.* comatoso, in coma.
**comb** *n.* pettine *m.*; pettinata; (industr.) pettinatura; *horse* —, striglia; cresta.
**comb** *tr.* pettinare; *to — one's hair*, pettinarsi, darsi una pettinata; *to — down a horse*, strigliare un cavallo; (fig.) perlustrare, rastrellare.
**com·bat** *n.* combattimento; conflitto; lotta; *single* —, duello; *unarmed* —, combattimento inerme.
**combat** *tr.* combattere, lottare contro, contrastare. **-ant** *adj., n.* combattente *m., f.* **-ive** *adj.* battagliero, combattivo, aggressivo. **-iveness, -ivity** *n.* combattività; aggressività.
**comb(e)** *n.* (geog.) valle stretta ed allungata, comba.
**comber** *n.* (text.) pettinatore, cardatore; (machine) pettinatrice, cardatrice; (breaking wave) frangente *m.*
**combination** *n.* combinazione; — *lock*, serratura con segreto; — *room*, (Cambridge) sala di ritrovo; (motor.) motocarrozzetta, 'sidecar' *m. indecl.*
**combine** *n.* associazione; gruppo di aziende; cartello; consorzio; *tr.* combinare; unire; congiungere; abbinare; *-d efforts*, sforzi combinati; *intr.* unirsi; congiungersi; combinarsi; contribuire.
**combine-harvester** *n.* (agric.) mietitrebbiatrice.
**combing** *n.* pettinatura; pettinata; *pl.* capelli strappati dal pettine, (industr.) fili strappati dalla cardatrice.
**combustib-le** *adj.* combustibile; infiammabile; accendibile; *n.* combustibile *m.* **-ility** *n.* combustibilità.
**combustion** *n.* combustione; — *chamber*, camera di combustione; *spontaneous* —, autocombustione; *internal — engine*, motore *m.* a combustione interna.
**come** *intr.* venire; arrivare; accadere; avvenire; succedere; (fig.) giungere; — *here!*, vieni qua!; *I'm coming*, vengo; —, —*!*, ma andiamo!, macchè!; — *then!*, su! allora!; *to — running*, venire di corsa; — *what may*, accada quel che accada, qualunque cosa avvenga; *to — of a good family*, essere di buona famiglia; *what does the bill — to?*, quanto viene il conto?; *it doesn't — to much*, non è gran cosa poca roba; *what are things coming to?*, dove andiamo a finire?; *has it — to this?*, siamo giunti a questo?; *I have — to believe that*, sono giunto a credere che; *in days to* —, nei giorni futuri; *the life to* —, la vita futura, l'al di là; *when it -s to . . .*, quanto a . . ., quando si tratta di . . .; *when I — to think of it*, ora che ci penso; *to — easy*, riuscire facile; *to — right*, aggiustarsi, finire bene; *to — true*,

avverarsi; *to — undone*, slegarsi, disfarsi; *to — unsewn*, scucirsi; *to — unstuck*, distaccarsi, (fig.) trovarsi nei guai; *to — to an agreement*, addivenire ad un accordo; *to — to be*, diventare, divenire; *to — to blows*, venire alle mani; *to — to grief*, finire male; *to — to a halt*, fermarsi; *to — to light*, venire alla luce, rivelarsi; *to — to pass*, adempirsi, avverarsi, accadere; *to — to pieces*, andare in pezzi, disfarsi; *to — to one's senses*, riprendere i sensi, rinvenire; *to — to terms with*, venire ai patti con. FOLLOW. BY ADV. OR PREP.: *to — about*, accadere, succedere, (naut.) virare di bordo, (of wind) mutare, cambiare direzione; *to — across*, incontrare per caso, imbattersi in, trovare per caso; *to — after*, seguire, succedere a; *to — again*, tornare; *— again soon!*, arriverderci presto!; *to — along* (*with*), venire (con); *to — alongside*, (naut.) accostare, accostarsi; *to — away*, venire via, distaccarsi; *to — back*, ritornare; *it all —s back to me*, mi ritorna tutto alla mente; *to — before*, precedere, venire prima di; comparire davanti a; essere presentato a; *to — between*, avvenire fra; (fig.) interporsi fra; *to — by*, passare (vicino a); passare da; ottenere, avere; *to — down*, scendere; essere tramandato; essere demolito; abbassarsi, calare; *to — down upon someone*, dare una lavata di testa a qualcuno; *to — forward*, venire avanti, presentarsi, affacciarsi; *to — home*, ritornare a casa, rientrare; (fig.) *to — home to*, toccare sul vivo; *to — in*, entrare; *— in!*, avanti!; *please — in, please — this way*, s'accomodi; (of tide) salire; (of season) cominciare; (of fashion) essere lanciato; (be useful) servire; (sport) *to — in first*, arrivare per primo; (fam.) *that's where I — in*, ecco dove entro in ballo io; *to — in for*, (praise, blame) ricevere; *to — into*, entrare in; ereditare, entrare in possesso di; (of law) *to — into force*, entrare in vigore; *to — in(to) sight of*, giungere in vista di; *to — near* (*to*), avvicinarsi (a); (fig.) mancare poco (che), correre il rischio (di); *to — off*, cadere da; aver luogo; riuscire; *to — off well*, cavarsela brillantemente; *to — off badly*, avere la peggio, cavarsela malamente; (fam.) *— off it!*, basta!, ma va là; *to — on*, venire avanti; *— on!*, avanti!, presto!, andiamo; forza!, dai! dai!; (of rain, illness) sopraggiungere, venire; (theatr.) entrare in scena; far progressi, crescere; *to — on well*, venire su bene; *to — out*, venire fuori, uscire; essere pubblicato; (of flower) sbocciare; (of stain) stingere; *at last the truth is coming out*, finalmente la verità viene a galla; (in society) debuttare; (on strike) scioperare; risultare, rivelarsi; *to — over*, venire; attraversare; *to — over to someone's side*, passare dalla parte di qualcuno; *what has — over you?*, che cosa ti prende?; *to — round*, girare intorno a; (of wind) cambiare direzione, mutare; *— round and see me one day*, vieni a trovarmi un giorno; (after a faint) riaversi, riprendere i sensi; (fig.) *to — round to someone's way of thinking*, aderire al modo di pensare di qualcuno; *to — through*, passare attraverso, attraversare, superare; *to — through without a scratch*, uscirne indenne; *to — together*, riunirsi, incontrarsi, radunarsi; *to — under*, passare sotto; *to — under someone's influence*, essere soggetto all'influenza di qualcuno; *to — under the heading of*, trovarsi sotta la rubrica di; *to — up*, venire su, salire; venire a galla; (of plant) crescere, spuntare; (of tide) salire; *to — up to someone* (*in street*), avvicinarsi a qualcuno; *to — up against something*, urtare, cozzare contro qualcosa; *to — up to expectations*, corrispondere all'aspettativa; *to — within someone's duties*, rientrare nei doveri di qualcuno.

**comeback** *n.* ritorno; risposta arguta, battuta.

**comedian** *n.* comico; (fig.) commediante *m., f.*; buffone *m.*

**comedown** *n.* rovescio; umiliazione.

**comedy** *n.* commedia; *musical —*, operetta.

**comel-y** *adj.* bello; avvenente; grazioso. **-iness** *n.* bellezza; avvenenza; bell'aspetto.

**comer** *n.* chi viene; *the first —*, il primo venuto; *late —*, ritardatario; *open to all —s*, aperto a tutti.

**comestible** *adj., n.* commestibile *m.*

**comet** *n.* cometa.

**comfort** *n.* agio; comodità; conforto; agiatezza; benessere *m.*; *to live in —*, vivere nell'agiatezza; consolazione; *cold —*, una magra consolazione; (rel.) *the —s of religion*, i conforti della religione; *tr.* consolare; confortare; ridare coraggio a.

**comfortabl-e** *adj.* comodo; di conforto; confortevole; all'agio; agevole; *to be —*, stare a proprio agio, star bene; *to make oneself —*, mettersi a proprio agio, non fare complimenti; sufficiente, adeguato. **-y** *adv.* comodamente; a proprio comodo, a bell'agio; *-ly off*, in buone condizioni finanziarie, agiato, benestante.

**comfort-er** consolatore, consolatrice; confortatore, confortatrice. **-ing** *adj.* consolante; confortante; rassicurante. **-less** *adj.* scomodo; disadorno; poco accogliente; squallido.

**comfrey** *n.* (bot.) consolida maggiore.

**comic(al)** *adj.* comico; buffo; ridicolo; umoristico; (theatr.) *— actor*, comico; *— quality*, comicità; *— opera*, opera buffa; *— paper*, giornale umoristico; *— strip*, racconto umoristico a fumetti, fumetto; *n. comic*, fumetto.

**coming** *adj.* prossimo; futuro; da venire; venturo; (fig.) *a — man*, un uomo promettente; *n.* venuta; arrivo; avvento; *— of age*, il diventar maggiorenne; *— and going*, andirivieni *m. indecl.*; *— back*, ritorno; *— down*, discesa; *— in*, entrata; *— on*, inizio; *— out*, uscita, (in society) debutto; *— together*, riunione.

**comity** *n. the — of nations*, le nazioni amiche, rispetto reciproco di leggi e costumi.

**comma** *n.* virgola; *inverted —s*, virgolette *f.pl.*; (mus.) comma *m.*

**command** *n.* comando; ordine *m.*; *under the — of*, agli ordini di sotto il comando di; *to be in — of*, avere il comando di; (mil.) comando; *Higher Command*, Comando Supremo; *— of the sea*, dominio dei mari; *— of a language*, padronanza di una lingua.

**command** *tr.* comandare; ordinare; *to — someone to do something*, ordinare a qualcuno di fare qualcosa; (mil.) comandare, essere comandante, avere il comando di; dominare; controllare; *to — a view over a valley*, dominare una vallata; *to — admiration*, ispirare ammirazione.

**commandant** *n.* comandante, *m.*, capo.

**commandeer** *tr.* requisire. **-ing** *n.* requisizione.

**commander** *n.* (mil.) comandante *m.*; capo; (naval) capitano di fregata.

**commander-in-chief** *n.* comandante *m.* in capo, generalissimo.

**commanding** *adj.* che comanda; *— officer*, comandante *m.*; (fig.) *— position*, posizione dominante; imperioso, imperativo, autoritario.

**commandment** *n.* comandamento; precetto; *the Ten Commandments*, i dieci Comandamenti, il Decalogo.

**commando** *n.* (mil.) reparto di truppe d'assalto, di commando.

**comme il faut** *attrib.* ammodo.

**commemorat-e** *tr.* commemorare; ricordare; onorare la memoria di; rammentare. **-ion** *n.* commemorazione.

**commence** *tr.* cominciare; iniziare; *intr.* cominciare; esordire.

**-ment** *n.* principio; inizio; esordio; debutto.
**commend** *tr.* raccomandare; lodare; encomiare; (rel.) *to — one's soul to God*, raccomandar l'anima a Dio; *to — itself to*, riscuotere l'approvazione di. **-able** *adj.* lodevole; encomiabile. **-ation** *n.* lode *f.*; elogio; encomio. **-atory** *adj.* laudativo; di lode; elogiativo.
**commensur-able** *adj.* commensurabile; proporzionale. **-ate** *adj.* commisurato; proporzionato.
**comment**[1] *n.* commento; osservazione; apprezzamento; rilievo; *no —*, niente da dire; *to call for —*, richiedere commenti.
**comment**[2] *intr.* commentare; fare qualche osservazione; *to — on a text*, commentare un testo; *to — on someone's behaviour*, criticare la condotta di qualcuno.
**commentary** *n.* commentario; (liter.) chiosa; *running —*, commento particolareggiato; cronaca.
**commentator** *n.* commentatore; chiosatore; (radio) radiocronista *m.*
**commerce** *n.* commercio; traffico; scambi, *m.pl.*; *attrib.* mercantile.
**commercial** *adj.* commerciale; di commercio; *— traveller*, commesso di commercio, viaggiatore di commercio; *n.* pubblicità commerciale. **-ism** *n.* spirito commerciale; mercantilismo.
**comminatory** *adj.* (leg.) comminatorio.
**commingle** *tr.* mescolare insieme; *intr.* mescolarsi insieme.
**commiserat-e** *tr.*, *intr.* commiserare; provare pietà (di); dolersi (di). **-ion** *n.* commiserazione; compassione.
**commissariat** *n.* (mil.) commissariato; intendenza; (Russia) ministero.
**commissar(y)** *n.* commissario; delegato.
**commission** *n.* commissione; comitato; delegazione; incarico; mandato; *to carry out a —*, eseguire una commissione; *to have a roving —*, aver libertà di manovra, lavorare indipendentemente; (comm.) *5% —*, provvigione del cinque per cento; *— agent*, commissionario; (leg.) perpetrazione; (mil.) brevetto da ufficiale; *Queen's —*, nomina reale; *to get a —*, essere nominato ufficiale; *to resign one's —*, dare le dimissioni da ufficiale; (naut.) *ship in —*, nave armata.
**commission** *tr.* incaricare; *to — someone to do something*, incaricare qualcuno di fare qualcosa; ordinare; commissionare; commettere; nominare; (ship) armare, equipaggiare.
**commissionaire** *n.* fattorino; portiere *m.*
**commissioned** *adj.* delegato; munito di autorità; *— officer*, ufficiale *m.*; *non-commissioned officer*, sottufficiale *m.*
**commissioner** *n.* commissario; membro di una commissione; *— for oaths*, commissario di dichiarazione sotto giuramento, notaio pubblico; *— of police* questore.
**commit** *tr.* affidare; rimettere; commettere; fare; perpetrare; *to — oneself*, impegnarsi, compromettersi; *to — to memory*, imparare a memoria; *to — to writing*, mettere per iscritto; (leg.) *to — for trial*, rinviare a giudizio; *to — to prison*, mandare in prigione; *— no nuisance*, vietato lordare.
**commitment** *n.* impegno; see also **committal.**
**committal** *n.* mandato; incarico; perpetrazione; sepoltura; (leg.) rinvio.
**committee** *n.* comitato; commissione; delegazione; *advisory —*, comitato consultivo; *joint —*, commissione mista; *standing —*, commissione permanente; *reception —*, comitato per l'ospitalità; *selection —*, commissione delle proposte.
**committee-meeting** *n.* seduta, riunione di comitato. **-room** *n.* sala del comitato.
**commixture** *n.* miscuglio.
**commode** *n.* cassettone *m.*; canterano; seggetta.
**commodious** *adj.* ampio; spazioso; comodo. **-ness** *n.* ampiezza; spaziosità; comodità.
**commodity** *n.* derrata; merce *f.*; genere *m.*; *staple —*, prodotto base.
**commodore** *n.* (naut.) commodoro, comandante *m.* di divisione; (of yacht club) presidente *m.*
**common** *adj.* comune; ordinario, volgare; solito, abituale, corrente; *the — good*, il bene comune; *— property*, proprietà comune; *— law*, legge consuetudinaria; *European Common Market*, Mercato Comune Europeo (MCE); *— occurrence*, fatto normale, fatto di tutti i giorni, casa di ordinaria amministrazione; *— people*, il popolo, il volgo, (pejor.) gente ordinaria; *the Book of Common Prayer*, la liturgia anglicana; *— talk*, voce diffusa; *the — weal*, la cosa pubblica, lo stato, il benessere pubblico; *— or garden*, comune, solito, banale; *in — use*, d'uso corrente; *out of the —*, fuori del comune, straordinario; *to share in —*, *to make —*, accomunare; (gramm.) *— noun*, nome *m.* comune; *— gender*, genere *m.* comune; *n.* (hist.) pascolo demaniale; parco.
**commonalty** *n.* popolo; volgo; comunità.
**commoner** *n.* cittadino.
**commonness** *n.* banalità; volgarità; frequenza.
**commonplace** *adj.* banale, ordinario, trito; *n.* banalità; luogo comune; *— book*, zibaldone *m.*
**commons** *n.* il popolo, il Terzo Stato; *House of Commons*, Camera dei Comuni; razioni *f.pl.*; *to be on short —*, essere a stecchetto, fare un pasto magro.
**commonsense** *n.* buon senso; *adj.* assennato, sensato.
**commonwealth** *n.* benessere pubblico; repubblica; (hist.) *the Commonwealth* (1649–60), la Repubblica inglese; *the British —*, la Comunità Britannica, il 'Commonwealth'; *the — of Australia*, la Federazione Australiana.
**commotion** *n.* confusione; subbuglio; tumulto *m.*; finimondo; *to cause a —*, mettere tutto il campo a rumore, suscitare un vespaio.
**communal** *adj.* comunale; della comunità.
**com·mune** *n.* (admin.) comune *m.*
**commune** *intr.* intrattenersi; conferire.
**communicable** *adj.* comunicabile; (med.) contagioso.
**communicant** *n.* (eccl.) comunicando, comunicanda; (after Communion) comunicato, comunicata *f.*
**communicat-e** *tr.* comunicare; trasmettere; partecipare; far conoscere, diffondere; *intr. to — with*, essere in comunicazione con. **-ing** *adj.* comunicante. **-ion** *n.* comunicazione; informazione; relazione; rapporto; *to get into -ion with*, mettersi in relazione con; *to break off all -ions with*, rompere ogni rapporto con; (rlwy.) *-ion cord*, segnale d'allarme; (mil.) *-ion trench*, camminamento; *lines of -ion*, retrovie *f.pl.*, linee *f.pl.* di comunicazione. **-ive** *adj.* comunicativo; espansivo; loquace.
**communion** *n.* comunione; comunanza; intima relazione; (rel.) *the Anglican —*, la confessione anglicana; (liturg.) sunzione; (as part of Mass) comunione; (antiphon) communio; (as given in church or taken to sick and dying), la Santa Comunione; L'Eucaristia; *the priest is taking Holy Communion to a dying parishioner*, il parroco porta il viatico (la comunione, il Santissimo) a un fedele moribondo; *to make one's —*, to go to —, comunicarsi; *to go to confession and —*, far le sue devozioni; *the priest gave him —*, il prete lo comunicò, gl'impartì la comunione.

**communiqué** *n.* comunicato ufficiale.
**commun-ism** *n.* comunismo. **-ist** *adj., n.* comunista *m., f.*; *the Italian -ist Party*, il Partito Comunista Italiano (P.C.I.).
**community** *n.* comunità; comunanza; — *centre*, sala di ricreazione; — *singing*, canto in coro.
**commutable** *adj.* permutabile; (leg.) commutabile.
**commute** *tr.* (electr.; leg.) commutare; *intr.* viaggiare come abbonato.
**commuter** *n.* abbonato.
**Como** *pr.n.* Como *f.*; *of* —, comasco; *Lake* —, il Lago di Como, il Lario.
**compact**[1] *adj.* compatto; serrato; *tr.* consolidare; rendere compatto; *to be -ed of*, essere composto di.
**com·pact**[2] *n.* patto; accordo; convenzione; portacipria *m. indecl.*
**compactness** *n.* compattezza; (fig.) concisione.
**companion** *n.* compagno; camerata *m., f.*; socio *m.*; accompagnatore; *boon* —, compagno di svaghi; *travelling* —, compagno di viaggio; — *in arms*, commilitone *m.*; *lady* —, dama di compagnia; *to be a — to*, accompagnare; vademecum *m.*; — *picture*, ribattimento; (naut.) cappa di boccaporto.
**companion-able** *adj.* socievole. **-ship** *n.* compagnia; amicizia; cameratismo. **-way** *n.* (naut.) scaletta di boccaporto.
**company** *n.* compagnia; *good* —, buona compagnia; *bad* —, cattiva compagnia; *for the sake of* —, per il piacere della compagnia, per non rimanere solo; *in the — of*, accompagnato da; *present — excepted*, esclusi i presenti; *to keep — with*, accompagnarsi, tener compagnia a, andare insieme con; *to part — with*, separarsi da; (provb.) *two's —, three's none*, poca brigata, vita beata; comitiva, brigata; (mil.) compagnia; (naut.) *ship's* —, equipaggio, ciurma; (comm.) società, compagnia, ditta; *limited* —, società anonima.
**comparable** *adj.* pargonabile; comparabile.
**comparative** *adj.* comparativo; comparato; (fig.) relativo; *n.* (gramm.) comparativo.
**compare** *tr.* paragonare; confrontare; agguagliare; collazionare; (gramm.) formare il comparativo di; *to — with, tr.* confrontare a, *intr.* essere paragonabile a, sostenere il confronto con; *-d with*, in confronto di, rispetto a, di fronte a; *to — notes with*, scambiare idee con.
**comparison** *n.* confronto; paragone *m.*; accostamento; (gramm.) comparazione; *by — with*, in confronto di, rispetto a, di fronte a; *beyond* —, senza paragone, imparagonabile; *to bear — with*, sostenere il confronto con, essere paragonabile a, stare di fronte a.
**compartment** *n.* compartimento; suddivisione; casella; (rlwy.) scompartimento; (naut.) *watertight* —, compartimento stagno, paratia stagna; (mech.) locale *m.*; camera.
**compass** *n.* circonferenza; spazio; ambito; portata; limiti *m.pl.*; (of arch) sesto; (mus.) registro; estensione; diapason *m. indecl.*; *mariner's* —, bussola nautica; *to take a — bearing*, fare un rilevamento con la bussola; *a pair of -es*, compasso, seste *f.pl.*
**compass** *tr.* cingere; circondare; accerchiare; ottenere, raggiungere; complottare, tramare.
**compass-box** *n.* (naut.) abitacolo; chiesuola. **-card** *n.* (naut.) rosa dei venti.
**compassion** *n.* compassione; pietà; misericordia. **-ate** *adj.* pieno di compassione; pietoso; misericordioso; compassionevole; (mil.) *-ate leave*, congedo straordinario per motivi familiari.
**compatib-le** *adj.* compatibile. **-ility** *n.* compatibilità.
**compatriot** *n.* compatriota *m., f.*
**compeer** *n.* uguale *m.*; pari *m. indecl.*
**compel** *tr.* costringere; obbligare; forzare; *to — someone to do something*, costringere qualcuno a fare qualcosa; *to be -led to*, essere costretto a, dovere per forza; (fig.) *to — respect*, esigere rispetto, farsi rispettare.
**compelling** *adj.* irresistibile; impellente.
**compendious** *adj.* compendioso; sommario; conciso; succinto.
**compendium** *n.* compendio; sunto; riassunto.
**compensat-e** *tr.* compensare, ricompensare; indennizzare; risarcire; *to — someone for something*, indennizzare qualcuno per qualcosa; *intr. to — for*, supplire a. **-ion** *n.* compenso, ricompenso; indennizzo; risarcimento dei danni; *by way of -ion for*, per compenso di. **-ory** *adj.* compensativo; compensatore.
**compère** *n.* (theatr.) presentatore.
**compete** *intr.* concorrere; gareggiare; partecipare; *to — for*, concorrere a; *to — with*, fare concorrenza a, sostenere la concorrenza di.
**compet-ence** *n.* competenza; abilità; capacità; (leg.) competenza, pertinenza; (fig.) ambito. **-ent** *adj.* competente; capace; abile; atto; (leg.) competente idoneo.
**competition** *n.* gara; competizione; agone *m.*; concorso; concorrenza; *to go in for a* —, concorrere; *to enter into — with*, mettersi in gara con, gareggiare con; *to face* —, far fronte alla concorrenza.
**competitive** *adj.* di gara; di competizione; — *prices*, prezzi di concorrenza; — *examination*, concorso; — *spirit*, spirito agonistico.
**competitor** *n.* concorrente *m., f.*; competitore; agonista *m., f.*; (fig.) emulo; rivale *m., f.*
**compilation** *n.* compilazione.
**compile** *tr.* compilare; comporre; mettere insieme.
**complac-ency** *n.* compiacenza di sè; compiacimento; autosufficienza. **-ent** *adj.* compiaciuto; soddisfatto di sè; auto sufficiente.
**complain** *intr.* lamentarsi; lagnarsi; querelarsi; *to — of a pain*, accusare un dolore; *to be always -ing*, lamentarsi sempre; *to — about*, lagnarsi di.
**complainant** *n.* (leg.) querelante *m., f.*
**complaint** *n.* lamento; lagnanza; reclamo; *to have no cause for* —, non aver alcuna ragione di cui lamentarsi; *to make a* —, lagnarsi, formulare un reclamo; (med.) malattia; affezione; *mild* —, disturbo.
**complaisant** *adj.* compiacente; cortese.
**complement** *n.* complemento; il necessario per completare; dotazione; *with its full — of*, al completo di; (mil.; naut.) effettivi *m.pl.*
**complementary** *adj.* complementare.
**complete** *adj.* completo; intero; totale; finito; perfetto; *tr.* completare; compire, terminare, finire, perfezionare; riempire. **-ness** *n.* completezza; compiatezza; pienezza.
**completion** *n.* completamento; compimento; terminazione; perfezionamento.
**complex** *adj.* complesso; complicato; intricato; *n.* complesso; insieme *m.*; *inferiority* —, complesso d'inferiorità.
**complexion** *n.* carnagione *f.*; colorito; carattere *m.*; aspetto; *to put a good — on*, presentare sotto un aspetto favorevole. **-ed** *adj.* di carnagione.
**complexity** *n.* complessità; complicatezza.
**compliance** *n.* acquiescenza; osservanza; condiscendenza; *in — with*, in conformità a, conforme a.
**compliant** *adj.* accomodante; compiacente; accondiscente; servile.
**complic-ate** *tr.* complicare; rendere difficile. **-ated** *adj.* complicato; complesso; difficile; *to become -ated*, complicarsi, diventare difficile. **-ation** *n.* complicazione; difficoltà.
**complicity** *n.* complicità; (leg.) correità.
**compliment** *n.* complimento; *to*

*pay a — to*, fare un complimento a; *to pay one's -s to*, fare una visita di cortesia a; saluto; ossequio; *with the publisher's -s*, con gli ossequi dell'editore; *the -s of the season*, i migliori auguri; *tr.* complimentare, congratularsi con, felicitarsi con. **-ary** *adj.* complimentare; *-ary seats*, entrate di favore; *-ary ticket*, biglietto di omaggio.

**compline** *n.* (liturg.) compieta.

**comply** *intr.* ubbidire; acconsentire; *to — with*, conformarsi a, osservare, rispettare.

**component** *adj.*, *n.* componente *m.*; *— part*, pezzo staccato.

**comport** *rfl.* *to — oneself*, comportarsi.

**compos-e** *tr.* comporre; costituire; *to be -d of*, essere composto di, comporsi di, consistere di; (fig.) ricomporre, raccogliere, calmare; *to — a quarrel*, comporre una vertenza. **-ed** *adj.* composto; calmo; tranquillo. **-er** *n.* (mus.) compositore; istrumentatore. **-ing** *n.* il comporre; (typ.) composizione.

**composite** *adj.* composto; a struttura mista; *n.* corpo composto.

**composition** *n.* composizione; opera; composto; miscela; concordato; accomodamento; transazione.

**compositor** *n.* (typ.) compositore.

**compos mentis** *adj.* (leg.) sano di mente.

**compost** *n.* composto; concime *m.*

**composure** *n.* compostezza; calma; sangue freddo.

**com'pound** *adj.* composto; *— interest*, interessi composti; *— word*, parola composta; (surg.) *— fracture*, frattura composta; *n.* miscela; composto.

**compound** *tr.* comporre; mescolare; combinare; (of debt) regolare; *intr.* venire ad un accordo; transigere.

**comprehend** *tr.* capire; comprendere; includere; comprendere; contenere.

**comprehensib-le** *adj.* intelligibile; comprensibile. **-ility** *n.* intelligibilità; comprensibilità.

**comprehension** *n.* comprensione.

**comprehensive** *adj.* comprensivo; di vasta portata. **-ness** *n.* comprensiva.

**com'press** *n.* (med.) compressa.

**compress** *tr.* comprimere; serrare; (fig.) condensare. **-ion** *n.* compressione; (fig.) condensazione. **-or** *n.* compressore.

**comprise** *tr.* comprendere; includere; contenere; abbracciare.

**compromis-e** *n.* compromesso; accomodamento; transazione; *tr.* compromettere; *to — oneself*, compromettersi; *intr.* giungere a un compromesso; transigere. **-ing** *adj.* compromettente; imbarazzante.

**Comptroller** *n.* *— of the Royal Household*, Sovrintendente della Casa Reale.

**compulsion** *n.* costrizione; obbligo; *under —*, per costrizione, per forza.

**compulsive** *adj.* coercitivo.

**compulsory** *adj.* d'obbligo; obbligatorio; forzato; forzoso.

**compunction** *n.* rimorso; compunzione.

**computation** *n.* computo; calcolo; computazione.

**compute** *tr.* computare; calcolare; contare; abbacare.

**computer** *n.* calcolatrice.

**comrade** *n.* camerata *m.*, *f.*; compagno. **-ly** *adj.* cameratesco; affratellevole. **-ship** *n.* cameratismo.

**con** *tr.* studiare attentamente, ripassare.

**concatenation** *n.* concatenazione.

**concav-e** *adj.* concavo; incavato. **-ity** *n.* concavità.

**conceal** *tr.* celare; nascondere; tener segreto; dissimulare; (leg.) ricettare; *to keep -ed*, nascondere, tener nascosto. **-ment** *n.* celamento; nascondimento; dissimulazione; nascondiglio; (leg.) ricettazione.

**concede** *tr.* concedere; cedere; ammettere; acconsentire.

**conceit** *n.* vanità; presunzione; boria; albagia; ricercatezza; concettino; (fam.) *puffed up with —*, gonfio come una rana.

**conceited** *adj.* vanitoso; vanesio; presuntuoso; borioso; affettato; pieno di sè. **-ness** *n.* vanità; presunzione; albagia.

**conceivab-le** *adj.* concepibile; immaginabile; (fam.) *every — thing*, ogni ben di Dio. **-ility** *n.* concepibilità.

**conceive** *tr.* concepire; generare; *intr.* concepire; ingravidarsi; (fig.) immaginare; ideare; concepire.

**concentrate** *n.* concentrato; *tr.* concentrare; far convergere; (chem.) condensare; *intr.* concentrarsi; *to — on*, concentrare la propria attenzione su, dedicarsia.

**concentration** *n.* concentrazione; concentramento; *— camp*, campo di concentramento.

**concentric** *adj.* concentrico. **-ity** *n.* l'essere concentrico.

**concept** *n.* concetto; nozione.

**conception** *n.* concezione; concepimento; (theol.) *the Immaculate Conception*, l'Immacolata Concezione, la Concezione di Maria; (fam.) *I haven't the remotest —*, non ne ho la minima idea.

**concern**[1] *n.* sollecitudine *f.*; ansietà; preoccupazione; inquietudine *f.*; interesse *m.*; faccenda; affare *m.*; arnese *m.*; cosa; (comm.) ditta, azienda, società; negozio; *a going —*, un negozio bene avviato; *to show —*, inquietarsi, preoccuparsi; *it's no — of mine*, non mi riguarda, non ci entro.

**concern**[2] *tr.* riguardare; toccare; interessare; concernere; *it does not — me*, non mi riguarda; *to whomsoever it may —*, a chiunque riguardi; inquietare, preoccupare. **-ed** *adj.* interessato; in questione; *the people -ed*, gli interessati; *the firm -ed*, la ditta in questione; preoccupato; ansioso; *to look -ed*, avere l'aria preoccupata; *to be much -ed about*, essere molto preoccupato per. **-ing** *prep.* riguardo a; circa; in merito a.

**concert** *n.* concerto; *— hall*, sala da concerto; *— performer*, concertista *m.*, *f.*; (fig.) accordo; armonia; concerto; *to act in —*, agire di comune accordo.

**concerted** *adj.* (mus.) concertato; (fig.) convenuto, predisposto, concertato, congiunto.

**concertina** *n.* (mus.) fisarmonica, concertina; (motor.) *— connexion*, connessione a mantice; (rlwy.) *— vestibule*, passaggio a soffietto.

**concerto** *n.* (mus.) concerto; *violin —*, concerto per violino.

**concert-pitch** *n.* diapason *m.* *indecl.* da concerto.

**concession** *n.* concessione; rilascio; agevolazione.

**conch** *n.* conchiglia; (zool.) mollusco; crostaceo; (archit.) conca.

**concierge** *n.* portinaio.

**conciliar** *adj.* (eccl.) conciliare.

**concili-ate** *tr.* conciliare; comporre. **-ation** *n.* conciliazione. **-ative, -atory** *adj.* conciliante, conciliativo.

**concis-e** *adj.* conciso; succinto; breve. **-eness, -ion** *n.* concisione; brevità.

**conclave** *n.* (eccl.) conclave *m.*; (fam.) riunione segreta; *to be in — with*, consigliarsi a quattr'occhi con.

**conclud-e** *tr.*, *intr.* finire, terminare, chiudere; concludere; dedurre, desumere; decidere. **-ing** *adj.* ultimo; finale; di chiusura.

**conclusion** *n.* conclusione; fine *f.*, chiusura; *in —*, in fine, insomma, in sostanza; *to draw -s*, tirare le conclusioni; *to try -s with*, misurarsi con.

**conclusive** *adj.* conclusivo; definitivo; decisivo.

**concoct** *tr.* confezionare; mescolare; (fig.) inventare; architettare; macchinare; tramare. **-ion** *n.* intruglio; decotto; (fig.) macchinazione; elaborazione; panzana.

**concomit-ance** concomitanza. **-ant** *adj.* concomitante.

**concord** *n.* concordia; armonia;

accordo; (mus.) consonanza, concordanza.
**concord-ance** *n.* accordo; armonia; (gramm.; mus.) concordanza; indice analitico. **-ant** *adj.* concordante; concorde; armonioso.
**concordat** *n.* (hist.) concordato.
**concourse** *n.* concorso; affluenza; (archit.) atrio.
**concrete** *adj.* concreto; *n. the —*, il concreto; (bldg.) betone *m.*, calcestruzzo; conglomerato; *reinforced —*, cemento armato; *to set in —*, annegare nel calcestruzzo.
**concrete-mixer** *n.* (bldg.) betoniera.
**concreteness** *n.* concretezza.
**concretion** *n.* (geol.) concrezione.
**concubin-e** *n.* concubina. **-age** *n.* concubinato.
**concupiscence** *n.* concupiscenza.
**concur** *intr.* concorrere; coincidere; andare d'accordo, accordarsi; *to — with someone in an opinion*, condividere l'opinione di qualcuno.
**concurr-ence** *n.* concorso; simultaneità; consenso; (geom.) convergenzo. **-ent** *adj.* concorrente; simultaneo; concorde, concordante; (geom.) convergente.
**concussion** *n.* scossa; urto; (med.) commozione cerebrale.
**condemn** *tr.* condannare; *to be -ed to death*, essere condannato a morte; *-ed man*, condannato; *-ed cell*, cella dei condannati a morte; (fig.) censurare, biasimare, stroncare. **-ation** *n.* condanna; (fig.) censura; biasimo. **-atory** *adj.* condannatorio; (fig.) sfavorevole.
**condensable** *adj.* condensabile.
**condensate** *n.* (chem.) condensato.
**condensation** *n.* condensazione.
**condens-e** *tr.* condensare; addensare; *intr.* condensarsi, addensarsi; *-d milk*, latte condensato; (fig.) abbreviare; compendiare. **-er** *n.* condensatore.
**condescend** *intr.* condiscendere; degnarsi. **-ing** *adj.* condiscendente; dall'alto in basso.
**condescension** *n.* condiscendenza; degnazione.
**condign** *adj.* giusto; meritato; adeguato.
**condiment** *n.* condimento.
**condition** *n.* condizione; obbligo; *-s of sale*, modalità di vendita; *n. weather -s*, condizioni meteorologiche; *on — that*, a condizione che, purchè, premesso che; stato; condizioni *f.pl.*; *in good —*, in perfetta salute, (sport) in forma, allenato; in buone condizioni; *tr.* condizionare. **-al** *adj., n.* condizionale *m.*
**condole** *intr. to — with*, condolersi con, esprimere le proprie condoglianze a.
**condolence** *n.* condoglianze *f.pl.*
**condom** *n.* condon *m. indecl.*, goldone *m.*
**condominium** *n.* condominio.
**condon-e** *tr.* condonare; passar sopra; perdonare; scusare. **-ation** *n.* condono.
**condor** *n.* (orn.) condore *m.*
**condottiere** *n.* condottiero, condottiere *m.*
**conduc-e** *intr.* condurre; contribuire, tendere. **-ive** *adj.* contribuente; tendente.
**con·duct** *n.* condotta; comportamento; contegno; direzione; *safe —*, salvacondotto.
**conduct** *tr.* condurre; guidare; dirigere; menare; accompagnare; (mus.) dirigere; (phys.) condurre, trasmettere; *to — oneself*, comportarsi; *-ed tour*, gita accompagnata. **-ing** *n.* direzione. **-ion** *n.* (phys.) conduzione; convogliamento. **-ivity** *n.* (phys.) conducibilità; conduttività.
**conduct-or** *n.* (mus.) dirigente *m.*, maestro; (of tour) accompagnatore; (bus, tram) bigliettario; (phys.) conduttore. **-ress** *n.* bigliettaria.
**conduit** *n.* condotto; alveo.
**cone** *n.* (geom.) cono; (fir, pine) pigna; (ice-cream) cialdone *m.*, cono; (bot.) strobilo, strobile *m.*
**confabulat-e** *intr.* confabulare. **-ion** *n.* confabulazione; discussione.
**confection** *n.* confezione. **-er** *n.* pasticciere *m.*; *-er's shop*, pasticceria. **-ery** *n.* dolci, dolciumi, confetti *m.pl.*; *-ery shop* pasticceria.
**confederacy** *n.* confederazione; complotto; cospirazione.
**confederat-e** *adj.* confederato; alleato; *n.* confederato; complice *m., f.*; correo; compare *m.*; *tr.* confederare; *intr.* confederarsi; allearsi. **-ion** *n.* confederazione.
**confer** *tr.* conferire; accordare; *to — a title on*, conferire un titolo a; *intr.* conferire; consultarsi; abboccarsi. **-ence** *n.* conferenza; consultazione; abboccamento; (industr.) congresso; (med.) consulto; *press —*, conferenza stampa. **-ment** *n.* conferimento.
**confess** *tr., intr.* confessare; riconoscere; ammettere; *to — a penitent*, confessare un penitente; *to — to a priest*, confessarsi da un sacerdote.
**confessedly** *adv.* per confessione propria; apertamente.
**confession** *n.* confessione; ammissione; professione; *to make one's —*, far la confessione, confessarsi; *he goes to the parish priest for —*, si confessa dal parroco; *the priest heard his —* il prete lo confessò; *the seal of —*, il segreto della confessione. **-al** *n.* (eccl.) confessionale *m.*, confessionario.
**confessor** *n.* confessore.
**confetti** *n.* coriandoli *m.pl.*
**confidant(e)** *n.* confidente *m., f.*
**confide** *tr.* affidare; confidare; *intr. to — in*, confidare in, confidarsi con, aver fiducia in.
**confidence** *n.* fiducia; fede *f.*; sicurezza; *vote of —*, voto di fiducia; *motion of no —*, mozione di sfiducia; *with complete —*, ad occhi chiusi; *— trick*, truffa all'americana; *to gain —*, affrancarsi; *to inspire —*, dare affidamento; confidenza; *in strict —*, con la massima riservatezza; *to take someone into one's —*, confidarsi con qualcuno; *to tell in —*, dire in confidenza.
**confident** *adj.* fiducioso; sicuro; *to be — of*, avere fiducia in; *to be — that*, essere fiducioso che, sentirsi sicuro che; baldanzoso, sicuro di sè, presuntuoso.
**confidential** *adj.* confidenziale; riservato; privato; *— letter*, lettera riservata.
**confiding** *adj.* fiducioso; ingenuo; senza sospetti.
**configuration** *n.* configurazione; conformazione.
**con·fine**[1] *n.* confine *m.*; limite *m.*; *within the -s of*, entro i confini di.
**confin-e**[2] *tr.* relegare; imprigionare; rinchiudere; internare; *to be -d to bed*, essere costretto a letto; (mil.) *to — to barracks*, consegnare; *to be -d*, partorire; *to — oneself to*, limitarsi a.
**confinement** *n.* imprigionamento; prigionia; reclusione; *solitary —*, segregazione cellulare; (mil.) *— to barracks*, consegna; (of woman) parto, puerperio; limitazione, restrizione *f.*
**confirm** *tr.* confermare; corroborare; ratificare; (leg.) confermare, omologare, avallare; (eccl.) cresimare, confermare. **-ation** *n.* conferma; corroborazione; ratificazione; (eccl.) cresima, prima comunione. **-ative, -atory** *adj.* confermativo; affermativo. **-ed** *adj.* confermato; (eccl.) cresimato; (fam.) inveterato, impenitente, matricolato.
**confiscat-e** *tr.* confiscare; sequestrare. **-ion** *n.* confisca; sequestro.
**conflagration** *n.* incendio; conflagrazione.
**con·flict** *n.* conflitto; contrasto; lotta; scontro; *to come into — with*, venire a conflitto con, scontrarsi con.
**conflict** *intr. to — with*, essere in conflitto con, contrastare con, discordare da. **-ing** *adj.* contrario; contrastante; in contrasto, contradditorio; *-ing interests*, interessi contrastanti; *-ing evidence*, prove contradditorie.
**confluence** *n.* confluenza; (of roads) incrocio.
**conform** *tr.* conformare; uniformare; *intr.* conformarsi; uniformarsi; ubbidire; adattarsi.

**conformab-le** *adj.* conforme. **-ility** *n.* conformità.
**conformation** *n.* conformazione; configurazione; (fig.) adattamento.
**conform-ist** *n.* conformista *m., f.* **-ity** *n.* conformità; accordo; uniformità; *in -ity with*, conformemente a; (rel.) conformismo.
**confound** *tr.* sconcertare; disorientare; sconvolgere; *to be -ed*, essere stupefatto; *— you!*, va' al diavolo! **-ed** *adj.* (fam.) maledetto; insopportabile.
**confraternity** *n.* (rel.) confraternità, congrega.
**confrère** *n.* confratello; collega *m.*
**confront** *tr.* affrontare; trovarsi di fronte a; collazionare; (leg.) mettere a confronto.
**Confuc-ius** *pr.n.* Confucio. **-ianism** *n.* confucianismo.
**confus-e** *tr.* confondere; sconcertare; disorientare; mescolare; scambiare; *to get -d*, confondersi; scambiare, prendere per. **-ed** *adj.* confuso; sconcertato; perplesso; disorientato; disordinato; alla rinfusa; aggrovigliato. **-ing** *adj.* sconcertante; abbagliante; che confonde; che rende perplesso.
**confusion** *n.* confusione; disordin e*m.*; scompiglio; babele *f.*; *in —*, confuso, alla rinfusa; *to throw into —*, scompigliare, sbaragliare; *to drink to the — of one's enemies*, bere alla sconfitta dei propri nemici; imbarazzo; turbamento; scambio.
**confut-e** *tr.* confutare. **-ation** *n.* confutazione.
**congeal** *tr.* coagulare; cagliare; congelare, agghiacciare; *intr.* coagularsi, cagliarsi; congelarsi, agghiacciarsi.
**congenial** *adj.* affine; congeniale; simpatico; amabile.
**congenital** *adj.* congenito; innato
**conger** *n.* (ichth.) gongro.
**congest-ed** *adj.* congestionato; sovrappopolato; sovraffollato. **-ion** *n.* congestione; *-ion of the lungs*, congestione polmonare.
**conglomerat-e** *adj., n.* conglomerato; *tr.* conglomerare; *intr.* conglomerarsi. **-ion** *n.* conglomerazione; (fig.) guazzabuglio.
**conglutination** *n.* agglutinazione.
**Congo** *pr.n.* (geog.) Congo. **-lese** *adj., n.* congolese *m., f.*
**congratulat-e** *tr.* congratularsi con; rallegrarsi con; complimentare; fare i propri complimenti a, felicitarsi con; *I — you on your success*, mi congratulo con te per il tuo successo. **-ion** *n.* congratulazione, felicitazione; complimenti *m.pl.*; *-ions!*, i miei complimenti! **-ory** *adj.* gratulatorio, di felicitazione.
**congregate** *tr.* congregare; riunire; adunare; *intr.* congregarsi; riunirsi; adunarsi.
**congregation** *n.* riunione; adunata; assemblea; (rel.) congregazione; fedeli *m.pl.* **-al** *adj.* della congregazione; *-al worship*, culto pubblico; *-al church*, chiesa congregazionalista. **-alism** *n.* congregazionalismo. **-alist** congregazionalista *m., f.*
**congress** *n.* congresso; riunione; (USA) *Congress*, il Congresso. **-ional** *adj.* di congresso. **-man** *n.* (pol.) membro del Congresso.
**congruence** *n.* congruenza.
**congruity** *n.* congruità; conformità.
**congruous** *adj.* congruo, congruente; conforme.
**conic, conic-al** *adj.* conico. **-alness, -ity** *n.* conicità.
**conifer** *n.* (bot.) conifero. **-ous** *adj.* conifero.
**conjectur-e** *n.* congettura; supposizione; *tr., intr.* congetturare; supporre. **-able** *adj.* congetturabile. **-al** *adj.* congetturale.
**conjoin** *tr.* congiungere; combinare; annettere.
**conjoint** *adj.* congiunto; (herald.) accollato.
**conjugal** *adj.* coniugale; matrimoniale.
**conjugat-e** *tr.* coniugare. **-ion** *n.* coniugazione.
**conjunct** *adj.* congiunto. **-ion** *n.* congiunzione; *in -ion with*, insieme con. **-ive** *adj., n.* congiuntivo.
**conjunctivitis** *n.* (med.) congiuntivite *f.*
**conjuncture** *n.* congiuntura; circostanza.
**conjur-e** *tr.* scongiurare; ammaliare; incantare; *to — away*, esorcizzare, far scomparire per incanto; *to — up*, evocare, richiamare; *intr.* fare il prestigiatore, fare giuochi di prestigio. **-er, -or** *n.* prestigiatore. **-ing** *n.* prestidigitazione; giuoco di prestigio; *-ing trick*, giuoco di prestigio.
**conk** *n.* (slang) naso; colpo; *tr.* colpire; *intr. to — out*, far cilecca.
**conker** *n.* (fam.) castagnino; *pl.* giuoco infantile con castagnini.
**connate** *adj.* (bot.) connato.
**connatural** *adj.* connaturale.
**connect** *tr.* connettere, collegare, unire, allacciare, congiungere; (electr.) accoppiare; (fig.) associare, ricollegare; *to be -ed with*, aver rapporti con, far parte di; (fig.) ricollegarsi a; *intr.* (of trains, *etc.*) far coincidenza. **-ed** *part. adj.* congiunto; unito; allacciato; connesso, coerente; *well -ed*, bene imparentato.
**connecting-rod** *n.* (mech.) biella; (bldg.) ferro di sovrapposizione.
**connection, connexion** *n.* connessione; collegamento; comunicazione; (electr.) accoppiamento; rapporto; relazione; *in — with*, in relazione a, in merito a; in occasione di; parente *m., f.*; congiunto; (comm.) clientela; (rlwy.; bus) coincidenza; *to run in — with*, far coincidenza con.
**connective** *adj.* connettivo.
**conning-tower** *n.* (naut.) torretta di comando.
**conniv-e** *intr. to — at*, essere connivente a, essere complice di; (fig.) tollerare. **-ance** connivenza; complicità.
**connoisseur** *n.* intenditore, conoscitore, amatore; buongustaio.
**connot-e** *tr.* denotare; significare implicitamente. **-ation** *n.* significato implicito.
**connubial** *adj.* coniugale; matrimoniale.
**conquer** *tr.* conquistare; soggiogare; vincere; (fig.) superare; sormontare; *intr.* vincere. **-ing** *adj.* vittorioso. **-or** *n.* conquistatore; vincitore; *William the Conqueror*, Guglielmo il Conquistatore.
**conquest** *n.* conquista; vittoria.
**Conrad** *pr.n.* Corrado.
**consanguin-eous** *adj.* consanguineo. **-ity** *n.* consanguineità.
**conscience** *n.* coscienza; *accommodating —*, coscienza elastica; *case of —*, caso di coscienza; *to have a guilty —*, avere la coscienza sporca; *to have on one's —*, aver sull'anima; *— money*, restituzione anonima di somma dovuta.
**conscience-stricken** *adj.* preso dal rimorso; *to be —*, sentirsi rimordere la coscienza.
**conscientious** *adj.* coscienzioso; scrupoloso; zelante; accurato; diligente; *— objector*, obiettore di coscienza. **-ness** *n.* coscienziosità; zelo; accuratezza; amor proprio.
**conscious** *adj.* consapevole; conscio; compreso; cosciente; *to be — of*, essere consapevole di, accorgersi di, sentire; *to become —*, tornare in sè, riprendere conoscenza. **-ness** *n.* coscienza; consapevolezza; (med.) conoscenza.
**con·script** *n.* (mil.) coscritto, soldato di leva; (hist.) *the — fathers*, i padri coscritti.
**conscript** *tr.* coscrivere, chiamare alle armi. **-ion** *n.* leva; coscrizione.
**consecrat-e** *tr.* (rel.) consacrare; (fig.) dedicare. **-ion** *n.* consacrazione; (fig.) dedizione.
**consecutive** *adj.* consecutivo; successivo.
**consensual** *adj.* consensuale.
**consensus** *n.* consenso unanime; accordo.
**consent** *n.* consenso; acconsentimento; accordo; *by mutual —*, di comune accordo; *intr.* acconsentire; annuire; dire di sì.
**consequence** *n.* conseguenza; effetto; *in —*, per conseguenza; *in — of*, a causa di, in seguito a,

per effetto di; *to suffer the ~s*, sopportare le conseguenze, andare di mezzo; rilievo; importanza; *of* —, importante; *it is of no* —, non importa, non ha nessuna importanza.

**consequent** *adj.* conseguente; risultante; che deriva. **~ly** *adv.* di conseguenza perciò; dunque; quindi. **~ial** *adj.* che consegue; che deriva; pieno di sè, prepotente, borioso. **~iality** *n.* conseguenza; coerenza; (fig.) prepotenza, boria.

**conservable** *adj.* conservabile.

**conservancy** *n.* conservazione; commissione di controllo.

**conservation** *n.* conservazione; tutela; preservazione.

**conservative** *adj.* conservativo; cauto; prudenziale; (pol.) *adj.*, *n.* conservatore.

**conservatoire** *n.* (mus.) conservatorio liceo musicale.

**conservator** *n.* preservatore; tutore; direttore, sovrintendente.

**conservatory** *n.* serra.

**conserve** *n.* (cul.) conserva di frutta; marmellata; *tr.* conservare; preservare.

**consider** *tr.* considerare; reputare; giudicare; ritenere; *to — something as done*, considerare qualcosa bello e fatto; *to — it one's duty to do something*, ritenere il proprio dovere far qualcosa; *to — what to do*, riflettere sul da farsi; aver riguardo di, rispettare; tener conto di; pensare su, riflettere su, ponderare; guardare, contemplare.

**considerab~le** *adj.* considerevole; notevole; discreto, vistoso; degno di considerazione. **~ly** *adv.* considerevolmente; discretamente; alquanto; assai.

**considerate** *adj.* riguardoso; sollecito; rispettoso dei sentimenti altrui. **~ness** *n.* riguardo; sollecitudine *f.*; delicatezza.

**consideration** *n.* considerazione; riflessione; *after due* —, dopo dovuta riflessione; *in — of*, in considerazione di, dato, visto, in vista di; *under* —, in esame; *to take into* —, prendere in considerazione, tenere conto di; riguardo; sollecitudine *f.*; delicatezza; compenso; *for a* —, dietro compenso; fattore *m.*; motivo.

**consider~ed** *part.* of **consider**, *q.v.*; *adj.* ponderato, meditato; *— opinion*, opinione ben ponderata. **~ing** *part.*, *ger.*, *prep.* tenuto conto di, dato, visto, in considerazione di; *~ing that*, dato che, visto che.

**consign** *tr.* consegnare; spedire; (fig.) affidare; rimettere; (leg.) *to — to prison*, associare alle carceri. **~ee** *n.* consegnatario; destinatario. **~er** *n.* mittente *m.*, *f.* **~ment** *n.* spedizione; consegna; invio; partita di merce; (comm.) *on ~ment*, in deposito; *~ment note*, nota di spedizione.

**consist** *intr.* constare (di); essere composto (di); consistere (in); essere costituito (da). **~ence, ~ency** *n.* consistenza; densità; solidità; (fig.) coerenza; costanza. **~ent** *adj.* compatibile; in armonia; (fig.) coerente; costante.

**consistor~y** *n.* (eccl.) concistoro; *— court*, tribunale diocesano. **~ial** *adj.* concistoriale.

**con·sole**[1] *n.* (archit.) mensola; consolle *f.*

**consol~e**[2] *tr.* consolare; confortare; *to — oneself*, mettersi l'animo in pace. **~able** *adj.* consolabile. **~ation** *n.* consolazione; *words of ~ation*, parole consolatrici; *~ation prize*, premio di consolazione. **~atory** *adj.* consolatorio, consolante, di conforto.

**consolidat~e** *tr.* consolidare; rafforzare; *intr.* consolidarsi; rafforzarsi; (comm.) *to — a debt*, unificare un debito; fondere; combinare. **~ion** *n.* consolidazione; rafforzamento; (comm.) fusione, riunione.

**consols** *n.* (finan.) consolidato.

**consommé** *n.* (cul.) brodo ristretto, minestrina.

**conson~ance** *n.* (mus.) consonanza, corrispondenza. **~ant** *adj.* consono (a); conforme (a); (mus.) consonante; *n.* (gramm.) consonante *f.* **~antal** *adj.* consonantico.

**con·sort** *n.* consorte, coniuge *m.*; consorte *f.*; *Prince Consort*, principe consorte; (mus.) accordo.

**consort** *intr. to — with*, associarsi con; frequentare.

**consortium** *n.* consorzio.

**conspectus** *n.* panorama *m.*; rassegna; tabella sinottica.

**conspicuous** *adj.* cospicuo, vistoso, notevole; evidente, bene in vista; *to be — by one's absence*, brillare per l'assenza. **~ness** *n.* cospicuità, vistosità; evidenza.

**conspir~acy** *n.* cospirazione; congiura; complotto. **~ator** *n.* cospiratore; congiurato.

**conspire** *intr.* cospirare; congiurare; complottare; far cabala.

**constable** *n.* (hist.) con(n)estabile *m.*; poliziotto, vigile *m.*; appuntato (dei carabinieri); *Chief* —, Capo della Polizia, (in Italy) Questore; *special* —, tutore volontario dell'ordine.

**constabulary** *n.* corpo della polizia.

**Constance** *pr.n.* Costanza.

**constancy** *n.* costanza; fermezza; fedeltà.

**constant** *adj.* costante; fedele; continuo; (math.; phys.) costante, invariabile; *n.* (math.) costante *f.*

**Constantine** *pr.n.* Costantino; (geog.) Costantina.

**Constantinople** *pr.n.* (geog.) Costantinopoli *f.*

**constellation** *n.* costellazione.

**consternat~e** *tr.* costernare; atterrire. **~ion** *n.* costernazione; atterrimento, allibimento.

**constipat~ed** *adj.* stitico. **~ion** *n.* stitichezza; (med.) costipazione intestinale.

**constituency** *n.* collegio elettorale.

**constituent** *adj.* costituente; che compone; *— parts*, componenti *f.pl.*; *n.* elemento; componente; (pol.) elettore.

**constitute** *tr.* costituire, formare, essere; nominare, eleggare; *to be ~d as a republic*, reggersi a repubblica.

**constitution** *n.* costituzione; formazione; (pol.) costituzione, statuto; (med.) salute *f.*, abito. **~al** *adj.* costituzionale; *n.* passeggiata igienica.

**constitutive** *adj.* costitutivo.

**constrain** *tr.* costringere; forzare; obbligare. **~ed** *part. adj.* costretto; forzato; (fig.) impacciato, imbarazzato.

**constraint** *n.* costrizione; coercizione; (fig.) imbarazzo, soggezione.

**constrict** *tr.* stringere; comprimere; restringere. **~ion** *n.* stringimento; compressione. **~or** *n.* (anat.) muscolo costrittore.

**construct** *tr.* costruire; edificare; alzare; formulare.

**construction** *n.* costruzione; edificio; interpretazione, senso. **~al** *adj.* strutturale; di costruzione.

**constructive** *adj.* costruttivo; positivo; (leg.) implicito, indiziario.

**constructor** *n.* costruttore.

**construe** *tr.* tradurre; interpretare, spiegare; (gramm.) *to be ~d with*, reggere.

**consubstantial** *adj.* (theol.) consustanziale.

**consuetud~e** *n.* consuetudine *f.* **~inary** *adj.* consuetudinario.

**consul** *n.* console *m.* **~ar** *adj.* consolare. **~ate** *n.* consolato.

**consul-general** *n.* console generale.

**consult** *tr.* consultare; tener conto di, avere riguardo a; *intr.* consultarsi, concertarsi. **~ant** *n.* consulente *m.*; esperto; (med.) consulente medico. **~ation** *n.* consultazione; (med.) consulto; *in ~ation with*, previa consultazione con. **~ing** *adj.* consulente; *~ing room*, consultorio; (med.) ambulatorio, studio; *~ing hours*, orario di visita.

**consum~e** *tr.* consumare; distruggere; (fig.) *to be ~ed by*, consumarsi di, essere consumato da, struggersi da. **~able** *adj.* consumabile. **~er** *n.* consumatore; utente *m.*, *f.*; abbonato; *~er goods*, generi *m.pl.* di consumo.

**consum'mate** *adj.* consumato; perfetto.
**consummat-e** *tr.* compiere; (eccl.; leg.) consumare. **-ion** *n.* completamento; coronamento; (of marriage) consumazione.
**consumption** *n.* consumo; spreco, sciupìo; (med.) consunzione, tisi *f.*, tubercolosi *f.*
**consumptive** *adj.* che consuma; *n.* (med.) tisico, tuberculotico, tubercoloso.
**contact** *n.* contatto; punto d'incontro; — *lenses*, lenti *f.pl.* a contatto; (electr.) — *to earth*, messa a terra; — *breaker*, interruttore; conoscenza, amicizia; *to establish — with*, mettersi in contatto con, aprire un dialogo con; *tr.* mettersi in contatto con, avvicinare.
**contag-ion** *n.* contagio. **-ious** *adj.* contagioso. **-iousness** *n.* contagiosità.
**contain** *tr.* contenere; racchiudere; comprendere; includere; trattenere; frenare; (fig.) *to — oneself*, contenersi; controllarsi. **-er** *n.* recipiente *m.*; contenitore; (rlwy.) cassa mobile.
**contaminat-e** *tr.* contaminare; inquinare; adulterare; (fig.) corrompere. **-ion** *n.* contaminazione; inquinamento; (fig.) corruzione.
**contango** *n.* (finan.) premio di riporto.
**contemn** *tr.* spregiare; disprezzare.
**contemplat-e** *tr.* contemplare; meditare; proporsi; attendersi; avere intenzione di; guardare attentamente; *intr.* meditare, riflettere. **-ion** *n.* contemplazione; meditazione; raccoglimento. **-ive** *adj.* contemplativo; meditativo.
**contemporan-eity** *n.* contemporaneità. **-eous** *adj.* contemporaneo; simultaneo.
**contemporary** *adj.* contemporaneo, coetaneo; coevo; *n.* coetaneo; compagno.
**contempt** *n.* disprezzo; dispregio; (leg.) — *of court*, oltraggio alla corte.
**contemptib-le** *adj.* spregevole; disprezzabile; *n.* (hist.) *the old -s*, l'esercito regolare britannico del 1914; l'associazione dei reduci della prima guerra mondiale. **-ility, -leness** *n.* spregevolezza.
**contemptuous** *adj.* sprezzante; sdegnoso, insolente; altero. **-ness** *n.* disprezzo; sdegno; insolenza; alterigia.
**contend** *tr., intr.* contendere; combattere; gareggiare; contrastare; affermare; sostenere; *-ing passions*, passioni *f.pl.* contrastanti.
**content**[1] *adj.* contento; soddisfatto; lieto; pago; *to be — with*, essere contento di, accontentarsi di; *n.* contentezza; soddisfazione; letizia; *to one's heart's —*, a sazietà; *tr.* accontentare; soddisfare; appagare; *to — oneself with*, contentarsi di.
**con'tent**[2] *n.* contenuto, capacità; *table of -s*, indice sommario.
**contented** *adj.* contento; di contentezza; soddisfatto. **-ness** *n.* contentezza; soddisfazione.
**contention** *n.* contesa; disputa; opinione; *my — is that*, sostengo che; *the bone of —*, il pomo della discordia.
**contentious** *adj.* polemico; controverso; (leg.) contenzioso. **-ness** *n.* polemicità; litigiosità.
**contentment** *n.* contentezza; soddisfazione.
**contermin-al, -ous** *adj.* contermine; limitrofo.
**con'test** *n.* contesa; contrasto; lotta; (sport) gara, competizione, concorso.
**contest** *tr.* contestare; contrastare; contendere; disputare; *to — every inch of the ground*, contendere ogni palmo di terreno; (leg.) *to — a will*, impugnare un testamento; (pol.) *to — a seat*, presentarsi candidato a un seggio. **-ant** *n.* concorrente *m., f.*; competitore. **-ation** *n.* contestazione; contrasto; contesa.
**context** *n.* contesto.
**contigu-ous** *adj.* contiguo. **-ity** *n.* contiguity.
**contin-ent**[1] *adj.* continente; casto. **-ence** *n.* continenza; castità.
**continent**[2] *n.* (geog.) continente *m.*; *the Continent*, l'Europa continentale, il continente. **-al** *adj.* continentale; *n.* abitante *m., f.* del continente europeo.
**conting-ency** *n.* contingenza; eventualità; evenienza; alea; (comm.) — *fund*, riserva speciale. **-ent** *adj.* eventuale; accidentale; fortuito; imprevisto; condizionato; *to be -ent on*, dipendere da; *n.* contingenza; (mil.) contingente *m.*; reparto.
**continual** *adj.* continuo; ininterrotto; incessante. **-ly** *adv.* sempre; di continuo; continuamente, ininterrottamente; incessantemente.
**continue** *tr.* continuare; proseguire; riprendere; *to — doing something*, continuare a fare qualcosa; '*to be -d*', il seguito alla prossima puntata, continua al prossimo numero; *intr.* continuare; proseguire; durare; restare, rimanere. **-d** *part. adj.* continuo; ininterrotto; incessante.
**continuity** *n.* continuità; (cinem.) sceneggiatura; — *man*, dialoghista *m.*
**continuous** *adj.* continuo; continuato; ininterrotto.
**contort** *tr.* contorcere; storcere; (fig.) stravolgere. **-ion** *n.* contorsione; storcimento. **-ionist** *n.* contorsionista *m., f.*
**contour** *n.* contorno; profilo; — *lines*, curve *f.pl.* di livello, linee *f.pl.* ipsometriche.
**contraband** *n.* contrabbando; — *goods*, merci *f.pl.* di contrabbando.
**contrabass** *n.* (mus.) contrabbasso.
**contracept-ion** *n.* pratiche *f.pl.* antifecondative. **-ive** *n.* anticoncettivo, anticoncezionale *m.*, antifecondativo.
**con'tract** *n.* patto; accordo; (leg.) contratto; (comm.) appalto; *to enter into a — with*, stipulare un contratto con; *breach of —*, rottura di contratto; *to secure a —*, ottenere un appalto; (cards) impegno.
**contract** *tr.* contrarre; restringere; *intr.* contrarsi, restringersi; *to — out of*, liberarsi per mezzo di contratto da; *-ing parties*, parti *f.pl.* contraenti. **-ion** *n.* contrazione. **-or** *n.* (leg.) contraente *m., f.*; (comm.) fornitore; appaltatore, imprenditore.
**contradict** *tr.* contraddire; smentire. **-ion** *n.* contraddizione; smentita. **-ory** *adj.* contraddittorio.
**contraption** *n.* arnese *m.*; aggeggio; congegno.
**contrariety** *n.* antagonismo; discordanza.
**contrariness** *n.* spirito di contraddizione.
**contrariwise** *adv.* al contrario; in senso contrario.
**contrary** *adj.* contrario; avverso; sfavorevole; opposto; cattivo, testardo; *adv. — to*, contrariamente a, all'opposto di, contro; *n.* contrario; opposto; *on the —*, al contrario, anzi, invece; *to the —*, in contrario; (comm.) *unless we hear from you to the —*, salvo contrordini.
**con'trast** *n.* contrasto; antitesi *f. indecl.*; *a striking —*, un vivo contrasto; *in — with*, in antitesi con.
**contrast** *tr.* mettere in contrasto; confrontare; contrapporre; *intr.* far contrasto; contrastare. **-ing** *adj.* contrastante, di contrasto.
**contraven-e** *tr.* contravvenire a; trasgredire; contraddire; opporsi a. **-tion** *n.* contravvenzione; trasgressione; infrazione.
**contribut-e** *tr., intr.* contribuire; fornire; (journ.) scrivere. **-ion** *n.* contributo; contribuzione; (journ.) articolo; (comm.) apporto. **-or** *n.* contributore; (journ.) collaboratore. **-ory** *adj.* contribuente, che ha contribuito a.
**contrit-e** *adj.* contrito; pentito; compunto. **-ion** *n.* contrizione; pentimento; compunzione.
**contrivance** *n.* invenzione; escogitazione; congegno, arnese *m.*, dispositivo.
**contrive** *tr.* escogitare; trovare; macchinare; fare in modo di, riuscire a.

**control** *n.* autorità; giurisdizione; padronanza; dominio; controllo; sorveglianza; disciplina; limitazione; (mech.) dispositivo di comando; *to be out of —*, non rispondere ai comandi; regolatore *m.*; *remote —*, comando a distanza, telecomando; *circumstances beyond our —*, circostanze che non dipendono da noi; *— of the seas*, dominio dei mari; *to be in —*, comandare, dominare, dirigere, (fam.) stare a cassetta; *to have — of*, dirigere, avere autorità su; (fig.) dominare, domare; *to have no — over*, non aver nessuna autorità su; *to get under —*, domare, frenare.

**control** *tr.* esercitare autorità su, dominare; dirigere; regolare; controllare; verificare; frenare; reprimere; trattenere; domare; *to — oneself*, frenarsi, stare calmo.

**controller** *n.* controllore; verificatore; (electr.) combinatore.

**control-room** *n.* (in submarine) camera di manovra. **-tower** *n.* (aeron.) torre *f.* di comando.

**controvers-y** *n.* polemica; controversia; vertenza. **-ial** *adj.* controverso; discutibile; polemico.

**contumacious** *adj.* insubordinato; (leg.) contumace.

**contumaciousness, contumacy** *n.* insubordinazione; (leg.) contumacia.

**contumely** *n.* contumelia; ingiuria; insolenza.

**contusion** *n.* contusione; ammaccatura.

**conundrum** *n.* indovinello; enigma *m.*

**convalesc-e** *intr.* migliorare; rimettersi in salute. **-ence** *n.* convalescenza. **-ent** *adj.*, *n.* convalescente *m.*, *f.*; *-ent home*, convalescenziario.

**convec-tion** *n.* (phys.) convezione. **-tor** *n.* convettore *m.*

**conven-e** *tr.* convocare; adunare; riunire; (leg.) citare; convenire; *intr.* radunarsi; incontrarsi. **-er** *n.* convocatore.

**convenience** *n.* comodo; comodità; convenienza; *a marriage of —*, un matrimonio d'interesse; *modern -s*, comodità moderne; *public —*, gabinetti pubblici; *at your —*, con Suo comodo; *at your earliest —*, il più presto possibile, alla prima occasione.

**convenient** *adj.* comodo; adatto; conveniente; utile; che va bene; *to be —*, far comodo, convenire.

**convent** *n.* convento; *to enter a —*, entrare in convento, farsi monaca.

**convention** *n.* patto; accordo; convegno, convenzione; consuetudine *f.*; convenzione. **-al** *adj.* convenzionale; tradizionale; formale. **-alism** *n.* convenzionalismo; formalismo.

**converg-e** *tr.* far convergere; *intr.* convergere **-ence** *n.* convergenza. **-ent, -ing** *adj.* convergente.

**convers-ant** *adj.* *— with*, versato in, pratico di, al corrente di. **-ance** *n.* dimestichezza; familiarità; conoscenza.

**conversation** *n.* conversazione; discorso. **-al** *adj.* loquace; che ama conversare; familiare.

**con'verse**[1] *adj.*, *n.* inverso; contrario. **-ly** *adv.* al contrario; viceversa.

**con'verse**[2] *n.* conversazione; (fig.) comunione spirituale.

**converse**[3] *intr.* conversare; parlare; discorrere.

**conversion** *n.* conversione; trasformazione; cambiamento.

**con'vert**[1] *n.* convertito; convertita; *to become a — to*, convertirsi a; *to make a — of*, convertire.

**convert**[2] *tr.* convertire; trasformare; cambiare; *to — a room as a kitchen*, adibire una stanza ad uso di cucina. **-ible** *adj.* convertibile; (motor.) decapottabile; *n.* macchina decapottabile.

**convex** *adj.* convesso. **-ity** *n.* convessità.

**convey** *tr.* portare; trasportare; convogliare; trasmettere; comunicare; rendere; *it -s nothing to me*, non mi dice niente; (leg.) trasferire.

**conveyance** *n.* mezzo di trasporto; veicolo; trasmissione; comunicazione; (tech.) convogliamento; (leg.) trasferimento, cessione; atto di cessione.

**conveyancer** *n.* notaio; legale *m.* che prepara un atto di cessione.

**convey-er, -or** *n.* portatore; latore; (mech.) trasportatore, convogliatore.

**con'vict** *n.* forzato, galeotto; ergastolano; *— prison*, penitenziario, bagno penale, ergastolo.

**convict** *tr.* dichiarare colpevole, condannare.

**conviction** *n.* persuasione; convinzione; *it is my — that*, sono convinto che; *to be open to —*, essere pronto a lasciarsi convincere; (leg.) dichiarazione di colpevolezza, condanna; *previous -s*, condanne *f.pl.* precedenti.

**convinc-e** *tr.* convincere; persuadere. **-ing** *adj.* convincente; persuasivo.

**convivial** *adj.* gioviale; allegro; festevole; conviviale. **-ity** *n.* giovialità, allegria.

**convocation** *n.* convocazione; assemblea; (eccl.) sinodo; (Oxford) consiglio accademico.

**convoke** *tr.* convocare; adunare.

**convolution** *n.* spira; (anat.) circonvoluzione.

**convolvulus** *n.* (bot.) convolvolo.

**convoy** *n.* convoglio; scorta; *tr.* convogliare, scortare.

**convuls-e** *tr.* sconvolgere; scuotere; *to be -ed with laughter*, contorcersi dalle risa. **-ion** *n.* convulsione; spasimo; (fig.) sconvolgimento.

**cony** *n.* coniglio; pelle *f.* di coniglio.

**coo** *intr.* tubare; *to bill and —*, tubare.

**cook** *n.* cuoco, cuoca; (provb.) *too many -s spoil the broth*, troppi cuochi guastano il pranzo.

**cook** *tr.* far cuocere, cucinare; (fig.) *to — the accounts*, falsificare i conti; *to — someone's goose*, conciare qualcuno per le feste; *to — up*, inventare; *intr.* cuocere, fare la cucina, cucinare; cuocersi; (fam.) *what's -ing ?*, che cosa bolle in pentola ?

**cooker** *n.* cucina economica; fornello; *electric —*, fornello elettrico; *gas —*, fornello a gas; *steam —*, bagnomaria; (of apples) *to be good -s*, essere buoni da cuocere, cuocersi bene.

**cookery** *n.* arte culinaria; cucina; *— book* libro di cucina, ricettario.

**cookhouse** *n.* (mil.) cucina da campo.

**cooking** *n.* cucina; *Italian —*, la cucina italiana; *plain —*, cucina casalinga; *to do the —*, fare la cucina, (fam.) stare ai fornelli; *attrib.* da cucinare.

**cookshop** *n.* rosticceria.

**cool** *adj.* fresco; leggero; (fig.) calmo, tranquillo; freddo; *— as a cucumber*, fresco come una rosa, sfacciato; *a — reception*, un'accoglienza molto fredda; *to get —*, rinfrescarsi, prendere il fresco; *to keep —*, mantenersi fresco, (fig.) conservare la calma; *to have a — head*, avere molto sangue freddo; (fam.) *a — thousand pounds*, la bellezza di mille sterline; *n.* fresco, frescura.

**cool** *tr.* rinfrescare; raffreddare; (fig.) calmare; refrigerare; *to — down*, calmare, fare una doccia fredda a; (fam.) *to — one's heels*, stare ad aspettare, fare anticamera; *intr.* rinfrescarsi; raffreddarsi; *to — down*, rinfrescarsi, (fig.) calmarsi; (of anger) sbollire.

**coolant** *n.* (industr.) refrigerante *m.*

**cooler** *n.* (industr.) refrigerante *m.*; (for wine), refrigeratore; (slang) *in the —*, in gattabuia, al fresco.

**cool-headed** *adj.* imperturbabile; calmo. **-ness** *n.* sangue freddo; calma.

**cooling** *adj.* rinfrescante; (industr.) refrigerante; *n.* abbassamento di temperatura; (industr.) raffreddamento; *— tower*, torre *f.* di raffreddamento.

**coolness** *n.* fresco; frescura; refrigerio; (fig.) freddezza; frigidezza; sangue freddo; calma.

**coomb** *n.* valletta, comba.

**coon** *n.* (zool.) procione *m.*; (derog.) negro.

**coop** *n.* stia; *tr.* *to — up*, mettere

nella stia; rinchiudere, chiudere in gabbia, stipare.
**cooper** *n.* bottaio. **-age** *n.* mestiere *m.* del bottaio.
**co-operat-e** *intr.* cooperare; collaborare; contribuire. **-ion** *n.* cooperazione; collaborazione. **-ive** *adj.* cooperativo; *n.* *-ive* (*society*), cooperativa (di consumo). **-or** *n.* cooperatore; collaboratore.
**co-opt** *tr.* eleggere (un nuovo membro).
**co-ordinat-e** *adj.* coordinato, dello stesso ordine; *n.* (math.) coordinata; *tr.* coordinare. **-ion** *n.* coordinazione.
**coot** *n.* (orn.) folaga; (fam.) *as bald as a —*, pelato come un uovo; *as queer as a —*, molto strambo
**co-owner** *n.* comproprietario, condomino. **-ship** *n.* comproprietà, condominio.
**cop**[1] *n.* (text.) bobina, rocchetto; *tr.* incannare.
**cop**[2] *n.* (slang) see **copper.**
**cop**[3] *tr.* (slang) pescare; *to — it*, prenderle, buscarne; *n. it's a fair —*, mi hai pescato.
**copal** *n.* copale *f.*
**co-partner** *n.* consocio.
**cope**[1] *n.* (eccl.) piviale *m.*; (fig.) cappa.
**cope**[2] *intr. to — with*, far fronte a, tener testa a, lottare contro; *I just can't —*, non ci arrivo.
**Copenhagen** *pr.n.* (geog.) Copenhagen.
**Copernicus** *pr.n.* Copernico.
**co-pilot** *n.* (aeron.) secondo pilota.
**coping** *n.* (archit.) cimasa, coronamento.
**coping-stone** *n.* (archit.) pietra per cimasa.
**copious** *adj.* copioso; abbondante; ampolloso. **-ness** *n.* copiosità; abbondanza.
**copper**[1] *n.* (metall.) rame *m.*; (coin) moneta di rame; *pl.* spiccioli *m.pl.*; (colour) color rame; *— beech*, faggio rosso; *attrib.* di rame; (boiler) caldaia di rame; *tr.* rivestire di rame, ramare.
**copper**[2] *n.* poliziotto; *-'s nark*, birro, sbirro.
**copper-coloured** *adj.* color rame.
**copperplate** *n.* lastra di rame; *— engraving*, incisione su rame, calcografia; *— handwriting*, bella scrittura, calligrafia.
**coppersmith** *n.* ramaio.
**coppice** *n.* boschetto; macchia.
**copra** *n.* copra.
**copse** *n.* bosco ceduo.
**Copt** *pr.n.* Copto. **-ic** *adj.* copto; *n.* lingua copta.
**copulat-e** *intr.* accoppiarsi. **-ion** *n.* accoppiamento, copulazione.
**copy** *n.* copia; trascrizione; riproduzione; *certified true —*, per copia conforme; *fair —*, bella copia; *rough —*, brutta copia, minuta, abbozzo; *to make a — of*, copiare; esemplare *m.*; copia; numero; imitazione, copia; replica, copia; (theatr.) copione *m.*; (typ.) originale *m.*, materiale *m.*
**copy** *tr.* copiare; riprodurre; *to — down*, trascrivere; imitare; seguire l'esempio di.
**copybook** *n.* quaderno.
**copying** *n.* copiare *m.* trascrizione; riproduzione; *— ink*, inchiostro copiativo.
**copyist** *n.* copista *m.*, *f.*
**copyright** *n.* diritti *m.pl.* d'autore; *attrib.* tutelato da diritto d'autore; *no longer —*, di dominio pubblico; (on verso of title-page) 'copyright', proprietà letteraria riservata, riproduzione vietata.
**copy-writer** *n.* redattore pubblicitario.
**coquet-te** *n.* civetta. **-ry** *n.* civetteria. **-tish** *adj.* civettuolo.
**coracle** *n.* barca di vimini.
**coral** *n.* corallo; *attrib.* corallino.
**corbel** *n.* (archit.) modiglione *m.*; mensola.
**cord** *n.* corda; cordone *m.*; cordoncino; funicella; spago; (fig.) legame *m.*; (electr.) cordone, filo; (friar's) cordiglio, cordone; (anat.) *spinal —*, midollo spinale; *umbilical —*, cordone ombilicale; *vocal -s*, corde *f.pl.* vocali; (text.) costa; *tr.* legare con corda. **-age** *n.* cordame *m.*; (naut.) sartiame *m.* **-elier** *n.* (eccl.) cordigliere *m.*
**cordial** *adj.* cordiale; caloroso; *n.* cordiale *m.* **-ity** *n.* cordialità.
**cordon** *n.* cordone *m.*
**corduroy** *n.* velluto a coste; fustagno.
**core** *n.* torsolo; (of metal) anima; (fig.) centro; cuore *m.*; nocciolo; *English to the —*, inglese fino in fondo all'anima.
**co-religionist** *n.* correligionario. **-respondent** *n.* correo in adulterio.
**coriander** *n.* (bot.) coriandolo.
**Corinth** *pr.n.* (geog.) Corinto *f.* **-ian** *adj.*, *n.* corinzio, di Corinto.
**cork** *n.* sughero; *— tree*, quercia da sughero; turacciolo, tappo; *to draw the —*, levare il tappo, sturare, stappare; *— jacket*, giubbetto di salvataggio; *to bob like a —*, ballonzolare; *tr.* mettere il tappo a, turare, tappare. **-age** *n.* compenso dovuto a un albergo per bottiglie acquistate altrove. **-ed** *adj.* turato, tappato; (of wine) che sa di turacciolo. **-ing** *n.* turamento; *attrib.* (fam.) meraviglioso, strabiliante. **-screw** *n.* cavaturaccioli, cavatappi *m. indecl.* *-screw dive*, picchiata in spirale; *-screw staircase*, scala a chiocciola.
**cork-tipped** *adj.* con bocchino di sughero.
**cormorant** *n.* (orn.) cormorano, marangone *m.*
**corn**[1] *n.* grano; frumento; cereali *m.pl.*; (Scotland) avena; (U.S.A.) granturco; *Indian —*, granturco, granone *m.*, mais *m.*; *— exchange*, borsa dei cereali. (fam. *-y adj.*) rifritto, trito.
**corn**[2] *n.* callo, durone *m.*; *soft —*, occhio di pernice; *to tread on someone's -s*, pestare i calli a qualcuno.
**corn-cob** *n.* pannocchia, tutolo. **-chandler** *n.* rivenditore di grano.
**cornea** *n.* (anat.) cornea.
**corned** *adj.* conservato sotto sale.
**cornelian** *n.* (miner.) corniuola, cornalina.
**corner** *n.* angolo; canto; cantuccio; *a — house*, una casa che fa angolo; *a — seat*, un posto d'angolo; (football) *— kick*, calcio d'angolo; *a tight —*, una situazione difficile, un pasticcio; *to cut off a —*, prendere una scorciatoia; *to drive someone into a —*, mettere qualcuno con le spalle al muro; *to hide in a —*, rincantucciarsi; *to turn the —*, voltare l'angolo, (fig.) superare la crisi; (comm.) *to make a — in*, accaparrare, bagarinare.
**corner** *tr.* spingere in un angolo; (fig.) mettere alle strette; (comm.) accaparrare, incettare, bagarinare.
**cornerstone** *n.* pietra angolare.
**cornet** *n.* (mus.) cornetta; (for ice-cream) cartoccio, cono.
**cornflakes** *n. pl.* fiocchi di granturco.
**corn-flour** *n.* farina di granturco.
**cornflower** *n.* (bot.) fiordaliso.
**cornice** *n.* (archit.) cornice *f.*; cornicione *m.*
**Cornish** *adj.* della Cornovaglia, cornovagliese. **-man, -woman** *n.* cornovagliese *m.*, *f.*
**corn-plaster** *n.* callifugo, cerotto per calli.
**corn-sheaf** *n.* covone *m.*
**cornucopia** *n.* cornucopia, corno dell'abbondanza.
**Cornwall** *pr.n.* (geog.) Cornovaglia.
**corny** *adj.* see under corn.[1]
**corollary** *n.* corollario.
**coronary** *adj.* (anat.) coronario.
**coronation** *n.* incoronazione.
**coroner** *n.* magistrato incaricato dell'inchiesta nei casi di morte sospetta o di tesoro trovato.
**coronet** *n.* corona gentilizia; diadema *m.*
**corporal** *adj.* corporale; corporeo; *n.* (mil.) caporale *m.*
**corporate** *adj.* corporativo.
**corporation** *n.* ente *m.* morale; corporazione; (comm.) società anonima; consiglio comunale; (joc.) pancia.
**corporative** *adj.* corporativo.
**corporeal** *adj.* corporeo.
**corps** *n.* (mil.) corpo, reparto; *army —*, corpo d'armata; *esprit de —*, spirito di corpo; *— de ballet*, corpo di ballo.

**corpse** *n.* cadavere *m.*; salma.
**corpul-ent** *adj.* corpulento; obeso; adiposo. **-ence, -ency** *n.* corpulenza; obesità; adipe *m.*
**corpus** *n.* corpus *m.*, raccolta di scritti; (leg.) — *delicti*, corpo del reato; (eccl.) *Corpus Christi*, Corpus Domini.
**corpuscle** *n.* corpuscolo; globulo.
**corral** *n.* recinto; (hist.) cerchio di carri.
**correct** *adj.* corretto; retto; giusto; esatto; preciso; adatto, appropriato; *tr.* correggere; rettificare; regolare; aggiustare; mettere a posto. **-ion** *n.* correzione; rettifica. **-ive** *adj.*, *n.* correttivo. **-ness** *n.* correttezza; esattezza. **-or** *n.* correttore *m.*
**correlat-e** *tr.* mettere in correlazione. **-ion** *n.* correlazione.
**correspond** *intr.* corrispondere, scambiare lettere, essere in relazione epistolare; *to* — *to*, corrispondere a, equivalere a; rispondere a. **-ence** *n.* corrispondenza. **-ent** *adj.*, *n.* corrispondente *m.*, *f.*; *special -ent*, inviato speciale; *war -ent*, corrispondente di guerra. **-ing** *adj.* corrispondente.
**corridor** *n.* corridoio; andito.
**corrigenda** *n.* errata-corrige *m.*
**corrobor-ate** *tr.* corroborare; confermare; avvalorare. **-ant** *adj.*, *n.* corroborante *m.* **-ation** *n.* corroborazione; conferma; avvaloramento. **-ative** *adj.* corroborativo.
**corr-ode** *tr.* corrodere; (fig.) rodere; *intr.* corrodersi. **-osion** *n.* corrosione. **-osive** *adj.* corrosivo.
**corrugat-e** *tr.* corrugare; *intr.* corrugarsi; *-ed iron*, lamiera di ferro ondulato; *-ed cardboard*, cartone increspato.
**corrupt** *adj.* corrotto; guasto, contaminato; — *practices*, forme *f.pl.* di corruzione; *tr.* corrompere; guastare; contaminare. **-ion** *n.* corruzione; corruttela.
**corsage** *n.* corpetto.
**corsair** *n.* corsaro; (ship) nave corsara.
**corset** *n.* busto; guaina; *tr.* mettere in busto; (fig.) costringere.
**Corsic-a** *pr.n.* (geog.) Corsica. **-an** *adj.*, *n.* corso.
**cortège** *n.* corteggio, corteo.
**cortex** *n.* corteccia.
**cortisone** *n.* (pharm.) cortisone *m.*
**coruscat-e** *intr.* corruscare; scintillare. **-ion** *n.* corruscazione; scintillio.
**corvette** *n.* (naut.) corvetta.
**Cos**[1] *pr.n.* (geog.) Cos *f.*
**cos**[2] *n.* (bot.) lattuga romana.
**cosh** *n.* randello; *tr.* colpire con un randello, randellare.
**cosine** *n.* (math.) coseno.
**cosiness** *n.* agio; comodità; intimità.
**cosmetic** *adj.*, *n.* cosmetico.
**cosm-ic** *adj.* cosmico. **-ography** *n.* cosmografia. **-onaut** *n.* cosmonauta *m.* **-opolitan** *adj.*, *n.* cosmopolita *m.*, *f.*
**cosmos** *n.* cosmo.
**cossack** *n.* cosacco.
**cosset** *tr.* vezzeggiare.
**cost** *n.* costo; prezzo; spesa; — *price*, prezzo di costo; *the* — *of living*, il costo della vita; — *of living bonus*, carovita *m.*, caroviveri *m.*; *at all -s*, a tutti i costi, a ogni costo; *at the* — *of many lives*, con grave perdita di vite; *to learn to one's* —, imparare a proprie spese; (leg.) *the -s*, le spese processuali.
**cost** *tr.*, *intr.* costare; — *what it may*, costi quel che costi; *how much does it* —?, quanto costa?
**coster(monger)** *n.* venditore ambulante di frutta e legumi.
**costing** *n.* valutazione dei costi; — *department*, reparto costi.
**costive** *adj.* stitico. **-ness** *n.* stitichezza.
**costl-y** *adj.* costoso; carissimo; sontuoso; ricco. **-iness** *n.* prezzo eccessivo; alto costo; sontuosità; ricchezza.
**costum-e** *n.* costume *m.*; vestito; abito; foggia; — *play*, dramma storico. **-ier** *n.* sarta; venditrice di costumi; vestiarista *m.*, *f.*
**cosy** *adj.* intimo; gradevole; accogliente; raccoltino.
**cot** *n.* lettino, branda; (naut.) cuccetta, amaca.
**coterie** *n.* cricca; brigata; *literary* —, cenacolo letterario.
**cottage** *n.* casetta di campagna, casa contadinesca, villino; — *hospital*, casa di salute; — *loaf*, pagnotta.
**cotton**[1] *n.* cotone *m.*; *sewing* —, filo da cucire; — *mill*, cotonificio, filatura; — *waste*, cascame *m.* di cotone, stoppaccio.
**cotton**[2] *intr.* (fam.) *to* — *on to somebody*, affezionarsi a qualcuno; *to* — *on to something*, capire qualcosa.
**cotton-wool** *n.* cotone idrofilo; bambagia; ovatta.
**cotyledon** *n.* (bot.) cotiledone *m.*
**couch** *n.* divano; canapè *m.*; giaciglio; letto.
**couch** *tr.* *to* — *a lance*, mettere in resta una lancia; esprimere, redigere; *intr.* coricarsi, accucciarsi.
**couchant** *adj.* (herald.) coricato.
**couch-grass** *m.* (bot.) gramigna dente canino.
**cougar** *n.* (zool.) coguaro.
**cough** *n.* tosse *f.*; *to have a bad* —, avere una forte tosse; *to give a slight* —, tossire leggermente, tossicchiare; *intr.* tossire; *tr.* *to* — *up*, espettorare, espellere tossendo, (fam.) sputare, tirar fuori.
**cough-lozenge** *n.* pasticcia per la tosse. **-mixture** *n.* sciroppo per la tosse.
**could** *past def.* of **can**, *q.v.*
**council** *n.* consiglio; (eccl.) concilio; *town* —, consiglio comunale, consiglio municipale; giunta; *county* —, consiglio provinciale; *Privy Council*, Consiglio privato della Corona; — *house*, casa popolare. **-lor** *n.* consigliere, membro di un consiglio; assessore.
**counsel** *n.* consiglio; *to take* — *with someone*, consultarsi con qualcuno; *to keep one's own* —, serbare il proprio segreto, non rivelare le proprie opinioni; *evangelical -s*, — *of perfection*, consigli evangelici (also iron.); (leg.) avvocato patrocinatore, patrono; — *for the defence*, (avvocato) difensore *m.*; — *for the prosecution*, pubblico ministero; *tr.* consigliare, raccomandare. **-lor** *n.* consigliere *m.*, chi dà consigli.
**count**[1] *n.* conto; conteggio; calcolo; scrutinio; *to keep* — *of*, riuscire a contare; *to lose* — *of*, perdere il conto di; *to take no* — *of*, non tenere in nessuna considerazione, non badare a; (boxing) *to take the* —, essere sconfitto per k.o.; (leg.) capo d'accusa; (text.) titolo.
**count**[1] *tr.* contare; calcolare; conteggiare; (fig.) annoverare; includere; considerare; (provb.) *don't* — *your chickens before they're hatched*, non dir quattro se non è nel sacco; *to* — *in*, includere, comprendere, non lasciar fuori; (pol.) *to* — *out*, aggiornare per mancanza del numero legale; (boxing) *to be -ed out*, essere sconfitto per k.o.; *to* — *up*, sommare, conteggiare, fare il conteggio di; *intr.* contare, valere, importare; *to* — *for little*, valere poco; *to* — *(up)on*, contare su, far assegnamento su.
**Count**[2] *n.* Conte *m.* **-ess** *n.* Contessa.
**countenance** *n.* espressione del viso; faccia; volto; aspetto; *to change* —, cambiare volto; *to keep one's* —, rimanere composto, restare serio; *to lose* —, perdere il dominio di sè, tradirsi; *to lend* — *to*, prestare appoggio a, favorire.
**countenance** *tr.* approvare; autorizzare; favorire; tollerare.
**counter**[1] *adj.* contrario; opposto; *to run* — *to*, opporsi a, andare contro; *tr.*, *intr.* controbattere; parare; (fig.) reagire a; rispondere a, contraddire; (mech.) invertire.
**counter**[2] *n.* contatore; calcolatore; sportello; banco; *under the* —, sottobanco; gettone *m.*, fiche *f.*; (naut.) volta di poppa.
**counteract** *tr.* mitigare gli effetti di; contrapporsi a; neutralizzare.

**counter-attack** *n.* contrattacco; *tr., intr.* contrattaccare.
**counter-attraction** *n.* attrazione in concorrenza.
**counterbalance** *n.* contrappeso; (mech.) controbilanciere *m.*; *tr.* fare da contrappeso a; bilanciare; equilibrare; (mech.) controbilanciare.
**counter-blast** *n.* risposta energica. **-claim** *n.* controreclamo; (leg.) controquerela; domanda riconvenzionale; *tr., intr.* fare un controreclamo; (leg.) sporgere una controquerela. **-clockwise** *adv.* in senso antiorario. **-espionage** *n.* controspionaggio.
**counterfeit** *adj.* contraffatto; falso; falsificato; (fig.) simulato; *n.* contraffazione, falsificazione; *tr.* contraffare; falsificare; imitare; (fig.) simulare; fingere. **-er** *n.* falsario; contraffattore; (fig.) simulatore.
**counterfoil** *n.* (comm.) matrice *f.*; — *book*, registro a madre e figlia.
**counter-instruction** *n.* contrordine *m.* **-irritant** *adj., n.* (med.) revulsivo.
**counter-mand** *tr.* revocare; annullare; richiamare. **-pane** *n.* copriletto. **-part** *n.* copia esatta; duplicato; ritratto; sosia *m.*; complemento; contropartita. **-point** *n.* (mus.) contrappunto. **-poise** *n.* contrappeso; *tr.* contrappesare; controbilanciare.
**Counter-Reformation** *n.* (hist.) controriforma.
**counter-sign** *n.* contrassegno; controfirma; (mil.) parola d'ordine; *tr., intr.* contrassegnare; controfirmare. **-sink** *tr.* (mech.) fresare, smussare, accecare. **-sinking** *n.* accecatura; *-sinking drill*, accecatoio. **-stroke** *n.* contraccolpo. **-vail** *tr., intr.* controbilanciare; prevalere.
**Countess** *n.* Contessa.
**counting** *n.* conteggio; contare *m.*; (of votes) scrutinio.
**counting-house** *n.* ufficio di contabilità; amministrazione.
**countless** *adj.* innumerevole.
**countrified** *adj.* rurale; campagnuolo; rustico.
**country** *n.* paese *m.*; stato; patria; campagna; contrada; *in the* —, in campagna; *to go to the* —, andare in campagna, (pol.) fare appello al paese, indire le elezioni generali; *to go back to one's own* —, rimpatriare, tornare in patria; *to live in the* —, vivere in campagna; — *folk*, gente *f.* di campagna; — *gentleman*, signore di campagna, proprietario terriero; — *house*, villa di campagna, castello; — *town*, città di provincia.
**country-dance** *n.* danza campestre.
**country-man** *n.* contadino; compatriota *m., f.*; compaesano; concittadino. **-side** *n.* campagna.
**county** *n.* contea; provincia; — *borough*, città di provincia; — *council*, consiglio di provincia; — *town*, capoluogo di contea; *the* —, la nobiltà di campagna, l'alta società provinciale; *the Home Counties*, le sei contee intorno a Londra.
**coup** *n.* colpo; — *d'état*, colpo di stato; — *de grâce*, colpo di grazia.
**couple** *n.* coppia; paio; *a* — *of*, due, una coppia di, qualche, un paio di; *a married* —, una coppia di sposi, due coniugi; *to hunt in -s*, correre a copie, correre a due a due; *tr.* accoppiare; appaiare; abbinare; (rlwy.) agganciare.
**couplet** *n.* distico.
**coupling** *n.* accoppiamento; attacco; (rlwy.) agganciamento.
**coupon** *n.* cedola; tagliando; scontrino; (comm.) buono.
**courage** *n.* coraggio; ardire *m.*; anima; *to pluck up* —, farsi coraggio.
**courageous** *adj.* coraggioso; animoso; audace.
**courier** *n.* corriere *m.*; messaggero; accompagnatore.
**course** *n.* corso; serie *f.*; decorso, andamento; (sport) percorso, pista, campo; (cul.) portata, piatto; direzione, via, linea; (naut.; aeron.) rotta; *a matter of* —, una cosa naturale; *in due* —, a tempo debito; *in the* — *of*, durante, nel corso di; *in* — *of construction*, in via di costruzione; *of* —, naturalmente, già, sicuro, va da sè, ben inteso, s'intende; *to let things take their* —, lasciar andare l'acqua alla china.
**courser** *n.* destriere *m.*
**coursing** *n.* caccia alla lepre con levrieri.
**court** *n.* corte *f.*; cortile *m.*; *the Court of St. James*, la corte di San Giacomo; (fig.) *to pay* — *to*, fare la corte a; *friends at* —, amici in alto; (leg.) corte *f.*; tribunale *m.*; palazzo di giustizia; *to settle a case out of* —, comporre una controversia in via amichevole; (mil.) — *of inquiry*, commissione d'inchiesta; (sport) campo.
**court** *tr.* corteggiare, fare la corte a; (fig.) sollecitare, cercare; *to* — *danger*, andare in cerca di un pericolo.
**court-card** *n.* figura.
**courteous** *adj.* cortese, gentile, affabile.
**courtesan** *n.* cortigiana.
**courtesy, courteousness** *n.* cortesia, gentilezza.
**courtier** *n.* cortigiano, gentiluomo di corte.
**courting** *n.* corteggiamento.
**courtly** *adj.* cortigianesco, cerimonioso, cortese, distinto.
**court-martial** *n.* tribunale *m.* militare, corte *f.* marziale; *tr.* deferire al tribunale militare.
**courtship** *n.* corteggiamento.
**courtyard** *n.* cortile *m.*
**cousin** *n.* cugino, cugina.
**cove**[1] *n.* (geog.) insenatura, cala.
**cove**[2] *n.* (slang) tipo, tizio.
**coven** *n.* (of witches) congrega.
**covenant** *n.* convenzione; patto; (bibl.) *Ark of the* —, arca del Testamento.
**Coventry** *pr.n.* (geog.) Coventry; (fig.) *to send to* —, dare l'ostracismo a.
**cover** *n.* coperta; coperchio; copertura; (of book) copertina; *from* — *to* —, dal principio alla fine; plico, busta; *under separate* —, in plico a parte; dossale *m.*; riparo, ricovero; *under* — *of*, al riparo di; *to take* —, mettersi al coperto, nascondersi; (fig.) velo, mantello; *under the* — *of darkness*, col favore delle tenebre; (industr.) coperchio, calotta, cuffia; (comm.) copertura; — *charge*, prezzo del coperto.
**cover** *tr.* coprire; ricoprire; rivestire; nascondere; comprendere; percorrere; (journ.) riferire, fare la cronaca di; (mil.) dominare, tenere sotto il fuoco; (sport) sostenere, star dietro a; (of animals) montare, coprire; *to* — *up*, coprire completamente; (fig.) nascondere, celare.
**coverage** *n.* (comm.) copertura; (journ.) trattazione, ampio servizio d'informazioni.
**covering** *n.* copertura; (fig.) protezione; *attrib.* di copertura; — *letter*, lettera d'accompagnamento.
**coverlet** *n.* copriletto.
**covert** *adj.* velato; finto; di sfuggita; *n.* ricovero, nascondiglio.
**covet** *tr.* agognare; ambire; adocchiare. **-ous** *adj.* avido; cupido; ambizioso. **-ousness** *n.* cupidigia; avidità.
**covey** *n.* covata; stormo.
**cow**[1] *n.* vacca; mucca; (of elephant, etc.) femmina.
**cow**[2] *tr.* intimidire; intimorire; costringere.
**coward** *n.* vigliacco; codardo. **-ice** *n.* vigliaccheria; codardia; pusillanimità. **-ly** *adj.* vigliacco; vile; codardo; pusillanime.
**cowboy** *n.* buttero; bovaro; cowboy *m. indecl.*
**cow-catcher** *n.* (rlwy.) cacciapietre *m. indecl.*
**cower** *intr.* acquattarsi; rintuzzarsi; farsi piccino.
**cow-herd** *n.* vaccaro. **-hide** *n.* cuoio di vacca, vacchetta.
**cowl** *n.* cocolla; tonaca; (on chimney) comignolo metallico; (aeron.; motor.) confano; (naut.) manica a vento, cuffia, tromba.
**cowshed** *n.* vaccheria; stalla.
**cowslip** *n.* (bot.) primula gialla, primavera.

**cox** *n.* (rowing) timoniere *m.*; *tr.* governare; *-ed four*, quattro con; *intr.* fare da timoniere.
**coxcomb** *n.* bellimbusto, damerino.
**coxswain** *n.* (naut.) nocchiere, timoniere *m.* **-less** *adj.* *-less four*, quattro senza.
**coy** *adj.* ritroso; schivo; timido; *to be — of*, rifuggire da. **-ness** *n.* ritrosia; modestia; timidezza.
**cozen** *tr.* gabbare; frodare.
**crab** *n.* (zool.) granchio; (astron.) Cancro; (mech.) verricello, argano; (rowing) *to catch a —*, pigliare un granchio; (fam.) see **crab-louse.**
**crab** *intr.* andare a pesca di granchi; *tr.* (fam.) demolire, sabotare, mettere i bastoni tra le ruote a.
**crab-apple** *n.* mela selvatica.
**crabbed** *adj.* arcigno; burbero; acido; contorto.
**crab-louse** *n.* pidocchio inguinale, piattola.
**crabwise** *adv.* da granchio, diagonalmente.
**crack** *n.* scoppio, schianto; (of whip) schiocco; fęnditura, incrinatura, crepa, screpolatura; botta, scappellotto; (fam.) *to have a — at something*, provare a far qualcosa; *excl.*, *onom.* crac!, pum!; *adj.* (fam.) scelto; famoso; fuori classe; *— shot*, tiratore scelto.
**crack** *tr.* far schioccare; far incrinare, fendere, rompere, spaccare; schiacciare; *to — a joke*, raccontare una barzelletta; (slang) *to — a crib*, penetrare in una casa con scasso; (chem.) sottoporre al processo di piroscissione; *intr.* schioccare; scoppiare, schiantare; incrinarsi, fendersi, spaccarsi, screpolarsi; *to — up*, elogiare, portare alle stelle, *intr.* andare in pezzi, accasciarsi.
**crack-brained** *adj.* scervellato; balzano; matto.
**cracked** *adj. part.* of **crack,** *q.v.*; fesso; (slang) matto, pazzo.
**cracker** *n.* gallettina, 'cracker' *m.*; (firework) petardo, mortaretto; *Christmas —*, confezione natalizia a sorpresa; (for nuts) schiaccianoci *m. indecl.*
**cracking** *adj.* crepitante, scoppiettante; *n.* crepitìo, scoppiettìo; fessura, screpolatura; (chem.) piroscissione, cracking; *— plant*, impianto di cracking; (slang) magnifico, ottimo.
**crackl-e** *n.* crepitìo; scricchiolìo; *intr.* crepitare; scricchiolare. **-ing** *n.* scoppiettìo; crepitìo; (cul.) rosolato; ciccioli *m.pl.*
**Cracow** *pr.n.* (geog.) Cracovia.
**cradle** *n.* culla; alzacoperte *m. indecl.*; (bldg.) centina; (naut.) *launching —*, invasatura; *tr.* cullare; tenere nella culla.
**craft** *n.* mestiere *m.*; arte *f.*; professione; *arts and -s*, arti e mestieri; abilità, destrezza, bravura; astuzia, furberia; (naut.) imbarcazione, naviglio; *landing —*, mezzo da sbarco.
**craftiness** *n.* astuzia; furberia.
**craftsman** *n.* artigiano; artefice *m.* **-ship** *n.* abilità; padronanza del mestiere; esecuzione; fattura.
**crafty** *adj.* astuto; furbo; accorto.
**crag** *n.* dirupo; picco; roccia. **-gy** *adj.* dirupato; roccioso; scosceso.
**cram** *tr.* ficcare; stipare; cacciare; rimpinzare, ingozzare; *intr.* stiparsi; (for exam.) sgobbare; *-med full* pieno zeppo.
**cramp** *n.* (med.) crampo; *writer's —*, crampo degli scrittori; *to get —*, aggranchirsi, prendere i crampi; (mech.) morsetto, grappa; *tr.* impacciare, ostacolare; (fig.) paralizzare, bloccare. **-ed** *adj.* aggranchito; rattrappito; ristretto; impacciato, legato.
**crampon** *n.* (techn.) braga a ganci; (climbing) rampone *m.*
**cranberry** *n.* (bot.) mirtillo rosso, mortella di palude.
**crane**[1] *n.* (orn.; mech.) gru *f. indecl.*
**crane**[2] *tr.* allungare; *intr.* allungare il collo, spingersi avanti.
**cran-ium** *n.* (anat.) cranio. **-ial** *adj.* cranico.
**crank** *n.* (mech.) gomito, manubrio, manovella; (on bicycle) pedivella; (fam.) eccentrico, maniaco; *tr.* piegare a gomito; mettere in moto con manovella; *to — up an engine*, avviare un motore a mano.
**crankshaft** *n.* albero a manovella, albero a gomito.
**crank-y** *adj.* eccentrico, originale, matto; stizzoso; instabile, che non funziona. **-iness** *n.* eccentricità; cattivo funzionamento.
**cranny** *n.* fessura, crepa; buco.
**crape** *n.* crespo; *— band*, bracciale *m.* da lutto.
**crash** *n.* fracasso; fragore *m.*; scontro, incidente *m.* grave; (comm.) crollo, fallimento; *— dive* (of submarine) immersione rapida; (aeron.) caduta; *— landing*, atterraggio di fortuna.
**crash** *intr.* crollare; scontrarsi; precipitare; *to — into*, scontrarsi con, urtare violentemente contro, sfondare; (comm.) crollare, andare in malora; (aeron.) precipitare.
**crash-helmet** *n.* casco di protezione.
**crass** *adj.* crasso; grossolano; madornale.
**crate** *n.* cassa (da imballaggio); *tr.* imballare.
**crater** *n.* cratere *m.*; cavità.
**cravat** *n.* cravatta.
**crave** *tr.* implorare; chiedere insistentemente; scongiurare; bramare, desiderare ardentemente.
**craven** *adj.* vigliacco; pusillanime.
**craving** *n.* brama; smania; desiderio ardente.
**craw** *n.* gozzo.
**crawl** *n.* movimento strisciante, strisciamento; (swimming) crawl *m.*; *at a —*, molto lentamente, (of car) a passo d'uomo; *intr.* andare carponi; strisciare; trascinarsi; procedere lentamente; (fig.) *to be -ing with*, brulicare di.
**crayfish** *n.* gambero d'acqua dolce.
**crayon** *n.* pastello; carboncino; matita colorata.
**craz-e** *n.* voga; mania, smaniai *to be the —*, essere la voga del momento. **-ed** *adj.* pazzo; matto; folle.
**craziness** *n.* pazzia; follia; (fig.) instabilità; irregolarità; eccentricità.
**crazy** *adj.* matto; pazzo; folle; da matti; *— with*, pazzo di; (fig.) stravagante, irregolare; *to be — about*, andare matto per; *a — affair*, roba da matti; *to drive —*, far impazzire; *to go —*, impazzire, diventar matto; *— pavement*, *— paving*, lastricato rustico.
**creak, -ing** *n.* cigolìo, stridìo; *intr.* cigolare; stridere; scricchiolare.
**cream** *n.* panna; crema; (fig.) fior fiore *m.*; (colour) color crema; *whipped —*, panna montata; (chem.) *— of tartar*, cremore *m.* di tartaro; *attrib.* alla crema; *tr.* scremare; *-ed potatoes*, purè di patate. **-ery** *n.* caseificio; latteria. **-y** *adj.* ricco di panna; (fig.) vellutato; morbido.
**crease** *n.* piega; sgualcitura; piegatura; grinza; (cricket) linea bianca; *tr.* fare la piega a; *well -d trousers*, calzoni con la piega a posto; *intr.* sgualcirsi, raggrinzarsi.
**create** *tr.* creare; fare; produrre; provocare; nominare; *to — a scandal*, suscitare uno scandalo; *to — a disturbance*, disturbare l'ordine pubblico.
**creation** *n.* creazione; atto creativo; nomina; *Creation*, l'Universo, il Creato.
**creativ-e** *adj.* creativo; originale; produttivo. **-ity, -eness** *n.* facoltà creativa.
**creator** *n.* creatore.
**creature** *n.* creatura; essere vivente; *dumb -s*, gli animali, le bestie; *— comforts*, benessere *m.* materiale; (fam.) *poor —*, poveretto, poveretta.
**crèche** *n.* asilo infantile; (rel.) presepio.
**credence** *n.* fede *f.*; fiducia; credenza; *worthy of —*, degno di fiducia; *to attach — to*, prestare fede a; *letter of —*, lettera di presentazione; (rel.) *— table*, credenza.
**credentials** *n.* credenziali *f.pl.*
**credib-le** *adj.* credibile; degno

di fede; verosimile. **-ility** *n.* credibilità.
**credit** *n.* (comm.) credito; *to buy on —*, comprare a credito; *no — is given in this shop*, in questo negozio non si fa credito; *— balance*, saldo attivo, differenza a credito; *— side*, avere *m.*, attivo; (fig.) *to be a — to*, fare onore a; *to give — to someone for*, attribuire a qualcuno il merito per; *to take — for someone else's work*, attribuirsi il merito del lavoro altrui.
**credit** *tr.* (comm.) accreditare; credere, prestare fede a; attribuire, riconoscere. **-able** *adj.* lodevole; degno di lode; che fa onore. **-or** *n.* creditore.
**credo** *n.* credo, professione di fede.
**credulity** *n.* credulità; dabbenaggine *f.*
**credulous** *adj.* credulo.
**creed** *n.* credo; confessione; credenza, fede.
**creek** *n.* insenatura; cala.
**creel** *n.* nassa, cesta per la pesca.
**creep** *n.* strisciamento; (geol.) scorrimento; (metall.) deformazione permanente; *pl.* (fam.) *it gives me the -s*, mi fa venire i brividi.
**creep** *intr.* strisciare; trascinarsi; avvicinarsi lentamente; insinuarsi; infilarsi; (of flesh) accapponarsi; (of plants) arrampicarsi; (metall.) deformarsi permanentemente; *to — away*, allontanarsi furtivamente; *to — down*, scendere lentamente; *to — up*, salire lentamente; *to — on*, avanzare a passi lenti, passare insensibilmente.
**creeper** *n.* (bot.) pianta rampicante, liana; *Virginia —*, vite *f.* del Canadà.
**creeping** *adj.* (bot.) strisciante; (fig.) lento; (med.) *— paralysis*, paralisi progressiva; (mil.) *— barrage*, tiro di sbarramento che si sposta con l'avanzare delle truppe.
**creepy** *adj.* che striscia, strisciante; (fig.) che dà i brividi, orripilante.
**cremat-e** *tr.* cremare. **-ion** *n.* cremazione. **-orium** *n.* crematoio, forno crematorio.
**crenellated** *adj.* (archit.) merlato; ammorsato.
**creole** *adj.*, *n.* creolo.
**creosote** *n.* (chem.) creosoto.
**crêpe** *n.* crespo; *— de Chine*, crespo di Cina; *— rubber*, gomma crespata.
**crepitation** *n.* crepitio.
**crept** *p.def. part.* of **creep**, *q.v.*
**crepuscular** *adj.* crepuscolare.
**crescendo** *n.* (mus.) crescendo.
**crescent** *adj.* crescente; *n.* luna crescente; mezzaluna; fila ricurva di case.
**cress** *n.* (bot.) crescione *m.*
**crest** *n.* cresta; ciuffo; pennacchio; (herald.) cimiero, timbro; insegna nobiliare; (archit.) linea di displuvio; *tr.* munire di pennacchio; raggiungere la cima di. **-fallen** *n.* mortificato; abbattuto; con la coda fra le gambe.
**cretaceous** *adj.* (geol.) cretaceo.
**Cretan** *adj.*, *n.* cretese *m.*, *f.*
**Crete** *pr.n.* (geog.) Creta; Candia.
**cretin** *n.* cretino. **-ism** *n.* cretinismo.
**cretonne** *n.* cotonina stampata.
**crevasse** *n.* crepaccio.
**crevice** *n.* crepa; fessura; interstizio.
**crew**[1] *n.* equipaggio; serventi *m.pl.*; squadra, gruppo; (pejor.) ciurma, masnada.
**crew**[2] *p.def.* of **crow**, *q.v.*
**crib** *n.* greppia; mangiatoia; presepio; lettino a sbarre; (archit.) puntellatura di sostegno; (slang) bigino; *tr.* (slang) copiare, plagiare.
**crick** *n.* crampo; torcicollo; *tr.* provocare un crampo; *to — one's neck*, prendersi un torcicollo.
**cricket** *n.* (ent.) grillo; (sport) cricket *m.*; *it isn't —*, non è sportivo, non è leale. **-er** *n.* giuocatore di cricket.
**crier** *n.* piagnucolone, piagnone *m.*; (leg.) usciere *m.*; banditore.
**crime** *n.* delitto; fatto delittuoso; reato; crimine *m.*; (mil.) *— sheet*, foglio delle punizioni.
**criminal** *adj.* delittuoso, criminale; criminoso; *— law*, diritto penale; *— investigation department, C.I.D.*, polizia giudiziaria; *n.* delinquente *m.*, *f.*; criminale *m.*, *f.*; *habitual —*, recidivo, pregiudicato; *— lawyer*, avvocato penalista.
**criminolog-y** *n.* criminologia. **-ist** *n.* criminologo; penalista *m.*
**crimp** *tr.* pieghettare, sgualcire; increspare, arricciare.
**crimson** *adj.* cremisi; *n.* cremisi *m.*; (fig.) rossore *m.*; *tr.* tingere di cremisi; *intr.* arrossire.
**cring-e** *intr.* acquattarsi; piegare la schiena; farsi piccolo. **-ing** *adj.* servile.
**cringle** *n.* (naut.) brancarella, gassa.
**crinkl-e** *n.* crespa; grinza; ruga; *tr.* increspare; spiegazzare; arricciare; *intr.* incresparsi; arricciarsi. **-y** *adj.* increspato; spiegazzato.
**crinoline** *n.* crinolina; guardinfante *m.*
**cripple** *n.* storpio; storpiato; mutilato; *tr.* storpiare; mutilare; (fig.) danneggiare; paralizzare.
**crisis** *n.* crisi *f.*
**crisp** *adj.* crespo; ricciuto; arricciato; croccante; frizzante; vivace; nitido; *n. potato -s* patatine *f.pl.* fritte croccanti.
**criss-cross** *adj.* incrociato; a linee incrociate; *tr.* incrociare, incrociarsi.
**criterion** *n.* criterio.
**critic** *n.* critico; *art —*, critico d'arte; *dramatic —*, critico teatrale. **-al** *adj.* critico; decisivo. **-ism** *n.* critica; (philos.) criticismo.
**criticiz-e** *tr.* criticare; censurare; riprendere; esprimere un giudizio su. **-able** *adj.* censurabile; biasimevole.
**critique** *n.* saggio critico; critica.
**croak** *n.* gracchiamento; gracidìo; *intr.* gracchiare; gracidare; (fig.) brontolare, predire malanni; (slang) morire. **-er** *n.* brontolone *m.*; uccello di malaugurio.
**Croatia** *pr.n.* (geog.) Croazia.
**Croat(ian)** *adj.*, *n.* croato.
**crochet** *n.* lavoro all'uncinetto; *tr.* lavorare all'uncinetto.
**crock** *n.* vaso; pentola; (fig.) rottame *m.*, rudere *m.* (also fig., of person); (horse) ronzino; (car) macchina stravecchia; *tr.* rendere inabile; *intr. to — up*, ammalarsi. **-ery** *n.* stoviglie *f.pl.*; vasellame *m.*
**crocodile** *n.* (zool.) coccodrillo; *— tears*, lacrime *f. pl.* di coccodrillo; coda, fila.
**crocus** *n.* (bot.) croco, zafferano.
**Croesus** *pr.n.* (myth.) Creso.
**croft** *n.* podere *m.*; campicello. **-er** *n.* affittuario di un podere; contadino; mezzadro.
**cron-e** *n.* vecchiaccia; vecchia megera; comare *f.* **-y** *n.* amico intimo; compagno.
**crook** *n.* uncino, raffio; curva, piega; *shepherd's —*, bastone *m.* da pastore; *bishop's —*, pastorale *m.*; truffatore; imbroglione *m.*; delinquente *m.*, *f.*; *by hook or by —*, di riffa o di raffa; *tr.* piegare; curvare.
**crooked**[1] *p.def. part.* of **crook**.
**crook·ed**[2] *adj.* curvo; storto; ricurvo; a sghembo; (fig.) tortuoso; di traverso; disonesto; truffaldino.
**croon** *intr.* canticchiare; cantare in tono sentimentale. **-er** *n.* cantante di canzoni sentimentali.
**crop** *n.* raccolta; raccolto; messe *f.*; *rotation of -s*, rotazione delle colture; *under —*, coltivato; *out of —*, a maggese; (of bird) gozzo; (of whip) manico; (of hair) rapata; *close —*, rapata a zero; (fig.) mucchio; *a — of lies*, un sacco di bugie; (fam.) *neck and —*, armi e bagagli.
**crop** *tr.* raccogliere; tagliar via, mozzare, rapare, tosare; (of sheep) *to — the grass*, brucare l'erba; *intr. to — up*, affiorare; (fam.) saltar fuori, capitare.
**cropper** *n.* potatore; tosatore; (tenant-farmer) mezzadro, coltivatore; (slang) capitombolo. ruzzolone *m.*; *to come a —*, fare un capitombolo, (fig.) far fiasco.
**croquet** *n.* pallamaglio, croquet *m.*
**croquette** *n.* (cul.) polpettina fritta, crocchetta.

**crosier** *n.* (eccl.) pastorale *m.*

**cross** *adj.* trasversale, obliquo; incrociato; contrario, avverso; *to be at — purposes,* fraintendersi; arrabbiato, imbronciato, adirato.

**cross** *n.* (rel.) croce *f.*; *the way of the —,* la via crucis, il calvario; *to bear one's —,* portare la propria croce; *to make the sign of the —,* fare il segno della croce, segnarsi; (hist.) *to take the —,* andar crociato; (on letter 't') taglio.

**cross** *tr.* attraversare, varcare, passare; intersecare; incrociarsi con, incrociare; *to — one's arms,* incrociare le braccia; *to — one's legs,* accavallare le gambe; *to — a cheque,* sbarrare un assegno; *to — one's 't's',* tagliare le 't'; *to — out,* cancellare; (fig.) *to — someone's plans,* contrastare i piani di qualcuno; *to — someone's path,* trovarsi sulla strada di qualcuno; *to — swords with,* misurarsi con, discutere con; *to — one's mind,* venire in mente a uno; (rel.) *to — oneself,* segnarsi; *intr.* fare una traversata; incrociarsi.

**cross-bar** *n.* traversa. **-beam** *n.* (bldg.) trave *f.* trasversale. **-bearer** *n.* (eccl. crocifero. **-belt** *n.* (mil.) cartucciera a tracollo.

**crossbill** *n.* (orn.) crociere. *m.*

**cross-bones** *n.* ossa *f. pl.* incrociate. **-bow** *n.* balestra. **-bred** *adj.* di razza incrociata, ibrido. **-breed** *n.* incrocio di razze.

**cross-country** *adj.* attraverso i campi; *— race,* 'cross' *m. indecl.*

**cross-examin-e** *tr., intr.* (leg.) interrogare in contraddittorio; (fig.) interrogare a fondo. **-ation** *n.* (leg.) interrogatorio in contraddittorio.

**cross-eyed** *adj.* strabico. **-fire** *n.* (mil.) fuoco incrociato.

**crossing** *n.* traversata; varco; passaggio; *a rough —,* una traversata tempestosa; (rlwy.) *level —,* passaggio a livello; incrocio; (archit.) crociata.

**cross-legged** *adj.* con le gambe accavallate.

**crossness** *n.* malumore *m.*

**cross-piece** *n.* traversa. **-question** *tr.* interrogare severamente. **-reference** *n.* rimando, rinvio.

**crossroad** *n.* strada trasversale, traversa; *pl.* bivio; crocicchio; crocevia *m.*; incrocio.

**cross-section** *n.* spaccato; sezione trasversale; (fig.) rappresentanza; settore rappresentativo.

**cross-stitch** *n.* punto in croce.

**crosswise** *adv.* per traverso, di traverso.

**crossword** *n.* — *puzzle,* giuoco delle parole incrociate, cruciverba *m.*

**crotchet** *n.* uncinetto; capriccio, ubbia; (mus.) semiminima. **-y** *adv.* **bizzarro, capriccioso.**

**crouch** *intr.* acquattarsi; rannicchiarsi; accucciarsi.

**croup**[1] *n.* groppa.

**croup**[2] *n.* (med.) crup(pe) *m.*

**crow**[1] *n.* (orn.) cornacchia; corvo; *carrion —,* cornacchia nera; *hooded —,* cornacchia grigia; *as the — flies,* in linea d'aria; *-'s foot,* zampa di gallina, ruga, (naut.) patta d'oca; *-'s nest,* coffa, gabbia.

**crow**[2] *n.* canto del gallo; (fig.) grido di gioia; *intr.* cantare; (fig.) fare gridi di gioia; *tr. to — victory over,* cantar vittoria su.

**crowbar** *n.* palanchino, piede *m.* di porco.

**crowd** *n.* folla; calca; ressa; moltitudine *f.*; masse *f.pl.*; (fig.) *to go with the —,* seguire la corrente, fare quello che fanno gli altri; (pejor.) combriccola, compagnia.

**crowd** *tr.* affollare; stipare; spingere; ammassare; *intr.* affollarsi; accalcarsi; assembrarsi; pigiarsi; *to — into,* entrare in folla; *to — round,* affollarsi intorno a; *to — together,* accalcarsi, stringersi insieme; (naut.) *to — on sail,* mettere tutte le vele al vento. **-ed** *adj.* affollato; stipato; pieno zeppo.

**crown** *n.* corona; *— prince,* principe ereditario; *— lands,* terre *f.pl.* demaniali; *— of the head,* calotta cranica; *— of a hat,* cocuzzolo di un cappello; *— of the road,* colmo.

**crown** *tr.* incoronare; (draughts) damare; (fig.) coronare; ricompensare; (fam.) *to — all,* per colmo di disgrazia. **-ing** *adj.* supremo, finale, ultimo; *n.* incoronazione; (fig.) coronamento.

**crozier** *n.* see **crosier.**

**crucial** *adj.* decisivo; critico; (anat.) crociato; (fam.) *at the — moment,* sul più bello.

**crucible** *n.* crogiuolo.

**crucifix** *n.* crocifisso. **-ion** *n.* crocifissione.

**cruciform** *adj.* crociforme.

**crucify** *tr.* crocifiggere; mettere in croce; (fig.) mortificare.

**crud-e** *adj.* grossolano; rozzo; brutale; immaturo; sommario; crudo; (chem.) grezzo, greggio, non raffinato; *— oil,* petrolio grezzo. **-eness, -ity** *n.* rozzezza; asprezza; brutalità; crudezza.

**cruel** *adj.* crudele; efferato, disumano; *to be — to,* maltrattare. **-ty** *n.* crudeltà; efferatezza; disumanità; *society for the prevention of* **-ty** *to animals,* società protettrice degli animali.

**cruet** *n.* ampolla, ampollina, acetoliera.

**cruise** *n.* crociera; *to go on a —,* fare una crociera; *intr.* incrociare; fare una crociera; girare a velocità di crociera.

**cruiser** *n.* incrociatore; motoscafo da crociera.

**cruising** *adj.* da crociera; *n.* crociera; incrociare *m.*; *— speed,* velocità di crociera.

**crumb** *n.* briciola; mollica; *tr.* panare.

**crumbl-e** *tr.* sbriciolare; (fig.) sgretolare; *intr.* sbriciolarsi; (fig.) sgretolarsi, crollare. **-ing, -y** *adj.* friabile; sgretoloso; (fig.) cadente.

**crumby** *adj.* midolloso; (fig.) soffice, molle.

**crumple** *tr.* spiegazzare; sgualcire; raggrinzire; *intr.* spiegazzarsi; sgualcirsi; raggrinzirsi; *to — up,* sfasciarsi; accartocciarsi; crollare, accasciarsi.

**crunch**[1] *n.* sgretolio; tritamento; scricchiolio; *tr.* schiacciare; masticare; sgretolare; *intr.* sgretolarsi; stridere, scricchiolare.

**crupper** *n.* sottocoda, posolino.

**crusad-e** *n.* crociata; *intr.* bandire, partecipare a una crociata. **-er** *n.* (hist.) crociato; (fig.) partecipante a una crociata.

**crush** *n.* schiacciamento; calca, folla, ressa; (fam.) *to have a — on,* avere una cotta per; *tr.* schiacciare, spiaccicare; pigiare; stipare; spiegazzare, sgualcire; (fig.) *to be -ed by,* essere affranto da; annientare, annichilire; (industr.) frantumare, triturare; *to — to death,* schiacciare a morte; *to — to pieces,* stritolare; *to — out,* spremere. **-er** *n.* (mech.) frantumatore, frantoio. **-ing** *adj.* schiacciante; *n.* schiacciamento; frantumazione; *-ing plant,* frantoio.

**crust** *n.* crosta; (fig.) incrostazione; (geol.) corteccia; *tr.* incrostare; coprire di crosta; *intr.* incrostarsi; coprirsi di crosta; aggrumarsi.

**crustacean** *n.* (zool.) crostaceo.

**crusty** *adj.* crostoso; (fig.) burbero, uggioso.

**crutch** *n.* gruccia, stampella; (fig.) sostegno; *to walk on -es,* camminare con le grucce; (anat.) inforcatura; (naut.) scalmiera.

**crux** *n.* momento decisivo, punto cruciale, nodo; *the — of the matter is,* qui sta il nodo della questione.

**cry** *n.* grido; urlo; pianto; strillo; *to have a good —,* farsi un bel pianto, sfogarsi col pianto; *to be in full —,* (of hounds) abbaiare forte, (fig.) essere in piena corsa; *it's a far — between,* c'è una bella differenza fra.

**cry** *tr., intr.* gridare; urlare; piangere; strillare; *stop -ing,* smettila di piangere; *to — one's eyes out,* consumarsi gli occhi dal piangere; *to — oneself to sleep,* addormentarsi a forza di piangere; *to — quits,* riconoscere che la partita è pari, riconciliarsi; *to — shame on someone,* additare qualcuno a vergogna; *to — stinking fish,* darsi la zappa sui piedi; *to — for,* chiedere, im-

plorare, reclamare; *to — out*, gridare, urlare, lamentarsi a gran voce; *to — out for*, reclamare, chiedere, implorare; *to — up*, portare alle stelle; *to — down*, denigrare, screditare; *to — off*, tirarsi indietro; (provb.) *it's no use ~ing over spilt milk*, cosa fatta capo ha, non serve piangere sul latte versato.

**crying** *adj.* gridante; piangente; (fig.) *a — need*, un bisogno urgente; *a — shame*, una palese vergogna; *n.* gridìo; pianto.

**crypt** *n.* cripta.

**cryptic** *adj.* ermetico, occulto, ambiguo.

**crypto-gram** *n.* crittogramma *m.* **~graphy** *n.* crittografia.

**crystal** *adj.* cristallino; *n.* cristallo.

**crystal-clear, crystalline** *adj.* cristallino.

**crystal-gazing** *n.* divinazione per mezzo di un globo di cristallo.

**crystalliz-e** *tr.* cristallizzare; (cul.) *~d fruits*, frutta candita; *intr.* cristallizzarsi; (fig.) concretarsi, assumere un aspetto ben definito. **~ation** *n.* cristallizzazione.

**crystalloid** *n.* (chem.) cristalloide *m.*

**cub** *n.* (of wild animal) cucciolo, piccolo; (of fox) volpacchiotto; (pejor., boy) ragazzaccio, giovinastro.

**Cub-a** *pr.n.* (geog.) Cuba. **~an** *adj.*, *n.* cubano.

**cubbyhole** *n.* angolo intimo; nido; tana.

**cube** *n.* cubo; *— root*, radice cubica; *tr.* (math.) elevare al cubo, fare la cubatura di.

**cub-hunting** *n.* caccia ai volpacchiotti.

**cubic** *adj.* cubico, cubo; *— centimetre*, centimetro cubo; *— foot*, piede cubo. **~al** *adj.* cubico, a forma di cubo.

**cubicle** *n.* cubicolo; scompartimento separato.

**cub-ism** *n.* cubismo. **~ist** *adj.*, *n.* cubista *m.*, *f.*

**cubit** *n.* cubito.

**cuckold** *n.* cornuto, becco; *tr.* fare le corna a, far becco.

**cuckoo** *n.* (orn.) cuculo, cuccù *m. indecl.*; (fig.) semplicione *m.*

**cuckoo-clock** *n.* orologio a cuccù.

**cucumber** *n.* (bot.) cetriolo; (fig.) *cool as a —*, imperturbabile, fresco come una rosa.

**cud** *n.* bolo alimentare; *to chew the —*, ruminare.

**cuddle** *tr.* coccolare; abbracciare teneramente; stringere al seno; *intr. to — up*, rannicchiarsi.

**cuddy** *n.* (naut.) cabina del comandante; cambusa.

**cudgel** *n.* randello; bastone *m.*; (fig.) *to take up the ~s for*, difendere a spada tratta; *tr.* bastonare; picchiare; (fig.) *to — one's brains*, lambiccarsi il cervello.

**cue** *n.* (billiards) stecca; (theatr.) attacco, spunto, battuta d'entrata; (fig.) *to take one's — from someone*, ricevere l'imbeccata da qualcuno.

**cue-rack** *n.* (billiards) portastecche *m. indecl.*

**cuff**[1] *n.* polsino, risvolto; (slang) *off the —*, a braccio; scapaccione *m.*, schiaffo; *tr.* schiaffeggiare.

**cuff-links** *n.* gemelli *m.pl.*

**cuirass** *n.* corazza.

**cuisine** *n.* cucina.

**cul-de-sac** *n.* vicolo cieco.

**culinary** *adj.* culinario; gastronomico.

**cull** *tr.* cogliere; (fig.) scegliere, fare una cernita di.

**culminat-e** *intr.* culminare; giungere al culmine; (fig.) concludersi; *~ing point*, apice *m.*, apogeo. **~ion** *n.* (astron.) culminazione; (fig.) culmine *m.*, apice *m.*, apogeo.

**culotte(s)** *n.* gonna pantalone.

**culpab-le** *adj.* colpevole; (leg.) colposo; *— negligence*, negligenza colposa. **~ility** *n.* colpevolezza.

**culprit** *n.* colpevole *m.*, *f.*

**cult** *n.* culto; (fig.) *to make a — of*, avere un culto per.

**cultivat-e** *tr.* coltivare; valorizzare. **~ed** *adj.* coltivato; (fig.) raffinato; colto. **~ion** *n.* coltivazione; (fig.) coltura. **~or** *n.* coltivatore; (fig.) cultore.

**cultur-e** *n.* coltivazione; coltura; (fig.) cultura; *a man of —*, un uomo colto; civilità. **~al** *adj.* culturale. **~ed** *adj.* coltivato; *~ed pearl*, perla coltivata, (fig.) colto; dotto.

**cultus** *n.* (rel.) culto.

**culverin** *n.* colubrina.

**culvert** *n.* chiavica, fogna, condotto sotterraneo.

**cumber** *tr.* ingombrare; ostruire. **~some** *adj.* ingombrante, incomodo.

**cumin** *n.* (bot.) comino.

**cumulative** *adj.* cumulativo; composto.

**cumulus** *n.* cumulo.

**cuneiform** *adj.* cuneiforme.

**cunning** *adj.* furbo; astuto; scaltro; accorto; abile; *n.* furberia; astuzia; accortezza.

**cunt** *n.* (fam.) fica.

**cup** *n.* tazza; (bot.; eccl.) calice *m.*; *a — of tea*, una tazza di tè; *~s and saucers*, tazze con piattini; (sport; mech.) coppa; *— final*, finale *f.* di coppa; (of barometer) vaschetta; (surg.) coppetta; (fig.) *the — is full*, la misura è colma; *to be in one's ~s*, avere alzato il gomito; (fam.) *that's another — of tea*, è un altro paio di maniche; *it's not your — of tea*, non è cibo per i tuoi denti.

**cup** *tr.* (surg.) applicare le coppette a; *to — one's hands*, unire le mani a guisa di coppa.

**cup-bearer** *n.* coppiere *m.*

**cupboard** *n.* armadio; credenza; *— love*, amore interessato; *the skeleton in the —*, il segreto di famiglia.

**cupful** *n.* tazza piena.

**Cupid** *pr.n.* (myth.) Cupido, Amore *m.*; *~'s bow*, l'arco di Cupido; (art) amorino, putto.

**cupidity** *n.* cupidigia, cupidità.

**cupola** *n.* (archit.) cupola, cupoletta; (on an octagonal base) tiburio.

**cupric** *adj.* (chem.) cuprico, ramico.

**cur** *n.* cagnaccio, cane bastardo; (fig.) vigliacco, mascalzone *m.*

**curable** *adj.* guaribile.

**curacy** *n.* vicariato; cura.

**curare** *n.* (pharm.) curaro.

**curate** *n.* (eccl.) viceparroco, vicario parrocchiale, cappellano, coadiutore del parroco.

**curative** *adj.* curativo; terapeutico.

**curator** *n.* curatore; amministratore; conservatore, direttore di museo.

**curb** *n.* (equit.) barbazzale *m.*; (of pavement) cordone *m.*; (fig.) freno; *to keep a — on*, tenere a freno, frenare; *tr.* frenare; tenere a freno; reprimere.

**curds** *n.* latte cagliato; giuncata; quagliata; *— and whey*, latte cagliato e siero.

**curdle** *tr.* far cagliare, aggrumare, coagulare; *intr.* accagliarsi, aggrumarsi, cagliare; (fig.) *it made my blood —*, mi si gelò il sangue.

**cure** *n.* rimedio, cura; *to take a —*, fare una cura; *to guarantee a —*, garantire la guarigione; (eccl.) *— of souls*, cura d'anime; *tr.* guarire, sanare; (fig.) rimediare a; affumicare; marinare; salare; conservare.

**curer** *n.* guaritore; salatore.

**curette** *n.* (surg.) raschiatoio.

**curfew** *n.* coprifuoco.

**curio** *n.* oggetto d'arte; ricordo di viaggio.

**curiosity** *n.* curiosità; desiderio di sapere; invadenza; curiosità, rarità; anticaglia; *the old — shop*, la bottega dell'antiquario.

**curious** *adj.* strano, singolare, insolito, curioso; *the — thing is that*, lo strano è che; incuriosito, indiscreto, curioso; *a — man*, un curioso. **~ness** *n.* singolarità; stranezza.

**curl** *n.* ricciolo, riccio; spirale, voluta; curva; (fig.) *a — of the lips*, una smorfia di sdegno; (bot.) arricciamento, bolla.

**curl** *tr.* arricciare; arrotolare; avvolgere a spirale; torcere; *to — one's lips*, torcere le labbra; (fig.) *to — oneself up*, rannicchiarsi, raggomitolarsi; *intr.* (of hair) arricciarsi; (of smoke) salire in spire; *to — up*, rannicchiarsi; (of

animal) accucciarsi. **-er** *n.* bigodino.
**curlew** *n.* (orn.) chiurlo.
**curl-iness** *n.* ricciutezza. **-ing** arricciatura; (game) giuoco di bocce sul ghiaccio.
**curling-pin** *n.* forcina per arricciare. **-paper** *n.* bigodino di carta.
**curly** *adj.* ricciuto, ricciolutο, riccio.
**curmudgeon** *n.* spilorcio, burbero.
**currant** *n.* (red, white or black) ribes *m. indecl.*; (dried) uva passa.
**currency** *n.* valuta, divisa, moneta (legale); *paper —*, moneta cartacea; (comm.) decorrenza; circolazione, corso; (fig.) *to gain —*, acquistare larga diffusione; *to give — to*, diffondere, avallare.
**current** *adj.* corrente; attuale; *— account*, conto corrente; *— events*, attualità *f.pl.*; *n.* corrente *f.*; *against the —*, contro corrente.
**curriculum** *n.* programma *m.* di studi, corso.
**curried** *adj.* (cul.) al curry.
**currier** *n.* conciapelli *m. indecl.*
**curry**[1] *n.* (cul.) polvere *f.* di radice di curcuma.
**curry**[2] *tr.* (leather) conciare; (horses) strigliare; *to — favour with someone*, cercare d'ingraziarsi qualcuno, (fam.) leccare i piedi a qualcuno.
**curry-comb** *n.* striglia.
**curse** *n.* maledizione; anatema *m.*; bestemmia, imprecazione; *a — upon him!*, sia maledetto!; *to call down -s upon*, invocare la maledizione di Dio su; (fig.) disastro, sciagura, flagello.
**curse** *tr.* maledire; imprecare contro; (fam.) *— it!*, maledizione!; *intr.* bestemmiare, imprecare.
**cursed** *part. adj.* maledetto; *to be — with*, essere afflitto da.
**cursive** *adj.*, *n.* corsivo.
**cursor-y** *adj.* frettoloso; superficiale; rapido; *a — glance*, una scorsa. **-iness** *n.* superficialità; rapidità.
**curt** *adj.* brusco; secco; reciso; asciutto.
**curtail** *tr.* accorciare; tagliare; abbreviare; decurtare; limitare; ridurre. **-ment** *n.* accorciamento; decurtazione; abbreviazione; limitazione; riduzione.
**curtain** *n.* tenda; tendina; (fig.) cortina; *to draw the -s*, tirare le tende; (fig.) *to draw a — over*, stendere un velo su; (pol.) *iron —*, cortina di ferro; (theatr.) sipario, tela; *the — rises*, s'alza il sipario; *the — falls*, cala il sipario; *to take a — call*, presentarsi alla ribalta; *safety —*, sipario anti-incendio; *tr.* provvedere di tende; *to — off*, separare con una tenda.
**curtain-raiser** *n.* (theatr.) avanspettacolo.
**curtness** *n.* tono brusco; asprezza.
**curts(e)y** *n.* inchino, riverenza; *intr.* fare una riverenza, inchinarsi.
**curvature** *n.* curvatura.
**curve**[1] *n.* curva; svolta; (of river) ansa; *tr.* curvare; piegare; *intr.* curvarsi; piegarsi, descrivere una curva; svoltare.
**curvet** *intr.* corvettare, fare una falcata.
**curvilinear** *adj.* curvilineo.
**cushion** *n.* cuscino; guanciale *m.*; (of billiard-table) sponda elastica; *tr.* munire di cuscini; imbottire; (fig.) assorbire, smorzare.
**cushy** *adj.* (fam.) comodo.
**cusp** *n.* cuspide *f.*
**cuspidor** *n.* sputacchiera.
**cuss, cussed** *see* **curse, cursed.**
**cussedness** *n.* (fam.) perversità; malvagità.
**custard** *n.* crema di uova e latte; *— apple*, anona.
**custodian** *n.* custode *m.*; conservatore; guardiano, portiere *m.*
**custody** *n.* custodia, guardia, tutela; *in safe —*, sotto buona guardia; *to grant — of a child to the father*, affidare al padre la custodia del figlio; arresto, detenzione; *to take into —*, arrestare; *to be in —*, essere in stato d'arresto.
**custom** *n.* costume *m.*; abitudine *f.*; consuetudine *f.*; usanza; *according to —*, secondo il costume; *the -s of a country*, le usanze di un paese; (comm.) clientela; *to lose one's —*, perdere la clientela; *to discontinue one's — at a shop*, smettere di servirsi in un negozio.
**customary** *adj.* abituale, d'uso, consueto, solito; *it is —*, è d'uso, si usa.
**customer** *n.* cliente *m.*, *f.*; avventore; (fam.) *a queer —*, un tipo strano.
**custom-house** *n.* dogana.
**Customs** *n.* la Dogana; *— officer*, funzionario della Dogana, doganiere *m.*; *— examination*, doganale.
**cut** *n.* taglio; incisione; ferita; ribasso, riduzione; (cards) alzata; (with sword) fendente *m.*; (sport) colpo tagliato; (fig.) *— and thrust*, botta e risposta; *a short —*, una scorciatoia; *to give someone the — direct*, fingere di non conoscere qualcuno; (fam.) *to be a — above*, valere più di.
**cut** *tr.* tagliare; recidere; intagliare, incidere; (fig.) fingere di non conoscere, togliere il saluto a; *— and dried*, bell'e fatto; *— flowers*, fiori recisi; *to — a poor figure*, fare una brutta figura; *to — the cards*, alzare le carte; *to — one's nails*, tagliarsi le unghie; *to have one's hair —*, farsi tagliare i capelli; (fam.) *to — one's lessons*, saltare le lezioni, marinare la scuola; *to — one's losses*, ridurre le perdite, rinunciare a un cattivo affare; *to — a tooth*, mettere un dente; *to — in half*, tagliare a metà; *to — to pieces*, tagliare a pezzi, tagliuzzare; *to — into slices*, affettare; *to — to the quick*, pungere sul vivo; *not to — much ice*, fare poco effetto, non cavare un ragno dal buco; *to — across*, attraversare; *to — away*, tagliare via, recidere; *to — back*, recidere; *to — down*, abbattere; *to — down expenses*, ridurre le spese; *to — off*, tagliare, mozzare, troncare; (fig.) interrompere, sospendere; *to — off a corner*, tagliar dritto; *to — off the gas supply*, sospendere l'erogazione del gas; *to be — off with a shilling*, essere diseredato; (mil.) *the battalion was — off*, il battaglione fu tagliato fuori; *to — out*, (ri)tagliare; tralasciare; *he's got his work — out*, avrà il suo daffare; *to — up*, tagliare, fare a pezzi; *to — up rough*, aversene a male; *to be very — up about something*, essere profondamente ferito da qualcosa; *to — loose*, liberare, liberarsi; *to — open*, aprire tagliando; *to — short*, interrompere, troncare; *to — a long story short*, per farla breve; *to — someone short*, troncare la parola in bocca a qualcuno; *intr.* *to — and run*, tagliare la corda; *to — in*, interrompere, intervenire, (in front of another car) tagliare la strada (a un'altra macchina).
**cutaneous** *adj.* cutaneo.
**cutaway** *n.* giacca del 'tight'; (drawing) spaccato.
**cute** *adj.* fino, astuto, furbo, in gamba; ingegnoso. **-ness** *n.* (of person) astuzia, furberia; (of thing) ingegnosità.
**cuticle** *n.* cuticola; epidermide *f.*
**cutlass** *n.* (naut.) sciabola curva da arrembaggio.
**cutler** *n.* coltellinaio.
**cutlery** *n.* posateria; coltelleria.
**cutlet** *n.* (cul.) costoletta.
**cut-out** *n.* ritaglio; (electr.) interruttore; (motor.) valvola di scappamento libero.
**cutter** *n.* (tailor.) tagliatore *m.*; (mech.) fresa; (naut.) lancia di bordo, 'cutter' *m.*; *revenue —*, nave guardacoste.
**cut-throat** *n.* tagliagole *m. indecl.*; assassino; (fig., attrib.) spietato.
**cutting** *adj.* tagliente; (fig.) sferzante; *n.* il tagliare, taglio; ribasso; incisione; (from newspaper) ritaglio; (bot.) margotta; (rlwy.) trincea.
**cuttlefish** *n.* seppia.
**cutwater** *n.* (of bridge) sprone *m.*, pigna, tagliacqua *m. indecl.*; (naut.) tagliamare *m. indecl.*
**cyanide** *n.* (chem.) cianuro.
**cyan-osis** *f.* (med.) cianosi *f.* **-otic** *adj.* cianotic.
**cybernetics** *n.* (scient.) cibernetica.

**Cyclades** *pr.n.* (geog.) Cicladi *f.pl.*
**cyclamen** *n.* (bot.) ciclamino.
**cycle** *n.* ciclo; (electr.) periodo; bicicletta; *intr.* andare in bicicletta; pedalare.
**cycle-car** *n.* motofurgone *m.*, motocarrozzetta. **-race** *n.* corsa ciclistica.
**cyclical** *adj.* ciclico.
**cycl-ing** *n.* ciclismo; l'andare in bicicletta; *no* —, vietato ai ciclisti. **-ist** *n.* ciclista *m.*, *f.*
**cyclone** *n.* ciclone *m.*
**Cyclops** *pr.n.* (myth.) Ciclope.
**cyclostyle** *n.* ciclostile *m.*; *tr.* ciclostilare.
**cygnet** *n.* cigno giovane.
**cylind-er** *n.* (mech.) cilindro, rullo; (of revolver) tamburo; (containing liquid gas) bombola. **-rical** *adj.* cilindrico.
**cyma** *n.* (archit.) gola.
**cymbal** *n.* (mus.) piatto, cembalo.
**cymric** *adj.* gallese, cimro.
**cynic** *n.* cinico. **-al** *adj.* cinico. **-ism** *n.* cinismo.
**cynosure** *n.* (astron.) cinosura; (fig.) centro d'attrazione, punto di mira.
**Cynthia** *pr.n.* Cinzia.
**cypress** *n.* cipresso.
**Cypr-us** *pr.n.* (geog.) Cipro. **-ian, -iot** *adj.*, *n.* cipriota *m.*, *f.*
**Cyril** *pr.n.* Cirillo.
**cyrillic** *adj.* cirillico.
**cyst** *n.* (med.) ciste, cisti *f.*
**Cytherea** *pr.n.* (myth.) Citerea.
**Czar** *n.* Zar. **-ism** *n.* zarismo.
**Czech** *adj.*, *n.* ceco. **-oslovak** *adj.*, *n.* cecoslovacco. **-oslovakia** *pr.n.* (geog.) Cecoslovacchia.

**D** *n.* di *m.*, *f.*; (teleph.) — *for David*, d come Domodossola; (mus.) re *m.*; *D-shaped*, a forma di D.
**dab**[1] *n.* colpettino; macchietta; tocco; *a — of butter*, un pezzettino di burro.
**dab**[1] *tr.* toccare leggermente, picchiettare; *to — one's eyes*, passarsi un fazzoletto sugli occhi; *to — paint on something*, stendere vernice *f.* su qualcosa.
**dab**[2] *n.* (ichth.) passerino.
**dab**[3] *adj.*, *n.* (slang) cannone *m.*, asso; *a — hand*, un asso.
**dabbl-e** *tr.* tuffare; inumidire, guazzare; *intr.* (fig.) fare il dilettante; *to — in*, dilettarsi in; *to — on the stock exchange*, fare piccole specolazioni in borsa. **-er** *n.* dilettante *m.*, *f.*
**dabchick** *n.* (orn.) tuffetto.
**dace** *n.* (ichth.) lasca.
**dachshund** *n.* cane bassotto.
**dactyl** *n.* (prosod.) dattilo.
**dad, daddy** *n.* babbo, papà; (fam.) *sugar* —, protettore.
**daddy-long-legs** *n.* (ent.) tipula.
**dado** *n.* (archit.) dado, zoccolo.
**daffodil** *n.* narciso.
**daft** *adj.* (fam.) matto, squilibrato.
**dagger** *n.* stiletto, pugnale *m.*; *cloak and — novel*, romanzo di cappa e spada; (fig.) *to be at -s drawn*, essere ai ferri corti; *to look -s at*, lanciare uno sguardo furibondo a; (typ.) croce *f.*
**dago** *n.* (pejor.) individuo di razza latina; meridionale *m.*, *f.*
**dahlia** *n.* (bot.) dalia.
**daily** *adj.* giornaliero, diurno; *our — bread*, il nostro pane quotidiano; — *newspaper*, quotidiano; domestica a giornata, donna a ore; *adv.* giornalmente, ogni giorno; al giorno.
**daint-y** *adj.* delicato, squisito, grazioso; schizzinoso; *n.* leccornia. **-iness** *n.* delicatezza, squisitezza; ricercatezza.
**dairy** *n.* latteria; cascina; — *butter*, burro di cascina.
**dairy-farming** *n.* industria dei latticini; caseificio.
**dairymaid** *n.* lattaia.
**dairyman** *n.* lattaio, lattivendolo.
**dais** *n.* palco, impalcatura.
**daisy** *n.* margheritina dei prati, pratolina.
**daisy-chain** *n.* ghirlanda di margheritine.
**dale** *n.* valle, vallata *f.*; *up hill and down* —, per monti e per valli.
**dalesman** *n.* valligiano.
**dalliance** *n.* indugio, esitazione; amoreggiamento.
**dally** *intr.* indugiare, sprecare tempo; esitare; *to — with a woman's affections*, scherzare con i sentimenti di una donna; *to — with an idea*, trastullarsi con una idea; *tr. to — the time away*, sprecare il tempo.
**Dalmatia** *pr.n.* (geog.) Dalmazia. **-n** *adj.*, *n.* dalmata *m.*, *f.*; *a -n dog*, un cane dalmata.
**dam**[1] *n.* sbarramento, argine *m.*; diga; *tr.* sbarrare, arginare, chiudere con dighe; (fig.) bloccare.
**dam**[2] *n.* (of animals) madre *f.*
**damag-e** *n.* danno, guasto; avaria; (leg.) indennizzo; *to be liable for -s*, essere responsabile per i danni e gli interessi; (fam.) prezzo, costo; *tr.* danneggiare, guastare, avariare; (fig.) nuocere a. **-ing** *adj.* dannoso, nocivo.
**damask** *adj.* damaschino; *n.* (text.) damasco; color rosa carico e cupo.
**dame** *n.* dama, signora; (as title) Donna.
**damn** *n.* (slang) un bel niente, nulla; *I don't care a* —, non mi importa un bel niente; *it isn't worth a* —, non vale un fico secco; *tr.* dannare; censurare; (slang) maledire, imprecare contro, mandare al diavolo; —*!*, maledizione!; — *you!*, va all'inferno!; *well I'm -ed!*, perdinci!, caspita!; *I'll be -ed if I will!*, nemmeno per sogno!; — *it all!*, al diavolo tutto quanto!; (fig.) rovinare. **-able** *adj.* dannabile; (slang) maledetto. **-ation** *n.* dannazione; *-ation!*, maledizione!, diavolo! **-atory** *adj.* condannatorio. **-ed** *adj.* dannato; *the -ed*, dannati. **-ing** *adj.* che porta alla condanna; *-ing evidence*, prove *f.pl.* schiaccianti.
**damp** *adj.* umido, bagnato; molle; madido; — *clothes*, vestiario bagnato; *forehead — with perspiration*, fronte madida di sudore; *n.* umidità; (fig.) depressione; abbattimento; *tr.* inumidire, bagnare; (fig.) soffocare, smorzare, estinguere; *to — the ardour of*, raffreddare l'ardore di; *to — down the fire*, smorzare il fuoco.
**dampen** see **damp** *tr.*
**damper** *n.* valvola di tiraggio; (mus.) smorzatoio, sordina; (for wetting stamps) spugnetta; (fig.) doccia fredda.
**dampness** *n.* umidità.
**damp-proof** *adj.* impermeabile.
**damsel** *n.* fanciulla, donzella.
**damson** *n.* susina damascena.
**dance** *n.* danza, ballo; festa da ballo; *may I have the next — with you?*, mi concede il prossimo ballo?; (fig.) *to lead someone a* —, dare del filo da torcere a qualcuno.
**dance** *tr.*, *intr.* ballare, danzare; *to — attendance*, fare anticamera; *to — out of the room*, uscire dalla stanza ballando; *to — for joy*, saltare dalla gioia; *to — a baby up and down*, dondolare un bambino.
**dance-band** *n.* orchestrina da ballo. **-hall** *n.* sala da ballo; dancing *m. indecl.* **-music** *n.* musica da ballo.
**dancer** *n.* danzatore, danzatrice; ballerino, ballerina.
**dancing** *n.* il ballo, la danza; *my — days are over*, i miei bei giorni sono passati.
**dancing-master** *n.* maestro di ballo. **-partner** *n.* cavaliere *m.*, dama *f.* **-school** *n.* scuola di danza.
**dandelion** *n.* (bot.) tarassico; (pop.) dente *m.* di leone.
**dandified** *adj.* attillato; affettato.
**dandle** *n.* dondolare.
**dandruff** *n.* forfora.
**dandy** *n.* zerbinotto, bellimbusto.
**Dane** *n.* danese *m.*, *f.*; *great* —, cane danese.

**danger** *n.* pericolo rischio; *to be in — of*, correre il pericolo di; *out of —*, fuori pericolo; *—, road up!*, attenzione, lavori stradali!; *— signal*, segnale *m.* d'allarme; *in — of one's life*, in pericolo di vita.
**dangerous** *adj.* pericoloso; rischioso; (fig.) *to be on — ground*, essere su terreno infido; *to be in a — mood*, avere un diavolo per capello; *a — example*, un esempio pernicioso.
**dangle** *tr.*, *intr.* dondolare, ciondolare, penzolare.
**Daniel** *pr.n.* Daniele.
**Danish** *adj.* danese; (language) il danese.
**dank** *adj.* umido, umidiccio; malsano.
**Dantean, Dantesque** *adj.* dantesco.
**Dantist** *n.* dantista *m.*, *f.*
**dapper** *adj.* attillato, elegante; lindo; vivace; *a — little man*, un omino vivace e ben vestito.
**dapple** *n.* chiazza; *attrib. dapple-grey horse*, cavallo chiazzato di grigio; *tr.* chiazzare, macchiettare; *~d horse*, cavallo pomellato; *~d sky*, cielo a pecorelle.
**Darby** *pr.n.* (fam.) *— and Joan*, Filemone e Bauci.
**Dardanelles** *pr.n.* (geog.) Dardanelli *m.pl.*
**dare** *tr.* osare; affrontare; rischiare; sfidare; *intr.* avventurarsi; *how — you!*, ma come osi fare una cosa simile!; *I — say that*, suppongo che; *I — say*, può darsi, credo bene.
**daredevil** *n.* scavezzacollo, temerario.
**daring** *adj.* audace, temerario, intrepido; ardito; *n.* audacità, temerarietà; ardimento.
**dark** *adj.* buio; scuro; tenebroso; *to get —*, farsi notte; *a — night*, una notte buia; *the sky is getting —*, il cielo si oscura; *— red*, rosso cupo; *— grey*, grigio scuro; *— man*, uomo bruno; (fig.) triste, nero; *to see the — side of things*, vedere tutto nero; misterioso, segreto; *to keep —*, tenere celato; *— horse*, vincitore imprevisto; *the Dark Ages*, l'Alto Medio Evo; *the Dark Continent*, il Continente Nero.
**dark** *n.* buio, oscurità; tenebre *f.pl.*; *in the —*, al buio; *after —*, a notte calata; *before —*, prima che si faccia notte; (fig.) *a leap in the —*, un salto nel buio; *to be in the — about*, essere all'oscuro di.
**dark-complexioned** *adj.* bruno.
**darken** *tr.* oscurare; rendere cupo; (fig.) diffamare; *intr.* oscurarsi; annuvolarsi; annerirsi; imbrunire; (fig.) *never — my door again!*, non rimettere mai più piede in casa mia!
**dark-eyed** *adj.* dagli occhi scuri.
**darkness** *n.* oscurità; tenebre *f.pl.*; (fig.) ignoranza, cecità; silenzio; trestezza; *— of complexion*, colorito bruno.
**darling** *adj.* caro; prediletto; simpaticissimo, carissimo; *n.* prediletto, favorito; *my —*, tesoro mio, gioia mia; *mother's —*, beniamino della mamma; *Fortune's —*, favorito della Fortuna.
**darn**[1] *tr.* rammendare; *to — socks*, accomodare i calzini; *n.* rammendatura.
**darn**[2] euphemism for **damn.**
**darnel** *n.* (bot.) loglio.
**darning** *n.* rammendo, rammendatura.
**darning-needle** *n.* ago da rammendo.
**dart** *n.* dardo; strale *m.*; *game of ~s*, tirassegno con frecce metalliche; slancio, guizzo; *to make a — at*, precipitarsi su; *tr.* scagliare, lanciare; *intr.* guizzare, balzare; slanciarsi, precipitarsi; *to — past*, passare come una freccia.
**dash**[1] *n.* slancio, impeto; foga; *to make a — for*, slanciarsi verso; colpo; spruzzo; *coffee with a — of brandy*, caffè con un goccio di acquavita; *a — of the pen*, un tratto di penna; *a — of colour*, una chiazza; (typ.) lineetta *f.*; (fam.) *to cut a —*, fare bella figura.
**dash**[1] *tr.* urtare, cozzare; buttare, gettare; *to — to pieces*, frantumare; *to — water over*, buttare acqua su; *to — one's head against a wall*, urtare con la testa contro il muro; sconcertare, confondere; *his hopes were ~ed*, le sue speranze furono infrante; *to — away a tear*, asciugarsi furtivamente una lagrima; *to — off a letter*, buttar giù una lettera; *to — out one's brains*, fracassarsi la testa; *intr.* precipitarsi; *to — along*, procedere a grande velocità; *to — off*, scappar via; *to — out*, precipitarsi fuori.
**dash**[2] *excl.* euphem. for **damn.**
**dashboard** *n.* parafango; (instrument panel) cruscotto.
**dashed** *adj.* euphem. for **damned.**
**dashing** *adj.* impetuoso, focoso; elegante.
**dastard** *n.* vigliacco, vile *m.* **~ly** *adj.* vigliacco, vile, ignobile.
**data** *n. pl.* see **datum.**
**datable** *adj.* databile.
**date**[1] *n.* (bot.) dattero.
**date**[2] *n.* data; *to —*, fino ad oggi; *up to —*, al corrente, aggiornato; all'ultima moda; *out of —*, antiquato, fuori moda; periodo, epoca; (comm.) scadenza; *to make a — with*, fissare un appuntamento con; *to have a —*, essere impegnato; *tr.* datare; fare appuntamento con; *intr. to — from*, datare da, risalire a; (fam.) essere fuori moda.
**dated** *adj.* fuori moda.
**date-line** *n.* (geog.) linea di cambiamento di data.
**dative** *adj.*, *n.* (gramm.) dativo.
**datum** *n.*, *pl.* **data**; dato, fatto; notizia; premessa; (geog.) *— point*, punto di riferimento.
**daub** *n.* sgorbio, imbratto; intonaco; scarabocchio; *tr.*, *intr.* imbrattare; impiastrare; impiastricciare.
**dauber** *n.* imbrattatele *m. indecl.*
**daughter** *n.* figlia, figliuola; *only —*, figlia unica.
**daughter-in-law** *n.* nuora.
**daunt** *tr.* intimidire, intimorire.
**dauntless** *adj.* intrepido, impavido. **~ness** *n.* intrepidezza.
**Dauphin** *n.* (hist.) delfino.
**David** *pr.n.* Davide.
**davit** *n.* (naut.) gru *f. indecl.* di imbarcazione.
**dawdle** *intr.* oziare, bighellonare; *to — away one's time*, sprecare il tempo; *don't —!*, sbrigatevi! **~r** *n.* perdigiorno, bighellone *m.*
**dawn** *n.* alba, aurora; *from — till dusk*, dall'alba al tramonto; *at first —*, allo spuntar del giorno; (fig.) alba, inizio, principio; primo apparire; *intr.* albeggiare, spuntare, far giorno; (fig.) apparire, manifestarsi; *at length it ~ed on me*, finalmente cominciai a capire. **~ing** *adj.* nascente; *n.* alba; lo spuntar del giorno.
**day** *n.* giorno; giornata; (poet.) dì *m. indecl.*; *by —*, di giorno; *three times a —*, tre volte al giorno; *all — long*, tutto il giorno; *some —*, un giorno o l'altro; *the — after tomorrow*, dopodomani; *the — before yesterday*, avantieri; *the other —*, l'altro giorno; *every other —*, a giorni alterni; *this very —*, oggi stesso; *this — week*, oggi a otto; *— off*, giorno di riposo; *it's all in the ~'s work*, capita a tutti; *to end one's ~s*, morire; (fam.) *every dog has his —*, ognuno ha il suo raggio di sole; *I've had my —*, ho avuto anch'io i miei giorni di prosperità; *let's make a — of it!*, spassiamocela!; *the good old ~s*, i bei tempi passati; *in ~s to come*, in avvenire; *to win the —*, vincere; *the — is ours*, la vittoria è nostra; *to pass the time of — with*, scambiare due parole con; *he's sixty if he's a —*, ha sessant'anni ben contati; *let's call it a —*, smettiamo di lavorare.
**day-boarder** *n.* (schol.) semiconvittore. **-book** *n.* (comm.) brogliaccio. **-boy** *n.* allievo esterno.
**daybreak** *n.* alba, lo spuntar del giorno.
**daydream** *n.* sogno ad occhi aperti; fantasticheria; *intr.* sognare ad occhi aperti; fare castelli in aria.
**day-labourer** *n.* lavoratore a giornata, giornaliero.
**daylight** *n.* luce *f.* del giorno,

giorno; alba; *before* —, prima dell'alba; *by* —, di giorno; *in broad* —, in pieno giorno; (fig.) *I begin to see* —, comincio a vederci chiaro.

**daylong** *adj.* che dura per tutta la giornata.

**day-nurse** *n.* infermiera che presta servizio di giorno. **-nursery** *n.* sala di soggiorno per bambini; asilo diurno per bambini. **-return, -ticket** *n.* (rlwy.) biglietto di andata e ritorno valido solo per la giornata. **-school** *n.* (schol.) scuola per allievi esterni.

**daytime** *n.* giorno; giornata.

**daze** *n.* sbalordimento, intontimento, stordimento; *to be in a* —, essere inebetito; *tr.* sbalordire, intontire; inebetire, stordire.

**dazzl-e**[1] *n.* abbagliamento; (mil.; naut.) mimetizzazione; *tr.* abbagliare, abbacinare; *to be ~d*, essere abbagliato. **~ing** *adj.* abbagliante, abbacinante.

**deacon** *n.* (eccl.) diacono. **~ry, ~ship** *n.* diaconato.

**dead** *adj.* morto; defunto; estinto; — *man*, morto; — *woman*, morta; *the Dead Sea*, il Mar Morto; — *march*, marcia funebre; — *and gone*, morto e sepolto; — *as a doornail*, morto stecchito; *to drop down* —, cadere a terra morto; (fig.) inerte; letargico; assoluto, completo; — *certainty*, certezza assoluta; — *loss*, perdita completa; — *silence*, silenzio di tomba; — *stop*, fermata brusca; *to be — on time*, essere in perfetto orario; *to be in — earnest*, fare proprio sul serio; *adv.* assolutamente; — *tired*, stanco morto; — *easy*, facilissimo; — *drunk*, ubriaco fradicio; (traffic sign) — *slow*, a passo d'uomo.

**dead** *n. the* —, i morti; (eccl.) *office for the* —, ufficio funebre; *to rise from the* —, risorgere; (fig.) silenzio di tomba; *in the — of night*, nel cuore della notte.

**dead-and-alive** *adj.* poco interessante, noioso.

**deaden** *tr.* attutire, smorzare.

**dead-end** *n.* vicolo cieco; *attrib. a — job*, un impiego senza possibilità di sviluppo.

**dead-letter** *n.* lettera ritornata al mittente; *adj.* — *office*, ufficio postale per lettere non recapitate; (fig.) non più valido.

**deadline** *n.* termine definitivo.

**deadliness** *n.* micidialità, velenosità.

**deadlock** *n.* punto morto, imbroglio inestricabile.

**deadly** *adj.* micidiale, velenoso, mortifero; — *insult*, insulto mortale; — *sin*, peccato capitale; (fig.) — *hatred*, odio implacabile; (of aim) infallibile; (fam.) noioso, insopportabile; (bot.) — *nightshade*, belladonna; *adv.* come la morte, da morto.

**deadweight** *n.* peso morto; (naut.) portata lorda.

**deaf** *adj.* sordo; — *and dumb*, sordomuto; — *as a post*, sordo come una campana; *to turn a — ear*, fare orecchi da mercante.

**deafen** *tr.* assordare, rendere sordo, stordire; intontire; *a ~ing noise*, un rumore assordante.

**deaf-mute** *n.* sordomuto.

**deafness** *n.* sordità; (fig.) disattenzione.

**deal**[1] *n.* quantità; *a great* —, moltissimo; *to have a good — to do*, aver molto da fare; *to read a great* —, leggere assai; *a great — better*, molto meglio; (iron.) *that's saying a good —!*, non è dire poco!

**deal**[2] *n.* (comm.) affare *m.*; *it's a —!*, affare fatto!, d'accordo!; *to give someone a fair* —, agire lealmente verso qualcuno; (pol.) accordo; *new* —, riforma economica; (cards) data; *whose — is it?*, a chi tocca dare?

**deal**[2] *intr.* trattare, negoziare, mercanteggiare; *to — in*, commerciare in; (fig.) immischiarsi di; *to — with*, trattare; occuparsi di; *an easy man to — with*, un uomo accomodante; *tr.* distribuire, ripartire; *to — a blow*, assestare un colpo; (cards) dare le carte; *he was ~t four aces*, gli sono toccati quattro assi.

**deal**[3] *m.* legno d'abete, legno di pino.

**dealer** *n.* commerciante, negoziante *m.*; *retail* —, dettagliante *m.*; *wholesale* —, grossista *m.*; (cards) chi dà le carte, datore.

**dealing** *n.* commercio; distribuzione; — *out*, ripartizione; (cards) data; *pl.* rapporti, relazioni; *to have ~s with*, avere rapporti con; (fig.) condotta.

**dean** *n.* (eccl.) decano, diacono; arciprete *m.*; *rural* —, vicario foraneo; (in University) preside *m.* di facoltà, preside di collegio. **~ship** *n.* diaconato; presidenza.

**dear**[1] *adj.* caro, amato, diletto; *to hold someone* —, voler bene a qualcuno; *my — fellow*, caro mio; *Dear Sir*, Egregio Signore; *Dear Madam*, Gentile Signora; *Dearest Mary*, Carissima Maria; *to run for — life*, correre per salvare la pelle; caro, costoso; *to get ~er*, rincarare; *n.* caro; cara *f.*; *he's an old* —, è una persona tanto cara; *help me, there's a* —, aiutami, su, da bravo!; *adv.* a caro prezzo; *it cost him* —, gli costò caro.

**dear**[2] *excl. oh —!*, Dio mio!; — *me!*, ohimè; *oh — no!*, certamente no!

**dearie, deary** *n.* caro, cara.

**dearly** *adv.* caramente, teneramente; (eccl.) — *beloved brethren!*, miei cari fratelli!; (of cost) a caro prezzo.

**dearness** *n.* caro prezzo, l'essere caro.

**dearth** *n.* carestia, scarsità, penuria; povertà; mancanza, assenza.

**death** *n.* morte *f.*; decesso, trapasso; scomparsa; fine *f.*; *at the point of* —, in punto di morte; *to die a violent* —, morire di morte violenta; *to starve to* —, morire di fame; *to be frozen to* —, morire assiderato; *to put to* —, far giustiziare; *to be in at the* —, essere presente all'uccisione della preda; *to catch one's — of cold*, prendersi un malanno; (admin.) *to notify a* —, notificare un decesso; (fig.) rovina, perdita; *the — of one's ambitions*, il crollo delle proprie ambizioni.

**death-agony** *n.* agonia.

**deathbed** *n.* letto di morte.

**death-blow** *n.* colpo mortale. **-cap** *n.* amanite (velenosa). **-chamber** *n.* camera mortuaria. **-dealing** *adj.* mortale, ferale, mortifero, letale. **-duties** *n.* diritti *m.pl.* di successione.

**deathless** *adj.* immortale, imperituro. **~ness** *n.* immortalità.

**deathlike** *adj.* simile alla morte, cadaverico.

**deathly** *adj.* mortale, come la morte; — *silence*, silenzio di tomba; *adv.* — *pale*, pallido come un morto, cadaverico.

**death-mask** *n.* maschera mortuaria. **-rate** *n.* indice *m.* di mortalità. **-rattle** *n.* rantolo. **-roll** *n.* elenco dei morti.

**death's-head** *n.* teschio.

**death-throes** *n.* agonia.

**deathtrap** *n.* luogo pericoloso; tranello.

**death-warrant** *n.* ordine *m.* di esecuzione della sentenza di morte; (fig.) sentenza di morte.

**death-watch** *n.* veglia al capezzale di un morto; (ent.) — *beetle*, anobio.

**deb** *n.* (fam.) abbrev. of **débutante,** *q.v.*

**débacle** *n.* crollo, sfacelo.

**debar** *tr.* escludere, privare; impedire, vietare.

**debase** *tr.* avvilire; abbassare; degradare; (of currency) svalutare. **~ment** *n.* avvilimento; degradazione; abiezione; (of currency) svalutazione.

**debatable** *adj.* discutibile, contestabile.

**debate** *n.* dibattito, dibattimento; discussione; *the question is still under* —, si sta ancora discutendo la questione; *tr., intr.* dibattere, discutere; *to — about*, disputare su; (fig.) considerare, ponderare.

**debating** *n.* dibattito, discussione; — *society*, circolo che organizza dibattiti.

**debauch** *n.* orgia, dissolutezza; bagordo; *tr.* pervertire, corrompere, traviare, sedurre. **-ee** *n.* libertino, uomo dissoluto. **-ery** *n.* dissolutezza; libertinaggio.
**debenture** *n.* (finan.) obbligazione.
**debilitate** *tr.* debilitare, indebolire.
**debility** *n.* debolezza; (med.) astenia.
**debit** *n.* debito; *the — side (of account)*, il dare; *— entry*, addebito; *— balance*, bilancio passivo; *to enter on the — side*, addebitare; *tr.* addebitare, segnare a carico.
**debonair** *adj.* bonario, disinvolto; di modi gentili.
**Deborah** *pr.n.* Debora.
**debouch** *intr.* sboccare, sfociare.
**debris** *n.* detriti *m.pl.*; macerie *f.pl.*
**debt** *n.* debito; *bad —*, credito inesigibile; *to get into —*, contrarre dei debiti; *up to one's eyes in —*, nei debiti fino al collo; oberato; (fig.) obbligo.
**debt-collector** *n.* esattore.
**debtor** *n.* debitore, debitrice.
**debunk** *tr.* (fam.) sgonfiare, ridurre alle giuste proporzioni. **-ing** *n.* sgonfiamento.
**début** *n.* debutto, esordio; ingresso in società; *to make one's —*, esordire.
**débutant(e)** *n.* esordiente *m., f.*; debuttante *f.*
**decade** *n.* decennio; diecina; decade *f.*
**decad-ence** *n.* decadenza. **-ent** *adj., n.* decadente *m., f.*
**decalogue** *n.* decalogo.
**decamp** *intr.* levare le tende; (fig.) svignarsela, scappare.
**decant** *intr.* decantare, travasare.
**decanter** *n.* caraffa.
**decapitat-e** *tr.* decapitare, decollare. **-ion** *n.* decapitazione, decollazione.
**decarboniz-e** *tr.* decarburare. **-ation** *n.* decarburazione.
**decasyllabic** *adj.*, **decasyllable** *n.* decasillabo.
**decay** *n.* decadenza; deperimento; *dental —*, carie *f.*; (fig.) rovina; sfacelo; *senile —*, decadimento senile; *intr.* decadere; deperire; disfarsi, putrefarsi; *-ed tooth*, dente cariato; (fig.) andare in rovina; *-ed gentlewoman*, signora decaduta.
**decease** *n.* decesso.
**deceased** *adj.* deceduto, defunto; *n.* defunto, defunta.
**deceit** *n.* inganno; truffa, frode *f.*; astuzia.
**deceitful** *adj.* ingannevole; fallace; falso, perfido, menzognero. **-ness** *n.* duplicità, perfidia.
**deceive** *tr.* ingannare; imbrogliare, abbindolare; *rfl. to — oneself*, illudersi; *I may be -d*, forse m'inganno.
**deceiver** *n.* ingannatore, imbroglione *m.*; seduttore.
**decelerate** *tr., intr.* rallentare.
**December** *pr. n.* dicembre *m.*
**decency** *n.* decenza; pudore *m.*; decoro; *in common —*, per riguardo alla decenza; creanza, convenienza.
**decennial** *adj.* decennale.
**decent** *adj.* decoroso, decente; convenevole; (fam.) *a — meal*, un pranzo discreto; bravo, gentile; *a — fellow*, un tipo simpatico, un bravo ragazzo; *quite —*, passabile.
**decentraliz-e** *tr., intr.* decentrare. **-ation** *n.* decentramento.
**deception** *n.* inganno; doppiezza; insidia.
**deceptive** *adj.* ingannevole, illusorio; fallace; *appearances are —*, le apparenze ingannano.
**decide** *tr.* decidere; stabilire; risolvere; *intr.* decidere, decidersi; prendere il partito; venire ad una decisione.
**decided** *adj.* deciso, risoluto; chiaro, positivo. **-ly** *adv.* decisamente, definitivamente, indubbiamente.
**deciduous** *adj.* (bot.) deciduo.
**decimal** *adj., n.* decimale *m.*; *— point*, virgola; *— system*, sistema decimale; *recurring —*, numero decimale periodico.
**decimat-e** *tr.* decimare. **-ion** *n.* decimazione.
**decimetre** *n.* decimetro ( = 3·937 inches).
**decipher** *tr.* decifrare; (fig.) svelare. **-able** *adj.* decifrabile. **-ing** *n.* decifrazione.
**decision** *n.* decisione; deliberazione, risoluzione; risolutezza, fermezza; *a man of —*, un uomo risoluto.
**decisive** *adj.* decisivo; fermo, deciso. **-ness** *n.* risolutezza; fermezza; decisione.
**deck**[1] *n.* (naut.) ponte *m.*, coperta; *all hands on — !*, tutti in coperta!; (of bus) *top —*, imperiale *m.*; (aeron.) *flight —*, ponte di volo.
**deck**[2] *tr.* ornare; adornare; parare; rivestire; *to — with flags*, imbandierare; *rfl. to — oneself out*, farsi bello, addobbarsi.
**deck-chair** *n.* sedia a sdraio.
**deckle-edged** *adj.* (paperm.) a bordo intonso, con la barba.
**declaim** *tr., intr.* declamare; recitare.
**declama-tion** *n.* declamazione. **-tory** *adj.* declamatorio.
**declaration** *n.* dichiarazione; proclama *m.*; (hist.) *Declaration of Independence*, Proclamazione di Indipendenza.
**declare** *tr.* dichiarare; proclamare; rendere noto; *to — war*, dichiarare la guerra; *to — a strike*, proclamare uno sciopero; *to — the result*, rendere noto il risultato; (customs) *have you anything to — ?*, avete qualcosa da dichiarare?; (finan.) *to — a dividend* stabilire un dividendo; (fig.) affermare, assicurare; *he -d he had seen you*, assicurò di averti visto; (fam.) *well, I — !*, davvero!; (cards) dichiarare; *rfl. to — oneself*, rivelare i propri sentimenti; (of illness) manifestarsi. **-d** *part.* declared; *adj.* aperto.
**declension** *n.* declino; (gramm.) declinazione.
**declinable** *adj.* (gramm.) declinabile.
**declination** *n.* inclinazione; pendenza; (astron.) declinazione; *magnetic —*, declinazione magnetica.
**decline** *n.* declino; decadimento, decadenza; deperimento; *to fall into a —*, perdere le forze; (of prices) ribasso; (of business) rallentamento; (fig.) tramonto.
**decline** *tr.* declinare, rifiutare, non accettare; (gramm.) declinare; *intr.* diminuire, venir meno, deperire; (of prices) diminuire; (fig.) tramontare.
**declivity** *n.* pendìo, declivio.
**declutch** *intr.* (motor.) disinnestarsi.
**decoction** *n.* decozione, decotto.
**decod-e** *tr.* decifrare; (fig.) svelare. **-ing** *n.* deciframento, trascrizione in chiaro.
**décolleté** *adj.* scollato; *n.* scollatura.
**decompos-e** *tr.* decomporre, scomporre; *intr.* decomporsi, scomporsi, disfarsi. **-ition** *n.* decomposizione, putrefazione; disfacimento.
**deconsecrate** *tr.* sconsacrare, secolarizzare.
**decontaminat-e** *tr.* togliere il contagio da, disinfettare. **-ion** *n.* disinfezione.
**decontrol** *tr.* liberalizzare, liberare dalle restrizioni.
**décor** *n.* (theatr.) messa in scena.
**decorat-e** *tr.* decorare, ornare, parare; conferire un titolo onorifico a. **-ed** *adj.* decorato, ornato, parato; (archit.) gotico fiammeggiante. **-ion** *n.* decorazione; ornamento, abbellimento; onorificenza; *holders of -ions*, decorati. **-ive** *adj.* decorativo; ornamentale. **-or** *n.* decoratore; *interior -or*, arredatore.
**decor-ous** *adj.* decoroso. **-um** *n.* decoro; buona creanza.
**decoy** *n.* esca; richiamo; *— duck*, anitra da richiamo; *tr.* adescare; allettare; abbindolare; attirare.
**decrease** *n.* diminuzione; decrescimento; ribasso; *tr., intr.* diminuire, decrescere.
**decree** *n.* decreto; editto; ordinanza; *— nisi*, sentenza prov-

visoria di divorzio; *tr.* decretare, ordinare.
**decrepit** *adj.* decrepito; decaduto. **-ude** *n.* decrepitezza; senilità.
**decrial** *n.* denigrazione; discredito.
**decrier** *n.* denigratore.
**decry** *tr.* denigrare; deprezzare; screditare.
**dedicat-e** *tr.* dedicare, consacrare; inaugurare; intitolare. **-ion** *n.* consacrazione, dedicazione; inaugurazione; dedica. **-ory, -ive** *adj.* dedicatorio.
**deduc-e** *tr.* dedurre; inferire, desumere; argomentare, concludere. **-ible** *adj.* deducibile.
**deduct** *tr.* dedurre; detrarre; sottrarre; trattenere; defalcare; *after -ing...*, dedotto.... **-ion** *n.* deduzione; sottrazione; trattenuta; sconto.
**deed** *n.* fatto, atto; azione; gesto; *good -s*, buone azioni; *charitable -s*, opere di carità; *-s, not words*, fatti, non parole; (fig.) impresa; (leg.) atto notarile; *— of gift*, atto di donazione.
**deed-box** *n.* cofanetto per conservare documenti. **-poll** *n.* atto unilaterale contratto a titolo gratuito.
**deem** *tr.* giudicare; stimare; considerare; ritenere.
**deep** *adj.* profondo, alto; *snow a foot —*, neve alta trenta centimetri; *four —*, in quattro file; *— red*, rosso cupo; (fig.) oscuro, astruso; *— in thought*, sprofondato nei pensieri; *— mourning*, lutto stretto; (fam.) *to go off the — end*, arrabbiarsi; (slang) *a — one*, un furbo; *adv.* profondamente; *— into the night*, fino a notte inoltrata; *to drink —*, bere copiosamente; (provb.) *still waters run —*, le acque chete rovinano i ponti; *— in my heart*, nel profondo del mio cuore; *n.* mare *m.*; oceano; *out of the —*, dagli abissi del mare.
**deepen** *tr.*, *intr.* approfondire, approfondirsi; (of colour) incupirsi.
**deep-freeze** *n.* surgelamento.
**deeply** *adv.* profondamente; *to go — into*, approfondirsi in; *— hurt*, gravemente ferito; *— in love*, innamoratissimo.
**deepness** *n.* profondità.
**deep-rooted** *adj.* dalle radici profonde, radicato. **-seated** *adj.* radicato; stabilito. **-set** *adj.* incavato, infossato.
**deer** *n.* cervo; *fallow —*, daino. **-hound** *n.* cane cerviero. **-skin** *n.* pelle *f.* di daino.
**deer-stalker** *n.* cacciatore di cervi; *— hat*, berretto da cacciatore.
**deface** *tr.* sfregiare; mutilare; guastare; imbrattare; *to — a stamp*, annullare un francobollo. **-ment** *n.* sfregio; mutilazione; annullamento.
**defalcat-e** *intr.* defalcare, sottrarre beni. **-ion** *n.* defalco; appropriazione indebita di beni; (leg.) concussione.
**defam-e** *tr.* diffamare; denigrare, parlar male di. **-ation** *n.* diffamazione; calunnia. **-atory** *adj.* diffamatorio.
**default** *n.* mancanza, omissione; *in — of*, in difetto di; (leg.) mancata comparizione; *judgment by —*, condanna in contumacia; (comm.) inadempienza; *intr.* venire meno agli obblighi; (leg.) rendersi contumace. **-er** *n.* imputato contumace; reo di appropriazione indebita; debitore moroso; (mil.) soldato consegnato.
**defeat** *n.* sconfitta, disfatta; (fig.) insuccesso, fallimento; *tr.* sconfiggere; sbaragliare; vincere; (fig.) far fallire. **-ism** *n.* disfattismo. **-ist** *n.* disfattista *m.*, *f.*
**defecat-e** *intr.* defecare. **-ion** *n.* defecazione.
**defect** *n.* difetto; mancanza; imperfezione; magagna. **-ion** *n.* defezione; diserzione; rinnegamento; (rel.) apostasia.
**defective** *adj.* difettoso; imperfetto; anormale; deficiente; (gramm.) difettivo. **-ness** *n.* difettosità; manchevolezza; imperfezione.
**defence** *n.* difesa; (leg.) *counsel for the —*, difensore; *pl.* (mil.) fortificazioni *f.pl.*, opere *f.pl.* di difesa. **-less** *adj.* senza difesa, indifeso, inerme.
**defend** *tr.* difendere, proteggere; (leg.) patrocinare; *rfl.* difendersi; (fig.) *to — oneself* (against), discolparsi (da). **-ant** *n.* (leg.) imputato, convenuto. **-er** *n.* difensore; campione *m.*
**defensib-le** *adj.* difensibile; giustificabile. **-ility** *n.* difendibilità.
**defensive** *adj.* difensivo; *n.* difensiva; *to be on the —*, stare sulle difese.
**defer** *tr.* differire, rimandare; rinviare, prorogare; *intr.* tardare; essere deferente, sottoporsi.
**deference** *n.* deferenza; rispetto; *in — to*, per deferenza verso; *with all due —*, con tutto il rispetto dovuto.
**deferent**[1], **deferential** *adj.* deferente, rispettoso.
**deferent**[2] *n.* (astron.) circolo deferente.
**deferment** *n.* diferimento; dilazione, rinvio; proroga.
**defiance** *n.* sfida; dispetto; *in — of*, a dispetto di.
**defiant** *adj.* provocante, insolente; sfrontato; ardito.
**deficiency** *n.* deficienza, mancanza; difetto; (comm.) disavanzo; (med.) carenza.
**deficient** *adj.* deficiente; incompleto, insufficiente; *to be — in*, mancare di; *mentally —*, infermo di mente, anormale.
**deficit** *n.* disavanzo, ammanco; *to make good the —*, colmare il disavanzo.
**de·file**[1] *n.* gola; stretto passo.
**defile**[2] *intr.* (mil.) marciare in file, sfilare.
**defile**[3] *tr.* insozzare, lordare; (fig.) profanare, violare.
**defin-e** *tr.* definire; determinare, delineare; (fig.) precisare. **-able** *adj.* definibile.
**definite, definitive** *adj.* definito; determinato, preciso; (comm.) fermo; (gramm.) definito; *past —*, passato remoto; (fig.) nitido.
**definition** *n.* definizione; determinazione; (fig.) nitidezza, chiarezza.
**deflate** *tr.* sgonfiare; (finan.) deflazionare; *intr.* sgonfiarsi.
**deflation** *n.* sgonfiamento; (finan.) deflazione. **-ary** *adj.* (finan.) deflazionistico.
**deflect** *tr.*, *intr.* deflettere, deviare. **-ion** *n.* flessione; deviazione.
**defloration** *n.* deflorazione, stupro, sverginamento.
**deflower** *tr.* deflorare, stuprare; sfiorire.
**deforestation** *n.* disboscamento.
**deform** *tr.* deformare, sfigurare. **-ation** *n.* deformazione; (med.) malformazione, deformità. **-ed** *adj.* deforme. **-ity** *n.* deformità.
**defraud** *tr.* frodare; defraudare. **-er** *n.* frodatore; peculatore.
**defray** *tr.* coprire; compensare; *to — expenses*, rimborsare le spese.
**defroster** *n.* (motor.) decongelatore.
**deft** *adj.* destro; lesto; agile; abile. **-ness** *n.* destrezza; abilità.
**defunct** *adj.* defunto.
**defy** *tr.* sfidare, provocare; (fig.) ostacolare; *it defies description*, è impossibile descriverlo.
**degeneracy** *n.* degenerazione, tralignamento; pervertimento.
**degenerat-e** *adj.* degenerato, degenere; basso, vile; *intr.* degenerare; declinare. **-ion** *n.* degenerazione; deterioramento.
**degrad-e** *tr.* degradare; avvilire, umiliare. **-ation** *n.* degradazione; umiliazione; abbrutimento.
**degree** *n.* grado; livello; *to some —*, fino ad un certo punto; *by -s*, poco a poco; rango, condizione; *University —*, laurea; *to take one's —*, laurearsi; (leg.) grado; (fam.) *third —*, interrogatorio severo; *third — methods*, sevizie *f.pl.*
**dehumanize** *tr.* disumanare.
**dehydrat-e** *tr.* (chem.) disidratare. **-ion** *n.* (chem.) disidratazione.
**de-icer** *n.* (aeron.) dispositivo antighiaccio.
**deif-y** *tr.* deificare; divinizzare. **-ication** *n.* deificazione.

**deign** *intr.* degnarsi; accondiscendere.
**deis-m** *n.* deismo. **-t** *n.* deista *m.*
**deity** *n.* dio *m.*; dea *f.*; deità, divinità *f. indecl.*; essere divino.
**dejected** *adj.* abbattuto; avvilito, scoraggiato, accasciato.
**dejection** *n.* abbattimento; accasciamento, avvilimento.
**delay** *n.* ritardo, indugio; rinvio; lungaggine *f.*; *without further —*, senza ulteriore ritardo; (comm.) proroga, dilazione; *tr.* ritardare, differire; ostacolare; *-ed action*, azione ritardata; (mil.) *-ing action*, azione ritardatrice; *intr.* indugiare; temporeggiare; tardare.
**delectable** *adj.* dilettevole; piacevole; gustoso.
**delectation** *n.* diletto.
**delegat-e** *n.* delegato; commissario; *tr.* delegare; autorizzare. **-ion** *n.* delegazione; *by -ion*, per delega.
**delete** *tr.* cancellare, sopprimere; biffare.
**deleterious** *adj.* nocivo; micidiale; deleterio.
**deletion** *n.* cancellatura; soppressione.
**deliberate** *adj.* ponderato, prudente; intenzionale, premeditato, voluto; *tr.*, *intr.* ponderare; riflettere; deliberare. **-ly** *adv.* apposta; prudentemente. **-ness** *n.* ponderatezza; misura; precauzione.
**delibera-tion** *n.* decisione ponderata; riflessione; deliberazione, dibattito. **-tive** *adj.* deliberativo; deliberante.
**delicacy, delicateness** *n.* delicatezza; finezza; sensibilità; gracilità; cibo ghiotto, leccornia.
**delicate** *adj.* delicato; fine; sensibile; *of — health*, di salute gracile; (fig.) *to tread on — ground*, toccare argomenti delicati.
**delicious** *adj.* delizioso; squisito; gustoso. **-ness** *n.* delizia; squisitezza; gusto squisito.
**delight** *n.* delizia; diletto; contentezza; *to take — in*, dilettarsi di; *tr.* deliziare, dilettare; *intr.* dilettarsi, compiacersi, rallegrarsi (di). **-ed** *adj.* lieto, lietissimo, contentissimo; *to be -ed with*, rallegrarsi di; *to be -ed to*, essere ben lieto di. **-edly** *adv.* lietamente; con sommo piacere. **-ful** *adj.* dilettevole; incantevole; delizioso; simpaticissimo.
**Delilah** *pr.n.* Dalila.
**delimit** *tr.* delimitare. **-ation** *n.* delimitazione.
**delineat-e** *tr.* delineare, tracciare; abbozzare. **-ion** *n.* delineazione; abbozzo.
**delinqu-ent** *adj.*, *n.* delinquente *m.*, *f.* **-ency** *n.* delinquenza; *juvenile -ency*, delinquenza minorile.
**delirious** *adj.* delirante, farneticante; (fig.) *— with joy*, ebro di gioia.
**delirium** *n.* delirio; furore *m.*
**deliver** *tr.* liberare; salvare; consegnare; recapitare; trasmettere; *to — a blow*, lanciare un colpo; *to — a speech*, pronunciare un discorso; *to — an opinion*, emettere un'opinione; *to be -ed of a child*, partorire; *rfl. to — oneself up to*, abbandonarsi a.
**deliverance** *n.* liberazione.
**deliverer** *n.* liberatore, salvatore; oratore, espositore.
**delivery** *n.* consegna; *postal —*, distribuzione postale; *cash on —*, pagamento contro assegno; dizione; *to have a good —*, saper parlare bene; (mil.) resa; (med.) parto.
**delivery-note** *n.* bollettino di consegna. **-van** *n.* furgoncino per consegna merce.
**dell** *n.* valletta.
**delouse** *tr.* spidocchiare; disinfestare.
**delphinium** *n.* (bot.) fiorcappuccio.
**delta** *n.* delta *m.*
**delude** *tr.* deludere, illudere; ingannare; *rfl.* illudersi.
**deluge** *n.* diluvio; inondazione; (bibl.) *the Deluge*, il diluvio universale; *tr.* diluviare; inondare; (fig.) sopraffare.
**delus-ion** *n.* illusione, allucinazione; inganno. **-ive** *adj.* illusorio, fallace; ingannevole.
**delve** *tr.*, *intr.* scavare, vangare; (fig.) far ricerche; *to — into the past*, rivangare il passato.
**demagnetize** *tr.* demagnetizzare, smagnetizzare.
**demago-gue** *n.* demagogo. **-gy** *n.* demagogia.
**demand** *n.* richiesta; *supply and —*, domanda e offerta; *in —*, ricercato; pretesa, esigenza; *to make -s*, esigere; (comm.) *on —*, a vista, dietro domanda; *tr.* esigere, pretendere; chiedere; domandare.
**demarcat-e** *n.* demarcare, delimitare. **-ion** *n.* demarcazione, delimitazione; *-ion line*, linea di demarcazione.
**demean** *tr.* abbassare, avvilire, umiliare.
**demeanour** *n.* contegno, modo di comportarsi.
**demented** *adj.* demente, impazzito, pazzo.
**dementia** *n.* (med.) demenza; *— praecox*, demenza precoce.
**demerit** *n.* demerito.
**demesne** *n.* dominio; proprietà fondiaria.
**demigod** *n.* semidio.
**demijohn** *n.* damigiana.
**demilitariz-e** *tr.* smilitarizzare. **-ation** *n.* smilitarizzazione.
**demise** *n.* decesso; (leg.) cessione.
**demisemiquaver** *n.* (mus.) biscroma.
**demission** *n.* dimissione.
**demit** *tr.* dimettere; *intr.* dimettersi.
**demiurge** *n.* demiurgo.
**demob** *tr.* (mil. slang) smobilitare.
**demobiliz-e** *tr.*, *intr.* smobilitare. **-ation** *n.* smobilitazione.
**democracy** *n.* democrazia.
**democrat** *n.* democratico; (Ital. pol.) *Christian —*, democristiano. **-ic(al)** *adj.* democratico.
**demoded** *adj.* fuori moda, antiquato.
**demography** *n.* demografia.
**demol-ish** *tr.* demolire; abbattere, distruggere. **-ition** *n.* demolizione.
**demon** *n.* demone *m.*, demonio; diavolo. **-iacal** *adj.* demoniaco. **-ic** *adj.* demonico, demoniaco. **-ology** *n.* demonologia.
**demonstrab-le** *adj.* dimostrabile. **-ility** *n.* dimostrabilità.
**demonstrat-e** *tr.* dimostrare, spiegare; *intr.* (pol.) fare una dimostrazione. **-ion** *n.* dimostrazione; prova. **-ive** *adj.* dimostrativo; (fig.) espansivo; affettuoso. **-or** *n.* dimostratore; chi dimostra; (techn.) assistente *m.*, *f.*
**demoraliz-e** *tr.* demoralizzare; scoraggiare; *to become -ed*, scoraggiarsi, avvilirsi. **-ation** *n.* demoralizzazione; scoraggiamento.
**Demosthenes** *pr.n.* Demostene.
**demote** *tr.* far retrocedere a grado inferiore; *-d to corporal*, retrocesso a caporale
**demur** *n.* obiezione; *without —*, senza esitazione; *to make no —*, non sollevare obiezioni; *intr.* esitare, sollevare obiezioni.
**demure** *adj.* contegnoso; pudico; *— look*, aria da santa.
**demurrage** *n.* (comm.) controstallia; sosta in magazzino.
**demy** *n.* (paperm.) formato mezzo folio; quadrato.
**den** *n.* tana; covile *m.*; *— of thieves*, covo di ladri; (bibl.) *— of lions*, fossa dei leoni; (fam.) stanzetta, studiolo.
**denationaliz-e** *tr.* snazionalizzare. **-ation** *n.* snazionalizzazione.
**denaturaliz-e** *tr.* privare della cittadinanza. **-ation** *n.* privazione della cittadinanza.
**denature** *tr.* snaturare.
**dene** *n.* valletta boscosa; duna.
**denial** *n.* diniego; negazione; rifiuto; smentita.
**denizen** *n.* abitante *m.*, *f.*; cittadino.
**Denmark** *pr.n.* (geog.) Danimarca.
**denominat-e** *tr.* denominare; chiamare. **-ion** *n.* denominazione; nome *m.*; (rel.) setta; (math.) unità di misura. **-ional** *adj.* (rel.) settario, confessionale. **-or** *n.* (math.) denominatore.
**denot-e** *tr.* denotare, indicare;

significare. **-ation** *n.* indicazione; segno; significato.
**dénouement** *n.* scioglimento, esito; compimento.
**denounce** *tr.* denunziare; accusare; inveire contro.
**dense** *adj.* denso, spesso, fitto; ottuso, stupido, duro.
**denseness, density** *n.* densità; ottusità, stupidità.
**dent** *n.* tacca; ammaccatura; incavo; impronta; *tr.* intaccare; ammaccare; dentellare.
**dental** *adj.* dentale; dentistico; *— surgeon,* medico dentista; *n.* dentale *m.*; (ling.) dentale *f.*
**dentat-e** *adj.* (bot.) dentellato; (zool.) dentato. **-ion** *n.* dentellatura.
**dentifrice** *n.* dentifricio.
**dentist** *n.* dentista *m.*; odontoiatra *m.* **-ry** *n.* professione del dentista; odontoiatria.
**dent-ition** *n.* dentizione. **-ure** *n.* dentiera.
**denud-e** *tr.* denudare; spogliare; (fig.) privare. **-ation** *n.* denudazione.
**denunciation** *n.* denunzia; accusa.
**deny** *tr.* negare, smentire; rinnegare, non riconoscere; rifiutare, recusare; *rfl. to — oneself,* privarsi di.
**deodorant** *n.* deodorante *m.*
**deodoriz-e** *tr.* deodorare. **-ation** *n.* deodorizzazione.
**depart** *intr.* partire; andarsene, allontanarsi; (fig.) *to — from,* abbandonare, non mantenere, derogare a; *tr. to — this life,* morire. **-ed** *adj.* svanito; *n. the —,* il defunto.
**department** *n.* reparto; ufficio; sezione; ministero; dicastero; *— store,* grande magazzino; (geog.) dipartimento; (University) sezione. **-al** *adj.* dipartimentale; di reparto.
**departure** *n.* partenza; *to take one's —,* andarsene, congedarsi; (fig.) allontanamento; *a new —,* un nuovo orientamento; *a — from duty,* una mancanza al dovere.
**depend** *intr.* dipendere (da); essere subordinato (a); *it all -s on circumstances,* tutto dipende dalle circostanze; (fig.) essere mantenuto (da); fidarsi (di), contare (su); *we cannot — on him,* non possiamo far assegnamento su di lui; *I — on my work for a living,* vivo dal mio lavoro.
**dependab-le** *adj.* fidato, sicuro; attendibile. **-leness, -ility** *n.* fidatezza, attendibilità; sicuro funzionamento.
**dependant** *n.* dipendente *m., f.*; domestico.
**dependenc-e** *n.* dipendenza; fiducia. **-y** *n.* dipendenza.
**dependent** *adj.* dipendente (da), a carico (di).
**depict** *tr.* dipingere; descrivere, rappresentare.
**depilatory** *adj. n.* depilatorio.
**deplenish** *tr.* vuotare, sgombrare.
**deplet-e** *tr.* esaurire; intaccare. **-ion** *n.* esaurimento; diminuzione.
**deplor-e** *tr.* deplorare; lamentarsi di. **-able** *adj.* deplorevole, deplorabile.
**deploy** *tr.* (mil.) spiegare; *intr.* spiegarsi. **-ment** *n.* spiegamento.
**depolarize** *tr.* (electr.) depolizzare.
**deponent** *adj.* (gramm.) deponente; *n.* (leg.) teste, testimone *m.*
**depopulat-e** *tr.* spopolare. **-ion** *n.* spopolamento.
**deport** *tr.* deportare; espellere; esiliare; *rfl.* comportarsi. **-ation** *n.* deportazione; espulsione. **-ment** *n.* contegno; portamento; condotta.
**depose** *tr.* deporre; destituire; *intr.* (leg.) deporre, testimoniare.
**deposit** *n.* (finan.) deposito, versamento; *— account,* conto vincolato; pegno, cauzione; anticipo; caparra sedimento; (geol.) giacimento; *tr.* depositare; posare, deporre. **-ary** *n.* depositario.
**deposition** *n.* deposizione; (leg.) testimonianza; deposito; (art) *the Deposition from the Cross,* la Deposizione dalla Croce.
**deposit-or** *n.* depositante *m., f.* **-ory** *n.* deposito; magazzino.
**depot** *n.* deposito; magazzino; (mil.) deposito; (rlwy.) stazione ferroviaria.
**deprav-e** *tr.* depravare; corrompere. **-ation** *n.* depravazione. **-ity** *n.* depravazione; pervertimento morale.
**deprecat-e** *tr.* disapprovare; condannare, biasimare. **-ion** *n.* disapprovazione; condanna, biasimo.
**depreciat-e** *tr.* svalutare; deprezzare; ammortare; *intr.* diminuire di valore; scadere di prezzo. **-ing** *adj.* sprezzante, spregiativo. **-ion** *n.* svalutazione; deprezzamento; rinvilio; (comm.) ammortamento; *-ion allowance,* quota di ammortamento. **-ive, -ory** *adj.* sprezzante, spregiativo; (gramm.) *-ory suffix,* suffisso peggiorativo.
**depredation** *n.* saccheggio, rapina; devastazione.
**depress** *tr.* deprimere; abbassare; metter sotto. **-ed** *adj.* depresso; abbattuto, accasciato, demoralizzato; *he is easily -ed,* si abbatte facilmente; (finan.) basso, languente, fiacco; (archit.) abbassato; *-ed area,* zona di disoccupazione. **-ing** *adj.* deprimente; rattristante. **-ion** *n.* depressione; abbattimento, scoraggiamento; (meteor.) depressione; (comm.) crisi *f. indecl.*, ristagno.
**depriv-e** *tr.* privare, spogliare; *to be -d of one's office,* essere rimosso dalla carica; (eccl.) deporre; *rfl.* imporsi delle privazioni. **-al** *n.* privazione. **-ation** *n.* privazione, revoca; (eccl.) deposizione.
**depth** *n.* profondità; altezza; *to be out of one's —,* non toccare più fondo, (fig.) non essere all'altezza; (of colour) intensità; (fig.) *in the — of,* nel cuore di; *pl.* abissi *m.pl.*; (fig.) *in the -s of despair,* nella disperazione più nera; *in the -s of one's heart,* nel più profondo del cuore.
**depth-charge** *n.* (naut.) bomba antisommergibili, bomba di profondità. **-finder** *n.* (naut.) scandaglio.
**depuration** *n.* depurazione.
**deput-e** *tr.* deputare, delegare. **-ation** *n.* deputazione, delegazione. **-ize** *intr.* sostituire, fare le veci (di).
**deputy** *n.* delegato, sostituto, supplente *m.*; (pol.) deputato, rappresentante *m.*; *Chamber of Deputies,* Camera dei Deputati.
**deputy-chairman** *n.* vicepresidente *m.* **-mayor** *n.* vicesindaco.
**deracinate** *tr.* sradicare.
**derail** *tr.* deragliare; *intr.* uscire dalle rotaie. **-ment** *n.* deragliamento.
**derange** *tr.* sconvolgere, scompigliare; (fig.) *to be -d,* essere pazzo. **-ment** *n.* sconvolgimento, scompiglio; (fig.) alienazione mentale.
**derelict** *adj.* derelitto, abbandonato; *n.* (naut.) relitto. **-ion** *n.* abbandono; omissione; mancanza.
**deride** *tr.* deridere, schernire, beffare.
**deris-ion** *n.* derisione; scherno; *howls of —,* urlate *f.pl.*; *to bring into —,* mettere in ischerno. **-ive** *adj.* derisivo, derisorio; (fig.) irrisorio.
**deriv-e** *tr.* derivare; trarre; *intr.* derivare; scaturire, provenire. **-ation** *n.* derivazione; etimologia, origine *f.* **-ative** *adj., n.* derivato.
**dermatitis** *n.* (med.) dermatite *f.*
**dermatolog-ist** *n.* (med.) dermatologo. **-y** *n.* dermatologia.
**derogat-e** *intr.* derogare; detrarre; far torto; venir meno. **-ion** *n.* derogazione, deroga. **-ory** *adj.* derogatorio; sprezzante, spregiativo.
**derrick** *n.* argano; gru *f. indecl.*; (naut.) falcone *m.*, picco da carico.
**derring-do** *n.* audacia.
**dervish** *n.* derviscio.
**descant**[1] *intr.* discorrere, dissertare.
**des'cant**[2] *n.* (mus.) contrappunto.

**descend** *intr.* scendere, discendere; *to — on*, calare su; *to — to someone's level*, abbassarsi al livello di qualcuno; *-ing from father to son*, passando di padre in figlio. **-ance, -ence** *n.* discendenza. **-ant** *n.* discendente *m., f.*; pronipote *m., f.*; *to be a -ant of*, discendere da.

**descent** *n.* discesa, scesa; pendìo; china; (mil.) incursione; lignaggio; nascita; (art.) *Descent from the Cross*, Deposizione dalla Croce; (fig.) caduta, rovina.

**describ-e** *tr.* descrivere; raccontare, narrare; *to — a circle*, tracciare un cerchio. **-able** *adj.* descrivibile.

**descript-ion** *n.* descrizione; *beyond —*, indescrivibile; connotati *m.pl.*; (fam.) genere *m.*, specie *f.*; *of every —*, di ogni genere. **-ive** *adj.* descrittivo; *-ive catalogue*, catalogo ragionato.

**descry** *tr.* scorgere, distinguere, riuscire a vedere.

**desecrat-e** *tr.* profanare, sconsacrare. **-ion** *n.* profanazione, sconsacrazione.

**de·sert**[1] *adj.* deserto, sterile, desolato; *a — island*, un'isola disabitata; *n.* (geog.) deserto; (fig.) luogo inculto; solitudine *f.*

**desert**[2] *n.* merito; *to get one's -s*, aver ciò che si merita; *a man of high -s*, un uomo benemerito.

**desert**[3] *tr.* disertare, abbandonare; *intr.* (mil.) disertare. **-er** *n.* (mil.) disertore. **-ion** *n.* diserzione; defezione; abbandono; (leg.) abbandono del tetto coniugale.

**deserv-e** *tr.* meritare, essere degno di; *he -d it*, se l'è meritato. **-edly** *adv.* meritatamente. **-ing** *adj.* meritevole, meritorio.

**desiccat-e** *tr.* essicare. **-ion** *tr.* essicazione. **-ive** *adj., n.* essicativo.

**desiderative** *adj.* desiderativo.

**desideratum** *n.* cosa desiderata.

**design** *n.* disegno; progetto; (comm.) modello; scopo, proposito; intenzione; *by accident or by —*, per caso o di proposito; (fig.) *to have -s on*, aver delle mire su; *tr.* progettare, disegnare, meditare; destinare; *intr.* deliberare, divisare.

**designat-e** *adj.* (eccl.) designato; *tr.* designare, nominare; indicare. **-ion** *n.* designazione.

**designedly** *adj.* di proposito; apposta; con intenzione.

**designer** *n.* disegnatore; costruttore; progettista *m., f.*; modellista *m., f.*, costumista *m., f.*

**designing** *adj.* (pejor.) intrigante, astuto, malintenzionato; *n.* disegno; creazione; *— department*, ufficio progetti.

**desinence** *n.* desinenza.

**desirab-le** *adj.* desiderabile; attraente, piacevole; consigliabile. **-ility, -leness** *n.* l'essere desiderabile; attrattiva; vantaggio.

**desir-e** *n.* desiderio; speranza; voglia; passione; brama; preghiera; *by general —*, a richiesta generale; *tr.* desiderare; volere, aver voglia di; tenere a; bramare; *it leaves much to be -d*, lascia molto a desiderare; pregare, chiedere. **-ous** *adj.* desideroso; *to be -ous of*, desiderare.

**desist** *intr.* desistere, smettere; *to — from*, rinunciare a.

**desk** *n.* scrivania; scrittoio; (schol.) banco; cattedra; *to pay at the —*, pagare alla cassa; (mus.) leggìo.

**desk-lamp** *n.* lampada da tavolo.

**desolat-e** *adj.* solitario, abbandonato, deserto; (fig.) sconsolato; *tr.* devastare, rendere inabitabile; (fig.) affliggere. **-eness, -ion** *n.* desolazione; devastazione; (fig.) afflizione, disperazione.

**despair** *n.* disperazione; *in —*, disperato; *to drive to —*, spingere alla disperazione, (fig.) essere la disperazione di; *to give way to —*, abbandonarsi alla disperazione; *intr.* disperare, perdere ogni speranza. **-ing** *adj.* disperato.

**despatch** see **dispatch.**

**desperado** *n.* disperato; uomo capace di tutto; anima dannata.

**desperate** *adj.* disperato, senza speranza; accanito; (fig.) *— remedies*, rimedi *m.pl.* estremi; *— energy*, la forza della disperazione. **-ly** *adv.* disperatamente; accanitamente. **-ness** *n.* disperazione; accanimento; inutilità.

**desperation** *n.* disperazione; esasperazione.

**despicable** *adj.* disprezzabile; spregevole; abietto.

**despise** *tr.* disprezzare, sprezzare; spregiare; *not to be -d*, non disprezzabile, tutt'altro che trascurabile.

**despite** *prep.* malgrado; *in — of*, a dispetto di.

**despoil** *tr.* spogliare; violare. **-er** *n.* spogliatore; saccheggiatore.

**despoliation, despoilment** *n.* spogliazione; saccheggio; depredazione.

**despond** *n.* disperazione; abbattimento; *the slough of —*, l'abisso della disperazione. **-ency** *n.* abbattimento; sconforto; accasciamento; depressione. **-ent** *adj.* abbattuto; scoraggiato; accasciato.

**despot** *n.* despota *m.*; tiranno. **-ic** *adj.* dispotico; arbitrario. **-ism** *n.* dispotismo; tirannide *f.*

**dessert** *n.* frutta; dolce *m.*; dessert *m.*

**dessert-spoon** *n.* cucchiaio da dessert.

**destination** *n.* destinazione.

**destine** *tr.* destinare; assegnare, adibire; *-d for*, diretto a.

**destiny** *n.* destino, fato; sorte *f.*; *man of —*, uomo fatale.

**destitut-e** *adj.* indigente; povero; *— of*, privo di, senza. **-ion** *n.* indigenza; povertà; miseria.

**destroy** *tr.* distruggere, annientare; *to have an animal -ed*, far uccidere un animale; (fig.) demolire; rendere inutile. **-er** *n.* distruttore; demolitore; (naut.) cacciatorpediniere *m.*

**destruct-ible** *adj.* distruttibile. **-ion** *n.* distruzione; rovina.

**destructive** *adj.* distruttivo, distruttore; rovinoso; nocivo; *— person*, rompitutto *m., f.* **-ness** *n.* mania distruttiva; potenza distruttiva.

**destructor** *n.* distruttore; *refuse —*, bruciatore di rifiuti.

**desuetude** *n.* dissuetudine *f.*; disuso.

**desultor-y** *adv.* saltuario; sconnesso, a sbalzi; senza metodo; *— reading*, letture *f.pl.* occasionali. **-iness** *n.* sconnessione; mancanza di metodo; disordine *m.*

**detach** *tr.* staccare, distaccare; separare; *to become -ed*, staccarsi; (mil.) distaccare. **-able** *adj.* staccabile, smontabile.

**detached** *adj.* staccato, separato; *a — house*, una casa isolata; (fig.) distaccato, disinteressato; senza pregiudizi; *a — view*, un punto di vista obiettivo; *to live — from the world*, vivere lontano dal mondo.

**detachment** *n.* distacco; separazione; (mil.) distaccamento; (fig.) indifferenza; disinteressamento; *— of mind*, libertà di spirito.

**de·tail** *n.* particolare *m.*, dettaglio; *further -s*, ulteriori ragguagli *m.pl.*; *in —*, dettagliatamente, per disteso; *to go into -s*, entrare nei particolari; *minor —*, minuzia; (mil.) drappello.

**detail** *tr.* particolareggiare, esporre minuziosamente, raccontare punto per punto; (mil.) comandare per servizio. **-ed** *adj.* particolareggiato; dettagliato; (mil.) comandato per servizio.

**detain** *tr.* detenere, trattenere; far ritardare; (leg.) fermare. **-er** *n.* (leg.) detentore; *writ of -er*, mandato di sequestro di persona.

**detect** *tr.* scoprire, scovare; scorgere, intravvedere; individuare; *to — someone in the act*, sorprendere qualcuno sul fatto. **-ion** *n.* scoperta; *to escape -ion*, sfuggire alla ricerca, (of a mistake) passare inosservato.

**detective** *adj.* rivelatore; *n.* detective *m.*, investigatore; agente investigativo; *private —*, investigatore privato; *— novel*, romanzo poliziesco, (fam.) un giallo.

**detector** *n.* scopritore; (radio) rivelatore.
**detention** *n.* fermo; detenzione; prigionia; — *camp*, campo di internamento; (schol.) punizione.
**deter** *tr.* trattenere, scoraggiare, fermare, dissuadere, rimuovere, distogliere.
**detergent** *adj.*, *n.* detergente *m.*, detersivo.
**deteriorat-e** *intr.* deteriorarsi, guastarsi, logorarsi; degenerare, peggiorare. **-ion** *n.* deterioramento; logorìo; peggioramento.
**determinate** *adj.* determinato, definito; preciso; risoluto.
**determination** *n.* determinazione; decisione; risolutezza; *air of* —, aria risoluta; (of frontier) delimitazione.
**determinative** *adj.* determinativo, definitivo; *n.* (gramm.) determinativo.
**determine** *tr.* determinare; fissare, stabilire, definire; decidere, risolvere; terminare; *intr.* decidersi, risolversi. **-d** *adj.* determinato; fisso, stabilito; deciso, risoluto.
**deterrent** *adj.* che trattiene, che dissuade; *n.* cosa che dissuade, che trattiene; *to act as a* —, esercitare un effetto preventivo; deterrente *m.*
**detest** *tr.* detestare; odiare, abominare. **-able** *adj.* detestabile; odioso, abominabile. **-ation** *n.* detestazione; odio; abominazione.
**dethrone** *tr.* detronizzare, deporre dal trono. **-ment** *n.* detronizzazione, deposizione.
**detonat-e** *tr.* far scoppiare, far detonare; *intr.* scoppiare, detonare. **-ion** *n.* detonazione; scoppio; esplosione. **-or** *n.* detonatore.
**detour** *n.* giro; deviazione; digressione.
**detract** *tr.* detrarre; *to — from*, diminuire; (fig.) diffamare, denigrare. **-ion** *n.* detrazione; diffamazione, denigrazione.
**detriment** *n.* detrimento; danno; pregiudizio; *to the — of*, a scapito di. **-al** *adj.* pregiudizievole, nocivo, dannoso.
**detritus** *n.* (geol.) detrito.
**deuce**[1] *n.* (cards, dice,) due *m.*; (lawn tennis) quaranta pari.
**deuce**[2] *n.* diavolo, diamine *m.*; *what the — do you mean?*, che diavolo volete dire?; *it's raining like the* —, piove che Dio la manda. **-d** *adj.* (fam.) diabolico; maledetto; *what -d bad luck!*, che razza di sfortuna!
**Deuteronomy** *pr.n.* Deuteronomio.
**devaloriz-e** *tr.* deprezzare; svalutare. **-ation** *n.* deprezzamento; svalutazione.
**devalu-e** *tr.* svalutare, deprezzare. **-ation** *n.* svalutazione; deprezzamento.
**devastat-e** *tr.* devastare; rovinare. **-ing** *adj.* devastante; rovinoso; (fam.) schiacciante. **-ingly** *adv.* (fam.) in modo schiacciante; *-ingly funny*, da far ridere a crepapelle. **-ion** *n.* devastazione; rovina.
**develop** *tr.* sviluppare, svolgere; (town-planning) valorizzare; generare; *to — an illness*, contrarre una malattia; (photog.) sviluppare; *intr.* svilupparsi, formarsi; *to — into*, divenire, degenerare in. **-er** *n.* (photog.) sviluppatore. **-ment** *n.* sviluppo; evoluzione; svolgimento; sfruttamento; (town-planning) valorizzazione.
**deviat-e** *intr.* deviare; allontanarsi. **-ion** *n.* deviazione; (naut.) dirottamento; (fig.) scostamento; errore *m.*
**device** *n.* espediente *m.*; mezzo; (fig.) stratagemma *m.*; (mech.) dispositivo, congegno; (herald.) divisa, impresa; *pl.* inclinazione; capricci *m.pl.* *to leave someone to his own -s*, lasciare libero qualcuno di agire come vuole.
**devil**[1] *n.* diavolo; demonio; *to cast out a* —, esorcizzare un demonio; *she* —, diavolessa, strega; (fam.) *the —!*, diamine!, che diavolo!; *to play the very* —, fare il diavolo a quattro; *a — of a row*, un baccano infernale; *to work like the* —, lavorare come un cane; *to be between the — and the deep sea*, trovarsi fra l'incudine e il martello; *to give the — his due*, rendere giustizia anche a chi non la merita; *to have the -'s own luck*, avere il diavolo nell'ampolla; *printer's* —, apprendista *m.*
**devil**[2] *tr.* (cul.) cuocere alla graticola con spezie; *intr.* lavorare per un altro.
**devil-fish** *n.* (ichth.) piovra.
**devilish** *adj.* diabolico; infernale; *adv.* diabolicamente; (fam.) *it's — hot*, fa un caldo infernale. **-ly** *adv.* see **devilish.** **-ness** *n.* natura diabolica.
**devil-may-care** *adj.* (fam.) strafottente.
**devilment, devilry** *n.* diavoleria; *to be full of* —, avere il diavolo in corpo.
**devil-worship** *n.* demonolatria.
**devious** *adj.* remoto, erratico; tortuoso, vagante.
**devis-e** *tr.* escogitare, progettare; combinare, elaborare, inventare; (leg.) disporre per testamento. **-able** *adj.* immaginabile, escogitabile; (leg.) trasmissibile.
**devitalize** *tr.* indebolire; (med.) devitalizzare.
**devoid** *adj.* privo, sprovvisto; *— of*, privo di, senza.
**devolution** *n.* devoluzione del potere; (admin.) decentramento.
**devolve** *tr.* trasmettere, trasferire; *intr.* devolvere, ricadere, incombere.
**devot-e** *tr.* dedicare, consacrare; *rfl.* votarsi, dedicarsi. **-ed** *adj.* devoto, dedito; affezionato. **-edness** *n.* devozione; affetto. **-ee** *n.* devoto; fedele *m.*, *f.*; (sport) tifoso; (pejor.) bigotto.
**devotion** *n.* devozione; dedizione; affetto; *pl.* (rel.) preghiere *f.pl.* **-al** *adj.* devoto, religioso.
**devour** *tr.* divorare; (fig.) dilapidare, distruggere. **-ing** *adj.* vorace, edace, rapace.
**devout** *adj.* devoto, pio; fervente, sincero. **-ness** *n.* devozione; pietà.
**dew** *n.* rugiada.
**dewlap** *n.* giogaia; (fig.) doppio mento.
**dew-pond** *n.* stagno artificiale alimentato dalla rugiada.
**dewy** *adj.* rugiadoso.
**dexter** *adj.* destro; *n.* (herald.) destra.
**dexter-ous** *adj.* destro; lesto; abile. **-ity, -ousness** *n.* destrezza; sveltezza.
**diabet-es** *n.* (med.) diabete *m.* **-ic** *adj.*, *n.* diabetico.
**diabolic(al)** *adj.* diabolico.
**diacon-al** *adj.* (eccl.) diaconale. **-ate** *n.* diaconato.
**diacritic(al)** *adj.*, *n.* (ling.) segno diacritico.
**diadem** *n.* diadema *m.*
**diaeresis** *n.* (gramm.) dieresi *f.*
**diagnos-e** *tr.* diagnosticare; fare la diagnosi di. **-is** *n.* diagnosi *f.*
**diagonal** *adj.* diagonale; *n.* diagonale *f.*
**diagram** *n.* diagramma *m.*, grafico; schema *m.* **-matic** *adj.* diagrammatico.
**dial** *n.* quadrante *m.*; (teleph.) disco combinatore; (slang) muso; *tr.* (teleph.) *to — a number*, formare un numero.
**dialect** *n.* dialetto; *adj.* di dialetto. **-al** *adj.* dialettale.
**dialectic** *adj.* (philos.) dialettico; (ling.) dialettale; *n.* dialettica.
**dialectics** *n.* dialettica.
**dialogue** *n.* dialogo; conversazione.
**diamet-er** *n.* diametro. **-rical** *adj.* diametrale.
**diamond** *n.* diamante *m.*; *cut* —, brillante *m.*; *rough* —, diamante grezzo; (fig.) uomo rozzo ma sincero; *— cut* —, astuzia per astuzia; *— wedding*, nozze *f.pl.* di diamante; losanga, rombo; *— panes*, vetri *m.pl.* romboidali; (typ.) corpo quattro e mezzo; *pl.* (cards) quadri *m.pl.*
**diaper** *n.* tela damascata; pannolino per bambini.
**diaphanous** *adj.* diafano; trasparente.
**diaphragm** *n.* (anat.) diaframma *m.*; (electr.) membrana.
**diarist** *n.* diarista *m.*, *f.*
**diarrhoea** *n.* (med.) diarrea.

**diary** *n.* diario; agenda; taccuino.
**diatribe** *n.* diatriba.
**dice** *n.* dadi *m.pl.*; *to play —*, giocare a dadi; *intr.* giocare a dadi; *tr.* (cul.) tagliare a dadini.
**dice-box** *n.* bossolo per dadi.
**dichotomy** *n.* dicotomia.
**dichromatic** *adj.* dicromatico.
**dickens** *n.* (fam.) *what the —!*, che diamine!
**dickey** *adj.* (fam.) malsicuro, barcollante; malaticcio.
**dick(e)y** *n.* finto sparato di camicia; (motor.) sedile *m.* posteriore.
**dick(e)y-bird** *n.* (fam.) uccellino.
**dictaphone** *n.* dittafono.
**dic·tate** *n.* dettame *m.*; comando; *the -s of conscience*, i dettami della coscienza.
**dictat-e** *tr.* dettare; (fig.) imporre; (fam.) *I won't be -ed to*, non voglio imposizioni. **-ion** *n.* dettato, dettatura.
**dictator** *n.* dittatore; (fig.) *— of fashion*, arbitro della moda. **-ial** *adj.* dittatoriale, dittatorio. **-ship** *n.* dittatura.
**diction** *n.* dizione; stile *m.*
**dictionary** *n.* dizionario, vocabolario; lessico.
**dictograph** *n.* dittografo.
**dictum** *n.* detto; massima; affermazione.
**didactic** *adj.* didattico.
**didactics** *n.* didattica.
**diddle** *tr.* (pop.) gabbare; imbrogliare.
**die**[1] *n.* (sing. of **dice**) dado; *the — is cast*, il dado è tratto; (archit.) dado; plinto; (typ.) stampo; matrice *f.*; filiera.
**die**[2] *intr.* morire; perire; decedere; trapassare; spegnersi; (fam.) crepare; *to — a natural death*, morire di morte naturale; *to — in one's shoes*, morire sulla breccia; *to — the death of a hero*, morire da eroe; *to — of a broken heart*, morire di crepacuore; *to — of starvation*, morire di fame; *to — a Christian death*, addormentarsi nel Signore; *never say —*, non disperare; (fig.) *to — with laughter*, morire dal ridere; *I'm dying to go to Italy*, non vedo l'ora di andare in Italia; *his secret -d with him*, si è portato il suo segreto nella tomba; *to — away*, affievolirsi, svanire, sparire lentamente; *to — down*, spegnersi lentamente; venir meno; *to — off*, estinguersi, scomparire.
**die-casting** *n.* pressofusione.
**diehard** *n.* (fam.) chi non si dà mai per vinto; duro a morire; (pol.) intransigente *m., f.*
**diesel** *adj.* *— engine*, motore *m.* diesel; *— oil*, nafta; *n.* diesel *m.*
**diet**[1] *n.* (pol.) dieta; assemblea.
**diet**[2] *n.* nutrimento; alimentazione; vitto; (med.) dieta; regime *m.*; *to be on a —*, essere a regime, stare a dieta; *tr.* mettere a regime; prescrivere una dieta a; *intr.* stare a dieta, essere a regime. **-ary** *adj.* dietetico; *n.* regime alimentare. **-etics** *n.* dietetica. **-etician** *n.* dietologo.
**differ** *intr.* essere diverso, essere dissimile; differire, non essere d'accordo, dissentire; *to agree to —*, rimanere ciascuno della propria opinione; *I beg to —*, mi permetto di essere d'opinione diversa; *opinions —*, i pareri sono discordi.
**difference** *n.* differenza; divergenza; *— in age*, disparità d'età; *it makes a great —*, c'è una bella differenza; *to split the —*, dividere a metà la differenza; *— of opinion*, divario, dissidio; *to settle a —*, appianare una divergenza, mettersi d'accordo.
**different** *adj.* differente; diverso, dissimile; altro; vario; *that's quite a — matter*, è tutt'altra cosa; *at — times*, in momenti diversi.
**differential** *adj.* differenziale; *n.* (motor.) differenziale *m.*
**differentiat-e** *tr.* differenziare; distinguere. **-ion** *n.* differenziazione.
**differently** *adv.* diversamente; altrimenti.
**difficult** *adj.* difficile; *— to please*, di difficile contentatura; *— to live with*, di carattere difficile; *to find it — to...*, trovare difficoltà a . . . .
**difficulty** *n.* difficoltà; *to have — in*, trovare difficoltà a; *to make no — about*, non fare nessuna difficoltà a; *to get over a —*, sormontare un ostacolo; *to be in a —*, trovarsi in una situazione difficile; *to be in financial difficulties*, essere a corto di denaro; (fam.) *that's the —*, qui sta il busillis; *to see no way out of a —*, non sapere come cavarsela.
**diffid-ence** *n.* timidezza; mancanza di fiducia in se stesso. **-ent** *adj.* timido, esitante; *to be -ent*, dubitare di se stesso.
**diffuse** *adj.* diffuso; (of style) prolisso. **-ness** *n.* prolissità.
**diffus-e** *tr.* diffondere; spargere, propagare. **-ion** *n.* diffusione; propagazione.
**diffusive** *adj.* diffusivo; prolisso.
**dig** *n.* vangata; scavo; (fam.) *to have a — at*, dare una stoccata a; *pl.* (fam.) *to live in -s*, alloggiare presso un affittacamere.
**dig** *tr.* vangare; scavare; *to — a hole*, scavare un buco; *to — for*, scavare per trovare; (fam.) *to — someone in the ribs*, dare una gomitata nelle costole a qualcuno; *to — up*, dissodare, rivangare; estrarre dal terreno; (fig.) tirare fuori, disseppellire; scovare; (fam.) *to — into*, fare una breccia in; *to — one's toes in*, tenersi saldo; (slang) capire, apprezzare; *rfl.* (mil.) *to — oneself in*, trincerarsi (also fig.).
**di·gest** *n.* sommario, riassunto; *Reader's Digest*, Selezione; (leg.) digesto.
**digest** *tr.* digerire; (fam.) assimilare.
**digestib-le** *adj.* digeribile. **-ility** *n.* digeribilità.
**digest-ion** *n.* digestione; (fam.) stomaco; *to have the — of an ostrich*, avere uno stomaco di struzzo. **-ive** *adj.* digestivo; digerente; *-ive system*, apparato digerente.
**digg-er** *n.* zappatore, scavatore; (pop.) australiano; *n.* soldato australiano; (machine) escavatrice. **-ing** *n.* vangatura; scavo; *pl.* (slang) alloggio presso un affittacamere.
**digit** *n.* dito; (math.) numero semplice. **-al** *adj.* digitale, delle dita.
**digitalis** *n.* (bot.) digitale *f.*
**dignif-y** *tr.* conferire dignità a, nobilitare, onorare; (fig.) fregiare. **-ied** *adj.* dignitoso; austero, nobile; maestoso.
**dignitary** *n.* dignitario; (eccl.) prelato.
**dignity** *n.* dignità; *to preserve one's —*, conservare la propria dignità; *an air of —*, un portamento dignitoso; *to stand on one's —*, mantenere la propria dignità; elevatezza; rango; ufficio.
**digress** *intr.* fare una digressione; deviare, divagare; *to — from*, allontanarsi da. **-ion** *n.* digressione; *this by way of -ion*, sia detto fra parentesi, questo per inciso. **-ive** *adj.* digressivo.
**dike** *n.* diga; argine *m.*; fossa.
**dilapidate** *tr.* dilapidare; sciupare; rovinare. **-d** *adj.* decrepito; sconquassato; sgangherato.
**dilapidation** *n.* dilapidazione; sfacelo.
**dilat-e** *tr.* dilatare; diffondere, dilungare; *intr.* dilatarsi; (fig.) diffondersi, dilungarsi. **-ation, -ion** *n.* dilatazione.
**dilator-y** *adj.* lento, tardivo; (leg.) dilatorio. **-iness** *n.* lentezza; dilazione; ritardo.
**dilemma** *n.* dilemma *m.*; *the horns of the —*, le corna del dilemma; (fam.) imbarazzo.
**dilettant-e** *n.* dilettante *m., f.* **-ist** *adj.* da dilettante. **-ism** *n.* dilettantismo.
**dilig-ence** *n.* diligenza; assiduità; cura; corriera. **-ent** *adj.* diligente; assiduo; industrioso; accurato.
**dill** *n.* (bot.) aneto.
**dilly-dally** *intr.* gingillarsi, tentennare; sciupare tempo.
**dilut-e** *adj.* diluito; stemperato, annacquato; (of colour) smorzato; (fig.) attenuato; *tr.* diluire; stemperare, allungare, annacquare; (fig.) attenuare, indebolire. **-ed** *part. adj.* diluito. **-ion** *n.* diluizione; stempera-

mento, annacquamento; sostanza diluita.

**dim** *adj.* pallido; debole; sordo; ottuso; smorzato; (fig.) vago, indistinto; appannato, offuscato, oscuro; *eyes — with tears,* occhi velati di lacrime; (fam.) *a — view,* una visione pessimistica; *to take a — view of,* disapprovare; *tr.* offuscare, oscurare; appannare; affievolire; (motor.) *to — headlights,* commutare; (fig.) velare.

**dimension** *n.* dimensione; grandezza; misura.

**diminish** *tr.* diminuire; ridurre, impicciolire; *intr.* diminuire; scemare, calare. **-ing** *adj.* diminuente; calante.

**diminution** *n.* diminuzione; riduzione; (archit.) rastremazione.

**diminutive** *adj.* minuscolo, piccolissimo; *n.* (gramm.) diminutivo. **-ness** *n.* piccolezzo.

**dimmer** *n.* (motor.) commutatore delle luci; (cinem.) oscuratore.

**dimness** *n.* debolezza; offuscamento; oscurità; imprecisione; (fig.) ottusità.

**dimple** *n.* (on cheek) fossetta; (fig.) increspatura; *intr.* illeggiadrirsi da fossette; (fig.) incresparsi.

**din** *n.* baccano, strepito, chiasso; fragore *m.*; *intr.* far baccano, strepitare; *to — into someone's ears,* far rintronare negli orecchi di qualcuno.

**dine** *intr.* pranzare; desinare; *to — on,* fare un pranzo a base di; *to — in,* pranzare a casa; *tr.* offrire un pranzo a.

**diner** *n.* commensale *m., f.,* (rlwy.) vagone *m.* ristorante.

**diner-out** *n.* chi pranza spesso fuori casa.

**ding** *intr., tr.* far risuonare; risuonare; (fam.) *to — into someone's head,* far capire a qualcuno.

**ding-dong** *adj.* oscillante; tintinnìo.

**dingey, dinghy** *n.* (naut.) dinghy *m.*; lancia.

**dinginess** *n.* squallore *m.*; aspetto povero; miseria.

**dingle** *n.* valletta ombrosa.

**dingo** *n.* (zool.) dingo.

**dingy** *adj.* squallido; sudicio, fosco; *— white,* bianco sporco.

**dining-car** *n.* vagone ristorante. **-hall** *n.* sala da pranzo; (schol.) refettorio. **-room** *n.* sala da pranzo. **-table** *n.* tavola da pranzo.

**dinky** *adj.* (fam.) carino, bellino, grazioso.

**dinner** *n.* pranzo; desinare *m.*; *to have —,* pranzare; *public —,* banchetto.

**dinner-dance** *n.* pranzo seguito da ballo. **-jacket** *n.* smoking *m.*

**dinnerless** *adj. to go —,* saltare il pranzo, stare a digiuno.

**dinner-party** *n.* pranzo con invitati; *to give a —,* offrire un pranzo. **-time** *n.* ora del pranzo. **-wagon** *n.* carrello; portavivande *m. indecl.*

**dinosaur** *n.* dinosauro.

**dint** *n.* tacca; segno; *by — of,* a forza di.

**diocesan** *adj.* diocesano.

**diocese** *n.* diocesi *f. indecl.*

**dioxide** *n.* (chem.) biossido.

**dip** *n.* tuffo; immersione; (fam.) bagno, nuotata; *lucky —,* tombola; inclinazione; (in ground) pendenza, abbassamento.

**dip** *tr.* tuffare, immergere, bagnare; intingere; *to — one's hand into one's purse,* mettere mano alla borsa; *to — a flag,* abbassare una bandiera in segno di saluto; (motor.) *to — the headlights,* abbassare i fari; *intr.* inclinarsi, abbassarsi; attingere; (aeron.) perdere quota; *to — into a book,* sfogliare un libro; *to — into one's capital,* attingere ai propri capitali.

**diphtheria** *n.* (med.) difterite *f.*

**diphthong** *n.* dittongo.

**diploma** *n.* diploma *m.*; diploma d'abilitazione.

**diplomacy** *n.* diplomazia.

**diplomat** *n.* diplomatico. **-ic** *adj.* diplomatico; *to enter the -ic service,* entrare nella carriera diplomatica.

**dipper** *n.* chi si immerge, tuffatore; mestolo; (pop. astron.) *the Dipper,* l'Orsa maggiore; (orn.) acquaiola.

**dipping** *n.* immersione.

**dipsomani-a** *n.* (med.) dipsomania. **-ac** *adj., n.* dipsomane *m., f.*; alcoolizzato.

**diptych** *n.* dittico.

**dire** *adj.* terribile, orrendo, atroce; *to be in — need of,* avere urgente bisogno di; *— poverty,* miseria nera.

**direct** *adj.* diretto, diritto; immediato; *to be a — descendant of,* discendere in linea diretta da; *— taxation,* imposte *f.pl.* dirette; *— control,* comando diretto; (gramm.) *— speech,* discorso diretto; (electr.) *— current,* corrente continua; (teleph.) *— dialling,* teleselezione; (fig.) franco, schietto, sincero; *adv.* direttamente, diretto.

**direct** *tr.* dirigere; amministrare; (theatr.; mus.) dirigere; indirizzare; ordinare; indicare; (leg.) istruire, *as -ed,* secondo le istruzioni ricevute.

**direction** *n.* direzione; amministrazione; indirizzo; senso; *in every —,* in ogni senso; *in the opposite —,* nel senso contrario; *in which —?,* verso dove?; *to lose one's sense of —,* perdere l'orientamento, disorientarsi; *pl.* istruzioni, indicazioni, direttive *f.pl.*; *-s for use,* indicazioni per l'uso; (theatr.) *stage -s,* didascalie *f.pl.*

**directional** *adj.* direttivo; (radio) direzionale.

**direction-finder** *n.* (radio) radiogoniometro.

**directive** *adj.* direttivo; *n.* direttiva.

**directly** *adv.* direttamente; immediatamente, subito; *conj.* appena.

**directness** *n.* franchezza; schiettezza; sincerità; fonte diretta.

**director** *n.* direttore; amministratore; *managing —,* amministratore delegato; *board of -s,* consiglio di amministrazione; (eccl.) direttore spirituale; (cinem.) regista *m.*

**directorate** *n.* direzione; consiglio di amministrazione.

**directorial** *adj.* direttorio, direttivo.

**directorship** *n.* direttorato; carica di amministratore.

**directory** *n.* indicatore; annuario; guida; *telephone —,* elenco telefonico; (Fr. hist.) Direttorio.

**directress** *n.* direttrice; amministratrice.

**direful** *adj.* orrendo, funesto.

**dirge** *n.* canto funebre; trenodia.

**dirk** *n.* (Scot.) daga; pugnale *m.*

**dirt** *n.* immondizia; sudiciume *m.*; sporcizia; fango; *to wash the — off,* lavar via la sporcizia; (fig.) *to throw — at,* sparlare di, diffamare; *to treat someone like —,* bistrattare qualcuno, *as cheap as —,* a prezzo bassissimo.

**dirtily** *adv.* sporcamente, sudiciamente; (fig.) vilmente.

**dirtiness** *n.* sporcizia; sozzura; (fig.) bassezza, viltà.

**dirty** *adj.* sporco, sudicio; sozzo; infangato, fangoso; (fig.) losco, lurido, osceno; *it's a — business,* è un affare losco; (vulg.) *to do the — on someone,* dare a qualcuno un colpo mancino; *— mind,* mente sporca; *— story,* storiella sboccata, barzelletta lurida; *— trick,* brutto tiro; *— work,* porcherie *f.pl.*; *— pig,* sporcaccione, sozzone *m.*

**dirty** *tr.* sporcare, insudiciare, insozzare; *rfl.* sporcarsi.

**disability** *n.* incapacità; infermità; *— pension,* pensione *f.* d'invalidità.

**disable** *tr.* rendere incapace, rendere inabile, mutilare; *-d soldier,* invalido, mutilato di guerra. **-ment** *n.* incapacità.

**disabuse** *tr.* disingannare.

**disaccord** *n.* disaccordo; dissenso.

**disaccustom** *tr.* disabituare.

**disadvantage** *n.* svantaggio; detrimento; perdita. **-ous** *adj.* svantaggioso; sfavorevole.

**disaffect-ed** *adj.* malcontento, maldisposto, sovversivo. **-edness, -ion** *n.* disaffezione, scontentezza; spirito di ribellione.

**disagree** *intr.* non andare d'accordo, essere in disaccordo; (fig.) non essere confacente, non convenire. **-able** *adj.* spiacevole, sgradevole, antipatico. **-ment** *n.* disaccordo; dissenso, dissidio, dissapore *m.*; discordanza.

**disallow** *tr.* non ammettere, disapprovare, disconoscere, non riconoscere; (sport) *to — a goal*, annullare un gol.

**disappear** *intr.* sparire, scomparire, svanire, (fig.) eclissarsi. **-ance** *n.* scomparsa, sparizione.

**disappoint** *tr.* deludere, frustrare. **-ed** *adj.* deluso; scontento, insoddisfatto. **-ing** *adj.* deludente; spiacevole; *how -ing !*, che disdetta! **-ment** *n.* delusione; contrattempo, disappunto.

**disapprobation, disapproval** *n.* disapprovazione; riprensione.

**disapprove** *tr.*, *intr.* disapprovare, trovare a ridire (su).

**disarm** *tr.* disarmare; *a -ing smile*, un sorriso disarmante; *intr.* disarmarsi. **-ament, -ing** *n.* disarmo.

**disarrange** *tr.* disordinare; scompigliare.

**disarrangement, disarray** *n.* disordine *m.*; scompiglio; confusione.

**disassemble** *tr.* smontare.

**disast-er** *n.* disastro; calamità; catastrofe *f.*, sinistro; (fam.) guaio. **-rous** *adj.* disastroso; calamitoso.

**disavow** *tr.* ripudiare, disconoscere, rinnegare; sconfessare.

**disband** *tr.* sbandare; licenziare; sciogliere; congedare; *intr.* sbandarsi, sciogliersi. **-ment** *n.* sbandamento; licenziamento; dispersione.

**disbar** *tr.* radiare dall'albo degli avvocati.

**disbelief** *n.* incredulità; scetticismo; (rel.) miscredenza.

**disbeliev-e** *tr.*, *intr.* non credere, non prestar fede (a). **-er** *n.* incredulo, scettico; (rel.) miscredente *m.*, *f.*

**disburs-e** *tr.* sborsare. **-ement, -al** *n.* sborso; pagamento; spese *f.pl.*

**discard** *tr.* scartare; mettere da parte; smettere; *intr.* (cards) fare uno scarto.

**discern** *tr.* discernere; distinguere; scorgere. **-ible** *adj.* discernibile; percepibile, percettibile; visibile. **-ment** *n.* discernimento; giudizio; acume *m.*; oculatezza.

**discharge** *n.* adempimento; pagamento, quietanza; riabilitazione; scarica, sparo; scarico, scaricamento; congedo; licenziamento, esonero; scarcerazione, liberazione; (electr.) scarica; (phys.) liberazione, efflusso; emissione; (med.) suppurazione.

**discharge** *tr.* scaricare; *to — a duty*, adempiere un dovere; *to — a debt*, saldare un debito; sparare; (mil.) congedare; riformare; *to — from hospital*, dimettere dall'ospedale; *to — as unfit*, licenziare, esonerare; scarcerare, liberare; (leg.) assolvere; (electr.) scaricare; (phys.) liberare, emettere; *intr.* (electr.) scaricarsi; (med.) suppurare, essudare.

**disciple** *n.* discepolo.

**disciplin-e** *n.* disciplina; addestramento; punizione; *tr.* disciplinare; addestrare; castigare; (fig.) formare. **-arian** *n.* disciplinatore. **-ary** *adj.* disciplinare.

**disclaim** *tr.* rifiutare; sconfessare, ripudiare; negare; rinunciare. **-er** *n.* rifiuto; rinuncia; sconfessamento.

**disclos-e** *tr.* svelare, scoprire; schiudere; divulgare, propagare. **-ure** *n.* rivelazione; scoperta; divulgazione, propagazione.

**discolour** *tr.* decolorare, scolorire; *intr.* scolorirsi; sbiadire.

**discolo(u)ration** *n.* scoloramento

**discomfit** *tr.* sconfiggere, sconfortare; sconcertare, frustrare. **-ure** *n.* sconfitta; sconforto; turbamento.

**discomfort** *n.* disagio; incomodo; *tr.* mettere a disagio; incomodare.

**discompos-e** *tr.* scomporre; turbare; scompigliare. **-ure** *n.* scompostezza; turbamento; alterazione.

**disconcert** *tr.* sconcertare; turbare; disorientare. **-ing** *adj.* sconcertante.

**disconnect** *tr.* sconnettere; disgiungere; separare, staccare; (electr.) disinserire, interrompere; (mech.) disinnestare; (motor) *to — the clutch*, debraiare. **-ed** *adj.* sconnesso; incoerente. **-edness** *n.* incoerenza. **-ion** *n.* sconnessione; incoerenza; (mech.) disinnesto.

**disconsolate** *adj.* sconsolato; addolorato; desolato; affranto.

**discontent** *n.* scontento, scontentezza; malcontento. **-ed** *adj.* scontento, malcontento; insoddisfatto. **-edness** *n.* scontentezza.

**discontinu-e** *tr.* cessare; sospendere; interrompere; *intr.* cessare; essere interrotto. **-ance** *n.* cessazione; sospensione, interruzione. **-uity** *n.* discontinuità.

**discord** *n.* discordia; disaccordo, dissidio, dissenso; (mus.) dissonanza, disarmonia. **-ance** *n.* dissenso; disaccordo; discordanza. **-ant** *adj.* discorde, dissenziente; (of sounds) discordante.

**dis·count** *n.* sconto; ribasso; riduzione; abbuono (fig.) *at a —*, sottoprezzo; non richiesto.

**discount** *tr.* scontare; (fig.) non credere a.

**discountenance** *tr.* disapprovare; scoraggiare, veder male, opporsi a; mettere in imbarazzo.

**discourag-e** *tr.* scoraggiare; abbattere; dissuadere, stornare. **-ement** *n.* scoraggiamento. **-ing** *adj.* scoraggiante; deprimente.

**dis·course** *n.* discorso; orazione; dissertazione; *to hold — with*, conferire con.

**discourse** *tr.* discorrere; dissertare; ragionare; intrattenersi.

**discourte-ous** *adj.* scortese. **-sy** *n.* scortesia.

**discover** *tr.* scoprire; trovare; inventare; palesare; accorgersi di, rendersi conto di. **-er** *n.* scopritore. **-y** *n.* scoperta; rivelazione.

**discredit** *n.* scredito, discredito; dubbio; obbrobrio; *tr.* screditare; diffamare; mettere in dubbio. **-able** *adj.* disonorevole; indegno; che porta discredito.

**discreet** *adj.* prudente, circospetto, discreto; riservato.

**discrep-ancy** *n.* discrepanza; divario; divergenza; contraddizione. **-ant** *adj.* discrepante; discorde, diverso.

**discrete** *adj.* separato, distinto; astratto.

**discretion** *n.* discrezione; prudenza; discernimento, giudizio; arbitrio; libertà di azione; *years of —*, età della ragione. **-ary** *adj.* discrezionale; lasciato a discrezione.

**discriminat-e** *tr.*, *intr.* discriminare, distinguere, differenziare. **-ing** *adj.* perspicace, penetrante; giudizioso; *-ing taste*, gusto fino. **-ion** *n.* discriminazione; distinzione; discernimento; giudizio.

**discursive** *adj.* saltuario, sconnesso; scucito.

**discus** *n.* disco.

**discuss** *tr.* discutere, deliberare, dibattere; ragionare di, trattare, studiare.

**discussion** *n.* discussione; dibattimento; disputa.

**disdain** *n.* sdegno; disprezzo; *tr.* sdegnare; disprezzare. **-ful** *adj.* sdegnoso; sprezzante; altero.

**disease** *n.* malattia; morbo; affezione. **-d** *adj.* ammalato, malato; infetto; (fig.) morboso.

**disem-bark** *tr.*, *intr.* sbarcare. **-barcation** *n.* sbarco.

**disembarrass** *tr.* sbarazzare; liberare, sgombrare.

**disembod-y** *tr.* liberare dal corpo, disincarnare; (mil.) congedare. **-iment** *n.* liberazione dal corpo; (mil.) congedo.

**disembowel** *tr.* sbudellare, sventrare.

**disenchant** *tr.* disincantare.

**-ment** *n.* disincanto; disillusione; disinnamoramento.
**disencumber** *tr.* sgombrare, sgravare, sbarazzare.
**disengage** *tr.* disimpegnare, liberare; (mech.) disinnestare, disingranare; *intr.* disimpegnarsi, liberarsi. **-d** *adj.* libero; disponibile; disinnestato.
**disentangle** *tr.* districare, sbrogliare, dipanare; (fig.) appianare, chiarire. **-ment** *n.* districamento.
**disentomb** *tr.* disseppellire, esumare.
**disfavour** *n.* disfavore, sfavore *m.*; disapprovazione.
**disfigure** *tr.* sfigurare, deformare; (fig.) deturpare. **-ment** *n.* deformazione; sfregio; deturpazione.
**disfranchise** *tr.* privare del diritto di suffragio. **-ment** *n.* privazione del diritto di suffragio.
**disgorge** *tr.* rigettare; (fig.) restituire.
**disgrace** *n.* disfavore, disonore *m.*; vergogna, onta; (fam.) *it's a —!*, è uno scandalo!; *tr.* disonorare; destituire. **-ful** *adj.* vergognoso; disonorevole; scandaloso. **-fulness** *n.* vergogna; onta; infamia.
**disgruntled** *adj.* seccato; malcontento; di cattivo umore.
**disguise** *n.* travestimento; *in the — of a priest*, travestito da prete; *under the — of*, sotto la maschera di; *tr.* travestire; (fig.) camuffare, mascherare, *to — one's feelings*, nascondere i propri sentimenti; *there is no disguising the fact that*, è inutile negare che.
**disgust** *n.* disgusto, schifo; ripugnanza; ribrezzo; stizza; *much to my —*, con mio grande disappunto; *tr.* disgustare; far schifo a; nauseare; (fig.) scandalizzare, spiacere a. **-ing** *adj.* disgustoso; nauseabondo; ripugnante; schifoso; scandaloso; *it's -ing!*, fa schifo!
**dish** *n.* piatto, scodella; *to wash the -es*, rigovernare; (at a meal) piatto, pietanza; *a — fit for a king*, un boccone da cardinale; (photog.) bacinella; *tr.* scodellare, mettere in piatto; *to — up*, servire; (fig.) presentare; (slang) *we're -ed!*, siamo fregati!
**disharmony** *n.* disarmonia; dissonanza.
**dishcloth** *n.* strofinaccio per piatti.
**dish-cover** *n.* copripiatto.
**dishearten** *tr.* scoraggiare; sconfortare. **-ing** *adj.* scoraggiante.
**dishevelled** *adj.* scapigliato; arruffato, disordinato.
**dishonest** *adj.* disonesto; sleale. **-y** *n.* disonestà.
**dishonour** *n.* disonore *m.* infamia; *to bring — on*, disonorare; *tr.* disonorare, far disonore a; (fig.) mancare a, venir meno a; (comm.) *-ed cheque*, assegno a vuoto. **-able** *adj.* disonesto; disonorevole, ignobile.
**dish-warmer** *n.* scaldapiatti *m. indecl.*
**dishwasher** *n.* lavapiatti *m. indecl.*
**dishwater** *n.* acqua di rigovernatura; (fam.) *it tastes like —*, sa di risciacquatura.
**disillusion** *n.* disillusione; disinganno; *tr.* disilludere; disincantare, disingannare. **-ment** *n.* disillusione; disinganno.
**disinclin-ation** *n.* riluttanza; avversione. **-ed** *adj.* riluttante; avverso, alieno; *to be -ed to*, aver poca voglia di.
**disinfect** *tr.* disinfettare. **-ant** *n.* disinfettante, detergente *m.* **-ion** *n.* disinfezione; sterlizzazione.
**disingenuous** *adj.* insincero, falso. **-ness** *n.* insincerità.
**disinherit** *tr.* diseredare.
**disintegrat-e** *tr.* disintegrare, disgregare; *intr.* disintegrarsi, disfarsi. **-ion** *n.* disintegrazione; disfacimento.
**disinter** *tr.* disseppellire, disumare, esumare.
**disinterest** *tr.* disinteressare. **-ed** *adj.* imparziale. disinteressato; indifferente. **-edness** *n.* disinteresse *m.*; imparzialità, indifferenza.
**disinterment** *n.* esumazione.
**disjoin** *tr.* disgiungere, disunire, distaccare.
**disjoint** *tr.* slogare, smembrare, disarticolare. **-ed** *adj.* disarticolato, slogato; (fig.) sconnesso, incoerente. **-edness** *n.* incoerenza, sconnessione.
**disjunctive** *adj.* (gramm.) disgiuntivo.
**disk** *n.* disco; (mil.) *identity —*, piastrina d'identità; (med.) *slipped —*, ernia del disco.
**dislike** *n.* antipatia, avversione; *likes and -s*, simpatie e antipatie; *to take a — to*, prendere in uggia; *tr.* provare antipatia per, non amare; detestare; *he -s you*, tu gli sei antipatico; *I — it*, non mi piace; *I don't — it*, non mi dispiace; *to be -d*, essere mal visto.
**dislocat-e** *tr.* slogare, dislocare; spostare; (med.) lussare; (fig.) disorganizzare. **-ion** *n.* slogatura; spostamento, dislocamento; (med.) lussazione; (fig.) disorganizzazione.
**dislodge** *tr.* sloggiare, scacciare, rimuovere; *to become -d*, staccarsi.
**disloyal** *adj.* sleale; infedele; perfido. **-ty** *n.* slealtà; infedeltà; perfidia.
**dismal** *adj.* triste; lugubre; cupo; tetro; fosco.
**dismantl-e** *tr.* smantellare; smontare; (naut.) disarmare. **-ing, -ement** *n.* smantellamento, smontaggio; (naut.) disarmo.
**dismast** (naut.) disalberare.
**dismay** *n.* costernazione; sgomento; *in —*, costernato, allibito; *tr.* sgomentare; costernare. **-ed** *adj.* costernato, allibito.
**dismember** *tr.* smembrare. **-ment, -ing** *n.* smembramento.
**dismiss** *tr.* mettere da parte, scartare, allontanare; *to — something from one's mind*, scacciare qualcosa dalla mente; *let us — the subject*, non ne parliamo più; congedare, licenziare; (mil.) *to be -ed from the service*, essere radiato dai ranghi; (order) —!, rompete le file!; respingere, rigettare; (leg.) prosciogliere; *to — a case*, emettere ordinanza di non luogo a procedere. **-al** *n.* rinvio; congedo, licenziamento; destituzione; (leg.) proscioglimento.
**dismount** *tr.* smontare, far scendere da; (mil.) appiedare; *intr.* scendere, smontare. **-ed** *adj.* smontato; a piedi.
**disobedi-ence** *n.* disubbidienza. **-ent** *adj.* disubbidiente; indisciplinato; *to be -ent to*, disubbidire a.
**disobey** *tr.* disubbidire a; trasgredire.
**disoblig-e** *tr.* usare scortesia verso; *I am sorry to have to — you*, mi rincresce di non poter accontentarti. **-ing** *adj.* scortese; scompiacente; sgarbato. **-ingness** *n.* scortesia; sgarbatezza.
**disorder** *n.* disordine *m.*; confusione; *to flee in —*, fuggire disordinatamente; sommossa; tumulto, disordine *m.*; (med.) disturbo, indisposizione; *tr.* mettere in disordine, disordinare, scompigliare.
**disorderl-y** *adj.* disordinato, sregolato; confusionario; indisciplinato, turbolento; (leg.) *charged with being drunk and —*, imputato di ubriachezza molesta. **-iness** *n.* disordine *m.*; confusione; indisciplina, turbolenza.
**disorganiz-e** *tr.* disorganizzare; scomporne la compagine; *to become -ed*, disorganizzarsi. **-ation** *n.* disorganizzazione.
**disorientation** *n.* disorientamento.
**disown** *tr.* rinnegare, ripudiare, sconfessare; non riconoscere.
**disparage** *tr.* deprezzare; screditare; denigrare. **-ment** *n.* denigrazione; deprezzamento; scredito.
**disparaging** *adj.* sprezzante, spregiativo.
**disparate** *adj.* disparato.
**disparity** *n.* disparità; differenza, disuguaglianza.
**dispassionate** *adj.* spassionato; imparziale. **-ness** *n.* calma; imparzialità.
**dispatch** *n.* spedizione, invio;

(mil.) dispaccio; *mentioned in ~es*, citato all'ordine del giorno; celerità, prontezza; rapido disbrigo; *with the utmost —*, con la massima sollecitudine; *tr.* spedire; inviare; sbrigare; spacciare, dare il colpo di grazia a.
**dispatch-bag** *n.* valigia diplomatica. **-box** *n.* cassetta per documenti ufficiali. **-case** *n.* valigetta; borsa. **-rider** *n.* (mil.) staffetta.
**dispel** *tr.* dissipare, disperdere; scacciare.
**dispensable** *adj.* non necessario; dispensabile.
**dispensary** *n.* farmacia.
**dispensation** *n.* dispensa; distribuzione; (eccl.) dispensa, dispensazione; *the ~s of Providence*, i decreti della Provvidenza.
**dispens-e** *tr.* dispensare, distribuire; *to — justice*, amministrare la giustizia; (eccl.) dispensare; *intr. to — with*, fare a meno di, eliminare; (pharm.) preparare medicinali. **~er** *n.* farmacista *m.*; (in hospital) addetto alla preparazione dei medicinali; amministratore. **~ing** *adj.* che dispensa; *~ing chemist*, farmacista autorizzato a preparare le ricette; *n.* preparazione delle ricette.
**dispers-e** *tr.* disperdere; spargere; sparpagliare; *intr.* disperdersi; diradarsi. **~al** *n.* dispersione. **~ion** *n.* dispersione; *~ion of heat*, diffusione di calore.
**dispirited** *adj.* scoraggiato, abbattuto; demoralizzato, depresso.
**displace** *tr.* spostare, rimuovere; soppiantare; sostituire. *~d person*, apolide *m., f.* **~ment** *n.* spostamento; sostituzione da altro; (naut.) dislocamento.
**display** *n.* mostra, esposizione; (pejor.) ostentazione, pompa; *to be fond of—*, aver piacere di mettersi in mostra; spettacolo; *fashion —*, sfilata della moda; *tr.* mostrare, mettere in mostra; esibire, esporre; ostentare; manifestare, rivelare.
**displeas-e** *tr.* dispiacere a, spiacere a; scontentare; seccare; *to be ~ed*, essere malcontento. **~ing** spiacevole; sgradevole, sgradito. **~ure** *n.* dispiacere *m.*; malcontento; *to incur someone's ~ure*, attirarsi l'ira di qualcuno.
**disport** *rfl.* spassarsi; sgambettare.
**disposable** *adj.* disponibile.
**disposal** *n.* disposizione; *to place oneself at someone's —*, mettersi a disposizione di qualcuno; sistemazione; *— of refuse*, eliminazione dei rifiuti; (comm.) vendita; cessione; *for —*, da vendere; (mil.) collocamento; *bomb — unit*, reparto addetto al disinnescamento delle bombe.
**dispose** *tr.* disporre, sistemare, mettere in ordine; *man proposes, God ~s*, l'uomo propone e Dio dispone; rendere propenso, persuadere; *to — of*, disfarsi di, sbarazzarsi di; vendere.
**disposed** *adj.* disposto; incline; intenzionato; *are you — to go ?*, ti senti di andare ?; *well —*, bene intenzionato.
**disposition** *n.* disposizione; ordine *m.*; predisposizione, tendenza; indole *f.*; temperamento.
**dispossess** *tr.* spossessare; spodestare; espropriare; spogliare. **~ion** *n.* esproprio, espropriazione; spogliazione.
**disproof** *n.* confutazione.
**disproportion** *n.* sproporzione. **~ate** *adj.* sproporzionato.
**disprove** *tr.* confutare; dimostrare la falsità di.
**disputable** *adj.* disputabile; discutibile.
**disputat-ion** *n.* disputa; discussione. **~ious** *adj.* cavilloso, contenzioso.
**dispute** *n.* disputa, vertenza, controversia; diverbio; lite *f.*; *beyond —*, fuori discussione; *tr.* contestare; contrastare; *intr.* disputare, discutere; litigare.
**disqualif-y** *tr.* incapacitare, inabilitare; (leg.) interdire; (sport) squalificare. **~ication** *n.* incapacità, inabilità; (leg.) interdizione; (sport) squalifica.
**disquiet** *n.* inquietudine; ansietà; *tr.* inquietare; turbare. **~ing** *adj.* inquietante; allarmante. **~ude** *n.* inquietudine *f.*
**disquisition** *n.* disquisizione; dissertazione.
**disregard** *n.* noncuranza; mancanza di riguardo; disprezzo; *— of the law*, inosservanza della legge; *tr.* trascurare; non badare a, non fare caso di; disconoscere. **~ful** *adj.* noncurante; poco riguardoso.
**disrepair** *n.* sfacelo; cattivo stato; rovina.
**disreputable** *adj.* malfamato; screditato; disonorevole; (fig.) logoro, sciupato.
**disreputable-looking** *adj.* di aspetto losco.
**disrepute** *n.* cattiva reputazione; discredito; disistima; *to fall into —*, acquistarsi una cattiva fama, cadere in discredito.
**disrespect** *n.* mancanza di rispetto; sgarbatezza, irreverenza. **~ful** *adj.* poco rispettoso, irreverente; sgarbato.
**disrobe** *tr.* svestire; *intr.* svestirsi.
**disrupt** *tr.* spezzare, rompere; (fig.) mettere in disordine, scompigliare. **~ion** *n.* rottura; scisma *m.*; disordine *m.*; scompiglio.
**dissatisfaction** *n.* insoddisfazione; malcontento.
**dissatisfy** *tr.* scontentare, non soddisfare.
**dissect** *tr.* dissezionare, sezionare; (fig.) analizzare. **~ion** *n.* dissezione; sezionamento; (fig.) analisi *f. indecl.*
**dissemble** *tr.*, *intr.* dissimulare; fingere. **~r** *n.* simulatore; ipocrita *m., f.*
**disseminat-e** *tr.* disseminare; (fig.) diffondere. **~ion** *n.* disseminazione; (fig.) divulgazione; diffusione.
**dissension** *n.* divergenza; dissenso; dissidio; *to sow —*, seminare dissidio.
**dissent** *n.* dissenso, dissidio; *intr.* dissentire. **~er** *n.* dissidente *m.,f.*; *pl.* (hist.) *the Dissenters*, i Dissidenti. **~ient** *adj.* dissidente.
**dissertation** *n.* dissertazione.
**disservice** *n.* cattivo servizio, danno.
**dissid-ence** *n.* dissidio; disaccordo. **~ent** *adj.*, *n.* dissidente *m., f.*
**dissimilar** *adj.* dissimile, diverso. **~ity** *n.* dissomiglianza, dissimilitudine *f.*
**dissimulat-e** *tr.* dissimulare, fingere. **~ion** *n.* dissimulazione, finzione.
**dissipat-ed** *adj.* dissoluto (also fig.). **~ion** *n.* dispersione; (fig.) dissipazione, dissolutezza.
**dissociat-e** *tr.* disassociare, separare; (psych.) sdoppiarsi. **~ion** *n.* dissociazione, separazione; (psych.) sdoppiamento.
**dissoluble** *adj.* dissolubile.
**dissolute** *adj.* dissoluto, licenzioso. **~ness** *n.* dissolutezza.
**dissolution** *n.* dissoluzione; liquefazione; (leg.) scioglimento; (fig.) morte *f.*
**dissolve** *tr.* sciogliere; dissolvere; *intr.* sciogliersi; *to — into thin air*, andare in fumo.
**disson-ance** *n.* dissonanza; discordanza. **~ant** *adj.* dissonante; discorde.
**dissu-ade** *tr.* dissuadere, distogliere. **~asion** *n.* dissuasione. **~asive** *adj.* dissuasivo.
**distaff** *n.* canocchia, rocca; *the — side*, il ramo femminile.
**distance** *n.* distanza; lontananza; *within striking —*, a portata di mano; *from a —*, da lontano; (fig.) riservatezza, riserbo; *to keep one's —*, mantenere le distanze; *tr.* distanziare.
**distant** *adj.* distante, lontano; discosto, remoto; *a — relation*, un parente lontano; *a — resemblance*, una vaga rassomiglianza; (fig.) riservato, freddo.
**distaste** *n.* avversione, antipatia. **~ful** *adj.* antipatico, sgradevole. **~fulness** *n.* sgradevolezza.
**distemper**[1] *n.* (paint.) tempera; intonaco; *tr.* (paint.) dipingere a tempera; intonacare.
**distemper**[2] *n.* (vet.) cimurro.
**distend** *tr.* distendere; dilatare;

gonfiare; *intr.* distendersi, dilatarsi; (fig.) allargarsi.
**distension** *n.* distensione, dilatazione; gonfiamento.
**distich** *n.* (prosod.) distico.
**distill** *tr.* distillare. **-ation** *n.* distillazione. **-er** *n.* distillatore. **-ery** *n.* distilleria.
**distinct** *adj.* differente, diverso; distinto, chiaro, nitido, netto. **-ion** *n.* distinzione; superiorità; *a person of -ion*, una persona distinta; diversità; differenza; *without -ion*, indistintamente; onorificenza. **-ive** *adj.* distintivo, caratteristico, proprio. **-ness** *n.* chiarezza, nitidezza.
**distinguish** *tr.* distinguere, differenziare; individuare, vedere, notare; *to — onself*, farsi notare. **-able** *adj.* distinguibile. **-ed** *adj.* distinto; insigne, illustre; eletto; *to look -ed*, avere un'aria di distinzione.
**distort** *tr.* storcere, distorcere; (fig.) alterare; *-ing mirror*, specchio deformante. **-ion** *n* distorsione; deformazione; alterazione. **-ionist** *n.* contorsionista *m.*, *f.*
**distract** *tr.* distarrre, distogliere; (fig.) turbare, far impazzire, far disperare. **-ion** *n.* distrazione; diversivo; divertimento, svago; (fig.) pazzia, follia; *to love to -ion*, amare alla follia.
**distrain** *tr.*, *intr.* (leg.) pignorare.
**distraught** *adj.* turbato.
**distress** *n.* angoscia; preoccupazione; *ship in —*, nave *f.* in pericolo; miseria; *tr.* affliggere; angustiare; preoccupare; disturbare; contristare; accorare. **-ed** *adj.* afflitto; dolente; angustiato; indigente; *-ed areas*, zone *f.pl.* di disoccupazione; *-ed gentlewoman*, signora decaduta. **-ful**, **-ing** *adj.* penoso; doloroso.
**distribut-e** *tr.* distribuire; dividere; ripartire. **-ion** *n.* distribuzione; ripartizione; divisione. **-ive** *adj.* distributivo. **-or** *n.* distributore.
**district** *n.* distretto; quartiere, rione *m.*; zona, regione; *the Lake District*, la zona dei laghi; *attrib.* distrettuale.
**distrust** *n.* diffidenza; sospetto; *tr.* diffidare di; sospettare; non avere fiducia in; *to — one's own eyes*, non credere ai propri occhi. **-ful** *adj.* diffidente; sospettoso.
**disturb** *tr.* disturbare, turbare; importunare; incomodare. **-ance** *n.* disturbo; disordine *m.*; tumulto; sommossa; (meteor.) perturbazione.
**disunion** *n.* disunione.
**disunite** *tr.* disunire; *intr.* disunirsi.
**disuse** *n.* disuso. **-d** *adj.* non più usato, fuori uso.
**disyllable** *n.* disillabo.
**ditch** *n.* fossa; fosso, fossato; trincea; (mil.) *anti-tank —*, fosso anticarro; *tr.* munire di fossi; prosciugare; (fam.) *to — a car*, finire con la macchina in un fosso; (slang) piantare in asso. **-er** *n.* sterratore, affossatore.
**ditch-water** *n.* acqua stagnante; (fam.) *as dull as —*, noioso da morire.
**dither** *n.* (fam.) eccitazione; *to be in a —*, essere eccitato; *intr.* vacillare, titubare.
**ditto** *adj.*, *n.* idem, lo stesso, detto; *to say — to everything*, dire sì a tutto.
**ditty** *n.* (mus.) canzoncino.
**diuretic** *adj.*, *n.* (med.) diuretico.
**diurnal** *adj.* diurno, quotidiano.
**divagat-e** *intr.* divagare; digredire. **-ion** *n.* divagazione; digressione.
**divan** *n.* divano; ottomana; *— bed*, divano-letto.
**divaricat-e** *intr.* divaricare; divergere. **-ion** *n.* divaricazione.
**dive** *n.* tuffo; tuffata; immersione; (fam.) taverna sotterranea; *intr.* tuffarsi; fare un tuffo; immergersi; *to — into one's pocket*, pescare nelle proprie tasche. **-r** *n.* tuffatore; (professional) palombaro; (orn.) tuffetto.
**diverg-e** *intr.* divergere. **-ence**, **-ency** *n.* divergenza. **-ent**, **-ing** *adj.* divergente.
**divers** *adj.*, *pl.* diversi; parecchi.
**diverse** *adj.* diverso, differente.
**diversify** *tr.* diversificare, differenziare.
**diversion** *n.* diversione; divertimento; passatempo.
**diversity** *n.* diversità; varietà.
**divert** *tr.* deviare, sviare, stornare; divertire. **-ing** *adj.* divertente.
**Dives** *pr.n.* (bibl.) il ricco epulone.
**divest** *tr.* spogliare, svestire; (fig.) privare.
**divid-e** *tr.* dividere; separare, spartire; *to — off*, separare; *to — out*, distribuire; *to — up*, separare in tante parti; *intr.* (math.) dividere, essere divisible; *n.* (geog.) spartiacque *m.*; displuvio. **-ed** *adj.* diviso; *-ed skirt*, gonna pantalone. **-end** *n.* (math.; finan.) dividendo; *interim -end*, dividendo provvisorio. **-ers** *n.pl.* compasso a punte fisse.
**divin-e** *adj.* divino; (fig.) mirabile; *n.* teologo, ecclesiastico; *tr.* indovinare, presagire; (fig.) intuire. **-ation** *n.* divinazione, profezia; (fig.) intuizione. **-er** *n.* indovino, mago; *water-diviner*, rabdomante *m.*, *f.*
**diving** *n.* il tuffarsi; immersione.
**diving-bell** *n.* campana subacquea. **-board** *n.* trampolino. **-helmet** *n.* casco da palombaro. **-suit** *n.* scafandro.
**divining** *n.* divinazione. **-rod** *n.* verga divinatoria.
**divinity** *n.* divinità; dio; teologia.
**divisib-le** *adj.* divisibile. **-ility** *n.* divisibilità.
**division** *n.* divisione; ripartizione, distribuzione; differenza; *— of opinion*, discordia; (Parliament) votazione. **-al** *adj.* divisionale; (mil.) di divisione.
**divisor** *n.* (math.) divisore.
**divorce** *n.* divorzio; (fig.) separazione; *tr.* divorziare; far divorzio da; *they are -d*, hanno divorziato; (fig.) separare. **-ment** *n.* divorzio.
**divulg-e** *tr.* divulgare; rivelare; diffondere, far conoscere. **-ation**, **-ement**, **-ence** *n.* divulgazione.
**dizz-y** *adj.* preso da vertigine, vertiginoso; *to feel —*, sentirsi girare la testa; *to make —*, far venire le vertigini. **-iness** *n.* vertigine *f.*; capogiro; stordimento.
**do**[1] *n.* (mus.) ut *m.*
**do**[2] *n.* (fam.) festa; trattenimento; (slang) *a fair —*, un buon affare; *that's not a fair —* non è giusto.
**do**[3] *aux. verb.* In interrogative and negative forms not translated in Italian; e.g. *— you speak German? No, I don't*, parlate il tedesco? No. In emphatic forms rendered by use of augmentatives; e.g. *I — believe it*, ci credo davvero, sì che ci credo, ci credo e come! Repetitive negative forms after questions (*don't you, doesn't he, didn't they*, etc.) usually omitted or rendered by 'vero' or 'non è vero'; e.g. *you play bridge, don't you?*, sai giocare al bridge, vero? **do-it-yourself** *adj.* di cosa fatta da dilettante.
**do**[4] *tr.* fare; *to — one's duty*, fare il proprio dovere; *what is he -ing?*, che cosa sta facendo?; *what does he —?*, che mestiere fa?; *what's that got to — with it?*, che c'entra?; *to — nothing*, non fare nulla; *nothing -ing!*, niente da fare!; *to — good*, fare del bene; *no sooner said than done*, detto fatto; *how — you —?*, come stai?; *that will —*, basta così; *will £5 —?*, basteranno cinque sterline?; *to — a room*, rassettare una stanza; *to — one's hair*, pettinarsi; *I've been done*, mi hanno ingannato; (cul.) cuocere; *well done*, ben cotto; *to — away with*, togliere di mezzo, abolire, (euphem.) uccidere; *to be done for*, essere rovinato; *to — someone in*, accoppare qualcuno; *to — out of*, togliere con inganno; *to — up*, fare un pacco di; *to — up one's clothes*, abbottonarsi; *to — up a house*, rimettere a nuovo una casa; (fig.) *to feel done up*, sentirsi sfinito; *to — without*, fare a meno di.

**docil-e** *adj.* docile; mansueto, ammansito. **-ity** *n.* docilità; mansuetudine *f.*
**dock**[1] *n.* (naut.) bacino; *the -s*, le banchine *f.pl.*, la zona portuale; *dry* —, bacino di carenaggio; *wet* —, darsena; (fam.) *to be in* —, essere in riparazione. *tr.* (naut.) far entrare in bacino; *intr.* entrare in bacino, attraccare.
**dock**[2] *n.* (in court) banco degli imputati, gabbia.
**dock**[3] *n.* mozzicone, troncone *m.*; sottocoda; *tr.* mozzare, troncare; (fig.) *to — someone of*, privare qualcuno di.
**dock**[4] *n.* (bot.) romice *m.*; lapazio; erba pazienza.
**dockage** *n.* (naut.) diritti *m.pl.* di banchina, diritti portuali.
**docker** *n.* stivatore, facchino del porto.
**docket** *n.* bolletta; etichetta; *tr.* munire di etichette, classificare; fare un sommario di.
**dock-land** *n.* zona del porto.
**dockyard** *n.* cantiere navale, arsenale *m.*; *naval* —, porto militare.
**doctor** *n.* dottore; *woman* —, dottoressa; medico; *to see a* —, consultare un medico; *to send for a* —, chiamare un medico; *ship's* —, medico di bordo; *-'s degree*, dottorato, (in Italy) laurea; *tr.* curare, medicare; (of male cat or dog) castrare; (fig.) adulterare, sofisticare, falsificare. **-ing** *n.* cura; (fam.) professione di medico; (fig.) adulterazione, falsificazione.
**doctrin-e** *n.* dottrina. **-aire** *adj.*, *n.* dottrinario. **-al** *adj.* dottrinale.
**document** *n.* documento; certificato; attestato; (leg.) atto; *tr.* documentare. **-ary** *adj.* documentario; *n.* (cinem.) documentario. **-ation** *n.* documentazione.
**dodder**[1] *n.* (bot.) cuscuta.
**dodder**[2] *intr.* barcollare, vacillare; tremare. **-er** *n.* (fam.) vecchio decrepito. **-ing** *adj.* senile.
**dodecasyllable** *n.* (prosod.) dodecasillabo.
**dodge** *n.* scarto; (fig.) stratagemma *m.*, sotterfugio, trucco; *tr.* eludere, schivare, scansare; *intr.* spostarsi, saltellare, scansarsi. **-r** *n.* (fam.) furbo; sornione *m.*; (naut.) riparo contro gli spruzzi.
**dodo** *n.* (orn.) dronte *m.*; (fam.) *as dead as the* —, vecchio come il cucco.
**doe** *n.* (deer) daina; (hare) lepre femmina; (rabbit) coniglia. **-skin** *n.* pelle *f.* di daina.
**doer** *n.* che fa, che agisce; fattore; autore.
**doff** *tr.* togliersi, cavare; disfarsi.
**dog** *n.* cane *m.*; *she* —, cagna *f.*; *sporting* —, cane da caccia; (fam.) *to lead a -'s life*, fare una vita da cani; *to die a -'s death*, morire come un cane; *to go to the -s*, andare in malora; *to throw discretion to the -s*, mettere da parte ogni discrezione; *to rain cats and -s*, piovere a catinelle; *a -'s chance*, pochissima probabilità; *a — in the manger*, uno che non vuol spartire con gli altri; (provb.) *every — has his day*, ognuno ha il suo raggio di sole; *let sleeping -s lie*, non disturbare il cane che dorme; (fam., fig.) individuo, *dirty* —, sporcaccione *m.*; *gay* —, bontempone *m.*, *lucky* —, uomo fortunato; *sly* —, furbacchione *m.*; *top* —, pezzo grosso, vincitore; *attrib.* — *Latin*, latino maccheronico; (astron.) *Dog Star*, Sirio; (mech.) gancio, rampone *m.*
**dog** *tr.* pedinare, spiare; *to — someone's footsteps*, pedinare qualcuno; *to be -ged by*, essere perseguitato da.
**dog-biscuit** *n.* biscotto per cani. **-cart** *n.* biroccino. **-catcher** *n.* accalappiacani *m. indecl.* **-collar** *n.* collare *m.* per cani; (fam., eccl.) collarino dei preti. **-days** *n.* giorni *m.pl.* della canicola.
**doge** *n.* (hist.) doge *m.*; *-'s wife*, dogaressa.
**dog-eared** *adj.* con orecchie alle pagine. **-fancier** *n.* venditore di cani; (dog-lover) cinofilo.
**dogfight** *n.* combattimento di cani; (mil. slang) mischia generale; (aeron.) combattimento aereo.
**dogfish** *n.* (ichth.) alopia.
**dogged** *adj.* accanito; ostinato, tenace; — *does it*, chi la dura la vince. **-ness** *n.* accanimento; ostinazione, tenacia.
**doggerel** *n.* poesia burlesca; filastrocca; brutti versi *m.pl.*
**doggie** *n.* (fam.) canino, cagnolino.
**doggo** *adv.* (fam.) *to lie* —, fare il morto.
**doggy** *adj.* da cane, cagnesco.
**dog-house** *n.* (fam.) *to be in the* —, essere in cattivo odore presso la moglie.
**dog-kennel** *n.* canile *m.* **-lead** *n.* guinzaglio. **-like** *adj.*, *adv.* da cane, come un cane. **-lover** *n.* cinofilo; chi ama i cani.
**dogma** *n.* dogma, domma *m.* **-tic** *adj.* dogmatico. **-tism** *n.* dogmatismo. **-tist** *n.* dogmatista, dommatista *m.*, *f.* **-tize** *intr.* dogmatizzare.
**do-gooder** *n.* (iron.) benefattore.
**dog-racing** *n.* corse *f.pl.* di levrieri; — *track*, cinodromo. **-rose** *n.* (bot.) rosa canina. **-show** *n.* mostra cinofila. **-tired** *adj.* stanco morto. **-tooth** *n.* dente canino.
**doily** *n.* tovagliolino; sottocoppa.
**doing** *n.* il fare; opera, azione; *that's his* —, è colpa sua; *it takes some* —, ce ne vuole per farlo; avvenimento; vicenda; *great -s*, avvenimenti importanti; *tell me about your -s*, dimmi che cosa hai fatto; *pl.* (fam.) *the -s*, il necessario, gli arnesi.
**doldrums** *n.* (naut.) zona delle calme equatoriali; (fig.) *to be in the* —, essere d'umore nero.
**dole** *n.* elemosina, carità; sussidio di disoccupazione, *to be on the* —, essere disoccupato (e ricevere il sussidio); *tr. to — out*, distribuire in piccole quantità; ripartire.
**doleful** *adj.* doloroso, triste, lugubre. **-ness** *n.* tristezza, melanconia.
**doll** *n.* bambola; pupa; *rag* —, bamboccio; *-'s house*, casa di bambola; *tr.* (fam.) *to — up*, agghindare; *rfl.* agghindarsi.
**dollar** *n.* dollaro.
**dolly** *n.* (fam.) bambola. **-bird** *n.* (fam.) ragazza leggiera.
**Dolomite** (miner.) dolomite *f.*; (geog.) *the Dolomites* le Dolomiti.
**dolorous** *adj.* doloroso.
**dolour** *n.* dolore *m.*
**dolphin** *n.* (zool.) delfino; (ichth.) corifena.
**dolt** *n.* allocco; stupido. **-ish** *adj.* stupido, ottuso, sciocco.
**domain** *n.* demanio; proprietà terriera; (fig.) dominio.
**dome** *n.* (archit.) cupola; (fig.) duomo. **-d** *adj.* a cupola.
**Domesday** *n.* giorno del giudizio; — *Book*, il Libro del Catasto d'Inghilterra (1086).
**domestic** *adj.* domestico, casalingo; — *animal*, animale domestico; — *life*, vita di famiglia; — *servant*, domestico *m.*, domestica *f.*; — *help*, donna a ore; (fig.) interno; nazionale.
**domesticat-e** *tr.* addomesticare; abituare alla vita casalinga. **-ion** *n.* addomesticamento; attaccamento alla vita familiare.
**domesticity** *n.* domesticità; amore per il focolare domestico.
**domicile** *n.* domicilio; *tr.* domiciliare; *intr.* stabilirsi, risiedere.
**domin-ance** *n.* predominio; dominazione; ascendente *m.* **-ant** *adj.* dominante; prevalente.
**dominat-e** *tr.*, *intr.* dominare, prevalere, reggere; (fig.) sovrastare. **-ion** *n.* dominazione; dominio; ascendente *m.*
**domineer** *intr.* spadroneggiare, signoreggiare, dominare. **-ing** *adj.* prepotente; imperioso; tirannico. **-ingly** *adv.* imperiosamente; da tiranno.
**Dominican** *adj.*, *n.* domenicano.
**dominion** *n.* dominio; impero; (fig.) autorità; ascendente *m.*
**domino** *n.* domino.
**don**[1] *n.* (title) don *m.*; *a — Juan*, un Don Giovanni; (schol.) docente universitario.

**don**[2] *tr.* indossare, vestire.

**donat-e** *tr.* donare, elargire. **-ion** *n.* dono; donazione, elargizione.

**done** *part.* of **do**, *q.v.*; *well —!*, bravo!; *— for*, spacciato; *newly — up*, rimesso a nuovo; *easier said than —*, fra il dire e il fare c'è di mezzo il mare; *no sooner said than —*, detto fatto.

**donkey** *n.* asino, asinello, ciuco, somaro; (fig.) imbecille *m.*

**donkey-engine** *n.* motore ausiliario.

**donnish** *adj.* pedantesco, professorale.

**donor** *n.* donatore, donatrice.

**doodle** *intr.* (fam.) scarabocchiare, fare ghirigori.

**doom** *n.* condanna; sorte *f.*; destino; *to meet one's —*, trovare la morte; *the day of —*, il giorno del giudizio universale; *until the crack of —*, fino al giudizio universale; *tr.* condannare; destinare. **-ed** *adj.* condannato; votato alla distruzione. **-watch** *n.* la sentinella del destino.

**doomsday** *n.* giudizio universale, finimondo; *to put off till —*, rimandare alle calende greche.

**door** *n.* porta; uscio; ingresso; *out of -s*, all'aria aperta; *within -s*, in casa; *to show to the —*, accompagnare alla porta; *to show the — to*, mettere alla porta; *next —*, la casa vicina; *front —*, porta principale; *back —*, porta posteriore; *revolving —*, porta girevole; *sliding —*, porta scorrevole; (of car, train) sportello; portiera.

**doorbell** *n.* campanello.

**door-frame** *n.* telaio della porta.

**door-keeper** *n.* portinaio, portiere *m.* **-knocker** *n.* battaglio, battiporta *m.* **-man** *n.* portiere. **-mat** *n.* stuoia; zerbino. **-nail** *n.* (fam.) *as dead as a -nail*, morto stecchito. **-post** *n.* stipite *m.* **-step** *n.* gradino della porta; (fig.) soglia. **-way** *n.* entrata; portone *m.*

**dope** *n.* narcotico, stupefacente *m.*; (aeron.) vernice *f.*; (slang) notizie *f.pl.* segrete; *tr.* somministrare un narcotico a, narcotizzare.

**dope-fiend** *n.* morfinomane *m.*, *f.*

**doping** *n.* somministrazione di stupefacenti.

**dopy** *adj.* (slang) inebetito.

**doric** *adj.*, *n.* (archit.; ling.) dorico.

**dormant** *adj.* addormentato, assopito, latente; inattivo, caduto in disuso.

**dormer(-window)** *n.* abbaino.

**dormitory** *n.* dormitorio; *— town*, sobborgo.

**dormouse** *n.* (zool.) ghiro.

**dorsal** *adj.* dorsale.

**dory** *n.* (ichth.) pesce *m.* San Pietro.

**dosage** *n.* dosatura; dosaggio.

**dose** *n.* dose *f.*; (fig.) *to strengthen the —*, rincarare la dose; *to give someone a — of his own medicine*, far assaggiare a qualcuno il propro rimedio; *tr.* dosare, somministrare una dose a; (fig.) sofisticare, adulterare.

**doss** *intr.* (fam.) *to — down*, coricarsi.

**doss-house** *n.* dormitorio pubblico.

**dossier** *n.* incartamento.

**dot** *n.* punto, puntino; (of a child) *a little —*, un piccino; *-s and dashes*, punti e linee; (fam.) *on the —*, puntualmente, in orario; *tr.* punteggiare; macchiare; *to — one's i's*, mettere i punti sugli i; *to sign on the -ted line*, firmare sulla riga punteggiata, (fig.) accettare senza discutere.

**dot-age** *n.* rimbambimento; senilità. **-ard** *n.* vecchio rimbambito.

**dote** *intr.* essere rimbambito; *to — on*, amare follemente, essere infatuato di.

**dotty** *adj.* punteggiato, macchiato; (slang) tocco.

**double** *adj.* doppio, duplice; *— chin*, doppio mento, pappagorgia; *— bed*, letto matrimoniale; *— room*, camera a due letti; *— meaning*, doppio senso; *adv.* doppiamente, due volte tanto; *to see —*, vedere doppio;

**double** *n.* doppio; (person) sosia *m.*; (cinem.) controfigura *m.*, *f.*; *— or quits*, lascia o raddoppia; (mil.) *at the —*, a passo di corsa; (sport) *men's —*, doppio maschile; *women's —*, doppio femminile; *mixed —*, doppio misto; (betting) accoppiata.

**double** *tr.* raddoppiare, moltiplicare per due; *to — up*, piegare in due; (naut.; cinem.) doppiare; *intr.* (mil.) marciare a passo di corsa; (theatr.) sostenere due ruoli; (fig.) cambiare direzione, piegarsi; *to — back*, ritornare sui propri passi; *to — up in pain*, contorcersi dal dolore.

**double-barrelled** *adj.* (of gun) a doppia canna; (of surname) doppio. **-bass** *n.* (mus.) contrabbasso. **-bedded** *adj.* a due letti. **-breasted** *adj.* a doppio petto. **-cross** *n.* doppio giuoco; *tr.* fare il doppio giuoco a. **-dealing** *n.* duplicità. **-decker** *n.* bus a due piani. **-dyed** *adj.* tinto due volte; (fam.) matricolato. **-edged** *adj.* a doppio taglio. **-entry** (bookkeeping) *n.* partita doppia. **-faced** *adj.* a due facce; (fig.) falso, ipocrita. **-lock** *tr.* chiudere a doppia mandata. **-quick** *adj.* *in -quick time*, prestissimo, a passo di corsa.

**doublet** *n.* (cost.) farsetto; giubba; (fig.) doppione *m.*

**doubly** *adv.* doppiamente, due volte.

**doubt** *n.* dubbio; incertezza; *to be in —*, dubitare; essere incerto; *no —*, non c'è dubbio; *beyond all —*, indubbiamente; *to raise -s*, sollevare dei dubbi; *to throw — on*, mettere in forse; *tr.* mettere in dubbio, dubitare di; *I — it*, ne dubito; *to — one's eyes*, non credere ai propri occhi; *intr.* stare in dubbio; essere incerto.

**doubtful** *adj.* dubbio; incerto; *in — taste*, di dubbio gusto; irresoluto, titubante; *to be — what to do*, essere in dubbio sul da farsi; *of — reputation*, ambiguo. **-ness** *n.* dubbiosità; incertezza; irresolutezza.

**doubtless** *adj.* indubbio, certo; *adv.* indubbiamente, senza dubbio.

**douche** *n.* doccia; (fig.) *a cold —*, una doccia fredda; (med.) irrigazione.

**dough** *n.* pasta di pane; (slang) quattrini *m.pl.*

**dought-y** *adj.* prode; valoroso. **-iness** *n.* prodezza; valore *m.*

**dour** *adj.* duro; severo, austero. **-ness** *n.* durezza; severità; austerità.

**dous-e** *tr.* gettare acqua su; immergere; *to — the light*, spegnere la luce. **-ing** *n.* doccia.

**dove** *n.* colomba; tortora; (fam.) *my —*, tesoro mio, amor mio; *to coo like a —*, tubare.

**dove-coloured** *adj.* di color tortora.

**dovecot(e)** *n.* colombaia, piccionaia.

**dovetail** *tr.* incastrare a coda di rondine; (fig.) collegare; *intr.* incastrarsi; (fig.) collegarsi.

**dowager** *n.* vedova (di principe, nobile); *queen —*, regina madre; (fam.) vecchia signora.

**dowdy** *adj.* malvestito, sciatto.

**dowel** *n.* (mech.) cavicchio.

**dower** *n.* dote *f.*; doario; *tr.* dotare.

**down**[1] *adv.* giù, abbasso, di sotto, a terra, per terra; *cash —*, pronto cassa; (fam.) *— and out*, al verde, ridotto alla miseria; *— in the mouth*, giù di morale; *— at heel*, scalcagnato; (to a dog) *—!*, cuccia!; *— under*, agli antipodi, in Australia; *— with...!*, abbasso...!; *adj.* discendente; (rlwy.) *— train*, treno proveniente da Londra; (fam.) abbattuto, depresso; *n.* basso; *ups and -s*, alti e bassi; (slang) *to have a — on someone*, avercela con qualcuno; *tr.* mettere giù, abbattere, buttare a terra; *to — tools*, abbandonare il lavoro; (slang) *to — a drink*, tracannare un bicchiere.

**down**[2] *n.* duna, collina erbosa.

**down**[3] *n.* lanugine *f.*; peluria; piumino.
**down-cast** *adj.* scoraggiato, abbattuto. **-fall** *n.* caduta, crollo; rovescio; rovina. **-grade** *tr.* retrocedere, abbassare di grado. **-hearted** *adj.* scoraggiato, abbattuto, accasciato. **-hill** *adj.* discendente; *adv.* in pendìo, in discesa; (fig.) *to go -hill*, andare declinando, andare a rotoli; (sport) *-hill race*, discesa libera. **-most** *adj.* il più basso. **-pour** *n.* acquazzone *m.*; pioggia dirotta. **-right** *adj.* vero; schietto, franco; *adv.* nettamente, categoricamente, addirittura. **-rightness** *n.* franchezza; sincerità. **-stairs** *adj.* di sotto, al piano inferiore; *adv.* giù, abbasso, al pianterreno; *to go -stairs*, scendere le scale. **-stream** *adv.* a valle. **-trodden** *adj.* calpestato, oppresso.
**downward** *adj.* discendente.
**downward(s)** *adv.* verso il basso, in giù.
**dowry** *n.* dote *f.*
**dowser** *n.* rabdomante *m.*, *f.*; (cinem.) schermo paraluce.
**doxology** *n.* (liturg.) dossologia.
**doyen** *n.* decano.
**doz-e** *n.* sonnellino, pisolino; *intr.* sonnecchiare, dormicchiare; *to — off*, assopirsi. **-y** *adj.* sonnolento; neghittoso.
**dozen** *n.* dozzina; (fig.) diecina; *baker's —*, dozzina abbondante; (fam.) *to talk nineteen to the —*, chiacchierare a non finire. **-th** *adj.* dodicesimo; (fam.) ennesimo.
**drab** *adj.* squallido, scialbo; *n.* sgualdrina.
**drachma, drachm** *n.* dramma.
**draft** *n.* (comm.) tratta; cambiale *m.*; effetto; *banker's —*, assegno circolare; brutta copia, prima stesura; abbozzo; (leg.) progetto, schema *m.*; (mil.) distaccamento; *tr.* redigere, stendere; (mil.) distaccare.
**drag** *n.* trazione; traino; (agric.) erpice *m.*; (hunt.) odore *m.* di selvaggina sparso sul terreno; (fishing) rete *f.* a strascico; (mech.) resistenza; (fig.) peso, impedimento; (theatr.; slang) *in —*, (uomo) vestito da donna.
**drag** *tr.* trascinare; tirare con sforzo; strappare; *to — one's feet*, strascicare i piedi; *to — a pond*, dragare uno stagno; *to — the truth out of someone*, strappare la verità a qualcuno; *to — up an old story*, tirar fuori una vecchia storia; *intr.* trascinarsi; *to — on*, scorrere lentamente.
**drag-anchor** *n.* (naut.) ancora flottante. **-net** *n.* giacchio; rete *f.* a strascico; (fig.) rastrellamento.
**draggle** *tr.* strascicare nel fango; inzaccherare.
**dragon** *n.* drago; (astron.) Dragone *m.*; (fig.) *female —* dragonessa, donna di rigidi principi.
**dragon-fly** *n.* (ent.) libellula.
**dragoon** *n.* (mil.) dragone *m.*; *tr.* soggiogare con la forza militare; (fig.) intimidire, costringere.
**drain** *n.* canale *m.* di scolo; fogna; *pl. the -s*, la fognatura; (fig.) *to throw down the —*, sprecare; (med.) tubo di drenaggio; (mech.) tubo di scarico; (fig.) fuga, perdita; *the brain —*, la fuga dei cervelli; *— on resources*, perdita di risorse; (fam.) goccia.
**drain** *tr.* far scolare; prosciugare; (med.) drenare; (fig.) esaurire; bere fino all'ultimo; *intr.* scolare; defluire.
**drainage** *n.* scolo, scarico; fognatura; (med.) drenaggio.
**drain-pipe** *n.* tubo di scarico, canale *m.* di scolo.
**drake** *n.* maschio dell'anitra.
**dram** *n.* dramma *m.* (=1.772 grammi); (fam., Scot.) *a wee —*, una gocciolina, un dito.
**drama** *n.* dramma *m.*; the —, il teatro. **-tic** *adj.* drammatico; teatrale; (fig.) impressionante. **-tics** *n.* drammatica; teatro; *amateur -tics*, produzioni *f.pl.* drammatiche di dilettanti; *amateur -tics society*, società filodrammatica. **-tist** *n.* drammaturgo.
**dramatiz-e** *tr.* drammatizzare, ridurre per il teatro; (fig.) esagerare. **-ation** *n.* riduzione per il teatro; (fig.) esagerazione.
**drape** *tr.* drappeggiare, parare con drappi; *-d in mourning*, parato a lutto.
**draper** *n.* negoziante *m.* di tessuti, merciaio.
**drapery** *n.* tessuti *m.pl.*; stoffe *f.pl.* (art) panni *m.pl.*; panneggio.
**drastic** *adj.* drastico; energico; *— alteration*, cambiamento fondamentale.
**draught** *n.* tiro; trazione; traino; *— animal*, bestia da tiro; (of liquid) dose *f.*; sorso; *— beer*, birra alla spina; *to drink at one —*, bere in un solo sorso; corrente *f.* d'aria; (naut.) pescaggio, profondità di immersione; (of fishes) retata.
**draughtboard** *n.* scacchiera.
**draughtiness** *n.* l'essere esposto alle correnti d'aria.
**draughts** *n.* giuoco della dama.
**draught-screen** *n.* paravento.
**draughtsman** *n.* disegnatore; (in game of draughts) pedina. **-ship** *n.* arte *f.* del disegno.
**draughty** *adj.* esposto a correnti d'aria.
**draw** *n.* tiro; *to be quick on the —*, essere veloce nell'estrarre (un'arma); (lottery) estrazione; sorteggio; (sport) partita nulla, punteggio pari; (fig.) attrazione.
**draw** *tr.* tirare; trarre, trascinare; attrarre, attirare; estrarre, cavare, strappare, estorcere; *to — money*, riscuotere del denaro; *to — a cheque*, emettere un assegno; (art) disegnare, tracciare; (metall.) trafilare; *to — the blinds*, tirare le tende; *to — breath*, respirare; *to — lots*, tirare a sorte; *to — a prize*, vincere un premio; (sport) *to — a game*, far pari, pareggiare; (mil.) *to — rations*, ritirare le razioni; (naut.) pescare; (fig.) *to — a blank*, restare con un pugno di mosche; *to — it mild*, non esagerare; *to — the long bow*, esagerare, dirle grosse; *to — a distinction*, fare una distinzione; *to — down*, abbassare, (fig.) atterrarsi; *to — forth*, tirar fuori; *to — on*, calzare, infilarsi, (finan.) attingere a; *to — out*, estrarre, (fig.) far parlare; *to — together*, riunire; *to — up*, tirar su, elaborare, redigere; *intr.* *to — aside*, scostarsi; *to — away*, allontanarsi; *to — back*, tirarsi indietro; *to — in* (of days) accorciarsi; *to — on*, avanzare; *to — out*, prolungarsi; *to — up*, fermarsi.
**drawback** *n.* inconveniente *m.*; svantaggio, difetto, ostacolo.
**drawbridge** *n.* ponte levatoio.
**drawee** *n.* (comm.) trattario.
**drawer**[1] *n.* chi tira, chi attinge; (art) disegnatore.
**drawer**[2] *n.* cassetto; tiretto; *chest of -s*, cassettone, comò *m.*; (cost.) *-s*, mutandine *f.pl.*
**drawing** *n.* il tirare, tiraggio; estrazione; (art) disegno; (comm.) prelevamento; (metall.) trafilatura.
**drawing-board** *n.* tavola per disegno. **-master** *n.* professore di disegno. **-paper** *n.* carta da disegno. **-pin** *n.* puntina da disegno. **-room** *n.* salotto.
**drawl** *n.* pronuncia lenta e strascicante; voce affettata; *tr.* pronunciare con voce strascicata ed affettata; *intr.* strascicare le parole.
**drawn** *adj.* tratto, tirato; indeciso; disegnato.
**dray** *n.* carro pesante. **-man** *n.* carrettiere *m.*
**dread** *adj.* spaventoso; augusto, venerabile; *n.* timore *m.*; paura; terrore *m.*; *holy —*, sacro terrore; *to be in — of*, temere; (fam.) fobia; *tr.* temere, avere paura di. **-ful** *adj.* terribile; spaventevole; formidabile. **-fulness** *n.* spaventosità.
**dream** *n.* sogno; *to have a —*, sognare; (fig.) visione; fantasmagoria; *tr.* *to — about*, sognare; (fig.) immaginare, vagheggiare; (fam.) *I wouldn't — of doing it*, non lo farei nemmeno

per sogno. **-er** *n.* sognatore; (fig.) visionario; *intr.* fare un sogno; (fig.) vaneggiare. **-ily** *adv.* vagamente; come in sogno. **-iness** *n.* stato di sogno; tendenza a fantasticare. **-land** *n.* terra dei sogni. **-less** *adj.* senza sogni; *-less sleep*, sonno profondo. **-y** *adv.* sognante; languido; (fig.) vago.

**drear, drear-y** *adj.* triste, tetro, cupo; (fig.) monotono, noioso. **-iness** *n.* desolazione; tristezza; monotonia.

**dredg-e** *n.* draga; *tr.* dragare. **-er** *n.* draga. **-ing** *n.* dragaggio.

**dregs** *n.* feccia; sedimento; (fig.) *the — of society*, i bassifondi della società.

**drench** *tr.* bagnare, inzuppare; *-ed to the skin*, inzuppato fino alle ossa; *-ed with blood*, imbrattato di sangue. **-ing** *n.* bagnatura.

**Dresden** *pr.n.* (geog.) Dresda.

**dress** *n.* abbigliamento; veste *f.*; (mil.) tenuta, divisa; abito; vestito; *morning —*, abito da mattina; (men's) finanziera; 'tight' *m. indecl.*; *evening —*, abito da sera; *full evening —*, abito da cerimonia, (men's) marsina; frac *m. indecl.*; (fig.) forma.

**dress** *tr.* vestire, abbigliare; decorare; *to — one's hair*, pettinarsi; *to — a shop-window*, allestire una vetrina; (naut.) *to — a ship overall*, pavesare una nave; (med.) medicare, bendare; (cul.) guarnire, condire; (agric.) concimare; (industr.) rifinire, dare l'appretto a; (tan.) conciare; (fam.) *to — someone down*, dare una lavata di capo a qualcuno; *rfl.*, *intr.* abbigliarsi, vestirsi; *to — for dinner*, cambiarsi; (fam.) *to — up*, mettersi in ghingheri; travestirsi.

**dressage** *n.* (equit.) dressage *m.*, addestramento.

**dress-circle** *n.* (theatr.) prima galleria. **-coat** *n.* marsina; frac *m.* **-designer** *n.* couturier *m.*; direttore di una casa di moda; (theatr.) costumista *m.*, *f.*

**dresser**[1] *n.* (med.) assistente *m.*, *f.*; (theatr.) vestiarista *m.*, *f.*; (industr.) conciatore.

**dresser**[2] *n.* (furniture) credenza, dispensa.

**dressiness** *n.* ricercatezza nel vestirsi; eleganza esagerata.

**dressing** *n.* il vestirsi; allestimento; (med.) medicazione, benda; (cul.) condimento; (agric.) concime *m.*; (industr.) appretto, rifinitura; (tan.) concia.

**dressing-case** *n.* astuccio da toletta. **-down** *n.* (fam.) sgridata, lavatura di capo. **-gown** *n.* vestaglia. **-room** *n.* camera da toletta; (theatr.) camerino; (sport) spogliatoio. **-table** *n.* tavola da toletta.

**dressmak-er** *n.* sarta da donna. **-ing** *n.* sartoria; confezioni *f.pl.* per donna.

**dress-preserver, dress-shield** *n.* sottoascella. **-rehearsal** *n.* (theatr.) prova generale, prova in costume. **-shirt** *n.* camicia da sera, sparato. **-shoes** *n. pl.* scarpe *f.pl.* da ballo. **-suit** *n.* abito da sera, da cerimonia.

**dressy** *adj.* troppo elegante nell'abbigliamento.

**dribble** *n.* gocciolamento, sbavamento *m.*; (sport) palleggio; *intr.* gocciolare, sbavare; (sport) palleggiare.

**driblet** *n.* gocciolina, piccolissima quantità.

**dried** *p.def.*, *part.* of **dry**, *q.v.*; *adj.* secco, essiccato, asciutto.

**drift** *n.* deriva; l'andare alla deriva; flusso, corrente *f.* (also fig.); spinta della corrente; (of tide, *etc.*) direzione; (of snow) cumulo; (fig.) portata, piega; *policy of —*, politica del lasciar fare.

**drift** *intr.* andare alla deriva; essere trasportato dalla corrente (also fig.); (of snow) ammucchiarsi; (fig.) *to — apart*, perdersi a poco a poco di vista, allontanarsi spiritualmente l'uno dall'altro; *to let oneself —*, lasciarsi andare.

**drifter** *n.* (naut.) peschereccio con tramaglio; (fig.) fannullone *m.*

**driftwood** *n.* pezzi *m.pl.* di legno galleggianti.

**drill**[1] *n.* trivella, sonda; (dentist's) trapano; *tr.* trapanare, sondare, perforare; *to — a hole*, fare un buco.

**drill**[2] *n.* (agric.) solco; (machine) seminatrice; *tr.* (agric.) seminare a solchi.

**drill**[3] *n.* (text.) traliccio di stoffa.

**drill**[4] *n.* (mil., etc.) esercitazioni *f.pl.*, addestramenti *m.pl.*; (fig.) esercizio; *tr.* (mil., etc.) esercitare; addestrare; *intr.* far esercitazioni.

**drill**[5] *n.* (zool.) babbuino dell'Africa dell'ovest, più piccolo del mandrello.

**drill-ground** *n.* (mil.) piazza d'armi. **-sergeant** *n.* (mil.) sergente *m.* istruttore.

**drink** *n.* bevanda, bibita; bevuta, sorsata; *food and —*, il bere e il mangiare; *soft —*, bibita analcoolica; *strong —*, bevanda alcoolica; *would you like a —?*, vuol bere qualcosa?; *to stand someone a —*, pagare da bere a qualcuno; (fam.) alcoolismo; *to take to —*, darsi al bere; (naut. slang) il mare.

**drink** *tr.* bere; *what will you —?*, che cosa bevi?; *fit to —*, bevibile, (of water) potabile; (fig.) *to — in*, assorbare, ascoltare con piacere; *intr.* bere; (pejor.) ubriacarsi, essere dedito al bere; *to — like a fish*, bere come una spugna; *to — oneself to death*, rovinarsi la salute a forza di bere.

**drink-able** *adj.* bevibile; (of water) potabile; *n.pl.* *-s*, bevande *f.pl.* **-er** *n.* bevitore. **-ing** *n.* il bere; (pejor.) alcoolismo; ubriachezza.

**drinking-bout** *n.* bevuta. **-fountain** *n.* fontanella. **-song** *n.* canzone bacchica. **-trough** *n.* abbeveratoio. **-water** *n.* acqua potabile.

**drink-money** *n.* mancia.

**drip**[1] *n.* gocciolamento; stillicidio; (archit.) gocciolatoio; *tr.* grondare; *intr.* gocciolare, stillare.

**dripping** *adj.* gocciolante, grondante; *to be — wet*, essere inzuppato; *n.* gocciolio; stillicidio; (cul.) sugo d'arrosto.

**dripstone** *n.* (archit.) gocciolatoio di pietra; grondaia.

**drive** *n.* passeggiata; giro; *to go for a —*, fare una gita in macchina; *—(way)*, viale *m.*; (sport) colpo forte; (mech.) propulsione; trasmissione; (motor.) guida; (fig.) energia; *a — to raise funds*, una campagna per raccogliere fondi; *a whist —*, una partita di whist.

**drive** *tr.* condurre; (motor.) guidare; (mech.) azionare; (sport) colpire con energia; (fig.) spingere, forzare; *to — a bargain*, concludere un buon affare; (fam.) *what is he driving at?*, che cosa intende?; *to — away*, scacciare; *to — in*, conficcare; *to — under*, reprimere; *intr.* (motor.) *does he know how to —?*, sa guidare?; *shall we — or walk?*, andiamo in macchina oppure a piedi?; (of rain) battere; *to — away*, andare via in macchina; *to — in*, entrare con un veicolo.

**drivel** *n.* bava; (fig.) *to talk —*, dire sciocchezze *f.pl.*; *intr.* sbavare; (fig.) dire sciocchezze; *drivelling*, imbecille.

**driven** *part.* of **drive**, *q.v.*; *adj.* spinto; (mech.) azionato, comandato.

**driver** *n.* (motor.) conducente, guidatore; autista *m.*; *-'s licence*, patente *f.* di guida; (rlwy.) macchinista *m.*; (of horse vehicle) cocchiere *m.*; carettiere *m.*; (golf) mazza.

**driving** *adj.* (of rain, *etc.*) che sbatte, sferzante; (mech.) che fa funzionare, di comando; *— force*, forza motrice; *n.* (motor.) guida; *— licence*, patente *f.* di guida, *— school*, scuola di guida; *— test*, esame *m.* per ottenere la patente di guida.

**driving-belt** *n.* (mech.) cinghia

motrice. **-mirror** *n.* (motor.) specchietto retrovisivo. **-shaft** *n.* albero motore. **-wheel** *n.* (mech.) ruota motrice; (motor.) volante *m.*

**drizzl-e** *n.* pioggerella; pioggia fine; *intr.* piovigginare. **-ing** *adj.* piovigginoso.

**droll** *adj.* buffo, comico, ameno. **-ery** *n.* buffoneria; facezia.

**dromedary** *n.* (zool.) dromedario.

**dron-e** *n.* (ent.) fuco, pecchione *m.*; (fam.) fannullone *m.*; (sound) ronzìo; (mus.) bordone *m.*; *intr.* ronzare; (fig.) salmodiare; biascicare. **-ing** *adj.* ronzante, monotono; *n.* ronzìo.

**droop** *n.* posizione abbassata; (fig.) accasciamento; *tr.* abbassare; *intr.* abbassarsi; (of flowers) languire, appassire. **-ing** *adj.* pendente, piegato in giù; (fig.) languente, accasciato.

**drop** *n.* goccia; *to the last —*, fino all'ultima goccia; sorso; *a little — of wine*, un dito di vino; *to take a —*, bere un bicchierino; (sweet) caramella; caduta; discesa; (of prices) abbassamento, diminuzione, calo; (aeron.) *parachute —*, lancio col paracadute.

**drop** *tr.* lasciar cadere; *to — a tear*, versare una lacrima; *to — a hint*, fare un suggerimento; *to — someone a line*, scrivere due righe a qualcuno; *to — one's voice*, abbassare la voce; *to — one's aitches*, non pronunciare l'acca; *to — a parcel at someone's house*, consegnare un pacco a casa di qualcuno; *to — someone* (from a car), fare scendere qualcuno; *to — an acquaintance*, togliere il saluto a qualcuno; (to a dog) *— it !*, lascia!; (fam.) *to — a brick*, fare una gaffe; (aeron.) *to — bombs*, sganciare delle bombe; (naut.) *to — anchor*, gettare l'ancora; *intr.* cadere, cascare, lasciarsi cadere; *to — into a chair*, abbandonarsi in una poltrona; *to be ready to —*, cascare della stanchezza; *to — asleep*, addormentarsi; (of wind, temperature) cadere, diminuire; (of prices) abbassarsi, calare; *to — behind*, rimanere indietro; *to — in*, capitare per una breve visita; *to — out*, ritirarsi.

**drop-bottle** *n.* (med.) contagocce *m. indecl.* **-curtain, -scene** *n.* (theatr.) sipario.

**droplet** *n.* gocciolina.

**dropper** *n.* contagocce *m. indecl.*

**dropping-off** *n.* diminuzione.

**droppings** *n. pl.* sterco, escremento.

**drops-y** *n.* (med.) idropisia. **-ical, -ied** *adj.* (med.) idropico.

**dross** *n.* scoria; (fig.) scarto.

**drought** *n.* siccità.

**drove**[1] *n.* branco, gregge *m.*, mandria; (fig.) turba, folla.

**drove**[2] *p. def.* of **drive**, *q.v.*

**drover** *n.* boaro, mandriano.

**drown** *tr.* annegare, affogare; *to be -ed*, annegare; (fam.) *to — one's sorrow in drink*, annegare il dolore nel vino; (fig.) sommergere, bagnare; (of sound) coprire, smorzare; *intr.* annegare, annegarsi, affogare. **-ed** *adj.* *a -ed man*, un annegato; (fam.) *to look like a -ed rat*, sembrare un pulcino bagnato; (of sound) smorzato. **-ing** *adj.* che sta per annegare; (provb.) *a -ing man will clutch at a straw*, un annegato si aggrappa ai fuscelli; *n.* annegamento, affogamento.

**drowse** *tr.* *to — the time away*, passare il tempo a sonnecchiare; *intr.* sonnecchiare, assopirsi, dormicchiare.

**drows-y** *adj.* sonnolento, sonnacchioso, assopito. **-iness** *n.* sonnolenza; assopimento; dormiveglia *m.*

**drub** *tr.* bastonare, picchiare; *to — something into someone's head*, ficcare qualcosa nella testa di qualcuno. **-bing** *n.* bastonatura.

**drudg-e** *n.* chi sfacchina; (fig.) schiavo; donna di servizio sfruttata dai padroni; *intr.* lavorare come un negro, sfacchinare; tirare la carretta. **-ery** *n.* lavoro faticoso; sfacchinata.

**drug** *n.* farmaco; medicinale *m.*; droga; narcotico, stupefacente *m.*; *— habit*, morfinomania; *— traffic*, traffico degli stupefacenti; (fig.) *a — on the market*, merce *f.* invendibile; *tr.* narcotizzare, somministrare narcotici a; adulterare con sostanze narcotiche.

**drug-addict, -fiend** *n.* morfinomane *m., f.*

**drugged** *adj.* narcotizzato; (fig.) ebbro.

**drugget** *n.* bigello.

**druggist** *n.* farmacista *m.*

**druid** *n.* druido. **-ess** *n.* druidessa. **-ism** *n.* druidismo, religione dei druidi.

**drum** *n.* tamburo *m.*; *big —*, grancassa; (fam.) *to beat the big —*, battere la grancassa; (anat.; archit.) timpano; (mech.) cilindro; *intr.* suonare il tamburo; (with fingers) tambureggiare, tamburellare; *tr.* (fig.) *to — something into the head of*, far entrare qualcosa nella testa di; (of insects) ronzare. **-head** *n.* pelle *f.* di tamburo. **-mer** *n.* tamburo; *-mer boy*, tamburino. **-ming** *n.* rullo del tamburo; (of insects) ronzìo. **-stick** *n.* bacchetta da tamburo; (cul., fam.) gamba di pollo, anca.

**drunk** *adj.* ubriaco; *to get —*, ubriacarsi; *dead —*, ubriaco fradicio; (fig.) ebbro. **-ard** *n.* ubriacone, beone *m.*

**drunken** *adj.* ubriaco; *a — brawl*, una rissa fra ubriachi; **-ness** *n.* ubriachezza, ebbrezza.

**dry** *adj.* secco, asciutto; *— dock*, bacino di carenaggio; *— goods*, gli aridi *m.pl.*; *— land*, terraferma; *— rot*, carie *f.* del legno; *— shampoo*, frizione; monotono, arido; mordace; *a — laugh*, un riso ironico; (fam.) *to be left high and —*, rimanere all'asciutto; (slang) *to feel —*, aver sete.

**dry** *tr.* asciugare, seccare, disseccare; (industr.) essiccare; *intr.* asciugarsi; (fam.) *to — up*, smettere di parlare.

**dryad** *m.* (myth.) driade *f.*

**dryasdust** *adj.* noioso; *n.* pedante *m.*

**dry-clean** *tr.* pulire, lavare a secco. **-ing** *n.* pulitura a secco.

**dryer** *n.* essiccatore, essiccatoio; (chem.) essiccativo.

**drying** *adj.* essiccante, essiccativo; *n.* l'asciugarsi; essiccazione, essiccamento.

**dryly, drily** *adv.* seccamente.

**dryness** *n.* secchezza; aridità; (meteor.) siccità.

**dual** *adj.* doppio, duplice; (gramm.) duale; *— carriageway*, strada a doppia carreggiata. **-ism** *n.* dualismo; dualità.

**dub** *tr.* (hist.) creare (cavaliere); (fam.) dare un soprannome a, qualificare; (industr.) addobbare; (cinem.) doppiare.

**dubbin** *n.* grasso da stivali.

**dubbing** *n.* (industr.) addobbamento; (cinem.) doppiaggio.

**dubiety** *n.* dubbiosità; incertezza.

**dubious** *adj.* dubbio; incerto, poco chiaro; equivoco. **-ness** *n.* dubbiosità; incertezza.

**ducal** *adj.* ducale.

**ducat** *n.* (coin) ducato.

**duchess** *n.* duchessa.

**duchy** *n.* ducato.

**duck**[1] *n.* (orn.) anitra, anatra; (fam.) *to play -s and drakes*, giuocare a rimbalzello; *like a — to water*, senza esitazione, senza difficoltà; *it's like pouring water on a -'s back*, è tutta fatica sprecata; (fig.) *a lame —*, un debole, un incompetente; (term of affection) cocco, amore *m.*

**duck**[2] *n.* (text.) tela olona, tela da vela; *pl.* calzoni *m.pl.* di tela bianca.

**duck**[3] *n.* tuffo; inchino; *tr.* buttare in acqua; *to — one's head*, abbassare di colpo la testa; *intr.* inchinarsi, tuffarsi.

**duckbill** *n.* (zool.) ornitorinco.

**duckboard(s)** *n.* ponte *m.* di tavole.

**ducking** *n.* immersione; bagnatura; *to give someone a —*, buttare qualcuno nell'acqua.

**duckling** *n.* anatroccolo.

**duckpond** *n.* stagno per anitre; (joc.) l'oceano Atlantico.

**duckweed** *n.* (bot.) lente *f.* di palude, anitrina.
**ducky** *n.* (fam.) cocco.
**duct** *n.* condotto; (anat.) canale *m.*; vaso.
**ductile** *adj.* duttile; (fig.) docile.
**dud** *n.* (mil.) proiettile *m.* che fa cilecca; *adj.* (fam.) che non vale nulla, inutile; — *cheque*, assegno a vuoto.
**dude** *n.* zerbinotto, bellimbusto.
**dudgeon** *n.* sdegno; risentimento.
**due** *adj.* dovuto, da pagarsi; *to fall* —, scadere; conveniente, giusto; che spetta; *in — time*, a tempo debito; *the ship is — tomorrow*, la nave è attesa per domani; (rlwy.) in arrivo; *adv.* — *north*, direttamente a nord; *n.* il dovuto, il debito, ciò che spetta; *to give the devil his* —, dare a ciascuno quel che gli spetta; *pl.* diritti *m.pl.*; quota; dazio.
**duel** *n.* duello; (fig.) lotta; *intr.* battersi in duello. **-ling** *n.* il duellare. **-list** *n.* duellante *m.*
**duenna** *n.* governante *f.*; dama di compagnia.
**duet** *n.* duetto; duo *m.*
**duffel, duffle,** *n.* (text.) stoffa pesante, mollettone *m.*; — *coat*, montgomery *m. indecl.*
**duffer** *n.* (fam.) ignorante *m.*, *f.*; inetto; somaro.
**dug**[1] *n.* capezzolo; mammella.
**dug**[2] *p. def.*, *part.* of **dig,** *q.v.*
**dugout** *n.* canoa ricavata da un tronco d'albero; (shelter) rifugio sotterraneo.
**duke** *n.* duca *m.* **-dom** *n.* ducato.
**dulcet** *adj.* dolce; soave.
**dulcify** *tr.* addolcire, dolcificare.
**dulcimer** *n.* (mus.) zimbalon *m.*
**dull** *adj.* ottuso, lento, poco intelligente; triste, depresso; noioso, tedioso; grigio, fosco; sordo; cupo; opaco; offuscato; poco brillante; non tagliente, spuntato; (comm.) fiacco, inattivo; *the — season*, la stagione morta.
**dull** *tr.* smussare, spuntare; appannare, offuscare; attutire, intorpidire, alleviare; smorzare, attenuare.
**dullard** *n.* stupido; imbecille *m.*
**dul(l)ness** *n.* lentezza; ottusità; mancanza di colore, opacità; monotonia; noia; (comm.) fiacchezza; ristagno.
**dull-witted** *adj.* ottuso; tardo di mente.
**dully** *adv.* lentamente; ottusamente.
**duly** *adv.* debitamente; a tempo debito; regolarmente.
**dumb** *adj.* muto; *deaf and* —, sordomuto; — *animals*, le bestie; (fig.) ammutolito, reticente; *to be struck — with*, ammutolire per; *tr.* attutire; rendere sordo.
**dumb-bell** *n.* manubrio per ginnastica.
**dumbfound** *tr.* confondere, stupire, stordire.
**dumbly** *adv.* senza pronunciare parola, in silenzio.
**dumbness** *n.* mutismo; (fig.) silenzio.
**dumb-show** *n.* pantomima; scena muta. **-waiter** *n.* (furniture) carrello; (lift) montavivande *m. indecl.*
**dummy** *adj.* finto, pasticcio, falso; (mil.) — *cartridge*, cartuccia a salve; *n.* manichino, fantoccio; (comm.) articolo finto; (fig.) uomo di paglia; prestanome *m.*; (cards) morto.
**dump** *n.* luogo di scarico, deposito: ammasso, mucchio; (slang) brutto posto; bettola; *tr.* scaricare; formare un deposito di; (comm.) esportare a prezzi rovinosi a scopo di concorrenza; (fam.) *you can — your suitcase here*, puoi buttar qui la tua valigia; *to — down*, mettere giù con rumore sordo. **-ing** *n.* scarico; (comm.) dumping *m.*; esportazione di merce a prezzi rovinosi.
**dumpiness** *n.* aspetto tarchiato.
**dumps** *n.* (fam.) *to be in the* —, essere di umore nero.
**dumpy** *adj.* tarchiato e rotondetto; grassotto.
**dun**[1] *adj.* bruno grigiastro.
**dun**[2] *n.* creditore importuno, esattore di debiti; sollecitazione di pagamento; *tr.* sollecitare; *dunning letter*, lettera che sollecita il pagamento di un debito.
**dunce** *n.* ignorante *m.*; asino.
**dunderhead** *n.* stupido.
**dune** *n.* duna.
**dung** *n.* sterco; letame *m.*; escrementi *m.pl.* animali.
**dungarees** *n. pl.* tuta.
**dungeon** *n.* prigione sotterranea.
**dunghill** *n.* letamaio.
**Dunkirk** *pr.n.* (geog.) Dunkerque.
**dunnage** *n.* (comm.) pagliuolo; (fam.) bagagli *m.pl.*
**duodenal** *adj.* (med.; anat.) duodenale.
**dupe** *n.* gonzo; vittima di un inganno; *to be the ready — of*, lasciarsi facilmente ingannare da; *tr.* gabbare, ingannare, abbindolare.
**duplicat-e** *adj.* doppio; di ricambio; *n.* duplicato, doppione *m.*; *in* —, in doppia copia; *tr.* duplicare, ciclostilare; copiare. **-ion** *n.* raddoppiamento; duplicazione. **-or** *n.* duplicatore, ciclostile *m.*
**duplicity** *n.* duplicità; doppiezza; malafede *f.*
**durab-le** *adj.* durevole; duraturo; resistente. **-ility** *n.* durabilità; durata.
**durance** *n.* prigionia.
**duration** *n.* durata.
**duress** *n.* prigionia; arresto; violenza; *to act under* —, cedere alla forza.
**during** *prep.* durante, nel corso di.
**dusk** *n.* crepuscolo; l'imbrunire *m.*
**dusk-y** *adj.* oscuro, fosco, tetro; (of complexion) bruno. **-iness** *n.* oscurità, colore scuro.
**dust** *n.* polvere *f.*; (fig.) *to shake the — off one's feet*, andarsene indignato; (fam.) *to throw — in someone's eyes*, gettar polvere negli occhi a qualcuno; (fam.) *to kick up a* —, fare una scenata; (of the dead) ceneri *f.pl.*; *tr.* spolverare; impolverare; cospargere.
**dustbin** *n.* bidone *m.* per la spazzatura; pattumiera; portaimmondizie *m. indecl.*
**dust-cover** *n.* spolverina; (of book) sopraccopertina.
**duster** *n.* strofinaccio, spolverino.
**dustiness** *n.* l'essere polveroso.
**dusting** *n.* lo spolverare; (fam., fig.) bastonata.
**dust-jacket** *n.* sopraccopertina.
**dust-man** *n.* spazzino; incaricato del servizio di nettezza urbana. **-pan** *n.* paletta per la spazzatura.
**dust-sheet** *n.* lenzuolo per coprire i mobili. **-up** *n.* (fam.) lite *f.*; bisticcio.
**dusty** *adj.* polveroso; coperto di polvere; (fam.) *it's not so* —, non c'è male, è discreto.
**Dutch** *adj.* olandese; — *courage*, finto coraggio, coraggio dovuto all'alcool; (geog.) — *East Indies*, Indie Orientali Olandesi *f.pl.*; *to go* —, fare alla romana; *n.* la lingua olandese; *pl. the* —, gli olandesi; *double* —, lingua incomprensibile, ostrogotica; (slang) *my old* —, mia moglie. **-man** *n.* olandese; (fam.) *well, I'm a Dutchman!*, non ci credo!
**dutiable** *adj.* soggetto a dogana.
**dutiful** *adj.* rispettoso; ubbidiente; sottomesso; premuroso.
**duty** *n.* dovere *m.*; *to do one's* —, fare il proprio dovere; *to fail in one's* —, mancare al dovere; *as in — bound*, come si deve; mansione *f.*; competenze *f.pl.*; incarico; compito; servizio; *on* —, di servizio; *off* —, libero; (mil.) — *officer*, ufficiale di giornata; (customs) diritto doganale, dogana, dazio; imposta; *estate* —, imposta di successione; *stamp* —, tassa di bollo.
**dwarf** *adj.*, *n.* nano; *tr.* rimpicciolire.
**dwell** *intr.* dimorare, abitare, risiedere; (fig.) rimanere; *to — on*, soffermarsi su, insistere su, pensare sempre a; dilungarsi su. **-er** *n.* abitante *m.*, *f.*, residente *m.*, *f.*
**dwelling** *n.* abitazione; casa;

dimora; residenza; (fig.) insistenza.
**dwelling-house** *n.* cosa d'abitazione. **-place** *n.* dimora; residenza.
**dwelt** *p.def., part.* of **dwell,** *q.v.*
**dwindl-e** *intr.* diminuire; scemare; affievolirsi; (fig.) deperire; *to — away,* diminuire poco alla volta; *to — to nothing,* ridursi a nulla. **-ing** *adj.* che diminuisce; *n.* diminuzione; (fig.) deperimento.
**dye** *n.* tinta; tintura; materia colorante; (fig.) *a villain of the deepest —,* un furfante matricolato; *tr.* tingere; *to — one's hair,* tingersi i capelli; *to have a dress -d,* farsi tingere un vestito; *-d in the wool,* di lana tinta prima della tessitura; (fig.) *a -d-in-the-wool socialist,* un socialista sfegatato. **-ing** *n.* il tingere; tintura.
**dyer** *n.* tintore; (comm.) *-s and cleaners,* tintoria e lavanderia.
**dying** *adj.* morente, moribondo; *n.* il morire; morte *f.*; *the — day,* il giorno che muore; *his — day,* il giorno della sua morte; *the —,* i morenti; *a — man,* un moribondo; *— words,* ultime parole *f.pl.*
**dyke** *n.* see **dike.**
**dyn-amic(al)** *adj.* dinamico. **-amics** *n.* dinamica. **-amism** *n.* dinamismo.
**dynamite** *n.* dinamite *f.*; *tr.* far saltare con la dinamite.
**dynamo** *n.* dinamo *f.*
**dynast** *n.* dinasta *m.* **-ic** *adj.* dinastico. **-y** *n.* dinastia.
**dysentery** *n.* dissenteria.
**dyspep-sia** *n.* (med.) dispepsia. **-tic** *adj. n.* dispeptico.

**E** *n.* e *f.*; (teleph.) *— for Edward,* e come Emilia; (mus.) mi *m.*
**each** *adj.* ogni; *— one,* ciascuno; *prn.* ognuno; *they cost a pound —,* costano una sterlina l'uno; *— other,* l'un l'altro, *pl.* gli uni e gli altri; *we love — other,* ci amiamo; *they love each —,* si amano.
**eager** *adj.* ardente; avido; alacre; impetuoso, premuroso; *an — student of English,* uno studente appassionato dell'inglese; *— to,* desideroso di; *to be — for,* desiderare ardentemente. **-ness** *n.* ardore *m.*; premura; zelo; impazienza; brama.
**eagle** *n.* (orn.) aquila; (herald.) *double-headed —,* aquila bicipite.
**eaglet** *n.* aquilotto.
**ear** *n.* orecchio; *to prick up one's -s,* stare ad orecchi tesi; *to be all -s,* essere tutt'orecchi; *to turn a deaf —,* fare l'orecchio di mercante; *by —,* a orecchio; (*also* orecchia, *usu.* of ear-shaped objects); *— of corn,* spiga.
**earache** *n.* mal *m.* d'orecchi.
**ear-drop** *n.* pendente *m.* **-drum** *n.* timpano.
**earl** *n.* conte *m.* **-dom** *n.* contea; dignità di conte.
**earliness** *n.* prestezza; precocità.
**early** *adj.* primo; *— childhood,* prima infanzia; *the — nineteenth century,* i primi anni del secolo decimonono; *in — June,* ai primi di giugno; *in — summer,* al principio dell'estate; *in the — morning,* di buon mattino; mattutino, mattiniero; *at this — hour,* a quest'ora mattutina; *an — riser,* una persona mattiniera; *the — train,* il treno della mattina; *in its — stages,* allo stato embrionale; prematuro; precoce; *— peas,* piselli primaticci; *an — winter,* un inverno precoce; antico; *earliest times,* i tempi più remoti; *at an — date,* fra poco, prossimamente; *at your earliest convenience,* con cortese sollecitudine.
**early** *adv.* presto, di buon'ora, per tempo; *to arrive too —,* arrivare in anticipo; *not earlier than,* non prima di.
**early-closing** *n.* chiusura anticipata; *— day,* giorno in cui i negozi sono chiusi nel pomeriggio; sabato inglese.
**earmark** *tr.* apporre il marchio di proprietà sull'orecchio di; (fig.) accantonare; assegnare a scopo speciale; devolvere.
**earn** *tr.* guadagnare, guadagnarsi; meritarsi; *to — one's living,* guadagnarsi da vivere.
**earnest**[1] *adj.* serio, zelante; coscienzioso; fervido, caloroso; *to be in —,* fare sul serio; *— request,* richiesta urgente.
**earnest**[2] *n.* pegno; caparra.
**earnestness** *n.* serietà; diligenza; fervore *m.*
**earnings** *n.pl.* guadagni *m.pl.*; salario; stipendio; reddito; (comm.) utile *m.*
**ear-phone** *n.* cuffia. **-piercing** *adj.* penetrante; squillante. **-plug** *n.* tappo per orecchi. **-ring** *n.* orecchino.
**earshot** *n.* *within —,* a portata d'orecchio, a portata di voce.
**ear-specialist** *n.* otoiatra *m.* **-splitting** *adj.* assordante.
**earth**[1] *n.* terra, mondo, globo terrestre; (fig.) *to move heaven and —,* muovere cielo e terra; *to come back to —,* scendere dalle nuvole; *how on —?,* come mai?; *nothing on —,* nulla al mondo; terreno, suolo, terra; (of fox) tana; (electr.) massa, terra.
**earth**[2] *tr.* (agric.) coprire di terra; (electr.) mettere a terra.
**earth-born** *adj.* mortale. **-bound** *adj.* legato alle cose terrene.
**earthen** *adj.* di terra, di terra cotta. **-ware** *n.* terraglie *f.pl.*; stoviglie *f.pl.*
**earthliness, earthiness** *n.* terrenità; attaccamento alle cose terrene; mondanità.
**earthly** *adj.* terrestre, della terra; terreno, mondano; (fam.) *for no — reason,* per nessuna ragione al mondo; *no — use,* affatto inutile.
**earth-quake** *n.* terremoto; *— shock,* scossa sismica; *submarine —,* maremoto. **-work** *n.* terrapieno; (mil.) fortificazione. **-worm** *n.* lombrico.
**earthy** *adj.* di terra, terroso; (fig.) grossolano.
**ear-trumpet** *n.* cornetto acustico.
**earwig** *n.* (ent.) forfecchia.
**ease** *n.* agio, comodo; benessere; riposo; tranquillità; *to be at —,* essere tranquillo; *to be ill at —,* essere a disagio; *a life of —,* una vita comoda; *with —,* con facilità; *— of manner,* disinvoltura, naturalezza; (mil.) *stand at —!,* riposo!
**ease** *tr.* sollevare, allievare, alleggerire; agevolare; *intr.* attenuarsi, calmarsi; *to — off,* rilassarsi; *to — up,* rallentare.
**easel** *n.* cavalletto, leggìo.
**easily** *adv.* facilmente, senza difficoltà, agevolmente, comodamente; (fig.) *to take life —,* prendere la vita come viene.
**easiness** *n.* facilità; agevolezza; comodità; bontà; disinvoltura.
**easing** *n.* sollievo, alleviamento; *— of tension,* allentamento della tensione.
**east** *adj.* orientale, dell'est; *— wind,* vento dell'est; *adv.* ad est, verso est; *n.* est, oriente, levante *m.*; *the Middle East,* il Medio Oriente; *the Far East,* l'Estremo Oriente; *the East Indies,* le Indie Orientali. **-bound** *adj.* diretto verso l'est.
**Easter** *n.* Pasqua; *— Day,* la domenica di Pasqua; *— Monday,* il Lunedì di Pasqua; *— Eve,* il sabato santo; *— egg,* uovo pasquale.
**easterly** *adj.* dall'est, dell'est.
**eastern** *adj.* orientale, dell'est.
**eastertide** *n.* tempo pasquale, la pasqua.
**eastward** *adj., adv.* ad est, verso est, verso oriente.
**easy** *adj.* facile; semplice, elementare; agevole; tranquillo; *within — reach,* facile a raggiungersi; *— conscience,* coscienza tranquilla; *to make one's mind —*

*about*, rassicurarsi su; *to travel by — stages*, viaggiare a piccole tappe; *to take it —*, prendersela con comodo; (comm.) *on — terms*, con facilitazioni di pagamento; (provb.) *easier said than done*, altro è dire altro è fare.
**easy-chair** *n.* poltrona. **-going** *adj.* incurante, compiacente, accomodante; affabile.
**eat** *tr.*, *intr.* mangiare; *to — too much*, eccedere nel mangiare; *to — up*, mangiare fino all'ultima briciola; (fig.) *to — one's heart out*, mangiarsi il fegato; *to — one's words*, rimangiarsi la parola; *to — (away)*, corrodere, attaccare.
**eatable** *adj.* mangiabile; mangereccio; commestibile; *n.pl.* vivande *f.pl.*, viveri *m.pl.*, commestibili *m.pl.*
**eater** *n.* mangiatore; (fam.) *a hearty —*, una buona forchetta.
**eau-de-cologne** *n.* acqua di Colonia.
**eaves** *n. pl.* gronda; cornicione *m.* **-drop** *intr.* origliare. **-dropper** *n.* chi origlia alla porta.
**ebb**[1] *n.* riflusso; *— and flow*, flusso e riflusso; *— tide*, bassa marea; *intr.* rifluire, abbassarsi; (fig.) declinare.
**ebonite** *n.* ebanite *f.*
**ebony** *n.* ebano; *colour of —*, nero d'ebano.
**ebullient** *adj.* bollente; (fig.) esuberante.
**eccentric** *adj.* (geom.) eccentrico; (fig.) eccentrico; stravagante, originale; *n.* eccentrico. **-ity** *n.* (geom.) eccentricità; (fig.) originalità, stravaganza, eccentricità.
**Ecclesiastes** *pr.n.* Ecclesiaste *m.*
**ecclesiastic** *adj.*, *n.* ecclesiastico. **-al** *adj.* ecclesiastico.
**Ecclesiasticus** *pr.n.* l'Ecclesiastico.
**echelon** *n.* scaglione *m.*
**echo** *n.* eco *m.*, *f.*; *tr.* far eco a, ripetere; *intr.* echeggiare, risuonare.
**echo-sounder** *n.* (naut.) scandaglio acustico.
**eclectic** *adj.*, *n.* eclettico. **-ism** *n.* eclettismo.
**eclipse** *n.* eclissi *f.*; *tr.* eclissare.
**eclogue** *n.* (lit.) egloga.
**ecology** *n.* ecologia.
**economic** *adj.* economico; *— system*, economia. **-al** *adj.* economo, frugale, parsimonioso; *to be -al of*, non sciupare. **-s** *n.* scienza economica, economia.
**economist** *n.* economista *m.*, *f.*; persona economica.
**economize** *tr.* economizzare; risparmiare; *intr.* fare economia.
**economy** *n.* economia; *planned —*, economia pianificata; *to practise —*, economizzare.
**ecst-asy** *n.* estasi *f indecl.*; rapimento, trasporto; *to be in —*, estasiarsi; *to go into ecstasies*, andare in brodo di giuggiole. **-atic** *adj.* estatico.
**Ecuador** *pr.n.* (geog.) Ecuador *m.*, la Repubblica dell'Equatore.
**ecumenical** *adj.* ecumenico; universale.
**eczema** *n.* eczema *m.*
**eddy** *n.* vortice *m.*; mulinello; turbine *m.*; risucchio; *intr.* turbinare; risucchiare; mulinare.
**Eden** *pr.n.* Eden *m.*, paradiso terrestre.
**edge** *n.* orlo, bordo; margine, limite *m.*; sponda; *— of the road*, ciglio della strada; (weapon) taglio; filo; *with a sharp —*, molto affilato; *to put an — on*, affilare; *to take the — off*, smussare; (fam.) *to be on —*, avere i nervi a fior di pelle; *to set one's teeth on —*, far allegare i denti; (of book) *gilt —*, taglio dorato.
**edge** *tr.* orlare, bordare; affilare, aguzzare; muovere poco a poco; *to — one's way into*, intrufolarsi in; *to — one's way through*, farsi strada attraverso; *intr. to — away*, allontanarsi poco a poco.
**edg-ed** *adj.* orlato; affilato, tagliente. **-eways, -ewise** *adv.* dalla parte del taglio, di sbieco, di traverso; (fam.) *not to be able to get a word in -eways*, non riuscire a infilare una parola nella conversazione. **-iness** *n.* (fam.) nervosismo. **-ing** *n.* orlatura; bordo; frangia **-y** *n.* affilato; (fam.) nervoso.
**edib-le** *adj.* mangiabile; commestibile, mangereccio. **-les** *n.pl.* commestibili *m.pl.* **-ility** *n.* mangiabilità.
**edict** *n.* editto.
**edification** *n.* edificazione.
**edifice** *n.* edificio.
**edify** *tr.* edificare. **-ing** *adj.* edificante; elevato.
**Edinburgh** *pr.n.* (geog.) Edimburgo *f.*
**edit** *tr.* curare, commentare; curare l'edizione di; *-ed by*, a cura di; (journ.) dirigere; *-ed by*, sotto la direzione di.
**Edith** *pr.n.* Editta.
**editing** *n.* redazione; commento; (journ.) direzione.
**edition** *n.* edizione; *limited —*, edizione a tiratura ristretta; *revised —*, edizione riveduta; *unabridged —*, edizione integrale.
**editor** *n.* curatore; *newspaper —*, direttore; *section —*, redattore; *city —*, redattore finanziario; *sporting —*, redattore sportivo. **-ial** *adj.* editoriale; *-ial staff*, redazione; *n.* articolo di fondo.
**Edmund** *pr.n.* Edmondo.
**educate** *tr.* educare, istruire; provvedere all'educazione di; *he was -d in Italy*, ha compiuto i suoi studi in Italia; (fig.) addestrare; *to — one's memory*, esercitare la memoria. **-d** *adj.* istruito; colto.
**education** *n.* educazione; coltura; istruzione; insegnamento; *Ministry of —*, Ministero della Pubblica Istruzione. **-al** *adj.* educativo; scolastico.
**educative** *adj.* educativo; istruttivo.
**educator** *n.* educatore; pedagogo.
**Edward** *pr.n.* Edoardo.
**eel** *n.* (ichth.) anguilla; *to be as slippery as an —*, guizzare di mano come un'anguilla.
**eel-basket, eel-trap** *n.* nassa. **-pond,** anguillara. **-shaped** *adj.* anguillare, anguilliforme.
**e'en** *adv.* (poet.). See **even.**
**e'er** *adv.* (poet.). See **ever.**
**eer-ie, -y** *adj.* misterioso; fantastico; strano; che fa rabbrividire. **-iness** *n.* stranezza, misteriosità.
**efface** *tr.* cancellare; far scomparire; obliterare; *rfl. to — oneself*, tenersi in disparte. **-ment** *n.* cancellamento; obliterazione.
**effect** *n.* effetto; risultato; conseguenza; *in —*, in realtà; *to have a good — on*, giovare a; *to have a bad — on*, nuocere a, essere deleterio a; *to give — to*, effettuare; *to take —*, entrare in vigore; *with — from today*, a partire da oggi; senso, significato; *or words to that —*, o qualcosa del genere; *to the — that*, dicendo che; impressione, effetto, *personal -s*, effetti personali, beni *m.pl.*
**effect** *tr.* effettuare; compiere; eseguire; realizzare; *to — an entrance*, entrare di forza.
**effective** *adj.* efficace, efficiente; *to become —*, entrare in vigore; che colpisce. **-ness** *n.* efficacia.
**effectual** *adj.* efficace; valido.
**effectuate** *tr.* effettuare.
**effeminacy, effeminateness** *n.* effeminatezza.
**effeminate** *adj.* effeminato.
**effervesc-e** *intr.* essere in effervescenza; spumeggiare; (fig.) essere vivace. **-ence** *n.* effervescenza. **-ent** *adj.* effervescente; spumeggiante; (fig.) vivace.
**effete** *adj.* indebolito; che ha fatto il suo tempo; esausto. **-ness** *n.* debolezza; mancanza di efficacia.
**efficacious** *adj.* efficace.
**efficacy, efficacity** *n.* efficacia; (industr.) rendimento.
**effici-ency** *n.* efficienza; capacità; abilità; (industr.) rendimento. **-ent** *adj.* efficiente; capace, abile; (industr.) ad alto rendimento.
**effigy** *n.* effigie *f.*
**effloresc-e** *intr.* fiorire, essere efflorescente. **-ence** *n.* efflorescenza; fioritura. **-ent** *adj.* efflorescente; fiorente.
**effluent** *adj.* defluente; *n.* canale *m.* di scarico; emissario.

**effluvium** *n.* effluvio; odore *m.*; esalazione.
**efflux** *n.* efflusso; emanazione.
**effort** *n.* sforzo; fatica; *to make an* —, sforzarsi; durare fatica; fare di tutto, scuotersi; (fam.) *my latest* —, il mio ultimo lavoro; *quite a good* —, riuscito abbastanza bene. **-less** *adj.* senza sforzo; fatto con facilità.
**effrontery** *n.* sfrontatezza; sfacciataggine *f.*
**effulg-ence** *n.* splendore, fulgore *m.* **-ent** *adj.* splendente; risplendente; lucente.
**effus-e** *tr.* effondere; spargere; *intr.* effondersi. **-ion** *n.* effusione; (of blood) versamento; (fig.) effusione, espansività. **-ive** *adj.* espansivo, esuberante. **-iveness** *n.* effusione, espansività.
**egg**[1] *n.* uovo (*pl.* **uova** *f.*); *a bad* —, un uovo marcio, (fig.) un buono a nulla; *a good* —, (fig.) un buon diavolo; *hard-boiled* —, uovo sodo; *new-laid* —, uovo fresco; *raw* —, uovo da bere; *china* —, endice *m.*; *to put all one's -s in one basket*, rischiare il tutto per il tutto; (slang) *as sure as -s is -s*, sicuro come due più due fanno quattro; *to teach one's grandmother to suck -s*, dare consigli a chi ne sa di più.
**egg**[2] *tr. to — on*, aizzare, incitare.
**egg-cup** *n.* portauovo *m.* **-flip, -nog** *n.* zabaione *n.* **-head** *n.* (slang) testa d'uovo. **-plant** *n.* (bot.) melanzana. **-shaped** *adj.* ovale.
**eggshell** *n.* guscio d'uovo.
**egg-timer** *n.* clessidra per uova. **-whisk** *n.* frullino.
**eglantine** *n.* (bot.) rosa canina.
**egocentric** *adj.* egocentrico.
**ego-ism** *n.* egoismo. **-ist** *n.* egoista *m.*, *f.* **-istic(al)** *adj.* egoistico.
**ego-tism** *n.* egotismo; autoesaltazione. **-tist** *n.* egotista *m.*, *f.* **-tistic(al)** *adj.* egotistico.
**egregious** *adj.* egregio; (pejor.) grossolano; — *blunder*, errore *m.* madornale.
**egress** *n.* uscita.
**egret** *n.* (orn.) airone bianco; (tuft) ciuffo, pennacchio.
**Egypt** *pr.n.* (geog.) Egitto. **-ian** *adj.*, *n.* egiziano; (liter.) egizio, egiziaco.
**egyptolog-y** *n.* egittologia. **-ist** *n.* egittologo.
**eider** *n.* (orn.) — *duck*, anatra dal piumino. **-down** *n.* piumino; *-down quilt*, piumino, trapunta.
**eight** *adj.*, *n.* otto *m.*; *at — o'clock*, alle otto; *half-past* —, le otto e mezzo; (fam.) *to have had one over the* —, aver bevuto troppo; (sport) canotto a otto rematori.
**eighteen** *card. num.* diciotto; *eighteen-year-old*, diciottenne *m.*, *f.* **-th** *ord. num.* diciottesimo, decimottavo; *the -th* (day of month), il diciotto; *the -th century*, il settecento, il secolo decimottavo.
**eightfold** *adj.* ottuplo; *adv.* per otto volte.
**eighth** *ord. num.* ottavo; *the* —, (day of month) l'otto; *Edward the* —, Eduardo ottavo.
**eightieth** *ord. num.* ottantesimo.
**eight-syllabled** *adj.* (prosod.) ottonario.
**eighty** *card. num.* ottanta; *in the eighties*, tra il 1880 e il 1889, nella nona decade del secolo decimonono; *he is in his eighties*, ha più di ottant'anni, è ottantenne.
**eighty-first** *ord num.*, *adj.* ottantunesimo, ottantesimo primo. **-one** *card. num.*, *adj.* ottantuno. **-second** *ord. num.* ottantaduesimo, ottantesimo secondo. **-two** *card. num.* ottantadue.
**Eileen** *pr.n.* Elona.
**Eire** *pr.n.* Irlanda, la Repubblica Irlandese, l'Irlanda del Sud.
**either** *adj.*, *prn.* o l'uno o l'altro; ciascuno dei due; tutti e due; *on — side of the street*, su ciascun lato della strada; *without taking — side*, senza prendere le parti dell'uno o dell'altro; (in neg. phrases) nè l'uno nè l'altro; — *way*, in un modo o nell'altro; *at — end*, a tutte e due le estremità; *adv.* (after neg.) neanche, neppure, nemmeno; *can't you tell me —?*, nemmeno tu puoi dirmelo?; *conj.* o, oppure, ovvero; *either . . . or*, o . . . o, sia . . . sia.
**ejaculat-e** *tr.* esclamare; eiaculare. **-ion** *n.* esclamazione; eiaculazione **-ory** *adj.* esclamativo; giaculatorio.
**eject** *tr.* gettare fuori, espellere, emettere; *to — from* (*a house*), sfrattare; (mech.) eiettere. **-ion** *n.* espulsione; (from house) sfratto; (mech.) eiezione.
**eke** *tr. to — out*, supplire all'insufficienza di; consumare economicamente; *to — out a living*, sbarcare il lunario.
**elaborate** *adj.* elaborato; minuzioso; lavorato con cura; — *style*, stile ammanierato; (fig.) *the whole — structure*, tutto l'edificio; *tr.* elaborare; sviluppare; ammanierare. **-ness** *n.* elaboratezza; minuziosità; accuratezza.
**elaboration** *n.* elaborazione.
**élan** *n.* slancio; dinamismo.
**elapse** *intr.* passare; trascorrere; decorrere.
**elastic** *adj.*, *n.* elastico; — *band*, fettuccia elastica, nastro elastico. **-ity** *n.* elasticità.
**elat-e** *tr.* esaltare, rallegrare, entusiasmare. **-ed** *adj.* esaltato, esultante; allegro; *to be -ed*, esultare. **-ion** *n.* esaltazione, esultanza; ebbrezza.
**Elba** *pr.n.* (geog.) l'Isola d'Elba.
**elbow** *n.* gomito; *to be out at -s*, essere poveramente vestito; (fam.) *to raise one's* —, alzare il gomito; (of chair) bracciuolo; *tr.* dare gomitate a, urtare col gomito; *to — one's way*, avanzare a gomitate.
**elbow-grease** *n.* (fam.) olio di gomito. **-rest** *n.* bracciuolo. **-room** *n.* (fig.) libertà di movimento; spazio.
**elder**[1] *adj.* più vecchio, anziano, maggiore; — *brother*, fratello maggiore, — *son*, figlio maggiore, figlio primogenito; *n.* maggiore *m.*, *f.*; anziano.
**elder**[2] *n.* (bot.) sambuco. **-berry** *n.* bacca di sambuco.
**elderly** *adj.* attempato, anziano, di una certa età.
**eldest** *adj.* maggiore, primogenito.
**Eleanor** *pr.n.* Eleanora, Leonora.
**elect** *adj.* eletto, scelto; designato; *tr.* eleggere, scegliere, *to — to do something*, decidersi di far qualcosa, optare per qualcosa.
**election** *n.* elezione; scelta; *general* —, elezioni generali; *municipal* —, elezioni amministrative; — *campaign*, propaganda elettorale; *to stand for* —, presentarsi come candidato. **-eering** *n.* campagna elettorale, propaganda elettorale.
**elector** *n.* elettore. **-ate** *n.* elettorato; gli elettori.
**Electra** *pr.n.* (myth.) Elettra.
**electric** *adj.* elettrico; — *fire*, stufetta elettrica; *household — appliances*, elettrodomestici *m.pl.*; — *motor*, elettromotore *m.*; — *shock*, scossa elettrica; — *torch*, 'flash' *m. indecl.*, lampadina tascabile; (ichth.) — *eel*, ginnoto. **-al** *adj.* elettrico; *-al engineer*, elettrotecnico.
**electrician** *n.* elettricista *m.*; elettrotecnico.
**electricity** *n.* elettricità; energia elettrica.
**electrification** *n.* elettrificazione.
**electrif-y** *tr.* elettrificare; (fig.) elettrizzare. **-ied** *adj.* elettrificato; (fig.) elettrizzato. **-ying** *adj.* elettrizzante.
**electro-** *pref.* elettro-
**electrocut-e** *tr.* fulminare (mediante l'elettricità); *to be -d*, essere fulminato, (of criminal) morire sulla sedia elettrica. **-ion** *n.* fulminazione; (of criminal) elettroesecuzione, morte *f.* sulla sedia elettrica.
**electrode** *n.* elettrodo.
**electrodynamics** *n.* elettrodinamica.
**electrolysis** *n.* elettrolisi *f.*
**electron** *n.* elettrone *m.* **-ic** *adj.* elettronico. **-ics** *n.* elettronica.
**electroplate** *n.* articoli *m.pl.* placcati elettroliticamente; *tr.* placcare elettrolitamente.

**electrotype** *n.* (typ.) galvano.
**eleg-ance** *n.* eleganza; stile squisito; finezza. **-ant** *adj.* elegante; raffinato; fino.
**eleg-y** *n.* elegia. **-iac** *adj.* elegiaco.
**element** *n.* elemento; (fig.) fattore *m.* **-al** *adj.* fondamentale; rudimentale. **-ary** *adj.* elementare; rudimentale; *-ary principles*, elementi *m.pl.*
**elephant** *n.* elefante *m.*; *female —*, elefantessa. **-iasis** *n.* (med.) elefantiasi *f.* **-ine** *adj.* elefantesco, elefantino.
**elevat-e** *tr.* elevare; innalzare, alzare; (fig.) esaltare. **-ed** *adj.* elevato; eminente; *-ed railway*, ferrovia sopraelevata. **-ing** *adj.* che eleva, edificante.
**elevation** *n.* elevazione; *— above sea level*, altezza sul livello del mare; altura; (astron.) altezza; (archit.) proiezione ortogonale, alzata; (fig.) elevatezza.
**elevator** *n.* elevatore *m.*; montacarichi *m. indecl.*; ascensore.
**eleven** *card. num.* undici; *— o'clock*, le undici; *n.* squadra di undici giocatori, undici *f.* **-ses** *pl.* (fam.) caffè alle undici. **-th** *ord. num.* undicesimo, decimoprimo; *at the -th hour*, all'ultimo momento; *the -th of May*, l'undici maggio; *n.* undicesimo; undicesima parte.
**elf** *n.* elfo; folletto. **-in** *adj.* di elfo; di folletto; (fig.) da fiaba.
**elicit** *tr.* trarre fuori; provocare.
**elide** *tr.* (gramm.) elidere.
**eligib-le** *adj.* eleggibile; vantaggioso; *an — young man*, un buon partito. **-ility** *n.* eleggibilità.
**Elijah** *pr.n.* (bibl.) Elia *m.*
**eliminat-e** *tr.* eliminare; togliere, scartare; (euph.) togliere dalla circolazione. **-ion** *n.* eliminazione. **-ive, -ory** *adj.* eliminatorio; (sport) *-ory round*, eliminatoria.
**elision** *n.* (gramm.) elisione.
**Elisha** *pr.n.* (bibl.) Eliseo.
**élite** *n.* fior fiore *m.*, élite *f.*
**elixir** *n.* elisir(e) *m.*
**Eliza** *pr.n.* Elisa, Lisa.
**Elizabeth** *pr.n.* Elisabetta. **-an** *adj.*, *n.* (hist.) elisabettiano.
**elk** *n.* (zool.) alce *m.*
**Ellen** *pr.n.* Elena.
**ellipse** *n.* (geom.) el(l)isse *f.*
**ellipsis** *n.* (gramm.) ellissi *f.*
**elliptic(al)** (gramm.; geom.) el(l)ittico.
**elm** *n.* olmo.
**elocution** *n.* elocuzione; dizione. **-ist** *n.* maestro di dizione, dicitore.
**elongat-e** *tr.* allungare. **-ed** *adj.* allungato; affusolato. **-ion** *n.* allungamento.
**elope** *intr.* sposarsi senza il consenso dei genitori; (of wife) scappare con l'amante. **-ment** *n.* fuga (con la persona amata); matrimonio clandestino.
**eloqu-ence** *n.* eloquenza; retorica. **-ent** *adj.* eloquente; retorico.
**else** *adj.* altro; *what —*, che altro; *everybody —*, tutti gli altri; *nothing —*, nulla più; *who —?*, chi altro?; *adv.* altrimenti, oppure. **-where** *adv.* altrove.
**Elsie** *pr.n.* Lisa.
**elucidat-e** *tr.* dilucidare; chiarire, spiegare. **-ion** *n.* elucidazione; spiegazione; chiarimento.
**elucubration** *n.* elucubrazione.
**elude** *tr.* eludere; schivare, evitare; sfuggire a.
**elusive** *adj.* elusivo; evasivo; sfuggevole; inafferrabile.
**Elysi-um** *pr.n.* (myth.) Eliso, Elisio. **-an** *adj.* elisio; *the -an fields*, i campi elisi.
**em** *n.* (letter) emme *m.*, *f.*; (typ.) riga.
**emaciat-ed** *adj.* emaciato; allampanato, smagrito. **-ion** *n.* emaciazione; dimagramento.
**emanat-e** *intr.* emanare. **-ion** *n.* emanazione; effluvio.
**emancipat-e** *tr.* emancipare; liberare. **-ion** *n.* emancipazione.
**emasculate** *tr.* castrare, evirare; (fig.) snervare.
**embalm** *tr.* imbalsamare; (fig.) conservare; profumare. **-ment, -ing** *n.* imbalsamazione.
**embankment** *n.* argine *m.*; diga, alzaia; strada lungo un fiume.
**embargo** *n.* embargo; sequestro; divieto; proibizione.
**embark** *tr.* imbarcare; *intr.* imbarcarsi; (fig.) *to — on*, intraprendere. **-ation** *n.* imbarco.
**embarrass** *tr.* imbarazzare; mettere in imbarazzo; *to feel -ed*, trovarsi a disagio. **-ing** *adj.* imbarazzante; sconcertante. **-ment** *n.* imbarazzo; disagio; difficoltà; perplessità.
**embassy** *n.* ambasciata; (mission) ambasceria.
**embattled** *adj.* (archit.) merlato; (mil.) schierato.
**embed** *tr.* incastrare; conficcare; piantare.
**embellish** *tr.* abbellire; ornare, decorare. **-ment** *n.* abbellimento; migliorie *f.pl.*; (mus.) fiore *m.*
**ember(s)** *n.* tizzone *m.*; brace *f.*; ceneri *f.pl.*; (eccl.) *Ember Days*, Quattro Tempora.
**embezzle** *tr.* malversare; appropriarsi indebitamente. **-ment** *n.* (leg.) malversazione, appropriazione indebita, concussione.
**embitter** *tr.* rendere amaro; (fig.) amareggiare, inasprire. **-ment** *n.* inasprimento; amerezza.
**emblazon** *tr.* blasonare.
**emblem** *n.* emblema *m.*; simbolo; segnacolo. **-atic(al)** *adj.* emblematico; simbolico.
**embod-y** *tr.* incorporare; dar corpo a; incarnare; (fig.) personificare. **-iment** *n.* incorporazione; personificazione; incarnazione.
**embolden** *tr.* incoraggiare, imbaldanzire.
**embolism** *n.* (med.) embolia; (astron.) embolismo.
**emboss** *tr.* (metall.) sbalzare, intagliare; (typ.) stampare in rilievo. **-ed** *adj.* fatto in rilievo; sbalzato, a sbalzo.
**embrace** *n.* abbraccio, abbracciamento; amplesso; *tr.* abbracciare; cingere, stringere; comprendere; *recip. rfl.* abbracciarsi.
**embrasure** *n.* strombatura; (mil.) cannoniera; feritoia.
**embrocation** *n.* embrocazione; linimento.
**embroider** *tr.* ricamare; (fig.) abbellire. **-y** *n.* ricamo; *-y frame*, telaio da ricamo; (fig.) abbellimento.
**embroil** *tr.* imbrogliare; coinvolgere; confondere; seminare discordia fra.
**embryo** *n.* embrione *m.*; *in —*, allo stato embrionale; (fig.) *poet in —*, poeta in erba. **-nic** *adj.* embrionale, embrionico, in embrione.
**emend, -ate** *tr.* emendare; correggere. **-ation** *n.* emendazione; correzione.
**emerald** *n.* smeraldo; (joc.) *the Emerald Isle*, la verde Irlanda.
**emerge** *intr.* emergere; affiorare; sorgere; (fig.) risultare, apparire, riuscire.
**emergence** *n.* emersione; apparizione.
**emergency** *n.* emergenza; contingenza; caso imprevisto; crisi *f. indecl.*; stato di emergenza; *in case of —*, in caso di urgenza; *to meet an —*, far fronte ad una situazione critica; *to rise to an —*, mostrarsi all'altezza della situazione; *— exit*, uscita di sicurezza; (aeron.) *— landing*, atterraggio di fortuna.
**emergent** *adj.* emergente.
**emersion** *n.* emersione.
**emery** *n.* smeriglio; *— paper*, carta smerigliata.
**emetic** *adj.*, *n.* (pharm.) emetico.
**emigrant** *adj.*, *n.* emigrante *m.*, *f.* emigrato.
**emigrat-e** *intr.* emigrare. **-ion** *n.* emigrazione.
**Emilia** *pr.n.* Emilia; (geog.) Emilia. **-n** *adj.*, *n.* (geog.) emiliano.
**Emily** *pr.n.* Emilia.
**emin-ence** *n.* eminenza; altura; (eccl.) Eminenza. **-ent** *adj.* eminente; prominente, distinto.
**emissary** *n.* emissario.
**emission** *n.* emissione.

**emit** *tr.* emettere; esalare, emanare; (fig.) esprimere.
**Emmanuel** *pr.n.* Emanuele.
**emollient** *adj.*, *n.* emolliente *m.*
**emolument** *n.* rimunerazione; stipendio.
**emotion** *n.* emozione; commozione; *to appeal to the -s*, fare appello ai sentimenti; *to betray one's —*, mostrarsi commosso. **-al** *adj.* emotivo; impressionabile; emozionante, commovente. **-alism** *n.* emotività; impressionabilità.
**emotive** *adj.* emotivo.
**empanel** *tr.* iscrivere nella lista dei giurati; *to — a jury*, formare la lista dei giurati.
**emperor** *n.* imperatore.
**emphasis** *n.* enfasi *f.*; vigore *m.*; accentuazione; rilievo; (fig.) importanza.
**emphasize** *tr.* accentuare; dare rilievo a, sottolineare; (mus.) marcare.
**emphatic** *adj.* accentuato; sottolineato; vigoroso, energico; risoluto, reciso.
**empire** *n.* impero.
**empiric** *adj.* empirico; *n.* empirista *m.* **-al** *adj.* empirico. **-ism** *n.* empirismo. **-ist** *n.* empirista *m.*
**emplacement** *n.* (mil.) piazzuola, postazione.
**employ** *n.* impiego; *to be in the — of*, essere impiegato presso; *tr.* impiegare; adoperare; usare; servirsi di; assumere al proprio servizio; *rfl. to — oneself in*, occuparsi di. **-ee** *n.* impiegato; salariato; elemento. **-er** *n.* padrone *m.*, *f.* principale *m.*; datore di lavoro. **-ment** *n.* impiego; occupazione; lavoro; *-ment agency*, ufficio di collocamento.
**emporium** *n.* emporio; negozio.
**empower** *tr.* autorizzare; conferire poteri a; (leg.) abilitare.
**empress** *n.* imperatrice.
**emptiness** *n.* vuoto; vacuità.
**empty** *adj.* vuoto; deserto; disabitato; vacante; (fig.) vano, vuoto; *— of meaning*, privo di senso; (fam.) a digiuno; *to be taken on an — stomach*, da prendersi a digiuno.
**empty** *tr.* vuotare, svuotare; scaricare, sgombrare; *intr.* vuotarsi, scaricarsi; (geog.) sfociare, sboccare.
**empty-handed** *adj.* a mani vuote, a denti asciutti. **-headed** *adj.* scervellato.
**empurple** *tr.* imporporare.
**Empyrean** *adj.*, *n.* empireo.
**emu** *n.* (orn.) emù *m. indecl.*
**emulat-e** *tr.* emulare; gareggiare con. **-ion** *n.* emulazione.
**emulous** *adj.* emulo; desideroso, bramoso.
**emulsify** *tr.* emulsionare; *intr.* emulsionarsi.
**emulsion** *n.* emulsione.
**en** *n.* (letter) enne *f.*; (typ.) mezza riga.
**enable** *tr.* mettere in grado di; rendere capace di; permettere; (leg.) abilitare.
**enact** *tr.* decretare; promulgare; mettere in esecuzione; ordinare; (theatr.) recitare, rappresentare. **-ment** *n.* promulgazione; ordine *m.*
**enamel** *n.* smalto; lacca; vernice *f.*; *— ware*, vasellame smaltato; *tr.* smaltare.
**enamelled** *adj.*, smaltato, a smalto.
**enamour** *tr.* innamorare, affascinare; *to become -ed of*, innamorarsi di.
**encamp** *tr.* accampare; *intr.* accamparsi. **-ment** *n.* campeggio, accampamento.
**encase** *tr.* rinchiudere in astuccio; (fig.) rivestire.
**encash** *tr.* incassare, convertire in denaro.
**encaustic** *adj.* (art.) encaustico, ad encausto; *n.* encausto.
**enchain** *tr.* incatenare.
**enchant** *tr.* incantare; ammaliare, affascinare. **-er** *n.* incantatore *m.*; mago. **-ing** *adj.* incantevole; affascinante. **-ment** *n.* incanto, incantesimo; fascino. **-ress** *n.* incantatrice, ammaliatrice.
**encircle** *tr.* cingere, circondare. **-ment** *n.* accerchiamento; *policy of -ment*, politica di accerchiamento.
**enclasp** *tr.* abbracciare, stringere.
**enclave** *n.* zona circondata da territori stranieri.
**enclitic** *adj.* (gramm.) enclitico; *n.* enclitica.
**enclos-e** *tr.* chiudere, rinchiudere; cingere, circondare; *to — in a letter*, allegare, accludere, unire ad una lettera. **-ed** *adj.* chiuso, rinchiuso; cinto, circondato; (in letter) allegato, accluso, unito. **-ure** *n.* recinto; cinta; (in letter) allegato; (eccl.) clausura.
**encomiast** *n.* encomiatore; lodatore. **-ic(al)** *adj.* encomiastico; elogistico.
**encomium** *n.* encomio; elogio; lode *f.* solenne.
**encompass** *tr.* circondare, attorniare; racchiudere; procurare.
**encore** *n. excl.* (theatr.) bis *m.*; *to get an —*, avere un bis; *to give an —*, concedere un bis; *tr.* (theatr.) chiedere un bis, bissare.
**encounter** *n.* incontro, scontro; duello; *tr.* incontrare; imbattersi in; *to — dangers*, affrontare pericoli.
**encourag-e** *tr.* incoraggiare; incitare; animare; stimolare; favorire. **-ement** *n.* incoraggiamento; incitamento. **-ing** *adj.* incoraggiante.
**encroach** *intr. to — on*, invadere, usurpare, intaccare; guadagnare terreno; (fig.) *to — on someone's time*, abusare del tempo di qualcuno. **-ment** *n.* usurpazione; invasione; (leg.) lesione; erosione; (fig.) abuso.
**encrust** *tr.* incrostare; rivestire. **-ation, -ment** *n.* incrostazione.
**encumber** *tr.* ingombrare; imbarazzare; impacciare; *to be -ed with*, essere carico di; (leg.) gravare.
**encumbrance** *n.* ingombro; imbarazzo, impaccio; carico; (leg.) debito; ipoteca.
**encyclical** *adj.* enciclico; *n.* enciclica.
**encyclopaed-ia** *n.* enciclopedia; (fam.) *he's a walking —*, è una biblioteca ambulante. **-ic** *adj.* enciclopedico. **-ist** *n.* enciclopedista *m.*
**end** *n.* **1.** fine *f.*; estremità; termine *m.*; conclusione; *from — to —*, dal principio alla fine, da un capo all'altro; *in the —*, infine; *on —*, in piedi, dritto; *ten on —*, dieci di fila; *his hair stood on —*, gli si rizzarono i capelli; *to come to a bad —*, finire male; *to draw to an —*, volgere al termine; *the — house*, l'ultima casa; *odds and -s*, cianfrusaglie *f.pl.*; (fam.) *to be at a loose —*, essere disoccupato; *to be at one's wit's —*, non sapere che cosa fare; *to have the right — of the stick*, avere il coltello per il manico; *to get hold of the wrong — of the stick*, capire male, avere una idea sbagliata; *to make both -s meet*, sbarcare il lunario; *to have no — of money*, avere un sacco di soldi; *to keep one's — up*, tener duro, non cedere. **2.** fine *m.*, scopo; mira; intento; *to what —?*, a che scopo?, *to the — that*, affinchè; *the — justifies the means*, il fine giustifica i mezzi.
**end** *tr.* finire; terminare; concludere; *intr.* finire; concludere; *to — up*, riuscire; chiudersi.
**endanger** *tr.* mettere in pericolo, rischiare; compromettere.
**endear** *tr.* rendere caro, affezionare; rendersi caro. **-ing** *adj.* simpatico; grato; amabile; tenero, affettuoso. **-ment** *n.* tenerezza; vezzo; *term of -ment*, vezzeggiativo.
**endeavour** *n.* sforzo, tentativo; *intr.* cercare, sforzarsi, adoperarsi.
**endemic** *adj.* (med.) endemico.
**ending** *n.* fine *f.*; termine *m.*; *a happy —*, una felice conclusione; (gramm.) desinenza.
**endive** *n.* (bot.) indivia.
**endless** *adj.* senza fine; infinito; interminabile; continuo; *— task*, tela di Penelope. **-ness** *n.* infinità; perpetuità.
**endors-e** *tr.* vistare, firmare; (comm.) girare; (fig.) approvare, appoggiare. **-ement** *n.* visto; (comm.) girata; (fig.) approvazione. **-er** *n.* girante *m.*, *f.*

**endow** *tr.* dotare; sussidiare; (fig.) provvedere, fornire; *to be -ed with,* essere dotato di. **-ment** *n.* dotazione, donazione; costituzione di dote; (eccl.) dote *f.*
**end-paper** *n.* (bookb.) risguardo.
**endue** *tr.* (lit.) investire, rivestire; dotare.
**endur-e** *tr.* sopportare, tollerare; soffrire; *intr.* durare; restare; resistere. **-able** *adj.* sopportabile, tollerabile. **-ance** *n.* tolleranza; pazienza; resistenza; (sport) *-ance test,* prova di regolarità. **-ing** *adj.* tollerante; paziente; resistente; stabile, durevole.
**endways, endwise** *adv.*; perpendicolarmente; capo a capo.
**enema** *n.* (med.) clistere *m.*
**enemy** *n.* nemico; avversario.
**energetic** *adj.* energico, dinamico.
**energiz-e** *tr.* infondere energia a, stimolare. **-ing** *adj.* energetico.
**energy** *n.* energia; forza; vigore *m.*
**enervat-e** *tr.* snervare; rendere fiacco, debilitare. **-ing** *adj.* snervante; *an -ing climate,* un clima debilitante. **-ion** *n.* infiacchimento; mollezza.
**enfeeble** *tr.* affievolire; indebolire; debilitare. **-ment** *n.* indebolimento.
**enfold** *tr.* avviluppare, avvolgere; cingere.
**enforce** *tr.* imporre; far rispettare, far valere. **-d** *adj.* forzato; imposto; obbligatorio. **-ment** *n.* imposizione; esecuzione; applicazione.
**enfranchise** *tr.* affrancare, emancipare; accordare il diritto di suffragio a. **-ment** *n.* affrancamento; emancipazione; diritto di suffragio.
**engage** *tr.* impegnare; occupare; prendere; ingaggiare, noleggiare; assumere; *to — a room,* prenotare una camera; (mil.) impegnare battaglia; attaccare; (mech.) ingranare, innestare; *to — gears,* innestare la frizione; (fig.) attirare, attrarre, trattenere; *to — in,* impegnarsi in, prendere parte in.
**engaged** *adj.* impegnato, occupato; *— to be married,* fidanzato; *the — couple,* i fidanzati; (theatr.) scritturato; (teleph.) *line —,* linea occupata; (mech.) ingranato, innestato.
**engagement** *n.* impegno; *to enter into an —,* impegnarsi; *to free oneself from an —,* disimpegnarsi; fidanzamento; *— ring,* anello di fidanzamento; appuntamento; *— of staff,* assunzione; (mil.) scontro, combattimento.
**engaging** *adj.* attraente, seducente, simpatico.
**engender** *tr.* generare, far nascere; (fig.) causare, produrre.
**engine** *n.* macchina; *railway —,* locomotiva; *diesel —,* locomotore; (motor.) motore; *internal combustion —,* motore a combustione interna; *— trouble,* guasto al motore; (fig.) mezzo, strumento.
**engine-driver** *n.* macchinista *m.*
**engineer** *n.* ingegnere *m.*; meccanico, tecnico; (mil.) geniere *m.*; *the Engineers,* il genio militare; (naut.) macchinista *m.*; (fig.) promotore.
**engineer** *tr.* costruire; dirigere la costruzione di; (fam.) combinare, macchinare.
**engineering** *n.* ingegneria; costruzione meccanica.
**engine-room** *n.* sala macchine. **-shed** *n.* (rlwy.) rimessa per locomotive.
**England** *pr.n.* Inghilterra; *New —,* la Nuova Inghilterra; *the Church of —,* la chiesa anglicana.
**English** *adj.* inglese; *in the — manner,* all'inglese; *the — language,* la lingua inglese, l'inglese *m.*; *the — Channel,* la Manica; *n. the —,* gli inglesi; l'inglese; *King's (or Queen's) —,* l'inglese delle classi colte; *standard —,* l'inglese normale; (fam.) *in plain —,* in buon latino, chiaro e tondo; *tr.* tradurre in inglese; anglicizzare.
**English-born** *adj., n.* inglese di nascita.
**Englishman** *n.* inglese *m.*
**English-speaking** *adj.* che parla inglese.
**Englishwoman** *n.* inglese *f.*
**engraft** *tr.* innestare; (fig.) inculcare.
**engrain** *tr.* tingere a forte tinta; (fig.) penetrare profondamente in.
**engrav-e** *tr.* incidere, intagliare; (fig.) imprimere. **-er** *n.* incisore, intagliatore; (industr.) calcografo. **-ing** *n.* incisione, l'arte *f.* dell'incisione.
**engross** *tr.* scrivere (a grossi caratteri); copiare; (fig.) assorbire; *to be -ed in,* essere assorbito da. **-ing** *adj.* interessantissimo. **-ment** *n.* copiatura di documenti, bella copia.
**engulf** *tr.* inghiottire, ingolfare.
**enhance** *tr.* accrescere, intensificare; abbellire; aumentare. **-ment** *n.* abbellimento; intensificazione; aumento.
**enigma** *n.* enigma, enimma *m.* **-tic(al)** *adj.* enigmatico.
**enjoin** *tr.* ingiungere, imporre; intimare, raccomandare.
**enjoy** *tr.* godere; assaporare, gustare; provar piacere in; *to — good health,* godere buona salute; *to — a meal,* mangiare con appetito; *he -s reading,* gli piace leggere; *rfl. to — oneself,* divertirsi; *— yourself!,* buon divertimento! **-able** *adj.* piacevole, gradevole; divertente. **-ment** *n.* godimento; piacere *m.*; diletto; il divertirsi.
**enkindle** *tr.* infiammare, accendere.
**enlarge** *tr.* allargare; estendere; ampliare; (photog.) ingrandire; (fig.) *to — upon,* dilungarsi su. **-ment** *n.* allargamento; amplificazione; (photog.) ingrandimento; (med.) ipertrofia.
**enlighten** *tr.* illuminare, rischiarare; chiarire; istruire. **-er** *n.* (lit. hist.) illuminista *m., f.* **-ment** *n.* schiarimento; illuminazione; (lit. hist.) illuminismo.
**enlist** *tr.* arruolare; reclutare; ingaggiare; (fig.) assicurarsi l'aiuto di; *intr.* (mil.) arruolarsi come volontario. **-ment** *n.* (mil.) arruolamento; ingaggio.
**enliven** *tr.* animare; ravvivare.
**enmesh** *tr.* irretire; inviluppare.
**enmity** *n.* inimicizia; ostilità.
**ennoble** *tr.* nobilitare, rendere nobile. **-ment** *n.* nobilitazione; (fig.) esaltazione.
**ennui** *n.* noia; tedio.
**enormity** *n.* enormità; mostruosità.
**enormous** *adj.* enorme; immenso; smisurato. **-ness** *n.* enormità.
**enough** *adj.* abbastanza, bastante, sufficiente; *that's —!,* basta!; *— to live on,* tanto da vivere; *to have — and to spare,* avere più che abbastanza; *adv.* abbastanza; sufficientemente; discretamente; *sure —,* sicurissimo; *n.* il necessario; (provb.) *— is as good as a feast,* chi si contenta gode.
**enounce** *tr.* enunciare; pronunciare. **-ment** *n.* enunciazione; dichiarazione.
**enquire** *intr.* See **inquire.**
**enquiry** *n.* See **inquiry.**
**enrage** *tr.* far arrabbiare; *to be -d,* essere arrabbiato.
**enrapture** *tr.* rapire; estasiare; incantare; entusiasmare.
**enrich** *tr.* arricchire; (fig.) abbellire; impreziosire. **-ing, -ment** *n.* arricchimento; abbellimento.
**enrol(l)** *tr.* (mil.) arruolare; (industr.) ingaggiare; *intr.* arruolarsi; ingaggiarsi.
**ensconce** *tr.* mettere al sicuro; *to — oneself in a corner,* nascondersi in un angolo; *to — oneself in an armchair,* sprofondarsi in una poltrona.
**ensemble** *n.* complesso; insieme *m.*
**enshrine** *tr.* rinchiudere in un reliquiario, custodire come cosa sacra.
**enshroud** *tr.* avolgere; nascondere.
**ensign** *n.* bandiera; stendardo; insegna; distintivo; (mil. hist.) alfiere *m.*
**enslave** *tr.* asservire; assoggettare; far schiavo; (fig.) *to be -d by,* essere schiavo di.
**ensnare** *tr.* prendere al laccio, irretire.

**ensu-e** *intr.* seguire; derivare, risultare; succedere. **-ing** *adj.* seguente, successivo; conseguente.
**ensure** *tr.* assicurare; garantire.
**entablature** *n.* (archit.) trabeazione.
**entail** *n.* (leg.) assegnazione, eredità inalienabile; *tr.* (leg.) assegnare con limitazioni; (fig.) comportare, implicare.
**entangle** *tr.* imbrogliare; aggrovigliare; impigliare; (fig.) coinvolgere; *to become -d*, impigliarsi. **-ment** *n.* imbroglio; garbuglio; impiccio; (mil.) reticolato.
**entente** *n.* intesa.
**enter** *tr.* entrare in, entrare a far parte di; *to — a street*, imboccare una via; *to — the army*, entrare nell'esercito; *to — one's name*, iscriversi; (comm.) registrare, notare; *intr.* entrare; (theatr.) — *Hamlet*, entra Amleto; *to — into*, entrare in; iniziare; *to — into possession*, prendere possesso; *to — upon*, iniziare; *to — upon a discussion*, intavolare una discussione.
**enteric** *adj.* (med.) enterico, intestinale.
**entering** *n.* entrata; iscrizione, registrazione.
**enteritis** *n.* enterite *f.*
**enterpris-e** *n.* impresa; (fig.) iniziativa, spirito intraprendente; *to show —*, mostrarsi intraprendente. **-ing** *adj.* intraprendente, pieno d'iniziativa.
**entertain** *tr.* accogliere, ospitare, ricevere; divertire, intrattenere; (fig.) accarezzare, nutrire, avere, concepire; accettare, prendere in considerazione.
**entertainer** *n.* canzonettista *m.*, *f.*; comico.
**entertaining** *adj.* divertente; piacevole, ameno.
**entertainment** *n.* trattenimento; divertimento, spettacolo; *place of —*, luogo di divertimento; (comm.) — *allowance*, spese *f.pl.* di rappresentanza; — *tax*, tassa sugli spettacoli.
**enthral(l)** *tr.* incantare, affascinare, ammaliare. **-ling** *adj.* incantevole.
**enthrone** *tr.* mettere sul trono, incoronare; (eccl.) intronizzare. **-ment** *n.* incoronazione; intronizzazione; insediamento.
**enthuse** *intr.* entusiasmarsi.
**enthusi-asm** *n.* entusiasmo; *to be moved to —*, entusiasmarsi, appassionarsi. **-ast** *n.* entusiasta *m.,f.*; appassionato; tifoso. **-astic** *adj.* entusiastico; appassionato; *to become -astic*, entusiasmarsi.
**entic-e** *tr.* allettare; sedurre; adescare. **-ement** *n.* adescamento; allettamento; seduzione; lusinga; attrazione. **-er** *n.* seduttore; tentatore. **-ing** *adj.* seducente; attraente; lusinghevole.
**entire** *adj.* intero, completo, tutto; assoluto, perfetto. **-ly** *adv.* interamente, completamente; in tutto e per tutto. **-ty** *n.* interezza, totalità; *in its -ty*, per intero, nell'insieme.
**entitle** *tr.* intitolare; nominare; qualificare; dare diritto a; *to be -d to*, aver diritto a. **-ment** *n.* titolo; stile *m.*; diritto.
**entity** *n.* entità.
**entomb** *tr.* seppellire, mettere nella tomba; servire da tomba a. **-ment** *n.* sepoltura; seppellimento.
**entomolog-y** *n.* entomologia. **-ical** *adj.* entomologico. **-ist** *n.* entomologo.
**entrails** *n.pl.* viscere *f.pl.*; intestini *m.pl.*
**entrain** *tr.* far salire in treno; *intr.* salire in treno.
**entrammel** *tr.* impigliare, imbrogliare.
**entrance**[1] *n.* entrata; ingresso; accesso; adito; *to make one's —*, entrare; *to force an —*, entrare di forza; — *examination*, esame *m.* d'ammissione; — *free*, ingresso libero; *main —*, ingresso principale; *side —*, ingresso laterale.
**entranc-e**[2] *tr.* incantare; estasiare; rapire; ipnotizzare. **-ement** *n.* incanto; estasi *f.*; rapimento.
**entrancing** *adj.* incantevole.
**entrance-fee** *n.* tassa d'ammissione; tassa d'iscrizione; (theatr.) ingresso; (sport) entratura.
**entrant** *n.* chi entra; candidato; (sport) concorrente *m.*, *f.*; competitore.
**entrap** *tr.* prendere in trappola; raggirare.
**entreat** *tr.* supplicare; pregare; implorare. **-ing** *adj.* supplichevole. **-y** *n.* supplica, preghiera; istanza.
**entrée** *n.* entrata; (cul.) seconda portata.
**entrench** *tr.* trincerare, fortificare; *intr.* — *upon*, usurpare. **-ment** *n.* trinceramento; trincea.
**entresol** *n.* (archit.) mezzanino.
**entrust** *tr.* affidare, commettere, consegnare; *he has been -ed with the task*, gli è stato affidato il compito.
**entry** *n.* entrata; ingresso; accesso; (motor.) *no —*, senso unico, senso vietato; annotazione; (bookkeeping) partita; *double —*, partita doppia; (comm.) articolo registrato; (sport) iscrizione; elenco degli iscritti.
**entwine** *tr.* intrecciare, intessere; (fig.) stringere.
**enumerat-e** *tr.* enumerare; elencare; contare; annoverare. **-ion** *n.* enumerazione.
**enunciat-e** *tr.* enunciare, pronunciare, articolare. **-ion** *n.* enunciazione; dizione; pronuncia.
**envelop** *tr.* avviluppare, avvolgere; (mil.) circondare, accerchiare. **-ment** *n.* avvolgimento.
**envelope** *n.* busta; plico; *pay —*, busta paga; (biol.) involucro.
**envenom** *tr.* avvelenare; (fig.) amareggiare.
**enviable** *adj.* invidiabile.
**envious** *adj.* invidioso.
**environment** *n.* ambiente *m.*; condizioni ambientali. **-al** *adj.* ambientale.
**environs** *n.* dintorni *m.pl.*; vicinato.
**envisage** *tr.* contemplare; considerare; affrontare.
**envoi, envoy**[1] *n.* (prosod.) commiato.
**envoy**[2] inviato; legato; ministro plenipotenziario.
**envy** *n.* invidia; gelosia; *green with —*, verde d'invidia; *to excite —*, suscitare invidia; *to feel —*, invidiare; *to be the — of*, essere l'invidia di; *tr.* invidiare; *to be envied by*, fare invidia a.
**enwrap** *tr.* avvolgere, avvoltolare.
**enzyme** *n.* (biol.) enzima *m.*
**eocene** *adj.* (geol.) eocenico; *n.* eocene *m.*
**eolithic** *adj.* (geol.) eolitico.
**epaulette** *n.* (mil.) spallina.
**épergne** *n.* alzata da tavola.
**ephemeral** *adj.* effimero; passeggero.
**epic** *adj.* epico; *n.* epopea, poema epico.
**epicentre** *n.* (geol.) epicentro.
**epicure** *n.* epicureo; (fam.) buongustaio.
**Epicure-an** *adj.* epicureo. **-eanism** *n.* epicurismo.
**epicycle** *n.* (astron.) epiciclo.
**epidemic** *adj.* epidemico; *n.* epidemia. **-al** *adj.* epidemico.
**epidermis** *n.* epidermide *f.*
**epigram** *n.* epigramma *m.* **-matic(al)** *adj.* epigrammatico. **-matist** *n.* epigrammista *m.*
**epigraph** *n.* epigrafe *f.*
**epilep-sy** *n.* epilessia; mal caduco. **-tic** *adj.* epilettico; *-tic fit*, accesso epilettico; *n.* epilettico.
**epilogue** *n.* epilogo.
**Epiphany** *n.* (rel.) Epifania; (fam.) Befana.
**episcop-acy** *n.* episcopato. **-al** *adj.* episcopale, vescovile. **-ate** *n.* vescovato, episcopato.
**episod-e** *n.* episodio; incidente *m.* **-ic(al)** *adj.* episodico.
**epist-le** *n.* epistola. **-olary** *adj.* epistolare.
**epitaph** *n.* epitaffio.
**epithet** *n.* epiteto.
**epitom-e** *n.* epitome *m.*; (fig.) sunto; compendio. **-ize** *tr.* epitomare; (fig.) riassumere, compendiare.
**epoch** *n.* epoca; età.
**epoch-making** *adj.* che fa epoca, storico.
**epos** *n.* epos *m. indecl.*; epopea.
**Epsom** *pr.n.* (geog.) Epsom; — *salts*, sale *m.* inglese.

**equab-le** *adj.* uniforme; costante; equanime. **-ility** *n.* uniformità; equanimità, serenità.

**equal** *adj.* eguale, uguale; pari; *other things being —*, a parità di condizioni; *of — value*, dello stesso valore; *an — contest*, una lotta serrata; *to be — to*, essere pari a, equivalere; *to be — to the occasion*, essere all'altezza della situazione; *to feel — to*, sentirsi capace di; (fam.) *to get — with someone*, rendere pan per focaccia; *n.* pari *m. indecl.*; simile *m., f.*; *to treat as an —*, trattare da pari a pari; *to find one's —*, incontrare un degno avversario; *tr.* uguagliare, equivalere a; *two plus two -s four*, due più due fa quattro; *there is nothing to — it*, non c'è nulla che lo possa uguagliare.

**equality** *n.* uguaglianza; parità; *on a footing of —* su un piede di parità.

**equaliz-e** *tr.* agguagliare, ragguagliare; parificare; equiparare, uniformare; (sport) pareggiare. **-ation** *n.* parificazione; livellamento; perequazione; (finan.) compensazione. **-er** *n.* (sport) pareggio.

**equally** *adv.* egualmente; parimenti.

**equanimity** *n.* equanimità; serenità.

**equate** *tr.* rendere uguale; (math.) uguagliare; (fig.) paragonare.

**equation** *n.* (math.) equazione.

**equator** *n.* (geog.) equatore *m.* **-ial** *adj.* (geog.) equatoriale.

**equerry** *n.* (hist.) scudiero; (modern) gentiluomo di servizio a corte.

**equestrian** *adj.* equestre; — *sports*, equitazione; *n.* cavallerizzo, cavaliere *m.*

**equidistant** *adj.* equidistante.

**equilateral** *adj.* (geom.) equilaterale, equilatero.

**equilibrat-e** *tr.* equilibrare; bilanciare; *intr.* equilibrarsi, bilanciarsi. **-ion** *n.* equilibrazione.

**equilibrist** *n.* equilibrista *m.*; funambolo.

**equilibrium** *n.* equilibrio; *to keep one's —*, mantenersi in equilibrio.

**equine** *adj.* equino, ippico.

**equi-nox** *n.* equinozio. **-noctial** *adj.* equinoziale.

**equip** *tr.* equipaggiare, allestire; dotare; arredare; attrezzare; *to — with*, fornire di; *to be -ped with*, avere in dotazione; (mil.) armare. **-ment** *n.* equipaggiamento; *the necessary -ment*, il necessario; arredamento; attrezzatura; attrezzi *m.pl.*; (electr.) apparecchiatura; (mil.) armamento.

**equipoise** *n.* equilibrio; contrappeso; *tr.* equilibrare; bilanciare.

**equitable** *adj.* equo; giusto; imparziale. **-ness** *n.* equità.

**equitation** *n.* equitazione.

**equity** *n.* equità; giustizia; (finan.) azioni ordinarie a reddito variabile.

**equival-ence** *n.* equivalenza. **-ent** *adj.* equivalente; *to be -ent to*, equivalere a; *n.* equivalente *m.*

**equivocal** *adj.* equivoco; ambiguo. **-ity** *n.* equivocità; ambiguità.

**equivocat-e** *intr.* equivocare; cavillare. **-ion** *n.* equivoco; giuoco di parole.

**era** *n.* era; epoca.

**eradicable** *adj.* sradicabile; estirpabile.

**eradicat-e** *tr.* sradicare; estirpare; divellere. **-ion** *n.* sradicamento; estirpazione.

**eras-e** *tr.* cancellare, raschiare. **-er** *n.* raschino; gomma per cancellare. **-ure** *n.* cancellatura, raschiatura.

**ere** *prep.* prima di; *conj.* prima che, piuttosto che.

**Erebus** *pr.n.* (myth) Erebo.

**erect** *tr.* erigere; innalzare, rizzare; costruire; *adj.* eretto; dritto, ritto; in piedi. **-ion** *n.* erezione; costruzione; edificio; (mech.) montaggio.

**erewhile** *adv.* (poet.) poco fa.

**ergot** *n.* (bot.) segala cornuta.

**Erin** *pr.n.* (poet.) Irlanda.

**Eritre-a** *pr.n.* (geog.) Eritrea. **-an** *adj., n.* eritreo.

**ermine** *n.* ermellino; *attrib.* di ermellino.

**Ernest** *pr.n.* Ernesto.

**ero-de** *tr.* erodere; corrodere; consumare. **-sion** *n.* erosione; corrosione.

**erotic** *adj.* erotico. **-ism** *n.* erotismo.

**err** *intr.* fare errori; sbagliare; peccare; (fig.) allontanarsi.

**errand** *n.* commissione; ambasciata; *to run -s*, fare commissioni; (fig.) incarico; *fool's —*, impresa inutile.

**errand-boy** *n.* fattorino.

**errant** *adj.* errante.

**erratic** *adj.* erratico; irregolare; intermittente; discontinuo.

**erring** *adj.* che sbaglia; traviato; che si allontana dalla retta via.

**erroneous** *adj.* erroneo; sbagliato.

**error** *n.* errore *m.*; sbaglio; abbaglio; *clerical —*, errore di trascrizione; *printer's —*, errore di stampa; *-s and ommissions excepted*, salvo errori ed omissioni; *to be in —*, aver torto.

**erstwhile** *adv.* (poet.) tempo fa; *adj.* — *president*, ex presidente *m.*

**eruct, -ate** *tr., intr.* eruttare, ruttare. **-ation** *n.* eruttazione; rutto.

**erudit-e** *adj.* erudito; dotto. **-ion** *n.* erudizione; dottrina.

**erupt** *intr.* erompere; eruttare. **-ion** *n.* eruzione; (fig.) scoppio.

**escalat-e** *intr.* crescere rapidamente, aumentarsi. **-ion** *n.* aumento, sviluppo rapidissimo.

**escalator** *n.* scala mobile.

**escapade** *n.* scappatella; birichinata.

**escape** *n.* fuga; evasione; scampo; — *of gas*, fuga di gas; *to make one's —*, fuggire, evadere, scappare; *to have a narrow —*, cavarsela per miracolo; *means of —*, scampo; (mech.) scappamento.

**escape** *tr.* sfuggire, evitare, scansare, schivare; *intr.* fuggire, evadere, scappare, scampare; *an attempt to —*, un tentativo di evasione; *an -d prisoner*, un evaso; *to — by the skin of one's teeth*, farcela per un pelo.

**escapement** *n.* (mus.; mech.) scappamento.

**escap-ism** *n.* evasione dalla realtà. **-ist** *n.* chi cerca di sfuggire alla realtà; *attrib.* *-ist literature*, letteratura d'evasione.

**escarpment** *n.* scarpata.

**eschatolog-y** *n.* escatologia. **-ical** *adj.* escatologico.

**eschew** *tr.* evitare; astenersi da.

**e'scort** *n.* (mil.) scorta; *to conduct under —*, scortare; accompagnatore.

**escort** *tr.* scortare; accompagnare.

**escutcheon** *n.* (herald.) scudo; (fig.) *a blot on one's —*, una macchia sulla propria reputazione.

**Eskimo** *adj., n.* eschimese *m., f.*

**esophagus** *n.* (anat.) esofago.

**esoteric(al)** *adj.* esoterico.

**espalier** *n.* spalliera.

**esparto** *n.* — *grass*, sparto.

**especial** *adj.* notevole; particolare; speciale. **-ly** *adv.* specialmente; soprattutto; specie.

**espionage** *n.* spionaggio.

**esplanade** *n.* spianata, passeggiata; lungomare *m.*

**espous-e** *tr.* sposare; (fig.) abbracciare; appoggiare. **-al** *n.* sposalizio; (fig.) adozione.

**espy** *tr.* scorgere; scoprire.

**esquire** *n.* (hist.) scudiero; (as courtesy title) signore; nobiluomo.

**es'say** *n.* prova, saggio, tentativo; (lit.) saggio; (schol.) componimento.

**essay** *tr.* provare, provarsi in tentare.

**essayist** *n.* saggista *m., f.*

**essence** *n.* essenza; sostanza; (fig.) nocciolo; quintessenza.

**essential** *adj.* essenziale; sostanziale; indispensabile, di prima necessità; *the — thing*, l'essenziale; *n.* essenziale *m.* **-ity, -ness** *n.* essenzialità.

**establish** *tr.* stabilire; constatare; provare; fondare, istituire, instaurare; *to — relations with*, stringere rapporti con; (leg.) confermare.

**established** *adj.* stabilito; constatato; fondato; istituito; *the*

*Established Church*, la religione di Stato.
**establishment** *n.* lo stabilire; constatazione; fondazione; costituzione; azienda; casa, famiglia; personale *m.*; (mil.) personale effettivo; (fam.) *the* —, la cricca dominante, le eminenze grigie.
**estate** *n.* stato, condizione; tenuta, proprietà; rango; classe *f.*; *man's* —, l'età virile; beni *m.pl.*, patrimonio; — *duty*, imposta sul patrimonio; *personal* —, beni mobili; *real* —, beni immobili.
**estate-agent** *n.* mediatore; fattore.
**esteem** *n.* stima, considerazione; *to hold in* —, aver grande stima di; *tr.* stimare, tenere in gran conto, apprezzare; considerare; (comm.) *your -ed order*, vostro ambito ordine.
**estimable** *adj.* stimabile; pregevole.
**estimat-e** *n.* stima; valutazione; (comm.) preventivo; (fig.) calcolo; *tr.* stimare, fare la stima di, valutare; (comm.) preventivare; (fig.) calcolare. **-ion** *n.* stima; valutazione; apprezzamento; considerazione.
**estrange** *tr.* alienare; allontanare; disaffezionare; *to become -d from*, allontanarsi da, staccarsi da. **-ment** *n.* alienazione; allontanamento; distacco; discordia; disinnamoramento.
**estuary** *n.* estuario.
**etcetera, etc.** eccetera, ecc.; *n.pl.* (fam.) annessi e connessi.
**etch** *tr.* incidere all'acquaforte; (chem.) attaccare. **-er** *n.* acquafortista, incisore *m.* **-ing** *n.* incisione all'acquaforte, acquaforte *f.*
**eternal** *adj.* eterno; (fig.) incessante; *n. the Eternal*, l'Eterno.
**eternity** *n.* eternità.
**ether** *n.* (chem.) etere *m.*; (fig.) aria; cielo.
**ethereal** *adj.* etereo, del cielo; (fig.) impalpabile; spirituale; (chem.) volatile.
**ethic(al)** *adj.* etico; morale.
**ethics** *n.* etica.
**Ethiopia** *pr.n.* (geog.) Etiopia. **-n** *adj.* etiopico; *n.* etiope *m., f.*
**ethnic(al)** *adj.* etnico.
**ethnograph-y** *n.* etnografia. **-er** *n.* etnografo. **-ic(al)** *adj.* etnografico.
**ethnolog-y** *n.* etnologia. **-ical** *adj.* etnologico. **-ist** *n.* etnologo.
**ethyl** *n.* (chem.) etile *m.*
**etiquette** *n.* etichetta; protocollo; usi *m.pl.* convenzionali; galateo.
**Etruscan** *adj., n.* etrusco.
**etymolog-y** *n.* etimologia. **-ical** *adj.* etimologico. **-ist** *n.* etimologista *m., f.*
**eucalyptus** *n.* eucalipto.
**eucharist** *n.* (theol.) eucaristia. **-ic** *adj.* (theol.) eucaristico.
**Euclid** *pr.n.* Euclide; (fam.) geometria.
**Euganean** *adj.* (geog.) euganeo; — *hills*, Colli Euganei.
**Eugene** *pr.n.* Eugenio.
**eugenic** *adj.* eugenico. **-s** *n.pl.* eugenetica.
**eulog-y** *n.* elogio; panegirico. **-ise** *tr.* fare l'elogio di; laudare. **-ist** *n.* elogiatore; panegirista *n.* **-istic(al)** *adj.* elogiativo; laudativo.
**Eumenides** *n.pl.* (myth.) Eumenidi *f.pl.*
**eunuch** *n.* eunuco.
**euphem-ism** *n.* eufemismo. **-istic** *adj.* eufemistico.
**euphon-y** *n.* eufonia; *for the sake of* —, per eufonia. **-ic** *adj.* eufonico; armonioso.
**Euphrates** *pr.n.* (geog.) Eufrate *m.*
**euphuism** *n.* (lit.) eufuismo.
**Eurasian** *adj., n.* eurasiatico.
**eurhythmic** *adj.* euritmico; regolare. **-s** *n.pl.* euritmia.
**Euripides** *pr.n.* Euripide.
**Europ-e** *pr.n.* Europa. **-ean** *adj., n.* europeo. **-eanize** *tr.* europeizzare.
**Eustace** *pr.n.* Eustachio.
**euthanasia** *n.* eutanasia.
**Eva** *pr.n.* Eva.
**evacuat-e** *tr., intr.* evacuare; sfollare; (mil.) ritirarsi; (med.) evacuare. **-ion** *n.* evacuazione.
**evacuee** *n.* sfollato, sfollata.
**evade** *tr.* evadere a; evitare, eludere, schivare; sottrarsi a.
**evaluat-e** *tr.* valutare. **-ion** *n.* valutazione.
**evanesc-e** *intr.* svanire. **-ence** *n.* evanescenza. **-ent** *adj.* evanescente.
**evangel-ic(al)** *adj.* evangelico. **-ism** *n.* predicazione del vangelo. **-ist** *n.* evangelista *m.* **-ize** *tr.* evangelizzare.
**evaporat-e** *tr.* far evaporare; *intr.* evaporare; *-ed milk*, latte evaporato. **-ion** *n.* evaporazione.
**evas-ion** *n.* evasione; *tax* —, evasione fiscale; sotterfugio; pretesto. **-ive** *adj.* evasivo.
**Eve**[1] *pr.n.* Eva.
**eve**[2] *n.* vigilia; *on the — of*, (al)la vigilia di (also fig.); *Christmas Eve*, la vigilia di Natale; *New Year's Eve*, il San Silvestro, l'ultimo dell'anno; (poet.) sera; *at* —, di sera.
**even** *adj.* uguale, uniforme; piano, liscio, piatto; regolare; pari; *odds and -s*, pari e dispari; — *with*, a livello di; *to get — with*, prendere la rivincita su; — *chance*, probabilità discreta; *an — contest*, una lotta ad armi pari; *to back a horse at -s*, scommettere su un cavallo alla pari; *tr.* appianare, livellare; uguagliare, rendere uguale; *to — up*, pareggiare, bilanciare; *adv.* ancora, perfino, anche, proprio; — *if*, anche se, seppure; — *so*, anche se è così; *not* —, neppure. neanche; — *though*, seppure, quand'anche; — *as*, proprio mentre.
**evenfall** *n.* (poet.) crepuscolo.
**evening** *n.* sera; serata; *this* —, stasera; *yesterday* —, ieri sera, iersera; *good* —, buona sera; *in the* —, di sera; *a musical* —, una serata musicale; *to spend the* —, passare la serata; — *dress*, abito da sera; (men's) frac *m. indecl.*; — *paper*, giornale *m.* della sera; — *star*, stella della sera, vespero; (rel.) — *prayer*, vespro; (fig.) declino; fine *f.*; tramonto.
**evenly** *adv.* ugualmente, in modo uguale, parimente; imparzialmente, equamente.
**even-minded** *adj.* equilibrato, imparziale.
**evenness** *n.* uguaglianza; regolarità; uniformità; (of temper) serenità.
**even-numbered** *adj.* avente i numeri pari.
**evensong** *n.* (rel.) vespro.
**event** *n.* caso; avvenimento; eventualità; *current -s*, attualità *f.pl.*; (sport) prova, gara.
**eventful** *adj.* ricco di avvenimenti, memorabile; (fig.) movimentato. **-ness** *n.* ricchezza di avvenimenti.
**eventide** *n.* (poet.) sera, tramonto.
**eventual** *adj.* ultimo, finale; conclusivo, decisivo; definitivo. **-ity** *n.* eventualità. **-ly** *adv.* alla fine, finalmente, in ultimo.
**eventuate** *intr.* risultare; avverarsi.
**ever** *adv.* mai; *hardly* —, quasi mai; — *and again.* ogni tanto; sempre; *for* —, per sempre; *yours* —, sempre tuo; — *after*, da allora in poi; — *since*, (*adv.*) da allora, (*conj.*) da quando; — *so much easier*, infinitamente più facile; (fam.) *did you —!*, caspita!; *he is — so nice!*, è tanto gentile!
**evergreen** *adj., n.* (bot.) sempreverde *m.*; che ha sempre d'attualità.
**everlasting** *adj.* eterno, sempiterno, perpetuo, perenne.
**evermore** *adv.* sempre, perpetuamente; *for* —, per sempre.
**every** *adj.* ogni, ognuno, ciascuno, tutti; — *other day*, ogni due giorni, un giorno sì un giorno no; — *now and then*, ogni tanto, di quando in quando; — *one*, ciascuno, ognuno, tutti; — *man for himself*, ciascuno per sè, si salvi chi può.
**every-body** *pr.n.* ognuno, tutti; — *else*, tutti gli altri. **-day** *adj.* quotidiano, di tutti i giorni; (fig.) normale, all'ordine del giorno; *adv.* ogni giorno. **-man** *n.* ogni uomo, ognuno; chiunque. **-one** *pr.n.* ciascuno, ognuno, tutti; *-one else*, tutti gli

altri, tutti quanti. **-thing** *pr.n.* ogni cosa; tutto; (fig.) tutto, cosa di massima importanza. **-where** *adv.* dovunque, dappertutto, in qualsiasi luogo, per ogni dove.

**evict** *tr.* sfrattare; espellere. **-ion** *n.* sfratto.

**evidence** *n.* evidenza; prova; *external —*, prova estrinseca; *internal —*, prova intrinseca; *to give — of*, dar prova di; *to be in —*, essere in vista, farsi vedere; *to fly in the face of —*, rifiutare di riconoscere la verità; (leg.) testimonianza, deposizione; indizio; *to give —*, testimoniare, deporre; *circumstantial —*, prove indirette.

**evidence** *tr.* dimostrare; provare; manifestare.

**evident** *adj.* evidente; manifesto; ovvio; chiaro. **-ial** *adj.* probativo, indicativo. **-ly** *adv.* evidentemente; ovviamente.

**evil** *adj.* cattivo, malvagio, perverso; (fig.) brutto, sfortunato; *the Evil one*, il demonio, il diavolo; *— reputation*, cattiva reputazione; *— tongue*, mala lingua; *— eye*, malocchio; *to fall on — days*, trovarsi in difficoltà.

**evil** *n.* male *m.*; peccato; *to do —*, fare del male, peccare; *to speak — of*, parlar male di; *to return good for —*, rendere bene per male; *King's —*, scrofola.

**evil-doer** *n.* malfattore, malvivente *m.*

**evilly** *adv.* male; malvagiamente.

**evil-looking** *adj.* losco; sinistro. **-minded** *adj.* malintenzionato. **-speaking** *adj.* maldicente; *n.* maldicenza.

**evince** *tr.* mostrare, manifestare, dimostrare.

**eviscerate** *tr.* sviscerare, sventrare.

**evocat-ion** *n.* evocazione. **-ive, -ory** *adj.* evocatore; evocativo.

**evoke** *tr.* evocare.

**evolution** *n.* evoluzione; svolgimento, sviluppo. **-ary** *adj.* (per mezzo) di evoluzione. **-ist** *n.* evoluzionista *m.*

**evolve** *tr.* evolvere; svolgere; elaborare; sviluppare; *intr.* svolgersi; svilupparsi.

**ewe** *n.* pecora.

**ewe-lamb** *n.* agnella; (fig.) tesorino.

**ewer** *n.* brocca; boccale *m.*

**ex-** *pref.* ex; già; un tempo; quondam; fu.

**exacerbate** *tr.* esacerbare; esasperare, irritare; dare noia a.

**exact** *adj.* esatto; preciso; giusto; puntuale; *tr.* esigere; chiedere; richiedere. **-ing** *adj.* esigente; impegnativo; che richiede attenzione. **-ion** *n.* esazione; estorsione; (leg.) concussione. **-itude, -ness** *n.* esattezza; precisione.

**exaggerat-e** *tr.*, *intr.* esagerare, eccedere; rincarare la dose; essere eccessivo. **-ion** *n.* esagerazione.

**exalt** *tr.* esaltare; elevare, innalzare, vantare, lodare; *to — to the skies*, portare al settimo cielo. **-ation** *n.* esaltazione; eccitazione. **-ed** *adj.* elevato; di alto rango; esaltato, eccitato.

**exam** *n.* (schol.) esame *m.*

**examination** *n.* esame; verifica, ispezione; *on —*, all'esame; *after thorough —*, dopo accurata disamina; *the matter is under —*, si sta studiando la questione; *customs —*, visita doganale; *medical —*, visita medica; (leg., of witnesses) interrogatorio; (schol.) esame, prova; *competitive —*, concorso; *entrance —*, esame di ammissione; *oral —*, prova orale; *written —*, prova scritta; *to take an —*, dare un esame; *to pass an —*, superare un esame; *to fail in an —*, essere rimandato, (fam.) essere bocciato.

**examin-e** *tr.* esaminare; verificare; ispezionare; (med.) visitare; (leg.) *to — a case*, istruire un processo; *to — a witness*, interrogare un testimonio; *examining magistrate*, giudice istruttore. **-ee** *n.* candidato. **-er** *n.* ispettore; verificatore; esaminatore; *board of -ers*, commissione d'esame.

**example** *n.* esempio; esemplare *m.*; tipo; precedente *m.*; *to set an —*, dare l'esempio; *to make an — of*, dare una punizione esemplare a; *for —*, per esempio, ad esempio.

**exasperat-e** *tr.* esasperare; inasprire, eccitare, irritare; *to become -d*, irritarsi, accalorarsi; provocare; (fig.) *to — a situation*, aggravare una situazione. **-ing** *adj.* esasperante; irritante. **-ion** *n.* esasperazione; irritazione; (fig.) aggravamento, peggioramento.

**excavat-e** *tr.* scavare. **-ion** *n.* scavo; lo scavare; (bldg.) sterro. **-or** *n.* scavatore; sterratore; (machine) escavatore; scavatrice.

**exceed** *tr.* eccedere; superare, oltrepassare; andare oltre; esorbitare da; *not -ing*, non oltre; (motor.) *-ing the speed limit*, eccesso di velocità. **-ingly** *adv.* molto; estremamente.

**excel** *tr.* superare, essere superiore a; *intr.* primeggiare, eccellere.

**excellenc-e** *n.* eccellenza; pregio; superiorità; perfezione; *par —*, per eccellenza. **-y** *n.* (title) Eccellenza.

**excellent** *adj.* eccellente; ottimo; buonissimo, bravo.

**except** *prep.* eccetto; salvo, tranne, ad eccezione di, eccettuato, all'infuori di; *conj.*; *— that*, salvo che, senonchè; *tr.* eccettuare; escludere; *intr.* eccepire.

**excepting** *prep.* See **except.**

**exception** *n.* eccezione; *with the — of*, ad eccezione di; *the — proves the rule*, l'eccezione conferma la regola; *to take — to*, eccepire a, trovare a ridire su, criticare. **-able** *adj.* eccepibile; criticabile. **-al** *adj.* eccezionale; singolare; insolito; raro; d'eccezione.

**excerpt** *n.* estratto, brano scelto; citazione.

**excess** *n.* eccesso; eccedenza; sovrabbondanza; eccedente *m.*; intemperanza; *in — of*, in eccesso di, eccedente, oltre; *to be in — of*, superare, oltrepassare; *to eat to —*, mangiare troppo; *to carry to —*, portare all'eccesso, esagerare; *attrib. — fare*, supplemento, differenza; *— luggage*, bagaglio eccedente; *— profits duty*, tassa sui soprapprofitti; *— weight*, soprappeso. **-ive** *adj.* eccessivo; esagerato; smoderato. **-iveness** *n.* eccessività; smoderatezza.

**exchange** *n.* cambio; scambio; *— and barter*, baratto; *in — for*, in cambio di; *to take in —*, prendere in cambio; *an — of compliments*, uno scambio di complimenti; (finan.) cambio; *— office*, ufficio cambio, cambiavalute *m. indecl.*; *par of —*, parità di cambio; *rate of —*, tasso di cambio; *bill of —*, cambiale *f.*; *telephone —*, centrale *f.*; *labour —*, ufficio di collocamento.

**exchange** *tr.* scambiare; cambiare; barattare; *to — greetings*, scambiare saluti.

**exchangeab-le** *adj.* scambiabile, cambiabile. **-ility** *n.* possibilità di scambio.

**exchequer** *n.* scacchiere *m.*; *Chancellor of the —*, Cancelliere dello Scacchiere, Ministro delle Finanze; erario; tesoro; (fam.) risorse *f.pl.*

**ex'cise**[1] *n.* imposte indirette; dazio di consumo; *tr.* tassare. **-man** *n.* daziere *m.*

**excis-e**[2] *tr.* tagliar via; recidere. **-ion** *n.* taglio; recisione.

**excitab-le** *adj.* eccitabile; impressionabile; emotivo. **-ility** *n.* eccitabilità.

**excit-e** *tr.* eccitare; elettrizzare; stimolare; provocare; *to — suspicion*, suscitare sospetto; *easily -d*, eccitabile, molto impressionabile. **-ed** *adj.* eccitato; commosso; emozionato; *to get -ed*, eccitarsi; commuoversi. **-ement** *n.* eccitazione; agitazione; emozione; sensazione; orgasmo. **-ing** *adj.* emozionante.

**exclaim** *intr.* esclamare; gridare.

**exclamat-ion** *n.* esclamazione; grido; *— mark*, punto esclamativo. **-ive, -ory** *adj.* esclamativo.

**exclud-e** *tr.* escludere; scartare; *to — someone from entering*, vietare a qualcuno l'ingresso. **-ing** *prep.* escluso; eccettuato; senza contare.

**exclusion** *n.* esclusione.
**exclusive** *adj.* esclusivo; — *rights*, diritti *m.pl.* esclusivi, esclusiva; — *of*, escluso, senza contare, all'infuori di; solo, unico; chiuso, scelto, riservato a poche persone; che accoglie una clientela scelta; signorile. **-ness** *n.* esclusività.
**excogitate** *tr.* escogitare; architettare.
**excommunicat-e** *tr.* (eccl.) scomunicare. **-ion** *n.* (eccl.) scomunica; anatema *m.*
**excoriat-e** *tr.* escoriare; scorticare. **-ion** *n.* escoriazione; scorticatura.
**excrement** *n.* escremento; sterco.
**excrescence** *n.* escresenza; protuberanza.
**excretion** *n.* escrezione.
**excruciat-e** *tr.* tormentare, straziare. **-ing** *adj.* atroce, straziante. **-ingly** *adv.* atrocemente; (fam.) *-ingly funny*, buffo da far scoppiare.
**exculpat-e** *tr.* scolpare; assolvere; giustificare. **-ion** *n.* discolpa; giustificazione.
**excursion** *n.* escursione; gita; *to go on an* —, fare una gita; — *train*, treno popolare; (fig.) digressione, divagazione. **-ist** *n.* escursionista *m., f.*; gitante *m., f.*
**excursive** *adj.* digressivo, divagante; errante.
**excursus** *n.* dissertazione.
**excusable** *adj.* scusabile; perdonabile.
**excuse** *n.* scusa; giustificazione; *to make -s*, scusarsi; *lame -s*, magre scuse; *a poor* —, una meschina scusa; pretesto; *to find an* —, trovare un pretesto.
**excuse** *tr.* scusare; perdonare; giustificare; — *me!*, scusi!, permesso!; *to — from*, dispensare da, esentare da; *to — someone on the grounds of youth*, scusare con l'età giovanile.
**execrable** *adj.* esecrabile; esecrando.
**execrat-e** *tr.* esecrare; detestare, maledire. **-ion** *n.* esecrazione; maledizione.
**executant** *n.* esecutore.
**execute** *tr.* eseguire; mettere in esecuzione; (comm.) dare esecuzione a, mandare ad effetto, effettuare; (art) creare, eseguire; (leg.) eseguire, convalidare; *to — a criminal*, giustiziare un condannato.
**execution** *n.* esecuzione; adempimento; *to put in* —, dar corso a; attuazione; (art) esecuzione; (of criminal) esecuzione capitale, esecuzione di una sentenza di morte; (leg.) convalidazione; sequestro. **-er** *n.* boia *m.*, carnefice *m.*
**executive** *adj.* esecutivo; *n.* potere esecutivo, direzione; dirigente *m.*; funzionario.
**executor** *n.* (leg.) esecutore testamentario; *literary* —, curatore di opere postume.
**executrix** *n.* (leg.) esecutrice testamentaria.
**exegesis** *n.* esegesi *f.*
**exegete** *n.* esegeta *m.*
**exemplar** *n.* esemplare *m.*; modello; tipo. **-iness, -ity** *n.* esemplarità. **-y** *adj.* esemplare; che serve da modello.
**exemplif-y** *tr.* esemplificare; illustrare con esempi; servire d'esempio a. **-ication** *n.* esemplificazione.
**exempt** *adj.* esente; dispensato; esonerato; *tr.* esentare; dispensare; esonerare. **-ion** *n.* esenzione; dispensa; esonero.
**exequies** *n.pl.* esequie *f.pl.*
**exercise** *n.* esercizio; uso; esercizio fisico, moto; *to take* —, fare del moto; (schol.) tema *m.*; compito; (mil.) esercitazione; manovre *f.pl.*
**exercise** *tr.* esercitare; usare; praticare; allenare; preoccupare.
**exercise-book** *n.* quaderno.
**exert** *tr.* esercitare, adoperare, impiegare; *rfl.* sforzarsi, darsi da fare, adoperarsi. **-ion** *n.* esercizio; uso; impiego; sforzo.
**exhal-e** *tr.* esalare; emanare; *intr.* spirare. **-ation** *n.* esalazione.
**exhaust** *n.* (mech.) scappamento, scarico; — *pipe*, tubo di scarico; *tr.* esaurire; stancare; spossare; vuotare; *rfl.* esaurirsi. **-ed** *adj.* esaurito, esausto; sfinito; spossato; stanco; vuoto. **-ible** *adj.* esauribile. **-ing** che esaurisce; che stanca; spossante; faticoso. **-ion** *n.* esaurimento; *state of -ion*, spossatezza. **-ive** *adj.* esauriente; completo; approfondito.
**exhibit** *n.* oggetto esposto in una mostra; (leg.) documento, oggetto di appoggio; *tr.* esibire; esporre; mostrare.
**exhibition** *n.* presentazione; produzione; esposizione, mostra; (comm.; industr.) fiera; (fig.) *to make an — of oneself*, dare spettacolo di sè. **-ism** *n.* esibizionismo.
**exhibitor** *n.* esibitore, espositore.
**exhilarat-e** *tr.* esilarare; rallegrare. **-ing** *adj.* esilarante. **-ion** *n.* esilaramento; allegrezza; ilarità.
**exhort** *tr.* esortare; raccomandare. **-ation** *n.* esortazione. **-atory** *adj.* esortatorio.
**exhum-e** *tr.* esumare, disumare. **-ation** *n.* esumazione; disseppellimento.
**exig-ence, -ency** *n.* esigenza; necessità; bisogno; situazione critica; crisi *f. indecl.* **-ent** *adj.* esigente; pressante; urgente.
**exiguity, exiguousness** *n.* esiguità; piccolezza.
**exiguous** *adj.* esiguo; piccolo.
**exile** *n.* esilio; bando; esule *m., f.*; esiliato; fuoruscito; *tr.* esiliare, condannare all'esilio; mettere al bando; proscrivere.
**exist** *intr.* esistere; essere; vivere.
**existence** *n.* esistenza; vita; *to be in* —, esistere; *to come into* —, nascere; *to bring into* —, far nascere, creare; *the biggest in* —, il più grande che esista.
**existent** *adj.* esistente.
**existential** *adj.* (philos.) esistenziale. **-ism** *n.* esistenzialismo. **-ist** *n.* esistenzialista *m.*
**existing** *adj.* esistente; attuale.
**exit** *n.* uscita; *to make one's* —, uscire; (fig.) morire; *emergency* —, uscita di sicurezza; *intr.* uscire.
**exodus** *n.* esodo; partenza; (bibl.) Esodo.
**exonerat-e** *tr.* esonerare; dispensare; assolvere; discolpare. **-ion** *n.* esonero; discolpa; assoluzione.
**exorbit-ance** *n.* esorbitanza; esagerazione. **-ant** *adj.* esorbitante; esagerato; eccessivo.
**exorc-ism** *n.* esorcismo; scongiuro. **-ist** *n.* esorcista *m.* **-ize** *tr.* esorcizzare; scongiurare.
**exordium** *n.* esordio.
**exotic** *adj.* esotico; *n.* pianta esotica. **-ism** *n.* esotismo.
**expand** *tr.* espandere; estendere; dilatare; allargare; spiegare; *intr.* espandersi; estendersi; (fig.) diventare espansivo.
**expanse** *n.* distesa; spazio; estensione.
**expansion** *n.* espansione; estensione; allargamento; sviluppo. **-ism** *n.* (econ.) espansionismo.
**expansive** *adj.* espansivo; esteso; ampio; esuberante. **-ness** *n.* espansività; esuberanza.
**expatiat-e** *intr.* diffondersi, dilungarsi, dissertare. **-ion** *n.* dissertazione; discorso lungo.
**expatriat-e** *adj.*, *n.* espatriato; *tr.*, *intr.* espatriare. **-ion** *n.* espatrio.
**expect** *tr.* aspettare, aspettarsi, attendere; *I -ed him yesterday*, lo aspettavo ieri; *I -ed that he would come*, mi aspettavo che sarebbe venuto; *to be -ing a baby*, essere in attesa di un bambino; *to — the worst*, aspettarsi il peggio; esigere, pretendere; pensare, credere, supporre; *what can you —?*, che vuoi?
**expectancy** *n.* aspettativa; attesa.
**expectant** *adj.* che attende, che aspetta; — *mother*, donna incinta. **-ly** *adv.* in attesa.
**expectation** *n.* aspettazione, aspettativa; attesa; *in — of*, in attesa di; *to come up to -s*, rispondere all'aspettativa; *to fall short of -s*, non corrispondere all'aspettativa, deludere; — *of life*, probabilità di vita; *pl.* speranze *f.pl.*; prospettiva di eredità.

**expectorate** *tr.*, *intr.* espettorare; sputare.
**expedience, expediency** *n.* convenienza, opportunità; vantaggio; utilità.
**expedient** *adj.* conveniente, opportuno, utile, vantaggioso; *n.* espediente *m.*; accorgimento; mezzo; ripiego; *to resort to -s*, ricorrere ad espedienti.
**expedite** *tr.* sbrigare; accelerare; sollecitare.
**expedition** *n.* spedizione; prontezza; sollecitudine *f.*
**expeditionary** *adj.* (mil.) di spedizione; — *force*, corpo di spedizione.
**expeditious** *adj.* speditivo; sbrigativo; pronto, sollecito. **-ness** *n.* prontezza; sollecitudine *f.*
**expel** *tr.* espellere; scacciare; radiare; *to be -led* (from school, *etc.*), essere rimosso.
**expend** *tr.* spendere; consumare; esaurire. **-iture** *n.* spesa; dispendio; consumo.
**expense** *n.* spesa; *at one's own* —, a proprie spese; *at the firm's* —, a spese della ditta; *entertainment -s*, spese di rappresentanza; *incidental -s*, spese varie; *overhead -s*, spese generali; — *account*, conto spese; costo, prezzo; *at the — of his life*, a prezzo della vita; *a useless — of time*, uno spreco inutile di tempo; *to laugh at someone's* —, ridere alle spalle di qualcuno.
**expensive** *adj.* costoso, caro; dispendioso; *to be* —, costare molto. **-ness** *n.* alto costo; carezza.
**experience** *n.* esperienza; pratica; *to speak from* —, parlare da pratico; incidente *m.*; avventura; *an unpleasant* —, una brutta esperienza; *tr.* provare; fare l'esperienza di; esperimentare; *to — hard times*, attraversare tempi difficili. **-d** *adj.* esperto; perito; pratico; di (molta) esperienza.
**experiment** *n.* esperimento; esperienza; prova; *by way of* —, a titolo di prova; *tr.* sperimentare; provare; *intr.* fare esperimenti. **-al** *adj.* sperimentale. **-ation** *n.* esperimento; lo sperimentare.
**expert** *adj.* esperto; abile; competente; *n.* perito; tecnico; specialista *m.*; esperto; conoscitore; *to pose as an* —, farsi passare per esperto. **-ise, -ness** *n.* perizia; abilità; destrezza.
**expiable** *adj.* espiabile.
**expi-ate** *tr.* espiare; (rel.) purgare. **-ation** *n.* espiazione; (rel.) *-ation of sins*, purgazione dei peccati. **-atory** *adj.* espiatorio.
**expiration** *n.* fine *f.*; termine *m.*; (finan.) scadenza; (med.; bot.) espirazione.
**expire** *intr.* scadere, finire, cessare; spirare, morire; *tr.* (med.; bot.) espirare, esalare.
**expiry** *n.* scadenza; fine *f.*; termine *m.*
**explain** *tr.* spiegare; chiarire; dilucidare; giustificare; *to — away*, dare una spiegazione plausibile di. **-able** *adj.* spiegabile.
**explanat-ion** *n.* spiegazione; schiarimento; giustificazione; *to give an — of*, giustificare, rendere ragione di. **-ory** *adj.* esplicativo; *-ory notes*, commento.
**expletive** *n.* particella espletiva; pleonasmo; (fam.) bestemmia.
**explic-able** *adj.* spiegabile. **-ative, -atory** *adj.* esplicativo.
**explicit** *adj.* esplicito; chiaro; categorico. **-ness** *n.* chiarezza.
**explode** *tr.* esplodere, far scoppiare; far saltare; (fig.) *to — a theory*, screditare una teoria; *intr.* esplodere; scoppiare.
**ex'ploit** *n.* impresa, prodezza; azione eroica; *pl.* gesta *f.pl.*
**exploit** *tr.* sfruttare, utilizzare; valorizzare; trarre partito da. **-ation** *n.* sfruttamento; utilizzazione; valorizzazione. **-er** *n.* sfruttatore.
**exploration** *n.* esplorazione; (fig.) studio.
**explorat-ory, -ive** *adj.* esploratorio, esplorativo.
**explor-e** *tr.* esplorare; (fig.) studiare. **-er** *n.* esploratore.
**explosion** *n.* esplosione; scoppio.
**explosive** *adj.* esplosivo; (fig.) che provoca una esplosione; *n.* esplosivo; (mil.) *high* —, esplosivo dirompente. **-ness** *n.* esplosività.
**exponent** *n.* esponente *m.*; interprete *m.*, rappresentante *m.*
**ex'port** *n.* esportazione; *pl.* merci *f.pl.* di esportazione; — *trade*, commercio di esportazione.
**export** *tr.* esportare. **-ation** *n.* esportazione. **-er** *n.* esportatore.
**expose** *tr.* esporre; mostrare; (fig.) svelare, palesare, smascherare; (photog.) esporre.
**exposition** *n.* esposizione; interpretazione; commento.
**expositor** *n.* espositore; commentatore.
**expostulat-e** *intr.* far rimostranze; lagnarsi. **-ion** *n.* rimostranza; lagnanza.
**exposure** *n.* esposizione; divulgazione; denunzia; rivelazione; scoperta; smascheramento; *to die of* —, morire per assideramento; (photog.) esposizione, posa.
**expound** *tr.* esporre; interpretare; spiegare.
**express** *adj.* espresso; esplicito; preciso; *n.* espresso; *by* —, per espresso; — *letter*, espresso; — *train*, direttissimo; *tr.* esprimere, manifestare; mandare per espresso; *rfl.* esprimersi. **-ible** *adj.* esprimibile.
**expression** *n.* espressione; manifestazione; *to give — to*, esprimere; *power of* —, eloquenza; locuzione, modo di dire. **-less** *adj.* senza espressione; impassibile; inespressivo.
**expressive** *adj.* espressivo; significativo. **-ness** *n.* efficacia espressiva.
**expressly** *adv.* espressamente; esplicitamente; apposta.
**expropriat-e** *tr.* espropriare. **-ion** *n.* espropriazione.
**expulsion** *n.* espulsione; eliminazione; (from school) rimozione.
**expunge** *tr.* espungere; cancellare.
**expurgat-e** *tr.* espurgare. **-ion** *n.* espurgazione.
**exquisite** *adj.* squisito; finissimo; ricercato; raffinato; elegantone *m.* **-ness** *n.* squisitezza; finezza; ricercatezza.
**ex-serviceman** *n.* excombattente *m.*
**extant** *adj.* ancora esistente; *to be* —, esistere.
**extempor-aneous, -ary, -e** *adj.* estemporaneo; improvvisato.
**extemporiz-e** *tr.*, *intr.* improvvisare. **-ation** *n.* improvvisazione.
**extend** *tr.* estendere, stendere; tendere; allungare, prolungare; allargare, dilatare, ampliare; ingrandire; accordare, offrire; *intr.* estendersi; prolungarsi; allargarsi.
**extensible** *adj.* estensibile, estendibile; allungabile.
**extension** *n.* estensione; prolungamento; allargamento; ampliamento; (comm.) proroga, estensione; (teleph.) telefono interno.
**extensive** *adj.* estensivo, esteso; ampio; vasto. **-ness** *n.* estensione; larghezza.
**extent** *n.* estensione; volume *m.*; grado; entità; punto; limite *m.*; *to a certain* —, fino a un certo punto; *to a great* —, in larga misura; *to what* —?, fin dove?, fino a che punto?
**extenuat-e** *tr.* attenuare; (leg.) *-ing circumstances*, circostanze attenuanti; estenuare, indebolire. **-ion** *n.* attenuazione; indebolimento.
**exterior** *adj.* esteriore, esterno; *n.* esterno; aspetto.
**exterminat-e** *tr.* sterminare; annientare; estirpare. **-ion** *n.* sterminio; annientamento.
**external** *adj.* esterno; esteriore; *n. to judge by -s*, giudicare dall'apparenza.
**extinct** *adj.* estinto; scomparso; morto; (fig.) spento; *to become* —, spegnersi. **-ion** *n.* estinzione; (comm.) ammortamento, ammortizzazione.
**extinguish** *tr.* spegnere, estinguere; (comm.) ammortizzare;

(fig.) eclissare, oscurare. **-er** *n.* estintore; spegnitoio.
**extirpat-e** *tr.* estirpare; sradicare; distruggere. **-ion** *n.* estirpazione; sradicamento.
**extol** *tr.* estollere; esaltare; lodare; magnificare; celebrare.
**extort** *n.* estorcere; togliere a forza; strappare. **-ion** *n.* estorsione. **-ionate** *adj.* esorbitante; esagerato; eccessivo; oppressivo.
**extra** *adj.* straordinario; supplementare; in più, extra; — *charge*, supplemento; — *postage*, soprattassa; —*pay*, soprassoldo; *n.* extra *m. indecl.*, cosa insolita; (theatr.) trapelo; (cinem.) comparsa.
**ex'tract** *n.* estratto; citazione; brano.
**extract** *tr.* estrarre; togliere; strappare; estorcere; *to — a tooth*, cavare un dente. **-ion** *n.* estrazio ne; *of Italian -ion*, di origine italiana. **-ive** *adj.* estrattivo. **-or** *n.* estrattore.
**extradit-e** *tr.* (leg.) estradare. **-able** *adj.* (leg.) passibile di estradizione. **-ion** *n.* (leg.) estradizione.
**extra-judicial** *adj.* (leg.) extragiudiziale. **-mundane** *adj.* fuori del nostro mondo, ultraterreno. **-mural** *adj.* estramurale, fuori le mura.
**extraneous** *adj.* estraneo; alieno; estrinseco.
**extraordinary** *adj.* straordinario; singolare; eccezionale; (fam.) fenomenale; *excl.* —*!*, strano!
**extraterritorial** *adj.* estraterritoriale.
**extravag-ance** *n.* prodigalità; stravaganza. **-ant** *adj.* stravagante; prodigo; spendereccio; esagerato; eccessivo; ridicolo.
**extreme** *adj.* estremo; ultimo; grave; eccezionale; severo; (rel.) — *unction*, estrema unzione; *n.* estremo; estremità; fine *f.*; *in the —*, all'estremo; *to go to -s*, eccedere; (provb.) *-s meet*, gli estremi si toccano. **-ly** *adv.* estremamente; sommamente; molto. **-ism** *n.* estremismo. **-ist** *n.* estremista *m.*; ultra *m.* **-ity** *n.* estremità; imbarazzo; pericolo; situazione critica.
**extricat-e** *tr.* districare; trarre d'impaccio, liberare. **-ion** *n.* districamento; liberazione.
**extrinsic** *adj.* estrinseco; non essenziale.
**extrovert** *n.* estroverso. **-ed** *adj.* estroverso.
**extr-ude** *tr.* estrudere; espellere; spingere fuori. **-usion** *n.* estrusione; espulsione.
**exuber-ance** *n.* esuberanza; sovrabbondanza. **-ant** *adj.* esuberante; sovrabbondante; rigoglioso. **-ation** *n.* essudazione; trasudazione.
**exud-e** *tr.*, *intr.* essudare; trasudare.
**exult** *intr.* esultare; trionfare; gioire. **-ance, -ancy** *n.* esultanza; trionfo. **-ant** *adj.* esultante; trionfante. **-ation** *n.* esultazione; ebrezza; giubilio; trionfo.
**eye** *n.* occhio; (fig.) vista; sguardo; *— of a needle*, cruna; (of peacock's tail) occhio, macchia; (bot.) gemma; bottone *m.*; (naut.) occhiello, gassa; *to the naked —*, a occhion udo; *evil —*, malocchio; *expert —*, occhio indagatore, occhio clinico; *further than the — can reach*, a perdita d'occhio; *with -s staring out of one's head*, con gli occhi fuori dell'orbita; *in the twinkling of an —*, in un batter d'occhio; *to be the apple of someone's —*, essere la pupilla dell'occhio di qualcuno; *to be up to one's -s in work*, avere lavoro fin sopra i capelli; (fam.) *to have a black —*, avere un occhio pesto *to have a good — for business*, aver buon fiuto per gli affari; *to have -s at the back of one's head*, avere gli occhi di Argo; *to keep an — on*, badare a; *to make -s at someone*, fare gli occhi di triglia a qualcuno; *to run an — over*, dare un'occhiata a; *to screw up one's —*, strizzare gli occhi; *to set -s on*, adocchiare, vedere, mettere gli occhi su; *to strike the —*, dare nell'occhio; *to turn a blind —*, chiudere un occhio.
**eye** *tr.* adocchiare; squadrare; sbirciare; *to — greedily*, divorare con gli occhi.
**eye-ball** *n.* bulbo oculare. **-brow** *n.* sopracciglio; *to knit one's -brows*, aggrottare le ciglia.
**eye-bath** *n.* bacinella oculare.
**eye-doctor** *n.* oculista *m.*
**eye-glass** *n.* monocolo, (fam.) caramella; *pl.* occhiali *m.pl.* **-lash** *n.* ciglio. **-less** *adj.* senza occhi; cieco. **-let** *n.* occhiello. **-lid** *n.* palpebra.
**eye-opener** *n.* (fam.) fatto sorprendente, fatto rivelatore. **-shade** *n.* visiera. **-shadow** *n.* bistro.
**eyeshot** *n.* campo visivo; *within —*, a portata d'occhi.
**eyesight** *n.* vista; visione; capacità visiva.
**eyesore** *n.* cosa brutta.
**eye-strain** *n.* stanchezza degli occhi. **-tooth** *n.* dente canino.
**eyewash** *n.* collirio; (slang) il dare da bere a; balle *f.pl.*
**eye-witness** *n.* testimonio oculare.
**eyot** *n.* isolotto.
**eyrie** *n.* nido di uccello da preda; (fig.) castello in cima ad un picco.
**Ezekiel** *pr.n.* (bibl.) Ezechiele.
**Ezra** *pr.n.* Esdra.

**F, f** *n.* effe *f.*, *m.*; (teleph.) — *for Frederick*, effe come Firenze; (mus.) fa *m.*
**fabl-e** *n.* favola, fiaba; mito; (fig.) frottola; pura invenzione; *intr.* favoleggiare, raccontar favole. **-d** *adj.* favoloso, leggendario.
**fabric** *n.* (text.) tessuto; stoffa; intelaiatura; edificio; struttura.
**fabricat-e** *tr.* fabbricare; (fig.) inventare, falsificare. **-ion** *n.* invenzione; falsificazione; menzogna.
**fabulous** *adj.* favoloso; fiabesco; leggendario; mitico.
**façade** *n.* (archit.) facciata; fronte *f.*; (fig.) facciata, apparenza.
**face** *n.* faccia; volto; viso; (slang) muso; (of coin) faccia; (of clock) quadrante *m.*; (typ.) carattere *m.*; (fig.) aspetto, apparenza; (fam.) faccia tosta, sfrontatezza; *— to — with*, a faccia a faccia con; *on the — of it*, a prima vista; *in the — of*, di fronte a; *— value*, valore *m.* nominale; *to fly in the — of*, sfidare; *to look facts in the —*, affrontare la realtà; *to pull -s*, far boccacce; *to set one's — against*, opporsi a; *to show one's —*, farsi vedere.
**face** *tr.* fronteggiare, essere di fronte a; (fig.) affrontare, opporsi a; (bldg.) rivestire, ricoprire; *to — the sea*, dare sul mare, (fam.) *to — the music*, accettare con coraggio le conseguenze delle proprie azioni; *intr. to — both ways*, guardare nei due sensi, *to — about*, voltarsi.
**face-ache** *n.* nevralgia facciale. **-cream** *n.* crema per il viso. **-lift(ing)** *n.* plastica facciale. **-powder** *n.* cipria.
**facer** *n.* (fam.) difficoltà inattesa.
**facet** *n.* faccetta; *tr.* sfaccettare.
**facetiae** *n.* facezie *f.pl.*
**facetious** *adj.* faceto. **-ness** *n.* lepidezza; piacevolezza; facezie *f.pl.*
**facial** *adj.* facciale; — *massage*, massaggio al viso.
**facile** *adj.* facile, ottenuto facilmente; remissibile, accomodante; superficiale.
**facilitate** *tr.* facilitare, agevolare.
**facility** *n.* facilità; facilitazione.
**facing** *adj.*, *n.* (bldg.) che sta di

fronte a, che dà su; rivestimento; *pl.* (mil.) risvolti *m.pl.*, mostrine *f.pl.*
**facsimile** *n.* facsimile *m.*
**fact** *n.* fatto; verità, realtà; *an accomplished —*, un fatto compiuto; *in —*, di fatto, infatti; *in point of —*, in verità, in effetto; *the — of the matter is*, il fatto sta; *as a matter of —*, per dire la verità.
**fact-finding** *adj.* di inchiesta; *— committee*, commissione di inchiesta.
**faction** *n.* fazione; partigianeria; discordia; dissenso.
**factious** *adj.* fazioso; partigiano. **-ness** *n.* spirito di parte; faziosità; partigianeria.
**factitious** *adj.* fittizio, artificiale, falso. **-ness** *n.* artificialità.
**factor** *n.* fattore *m.*; agente *m.*; commissionario; elemento; (math.) fattore.
**factory** *n.* fabbrica; officina; stabilimento; opificio; *— farming*, allevamento in batteria.
**factual** *adj.* fattivo; positivo; effettivo.
**facultative** *adj.* facoltativo.
**faculty** *n.* facoltà; capacità; attitudine *f.*
**facundity** *n.* facondia, eloquenza.
**fad** *n.* capriccio; ghiribizzo; ubbia; mania; moda bizzarra. **-diness, -dishness** *n.* tendenza a seguire le proprie manie. **-dy** *adj.* capriccioso.
**fade** *intr.* scolorirsi, sbiadire; appassire, languire; (fig.) deperire; svanire; scomparire; dileguarsi; *to — away*, affievolirsi; *tr.* scolorire, far sbiadire. **-d** *part. adj.* scolorito; sbiadito; appassito; stinto.
**fade-out** *n.* (cinem.) dissolvenza.
**faeces** *n.* (med.) feci *f.pl.*
**faerie, faery** *adj.* (poet.) fiabesco, delle fate.
**fag** *n.* (fam.) lavoro pesante, sfacchinata; (slang) sigaretta; *intr.* (fam.) sgobbare, sfacchinare.
**fag-end** *n.* (slang) mozzicone di sigaretta; (fig.) fine *f.*
**fagged** *adj.* (fam.) stanco; *— out*, stanco morto.
**faggot** *n.* fascina; fascio; fastello; (cul.) salsiccia; (fam., derog.) vecchiaccia; (slang, derog.) omosessuale; *tr.* affastellare, legare in fascina.
**fail** *n.* *without —*, senza fallo; senz'altro; *intr.* fallire, non riuscire, abortire; mancare; venire meno; diminuire, indebolirsi; (mech.) fermarsi, far cilecca; non superare un esame, essere respinto; *tr.* abbandonare, lasciare in asso; bocciare, respingere (un candidato).
**failing** *adj.* debole, che viene meno; *— health*, salute cagionevole; *prep.* in mancanza di, salvo; *n.* mancanza; difetto.
**failure** *n.* insuccesso; fallimento; mancanza; omissione; insufficienza; incapacità; (mech.) guasto; avaria; *he is a —*, è un fallito.
**fain** *adj.* disposto, contento; *adv.* volentieri.
**faint** *adj.* debole; fiacco; appena percettibile; pallido; *to feel —*, sentirsi venir meno; *to be — with hunger*, cascare dalla fame; indistinto, vago; (fig.) *I haven't the -est idea*, non ho la più pallida idea; timido, pauroso; *n.* svenimento; deliquio; *intr.* svenire, venir meno; cadere in deliquio; *to — away*, affievolirsi, dileguarsi.
**faint-hearted** *adj.* timido, pusillanime. **-ness** *n.* timidezza, pusillanimità.
**faint-ly** *adv.* debolmente. **-ness** *n.* debolezza; languore *m.*; fiacchezza; (fig.) pallidezza.
**fair**[1] *adj.* bello; *the — sex*, il bel sesso; *my — lady*, la mia bella; *— weather*, bel tempo; *— wind*, vento propizio; *— copy*, bella copia; giusto, imparziale; leale, onesto; *it isn't —*, non è giusto; *a — share*, una giusta parte; *by — means or foul*, con le buone o con le cattive; *— play*, comportamento leale, (sport) giuoco leale; *all's — in love and war*, in amore e in guerra tutto è lecito; *— hair*, capelli biondi; *of — complexion*, di carnagione chiara; discreto, passabile; *a — chance*, una buona probabilità; *adv.* lealmente, secondo le regole, con precisione; *to bid —*, promettere bene, augurare bene.
**fair**[2] fiera; mercato; *Vanity —*, la Fiera delle Vanità.
**fair-haired, -headed** *adj.* biondo, dai capelli biondi.
**fairly** *adv.* lealmente, imparzialmente; abbastanza, discretamente.
**fair-minded** *adj.* equo; imparziale. **-ness** *n.* imparzialità.
**fairness** *n.* bellezza; lealtà, equità, imparzialità; color biondo; chiarezza; *in all —*, in tutta franchezza, per essere giusto.
**fair-sized** *adj.* di grandezza discreta, discretamente grande.
**fairway** *n.* canale *m.* navigabile; (golf) via tagliata.
**fairy** *n.* fata, maga; (fig.) *— godmother*, buona fata.
**fairy-lamp** *n.* lampioncino alla veneziana.
**fairyland** *n.* paese *m.* delle fate; (fig.) paesaggio incantevole.
**fairy-story, -tale** *n.* fiaba; (fig.) menzogna.
**faith** *n.* fede *f.*; fiducia; (rel.) fede, credenza; *in bad —*, in malafede; *in good —*, in buona fede; *to put one's — in*, fidarsi di, porre fiducia in; *breach of —*, mancanza alla parola.
**faithful** *adj.* fedele; leale; costante; esatto, conforme; *n.* *the —*, i fedeli, i credenti, i devoti. **-ly** *adv.* fedelmente, lealmente; (comm.) *yours -ly*, con distinti saluti. **-ness** *n.* fedeltà; lealtà; esattezza.
**faith-healer** *n.* guaritore. **-healing** *n.* guarigione per suggestione.
**faithless** *adj.* che non ha fede; perfido; infedele; sleale. **-ness** *n.* infedeltà; mancanza di fede; perfidia; slealtà.
**fake** *n.* articolo fasullo; contraffazione; falsificazione; *tr.* contraffare; falsificare; (fam.) *to — up*, inventare.
**fakir** *n.* fachiro.
**falcon** *n.* (orn.) falcone *m.* **-er** *n.* falconiere *m.* **-ry** *n.* falconeria.
**faldstool** *n.* (liturg.) faldistorio, inginocchiatoio.
**fall**[1] *n.* caduta; (fig.) rovina; decadenza; *the — of man*, la caduta dell'uomo; *a — of snow*, una nevicata; declivio; ribasso; abbassamento; cascata, cateratta; (fam.) *to be riding for a —*, andare a rompicollo.
**fall**[1] *intr.* cadere, cascare; crollare; abbattersi; diminuire; inclinarsi, scendere; abbassarsi; accadere; *it fell to my lot*, mi toccò in sorte; *to let —*, lasciar cadere; *to — asleep*, addormentarsi; *to — due*, scadere; *to — foul of*, inimicarsi con; *to — ill*, ammalarsi; *to — in love with*, innamorarsi di; *to — back*, rinculare, indietreggiare; *to — back on*, ricorrere a; *to — behind*, rimanere indietro; *to — in*, crollare, (mil.) formare le righe; *to — in with*, incontrare per caso, (agree) andare d'accordo con; *to — out*, litigare, (mil.) rompere le righe; *to — short*, difettare, mancare; *to — through*, fallire, andare a monte; *to — to*, cominciare, darci dentro; *to — upon*, attaccare.
**Fall**[2] *n.* (Amer.) autunno.
**fallacious** *adj.* fallace; erroneo; falso. **-ness** *n.* fallacia; falsità.
**fallacy** *n.* sofisma *m.*; errore *m.*; fallacia.
**fallen** *p. part.* of **fall**, *q.v.*; *adj.* caduto; *pl.* *the —*, i caduti in guerra.
**fallib-le** *adj.* fallibile. **-ility** *n.* fallibilità.
**falling** *adj.* cadente; *n.* caduta; crollo; *— away*, deperimento; *— back*, ripiegamento; *— off*, diminuzione; *— out*, dissidio.
**fall-out** *n.* (phys.) pioggia radioattiva.
**fallow** *adj.* (agric.) a maggese; *to lie —*, rimanere incolto; *n.* maggese *m.*; *adj.* fulvo, rossiccio.
**false** *adj.* falso; erroneo; sbagliato; *to be — to*, tradire; (mus.) stonato; contraffatto, falsificato, finto, artificiale; *— hair*, capelli *m.pl.* posticci; *— teeth*, denti *m.pl.* finti; *— bottom*, doppio fondo; *— modesty*, finta umiltà.

**-hood** *n.* menzogna, bugia; *to distinguish truth from -hood*, distinguere il vero dal falso. **-ness** *n.* falsità; perfidia; doppiezza.
**falsif-y** *tr.* falsificare; contraffare; alterare; provare la falsità di, smentire. **-ication** *n.* falsificazione; contraffazione. **-ier** *n.* falsificatore, falsario; contraffattore.
**falsity** *n.* falsità; disonestà.
**falter** *intr.* vacillare, esitare; balbettare, impappinarsi. **-ing** *adj.* esitante, vacillante, titubante; balbettante.
**fame** *n.* fama; rinomanza; reputazione; celebrità; gloria. **-d** *adj.* rinomato.
**familiar** *adj.* familiare; intimo; *to be on — terms with*, conoscere bene, aver dimestichezza con; conosciuto, noto; *to be on — ground*, essere nel proprio elemento; (pejor.) impudente, sfacciato. **-ity** *n.* familiarità; intimità; confidenza; dimestichezza; (pejor.) impudenza; sfacciataggine *f.*; *-ity breeds contempt*, cosa troppo vista perde grazia e vista. **-ize** *tr.* familiarizzare; far conoscere.
**family** *n.* famiglia; *the Holy Family*, la Sacra Famiglia, (paint.) Sacra Conversazione; *my —*, i miei; *a — man*, un padre di famiglia; *a friend of the —*, un amico di casa; *to be one of the —*, essere di famiglia; *— tree*, albero genealogico; *— allowances*, assegni *m.pl.* familiari; *— troubles*, noie *f.pl.* domestiche.
**famine** *n.* carestia; *to die of —*, morire di fame.
**famish** *tr.* affamare; far morire di fame. **-ed, -ing,** *adj.* affamato.
**famous** *adj.* famoso; rinomato; celebre; (fam.) ottimo; meraviglioso.
**fan** *n.* ventaglio; (mech.) ventilatore; (agric.) vaglio; (fam.) ammiratore appassionato; (sport) tifoso; *tr.* sventolare, fare vento a, ventilare; *to — oneself*, farsi vento; *to — the flame*, soffiare nel fuoco; (agric.) vagliare; (fig.) eccitare, stimolare; *intr. to — out*, spiegarsi a ventaglio.
**fanatic, -al** *adj.*, *n.* fanatico. **-ism** *n.* fanatismo.
**fancied** *adj.* immaginato; immaginario; supposto.
**fancier** *n.* amatore; conoscitore; collezionista *m.*, *f.*; *dog —*, allevatore di cani.
**fanciful** *adj.* fantastico; fantasioso; capriccioso, bizzarro. **-ness** *n.* fantasia; capriccio; fantasticheria.
**fancy** *adj.* di fantasia, fantastico; *— cakes*, pasticcini *m.pl.*; *— goods*, articoli *m.pl.* di fantasia; (fam.) esagerato; *n.* fantasia; idea; pensiero; gusto, capriccio; simpatia; *to take a — to*, invaghirsi di; *a passing —*, una simpatia passeggera; *tr.* immaginare, immaginarsi; figurarsi; *just —!*, figùrati!; pensare, credere, avere l'impressione che; gustare, avere desiderio di; *what do you — for dinner*, che cosa ti piacerebbe per cena?
**fancy-dress** *n.* costume *m.*; *— ball*, ballo in maschera
**fane** *n.* (poet.) fano; tempio.
**fanfare** *n.* fanfara; squillo.
**fang** *n.* zanna; dente *m.*
**fanlight** *n.* (archit.) lunetta, sopraffinestra.
**fan-mail** *n.* posta degli ammiratori.
**fantail** *n.* (orn.) piccione *m.* con coda a ventaglio, piccione pavonino.
**fantastic** *adj.* fantastico; bizzarro; strano; capriccioso.
**fantasy** *n.* fantasia; capriccio; idea fantastica; visione.
**far** *adj.* lontano, distante, remoto; *the Far East*, l'Estremo Oriente; *a — way from*, lontano da; *the — side*, la parte opposta; *the — end*, l'altra estremità; *adv.* lontano, distante; *as — as the station*, fino alla stazione; *as — as I know*, per quanto mi risulta; *in so — as*, in quanto; *by —*, di gran lunga; *— from it!*, al contrario!, tutt'altro!; *— better*, molto meglio; *how — is it to Milan?*, quanto dista Milano?; *so — so good*, fin qui va bene; *to go too —*, esagerare; *— from perfect*, lungi dall'essere perfetto.
**far-away** *adj.* lontano; distante; (fig.) distratto.
**farc-e** *n.* farsa; buffonata. **-ical** *adj.* farsesco, buffo; comico; burlesco.
**fare** *n.* prezzo del biglietto; tariffa; *full —*, tariffa intera; *single —*, andata; *return —*, andata e ritorno; *excess —*, supplemento; viaggiatore; cliente *m.*, *f.*; vitto, cibo; *bill of —*, lista delle vivande; menù *m.*; *intr.* vivere, trovarsi; *how did you —?*, come ti sei trovato?; *to — sumptuously*, vivere come il papa; andare fuori, partire; *— thee well!*, addio!
**farewell** *excl.* addio!; arrivederci; *— for ever!*, addio per sempre!; buon viaggio!; *attrib.* d'addio; *— performance*, serata d'addio; *n.* addio; congedo; *to bid — to*, dire addio a, congedarsi da, prendere congedo da.
**far-famed** *adj.* celebre, rinomato; conosciuto in tutto il mondo. **-fetched** *adj.* ricercato, affettato, forzato; (fam.) stiracchiato.
**farm** *n.* fattoria; masseria; podere *m.*; azienda agricola; casa colonica; *— buildings*, edifici di una fattoria; *— produce*, prodotti agricoli; *tr.* coltivare; *to — out*, dare in appalto; *intr.* fare l'agricoltore.
**farmer** *n.* agricoltore; mezzadro; fittavolo; (finan.) appaltatore.
**farmhouse** *n.* casa colonica; masseria; fattoria; *— dairy*, cascina.
**farming** *n.* agricoltura; coltivazione; lavoro di una fattoria; *factory —*, allevamento in batteria.
**farm-labourer** *n.* bracciante *m.*; contadino.
**farm-stead** *n.* fattoria; masseria; cascinale *m.* **-yard** *n.* corte *f.*; cortile *m.*, aia; *-yard animals*, animali *m.pl.* da basso cortile.
**far-off** *adj.* lontano, distante, remoto.
**farouche** *adj.* timido, ritroso, selvatico.
**farrago** *n.* faraggine *f.*; miscuglio.
**far-reaching** *adj.* di gran portata.
**farrier** *n.* maniscalco.
**farrow** *n.* (of sow) figliata; *intr.* (of sow) figliare.
**far-seeing** *adj.* preveggente, previdente, perspicace. **-sighted** *adj.* previdente, (med.) presbite.
**fart** *n.* (vulg.) peto *m.*, scoreggia; *intr.* (vulg.) far peti, scoreggiare.
**farther** *adj.*, *adv.* più lontano, più in là; *— back*, più indietro; *— off*, più lontano; *— on*, più avanti; *— up*, più in sù; *on the — bank*, sulla riva opposta; cf. **further.** **-most** *adj.* il più lontano, il più distante; *at the — ends*, alle estremità.
**farthest** *adj.* il più lontano; *adv. at the —*, al più, al massimo.
**farthing** *n.* quarto di un vecchio penny; quattrino; (fig.) cosa di nessun valore.
**fascinat-e** *tr.* affascinare; incantare; ammaliare. **-ing** *adj.* affascinante; avvincente; incantevole. **-ion** *n.* fascino; attrattiva; incanto.
**fasc-ism** *n.* fascismo. **-ist** *n.*, *adj.* fascista *m.*, *f.*
**fash** *tr.* (Scot.) seccare, infastidire.
**fashion** *n.* modo; maniera; *after a —*, in un certo modo; *after the — of*, alla maniera di; *in the Italian —*, all'italiana; moda; stile *m.*; voga; *in —*, alla moda; *out of —*, fuori moda; *to be the —*, essere di moda; *to set the —*, creare la moda; *the latest —*, l'ultima voga; *tr.* foggiare; forgiare; modellare; fare. **-able** *adj.* alla moda, di moda, in voga; elegante; *-able society*, il bel mondo, il gran mondo; *-able audience*, un uditorio scelto. **-ableness** *n.* eleganza; voga.
**fashion-plate** *n.* figurino di moda.
**fast**[1] *adj.* fermo, saldo, fisso; stretto; solido; inalterabile; *— colours*, colori resistenti; *to*

*make* —, legare bene, chiudere bene, (naut.) ormeggiare; *hard and — rule*, regolamento immutabile; —*friends*, amici stretti; *adv.* fermamente, saldamente; strettamente; — *asleep*, profondamente addormentato; *to stand* —, star fermo; *to play — and loose with*, fare a tiremmolla con.

**fast**[2] *adj.* rapido, veloce, svelto; *a — train*, un treno diretto; *my watch is five minutes* —, il mio orologio è avanti di cinque minuti; (pejor.) dissoluto, amante dei piaceri; *the — set*, quelli che fanno la dolce vita; *a — woman*, una donna allegra; *adv.* velocemente, rapidamente, presto; *to talk* —, parlare frettolosamente; *to walk* —, camminare veloce; *it is raining* —, piove a dirotto; *not so —!*, adagio!

**fast**[3] *n.* digiuno; *to break one's* —, rompere il digiuno; *to keep a* —, mangiar magro, digiunare; *intr.* digiunare; osservare il digiuno.

**fast-day** *n.* giorno di digiuno, giorno di magro.

**fasten** *tr.* fissare, legare; attaccare; stringere; agganciare, abbottonare; *to — one's shoes*, allacciarsi le scarpe; chiudere; *to — one's eyes on*, fissare gli occhi su; *to — a crime on*, incolpare di un delitto; *to — one's attention on*, concentrare l'attenzione su; *to — down*, assicurare, legare; (letter) sigillare; *intr.* attaccarsi; agganciarsi; allacciarsi; chiudersi; *to — upon*, appigliarsi a. **-er, -ing** *n.* fermaglio; legaccio; laccio; gancio; chiusura.

**fastidious** *adj.* meticoloso; esigente; pignolo, schifiltoso. **-ness** *n.* meticolosità; pignoleria, schifiltosità.

**fastness** *n.* fermezza; solidità; velocità; (mil.) fortezza, cittadella.

**fat** *adj.* grasso, pingue, corpulento; — *woman* (*at fair*), donna cannone; *to get* —, ingrassare; grosso; fertile, ricco; (fam.) *a — job*, un lavoro ben rimunerato; (slang) *a — lot*, un bel niente; *that's a — lot of good!*, che bel consiglio!; *n.* grasso; pinguedine *f.*, corpulenza; *to put on* —, ingrassare; *to remove — from*, sgrassare; (fig.) *the — is in the fire*, ormai il male è fatto; *to live on the — of the land*, vivere come un papa.

**fatal** *adj.* fatale; inevitabile, ineluttabile; decisivo; mortale, funesto. **-ism** *n.* fatalismo. **-ist** *n.* fatalista *m.*, *f.* **-ity** *n.* fatalità; destino; morte *f.* accidentale.

**fat-e** *n.* fato; destino; nemesi *f.*; sorte *f.*; *to meet one's* —, morire; (myth.) Parca; *the Fates*, le Parche. **-ed** *adj.* fatale; destinato; condannato. **-eful** *adj.* funesto; decisivo.

**fathead** *n.* (fam.) zuccone *m.*; testa dura; asino; (vulg.) coglione *m.* **-ed** *adj.* stupido; imbecille.

**father** *n.* padre; (fam.) papà, babbo; *from — to son*, da padre in figlio; *to act as a — to*, far da padre a; (priest) reverendo; (monk, friar) padre; *the Holy* —, il Santo Padre; — *confessor*, padre spirituale; *like — like son*, tale il padre tale il figlio; *the wish is — to the thought*, il desiderio guida il pensiero; *pl.* gli anziani; *our -s*, i nostri antenati; *tr.* procreare; (fig.) fare da padre a, concepire; addossarsi la paternità di; *to — on*, attribuire a. **-hood** *n.* paternità. **-ing** *n.* generazione; adottamento; il fare da padre; (fig.) attribuzione.

**father-in-law** *n.* suocero.

**father-land** *n.* patria. **-less** *adj.* senza padre, orfano di padre. **-liness** *n.* affetto paterno; (fig.) paternalismo. **-ly** *adj.* paterno, di padre.

**fathom** *n.* (naut.) braccio; *ten -s deep*, a dieci braccia di profondità; *tr.* (naut.) sondare, scandagliare; (fig.) approfondire, penetrare; indagare; indovinare. **-less** *adj.* incommensurabile; (fig.) incomprensibile.

**fatigu-e** *n.* stanchezza; esaurimento; fatica; (mil.) corvée *f.*; — *dress*, tenuta di fatica; — *party*, distaccamento per servizio comandato; *tr.* affaticare; stancare. **-ing** *adj.* faticoso, affaticante.

**fatness** *n.* grassezza, corpulenza. pinguedine *f.*

**fatted** *adj.* ingrassato; *to kill the — calf*, uccidere il vitello grasso, far festa a chi ritorna.

**fatten** *tr.*, *intr.* ingrassare, impinguare. **-ing** *n.* ingrassamento.

**fatty** *adj.* grasso, adiposo; untuoso; *n.* (joc.) grassoccio.

**fatuity, fatuousness** *n.* fatuità; stoltezza.

**fatuous** *adj.* fatuo; stolto.

**fault** *n.* difetto; vizio; mancanza; imperfezione; *to find — with*, trovare a ridire sul conto di; fallo; errore *m.*; *to be at* —, essere colpevole; *it wasn't his* —, non era colpa sua; *to a* —, fin troppo; (geol.) faglia; (tennis) fallo; (electr.) difetto.

**fault-finder** *n.* critico pignolo. **-finding** *n.* critica pedante.

**faultiness** *n.* imperfezione.

**faultless** *adj.* perfetto; impeccabile; senza colpa; irreprensibile. **-ness** *n.* perfezione; impeccabilità; irreprensibilità.

**faulty** *adj.* difettoso; imperfetto.

**faun** *n.* (myth.) fauno.

**fauna** *n.* (zool.) fauna.

**favour** *n.* favore *m.*; piacere *m.*; *to do someone a* —, favorire qualcuno; *in — of*, a favore di; *to find — in someone's eyes*, essere nelle buone grazie di qualcuno; *to win the — of*, conquistarsi la benevolenza di; *to curry — with*, insinuarsi nelle grazie di; (comm.) *your — of the 5th inst.*, la vostra pregiata del cinque corrente; distintivo; (fig.) aiuto; *under — of night*, col favore della notte.

**favour** *tr.* favorire, favoreggiare; aiutare; preferire; appoggiare, approvare; *fortune -s the brave*, la fortuna sorride ai coraggiosi; *she -s her mother*, lei rassomiglia alla madre.

**favourable** *adj.* favorevole; propizio; vantaggioso; *a — reception*, una buona accoglienza; *to look with a — eye on*, guardare benevolmente; — *terms*, condizioni vantaggiose.

**favourit-e** *adj.* preferito; prediletto; *n.* favorito; beniamino; *he is a general* —, tutti gli vogliono bene; (sport) favorito. **-ism** *n.* favoritismo.

**fawn**[1] *adj.* fulvo.

**fawn**[2] *n.* (zool.) cerbiatto, daino.

**fawn**[3] *intr.* (of deer) figliare; (fig.) strisciare; *to — upon*, adulare, corteggiare; (of dog) far festa a.

**fealty** *n.* fedeltà.

**fear** *n.* paura; timore *m.*; terrore *m.*; *for — of*, per timore di; *for — that*, per timore che; *wild with* —, pazzo di terrore; *to stand in — of*, temere; (fam.) *no —!*, non c'è pericolo!, sfido!; *to put the — of God into someone*, dare a qualcuno una lavata di capo da far paura; *tr.* dubitare; temere; aver paura di; *I — I am late*, temo di essere in ritardo; *a man to be -ed*, un uomo temibile; *to — to speak*, aver paura di parlare; *never —!*, niente paura! **-ful** *adj.* terribile, spaventoso; pauroso, pavido; *to be -ful of*, temere. **-fully** *adv.* terribilmente; timidamente; (fam.) tremendamente; *I'm -fully sorry*, mi dispiace tanto. **-fulness** *n.* aspetto terribile; timore *m.* **-less** *adj.* intrepido, senza paura; *to be -less of*, non aver paura di. **-lessness** *n.* intrepidezza; coraggio. **-some** *adj.* spaventoso, temibile, terribile.

**feasib-le** *adj.* praticabile; fattibile; verosimile. **-ility** *n.* praticabilità.

**feast** *n.* festa; banchetto, convito; (provb.) *enough is as good as a* —, il troppo stroppia; (fig.) gaudio; abbondanza; *tr.* festeggiare; trattare in modo principesco; (fig.) *to — one's eyes on*, rallegrarsi gli occhi alla vista di; *intr.* far festa, banchettare. **-ing** *n.* festeggiamento; baldoria.

**feast-day** *n.* giorno di festa.

**feat** *n.* impresa, azione insigne; gesta *f.pl.*; — *of arms*, fatto d'arme;

— *of engineering*, trionfo dell'ingegneria.

**feather** *n.* penna, piuma; (mil.) pennacchio; *pl.* piumaggio; penne *f.pl.*; (fig.) *in high* —, di ottimo umore; *in full* —, in grande toletta; *birds of a* —, gente della stessa risma; (provb.) *birds of a — flock together*, ogni simile ama il suo simile; *to make the* -*s fly*, scatenare un putiferio. **-less** *adj.* senza penne, implume. **-y** *adj.* piumato, pennato; soffice.

**feather** *tr.* mettere penne a, ornare di piume; (fig.) *to — one's own nest*, arricchirsi a spese degli altri; (rowing) *to — oars*, spalare i remi. **-ed** *part. adj.* pennuto; ornato di piume.

**feather-bed** *n.* letto di piume.

**feather-brained** *adj.* leggero, sventato; *to be -brained*, aver un cervello di gallina.

**feature** *n.* fattezza; lineamento; tratto; *pl.* fisionomia; caratteristica, aspetto, tratto distintivo; (journ.) elzeviro; specialità; rilievo; (geog.) configurazione. **-less** *adj.* privo di tratti caratteristici; (fig.) monotono, poco interessante.

**feature** *tr.* caratterizzare, rappresentare, ritrarre; (theatr.; cinem.) dare rilievo a, mettere in evidenza; *featuring Sophia Loren*, con Sophia Loren come protagonista.

**feature-writer** *n.* (journ.) elzevirista *m.*

**febr-ifuge** *n.* (med.) febbrifugo. **-ile** *adj.* febbrile.

**February** *pr.n.* febbraio.

**feckless** *adj.* incapace, inabile, inetto; neghittoso; spensierato. **-ness** *n.* incapacità; inettitudine *f.*; sbadataggine *f.*

**fecund** *adj.* fecondo, prolifico. **-ate** *tr.* fecondare. **-ity** *n.* fecondità.

**federal** *adj.* federale. **-ism** *n.* federalismo. **-ist** *n.* federalista *m.*; (U.S.A., hist.) nordista *m.*

**federat-e** *tr.* unire; confederare; *intr.* unirsi; confederarsi. **-ion** *n.* federazione; confederazione.

**fee** *n.* onorario; competenza; parcella; emolumento; *entrance* —, tassa d'iscrizione; *school* -*s*, retta; (hist.) feudo, beneficio feudale.

**feeble** *adj.* debole; fievole; fiacco; infermo. **-ness** *n.* debolezza; fiacchezza; infermità.

**feeble-minded** *adj.* debole di mente; ebete; cretino; rammollito. **-mindedness** *n.* debolezza di mente.

**feed** *n.* alimentazione; nutrimento; mangime *m.*; (joc.) *to be off one's* —, non aver appetito; *a good* —, un buon pasto; (of baby) allattamento, poppata; (mech.) alimentazione.

**feed** *tr.* nutrire; cibare; alimentare; allattare; (fig.) rifornire, nutrire; (mech.) alimentare; *to — up*, ingrassare, sottoporre a superalimentazione; (fam.) *fed up*, stufo; *intr.* mangiare; cibarsi; nutrirsi; (baby) poppare; *to — on*, cibarsi di. **-er** *n.* chi si nutre, chi mangia; mangiatore; (for baby) poppatoio; (bib) bavaglino; (geog.) affluente *m.* **-ing** *adj.* nutriente; *n.* il mangiare; alimentazione.

**feeding-bottle** *n.* poppatoio.

**feel** *n.* tatto; tocco; *to judge by the — of*, giudicare toccando; (fig.) sensazione; *to get the — of*, abituarsi a.

**feel** *tr.* tastare; palpare; toccare; sentire con il tatto; sentire; avvertire; risentire; *to — the heat*, risentire il caldo; *to — a pain*, avvertire un dolore; (fig.) *to — pity*, sentire pietà; *to — a dislike for*, provare antipatia per; *to — one's way*, procedere a tastoni; (fam.) *I don't — quite the thing*, non mi sento troppo bene; pensare, aver la sensazione che, giudicare; *I — that I am right*, penso di aver ragione; *intr.* risultare al tatto, sembrare; sentirsi; *I — well*, mi sento bene; *to — hot*, aver caldo; *to — hungry*, aver fame; *I — angry*, sono arrabbiato; *to — up to*, sentirsi di; *to — like*, sentirsi disposto a; *to — at home*, sentirsi come a casa. **-er** *n.* chi sente; che sente; (fig.); *to throw out a -er*, tastare il terreno.

**feeling** *adj.* sensibile; che si commuove; *n.* tatto, il tastare; sentimento; senso; sensazione; affetto; *to have no* —, mancare dì sensibilità; *to hurt the* -*s of*, urtare le suscettibilità di; opinione. **-ly** *adv.* con sentimento; con commozione.

**feign** *tr.* fingere; simulare; ostentare; far vista di; *to — indifference*, ostentare indifferenza; *to — death*, simulare la morte; *intr.* fingersi. **-ing** *n.* dissimulazione; finta.

**feint** *n.* finta; (mil.) finto attacco; *intr.* fare finta; (mil.) fare un finto attacco.

**feldspar** *n.* (miner.) feldspato.

**felicitat-e** *tr.* felicitare, congratularsi con. **-ion** *n.* felicitazione, congratulazione.

**felicitous** *adj.* felice; adatto; appropriato.

**felicity**[1] *n.* felicità; contentezza.

**Felicity**[2] *pr.n.* Felicità.

**feline** *adj.* felino; gattesco; di gatto; *n.* felino.

**Felix** *pr.n.* Felice.

**fell**[1] *adj.* feroce; crudele; truce; fiero; funesto.

**fell**[2] *n.* pelle *f.*; vello; pellame *m.*

**fell**[3] *n.* (geog.) monte roccioso.

**fell**[4] *tr.* abbattere; atterrare. **-ing** *n.* abbattimento; taglio.

**fell**[5] *p. def.* of **fall**, *q.v.*

**felloe** *n.* gavello di ruota.

**fellow** *n.* persona; individuo; tizio; tipo; *my dear —!*, caro mio!; *a good* —, un tipo simpatico; *a poor* —, un povero diavolo; laureato aggregato a un collegio universitario; membro; compagno.

**fellow-being** *n.* simile *m.*, *f.* **-citizen** *n.* concittadino. **-countryman** *n.* compatriotta *m.*, *f.* **-creature** *n.* simile *m.*, *f.* **-feeling** *n.* simpatia; comprensione. **-helper** *n.* collaboratore; coadiutore. **-prisoner** *n.* compagno di prigionia.

**fellowship** *n.* compagnia; amicizia; *good* —, cameratismo; corporazione; confraternita; posizione di un fellow universitario.

**fellow-soldier** *n.* compagno d'armi, commilitone *m.* **-student** *n.* compagno di studi. **-sufferer** *n.* compagno di sventura. **-thinker** *n.* (rel.) correligionario. **-townsman** *n.* concittadino, compaesano. **-traveller** *n.* compagno di viaggio. **-worker** *n.* compagno di lavoro; collega *m.*, *f.*

**felo de se** *n.* (leg.) suicidio.

**felon** *n.* (leg.) delinquente *m.*, *f.*; criminale *m.*, *f.*

**felon-y** *n.* (leg.) crimine *m.* **-ious** *adj.* criminoso.

**felt**[1] *n.* feltro; *tr.* feltrare, infeltrire. **-ing** *n.* feltratura.

**felt**[2] *p. def.*, *part.* of **feel**, *q.v.*

**felucca** *n.* (naut.) feluca.

**female** *adj.* femminile, di sesso femminile; — *child*, bambina; — *companion*, compagna; (mech.) — *screw*, vite femmina; *n.* femmina.

**feminin-e** *adj.* femminile; femminina, muliebre. **-eness, -ity** *n.* femminilità.

**femin-ism** *n.* femminismo. **-ist** *n.* femminista *m.*, *f.* **-ize** *tr.* femminizzare; effemminare.

**femoral** *adj.* (anat.) femorale.

**femur** *n.* (anat.) femore *m.*

**fen** *n.* palude *f.*; maremma.

**fence**[1] *n.* steccato; palizzata; stecconato; recinto; siepe *f.*; (fig.) *to sit on the* —, esitare, essere indeciso, (pol.) mantenersi neutrale; (slang) ricettatore.

**fence**[2] *tr.* cintare; circondare con steccato; *to — in*, chiudere in un recinto; *to — off*, dividere a mezzo di un recinto; *intr.* tirar di scherma; (fig.) schermirsi.

**fencer** *n.* schermidore.

**fencing** *n.* recinto; materiale *m.* per cintare; (sport) scherma.
**fencing-master** *n.* maestro di scherma, maestro d'armi. **-match** *n.* torneo, gara di scherma.
**fend** *tr.*, *intr.* (poet.) difendere; *to — off*, parare, stornare; *to — for oneself*, saper badare a se stesso, arrangiarsi; *left to — for oneself*, lasciato in balìa di se stesso.
**fender** *n.* paracenere *m.*; (motor.) paraurti *m.*; (naut.) parabordo.
**fenestration** *n.* (archit.) disposizione delle finestre.
**fennel** *n.* (bot.) finocchio.
**fenny** *adj.* palustre; pantanoso.
**Ferdinand** *pr.n.* Ferdinando.
**fer·ment** *n.* fermento; lievito; (fig.) tumulto; fermento; agitazione.
**ferment** *tr.* far fermentare; *intr.* fermentare. **-ation** *n.* fermentazione.
**fern** *n.* (bot.) felce *f.*; *maidenhair —*, capelvenere *m.* **-ery** *n.* felceto, vivaio di felci.
**feroc-ious** *adj.* feroce; fiero; crudele. **-ity, -iousness** *n.* ferocia; crudeltà.
**ferret** *n.* (zool.) furetto; *intr.* cacciare col furetto; (fam.) *to — about*, frugare, cercare; *to — out*, scovare, scoprire.
**ferric** *adj.* (chem.) ferrico.
**ferriferous** *adj.* ferrifero.
**ferro-concrete** *n.* cemento armato.
**ferruginous** *adj.* ferruginoso.
**ferrule** *n.* ghiera; puntale *m.*; anello.
**ferry** *n.* traghetto; barca da traghetto, nave traghetto; *tr.* traghettare; *to — across*, far passare, traghettare; (aeron.) trasportare per via aerea.
**ferry-boat** *n.* barca da traghetto, nave traghetto. **-bridge** *n.* ponte *m.* trasbordatore.
**ferryman** *n.* traghettatore; (lit.) *the — of the Styx*, il nocchiero dello Stige.
**fertil-e** *adj.* fertile; fecondo. **-ity** *n.* fertilità; fecondità; feracità.
**fertiliz-e** *tr.* fertilizzare; fecondare. **-ation** *n.* fertilizzazione; fecondazione. **-er** *n.* concime *m.*; fertilizzante *m.*; *artificial -er*, concime chimico.
**ferv-ent** *adj.* fervente; ardente; caloroso; zelante. **-ency** *n.* ardore *m.*; calore *m.*; fervore *m.*; zelo.
**fervid** *adj.* fervido; ardente; caloroso.
**fervour** *n.* ardore *m.*; fervore *m.*; passione; zelo.
**fess(e)** *n.* (herald.) fascia.
**festal** *adj.* festivo; festoso; di festa.
**fester** *n.* (med.) ascesso; postema; *intr.* suppurare; (fig.) corrompersi.
**festival** *n.* festa; celebrazione; festival *m.*
**festiv-e** *adj.* festivo; festoso; lieto, allegro. **-ity** *n.* festa; festività; festeggiamento.
**festoon** *n.* festone *m.*; ghirlanda; *tr.* ornare di festoni.
**fetch** *tr.* andare a prendere; *to — the doctor*, andare a cercare il medico; *to — water from the river*, attingere acqua al fiume, *to — and carry*, far commissioni, sfacchinare; prendere, trarre; *to — one's breath*, prendere fiato; *to — a sigh*, trarre un sospiro; rendere, raggiungere; *to — a high price*, raggiungere un prezzo elevato; (fam.) *to — someone a box on the ear*, dare uno schiaffo a qualcuno; *that'll — him*, vedrai che questo lo farà accorrere; *to — back*, riportare, ricondurre; *to — down*, far scendere; *to — up*, vomitare; *to — up at*, giungere finalmente a; *intr.* (naut.) virare, tenere rotta verso.
**fetching** *adj.* attraente; *a — smile*, un sorriso seducente.
**fête** *n.* festa; *tr.* festeggiare; celebrare.
**fetid** *adj.* fetido; puzzolente. **-ity, -ness** *n.* fetore *m.*; fetidume *m.*
**fetish, fetich(e)** *n.* feticcio; (fig.) idolo. **-ism** *n.* feticismo.
**fetlock** *n.* barbetta, pastoia.
**fetter** *n.* catena; (fig.) legame *m.*; vincolo; *pl.* ceppi *m.pl.*, manette *f.pl.*; (fig.) schiavitù *f.*; *tr.* incatenare; ammanettare; (fig.) intralciare; legare.
**fettle** *n.* stato; condizione; (fam.) *to be in high —*, sentirsi proprio bene, stare benone.
**feud** *n.* feudo; (fig.) ostilità; lite *f.*; contrasto; *blood —*, faida; *deadly —*, guerra a morte, vendetta.
**feudal** *adj.* feudale. **-ism** *n.* (hist.) feudalismo.
**fever** *n.* febbre *f.*; *to have a —* essere febbricitante, aver la febbre; (fig.) sovraeccitazione; *to be in a —*, essere sovraeccitato; *a — of impatience*, impazienza febbrile.
**feverfew** *n.* (bot.) camomilla.
**feverish** *adj.* febbricitante; *to be —*, aver la febbre; (fig.) febbrile, affannoso. **-ness** *n.* stato febbrile.
**few** *adj.* pochi *m.pl.*, poche *f.pl.*; *a —*, alcuni *m.pl.*, alcune *f.pl.*, qualche *m.*, *f.* (followed in Italian by sing.); *some —*, alcuni; *very —*, pochissimi; *a good —*, parecchi; *prn.*, *n.* pochi; *the —*, i pochi, la minoranza; *— people*, pochi.
**fewer** *comp. adj.* meno; non tanti; *the — the better*, in meno si è e meglio si sta.
**fianc-é** *n.* fidanzato. **-ée** *n.* fidanzata.
**fiasco** *n.* fallimento; insuccesso; fiasco.
**fiat**[1] *n.* autorizzazione; decreto.
**Fiat**[2] *pr.n.* (motor.) Fiat *f.*
**fib** *n.* (fam.) bugia; frottola; *intr.* dire bugie.
**fibr-e** *n.* fibra; *man-made —*, fibra artificiale; (fig.) fibra, natura. **-ous** *adj.* fibroso; fibrato.
**fichu** *n.* fisciù *m.*; scialletto.
**fickle** *adj.* mobile; incostante; volubile; variabile. **-ness** *n.* incostanza; volubilità.
**fiction** *n.* finzione; invenzione; (lit.) prosa narrativa, novellistica; *writer of —*, narratore, romanziere *m.*; *works of —*, romanzi *m.pl.* **-al** *adj.* immaginario; finto; romanzesco.
**fictitious** *adj.* fittizio; finto; falso; immaginario.
**fiddle** *n.* violino; (fig.) *to play second —*, avere una parte secondaria; (naut.) tavola di rullìo; trucco; *intr.* suonare il violino; (fig.) giocherellare, trastullarsi; (pejor.) *to — with*, manipolare, falsificare; *tr.* truccare; *to — away one's time*, perdere il tempo in sciocchezze.
**fiddlededee** *excl.* sciocchezze!
**fiddle-faddle** *n.* sciocchezze *f.pl.*; *intr.* dire sciocchezze; giocherellare, perdere tempo.
**fiddler** *n.* violinista *m.*, *f.*; suonatore di violino.
**fiddlestick** *n.* archetto *m.*; *pl. excl. -s!*, sciocchezze!
**fiddling** *adj.* frivolo; sciocco; fatuo; futile; *a — job*, lavoro inutile che pur richiede molta attenzione.
**fidelity** *n.* fedeltà; esattezza.
**fidget** *n.* persona nervosa, che non sta mai fermo; (fam.) *to give someone the -s*, dare sui nervi a qualcuno; *intr.* agitarsi, dar fastidio; *don't —!*, sta fermo! **-y** *adj.* irrequieto; nervoso.
**Fido** *pr.n.m.* (dog's name) Fido.
**fiduciary** *adj.* fiduciario.
**fie** *excl.* vergogna!; oibò!
**fief** *n.* (hist.) feudo.
**field** *n.* campo; campi *m.pl.*; campagna; (mil.) campo; *— of fire*, campo di tiro; *to take the —*, iniziare una campagna; (fig.) campo, teatro d'azione, settore *m.*; (comm.) mercato; (sport) campo, terreno sportivo, stadio; (racing) tutti i cavalli.
**field-artillery** *n.* artiglieria campale. **-day** *n.* (mil.) giorno di manovre, giornata campale; (fam.) grande occasione, successo.
**fielder** *n.* (cricket) giuocatore che rincorre e rilancia la palla.
**fieldfare** *n.* (orn.) tordela.
**field-glass** *n.* binocolo. **-gun** *n.*

(mil.) cannone *m.* di artiglieria campale. **-hospital** *n.* ospedale *m.* da campo. **-marshal** *n.* feldmaresciallo; (in Italy) Maresciallo d'Italia. **-mouse** *n.* topolino di campagna. **-officer** *n.* (mil.) ufficiale col grado di maggiore, tenente colonnello o colonnello. **-sports** *n.* caccia e pesca.

**fiend** *n.* demonio; spirito maligno; persona crudele; diavolo. **-ish** *adj.* diabolico; infernale.

**fierce** *adj.* feroce; fiero; crudele; (fig.) ardente; intenso. **-ness** *n.* ferocia; violenza; ardore *m.*

**fier-y** *adj.* focoso; ardente. **-iness** *n.* foga; ardore *m.*; irascibilità.

**fife** *n.* (mus.) piffero.

**fifteen** *card. num.* quindici. **-th** *ord. num.* quindicesimo, decimoquinto; *the -th of August*, il quindici agosto.

**fifth** *ord. num.* quinto; *— column*, quinta colonna; *Henry the —*, Enrico Quinto; *the — of May*, il cinque maggio; *n.* quinto; quinta parte. **-ly** *adv.* in quinto luogo.

**fifth-rate** *adj.* di pessima qualità, infimo.

**fiftieth** *ord. num.* cinquantesimo; *— anniversary*, cinquantenario.

**fifty** *card. num.* cinquanta; *about —*, una cinquantina; *fifty-fifty*, a metà, diviso in parti eguali; *fifty-one*, *fifty-two*, cinquantuno, cinquantadue; *fifty-first*, cinquantunesimo, cinquantesimo primo; *fifty-second*, cinquantaduesimo, cinquantesimo secondo.

**fig** *n.* fico; *dried —*, fico secco; *it isn't worth a —*, non vale un fico.

**fight** *n.* combattimento; zuffa; rissa; lotta; *free —*, mischia; *sham —*, finta battaglia; *to put up a good —*, battersi bene, lottare coraggiosamente; *to have a — with someone*, prendere a pugni qualcuno.

**fight** *tr.* combattere; lottare contro; dar battaglia a; *to — the good —*, combattere per una buona causa; *to — one's way* (*out*), aprirsi un varco; *to — a disease*, lottare contro una malattia; *to — corruption*, dar battaglia alla corruzione; *to — a duel*, battersi in duello; *to — it out*, battersi fino alla fine; *to — an election*, presentarsi come candidato ad una elezione; *to — off*, scacciare; *intr.* combattere; battersi; *to — shy of*, vincere; *to — for*, combattere per.

**fighter** *n.* combattente *m.*; *he is no —*, non è un eroe, non ha voglia di battersi; (aeron.) caccia *m. indecl.*

**fighting** *adj.* combattente; (fig.) combattivo; *— spirit*, spirito combattivo; *— ships*, navi *f.pl.* di guerra; *— line*, prima linea; *— cock*, gallo da combattimento, (fig.) galletto; *to live like a — cock*, vivere come un papa; *n.* combattimento; lotta; tafferuglio; rissa; *hand-to-hand —*, lotta corpo a corpo.

**fig-leaf** *n.* foglia di fico; (art) foglia d'acanto. **-tree** *n.* fico.

**figment** *n.* finzione; invenzione; fantasia.

**figuration** *n.* figurazione; rappresentazione.

**figurative** *adj.* figurativo; figurato; allegorico; metaforico; simbolico.

**figure** *n.* figura; forma; *to cut a sorry —*, fare brutta figura; *to keep one's —*, mantenere la linea; (art) figura, immagine *f.*; *lay —*, manichino; illustrazione, tavola, rappresentazione figurata; diagramma *m.*; *— of speech*, metafora, modo di dire; cifra, numero; *a round —*, una cifra rotonda; *to be quick at -s*, essere bravo in aritmetica; prezzo, ammontare *m.*; *a high —*, un prezzo elevato; *to add up the -s*, fare la somma.

**figure** *tr.* raffigurare; rappresentare; immaginare, figurarsi; *to — out*, calcolare; *intr.* apparire; figurare; trovarsi.

**figurehead** *n.* polena; (fig.) uomo di paglia, prestanome *m.*

**figurine** *n.* figurina, statuetta.

**Fiji** *pr.n.* (geog.) le isole Figi.

**filament** *n.* filamento; fibrilla.

**filbert** *n.* avellana, nocciuola; *—* (*tree*), avellano, nocciuolo.

**filch** *tr.* rubacchiare; sgraffignare. **-er** *n.* ladruncolo. **-ing** *n.* furterello.

**file**[1] *n.* lima; *tr.* limare; levigare; *to — away*, togliere con la lima; *to — down*, levigare.

**file**[2] *n.* filza; schedario; (comm.) raccoglitore; *— number*, numero di riferimento; *pl.* archivio; *to be on —*, trovarsi in archivio, (fig.) essere noto; fila; *single —*, fila indiana; (mil.) *the rank and —*, la bassa forza, (fig.) l'uomo qualunque.

**file**[2] *tr.* infilzare; archiviare; ordinare; registrare; (leg.) *to — a statement*, deporre una dichiarazione; *to — a suit for divorce*, far istanza di divorzio; *intr. to — off*, allontanarsi marciando in fila; *to — out*, uscire in fila; *to — past*, sfilare.

**file-card** *n.* scheda; cartellino. **-copy** *n.* copia da archiviare.

**filial** *adj.* filiale.

**filibuster** *n.* filibustiere *m.*; (pol.) ostruzionista *m.* **-ing** *n.* (pol.) ostruzionismo.

**filigree** *n.* filigrana.

**filing**[1] *n.* limatura.

**filing**[2] *n.* archiviazione; ordinamento in raccoglitori; *— system*, sistema di raccolta.

**filing-cabinet** *n.* schedario; casellario.

**fill** *n.* quantità sufficiente per riempire; pieno; sufficienza; sazietà; *to eat one's —*, mangiare a sazietà.

**fill** *tr.* riempire; colmare; caricare; *to — to the brim*, riempire sino all'orlo; *to — a gap*, colmare una lacuna; (dentistry) otturare, impiombare; (comm.) *to — an order*, eseguire un ordine; coprire, occupare, tenere; (theatr.) *to — a role*, interpretare una parte; (fam.) *to — someone's shoes*, prendere il posto di qualcuno; *to — in*, compilare, completare, inserire; *to — in a form*, riempire un modulo; *to — out*, gonfiare, ingrassare; *to — up*, riempire, completare, *intr.* riempirsi, diventare pieno, (motor.) fare il pieno; *to — out*, gonfiarsi, ingrassarsi.

**filler-cap** *n.* (motor.) bocchettone *m.* di riempimento.

**fillet** *n.* fascia; benda; (archit.) listello; lesena; (cul.) filetto, fetta; *tr.* (archit.) ornare di listelli; (cul.) tagliare a fette.

**filling** *adj.* sazievole, che sazia; *n.* riempitura; (dentistry) otturazione, impiombatura; mastice *m.* per otturazioni; (cul.) ripieno.

**filling-station** *n.* (motor.) stazione di rifornimento

**fillip** *n.* colpo col dito; (fig.) sprone *m.*; stimolo; *to give a — to*, stimolare.

**filly** *n.* puledra; (joc.) ragazza.

**film** *n.* strato sottile; (fig.) velo; patina; (anat.) membrana; (photog.) pellicola; (cinem.) film *m.*; pellicola; *to shoot a —*, girare un film; *silent —*, film muto; *talking —*, film parlato, film sonoro; *news —*, cinegiornale *m.*; *pl. the -s*, il cinema; *tr.* filmare; girare un film; riprodurre cinematograficamente; *intr.* coprirsi di uno strato sottile. **-goer** *n.* amante *m.*, *f.* del cinema.

**filminess** *n.* trasparenza; leggerezza.

**film-star** *n.* divo, diva del cinema. **-test** *n.* provino.

**filmy** *adj.* tenue; sottile; vaporoso; annebbiato; trasparente.

**filter** *n.* filtro; *tr.* filtrare; *intr.* infiltrarsi; (fig.) trapelare; *to — out*, diffondersi.

**filter-bed** *n.* strato filtrante. **-tip** *n.* filtro.

**filth** *n.* sporcizia; sudiciume *m.*; immondizia; sozzura; lordura. **-iness** *n.* sozzura; sporcizia; (fig.) oscenità. **-y** *adj.* sporco; sudicio; sozzo; osceno; *-y language*, turpiloquio; (joc.) *-y lucre*, il vile denaro.

**filtration** *n.* filtrazione.

**fin** *n.* pinna; (aeron.) piano stabilizzatore; (mech.) aletta.

**final** *adj.* finale; ultimo; (fig.) definitivo, decisivo; *n.* (sport) gara finale, finale *f.*; (schol.) esame *m.* finale; (of newspaper) ultima edizione.

**finale** *n.* (mus.) finale *m.*; *grand –*, gran finale, (fig.) apoteosi *f.*

**finalist** *n.* (sport) finalista *m., f.*

**finality** *n.* finalità; carattere definitivo.

**finally** *adv.* infine, alla fine, finalmente.

**finance** *n.* finanza; *tr.* finanziare; sovvenzionare; coprire le spese di.

**financial** *adj.* finanziario; *– year*, (comm.) anno di gestione, (admin.) anno fiscale.

**financier** *n.* finanziere, finanziatore *m.*

**finch** *n.* (orn.) fringuello.

**find** *n.* scoperta; ritrovamento; (fam.) *a great –*, una bella scoperta.

**find** *tr.* trovare; ritrovare; scoprire; *to be found*, trovarsi; *to – one's bearings*, orientarsi; *to – one's feet*, sistemarsi, abituarsi a; *to – one's way*, trovare la strada; *to – time*, trovare tempo; provare; *to – difficulty*, provare difficoltà; *to – fault with*, criticare, lamentarsi di; constatare, trovare; *I found that it was not at all easy*, ho constatato che non era mica facile; provvedere, fornire; *to – money*, fornire denaro; (mil.) fornire; *all found*, vitto e alloggio gratis; (leg.) dichiarare, sentenziare; *to – guilty*, dichiarare colpevole; (fig.) *to – out*, scoprire, cercare di scoprire; *to – someone out*, non trovare qualcuno in casa, (fig.) smascherare qualcuno, scoprire il vero carattere di qualcuno.

**find-er** *n.* chi trova; ritrovatore, scopritore, inventore. **-ing** *n.* ritrovamento; (leg.) sentenza.

**fine[1]** *adj.* fine; puro; raffinato, pregiato; *– sand*, sabbia fine; *– workmanship*, lavorazione raffinata; *a – distinction*, una distinzione sottile; bello; *– weather*, bel tempo; *wet or –*, con qualunque tempo; *one of these – days*, un bel giorno; *that's – !*, benissimo!; *the – arts*, le belle arti; *a – intellect*, un bell'ingegno; *– feelings*, sentimenti elevati; *adv.* bene; (fam.) *it suits me –*, mi va benone; *to cut it –*, farcela per un pelo.

**fine[2]** *n.* (leg.) multa, ammenda; *to inflict a –*, condannare a pagare una multa, multare; *to pay a –*, pagare una multa; *tr.* multare; *to be -d*, essere multato, essere condannato a pagare una multa.

**fineness** *n.* finezza; bellezza; raffinatezza; finitezza.

**finery** *n.* eleganza vistosa; fronzoli *m.pl.*; bei vestiti *m.pl.*

**finesse** *n.* finezza; sottigliezza; astuzia; (cards) finezza; *intr.* giuocare d'astuzia, sottilizzare; (cards) *to – the queen*, far finezza con la dama.

**finger** *n.* dito; *index –*, indice *m.*; *middle –*, dito medio; *ring –*, (dito) anulare; *little –*, mignolo; *to eat with one's -s*, mangiare con le mani; *to lay one's – on*, mettere il dito su; *to twist someone round one's little –*, rigirare qualcuno come si vuole; *to have a – in the pie*, aver le mani in pasta, metterci lo zampino; *to cross one's -s*, toccar ferro; *to burn one's -s*, rimanere scottato; *my -s itch to do it*, ho una voglia matta di farlo; *a – of whisky*, un dito di whisky; (mech.) lancetta; (biscuit) lingua di suocera.

**finger** *tr.* toccare; tastare; palpare; brancicare; rubacchiare; (mus.) diteggiare; *to – the keys*, tasteggiare. **-ing** *n.* il tasteggiare; (mus.) diteggiatura.

**finger-board** *n.* (mus.) (of piano) tastiera; (of violin) manico. **-bowl** *n.* vaschetta lavadita. **-mark** *n.* ditata. **-nail** *n.* unghia. **-post** *n.* palo segnavia. **-print** *n.* impronta digitale. **-stall** *n.* copridito. **-tip** *n.* punta del dito; *to have something at one's -tips*, sapere a menadito, avere sulla punta delle dita.

**finial** *n.* (archit.) guglietta ornamentale, cuspide *f.*

**finicking, finicky, finikin** *adj.* (fam.) meticoloso, pignolo.

**finis** *n.* fine *f.*

**finish[1]** *n.* fine *f.*; conclusione; *to fight to a –*, combattere fino all'ultimo; (sport) fine della partita, ultima volata; finezza, finitura; (text.) appretto.

**finish[2]** *tr., intr.* finire; terminare; concludere; porre fine a; (text.) apprettare; *to – off*, dare l'ultimo tocco a, dare il colpo di grazia a.

**finishing** *n.* rifinitura; (text.) appretto; *– school*, scuola di perfezionamento; *– touch*, ultimo tocco; (fam.) il becco all'oca.

**finishing-post** *n.* (sport) traguardo.

**finite** *adj.* limitato; circoscritto; determinato; (gramm.) finito.

**Finland** *pr.n.* (geog.) Finlandia.

**Finn** *n.* finno *m.*; finlandese *m., f.* **-ish** *adj.* finlandese; *n.* (language) la lingua finnica.

**fir, fir-tree** *n.* abete *m.* **-cone** *n.* pigna.

**fire** *n.* fuoco; *electric –*, stufa elettrica; *gas –*, stufa a gas; *to lay the –*, preparare il fuoco; *to light a –*, accendere il fuoco; *to poke the –*, attizzare il fuoco; *to sit by the –*, sedersi accanto al fuoco; *to fall out of the frying-pan into the –*, cadere dalla padella nella brace; (provb.) *there's no smoke without –*, non c'è fumo senza arrosto; *to add fuel to the –*, gettare olio sul fuoco; incendio; *to catch –*, prendere fuoco, accendersi; *to set – to*, appiccare il fuoco a, incendiare; *to set the Thames on –*, far qualcosa di straordinario; *a house on –*, una casa in fiamme; (mil.) tiro; *under –*, sotto il fuoco; *to be between two -s*, essere tra due fuochi; (fig.) ardore *m.*; foga; entusiasmo; *to hang –*, far cilecca.

**fire** *tr., intr.* dar fuoco a; incendiare; prendere fuoco; sparare; far fuoco; (fig.) *to – a question*, fare una domanda a bruciapelo; cuocere; scaldare, accendere; (fig.) infiammare, eccitare; infiammarsi, riscaldarsi; (slang) licenziare, silurare, mettere alla porta.

**fire-alarm** *n.* segnalatore, allarme *m.* d'incendio. **-arm** *n.* arma da fuoco; *-arms permit*, porto d'armi.

**fire-box** *n.* (rlwy.) focolaio, camera di combustione. **-brand** *n.* tizzone *m.*; (fig.) testa calda; agitatore. **-brick** *n.* mattone refrattario.

**fire-brigade** *n.* corpo dei pompieri. **-bucket** *n.* secchio per incendio.

**fire-clay** *n.* argilla refrattaria. **-damp** *n.* grisù *m.* **-dog** *n.* alare *m.*

**fire-eater** *n.* mangiatore di fuoco; (fig.) attaccabrighe *m. indecl.*

**fire-engine** *n.* pompa antincendio. **-escape** *n.* scala da pompieri; uscita di sicurezza. **-extinguisher** *n.* estintore *m.*

**firefly** *n.* (ent.) lucciola.

**fireguard** *n.* parafuoco.

**fire-hydrant** *n.* bocca da incendio. **-insurance** *n.* assicurazione contro gli incendi.

**firelight** *n.* luce *f.* del focolare. **-er** *n.* accendifuoco.

**fire-man** *n.* pompiere *m.* **-place** *n.* focolare *m.*; camino. **-proof** *adj.* incombustibile, resistente al fuoco, refrattario.

**fire-raiser** *n.* incendiario. **-raising** *n.* incendio doloso.

**fire-screen** *n.* parafuoco.

**fireside** *n.* focolare *m.*; (fig.) intimità domestica.

**fire-station** *n.* caserma dei pompieri.

**firewood** *n.* legna da ardere.

**firework** *n.* fuoco d'artificio; *-s display*, spettacolo di fuochi d'artificio; *to let off -s*, accendere fuochi d'artificio, (fig.) sfogarsi.

**firing** *n.* l'appiccare il fuoco; sparo; sparatoria; cottura;

alimentazione, caricamento; combustibile *m.*
**firing-line** *n.* (mil.) prima linea. **-party, -squad** *n.* plotone *m.* d'esecuzione.
**firm**[1] *adj.* stabile; saldo; solido; (fig.) fermo, deciso; *to remain —*, tener duro.
**firm**[2] *n.* (comm.) ditta; azienda; società; casa.
**firmament** *n.* firmamento; cielo.
**firmness** *n.* fermezza; saldezza; stabilità.
**first** *adj.* primo; *— but one*, secondo; *in the — place*, in primo luogo; (fig.) primario, il più importante; *— cousin*, cugino germano; *adv.* prima; in primo luogo; anzitutto; per la prima volta; piuttosto; *— come — served*, chi tardi arriva male alloggia.
**first-aid** *n.* pronto soccorso.
**firstborn** *adj., n.* primogenito.
**first-class** *adj.* di primo ordine, di prima qualità, primario; (rlwy.) prima classe. **-fruits** *n.* primizie *f.pl.*; (fig.) primi risultati. **-hand** *adj.* di prima mano; diretto. **-night** *n.* (theatr.) prima. **-rate** *adj.* ottimo, eccellente.
**firth** *n.* (Scot., geog.) estuario.
**fiscal** *adj.* fiscale.
**fish** *n.* pesce *m.*; *— and chips*, pesce fritto con patatine; (fig.) *neither — flesh nor fowl*, nè pesce nè carne; *a pretty kettle of —*, un bel pasticcio; *like a — out of water*, come un pesce fuor d'acqua; *to drink like a —*, bere come una spugna; *to have other — to fry*, avere altri affari cui badare; *a queer —*, un tipo strano.
**fish** *tr., intr.* pescare; *to — for trout*, pescare trote; (fig.) *to — in troubled waters*, pescare nel torbido; *to — for*, cercare di farsi dare; *to — in one's pockets*, frugare nelle proprie tasche; *to — out*, tirar fuori.
**fish-ball, -cake** *n.* (cul.) polpetta di pesce. **-bone** *n.* lisca; spina.
**fisher, fisherman** *n.* pescatore.
**fishery** *n.* (industr.) pesca; riserva di pesca, luogo dove si pesca.
**fish-fingers** *n.pl.* bastoncini *m.pl.* di pesce. **-glue** *n.* colla di pesce. **-hook** *n.* amo.
**fishing** *n.* pesca.
**fishing-boat** *n.* peschereccio. **-rod** *n.* canna da pesca.
**fish-market** *n.* mercato del pesce, pescheria.
**fishmonger** *n.* pescivendolo. **-plate** *n.* coprigiunto. **-pond** *n.* vivaio, peschiera. **-wife** *n.* pescivendola; (fig.) donna da trivio.
**fishy** *adj.* di pesce; pescoso; *to smell —*, saper di pesce; (fig.) equivoco, losco, sospetto; *there is something — about it*, è un affare sospetto.
**fissile** *adj.* fissile.
**fission** *n.* scissione; (phys.) fissione.
**fissure** *n.* fessura; screpolatura, fenditura.
**fist** *n.* pugno; *clenched —*, pugno chiuso; *mailed —*, pugno di ferro; (fam.) mano *f.*, calligrafia. **-icuffs** *n.* pugilato.
**fistula** *n.* (med.) fistola.
**fit**[1] *adj.* adatto; idoneo; capace; opportuno, conveniente; *— to eat*, commestibile; *— to drink*, potabile; *— to be seen*, presentabile; *— for publication*, pubblicabile; *— to do something*, capace di far qualcosa; *— for nothing*, buono a niente; *— for a dog*, da cani; *to think —*, pensare che sia opportuno; degno; sano; *— as a fiddle*, sano come un pesce; *— for military service*, abile al servizio militare; (sport) allenato, in forma; *to keep —*, mantenersi in forma.
**fit**[1] *n.* aderenza; misura; *a tight —*, una misura stretta; *a perfect —*, una misura perfetta; (mech.) accoppiamento.
**fit**[1] *tr.* accomodare; aggiustare; adattare; *to make the punishment — the crime*, adeguare la pena al delitto; andare bene; convenire; *the example does not — the case*, l'esempio non conviene al caso; (mech.) *to — a machine together*, montare una macchina; *rfl.* adattarsi a, prepararsi per; *intr.* andare bene, stare bene, convenire; *to — in*, *tr.* incastrare, *intr.* andar bene, accordarsi; *to — on*, provare, (mech.) montare; *to — out*, allestire, provvedere al necessario; *to — up*, arredare, allestire.
**fit**[2] attacco; accesso; parossismo; convulsione; *to have a —*, essere preso da convulsioni, (fig.) essere molto sorpreso; (fam.) *she'll have a —, when you tell her*, quando glielo dirai, le verrà un accidente; *to give someone a —*, far venire un colpo a qualcuno; capriccio; ticchio; *if the — takes me*, se mi salta il ticchio; *by -s and starts*, a sbalzi.
**fitful** *adj.* spasmodico; capriccioso; irregolare.
**fit-ly** *adv.* convenevolmente; giustamente; a proposito. **-ness** *n.* capacità; attitudine *f.*; convenienza; l'essere adatto; *physical -ness*, buona salute.
**fitter**[1] *adj. comp.* of **fit**[1], *q.v.*
**fitter**[2] *n.* (mech.) aggiustatore, montatore, meccanico; (of clothes) sarto che fa la prova.
**fitting** *adj.* conveniente; adatto; che si addice; *n.* adattamento, aggiustamento; (tailor.) prova; *pl.* accessori *m.pl.*; attrezzi *m.pl.*; equipaggiamento; (in house) suppellettili *f.pl.*, arredi *m.pl.*; (mech.) guarnizioni *f.pl.*
**five** *card. num.* cinque. **-fold** *adj.* quintuplice, quintuplo.
**fiver** *n.* (fam.) banconota da cinque sterline.
**fives** *n.* (sport) giuoco della palla al muro.
**fix** *tr.* fissare; stabilire; determinare; (paint.) raffermare; (photog.) fissare; (fam.) *we'll — him!*, l'aggiusteremo!; *to — up*, sistemare, regolare, accomodare, mettere in ordine; *intr. to — on*, stabilire, decidersi per, sistemare.
**fix** *n.* difficoltà *f. indecl.*; dilemma *m.*; *to be in a —*, essere nei guai; (naut.) rilievo, punto nave.
**fix-ation** *n.* fissazione. **-ative** *adj., n.* fissativo.
**fixed** *adj.* fisso; fissato; stabile; stabilito. **-ness, fixity** *n.* fissità; stabilità.
**fixing** *n.* fissaggio.
**fixture** *n.* ciò che è fisso; *pl.* installazioni fisse; (sport) avvenimento sportivo, incontro; (fam. of person) istituzione. **-list** *n.* (sport) calendario.
**fizz** *n.* effervescenza; sibilo; (fam.) spumante *m.*, sciampagna *m.*; *intr.* frizzare; spumeggiare; sibilare.
**fizzle** *intr.* spumeggiare; (fam.) *— out*, fare fiasco, andare a monte.
**fizzy** *adj.* (fam.) gassoso, effervescente, frizzante.
**flabbergast** *tr.* (fam.) stupire; sbalordire. **-ed** *part. adj.* stupito; sbalordito.
**flabb-y** *adj.* floscio; fiacco; flaccido; molle. **-iness** *n.* flaccidezza; mollezza; fiacchezza.
**flaccid** *adj.* flaccido; molle; floscio. **-ity** *n.* flaccidezza; fiacchezza; languidezza.
**flag**[1] *n.* (bot.) acoro, giaggiolo.
**flag**[2] *n.* pietra per lastricare; *pl.* lastrico; *tr.* lastricare.
**flag**[3] *n.* bandiera; stendardo; *— of truce*, bandiera bianca; *to hoist the —*, issare la bandiera; *to strike the —*, ammainare la bandiera; *to fly the Italian —*, battere bandiera italiana; *to keep the — flying*, resistere ad oltranza, (fig.) non lasciarsi abbattere; *— of convenience*, bandiera di convenienza; (taxi) banderuola; *tr.* segnalare con bandiera; imbandierare.
**flag**[4] *intr.* penzolare, illanguidire, affievolirsi.
**flag-bearer** *n.* portabandiera *m.* **-captain** *n.* capitano di nave ammiraglia. **-day** *n.* giorno di questua per un'opera di beneficenza.
**flagell-ate** *tr.* flagellare. **-ant** *adj.* flagellante; *n.* flagellatore. **-ation** *n.* flagellazione.

**flageolet** *n.* (mus.) zufolo; (cul.) faggiolino.
**flag-lieutenant** *n.* (naval) aiutante di bandiera. **-officer** *n.* (naval) ufficiale ammiraglio.
**flagon** *n.* bottiglione *m.*; bricco.
**flagr-ant** *adj.* scandaloso; odioso; flagrante; vistoso; evidente. **-ancy** *n.* enormità; vistosità.
**flag-ship** *n.* nave ammiraglia. **-staff** *n.* asta di bandiera.
**flagstone** *n.* lastra di pietra, lastrico.
**flag-wagging** *n.* il segnalare con bandiere; (fig.) sciovinismo.
**flail** *n.* (agric.) correggiato.
**flair** *n.* fiuto; intuito; (fam.) bernoccolo.
**flak-e** *n.* fiocco; scaglia; squama lamina; *intr.* cadere in fiocchi; scagliarsi; sfaldarsi; squamarsi. **-y** *adj.* a scaglie; a lamine; (cul.) sfogliato.
**flamboy-ant** *adj.* sgargiante, fastoso; (archit.) fiammeggiante. **-ance** *n.* vistosità; fasto.
**flame** *n.* fiamma; vampa; fuoco; sfolgorìo; *to burst into -s*, divampare; (fam.) *she was an old — of mine*, era una mia antica fiamma; *intr.* fiammeggiare; divampare; (fig.) prorompere, splendere; arrossire.
**flaming** *adj.* fiammeggiante; infuocato; accesso; (fig.) violento, focoso; (slang) maledetto.
**flamingo** *n.* (orn.) fenicottero.
**flan** *n.* (cul.) sformato; (typ.) flano.
**Flanders** *pr.n.* (geog.) Fiandra.
**flange** *n.* flangia; bordo; orlo; (eng.) ala.
**flank** *n.* fianco; lato; *tr.* fiancheggiare, affiancare.
**flannel** *n.* flanella; *pl.* completo sportivo.
**flannelette** *n.* flanella di cotone.
**flap** *n.* lembo; risvolto; labbro; lobo; (of envelope) linguetta; (of hat) tesa; (of pocket) patta; (of bird's wing) alata, colpo d'ala; (of table, *etc.*) ribalta; (slang) *to be in a —*, essere in preda al panico, aver la fifa.
**flap** *tr.* sventolare; agitare; battere le ali; *intr.* battere; penzolare; (slang) agitarsi, perdere le staffe.
**flapdoodle** *n.* sciocchezze, frottole *f.pl.*
**flapjack** *n.* portacipria *m. indecl.*; (cul.) frittella.
**flapper** *n.* (1920s slang) ragazza.
**flare** *n.* fiammata; vampa; chiarore *m.*; razzo; segnale luminoso; *intr.* fiammeggiare; brillare; *to — up*, divampare, (fig.) arrabbiarsi, esplodere.
**flash** *n.* lampo; baleno; bagliore *m.*; sprazzo; *in a —*, in un lampo; *— of lightning*, lampo; *a — in the pan*, fuoco di paglia; *— of wit*, tratto di spirito; (radio; journ.) messaggio breve, notizia breve; *tr.* far balenare; proiettare luce; (news, message) diffondere rapidamente; *intr.* lampeggiare; balenare; scintillare; *to — past*, passare come un bolide.
**flash** *adj.* sgargiante; vistoso.
**flash-back** *n.* (cinem.) scena retrospettiva. **-lamp** *n.* lampada per segnalazioni; lampadina tascabile.
**flashlight** *n.* (naut.) luce *f.* intermittente; (photog.) lampo di magnesio.
**flash-point** *n.* (phys.) punto di infiammabilità.
**flashy** *adj.* vistoso; appariscente; sgargiante.
**flask** *n.* flacone *m.*; fiaschetta; *thermos —*, termos *m. indecl.*; pallone *m.*
**flat** *adj.* piatto; piano; liscio; disteso; *to fall —*, cadere disteso, (fig.) fallire, non riscuotere applausi; *to have — feet*, avere i piedi dolci; (of beer, wine) svanito; (of tyre) sgonfio; (fig.) monotono, uniforme, scialbo; deciso, reciso, netto, perentorio; (racing) *— race*, corsa piana; (fam.) *— out, adv.* a briglia sciolta; *adj.* stanco; morto.
**flat** *n.* parte piatta; pianura; appartamento; *block of -s*, palazzo diviso in appartamenti; (mus.) bemolle *m.*
**flatfoot** *n.* (slang, derog.) poliziotto.
**flat-footed** *adj.* dai piedi piatti; (slang) come un poliziotto. **-iron** *n.* ferro da stiro.
**flatlet** *n.* appartamentino.
**flatness** *n.* pianezza; uniformità; monotonia; (of refusal, etc.) l'essere netto.
**flat-nosed** *adj.* camuso.
**flatten** *tr.* appiattire; rendere piatto; spianare; livellare; *to — oneself against the wall*, schiacciarsi contro il muro.
**flatter** *tr.* adulare; lusingare; blandire; abbellire; *rfl. to — oneself*, lusingarsi; sperare. **-er** *n.* adulatore. **-ing** *adj.* lusinghiero; adulatorio. **-y** *n.* adulazione; lusinga; blandizie *f.pl.*
**flatul-ent** *adj.* (med.) flatulento; (fig.) pretenzioso, pomposo. **-ence** *n.* (med.) flatulenza.
**flaunt** *tr.* ostentare; sfoggiare; sventolare; *intr.* pavoneggiarsi. **-ing** *adj.* sfarzoso; vistoso; (of flag) sventolante.
**flautist** *n.* (mus.) flautista *m., f.*
**flavour** *n.* sapore *m.*; gusto; *tr.* condire; rendere saporito; dare sapore a. **-ing** *n.* condimento. **-less** *adj.* insipido.
**flaw** *n.* difetto; vizio; pecca; tacca; screpolatura; incrinatura; *tr.* trovare da ridire a. **-less** *adj.* senza difetto; impeccabile; perfetto; intatto.
**flax** *n.* lino; tela di lino. **-en** *adj.* di lino; (of hair) biondo, biondissimo.
**flay** *tr.* scorticare; pelare; scuoiare; (fig.) criticare vivamente; sferzare; bistrattare.
**flea** *n.* pulce *f.*; (fam.) *to have a — in one's ear*, avere dei sospetti; *to send someone away with a — in his ear*, licenziare bruscamente qualcuno.
**fleabane** *n.* (bot.) pulicaria, incensaria.
**flea-bite** *n.* morso di pulce; (fam.) bagatella, inezia. **-bitten** *adj.* morso dalle pulci; macchiato; (fig.) meschino. **-pit** *n.* (fam.) teatro o cinema cadente.
**fleck** *n.* macchia; chiazza; granello; *tr.* macchiare; chiazzare.
**fled** *p. def., part.* of **flee,** *q.v.*
**fledg-e** *tr.* fornire di penne; aver cura di, insegnare a volare. **-ed** *adj.* piumato, pennuto. **-(e)ling** *n.* uccellino; *adj.* (fig.) pivellino; *-ling poet*, poeta in erba.
**flee** *intr.* fuggire; scappare; *tr.* fuggire; abbandonare; schivare.
**fleec-e** *n.* vello; tosone *m.*; *the Golden —*, (myth.) il vello d'oro, (herald.) il toson d'oro; (text.) *— lining*, fodera di lana; *tr.* tosare; (fig.) spogliare, spennacchiare. **-y** *adj.* velloso; lanoso; (fig.) *-y clouds*, pecorelle *f.pl.*
**fleeing** *adj.* in fuga; *n.* fuga.
**fleet**[1] *n.* flotta; marina di guerra; (fig.) gruppo; flottiglia.
**fleet**[2] *adj.* rapido; veloce; agile; lesto. **-ing** *adj.* fugace; transitorio; effimero. **-ness** *n.* velocità; agilità.
**Fleet Street** *pr.n.* strada londinese in cui si trovano le redazioni di molti giornali; (fig.) la stampa.
**Fleming** *n.* fiammingo.
**Flemish** *adj.* fiammingo; *n.* (language) lingua fiamminga, il fiammingo.
**flesh** carne *f.*; *in the —*, in carne ed ossa; *one's own — and blood*, i propri figli; *to go the way of all —*, morire; *to mortify the —*, mortificare il corpo; *the spirit is willing but the — is weak*, lo spirito è forte ma la carne è debole; *the sins of the —*, i peccati carnali; *to put on —*, ingrassare, rimettersi in carne; *to make someone's — creep*, far venire la pelle d'oca a qualcuno; (med.) *— wound*, ferita superficiale; *proud —*, granulazione esuberante; (paint.) carne *f.*, incarnato; (of fruit) polpa; *tr.* (tan.) scarnire. **-iness** *n.* carnosità; obesità. **-less** *adj.* scarno; magro. **-ly** *adj.* carnale, sensuale. **-pots** *n. pl.* (fig.) vita comoda, lusso.

**fleur-de-lis, -lys** *n.* fiordaliso; giglio.
**flew** *p.def.* of **fly,** *q.v.*
**flex** *n.* (electr.) filo; cordone *m.*; *tr.* piegare; flettere.
**flexi-ble** *adj.* flessibile; pieghevole; elastico; (mus.) pastoso; (fig.) trattabile, arrendevole, docile, compiacente; versatile. **-bility** *n.* flessibilità; elasticità; (fig.) docilità; (mus.) pastosità.
**flexion** *n.* flessione; curvatura.
**flick** *n.* colpetto; buffetto; schiocco; *pl.* (slang) cinema *m.*; *tr.* colpire leggermente; *to — off,* far volare via.
**flicker** *n.* guizzo; tremolio; (of eyelid) battito; *intr.* tremolare; guizzare; vacillare; svolazzare; *to — out,* spegnersi.
**flight** *n.* **1.** volo; volata; *in —,* durante il volo; (fig.) slancio; *— of steps,* rampa, ramo; (artill.) traiettoria; (aeron.) *formation —,* stormo. **2.** fuga; *the — into Egypt,* la fuga in Egitto; *to take to —,* darsi alla fuga; *to put to —,* mettere in fuga.
**flight-y** *adj.* frivolo; incostante; volubile. **-iness** *n.* leggerezza; incostanza; volubilità.
**flims-y** *adj.* tenue; fragile; debole; frivolo, senza consistenza, poco convincente; *n.* carta velina. **-iness** *n.* tenuità; fragilità; (fig.) frivolezza; inconsistenza.
**flinch** *intr.* indietreggiare; rinculare; sussultare; *without -ing,* senza battere ciglio; (fig.) *I shall not — from my duty,* non esiterò a compiere il mio dovere.
**fling** *n.* getto; lancio; (fig.) *in full —,* a tutto andare; *to have a — at someone,* canzonare qualcuno; *to have a — at something,* provare di far qualcosa; (fam.) *to have one's —,* correre la cavallina; *Highland —,* giga, danza movimentata scozzese.
**fling** *tr.* lanciare; scagliare; gettare; buttare; *to — a window open,* spalancare una finestra; *to — one's arms round someone,* stringere qualcuno fra le braccia; (fig.) *to — caution to the winds,* buttare al vento la prudenza; *to — mud at someone,* sparlare di qualcuno; *to — aside,* scartare; *to — away,* buttar via, sprecare; *to — back,* respingere; *to — down,* abbattere, gettare in terra; *to — off,* gettare via, sbarazzarsi di; *to — on one's clothes,* vestirsi in fretta e furia; *to — out,* buttar fuori; *to — out one's arms,* allargare le braccia; *to — up one's arms,* alzare le braccia; *intr. to — out of the room,* uscire bruscamente dalla stanza.
**flint** *n.* selce, silice *f.*; (for lighter) pietra focaia.
**flip** *n.* buffetto; colpetto; (slang) piccolo giro in aereo; *tr.* dare un colpetto a; colpire leggermente; schioccare.
**flipp-ant** *adj.* poco serio; disinvolto, frivolo; irriverente. **-ancy** *n.* leggerezza; mancanza di serietà.
**flipper** *n.* pinna; ala natatoria; (slang) mano *f.*; zampa.
**flirt** *n.* (man) vagheggino, dongiovanni *m.*; (woman) civetta; *intr.* amoreggiare; flirtare; civettare. **-ation** *n.* amoreggiamento; flirt *m.* **-atious** *adj.* civettuolo; galante; incline a flirtare.
**flit** *n.* (fam.) trasloco clandestino (per non pagare l'affitto); *to do a midnight —,* far il San Martino; *intr.* svolazzare; volteggiare; (fam.) andarsene alla chetichella; (fig.) scorrere, passare.
**flitch** *n.* (cul.) lardone *m.*; (of wood) travetto.
**flitter** *intr.* volteggiare; svolazzare.
**float** *n.* (naut.) galleggiante *m.*; gavitello; (fishing) sughero; (carnival car) carro; (comm.) quota di spiccioli, riserva di cassa; (bldg.) pialletto; (theatr.) luci *f.pl.* della ribalta.
**float** *tr.* far galleggiare, trasportare per via acquea; (agric.) inondare; (comm.) *to — a company,* costituire una società; *intr.* galleggiare, stare a galla; scendere lentamente; (swimming) fare il morto; (fig.) fluttuare; *to — down,* scendere lentamente. **-ing** *adj.* galleggiante; fluttuante; (comm.) *-ing debt,* debito fluttuante; (med.) *-ing kidney,* rene *m.* mobile.
**floccul-ar, -ent** *adj.* fioccoso.
**flock**[1] *n.* fiocco; bioccolo; (in mattress) borra; *pl.* (chem.) precipitati *m.pl.*
**flock**[2] *n.* gregge *m.*; mandria; branco; *— of birds,* stormo di uccelli; (fig.) folla; turba; (eccl.) gregge; *intr.* accorrere in massa; affollarsi, accalcarsi; affluire; *to — together,* riunirsi, radunarsi; (provb.) *birds of a feather — together,* ogni simile ama il suo simile.
**floe** *n.* banchisa.
**flog** *tr.* battere; fustigare; bastonare; (fam.) *to — something into someone,* insegnare qualcosa a qualcuno a suon di busse; *to — a dead horse,* pestare l'acqua nel mortaio, sprecare energia; (fishing) *to — a stream,* gettare la lenza ripetutamente su un corso d'acqua; (slang) vendere. **-ging** *n.* bastonatura; staffilata.
**flood** *n.* inondazione; allagamento; alluvione; diluvio; *— victims,* alluvionati *m.pl.*; (bibl.) *the Flood,* il diluvio universale; flusso; (of river) piena, straripamento; (fig.) fiume *m.*, torrente *m.*; ondata; *a — of tears,* un rio di lagrime.
**flood** *tr.* inondare; allagare; riempire fino a far straripare; sommergere; *to be -ed out,* essere costretto a fuggire da un'alluvione; *intr.* affluire.
**flood-gate** *n.* (hydr. eng.) paratoia, chiusa. **-light** *tr.* illuminare con riflettori; (fig.) illuminare a giorno, gettare luce su. **-lighting** *n.* illuminazione con riflettori.
**flood-mark** *n.* guardia; (on seashore) battigia. **-tide** *n.* flusso di marea, alta marea.
**floor** *n.* pavimento; solaio; *stone —,* pavimento di pietra; *wooden —,* pavimento in legno, palchetto; piano; *ground —,* pianterreno; *first —,* primo piano, piano nobile; *top —,* ultimo piano; (fig.) fondo; *to take the —,* prendere la parola; ballare; *to hold the —,* tenere il bandolo della conversazione, accaparrarsi l'attenzione di tutti; (fam.) *to wipe the — with someone,* aver la meglio su qualcuno.
**floor** *tr.* pavimentare; (fam.) sbaragliare, atterrare; *the question -ed me,* non sapevo rispondere alla domanda.
**floor-board** *n.* asse *f.* di palchetto. **-cloth** *n.* straccio di cucina.
**floor-polish** *n.* lucido per palchetto, cera.
**flop** *n.* tonfo; *to fall with a —,* cadere di schianto; (slang) insuccesso, fiasco; *to be a —,* far fiasco; *intr.* cadere di schianto; muoversi in modo sgraziato; *to — down,* lasciarsi cadere.
**floppy** *adj.* floscio; molle.
**Flora**[1] *pr.n.* Flora.
**flora**[2] *n.* (bot.) flora.
**floral** *adj.* floreale.
**Florence**[1] *pr.n.* Fiorenza.
**Florence**[2] *pr.n.* (geog.) Firenze.
**Florentine** *adj.*, *n.* fiorentino.
**florescence** *n.* fioritura; infiorescenza.
**florid** *adj.* florido; (of style) fiorito.
**florist** *n.* fioraio.
**floss** *n.* (bot.) lanuggine *f.*; (of silk) bavella, borra; (metall.) scoria galleggiante.
**flotation** *n.* (comm.) lancio di una società.
**flotilla** *n.* flottiglia.
**flotsam** *n.* relitti *m.pl.* galleggianti sul mare; (fig.) relitto.
**flounce**[1] *n.* gesto rapido d'impazienza; *intr.* dimenarsi; *to — out,* uscire con un gesto d'impazienza.
**flounce**[2] *n.* (dressm.) balza; volante *m.*; *tr.* (dressm.) ornare di balze.
**flounder**[1] *n.* (ichth.) passera.
**flounder**[2] *intr.* dibattersi; sguazzare; (fig.) impappinarsi.

**flour** *n.* farina; fior di farina.
**flourish** *n.* svolazzo; ghirigoro; paraffa; (of trumpets) squillo; gesto largo; fioritura, fiorettatura; *tr.* agitare; brandire; *intr.* fiorire, prosperare; (fig.) vivere, essere attivo. **-ing** *adj.* fiorente; prospero; rigoglioso.
**flour-mill** *n.* mulino.
**floury** *adj.* farinoso, infarinato.
**flout** *tr.* schernire; beffarsi di; far poco caso di; (fig.) sfidare.
**flow** *n.* flusso; afflusso; efflusso; movimento; (fig.) caduta, linea; *intr.* scorrere; fluire; colare; circolare; (drapery) scendere, ricadere; *to — away,* scolare; *to — back,* rifluire; *to — in,* affluire, entrare; *to — into,* (of river) sboccare in; *to — out of,* sgorgare da; (fig.) *to be -ing with,* abbondare di.
**flower** *n.* fiore *m.*; *a bunch of -s,* un mazzetto di fiori; *wild -s,* fiori di campo; *to burst into —,* sbocciare; *no -s by request,* si prega di non inviare fiori; *say it with -s,* fate i vostri auguri inviando fiori; (fig.) *-s of speech,* fiori della retorica; *in the — of one's age,* nel fiore degli anni; (chem.) fiore; *-s of sulphur,* fiori di zolfo.
**flower** *intr.* fiorire; essere in fiore; produrre fiori; (fig.) fiorire; (art) ornare di motivi floreali. **-ed** *adj.* fiorito; a fiori; a fiorami; ornato di fiori.
**flowerbed** *n.* aiuola.
**flower-girl** *n.* fioraia. **-holder** *n.* portafiori *m. indecl.* **-piece** *n.* quadro raffigurante fiori. **-pot** *n.* vaso da fiori. **-shop** *n.* negozio di fioraio. **-show** *n.* esposizione di fiori. **-stalk** *n.* stelo di fiore. **-stand** *n.* portafiori *m.*
**flowering** *adj.* in fiore; *— plants,* piante *f.pl.* che producono fiori.
**flower-y** *adj.* fiorito (also fig.). **-iness** *n.* stile fiorito.
**flowing** *adj.* fluente, corrente; fluido, scorrevole; (of tide) crescente; *n.* flusso; scolo.
**flown** *p. part.* of **fly,** *q.v.*
**flu** *n.* (pop.) influenza; grippe *f.*; spagnuola.
**fluctu-ate** *intr.* fluttuare; oscillare. **-ation** *n.* oscillazione; variazione.
**flue** *n.* gola di tiraggio (del camino).
**flu-ent** *adj.* corrente; scorrevole; fluido; *to speak — Italian,* parlare correntemente l'italiano. **-ency** *n.* scioltezza; scorrevolezza; *to speak with -ency,* parlare correntemente.
**flue-pipe** *n.* (mus.) canna d'organo.
**fluff**[1] *n.* borra; peluria; lanugine *f.*; (theatr.) papera.
**fluff**[2] *tr.* arruffare; (theatr.) impaperarsi su.
**fluff-y** *adj.* lanuginoso, cotonoso; morbido, soffice; vaporoso; arruffato. **-iness** *n.* l'essere arruffato; morbidezza.
**fluid** *adj.* fluido; liquido; (fig.) instabile; (of style) facile, corrente. **-ity** *n.* fluidità.
**fluke**[1] *n.* (naut.) patta, marra; (of whale) coda.
**fluke**[2] *n.* (fam.) colpo fortunato, successo inaspettato; caso fortuito; *by a —,* per puro caso; *intr.* (fam.) fare un colpo fortunato.
**flummox** *tr.* (fam.) sconcertare, confondere.
**flump** *n.* (fam.) tonfo; *intr.* fare un tonfo; muoversi pesantemente.
**flung** *p.def., part.* of **fling,** *q.v.*
**flunkey** *n.* lacchè *m.*; (fig.) parassita *m.*; persona servile.
**fluoresc-ent** *adj.* fluoroescente. **-ence** *n.* fluorescenza.
**fluorine** *n.* (chem.) fluorina.
**flurry** *n.* turbine *m.*; tormento; (fig.) agitazione; trambusto; nervosismo; *to be in a —,* essere innervosito; *tr.* innervosire; confondere; *to get flurried,* perdere la testa.
**flush** *adj.* ripieno; traboccante; rigurgitante; *— with,* a livello di, rasente a; (fam.) ben fornito; *to be — of money,* essere pieno di soldi; *to be — with money,* spendere liberamente.
**flush** *n.* flusso; rossore *m.*; vampa; (fig.) *in the — of victory,* nell'ebbrezza della vittoria; *the first — of dawn,* lo spuntar del giorno; (cards) cinque carte dello stesso seme.
**flush** *tr.* lavare per mezzo di un forte getto; *to — the closet,* vuotare la vasca del gabinetto tirando la catena; (bldg.) livellare; *intr.* arrossire, diventar rosso in viso, avvampare, accendersi. **-ed** *adj.* lavato; rosso in viso, acceso, accaldato; (fig.) ebbro.
**Flushing** *pr.n.* (geog.) Vlessinga, Flessinga.
**fluster** *n.* agitazione; confusione; *tr.* turbare; confondere; far perdere la testa a; *to get -ed,* turbarsi, perdere la testa.
**flute**[1] *n.* (mus.) flauto; *intr.* suonare il flauto; (fig.) parlare con voce esile.
**flute**[2] *n.* (archit.) scanalatura; *tr.* scanalare.
**flutter** *n.* battito; frullìo; (fig.) confusione; (fam.) *to be all of a —,* essere agitato, essere commosso; *to have a little —,* fare qualche scommessa, fare una piccola speculazione.
**flutter** *tr.* battere; (fig.) turbare, sconvolgere, innervosire; (fam.) *to — the dovecots,* gettare scompiglio, suscitare un putiferio; *intr.* svolazzare, aleggiare; (of flag) sventolare; (fig.) palpitare, muoversi in giro con agitazione; *to — to the ground,* cadere lentamente a terra.
**flux** *n.* flusso; afflusso; (med.) sbocco; (fig.) *in a state of —,* soggetto a cambiamenti continui.
**fly**[1] *n.* mosca; *to die like flies,* morire come le mosche; (fig.) *a — in amber,* una cosa rara; *there's always a — in the ointment,* non c'è carne senz'osso; *there are no flies on him,* non è mica un fesso; (fishing) esca artificiale; *to rise to the —,* prendere l'esca, abboccare; (pharm.) *Spanish —,* cantaride *f.*
**fly**[2] *intr.* volare; viaggiare in aeroplano; *to — high,* volare alto, (fig.) essere ambizioso, mirare in alto; *a rumour is -ing around,* circola una voce; svolazzare; sventolare; *to — open,* spalancarsi; (fig.) *to — to pieces,* spezzarsi; *to — into a passion,* dare in eccessi; *to — off the handle,* uscir del manico; *to let — (at),* sparare (contro); *to make the feathers —,* suscitare un putiferio; fuggire, correre; *time flies,* il tempo fugge; *to — to arms,* correre alle armi; *to — to someone for help,* ricorrere a qualcuno per aiuto; (fam.) *they flew out of the room,* uscirono di corsa dalla stanza; *it is late, I must —,* è tardi, debbo scappare; *to — from justice,* sottrarsi alla giustizia; *to — back,* tornare in aereo, (fig.) rimbalzare; *to — by,* passare rapidamente; *to — off,* volare via, saltare via; *to — over,* sorvolare; *to — past,* passare volando; *to — up,* salire rapidamente; *tr.* far volare; trasportare per via aerea; *to — the Italian flag,* battere bandiera italiana; *to — the Atlantic,* attraversare l'Atlantico in aeroplano; *to — a kite,* lanciare un aquilone, (fig.) saggiare l'opinione pubblica, vedere che vento tira.
**fly**[3] *n.* fiacchere *m.*; (mech.) volano; *pl.* (theatr.) culisse *f.*; spazio sopra il proscenio; (cost.) striscia di stoffa per nascondere l'abbottonatura.
**fly**[4] *adj.* (slang) svelto, sveglio, scaltro.
**fly-blown** *adj.* insudiciato dalle mosche.
**fly-by-night** *n.* nottambulo.
**flycatcher** *n.* (orn.) muscicapa *f.*, pigliamosche *m.*
**flyer** *n.* aviatore, aeronauta *m.*; (sport) velocista *m.*; (rlwy.) rapido; (bird) volatile *m. indecl.*
**flying** *adj.* volante, che vola; (mil.) veloce; (of flag) sventolante; *the Flying Dutchman,* il vascello fantasma; (fig.) *with —*

*colours*, con le bandiere spiegate; breve, rapido; *a — visit*, una visita breve; — *bomb*, bomba volante; (archit.) — *buttress*, arco rampante; — *saucer*, disco volante; — *squad*, squadra mobile; *n.* il volare, volo.

**flying-boat** *n.* idrovolante *m.* **-field** *n.* campo di aviazione. **-fish** *n.* pesce *m.* volante, rondine *f.* di mare.

**flyleaf** *n.* (typ.) risguardo, occhiello.

**fly-over** *n.* cavalcavia *m. indecl.* **-paper** *n.* carta moschicida.

**fly-past** *n.* (aeron.) sfilata di aeroplani. **-sheet** *n.* foglio volante.

**fly-wheel** *n.* volano. **-whisk** *n.* scacciamosche *m. indecl.*

**foal** *n.* puledro; *intr.* figliare.

**foam** *n.* schiuma, bava; *intr.* spumeggiare, spumare; far bava; *to — at the mouth*, aver la bava alla bocca; (fig.) *to — with rage*, essere furioso. **-ing** *adj.* spumeggiante, spumante.

**fob**[1] *n.* taschino per orologio; catena per orologio.

**fob**[2] *tr.* imbrogliare; *to — something off on*, appioppare qualcosa a; *to — off*, rimandare.

**focal** *adj.* focale.

**foc'̓s'le** *n.* See **forecastle.**

**focus** *n.* fuoco; *in —*, a fuoco; *out of —*, fuori fuoco, sfocato; (fig.) centro; (med.) focolaio; *tr.* mettere a fuoco; (fig.) concentrare; *intr.* convergere.

**fodder** *n.* foraggio; mangime *m.*

**foe, foeman** *n.* nemico; avversario.

**foetus** *n.* (med.) feto.

**fog** *n.* nebbia; bruma; *sea —*, foschia; *dense —*, nebbione *m.*; (photog.) velatura.

**fog-bank** *n.* banco di nebbia. **-bound** *adj.* avvolto nella nebbia, fermo per la nebbia.

**foggy** *adj.* nebbioso; brumoso; *a — day*, una giornata di nebbia; *it's —*, c'è nebbia; *to become —*, annebbiarsi; (fig.) *to have only a — idea of*, aver soltanto un'idea vaga di; *I haven't the foggiest idea*, non ne so proprio niente.

**foghorn** *n.* (naut.) sirena da nebbia; (fig.) *a voice like a —*, una voce stentorea.

**fog-signal** *n.* (rlwy.) petardo.

**fogy, fogey** *n.* persona all'antica, vecchio barbogio.

**foible** *n.* debole *m.*

**foil**[1] *n.* lamina di metallo; (fig.) contrappeso; *to serve as a —*, servire a far risaltare; (archit.) fogliame *m.*; (fencing) fioretto.

**foil**[2] *tr.* frustrare, sventare.

**foist** *tr.* rifilare; appioppare; attribuire; inserire; interpolare.

**fold**[1] *n.* ovile *m.*; *to bring a lost sheep back to the —*, ricondurre all'ovile una pecora smarrita.

**fold**[2] *n.* piega; ripiegatura; spira; *tr.* piegare; avvolgere; *to — one's hands*, congiungere le mani; *to — one's arms*, incrociare le braccia; *to — up*, avvolgere; *to — up an umbrella*, chiudere un ombrello; *intr.* piegarsi; (fam.) *to — up*, far fiasco, cessare l'attività.

**folder** *n.* piegatore; (machine) piegatrice; (typ.) piegafoglio; (for papers) cartella; (leaflet) volantino

**folding** *adj.* pieghevole, ripiegabile; — *bed*, letto da campo, branda; letto pieghevole; — *chair*, sedia pieghevole; *n.* piegatura; avvolgimento; (geol.) corrugamento.

**foliage** *n.* fogliame *m.*; (paint.) frappa.

**foliate** *adj.* fronzuto; (archit.) sfogliato; (bot.) foliaceo.

**folio** *n.* folio; *first —*, primo in folio.

**folk** *n.* gente *f.*; popolo; nazione; *the old —*, i vecchi; *my —*, i miei; *your —*, i tuoi; *fine —*, il bel mondo, i signori; *country —*, la gente di campagna, i contadini; (pop.) *the little —*, le fate, i folletti.

**folk-danc-e** *n.* danza rustica; ballo popolare. **-ing** *n.* culto moderno delle danze antiche.

**folklor-e** *n.* folclore *m.* **-ist** *n.* folclorista *m., f.*

**folk-song** *n.* canto popolare.

**follicle** *n.* follicolo.

**follow** *tr.* seguire; inseguire; tenere dietro a; accompagnare; — *me*, seguitemi; *to — a road*, seguire una strada; *to — one's nose*, andare a casaccio, affidarsi alla fortuna; *to — the advice of*, seguire i consigli di; *to — in the footsteps of*, seguitare le orme di; *to — a trade*, esercitare un mestiere; *to — with one's eyes*, accompagnare con gli occhi; *to — as chairman*, succedere come presidente; *night -s day*, la notte succede al giorno; *to — the drum*, andare a fare il soldato; *to — the plough*, fare il contadino; *to — the hounds*, andare a caccia (della volpe); *to — suit*, (cards) giuocare una carta dello stesso seme, (fig.) fare lo stesso: comprendere; capire; *I don't — you*, non capisco ciò che vuoi dire; *to — out*, eseguire, proseguire; *to — up*, seguire, star dietro a; *intr.* seguire; conseguire; risultare; *silence -ed*, seguì un silenzio; *it -s that*, consegue che; *it doesn't —*, non vuol dire; *as -s*, come segue.

**follower** *n.* seguace *m.*; discepolo; aderente *m.*; partigiano.

**following** *adj.* seguente; susseguente; successivo; *the — day*, il giorno dopo; *n.* seguito; seguaci *m.pl.*

**follow-my-leader** *n.* giuoco del papasso.

**folly** *n.* follia; pazzia; *the height of —*, il colmo della pazzia; *an act of —*, una pazzia.

**foment** *tr.* fomentare; istigare; (med.) applicare fomenti a. **-ation** *n.* fomentazione; istigazione; fomento.

**fond** *adj.* affettuoso; affezionato; tenero; *to be — of*, voler bene a, amare; *he is very — of his sister*, vuol molto bene a sua sorella; *to become — of*, affezionarsi a, prendere affetto a; *are you — of music?*, ti piace la musica?; *to be — of games*, essere appassionato dello sport; *a — mother*, una madre indulgente; (fig.) vano; — *hopes*, speranze vane, speranze ingenue.

**fondant** *n.* (cul.) fondente *m.*

**fondle** *tr.* vezzeggiare; coccolare; accarezzare.

**fondness** *n.* tenerezza; affetto; indulgenza; (fig.) inclinazione; gusto; predisposizione.

**font** *n.* fonte *f.* battesimale; (eccl.) piscina battesimale; (poet.) fonte, sorgente *f.*

**food** *n.* cibo; vitto; vivanda; mangime *m.*; — *and lodging*, vitto e alloggio; — *and drink*, mangiare e bere; alimento; nutrimento; — *products*, prodotti alimentari; (fig.) — *for thought*, roba da far pensare. **-stuffs** *n.* alimentari *m.pl.*, derrate alimentari *f.pl.*; cibarie *f.pl.*

**fool** *n.* sciocco; stupido; scemo; allocco; cretino; idiota *m.*; imbecille *m.*; scimunito; coglione *m.*, minchione *m.*, fesso; (hist.) buffone *m.*; *to play the —*, far sciocchezze, far stupidaggini; *to call someone a —*, dare dello sciocco a qualcuno; *to make a — of oneself*, rendersi ridicolo; *to make a — of*, beffarsi di, prendere in giro; *-'s errand*, impresa inutile; *-'s paradise*, sciocca illusione; *April —*, vittima di un pesce d'aprile; *All Fools' Day*, il primo aprile, il giorno dei pesci d'aprile; (provb.) *no — like an old —*, nessuno è più stolto di un vecchio innamorato.

**fool** *tr.* prendere in giro; beffarsi di; ingannare; *to — someone out of money*, scroccare denaro a qualcuno; *to — someone into believing that*, far credere a qualcuno che; *to — away*, sciupare scioccamente; *intr.* scherzare; fare l'imbecille; *to — about*, far niente, stare in ozio.

**foolery** *n.* azione sciocca; stupidaggine *f.*; stravaganza; buffonata.

**foolhard-y** *n.* temerario; sventato; incurante. **-iness** *n.* temerarietà; sventataggine *f.*

**foolish** *adj.* sciocco; ridicolo; assurdo; insensato; *a — thing*,

una sciocchezza; *to look —*, sembrare ridicolo; (bibl.) *the — Virgins*, le Vergini folli. **-ness** *n.* sciocchezza; assurdità; insensatezza.

**foolproof** *adj.* facilissimo; sicurissimo; che un imbecille qualsiasi può fare.

**foolscap** *n.* carta formato protocollo.

**foot** *n.* piede *m.*; (of animal) zampa; (hoof) zoccolo; *on —*, a piedi; *on one's feet*, in piedi; *to fall on one's feet*, essere fortunato, cavarsela bene; *to find one's feet*, sistemarsi; *to go on —*, andare a piedi; *to have one — in the grave*, avere un piede nella fossa; *to jump to one's feet*, saltare su; *to keep one's feet*, mantenersi in equilibrio; *to knock someone off his feet*, far perdere l'equilibrio a qualcuno; *to put one's — down*, farsi valere, imporsi; *to set on —*, organizzare, avviare; *to set — on*, mettere piede su; *to shake the dust from off one's feet*, andarsene indignato, (fam.) baciare il chiavistello; *to trample under —*, calpestare; (slang) *my — !*, balle!; *to put one's — in it*, fare una gaffe; *to get cold feet*, aver la fifa; (math.; prosod.) piede; *square —*, piede quadrato; *cubic —*, piede cubico; (mil.) fanteria; (vet.) *— and mouth disease*, afta epizootica; (lower portion) base *f.*; zoccolo; fondo.

**foot** *tr.* (fam.) *to — it*, andare a piedi, camminare; (fam.) *to — the bill*, saldare il conto.

**football** *n.* palla; pallone *m.*; *association —*, calcio; *— association*, federazione del calcio; (rugby) pallovale *f.*; *Italian —*, pallone *m.* **-er** *n.* giuocatore del calcio, calciatore.

**foot-bath** *n.* pediluvio; vaschetta per pediluvio.

**footboard** *n.* predellino; pedana.

**foot-brake** *n.* (motor.) freno a pedale.

**foot-bridge** *n.* passerella. **-fall** *n.* passo; rumore *m.* di passo. **-gear** *n.* calzatura. **-hills** *n.pl.* bassa montagna; colline *f.pl.*; (of Alps) Prealpi *f.pl.* **-hold** *n.* punto d'appoggio; *to get a -hold*, prendere piede; *to lose one's -hold*, scivolare.

**footing** *n.* posizione del piede; (fig.) punto d'appoggio; *to miss one's —*, mettere un piede in fallo; *to be on a friendly — with*, avere relazioni amichevoli con; *to treat everyone on an equal —*, non fare distinzione da persona a persona; *on a war —*, sul piede di guerra; (archit.) fondamento.

**footl-e** *intr.* (fam.) gingillarsi; *to — away*, sprecare. **-ing** *adj.* insignificante; frivolo.

**footlights** *n.* luci *f.pl.* della ribalta, ribalta.

**footman** *n.* lacchè *m.*; valletto; staffiere *m.*

**foot-mark** *n.* orma, impronta del piede. **-note** *n.* postilla; nota a piè di pagina; annotazione. **-pad** *n.* ladro; grassatore; (hist.) bandito. **-path** *n.* (in country) sentiero; (in town) marciapiede *m.* **-print** *n.* orma, impronta di piede. **-race** *n.* corsa podistica. **-rest** *n.* poggiapiedi *m. indecl.*

**foot-rot** *n.* (vet.) ulcera alle zampe.

**footrule** *n.* regolo lungo un piede.

**foot-slog** *intr.* (slang) andare a piedi; (mil.) marciare. **-ger** *n.* pedone *m.*; (mil.) fante *m.*

**foot-soldier** *n.* (mil.) fante *m.*

**foot-sore** *adj.* che ha male ai piedi; (fig.) stanco dopo una lunga camminata. **-step** *n.* passo; pedata; orma; *to follow in the -steps of*, ricalcare le orme di. **-stool** *n.* sgabellino; posapiedi *m. indecl.*

**foot-warmer** *n.* scaldapiedi *m. indecl.*

**footway** *n.* See **footpath.**

**footwear** *n.* calzatura.

**fop** *n.* bellimbusto, zerbinotto; ganimede *m.* **-pish** *adj.* fatuo; affettato. **-pishness** *n.* fatuità; affettazione.

**for** *conj.* chè; perchè; poichè; giacchè; *prep.* per; a favore di; in cambio di; da; di; *as —*, quanto a; *— all that*, ciò nonostante; *— and against*, pro e contro; *— love of*, per amor di; *but —*, senza, se non fosse per. When followed in English by accusative and infinitive, translated in Italian by conjunctive clause; e.g. *I am waiting for you to help me*, aspetto che tu mi aiuti. For use in other phrases, see under respective verbs and nouns.

**forage** *n.* foraggio; *intr.* foraggiare; raccogliere foraggi; (fig.) cercare.

**forage-cap** *n.* (mil.) bustina.

**forager** *n.* foraggiere *m.*

**forasmuch as** *conj.* in quanto che; visto che; poichè.

**foray** *n.* incursione; scorreria.

**forbade** *p.def.* of **forbid,** *q.v.*

**forbear** *tr.* astenersi da; evitare; fare a meno di; *intr.* pazientare; essere indulgente. **-ance** *n.* pazienza; tolleranza.

**forbid** *tr.* vietare; interdire; proibire; *to — someone the house*, vietare a qualcuno l'accesso alla casa; *he had been -den to go out*, gli era stato proibito di uscire; *the doctor has -den him wine*, il medico gli ha proibito il vino; *God — !*, Dio ce ne guardi! **-den** *part. adj.* vietato, proibito; *-den fruit*, frutto proibito; *smoking -den*, vietato fumare. **-ding** *adj.* severo; austero; aspro; formidabile; (of sky) minaccioso.

**forbore, forborne** *p.def.*, *part.* of **forbear,** *q.v.*

**force** *n.* forza; violenza; vigore *m.*; *by sheer —*, a viva forza; *by — of circumstances*, per forza delle circostanze; *to resort to —*, ricorrere alla forza; (leg.) *laws in —*, leggi vigenti; *to come into —*, entrare in vigore; (mil.) *armed -s*, forze armate; *landing —*, truppe da sbarco; *the Air Force*, l'aeronautica militare; *the police —*, la forza pubblica, la polizia; (scient.) *the — of gravity*, la forza della gravità; (electr.) energia; (fig.) esatto significato, senso.

**force** *tr.* forzare; sforzare; costringere; *to — open a door*, forzare una porta; *to — an entry*, entrare con la forza, penetrare a forza; *to — back*, respingere; *to — down*, far discendere; *to — out*, spingere fuori; *to — up*, far salire; *rfl. to — oneself to do something*, sforzarsi di far qualcosa.

**forced** *part. adj.* forzato; inevitabile; obbligatorio; *a — smile*, un sorriso forzato; (aeron.) *— landing*, atterraggio di fortuna; (mil.) *— march*, marcia forzata.

**forceful** *adj.* forte; energico; vigoroso; aggressivo.

**forcemeat** *n.* (cul.) carne trita; *— ball*, crocchetta di carne.

**forceps** *n.* (surg.) forcipe *m.*; (dental) pinza.

**forcible** *adj.* energico; vigoroso; (fig.) efficace.

**ford** *n.* guado; *tr.* guadare; passare a guado. **-able** *adj.* guadabile.

**fore**[1] *adj.* anteriore; (naut.) di prua; *n. to come to the —*, venire alla ribalta, divenire d'attualità.

**fore**[2] *excl.* (golf) attenti!, attenzione!

**fore·arm**[1] *n.* avambraccio.

**forearm**[2] *tr.* premunire; (provb.) *forewarned is -ed*, uomo avvertito, mezzo munito.

**fore-bode** *tr.* presagire; presentire; preannunziare. **-boding** *n.* presentimento; presagio.

**forecast**[1] *n.* previsione; pronostico.

**forecast**[2] *tr.* prevedere; pronosticare.

**fore-castle** *n.* (naut.) castello di prua. **-close** *tr.* (leg.) precludere il riscatto di (una ipoteca). **-court** *n.* anticorte *f.*; primo cortile. **-doom** *tr.* condannare in anticipo; predestinare. **-father** *n.* antenato; avo. **-finger** *n.* indice *m.* **-foot** *n.* zampa anteriore. **-front** *n.* parte *f.* anteriore; davanti *m.*; (mil.) prima linea.

**fore-go** *tr.*, *intr.* precedere. **-going** *adj.* precedente; antecedente; *the -going*, quanto sopra. **-gone** *adj.* predeterminato; sicuro; *a -gone con-*

*clusion*, un risultato inevitabile, una decisione già scontata.

**fore-ground** *n.* primo piano; *in the* —, in primo piano, (fig.) molto in vista. **-hand** *n.* posizione superiore; (of horse) parte *f.* dal garrese alla testa; (sport) *-hand stroke*, colpo diritto. **-head** *n.* fronte *f.*

**foreign** *adj.* straniero; forestiero; estero; — *correspondent*, corrispondente per l'estero; — *trade*, commercio coll'estero; — *travel*, viaggi all'estero; *in — parts*, all'estero, in terra straniera; *Foreign Office*, Ministero degli Affari Esteri; — *money order*, vaglia internazionale; (fig.) estraneo; alieno; *a — body*, un corpo estraneo.

**foreigner** *n.* straniero; forestiere *m.*

**fore-judge** *tr.* giudicare a priori. **-knowledge** *n.* prescienza; preconoscenza; prenozione. **-land** *n.* (geog.) promontorio; capo. **-leg** *n.* zampa anteriore. **-lock** *n.* ciuffo sulla fronte; (fig.) *to take time by the -lock*, cogliere l'occasione; (mech.) copiglia.

**foreman** caposquadra *m.*; caporeparto; *works* —, capo-officina; (in printing works) proto; (leg.) — *of the jury*, presidente *m.*, capo della giuria.

**foremast** *n.* (naut.) albero di trinchetto.

**fore-mentioned** *adj.* suddetto; summenzionato.

**foremost** *adj.* primo; principale; più importante; *adv.* in primo luogo; *first and* —, anzitutto; *head* —, a capo all'ingiù, a testa in avanti.

**fore-name** *n.* nome di battesimo. **-noon** *n.* mattina; mattinata; *in the -noon*, prima di mezzogiorno, nelle ore antimeridiane.

**forensic** *adj.* forense; del foro; — *medicine*, la medicina legale.

**fore-part** *n.* parte *f.* anteriore. **-paw** *n.* zampa anteriore. **-peak** *n.* (naut.) gavone *m.* di prua.

**fore-quarter** *n.* (butcher.) quarto anteriore; *pl.* parte *f.* anteriore.

**fore-runner** *n.* precursore; antesignano. **-sail** *n.* (naut.) vela di trinchetto. **-see** *tr.* prevedere. **-seeable** *adj.* prevedibile. **-seeing** *adj.* preveggente, previdente; *n.* preveggenza, previdenza. **-shadow** *tr.* adombrare; presagire. **-shore** *n.* lido litorale.

**foreshorten** *tr.* (art) scorciare; disegnare in prospettiva. **-ed** *adj.* scorciato; di scorcio. **-ing** *n.* scorciatura, scorcio.

**fore-sight** *n.* previdenza, preveggenza; *lack of* —, improvvidenza; (of gun) mirino. **-skin** *n.* prepuzio.

**forest** *n.* foresta; bosco; (fig.) selva; *attrib.* — *tree*, albero di alto fusto; *adj.* forestale.

**fore-stall** *tr.* anticipare; prevenire. **-stay** *n.* (naut.) straglio di trinchetto.

**forester, forest ranger** *n.* guardia forestale, guardaboschi *m. indecl.*

**forestry** *n.* silvicoltura; *school of* —, scuola forestale.

**fore-taste** *n.* pregustazione; *to have a — of*, pregustare; *tr.* pregustare; assaggiare. **-tell** *tr.* predire; pronosticare; annunziare. **-thought** *n.* premeditazione; previdenza. **-token** *tr.* presagire; preannunziare. **-told** *p.def.*, *part.* of **foretell,** *q.v.*

**forever, forevermore, for ever** *adv.* per sempre.

**fore-warn** *tr.* avvertire; preavvisare; prevenire; *-warned is forearmed*, uomo avvertito, mezzo munito. **-warning** *n.* preavviso; avvertimento.

**fore-went** *p.def.* of **forego,** *q.v.* **-woman** *n.* (industr.) prima lavorante; direttrice; (of jury) capo. **-word** *n.* prefazione; proemio.

**forfeit** *n.* fio, pegno; multa, ammenda; confisca, sequestro; *pl.* (game) pegni *m.pl.*, penitenza; *tr.* pagare il fio con; perdere per confisca; perdere, dover abbandonare. **-ure** *n.* perdita; confisca.

**forgather** *intr.* adunarsi; raccogliersi.

**forgave** *p.def.* of **forgive,** *q.v.*

**forge** *n.* fucina; officina di fabbro ferraio; *tr.* fucinare, forgiare; (fig.) fabbricare; (leg.) contraffare, falsificare; *to — a cheque*, apporre una firma falsa ad un assegno; *intr. to — ahead*, avanzare, farsi strada; (naut.) andare avanti a tutta velocità; (sport) distanziare gli altri concorrenti, staccarsi.

**forg-ed** *part. adj.* (metall.) fucinato, forgiato; (cheque, coin) falsificato, contraffatto. **-er** *n.* falsario, contraffattore. **-ery** *n.* contraffazione, falsificazione; (leg.) falso.

**forget** *tr.*, *intr.* dimenticare, dimenticarsi (di); scordare, scordarsi (di); non ricordare (di); *to — to do something*, dimenticare di far qualcosa; *to — how to do something*, non ricordarsi più come fare qualcosa; *that never-to-be-forgotten day*, quel giorno indimenticabile; *I shall not* —, me ne ricorderò, non (lo) dimenticherò; (fam.) *and don't you — it !*, badatevi bene!; *don't — to . . .*, non mancare di . . .; *let's — (about) it !*, non ne parliamo più; *rfl.* (fig.) *to — oneself*, perdere la padronanza di se stesso, lasciarsi andare, venir meno alle usanze convenzionali.

**forgetful** *adj.* immemore; smemorato; noncurante; negligente. **-ness** *n.* dimenticanza; smemorataggine *f.*; oblìo; negligenza.

**forget-me-not** *n.* (bot.) miosotide *f.*; (pop.) non-ti-scordar-di-me *m.*

**forgivable** *adj.* scusabile; perdonabile.

**forgive** *tr.* perdonare; rimettere; condonare; *God — me !*, Dio mi perdoni!; — *me*, mi perdoni, perdonami; — *us our sins*, rimetti i nostri peccati; *to — a debt*, rimettere un debito.

**forgiveness** *n.* perdono; remissione; *to ask for* —, chiedere perdono, chiedere scusa; (fig.) indulgenza.

**forgiving** *adj.* clemente; pronto a perdonare; indulgente; comprensivo. **-ness** *n.* indulgenza; comprensione.

**forgo** *tr.* rinunciare a; astenersi da.

**forgot, forgotten** *p.def.*, *part.* of **forget,** *q.v.*

**fork** *n.* (agric.) forca; forcone *m.*; tridente *m.*; (table) —, forchetta; (in road) bivio, biforcazione; (anat.; tailor.) forcatura; (bot.; mech.) forcella.

**fork** *tr.* (agric.) trasportare con un forcone; *intr.* (of road) biforcarsi; — *right for Cambridge*, prendere a destra per Cambridge; (slang) *to — out*, mettere mano alla borsa, tirar fuori. **-ed** *adj.* forcuto; biforcato; a forcella. **-ful** *n.* (agric.) forcata; (table) forchettata.

**forlorn** *adj.* derelitto, abbandonato, sconsolato; solitario; disperato; *a — hope*, un'impresa disperata, una speranza vana.

**form** *n.* forma; figura; foggia; aspetto; apparenza; *good* —, buona creanza; *bad* —, cattive maniere; *for the sake of* —, per riguardo all'etichetta; modulo; *to fill in a* —, riempire un modulo; panca, banco; classe *f.*; stato di salute; *in (good)* —, in forma; *out of* —, giù di forma; (industr.) forma, stampo, matrice *f.*; (of hare) covo.

**form** *tr.* formare; fare; modellare; sviluppare; articolare; (comm.) *to — a company*, costituire una società; (fig.) *to — an idea of*, farsi un'idea di, concepire; *to — part of*, far parte di; (mil.) disporsi in; *to — column*, incolonnarsi; *intr.* formarsi, prendere forma; (mil.) *to — up*, mettersi in fila.

**formal** *adj.* formale; positivo; esplicito; ufficiale; convenzionale; cerimonioso; — *dress*, abito da cerimonia; (fig.) rigido; preciso.

**formaldehyde** *n.* (chem.) formaldeide *f.*

**formalin** *n.* (chem.) formalina.
**formal-ism** *n.* formalismo *m.* **-ist** *n.* formalista *m., f.*
**formality** *n.* formalità; cerimonia; convenzionalismo; *to dispense with formalities,* bandire le cerimonie, lasciar stare i complimenti.
**formalize** *tr.* formulare; dar forma a; formalizzare.
**format** *n.* formato.
**formation** *n.* formazione; costituzione; sviluppo.
**formative** *adj.* formativo; plastico.
**forme** *n.* (typ.) forma.
**former**[1] *adj.* precedente; primo; anteriore; anziano; antico; *a — pupil,* un antico allievo; di un tempo; già, ex; *Mr. B, — manager of the firm,* il signor B, già (*or* ex) direttore della ditta; (if dead) fu; *prn. the — and the latter,* il primo e il secondo, quello e questo. **-ly** *adv.* già; altre volte; anticamente; un tempo; in altri tempi.
**former**[2] *n.* formatore; creatore; artefice *m.*
**formic** *adj.* (chem.) formico.
**Formica** *n.* (industr.) for·mica.
**formidable** *adj.* formidabile; spaventoso; enorme.
**formless** *adj.* informe; amorfo.
**formul-a** *n.* formula. **-ary** *n.* formulario. **-ate** *tr.* formulare. **-ation** *n.* formulazione; esposizione.
**fornicat-e** *intr.* fornicare. **-ion** *n.* fornicazione.
**forsak-e** *tr.* abbandonare; lasciare; rinunciare a; *to — one's religion,* apostatare. **-en** *adj.* abbandonato; deserto.
**forsook** *p.def.* of **forsake,** *q.v.*
**forsooth** *adv.* davvero; veramente.
**forswear** *tr.* abiurare; rinnegare; rinunciare a; (leg.) spergiurare, giurare il falso.
**forswore, forsworn** *p.def., part.* of **forswear,** *q.v.*
**fort** *n.* fortezza; forte *m.*; posto fortificato.
**forte** *n.* forte *m.*; attitudine spiccata.
**forth** *adv.* avanti, in poi; *from this day —,* d'ora in poi; *and so —,* e così via, eccetera; fuori; *to go —,* uscire; *to set —,* mettersi in viaggio; *to hold —,* declamare. **-coming** *adj.* imminente; che sta per venire; prossimo, pronto; (fig.) *he is not very -coming,* è molto riservato, non ha voglia di parlare. **-right** *adj.* franco, schietto; esplicito. **-with** *adv.* subito; immediatamente; senz'altro; seduta stante.
**fortieth** *ord. num.* quarantesimo.
**fortification** *n.* fortificazione; (of wine) aumento dell'alcoolicità.
**fortify** *tr.* fortificare; (fig.) rinvigorire, rafforzare, incoraggiare; (eccl.) *fortified with the rites of the Church,* munito dei conforti religiosi; (wines) aumentare l'alcoolicità di.
**fortitude** *n.* forza d'animo; coraggio; (rel.) fortezza.
**fortnight** *n.* quindici giorni *m.pl.*, quindicina; due settimane *f.pl.*; *a — ago,* due settimane fa, quindici giorni fa; *this day —,* oggi a quindici. **-ly** *adj.* quindicinale, bimensile; *adv.* ogni quindici giorni, ogni due settimane, due volte al mese, bimensilmente.
**fortress** *n.* fortezza; piazzaforte.
**fortuitous** *adj.* fortuito; casuale; accidentale. **-ness** *n.* casualità.
**fortunate** *adj.* fortunato, felice; propizio, favorevole; *how —!*; che fortuna! **-ly** *adv.* fortunatamente, per fortuna.
**fortune** *n.* fortuna; *good —,* fortuna; *bad —,* sfortuna; *a stroke of (good) —,* un colpo di fortuna; sorte *f.*; destino; futuro; *to have one's — told,* farsi dire il futuro, farsi fare l'oroscopo; ricchezza, patrimonio; *a man of —,* un uomo ricchissimo; *to make a —,* diventar ricco; *to come into a —,* ereditare un patrimonio; *born to —,* nato con la camicia; *a soldier of —,* un soldato di ventura.
**fortune-hunter** *n.* cacciatore di dote. **-teller** *n.* chiromante *m., f.*; indovino; pitonessa. **-telling** *n.* chiromanzia; sortilegio; predizione dell'avvenire.
**forty** *card. num.* quaranta; *forty-one,* quarantuno; *forty-two,* quarantadue; *forty-first,* quarantunesimo, quarantesimo primo; *forty-second,* quarantaduesimo, quarantesimo secondo; (fig.) *— winks,* pisolino, sonnellino; *to have — winks,* schiacciare un pisolino; *the forties,* gli anni dal 40 al 50, la quinta decade.
**forum** *n.* foro.
**forward** *adj.* avanzato, primo, in avanti; (fig.) progressista; precoce; primaticcio; presuntuoso, prepotente, impertinente; (comm.) futuro.
**forward, forwards** *adv.* avanti, in avanti; *backwards and forwards,* avanti e indietro; *from that time forward,* a partire da quel giorno; *to put forward,* proporre; anticipare; mettere avanti; to *push forward,* mettersi in evidenza, farsi avanti; *to step forward,* fare un passo avanti; *to look forward to,* anticipare con piacere.
**forward** *n.* (sport) attaccante *m.*; avanti *m.*; *centre —,* centravanti *m.*; *wing —,* ala.
**forward** *tr.* spedire; mandare; inoltrare; rispedire; *please —,* si prega di rispedire; (fig.) promuovere, secondare, essere fautore di. **-ing** *n.* spedizione; *-ing agent,* spedizioniere. **-ness** *n.* progresso; precocità; prepotenza, impertinenza.
**forwent** *p.def.* of **forego,** *q.v.*
**fossil** *n.* fossile. **-ization** *n.* fossilizzazione. **-ize** *tr.* fossilizzare; *intr.* fossilizzarsi.
**foster** *tr.* allevare; nutrire; (fig.) incoraggiare; favorire; alimentare; *to — class hatred,* alimentare l'odio di classe.
**foster-brother** *n.* fratello di latte. **-father** *n.* padre adottivo. **-mother** *n.* nutrice, balia; madre adottiva. **-sister** *n.* sorella di latte.
**fought** *p.def., part.* of **fight,** *q.v.*
**foul** *adj.* sporco; lurido; puzzolente; tempestoso; brutto; *— language,* turpiloquio; *— play,* (leg.) delitto, omicidio; (sport) giuoco falloso; *by fair means or —,* con mezzi leciti o illeciti, in un modo o nell'altro; *to run — of,* (naut.) entrare in collisione con (un'altra nave), (fig.) imbattersi in, venire a lite con; *n.* (sport) fallo, irregolarità.
**foul** *tr.* sporcare; insudiciare; (naut.) impigliarsi, entrare in collisione con.
**foul-mouthed** *adj.* sboccato; incline al turpiloquio.
**found**[1] *p.def., part.* of **find,** *q.v.*
**found**[2] *tr.* fondare; istituire; stabilire; (fig.) basare.
**found**[3] *tr.* (metall.) fondere, gettare.
**foundation** *n.* fondazione; istituto; fondamento; (fig.) base *f.*; motivo; *— cream,* crema base; *— stone,* prima pietra.
**founder**[1] *n.* fondatore; (metall.) fonditore.
**founder**[2] *intr.* andare a picco, affondarsi, colare a picco.
**foundling** *n.* trovatello; *— hospital,* brefotrofio.
**foundry** *n.* (metall.) fonderia.
**fount** *n.* sorgente *f.*; fonte *f.*; (typ.) serie *f.* di caratteri, alfabeto; *wrong —,* rifuso.
**fountain** *n.* fontana; getto d'acqua.
**fountain-head** *n.* sorgente *f.*; origine *f.* **-pen** *n.* penna stilografica.
**four** *card. num.* quattro; *n. on all -s,* carponi. **-fold** *adj.* quadruplo; *adv.* quattro volte.
**four-cornered** *adj.* quadrangolare. **-footed** *adj., n.* quadrupede *m.* **-in-hand** *n.* tiro a quattro. **-poster** *n.* letto a quattro colonne. **-seater** *n.* vettura a quattro posti.
**fourscore** *adj.* ottanta; *— and ten,* novanta.
**foursome** *n.* partita in quattro, quattro *m.*
**fourteen** *card. num.* quattordici.

**-th** *ord. num.* quattordicesimo, decimo quarto; *the -th of April*, il quattordici aprile.
**fourth** *ord. num.* quarto; *n.* quarto, quarta parte; *the — of April*, il quattro aprile; *three -s*, tre quarti; (games) *to make a —*, fare il quarto. **-ly** *adv.* in quarto luogo.
**four-wheeler** *n.* vettura a quattro ruote.
**fowl** *n.* pollo; (cul.) *roast —*, pollo arrosto; *boiled —*, pollo a lesso; volatile *m.*; (bibl.) *the -s of the air*, gli uccelli del cielo. **-er** *n.* uccellatore. **-house** *n.* pollaio. **-ing** *n.* uccellagione *f.*
**fowling-piece** *n.* fucile da caccia.
**fox** *n.* volpe *f.*; *dog —*, volpe maschio; (fig.) *a sly old —*, un volpone, un furbone; *tr.* ingannare, truffare; sconcertare. **-ed** *part. adj.* perplesso; (of books) chiazzato.
**fox-cub** *n.* volpacchiotto.
**foxglove** *n.* (bot.) digitale *f.*
**foxhound** *n.* cane *m.* da caccia, bracco.
**fox-hunting** *n.* caccia alla volpe.
**foxiness** *n.* furberia; astuzia; scaltrezza.
**fox-terrier** *n.* fox *m.*; *wire-haired —*, fox a pelo ruvido.
**foxy** *adj.* furbo; scaltro; astuto.
**foyer** *n.* (theatr.) ridotto.
**fracas** *n.* baruffa; rissa; fracasso.
**fraction** *n.* frazione; (fig.) piccola parte. **-al** *adj.* frazionario.
**fractious** *adj.* indisciplinato, litigioso; permaloso, piagnucoloso. **-ness** *n.* indisciplina; permalosità.
**fracture** *n.* frattura; rottura; *to set a —*, ridurre una frattura; *tr.* spaccare; rompere; fratturare; *to — one's leg*, rompersi la gamba.
**fragil-e** *adj.* fragile; debole, gracile. **-ity** *n.* fragilità; debolezza; gracilità.
**fragment** *n.* frammento; coccio; scheggia. **-ary** *adj.* frammentario; incompleto.
**fragr-ance** *n.* fragranza; profumo. **-ant** *adj.* fragrante; profumato.
**frail** *adj.* fragile; debole, gracile; *of — health*, caduco. **-ty** *n.* fragilità; debolezza; gracilità.
**frame** *n.* telaio; intelaiatura; cornice *f.*; ossatura; (fig.) struttura; *— of mind*, disposizione d'animo, umore *m.*; (hortic.) cassa di vetri; (eng.) affusto.
**frame** *tr.* formare; costruire; incorniciare; redigere; (slang) architettare un'accusa contro, imbrogliare; falsificare.
**framework** *n.* intelaiatura; (naut.) membratura; (fig.) schema *m.*, abbozzo, struttura.
**franc** *n.* franco.
**France** *pr.n.* (geog.) Francia.
**Frances** *pr.n.* Francesca.
**franchise** *n.* diritto di voto; (comm.) franchigia.
**Francis** *pr.n.* Francesco.
**Franciscan** *adj.*, *n.* francescano.
**Franco-phile** *n.*, *adj.* francofilo. **-phobe** *n.*, *adj.* francofobo.
**Frank** *pr.n.* Franco; (hist.) *the -s*, i Franchi.
**frank** *tr.* affrancare, timbrare.
**Frankfurt** *pr.n.* (geog.) Francoforte *f.*
**frankincense** *n.* incenso.
**frankness** *n.* franchezza; schiettezza; sincerità.
**frantic** *adj.* frenetico; pazzo.
**fraternal** *adj.* fraterno.
**fraternity** *n.* fraternità; fratellanza; confraternita.
**fraterniz-e** *intr.* fraternizzare; intrattenersi amichevolmente. **-ation** *n.* affratellamento; l'intrattenersi amichevolmente.
**fratricid-e** *n.* (crime) fratricidio; (perpetrator) fratricida *m.* **-al** *adj.* fratricida.
**fraud** *n.* frode *f.*; inganno; (person) impostore, truffatore *m.* **-ulence** *n.* frode *f.* **-ulent** *adj.* fraudolento doloso.
**fraught** *adj.* carico; pieno; *— with danger*, pericolosissimo; (slang) nervoso.
**fray**[1] *n.* mischia; combattimento; (fig.) lotta.
**fray**[2] *tr.* logorare; consumare; (fig.) *his nerves are -ed*, ha i nervi scoperti; *intr.* sfilacciarsi; *to get -ed*, diventare liso.
**freak** *n.* capriccio; *-s of fashion*, capricci della moda; fenomeno; anormalità; macchietta, persona anormale, figura grottesca; aborto. **-ish** *adj.* capriccioso. **-ishness** *n.* capricciosità.
**freckl-e** *n.* lentiggine *f.*; (med.) efelide *f.* **-ed** *adj.* lentigginoso, coperto di lentiggini.
**Frederick** *pr.n.* Federico.
**free** *adj.* libero, in libertà; *to set —*, liberare, ridonare la libertà a; *to make — use of*, fare libero uso di; *to have one's hands —*, avere le mani libere, non aver impegni; *to give someone a — hand*, dare carta bianca a qualcuno; libero, gratuito, gratis; *— admission*, entrata libera; *— ticket*, biglietto gratuito, biglietto di omaggio; (comm.) franco; *— on board*, franco bordo; esente; *— of tax*, esente da tutte le tasse; disinvolto, sciolto, spigliato; sconveniente, licenzioso; copioso, generoso; (mech.) folle, libero; *— enterprise*, iniziativa privata; *— fight*, mischia generale; *— speech*, libertà di parola; *— trade*, libero scambio; *— will*, volontà spontanea, (theol.) libero arbitrio; *adv.* gratis; gratuitamente.
**free** *tr.* liberare; sciogliere; *to — oneself of*, liberarsi da, sbarazzarsi di.
**freebooter** *n.* pirata *m.*; predone *m.*
**freeborn** *adj.* nato libero.
**freedman** *n.* (hist.) liberto.
**freedom** *n.* libertà; *— of the seas*, libertà dei mari; *to give someone the — of the house*, mettere la propria casa a disposizione di qualcuno; *— of a city*, cittadinanza onoraria; (fig.) franchezza; disinvoltura; familiarità.
**free-hand** *adj.* ordinario, non dattilografato, scritto a mano; *— drawing*, disegno a mano libera.
**free-handed** *adj.* liberale, generoso.
**freehold** *n.* proprietà fondiaria assoluta.
**free-lance** *adj.* indipendente.
**freely** *adv.* liberamente; gratuitamente.
**freeman** *n.* cittadino onorario.
**freemason** *n.* massone, frammassone *m.* **-ry** *n.* massoneria; frammassoneria; (fig.) fratellanza, fraternità.
**freesia** *n.* (bot.) fresia.
**free-spoken** *adj.* franco, aperto nel parlare.
**freethinker** *n.* libero pensatore.
**free-trader** *n.* liberoscambista *m.*
**freeze** *n.* gelo; congelamento; *tr.* congelare; (comm.) bloccare, congelare; (fig.) agghiacciare; *intr.* gelare, coprirsi di ghiaccio; (of temperature) essere sotto zero; (fam.) aver molto freddo, sentire il freddo.
**freezing** *adj.* glaciale; *n.* congelamento; *— mixture*, miscela congelante.
**freezing-point** *n.* punto di congelamento, zero.
**Freiburg** *pr.n.* (geog.) Friburgo in Brisgovia.
**freight** *n.* nolo; carico; (rlwy.) *— car*, carro merci; *tr.* noleggiare. **-er** *n.* noleggiatore; nave *f.* da carico.
**French** *adj.* francese; *— leave*, andarsene all'inglese, eclissarsi; *— beans*, fagiolini verdi; *— letter*, condon *m.*, goldone *m.*; *— window*, porta-finestra; *— polish*, vernice *f.* francese; *French-speaking Switzerland*, la Svizzera francese; *n.* la lingua francese, il francese; *the —*, i francesi, il popolo francese.
**French-man** *n.* francese *m.* **-woman** *n.* francese *f.*
**frenz-y** *n.* frenesia; (fig.) trasporto. **-ied** *adj.* frenetico, accanito.
**frequency** *n.* frequenza.
**fre'quent** *adj.* frequente; ripetuto; diffuso.
**frequent** *tr.* frequentare.
**frequentative** *adj.* (gramm.) frequentativo.
**fresco** *n.* (paint.) affresco; *tr.* affrescare, dipingere in affresco.
**fresh** *adj.* fresco; *— air*, aria fresca, aria pura; nuovo; *to*

*break — ground*, iniziare un'attività nuova; — *water*, acqua dolce; brillante, splendente; (fig.) vigoroso, non ancora stanco; *to be — from school*, essere appena uscita dalla scuola; (fam., pejor.) insolente, impertinente.

**freshen** *tr.* rinfrescare; rinnovare; *intr.* rinfrescarsi, diventare fresco; (of wind) diventare più forte.

**freshman** *n.* matricola *f.*

**freshness** *n.* freschezza; novità; vigore *m.*

**fresh-water** *adj.* d'acqua dolce.

**fret**[1] *n.* irrequietezza, inquietudine *f.*; *tr.*, *intr.* inquietarsi; crucciarsi; piagnucolare; *to — over trifles*, inquietarsi per cose futili; *to — and fume*, mordere il freno.

**fret**[2] *n.* (archit.) fregio; lavoro ad intaglio; *tr.* ornare con fregi, intagliare.

**fretful** *adj.* permaloso, piagnucoloso.

**fret-saw** *n.* sega da traforo. **-work** *n.* lavoro di traforo.

**friab-le** *adj.* friabile. **-leness, -ility** *n.* friabilità.

**friar** *n.* frate *m.*; monaco; *Austin —*, agostiniano; *black —*, domenicano; *grey —*, francescano; *white —*, carmelitano. **-y** *n.* convento di frati.

**fricassee** *n.* (cul.) fricassea; piatto alla cacciatora.

**friction** *n.* frizione; attrito.

**Friday** *pr.n.* venerdì *m.*; *Good —*, venerdì santo.

**fridge** *n.* (fam.) frigorifero.

**fried** *p.def.*, *part.* of **fry**, *q.v.*; fritto.

**friend** *n.* amico; amica; *to make -s with*, fare amicizia con; *to part as -s*, separarsi senza rancore; *to make -s again*, rappacificarsi; (provb.) *a — in need is a — indeed*, un vero amico si conosce nel bisogno; *the Society of Friends*, i quacqueri.

**friendless** *adj.* senza amici. **-ness** *n.* mancanza di amicizie; solitudine *f.*

**friendliness** *n.* amichevolezza; cordialità.

**friendly** *adj.* amichevole, gentile, cordiale, amico; benevolo, ben disposto, cortese; (sport) *a — match*, un incontro amichevole; *to be — with*, essere amico di; *to be on — terms*, essere in relazioni amichevoli; *Friendly Society*, società di mutuo soccorso; (fig.) propizio, favorevole.

**friendship** *n.* amicizia.

**Friesland** *pr.n.* (geog.) Frisia.

**frieze** *n.* (archit.) fregio; (text.) tela di Frisia.

**frigate** *n.* (naut.) fregata.

**fright** *n.* paura; spavento; allarme *m.*; *to take —*, aver paura; spaventarsi; allarmarsi; (fam.) persona grottesca, persona brutta, macchietta.

**frighten** *tr.* spaventare; far paura a; allarmare; *to feel -ed*, aver paura; *to — someone to death*, far morire qualcuno di paura.

**frightening, frightful** *adj.* spaventevole; terribile; orribile; (fig.) brutto.

**frightfully** *adv.* terribilmente; spaventevolmente; (fam.) molto, infinitamente; *I'm — sorry*, mi dispiace tanto.

**frightfulness** *n.* spavento; terrore *m.*; (hist.) *policy of —*, politica di terrore.

**frigid** *adj.* frigido; glaciale; freddo.

**frigidarium** *n.* frigidario.

**frigidity, frigidness** *n.* freddezza; frigidità.

**frill** *n.* fronzolo; gala increspata; *pl.* (fig.) ornamenti superflui, ninnoli *m.pl.*; *tr.* ornare di gale; increspare.

**fringe** *n.* frangia; frangetta; orlo; bordo; limite *m.*; margine *m.*; estrema periferia; *tr.* ornare di frangia; orlare; fiancheggiare.

**frippery** *n.* fronzoli, ninnoli *m.pl.*

**Frisian** *adj.*, *n.* frisone *m.*, *f.*

**frisk** *n.* capriola; salto; scodinzolìo, colpo di coda; *intr.* saltellare, far capriole, giuocare; *tr.* (slang) perquisire.

**frisk-y** *adj.* vispo; vivace; saltellante. **-iness** *n.* vivacità; vispezza; il saltellare.

**fritillary** *n.* (bot.) fritillaria.

**fritter**[1] *n.* (cul.) frittella.

**fritter**[2] *tr. to — away*, sprecare, sciupare.

**Fritz** *pr.n.* Federico; (slang) tedesco.

**frivol** *tr. to — away*, sprecare, sciupare, sperperare; *intr.* frivoleggiare. **-ity** *n.* frivolezza; leggerezza; allegria; baldoria. **-ous** *adj.* frivolo; leggero.

**frizz** *n.* (fam.) ricciolo. **-iness** *n.* (fam.) l'essere ricciuto. **-le** *tr.* (fam.) arricciare; *intr.* arricciarsi; (cul.) crepitare, sfrigolare. **-y** *adj.* crespo; ricciuto.

**fro** *adv. to and —*, avanti e indietro; su e giù.

**frock** *n.* (man's) giubbotto; grembialone *m.*; vestito; costume *m.*; gonna; (eccl.) tonaca, sottana.

**frog**[1] *n.* rana; ranocchio; (of horse) fettone *m.*; (med.) afta.

**frog**[2] *n.* (mil., of sword) dragona; (on tunic) alamaro.

**froggy** *n.* (fam.) ranocchio; (pejor.) francese *m.*, *f.*

**frogman** *n.* sommozzatore.

**frog-march** *tr.* trascinare un recalcitrante in quattro, tenendolo per le gambe e le braccia.

**frolic** *n.* scherzo; scappata; monelleria; folleggiamento; *intr.* far scherzi; folleggiare; trastullarsi. **-some** *adj.* allegro; pazzerello.

**from** *prep.* da; — *bad to worse*, di male in peggio; — *day to day*, di giorno in giorno; — *time to time*, di quando in quando; *as — today*, a datare da oggi; a causa di, per. For other uses see under respective verbs and nouns.

**frond** *n.* fronda; foglia.

**front** *adj.* anteriore; — *page*, prima pagina; — *row*, prima fila; — *wheel*, ruota anteriore; *n.* parte *f.* anteriore; fronte *f.*; (archit.) facciata; *to come to the —*, farsi conoscere, mettersi in evidenza; (pol.; mil.) fronte *m.*; *to put a bold — on*, affrontare; lungomare *m.*; passeggiata a mare; *prep. phrs. in —*, avanti; *in — of*, davanti a; *to go in — of*, andare avanti a.

**front** *tr.* essere davanti a, essere in faccia di; guardare su; (bldg.) fare una nuova facciata a.

**frontage** *n.* lunghezza della facciata, lunghezza di un terreno situato lungo una strada; facciata; esposizione.

**frontal** *adj.* frontale; *n.* facciata; (of altar) paliotto, dossale *m.*; (cost.) benda per la fronte. **-ly** *adv.* di fronte.

**front-door** *n.* porta d'entrata, portone *m.*

**frontier** *adj.* limitrofo, di confine; *n.* frontiera; confine *m.*; (fig.) limite *m.*

**frontispiece** *n.* illustrazione a capo di un libro, frontespizio illustrato; (archit.) facciata.

**fronton** *n.* (archit.) frontone *m.*

**front-ranking** *adj.* di primo piano, ben noto.

**front-room** *n.* stanza che dà sulla strada. **-view** *n.* veduta frontale; modello visto da fronte; (archit.) elevazione.

**frost** *n.* gelo; brina; *black —*, freddo intenso senza brina; *white —*, brina; (slang) fiasco, insuccesso clamoroso; *tr.* far gelare, coprire di brina; (cul.) glassare; *-ed glass*, vetro smerigliato.

**frost-bite** *n.* (med.) congelamento. **-bitten** *adj.* (med.) congelato; (agric.) danneggiato dal gelo.

**frostiness** *n.* freddo glaciale; (fig.) freddezza.

**frosting** *n.* (cul.) glassatura; (of glass) smerigliatura.

**frosty** *adj.* glaciale; gelido.

**froth** *n.* schiuma; (on mouth) bava; (fig.) sciocchezza; *intr.* far schiuma, spumare; *-ing at the mouth*, con la bava alla bocca.

**froth-y** *adj.* schiumoso; spumante; (fig.) leggero; frivolo.

**-iness** *n.* spumosità; (fig.) futilità.

**frown** *n.* aggrottamento delle ciglia; cipiglio; viso arcigno; *intr.* aggrottare le ciglia; accigliarsi; corrugare la fronte; *to — upon,* disapprovare; *to — at,* guardare in cagnesco. **-ing** *adj.* accigliato; arcigno; annuvolato.

**frowst** *n.* tanfo di rinchiuso. **-y** *adj.* ammuffito; che sa di rinchiuso.

**frowsy** *adj.* (of person) mal vestito, trascurato.

**frozen** *part.* of **freeze,** *q.v.*; *adj.* congelato, gelato; (fig.) *to feel —,* aver molto freddo, gelare; (finan.) bloccato.

**fructiferous** *adj.* fruttifero.

**fructif-y** *tr.* fecondare; fertilizzare; *intr.* fruttificare. **-ication** *n.* fruttificazione.

**frugal** *adj.* frugale; parco; sobrio; economo. **-ity** *n.* frugalità; parsimonia; sobrietà; economia.

**fruit** *n.* frutto; prodotto della terra; (at table) frutta; *first -s,* primizie *f.pl.*; *dried —,* frutta secca; *stewed —,* composta di frutta; *— salad,* macedonia di frutta; *to bear —,* fruttare; (fig.) frutto; risultato; *tr.* far fruttificare; *intr.* fruttare, dar frutti.

**fruitarian** *n.* persona che si nutre di frutta.

**fruit-basket** *n.* cestino per frutta. **-bearing** *adj.* fruttifero. **-bowl** *n.* fruttiera. **-cake** *n.* panfrutto.

**fruiterer** *n.* fruttivendolo; commerciante *m.* di frutta.

**fruit-farmer, -grower** *n.* frutticultore. **-farming, -growing** *n.* frutticultura.

**fruitful** *adj.* fruttifero; fertile; prolifico; fecondo; (fig.) redditizio; rimunerativo. **-ness** *n.* fertilità; fecondità; (fig.) utilità.

**fruition** *n.* fruizione; realizzazione.

**fruitless** *adj.* senza frutto; infruttuoso; sterile; (fig.) inutile, vano. **-ness** *n.* sterilità; (fig.) inutilità.

**fruit-stand** *n.* fruttiera. **-tree** *n.* albero da frutta.

**fruity** *adj.* che sa di frutto; gustoso, saporito; (fig.) piccante; (of complexion) rosso per aver bevuto troppo, vinoso.

**frump** *n.* (fam.) donna malvestita, donna vestita con abiti fuori moda, sciattona.

**frustrat-e** *tr.* deludere; rendere vano; frustrare; attraversare. **-ion** *n.* frustrazione; delusione.

**fry** *n.* (ichth.) avannotti *m.pl.*; pesciolini appena nati; *small —,* pesciolini, (fig.) persona di poca importanza, nonnulla *m.*

**fry** *tr.* friggere; far friggere; *intr.* friggere, friggersi, *n.* frittura; fritto.

**frying-pan** *n.* padella; *to jump out of the — into the fire,* cadere dalla padella nella brace.

**fry-up** *n.* (cul., fam.) frittata.

**fuchsia** *n.* (bot.) fucsia.

**fuck** *tr., intr.* fottere.

**fuddle** *n.* confusione mentale; annebbiamento; *tr.* confondere; annebbiare; intontire.

**fudge** *excl.* frottole!; *n.* (cul.) dolce caramellato con cioccolata; *tr.* rattoppare alla meglio; (slang) falsificare.

**fuel** *n.* combustibile *m.*; (motor.; aeron.) carburante *m.*; *— oil,* nafta; *— tank,* serbatoio di benzina; (fig.) alimento; esca; *to add — to the flames,* soffiare sul fuoco; *tr.* alimentare di combustibile, rifornire di carburante; *intr.* rifornirsi di carburante; (fam.) fare il pieno.

**fug** *n.* (fam.) tanfo di rinchiuso; aria viziata. **-gy** *adj.* (fam.) stantio, che sente di rinchiuso.

**fugitive** *adj.* fugace; effimero; *n.* fuggiasco, fuggitivo; profugo.

**fugue** *n.* (mus.) fuga; (med.) amnesia.

**fulcrum** *n.* fulcro.

**fulfil** *n.* adempiere; compiere; effettuare; esaudire; soddisfare; *to — an engagement,* mantenere un impegno. **-ment** *n.* adempimento; compimento; esaudimento; realizzazione; effettuazione; osservanza.

**fulgent, fulgid** *adj.* fulgido.

**fuliginous** *adj.* fuligginoso.

**full**[1] *adj.* pieno; ripieno; colmo; ricolmo; *half —,* mezzo vuoto; *— up,* pieno zeppo, (bus, etc.) completo, (theatr.) esaurito; intero, completo, integrale; *— text,* testo integrale; *to give one's — name,* dare nome e cognome, scrivere il proprio nome per intero; *— details,* particolari esaurienti; (pol.) *— session,* seduta plenaria; *to be of — age,* essere di età maggiore, essere maggiorenne; *— house,* (theatr.) piena, (poker) full *m.*, tris e coppia; *a — day,* una giornata intera; *— dress,* abito da cerimonia; *— fare,* prezzo intero del biglietto; *— moon,* luna piena, plenilunio; *to give someone — scope,* dare piena libertà d'azione a qualcuno; *— score,* (mus.) partitura, (sport) risultato finale; *— size,* grandezza naturale; *at — speed,* a tutta velocità; *— statement,* dichiarazione particolareggiata; *in —,* per disteso; *in — swing,* in pieno sviluppo, in piena attività; *— uniform,* alta tenuta; *a — voice,* una voce sonora; *— weight,* peso giusto; *— of years,* carico di anni; (fig.) tutto preso da; *to be — of oneself,* essere pieno di sè; (fam.) *— of beans,* pieno di energia; *— of guts,* coraggiosissimo, pieno di fegato.

**full**[1] *adv.* completamente; direttamente; *— well,* perfettamente; *to hit someone — on the nose,* colpire qualcuno in pieno viso; (poet.) molto; *— many a time,* ben spesso; *— many a flower,* moltissimi fiori.

**full**[1] *n.* pieno; pienezza; totale *m.*; *to the —,* al massimo.

**full**[2] *tr.* (tailor.) rendere ampio; (text.) follare.

**full-back** *n.* (soccer) terzino; (rugby) portiere *m.* **-blooded** *adj.* di razza pura; sanguigno; vigoroso; esuberante. **-blown** *adj.* (bot.) completamente sbocciato; (fig.) brevettato; abilitato; competente. **-bodied** *adj.* corpulento; (of voice) sonoro; (of wine) che ha corpo.

**fuller** *n.* (text.) follatore, follone *m.*; (pharm.) *-'s earth,* argilla saponifera.

**full-grown** *adj.* cresciuto, fatto, adulto.

**fulling** *n.* (text.) follatura, gualcamento.

**full-length** *adj.* in tutta la lunghezza; (of portrait) a tutta figura; *lying —,* bocconi. **-page** *adj.* fuori testo. **-sized** *adj.* di grandezza naturale. **-stop** *n.* punto fermo. **-time** *adj.* che ha il contratto, salariato, stipendiato; *a -time job,* un lavoro che occupa tutto il tempo disponibile.

**fullness** *n.* pienezza; abbondanza; ampiezza; *in the — of time,* a tempo opportuno, a cose mature.

**fully** *adv.* pienamente; completamente; interamente; non meno di, almeno. **-fledged** *adj.* avente tutte le penne; (fig.) cresciuto; fatto; abilitato; brevettato.

**fulminat-e** *tr.* fulminare; detonare; *intr.* (fig.) imprecare; inveire. **-ion** *n.* fulminazione; (fig.) imprecazione.

**fulsome** *adj.* insincero; esagerato; servile; nauseante; *— flattery,* adulazione nauseante, incensatura. **-ness** *n.* insincerità; servilità.

**fumble** *tr.* lasciarsi sfuggire; *intr.* cercare tastando; andare a tastoni; annaspare, muovere goffamente le mani.

**fumbler** *n.* persona maldestra; pasticcione *m.*; confusionario.

**fume** *n.* fumo; vapore *m.*; esalazione; (fig.) stato di agitazione; collera; *tr.* esporre al fumo; affumicare; profumare; *-d oak,* quercia patinata; *intr.* emettere fumo; esalare vapori; (fig.) arrabbiarsi; imprecare; esplodere.

**fumigat-e** *tr.* suffumigare;

profumare; purificare; disinfettare. **-ion** *n.* suffumigio.
**fuming** *adj.* che emette fumo; fumante; (fig.) arrabbiato, furibondo.
**fun** *n.* spasso; divertimento; scherzo; *to make — of*, canzonare, prendere in giro, farsi beffe di; *for —, in —*, per ridere, per scherzo, per divertimento; *to be full of —*, essere pieno di allegria; *what —!*, che spasso!, che buffo!; *he is great —*, è molto divertente, è tanto simpatico; *— fair*, Luna Park *m.*
**funambul-ism** *n.* funambolismo. **-ist** *n.* funambolo.
**function** *n.* funzione; scopo; mansione; incombenza; cerimonia; *intr.* funzionare; fungere; agire. **-al** *adj.* funzionale. **-ary** *n.* funzionario.
**fund** *n.* fondo; riserva; capitale *m.*; *sinking —*, fondo di ammortamento; (finan.) *the -s*, i titoli di stato; (fig.) quantità; *to have a — of patience*, essere infinitamente paziente; *pl.* (fam.) denaro, soldi *m.pl.*; *to be in -s*, aver soldi in tasca; *tr.* investire nei titoli di stato; accumulare una riserva; consolidare.
**fundament** *n.* (lit., joc.) deretano.
**fundamental** *adj.* fondamentale; basilare; essenziale; *n.* principio; essenziale *m.*; base *f.* **-ist** *n.* chi crede al senso letterale della Bibbia.
**funeral** *adj.* funereo, funebre; *n.* funerale *m.*; esequie *f.pl.*; *— march*, marcia funebre; *— procession*, corteo funebre; *— service*, ufficio funebre, ufficio dei defunti; (fam.) *that's your —*, è affar tuo, tocca a te.
**funerary** *adj.* funereo, funebre, funerario.
**funereal** *adj.* funereo, lugubre, triste.
**fungicidal** *adj.* anticrittogamico.
**fungiform** *adj.* fungiforme.
**fungous** *adj.* fungoso.
**fungus** *n.* fungo; crittogama; *edible —*, fungo commestibile.
**funicle** *n.* (bot.) funicolo.
**funicular** *adj.* funicolare; *— railway*, funicolare *f.*
**funk** *n.* (fam.) fifa; *to be in a —*, aver la fifa; (person) vigliacco; *tr.* aver paura di.
**funk-hole** *n.* rifugio; nascondiglio.
**funnel** *n.* imbuto; pevera; (of ship, locomotive) ciminiera, fumaiolo. **-led** *adj.* munito di ciminiera; imbutiforme.
**funn-y** *adj.* divertente; comico; buffo; *— story*, barzelletta; strano; singolare; bizzarro; *the — thing is*, il bello è; (fam.) *to feel —*, sentirsi male. **-iness** *n.* comicità; stranezza.
**funnybone** *n.* (fam.) punta del gomito.
**fur** *n.* pelo; pelame *m.*; (cost.) pelliccia; guarnizione di pelo; (on tongue) patina; (fig.) incrostazione; *to make the — fly*, suscitare un putiferio, combattere come cane e gatto; *tr.* foderare di pelliccia; *intr.* incrostarsi; (of tongue, teeth) coprirsi di patina.
**furbish** *tr.* lucidare; forbire; (fig.) *to — up*, rinfrescare.
**fur-coat** *n.* pelliccia.
**furious** *adj.* furioso; furibondo; infuriato; rabido, arrabbiato; *to be —*, essere arrabbiatissimo; *to get —*, montare su tutte le furie; (fig.) eccessivo; pazzo; *at a — pace*, a velocità pazza.
**furl** *tr.* piegare; chiudere; (naut.) serrare; *to — a flag*, ammainare una bandiera.
**fur-lined** *adj.* foderato di pelliccia.
**furlough** *n.* (mil.) licenza, permesso; *on —*, in licenza; (naval) franchigia.
**furnace** *n.* caldaia; (industr.) fornace *f.*; forno; *blast —*, altoforno (fig.); luogo caldissimo, caldo infernale.
**furnish** *tr.* fornire; munire; dotare; ammobiliare, arredare. **-ed** *adj.* ammobiliato; arredato; *— with*, munito di. **-er** *n.* fornitore; mobiliere *m.* **-ing** *n.* fornitura; *pl.* mobilio, mobili *m.pl.*, suppellettili *f.pl.*, arredi *m.pl.*
**furniture** *n.* mobilio; mobili *m.pl.*; arredamento; *a piece of —*, un mobile; *a suite of —*, mobilia per una stanza; (industr.) attrezzatura; (typ.) marginatura.
**furniture-dealer** *n.* mobiliere *m.*, commerciante *m.* in mobili. **-polish** *n.* lucido per mobili. **-remover** *n.* agenzia di traslochi. **-shop** *n.* negozio di mobili. **-van** *n.* furgone *m.* per traslochi.
**furore** *n.* entusiasmo; *to create a —*, far furore.
**furred** *adj.* guarnito di pelliccia; (fig., *e.g.* of tongue) patinato; incrostato.
**furrier** *n.* pelliciaio.
**furrow** *n.* (agric.) solco; (on face) ruga profonda, grinza; (fig.) scanalatura; *tr.* (agric.) arare; solcare.
**furry** *adj.* peloso.
**further** *adj.* più lontano; cf. **farther**; ulteriore; nuovo; *without — delay*, senza ulteriore indugio; *— details*, più ampi dettagli; *until — notice*, fino a nuovo avviso; *without — ado*, senz'altro; *adv.* più lontano, più in là, oltre; ancora, inoltre; *tr.* promuovere; favorire; secondare; agevolare. **-ance** *n.* avanzamento; appoggio; agevolazione. **-more** *adv.* inoltre; di più ancora. **-most** *adj.* il più lontano; il più remoto.
**furthest** *adj.* il più lontano; estremo.
**furtive** *adj.* furtivo; di soppiatto.
**fury** *n.* furia; furore *m.*; (fig.) *to work like —*, lavorare con accanimento; (myth.) *the Furies*, le Furie, le Eumenidi; (fam.) donna violenta, virago *f.*
**furze** *n.* (bot.) ginestrone *m.*
**fuse** *n.* (electr.) valvola; fusibile *m.*; (mil.) miccia; (detonator) spoletta, detonatore; *tr.* fondere; amalgamare; unire; *intr.* fondersi; (electr.) saltare; munire di spoletta; munire di miccia; armare.
**fuselage** *n.* (aeron.) fusoliera.
**fusib-le** *adj.* fusibile. **-ility** *n.* fusibilità.
**fusilier** *n.* (mil.) fuciliere *m.*
**fusillade** *n.* fucilata; fucileria; sparatoria.
**fusion** *n.* fusione; amalgamazione.
**fuss** *n.* scalpore *m.*; clamore *m.*; baccano; *to kick up a —*, lamentarsi; (fig.) *to make a — of*, avere delle cure esagerate per, colmare di cortesie esagerate; *intr.* preoccuparsi per nulla; agitarsi; lamentarsi; aver cure esagerate; far delle storie. **-pot** *n.* (fam.) persona pignola, che fa delle storie, che si preoccupa per nulla.
**fuss-y** *adj.* pignolo; meticoloso. **-iness** *n.* pignoleria; meticolosità.
**fustian** *n.* (text.) fustagno; (fig.) ampollosità; magniloquenza.
**fustigat-e** *tr.* fustigare. **-ion** *n.* fustigazione.
**fust-y** *adj.* che sa di rinchiuso; (of bread) raffermo; (fig.) antiquato; sorpassato. **-iness** *n.* tanfo; odore *m.* di muffa; (fig.) l'essere antiquato.
**futil-e** *adj.* futile; inutile; vano; frivolo. **-ity** *n.* futilità; inutilità.
**future** *adj.* futuro; *n.* futuro; avvenire *m.*; (gramm.) futuro. **-less** *adj.* senza avvenire; senza possibilità di successo.
**futur-ism** *n.* futurismo. **-ist** *adj.*, *n.* futurista *m.*, *f.* **-istic** *adj.* futuristico.
**futurity** *n.* avvenire *m.*
**fuzz** *n.* lanugine *f.*; peluria; increspatura; (slang) polizia. **-iness** *n.* increspatura; (photog.) sfocatura. **-y** *adj.* peloso; increspato; arruffato; (fig.) indistinto; confuso; (photog.) sfocato.

**G** *n.* gi *m.*, *f.* (teleph.) — *for George*, gi come Genova; (mus.) sol *m.*

**gab** *n.* chiacchiera; parlantina; *to have the gift of the* —, avere la parlantina sciolta.

**gabble** *n.* (of geese) schiamazzo; (fig.) chiacchierìo, cicaleccio; discorso pronunciato frettolosamente; *tr.* recitare meccanicamente, pronunciare indistintamente; *intr.* (of geese) schiamazzare; (fig.) chiacchierare, cicalare; parlare frettolosamente. **-r** *n.* chiacchierone *m.*; chiacchierona *f.*

**gaberdine** *n.* (cost.) gabbano; (text.) gaberdina.

**gable** *n.* (archit.) pigna; frontone *m.*; timpano; tetto a due spioventi su timpano.

**gad**[I] *n.* (excl.) *by* —*!*, per Dio!

**gad**[2] *intr.* gironzolare, bighellonare; *to* — *about*, correre qua e là, vagabondare. **-about** *n.* (fam.) bighellone *m.*; bighellona *f.* **-fly** *n.* (ent.) tafano; (fig.) seccatore.

**gadget** *n.* congegno; dispositivo; (fam.) aggeggio.

**gael** *n.* gaelico. **-ic** *adj.* gaelico; *n.* (ling.) gaelico; lingua gaelica.

**gaff** *n.* (fishing) uncino; graffio; fiocina; (naut.) picco; (fig.) *to blow the* —, rivelare un segreto, (fam.) cantare; *tr.* (fishing) uncinare, fiocinare.

**gaffer** *n.* compare *m.*; vecchio; mastro.

**gag** *n.* bavaglio; (surg.) apribocca *m.*; (theatr.) battuta spiritosa, motto, frizzo; *tr.* imbavagliare; *intr.* (theatr.) improvvisare battute.

**gaga** *adj.* (slang) gagà; rimbambito, imbecille.

**gage** *n.* pegno; garanzia; arra, caparra; *to throw down the* —, sfidare; *tr.* impegnare, dare in pegno; sfidare.

**gaggle** *n.* (of geese) branco; (noise) schiamazzo di oche; (fig.) gruppo di donne; *intr.* schiamazzare.

**gaiety** *n.* gaiezza; allegria; giocondità.

**gaily** *adv.* gaiamente, allegramente.

**gain** *n.* guadagno; profitto; vantaggio; *ill-gotten -s*, guadagni illeciti, proventi disonesti; aumento, crescita; (pol.) vincita; *Labour* —, seggio già di un altro partito vinto dai laburisti; *tr.* guadagnare, ottenere; acquistare; vincere; raggiungere; aumentare; *intr.* progredire; beneficiare; profittare; (of watch) avanzare, andare avanti; *to* — *upon*, raggiungere, raccorciare le distanze. **-er** *n.* beneficiario; vincitore; *to be the -er by*, beneficiare di. **-ful** *adj.* lucroso, lucrativo; rimunerativo.

**gainsay** *tr.* contraddire; negare.

**gait** *n.* andatura; portamento; passo.

**gaiter** *n.* ghetta; uosa.

**gal** *n.* (pop.) ragazza, tosa.

**gala** *n.* gala, festa.

**galantine** *n.* (cul.) galantina.

**galaxy** *n.* (astron.) galassia, Via Lattea; (fig.) costellazione, riunione di persone brillanti.

**gale**[I] *n.* burrasca; tempesta; bufera di vento; fortunale *m.*; (fig.) *a* — *of laughter* un gran scoppio di risa.

**gale**[2] *n.* (bot.) mirica.

**gall**[I] *n.* fiele *m.*; bile *f.*; (fig.) rancore *m.*, livore *m.*; *pen dipped in* —, penna intinta nel fiele; (bot.) galla; (vet.) pustola; escoriazione; *tr.* scorticare; irritare.

**gallant** *adj.* coraggioso, valoroso, prode, bravo; (to women) galante, cavalleresco, cortese; *n.* galante *m.*; amoroso; cavaliere *m.* damerino. **-ry** *n.* prodezza; coraggio; valore *m.*; *decorated for* —, decorato al valore; galanteria, intrigo amoroso.

**gall-bladder** *n.* vescicola del fiele; (med.) cistifellea.

**galleon** *n.* galeone *m.*

**gallery** *n.* galleria; tribuna; loggia; (of pictures) pinacoteca; (theatr.) loggione *m.*, piccionaia; (fig.) *to play to the* —, cercare di cattivarsi la simpatia del grosso pubblico.

**galley** *n.* (hist.) galea, galera; (naut.) *cook's* —, cambusa; (typ.) vantaggio; (proof) bozza in colonna.

**galley-slave** *n.* galotto.

**Gallic**[I] *adj.* gallico, francese.

**gallic**[2] *adj.* (chem.) gallico.

**gallican** *adj.*, *n.* (eccl.) gallicano. **-ism** *n.* (eccl.) gallicanismo.

**gallic-ism** *n.* gallicismo, francesismo *m.* **-ize** *intr.* gallicizzare, francesizzare.

**galling** *adj.* scorticante; irritante; fastidioso.

**gallivant** *intr.* bighellonare; fare il galante.

**gall-nut** *n.* noce *f.* di galla.

**gallon** *n.* gallone *m.* (= 4·54 litri).

**gallop** *n.* galoppo, galoppata; *at full* —, a gran galoppo, a briglia sciolta; *hand* —, piccolo galoppo; *to break into a* —, mettersi a galoppare; *intr.* galoppare, andare al galoppo (fig.) *to* — *through a book*, leggere un libro di volata. **-ing** *part.* che galoppa; (fig.) rapido; *-ing inflation*, inflazione galoppante.

**Gallo-phile** *adj.*, *n.* gallofilo, francofilo. **-phobe** *adj.*, *n.* gallofobo.

**gallows** *n.* forca; patibolo; *to cheat the* —, sfuggire alla forca.

**gallows-bird** *n.* (fam.) avanzo da, di galera.

**gallstone(s)** *n.* (med.) calcolo biliare.

**Gallup** *pr.n.* — poll, sondaggio Gallup.

**galop** *n.* (dance) galoppo.

**galore** *adv.* (fam.) in abbondanza, a bizzeffe, a iosa.

**galosh** *n.* galoscia, soprascarpa di gomma.

**galvanic** *adj.* galvanico.

**galvaniz-e** *tr.* galvanizzare. **-ation** *n.* galvanizzazione.

**gambit** *n.* gambitto.

**gambl-e** *n.* giuoco di azzardo; (fig.) speculazione, impresa rischiosa; *tr.*, *intr.* giuocare d'azzardo; (fig.) speculare, arrischiare; *to* — *away*, perdere al giuoco. **-er** *n.* giuocatore d'azzardo; (on stock exchange) speculatore; (fig.) chi ama il rischio. **-ing** *n.* giuoco d'azzardo; *-ing debts*, debiti *m.pl.* di giuoco; *-ing den*, bisca.

**gamboge** *n.* (paint.) gommagutta di color arancione.

**gambol** *n.* capriola; salto; *intr.* saltellare; far capriole.

**game**[I] *n.* giuoco; *the* — *of football*, il giuoco del calcio; *the Olympic Games*, i Giuochi Olimpici; *pl.* sport *m.*; *he is fond of -s*, gli piace lo sport; (match) partita; *a* — *of football*, una partita di calcio; *to play a good* —, giuocare bene; *to play the* —, stare al giuoco, osservare le regole, comportarsi lealmente; *to have the* — *in one's hands*, essere sicuro del successo; *to be off one's* —, non essere in vena; (fig.) scherzo, trucco; *to make* — *of*, farsi beffe di; *fun and -s*, scherzi; *what's the* —*?*, è uno scherzo?; *what a* —*!*, che pasticcio!; *to spoil someone's* —, rovinare i piani di qualcuno; *the* — *is up*, il giuoco è fallito; *intr.* giuocare (d'azzardo); *tr. to* — *away*, sciupare, sprecare.

**game**[2] *n.* (hunt.) selvaggina; *big* —, caccia grossa.

**game**[3] *adj.* coraggioso; che ha del fegato; *to die* —, morire da eroe; *to be* — *for anything*, essere pronto a tutto.

**game**[3] *adj.* see **gammy**

**game-bag** *n.* carniera.

**gamecock** gallo da combattimento.

**gamekeeper** *n.* guardacaccia *m. indecl.*

**game-laws** *n.* leggi *f.pl.* per la caccia. **-licence** *n.* licenza da caccia.

**game-ly** *adv.* coraggiosamente, arditamente. **-ness** *n.* coraggio.

**game-preserve** *n.* riserva di caccia.

**gamester** *n.* giuocatore d'azzardo.

**gaming** *n.* giuoco d'azzardo.

**gaming-house** *n.* bisca. **-table** *n.* tavolo da giuoco; (fam.) tappeto verde.

**gamma** *n.* gamma.

**gammer** *n.* (fam.) vecchia comare.

**gammon** *n.* (cul.) prosciutto salato; (fam.) sciocchezza.
**gamp** *n.* (fam.) ombrello.
**gammy** *adj.* (fam., of leg) zoppo, storto, rattrapito; ferito.
**gamut** *n.* gamma; (mus.) scala diatonica.
**gander** *n.* papero, maschio dell'oca; (fig.) semplicione *m.*
**gang**[1] *intr.* (Scot.) See **go.**
**gang**[2] *n.* squadra; gruppo; masnada; *intr.* (fam.) *to — up*, formare una combriccola, allearsi.
**ganger** *n.* caposquadra *m. indecl.*
**gang-plank** *n.* passerella; ponticello di sbarco.
**Ganges** *pr.n.* (geog.) Gange *m.*
**gangling** *adj.* allampanato.
**ganglion** *n.* (anat.) ganglio; (fig.) centro di attività.
**gangren-e** *n.* (med.) cancrena. **-ous** *adj.* cancrenoso.
**gangster** *n.* gangster *m.*; bandito; malvivente *m.*
**gangway** *n.* corridoio; passaggio; corsia; (on ship) barcarizzo; passavanti *m. indecl.*; (ship to shore) passerella; *excl.* *—!*, indietro!
**gannet** *n.* (orn.) sula.
**gantry** *n.* (for cask) cavalletto; (for crane) piattaforma.
**gaol** *n.* carcere *m.*, prigione *f.*; *tr.* mettere in prigione, incarcerare; condannare a prigionia.
**gaol-bird** *n.* forzato; galeotto; avanzo di galera.
**gaoler** *n.* carceriere *m.*
**gap** *n.* breccia; apertura; squarcio; buco; (fig.) vuoto; lacuna, distacco; *to fill a —*, colmare una lacuna; *to leave a —*, lasciare un vuoto; divergenza.
**gap-e** *n.* sbadiglio; sguardo fisso a bocca aperta; *pl.* (vet.) difterite dei polli; *intr.* sbadigliare; spalancare la bocca, guardare a bocca aperta; (fam.) badaluccare. **-ing** *adj.* a bocca aperta, in atto di sbadigliare; (fig.) stupito, stordito; *-ing wound*, ferita aperta.
**garage** *n.* autorimessa; garage *m. indecl.*; *tr.* mettere in rimessa.
**garb** *n.* costume *m.*; abito; abbigliamento; (fig.) forma; aspetto; *tr.* rivestire; abbigliare.
**garbage** *n.* immondizie *f.pl.*; rifiuti *m.pl.*; *— heap*, mondezzaio; (fig.) cosa di nessun valore; (fam.) porcheria.
**garble** *tr.* storpiare; mutilare; troncare.
**garden** *n.* giardino; *vegetable —*, orto; *public -s*, giardini pubblici; *the Garden of Eden*, Eden *m.*, il paradiso terrestre; *— city*, città giardino; (fig.) regione fertile; (fam.) *to lead someone up the — path*, adescare qualcuno; *intr.* lavorare in giardino, fare del giardinaggio. **-er** *n.* giardiniere *m.*; *market -er*, ortolano.
**gardenia** (bot.) gardenia.
**gardening** *n.* giardinaggio; lavoro in giardino; orticultura.
**garden-party** *n.* ricevimento in giardino.
**gargantuan** *adj.* gigantesco; enorme.
**gargle** *intr.* gargarizzare; *n.* liquido per gargarismo.
**gargoyle** *n.* (archit.) grondone *m.*; doccione *m.*; garguglia; figura grottesca; macchietta.
**garish** *adj.* sgargiante; squillante; vistoso; (of light) abbagliante.
**garland** *n.* ghirlanda; serto; *tr.* inghirlandare.
**garlic** *n.* aglio; *a clove of —*, uno spicco d'aglio.
**garment** *n.* indumento; capo di vestiario.
**garn** *excl.* (slang = go on), va là!
**garner** *n.* granaio; *tr.* raggranellare; raccogliere.
**garnet** *n.* (miner.) granato; (naut.) paranco.
**garnish** *n.* ornamento; guarnizione; (cul.) contorno; *tr.* adornare, guarnire, abbellire. **-ing** *n.* guarnizione; (cul.) contorno.
**garret** *n.* soffitta; solaio; abbaino.
**garrison** *n.* guarnigione; presidio; *— artillery*, artiglieria di piazza; *tr.* fornire di guarnigione, presidiare.
**garrotte** *n.* garrotta; *tr.* strangolare, giustiziare strangolando.
**garrul-ous** *adj.* garrulo, loquace, ciarliero, verboso. **-ity, -ousness** *n.* garrulità, loquacità, verbosità.
**garter** *n.* giarrettiera; legaccio; *Order of the —*, Ordine *m.* della Giarrettiera.
**gas** *n.* gas *m.*; (Amer.) benzina, carburante *m.*; *poison —*, gas asfissiante; *laughing —*, gas esilarante; *tear —*, gas lacrimogeno; *to turn up the —*, accendere il gas; *to turn off the —*, spegnere il gas; (fam.) *to step on the —*, accelerare; *tr.* (chem.) gasare; (mil.) lanciare un attacco con gas; *to be -sed*, essere esposto all'azione del gas; *intr.* (fam.) chiacchierare, ciarlare.
**gas-bag** *n.* pallone *m.* a gas; (fam.) chiacchierone *m.*, chiacchierona *f.* **-burner** *n.* becco a gas. **-chamber** *n.* camera a gas.
**Gascon** *n.*, *adj.* guascone *m.*, *f.* **-ade** *n.* guasconata, spacconata. **-y** *pr.n.* (geog.) Guascogna.
**gas-cooker** *n.* fornello a gas. **-engine** *n.* motore *m.* a gas.
**gaseous** *n.* gassoso.
**gas-fire** *n.* stufa a gas. **-fitter** gasista *m.*
**gasman** *n.* gasista *m.*
**gash** *n.* sfregio; taglio; *tr.* tagliare; sfregiare; incidere.
**gas-holder** *n.* gasometro.
**gasif-y** *tr.* convertire in gas; volatilizzare; *intr.* volatilizzarsi. **-ication** *n.* gasìficazìone.
**gas-jet** *n.* becco a gas.
**gasket** *n.* (mech.) guarnizione; (naut.) gaschetto; premibaderna, premistoppa *m. indecl.*
**gas-lamp** *n.* (in street) lampada a gas. **-light** *n.* illuminazione a gas, lume *m.* a gas. **-lighting** *n.* illuminazione a gas.
**gas-main** *n.* condotta del gas.
**gas-mantle** *n.* reticella a incandescenza.
**gas-mask** *n.* maschera antigas.
**gas-meter** *n.* contatore del gas.
**gasogene** *n.* gasogeno.
**gasolene, gasoline** *n.* (chem.) gasolina; (motor.) benzina.
**gasometer** *n.* gasometro.
**gas-oven** *n.* fornello a gas, cucina a gas.
**gasp** *n.* respiro affannoso, anelito, rantolo; *to be at one's last —*, essere in punto di morte; *intr.* ansare, ansimare, anelare; respirare affannosamente; boccheggiare; rimanere senza fiato; (fam.) *I am -ing for a drink*, muoio di sete. **-er** *n.* (slang) sigaretta.
**gas-pipe** *n.* conduttura del gas. **-ring** *n.* fornello a gas. **-stove** *n.* cucina a gas.
**gassy** *adj.* gassoso; (fam.) verboso.
**gastr-ic** *adj.* gastrico. **-itis** *n.* gastrite *f.*
**gastronom-y** *n.* gastronomia. **-e, -er** *n.* gastronomo. **-ic(al)** gastronomico.
**gasworks** *n.* officina del gas.
**gate** *n.* porta; portone *m.*; cancello; barriera; (sport) numero di spettatori paganti; incasso; *tr.* (hist.) togliere (a uno) il permesso di libera uscita. **-crash** *tr.*, *intr.* entrare senza pagare in, assistere senza essere invitato a; (fam.) bucherare. **-crasher** *n.* intruso; (fam.) portoghese *m.*, *f.* **-house** *n.* portineria; corpo di guardia, casello. **-keeper** *n.* portiere *m.*; portinaio; guardiano; (rlwy.) cantoniere *m.*
**gate-legged** *adj.* a gambe mobili. **-money** *n.* prezzo d'ingresso; incasso.
**gate-post** *n.* cardine *m.*; montante *m.* **-way** *n.* portone *m.*; passaggio, ingresso; entrata.
**gather** *tr.* cogliere, raccogliere, riunire, radunare; *rfl.* raccogliersi, riprendersi; *to — flowers*, cogliere fiori; *to — oneself together*, raccogliere le proprie energie; *to — speed*, aumentare di velocità, avviarsi; (naut.) *to — way*, mettersi in moto; (provb.) *a rolling stone -s no moss*, sasso che rotola non raccoglie muschio; dedurre, capire; *so I —*, così mi pare; (needlew.) pieghettare, increspare; *intr.* raccogliersi, riunirsi, radunarsi; (med.) formare un ascesso, suppurare. **-ing** *n.* raccolta; riunione; adunata; assembra-

mento; congregazione; (med.) ascesso; suppurazione.
**gauche** *adj.* goffo; sgarbato.
**gaud-y** *adj.* sfarzoso; fastoso; vistoso. **-iness** *n.* vistosità; sfarzo; fasto.
**gauge** *n.* misura; (mech.) calibro; indicatore; (naut.) pescaggio; (rlwy.) scartamento; *tr.* misurare; (mech.) calibrare; (naut.) pescare; (fig.) stimare, calcolare. **-able** *adj.* misurabile.
**Gaul** *pr.n.* (geog.) Gallia; (person) Gallo.
**gaunt** *adj.* scarno, magro, sparuto, macilento; (fig.) ruvido, desolato. **-ness** *n.* magrezza; (fig.) desolazione.
**gauntlet** *n.* (hist.) manopola; (fig.) sfida; (motor.) guanto per automobilista; (mil.) punizione delle bacchette; *to run the —*, passare sotto le bacchette; (fig.) esporsi agli attacchi, sfidare la critica.
**gauze** *n.* garza; *wire —*, reticella metallica; (fig.) velo.
**gave** *p.def.* of **give,** *q.v.*
**gavel** *n.* martelletto.
**gavotte** *n.* gavotta.
**gawk** *n.* persona goffa; balordo; (fam.) cero; *intr. to — at*, fissare con aria sciocca. **-iness** *n.* goffaggine *f.* **-y** *adj.* goffo; sgraziato; balordo.
**gay** *adj.* gaio; allegro; giulivo; vivace, brillante; *to become —*, animarsi, rallegrarsi; *to lead a — life*, godersi la vita, vivere in allegria; (fam.) *to go —*, darsi alla vita allegra; (fam.) omosessuale; *— Lib.*, Movimento di Liberazione degli Invertiti.
**gaze** *n.* sguardo fisso; *exposed to the public —*, esposto agli occhi di tutti; (fig.) contemplazione; *intr.* guardar fissamente, mirare, contemplare; *to — at*, fissare; *to — covetously at*, divorare con gli occhi.
**gazebo** *n.* belvedere *m.*
**gazelle** *n.* gazzella.
**gazette** *n.* gazzetta ufficiale; giornale *m.*; *tr.* pubblicare nella gazzetta ufficiale; (mil., of officer) nominare, destinare. **-er** *n.* dizionario geografico, atlante *m.*
**gear** *n.* arnesi, attrezzi, utensili *m.pl.*; attrezzatura; equipaggiamento; (fam.) roba; vestiario; (mech.) meccanismo, dispositivo; ingranaggio; (motor.) cambio; *bottom —*, prima velocità; *top —*, quarta velocità; *neutral —*, cambio in folle; *differential —*, differenziale *m.*; *to change —*, cambiare velocità; *to throw out of —*, (mech.) disingranare, disinnestare; (fig.) disturbare, sconvolgere, guastare; *tr.* (mech.) ingranare; (fig.) disporre; combinare.
**gear-box, -case** *n.* scatola del cambio, carter *m. indecl.* **-lever** *n.* leva del cambio, leva di comando. **-wheel** *n.* ruota dentata.
**gecko** *n.* (zool.) geco.
**gee-gee** *n.* (fam.) cavallino. **-up** *excl.* arri!, ih!; (joc.) avanti!
**geese** *n.pl.* of **goose,** *q.v.*
**gelatine** *n.* gelatina.
**gelatin-ize** *tr.* gelatinizzare; *intr.* gelatinizzarsi. **-ous** *adj.* gelatinoso.
**geld** *tr.* castrare. **-ing** *n.* cavallo castrato.
**gelid** *adj.* gelido.
**gelignite** *n.* nitroglicerina.
**gem** *n.* gemma; gioiello; pietra preziosa; (fig.) perla; (fam.) errore *m.* madornale, perla.
**geminate** *adj.* accoppiato; *n.* (gramm.) doppio; *tr.* (archit.; art) accoppiare; (gramm.) raddoppiare, duplicare.
**gemmed** *adj.* ingemmato.
**gender** *n.* (gramm.) genere *m.*; (fam.) sesso.
**genealog-y** *n.* genealogia. **-ical** *adj.* genealogico. **-ist** *n.* genealogista *m.*
**general** *adj.* generale; comune; prevalente; generico; *— post office*, posta centrale; *— practitioner*, medico generico; (mil.) *— headquarters*, gran quartiere generale; vago, generale; *to have a — idea of*, avere un'idea generica di.
**general** *n.* (mil.; eccl.) generale *m.*; *the — public*, il pubblico.
**generality** *n.* generalità; maggioranza.
**generaliz-e** *tr.*, *intr.* generalizzare; rendere generale. **-ation** *n.* generalizzazione.
**generally** *adv.* generalmente; in genere; comunemente; di solito.
**generalship** *n.* generalato; grado di generale; abilità militare; (fig.) abilità organizzativa; autorità.
**generat-e** *tr.* generare; procreare; produrre. **-ing** *adj.* generativo, generatore, produttore; *-ing station*, centrale elettrica. **-ion** *n.* generazione; *spontaneous -ion*, generazione spontanea; the *rising -ion*, la nuova generazione, la gioventù, i giovani. **-ive** *adj.* generativo, generatore, produttivo. **-or** *n.* generatore; (electr.) generatore, dinamo *f.*, alternatore.
**generic(al)** *adj.* generico.
**gener-ous** *adj.* generoso; liberale; munifico; magnanimo; (fig.) fertile; ampio, abbondante, copioso; *to be — with*, effondere. **-osity** *n.* generosità; liberalità; magnanimità.
**genesis** *n.* genesi *f.*; origine *f.*; (bibl.) Genesi *f.*
**genet** *n.* (zool.) genetta.
**genetic** *adj.* genetico. **-s** *n.* genetica.
**Genev-a** *pr.n.* Ginevra; *the Lake of —*, il Lago di Ginevra, il Lemano. **-an, -ese** *adj.*, *n.* ginevrino.
**Genevieve** *pr.n.* Ginevra.
**genial** *adj.* gioviale, socievole; mite, benigno. **-ity** *n.* giovialità, cordialità; mitezza.
**genie** *n.* genio; spirito; demonio.
**genital** *adj.* genitale; *n. pl.* genitali *m.pl.*
**genitive** *adj.*, *n.* (gramm.) genitivo.
**genius** *n.* genio; ingegno; *a man of —*, un uomo d'ingegno; *a work of —*, un'opera di genio; *to be a —*, essere un genio; (fam.) *he's no —*, non è un'aquila; talento; abilità; *to have a — for doing the wrong thing*, aver la specialità di far le cose sbagliate; spirito, genio particolare; (fig.) *good —*, angelo custode; *evil —*, spirito maligno; *— loci*, dio locale.
**Geno-a** *pr.n.* (geog.) Genova; (fam.) la Superba. **-ese** *adj.*, *n.* genovese *m.*, *f.*
**genocide** *n.* genocidio.
**genre** *n.* genere *m.*
**gent** *n.* (pop.) *abbrev.* of **gentleman,** *q.v.*
**genteel** *adj.* manieroso, che ha pretese di signorilità; eufemistico; *— poverty*, povertà che cerca di salvare le apparenze.
**gentian** *n.* (bot.) genziana.
**gentile** *adj.*, *n.* gentile *m.*, *f.*, pagano.
**gentility** *n.* signorilità; distinzione; nascita elevata.
**gentle** *adj.* tenero, affettuoso; mite, dolce, moderato; nobile, distinto; facile, non faticoso, non violento.
**gentlefolk(s)** *n.* gente *f.* dell'alta società, i signori.
**gentleman** signore; *ladies and gentlemen*, signore e signori; (of good family) gentiluomo; (in moral sense) gentiluomo; *a perfect —*, un perfetto gentiluomo; (fam.) *he's no —*, è un mascalzone, è un tizio qualunque; *to lead a —'s life*, vivere da signore; *a — at large*, un disoccupato; *—'s agreement*, accordo sulla parola.
**gentleman-farmer** *n.* gentiluomo di campagna che fa l'agricoltore.
**gentlemanl-y** *adj.* distinto; signorile. **-iness** *n.* modi gentili; signorilità.
**gentleness** *n.* dolcezza, mitezza; tenerezza; affettuosità.
**gentlewoman** *n.* gentildonna; signora.
**gently** *adv.* dolcemente; soavemente; teneramente; adagio.
**gentry** *n.* piccola nobilità; gente per bene; *landed —*, proprietari terrieri; (iron. pejor.) gente *f.*; *the light-fingered —*, i signori borsaiuoli.
**genuflect** *intr.* fare genuflessione, genuflettersi. **-ion** *n.* genuflessione.
**genuine** *adj.* genuino, autentico;

(fig.) schietto, sincero. -**ly** *adv.* sinceramente; veramente. -**ness** *n.* genuinità; autenticità.
**genus** *n.* genere *m.*
**geode-sy** *n.* geodesia. -**tic** *adj.* geodesico.
**Geoffrey** *pr.n.* Goffredo.
**geograph-y** *n.* geografia. -**er** *n.* geografo. -**ic(al)** *adj.* geografico.
**geolog-y** *n.* geologia. -**ical** *adj.* geologico. -**ist** *n.* geologo.
**geomancy** *n.* geomanzia.
**geometr-y** *n.* geometria. -**ic(al)** *adj.* geometrico. -**ician** *n.* geometro.
**geophysics** *n.* geofisica.
**George** *pr.n.* Giorgio; — *medal*, medaglia al valore civile; — *cross*, medaglia al valore militare; *excl. by —!*, per bacco!
**Georgia** *pr.n.* (geog.) Georgia.
**Georgian** *adj.* (Britain) dell'epoca georgiana (1714-1830); (USA, USSR) georgiano, della Georgia; *n.* georgiano.
**Georgiana** *pr.n.* Giorgiana.
**georgic** *adj.* georgico; *n.* (lit.) *the -s*, le Georgiche.
**Gerald, Gerard** *pr.n.* Gherardo, Gerardo.
**Geraldine** *pr.n.* Geraldina.
**geranium** *n.* geranio, pelargonio.
**gerfalcon** *n.* (orn.) girofalco.
**geriatr-ic** *adj.* geriatrico. -**ics**, -**y** *n.* (med.) geriatria.
**germ** *n.* germe *m.*; germoglio; embrione *m.*; (fig.) principio; origine *f.*; *intr.* germinare; (fig.) sorgere; nascere.
**german**[1] *adj.* germano; *cousin —*, cugino germano, cugino di primo grado.
**German**[2] *adj.*, *n.* tedesco; — *woman*, tedesca; — *language*, tedesco, lingua tedesca; — *measles*, rosolia; — *silver*, argentone *m.*
**germane** *adj.* pertinente, relativo.
**German-y** *pr.n.* (geog.) Germania. -**ic** *adj.* germanico, teutonico.
**germicide** *n.* germicida *m.*
**germinal** *adj.* germinale.
**germinat-e** *tr.* far germinare; *intr.* germinare; nascere. -**ion** *n.* germinazione. -**ive** *adj.* germinativo.
**gerontocracy** *n.* gerontocrazia.
**gerontology** *n.* (med.) gerontologia.
**Gertrude** *pr.n.* Geltrude.
**gerund** *n.* (gramm.) gerundio. -**ial**, -**ival** *adj.* (gramm.) gerundivo. -**ive** *adj.*, *n.* gerundivo.
**gestation** *n.* gestazione.
**gestatorial** *adj.* (eccl.) gestatoria; — *chair*, sedia gestatoria.
**gesticulat-e** *intr.* gesticolare, gestire. -**ion** *n.* gesticolazione; gesto.
**gesture** *n.* gesto; (fig.) atto, azione, mossa; *intr.* gesticolare, esprimersi a gesti.
**get** *tr.* 1. OBTAIN: ottenere; ricavare; procurare, procurarsi; acquistare; comprare. 2. FETCH: andare a prendere; cercare. 3. RECEIVE: ricevere, avere. 4. TAKE: prendere; contrarre. 5. UNDERSTAND: capire. 6. FOLLOW. BY ACC. AND INF.: far fare, fare in modo che; *to — someone to do something*, far fare qualcosa a qualcuno. 7. TO HAVE GOT: avere, possedere; *to have — to do something*, dover far qualcosa, essere costretto a far qualcosa. 8. *intr.* TO BECOME: divenire, diventare; (when followed by *adj.* or *part.* usually translated by *rfl.* verb; see under respective adjectives). 9. BEGIN: mettersi a, cominciare a. 10. REACH: andare a, raggiungere, arrivare a; *where did we — to?*, dove siamo rimasti? 11. FOLLOW. BY ADV. OR PREP.: *to — about*, circolare, viaggiare, (of news) diffondersi, correre; *to — abroad*, andare all'estero, (of news) diffondersi; *to — above oneself*, diventare prepotente; *to — across*, *tr.* far capire, far riuscire, *intr.* attraversare, passare, (fig.) riuscire; *to — ahead*, far progressi; *to — ahead of*, superare; *to — along*, andare avanti; *to — along with someone*, andare d'accordo con qualcuno; (fam.) *— along with you!*, ma va là!, vattene!; *to — along without*, fare a meno di; *to — at*, riuscire a capire, raggiungere, arrivare a; *to — away*, *tr.* strappare, allontanare, far partire *intr.* fuggire, allontanarsi; (fam.) *there is no -ting away from the fact that*, non c'è dubbio che; *to — away with it*, farla franca; *to — back*, *tr.* riavere, farsi restituire; (fam.) *to — one's own back*, vendicarsi; *intr.* ritornare, (into car, etc.) risalire; *to — behind*, rimanere indietro, mettersi dietro a; *to — by*, passare; *to — down*, *tr.* tirare giù, (in writing) mettere in iscritto, *intr.* scendere; (to dog) *— down!*, cuccia!, giù!; *to — down on one's knees*, inginocchiarsi; *to — down to one's work*, mettersi a lavorare sul serio; *to — in*, *tr.* far venire, far entrare; *to — one's hand in*, farsi la mano; *to — a word in*, riuscire a dire una parola; *intr.* tornare, rientrare; entrare, penetrare; (train, car) salire, arrivare, (pol.) essere eletto; (fam.) *to — in with someone*, stabilire buoni rapporti con qualcuno; *to — into*, *tr.* far entrare, introdurre, *intr.* entrare in, penetrare in, (car, train) salire, (club) farsi eleggere socio di, abituarsi a, acquistare, pigliare; *to — into trouble*, cacciarsi nei pasticci; *to — into a rage*, arrabbiarsi; *to — off*, *tr.* togliere, levare; spedire; sbarazzarsi di; far assolvere, *intr.* scendere (da), andarsene, partire; *to — off to sleep*, addormentarsi; *to — off with a fine*, cavarsela con una multa; (fam.) *to — off with a girl*, intendersi con una ragazza; *to — on*, *tr.* mettere; *to — one's shoes on*, mettersi le scarpe; (fam.) *to — a move on*, spicciarsi, far presto, affrettarsi; *intr.* salire (su), montare (su, in, a), mettersi (in, su), far progressi, far carriera, andare avanti; andare d'accordo, intendersi; *to be -ting on*, star invecchiando; *to be -ting on for thirty*, andare per i trenta; (fam.) *to — on to something*, scoprire qualcosa di buono; *to — out*, *tr.* tirar fuori, cavare, far uscire, elaborare, preparare, *intr.* uscire (da), (of car, train, etc.) scendere (da); fuggire (da), (of habit, etc.) perdere; schivare, farsi dispensare da; (of difficulty) cavarsi di; *to — out of hand*, diventare incontrollabile; *to — over*, *tr.* far passare sopra, portare a termine, *intr.* scavalcare, superare; rimettersi da; *to — round*, aggirare, eludere, (person) persuadere, lusingare; *to — through*, *tr.* far superare, far giungere a destinazione, far passare, *intr.* giungere a destinazione, (teleph.) ottenere la comunicazione, passare (per), attraversare, finire, (money) sprecare, (of law) essere approvato; *to — together*, *tr.* radunare, riunire, raccogliere, *intr.* radunarsi, riunirsi; *to — under*, *tr.* mettere sotto, dominare, *intr.* passare sotto; *to — up*, *tr.* far salire; organizzare, promuovere, *intr.* alzarsi; salire; (fig.) *to — up to mischief*, combinarne una di grossa, *rfl.* *to — oneself up as*, travestirsi da; *tr.* *to — with child*, fare incinta.
**get** *n.* (slang) bambino illegittimo.
**get-at-able** *adj.* (fam.) accessibile, raggiungibile. -**ness** *n.* (fam.) accessibilità.
**getaway** *n.* fuga; evasione; *to make a —*, fuggire, scappare, svignarsela.
**get-up** *n.* costume *m.*; truccatura; presentazione.
**gewgaw** *n.* ninnolo, gingillo, fronzolo.
**geyser** *n.* (geol.) geyser *m.*; sorgente calda; scaldabagno.
**ghastl-y** *adj.* orrendo, spaventoso; (fam.) *a — mistake*, un errore madornale; pallido, spettrale, smunto. -**iness** *n.* orrore *m.*; pallore *m.*
**Ghent** *pr.n.* (geog.) Gand.
**gherkin** *n.* cetriuolo, cetriolino.
**ghetto** *n.* ghetto.
**ghost** *n.* (rel.) spirito; *the Holy Ghost*, lo Spirito Santo; *to give up the —*, rendere l'anima a Dio, morire; spettro; fantasma *m.*; ombra; apparizione; (fig.) — *town*, città abbandonata; —

*writer*, collaboratore anonimo 'negro'; (fam.) *not the — of a chance*, neanche l'ombra di una probabilità; *the — of a smile*, un sorriso vago. **-like, -ly** *adj.* spettrale; (rel.) spirituale.

**ghoul** *n.* (myth.) demone *m.* che divora i cadaveri, (fig.) spogliatore di tombe. **-ish** *adj.* mostruoso; macabro.

**ghurka** *n.* gurkha *m.*

**giant** *adj.* gigantesco; *n.* gigante *m.* **-ess** *n.* gigantessa.

**gibber** *intr.* borbottare; farfugliare; parlare rapidamente ed incoerentemente. **-ish** *n.* borbottìo; farfuglio; discorso inintelligibile.

**gibbet** *n.* forca, patibolo.

**gibbon** *n.* (zool.) gibbone *m.*

**gibb-ose, -ous** *adj.* gibboso; (of pers.) gobbo. **-osity** *n.* gibbosità.

**gib-e** *n.* beffa; scherno; sarcasmo; *intr.* schernire, beffare; *to — at someone*, beffarsi di qualcuno. **-ing** *adj.* derisorio; beffardo.

**giblets** *n.pl.* (of a fowl) frattaglie *f.pl.*; rigaglie *f.pl.*

**Gibraltar** *pr.n.* (geog.) Gibilterra.

**gibus** *n.* cappello a cilindro pieghevole; gibus *m. indecl.*

**gidd-y** *adj.* preso da vertigini; *to feel —*, aver le vertigini; (fig.) vertiginoso; spensierato, scervellato, frivolo; (fam.) *to play the — goat*, fare il buffone. **-iness** *n.* vertigine *f.*; capogiro; spensieratezza; frivolezza.

**gift** *n.* dono; regalo; donazione; *Christmas* (*or New Year's*) *—*, strenna; (rel.) oblazione; *deed of —*, atto di donazione; (fam.) *— of the gab*, dono della favella, parlatina sciolta; (provb.) *never look a — horse in the mouth*, a cavallo donato non si guarda in bocca; dono, talento, dote *f.*

**gift** *tr.* dotare, donare. **-ed** *adj.* dotato; fornito di talento; geniale.

**gig** *n.* baroccino, calessino; (naut.) lancia.

**gigantic** *adj.* gigantesco.

**giggle** *n.* risatina sciocca, ridarella; *intr.* ridere scioccamente, ridacchiare.

**gigue** *n.* (mus.) giga.

**Gilbert** *pr.n.* Gilberto.

**gild** *tr.* indorare, dorare; *to — the pill*, addolcire la pillola. **-ed** *adj.* dorato. **-er** *n.* doratore; (art) argentatore. **-ing** *n.* doratura.

**Giles** *pr.n.* Egidio.

**gill**[1] *n.* branchia; (bot.) lamella; (joc.) goti *f.pl.*, pappagorgia; *to turn green about the -s*, impallidire.

**gill**[2] *n.* (measure) quarto di pinta (=0·142 litri).

**gillyflower** *n.* (bot.) garofano; (pop.) violaciocca.

**gilt** *adj.* dorato, indorato; *n.* doratura, indoratura *f.*; (fam.) *to take the — off the gingerbread*, spogliare di ogni attrattiva.

**gilt-edged** *adj.* a taglio dorato *n.* (Stock Exchange) titoli di stato.

**gimbals** *n.* (naut.) sospensione cardanica, cardana.

**gimcrack** *adj.* vistoso, appariscente; *n.* cianfrusaglia.

**gimlet** *n.* succhiello; *tr.* succhiellare.

**gimlet-eyed** *adj.* dagli occhi penetranti.

**gimmick** *n.* arnese *m.*; aggeggio; (slang) trucco.

**gimp** *n.* (text.) cordoncino, passamano.

**gin**[1] *n.* trappola; (mech.) argano; capra; (naut.) paranco.

**gin**[2] *n.* gineprella, ginepro; gin *m.*

**gin**[3] *tr.* (text.) sgranare; *n.* sgranatrice.

**ginger** *adj.* (colour) fulvo; rosso; *n.* (bot.) zenzero; (fig.) vivacità, energia; (fam.) persona dai capelli rossi; *tr.* aggiungere zenzero a; (fig.) *to — up*, stimolare, incitare.

**ginger-ale, -beer, -pop** *n.* bibita al zenzero.

**gingerbread** *n.* pan di zenzero.

**ginger-haired** *adj.* dai capelli rossicci.

**gingerly** *adj.* guardingo; cauto; a passi felpati.

**gingery** *adj.* che sa di zenzero, aromatizzato con zenzero; (of hair) rossiccio; (of temper) focoso, irritabile.

**gingham** *n.* (text.) percallina; (fam.) ombrellaccio.

**gingiv-al** *adj.* (anat.) gengivale. **-itis** *n.* (med.) gengivite *f.*

**ginkgo** *n.* (bot.) ginco, albero da quaranta soldi.

**ginnery** *n.* (text.) filatura di cotone.

**Giorgionesque** *adj.* (art) giorgionesco.

**gippo** *adj.*, *n.* (slang) egiziano.

**gipsy** *n.* zingaro, gitano.

**giraffe** *n.* giraffa.

**gird** *tr.* cingere, fasciare, circondare; *to — on one's sword*, cingere la spada; (fig.) *to — up one's loins*, accingersi, prepararsi alla lotta.

**girder** *n.* (bldg.) trave maestra; (mech.) sbarra.

**girdle** *n.* cintura; fascia; cinturino; cintola; cerchia, cinta; (cost.) reggicalze *m.*; ventriera; *tr.* cingere, fasciare; circondare, racchiudere.

**girl** *n.* ragazza; fanciulla, giovinetta; giovane donna; *little —*, bambina, ragazzina; *Girl Guide*, Giovane Esploratrice; fidanzata; (fam.) *old —*, cara mia; *au pair —*, ragazza alla pari; *pin-up —*, ragazza da copertina; *pick-up —*, peripatetica; *call —*, ragazza da squillo.

**girl-child** *n.* bambina, femmina; figlia. **-friend** *n.* amica.

**girlhood** *n.* fanciullezza, giovinezza, adolescenza.

**girlish** *adj.* da ragazza. **-ness** *n.* aspetto di fanciulla; modi da ragazza.

**Girondist** *adj.*, *pr.n.* (hist.) girondino.

**girth** *n.* (of horse) cinghia; sottopancia *m.*; (of person) circonferenza; giro; *tr.* cingere (un cavallo), assicurare (la sella) con una cinghia; (measure) circondare per prendere la misura.

**gist** *n.* quintessenza; nocciolo.

**give** *n.* elasticità; cedimento, flessione; *— and take*, concessione reciproca, compromesso.

**give** *tr.* dare; donare; regalare; consegnare; concedere, accordare, offrire; *to — a present to*, fare un regalo a; *to — a dinner*, offrire un pranzo; *to — a sigh*, dare un sospiro, sospirare; *to — birth to*, dare alla luce, (fig.) dare origine a; *to — details*, fornire particolari; *to — ear*, prestare orecchio; *to — evidence*, testimoniare; *to — liberally*, elargire; *to — a receipt*, rilasciare una ricevuta; *to — rise to*, provocare, causare; *to — thanks*, rendere grazie; *to — tongue*, latrare, (of person) gridare, parlare; *to — vent to*, dare sfogo a; *to — way*, cedere, (to emotion) abbandonarsi; *to — someone a cold*, attaccare un raffreddore a qualcuno; (fam.) *— him my love*, salutalo da parte mia; *to — as good as one gets*, rendere pan per focaccia; *to — someone a bit of one's mind*, dirne quattro a qualcuno; *to — someone what for*, conciare qualcuno per le feste; *to — someone the slip*, evitare qualcuno, andarsene alla chetichella. FOLLOW. BY DAT. AND INF.: *to — someone to believe*, far credere a qualcuno; *rfl. to — oneself to*, darsi a, dedicarsi a, consacrarsi a; *intr.* cedere, piegarsi, allentarsi; FOLLOW. BY ADV. OR PREP.: *to — away*, dar via, regalare, distribuire, rivelare, tradire; *to — away the bride*, accompagnare la sposa all'altare; *to — back*, rendere, restituire, dare indietro; *to — forth*, mettere; *to — in*, cedere, arrendersi, abbandonarsi; *to — something in*, consegnare qualcosa; *to — one's name in*, farsi annunciare, farsi iscrivere; *to — off*, emettere, liberare; *to — out*, annunciare, distribuire, esaurirsi, venire a mancare, spegnersi; *to — oneself out as*, farsi passare per; *to — over*, smettere, consegnare; *to — up*, cedere, abbandonare, smettere; *to — oneself up*, costituirsi; *to — oneself up to*, abbandonarsi a, dedicarsi a.

**given** *p. part.* of **give,** *q.v.*; *adj.* dato; — *name,* nome di battesimo; *at a — time,* ad ora stabilita; — *to,* dedito a, incline a.
**giver** *n.* donatore; datore; dispensatore.
**gizzard** *n.* (anat.) ventriglio; (fam.) stomaco; *to stick in one's —,* rimanere sullo stomaco.
**glabrous** *adj.* glabroso, liscio.
**glacial** *adj.* glaciale.
**glaciation** *n.* (geol.) glaciazione.
**glacier** *n.* ghiacciaio.
**glacis** *n.* (mil. archit.) antispalto.
**glad** *adj.* lieto; contento; felice; *to be —,* rallegrarsi, essere lieto; *I should be — to know,* mi piacerebbe sapere; (fam.) — *rags,* abiti da festa. **-den** *tr.* rallegrare; allietare; dilettare; accontentare, rendere felice.
**glade** *n.* radura.
**gladiator** *n.* gladiatore *m.* **-ial** *adj.* gladiatorio.
**gladiolus** *n.* (bot.) gladiolo.
**glad-ness** *n.* contentezza; allegrezza; letizia; gioia. **-some** *adj.* lieto; gaio; giocondo.
**glaive** *n.* (lit.) spada.
**glamour** *n.* incanto; fascino. **-ize** *tr.* esagerare il fascino di; prestare incanto a. **-ous** *adj.* attraente; affascinante; incantevole.
**glanc-e** *n.* sguardo; occhiata; *at a —, at first —,* a prima vista; colpo obliquo; bagliore *m.*; *intr.* lanciare uno sguardo, dare un'occhiata (a); *to — over,* scorrere rapidamente; *to — up from,* distogliere lo sguardo da; (fig.) *to — at,* alludere a; sfiorare, toccare fugacemente; balenare; *to — off,* guizzare via da, deviare da, sfiorare. **-ing** *adj.* fugace; rapido; *a -ing blow,* un colpo che rimbalza.
**gland** *n.* (anat.; bot.) ghiandola; *he has something wrong with his -s,* ha una disfunzione ghiandolare.
**glanders** *n.* (vet.) morva; barbiglioni *m.pl.*
**glandular** *adj.* (anat.) glandolare, adenoso.
**glar-e** *n.* bagliore *m.*; riverbero, luce *f.* abbagliante; sguardo truce, sguardo minaccioso; *intr.* splendere di luce abbagliante, rifulgere, sfolgorare; (fam.) guardare con occhio truce; *to — at,* guardare in cagnesco. **-ing** *adj.* abbagliante; accecante; sfolgorante; (fam.) truce, torvo; (fig.) *a -ing mistake,* un errore madornale.
**glass** *n.* vetro; cristallo; — *door,* porta a vetri; — *eye,* occhio di vetro; bicchiere *m.*; calice *m.*; specchio; barometro; lente *f.*; *pl.* occhiali *m.pl.*; binocolo; (provb.) *those who live in — houses shouldn't throw stones,* chi ha tegoli di vetro non tiri sassi al vicino.
**glass-blower** *n.* soffiatore di vetro, vetraio. **-blowing** *n.* soffiatura del vetro.
**glass-ful** *n.* bicchiere pieno, contenuto di un bicchiere. **-house** *n.* (hortic.) serra; (mil. slang) carcere militare. **-ware** *n.* vetrame *m.*; vetrerie *f.pl.*; articoli di vetro. **-works** *n.* vetreria.
**glassy** *adj.*: vitreo, di vetro, cristallino; (fig.) trasparente, limpido.
**glaucoma** *n.* (med.) glaucoma *m.*
**glaucous** *adj.* glauco.
**glaz-e** *n.* (ceram.) vernice *f.* trasparente; smalto; patina; (fig.) superficie vetrosa, aspetto vitreo; (cul.) gelatina, biuta; *tr.* fornire di vetri, mettere vetri a; (ceram.) smaltare, verniciare, stendere vernice su; (fig.) levigare, lucidare; (cul.) biutare; *intr.* diventare vitreo. **-er** *n.* verniciatore. **-ier** *n.* vetraio.
**gleam** *n.* barlume *m.*; sprazzo di luce; raggio; *intr.* scintillare; luccicare; brillare; lampeggiare.
**glean** *tr.* spigolare; racimolare; (fig.) raccogliere. **-er** *n.* spigolatore *m.* **-ing** *n.* spigolatura; racimolatura; (fig.) raccolta.
**glebe** *n.* gleba.
**glee** *n.* gaiezza; allegria; gioia; (mus.) canone per sole voci maschili. **-ful** *adj.*, gaio; allegro; lieto.
**glen** *n.* valletta; forra.
**glib** *adj.* loquace, facondo, scorrevole; pronto. **-ness** *n.* loquacità; facilità di parola; scioltezza di lingua; prontezza.
**glid-e** *n.* scivolata; sdrucciolamento; (dancing) passo strisciato; (mus.) legamento; (ling.) suono transitorio; (aeron.) volo planato; *intr.* scivolare; strisciare; sdrucciolare; passare scivolando; *to — away,* allontanarsi scivolando, passare; (aeron.) librarsi in aria, planare. **-er** *n.* (aeron.) aliante *m.* **-ing** *n.* scivolamento; (aeron.) volo a vela.
**glim** *n.* (pop.) lume *m.*; lanterna; (joc.) *to douse the —,* spegnere la luce.
**glimmer** *n.* barlume *m.*; luccichìo; scintillìo; luce *f.* debole, chiarore *m.*; *intr.* luccicare; (of dawn) albeggiare.
**glimpse** *n.* breve visione; occhiata rapida; *to catch a — of,* vedere di sfuggita, intravedere, adocchiare; (fig.) pallida idea; *tr.* intravvedere; vedere di sfuggita; *intr.* *to — at,* scorrere rapidamente.
**glint** *n.* riflesso; scintillìo; lucentezza; *intr.* scintillare; brillare.
**glissade** *n.* scivolata; *intr.* scivolare; slittare;
**glissando** *adv.* (mus.) strisciando, portato.
**glisten** *intr.* luccicare; sfavillare; brillare. **-ing** *n.* luccichìo; scintillìo; lucentezza.
**glitter** *n.* luccichìo; scintillìo; lucentezza; *intr.* brillare; rifulgere; risplendere; scintillare; luccicare; (provb.) *all is not gold that -s,* non è tutt' oro quel che riluce.
**gloaming** *n.* crepuscolo.
**gloat** *intr.* gongolare, congratularsi con se stresso; *to — over,* guardare avidamente, divorare con gli occhi; godere (delle disgrazie altrui).
**global** *adj.* globale.
**globe** *n.* globo; sfera; orbe *m.*; *the —* (Earth), la terra; (chart) mappamondo; pianeta *m.*; (for fish) vaschetta.
**globe-trotter** *n.* giramondo.
**globul-e** *n.* globulo; goccia. **-ar** *adj.* globulare; sferico.
**gloom** *n.* oscurità; buio; tenebre *f.pl.*; (fig.) tristezza; malinconia. **-iness** *n.* oscurità; (fig.) tristezza, depressione morale. **-y** *adj.* cupo; oscuro; fosco, annuvolato; *to become -y,* annuvolarsi; (fig.) lugubre, triste, malinconico; *to feel -y,* essere triste; *the -y side of things,* il lato peggiore delle cose.
**glorif-y** *tr.* glorificare, esaltare, celebrare, divinizzare. **-ication** *n.* glorificazione; (fam.) festeggiamento. **-ier** *n.* glorificatore *m.*
**gloriole** *n.* aureola.
**glorious** *adj.* glorioso; illustre; (fam.) bellissimo, splendido, stupendo; (iron.) *a — muddle,* un bel pasticcio.
**glory** *n.* gloria; fama; onore *m.*; — *to God!,* gloria a Dio!; (fig.) splendore *m.*; bellezza; maestà; (halo) aureola; (bot.) *morning —,* ipomea *f.*; (USA) *Old Glory,* la bandiera nazionale degli Stati Uniti; (iron.) *to go to —,* crepare, andare all'altro mondo; *intr.* esultare; gloriarsi; vantarsi.
**gloss**[1] *n.* lucentezza; (fig.) apparenza esteriore; *to take the — off something,* ridurre alle giuste proporzioni qualcosa; *a — of respectability,* un soffio di rispettabilità; *tr.* lucidare; (fig.) *to — over one's mistakes,* sorvolare sui propri errori.
**gloss**[2] *n.* chiosa; glossa; commento; *tr.* chiosare; commentare; interpretare. **-ary** *n.* glossario; vocabolario; lessico.
**glossiness** *n.* lucidezza; lucentezza.
**glossitis** *n.* (med.) glossite *f.*
**glossographer** *n.* glossografo.
**glossology** *n.* glossologia; filologia comparativa.
**glossy** *adj.* lucido, lucente, liscio; (paperm.) — *paper,* carta patinata.
**glottis** *n.* (anat.) glottide *f.*
**glove** *n.* guanto; (boxing) guantone *m.*; *to fit like a —,* calzare a

pennello, (fam.) stare dipinto; *to be hand in —*, esser pane e cacio; *tr.* inguantare, mettere guanti a, fornire di guanti.
**glove-maker, glover** *n.* guantaio.
**glove-stretcher** *n.* allargaguanti *m. indecl.*
**glow** *n.* calore *m.*; incandescenza; scintillìo; splendore *m.*; rossore *m.*; colorito vivo; colore acceso; (fig.) ardore *m.*; entusiasmo; *intr.* essere incandescente; scintillare, risplendere; avvampare; (fig.) ardere.
**glower** *intr.* guardare in cagnesco, fare un viso minaccioso, rabbuiarsi in volto. **-ing** *adj.* torvo, minaccioso, rabbuiato.
**glowing** *adj.* incandescente; ardente; *a — sky*, un cielo di fuoco; raggiante; entusiastico fervente.
**glow-lamp** *n.* lampada incandescente. **-worm** *n.* lucciola.
**gloxinia** *n.* (bot.) glossinia.
**gloze** *tr.* palliare; velare.
**glucose** *n.* glucosio; destroso.
**glue** *n.* colla; glutine *m.*; *tr.* incollare, appiccicare insieme; attaccare con colla; (fig.) attaccare, fissare. **-y** *adj.* colloso; attaccaticcio, appiccicaticcio.
**glum** *adj.* tetro; cupo; accigliato; triste; *to look —*, aver l'aria triste. **-ness** *n.* l'essere accigliato; tristezza.
**glut** *n.* sovrabbondanza; ingorgo; eccedenza; (fig.) saturazione; *tr.* saturare; *to — the market*, inondare il mercato; *to — oneself*, saziarsi; *to — one's eyes*, saziare la vista.
**gluten** *n.* glutine *m.*
**gluteus** *n.* (anat.) gluteo.
**glutin-ous** *adj.* glutinoso. **-ize** *tr.* rendere glutinoso. **-osity, -ousness** *n.* glutinosità.
**glutton** *n.* ghiotto, ghiottone *m.*; goloso; (fig.) divoratore; (zool.) ghiottone. **-ous** *adj.* ghiotto; goloso; ingordo. **-y** *n.* ghiottoneria; golosità; ingordigia; gola.
**glycerin(e)** *n.* (chem.) glicerina.
**glycol** *n.* (chem.) glicole *m.*
**glyph** *n.* (archit.) glifo.
**glypt-ics** *n.* glittica. **-ography** *n.* glittografia.
**gnarl** *n.* nodo; nocchio. **-ed** *adj.* nodoso; nocchiuto.
**gnash** *tr. to — one's teeth*, digrignare i denti.
**gnat** *n.* (ent.) culice *m.*; (pop.) moscerino; (fig.) *to strain at a —*, dare importanza a delle inezie.
**gnaw** *tr., intr.* rodere; rosicchiare; (fig.) corrodere; consumare.
**gnome**[1] *n.* gnomo.
**gnom-e**[2] *n.* (Gk. lit) massima; aforisma *m.* **-ic** *adj.* gnomico; sentenzioso.
**gnomon** *n.* gnomone *m.*; ago.
**gnosis** *n.* gnosi *f.*
**gnosticism** *n.* gnosticismo.
**gnu** *n.* (zool.) gnù *m. indecl.*
**go** *n.* moto; *to be always on the —*, essere sempre in giro, essere sempre occupato; energia; *to be full of —*, essere dinamico, essere pieno di energia; tentativo; *to have a — at*, tentare di fare; *let's have a — !*, proviamo!; *at one —*, in un sol colpo; *it's no — !*, è inutile!; *all the —*, di moda, in voga.
**go** *intr.* andare; *you may —*, potete andare; *to — on foot*, andare a piedi; *to — by* (car, train), andare in. FOLLOW. BY 'AND' OR 'TO', PLUS INFIN.: andare a; *to — and see*, andare a vedere. FOLLOW. BY GERUND; andare a; *to — hunting*, andare a caccia. WITH FUTURE SENSE, FOLLOW. BY INFIN.: *to be -ing to*, essere in procinto di, avere l'intenzione di, stare per; diventare, divenire, farsi. FOLLOW BY ADJ. see under respective adjectives. FOLLOW. BY ADV.: *to — about*, girare, circolare, (naut.) virare di bordo; *to — ahead*, andare avanti, far progressi; *to — ahead of*, superare; *to — along*, procedere; (fam.) *— along with you!*, ma va la!; *to — ashore*, andare a terra, sbarcare, incagliarsi; *to — astray*, smarrirsi; *to — away*, andarsene, partire; *to — back*, ritornare; *to — back to bed*, rimettersi a letto; *to — back to* (date from) rimontare a *to — by*, passare; *to — down*, scendere, (of ship) affondare; *to — forth*, uscire; *to — forward*, avanzare; *to — in*, entrare; *to — in for*, dedicarsi a; *to — off*, andarsene; esplodere; *to — on*, continuare, passare; succedere; *to — out*, uscire, andar fuori, (of light) spegnersi; *to — up*, salire, montare. FOLLOW. BY PREP.: *to — about*, occuparsi di; *to — after*, correre dietro, cercare; *to — against*, andare contro, opporsi a; *to — by*, regolarsi su; andare sotto; *to — for*, andare a cercare; aggredire, lanciarsi contro; *to — into*, esaminare, studiare, entrare in; *to — off*, deviare da, uscire da; *to — off one's head*, impazzire; *to — over*, esaminare, ritoccare; *to — round*, girare; *to — through*, attraversare, esaminare; *to — with*, accompagnare; *to — without*, fare a meno di; *it -es without saying that*, va da sè che.
**goad** *n.* pungolo; aculeo; (fig.) stimolo; sprone *m.*; incitamento; *tr.* pungere, pungolare; (fig.) spronare; aguzzare; incitare; spingere.
**go-ahead** *adj.* intraprendente; attivo; progressista; *n.* permesso di passare all'azione; benestare *m.*
**goal** *n.* meta; scopo; traguardo; obiettivo; (sport) porta; rete *f.*; gol *m. indecl.*; *to score a —*, segnare una rete. **-keeper** *n.* portiere *m.*
**goal-kick** *n.* (sport) rimessa. **-post** *n.* (sport) palo.
**goat** *n.* capra; *he-goat*, capro, caprone *m.*, becco; (astron.) *the Goat*, il Capricorno; *to separate the sheep from the -s*, separare i buoni dai cattivi; (fam.) *to play the —*, fare lo sciocco, fare buffonate; *to get someone's —*, irritare qualcuno; uomo lascivo. **-ee** *n.* barbetta a punta, pizzo. **-herd** *n.* capraio. **-skin** *n.* pelle di capra; (bookb.) marocchino; otre *m.* **-sucker** *n.* (orn.) caprimulgo.
**gobble** *n.* (turkey) gloglò *m.*; *tr.* inghiottire, ingoiare, trangugiare in fretta; (fig.) divorare, impadronirsi di; *intr.* (of turkey) gloglottare. **-r** *n.* ghiottone *m.*; chi ingoia in fretta; (fam.) tacchino.
**go-between** *n.* intermediario, mediatore, mezzano.
**goblet** *n.* calice *m.*; coppa; bicchiere *m.*
**goblin** *n.* folletto; demonio; spirito maligno.
**go-cart** *n.* carrozzella per bambini, girello.
**god** *n.* dio; nume *m.*; divinità; (fig.) idolo; *pl. the -s*, gli dei; *household -s*, i Penati; (fam.) *a sight for the -s*, uno spettacolo da far ridere; (theatr., gallery), Olimpo, loggione *m.*
**God** *n.* Dio; *the Lord —*, il Signor Iddio; *thank — !*, grazie a Dio, come Dio volle; *— willing*, se Dio vuole; *— help you*, che Dio ti aiuti; *—'s acre*, cimitero, camposanto.
**god-child** *n.* figlioccio. **-daughter** *n.* figlioccia.
**goddess** *n.* dea.
**godfather** *n.* padrino.
**god-fearing** *adj.* timorato di Dio. **-forsaken** *adj.* abbandonato da Dio; (fig.) sperduto; *a forsaken place*, un luogo incolto e senza conforti.
**Godfrey** *pr.n.* Goffredo.
**godhead** *n.* divinità; nume *m.*
**godless** *adj.* (fig.) ateo; empio; malvagio. **-ness** *n.* ateismo; empietà.
**godlike** *adj.* divino, simile a un dio.
**godl-y** *adj.* pio; devoto. **-iness** *n.* devozione; santità; pietà.
**godmother** *n.* madrina.
**godparent** *n.* padrino, madrina; *to be — to*, tenere a battesimo, far da padrino a.
**godsend** *n.* dono del cielo; fortuna inaspettata; manna.
**godson** *n.* figlioccio.
**godspeed** *n. to wish — to*, augurare buon viaggio a.
**goer** *n.* chi va; *comers and -s*, chi va e chi vieno; camminatore; (sport) velocista *m.*; (of horse) che corre bene; (fig.) uomo energico.

**goffer** *n.* (cost.) gala a pieghe; ferro per pieghettare; *tr.* pieghettare, increspare, stirare a cannoncini; (bookb.) goffrare.
**go-getter** *n.* (slang) uomo intraprendente; arrivista *m.*
**goggle** *intr.* roteare gli occhi; stralunare; guardare con occhi stralunati. **-s** *n.* occhialoni *m.pl.*; occhiali di protezione.
**goggle-eyed** *adj.* dagli occhi bovini.
**going** *adj.* che va, che cammina; (comm.) *a — concern*, un'azienda in piena attività; *n.* andare *m.*, andatura, andata; *comings and -s*, viavai *m. indecl.*; terreno; *— away*, partenza; *— back*, ritorno; *— down*, discesa, calata; (of sun) tramonto; *— out*, uscita, uscire *m.*
**goitre** *n.* (med.) gozzo.
**gold** *adj.* d'oro; aureo; *n.* oro; *Dutch —*, similoro; (colour) giallo oro, dorato; (fig.) denaro, ricchezza; *— plate*, vasellame d'oro; *— standard*, base aurea; (geog.) *Gold Coast*, Costa d'Oro.
**gold-bearing** *adj.* aurifero. **-beater** *n.* battiloro. **-digger** *n.* cercatore d'oro; (of woman) donna che spilla denaro agli uomini.
**gold-dust** *n.* polvere *f.* d'oro.
**golden** *adj.* d'oro; dorato; (of hair) biondo oro; (fig.) prezioso; *— age*, età dell'oro; *— fleece*, vello d'oro; *Golden Horn*, Corno d'oro; *— mean*, giusto mezzo; *— number*, numero aureo; *— rule*, regola aurea; *— syrup*, melassa; *— wedding*, nozze *f.pl.* d'oro.
**goldenrod** *n.* (bot.) verga d'oro.
**gold-field** *n.* zona aurifera. **-finch** *n.* (orn.) cardellino. **-fish** *n.* pesce rosso.
**gold-leaf** *n.* oro laminato. **-mine** *n.* miniera d'oro.
**goldsmith** *n.* orefice *m.*; *-'s work*, oreficeria.
**golf** *n.* golf *m.*; *a round of —*, una partita di golf; *to play —*, giuocare al golf.
**golf-ball** *n.* palla da golf. **-club** *n.* circolo del golf; (implement) bastone, mazza da golf. **-course, -links** *n.* campo di golf.
**golf-er** *n.* giuocatore di golf. **-ing** *n.* il giuocare al golf.
**Goliath** *pr.n.* (bibl.) Golia.
**golosh** *n.* See **galosh.**
**gondol-a** *n.* gondola; (aeron.) navicella. **-ier** *n.* gondoliere *m.*
**gone** *part.* of **go**, *q.v.*; *adj.* passato; andato; *these ten years —*, dieci anni fa; *far —*, in uno stato avanzato; (of woman) *five months —*, incinta da cinque mesi; *dead and —*, morto e sepolto; (fam.) *to be — on*, essere innamorato di. **-r** *n.* (slang) *to be a -r*, essere spacciato.
**gonf-alon, -anon** (hist.) gonfalone *m.* **-alonier** *n.* (hist.) gonfaloniere *m.*
**gong** *n.* gong *m.*, tam-tam *m.*; (slang) medaglia al valore; *tr.*, *intr.* suonare il gong; *to be -ed*, (boxing) essere messo fuori combattimento; (motor.) essere fermato dalla polizia stradale, subire una contravvenzione.
**gonorrhoea** *n.* (med.) gonorrea, blenorragia.
**goo** *n.* (fam.) dolciume *m.*
**good** *adj.* buono; virtuoso; gentile; bello; bravo, forte; valido; bravo, saggio; *Good Friday*, Venerdì Santo; *— humour*, buon umore; *— looks*, bellezza; *— nature*, bontà di cuore; *— temper*, bontà, buon umore; *— will*, buona volontà; *— works*, opere di bene; *to have a — time*, divertirsi; *a — deal of*, molto, assai; *a — many*, molti; *a — while*, molto tempo; *a — three miles*, tre miglia abbondanti; *as — as*, quasi; *a — turn*, un servizio, un favore; *excl. — !*, bene!; *very — !*, benissimo!
**good** *n.* bene *m.*; *to do —*, fare del bene; vantaggio; utilità; *it's no —*, non serve, è inutile, non vale la pena; *what's the — of?*, a che serve?; *for —*, per sempre; *it's all to the —*, è tanto di guadagnato. *Cf.* **goods.**
**goodbye** *exl.*, *n.*, addio, arrivederci; *to say — to*, dire addio a; salutare; *I must say —*, devo andare.
**good-fellowship** *n.* socievolezza; cordialità.
**good-for-nothing** *adj.* inutile; di nessun valore; *n.* buon a nulla.
**good-hearted** *adj.* di buon cuore, buono. **-ness** *n.* bontà.
**good-humoured** *adj.* di buon umore; buono; gentile; affabile.
**goodish** *adj.* discreto, abbastanza buono; *a — number*, un numero abbastanza grande; *a — step*, abbastanza lontano.
**good-looking** *adj.* bello, di bell'aspetto.
**goodl-y** *adj.* bello, buono, grande; *a — sum*, una bella somma. **-iness** *n.* bellezza; bella sembianza.
**good-natured** *adj.* buono, gentile, bonario.
**goodness** *n.* bontà; gentilezza; benevolenza; probità; virtù; *have the — to*, abbia la gentilezza di; qualità; *excl. my — !*, Dio mio!; *for — sake!*, per carità!; *— knows what I must do*, Dio sa che cosa devo fare.
**goods** *n.* merce *f.*; beni *m.pl.*; *to deliver the —*, consegnare la merce, (fig.) adempiere i propri impegni; *capital —*, beni di produzione; *consumer —*, beni di consumo; *manufactured —*, manufatti *m.pl.*; (leg.) beni mobili; *— and chattels*, beni personali.
**goods-station** *n.* (rlwy.) scalo merci. **-train** *n.* (rlwy.) treno merci. **-truck** *n.* (rlwy.) vagone *m.* merci.
**good-tempered** *adj.* di carattere buono, buono, bonario.
**goodwill** *n.* benevolenza; carità; gentilezza; clientela; (comm.) avviamento.
**goody** *n.* (fam.) dolce *m.*; leccornia.
**goody-goody** *adj.* troppo buono; *n.* santarellino, santarellina.
**gooey** *adj.* dolciastro.
**goofy** *adj.* (slang) scemo, sciocco.
**goose** *n.* oca; *a flock of geese*, un branco di oche; *wild —*, oca selvatica; (fam.) emigrante irlandese; *wild — chase*, impresa sciocca; (fam.) *to cook someone's —*, dare il colpo di grazia a qualcuno, servire qualcuno; (provb.) *what is sauce for the — is sauce for the gander*, non si possono usare due pesi e due misure.
**gooseberry** *n.* uva spina; (fam.) *to play —*, reggere il lume, reggere il moccolo; (cul.) *— fool*, crema di uva spina. **-bush** *n.* arbusto di uva spina.
**gooseflesh** *n.* pelle d'oca, pelle accaponata.
**gooseherd** *n.* guardiano di oche.
**goose-neck** *n.* (mech.) collo d'oca. **-quill** *n.* penna d'oca.
**goosestep** *n.* passo dell'oca, passo romano.
**Gordian** *adj.* gordiano; *to cut the — knot*, tagliare il nodo gordiano.
**gore**[1] *n.* (dressm.) gherone *m.*; (of umbrella) spicchio.
**gore**[2] *n.* sangue coagulato.
**gore**[3] *tr.* colpire con le corna, trafiggere.
**gorge** *n.* (anat.) gola; fauci *f.pl.*; (fig.) *to make one's — rise*, far venire la nausea; (geol.) gola; burrone *m.*; *tr.* satollare; rimpinzare; *intr.* rimpinzarsi; mangiare con ingordigia.
**gorgeous** *adj.*, sfarzoso; sgargiante; magnifico. **-ness** *n.* sontuosità; fastosità; magnificenza.
**Gorgon** *n.* (myth.) Gorgone *f.*
**gorilla** *n.* (zool.) gorilla *m.*
**gormandize** *intr.* impinzarsi; mangiare golosamente. **-r** *n.* ghiottone *m.*
**gorse** *n.* ginestrone *m.*, ginestra spinosa.
**gory** *adj.* insanguinato; cruento.
**gosh** *excl.* caspita!, Dio mio!
**goshawk** *n.* (orn.) astore *m.*
**gosling** *n.* paperino.
**go-slow** *adj.* *— strike*, sciopero del regolamento.
**gospel** *n.* vangelo; *— truth*, verità inconfutabile; (fam.) *to take something for —*, credere a qualcosa come se fosse vangelo.
**gossamer** *n.* ragnatela; filo di

ragnatela; (fig.) garza, tessuto finissimo.
**gossip** *n.* pettegolezzo; diceria; chiacchiere *f.pl.*; ciarle *f.pl.*; *it's only —*, è soltanto un si dice; (person) pettegolo; chiacchierona *f.*; *intr.* chiacchierare; ciarlare; far pettegolezzi. **-er** *n.* chiacchierone *m.*; pettegolo. **-y** *adj.* (of style) aneddotico; *-y old woman*, vecchia pettegola.
**got** *p.def.*, *part* of **get**, *q.v.*
**Goth** *n.* (hist.) Goto. **-ic** *adj.* gotico; (archit.; art) gotico, ogivale; *n.* architettura gotica, stile gotico.
**gouache** *n.* (art) guazzo; pittura a guazzo.
**gouge** *n.* sgorbia; scalpello; *tr.* sgorbiare; scalpellare; (eng.) alesare; (fig.) *to — out someone's eyes* cavare gli occhi a qualcuno.
**goulash** *n.* (cul.) gulash all'ungherese.
**gourd** *n.* zucca; cucurbita; (bottle) caravazza, zucca.
**gourmand** *adj.*, *n.* ghiotto, ghiottone *m.*; goloso.
**gourmet** *n.* buongustaio.
**gout** *n.* (med.) gotta, podagra. **-y** *adj.* gottoso, podagroso.
**govern** *tr.* governare; reggere; dirigere; amministrare; controllare; influenzare; (gramm.) reggere. **-able** *adj.* governabile. **-ance** *n.* governo; direzione; controllo.
**governess** *n.* istitutrice.
**governing** *part. adj.* governante; dirigente; dominante; *— body*, organo direttivo; *— principle*, norma; *the — class*, i dirigenti.
**government** *n.* governo; amministrazione; regime *m.*; ministero; *to form a —*, formare un ministero; *— department*, dicastero; *— offices*, uffici governativi, ministeri *m.pl.*; *— organ*, giornale ufficiale del governo; *petticoat —*, matriarcato, regime delle donne; *temporal —*, principato temporale. **-al** *adj.* governativo, del governo.
**governor** *n.* governatore; amministratore; governante *m.*; *board of -s*, consiglio di amministrazione; (fam.) babbo; (pop.) signore, signor padrone; (mech.) regolatore.
**governor-general** *n.* governatore generale.
**governorship** *n.* governatorato.
**grab** *n.* strappo; stretta; (pol.) *policy of —*, politica rapace; (fam.) *smash and — raid*, operazione lampo; (mech.) benna; *tr.* afferrare; arraffare; agguantare; strappare; acchiappare; *intr. to — at*, cercare di afferrare; (mech.) prendere con la benna.
**grace** *n.* grazia; *the three Graces*, le tre Grazie; leggiadria; avvenenza; eleganza; favore *m.*; perdono; grazia; (theol.) *grazia divina*; benedicite *m.*; *to say —*, recitare il benedicite; (mus.) ornamento; (comm.) *days of —*, giorni di grazia; (title) *His Grace*, Sua Eccellenza.
**grace** *tr.* adornare; abbellire; favorire; *to — with one's presence*, onorare della propria presenza.
**graceful** *adj.* grazioso, leggiadro, elegante; (fig.) *a — act*, un atto gentile. **-ness** *n.* grazia; leggiadria; eleganza.
**graceless** *adj.* sgarbato; sgraziato; (theol.) non in stato di grazia; (fig.) perverso; scellerato. **-ness** *n.* mancanza di grazia; sgarbataggine *f.*; (fig.) perversità.
**grace-note** *n.* (mus.) notina; appoggiatura; nota di passaggio.
**gracious** *adj.* benevolo; benigno; amabile; condiscendente; clemente; grazioso; (fam.) *my —!*, *goodness —!*, caspita!, Dio mio! **-ness** *n.* benevolenza; benignità; condiscendenza; gentilezza.
**gradation** *n.* gradazione; (art) digradazione; sfumatura; (ling.) apofonia. **-al** *adj.* graduale; a gradi.
**grade** *n.* grado; rango; livello; qualità; *on the up —*, in rialzo, in salita; *to be on the down —*, essere in declino; (fam.) *to make the —*, riuscire, raggiungere la meta; *tr.* graduare; classificare; livellare; (art) sfumare.
**gradient** *n.* (up) salita; (down) pendenza, china; (up or down) inclinazione; (phys.; electr.) gradiente *m.*
**gradual** *adj.* graduale; dolce; moderato; *n.* graduale *m.* **-ly** *adv.* gradualmente; gradatamente; poco a poco.
**graduat-e** *n.* laureato; *tr.* graduare; proporzionare; *intr.* laurearsi, conseguire la laurea. **-ion** *n.* graduazione; sfumatura; (schol.) il laurearsi; (ceremony) consegna delle lauree.
**graec-ism** *n.* grecismo, ellenismo. **-ize** *tr.*, *intr.* grecizzare.
**graeco-roman** *adj.* greco-romano.
**graft** *n.* (hortic.) innesto; (surg.) trapianto; (slang) corruzione, concussione; camorra; *tr.* (bot.) innestare; (surg.) trapiantare; (slang) sbracciare. **-er** *n.* innestatore.
**Grail** *n.* *the Holy —*, il santo gradale.
**grain** *n.* (agric.) grano; biada; frumento; granaglie *f.pl.*; cereali *m.pl.*; (sand) granello, (coffee, rice) chicco; (fig.) granello, pizzico, briciolo; (in wood) filo, venatura; (in leather) grana; (of precious stones) acqua; (fig.) *against the —*, contro pelo, a malavoglia, a malincuore.
**grain** *tr.* granire, granulare, tingere in grana; (leather, etc.) zigrinare; (hides) depilare, pelare; (paint) marmorare, venare, marezzare.
**gramin-aceous** *adj.* (bot.) graminaceo. **-ivorous** *adj.* erbivoro.
**grammar** *n.* grammatica; *— school*, scuola media. **-ian** *n.* grammatico.
**grammatical** *adj.* grammaticale.
**gramme** *n.* grammo.
**gramophone** *n.* grammofono; *— needle*, puntina per grammofono; *— record*, disco; *collection of — records*, discoteca.
**grampus** *n.* (zool.) orca; (fam.) *to puff like a —*, sbuffare come una locomotiva.
**Granada** *pr.n.* (geog.) Granata.
**granary** *n.* granaio.
**grand** *adj.* grande; grandioso; sublime; *the Grand Canal*, il Canal Grande; *Grand Duke*, granduca *m.*; *Grand Duchess*, granduchessa; *Grand Duchy*, granducato; *— opera*, opera lirica, melodramma *m.*; *— piano*, pianoforte *m.* a coda; (math.) completo; *— total*, totale assoluto, somma; (fam.) magnifico, bellissimo; *to have a — time*, divertirsi un mondo e mezzo; *I'm not feeling very —*, non mi sento tanto bene; *n.* (USA, slang) *a —*, un biglietto da mille dollari.
**grandad** *n.* (fam.) nonno.
**grand-child** *n.* nipote *m.*, *f.*; nipotino; abiatico. **-daughter** *n.* nipote *f.*, nipotina.
**grandee** *n.* Grande di Spagna, gran signore *m.*
**grandeur** *n.* grandiosità, grandezza; magnificenza; altezza; elevatezza.
**grandfather** *n.* nonno; avo; *— clock*, orologio a pendolo.
**grandiloqu-ence** *n.* grandiloquenza; magniloquenza. **-ent** *adj.* magniloquente; ampolloso.
**grandios-e** *adj.* grandioso magnifico; pomposo; fastoso. **-ity** grandiosità; fastosità.
**grand(mam)ma** *n.* (fam.) nonna.
**grandmother** *n.* nonna; ava; (fam.) *to teach one's — to suck eggs*, insegnare agli uccelli a volare. **-ly** *adj.* da nonna; (fig.) eccessivamento materno.
**grandness** *n.* grandezza; grandiosità; magnificenza.
**grand(pa)pa** *n.* (fam.) nonno.
**grand-parent** *n.* nonno, nonna. **-sire** *n.* (lit.) nonno; avo. **-son** *n.* nipote *m.*; nipotino; abiatico.
**grandstand** *n.* tribuna d'onore.
**grange** *n.* fattoria; masseria; casa colonica.
**granit-e** *n.* granito. **-ic** *adj.* granitico.
**granivorous** *adj.* granivoro.
**grannie, granny** *n.* (fam.) nonna, nonnina; *— knot*, nodo falso.
**grant** *n.* concessione; dono; sovvenzione; assegnazione; (schol.) *State —*, borsa di studio statale; *tr.* accordare; con-

cedere; assegnare; elargire; rilasciare; *to — a pardon*, concedere la grazia; *to — a pension*, assegnare una pensione; *to — that*, ammettere che; *-ed that*, supposto che; *to take for -ed*, ritenere per certo, assumere. **-ee** *n.* concessionario; beneficiario. **-or, -er** *n.* (leg.) concedente *m., f.*

**granular** *adj.* granulato, granuloso, granulare. **-ity** *n.* granulosità.

**granulat-e** *tr.* granulare, cristallizzare, granire; *intr.* granularsi, cristallizzarsi, granire. **-ion** *n.* granulazione, granitura, cristallizzazione.

**granul-e** *n.* granulo, granello. **-ose, -ous** *adj.* granuloso.

**grape** *n.* chicco d'uva, acino; *pl.* uva; *a bunch of -s*, un grappolo d'uva; *sour -s*, uva acerba.

**grapefruit** *n.* pompelmo.

**grape-growing** *n.* viticoltura.

**grapeshot** *n.* (mil.) mitraglia.

**grape-stone** *n.* vinacciuolo. **-sugar** *n.* glucosio, destroso.

**grape-vine** *n.* vite *f.*; (fig.) canali *m.pl.* confidenziali.

**graph** *n.* grafico; diagramma *m.*; *— paper*, carta a quadretti, carta millimetrata. **-ic** *adj.* grafico; (fig.) pittoresco, vivace, vivido.

**graphite** *n.* grafite *f.*

**graphology** *n.* grafologia.

**grapnel** *n.* uncino; grappino.

**grapple** *tr.* abbrancare; aggrappare; afferrare; *intr.* aggrapparsi; *to — with*, venire alle prese con.

**grappling-iron** *n.* (naut.) graffino; uncino.

**grasp** *n.* presa; stretta; *to wrest from the — of*, strappare dalle mani di; (fig.) comprensione; intendimento; *tr.* afferrare; impugnare; agguantare; stringere; (fig.) capire; comprendere; *intr.* aggrapparsi attaccarsi, *to — at a straw*, attaccarsi ad una pagliuzza. **-ing** *adj.* tenace; avido; cupido; avaro.

**grass** *n.* erba; *a blade of —*, un filo d'erba; (lawn) prato; *keep off the —!*, vietato calpestare il prato!; *to let the — grow under one's feet*, perdere tempo; pascolo; *to put out to —*, mandare al pascolo; *tr.* ricoprire d'erba; *intr.* (slang) cantare.

**grass-covered** *adj.* erboso. **-green** *adj.* verde prato.

**grasshopper** *n.* (ent.) cavalletta.

**grassland** *n.* prateria; terreno erboso.

**grass-snake** *n.* (zool.) biscia. **-widow** *n.* moglie il cui marito è assente.

**grassy** *adj.* erboso.

**grate** *n.* griglia; inferriata; grata; (fireplace) focolare *m.*, camino; (cul.) graticola; *tr.* fornire di griglia; (cul.) grattugiare; (fig.) *to — one's teeth*, digrignare i denti; *intr.* stridere, cigolare; (fig.) *to — on the ear*, straziare gli orecchi; *to — on the nerves*, dare sui nervi.

**grateful** *adj.* grato; riconoscente; gradito, gradevole. **-ly** *adv.* con gratitudine, con riconoscenza. **-ness** *n.* gratitudine *f.*; riconoscenza.

**grater** *n.* grattugia.

**gratif-y** *tr.* appagare, accontentare, soddisfare, compiacere a; gratificare, compensare. **-ication** *n.* soddisfacimento; diletto; ricompensa; gratifica. **-ying** *adj.* soddisfacente, gradito, piacevole.

**grating** *adj.* aspro, stridente; *n.* stridore *m.*; griglia inferriata.

**gratis** *adv.* gratis, gratuitamente.

**gratitude** *n.* gratitudine, riconoscenza, riconoscimento.

**gratuitous** *adj.* gratuito ingiustificato. **-ness** *n.* gratuità.

**gratuity** *n.* mancia; gratifica.

**gravamen** *n.* gravame *m.*

**grave**[1] *adj.* grave; serio; severo; austero; solenne; (gramm.) *— accent*, accento grave.

**grave**[2] *n.* tomba; fossa; sepolcro; (fig.) morte *f.*

**grave**[3] *tr.* scolpire; incidere.

**grave-clothes** *n.* sudario. **-digger** *n.* beccamorti *m. indecl.*; becchino; affossatore.

**gravel** *n.* ghiaia; ghiaietto; *to strew with —*, inghiaiaro; (med.) renella; *tr.* inghiaiare.

**gravel-pit** *n.* cava di ghiaia.

**gravelly** *adj.* ghiaioso, ghiaiato.

**graven** *adj.* scolpito; inciso; *— image*, idolo.

**graveness** *n.* gravità; serietà; austerità.

**grave-stone** *n.* lapide funeraria, pietra tombale. **-yard** *n.* camposanto, cimitero.

**gravid** *adj.* gravido.

**graving-dock** *n.* (naut.) bacino di carenaggio. **-tool** *n.* bulino.

**gravitat-e** *intr.* gravitare. **-ion** *n.* gravitazione.

**gravity** *n.* gravità; serietà; austerità; *to keep one's —* mantenersi serio; (phys.) gravità; *centre of —*, baricentro; *specific —*, peso specifico.

**gravy** *n.* (cul.) sugo di carne, salsa.

**gravy-boat** *n.* salsiera.

**gray** *adj., n.* see **grey**.

**grayling** *n.* (ichth.) temolo.

**graz-e**[1] *n.* scalfittura; escoriazione; colpo di striscio; *tr.* scalfire; escoriare; sfiorare; rasentare. **-ing** *adj.* radente.

**graz-e**[2] *intr.* (agric.) pascere, pascolare. **-ier** *n.* allevatore di bestiane. **-ing** *n.* pascolo, pastura.

**grease** *n.* grasso; unto; sugna; grasso animale; lubrificante *m.*; olio denso; *to remove — stains from*, sgrassare; *tr.* ungere; ingrassare; lubrificare; *to — the wheels*, ungere le ruote; *to — someone's palm*, ungere la palma a qualcuno; sporcare d'unto.

**grease-cup, -cap** *n.* (mech.) ingrassatore. **-gun** *n.* (mech.) pompa per ingrassaggio.

**greasepaint** *n.* (theatr.) cerone *m.*

**grease-proof** *adj.* *— paper*, carta impermeabile al grasso.

**greaser** *n.* ingrassatore.

**greas-y** *adj.* grasso; unto; oleoso; macchiato di grasso, sudicio; sdruccievole, viscido; *— pole*, albero della cuccagna. **-iness** *n.* grassume *m.*; untume *m.*; untuosità; grassezza; oleosità; (fig.) untuosità.

**great** *adj.* grande; grosso; *a — man*, un grande; *Great Britain*, Gran Bretagna; (astron.) *Great Bear*, Orsa Maggiore; (emphatic) grandissimo, grossissimo; (quantitative) *a — deal of*, molto; *a — many*, moltissimi; *a — while ago*, molto tempo fa; *to reach a — age*, arrivare a tarda età; *to a — extent*, in via di massima, notevolmente; *no — matter*, una cosa di poca importanza; (fam.) magnifico, fantastico, divertente; *to have a — time*, divertirsi moltissimo; *to feel —*, sentirsi benissimo; bravo in, forte in; *n. the —*, i grandi; *— and small*, grandi e piccoli.

**great-aunt** *n.* prozia.

**greatcoat** *n.* soprabito; (mil.) cappotto.

**greater** *adj.* più grande, maggiore; *to grow — and —*, diventar sempre più grande.

**great-grandchild** *n.* pronipote *m., f.* **-granddaughter** *n.* pronipote *f.* **-grandfather** *n.* bisnonno, bisavolo. **-grandmother** *n.* bisnonna, bisavola. **-great-grandfather** *n.* trisavolo, bisarcavolo. **-great-grandmother** *n.* trisavola. **-hearted** *adj.* di gran cuore, generoso, magnanimo. **-heartedness** *n.* generosità, magnanimità.

**greatly** *adv.* molto; grandemente; altamente.

**great-nephew** *n.* pronipote *m.*

**greatness** *n.* grandezza; grossezza; altezza; elevatezza.

**great-niece** *n.* pronipote *f.* **-uncle** *n.* prozio.

**greave** *n.* (hist.) gambale *m.*

**grebe** *n.* (orn.) colimbo.

**Grecian** *adj., n.* greco.

**Greece** *pr.n.* Grecia.

**greed** *n.* cupidigia; avidità; bramosia; golosità; ingordigia. **-iness** *n.* avidità; golosità; ingordigia. **-y** *adj.* cupido; avido; goloso; ingordo.

**Greek** *adj.* greco; *the — Church*, la Chiesa ortodossa; *n.* greco *m.*, greca *f.*; (ling.) greco, lingua

greca; — *scholar*, grecista *m.*, *f.*, ellenista *m.*, *f.*; (fam.) *it's all — to me*, non ci capisco un'acca, questo è arabo per me.

**green** *adj.* verde; *to turn —*, inverdire; (of tree) coperto di foglie; — *Christmas*, Natale senza neve; — *belt*, zona verde; acerbo; fresco, vegeto; *to keep someone's memory —*, tener vivo il ricordo di qualcuno; — *old age*, vecchiaia vegeta; (fam.) ingenuo, semplice; *n.* verde *m.*; prato pubblico; (golf) praticello; *pl.* (cul.) verdura; *intr.* inverdire, verdeggiare.

**greenery** *n.* vegetazione, verdura.

**green-eyed** *adj.* dagli occhi verdi; (fig.) geloso; (fam.) *the — monster*, la gelosia.

**green-finch** *n.* (orn.) verdone *m.* **-fly** *n.* (ent.) afide *m.*, gorgoglione *m.* **-gage** *n.* susina verde, susina claudia. **-grocer** *n.* erbivendolo, fruttivendolo. **-grocery** *n.* frutta e verdura; ortaggi *m.pl.* **-horn** *n.* (fam.) pivello, sbarbatello. **-house** *n.* (hortic.) serra.

**greenish** *adj.* verdastro, verdognolo.

**Greenland** *pr.n.* (geog.) Groenlandia. **-er** *n.* groenlandese *m.*, *f.*

**greenness** *n.* verde *m.*; vegetazione; acerbezza; (fig.) immaturita, inesperienza.

**green-room** *n.* (theatr.) camerino degli artisti. **-sward** *n.* prato erboso. **-wood** *n.* bosco; foresta.

**greet**[1] *tr.* salutare; rivolgere il saluto a; dare il benvenuto a; (fig.) offrirsi alla vista di. **-ing** *n.* saluto; *pl.* saluti, auguri *m.pl.*

**greet**[2] *intr.* (Scot.) piangere.

**gregarious** *adj.* gregario; socievole.

**Gregorian** *adj.* gregoriano.

**Gregory** *pr.n.* Gregorio.

**gremlin** *n.* spiritello maligno.

**Grenada** *pr.n.* (geog.) Granata.

**grenad-e** *n.* (mil.) granata. **-ier** *n.* (mil.) granatiere *m.*

**grew** *p.def.* of **grow**, *q.v.*

**grey** *adj.* grigio; bigio; — *friar*, francescano; (fig.) tetro, grigio; (fam.) — *matter*, cervello; (provb.) *all cats are — in the twilight*, la sera tutti i gatti sono grigi; *n.* grigio; cavallo grigio; *hair touched with —*, capelli brizzolati; *tr.* rendere grigio; *intr.* diventar grigio. **-beard** *n.* vecchione *m.* **-hound** *n.* levriere *m.*; *-hound racing*, corse di levrieri. **-ish** *adj.* grigiastro. **-lag** *n.* (orn.) oca selvatica. **-ness** *n.* grigiore *m.*; (fig.) tristezza.

**grid** *n.* grata; griglia; (on map) quadrettatura; (electr.) rete *f.* nazionale.

**griddle** *n.* (cul.) gratella tegamino; vaglio; *tr.* cucinare in tegamino.

**gridiron** *n.* graticola, gratella.

**grief** *n.* dolore *m.*; angoscia; afflizione; accoramento; (fam.) *to come to —*, far fiasco, andare in malora.

**grief-stricken** *adj.* affranto dal dolore.

**grievance** *n.* motivo di lagnanza; rancore *m.*; torto; ingiustizia.

**grieve** *tr.* affliggere; addolorare; accorare; attristare; *intr.* affliggersi; addolorarsi; accorarsi.

**grievous** *adj.* doloroso; penoso; amaro; grave. **-ness** *n.* gravità.

**griffin, griffon, gryphon** *n.* grifo, grifone *m.*

**grill** *n.* griglia; inferriata; cancello; (cul.) griglia, graticola; *mixed —*, misto di carne ai ferri; *tr.* (cul.) cuocere ai ferri; arrostire; (slang) interrogare severamente a lungo, sottoporre al terzo grado.

**grille** *n.* See **grill**; (in convent) grata, graticola.

**grim** *adj.* torvo; fosco; sinistro; feroce; orrendo; *a — smile*, un sorriso sardonico; *to hold on like — death*, aggrapparsi disperatamente.

**grimace** *n.* smorfia; *intr.* far smorfie.

**grimalkin** *n.* vecchia gatta; (fig.) megera.

**grime** *n.* sudiciume *m.*; fuliggine *f.*; *tr.* sporcare; insudiciare.

**griminess** *n.* sporcizia sudiciume *m.*

**grimness** *n.* aspetto torvo; ferocia; carattere orrendo.

**grimy** *adj.* sporco; sudicio; fuligginoso.

**grin** *n.* sogghigno; ghigno; smorfia; *a broad —*, un largo sorriso; *intr.* fare un largo sorriso; sogghignare; ridacchiare; *to — and bear it*, far buon viso a cattivo giuoco.

**grind** *n.* fatica; lavoro pesante, lavoro monotono; (fam.) *the daily —*, le faccende quotidiane, il trantran quotidiano; (slang) corsa ad ostacoli; *tr.* macinare; tritare; triturare; frantumare; maciullare; polverizzare; affilare, arrotare; levigare, molare; *to — one's teeth*, digrignare i denti; (fig.) schiacciare, opprimere; *intr.* frantumarsi, polverizzarsi, spezzarsi; (slang) sgobbare.

**grinder** *n.* macina; (machine) molatrice, affilatrice *f.*; (tooth) molare *m.*; (person) arrotino; (of musical instrument) suonatore.

**grinding** *n.* macinatura; affilatura; levigatura; molatura; (of teeth) digrignamento, stridore *m.*; (fig.) oppressione.

**grinding-wheel** *n.* mola.

**grindstone** *n.* macina, mola; *to keep someone's nose to the —*, far lavorare qualcuno indefessamente.

**grip** *n.* presa; stretta; *to come to -s with*, venire alle prese con; (fig.) *to be in the — of*, essere in preda a; (fig.) padronanza, controllo; *to have a firm — on*, avere in pugno; *to loose one's —*, perdere il controllo; manico, impugnatura; (mech.) gancio, agganciatore; (USA) valigetta; (motor., of tyres) aderenza.

**grip** *tr.* afferrare; stringere; impugnare; (fig.) *to — the attention of*, imporsi all'attenzione di.

**gripe(s)** *n.* (med.) colica; *intr.* (slang) avere sempre qualcosa da lagnarsi.

**gripping** *adj.* avaro; rapace; lacerante, acuto.

**grisaille** *n.* (art) grisaille *f.*; chiaroscuro; (text.) bianconero.

**grisl-y** *adj.* orribile; spaventoso; macabro; raccapricciante. **-iness** *n.* orribilità; spaventosità.

**Grisons** *pr.n. pl.* (geog.) *the —*, i Grigioni *m.pl.*

**grist** *n.* grano da macinare; frumento; (fig.) *to bring — to the mill*, far venire l'acqua al molino.

**gristl-e** *n.* (anat.) cartilagine *f.* **-y** *adj.* cartilaginoso; tiglioso.

**grit** *n.* arenaria; sabbia; graniglia; (fig.) coraggio; (fam.) fegato; *intr.* scricchiolare.

**gritt-y** *adj.* sabbioso; renoso; ghiaioso; granuloso. **-iness** *n.* l'essere sabbioso.

**grizzl-e** *intr.* piagnucolare; brontolare. **-ed** *adj.* grigio; brizzolato. **-y** *adj.* grigio; *-ly bear*, orso grigio.

**groan** *n.* gemito; lamento; *intr.* gemere; lamentarsi; brontolare; (fig.) gemere; dire fra i gemiti.

**groats** *n.pl.* fiocchi *m.pl.* d'avena.

**grocer** *n.* droghiere *m.*; negoziante di generi alimentari; *T's (shop)*, drogheria, negozio di generi alimentari. **-y** *n.* generi alimentari *m.pl.*

**grog** *n.* grog *m.*, ponce *m.*

**grog-shop** *n.* bettola.

**groggy** *adj.* debole; malfermo; vacillante; *to feel —*, sentirsi poco bene; brillo.

**groin** *n.* (anat.) inguine *m.*; anguinaia; (archit.) costolone *m.* **-ed** *adj.* (archit.) a costoloni.

**groom** *n.* staffiere *m.*; palafreniere *m.*; gentiluomo; sposo; *tr.* strigliare; governare; (fig.) rassettare; pulire; preparare; istruire.

**groove** *n.* scanalatura; solco; (fig.) vecchia abitudine; trantran *m.*; *tr.* scanalare; incavare; solcare.

**grop-e** *intr.* brancolare; andare a tastoni; *to — for*, cercare andando a tastoni. **-ing** *adj.*, **-ingly** *adv.* a tastoni.

**gross** *adj.* grossolano; rozzo; volgare; madornale, flagrante;

(comm.) lordo; — *weight*, peso lordo; — *income*, reddito imponibile; *n.* grossa, dodici dozzine *f.pl.* **-ly** *adv.* grossolanamente; volgarmente; enormente; esageratamente. **-ness** *n.* grossolanità; rozzezza; volgarità; enormità.

**grotesque** *adj.* grottesco; stravagante; assurdo; *n.* (art) grottesco. **-ness** *n.* stravaganza, bizzarria.

**grotto** *n.* grotta.

**ground**[1] *n.* terreno; terra; suolo; superficie della terra; *on the* —, per terra, in terra; — *rent*, affitto del terreno; *to break fresh* —, coltivare un terreno incolto; (fig.) tentare qualcosa di nuovo; *to be on sure* —, conoscere il terreno, (fig.) essere sicuro del proprio fatto; *to cover a lot of* —, percorrere molta strada; *to fall to the* —, cadere a terra, (fig.) fallire; *to gain* —, guadagnare terreno; *to lose* —, perdere terreno, cedere; *to shift one's* —, cambiare il proprio punto di vista; *to stand one's* —, tener duro; *to till the* —, coltivare il suolo; *pl.* terreni, parco, giardino; *house and -s*, casa e terreni; *the -s of a country house*, il parco di una villa; *sports* —, campo sportivo, stadio; fondi *m.pl.*; fondo; *to touch* —, toccare il fondo, (of ship) arenarsi; (paint.) fondo; piano; sfondo; (fig.) ragione *f.*, motivo; base *f.*; *to have good -s*, aver buone ragioni; *without any -s*, senza alcun motivo.

**ground**[2] *tr.* fondare, basare; (fig.) insegnare i primi elementi a; (aeron.) vietare il volo a (un aeroplano); *intr.* (naut.) arenarsi, incagliarsi; (aeron.) atterrare.

**ground**[3] *p.def.*, *part.* of **grind**, *q.v.*

**ground-floor** *n.* pianterreno.

**grounding** *n.* fondamento; base *f.*; (naut.) arenamento; (aeron.) atterraggio; (paint.) fondo, prima mano.

**groundless** *adj.* infondato. **-ness** *n.* infondatezza.

**ground-nut** *n.* (bot.) arachide *f.* **-plan** *n.* pianta sezione orizzontale.

**groundsman** *n.* (sport) inserviente di campo sportivo.

**groundwork** *n.* fondamento; base *f.*; preparativi *m.pl.*

**group** *n.* gruppo; raggruppamento; comitiva; brigata; crocchio; *literary* —, cenacolo, scuola; (chem.) radicale *m.*; *tr.* raggruppare, aggruppare; radunare; classificare; disporre in gruppi; *intr.* raggrupparsi; radunarsi. **-ing** *n.* raggruppamento; disposizione in gruppi.

**grouse**[1] *n.* (orn.) tetraone *m.*, gallo cedrone.

**grouse**[2] *n.* (fam.) brontolìo; lagnanza; *intr.* brontolare, lagnarsi. **-r** *n.* brontolone *m.*, brontolona *f.*

**grout** *n.* (bldg.) malta liquida, boiacca.

**grove** *n.* boschetto; piantagione *f.*; *oak* —, querceto; *olive* —, uliveto; *orange* —, aranceto.

**grovel** *intr.* strisciare; strascicarsi; (fig.) umiliarsi; *to — before someone*, leccare i piedi a qualcuno. **-ler** *n.indecl.* adulatore; leccapiedi *m. indecl.* **-ling** *adj.* abietto; *gerund.* strisciamento; adulazione.

**grow** *tr.* coltivare; lasciar crescere; far crescere; *intr.* crescere; fiorire; ingrandire; svilupparsi; diventare, divenire; *to — angry*, arrabbiarsi; *to — better*, migliorare; *to — bigger*, ingrossare; *to — less*, diminuire; *to — old*, invecchiare; *to — red*, arrossire; *to — rich*, arricchirsi; *to — smaller*, rimpicciolire; *to — thin*, dimagrire; *to — tired*, stancarsi; *to — young again*, ringiovanire; *to — worse*, peggiorare; *to — out of a habit*, perdere un'abitudine; *to — up*, crescere, diventare adulto. **-er** *n.* coltivatore. **-ing** *adj.* crescente; che aumenta, che ingrandisce; *n.* crescita; aumento; coltivazione.

**growl** *n.* ringhio; grugnito; (fig.) brontolìo; *intr.* ringhiare; grugnire; brontolare. **-er** *n.* borbottone, brontolone *m.*; (hist.) carrozza a quattro ruote.

**crown** *adj.* cresciuto; adulto; fatto.

**grown-up** *n.* adulto; (fam.) *the -s*, i grandi.

**growth** *n.* crescita; aumento; sviluppo; progresso; espansione; (med.) tumore *m.*; ulcera; escrescenza.

**groyne** *n.* frangiflutti *m. indecl.*; (river) pennello; (archit.) sprone *m.*

**grub** *n.* bruco; lombrico; verme *m.*; larva; (pop.) mangiare, mangime *m.*; *intr.* scavare; zappare; (pop.) *to — along*, vivacchiare; *to — away*, sgobbare. **-by** *adj.* verminoso; bacato; (fig.) sporco; sudicio.

**grudg-e** *n.* rancore *m.*; astio; *to have a — against someone*, avercela con qualcuno, pagarsela al dito, serbare rancore contro qualcuno; *to bear no* —, non invidiare, non nutrire rancore; *to pay off old -s*, soddisfare vecchi rancori; *tr.* dare di malavoglia; invidiare. **-ing** *adj.* dato controvoglia; riluttante; invidioso; avaro. **-ingly** *adv.* controvoglia; malvolentieri; a malincuore; a suo disgrado.

**gruel** *n.* farinata d'avena.

**gruelling** *adj.* dura; faticosa; estenuante.

**gruesome** *adj.* macabro; raccapricciante.

**gruff** *adj.* burbero; aspro; arcigno; (of voice) rauco. **-ness** *n.* asprezza; sgarbatezza; tono burbero; rudezza.

**grumbl-e** *n.* brontolìo; borbottìo; lagnanza; *intr.* borbottare; brontolare; lagnarsi; dir male. **-er** *n.* brontolone *m.*; borbottona *f.*

**grumbl-ing** *n.* brontolìo; borbottamento; mormorìo. **-ingly** *adv.* brontolando, di mala voglia.

**grump-y, -ish** *adj.* arcigno; burbero; scontroso; irritabile. **-iness** *n.* cattivo umore; irritabilità.

**grunt** *n.* grugnito; brontolìo; *to give a* —, grugnire; borbottare; *intr.* grugnire; borbottare.

**gruyère** *n.* (cheese) gruviera; (pop.) emmental *m.*

**guarant-ee** *n.* garanzia; pegno; (comm.) avallo; (person) garante *m.*, *f.*; *tr.* garantire; farsi garante di, rispondere di; (comm.) avallare. **-or** *n.* garante *m.*, *f.*; mallevadore *m.*; (comm.) avallante *m.*

**guard** *n.* guardia; *to be on one's* —, stare in guardia; *to catch someone off his* —, cogliere qualcuno di sorpresa; *to put someone on his — against*, premunire qualcuno contro; (fencing) posizione di guardia; *on* —, in guardia; (mil.) guardia, scorta; *to be on* —, essere di guardia; *to come off* —, smontare di guardia; *the old* —, la vecchia guardia; — *of honour*, guardia d'onore; *the changing of the* —, il cambio della guardia; *the Guards*, la Guardia Reale; custode *m.*; guardiano; (rlwy.) capotreno; *—'s van*, bagagliaio; (of sword) guardamano, guardia; parafuoco.

**guard** *tr.* custodire; difendere; proteggere; sorvegliare; *intr.* stare in guardia; badare a; premunirsi. **-ed** *adj.* guardingo; cauto; prudente; circospetto. **-edly** *adv.* cautamente. **-edness** *n.* cautela; prudenza; circospezione.

**guardian** *n.* guardiano; custode *m.*; — *angel*, angelo custode; (leg.) tutore *m.*; (eccl.) guardiano. **-ship** *n.* (leg.) tutela; (eccl.) guardianato.

**guard-rail** *n.* ringhiera; (rlwy.) controrotaia; (naut.) battagliola, orlo di murata. **-room** *n.* (mil.) corpo di guardia; sala di disciplina.

**guardsman** *n.* membro dei reggimenti della Guardia Reale.

**gudgeon** *n.* (ichth.) ghiozzo; (mech.) perno.

**Guelf, Guelph** *n.* (hist.) guelfo.

**guerdon** *n.* guiderdone *m.*

**guer(r)illa** *n.* guerriglia; (person) guerrigliere *m.*, partigiano.

**guess** *n.* congettura; supposizione; *to have a* —, indovinare, congetturare, azzardare un'ipotesi; *to make a good* —, cogliere nel segno; *at a rough* —, a occhio e croce, a lume di naso, su per giù;

*tr., intr.* indovinare; congetturare, supporre; (USA) credere. **-work** *n.* congettura; *by -work*, a occhio e croce.

**guest** *n.* ospite *m., f.*; invitato; convitato; (of hotel) cliente *m., f.*; ospite *m., f.*; *paying* —, ospite pagante, dozzinante *m., f.*, pensionante *m., f.*

**guest-house** *n.* pensione; locanda. **-room** *n.* camera degli ospiti.

**guffaw** *n.* risata fragorosa; sghignazzata; *intr.* scoppiare in una grossa risata; sghignazzare.

**guidance** *n.* guida; direzione; *for your* —, per vostra norma, a titolo indicativo.

**guide** *n.* guida; cicerone *m.*; giovane esploratrice; consigliere *m.*; mentore *m.*; manuale *m.*; *railway* —, orario ferroviario; (fig.) insegnamento; direttiva; *tr.* guidare; condurre; dirigere; (fig.) *to be -d by*, seguire il consiglio di; (mil.) *-d missile*, missile teleguidato.

**guide-post** *n.* indicatore stradale; (fig.) indizio.

**guild** *n.* corporazione; associazione; (eccl.) confraternita; compagnia; (hist.) gilda; arte *f.*; scuola.

**guildhall** *n.* sede *f.* di corporazione; municipio.

**guile** *n.* astuzia; scaltrezza; insidia. **-ful** *adj.* astuto; scaltro; insidioso. **-less** *adj.* candido; semplice; ingenuo; senza dolo. **-lessness** *n.* candore *m.*; ingenuità; semplicità.

**guillemot** *n.* (orn.) uria.

**guillotine** *n.* ghigliottina; (paper) taglierina; *tr.* ghigliottinare; decapitare.

**guilt** *n.* colpa; colpevolezza. **-ily** *adv.* colpevolmente; come un colpevole. **-iness** *n.* colpevolezza. **-less** *adj.* senza colpa, innocente; (fig.) ignaro. **-lessness** *n.* innocenza.

**guilty** *adj.* colpevole; reo; *not* —, innocente; *to find someone* —, riconoscere qualcuno colpevole; *to find someone not* —, assolvere qualcuno; *to plead* —, confessarsi reo, ammettere la propria colpa; (fig.) che si sente colpevole, responsabile; — *conscience*, coscienza tormentata; — *of a mistake*, responsabile di un errore.

**guinea** *n.* ghinea; *half a* —, mezza ghinea.

**guinea-fowl, -hen** *n.* (orn.; cul.) faraona. **-pig** *n.* porcellino d'India, cavia *m.*

**Guinevere** *pr. n.* Ginevra.

**guise** *n.* aspetto; sembianza; guisa; foggia, abito; *under the — of*, sotto la maschera di; *in the — of*, in veste di.

**guitar** *n.* chitarra. **-ist** *n.* chitarrista *m., f.*

**gulch** *n.* burrone *m.*

**gules** *adj., n.* (herald.) rosso.

**gulf** *n.* (geog.) golfo; insenatura; *the Gulf Stream*, la Corrente del Golfo; abisso; (fig.) baratro; divergenza.

**gull** *n.* (orn.) gabbiano; *tr.* (fam.) ingannare, truffare, darla a bere a.

**gullet** *n.* gola; esofago.

**gullib-le** *adj.* credulo; ingenuo. **-ility** *n.* credulità; ingenuità.

**gully** *n.* burrone *m.*; gola; condotto di scolo, cunetta.

**gulp** *n.* sforzo nell'ingoiare; sorso; boccata; *at one* —, d'un fiato, d'un tratto; *tr.* ingoiare; trangugiare; tracannare; mandar giù; (fig.) inghiottire; soffocare; *intr.* singhiozzare.

**gum** *n.* gomma; — *arabic*, gomma arabica; — *elastic*, caucciù *m.*, gomma; (anat.) gengiva; (on eyes) cispa; *tr.* ingommare; incollare.

**gum-bearing** *adj.* gommifero.

**gumboil** *n.* ascesso alle gengive.

**gum-boots** *n.pl.* stivali di gomma.

**gumm-y** *adj.* gommoso; vischioso; aderente; appiccicoso; (of eyes) cisposo. **-iness** *n.* gommosità; viscosità.

**gumption** *n.* buon senso; praticità; spirito d'iniziativa.

**gum-shoes** *n.* scarpe di gomma, galosce *f.pl.* **-tree** *n.* albero della gomma; (slang) *to be up a -tree*, essere nei guai.

**gun** *n.* fucile *m.*; moschetto; schioppo; arma; rivoltella; pistola; cannone *m.*; pezzo d'artiglieria; bocca da fuoco; cacciatore; (slang) *a big* —, un pezzo grosso; *son of a* —, figlio d'un cane; (fig.) *to stick to one's -s*, tener duro; (of wind) *to blow great -s*, soffiiar forte; *intr.* (slang) *to be -ning for someone*, avercela con qualcuno.

**gun-barrel** *n.* canna di fucile. **-boat** *n.* (naut.) cannoniera. **-carriage** *n.* affusto di cannone. **-case** *n.* custodia per fucile. **-cotton** *n.* fulmicotone, nitrocotone. **-dog** *n.* cane *m.* da caccia.

**gunfire** *n.* sparatoria; fuoco d'artiglieria; cannoneggiamento, bombardamento; colpi *m.pl.* di cannoni; (mil., slang) sveglia.

**gun-licence** *n.* licenza di caccia.

**gun-man** *n.* (pop.) bandito armato, terrorista *m.* **-metal** *n.* bronzo rosso.

**gunner** *n.* artigliere, cannoniere *m.* **-y** *n.* arte di maneggiare cannoni; artiglieria.

**gunpowder** *n.* polvere *f.* da sparo; esplosivo; (hist.) *the Gunpowder Plot*, la Congiura delle Polveri.

**gun-runner** *n.* contrabbandiere *m.* di armi. **-running** *n.* contrabbando di armi.

**gunshot** *n.* colpo di fucile; *within* —, a portata di fucile, a un tiro di schioppo; — *wound*, ferita d'arma da fuoco.

**gun-shy** *adj.* che teme gli spari.

**gunsmith** *n.* armaiuolo.

**gun-stock** *n.* fusto di fucile.

**gunwale** *n.* (naut.) capo di banda, bastingaggio.

**gurgle** *n.* gorgoglio; mormorìo; *intr.* gorgogliare; mormorare.

**gush** *n.* sgorgo; rigorgo; zampillo; fiotto; getto; (fig.) effusione; torrente *m.*; *intr.* sgorgare; scaturire; zampillare; effondere; (fam.) entusiasmarsi, intenerirsi, parlare con effusione; *tr.* emettere a fiotti.

**gust** *n.* raffica; scroscio; colpo; (fig.) scoppio.

**gustation** *n.* degustazione.

**gusto** *n.* fervore *m.*; entusiasmo; slancio; piacere *m.*

**gusty** *adj.* burrascoso; ventoso; tempestoso; che soffia a raffiche.

**gut** *n.* budello; (mus.) minugia; *pl.* budella *f.*, intestini *m.*; (fig.; fam.) coraggio, fegato; *tr.* sventrare; sbudellare; (fig.) distruggere.

**gutta-percha** *n.* guttaperca.

**gutter** *n.* grondaia; scaricatoio; cunetta; rigagnolo; condotto; (fig.) strada, bassifondi *m.pl.*; *language of the* —, linguaggio della strada; *brought up in the* —, cresciuto nel fango; *to raise from the* —, raccogliere dalla strada; *the — press*, la stampa gialla; *tr.* fornire di grondaie, scanalare; *intr.* (of candle) scolare. **-snipe** *n.* monello; (in Naples) scugnizzo.

**guttural** *adj., n.* gutturale *f.*

**Guy**[1] *pr.n.* Guido.

**guy**[2] *n.* fantoccio di Guy Fawkes che si brucia la notte del 5 novembre; (fig.) spauracchio; macchietta; (USA) tipo, individuo; (rope) tirante *m.* a fune, corda di fissaggio.

**guzzl-e** *tr.* ingoiare; *intr.* gozzovigliare. **-ing** *n.* golosità. **-er** *n.* crapulone *m.*

**Gwendolen** *pr.n.* Guendalina.

**gym** *n. abbrev. of* **gymnasium, gymnastics** *q.v.*

**gymkana** *n.* gincana.

**gymnasium** *n.* palestra.

**gymnast** *n.* ginnasta *m., f.* **-ic** *adj.* ginnastico. **-ics** *n.* ginnastica.

**gynaecolog-y** *n.* (med.) ginecologia. **-ical** *adj.* (med.) ginecologico. **-ist** *n.* (med.) ginecologo.

**gypsum** *n.* gesso idrato.

**gyrat-e** *intr.* girare; roteare. **-ory** *adj.* giratorio; rotatorio.

**gyroscope** *n.* giroscopio.

**H, h** *n.* acca; (teleph.) — *for Harry,* acca come hotel; *H bomb,* bomba H; *to drop one's —'s,* non aspirare l'acca.

**ha** *excl.* ah!

**Habeas Corpus** *n.* (leg.) ordine *m.* (al direttore di un carcere) di far comparire un arrestato davanti a un giudice.

**haberdasher** *n.* merciaio. **-y** *n.* merceria; articoli di merceria.

**habiliment** *n.* abbigliamento, vestiario.

**habilitation** *n.* abilitazione.

**habit** *n.* abitudine *f.*; consuetudine *f.*; *to be in the — of, to make a — of,* avere l'abitudine di; *to break oneself of a —,* vincere un'abitudine, disabituarsi; *to get into the — of,* prendere l'abitudine di, abituarsi a; *to grow out of a —,* perdere un'abitudine con l'età; *drug —,* oppiomania, morfinomania; temperamento; costituzione; (eccl.) abito, tonaca; *lady's riding —,* amazzone *f.*; *tr.* vestire; *-ed in white,* vestito di bianco.

**habitab-le** *adj.* abitabile. **-ility, -leness** *n.* abitabilità.

**habitat** *n.* (bot.; zool.) habitat *m.*; ambiente *m.*

**habitation** *n.* abitazione; dimora; *fit for —,* abitabile.

**habitual** *adj.* abituale; consueto; solito; — *criminal,* recidivo; pregiudicato. **-ly** *adv.* di solito; abitualmente.

**habituate** *tr.* abituare; avvezzare.

**habitude** *n.* abitudine *f.*; consuetudine *f.*

**hack**[1] *n.* tacca; taglio; intaccatura; (football) calcio allo stinco; (tool) piccone *m.*; *tr.* tagliuzzare, tagliare, sminuzzare; *to — to pieces,* tagliare a pezzi; (football) colpire nello stinco.

**hack**[2] *n.* cavallo da nolo; ronzino; (fam.) scribacchino, imbrattacarte *m.*; *intr.* cavalcare al passo; cavalli da nolo; (fam.) fare un lavoro mal retribuito.

**hacking** *adj.* — *cough,* tosse secca.

**hackle** *n.* (text.) pettine da cardare; (of cock) penne del collo; (fishing) tipo di mosca artificiale; *tr.* (text.) pettinare.

**hackney** *n.* cavallo da nolo.

**hackney-carriage** *n.* vettura pubblica.

**hackneyed** *adj.* banale, comune, trito, molto usato.

**hack-saw** *n.* seghetto, sega per metalli.

**hackwork** *n.* lavoro faticoso e noioso.

**had** *p.def., part. of* **have,** *q.v.*

**haddock** *n.* (ichth.) *fresh —,* specie di merluzzo; *dried —,* baccalà *m.*

**Hades** *pr.n.* (myth.) Ade *m.*; Inferno.

**Hadrian** *pr.n.* Adriano.

**haematic** *adj.* (phys.) ematico; (pharm.) rimedio antianemico.

**haemo-globin** *n.* (phys.) emoglobina. **-philia** *n.* emofilia. **-rrhage** *n.* emorragia. **-rrhoids** *n.* (med.) emorroidi *f.pl.* **-static** *adj., n.* emostatico, antiemorragico.

**haft** *n.* manico; impugnatura; elsa; *tr.* fornire di manico.

**hag** *n.* vecchiaccia; megera; strega; lampreda.

**haggard** *adj.* sparuto; macilento; sofferente; (of hawk) non addomesticato.

**haggis** *n.* (cul., Scot.) frattaglie tritate, contenute in unsacco a modo di un salsiccione.

**haggle** *intr.* mercanteggiare, tirare sul prezzo; (fig.) cavillare.

**hagiograph-y** *n.* agiografia. **-er** *n.* agiografo. **-ic(al)** *adj.* agiografico.

**hagiolog-y** *n.* agiologia. **-ist** *n.* agiologo.

**hag-ridden** *adj.* tormentato dalle streghe, oppresso da incubi.

**Hague** *pr.n.* (geog.) *The —,* l'Aia.

**hail**[1] *n.* (meteor.) grandine *f.*, gragnuola; (fig.) *a — of bullets,* una raffica di pallottole; *tr.* far cadere come grandine; *intr.* grandinare.

**hail**[2] *n.* saluto; chiamata; appello; *within —,* a portata di voce; *excl.* ave!, salve!, salute!; *tr.* salutare; chiamare; *to — a taxi,* chiamare un tassì che passa; *intr. to — from,* essere oriundo di, essere nato a; *to — from Milan,* essere milanese.

**hail-fellow-well-met** *adj.* cordiale con tutti, espansivo.

**hail-stone** *n.* chicco di grandine. **-storm** *n.* grandinata.

**hair** *n.* capello; pelo; (collect.) capelli *m.pl.*; capigliatura; chioma; (of animals) pelo; (of horse) crine *m.*; *to do one's —,* pettinarsi; *to get one's — cut,* farsi tagliare i capelli; *to let one's — down,* sciogliersi i capelli, (fam.) sfogarsi; *to put one's — up,* raccogliere i capelli sulla nuca; *to lose one's —,* perdere i capelli; (fam.) *to keep one's — on,* mantenersi calmo; *to make someone's — stand on end,* far rizzare i capelli a qualcuno; *to tear one's —,* strapparsi i capelli, mettersi le mani nei capelli; *to split -s,* spaccare un capello in quattro, cercare il capello nell'uovo, cavillare; *not to turn a —,* restare impassibile, non battere ciglio. **-brush** *n.* spazzola per capelli. **-cut** *n.* taglio dei capelli; *to have a -cut,* farsi tagliare i capelli.

**hair-do** *n.* (fam.) acconciatura.

**hairdresser** *n.* parucchiere *m.*, parucchieria *f.*; barbiere *m.*

**hair-dryer** *n.* asciugacapelli *m.*; casco. **-dye** *n.* tintura per capelli.

**hairiness** *n.* pelosità.

**hairless** *adj.* senza capelli, calvo; glabro; (of animals) senza peli.

**hairpin** *n.* forcina; (fig.) — *bend,* brusca svolta, curva a forcella.

**hair-raising** *adj.* da far rizzare i capelli, emozionante. **-restorer** *n.* rigeneratore per capelli.

**hairsbreadth** *n.* spessore di un capello; (fig.) *to have a — escape,* salvarsi per miracolo; *to be within a — of,* essere a un pelo da.

**hair-shirt** *n.* cilicio. **-wash** *n.* lozione per capelli. **-wave** *n.* ondulazione.

**hairy** *adj.* peloso; irsuto; villoso.

**hake** *n.* (ichth.) nasello.

**halberd** *n.* alabarda. **-ier** *n.* alabardiere *m.*

**halcyon** *n.* (myth.; orn.) alcione *m.*; — *days,* giorni dell'alcione, (fig.) giorni sereni.

**hale** *adj.* sano; gagliardo; vegeto; robusto; *tr.* trascinare; tirare a forza.

**half** *adj.* mezzo; — *an hour,* una mezz'ora; (numis.) — *a crown,* una mezza corona; *adv.* (a) mezzo, a metà; — *past five,* le cinque e mezzo; — *as much again,* un'altra metà in più; — *asleep,* quasi addormentato; — *cooked,* cotto a metà; (slang) *it isn't — bad,* non è mica male; *not —!,* sfido!

**half** *n.* metà; mezzo; — *of the work,* metà del lavoro; *two and a —,* due e mezzo; — *and —,* mezzo e mezzo; (joc.) *my better —,* mia moglie, la mia metà; *to do things by halves,* fare le cose a metà; *to go halves with,* fare a metà con; *to fold in —,* piegare in due; (rlwy.) *return —,* biglietto di ritorno; (sport) *first —,* primo tempo; *second —,* secondo tempo, ripresa.

**half-back** *n.* (sport) mediano, sostegno **-baked** *adj.* cotto a metà; (fig.) inesperto, bazzotto; crudo, indigesto. **-binding** *n.* rilegatura in mezza pelle, in mezza tela. **-breed** *n.* meticcio. **-brother** *n.* fratellastro. **-caste** *n.* (numis.) mulatto. **-crown** *n.* mezza corona. **-hearted** *adj.* tiepido; esitante; abulico. **-holiday** *n.* mezza festa; sabato inglese. **-length** *n.* mezza lunghezza; ritratto a mezzo busto. **-light** *n.* penombra. **-mast** *n.* *at —,* a mezz'asta; *flag at -mast,* bandiera abbrunata. **-measure** *n.* mezza misura; provvedimento inadeguato. **-monthly** *adj.* bimensile; quindicinale; due volte al mese. **-moon** *n.* mezzaluna. **-pay** *n.* mezza paga, mezzo stipendio.

**halfpenny** *n.* mezzo penny; soldo; (fam.) *to get more kicks than halfpence,* ricevere più calci che carezze; *to be not a — the worse,* cavarsela a buon mercato.

**half-price** *n.* metà prezzo. **-seas-over** *adj.* (pop.) alticcio, mezzo brillo. **-sister** *n.* sorellastra. **-time** *n.* (sport) intervallo.

**-title** *n.* (typ.) occhiello, falso titolo *m.* **-tone** *n.* (typ.) mezzatinta.

**half-way** *adj., adv.* a mezza strada, a metà del cammino; *to meet someone —,* giungere ad un compromesso con qualcuno. **-witted** *adj.* scemo; cretino; ebete. **-year** *n.* semestre *m.* **-yearly** *adj.* semestrale; *adv.* semestralmente; ogni sei mesi, due volte all'anno.

**halibut** *n.* (ichth.) sogliola atlantica, ippoglosso.

**hall** *n.* sala; salone *m.*; aula; entrata; androne *m.*; vestibolo; atrio; *town —,* municipio, palazzo municipale; (country house) villa, casa signorile, maniero; (at university) collegio, casa dello studente; (dining) —, refettorio.

**hallelujah** *excl., n.* alleluia *m.*

**halliard** *n.* see **halyard.**

**hallmark** *n.* punzonatura (su oggetti d'oro e d'argento); (fig.) garanzia.

**hallo** *excl.* ehi, ohè, olà; (teleph.) pronto!; (on meeting friend) ciao.

**halloo** *intr.* gridare; vociare; *to — to someone,* chiamare qualcuno a gran voce; *tr.* (hunt.) aizzare (i cani).

**Hallow**[1] *n. All ~s,* Ognissanti *m.*; *~e'en,* vigilia d'Ognissanti.

**hallow**[2] *tr.* santificare; consacrare.

**hall-porter** *n.* (hotel) portiere *m.*; (block of flats) portinaio.

**hall-stand** *n.* attaccapanni *m. indecl.*

**hallucinat-e** *tr.* allucinare. **-ion** *n.* allucinazione; illusione; *to suffer from ~ions,* allucinarsi. **-ory** *adj.* allucinante; illusorio.

**halo** *n.* alone *m.*; aureola; gloria; *tr.* circondare di un'aureola.

**halt**[1] *adj.* zoppo; *intr.* zoppicare; (fig.) esitare; *~ing speech,* parlare esitante.

**halt**[2] *n.* sosta; fermata; tappa; *to come to a —,* fermarsi; (rlwy.) fermata; (mil.) alto; *tr.* fermare; arrestare; (mil.) far fare tappa a; *intr.* fermarsi; arrestarsi; (mil.) far tappa; fare alto; *—!,* alt!, alto!

**halter** *n.* cavezza; capestro.

**halve** *tr.* dividere a metà; ridurre alla metà.

**halyard** *n.* (naut.) amante *m.*; drizza.

**Ham**[1] *pr.n.* (bibl.) Cam.

**ham**[2] *n.* (anat.) natica; (cul.) prosciutto; *cooked —,* prosciutto cotto; *raw —,* prosciutto crudo; (slang) *— actor,* gigione *m.*; *intr.* (theatr.) interpretare in modo esagerato, esagerare; *tr. to — a part,* sovraccaricare un ruolo.

**hamadryad** *n.* (myth.; zool.) amadriade *f.*

**Hamburg** *pr.n.* (geog.) Amburgo. **~er** *n.* amburghese *m., f.*; (cul.) polpetta di carne di manzo e cipolla, hamburger *m. indecl.*

**hamitic** *adj.* camitico.

**Hamlet**[1] *pr.n.* Amleto.

**hamlet**[2] *n.* piccolo villaggio; frazione; paesino.

**hammer** *n.* martello; maglio; (of gun) cane *m.*; (of piano) martelletto; (auctioneer's) martello; *to come under the —,* essere venduto all'asta; (fam.) *hammer-and-tongs,* violentemente, con energia; *tr.* martellare; battere; picchiare; (Stock Exchange) dichiarare fallito; (fam.) dare una batosta a; *to — into one's head,* mettersi bene in testa; *to — out,* formulare, progettare; *intr. to — away at,* lavorare sodo a.

**hammock** *n.* amaca.

**hamper** *n.* paniere *m.*; cesto; canestro; (naut.) sovrastruttura, accessori ingombranti; *tr.* imbarazzare; intralciare; ostacolare.

**hamster** *n.* (zool.) criceto.

**hamstring** *n.* tendine del garetto; *tr.* azzoppare tagliando i tendini; (fig.) impedire.

**hand** *n.* mano *f.*; *clenched —,* pugno; *~'s breadth,* palmo; *at —,* a portata di mano, vicino, *by —,* a mano; *in —,* in mano, (fig.) in corso, a disposizione; *on —,* disponibile; *on the one —,* da un lato, da una parte; *on the other —,* d'altra parte, d'altronde; *~s off!,* via le mani!, non toccare!; *~s up!,* mani in alto!; *— in —,* mano in mano; *— to —,* corpo a corpo; *— over fist,* rapidamente; *from — to mouth,* alla giornata; *by show of ~s,* per alzata di mano; *to be a good — at,* essere bravo a; *to be — in glove with,* esser pane e cacio con, essere corpo e anima con; *to bind someone — and foot,* legare qualcuno mani e piedi; *to change ~s,* cambiare mano, passare in altre mani; *to force someone's —,* calcare la mano a qualcuno; *to get one's — in,* impratichirsi, farsi la mano; *to get something off one's ~s,* liberarsi di qualcosa; *to get the upper —,* prendere il sopravvento; *to get out of —,* diventare incontrollabile; *to keep one's — in,* tenersi in esercizio; *to lay ~s on someone,* mettere le mani addosso a qualcuno; *to lay ~s on something,* impadronirsi di qualcosa; *to lend a —,* dare una mano, aiutare; *to shake ~s with,* stringere la mano a; *to take a — in,* prendere parte a, partecipare a; *to win ~s down,* vincere facilmente; operaio, lavoratore, braccio; *pl.* personale *m.*; manodopera, (naut.) equipaggio; *all ~s on deck!,* tutti sul ponte!; calligrafia, mano; firma; (measure = 10·16 cm.) palmo, spanna; (cards) mano; (of clock) lancetta.

**hand** *tr.* dare; consegnare; porgere; passare; *to — down,* far scendere, aiutare a scendere, (fig.) trasmettere, tramandare; *to — in,* consegnare, rassegnare; *to — out,* distribuire; *to — over,* consegnare; *to — round,* distribuire, far circolare.

**handbag** *n.* borsetta.

**hand-barrow** *n.* carretto a mano.

**hand-bill** *n.* volantino; circolare *f.*; prospetto; programma *m.*; depliant *m. indecl.* **-book** *n.* manuale *m.*; guida.

**hand-brake** *n.* (motor.) freno a mano.

**handcuff** *tr.* ammanettare, mettere le manette a. **~s** *n.* manette *f.pl.*

**handful** *n.* manata; manciata, manipolo; (fig.) *only a — of people,* pochissima gente; (fam.) persona incontrollabile, bambino terribile.

**hand-gallop** *n.* piccolo galoppo.

**handgrip** *n.* stretta di mano; (on bicycle) manopola.

**handicap** *n.* svantaggio; aggravio; impedimento; (sport) handicap *m.,* abbuono; *tr.* intralciare; aggravare; impedire; (sport) (h)andicappare, assegnare l'handicap a.

**handicraft** *n.* mestiere *m.*; arte *f.*; lavoro manuale, artigianato. **-sman** *n.* artigiano.

**handiness** *n.* l'essere maneggevole; comodità; (naut.) manovrabilità.

**handiwork** *n.* lavoro fatto a mano; (pejor.) *that's his —,* ci ha messo la zampa lui, è una delle sue.

**handkerchief** *n.* fazzoletto.

**handle** *n.* manico; impugnatura; maniglia; ansa; (mech.) manovella, manubrio; (fig.) pretesto, occasione; (fam.) *to fly off the —,* montare su tutte le furie; *tr.* maneggiare; toccare con le mani; tastare; (fig.) trattare; *to — roughly,* manomettere, maltrattare; (comm.) commerciare in, trattare; (naut.) manovrare. **-bar** *n.* manubrio.

**handling** *n.* maneggiamento; manipolazione; trattamento; (fig.) svolgimento.

**handmaid(en)** *n.* ancella.

**hand-organ** *n.* organetto di Barberia. **-out** *n.* distribuzione; (journ.) comunicato alla stampa. **-press** *n.* (typ.) torchio a mano.

**handrail** *n.* ringhiera; corrimano; balaustrata.

**handshake** *n.* stretta di mano; (fig.) *golden —,* liquidazione generosa, compenso generoso per perdita d'impiego.

**handsome** *n.* bello; ben fatto; (fig.) generoso, liberale; discreto, considerevole. **-ness** *n.* bellezza; eleganza; (fig.) generosità.

**handwork** *n.* lavoro a mano; lavoro manuale; artigianato.
**handwriting** *n.* caligrafia, mano *f.*
**hand-written** *adj.* manoscritto, scritto a mano.
**handy** *adj.* (of person) abile, destro; (of things) maneggevole, comodo, utile; *to keep something —*, tenere qualcosa a portata di mano. **-man** *n.* uomo; impiegato manuale; chi sa fare un po' di tutto.
**hang** *n.* ricaduta; *to get the — of*, afferrare il senso di; *tr.* appendere; sospendere; attaccare; tappezzare; abbassare, chinare; montare; *to — a picture at an exhibition*, esibire un quadro ad una mostra; *to — (by the neck)*, impiccare; (fam.) *— it!*, all'inferno!; *I'll be -ed if*, che mi venga un accidente se; *intr.* pendere; penzolare; essere sospeso; attaccarsi; abbassarsi; (on gallows) essere impiccato; *to — by a thread*, essere sospeso a un filo; *to — fire*, svolgersi lentamente; *to — on to someone's arm*, attaccarsi al braccio di qualcuno; *to — around*, bazzicare intorno, gironzolare; *to — back*, restare indietro, (fig.) esitare; *to — on* (be dependent on), dipendere da, (persist) perseverare, (teleph.) rimanere all'apparecchio; *to — out*, *tr.* stendere, esporre, *intr.* sporgersi, (slang) abitare; *to — over*, incombere su, minacciare, (of smell) stagnare; *to — together*, mantenersi uniti; *to — up*, appendere, sospendere, (teleph.) riagganciare, riattaccare.
**hangar** *n.* hangar *m.*, aviorimessa, capannone *m.*
**hang-dog** *adj.* (fam.) abbattuto; *— look*, faccia patibolare.
**hanger** *n.* gancio; uncino; attaccapanni *m. indecl.*; coltellaccio.
**hanger-on** *n.* (fam.) scroccone *m.*, parassita *m.*
**hanging** *adj.* pendente; pensile; appeso; sospeso; *— garden*, giardino pensile; *n.* sospensione; (art) *— committee*, giuria di una esposizione; (on gallows) impiccagione *f.*; *pl.*, (in room) tappezzerie *f.pl.*, arazzi *m.pl.*, tendine *f.pl.*; (in church) paramenti *m.pl.*, addobbi *m.pl.*
**hangman** *n.* boia *m.*, carnefice *m.*
**hang-out** *n.* (fam.) ritrovo, abitazione; tana. **-over** *n.* (fam.) malessere *m.* dopo una sbornia.
**hank** *n.* matassa.
**hanker** *intr. to — after*, bramare, ambire, agognare a. **-ing** *n.* brama; forte desiderio; *to have a -ing for*, agognare.
**hanky** *n.* (fam.) fazzoletto.
**hanky-panky** *n.* (fam.) imbroglio; qualcosa di poco chiaro.
**Hannibal** *pr.n.* Annibale.
**Hanover** *pr.n.* (geog.) Annover *f.*, *m.* **-ian** *adj.* (h)annoveriano.
**Hanseatic** *adj.* (hist) anseatico.
**haphazard** *adj.* casuale; accidentale; (fig.) disordinato.
**hapless** *adj.* sfortunato; infelice.
**happen** *intr.* succedere; accadere; avvenire; *whatever -s*, qualunque cosa avvenga, in ogni modo; *as it -s*, per caso; *should it so —*, caso mai; *he -ed to tell me*, ebbe a dirmi; *to — again*, succedere un'altra volta; *to — upon*, trovare per caso; *do you — to have a pencil?*, hai per caso una matita? **-ing** *n.* avvenimento.
**happ-y** *adj.* felice; contento; lieto; beato; fortunato; propizio; *a — event*, un lieto evento *to be as — as the day is long*, essere felice come una Pasqua; *— Christmas!*, buon Natale!; *a — idea*, un'ottima idea. **-ily** *adv.* felicemente; fortunatamente, per fortuna. **-iness** *n.* felicità.
**happy-go-lucky** *adj.* casuale; spensierato; che prende il mondo come viene.
**Hapsburg** *pr.n.* (hist.) Absburgo, Asburgo.
**harangue** *n.* arringa; allocuzione; *tr.* arringare; *intr.* pronunciare un'arringa.
**harass** *tr.* molestare; tormentare; vessare; (mil.) bersagliare con continui attacchi. **-ing** *adj.* molesto; opprimente; vessatore.
**harbinger** *n.* precursore; foriere *n.*; messaggiero; annunziatore; *to be the — of*, annunciare; precedere.
**harbour** *n.* porto; *— station*, stazione marittima; (fig.) asilo; rifugio; *tr.* accogliere, dare asilo a; (leg.) *to — a criminal*, dare ricetto a un criminale; (fig.) nutrire. **-age** rifugio; asilo.
**harbour-master** *n.* capitano del porto.
**hard** *adj.* duro; *to become —*, indurirsi; *to be — of hearing*, essere duro d'orecchio; *to strike a — blow*, colpire duramente; (fam.) *to be as — as nails*, essere sano, avere poca sensibilità; *a — nut to crack*, un osso duro; (fig.) duro, severo, spietato; *a — man*, un uomo severo; *a — winter*, un inverno rigido; *— luck*, sfortuna; *— times*, tempi difficili; *— and fast*, rigido, immutabile; *to be — on*, essere severo con; *a — task*, un compito difficile; *— to please*, incontentabile; *— to understand*, difficile da capire, incomprensibile; *the — facts*, i semplici fatti; *— drinker*, bevitore accanito; *— battle*, combattimento strenuo; *— work*, lavoro faticoso; (leg.) *— labour*, lavori forzati; *adv.* forte; energicamente; *to work —*, lavorare sodo; *to look — at*, guardare fissamente; *to think —*, riflettere profondamente; *to try —*, provare e riprovare; *to rain —*, piovere dirottamente; *to drink —*, bere troppo; *to follow — after*, seguire da vicino; (fam.) *to be — up for*, essere a corto di; *— up*, al verde.
**hard-bitten** *adj.* tenace; duro. **-boiled** *adj.* (of egg) sodo; (fig.) sofisticato.
**harden** *tr.* indurire; temprare; *intr.* indurirsi; assodarsi; diventare duro.
**hard-fisted** *adj.* avaro. **-headed** *adj.* pratico, positivo. **-hearted** *adj.* duro; crudele; insensibile.
**hard-ihood** *n.* ardore *m.*; audacia; sfrontatezza. **-iness** *n.* vigore *m.*; robustezza; resistenza.
**hardly** *adv.* duramente; severamente; appena, a stento, a malapena, difficilmente; *I had — arrived*, ero appena arrivato; *he can — do that*, è difficile che faccia così; *— anyone*, quasi nessuno; *— anything*, quasi niente; *— ever*, quasi mai.
**hard-ness** *n.* durezza; fermezza; rigore *m.*; severità; difficoltà. **-ship** *n.* privazione; avversità; stento; disagio. **-ware** *n.* ferramenta *f.pl.*
**hard-wearing** *adj.* duraturo, durevole; resistente. **-working** *adj.* laborioso; diligente.
**hardy** *adj.* ardito, coraggioso; robusto, resistente, vigoroso.
**hare** *n.* lepre *f.*; *a young —*, un leprotto; (cul.) *jugged —*, lepre in salmì; (fam.) *as mad as a March —*, matto da legare; *to start a —*, dare una nuova svolta alla conversazione, creare un diversivo; *to run with the — and hunt with the hounds*, tenere il piede in due scarpe, fare il doppio giuoco; (provb.) *first catch your —*, non dir quattro se non l'hai nel sacco; *intr.* (fam.) correre come una lepre; *to — off*, scappare.
**harebell** *n.* (bot.) campanula turchina.
**hare-brained** *adj.* scervellato; sventato; insensato. **-lip** *n.* labbro leporino.
**harem** *n.* harem *m.*; gineceo.
**haricot** *n.* fagiuolo secco.
**hark** *intr.* ascoltare; *excl.* ascolta!, ascoltate!; (fam.) *— at him!*, ma sentire che cosa dice!; *to — back to something*, ritornare su qualcosa, tornare indietro col pensiero.
**harlequin** *n.* arlecchino, buffone *m.* **-ade** *n.* arlecchinata.
**harlot** *n.* meretrice *f.*, puttana; *to play the —*, fare la puttana, prostituirsi. **-ry** *n.* prostituzione.
**harm** *n.* male *m.*; danno; torto; *to do — to*, far male a, danneggiare; *no — done*, niente di male; *out of -'s way*, in luogo sicuro; *I meant no —*, non intendevo far male; *there's no — in trying*, si può sempre provare; *it will do more — than good*, ciò farà più male che

bene; (leg.) *bodily* —, vie di fatto; *tr.* nuocere a; far male a; danneggiare; far torto a; *not to — a hair of a person's head*, non torcere un capello a. **-ful** *adj.* nocivo; dannoso. **-less** *adj.* innocuo; inoffensivo.

**harmonic** *adj.*, *n.* armonico; *pl.* armonia. **-a** *n.* (mus.) armonica. **-on** *n.* armonica a bocca.

**harmoni-ous** *adj.* armonioso; melodioso. **-um** *n.* armonio, armonium *m.*

**harmonize** *tr.* armonizzare; mettere d'accordo; *intr.* armonizzare; andare bene insieme.

**harmony** *n.* armonia; accordo; *to be in — with*, essere d'accordo con; *to bring into* —, concordare.

**harness** *n.* bardatura; finimenti *m.pl.*; armatura; (for child) dande *f.pl.*; *to die in* —, morire sulla breccia, morire in pieno lavoro; *tr.* bardare, mettere i finimenti a; attaccare ad una carrozza; (eng.) *to — a waterfall*, imbrigliare una cascata. **-maker** *n.* sellaio.

**Harold** *pr.n.* Aroldo.

**harp** *n.* arpa; *intr.* suonare l'arpa, arpeggiare; (fam.) *to be always -ing on the same string*, toccare sempre lo stesso tasto, ripetere sempre la stessa cosa. **-er, -ist** *n.* arpista *m.*, *f.*, arpeggiatore.

**harpoon** *n.* rampone *m.*, fiocina; *tr.* colpire con la fiocina; ramponare. **-er** *n.* ramponiere *m.*

**harpsichord** *n.* clavicembalo.

**harpy** *n.* (myth.) arpia; (fam.) *old* —, vecchia megera.

**harridan** *n.* (fam.) vecchiaccia, megera.

**harrier** *n.* predatore; (dog) levriere *m.*; (fig., sport) corridore, atleta *m.*; (bot.) albanella.

**harrow** *n.* erpice *m.*; *tr.* (agric.) erpicare; (fig.) straziare; tormentare. **-ing** *adj.* straziante; atroce.

**Harry**[1] *pr.n.* Arrigo.

**harry**[2] *tr.* depredare; saccheggiare; *to — the enemy*, non lasciare al nemico nessuna tregua.

**harsh** *adj.* aspro; duro; agro; ruvido; severo; discordante, sgradevole. **-ness** *n.* asprezza; durezza; severità, crudeltà.

**hart** *n.* cervo; (bot.) *-'s tongue*, lingua cervina. **-shorn** *n.* corno di cervo; *(spirit of)* —, ammoniaca liquida.

**harum-scarum** *adj.*, *n.* (fam.) sventato; irresponsabile.

**harvest** *n.* raccolto; messe *f.*; mietitura; (of grapes) vendemmia; (fig.) frutti *m.pl.*; *— festival*, *— home*, festa della mietitura; *— moon*, luna di settembre; *— mouse*, arvicola, topo dei campi; *to get the — in*, fare il raccolto, mettere al riparo il raccolto; *to reap the* —, mietere; *tr.* mietere; raccogliere; fare il raccolto di. **-er** *n.* mietitore, mietitrice; (machine) mietitrice; *combine(d) -er*, mietitrebbia.

**hash** *n.* (cul.) carne tritata; (fig.) guazzabuglio, pasticcio; (fam.) *to make a — of*, fare un pasticcio di; *to settle someone's* —, mettere qualcuno a posto; *tr.* (cul.) tritare, impastare; (fam.) *to — up*, fare un guazzabuglio di; inventare, architettare.

**hasheesh, hashish** *n.* hascisc *m.*

**hasp** *n.* (on window) spagnoletta; (of padlock) cerniera; (text.) matassa; *tr.* agganciare, chiudere a lucchetto.

**hassock** *n.* poggiapiedi *m. indecl.*; (church) inginocchiatoio; (turf) zolla erbosa.

**haste** *n.* fretta; precipitazione; premura; *make —!*, fa presto!; *in great* —, in gran fretta; (provb.) *more — less speed*, chi ha fretta vada adagio.

**hasten** *tr.* affrettare; sollecitare; precipitare; accelerare; *intr.* affrettarsi; far fretta; precipitarsi; spicciarsi; *to — away*, partire in fretta; *to — back*, tornare in fretta.

**hast-y** *adj.* frettoloso; affrettato; rapido; pronto; irritabile, irascibile. **-ily** *adv.* in fretta; frettolosamente; precipitosamente. **-iness** *n.* precipitazione; fretta; irritabilità.

**hat** *n.* cappello; *bowler* —, bombetta; *top* —, *silk* —, cilindro, tuba; *straw* —, paglietta; *to keep one's — on*, rimanere coperto; *to put on one's* —, coprirsi, mettersi il cappello; *to raise one's* —, salutare levandosi il cappello; *to take one's — off*, levarsi il cappello, scoprirsi; *— in hand*, col cappello in mano, con deferenza; *-s off!*, giù il cappello!; (fam.) *to keep something under one's* —, mantenere segreto qualcosa, star zitto; *to send the — round*, fare una colletta; *to talk through one's* —, dire sciocchezze, vantarsi; (slang) *a bad* —, un farabutto; *my —!*, macchè! **-band** *n.* nastro da cappello. **-box** *n.* cappelliera. **-brush** *n.* spazzola per cappelli.

**hatch**[1] *n.* portello, sportello; (naut.) boccaporto; *under -es*, sotto coperta.

**hatch**[2] *tr.* (of birds) covare, far schiudere; (fig.) tramare, macchinare; *intr.* nascere; (provb.) *don't count your chickens before they are -ed*, non dire quattro finchè non l'hai nel sacco. **-er** *n.* incubatrice. **-ery** *n.* vivaio.

**hatch**[3] *tr.* (on map) tratteggiare, ombreggiare.

**hatchet** *n.* accetta; ascia; (fig.) *to bury the* —, riconciliarsi, far la pace.

**hatchment** *n.* (herald.) stemma *m.* funebre.

**hate** *n.* odio; *tr.* odiare; avere in odio; detestare; *to — doing*, fare malvolentieri; *I should — to be late*, mi dispiacerebbe essere in ritardo. **-ful** *adj.* odioso; detestabile. **-fulness** *n.* odiosità. **-r** *n.* odiatore; nemico.

**hat-ful** *n.* cappellata. **-less** *adj.* senza cappello; a testa nuda; scoperto. **-pin** *n.* spillone *m.*, da cappello. **-rack** *n.* rastrelliera per cappelli.

**hatred** *n.* odio; avversione; inimicizia; astio.

**hat-shop** *n.* cappelleria; (for women) modisteria.

**hatt-ed** *adj.* fornito di cappello, che porta un cappello. **-er** *n.* cappellaio; (fam.) *as mad as a -er*, matto da legare.

**hauberk** *n.* usbergo.

**haught-y** *adj.* altero; altezzoso, arrogante; borioso; superbo. **-iness** *n.* alterigia; arroganza; boria; superbia.

**haul** *n.* trazione; tiro; (of fish) retata; (fig.) guadagno, colpo; *tr.* tirare; trainare; rimorchiare; trasportare; (naut.) alare; (fig.) *to — over the coals*, criticare severamente, dare una lavata di testa a; *to — down the flag*, ammainare la bandiera; *to — up*, tirare su, issare, (fig.) citare davanti al tribunale, far comparire in giudizio; *intr.* (naut.) accostare; (of wind) cambiare, girare. **-age** *n.* trazione; trasporto; *-age contractor*, imprenditore di trasporti; (naut.) alaggio. **-ier** *n.* carrettiere *m.*; imprenditore di trasporti.

**haunch** *n.* anca; fianco; *to sit on one's -es*, accoccolarsi; (cul.) coscia, quarto.

**haunt** *n.* ricovero; ritrovo; luogo frequentato; (pejor.) covo; tana; *tr.* frequentare; praticare; visitare; *a -ed house*, una casa frequentata dagli spettri; (fig.) tormentare, perseguitare, ossessionare; *a -ed look*, un'aria allucinata. **-ing** *adj.* ossessionante; *a -ing melody*, una melodia che ricorre continuamente alla memoria.

**hautboy** *n.* (mus.) oboe *m.*

**Havana** *pr.n.* (geog.) Avana; *— cigar*, avana, sigaro avana.

**have** **1.** *aux.* avere; (with some verbs) essere; *to — got*, avere (*cf.* **get**). **2.** *tr.* avere, possedere; (foll. by *acc.* and *p. part.*), fare; *to — something repaired*, far riparare qualcosa; *to — to*, (foll. by *inf.*) dovere, avere da; *I — to go*, devo andare; *I — so many things to do*, ho tante cose da fare; prendere; ricevere; *I had rather*, preferirei; *you had better*, sarebbe meglio che tu; *to — a good time*, divertirsi; *to — a cold*, essere raffreddato; *to — had it*, essere spacciato; *to — it off with*, avere dei rapporti sessuali con; *to — it out with someone*, mettere

fine ad una disputa con qualcuno; *to — the worst of it*, avere la peggio; *to — someone in*, far entrare qualcuno, invitare qualcuno; *to — someone on*, canzonare qualcuno; *to — nothing on*, non aver niente da fare; (no clothes) essere nudo; *to be had*, lasciarsi ingannare; *I'm not having any*, non me la danno da bere; *you — me there!*, mi hai colto in fallo!, non so che dire; *to — someone up*, far comparire in giudizio. For other uses with nouns, adjectives and verbs see under respective headwords.
**have** *n.* (fam.) truffa; *pl. the -s*, gli abbienti; *the have-nots*, i non abbienti, i diseredati.
**haven** *n.* porto; rada; (fig.) asilo, rifugio, riparo.
**have-not** *n. the -s*, i diseredati (della sorte), i non abbienti.
**haversack** *n.* bisaccia; tascapane *m.*
**havoc** *n.* distruzione; strage *f.*; *to make — of, to play — with*, far strage di, distruggere, rovinare.
**haw** *n.* (bot.) bacca di biancospino.
**Hawaii** *pr.n.* (geog.) le isole Havai. **-an** *adj.*, *n.* havaiano.
**hawk**[1] *n.* (orn.) falco, sparviero; *eyes like a —*, occhi di lince; (fig.) persona rapace; *intr.* (hunt.) cacciare col falco; *to go -ing*, andare a caccia col falco. **-er** *n.* falconiere *m.*
**hawk**[2] *tr.* portare in giro per vendere; (fig.) mettere in giro; *intr.* fare il venditore ambulante. **-er** *n.* venditore ambulante.
**hawk**[3] *intr.* raschiarsi la gola.
**hawk-eyed** *adj.* dagli occhi di lince, di vista acuta.
**hawking** *n.* caccia col falco.
**hawk-moth** *n.* (ent.) smerinto. **-nosed** *adj.* dal naso aquilino, dal naso adunco.
**hawse** *n.* (naut.) cubia.
**hawser** *n.* (naut.) gomena, alzaia.
**hawthorn** *n.* (bot.) biancospino.
**hay** *n.* fieno; *to make —*, falciare ed esporre il fieno al sole; (fig.) *to make — while the sun shines*, approfittare di una buona occasione, battere il ferro finchè è caldo; *to make — of something*, mettere qualcosa in disordine, demolire qualcosa.
**haycock** *n.* meta; mucchio di fieno.
**hay-fever** *n.* febbre *f.* del fieno.
**hayfield** *n.* prato da falciare.
**hay-fork** forcone *m.* **-harvest** *n.* fienagione *f.* **-loft** *n.* fienile *m.*
**hay-making** *n.* falciatura; fienagione *f.* **-rick, -stack** *n.* fienile *m.*; pagliaio. **-seed** *n.* seme *m.* di erba. **-wire** *adj.* matto; (fam.) *to go -wire*, perdere le staffe.
**hazard** *n.* azzardo; rischio; pericolo; *game of —*, giuoco di azzardo; *to run the —*, correre il rischio; *at all -s*, ad ogni costo; (golf) ostacolo naturale; *tr.* arrischiare; azzardare. **-ous** *adj.* rischioso; azzardato; pericoloso.
**haze** *n.* foschìa; nebbia prodotta dal caldo; (fig.) confusione mentale.
**hazel** *n.* (bot.) nocciuolo, avellano, corilo; (colour) color nocciuolo.
**hazel-nut** *n.* (bot.) nocciuola, avellana.
**haz-y** *adj.* nebbioso; (fig.) vago; confuso; indistinto; nebuloso. **-ily** *adv.* confusamente; indistintamente. **-iness** *n.* foschìa; nebbiosità; (fig.) confusione; nebulosità.
**he** *pers. prn.* egli, esso; (emphatic) lui; (antecedent of *rel. prn.*) colui; *— who*, colui che; *— himself*, egli stesso, lui stesso; *attrib.* maschio; *n.* (fam.) maschio.
**head** *n.* testa, capo; *— of hair*, capigliatura; *to nod one's —*, annuire; *to shake one's —*, far cenno di no; *to keep one's —*, mantenersi calmo; *to lose one's —*, perdere la testa, (fam.) perdere la bussola; *a pound a —*, una sterlina a testa; *twenty — of cattle*, venti capi di bestiame; (leader) capo, dirigente *m.*, direttore, gerente *m.*; *attrib. — office*, sede *f.*; (on coin) testa; *-s or tails*, testa o croce; (geog.) capo, promontorio; (bot.) capolino; (naut.) prora; (of bed) capezzale *m.*; (of cane, etc.) pomo; (on liquid) schiuma; (of nail, etc.) capocchia; (of spear, etc.) punta; (of steam) pressione; (heading) rubrica, capitolo; (typ.) *running -s*, testate *f.pl.*; (fam.) *to be — over heels in love with*, essere innamorato alla follia di; *to be off one's —*, essere matto; *to be unable to make — or tail of*, non riuscire a raccapezzarsi; (provb.) *two -s are better than one*, quattro occhi valgono più di due.
**head** *tr.* colpire con la testa; dirigere, capeggiare, essere a capo di, essere in testa a; *to be — of the poll*, essere primo nello scrutinio; (letter, article, etc.) intestare, intitolare; *to — off*, intercettare, far deviare; *intr. to — (for)*, dirigersi (verso); (fig.) *to be -ing straight for*, andare diritto diritto verso.
**headache** *n.* mal di capo, mal di testa, emicrania; (fig.) preoccupazione; seccatura; guaio.
**headband** *n.* fascia; benda; (bookb.) capitello.
**head-dress** *n.* copricapo; acconciatura.
**headed** *adj.* munito di testa; (fig.) capeggiato (da); intitolato; (journ.) intestato.
**header** *n.* tuffo; caduta con la testa in avanti; (bldg.) mattone *m.* di punta.
**headgear** *n.* copricapo *m.*; (min.) incastellatura.
**head-hunter** *n.* cacciatore di teste.
**headiness** *n.* impetuosità; violenza; (of wine) qualità inebriante.
**heading** *n.* intestazione; rubrica; voce *f.*; titolo; categoria; capitolo.
**headland** *n.* (geog.) capo, promontorio.
**headless** *adj.* senza testa, senza capo; acefalo.
**head-light, -lamp** *n.* (motor.) faro anteriore, fanale *m.*; *to dip the -s*, abbassare i fari; *to turn on the -s*, accendere i fari.
**headline** *n.* titolo; intestazione; testata; (radio) *-s of the news*, sommario delle notizie.
**headlong** *adj.* precipitoso; *adv.* a capofitto, precipitosamente, a dirotto.
**headman** *n.* capo tribù.
**head-master** *n.* direttore didattico, preside *m.* **-mistress** *n.* direttrice di scuola.
**headmost** *adj.* primo; più avanzato.
**head-on** *adj.* frontale.
**head-phones** *n.* cuffia.
**headpiece** *n.* (fam.) testa, cervello; (helmet) elmo; (typ). testata.
**headquarters** *n.* (mil.) quartiere *m.* generale; (comm.) sede *f.*; direzione.
**head-rest** *n.* poggiacapo.
**headship** *n.* direttorato, primato.
**headsman** *n.* carnefice *m.*; boia *m.*
**head-stone** *n.* pietra tombale; (archit.) pietra angolare. **-strong** *adj.* testardo; caparbio; ostinato. **-way** *n.* progresso; cammino; (anat.) abbrivo; (of arch) altezza; *to make -way*, progredire, far strada. **-word** *n.* voce *f.*; rubrica.
**heady** *adj.* (of person) impetuoso; (of wine) che dà alla testa, inebriante.
**heal** *tr.* guarire; (fig.) sanare, rimediare; comporre; *intr.* guarire; (of wound) cicatrizzarsi. **-er** *n.* guaritore. **-ing** *adj.* curativo; salutare; salubre; *n.* guarigione; (of wound) cicatrizzazione.
**heal-all** *n.* panacea.
**health** *n.* salute *f.*; *— resort*, stazione climatica, luogo di cura; *— insurance*, assicurazione contro le malattie; *National Health Service*, Servizio Sanitario Statale, mutua. **-ful** *adj.* sano; salubre; salutare.
**health-y** *adj.* sano, in buona salute; robusto, vigoroso; salubre; (fig.) salutare. **-iness** *n.* (of person) salute *f.*; (of place) salubrità.
**heap** *n.* mucchio; cumulo; catasta;

ammasso; accumulazione; (fam.) gran numero, mucchio; *a — of*, molto, moltissimo, un mucchio di; *-s of*, moltissimi; *tr.* ammucchiare; accumulare; ammassare; accatastare; *to — on the measure*, colmare la misura; *to — praises on*, colmare di lodi; *to — a plate with cherries*, riempire un piatto di ciliegie.

**hear** *tr.*, *intr.* udire; sentire; intendere; sentir dire, venire a sapere; ascoltare; esaudire; (leg.) dare udienza a; *to — about*, aver notizie di; *to — from*, ricevere notizie da; *to — of*, sentir parlare di; *to — Mass*, ascoltare la messa; *excl.* *—! —!*, bene!, bravo! **-er** *n.* uditore; ascoltatore; *pl.* uditori *m.pl.* **-ing** *n.* udito; *within -ing*, a portata d'orecchio; *hard of -ing*, duro d'orecchi; udienza; (fig.) attenzione; il venire a sapere.

**hearken** *intr.* ascoltare; stare attento; prestare attenzione.

**hearsay** *n.* sentito dire; voce *f.*; diceria; *by —*, per sentito dire.

**hearse** *n.* carro funebre.

**heart** *n.* cuore *m.*; anima; animo; *his — is in the right place*, è un uomo di cuore; *to break one's — over*, crucciarsi per; *to break someone's —*, spezzare il cuore a qualcuno; *to have one's — in one's mouth*, avere il cuore in gola; *to put one's — and soul into something*, darsi anima e corpo a qualcosa; *to set one's — at rest*, mettersi il cuore in pace; *to take —*, farsi animo; *to lose —*, perdersi d'animo; *to take things to —*, amareggiarsi; (fig.) *at —*, in fondo; *by —*, a memoria; (med.) *— attack*, attacco cardiaco; *— disease*, malattia del cuore; *— failure*, collasso cardiaco; (cards) cuore.

**heartache** *n.* mal di cuore; (fig.) crepacuore *m.*; angoscia; accoramento.

**heart-beat** *n.* pulsazione del cuore; (fig.) batticuore *m.*; emozione.

**heartbreak** *n.* crepacuore *m.* **-ing** *adj.*straziante; faticosissimo, noiosissimo.

**heartbroken** *adj.* straziato; accorato, accasciato dal dolore; *to be —*, essere accorato, accorarsi.

**heartburn** *n.* (med.) anticuore *m.*; bruciore *m.* di stomaco. **-ing** *n.* rancore *m.*; malcontento; gelosia; invidia; risentimento.

**hearten** *tr.* incoraggiare; rincuorare; *intr.* prendere coraggio; rincuorarsi. **-ing** *adj.* incoraggiante.

**heartfelt** *adj.* cordiale; di cuore; sincero; schietto.

**heart-free** *adj.* che ha il cuore libero, illibato.

**hearth** *n.* focolare *m.*; camino; (industr.) suola, crogiulo.

**hearth-rug** *n.* tappeto steso davanti al camino.

**hearthstone** *n.* pietra del focolare; pietra pomice.

**hearti-ly** *adv.* di cuore, cordialmente; sinceramente; (fig.) assai, abbondantemente; *to eat —*, mangiare con appetito; (fam.) *to be — sick of*, essere più che stufo di. **-ness** *n.* cordialità, sincerità; (fig.) vigore *m.*; vigoria; espansività.

**heartless** *adj.* senza cuore; insensibile, spietato. **-ness** *n.* mancanza di cuore, insensibilità.

**heart-rending** *adj.* straziante; accorante. **-searching** *n.* esame *m.* di coscienza; lunga riflessione.

**heartease** *n.* (bot.) viola del pensiero.

**heart-shaped** *adj.* a forma di cuore.

**heart-sick** *adj.* abbattuto; scoraggiato. **-sore** *adj.* addolorato; accorato.

**heart-stirring** *adj.* commovente; emozionante. **-strings** *n.* legami affettivi. **-to-heart** *adj.* a cuore aperto, sincero; *n.* conversazione a cuore aperto.

**hearty** *adj.* cordiale; sincero; di cuore; caloroso; sano, vegeto; copioso; (effusive) espansivo.

**heat** *n.* calore *m.*; caldo; calura; *in the — of the day*, nelle ore calde; (fig.) fuoco; foga, vivacità; *in the — of the moment*, nella foga del momento; *to reply with —*, rispondere con vivacità; (of animals) foia, fregola; (med.) *prickly —*, volatica, lichene *m.*; (sport) eliminatoria; *dead —*, gara alla pari; *tr.* scaldare; riscaldare; *to — up*, riscaldare; (fig.) infiammare; *to — the imagination*, stimolare l'immaginazione, *intr.* scaldarsi; animarsi; *to get -ed*, accalorarsi.

**heat-absorbing** *adj.* assorbente del calore. **-conveying** *adj.* calorifero, conduttore del calore.

**heated** *adj.* riscaldato; (fig.) caloroso, caldo; animato, vivace.

**heater** *n.* riscaldatore, calorifero; scaldabagno; scaldino, scaldapiedi *m. indecl.*; scaldapiatti *m. indecl.*; *electric —*, stufa elettrica; *electric immersion —*, resistenza corazzata.

**heath** *n.* brughiera, landa; (bot.) erica, scopa.

**heathen** *adj.*, *n.* pagano; (collect.) *the —*, i pagani; (fam.) birbante *m.*, birichino. **-dom** *n.* paganesimo. **-ish** *adj.* paganeggiante; barbaro; incivile. **-ism** *n.* paganesimo; idolatria.

**heather** *n.* (bot.) erica, scopa.

**heating** *n.* riscaldamento; *central —*, termosifone, riscaldamento centrale; *to turn off the —*, spegnere il termosifone; *steam —*, riscaldamento a vapore.

**heat-stroke** *n.* colpo di sole. **-wave** *n.*ondata di calore; periodo di gran caldo, calura.

**heave** *n.* sollevamento; sforzo; ondeggiamento; (fam.) conato di vomito; *tr.* sollevare; alzare; buttare, gettare; emettere; (naut.) alare; *to — overboard*, gettare a mare; *intr.* (of sea) ondeggiare, gonfiarsi; (naut.) *to — in sight*, apparire all'orizzonte; *to — to*, mettersi in panna; *—!*, issa!; (fam.) recere, avere conati di vomito.

**heaven** *n.* cielo; paradiso; *to go to —*, andare in paradiso; *the seventh —*, il settimo cielo, il colmo della felicità; (fam.) *for -'s sake*, per amor del cielo; *good -s!*, santo cielo!; *thank —!*, grazie al cielo!; *to move — and earth*, fare sforzi inauditi. **-ly** *adj.* celeste, del cielo; divino; (fam.) delizioso. **-ward(s)** *adv.* verso il cielo.

**heaven-sent** *adj.* inviato dal cielo, provvidenziale.

**heavily** *adv.* pesantemente; fortemente; molto; assai; *— loaded*, sovraccarico; *to be fined —*, pagare una grossa multa; *to breathe —*, ansare; *to drink —*, bere molto; *to lose —*, perdere una forte somma; *to sleep —*, dormire profondamente; *to weigh — on*, pesare su; (of time) *to hang —*, passare lentamente.

**heaviness** *n.* pesantezza; gravezza; (fig.) tristezza; malinconia; languore *m.*

**heaving** *adj.* ondeggiante; palpitante; *n.* ondeggiamento; palpitazione.

**heavy** *adj.* pesante; (fig.) triste; grave; noioso; forte, violento; *— sea*, mare grosso; *to lie — on*, pesare su; *a — meal*, un pasto abbondante; *— rain*, pioggia dirotta; *— shower*, rovescio d'acqua; (chem.) *— water*, acqua pesante.

**heavy-handed** *adj.*, maldestro; severo. **-hearted** *adj.* malinconico; triste. **-laden** *adj.* sovraccarico; (fig.) oppresso.

**heavyweight** *n.* (boxing) peso massimo.

**hebdomadal** *adj.* ebdomadario, settimanale.

**Hebe** *pr.n.* (myth.) Ebe.

**hebetude** *n.* ebetismo; stupidità.

**Hebra-ic** *adj.* ebraico, ebreo. **-ism** *n.* ebraismo.

**Hebrew** *adj.* ebreo, ebraico; *n.* ebreo, israelita *m.*; ebraico, lingua ebraica; *— scholar*, ebraista *m.*

**Hebrides** *pr.n.* (geog.) Ebridi *f.pl.*

**Hecate** *pr.n.* (myth.) Ecate.

**hecatomb** *n.* ecatombe *f.*

**heckl-e** *tr.* (text.) pettinare; (pol.) sottoporre a domande imbarazzanti, interrompere. **-er** *n.*

(text.) pettinatore; (pol.) interruttore. **-ing** *n.* interruzioni imbarazzanti, domande rivolte ad un oratore per impedirlo di continuare.
**hectare** *n.* (=2·471 acres) ettaro.
**hectic** *adj.* etico, tisico; (fam.) movimentato.
**hecto-gram** *n.* (=3·527 oz.) ettogrammo, (fam.) etto. **-litre** *n.* (=22 gallons) ettolitro. **-metre** *n.* (=109·36 yds) ettometro.
**Hector**[1] *pr.n.* Ettore; (fig.) fanfarone, spaccone, prepotente *m.*
**hector**[2] *tr.*, *intr.* fare il prepotente, malmenare. **-ing** *adj.* prepotente, insolente.
**Hecuba** *pr.n.* (myth.) Ecuba.
**hedge** *n.* siepe *f.*; *quickset* —, siepe viva; (fig.) barriera, protezione, riparo; *tr.* assiepare; circondare con una siepe; (fig.) *to — a bet*, scommettere pro e contro; *intr.* (fig.) evadere a una domanda, evitare di compromettersi.
**hedge-hog** *n.* riccio, porcospino. **-hop** *intr.* (aeron.) sorvolare a quota minima. **-row** *n.* siepe divisoria.
**hedge-sparrow** *n.* (orn.) passera scopaiola.
**hedon-ism** *n.* edonismo, epicureismo. **-ist** *n.* edonista *m.*, *f.* **-istic** *adj.* edonistico.
**heed** *n.* cura; attenzione; *to pay — to*, fare attenzione a, badare a; *to take — of*, badare a, tener conto di; *tr.* badare a, prestare attenzione a, dare retta a. **-ful** *adj.* attento; accorto; vigile; *to be -ful of*, badare a. **-fulness** *n.* attenzione; cura.
**heedless** *adj.* disattento; stordito; noncurante; sbadato. **-ness** *n.* disattenzione; sbadataggine *f.*; negligenza.
**hee-haw** *n.* raglio d'asino; *intr.* ragliare.
**heel** *n.* calcagno; tallone *m.*; *Achilles'* —, tallone d'Achille; (of shoe) tacco; (of stocking) calcagno; *rubber* —, tacco di gomma; *stiletto* —, tacco a spillo; *down at* —, scalcagnato; *under the — of*, sotto il tacco di; *head over -s*, sottosopra, a capitombolo; *to turn head over -s*, fare i capitomboli; *to bring to* —, farsi ubbidire da; *to come to* —, (of dog) seguire (il padrone), ubbidire; *to cool*, (*to kick*) *one's -s*, aspettare a lungo; *to lay someone by the -s*, far imprigionare qualcuno; *to take to ones -s*, darsela a gambe, alzare il tacco; *to tread on someone's -s*, stare ai calcagni di qualcuno; *to turn on one's* —, girare sul tacco; (fam.) *-s up!*, vuotate i bicchieri!; (slang) farabutto, mascalzone *m.*
**heel** *tr.* colpire col tacco; (shoem.) mettere i tacchi a; seguire da presso; *intr.* (naut.) *to — over*, sbandare, coricarsi sul fianco.
**heel-tap** *n.* sopratacco; (fam.) residuo in fondo al bicchiere.
**hefty** *adj.* forte; gagliardo; robusto.
**Hegelian** *adj.* hegeliano, di Hegel.
**hegemony** *n.* egemonia.
**hegira** *n.* (hist.) egira.
**heifer** *n.* giovenca.
**heigh** *excl.* ehi!, eh!
**heigh-ho** *excl.* ahimè!, ohimè!
**height** *n.* altezza; altitudine *f.*; *six feet in* —, alto sei piedi; *what is your — ?*, quanto sei alto?; *— above sea level*, altitudine s. l. m. (sul livello del mare); altura, collina; cima; (fig.) più alto grado; colmo; culmine *m.*; apogeo; *the — of folly*, il colmo della follia; *the — of the season*, il culmine della stagione. **-en** *tr.* alzare, innalzare; (fig.) accrescere, aumentare; intensificare; far spiccare, mettere in rilievo; *intr.* crescere, aumentare; intensificarsi.
**heinous** *adj.* atroce; nefando; odioso. **-ness** *n.* atrocità; nefandezza; odiosità.
**heir** *n.* erede *m.* *— apparent*, erede in linea diretta; *— presumptive*, erede presunto; *sole* —, erede unico, erede universale. **-ess** *n.* erede *f.*, ereditiera. **-loom** *n.* (leg.) bene mobile spettante all'erede di famiglia; (fam.) *family -loom*, cimelio di casa.
**held** *p.def.*, *part.* of **hold,** *q.v.*
**Helen, Helena** *pr.n.* Elena.
**helic-al** *adj.* ad elica, a spirale, spiraliforme. **-oid** *adj.* elicoidale.
**Helicon** *pr.n.* (geog.) Elicona.
**helicopter** *n.* elicottero.
**helio-centric** *adj.* eliocentrico. **-graph** *n.* eliografo. **-graphy** *n.* eliografia. **-gravure** *n.* fotoincisione. **-therapy** *n.* (med.) elioterapia. **-trope** *n.* (bot.) eliotropio; (colour) porpora.
**helium** *n.* (chem.) elio.
**Hell** *n.* Inferno; (fig.) *gambling* —, bisca; (fam.) *go to — !*, va all'inferno!; *what the — is he doing?*, che diavolo fa?; *— for leather*, a spron battuto; *a — of a noise*, un fracasso infernale; *to make someone's life a* —, rendere un inferno la vita di qualcuno; *to raise* —, sollevare un putiferio; *to work like* —, lavorare accanitamente, sgobbare; (provb.) *the way to — is paved with good intentions*, la via dell'Inferno è lastricata di buone intenzioni.
**hell-cat** *n.* (fam.) megera, furia.
**hellebore** *n.* (bot.) elleboro, veratro.
**Hellen-e** *n.* greco, ellene *m.* **-ic** *adj.* greco, ellenico. **-ism** *n.* ellenismo. **-ist** *n.* ellenista *m.* **-istic** *adj.* ellenistico.
**hell-fire** *n.* fuoco d'inferno; pene *f.pl.* dell'inferno; *to go through* —, patire l'inferno. **-ish** *adj.* infernale, diabolico.
**hello** *excl.* olà!; (teleph.) pronto!
**helm** *n.* elmo; casco; (naut.) timone *m.*; *the man at the* —, il timoniere, (fig.) il direttore dell'impresa; *to take the* —, assumere la direzione; *the — of State*, il governo.
**helmet** *n.* elmo, elmetto; casco; *crash* —, casco da guidatore; *flying* —, casco da aviatore. **-ed** *adj.* con l'elmo in capo.
**helmsman** *n.* timoniere *m.*
**helot** *n.* (hist.) ilota *m.* **-ry** *n.* (hist.) ilotismo.
**help** *n.* aiuto; assistenza; soccorso; *to call for* —, invocare aiuto; *to be a great* —, essere di grande aiuto; rimedio; *there's no — for it*, non c'è rimedio; donna di servizio; *daily* —, donna a ore; *lady* —, governante *f.* di casa.
**help** *tr.* aiutare; assistere; soccorrere; dare una mano a; *can I — you?*, posso aiutar La?; *to — someone across the road*, aiutare qualcuno ad attraversare la strada; *to — the wounded*, soccorrere i feriti; (provb.) *God -s those who — themselves*, aiùtati che Dio t'aiuta; *so — me God!*, Dio è il mio testimone!; *to — down*, aiutare a scendere; *to — on*, aiutare ad andare avanti; *to — someone on with his coat*, aiùtare qualcuno ad indossare il capotto; *to — out*, aiutare a uscire, prestare aiuto; *to — over*, aiutare a sormontare; *to — up*, aiutare a salire, aiutare ad alzarsi; servire, dare; *can I — you to ...?*, posso darti ...?; *to — oneself to*, servirsi di, (pejor.) rubare; (fig.) evitare, fare a meno di; *it can't be -ed*, è inevitabile, non c'e rimedio; *I can't — laughing*, non posso fare a meno di ridere; *I can't — it*, non posso farci nulla; *I don't do more than I can* —, faccio solo ciò che è assolutamente necessario.
**helper** *n.* aiutante *m.*, *f.*, aiuto; assistente *m.*, *f.*; collaboratore; soccorritore; *voluntary* —, attivista *m.*, *f.*
**helpful** *adj.* utile; giovevole; vantaggioso; servizievole. **-ness** *n.* utilità; prontezza a dare aiuto, buona voglia.
**helping** *adj.* *a — hand*, una mano soccorritrice; *n.* il prestare aiuto; porzione; *second* —, porzione supplementare.
**helpless** *adj.* debole; impotente; senza aiuto; indifeso; *to be — in a matter*, non poterci far niente. **-ness** *n.* debolezza; incapacità; impotenza; mancanza d'iniziativa.
**help-mate, -meet** *n.* collaboratore; compagno; consorte *m.*, *f.*
**helter-skelter** *adv.* alla rinfusa,

alla diavola, disordinatamente, in disordine.

**helve** *n.* manico.

**Helvet-ia** *pr.n.* (geog.) Elvezia, Svizzera. **-ian, -ic** *adj.* elvetico, svizzero.

**hem**[1] *n.* orlo; orlatura; contorno; bordura; *tr.* orlare; fregiare; (fig.) *to — in*, cingere, rinchiudere, circondare, attorniare, accerchiare.

**hem**[2] *intr.* schiarirsi la voce; *to — and haw*, esitare, titubare.

**he-man** *n.* (fam.) uomo virile, vero uomo.

**hemi-** *pref.* emi-.

**hemi-cycle** *n.* emiciclo. **-demisemiquaver** *n.* (mus.) quarticroma, semibiscroma. **-sphere** *n.* emisfero. **-spheric(al)** *adj.* emisferico. **-stich** *n.* (prosod.) emistichio.

**hemlock** *n.* (bot.) cicuta.

**hemorr-hage** *n.* see **haemorrhage**. **-hoids** *n.pl.* see **haemorrhoids.**

**hemp** *n.* canapa; — *rope*, canapo; *Indian —*, cannacoro. **-en** *adj.* di canapa, canapino.

**hem-stitch** *n.* orlo a giorno; *tr.* fare l'orlo a giorno.

**hen** *n.* gallina; chioccia; — *bird*, uccello femmina; (joc.) *an old —*, una vecchia.

**henbane** *n.* (bot.) giusquiamo.

**hence** *adv.* di qui a; *six months —*, di qui a sei mesi; donde, quindi, perciò; *get thee —!*, via! **-forth, -forward** *adv.* d'ora innanzi, per l'avvenire, ormai.

**henchman** *n.* (hist.) paggio; (pol.) seguace *m.*; accolito; uomo di fiducia.

**hen-coop** *n.* stia; gabbia.

**hendecasyllab-le** *n.* endecasillabo. **-ic** *adj.* endecasillabo.

**hendiadys** *n.* (gramm.) endiadi *f.*

**hen-house** *n.* pollaio.

**henna** *n.* (bot.) alcanna; (cosmetic) ennè *m.*

**hen-party** *n.* convegno di sole donne.

**henpeck** *tr.* (of wife) malmenare (il marito). **-ed** *adj.* (fam.) dominato dalla moglie.

**Henrietta** *pr.n.* Enrica, Enrichetta.

**hen-roost** *n.* pollaio.

**Henry** *pr.n.* Enrico.

**hepatitis** *n.* epatite *f.*

**hepta-chord** *n.* (mus.) ettacordo. **-gon** *n.* (geom.) ettagono. **-gonal** *adj.* ettagonale. **-hedron** *n.* (geom.) ettaedro.

**Heptameron** *pr.n.* (lit. hist.) Eptamerone *m.*

**heptameter** *n.* (prosod.) ettametro.

**heptarchy** *n.* eptarchia.

**heptasyllabic** *adj.* eptasillabo.

**Heptateuch** *pr.n.* (bibl.) Eptateuco.

**her** *pers. prn.* (acc.) la; (dat.) le; (fam.) *it's —*, è lei; (after *prep.*) lei; *rfl.* si, se; *poss. adj.* suo, sua, suoi, sue.

**Heracles** *pr.n.* (myth.) Eracle.

**herald** *n.* (hist.) araldo; (fig.) messaggero nunzio; precursore; foriero; *tr.* annunziare; proclamare. **-ic** *adj.* araldico; *-ic bearings*, stemma gentilizio, divisa. **-ry** *n.* araldica.

**herb** *n.* erba; pianta erbacea; erba medica; — *shop*, negozio di erborista; — *tea*, tisana, infusione di erbe; — *of grace*, ruta. **-aceous** *adj.* erbaceo. **-al** *adj.* di erba, erbaceo; *n.* erbario. **-alist** *n.* erborista *m.* **-arium** *n.* erbario.

**Herbert** *pr.n.* Erberto.

**Herculaneum** *pr.n.* (geog.) Ercolano.

**Hercule-s** *pr.n.* Ercole; *the labours of —*, le fatiche d'Ercole; *the Pillars of —*, le Colonne d'Ercole. **-ean** *adj.* erculeo.

**herd** *n.* gregge *m.*; mandria; branco; (fig.) massa; moltitudine *f.*; *the — instinct*, l'istinto gregario; *the common —*, il volgo, la plebe; (person) mandriano, pastore; *tr.* condurre il bestiame, pascolare; (fig.) guidare, far entrare; *intr.* formare gregge; *to — together*, riunirsi in gregge. **-sman** *n.* mandriano, pastore *m.*

**here** *adv.* qui, qua, quaggiù; *from —*, da qui; *in —*, qui dentro; *up —*, qui su, quassù; (answering roll-call) presente!; — *I am*, son qui, eccomi qua; — *you are*, ecco qua, to'; — *it is*, eccolo; — *we are*, eccoci; *look —*, guarda!, senti!; — *goes*, ecco, si comincia; — *lies*, qui giace; — *and there*, qua e là; *that's neither — nor there*, ciò non importa; — *there and everywhere*, dovunque; — *and now*, subito; *-'s to you*, salute!, alla tua!; *my friend —*, questo mio amico; (excl.) *—!*, eh! **-abouts** *adv.* qui vicino, qui presso, all'intorno; *he doesn't belong -abouts*, non è di queste parti. **-after** *adv.* d'ora innanzi, in futuro; in seguito; *n. the -after*, l'altro mondo, l'al di là *m.*, la vita futura. **-at** *adv.* su ciò, al che, quando avvenne questo. **-by** *adv.* con questo mezzo, con la presente.

**heredit-y** *n.* eredità, ereditarietà. **-ary** *adj.* ereditario.

**herein** *adv.* in questo, qui; (comm.) qui accluso, qui allegato. **-after** *adv.* dopo; più avanti, qui sotto.

**hereof** *adv.* di questo; *upon receipt —*, ricevuta questa lettera.

**heresiarch** *n.* eresiarca *m.*

**here-sy** *n.* eresia **-tic** *n.* eretico. **-tical** *adj.* eretico.

**hereto** *adv.* fin qui, a questo; *annexed —*, qui allegato. **-fore** *adv.* prima, prima d'ora, fin qui; *as -fore*, come prima.

**here-under** *adv.* qui sotto, qui in calce. **-upon** *adv.* su questo, allora, con ciò. **-with** *adv.* qui accluso, con questo, con la presente.

**heritage** *n.* eredità; patrimonio; (fig.) retaggio.

**hermaphrodit-e** *adj.*, *n.* ermafrodite *m.* **-ic(al)** *adj.* ermafrodite, androgino.

**hermeneut-ic(al)** *adj.* ermeneutico. **-ics** *n.* ermeneutica.

**Hermes** *pr.n.* Ermes, Ermete.

**hermetic** *adj.* ermetico.

**hermit** *n.* eremita *m.*, *f.*, anacoreta *m.*, *f.*, romito. **-age** *n.* eremo, eremitaggio, romitorio.

**hermit-crab** *n.* (zool.) paguro.

**hernia** *n.* (med.) ernia.

**Hero**[1] *pr.n.* (myth.) Ero.

**hero**[2] *n.* eroe *m.*; (of novel etc.) protagonista *m.*; (fig.) persona celebre; — *worship*, culto degli eroi; ammirazione; (fam.) cotta.

**Herod** *pr.n.* (hist.) Erode.

**heroic** *adj.* eroico, di eroe; *n.* (prosod.) verso eroico; *pl.* (fig.) linguaggio pomposo; teatralità, stravaganza. **-al** *adj.* eroico.

**heroi-comic(al)** *adj.* eroicomico.

**heroin** *n.* (chem.) eroina.

**heroine** *n.* eroina; (liter.) protagonista *f.*

**heroism** *n.* eroismo.

**heron** *n.* (orn.) airone *m.*

**herpes** *n.* (med.) erpete *m.*

**herring** *n.* (ichth.) aringa; (fig.) *red —*, diversivo; *to draw a red —, across the trail*, menare il can per l'aia.

**herring-bone** *adj.* a lisca di pesce. **-pond** *n.* (joc.) l'Atlantico.

**hers** *poss. prn.* il suo, la sua, i suoi, le sue; *a book of —*, un suo libro.

**herself** *rfl. prn. nom. she —*, lei stessa, ella stessa; *acc.* si, (after *prep.*) se, se stessa; *by —*, da sola; (fig.) *she was not —*, non era in sè.

**Hertzegovina** *pr.n.* (geog.) Erzegovina.

**hertzian** *adj.* (phys.) hertziano.

**hesit-ancy** *n.* esitazione; titubanza. **-ant** *adj.* esitante; irresoluto; titubante.

**hesitat-e** *intr.* esitare, titubare, essere incerto; *not to — to*, non disdegnare di. **-ing** *adj.* esitante, incerto, titubante. **-ion** *n.* esitazione; *without -ion*, senza esitare, senz'altro.

**Hesperides** *pr.n.* (geog.) Esperidi *f.pl.*

**Hesperus** *pr.n.* (astron.) Espero.

**Hess-e** *pr.n.* (geog.) Assia. **-ian** *adj.* di Assia; (text.) tela di canapa.

**het** *adj.* (slang) *to be — up*, essere fuori di sè; *to get — up*, arrabbiarsi, uscire dai gangheri.

**hetero-dox** *adj.* eterodosso. **-doxy** *n.* eterodossia. **-geneity** *n.* eterogeneità. **-geneous** *adj.* eterogeneo. **-nomy** *n.* etero-

nomia. -**sexual** *adj.* eterosessuale. -**zygote** *n.* eterozigote *m.*
**heteronomy** *n.* eteronomia.
**hew** *tr.* tagliare; spaccare, fendere; *to — down*, abbattere; *to — out*, sbozzare. -**er** *n.* tagliatore; spaccalegna *m. indecl.* -**n** *p. part.* of **hew**; *adj.* tagliato; sbozzato; *-n timber*, legname rifilato.
**hexagon** *n.* esagono. -**al** *adj.* esagonale.
**hexahedron** *n.* (geom.) esaedro.
**hexameter** *n.* (prosod.) esametro.
**heyday** *n.* apogeo; apice *m.*; bei giorni *m.pl.*; fiore *m.*
**hiatus** *n.* (gramm.) iato; lacuna.
**hibernat-e** *intr.* svernare; essere in ibernazione; (fig.) passare l'inverno. -**ion** *n.* ibernazione; svernamento.
**hibernian** *adj.*, *n.* irlandese *m.*, *f.*
**hibiscus** *n.* (bot.) ibisco.
**hiccough, hiccup** *n.* singulto, singhiozzo; *to have (got) -s*, avere il singhiozzo; *intr.* avere il singhiozzo; *he -ed out an apology*, si scusò fra i singulti.
**hickory** *n.* noce *m.* d'America; legno di noce d'America.
**hid, hidden** *p. def.*, *part.* of **hide**; nascosto, celato.
**hide**[1] *n.* pelle *f.*; cuoio; pellame *m.*; (joc.) *to save one's —*, salvare la pelle; *to have a thick —*, aver la pelle dura, essere insensibile; *tr.* (tan.) spellare, scorticare.
**hide**[2] *tr.* nascondere; celare; *intr.* nascondersi; celarsi; *n.* nascondiglio.
**hide-and-seek** *n.* rimpiattino.
**hide-bound** *adj.* con la pelle aderente; (fig.) di mente ristretta; burocratico.
**hideous** *adj.* bruttissimo; orribile; orrendo. -**ness** *n.* bruttezza; spaventosità.
**hide-out** *n.* nascondiglio.
**hiding**[1] *n.* bastonatura, legnata; (sport) sconfitta, batosta.
**hiding**[2] *n.* il nascondere; *to go into —*, nascondersi, darsi alla macchia; *— place*, nascondiglio.
**hie** *intr.* correre; andare in fretta.
**hierarch** *n.* gerarca *m.* -**y** *n.* gerarchia.
**hieratic** *adj.* ieratico.
**hieroglyph** *n.* geroglifico. -**ic(al)** *adj.* geroglifico.
**Hieronymus** *pr.n.* Geronimo, Gerolamo.
**higgle** *intr.* lesinare sul prezzo; stiracchiare; cavillare.
**higgledy-piggledy** *adv.* alla rinfusa, a catafascio.
**high** *adj.* alto; elevato; (fig.) grande; sublime; eminente; superiore; *— altar*, altare maggiore; *the -est bidder*, il miglior offerente; *— colour*, colore acceso; *— gear*, quarta velocità; *— jump*, salto in alto; *— life*, gran mondo; *— Mass*, messa solenne; *— relief*, altorilievo; *— road*, strada maestra; *— school*, scuola media; *— sea*, mare grosso; *on the — seas*, in alto mare; *— speed*, alta velocità; *— spirits*, allegria; *— street*, via principale; *— tide*, alta marea; *— treason*, alto tradimento; *— wind*, vento forte; *— words*, parole grosse, parolacce *f.pl.*; *— and dry*, al secco, (fig.) a bocca asciutta; *— and mighty*, altezzoso; *with a — hand*, arbitrariamente; (of price) alto, caro, costoso; (of time) pieno, avanzato; (of voice) alto, acuto; *— summer*, piena estate; *it is — time for me to go*, è ora che me ne vada; (of food) frollo, alterato; *to smell —*, puzzare; (slang) *to get — (on)*, esaltarsi (a mezzo di).
**high** *adv.* alto, in alto; *to aim —*, mirare in alto; *to rise — in the esteem of*, crescere nella stima di; *— and low*, dovunque; *to play —*, giuocare forte; (of sea) *to run —*, essere grosso, (fig., of feeling) essere scosso; *— up*, in alto, *-er up the river*, a monte.
**high** *n.* il Cielo; l'Alto; *on —*, in Cielo; (meteor.) anticiclone *m.*, area anticiclonica.
**highball** *n.* whisky con ghiaccio.
**high-born** *adj.* nobile di nascita, di alto lignaggio.
**highbrow** *n.* intellettuale *m.*, *f.*, saccentone *m.*
**high-class** *adj.* superiore, di prima qualità, di prim'ordine.
**highfalutin(g)** *n.* (fam.) ampolloso.
**high-flown** *adj.* ampolloso, turgido. -**handed** *adj.* prepotente, arbitrario. -**jump** *n.* (slang.) *to be for the — jump*, prenderle.
**highland** *n.* altipiano, regione montuosa; *pl. the Highlands*, la Scozia settentrionale. -**er** *n.* montanaro, montanaro scozzese.
**highlight** *n.* (fig.) culmine *m.*, clou *m. indecl.*
**highly** *adv.* altamente, molto, assai; *— paid*, ben pagato; *to think — of*, tenere in molta considerazione.
**high-minded** *adj.* magnanimo, di mente elevata. -**ness** *n.* magnanimità; nobilità.
**high-necked** *adj.* accollato.
**highness** *n.* altezza; elevatezza; (title) Altezza; *His Royal Highness*, Sua Altezza Reale.
**high-pitched** *adj.* (of sound) acuto; (of roof) ripido. -**priced** *adj.* costoso, caro, dal prezzo alto. -**priest** *n.* sommo sacerdote; (fig.) pontefice *m.*; capo riconosciuto. -**principled** *adj.* di alti principi. -**ranking** *adj.* altolocato, importante. -**sounding** *adj.* pomposo, altisonante. -**spirited** *adj.* audace, ardito, vivace; (of horse) focoso.
**highway** *n.* strada pubblica, strada maestra, arteria; *— code*, codice *m.* stradale; *— robbery*, grassazione, rapina.
**highwayman** *n.* bandito; rapinatore; grassatore.
**hijack** *tr.* dirottare. -**er** *n.* dirottatore, pirata *m.* dell'aria. -**ing** *gerund* dirottamento (aereo).
**hik-e** *intr.* fare un'escursione a piedi, camminare. -**ing** *n.* escursione a piedi; *to go -ing*, fare una camminata, fare una escursione a piedi. -**er** *n.* escursionista *m.*, *f.* a piedi.
**hilari-ous** *adj.* ilare; allegro. -**ty**, -**ousness** *n.* ilarità; allegria.
**Hilary** *pr.n.* Ilario.
**hill** *n.* collina; colle *m.*; poggio; altura; *up — and down dale*, per monti e per valli, dovunque.
**hilliness** *n.* natura collinosa.
**hillock** *n.* monticello, collinetta, poggio.
**hill-side** *n.* pendìo di collina, pendenza. -**top** *n.* sommità di collina.
**hilly** *adj.* collinoso; montuoso; *— road*, strada a saliscendi.
**hilt** *n.* elsa; impugnatura; guardia di spada; *to prove up to the —*, dimostrare pienamente; *mortgaged up to the —*, gravato da fortissime ipoteche.
**hilum** *n.* (bot.) ilo.
**him** *pers. prn. acc.* lo, lui; *dat.* gli, a lui; (after *prep.*) lui; (with *rfl.* force) si, sè; *— who*, colui che.
**Himalaya** *pr.n.* (geog.) Imalaia.
**himself** *rfl. prn.* si, sè, se stesso; *he —*, egli stesso; *Michelangelo —*, lo stesso Michelangelo; *by —*, da solo.
**hind**[1] *adj.* posteriore.
**hind**[2] *n.* (zool.) cerva, daina.
**hind**[3] *n.* (poet.) contadino, villico.
**hinder**[1] *adj.* posteriore; *— part*, parte posteriore.
**hinder**[2] *tr.* impedire, ostacolare.
**hind-legs** *n.* gambe posteriori; (fam.) *to get up one's —*, alzarsi per protestare; sputare sentenze.
**hind-most, -ermost** *adj.* ultimo; ultimo di tutti; *everyone for himself and the devil take the hindmost*, si salvi chi può.
**Hindoo** see **hindu.**
**hindquarters** *n.* posteriore *m.*; anche *f.pl.*
**hindrance** *n.* impedimento; ostacolo; impaccio; (leg.) *without let or —*, senza impedimenti, liberamente.
**hindsight** *n.* (on gun) alzo, tacco; (fig.) senno di poi.
**Hind-u** *adj.*, *n.* indù *m.*, *f.* -**ustani** *n.* indostano.
**hinge** *n.* cardine *m.*; cerniera; ganghero; *off its -s*, scardinato; (fig.) perno; *tr.* incardinare, munire di cardini; *intr.* incardinarsi, imperniarsi; (fig.) dipendere.
**hinny**[1] *n.* (zool.) bardotto.
**hinny**[2] *intr.* nitrire.
**hint** *n.* accenno, cenno; indizio; allusione; *broad —*, allusione

evidente; *gentle* —, lieve accenno; *to drop someone a* —, dare un suggerimento a qualcuno, fare un accenno a qualcuno; *to give someone a few -s about*, fare a qualcuno degli accenni a proposito di; *to take a* —, intendere a volo; *pl. -s for housewives*, consigli per le massaie; *intr.* accennare; alludere; suggerire; insinuare; *to — at*, lasciar intendere, far intravvedere, accennare a.

**hinterland** *n.* retroterra, entroterra *m.*

**hip**[1] *n.* (anat.) anca; fianco; *to swing one's -s*, camminare ancheggiando; — *measurement*, misura delle anche; (lit., joc.) *to smite — and thigh*, bussare a santa ragione; (archit.) spigolo, displuvio.

**hip**[2] *n.* (bot.) ballerina.

**hip**[3] *n.* (fam.) depressione; *to have the* —, essere d'umore nero; *tr.* (fam.) seccare, rattristare.

**hip-bath** *n.* semicupio, mezza vasca da bagno. **-flask** *n.* fiaschetta tascabile. **-joint** *n.* giuntura conofemorale.

**hipparch** *n.* (Gk. antiq.) ipparco.

**hippety-hop** *adv.* balzelloni, saltellando.

**hippo-camp** *n.* (myth.) ippocampo; (ichth.) cavalluccio marino, ippocampo. **-centaur** *n.* (myth.) ippocentauro.

**Hippocrat-es** *pr.n.* Ippocrate. **-ic** *adj.* ippocratico.

**hippo-drome** *n.* ippodromo. **-griff** *n.* (myth.) ippogrifo. **-potamus** *n.* ippopotamo.

**hire** *n.* nolo, noleggio; affitto; *for* —, a nolo, (on taxi) libero; *to let out on* —, noleggiare; salario; *tr.* noleggiare, prendere a nolo; prendere in affitto; (let out) noleggiare, dare a nolo, dare in affitto; pagare, prezzolare; *-d assassin*, sicario; *-d ruffian*, guappo; (USA) *-d girl*, domestica; *-d man*, bracciante *m.*

**hireling** *n.* mercenario; prezzolato.

**hire-purchase** *n.* vendita a rate; *to buy on* —, comprare a rate.

**hir-er** *n.* noleggiatore. **-ing** *n.* noleggio; affitto.

**hirsute** *adj.* irsuto, peloso, ispido. **-ness** *n.* pelosità.

**his** *poss. adj.* il suo, la sua, i suoi, le sue, di lui; *poss. prn.* suo, sua, suoi, sue, di lui; *a book of* —, un suo libro; *it's no business of* —, è una faccenda che non lo riguarda.

**Hispanic** *adj.* ispanico.

**hiss** *n.* fischio, fischiata; sibilo; *tr., intr.* fischiare, sibilare; *to — off the stage*, far uscire dal palcoscenico con fischi. **-ing** *adj.* sibilante, fischiante; *n.* sibilio; fischiata.

**histolog-y** *n.* istologia. **-ic(al)** *adj.* istologico.

**historian** *n.* storico; storiografo.

**historiated** *adj.* istoriato.

**historic** *adj.* storico. **-al** *adj.* storico; basato sulla storia; *-al novel*, romanzo storico.

**historiograph-y** *n.* storiografia. **-er** *n.* storiografo. **-ic(al)** *adj.* storiografico.

**history** *n.* storia; manuale *m.* di storia; *ancient* —, storia antica, (fam.) roba vecchia; *natural* —, storia naturale; (fig.) passato; *to know the inner — of*, conoscere la verità su.

**histrion-ic(al)** *adj.* istrionico; teatrale, drammatico. **-ics** *n.pl.* istrionica; (fig.) teatralità, commedia.

**hit** *n.* colpo; botta; (fig.) successo; *to make a* —, avere un grande successo; *tr.* colpire; percuotere; battere; *to — someone a blow*, dare un pugno a qualcuno; *to — below the belt*, colpire a tradimento; *to — the nail on the head*, cogliere nel segno, indovinare; *to — the mark*, dare nel segno; *— or miss*, in ogni caso, alla buona; (slang) *to — the hay*, andare a dormire; *to — the right path*, trovare la giusta stada; *intr. to — against*, urtare contro, *to — back*, reagire, difendersi; *to — off*, imitare; *to — it off with*, andare d'accordo con; *to — on*, azzeccare; *to — out*, dare grandi colpi.

**hitch** *n.* colpo; strattone *m.*; balzo; intoppo, difficoltà; *without a* —, senza intoppi; (naut.) nodo; *tr.* tirare; *to — up one's trousers*, aggiustarsi i calzoni; legare, attaccare; *to — a horse to a carriage*, attaccare un cavallo alla carrozza; (fig.) *to — one's wagon to a star*, entrare nella scia di persona altolocata; (naut.) legare con gomene; *to — up*, attaccare; (fam.) *to get -ed*, sposarsi; *intr.* rimanere impigliato; *to — on to*, attaccarsi a (slang) fare l'autostop.

**hitch-hike** *intr.* fare l'autostop, viaggiare col sistema dell'autostop. **-hiking** *n.* autostop *m.*

**hither** *adj.* (geog.) citeriore; *adv.* (verso) qui, per di qua; *— and thither*, qua e là, su e giù. **-to** *adv.* finora, sinora; *as -to*, come per il passato, come prima.

**hitter** *n.* (sport) giuocatore che colpisce forte.

**hive** *n.* alveare *m.* (also fig.); arnia, bugno; (swarm) sciame *m.*; *tr.* far entrare, immagazzinare nell'arnia; *intr.* entrare nell'arnia; (fig.) *to — off*, separarsi dal gruppo, (comm.) dividere i beni di una società creando diverse società consociate.

**ho** *excl.* oh!, olà!, ohè!; (naut.) issa!; *westward* —, verso l'ovest.

**hoar** *adj.* (poet.) canuto, bianco.

**hoard** *n.* gruzzolo, peculio, tesoro; (fig.) scorta, mucchio; *tr.* ammassare, tesaurizzare; incettare, accaparrare. **-er** *n.* avaro; incettatore, accaparratore.

**hoarding**[1] gerund of **hoard,** *q.v.*

**hoarding**[2] *n.* palizzata; recinto provvisorio; *advertisement* —, tabellone *m.* d'affissione.

**hoarfrost** *n.* brina.

**hoariness** *n.* vetustà; candore *m.*; canizie *f.pl.*

**hoarse** *adj.* rauco, fioco; *to shout oneself* —, diventar rauco a forza di gridare. **-ness** *n.* raucedine, fiocaggine *f.*

**hoary** *adj.* bianco, canuto, dai capelli bianchi; vecchio, venerabile.

**hoax** *n.* burla, beffa; tiro birbone; mistificazione; *tr.* burlare, beffare; mistificare; giuocare un tiro a; (fam.) piantar carote. **-er** *n.* burlone *m.*; mistificatore.

**hob** *n.* mensola del focolare; (mech.) creatore.

**hobble** *n.* (for horse) pastoia; (fig.) zoppicamento; *tr.* mettere le pastoie a; *intr.* zoppicare, procedere a fatica (also fig.); *to — along*, avanzare zoppicando. **-dehoy** *n.* giovanotto goffo, zoticone *m.*

**hobby** *n.* hobby *m.*; passatempo; svago preferito.

**hobby-horse** *n.* cavalluccio di legno; (fig.) cavallo di battaglia.

**hobgoblin** *n.* folletto; spauracchio; babau *m. indecl.*

**hobnail** *n.* grosso chiodo da scarpe; bulletta. **-ed** *adj.* chiodato.

**hobnob** *intr.* (fam.) bere insieme, intrattenersi amichevolmente; *to — with*, frequentare.

**hobo** *n.* (USA) vagabondo.

**Hobson** *pr.n.* *-'s choice*, scelta forzata, mancanza di alternativa.

**hock**[1] *n.* (anat.) garretto.

**hock**[2] *n.* vino bianco del Reno.

**hock**[3] *tr.* (slang) impegnare.

**hockey** *n.* hockey *m.*; *ice* —, disco sul ghiaccio.

**hocus** *tr.* ingannare, imbrogliare, mistificare; drogare.

**hocus-pocus** *n.* gherminella; formula magica; abracadabra *m. indecl.*

**hod** *n.* (bldg.) giornello.

**hoe** *n.* zappa; sarchio, sarchiello; *rotary* —, erpice *m.* a stella; *tr.* zappare; sarchiare; (fam.) *to have a hard row to* —, avere una gatta da pelare. **-ing** *n.* zappatura; sarchiatura.

**hog** *n.* maiale *m.*; porco; *road* —, pirata *m.* della strada; *to go the whole* —, andare fino in fondo, arrischiare tutto; *tr.* inarcare; (horse's mane) tagliare; (fam.) mangiare ghiottamente; *to — the whole lot*, prendere tutto per sè. **-back, hog's back,** *n.* schiena d'asino; dorsale *f.* **-ged** *adj.* inarcato; (of horse's mane) tagliata corta. **-gish** *adj.* porcino, da porco, (fig.) bestiale; sporco.

**-gishness** *n.* porcheria; sudiceria.
**Hogmanay** *n.* (Scot.) vigilia di capo d'anno.
**hogshead** *n.* botte *f.* (della capacità di 54 galloni = 238 litri).
**hogwash** *n.* avanzi *m.pl.* di cucina per i porci; (fig.) robaccia.
**hoick** *tr.* (fam.) tirar su di scatto; (aeron.) far impennare.
**hoist**[1] *n.* montacarichi *m. indecl.*; ascensore; (naut.) ghinda; (fam.) spinta verso l'alto; *tr.* alzare, innalzare; levare, sollevare; *to — the anchor*, levare l'ancora; issare; (naut.) *-ing tackle*, paranco.
**hoist**[2] *part.* of **hoist**; *to be — with one's own petard*, tirarsi la zappa sui piedi.
**hoity-toity** *adj.* che si dà delle arie; altero; petulante; *excl.* chibò!
**hokey-pokey** *n.* see **hocus-pocus.**
**hold** *n.* presa; stretta; *to catch — of*, afferrare; *to get — of*, afferrarsi a, ottenere, trovare, capire; *to lay — of*, acchiappare; *to let go one's —*, abbandonare la presa; (fig.) ascendente *m.*; influenza; *to have a — over*, avere un ascendente su; punto d'appoggio, sostegno, impugnatura; (climbing) abbricagnolo; (naut.) stiva.
**hold** *tr.* tenere; *to — hands*, tenersi per mano; *to — oneself ready*, tenersi pronto; contenere; ritenere, credere, pensare; *to — one's breath*, trattenere il respiro; *to — one's tongue*, tacere; *to — at bay*, tenere a bada; difendere; *to — one's ground*, mantenere le proprie posizioni; occupare; *to — an office*, occupare una carica; *to — shares in*, avere delle azioni in; dirigere; *to — a meeting*, riunirsi; (teleph.) *to — the line*, rimanere all'apparecchio, non interrompere la comunicazione; *intr.* resistere, tenere; *the rope won't —*, la corda non resisterà; *— tight!*, tenetevi saldi; perdurare, continuare; *the fine weather won't —*, il bel tempo non perdurerà; *to — good*, restare valido; *to — by*, mantenere; *to — with*, approvare. FOLLOW. BY ADV. OR PREP.: *to — aloof*, tenersi in disparte; *to — back*, *tr.* trattenere, nascondere, *intr.* trattenersi, starsene indietro, esitare; *to — down*, abbassare, tenere in soggezione; *to — forth*, *tr.* offrire, stendere, *intr.* declamare, fare una dissertazione; *to — in*, imbrigliare, frenare; *to — off*, *tr.* tenere a distanza, respingere, *intr.* tenersi in disparte; *to — on*, non cedere, persistere, (teleph.) rimanere all'apparecchio, restare in linea; *to — on to*, aggrapparsi a; *to — out*, *tr.* stendere, offrire, *intr.* resistere, tener duro; *to — over*, tenere in sospeso; *to — together*, *tr.* tenere insieme, *intr.* restare uniti; *to — up*, elevare, alzare, fermare, ostacolare, ostruire, (with intent to rob) fermare per derubare.
**holdall** *n.* borsa, sacca.
**holder** *n.* proprietario; possessore; detentore; incaricato; recipiente *m.*; fodero, astuccio; manico.
**holding** *n.* proprietà, podere *m.*, tenuta; (of shares) pacchetto; *— company*, società finanziaria.
**hold-up** *n.* intoppo, intralcio, ingorgo; ritardo; rapina a mano armata.
**hole** *n.* foro; buco, buca; spiraglio; pertugio; apertura; breccia; *to bore a — in*, forare, bucare; (fam.) *to make a — in one's capital*, attingere ai propri capitali; *a square peg in a round —*, una persona inadatta al suo ambiente; (slang) *to put a — through someone*, ammazzare qualcuno; (of animal) tana, antro, covo; (pejor.) luogo noioso, brutto posto; *a godforsaken —*, un luogo sperduto; (fam.) *to find oneself in a —*, trovarsi nei guai; (mech.) *inspection —*, spia; (golf) buca; *tr.* bucare, forare; *intr.* bucarsi; (golf) fare una buca.
**holiday** *n.* giorno festivo, festa; *Bank —*, festa legale; vacanza; *pl.* le vacanze, le ferie; villeggiatura; *to take a —*, prendersi una vacanza; *to spend one's -s*, trascorrere le vacanze; *— camp*, campeggio; *— resort*, luogo di villeggiatura, stazione balneare, stazione marittima; *intr.* (fam.) trascorrere le vacanze, andare in vacanza. **-maker** *n.* gitante *m.*, *f.*; escursionista *m.*, *f.*; villeggiante *m.*, *f.*, turista *m.*, *f.*
**holiness** *n.* santità *f.*; *His —*, Sua Santità, il Santo Padre.
**Holland** *pr.n.* (geog.) Olanda; (text.) *holland n.* tela d'Olanda; *brown —*, lino grezzo. **-er** *n.* olandese *m.*, *f.*
**holler** *tr.*, *intr.* (fam.) gridare, urlare.
**hollow** *adj.* cav., concavo; vuoto; cupo, sordo, cavernoso; (fig.) vano, vuoto, falso, irreale; *— cheeks*, guance infossate; *adv. to beat someone —*, stravincere qualcuno; *n.* cavo; cavità; *— of the hand*, cavo della mano; (geol.) buca, depressione, avvallamento, vallata; *tr.* scavare, incavare; *-ed out*, sgusciato; *intr.* scavarsi, incavarsi. **-ness** *n.* cavità; (of voice) timbro cavernoso; (fig.) falsità, insincerità.
**holly** *n.* agrifoglio, leccio spinoso. **-hock** *n.* malvone *m.*; alcea.
**holm**[1] *n.* isoletta, golena.
**holm-(oak)**[2] *n.* (bot.) leccio.
**holocaust** *n.* olocausto.
**Holofernes** *pr.n.* (bibl.) Oloferne.
**holograph** *n.* documento olografo.
**holster** *n.* fondina.
**holy** *adj.* santo, sacro; consacrato, benedetto; *— orders*, ordini *m.pl.* sacri; *— water*, acqua santa, acqua benedetta; *Holy Ghost*, Spirito Santo; *Holy Land*, Terra Santa; *Holy See*, Santa Sede; *Holy Trinity*, Santa Trinità; *Holy Writ*, Sacra Scrittura; *the Holy of Holies*, il Santo dei Santi; (fig., pop.) Santo, sacro; *to have a — fear of*, avere una santa paura di; *a — terror*, un'ira di Dio; (of child) un piccolo diavolo; (of adult) *he's a — terror for women*, corre sempre dietro alle donne.
**holystone** *n.* pietra pomice.
**holy-water** *attrib.*, *adj.* *— basin*, acquasantiera; *— sprinkler*, aspersorio.
**homage** *n.* omaggio; atto di reverenza; *to pay — to*, rendere omaggio.
**home** *adj.* domestico, casalingo, familiare; nazionale; *— address*, indirizzo personale, domicilio; *for — consumption*, ad uso nazionale; *— industries*, industrie nazionali; *— journey*, viaggio di ritorno; *— life*, vita casalinga, vita di famiglia; *— news*, notizie nazionali; *— products*, prodotti nazionali; *— trade*, commercio interno; *— town*, città natia, luogo di nascita; *— truth*, verità spiacevole; (sport) *— ground*, terreno amico; *— match*, partita in casa; *the — team*, gli ospitanti, i padroni di casa; *adv.* a casa, in patria; *to come —*, tornare a casa, (from abroad) rimpatriare; *to get —*, arrivare a casa; *to see someone —*, accompagnare qualcuno a casa; *on the way —*, tornando a casa; (fam.) *that's nothing to write — about*, non è niente di cui vantarsi; (fig.) *to bring something — to someone*, aprire gli occhi a qualcuno; *to bring a charge — to someone*, accusare qualcuno; *it will come — to him some day*, un giorno se ne pentirà; *curses come — to roost*, le maledizioni ricadono su chi le lancia; *to go —*, andare a segno; *to screw —*, avvitare a fondo; *to strike —*, colpire nel vivo.
**home** *n.* casa, dimora, domicilio, abitazione, residenza, focolare domestico, famiglia; paese *m.*; patria; *at —*, a casa; *at — and abroad*, in patria e all'estero; *to be at —*, essere in casa, *to be at — on Wednesdays*, ricevere il mercoledì; *to be away from —*, essere fuori, essere in viaggio; *ancestral —*, casa paterna, casa degli antenati; *a — from —*, una seconda casa; *to feel at —*, sentirsi a proprio agio, sentirsi come a casa propria; *to give someone a —*, accogliere qualcuno in casa; *to have a — of one's own*, avere casa propria; *to go to one's last —*, morire, partire per

l'ultima dimora; *to keep the — going*, mandare avanti la baracca; *to leave* —, lasciare la casa paterna, abbandonare il tetto coniugale; *to make one's — with somebody* andare ad abitare con qualcuno; *to make oneself at* —, fare come a casa propria; *to set up a — of one's own*, mettere su casa propria; *to stay at* —, restare in casa, badare alle faccende domestiche; —, *sweet —!*, casa, dolce casa!; (provb.) *be it ever so humble there's no place like* —, casa mia, casa mia, per piccina che tu sia, tu mi sembri una badia; (provb.) *charity begins at* —, la carità incomincia a casa propria; *the — counties*, le contee intorno a Londra; *the Home Fleet*, la flotta metropolitana; *the Home Office*, il Ministero dell'Interno; *the Home Secretary*, il Ministro dell'Interno; *Home Rule*, autonomia, indipendenza; asilo, rifugio, ricovero, ospizio; — *for the blind*, ospizio dei ciechi; — *for dogs*, canile *m.*, pensione per i cani; — *of rest*, casa di riposo; *old people's* —, ricovero per i vecchi; *sailors'* —, casa della gente di mare; *Greece is the — of the arts*, la Grecia è la patria delle arti; *Oxford is the — of lost causes*, Oxford è l'asilo delle cause perse; (fig.) *to be at — with a subject*, essere pratico di una materia, avere una materia sulla punta delle dita; *to eat someone out of house and* —, vivere alle spalle di qualcuno; *nearer* —, più vicino; *to take an example nearer* —, senza andare a cercare più lontano; (bot.; zool.), ambiente *m.* naturale, elemento, habitat *m.*

**home** *intr.* (of pigeons) trovare la via di casa, tornare alla colombaia; (aeron.) tornare; cogliere nel segno.

**homecoming** *n.* ritorno a casa; ritorno in patria.

**home-grown** *adj.* nostrano, indigeno.

**homeland** *n.* patria, paese natio.

**homeless** *adj.* senza casa, senza tetto; *pl. the* —, i senza tetto. **-ness** *n.* l'essere senza tetto.

**homelike** *adj.* domestico, intimo, familiare.

**homeliness** *n.* modi casalinghi; semplicità; (USA) bruttezza.

**home-lover** *n.* casalingo, chi preferisce la vita di famiglia.

**homely** *adj.* casalingo; domestico; semplice; (USA) bruttino.

**home-made** *adj.* fatto in casa; casalingo.

**Homer**[1] *pr.n.* Omero. **-ic** *adj.* omerico; *-ic laughter*, risata omerica.

**homer**[2] *n.* piccione *m.* viaggiatore.

**home-sick** *adj.* nostalgico. **-ness** *n.* nostalgia. **-spun** *adj.* tessuto in casa; casalingo; (fig.) semplice, grossolano; *n.* stoffa tessuta in casa, panno grosso. **-stead** *n.* casa colonica; cascina; fattoria. **-ward** *adj.* di ritorno, che conduce a casa; *adv. -ward bound*, diretto in patria. **-wards** *adv.* verso casa, verso il proprio paese. **-work** *n.* compiti *m.pl.* fatti a casa.

**homicid-e** *n.* (person) omicida *m., f.*; (crime) omicidio. **-al** *adj.* omicida, micidiale.

**homily** *n.* omelia; (fam.) sermoncino.

**homing** *adj.* che torna a casa; — *pigeon*, piccione *m.* viaggiatore.

**homoeopathic** *adj.* (med.) omeopatico.

**homo-geneity, -geneousness** *n.* omogeneità. **-geneous** *adj.* omogeneo.

**homolog-y** *n.* omologia. **-ous** *adj.* omologo.

**homonym** *n.* (ling.) omonimo. **-ous** *adj.* omonimo. **-y** *n.* omonimia.

**homosexual** *adj., n.* omosessuale *m., f.* **-ity** *n.* omosessualità.

**homuncule, homunculus** *n.* omuncolo.

**hone** *n.* cota; *tr.* affilare; (mech.) levigare; smerigliare.

**honest** *adj.* onesto; integro; probo; bravo; leale; franco, sincero; — *people*, brava gente; (fig.) giusto; (of woman) casta, virtuosa. **-ly** *adv.* onestamente; *excl. -ly!*, davvero!; questo è il colmo! **-y** *n.* probità; onestà; integrità; buona fede; lealtà; sincerità; (bot.) lunaria.

**honey** *n.* miele *m.*; (fig.) dolcezza; (term of affection) tesoro. **-comb** *n.* favo; (metall.) falla; *tr.* crivellare. **-combed** *adj.* bucherellato, crivellato, reticolato. **-dew** *n.* melata. **-ed** *adj.* (fig.) dolce come il miele, sdolcinato, mellifluo. **-moon** *n.* luna di miele, viaggio di nozze; *intr.* trascorrere la luna di miele. **-suckle** *n.* caprifoglio, madreselva. **-wort** *n.* (bot.) cerinte *f.*

**honing** *n.* affilatura.

**honk** *intr.* (of wild duck) anatare; (motor.) suonare il clacson.

**honorarium** *n.* onorario.

**honorary** *adj.* onorario, onorifico, non retribuito; — *degree*, laurea ad honorem; — *member*, socio onorario.

**honorific** *adj.* onorifico; *n.* formula di cortesia.

**honour** *n.* onore *m.*; buon nome *m.*; *in — of*, in onore di, in omaggio a; *word of* —, parola d'onore; *to be an — to*, fare onore a; *to be on one's* —, essere legato dalla parola d'onore; *seat of* —, posto d'onore; *to consider something an* —, recarsi ad onore qualcosa; (provb.) *there is — among thieves*, cane non mangia cane; stima; considerazione; *to hold someone in* —, tenere qualcuno in grande considerazione; reputazione, castità; onorificenza; (leg.) *Your Honour*, Signor Giudice; (cards) onore; *pl.* onorificenze *f.pl.*, titoli *m.pl.*, decorazioni *f.pl.*; *-s list*, elenco delle onorificenze concesse; *military -s*, onori militari; *last -s*, onoranze funebri; *with -s*, con lode; *to take an -s degree*, laurearsi (specializzandosi in conformità con certi criteri); (fam.) *to do the -s of the house*, fare gli onori di casa.

**honour** *tr.* onorare, far onore a; stimare; venerare; *to — one's signature*, far onore alla propria firma; (comm.) accettare, accogliere. **-able** *n.* onorevole; venerando; onorato; spettabile, stimato; onesto; d'onore; *the -able member*, l'onorevole deputato; *right -able*, onorevolissimo; (courtesy title of peer's younger son) conte *m.* **-ableness** *n.* onorabilità, onorevolezza; probità.

**hood** *n.* (cost.) cappuccio; (motor.) cappotta; (photog.) paraluce *m.*; (of carriage) mantice *m.*; *tr.* incappucciare, fornire di cappuccio. **-ed** *adj.* cappucciato, incappucciato, a cappuccio; (fig.) coperto, nascosto.

**hoodlum** *n.* (slang) teppista *m.*

**hoodwink** *n.* (fam.) abbindolare, ingannare.

**hooey** *n.* (slang) *that's all —!*, sono frottole!

**hoof** *n.* zoccolo, unghia; *cloven* —, piede caprino; *tr.* colpire con lo zoccolo; (joc.) *to — it*, andare a piedi; *to — out*, scacciare a calci. **-ed** *adj.* che ha zoccoli, ungulato, unghiato.

**hook** *n.* uncino, gancio; — *and eye*, allacciatura a gancio; (fam.) *by — or by crook*, di riffa o di raffa; (slang) *to sling one's* —, andarsene; (fishing) amo; (agric.) falce *f.*; (naut.) gaffa, gancio; (boxing) gancio; *tr.* agganciare; prendere all'amo; (fam.) *to — a husband*, pescare un marito; *intr.* agganciarsi.

**hookah** *n.* narghilè *m.*

**hook-nose** *n.* naso aquilino, naso ricurvo. **-up** *n.* (radio) relais *m.*; (fam.) legame *m.*; alleanza.

**hookworms** *n.* (zool.) acantocefali *m.pl.*

**hooligan** *n.* teppista *m.*, giovinastro. **-ism** *n.* teppismo.

**hoop** *n.* cerchio; collare *m.*; (on gun) cerchiatura; (toy) cerchio; (cost.) guardinfante *m.*, crinolina; *tr.* cerchiare. **-er** *n.* bottaio.

**hoopoe** *n.* (orn.) upupa.

**hoot** *n.* ululo; fischio; (slang) *I don't care two -s*, non m'importa un fico secco; *tr.* fischiare; *intr.* ululare; chiurlare; fischiare; (motor.) suonare il clacson.

**hooter** *n.* sirena; (motor.) clacson *m. indecl.*
**hop**[1] *n.* (bot.) luppolo.
**hop**[2] *n.* salto; salterello; —, *skip and jump*, salto triplo; (fam.) *to be on the* —, essere in continuo movimento, essere in fuga; *to catch on the* —, balzellare; (aeron.) tappa; (pop.) ballo, ballonchio; *intr.* saltare, saltellare; *to — away*, andarsene saltellando; *to — over to Milan*, fare un salto a Milano; (fam.) *to — off, to — it*, svignarsela; (aeron.) decollare.
**hope** *n.* speranza; fiducia; attesa; *a ray of* —, un barlume di speranza; *to live on* —, cibarsi di speranza; *to live in — that*, vivere sperando che; *to give up* —, disperare; *to give up all* —, mollare; *forlorn* —, speranza vana, (fig.) impresa disperata; (provb.) *while there's life there's* —, finchè c'è vita c'è speranza; *what a —!*, magari!; *a pious* —, un pio desiderio; *tr., intr.* sperare, confidare, aspettarsi; *to — for something*, sperare qualcosa; *it is -d to*, si spera di; *to — for the best*, sperare per la meglio; *to — against* —, sperare fino all'ultimo; (comm.) *hoping to receive your reply*, nell'attesa di leggervi.
**hopeful** *adj.* pieno di speranza, fiducioso; promettente. **-ly** *adv.* fiduciosamente; con buone speranze. **-ness** *n.* fiducia; buona speranza.
**hopeless** *adj.* senza speranza; disperato; irrimediabile, irreparabile; *to give up as* —, rinunciare (a qualcosa) perchè impossibile; (fam.) *you're* —, sei incorreggibile. **-ness** *n.* disperazione; irreparabilità.
**hop-field, -garden** *n.* luppolaia, luppoliera.
**hoplite** *n.* (Gk. antiq.) oplite *m.*
**Hop-o'-my-thumb** *n.* Pollicino; (fig.) persona piccolissima, nano.
**hopper** *n.* chi salta; (mech.) tramoggia; (agric.) seminatoio; (naut.) chiatta.
**hop-picker** *n.* raccoglitore di luppolo. **-picking** *n.* raccolta del luppolo.
**hopscotch** *n.* giuoco del mondo.
**Hora-ce** *pr.n.* Orazio. **-tian** *adj.* oraziano.
**horde** *n.* orda; schiera, banda; (fig.) moltitudine *f.*
**horehound** *n.* (bot.) erba apiola; marrobbio.
**horizon** *n.* orizzonte *m.* **-tal** *adj.* orizzontale; (gymn.) *-tal bars*, sbarre *f.pl.* orizzontali. **-tality** *n.* orizzontalità.
**hormone** *n.* (phys.) ormone *m.*
**horn** *n.* corno; antenna; tentacolo; (mus.) corno; cornetto; tromba; (motor.) clacson *m.*, tromba; *to sound the* —, strombettare; — *of plenty*, cornucopia; *the -s of a dilemma*, i corni di un dilemma; (fig.) *to take the bull by the -s*, prendere il toro per le corna; *to draw in one's -s*, ritirarsi, ripiegar le ali.
**hornbeam** *n.* (bot.) carpino.
**hornbill** *n.* (orn.) bucero.
**hornblende** *n.* (miner.) anfibolo, orneblenda.
**horned** *adj.* cornuto, fornito di corna; a forma di corno.
**hornet** *n.* (ent.) calabrone *m.*; *to bring a -s' nest about one's ears, to stir up a -s' nest*, suscitare un vespaio.
**horniness** *n.* carattere corneo; callosità.
**hornpipe** *n.* danza di marinai.
**horn-player** *n.* (mus.) cornista *m., f.*
**horn-rimmed** *adj.* — *spectacles*, occhiali *m.pl.* cerchiati di corno.
**horny** *adj.* corneo, di corno; calloso, indurito.
**horo-graphy** *n.* gnonica. **-logy** *n.* orologeria. **-scope** *n.* oroscopo; *to cast the -scope*, fare l'oroscopo.
**horrible** *adj.* orribile; orrendo; spaventoso; (fam.) fastidioso, spiacevole. **-ness** *n.* orribilità.
**horrid** *adj.* orrido; orrendo; spaventoso; (fam.) antipatico, cattivo.
**horrif-y** *tr.* far inorridire; incutere terrore a; (fig.) scandalizzare, offendere; *to be -ed*, raccapricciarsi. **-ic, -ying** *adj.* orribile; orripilante.
**horror** *n.* orrore *m.*; spavento; disgusto; *the -s of war*, gli orrori della guerra; *to have a — of being . . .*, aver paura di essere . . .; *to have a — of doing something*, avere in odio di far qualcosa; (fam.) *a perfect* —, un orrore; *it gives me the -s*, mi fa venire i brividi.
**horror-stricken, -struck,** *adj.* atterrito; colpito da orrore.
**hors-d'œuvre** *n.* antipasto.
**horse** *n.* cavallo; *saddle* —, cavallo da sella; *draught* —, cavallo da tiro; *to ride a* —, cavalcare; *to mount a* —, montare a cavallo; *to let a — have its head*, dar la briglia a un cavallo; (fig.) *dark* —, vincitore inaspettato, acqua cheta; *to flog a dead* —, battere l'acqua nel mortaio; *to put the cart before the* —, mettere il carro innanzi ai buoi; *that's a — of a different colour*, quello è un altro paio di maniche; *to get on one's high* —, montare sul cavallo d'Orlando; *to work like a* —, lavorare come un cane; (provb.) *never look a gift — in the mouth*, a caval donato non si guarda in bocca; (mil.) cavalleria; *light* —, cavalleria leggera; (furniture) cavalletto; *tr.* fornire di cavalli; *to be well -d*, essere ben montato, avere un buon cavallo; *to — a mare*, far fare la monta a una cavalla.
**horse-artillery** *n.* artiglieria a cavallo.
**horseback** *adv. on* —, a cavallo.
**horse-box** *n.* stalla; (rlwy.) carro per trasporto cavalli. **-chestnut** *n.* ippocastano, castagno d'India.
**horsecloth** *n.* coperta da cavallo, gualdrappa.
**horse-dealing** *n.* traffico di cavalli; (fam., politics) compromesse *f.pl.*
**horse-doctor** *n.* veterinario.
**horseflesh** *n.* carne *f.* di cavallo; *to be a judge of* —, essere conoscitore di cavalli.
**horsefly** *n.* tafano.
**horse-guard(s)** *n.* guardia a cavallo.
**horsehair** *n.* crine *m.* (di cavallo).
**horse-laugh, -laughter** *n.* riso sgangherato, risata grassa.
**horseman** *n.* cavaliere *m.* **-ship** *n.* equitazione; maneggio.
**horseplay** *n.* giuoco scatenato; teppismo.
**horse-pond** *n.* abbeveratoio. **-power** *n.* cavallo vapore; potenza in cavalli vapore; *a ten horse-power car*, una macchina da dieci cavalli. **-race** *n.* corsa di cavalli, corsa ippica. **-racing** *n.* corse di cavalli, ippica. **-radish** *n.* (bot.) rafano; (cul.) cren *m.*, crenno. **-sense** *n.* buon senso.
**horseshoe** *n.* ferro di cavallo.
**horse-show** *n.* concorso ippico; mostra equina. **-tail** *n.* (bot.) coda di cavallo, equiseto. **-trainer** *n.* allenatore di cavalli. **-trough** *n.* abbeveratoio per cavalli.
**horsewhip** *n.* frusta, frustino, sferza; *tr.* sferzare, frustare.
**horsewoman** *n.* amazzone *f.*, cavallerizza.
**horsy** *adj.* di cavallo, cavallino; che affetta le usanze dei fantini.
**hortative, hortatory** *adj.* esortativo, esortatorio.
**horticultur-e** *n.* orticultura. **-al** *adj.* attinente all'orticultura; *-al show*, mostra d'orticultura. **-ist** *n.* orticultore.
**hosanna** *n.* osanna.
**hose** *n.* tubo per inaffiare; manichetta, naspo; (cost.) calze *f.pl.* **-pipe** *n.* tubo flessibile; manichetta.
**hosier** *n.* commerciante *m.* in calze. **-y** *n.* maglieria.
**hospice** *n.* ospizio, ricovero.
**hospitable** *adj.* ospitale.
**hospital** *n.* ospedale *m.*, nosocomio; clinica; — *attendant*, infermiere *m.*, — *nurse*, infermiera; — *ship*, nave *f.* ospedale.
**hospitality** *n.* ospitalità.

**hospitaliz-e** *tr.* far ricoverare in ospedale. **-ation** *n.* ricovero in ospedale.
**hospita(l)ler** *n.* (hist.) Ospitaliere *m.*
**host**[1] *n.* moltitudine *f.*; folla; schiera; armata; *the heavenly -s*, le milizie celesti; (fam.) *a — of people*, una folla di gente; *he is a — in himself*, è una persona che ne vale dieci.
**host**[2] *n.* ospite *m.*; anfitrione *m.*; oste *m.*, albergatore; (fam.) *to reckon without one's —*, fare i conti senza l'oste; (joc.) *mine —*, il padrone di un'osteria.
**host**[3] *n.* (eccl.) ostia consacrata.
**hostage** *n.* ostaggio; (fig.) pegno.
**hostel** *n.* ospizio, ostello, pensionato; dormitorio pubblico; *youth —*, ostello della gioventù. **-ry** *n.* osteria; albergo.
**hostess** *n.* ospite *f.*; padrona di casa; ostessa, locandiera; (aeron.) hostess *f.*; (in a night club) entraineuse *f.*
**hostil-e** *adj.* ostile; nemico; contrario; avverso. **-ity** *n.* ostilità; inimicizia; antagonismo; *pl.* (mil.) ostilità *f.pl.*
**hot** *adj.* caldo; ardente; *to be —*, (of person) aver caldo, (of thing) essere caldo, (of temperature) far caldo; *to get —*, scaldarsi, riscaldarsi; (fam.) *to get into — water*, mettersi nei guai; *piping —*, caldo bollente; forte, piccante; (fig.) ardente, impetuoso, veemente; *— news*, notizie recentissime; *— scent*, traccia fresca; *— temper*, temperamento impetuoso; *to be — on the track of*, stare alle calcagna di; *— war*, guerra calda; *adv.* ad alta temperatura; (fig.) *to blow — and cold*, cambiare continuamente opinione; *to go — all over*, avere delle vampate di caldo; (fam.) *he gave it me —*, mi ha fatto una strapazzata; *tr.* (fam.) *to — up*, riscaldare.
**hotbed** *n.* (hortic.) letto caldo, concimaia; (fig.) focolaio, fomite *m.*
**hot-blooded** *adj.* dal sangue caldo, ardente, impetuoso.
**hotchpotch** *n.* (cul.) carne *f.* in umido con cavoli; (fig.) miscuglio, guazzabuglio.
**hot-dog** *n.* (cul.) panino imbottito con salsiccia.
**hotel** *n.* albergo; *private —*, pensione; *— industry*, industria alberghiera; *— orchestra*, orchestrina.
**hotel-keeper** *n.* albergatore.
**hot-foot** *adv.* a gran velocità, in fretta. **-head** *n.* testa calda; *young -head*, giovane impetuoso. **-house** *n.* (hortic.) serra.
**hotly** *adv.* caldamente; vivamente; ardentemente; violentemente.
**hotness** *n.* calore *m.*
**hot-plate** *n.* scaldapiatti, scaldavivande *m. indecl.*
**hotpot** *n.* (cul.) spezzatino di carne con patate.
**hot-tempered** *adj.* irascibile, eccitabile; scalmenato; violento.
**hottentot** *n.* ottentotto.
**hound** *n.* cane da caccia, bracco, segugio; *a pack of -s*, una muta di cani; (fig.) canaglia; *tr.* cacciare con i cani; (fig.) perseguitare *to — on*, incitare, aizzare; *to - out*, cacciar via.
**hour** *n.* ora; *quarter of an —*, quarto d'ora; *half an —*, mezz'ora; *an — and a half*, un'ora e mezzo; *in an -'s time*, fra un'ora; *— by —*, d'ora in ora; *by the —*, all'ora; *three -s' journey*, viaggio di tre ore; *sixty miles an —*, cento chilometri all'ora; *pl.* orario; *office -s*, orario d'ufficio; *out of -s*, fuori delle ore di lavoro; *forty-hour week*, settimana lavorativa di quarant'ore; *the small -s*, le ore piccole; *to keep late -s*, andare a letto tardi; *to keep regular -s*, condurre una vita regolata; (eccl.) *book of -s*, libro d'ore; (fig.) momento, periodo; *the — has come*, il momento è giunto; *in an evil —*, in un brutto momento; *at the eleventh —*, all'ultimo momento; *the happiest -s of my life*, il periodo più bello della mia vita.
**hourglass** *n.* clessidra.
**hour-hand** *n.* lancetta delle ore.
**houri** *n.* uri *f. indecl.*
**hourly** *adj.* orario; ad ogni ora; *— train service*, servizio ferroviario con partenze ad ogni ora; (fig.) continuo; *in — dread*, nel continuo terrore; *adv.* ogni ora, una volta all'ora; d'ora in ora; (fig.) continuamente.
**house** *n.* casa; dimora; abitazione; *town —*, casa in città, palazzo; *country —*, villa; *apartment —*, palazzo; *public —*, osteria, bar *m.*; famiglia, casato; (pol.) *House of Commons*, Camera dei Comuni, (Ital. equiv.) Camera dei Deputati; *House of Lords*, Camera dei Pari (dei Lordi), (Ital. equiv.) Senato; (comm.) ditta, azienda, società; (theatr.) sala; pubblico; *empty —*, sala vuota; *full —*, pubblico numeroso, tutto esaurito; *second —*, secondo spettacolo; (poker) *full —*, full *m.*; (game) giuoco del lotto.
**house** *tr.* albergare; alloggiare; ricevere in casa; fornire di case, trovare alloggio per; immagazzinare, mettere al sicuro; (carpen.) incastrare.
**house-agent** *n.* mediatore di immobili.
**houseboat** *n.* casa galleggiante.
**housebreak-er** *n.* scassinatore; (bldg.) demolitore di case vecchie. **-ing** *n.* scasso; (leg.) effrazione, violazione di domicilo; (bldg.) demolizione di case vecchie.
**house-dog** *n.* cane *m.* da guardia. **-fly** *n.* mosca domestica.
**houseful** *n.* casa piena; *a — of children*, una nidiata di bambini.
**household** *n.* famiglia, casa; *attrib.* casalingo, di casa, domestico; *— expenses*, spese domestiche, spese di casa; *— goods*, lari, penati *m.pl.*; *— goods*, masserizie *f.pl.*; *— word*, parola sulla bocca di tutti; (mil.) *— troops*, i reggimenti della guardia reale. **-er** *n.* capo di famiglia, locatario di casa.
**housekeep-er** *n.* massaia; governante *f.* **-ing** *n.* governo della casa; faccende domestiche; economia domestica.
**housemaid** *n.* domestica; cameriera; donna di servizio; (med.) *-'s knee*, borsite *f.* prepatellare, (pop.) ginocchio della lavandaia.
**house-painter** *n.* decoratore; imbianchino; pittore edile. **-property** *n.* proprietà immobiliare, beni immobili. **-surgeon** *n.* chirurgo interno di ospedale.
**house-to-house** *attrib. adj.* di porta in porta.
**house-top** *n.* tetto; *to proclaim from the -s*, gridare dal tetto, annunciare pubblicamente.
**housewarming** *n.* festa per l'inaugurazione di una casa.
**housewife** *n.* massaia; donna di casa; (admin.) casalinga; (pronoun. hussif) astuccio da lavoro. **-ly** *adj.* di massaia, di padrona di casa, domestico.
**housing** *n.* alloggio, alloggiamento; *— estate*, quartiere *m.* residenziale; *— problem*, crisi *f. indecl.* degli alloggi; (mech.) custodia, gabbia; (motor.) scatola.
**hovel** *n.* casupola; tugurio; baracca; capanna; abituro.
**hover** *intr.* volteggiare, librarsi; svolazzare; *to — over*, librarsi sopra, sorvolare; (fig.) *to — round*, ronzare intorno; *to — on the brink*, esitare. **-craft** *n.* veicolo a cuscinetti d'aria.
**how** *adv.* come, in che modo; *— do you do?*, come sta?, (after introd.) piacere!, buon giorno!; *— much?*, quanto?; *— many?*, quanti?; *— often?*, quante volte?; *— far is it?*, quanto è lontano?; *— long does it take?*, quanto tempo ci vuole?; *— ever?*, *— on earth?*, come mai?; *— about a glass of wine?*, che ne dici di bere un po' di vino?; *conj.* che; (fam.) *he told us — he had seen you*, ci disse che ti aveva visto; *n. the — and the why*, il come ed il perchè. **-beit** *conj.* nondimeno; tuttavia.
**howdah** *n.* portantina fissata sul dorso di un elefante, castello.
**however** *adv.* comunque, per quanto, però, tuttavia, ciononо-

stante; *conj.* pure, nondimeno, tuttavia, però.

**howitzer** *n.* (artill.) obice *m.*

**howl** *n.* urlo; ululato; mugolio; lamento; grido lamentoso; *to give a — of rage*, urlare di rabbia; *— of pain*, grido di dolore; *intr.* urlare; ululare; gridare; mugolare; lamentarsi; piangere; gemere; *to — with laughter*, ridere a squarciagola; *tr. to — defiance*, lanciare una sfida; (fam.) *to — someone down*, costringere qualcuno di tacere a forza di interruzioni. **-er** *n.* urlatore; piagnone *m.*; (zool.) *-er monkey*, micete *m.*; (fig.) errore pacchiano, perla, strafalcione *m.* **-ing** *adj.* che urla, urlante; (fig.) terribile; *a -ing success*, un successo strepitoso.

**howsoever** *adv.* See **however.**

**hoyden** *n.* monella, ragazzaccia, maschietta.

**hub** *n.* mozzo (di ruota); (fig.) punto centrale, epicentro.

**hubbub** *n.* baccano; chiasso; schiamazzo; baraonda; un casa del diavolo.

**hubby** *n.* (fam., dimin. of **husband**) maritino.

**Hubert** *pr.n.* Uberto.

**huckaback** *n.* tela ruvida (per asciugamani).

**huckleberry** *n.* (bot., USA) mirtillo.

**huckster** *n.* rigattiere *m.*, rivendugliolo, trafficante *m.*

**huddle** *n.* folla, calca, confusione; *to go into a —*, affollarsi, accalcarsi; *tr.* ammucchiare, mettere insieme alla rinfusa; *to — oneself up*, raggomitolarsi; *intr. to — together*, accalcarsi, raggruzzolarsi.

**hue**[1] *n.* colore *m.*; tinta; sfumatura.

**hue**[2] *n.* clamore *m.*; *— and cry*, grido d'allarme; *to raise a — and cry against*, organizzare una campagna contro.

**huff** *n.* stizza; *to be in a —*, stizzirsi. **-iness** *n.* suscettibilità; petulanza. **-y** *adj.* suscettibile; stizzoso; stizzito.

**hug** *n.* abbraccio; amplesso; stretta; *to give someone a —*, stringere qualcuno fra le braccia; *tr.* abbracciare; stringere fra le braccia; (fig.) restare attaccato a; *to — oneself*, congratularsi con se stesso; (naut.) costeggiare.

**huge** *adj.* enorme; immenso; smisurato; vasto; madornale. **-ness** *n.* vastità; immensità; grandezza smisurata.

**hugger-mugger** *n.* confusione; segretezza.

**Hugh, Hugo** *pr.n.* Ugo.

**Huguenot** *pr.n.* (hist.) Ugonotto.

**hulk** *n.* carcassa; scafo di nave smantellata; (hist.) *the -s*, galera, bagno penale; (of person) grosso individuo; fannullone *m.*; (naut.) pontone *m.* **-ing** *adj.* (fam.) grosso, goffo, grossolano.

**hull** *n.* guscio; baccello; mallo; (of ship) scafo; *— down*, nave il cui scafo è ancora invisibile; *tr.* sgusciare, sbucciare, sgranare; (naut.) forare (lo scafo di una nave).

**hullabaloo** *n.* baccano, schiamazzo.

**hullo** *excl.* oh!; (fam., as greeting) salve!, buon giorno!, ciao!; *to say — to*, salutare; (teleph.) pronto!

**hum** *excl.* ehm!, uhm!

**hum** *n.* ronzio; mormorio; *tr.* canticchiare, cantare a bocca chiusa; *intr.* canticchiare, ronzare, mormorare; (fig.) *to make things —*, far frullare una faccenda; (fam.) *to — and haw*, esitare, titubare.

**human** *adj.* umano; *— being*, essere umano; (fam.) gentile; comprensivo.

**humane** *adj.* umano; umanitario; compassionevole; mite; (schol.) umanistico. **-ness** *n.* umanità; benevolenza; pietà.

**human-ism** *n.* (lit. hist.; philos.) umanesimo, umanismo. **-ist** *n.* umanista *m., f.* **-istic** *adj.* umanistico.

**humanitarian** *adj., n.* umanitario; filantropico. **-ism** *n.* umanitarismo; filantropia.

**humanity** *n.* umanità; il genere umano; gli uomini; bontà; benevolenza; clemenza; *pl. the humanities*, le discipline classiche.

**humaniz-e** *tr.* umanizzare; rendere umano; adattare all'uso umano. **-ation** *n.* umanizzazione.

**humankind** *n.* il genere umano, l'umanità.

**humanly** *adv.* da uomo, umanamente; *— speaking*, parlando da uomo.

**Humbert** *pr.n.* Umberto.

**humble** *adj.* umile, modesto, dimesso; *in my — opinion*, secondo il mio umile parere; *of — origin*, di origini umili; (fam.) *to eat — pie*, andare a Canossa; *tr.* umiliare, avvilire, mortificare; *to — oneself*, umiliarsi, abbassarsi. **-ness** *n.* umilità.

**humble-bee** *n.* see **bumble-bee.**

**humbug** *n.* (fam.) frottola, mistificazione, baia; (person) gabbamondo, ciarlatano; caramella alla menta; *tr.* corbellare, mistificare, abbindolare.

**humdrum** *adj.* monotono, banale; tedioso, noioso.

**humectation** *n.* umettazione.

**humid** *adj.* umido. **-ify** *tr.* inumidire. **-ity** *n.* umidità, umidezza.

**humiliat-e** *tr.* umiliare; mortificare. **-ing** *adj.* umiliante; mortificante. **-ion** *n.* umiliazione; mortificazione.

**humility** *n.* umiltà; sottomissione.

**humming** *adj.* ronzante; *n.* ronzio; mormorio.

**humming-bird** *n.* (orn.) colibrì *m. indecl.* **-top** *n.* trottola.

**hummock** *n.* poggio; altura; cresta di banchisa.

**humorist** *n.* umorista, *m., f.*; persona faceta, persona spiritosa.

**humorous** *adj.* arguto; dotato di senso dell'umorismo, spiritoso, divertente. **-ness** *n.* arguzia; umorismo.

**humour** *n.* umore *m.*; disposizione; stato d'animo; *good —*, buon umore; *bad —*, malumore *m.*; *to be in the — to*, aver voglia di, essere in vena di; *when the — takes me*, quando mi prende il capriccio; umorismo; comicità; senso dell'umorismo; *the — of the situation*, il lato comico della situazione; *broad —*, comicità grossolana; (med.) umore; *tr.* compiacere; assecondare; lasciar fare a. **-less** *adj.* privo di senso dell'umorismo.

**hump** *n.* gobba; bernoccolo; gibbosità; (geol.) collinetta, cresta; (fam.) *it gives me the —*, mi dà la malinconia; *tr.* curvare a forma di gobba; (fam.) portare sulle spalle. **-back, hunchback,** *n.* gobbo *m.*, gobba *f.* **-backed, hunchbacked** *adj.* gobbo, gibboso.

**humus** *n.* (hortic.) humus *m.*

**Hun** *n.* (hist.) Unno; barbaro; (pejor.) tedescaccio.

**hunch** *n.* gobba, gibbosità; (slang) *to have a — that*, avere il sospetto che; *tr.* incurvare, arcuare; (fam.) *to sit -ed up*, accovacciarsi.

**hundred** *card. num.* cento; centinaio; *two —*, duecento; *a — and one*, cent(o)uno; *— and first*, centunesimo, centesimo primo; *about a —*, circa un centinaio (di); *-s*, centinaia; *in (the year) 1900*, nel(l'anno) millenovecento; *to live to be a —*, campare cent'anni; *a — per cent*, al cento per cento. **-fold** *adj., n.* centuplo; *adv.* cento volte. **-th** *ord. num.* centesimo. **-weight** *n.* (approx.) mezzo quintale (50 kg.), cinquanta chili.

**hung** *p.def., part.* of **hang,** *q.v.*

**Hungar-y** *pr.n.* (geog.) Ungheria. **-ian** *adj., n.* ungherese *m., f.*; magiaro.

**hunger** *n.* fame *f.*; *to be faint with —*, cascare dalla fame; *to feel the pangs of —*, sentire lo stimolo della fame; appetito; (fig.) sete *f.*; *intr.* aver fame; (fig.) *to — for*, bramare, desiderare ardentemente.

**hunger-strike** *n.* sciopero della fame.

**hungrily** *adv.* con grande appetito; (fig.) avidamente.

**hungry** *adj.* affamato, famelico; *to be —*, aver fame; *to feel —*,

avere appetito, aver voglia di mangiare qualcosa; *the* —, gli affamati; (fig.) bramoso, assetato.
**hunk** *n.* grosso pezzo; tozzo.
**Hunnish** *adj.* unnico, degli Unni; (pejor.) barbaro.
**hunt** *n.* caccia; insieme *m.* dei cacciatori; (fig.) ricerca affannosa; *tr.* cacciare, andare a caccia di; (fig.) inseguire, scacciare; *to — down*, perseguitare, dar la caccia a; *to — for*, cercare affannosamente; *to — out*, scovare; *to — up*, frugare, cercare; *to have a -ed look*, avere l'aspetto di chi si sente inseguito. **-er** *n.* cacciatore; cavallo da caccia; orologio con calotta. **-ing** *n.* caccia; arte venatoria; *to go -ing*, andare alla caccia; (fig.) ricerca.
**hunting-box** *n.* casino da caccia. **-crop** *n.* frustino da caccia. **-ground** *n.* terreno da caccia; (fig.) *happy -ground*, paradiso.
**huntress** *n.* cacciatrice.
**huntsman** *n.* cacciatore; capocaccia *m.*, bracchiere *m.*
**hurdle** *n.* graticcio; barriera; siepe *f.* mobile; *pl.* (sport) corsa a ostacoli; *tr.* ingraticciare; *intr.* fare una corsa a ostacoli. **-r** *n.* fabbricante di graticci; (sport) ostacolista *m., f.*
**hurdy-gurdy** *n.* (mus.) organetto a manovella, ghironda; organetto di Barberia.
**hurl** *tr.* scagliare, scaraventare, lanciare; *to — back*, respingere.
**hurly-burly** *n.* (fam.) subbuglio, tafferuglio, baraonda.
**hurrah, hurray** *excl.* urrah!, evviva!, viva!
**hurricane** *n.* uragano; ciclone *m.*; (fig.) *a — of applause*, uno scroscio di applausi.
**hurricane-lamp** *n.* lampada chiusa, lanterna di sicurezza.
**hurried** *adj.* affrettato; frettoloso; precipitoso. **-ly** *adv.* in fretta frettolosamente.
**hurry** *n.* fretta; premura; *to be in a* —, aver fretta; *to write in a* —, scrivere in fretta; *no* —, non c'è fretta; (fam.) *you won't see him again in a* —, ci vorrà del tempo prima di rivederlo; *tr.* affrettare; sollecitare; far premura a; spronare; *intr.* affrettarsi, andare in fretta; sbrigarsi; *to — along*, camminare in fretta; *to — away*, scappare, andarsene in fretta; *to — back*, tornare in fretta; (fam.) *— up!*, sbrigati!
**hurt** *n.* dolore *m.*; male *m.*; ferita; lesione; (fig.) danno; offesa; *tr.* recare dolore a, far male a; ferire, offendere; *to get* —, essere ferito; *to — oneself*, farsi male; *to — someone's feelings*, offendere le suscettibilità di qualcuno; *to feel* —, rimanere offeso; *intr.* dolere, far male; *my foot -s*, mi duole il piede, mi fa male il piede; (fam.) *it won't — if*, non fa niente se. **-ful** *adj.* nocivo; dannoso; offensivo. **-fulness** *n.* dannosità; perniciosità.
**hurtle** *tr.* scagliare; lanciare; *intr.* scagliarsi; precipitarsi come un bolide.
**husband** *n.* marito, sposo, coniuge *m.*; *tr.* risparmiare, usare con frugalità, amministrare con parsimonia. **-man** *n.* agricoltore, colono. **-ry** *n.* agricoltura; lavoro dei campi; (fig.) frugalità; economia; *good -ry*, buona amministrazione.
**hush** *excl.* zitto!, silenzio!; *n.* silenzio; calma; quiete *f.*; *tr.* far tacere; imporre silenzio a; chetare; (fig.) calmare; ninnare; *to — up*, soffocare, far tacere; *intr.* tacere, star zitto.
**hush-hush** *adj.* (fam.) segretissimo. **-money** *n.* prezzo del silenzio.
**husk** *n.* guscio; buccia; loppa; *rice in the* —, risone *m.*; (fig.) involucro; *tr.* sgusciare; sbucciare; mondare; scartocciare.
**husk-y**[1] *adj.* pieno di bucce; secco; (of voice) rauco, fioco, velato. **-iness** *n.* raucedine *f.*
**husky**[2] *n.* cane *m.* esquimese.
**hussar** *n.* ussaro.
**Hussite** *pr.n.* (rel. hist.) Ussita *m.*
**hussy** *n.* (fam.) sgualdrina, sfacciatella.
**hustings** *n.* tribuna elettorale.
**hustle** *n.* spinta; spintone *m.*; *to get a — on*, sbrigarsi; *tr.* spingere; *intr.* affrettarsi, sbrigarsi, spingersi avanti, aprirsi la via a forza di spintoni. **-r** *n.* persona sbrigativa.
**hut** *n.* capanna; baracca; casupola; *Alpine* —, rifugio alpino, baita.
**hutch** *n.* conigliera; gabbia, (joc.) baracca.
**hutment** *n.* (mil.) baraccamento.
**hyacinth** *n.* (bot.) giacinto.
**hybrid** *adj.* ibrido; eterogeneo; *n.* ibrido. **-ism, -ity** *n.* ibridismo.
**hydra** *n.* (myth.) idra.
**hydrangea** *n.* (bot.) ortensia, idrangea.
**hydrant** *n.* idrante *m.*, bocca d'incendio.
**hydrat-e** *n.* (chem.) idrato. **-ion** *n.* (chem.) idratazione.
**hydraulic** *adj.* idraulico. **-s** *n.* idraulica.
**hydro** *n.* (fam.) see **hydropathic**.
**hydro-carbon** *n.* (chem.) idrocarburo. **-chlorate** *n.* (chem.) idroclorato. **-chloride** *n.* (chem.) idrocloruro. **-chloric** *adj.* (chem.) cloridrico. **-dynamic(al)** *adj.* idrodinamico. **-dynamics** *n.* idrodinamica. **-electric** *adj.* idroelettrico. **-foil** *n.* (naut.) aliscafo.
**hydrogen** *n.* (chem.) idrogeno; *— bomb*, bomba all'idrogeno; *— peroxide*, acqua ossigenata.
**hydrograph-y** *n.* idrografia. **-er** *n.* idrografo. **-ic(al)** idrografico.
**hydrolog-y** *n.* idrologia. **-ic(al)** *adj.* idrologico.
**hydro-lysis** *n.* (chem.) idrolisi *f.* **-mania** *n.* (med.) idromania. **-mancy** *n.* idromanzia. **-mel** *n.* idromele *m.* **-meter** *n.* (phys.) idrometro. **-pathic** *adj.* (med.) idroterapico; *n.* stabilimento idroterapico. **-pathy** *n.* idroterapia. **-phobia** *n.* (med.) idrofobia; (pop.) rabbia. **-phobic** *adj.* (med.) idrofobo. **-phone** *n.* (naut.) idrofono. **-plane** *n.* idroplano; idrovolante *m.*; (naut.) timone *m.* di profondità. **-sphere** *n.* (geog.) idrosfera. **-stat** *n.* idrostato, regolatore di livello. **-static(al)** *adj.* idrostatico. **-statics** *n.* idrostatica. **-therapeutic** *adj.* (med.) idroterapeutico. **-therapeutics** *n.* (med.) idroterapia. **-thermal** *adj.* idrotermale.
**hydrozoa** *n.* (zool.) idrozoi *m.pl.*
**hyena** *n.* (zool.) iena.
**hygien-e** *n.* igiene *f.* **-ic(al)** *adj.* igienico. **-ics** *n.* igiene *f.* **-ist** *n.* igienista *m., f.*
**Hymen** *pr.n.* (myth.) Imene; (anat.) imene *m.* **-eal** *adj.* imeneo, nuziale.
**hymn** *n.* inno, canto sacro, carme *m.*; laude *f.*; *tr.* inneggiare; *intr.* cantare inni. **-al** *n.* libro di inni; (eccl.) innario. **-ary** *n.* (eccl.) innario.
**hymn-book** *n.* libro di inni.
**hymn-ody** *n.* innodia. **-ographer** *n.* innografo. **-ologist** *n.* (mus.) innologo. **-ology** *n.* innologia.
**hyperbol-e** *n.* (rhet.) iperbole *f.* **-ic(al)** *adj.* (rhet.) iperbolico. **-ism** *n.* iperboleggiamento.
**hyperborean** *adj.*, *n.* iperboreo.
**hypercritical** *adj.* ipercritico.
**Hyperion** *pr.n.* (myth.) Iperione.
**hyper-sensitive** *adj.* ipersensibile. **-sonic** *adj.* supersonico. **-tension** *n.* (med.) ipertensione. **-thyroidism** *n.* (med.) ipertiroidismo. **-trophy** *n.* (med.) ipertrofia.
**hyphen** *n.* lineetta; trattino; (typ.) divisione. **-ate** *tr.* unire con lineetta, scrivere con lineetta.
**hypno-sis** *n.* ipnosi *f.* **-tic** *adj.* ipnotico. **-tism** *n.* ipnotismo. **-tist** *n.* ipnotizzatore. **-tize** *tr.* ipnotizzare.
**hypo** *n.* (photog.) iposolfito di soda.
**hypocaust** *n.* (Rom. antiq.) ipocausto.
**hypochondria** *n.* (med.) ipocondria. **-c** *adj.*, *n.* ipocondriaco.
**hypocr-isy** *n.* ipocrisia;

doppiezza. **-ite** *n.* ipocrita *m., f.* **-itic(al)** *adj.* ipocrito.
**hypodermic** *adj.* ipodermico; — *syringe*, siringa ipodermica.
**hypotenuse** *n.* (geom.) ipotenusa.
**hypothe-sis** *n.* ipotesi *f. indecl.* **-size** *tr., intr.* supporre, fare ipotesi. **-tic(al)** *adj.* ipotetico.
**hyssop** *n.* (bot.) issopo.
**hyster-ia** *n.* isteria; isterismo. **-ic(al)** *adj.* isterico. **-ics** *n.* attacco isterico; *to fall into -ics*, avere una crisi di nervi; *to fly into -ics*, dare in eccessi.

**I,**[1] **i** *n.* i *m., f.*; (teleph.) — *for Isaac*, i come Imola; *to dot one's -'s*, mettere i puntini sugli i.
**I**[2] *pers. prn.* io (but often omitted in Italian, when not emphatic); *it is* —, sono io; *I who*, io che; *here — am*, eccomi; (when Eng. conj. is rendered by Ital. prep.) me; *he eats more than — (do)*, mangia più di me (fam.) — *say !*, senta!; *n.* io *m.*
**iamb, iambus** *n.* (prosod.) giambo. **-ic** *adj.* (prosod.) giambo. **-ic** *adj.* (prosod.) giambico; *n.* giambo, verso giambico.
**Iberia** *pr.n.* (geog.) Iberia. **-n** *adj.* iberico; *n.* ibero.
**ibex** *n.* (zool.) stambecco.
**Icarus** *pr.n.* (myth.) Icaro.
**ice** *n.* ghiaccio; — *age*, epoca glaciale; *my feet are like* —, ho piedi di ghiaccio; *to turn to* —, agghiacciarsi; (fig.) *to skate on thin* —, toccare un argomento delicato; *to break the* —, rompere il ghiaccio; (fam.) *to cut no — with*, non fare impressione su; (cul.) gelato.
**ice** *tr.* ghiacciare, gelare, congelare; *to be -d over*, essere coperto di ghiaccio; *to be -d up*, essere bloccato dai ghiacci; mettere in ghiaccio; (cul.) glassare, candire.
**ice-axe** *n.* piccozza da alpinisti.
**ice-berg** *n.* iceberg *m.* **-blink** *n.* riverbero del ghiaccio.
**ice-block** *n.* (geog.) seracco. **-box** ghiacciaia, frigorifero. **-bound** *adj.* chiuso fra i ghiacci. **-breaker** *n.* nave *f.* rompighiaccio. **-cold** *adj.* freddo come il ghiaccio, glaciale, diaccio. **-cream** *n.* gelato; *-cream seller*, gelatiere *m.* **-fall** *n.* cascata di seracchi. **-floe** *n.* banchisa, banchiglia. **-hockey** *n.* disco sul ghiaccio. **-house** ghiacciaia; frigorifero; (fam.) *this room is like an -house*, in questa stanza si gela.
**Iceland** *pr.n.* (geog.) Islanda. **-er** *n.* islandese *m., f.* **-ic** *adj.* islandese; *n.* (ling.) islandese *m.*, lingua islandese.
**ice-pack** *n.* (geol.) banchisa; (med.) impacco di ghiaccio. **-pail** *n.* secchiello da ghiaccio. **-plant** *n.* (bot.) erba cristallina. **-rink** *n.* pista di pattinaggio.
**ichneumon** *n.* (zool.) icneumone *m.*
**ichnograph-y** *n.* icnografia. **-ic(al)** *adj.* icnografico.
**ichthyology** *n.* ittiologia.
**icicle** *n.* ghiacciuolo.
**iciness** *n.* gelidezza; freddo glaciale; frigidezza.
**icing** *n.* (cul.) glassa.
**icon** *n.* icona, icone *f.* **-oclasm** *n.* iconoclastia. **-oclast** *n.* iconoclasta *m.* **-oclastic** *adj.* iconoclastico. **-ographer** *n.* iconografo. **-ographic(al)** *adj.* iconografico. **-ography** *n.* iconografia. **-olatry** *n.* iconolatria. **-ology** *n.* iconologia. **-oscope** *n.* iconoscopio.
**ictus** *n.* (prosod.) arsi *f.*; accento ritmico; (med.; mus.) ictus *m.*
**icy** *adj.* gelido, gelato, ghiacciato; (poet.; med.) algido.
**idea** *n.* idea; concetto; nozione; opinione; impressione; *what a good — !*, che bell'idea!; *I hit upon the — of*, mi venne l'idea di; *I've no* —, non saprei; *to have got an — that*, aver l'impressione che; *strange -s*, opinioni strambe; intenzione; *the young* —, i giovani, la gioventù.
**ideal** *adj., n.* ideale *m.* **-ism** *n.* idealismo. **-list** *n.* idealista *m., f.* **-istic** *adj.* idealistico. **-ity** *n.* idealità. **-ization** *n.* idealizzazione. **-ize** *tr.* idealizzare.
**identical** *adj.* identico; uguale; (med.) — *twins*, gemelli *m.pl.* monozigotici.
**identif-y** *tr.* identificare; constatare l'identità di; *to — oneself with*, identificarsi con, associarsi strettamente con. **-iable** *adj.* identificabile. **-ication** *n.* identificazione; riconoscimento; *-ication card*, carta d'identità; *-ication mark*, contrassegno; *-ication parade*, confronto all'americana.
**identity** *n.* identità; *to prove one's* —, stabilire la propria identità; *mistaken* —, errore *m.* di persona; — *card*, carta d'identità, documento di legittimazione; (mil.) — *disc*, piastrina di riconoscimento.
**ideo-gram, -graph** *n.* ideogramma *m.* **-graphic(al)** *adj.* ideografico. **-graphy** *n.* ideografia. **-logic(al)** *adj.* ideologico. **-logist** *n.* ideologista *m., f.*, ideologo.
**ideology** *n.* ideologia.
**Ides** *n.* (hist.) Idi *m.pl.*; *the — of March*, gli Idi di Marzo.
**idiocy** *n.* idiozia; ebetismo; cretinismo.
**idiom** *n.* idioma *m.*; dialetto; idiotismo, modo di dire, locuzione.
**idiomatic(al)** *adj.* idiomatico; — *expression*, idiotismo.
**idiosyncrasy** *n.* idiosincrasia.
**idiot** *n.* idiota *m., f.*, cretino, ebete *m., f.*; *the village* —, il cretino del paese; (fam.) *don't be an — !*, non fare lo stupido! **-ic** *adj.* idiota, imbecille, stupido; (fam.) *don't be -ic*, non fare lo stupido.
**idle** *adj.* ozioso; pigro; indolente; sfaccendato; *to be* —, stare senza far niente; disoccupato; (of machinery) fermo; *to run* —, girare a folle; (fig.) vano, futile, inutile, senza scopo; *intr.* oziare; stare senza far niente; gironzolare; (mech.) girare a folle; *tr. to — the time away*, perdere il tempo oziando. **-ness** *n.* ozio; pigrizia; infingardaggine *f.*; indolenza; (fig.) inutilità; futilità; frivolezza. **-r** *n.* ozioso; pigro; fannullone *m.*; infingardo.
**idol** *n.* idolo; *the — of the family*, il beniamino della famiglia. **-ater, -atress** *n.* idolatra *m., f.* **-atrous** *adj.* da idolatra, idolatrico. **-atry** *n.* idolatria. **-ize** *tr.* idolatrare, idoleggiare, fare un idolo di.
**idyl(l)** *n.* idillio. **-ic** *adj.* idilliaco, idillico. **-ist** *n.* scrittore di idilli.
**if** *conj.* se, seppure; *as* —, come se; *even* —, anche se, quand'anche; — *anything*, se mai; — *not*, se no; a meno che (non); — *only*, se solo, se non altro, magari; — *you please*, per piacere, per cortesia; *n.* se *m.*; *the -s and the buts*, i se e i ma.
**igloo** *n.* igloo *m. indecl.*
**Ignatious** *pr.n.* Ignazio.
**ign-eous** *adj.* igneo. **-iferous** *adj.* ignifero. **-itable** *adj.* accensibile, infiammabile. **-ite** *tr.* accendere, incendiare, dar fuoco a; *intr.* accendersi, prendere fuoco, bruciare. **-ition** accensione; ignizione; (motor.) *-ition key*, chiavetta dell'accensione.
**ignob-le** *adj.* ignobile; vile; turpe. **-ility, -leness** *n.* ignobilità; bassezza.
**ignomin-y** *n.* ignominia; infamia; disonore *m.* **-ious** *adj.* ignominioso; infamante.
**ignoramus** *n.* ignorante *m., f.*; ignorantone *m.*
**ignor-ance** *n.* ignoranza; *to keep someone in — of*, tenere qualcuno all'oscuro di. **-ant** *adj.* ignorante;

illetterato; ignaro; *to be -ant of*, ignorare. **-antly** *adv.* per ignoranza.

**ignore** *tr.* trascurare, fingere di non sapere, non tenere conto di; fingere di non riconoscere, non voler riconoscere.

**iguan-a** *n.* (zool.) iguana. **-odon** *n.* (zool.) iguanodonte *m.*

**ikon** *n.* see **icon**.

**ilex** *n.* (bot.) elce *m.*, ilice *f.*, leccio.

**iliac** *adj.* (anat.) iliaco.

**Iliad** *pr.n.* Iliade *f.*

**ilk** *adj.* (Scot.) stesso; *n. of that* —, dello stesso genere, dello stesso luogo.

**ill** *adj.*, ammalato, malato; *to be* —, essere ammalato; *to fall, get, be taken* —, ammalarsi; *to feel* —, sentirsi male; *to look* —, avere una brutta cera; cattivo, nocivo, dannoso; — *deed*, cattiva azione; — *fame*, cattiva fama, brutta reputazione; — *news*, brutte notizie *f.pl.*; — *omen*, malaugurio; (provb.) *it's an — wind that blows nobody any good*, non tutto il male viene per nuocere; *adv.* male, malamente, malauguratamente; *to behave* —, comportarsi male; *it — becomes you*, non si addice a te; *to take something* —, prendere qualcosa in mala parte; — *at ease*, a mal agio, imbarazzato; *I can — afford the expense*, non posso sobbarcarmi alle spese; *n.* male *m.*; *to do* —, fare del male; *to speak — of*, dire male di; torto, danno; *pl. the -s of life*, le avversità della vita; *a cure for all -s*, una panacea.

**ill-advised** *adj.* (of pers.) malavveduto, malaccorto; sconsiderato, imprudente, inopportuno. **-behaved** *adj.* sgarbato, maleducato. **-bred** *adj.* maleducato, sgarbato, senza educazione. **-breeding** *n.* mancanza di educazione; sgarbatezza; scorrettezza. **-deserved** *adj.* immeritato. **-disposed** *adj.* maldisposto, malevolo.

**illegal** *adj.* illegale, illecito. **-ity** *n.* illegalità.

**illegib-le** *adj.* illeggibile; indecifrabile. **-ility** *n.* illeggibilità.

**illegitim-acy** *n.* illegittimità. **-ate** *adj.* illegittimo.

**ill-famed** *adj.* malfamato. **-fated** *adj.* malaugurato; disgraziato; sfortunato. **-favoured** *adj.* brutto; sgraziato; deforme. **-feeling** *n.* rancore *m.*; inimicizia; malevolenza. **-gotten** *adj.* mal acquisito; illecito. **-health** *n.* salute cagionevole, cattiva salute. **-humour** *n.* malumore *m.*; malanimo. **-humoured** *adj.* di malumore; bisbetico.

**illiberal** *adj.* illiberale; meschino; poco generoso. **-ity** *n.* illiberalità; grettezza.

**illicit** *adj.* illecito; vietato; abusivo.

**illimitab-le** *adj.* non limitabile; illimitato; sconfinato. **-leness** *n.* illimitatezza. **-ly** *adj.* illimitatamente.

**ill-informed** *adj.* male informato; ignorante.

**illiter-acy** *n.* analfabetismo; mancanza di coltura. **-ate** *adj.*, *n.* analfabeta *m.*, *f.*; illetterato; ignorante *m.*, *f.*

**ill-judged** *adj.* inopportuno; sconsiderato; sconsigliato. **-luck** *n.* mala fortuna; mala sorte; sfortuna; *as -luck would have it*, disgrazia volle (che); *a run of -luck*, una serie di disgrazie; *to bring -luck*, portare sfortuna. **-mannered** *adj.* maleducato; sgarbato. **-matched** *adj.* disperato; *-matched couple*, sposi mal assortiti. **-natured** *adj.* cattivo, malizioso, bisbetico.

**illness** *n.* malattia; indisposizione; infermità.

**illogical** *adj.* illogico. **-ity, -ness** *n.* illogicità.

**ill-omened** *adj.* di cattivo augurio; nefasto; sinistro. **-qualified** *adj.* incompetente; inetto. **-repute** *n.* cattiva reputazione. **-requited** *adj.* mal ricompensato. **-starred** *adj.* sfortunato; nato sotto una cattiva stella. **-timed** *adj.* inopportuno; intempestivo; fuor di proposito. **-treat** *tr.* maltrattare, bistrattare; malmenare. **-treatment** *n.* maltrattamento.

**illuminat-e** *tr.* illuminare; rischiarare; (art) miniare, illuminare, istoriare. **-ing** *adj.* illuminante; chiarificante. **-ion** *n.* illuminazione; *pl.* luminaria; (art) miniatura, illuminazione. **-ive** *adj.* illuminativo. **-or** *n.* illuminatore; (art) miniatore.

**ill-use** *tr.* maltrattare; malmenare.

**illusion** *n.* illusione; *to be under an* —, illudersi. **-ist** *n.* illusionista *m.*

**illusive** *adj.* illusorio; ingannevole. **-ness** *n.* illusorietà.

**illusory** *adj.* illusorio.

**illustrat-e** *tr.* illustrare; spiegare, delucidare, interpretare, schiarire. **-ion** *n.* illustrazione; spiegazione; esempio. **-ive** *adj.* illustrativo; esplicativo. **-or** *n.* illustratore.

**illustrious** *adj.* illustre; insigne; celebre. **-ness** *n.* celebrità; fama; rinomanza.

**ill-will** *n.* malvolere *m.*; malanimo; malevolenza; rancore *m.*

**Illyria** *pr.n.* (geog.) Illiria. **-n** *adj.* illirico.

**image** *n.* immagine *f.*; effigie *f.*; idolo; figura; metafora; (fig.) ritratto; *she is the very — of her mother*, è proprio il ritratto di sua madre.

**imagery** *n.* immagini *f.pl.*; statuaria; metafora, linguaggio figurato.

**imagin-able** *adj.* immaginabile, che si può immaginare. **-ary** *adj.* immaginario. **-ation** *n.* immaginazione; fantasia; immaginativa. **-ative** *adj.* immaginoso, immaginativo.

**imagin-e** *tr.* figurarsi, immaginare, immaginarsi, farsi un'idea di. **-ing** *n.* immaginazione; fantasia.

**imago** *n.* (ent.) imagine *f.*

**imbecil-e** *adj.* imbecille; scemo; *n.* imbecille *m.*, *f.*, ebete *m.*, *f.*; scemo. **-ic** *adj.* imbecille. **-ity** imbecillità; atto da imbecille.

**imbibe** *tr.* bere, imbevere; (fig.) assorbire, assimilare.

**imbue** *tr.* imbevere; impregnare.

**imitable** *adj.* imitabile.

**imitat-e** *tr.* imitare; contraffare; opiare; *to — someone's voice*, rifare la voce di qualcuno. **-ion** *n.* imitazione; contraffazione; copia; *attrib.* falso, finto, artificiale. **-ive** *adj.* imitativo; imitatore. **-or** *n.* imitatore; contraffattore.

**immaculate** *adj.* immacolato; incontaminato; puro; (fam.) impeccabile. **-ness** *n.* immacolatezza; purità, purezza; (fam.) impeccabilità.

**imman-ence** *n.* immanenza. **-ent** *adj.* immanente.

**immaterial** *adj.* immateriale; incorporeo; (fig.) indifferente; di nessuna importanza. **-ism** *n.* immaterialismo. **-ity** *n.* immaterialità; irrilevanza.

**immatur-e** *adj.* immaturo; prematuro; embrionale. **-eness, -ity** *n.* immaturità.

**immeasurab-le** *adj.* incommensurabile; smisurato; immenso. **-ility, -leness** *n.* immensurabilità; immensità.

**immediacy** *n.* immediatezza; urgenza; rapporto diretto.

**immediate** *adj.* immediato; istantaneo; diretto; *the — future*, il prossimo avvenire; *for — delivery*, urgente. **-ly** *adv.* immediatamente; subito; direttamente; *conj.* (non) appena. **-ness** *n.* immediatezza, subitaneità; istantaneità.

**immemorial** *adj.* immemorabile; *from time* —, da tempo immemorabile.

**immens-e** *adj.* immenso; smisurato. **-eness, -ity** *n.* immensità; smisuratezza.

**immensurable** *adj.* immensurabile.

**immerse, immerge** *tr.* immergere; tuffare; (fig.) *to be -d in one's work*, essere assorto nel lavoro.

**immersion** *n.* immersione; battesimo per immersione;

(electr.) – *heater*, riscaldatore ad immersione, resistenza corazzata.
**immigr-ant** *adj.*, *n.* immigrante *m.*, *f.* **-ate** *intr.* immigrare. **-ation** *n.* immigrazione.
**immin-ence,** *n.* imminenza. **-ent** *adj.* imminente; prossimo.
**immobil-e** *adj.* immobile; stazionario; fermo. **-ity** *n.* immobilità.
**immobiliz-e** *tr.* immobilizzare; fermare; mettere fuori dalla circolazione. **-ation** *n.* immobilizzazione.
**immoderate** *adj.* immoderato, smoderato; sfrenato; eccessivo; *to be* –, eccedere. **-ness, immoderation** *n.* immoderatezza; eccesso.
**immodest** *adj.* immodesto; impudico; spudorato; sfacciato. **-ly** *adv.* spudoratamente; sfacciatamente. **-y** *n.* immodestia; impudicizia; spudoratezza.
**immolat-e** *tr.* immolare; sacrificare. **-ion** *n.* immolazione.
**immoral** *adj.* immorale; dissoluto; vizioso; disonesto. **-ity** *n.* immoralità; dissolutezza.
**immortal** *adj.* immortale; eterno; perenne; *n.* spirito; *the -s*, gli immortali. **-ity** *n.* immortalità; perpetuità.
**immortalize** *tr.* immortalizzare, immortalare.
**immovab-le** *adj.* irremovibile; immobile; fermo; fisso; (fig.) insensibile; impassibile; (leg.) immobile. **-ility, -leness** *n.* irremovibilità; immobilità; (fig.) impassibilità.
**immun-e** *adj.* immune, libero (da), esente; (med.) immune. **-ity** *n.* immunità; *diplomatic -ity*, immunità diplomatica.
**immuniz-e** *tr.* immunizzare. **-ation** *n.* immunizzazione.
**immure** *tr.* (fig.) murare; rinchiudere; imprigionare.
**immutab-le** *adj.* immutabile; invariabile. **-ility** *n.* immutabilità; invariabilità.
**imp** *n.* folletto; diavoletto; demonietto; (of child) birichino.
**impact** *n.* urto; cozzo; collisione; (artill.) impatto.
**impair** *tr.* menomare; danneggiare; indebolire; intaccare; alterare; *to become -ed*, deperire, deteriorare, alterarsi.
**impale** *tr.* impalare; trafiggere; infiggere.
**impalpab-le** *adj.* impalpabile. **-ility** *n.* impalpabilità.
**impart** *tr.* impartire; comunicare; trasmettere; dispensare; (fig.) dare; infondere.
**impartial** *adj.* imparziale; equo; disinteressato. **-ity** *n.* imparzialità; equità.
**impassable** *adj.* invalicabile, impraticabile; (of river) inguadabile.
**impasse** *n.* (fig.) vicolo cieco.
**impassib-le** *adj.* impassibile; imperturbabile. **-ility, -leness** *n.* impassibilità; imperturbabilità.
**impassioned** *adj.* appassionato; caloroso.
**impassive** *adj.* impassibile; insensibile. **-ness** *n.* impassibilità; insensibilità.
**impati-ence** *n.* impazienza; insofferenza; ansia. **-ent** *adj.* impaziente; insofferente; intollerante; *to be -ent of*, non poter sopportare; *to get -ent*, impazientirsi, perdere la pazienza.
**impavid** *adj.* impavido.
**impeach** *tr.* (leg.) accusare; incriminare; (fig.) mettere in dubbio, screditare. **-ment** *n.* imputazione; incriminazione; (fig.) denigrazione.
**impeccab-le** *adj.* impeccabile. **-ility** *n.* impeccabilità.
**impecuni-ous** *adj.* senza denaro; indigente. **-osity** *n.* mancanza di denaro; indigenza.
**impede** *tr.* impedire; intralciare; ostacolare; ritardare.
**impediment** *n.* impedimento; ostacolo; ingombro; difficoltà; *to have an – in one's speech*, avere un difetto di pronuncia.
**impedimenta** *n.* bagagli *m.pl.*; (fam.) roba.
**impel** *tr.* spingere; costringere; forzare.
**impend** *intr.* sovrastare; incombere; essere imminente. **-ing** *adj.* imminente; sovrastante; incombente.
**impenetrab-le** *adj.* impenetrabile. **-ility** *n.* impenetrabilità.
**impenit-ence** *n.* impenitenza. **-ent** *adj.* impenitente; incorreggibile.
**imperative** *adj.* imperativo; urgente; imperioso; (gramm.) *adj.*, *n.* imperativo. **-ness** *n.* urgenza; imperiosità.
**imperatorial** *adj.* imperatorio, imperiale.
**imperceptib-le** *adj.* impercettibile. **-ility, -leness** *n.* impercettibilità.
**imperfect** *adj.* imperfetto; difettoso; incompleto; (gramm.) *adj.*, *n.* imperfetto. **-ion, -ness** *n.* imperfezione; difetto; incompiutezza.
**imperforable** *adj.* imperforabile.
**imperial** *adj.* imperiale; maestoso; grandioso; *n.* (beard) pizzo, imperiale *m.* **-ism** *n.* imperialismo. **-ist** *n.* imperialista *m.*, *f.* **-istic** *adj.* imperialistico.
**imperil** *tr.* mettere in pericolo, mettere a repentaglio; (fig.) compromettere.
**imperious** *adj.* imperioso; prepotente; altero; urgente.
**imperishab-le** *adj.* imperituro; indistruttibile. **-ility, -leness** *n.* l'essere imperituro; indistruttibilità.
**imperman-ence** *n.* temporaneità. **-ent** *adj.* non permanente; temporaneo.
**impermeab-le** *adj.* impermeabile. **-ility, -leness** *n.* impermeabilità.
**impermissible** *adj.* non permissibile.
**impersonal** *adj.* impersonale. **-ity** *n.* impersonalità.
**impersonat-e** *tr.* impersonare, personificare; assumere una personalità fittizia; (theatr.) interpretare. **-ion** *n.* personificazione; l'assumere una personalità fittizia; (theatr.) interpretazione.
**impersonator** *n.* chi assume una personalità fittizia; (theatr.) interprete *m.*, *f.*
**impertin-ence** *n.* impertinenza; insolenza; impudenza; *a piece of* –, un'impertinenza. **-ent** *adj.* impertinente; impudente; insolente; non pertinente, inappropriato.
**imperturbab-le** *adj.* imperturbabile; calmo; flemmatico. **-ility** *n.* imperturbabilità; calma.
**impervious** *adj.* impervio; impermeabile; impenetrabile; (fig.) sordo. **-ness** *n.* impermeabilità; impenetrabilità.
**impetigo** *n.* (med.) impetigine *f.*
**impetu-ous** *adj.* impetuoso; irruente. **-osity, -ousness** *n.* impetuosità; irruenza; slancio.
**impetus** *n.* impeto; spinta; impulso.
**impiety** *n.* empietà.
**impinge** *intr.* *to – (up)on*, urtare contro, percuotere; (fig.) usurpare, invadere. **-ment** *n.* urto; (fig.) invadenza.
**impious** *adj.* empio; irreligioso.
**impish** *adj.* malizioso; (of child) birichino. **-ness** *n.* malizia; carattere birichino.
**implacab-le** *adj.* implacabile; spietato. **-ility** *n.* implacabilità.
**implant** *tr.* piantare; fissare; (fig.) inculcare; instillare; imprimere. **-ation** *n.* impianto; (fig.) inculcazione.
**implement** *n.* attrezzo; utensile *m.*; strumento; (leg.) adempimento; *tr.* effetturare; adempiere; completare; (comm.) rendere effettivo. **-ation** *n.* adempimento; messa in vigore.
**implicat-e** *tr.* implicare; coinvolgere; compromettere. **-ion** *n.* implicazione; insinuazione.
**implicit, implied** *adj.* implicito; tacito; sottinteso.
**implor-e** *tr.* implorare; suppli-

care; impetrare. **-ing** *adj.* supplichevole.
**impluvium** *n.* (Rom. antiq.) impluvio.
**imply** *tr.* implicare; significare; voler dire; insinuare.
**impolite** *adj.* scortese, sgarbato, maleducato. **-ness** *n.* scortesia, sgarbatezza.
**impolitic** *adj.* impolitico, inopportuno, imprudente.
**imponderab-le** *adj.* imponderabile. **-ility** *n.* imponderabilità.
**im'port** *n.* importanza; valore *m.*; significato; senso; (comm.) importazione; articolo d'importazione; — *duty,* dazio di importazione.
**import** *tr.* essere importante; significare; indicare; (comm.) importare; introdurre. **-able** *adj.* importabile.
**import-ance** *n.* importanza; rilievo; entità; *to attach — to,* attribuire importanza a, dare rilievo a; (fam.) *full of his own —,* pieno di sè. **-ant** *adj.* importante, d'importanza; rilevante; ragguardevole.
**importation** *n.* importazione.
**importer** *n.* importatore.
**importunate** *adj.* importuno; molesto; insistente.
**importun-e** *tr.* importunare; molestare; sollecitare insistentemente. **-ity** *n.* importunità; insistenza.
**impose** *tr.* imporre; prescrivere, dettare; *to — a tax,* imporre una tassa; infliggere; *intr. to — (up)on,* ingannare, abusare di.
**imposing** *adj.* imponente; grandioso. **-ness** *n.* imponenza.
**imposition** *n.* imposizione; imposta; inganno; impostura.
**impossib-le** *adj.* impossibile; (fam.) assurdo, intollerabile; *to attempt the —,* raddrizzare le gambe ai cani. **-ility** *n.* impossibilità; cosa impossibile. **-ly** *adv.* impossibilmente; *not -ly,* può darsi.
**impost** *n.* imposta; tassa; (archit.) imposta, piedritto.
**impost-or** *n.* impostore; imbroglione *m.* **-ure** *n.* impostura; inganno.
**impot-ence, -ency** *n.* impotenza; incapacità. **-ent** *adj.* impotente; debole; incapace.
**impound** *tr.* sequestrare; confiscare; rinchiudere in un recinto.
**impoverish** *tr.* impoverire; (fig.) esaurire. **-ment** *n.* impoverimento; (fig.) esaurimento.
**impracticab-le** *adj.* inattuabile; impossibile; impraticabile; intrattabile. **-ility, -leness** *n.* impraticabilità; inattuabilità; impossibilità.
**imprecat-e** *tr.* imprecare; maledire. **-ion** *n.* imprecazione; maledizione; bestemmia. **-ory** *adj.* imprecativo, imprecatorio.
**impregn-able** *adj.* imprendibile; inespugnabile; (fig.) insuperabile. **-ate** *tr.* (biol.) fecondare, rendere fecondo, fertilizzare; impregnare; imbevere; saturare. **-ated** *adj.* (biol.) pregno; fecondato; gravido; saturo; impregnato. **-ation** *n.* fecondazione; impregnazione.
**imprescriptible** *adj.* imprescrittibile.
**impress** *n.* impronta; impressione; marchio; *tr.* (typ.) imprimere, stampare; (fig.) impressionare, fare impressione su; edificare; colpire; inculcare; infondere; (hist.) arruolare forzatamente, requisire.
**impression** *n.* impressione; (typ.) ristampa; *to give the — of,* dare a divedere di, *to make an —,* fare effetto.
**impressionab-le** *adj.* impressionabile; sensibile. **-ility** *n.* impressionabilità; sensibilità.
**impression-ism** *n.* (art) impressionismo. **-ist** *n.* (art) impressionista *m., f.*; macchiaiuolo. **-istic** *adj.* (art) impressionistico.
**impressive** *adj.* impressionante; imponente; commovente; solenne. **-ly** *adv.* in modo impressionante; solennemente. **-ness** *n.* imponenza; solennità; forza.
**impressment** *n.* (hist.) arruolamento forzato, leva; requisizione.
**imprest** *n.* (comm.; admin.) anticipo; prestito (concesso a pubblico funzionario).
**imprimatur** *n.* (typ.) visto; (fam.) si stampi *m.*; (eccl.) imprimatur *m.*; (fig.) approvazione.
**im'print** *n.* impressione; impronta; (typ.) *no —,* senza indicazione dell'editore; *publisher's —,* nome *m.* dell'editore; *under the — of,* coi tipi di; *printer's —,* emblema *m.*, divisa di stampatore.
**imprint** *tr.* (typ.) imprimere (also fig.)
**imprison** *tr.* imprigionare; incarcerare; (fig.) rinchiudere; confinare. **-ment** *n.* imprigionamento; prigionia; carcerazione; (leg.) reclusione, detenzione.
**improbab-le** *adj.* improbabile; inverosimile. **-ility** *n.* improbabilità; inverosimiglianza.
**improbity** *n.* disonestà; malvagità.
**impromptu** *adj.* improvvisato, estemporaneo; *adv.* estemporaneamente, all'improvviso; *n.* improvvisazione.
**improp-er** *adj.* improprio; abusivo; sconveniente; sconcio; indecente; erroneo; disadatto. **-riety** *n.* improprietà; sconvenienza; indecenza; erroneità; scorrettezza.
**improve** *tr.* migliorare; perfezionare; valorizzare; apportare delle migliorie a; emendare; abbellire; (fig.) approfittare di, sfruttare; *intr.* migliorare, star meglio, andare meglio, far progressi; (of weather) aggiustarsi, migliorare; *to — (up)on,* perfezionare. **-ment** *n.* miglioramento; miglioria; perfezionamento; progresso; *to effect -ments in,* migliorare, apportare delle migliorie a; *to be an -ment on,* superare, rappresentare un miglioramento in confronto a; *to leave room for -ment,* essere suscettibile di miglioramento.
**improver** *n.* perfezionatore; valorizzatore; (industr.) apprendista *m.*
**improvident** *adj.* imprevidente; imprudente; prodigo.
**improving** *adj.* che migliora; edificante.
**improvidence** *n.* improvvidenza; imprudenza.
**improvis-e** *tr.* improvvisare; preparare in fretta. **-ation** *n.* improvvisazione. **-er** *n.* improvvisatore.
**imprud-ence** *n.* imprudenza; imprevidenza; avventatezza. **-ent** *adj.* imprudente; incauto; imprevidente; avventato.
**impud-ence** *n.* impudenza; sfacciataggine; sfrontatezza; *what —!,* ci vuole una bella sfacciataggine! **-ent** *adj.* impudente; sfacciato; sfrontato.
**impugn** *tr.* impugnare; oppugnare; mettere in dubbio.
**impuissance** *n.* impotenza; debolezza.
**impulse** *n.* impulso; impeto; spinta; stimolo; istinto; *to act upon —,* agire d'impulso; *to feel an — to,* sentirsi spinto a; *to give way to an —,* secondare un impulso; (electr.) impulso.
**impulsion** *n.* impulso; impeto; spinta; (mech.) propulsione.
**impulsive** *adj.* impulsivo; (mech.) propulsore. **-ness** *n.* impulsività.
**impunity** *n.* impunità.
**impur-e** *adj.* impuro; immondo; contaminato; viziato; adulterato. **-ity** *n.* impurità; (chem.) corpo estraneo.
**imputab-le** *adj.* imputabile; attribuibile. **-ility** *n.* imputabilità.
**imput-e** *tr.* imputare, ascrivere, attribuire, addebitare, accagionare. **-ation** *n.* imputazione; attribuzione; accusa; addebito. **-ative** *adj.* d'imputazione.
**in** *prep.* in; dentro; *— the,* nel, nello, nella, *pl.* nei, negli, nelle; entro, fra, tra. FOLLOW. BY GERUND: a, di; *— all,* in tutto; *— that,* in quanto che. (For adverbial and idiomatic uses, see under various adjectives, nouns and verbs.)
**inability** *n.* incapacità; inabilità.
**inaccessib-le** *adj.* inaccessibile;

irraggiungibile. **-ility, -leness** *n.* inaccessibilità; irraggiungibilità.
**inaccur-acy** *n.* inesattezza; imprecisione. **-ate** *adj.* inesatto; impreciso; infedele.
**inaction** *n.* inattività; inazione; (phys.; chem.) inerzia.
**inactiv-e** *adj.* inattivo; inoperoso; inerte; passivo. **-ity** *n.* inattività; inoperosità; inerzia; passività.
**inadaptab-le** *adj.* inadattabile. **-ility** *n.* inadattabilità.
**inadequ-acy** *n.* inadeguatezza; insufficienza. **-ate** *adj.* inadeguato; insufficiente; inetto.
**inadmissib-le** *adj.* inammissibile. **-ility** *n.* inammissibilità.
**inadvert-ence, -ency** *n.* inavvertenza; disattenzione; sbadataggine *f.* **-ent** *adj.* disattento; sbadato; involontario.
**inadvisable** *adj.* See **unadvisable.**
**inalienab-le** *adj.* inalienabile. **-ility** *n.* inalterabilità; immutabilità.
**inalterable** *adj.* inalterabile; immutabile.
**inane** *adj.* inane; vacuo; futile; insensato; sciocco.
**inanimate** *adj.* inanimato; senza vita; esanime; (fig.) fiacco.
**inanity** *n.* inanità; vacuità; futilità.
**inappeasable** *adj.* implacabile; insaziabile.
**inapplicab-le** *adj.* inapplicabile; inadatto. **-ility** *n.* inapplicabilità.
**inapposite** *adj.* improprio; fuori luogo. **-ness** *n.* improprietà.
**inappreciable** *adj.* inapprezzabile; impercettibile; trascurabile; di nessun conto.
**inappropriate** *adj.* improprio; inappropriato, disadatto; incompatibile.
**inapt** *adj.* inadatto; improprio; maldestro; inabile. **-itude, -ness** *n.* inattitudine *f.*; incapacità.
**inarticulate** *adj.* inarticolato; indistinto; che non sa esprimersi; (fig.) muto; (zool.) disarticolato. **-ness** *n.* poca chiarezza; afonia; incapacità di esprimersi; (zool.) disarticolazione.
**inartistic** *adj.* non artistico; brutto; non portato all'arte.
**inasmuch** *conj.* — *as*, in quanto che, dacchè.
**inattent-ion** *n.* disattenzione; inattenzione; distrazione. **-ive** *adj.* disattento; distratto; sbadato. **-iveness** *n.* disattenzione; distrazione.
**inaudib-le** *adj.* impercettibile; inafferrabile; inaudibile; *he was quite* —, era impossible afferrare le sue parole. **-ility** *n.* impercettibilità; inafferrabilità. **-ly** *adv.* in modo non udibile.
**inaugur-al** *adj.* inaugurale. **-ate** *tr.* inaugurare. **-ation** *n.* inaugurazione; (fig.) apertura.
**inauspicious** *adj.* malaugurato; infausto; funesto. **-ness** *n.* cattivi auspici *m.pl.*; malaugurio.
**inboard** *adj.*, *adv.* (naut.) entrobordo.
**inborn** *adj.* innato; congenito; naturale.
**inbred** *adj.* innato; congenito; naturale; (of horses, *etc.*) consanguineo.
**in-breeding** *n.* (biol.) indogamia; incrocio tra affini.
**Inca** *n.* (hist.) Inca *m. indecl.*
**incalculab-le** *adj.* incalcolabile; imprevedibile; incerto, inattendibile. **-ility** *n.* incalcolabilità; imprevedibilità.
**incandesc-ence** *n.* incandescenza. **-ent** *adj.* incandescente; *-ent burner*, becco incandescente.
**incantation** *n.* incanto, incantesimo.
**incapab-le** *adj.* incapace; inabile; inetto; (leg.) inabilitato. **-ility** *n.* incapacità; inettitudine; inabilità.
**incapacit-ate** *tr.* rendere incapace; inabilitare; (leg.) dichiarare incapace; inabilitare. **-y** *n.* incapacità; inabilità; incompetenza.
**incarcerat-e** *tr.* incarcerare. **-ion** *n.* incarcerazione, incarceramento.
**incarnadine** *adj.* incarnatino, color cremisi.
**incarnat-e** *adj.* incarnato; *to be* —, umanarsi, incarnarsi; (colour) incarnato, incarnatino; *tr.* incarnare, personificare. **-ion** *n.* incarnazione; personificazione.
**incautious** *adj.* incauto; imprudente; sconsiderato. **-ness** *n.* imprudenza; sconsideratezza.
**incendiar-ism** *n.* incendio doloso; sobillazione. **-y** *adj.* incendiario; (fig.) sovversivo, sedizioso; *n.* incendiario; sovversivo.
**in·cense**[1] *n.* incenso; (fig.) incensamento.
**incense**[1] *tr.* incensare; profumare di incenso.
**incense**[2] *tr.* irritare; esasperare; stizzire, provocare; *to become -d*, irritarsi.
**incense-burner** *n.* incensiere *m.*, turibolo.
**incentive** *n.* incentivo; stimolo; motivo.
**inception** *n.* inizio; principio.
**incertitude** *n.* incertezza; dubbio; indecisione.
**incessant** *adj.* incessante; continuo; ininterrotto.
**incest** *n.* incesto. **-uous** *adj.* incestuoso.
**inch** *n.* pollice *m.* (=2.54 cm.); *cubic* —, pollice cubico (=16.388 $cm.^3$); *square* —, pollice quadrato (=6.4516 $cm.^2$); — *by* —, a poco a poco; *every* — *a king*, re da capo a piedi; (fig.) *an* — *of*, a un pelo da; *pl.* statura; *intr.* muoversi poco alla volta; *to* — *forward*, andare avanti a poco a poco.
**inchoat-e** *adj.* appena cominciato; rudimentale. **-ive** *adj.* incoative; incipiente; iniziale.
**incid-ence** *n.* incidenza. **-ent** *adj.* inerente; *n.* caso; avvenimento; episodio.
**incidental** *adj.* casuale; fortuito; accidentale; secondario; (comm.) — *expenses*, spese varie. **-ly** *adv.* incidentalmente; fortuitamente; tra parentesi.
**incinerat-ion** *n.* incenerimento. **-or** *n.* forno per rifiuti, bruciatore di rifiuti.
**incipi-ent** *adj.* incipiente; nascente. **-ence, -ency** *n.* incipienza; inizio.
**incis-e** *tr.* incidere; intagliare. **-ion** *n.* incisione; taglio.
**incisive** *adj.* incisivo; tagliente; (fig.) acuto, penetrante. **-ness** *n.* acutezza; tono incisivo.
**incisor** *n.* dente incisivo.
**incite** *tr.* incitare; aizzare; spronare; spingere; istigare. **-ment** *n.* incitamento; eccitamento; istigazione; stimolo.
**incivility** *n.* scortesia; sgarbatezza; inciviltà.
**inclem-ency** *n.* inclemenza; asprezza; rigore *m.* **-ent** *adj.* inclemente; aspro; duro.
**inclination** *n.* inclinazione; pendenza; disposizione; propensione, propensità; tendenza; predilezione; voglia.
**incline** *n.* piano inclinato; pendìo; declivio; china; salita; rampa; *tr.* inclinare; piegare; chinare; (fig.) *to* — *one's ear to*, ascoltare con benevolenza; indurre; persuadere; *intr.* tendere, essere propenso a. **-d** *adj.* inclinato; propenso; proclive; tendente; *to feel -ed for*, aver voglia di.
**inclose, inclosure.** See **enclose, enclosure.**
**include** *tr.* includere; accludere, annettere; comprendere; contare, annoverare; *service -d*, servizio compreso; *up to and including 31st May*, a tutto il trentun maggio; *not including*, escluso, senza contare.
**inclus-ion** *n.* inclusione. **-ive** *adj.* inclusivo, compreso; *-ive terms*, tutto compreso; *-ive charge*, prezzo complessivo; *to 31st May -ive*, fino a tutto il trentun maggio.
**incognito** *adj. n.* incognito; *to remain* —, conservare l'anonimo; *to travel* —, viaggiare in incognito.
**incognizant** *adj.* inconscio; *to be* — *of something*, ignorare qualcosa.
**incoher-ent** *adj.* incoerente; incongruo. **-ence, -ency** *n.* incoerenza; incongruità.
**incohesion** *n.* mancanza di coesione.
**incombustib-le** *adj.* incombustibile; ininfiammabile. **-ility** *n.* incombustibilità.
**income** *n.* reddito; entrate *f.pl.*;

*earned* —, reddito professionale, stipendio, salario; *assessable* —, reddito imponibile; *to live on a fixed* —, vivere di rendita, vivere del proprio; *to live within one's* —, vivere secondo le proprie possibilità; *to live beyond one's* —, vivere al di sopra dei propri mezzi; — *tax*, imposta sul reddito, ricchezza mobile; — *tax return*, dichiarazione del reddito; — *tax form*, modulo per la denuncia del reddito; *rate of* — *tax*, aliquota dell'imposta sul reddito.

**incomer** *n.* chi entra; successore; sopravvenuto.

**incoming** *adj.* entrante, in arrivo; — *mail*, posta in arrivo; — *tenant*, inquilino subentrante; — *tide*, marea montante.

**incommensur-able** *adj.* incommensurabile; smisurato. **-ate** *adj.* sproporzionato; insufficiente; inadequato.

**incommode** *tr.* incomodare; scomodare; disturbare.

**incommodious** *adj.* incomodo, scomodo. **-ness, incommodity** *n.* incomodità, scomodità.

**incommunicab-le** *adj.* incomunicabile, indicibile. **-ility** *n.* incomunicabilità. **-leness** *n.* incomunicabilità.

**incommunicative** *adj.* riservato. **-ness** *n.* riservatezza; riserbo.

**incommutab-le** *adj.* incommutabile. **-ility** *n.* incommutabilità.

**incomparable** *adj.* incomparabile; impareggiabile. **-ness** *n.* incomparabilità; impareggiabilità.

**incompatib-le** *adj.* incompatibile. **-ility** *n.* incompatibilità.

**incompet-ent** *adj.* incompetente, incapace, inetto. **-ence, -ency** *n.* incompetenza; incapacità.

**incomplet-e** *adj.* incompleto; incompiuto; imperfetto. **-eness, -iontion** *n.* incompletezza; imperfezione.

**incomprehensib-le** *adj.* incomprensibile; inintelligibile. **-ility, -leness** incomprensibilità.

**incompressib-le** *adj.* incompressibile. **-ility** *n.* incompressibilità.

**incomputable** *adj.* incalcolabile.

**inconceivab-le** *adj.* inconcepibile; incredibile. **-ility** *n.* inconcepibilità.

**inconclusive** *adj.* inconcludente; sconclusionato. **-ness** *n.* inconcludenza.

**incongr-uent** *adj.* incongruo; incongruente. **-uity** *n.* incongruità; assurdità.

**incongruous** *adj.* incongruo, incongruente; assurdo. **-ness** *n.* See **incongruity.**

**inconsequ-ence** *n.* inconseguenza; illogicità. **-ent** *adj.* inconseguente; illogico; irrilevante; non pertinente.

**inconsequential** *adj.* inconseguente; illogico. **-ity** *n.* inconseguenza; illogicità.

**inconsiderable** *adj.* trascurabile; insignificante; di poco valore.

**inconsiderate** *adj.* sconsiderato; senza considerazione, senza riguardi. **-ness, inconsideration** *n.* inconsideratezza; irriflessione, sbadatezza; mancanza di riguardo.

**inconsist-ency** *n.* inconsistenza; discordanza; incompatibilità. **-ent** *adj.* inconsistente; incompatibile; contraddittorio; *to be -ent with*, essere contrario a, essere incompatibile con.

**inconsolable** *adj.* inconsolabile.

**inconsonant** *adj.* non consono; discorde; *to be* — *with*, non essere d'accordo con.

**inconspicuous** *adj.* incospicuo; insignificante; *to be* —, non dare nell'occhio. **-ness** *n.* il passare inosservato; l'essere insignificante.

**inconst-ancy** *n.* incostanza; instabilità; mutabilità. **-ant** *adj.* incostante; instabile; mutabile; variabile.

**inconsumable** *adj.* inconsumabile.

**incontestable** *adj.* incontestabile; incontrastabile.

**incontin-ent** *adj.* incontinente; smoderato. **-ence, -ency** *n.* incontinenza.

**incontrovertible** *adj.* incontrovertibile; incontestabile.

**inconveni-ence** *n.* incomodo; disturbo; *to cause* —, *to be an* — *to*, incomodare, dare disturbo a; *without the slightest* —, senza il minimo disturbo; scomodità; inconveniente *m.*; *tr.* incomodare, scomodare; disturbare, dare disturbo a. **-ent** *adj.* incomodo, scomodo, disagevole; *to be -ent to*, recare disturbo a.

**inconvertible** *adj.* inconvertibile.

**inconvincible** *adj.* inconvincibile.

**incorporate** *adj.* See **incorporeal, incorporated.**

**incorporat-e** *tr.* incorporare; fondere; (comm.) costituire in società, erigere in ente morale; *intr.* incorporarsi, associarsi. **-ed** *adj.* incorporato, unito in corporazione, eretto in ente morale; (USA) società per azioni. **-ion** *n.* incorporamento, incorporazione; costituzione (di una società).

**incorporeal** *adj.* incorporeo; privo di corpo. **-ity** *n.* incorporeità.

**incorrect** *adj.* inesatto, erroneo; — *behaviour*, modo scorretto di comportarsi. **-ness** *n.* inesattezza; scorrettezza.

**incorrigib-le** *adj.* incorreggibile; impenitente. **-ility** *n.* incoreggibilità.

**incorrodible** *adj.* inattaccabile, che non si può corrodere.

**incorrupt** *adj.* incorrotto; integro; (text) corretto. **-ibility** *n.* incorruttibilità. **-ible** *adj.* incorruttibile.

**increasable** *adj.* aumentabile; accrescibile.

**in·crease** *n.* aumento; accrescimento; crescita; incremento; *to be on the* —, essere in aumento.

**increase** *tr.* aumentare; accrescere; *to* — *prices*, aumentare i prezzi; *to* — *one's efforts*, raddoppiare i propri sforzi; *to* — *speed*, aumentare la velocità; *intr.* crescere; aumentare; ingrandirsi; *to* — *in power*, aumentare di potenza; *to* — *threefold, fivefold*, triplicarsi, quintuplicarsi; *-d cost of living*, rincaro della vita.

**increasing** *adj.* crescente; in aumento, che aumenta. **-ly** *adv.* in aumento; sempre più.

**incredib-le** *adj.* incredibile. **-ility** *n.* incredibilità.

**incredul-ous** *adj.* incredulo. **-ity, -ousness** *n.* incredulità.

**increment** *n.* incremento; aumento; plusvalore *m.*; *unearned* —, profitto congiunturale.

**incriminat-e** *tr.* incriminare; incolpare; imputare. **-ion** *n.* incriminazione.

**incrustation** *n.* incrostazione, incrostatura; rivestimento

**incubat-e** *tr.* covare; incubare; (fig.) meditare. **-ion** *n.* incubazione. **-or** *n.* incubatrice.

**incubus** *n.* incubo; (fig.) peso.

**inculcat-e** *tr.* inculcare; imprimere. **-ion** *n.* inculcazione.

**inculpat-e** *tr.* incolpare; incriminare; accusare; accagionare. **-ion** *n.* incolpazione; imputazione; accusa. **-ory** *adj.* incolpatore; accusatore; d'accusa.

**incumbent** *adj.* incombente; sovrastante; obbligatorio; *to be* — *upon*, incombere a, toccare a; *n.* (eccl.) beneficiario.

**incunabulum** *n.* incunabolo.

**incur** *tr.* incorrere in; contrarre; esporsi a; attirarsi addosso.

**incurab-le** *adj.* inguaribile; cronico; incurabile; insanabile; che non ha rimedio. **-ility** *n.* incurabilità.

**incuri-ous** *adj.* non curioso; indifferente; negligente; noncurante. **-osity, -ousness** *n.* mancanza di curiosità; indifferenza.

**incursion** *n.* incursione; irruzione; scorreria.

**incurvation** *n.* incurvatura, incurvamento.

**indebted** *adj.* indebitato; (fig.) obbligato; tenuto grato; *to be* — *to*, essere debitore di, dovere a. **-ness** *n.* l'essere indebitato; debito.

**indec-ency** *n.* indecenza; scon-

venienza; (leg.) oltraggio al pudore. **-ent** *adj.* indecente; sconveniente; sconcio, indecoroso; (leg.) *-ent behaviour,* oltraggio al pudore.

**indecipherable** *adj.* indecifrabile; illeggibile.

**indecis-ion** *n.* indecisione; irresolutezza; esitazione. **-ive** *adj.* non decisivo; indeciso, irresoluto. **-iveness** *n.* indecisione; incertezza.

**indeclinable** *adj.* (gramm.) indeclinabile.

**indecorous** *adj.* indecoroso; sconveniente. **-ness, indecorum** *n.* mancanza di decoro; sconvenienza.

**indeed** *adv.* difatti; in effetti; in verità; davvero; veramente; a dire il vero; anzi, in realtà, realmente; (excl.) davvero!; (when used with *adj.* as intensive) rendered by -issimo; *I am glad —,* sono lietissimo.

**indefatigable** *adj.* infaticabile; instancabile, indefesso. **-ness** *n.* infaticabilità; instancabilità.

**indefensible** *adj.* indifendibile; insostenibile; in(e)scusabile.

**indefinable** *adj.* indefinibile.

**indefinite** *adj.* indefinito; vago; indeterminato; illimitato; (gramm.) *adj., n.* indefinito. **-ly** *adv.* vagamente; senza limite. **-ness** *n.* indefinitezza; indeterminatezza.

**indelib-le** *adj.* indelebile; incancellabile; *— pencil,* matita copiativa. **-ility** *n.* indelebilità.

**indelic-acy** *n.* indelicatezza; sconvenienza, grossolanità. **-ate** *adj.* indelicato; grossolano, sconveniente.

**indemnif-y** *tr.* indennizzare, risarcire; garantire, assicurare. **-ication** *n.* indennizzo, risarcimento; garanzia.

**indemnity** *n.* indennità, indennizzo, risarcimento.

**indent** *n.* incavo; ordinazione, richiesta, requisizione; (typ.) capoverso, accapo, indentro; (mech.) indentura; *tr.* incavare; frastagliare; (typ.) cominciare indentro; (mech.) dentellare, intaccare; *intr. to — for,* ordinare, requisire. **-ation** *n.* incavo; dentellatura, indentatura; (typ.) capoverso; (geog.) insenatura. **-ed** *adj.* dentellato; frastagliato.

**indenture** *n.* (leg.) controscritta, contratto bilaterale; *pl.* contratto di apprendistato; *tr.* vincolare con contratto; collocare come apprendista, mettere a far pratica.

**independ-ence** *n.* indipendenza; autonomia. **-ent** *adj.* indipendente; autonomo; *of -ent means,* benestante. **-ently** *adv.* indipendentemente; separatamente; *-ently of,* all'infuori di, oltre.

**indescribable** *adj.* indescrivibile; indicibile.

**indestructib-le** *adj.* indistruttibile. **-ility, -leness** *n.* indistruttibilità.

**indetermin-able** *adj.* indeterminabile. **-ate** *adj.* indeterminato; non precisato; vago, indefinito. **-ateness** *n.* indeterminatezza. **-ation** *n.* indeterminazione; irresolutezza.

**index** *n.* indice *m.*; rubrica; elenco; *card —,* schedario; (eccl.) *the Index,* l'Indice (dei libri proibiti); *— finger,* indice; *cost of living —,* indice del costo della vita; (fig.) indizio; indicazione; coefficiente *m.*; *tr.* fare l'indice di, rubricare; (eccl.) mettere all'Indice; (mech.) graduare. **-er** *n.* compilatore di un indice.

**India** *pr.n.* (geog.) India; (paperm.) *— paper,* carta d'India, carta Oxford. **-n** *adj.* indiano; *-n club,* clava; *-n corn,* granturco; *in -n file,* in fila indiana; *-n ink,* inchiostro di China; *-n summer,* estate di San Martino; *n.* indiano *m.,* indiana *f.*; *Red -n,* pellirossa *m., f.*

**india-rubber** *n.* caucciù *m.*; gomma; *— stamp,* timbro di gomma.

**indicat-e** *tr.* indicare; segnalare, segnare; additare; denotare. **-ion** *n.* indicazione; indizio; segno; *to give an -ion of,* indicare, suggerire. **-ive** *adj.* indicativo; che indica; che donota; (gramm.) *adj., n.* indicativo. **-or** *n.* indicatore. **-ory** *adj.* indicativo.

**indict** *tr.* accusare, mettere in stato d'accusa. **-able** *adj.* accusabile, imputabile; *an -able offence,* un atto passibile di pena. **-ment** *n.* accusa; imputazione; *bill of -ment,* atto d'accusa.

**Indies** *pr.n.* (geog.) *East —,* Indie orientali; *West —,* Indie occidentali.

**indiffer-ence** *n.* indifferenza; apatia; mancanza d'interesse; *a matter of —,* una cosa di nessuna importanza. **-ent** *adj.* indifferente; apatico; imparziale; insensibile; mediocre, poco importante; *-ent health,* salute cagionevole.

**indigenous** *adj.* indigeno, nativo.

**indig-ent** *adj.* indigente; povero, bisognoso. **-ence, -ency** *n.* indigenza, miseria.

**indigestib-le** *adj.* indigesto, indigeribile, indigestibile. **-ility** *n.* indigeribilità.

**indigestion** *n.* indigestione; dispepsia; (pop.) mal di pancia.

**indignant** *adj.* indignato, sdegnato, sdegnoso; *to feel —,* indignarsi. **-ly** *adv.* con indignazione; con sdegno.

**indignation** *n.* indignazione; sdegno; *— meeting,* comizio di protesta.

**indignity** *n.* trattamento indegno; offesa; umiliazione.

**indigo** *n.* indaco; *— plant,* indigofera.

**indirect** *adj.* indiretto; obliquo, traverso; (gramm.) indiretto. **-ly** *adv.* indirettamente; di riflesso. **-ness** *n.* obliquità; tortuosità.

**indiscernible** *adj.* indiscernibile; impercettibile; indistinguibile.

**indiscipline** *n.* indisciplina.

**indiscreet** *adj.* imprudente; incauto; irriflessivo; indiscreto. **-ness** *n.* inopportunità; indiscretezza.

**indiscretion** *n.* imprudenza; sconsideratezza; indiscrezione.

**indiscriminat-e** *adj.* confuso, indiscriminato, non differenziato; promiscuo. **-ely** *adv.* confusamente; a casaccio; senza distinzione alcuna. **-ing** *adj.* senza discernimento; che non fa distinzioni.

**indispensab-le** *adj.* indispensabile; essenziale, necessario. **-ility, -leness** *n.* indispensabilità; necessità.

**indispos-e** *tr.* indisporre; rendere indisposto; distogliere. **-ed** *adj.* maldisposto; avverso; indisposto; *to feel -ed,* sentirsi poco bene. **-ition** *n.* avversione; indisposizione; malessere *m.*

**indisputab-le** *adj.* indisputabile, incontestabile, indiscutibile. **-ility, -leness** *n.* incontestabilità; indiscutibilità.

**indissolub-le** *adj.* indissolubile. **-ility** *n.* indissolubilità.

**indistinct** *adj.* indistinto; poco chiaro; vago, confuso. **-ness** *n.* indistinzione; mancanza di chiarezza.

**indistinguishable** *adj.* indistinguibile; indiscernibile; impercettibile.

**indite** *tr.* (lit., joc.) redigere; comporre; scrivere.

**individual** *adj.* individuale; singolo; personale; particolare; *n.* individuo; persona; (fam.) tipo. **-ism** *n.* individualismo. **-ist** *n.* individualista *m., f.* **-istic** *adj.* individualistico. **-ity** *n.* individualità.

**individualiz-e, individuate** *tr.* individualizzare, individuare. **-ation** *n.* individualizzazione, individuazione.

**indivisib-le** *adj.* indivisibile; inseparabile. **-ility** *n.* indivisibilità.

**Indo-aryan** *adj., n.* (ethn.; ling.) indoariano. **-China** *pr.n.* (geog.) Indocina.

**indocil-e** *adj.* indocile; ricalcitrante. **-ity** *n.* indocilità.

**indoctrinat-e** *tr.* addottrinare. **-ion** *n.* addottrinamento; *political -ion,* istruzione politica, propaganda politica.

**indol-ence** *n.* indolenza; pigrizia; (theol.) accidia; (med.) insen-

sibilità. **-ent** *adj.* indolente; neghittoso; pigro, infingardo; (med.) indolore.

**indomitable** *adj.* indomabile; indomito; ferreo.

**Indonesia** *pr.n.* (geog.) Indonesia. **-n** *adj., n.* indonesiano.

**indoor** *adj.* di casa, casalingo, domestico; interno; — *games*, giuochi di società; — *clothes*, vestiti da casa. **-s** *adv.* in casa; al coperto, all'interno; *-s and out*, dentro e fuori; *to stay -s*, rimanere in casa.

**indorse** see **endorse.**

**indubitable** *adj.* indubitabile; indubbio; certo.

**induce** *tr.* indurre; persuadere; spingere; produrre, causare. **-ment** *n.* allettamento; lusinga; persuasione; motivo; stimolo.

**induct** *tr.* installare; investire; (eccl.) mettere in possesso (di un beneficio); (electr.) indurre. **-ion** *n.* induzione; insediamento; investitura; (eccl.) presa di possesso; (electr.) induzione, ammissione; *-ion coil*, bobina d'induzione. **-ive** *adj.* induttivo.

**indulge** *tr.* essere indulgente con; compiacere, abbandonarsi a; (eccl.) concedere un'indulgenza a; *intr.* lasciarsi andare; (fam.) bere troppo; *to — in*, permettersi, concedersi.

**indulgence** *n.* indulgenza; compiacenza; (pejor.) vizio; l'abbandonarsi a, il concedersi; (eccl.) indulgenza.

**indulgent** *adj.* indulgente; compiacente; benevolo.

**Indus** *pr.n.* (geog.) Indo.

**industrial** *adj.* industriale; (comm.) — *spirit*, alcool denaturato; *n.pl.* (finan.) azioni di ditte industriali. **-ism** *n.* industrialismo. **-ist** *n.* industriale *m.*

**industrializ-e** *tr.* industrializzare. **-ation** *n.* industrializzazione.

**industrious** *adj.* diligente; laborioso; zelante; alacre; (pejor.) industrioso. **-ness** *n.* diligenza.

**industry** *n.* industria; manifattura; diligenza, operosità, zelo.

**indweller** *n.* abitante *m., f.*

**inebriant** *adj.* inebriante; *n.* sostanza inebriante.

**inebriat-e** *tr.* inebriare, ubriacare; *n.* alcoolizzato. **-ed** *adj.* ubriaco; (fig.) ebbro. **-ion, inebriety** *n.* ubriachezza; (fig.) ebbrezza.

**inedible** *adj.* immangiabile.

**ineffab-le** *adj.* ineffabile. **-ility, -leness** *n.* ineffabilità.

**ineffaceable** *adj.* incancellabile, indelebile.

**ineffective** *adj.* inefficace; (art; archit.) di scarso effetto; incapace, poco efficiente. **-ness** *n.* inefficacia.

**ineffectual** *adj.* inutile, vano; inefficace. **-ness** *n.* inefficacia; inutilità.

**inefficacious** *adj.* inefficace. **-ness, inefficacity, inefficacy** *n.* inefficacia.

**ineffici-ency** *n.* inefficienza; incapacità, scarsa attitudine. **-ent** *adj.* inefficiente; incapace, poco capace.

**ineleg-ant** *adj.* poco elegante. **-ance, -ancy** *n.* ineleganza.

**ineligib-le** *adj.* ineleggibile; inabile (al servizio militare). **-ility** *n.* ineleggibilità; inabilità (al servizio militare).

**ineluctable** *adj.* ineluttabile; inevitabile.

**inept** *adj.* inetto; incapace; fatuo, sciocco. **-itude, -ness** *n.* inettitudine *f.*; incapacità; fatuità, schiocchezza; dappocaggine *f.*

**inequable** *adj.* non uniforme, mutevole.

**inequal** *adj.* See **unequal.**

**inequality** *n.* ineguaglianza; disuguaglianza; irregolarità.

**inequitable** *adj.* ingiusto, non equo.

**inequity** *n.* ingiustizia.

**ineradicable** *adj.* inestirpabile.

**inert** *adj.* inerte; apatico; pigro; indolente; (chem.) inerte. **-ia** *n.* inerzia; apatia; (chem.) inerzia. **-ness** *n.* inerzia.

**inescapable** *adj.* inevitabile.

**inessential** *adj.* non essenziale.

**inestimable** *adj.* inestimabile; incalcolabile.

**inevitab-le** *adj.* inevitabile; immancabile, certo; (fam.) solito; *n. to accept the —*, rassegnarsi. **-ility, -leness** *n.* inevitabilità.

**inexact** *adj.* inesatto; impreciso. **-itude, -ness** *n.* inesattezza; imprecisione.

**inexcusable** *adj.* in(e)scusabile, imperdonabile; ingiustificabile.

**inexhaustib-le** *adj.* inesauribile. **-ility, -leness** *n.* inesauribilità.

**inexistent** *adj.* inesistente.

**inexorab-le** *adj.* inesorabile; implacabile; accanito. **-ility, -leness** *n.* inesorabilità.

**inexpedi-ent** *adj.* inopportuno, non conveniente; svantaggioso. **-ence, -ency** *n.* inopportunità.

**inexpensive** *adj.* poco costoso, di poco prezzo, a buon mercato. **-ness** *n.* basso prezzo.

**inexperience** *n.* inesperienza; imperizia; mancanza di esperienza. **-d** *adj.* inesperto, senza esperienza; ingenuo, semplice.

**inexpert** *adj.* inesperto; inabile.

**inexpiable** *adj.* inespiabile.

**inexplicable** *adj.* inesplicabile, inspiegabile.

**inexplicit** *adj.* non esplicito non chiaro.

**inexplosive** *adj.* inesplodibile, non esplosivo.

**inexpressible** *adj.* inesprimibile, indicibile.

**inexpressive** *adj.* inespressivo, senza espressione.

**inexpugnable** *adj.* inespugnabile, invincibile.

**inextensible** *adj.* inestensibile.

**inextinguishable** *adj.* inestinguibile.

**inextricab-le** *adj.* inestricabile. **-leness, -ility** *n.* inestricabilità.

**infallib-le** *adj.* infallibile. **-ility -leness** *n.* infallibilità.

**infam-ous** *adj.* infame; scellerato; tristo. **-y** *n.* infamia; scelleratezza; disonore *m.*

**infancy** *n.* infanzia; *from —*, dalla più tenera età; (leg.) minorità; (fig.) periodo iniziale; inizi *m.pl.*

**infant** *adj.* infantile; (fig.) nuovo, nascente; *n.* neonato, bambino, infante *m.*; — *prodigy*, bambino prodigio; *the Infant Jesus*, il Bambino Gesù; — *school*, asilo infantile, giardino d'infanzia; (leg.) minorenne *m., f.*

**Infant-a** *n.* (hist.) infanta (di Spagna) **-(e)** *n.* (hist.) infante *m.* (di Spagna).

**infanticid-e** *n.* (person) infanticida *m., f.*; (crime) infanticidio *m.* **-al** *adj.* infanticida.

**infantil-e** *adj.* infantile, bambinesco, puerile; (med.) — *paralysis*, poliomielite *f.* **-ism** *n.* (med.) infantilismo.

**infantry** *n.* fanteria. **-man** *n.* fante *m.*, soldato di fanteria.

**infatuat-e** *tr.* infatuare; far impazzire; affascinare. **-ion** *n.* infatuazione.

**infect** *tr.* infettare; contagiare; ammorbire; appestare; (fig.) comunicarsi a; (phon.) modificare. **-ed** *adj.* infetto. **-ion** *n.* infezione; contagio; (fig.) contaminazione morale. **-ious** *adj.* infettivo; contagioso; (fam.) attaccaticcio. **-iousness** *n.* natura infettiva; contagio.

**infelicit-ous** *adj.* infelice; improprio; stonato. **-y** *n.* infelicità; sventura; (fig.) improprietà.

**infer** *tr.* inferire; dedurre; desumere; arguire; implicare; significare. **-able** *adj.* desumibile; deducibile. **-ence** *n.* inferenza; deduzione; conclusione. **-ential** *adj.* deduttivo.

**inferior** *adj.* inferiore; scadente, deteriore; *n.* inferiore *m., f.*; subalterno. **-ity** *n.* inferiorità; *-ity complex*, complesso d'inferiorità; *-ity in numbers*, inferiorità numerica.

**infernal** *adj.* infernale; *the — regions*, gl'inferi; (fig.) infernale, diabolico. **-ly** *adv.* infernalmente, diabolicamente; (fam.) *it is -ly hot*, fa un caldo infernale.

**infertil-e** *adj.* infertile; infecondo; sterile. **-ity** *n.* infertilità; sterilità.

**infest** *tr.* infestare.

**infidel** *adj., n.* (hist.) infedele *m., f.*; miscredente *m., f.* **-ity** *n.* infedeltà; miscredenza; (leg.) *conjugal -ity*, infedeltà coniugale.

**infighting** *n.* (boxing) lotta corpo a corpo.

**infiltrat-e** *tr.* infiltrare, filtrare;

*intr.* infiltrarsi. **-ion** *n.* infiltrazione.
**infinite** *adj.* infinito; illimitato; immenso; *an — number of*, un'infinità di; (gramm.) infinito, indefinito; *n.* infinito. **-ness** *n.* infinità; immensità.
**infinitesimal** *adj.* infinitesimale; *n.* infinitesimo, quantità infinitesimale.
**infinitive** *adj.*, *n.* (gramm.) infinito; *in the —*, all'infinito.
**infinit-y** *n.* infinità; immensità; (math.; photog.) infinito. **-ude** *n.* infinità, infinitudine *f.*
**infirm** *adj.* infermo; cagionevole; malaticcio; debole; acciaccoso; (fig.) irresoluto, incerto.
**infirm-ary** *n.* infermeria; ambulatorio; ospedale *m.* **-ity** *n.* infermità; debolezza; acciacco; (fig.) irresolutezza.
**inflame** *tr.* infiammare; accendere; (fig.) eccitare; attizzare; *intr.* infiammarsi; ardere; bruciare; prendere fuoco; (med.) infiammarsi.
**inflammab-le** *adj.* infiammabile. **-ility, -leness** *n.* infiammabilità.
**inflammat-ion** *n.* (med.) infiammazione; *— of the lungs*, polmonite *f.* **-ory** *adj.* infiammatorio.
**inflat-e** *tr.* gonfiare; enfiare; (finan.) inflazionare, provocare l'inflazione. **-ed** *adj.* gonfiato, gonfio; enfio; (fig.) ampolloso, altisonante; *-ed price*, prezzo esagerato. **-er** *n.* (motor.) pompa (per pneumatici).
**inflation** *n.* gonfiatura; (med.) enfiagione *f.*, gonfiore *m.*; (finan.) inflazione. **-ary** *adj.* (finan.) inflazionario. **-ism** *n.* (finan.) inflazionismo. **-ist** *n.* (finan.) inflazionista *m.*
**inflect** *tr.* flettere; piegare; (gramm.) flettere, inflettere; modulare. **-ion, inflexion** *n.* flessione, inflessione; (of voice) modulazione. **-ive** *adj.* (ling.) flessivo.
**inflexib-le** *adj.* inflessibile; rigido. **-ility, -leness** *n.* inflessibilità; rigidezza.
**inflict** *tr.* infliggere. **-ion** *n.* inflizione; (fam.) fastidio; seccatura.
**inflorescence** *n.* (bot.) infiorescenza.
**inflow** *n.* afflusso; cf. **influx.**
**influence** *n.* influenza; influsso; ascendente *m.*; *a person of —*, una persona autorevole; *to exert — on*, influenzare, esercitare il proprio ascendente su; (leg.) *undue —*, captazione; *tr.* influire su, influenzare; esercitare un ascendente su.
**influent** *adj.*, *n.* (geog.) affluente *m.*
**influential** *adj.* influente; autorevole; *— friends*, amici altolocati.
**influenza** *n.* influenza; grippe *m.*, *f.*; (pop.) forte raffreddore.
**influx** *n.* afflusso; affluenza; (geog.) confluenza; (fig.) invasione; concorso.
**inform** *tr.* informare; avvertire; avvisare, ragguagliare; rendere edotto; far sapere a; *to — of*, avvisare di; *to keep -ed*, ragguagliare, tenere al corrente; (lit.) dare forma a, ispirare; *intr. to — against*, denunciare.
**informal** *adj.* non ufficiale, senza cerimonia, senza formalità, alla buona; (leg.) irregolare. **-ity** *n.* mancanza di formalità; carattere *m.* intimo; (leg.) irregolarità.
**informant** *n.* informatore; (leg.) accusatore, querelante *m.*; (fam.) *who is your —?*, chi ti ha detto questo ?
**information** *n.* informazioni, notizie *f.pl.*; ragguagli *m.pl.*; *a piece of —*, un'informazione, una notizia; *to give someone — about*, informare qualcuno su; *to ask for —*, informarsi; *for your —*, a titolo d'informazione; *— bureau*, ufficio informazioni; (fam.) *a mine of —*, una miniera di notizie; (leg.) accusa, denuncia, delazione.
**informat-ive, -ory** *adj.* informativo; istruttivo.
**informer** *n.* delatore; spia; *to turn —*, denunciare i propri complici.
**infraction** *n.* infrazione.
**infra-dig** *adj.* (pop.) poco dignitoso.
**infrangible** *adj.* infrangibile.
**infra-red** *adj.* infrarosso.
**infrequ-ency** *n.* infrequenza; rarità. **-ent** *adj.* infrequente; raro; rado. **-ently** *adv.* raramente; *not -ently*, ogni tanto.
**infringe** *tr.* contravvenire a, violare; contraffare; *intr. to — upon*, usurpare. **-ment** *n.* infrazione; violazione; contraffazione; *-ment of copyright*, violazione delle leggi sui diritti d'autore; *to commit an -ment of*, violare. **-r** *n.* violatore; contraffatore; trasgressore.
**infuriate** *tr.* far infuriare; far arrabbiare; *to be -d*, essere furibondo; arrabbiarsi.
**infus-e** *tr.* infondere; instillare; ispirare; fare un'infusione di. **-ion** *n.* infusione; decotto.
**ingathering** *n.* raccolto, raccolta.
**ingen-ious** *adj.* ingegnoso; abile; geniale. **-iousness, -uity** *n.* ingegnosità; genialità; abilità inventiva; *to tax one's -uity*, ingegnarsi.
**ingenuous** *adj.* ingenuo, candido; schietto, sincero. **-ness** *n.* ingenuità; candore *m.*; semplicità.
**ingest** *tr.* ingerire. **-ion** *n.* ingerimento.
**ingle-nook** *n.* cantuccio presso il focolare.
**inglorious** *adj.* poco glorioso, inglorioso; ignominioso; umile, oscuro, sconosciuto.
**ingoing** *adj.* entrante, nuovo, in arrivo; *— tenant*, inquilino subentrante.
**ingot** *n.* (of gold, silver) lingotto; (of iron) pane *m.*
**ingrain** see **engrain.**
**ingrained** *adj.* radicato; inveterato.
**ingrate** *n.* ingrato *m.*, ingrata *f.*
**ingratiat-e** *tr.* ingraziare; *to — oneself with someone*, ingraziarsi qualcuno, insinuarsi nelle buone grazie di qualcuno. **-ing, -ory** *adj.* insinuante.
**ingratitude** *n.* ingratitudine *f.*
**ingredient** *n.* ingrediente *m.*; elemento.
**ingress** *n.* ingresso entrata.
**ingrowing** *adj.* che cresce internamente; *— toenail*, unghia incarnita.
**inguinal** *adj.* (anat.) inguinale.
**inhabit** *tr.* abitare; stare in; occupare. **-able** *adj.* abitabile. **-ant** *n.* abitante *m.*, *f.*
**inhalation** *n.* inalazione; aspirazione.
**inhal-e** *tr.* inalare; aspirare; *intr.* aspirare il fumo (di tabacco). **-ing** *n.* inalazione; aspirazione.
**inharmonious** *adj.* inarmonioso; disarmonico; discordante. **-ness** *n.* inarmonia; discordanza.
**inher-e** *intr.* essere inerente; inerire, essere proprio (di). **-ence, -ency** *n.* inerenza. **-ent** *adj.* inerente; innato; intrinseco; *to be -ent*, inerire.
**inherit** *tr.* ereditare. **-able** *adj.* ereditario, ereditabile. **-ance** *n.* eredità; successione; patrimonio; retaggio. **-or** *n.* erede, *m.*, *f.*
**inhibit** *tr.* inibire; sopprimere; (eccl.; leg.) interdire. **-ion** *n.* inibizione; (eccl.; leg.) interdizione. **-ive, -ory** *adj.* inibitorio.
**inhospitable** *adj.* inospitale. **-ness, inhospitality** *n.* inospitalità.
**inhuman** *adj.* inumano; barbaro; crudele. **-ity** *n.* inumanità; crudeltà.
**inhumation** *n.* inumazione; seppellimento.
**inhume** *tr.* inumare; seppellire; sotterrare.
**inimical** *adj.* ostile; avverso; contrario, nemico; *to be — to*, osteggiare. **-ity, -ness** *n.* inimitabilità.
**inimitable** *adj.* inimitabile.
**iniquitous** *adj.* iniquo; ingiusto; malvagio; *an — deed*, un'iniquità.
**iniquity** *n.* iniquità, ingiustizia; *a den of —* un baratro.
**initial** *adj.* iniziale; primo; *n.* iniziale *f.*; *pl.* sigla, parafa; *tr.* firmare con le iniziali siglare, parafare. **-ly** *adv.* nel principio, all'inizio.

**initiat-e** *adj.*, *n.* iniziato; *tr.* iniziare; istituire; introdurre. **-ion** *n.* iniziazione; inizio. **-ive** *n.* iniziativa; *to lack -ive*, mancare di iniziativa; *on one's own -ive*, di propria iniziativa. **-or** *n.* iniziatore. **-ory** *adj.* iniziativo; preliminare.

**inject** *tr.* immettere; (med.) iniettare. **-ion** *n.* immissione; (mech.; med.) iniezione; *hyperdermic -ion*, iniezione sottocutanea; *intramuscular -ion*, iniezione per via intramuscolare; *intravenous -ion*, iniezione per endovena; *to have an -ion*, farsi fare un'inezione. **-or** *n.* iniettore.

**injudicious** *adj.* poco giudizioso; imprudente. **-ness** *n.* mancanza di giudizio; imprudenza.

**injunction** *n.* ingiunzione; ordine *m.*; *to give -s to*, ingiungere a.

**injur-e** *tr.* ledere; nuocere a; danneggiare; far male a, far torto a; ferire; offendere. **-ed** *adj.* leso; danneggiato; (leg.) *-ed party*, parte lesa; offeso; ferito; *n.pl. the -ed*, i feriti. **-ious** *adj.* nocivo; dannoso; lesivo. **-y** *n.* lesione; torto; male *m.*; danno; offesa; ferita; infortunio; (comm.) avaria.

**injustice** *n.* ingiustizia; torto.

**ink** *n.* inchiostro; *copying —*, inchiostro copiativo; *Indian —*, inchiostro di China; *invisible —* inchiostro simpatico; *marking —*, inchiostro indelebile; *printing —*, inchiostro da stampa; *tr.* imbrattare d'inchiostro; (typ.) inchiostrare; *to — in*, ripassare ad inchiostro.

**ink-eraser** *n.* gomma da inchiostro. **-feed** *n.* (of fountain-pen) serbatoio. **-fish** *n.* (ichth.) seppia. **-horn** *n.* calamaio di corno.

**inkiness** *n.* nerezza; nero d'inchiostro.

**inking** *n.* (typ.) inchiostrazione.

**inkling** *n.* sospetto; sentore *m.*; indizio.

**ink-pad** *n.* tampone *m.*, cuscinetto per timbri.

**inkpot** *n.* calamaio.

**ink-slinger** *n.* imbrattacarte *m. indecl.* **-slinging** *n.* scambio di articoli ingiuriosi.

**inkstand** *n.* calamaio da scrittoio.

**ink-well** *n.* calamaio infisso.

**inky** *adj.* macchiato d'inchiostro; (fig.) nero come l'inchiostro.

**inlaid** *adj.* intarsiato, intavolato; *— work*, lavoro d'intarsio.

**inland** *adj.* interno; *— revenue*, fisco, erario; *adv.* all'interno, nell'interno; *n.* interno, entroterra *m.*

**in-laws** *n.* (fam.) parenti acquisiti.

**inlay** *n.* intarsiatura; intarsio; (archit.) incrostatura; *tr.* intarsiare; (archit.) incrostare.

**inlet** *n.* (geog.) insenatura; (needlew.) inserzione; (mech.) ammissione, presa.

**inmate** *n.* abitante *m.*, *f.*; coinquilino; (of hotel) pensionante *m.*, *f.*, ospite *m.*, *f.*; (of hospital) degente *m.*, *f.*; (of asylum, prison) internato.

**inmost, innermost,** *adj.* intimo; interiore; il più profondo; il più recondito.

**inn** *n.* albergo, locanda; *Inns of Court*, collegi degli avvocati.

**innate** *adj.* innato; ingenito, congenito; istintivo. **-ly** *adv.* istintivamente.

**innavigable** *adj.* innavigabile, non navigabile.

**inner** *adj.* interiore, interno; (fig.) intimo, segreto; (motor.) *— tube*, camera d'aria; (fam.) *— man*, appetito, stomaco.

**innermost** *adj.* See **inmost.**

**innings** *n.* (cricket) turno; (fig.) periodo di preminenza.

**innkeeper** *n.* albergatore; locandiere *m.*

**innoc-ence** *n.* innocenza; semplicità; candore *m.* **-ent** *adj.* innocente; semplice; ingenuo; *-ent of*, privo di, senza; *n.* innocente *m.*, *f.*; ingenuo; (bibl.) *slaughter of the -s*, strage degli innocenti. **-ently** *adv.* innocentemente, ingenuamente.

**innocu-ous** *adj.* innocuo; inoffensivo. **-ity, -ousness**; *n.* innocuità.

**innovat-e** *intr.* fare innovazione; introdurre novità. **-ion** *n.* innovazione; novità. **-or** *n.* innovatore.

**innuendo** *n.* insinuazione; allusione.

**innumerable** *adj.* innumerevole, innumerabile.

**inobservance** *n.* inosservanza.

**inoculat-e** *tr.* (med.) inoculare, vaccinare; (agric.) innestare; (fig.) inculcare. **-ion** *n.* (med.) inoculazione, vaccinazione; (agric.) innesto.

**inodorous** *adj.* inodoro.

**inoffensive** *adj.* inoffensivo, innocuo. **-ness** *n.* innocuità.

**inoperative** *adj.* inefficace; senza effetto.

**inopportun-e** *adj.* inopportuno; intempestivo. **-eness, -ity** *n.* inopportunità.

**inordinate** *adj.* smoderato; eccessivo; sregolato; disordinato. **-ly** *adv.* smoderatamente; eccessivamente. **-ness** *n.* smoderatezza; eccesso *m.*; sregolatezza; disordine *m.*

**inorganic** *adj.* inorganico.

**inornate** *adj.* disadorno, senza ornamento.

**inosculation** *n.* (anat.) anastomosi *f.*

**in-patient** *n.* (med.) degente *m.*, *f.*, ricoverato. **-pouring** *n.* afflusso.

**input** *n.* (mech.) energia assorbita; (electr.) alimentazione, entrata.

**inquest** *n.* inchiesta, istruttoria; *coroner's —*, inchiesta giudiziaria in caso di morte improvvisa.

**inquietude** *n.* inquietudine *f.*

**inquir-e** *tr.* chiedere; domandare; *to — the way*, chiedere la strada; *to — whether*, domandare se; *intr.* informarsi, chiedere notizie; *to — about*, chiedere notizie su; *to — after someone*, domandare di qualcuno; *to — into*, indagare, fare indagini su; *— within*, rivolgersi qui. **-er** *n.* indagatore; investigatore; chi cerca informazioni. **-ing** *adj.* curioso; indagatore.

**inquiry** *n.* domanda; informazione; *to make inquiries about*, assumere informazioni su; *— office*, ufficio informazioni; (leg.) inchiesta; *court of —*, commissione d'inchiesta; *to hold an — into*, procedere a un'inchiesta su.

**inquisition** ricerca; inchiesta; (eccl.) Inquisizione, Sant'Ufficio. **-al** *adj.* inquisitorio.

**inquisitive** *adj.* curioso; indagatore. **-ness** *n.* curiosità.

**inquisitor** *n.* (leg.) magistrato inquirente; (eccl.) inquisitore. **-ial** *adj.* inquisitoriale.

**inroad** *n.* incursione; irruzione; invasione; (fig.) *to make -s on someone's time*, far perdere tempo a qualcuno.

**inrush** *n.* irruzione; afflusso.

**insalubr-ious** *adj.* insalubre, malsano. **-ity** *n.* insalubrità.

**insane** *adj.* pazzo, matto; alienato; (fig.) insensato, folle.

**insanitary** *adj.* insalubre; antigienico; malsano.

**insanity** *n.* pazzia; demenza; alienazione mentale; (fig.) insensatezza; follia.

**insatiab-le** *adj.* insaziabile; ingordo. **-ility, -leness** *n.* insaziabilità.

**inscribe** *tr.* iscrivere; incidere, scolpire; (geom.) inscrivere; dedicare; *-d stock*, titoli *m.pl.* nominativi.

**inscription** *n.* iscrizione; soprascritta; epitaffio; dedica.

**inscrutab-le** *adj.* inscrutabile; imperscrutabile; impenetrabile. **-ility, -leness** *n.* inscrutabilità; impenetrabilità.

**insect** *n.* insetto. **-icide** *n.* insetticida *m.*

**insect-powder** *n.* polvere *f.* insetticida.

**insecur-e** *adj.* malsicuro; malfermo; incerto; instabile. **-ity** *n.* instabilità; mancanza di sicurezza; incertezza.

**insemination** *n.* (med.) fecondazione.

**insensate** *adj.* insensato.

**insensib-le** *adj.* insensitivo; indifferente; impassibile; impercettibile; svenuto, in stato di incoscienza, in deliquio. **-ility** *n.* insensibilità; indifferenza; incoscienza.

**insensitive** *adj.* insensibile. **-ness** *n.* insensibilità.

**insentient** *adj.* inanimato, insensibile.

**inseparab-le** *adj.* inseparabile. **-ility, -leness** *n.* inseparabilità.

**in·sert** *n.* inserzione; aggiunta; (mech.) guarnizione.

**insert** *tr.* inserire; introdurre; intercalare; *to — an advertisement in a newspaper*, fare un'inserzione su un giornale.

**insertion** *n.* inserzione; aggiunta.

**in·set** *n.* aggiunta; inserto; flusso; (typ.) fuori testo, aggiunta.

**inset** *tr.* inserire; (typ.) accavallare.

**inside** *adj.* interno, interiore; *— information*, informazioni confidenziali; (motor.) *— drive*, guida interna; *adv.* internamente, dentro, addentro; *— out*, a rovescio; *to turn — out*, rivoltare, rovesciare; *— and out*, dentro e fuori; *— of*, in meno di; *n.* interno, interiore *m.*; *on the —*, all'interno; (anat.) interiora *f.pl.*; (fam.) stomaco; *prep.* in, dentro, nell'interno di.

**insidious** *adj.* insidioso; perfido. **-ness** *n.* insidia; perfidia.

**insight** *n.* discernimento; intuito; acume *m.*; *to afford an — into*, lasciar intravvedere; *to get an — into*, riuscire a vedere a fondo in.

**insignia** *n.* insegne *f.pl.*; distintivo.

**insignific-ance** *n.* scarsa importanza; piccolezza; futilità. **-ant** *adj.* insignificante; di nessun conto; trascurabile.

**insincer-e** *adj.* insincero, poco sincero; falso; affettato. **-ity** *n.* insincerità; mancanza di sincerità; falsità.

**insinuat-e** *tr.* insinuare; introdurre; dare ad intendere; far credere. **-ing** *adj.* insinuante; subdolo; persuasivo. **-ion** *n.* insinuazione.

**insipid** *adj.* insipido; scipito; (fig.) insulso; sciocco. **-ity, -ness** *n.* insipidezza; scipitaggine *f.*; (fig.) insulsaggine *f.*; sciocchezza.

**insist** *intr.* insistere, persistere; *to — on*, insistere su; *to — on someone doing something*, insistere perchè qualcuno faccia qualcosa; *to — on knowing*, insistere per sapere. **-ence, -ency** *n.* insistenza; (fam.) *by dint of -ence*, batti e ribatti. **-ent** *adj.* insistente, persistente.

**insobriety** *n.* intemperanza.

**insolat-e** *tr.* insolare, soleggiare, esporre al sole. **-ion** *n.* insolazione; colpo di sole.

**insole** *n.* (shoem.) suola interna, sottopiede *m.*

**insol-ence** *n.* insolenza; impertinenza; alterigia; arroganza. **-ent** *adj.* insolente; impertinente; arrogante; *an -ent fellow*, un insolente.

**insolub-le** *adj.* insolubile. **-ility, -leness** *n.* insolubilità.

**insolvable** *adj.* insolubile.

**insolv-ency** *n.* insolvenza; insolvibilità. **-ent** *adj.* insolvente, insolvibile; *n.* debitore insolvente.

**insomnia** *n.* insonnia. **-c** *n.* insonne *m., f.*

**insomuch** *adv.* tanto; *— as*, tanto che, visto che; *— that*, fino al punto che, tanto che.

**insouci-ance** *n.* noncuranza. **-ant** *adj.* noncurante.

**inspect** *tr.* ispezionare; esaminare; visitare; verificare; (mil.) passare in rivista; (industr.) controllare, collaudare.

**inspection** *n.* ispezione; verifica; esame *m.*; (mil.) rivista; (industr.) controllo, collaudo.

**inspector** *n.* ispettore; verificatore; (of police) commissario; (rlwy.) controllore; (industr.) collaudatore. **-ship** *n.* ispettorato.

**inspiration** *n.* (of air) inspirazione, aspirazione; *to draw — from*, ispirarsi a, da; *poetic —*, vena poetica.

**inspire** *tr.* inspirare, aspirare; ispirare, (fig.) infondere; *an inspiring example*, un esempio ispiratore; *to — with confidence*, infondere fiducia in; *to be -d by nature*, ispirarsi alla natura, trarre ispirazione dalla natura; (pejor.) suggerire.

**inspirit** *tr.* animare; incoraggiare.

**inspissate** *tr.* inspessire; condensare.

**instability** *n.* instabilità; incostanza.

**instal(l)** *tr.* installare; impiantare; insediare; (eccl.) investire; insediare; (fam.) *to — oneself*, sedersi, mettersi. **-llation** *n.* installazione; insediamento; impianto.

**instalment** *n.* acconto, rata; *payment by -s*, pagamento rateale; dispensa, puntata.

**instance** *n.* esempio; caso; *for —*, per esempio; *in the first —*, in primo luogo; *at the — of*, a richiesta di; (leg.) istanza, domanda; *court of first —*, tribunale *m.* di prima instanza; *tr.* citare; addurre ad esempio.

**instancy** *n.* urgenza; insistenza; persistenza.

**instant** *adj.* immediato; istantaneo; urgente; (comm.) del corrente mese; *on the 5th inst.*, il cinque corrente; *n.* istante *m.*; momento; attimo; *in an —*, in un batter d'occhio; *at that very —*, in quel preciso momento; *the — (that)*, non appena (che).

**instantaneous** *adj.* istantaneo. **-ness** *n.* istantaneità.

**instanter** *adv.* (fam.) subito; all'istante.

**instantly** *adv.* immediatamente; subito; all'istante.

**instaurat-ion** *n.* restaurazione; rinnovamento. **-or** *n.* restauratore, rinnovatore.

**instead** *adv.* invece; in luogo; anzi, anzichè.

**instep** *n.* (anat.) collo del piede; (of shoe) collo della scarpa.

**instigat-e** *tr.* istigare; incitare; fomentare; aizzare. **-ion** *n.* istigazione; incitamento; *at the -ion of*, per istigazione di. **-or** *n.* istigatore; incitatore.

**instil(l)** *tr.* instillare; infondere; inculcare. **-lation** *n.* instillazione.

**in·stinct** *n.* istinto; impulso; *by —*, per istinto, istintivamente.

**instinct** *adj.* imbevuto, pieno.

**instinctive** *adj.* istintivo; spontaneo.

**institute** *n.* istituto; scuola; accademia; (leg.) istituzione; *tr.* istituire; stabilire; fondare; (leg.) *to — proceedings*, intentare processo; *to — an heir*, nominare un erede; (eccl.) investire.

**institution** *n.* istituzione; creazione, fondazione; istituto; ente *m.*; associazione; *charitable —*, istituto di beneficenza; (eccl.) nomina. **-al** *adj.* istituzionale. **-or** *n.* istitutore; fondatore.

**instruct** *tr.* istruire; dare istruzioni a; insegnare; informare; incaricare, dare ordini a, dare disposizioni a. **-ion** *n.* istruzione; insegnamento; ordine *m.*; disposizione. **-ional** *adj.* d'istruzione; educativo. **-ive** *adj.* istruttivo. **-or** *n.* istruttore; precettore; insegnante *m., f.*

**instructress** *n.* istruttrice; insegnante *f.*

**instrument** *n.* strumento; arnese *m.*; (mus.) strumento; (comm.) documento, titolo; (leg.) atto; (fig.) agente *m., f.*, strumento, mezzo. **-al** *adj.* strumentale; (fig.) attivo; *to be -al in doing something*, contribuire a far qualcosa; (mus.) *-al performer*, strumentista *m., f.* **-alist** *n.* (mus.) strumentista *m., f.*, concertista *m., f.* **-ality** *n.* mezzo; opera; aiuto. **-ation** *n.* (mus.) istrumentazione, istrumentatura, orchestrazione.

**instrument-board, -panel** *n.* (aeron.; motor.) cruscotto.

**insubordinat-e** *adj.* insubordinato; indisciplinato. **-ion** *n.* insubordinazione; indisciplinatezza.

**insubstantial** *adj.* incorporeo; inconsistente; irreale.

**insuccess** *n.* insuccesso.

**insufferable** *adj.* insopportabile; intollerabile; insoffribile.

**insuffici-ent** *adj.* insufficiente; inadeguato. **-ence -ency,** *n.* insufficienza; inadeguatezza.

**insufflat-ion** *n.* insufflazione; (med.) inalazione. **-or** *n.*

(industr.) soffiatore; (med.) inalatore.
**insular** *adj.* insulare; (fig.) — *mind*, mentalità ristretta. **-ism, -ity** *n.* insularità; (fig.) ristrettezza mentale; (pop.) campanilismo.
**insulat-e** *tr.* isolare; separare; staccare; (electr.) isolare. **-ion** *n.* isolamento; separazione; (electr.) isolamento. **-or** *n.* (electr.) isolatore.
**insulin** *n.* (pharm.) insulina.
**in'sult** *n.* insulto; affronto; oltraggio; ingiuria; offesa.
**insult** *tr.* insultare; ingiuriare; oltraggiare; offendere; *to feel -ed*, ritenersi offeso. **-ing** *adj.* insultante; ingiurioso; offensivo.
**insuperab-le** *adj.* insuperabile; invincibile; insormontabile. **-ility** *n.* insuperabilità.
**insupportable** *adj.* insopportabile; insoffribile; intollerabile. **-ness** *n.* insopportabilità.
**insuppressible** *adj.* insopprimibile; irrepressibile.
**insurable** *adj.* assicurabile.
**insurance** *n.* assicurazione; *accident* —, assicurazione contro gli infortuni; *fire* —, assicurazione contro gli incendi; *life* —, assicurazione sulla vita; *national* —, previdenza sociale; — *company*, società di assicurazione; — *policy*, polizza di assicurazione.
**insure** *tr.* assicurare; (fig.) garantire. **-d** *adj.*, *n.* assicurato. **-r** *n.* assicuratore.
**insurg-ence, -ency** *n.* insurrezione; rivolta. **-ent** *adj.*, *n.* insorto; ribelle *m.*, *f.*
**insurmountable** *adj.* insormontabile; insuperabile.
**insurrection** *n.* insurrezione; sollevazione; rivolta; *to rise in* —, insorgere. **-al, -ary** *adj.* insurrezionale. **-ist** *n.* insorto; rivoltoso.
**insusceptib-le** *adj.* non suscettibile, insensibile. **-ility** *n.* mancanza di suscettibilità, insensibilità.
**intact** *adj.* intatto; intero; integro.
**intaglio** *n.* intaglio; incisione; *to do — work*, incidere.
**intake** *n.* assorbimento; (hydr. eng.) presa, immissione; (of pump) aspirazione; (min.) pozzo d'aerazione; (of tube) strozzatura.
**intangib-le** *adj.* intangibile; inafferrabile. **-ility** *n.* intangibilità.
**integer** *n.* (math.) numero intero.
**integral** *adj.* integro, integrale; compiuto; totale; (math.) integrale. **-ity** *n.* integralità.
**integrat-e** *tr.* integrare; completare; (math.) integrare. **-ion** *n.* integrazione.
**integrity** *n.* integrità; probità.
**integument** *n.* (bot.) tegmine *m.*, tegumento; *external* —, primina.
**intellect** *n.* intelletto; intendimento; intelligenza; (fam.) mente *f.*
**intellectual** *adj.* intellettuale; intelligente; *n.* intellettuale *m.*, *f.* **-ity** *n.* intellettualità.
**intelligence** *n.* intelligenza; sagacia; perspicacia; intesa; notizie *f.pl.*, informazioni *f.pl.*; (*Italian*) *Military Intelligence*, Servizio Informazioni Militari (S.I.M.); *Naval Intelligence*, Servizio Informazioni Navali (S.I.N.); *Air Intelligence*, Servizio Informazioni Aeronautiche (S.I.A.).
**intelligent** *adj.* intelligente; perspicace; sagace. **-sia** *n.* intelligenzia; intellettuali *m.pl.*
**intelligib-le** *adj.* intelligibile; comprensibile. **-ility, -leness** *n.* intelligibilità; chiarezza.
**intemperance** *n.* intemperanza; smoderatezza; abuso.
**intemperate** *adj.* intemperato; sfrenato; smoderato; eccessivo; dedito al bere; (of climate) rigido.
**intend** *tr.* intendere; aver l'intenzione (di); prefiggersi; proporsi; avere in mente (di); destinare, designare; intendere (dire), significare. **-ance, -ancy** *n.* intendenza. **-ant** *n.* intendente *m.*, sovraintendente *m.* **-ed** *adj.* intenzionale; premeditato; deliberato; progettato; voluto; *n.* (fam.) fidanzato *m.*, fidanzata *f.*
**intense** *adj.* intenso; profondo; vivo, veemente; — *pain*, dolore acuto; (fig.) teso; emotivo.
**intensif-y** *tr.* intensificare; rinforzare. **-ication** *n.* intensificazione.
**intens-ity, -eness** *n.* intensità; veemenza; vigore *m.*; (photog.) forza, intensità.
**intensive** *adj.* intenso, intensivo; concentrato; — *work*, lavoro indefesso; (gramm.) intensivo, enfatico.
**intent** *adj.* intento, attento assorto; *to be — on*, essere tutto intento a, aver l'intenzione di; — *gaze*, sguardo fisso; *n.* intento; scopo deliberato; proposito; *with good* —, con buone intenzioni; *with — to kill*, con lo scopo deliberato di uccidere; *to all -s and purposes*, virtualmente, effettivamente, a tutti gli effetti.
**intention** *n.* intenzione; intento; proposito; scopo; fine *m.*; *to have the — of*, avere l'intenzione di, intendere di; *with the best -s*, a fin di bene; *what are his -s ?*, che intenzioni ha ?, che cosa intende fare ?; (provb.) *the road to hell is paved with good -s*, di buone intenzioni è lastricato l'inferno. **-al** *adj.* intenzionale, premeditato, deliberato. **-ally** *adv.* apposta; deliberatamente.
**intently** *adv.* intentamente; attentamente.
**inter** *tr.* seppellire; sotterrare; inumare.
**inter-** *pref.* inter-.
**interact** *intr.* reagire reciprocamente, esercitare un'azione reciproca **-ion** *n.* azione reciproca.
**inter-allied** *adj.* interalleato. **-breed** *tr.* incrociare; *intr.* incrociarsi. **-calate** *tr.* intercalare; interpolare. **-cede** *intr.* intercedere. **-cellular** *adj.* (biol.) intercellulare.
**intercept** *n.* intercettamento; messaggio intercettato; (geom.) segmento; *tr.* intercettare; interrompere; arrestare, fermare. **-ion** *n.* intercettamento, intercettazione.
**inter-cession** *n.* intercessione; intervento. **-cessor** *n.* intercessore, intermediario.
**interchange** *n.* scambio; baratto; avvicendamento; *tr.* intercambiare, scambiare; alternare; avvicendare; *intr.* scambiarsi; avvicendarsi. **-ability** *n.* intercambiabilità; scambievolezza. **-able** *adj.* intercambiabile; scambievole; vicendevole.
**intercolonial** *adj.* intercoloniale.
**intercommunicat-e** *intr.* intercomunicare; essere intercomunicante. **-ion** *n.* intercomunicazione.
**inter-continental** *adj.* intercontinentale. **-costal** *adj.* intercostale. **-course** *n.* comunicazione; relazioni *f.pl.*; rapporti *m.pl.*; *sexual* —, rapporti sessuali, coito. **-current** *adj.* intercorrente. **-departmental** *adj.* interdipartimentale.
**interdepend** *intr.* dipendere l'uno dall'altro. **-ence** *n.* interdipendenza. **-ent** *adj.* interdipendente.
**interdict** *n.* divieto; interdizione; (eccl.) interdetto; *tr.* interdire; proibire; vietare. **-ion** *n.* interdizione; divieto.
**interest** *n.* interesse *m.*; interessamento; *of* —, interessante; *to take an — in*, interessarsi di; *to lose — in*, disinteressarsi di; interesse, vantaggio, profitto; (finan.) interesse; *compound* —, interesse composto; *rate of* — tasso di interesse; *at 3%* — all'interesse del tre per cento; (fig.) *to repay with* —, restituire ad usura; *tr.* interessare; destare interesse in; *to be -ed*, interessarsi. **-ed** *adj.* *the -ed parties*, le parti interessate, gli interessati; *-ed motives*, motivi interessati. **-ing** *adj.* interessante; emozionante; (fam.) *in an -ing condition*, in stato interessante, incinta.
**interfer-e** *intr.* intervenire; intromettersi; immischiarsi; infram(m)ettersi; *to — with*, ostacolare; (phys.; radio) interferire. **-ence** *n.* inframmettenza; ingerenza; intromissione;

intervento; (phys.; radio) interferenza.
**interim** *adj.* provvisorio; ad interim; (pol.) interinale; (finan.) — *dividend*, dividendo provvisorio; — *statement*, relazione interinale; *n.* interim *m.*; intervallo; (pol.) interinato; *in the* —, nel frattempo.
**interior** *adj.* interiore, interno; *n.* interiore *m.*, interno; (geog.) entroterra *m.*, *f.*; (art) interno; — *decorator*, arredatore.
**interject** *tr.* interloquire con. **-ion** *n.* (gramm.) interiezione.
**inter-knit** *tr.* intrecciare; *intr.* intrecciarsi. **-lace** *tr.* intrecciare; allacciare; *intr.* intrecciarsi. **-lard** *tr.* infiorare. **-leave** *tr.* interfogliare. **-linear** *adj.* interlineare. **-lineation** *n.* interlineazione. **-link** *tr.* concatenare. **-lock** *tr.* allacciare; unire; congiungere; (cinem.) sincronizzare; *intr.* allacciarsi, congiungersi, unirsi; (mech.) combaciare.
**interlocut-ion** *n.* interlocuzione. **-or** *n.* interlocutore. **-ory** *adj.* interlocutorio.
**interloper** *n.* intruso.
**interlude** *n.* (theatr.) intervallo; (mus.) intermezzo, interludio.
**intermarr-iage** *n.* matrimonio fra consanguinei; matrimonio fra razze diverse. **-y** *intr.* imparentarsi per mezzo di matrimonio.
**intermediary** *adj.* intermedio; *n.* mediatore, intermediario.
**intermediate** *adj.* intermedio; frapposto; medio; — *examinations*, esami *m.pl.* preliminari di laurea; *intr.* fare da mediatore; interporsi.
**interment** *n.* sepoltura, seppellimento; sotterramento; inumazione.
**interminable** *adj.* interminabile; senza fine.
**intermingle** *tr.* mescolare; frammischiare; *intr.* mescolarsi insieme.
**intermission** *n.* intermissione; interruzione; sosta; pausa.
**intermit** *tr.* interrompere; sospendere; *intr.* interrompersi; essere intermittente. **-tence** *n.* intermittenza, pausa. **-tent** *adj.* intermittente.
**intermix** *tr.* frammischiare; *intr.* frammischiarsi. **-ture** *n.* miscuglio, mescolanza.
**in'tern** *n.* (med.) medico interno.
**intern** *tr.* internare.
**internal** *adj.* interno, interiore; (fig.) intimo, intrinseco; (mech.) — *combustion engine*, motore *m.* a scoppio.
**international** *adj.* internazionale; (sport) — *player*, (giocatore) nazionale *m.*; *n.* (pol.) Internazionale *f.* **-ism** *n.* internazionalismo. **-ist** *n.* internazionalista *m.*, *f.* **-ize** *tr.* internazionalizzare; rendere internazionale.
**internecine** *adj.* micidiale; reciprocamente nocivo.
**intern-ee** *n.* internato. **-ment** *n.* internamento; *-ment camp*, campo di concentramento.
**inter-oceanic** *adj.* interoceanico. **-page** *tr.* interfogliare. **-parietal** *adj.* (anat.) interparietale.
**interpellat-e** *tr.* interpellare; fare una interpellanza. **-ion** *n.* interpellanza. **-or** *n.* interpellante *m.*, *f.*
**interpenetrat-e** *tr.* compenetrare; *intr.* compenetrarsi. **-ion** *n.* compenetrazione.
**inter-phone** *n.* citofono. **-planetary** *adj.* interplanetario. **-play** *n.* azione reciproca; *-play of colours*, giuoco di colori.
**interpolat-e** *tr.* interpolare; inserire; intercalare; *-ed clause*, inciso. **-ion** *n.* interpolazione.
**interpos-e** *tr.* interporre, frapporre; *intr.* interporsi, frapporsi; intervenire. **-ition** *n.* interposizione; intervento.
**interpret** *tr.* interpretare; spiegare; (theatr.) *to — a part*, creare una parte; *intr.* fare l'interprete. **-ation** *n.* interpretazione; spiegazione; *to give an -ation of*, interpretare. **-ative** *adj.* interpretativo. **-er** *n.* interprete *m.*, *f.*; *to act as -er*, fare da interprete. **-ership** *n.* funzione di interprete. **-ress** *n.* interprete *f.*
**inter-racial** *adj.* comune a più razze; (of marriage) fra persone di razze diverse. **-regnum** *n.* interregno; (fig.) intervallo. **-relation** *n.* relazione, rapporto. **-relationship** *n.* interdipendenza.
**interrogat-e** *tr.* interrogare; (leg.) esaminare. **-ion** *n.* interrogazione *f.*; note (*or mark*) *of* —, punto interrogativo. **-ive** *adj.* interrogativo; *n.* interrogativo, parola interrogativa. **-or** *n.* interrogatore; interrogante *m.*, *f.*; esaminatore.
**interrupt** *tr.* interrompere; troncare, sospendere; bloccare; disturbare. **-er** *n.* interruttore. **-ion** *n.* interruzione; sospensione. **-ive** *adj.* interrompente.
**intersect** *tr.* intersecare; tagliare; incrociare; *intr.* intersecarsi; incrociarsi. **-ion** *n.* intersecazione; (geom.) intersezione, intersecamento; (archit.) incrociata.
**interspace** *n.* intervallo, spazio.
**interspers-e** *tr.* cospargere, spargere qua e là; disseminare. **-ion** *n.* cospargimento.
**inter-state** *adj.* fra stati.
**interstellar** *adj.* interstellare.
**intersti-ce** *n.* interstizio. **-tial** *adj.* interstiziale.
**inter-tangle** *tr.* intrecciare insieme; *to become -tangled* impigliarsi, attorcigliarsi. **-tribal** *adj.* comune a parecchie tribù; fra tribù. **-twine** *tr.* intrecciare; attorcigliare; aggraticciare; aggrovigliare; *intr.* intrecciarsi; attorcigliarsi; aggrovigliarsi.
**interval** *n.* intervallo; intermezzo, spazio; pausa, intermissione; (meteor.) *bright -s*, schiarite *f.pl.*
**intervene** *intr.* intervenire; frapporsi, intromettersi; accadere, avvenire; (of time) trascorrere.
**intervention** *n.* intervento; interposizione; mediazione. **-ist** *n.* (pol.) interventista *m.*, *f.*
**interview** *n.* intervista; abboccamento; colloquio.
**interview** *tr.* abboccarsi con; (journ.) intervistare. **-er** *n.* (journ.) intervistatore.
**inter-weave** *tr.* intessere; intrecciare; *intr.* intrecciarsi. **-wove**, **-woven** *p.def.*, *part.*
**intest-acy** *n.* (leg.) successione ab intestato. **-ate** *adj.* (leg.) intestato.
**intestin-e** *adj.* intestino; interno; domestico; *n.* (anat.) intestino, budello; *pl.* *-s*, viscere *f.pl.*, budella *f.pl.* **-al** *adj.* (anat.) intestinale.
**intimacy** *n.* intimità; domestichezza, dimestichezza; *sexual* —, rapporti *m.pl.* sessuali.
**intimate**[1] *adj.* intimo; familiare; a tu per tu; *to be on — terms with*, essere in rapporti intimi con; (fig.) profondo; *n.* amico intimo.
**intimat-e**[2] *tr.* intimare; far sapere; notificare; dichiarare; accennare (a); suggerire. **-ion** *n.* intimazione; avviso; cenno; indizio.
**intimidat-e** *tr.* intimidire; intimorire. **-ion** *n.* intimidazione. **-ory** *adj.* intimidatorio.
**into** *prep.* in, dentro, entro; *far — the night*, fino a tarda notte; *to grow* —, diventare.
**intolerable** *adj.* intollerabile; insopportabile; insoffribile. **-ness** *n.* intollerabilità; insopportabilità.
**intoler-ance** *n.* intolleranza. **-ant** *adj.* intollerante; intransigente; *to be -ant of*, non poter soffrire.
**intonation** *n.* intonazione; modulazione; (eccl.) cantilena; (fig.) cadenza; ritmo.
**intone** *tr.* intonare; (eccl.) recitare cantando, cantilenare.
**intoxic-ant** *adj.* inebriante; alcoolico; intossicante; *n.* bevanda alcoolica. **-ate** *tr.* inebriare, ubriacare; intossicare; (fig.) eccitare; esaltare. **-ated** *adj.* ubriaco, inebriato; (fig.) ebbro, eccitato. **-ation** *n.* ubriachezza, ebbrezza; (fig.) eccitazione.
**intractab-le** *adj.* intrattabile, indocile, scontroso. **-ility**, **-leness** *n.* intrattabilità, indocilità.

**intransig-ence, -ency** *n.* intransigenza. **-ent** *adj.* intransigente.
**intransitive** *adj., n.* (gramm.) intransitivo.
**intravenous** *adj.* (med.) endovenoso; — *injection*, endovenosa.
**intreat** *tr.* See **entreat.**
**intrepid** *adj.* intrepido; impavido. **-ity** *n.* intrepidezza, intrepidità; coraggio.
**intric-acy** *n.* groviglio; viluppo; complicazione; (fig.) labirinto. **-ate** *adj.* intricato; involuto, aggrovigliato; complicato; difficile.
**intrigu-e** *n.* intrigo; raggiro; macchinazione; maneggio; tresca; (theatr.) intreccio; *intr* intrigare, fare cabala, complottare; *tr.* (fam.) interessare; incuriosire; affascinare. **-er** *n.* intrigante *m., f.* **-ing** *adj.* intrigante; (fam.) interessante; affascinante; curioso.
**intrinsic** *adj.* intrinseco; essenziale; reale.
**intro-** *pref.* intro-.
**introduce** *tr.* introdurre; far entrare; presentare; far conoscere. **-r** *n.* introduttore; presentatore.
**introduction** *n.* introduzione; presentazione; *letter of* —, lettera di presentazione, lettera di raccomandazione; esordio; prefazione; manuale elementare.
**introductory** *adj.* introduttivo; preliminare.
**introit** *n.* (eccl.) introito.
**intro-mission** *n.* intromissione. **-spection** *n.* introspezione. **-spective** *adj.* introspettivo. **-version** *n.* introversione. **-vert** *adj., n.* introvertito.
**intrude** *tr.* intromettere; imporre; *to — one's opinions on*, far accettare le proprie opinioni a; *intr.* intromettersi arbitrariamente; (fam.) disturbare. **-r** *n.* intruso; (fam.) importuno, seccatore.
**intrusion** *n.* intrusione; (leg.) usurpazione; (geol.) filone *m.*
**intrusive** *adj.* intruso; importuno; invadente; (geol.) intrusivo. **-ness** *n.* importunità; indiscrezione.
**intuit-ion** *n.* intuito, intuizione. **-ive** *adj.* intuitivo.
**intumesc-ence** *n.* tumefazione, intumescenza. **-ent** *adj.* intumescente.
**inundat-e** *tr.* inondare; allagare. **-ion** *n.* inondazione; allagamento.
**inurban-e** *adj.* inurbano; scortese. **-ity** *n.* inurbanità; scortesia.
**inure** *tr.* abituare; avvezzare; assuefare; agguerrire; *to become -d to*, agguerrirsi a.
**inutility** *n.* inutilità; futilità.
**invade** *tr.* invadere; assalire; violare. **-r** *n.* invasore.
**inva·lid** *adj.* invalido; non valevole; nullo; *tr.* rendere invalido; dichiarare inabile per invalidità.
**invalid** *n.* malato; invalido; infermo; cronico; (mil.) *to be -ed out of the army*, essere riformato.
**invalid-ate** *tr.* invalidare; infirmare; annullare. **-ity** *n.* invalidità.
**invaluable** *adj.* inestimabile; impagabile.
**invariabl-e** *adj.* invariabile; (math.) costante. **-y** *adv.* sempre; invariabilmente.
**invasion** *n.* invasione; (fig.) intrusione; (leg.) violazione.
**invective** *n.* invettiva; ingiuria.
**inveigh** *intr.* inveire; declamare (contro).
**inveigle** *tr.* adescare; allettare; indurre; *to — someone into doing something*, indurre qualcuno a far qualcosa. **-ment** *n.* adescamento; allettamento.
**invent** *tr.* inventare; trovare. **-ion** *n.* invenzione; scoperta; (provb.) *necessity is the mother of* —, la necessità è il miglior maestro. **-ive** *adj.* inventivo; ingegnoso. **-iveness** *n.* inventiva; fantasia. **-or** *n.* inventore.
**inventory** *n.* inventario; *tr.* inventariare, fare l'inventario di, elencare.
**invers-e** *adj.* inverso; opposto; contrario; *in — ratio*, in ragione inversa. **-ion** *n.* inversione; rovesciamento.
**invert** *tr.* invertire; rovesciare; capovolgere; trasporre. **-ed** *adj.* invertito; rovesciato; (typ.) *-ed commas*, virgolette *f.pl.*
**invertebrate** *adj., n.* invertebrato.
**invest** *tr.* rivestire, investire; (finan.) investire; *intr.* fare investimenti; (fam.) *to — in*, comprare; (mil.) investire, cingere d'assedio, circondare.
**investigat-e** *tr.* investigare; indagare; esplorare. **-ion** *n.* investigazione; indagine *f.*; *to cause an -ion to be made*, far fare delle indagini. **-ive** *adj.* investigativo. **-or** *n.* investigatore; indagatore. **-ory** *adj.* investigativo; indagatore.
**investiture** *n.* investitura.
**investment** *n.* (finan.) investimento; — *trust*, società finanziaria di investimento; (mil.) assedio, investimento.
**investor** *n.* investitore; chi investe capitali; *small* —, piccolo risparmiatore.
**inveterate** *adj.* inveterato; accanito; (med.) inguaribile, cronico.
**invidious** *adj.* sgradevole; irritante, odioso; antipatico. **-ness** *n.* odiosità; spiacevolezza.
**invigilat-e** *tr., intr.* sorvegliare. **-ion** *n.* sorveglianza. **-or** *n.* sorvegliante *m., f.*; assistente *m., f.*
**invigorat-e** *tr.* rinvigorire; rinforzare; rianimare. **-ing** *adj.* rinforzante; fortificante; salubre, corroborante. **-ion** *n.* rinvigorimento.
**invincib-le** *adj.* invincibile. **-ility** *n.* invincibilità.
**inviolab-le** *adj.* inviolabile; sacrosanto. **-ility** *n.* inviolabilità.
**inviolate** *adj.* inviolato; illeso; integro; intatto.
**invisib-le** *adj.* invisibile; impercettibile; — *mending*, rammendo invisibile; — *ink*, inchiostro simpatico. **-ility, -leness** *n.* invisibilità.
**invit-e** *tr.* invitare; convitare; *-d guests*, i convitati, gli invitati; *to — in*, invitare ad entrare; *to — out*, invitare a uscire; (fig.) provocare; esporsi a; *to — criticism*, esporsi a critiche. **-ation** *n.* invito. **-ing** *adj.* attraente; seducente; invitante.
**invocat-ion** *n.* invocazione; appello. **-ory** *adj.* invocativo; invocante.
**invoice** *n.* (comm.) fattura; *tr.* fatturare.
**invoke** *tr.* invocare; chiedere; impetrare; evocare; (fig.) appellarsi a.
**involuntar-y** *adj.* involontario. **-iness** *n.* involontarietà.
**involution** *n.* involuzione; (math.) elevazione a potenza.
**involv-e** *tr.* attorcigliare; avvolgere a spirale; complicare; involvere; coinvolgere; compromettere; implicare; *to be -d in a scandal*, essere coinvolto in uno scandalo; richiedere; comportare; *to — expense*, comportare spese; (math.) elevare a potenza. **-ed** *adj.* complicato; aggrovigliato; *-ed style*, stile involuto. **-ement** *n.* l'essere coinvolto; implicazione.
**invulnerab-le** *adj.* invulnerabile. **-ility** *n.* invulnerabilità.
**inward** *adj.* interiore, interno; (fig.) intimo. **-ly** *adv.* interiormente; nell'intimo dell'anima; fra sè. **-ness** *n.* interiorità; intimità; spiritualità.
**inward(s)** *adv.* verso l'interno; all'interno; internamente, interiormente; (naut.) — *bound*, in viaggio di ritorno.
**inwrought** *adj.* intessuto; ricamato; lavorato.
**iod-ide** *n.* (chem.) ioduro. **-ine** *n.* (chem.) iodio. **-ize** *tr.* (chem.) iodare. **-oform** *n.* (chem.) iodoformio.
**ion** *n.* (phys.) ione *m.*
**Ionian** *adj.* (geog.) Ionio; — *Sea*, Mare Ionio.
**Ionic** *adj.* (archit.) ionico.
**ionium** *n.* (chem.) ionio.
**ionosphere** *n.* ionosfera.
**iota** *n.* iota *m.*
**I.O.U.** *n.* (contr. for **I owe you**) dichiarazione di debito.
**ipecacuanha** *n.* (bot.; pharm.) ipecacuana.
**Iphigenia** *pr.n.* Ifigenia.

**Iran** *pr.n.* (geog.) Iran *m.* **-ian** *adj.* iranico.
**Iraq** *pr.n.* (geog.) Irak *m.* **-ui** *adj.*, *n.* iracheno.
**irascib-le** *adj.* irascibile; iracondo; irritabile; collerico. **-ility** *n.* irascibilità; iracondia.
**irate** *adj.* adirato; iroso; incollerito; arrabbiato.
**ire** *n.* ira; collera; sdegno.
**Ireland** *pr.n.* (geog.) Irlanda.
**iridesc-ence** *n.* iridescenza. **-ent** *adj.* iridescente.
**Iris**[1] *pr.n.* Iride.
**iris**[2] *n.* (anat.) iride *f.*; (bot.) giaggiolo, iris *m. indecl.*
**Irish** *adj.* irlandese; — *Free State*, Stato Libero d'Irlanda; la Repubblica irlandese.; *n. pl. the* —, gli Irlandesi. **-man** *n.* irlandese *m.* **-woman** *n.* irlandese *f.*
**irk** *tr.* infastidire; ripugnare; annoiare; dar noia a. **-some** *adj.* noioso; fastidioso; seccante; molesto, tedioso. **-someness** *n.* fastidio; noia; tedio.
**iron** *adj.* di ferro; ferreo; ferruginoso; (colour) color ferro; *n.* ferro; — *age*, età del ferro; — *curtain*, cortina di ferro; — *industry*, industria metallurgica; — *lung*, polmone *m.* d'acciaio; — *ore*, minerale *m.* di ferro; (mil.) — *rations*, razioni di riserva; *cast* —, ghisa; *corrugated* —, lamiera di ferro ondulato; *wrought* —, ferro battuto; *flat* —, ferro da stiro; (golf) mazza; *pl.* *-s*, catene *f.pl.*, ceppi *m.pl.*; *to have too many -s in the fire*, avere troppa carne al fuoco; (provb.) *strike while the -'s hot*, battere il ferro mentre è caldo; *tr.* stirare; (fig.) *to — out*, spianare; rivestire di ferro; ferrare.
**iron-bound** *adj.* cinto di ferro, ferrato; (fig.) — *coast*, costa rocciosa.
**ironclad** *adj.* corazzato; *n.* (naut.) corazzata.
**ironer** *n.* stiratore *m.*, stiratrice *f.*
**iron-foundry** *n.* ferriera, fonderia. **-handed** *adj.* dal pugno di ferro; severo; inflessibile.
**ironic(al)** *adj.* ironico.
**ironing** *n.* stiratura.
**ironist** *n.* ironista *m.*, *f.*
**iron-master** *n.* padrone *m.* di ferriera. **-monger** *n.* negoziante *m.* in ferramenta. **-mongery** *n.* ferramenta *f.pl.*, ferrame *m.*
**iron-mould** *n.* macchia di ruggine.
**iron-smith** *n.* fabbro ferraio. **-ware** *n.* See **ironmongery.**
**irony** *n.* ironia.
**iroquois** *adj.*, *n.* (ethn.) irochese *m.*, *f.*
**irradi-ance** *n.* irradiazione; irraggiamento. **-ate** *tr.* irradiare; illuminare; rischiarare; *intr.* irradiare; risplendere. **-ation** *n.* irradiazione; irraggiamento; illuminazione.
**irrational** *adj.* irrazionale, irragionevole; illogico, assurdo; *n.* (math.) numero irrazionale. **-ity** *n.* irrazionalità; irragionevolezza; assurdità.
**irreclaimable** *adj.* incorreggibile; non bonificabile.
**irreconcilab-le** *adj.* irreconciliabile; incompatibile. **-ility** *n.* irreconciliabilità; inconciliabilità; incompatibilità.
**irrecoverable** *adj.* irrecuperabile; inesigibile; irreparabile.
**irredeemable** *adj.* irredimibile; incorreggibile.
**irredent-ism** *n.* (pol.) irredentismo. **-ist** *adj.*, *n.* (pol.) irredentista *m.*, *f.*
**irreducib-le** *adj.* irriducibile. **-ility, -leness** *n.* irriducibilità.
**irrefragable** *adj.* irrefragabile.
**irrefrangible** *adj.* irrefrangibile; inviolabile.
**irrefutab-le** *adj.* irrefutabile. **-ility** *n.* irrefutabilità.
**irregular** *adj.* irregolare; anormale; asimmetrico; accidentato; sregolato, disordinato; (gramm.) irregolare; *n.pl.* (mil.) truppe irregolari. **-ity** *n.* irregolarità; anormalità.
**irrelev-ance, -ancy** *n.* non pertinenza. **-ant** *adj.* non pertinente; non appropriato; alieno; irrilevante, insignificante; *to make -ant remarks*, divagare.
**irreligi-ous** *adj.* irreligioso; empio. **-on, -ousness** *n.* irreligione, irreligiosità.
**irremediable** *adj.* irrimediabile; irreparabile.
**irremissible** *adj.* irremissibile; imperdonabile.
**irremovable** *adj.* irremovibile, inamovibile.
**irreparab-le** *adj.* irreparabile; irrimediabile. **-ility, -leness** *n.* irreparabilità.
**irreplaceable** *adj.* insostituibile.
**irreprehensible** *adj.* irreprensibile. **-ness** *n.* irreprensibilità.
**irrepressible** *adj.* irreprimibile, irrefrenabile.
**irreproachable** *adj.* irreprensibile, incensurabile.
**irresistib-le** *adj.* irresistibile. **-ility, -leness** *n.* irresistibilità.
**irresolute** *adj.* irresoluto; indeciso; dubitoso. **-ness, irresolution** *n.* irresolutezza; irresoluzione; indecisione.
**irresolvable** *adj.* insolubile.
**irrespective** *adj.* — *of*, senza riguardo a, noncurante di, senza preoccuparsi di. **-ly** *adv.* senza riguardo.
**irresponsib-le** *adj.* irresponsabile. **-ility** *n.* irresponsabilità.
**irresponsive** *adj.* che non risponde; che non reagisce; flemmatico; insensibile. **-ness** *n.* riservatezza; insensibilità.
**irretrievab-le** *adj.* irrecuperabile; irreparabile; irrimediabile. **-ility** *n.* irrecuperabilità; irreparabilità.
**irrever-ence** *n.* irriverenza; irreligiosità; empietà; insolenza. **-ent** *adj.* irriverente; irreligioso; empio; insolente.
**irrevocab-le** *adj.* irrevocabile. **-ility, -leness** *n.* irrevocabilità.
**irrigat-e** *tr.* irrigare; irrorare; bagnare. **-ion** *n.* irrigazione; *attrib.* irrigatore.
**irritab-le** *adj.* irritabile; permaloso; che prude, pruriginoso. **-ility, -leness** irritabilità; permalosità.
**irritat-e** *tr.* irritare; stuzzicare; seccare; *to be -ed*, irritarsi, adirarsi, arrabbiarsi; *intr.* prudere. **-ing** *adj.* irritante; stuzzicante; seccante. **-ion** *n.* irritazione; provocazione; prurito, prurigine *f.*
**irrupt** *intr.* irrompere. **-ion** *n.* irruzione; incursione; scorreria.
**is** See **be.**
**Isaac** *pr.n.* Isacco.
**Isabel, Isabella** *pr.n.* Isabella.
**Isaiah** *pr.n.* Isaia *m.*
**Iscariot** *pr.n.* *Judas* —, Giuda Iscariota *m.*
**Iseult** *pr.n.* Isotta.
**Ishmael** *pr.n.* Ismaele **-ite** *n.* ismaelita *m.*, *f.*
**Isidorus, Isidore** *pr.n.* Isidoro.
**isinglass** *n.* colla di pesce; gelatina; (miner.) mica.
**Isis** *pr.n.* (myth.) Iside.
**Islam** *n.* Islam *m.*, Islamismo. **-ic** *adj.* islamico.
**island** *n.* isola; *traffic* —, salvagente *m.*, spartitraffico. **-er** *n.* isolano.
**isl-e** *n.* isola; *the British Isles*, le Isole Britanniche. **-et** *n.* isoletta, isolotto.
**isobar** *n.* (meteor.) linea isobara; (chem.) isobaro. **-ic** *adj.* isobarico, isobaro.
**isolat-e** *tr.* isolare; separare. **-ion** *n.* isolamento; *-ion hospital*, ospedale *m.* per malattie contagiose, lazzaretto. **-ionism** *n.* (pol.) isolazionismo. **-ionist** *n.* (pol.) isolazionista *m.*, *f.*
**Isolde** *pr.n.* Isotta.
**isometric(al)** *adj.* (geom.) isometrico.
**isosceles** *adj.* (geom.) isoscele.
**isotherm** *n.* (meteor.) isoterma.
**isotop-e** *n.* (chem.) isotopo. **-ic** *adj.* isotopico.
**Israel** *pr.n.* Israele *m.* **-i** *adj.*, *n.* israeliano. **-ite** *adj.*, *n.* israelita *m.*, *f.* **-itic, -itish** *adj.* israelita, israelitico.
**issue** *n.* uscita; sbocco; esito; risultato; conclusione; prole *f.*, discendenza; *without* —, senza prole; questione, problema *m.*, punto in discussione; *to join — about*, discutere; (finan.) emissione; pubblicazione, edizione; numero; (mil.) fornitura, distribuzione; *attrib.* di commissariato; *tr.* (finan.) emettere; rilasciare; pubblicare; (mil.) fornire, distribuire; *intr.*

uscire, emanare; (of blood) sgorgare.
**Istambul, Istanbul** *pr.n.* (geog.) Istanbùl.
**isthmus** *n.* (geog.) istmo.
**it**[1] *prn. nom.* (generally omitted in Italian) esso *m.*, essa *f.*, ciò *m.*, *f.*; *acc.* lo *m.*, la *f.*, ci; (after prep.) esso *m.*, essa *f.*, ciò *m.*; *dat.* gli *m.*, le *f.*, ci *m.*, *f.*, vi *m.*, *f.*; *gen.* ne *m.*, *f.*, di ciò, di esso, di essa; *who is —?*, chi è?; *it's me(I)*, sono io; *far from —*, tutt'altro; *— doesn't matter*, non importa; *— is raining*, piove; *— is three o'clock*, sono le tre; (fam.) il non plus ultra; fascino, attrattiva.
**it**[2] *n.* (abbrev. of **Italian**) *gin and —*, gin con vermut italiano.
**itacism** *n.* (ling.) itacismo.
**Italian** *adj.* italiano, d'Italia; *n.* italiano *m.*, italiana *f.*; *the ~s*, gli Italiani; (language) italiano, lingua italiana.
**Italianism** *n.* italianismo.
**Italianiz-e** *tr.* italianizzare; *to become ~ed*, italianizzarsi. **-ation** *n.* italianizzazione.
**italic** *adj.* italico; (typ.) corsivo; *n.pl.* corsivo, caratteri *m.pl.* corsivi; *in ~s*, in corsivo. **-ize** *tr.* (typ.) stampare in corsivi; (in MS.) sottolineare.
**italo-american** *adj.*, *n.* italo-americano. **-byzantine** *adj.* italo-bizantino.
**Italy** *pr.n.* Italia; (poet.) Ausonia, Esperia; (fig.) il bel paese.
**itch** *n.* prurito; prurigine *f.*; pizzicore *m.*; rogna, scabbia; (fig.) voglia, desiderio irresistibile; *intr.* prudere, pizzicare; sentire prurito; (fig.) *to — to do something*, morire dalla voglia di far qualcosa. **-iness** *n.* prurito, prurigine *f.* **-ing** *adj.* pruriginoso. **-y** *adj.* che prude; rognoso.
**item** *n.* voce *f.*; capo; dettaglio; *~s of news*, notizie *f.pl.*, fatti *m.pl.* del giorno; (theatr.) numero; *~s on the agenda of a meeting*, questioni all'ordine del giorno di un'assemblea. **-ize** *tr.* dettagliare; elencare.
**iterat-e** *tr.* reiterare; ripetere. **-ion** *n.* reiterazione; ripetizione. **-ive** *adj.* (gramm.) iterativo; frequentativo.
**Ithaca** *pr.n.* (geog.) Itaca.
**itinerant** *adj.* ambulante; errante; girovago; viaggiante.
**itinerary** *adj.* itinerario; di viaggio; *n.* itinerario.
**its** *poss. adj.* il suo, la sua; *pl.* i suoi, le sue.
**itself** *rfl. prn.* si, (after prep.) sè; *all by —*, da solo; *of —*, da sè; (emphatic) *nom.* esso stesso, essa stessa; *acc.* se stesso, se stessa.
**Ivanhoe** *pr.n.* Ivanoe.
**ivied** *adj.* coperto di edera.
**ivory** *n.* avorio; *attrib.* eburneo.
**ivy** *n.* (bot.) edera, ellera; *poison —*, tossicodendro.
**Ixion** *pr.n.* (myth.) Issione.

**J, j** *n.* now no longer used in Italian; as initial consonant replaced by I or Gi; in terminations formerly used following i, ij, now written ii) I lungo; (teleph.) *— for Jack*, i lungo come jersey.
**jab** *n.* stoccata; stilettata; puntata; *tr.* dare una stoccata con; conficcare.
**jabber** *n.* borottamento; chiacchierio; ciarla; *intr.* barbugliare; farfugliare; borbottare; chiacchierare; ciarlare.
**jack**[1] *n.* bandiera (di nave); (cards) fante *m.*; (cul.) girarrosto; (bowls) boccino; (mech.) cricco, martinetto, arganetto; *tr.* (motor.) sollevare con un cricco.
**Jack**[2] *pr.n.* (dimin. of **John**) Giovannino; *— Frost*, Mastro Gelo; *— Tar*, marò *m. indecl.*; *before you could say — Robinson*, in un batter d'occhio, in men che non si dice; *I'm all right —*, io sto bene.
**jackal** *n.* sciacallo.
**jackanapes** *n.* vanesio, sfacciatello.
**jackass** *n.* asino; ciuco; somaro; (fig.) imbecille *m.*; (orn.) *laughing —*, dacelide *f.*
**jackboot** *n.* stivalone *m.*
**jackdaw** *n.* (orn.) taccola.
**jacket** *n.* (cost.) giacca, giacchetta; giubba; (of book) sopracopertina; (of potato) buccia; *potatoes in their ~s*, patate in camicia; (mech.) rivestimento; *tr.* (mech.) rivestire con materiale isolante.
**jack-in-the-box** *n.* saltamartino, fantoccio a molla. **-knife** *n.* coltello a serramanico. **-o'-lantern** *n.* fuoco fatuo. **-plane** *n.* pialletto.
**jackpot** *n.* (cards) posta, insieme delle poste; (pop.) grossa vincita.
**Jacob** *pr.n.* Giacobbe; *~'s ladder*, scala di Giacobbe, (naut.) biscaglina.
**Jacobean** *adj.*, *n.* del regno di Giacomo I (1603–25).
**Jacobin** *adj. n.* (hist.) giacobino.
**jacobin-ic(al)** *adj.* (hist.) giacobino. **-ism** *n.* (hist.) giacobinismo.
**Jacobite** *adj.*, *n.* (hist.) giacobita *m.*
**jade**[1] *n.* rozza, brenna, ronzino; (woman) donnaccia, sgualdrina, ragazzaccia.
**jade**[2] *n.* giada; (colour) verde giada.
**jaded** *adj.* spossato, stanco.
**Jael** *pr.n.* (bibl.) Giaele.
**Jaffa** *pr.n.* (geog.) Giaffa.
**jagged** *adj.* intaccato; dentellato; seghettato; frastagliato; scabroso; (bot.) lanceolato. **-ness** *n.* frastagliamento; dentellatura; scabrosità.
**jaguar** *n.* (zool.) giaguaro.
**jail, jailer** *n.* See **gaol, gaoler.**
**jam**[1] *n.* (cul.) marmellata; conserva di frutta; (fam.) *it's money for —!*, è un regalo!
**jam**[2] *n.* inceppamento; intralcio; ingorgo; *traffic —*, ingorgo della circolazione; (fam.) pasticcio; *adv. — full*, pieno zeppo; *tr.* pigiare; serrare; comprimere; bloccare; *to — on the brakes*, bloccare i freni; (radio) disturbare; *intr.* bloccarsi; fermarsi; incepparsi.
**Jamaica** *pr.n.* (geog.) Giamaica. **-n** *adj.*, *n.* giamaicano.
**jamb** *n.* (of door) stipite *m.*; montante *m.*
**jamboree** *n.* (of boy-scouts) raduno di Giovani Esploratori; (fig.) baldoria.
**James** *pr.n.* Giacomo.
**jam-jar, -pot** *n.* barattolo per marmellata.
**jammy** *adj.* imbrattato di marmellata; attaccaticcio.
**Jane** *pr.n.* Giovanna, Gianna.
**jangl-e** *n.* suono stonato; *tr.* far emettere suoni stonati; *intr.* stonare. **-ing** *adj.* stonato, discordante.
**janissary** *n.* (hist.) giannizzero.
**janit-or** *n.* portinaio, portiere, custode *m.* **-ress** *n.* portinaia.
**Jansen-ism** *n.* (rel. hist.) giansenismo. **-ist** *n.* (rel. hist.) giansenista *m.*, *f.*
**January** *pr.n.* gennaio.
**Japan** *pr.n.* (geog.) Giappone *m.*; *n.* oggetto laccato; lacca giapponese; *tr.* verniciare con lacca giapponese, laccare. **-ese** *adj.*, *n.* giapponese *m.*, *f.*, *~ese vellum*, carta Giappone.
**japanning** *n.* laccatura; verniciatura.
**japonica** *n.* (bot.) cotogno del Giappone.
**jar**[1] *n.* vibrazione; scossa; urto; discordanza; stonatura; *intr.* stonare; discordare; scordare; *to — upon*, offendere, irritare, urtare; *tr.* far vibrare; scuotere; urtare.
**jar**[2] vaso; giara; orcio; brocca; anfora.
**jargon** *n.* gergo; linguaggio professionale.
**jarring** *adj.* stonato; stridente; scordato; dissonante; che scuote.
**jasmin(e)** *n.* (bot.) gelsomino.

**Jason** *pr.n.* (myth.) Giasone.
**jasper** *n.* (miner.) diaspro.
**jaundice** *n.* (med.) itterizia; (fig.) invidia, gelosia. **-d** *adj.* (med.) itterico; (fig.) invidioso, geloso.
**jaunt** *n.* gita; scampagnata; escursione; *intr.* fare una gita, andare a spasso.
**jaunt-y** *adj.* gaio; vivace; disinvolto; baldanzoso. **-ily** *adv.* gaiamente; vivacemente; baldanzosamente; con disinvoltura. **-iness** *n.* gaiezza; vivacità; disinvoltura; baldanza.
**Java** *pr.n.* (geog.) Giava. **-nese** *adj.*, *n.* giavanese *m.*, *f.*
**javelin** *n.* giavellotto.
**jaw** *n.* mascella; mandibola; ganascia; *his — dropped*, restò a bocca aperta; *pl.* (of animal), fauci *f.pl.*; (fam.) *to hold one's —*, chiudere il becco, star zitto; (slang) chiacchiere *f.pl.*, sermoncino; (mech.) morsa, ganascia; *intr.* (fam.) ciarlare, chiacchierare; far la predica a.
**jaw-bone** *n.* osso mandibolare, mascella. **-breaker** *n.* (fam.) parola difficile da pronunciare, parola ostrogotica.
**jay** *n.* (orn.) ghiandaia.
**jay-walker** *n.* pedone disattento.
**jealous** *adj.* geloso; invidioso; sospettoso; zelante, *to become —*, ingelosirsi; *to make —*, far ingelosire. **-y,** *n.* gelosia; invidia; zelo.
**Jean** *pr.n.* Giovanna.
**jeans** *n.* (cost.) *blue —*, blue jeans *m.pl.*, calzoni di tela grossa.
**jeep** *n.* camionetta, jeep *m. indecl.*
**jeer** *n.* scherno; canzonatura; dileggio; *intr. to — at*, schernire; canzonare; fischiare; dileggiare. **-ing** *adj.* derisorio; derisivo; beffardo; canzonatorio.
**Jehovah** *pr.n.* Geova, Ieova.
**jejune** *adj.* magro; gramo; arido, sterile; privo d'interesse; semplicione.
**jell-y** *n.* gelatina; (pharm.) *petroleum —*, vasellina. **-ied** *adj.* in gelatina.
**jellyfish** *n.* medusa.
**jemmy** *n.* grimaldello.
**jennet** *n.* ginnetto.
**jenny**[1] *n.* (text.) filatoio; (crane) gru *f.* mobile.
**Jenny**[2] *pr.n.* Gianna.
**jeopard-y** *n.* rischio; repentaglio; pericolo. **-ize** *tr.* mettere a repentaglio; arrischiare; mettere in pericolo.
**jeremiad** *n.* geremiade *f.*
**Jeremiah, Jeremy** *pr.n.* Geremia.
**Jericho** *pr.n.* Gerico; (fam.) *go to — !*, va a farti benedire.
**jerk** *n.* scossa; scatto; strattone; strappo; (med.) riflesso; (fam.) *physical -s*, ginnastica; *tr.* scuotere; dare uno strattone a; spingere; *to — out*, far uscire a scatti; parlare a scatti; *to — up*, alzare di scatto; *intr.* scattare, balzare; *to — along*, avanzare a scatti. **-ily** *adv.* a sbalzi, a scatti, spasmodicamente.
**jerkin** *n.* (cost.) giacchetta di cuoio, giustacuore *m.*
**jerky** *adj.* a scatti, a scosse, sussultante; (fig.) *— style*, stile desultorio.
**Jerome** *pr.n.* Gerolamo.
**jerry** *n.* (pop.) soldato tedesco; (vulg.) vaso da notte.
**jerry-built** *adj.* (pop.) costruito con materiale scadente, costruito in fretta.
**jersey** *n.* (sport) maglia.
**Jerusalem** *pr.n.* (geog.) Gerusalemme *f.*; (bot.) *— artichoke*, topinamburo.
**jess** *n.* (falconry) geto.
**jessamine** *n.* See **jasmin(e).**
**Jesse** *pr.n.* Jesse *m.*; *tree of —*, albero di Jesse.
**jest** *n.* scherzo; motteggio; burla; beffa, facezia; frizzo; celia; *half in —, half in earnest*, tra il serio e il faceto; *to say something in —*, dire qualcosa per scherzo; (provb.) *there's many a true word spoken in —*, scherzando Arlecchino si confessa; (fig.) *he is a standing —*, è lo zimbello di tutti; *intr.* scherzare; motteggiare; celiare; burlare; farsi beffe. **-er** *n.* beffatore; burlone, celiatore *m.*; (slang) freddurista *m.*; (hist.) buffone *m.* **-ingly** *adv.* per scherzo; per burla.
**Jesuit** *n.* Gesuita *m.*; (pejor.) ipocrita *m.* **-ical** *adj.* (pejor.) gesuitico, da Gesuita. **-ism, -ry** *n.* gesuitismo.
**Jesus** *pr.n.* Gesù.; *— Christ*, Gesù Cristo; *Society of —*, compagnia di Gesù.
**jet**[1] *n.* (miner.) giaietto, glavazzo, gè *m.*; ambra nera; (colour) giaietto.
**jet**[2] *n.* (of liquid) getto, zampillo, spruzzo; (gas) becco; (sprinkler) spruzzatore; (of whale) sfiatatoio; (aeron.) aviogetto, jet *m.*, aeroplano a reazione; *— engine*, reattore; *intr.* zampillare, schizzare.
**jet-black** *adj.* nero come ebano, nero lucente, giaetto.
**jetsam** *n.* relitti di mare, gettito.
**jettison** *tr.* gettare in mare, fare gettito; (fig.) disfarsi di, buttar via.
**jetty** *n.* molo; gettata; calata; *landing —*, imbarcadero, pontile *m.*
**Jew** *n.* ebreo; giudeo; israelita, *-'s harp*, scacciapensieri *m. indecl.*; *the wandering —*, l'Ebreo errante; **-baiting** *n.* persecuzione degli ebrei, antisemitismo.
**jewel** *n.* gioia, gioiello; pietra preziosa; (in a watch) rubino; (fig.) perla, tesoro; *tr.* ingioiellare, ingemmare; ornare di pietre preziose; (watchm.) montare su rubini.
**jewel-box, -case** *n.* scrigno; astuccio per gioielli; cofanetto.
**jeweller** *n.* gioielliere *m.*; *-'s shop*, gioielleria.
**jewel(le)ry** *n.* gioielli *m.pl.*; gioie *f.pl.*; (art, trade) gioielleria.
**jewel-stand** *n.* portagioielli *m. indecl.*
**Jewess** *n.* ebrea, israelita.
**Jewish** *adj.* ebreo, ebraic , giudaico, israelitico.
**Jewry** *n.* gli ebrei *m.pl.*, il popolo ebraico; ghetto.
**Jezebel** *pr.n.* Gezabele; (fig.) megera.
**jib** *n.* (naut.) fiocco; (mech.) braccio; (slang) *the cut of one's —*, l'aspetto del viso; *intr.* impennarsi, impuntarsi, recalcitrare, essere restìo; (fig.) *to — at*, mostrare ripugnanza per, mostrarsi riluttante a.
**jib-boom** *n.* (naut.) asta di fiocco.
**jibe.** See **gibe.**
**jiffy** *n.* (fam.) batter d'occhio; istante *m.*, momentino.
**jig** *n.* (dance) giga; (mech.) maschera di montaggio; (min.) crivello oscillante; *tr.* crivellare; *intr.* ballare la giga; *to — up and down*, saltare su e giù; (mech.) lavorare con maschere.
**jig-saw** *n.* sega da traforo; *— puzzle*, giuoco di pazienza; (fig.) mosaico.
**jilt** *tr.* piantare in asso (un innamorato), rompere il fidanzamento.
**Jim** *pr.n.* (dimin. of **James**) Giacomino.
**jingle** *n.* tintinnìo; cantilena; allitterazione; *tr.* far tintinnare; *intr.* tintinnare.
**jingo** *n.* (fam.) sciovinista *m.*; nazionalista fanatico; *excl. by — !*, per Bacco! **-ism** *n.* sciovinismo. **-istic** *adj.* sciovinista.
**jinn** *n.* (myth.) genio; demone *m.*
**jitter-y** *adj.* (fam.) nervoso. **-iness** *n.* nervosismo; (pop.) fifa. **-s** *n.* (pop.) *to have the -s*, aver i nervi a fior di pelle, aver la fifa.
**Jo** *pr.n.* (dimin. of **Josephine**) Gianna.
**Joachim** *pr.n.* Gioacchino.
**Joan** *pr.n.* Giovanna; *— of Arc*, Giovanna d'Arco; *Pope —*, Papessa Giovanna.
**Job**[1] *pr.n.* Giobbe; *-'s comforter*, amico di Giobbe.
**job**[2] *n.* lavoro; impiego; posto; *full-time —*, impiego a orario completo; *part-time —*, impiego a mezza giornata; *odd -s*, lavori vari; *to be out of a —*, essere disoccupato; *to know one's —*, conoscere il mestiere; (iron.) *a put-up —*, una commedia; (comm.) *a — lot*, un lotto di merci varie; (fam.) faccenda; affare *m.*; *a bad —*, un affare serio, una brutta faccenda; *a good —*, una bella cosa; *and a good — too!*, meno male!; *it's a good — that*, meno male che;

*to give something up as a bad* —, rinunciare a un'impresa impossibile; *to have a — finding the way*, trovare la strada dopo molte peripezie; *to make a good — of*, fare bene; *to make the best of a bad* —, cavarsela alla meno peggio; *tr.* (horses, *etc.*) dare a nolo; *intr.* lavorare a cottimo.

**jobber** *n.* (stock exchange) agente di borsa, borsista *m.*; (pejor.) intrigante, trafficante *m.* **-y** *n.* baratteria; peculato; intrigo; manovra; macchinazione.

**jobbing** *adj.* a cottimo; avventizio.

**jobless** *adj.* senza lavoro, disoccupato.

**jockey** *n.* fantino; *disk* —, annunciatore di programma di dischi; *tr.*, *intr.* intrigare; ingannare; manovrare; *to — into*, costringere a fare.

**jocos-e** *adj.* giocoso; faceto; gioviale. **-eness, -ity** *n.* giovialità; giocondità.

**jocular** *adj.* faceto; scherzoso; lepido; allegro. **-ity** *n.* lepidezza; giocondità; allegria.

**jocund** *adj.* giocondo; gaio; allegro. **-ity** *n.* giocondità; allegria.

**Joe** *pr.n.* (dimin. of **Joseph**) Beppe, Peppino.

**jog** *n.* scossa; spinta; gomitata; *tr.* spingere; scuotere leggermente; dar di gomito; *to — someone's memory*, rinfrescare la memoria di qualcuno; *intr. to — along*, trotterellare, andare al piccolo trotto, camminare lentamente; (fig.) seguire il solito trantran, tirare avanti.

**jog-trot** *n.* mezzo trotto; (fig.) andatura lenta.

**John** *pr.n.* Giovanni; — *Bull*, l'Inglese tipico, gli Inglesi.

**Johnny** *n.*, *pr.n.* Nino; (pop.) individuo, tipo.

**join** *n.* punto di congiunzione; giuntura; ricommettitura; *tr.* unire; congiungere; congiungersi con; collegare; legare; *to — in marriage*, congiungere in matrimonio; *to — hands with someone*, prendere qualcuno per mano, (fig.) unirsi a qualcuno; raggiungere; (mil.) *to — one's unit*, raggiungere il reparto; accompagnare; associarsi a; diventar socio di, iscriversi a, entrare in; *to — battle*, attaccare battaglia; *to — issue with*, venire a discussione con; *intr.* unirsi, congiungersi; *to — in*, entrare a far parte (di), unirsi (a); (mil.) *to — up*, arruolarsi come volontario.

**joiner** *n.* falegname *m.*; legnaiuolo; fabbricante *m.* di mobili. **-y** *n.* falegnameria.

**joint** *adj.* comune; in comune; unito; — *account*, conto intestato a due o più persone, conto comune; — *action*, azione collettiva; — *author*, coautore; — *commission*, commissione mista; — *efforts*, sforzi comuni; — *heir*, coerede *m.*, *f.*; — *liability*, responsabilità collettiva; — *manager*, condirettore; — *owner*, comproprietario; — *tenant*, coinquilino; — *undertaking*, impegno collettivo.

**joint** *n.* giuntura; congiunzione; (anat.) articolazione, giuntura; (bot.) nodo; (mech.) giunto, giunzione; (cul.) trancio di carne; (slang) bettola, locale di infima categoria, spaccio clandestino; *tr.* unire; congiungere; (mech.) connettere, raccordare.

**jointly** *adv.* unitamente, in comune, collettivamente; (leg.) — *and severally*, congiuntamente e separatamente.

**jointure** *n.* (leg.) appannaggio vedovile.

**joist** *n.* (archit.) trave *f.*; travicello, palco; *tr.* munire di travicelli.

**joke** *n.* scherzo; facezia; arguzia; motto spiritoso; barzelletta; *practical* —, burla, beffa, tiro mancino; *to crack -s*, dir facezie; *to play a practical — on*, giocare una beffa a; *no* —, un affare serio; *to be unable to see the* —, non vedere il lato comico, non avere il senso dell'umorismo; *the — is*, il buffo è.

**joke** *intr.* scherzare; celiare; dire facezie; raccontare barzellette; *to — about something*, prendere qualcosa come uno scherzo, dire qualcosa per ridere; *I was only joking*, era solo uno scherzo.

**joker** *n.* burlone *m.*; celione *m.*; motteggiatore; tipo ameno; (cards) matta, jolly *m. indecl.*

**joking** *adj.* faceto; scherzoso; *this is no — matter*, è un affare serio, non c'è da ridere; *n. — apart*, sul serio. **-ly** *adv.* per scherzo; scherzando; ridendo.

**jollification** *n.* (fam.) festa; baldoria, allegria.

**jolliness, jollity** *n.* allegria, allegrezza; baldoria; ilarità; *to be in no mood for jollity*, non aver nessuna voglia di far baldoria.

**jolly** *adj.* allegro; gaio; ameno; divertente; festoso; *n.* (slang, naut.) fante *m.* di marina; *adv.* (pop.) molto, moltissimo; *I'm — glad*, sono contentissimo; *a — good fellow*, un ottimo ragazzo; *you've — well got to*, devi assolutamente.

**jollyboat** *n.* (naut.) iole *f.*

**jolt** *n.* scossa; sobbalzo; sbalzo; (fam.) *a nasty* —, una sorpresa sgradevole; *tr.* scuotere; far sobbalzare; *intr.* sobbalzare.

**Jonah** *pr.n.* (bibl.) Giona; (fig.) iettatore.

**Jonathan** *pr.n.* Gionata.

**jonquil** *n.* (bot.) giunchiglia.

**Jordan** *pr.n.* (river) Giordano; (state) Giordania.

**Joseph** *pr.n.* Giuseppe.

**Josephine** *pr.n.* Giuseppina.

**Joshua** *pr.n.* Giosuè.

**Josiah** *pr.n.* Giosia.

**joss** *n.* idolo cinese.

**joss-house** *n.* tempio cinese. **-stick** *n.* bastoncino d'incenso.

**jostle** *n.* spinta; urto; gomitata; *tr.*, *intr.* spingere; dar di gomito; farsi strada a gomitate; (fig.) lottare.

**jot** *n.* iota, ette *m.*; (fam.) *I don't care a* —, me n'infischio; *tr. to — down*, prendere nota di, (fam.) buttare giù. **-ter** *n.* taccuino. **-ting** *n.* annotazione; appunto.

**journal** *n.* giornale *m.*; periodico; rivista; diario.

**journalese** *n.* (fam.) gergo giornalistico.

**journal-ism** *n.* giornalismo. **-ist** *n.* giornalista *m.*, *f.* **-istic** *adj.* giornalistico.

**journey** *n.* viaggio; *pleasant —!*, buon viaggio!; *outward* —, viaggio di andata; *return* —, viaggio di ritorno; *on a* —, in viaggio; *to go on a* —, mettersi in viaggio; *—'s end*, la fine del viaggio; *intr.* viaggiare; fare un viaggio.

**journeyman** *n.* operaio a giornata, avventizio; artigiano, operaio qualificato.

**joust** *n.* giostra; torneo; *intr.* giostrare; torneare; partecipare a un torneo.

**Jove** *pr.n.* (myth.) Giove; (fam.) *by —!*, per Bacco!, per Giove!

**jovial** *adj.* gioviale; lieto; allegro. **-ity, -ness** *n.* giovialità; gaiezza; allegrezza.

**Jovian** *adj.* di Giove.

**jowl** *n.* mascella; gota, guancia; *cheek by* —, guancia a guancia.

**joy** *n.* gioia; allegrezza; letizia; gaudio; *to jump for* —, saltare dalla gioia; *to be beside oneself with* —, non stare in sè dalla gioia; *pl.* piaceri *m.pl.*; delizie *f.pl.*

**joy-bells** *n.pl.* campane *f.pl.* a festa.

**joyful** *adj.* gioioso; giulivo; lieto; allegro. **-ness** *n.* gioia; allegrezza.

**joyless** *adj.* senza gioia; triste; mesto. **-ness** *n.* tristezza; mestizia.

**joyous** *adj.* gioioso; gaudioso; giulivo; allegro. **-ness** *n.* gioia; allegrezza.

**joy-ride** *n.* gita in macchina. **-stick** *n.* (aeron.) leva di comando.

**Juan** *pr.n.* Giovanni; *Don* —, Don Giovanni, (fig.) dongiovanni *m.*

**jubilant** *adj.* giubilante; esultante; trionfante. **-ly** *adv.* con giubilo; trionfalmente.

**jubilation** *n.* giubilo; esultanza.

**jubilee** *n.* giubileo; cinquantenario; *diamond* —, sessantesimo anniversario.

**Judaea** *pr.n.* (geog.) Giudea.

**Jud-aic(al)** *adj.* giudaico; ebraico. **-aism** *n.* giudaismo.

**Judas** *pr.n.* Giuda; — *Iscariot*, Giuda Iscariota; — *kiss*, bacio di Giuda; (fig.) traditore; (bot.) — *tree*, siliquastro, albero di Giuda; (spyhole) spia.

**Jude** *pr.n.* Giuda.

**judge** *n.* giudice *m.*; arbitro; (at competition) membro della giuria; *the -s*, la giuria; (bibl.) *Judges*, Giudici *m.pl.*; (fig.) conoscitore, intenditore; *to be a good — of*, intendersi di, essere conoscitore di; *tr.* giudicare; stimare, ritenere, considerare; *intr.* giudicare; decidere.

**judg(e)ment** *n.* giudizio; *the Last —*, il Giudizio Universale; (leg.) sentenza; *to pass —*, pronunciare la sentenza; punizione; castigo; (fig.) giudizio; parere *m.*, discernimento; *in my —*, a mio giudizio; *to have good —*, essere conoscitore; *an error of —*, un errore di calcolo.

**judg(e)ment-hall** *n.* aula delle udienze. **-seat** *n.* tribunale *m.*; banco dei giudici.

**judicature** *n.* magistratura, giudicatura, giustizia; corte *f.* di giustizia, ordinamento giudiziario.

**judicial** *adj.* giudiziario, giudiziale, giuridico; — *separation*, separazione legale; (fig.) imparziale.

**judiciary** *adj.* giudiziario; *n.* magistratura.

**judicious** *adj.* giudizioso; ragionativo; savio; accorto; prudente. **-ness** *n.* giudizio; assennatezza; prudenza.

**Judith** *pr.n.* Giuditta.

**Judy** *pr.n.* Giuditta; *Punch and —*, Pulcinella e sua moglie; *Punch and — show*, teatrino dei burattini.

**jug** *n.* brocca; bricco; caraffa; anfora; boccale *m.*; (slang), gattabuia; *tr.* (cul.) cuocere in salmì; *-ged hare*, lepre in salmì; (slang) mettere in gattabuia.

**juggl-e** *intr.* fare il prestigiatore, fare giuochi di destrezza; (fig.) truffare; *to — with*, svisare. **-er** *n.* prestigiatore, giocoliere; (fig.) impostore. **-ery, -ing** *n.* giuochi *m.pl.* di prestigio.

**Jugoslav** *adj.*, *n.* iugoslavo. **-ia** *pr.n.* (geog.) Iugoslavia.

**jugular** *adj.*, *n.* (anat.) giugulare *f.*

**juice** *n.* succo; sugo; (anat.) *gastric —*, succo gastrico; (pop.) benzina; (electr.) corrente elettrica; (fam.) *to let someone stew in his own —*, lasciar bollire qualcuno nel proprio brodo.

**juic-y** *adj.* succoso, sugoso, succulento; (fam.) interessante, piccante. **-iness** *n.* succosità, sugosità.

**jujube** *n.* (bot.) giuggiola; — *tree*, giuggiolo; giuggiola, pasticca di gomma.

**julep** *n.* giulebbe *m.*; *mint —*, bibita alla menta.

**Julia** *pr.n.* Giulia.

**Julian**[1] *adj.* giuliano, di Giulio Cesare; (geog.) *the — Alps*, le Alpi Giulie.

**Julian**[2] *pr.n.* Giuliano.

**Juliana** *pr.n.* Giuliana.

**Juliet** *pr.n.* Giulietta; *Romeo and —*, Giulietta e Romeo.

**Julius** *pr.n.* Giulio.

**July** *pr.n.* luglio.

**jumble** *n.* miscuglio; guazzabuglio; confusione; — *sale*, vendita di merci varie per beneficenza; bazar *m.*; *tr.* confondere; mescolare; mischiare; accozzare; affastellare; mettere alla rinfusa; *to — up*, mescolare, far confusione.

**jumbo** *n.* (pop.) elefante *m.*; (fig.) colosso, pachiderma *m.*; (aeron.) *Jumbo jet*, aviogetto.

**jump** *n.* salto; balzo; (fam.) sussulto; (sport) *high —*, salto in alto; *long —*, salto in lungo; *running —*, salto con rincorsa; *pole —*, salto coll'asta; (racing) ostacolo; *to put a horse over a —*, far saltare un ostacolo a un cavallo.

**jump** *tr.* saltare; superare con un salto; scavalcare; (rlwy.) *to — the rails*, deragliare; (fam.) *to — a claim*, usurpare i diritti su un terreno; *intr.* saltare; fare un salto; (fam.) sussultare; trasalire; (fig.) *to — to conclusions*, giungere a conclusioni affrettate; *to — down someone's throat*, ricacciare le parole in gola a qualcuno, rompere la parola in bocca a qualcuno; *to — out of one's skin*, trasalire per la paura; *to — at*, accettare con entusiasmo; *to — in*, balzar dentro, salire (in macchina); *to — on*, sgridare; *to — off*, partire con un balzo, lanciarsi; *to — over*, scavalcare.

**jumped-up** *adj.* (fam.) promosso troppo rapidamente.

**jumper** *n.* saltatore; (cost.) golf *m. indecl.*; maglione *m.*; (naut.) camiciotto da marinaio.

**jumpiness** *n.* (fam.) nervosismo.

**jumping** *n.* il saltare *m.*; — *jack*, fantoccio legato a un elastico.

**jumping-board** *n.* trampolino.

**jumping-off place** *n.* (fam.) punto di partenza.

**jumpy** *adj.* nervoso; eccitato; (fam., of market) instabile.

**junction** *n.* congiunzione; punto di riunione; (of roads) bivio; *railway —*, nodo ferroviario, biforcazione.

**juncture** *n.* congiuntura; frangente *m.*; momento critico; *at this —*, in questo frangente; (anat.) articolazione.

**June** *pr.n.* giugno.

**jungle** *n.* giungla.

**junior** *adj.* più giovane, minore, iuniore; meno anziano; cadetto; figlio; (mil.) — *officers*, ufficiali subalterni; (comm.) — *partner*, socio giovane; — *clerk*, impiegato giovane; *n.* il più giovane; *he is my —*, è più giovane di me; *our -s*, i giovani, la gioventù. **-ity** *n.* minorità; qualità di iuniore.

**juniper** *n.* (bot.) ginepro.

**junk**[1] *n.* (naut.) giunca.

**junk**[2] *n.* (naut.) stoppa; (salt meat) carne salata; (fig.) avanzi *m.pl.*; anticaglie *f.pl.*; rifiuti *m.pl.*; roba vecchia.

**junket** *n.* (cul.) giuncata.

**junketing** *n.* (fam.) festa; banchetto; baldoria.

**Juno** *pr.n.* Giunone.

**junta** *n.* (hist.) giunta; consiglio.

**Jupiter** *pr.n.* (myth.) Giove.

**jurassic** *adj.* (geol.) giurassico.

**juridical** *adj.* giuridico.

**juris-diction** *n.* giurisdizione; competenza. **-prudence** *n.* giurisprudenza.

**jurist** *n.* giurista *m.*

**juror, juryman** *n.* giurato, membro della giuria; (in Italy) giudice *m.* popolare.

**jury** *n.* giurati *m.pl.*; giuria; *foreman of the —*, presidente *m.* della giuria.

**jury-box** *n.* banco dei giurati.

**juryman** *n.* See **juror.**

**jury-mast** *n.* (naut.) albero di fortuna.

**just** *adj.* giusto; retto, onesto; equo, imparziale; preciso, giusto, dovuto; *n.pl. the —*, i giusti; *adv.* esattamente, precisamente, giusto, appunto, proprio, lì lì; — *in time*, proprio al momento buono, tempestivamente; — *now*, proprio ora, un momento fa, or ora; — *so*, precisamente, proprio così, già; — *as*, proprio mentre, proprio quando; *it is — six o'clock*, sono le sei precise; appena, per poco; *he is — twenty*, ha appena vent'anni; *he has — come*, è appena arrivato; — *enough*, appena abbastanza; soltanto; — *one*, soltanto uno; — *a little*, soltanto un pochino; — *to please me*, soltanto per farmi un piacere; — *this once*, una volta tanto; — *a moment!*, un momento!; (emphatic) — *listen to him!*, ma statelo a sentire!; — *fancy!*, ma figurati!; — *look at this!*, ma guarda un po'!

**justice** *n.* giustizia; *court of —*, tribunale *m.*; *to bring to —*, processare; giudice *m.*; *Lord Chief Justice*, (in England) Capo della Magistratura, (Italian equivalent) Presidente della Corte di Cassazione; — *of the peace*, (in England) magistrato, (Italian equivalent) pretore *m.*, giudice conciliatore; (fig.) giustizia; imparzialità; *to do — to a meal*, far onore a un pasto; *to do oneself —*, fare bella figura.

**justiciary** *adj.* giudiziario; *n.* giudice *m.*
**justifiab-le** *adj.* giustificabile; scusabile; (leg.) legittimo; — *homicide*, omicidio per legittima difesa. **-ility, -leness** *n.* giustificabilità; (leg.) legittimità.
**justification** *n.* giustificazione; scusa; (typ.) giustezza.
**justificative, justificatory** *adj.* giustificativo, giustificatorio.
**justify** *tr.* giustificare; motivare; scusare; (typ.) allineare.
**Justin** *pr.n.* Giustino.
**Justina, Justine** *pr.n.* Giustina.
**Justinian** *pr.n.* Giustiniano.
**justly** *adv.* giustamente; con giustizia.
**justness** *n.* giustizia; giustezza; precisione; esattezza.
**Justus** *pr.n.* Giusto.
**jut** *n.* proiezione; sporgenza; (bldg.) aggetto; *intr. to* — (*out*), sporgere, protendersi; (bldg.) aggettare.
**jute** *n.* iuta.
**jutting** *adj.* sporgente.
**Juvenal** *pr.n.* Giovenale.
**juvenile** *adj.* giovanile; giovane; — *books*, libri per ragazzi; (theatr.) — *lead*, giovane primo, giovane prima; — *court*, tribunale dei minorenni; — *delinquent*, imputato minorenne; *n.* giovane *m.*, *f.*, minorenne *m.*, *f.*
**juvenilia** *n.* opere *f.pl.* giovanili.
**juvenility** *n.* giovinezza; aspetto giovanile.
**juxtapos-e** *tr.* giustapporre; affiancare. **-ition** *n.* giustapposizione; accostamento.

**K, k,** *n.* (in Italian occurs only in words of foreign origin) cappa; (teleph.) *K for king*, cappa come kursaal.
**Kaffir** *adj.*, *n.* cafro; (stock exchange) *-s*, azioni delle miniere sudafricane.
**Kaiser** *n.* Kaiser *m.*
**kale** *n. curly* —, cavolo riccio; *sea* —, cavolo marino.
**kaleidoscop-e** *n.* caleidoscopio. **-ic(al)** *adj.* caleidoscopico.
**kalends** *n. Greek* —, calende greche.
**kali** *n.* (bot.) cali *m.*
**kangaroo** *n.* canguro; (fam.) — *court*, processo illegale.
**Kantian** *adj.* (philos.) kantiano, cantiano, di Kant. **-ism** *n.* kantismo; neocriticismo.
**kaolin** *n.* caolino.
**kapok** *n.* capoc.
**Kashmir** (geog.) Cascemir.
**Katharine, Katherine, Kathleen, Kate** *pr.n.* Caterina.
**kayak** *n.* caiacco.
**kedge(-anchor)** *n.* (naut.) ancorotto, andrivello.
**kedge** *tr.*, *intr.* (naut.) tonneggiare.
**keel** *n.* (naut.) chiglia, carena; *false* —, sottochiglia; (fig.) nave *f.*; *intr. to* — (*over*), capovolgere.
**keen** *adj.* acuminato, affilato, tagliente; pungente, penetrante; *to get -er*, rincrudire; acuto; (fig.) vivo, forte, intenso; *a — appetite*, un appetito vorace; *a — disappointment*, una forte delusione; — *interest*, vivo interesse; — *competition*, aspra concorrenza; mordace; appassionato; entusiasta; zelante; (fam.) *to be — on doing something*, aver gran voglia di far qualcosa; *to be — on games*, essere appassionato dello sport; — *as mustard*, appassionatissimo; *to be — on a girl*, aver preso una cotta per una ragazza.
**keening** *n.* lamentazione di un morto, lamento funebre.
**keenly** *adv.* acutamente; intensamente; vivamente; avidamente; con perspicacia; in modo penetrante.
**keenness** *n.* sottigliezza; rigore *m.*; acutezza, finezza; (fig.) intensità; ardore *m.*; vivo desiderio; avidità; entusiasmo.
**keen-witted** *adj.* acuto, scaltro.
**keep** *n.* (archit.) maschio, torrione *m.*; cittadella; (fig.) sostentamento, mantenimento; *to earn one's* —, mantenersi, guadagnare da vivere; *he isn't worth his* —, il suo lavoro non vale le spese di mantenerlo; *board and* —, vitto e alloggio; (fam.) *for -s*, per sempre.
**keep** *tr.* tenere; mantenere; conservare; custodire; *to — house for*, tenere la casa per; *to — the books*, tenere la contabilità; *to — in mind*, tenere a mente; *to — to oneself*, tenere per sè; *to — under lock and key*, tenere sotto chiave; (mus.) *to — time*, tenere il tempo; (of watch) funzionare bene; *to — open house*, tenere corte bandita; *to — watch on*, tener d'occhio; *to — a large family*, mantenere una famiglia numerosa; *to — one's word*, mantenere la parola; *to — one's countenance*, mantenersi calmo; *to — one's temper*, controllarsi, non arrabbiarsi; *to — one's head*, non perdere la testa; *to — one's balance*, mantenersi in equilibrio; avere, tenere; *to — a car*, avere la macchina; gestire, esercire, dirigere; *to — a shop*, gestire un negozio, fare il negoziante; osservare, rispettare; *to — the Commandments*, osservare i Comandamenti; *to — the law*, rispettare la legge; festeggiare, celebrare; *to — Christmas*, festeggiare il Natale; proteggere, difendere; *God — you!*, Dio ti protegga; riservare, destinare; *intr.* tenersi, mantenersi; stare, restare, rimanere; continuare; conservarsi; durare; *to — afloat*, mantenersi a gallo, galleggiare; *to — aloof*, tenersi in disparte, non immischiarsi; *to — awake*, star sveglio. FOLLOW. BY ACC. AND GERUND: *to — someone waiting*, far aspettare qualcuno; *to — the conversation going*, tener vivo il discorso. FOLLOW. BY ADV. OR PREP.: *to — away*, *tr.* tenere lontano, allontanare, *intr.* stare lontano, tenersi a distanza; *to — back*, *tr.* trattenere, (fig.) nascondere, *intr.* stare indietro, tenersi in disparte; *to — down*, *tr.* contenere, reprimere, mantenere basso; *intr.* stare giù; *to — from*, *tr. to — someone from doing something*, impedire che qualcuno faccia qualcosa; *intr.* astenersi da; *to — in*, *tr.* tenere rinchiuso, (schol.) trattenere a scuola; (fam.) *to — one's hand in*, tenersi in esercizio; *intr. to — in with*, mantenersi in buoni rapporti con; *to — in touch*, mantenersi a contatto; *to — off*, *tr.* tenere a distanza, respingere; — *your hands off!*, non toccare!; *intr.* tenersi lontano, evitare; — *off the grass!*, è vietato calpestare l'erba!; *to — on*, *tr.* continuare a tenere, non disfarsi di; *to — one's hat on*, rimanere coperto, non togliersi il cappello; *intr.* continuare, non fare che, non cessare; (fam.) *to — on at someone*, stare dietro a qualcuno; *to — out*, *tr.* non lasciar entrare; *intr.* restare fuori, tenersi lontano, non immischiarsi; *to — together*, *tr.* tenere insieme; *intr.* restare uniti; *to — under*, *tr.* reprimere, tenere a freno; *to — up*, *tr.* tenere su, tenere alto, mantenere; *to — up appearances*, salvare le apparenze; (fam.) *to — one's tail up*, non scoraggiarsi; *intr.* continuare; *to — up with*, seguire da vicino.
**keeper** *n.* guardiano, custode *m.*, sorvegliante *m.*; conservatore, direttore, intendente *m.*; *Keeper of the Seal*, Guardasigilli *m.*; (of hotel) padrone *m.*, oste *m.*; (electr.) ancora, armatura.
**keeping** *n.* custodia; guardia; sorveglianza; *in safe* —, sotto sicura custodia; conservazione; mantenimento; osservanza; adempimento; (fig.) *in — with*, conforme a, consono a, in

armonia con; *out of — with*, dissonante da.
**keepsake** *n.* ricordo; pegno.
**keg** *n.* barilotto; botticello.
**kelp** *n.* (bot.) varecchi *m.pl.*; fuco.
**kelt**[1] *n.* (ichth.) salmone *m.* che ha deposto le uova.
**kelt**[2], **keltic** *n., adj.* See **celt, celtic.**
**ken** *n.* conoscenza; percezione; *to be out of one's —*, essere al di là della propria comprensione; *tr.* (Scot.). See **know.**
**kennel**[1] *n.* canile *m.*; covo; *pl.* allevamento di cani.
**kennel**[2] *n.* cunetta, rigagnolo.
**Kent** *pr.n.* (geog.) la contea del Kent; *man of —*, nativo della parte orientale del Kent. **-ish** *adj.* del Kent; *-ish man*, nativo della parte occidentale del Kent.
**Kenya** *pr.n.* (geog.) Kenia, Chenia.
**kept** *p.def., part.* of **keep,** *q.v.*
**keratose** *adj.* (chem.) corneo.
**kerb** *n.* cordone *m.*; orlo. **-stone** *n.* cordonatura.
**kerchief** *n.* fazzoletto.
**kermess** *n.* chermessa.
**kernel** *n.* mandorla; nocciolo; gheriglio; acino; (fig.) nucleo; essenza.
**kerosene** *n.* petrolio raffinato.
**kestrel** *n.* (orn.) gheppio; accertello.
**ketch** *n.* (naut.) tartana.
**ketchup** *n.* salsa piccante.
**kettle** *n.* bollitore; brico; *camp —*, marmitta; (fig.) *a pretty — of fish*, un bel pasticcio; (provb.) *that's the pot calling the — black*, quello è un vedere i bruscoli altrui e non le sue travi.
**kettledrum** *n.* (mus.) nacchera; timballo; timpano.
**key**[1] *n.* chiave *f.*; (piano, typewriter) tasto; (watch) chiavetta; (mus.) chiave, tono; (mech.) bietta; *tr.* (mus.) accordare; (mech.) inchiavettare; (fig.) *to — up*, stimolare, incitare; *-ed up*, teso, entusiasmato.
**key**[2] *n.* (geog., USA) isoletta bassa, scogliera.
**key-board** *n.* tastiera. **-hole** *n.* buco della serratura.
**key-money** *n.* buonuscita. **-note** *n.* (mus.) tonica; (fig.) nota dominante. **-ring** *n.* anello portachiavi.
**keystone** *n.* (archit.) chiave *f.* di volta.
**khaki** *adj., n.* cachi *m.*; (Italian equivalent) grigio-verde *m.*
**kibosh** *n.* (pop.) sciocchezza; fandonia; *to put the — on*, mettere fine a.
**kick** *n.* calcio; pedata; (football) *corner —*, calcio d'angolo; *free —*, (calcio di) punizione; *drop —*, drop *m.*; *goal —*, rimessa; *penalty —*, (calcio di) rigore; (of gun) rinculo; (fig.) forza, effetto stimolante; *with a — in it*, stimolante, forte; *to have no — left*, essere completamente a terra.
**kick** *tr.* dare una pedata a; spingere a calci; (fam.) *to — someone out*, buttar fuori qualcuno; *to — someone downstairs*, scaraventare qualcuno dalle scale; *to — someone upstairs*, liberarsi di qualcuno facendolo promuovere; (pop.) *to — the bucket*, crepare, tirare le cuoia; *to — one's heels*, attendere a lungo, non aver niente da fare; *intr.* dar calci; (of gun) rinculare; (fig.) reagire, protestare; *to — off*, *tr.* liberarsi con un calcio di, *intr.* (football) dare il calcio d'inizio; *to — up*, sollevare; *to — up a fuss*, scatenare un putiferio; *to — up a row*, far baccano.
**kicker** *n.* calciatore; cavallo che tira calci.
**kick-off** *n.* (football) calcio d'inizio.
**kid** *n.* capretto; pelle *f.* di capretto; (fam.) piccino, bimbo; *tr., intr.* partorire; (pop.) gabbare, prendere in giro, ingannare.
**kiddie, kiddy** *n.* (fam.) bambino.
**kid-gloves** *n.* guanti di pelle di capretto; (fig.) *to handle someone with —*, trattare qualcuno coi guanti.
**kidnap** *tr.* rapire, portare via a forza. **-per** *n.* rapitore. **-ping** *n.* ratto.
**kidney** *n.* (anat.) rene *m.*; (cul.) rognone *m.*; (bot.) *— bean*, fagiuolo, fagiuolino; (fig.) tempra, sorta.
**kill** *n.* uccisione; (hunt.) cacciagione *f.*; *tr.* uccidere; ammazzare; far morire; *to get -ed*, essere ucciso, rimanerci, *-ed in action*, morto in combattimento; (fig.) *to — time*, ammazzare il tempo; distruggere; sopprimere; *to — with kindness*, soffocare di gentilezze; (pop.) *to — a bottle*, vuotare una bottiglia; (provb.) *to — two birds with one stone*, prendere due piccioni con una fava. **-er** *n.* uccisore; assassino; (zool.) *-er whale*, orca marina. **-ing** *adj.* mortale, micidiale, che ammazza; (fam.) affascinante, irresistibile; da far crepare; *n.* uccisione; assassinio.
**kill-joy** *n.* guastafeste *m. indecl.*
**kiln** *n.* forno; fornace *f.*
**kilo, -gram(me)** *n.* chilo, chilogramma *m.* (2.204 lbs.). **-metre** *n.* chilometro (0.621 mile). **-metric** *adj.* chilometrico. **-watt** *n.* (electr.) chilowatt *m.*
**kilt** *n.* (cost.) gonnella alla scozzese.
**kimono** *n.* (cost.) chimono.
**kin** *adj.* consanguineo; affine; *n.* parenti, congiunti *m.pl.*; parentela; *next of —*, parente prossimo; *kith and —*, amici e parenti.
**kind**[1] *adj.* gentile; cortese; amabile, affabile; benevolo; *that's very — of you*, sei molto gentile; *be so — as to*, abbia la gentilezza di; *— regards*, cordiali saluti *m.pl.*; *— people*, buona gente; *— words*, parole *f.pl.* gentili.
**kind**[2] *n.* specie; razza; genere *m.*; *what — of flower is this?*, che specie di fiore è questo?; *he is a — of writer*, è una specie di scrittore; *human —*, il genere umano; *of all -s*, di tutti i generi; *nothing of the —*, niente del genere; natura, carattere *m.*; *payment in —*, pagamento in natura; *to repay someone in —*, ripagare qualcuno della stessa moneta; (fam.) *— of*, quasi, piuttosto; *I — of expected it*, quasi me lo aspettavo.
**kindergarten** *n.* giardino d'infanzia, asilo infantile.
**kind-hearted** *adj.* di cuore buono; benevolo; gentile. **-ness** *n.* bontà di cuore; benevolenza.
**kindle** *tr.* accendere; dar fuoco a; (fig.) eccitare, provocare; *intr.* accendersi; prendere fuoco.
**kindliness** *n.* gentilezza; amorevolezza; amabilità; bontà di cuore; mitezza.
**kindling** *n.* accensione; legna minuta per accendere il fuoco.
**kindly** *adj.* gentile; amabile; amorevole; buono; benevolo; *adv.* gentilmente; cortesemente; per favore, per cortesia; *to take — to someone*, trovare simpatico qualcuno.
**kindness** *n.* gentilezza; bontà; benevolenza; *to do someone a —*, fare un piacere a qualcuno.
**kindred** *n.* parentela; parenti *m.pl.*; congiunti *m.pl.*; *attrib.* imparentato, affine, simile; *a — spirit*, un'anima gemella.
**kine** *n.* bestiame *m.*; vacche *f.pl.*
**kinema** *n.* See **cinema.**
**kinetic** *adj.* (phys.) cinetico.
**king** *n.* re *m.*; sovrano; monarca *m.*; *the three -s*, i Re Magi; *the book of Kings*, il Libro dei Re; (cards, chess) re; (draughts) dama; (fig.) magnate *m.*; *the — of beasts*, il re degli animali; *the -'s English*, l'inglese come parlato dalle classi colte; *-'s evidence*, imputato che testimonia contro i complici; *-'s evil*, scrofola; *-'s highway*, le strade nazionali; *a dish fit for a —*, un boccone da cardinale.
**kingcup** *n.* (bot.) calta palustre.
**kingdom** *n.* regno; reame *m.*; *the United —*, il Regno Unito; *the animal —*, il regno animale; (pop.) *— come*, il mondo dell'al di là; *till — come*, per sempre.
**kingfisher** *n.* (orn.) alcione *m.*, martin pescatore.
**kinglike** *adj.* da re, reale.
**kingl-y** *adj.* regale, regio, reale. **-iness** *n.* maestà, regalità.
**king-of-arms** *n.* (herald.) primo araldo. **-pin** *n.* (mech.) perno di sterzaggio; (fig.) uomo chiave. **-post** *n.* (bldg.) monaco, ometto.

**kingship** *n.* regalità; potere sovrano.
**kink** *n.* nodo; cappio; cocca; ghiribizzo; grillo; *intr.* attorcigliarsi; annodarsi. **-y** *adj.* attorcigliato; ricciuto; (fam.) eccentrico, strambo; originale; (of sex) alquanto pervertito.
**kinless** *adj.* senza parenti; solo.
**kins-folk** *n.* parenti *m.pl.*; congiunti *m.pl.*; parentela. **-hip** *n.* parentela; (fig.) affinità. **-man** *n.* parente *m.*; congiunto. **-woman** *n.* parente *f.*; congiunta.
**kiosk** *n.* chiosco; edicola.
**kip** *n.* (pop.) pisolino; letto.
**kipper** *n.* aringa affumicata.
**kirk** *n.* (Scot.) chiesa.
**kismet** *n.* fato, destino.
**kiss** *n.* bacio; *to give someone a —*, baciare qualcuno; *to blow someone a —*, mandare un bacio a qualcuno; (billiards) rimpallo; *— of life*, il bacio della vita; *tr.* baciare; *to — goodbye*, accomiatarsi con un bacio da; *to — one's hand to*, mandare un bacio con la mano a; *to — away*, asciugare con baci; (fig.) *to — the dust*, mordere la polvere; *intr.* baciarsi; *to — and be friends*, riconciliarsi con un bacio; (billiards) rimpallare.
**kit** corredo; roba; arnesi *m.pl.*; attrezzi *m.pl.*; utensili *m.pl.*; *to pack one's —*, fare i bagagli; (mil.) equipaggiamento. **-bag** *n.* sacca sportiva; (mil.) sacco militare.
**kitchen** *n.* cucina; *— garden*, orto, orticello; *— range*, fornello; *— sink*, acquaio; *— utensils*, batteria da cucina. **-ette** *n.* cucinino.
**kite** *n.* (orn.) nibbio; aquilone *m.*, cervo volante; *to fly a —*, lanciare un aquilone, (fig.) saggiare l'opinione pubblica; (aeron.) pallone drago.
**kith** *n.* parentela; *— and kin*, amici e parenti *m.pl.*
**kitsch** *adj.* pacchiano.
**kitten** *n.* gattino; micio, micino; *to have -s*, fare dei gattini, (fig.) emozionarsi; *intr.* fare dei gattini. **-ish** *adj.* da gattino; vivace; vispo.
**kittiwake** *n.* (orn.) gabbiano tridattilo.
**kiwi** *n.* (orn.) atterige *f.*
**klaxon (horn)** clackson *m.*; tromba.
**kleptomani-a** *n.* cleptomania. **-ac** *adj.*, *n.* cleptomane *m.*, *f.*
**knack** *n.* destrezza; abilità; arte *f.*; abitudine *f.* **-er** *n.* macellatore di cavalli inabili, macellaio; *-er's yard*, macello; *pl.* (slang) balle *f.pl.*
**knapsack** *n.* zaino, sacco.
**knav-e** *n.* briccone *m.*; furfante *m.*; mariuolo; (cards) fante *m.* **-ery, -ishness** *n.* bricconeria; furfanteria; mariuoleria; disonestà. **-ish** *adj.* furbo; losco; disonesto; da mariuolo; *-ish trick*, bricconeria; malvagità.
**knead** *tr.* intridere; impastare; (fig.) mescolare; massaggiare. **-ing** *n.* impastatura; *-ing trough*, madia; *-ing machine*, gramolatrice.
**knee** *n.* ginocchio; *on one's -s*, in ginocchio, ginocchioni; *to go down on one's -s*, inginocchiarsi; *to sit with one's -s crossed*, tenere le gambe incrociate; (med.) *housemaid's —*, borsite *f.* prepatellare, (pop.) ginocchio della lavandaia; (fig.) *to bend the — before*, piegare il ginocchio davanti a; *to bring someone to his -s*, ridurre qualcuno a completa sottomissione; (mech.) tubo a gomito.
**knee-breeches** *n.* calzoni corti; calzoni alla zuava. **-cap** *n.* (anat.) rotella; rotula; (pad) ginocchiera. **-deep, -high** *adj.* (che arriva) fino al ginocchio. **-joint** *n.* articolazione del ginocchio.
**kneel** *intr.* inginocchiarsi; mettersi in ginocchio; genuflettersi; *to — on one knee*, mettere un ginocchio a terra. **-er** *n.* chi s'inginocchia; inginocchiatoio.
**knell** *n.* rintocco funebre; campana a morto; (fig.) triste presagio; *intr.* suonare a morto.
**knelt** *p.def.*, *part.* of **kneel**, *q.v.*
**knew** *p.def.* of **know**, *q.v.*
**knickerbockers** *n.* calzoni corti, calzoncini *m.pl.*
**knickers** *n.* calzoni corti, calzoncini *m.pl.*; (women's) mutande, mutandine *f.pl.*
**knick-knack** *n.* ninnolo; gingillo.
**knife** *n.* coltello; *—, fork and spoon*, posate *f.pl.*, coperto; (art) *palette —*, mestichino; (surg.) bisturi *m.*; (fig.) *war to the —*, guerra ad oltranza; (fam.) *to have one's — into*, avercela a morte con; *before one could say —*, in un batter d'occhio; *tr.* accoltellare; pugnalare.
**knife-blade** *n.* lama di coltello. **-edge** *n.* filo di lama. **-grinder** *n.* arrotino; (machine) arrotatrice, affilatrice. **-rest** *n.* posaposate *m.*
**knight** *n.* cavaliere *m.*; *— errant*, cavaliere errante; (chess) cavallo; *tr.* creare cavaliere. **-hood** *n.* rango di cavaliere; (collect.) cavalleria. **-ly** *adj.* cavalleresco, da cavaliere.
**knit** *tr.*, *intr.* lavorare a maglia; sferruzzare; *to — socks*, fare la calza; saldare, saldarsi; unire, unirsi; *— together by*, uniti da; (fig.) *to — one's brows*, aggrottare le ciglia, corrugare la fronte. **-ter** *n.* chi lavora a maglia; (text.) telaio per maglieria. **-ting** *n.* lavoro a maglia, maglieria. **-ting-needle** *n.* ferro, ago da calza. **-wear** *n.* maglieria.
**knob** *n.* bozza; protuberanza; bernoccolo; nodo; pomo; maniglia; (on radio set) manopola; (pop.) zucca.
**knobb-ly, -y** *adj.* pieno di protuberanze; nodoso; biturzoluto. **-iness** *n.* nodosità.
**knock** *n.* colpo; urto; percossa; bussa; (at door) bussata, picchio; (fam.) *to get a nasty —*, subire una batosta; (motor.) battito in testa.
**knock** *tr.* colpire; battere; dare un colpo a; urtare; *to — someone senseless*, tramortire qualcuno con un colpo; (fam.) denigrare; *to — one's head against the wall*, battere con la testa contro il muro; (fig.) *to — one's head against a brick wall*, arrampicarsi sui vetri; *our plans have been -ed on the head*, i nostri progetti sono andati a monte; *intr.* (on door) bussare, picchiare; *to — against*, urtare; (of engine), battere in testa; FOLLOW. BY PREP. OR ADV.: *to — about*, *tr.* malmenare, bistrattare, *intr.* vagabondare, fare vita randagia; *to — down*, *tr.* abbattere, atterrare; *to be -ed down by a car*, essere travolto da una macchina; (at auction) aggiudicare, (prices) abbassare; (house, *etc.*) demolire; *to — in*, *tr.* conficcare, far penetrare; *to — off*, *tr.* far cadere; (work) fare rapidamente, *to — something off the price*, detrarre dal prezzo, (slang) rubare, *intr.* smettere di lavorare, *to — out*, *tr.* far uscire, vuotare colpendo; *to — out of the hand of*, far cadere dalla mano di, (sport) sconfiggere, eliminare, mettere fuori combattimento, (boxing) mettere knock-out; *to — over*, rovesciare; *to — together*, *tr.* mettere insieme in fretta, *intr.* urtarsi a vicenda, battere insieme; *to — up*, *tr.* (work) abborracciare, svegliare, (slang, USA) fare incinta, *rfl.* sfinirsi da troppo lavoro; *intr. to — up against*, imbattersi in.
**knocker** *n.* (on door) battente *m.*; picchiotto; martello.
**knock-kneed** *adj.* dalle gambe ad X, dalle gambe storte. **-out** *n.* *attrib.* *-out blow*, colpo di grazias colpo che mette fuori combattimento; (boxing) knockout *m.*
**knoll** *n.* monticello, poggio; collinetta.
**knot** *n.* nodo; annodatura; viluppo; groviglio; *to tie a —*, fare un nodo; *to untie a —*, disfare un nodo; (bot.) nocchio, nodo; (anat.) ganglio; (naut.) nodo, miglio marino; (fig.) gruppo, crocchio; *tr.* annodare; legare; aggrovigliare; *intr.* annodarsi; aggrovigliarsi. **-ted** *adj.* pieno di nodi; nodoso; annodato; intrecciato; ingarbugliato. **-tiness** *n.* nodosità; (fig.) difficoltà; complessità. **-ty** *adj.* nodoso; nocchiuto; (fig.) difficile; spinoso; scabroso.

**know** *n.* (fam.) *to be in the —* essere al corrente. **know** *tr.* sapere; conoscere; riconoscere; distinguere; *he -s he is right,* sa di aver ragione; *I do not — him,* non lo conosco; *he knew me by my voice,* mi riconobbe dalla voce; *to — good from evil,* distinguere il bene dal male; *to — by name, not by sight,* conoscere di nome, non di vista; *to — for certain,* sapere per certo; *to — how to,* sapere (come), saper fare; *to — inside out,* conoscere a fondo, a menadito; *to — the ropes,* essere pratico, conoscere tutti i segreti; *to get to —,* venire a sapere, fare la conoscenza di; *to let someone —,* far sapere a qualcuno, avvisare qualcuno; *as far as I —,* per quel che ne so, per quanto sappia; *to — about,* essere al corrente di, essere informato su; *what do you — about that ?,* cosa hai da dire in proposito ?; *to — of,* sapere, aver sentito parlare di; *not that I — of,* no, che io sappia; (fam.) *I don't — him from Adam !,* mai visto!, mai conosciuto!; *how should I — ?,* come faccio a sapere ?, *don't I — it !,* lo dici a me!; *not if I — it !,* per nulla al mondo!; *to — what's what, to — a thing or two,* saperla lunga.

**knowable** *adj.* conoscibile; scibile; comprensibile; apprendibile.

**know-all** *n.* sapientone *m.*; barbassoro. **-how** *n.* (fam.) conoscenza pratica; abilità tecnica.

**knowing** *adj.* intelligente; abile; sagace; furbo; furbesco; astuto; *n.* conoscenza; conoscimento; (fam.) *there is no —,* non si può sapere, è impossibile dire. **-ly** *adv.* coscientemente; intenzionalmente; furbamente; furbescamente; astutamente.

**knowledge** *n.* conoscenza; cognizione; *lack of —,* ignoranza; *to the best of my —,* per quanto sappia; *it is a matter of common — that,* è notorio che; *to be public —,* essere di pubblico dominio; *it has come to my — that . . .,* ho saputo che . . .; *without my —,* a mia insaputa; *to have (a) — of,* conoscere; *to have a working — of,* essere pratico di; *to have no — of,* non sapere, ignorare; *to keep something from someone's —,* nascondere qualcosa a qualcuno; *to speak with full —,* parlare con cognizione di causa; sapere *m.*; scienza; erudizione; scibile *m.*; (provb.) *— is power,* sapere è potere; (bibl.) *the tree of — of good and evil,* l'albero della scienza del bene e del male; (leg.) *carnal —,* conoscenza carnale. **-able** *adj.* bene informato; istruito.

**known** *adj.* noto; conosciuto; saputo; *to make —,* far conoscere, far sapere, divulgare, rendere noto; *to make oneself —,* farsi conoscere; *to be — as,* chiamarsi.

**knuckle** *n.* nocca; *to rap over the -s,* battere sulle nocche a, (fig.) sgridare; (cul.) garretto; *tr.* battere con le nocche; *intr.* (fig.) *to — under,* cedere, sottomettersi; *to — under to,* chinare la testa a, piegarsi a.

**knuckle-bone** *n.* falange *f.* **-duster** *n.* (slang) pugno di ferro.

**kohl** *n.* polvere *f.* d'antimonio.

**Koran** *n.* Corano. **-ic** *adj.* del Corano.

**Korea** *pr.n.* (geog.) Corea. **-n** *adj., n.* coreano.

**kosher** *adj.* puro secondo la legge ebraica; *n.* cibo preparato secondo la legge ebraica.

**kowtow** *intr.* prostrarsi (alla maniera cinese); (fig.) umiliarsi, strisciare.

**Kremlin** *pr.n.* Cremlino.

**kudos** *n.* (pop.) fama, gloria.

**kurd** *adj., n.* (ethn.) curdo. **-ish** *adj.* (ethn.) curdo; *n.* (ling.) curdo.

**kursaal** *n.* stabilimento termale; casinò *m. indecl.*

**L, l** *n.* elle *m., f.*; (teleph.) *— for Lucy,* elle come Livorno.

**lab** *n.* (fam.) abbrev. of **laboratory,** *q.v.*

**label** *n.* etichetta; cartellino; marca; (herald.) lambello; *tr.* mettere l'etichetta a, contrassegnare con etichetta; (fig.) classificare, catalogare, definire.

**labial** *adj., n.* (ling.) labiale *f.* **-ize** *tr.* (ling.) rendere labiale.

**labiodental** *adj., n.* (ling.) labiodentale *f.*

**laboratory** *n.* laboratorio.

**laborious** *adj.* laborioso; faticoso; arduo; operoso, solerte. **-ness** *n.* laboriosità; fatica.

**labour** *n.* lavoro; fatica; sforzo; *the -s of Hercules,* le fatiche d'Ercole; (leg.) *hard —,* lavori forzati, carcere duro; (industr.) manodopera; *shortage of —,* mancanza di manodopera; *— exchange,* ufficio collocamento; *skilled —,* manodopera specializzata; (pol.) i lavoratori, la classe operaia; *Labour Party* (in Britain) partito laburista, (elsewhere) partito del lavoro; *to vote —,* votare per i laburisti; (med.) doglie *f.pl.*, travaglio; *tr.* elaborare; insistere su; *intr.* lavorare; faticare; avanzare a fatica; *to — at,* affaticarsi a, occuparsi di; *to — under,* soffrire per, lottare contro. **-ed** *adj.* elaborato; pesante; stentato; *-ed breathing,* respiro affannoso. **-er** *n.* lavoratore; manovale *m.*; bracciante *m.*; uomo di fatica. **-ing** *adj.* lavorante; *the -ing class,* la classe operaia. **-ite** *n.* (pol.) laburista *m., f.*

**labour-pains** *m.pl.* doglie del parto. **-saving** *adj.* che risparmia fatica.

**laburnum** *n.* (bot.) laburno, avorno, citiso.

**labyrinth** *n.* labirinto; dedalo; (fig.) ginepraio. **-an, -ine** *adj.* labirintico; intricato.

**lac** *n.* lacca.

**lace** *n.* (of shoe) laccio, stringa; (dressm.) pizzo, merletto, trina, gallone *m.*, passamaneria; *— trimming,* guarnizione in pizzo; (archit.) dentello; *tr.* allacciare; ornare di pizzi, gallonare; *to — wine,* correggere il vino; *coffee -d with cognac,* caffè corretto con cognac; *intr.* allacciarsi.

**lace-maker** *n.* merlettaia, trinaia, fabbricante *m., f.* di merletti.

**lacerat-e** *tr.* lacerare; strappare. **-ion** *n.* lacerazione.

**lace-work** *n.* merletti, pizzi *m.pl.*

**lachrym-al** *adj.* lacrimale, lacrimatorio. **-ose** *adj.* lacrimoso.

**lack** *n.* mancanza; insufficienza; deficienza; scarsità; *for — of,* per mancanza di; *there is a — of,* manca, c'è difetto di; *there is no — of,* non manca; *tr.* mancare di; *he -s courage,* manca di coraggio, gli manca il coraggio; *intr.* mancare; occorrere.

**lackadaisical** *adj.* apatico; svogliato; indolente; affettato, lezioso. **-ness** *n.* apatia; indolenza; affettazione.

**lackey** *n.* lacchè *m. indecl.*; valletto; (fig.) adulatore.

**lack-lustre** *adj.* opaco; appannato; matto; che non rifulge.

**laconic** *adj.* laconico; conciso.

**lacquer** *n.* lacca; *tr.* verniciare, laccare. **-ing** *n.* laccatura.

**lact-ation** *n.* lattazione, allattamento. **-ic** *adj.* lattico. **-iferous** *adj.* lattifero.

**lacuna** *n.* lacuna; vuoto.

**lacustr-ian, -ine** *adj.* lacustre.

**lad** *n.* giovinetto, giovanotto; ragazzo.

**ladder** *n.* scala a piuoli; (fig). scala; (in stocking) smagliatura; *to go into -s,* smagliarsi; *tr.* munire di scale; *intr.* (of stocking) smagliarsi.

**ladder-proof** *adj.* (of stocking) indemagliabile.
**lade** *tr.* caricare.
**laden** *adj.* caricato, carico; (fig.) oppresso.
**ladin** *n.* (ling.) ladino
**lading** *n.* carico, caricamento; *bill of –*, polizza di carico.
**ladle** *n.* mestolo, ramaiuolo, cucchiaione *m.*; (industr.) siviera, secchione *m.*
**ladle** *tr.* scodellare, versare con un mestolo; (fig.) riversare, distribuire; declamare; (industr.) colare.
**lady** *n.* signora, dama; (of nobility) nobildonna; *young –*, signorina; *old –*, vecchia signora; *– of the house*, padrona di casa; *ladies and gentlemen*, signore e signori; (wife) moglie *f.*, signora; *– friend*, amica, amante *f.*; *ladies' man*, damerino; *– help*, governante *f.*; (as title) milady *f.*, contessa, marchesa, baronessa; *Lady Bountiful*, fata benefica; (rel.) *Our Lady*, Nostra Signora, la Madonna; *Lady Day*, l'Annunciazione; *Lady Chapel*, cappella della Madonna. When used attributively, is rendered by feminine form of noun, e.g. *– doctor*, dottoressa; *– reader*, lettrice; *– dog*, cagna.
**ladybird** *n.* (ent.) coccinella, gallinetta.
**lady-in-waiting** *n.* dama di corte.
**lady-killer** *n.* dongiovanni *m.*, rubacuori *m. indecl.*
**ladylike** *adj.* da signora; distinto, signorile; (of man) effeminato.
**ladyship** *n.* signoria; *your –*, Signora, Contessa, la Signoria Vostra.
**lag**[1] *n.* ritardo; intervallo; *intr.* ritardare, avanzare lentamente; *to – behind*, rimanere indietro.
**lag**[2] *n.* (slang) avanzo di galera; pregiudicato.
**lag**[3] *tr.* (industr.) rivestire con materiale isolante; isolare; blindare.
**lager**[1] *n.* birra tedesca chiara.
**lager**[2] *n.* campo di prigionieri di guerra, campo di concentramento.
**laggard** *n.* ritardatario; individuo che resta sempre indietro.
**lagging**[1] *gerund.* of **lag**[1]; il ritardare.
**lagging**[2] *n.* (industr.) rivestimento isolante.
**lagoon** *n.* laguna; valle *f.*
**laicize** *tr.* laicizzare.
**laid** *p.def.*, *part.* of **lay,** *q.v.*
**lain** *part.* of **lie,** *q.v.*
**lair** *n.* tana; covo; antro; (fig.) nascondiglio.
**laird** *n.* (Scot.) proprietario terriero, possidente *m.*
**laity** *n.* i laici; laicato; (fig.) i profani.
**lake**[1] *n.* lago; *the Lake District*, la zona dei laghi; *the Lake poets*, i poeti laghisti.
**lake**[2] *n.* (colour) rosso lacca.
**lam** *tr.* (pop.) battere, bastonare, picchiare; *to – something into someone*, cacciare qualcosa in testa a qualcuno.
**lama** *n.* (rel.) lama *m.*; *the Grand –*, il Gran Lama.
**lamb** *n.* agnello; (fam.) persona ubbidiente; *to go like a –*, andare senza protestare; (term of affection) *my –*, tesoro mio; *intr.* (of ewe) figliare. **-ing** *n.* agnellatura; *-ing season*, agnellatura.
**lambent** *adj.* lambente, che lambisce; guizzante; blando, diffuso.
**lambkin** *n.* agnellino, agnelletto.
**lamb-like** *adj.* timido, come un agnello, mansueto.
**lambrequin** *n.* (herald.) lambrecchino.
**lambskin** *n.* pelle *f.* d'agnello.
**lame** *adj.* zoppo, zoppicante; storpio; claudicante; *to be –*, zoppicare; (fig.) zoppicante; debole; cattivo; insufficiente; (fam.) *a – duck*, un fallito, una persona debole; *tr.* storpiare, azzoppare. **-ness** *n.* zoppaggine *f.*; claudicazione; (fig.) debolezza.
**lament** *n.* lamento; pianto; elegia funebre; *tr.*, *intr.* lamentare; deplorare; lamentarsi (di), dolersi (di); piangere. **-able** *adj.* lamentevole; deplorevole. **-ation** *n.* lamentazione; lamento. **-ed** *adj.* deplorato; compianto; *late -ed*, compianto, rimpianto.
**lamin-a** *n.* lamina; piastra di metallo; (bot.) lobo; (geol.) strato. **-ate** *adj.* laminato, in lamine, a strati; *tr.* laminare; ridurre in lamine; coprire di lamine; *intr.* dividersi in lamine. **-ation** *n.* laminatura; (geol.) stratificazione.
**lammergeyer** *n.* (orn.) gipeto, avvoltoio barbuto.
**lamp** *n.* lampada, lampadina; lanterna; lucerna; *reading –*, lampada da tavolo; (on ship, car) fanale *m.*, faro.
**lamp-black** *n.* nero fumo; (paint.) fuliggine *f.* **-bracket** *n.* braccio portalampada.
**lamplight** *n.* luce *f.* di lampada, luce artificiale. **-er** *n.* lampionaio, accendilume *m.*
**lampoon** *n.* libello satirico, pasquinata; *tr.* satireggiare, denigrare con libelli. **-er, -ist** *n.* libellista *m.*, scrittore di pasquinate.
**lamp-post** *n.* sostegno del lampione; *tall as a –*, allampanato, spilungato; (fam.) *between you and me and the –*, in gran segreto, in confidenza.
**lamprey** *n.* (ichth.) lampreda.
**lampshade** *n.* paralume *m.*
**lance** *n.* lancia; (fig.) *to break a – with*, spezzare una lancia con; *tr.* ferire con una lancia; (surg.) incidere col bisturi, lancettare.
**lance-corporal** *n.* (mil.) vice-caporale *m.*; (of carabinieri) appuntato.
**Lancelot** *pr.n.* Lancillotto.
**lancer** *n.* lanciere *m.*; *pl.* (dance) i lancieri.
**lance-sergeant** *n.* (mil.) caporale *m.* maggiore.
**lancet** *n.* (surg.) bisturi *m. indecl.*, lancetta; (archit.) finestra ad ogiva.
**lancinating** *adj.* lancinante, acuto.
**land** *n.* terra; *dry –*, terra ferma; *to travel by –*, viaggiare per terra; paese *m.*; contrada; *native –*, patria; *– of plenty*, paese di cuccagna; *the promised –*, la terra promessa; *Holy Land*, Terra Santa; terreno, suolo, terre *f.pl.*, campi *m.pl.*, campagna; *to work on the –*, lavorare nei campi; *the flight from the –*, la fuga dai campi; *to own –*, essere proprietario di terreni; *waste –*, terreno incolto; *no man's –*, terra di nessuno; *attrib.* terrestre; (mil.) *– forces*, forze terrestri; *the – question*, la questione agraria; (fig.) *the – of the living*, questo mondo; *to see how the – lies*, tastare il terreno.
**land** *tr.*, *intr.* sbarcare; approdare; (aeron.) atterrare; *to – a fish*, tirare alla riva un pesce; (fig.) *to – a prize*, pescare un premio; *to – in prison*, finire in prigione; *to – someone in difficulties*, porre qualcuno nelle difficoltà; *to – on one's feet*, cadere in piedi, cavarsi d'impaccio; *I have been -ed with a false thousand lire note*, mi hanno appioppato un biglietto falso da mille lire; *to – a blow on someone's nose*, assestare a qualcuno un colpo sul naso.
**land-agent** *n.* fattore; amministratore di campagne.
**landed** *adj.* fondiario; *– gentry*, piccola nobiltà di campagna.
**landfall** *n.* (naut.) approdo.
**landholder** *n.* possidente *m.*; proprietario terriero; fittaiuolo.
**landing** *n.* sbarco; (naut.) approdo; (aeron.) atterraggio; (of seaplane) ammaraggio; (archit.) pianerottolo, piano, ripiano.
**landing-card** *n.* contrassegno per lo sbarco. **-craft** *n.* (mil.) mezzo da sbarco. **-ground** *n.* (aeron.) campo di atterraggio. **-net** *n.* (fishing) vangaiuola, negossa. **-party** *n.* (naut.) reparto da sbarco. **-place** *n.* approdo, scalo, punto di sbarco. **-stage** *n.* imbacadero, pontile *m.*, scalo, scalandrone *m.*
**landlady** *n.* proprietaria; (of hotel) albergatrice, proprietaria; (of inn) locandiera, ostessa;

(of café) padrona; (of lodging-house) affittacamere *f. indecl.*
**landlocked** *adj.* circondato da terre; sicuro, riparato; (geog.) mediterraneo.
**landlord** *n.* proprietario terriero, possidente *m.*; *absentee* —, latifondista *m.*; (of house) proprietario; (of hotel) albergatore, proprietario; (of inn) locandiere *m.*, oste *m.*; (of café) padrone *m.*; (of lodging-house) affittacamere *m. indecl.*
**landlubber** *n.* abitante di terra ferma, marinaio di acqua dolce.
**landmark** *n.* pietra di confine; punto di riferimento; (fig.) pietra miliare, segnacolo.
**landowner** *n.* proprietario fondiario; possidente *m.*; (pejor.) latifondista *m.*
**landscape** *n.* paesaggio.
**landscape-garden** *n.* giardino all'inglese. **-painter** *n.* paesaggista, paesista, pittore di paesaggi.
**land-slide** *n.* frana; franamento; (s)lavina; (fig., pol.) vittoria schiacciante, valanga, rovesciamento della situazione. **-slip** *n.* frana; franamento; (s)lavina. **-sman** *n.* uomo di terra ferma.
**land-surveying** *n.* agrimensura. **-surveyor** *n.* agrimensore, geometra *m.*
**landward(s)** *adj.*, *adv.* verso terra.
**lane** *n.* viottolo; sentiero; stradicciuola; vicolo, vico; (on motor road) corsia, carreggiata; (*shipping*) —, rotta; (fig.) *to form a* —, fare ala.
**language** *n.* lingua; favella; idioma *m.*; linguaggio; *bad* —, turpiloquio.
**languedoc** *pr.n.* (geog.) Linguadoca.
**languid** *adj.* languido; (fig.) fiacco, debole. **-ness** *n.* languidezza; languore *m.*; fiacchezza.
**languish** *intr.* languire; indebolirsi; affievolirsi; (fig.) struggersi; appassire. **-ing** *adj.* languido, languente; pieno di languore; (fig.) tenero, dolce.
**languor** *n.* languore *m.*; (fig.) apatia; indifferenza. **-ous** *adj.* languido; pieno di languore.
**langur** *n.* (zool.) entello.
**lani-ferous, -gerous** *adj.* lanifero, lanigero.
**lank** *adj.* alto e magro; sparuto; allampanato; (of hair) liscio, piatto. **-iness, -ness** *n.* magrezza; sparutezza. **-y** *adj.* alto e magro; sparuto; allampanato; dinoccolato.
**lantern** *n.* lanterna; fanale *m.*; faro; *dark* —, lanterna cieca; *magic* —, lanterna magica; — *lecture*, conferenza con proiezioni; — *slide*, diapositiva, lastra; *Chinese* —, lampioncino veneziano; (archit.) lanterna, capannuccio, pergamena.
**lantern-jawed** *adj.* dalle guancie infossate, dal viso sparuto.
**lanuginous** *adj.* lanuginoso.
**lanyard** *n.* cordone *m.*; (naut.) collatore.
**Laocoon** *pr.n.* (myth.) Laocoonte.
**lap**[1] *n.* grembo; *to sit on someone's* —, sedere in grembo a qualcuno; *in the* — *of luxury*, nel lusso; *in the* — *of Providence*, nelle mani di Dio; piega, falda, parte sovrapposta; (sport) giro; *last* —, ultimo giro, (fig.) ultima tappa; *tr.* avvolgere; ricoprire; piegare; (text.) infaldare; (mech.) incastrare; sovrapporre; (sport) superare (uno) di uno o più giri, doppiare.
**lap**[2] *n.* atto del bere con la lingua; (fig.) sciabordìo, sciacquìo; *tr.* bere avidamente; lappare; (fig.) lambire; *to* — *up*, bere, (fig.) credere a.
**lapdog** *n.* cagnolino di lusso, cagnolino da salotto.
**lapel** *n.* (cost.) risvolto, risvolta, rovescio.
**lapful** *n.* grembialata.
**lapidary** *adj.*, *n.* lapidario.
**lapidat-e** *tr.* lapidare. **-ion** *n.* lapidazione.
**lapis lazuli** *n.* lapislazzuli *m.*
**Lapland** *pr.n.* (geog.) Lapponia. **-er** *n.* lappone *m.*, *f.*
**Lapp** *n.* lappone *m.*, *f.*
**lappet** *n.* falda; risvolto; lembo; (of ear) lobo; (of mitre) infula, bendone *m.*; (of keyhole), copriserratura.
**lapse** *n.* errore *m.*; sbaglio; passo falso; (fig.) ricaduta; decorrenza, decorso; intervallo; lasso; (leg.) scadimento, scadenza; *intr.* mancare; decadere; venir meno; (fig.) cadere; abbandonarsi; scivolare; decorrere, trascorrere; scadere, cadere in prescrizione.
**lapwing** *n.* (orn.) pavoncella.
**larboard** *n.* (naut.) babordo.
**larceny** *n.* ladrocinio; furto.
**larch** *n.* (bot.) larice *m.*
**lard** *n.* strutto, sugna; *tr.* (cul.) ungere con strutto; (fig.) arricchire, condire.
**larder** *n.* dispensa; credenza.
**Lares** *pr.n.pl.* Lari *m.pl.*
**large** *adj.* grande; vasto; spazioso; ampio; largo; *a* — *number*, un gran numero; *a* — *family*, una famiglia numerosa; *a* — *sum*, una somma considerevole; *as* — *as life*, al naturale; *on a* — *scale*, su vasta scala; *in a* — *measure*, in gran parte; *to grow* —, ingrandire, ingrossarsi; *n. to be at* —, essere in libertà; *to set at* —, liberare; *the world at* —, il mondo in genere; *by and* —, in genere, nel complesso.
**large-hearted** *adj.* generoso; magnanimo. **-ness** *n.* generosità; magnanimità.
**largely** *adv.* largamente; ampiamente; in gran parte.
**largeness** *n.* grandezza; ampiezza; larghezza.
**large-sized** *adj.* grande; di grandi dimensioni.
**largesse** *n.* liberalità; dono; regalo; mancia.
**largish** *adj.* piuttosto grande.
**lariat** *n.* laccio.
**lark**[1] *n.* (orn.) allodola; *to rise with the* —, alzarsi presto.
**lark**[2] *n.* scherzo; burla; birichinata; *what a* — *!*, che spasso!; *intr.* fare scherzi, fare delle burle; *to* — *about*, divertirsi.
**larkspur** *n.* (bot.) fiorcappuccio, speronella.
**larva** *n.* (ent.) larva; (fig.) spettro; fantasma *m.*
**laryngitis** *n.* (med.) laringite *f.*
**larynx** *n.* (anat.) laringe *f.*
**lascivious** *adj.* lascivo; lussurioso. **-ness** *n.* lascivia; lussuria.
**lash** *n.* colpo di frusta; frustata; frustino; cordicella; (of eye) ciglio; *tr.* frustare, sferzare, flagellare; (of animal) *to* — *its tail*, agitare, dimenare la coda; (fig.) *to* — *oneself into a fury*, andar su tutte le furie, infuriarsi; *intr. to* — *out*, menar colpi alla cieca, (of horse) sferrare calci, (fig.) inveire; legare, allacciare.
**lashing** *n.* sferzata; staffilata; legatura; allacciatura; *pl.* (pop.) profusione; mucchio.
**lass, lassie** *n.* ragazza, fanciulla, giovinetta.
**lassitude** *n.* lassitudine *f.*; stanchezza; accasciamento.
**lasso** *n.* laccio; accappiatura; *tr.* prendere col laccio; accappiare.
**last**[1] *adj.* ultimo, finale; estremo; — *but one*, penultimo; — *but two*, terzultimo; *the* — *two*, gli ultimi due; — *but not least*, ultimo ma non meno inportante; *the Last Judgement*, l'Ultimo Giudizio, il Guidizio Supremo; *to breathe one's* —, spirare, esalare l'ultimo respiro; — *will and testament*, ultime volontà; *to pay one's* — *respects*, rendere gli estremi onori; (fam.) *on one's* — *legs*, (dying) vicino a morire, (in difficulties) all'estremo delle proprie risorse; *the* — *straw*, il colmo, la goccia che fa traboccare il vaso; — *thing at night*, l'ultima cosa prima di coricarsi; andato, scorso, passato; — *Monday*, lunedì scorso; — *week*, la settimana passata; — *night*, la notte passata, ieri sera; — *night but one*, l'altro ieri sera; *this day* — *week*, oggi fa otto giorni; *adv.* in ultimo, per l'ultimo, l'ultima volta; *at* —, alla fine, finalmente.
**last**[2] *n.* (shoem.) forma di scarpa; (provb.) *let the cobbler stick to his* —, a ciascuno il proprio mestiere.
**last**[3] *intr.* durare; resistere; conservarsi. **-ing** *adj.* durevole, duraturo.

**lastly** *adv.* in ultimo luogo; finalmente, alla fine; per ultimo; in conclusione.
**latch** *n.* saliscendi *m.*; chiavistello; nottola; scatto; (on gate) stanghetta; *tr.* chiudere con saliscendi.
**latchet** *n.* laccio, stringa, cordone *m.*
**latch-key** *n.* chiave *f.* di casa, chiave per serratura a molle.
**late** *adj.* tardo; tardivo; avanzato; inoltrato; *the — Mr. Brown*, il fu Signor Bruni; defunto; già, ex, precedente; recente; *of —*, recentemente; *adv.* in ritardo, tardi; *it's too —*, è troppo tardi; *to be twenty minutes —*, essere in ritardo di venti minuti, avere venti minuti di ritardo; (provb.) *better — than never*, meglio tardi che mai.
**late-comer** *n.* ritardatario.
**lateen** *adj.* — *sail*, vela latina.
**lately** *adv.* recentemente; ultimamente; di recente; poco fa; *what have you been doing —?*, che cosa hai fatto in questi ultimi tempi?; *until —*, fino a poco tempo fa; *as — as yesterday*, ieri ancora.
**lateness** *n.* ritardo; indugio; *the — of the hour*, l'ora avanzata.
**latent** *adj.* latente; nascosto; potenziale.
**later** *adj.* posteriore; più tardo; ulteriore; più recente; successivo; *adv.* più tardi, dopo; *— on*, più tardi; in seguito; *sooner or —*, prima o poi; *not — than Monday* entro lunedì; (fam.) *see you —*, a più tardi.
**lateral** *adj.* laterale.
**Lateran** *pr.n.* Laterano; *adj.* lateranense; *St. John —*, San Giovanni in Laterano.
**latest** *adj.* ultimo; recentissimo; *at the —*, al più tardi; *the — date*, il termine *m.*
**latex** *n.* (bot.) latte *m.*, lattice *m.*
**lath** *n.* assicella; listello; canniccio; (of blind) stecca; (fig.) *thin as a —*, magro come un chiodo.
**lathe** *n.* (mech.) tornio.
**lather** *n.* schiuma; *tr.* insaponare; coprire di schiuma di sapone; *intr.* far schiuma; (of horse) ricoprirsi di schiuma.
**lath-work** *n.* incannicciatura.
**Latin** *adj.*, *n.* latino; *dog —*, latino maccheronico. **-ism** *n.*, latinismo. **-ist** *n.* latinista *m.*, *f.* **-ity** *n.* latinità *f.* **-ize** *tr.*, *intr.* latinizzare, latineggiare.
**latitud-e** *n.* (geog.) latitudine *f.*; altezza; *pl.* regioni *f.pl.*, climi *m.pl.*; (fig.) larghezza; libertà. **-inal** *adj.* latitudinale. **-inarian** *adj.*, *n.* latitudinario. **-inarianism** *n.* latitudinarianismo; tolleranza.
**Latium** *pr.n.* (geog.) Lazio.
**latrine** *n.* latrina.
**latter** *adj.* posteriore; ultimo; secondo; *the — half of the century*, la seconda metà del secolo; *the — end*, la parte finale; *the former . . . the —*, quello . . . questo, quegli . . . questi. **-ly** *adv.* recentemente, ultimamente. **-most** *adj.* See **last.**
**lattice** *n.* traliccio; graticciata; grata. **-d** *adj.* munito di grata; ammandorlato.
**lattice-work** *n.* intelaiatura a traliccio, ammandorlato.
**laud** *n.* lode *f.*; (chant) lauda, laude *f.*; *tr.* lodare; encomiare; *to — to the skies*, portare alle stelle.
**laudab-le** *adj.* lodevole; degno di elogio. **-ility** *n.* lodabilità.
**laudanum** *n.* (pharm.) laudano.
**laudat-ory, -ive** *adj.* laudativo; elogiativo; encomiastico.
**laugh** *n.* riso; risata; *a loud —*, una risata sonora; *to give a forced —*, ridere a denti stretti; *to raise a —*, destare ilarità; *to have the — of someone*, ridere a spese di qualcuno; *intr.* ridere; *to — at*, ridere di, ridersi di, burlarsi di; *to — heartily*, ridere di cuore; *to burst out -ing*, scoppiare a ridere; *you make me —*, mi fai ridere; *there's nothing to — at*, non c'è da ridere; *what are you -ing at?*, perchè ridi?; *to — up one's sleeve*, ridere sotto i baffi; *to — in someone's face*, ridere in faccia a qualcuno; *I don't like being -ed at*, non mi piace che si rida di me; *to make someone — on the wrong side of his face*, far passare a qualcuno la voglia di ridere; (fam.) *it's enough to make a cat —*, è roba da far ridere i polli; (provb.) *he -s best who -s last*, ride bene chi ride ultimo; *tr. to — away*, allontanar ridendo; *to — off*, buttare in ridere, cavarsela con spirito da. **-able** *adj.* risibile; ridicolo; comico. **-ableness** *n.* comicità. **-ing** *adj.* che ride, allegro; ridente; *it's no -ing matter*, non c'è da ridere; *n.* risata; ridere; *stop —!*, basta con le risate! **-ingly** *adv.* ridendo; con risa.
**laughing-gas** *n.* gas *m.* esilarante. **-stock** zimbello; *to make a -stock of oneself*, rendersi ridicolo.
**laughter** *n.* risata; riso; ridere; ilarità; *a burst of —*, uno scoppio di riso; *a fit of —*, un riso irrefrenabile; *to split one's sides with —*, sbellicarsi dalle risa.
**launch** *n.* lancia, scialuppa; motolancia, motoscafo; *n.* (of ship) varo; (of missile) lancio; *tr.* lanciare; scagliare; *to — an attack*, sferrare un attacco; *to — an enterprise*, lanciare un'impresa; (naut.) varare; *intr. to — out*, lanciarsi, darsi, avventurarsi. **-ing** *n.* (of ship) varo; (of enterprise) varo; (of missile) lancio.
**launching-site** *n.* pista di lancio.
**launder** *tr.* lavare e stirare; *freshly -ed*, di bucato. **-ette** *n.* lavanderia automatica.
**laund-ress** *n.* lavandaia, stiratrice. **-ry** *n.* lavanderia; bucato.
**laureate** *adj.* coronato d'alloro; *poet —*, (in England) poeta di corte, (hist.) poeta cesareo.
**laurel** *n.* alloro, lauro; *— wreath*, corona di alloro; *pl.* (fig.) allori; *to rest on one's -s*, addormentarsi sugli allori.
**Laurence, Lawrence** *pr.n.* Lorenzo.
**Laurentian** *adj.* laurenziano, di Lorenzo.
**Lausanne** *pr.n.* (geog.) Losanna.
**lava** *n.* lava.
**lavatory** *n.* gabinetto, ritirata, toeletta; (pop.) cesso; *public —*, gabinetti *m.pl.* di decenza.
**lave** *tr.* lavare, bagnare.
**lavender** *n.* lavanda. **-water** *n.* acqua di lavanda.
**lavish** *adj.* prodigo, profuso; generoso, liberale; *tr.* prodigare, profondere; dare largamente. **-ness** *n.* prodigalità, profusione.
**law** *n.* legge *f.*; decreto legge; ordinanza; *to lay down the —*, dettar legge; *to enforce a —*, far osservare la legge; *to keep the —*, osservare la legge; *— and order*, ordine pubblico; *martial —*, legge marziale; (jurisprudence) diritto, giurisprudenza; (justice) giustizia, vie legali; *to go to —*, ricorrere alle vie legali; *to take the — into one's own hands*, farsi giustizia da sè; *— of nature*, legge di natura; *Kepler's -s*, le leggi di Keplero; avvocatura professione legale; *pl.* regole *f.pl.*; regolamento.
**law-abiding** *adj.* osservante della legge; disciplinato. **-court** *n.* tribunale *m.*; *pl.* palazzo di giustizia.
**lawful** *adj.* legittimo, lecito, legale. **-ly** *adv.* secondo la legge, legittimamente, legalmente. **-ness** *n.* legittimità, legalità.
**lawgiver** *n.* legislatore.
**lawless** *adj.* senza legge, illegale; arbitrario; sfrenato. **-ness** *n.* licenza; sfrenatezza; disordine *m.*; anarchia.
**lawn**[1] *n.* (text.) batista, rensa.
**lawn**[2] *n.* (hortic.) prato rasato, praticello.
**lawn-mower** *n.* falciatrice per prati erbosi.
**lawn-tennis** *n.* tennis *m.*
**Lawrence** *pr.n.* See **Laurence.**
**lawsuit** *n.* causa; processo.
**lawyer** *n.* avvocato; legale, giurista *m.*, *f.*
**lax** *adj.* trascurato, negligente, inesatto; fiacco, molle, rilassato.
**laxative** *adj.*, *n.* (pharm.) lassativo.
**laxity, laxness** *n.* rilassatezza; fiacchezza; trascuratezza, inesattezza.

**lay**[1] *adj.* (eccl.) laico, laicale, secolare; — *brother*, converso; — *sister*, conversa; — *clerk*, cantore; (fig.) non professionale, profano.

**lay**[2] *n.* (poet.) lai *m. indecl.*

**lay**[3] *n.* situazione, disposizione, configurazione; (of animal) tana.

**lay**[3] *tr.* posare; mettere; stendere; reclinare; adagiare; collocare; (fam.) giacere con; *to — bare*, mettere a nudo, rivelare; *to — the blame on*, addossare la colpa a; *to — claim to*, rivendicare; *to — dead*, uccidere; *to — hands on*, trovare, impadronirsi di, (assault) mettere le mani addosso a, (eccl.) imporre le mani a; *to — hold of*, afferrare; *to — siege to*, porre l'assedio a; *to — stress on*, accentuare, rilevare l'importanza di; *to — a trap for*, tendere un'insidia a; (of birds) *to — eggs* deporre le uova; disporre, preparare; *to — the fire*, preparare il fuoco; *to — the table*, apparecchiare la tavola; sottoporre; *to — something before someone*, sottoporre qualcosa a qualcuno; imporre, infliggere; *to — a tax on*, imporre una tassa su; progettare; svolgersi; *the scene is laid in Rome*, l'azione si svolge a Roma; *to — a ghost*, esorcizzare uno spirito; *to — a bet*, scommettere, fare una scommessa; *to — money on*, scommettere denaro su; (mil.) *to — a gun*, puntare un cannone. FOLLOW. BY ADV. OR PREP.: *to — aside*, mettere da parte, serbare, abbandonare; *to — down*, mettere a terra, (conditions) stabilire, (rules) formulare, (arms) deporre, (one's life) sacrificare, (wine) mettere in cantina, (cards) mettere sulla tavola, scoprire; *to — in*, mettere in serbo, farsi una provvista di; (pop.) *to — into*, picchiare; *to — off* (*workmen*), licenziare temporaneamente, sospendere; *to — on*, disporre, installare, improvvisare; (fam.) *to — it on thick*, esagerare; *to — out*, stendere, spendere, sborsare; *to — out a corpse*, comporre una salma; (fam.) *to — someone out*, mettere fuori combattimento qualcuno; *to — low*, abbattere; *to — up*, mettere in serbo, accumulare, (naut.) mettere in disarmo (una nave); *to be laid up*, essere costretto a stare a letto.

**lay**[4] *p.def.* of **lie**, *q.v.*

**lay-by** *n.* (on road) piazzuola; (on river) punto di sbarco.

**layer** *n.* strato; (agric.) margotta, propaggine *f.*; (hen) che fa molte uova, ovaiola; scommettitore, allibratore di scommesse; (artill.) puntatore.

**layette** *n.* corredino da neonato.

**lay-figure** *n.* manichino, fantoccio (also fig.).

**layman** *n.* (eccl.) laico, secolare *m.*; (fig.) profano.

**lay-out** *n.* disposizione; ordinamento; tracciato, pianta; (typ.) disposizione tipografica; menabò *m. indecl.*

**lazaret(to)** *n.* lazzaretto.

**Lazarus** *pr.n.* (bibl.) Lazzaro.

**laze** *n.* (fam.) *an hour's —*, un'ora di ozio; *intr.* oziare, fare il pigro; *tr. to — away one's time*, passare il tempo nell'ozio.

**laz-y** *adj.* pigro; indolente; infingardo; neghittoso. **-iness** *n.* pigrizia; indolenza; infingardaggine *f.*

**lazy-bones** *n.* (fam.) pigrone *m.*

**lea**[1] *adj.* (of land) a maggese.

**lea**[2] *n.* (poet.) prato, campo, prateria.

**lea**[3] *n.* (text.) misura per filati, matassa.

**leach** *tr.* (geol.) dilavare; (chem.) liscivare; (bldg.) percolare.

**lead**[1] *n.* piombo; *black —*, piombaggine *f.*, grafite *f.*; *red —*, minio; *white —*, biacca; piombino, scandaglio; *to heave the —*, scandagliare; (typ.) interlinea; (pop.) *to swing the —*, scansare fatiche, (mil.) marcare visita; *tr.* piombare, impiombare; (typ.) interlineare; *intr.* incrostarsi di piombo. **-ed** *adj.* piombato; (typ.) interlineato. **-en** *adj.* di piombo; (of colour) plumbeo; (fig.) pesante. **-ing** *n.* impiombatura; lavoro in piombo; (typ.) interlineazione.

**lead**[2] *n.* direzione; comando; guida; condotta; esempio; *to take the —*, prendere la direzione, (sport) essere in testa, prendere il primo posto; *to follow the — of*, seguire l'esempio di, lasciarsi guidare da; (theatr.) primo attore; *juvenile —*, primo attore giovane; *dogs must be kept on the —*, i cani devono essere tenuti a guinzaglio; (cards) mano, data; (electr.) conduttore isolato; *tr.* condurre; guidare; menare; dirigere; capeggiare; *to — to the altar*, condurre all'altare; *to — the way*, mostrare la strada, guidare; *to — an expedition*, capeggiare una spedizione; *to — astray*, sviare; *to — away*, condurre via, (fig.) *to be led away*, essere trascinato; *to — back*, ricondurre; (fig.) *to — someone a dance*, dar del filo da torcere a qualcuno; *to — someone by the nose*, menare qualcuno per il naso; *to — a busy life*, fare una vita attiva; *to — a double life*, condurre una doppia vita; indurre, persuadere, fare; *to — into temptation*, indurre nella tentazione; *to — someone to believe*, indurre qualcuno a credere, far credere a qualcuno; *intr.* condurre; menare; portare; andare davanti; *all roads — to Rome*, tutte le strade conducono a Roma; (fig.) portare (a), dar adito (a); (sport) essere in testa; *to — by two lengths*, condurre per due lunghezze; (cards) essere di mano, aver la data.

**leader** *n.* capo; conduttore; dirigente *m.*; comandante *m.*; capofila *m.*; (pol.) capopartito; (leg.) avvocato principale (in una causa); (of orchestra) primo violino; (journ.) editoriale *m.*, articolo di fondo; (sport) chi è in testa; (min.) vena secondaria; (mech.) conduttore. **-less** *adj.* senza guida, senza capo. **-ship** *n.* condotta; direzione; comando; arte *f.* di comandare; primato; supremazia.

**leading**[2] *adj.* che guida, che dirige, che è in testa; dominante, principale, primo; *a — London surgeon*, uno dei primi chirurghi di Londra; (theatr.) — *lady*, prima attrice; (journ.) — *article*, editoriale *m.*, articolo di fondo; (naut.) — *seaman*, marinaio scelto; (sport) primo, in testa; (fig.) — *question*, domanda capziosa, domanda insidiosa; *n.* direzione; condotta; guida.

**leading-strings** *n.* dande *f.pl.*; (fig.) *to be in —*, essere sotto tutela.

**lead-line** *n.* (naut.) sagola per scandaglio. **-pencil** *n.* matita. **-poisoning** *n.* saturnismo, malattia del piombo. **-swinger** *n.* (pop.) scansafatiche *m. indecl.*

**leaf** *n.* foglia; (collect.) fogliame *m.*, fronde *f.pl.*; *in —*, in foglia, coperto di foglie; *to put forth leaves*, mettere le foglie, frondeggiare; *to shed leaves*, perdere le foglie, sfogliarsi; (fig.) *to shake like a —*, tremare come una canna; (of paper, metal) foglio; (of book) foglio, pagina; *to turn over the leaves of a book*, sfogliare un libro; (fig.) *to turn over a new —*, cambiare vita, migliorare; *to take a — out of someone's book*, seguire l'esempio di qualcuno; battente *m.*, imposta; (of table) asse *f.*, ribalta; (mech., of wheel) paletta; (of spring) lamina; *intr.* frondeggiare; (fig.) *to — through a book*, sfogliare un libro. **-age** *n.* fogliame *m.*

**leaf-green** *adj.*, *n.* verde prato; clorofilla.

**leafiness** *n.* ricchezza di foglie, frondosità.

**leaf-insect** *n.* (ent.) fillio.

**leafless** *adj.* senza foglie; spoglio, sfrondato; (bot.) afillante.

**leaflet** *n.* volantino, volante *m.*, manifestino.

**leaf-mould** *n.* terriccio. **-stalk** *n.* picciuolo

**leafy** *adj.* fronzuto, foglioso, coperto di foglie.

**league**[1] *n.* (measure) lega.

**league**[2] *n.* lega, associazione, confederazione; *the — of Nations*,

la Società delle Nazioni; (football) lega; — *table*, classifica; *tr.* unire in lega; *intr.* allearsi, confederarsi, far lega.

**Leah** *pr.n.* Lia, Lea.

**leak** *n.* fessura; fuga, perdita; (naut.) falla; *to spring a —*, aprire una falla; (electr.) dispersione; *intr.* perdere, colare, lasciar uscire liquido; (of boat) far acqua; (fig.) *to — out*, trapelare. **-age** *n.* perdita, scolo, colatura; fuga; (fig.) trapelamento.

**lean**[1] *adj.* magro, scarno, sparuto; — *as a rake*, magro come un chiodo; *to grow —*, dimagrire; (fig.) povero, scarso; — *years*, anni di carestia; *n.* parte magra; carne magra.

**lean**[2] *n.* inclinazione; *on the —*, inclinato; *tr.* inclinare, far pendere; appoggiare; *intr.* inclinarsi, pendere; appoggiarsi; *to — against*, appoggiarsi a; *to — back*, inclinarsi indietro, sdraiarsi; *to — forward*, piegarsi in avanti; *to — out*, sporgersi; *it is dangerous to — out of the window*, è pericoloso sporgersi; (fig.) *to — (up)on*, dipendere da, affidarsi a; *to — towards*, tendere verso, avere un'inclinazione verso.

**Leander** *pr.n.* Leandro.

**leaning** *adj.* inclinato; pendente; *the — tower of Pisa*, la torre pendente di Pisa; *n.* inclinazione, propensione, tendenza.

**leanness** *n.* magrezza; sparutezza.

**leant** *p.def.*, *part.* of **lean**[2], *q.v.*

**lean-to** *adj.* appoggiato a un muro; *n.* barchessa, tettoia.

**leap** *n.* salto; balzo; *a — in the dark*, un salto nel buio; *by -s and bounds*, a balzelloni, a passi da gigante; *tr.* saltare; *to — a horse*, far saltare un cavallo; *intr.* saltare, balzare; dare un balzo; spiccare un salto; *to — to one's feet*, balzare in piedi; *to — out*, saltar fuori, uscire con un balzo; *to — over something*, scavalcare qualcosa con un salto; (provb.) *look before you —*, prima di agire pensaci. **-er** *n.* saltatore.

**leap-frog** *n.* cavalletta, saltamontone *m.*

**leaping** *adj.* saltante, saltellante.

**leap-year** *n.* anno bisestile.

**learn** *tr.*, *intr.* imparare; studiare; *to — how to do something*, imparare a far qualcosa; *to — by heart*, imparare a memoria; venire a sapere, apprendere, sentire.

**learned**[1] *part. adj.* imparato; studiato; sentito.

**learne·d**[2] *adj.* dotto, erudito, istruito; *a — man*, un erudito, un dotto. **-ness** *n.* erudizione.

**learner** *n.* allievo; scolaro; chi impara; apprendista *m.*, *f.*, novizio, principiante *m.*, *f.*

**learning** *n.* cultura; erudizione; sapere *m.*; dottrina; studio; *branch of —*, disciplina.

**lease** *n.* contratto d'affitto; affitto; allogazione; *long —*, enfiteusi *f.*; (fam.) *to take a new — of life*, cominciare una vita nuova; *tr.* affittare; dare in affitto; prendere in affitto. **-hold** *n.* proprietà in affitto; durata di un contratto d'affitto. **-holder** *n.* affittuario, locatario.

**leash** *n.* guinzaglio, legaccio, laccio; *on the —*, al guinzaglio; (fig.) *to hold in —*, tenere a freno.

**leash** *tr.* tenere al guinzaglio; allacciare.

**least** *adj.* minimo; più piccolo; *last but not —*, ultimo ma non il meno importante; *to be not the — bit musical*, non aver alcun senso musicale; (math.) — *common multiple*, minimo comune multiplo; *n.* (il) meno; *not in the —*, per niente, affatto; *at (the) —*, almeno; *to say the —*, per non dirne più, a dir poco; *adv.* (il) meno, minimamente; — *of all*, meno di tutti; soprattutto; tanto meno.

**leather** *n.* cuoio; pelle *f.*; *artificial —*, pelle finta; *Morocco —*, marocchino; *patent —*, cuoio verniciato, copale *f.*; — *bottle*, otre *m.*; — *gloves*, guanti di pelle; *fancy — goods*, articoli di pelletteria; (pop.) palla; *tr.* (fam.) conciare per le feste.

**leather-bound** *adj.* rilegato in cuoio. **-dresser** *n.* conciatore *m.*, conciapelle *m.* **-dressing** *n.* concia di pelli.

**leathern** *adj.* di cuoio, di pelle.

**leathery** *adj.* come il cuoio, coriaceo; (fig.) duro.

**leave** *n.* permesso; autorizzazione; licenza; *by your —*, col vostro permesso; *without saying 'by your —'*, senza chiedere permesso; *to take — to do something*, permettersi di far qualcosa; congedo; commiato; *to take one's —*, prendere congedo, accommiatarsi; *to take French —*, andarsene all'inglese; (fig.) *to take — of one's senses*, impazzire; licenza; congedo; permesso; *to be on —*, essere in licenza; *ticket of —*, libertà provvisoria.

**leave** *tr.* lasciare; abbandonare; *to — a wife and three children*, lasciare moglie e tre figli; *to — one's wife*, abbandonare la moglie; *it -s much to be desired*, lascia molto a desiderare; *to — the table*, alzarsi da tavola; *to — hold of*, lasciar andare; *to — in the lurch*, piantare; *let us — it at that*, basta!, non ne parliamo più; *to — something unsaid*, tacere qualcosa; *to — alone*, lasciar stare, lasciare in pace; *to — behind*, lasciare indietro, dimenticare; *to — off*, smettere, cessare; *to — out*, omettere, trascurare; affidare, consegnare; *I — the matter to you*, affido la cosa a te; — *it to me!*, lascia fare a me!; *to — something to time*, affidare qualcosa al tempo; partire da, uscire da; *to — the room*, uscire dalla stanza; *we — Paris at six*, partiamo da Parigi alle sei; *to — the rails*, uscire dalle rotaie, deragliare; *to — home*, andare via; *to be left*, rimanere, restare; *there is no bread left*, non c'è più pane; *to be left over*, avanzare; *intr.* partire; *the train -s at three*, il treno parte alle tre.

**leaven** *n.* lievito; (fig.) fermento; *tr.* far lievitare; fermentare; (fig.) temperare, modificare.

**leave-taking** *n.* commiato; congedo; distacco; addio.

**leaving** *n.* partenza; — *certificate*, certificato di studi; — *examination*, esame *m.* di licenza; *pl.* avanzi, rimasugli, rifiuti *m.pl.*

**Leban-on** *pr.n.* (geog.) Libano. **-ese** *adj.*, *n.* libanese *m.*, *f.*

**lecher** *n.* libertino. **-ous** *adj.* lascivo, libertino, libidinoso. **-ousness, -y** *n.* lascivia; libertinaggio.

**lectern** *n.* (eccl.) leggìo.

**lectionary** *n.* (eccl.) lezionale *m.*, lezionario.

**lector** *n.* lettore *m.*, lettrice *f.*

**lecture** *n.* conferenza; lezione; *to attend -s*, seguire un corso di lezioni; *to give (deliver) a —*, tenere una conferenza; (fam.) *to give someone a —*, rimproverare qualcuno, fare una ramanzina a qualcuno; *intr.* tenere conferenze, tenere un corso di lezioni; (fam.) predicare; *tr.* ammonire, rimproverare, fare una paternale a.

**lecture-hall, -room** *n.* sala da conferenze; aula universitaria.

**lecturer** *n.* conferenziere *m.*; docente universitario.

**led** *p.def.*, *part.* of **lead**, *q.v.*

**Leda** *pr.n.* (myth.) Leda.

**ledge** *n.* sporgenza; cornice *f.*; (under water) scoglio; (of window) davanzale *m.*

**ledger** *n.* libro mastro; (archit.) traversa.

**lee** *n.* (naut.) sottovento, lato di sottovento; (fig.) luogo riparato; *under the — of*, riparto da.

**leech** *n.* (zool.) sanguisuga, mignatta; chirurgo, flebotomo.

**leek** *n.* (bot.) porro.

**leer** *n.* sguardo bieco; sbirciata; occhiata maliziosa; *intr.* guardare sbiecamente; guardare sott'occhio; guardare con occhio malizioso. **-ing** *adj.* sbieco, di traverso.

**lees** *n.* feccia, sedimento; fondo.

**leeward** *adj.*, *adv.* sottovento, verso sottovento.

**Leeward Islands** *pr.n.* (geog.) Isole di Sottovento.

**leeway** *n.* (naut.; aeron.) deriva; scarroccio; (fig.) lavoro arre-

trato, tempo perduto; *to make up —*, rifarsi del tempo perduto.

**left**[1] *adj.* sinistro; manco; *adv.* a sinistra, sulla sinistra, verso sinistra; *n.* sinistra; *on the —*, a sinistra, sulla sinistra; *to walk on the — of*, cedere la destra a; (pol.) *the Left*, la Sinistra.

**left**[2] *p.def.*, *part.* of **leave**, *q.v.*; *adj. left-luggage office*, deposito bagagli.

**left-hand** *adj.* sinistro; mancino; *on the — side*, a sinistra, sul lato sinistro; *— blow*, colpo mancino; *— page*, verso. **-ed** *adj.* mancino, sinistrorso; con la mano sinistra; (fig.) ambiguo, equivoco; *-ed compliment*, complimento ambiguo; *-ed marriage*, matrimonio morganatico. **-edness** *n.* uso della mano sinistra; (fig.) goffaggine *f.* **-er** *n.* mancino; colpo con la mano sinistra.

**left-off** *adj.* *— clothing*, vestiti usati, abiti smessi. **-overs** *n.* avanzi *m.pl.* **-winger** *n.* (pol.) uomo di sinistra, simpatizzante della sinistra; (football) ala sinistra.

**leftward(s)** *adj.*, *adv.* verso sinistra.

**leg** *n.* gamba; *wooden —*, gamba di legno; *to stretch one's -s*, sgranchirsi le gambe; zampa; (of poultry) coscia; (of mutton, beef) coscio, cosciotto; (of furniture, etc.) gamba, piede *m.*; (of boot, etc.) gambale *m.*; (fam.) tappa; (fig.) *to be on one's last -s*, essere vicino alla morte, essere alla fine delle proprie risorse, (of things) essere vicino alla fine; *not to have a — to stand on*, non aver nessuna ragione convincente; *to run someone off his -s*, far correre qualcuno; *to pull someone's —*, prendere qualcuno in giro; (fam.) *to shake a —*, ballare; *show a —!*, alzatevi!; *tr.* (fam.) *to — it*, fare la strada a piedi; scappare.

**legacy** *n.* legato, lascito; (fig.) eredità, patrimonio.

**legal** *adj.* legale, legittimo, lecito; giuridico; *to take — advice*, consultare un avvocato; *to be — tender*, aver corso legale. **-ity** *n.* legalità.

**legaliz-e** *tr.* legalizzare; legittimare; autenticare; regolarizzare. **-ation** *n.* legalizzazione.

**legate** *n.* legato. **-ship** *n.* carica di legato, legazione.

**legatee** *n.* legatario.

**legation** *n.* legazione.

**legend** *n.* leggenda; mito; iscrizione; didascalia. **-ary** *adj.* leggendario; mitico.

**legerdemain** *n.* prestidigitazione; giuoco di prestigio, giuoco di mano.

**leggings** *n.* (cost.) gambali *m.pl.*, ghette *f.pl.*, uose *f.pl.*

**Leghorn** *pr.n.* (geog.) Livorno; *— hen*, gallina di razza livornese.

**legib-le** *adj.* leggibile. **-ility** *n.* leggibilità.

**legion** *n.* legione; *British Legion*, associazione degli ex combattenti britannici; (fig.) schiera; moltitudine *f.* **-ary** *adj.*, *n.* legionario.

**legislat-e** *intr.* far leggi, legiferare; *tr.* dar leggi a. **-ion** *n.* legislazione. **-ive** *adj.* legislativo. **-or** *n.* legislatore. **-ure** *n.* legislatura; corpo legislativo; parlamento.

**legist** *n.* giureconsulto, legista *m.*

**legitim-acy** *n.* legittimità, legalità. **-ate** *adj.* legittimo, legale, lecito; giusto; *tr.* legittimare, dichiarare legittimo. **-ation** *n.* legittimazione. **-atize** *tr.* See **legitimate.** **-ist** *adj.*, *n.* legittimista *m.*, *f.*

**leg-pull** *n.* presa in giro, canzonatura.

**legum-e, -en** *n.* (bot.) legume *m.* **-inous** *adj.* leguminoso.

**Leipzig** *pr.n.* (geog.) Lipsia.

**leisure** *n.* ozio; agio; riposo; *— hours*, ore libere, ore di riposo; comodo; *at your —*, con vostro comodo. **-d** *adj.* libero; sfaccendato; *the -d classes*, le classi agiate. **-ly** *adj.* fatto con agio, fatto con comodo; *a -ly journey*, un viaggio comodo; *in a -ly way*, senza fretta; lento.

**Lemberg** *pr.n.*(geog.). See **Lwow.**

**lemming** *n.* (zool.) topo artico, lemming *m. indecl.*

**Lemnos** *pr.n.* (geog.) Lemno.

**lemon** *n.* limone *m.*; (colour) giallo limone; (pharm.) *salts of —*, sale *m.* di acetosella, ossalato di potassa. **-ade** *n.* limonata; *fizzy -ade*, limonata gassosa.

**lemon-juice** *n.* spremuta di limone. **-squash** *n.* limonata. **-squeezer** *n.* spremilimoni *m. indecl.*

**lemur** *n.* (Rom. myth.; zool.) lemure *m.*

**lend** *tr.* prestare; dare in prestito; fare dei prestiti. **-er** *n.* prestatore. **-ing** *n.* l'imprestare; prestito; *-ing library*, biblioteca circolante.

**length** *n.* lunghezza; estensione; *ten miles in —*, lungo dieci miglia; *at arm's —*, alla distanza di un braccio, (fig.) a debita distanza; *at full —*, lungo disteso, (fig.) per esteso; durata, periodo, spazio; (of cloth) taglio; (of rope, etc.) pezzo; (prosod.) quantità; (fig.) *— of service*, anzianità; *at —*, finalmente, alla fine, (in detail) per disteso; *to go to the — of*, arrivare fino a; *to go to great -s to*, fare tutto il possibile per. **-en** *tr.* allungare; prolungare; stendere; *intr.* allungarsi; prolungarsi; stendersi. **-ening** *n.* allungamento; prolungamento. **-ily** *adv.* per disteso, in modo prolisso. **-iness** *n.* prolissità; lunghezza eccessiva. **-ways, -wise** *adv.* per il lungo, nel senso della lunghezza, longitudinalmente. **-y** *adj.* lungo; (fig.) prolisso.

**leni-ency** *n.* indulgenza; mitezza; clemenza. **-ent** *adj.* indulgente; mite; clemente.

**Leningrad** *pr.n.* (geog.) Leningrado *f.*

**Leninism** *n.* (pol.) leninismo.

**lenitive** *adj.* lenitivo; calmante; (med.) palliativo, addolcitivo.

**lens** *n.* lente *f.*; (of camera, microscope) obiettivo; (of eye) cristallino.

**lent**[1] *p.def.*, *part.* of **lend,** *q.v.*

**Lent**[2] *n.* (eccl.) quaresima; *of —*, quaresimale; *first Sunday in —*, Quadragesima; *to keep —*, far quadresima. **-en** *adj.* di quaresima, quaresimale; *-en fare*, il mangiare magro.

**lenti-cular, -form** *adj.* lenticolare.

**lentil** *n.* (bot.) lente *f.*, lenticchia.

**Leo** *pr.n.* Leone.

**Leonard** *pr.n.* Leonardo.

**leonine** *adj.* leonino.

**leopard** *n.* leopardo; gattopardo. **-ess** *n.* femmina del leopardo.

**Leopold** *pr.n.* Leopoldo.

**leper** *n.* lebbroso; *— hospital*, lebbrosario.

**lepidopter** *n.* (ent.) lepidottero.

**leporine** *adj.* leporino.

**leprechaun** *n.* (Irish myth.) spiritello, folletto.

**lepr-osy** *n.* lebbra. **-ous** *adj.* lebbroso.

**lesbian** *adj.* lesbico; *n.* lesbica, tribade *f.* **-ism** *n.* lesbismo, tribadismo, amore saffico.

**Lesbos** *pr.n.* (geog.) Lesbo.

**lèse-majesty** *n.* (leg.) delitto di lesa maiestà.

**lesion** *n.* lesione.

**less**[1] *adj.* minore; più piccolo; inferiore; meno; *to grow —*, diminuire, diventar meno, rimpicciolirsi; *adv.* meno, di meno; *— and —*, di meno in meno; *n.* meno; *so much the —*, tanto meno; *in — than no time*, in men che non si dica; *prep.* meno.

**-less**[2] *suff.* senza, privo di.

**lessee** *n.* affittuario; locatario; concessionario.

**lessen** *tr.* diminuire; rimpicciolire; abbassare; *intr.* diminuire; scemare; rimpicciolirsi; abbassarsi. **-ing** *n.* diminuzione; rimpicciolimento; attenuazione.

**lesser** *adj.* minore; inferiore; più piccolo; *the — evil*, il male minore; *in a — degree*, in minor grado.

**lesson** *n.* lezione; ripetizione.

**lessor** *n.* locatore, allogatore.

**lest** *conj.* per paura che, per tema che, affinchè non.

**let**[1] *n.* impedimento, ostacolo; *without — or hindrance*, senza impedimenti; (lawn-tennis) colpo nullo.

**let**[2] *n.* locazione, affitto.

**let**[2] *tr.* lasciare; permettere; fare; — *me do what I like*, lasciami fare quello che voglio; — *me tell you*, lascia che ti dica; — *me know as soon as you are ready*, fammi sapere quando sarai pronto; *to — oneself be swindled*, lasciarsi ingannare; *to — bygones be bygones*, dimenticare il passato; *to — someone have something*, far avere qualcosa a qualcuno; *to — alone*, lasciar stare, non fare attenzione a; (fig.) — *alone the price*, senza parlare del prezzo; *to — blood*, cavar sangue, salassare; *to — fall*, lasciar cadere, abbandonare; *to — fly*, lasciar andare, scagliare, (fam.) sfogarsi; *to — go*, lasciare, mollare; *to — oneself go*, sfogarsi; (naut.) *to — go the anchor*, affondare l'ancora; *to — slip*, lasciar sfuggire. AS AUX., NOT TRANSLATED: — *us go*, andiamo; — *him go*, (che) vada, vada pure; — *them go*, che vadano; — *it be so*, così sia. FOLLOW. BY ADV. OR PREP.: *to — down*, abbassare, far scendere, calare, (hair) sciogliere, (dress) allungare; (fig.) *to — someone down*, abbandonare qualcuno nei guai, deludere qualcuno; *I won't — you down*, puoi contare su di me; *to — someone down gently*, usare tatto nel rifiutare qualcosa a qualcuno; *to — in*, far entrare, lasciar entrare, inserire, incastrare; (fig.) *to — oneself in for something*, esporsi a qualcosa, lasciarsi persuadere a far qualcosa; *to — into*, lasciar penetrare; *to — someone into a secret*, mettere a parte qualcuno di un segreto; *to — off*, far partire, sparare; lasciar andare, perdonare; *to be — off with a fine*, cavarsela con una multa; *to — someone off from doing something*, dispensare qualcuno dal fare qualcosa; (fam.) *to — off steam*, sfogarsi; (fam.) *to — on*, *intr.* cantare; *to — out*, far uscire, accompagnare alla porta, liberare, mettere in libertà, (secret) lasciar sfuggire, (dress) allargare; (fig.) *to — the cat out of the bag*, svelare un segreto; *intr.* sferrare un colpo; *to — through*, lasciar passare; *to — up*, far salire, *intr.* (fam.) smettere. RENT: affittare, dare in affitto, *flat to —*, appartamento da affittare; *to — out*, affittare.

**let-down** *n.* (fam.) delusione, disappunto.

**lethal** *adj.* letale, micidiale.

**letharg-y** *n.* letargia, letargo. **-ic(al)** *adj.* letargico.

**Lethe** *pr.n.* (myth.) Lete *m.*; (fig.) oblio.

**letter** *n.* lettera; *capital —*, maiuscola; *small —*, minuscola; (typ.) carattere *m.*; lettera, missiva, epistola; (comm.) — *of credit*, lettera di credito; (fig.) *the — and the spirit*, la forma e la sostanza; *pl.* letteratura, lettere *f.pl.*; carteggio, lettere; *tr.* imprimere il titolo su; classificare in ordine alfabetico. **-ed** *part. adj.* impresso con lettere; letterato, dotto.

**letter-book** *n.* (comm.) copialettere *m.* **-box** *n.* buca delle lettere, cassetta postale. **-card** *n.* biglietto postale. **-file** *n.* raccoglitore di corrispondenza. **-head** *n.* intestazione, testata di lettera.

**lettering** *n.* lettere impresse; titolo; (art) disegno di caratteri.

**letter-paper** *n.* carta da lettere.

**letterpress** *n.* (typ.) testo di un libro stampato (escluse le illustrazioni).

**letter-weight** *n.* fermacarte *m. indecl.*

**letting** *n.* affitto; — *value*, valore locativo.

**lettuce** *n.* (bot.; cul.) lattuga.

**leukemia** *n.* (med.) leucemia.

**Levant** *pr.n.* (geog.) Levante *m.*; vento di levante. **-ine** *adj.*, *n.* levantino.

**levee**[1] *n.* ricevimento; udienza.

**levee**[2] *n.* (USA) diga; argine *m.*

**level** *adj.* piatto, piano, uniforme; — *ground*, terreno piano; — *with the ground*, a livello di terra; *to make —*, spianare, livellare; (rlwy.) — *crossing*, passaggio a livello; (fig.) equilibrato, regolare; *to keep a — head*, conservare il sangue freddo; *to do one's — best*, fare tutto il possibile; (sport) a parità di punti, alla pari; *n.* superficie piana, spianata; livello, piano; *difference of —*, dislivello; *sea —*, livello del mare; *on a — with*, a livello con; *to be on the same — as*, essere sullo stesso piano di; (fig.) *to rise to someone's —*, innalzarsi al livello di; (fam.) *to be on the —*, essere onesto; (instrument) livella; *tr.* livellare, spianare; rendere uguale, uguagliare; *to — to the ground*, radere al suolo; *to — a gun at*, puntare un fucile contro; (fig.) *to — an accusation against*, lanciare un'accusa contro. **-ler** *n.* livellatore; agguagliatore.

**level-headed** *adj.* equilibrato; assennato; con la testa quadrata. **-ness** *n.* buon senso; equilibrio; assennatezza.

**levelling** *n.* livellamento; spianamento; (of gun) puntamento, mira.

**levelness** *n.* uniformità; parità; condizione di essere a livello.

**lever** *n.* leva; (motor.) *gear —*, leva del cambio di velocità; manubrio; (clockm.) ancora; (fig.) mezzo, stimolo; *tr.* alzare con una leva, muovere con una leva, far leva a. **-age** *n.* potenza di una leva; giuoco di una leva; (fig.) influenza; potere *m.*

**leveret** *n.* leprotto.

**leviable** *adj.* imponibile, tassabile.

**leviathan** *n.* leviatano.

**levigat-e** *tr.* levigare; lisciare; polverizzare. **-ion** *n.* levigazione; polverizzazione.

**levitat-e** *tr.* alzare in aria; *intr.* alzarsi in aria, fluttuare nell'aria. **-ion** *n.* levitazione.

**Levite** *n.* levita *m.*

**Leviticus** *pr.n.* Levitico.

**levity** *n.* leggerezza; frivolezza; spensieratezza.

**levy** *n.* imposta; tributo; contributo; (mil.) leva; *tr.* imporre, esigere; *to — war on*, fare la guerra a; *to — blackmail on*, fare un ricatto a; (mil.) arruolare.

**lewd** *adj.* impudico; lascivo; pornografico. **-ness** *n.* impudicizia, lascivia.

**Lewis**[1] *pr.n.* Luigi; (mil.) — *gun*, mitragliatrice Lewis.

**lewis**[2] *n.* (bldg.) ulivella, campanella.

**lexical** *adj.* lessicale.

**lexicograph-y** *n.* lessicografia. **-er** *n.* lessicografo, dizionarista *m.*, *f.* **-ic(al)** *adj.* lessicografico.

**lexicology** *n.* lessicologia.

**lexicon** *n.* lessico; dizionario.

**Leyden** *pr.n.* (geog.) Leida.

**liab-le** *adj.* soggetto; *to be — to make mistakes*, essere soggetto a fare errori; (leg.) responsabile; — *for damages*, responsabile dei danni; — *to a fine*, passibile di multa. **-ility** *n.* obbligo; impegno; (leg.) responsabilità; (comm.) passività, passivo, debito; *assets and -ilities*, attivo e passivo; *to meet one's -ilities*, soddisfare ai propri impegni; *limited -ility*, responsabilità limitata; (fig.) disposizione, tendenza.

**liaise** *intr.* (mil. slang) fare il collegamento con.

**liaison** *n.* legame *m.*; (phon.) legamento; (fam.) relazione amorosa; (mil.) collegamento; — *officer*, ufficiale *m.* di collegamento.

**liar** *n.* bugiardo, mentitore.

**lib.** *ad —*, a discrezione.

**libation** *n.* libagione.

**libel** *n.* libello; calunnia; (leg.) diffamazione; *action for —*, querela per diffamazione; *tr.* diffamare; calunniare. **-ler** *n.* diffamatore; calunniatore. **-lous** *adj.* diffamatorio; calunnioso.

**liberal** *adj.* liberale; *the — arts*, le arti liberali; — *education*, educazione umanistica; (pol.) — *party*, partito liberale; generoso, prodigo, largo; — *offer*, offerta generosa, — *of promises*, prodigio di promesse; abbondante, ampio, copioso; *n.* (pol.) liberale *m.*, *f.* **-ism** *n.* (pol.) liberalismo. **-ity** *n.* liberalità; munificenza, generosità.

**liberat-e** *tr.* liberare, mettere in

libertà; affrancare; (chem.) liberare. **-ion** *n.* liberazione; affrancamento. **-or** *n.* liberatore.
**libertin-e** *adj.*, *n.* libertino. **-age, -ism** *n.* libertinaggio; dissolutezza.
**liberty** *n.* libertà; *to be at* —, essere libero, essere in libertà; *to set at* —, mettere in libertà, liberare; *to take the* — *of doing something*, prendersi la libertà di far qualcosa; *to take liberties with someone*, permettersi delle libertà con qualcuno.
**libidinous** *adj.* libidinoso; lascivo. **-ness, libido** *n.* libidine *f.*, lascivia.
**librarian** *n.* bibliotecario. **-ship** *n.* carica di bibliotecario.
**library** *n.* biblioteca; *free* —, biblioteca pubblica; *lending* —, biblioteca che dà libri in prestito, biblioteca circolante.
**librat-e** *intr.* librarsi; oscillare; bilanciarsi. **-ion** *n.* librazione; oscillazione. **-ory** *adj.* oscillatorio.
**librett-o** *n.* (theatr.) libretto d'opera. **-ist** *n.* (theatr.) librettista *m.*
**Libya** *pr.n.* (geog.) Libia. **-n** *adj.* libico.
**lice** *pl.* of **louse,** *q.v.*
**licence** *n.* licenza; permesso; autorizzazione; patente *f.*; *arms* —, porto d'armi; (motor.) *driving* —, patente di guida; *car* —, bolla di circolazione; (eccl.) *special* —, dispensa di pubblicazioni matrimoniali; (fig.) *poetic* —, licenza poetica; (pejor.) scostumatezza.
**licens-e** *tr.* autorizzare; rilasciare una patente a. **-ed** *adj.* autorizzato; patentato. **-ee** *n.* gestore autorizzato; detentore di una licenza; concessionario.
**licentiate** *n.* licenziato, diplomato.
**licentious** *adj.* licenzioso, scostumato, dissoluto. **-ness** *n.* dissolutezza; scostumatezza; licenziosità.
**lichen** *n.* (bot.) lichene *m.*, (med.) impetigine *f.*
**licit** *adj.* lecito; permesso.
**lick** *n.* leccata, leccatura; (slang) *at a great* —, a rotta di collo; *tr.* leccare; *to* — *up*, leccare, pulire leccando; lambire; (fig.) *to* — *the dust*, mordere la polvere; (fam.) *to* — *into shape*, dar forma a, foggiare, rendere presentabile; *to* — *someone's boots*, leccare i piedi a qualcuno; (slang) picchiare, battere, superare. **-ing** *n.* leccata, leccatura; (slang) bastonatura, batosta.
**lickspittle** *n.* (fam.) leccapiedi *m.*
**lid** *n.* coperchio; (bot.) copercolo; (pop.) *that puts the* — *on it!*, ci mancava questo!; (slang) cappello.
**lido** *n.* piscina pubblica.
**lie**[1] *n.* menzogna, bugia; *white* —, bugia pietosa; *a pack of* -*s*, un tessuto di menzogne; *to tell a* —, mentire, dire una bugia; *to give the* — *to something*, smentire qualcosa; *to give someone the* —, ricacciare una menzogna in gola a qualcuno, far bugiardo qualcuno; *intr.* mentire, dir bugie.
**lie**[2] *n.* posizione, situazione; disposizione; configurazione; *intr.* giacere; stare disteso; stare sdraiato; *here* -*s*, qui giace; *to* — *ill in bed*, giacere ammalato a letto; *to* — *in wait*, stare in agguato; *let sleeping dogs* —, non svegliare il can che dorme; *to* — *doggo*, fare l'indiano; *to* — *low*, tenersi nascosto, non immischiarsi; (fig.) *to* — *heavy upon*, pesare su; essere, stare, trovarsi, rimanere, restare; *to* — *in prison*, essere in prigione; *to* — *in bed*, stare a letto; *to* — *idle*, rimanere inoperoso; *as far as in me* -*s*, per quel che sta in me, *it* -*s with me*, sta a me, spetta a me; *to find out how the land* -*s*, scoprire come stanno le cose; estendersi, allargarsi; *the plain lay before us*, la pianura si estendeva dinanzi a noi; *to* — *about*, essere sparso qua e là; *to* — *down*, coricarsi, sdraiarsi; (to dog) — *down!*, cuccia!; (fig.) *to take something lying down*, subire qualcosa senza protestare; *to* — *in*, partorire; *to* — *up*, rimanere a letto, tenere il letto.
**lie-abed** *n.* (fam.) pigrone *m.*, dormiglione *m.*
**lie-detector** *n.* macchina della verità.
**lief** *adv.* (poet., lit.) volentieri; *I would as* — *go as stay*, andare o restare mi è indifferente. **-er** *adv.* tanto volentieri quanto; piuttosto.
**liege** *adj.* ligio, fedele; *n.* vassallo.
**Liège** *pr.n.* (geog.) Liegi *f.*
**lien** *n.* pegno; garanzia.
**lieu** *n.* *in* — *of*, in luogo di, invece di.
**lieutenant** *n.* (mil.; naval) tenente *m.*; *second* —, sottotenente *m.*; *Lord Lieutenant*, luogotenente della Regina. **-ancy** *n.* luogotenenza.
**lieutenant-colonel** *n.* (mil.) tenente colonnello. **-commander** *n.* (naut.) capitano di corvetta. **-general** *n.* (mil.) generale di corpo d'armata. **-governor** *m.* vice-governatore.
**life** *n.* vita; esistenza; modo di vivere; *spiritual* —, vita interiore; *manner of* —, modo di vivere; *a matter of* — *and death*, una questione di vita o di morte; *many lives were lost*, ci furono molti morti; *early* —, infanzia; *married* —, vita matrimoniale; *at my time of* —, alla mia età; *high* —, vita elegante; *low* —, i bassifondi; *an easy* —, una vita da canonico; *a dog's* —, una vita da cane; *expectation of* —, media normale della vita; — *annuity*, vitalizio; *a* — *sentence*, una condanna a vita; *such is* —*!*, la vita è così!; *to bring to* —, rianimare, far rinvenire; *to depart this* —, passare a miglior vita; *to escape with one's* —, salvarsi la pelle; *to give* — *to*, animare; *to have the time of one's* —, divertirsi come non mai; *to have as many lives as a cat*, aver la pelle dura; *to lay down one's* —, dar la vita, morire; *to lead a gay* —, fare la dolce vita; *to run for one's* —, cercare la salvezza nella fuga; *to sell one's* — *dearly*, vendere cara la vita; *to take someone's* —, uccidere qualcuno; *to take one's own* —, suicidarsi; (provb.) *while there's* — *there's hope*, finchè c'è vita c'è speranza; vivacità; *to be full of* —, essere molto vivace; *the* — *and soul of the party*, l'anima della compagnia; *to put new* — *into*, rinvigorire; realtà; (fam.) *never in my* —, mai in vita mia; *not on your* —, nemmeno per sogno!; *for the* — *of me*, per quanti sforzi faccia; (art) vivo, naturale *m.*, vero; *larger than* —, più grande del naturale; *to draw from* —, disegnare dal vivo; *still* —, natura morta.
**life-belt** *n.* cintura di salvataggio, salvagente *m.* **-boat** *n.* scialuppa di salvataggio. **-buoy** *n.* salvagente *m.*, boa di salvataggio.
**life-guard** *n.* (mil.) guardia del corpo. **-insurance** *n.* assicurazione sulla vita. **-interest** *n.* rendita vitalizia; usufrutto. **-jacket** *n.* cintura di salvataggio.
**lifeless** *adj.* esanime; senza vita; (fig.) fiacco. **-ness** *n.* mancanza di vita; inerzia; mancanza di movimento; fiacchezza.
**lifelike** *adj.* naturale; vivido; realistico; vivente, parlante.
**life-line** *n.* (naut.) sagola di salvataggio; (fig.) linea di comunicazione vitale.
**lifelong** *adj.* di tutta la vita, che dura tutta la vita.
**life-member** *n.* socio vitalizio. **-preserver** *n.* sfollagente *m.*, manganello; (naut.) salvagente *m.* **-size(d)** *adj.* di grandezza naturale, al naturale.
**lifetime** *n.* vita, durata della vita.
**lift** *n.* sollevamento; innalzamento; spinta; ascensore, elevatore; montacarichi *m. indecl.*; *service* —, montavivande *m. indecl.*; *chair* —, seggiovia; *ski* —, sciovia; *to give someone a* —, dare un passaggio a qualcuno; *to thumb a* —, fare l'autostop; *tr.* sollevare, alzare, innalzare; plagiare; (slang) rubare, arraffare; *intr.* (of weather) schiarirsi, diradarsi; (of clouds, fog) dissiparsi.

**lift-attendant, -boy, liftman** *n.* addetto all'ascensore.

**lift-up** *attrib. adj.* ribaltabile.

**liga-ment** *n.* (anat.) legamento. **-ture** *n.* nesso; legatura.

**light**[1] *adj.* chiaro, pieno di luce, luminoso; *to become —,* rischiararsi, far giorno; (hair) biondo; leggero, lieve, non pesante; *— music,* musica leggera; *— opera,* operetta; *— reading,* letture amene; non importante, insignificante; *to make — of,* non dare importanza a; (fig.) leggero, frivolo, incostante.

**light**[2] *n.* luce *f.*, lume *m.*; *by the — of the sun,* alla luce del sole; *by the — of the moon,* al chiaro di luna; *at first —,* all'alba; *against the —,* controluce; *to turn on the —,* accendere la luce; *to put out the —,* spegnere la luce; illuminazione; chiarore *m.*; (fig.) *to come to —,* venire alla luce; *under a new —,* sotto un altro aspetto; fiammifero, fuoco; (motor.; naut.) fanale *m.*; (paint.) chiaro; *— and shade,* chiaroscuro; (archit.) apertura; *window with three -s,* trifora; *traffic -s,* semaforo; *flashing —,* luce intermittente; (fig.) *to see the red —,* rendersi conto del pericolo.

**light**[2] *tr.* accendere, dar fuoco a; illuminare, rischiarare, far lume a; (fig.) animare, accendere; *intr.* accendersi, illuminarsi; *to — up,* illuminarsi, (fig.) accendere una sigaretta; (pop.) *lit up,* brillo.

**light**[3] *intr.* scendere; posarsi; (fig.) *to — (up)on,* imbattersi in, trovare per caso.

**lighten** *tr.* alleggerire, sgravare; (fig.) alleviare, mitigare; illuminare, rischiarare; *to — the darkness,* illuminare le tenebre; *to — a colour,* rischiarare un colore, chiarire un colore; *intr.* illuminarsi, diventare più chiaro; (of weather) rischiararsi, schiarirsi; (of lightning) lampeggiare.

**lighter**[1] *adj. comp.* of **light**[1], *q.v.*

**lighter**[2] accenditore; (for cigars, cigarettes) accendisigaro, accendino.

**lighter**[3] *n.* (naut.) chiatta, maona, bettolina. **-age** *n.* (naut.) spese per trasporto su chiatta. **-man** *n.* chiattaiuolo.

**light-headed** *adj.* sventato, frivolo, scervellato; delirante; *to be —,* delirare. **-ness** *n.* sventatezza; stato di delirio.

**light-hearted** *adj.* gaio, allegro; ottimista. **-ness** *n.* gaiezza, allegria; ottimismo.

**lighthouse** *n.* faro.

**lighting** *n.* accensione; illuminazione; *-up time,* l'ora fissata per l'accensione delle luci.

**lightly** *adv.* leggermente, alla leggera; poco; (fam.) *to get off —,* cavarsela a buon mercato.

**lightness** *n.* chiarezza; luminosità; leggerezza.

**lightning** *n.* fulmine *m.*; *a flash of —,* un lampo; *struck by —,* fulminato; *as quick as —, with — speed,* veloce come un lampo, fulmineo; (fig.) *— strike,* sciopero lampo.

**lightning-conductor** *n.* parafulmine *m.*

**light-o'-love** *n.* amante *f.*, donna leggera.

**lights** *n.* (animal food) corata; polmoni *m.pl.*

**lightship** *n.* battello faro.

**lightsome** *adj.* (poet.) leggero, grazioso; allegro, giocondo.

**light-weight** *n.* (boxing) peso leggero.

**ligneous** *adj.* ligneo, legnoso.

**lignify** *tr.* trasformare in legno; *intr.* lignificarsi, trasformarsi in legno.

**lignite** *n.* lignite *f.*

**Ligurian** *adj.*, *n.* (geog.) ligure *m.*, *f.*

**like**[1] *adj.* simile; somigliante; analogo; pari, uguale, tale; *to be —,* (ras)somigliare; *to be — each other,* (ras)somigliarsi; *to be as — as two peas,* somigliarsi come due gocce d'acqua; *what is he — ?,* che tipo è?; *there is nothing like ...,* non c'è niente di meglio di ...; *something — ...,* qualcosa come ...; *that's more — it,* questo va meglio; *that's just — him!,* è fatto così!; *just — a woman!,* tipicamente femminile!, le donne son così!; *to feel —,* sentirsi di; *I feel — a cup of tea,* prenderei volentieri una tazza di tè; *it looks — rain,* sembra che voglia piovere; *to look —,* rassomigliare; (provb.) *— father — son,* tale padre tale figlio; *adv. — enough,* probabilmente; *conj.* come; *do — me,* fa come me, fa come faccio io; *prep.* come; da; *— that,* così; *to run — a madman,* correre come un pazzo; *to fit — a glove,* calzare come un guanto; *to swear — a trooper,* bestemmiare come un turco.

**like**[1] *n.* simile *m.*, pari *m.*, uguale *m.*, cosa simile; *did you ever hear the — ?,* hai mai sentito una cosa simile?; *you and the -s of you,* tu e i tuoi pari; *and the —,* e simili, e così via; *to give — for —,* rendere pan per focaccia; (provb.) *— draws to —* chi si somiglia si piglia.

**like**[2] *tr.* aver simpatia per, gradire, preferire; *I — strawberries,* mi piacciono le fragole; *I — him,* mi è molto simpatico; *do you — wine ?,* ti piace il vino?; *would you — a glass of wine ?,* gradiresti un bicchiere di vino?; *how do you — your tea ?,* come preferisci il tè?; *I — it strong,* mi piace forte; *to — better,* preferire; volere, desiderare; *as you —,* come vuoi; *if you —,* se vuoi, se lo desideri; *take as many as you —,* prendine quanti ne vuoi; *I should — them to know,* vorrei che (essi) sapessero; *I would — some bread,* voglio del pane; *I would — to speak to Mr.X,* vorrei parlare col Signor X; *whether you — it or not,* volente o nolente; *n.* (fam.) *-s and dislikes,* simpatie e antipatie; gusti *m.pl.*

**likeable** *adj.* simpatico; amabile; piacevole. **-ness** *n.* amabilità; piacevolezza.

**likel-y** *adj.* probabile; verosimile; adatto; promettente; *adv.* probabilmente, verosimilmente. **-ihood, -iness** *n.* probabilità; verosimiglianza; *in all -ihood,* con tutta probabilità.

**like-minded** *adj.* della stessa opinione.

**liken** *tr.* paragonare.

**likeness** *n.* somiglianza, rassomiglianza; *this portrait is a good —,* questo ritratto è molto somigliante; immagine *f.*; sembianza, aspetto; ritratto; fotografia; *to have one's — taken,* farsi fare un ritratto, farsi fotografare.

**likewise** *adv.* parimenti, similmente, altresì, anche; *to do —,* fare altrettanto.

**liking** *n.* gusto; predilezione; preferenza; simpatia; *to take a — for,* prendere gusto a, trovare simpatico; *to be to someone's —,* essere gradito a qualcuno, andare a genio a qualcuno, piacere a qualcuno.

**lilac** *adj.* lilla, di color lilla; *n.* (bot.) lilla *m.*, serenella, siringa.

**Lilian** *pr.n.* Liliana.

**Lille** *pr.n.* (geog.) Lilla.

**Lilliputian** *adj.*, *n.* lillipuziano.

**lilt** *n.* ritmo, cadenza; *tr.*, *intr.* cantare, gorgheggiare. **-ing** *adj.* cadenzato.

**lily** *n.* (bot.) giglio; *— of the valley,* mughetto, giglio delle valli; *madonna —,* lirio, giglio di Sant'Antonio; (fig.) *white as a —,* bianco come un giglio.

**limb** *n.* arto, membro; *the lower -s,* gli arti inferiori; *to tear — from —,* smembrare; ramo; (of building) ala; (fam.) *— of the law,* rappresentante *m.* della legge.

**limber**[1] *adj.* flessibile, pieghevole; agile; *tr.* rendere flessibile; *intr.* (sport) *to — up,* scaldarsi i muscoli.

**limber**[2] *n.* (artill.) avantreno; *tr.* (artill.) attaccare all'avantreno.

**Limbo** *pr.n.* (theol.) Limbo; (fam.) dimenticatoio.

**Limburg** *pr.n.* (geog.) Limburgo.

**lime**[1] *n.* (chem.) calce *f.*, calcina; *quick —,* calce viva; *slaked —,* calce spenta; *bird —,* pania,

vischio; *tr.* (bldg.) cementare; (agric.) calcinare; invischiare, impaniare, tendere panie a.
**lime**² *n.* (citrus) cedro.
**lime**³ *n.* (bot.) tiglio.
**lime-juice** *n.* succo di cedro, cedrata.
**lime-kiln** *n.* fornace *f.* da calce.
**limelight** *n.* (theatr.) luce *f.* della ribalta; (fig.) *in the —*, assai in vista, alla ribalta.
**limestone** *adj.* calcareo; *n.* calcare *m.*
**limit** *n.* limite *m.*; confine *m.*; ambito; *within -s*, fino a un certo punto; *within the -s of possibility*, nell'ambito del possibile; (motor.) *speed —*, velocità permessa, limite di velocità; (fam.) *that's the —* è il colmo, ci mancava questo; *he's the —!*, è una persona impossibile!; *tr.* limitare; confinare; restringere; (fig.) frenare. **-able** *adj.* limitabile. **-ary** *adj.* limitativo; restrittivo; (geog.) situato alla frontiera. **-ation** *n.* limitazione; restrizione; limite *m.* **-ative** *adj.* limitativo. **-ed** *adj.* limitato; ristretto; (fig.) angusto; *-ed monarchy*, monarchia costituzionale; (comm.) *-ed company*, società a responsabilità limitata, società anonima. **-less** *adj.* illimitato, senza limiti.
**limn** *tr.* ritrarre, disegnare; dipingere; illuminare; miniare.
**limousine** *n.* (motor.) berlina.
**limp**¹ *adj.* flaccido; floscio; molle; debole; *to feel as — as a rag*, sentirsi debole come uno straccio; (bookb.) flessibile, pieghevole.
**limp**² *n.* zoppicamento; *to walk with a —*, zoppicare; *intr.* zoppicare, camminare zoppicando; *to — off*, allontanarsi zoppicando; (fig.) avanzare con fatica, camminare a stento.
**limpet** *n.* (zool.) patella; (fig.) *to stick to someone like a —*, appiccicarsi a qualcuno come una mignatta.
**limpid** *adj.* limpido; chiaro; terso; trasparente. **-ity, -ness** *n.* limpidezza.
**limpness** *n.* flaccidità; mollezza; debolezza; flessibilità.
**linch-pin** *n.* acciarino; (fig.) chiave *f.* di volta.
**linden(-tree)** *n.* tiglio.
**line**¹ *n.* linea; tratto; *a straight —*, una linea retta; *all along the —*, su tutta la linea; *to form a —*, allinearsi, *to set in —*, allineare; allineamento; contorno; ruga; riga; *to drop someone a —*, scrivere due righe a qualcuno; *to read between the -s*, leggere tra le righe; (poet.) verso; *-s of communication*, linee di comunicazione; *railway —*, linea ferroviaria, binari *m.pl.*; *branch —*, linea secondaria, diramazione; *main —*, linea principale; *up —*, binario ascendente; *down —*, binario discendente; *shipping —*, società di navigazione; *air —*, aviolinea, società di navigazione aerea; *Italian Air Line*, Alitalia; (teleph.) linea; *hold the —*, rimanga all'apparecchio; *— engaged*, linea occupata; (geog.) *the Line*, l'equatore; *demarcation —*, linea di demarcazione, confine *m.*; filo, cordicella, corda; *to hang out the washing on the —*, stendere la biancheria sulla corda; fila, coda, ala; linea, stirpe *f.*, dinastia, discendenza; *marriage -s*, certificato di matrimonio; (fig.) *the — of least resistance*, il sistema più facile; *on modern -s*, con criteri moderni; *a — of conduct*, una linea di condotta; *to come into —*, conformarsi, mettersi d'accordo; *to draw the —*, stabilire il limite; *one must draw the — somewhere*, ci deve essere un limite; *to know what — to take*, sapere come regolarsi; *to overstep the —*, oltrepassare il limite; *to toe the —*, sottomettersi, ubbidire; mestiere *m.*, ramo, attività; *what's his —?*, che mestiere fa?; *that's not in my —*, non è cosa di cui mi occupo, non sono competente in materia; *to take up a — of one's own*, seguire la propria direttiva; *to take a strong —*, mostrarsi duro; *something in that —*, qualcosa del genere; *a new — in shirts*, un nuovo tipo di camicie; (fam.) *hard -s!*, che sfortuna!, che scalogna!; *to get a — on something* farsi un'idea di qualcosa.
**line**¹ *tr.* rigare; delineare; *-d with grief*, segnato dal dolore; allineare, fiancheggiare, affiancare; *street -d with trees*, strada fiancheggiata da alberi; *to — the path of a procession*, far ala ad un corteo; *to — in*, abbozzare; *to — up*, *tr.* allineare, mettere in fila; *intr.* allinearsi, mettersi in fila, far la coda.
**line**² *tr.* foderare; *-d with fur*, foderato di pelle; (industr.) rinforzare, foderare; (fam.) *to — one's stomach*, riempirsi la pancia; *to — one's purse*, far soldi.
**lineage** *n.* lignaggio; casato; stirpe *f.*
**lineal** *adj.* lineare; in linea diretta; diretto; *a — descendant*, un discendente diretto.
**lineament** *n.* lineamento; fattezza; tratto; caratteristico.
**linear** *adj.* lineare.
**lineate** *adj.* lineato, rigato, a striscie.
**line-block** *n.* (typ.) cliché *m.*; zincografia. **-drawing** *n.* disegno al tratto. **-engraver** *n.* incisore. **-engraving** *n.* incisione. **-fishing** *n.* pesca alla lenza.
**linen** *adj.* di lino; *n.* lino, tela di lino, pannolino; biancheria; *to wash one's dirty — in public*, lavarsi i panni sudici in pubblico.
**linen-draper** *n.* negoziante *m.* di teleria. **-drapery** *n.* teleria.
**liner**¹ *n.* (naut.) nave *f.* di linea, transatlantico; (aeron.) aeroplano di linea.
**liner**² *n.* foderatore; (mech.) canna, camicia smontabile.
**line-space** *n.* (typ.) interlinea.
**linesman** *n.* (telegr.) guardafili *m. indecl.*; (sport) guardalinea *m. indecl.*
**line-up** *n.* allineamento, schieramento.
**ling**¹ *n.* (bot.) grecchia, erica.
**ling**² *n.* (ichth.) molva allungata.
**linger** *intr.* indugiare; attardarsi; restare indietro; languire, struggersi; *to — about*, bighellonare; *to — over something*, tirare in lungo qualcosa. **-ing** *adj.* indugiante, che si indugia; lento, protratto.
**lingo** *n.* (fam.) linguaggio, gergo; lingua straniera.
**lingual** *adj.* (anat.; ling.) linguale.
**linguiform** *adj.* linguiforme.
**linguist** *n.* linguista *m.*, *f.*; poliglotta *m.*, *f.* **-ic** *adj.* linguistico. **-ics** *n.* linguistica.
**liniment** *n.* linimento; balsamo.
**lining**¹ *n.* allineamento; rigatura.
**lining**² *n.* fodera; (provb.) *every cloud has a silver —*, non tutto il male viene a nuocere; (industr.) rivestimento interno, incamiciatura.
**link**¹ *n.* anello; maglia; *the missing —*, l'ipotetico anello di congiunzione; vincolo; legame *m.*; collegamento; congiunzione; *pl.* (for cuffs) gemelli *m.pl.*; *tr.* legare, collegare; congiungere; unire; *to — arms*, prendersi a braccetto; *intr.* *to — up with*, unirsi a.
**link**² *n.* (Scot.) duna; *pl.* (golf) campo da golf.
**link-boy, -man** *n.* (hist.) portafiaccola *m. indecl.*
**linnet** *n.* (orn.) fanello.
**linoleum** *n.* linoleum *m.*; tela cerata.
**linotype** *n.* linotipo, linotipia. **-operator** *n.* linotipista *m.*
**linseed** *n.* semi *m.pl.* di lino, linosa.
**lint** *n.* filaccia.
**lintel** *n.* (archit.) architrave *m.*; soprassoglio; mensola.
**lion** *n.* (zool.; astron.) leone *m.*; (fig.) persona coraggiosa, leone; *the -'s share*, la parte del leone; *to put one's head into the -'s mouth*, incorrere in gravi pericoli; *the British Lion*, il leone britannico; *to twist the -'s tail*, torcere la coda al leone (britannico); (fam.) celebrità.
**lion-cub, -whelp** *n.* leoncello.
**Lionel** *pr.n.* Lionello.
**lioness** *n.* leonessa.
**lion-heart** *n.* cuor di leone, uomo coraggioso. **-ed** *adj.* coraggioso, dal cuor di leone.

**lionize** *tr.* (fam.) trattare da celebrità; adulare.

**lip** *n.* labbro; *to bite one's -s,* mordersi le labbra; *to curl one's -s,* atteggiare le labbra a disprezzo; *to hang on the -s of,* pendere dalle labbra di; *to keep a stiff upper —,* non battere ciglio, restare imperterrito; *to purse one's -s,* serrare le labbra; *to smack one's -s,* schioccare le labbra; *to open one's -s,* aprire la bocca; *to be on everyone's -s,* essere sulla bocca di tutti; (fam.) *none of your —!;* basta con le tue impertinenze!; (fig.) orlo, margine *m.*; (of wound) labbro; (bot.) labello.

**lip-read** *intr.* capire dal moto delle labbra. **-ing** *n.* il capire dal moto delle labbra, metodo orale per sordomuti.

**lip-salve** *n.* burro di cacao per le labbra. **-service** *n.* rispetto non sentito, mancanza di sincerità.

**lipstick** *n.* rossetto per le labbra.

**liquef-y** *tr.* liquefare; sciogliere; *intr.* liquefarsi; sciogliersi. **-action** *n.* liquefazione.

**liquescent** *adj.* liquescente.

**liqueur** *n.* liquore *m.*

**liquid** *adj.* liquido; fluido; scorrevole; (comm.) — *assets,* attività liquida, disponibilità finanziaria; (fig.) chiaro, limpido, trasparente; fluttuante; instabile; *n.* liquido; (ling.) liquida. **-ate** *tr.* liquidare, saldare, pagare; (fig.) eliminare, uccidere. **-ation** *n.* (comm.) liquidazione; *to go into -ation,* andare in liquidazione; (fig.) eliminazione. **-ator** *n.* liquidatore. **-ity, -ness** *n.* liquidità.

**liquor** *n.* bevanda alcoolica; *in —,* ubriaco; (chem.) sostanza liquida, soluzione.

**liquorice** *n.* liquirizia, adipso.

**Lisbon** *pr.n.* (geog.) Lisbona.

**lisp** *n.* pronuncia blesa; *to speak with a —,* parlare bleso; *he has a —,* gli manca l'erre; (fig.) fruscio, mormorio; *intr.* parlare bleso; balbettare.

**lissom(e)** *adj.* svelto; pieghevole, flessibile. **-ness** *n.* sveltezza; pieghevolezza.

**list**[1] *n.* lista; elenco, catalogo; *black —,* lista nera; *waiting —,* elenco di riserva; *wine —,* carta dei vini; *to make a — of,* elencare; (mil.) *active —,* ruolo attivo; *tr.* elencare; catalogare; registrare; (mil.) arruolare.

**list**[2] (naut.) sbandamento; *intr.* sbandare.

**list**[3] *n.* (text.) lista, striscia, cimosa, vivagno; (archit.) lista, listello; *pl.* recinto; (fig.) *to enter the -s,* entrare in lizza; *tr.* (text.) listare, tagliare a listelli.

**list**[4] *tr., intr.* (poet.) aver voglia, desiderare.

**list**[5] *tr., intr.* (poet.). See **listen.**

**listel** *n.* (archit.) listello.

**listen** *tr., intr.* ascoltare; prestare ascolto (a); badare (a); *to — for,* stare ad ascoltare; *to — in,* captare una comunicazione, (radio) ascoltare la radio; (fig.) *to — to advice,* seguire un consiglio; *to — to reason,* intendere ragione. **-er** *n.* ascoltatore; uditore; *to be a good —,* saper ascoltare; (radio) radioascoltatore. **-ing** *n.* ascolto; (mil.) *-ing post,* posta di ascolto, (aeron.) aerofono.

**listless** *adj.* languido; indifferente; svogliato. **-ness** *n.* noncuranza; indifferenza; svogliatezza.

**lit** *p.def., part.* of **light**[1], *q.v.*

**litany** *n.* litania.

**literacy** *n.* il saper leggere e scrivere, grado di istruzione.

**literal** *adj.* letterale; alla lettera; testuale; reale; (fig.) prosaico; privo di immaginazione; *n.* (typ.) rifuso.

**literary** *adj.* letterario; — *man,* letterato, uomo di lettere.

**literate** *adj.* capace di leggere e scrivere; letterato.

**literature** *n.* letteratura; *light —,* letteratura amena; (comm.) opuscoli *m.pl.* pubblicitari.

**lithe** *adj.* snello; svelto; agile; flessibile. **-ness** *n.* pieghevolezza; flessibilità; agilità.

**lithium** *n.* (chem.) litio.

**lithograph** *n.* litografia; *tr.* litografare. **-er** *n.* litografa *m.* **-ic(al)** *adj.* litografico. **-y** *n.* litografia.

**litig-ant** *adj., n.* (leg.) contendente *m., f.* **-ate** *tr., intr.* (leg.) essere in causa; litigare, disputare. **-ation** *n.* (leg.) lite *f.*, causa.

**litigious** *adj.* litigioso; contenzioso. **-ness** *n.* litigiosità; contenziosità.

**litmus** *n.* (chem.) tornasole *m.*; laccamuffa; — *paper,* cartina di tornasole.

**litre** *n.* litro.

**litter** *n.* lettiga, barella; (in stables) lettiera, strame *m.*; (young animals) figliata, allevata; (rubbish) rifiuti *m.pl.*, immondizie *f.pl.*; (fig.) disordine *m.*; *tr., intr.* preparare la lettiera, stendere strame; (of animals) figliare, proliferare; (fig.) sparpagliare, lasciare in disordine, ingombrare.

**little** *adj.* piccolo, piccino; (frequently rendered in Italian by diminutive suffix); *my — sister,* mia sorellina; *a — room,* una stanzetta; poco, un po' di; — *milk,* poco latte; *a — milk,* un po' di latte; *a — way,* un breve tratto di strada; *a — while,* un po' di tempo, un momentino; *a — less noise,* un po' meno rumore; (pejor.) insignificante, meschino, gretto; *a — mind,* una menta meschina; (anat.) — *finger,* (dito) mignolo; (astron.) *the Little Bear,* l'Orsa Minore; *the — people,* le fate; *adv.* poco, alquanto, piuttosto; — *by —,* a poco a poco; — *known,* poco conosciuto; *as — as possible,* il meno possibile; *a — too large,* un po' troppo grande; *a — afraid,* piuttosto spaventato; — *did he think that,* era ben lontano del pensare che.

**little** *n.* poco, pochino, poca cosa, piccola quantità; *he knows a — of everything,* sa un po' di tutto; — *or nothing,* poco o nulla; *the — I know,* il poco che ne so (io); *what — I could,* quel poco che potei; *wait a —,* aspetta un po'; *after a —,* dopo un po' (di tempo); *just a —,* un pochino; *however —,* per poco che; *very —,* pochissimo; (fig.) *to come to —,* riuscire piuttosto male; *to think — of,* non tenere in gran conto, non dar peso a; (provb.) *every — helps,* tutto fa brodo. **-ness** *n.* piccolezza; pochezza; (pejor.) mediocrità, meschinità.

**littoral** *adj.* li(t)orale, littoraneo; *n.* li(t)torale *m.*

**liturg-y** *n.* liturgia. **-ic(al)** *adj.* liturgico.

**live**[1] *adj.* vivo, vivente; (fam.) in carne ed ossa; ardente; carico, inesploso; (electr.) *a — wire,* un filo sotto tensione, (fam.) un tipo dinamico; (fig.) *a — question,* una questione di attualità.

**live**[2] *tr., intr.* vivere, esistere; — *and let —,* vivere e lasciar vivere; *as long as he -s,* finch'è vivo; *to — to be a hundred,* campare cent'anni; *long — the Queen!,* viva la Regina!; abitare, stare, dimorare; *where does he —?,* dove sta di casa?; *he -s in Milan,* abita a Milano; *to — in, to — by,* vivere di; *to — on one's income,* vivere delle proprie entrate; *to — on,* continuare a vivere, (fig.) perdurare; *to — by one's wits,* vivere d'espedienti; *to — from hand to mouth,* vivere alla giornata; (fig.) *to — down,* far dimenticare; (schol.) *to — in,* essere interno; *to — out,* essere esterno; *to — through,* sopravvivere a; *to — up to one's reputation,* giustificare la propria reputazione; *is life worth living?,* vale la pena di vivere?

**liveable** *adj.* abitabile; sopportabile.

**livelihood** *n.* vita; mezzi di sussistenza; *to earn a —,* guadagnarsi la vita; *to deprive someone of his —,* togliere il pane di bocca a qualcuno.

**liveliness** *n.* vivacità; gaiezza; animazione; brio; anima.

**livelong** *adj.* che dura per tutta la vita; (fam.) *all the — day,* tutta la santa giornata.

**lively** *adj.* vivo, vivace; animato;

movimentato; dinamico; vispo, pieno di vita; vivo, intenso; *to grow —*, animarsi; *to take a — interest in something*, interessarsi vivamente a qualcosa; *to make things — for someone*, dare del filo da torcere a qualcuno; *as — as a cricket*, allegro come un grillo.

**liven** *tr. to — (up)*, ravvivare, animare, rallegrare; *intr.* ravvivarsi, animarsi.

**liver**[1] *n.* (anat.) fegato; *— attack*, colica epatica; *— complaint*, mal di fegato; (colour) rosso bruno.

**liver**[2] *n.* vivente *m., f.*; persona che conduce un certo genere di vita; *luxurious —*, epulone *m.*; *loose —*, libertino.

**liveried** *adj.* che porta una livrea.

**liverish** *adj.* (fam.) sofferente di fegato, bilioso; (fig.) irritabile, stizzoso.

**liverwort** *n.* (bot.) fegatella, epatica.

**livery** *adj.* del color del fegato; (fam.) bilioso, irritabile, stizzoso.

**livery** *n.* livrea; *— company*, corporazione londinese, arte *f.*

**livery-stable** *n.* stallaggio, stallatico.

**livestock** *n.* bestiame *m.*

**livid** *adj.* livido, bluastro; (fam.) furioso, arrabbiato. **-ity, -ness** *n.* lividezza.

**living** *adj.* vivo, vivente, esistente, in vita; *pl. the —*, i viventi; *not a — soul is to be seen*, non si vede anima viva; *no — man could do better*, nessuno al mondo potrebbe far meglio; *within — memory*, a memoria d'uomo; *n.* vita; vivere *m.*; esistenza; mezzi di sussistenza; *the art of —*, l'arte del vivere; *standard of —*, livello della vita; *to earn one's —*, guadagnarsi la vita; *a — wage*, un salario che basta per vivere; *— expenses*, spese *f.pl.* di soggiorno e vitto; (eccl.) beneficio, prebenda.

**living-room** *n.* stanza di soggiorno; (fig.) spazio vitale.

**Livy** *pr.n.* Tito Livio.

**lizard** *n.* (zool.) lucertola.

**llama** *n.* (zool.) lama *m.*

**lo** *excl.* (poet.) guarda!, ecco!

**load** *n.* carico; peso; soma; *maximum —*, portata massima; (mech.) carico, pressione; (electr.) carica, tensione; (fig.) *to take a — off someone's mind*, togliere un gran peso dal cuore di qualcuno; *to get a — off one's chest*, sfogarsi; *pl.* (fam.) *-s of*, un sacco di; *tr.* caricare; colmare; fare il carico di; *rfl. to — oneself up with*, caricarsi di; (fig.) caricare, colmare, gravare; *to — the dice*, falsare i dadi; *intr. to — up*, fare il carico. **-ed** *adj.* caricato, carico; *a -ed revolver*, una rivoltella carica; *to be -ed*, essere carico, (fam.) ubbriaco; ricco; *-ed stick*, bastone piombato; *-ed question*, domanda insidiosa. **-er** *n.* caricatore. **-ing** *n.* carico, caricamento.

**loadstone** *n.* calamita; (miner.) magnetite *f.*

**loaf**[1] *n.* pane; pan carrè; *round —*, pagnetta; *French —*, bastoncino di pane; *to slice a —*, affettare un pane; (fam.) cocuzza; *use your —!*, svegliati!; (provb.) *half a — is better than no —*, meglio poco che nulla.

**loaf**[2] *intr.* oziare, andare a zonzo, far niente; *tr. to — the time away*, passare il tempo nell'ozio. **-er** *n.* (fam.) fannullone, bighellone *m.*

**loaf-sugar** *n.* zucchero in pani.

**loam** *n.* terra grassa, argilla, terriccio, marna; *tr.* ricoprire di terriccio. **-y** *adj.* grasso, argilloso.

**loan** *n.* prestito; mutuo; *on —*, a prestito; *to ask for the — of*, chiedere in prestito; *to raise a —*, emettere un prestito, (fam.) farsi prestare soldi; *tr.* prestare, imprestare, dare in prestito, dare a mutuo.

**loan-word** *n.* (ling.) parola introdotta da altra lingua.

**loath, loth** *adj.* avverso; poco disposto; restìo; riluttante; *to be — to do something*, esser poco disposto a far qualcosa; *nothing —*, ben volentieri.

**loath-e** *tr.* aborrire; detestare; odiare; avere a schifo; *to — wine*, sentire ripugnanza per il vino; *to — doing something*, aver ripugnanza di far qualcosa. **-ing** *n.* disgusto; aborrimento; ripugnanza; schifo. **-some** *adj.* ripugnante; detestabile; odioso; schifoso. **-someness** *n.* schifosità.

**lob** *n.* (sport) pallonetto, palla lanciata in alto; *intr.* passeggiare pesantemente; *tr., intr.* (sport) fare pallonetti, lanciare la palla in alto.

**lobate** *adj.* lobato.

**lobby** *n.* anticamera, corridoio, vestibolo; (pol.) corridoio dove si passa per votare, (in Chamber of deputies in Rome) transatlantico; (theatr.) ridotto; *tr., intr.* (pol.) cercare di influenzare i colleghi frequentando i corridoi, far manovre di anticamera.

**lobe** *n.* lobo. **-d** *adj.* lobato; (archit.) *three-lobed*, trilobo.

**lobelia** *n.* (bot.) lobelia.

**lobster** *n.* aragosta.

**lobster-pot** *n.* nassa.

**lobular** *adj.* lobulare.

**lob-worm** *n.* (zool.) arenicola.

**local** *adj.* locale, del luogo, nostrano; *— train*, treno locale, accelerato; *— colour*, colore *m.* locale; (med.) *— anaesthetic*, anestesia locale; (admin.) *— elections*, elezioni amministrative; *n.* abitante del luogo; (fam.) osteria, taverna. **-ity** *n.* località; luogo; (fam.) *to have the bump of -ity*, sapersi orientare. **-ize** *tr.* localizzare; determinare la posizione di.

**locat-e** *tr.* indicare; individuare; *to be -d*, essere situato, trovarsi. **-ion** *n.* situazione, posizione, sito, locazione; (cinem.) set *m.* all'aperto. **-ive** *adj., n.* (gramm.) locativo.

**loch** *n.* (Scot.) lago; *sea —*, braccio di mare.

**lock**[1] *n.* serratura; toppa; *double —*, serratura a doppia mandata; *under — and key*, sotto chiave; (fig.) *—, stock and barrel*, con armi e bagali; otturatore; (mech.) chiavetta, copiglia, bloccaggio; (eng.) camera di equilibrio; *tr.* chiudere a chiave, serrare; (fig.) serrare, rinchiudere, stringere; (provb.) *to — the stable door after the horse has bolted*, chiudere la stalla quando i buoi sono scappati; (mech.) bloccare, immobilizzare; *to — away*, chiudere sotto chiave, mettere al sicuro, (fig.) custodire; *to — in*, rinchiudere, mettere sotto chiave; *to — out*, chiudere fuori, chiudere la porta in faccia a, (industr.) fare una serrata; *to — up*, mettere al sicuro, chiudere a chiave, rinchiudere, (finan.) immobilizzare; *intr.* chiudersi a chiave; (mech.) incepparsi incantarsi, bloccarsi.

**lock**[2] *n.* (of hair) ciocca, ricciolo; *pl.* capelli *m.pl.*, trecce *f.pl.*; (of wool) fiocco.

**lock**[3] *n.* (on canal, river) chiusa, conca, diga; cateratta.

**lock-chain** *n.* catena per bloccare una ruota.

**locker** *n.* armadietto a chiave, casellario chiuso; (naut.) bauletto, cassone *m.*

**locket** *n.* medaglione *m.*

**lock-hospital** *n.* (hist.) ospedale *m.* di malattie veneree.

**lockjaw** *n.* (med.) tetano.

**lock-keeper** *n.* guardiano di una chiusa, guardaconca. *m. indecl.*

**lock-nut** *n.* controdado.

**lock-out** *n.* (industr.) serrata.

**locksmith** *n.* fabbro, magnano.

**lock-up** *n.* (at police station) guardina, cella; (finan.) investimento a lunga scadenza; *attrib. adj. — shop*, bottega senza abitazione.

**locomot-ion** *n.* locomozione. **-ive** *adj.* locomotivo; locomotore; *n.* (steam) locomotiva; (electric, Diesel) locomotrice. **-or** *adj.* locomotore; (med.) *-orataxy*, atassia locomotrice.

**locum(-tenens)** *n.* supplente *m.*, interino, sostituto; *to act as — to*, sostituire.

**locust** *n.* (ent.) locusta, cavalletta, acridio.

**locust-bean** *n.* (bot.) carruba. **-tree** *n.* (bot.) carrubo, robinia.

**locution** *n.* locuzione; modo di dire.
**lode** *n.* (miner.) vena; filone *m.*
**lodestar** *n.* stella polare.
**lodge** *n.* casa; residenza; (masonic) loggia; *porter's —*, portineria; *shooting —*, padiglione *m.* di caccia; (of animal) tana; *tr.* alloggiare, albergare, ospitare, dare alloggio a; deporre, depositare, collocare; presentare; (leg.) sporgere (querela); *intr.* alloggiare, abitare; conficcarsi, piantarsi.
**lodg(e)ment** *n.* (comm.) deposito, versamento; (leg.) presentazione; (mil.) posizione stabile.
**lodger** *n.* inquilino, pigionante *m.*, *f.*
**lodging** *n.* alloggio; camera ammobiliata; *pl.* camere in affitto; *to give — to*, alloggiare; *board and —*, vitto e alloggio.
**lodging-house** *n.* alloggio; pensione; *— keeper*, affittacamere *m.*, *f.*, alloggiatore.
**loft** *n.* solaio; soffitta; (hay) fienile *m.*; (organ) tribuna, cantoria; (for pigeons) piccionaia; *tr.* (pigeons) tenere in piccionaia; (golf) alzare.
**loft-y** *adj.* alto; elevato; (fig.) nobile, eminente, eccelso, grande, sublime; (pejor.) superbo, altero, altezzoso. **-iness** *n.* altezza, elevatezza; (fig.) nobiltà; grandezza; superbia.
**log** *n.* ceppo, ciocco, tronco; (fig.) *to sleep like a —*, dormire come un ghiro; *as easy as falling off a —*, come bere un uovo; *King —*, Re Travicello; (naut.) solcometro; registro, giornale di bordo; *tr.* far legname; (fig.) registrare; (naut.) registrare su giornale di bordo.
**loganberry** *n.* lampone *m.*
**logarithm** *n.* logaritmo. **-ic(al)** *adj.* logaritmico.
**log-book** *n.* giornale di bordo. **-cabin** *n.* capanna di legno.
**loggerhead** *n.* (zool.) tartaruga marina; (fig.) *to be at -s*, essere come cane e gatto, essere in lite; *to set people at -s*, mettere la discordia fra la gente, seminare zizzania.
**loggia** *n.* (archit.) loggia, terrazzo, altana.
**logic** *n.* logica. **-al** *adj.* logico; ragionatore. **-ality** *n.* logicità. **-ian** *n.* logico; ragionatore.
**logist-ic(al)** *adj.* logistico. **-ics** *n.* logistica.
**logwood** *n.* (bot.) campeggio.
**loin** *n.* (cul.) lonza, lombata; *pl.*, (anat.) reni *f.pl.*; (fig.) lombi *m.pl.*, fianchi *m.pl.*; *to gird up one's -s*, cingersi i lombi, apprestarsi. **-cloth** *n.* perizoma *m.*
**Loire** *pr.n.* (geog.) Loira.
**loiter** *intr.* indugiare, gironzolare, bighellonare, andare a zonzo; *tr. to — away the hours*, passare le ore oziando. **-er** *n.* bighellone *m.*; perdigiorno. **-ing** l'indugiare, l'andare a zonzo; (leg.) *-ing with intent*, atteggiamento sospetto.
**loll** *intr.* ciondolare, penzolare; *tr. to — (out) its tongue*, lasciar penzolare la lingua.
**lollipop** *n.* lecca-lecca *m.*
**lollop** *intr.* muoversi goffamente, bighellonare.
**Lombard** *adj.*, *n.* lombardo; (hist.) longobardo. **-ic** *adj.* lombardo, longobardo. **-y** *pr.n.* (geog.) Lombardia.
**London** *pr.n.* Londra; *attrib.* di Londra; londinese; (bot.) *— pride*, sassifraga ombrosa. **-er** *n.* londinese *m.*, *f.*
**lone** *adj.* solitario, solo, isolato; (fig.) *to play a — hand*, fare da solo.
**lonel-y** *adj.* solitario, solo, solingo, isolato; remoto, fuor di mano. **-iness** *n.* solitudine *f.*, isolamento; malinconia
**lonesome** *adj.* (poet., fam.) solitario, solingo; malinconico.
**long**[1] *adj.* lungo; *four miles —*, lungo quattro miglia; *a — four miles*, quattro buone miglia; *how — is it?*, quanto è lungo?; *how — are the holidays?*, quanto durano le vacanze?; *to take a — chance*, rischiare molto; *a — dozen*, tredici; *a — drink*, una bibita allungata; *a — face*, un muso imbronciato, una faccia da funerale; *a — job*, un affare lungo; *— memory*, memoria tenace; *in the — run*, a lungo andare; *of — standing*, di vecchia data; *to have a — talk*, parlare a lungo; *a — time*, molto tempo; *it will take a — time*, ci vorrà molto tempo; *they are a — time coming*, tardano molto; *— in the tooth*, non più tanto giovane; *— vacation*, vacanze estive; *it's a — way to the town*, la città è distante; *to take the -est way round*, fare la strada più lunga; *by a — way*, *by a — chalk*, di gran lunga; *to get -er*, allungarsi; *to make -er*, allungare; *at the -est*, al massimo; (sport) *— jump*, salto in lungo; (betting) *— odds*, quota alta; *to lay — odds on*, puntare forte su; (typ.) *— primer*, corpo dieci; *n. the — and the short of it*, tutti i particolari; *the — and the short of it is*, per dirla in breve; (phon.) vocale lunga; molto tempo; *he hasn't — to live*, non ha molto tempo da vivere; *before —*, fra breve; *it won't take —*, non ci vorrà molto tempo; *to have just — enough to do something*, avere appena il tempo per fare qualcosa.
**long**[1] *adv.* lungamente, a lungo, per lungo tempo; *— after*, molto tempo dopo; *— before*, molto tempo prima; *all night —*, per tutta la notte; *how — does it take?*, quanto tempo ci vuole?; *how — have you been here?*, da quanto tempo sei qui?; *does it last —?*, dura molto?; *not very —*, pochissimo tempo; *a week -er*, ancora una settimana; *no -er*, non più; *as — as*, finquanto, finchè, purchè; *— live the Queen!*, viva la Regina!; (fam.) *so —!*, ciao!
**long**[2] *intr.* bramare; desiderare fortemente; aver gran voglia; *I — to go back to Italy*, non vedo l'ora di tornare in Italia; *to — for*, desiderare ardentemente, aver nostalgia di.
**long-ago** *adj.* lontano (nel tempo); *adv. long ago*, molto tempo fa; *n. in the days of long ago*, nei tempi lontani.
**longboat** *n.* (naut.) scialuppa, lancia.
**long-bow** *n.* arco; (fig.) *to draw the —*, raccontare frottole. **-dated** *adj.* a lunga scadenza. **-distance** *attrib. adj.* a lunga distanza, (teleph.) *-distance call*, telefonata interurbana. **-drawn(-out)** *adj.* prolungato, protratto; (fig.) *to be long-drawn-out*, andare per le lunghe.
**longevity** *n.* longevità.
**long-felt** *adj.* risentito da molto tempo. **-hand** *n.* (as opposed to short-hand) scrittura ordinaria. **-headed** *adj.* dolicocefalo; (fig.) sagace, scaltro.
**longing** *adj.* bramoso; ardente; smanioso; *n.* brama; vivo desiderio; voglia.
**longish** *adj.* lunghetto, piuttosto lungo.
**longitud-e** *n.* longitudine *f.* **-inal** *adj.* longitudinale.
**long-legged** *adj.* dalle gambe lunghe. **-lived** *adj.* longevo; (fig.) duraturo. **-playing** *adj.* *-playing record*, (disco) microsolco. **-range** *adj.* a grande portata.
**longshore** *adj.* attiguo alla riva. **-man** *n.* scaricatore, facchino del porto.
**long-sighted** *adj.* presbite; (fig.) preveggente, perspicace. **-standing** *adj.* di vecchia data. **-suffering** *adj.* longanime, paziente, che soffre in silenzio. **-term** *adj.* a lunga scadenza. **-wave** *adj.* (radio) a onde lunghe. **-winded** *adj.* prolisso, barboso; interminabile.
**loo** *n.* (fam.) gabinetto.
**loofah** *n.* luffa, spugna vegetale.
**look** *n.* sguardo; colpo d'occhio; occhiata; *to have a — at*, dare un'occhiata a; *to have a good — at*, esaminare attentamente; *may I have a —?*, posso vedere?; aria, aspetto, espressione; *a vacant —*, un'aria distratta; *I don't like the — of him*, il suo aspetto non mi piace; *an ugly —*, un'espressione di cattiveria, un brutto aspetto;

*to have an Italian* —, sembrare italiano; *pl.* *to judge by* ~*s*, giudicare dalle apparenze; *good* ~*s*, bellezza, bella presenza.

**look** *intr.* guardare; vedere; — *here!*, ma guarda un po!, di' un po', vedi un po'!; *to — the other way*, guardare altrove; *to — someone in the face*, guardare qualcuno in viso; *to — askance at*, guardare di sbieco; *to — one's last on*, dare un'ultima occhiata a; — *who's here!*, ma chi si vede?; — *sharp!*, sbrigati, fa presto!; *the house* ~*s south*, la casa è esposta a mezzogiorno; sembrare, aver l'aria (di), parere; *it* ~*s as if*, sembra che, pare che; *to — happy*, aver l'aria felice; *to — well*, aver buona cera; *she* ~*s well in black*, il nero le dona; *to — ill*, aver brutta cera; *to — off colour*, aver l'aria di non star troppo bene; *to — promising*, promettere bene; *to — like*, sembrare, fare l'effetto di; *it* ~*s like rain*, sembra che voglia piovere, deve piovere; *he* ~*s like winning*, è probabile che vinca; *what does he — like?*, che tipo è?, com'è?; *he* ~*s like his father*, assomiglia al padre; *to — one's best*, apparire in piena bellezza; *to make someone — small*, mortificare qualcuno; *to — daggers at*, lanciare sguardi di odio a; *to — one's age*, dimostrare i propri anni; *she's fifty but she doesn't — it*, ha cinquant'anni ma non li dimostra; (provb.) — *before you leap*, prima di agire pensaci. FOLLOW. BY PREP. OR ADV.: *to — about*, guardare in giro; *to — about for*, cercare; *to — after*, badare a, curare, occuparsi di, seguire con gli occhi; — *after yourself!*, stia bene!; *to — ahead*, guardare avanti, (fig.) guardare al futuro; — *ahead!*, guarda dove vai!, attento!; *to — at*, guardare, considerare, contemplare; *to — at the shops*, guardare nelle vetrine dei negozi; *to — at him you would say . . .*, a vederlo si direbbe . . .; *she won't — at him*, ella non ne vuol sapere; *whichever way you — at it*, da qualunque punto di vista si consideri; *the hotel is not much to — at*, da fuori l'albergo non sembra gran chè; *to — away*, guardare dall'altra parte, guardare altrove; *to — back*, guardare indietro; *from that day he has never* ~*ed back*, da quel giorno è sempre andato avanti; *to — back on*, ricordare; *to — down*, abbassare gli occhi; *to — down on*, guardare con disprezzo, disprezzare; *to — for*, cercare, aspettarsi; *to — forward*, guardare al futuro; *to — forward to*, attendere con impazienza, non veder l'ora di, rallegrarsi in anticipo; (comm.) ~*ing forward to hearing from you*, in attesa di una cortese risposta; *to — in*, guardare dentro, (fam.) fare una visitina; guardare la televisione; *to — in again*, ripassare; *to — in at the window*, dare un'occhiata attraverso la finestra; *to — into*, esaminare attentamente, indagare; *to — on*, stare a guardare, assistere; essere spettatore; *to — on something as*, considerare qualcosa come; *to — on(to)* (of window, *etc.*), dare su, essere prospiciente a; *to — out*, guardare fuori, affacciarsi, stare attento, badare; *to — out for*, cercare, restare in attesa di, stare in guardia per; *to — over*, esaminare, dare una scorsa a, ripassare; *to — over a house*, ispezionare una casa prima di prenderla in affitto; *to — round*, guardare intorno, guardare indietro, cercare dappertutto; *to — round for*, cercare con gli occhi; *to — through*, guardare attraverso, scrutare, scorrere, sfogliare; *to — up*, alzare gli occhi; (fam.) *things are* ~*ing up*, le cose vanno meglio; *to — something up*, cercare qualcosa, consultare un dizionario, ecc., per trovare qualcosa; *to — someone up*, passare da qualcuno, andare a trovare qualcuno; *to — someone up and down*, squadrare qualcuno; *to — up to*, rispettare, venerare; *to — upon*, considerare, contemplare.

**looker-on** *n.* spettatore; astante *m.*, *f.*

**look-in** *n.* (fam.) visitina; *he won't get a* —, non ha nessuna speranza di riuscire.

**looking-glass** *n.* specchio.

**look-out** *n.* guardia; *to be on the — for*, stare in guardia per, cercare; *to keep a good* —, stare all'erta; (mil.) osservatore; (naut.) alberante *m.*; (fig.) *it's a bad* —, è una brutta prospettiva; *that's my —!*, spetta a me!, è affare mio! **-over** *n.* *to give something a* ~*over*, dare un'occhiata a qualcosa.

**loom**[1] *n.* (text.) telaio.

**loom**[2] *intr.* apparire indistintamente, disegnarsi in lontananza; (fig.) incombere; *dangers* ~*ing ahead*, pericoli incombenti; *to — large*, essere imminente, assumere importanza.

**loon** *n.* (orn.) tuffetto, colimbo.

**loony** *adj.*, *n.* (pop.) matto. **-bin** *n.* (pop.) manicomio, casa dei matti.

**loop** *n.* cappio; anello; laccio; (of braid) alamaro; (needlew.) maglia; (in writing) occhiello; (in river, road) ansa; (rlwy.) raccordo; *tr.*, *intr.* fare un cappio; annodare, affibbiare; (aeron.) *to — the* —, fare il cerchio della morte. **-hole** *n.* (archit.) feritoia, merletto; (fig.) scappatoia.

**loop-line** *n.* (rlwy.) raccordo. **-stitch** *n.* (needlew.) punto a maglia.

**loose** *adj.* sciolto; slegato; staccato; libero; — *cash*, spiccioli; — *earth*, terriccio; *on a — rein*, con redini lente, (fig.) con indulgenza; *a — tooth*, un dente che dondola; *a — tongue*, una lingua sciolta; *to break* —, staccarsi, scappare, evadere, (fig.) scatenarsi; *to come, to get* —, sciogliersi, disfarsi, allentarsi; *to hang* —, pendere; *to let* —, liberare, dar libero corso a, lasciar andare; *to let a dog* —, sguinzagliare un cane; *to work* —, allentarsi; (fam.) *to have a screw* —, mancare di una rotella; ampio, largo; vago, sconnesso, approssimativo; licenzioso, dissoluto; *a — woman*, una donna di facili costumi; (fam.) *at a — end*, sfaccendato, a zonzo; *tr.* sciogliere; slegare; slacciare; snodare; (fig.) liberare, lasciar andare; *tr.*, *intr.* *to — off*, sparare.

**loose-box** *n.* box *m.* **-fitting** *adj.* ampio, largo. **-knit** *adj.* dinoccolato. **-leaf** *adj.* ~*leaf ledger*, mastro a fogli staccati; ~*leaf notebook*, quaderno a fogli staccati.

**loosely** *adv.* scioltamente; mollemente; approssimativamente; imprecisamente; in senso lato.

**loosen** *tr.* sciogliere; allentare; *to — someone's tongue*, far sciogliere la lingua a qualcuno; *to — one's grip*, allentare la presa; *intr.* sciogliersi; allentarsi. ~**er** *n.* (pharm.) lassativo.

**looseness** *n.* scioltezza; ampiezza, imprecisione; dissolutezza.

**loosestrife** *n.* (bot.) *purple* —, riparella; *yellow* —, mazza d'oro.

**loot** *n.* bottino; *tr.* saccheggiare, far man bassa di; *intr.* darsi ai saccheggi. ~**er** *n.* saccheggiatore, predone *m.* ~**ing** *n.* saccheggio.

**lop** *n.* potatura; rami potati; *tr.* tagliare, potare; (bot.) diradare; *to — off*, mozzare; *intr.* pendere.

**lope** *n.* lungo salto, balzo; *intr.* muoversi a lunghi balzi; camminare dinoccolato.

**lop-eared** *adj.* dalle orecchie pendenti. **-sided** *adj.* asimmetrico; sbilenco; pendente da una parte; male equilibrato.

**loquacious** *adj.* loquace; garrulo. ~**ness, loquacity** *n.* loquacità; garrulità.

**lord** *n.* signore *m.*; — *of the manor*, signore del castello; (rel.) *Our Lord*, Nostro Signore; *the Lord's Prayer*, il paternostro; *the Lord's Day*, la domenica; (Earl) conte *m.*, (Baron) barone *m.*, (Marquess) marchese *m.*; *House of Lords*, camera dei lords, camera alta; *my Lord*, signor conte, ecc.; (leg.) signor giudice, (eccl.) monsignore; *Lord Lieutenant* (of English county),

luogotenente *m.*, (Italian equiv.) prefetto (di una provincia); *Lord Mayor*, Sindaco; (fig.) *to live like a —*, vivere come un papa; *drunk as a —*, ubriaco fradice; (fam.) *Lord bless my soul!*, Dio mio!; *tr.*, *intr.* signoreggiare, dominare; *to — it over someone*, tiranneggiare qualcuno. **-liness** *n.* dignità, alterigia; sfarzo, magnificenza. **-ling** *n.* signorotto; tirannello. **-ly** *adj.* signorile, da gran signore; (pejor.) altero, superbo; magnifico; sfarzoso, fastoso. **-ship** *n.* signoria; *Your -ship*, vostra Signoria, Vossignoria; (leg.) signor giudice.

**lore** *n.* sapere *m.*; erudizione; corpo di tradizioni; cf. **folklore.**

**lorgn-ette, -on** *n.* occhialino; binocolo da teatro.

**lorn** *adj.* (poet.) abbandonato, solingo.

**Lorraine** *pr.n.* (geog.) Lorena.

**lorry** *n.* autocarro, camion *m.*; (with trailer) autotreno.

**lorry-driver** *n.* camionista *m.*

**lory** *n.* (orn.) lorichetto.

**losable** *adj.* perdibile.

**lose** *tr.* perdere; smarrire; rimettere; *to — one's character*, perdere la propria reputazione; *to — ground*, perdere terreno; *to — one's head*, perdere la testa; *to — heart*, scoraggiarsi; *to — one's heart to*, innamorarsi di; *to — interest*, non interessarsi più; *to — one's reason*, impazzire; *to — sight of*, perdere di vista; *to — strength*, perdere forza, accasciarsi; *to — one's temper*, arrabbiarsi, perdere la pazienza; *to — time*, perdere tempo, (of watch) ritardare; *to — the train*, perdere il treno; *to — one's way*, sbagliare strada, smarrirsi; *to — weight*, diminuire di peso; *to be lost*, smarrirsi, perdersi; *to be lost at sea*, perire in un naufragio; *the hint was lost upon him*, il consiglio fu sprecato con lui; *to get lost*, smarrirsi, perdere l'orientamento, (of thing) andare disperso; *to give something up as lost*, perdere la speranza di ritrovare qualcosa; *intr.* perdere, essere sconfitto; *to — heavily*, rimettere una forte somma, subire perdite gravissime.

**loser** *n.* perdente *m., f.*; *to be a —*, perdere, essere in perdita; *to be a good —*, saper perdere.

**losing** *adj.* perdente; *to play a — game*, non aver speranza di vincere; (sport) *the — side*, i vinti.

**loss** *n.* perdita; *— of appetite*, inappetenza; *a dead —*, una perdita totale; *to cut one's -es*, ridurre le perdite; (fig.) danno, svantaggio; *the — is mine*, il danno è mio; *he's no great —*, si può fare anche senza di lui; *to be at a —*, essere disorientato, non saper che fare; *I am at a — to explain*, non so spiegarmi.

**lost** *p.def.*, *part.* of **lose,** *q.v.*; *adj.* perduto, perso, smarrito; *a — cause*, una causa persa; *— property*, oggetti smarriti; *— souls*, anime dannate; *to give up for —*, dare per perso, abbandonare ogni speranza di ritrovare; (fig.) *— to*, insensibile a; *to look —*, aver l'aria spaesato.

**lot** *n.* sorte *f.*; destino; *by —*, per sorteggio; *to cast, to draw -s*, trarre a sorte; *to fall to someone's —*, toccare in sorte a qualcuno; *to throw in one's — with*, condividere la sorte di; lotto, appezzamento; (comm.) lotto, partita; (fam.) grande quantità, tutto; *a — of*, molto; *that's the —*, ecco tutto; *such a — of*, tanto; *what a — of*, quanto; *quite a — of*, assai; *the whole —*, tutto quanto; *he's a bad —*, è un pessimo soggetto; (iron.) *you're a nice —!*, siete dei bravi!; *a nice — of money*, una bella sommetta; *pl. -s of money*, un sacco di soldi; *-s of friends*, tanti amici; *I feel -s better*, mi sento di nuovo in gamba.

**loth** *adj.* See **loath.**

**Lothario** *pr.n.* *to be a gay —*, essere un dongiovanni, fare la bella vita.

**lotion** *n.* lozione.

**lottery** *n.* lotteria; estrazione a sorte; (fig.) caso; *marriage is a —*, il matrimonio è un salto nel buio.

**lottery-wheel** *n.* ruota della fortuna.

**lotto** *n.* (game) tombola.

**lotus** *n.* (bot.) loto; *— lily*, nelumbio.

**lotus-eater** *n.* lotofago; (fig.) mangiatore di loti; gaudente *m., f.*, fannullone *m.*

**loud** *adj.* alto, forte, rumoroso; *to speak in a — voice*, parlare alto; *— cheers, — applause*, applausi rumorosi, viva acclamazione; (of colour, dress) vistoso, sgargiante, chiassoso; (pejor.) volgare; (fig.) *to be — in one's praises of*, lodare calorosamente; *adv. out —*, ad alta voce; *— and long*, forte e a lungo, *don't speak so —*, parla più basso.

**louden** *tr.* rendere più forte, alzare; *intr.* diventare più forte; diventare più rumoroso.

**loudly** *adv.* alto, forte, fortemente, ad alta voce, rumorosamente.

**loud-mouthed** *adj.* rumoroso; da abbaione.

**loudness** *n.* forza, altezza di voce, rumorosità; (of dress) vistosità; (pejor.) volgarità.

**loud-sounding** *adj.* altisonante. **-speaker** *n.* altoparlante *m.*

**lough** *n.* (in Ireland) lago, braccio di mare.

**Louis** *pr.n.* Luigi.

**Louisa** *pr.n.* Luigia, Luisa.

**Louisiana** *pr.n.* (geog.) Luigiana.

**lounge** *n.* sala di ritrovo; salotto; (theatr.) ridotto; *intr.* gironzolare, bighellonare, dondolarsi; *tr. to — away the time*, passare il tempo in ozio.

**lounge-bed** *n.* canapè, letto a divano. **-chair** *n.* agrippina, poltrona a sdraio. **-lizard** *n.* (slang) gigolo.

**lounger** *n.* bighellone, fannullone *m.*; chi va a zonzo.

**lounge-suit** *n.* (cost.) abito da passeggio.

**lour** *n.* cipiglio; (of sky) oscuramento, minaccia di tempesta; *intr.* aggrottare le ciglia; (of sky) oscurarsi, annuvolarsi.

**louse** *n.* pidocchio.

**lous-y** *adj.* pidocchioso; (fig.) schifoso; *a — trick*, un brutto tiro; *to feel —*, sentirsi a terra. **-iness** *n.* l'essere pidocchioso; (fig.) schifosità.

**lout** *n.* zoticone *m.*; giovinastro; villano. **-ish** *adj.* zotico; grossolano; villano; rustico. **-ishness** *n.* grossolanità; rustichezza.

**Louvain** *pr.n.* (geog.) Lovanio *f.*

**louver, louvre** *n.* (archit.) abbaino, lucernario; (motor.) feritoia per ventilazione, sfinestratura.

**lovable** *adj.* amabile, simpatico. **-ness** *n.* amabilità.

**love**[1] *n.* amore *m.*; affetto; devozione; *to be in — with*, amare, essere innamorato di; *to fall in — with*, innamorarsi di; *to make — to*, corteggiare, fare all'amore con, amoreggiare con; *to marry for —*, fare un matrimonio d'amore; *there is no — lost between them*, essi si detestano; *not to be had for — or money*, impossibile a ottenere, introvabile; *a labour of —*, un lavoro grato sebbene mal retribuito; (provb.) *all's fair in — and war*, tutto è lecito in amore e in guerra; Amore, Cupido; (fam.) *my —*, caro *m.*, cara *f.*, amor mio; *for the — of God!*, per l'amor di Dio!; *give him my —*, salutalo da parte mia; *with —*, affettuosamente; *— to all*, saluti affettuosi a tutti, un'abbracciata a tutti.

**love**[1] *tr.* amare, voler bene a; dilettarsi di, essere appassionato di; *to — one another*, amarsi (l'un l'altro); (fam.) *he -s music*, gli piace la musica; *I — reading*, mi piace leggere; *I should — him to come*, mi piacerebbe tanto che venisse.

**love**[2] *n.* (sport) zero; *— all*, zero a zero.

**love-affair** *n.* relazione amorosa, amoruccio. **-bird** *n.* pappagallino verde. **-child** *n.* figlio naturale. **-feast** *n.* agape *f.* **-in-a-mist** *n.* (bot.) scapigliata, damigella.

**-in-idleness** *n.* (bot.) viola del pensiero.
**loveless** *adj.* senza amore, che non ama. **-ness** *n.* mancanza di amore.
**love-letter** *n.* biglietto amoroso, lettera d'amore. **-lies-bleeding** *n.* (bot.) code *f.pl.* rosse. **-life** *n.* vita amorosa.
**loveliness** *n.* (of woman) avvenenza, vaghezza, leggiadria, bellezza; (of things) bellezza.
**lovelock** *n.* tirabaci *m. indecl.*
**love-lorn** *adj.* (poet.) che si strugge d'amore, abbandonato.
**lovely** *adj.* bello, grazioso, vezzoso; incantevole, dilettevole; — *to look at*, bello a vedersi; (fam.) *to have a — time*, divertirsi un mondo.
**love-making** *n.* il fare all'amore. **-match** *n.* matrimonio d'amore. **-philtre, -potion** *n.* filtro d'amore.
**lover** *n.* amante *m., f.*; innamorato, amoroso, amico, amica; (of things) amatore, appassionato; *a — of music*, un appassionato della musica.
**lovesick** *adj.* malato d'amore, innamorato.
**love-token** *n.* pegno d'amore.
**loving** *adj.* amoroso, affettuoso, amorevole; d'amore, amante.
**loving-kindness** *n.* bontà; carità.
**low**[1] *adj.* basso; *-er*, più basso, inferiore; *-est*, il più basso, infimo; *in a — voice*, a bassa voce, sottovoce; *the Low Countries*, i Paesi Bassi; (eccl.) — *Sunday*, domenica in albis; — *mass*, messa bassa; (art) — *relief*, basso rilievo; — *tide*, bassa marea; — *water*, acqua bassa, (in river) magra, (fig.) *to find oneself in — water*, navigare in cattive acque; *to be of — birth*, essere di umile estrazione; *a — bow*, un profondo inchino; — *diet*, dieta scarsa; (motor.) — *gear*, prima velocità; volgare, grossolano; *the -er orders*, le classi inferiori, il volgo; (fig.) *in — spirits*, abbattuto; *to be feeling —*, essere giù di corda; *to have a — opinion of*, stimare poco.
**low**[1] *adv.* basso, in basso; *to fall —*, cadere in basso, decadere; *to lie —*, star quieto, aspettare il momento favorevole; *to be laid —*, essere abbattuto, essere ucciso, (fig.) essere costretto a letto; *to run —*, esaurirsi.
**low**[1] *n.* (meteor.) area ciclonica.
**low**[2] *n.* mugghio, muggito; *intr.* muggire, mugghiare.
**lowbrow** *adj.* popolare, volgare, grossolano; *n.* persona senza cultura, persona non molto intelligente; idiota *m., f.*
**low-class** *adj.* volgare, inferiore. **-down** *adj.* basso; (fig.) abietto, sleale; *a -down trick*, un tiro mancino; *n.* (slang) *to get the -down on*, farsi dire la verità su.
**lower** *adj. comp.* of **low**, *q.v.*; (geog.) basso; (pol.) *the Lower House*, la camera bassa, la Camera dei Comuni; *tr.* abbassare, calare, far discendere; diminuire, ridurre; (fig.) degradare, umiliare; (flags, *etc.*) ammainare; *intr.* abbassarsi. **-most** *adj.* il più basso.
**low-grade** *adj.* di qualità inferiore.
**lowing** *n.* muggito.
**lowland** *n.* terreno pianeggiante, bassopiano. **-er** *n.* abitante della pianura.
**lowl-y** *adj.* umile; dimesso; modesto. **-iness** *n.* umiltà; modestia.
**low-lying** *adj.* situato a bassa quota, in pianura.
**low-necked** *adj.* scollato.
**lowness** *n.* bassezza; modicità; gravità; debolezza; tono basso; (fig.) — *of spirits*, abbattimento.
**low-pitched** *adj.* (mus.) basso.
**loyal** *adj.* fedele, devoto; *to drink the — toast*, bere alla salute della Regina; sincero, leale. **-ist** *n.* suddito fedele; (pol.) monarchico. **-ty** *n.* fedeltà; devozione; lealtà.
**lozenge** *n.* (herald.) losanga; (geom.) rombo; (pharm.) pastiglia, pasticca.
**lubber** *n.* goffone *m.*; rustico; zoticone *m.*; (naut.) marinaio d'acqua dolce.
**Lubeck** *pr.n.* (geog.) Lubecca.
**lubric-ant** *adj., n.* lubrificante *m.* **-ate** *tr.* lubrificare. **-ating** *adj.* lubrificante. **-ation** *n.* lubrificazione. **-ator** *n.* lubrificatore.
**lubric-ious** *adj.* lubrico. **-ity** *n.* lubricità; viscosità.
**Lucan** *pr.n.* Lucano.
**luce** *n.* (ichth.) luccio.
**lucent** *adj.* lucente, luminoso.
**Lucerne**[1] *pr.n.* (geog.) Lucerna.
**lucern(e)**[2] *n.* (bot.) erba medica, erba spagna.
**Lucian** *pr.n.* Luciano.
**lucid** *adj.* limpido; terso; (fig.) chiaro; lucido; *a — interval*, intervallo di lucidità. **-ity** *n.* lucentezza; lucidità; (fig.) chiarezza.
**Lucifer** *pr.n.* Lucifero; — *(match)*, zolfanello, fiammifero.
**luck** *n.* ventura; sorte *f.*; caso; *good —*, buona fortuna; *(I wish you) good —!*, auguri!; *bad —*, sfortuna; *what rotten —!* che disdetta! che scalogna!; *to try one's —*, tentare la sorte; *to be down on one's —*, essere scalognato; *to be in —*, essere fortunato; *to be out of —*, essere sfortunato; *a run of —*, una serie di successi; *as ill — would have it*, il diavolo volle (che); *to push one's —*, tentare la fortuna.
**luckiness** *n.* fortuna; buona sorte.
**luckless** *adj.* sfortunato, sventurato; infelice, disgraziato. **-ness** *n.* sfortuna.
**lucky** *adj.* fortunato; *how —!*, che fortuna!; *to be born —*, essere nato con la camicia; *it was — for him he did*, meno male che abbia fatto così; *a — shot*, un colpo indovinato; *— beggar!*, *— dog!*, beato te!; propizio, favorevole; *a — day*, un giorno propizio.
**lucrative** *adj.* lucrativo; profittevole; redditizio.
**lucre** *n.* lucro; guadagno; (joc.) *filthy —*, il vile denaro.
**Lucretia** *pr.n.* Lucrezia.
**lucubrat-e** *intr.* elucubrare. **-ion** *n.* elucubrazione; disquisizione.
**Lucy** *pr.n.* Lucia.
**ludicrous** *adj.* ridicolo; comico; assurdo. **-ness** *n.* ridicolezza; comicità.
**luff** *n.* (naut.) orzata.
**lug**[1] *n.* (of ear) lobo; (fam.) ear; (of cap) paraorecchi *m. indecl.*; (mech.) aggetto, aletta.
**lug**[2] *n.* strappata, tirata; *tr.* tirare, trascinare, (fam.) rimorchiarsi dietro; *intr. to — at*, tirare con forza.
**luggage** *n.* bagaglio; *articles of —*, bagagli; *hand —*, bagaglio a mano; *— receipt*, scontrino del bagaglio.
**luggage-rack** *n.* (rlwy.) reticella. **-ticket** *n.* scontrino del bagaglio. **-van** *n.* (rlwy.) bagagliaio.
**lugger** *n.* (naut.) trabaccolo.
**lughole** *n.* (pop.) orecchio.
**lugubrious** *adj.* lugubre, cupo, tetro. **-ly** *adv.* lugubremente. **-ness** *n.* l'essere lugubre; tristezza.
**lugworm** *n.* verme *m.* da pesca.
**Luke** *pr.n.* Luca.
**lukewarm** *adj.* tiepiedo; (fig.) indifferente, poco zelante. **-ness** *n.* tiepidezza; (fig.) mancanza di entusiasmo, indifferenza.
**lull** *n.* momento di calma, bonaccia; (fig.) pausa, tregua; *tr.* cullare, far addormentare; *to — a child to sleep*, far addormentare un bambino cullandolo; (fig.) calmare, acquietare; *to — suspicion(s)*, dissipare i sospetti; *intr.* calmarsi, acquietarsi.
**lullaby** *n.* ninna-nanna; cantilena.
**lumbago** *n.* (med.) lombaggine *f.*
**lumbar** *adj.* (anat.) lombare.
**lumber** *n.* mobili di scarto; cianfrusaglie *f.pl.*; legname *m.*; *tr.* ingombrare, accatastare; *to — (up) a room with furniture*, ingombrare una stanza con mobili; tagliare (legname); *intr. to — about*, muoversi pesantemente. **-ing** *adj.* che si muove pesantemente.
**lumber-jack, -man** *n.* boscaiolo, abbattitore (di alberi). **-mill** *n.* segheria. **-room** *n.* ripostiglio. **-yard** *n.* deposito di legname.

**luminary** *n.* (astron.) astro, corpo luminoso; (fig.) luminare *m.*, personaggio autorevole.
**luminescence** *n.* luminescenza.
**luminosity, luminousness** *n.* luminosità.
**luminous** *adj.* luminoso; fulgente; (of paint) fosforescente.
**lump** *n.* protuberanza; bernoccolo; gonfiore *m.*; massa; zolla; (of sugar) zolletta; (in liquid) grumo; (in throat) nodo, groppo; (fig.) — *sum*, somma globale; (fam.) persona goffa; *tr.* ammassare; *to — together*, mettere insieme, (fig.) considerare alla stessa tregua; (fam.) *if you don't like it, you'll have to — it*, se non ti piace, pazienza; *intr.* (of material, liquid) raggrumarsi. **-ish** *adj.* massiccio; pesante; torvo. **-y** *adj.* pieno di protuberanze; grumoso, granulato.
**lunacy** *n.* alienazione (mentale), infermità di mente, demenza; (fig.) *it's sheer —*, è una pazzia.
**lunar** *adj.* lunare.
**lunate** *adj.* lunato, falcato.
**lunatic** *adj.* pazzo, da pazzo, matto; *n.* alienato, pazzo; — *asylum*, manicomio.
**lunch, -eon** *n.* (seconda) colazione, pasto del mezzogiorno; — *basket*, cestino da viaggio; *sandwich —*, colazione al sacco; *intr. to —*, far colazione. **-time** ora della (seconda) collazione; *attrib.* che ha luogo tra mezzogiorno e le due.
**lunette** *n.* (archit.) lunetta; (mil.) alone *m.*
**lung** *n.* (anat.) polmone *m.*; (med.) *iron —*, polmone d'acciaio; (fam.) *to have good -s*, avere una voce forte; *to shout at the top of one's -s*, urlare a squarciagola.
**lung-disease** *n.* malattia polmonare.
**lunge** *n.* stoccata, rapido movimento in avanti; (fencing) affondo, allungo; *intr.* dare una stoccata; *to — forward*, precipitarsi in avanti; (fam.) *to — out at*, allungare un pugno a; (fencing) fare un affondo.
**lung-power** *n.* potenza di voce.
**lupin** *n.* (bot.) lupino.
**lupine** *adj.* di lupo, lupesco.
**lurch** *n.* barcollamento, sbandamento, scarto; agguato; (naut.) rollìo violento; (fig.) *to leave someone in the —*, piantare in asso qualcuno, lasciare qualcuno nelle peste; *intr.* barcollare, sbandare, fare uno scarto; tenersi in agguato; *to — across the road*, attraversare la strada barcollando; (naut.) rollare violentemente. **-er** *n.* cane da caccia bastardo.
**lure** *n.* esca; (falconry) logoro; (fig.) allettamento, fascino; *the — of the sea*, il fascino del mare; *tr.* adescare, allettare, attirare; (falconry) richiamare col logoro; *to — away from*, distogliere da; *to — into doing something*, indurre a far qualcosa; *to be -d on*, lasciarsi trascinare.
**lurid** *adj.* fosco; spettrale; sinistro; livido; rosseggiante; molto colorito.
**lurk** *intr.* nascondersi, stare in agguato, tenersi da parte; (fig.) *-ing doubts*, vaghi dubbi; preoccupazioni nascoste.
**luscious** *adj.* succulento; delizioso; dolce; melato. **-ness** *n.* saporosità; estrema dolcezza; ridondanza; immaginosità.
**lush** *adj.* lussureggiante; rigoglioso. **-ness** *n.* esuberanza; rigoglio.
**lust** *n.* lussuria; concupiscenza; sensualità; (fig.) brama; sete *f.*; *intr. to — after*, bramare; concupire; agognare; (fig.) *to — for*, aver sete di. **-ful** *adj.* lascivo; sensuale; libidinoso; bramoso. **-fulness** *n.* bramosia; concupiscenza; sensualità.
**lustiness** *n.* vigoria; gagliardia.
**lustra-l** *adj.* lustrale. **-ation** *n.* lustrazione.
**lustre**[1] *n.* lucentezza, lucidezza, luminosità; lustro, splendore *m.*; lampadario a gocce; goccia; lustrina.
**lustre**[2] *n.* (Rom. antiq.) lustro.
**lustrous** *adj.* lucido; rilucente; splendente.
**lusty** *adj.* gagliardo; vigoroso; robusto.
**lute**[1] *n.* (mus.) liuto.
**lute**[2] *n.* (bldg.) luto.
**Luther** *pr.n.* Lutero. **-an** *adj.*, *n.* luterano. **-anism** *n.* luteranesimo.
**Luxembourg** *pr.n.* (geog., country) Lussemburgo *m.*; (city) Lussemburgo *f.*
**luxuri-ance** *n.* esuberanza; rigoglio. **-ant** *adj.* esuberante; rigoglioso; lussureggiante. **-ate** *intr.* lussureggiare; prosperare rigogliosamente; vivere nel lusso, godersela.
**luxurious** *adj.* lussuoso, di lusso; sontuoso; fastoso; voluttuoso; che ama il lusso. **-ness** *n.* lusso; amore per il lusso; fasto; sontuosità; sfarzo.
**luxury** *n.* lusso; sontuosità; *to live in —*, vivere nel lusso; articolo di lusso, lusso.
**Lwow** *pr.n.* (geog.) Leopoli *f.*
**lych-gate** *n.* portico coperto (all'entrata di un cimitero).
**lye** *n.* lisciva, ranno, soluzione alcalina.
**lying**[1] bugiardo, menzognero, mendace; *n.* il dir bugie; *cf.* **lie**[1].
**lying**[2] *adj.* giacente, situato; coricato, sdraiato; *n.* il giacere; *cf.* **lie**[2].
**lying-in-state** *n.* esposizione.
**lymph** *n.* linfa; (med.) vaccino. **-atic** *adj.* linfatico.
**lyncean** *adj.* linceo, di lince.
**lynch** *tr.* linciare. **-ing** *n.* linciaggio.
**lynx** *n.* lince *f.*, cerviere *m.*
**lynx-eyed** *adj.* dagli occhi di lince, linceo.
**Lyons** *pr.n.* (geog.) Lione *f.*
**lyre** *n.* lira, cetra.
**lyric** *adj.* lirico; *n.* poesia lirica; lirica; (theatr.) canzone *f.* **-al** *adj.* lirico. **-ism** *n.* lirismo.

**M, m** *n.* emme *m.*, *f.*; (teleph.) — *for Mary*, emme come Milano.
**macabre** *adj.* macabro.
**macadamize** *tr.* macadamizzare, pavimentare a macadam.
**macaron-i** *n.* pasta asciutta; maccheroni *m.pl.* **-ic** *adj.* maccheronico.
**macaroon** *n.* (cul.) amaretto.
**macaw** *n.* (orn.) macao.
**Maccabe-es** *pr.n.* (bibl.) Maccabei. **-an** *adj.* (bibl.) maccabeo.
**mace**[1] *n.* mazza. **-bearer** *n.* mazziere *m.*
**mace**[2] *n.* (cul.) macis *m.*, mace *f.*
**macedoine** *n.* (cul.) macedonia.
**macerat-e** *tr.* macerare; *intr.* macerarsi. **-ion** *n.* macerazione.
**mach** (aeron.) — *number*, numero mach. **-meter** *n.* (aeron.) metro mach.
**Machiavell-ian** *adj.* machiavellico. **-ism** *n.* machiavellismo.
**machicolation, machicoulis** *n.* (archit.) piombatoio, caditoia.
**machinat-e** *intr.* macchinare; tramare. **-ion** *n.* macchinazione; congiura; trama.
**machine** *n.* macchina; (fig.) *a mere —*, un automa; (pol.) *the party —*, l'organizzazione del partito; *tr.* lavorare a macchina, eseguire a macchina.
**machine-gun** *n.* mitragliatrice. *tr.* mitragliare. **-gunner** *n.* mitragliere. **-minder** *n.* (industr.) macchinista *m.*
**machinery** *n.* macchinario; impianto; meccanismo; congegno; (fig.) organizzazione; meccanismo.
**machine-tool** *n.* macchina utensile.
**machin-ing** *n.* lavorazione a macchina; (typ.) avviamento, messa in macchina. **-ist** *n.* macchinista *m.*, meccanico specializzato.
**mackerel** *n.* (ichth.) sgombro,

maccarello; (fig.) — *sky*, cielo a pecorelle.
**mackintosh** *n.* impermeabile *m.*; tessuto gommato.
**macro-cosm** *n.* macrocosmo. **-scopic** *adj.* macroscopico.
**mad** *adj.* pazzo, matto, folle; fobo, arrabbiato; (fig.) furibondo, arrabbiato, furioso; *to go* —, impazzire, diventare matto; *to drive someone* —, far impazzire, far disperare qualcuno; — *as a March hare, as a hatter*, matto da legare; *raving* —, pazzo furioso; *to get — with someone*, arrabbiarsi con qualcuno; *to be — on games*, andare pazzo per lo sport; *like* —, come un pazzo; *in — haste*, in fretta e furia.
**madam** *n.* signora.
**madcap** *n.* scervellato, testa matta.
**madden** *tr.* far impazzire, far diventare matto, far arrabbiare; (fam.) *it's -ing!*, è roba da far diventare matto!; *how -ing!*, che rabbia!
**madder** *n.* (bot.) robbia.
**Madeira** *pr.n.* (geog.) Madera; (wine) vino di Madera.
**madman** *n.* pazzo, folle *m.*, matto, forsennato.
**madness** *n.* pazzia; demenza; follia; furore *m.*; (of animal) rabbia.
**madrepore** *n.* (bot.) madrepora, acropora.
**madrigal** *n.* madrigale *m.*
**Maecenas** *pr.n.* Mecenate; (fig.) mecenate *m.*
**maenad** *n.* menade *f.*, baccante *f.*
**magazine** *n.* magazzino; deposito; fondaco; rivista, periodico; (mil.) polveriera; (of rifle) caricatore; (naut.) santabarbara.
**Magdalen(e)** *pr.n.* Maddalena.
**Magellan** *pr.n.* Magellano.
**maggot** *n.* verme *m.*; baco; bruco; (fig., lit.) grillo, idea fissa. **-y** *adj.* guasto, bacato.
**Magi** *n. the three* —, i Re Magi.
**magic** *adj.* magico; fatato; *n.* magia; incanto; *black* —, magia nera; (fam.) *like* —, come per incanto. **-al** *adj.* magico; incantevole. **-ian** *n.* mago; indovino; negromante *m.*
**magisterial** *adj.* di maestro, di magistrato; magistrale; autoritario, autorevole.
**magistr-ate** *n.* (in Britain) magistrato; (Italian equiv.) pretore *m.*; *examining* —, giudice istruttore. **-acy** *n.* magistratura.
**magnanim-ous** *adj.* magnanimo. **-ity** *n.* magnanimità.
**magnate** *n.* magnate *m.*, maggiorente *m.*; *industrial* —, grande industriale *m.*
**magnesi-a** *n.* magnesia. **-um** *n.* magnesio.
**magnet** *n.* calamita; magnete *m.* **-ic** *adj.* magnetico; (fig.) affascinante. **-ism** *n.* magnetismo. **-ist** *n.* magnetista *m.* **-ization** *n.* magnetizzazione. **-ize** *tr.* magnetizzare.
**magneto** *n.* (electr.; motor.) magnete *m.*; *hand-starting* —, magnete d'avviamento; *ignition* —, magnete d'accensione. **-meter** *n.* magnetometro.
**magnification** *n.* magnificazione; esaltazione; ingrandimento.
**magnific-ence** *n.* magnificenza; sfarzo. **-ent** *adj.* magnifico; sontuoso; splendido; eccelso.
**magnif-y** *tr.* magnificare; ingrandire; (fig.) esagerare, esaltare. **-ied** *adj.* ingrandito; magnificato; (fig.) esagerato. **-ier** *n.* magnificatore; esaltatore; (opt.) lente d'ingrandimento.
**magnifying-glass** *n.* lente *f.* d'ingrandimento.
**magniloqu-ence** *n.* magniloquenza; ampollosità. **-ent** *adj.* magniloquente; ampolloso.
**magnitude** *n.* grandezza; importanza.
**magnolia** *n* (bot.) magnolia.
**magnum** *n* bottiglione *m.* (da 2.28 litri).
**magnum opus** *n.* capolavoro.
**magpie** *n.* (orn.) gazza; *The Thieving* —, La Gazza Ladra; (shooting, on target) penultimo cerchio.
**Magyar** *adj.*, *n.* magiaro.
**Maharaja(h)** *n.* maragià *m.*
**mahlstick, maulstick** *n.* (paint.) appoggiamani *m. indecl.*, mazza.
**mahogany** *n.* mogano, acagiù *m.*
**Mahomet, Muhammad** *pr.n.* Maometto. **-an, mahommedan** *adj.*, *n.* maomettano; islamita *m.*, *f.* **-anism, mahommedanism** *n.* maomettismo; islamismo.
**mahout** *n.* guidatore di elefanti.
**maid** *n.* fanciulla; pulcella; ragazza; vergine *f.*; *the — of Orleans*, la Pulcella d'Orleans; *old* —, zitella; domestica, cameriera, donna di servizio, (fam.) servetta; *lady's* —, cameriera; — *of all work*, donna tutto fare.
**maiden** *n.* fanciulla; ragazza; *attrib.* virgineo, verginale; — *aunt*, zia nubile; — *lady*, signorina; — *name*, cognome da nubile, (fam.) cognome da ragazza; (fig.) — *speech*, primo discorso; — *voyage*, primo viaggio, viaggio inaugurale; (cricket) — *over*, serie di sei palle senza che il battitore riesca a segnare un solo punto. **-hair** *n.* (bot.) — *fern*, capelvenere *m.* **-head** *n.* verginità; (anat.) imene *m.* **-hood** *n.* fanciullezza; verginità. **-like, -ly** *adj.* verginale; pudico; modesto. **-liness** *n.* pudore *m.*; modestia.
**maidservant** *n.* domestica; cameriera; donna di servizio; (poet.) ancella.
**mail**[1] *n.* maglia di ferro; *coat of* —, cotta di maglia.
**mail**[2] *n.* posta; corrispondenza; servizio postale; *inward* —, corrispondenza in arrivo; *outward* —, corrispondenza in partenza; *air* —, posta aerea; *tr.* impostare; mandare per posta; *-ing list*, elenco di indirizzi per invio di materiale pubblicitario; *please add our name to your -ing list*, vogliate inviarci i vostri cataloghi e listini.
**mail-bag** *n.* sacco postale. **-boat, -steamer** *n.* battello postale. **-coach** *n.* diligenza postale, corriera. **-order** *n.* ordinazione per posta. **-train** *n.* (rlwy.) treno postale. **-van** *n.* vagone *m.* postale; (rlwy.) furgone *m.* postale.
**mailed** *adj.* rivestito di maglia; corazzato; *the — fist*, il pugno di ferro.
**maim** *tr.* mutilare; storpiare. **-ed** *part. adj.* mutilato; storpiato; *n.pl.* storpi *m.pl.*; *the halt and the -ed*, gli zoppi e gli storpi.
**main** *adj.* principale; più importante; essenziale; saliente; capitale; — *building*, edificio principale; — *feature*, tratto saliente; — *idea*, concetto generale; *the — issue*, l'essenziale, il nocciolo della questione; (rlwy.) — *line*, linea principale; — *station*, stazione centrale; — *road*, strada maestra; — *street*, via principale; (mil.) — *body*, grosso (dell'esercito); (fam.) *to have an eye to the — chance*, badare ai propri interessi; *n.* complesso; *in the* —, nel complesso, in genere; *with might and* —, con tutte le forze; mare, oceano; *the Spanish Main*, il Mar delle Antille; (water, gas, electr.) conduttura principale; (radio) *-s-operated set*, radio a corrente elettrica.
**mainbrace** *n.* (naut.) corda del pennone di maestra; *to splice the* —, distribuire una razione supplementare di rhum.
**main-deck** *n.* (naut.) ponte di batteria.
**mainland** *n.* continente *m.*; terra ferma.
**mainly** *adv.* principalmente; soprattutto; in genere, nel complesso.
**main-mast** *n.* (naut.) albero maestro. **-sail** *n.* (naut.) vela di maestra. **-spring** *n.* (watchm.) molla principale; (fig.) movente *m.* principale. **-stay** *n.* (naut.) straglio di maestra; (fig.) appoggio, sostegno; braccio destro.
**maintain** *tr.* mantenere; provvedere a; *to — one's rights*, asserire i propri diritti; (mil.) *to — a position*, conservare una posizione; affermare, asserire, pretendere, sostenere; *he -s that he is right*, sostiene di aver ragione. **-able** *adj.* mantenibile; sostenibile. **-er** *n.* mantenitore; sostenitore.

**maintenance** *n.* mantenimento; sostentamento; difesa; alimenti *m.pl.*; (industr.) manutenzione; — *staff*, personale addetto alla manutenzione.
**main-top** *n.* (naut.) gabbia di maestra. **-yard** *n.* (naut.) pennone di maestra.
**Mainz** *pr.n.* (geog.) Magonza.
**maiso(n)nette** *n.* appartamento a due piani, casetta.
**maize** *n.* mais *m.*, granturco.
**majest-y** *n.* maestà; *His, Her Majesty*, Sua Maestà. **-ic(al)** *adj.* maestoso.
**majolica** *n.* maiolica; *attrib.* di maiolica.
**major** *adj.* più grande; maggiore; superiore; *the — part*, la parte maggiore; (mus.) maggiore *m.*; *n.* (leg.) maggiorenne *m., f.*; (mil.) maggiore *m.*
**Majorca** *pr.n.* (geog.) Maiorca.
**major-domo** *n.* maggiordomo. **-general** *n.* generale *m.* di divisione.
**majority** *n.* maggioranza; *absolute —*, maggioranza assoluta; *to win by a narrow —*, vincere di stretta misura; *to join the —*, raggiungere il numero dei più; (leg.) maggiore età; *to attain one's —*, diventare maggiorenne; (mil.) grado di maggiore.
**majuscule** *adj.* maiuscolo; *n.* lettera maiuscola.
**make** *n.* forma; fattura; struttura; fabbricazione; (industr.) marca; (fam.) *to be on the —*, essere intento a far soldi.
**make** *tr., intr.* fare, creare, fabbricare; rendere; *God made the world*, Dio creò il mondo; *wine is made from grapes*, il vino è fatto con l'uva; *to have something made*, far fare qualcosa; *to — someone do something*, costringere qualcuno a far qualcosa, far fare qualcosa da qualcuno; *to — someone laugh*, far ridere qualcuno; *to — away with*, abolire, disfarsi di, ammazzare; *to — away with oneself*, suicidarsi; *to — a bed*, rifare un letto; *to — believe*, far credere, dare a intendere; *to — the best of*, trarre il massimo vantaggio da; *to — the best of a bad bargain*, fare buon viso a cattiva sorte; *to — bold*, permettersi, prendere la libertà di; *to — both ends meet*, sbarcare il lunario; *to — a clean breast*, confessare, vuotare il sacco; *to — clear*, chiarire, rendere chiaro; *to — do with*, arrangiarsi con, aiutarsi con; *to — faces*, far smorfie; *to — fast*, legare; *to — a fool of*, beffarsi di; *to — for*, dirigersi verso; *to — free with*, prendersi libertà con, abusare di; *to — friends with*, stringere amicizia con; *to — a fuss*, far storie, suscitare un pandemonio; *to — good*, *tr.* mantenere, risarcire; *intr.* far carriera, riuscire; *to — a habit of doing*, abituarsi a fare, prendere l'abitudine di fare; *to — haste*, affrettarsi; *to — hay*, raccogliere fieno; (fig.) *to — hay while the sun shines*, battere il ferro mentre è caldo; *to — hay of*, creare confusione in; *to — something hot*, riscaldare qualcosa; *to — it hot for someone*, rendere la vita difficile a qualcuno; *to — inquiries*, informarsi, assumere informazioni; *to — little of*, dare poca importanza a; *to — a living*, guadagnarsi la vita; *to — love to*, corteggiare, amoreggiare con; *to — merry*, far festa, far baldoria; *to — the most of*, profittare al massimo di; *to — much of*, dare molta importanza a; *to — much of someone*, festeggiare qualcuno; trattare qualcuno con ogni riguardo; *to — a noise*, far chiasso; *to — off*, svignarsela, andarsene in fretta; *to — off with*, andarsene con, rubare; *to — oneself understood*, farsi capire; *to — out*, distinguere, scorgere, redigere, capire, pretendere; (fam.) riuscire; *to — over*, trasferire; *to — ready*, preparare, (typ.) fare l'avviamento; *to — short work of*, sbrigare rapidamente; *to — sure*, assicurare, assicurarsi; *to — towards*, puntare verso; *to — trouble*, dare noia, far storie; *to — up*, inventare, trovare, comporre; *to — up one's face*, truccarsi; *to — up for*, compensare; *to — up for lost time*, riguadagnare, ricuperare il tempo perduto; *to — up one's mind*, decidersi; *to — up to someone*, adulare qualcuno; *to — water*, orinare, (naut.) imbarcare acqua; *to — way*, far largo, far ala; *to — one's way*, andare, recarsi; *to — way for*, cedere il posto a.
**make-believe** *n.* finzione; invenzione; *he lives in a world of —*, vive in un mondo di sogni; *adj.* finto di sogno, illusorio; *tr.* fingere, fare finta di; *intr.* illudersi, pascersi di sogni.
**maker** *n.* fattore; creatore; artefice *m.*; (comm.) fabbricante *m.*; costruttore.
**makeshift** *adj.* improvvisato, di fortuna; *n.* espediente *m.*; ripiego.
**make-up** composizione; confezione; fattura; formazione; (theatr.) truccatura; (typ.) impaginazione.
**makeweight** *n.* complemento di peso; aggiunta; riempitivo; (fam.) contentino; *as a —*, per far numero.
**making** *n.* fattura; lavorazione; confezione; (fig.) *military service was the — of him*, il servizio militare ha contribuito alla formazione del suo carattere; (fam.) *this is none of my —*, non l'ho mica fatto io; *to have the -s of a poet*, aver la stoffa di un poeta.
**malachite** *n.* (miner.) malachite *f.*
**maladjust-ed** *adj.* disadatto; mal assortito; incapace di adattarsi. **-ment** *n.* inadattabilità; incapacità di adattamento; regolazione difettosa.
**maladministration** *n.* malgoverno; cattiva amministrazione.
**maladroit** *adj.* malaccorto; maldestro; goffo. **-ness** *n.* malaccortezza; goffaggine *f.*
**malady** *n.* malattia.
**malaise** *n.* malessere *m.*
**Malapropism** *n.* sproposito; papera; strafalcione *m.*; (fam.) perla.
**malapropos** *adv.* a sproposito; inopportunamente.
**malaria** *n.* malaria. **-l** *adj.* malarico.
**Malaya, Malaysia** *pr.n.* Malesia. **-n** *adj., n.* malese *m., f.*
**malcontent** *adj., n.* malcontento; persona malcontenta.
**male** *adj.* maschio, maschile, di sesso maschile; *— child*, maschietto; *— nurse*, infermiere *m.*; (mech.) maschio; *n.* maschio.
**maledict-ion** *n.* maledizione. **-ory** *adj.* maldicente.
**malefact-ion** *n.* misfatto. **-or** *n.* malfattore.
**malefic** *adj.* malefico, maligno. **-ence** *n.* malvagità. **-ent** *adj.* malvagio, malefico, maligno.
**malevol-ence** *n.* malevolenza; malanimo. **-ent** *adj.* malevolo; maligno.
**malfeasance** *n.* condotta scorretta; misfatto.
**malform-ation** *n.* conformazione difettosa; deformità. **-ed** *adj.* malformato; deforme.
**malice** *n.* malizia; malignità; astio; rancore *m.*; *out of —*, maliziosamente; *to bear — towards*, covare astio per; *— aforethought*, premeditazione maliziosa.
**malicious** *adj.* malizioso, maligno, malevolo; (leg.) doloso; *— act*, dolo. **-ness** *n.* malignità; malanimo; cattiveria.
**malign, -ant** *adj.* maligno, malefico; nocivo; (med.) maligno; *tr.* diffamare; denigrare. **-ancy, -ity** *n.* malignità; malvagità; (med.) indole maligna.
**malinger** *intr.* fingersi ammalato, darsi malato; (fig.) sfuggire al dovere, scansare fatiche. **-er** *n.* finto malato; fiaccone *m.*; scansafatiche *m. indecl.*
**mall** *n.* viale *m.*; passeggiata.
**mallard** *n.* (orn.) anitra selvatica.
**malleab-le** *adj.* malleabile; (fig.) docile, mansueto. **-ility** *n.* malleabilità.
**mallet** maglio; martello di legno; mazzuolo.

**mallow** *n.* (bot.) malva; *marsh* —, alcea, altea.
**malmsey** *n.* malvasia.
**malnutrition** *n.* malnutrizione, denutrizione.
**malodorous** *adj.* puzzolente, maleolente.
**malpractice** *n.* malcostume *m.*; misfatto; pratica illecita.
**malt** *n.* malto, orzo tallito; — *liquor*, birra; *tr.* trasformare in malto, far germogliare.
**Malt-a** *pr.n.* (geog.) Malta. **-ese** *adj.*, *n.* maltese *m.*, *f.*; *-ese cross*, la croce di Malta.
**malthouse** *n.* malteria.
**Malthusian** *adj.*, *n.* maltusiano. **-ism** *n.* maltusianesimo.
**maltreat** *tr.* maltrattare, bistrattare; malmenare. **-ment** *n.* maltrattamento, bistrattamento.
**malversation** *n.* malversazione, amministrazione disonesta.
**mamma, mama** *n.* (fam.) mamma.
**mammal** *n.* (zool.) mammifero. **-ia** *n.pl.* mammiferi. **-ian** *adj.* mammifero.
**mammary** *adj.* (anat.) mammario, — *glands*, ghiandole *f.pl.* mammarie.
**Mammon** *pr.n.* Mammone; (fig.) mammona *m.*
**mammoth** *n.* mammut *m.*; *attrib.* enorme, mastodontico.
**man** *n.* uomo; *a — of letters*, un letterato; (when preceded by *adj.* often omitted in Italian): *an old* —, un vecchio, *a rich* —, un ricco; *a dead* —, un morto; l'uomo, gli uomini, l'umanità, il genere umano; *every* —, ognuno; *no* —, nessuno; *the — in the street*, l'uomo della strada, l'uomo qualunque; *-'s estate*, età virile, età maggiore; *as — to* —, da uomo a uomo; *they answered yes to a* —, tutti quanti risposero di sì; *pl. men*, gli uomini; *men say that*, si dice che, tutti dicono che; servo, domestico; operaio, lavoratore; (mil.) *officers, N.C.O.s and men*, ufficiali, sottufficiali e soldati; — *and wife*, marito e moglie; (fam.) *my young* —, il mio fidanzato; *old* —, vecchio mio, mio caro; *an Oxford* —, uno studente di Oxford, uno che ha studiato a Oxford.
**man** *tr.* munire di uomini; (mil.) presidiare; (naut.) equipaggiare (una nave); *to — the pumps*, far funzionare le pompe.
**manacle** *n.* manetta; *tr.* ammanettare; (fig.) trattenere.
**manage** *tr.* dirigere; amministrare; *to — a business*, dirigere un'impresa commerciale; maneggiare, manovrare; saper trattare; *intr.* (fam.) cavarsela, farcela; *I can — alone*, ce la faccio da solo; FOLLOW. BY INFIN.: riuscire (a), fare in modo (di); *I -d to find him*, sono riuscito a trovarlo; *to — without*, fare a meno di. **-able** *adj.* (of person) trattabile, docile; (of thing) maneggevole. **-ableness** *n.* (of person) trattabilità, docilità; (of thing) maneggiabilità.
**management** *n.* amministrazione; direzione; gestione; condotta; (collect.) direzione, i dirigenti; (of tools, horses) maneggio, governo; (fig.) abilità.
**manager** *n.* direttore; gerente *m.*; dirigente *m.*; *assistant* —, vicedirettore; *sales* —, direttore commerciale; *works* —, direttore di fabbrica; amministratore; (theatr.) impresario; (sport) direttore tecnico, accompagnatore; (fig.) *she's a good* —, è una brava massaia. **-ess** *n.* direttrice; (of shop, hotel) padrona. **-ial** *adj.* direttivo, di direttore. **-ship** *n.* direzione; amministrazione; gerenza.
**managing** *adj.* dirigente, che dirige; — *director*, consigliere delegato.
**man-at-arms** *n.* armigero; soldato. **-child** *n.* maschietto, ragazzo.
**manchu** *adj.*, *n.* manciù, mancese *m.*, *f.*
**Manchuria** *pr.n.* (geog.) Manciuria.
**manciple** *n.* economo.
**Mancunian** *adj.*, *n.* di Manchester.
**mandarin** *n.* (ling.) mandarino; (bot.) — *orange*, mandarino, arancia mandarina.
**mandat-e** *n.* (pol.; leg.) mandato; incarico; comando; ordine *m.*; *tr.* affidare ad un mandatario; *-d territory*, territorio sotto mandato. **-ory** *adj.* (pol.) mandatario; (leg.) ingiuntivo; *n.* mandatario.
**mandible** *n.* (anat.) mandibola.
**mandolin(e)** *n.* (mus.) mandolino. **-ist** *n.* (mus.) mandolinista *m.*, *f.*
**mandr-agora, -ake** *n.* (bot.) mandragora, mandragola.
**mandrel** *n.* mandrino; (metall.) anima metallica.
**mandrill** *n.* (zool.) mandrillo.
**manducat-e** *tr.* manducare, masticare. **-ion** *n.* manducazione, masticazione.
**mane** *n.* criniera.
**man-eater** *n.* antropofago; cannibale *m.*; mangiatore d'uomini. **-eating** *adj.* antropofago; *-eating shark*, pescecane *m.*
**manège** *n.* maneggio.
**manful** *adj.* virile; coraggioso; valoroso. **-ly** *adv.* da uomo; coraggiosamente, virilmente. **-ness** *n.* coraggio; valore *m.*; virilità.
**manganese** *n.* manganese *m.*
**mange** *n.* (vet.) rogna, scabbia.
**mangel-wurzel** *n.* barbabietola da foraggio.
**manger** *n.* mangiatoia, greppia; (eccl.) presepio.
**mangl-e** *n.* mangano; *tr.* manganare, passare al mangano; (fig.) sbranare, mutilare, lacerare; straziare, storpiare. **-ing** *n.* manganatura; cilindratura; *to do the -ing*, passare al mangano; (fig.) lacerazione, mutilazione; (fig.) storpiatura.
**mango** *n.* (bot.) mango.
**mangold** *n.* (bot.) bietola da foraggio.
**mangrove** *n.* (bot.) mangrovia.
**mangy** *adj.* rognoso, scabbioso.
**manhandle** *tr.* manovrare, muovere a mano; (fig.) maltrattare, mettere le mani addosso a.
**manhole** *n.* botola; bocca di accesso; — *cover*, tombino; (naut.) boccaportella.
**manhood** *n.* virilità; età virile; mascolinità; coraggio; umanità; *the — of a nation*, tutti gli uomini di una nazione.
**man-hour** *n.* (industr.) ora lavorativa.
**mania** *n.* (med.) mania; *persecution* —, mania di persecuzione; (fam.) entusiasmo esagerato; (for sport) tifo.
**maniac** *n.* maniaco; pazzo furioso, ossesso. **-al** *adj.* maniaco.
**manich-ee, -ean** *n.* (rel.) manicheo.
**manicur-e** *n.* manicure *f.*; cosmesi delle mani; *tr. to — someone's hands*, fare la manicure a qualcuno. **-ist** *n.* manicure *m.*, *f.*
**manifest** *adj.* manifesto; evidente; palese; chiaro; lampante; *n.* (comm.) manifesto di bordo, nota di carico; *tr.* manifestare; dimostrare; rivelare; *intr.* fare una manifestazione. **-ation** *n.* manifestazione; dimostrazione. **-o** *n.* proclama *m.*
**manifold** *adj.* molteplice; vario; diverso; numeroso; multiforme; — *writer*, poligrafo; — *book*, copialettere *m.*; *tr.* poligrafare, moltiplicare. **-ness** *n.* molteplicità; varietà.
**manikin** *n.* omino, ometto, omuncolo, nanerottolo; (model) manichino, fantoccio.
**Manilla** *pr.n.* (geog.) Manilla; *n.* manilla; — *hemp*, abacà.
**maniple** *n.* (Rom. antiq.) manipolo.
**manipulat-e** *tr.* manipolare; maneggiare; manovrare; (pejor.) falsificare. **-ion** *n.* manipolazione; lavorazione. **-or** *n.* manipolatore.
**mankind** *n.* il genere umano, l'umanità, gli uomini.
**manlike** *adj.* da uomo; virile; maschile; antropomorfo, antropoide.
**manl-y** *adj.* da uomo; virile; maschio; coraggioso. **-iness** *n.* coraggio virile; virilità; mascolinità.
**man-made** *adj.* (industr.) artificiale; manufatto; fabbricato.

**manna** *n.* manna.
**mannequin** *n.* manichino; indossatrice; — *parade*, sfilata di modelle.
**manner** *n.* maniera; guisa; modo; *in the Italian* —, all'italiana; *in what* —?, in che modo?; *in like* —, parimenti; *in a — of speaking*, per così dire; *as if to the — born*, come se non avesse fatto altro dalla nascita; *pl. good* -*s*, buone maniere; *bad* -*s*, cattive maniere; *to have no* -*s*, essere senza educazione; usanze *f.pl.*, abitudini *f.pl.*; contegno, atteggiamento; stile *m.*; *after the — of*, secondo lo stile di; *a — of one's own*, uno stile inconfondibile; *all — of people*, ogni sorta di gente. **-ed** *adj.* manierato; affettato; ricercato. **-ism** *n.* manierismo; affettazione; (fam.) abitudine *f.*; ticchio. **-ist** *n.* manierista, *m.*, *f.*; artista di maniera. **-less** *adj.* sgarbato; scortese; maleducato.
**mannerl-y** *adv.* garbato; cortese; educato. **-iness** *n.* cortesia; educazione; urbanità.
**mannish** *adj.* da uomo, maschile; poco femminile. **-ness** *n.* mascolinità, maschiezza.
**manoeuvrab-le** *adj.* manovrabile. **-ility** *n.* manovrabilità.
**manoeuvre** *n.* manovra; *intr.* far manovre; *tr.* far fare manovre; (fig.) manovrare, far in modo di, usare stratagemmi; *to — someone into doing something*, persuadere qualcuno con stratagemmi a fare qualcosa. **-r** *n.* stratega *m.*; (fig.) destreggiatore, intrigante *m.*
**man-of-war** *n.* nave da guerra.
**manor** *n.* maniero; casa signorile; castello; (hist.) feudo.
**manor-house** maniero, casa signorile.
**manorial** *adj.* feudale.
**manpower** *n.* manodopera effettiva; potenziale umano.
**mansard** *n.* (archit.) mansarda.
**manse** *n.* presbiterio.
**manservant** *n.* servitore, domestico.
**mansion** *n.* palazzo; grande casa, casa signorile; residenza.
**manslaughter** *n.* (leg.) omicidio colposo, omicidio preterintenzionale.
**mansuetude** *n.* mansuetudine *f.*
**mantel-piece** *n.* caminetto; frontale del caminetto. **-shelf** *n.* cappa del camino.
**mantilla** *n.* (cost.) mantiglia.
**mantis** *n.* (ent.) mantide *f.*; *praying* —, mantide religiosa, (pop.) pregadio.
**mantle** *n.* (cost.) manto; (for gas-lamp) reticella; *tr.* ammantare; velare; *intr.* coprirsi.
**mantlet** *n.* (cost.) mantellina; (mil. hist.) spaglione *m.*
**man-trap** *n.* trabocchetto, trappola.
**Mantua** *pr.n.* (geog.) Mantova. **-n** *adj.*, *n.* mantovano.
**manual** *adj.* manuale, fatto a mano; azionato a mano; — *labour*, lavoro manuale; *n.* manuale *m.*; libretto; guida; (mus.) tastiera, manuale; (mil.) — *exercise*, maneggio delle armi.
**manufactur-e** *n.* fabbricazione; manifattura; lavorazione; *tr.* fabbricare; confezionare; produrre; (fig.) *to — news*, fabbricare notizie. **-er** *n.* fabbricante *m.*; industriale *m.* **-ing** *adj.* manifatturiero; industriale; *-ing town*, città industriale; *n.* fabbricazione; manifattura; confezione.
**manum-ission** *n.* manomissione, emancipazione. **-it** *tr.* manomettere, emancipare, liberare.
**manure** *n.* concime *m.*; letame *m.*; ingrasso; *green* —, sovescio, appannume *m.*; *artificial* —, concime, fertilizzante *m.*; *tr.* concimare; ingrassare; fertilizzare.
**manure-heap** *n.* letamaio.
**manuring** *n.* concimazione; fertilizzazione.
**manuscript** *adj.* manoscritto; *n.* manoscritto; codice *m.*
**Manx** *adj.* dell'isola di Man; una razza di gatti che nascono senza coda. **-man** *n.* abitante *m.* dell'isola di Man.
**many** *pl. adj.* molti *m.*, molte *f.*; un gran numero di, più di uno; — *a*, più di uno; *ever so* —, *very* —, moltissimi; *how* —, quanti; *so* —, *a great* —, tanti; *as — again*, altrettanti; *as — . . . as*, tanti . . . quanti; *too* —, troppi; *prn.* molti; *how* —?, quanti?; *one too* —, uno di troppo; *n.* molti; *a great, a good* —, un gran numero, moltissimi; *the* —, la moltitudine, la folla. **-coloured** *adj.* multicolore, policromo. **-headed** *adj.* dalle molte teste. **-sided** *adj.* multilaterale, molteplice; complesso; (fig.) versatile. **-sidedness** *n.* complessità; diversità.
**map** *n.* carta geografica; mappa; pianta; — *of the world*, mappamondo; (fig.) *to put a place on the* —, far conoscere un luogo; *off the* —, remoto, sperduto; *tr.* fare una carta di, disegnare la carta di; *to — out a route*, tracciare un itinerario; *to — out a course of action*, tracciare un piano d'azione.
**maple(-tree)** *n.* (bot.) acero; — *syrup*, sciroppo di zucchero d'acero.
**map-maker** *n.* cartografo. **-making** *n.* cartografia. **-reading** *n.* interpretazione delle carte topografiche.
**mar** *tr.* guastare, rovinare; sfigurare, alterare; (fig.) *to make or — someone*, fare la fortuna di qualcuno o rovinarlo.
**marabou(t)** *n.* (orn.) marabù *m.*; (Moslem) marabutto.
**Marathon** *pr.n.* (geog.) Maratona; (sport) maratona.
**maraud** *tr.*, *intr.* predare, saccheggiare; far scorrerie. **-er** *n.* razziatore; predone *m.*; ladrone *m.* **-ing** *gerund* saccheggio; predamento; ladroneggio; *adj.* razziatore.
**marbl-e** *n.* marmo; — *industry*, industria marmorifera; — *quarry*, cava di marmo; *attrib.* di marmo, marmoreo; (fig.) *a heart of* —, un cuore di pietra; (glass ball) bilia, pallina; *pl.* bilie; *to play* -*s*, giuocare alle bilie; *tr.* (paperm., text.) marmorizzare, marezzare. **-ed** *part. adj.* marmorizzato, marezzato. **-ing** *n.* marmorizzazione, marezzatura.
**marble-edged** *adj.* (bookb.) con i margini marmorizzati. **-cutter, -mason** *n.* marmista *m.*
**March**[1] *pr.n.* marzo; *the seventh of* —, il sette marzo; *attrib.* marzolino.
**march**[2] *n.* frontiera; confine *m.*; marca, zona di confine; *pl. the Marches*, le Marche; *intr. to — with (upon)*, essere limitrofo di, confinare con.
**march**[3] *n.* (mus.) marcia; *funeral* —, marcia funebre; *wedding* —, marcia nuziale; (mil.) marcia, passo di marcia; *on the* —, in marcia; *a day's* —, una giornata di marcia; *route* —, marcia di addestramento; *forced* —, marcia forzata; (fig.) *the — of events*, lo svolgersi degli avvenimenti; *the — of progress*, il cammino del progresso; *the — of time*, il corso del tempo.
**march**[3] *tr.* far marciare; *intr.* marciare, mettersi in marcia; (mil.) *quick* —!, avanti marsch!; *to — past*, sfilare; *to — three abreast*, marciare a tre a tre; (fig.) camminare, avanzare; *to — away*, *tr.* allontanare a passo di marcia, *intr.* andarsene; *to — in*, *tr.* far entrare a passo di marcia, *intr.* entrare bruscamente; *to — off*, *tr.* condurre via, *intr.* partire bruscamente, allontanarsi; *to — out*, *tr.* far uscire a passo di marcia, *intr.* uscire bruscamente; *to — past*, (mil.) sfilare; *to — up*, avvicinarsi, avanzare.
**marching** *adj.* marciante, di marcia; (mil.) — *orders*, ordine di marcia; *to give someone his — orders*, licenziare qualcuno bruscamente.
**marchioness** *n.* marchesa.
**marchpane** *n.* See **marzipan.**
**march-past** *n.* sfilata.
**Marcus** *pr.n.* Marco.
**mare** *n.* cavalla, giumenta, puledra; *Shank's* —, il cavallo di San Francesco; (fig.) -*'s nest*, scoperta deludente.
**Margaret** *pr.n.* Margherita.

**margarine** *n.* margarina.
**margin** *n.* margine *m.*; bordo; orlo; (comm.) margine; (finan.) somma versata per coprire eventuali perdite. **-al** *adj.* marginale; *-al notes*, note in margine; (fig.) *-al case*, caso limite. **-alia** *n.pl.* note marginali.
**margrav-e** *n.* (hist.) margravio. **-ine** *n.* (hist.) margravia.
**Marguerite** *n.* Margherita.
**Maria** *pr.n.* Maria; (pop.) *black —*, furgone cellulare.
**Marian**[1] *pr.n.* Marianna.
**Marian**[2] *adj.* mariano, della Vergine.
**marigold** *n.* calendula, fiorrancio.
**marijuana** *n.* canapa indiana; marijuana.
**marina** *n.* lungomare *m.*; porticciuolo per panfili.
**marinade** *n.* (cul.) marinata; salsa di aceto; *tr.* (cul.) marinare.
**marine** *adj.* marino; marittimo; del mare; *— insurance*, assicurazione marittima; *— stores*, forniture per navi, rigatteria; *n.* marina; *mercantile —*, marina mercantile; soldato di fanteria marina; *pl.* fanteria marina; (fam.) *tell that to the -s!*, vallo a raccontare a un altro!
**mariner** *n.* marinaio; *master —*, capitano di lungo corso, capitano di nave mercantile.
**mariolatry** *n.* (theol.) mariolatria.
**marionette** *n.* marionetta.
**marital** *adj.* maritale, coniugale.
**maritime** *adj.* marittimo, marino, di mare.
**marjoram** *n.* (bot.) maggiorana, amaraco; *wild —*, acciughero.
**Mark**[1] *pr.n.* Marco.
**mark**[2] *n.* (currency) marco.
**mark**[3] *n.* segno; traccia; impronta; marchio; *punctuation —*, segno di interpunzione; croce *f.*; *manufacturer's —*, marchio di fabbrica; (schol.) voto, votazione; *dirty -s*, segnacci *m.pl.*; *-s of suffering*, segni della sofferenza; *to leave a —*, lasciare traccia di sè; *to make one's —*, farsi un nome; *wide of the —*, lontano dal bersaglio; (fam.) *I don't feel up to the —*, mi sento giù di corda; *saving the —*, con licenza parlando; *to be first off the —*, partire per primo; *to be quick off the —*, cogliere la palla al balzo; *to hit the —*, dare nel segno, far centro.
**mark**[3] *tr.* segnare; contrassegnare; marcare; indicare; (schol.) dare i voti a; *to — the rhythm*, battere il tempo; *to — time*, segnare il passo; (fig.) *to — one's approval*, manifestare la propria approvazione; notare, osservare, badare a, fare attenzione a; *— my words!*, bada alle mie parole!, dà retta a me!, te lo dico io!; *to — down*, prendere nota di; *to — down the price*, ridurre il prezzo; *to — off*, delimitare, (fig.) distinguere; *to — out*, tracciare; *to — up the score*, segnare i punti; *to — up the price*, aumentare il prezzo.
**marked** *adj.* segnato; contrassegnato; notevole, accentuato, spiccato; *a — improvement*, un miglioramento notevole; *to become more —*, accentuarsi; *a — foreign accent*, uno spiccato accento straniero; (fig.) *a — man*, un uomo noto, un uomo ricercato dalla polizia. **-ly** *adv.* segnatamente; marcatamente; notevolmente. **-ness** *n.* carattere marcato.
**marker** *n.* (sport) marcatore; segnatore; segnalibro; (mil.) capofila *m. indecl.*
**market** *n.* mercato; *— day*, giorno di mercato, *— square*, piazza del mercato; (comm.) mercato, compravendita; *home —*, mercato interno; *overseas —*, mercato d'oltremare; *black —*, borsa nera; *open —*, mercato libero; *to be in the —*, essere sul mercato per fare acquisti, essere in vendita; *to put on the —*, mettere in vendita, lanciare; *— price*, prezzo corrente; *to be good — value*, essere un buon affare; *tr.* mettere in vendita, vendere al mercato; *intr.* fare le spese, fare acquisti. **-able** *adj.* vendibile; smerciabile.
**market-garden** *n.* orto. **-er** *n.* ortolano.
**marketing** *n.* compravendita; *to go —*, andare a fare le spese; (of new product) lancio, messa in vendita; tecnica della vendita; *— board*, ufficio controllo vendite.
**market-place** *n.* piazza del mercato.
**marking** *adj.* che segna; *n.* segnatura, marcatura; *— ink*, inchiostro indelebile; *pl.* segni caratteristici, (on animals) strisce, macchie *f.pl.*
**marksman** *n.* tiratore scelto, buon tiratore. **-ship** *n.* abilità nel tiro, precisione di tiro.
**marl** *n.* (geol.) marna, marga; *tr.* (agric.) marnare, concimare con marna.
**marline** *n.* (naut.) merlino; *— spike*, caviglia da impiombare.
**marmalade** *n.* (cul.) marmellata d'arance; *lemon —*, marmellata di limoni.
**marmoreal, marmorean** *adj.* marmoreo.
**marmoset** *n.* (zool.) apale *f.*, uistiti *f.*
**marmot** *n.* (zool.) marmotta.
**Marne** *pr.n.* (geog.) Marna.
**maroon**[1] *adj.*, *n.* (colour) marrone rossastro.
**maroon**[2] *tr.* abbandonare in luogo deserto; (fam.) *to be -ed by floods*, essere circondato dalle acque di un'inondazione.
**maroon**[3] *n.* specie di fuoco d'artifizio di tipo razzo.
**marquee** *n.* grande tenda; padiglione *m.*
**marquess, marquis** *n.* marchese *m.*
**marquetry** *n.* intarsio, intarsiatura.
**marquisate** *n.* marchesato.
**marriage** *n.* matrimonio, nozze *f.pl.*; *to give in —*, dare in moglie; *to take in —*, prendere in moglie; *— service*, cerimonia nuziale; (fig.) unione; fusione; connubio. **-able** *adj.* nubile, da marito, maritabile.
**marriage-licence** *n.* dispensa di matrimonio. **-lines** *n.* certificato di matrimonio.
**married** *adj.* ammogliato, sposato; coniugato; sposata, maritata, coniugata; *to get —*, sposarsi; *a — couple*, una coppia di coniugi; coniugale, matrimoniale.
**marrow** *n.* (anat.) midollo; (hortic.) zucca. **-bone** *n.* osso con midollo, ossobuco.
**marry** *tr.* sposare; (of woman) maritare, accasare; (of man) ammogliare; *to get married*, sposarsi; *to — money*, fare un buon matrimonio; unire in matrimonio; *intr.* sposarsi; (of man) ammogliarsi; (of woman) maritarsi; *to — again*, risposarsi, ricollocarsi, passare a seconde nozze; *to — into a family*, imparentarsi con una famiglia.
**Mars** *pr.n.* (myth.; astron.) Marte.
**marseillaise** *n.* (mus.) marsigliese *f.*
**Marseilles** *pr.n.* (geog.) Marsiglia.
**marsh** *n.* palude *f.*; acquitrino; vallo; *the Pontine Marshes*, le paludi pontine, l'agro pontino.
**marshal**[1] *n.* (hist.) maresciallo; *Earl Marshal*, gran maresciallo.
**marshal**[2] *tr.* ordinare, disporre in ordine; (mil.) schierare; (fig.) condurre cerimoniosamente; *intr.* (mil.) schierarsi. **-ling** *n.* ordinamento; (mil.) schieramento. **-ling-yard** *n.* (rlwy.) stazione di smistamento.
**marsh-fever** *n.* malaria; paludismo. **-gas** *n.* metano.
**marshland** *n.* terreno paludoso.
**marsh-mallow** *n.* (bot.) alcea, altea, bismalva. **-marigold** *n.* (bot.) calta palustre.
**marshy** *adj.* palustre, paludoso, acquitrinoso.
**marsupial** *adj.*, *n.* marsupiale *m.*
**mart** *n.* fiera; emporio; sala di vendita all'asta.
**marten** *n.* (zool.) martora.
**Martha** *pr.n.* Marta.
**martial** *adj.* marziale, militare, guerresco; *— law*, legge *f.*

marziale, stato di assedio. **-ly** *adv.* in modo marziale.
**Martian** *adj.*, *n.* marziano.
**Martin**[1] *pr.n.* Martino.
**martin**[2] *n.* (orn.) rondicchio.
**martinet** *n.* (mil.) ufficiale rigoroso, (fam.) caporale *m.*; *to be a —*, comandare a bacchetta.
**martingale** *n.* martingala; (naut.) controstraglio.
**Martinique** *pr.n.* (geog.) Martinica.
**Martinmas** *pr.n.* il San Martino, la festa di San Martino.
**martlet** *n.* (orn.) rondone *m.*; (herald.) merlotto.
**martyr** *n.* martire *m.*, *f.*; (fig.) vittima; *to make a — of oneself*, fare il martire, atteggiarsi a martire; *to be a — to rheumatism*, essere vittima del reumatismo; *tr.* martirizzare, martoriare, condannare al martirio. **-dom** *n.* martirio. **-ize** *tr.* martirizzare, martoriare; tormentare. **-ology** *n.* martirologio.
**marvel** *n.* meraviglia; prodigio; *it is a — to me that ...*, mi stupisce che ...; *intr.* meravigliarsi; stupirsi; *to — at*, stupirsi di; ammirare. **-lous** *adj.* meraviglioso; mirabile; stupendo; prodigioso.
**marx-ism** *n.* marxismo. **-ist, -ian** *adj.*, *n.* marxista *m.*, *f.*
**Mary** *pr.n.* Maria.
**marzipan** *n.* (cul.) marzapane *m.*
**mascot** *n.* mascotte *f.*, portafortuna *m.*, *f.*, talismano.
**masculin-e** *adj.* maschile, mascolino; (gramm.) maschile; (fig.) maschio, virile. **-eness, -ity** *n.* mascolinità; maschiezza; virilità.
**mash** *n.* beverone *m.*, pastone *m.*; (cul.) purè *m.*, passata; (fig.) *to reduce to a —*, ridurre in polpa; *tr.* pestare; schiacciare; ridurre in polpa; (cul.) *to — potatoes*, fare un purè di patate. **-ed** *adj.* pestato; schiacciato; (cul.) *-ed potatoes*, purè di patate.
**mashie, mashy** *n.* (golf) mazza.
**mask** *n.* maschera (also fig.); *to throw off the —*, gettare la maschera; *tr.* mascherare; (fig.) celare, nascondere; *to — one's face*, mascherarsi. **-ed** *adj.* mascherato; (fig.) dissimulato; *-ed ball*, ballo in maschera.
**masoch-ism** *n.* masochismo. **-ist** *n.* masochista *m.*, *f.*
**mason** *n.* muratore; *master —*, capomastro; (freemason) massone *m.* **-ic** *adj.* massonico, della massoneria. **-ry** *n.* costruzione in muratura.
**masque** *n.* spettacolo allegorico.
**masquerade** *n.* mascherata; (fig.) montatura; *intr.* mascherarsi; travestirsi; presentarsi sotto mentite spoglie; *to — as*, farsi passare per. **-r** *n.* maschera; persona che si fa passare per un'altra.
**mass**[1] *n.* massa; ammasso; accumulazione; mole *f.*; quantità grande, gran numero; *pl. the -es*, il popolo, le masse; (fam.) *-es of*, un mucchio di; *attrib.* in massa; *a — attack*, un attacco in massa; *tr.* ammassare; accumulare; *intr.* ammassarsi; radunarsi.
**mass**[2] *n.* (eccl.) messa; *low —*, messa letta; *high —*, messa solenne; *sung —*, messa cantata; *— on behalf of*, messa in suffragio di; *requiem —*, messa per i defunti; *to go to —*, andare alla messa; *to hear —*, sentire la messa.
**massacre** *n.* massacro; strage *f.*; eccidio; *tr.* massacrare; trucidare; far strage di.
**massage** *n.* massaggio; *tr.* massaggiare.
**mass-box** *n.* messale *m.*
**mass-eur** *n.* massaggiatore. **-euse** *n.* massaggiatrice.
**massif** *n.* (geol.) massiccio.
**massive** *adj.* massiccio; compatto; solido; forte. **-ness** *n.* compattezza; solidità.
**mass-meeting** *n.* adunata popolare; comizio popolare. **-produced** *adj.* prodotto in serie. **-production** *n.* (industr.) produzione in serie.
**mast**[1] *n.* (naut.) albero; *to sail before the —*, fare il marinaio semplice, navigare; *jury —*, albero di fortuna; *pl.* alberatura; (radio) antenna; *tr.* (naut.) alberare.
**mast**[2] *n.* (bot.) ghianda, bacca.
**master** *n.* padrone *m.*; signore *m.*; signorino; padroncino; maestro; (university) *— of arts*, laureato, professore; (naut.) capitano; *attrib.* maestro; *tr.* aver la meglio su; vincere; sopprafare; dominare; (fig.) *to — a language*, conoscere a perfezione una lingua, impadronirsi di una lingua. **-ful** *adj.* imperioso; autoritario; prepotente; abile, magistrale.
**master-key** *n.* chiave maestra, passapertutto *m.*
**masterly** *adj.* magistrale, da maestro, abilissimo; *in a — manner*, magistralmente, con l'abilità di un maestro.
**masterpiece** *n.* capolavoro.
**master-singer** *n.* maestro cantore.**-stroke** *n.* colpo magistrale.
**mastery** *n.* padronanza; conoscenza; profonda; maestria; supremazia; signoria; dominio.
**mastic** *n.* (bot.) lentischio; (gum) mastice *m.*
**masticat-e** *tr.* masticare; (industr.) plastificare. **-ion** *n.* masticazione.
**mastiff** *n.* mastino, alano.
**mastitis** *n.* (med.) mastite *f.*
**mastodon** *n.* (zool.) mastodonte *m.* **-tic** *adj.* mastodontico.
**mastoid** *adj.* (med.) mastoideo; *n.* mastoide *f.*
**masturbat-e** *intr.* masturbarsi. **-ion** *n.* masturbazione.
**mat**[1] *adj.* appannato, opaco, matto, non brunito; *— paper*, carta patinata opaca; *tr.* rendere opaco, smerigliare.
**mat**[2] stuoia, stoino; zerbino; sottopiatto, sottovaso; (naut.) paglietto; (fam.) *to put someone on the —*, lavare la testa a qualcuno; *tr.* coprire di stuoie; intrecciare; *intr.* appiccicarsi.
**matador** *n.* matador *m.*
**match**[1] *n.* uguale *m.*; pari *m.*; simile *m.*; riscontro; *to be a good —*, andare bene insieme; *to be a — for*, essere uguale a, essere capace di competere con; *to be more than a — for*, essere superiore a; *to be no — for*, essere inferiore a, non poter competere con; *to meet one's —*, incontrare un degno avversario, trovar pane per i propri denti; matrimonio, partito; *to make a good —*, fare un buon matrimonio; *to make a — of it*, sposarsi; gara, partita, incontro; *return —*, partita di ritorno.
**match**[1] *tr.* uguagliare, pareggiare; armonizzare, assortire, uniformare; opporre; *to — oneself against*, misurarsi con; *to — one person against another*, opporre una persona a un'altra; *evenly -ed*, pressochè uguali di forza; (mech.) accoppiare, adattare; *intr.* armonizzare, accompagnarsi, andare bene insieme, corrispondere.
**match**[2] *n.* fiammifero; *safety —*, svedese *m.*; *wax —*, cerino; *sulphur —*, zolfanello; *a box of -es*, una scatola di fiammiferi (*cf.* **matchbox**); *a book of -es*, una bustina di fiammiferi; (fuse) miccia.
**matchable** *adj.* uguagliabile; accompagnabile; accoppiabile.
**matchboard(ing)** (carpen.) perlina.
**matchbox** *n.* scatola da fiammiferi.
**matchless** *adj.* impareggiabile; senza pari; incomparabile. **-ness** *n.* incomparabilità, impareggiabilità.
**matchlock** *n.* fucile a miccia.
**match-maker** *n.* (fam.) combinatore *m.*, combinatrice *f.* di matrimoni.
**matchwood** *n.* schegge di legno; (fig.) *to make — of*, fare a pezzi, frantumare.
**mate**[1] *n.* compagno *m.*, compagna *f.*; aiuto; assistente *m.*, *f.*; consorte *m.*, *f.*; (pop.) amico, capo; (naut.) secondo, ufficiale in seconda; *tr.* accoppiare; appaiare; unire; *intr.* (of animal) accoppiarsi; (joc.) sposarsi.
**mate**[2] *n.* (chess) scacco matto; *tr.* fare scacco matto a.

**mater** *n.* (fam.) mamma.
**material** *adj.* materiale, sostanziale; importante; essenziale; grossolano; *n.* materia; sostanza; materiale *m.*; *raw -s*, materie prime; stoffa, tessuto; *pl.* oggetti; roba. **-ism** *n.* materialismo. **-ist** *n.* materialista *m.*, *f.* **-istic** *adj.* materialistico. **-ity** *n.* materialità.
**materializ-e** *tr.* materializzare; *intr.* materializzarsi; avverarsi; prendere corpo; realizzarsi. **-ation** *n.* materializzazione; realizzazione.
**materially** *adv.* materialmente; fisicamente; essenzialmente.
**maternal** *adj.* materno.
**maternity** *n.* maternità; *— centre*, consultorio per gestanti; *— hospital*, maternità, clinica ostetricia; *— ward*, reparto ostetrico.
**matey** *adj.* (pop.) amico, amichevole; intimo.
**mathematic-s** *n.* matematica. **-al** *adj.* matematico, di matematica. **-ian** *n.* matematico.
**Matilda** *pr.n.* Matilde.
**matinée** *n.* (theatr.) mattinata; rappresentazione diurna.
**matins** *n. pl.* (eccl.) mattutino.
**matriarch** *n.* matrona; donna che predomina in una famiglia. **-al** *adj.* matriarcale. **-y** *n.* matriarcato.
**matricide** *n.* (crime) matricidio; (person) matricida *m.*, *f.*
**matriculat-e** *intr.* immatricolarsi; iscriversi (all'università); superare l'esame di ammissione; conseguire la licenza liceale. **-ion** *n.* immatricolazione; iscrizione (all università); (exam.) licenza liceale.
**matrimon-y** *n.* matrimonio. **-ial** *adj.* matrimoniale, coniugale.
**matrix** *n.* matrice *f.*; stampo; forma; (anat.) utero.
**matron** *n.* matrona; madre di famiglia; signora anziana; direttrice, capoinfermiera; (schol.) governante *f.* **-al, -ly** *adj.* da matrona, matronale; di età matura. **-hood** *n.* matronato.
**matt(e)** *adj.* See **mat**[1].
**matted** *part.* of **mat**[2], *q.v.* *— hair*, capelli appiccicati.
**matter** *n.* materia; sostanza; *vegetable —*, materia vegetale; (fig.) contenuto; argomento; materia; (med.) pus *m.*, materia; *printed —*, stampati *m.pl.*, stampe *f.pl.*; (fam.) cosa, faccenda, affare *m.*, questione; *a serious —, no laughing —*, una faccenda seria; *a — of course*, una faccenda di ordinaria amministrazione; *a — of money*, una questione di denaro; *as a — of fact*, in realtà, fatto sta che; *for that —*, per quanto riguarda ciò; *in the — of*, a proposito di; *to attend to, to look into a —*, occuparsi di una cosa; *to take -s easy*, prendere le cose alla leggera; *not to mince -s*, per parlare chiaro; *what's the — with you?*, che cosa hai?; *there's nothing the — with me*, non ho nulla, sto benissimo; *no — what*, non importa che cosa; *no — how*, non importa come, comunque; *no — where*, non importa dove, dovunque.
**matter** *intr.* importare, contare, premere; *what does it —?*, che importa?; *it doesn't —*, non importa, non fa niente; (med.) suppurare.
**Matterhorn** *pr.n.* (geog.) Cervino.
**matter-of-fact** *adj.* positivo, pratico.
**Matthew** *pr.n.* Matteo.
**Matthias** *pr.n.* Mattia *m.*
**matting** *n.* stuoia; materiale per stuoie.
**mattock** *n.* zappa; piccone *m.*
**mattress** *n.* materasso; *straw —*, paglericcio. **-maker** *n.* materassaio.
**matur-e** *adj.* maturo; (comm.) scaduto; *tr.*, *intr.* maturare; (comm.) scadere. **-ation** *n.* maturazione; sviluppo. **-ity** *n.* maturità; *years of -ity*, età matura; *to come to -ity* maturare; (comm.) scadenza.
**matutinal** *adj.* mattutino, mattinale.
**maudlin** *adj.* piagnucoloso; querulo; sdolcinato; scioccamente sentimentale.
**maul** *tr.* malmenare, maltrattare; battere; *to be -ed by a tiger*, essere ferito da un tigre; (fig.) bistrattare; (fam.) accarezzare goffamente.
**maulstick** *n.* See **mahlstick.**
**maunder** *intr.* *to — (along)*, vagare senza meta, andare a zonzo; *to — (on)*, parlare a vanvera, divagare.
**Maundy** *pr.n.* *— Thursday*, giovedì santo.
**Maurice** *pr.n.* Maurizio.
**Mauritius** *pr.n.* (geog.) Maurizio.
**mausoleum** *n.* mausoleo.
**mauve** *adj.*, *n.* malva.
**mavis** *n.* (poet.) tordo.
**maw** *n.* (of bird) gozzo; (of animal) stomaco; (fam.) bocca, mascella.
**mawkish** *adj.* sdolcinato, lezioso, insipido. **-ness** *n.* sdolcinatezza, leziosità, insipidezza.
**maxill-a** *n.* (anat.) mascella. **-ary** *adj.* mascellare.
**maxim** *n.* massima; sentenza; (fig.) norma; principio.
**maximal** *adj.* massimo, del massimo valore.
**Maximilian** *pr.n.* Massimiliano.
**maximum** *adj.*, *n.* massimo.
**May**[1] *pr.n.* maggio; *— Day*, il primo maggio, Festa del Lavoro; *the seventh of —*, il sette maggio; (fig.) primavera; (bot.) biancospino.
**May**[2] *pr.n.* Maria.
**may**[3] *aux.* *— I smoke?*, posso fumare?, permette ch'io fumiq.; *you — go*, potete andare; *he — come when he likes*, può venire quando vuole; *if I — say so*, se mi è concesso dirlo; *it — be that*, può darsi che, probabilmente; *it might be that*, potrebbe darsi che; *it — rain*, può darsi che piova, forse pioverà; *you — have read this book*, forse avrai letto questo libro; *it — be so*, può darsi; *you might have told me*, avresti potuto dirmelo; *that's as — be*, secondo; *be that as it —*, avvenga quello che avvenga, comunque; *we might as well go*, tanto varrebbe andare; *he recognized me as well he might*, mi riconobbe e non c'è meravigliarsi; *I will write so that you — know where I am*, scriverò affinchè tu possa sapere dove mi trovo; *— you be happy!*, che tu possa essere felice!
**maybe** *adv.* forse; può darsi; probabilmente; magari.
**Mayence** *pr.n.* (geog.) Magonza.
**may-flower** *n.* (bot.) biancospino. **-fly** *n.* (ent.) effimera.
**mayhem** *n.* (leg.) mutilazione, lesione.
**mayonnaise** *n.* (cul.) salsa maionese.
**mayor** *n.* sindaco; (hist.) podestà *m.* **-al** *adj.* del sindaco. **-alty** *n.* sindacato. **-ess** *n.* moglie del sindaco.
**maypole** *n.* albero di maggio.
**may-tree** *n.* (bot.) biancospino.
**maze** *n.* labirinto, dedalo; (fam.) perplessità.
**mazurka** *n.* mazurca.
**me** *pers. prn.* mi; (after prep. or followed by another prn.): me; *give — the book*, dammi il libro; *give it to —*, dammelo; *come with —*, vieni con me; (fam.) *dear —!*, caspita!; *ah —!*, povero me!; *it's —*, sono io.
**mead**[1] *n.* idromele *m.*
**mead**[2] *n.* (poet.) *cf.* **meadow.**
**meadow** *n.* prato, prateria, pascolo.
**meadow-grass** *n.* (bot.) erba maggenga. **-saffron** *n.* (bot.) colchico.
**meadowsheet** *n.* (bot.) regina dei prati.
**meagre** *adj.* magro; scarno; (fig.) scarso; frugale. **-ness** *n.* magrezza; scarsità; frugalità.
**meal**[1] *n.* (agric.) farina; *Indian —*, farina di mais.
**meal**[2] *n.* pasto; *a square —*, un pasto sostanzioso; *to make a — of*, cibarsi di.
**mealie** *n.* mais *m.*, granturco.
**meal-time** *n.* ora del pasto, ora di mangiare.
**meal-tub** *n.* madia.

**meal-y** *adj.* farinoso, cosparso di farina. **-iness** *n.* farinosità.

**mealy-mouthed** *adj.* mellifluo, insincero.

**mean**[1] *adj.* gretto, meschino, spilorcio, avaro, tirchio; basso, mediocre; *of — birth,* di bassi natali; *no — scholar,* uno studioso di valore; *no — city,* una città grandissima; squallido, vile; invidioso; di cattivo umore.

**mean**[2] *adj.* medio, intermedio; *Greenwich — time,* ora media di Greenwich.

**mean**[3] *n.* mezzo; punto intermedio; media; *the golden —* la sezione aurea, (fig.) l'ideale *m.*; *pl.* mezzi; *-s of communication,* mezzi di comunicazione; *to find the -s of doing something,* trovare i mezzi per fare qualcosa; *by -s of,* per mezzo di; *by all -s,* ma certo! faccia pure!; *by no -s,* niente affatto; *by some -s or other,* in qualche modo; *by fair -s or foul,* con le buone o con le cattive; mezzi; risorse *f.pl.*; *a man of -s,* un benestante; *to live beyond one's -s,* spendere più di quanto si guadagna; *-s test,* accertamento del reddito per il rilascio di un certificato.

**mean**[4] *tr.* significare, voler dire, intendere; *what does this word —?,* che cosa significa questa parola?; *what I — is this,* ciò che voglio dire è questo; *what do you — to do,* che cosa intendi fare?; *it -s nothing,* non significa niente; *you don't — to say so!,* davvero!; *I — what I say,* lo dico sul serio; *I — to be obeyed,* voglio che mi si ubbidisca; *I did not — you,* non mi riferivo a te; *to — business,* fare sul serio; *to — mischief,* meditare un brutto tiro; destinare, dirigere; *I -t it for you,* l'ho destinato a te; *my remarks weren't -t for him,* le mie osservazioni non furono dirette a lui; *he was never -t to be a doctor,* non era nato per fare il medico.

**meander** *intr.* serpeggiare; vagare; (fig.) divagare; parlare a vanvera. **-ing** *adj.* serpeggiante; sinuoso, tortuoso; (fig.) vago, sconnesso.

**meaning** *adj.* significativo, espressivo; *a — look,* uno sguardo significativo; *n.* significato; senso; *what's the — of this?,* che cosa significa questo?; *if you understand my —,* se capisci la mia idea; *double —,* doppio senso. **-less** *n.* senza significato; senza motivo. **-ly** *adv.* in modo significativo; eloquentemente.

**meanness** *n.* meschinità; grettezza; squallore *m*

**meant** *p.def., part.* of **mean,** *q.v.*

**mean-time, -while** *adv.* intanto; *n. in the —,* nel frattempo.

**measle** *n.* (vet.) tenia.

**measl-es** *n.* morbillo; *German —,* rosolia. **-y** *adj.* morbilloso; (vet.) infetto da tenia; (pop.) meschino, miserabile.

**measurab-le** *adj.* misurabile; *within — distance of,* a due passi da. **-ility** *n.* misurabilità.

**measure** *n.* misura; *made to —,* fatto su misura; *in some —,* in parte; (fig.) provvedimento; *to take -s,* provvedere; *tr.* misurare; prendere le misure; (fam.) *to — one's length,* cadere lungo disteso; (fig.) valutare, stimare; *rfl.* misurarsi; *intr.* avere una certa misura, misurare. **-d** *adj.* misurato; moderato; cadenzato, ritmico; *-ed tread,* passo cadenzato. **-less** *adj.* smisurato; incommensurabile; sconfinato.

**measurement** *n.* misura; misurazione; *pl.* misure, dimensioni *f.pl.*; volume *m.*

**measuring** *n.* misurazione; (pharm.) dosaggio. **-glass** *n.* vetro graduato. **-rod** *n.* asta di misurazione, metro. **-tape** *n.* nastro metrico.

**meat** *n.* carne *f.*; *boiled —,* lesso; *roast —,* arrosto; *canned —,* carne in scatola; *chilled —,* carne congelata; *minced —,* carne trita; *— and drink,* cibo e bevanda; (fig.) sostanza; (provb.) *one man's — is another man's poison,* ciò che giova all'uno nuoce all'altro; (fam.) *strong —,* roba forte, roba spinta.

**meat-chopper** *n.* mannaia. **-eating** *adj.* carnivoro.

**meatless** *adj.* senza carne; *— days,* giorni di magro.

**meat-safe** *n.* moschaiuola; guardavivande *m. indecl.*

**meaty** *adj.* carnoso, polposo; (fig.) sostanzioso.

**Mecca** *pr.n.* (geog.) Mecca; (fig.) mecca, meta.

**mechanic** *n.* meccanico; tecnico. **-al** *adj.* meccanico; automatico; *-al transport,* trasporto motorizzato; (fig.) istintivo; meccanico. **-ian** *n.* meccanico. **-s** *n.* meccanica; meccanismo.

**mechanism** *n.* meccanismo; congegno; dispositivo; tecnica.

**mechaniz-e** *tr.* meccanizzare. **-ation** *n.* meccanizzazione.

**medal** *n.* medaglia; decorazione; (fig.) *the reverse of the —,* il rovescio della medaglia. **-lion** *n.* medaglione *m.* **-list** *n* medagliaio; medaglista *m., f.*; (sport) vincitore di una medaglia.

**meddle** *intr.* immischiarsi; impicciarsi, intromettersi; ingerirsi; interferire; (fam.) *don't — with my books!,* non toccare i miei libri! **-r** *n.* intrigante *m.*; ficcanaso. **-some** *adj.* intrigante, che s'impiccia dei fatti altrui; *-some person,* ficcanaso. **-someness** *n.* ingerenza; intromissione.

**Mede** *pr.n.* (hist.) abitante della Media; *like the laws of the -s and Persians,* una legge immutabile.

**medi(a)eval** *adj.* medioevale, del medioevo. **-ist** *n.* studioso del medioevo.

**medial** *adj.* medio, mediano; (anat.; ling.) mediale.

**mediat-e** *tr., intr.* far da intermediario; intercedere; interporsi; pacificare; conseguire con la mediazione. **-or** *n.* mediatore; intermediario; intercessore; paciere.

**medical** *adj.* medico, della medicina; *a — man,* un medico; *— attention,* cure mediche, assistenza medica; *to take — advice,* riccorrere al medico, farsi curare da un medico; (mil.) *— corps,* corpo sanitario; *to go before a — board,* passare la visita medica; *— jurisprudence,* medicina legale; *— officer,* ufficiale sanitario; *— school,* scuola di medicina; *— student,* studente in medicina. **-ly** *adv.* da medico; per mezzo di medicine; *-ly speaking,* parlando da medico; *to be -ly examined,* farsi visitare da un medico.

**medicament** *n.* medicamento, farmaco.

**medicaster** *n.* medicastro, guaritore.

**medicat-e** *tr.* medicare; curare. **-ion** *n.* medicazione; cura. **-ive** *adj.* medicamentoso; curativo.

**Medicean** *adj.* (hist.) mediceo.

**medicin-e** *n.* medicina, scienza medica; medicina, farmaco, rimedio; *to practise —,* esecitare la professione di medico; (fam.) *to take one's —,* ingoiare una pillola amara; *to give someone a taste of his own —,* rendere pan per focaccia. **-al** *adj.* medicinale.

**medicine-case** *n.* cassetta farmaceutica. **-glass** *n.* vetro graduato. **-man** *n.* stregone *m.*

**medico** *n.* (fam.) medico, dottore.

**medieval** *adj.* See **mediaeval.**

**mediocr-e** *adj.* mediocre. **-ity** *n.* mediocrità.

**meditat-e** *intr.* meditare; riflettere; *tr.* macchinare; progettare. **-ion** *n.* meditazione. **-ive** *adj.* meditabondo, meditativo; pensoso. **-iveness** *n.* inclinazione alla meditazione.

**Mediterranean** *adj.* mediterraneo; *n. — Sea,* Mediterraneo.

**medium** *adj.* medio; *n.* medio, mezzo; *the happy —,* il giusto mezzo; *natural —,* elemento naturale; *advertising —,* mezzo pubblicitario; *through the — of,* tramite, per mezzo di; (finan.) media; (art) veicolo; (spiritualism) medium *m.*; (biol.) brodo di coltura.

**mediumistic** *adj.* medianico.

**medium-sized** *adj.* di grandezza media.

**medlar** *n.* nespola; — *tree,* nespolo.
**medley** *n.* miscuglio; guazzabuglio; accozzaglia; miscellanea; zibaldone *m.*; (mus.) pasticcio; selezione.
**meed** *n.* ricompensa; premio; — *of praise,* tributo di elogio.
**meek** *adj.* mansueto; remissivo; rimesso; — *as a lamb,* mansueto come un agnello; (bibl.) umile. **-ness** *n.* mansuetudine *f.*; docilità; remissività.
**meerschaum** *n.* sepiolite *f.*; (pop.) schiuma di mare; — *pipe,* pipa di schiuma.
**meet**[1] *adj.* conveniente; idoneo; appropriato; *to be* —, convenire.
**meet**[2] *n.* (hunt.) raduno di cacciatori.
**meet**[3] *tr.* incontrare; imbattersi in; trovare; venire incontro a; fare la conoscenza di, conoscere; *I met him in the street,* lo incontrai per strada; *the other day I met a friend of mine,* l'altro giorno mi sono imbattuto in un mio amico; *he met us with a smile,* ci venne incontro con un sorriso; *I think we met each other in Venice,* mi pare che ci siamo conosciuti a Venezia; *I will — you at the cafe,* verrò a trovarti al caffè; — *me at the station,* vieni a prendermi alla stazione; *buses — all trains,* ci sono autobus in coincidenza con tutti i treni; (fig.) *to — someone's wishes,* venire incontro ai desideri di qualcuno; *to — someone halfway,* venire ad un compresso con qualcuno; *to — one's debts,* far fronte ai propri debiti; *his hand met hers,* la sua mano incontrò quella di lei; *to — the eye,* attirare l'attenzione; *to meet someone's eye,* incontrare lo sguardo di qualcuno; *to — the case,* essere adeguato al caso; *intr.* incontrarsi, trovarsi, conoscersi; riunirsi; (fam.) *to make both ends —,* sbarcare il lunario; *to — with,* incontrare, trovare, subire; *to — with a cool reception,* trovare un'accoglienza fredda; *he met with an accident,* gli è capitato un incidente.
**meeting** *n.* incontro; *at first —,* al primo incontro; incrocio; confluenza; raduno, adunanza, riunione, convegno; assemblea; seduta; (pol.) comizio; (of bills) pagamento; (sport) riunione.
**meeting-place** *n.* luogo di riunione, ritrovo. **-point** *n.* punto d'intersezione.
**megaceph-alic, -alous** *adj.* (med.) megalocefalo.
**mega-cycle** *n.* (radio) megaciclo. **-lith** *n.* (archaeol.) megalito. **-lithic** *adj.* (archaeol.) megalitico. **-lomania** *n.* megalomania. **-lomaniac** *n.* megalomane *m.* **-phone** *n.* megafono, portavoce *m.*, altoparlante *m.*
**megrim** *n.* emicrania; (fig.) capriccio; *pl.* depressione; cattivo umore.
**melanchol-ia** *n.* (med.) melanconia; depressione psichica. **-ic** *adj.* melanconico; triste. **-y** *adj.* melanconico; triste; *n.* melanconia; tristezza.
**Melchisedec, Melchizedec** *pr.n.* (bibl.) Melchisedec.
**mêlée** *n.* mischia; confusione.
**meliorat-e** *tr.* migliorare. **-ion** *n.* miglioramento.
**melliflu-ence** *n.* mellifluità. **-ent, -ous** *adj.* mellifluo.
**mellow** *adj.* maturo; (of wine) amabile; (of soil) ricco, fertile; (fig.) stagionato; (of light) morbido, pastoso; (of person) pacato; (fam.) allegro, un po' brillo; *tr.* far maturare; stagionare; *intr.* maturare; stagionarsi; (of colour) ammorbidirsi; (of person) addolcirsi, intenerirsi. **-ness** *n.* maturità; (fig.) morbidezza; dolcezza; tenerezza.
**melodious** *adj.* melodioso. **-ness** *n.* melodiosità.
**melodrama** *n.* dramma sensazionale a lieto fine; (fig.) melodramma *m.* **-tic** *adj.* melodrammatico; sensazionale.
**melody** *n.* melodia; aria.
**melon** *n.* melone *m.*; *water —,* anguria.
**melt** *tr.* sciogliere; fondere; (fig.) intenerire; commuovere; *to — down,* fondere per utilizzare il metallo; *intr.* sciogliersi; fondersi; dileguarsi; liquefarsi; (fig.) intenerirsi, commuoversi; *to — away,* sciogliersi completamente, (fig.) svanire, (of crowd) disperdersi; *n.* (metall.) fusione, colata di metallo fuso. **-er** *n.* fonditore.
**melting-point** *n.* punto di fusione. **-pot** *n.* crogiuolo.
**member** *n.* (anat.) membro; (of club, society) membro, socio, associato, aggregato; (of Parliament) deputato, (pop.) onorevole *m.*; (of town council) consigliere *m.*; (archit.) membro, elemento; (mech.) parte *f.*; pezzo. **-ship** *n.* *to apply for -ship of a club,* chiedere di essere ammesso come socio di un club; *-ship is limited to 300,* il numero dei soci non deve superare trecento; *-ship card,* tessera di associazione.
**membran-e** *n.* membrana. **-aceous** *adj.* membranaceo.
**memento** *n.* ricordo, memento.
**memoir** *n.* nota biografica; *pl.* ricordi *m.pl.*, memorie *f.pl.*
**memorable** *adj.* memorabile; indimenticabile.
**memorandum** *n.* appunto; nota; memorandum *m.*; promemoria. **-book** *n.* taccuino; agenda. **-pad, -tablet** *n.* blocchetto per appunti.
**memorial** *adj.* commemorativo; *n.* monumento; cippo; *war —,* monumento ai caduti; — *table,* targa commemorativa; (fig.) ricordo; memoriale *m.*; supplica. **-ist** *n.* memorialista *m.*
**memorize** *tr.* imparare a memoria, sapere a mente, ricordare.
**memory** *n.* memoria; *to have a good —,* avere buona memoria; *to have a bad —,* ricordare poco e male; *to commit to —,* imparare a memoria; *loss of —,* amnesia; *to lose one's —,* perdere la memoria; *to the best of my —,* per quanto mi ricordo; *it has slipped my —,* mi è sfuggito di mente; *within living —,* a memoria d'uomo; *to quote from —,* citare a memoria; ricordo, ricordanza, rimembranza; *in — of,* a ricordo di; *of blessed —,* di buona memoria; *to have pleasant memories of,* aver buoni ricordi di; *to live on one's memories,* vivere di ricordi; *to keep someone's — alive,* tenere vivo il ricordo di qualcuno.
**Memphis** *pr.n.* (geog.) Menfi *f.*
**men** *n.pl.* of **man**, *q.v.*
**menac-e** *n.* minaccia; (fam.) *a public —,* un pericolo pubblico; *tr.* minacciare; (fig.) mettere in pericolo. **-ing** *adj.* minaccioso; torvo.
**menagerie** *n.* serraglio.
**mend** *n.* rammendo; rattoppo; (fam.) *to be on the —,* star rimettendosi (di salute); *tr.* rammendare; accomodare; rattoppare; aggiustare; (fig.) correggere; *to — one's ways,* ravvedersi; correggersi; (provb.) *least said soonest -ed,* un bel tacer non fu mai scritto; *intr.* correggersi; migliorare, rimettersi; (of weather) rasserenarsi; (provb.) *it's never too late to —,* non è mai troppo tardi per correggersi.
**mendacious** *adj.* mendace, menzognero. **-ness, mendacity** *n.* tendenza a mentire, mendacia.
**mender** *n.* riparatore; rammendatore.
**mendicant** *adj.* mendicante; *n.* mendicante *m., f.*; accattone *m.*; pezzente *m., f.*
**mendic-ity, -ancy** *n.* mendicità; accattonaggio.
**mending** *n.* rammendo; rattoppamento; *invisible —,* rammendo invisibile; roba da rammendare.
**menfolk** *n.* gli uomini.
**menial** *adj.* servile; umile; *n.* servo; (pejor.) lacchè *m. indecl.*
**meningitis** *n.* (med.) meningite *f.*
**menopause** *n.* (med.) menopausa.
**menstru-al** *adj.* (med.) mestruale; (astron.) mensile. **-ate** *intr.* mestruare. **-ation** *n.* mestruazione.
**mensurab-le** *adj.* misurabile. **-ility** *n.* misurabilità.

**mensuration** *n.* misurazione.
**mental** *adj.* mentale; intellettuale; — *reservation*, riserva mentale; — *arithmetic*, calcolo mentale; — *deficient*, deficiente *m.*, *f.*; — *home*, clinica psichiatrica; — *hospital*, ospedale psichiatrico; — *patient*, malato di mente, alienato; (pop.) *to be* —, essere un po' tocco. **-ity** *n.* mentalità; intelligenza.
**mention** *n.* menzione; cenno; allusione; riferimento; *to make no — of*, non fare cenno di, passare sotto silenzio; (mil.) citazione; (schol.) *honourable* —, accessit *m.*
**mention** *tr.* accennare a, far cenno di, mentovare, parlare di, nominare, citare; *the newspapers don't — it*, i giornali non ne fanno cenno; *I -ed the incident in my article*, nel mio articolo ho accennato a questa faccenda; *I will — it to him*, gliene parlerò; *you may — my name*, puoi citare il mio nome; *I must also — that . . .*, devo anche dire che . . .; *as already -ed*, come già detto; *not to — . . .*, per non parlare di . . .; *it isn't worth -ing*, non vale la pena di parlarne; *I heard my name -ed*, ho sentito pronunciare il mio nome; (mil.) *to be -ed in dispatches*, essere citato all'ordine del giorno; (fam.) *don't — it!*, si figuri!, prego!, non c'è di che!
**mentor** *n.* mentore, consigliere.
**menu** *n.* carta; lista delle vivande; pasto a prezzo fisso.
**Mephistophel-es** *pr.n.* Mefistofele. **-ean** *adj.* mefistofelico.
**mephitic** *adj.* mefitico.
**mercantile** *adj.* mercantile; commerciale; — *marine*, marina mercantile; (pejor.) venale; mercenario.
**Mercator** *pr.n.* Mercatore *-'s projection*, proiezione di Mercatore.
**mercenary** *adj.* mercenario; venale; prezzolato; *n.* (soldato) mercenario.
**mercer** *n.* negoziante di stoffe, merciaio. **-ize** *tr.* mercerizzare.
**merchandise** *n.* merce; mercanzia.
**merchant** *n.* commerciante all'ingrosso, mercante; (pop.) tipo, individuo; *attrib.* mercantile; — *service*, marina mercantile; — *ship*, nave mercantile. **-man** *n.* nave mercantile.
**merciful** *adj.* pietoso; clemente; misericordioso; *to be — to*, aver pietà di. **-ly** *adv.* pietosamente; misericordiosamente; (fam.) grazie a Dio. **-ness** *n.* pietà; misericordia.
**merciless** *adj.* spietato, senza pietà; crudele; implacabile. **-ness** *n.* spietatezza; crudeltà.
**mercurial** *adj.* mercuriale, a mercurio; (fig.) vivace, volubile.
**Mercury**[1] *pr.n.* Mercurio.
**Mercury**[2] *n.* mercurio, argento vivo; barometro; (bot.) mercorella.
**mercy** *n.* misericordia; pietà; carità; *divine* —, misericordia divina; *works of* —, opere di carità; *sister of* —, suora di carità; *without* —, senza pietà; *to ask for* —, implorare pietà; *to have — upon*, aver pietà di, dimostrare misericordia per; *excl.* misericordia!; (fig.) *at the — of*, alla mercè di, in balia di; *to be at someone's* —, essere alla mercè di qualcuno; (fam.) *what a —!*, che fortuna!; *to be thankful for small mercies*, essere grato di ogni piccolo benefizio.
**mercy-seat** *n.* propiziatorio, trono di Dio.
**mere**[1] *adj.* semplice; puro; mero; pretto; solo; nient'altro che; *by — chance*, per puro caso; *a — coincidence*, una mera coincidenza; *at the — thought of*, al solo pensiero di; *a — trifle*, nient'altro che una sciocchezza. **-ly** *adv.* semplicemente; puramente; meramente; soltanto; *not -ly . . . but also*, non solo . . . ma anche.
**mere**[2] *n.* lago, laghetto; stagno.
**meretricious** *adj.* fallace, falso; vistoso, pomposo. **-ness** *n.* fallacia, falsità; vistosità, pompositá.
**merganser** *n.* (orn.) smergo, mergone *m.*
**merge** *tr.* fondere; assorbire; (comm.) amalgamare, incorporare; *intr.* fondersi; amalgamarsi; (fig.) *twilight -d into darkness*, il crepuscolo si spense nell'oscurità. **-r** *n.* fusione; amalgamento.
**meridian** *n.* meridiano; — *line*, meridiana; (fig.) apogeo. **-al** *adj.*, *n.* meridionale *m.*, *f.*
**meringue** *n.* (cul.) meringa.
**merit** *n.* merito; valore; pregio; *tr.* meritare; essere degno di.
**meritorious** *adj.* meritorio; meritevole; benemerito. **-ness** *n.* merito; l'essere meritorio.
**Merlin**[1] *pr.n.* Merlino.
**merlin**[2] *n.* (orn.) smeriglio.
**mer-maid** *n.* sirena. **-man** *n.* tritone *m.*
**Merovingian** *adj.*, *n.* (hist.) merovingio.
**merriment** *n.* allegrezza, allegria; ilarità.
**merry** *adj.* allegro; gaio; giocondo; *always — and bright*, sempre allegro; — *as a cricket*, allegro come un passero; — *Christmas!*, buon Natale!; *to make* —, stare allegri, fare baldoria; *to make — over*, ridere di, burlarsi di; *the more the merrier*, più siamo tanto meglio è; *the — month of May*, il dolce mese di maggio; *Merry England*, la dolce Inghilterra, l'Inghilterra del secolo sedicesimo.
**merry-andrew** *n.* buffone *m.*; pagliaccio. **-go-round** *n.* carosello; giostra. **-making** *n.* festa; divertimento; baldoria.
**merrythought** *n.* forcella, sterno di pollo.
**mesenter-y** *n.* (anat.) mesenterio. **-ic** *adj.* mesenterico.
**mesh** *n.* maglia; rete *f.*; (fig.) *to be caught in the -(es)*, essere preso nella rete; (mech.) ingranaggio; *in* —, ingranato; *tr.* prendere nella rete, irretire; (mech.) ingranare.
**mesmer-ic** *adj.* mesmerico. **-ism** *n.* mesmerismo. **-ist** *n.* mesmerista *m.*; ipnotizzatore. **-ize** *tr.* mesmerizzare; ipnotizzare.
**mesozoic** *adj.* (geol.) mesozoico.
**mess** *n.* pasticcio; confusione; disordine *m.*; *what a —!*, che pasticcio!; *to be in a* —, (of person) essere nei guai, (of things) essere in disordine; *to make a — on the floor*, sporcare il pavimento; *to make a — of something*, rovinare qualcosa, fare un pasticcio di qualcosa; *to get into a* —, cacciarsi nei guai; *to clear up the* —, rimettere in ordine, fare pulizia; mensa; *officers'* —, mensa ufficiali; piatto; pappa.
**mess** *tr.* mettere in confusione; imbrogliare; *to — things up*, fare pasticci, guastare tutto; *intr.* mangiare insieme, far mensa comune; *to — about*, far stupidaggini, perdersi in cose inutili.
**message** *n.* messaggio; commissione; ambasciata; *to take a — to*, fare un'ambasciata, portare un messaggio; *to run -s*, fare commissioni; *to send someone with a* —, mandare qualcuno a fare una commissione.
**messenger** *n.* messaggero; messo; *Queen's* —, corriere diplomatico.
**messenger-boy** *n.* fattorino.
**Messiah** *pr.n.* Messia.
**messianic** *adj.* messianico.
**messiness** *n.* disordine *m.*; sporcizia.
**messmate** *n.* compagno di mensa, commensale *m.*
**messrs.** *n.* (on evelopes) Signori; (firm) Spettabile Ditta.
**mess-tin** *n.* (mil.) gavetta.
**messuage** *n.* podere *m.*
**mess-up** *n.* (fam.) imbroglio; pasticcio.
**messy** *adj.* (fam.) confuso; disordinato; imbrattato, sudicio.
**met** *p.def.*, *part.* of **meet**, *q.v.*
**metabol-ic** *adj.* metabolico. **-ism** *n.* metabolismo.
**metal** *n.* metallo; *precious* —, metallo prezioso; *base* —, metallo vile; (for roads) brecciame *m.*, pietrisco; *pl.* (rlwy.) rotaie *f.pl.*; *tr.* rivestire di metallo; (roads) macadamizzare, massicciare, inghiaiare.
**metall-ic** *adj.* metallico, di

metallo. **-ize** *tr.* metallizzare; vulcanizzare. **-ography** *n.* metallografia. **-oid** *adj.* metalloidico; *n.* metalloide *m.*
**metallurg-y** *n.* metallurgia. **-ic(al)** *adj.* metallurgico. **-ist** *n.* metallurgo.
**metamorphosis** *n.* metamorfosi *f. indecl.*, trasformazione.
**metaphor** *n.* metafora; traslato; *mixed —*, metafora incoerente. **-ic(al)** *adj.* metaforico.
**meta-phrase** *n.* metafrasi *f.*; traduzione letterale.
**metaphysic-s** *n.* metafisica. **-al** *adj.* metafisico; trascendentale. **-ian** *n.* metafisico.
**meta-plasm** *n.* (biol.) metaplasma *m.*; (gramm.) metaplasmo. **-stasis** *n.* (med.) metastasi *f.* **-tarsus** *n.* (anat.) metatarso. **-thesis** *n.* (ling.) metatesi *f.*; (med.) metastasi *f.*; (chem.) sostituzione.
**metayage** *n.* mezzadria.
**mete** *tr.* misurare; commisurare; dosare; *to — out*, distribuire, ripartire, dispensare.
**metempsychosis** *n.* metempsicosi *f.*
**meteor** *n.* meteora. **-ic** *adj.* meteorico; (fig.) transitorio, fugace, rapidissimo. **-ite** *n.* meteorite *f.*; aerolito.
**meteorolog-y** *n.* meteorologia. **-ical** *adj.* meteorologico. **-ist** *n.* meteorologo.
**meter** *n.* misuratore; contatore; *altitude —*, altimetro; *electric —*, contatore dell'elettricità; *slot —*, contatore a moneta. Cf. **metre**. **-age** *n.* misurazione a contatore.
**methane** (chem.) metano.
**methinks** *intr.* (poet.) mi sembra, mi pare.
**method** *n.* metodo; modo; modalità; *a man of —*, un uomo metodico; *— of payment*, modalità di pagamento; *with —*, con ordine, ordinatamente; (fig.) *there's — in his madness*, è meno pazzo di quanto sembra. **-ical** *adj.* metodico; ordinato; ben regolato; sistemato.
**Method-ism** *n.* (rel.) metodismo. **-ist** *n.* metodista *m.*, *f.*
**Methuselah, Methusalem** *pr.n.* (bibl.) Matusalemme.
**methyl** *n.* (chem.) metile *m.* **-ated** *adj.* (chem.) metilico, metilizzato; *-ated spirits*, alcool denaturato. **-ene** *n.* (chem.) metilene *m.*
**meticulosity** *n.* meticolosità.
**meticulous** *adj.* meticoloso, pignolo.
**metonym-y** *n.* (rhet.) metonimia. **-ical** *adj.* (rhet.) metonimico.
**metope** *n.* (archit.) metope *f.*
**metre**[1] *n.* (prosod.) metro; metrica, prosodia; *in —*, in versi; (mus.) tempo.
**metre**[2] *n.* (unit of length) metro (= 39·37 inches); *cubic —*, metro cubo; *square —*, metro quadrato.
**metric(al)** *adj.* metrico.
**metrolog-y** *n.* metrologia. **-ical** *adj.* metrologico.
**metronome** *n.* metronomo.
**metropol-is** *n.* metropoli *f.*, capitale *f.* **-itan** *adj.* metropolitano; *-itan railway* (London), sezione della ferrovia sotterranea londinese; *n.* (eccl.) vescovo metropolitano.
**mettle** *n.* ardore *m.*; coraggio; animo; *to put someone on his —*, mettere qualcuno alla prova; *to be on one's —*, voler dar prova del proprio valore; tempra; carattere *m.* **-some** *adj.* focoso, bizzarro.
**Meuse** *pr.n.* (geog.) Mosa.
**mew**[1] (of cat) miagolio, miao; *intr.* miagolare.
**mew**[2] (orn.) gabbiano.
**mew**[3] *n.* (hist.) gabbia per falchi; *pl.* scuderie *f.pl.*; vicolo cieco in cui si trovavano una volta le scuderie; *intr.* (of birds) mutare le penne, mudare, fare la muda; *tr. to — up*, rinchiudere (in gabbia).
**mewling** *adj.* piagnucoloso.
**Mexic-o** *pr.n.* (geog.) Messico; *— City*, Città del Messico. **-an** *adj.*, *n.* messicano.
**mezzanine** *n.* (archit.) mezzanino, ammezzato.
**mezzo-soprano** *n.* mezzosoprano.
**mezzotint** *n.* mezzatinta.
**miaow** *n.* miao; miagolio; *intr.* far miao, miagolare.
**miasm-a** *n.* miasma *m.* **-al, -atic** *adj.* miasmatico.
**mica** *n.* mica.
**Micah** *pr.n.* (bibl.) Michea.
**mice** *pl.* of **mouse**, *q.v.*
**Michael** *pr.n.* Michele *— Angelo*, Michelangelo.
**Michaelmas** *n.* il San Michele, giorno di San Michele; (bot.) *— daisy*, astro.
**Michelangelesque** *adj.* michelangiolesco, (nello stile) di Michelangelo.
**Mickey** *pr.n.*, *m.* (dimin. of **Michael**) Michelino; (cinem.) *— Mouse*, Topolino.
**Micky** *pr.n.*, *m.* (abbrev. of **Michael**) Michelino; (fam.) *to take the — (out of)*, burlare; *a — Finn*, una bibita drogata.
**microb-e** *n.* microbo. **-ial, -ic** *adj.* microbico. **-iology** *n.* microbiologia.
**micro-cosm** *n.* microcosmo. **-groove** *n.* microsolco. **-metry** *n.* micrometria. **-phone** *n.* microfono. **-photography** *n.* microfotografia. **-scope** *n.* microscopio. **-scopic(al)** *adj.* microscopico; *-scopic examination*, esame *m.* al microscopio; (fig.) minuscolo, piccolissimo. **-scopy** *n.* miscroscopia. **-seismograph** *n.* microsismografo. **-spore** *n.* (bot.) microspora. **-wave** *n.* (radio) microonda.
**mid** *adj.* medio; in mezzo; metà; *in — June*, a metà giugno; *in — air*, tra cielo e terra; *in his — fifties*, sui cinquanticinque anni; *in — Channel*, in mezzo alla Manica.
**Midas** *pr.n.* Mida.
**midday** *n.* mezzogiorno; mezzodì *m.*; *attrib. — meal*, pasto di mezzogiorno.
**midden** *n.* mucchio di letame; (archaeol.) *kitchen —*, chiocciolaio, cumulo di rifiuti di cucina.
**middle** *adj.* medio; intermedio, nel mezzo, centrale, di mezzo; *of — height*, di media statura; *— finger*, dito medio; *the — course*, la via di mezzo; *the — classes*, le classi medie, il ceto medio, la borghesia; *the Middle Ages*, il Medioevo; *the Middle East*, il Medio Oriente; *the Middle West* (USA), gli Stati della Prateria; *— English*, l'inglese medioevale; (paint.) *— ground*, secondo piano; (journ.) *— article*, elzeviro.
**middle** *n.* mezzo; centro; *in the — of*, in mezzo a, nel mezzo di; *in the very — of*, nel bel mezzo di; *to be in the — of doing something*, star facendo qualcosa; (anat.) vita, cintola.
**middle-aged** *adj.* di mezza età, di una certa età. **-class** *adj.* borghese, della borghesia.
**middleman** *n.* intermediario, mediatore.
**middlemost** *adj.* il più vicino al centro, centralissimo.
**middle-sized** *adj.* di media grandezza.
**middling** *adj.* medio; discreto; (pejor.) mediocre, passabile.
**midge** *n.* (ent.) moscerino.
**midget** *n.* nanerottolo; pigmeo; persona piccolissima; *attrib.* piccolissimo, tascabile.
**midland** *adj.* interno, centrale; *n.pl. the Midlands*, l'Inghilterra centrale.
**mid-Lent** *n.* mezza quaresima.
**midnight** *n.* mezzanotte *f.*; *attrib.* di mezzanotte, notturno.
**mid-ocean** *n.* alto mare *m.*; *attrib.* in alto mare.
**midrib** *n.* (bot.) rachide *f.*, nervo mediano.
**midriff** *n.* (anat.) diaframma *m.*
**mid-season** *n.* mezza stagione.
**midshipman** *n.* aspirante (di marina), guardiamarina *m.*
**midst** *n.* mezzo; centro; *in the — of*, nel mezzo di, fra, tra; *in our —*, fra noi.
**midstream** *n.* mezzo della corrente.
**midsummer** *n.* mezza estate; solstizio d'estate; *— day*, il San Giovanni; *A Midsummer Night's Dream*, Sogno di una notte di mezz'estate.
**midway** *adv.* a metà strada, nel

mezzo del cammino, a metà distanza.
**mid-week** *adj.* di metà settimana; *n.* il mezzo della settimana.
**midwife** *n.* levatrice, ostetrica. **-ry** *n.* ostetricia.
**midwinter** *n.* cuore dell'inverno; *in —*, in pieno inverno.
**mien** *n.* aria; aspetto; portamento.
**might**[1] *n.* forza; potenza; potere *m.*; *with all one's —, with — and main*, con tutte le forze, a bastalena, di lena; (provb.) *— is right*, la ragione è del più forte.
**might**[2] *p.def.* of **may**, *q.v.*
**might-have-been** *n.* ciò che sarebbe potuto essere; (person) uomo mancato.
**might-y** *adj.* forte; possente; potente; imponente; *pl. the —*, i potenti; (fam.) *high and —*, prepotente; *adv.* (fam.) estremamente. **-ily** *adv.* potentemente; fortemente; (fam.) estremamente. **-iness** *n.* potenza; potere *m.*
**mignonette** *n.* (bot.) reseda, amorino.
**migr-ant** *adj.* migratore, emigrante; *n.* migratore, emigrante *m.*, *f.*; nomade *m.* **-ate** *intr.* emigrare; trasmigrare. **-ation** *n.* migrazione; emigrazione. **-atory** *adj.* migratore, migratorio; di passo; nomade.
**Mike**[1] *pr.n.*, *m.* (dimin. of **Michael**) Michelino.
**mike**[2] *n.* (fam.) microfono.
**Milan** *pr.n.* (geog.) Milano; *the — football club*, il Milan. **-ese** *adj.*, *n.* milanese *m.*, *f.*; (fam.) ambrosiano.
**milch** *adj.* da latte. **-cow** *n.* mucca da latte; (fig.) fonte di denaro.
**mild** *adj.* mite; moderato; dolce; gentile; lieve; (of beer) leggero; (of medicine) blando; (of illness) benigno, leggero.
**mildew** *n.* muffa; macchia di umidità; (on plants) ruggine *f.*; (on vines) oidio. **-ed, -y** *adj.* ammuffito; coperto di muffa; *-y smell*, odore di muffa.
**mildness** *n.* mitezza; dolcezza; leggerezza; (of illness) benignità.
**mile** *n.* miglio (= 1609.3 metres); *square —*, miglio quadrato; *nautical —*, miglio marittimo; *a — away*, lontano un miglio; (fig.) *not to be within -s of*, non poter essere anche lontanamente paragonato a; *to be -s better than*, valere infinitamente di più di; *to be -s out*, essere a mille miglia dalla soluzione giusta; *to eat up the -s*, divorare la strada. **-age** *n.* distanza in miglia, distanza percorsa da un veicolo; (motor.) *-age recorder*, contachilometri *m.* **-stone** *n.* pietra miliare.
**milfoil** *n.* (bot.) millefoglie *m.*, achillea.
**milieu** *n.* ambiente *m.*
**milit-ancy** *n.* inclinazione alla lotta; (pol.) attivismo. **-ant** *adj.* militante, attivo; *n.* (pol.) attivista *m.*
**militar-ism** *n.* militarismo. **-ist** *n.* militarista *m.*
**militariz-e** *tr.* militarizzare. **-ation** *n.* militarizzazione.
**military** *adj.* militare; dell'esercito; *a — man*, un militare; *— service*, servizio militare; *— law*, codice militare; *of — age*, di leva; *n. the —*, l'esercito, i militari *m.pl.*
**militate** *intr.* militare (also fig.).
**militia** *n.* milizia, guardia nazionale. **-man** *n.* milite *m.*
**milk** *n.* latte *m.*; *land flowing with — and honey*, paese di Cuccagna; (fam.) *to come home with the —*, rientrare alle ore piccole; (provb.) *it's no use crying over spilt —*, cosa fatta capo ha; *tr.* mungere; *to — a cow*, mungere una mucca; (joc.) *to — a bull*, tentare l'impossibile; estrarre, cavare; (fig.) mungere, sfruttare, rubare; *to — the till*, rubare dalla cassa; *to — a lorry*, rubare nafta dal serbatoio di un camion; *intr.* dar latte; *the cows are -ing well*, le mucche danno molto latte.
**milk-and-water** *adj.* (fam.) insipido; annacquato; *a — Communist*, un comunista all'acqua di rosa. **-can** *n.* bidone da latte. **-crust** *n.* (med.) acore *m.*, crosta lattea.
**milker** *n.* (person) mungitore *m.*, mungitrice *f.*; (cow) mucca da latte; (machine) mungitrice.
**milk-fever** *n.* (med.) febbre lattea. **-float** *n.* furgone del latte.
**milkiness** *n.* lattescenza.
**milking** *n.* mungitura; *— machine*, mungitrice.
**milk-jug** *n.* lattiera.
**milk-maid** *n.* mungitrice. **-man** *n.* lattaio lattivendolo.
**milk-powder** *n.* latte in polvere. **-pudding** *n.* (cul.) budino al latte. **-shake** *n.* frullato di latte.
**milksop** *n.* (fam.) pulcino bagnato; individuo effeminato.
**milk-tooth** *n.* dente di latte. **-white** *adj.* bianco come il latte. **-woman** *n.* lattaia, lattivendola.
**milky** *adj.* latteo, lattiginoso; *the Milky Way*, la Via Lattea.
**mill** *n.* mulino; (fig.) *to bring grist to the —*, tirare l'acqua al proprio mulino; *to put through the —*, mettere a dura prova; *the -s of God grind slowly*, Dio non paga il sabato; (industr.) opificio, stabilimento; (mixer) mescolatore, molazza; (mech.) fresa; (rolling-mill) laminatoio; (for coffee) macinino; *tr.* macinare; tritare; frantumare; (text.) follare; (mech.) fresare; (roll) laminare; *intr.* (fig.) circolare disordinatamente, assieparsi.
**millen-ary** *adj.* millenario, millenne; *n.* millennio. **-nial** *adj.* millenne, di millennio. **-nium** *n.* millennio.
**miller** *n.* mugnaio; *-'s wife*, mugnaia; (mech.) operaio fresatore, (machine) fresatrice *f.*; (bot.) *dusty —*, coronaria, cotonella.
**millet** *n.* miglio, panico.
**mill-hand** *n.* operaio di fabbrica; operaio mugnaio.
**milliard** *n.* miliardo. **-aire** *n.* miliardario.
**milli-gram(me)** *n.* milligrammo. **-litre** *n.* millilitro. **-metre** *n.* millimetro.
**milliner** *n.* modista *f.* **-y** *n.* articoli di modisteria; *-y shop*, modisteria.
**milling** *n.* (of corn) macinatura; (mech.) fresatura; (of coin) granitura.
**million** *card. num.* milione *m.*; *to be worth -s*, essere miliardario. **-aire** *n.* milionario. **-th** *ord. num.* milionesimo.
**millowner** *n.* proprietario di mulino, proprietario di fabbrica.
**mill-pond** *n.* gora di mulino; (of sea) *smooth as a —*, liscio come uno specchio. **-race** *n.* gora di mulino, canale di adduzione.
**mill-stone** *n.* macina, pietra da mulino; (fig.) peso; onere *m.* **-wright** *n.* costruttore di mulini.
**milt** *n.* (anat.) milza; (ichth.) latte di pesce; *tr.* (ichth.) fecondare.
**Milton-ian, -ic** *adj.* miltoniano, di Milton.
**mime** *n.* (theatr.) mimo, mimica; (actor) mimo, mimico; *tr.* mimare, imitare.
**mimeograph** *n.* ciclostile *m.*; *tr.* ciclostilare.
**mim-esis** *n.* mimesi *f.* **-etic** *adj.* mimetico.
**mimic** *adj.* mimico, mimetico; imitativo; *n.* mimo, mimico, imitatore; *tr.* imitare; contraffare, scimmiottare. **-ry** *n.* mimica, pantomima; imitazione.
**mimosa** *f.* (bot.) acacia, erba mimosa; *— blossom*, gaggia.
**minaret** *n.* minareto.
**minatory** *adj.* minatorio; minaccioso.
**mince** *n.* carne tritata; *tr.* (cul.) tritare, tagliuzzare, sminuzzare; (fig.) attenuare; *to — one's words*, parlare eufemisticamente; *not to — matters*, parlare francamente; *intr.* camminare a passettini, camminare in modo affettato. **-d** *adj.* (cul.) tritato, sminuzzato. **-meat** *n.* (cul.) carne tritata; (for mince-pies) composta di frutta secca e mele; (fig., fam.) *to make -meat of*, fare polpette di, demolire.

**mince-pie** *n.* (cul.) pasticcio di frutta secca.
**minc-er** *n.* tritacarne *m.* **-ing** *adj.* affettato, lezioso; *-ing steps*, passettini *m.pl.*
**mind** *n.* mente *f.*; intelligenza; intelletto; spirito; animo; *one of the great -s*, una delle grandi menti; *a penetrating —*, una mente acuta; *state of —*, stato d'animo; *peace of —*, serenità; *presence of —*, presenza di spirito; *absence of —*, distrazione; *a turn of —*, mentalità, modo di pensare; *the -'s eye*, gli occhi della mente; *to give one's — to*, fare attenzione a; *to keep one's — on*, pensare continuamente a; *to take one's — off*, smettere di pensare a; *to have something on one's —*, essere preoccupato; *of sound —*, sano di mente; *to be out of one's —*, essere fuori di sè, essere pazzo; *to bear in —*, ricordare, tenere a mente; *to bring to —*, rammentare, far ricordare; *to put someone in — of something*, far ricordare qualcosa a qualcuno; *it never crossed my —*, non mi è mai venuto in mente; (provb.) *out of sight out of —*, lontan dagli occhi lontan dal cuore; *to my —*, secondo me, a mio parere; *to be in two -s*, esitare, essere indeciso; *to change one's —*, cambiare opinione, cambiare idea; *to speak one's —*, parlare chiaro e tondo; *to have a good — to*, avere quasi deciso di; *to make up one's —*, decidersi; *to be of one —*, essere dello stesso parere; (fam.) *to give someone a piece of one's —*, fare un ramanzino a qualcuno, dirne quattro a qualcuno.
**mind** *tr.*, *intr.* badare a, occuparsi di, aver cura di; *to — the baby*, badare al bambino; *to — the house*, occuparsi della casa; *to — one's own business*, badare ai fatti suoi; *— you!*, bada!; *to — someone's advice*, badare ai consigli di qualcuno; *— you do it*, non dimenticare di farlo; *— the step!*, attenzione al gradino!; *— your head!*, bada a non battere il capo!; *— you do!*, mi raccomando!; *if you don't —*, se non ti spiace; *do you — if I smoke?*, Le spiace se fumo?; *I don't — trying*, sono disposto a provare; *I wouldn't — a whisky*, non mi spiacerebbe un bicchierino di whisky; (fam.) *never —!*, non importa!, (to child) non piangere!
**minded** *adj.* disposto; incline; intenzionato; del parere; che si interessa; *if you are so —*, se siete di quel parere. For compounds, **absent-minded** *etc.*, see under first element.
**minder** *n.* sorvegliante *m.*, *f.*, guardiano; custode *m.*
**mindful** *adj.* attento memore.
**mindless** *adj.* noncurante, disattento; scervellato; stordito.
**mind-reading** *n.* lettura del pensiero.
**mine**[1] *n.* miniera; (mil.; naval) mina; *tr.*, *intr.* scavare; (min.) estrarre da una miniera; (mil.) minare, posare mine in; (fig.) minare; indebolire.
**mine**[2] *poss. prn.* il mio *m.*, la mia *f.*, i miei *m.pl.*, le mie *f.pl.*; *this is —*, questo è mio; *a friend of —*, un mio amico; (fam.) *me and —*, io ed i miei.
**mine-detector** *n.* (mil.) rilevatore di mine.
**mine-field** *n.* (mil.) campo minato. **-layer** *n.* (naut.) posamine *m. indecl.*
**miner** *n.* minatore.
**mineral** *adj.* minerale; *— water*, acqua minerale; *n.* minerale *m.*
**mineralog-y** *n.* mineralogia. **-ical** *adj.* mineralogico. **-ist** *n.* mineralogista *m.*
**Minerva** *pr.n.* (myth.) Minerva.
**minesweeper** *n.* (naut.) dragamine *m. indecl.*
**mingl-e** *tr.* mescolare, mischiare, confondere; accomunare; *intr.* mescolarsi, mischiarsi; confondersi; accomunarsi; unirsi. **-ing** *n.* mescolanza; miscuglio.
**miniature** *adj.* minuscolo, in miniatura, in scala ridotta; *n.* miniatura; *to paint -s*, *to illuminate -s*, miniare. **-painting** *n.* miniatura.
**miniaturist** *n.* miniaturista *m.*, miniatore.
**minim** *n.* (mus.) minima; (pharm.) goccia; (eccl.) minimo.
**minim-um** *adj.*, *n.* minimo. **-al** *adj.* minimo. **-ize** *tr.* ridurre al minimo, minimizzare; (fig.) sminuire, attribuire poca importanza a.
**mining** *adj.* minerario; *n.* scavo, estrazione; (mil.; naval) posa di mine.
**minion** *n.* (pejor.) favorito; tirapiedi *m.*; schiavo; (joc.) *the -s of the law*, i poliziotti.
**minister** *n.* (pol.) ministro; *Prime Minister*, primo ministro, (in Italy) capo del governo, presidente del consiglio; (eccl.) ministro del culto, pastore, sacerdote *m.*; (diplomacy) incaricato, ambasciatore *m.*; *intr.* portare aiuto; *to — to*, assistere, soccorrere; *to — to someone's needs*, provvedere ai bisogni di qualcuno; (fig.) lusingare; (eccl.) celebrare, ufficiare; *to — to a parish*, curare una parrocchia; (fig.) *-ing angel*, angelo di bontà. **-ial** *adj.* (pol.) ministeriale; (eccl.) sacerdotale.
**ministrant** *n.* (eccl.) celebrante, ufficiante *m.*
**ministration** *n.* cura; soccorso; assistenza; (eccl.) ministero, cura spirituale.
**ministry** *n.* governo; (offices) ministero *m.*; (eccl.) sacerdozio, ministero.
**minium** *n.* (chem.) minio.
**miniver** *n.* vaio, pelo di ermellino.
**mink** *n.* (animal, fur) visone *m.*
**minnow** *n.* pesciolino; (fig.) *a Triton among -s*, un gigante fra i pigmei.
**Minoan** *adj.* minoico, minossico.
**minor** *adj.* minore; più piccolo; di secondaria importanza; (eccl.) minore; *n.* (leg.) minorenne *m.*, *f.*; (eccl.) frate minore; (philos.) premessa minore; (mus.) minore *m.* **-ity** *n.* minoranza; (leg.) minorità, età minore; *attrib.* *-ity group*, gruppo dissenziente.
**Minos** *pr.n.* (myth.) Minosse, Minòs.
**Minotaur** *pr.n.* (myth.) Minotauro.
**minster** *n.* cattedrale, chiesa di una abbazia.
**minstrel** *n.* (hist.) menestrello, giullare *m.*; rapsodo; (theatr.) cantante (travestito da negro). **-sy** *n.* arte dei menestrelli, poesia giullaresca.
**mint**[1] *n.* (bot.) menta.
**mint**[2] *n.* zecca; (fig.) *in — condition*, in condizione perfetta, nuovo di zecca; (fam.) *to have a — of money*, avere un mucchio di soldi; *tr.* coniare, battere (monete). **-age** *n.* coniatura.
**mint-julep** *n.* sciroppo di menta. **-sauce** *n.* (cul.) salsa alla menta.
**minuet** *n.* minuetto.
**minus** *prep.* (math.) meno; (fam.) senza, privo di.
**minuscule** *adj.* minuscolo; *n.* minuscola.
**minute** *adj.* minuto; piccolissimo, minuscolo; minuzioso, meticoloso. **-ly** *adv.* minuziosamente, esattamente. **-ness** *n.* minutezza, piccolezza; minuziosità.
**mi·nute** *n.* minuto; *ten -s to five*, le cinque meno dieci; *ten -s past five*, le cinque e dieci; *to be five -s late*, essere in ritardo dicinque minuti; momento, istante *m.*; *wait a —*, aspetta un momento; *in a —!*, subito!; *half a —*, un momentino; *the — (that)*, non appena; *any —*, da un momento all'altro; *to the —*, puntualmente, in punto; (geom.) minuto; appunto, minuta; *pl.* *the -s of a meeting*, il verbale; *to enter in the -s*, mettere agli atti; *tr.* prendere nota di; stendere il verbale di.
**minute-hand** *n.* lancetta dei minuti.
**minute-ly, -ness** see under **minute.**
**minutiae** *n. pl.* minuzie *f.pl.*
**minx** *n.* (fam.) civetta, birichina, sfacciatella.
**Miocene** *adj.* (geol.) miocenico; *n.* miocene *m.*
**miracle** *n.* miracolo; prodigio;

*to work a* —, fare un miracolo; *by a* —, per miracolo; (theatr.) — *play*, sacra rappresentazione. **-monger, -worker** *n.* taumaturgo.

**miraculous** *adj.* miracoloso; prodigioso; meraviglioso. **-ness** *n.* miracolosità; miracoloso.

**mirage** *n.* miraggio.

**mire** *n.* melma; mota; fango; pantano; *to sink into the* —, affondare nel pantano; (fig.) *to drag through the* —, trascinare nel fango; *tr.* infangare; inzaccherare; sporcare di mota; *intr.* affondare nel pantano.

**mirror** *n.* specchio; (motor.) specchietto retrovisore; *tr.* specchiare; riflettere; (fig.) rispecchiare.

**mirth** *n.* ilarità; giubilo; allegria. **-ful** *adj.* ilare, gioioso; ridente; allegro. **-fulness** *n.* ilarità; gioia, allegrezza.

**mirthless** *adj.* senza allegria, triste; cupo.

**mirth-provoking** *adj.* che provoca ilarità.

**miry** *adj.* fangoso, melmoso.

**misadventure** *n.* contrattempo; disgrazia; infortunio; (leg.) *by* —, preterintenzionale.

**misalliance** *n.* matrimonio sconveniente.

**misanthrop-e, -ist** *n.* misantropo. **-ic(al)** *adj.* misantropico. **-y** *n.* misantropia.

**misappl-y** *tr.* applicare erroneamente, usare a sproposito; (leg.) stornare. **-ication** *n.* uso erroneo, applicazione sbagliata; (leg.) storno, appropriazione indebita.

**misapprehen-d** *tr.* fraintendere. **-sion** *n.* malinteso, equivoco.

**misappropriat-e** *tr.* appropriarsi indebitamente di, stornare. **-ion** *n.* appropriazione indebita, storno.

**misbecom-e** *tr.* sconvenire a, star male a. **-ing** *adj.* sconveniente, inadatto.

**misbegotten** *adj.* illegittimo, bastardo; (fig.) strampalato.

**misbehav-e** *intr.* comportarsi male. **-iour** *n.* cattiva condotta, villania.

**misbelie-f** *n.* miscredenza, falsa opinione; (rel.) infedeltà. **-ver** *n.* miscredente *m., f.*; (rel.) infedele *m., f.* **-ving** *adj.* miscredente, empio.

**miscalculat-e** *tr., intr.* calcolare male. **-ion** *n.* calcolo errato, errore di calcolo.

**miscall** *tr.* chiamare con nome sbagliato, chiamare impropriamente.

**miscarr-y** *intr.* smarrirsi, perdersi; (fig.) fallire, andare a rotoli; (med.) abortire. **-iage** *n.* disguido, smarrimento; (fig.) *-iage of justice*, errore giudiziario; (med.) disvio, aborto; *to have a -iage*, abortire.

**miscasting** *n.* errore di calcolo; (theatr.) errata distribuzione delle parti.

**miscegenation** *n.* incrocio di razze.

**miscellane-a** *n.* miscellanea; raccolta di scritti vari. **-ous** *adj.* miscellaneo; eterogeneo; misto. **-ously** *adv.* in modo eterogeneo.

**miscellany** *n.* raccolta di scritti vari, miscellanea; mescolanza.

**mischance** *n.* sfortuna, disgrazia, sventura, disdetta; *by* —, per disgrazia, per sventura.

**mischief** *n.* danno; male *m.*; torto; *to do someone a* —, far del male a qualcuno; fastidi, guai *m.pl.*; *the — of it is that . . .*, il guaio è che . . .; *to keep out of* —, tenersi lontano dai fastidi, non far dei guai; malizia, cattiveria; *full of* —, malizioso, cattivo; *out of pure* —, per pura cattiveria; brutto tiro, birichinata; *to be up to some* —, star meditando un brutto tiro, star combinandone una delle sue; *to get into* —, fare delle marachelle, cacciarsi nei guai; discordia, zizzania; *to make* —, creare discordia, metter male, intorbidire le acque.

**mischief-maker** *n.* mettimale *m., f.*, accattabrighe *m., f.*; seminatore di discordia; linguaccia.

**mischievous** *adj.* cattivo, malizioso, molesto; (of child) birichino; (of thing) dannoso, nocivo. **-ness** *n.* cattiveria, malizia, furberia; (of child) cattiveria; (of thing) l'essere nocivo.

**misconceive** *tr.* concepire male, intendere male, fraintendere, formarsi un'idea sbagliata di.

**misconception** *n.* concetto erroneo, idea sbagliata, fraintendimento.

**miscon·duct** *n.* cattiva condotta; cattiva amministrazione; (leg.) adulterio.

**misconduct** *tr.* dirigere male, amministrare male; *rfl. to — oneself*, comportarsi male; (leg.) commettere adulterio.

**misconstruction** *n.* falsa interpretazione; (gramm.) costruzione sbagliata.

**misconstrue** *tr.* interpretare male, fraintendere; tradurre male.

**miscount** *tr.* contar male, fare un conteggio sbagliato; *n.* conteggio sbagliato, errore di addizione.

**miscreant** *n.* (rel.) eretico; (fam.) furfante *m.*, malandrino, scellerato.

**misdate** *tr.* datare erroneamente.

**misdeal** *tr., intr.* (cards) distribuire male; *n.* distribuzione errata.

**misdeed** *n.* misfatto.

**misdemeanour** *n.* cattiva condotta; (leg.) misfatto, contravvenzione, reato.

**misdirect** *tr.* dare instruzioni errate a, dirigere male; mandare in direzione sbagliata; (letter) sbagliare l'indirizzo di. **-ion** *n.* indicazione sbagliata; indirizzo errato.

**misdoing** *n.* misfatto.

**mise-en-scène** *n.* (theatr.) allestimento scenico, regia; (fig.) messa in scena.

**miser** *n.* avaro; taccagno.

**miserabl-e** *adj.* misero; disgraziato; infelice; sventurato; *to feel* —, sentirsi depresso; *to make someone's life* —, rendere la vita intollerabile a qualcuno; (fig.) meschino, miserevole, irrisorio, pietoso, squallido; deprimente, penoso; — *weather*, tempaccio; *a — failure*, un fiasco deplorevole. **-eness** *n.* infelicità; abbattimento; sconforto. **-y** *adv.* miseramente; infelicemente; (fig.) meschinamente, miserevolmente.

**misericord** *n.* misericordia; pietà.

**miserl-y** *adj.* avaro; taccagno; gretto. **-iness** *n.* avarizia; taccagneria.

**misery** *n.* miseria, povertà, indigenza; sofferenze *f.pl.*, infelicità, afflizione; *to put an animal out of its* —, porre fine alle sofferenze di una bestia.

**misfire** *n.* cilecca, scatto a vuoto; (motor.) accensione difettosa; (brickmaking) mattone malcotto; *intr.* far cilecca, scattare a vuoto; (motor.) dare accensioni irregolari.

**misfit** *n.* abito che non si adatta bene; (fig.) pesce fuor d'acqua.

**misfortune** *n.* sfortuna, sventura, disgrazia; malanno; accidente *m.*; (provb.) *-s never come singly*, un male attira l'altro.

**misgiv-e** *tr.* ispirare diffidenza a, far presentire disgrazie a. **-ing** *n.* presentimento (di male); apprensione; dubbio; sospetto.

**misgovern** *tr.* governare male, amministrare male. **-ment** *n.* malgoverno, cattiva amministrazione.

**misguided** *adj.* fuorviato, sviato; — *zeal*, zelo eccessivo; scriteriato.

**mishandle** *tr.* maneggiare male; (fig.) malmenare, maltrattare.

**mishap** *n.* disgrazia; contrattempo; infortunio; disavventura.

**mishear** *tr.* udire male, intendere male.

**mishit** *tr.* colpire male (una palla).

**misinform** *tr.* informare male; fuorviare. **-ation** *n.* informazione sbagliata.

**misinterpret** *tr.* interpretare male; fraintendere. **-ation** *n.* interpretazione sbagliata; fraintendimento.

**misjudg-e** *tr.* giudicare male; calcolare male; farsi un'idea

sbagliata di. **-(e)ment** *n.* guidizio sbagliato.
**mislay** *tr.* smarrire.
**mislead** *tr.* sviare, fuorviare; (fig.) ingannare, indurre in errore. **-ing** *adj.* ingannevole; fallace.
**mismanage** *tr.* dirigere male, amministrare male. **-ment** *n.* cattiva amministrazione.
**misname** *tr.* chiamare con nome sbagliato.
**misnomer** *n.* errore di nome, termine improprio.
**misogyn-y** *n.* misoginia. **-ist** misogino.
**misplace** *tr.* collocare male; collocare al posto sbagliato.
**mis'print** *n.* errore di stampa, errore tipografico.
**misprint** *tr.* stampare con errori.
**mispronounce** *tr.* pronunciare scorrettamente; storpiare.
**mispronunciation** *n.* pronuncia scorretta; errore di pronuncia.
**misquot-e** *tr.* citare erroneamente. **-ation** *n.* citazione inesatta.
**misread** *tr.* leggere erroneamente; fraintendere. **-ing** *n.* lettura sbagliata; falsa interpretazione.
**misrepresent** *tr.* travisare; snaturare; esporre sotto una falsa luce; rappresentare erroneamente. **-ation** *n.* rappresentazione inesatta, esposizione erronea; (leg.) falsa dichiarazione.
**misrule** *n.* malgoverno; cattiva amministrazione; *tr.* governar male.
**miss**[1] *n.* (before name) signorina; *the Misses Smith,* le signorine Smith, le sorelle Smith; *thank you, Miss Smith,* grazie, signorina; (fam.) ragazzetta; *— Europe,* Miss Europa.
**miss**[2] *n.* colpo mancato, colpo andato a vuoto; *a lucky —,* una via d'uscita inaspettata; (fam.) *to give something a —,* tralasciare di far qualcosa; (provb.) *a — is as good as a mile,* per un punto Martin perse la cappa.
**miss**[2] *tr., intr.* mancare (il colpo), non colpire nel segno; *to — the target,* mancare il bersaglio; *to — a meal,* saltare un pasto; *to — an appointment,* mancare a un appuntamento; *he barely -ed being killed,* poco mancò che non fosse ucciso; *I was sorry to — you,* mi è spiaciuto di non averti trovato; *to — the point,* non afferrare l'essenziale; perdere; *to — the bus,* perdere l'autobus; *to — an opportunity,* perdere un'occasione; *to — one's footing,* mettere il piede in fallo; *I -ed my gloves,* non trovai più i miei guanti; *to — the most important thing of all,* andare a Roma e non vedere il papa; *I shall — you badly,* sentirò molto la tua mancanza; *he won't be -ed,* nessuno rimpiangerà la sua partenza; *to — out,* omettere, tralasciare.
**missal** *n.* messale *m.*
**missel** *n.* *— thrush,* tordella.
**misshapen** *adj.* deforme, deformato; mal fatto.
**missile** *n.* missile *m.*; proiettile *m.*; *guided —,* missile teleguidato.
**missing** *adj.* mancante; smarrito; perso; *to be —,* mancare; (mil.) disperso; *to be reported —,* essere dato per disperso.
**mission** *n.* missione; ambasciata; *to be sent on a —,* essere mandato in missione; (eccl.) missione. **-ary** *adj., n.* missionario.
**missis** *n.* (pop. for Mrs.) Signora, padrona; *my —, the —,* mia moglia, mia vecchia.
**missive** *n.* missiva.
**misspell** *tr.* sbagliare l'ortografia di, scrivere male.
**misspend** *tr.* spendere male, sprecare, impiegare male; *misspent youth,* gioventù passata nella dissipazione.
**misstate** *tr.* affermare erroneamente; riferir male; esporre inesattamente. **-ment** *n.* affermazione errata, dichiarazione inesatta, errore di fatto.
**missus** *n.* (pop.) see **missis.**
**mist** *n.* bruma, foschia; *Scotch —,* pioggerella, tempo inglese; (on glass) appannamento; (fig.) *to have a — before one's eyes,* avere un velo davanti agli occhi; *in the -s of time,* nella notte dei tempi; *tr.* appannare; *intr.* appannarsi.
**mistake** *n.* errore *m.*; sbaglio; equivoco; fallo; svista; abbaglio; *by —,* per errore, per isbaglio; *to make a —,* fare un errore, sbagliare; *there is some —,* ci dev'essere un errore; (fam.) *it is warm and no —,* fa caldo non c'è che dire; *tr.* confondere; scambiare; *to — one thing for another,* scambiare una cosa per un'altra, confondere due cose; sbagliare; *to be -n,* sbagliarsi; *there is no mistaking the fact that,* non si può sbagliare il fatto che; non capire, fraintendere.
**mistaken** *part.* of **mistake,** *q.v.*; *adj.* sbagliato, erroneo, falso; fuori posto; *a — idea,* un'idea falsa; *— identity,* errore di persona; *— zeal,* zelo fuori posto.
**Mister** *n.* signor(e) *m.*; *Mr. Smith,* il signor Smith; *Mr. Chairman,* Signor Presidente.
**mistime** *tr.* dire fuori luogo; fare intempestivamente. **-d** *adj.* inopportuno, intempestivo.
**mistiness** *n.* brumosità; foschia; (on glass) appannamento; (fig.) poca chiarezza.
**mistletoe** *n.* vischio.
**mistook** *p.def.* of **mistake,** *q.v.*
**mistral** *n.* maestrale *m.*
**mistranslat-e** *tr.* tradurre male; travisare il senso di. **-ion** *n.* traduzione scorretta; errore di traduzione.
**mistress** *n.* (of house) padrona, signora; *where is your —?,* dov'è la padrona?; *to be one's own —,* essere padrona di se stessa; (fig.) *to be — of,* dominare, essere padrona di, signoreggiare su; (schol.) insegnante *f.*, maestra; amante *f.*, amica; (pejor.) mantenuta.
**mistrust** *n.* diffidenza; sfiducia; sospetto; *tr.* diffidare di, sospettare di; non aver fiducia in. **-ful** *adj.* diffidente; sospettoso. **-fulness** *n.* diffidenza, sfiducia.
**misty** *adj.* nebbioso, brumoso, vaporoso; (fig.) oscuro, vago, confuso, indistinto.
**misunderstand** *tr.* fraintendere; capir male. **-ing** *n.* malinteso, equivoco; disaccordo, dissapore *m.*
**misunderstood** *part.* of **misunderstand,** *q.v., adj.* (of person) incompreso.
**misusage** *n.* maltrattamento.
**misuse** *n.* abuso, cattivo uso; maltrattamento.
**misuse** *tr.* abusare di, far cattivo uso di; adoperare male; maltrattare.
**mite**[1] *n.* (ent.) baco.
**mite**[2] *n.* somma piccolissima; (bibl.) *the widow's —,* l'obolo della vedova; piccino *m.*, piccina *f.*; piccola quantità, briciola.
**mitigat-e** *tr.* mitigare; moderare; lenire; alleviare; temperare; *to — a crime,* attenuare un delitto; (leg.) *-ing circumstances,* circostanze attenuanti. **-ion** *n.* mitigazione; lenimento; alleviamento; (of crime) attenuante *f.*
**mitre**[1] *n.* mitra, (pop.) mitria; (hist.) infula.
**mitre**[2] *n.* (carpen.) ugnatura; (techn.) giunto ad angolo.
**mitten, mitt** *n.* manopola, mezzo guanto; (boxing) guantone *m.*
**mix** *tr.* mescolare, mischiare; (in breeding) incrociare; (paint.) *to — colours,* mesticare colori; *to — the salad,* condire l'insalata; *to — up,* confondere; *to be -ed up in,* essere coinvolto in; *to get all -ed up,* confondersi, far confusione; *intr.* mescolarsi; *to — with,* frequentare, (of colours) accompagnarsi con. **-ed** *adj.* misto, mescolato, mischiato; eterogeneo; (cul.) *-ed grill,* misto di carne ai ferri; (sport) *-ed doubles,* doppi misti. **-er** *n.* (techn.) mescolatore, agitatore; (radio) variatore di frequenza; (of person) *to be a good -er,* essere affabile con tutti, essere socievole; *a bad -er,* un orso. **-ture** *n.* mescolanza, miscuglio; (fig.) misto; (chem.) miscuglio, miscela; (pharm.) mistura.
**mix-up** *n.* (fam.) confusione; parapiglia.
**mizzen** *adj.* (naut.) di mezzana; *n.* mezzana.
**mnemonic** *adj.* mnemonico. **-s** *n.pl.* mnemonica.
**moan** *n.* gemito; lamento; pianto;

*intr.* gemere; lamentarsi; piangere; emettere un flebile suono; (of wind, sea) ululare; *tr.* (poet.) lamentare.

**moat** *n.* fosso, fossato; *tr.* cingere di fossato.

**mob** *n.* folla; *the* —, la plebe, la plebaglia; — *law*, legge imposta dalla plebaglia; — *oratory*, oratoria da tribuno; — *psychology*, psicologia delle masse; (fam.) comitivia; *our* —, i nostri; *tr.* affollarsi intorno a; molestare.

**mobil-e** *adj.* mobile; spostabile; (fig.) instabile, volubile. **-ity** *n.* mobilità.

**mobiliz-e** *tr.* (mil.) mobilitare, mobilizzare; *intr.* ordinare la mobilitazione. **-ation** *n.* (mil.) mobilitazione.

**moccasin** *n.* mocassino.

**mock** *adj.* finto, falso; burlesco, *n. to make a — of*, deridere, prendere in giro; *tr.* deridere; ridere di; dileggiare; canzonare; schernire; *intr.* ridere; *to — at*, burlarsi di, deridere. **-er** *n.* beffeggiatore; burlone *m.*; schernitore. **-ery** *n.* derisione; dileggio; scherno; ludibrio; inganno, illusione, contraffazione.

**mock-heroic** *adj.* eroicomico.

**mocking** *adj.* beffardo; ironico; sarcastico. **-bird** *n.* mimo, tordo beffeggiatore.

**modal** *adj.* (mus.; gramm.) modale. **-ity** *n.* modalità.

**mode** *n.* modo; maniera; forma; genere *m.*; mezzo; sistema; moda; (mus.) modo.

**model** *n.* modello; (fig.) esempio; campione *m.*; *to take as a* —, prendere ad esempio; copia esatta; (industr.) modello; (couture) indossatrice *f.*; *artist's* —, modello *m.*; modella *f.*; *plastic* —, plastico; *working* —, modello funzionante; *attrib.* modello, che serve da modello; — *aeroplane*, aeromodello; *tr.* modellare; plasmare; formare; (sculp.) abbozzare; plasticare; (fig.) *to be -led on*, rifarsi a, essere ricalcato su, essere modellato a; *to — oneself on*, modellarsi su, seguire l'esempio di, prendere ad esempio; *intr.* fare un modello. **-ler** *n.* modellatore. **-ling** *n.* modellatura; creazione di modelli; (sculp.) plastica.

**moderat-e** *adj.* moderato; temperato; misurato; discreto; (of price) modico; (of person) assennato; (pejor.) mediocre, modesto, scarso; *n.* (pol.) moderato; *tr.* moderare; temperare; mitigare; calmare; *intr.* calmarsi, mitigarsi. **-ion** *n.* moderazione; misura; sobrietà; *in -ion*, moderatamente; senza esagerare. **-or** *n.* moderatore; (mech.) regolatore; (eccl.) ministro presbiteriano.

**modern** *adj.* moderno; recente; aggiornato; — *languages*, lingue moderne; — *times*, tempi presenti; *n.* moderno. **-ism** *n.* modernismo; (ling.) neologismo. **-ist** *n.* modernista *m.*, *f.* **-istic** *adj.* modernistico. **-ity** *n.* modernità.

**moderniz-e** *tr.* rimodernare, ammodernare, modernizzare; aggiornare; *to become -ed*, aggiornarsi. **-ation** *n.* rimodernamento *m.*, modernizzazione *f.*, aggiornamento.

**modernness** *n.* modernità.

**modest** *adj.* modesto, pudico; senza pretese, semplice; moderato, modico. **-y** *n.* modestia; pudore *m.*; semplicità.

**modicum** *n.* pochino, piccola quantità.

**modif-y** *tr.* modificare, cambiare, mutare; (gramm.) modificare; (fig.) trasformare, attenuare. **-iable** *adj.* modificabile. **-ication** *n.* modifica, adattamento. **-ier** *n.* modificatore. **-ying** *adj.* modificante; mitigante.

**modish** *adj.* alla moda, di moda. **-ness** *n.* conformità alla moda; modernità.

**modiste** *n.* modista *f.*, sarta.

**modulat-e** *tr.* modulare. **-ion** *n.* modulazione. **-or** *n.* modulatore.

**module** *n.* (archit.) modulo, modano.

**mogul** *n.* mogol *m.*, mongolo.

**mohair** *n.* pelo di capra d'Angora.

**Mohammed** *pr.n.* Maometto. **-an** *adj.*, *n.* maomettano. **-anism** *n.* maomettismo, islamismo.

**moiety** *n.* metà; mezzo; (fam.) piccola quantità.

**moil** *intr.* sgobbare, sfacchinare.

**moire, moiré** *adj.*, *n.* moerro, marezzatura; *moiré silk*, amoerro.

**moist** *adj.* umido, bagnato, madido, umidiccio; (meteor.) umido, piovoso. **-en** *tr.* umettare, inumidire, bagnare; *intr.* inumidirsi, bagnarsi. **-ness** *n.* umidità. **-ure** *n.* umidità, umidezza; madore *m.*; umore *m.*; vapore umido, appannamento.

**moke** *n.* (pop.) ciuco, somaro.

**molar** *adj.*, *n.* molare *m.*

**molasses** *n.* melassa.

**mole**[1] *n.* (on skin) neo.

**mole**[2] *n.* (zool.) talpa; (fig.) amico infedele.

**mole**[3] *n.* (breakwater) molo, diga; frangiflutti *m.*

**molecul-e** *n.* molecola; particella. **-ar** *adj.* molecolare; *-ar attraction*, aggregazione. **-arity** *n.* molecolarità.

**molehill** *n.* cumulo di terra sopra la tana di una talpa; (fam.) *to make a mountain out of a* —, fare d'una mosca un elefante, affogare in un bicchier d'acqua.

**moleskin** *n.* pelle di talpa; (text.) fustagno.

**molest** *tr.* molestare; infastidire. **-ation** *n.* molestia.

**mollif-y** *tr.* ammollire; ammorbidire; (fig.) rabbonire, placare. **-ication** *n.* ammollimento; (fig.) rabbonimento. **-ier** *n.* (chem.) emolliente *m.*; (fig.) paciere *m.*

**mollusc** *n.* mollusco.

**mollycoddle** *tr.* (fam.) coccolare, viziare, tenere sotto una campana di vetro, tenere nella bambagia.

**Moloch** *pr.n.* Moloc.

**molten** *adj.* fuso, liquefatto.

**moment** *n.* momento; attimo; istante *m.*; *one —!*, *wait a —!*, un momento!; *at any* —, da un momento all'altro; *at the (present)* —, ora, attualmente; *at odd -s*, a tempo perso; *a — ago*, or ora; *not for a* —, mai; *the very — that*, non appena che, proprio nell'attimo che; *in a* —, in un attimo, subito; *he never wastes a* —, non perde mai un istante; *to the* —, puntualmente; importanza; rilievo; *of great* —, di grande importanza. **-ary** *adj.* momentaneo; passeggero.

**momentous** *adj.* di gran momento, grave; importante. **-ness** *n.* importanza; gravità.

**momentum** *n.* (mech.; phys.) velocità acquisita; *to gather* —, aumentare di velocità; (fam.) impeto, slancio.

**Monaco** *pr.n.* (geog.) (Principato di) Monaco.

**monarch** *n.* monarca; sovrano. **-ic(al)** *adj.* monarchico. **-ism** *n.* monarchismo. **-ist** *adj.*, *n.* monarchico. **-y** *n.* monarchia; *limited -y*, monarchia costituzionale.

**monast-ery** *n.* monastero. **-ic(al)** *adj.* monastico; claustrale. **-icism** *n.* monachismo; vita monastica.

**Monday** *pr.n.* lunedì *m.*; *on -(s)*, il lunedì.

**monetary** *adj.* monetario.

**money** *n.* denaro, danaro; (fam.) soldi, quattrini *m.pl.*; *Italian* —, valuta italiana; *to be rolling in* —, nuotare nell'oro, avere un sacco di quattrini; *to be short of* —, essere a corto di denaro, essere senza soldi; *to get one's -'s worth*, spendere bene il proprio denaro; *for the* —, a quel prezzo; *a piece of* —, una moneta; *paper* —, moneta cartacea, biglietti *m.pl.*; *public* —, fondi pubblici; *ready* —, contanti *m.pl.*; *to be unwilling to part with* —, essere attaccato al denaro; *to make* —, far soldi, arricchirsi; *to raise* —, procurarsi del denaro, raccogliere soldi; — *thrown away*, denaro sprecato; *your — or your life!*, la borsa o la vita!; *time is* —, il tempo è denaro; (fam.) *not for love or* —, neanche dipinto.

**money-belt** *n.* cintura portadenari.

-**box** *n.* salvadanaio. -**ed** *adj.* danaroso, ricco; *the -ed classes*, i benestanti, i ricchi. -**changer** *n.* cambiavalute *m.*, agente *m.* di cambio. -**grubber** *n.* avaro, uno che s'interessa solo a fare soldi. -**lender** *n.* usuraio; strozzino. -**market** *n.* borsa valori. -**order** *n.* vaglia *m. indecl.*

**monger** *n.* mercante *m.*, venditore. -**ing** *n.* (derog.) traffico.

**Mongolia** *pr.n.* (geog.) Mongolia.

**Mongol, -ian** *adj.*, *n.* mongolo; (language) lingua mongolica. -**ic** *adj.* mongolico. -**oid** *adj.* mongoloido.

**mongoose** *n.* (zool.) mangusta.

**mongrel** *adj.* misto, ibrido; *n.* (dog) bastardo; (person) uomo di sangue misto, meticcio.

**mon-ism,** *n.* (philos.) monismo. -**ist** *n.* monista *m.* -**istic** *adj.* monistico.

**monitor** *n.* (am)monitore, consigliere; (schol.) capoclasse *m.*; (zool.) varano; (naut.) monitore, pontone *m.*, armato corazzato; (electr.) monitore, avvisatore; (radio) monitore; *tr.* (radio) controllare, ascoltare, intercettare; (teleph.) ascoltare segretamente. -**ing** *n.* (radio) servizio di ascolto. -**y** *adj.* ammonitore; (eccl.) monitorio; *-y letter*, monitorio.

**monk** *n.* monaco.

**monkey** *n.* scimmia; scimmiotto; (fam.) *you young —!*, birichino!; *— business*, imbroglio; (pop.) *to get someone's — up*, far andare qualcuno in bestia; *attrib.* scimmiesco; *tr.* scimmiottare; (pop.) *to — about with*, maneggiare maldestramente; immischiarsi in. -**ish** *adj.* scimmiesco.

**monkey-house** *n.* gabbia delle scimmie. -**jacket** *n.* (cost.) giacca corta. -**like** *adj.* scimmiesco. -**nut** *n.* arachide *f.*, babbagigi *m.pl.* -**puzzle** *n.* (bot.) araucaria. -**wrench** *n.* chiave inglese.

**monkfish** *n.* (ichth.) squadro, angelo.

**monkshood** *n.* (bot.) aconito, napello.

**monochord** *n.* (mus.) monocordo; (teleph.) monocorda.

**monochrom-e** *adj.* (art) monocromo; *n.* monocroma. -**atic** *adj.* monocromatico.

**monoc-le** *n.* monocolo, caramella. -**ular** *adj.* monoculare.

**monogam-y** *n.* monogamia. -**ic** *adj.* monogamico. -**ist** *n.* monogamo; fautore della monogamia. -**ous** *adj.* monogamo.

**monogram** *n.* monogramma *m.* -**matic(al)** *adj.* monogrammatico.

**monograph** *n.* monografia. -**er,** -**ist** *n.* monografista *m.*, scrittore di monografie.

**monolith** *n.* monolito. -**ic** *adj.* monolitico.

**monologue** *n.* monologo, soliloquio.

**monomania** *n.* monomania. -**c** *adj.* monomaniaco; *n.* monomane *m.*

**monoplane** *n.* (aeron.) monoplano.

**monopol-y** *n.* monopolio, possesso esclusivo. -**ist** *n.* monopolista *m.*; accaparratore, incettatore; fautore del monopolio. -**ization** *n.* monopolizzazione; accaparramento. -**ize** *tr.* monopolizzare; accaparrare. -**izer** *n.* monopolizzatore.

**mono-rail** *adj.* a una rotaia; *n.* monorotaia. -**syllabic(al)** *adj.* monosillabico, monosillabo. -**syllable** *n.* monosillabo. -**theism** *n.* (rel.) monoteismo. -**theist** *n.* (rel.) monoteista *m.* -**theistic** *adj.* (rel.) monoteistico.

**monoton-e** *adj.* monotono, senza modulazioni; *n.* uniformità di tono. -**ous** *adj.* monotono, uniforme. -**ousness,** -**y** *n.* monotonia.

**monotype** *n.* (typ.) monotipo; monotipia.

**monoxide** *n.* (chem.) monossido.

**monsignor(e)** *n.* monsignore *m.*

**monsoon** *n.* monsone *m.*

**monster** *n.* mostro; *attrib.* enorme, colossale.

**monstrance** *n.* (eccl.) ostensorio.

**monstrosity** *n.* mostruosità.

**monstrous** *adj.* mostruoso; atroce; enorme, colossale, prodigioso; incredibile. -**ly** *adv.* mostruosamente; prodigiosamente. -**ness** *n.* mostruosità; enormità.

**Mont Blanc** *pr.n.* (geog.) Monte Bianco.

**Mont Cenis** *pr.n.* (geog.) Moncenisio; *the — tunnel*, la galleria del Fréjus.

**Monte Carlo** *pr.n.* (geog.) Montecarlo.

**month** *n.* mese *m.*; *this day —*, fra un mese; *a — ago today*, un mese fa, oggi un mese; *by the —*, al mese; *from — to —*, di mese in mese; *-'s salary*, mensile *m.*, mensilità; (fam.) *a — of Sundays*, un'eternità. -**ly** *adj.* mensile; *adv.* mensilmente, al mese, una volta al mese; *n.* rivista mensile; *pl. monthlies*, mestruazione, (pop.) marchesa.

**monument** *n.* monumento; documento. -**al** *adj.* monumentale; colossale; imponente; *-al mason*, marmista *m.*

**moo** *n.* mugghio, muggito; *intr.* mugghire, muggire.

**mooch** *n.* fiacca; *intr.* (pop.) gironzolare, battere la fiacca; *tr.* (pop.) sgraffignare.

**mood**[1] *n.* (gramm.; mus.) modo.

**mood**[2] *n.* umore *m.*; stato d'animo; disposizione; *in a good —*, di buon umore; *in a bad —*, di cattivo umore; *in a generous —*, disposto ad essere generoso; *to feel in the — to*, sentirsi disposto a; *to feel in no laughing —*, non aver nessuna voglia di ridere; *pl.* capricci *m.pl.*, ubbie *f.pl.*; *a man of -s*, un uomo capriccioso. -**ily** *adv.* di malumore; tristemente; malinconicamente. -**iness** *n.* malinconia; malumore *m.*; tristezza; umore nero. -**y** *adj.* malinconico, triste; di malumore, imbronciato, cupo; capriccioso; *to be -y*, aver la luna.

**moon** *n.* luna; *full —*, luna piena, plenilunio; *half —*, mezza luna; *new —*, luna nuova, novilunio; *crescent —*, luna crescente, luna falcata; *waning —*, luna calante; *by the light of the —*, al chiaro di luna; *to land on the —*, allunare; (fig.) *to bay at the —*, abbaiare alla luna; *to cry for the —*, chiedere l'impossibile; *to promise someone the — and the stars*, promettere mari e monti a qualcuno; *to make someone believe that the — is made of green cheese*, far vedere la luna nel pozzo; *once in a blue —*, a ogni morte di vescovo; *tr. to — away the time*, perdere tempo sognando; *intr.* guardare con aria trasognata, sognare. -**beam** *n.* raggio di luna, raggio lunare. -**less** *adj.* senza luna, buio. -**light** *n.* chiaro di luna; *in (the) -light, by -light*, al chiaro di luna; *-light walk*, passeggiata al chiaro di luna; (fam.) *-light flit*, trasloco clandestino per non pagare l'affitto; *to do a -light flit*, fare il San Martino. -**lit** *adj.* illuminato dalla luna. -**rise** *n.* sorgere della luna. -**rock** *n.* roccia portata dalla luna. -**set** *n.* tramonto della luna. -**shine** *n.* chiaro di luna *m.*; (fam.) *it's all -shine!*, sono balle!; whisky distillato clandestinamente, whisky di contrabbando. -**stone** *n.* (miner.) pietra lunare, lunaria. -**struck** *adj.* lunatico. -**y** *adj.* di luna, simile alla luna; (fam.) distratto, trasognato, svagato.

**moor**[1], -**land** *n.* (heath) brughiera, landa.

**Moor**[2] *n.* Moro; Saraceno. -**ish** *adj.* moro, moresco.

**moor**[3] *tr.*, *intr.* (naut.) ormeggiare, ammarrare; ancorare. -**ing** *n.* (naut.) ormeggio, ammarraggio; ancoraggio; (fig.) *to loose one's -ings*, andare alla deriva.

**moorhen** *n.* (orn.) gallinella d'acqua.

**moose** *n.* (zool.) alce *m.*

**moot** *adj.* discutibile, controverso, dubbio; *— point*, punto controverso; *n.* (hist.) assemblea popolare; *— hall*, camera di consiglio; *tr.* sollevare; discutere.

**mop**[1] *n.* scopa di stracce, strofinaccio, straccio; (of hair) zazzera; (naut.) radazza; *tr.* pulire con uno strofinaccio; (fig.) *to — one's brow*, asciugarsi il sudore dalla fronte; (slang) *to*

— *the floor with*, aver la meglio su; *to — up*, asciugare, prosciugare, (slang) far piazza pulita di, (mil.) rastrellare.

**mop**[2] *n.* smorfia; *-s and mows*, boccacce *f.pl.*

**mope** *n.* musone *m.*; (fig.) *to have a fit of the -s*, veder tutto nero; *intr.* avvilirsi, imbronciarsi; immusonirsi.

**moped** *n.* micromotore, cucciolo.

**moppet** *n.* bambola fatta di cenci; (fam., of a woman) bambolina.

**mopy** *adj.* immusonito.

**morain-e** *n.* (geol.) morena. **-ic** *adj.* (geol.) morenico.

**moral** *adj.* morale; etico; — *philosophy*, filosofia morale, — *sense*, senso morale; virtuoso, onesto, serio; (fam.) virtuale, effettivo; *n.* morale *f.*; lezione; *pl.* moralità, buon costume, etica; *of easy -s*, di facili costumi; *of no -s*, amorale. **-e** *n.* morale *m.* **-ist** *n.* moralista *m.*, *f.* **-istic** *adj.* moralistico; didattico. **-ity** *n.* moralità; morale *f.*; buon costume; (theatr.) *-ity play*, sacra rappresentazione.

**moraliz-e** *tr.* moralizzare; rendere più morale; trarre la morale da; *intr.* moralizzare; moraleggiare. **-ation** *n.* moralizzazione; interpretazione morale.

**morally** *adv.* moralmente, in senso morale; virtuosamente; (fam.) effettivamente, virtualmente.

**morass** *n.* palude *f.*, pantano, acquitrino. **-ic, -y** *adj.* paludoso, acquitrinoso.

**moratorium** *n.* moratoria.

**Moravia** *pr.n.* (geog.) Moravia. **-n** *adj.*, *n.* (rel.) moravo; *-n Brethren*, Fratelli moravi.

**morbid** *adj.* morboso, malsano; (med.) morboso, patologico. **-ity, -ness** *n.* morbosità; (med.) stato patologico.

**mord-acity, -ancy** *n.* mordacità; asprezza; causticità. **-ant** *adj.* mordente; pungente; caustico; (chem.) corrosivo.

**mordent** *n.* (mus.) mordente *m.*

**more** *adj.*, *indef. prn.*, *n.* più, di più; una maggior quantità di, un maggior numero di; — *than*, più di, più che; *any —*, *some —*, di più, ancora, ancora un po' (di); *a little —*, ancora un po' (di); a few —, ancora qualche; *no —*, non . . . più; *nothing —*, nulla di più, non . . . più nulla; *the — . . . the —*, (quanto) più . . . (tanto) più; *all the —*, a più forte ragione; *adv.* più, di più, maggiormente, ancora; — *beautiful*, più bello; — *and —*, sempre più; — *or less*, più o meno, all'incirca; *neither — nor less*, nè più nè meno; *never —*, mai più; *so much the —*, tanto più, — *than once*, più di una volta; *once —*, ancora una volta.

**morel** *n.* (bot.) morchella esculenta.

**morello** *n.* (cherry) marasca.

**moreover** *adv.* inoltre, poi, per di più, daltronde.

**moresque** *adj.* moresco.

**morganatic** *adj.* morganatico.

**morgue** *n.* obitorio.

**moribund** *adj.* moribondo, morente.

**morisco** *adj.* moresco; (hist.) moro di Spagna; (Mexico) meticcio ispano-messicano; (dance) danza moresca.

**mormon** *adj.*, *n.* mormone *m.*, *f.* **-ism** *n.* mormonismo.

**morn** *n.* (poet.) mattino; cf. **morning**; indomani *m.*

**morning** *n.* mattino, mattina; mattinata; *good —!*, buon giorno!; *this —*, stamattina; *tomorrow —*, domani mattina; *in the —*, di mattina, in mattinata; *at four o'clock in the —*, alle quattro del mattino; *early in the —*, di buon mattino; *from — till night*, da mattina a sera, dal mattino alla sera; *to have the — off*, avere la mattinata libera; *attrib.* — *call*, visita di mattina; — *dress*, abito di mattino; — *gun*, tiro di diana; — *paper*, giornale del mattino; — *prayer*, preghiera mattutina; — *star*, stella del mattino, Venere, diana; — *tea*, tè bevuto prima di alzarsi; — *coffee*, caffè bevuto verso le undici del mattino; (fig.) *the — of life*, l'alba della vita; (bot.) — *glory*, ipomea.

**morning-coat** *n.* abito da cerimonia, finanziera, tight *m.* **-room** *n.* salottino.

**Morocc-o** *pr.n.* Marocco; (leather) marocchino. **-an** *adj.*, *n.* marocchino.

**moron** *n.* deficiente *m.*, *f.*; degenerato, scemo. **-ic** *adj.* stupido.

**morose** *adj.* tetro; cupo; sgarbato; misantropico. **-ness** *n.* tetraggine *f.*; sgarbatezza; mancanza di socievolezza.

**Morpheus** *pr.n.* (myth.) Morfeo; (joc.) *to be in the arms of —*, essere in braccio a Morfeo.

**morph-ia, -ine** *n.* morfina; *the — habit*, morfinomania.

**morpholog-y** *n.* morfologia. **-ical** *adj.* (ling.) morfologico.

**Morris Dance** *n.* danza moresca; danza campestre inglese.

**morrow** *n.* indomani *m.*

**morse**[1] *n.* (liturg.) pettorale *m.*

**morse**[2] *n. the — alphabet*, l'alfabeto Morse.

**morsel** *n.* bocconcino, pezzetto; tozzo.

**mortal** *adj.* mortale; *the — remains*, i resti mortali, le spoglie; mortale, letale, micidiale; (fig.) implacabile, fino alla morte; — *enemies*, nemici acerrimi; (fam.) *seven — days*, sette interminabili giorni; *to be in a — hurry*, avere molta fretta; *n.* mortale *m.*, *f.* **-ity** *n.* mortalità. **-ly** *adv.* mortalmente, a morte; (fam.) molto.

**mortar**[1] *n.* mortaio; *pestle and —*, pestello e mortaio; (artill.) mortaio.

**mortar**[2] *n.* (bldg.) malta, calcina; *to.* fissare con calcina.

**mortar-board** *n.* (bldg.) giornello; (schol.) tocco accademico.

**mortgag-e** *n.* ipoteca; *to raise a —*, accendere un'ipoteca; *to raise money on a —*, prendere denaro a prestito su garanzia ipotecaria; *to pay off a —*, estinguere un'ipoteca; *to be encumbered with -s*, essere gravato da ipoteche; *to redeem from —*, liberare da ipoteca; *tr.* ipotecare; (fig.) impegnare. **-ee** *n.* creditore ipotecario. **-er, -or** *n.* debitore ipotecario.

**mortice** *n.*, *tr.* see **mortise.**

**mortician** *n.* (USA) imprenditore di pompe funebri, necroforo.

**mortif-y** *tr.* mortificare; umiliare; (med.) incancrenire; *intr.* incancrenirsi. **-ication** *n.* mortificazione; (med.) cancrena, necrosi *f.*, ammortimento.

**mortise** *n.* (carpen.) mortasa, mortesa, incastro; *tr.* (carpen.) incastrare, congiungere a mortasa, addentare.

**mortmain** *n.* (leg.) manomorta.

**mortuary** *adj.* mortuario; *n.* obitorio, camera mortuaria.

**mosaic**[1] *adj.* (art) musivo, di mosaico; *n.* mosaico; *worker in —*, mosaicista *m.*; (photog.) mosaico aerofotografico, rilevamento fotopanoramico. **-ist** *n.* (art) mosaicista *m.*

**Mosaic**[2] *adj.* mosaico, di Mosè.

**moschatel** *n.* (bot.) adoxa, erba fumaria.

**Moscow** *pr.n.* (geog.) Mosca.

**Moselle** *pr.n.* (geog.) Mosella; (wine) vino della Mosella.

**Moses** *pr.n.* Mosè.

**Moslem** *adj.*, *n.* maomettano, musulmano.

**mosque** *n.* moschea.

**mosquito** *n.* (ent.) zanzara, anofele *f.* **-bite** *n.* puntura di zanzara. **-net** *n.* zanzariera. **-netting** *n.* garza per zanzariera.

**moss** *n.* (bot.) muschio, musco; (provb.) *a rolling stone gathers no —*, pietra che rotola non raccoglie muschio; terreno acquitrinoso; (peat) torbiera.

**moss-grown** *adj.* coperto di muschio.

**mossy** *adj.* muscoso, coperto di muschio.

**most** *adj.*, *n.* il più, il massimo, la maggior parte di, il maggior numero di; *at the —*, al massimo, tutt'al più; *in — cases*, nella generalità dei casi; — *of the time*, il più del tempo; *the — times*, il maggior numero di volte; *the — mistakes*, il maggior numero di errori; — *of us*, la maggior parte

di noi; *to make the — of*, trarre il meglio da, saper sfruttare al massimo; *adv.* molto, estremamente, — *likely*, molto probabilmente; *it is — kind of you*, sei molto gentile; soprattutto, maggiormente, di più; (superlative) il più *m.*, la più *f.*, i più *m.pl.*, le più *f.pl.* (N.B. The superlative is also expressed by adding -issimo, -issimamente, to *adj.* or *adv.*)

**mote** *n.* festuca, pagliuzza, bruscolo; granellino.

**motel** *n.* albergo per automobilisti, motel *m. indecl.*

**motet** *n.* (mus.) mottetto.

**moth** *n.* (ent.) falena; *clothes —*, tignola, tarma. **-balls** *n.* palline antitarma. **-eaten** *adj.* tarmato, roso dalle tarme; (fam.) vecchio, antiquato, malandato.

**mother** *n.* madre *f.*, (fam.) mamma; (eccl.) — *Superior*, (madre) superiora; *reverend —*, reverenda madre; — *country*, madrepatria; — *earth*, madreterra; — *tongue*, madrelingua; (fig.) madre, genitrice *f.*, maestra; (provb.) *necessity is the — of invention*, la necessità è il miglior maestro; (orn.) *Mother Carey's chickens*, procellaria; (pop.) donna anziana, vecchia; *tr.* curare come una madre, fare da madre a; dar vita a. **-craft** *n.* puericultura. **-hood** *n.* maternità.

**mothering** *n.* cure materne.

**mother-in-law** *n.* suocera.

**mother-land** *n.* madrepatria. **-less** *adj.* senza madre, orfano di madre.

**motherl-y** *adj.* materno, di madre, da madre; *in a — way*, maternamente. **-iness** *n.* tenerezza materna, atteggiamento materno.

**mother-naked** *adj.* nudo come un neonato, nudo come lo fece madre natura.

**mother-of-pearl** *n.* madreperla.

**mothproof** *adj.* antitarmico, inattaccabile dalle tarme.

**mothy** *adj.* tarmato, pieno di tarme.

**motif** *n.* (art; mus.) motivo; idea predominante, tema *m.*

**motion** *n.* moto; movimento; *the laws of —*, le leggi del moto; *perpetual —*, moto perpetuo; *to set in —*, mettere in moto, avviare; gesto, cenno; — *of the bowels*, andata di corpo; proposta; (pol.) mozione *f.*; *the — was carried*, la mozione fu approvata; *to reject a —*, respingere una mozione; *to put a — to the vote*, mettere una mozione ai voti; *tr.*, *intr.* far cenno, far segno; *to — someone away*, far cenno a qualcuno di allontanarsi; *to — someone to a chair*, invitare qualcuno a sedersi. **-less** *adj.* senza moto; immobile; fermo.

**motion-picture** *n.* pellicola cinematografica, — *theatre*, cinema. *m.*

**motivat-e** *tr.* motivare, dare un motivo a; essere il motivo di, causare, cagionare. **-ion** *n.* motivazione; motivo; movente *m.*

**motive** *adj.* motore; — *power*, forza motrice; *n.* motivo; movente *m.*; causa; ragione *f.*; *to have a — for doing something*, avere un motivo per fare qualcosa. **-less** *adj.* senza motivo.

**motley** *adj.* screziato, variopinto; *a — collection*, un miscuglio eterogeneo; *n.* (hist.) giubba variopinta (dei buffoni); *to wear the —*, fare il buffone.

**motor** *adj.* motore, motorio; *n.* (engine) motore *m.*; (car) automobile *f.*, macchina; *intr.* andare in macchina; *tr.* accompagnare in macchina. **-boat** *n.* motoscafo. **-bike, -cycle** *n.* motocicletta; *to -cycle*, andare a motocicletta. **-cycling** *n.* motociclismo. **-cyclist** *n.* motociclista. **-cade** *n.* sfilata di macchine. **-coach** *n.* pullman *m.*, torpedone *m.*

**motor-driven** *adj.* azionato a motore. **-fuel** *n.* carburante *m.* **-horn** *n.* clacson *m.*, tromba.

**motor-ing** *adj.* automobilistico; *n.* automobilismo. **-ist** *n.* automobilista *m.*

**motoriz-e** *tr.* motorizzare. **-ation** *n.* motorizzazione.

**motor-lorry** *n.* autocarro, camion *m.*; (with trailer) autotreno.

**motorman** *n.* macchinista *m.*, manovratore.

**motor-road** *n.* strada carrozzabile. **-scooter** *n.* moto, motoretta, vespa. **-spirit** *n.* carburante *m.*, benzina. **-vehicle** *n.* autoveicolo. **-vessel** *n.* (naut.) motonave *f.*

**motorway** *n.* autostrada.

**mottle** *n.* screziatura, chiazza; *tr.* marezzare, screziare, chiazzare. **-d** *adj.* chiazzato, screziato; venato.

**motto** *n.* motto; epigramma *m.*; detto; aforismo; (on crest) divisa; (in book) epigrafe *f.*

**moujik** *n.* mugik *m.*, contadino russo.

**mould**[1] *n.* (agric.) terriccio.

**mould**[2] *n.* muffa.

**mould**[3] *n.* (industr.) forma, stampo, modello; (fig.) stampo, tempra, carattere *m.*; (archit.) modanatura; (techn.) cassaforma; (geol.) impronta di fossile; (cul.) stampo, (pudding) budino, cucinato nello stampo; *tr.* modellare; formare; foggiare; plasmare; (metall.) fondere, gettare.

**moulder**[1] *intr.* ridursi in polvere; consumarsi; sgretolarsi.

**moulder**[2] *n.* modellatore; plasmatore.

**mouldiness** *n.* muffa; l'essere ammuffito; (fig.) stantio.

**moulding** *n.* modellatura; formazione; (industr.) stampaggio, formatura; (metall.) fusione, getto; (archit.) modanatura, cornice *f.*, cornicione *m.*

**mouldy** *adj.* muffito, ammuffito; *to turn —*, ammuffire; *to smell —*, sentire di muffa; (pop.) antiquato; *to feel —*, sentirsi a terra.

**moult** *n.* (of birds) muda; (of silkworms) muta; *intr.* mudare; mutare le penne. **-ing** *n.* (of birds) muda.

**mound** *n.* monticello; collinetta; tumulo; mucchio.

**mount**[1] *n.* monte *m.*; montagna; (bibl.) *the Sermon on the Mount*, il Sermone della Montagna.

**mount**[2] *n.* cavalcatura; (racing) monta; (opt.) montatura; (photog.) incorniciatura, montatura; sostegno, intelaiatura, affusto; (mech.) incastellatura.

**mount**[2] *tr.* salire (sopra, su); montare (su, a); *to — a hill*, salire su una collina; *to — a horse*, montare a cavallo; *to — someone*, fornire qualcuno di cavallo; (of animals) coprire; *to be -ed*, essere a cavallo; (mil.) *to — guard over*, fare la guardia a; *to — the guard*, cambiare la guardia; (artill.) *to — a gun*, mettere in posizione un cannone; (jewels, etc.) montare; incastonare; (photog.) incorniciare; (industr.) montare; (fig.) organizzare; mettere in scena; *intr.* salire, montare; (of blood) affluire; *to — up*, aumentare, crescere; *to — up to*, ammontare a.

**mountain** *n.* montagna; — *chain*, catena di montagne; — *pass*, valico, passo; — *sickness*, mal di montagna; *attrib.* di montagna; *to go to the -s*, andare in montagna; (fig.) *-s high*, altissimo; *a — of debts*, un mucchio di debiti; *to make a — out of a molehill*, affogare in un bicchier d'acqua. **-ash,** sorbo selvatico. **-eer** *n.* montanaro; (climber) alpinista *m.*; scalatore. **-eering** *n.* alpinismo. **-ous** *adj.* montagnoso, montuoso; alpestre; (fig.) enorme.

**mountebank** *n.* saltimbanco; (pejor.) ciarlatano.

**mounted** *part. adj.* (on horseback) a cavallo; (of photo *etc.*) incorniciato; (of jewel) incastonato; (mech.) montato.

**mounter** *n.* (industr.) montatore.

**mounting** *adj.* che sale, in salita; (fig.) in aumento; *n.* salita; (industr.) montaggio; (of photo, etc.) cornice *f.*; (of jewel) incastonatura, montatura; (theatr.) messa in scena, allestimento.

**mourn** *tr.*, *intr.* piangere, rim-

piangere, lamentare; *intr.* addolorarsi, lamentarsi, piangere. -**er** *n.* chi segue un funerale, chi è in lutto; *chief -s*, parenti stretti; (anthrop.) prefica.

**mournful** *adj.* triste; lamentoso; lugubre; funereo. -**ness** *n.* tristezza; dolore *m.*; malinconia; aspetto malinconico.

**mourning** *adj.* che lamenta, lamentoso; *n.* cordoglio; dolore *m.*; lutto; *to go into —*, mettere il lutto; *to wear —*, portare il lutto; *deep —*, lutto stretto; *half-mourning*, mezzo lutto; (fam.) *nails in —*, unghie a lutto.

**mourning-band** *n* fascia da lutto.

**mouse** *n.* sorcio, topo, topolino; (fig.) persona timida; *as poor as a church —*, povero in canna; *intr.* (of cat) far la caccia ai topi.

**mouse-coloured** *adj.* grigio topo.

**mouser** *n.* (cat) cacciatore di topi.

**mousetrap** *n.* trappola per topi; (fig.) trabocchetto.

**moustache** *n.* baffi *m.pl.*; mustacchi *m.pl.*; *toothbrush —*, baffi all'americana; *to wear a —*, portare i baffi. -**d** *adj.* baffuto.

**mousy** *adj.* (colour) grigio topo; che odora di topo; (fig.) timido, dimesso; silenzioso.

**mouth** *n.* bocca; (of animal) fauci *f.pl.*, gola; *from — to —*, di bocca in bocca; *by word of —*, a bocca, a voce; *useless —*, mangiapane *m.*, *f.*; *to have a nasty taste in one's —*, avere la bocca amara; *to live from hand to —*, vivere alla giornata; *to make someone's — water*, far venire l'acquolina in bocca a qualcuno; *to make a wry —*, storcere la bocca; *to put words into someone's —*, suggerire a qualcuno ciò che deve dire; *to take the words out of someone's —*, rubare le parole di bocca a qualcuno; (provb.) *don't look a gift horse in the —*, a caval donato non si guarda in bocca; (fam.) *to be down in the —*, essere depresso, essere giù di corda; *to make someone laugh on the wrong side of his —*, far passare la voglia di ridere a qualcuno; *shut your —!*, chiudi il becco!; (of river) foce *f.*, bocca, sbocco; (of tunnel) entrata, imbocco, ingresso; orifizio, apertura; smorfia.

**mouth** *tr.* declamare; *to — one's words*, pronunciare le parole con tono enfatico; *to — a horse*, abituare un cavallo al morso; (techn.) fare l'imboccatura a; *intr.* declamare; far smorfie.

**mouthful** *n.* boccone *m.*; boccata; *to swallow something at a —*, ingoiare qualcosa in un boccone; (fig.) parola lunga, frase roboante; sgridata.

**mouth-organ** *n.* armonica a bocca.

**mouthpiece** *n.* (mus.) imboccatura; becco; bocchetta; (of pipe) bocchino; (fig.) portavoce *m.*; organo.

**mouth-wash** *n.* acqua dentifricia.

**movab-le** *adj.* mobile, movibile; *— feast*, festa mobile; *pl.* beni mobili. -**ility** *n.* mobilità.

**move** *n.* movimento; *to be always on the —*, essere sempre in movimento; trasloco; (at games) mossa; (fig.) mossa, manovra, passo; *a bad —*, un passo falso, una manovra sbagliata; (fam.) *get a — on!*, sbrigati!; *to make a —*, andarsene; *what's the next —?*, cosa si fa adesso?

**move** *tr.* muovere; spostare; rimuovere; agitare; *to — one's head*, muovere la testa; *to — one's car*, spostare la macchina; *the wind -s the trees*, il vento agita gli alberi; *to — something from its place*, spostare qualcosa; (fig.) *to — heaven and earth*, muovere cielo e terra; commuovere, intenerire; *I was much -d*, fui molto commosso; *to — to tears*, commuovere fino alle lacrime; spingere, incitare, far cambiare idea a; *to be -d to act*, essere spinto ad agire; *nothing will — him*, niente gli farà cambiare idea; proporre; *to — a resolution*, proporre una mozione; *intr.* muoversi, mettersi in moto, spostarsi; *but it does —!*, eppur si muove!; *the train began to —*, il treno si mise in moto; *to — from one point to another*, spostarsi da un punto all'altro; *to keep moving*, spostarsi continuamente, circolare; traslocare, cambiar casa; *he has -d to Milan*, si è trasferito a Milano; (at games) fare una mossa; (fig.) *to — in good society*, frequentare l'alto mondo; *events are moving quickly*, gli avvenimenti si succedono rapidamente; *the action of the play -s slowly*, l'azione della commedia si svolge lentamente; *it's time we were moving*, è l'ora di andarsene. FOLLOW. BY ADV. OR PREP.: *to — about*, *tr.* spostare qua e là, *intr.* andare e venire, girare; *to — along*, *intr.* avanzare, circolare; *to — away*, *tr.* allontanare, portare via, *intr.* allontanarsi, andare via, partire; *to — back*, *tr.* far indietreggiare, spingere indietro, rimettere al posto di prima, *intr.* indietreggiare, rinculare, ritirarsi; *to — forward*, *tr.* far avanzare, *intr.* avanzare; *to — in*, *tr.* trasferire in, *intr.* entrare, traslocare in un nuovo alloggio; *to — off*, *intr.* allontanarsi, partire, mettersi in moto; *to — on*, *tr.* far circolare, *intr.* circolare; *to — out*, *tr.* far uscire, sgomberare, *intr.* sloggiare, traslocare; *to — towards*, *intr.* dirigersi verso; *to — up*, *tr.* far salire, *intr.* salire, avvicinarsi.

**movement** *n.* movimento; moto; gesto, cenno; (of prices) oscillazione; (mech.) meccanismo.

**mover** *n.* animatore; promotore; fautore; anima; (rel.) *the Prime Mover*, il Primo Motore; (of resolution) proponente *m.*, *f.*; (mech.) forza motrice.

**movie** *n.* (fam.) film *m.*; *pl. the -s*, il cinema; *— star*, stella del cinema; (woman) diva. -**land** *n.* (fam.) cinelandia, cinecittà.

**moving** *adj.* movente, mobile, in movimento, in moto; *a — train*, un treno in moto; *— staircase*, scala mobile; *— pictures*, cinema *m.*, cinematografo; *— spirit*, animatore; commovente, patetico, eloquente. -**ly** *adv.* eloquentemente; con passione.

**mow** *tr.* falciare; mietere, tagliare; (fig.) *to — down*, falciare, sterminare. -**er** *n.* (person) falciatore; mietitore; (machine) falciatrice; *lawn-mower*, falciatrice da prati. -**ing** *n.* falciatura; mietitura.

**mowing-machine** *n.* falciatrice.

**mown** *part.* of **mow**, *q.v.*

**much** *adj.* molto; *how —*, quanto; *so —*, tanto; *too —*, troppo; *very —*, moltissimo; *as — again*, altrettanto; *adv.* molto, assai, di gran lunga; *how —*, quanto; *so —*, tanto; *too —*, troppo; *— as*, per quanto; *as — as*, (tanto) quanto; *not so — as*, non tanto quanto; pressappoco; *— the same*, pressappoco lo stesso; *— to my astonishment*, con mio grande stupore.

**much** *n.* molto; gran parte; gran quantità; *I don't see — of him*, non lo vedo molto; *— of what he says*, gran parte di quello che dice; *it's not up to —* non vale gran che; *he is not — of an artist*, non è un grande artista; *to make — of someone*, festeggiare qualcuno, fare una grande accoglienza a; *to make — of something*, esagerare l'importanza di qualcosa; *to think — of*, avere una grande opinione di. -**ness** *n. to be much of a -ness*, essere pressappoco uguali, (fam.) darsela.

**mucilag-e** *n.* mucillaggine *f.* -**inous** *adj.* mucillagginoso.

**muck** *n.* (agric.) concime *m.*; letame *m.*; fango; fradiciume *m.*; (pejor.) porcheria, oscenità, sconcezza; cosa senza valore; *the food was awful —*, il cibo era una vera porcheria; *to write —*, scrivere libri osceni; (fam.) *to make a — of*, fare un pasticcio di; *tr.* (agric.) concimare; (pejor.) sporcare, lordare; *intr.* (pop.) *to — about*, bighellonare; *to — about with*, giocherellare con, fare delle carezze spinte a (una ragazza); *to — in with*, dividere la stessa camera con; *to — up*, fare un pasticcio di.

**muck-heap** *n.* letamaio; concimaia. -**rake** *n.* rastrello per il

concime. **-raking** *n.* (fam.) diffusione di notizie scandalose.

**mucky** *adj.* (fam.) fangoso, sporco; lurido, sudicio.

**muc-ous** *adj.* mucoso; viscoso; (anat.) — *membrane*, mucosa. **-us** *n.* muco.

**mud** *n.* fango; mota; melma; *river* —, limo; — *hut*, capanna di mota, tugurio; (fam.) *to be all over* —, essere tutto sporco di fango; *to get stuck in the* —, impantanarsi; (fig.) *to sling — at*, gettare fango su, denigrare, calunniare; (fam.) *his name is* —, il suo nome puzza.

**mud-bath** *n.* bagno di fango.

**muddied** *adj.* imbrattato di fango, infangato; torbido.

**muddiness** *n.* fangosità; torbidezza; (fig.) mancanza di chiarezza.

**muddl-e** *n.* confusione; disordine *m.*, pasticcio; imbroglio; *in a* —, confuso, in un pasticcio, in confusione; *to get into a* —, confondersi; *to make a — of*, fare un pasticcio di; *tr.* confondere; mettere confusione tra; affastellare; intontire, dare alla testa a; *to — up*, creare disordine in; *intr.* fare confusione; *to — about*, lavorare disordinatamente; *to — along*, tirare avanti alla meglio; *to — through*, cavarsela alla meno peggio, arrabattarsi. **-ed** *adj.* disordinato, in disordine; confuso; (with drink) intontito, alticcio. **-er** *n.* guastamestieri *m.*; pasticcione *m.*; confusionario. **-ing** *adj.* confusionario; che rende perplesso; imbarazzante.

**muddle-headed** *adj.* confusionario.

**muddy** *adj.* fangoso; melmoso; infangato; inzaccherato; ammelmato; torbido; opaco; (fig.) — *complexion*, brutta cera; *tr.* inzaccherare; imbrattare fango, infangare; intorbidare.

**mud-flap** *n.* (on bicycle) paraspruzzi *m. indecl.*

**mudguard** *n.* (motor.) parafango.

**mudlark** *n.* (fam.) monello, birichino.

**mud-pack** *n.* impiastro di fango. **-scraper** *n.* pulisciscarpe *m.*; **-slinger** *n.* denigratore, calunniatore; maldicente *m., f.*

**mud-stained** *adj.* imbrattato di fango.

**muezzin** *n.* muezzino.

**muff**[1] *n.* manicotto.

**muff**[2] *n.* (fam.) scimunito, persona maldestra; (sport) colpo mancato; *to make a — of*, mancare, sbagliare; *tr.* (fam.) mancare, sbagliare.

**muffin** *n.* tartina da tè.

**muffle** *n.* (techn.) muffola; (of animal) muso; *tr.* smorzare, attutire; soffocare, affogare; (drums) velare; (fig.) *to — up*, imbacuccare, avvolgere; *to — oneself up to the eyes*, imbacuccarsi fino alle orecchie.

**muffler** *n.* (cost.) sciarpa; (boxing) guantone *m.*; (in piano) feltro; (techn.) silenziatore, marmitta.

**mufti** *n.* (rel.) mufti *m.*; (mil.) abito civile; *in* —, in borghese.

**mug**[1] *n.* tazza, coppa.

**mug**[2] *n.* (slang) ceffo; gonzo, sempliciotto; *a -'s game*, roba per i gonzi; sgobbone, secchione *m.*; *tr.* (slang) *to — up*, sgobbare per imparare, studiare con lena.

**mug**[3] *tr.* (fam.) assalire.

**mugful** *n.* tazza piena.

**mugg-y** *adj.* umido e caldo; afoso; da scirocco; che sa di rinchiuso. **-iness** *n.* afa; calore umido; scirocco; aria viziata, odore di stantio.

**mugwort** *n.* (bot.) canapaccia, amareggiola, artemisia.

**mugwump** *n.* (slang) pezzo grosso.

**mulatto** *adj.*, *n.* mulatto.

**mulberry** *n.* mora, mora di gelso; — *tree*, moro, gelso.

**mulch** *n.* (hortic.) strame *m.*, terriccio, riparo di paglia umida; *tr.* (hortic.) riparare con terriccio.

**mulct** *tr.* multare, colpire di multa; *to — of*, privare di, far pagare.

**mule**[1] *n.* mulo *m.*, mula *f.*; *stubborn as a* —, testardo come un mulo; (text.) filatoio intermittente; (orn.) — *canary*, canarino ibrido.

**mule**[2] *n.* (slipper) ciabatta; pianella.

**mule-litter** *n.* lettiga.

**muleteer** *n.* mulattiere *m.*

**mule-track** *n.* mulattiera.

**mulish** *adj.* di mulo, da mulo, mulesco; (fig.) caparbio, ostinato, duro. **-ness** *n.* ostinazione; caparbietà; testardaggine *f.*

**mull**[1] *n.* (geog.) promontorio, capo.

**mull**[2] *n.* (fam.) confusione, pasticcio.

**mull**[3] *tr.* (text.) addocilire.

**mull**[4] *tr.* (fam.) non riuscire in, far fiasco in; *intr. to — over*, rimuginare.

**mull**[5] *tr.* riscaldare e condire con spezie; *-ed wine*, vino caldo, brûlè *m.*

**mullein** *n.* (bot.) tassobarbasso, coda di leone.

**muller** *n.* pestello; molazza.

**mullet**[1] *n.* (ichth.) *grey* —, muggine *m.*; *red* —, triglia.

**mullet**[2] *n.* (herald.) stella.

**mullion** *n.* (archit.) piantone *m.*, regolo.

**multi-colour(ed)** *adj.* multicolore, variopinto. **-farious** *adj.* multiforme, molteplice. **-fariousness** *n.* varietà; diversità; molteplicità. **-form** *adj.* multiforme; vario. **-lateral** *adj.* multilaterale. **-millionaire** *adj.*, *n.* multimilionario, miliardario.

**multiple** *adj.* multiplo, molteplice; — *store*, negozio a catena; *n.* (math.) multiplo; *least common* —, minimo comune multiplo; (electr.) parallelo.

**multiplex** *adj.* molteplice; (techn.) multiplo.

**multipli-able, -cable** *adj.* moltiplicabile. **-cand** *n.* moltiplicando. **-cation** *n.* moltiplicazione; *-cation table*, tavola pitagorica. **-cative** *adj.* moltiplicativo. **-cator** *n.* moltiplicatore. **-city** *n.* molteplicità; varietà.

**multipl-y** *tr.* moltiplicare; *intr.* moltiplicarsi. **-ier** *n.* (math.; electr.) moltiplicatore. **-ying** *n.* moltiplicazione, moltiplicarsi.

**multisyllable** *adj.* multisillabo, polisillabo.

**multitud-e** *n.* moltitudine *f.*; gran numero; massa, folla; molteplicità. **-inous** *adj.* molteplice; innumerevole; molto numeroso.

**mum**[1] *adj.*, *excl.* (fam.) zitto; *-'s the word!*, zitto!, acqua in bocca!; *to keep* —, tacere, non rifiatare.

**mum**[2] *n.* (fam.) mamma, mammina.

**mumble** *n.* borbottìo, mormorìo; *tr.*, *intr.* borbottare; mormorare; biascicare.

**mumbo-jumbo** *n.* (fam.) abracadabra *m.*

**mummer** *n.* (theatr.) mimo; (pejor.) guitto. **-y** *n.* (theatr.) mascherata, buffonata; (pejor.) cerimoniale ridicolo, abracadabra *m.*

**mummif-y** *tr.* mummificare; *intr.* mummificarsi. **-ication** *n.* mummificazione.

**mummy**[1] *n.* mummia.

**Mummy**[2] *n.* (fam.) mamma, mammina.

**mumps** *n.* (med.) parotite *f.*; (fam.) orecchioni *m.pl.*

**munch** *tr.* sgranocchiare; masticare; *intr.* ruminare.

**mundan-e** *adj.* mondano; terrestre. **-eness, -ity** *n.* mondanità.

**Munich** *pr.n.* (geog.) Monaco di Baviera; (pol.) cessione, compromessa (dal patto Anglo-tedesco del 1938).

**municipal** *adj.* municipale; comunale; — *buildings*, municipio; — *toll*, dazio. **-ism** *n.* municipalismo; (pejor.) campanilismo. **-ity** *n.* municipalità; comune *m.*

**munific-ence** *n.* munificenza. **-ent** *adj.* munificente, munifico.
**muniment** *n.* documento, atto; — *room*, archivio.
**munition(s)** *n.* munizioni *f.pl.*; rifornimenti, approvviggionamenti *m.pl.*
**munition** *tr.* fornire di munizioni.
**mural** *adj.* murale; *n.* murale *m.*, affresco.
**murder** *n.* (leg.) omicidio, (fam.) assassinio; *wilful* —, omicidio doloso, premeditato; (fig.) macello; *sheer* —, un vero macello; *tr.* ammazzare, assassinare, uccidere; (fig.) massacrare. **-er** *n.* (leg.) omicida *m.*, (fam.) assassino. **-ess** *n.* omicida *f.*, assassina. **-ous** *adj.* omicida, micidiale; sanguinario; feroce.
**murex** *n.* (zool.) murice *m.*
**murk-y** *adj.* buio, oscuro, fosco, tenebroso; — *darkness*, buio-fitto. **-iness** *n.* oscurità, buio (fig.) torbidezza.
**murmur** *n.* mormorìo; sussurro; borbottamento; (med.) soffio; *without a* —, senza fiatare, senza mormorare; *intr.*, *tr.* mormorare; sussurrare; borbottare; brontolare. **-er** *n.* mormoratore; brontolone *m.*, brontolona *f.*
**murrain** *n.* (vet.) epizoozia; (fam.) peste *f.*, moria, malanno.
**muscat, muscatel** *adj.*, *n.* (grape, wine) moscato.
**muscle** *n.* muscolo; (fam.) *without moving a* —, senza batter ciglia; muscolatura, forza muscolare; *man of* —, uomo muscoloso.
**Muscov-y** *pr.n.* (geog.; hist.) Moscovia. **-ite** *adj.*, *n.* moscovita *m.*, *f.*
**muscular** *adj.* (anat.) muscolare; — *man*, uomo muscoloso; (med.) — *injection*, iniezione intramuscolare. **-ity** *n.* muscolosità; vigore muscolare.
**Muse**[1] *pr.n.* Musa.
**muse**[2] *intr.* meditare, riflettere, fantasticare.
**museum** *n.* museo. **-piece** *n.* pezzo da museo.
**mush** *n.* (cul.) poltiglia, intriso, pappa; (pop.) stupidaggini *f.pl.*
**mushroom** *n.* fungo mangereccio; (bot.) agarico, fungo prataiuolo; *to spring up like -s*, venire su come i funghi; — *growth*, sviluppo rapido; *intr.* raccogliere funghi; (fig.) svilupparsi rapidamente, dilagare; (of bullet) schiacciarsi. **-bed** *n.* fungaia.
**mushy** *adj.* spappolato, molle; (fig.) sdolcinato, sentimentale.
**music** *n.* musica; *academy of* —, conservatorio; *chamber* —, musica da camera; *to set to* —, musicare, mettere in musica; *to write* —, comporre musica; (fig.) *the* — *of the spheres*, l'armonia celeste; (fam.) *to face the* —, affrontare le critiche, affrontare una sfuriata. **-al** *adj.* musicale; armonioso; melodioso; dotato per la musica; appassionato della musica, musicofilo; *to have a -al ear*, aver orecchio per la musica; *-al box*, cariglione *m.*; *-al comedy*, operetta; *-al instrument*, strumento; *-al director*, direttore d'orchestra; *n.* operetta, melodramma *m.* **-ality** *n.* musicalità; armonia.
**music-cabinet** *n.* portamusica *m.* **-hall** *n.* teatro di varietà. **-holder** *n.* leggìo.
**musician** *n.* musicista *m.*, musicante *m.*, *f.*, musico; *street* —, suonatore ambulante.
**music-lover** *n.* musicofilo, filarmonico.
**musicograph-y** *n.* musicografia. **-er** *n.* musicografo.
**musicolog-y** *n.* musicologia. **-ical** *adj.* musicologico.
**music-paper** *n.* carta pentagrammata. **-room** *n* sala da musica. **-stand** *n.* leggìo. **-stool** *n.* sgabello da pianoforte.
**musing** *adj.* meditabondo, pensoso; *n.* meditazione, riflessione, fantasticheria.
**musk** *n.* (zool.) muschio; (bot.) mimulo.
**musket** *n.* moschetto, fucile *m.* **-eer** *n.* moschettiere. **-ry** *n.* moschetteria, fucileria; (mil.) tiro.
**musk-ox** *n.* bue muschiato. **-rat** *n.* (zool.) topo muschiato, zibellino. **-rose** *n.* (bot.) rosa muschiata.
**musky** *adj.* muschiato, che odora di muschio.
**Muslim** *adj.*, *n.* musulmano.
**muslin** *n.* mussola, mussolina.
**musquash** *n.* topo muschiato, zibellino; pelliccia di topo muschiato.
**mussel** *n.* (zool.) mitillo; muscolo; cozza; *freshwater* —, anodonta.
**Mussulman** *adj.*, *n.* musulmano.
**must**[1] *n.* (of wine) mosto.
**must**[2] *n.* muffa.
**must**[3] *n.* (of animals) eccitazione periodica; — *elephant*, elefante infuriato.
**must**[4] *def. vb. he* — *go*, deve andare; *I* — *be more careful*, devo stare più attento; *it* — *be done*, deve essere fatto; bisogna che, è necessario che; *I* — *be going*, bisogna ch'io vada; *he* — *have left*, deve essere partito, sarà partito; *n.* (fam.) cosa essenziale, cosa che deve assolutamente essere fatta.
**mustang** *n.* mustango.
**mustard** *n.* (bot.) senape *f.*; (cul.) senape, mostarda.
**mustard-gas** *n.* iprite *f.* **-plaster** *n.* senapismo. **-pot** *n.* mostardiera. **-seed** *n.* seme di senape.
**muster** *n.* assembramento; riunione; (mil.) adunata, rivista; (fig.) *to pass* —, essere accettabile; *tr.* radunare; (mil.) passare in rassegna; (fig.) *to* — *up courage*, farsi coraggio, prendere il coraggio a due mani; *intr.* radunarsi. **-roll** *n.* ruolo, ruolino; (naval) appello.
**must-y** *adj.* ammuffito; stantio; rancido; *to grow* —, ammuffire; vecchio, superato. **-iness** *n.* muffa; odore di muffa.
**mutab-le** *adj.* mutabile, mutevole; incostante. **-ility** *n.* mutabilità; incostanza.
**mutation** *n.* mutamento; cambiamento; (biol.; mus.) mutazione.
**mute** *adj.* muto; ammutolito; silenzioso; taciturno; (phon.) muto, mutolo; *n.* muto; *undertaker's* —, beccamorto; (mus.) sordina; (theatr.) comparsa; *tr.* (mus.) mettere la sordina a. **-ness** *n.* mutezza, mutismo.
**mutilat-e** *tr.* mutilare; storpiare; mozzare; troncare. **-ion** *n.* mutilazione; mozzamento; troncamento. **-or** *n.* mutilatore.
**mutin-y** *n.* ammutinamento; rivolta; sedizione; *intr.* ammutinarsi; ribellarsi. **-eer** *n.* ammutinato; rivoltoso; rebelle *m.* **-ous** *adj.* ammutinato; rivoltoso; ribelle; sedizioso.
**mutism** *n.* mutismo.
**mutt** *n.* (slang) babbeo, scimunito.
**mutter** *n.* mormorìo; borbottìo; brontolamento; *intr.* mormorare; borbottare, brontolare; rumoreggiare; *tr. to* — *an oath*, borbottare un'imprecazione; *to* — *prayers*, biascicare paternostri. **-er** *n.* brontolone *m.* **-ing** *n.* mormorìo; borbottìo; brontolìo.
**mutton** *n.* (cul.) carne *f.* di montone *m.*; castrato; *leg of* —, cosciotto di montone; (fam.) *dead as* —, morto stecchito. **-chop** *n.* costoletta di montone; (fam.) *-chop whiskers*, favoriti, scopettoni *m.pl.*
**mutual** *adj.* reciproco; corrisposto; scambievole; — *benefit*, reciproco vantaggio; mutuo, comune; — *friend*, comune amico; *on* — *terms*, alla pari. **-ity** *n.* mutualità, reciprocità.
**muzzle** *n.* (of animal) muso; (for dogs, *etc.*) museruola; (of weapon) bocca, imboccatura; — *velocity*, velocità iniziale; *tr.* mettere la museruola a; (fig.) far tacere, tacitare, imbavagliare. **-loader** *n.* fucile ad avancarica, cannone ad avancarica.
**muzzy** *adj.* (fam.) intontito, inebetito; (fig.) confuso.
**my** *poss. adj.* il mio *m.*, la mia *f.*, i miei *m.pl.*, le mie *f.pl.*; — *book and* — *pen*, il mio libro e la mia penna; — *father and mother*, mio padre e mia madre; — *parents*, i miei genitori; *one of* — *friends*, un mio amico; *it's* — *turn*, tocca a me; *I have broken* — *arm*, mi son

rotto il braccio; — *goodness!*, santo cielo!, accipicchia!
**Mycenae** *pr.n.* (geog.) Micene. **-an** *adj.* micenico, miceneo.
**mycology** *n.* (bot.) micetologia.
**myelitis** *n.* (med.) mielite *f.*
**myocard-ium** *n.* (anat.) miocardio. **-itis** *n.* (med.) miocardite *f.*
**myop-ia** *n.* miopia. **-ic** *adj.* miope.
**myriad** *adj.* innumerevole; *n.* miriade *f.*
**Myrmidon** *n.* (hist.) mirmidone *m.*; (fig.) sbirro; *the -s of the law*, gli sbirri, i poliziotti.
**myrrh** *n.* mirra.
**myrtle** *n.* (bot.) mirto, mortella.
**myself** *prn.* (*nom.*) io stesso; (*acc.*, *dat.*) me stesso, mi, me; *I* —, io stesso; *I enjoyed* —, mi sono divertito; *I have hurt* —, mi sono fatto male; *for* —, per me; *as for* —, quanto a me; *by* —, da solo; *I was speaking to* —, parlavo tra me e me; *I am not quite* —, mi sento poco bene; *I am quite — again*, mi sono completamente rimesso.
**mystago-gue** *n.* mistagogo. **-gy** *n.* mistagogia.
**mysterious** *adj.* misterioso; arcano, strano. **-ness** *n.* misteriosità; mistero; segretezza.
**mystery** *n.* mistero; segreto; *wrapped in* —, avvolto nel mistero; *to make a — of*, fare un segreto di; (theatr.) — *play*, sacra rappresentazione, mistero.
**mystic** *adj.*, *n.* mistico. **-al** *adj.* mistico; misterioso. **-ism** *n.* misticismo, mistica.
**mystif-y** *tr.* mistificare; ingannare; disorientare. **-ication** *n.* mistificazione; disorientamento; inganno; burla.
**myth** *n.* mito. **-ical** *adj.* mitico; immaginario. **-icize** *tr.* volgere in mito; interpretare mitologicamente. **-ographer** *n.* mitografo. **-ography** *n.* mitografia.
**mytholog-y** *n.* mitologia. **-ic(al)** *adj.* mitologico; immaginario. **-ist** *n.* mitologo, mitologista *m.*
**myxomatosis** *n.* (med.) mixomatosi *f.*

**N, n** *n.* enne *m.*, *f.*; (teleph.) — *for Nellie*, enne come Napoli; (math) $n^{th}$, ennesimo; $n^{th}$ *power*, ennesima potenza.
**nab** *tr.* (fam.) arraffare, agguantare, acciuffare; (pop.) pescare; *to get -bed*, farsi pescare.
**nabob** nababbo.
**Naboth** *pr.n.* (bibl.) Nabot.
**nacelle** *n.* (aeron.) navicella, carlinga.
**nacre** *n.* madreperla. **-ous** *adj.* madreperlaceo.
**nadir** *n.* nadir *m.*; (fig.) punto di massima depressione.
**nag** *n.* (fam.) ronzino, cavalluccio; *tr.* rimbrottare; tormentare; cavare l'anima a; infastidire; *intr.* brontolare. **-ger** *n.* bisbetica, brontolona. **-ging** *adj.* (of wife) bisbetica, brontolona; (fig.) fastidioso; *n.* brontolio; (fig.) fastidio.
**naiad** *n.* (myth.) naiade *f.*
**nail** *n.* **1.** (anat.) unghia; *to bite one's -s*, mordersi le unghie; *to cut one's -s*, tagliarsi le unghie; (fig.) *tooth and* —, con accanimento. **2.** chiodo; *to drive a — home*, conficcare un chiodo, (fig.) guingere ad una conclusione, far valere la propria opinione; *to drive a — into someone's coffin*, affrettare la fine di qualcuno; (fam.) *hard as -s*, robustissimo, durissimo; severo; rigoroso; senza compassione; *to hit the — on the head*, colpire nel segno; *to pay on the* —, pagare in contanti.
**nail** *tr.* inchiodare; fissare con chiodi; mettere dei chiodi a; *to — a notice on the board*, fissare un avviso sul tabellone con chiodi; *to — up*, fissare con chiodi, chiudere con chiodi, inchiodare; (fig.) *to — one's colours to the mast*, persistere, irrigidirsi sulle proprie posizioni; *to — down*, chiudere con chiodi; (fig.) *to — down a lie*, dimostrare la falsità di un'affermazione; *to — someone down*, mettere qualcuno con le spalle al muro. **-ed** *adj.* fornito di chiodi; *-ed boots*, scarpe chiodate.
**nail-brush** *n.* spazzolino da unghie. **-drawer, -extractor** *n.* cacciachiodo. **-file** *n.* lima da unghie. **-head** *n.* capocchia di chiodo. **-polish** *n.* smalto per unghie. **-scissors** *n.pl.* forbici da unghie.
**naïve, naive** *adj.* ingenuo, semplice; candido. **-ty** *n.* ingenuità, semplicità; candore *m.*; dabbenaggine *f.*
**naked** *adj.* nudo; spogliato; *stark* —, nudo nudissimo; — *as the day of his birth*, nudo come mamma lo fece; *to strip* —, denudare, spogliare; (fig.) inerme, indifeso, non riparato, spoglio; *to the — eye*, a occhio nudo; *a — light*, una fiamma non riparata; — *sword*, spada sguainata; *the — truth*, la verità pura e semplice. **-ness** *n.* nudità.
**namby-pamby** *adj.* affettato, sentimentale, sdolcinato, insulso.
**name** *n.* nome *m.*; nominativo; *Christian* —, *first* —, nome (di battesimo); *family* —, cognome *m.*; *full* —, nome e cognome, generalità *f.pl.*; *to give one's full* —, declinare le generalità; *assumed* —, pseudonimo; *maiden* —, nome di signorina; *pet* —, vezzeggiativo; (mil.) —, *rank and number*, nome e cognome, grado e numero di matricola; *what is your* —?, Lei, come si chiama?; *my name is . . .*, mi chiamo . . .; *by* —, di nome; *in the — of*, a nome di; *in my* —, a mio nome; *another — for*, un sinonimo di; *to call by* —, chiamare per nome; *to go by the — of*, chiamarsi, farsi chiamare, andare sotto il nome di; *to lend one's — to*, prestare il proprio nome a, prestarsi a; *to put down one's* —, iscriversi, farsi iscrivere; *to put one's — to a document*, apporre la propria firma a un documento; *he hasn't a penny to his* —, non ha neanche un soldo; reputazione, fama, nome; *ill* —, brutta reputazione; *to have a — for*, essere noto come, godere fama di; *to make a — for oneself*, farsi un nome, affermarsi, emergere; (comm.) *trade* —, nome depositato; (theatr.) — *part*, ruolo del personaggio che dà il titolo all'opera, protagonista *m.*, *f.*; *to call someone -s*, dire delle insolenze a qualcuno, coprire qualcuno di ingiurie.
**name** *tr.* nominare; dare un nome a; chiamare; denominare; designare; *to be -d*, chiamarsi; fissare, scegliere; menzionare, accennare a, parlare di.
**nam(e)able** *adj.* nominabile; degno di essere nominato.
**name-day** *n.* onomastico.
**nameless** *adj.* senza nome; innominato; anonimo; ignoto.
**namely** *adv.* cioè, vale a dire; nominatamente.
**name-plate** *n.* targhetta.
**namesake** *n.* omonimo.
**Nancy** *pr.n.* (*dimin.* of **Anne**) Nina, Ninetta, Annetta; (slang) finocchio.
**nankeen** *n.* (text.) nanchino, anchina.
**Nanking** *pr.n.* (geog.) Nanchino.
**nanny** *n.* bambinaia, balia.
**nanny-goat** *f.* (fam.) capra, capretta.
**Naomi** *pr.n.* Noemi.
**nap**[1] *n.* sonnellino; pisolino; *to take a* —, schiacciare un pisolino, fare un sonnellino.
**nap**[2] *n.* (text.) peluria; pelo; *against the* —, a contrappelo; *tr.* (text.) felpare, cardare; spazzolare a contrappelo.

**nap**[3] *n.* (cards) napoleone *m.*
**nape** *n.* nuca.
**naphtha** *n.* nafta. **-lene** *n.* naftalina.
**napkin** *n.* tovagliuolo, salvietta; — *ring,* anello per tovagliuolo; (for baby) pannolino.
**Naples** *pr.n.* (geog.) Napoli *f.*
**Napoleon** *pr.n.* Napoleone; *n.* (coin) napoleone *m.*, marengo. **-ic** *adj.* napoleonico.
**napping** *adj. to catch someone* —, prendere qualcuno alla sprovvista.
**nappy** *n.* (fam.) pannolino.
**Narciss-us** *pr.n.* (myth.) Narciso; *n.* (bot.) narciso. **-ism** *n.* narcisismo.
**narco-sis** *n.* (med.) narcosi *f.* **-tic** *adj.*, *n.* narcotico.
**nard** *n* (bot.) nardo.
**nark** *n.* (slang) *copper's* —, spia della polizia, bivio.
**narrat-e** *tr.* narrare; raccontare. **-ion** *n.* narrazione; racconto; narrativa. **-ive** *adj.* narrativo; *n.* narrativa, racconto, resoconto. **-or** *n.* narratore; raccontatore.
**narrow** *adj.* stretto; ristretto; angusto; limitato; — *street,* vicolo stretto; — *circle,* ristretta cerchia; — *mind,* mente ristretta; — *majority,* maggioranza esigua; *to become -er,* restringersi; *to have a — escape,* scamparla bella, salvarsi per miracolo; minuzioso, rigoroso; — *inspection,* ispezione rigorosa; *n.* (geog.) stretta; *pl.* stretto.
**narrow** *tr.* restringere; limitare; *to — the gap between,* ridurre lo scarto fra; *to — down an argument,* restringere una discussione; *intr.* restringersi; contrarsi; *the road -s,* la strada si restringe. **-ly** *adv.* strettamente; ristrettamente; a stento; da vicino; (fig.) a fondo; minuziosamente; rigorosamente.
**narrow-gauge** *adj.* (rlwy.) a scartamento ridotto. **-minded** *adj.* di mente ristretta, di idee ristrette; gretto; retrogrado. **-mindedness** *n.* ristrettezza di mente; grettezza; povertà di spirito.
**narrowness** *n.* strettezza; ristrettezza; limitatezza; esiguità; meschinità; grettezza.
**narthex** *n.* (archit.) nartece *m.*
**narwhal** *n.* (zool.) narvalo.
**nasal** *adj.* nasale; (joc.) — *organ,* naso; *n.* (ling.) nasale *f.*, suono nasale; (of helmet) nasale *m.* **-ization** *n.* nasalizzazione. **-ize** *tr.* nasalizzare; *intr.* parlare con voce nasale.
**nascent** *adj.* nascente.
**nastily** *adv.* in modo disgustoso; sgradevolmente; con cattiveria.
**nastiness** *n.* schifosità; cattivo gusto; cattiveria.
**nasturtium** *n.* (bot.) nasturzio, fior cappuccino.
**nasty** *adj.* schifoso, disgustoso, ripugnante; cattivo, dispettoso, antipatico; *to turn* —, diventare cattivo; (of weather) brutto, cattivo; (fig.) *a — surprise,* una brutta sorpresa; (fam.) *a — one,* un colpo mancino; *a — piece of work,* un tipo antipatico; *a — mind,* una mente sporca.
**natal** *adj.* natale; — *day,* giorno natalizio.
**natation** *n.* nuoto.
**Nathaniel** *pr.n.* Nataniele.
**nation** *n.* nazione; popolo; *League of Nations,* Società delle Nazioni; *United Nations Organization* (UNO), Organizzazione delle Nazioni Unite (ONU).
**national** *adj.* nazionale; — *anthem,* inno nazionale; — *debt,* debito pubblico; — *insurance,* assicurazione di previdenza sociale; — *service,* servizio militare obbligatorio; *n.* cittadino; *pl.* connazionali *m.pl.*, compatrioti *m.pl.* **-ism** *n.* nazionalismo, patriottismo. **-ist** *n.* nazionalista *m.*, *f.* **-istic** *adj.* nazionalistico. **-ity** *n.* nazionalità; cittadinanza.
**nationaliz-e** *tr.* (pol.) nazionalizzare; (grant citizenship) naturalizzare. **-ation** *n.* (pol.) nazionalizzazione; (granting of citizenship) naturalizzazione.
**nationally** *adv.* nazionalmente; come nazione.
**national-socialism** *n.* (pol. hist.) nazionalsocialismo, nazismo. **-socialist** *n.* (pol. hist.) nazionalsocialista *m.*, *f.*, nazista *m.*, *f.*
**nation-wide** *adj.* diffuso in tutto il paese, nazionale.
**native** *adj.* indigeno; (pejor.) di razza non europea; nativo, oriundo, originario; natio; — *land,* terra natia; innato; (bot.) aborigene, autoctono; *n.* nativo; oriundo; indigeno; *to speak Italian like a* —, parlare italiano come uno del luogo; *to go* —, vivere da indigeno; (oyster) ostrica inglese.
**native-born** *adj.* nativo, di nascita; *a — Italian,* un italiano di nascita.
**nativity** *n.* natività; nascita; (astrol.) oroscopo.
**natter** *intr.* (fam.) brontolare; chiacchierare
**natt-y** *adj.* lindo; ben tenuto; svelto; *a — little gadget,* una piccola invenzione geniale. **-iness** *n.* lindezza, sveltezza.
**natural** *adj.* naturale; — *history,* storia naturale; — *law,* legge *f.* di natura; *death from — causes,* morte *f.* naturale; normale, genuino, non affettato; *in a — voice,* con voce normale, con voce per nulla affettata; innato, istintivo; — *enemies,* nemici *m.pl.* per istinto; — *gift,* dono innato; *f. a — mistake,* un errore comprensibile; *it comes — to me,* lo faccio per istinto; (of child) illegittimo, bastardo, naturale; (mus.) naturale, bequadro; *n.* cretino, mentecatto; *he's a* —, è un genio, lo fa per istinto; (mus.) nota naturale, bequadro; (cards) asso e dieci.
**natural-ism** *n.* (art) naturalismo. **-ist** *n.* (zool.; art) naturalista *m.*, *f.*; (phys.) fisicista *m.* **-istic** *adj.* naturalistico.
**naturaliz-e** *tr.* naturalizzare; (plants, animals) acclimatare. **-ation** *n.* naturalizzazione; (of plants, animals) acclimatamento.
**naturally** *adv.* naturalmente; istintivamente; (fig.) per forza; ben inteso.
**naturalness** *n.* naturalezza; disinvoltura; mancanza di affettazione.
**nature** *n.* natura; *the beauties of* —, le bellezze della natura; *human* —, la natura umana; *state of* —, stato naturale; *return to* —, ritorno allo stato primitivo; (art) *to paint from* —, dipingere dal vero; carattere *m.*, indole *f.*, temperamento, disposizione, inclinazione; (of things) essenza; *good* —, bonarietà; *ill* —, cattiveria; *second* —, seconda natura; *it is in the — of things that,* è naturale che; *things of this* —, roba di questo genere.
**natured** *adj.* (in compounds) di natura, di carattere.
**nature-lover** *n.* cultore *m.* della natura.
**naturism** *n.* naturismo, nudismo.
**naught** *n.* niente *m.*, nulla; *to come to* —, non riuscire, riuscire male, ridursi a zero; *to set at* —, non tenere in alcun conto. Cf. **nought.**
**naughtiness** *n.* (of child) cattiveria, cattiva condotta, disubbidienza; (wickedness) malvagità, (of story, *etc.*) carattere spinto.
**naughty** *adj.* (of child) cattivo, birichino, disubbidiente; (wicked) malvagio; (of story, etc.) spinto, grossolano.
**nausea** *n.* nausea; (fig.) avversione; fastidio, disgusto.
**nauseate** *tr.* nauseare, disgustare, stomacare.
**nauseating, nauseous** *adj.* nauseante, nauseabondo, disgustoso.
**nauseousness** *n.* nausea, carattere disgustoso.
**nautical** *adj.* nautico, marino, navale; — *mile,* miglio marittimo; — *science,* nautica.
**nautilus** *n.* (zool.) nautilo.
**naval** *adj.* navale, marittimo; della marina di guerra; — *officer,* ufficiale *m.* di marina; — *base,* base *f.* navale, porto militare.
**Navarre** *pr.n.* (geog.) Navarra.
**nave** *n.* (of church) navata

(centrale), nave *f.*; (of wheel) mozzo.
**navel** *n.* (anat.) ombelico; (fig.) punto centrale.
**navel-string** *n.* cordone *m.* ombelicale.
**navigab-le** *adj.* navigabile. **-ility, -leness** *n.* navigabilità.
**navigat-e** *tr.* navigare in, percorrere; governare, regolare la rotta di; *intr.* navigare, far rotta. **-ion** *n.* navigazione. **-or** *n.* navigatore; (aeron., naut.) ufficiale di rotta.
**navvy** *n.* terrazziere, sterratore, manovale *m.*
**navy** *n.* marina da guerra. **-blue** *n.* blu marino.
**nay** *adv.* no; anzi, anche, di più.
**Nazarene** *adj., n.* nazzareno.
**Nazareth** *pr.n.* (geog.) Nazaret *f.*
**Naz-i** *adj., n.* nazista *m., f.* **-ism** *n.* Nazismo.
**neap** *adj.* — *tide*, livello minimo raggiunto dall'alta marea al primo e al terzo quarto di luna, marea sizigia.
**Neapolitan** *adj., n.* napoletano; — *ice-cream*, cassata.
**near** *adj.* vicino; *-er*, più vicino; *-est*, prossimo, (il) più vicino; *the Near East*, il vicino oriente; *in the — distance*, vicino, in primo piano; *to take a -er view*, guardare da più vicino; (fam.) *a — miss*, un colpo mancato per un pelo; *to make a — guess*, quasi indovinare; *it was a — thing*, è quasi quasi successo, l'abbiamo scampata bella; *the -est way*, la strada più breve; (fig.) — *relations*, parenti stretti; *our -est and dearest*, i nostri cari; *a — resemblance*, una rassomiglianza stretta; approssimativo; *a — translation*, una traduzione approssimativa; avaro, tirchio; (motor., in Britain) *the — wheel*, la ruota sinistra; *to keep to the — side*, tenere la sinistra; *adv.* vicino, presso, accanto; — *at hand*, a portata di mano; — *by*, vicinissimo; *-er and -er*, sempre più vicino; *from — to*, da vicino; *as — as possible*, quanto vicino possibile; *to come —*, avvicinarsi; *to bring —*, avvicinare, accostare; quasi, circa; *prep.* vicino a, presso a, accanto a; — *me*, vicino a me; — *the town*, nei pressi della città; — *here*, qui vicino; *to be — the end*, avvicinarsi alla fine; *to come — to doing something*, essere sul punto di fare qualcosa; *tr.* avvicinare, avvicinarsi a.
**nearby** *adj.* vicino, accanto, adiacente; *adv.* vicino, dappresso, accanto; *prep.* vicino a, accanto a.
**nearly** *adv.* quasi; *very —*, quasi quasi, pressappoco; — *always*, quasi sempre; *not —*, affatto, tutt'altro che; *he — died*, poco mancò che non morisse; *not — enough*, tutt'altro che sufficiente, meno di quanto ci vuole.
**nearness** *n.* prossimità; vicinanza; intimità; esattezza; parsimonia, grettezza.
**near-sighted** *adj.* miope. **-ness** *n.* miopia.
**neat**[1] *adj.* pulito, lindo, ordinato, ben tenuto; elegante, di buon gusto; abile, destro; conciso, chiaro, epigrammatico; — *whisky*, whisky liscio.
**neat**[2] *n.* bovino; *-'s leather*, vacchetta; *-'s foot oil*, olio di piede di bue.
**neatly** *adv.* lindamente, pulitamente, ordinatamente; — *dressed*, vestito con buon gusto, elegante; abilmente, destramente; concisamente.
**neatness** *n.* pulizia; ordine; eleganza; buon gusto; abilità; concisione.
**Nebuchadnezzar** *pr.n.* (bibl.) Nabucodonosor, Nabucco.
**nebul-a** *n.* (astron.) nebulosa. **-ar** *adj.* (astron.) nebulare, di nebulosa. **-osity, -ousness** *n.* nebulosità. **-ous** *adj.* nebulare; nuvoloso; (fig.) nebuloso, vago, poco chiaro.
**necessarily** *adv.* necessariamente, di necessità.
**necessary** *adj.* necessario; indispensabile; richiesto; *to be —*, essere necessario, occorrere, bisognare, abbisognare; *to make all the — arrangements*, dare tutte le disposizioni utili; *more than is —*, più che non bisogna; *if —*, se mai, al bisogno; *a — evil*, un male inevitabile; *pl.* occorrente *m.*, fabbisogno; *the necessaries of life*, il necessario per vivere.
**necessitate** *tr.* necessitare, rendere necessario; richiedere.
**necessitous** *adj.* povero; bisognoso; indigente; *in — circumstances*, nell'indigenza. **-ness** *n.* indigenza; bisogno; penuria; miseria.
**necessity** *n.* necessità; *of —*, necessariamente, inevitabilmente; *a case of absolute —*, un caso di forza maggiore; *doctrine of —*, determinismo; *to be under the — of*, essere costretto a; *there is no — for you to do this*, non è necessario che tu faccia questo; *to make a virtue of —*, fare di necessità virtù; (provb.) — *is the mother of invention*, la necessità è il miglior maestro; — *knows no law*, la necessità non ha legge; urgenza, bisogno assoluto; *except in case of —*, salvo in caso di urgenza; necessario; indigenza, bisogno, miseria.
**neck** *n.* (anat.) collo; (of dress) scollatura; (of stringed instrument) manico; (geog., of land) lingua, istmo; (of sea) braccio, (in mountains) collo, col *m.*; *stiff —*, torcicollo; *to break one's —*, rompersi il collo; *to risk one's —*, rischiare la vita; *to save one's —*, sottrarsi alla morte, salvar la pelle; *to wring the — of*, tirare il collo a; (sport) *to win by a —*, vincere per un'incollatura; — *and —*, testa a testa; — *or nothing*, tutto per tutto; (fam.) — *and crop*, a capofitto; *to be up to one's — in work*, essere soffocato dal lavoro; *to get it in the —*, incassare un duro colpo, prendersi una lavata di capo; *intr.* (slang) sbaciucchiarsi.
**neck-band** *n.* collaretto, listino del collo. **-cloth** *n.* fazzoletto da collo; cravatta.
**neckerchief** *n.* fazzoletto da collo.
**neck-lace** *n.* collana. **-let** *n.* colletto, collo. **-tie** *n.* cravatta. **-wear** *n.* colletti *m.pl.*, cravatte *f.pl.*
**necrolog-y** *n.* necrologia; (obituary notice) necrologio. **-ical** *adj.* necrologico. **-ist** *n.* necrologista *m.*
**necroman-cer** *n.* negromante *m.* **-cy** *n.* negromanzia. **-tic** *adj.* negromantico.
**necropolis** *n.* necropoli *f.*
**nectar** *n.* (myth.) nettare *m.*
**nectarine** *n.* pesca noce.
**née** *adj.* nata.
**need** *n.* bisogno; necessità; *if — be, in case of —*, caso mai, al bisogno, se c'è bisogno; *there is no — to*, non occorre, non c'è bisogno di; *there is — for patience*, occorre pazienza, ci vuole pazienza; *to have — of, to be in — of*, aver bisogno di, abbisognare di; *to fill a —*, colmare un vuoto; *in the hour of —*, nei momenti difficili; (provb.) *a friend in — is a friend indeed*, nel bisogno si conoscono gli amici; miseria, indigenza.
**need** *tr.* aver bisogno di, abbisognare di, richiedere, volerci; *I — your help*, ho bisogno del tuo aiuto; *this -s patience*, questo richiede pazienza, ci vuole pazienza; *he -s a rest*, ha bisogno di riposarsi; (*aux.*) essere necessario, occorrere; — *he go?*, è proprio necessario che vada?; *she — not wait*, non occorre ch'essa aspetti; *we -n't have hurried*, non occorreva che ci affrettassimo; *he -n't have done it*, non c'era bisogno che lo facesse.
**needed** *adj.* necessario, che ci voleva, di cui c'era bisogno.
**needful** *adj.* necessario, abbisognevole; indispensabile; occorrente; *n. the —*, il necessario, (fam.) i soldi occorrenti. **-ness** *n.* necessità; bisogno.
**neediness** *n.* bisogno; indigenza; povertà.
**needle** *n.* ago; *eye of a —*, cruna; *to thread a —*, infilare un ago; *gramophone —*, puntina; (phys.) *space —*, ago spaziale, dipolo; (geog.) picco, guglia; (bot., of pine), ago; *shepherd's —*, acicula;

(fam.) *pins and -s*, formicolìo; *tr.* cucire; pungere con ago; (pop.) irritare, punzecchiare.
**needle-case** *n.* astuccio per aghi. agoraio.
**needleful** *n.* gugliata.
**needle-shaped** *adj.* a forma di ago, aghiforme; (bot.) acicolare.
**needless** *adj.* inutile; superfluo; non necessario. **-ly** *adv.* inutilmente, senza necessità. **-ness** *n.* inutilità; superfluità.
**needle-woman** *n.* cucitrice. **-work** *n.* lavoro ad ago, cucito; *to do —*, lavorare d'ago.
**needs** *adv.* (used only before or after 'must') necessariamente, per forza.
**needy** *adj.* indigente, bisognoso, povero.
**ne'er** *adv.* (poet. for **never**) mai, giammai, non . . . mai. **-do-well** *n.* buono a nulla, fannullone *m.*
**nefarious** *adj.* nefario, nefando; scellerato; losco; abbominevole. **-ness** *n.* nefandezza; scelleratezza.
**negat-e** *tr.* negare. **-ion** *n.* negazione.
**negative** *adj.* negativo; *n.* negazione; *to answer in the —*, rispondere di no; *two -s make an affirmative*, due negazioni affermano; (photog.) negativa; *tr.* respingere, porre il veto a; neutralizzare.
**neglect** *n.* negligenza; trascuratezza; noncuranza; disattenzione; omissione; abbandono; *tr.* trascurare; tralasciare; abbandonare; dimenticare; *to — to do something*, mancare di far qualcosa. **-ful** *adj.* negligente, noncurante; *to be -ful of*, trascurare.
**neglig-ence** *n.* negligenza; trascuratezza; indifferenza. **-ent** *adj.* negligente; trascurato; indifferente.
**negligible** *adj.* trascurabile.
**negotiab-le** *adj.* negoziabile; (on cheque) *not —*, non girabile. **-ility** *n.* negoziabilità.
**negotiat-e** *tr.* negoziare; trattare; (fam.) superare, passare; *intr.* negoziare; trattare. **-ion** *n.* negoziazione, negoziato; trattativa. **-or** *n.* negoziatore.
**negr-o** *adj.*, *n.* negro, nero; moro; *the — race*, la razza negra, i neri; *— spirituals*, canti religiosi dei negri d'America. **-ess** *n.* negra. **-oid** *adj.* negroide.
**neigh** *n.* nitrito; *intr.* nitrire.
**neighbour** *n.* vicino; prossimo; *my — at table*, il mio vicino di tavola; *next-door -s*, vicini di casa; (bibl.) *love thy — as thyself*, ama il tuo prossimo come ami te stesso. **-hood** *n.* vicinanza, vicinato; paraggi *m.pl.*, dintorni *m.pl.*, parti *f.pl.*; *residential -hood*, quartiere residenziale; (fig.) *in the -hood of*, circa, all'incirca. **-ing** *adj.* vicino; adiacente; contiguo; limitrofo. **-liness** *n.* rapporti di buon vicinato; socievolezza; cordialità. **-ly** *adj.* da buon vicino; socievole; cordiale; *to be -ly*, essere buon vicino; *in a -ly way*, da buon vicino.
**neighing** *gerund* nitrito.
**neither** *adj.* nè l'uno nè l'altro; *adv.* nè; *— . . . nor*, nè . . . nè; *conj.* neppure, nemmeno, nè; *prn.* nè l'uno nè l'altro, nessuno; *— of the two*, nessuno dei due.
**nelson** *n.* (wrestling) presa nella quale un braccio passa sotto quello dell'avversario e la mano gli preme contro la nuca.
**Nemesis** *pr.n.* (myth.) Nemesi *f.*; (fig.) nemesi.
**neo-** *pref.* neo-.
**neo-classical** *adj.* neoclassico. **-classicism** *n.* neoclassicismo.
**neo-lithic** *adj.* (geol.) neolitico. **-logism** *n.* (ling.) neologismo.
**neon** *n.* neon *m.*; *— lights*, luci al neon; *— signs*, insegne al neon.
**neophyte** *n.* neofito.
**neoplaton-ism** *n.* neoplatonismo. **-ist** *adj.*, *n.* neoplatonista *m.*
**nephew** *n.* nipote *m.* (di zio).
**nephritis** *n.* (med.) nefrite *f.*
**nepotism** *n.* nepotismo.
**Neptune** *pr.n.* (myth.) Nettuno.
**nereid** *n.* (myth.) nereide *f.*
**Nero** *pr.n.* Nerone. **-nian** *adj.* neroniano.
**nerve** *n.* (anat.) nervo; nerbo; *a fit of -s*, una crisi di nervi; *to have -s of steel*, avere dei nervi di acciaio; (fam.) *to get on the -s of*, dare sui nervi a; *to be a bundle of -s*, essere tutto nervi; *my -s are all on edge*, ho i nervi a fior di pelle; (bot.) nervatura; (fig.) coraggio, sangue freddo; *a man of —*, un uomo coraggioso; *to lose one's —*, perdere il proprio sangue freddo; *to strain every —*, fare ogni sforzo; *war of -s*, guerra psicologica; (pop.) sfacciataggine *f.*; *you've got a - !*, che sfacciataggine!, hai del fegato!; *tr.* rinvigorire, tonificare; (fig.) *to — oneself*, farsi coraggio.
**nerve-centre** *n.* centro nervoso.
**nerveless** *adj.* snervato; sfibrato; debole; fiacco; (bot.) senza nervature. **-ness** *n.* snervatezza; fiacchezza; inerzia.
**nerve-racking** *adj.* snervante; esasperante; che dà sui nervi. **-specialist** *n.* neurologo.
**nerviness** *n.* nervosità.
**nervous** *adj.* nervoso, di nervi; *— breakdown*, esaurimento nervoso; *— prostration*, nevrastenia; (fam.) timido, apprensivo, agitato, inquieto; *a — girl*, una ragazza timida; *to be —*, essere apprensivo, aver paura; *to get —*, inquietarsi, agitarsi; nerboruto, robusto; (fig.) vivace, spigliato. **-ness** *n.* nervosità; irritabilità; agitazione; timidezza; paura.
**nervy** *adj.* (fam.) nervoso; irritabile; isterico; (poet.) vigoroso.
**ness** *n.* (geog.) capo, promontorio.
**nest** *n.* nido; (fig.) covo, covile *m.*, tana; *to feather one's own —*, farsi un gruzzolo a spese altrui; *to foul one's own —*, tirar sassi in colombaia; *— of tables*, tavolini tipo cicogna; (naut.) *crow's —*, coffa, gabbia; *intr.* fare il nido, nidificare, annidarsi; *to go -ing*, andare in cerca di nidi di uccelli.
**nest-egg** *n.* nidiandolo, endice *m.*; (fig.) gruzzolo.
**nestful** *n.* nidiata.
**nesting** *adj.* nidificante; *n.* nidificazione.
**nestl-e** *intr.* annidarsi; (fig.) rannicchiarsi, accoccolarsi, stringersi affettuosamente. **-ing** *n.* uccellino di nido, nid(i)ace *m.*
**Nestor** *pr.n.* Nestore. **-ian** *adj.*, *n.* nestoriano.
**net**[1] *adj.* (comm.) netto; *— profit*, utile netto.
**net**[2] *n.* rete *f.*; reticella; *to spread a —*, stendere una rete; (text.) tulle *m.*; (fig.) laccio, trappola; *to be caught in the —*, essere preso in trappola; *tr.* cintare con reti; coprire con reti; catturare con reti; pescare con reti; (fig.) irretire; acchiappare; (comm.) guadagnare, incassare, ricavare; (sport) mandare in rete. **-ful** *n.* retata.
**nether** *adj.* inferiore; più basso; *— garments*, calzoni *m.pl.*; *— regions*, inferno, inferi *m.pl.*
**Netherland-s** *pr.n.* Paesi Bassi *m.pl.*, Olanda, Neerlandia. **-er** *n.* olandese *m.*, *f.*, abitante dei Paesi Bassi, neerlandese *m.*, *f.* **-ish** *adj.* olandese, dei Paesi Bassi, neerlandese.
**nethermost** *adj.* il più basso.
**nett** *adj.* see **net**[1].
**netting** *n.* lavoro a rete, reticella; reticolato.
**nettle** *n.* (bot.) ortica; *tr.* pungere; (fig.) irritare, seccare, ferire. **-rash** *n.* (med.) orticaria.
**network** *n.* rete *f.*; reticolato; (rlwy., roads; radio) rete.
**neuralg-ia** *n.* nevralgia. **-ic** *adj.* nevralgico.
**neurasthen-ia** *n.* nevrastenia. **-ic** *adj.* nevrastenico.
**neuritis** *n.* nevrite *f.*
**neurology** *n.* neurologia.
**neuro-sis** *n.* nevrosi *f.*, neurosi *f.* **-tic** *adj.*, *n.* nevrotico, neurotico.
**neuter** *adj.* (gramm.) neutro; intransitivo; (bot.; ent.) neutro; (of animal) castrato; *tr.* castrare.
**neutral** *adj.* (pol.) neutrale; (fig.) neutro, indeterminato; *n.* (stato) neutrale. **-ity** *n.* (pol.) neutralità.
**neutraliz-e** *tr.* neutralizzare; (fig.) rendere vano, annullare, elidere. **-ation** *n.* neutralizzazione.
**neutron** *n.* (phys.) neutrone *m.*
**never** *adv.* mai, giammai, non . . . mai; *— a*, nessuno, neppure uno; *— again*, mai più; *— before*, mai

prima, fin allora ... mai; *now or* —, adesso o mai più, ora o mai; (provb.) *better late than* —, meglio tardi che mai; (fam.) — *fear!*, niente paura!; — *mind!*, non importa!; *well I* —*!*, come mai!, chi l'avrebbe detto!; (emphatic) —*!*, impossibile!, giammai!, non può essere!; *I* — *slept a wink all night*, non ho chiuso occhio tutta la notte; *surely you* — *told him!*, è possibile che tu glielo abbia detto!; *he* — *so much as spoke*, non ha detto neppure una parola.

**never-ceasing** *adj.* incessante. **-ending** *adj.* interminabile, senza fine. **-failing** *adj.* infallibile.

**nevermore** *adv.* mai più.

**never-never** *n.* (fam.) *to buy on the* —, comprare a rate; (lit.) — *Land*, paese dei sogni.

**nevertheless** *adv.*, *conj.* nondimeno; tuttavia; ciononostante; ad ogni modo; pure.

**never-to-be-forgotten** *adj.* indimenticabile.

**new** *adj.* nuovo, novello; (fig.) nuovo, recente, moderno, originale; *as good as* —, quasi nuovo, come nuovo; *brand* —, nuovo di zecca, nuovo fiammante; *nothing* —, niente di nuovo; *I felt a* — *man*, mi sentii rinascere; — *bread*, pane fresco; — *potatoes*, patate novelle; — *wine*, vino nuovo; *a* — *boy*, allievo nuovo; — *moon*, luna nuova; *New Testament*, Nuovo Testamento; *the New World*, il Nuovo Mondo; *New Year*, l'anno nuovo, Capodanno; *New Year's Eve*, Santo Stefano, vigilia di Capodanno; *New Year's gift*, strenna; *New Year's wishes*, auguri di Capodanno; (geog.) *New England*, Nuova Inghilterra; *New South Wales*, Nuova Galles del Sud; *New York*, Nuova York, New York; *NewYorker*, nuovayorchese *m.*, *f.*; *New Zealand*, Nuova Zelandia; *New Zealander*, neozelandese *m.*, *f.*

**new-blown** *adj.* appena sbocciato.

**newborn** *adj.* neonato, nato da poco; — *baby*, neonato.

**Newcastle** *pr.n.* (geog.) Newcastle; (fig.) *to carry coals to* —, portare acqua al mare, portare legna al bosco.

**newcomer** *n.* nuovo venuto, neofito.

**newel** *n.* anima, colonna.

**newfangled** *adj.* (pejor.) di nuovo conio, modernistico, lontano dalle belle usanze antiche.

**Newfoundland** *pr.n.* (geog.) Terranova; — *dog*, cane di Terranova. **-er** *n.* abitante di Terranova.

**newish** *adj.* quasi nuovo, piuttosto nuovo.

**new-laid** *adj.* — *eggs*, uova fresche.

**newly** *adv.* nuovamente; recentemente, di recente, da poco, appena. **-wed** *adj.* appena sposato; *n.pl. the newly-weds*, gli sposi novelli.

**newness** *n.* novità; freschezza.

**news** *n.* notizie *f.pl.*; novità; nuove *f.pl.*; informazioni *f.pl.*; *good* —, notizie buone; *bad* —, brutta notizia; *piece of* —, notizia; *latest* —, ultimissime *f.pl.*; *stale* —, notizia con tanto di barba; *in the* —, sul giornale; *there is no* — *of*, mancano notizie di; *what's the* —*?*, che c'è di nuovo?; *that's* — *to me*, ecco una novità; *to break the* —, comunicare per primo le notizie, avvisare con la debita cautela (i congiunti); (provb.) *no* — *is good* —, niente nuove buone nuove, nessuna nuova buona nuova; *ill* — *flies apace*, le brutte notizie hanno le ali ai piedi.

**news-agency** *n.* agenzia d'informazioni.

**news-agent** *n.* giornalaio. **-boy** *n.* venditore di giornali, strillone *m.*

**news-bulletin** *n.* (radio) giornale radio.

**newsmonger** *n.* chiacchierone *m.*, pettegolo.

**newspaper** *n.* giornale *m.*; *daily* —, quotidiano; *evening* —, giornale della sera; *weekly* —, settimanale *m.*; *Sunday* —, giornale della domenica; — *man*, giornalista *m.*; — *stall*, edicola dei giornali.

**news-print** *n.* carta da giornale. **-reel** *n.* cinegiornale *m.*, film d'attualità. **-room** *n.* sala di lettura; (in offices of newspaper) sala redazione.

**news-sheet** *n.* foglio d'informazioni, giornale *m.* **-stall, -stand** *n.* edicola (per la vendita di giornali).

**newsvendor** *n.* see **newsagent.**

**news-writer** *n.* cronista *m.*, *f.*

**newsy** *adj.* (fam.) ricco di notizie, pieno di pettegolezze.

**newt** *n.* (zool.) tritone *m.*

**next** *adj.* prossimo; vicino; contiguo; adiacente; *we get out at the* — *stop*, scendiamo alla prossima fermata; *in the* — *room*, nella stanza vicina; *the house* — *door to ours*, la casa vicina alla nostra; più vicino; *the* — *town*, la città più vicina; *the* — *larger size*, una misura più grande; — *but one*, secondo; primo; *the* — *turning on the left*; la prima svolta a sinistra; prossimo, venturo; — *Sunday*, domenica prossima; — *week*, la settimana ventura; *this time* — *year*, d'oggi in un anno, fra un anno; *the* — *time I see him*, la prossima volta che lo vedo; *from one day to the* —, da un giorno all'altro; *what* —*?*, e poi?; *who's* —*?*, a chi tocca adesso?; seguente, dopo; *the* — *morning*, la mattina seguente, all'indomani, la mattina dopo; *adv.* dopo; poi; in seguito; appresso; la prossima volta; — *to London Birmingham is the largest city in England*, dopo Londra Birmingham è la più grande città d'Inghilterra; *what shall we do* —*?*, e poi cosa facciamo?; *when* — *you come*, la prossima volta che verrai; (fig.) — *to nothing*, quasi niente; *there is* — *to no proof*, non c'è quasi nessuna prova; *prep.* accanto a, vicino a.

**next-of-kin** *n.* parente più prossimo; *pl.* i congiunti.

**nexus** *n.* nesso; legame *m.*

**nib** *n.* pennino; punta.

**nibble** *n.* rosicchiamento; piccolo morso; bocconcino; *tr.*, *intr.* rosicchiare; mordicchiare; sgranocchiare; (of fish) abboccare; (of sheep, *etc.*) brucare.

**nice** *adj.* minuzioso; sottile; delicato; elegante; *a* — *distinction*, una distinzione sottile; *a* — *feeling for style*, un senso delicato dello stile; (fam.) gentile, simpatico; *to make oneself look* —, aggiustarsi benino; (of weather) bello; (of things) piacevole, grazioso; buono; (iron.) *this is a* — *mess!*, che bel pasticcio!; *you're a* — *one!*, sei proprio un bel tipo!

**Nice** *pr.n.* (geog.) Nizza.

**nicely** *adv.* esattamente; (fam.) proprio bene, benino, piacevolmente.

**Nicene** *adj.* di Nicea; *the* — *Creed*, il credo di Nicea.

**niceness** *n.* esattezza; scrupolosità; delicatezza; (fam.) bontà; gentilezza; piacevolezza.

**nicety** *n.* precisione; esattezza; finezza; *to a* —, esattamente, alla perfezione, a puntino; *pl. niceties*, minuzie, finezze, sfumature *f.pl.*

**niche** *n.* nicchia; ancona; (fig.) *to find a* — *for oneself*, intrufolarsi in un buon posto.

**Nicholas** *pr.n.* Nicola, Niccolò.

**nick**[1] *pr.n.* (*dimin.* of **Nicholas**), Niccolino, Nino; (fam.) *old* —, il Diavolo.

**nick**[2] *n.* tacca; intaccatura; (fig.) *in the* — *of time*, al momento giusto, all'ultimo istante; *tr.* intaccare, fare una tacca a; (slang) rubare, agguantare; *to get* -*ed*, essere arrestato.

**nickel** *n.* nichel *m.*, nichelio; (USA) moneta da cinque cents; *tr.* nichelare. **-plated** *adj.* nichelato. **-silver** *n.* argentone *m.*

**nickname** *n.* soprannome *m.*, nomignolo, vezzeggiativo; *tr.* soprannominare, chiamare col nomignolo; *to be* -*d*, avere il nomignolo di.

**Nicodemus** *pr.n.* Nicodemo.

**nicotine** *n.* nicotina.

**nict(it)ate** *intr.* battere le palpebre.

**niece** *n.* nipote *f.* (di zio).
**niffy** *adj.* (pop.) puzzolente, che sente di stantio.
**niggard** *n.* spilorcio, taccagno, avaro. **-liness** *n.* spilorceria, taccagneria, avarizia. **-ly** *adj.* spilorcio, taccagno, gretto, avaro; (fig.) meschino.
**nigger** *n.* (pejor.) negro.
**nigger-brown** *adj.* marrone scuro.
**niggl-e** *intr.* perdere tempo in inezie. **-ing** *adj.* insignificante; di poco valore; (fig.) meschino; *-ing handwriting*, calligrafia piccola e fitta.
**nigh** *adv.* vicino; — *unto*, vicino a; *well* —, quasi. Cf. **near.**
**night** *n.* notte *f.*; sera; *good —!*, buona notte!; *at* —, *by* —, di notte; *last* —, ieri sera, questa notte; *the — before*, l'altra notte; *all — long*, (per) tutta la notte; *far into the* —, fino a notte tarda; *late at* —, a notte inoltrata; *in the dead of* —, nel cuor della notte; *to have a good* —, dormire bene, passare una buona notte; *to have a bad* —, dormire male, passare una brutta notte; *to stay the* —, pernottare; *to turn — into day*, fare di notte giorno; (fam.) *to have a — out*, passare la serata fuori; *to make a — of it*, passare la notte facendo baldoria; *a dirty* —, una notte burrascosa; buio, oscurità, tenebre *f.pl.*; (theatr.) *first* —, prima recita, prima; *the Arabian Nights*, Le mille e una notte; *attrib.* — *flight*, volo notturno; — *porter*, portiere di notte; — *school*, scuola serale; — *shift*, turno di notte; — *work*, lavoro notturno.
**night-blindness** *n.* (med.) nictalopia.
**nightcap** *n.* berretto da notte; (fam.) ultimo bicchierino (prima di andare a letto).
**night-club** *n.* ritrovo notturno, night *m. indecl.*
**night-dress, -gown** *n.* camicia da notte (da donna).
**nightfall** *n.* tramonto, crepuscolo, sera; *at* —, al cader della notte, sul far della notte.
**nightingale** *n.* (orn.) usign(u)olo, lusignolo.
**nightjar** *n.* (orn.) nottolone *m.*, succiacapre *m.*, agotile *m.*
**night-lamp** *n.* lampada da notte.
**night-light** *n.* lumino. **-long** *adj.* che dura tutta la notte.
**nightly** *adj.* di notte, notturno; (di) tutte le sere, (di) ogni notte; *adv.* ogni notte, tutte le sere.
**nightmar-e** *n.* incubo. **-ish** *adj.* d'incubo; opprimente; (fam.) spaventoso.
**night-nurse** *n.* infermiera di notte.
**nightpiece** *n.* (art) notturno.
**night-prowler** *m.* nottambulo.
**nightshade** *n.* (bot.) solano; *deadly* —, belladonna.
**night-shelter** *n.* asilo di notte.
**nightshirt** *n.* camicia da notte (da uomo).
**night-stool** *n.* seggetta. **-time** *n.* notte *f.*; *in the -time*, di nottetempo, durante la notte. **-walker** *n.* nottambulo; (prostitute) passeggiatrice. **-watchman** *n.* guardiano notturno.
**nighty** *n.* (fam.) camicia da notte (da donna), canotte *f. indecl.*
**nihil-ism** *n.* nichilismo. **-ist** *n.* nichilista *m.*
**Nijmegen** *pr.n.* (geog.) Nimega.
**nil** *n.* niente *m.*, nulla *m.*, zero.
**Nil-e** *pr.n.* (geog.) Nilo. **-otic** *adj.* del Nilo, nilotico.
**nimble** *adj.* agile; svelto; lesto; (fig.) sveglio; pronto; elastico.
**nimble-fingered** *adj.* (pejor.) di mano lesta; (fam.) — *gentry*, borsaiuoli *m.pl.*
**nimbleness** *n.* agilità; sveltezza; lestezza.
**nimbus** *n.* (art) nimbo; aureola; (cloud) nembo.
**Nimrod** *pr.n.* Nembrotte; (fig.) cacciatore.
**nincompoop** *n.* sempliciotto; incompetente *m.*; baggeo.
**nine** *card. num.* nove; *it is — o'clock*, sono le nove; — *times out of ten*, nove volte su dieci; *a — days' wonder*, un fuoco di paglia; (fam.) *dressed up to the -s*, vestito a tutto punto. **-fold** *adj.* nonuplo, nove volte tanto. **-pins** *n.* birilli *m.pl.*
**nineteen** *card. num.* diciannove; (fam.) *to talk — to the dozen*, chiacchierare a non finire. **-th** *ord. num.* diciannovesimo, decimonono; *the -th of July*, il diciannove luglio; *n.* diciannovesimo.
**nineteen-year-old** *adj.*, *n.* diciannovenne.
**ninetieth** *ord. num.* novantesimo.
**ninety** *card. num.* novanta; — *years old*, novantenne; *the nineties*, l'ultima decade del secolo decimonono; *the naughty nineties*, gli anni scapestrati tra il 1890 e il 1900; *temperature in the nineties*, temperatura tra 90 e 100 F.; *an old man in his nineties*, un vecchio di oltre novant'anni. **-first** *ord. num.* novantunesimo, novantesimo primo. **-one** *card. num.* novantuno. **-nine** *card. num.* novantanove; (med.) *say -nine*, dica trentatre. **-second** *ord. num.* novantaduesimo, novantesimo secondo.
**Nineveh** *pr.n.* Ninive *f.*
**ninny** *n.* scioccherello, semplicione *m.*, zuccone *m.*
**ninth** *ord. num.* nono; *Piux IX*, Pio Nono; *the — of July*, il nove luglio. **-ly** *adv.* in nono luogo.
**Niobe** *pr.n.* (myth.) Niobe.
**nip**[1] *n.* pizzicotto, morso, stretta; (fig.) freddo mordente; (of liquor) bicchierino, sorso, porzioncina, dosatura; *tr.* pizzicare; pungere, morsicare; *to — in the bud*, recidere (un fiore) in boccio, (fig.) stroncare sul nascere; *intr.* correre qua e là, destreggiarsi; *to — in*, entrare lestamente, (fig.) intromettersi (in una conversazione); *to — off*, *tr.* levare pizzicando, *intr.* squagliarsela; *to — out*, *tr.* tirar fuori rapidamente, *intr.* uscire lestamente; *to — up*, *tr.* raccogliere lestamente, *intr.* salire lestamente; *to — up to London*, fare un salto a Londra.
**nipper** *n.* (fam.) ragazzino; *pl. pair of -s*, pinzette *f.pl.*, tenaglie *f.pl.*; (of crab, *etc.*) chele *f.pl.*
**nippiness** *n.* (fam.) agilità, sveltezza; (of air) freddo pungente.
**nipple** *n.* (of breast) capezzolo; (of feeding-bottle) poppatoio; (of hill) cocuzzolo; (mech.) cappuccio, capezzolo, rubinetto.
**nippy** *adj.* (fam.) agile, lesto, svelto; *to be* —, sbrigarsi; (of air) pungente, frizzante.
**nisi** *conj.* a meno che non; (leg.) *decree* —, sentenza provvisoria di divorzio.
**nit** *n.* lendine, uovo di parassita; (louse) pidocchio.
**nitrate** *n.* (chem.) nitrato.
**nitr-e** *n.* (chem.) nitro, salnitro, nitrato di potassio. **-ic** *adj.* (chem.) nitrico; *-ic acid*, acido nitrico, acquaforte *f.*
**nitrocellulose** *n.* nitrocellulosa.
**nitrogen** *n.* (chem.) azoto. **-ous** *adj.* (chem.) azotato.
**nitroglycerine** *n.* nitroglicerina.
**nitwit** *n.* (fam.) imbecille *m.*, *f.*, stupido.
**nix**[1] *n.* (pop.) niente *m.*
**nix**[2] *n.* (myth.) elfo acquatico. **-ie** *n.* (myth.) ninfa acquatica.
**no** *adj.* nessuno, non . . . alcuno, niuno, veruno, neppure uno; — *one*, nessuno; — *one person could do it*, nessuno potrebbe farlo da solo; — *other*, nessun altro; *there is — hope*, non c'è alcuna speranza; *I have — books at all*, non ho neppure un libro; *he made — reply*, non rispose niente; *he is — poet*, non è poeta; *this is — place for me*, questa non è aria per me; *there is — denying it*, è inutile negarlo; — *flowers by request*, si dispensa dall'inviare fiori; — *doubt*, senza dubbio; — *matter*, non importa; *by — means*, in nessun modo, non affatto; — *such thing!*, non è mica vero!; — *nonsense!*, non me ne fate!; *this is — joke*, non è uno scherzo; (pop.) — *go*, inutile; (bibliogr.) — *date* (n.d.), senza data (s.d.); — *admittance except on business*, vietato l'ingresso a chi non è addetto ai lavori; — *smoking*, vietato fumare; — *entry*, senso unico; — *parking*, divieto di sosta; — *overtaking*, divieto di sorpasso; — *thoroughfare*, divieto di transito, vicolo cieco; *adv.* no; *have you seen him?*, — *I haven't*, l'hai

visto?, no; *to say* —, dire di no; *whether or* —, ad ogni modo; *yes or* —, sì o no; (followed by *comp.*) non; — *later than*, non più tardi di; — *fewer than*, non meno di; — *more than*, non più di; — *sooner said than done*, detto fatto; *n.* no *m.*; rifiuto; *pl.* (pol.) *noes*, voti contrari.

**Noah** *pr.n.* (bibl.) Noè; *-'s Ark*, l'arca di Noè.

**nobble** *tr.* agguantare, acchiappare; rubare; (slang) *to — a horse*, drogare un cavallo da corsa.

**nobilitate** *tr.* nobilitare.

**nobility** *n.* nobiltà; nobili *m.pl.*; nobiltà, signorilità; generosità; sublimità; elevatezza.

**noble** *adj.* nobile; aristocratico; signorile; *of — birth*, di nobile nascita; (fig.) nobile, elevato, generoso; grandioso, sublime; *to do things on a — scale*, fare le cose in grande; *n.* see **nobleman**; (coin) ducato.

**nobleman** *n.* nobile *m.*; nobiluomo, gentiluomo, patrizio.

**noble-minded** *adj.* magnanimo; generoso; di sentimenti elevati. **-ness** *n.* magnanimità; generosità; nobiltà d'animo.

**nobleness** *n.* nobiltà, signorilità; magnanimità, generosità; grandezza, magnificenza; sublimità, elevatezza.

**noblewoman** *n.* nobile *f.*; nobildonna.

**nobody** *prn.* nessuno; *there was — present*, non c'era nessuno; — *else*, nessun altro; *n.* (fam.) nullità; zero; persona che non conta.

**nock** *n.* (of arrow) cocca.

**noctambul-ant** *adj.* nottambulo. **-ism** *n.* nottambulismo. **-ist** *n.* nottambulo.

**nocturn-al** *adj.* notturno, di notte. **-e** *n.* (mus.; paint.) notturno.

**nocuous** *adj.* nocivo, dannoso.

**nod** *n.* cenno del capo; inclinazione del capo; *to give a — of assent*, annuire; (fam.) *the land of Nod*, il paese dei sogni; *tr. to — assent*, annuire; *to — one's head*, fare un cenno col capo, chinare il capo; *intr.* fare un cenno col capo, inchinare il capo; *to — to a friend*, salutare un amico; chinare il capo nel sonno, sonnecchiare; (of plumes) svolazzare; *a -ding acquaintance*, una conoscenza superficiale, una persona conosciuta solo di vista.

**noddle** *tr.* (fam.) testa, zucca.

**nod-e** *n.* (bot.; astron.; electr.) nodo; (med.) nodosità; indurimento. **-ose** *adj.* nodoso, nocchioso. **-osity** *n.* nodosità.

**Noel** *pr.n.* Natale *m.*

**nog** *n.* (techn.) piuolo, cavicchio.

**noggin** *n.* piccolo boccale; (measure) 0.142 litri; (joc.) bibita (specialmente di birra).

**nohow** *adv.* in nessun modo.

**noise** *n.* rumore *m.*; clamore *m.*; fragore *m.*; strepito; baccano; chiasso, fracasso; (techn.) *background -s*, rumori di fondo; *to make a* —, far rumore, far chiasso; (fam.) *to make a — in the world*, far parlare di sè; *a big* —, un pezzo grosso; (pop.) *hold your —!*, sta zitto!; *tr. to — abroad*, diffondere, (fam.) strombazzare. **-less** *adj.* silenzioso; senza rumore; *with -less tread*, con passo felpato. **-lessness** *n.* silenzio; assenza di rumori; tranquillità.

**noisiness** *n.* rumorosità; fragore *m.*; chiasso; (of children) turbolenza.

**noisome** *adj.* fetido; disgustoso; puzzolente; nocivo. **-ness** *n.* miasma *m.*; fetore *m.*

**noisy** *adj.* rumoroso; strepitoso; chiassoso; turbolento; (fig.) chiassoso.

**nomad** *adj.*, *n.* nomade *m.*, *f.* **-ic** *adj.* nomade, vagante. **-ism** *n.* nomadismo; vita nomade.

**no-man's-land** *n.* terra di nessuno.

**nom-de-plume** *n.* pseudonimo.

**nomenclature** *n.* nomenclatura; terminologia.

**nominal** *adj.* nominale; simbolico; — *fee*, pagamento simbolico; nominativo; *to be the — head*, essere capo soltanto di nome. **-ism** *n.* (philos.) nominalismo. **-ist** *n.* (philos.) nominalista *m.*, *f.*

**nominat-e** *tr.* nominare; designare; (pol.) proporre come candidato. **-ion** *n.* nomina; designazione. **-ive** *adj.*, *n.* (gramm.) nominativo. **-or** *n.* designatore, nominatore.

**nominee** *n.* persona nominata, persona designata; candidato designato.

**non-** *pref.* non-.

**non-acceptance** *n.* mancata accettazione. **-accomplishment** *n.* mancato compimento. **-activity** *n.* inattività.

**nonage** *n.* minorità, età minore.

**nonagenarian** *adj.*, *n.* nonagenario, novantenne *m.*, *f.*

**non-alcoholic** *adj.* analcoolico. **-aligned** *adj.* non allineato; (pol.) non impegnato. **-appearance** *n.* assenza, mancata comparizione; (leg.) contumacia. **-arrival** *n.* mancato arrivo. **-attendance** *n.* assenza. **-catholic** *adj.*, *n.* acattolico.

**nonce** *n. for the* —, per il momento, questa volta.

**nonce-word** *n.* parola di circostanza, parola coniata per l'occasione.

**nonchal-ance** *n.* noncuranza; indifferenza. **-ant** *adj.* noncurante, indifferente.

**non-combatant** *adj.*, *n.* non combattente *m.* **-commissioned** *adj.* *-commissioned officer*, sottufficiale *m.* **-commital** *adj.* non impegnativo; cauto, prudente, che non vuol impegnarsi; *to be -commital*, non dire nè si nè no. **-compliance** *n.* mancato adempimento; rifiuto di ubbidire. **-conducting** *adj.* (electr.) non conduttore, coibente, isolante. **-conductor** *n.* (electr.) coibente *m.*, isolante *m.*

**nonconform-ist** *n.*, *adj.* anticonformista *m.*, *f.*; (rel.) dissidente *m.*, *f.* **-ism** *n.* (rel.) dissidenza. **-ity** *n.* anticonformismo.

**non-contributory** *adj.* (of pension scheme) senza trattenute dalla paga. **-delivery** *n.* mancata consegna.

**nondescript** *adj.* indefinito; non classificabile; qualunque; strambo, bizzarro; difficilmente classificabile.

**non-detachable** *adj.* non staccabile.

**none** *adj.* (bibl.) *thou shalt have — other gods but me*, non avrai altro Dio all'infuori di me; *adv.* affatto, niente affatto, punto; *to be — the worse off*, non stare affatto peggio; *the price is — too high*, il prezzo non è affatto troppo alto; *to be — the wiser*, non saperne più di prima; *prn.* nessuno, niuno, veruno, non uno, nemmeno uno; nulla, niente; *I have* —, non ne ho; — *but*, soltanto.

**none** *n.* (liturg.) nona.

**nonentity** *n.* (philos.) non essere *m.*; inesistenza; (fam.) nullità; zero.

**nones** *n.* (Rom. antiq.) none *f.pl.*

**non-existence** *n.* non essere *m.*; inesistenza. **-existent** *adj.* inesistente. **-fulfilment** *n.* mancato adempimento. **-member** *n.* non socio; *open to -members*, aperto al pubblico. **-observance** *n.* mancata osservanza, inosservanza.

**nonpareil** *adj.* senza pari, incomparabile; *n.* (typ.) corpo sei.

**non-payment** *n.* mancato pagamento.

**nonplus** *tr.* imbarazzare, sconcertare, rendere perplesso; *to be -sed*, essere perplesso.

**non-political** *adj.* apolitico. **-resident** *adj.* che non risiede nel luogo; esterno, estraneo; *n.* non residente *m.*, *f.*; *open to -residents*, aperto al pubblico.

**nonsens-e** *n.* nonsenso; controsenso; assurdità; (fam.) sciocchezze *f.pl.*, frottole *f.pl.*; (excl.) —!, macchè!, ma va là!, ma via!; *to talk* —, dire delle sciocchezze; — *rhyme*, filastrocca. **-ical** *adj.* assurdo; sciocco.

**non-smoker** *n.* chi non fuma; *I'm a —*, non fumo; (rlwy.) scompartimento in cui è vietato fumare. **-stop** *adj.* continuo; ininterrotto; (transport) senza fermate intermedie, direttissimo; *adv.* in-interrottamente. **-transferable** *adj.* personale; non cedibile; non trasferibile.

**noodle** *n.* baggeo; scimunito; semplicione *m.*, sempliciona *f.*; *pl.* (cul.) gnocchi *m.pl.*

**nook** *n.* angelo; cantuccio; *to explore every — and corner*, frugare dappertutto.

**noon** *n.* mezzogiorno, mezzodì *m.* **-day, -tide** *adj.* di mezzogiorno; *n.* meriggio, mezzogiorno.

**noose** *n.* laccio; cappio; nodo scorsoio; (fam.) *to put one's head in the —*, cadere in una trappola; *tr.* prendere al laccio; accalappiare.

**nor** *conj.* nè, neppure, nemmeno; *neither ... —*, nè ... nè; *he doesn't believe it and — do I*, non ci crede e nemmeno io.

**Nordic** *adj.* nordico.

**norm** *n.* norma; modello; tipo.

**normal** *adj.* normale; regolare; (geom.) perpendicolare; solito. **-cy, -ity** *n.* normalità.

**normaliz-e** *tr.* normalizzare. **-ation** *n.* normalizzazione.

**normally** *adv.* normalmente; (fam.) di solito, solitamente.

**Norman** *adj.* normanno; *— Conquest*, conquista normanna; (archit.) romanico; *n.* normanno.

**Normandy** *pr.n.* (geog.) Normandia.

**normative** *adj.* normativo.

**Norse** *adj.* norvegese; (hist.) scandinavo, dei vichinghi; *Old —*, la lingua scandinava antica. **-man** *n.* (hist.) scandinavo, vichingo.

**north** *adj.* del nord, settentrionale; *— wind*, vento del nord, tramontana; *North America*, America del Nord; *North Pole*, Polo Nord; *North Sea*, Mare del Nord; *with a — aspect*, esposto al nord; *n.* nord, settentrione *m.*

**north-bound** *adj.* diretto verso il nord. **-countryman** *n.* settentrionale *m.* **-east** *adj.* di nord-est; *n.* nord-est *m.* **-eastern** *adj.* di nord-est. **-eastward(s)** *adv.* verso nord-est.

**northerly** *adj.* (of wind) del nord.

**northern** *adj.* settentrionale; *— lights*, aurora boreale; *— Ireland*, Irlanda del Nord; *— Italy*, Alta Italia, Italia settentrionale. **-er** *n.* settentrionale *m.*, *f.* **-most, northmost** *adj.* il più al nord.

**northward(s)** *adv.* verso nord, in direzione nord.

**North-west** *adj.* di nord-ovest; *n.* nord-ovest *m.* **-western** *adj.* di nord-ovest. **-westward(s)** *adv.* verso nordovest.

**Norway** *pr.n.* (geog.) Norvegia.

**norwegian** *adj.*, *n.* norvegese *m.*, *f.*

**nose** *n.* naso; (of animal) muso; (of tool, *etc.*) becco; (of tube); apertura; (of cannon) volata; *to be as plain as the — on one's face*, essere chiaro come la luce del sole; *to bite someone's — off*, rispondere per le rime a qualcuno; *to blow one's —*, soffiarsi il naso; *to cut off one's — to spite one's face*, darsi del dito nell'occhio; *to follow one's —*, andare avanti diritto; *to lead by the —*, menare per il naso; *to look down one's — at*, guardare d'alto in basso; *to pay through the —*, pagare profumatamente; *to poke one's — into*, ficcare il naso in; *to put someone's — out of joint*, dare lo sgambetto a qualcuno; *to speak through one's —*, parlare nel naso; *to turn up one's — at*, arricciare il naso davanti a; *to make a long —*, (vulg.) fare maramao; fiuto; *to have a good —*, aver fiuto, avere un buon naso; (fam.) *to have a — round*, dare un'occhiatina intorno.

**nose** *tr.* fiutare; sentire l'odore di; *the steamer -d its way through the fog*, il piroscafo avanzò lentamente attraverso la nebbia; *to — out*, scovare, annusare; *intr. to — about*, andare intorno cercando, ficcare il naso negli affari altrui.

**nose-band** *n.* nasiera. **-bleeding** *n.* flusso di sangue (dal naso).

**nosegay** *n.* mazzolino di fiori.

**nose-rag** *n.* (pop.) fazzoletto. **-ring** *n.* anello da naso; nasiera.

**nostalg-ia** *n.* nostalgia, rimpianto. **-ic** *adj.* nostalgico.

**nostril** *n.* narice *f.*; (of horse) frogia.

**nostrum** *n.* panacea.

**nosy** *adj.* (fam.) curioso, indiscreto; *Nosy Parker*, ficcanaso.

**not** *adv.* non; *that is — true*, (ciò) non è vero; *I told him — to come*, gli dissi di non venire; *he said —*, disse di no; *he didn't say so*, non l'ha detto; (fam., after question) *don't you?*, *doesn't he?*, *can't you?*, non è vero?, vero?, no?; *it's raining, isn't it?*, piove, vero?; *you speak Italian, don't you?*, parli italiano, non è vero?; *he lives here, doesn't he?*, sta qui, no?; *why —?*, perchè no?; *if not*, se no; *— if*, non se; *— (but) that*, non già che, non è che non; *— at all*, niente affatto, non ... affatto, non ... mica; *— even*, neanche, neppure, nemmeno; *— everybody*, non tutti; *— exceeding*, che non supera; *— including*, non compreso; *— to mention*, per non parlare di; *— to be confused with*, da non confondersi con; (pharm.) *— to be taken*, per uso esterno; (emphatic) *— I!*, io no!; (pop.) *— bad*, non c'è male; *— half!*, sfido!

**notab-le** *adj.* notevole; degno di nota; notabile; insigne; percettibile, sensibile; *n.* notabile *m.*; maggiorente *m.* **-ility** *n.* notabilità, carattere notevole; maggiorente *m.* **-leness** *n.* carattere notevole, notabilità.

**notar-y** *n.* notaio; *— public*, notaio. **-ial** *adj.* notarile, di notaio.

**notation** *n.* (mus.) notazione; (math.) numerazione.

**notch** *n.* tacca, intaccatura; incavo; dentellatura; (on arrow) cocca; *tr.* fare delle tacche su, intaccare; dentellare; accoccare.

**note** *n.* nota; annotazione; appunto; *to take -s*, prendere appunti; *to take — of*, prendere atto di; biglietto; letterina; banconota; (mus.) nota, tono; (gramm.) punto, segno; commento, chiosa; *pl.* apparato critico; *diplomatic —*, nota diplomatica; importanza, eminenza; *men of —*, personaggi importanti; *nothing of —*, niente d'importante; *worthy of —*, degno di nota; *it is worthy of — that*, conviene notare che; (comm.) *— of hand*, cambiale *m.*; *promissory —*, pagherò *m.*, cambiario.

**note** *tr.* notare; prendere nota di, annotare; osservare, constatare, accorgersi di; (comm.) *we duly — that*, prendiamo buona nota che; *to — down* registrare.

**note-book** *n.* taccuino. **-case** *n.* portafogli *m.*

**noted** *adj.* ben conosciuto, noto, rinomato.

**notepaper** *n.* carta da lettere.

**noteworth-y** *adj.* degno di nota, notevole. **-iness** *n.* importanza; notevolezza.

**nothing** *adv.* per nulla, niente affatto; *— the worse*, per nulla male; *— like big enough*, assolutamente non abbastanza grande; *— loath*, ben volentieri; *— less than*, semplicemente; *— else than*, null'altro che; *n.* niente *m.*, nulla, zero; *to be a mere —*, essere uno zero, essere una nullità; *— good*, niente di buono; *next to —*, quasi nulla; *much ado about —*, molto rumore per nulla; *to have — to do with*, non avere niente a che fare con; *— doing*, niente da fare; *to work for —*, lavorare senza ricevere niente; *to think — of*, prendere alla leggera, disprezzare; (provb.) *— venture, — win*, chi non risica non rosica.

**nothingness** *n.* nullità; nulla; inesistenza.

**notice** *n.* avviso; avvertimento; preavviso; *until further —*, fino a nuovo avviso; *in absence of — to the contrary*, salvo avviso contrario; *without (previous) —*, senza

preavviso; *at a moment's —*, senza preavviso; (leg.) notifica, intimazione; *— to quit*, disdetta; *to give an employee a fortnight's —*, licenziare un dipendente con quindici giorni di preavviso; *to give —* (of intention to leave), licenziarsi, dare le dimissioni; nota, articolo; recensione; attenzione; *to take — of*, fare attenzione a, badare a; *to take no —*, non fare attenzione; *to attract —*, attirare l'attenzione; *to bring something to someone's —*, far notare qualcosa a qualcuno; *beneath one's —*, non degno di attenzione.
**notice** *tr.* notare, constatare, rilevare, osservare, accorgersi di; fare attenzione a, badare a; *to be -d*, attirare l'attenzione, dare nell'occhio, essere notato.
**noticeable** *adj.* apparente, percettibile, notevole, degno di nota; *it is not —*, non si vede.
**noticeboard** *n.* quadro per gli avvisi, tabellone per affissi.
**notif-y** *tr.* notificare; avvertire; intimare; denunciare; far sapere; *to — the police*, avvertire la polizia; *to — someone of the date of one's arrival*, far sapere a qualcuno la data del proprio arrivo. **-iable** *adj.* notificabile; da denunciarsi; da dichiarare. **-ication** *n.* notificazione; notifica.
**notion** *n.* nozione; idea; concetto; *a common —*, un'idea corrente; *he has no — of discipline*, non sa cos'è la disciplina; (fam.) *I haven't the faintest —*, non ho la più vaga idea. **-al** *adj.* speculativo; immaginario.
**notori-ety** *n.* notorietà. **-ous** *adj.* notorio; noto; famigerato.
**notwithstanding** *prep.* nonostante malgrado; *adv.* nondimeno, ciò nonostante, con tutto ciò.
**nougat** *n.* torrone *m.*
**nought** *n.* nulla *m.*; (math.) zero. Cf. **naught.**
**noun** *n.* (gramm.) nome *m.*; sostantivo.
**nourish** *tr.* nutrire; alimentare; *to be well -ed*, esser ben nutrito; (fig.) covare; nutrire; accarezzare. **-ing** *adj.* nutriente, nutritivo. **-ment** *n.* nutrimento; alimento; cibo.
**nous** *n.* nous *m.*; intelletto; (fam.) buon senso.
**Nova Scotia** *pr.n.* (geog.) Nuova Scozia.
**novel**[1] *adj.* nuovo, novello; originale; insolito, strano.
**novel**[2] *n.* romanzo; *detective —*, romanzo poliziesco. **-ette** *n.* romanzo breve; romanzo sentimentale. **-ist** *n.* romanziere *m.*; *woman -ist*, romanziera.
**novelty** *n.* novità.
**November** *pr.n.* novembre *m.*; *attrib.* di novembre.
**novic-e** *n.* principiante *m.*, *f.*, apprendista *m.*, *f.*; neofito; (eccl.) novizio, novizia. **-iate, novitiate** *n.* tirocinio; apprendistato; (eccl.) noviziato.
**now** *adv.* ora; adesso; attualmente; *— or never*, ora o mai; *just —*, or ora, proprio ora; *— and again*, di quando in quando, ogni tanto; *up to —, until —*, finora, fino adesso; *before —*, già; *from — on*, d'ora in avanti; (with verb in past tense) allora; *it — became clear*, allora divenne chiaro; (fam.) ebbene, dunque; *— what does that mean?*, ebbene cosa vuol dire?; *— then!*, ebbene!; *conj.* ora che, una volta che; *— (that) you mention it*, ora che lo dici.
**nowaday** *adj.* di oggi, odierno. **-s** *adv.* al giorno d'oggi, oggigiorno, oggidì, adesso.
**nowhere** *adv.* in nessun luogo, da nessuna parte; *— near as big*, di gran lungo non tanto grande; (fam.) *to get —*, fare un buco nell'acqua; (sport) *to be —*, non entrare in classifica, finire tra gli ultimi.
**nowise** *adv.* in nessun modo, niente affatto.
**noxious** *adj.* nocivo; dannoso; pernicioso; malsano. **-ness** *n.* l'essere nocivo; dannosità.
**nozzle** *n.* becco, beccuccio, boccaglio; (slang) muso.
**nuance** *n.* sfumatura; gradazione.
**nub** *n.* pezzetto; (fig.) nocciolo, l'essenziale.
**nubile** *adj.* nubile.
**nuclear** *adj.* nucleare; *— chain reaction*, reazione nucleare a catena; *— reactor*, reattore nucleare; *— warfare*, guerra atomica.
**nucleate** *adj.* avente un nucleo; *tr.* raccogliere in un nucleo; *intr.* formare un nucleo.
**nucleus** *n.* nucleo; (fig.) nucleo, nocciolo; gruppo.
**nude** *adj.* nudo; spoglio; *n.* (art) nudo, figura nuda; (fam.) *in the —*, nudo.
**nudge** *n.* piccola gomitata, colpetto; *tr.* dare un colpetto a.
**nud-ism** *n.* nudismo. **-ist** *n.* nudista *m.*, *f.*
**nudity** *n.* nudità.
**nugatory** *adj.* futile, vano, senza effetto; (leg.) nullo.
**nugget** *n.* pepita.
**nuisance** *n.* seccatura; fastidio; *what a —!*, che fastidio!, che garba!; *that child is an awful —*, quel bambino è un vero flagello; *to make a — of oneself*, seccare tutti; (leg.) infrazione dei regolamenti; *commit no —!*, non lordare!; (mil.) *— raid*, incursione di disturbo; *— value*, valore di disturbo.
**null** *adj.* nullo, non valido; *— and void*, senza valore legale; *tr.* annullare.
**nullif-y** *tr.* annullare, rendere nullo. **-ication** *n.* annullamento; abrogazione.
**nullity** *n.* (leg.) nullità; *— suit*, processo per annullamento; (fig.) nullità, zero.
**numb** *adj.* intirizzito, aggranchito, intorpidito; *to grow —*, intirizzirsi; (fig.) intontito; tramortito; paralizzato; *tr.* intirizzire, intorpidire, aggranchire, ammortire; (fig.) paralizzare.
**number** *n.* numero; cifra; *even -s*, numeri pari; *odd -s*, numeri dispari; *I live at — 5 Broad Street*, abito in Via Larga al numero cinque; *to the — of*, in numero di; *without —*, senza numero, innumerevole; *serial —*, numero d'ordine; *registration —*, numero di matricola; numero, fascicolo; *back —*, arretrato; (theatr.) numero; quantita; *a great — of*, un gran numero di, molti, numerosi; (bibl.) *Numbers*, Numeri; (fam.) *— one*, se stesso; *his -'s up*, è spacciato.
**number** *tr.* numerare; contare; *his days are -ed*, ha i giorni contati; ammontare a, contare; annoverare; *I — him among my friends*, lo annovero tra i miei amici.
**numbering** *n.* numerazione, enumerazione.
**numberless** *adj.* innumerevole.
**number-plate** *n.* (motor.) targa.
**numbness** *n.* torpore *m.* intirizzimento.
**numeral** *adj.* numerale; *n.* cifra, numero; numerale *m.*
**numerat-ion** *n.* numerazione. **-or** *n.* (math.) numeratore.
**numerical** *adj.* numerico.
**numerous** *adj.* numeroso; *pl.* numerosi, molti. **-ness** *n.* numerosità.
**numismatic** *adj.* numismatico. **-s** *n.* numismatica.
**numismatist** *n.* numismatico.
**numskull** *n.* (fam.) babbeo, testa dura.
**nun** *n.* monaca, religiosa, suora; *to become a —*, prendere il velo, monacarsi.
**nuncio** *n.* (eccl.) nunzio.
**nun-hood** *n.* monacato. **-nery** *n.* convento (per suore).
**nuptial** *adj.* nuziale; *n.pl.* nozze *f.pl.*
**Nuremberg** *pr.n.* (geog.) Norimberga.
**nurse** *n.* balia; nutrice; bambinaia; *wet —*, balia; *dry —*, balia asciutta; *to put out to —*, mettere a balia; infermiera; *male —*, infermiere; *tr.* allattare, nutrire; curare, prestare cure a; cullare, stringersi al seno; (fig.) nutrire, covare. **-maid** *n.* bambinaia.
**nursery** *n.* camera dei bambini; *day-nursery*, asilo infantile; *— rhyme*, poesia per bambini,

filastrocca; — *school*, giardino d'infanzia; (hortic.) vivaio; (fig.) *Florence, — of the arts*, Firenze, culla delle arti.

**nursery-garden** *n.* vivaio, orto. **-gardener** *n.* ortolano.

**nurseryman** *n.* ortolano, orticoltore.

**nursing** *adj.* che allatta; che cura; — *sister*, infermiera, suora; — *staff*, infermieri *m.pl.*, infermiere *f.pl.*; *n.* professione di infermiera; allattamento; il curare; *to go in for* —, farsi infermiera.

**nursing-home** *n.* casa di cura, clinica.

**nursling** *n.* lattante *m.*, *f.*, poppante *m.*, *f.*; (fig.) beniamino, prediletto.

**nurture** *n.* nutrimento, alimentazione; (fig.) allevamento, educazione; *tr.* nutrire; allevare, educare.

**nut** *n.* noce *f.*; nocciuola; — *tree*, noce *m.*; nocciuolo; *Brazil* —, noce del Perù; *to crack a* —, schiacciare una noce; (fig.) *a hard — to crack*, un osso duro, una gatta da pelare; (mech.) dado; (slang) *-s!*, balle!; zucca, testa; *to go off one's* —, diventare matto; *to be -s on something*, andare matto per qualcosa; *he can't sing for -s*, non sa affatto cantare; *intr. to go -ting*, andare a raccogliere noci.

**nut-brown** *adj.* color nocciuola. **-case** *n.* (fam.) tipo strambo.

**nutcracker** *n.* (*pair of*) *-s*, schiaccianoci *m.*; (orn.) ghiandaia, nocciolaia.

**nut-gall** *n.* galla di quercia.

**nutmeg** *n.* noce moscata. **-grater** *n.* grattugia per spezie.

**nutria** *n.* (zool.) nutria.

**nutri-ent** *adj.* nutriente, nutritivo. **-ment** *n.* nutrimento, alimento; cibo. **-tion** *n.* nutrizione, alimentazione *f.*

**nutritious** *adj.* nutritivo, nutriente. **-ness** *n.* efficacia nutritiva.

**nutritive** *adj.* nutritivo, nutriente; alimentare; *n.* cibo nutritivo.

**nutshell** *n.* guscio di noce; *in a* —, in poche parole.

**nutt-y** *adj.* che sa di noce; (fam.) strambo. **-iness** *n.* sapore di noce; (fam.) stramberia.

**nux vomica** *n.* (pharm.) noce vomica.

**nuzzle** *tr.*, *intr.* annusare, frugare col muso; (fig.) *to — up against*, rannicchiarsi vicino a.

**nylon** *n.* (text.) nailon *m.*; — *stockings*, *-s*, calze di nailon.

**nymph** *n.* ninfa; (ent.) ninfa, crisalide *f.*

**nymphomani-a** *n.* (med.) ninfomania, andromania; (pop.) furore uterino. **-ac** *n.* ninfomane *f.*

**O, o** *n.* o *m.*, *f.*; (teleph.) — *for Oliver*, O come Otranto; *my telephone number is four — five six*, il mio numero di telefono è quattro zero cinque sei.

**O, Oh** *excl.* oh!, (poet.) O!; — *for a glass of wine!*, oh poter bere un bicchiere di vino!

**oaf** *n.* tanghero, zoticone *m.* **-ish** *adj.* zotico, balordo. **-ishness** *n.* zoticaggine *f.*, rozzezza.

**oak** *n.* (bot.) quercia; *common* —, rovere *m.*, *f.*; *holm* —, leccio, ilice *f.*; legno di quercia, rovere; (fig.) *heart of* —, uomo coraggioso. **-apple, -gall** *n.* galla di quercia.

**oaken** *adj.* di quercia, di rovere.

**oakum** *n.* stoppa da calafato.

**oak-wood** *n.* querceto; legno di quercia.

**oar** *n.* remo; *to ply the -s, to pull at the -s*, remare; *to pull a good* —, essere un buon rematore; *to ship -s*, disarmare i remi; (fig.) *to rest on one's -s*, sospendere il lavoro, dormire sugli allori; (fam.) *to put in one's* —, intromettersi, intervenire a sproposito. **-sman** *n.* rematore, vogatore. **-smanship** *n.* arte del remare. **-swoman** *n.* rematrice.

**oasis** *n.* oasi *f. indecl.*

**oast** *n.* forno per asciugare il luppolo.

**oat(s)** *n.* avena; (fig.) *to sow one's wild -s*, correre la cavallina.

**oat-cake** *n.* (cul.) focaccia di avena.

**oaten** *adj.* di avena; (mus.) — *pipe*, avena.

**oath** *n.* giuramento; *to swear an* —, prestare giuramento, giurare; *on* —, sotto giuramento; (fam.) *I'll take my — on it*, lo giuro; bestemmia, imprecazione; *to rap out an* —, bestemmiare; *to utter a string of -s*, proferire una litania di bestemmie, dire il paternostro della bertuccia.

**oatmeal** *n.* farina d'avena.

**Obadiah** *pr.n.* (bibl.) Abdia.

**obdur-ate** *adj.* duro; inflessibile; ostinato; impenitente; incallito. **-acy, -ateness** *n.* inflessibilità; durezza; ostinazione; impenitenza.

**obedi-ence** *n.* ubbidienza; sottomissione; osservanza; *to enforce* —, esigere obbedienza; (comm.) *in — to your orders*, conformemente ai Vostri ordini; (eccl.) giurisdizione. **-ent** *adj.* ubbidiente; docile; mansueto; sottomesso; (in letters) *your -ent servant*, Vostro devotissimo, con osservanza.

**obeisance** *n.* riverenza; inchino; saluto rispettoso; (fig.) deferenza.

**obelisk** *n.* obelisco; (archit.) guglia; (typ.) crocetta, obelo.

**obelus** *n.* (typ.) crocetta, obelo.

**obes-e** *adj.* obeso, corpulento. **-ity, -eness** *n.* obesità.

**obey** *tr.* ubbidire a, obbedire a; sottomettersi a; osservare, rispettare; *intr.* ubbidire, obbedire.

**obfuscat-e** *tr.* offuscare, oscurare. **-ion** *n.* offuscamento.

**obituary** *adj.* necrologico; *n.* necrologia.

**ob·ject** *n.* oggetto, cosa; argomento, materia; scopo, fine *m.*, mira; obiettivo; (gramm.) oggetto; (photog.) obiettivo.

**object** *intr.* obiettare, sollevare delle obiezioni, protestare (contro); opporsi (a); trovare da ridire; *to — to doing something*, rifiutarsi di fare qualcosa; *I don't* —, non faccio nessuna obiezione, non ho niente in contrario.

**objectif-y** *tr.* oggettivare. **-ication** *n.* oggettivazione.

**objection** *n.* obiezione; protesta; *to raise an* —, sollevare un'obiezione, protestare; *to overrule an* —, non tener conto di un'obiezione; *to take — to*, protestare contro; *have you any —?*, hai da ridire?; *if you have no* —, se non hai nulla in contrario; avversione; *to have a strong — to*, sentire una forte avversione a; inconveniente *m.*; motivo di impedimento.

**objectionable** *adj.* ripugnante; spiacevole; riprensibile; biasimevole. **-ness** *n.* qualità riprensibile; qualità biasimevole.

**objective** *adj.* (philos.) obiettivo; (gramm.) — *case*, caso oggettivo; *n.* (philos.; photog.; mil.) obiettivo; scopo, proposito; (gramm.) oggettivo. **-ness, objectivity** *n.* obiettività, oggettività.

**objectivism** *n.* oggettivismo.

**object-lesson** *n.* (schol.) lezione visuale; esempio pratico; (fam.) esempio; lezione.

**objector** *n.* oppositore; confutatore; *conscientious* —, obiettore di coscienza.

**objurgation** *n.* rimprovero; riprensione.

**oblat-e** *n.* (eccl.) oblato. **-ion** *n.* (theol.) oblazione, offerta.

**obligate** *tr.* obbligare; costringere.

**obligation** *n.* obbligo; dovere *m.*; (leg.) obbligazione; *to be under an — to*, avere un obbligo verso; *to put someone under an* —, obbligare qualcuno a fare qualcosa (per gratitudine); impegno; *to*

*meet one's -s*, tener fede ai propri impegni; *to take an — upon oneself*, assumere l'impegno.
**obligatory** *adj.* obbligatorio, d'obbligo; *to make it — on someone to do something*, obbligare qualcuno a far qualcosa.
**oblige** *tr.* obbligare; costringere; *to be -d to*, essere obbligato a, avere il dovere di, avere da, dovere; fare un favore a, fare cosa grata a; *please — me by . . .*, fammi il favore di . . .; *can you — me with a light?*, può favorirmi un fiammifero?; (fam.) *anything to —!*, s'immagini!; *to be much -d to*, essere molto grato a.
**obliging** *adj.* compiacente; gentile; servizievole. **-ness** *n.* compiacenza; cortesia; gentilezza.
**obliqu-e** *adj.* obliquo; inclinato; (gramm.) indiretto. **-ity** *n.* obliquità.
**obliterat-e** *tr.* cancellare; obliterare; far sparire. **-ion** *n.* obliterazione; cancellazione; distruzione.
**oblivion** *n.* oblio, dimenticanza; *to fall into —*, cadere nell'oblio; *to rescue from —*, salvare dall'oblio.
**oblivious** *adj.* dimentico; immemore; incurante. **-ness** *n.* oblio, dimenticanza; incuranza.
**oblong** *adj.* oblungo, bislungo; (geom.) rettangolare; *n.* figura oblunga; rettangolo.
**obloquy** *n.* ingiuria, maldicenza; disonore *m.*, onta, infamia.
**obnoxious** *adj.* odioso; detestabile; sgradevole; molesto. **-ness** *n.* odiosità; molestia; sgradevolezza.
**obo-e** *n.* (mus.) oboe *m.* **-ist** *n.* oboista *m., f.*
**obscen-e** *adj.* osceno, turpe, impudico; *— language*, turpiloquio. **-eness, -ity** *n.* oscenità, turpitudine *f.*, impudicizia.
**obscurant-ism** *n.* oscurantismo. **-ist** *n.* oscurantista *m., f. indecl.*
**obscuration** *n.* oscuramento; (astron.) eclissi *f. indecl.*
**obscur-e** *adj.* oscuro, vago, ambiguo; scuro, tenebroso, fosco; poco noto; umile; poco chiaro, difficilmente comprensibile; *tr.* oscurare, ottenebrare, offuscare, velare; (fig.) eclissare; nascondere. **-eness** *n.* oscurità; umiltà. **-ity** *n.* oscurità; tenebre *f.pl.*; buio; (fig.) oscurità; *to live in -ity*, vivere sconosciuto.
**obsequies** *n.pl.* esequie *f.pl.*
**obsequious** *adj.* ossequioso, servile. **-ness** *n.* ossequiosità, servilità.
**observable** *adj.* percettibile; sensibile; visibile.
**observ-ance** *n.* osservanza; adempimento; pratica; (eccl.) osservanza, regola. **-ant** *adj.* osservante; rispettoso; attento, vigile; *n.* (eccl.) osservante *m.*
**observation** *n.* osservazione; attenzione; *to escape someone's —*, sfuggire all'attenzione di qualcuno; *to be under —*, essere sorvegliato, (med.) essere in osservazione; commento; (rlwy.) *— car*, vettura belvedere; *— post*, posto di osservazione.
**observatory** *n.* osservatorio; specola.
**observe** *tr.* osservare, scorgere; notare, rilevare; praticare, obbedire; *to — silence*, mantenere il silenzio; dire, osservare. **-r** *n.* osservatore; (mil.) vedetta; (aeron.) osservatore.
**obsess** *tr.* ossessionare. **-ed** *adj.* ossesso, ossessionato. *to be -ed by an idea*, essere ossessionato da un'idea. **-ion** *n.* ossessione; *suffering from -ions*, ossesso, ossessionato.
**obsidian** *n.* (miner.) ossidiana.
**obsolesc-ence** *n.* disuso; desuetudine *f.*; *to fall into —*, cadere in disuso. **-ent** *adj.* che sta cadendo in disuso; antiquato; logoro; non più utilizzabile.
**obsolete** *adj.* caduto in disuso, disusato; arcaico, antiquato, fuori moda. **-ness** *n.* l'essere in disuso, l'essere antiquato.
**obstacle** *n.* ostacolo; impedimento; difficoltà; *— race*, corsa ad ostacoli.
**obstetric-(al)** *adj.* (med.) ostetrico. **-ian** *n.* (med.) ostetrico. **-s** *n.* ostetricia.
**obstin-ate** *adj.* ostinato; caparbio; testardo; cocciuto; accanito. **-acy, -ateness** *n.* ostinatezza, ostinazione; caparbietà; accanimento.
**obstreperous** *adj.* strepitoso; riottoso; turbolento; ribelle; insofferente di disciplina; insubordinato. **-ness** *n.* turbolenza; indisciplinatezza; insubordinazione.
**obstruct** *tr.* ostruire; ostacolare; impedire; impacciare; bloccare; creare ostacoli a. **-ive** *adj.* ostruttivo, ostruente; che crea ostacoli.
**obstruction** *n.* ostruzione; ostacolo; impedimento; (fig.) difficoltà; (pol.) *to practise —* ricorrere all'ostruzionismo. **-ism** *n.* (pol.) ostruzionismo. **-ist** *n.* (pol.) ostruzionista *m., f.*
**obtain** *tr.* ottenere; procurare, procurarsi, acquistare; conseguire; raggiungere; *intr.* prevalere. **-able** *adj.* ottenibile; trovabile; conseguibile; raggiungibile. **-ment** *n.* ottenimento, conseguimento, raggiungimento.
**obtrude** *tr.* imporre, intrudere, intromettere; *to — oneself*, imporsi, farsi avanti, intromettersi; *intr.* imporsi, intromettersi.
**obtrus-ion** *n.* intrusione; invadenza. **-ive** *adj.* importuno; invadente; molesto. **-iveness** *n.* invadenza; intrusione; importunità.
**obtuse** *adj.* ottuso; smussato, spuntato; sordo; (fig.) ottuso, poco intelligente. **-ness** *n.* ottusità.
**obtuse-angled** *adj.* (geom.) ottusangolo, ad angoli ottusi.
**obverse** *adj.* opposto, inverso; *n.* opposto; (of medal) retto.
**obviate** *tr.* ovviare a; evitare; prevenire; rimediare; *to — a difficulty*, avviare a una difficoltà.
**obvious** *adj.* ovvio, evidente, manifesto, chiaro, che salta agli occhi; *it's — that*, va da sè che, ovviamente. **-ness** *n.* evidenza; chiarezza; l'essere ovvio.
**ocarina** *n.* (mus.) ocarina.
**occasion** *n.* occasione; *on one —*, una volta; *on the present —*, questa volta, in questo caso; *on rare -s*, rare volte; *should — arise*, al bisogno; *a great —*, un avvenimento; *to rise to the —*, mostrarsi all'altezza dell'occasione; *words appropriate to the —*, parole di circostanza; ragione, motivo; caso; *there is no —, to be angry*, non è il caso di arrabbiarsi; (fig.) *to go about one's lawful -s*, badare ai propri affari; *tr.* causare, cagionare, occasionare; dare luogo a.
**occasional** *adj.* occasionale, d'occasione; casuale; incidentale; *— verse*, versi d'occasione; *— showers*, pioggia sparsa. **-ly** *adv.* alle volte, di quando in quando, saltuariamente, ogni tanto.
**occident** *n.* occidente *m.* **-al** *adj.* occidentale.
**occipital** *adj.* occipitale.
**occiput** *n.* (anat.) occipite *m.*
**occlude** *tr.* occludere, chiudere.
**occlusion** *n.* occlusione.
**occult** *adj.* occulto; arcano; segreto; *the — sciences*, le scienze occulte. **-ism** *n.* occultismo.
**occup-ancy** *n.* occupazione; presa di possesso. **-ant** *n.* occupante *m., f.*; locatario; *the -ants of the car*, quanti viaggiavano sulla macchina.
**occupation** *n.* occupazione; *to be in — of*, occupare; *fit for —*, abitabile; (mil.) *army of —*, esercito d'occupazione; professione, mestiere *m.*, impiego; *what is his —?*, che mestiere fa? **-al** *adj.* professionale; *-al disease*, malattia professionale.
**occupier** *n.* occupante *m., f.*
**occupy** *tr.* occupare; abitare in; impiegare; *rfl. to — oneself with*, occuparsi di.
**occur** *intr.* accadere, avvenire, succedere, capitare; presentarsi; venire in mente; *it -red to me that*, mi venne in mente che.
**occurrence** *n.* avvenimento; evento; caso; incidente *m.*; *an everyday —*, un caso comune, un fatto di tutti i giorni.

**ocean** *n.* oceano, mare *m.*; *the Atlantic Ocean*, l'Oceano Atlantico; *attrib.* dell'oceano, oceanico; (fig.) immensità, mare; (fam.) *-s of time*, un'infinità di tempo.
**ocean-going** *adj.* di alto mare.
**oceanic** *adj.* oceanico.
**oceanograph-y** *n.* oceanografia, talassografia. **-ic(al)** *adj.* oceanografico.
**ochr-e** *n.* ocra. **-eous, -ous** *adj.* ocraceo, simile ad ocra.
**o'clock** *adv. phr.* dell'orologio; *it is two —*, sono le due.
**octagon** *n.* ottagono. **-al** *adj.* ottagonale.
**octahedron** *n.* ottaedro.
**octameter** *n.* (prosod.) ottametro.
**octane** *n.* (chem.) ottano.
**octave** *n.* ottava; (mus.) ottava; diapason *m. indecl.*
**Octavia** *pr.n.* Ottavia.
**Octavian** *pr.n.* Ottaviano.
**octavo** *adj.* (typ.) in-ottavo; *n.* ottavo.
**octennial** *adj.* ricorrente ogni otto anni; che dura otto anni.
**octet(te)** *n.* (mus.) ottetto.
**October** *pr.n.* ottobre *m.*; *adj.* di ottobre.
**octogenarian** *adj., n.* ottuagenario.
**octopus** *n.* (zool.) polipo, piovra.
**octoroon** *n.* persona che ha un ottavo di sangue negro.
**octosyllab-le** *n.* (prosod.) ottosillabo, ottonario; parola ottosillabica. **-ic** *adj.* ottosillabico, ottonario.
**octroi** *n.* dazio.
**octuple** *adj.* ottuplo.
**ocul-ar** *adj.* oculare. **-ist** *n.* oculista *m.*
**odalisque** *n.* odalisca.
**odd** *adj.* dispari, impari; *— numbers*, numeri dispari; spaiato, scompagnato; *— glove*, guanto spaiato; *— volumes*, volumi scompagnati; *at — moments*, a tempo perso; *— jobs*, lavori saltuari, lavoretti *m.pl.*; circa, in più, di resto; *forty —*, circa quaranta, una quarantina; *twenty pounds —*, venti sterline e rotti; *— money*, il resto; *— player*, giuocatore in più; (sport; cards) *the — game*, la bella; strano, originale, singolare, bizzarro; *how —!*, che strano!; *an — fellow*, un tipo originale; *in some — corner*, in qualche angolo impensato. Cf. **odds**.
**oddity** *n.* singolarità; stranezza; *an — (thing)*, una cosa strana, (person) originale *m.*, eccentrico, macchietta.
**odd-looking** *adj.* strano, bizzarro.
**oddly** *adv.* stranamente; *— enough he did not see me*, cosa strana, non si è accorto di me.
**odd-man-out** *n.* (sport, etc.) quello che viene eliminato; (fig.) una che sta o che viene lasciato da parte.
**oddments** *n. pl.* scampoli, rimasugli, avanzi *m.pl.*
**oddness** *n.* disparità; stranezza, singolarità.
**odd-numbered** *adj.* dispari.
**odds** *n. pl.* disparità; differenza; *— and ends*, cose varie, avanzi *m.pl.*; *the — are that*, è ben probabile che; *the — are against us*, abbiamo poca speranza di vincere; *to be at — with*, essere in disaccordo con, essere alle prese con; *to set at —*, seminare zizzania fra; *to fight against overwhelming —*, lottare contro forze enormemente superiori; posta; *the — are ten to one*, la posta è di dieci contro uno; *to lay — on*, scommettere che; *to lay — against*, scommettere che . . . non; (fam.) *what's the —?*, che importa?, che differenza fa?; *it makes no —*, non fa niente, è lo stesso.
**odd-shaped** *adj.* di forma bizzarra.
**ode** *n.* ode *f.*; *funeral —*, epicedio.
**Odin** *pr.n.* (myth.) Odino.
**odious** *adj.* odioso; detestabile.
**odium** *n.* odio; riprovazione generale.
**odontolog-y** *n.* odontoiatria, odontalgia. **-ist** *n.* odontoiatra *m.*
**odoriferous** *adj.* odorifero.
**odorous** *adj.* odoroso, fragrante.
**odour** *n.* odore *m.*; fragranza, profumo; (fig.) sentore, odore; *to be in bad — with*, essere mal visto da. **-less** *adj.* inodoro, senza odore.
**Odyssey** *pr.n.* Odissea.
**oecolog-y** *n.* ecologia. **-ical** *adj.* ecologico.
**oecumenical** *adj.* ecumenico; pancristiano; *— council*, concilio ecumenico.
**Oedipus** *pr.n.* Edipo; (psychol.) *— complex*, complesso di Edipo.
**oenolog-y** *n.* enologia. **-ist** *n.* enologo.
**of** *prep.* di; da; fra; tra; in; a; per.
**off** *adj.* esterno, più distante; destro; *on the — side*, a destra; *to be a bit —*, non essere più fresco; (fig.) *an — chance*, una possibilità remota; *a day —*, una giornata libera; *the — season*, la stagione morta; *— licence*, licenza di vendere bevande alcooliche per consumo fuori dallo stabile; chiuso; *the match is —*, la partita non avrà luogo; *the gas is —*, manca il gas; *the bet is —*, la scommessa non vale; *adv.* lontana, distante, discosto; *to be a long way —*, essere molto distante; *how far — is it?*, quanto dista?, quanto è lontano?; via; *I must be —*, devo andare via, devo partire; *be —!*, via!; *they're —!*, son partiti!; *hats —!*, giù i cappelli!; *prep.* lontano da, fuori di, al largo di; *just — the main road*, a poca distanza dalla strada maestra; *— Genoa*, al largo di Genova, nelle acque di Genova; *— the beaten track*, fuori mano; *— duty*, fuori servizio; *— one's head*, fuori di sè, matto; *to be — colour*, star poco bene; *— the point*, fuori di proposito; (theatr.) *— stage*, fuori scena.
**offal** *n.* (cul.) frattaglie, regaglie *f.pl.*; avanzi, rifiuti *m.pl.*
**off-day** *n.* (fam.) giorno in cui uno non si sente o non lavora bene.
**offence** *n.* offesa, ingiuria, oltraggio; *no — meant*, sia detto senza offesa; *to give — to*, offendere, dar ombra a; *to take —*, adontarsi, offendersi; *to take — at*, offendersi di, recarsi a offesa, prendere male, aversene a male; (leg.) delitto, reato; *an — against the law*, un'infrazione alla legge; (mil.) offesa, attacco. **-less** *adj.* inoffensivo, inocuo, innocente.
**offend** *tr.* offendere, oltraggiare, insultare; *to be -ed*, sentirsi offeso, offendersi, recarsi ad ingiuria; *to be easily -ed*, essere molto suscettibile; *intr.* commettere infrazioni; *to — against the law*, trasgredire la legge.
**offender** *n.* offensore; peccatore, colpevole *m., f.*; trasgressore; *first —*, incensurato; *juvenile —*, delinquente minorenne; *an old —*, un pregiudicato.
**offending** *adj.* offensivo; che reca offesa; nocivo.
**offensive** *adj.* offensivo, oltraggioso, ingiurioso, insultante; aggressivo, insolente; sgradevole, spiacevole, nauseante; *n.* (mil.) offensiva. **-ness** *n.* insolenza, aggressività; sgradevolezza.
**offer** *n.* offerta, proposta; *— of marriage*, proposta di matrimonio; (comm.) preventivo; *on —*, in vendita; *tr.* offrire, fare un'offerta di; *to — up*, offrire; proporre; *to — an apology*, presentare le proprie scuse; *to — resistance*, opporsi, opporre resistenza; *to — an opinion*, dare un'opinione; *intr.* offrirsi, presentarsi; *as occasion -s*, quando si presenti l'occasione. **-er** *n.* offerente *m., f.* **-ing** *n.* offerta; sacrificio; oblazione; *burnt -ing*, olocausto.
**offertory** *n.* (eccl.) offertorio; oblazione; colletta. **-box** *n.* (eccl.) cassetta delle elemosine.
**offhand-(ed)** *adj.* casuale, improvvisato; brusco, sbrigativo, disinvolto; *in an — manner*, bruscamente, senza complimenti. **-edly** *adv.* sbrigativamente, alla buona, bruscamente, senza complimenti. **-edness** *n.* spigliatezza; disinvoltura; modi bruschi.
**office** *n.* carica, incarico, funzione, impiego; *to be in —*, essere in carica; *to come into —*, entrare in carica; *term of —*, durata della carica; *to resign —*, dare le dimissioni; ufficio; studio, gabi-

netto; *branch* —, agenzia filiale; *head* —, sede *f.*, direzione generale; *manager's* —, direzione; *post* —, ufficio postale, posta; — *address*, recapito; — *hours*, orario, ore di ufficio; (theatr.) *box* —, camerino, botteghino; (admin.) *Foreign Office*, Ministero degli Affari Esteri; *Home Office*, Ministero dell'Interno; *War Office*, Ministero della Guerra; (eccl.) uffizio; *to say* —, recitare l'uffizio; *the Holy Office*, il Sant'Uffizio; (fig.) *through the good -s of*, con i buoni uffici di, grazie al gentile interessamento di.

**office-boy** *n.* fattorino.

**officer** *n.* ufficiale; funzionario; *customs* —, funzionario delle dogane, doganiere *m.*; *police* —, funzionario di polizia; (in Army, Navy, Air Force), ufficiale; *non-commissioned* —, *petty* —, sottufficiale *m.*; *staff* —, ufficiale di stato maggiore generale; *-s' training corps*, collegio militare; *tr.* (mil.) provvedere di ufficiali; comandare.

**official** *adj.* ufficiale, d'ufficio; *in an — capacity*, nell'esercizio della proprie funzioni; — *records*, archivi ministeriali, atti *m.pl.*; *n.* funzionario, ufficiale *m.*, incaricato; *high* —, alto funzionario, gerarca *m.* **-dom, -ism,** *n.* burocrazia; funzionarismo. **-ly** *adv.* ufficialmente, d'ufficio.

**officiant** *n.* (eccl.) ufficiante *m.*, ufficiatore.

**officiate** *intr.* esercitare le proprie funzioni; *to — as*, esercitare le funzioni di; *to — for*, sostituire; (eccl.) ufficiare, officiare; *officiating priest*, sacerdote ufficiante, celebrante *m.*

**officious** *adj.* ufficioso; inframmettente. **-ness** *n.* ufficiosità; inframmettenza; soverchia premura.

**offing** *n.* (naut.) largo; (fam.) *in the* —, in vista.

**off-load** *tr.* scaricare.

**offprint** *n.* (typ.) estratto.

**off-saddle** *tr.* dissellare; *intr.* scendere da cavallo, fare tappa.

**off-set** *n.* compenso, equivalente *m.*; (bot.) germoglio, rampollo; (mech.) deviazione; (typ.) offset *m.*, fotolito; *tr.* compensare, controbilanciare, fronteggiare; (mech.) deviare; *intr.* (bot.) germogliare, far dei rampolli. **-shoot** *n.* (bot.) germoglio, ramo, rampollo; (fig.) rampollo. **-shore** *adj.* (naut.) di terra; *adv.* al largo. **-side** *adj.*, *n.* (sport) fuori giuoco. **-spring** *n.* progenie *f.*, prole *f.*, figliolanza; discendenza; (fig.) prodotto, frutto; risultato.

**often** *adv.* (poet. **oft**) spesso, sovente, spesse volte, frequentemente; *how* —?, quante volte?; *too* —, troppe volte; *once too* —, una volta di troppo; *as — as*, ogni volta che; *as — as not*, quasi sempre, il più delle volte. **-times** *adv.* (lit.) spesse volte, sovente.

**ogee** *n.* (archit.) gola riversa; — *arch*, arco riverso; — *moulding*, modanatura a S.

**ogiv-e** *n.* (archit.) ogiva, sesto acuto. **-al** *adj.* (archit.) ogivale, a sesto acuto.

**ogle** *tr.* guardare amorosamente, lanciare occhiate amorose a.

**ogr-e** *n.* orco. **-ess** *n.* orchessa.

**oh!** *excl.* oh!, ah!, ahimè!, ahi!

**ohm** *n.* (electr.) ohm *m.*

**oil** *n.* olio; *olive* —, olio d'oliva; petrolio; *crude* —, petrolio grezzo; *fuel* —, nafta; *lubricating* —, olio lubrificante; *to strike* —, trovare il petrolio, (fig.) aver un successo; (paint.) *to paint in -s*, dipingere ad olio; (fig.) *to pour — on troubled waters*, gettar acqua sul fuoco; *to burn the midnight* —, lavorare fino a tarda notte; *tr.* ungere, lubrificare, ingrassare; *to — the wheels*, ungere le ruote; (fig.) *to — someone's palm*, ungere la palma a qualcuno; *intr.* diventare oleoso; (naut.) fare il pieno di nafta.

**oilcake** *n.* (industr.; agric.) pannello di sansa.

**oil-can** *n.* bidone *m.*, latta da petrolio; oliatore.

**oilcloth** *n.* tela cerata.

**oiled** *adj.* unto, lubrificato; — *silk*, seta impermeabilizzata; — *paper*, carta oliata; (fam.) *to be well* —, essere brillo.

**oiler** *n.* oliatore.

**oilfield** *n.* giacimento di petrolio, campo petrolifero.

**oil-fired** *adj.* a nafta.

**oiliness** *n.* untuosità; oleosità.

**oiling** *n.* lubrificazione; (text.) oliatura.

**oil-lamp** *n.* lampada ad olio.

**oil-mill** *n.* frantoio; oleificio.

**oil-painting** *n.* pittura ad olio.

**oil-seed** *n.* seme oleoso. **-skin** *n.* tela impermeabile; impermeabile *m.*

**oil-stove, -heater** *n.* stufa a petrolio. **-well** *n.* pozzo petrolifero.

**oily** *adj.* oleoso, untuoso, oleaginoso; (fig.) untuoso.

**ointment** *n.* unguento; pomata.

**old** *adj.* vecchio, antico, antiquato; usato; *an — man*, un vecchio; (fam.) — *man!*, vecchio mio!; *my — man*, mio babbo, *or* mio marito; *an — woman*, una vecchia; (fam.) *my — woman*, mia moglie; — *people*, i vecchi; — *maid*, zitella; *to grow* —, invecchiare; *how — is he?*, quanti anni ha?; *he is 40 years* —, ha quarant'anni; *how — do you think I am?*, Lei quanti anni mi dà?; — *age*, vecchiaia; *to live to a ripe — age*, campare tanti anni; *to look* —, sembrare vecchio; *he looks -er than he is*, sembra più vecchio di quanto è; *he is — enough to know better*, alla sua età dovrebbe vergognarsi di far così; *as — as Methuselah*, vecchio come Matusalemme; *a man forty years* — un uomo di quarant'anni; *an — friend of mine*, un mio vecchio amico; — *age pension*, pensione per la vecchiaia; — *age pensioner*, pensionato; *the good — times*, il buon tempo antico; *of* —, *in times of* —, nei tempi antichi, una volta; — *clothes*, vestiti usati; — *things*, anticaglia; — *iron*, rottami di ferro; — *salt*, vecchio lupo di mare; *an — stager*, un vecchio volpone; *an — hand*, un esperto; (fam.) *to have a fine — time*, divertirsi un mondo; *any — thing will do*, basta una cosa qualunque; *n. the* —, i vecchi.

**old-clothes-man** *n.* rigattiere. **-clothes-shop** *n.* bottega del rigattiere.

**olden** *adj.* (poet.) antico; remoto, trapassato; *in — times*, nei tempi antichi, anticamente.

**old-established** *adj.* fondato molti anni fa; che esiste da molti anni. **-fashioned** *adj.* antiquato, passato di moda, disusato; attaccato alle usanze antiche, reazionario; *an -fashioned child*, un bambino che sembra già vecchio.

**oldish** *adj.* vecchiotto, piuttosto vecchio, attempato.

**oldness** *n.* vecchiezza; antichità.

**oleaginous** *adj.* oleoso, oleaginoso; untuoso.

**oleander** *n.* (bot.) oleandro.

**oleography, oleography** *n.* oleografia.

**olfact-ion** *n.* olfatto. **-ory** *adj.* olfattivo, olfattorio; *n.* organo dell'olfatto.

**oligarch** *n.* oligarca *m.* **-ic(al)** *adj.* oligarchico. **-y** *n.* oligarchia.

**oliphant** *n.* (lit.) olifante *m.*

**olive** *adj.* d'oliva, olivastro; *n.* (bot.) oliva; — *tree*, olivo; (bibl.) *the Mount of Olives*, il Monte Oliveto.

**olive-branch** *n.* ramoscello d'olivo; (fig.) *to hold out the* —, portare un ramoscello d'olivo, portare proposte di pace. **-coloured** *adj.* verde oliva, olivastro. **-green** *adj.* verde oliva. **-grove** *n.* oliveto. **-oil** *n.* olio d'oliva.

**Oliver** *pr.n.* Oliviero.

**Olivia** *pr.n.* Olivia.

**Olympia** *pr.n.* Olimpia.

**olympiad** *n.* olimpiade *f.*

**olympian** *adj.* olimpico, dell'Olimpo.

**olympic** *adj.* olimpico, di Olimpia; (of victor at ancient Olympic games or competitor at modern) olimpionico; — *games*, giuochi olimpici, Olimpiadi *f.pl.*

**Olympus** *pr.n.* Olimpo.

**omega** *n.* (Gk. letter) omega.

**omelet(te)** *n.* frittata, omelette *f.*;

(provb.) *you cannot make an — without breaking eggs*, con niente non si fa niente.

**omen** *n.* presagio; augurio; pronostico; segno, indizio; *of good* —, di buon augurio; *of bad* —, di malaugurio; *tr.* presagire, pronosticare.

**ominous** *adj.* di malaugurio, sinistro, infausto; minaccioso, inquietante. **-ness** *n.* aspetto sinistro; malaugurio.

**omissible** *adj.* tralasciabile; che si può omettere.

**omission** *n.* omissione; negligenza; *sins of* —, peccati di omissione; (typ.) — *marks*, punti di reticenza.

**omit** *tr.* omettere, tralasciare, trascurare, dimenticare.

**omnibus** *n.* omnibus *m.*; *attrib.* — *volume*, volume *m.* contenente tutte le opere di un autore; — *clause*, clausola riguardante svariati argomenti. **-conductor** *n.* bigliettario. **-driver** *n.* conducente di autobus.

**omnipot-ence** *n.* onnipotenza. **-ent** *adj.* onnipotente.

**omnipres-ence** *n.* onnipresenza; ubiquità. **-ent** *adj.* onnipresente.

**omnisci-ence** *n.* onniscienza. **-ent** *adj.* onnisciente.

**omnivorous** *adj.* onnivoro; (fig.) — *reader*, lettore onnivoro.

**on** *adj.* (motor.; cricket) — *side*, lato sinistro; *adv.* su, sopra; indosso, addosso; *to have nothing* —, non aver niente addosso, non aver niente da fare, essere libero; *to be* —, essere in programma; *what is — at the cinema?*, che cosa danno al cinema?; (of gas, etc) essere acceso, (of tap) essere aperto; — *and* —, sempre avanti; *he went — and* —, fece un discorso interminabile; *off and* —, — *and off*, a intervalli, di quando in quando; *and so* —, e così via, eccetera; *later* —, più tardi; *from that day* —, da quel giorno in poi; *prep.* su, sopra; — *the table*, sulla, sopra la tavola; a, da; — *arrival*, all'arrivo; — *the right*, a destra; — *the other side*, dall'altra parte; (before date, not translated) — *the fifth of May*, il cinque maggio; — *Monday*, lunedì.

**onager** *n.* onagro.

**onanism** *n.* onanismo.

**once** *adv.* una volta; — *a month*, una volta al mese; — *more*, ancora una volta; *more than* —, più di una volta; *only* —, una volta sola; — *or twice*, una volta o due; — *in a while*, ogni tanto; — *for all*, una volta per sempre; *not* —, nemmeno una volta; *but* —, una sola volta; una volta che; una volta, un tempo, anticamente, già; *there was — upon a time*, c'era una volta; *a — famous writer*, uno scrittore già celebre; *we were all young* —, un tempo eravamo anche noi giovani; *at* —, subito; *all at* —, tutto d'un colpo, tutti insieme; *at — strong and gentle*, forte ma nello stesso tempo buono.

**once-over** *n.* (fam.) *to give something the* —, dare un rapido sguardo a qualcosa.

**oncoming** *adj.* che si avvicina, imminente; *n.* avvicinamento, imminenza.

**one** *card. num.* uno; — *man in a hundred*, un uomo su cento; — *hundred and* —, centuno; — *thousand and* —, mille uno; — *day last week*, un giorno della settimana scorsa; — *of these fine days*, un bel giorno; (provb.) — *swallow doesn't make a summer*, una rondine non fa primavera; un solo, unico; *with — voice*, ad una voce, ad una sola voce; *the — and only*, l'unico; stesso, medesimo; *in — direction*, nella stessa direzione; — *John Milton*, un certo Giovanni Milton; (number) uno; *two -s*, due uno; *chapter* —, capitolo uno, capitolo primo; *to be at* —, essere d'accordo; — (*o'clock*), l'una; (fam.) *a quick* —, un bicchierino; *pl. the little -s*, i piccini; *our dear -s*, i nostri cari.

**one** *prn.* uno, l'uno; — *another*, l'un l'altro, si; — *after another*, uno dopo l'altro; — *by* —, a uno a uno; *he is — of us*, è uno dei nostri; *many a* —, molti; *any — of these*, ognuno di questi; *no* —, nessuno; *demonstr. this* —, questo; *the* —, *that* —, quello; *which* —?, quale?; *impers.* uno, si; — *hears people say*, si sente dire; *if only — could know the future*, se solo si potesse conoscere il futuro; (in *acc.* case not translated); *it makes — think*, fa pensare; *it does — good*, fa bene; *gen.* -*'s*, proprio; *to give -'s opinion*, dare la propria opinione.

**one-armed** *adj.* monco (d'un braccio); — *man*, monco. **-class** *adj.* -*class liner*, trans-atlantico a classe unica. **-eyed** *adj.* ad un solo occhio, monocolo, cieco di un occhio; (fam.) -*eyed place*, posto fuori mano, cittadina di provincia.

**onefold** *adj.* semplice, singolo.

**one-man** *adj.* azionato da un solo uomo; (of woman, dog) che ama un uomo solo.

**oneness** *n.* unità, unicità; accordo; armonia.

**onerous** *adj.* oneroso; gravoso. **-ness** *n.* gravezza; onerosità.

**oneself** *prn.* se stesso, sè; *by* —, da solo; da sè; (with *rfl.* verb) si, se; *to keep — to* —, starsene sempre in disparte.

**one-sided** *adj.* unilaterale. **-ness** *n.* unilateralità.

**one-track** *adj.* (rlwy.) a un solo binario; (fig.) — *mind*, mente unilaterale. **-way** *adj.* in un solo senso; -*way street*, senso unico; -*way traffic*, circolazione a senso unico; (rlwy.) -*way ticket*, biglietto semplice.

**onion** *n.* cipolla; *spring* —, cipollina; *pickled -s*, cipolline sott'aceto; (pop.) testa, zucca; *to know one's -s*, essere molto in gamba, essere sveglio.

**onion-skin** *n.* buccia di cipolla; (paperm.) carta lucida.

**oniony** *adj.* di cipolla, che sa di cipolla.

**onlooker** *n.* spettatore; *pl.* gli astanti.

**only** *adj.* solo, unico; *my — hope*, la mia sola speranza; — *son*, — *child*, figlio unico; *adv.* solo, soltanto, solamente, unicamente, non . . . che; — *once*, una sola volta; — *just*, appena; *if* —, se almeno; — *to think of it*, soltanto a pensarci; *that — makes matters worse*, ciò non fa che peggiorare la situazione; *if — I had known!*, se almeno l'avessi saputo!; (fam.) *I am — too glad to accept your offer*, sono proprio contento di accettare la tua proposta; *conj.* ma, però, soltanto.

**only-begotten** *adj.* (theol.) unigenito.

**onomatopoe-ia** *n.* (ling.) onomatopeia. **-ic** *adj.* onomatopeico.

**on-rush** *n.* assalto, irruzione; impeto. **-set** *n.* assalto, attacco; (med.) accessione, accesso; (fig.) *from the -set*, dal principio. **-slaught** *n.* attacco violento, assalto.

**onto** *prep.* su, sopra; *cf.* **on** *prep.*

**ontolog-y** *n.* ontologia. **-ical** *adj.* ontologico.

**onus** *n.* onere *m.*; peso; obbligo; (leg.) — *of proof*, onere della prova.

**onward** *adj.* progressivo, che avanza, che progredisce.

**onward(s)** *adv.* avanti, in avanti; *from now* —, d'ora in poi, d'ora in avanti.

**onyx** *n.* onice *m.*

**oodles** *n.pl.* (slang) un sacco, un mucchio.

**oof** *n.* (slang) palanche *f.pl.*, schei *m.pl.*

**ooz-e** *n.* melma, fango; fanghiglia; *intr.* fluire, colare lentamente; trasudare, stillare; *to — away*, scomparire lentamente; *to — out*, esudare, (fig., of news) trapelare. **-y** *adj.* melmoso, fangoso.

**opacity** *n.* opacità.

**opal** *n.* opale *m.*

**opalesc-ence** *n.* opalescenza. **-ent, opalesque** *adj.* opalescente.

**opaque** *adj.* opaco. **-ness** *n.* see **opacity**.

**open** *adj.* aperto; dischiuso; *wide* —, spalancato; *in the — country*, in aperta campagna; *with — arms*, a braccia aperte, calorosamente; *with one's eyes* —, ad occhi aperti; *to keep one's ears*

—, tenere le orecchie aperte, tendere l'orecchio; *in the — air*, all'aria aperta; *on the — sea*, in alto mare; — *to the public*, aperto al pubblico; *an — boat*, una barca scoperta; *to fly* —, spalancarsi; *to throw* —, spalancare; *to keep — house*, tenere tavola imbandita; *to sleep in the — (air)*, dormire all'addiaccio; *to tear* —, aprire con uno strappo; (fig.) *an — contest*, una gara aperta a tutti, una gara libera; *an — question*, una questione non ancora risolta; *to leave a matter* —, lasciare in sospeso una faccenda; *an — secret*, un segreto di Pulcinella; (leg.) *an — verdict*, una sentenza di non luogo a procedere; *in — court*, a porte aperte; *an — enemy*, un nemico dichiarato; *an — scandal*, uno scandalo pubblico; — *to criticism*, esposto alle critiche; *to lay oneself — to*, esporsi a; — *to advice*, pronto ad accettare consigli; *the position is still* —, il posto è sempre libero; *to keep a day* —, lasciare un giorno libero; *an — port*, un porto franco; schietto, franco, aperto.

**open** *tr.* aprire; schiudere; *to — wide*, spalancare; *to — one's eyes*, spalancare gli occhi; *to — a bottle*, sturare, stappare una bottiglia; *to — fire*, aprire il fuoco, sparare; iniziare, avviare; *to — a campaign*, iniziare una campagna; *to — a discussion*, avviare una discussione; *to — an account with a bank*, accendere un conto presso una banca; inaugurare, dichiarare aperto; *to — out*, spiegare; *to — up*, schiudere, rendere accessibile; *intr.* aprirsi; *the shops — at nine*, i negozi si aprono alle nove; cominciare; (of flower) sbocciare; (fig.) schiudersi; *to — out*, allargarsi, svolgersi.

**open-air** *adj.* all'aria aperta, all'aperto, a cielo scoperto.

**opencast** *adj.* (min.) — *mining*, scavo a cielo aperto.

**opener** *n.* che apre, (cosa) che apre; (tins) apriscatole *m.*; (bottles) apribottiglie *m.*; (debate) primo oratore; (cards) apertura.

**open-handed** *adj.* generoso, largo (di mano), liberale. **-handedness** *n.* generosità, liberalità. **-hearted** *adj.* franco, sincero, cordiale, espansivo. **-heartedness** *n.* cordialità, franchezza.

**opening** *adj.* introduttivo; d'apertura; inaugurale; iniziale; — *medicine*, medicina lassativa; *n.* apertura; *formal* —, inaugurazione; inizio, principio, esordio; foro, breccia, apertura; (of window, door) vano; (comm.; pol.) apertura; (fig.) occasione.

**openly** *adv.* apertamente; pubblicamente; francamente; chiaro e tondo.

**open-minded** *adj.* spregiudicato; di larghe vedute; imparziale. **-mindedness** *n.* larghezza di vedute. **-mouthed** *adj.*, *adv.* a bocca aperta. **-necked** *adj.* scollato.

**openness** *n.* franchezza; sincerità; l'essere esposto.

**open-work** *adj.* a giorno, a traforo.

**opera** *n.* (theatr.) opera, opera lirica; melodramma *m.*; *comic* —, opera buffa; *light* —, operetta; *sacred* —, oratorio; — *season*, stagione lirica.

**operable** *adj.* (surg.) operabile.

**opera-cloak** *n.* mantello da sera. **-glass(es)** *n.* binocolo da teatro. **-hat** *n.* gibus *m.* **-house** *n.* teatro dell'opera. **-singer** *n.* artista lirico.

**operate** *tr.* operare; produrre; far funzionare, azionare; gestire, amministrare; (surg.) *to — on someone*, operare qualcuno; *to be -d on for appendicitis*, essere operato di appendicite; *intr.* operare, agire; funzionare; (mil.) eseguire delle operazioni, combattere.

**operatic** *adj.* di opera, operistico, lirico; — *singer*, artista lirico, cantante *m.*, *f.*

**operating** *adj.* operativo; attivo; operante; funzionante; *n.* funzionamento; azione; gestione; (surg.) operazione. **-theatre** *n.* (surg.) teatro operatorio, sala operatoria.

**operation** *n.* azione, attività; *in* —, in atto; *in full* —, in piena attività; *to come into* —, entrare in vigore; (comm.; math.; mil.) operazione; (surg.) operazione, intervento chirurgico; (surg.) *to perform an — on*, operare; (mech.) funzionamento. **-al** *adj.* relativo ad operazioni militari; *-al training*, addestramento.

**operative** *adj.* operativo; attivo; in vigore; efficace; (surg.) operatorio; *n.* operaio *m.*, operaia *f.*, lavorante *m.*, *f.*

**operator** *n.* (surg.; cinema) operatore; (mech.) macchinista *m.*; (teleph.) telefonista *m.*, *f.*, centralinista *m.*, *f.*; (radio) radiotelegrafista *m.*, marconista *m.*; (finan.) agente di borsa.

**Ophelia** *pr.n.* (lit.) Ofelia.

**ophicleide** *n.* (mus.) cimbasso, oficleide *f.*

**ophthalm-ia** *n.* oftalmia. **-ic** *adj.* oftalmico. **-ology** *n.* oftalmologia. **-oscope** *n.* oftalmoscopio. **-oscopy** *n.* oftalmoscopia.

**opiate** *adj.* oppiato, oppiaceo; *n.* oppiato narcotico.

**opine** *tr.* opinare, pensare, ritenere.

**opinion** *n.* opinione; parere *m.*; giudizio, modo di vedere; avviso; *in my* —, a mio avviso, secondo me; *in the — of*, secondo; *to be of the — that*, pensare che; *to give one's* —, esprimere il proprio parere; *to take someone's* —, consultare qualcuno; *a matter of* —, una cosa discutibile; stima. **-ated, -ative** *adj.* dogmatico, ostinato; tenace; intransigente; attaccato alle proprie idee. **-ativeness** *n.* ostinazione; attaccamento alle proprie idee.

**opium** *n.* oppio; — *addict*, oppiomane *m.*, *f.*; — *den*, fumeria d'oppio; *to drug with* —, alloppiare. **-eater** *n.* mangiatore di oppio, oppiomane *m.*, *f.* **-eating** *n.* oppiomania.

**Oporto** *pr.n.* (geog.) Porto.

**opossum** *n.* (zool.) opossum *m.*; (fam.) *to play 'possum*, fare l'indiano.

**opponent** *n.* avversario, antagonista *m.*, oppositore.

**opportune** *adj.* opportuno; tempestivo; a proposito; *at the — moment*, al momento giusto; *to be* —, convenire. **-ness** *n.* opportunità; tempestività.

**opportun-ism** *n.* opportunismo. **-ist** *n.* opportunista *m.*, *f.*

**opportunity** *n.* occasione; possibilità; *to take, to seize, the* —, cogliere l'occasione, approfittare dell'occasione; *to have an — of*, avere la possibilità di.

**oppos-e** *tr.* opporre, opporsi a; contrastare; essere contrario a; contrapporre. **-able** *adj.* opponibile. **-ed** *adj.* opposto; contrapposto; avverso, ostile, contrario. **-er** *n.* oppositore; avversario.

**opposite** *adj.* opposto; contrario; *in — directions*, in direzioni opposte; *the — sex*, l'altro sesso; — *number*, equivalente *m.*, *f.*, simile *m.*, *f.*; di fronte (a), di faccia (a), dirimpetto (a); *his house is — mine*, la sua casa è di fronte alla mia; *on the — side of the square*, dalla parte opposta della piazza; *n.* opposto; *quite the — of*, tutt'altro che.

**opposition** *n.* opposizione; resistenza; *leader of the* —, capo dell'opposizione; (astron.) opposizione; (comm.) *to set up in — to*, entrare in concorrenza con.

**oppress** *tr.* opprimere; (fig.) gravare; angustiare; *-ed peoples*, popoli oppressi. **-ion** *n.* oppressione; vessazione; (fig.) angoscia; ansia; abbattimento. **-ive** *adj.* oppressivo; tirannico; (of weather) opprimente, afoso, pesante. **-or** *n.* oppressore.

**opprobrious** *adj.* obbrobrioso; ingiurioso. **-ness** *n.* obbrobiosità.

**opprobrium** *n.* obbrobrio; vituperio; ignominia.

**oppugn** *tr.* oppugnare; combattere; opporsi a.

**opt** *intr.* optare.

**optative** *adj.* (gramm.) ottativo.

**optic** *adj.* ottico; *n.* (pop.) occhio. **-al** *adj.* ottico; *-al illusion*, illusione ottica. **-ian** *n.* ottico. **-s** *n.* ottica.

**optim-ism** *n.* ottimismo. **-ist** *n.* ottimista *m.*, *f.* **-istic** *adj.* ottimistico.

**option** *n.* opzione; scelta; facoltà; *with the — of*, con la facoltà di; *we had no — but to . . .*, non potevamo fare altro che . . .; (finan.) opzione; (fam.) *six months without the —*, sei mesi di prigione senza la facoltà di pagare una multa invece di scontare la sentenza. **-al** *adj.* facoltativo.

**opul-ence** *n.* opulenza; ricchezza. **-ent** *adj.* opulento; ricco; facoltoso; (fam., of a woman's charms) formoso.

**opuscule** *n.* opuscolo.

**or**[1] *n.* (herald.) oro.

**or**[2] *conj.* o, oppure, ossia, ovvero; (after negative) nè; *either —*, o . . . o, o . . . oppure; — (*else*), altrimenti; *a day — two*, qualche giorno, un paio di giorni.

**orac-le** *n.* oracolo; *to talk like an —*, parlare come un oracolo, pontificare; (fam.) *to work the —*, ottenere qualcosa per mezzo di influenze segrete. **-ular** *adj.* di oracolo, da oracolo; profetico; ambiguo, enigmatico.

**oral** *adj.* orale; — *examination*, esame orale. **-ly** *adv.* oralmente, a viva voce; (med.) per via orale.

**orange**[1] *adj.* di color arancio, simile all'arancio; *n.* arancia; (tree, colour) arancio; *blood —*, arancia sanguigna **-ade** *n.* aranciata.

**Orange**[2] *pr.n.* (geog.) Orange *f.*

**orange-blossom** *n.* fiore d'arancio. **-coloured** *adj.* arancio, arancino. **-ery** *n.* aranciera; (grove) aranceto. **-grove** *n.* aranceto. **-juice** *n.* succo d'arancia; (drink) spremuta d'arancia. **-squash** *n.* aranciata. **-water** *n.* acqua lanfa.

**orang-outan** *n.* (zool.) orangutan *m.*, orango.

**orate** *intr.* (joc.) arringare, fare un discorso.

**oration** *n.* orazione, arringa, allocuzione; (gramm.) discorso; *indirect —*, discorso indiretto.

**orator** *n.* oratore *m.*, oratrice *f.* **-ical** *adj.* oratorio; (pejor.) ampolloso, retorico.

**oratory** *n.* oratoria; eloquenza; retorica; *flight of —*, volo d'oratoria; (chapel) oratoria.

**orb** *n.* orbe, globo, sfera; (poet.) astro; occhio. **-ed** *adj.* a forma di orbe, sferico.

**orbit** *n.* (anat.; astron.) orbita; (fig.) zona di attività, ambito. **-al** *adj.* orbitale.

**orchard** *n.* frutteto, orto.

**orchestr-a** *n.* (mus.) orchestra; *string —*, orchestra d'archi; (theatr.) — *stall*, poltrona. **-al** *adj.* (mus.) orchestrale, d'orchestra; *-al score*, partitura. **-ate** *tr.* (mus.) orchestrare, instrumentare. **-ation** *n.* (mus.) orchestrazione, (i)strumentazione.

**orchid** *n.* (bot.) orchidea.

**ordain** *tr.* decretare, ordinare, stabilire; (eccl.) ordinare, consacrare; *to be -ed*, essere consacrato (sacerdote); (theol.) predestinare.

**ordeal** *n.* (hist.) giudizio di Dio, ordalia; — *by fire*, prova del fuoco; (fig.) dura prova, cimento.

**order** *n.* ordine *m.*; decreto; mandato; comando; regolamento; *by —*, per ordine; *in —*, in regola; *until further -s*, fino a nuovo ordine; *law and —*, l'ordine pubblico; *standing -s*, regole permanenti; *a question of —*, una questione di procedura; *to call to —*, richiamare all'ordine; *—!*, silenzio!, ordine!; *to give -s for something to be done*, ordinare di far qualcosa; *to keep —*, mantenere l'ordine; *in —*, per ordine, in ordine; *to put in —*, riordinare; (mil.) ordine; tenuta, divisa; classe *f.*, ceto, categoria; *of a high —*, di alto grado, di ottima qualità; *the lower -s*, le classi inferiori, il popolo; (of chivalry, monastic), ordine; (eccl.) *holy -s*, ordini sacri; *to be in holy -s*, essere sacerdote; (archit.) ordine; (mech.) *to be in —*, funzionare (bene); *out of —*, guasto; (comm.) ordinazione, commissione; *made to —*, fatto su ordinazione; *payable to —*, pagabile all'ordine; *standing —*, ordinazione fissa; *to give an — for*, ordinare; *postal —*, vaglia postale; (fam.) *to be all in —*, avere le carte in regola; *that's a tall —!*, ma questo è troppo!; *in — that*, affinchè, acciochè, perchè; *in — to*, per, onde, allo scopo di, a fine di.

**order** *tr.* ordinare; comandare; ingiungere; intimare; prescrivere; riordinare, mettere in ordine; (comm.) ordinare, commissionare, far fare; (eccl.) ordinare, consacrare; *to — about*, mandare qua e là; *to — away*, mandar via; *to — back*, richiamare, rimandare; *to — off*, mandar via, (sport) espellere; *to — out*, far uscire.

**order-form** *n.* modulo per ordinazioni.

**ordering** *n.* ordinamento: disposizione; (eccl.) ordinazione.

**orderless** *adj.* senz'ordine, disordinato.

**orderliness** *n.* ordine *m.*; regolarità; metodo; buona condotta; disciplina.

**orderly** *adj.* ordinato, regolato, regolare, metodico; tranquillo, disciplinato; *n.* (mil.) attendente *m.*; ordinanza; — *officer*, ufficiale di giornata; — *room*, sala di rapporto; (in hospital) inserviente *m.*, infermiere *m.*

**order-paper** *n.* testo dell'ordine del giorno.

**ordinal** *adj.* ordinale; *n.* numero ordinale; (eccl.) ordinale *m.*

**ordinance** *n.* ordinanza, decreto, legge *f.*, regolamento; (eccl.) rito.

**ordinand** *n.* (eccl.) ordinando, consacrando.

**ordinar-y** *adj.* ordinario; solito; consueto; normale; comune; (pejor.) ordinario, comune, volgare, mediocre, dozzinale; *the — reader*, il lettore comune, la generalità dei lettori; (naval) — *seaman* marinaio semplice, marò *m.*; *n.* (eccl.) ordinario; *above the —*, *out of the —*, fuori del comune, straordinario; *physician in —*, medico di corte. **-ily** *adv.* ordinariamente; comunemente; di solito. **-iness** *n.* carattere ordinario; banalità; mancanza di originalità.

**ordination** *n.* classificazione; (eccl.) ordinazione, consacrazione.

**ordnance** *n.* (artill.) artiglieria; *piece of —*, cannone *m.*; (mil.) — *depot*, ufficio approvvigionamento, sussistenza; — *survey map*, carta topografica militare.

**ordure** *n.* escremento; lordura, sporcizia; (fig.) oscenità.

**ore** *n.* minerale *m.*, metallo grezzo; *iron —*, minerale di ferro.

**organ** *n.* (anat.; mus.) organo; voce *f.*; (journ.) organo, giornale *m.*, portavoce *m.*; *street —*, *barrel —*, organetto di Barberia; *mouth —*, armonica. **-bellows** *n.* (mus.) mantice *m.* **-blower** *n.* tiramantici *m.* **-grinder** *n.* suonatore d'organetto di Barberia.

**organic(al)** *adj.* organico; (fig.) armonioso; *an — whole*, un insieme armonioso; fondamentale.

**organism** *n.* organismo.

**organist** *n.* organista *m.*, *f.*

**organiz-e** *tr.* organizzare; *intr.* organizzarsi. **-ation** *n.* organizzazione; organismo; ente *m.*; *charitable —*, istituto di beneficenza. **-er** *n.* organizzatore.

**organ-loft** *n.* tribuna dell'organo, cantoria. **-pipe** *n.* canna d'organo. **-stop** *n.* registro d'organo.

**orgasm** *n.* orgasmo.

**org-y** *n.* orgia; *bacchanalian —*, baccanale *m.*; (fig.) tripudio; *an — of colours*, una profusione di colori. **-iac, -iastic** *adj.* orgiastico.

**oriel** *n.* (archit.) — (*window*), finestra sporgente; (pop.) bovindo.

**Orient**[1] *adj.* (poet.) orientale, dell'est; (of sun) levante, nascente; *n.* oriente *m.*, est *m.*, levante *m.*
**orient**[2] *tr.* orientare; volgere verso est; *rfl.* orientarsi; volgersi verso est. **-ation** *n.* orientamento.
**oriental** *adj.* orientale; *n.* orientale *m., f.*; asiatico. **-ism** *n.* orientalismo. **-ist** *n.* orientalista *m., f.*
**orientate** see **orient**[2].
**orifice** *n.* orifizio; apertura; foro; bocca.
**oriflamme** *n.* (hist.) orifiamma.
**Origen** *pr.n.* Origene. **-ist** *n.* (eccl. hist.) origenista *m.*
**origin** *n.* origine *f.*; principio; provenienza; fonte *f.*; nascita, natali *m.pl.*, lignaggio.
**original** *adj.* originale, originario primo; nuovo; autentico; — *manuscript*, autografo; eccentrico, singolare; *n.* originale *m., f.* **-ity** *n.* originalità. **-ly** *adv.* in origine, originalmente, originariamente.
**originat-e** *tr.* originare, dar origine a; creare; far nascere; iniziare; *intr.* originare, aver origine; derivare; discendere; provenire. **-ion** *n.* origine *f.*; fonte *f.*; creazione; derivazione. **-ive** *adj.* creativo, inventivo. **-or** *n.* originatore, autore, creatore, iniziatore.
**oriole** *n.* (orn.) rigoglo.
**Orion** *pr.n.* (myth.; astron.) Orione.
**orison** *n.* preghiera, orazione.
**Orkney Islands** *pr.n.* (geog.) Isole Orcadi, le Orcadi.
**Orleans** *pr.n.* (geog.) Orléans; *New* —, Nuova Orleans; *the Maid of* —, la Pulcella d'Orléans.
**ormolu** *n.* bronzo dorato, similoro.
**ornament** *n.* ornamento; decorazione; adornamento; addobbo; ninnolo; (fig.) ornamento; lustro; *to be an — to one's profession*, onorare la propria professione; (mus.) abbellimento; (eccl.) *church -s*, suppellettili *f.pl.*, arredi sacri; *tr.* ornare, adornare; abbellire; decorare. **-al** *adj.* ornamentale; decorativo. **-ation** *n.* ornamentazione; abbellimento; decorazione.
**ornate** *adj.* ornato, riccamente decorato; elaborato. **-ness** *n.* ornatezza; elaboratezza.
**ornitholog-y** *n.* ornitologia. **-ist** *n.* ornitologo.
**orograph-y** *n.* orografia. **-ic(al)** *adj.* orografico.
**orphan** *n.* orfano *m.*, orfana *f.*; *to be left an* —, rimanere orfano; *tr.* rendere orfano; *to be -ed*, rimanere orfano. **-age, orphan-asylum** *n.* orfanotrofio. **-hood** *n.* condizione di orfano.
**Orphe-us** *pr.n.* (myth.) Orfeo. **-an** *adj.* orfico, di Orfeo.
**orphic** *adj.* orfico; (fig.) mistico, occulto; (mus.) melodioso.
**orrery** *n.* (astron.) planetario.
**orris**[1] *n.* (bot.) iris *m.*, giaggiuolo.
**orris**[2] *n.* (lace) ricamo in oro, passamaneria.
**orthodox** *adj.* ortodosso; *the Orthodox Church*, la Chiesa ortodossa. **-y** *n.* ortodossia.
**orthograph-y** *n.* ortografia; (geom.) proiezione ortogonale **-ic(al)** *adj.* ortografico; (geom.) ortogonale.
**orthopaed-ic** *adj.* ortopedico. **-ics, -y** *n.* ortopedia. **-ist** *n.* ortopedico.
**ortolan** *n.* (orn.) ortolano.
**oryx** *n.* (zool.) orice, orige.
**oscillat-e** *tr.* far oscillare; *intr.* oscillare; vacillare. **-ion** *n.* oscillazione; (fig.) esitazione; titubanza. **-or** *n.* (techn.) oscillatore. **-ory** *adj.* oscillatorio.
**osculat-e** *intr.* (joc.) baciare; (geom.) combaciare. **-ion** *n.* (joc.) bacio; (geom.) osculazione, tangenza. **-ory** *adj.* (geom.) combaciante, osculatore.
**osier** *n.* (bot.) vimine *m.*, vetrice *f.*, vinco. **-y** *n.* vincheto; (work) viminata.
**osier-bed** *n.* vincheto.
**Osiris** *pr.n.* (Egypt. myth.) Osiride.
**osmo-sis** *n.* (phys.) osmosi *f.* **-tic** *adj.* (phys.) osmotico.
**osprey** *n.* (orn.) ossifraga, aquila marina; egretta.
**ossature** *n.* (archit.) ossatura, ossame *m.*
**osseous** *adj.* (anat.) osseo.
**Ossianic** *adj.* (lit.) ossianico, di Ossian.
**ossicle** *n.* (anat.) ossicino.
**ossif-y** *tr.* ossificare; *intr.* ossificarsi. **-ication** *n.* ossificazione.
**ossuary** *n.* ossario.
**Ostend** *pr.n.* (geog.) Ostenda.
**ostens-ible** *adj.* ostensibile; preteso; finto. **-ive** *adj.* visibile; manifesto.
**ostentation** *n.* ostentazione; fasto; pompa.
**ostentatious** *adj.* ostentato; fastoso; pomposo; vanitoso. **-ness** *n.* ostentazione.
**osteolog-y** *n.* osteologia. **-ic(al)** *adj.* osteologico.
**osteopath** *n.* osteology; (pop.) conciaossa *m. indecl.*
**ostler** *n.* stalliere, mozzo di stalla.
**ostrac-ize** *tr.* ostracizzare, dar l'ostracismo a; mettere al bando; (joc.) *to be -ized*, essere all'indice. **-ism** *n.* ostracismo.
**ostrich** *n.* struzzo; *to have the digestion of an* —, avere uno stomaco da struzzo; (fig.) *to pursue an — policy*, fare lo struzzo.
**Ostrogoth** *adj., n.* ostrogoto.
**Oswald** *pr.n.* Osvaldo.
**Othello** *pr.n.* (lit.) Otello.
**other** *adj.* altro, diverso; *the — day*, l'altro giorno; *some day or* —, un giorno o l'altro; *every — day*, un giorno sì e l'altro no, ogni due giorni; *on the — hand*, d'altra parte; *at — times*, altre volte; *the — one*, l'altro; *— people*, gli altri, altrui (*follow.* by *sing.* verb); *— people's property*, la roba altrui; *— things*, altro, altre cose; *among — things*, fra altro; *the — world*, l'altro mondo; *the — side*, la parte opposta, (sport) gli avversari; *on the — side*, dall'altra parte; *in — respects*, sotto altri riguardi; *I would not have him — than he is*, non lo vorrei diverso da com'e; *for — reasons*, per ragioni ben diverse; *adv.* altrimenti.
**other** *prn.* l'altro; *pl.* altri, altrui (*foll.* by *sing.* verb); *the -s*, gli altri; *each* —, l'un l'altro; *some . . . -s*, gli uni . . . gli altri; *one after the* —, l'uno dopo l'altro; *no* —, nessun altro; *have you -s*, ne hai altri?; *I have -s*, ne ho altri; *this day of all -s*, proprio questo giorno.
**otherness** *n.* l'essere altro; diversità.
**otherwise** *adv.* altrimenti, in modo diverso; *he could not do — than obey me*, non poteva fare a meno di ubbidirmi; *— known as*, altrimenti detto, alias; *should it be* —, in caso contrario; *unless — stated*, salvo indicazione contraria; sotto altri riguardi, per il resto; (used as *conj.*) altrimenti, se no, d'altronde.
**otherworldl-y** *adj.* staccato dal mondo; (pop.) fra le nuvole. **-iness** *n.* distacco dalle cose terrene, spiritualità.
**otiose** *adj.* ozioso; inutile; futile.
**otitis** *n.* (med.) otite *f.*
**otter** *n.* (zool.) lontra. **-skin** *n.* pelle di lontra.
**Otto** *pr.n.* Ottone.
**Ottoman**[1] *adj., n.* ottomano; (furniture) ottoman, ottomana, divano.
**oubliette** *n.* (hist.) apertura a botola; (fig.) dimenticatoio.
**ought**[1] *n.* see **nought, aught.**
**ought**[2] *defect. verb*, rendered by conditional of **dovere**; *I — to go*, dovrei andare; *I — to have told you*, avrei dovuto dirti; *it — not to be allowed*, non si dovrebbe permetterlo; *it — not to have been allowed*, non si avrebbe dovuto permetterlo.
**ounce**[1] *n.* oncia (avoirdupois = gr. 28.35; troy = gr. 31,10; liquid = centilit. 2.8).
**ounce**[2] *n.* (zool.) irbis *f.*
**our** *poss. adj.* il nostro *m.*, la nostra *f.*, *pl.* i nostri *m.*, le nostre *f.*
**ours** *poss. prn.* il nostro *m.*, la nostra *f.*, *pl.* i nostri *m.*, le nostre *f.*; di noi; *a friend of* —, un nostro amico.
**ourselves** *rfl. prn.* (*nom.*) *we* —,

noi (stessi); (*acc.*) ci; *we have hurt* —, ci siamo fatti male; (after *prep.*) noi (stessi); *we did it by* —, l'abbiamo fatto da soli; *we are by* —, siamo soli; (emph.) noi stessi.

**oust** *tr.* soppiantare; espellere; sloggiare; (leg.) privare di.

**out** *adv.* fuori, al di fuori; — *and about*, in giro, fuori; — *and away*, di gran lunga; — *and* —, completamente; *attrib. an* — *and* — *rascal*, un briccone matricolato; — *at sea*, al largo, in alto mare; — *loud*, ad alta voce; — *there*, laggiù; *the voyage* —, il viaggio di andata; *day* —, scampagnata; *a night* —, una notte all'aperto; (fam.) una notte di baldoria; *to be* —, essere fuori, essere uscito, (of fire, light) essere spento, (of flower) essere sbocciato, (of sun, moon) splendere, (of tide) essere bassa, (of secret) essere noto, (be on strike) essere in sciopero; *to be* — *in one's reckoning*, aver sbagliato il calcolo; *to be* — *to do something*, essere deciso di far qualcosa; *to be* — *for*, andare alla caccia di qualcosa, cercare qualcosa; — *of*, fuori di, fuori da, da; — *of town*, fuori (di) città; — *of the window*, dalla finestra; senza; fra, tra; per; *made* — *of*, fatto di; *to be* — *of*, essere senza, essere a corto di; *to be well* — *of*, essersi cavato bene di; — *of action*, fuori servizio, guasto; — *of bounds*, fuori (dei) limiti; — *of breath*, senza fiato, ansimante; — *of commission*, (of ship) in disarmo, (mech.) fuori servizio; — *of countenance*, sconcertato, confuso; — *of date*, antiquato, non più usato, (of ticket, *etc.*) scaduto; — *of doors*, fuori, all'aperto; — *of fashion*, fuori moda; — *of favour*, in disgrazia; — *of hand*, indisciplinato, incontrollabile; incontinente; — *of kindness*, per gentilezza; — *of mind*, dimenticato; — *of one's mind*, pazzo; — *of number*, innumerevole; — *of one's element*, come un pesce fuor d'acqua; — *of order*, guasto, fuori servizio, (pol.) contrario al regolamento, non in regola; — *of place*, spostato, (fig.) male a proposito, inopportuno; — *of pocket*, in perdita; — *of pocket expenses*, sborsamenti *m.pl.*, spese incidentali; — *of practice*, fuori esercizio; — *of print*, esaurito; — *of reach*, distante, non a portata di mano; — *of shape*, sformato, storto; — *of sight*, fuori di vista; (provb.) — *of sight* — *of mind*, lontano dagli occhi, lontano dal cuore; — *of sorts*, indisposto, poco bene; — *of stock*, esaurito, non disponibile; — *of true*, storto; — *of tune*, stonato; — *of the way*, lontano, remoto, fuori mano, (fig.) insolito; — *of work*, disoccupato, senza lavoro; *to feel* — *of it*, sentirsi a disagio; *to get money* — *of*, spillare denaro da; *attrib.* esterno.

**out** *n. the ins and -s*, i minimi particolari.

**out** *tr.* (fam.) mandar fuori, mettere fuori; *intr.* venir fuori, venire a galla; *truth will* —, la verità verrà a galla; (provb.) *murder will* —, ogni nodo viene al pettine.

**out-act** *tr.* (theatr.) superare nella recitazione. **-balance** *tr.* superare di peso; (fig.) compensare. **-bid** *tr.* offrire di più di; fare un'offerta superiore; (cards, auction sale) rincarare su, rilanciare su. **-brave** *tr.* sfidare, sorpassare in coraggio. **-break** *n.* scoppio; esplosione; eruzione; sommossa; epidemia; *fresh -break*, recrudescenza, ricomparsa; *at the -break of war*, quando scoppiò la guerra, allo scoppio della guerra. *-building* *n.* dipendenza; annesso. **-burst** *n.* esplosione; scoppio. **-cast** *adj.* proscritto; bandito; *n.* reietto, proscritto; (fig.) paria *m.* **-caste** *adj., n.* (India) fuoricasta *m.*, paria *m.*, intoccabile *m.* **-class** *tr.* superare di gran lunga, essere un fuoriclasse di fronte a; *to be -classed*, non aver speranza di vincere. **-come** *n.* risultato; esito; conseguenza. **-crop** *n.* (geol.) affioramento; *intr.* affiorare. **-cry** *n.* grido; clamore *m.*; scalpore *m.*; *to make an -cry*, suscitare scalpore. **-dare** *tr.* sfidare, sorpassare in ardimento. **-distance** *tr.* distanziare, lasciare indietro. **-do** *tr.* sorpassare, superare, vincere; *not to be -done*, per non essere dammeno, non volendo essere dammeno. **-door** *adj.* esterno, all'aperto, all'aria aperta; *-door clothes*, abiti da passeggio. **-doors** *adv.* all'aperto, all'aria aperta, fuori.

**outer** *adj.* esterno, esteriore; — *garments*, abiti; (of tyre) — *cover*, copertone *m.*; (naut.) — *harbour*, avamporto; *n.* cerchio esteriore del bersaglio; (boring) colpo che mette fuori combattimento. **-most** *adj.* esterno, il più in fuori, il più lontano, estremo.

**out-face** *tr.* tener testa a, far abbassare gli occhi a, bravare. **-fall** *n.* (of river) foce *f.*; bocca; (of sewer) bocca di scarico. **-field** *n.* (agric.) terreno lontano dalla fattoria; (cricket) limiti del campo. **-fight** *tr.* vincere in combattimento; superare per tattica.

**outfit** *n.* corredo, occorrente *m.*, equipaggiamento; arnesi *m.pl.*; *first-aid* —, cassetta di primo soccorso; (mil.) — *allowance*, indennità di equipaggiamento; (slang) gruppo, squadra, (mil.) reparto. **-ter** *n.* negoziante in articoli di abbigliamento; provveditore, fornitore; *-ter's* (*shop*), negozio di confezioni per uomini.

**out-flank** *tr.* girare; circuire; (mil.) aggirare. **-flow** *n.* efflusso, deflusso; uscita; *intr.* defluire. **-flowing** *adj.* defluente, effluente, calante. **-fly** *tr.* sorpassare in volo. **-general** superare in strategia. **-going** *adj.* (of person) uscente, dimissionario; (of mail, *etc.*) in partenza; *-going tide*, marea calante; *n.* uscita; *pl.* (comm.) spese, uscite *f.pl.* **-grow** *tr.* (clothes) diventare troppo grande per; (become taller than) sorpassare in altezza; (fig.) perdere, disfarsi di. **-growth** *n.* escrescenza; (fig.) conseguenza; risultato.

**out-Herod** *tr. to out-Herod Herod*, superare Erode in crudeltà.

**outhouse** *n.* tettoia, capanna, rimessa, dipendenza.

**outing** *n.* scampagnata, gita, escursione; passeggiata.

**outlandish** *adj.* straniero, esotico, strano, bizzarro; remoto, fuori mano. **-ness** *n.* stranezza, bizzarria.

**outlast** *tr.* durare più a lungo di, sopravvivere a.

**outlaw** *n.* proscritto, bandito, fuorilegge *m., f.*; *tr.* proscrivere, bandire, mettere al bando. **-ry** *n.* proscrizione, bando.

**out-lay** *n.* spesa, sborsamento; sborsi *m.pl.*, dispendio. **-let** *n.* sbocco, sfogo, scarico; via d'uscita; foce *f.*; (fig.) sfogo.

**out·line** *n.* contorno; profilo; sagoma; *rough* —, abbozzo; (fig.) *brief* —, accenno; *in broad -s*, a grandi linee, a larghi tratti; *pl. -s of history*, elementi di storia.

**outline** *tr.* tracciare i contorni di, schizzare, abbozzare; *to be -d against*, staccarsi su, stagliarsi su; (fig.) delineare, tracciare a grandi linee.

**out-live** *tr.* sopravvivere a. **-look** *n.* vista; esposizione; prospettiva; modo di vedere; *breadth of -look*, larghezza di vedute; *a narrow -look*, un modo di vedere piuttosto ristretto. **-lying** *adj.* esterno, periferico, eccentrico, lontano; *-lying district*, zona periferica. **-manoeuvre** *tr.* superare nelle manovre, sventare, aver la meglio su. **-march** *tr.* superare nella marcia, lasciare indietro. **-moded** *adj.* fuori moda, antiquato. **-number** *tr.* superare in numero, essere più numerosi di.

**out-patient** *n.* malato esterno, malato non ricoverato; *-s' department*, ambulatorio.

**outplay** *tr.* giuocare meglio di, superare nel giuoco.

**out-post** *n.* avamposto, posto avanzato. **-pouring** *n.* effusione, sfogo. **-put** *n.* produzione; rendimento; (mech.) potenza sviluppata.

**out'rage** *n.* oltraggio, offesa; *an — upon decency*, un oltraggio al pudore; attentato.

**outrage** *tr.* oltraggiare, fare oltraggio a, violare.

**outrageous** *adj.* violento; offensivo; atroce, indegno; *it is — that*, è una vergogna che; eccessivo, esagerato. **-ness** *n.* enormità; esageratezza.

**outrance** *n.* oltranza.

**out-range** *tr.* (of gun) avere una portata maggiore di; (fig.) superare, sorpassare. **-ride** *tr.* superare (a cavallo), cavalcare più velocemente di; (of ship) superare (una tempesta). **-rider** *n.* battistrada *m.* **-rigger** *n.* (naut.) buttafuori *m.*; (boat) barca a scalmi; (aeron.) intelaiatura di sostegno.

**outright** *adj.* diretto, franco, schietto; (comm.) completo, in blocco; (of author) *to sell —*, vendere i diritti (di una pubblicazione) per una somma globale (rinunciando alla percentuale sulle vendite); *adv.* apertamente, schiettamente, senza ritegno; completamente, in blocco; al primo colpo, sul colpo. **-ness** *n.* franchezza, schiettezza; immediatezza.

**out-rival** *tr.* aver la meglio su, superare, battere. **-run** *tr.* correre più presto di; (fig.) superare. **-rush** *n.* fuga, fiotto. **-sail** *tr.* (naut.) oltrepassare; distanziare. **-set** *n.* principio, inizio; avviamento; *at the very -set*, al principio; *from the -set*, dal principio. **-shine** *tr.* eclissare, sorpassare in splendore.

**outside** *adj.* esterno, esteriore, estraneo; estremo, massimo; *— worker*, lavoratore a domicilio; *the — world*, il mondo di fuori; (fig.) *— influences*, influenze estranee; *an — opinion*, un'opinione indipendente; *an — chance*, una possibilità remota; (football) *— right*, ala destra; *adv.* fuori, all'esterno, all'aperto; superficialmente; (of bus) sull'imperiale, a cassetta; (fam.) *to get — of a good dinner*, mandar giù un buon pranzo; *prep.* fuori di, all'esterno di; all'infuori di, eccetto; (fig.) *to be — the scope of*, esulare da, essere estraneo a; *to stand — something*, essere estraneo a qualcosa; *n.* esterno, esteriore *m.*, parte esterna; superficie *f.*; massimo; *at the —*, al massimo, tutt'al più. **-r** *n.* estraneo; profano; (sport) concorrente con poche possibilità di vincere; (racing) cavallo non favorito.

**out-size** *n.* misura fuori dell'ordinario; taglia grande; *attrib.* fuori misura, grandissimo. **-skirts** *n.pl.* dintorni *m.pl.*; sobborghi *m.pl.*; periferia.

**outspoken** *adj.* franco, schietto; chiaro, esplicito; *to be —*, parlare chiaro. **-ly** *adv.* francamente; esplicitamente. **-ness** *n.* franchezza; schiettezza.

**out-spread** *adj.* steso, disteso; spiegato. **-standing** *adj.* prominente; sporgente; cospicuo; che spicca; (fig.) eminente, di rilievo, fuori del comune; non saldato, arretrato; in sospeso. **-stay** *tr.* restare più a lungo di; *to -stay one's welcome*, prolungare troppo una visita. **-stretched** *adj.* steso, disteso; spiegato; *with -stretched arms*, a braccia aperte. **-strip** *tr.* oltrepassare, distanziare; sorpassare, superare. **-vie** *tr.* sorpassare, superare. **-vote** *tr.* vincere nella votazione, mettere in minoranza; *to be -voted*, ricevere meno voti dell'avversario.

**outwalk** *tr.* camminare più lesto di; andare più lontano di.

**outward** *adj.* esterno, esteriore; (pharm.) *for — application*, per uso esterno; apparente, superficiale; *— journey*, viaggio di andata; *— mail*, posta in partenza. **-(s)** *adv.* esternamente, al di fuori, verso l'esterno; *— bound*, in viaggio di andata, in partenza. **-ly** *adv.* al di fuori, esternamente; in apparenza, apparentemente. **-ness** *n.* esteriorità; apparenza.

**out-wear** *tr.* consumare; sciupare; durare più a lungo di; cf. **outworn**. **-weigh** *tr.* pesare più di, superare in peso; (fig.) superare in importanza, prevalere su. **-wit** *tr.* superare in astuzia; (fam.) mettere nel sacco. **-work** *n.* (mil.) fortificazione esterna; *tr.* lavorare meglio di. **-worn** *adj.* logoro, sciupato, usato; (fig.) sorpassato, antiquato.

**ouzel** *n.* (orn.) merlo dal collare.

**oval** *adj.* ovale; *n.* ovale *m.*; (archit.) ovato.

**ovary** *n.* (anat.) ovaia; (bot.) ovario.

**ovate** *adj.* ovato.

**ovation** *n.* ovazione

**oven** *n.* forno, fornello; stufa; (cul.) *to cook something in a slow —*, cuocere qualcosa a forno modernato; *drying —*, stufa.

**over** *adv.* sopra, di sopra, al di sopra; *— here*, qui, da questa parte; *— there*, là, laggiù; tutto, completamente; *to be all — dust*, essere tutto coperto di polvere; in più, in eccesso; *children of ten and —*, bambini di dieci anni e più; *to have something —*, aver qualcosa in più; finito, passato; *it's (all) —*, è finito; *the storm is —*, il temporale è passato; *it's all — with him*, è spacciato; *— again*, un'altra volta; *to read — again*, leggere un'altra volta, rileggere; *six times —*, sei volte di seguito; *— and again*, più e più volte; *— against*, presso, dalla parte di; (teleph.) *— to you*, a voi. For verbal uses see under the respective verbs.

**over** *prep.* su, sopra; al di sopra di; dall'altra parte di, da una parte all'altra di, attraverso; al di là di; più di, oltre; *— and above*, oltre a; durante; in tutto, dappertutto; *all — Italy*, in tutta l'Italia, dappertutto in Italia; *all — the world*, in tutto il mondo; (math.) *three — four*, tre barra quattro.

**over** *n.* (comm.) eccedenza; (cricket) serie di palle; (shooting) colpo lungo; (knitting) aumento.

**over-** *pref.* (foll. by *adv.* or *adj.*) eccessivamente, troppo; (foll. by *n.*) eccessivo, troppo, sopra-, sovra-. Cf. below.

**over-act** *tr.*, *intr.* (theatr.) caricare (l'interpretazione); (fig.) esagerare, strafare. **-all** *adj.* globale, completo; *-all length*, lunghezza fuori tutto; *-all dimensions*, dimensioni di ingombro; *n.* (doctor's) camice *m.*; (woman's) grembiulone *m.*; (workman's) tuta. **-arm** *adj.* (swimming) a braccetto; (tennis) alto. **-awe** *tr.* intimidire, impaurire; incutere soggezione a. **-balance** *tr.* superare in peso, pesare più di, sbilanciare; *intr.* sbilanciarsi, perdere l'equilibrio, rovesciarsi.

**overbear** *tr.* dominare, soverchiare, sopraffare. **-ing** *adj.* prepotente, arrogante, altezzoso. **-ingness** *n.* prepotenza, altezzosità, arroganza.

**over-bid** *tr.* offrire un prezzo maggiore di, (at auction sale) rilanciare su; (cards) fare una dichiarazione superiore a. **-blown** *adj.* (of flower) troppo sbocciato. **-board** *adv.* fuori bordo, in mare, in acqua; *to fall -board*, cadere in acqua; *man -board!*, uomo in mare!; (fig.) *to throw a scheme -board*, rinunciare a un progetto. **-burden** *n.* sovraccarico; (min.) terreno di copertura; *tr.* sovraccaricare, aggravare. **-cast** *adj.* coperto, scuro, nuvoloso; (fig.) velato, offuscato; *n.* (needlew.) *-cast stitch*, sopraggitto. **-charge** *n.* sovraccarico; prezzo eccessivo; sovrapprezzo; *tr.* sovraccaricare; far pagare troppo caro. **-cloud** *tr.* rannuvolare, oscurare, offuscare; *intr.* rannuvolarsi, oscurarsi, offuscarsi. **-coat** *n.* soprabito, cappotto. **-come** *adj.* sopraffatto, commosso, emozionato; *tr.* superare, vincere, sopraffare; sormontare, debellare.

**overcrowd** *tr.* sovraffollare. **-ed** *adj.* sovraffollato, stipato. **-ing** *n.* sovraffollamento, sovrapopolamento.

**over-do** *tr.* esagerare, eccedere, strafare; (cul.) cuocere troppo; *rfl.* affaticarsi troppo, eccedere. **-done** *adj.* esagerato, eccessivo; (cul.) troppo cotto, stracotto. **-dose** *n.* dose eccessiva. **-draft** *n.* (at bank) scoperto; prestito, credito. **-draw** *tr., intr.* esagerare; (at bank) superare il credito consentito, emettere assegno a vuoto; *to be -drawn*, essere scoperto. **-dress** *tr.* vestire in modo troppo vistoso; *intr.* vestirsi con eccessivo lusso. **-drive** *tr.* strapazzare, affaticare, esaurire; sfruttare troppo; *intr.* (golf) mandare la palla troppo lontano. **-due** *adj.* in ritardo, tardivo; scaduto, arretrato. **-eat** *intr.* mangiare troppo, rimpinzarsi; *rfl. to -eat oneself*, rimpinzarsi, caricarsi lo stomaco, fare una scorpacciata. **-estimate** *tr.* sopravvalutare. **-excitement** *n.* sovraeccitazione.

**over-expose** *tr.* (photog.) sovraesporre.

**overexposure** *n.* sovraesposizione.

**ov'erflow** *n.* straripamento, traboccamento, allagamento; — *pipe*, tubo di scarico; — *meeting*, comizio suppletivo.

**over-flow** *tr.* inondare, allagare; *intr.* straripare, traboccare; (fig.) riversarsi. **-grow** *tr.* ricoprire, crescere sopra; *intr.* crescere troppo, diventare troppo grande. **-hand** *attrib. adj.* See **overarm.** **-hang** *n.* strapiombo; (archit.) aggetto, sporgenza; *tr.* sovrastare, strapiombare su, sporgere sopra, pendere sopra; (fig.) minacciare, incombere su. **-haul** *n.* ispezione, revisione, ripassata, visita, esame minuzioso; riparazione; *tr.* esaminare, ispezionare, ripassare, revisionare, verificare; raggiungere, sorpassare.

**overhead** *adj.* alto; aereo; (comm.) — *charges*, spese generali; *adv.* sopra la testa, in alto; in cielo, nel cielo; al piano di sopra. **-s** *n.* (comm.) spese generali.

**over-hear** *tr.* udire per caso, cogliere; *to — a conversation*, sorprendere una conversazione; *intr.* origliare. **-heat** *tr.* riscaldare troppo, surriscaldare; *rfl.* (fig.) eccitarsi, accaldarsi. **-joyed** *adj. to be -joyed*, essere lietissimo, essere pazzo di gioia; (fam.) toccare il cielo con un dito. **-laden** *adj.* sovraccarico, stracarico. **-land** *adj., adv.* per via di terra, per terra; *-land route*, via di terra. **-lap** *tr.* accavallare, sovrappore a, ricoprire; *intr.* sovrapporsi, coincidere; essere a meno di una lunghezza dall'avversario. **-lay** *n.* copertura; copriletto; *tr.* coprire, ricoprire; (archit.) incrostare. **-leaf** *adv.* sul verso, sul retro, alla pagina seguente; *see -leaf*, vedi retro; *tr.* saltare oltre, saltare al di là di; (fig.) omettere; *to -leap oneself*, saltare troppo lontano, oltrepassare lo scopo. **-lie** *tr.* coricarsi sopra, ricoprire; (a baby) soffocare coricandosi sopra. **-load** *n.* sovraccarico, carico eccessivo; *tr.* sovraccaricare, aggravare, ricolmare.

**overlook** *tr.* dare su; dominare; sorvegliare; non vedere; lasciarsi sfuggire; *I -ed the fact*, mi è sfuggito il fatto; tollerare, condonare, chiudere gli occhi a, passare sopra; stregare, gettare il malocchio su. **-er** *n.* (industr.) sorvegliante *m., f.*; ispettore.

**over-lying** *adj.* sovrapposto. **-mantel** *n.* specchiera, intelaiatura sopra il camino. **-much** *adv.* troppo, eccessivamente, oltre misura. **-night** *adj., adv.* durante la notte; per una notte; *to stay -night*, pernottare. **-pay** *tr.* pagare più del dovuto, ricompensare troppo largamente. **-payment** *n.* pagamento eccessivo. **-pitch** *tr.* (cricket) lanciare (la palla) troppo lontano; (fig.) esagerare; *to -pitch one's praise of someone*, lodare qualcuno smoderatamente.

**overpower** *tr.* sopraffare; soverchiare, soggiogare; vincere; dominare; opprimere; (fig.) *your kindness -s me*, la tua bontà mi confonde. **-ing** *adj.* (fig.) opprimente, schiacciante; irresistibile, prepotente.

**over-print** *tr.* (photog.; typ.) sovrastampare. **-production** *n.* (econ.) sovraproduzione. **-rate** *tr.* sopravvalutare; (fig.) far troppo caso di. **-reach** *tr.* oltrepassare; *to -reach oneself*, sopravvalutare le proprie forze, (fam.) darsi la zappa sui piedi.

**overrid-e** *tr.* passare a cavallo su; stancare, strapazzare; (fig.) calpestare, calcare, scartare, infrangere, annullare; non tenere conto di, passare sopra a. **-ing** *adj.* dominante.

**overrule** *tr.* dominare, governare; respingere, scartare; non tenere conto di; (leg.) annullare, cessare.

**overrun** *tr.* invadere; depredare, devastare; infestare; *to be — with*, essere infestato da; oltrepassare; (motor.) *to — the engine*, imballare il motore; *intr.* straripare, traboccare; (typ.) superare la giustezza; trasportare (caratteri). **-ner** *n.* invasore. **-ning** *n.* invasione; straripamento, traboccamento; (typ.) trasporto.

**oversea** *adj.* d'oltremare, straniero. **-(s)** *adv.* al di là del mare, oltremare.

**oversee** *tr.* sorvegliare, sopraintendere a. **-n** *adj. to be -n*, essere visto senza accorgersene. **-r** *n.* sorvegliante *m.*, soprintendente *m.*, ispettore; (typ.) proto.

**over-shadow** *tr.* ombreggiare, proiettare ombra su; (fig.) oscurare, adombrare, eclissare. **-shoe** *n.* soprascarpa. **-shoot** *tr., intr.* tirare al di là del bersaglio, sbagliare mira; (fig.) *to -shoot the mark*, passare il segno; (aeron.) *to -shoot the runway*, atterrare lungo. **-sight** *n.* svista, sbaglio, disattenzione; *through -sight*, per inavvertenza; sorveglianza, tutela. **-sleep** *intr.* dormire troppo a lungo, svegliarsi dopo l'ora fissata; (fam.) *rfl. to -sleep oneself*, dormire troppo a lungo. **-spread** *tr.* coprire; cospargere, spargersi sopra; diffondersi su; avvolgere. **-state** *tr.* esagerare. **-statement** *n.* esagerazione, affermazione esagerata. **-stay** *tr.* restare oltre i limiti di; (mil.) *to -stay one's leave*, tornare al reparto dopo la scadenza del permesso, mancare all'appello (dopo il permesso). **-step** *tr.* oltrepassare, eccedere, varcare, trasgredire; *to -step the mark*, eccedere, varcare i limiti. **-strain** *n.* sforzo eccessivo; (fig.) strapazzo; *tr.* affaticare, strapazzare, sforzare; *to -strain oneself*, strapazzarsi eccessivamente; (med.) sollecitare troppo. **-strung** *adj.* sovraeccitato, spossato; (mus.) *-strung piano*, pianoforte incrociato.

**overt** *adj.* manifesto, chiaro, palese, evidente; (leg.) pubblico.

**over-take** *tr.* raggiungere, superare; (fig.) sorprendere; (motor.) sorpassare. **-taking** *n.* raggiungimento; (motor.) sorpasso; *no -taking*, divieto di sorpasso. **-tax** *tr.* tassare eccessivamente; (fig.) abusare di. **-throw** *n.* rovesciamento; (fig.) sconvolgimento; rovina; (cricket) lancio troppo lungo (della palla); *tr.* rovesciare, capovolgere; (fig.) sconvolgere, rovinare, abbattere. **-time** *n.* ore straordinarie; (fam.) straordinario; *to work -time*, fare lo straordinario. **-tire** *tr.* stancare troppo, strapazzare.

**overtly** *adv.* apertamente, manifestamente; (leg.) pubblicamente.

**over-tone** *n.* (mus.) ipertono, suono armonico. **-top** *tr.* elevarsi al disopra di, superare, sovrastare, dominare; (fig.) eccedere, eclissare. **-trump** *tr., intr.* (cards) giuocare un atout che vale di più.

**overture** *n.* proposta, offerta; (pol.) apertura; (mus.) preludio, introduzione.

**over-turn** *tr.* rovesciare, capovolgere; (fig.) sconvolgere, abbattere, rovinare; *intr.* rovesciarsi, capovolgersi. **-weening** *adj.* arrogante, presuntuoso.

**-weight** *n.* eccesso di peso, sovrappeso; (rlwy., of luggage) eccedenza; *to be -weight,* passare il peso, pesare troppo, essere troppo grosso.

**overwhelm** *tr.* seppellire, sommergere; schiacciare, distruggere; (fig.) opprimere, sommergere, schiacciare, sopraffare; *-ed with grief,* affranto dal dolore; *-ed with work,* sommerso dal lavoro; *to — with kindness,* colmare di gentilezze. **-ing** *adj.* schiacciante; emozionante.

**over-work** *n.* lavoro eccessivo; *tr.* far lavorare troppo; (fig.) far eccessivo uso di; *rfl. to — oneself,* lavorare troppo; *intr.* lavorare troppo, sfacchinare, sgobbare. **-wrought** *adj.* teso, nervoso; (of thing) troppo ornato, tormentato.

**Ovid** *pr.n.* Ovidio.

**oviform** *adj.* oviforme, ovoide.

**ovi-parous** *adj.* oviparo. **-positor** *n.* (ent.) ovopositore.

**ovoid** *adj.* ovoide, ovale.

**owe** *tr.* dovere, essere debitore di.

**owing** *adj.* dovuto, non ancora pagato; *prep. — to,* dovuto a, a causa di, a motivo di, grazie a, in seguito a.

**owl** *n.* (orn.) gufo, civetta, allocco, barbagianni *m.*; (fig.) *a wise old —,* un vecchio savio; (fam.) *to look like a stuffed —,* sembrare un allocco. **-et** *n.* piccolo gufo. **-ish** *adj.* da gufo, barbagiannesco.

**own** *adj.* proprio (in Italian usually omitted; used only to give emphasis); *my —,* (il) mio, proprio mio; *in my — handwriting,* di mio pugno; *an idea of my —,* una idea mia personale; *n. on his — (initiative),* di propria iniziativa; *on his —,* da solo; *n. to come into one's —,* entrare in possesso dei propri beni, rientrare nei suoi; *to hold one's —,* mantenere le proprie posizioni, tener duro; (fam.) *to get one's — back,* vendicarsi, rendere pan per focaccia; *tr.* possedere, essere proprietario di; riconoscere; confessare, ammettere, concedere; *intr. to — up,* confessare.

**owner** *n.* proprietario, possessore; (comm.) *at —'s risk,* a rischio e pericolo del proprietario; (of ship) armatore; (fam.) padrone *m.*, padrona *f.* **-ship** *n.* proprietà, possesso; (comm.) *under new -ship,* cambiamento di proprietario.

**ox** *n.* bue *m.*, bove *m.*; *pl. -en,* buoi, bovini.

**oxal-ate** *n.* (chem.) ossalato. **-ic** *adj.* ossalico.

**Oxbridge** *n.* le due vecchie università inglesi (Oxford e Cambridge); also *adj.*

**ox-cart** *n.* carro a buoi. **-eye** *n.* (bot.) occhio di bove; (orn.) cinciallegra. **-eyed** *adj.* dagli occhi bovini.

**oxherd** *n.* mandriano (di buoi).

**oxhide** *n.* pelle di bue.

**oxid-e** *n.* (chem.) ossido. **-ation** *n.* ossidazione. **-ize** *tr.* ossidare; *intr.* ossidarsi.

**oxlip** *n.* (bot.) occhio di civetta, primula.

**Oxonian** *adj.* ossoniense, ossoniano, di Oxford; *n.* membro dell'università di Oxford.

**oxtail** *n.* coda di bue; (cul.) *— soup,* minestra con brodo di codino.

**ox-tongue** *n.* (cul.) lingua di bue.

**oxygen** *n.* ossigeno; *— mask,* maschera ad ossigeno; *— tent,* tenda ad ossigeno. **-ize** *tr.* ossigenare.

**oyez** *excl.* (as used by town-crier) udite!

**oyster** *n.* ostrica; (fig.) persona taciturna; (pop.) *close as an —,* muto come un pesce. **-bed** *n.* ostricaio, banco di ostriche. **-catcher** *n.* (orn.) ostralega. **-dealer** *n.* ostricaio, ostricaro.

**ozone** *n.* ozono.

**P, p** *n.* pi *m., f.*; (teleph.) *— for Peter,* pi come Palermo; (fam.) *to mind one's p's and q's,* badare al galateo, stare molto attento.

**pa** *n.* (fam.) papà *m. indecl.*, babbo.

**pabulum** *n.* pabolo, nutrimento.

**pace** *n.* passo; *ten -s off,* a dieci passi di distanza; passo, andatura, velocità; *at a walking —,* di passo, a passo d'uomo; *at a great —,* di buon passo; *to force the —,* forzare il passo; *to quicken one's —,* affrettare il passo; *to slacken one's —,* rallentare l'andatura; *to keep — with,* camminare di pari passo con; (fig.) *to keep — with the times,* tenersi al corrente; *to set the —,* dare l'andatura, fare da battistrada; (fam.) *to go the —,* bruciare le tappe; (of horse) ambio; *to put a horse through his -s,* fare bella mostra di un cavallo; (fig.) *to put someone through his -s,* mettere qualcuno alla prova.

**pace** *intr.* camminare, marciare, andare al passo; *to — up and down,* camminare su e giù; (of horse) ambiare; *tr.* misurare a passi, percorrere; *to — (off) a certain distance,* misurare a passi una certa distanza.

**pacemaker** *n.* (sport) battistrada *m. indecl.*

**pacer** *n.* cavallo addestrato al passo d'ambio; (sport) battistrada *m. indecl.*

**pachyderm** *n.* (zool.) pachiderma *m.*

**Pacific**[1] *pr.n.* (geog.) Pacifico.

**pacific**[2] *adj.* pacifico; tranquillo. **-ation** *n.* pacificazione.

**pacifier** *n.* paciere, pacificatore.

**pacif-ism** *n.* (pol.) pacifismo. **-ist** *n.* pacifista *m., f.*

**pacify** *tr.* pacificare, calmare; sedare, acchetare, abbonire.

**pack** *n.* pacco, involto; fardello, fagotto; soma; (comm.) imballo, imballaggio; (mil.) zaino; (med.) impacco, impiastro; (ice-pack) banchisa; (of cards) mazzo; (of hounds) muta; (fig., of thieves, *etc.*) banda, masnada; (fam.) *a — of lies,* un tessuto di bugie; *a — of nonsense,* una bubbolata; (rugby) attacanti *m.pl.*

**pack** *tr.* imballare, impaccare, impacchettare; incassare, inscatolare; *to — (up) one's things,* fare i bagagli, fare le valigie; pigiare, stipare; *to be -ed like sardines,* essere pigiati come acciughe; *to — passengers into a car,* stipare viaggiatori in una macchina; *the train was -ed,* il treno era pieno zeppo; *to — off,* spedire, mandare via; *to send someone -ing,* mandare qualcuno a farsi benedire, (mech.) guarnire, montare una guarnizione a; *intr.* fare i bagagli; stiparsi, stringersi; *to — up,* (fam.) andare via, far fagotto, (of motor) far cilecca, fermarsi.

**package** *n.* pacco, involto, collo; imballaggio; (industr.) *— deal,* accordo comprensivo.

**packer** *n.* imballatore, impaccatore.

**packet** *n.* pacchetto, pacco; *postal —,* pacco postale; *— of cigarettes,* pacchetto di sigarette; *— (boat),* (vapore) postale; (fam.) *to make a —,* guadagnare un sacco di soldi; (pop.) *to stop a —,* ricevere un colpo duro, essere colpito da una pallottola.

**pack-full** *adj.* (fam.) pieno zeppo. **-horse** *n.* cavallo da soma. **-ice** *n.* banchisa.

**packing** *n.* imballaggio; confezione; *to do one's —,* fare i bagagli; (mech.) guarnizione.

**packing-case** *n.* cassa da imballaggio. **-needle** *n.* agone *m.* **-paper** *n.* carta da imballaggio.

**packman** *n.* venditore ambulante.

**pack-saddle** *n.* basto.

**packthread** *n.* spago da imballaggio.

**pack-trail** *n.* mulattiera.

**pact** *n.* patto; convenzione.

**pad**[1] *n.* cuscinetto imbottito; tampone *m.*; batuffolo; imbottitura; (slang) alloggio; (for writing) notes *m. indecl.*; (artill.) borra; (of animal) zampa,

cuscinetto carnoso della zampa; (cricket) gambale *m.*; (mech.) flangia di attacco, cuscino ammortizzatore; *tr.* imbottire; tamponare; ovattare; (fig.) *to — (out)*, infarcire.

**pad**[2] *n.* (of feet, *etc.*) rumore *m.* (di assi), passo felpato; camminare a passi felpati.

**padd-ed** *adj.* imbottito. **-ing** *n.* imbottitura; ovatta; borra; (fig.) ripieno, borra, zeppa.

**paddle**[1] *n.* (for canoe) pagaia; (of wheel) pala; (of turtle, *etc.*) pinna, zampa palmata, natatoria; (industr.) spatola; (rowing) remata piana; *tr.*, *intr.* (canoe) spingere con la pagaia; (fig.) *to — one's own canoe*, sbrigarsi da sè, essere indipendente; (rowing) remare piano; (of turtle, duck, *etc.*) nuotare.

**paddle** *n.* lo sguazzare in acqua, pediluvio; *to go for a —*, sguazzare in acqua, fare un pediluvio; *intr.* sguazzare in acqua a piedi nudi.

**paddle-board** *n.* paletta di ruota. **-boat, -steamer** *n.* piroscafo a ruote. **-box** *n.* tamburo. **-wheel** *n.* ruota a pale.

**paddling-pool** *n.* piscina per bambini.

**paddock**[1] *n.* recinto, prato chiuso; (for racehorses) passeggiatoio; (min.) deposito per minerale.

**paddock**[2] *n.* (poet.) rospo.

**Paddy**[1] *pr.n.* (dimin. of **Patrick**) Patrizio; (fam.) irlandese *m.*

**paddy**[2] *n.* (fam.) accesso di rabbia.

**paddy**[3] *n.* riso vestito. **-field** *n.* risaia.

**padlock** *n.* lucchetto, catenaccio; *tr.* allucchettare, chiudere a catenaccio.

**padre** *n.* (mil.) cappellano militare; (fam.) prete, frate.

**Padua** *pr.n.* (geog.) Padova. **-n** *adj.*, *n.* padovano.

**paean** *n.* peana *m.*

**p(a)ederast** *n.* pederasta *m.* **-y** *n.* pederastia.

**paediatric** *adj.* (med.) pediatrico. **-ian** *n.* (med.) pediatra *m.*

**paeony** *n.* (bot.) peonia.

**pagan** *adj.*, *n.* pagano. **-ism** *n.* paganesimo, paganismo. **-ize** *tr.* paganizzare; *intr.* vivere da pagano.

**page**[1] *n.* (hist.) paggio, donzello; (in hotel) piccolo, fattorino; *tr.* (hotel) chiamare.

**page**[2] *n.* pagina; *right-hand —*, recto; *left-hand —*, verso; *on — 6*, a pagina sei; *tr.* numerare le pagine di; (typ.) impaginare.

**pageant** *n.* spettacolo all'aperto, corteo storico; parata, processione; (fig.) fasto. **-ry** *n.* fasto; pompa; sfarzo.

**page-boy** *n.* piccolo, fattorino.

**page-proof** *n.* (typ.) bozza impaginata.

**pagin-al** *adj.* di pagina; *— references*, rimandi alla pagina; pagina per pagina. **-ate** *tr.* (typ.) impaginare. **-ation, paging** *n.* numerazione delle pagine, paginatura; (typ.) impaginazione.

**pagoda** *n.* pagoda.

**paid** *p.def.*, *part.* of **pay**, *q.v.*; *adj.* pagato; retribuito; rimunerato; ricompensato.

**pail** *n.* secchia, secchio. **-ful** *n.* secchiata, una secchia piena.

**pain** *n.* dolore *m.*, male *m.*, sofferenza; angoscia, pena; (of childbirth) doglie *f.pl.*; (penalty) pena; *to give — to*, far male a, far soffrire; *to be out of one's —*, cessare di soffrire, morire; *to take — over*, fare con molta cura; *to take -s to do something*, sforzarsi di far qualcosa; *to have nothing for one's -s*, darsi pena per niente; *under — of death*, sotto pena di morte; *tr.* far male a, far soffrire; dolere, addolorare; *intr.* far male, dolere. **-ed** *adj.* addolorato, dolente.

**painful** *adj.* doloroso; penoso; gravoso; *it is — for me to have to say so*, mi fa pena dirlo; *to get —*, cominciare a far male. **-ness** *n.* dolore *m.*, dolorosità; pena.

**pain-killer** *n.* anodino, analgesico.

**painless** *adj.* indolore, senza dolore. **-ness** *n.* assenza di dolore.

**painstaking** *adj.* laborioso; diligente; coscienzioso; accurato; sollecito, premuroso; *n.* diligenza; cura; premura.

**paint** *n.* colore *m.*; vernice *f.*; *coat of —*, una mano di vernice; *wet —!*, vernice fresca!; *box of -s*, scatola di colori; (for face) belletto, rossetto; *tr.* dipingere, pitturare, verniciare, colorire; *to — something green*, verniciare qualcosa di verde; *to — out*, cancellare il già dipinto, cancellare passando sopra una mano di vernice; (fig.) *to — everything in rosy colours*, vedere tutto rosa; (fam.) *to — the town red*, fare baldoria; *intr. to — (one's face)*, imbellettarsi.

**paint-box** *n.* scatola di colori. **-brush** *n.* pennello.

**painter**[1] *n.* pittore *m.*, pittrice *f.*; *landscape —*, paesaggista *m.*, *f.*; *portrait —*, ritrattista *m.*; *house —*, decoratore, imbianchino, pittore edile.

**painter**[2] *n.* (naut.) cima da ormeggio, barba.

**painting** *n.* (art) pittura; quadro, dipinto; (of house, wall, *etc.*) verniciatura, il dipingere; *— on canvas*, tela; *— on wood*, tavola; *— on wall*, murale *f.*, affresco.

**paint-pot** *n.* vaso da colori. **-remover** *n.* solvente *m.* per vernice; (person) sverniciatore.

**pair** *n.* paio, coppia; *a — of shoes*, un paio di scarpe; (of horses, *etc.*) pariglia; *carriage and —*, vettura a due cavalli; (at wedding) *the happy —*, gli sposi; *au — girl*, ragazza alla pari; (cards) paio; (lottery) ambo; (fig.) *another — of shoes*, un altro paio di maniche; *tr.* appaiare, accoppiare; *intr.* appaiarsi, accoppiarsi, far paio; *to — off*, *tr.* mettere due per due, abbinare, *intr.* mettersi due per due, (fam.) sposarsi.

**pairing** *n.* appaiamento, abbinamento, accoppiamento.

**pajama** *n.* (USA) see **pyjama**.

**Pakistan** *pr.n.* (geog.) Pakistan. **-i** *adj.*, *n.* pachistano.

**pal** *n.* (pop.) camerata *m.*, compagno, amico; *intr.* (pop.) *to — up with someone*, fare amicizia con qualcuno.

**palace** *n.* palazzo; *royal —*, palazzo reale, reggia; *bishop's —*, vescovato.

**paladin** *n.* paladino.

**pal(a)eo-** *pref.* pale-, paleo-.

**palaeo-grapher** *n.* paleografo. **-graphic(al)** *adj.* paleografico. **-graphy** *n.* paleografia. **-lithic** *adj.* paleolitico.

**palafitte** *n.* (archaeol.) palafitta.

**palanquin** *n.* palanchino, lettiga.

**palatable** *adj.* saporito, gustoso, appetitoso; (fig.) gradevole; *to be — to*, gradire a, piacere a.

**palatal** *adj.* (anat.; ling.) palatale; *n.* (ling.) palatale *f.* **-ization** *n.* (ling.) palatalizzazione. **-ize** *tr.* (ling.) palatalizzare.

**palate** *n.* (anat.) palato; (fig.) gusto.

**palatial** *adj.* da palazzo; sontuoso, grandioso.

**Palatinate** *n.* (hist.) palatinato; (geog.) Palatinato.

**Palatine** *pr.n.* Palatino.

**palaver** *n.* abboccamento; (fam.) chiacchiere *f.pl.*; *intr.* confabulare; chiacchierare.

**pale**[1] *adj.* pallido; scialbo; allibito; *— as a ghost*, bianco come un cencio; *to grow —*, impallidire, allibire; biondo, chiaro; *— ale*, birra chiara; *tr.* far impallidire; *intr.* impallidire; allibire; diventare pallido.

**pale**[2] *n.* palo; confine *m.*; (herald.) palo, partito; *beyond the —*, fuori dei confini, (fig.) escluso dalla società, (fam.) impossibile.

**paleface** *n.* viso pallido, bianco.

**pale-faced** *adj.* dal volto pallido.

**paleness** *n.* pallore *m.*

**pale(o)-** *pref.* see **pal(a)eo-**.

**Palestin-e** *pr.n.* (geog.) Palestina. **-ian** *adj.*, *n.* palestinese *m.*, *f.*

**palette** *n.* (paint.) tavolozza, paletta. **-knife** *n.* (paint.) spatola, mestichino.

**palfrey** *n.* palafreno.

**palimpsest** *n.* palinsesto.

**palindrome** *n.* palindromo.

**paling** *n.* palizzata, stecconata.

**palinode** *n.* (lit.) palinodia.

**palisade** *n.* stecconata, palizzata; *tr.* stecconare, circondare con palizzata.

**palish** *adj.* pallidetto, palliduccio.
**pall**[1] *n.* drappo funebre; (eccl.) palla; (liturg.) animetta; (fig.) coltre *f.*, velo manto.
**pall**[2] *intr.* diventare insipido, non avere più sapore; *to — on*, saziare, stancare, satollare.
**Palladian** *adj.* (archit.) palladiano.
**palladium** *n.* palladio.
**Pallas** *pr.n.* (myth.) Pallade *f.*
**pall-bearer** *n.* chi regge i cordoni (a un funerale).
**pallet**[1] *n.* paglericcio, giaciglio.
**pallet**[2] *n.* (paint.) tavolozza; *cf.* **palette**; (watchm.) ancora; (pottery) spatola; (naut., of anchor) bocchetta; (herald.) verghetta.
**palliasse** *n.* paglericcio.
**palliat-e** *tr.* attenuare, mitigare, palliare; (med.) lenire. **-ing** *adj.* (med.) lenitivo; *-ing circumstances*, circostanze attenuanti. **-ion** *n.* attenuazione; mitigazione. **-ive** *adj.*, *n.* palliativo; lenitivo.
**pallid** *adj.* pallidetto, smunto, scialbo; (paint.) slavato. **-ness** *n.* pallore *m.*
**pallium** *n.* (eccl.) pallio; (zool.) mantello.
**pallor** *n.* pallore *m.*
**pallwise** *adv.* (herald.) in pergola.
**palm**[1] *n.* (bot.) palma, palmizio; *— Sunday*, Domenica delle Palme; (fig.) *to bear the —*, portare la palma, vincere; *to yield the —*, cedere la palma.
**palm**[2] *n.* (anat.) palmo; (fam.) *to grease someone's —*, corrompere qualcuno, ungere le ruote; *to hold someone in the — of one's hand*, tenere qualcuno nel proprio potere; (measure) palmo; (of oar) palma; (of anchor) patta; *tr.* toccare con la mano; nascondere nella mano; corrompere; (fam.) *to — off*, affibbiare, appioppare.
**palm-ar** *adj.* palmare. **-ate** *adj.* (bot.) palmato.
**palm-branch** *n.* ramo di palma.
**palmer** *n.* palmiere *m.*, pellegrino; (ent.) bruco peloso.
**palm-grove** *n.* palmeto. **-house** *n.* serra per palme.
**palmiped** *adj.*, *n.* (orn.) palmipede *m.*
**palmist** *n.* chiromante *m.*, *f.* **-ry** *n.* chiromanzia.
**palm-oil** *n.* olio di palma; (joc.) mancia.
**palmy** *adj.* (poet.) ricco di palme; (fig.) prosperoso, glorioso, felice.
**palpable** *adj.* palpabile; (fig.) evidente, manifesto.
**palpitat-e** *intr.* palpitare. **-ion** *n.* palpitazione; (fig.) affanno.
**pals-y** *n.* (bibl.) paralisi *f.* **-ied** *adj.* (bibl.) paralitico, paralizzato.
**palter** *intr.* equivocare, tergiversare.
**paltr-y** *adj.* meschino, gretto; miserabile, ridicolo. **-iness** *n.* meschinità, grettezza.
**paly** *adj.* (herald.) palato, verghettato.
**pampas** *n.* pampa; (bot.) *— grass*, ginereo, ginesio.
**pamper** *tr.* coccolare, viziare. **-ed** *adj.* viziato.
**pamphlet** *n.* opuscolo, libello. **-eer** *n.* autore di opuscoli, libellista *m.*
**Pan**[1] *pr.n.* (myth.) Pan, Pane; *pipes of —*, zampogna; *— pipes*, fistula.
**pan**[2] *n.* (cul.) tegame *m.*, casseruola, padella, scodellino, teglia; *pots and -s*, batteria da cucina; *to fall out of the frying-pan into the fire*, cadere dalla padella nella brace; *a flash in the —*, un fuoco di paglia; *lavatory —*, catino; (of scales) piatto; (mech.) coppa; (geol.) strato; *tr.* (min.) sottoporre a lavaggio; estrarre; *intr.* (fam.) *to — out*, risultare, finire; *how did it — out?*, com'è andato a finire?
**pan-** *pref.* pan-.
**panacea** *n.* panacea.
**panache** *n.* pennacchio; (fig.) ostentazione, spavalderia.
**Panama** *pr.n.* (geog.) Panama; *— hat*, cappello di paglia, panama *m.*
**Panamanian** *adj.*, *n.* (geog.) panamense *m.*, *f.*
**pan-american** *adj.* panamericano.
**pancake** *n.* (cul.) fritella; (fig.) *flat as a —*, completamente piatto, liscio come uno specchio; (geol.) *— ice*, ghiaccio a ciambelle; *intr.* (aeron. slang) scendere in picchiata.
**panchromatic** *adj.* (photog.) pancromatico.
**pancre-as** *n.* (anat.) pancreas *m.* **-atic** *adj.* pancreatico.
**panda** *n.* (zool.) panda.
**pandects** *n.* (leg.) pandette *f.pl.*
**pandemonium** *n.* pandemonio.
**pander** *n.* mezzano, ruffiano; *tr.*, *intr.* fare il mezzano (a); (fig.) *to — to*, favorire, prestarsi a.
**Pandora** *pr.n.* (myth.) Pandora; *—'s box*, il vaso di Pandora.
**pane** *n.* vetro, lastra di vetro; (bldg.) pannello; (text.) scacco; (of hammer) penna.
**panegyr-ic** *adj.*, *n.* panegirico. **-ist** *n.* panegirista *m.* **-ize** *tr.* elogiare, fare il panegirico di.
**panel** *n.* pannello; (archit.) formella, riquadro; (in ceiling) cassettone *m.*; (paint.) tavola, pannello; comitato, commissione; (of jury) lista; (min.) sezione; (aeron.; motor.) *instrument —*, cruscotto; *tr.* rivestire di pannelli; (min.) sezionare.
**panel-doctor** *n.* medico della mutua. **-envelope** *n.* busta a cellofane.
**panell-ed** *adj.* rivestito di legno, rivestito a pannelli; *— ceiling*, soffitto a cassettoni. **-ing** *n.* rivestimento a pannelli, pannelli *m.pl.*
**panful** *n.* padellata.
**pang** *n.* dolore acuto, spasimo, fitta; (fig.) angoscia; *to feel the -s of hunger*, sentire gli stimoli della fame.
**pan-german** *adj.* pangermanico. **-germanism** *n.* pangermanesimo. **-germanist** *n.* pangermanista *m.*
**pan-handle** *n.* manico di casseruola; (fig.) striscia di terra.
**panic** *adj.* panico; *n.* panico, terrore *m.*, allarme *m.*; *in a —*, colto dal panico; *intr.* essere in preda al panico, perdere la testa, allarmarsi. **-monger** *n.* allarmista *m.*, creatore di panico. **-stricken, -struck** *adj.* colto dal panico, spaventato, esterrefatto.
**panicky** *adj.* (fam.) soggetto al panico, pauroso.
**panjandrum** *n.* (fam.) funzionario arrogante, pezzo grosso.
**panification** *n.* panificazione.
**pannier** *n.* paniere *m.*, cesto; (on back) gerla.
**pannikin** *n.* tegamino; (mug) tazza di latta.
**panopl-y** *n.* (lit.) panoplia; armatura completa. **-ied** *adj.* armato da capo a piedi.
**panoram-a** *n.* panorama *m.*, vista. **-ic** *adj.* panoramico.
**pansy** *n.* (bot.) viola del pensiero; (joc.) finocchio.
**pant** *n.* anelito, ansito, palpito, respiro affannoso; sbuffo; *intr.* ansare, ansimare, anelare; sbuffare; *to — for breath*, anelare; *tr. to — out*, dire ansimando; (poet.) *to — for*, anelare a, bramare, aspirare a.
**Pantaloon** *pr.n.m.* (theatr.) Pantalone.
**pantaloons** *n.* (cost.) calzoni *m.pl.*, pantaloni *m.pl.*, braghe *f.pl.*
**pantechnicon** *n.* furgone da trasporto.
**panthe-ism** *n.* panteismo. **-ist** *n.* panteista *m.* **-istic(al)** *adj.* panteistico.
**Pantheon** *pr.n.* Panteon *m.*
**panther** *n.* pantera.
**panties** *n.* (fam.) mutandine *f.pl.*
**pantile** *n.* tegola alla fiamminga.
**panting** *adj.* ansante, ansimante, anelante; *n.* respiro affannoso, anelito, ansito, affanno; (fig.) bramosia.
**pantograph** *n.* pantografo, rapportatore.
**pantomim-e** *n.* mimica; (theatr.) pantomima. **-ic(al)** *adj.* pantomimico.
**pantry** *n.* dispensa.
**pants** *n.* (fam.) calzoni *m.pl.*; mutande *f.pl.*
**pap** *n.* (cul.) pappa; (of fruit) polpa.
**papa** *n.* papà *m.*, babbo.
**Papacy** *n.* Papato, Pontificato.
**papal** *adj.* papale, pontificio.

-**ism** *n.* papismo. -**ist** *n.* papista *m.*, papalino.
**papaverous** *adj.* di papavero, papaverico.
**papaw** *n.* (bot.) papaia.
**paper** *n.* carta; *on —*, sulla carta, in iscritto, (fig.) in teoria; *a sheet of —*, un foglio di carta; *a scrap of —*, un pezzo di carta; *airmail —*, carta da posta aerea; *blotting-paper*, carta assorbente; *brown —*, carta da imballaggio; *India —*, carta Oxford, carta India; *tissue —*, carta velina; *waste —*, carta straccia; *— bag*, sacchetto di carta; *— money*, valuta cartacea; *— work*, lavoro d'ufficio; documento; *pl.* incartamento, carteggio, documenti; *to send in one's -s*, dare le dimissioni; discorso; *to read a —*, fare un discorso; saggio; (schol.) prova, esame *m.*; *to set a —*, assegnare le domande, proporre il tema; giornale *m.*; *weekly —*, settimanale *m.*; *Sunday —*, giornale della domenica; *to read the -s*, leggere i giornali; *to write for the -s*, fare del giornalismo; *attrib.* di carta, cartaceo; *tr.* coprire di carta; tappezzare.
**paperback** *n.* libro brossato, libro in brossura.
**paper-backed, -bound** *adj.* (bookb.) in brossura, non rilegato. -**boy** *n.* strillone *m.* -**chase** *n.* corsa nella quale la pista consiste di pezzetti di carta. -**clip** *n.* fermaglino. -**hanger** *n.* tappezziere *m.* -**hanging** *n.* tappezzeria. -**knife** *n.* tagliacarte *m.* -**maker** *n.* fabbricante di carta. -**making, -manufacturing** *n.* fabbricazione dellacarta, industria cartiera. -**mill** *n.* cartiera.
**paperweight** *n.* fermacarte *m. indecl.*
**papery** *adj.* simile a carta.
**papier mâché** *n.* cartapesta.
**pap-ism** *n.* (derog.) papismo. -**ist** *n.* papista *m.*, *f.*, cattolico.
**pappy** *adj.* simile a pappa, molle.
**paprika** *n.* (cul.) paprica.
**papyrus** *n.* papiro.
**par** *n.* pari *f.*; parità; *at —*, alla pari; *above —*, sopra la pari; *below —*, sotto la pari; *— of exchange*, parità di cambio; *to be on a — with*, essere alla pari con; *to put on a — (with)*, accomunare; (fam.) *to feel below —*, sentirsi un po' giù.
**parable** *n.* parabola; *to speak in -s*, parlare per parabole.
**parabola** *n.* (geom.) parabola.
**parabolic(al)** *adj.* (geom.) parabolico; (fig.) allegorico.
**Paracelsus** *pr.n.* (hist.) Paracelso.
**parachut-e** *n.* paracadute *m.*; *intr. to — down*, scendere col paracadute. -**ist** *n.* paracadutista *m.*, *f.*
**parade** *n.* parata, mostra, sfoggio; *to make a — of*, fare sfoggio di, sfoggiare; (mil.) parata, adunata; corteo, processione; sfilata; (esplanade) spianata, passeggiata; (sea-front) lungomare *m.*; *tr.* far mostra di, ostentare, sfoggiare; (mil.) adunare, disporre in parata; *intr.* (mil.) adunarsi, sfilare; (fam.) *to — up and down*, passeggiare su e giù.
**paradigm** *n.* (gramm.) paradigma *m.*; modello.
**paradis-e** *n.* paradiso; (fig.) luogo di delizie; (fam.) *to live in a fool's —*, cullarsi in dolci speranze; (orn.) *bird of —*, uccello del paradiso. -**iac(al)** *adj.* paradisiaco.
**paradox** *n.* paradosso. -**ical** *adj.* paradossale.
**paraffin** *n.* petrolio (da illuminazione); (med.) paraffina. -**lamp** *n.* lampada a petrolio. -**oil** *n.* olio di petrolio. -**wax** *n.* paraffina.
**paragon** *n.* modello di perfezione, esemplare *m.*; (fig.) fenice *f.*; *a — of virtue*, un fiore di virtù; (typ.) corpo venti; *tr.* citare come esempio; (poet.) paragonare.
**paragraph** *n.* paragrafo, articolo, comma *m.*, capoverso; (journ.) trafiletto; (typ.) *new —*, (d)a capo; *tr.* dividere in paragrafi; *intr.* (journ.) scrivere un trafiletto. -**ing** *n.* divisione in paragrafi.
**Paraguay** *pr.n.* (geog.) Paraguai *m.* -**an** *adj.*, *n.* paraguaiano.
**parakeet** *n.* (orn.) parrocchetto.
**paralipomena** *n.* paralipomeni *m.pl.*
**parallax** *n.* (astron.) parallasse *f.*
**parallel** *adj.* parallelo; *to run — with*, correre parallelo a; *— ruler*, regolo per tracciare parallele; (gymn.) *— bars*, parallele *f.pl.*; (electr.) *— connection*, collegamento in paralleli; (fig.) simile, somigliante, analogo; *n.* (geom.; techn.) parallelo, parallela; (fig.) confronto, paragone *m.*; *to draw a — between two things*, fare un paragone fra due cose; *without —*, senza pari, senza precedenti; *tr.* essere parallelo a; collocare in parallelo; (fig.) paragonare (a), confrontare (con). -**epiped** *n.* (geom.) parallelepipedo. -**ism** *n.* parallelismo; confronto. -**ogram** *n.* parallelogrammo.
**paralys-e** *tr.* paralizzare. -**ation** *n.* immobilizzazione; paralisi *f.*
**paraly-sis** *n.* (med.) paralisi *f.*; *infantile —*, paralisi infantile. -**tic** *adj.*, *n.* paralitico; *-tic stroke*, attacco di paralisi; (fam.) ubriaco fradicio.
**paramount** *adj.* sovrano, dominante, supremo, sommo, eminente; *of — importance*, di somma importanza; *with him duty is —*, per lui il dovere conta più di ogni altra cosa.
**paramour** *n.* amante *m.*, *f.*, drudo *m.*, druda *f.*
**paranoia** *n.* (med.) paranoia *f.* -**c** *adj.*, *n.* paranoico.
**parapet** *n.* parapetto.
**paraphernalia** *n.* (leg.) paraferna, sopraddote *f.*; (fig.) roba personale, accessori *m.pl.*, armamentario; (pop.) bagagliume *m.*
**paraphras-e** *n.* parafrasi *f.*; *tr.*, *intr.* parafrasare, fare una parafrasi. -**tic** *adj.* parafrastico.
**parasit-e** *n.* parassita *m.* -**ic(al)** *adj.* parassitico. -**ism** *n.* parassitismo.
**parasol** *n.* parasole *m.*, ombrellino.
**paratroop-er** *n.* (mil.) paracadutista *m.* -**s** *n.* (mil.) reparti di paracadutisti *m.pl.*
**paratyphoid** *n.* (med.) paratifo.
**parboil** *tr.* (cul.) bollire parzialmente; (fig.) riscaldare troppo.
**Parcae** *pr.n.* (myth.) Parche *f.pl.*
**parcel** *n.* pacco, pacchetto, involto, collo; *— post*, servizio dei pacchi postali; *by — post*, a mezzo pacco postale; *-s office*, ufficio pacchi; *to do up a —*, confezionare un pacco; lotto; (fig.) *part and — of*, parte integrale di; *tr. to — out*, spartire, dividere, distribuire.
**parch** *tr.* essiccare, inaridire, bruciacchiare; *intr.* disseccarsi, inaridirsi. -**ed** *adj.* riarso, adusto; arido, sterile; *to be -ed with thirst*, bruciare dalla sete, avere la gola riarsa.
**parchment** *n.* pergamena, cartapecora; *— paper*, *imitation —*, carta pergamenata; *attrib.* pergamenaceo.
**pard** *n.* (poet.) pardo, leopardo.
**pardon** *n.* perdono; grazia; scusa; *to beg someone's —*, chiedere scusa a qualcuno; *I beg your —!*, mi scusi!; (eccl.) indulgenza; (leg.) *general —*, amnistia; *tr.* perdonare; accordare la grazia a; scusare; (leg.) graziare. -**able** *adj.* perdonabile; scusabile; remissibile. -**er** *n.* (eccl.) venditore di indulgenze.
**pare** *tr.* ritagliare, raffilare; (fruit) sbucciare; (vegetables) sbaccellare, mondare; (cloth, turf) tosare; *to — one's nails*, ritagliarsi le unghie.
**paregoric** *adj.*, *n.* (pharm.) paregorico.
**parent** *n.* genitore *m.*, padre *m.*, madre *f.*; *our first -s*, i nostri progenitori; (fig.) origine *f.*, fonte *f.*, sorgente *f.*; *attrib.* madre; *— firm*, casa madre. -**age** *n.* genitori *m.pl.*, antenati *m.pl.*; nascita, famiglia, lignaggio. -**al** *adj.* dei genitori; paterno, materno.
**parenthe-sis** *n.* parentesi *f.*; *in —*, tra parentesi; (fig.) pausa. -**tic(al)** *adj.* parentetico.
**parent-hood** *n.* paternità, maternità; *planned —*, pianificazione demografica. -**less** *adj.* senza genitori, orfano.
**parget** *n.* gesso, intonaco; *tr.* intonacare, decorare con gesso.

**parhelion** *n.* (astron.) parelio.
**pariah** *n.* paria *m., f.* (also fig.).
**Parian** *adj.* (geog.) di Paro; — *marble*, pario.
**parietal** *adj.* (anat.) parietale.
**Paris**[1] *pr.n.* (geog.) Parigi *f.*; — *white*, bianco di Parigi.
**Paris**[2] *pr.n.* (myth.) Paride; *the judgement of* —, il giudizio di Paride.
**parish** *n.* parrocchia; — *church*, pieve *f.*, chiesa parrocchiale; — *priest*, parroco, pievano, curato; (civil admin.) *country* —, comune *m.*, (in town) sezione; (fam.) *parish-pump politics*, campanilismo. **-ioner** *n.* parrocchiano; (eccl.) popolano; *pl.* il popolo.
**Parisian** *adj.* parigino, di Parigi; *n.* parigino.
**parisyllabic** *adj.* (ling.) parisillabo.
**parity** *n.* parità; uguaglianza.
**park** *n.* parco; *public* —, giardino pubblico; (mil.) parco; (motor.) posteggio, parcheggio; (game reserve) riserva di caccia; (oyster-bed) vivaio; *tr.*, *intr.* (motor.) parcheggiare, posteggiare, stazionare; (fig.) *to — oneself*, piantare le tende.
**Parker** *n.* (pop.) *Nosey* —, ficcanaso.
**parking** *n.* (motor.) parcheggio, posteggio; *no —!*, divieto di sosta!; — *on uneven dates*, è permesso il posteggio nei giorni dispari; — *meter*, contatore per parcheggio.
**parking-place** *n.* parcheggio, posteggio.
**park-keeper** *n.* custode *m.* (di un parco).
**parky** *adj.* (pop.) fresco.
**parlance** *n.* parlata, parlatura; gergo; *in common* —, nell'uso vivo, nel parlare comune; *in legal* —, in termini legali.
**parley** *n.* colloquio, abboccamento; *to hold a — with*, parlamentare con; *intr.* parlamentare, conferire, abboccarsi (con).
**parliament** *n.* parlamento; *the Houses of* —, il palazzo del Parlamento *m.*; *act of* —, decreto, legge *f.*; *member of* —, deputato, membro del parlamento; onorevole *m., f.*; *to dissolve* —, sciogliere il parlamento. **-arian** *n.* deputato esperto nelle tradizioni del Parlamento. **-ary** *adj.* parlamentare; *-ary constituency*, circoscrizione elettorale; *-ary election*, elezioni politiche; *-ary language*, linguaggio corretto.
**parlour** *n.* salotto, salottino; *bar* —, sala interna; (in convent) parlatorio; (comm.) *beauty* —, istituto di bellezza; — *games*, giuochi di società. **-maid** *n.* cameriera (che serve a tavola).
**parlous** *adj.* pericoloso, precario.
**Parm-a** *pr.n.* (geog.) Parma; *attrib.* parmense, parmigiano; — *violet*, viola di Parma. **-esan** *adj.*, *n.* parmigiano; *-esan cheese*, (formaggio) parmigiano.
**Parnass-us** *pr.n.* (geog.) Parnaso. **-ian** *adj.*, *n.* del Parnaso; (lit. hist.) parnassiano.
**parochial** *adj.* parrocchiale; comunale; (fig.) di campanile, campanilistico. **-ism** *n.* campanilismo, ristrettezza di vedute.
**parod-y** *n.* parodia; *tr.* parodiare. **-ist** *n.* parodista *m., f.*
**parole** *n.* parola, parola d'onore; parola d'ordine; *to be on* —, essere liberato sulla parola; *tr.* mettere in libertà sulla parola.
**paroquet** *n.* See **parakeet.**
**paroxysm** *n.* parossismo, accesso, orgasmo. **-al, -ic** *adj.* parossistico.
**parquet** *n.* pavimento in legno a tasselli. **-ry** *n.* pavimentazione in legno.
**parr** *n.* salmone giovane.
**parricid-al** *adj.* parricida. **-e** *n.* (person.) parricida *m., f.*; (crime) parricidio.
**parrot** *n.* pappagallo; (fig.) *to talk like a* —, fare il pappagallo; *in — fashion*, da pappagallo.
**parry** *n.* parata; *tr.* parare; (fig.) eludere, schivare; *to — a question*, eludere una domanda.
**parse** *tr.* (gramm.) analizzare.
**Parsee** *n.*, *adj.* Parso, Parsì *m.* **-ism** *n.* parsismo.
**parsimonious** *adj.* parsimonioso; parco; gretto. **-ness, parsimony,** *n.* parsimonia; grettezza; (fig.) economia.
**parsley** *n.* prezzemolo.
**parsnip** *n.* (bot.; cul.) pastinaca.
**parson** *n.* parroco; prete *m.*, curato; (cleric) ecclesiastico. **-age** *n.* canonica, presbiterio.
**part** *adv.* parzialmente, in parte; cf. **partly.**
**part** *n.* parte *f.*; porzione; — *of*, una parte di; *a great — of*, una gran parte di; *the greater — of*, la maggior parte di; *in* —, in parte, parzialmente; *for my* —, da parte mia; *to take — in*, prendere parte a; *to take someone's* —, parteggiare per qualcuno, prendere le parti di qualcuno; *to take something in good* —, prendere qualcosa filosoficamente; *I have done my* —, ho fatto quanto dovevo fare; *this is no — of my duties*, questo esula dalle mie competenze; (theatr.) parte, ruolo; *to take a* —, interpretare un ruolo, (fig.) *he is playing a* —, finge, fa commedia; (mus.) parte, voce *f.*; (of book) parte, tomo, (instalment) dispensa, fascicolo; quartiere *m.*, zona, località rione *m.*; *in foreign -s*, all'estero; *from all -s*, da ogni lato; *attrib.* parziale; — *payment*, pagamento in acconto; *pl.* talento, abilità; *a man of -s*, un uomo di talento, un uomo in gamba; (gramm.) *the -s of speech*, le parti del discorso; (fam.) *the privy -s*, i genitali; (mech.) *spare -s*, pezzi di ricambio.
**part** *tr.* separare, dividere, spartire; *to — company*, lasciarsi, separarsi; *to — one's hair*, farsi la scriminatura, farsi la riga; *intr.* lasciarsi, separarsi; (of lips) schiudersi; partire; spezzarsi; *the rope -ed*, la corda si spezzò; *to — from*, separarsi da, lasciare, dire addio a; *to — with*, disfarsi di, rinunciare a, dire addio a.
**partake** *intr.* *to — of*, prendere parte a, partecipare a; mangiare, consumare; condividere; (fig.) sapere di; *manners that — of insolence*, maniere che sanno d'insolenza.
**partaker** *n.* partecipante *m., f.*
**parted** *adj.* diviso, separato.
**parterre** *n.* aiuola; (theatr.) platea.
**parthenogenesis** *n.* (biol.; myth.) partenogenesi *f.*
**Parthenon** *pr.n.* (archit.) Partenone *m.*
**Parthenope** *pr.n.* (myth.) Partenope.
**Parthian** *adj.*, *n.* parto; — *shot*, freccia del Parto.
**partial** *adj.* parziale, in parte, non totale; propenso, parziale; *to be — to*, avere un debole per; *to be — to someone*, provare simpatia per qualcuno. **-ity** *n.* predilezione, inclinazione, preferenza; debole *m.*; favoritismo, parzialità. **-ly** *adv.* parzialmente, in parte.
**particip-ant** *adj.* partecipe; *n.* partecipante *m., f.* **-ate** *intr.* partecipare (a), prendere parte (a); condividere. **-ation** *n.* partecipazione. **-ator** *n.* partecipante *m., f.*
**particip-le** *n.* (gramm.) participio. **-ial** *adj.* (gramm.) participiale.
**particle** *n.* (gramm.) particella; (eccl.) particola; (fig.) *there is not a — of truth in the story*, non c'è ombra di verità in questa storia; *a — of common sense*, un grano di buon senso.
**particoloured** *adj.* multicolore, variopinto.
**particular** *adj.* particolare, speciale, determinato; *for no — reason*, per nessuna ragione speciale; *I have nothing — to do*, non ho niente di speciale da fare; *a — friend of mine*, un mio amico intimo; esatto, preciso, minuzioso; meticoloso, esigente, difficile, puntiglioso, pignolo; *he is — about his food*, è molto esigente per quanto riguarda il mangiare; *I'm not — about it*, non ho preferenze; *n.* dettaglio, particolare *m.*; *to give full -s*, dare ampi dettagli; *for further -s*, per ulteriori informazioni; *to go into -s*, entrare in particolari; *-s about oneself*, dati personali; *in* —, in particolare, specialmente. **-ity**

*n.* particolarità, peculiarità; singolarità, caratteristica; esigenza, meticolosità.

**particulariz-e** *tr.* particoleggiare, specificare, dettagliare. **-ation** *n.* particolarizzazione.

**particularly** *adv.* particolarmente, in particolare, specialmente, specie.

**parting** *adj.* d'addio, ultimo; — *directions*, ultime raccomandazioni; *a — word*, una parola d'addio; *a — kiss*, un ultimo bacio; (poet.) *the — day*, il giorno che muore; *n.* separazione, distacco, partenza; (fig.) *to find oneself at the — of the ways*, essere al bivio; (in hair) riga, scriminatura; rottura.

**partisan** *n.* partigiano, combattente della resistenza; (fig.) — *spirit*, spirito di partito; (weapon) partigiana. **-ship** *n.* partigianeria.

**partition** *n.* divisione, separazione; (pol.) spartizione; (bldg.) tramezzo, divisorio, assito; *tr.* separare, dividere in parti, spartire; *to — off*, dividere a mezzo muro divisorio.

**partitive** *adj.*, *n.* (gramm.) partitivo.

**partly** *adv.* in parte, parzialmente; (finan.) — *paid up*, versato in parte.

**partner** *n.* (comm.) socio; *sleeping* —, socio accomandante; *working* —, socio effettivo; (dancing) cavaliere *m.*, dama *f.*; (at games) partner *m.*, compagno; (husband) marito, compagno; (wife) moglie *f.*, compagna; *tr.* essere socio di, associarsi a; (at games) essere il partner di; (at dance) *to — a lady*, guidare una dama. **-ship** *n.* associazione, società; *to enter into -ship with*, entrare a far parte di una società con, associarsi con; *-ship agreement*, contratto di associazione; *industrial -ship*, partecipazione degli operai agli utili dell'azienda; *-ship in crime*, associazione a delinquere.

**partook** *p.def.* of **partake,** *q.v.*

**part-owner** *n.* comproprietario.

**partridge** *n.* (orn.) pernice *f.*

**part-song** *n.* (mus.) canto a più voci, villanella. **-time** *adj.* *-time job*, lavoro a mezza giornata.

**parturi-ent** *adj.*, *n.* partoriente *f.* **-tion** *n.* parto.

**party** *n.* comitiva, compagnia, brigata; *a big — of tourists*, una comitiva numerosa di turisti; riunione, trattenimento, festa; *to give a* —, fare una festa, offrire un trattenimento, invitare gli amici; *dinner* —, pranzo; *evening* —, serata; *garden* —, ricevimento all'aperto; *tea* —, tè *m.*; (pol.) partito, fazione; — *leader*, capo di partito; — *line*, politica del partito; — *man*, uomo di partito; — *politics*, politica dei partiti; *working* —, gruppo di lavoro; (leg.; comm.) parte *f.*; *injured* —, parte lesa; *to become — to an action*, costituirsi parte in un processo; *to be — to a crime*, essere complice in un delitto; *contracting parties*, parti contraenti; *third* —, terzi *m.pl.*; (mil.) plotone *m.*, pattuglia; *advance* —, avanguardia; *firing* —, plotone d'esecuzione; *landing* —, pattuglia di sbarco; *working* —, corvée *f.*; (bldg.) — *wall*, muro divisorio; (teleph.) — *line*, derivazione, duplex *m. indecl.*; (fig.) *to take the — line*, seguire le direttive del partito; (fam.) [*an old* —, un vecchio tipo.

**parvenu** *n.* nuovo ricco.

**parvis** *n.* (in front of church) sagrato.

**Paschal** *adj.* pasquale, di Pasqua.

**pasha** *n.* pascià *m. indecl.*

**Pasiphae** *pr.n.f.* (myth.) Pasife.

**pasquinade** *n.* pasquinata; *tr.* satireggiare.

**pass** *n.* passaggio; passo, valico, varco; stretto; passo, punto, situazione; *to such a — that*, a tal punto che; *a pretty* —, un bel pasticcio; lasciapassare *m.*, permesso, salvacondotto; (mil.) permesso, libera uscita; (rlwy.) *free* —, biglietto di viaggio gratuito, (theatr.) biglietto di favore; (schol.) promozione; — *degree*, laurea senza lode; (soccer) allungo; (rugby) apertura; (fencing) passata.

**pass** *tr.* passare, superare, oltrepassare; trascorrere; approvare; (schol.) *to — a candidate*, promuovere un candidato agli esami; esprimere, pronunciare; *to — an opinion*, esprimere un giudizio; *to — sentence*, pronunciare la condanna; (mil.) *to — in review*, passare in rivista; (sport) *to — the ball*, allungare la palla; (fam.) *to — the time of day with*, scambiare due parole con; *to — a dud coin*, rifilare una moneta falsa; *intr.* passare; *to let* —, lasciar passare; accadere, succedere; essere approvato, (schol.) essere promosso; (cards) passare. FOLLOW. BY ADV. OR PREP.: *to — across*, attraversare; *to — along*, *tr.* far passare da mano in mano, *intr.* passare oltre, circolare; *to — away*, *tr.* passare; *to — the time away*, passare il tempo; *intr.* passare, svanire, morire, trapassare; *to — between*, passare fra; *to — by*, *tr.* non curarsi di, lasciar passare, *intr.* passare oltre, passare davanti; *to — down*, *tr.* porgere, trasmettere, *intr.* — *down the car*, s'accomodino davanti; *to — for*, passare per; *to — in*, entrare; *to — into*, diventare, trasformarsi in; *to — off*, *tr.* far passare (per); *to — oneself off as*, passare sotto il nome di; *to — something off as a joke*, prendere qualcosa in ridere; *intr.* passare, svanire; *to — on*, *tr.* far circolare, trasmettere, *intr.* passare oltre, morire; *to — out*, *tr.* passare fuori, *intr.* uscire, svenire, (from college, etc.) superare l'ultimo esame; *to — over*, *tr.* omettere, sorvolare su, consegnare, *intr.* passare; (of storm, etc.) dileguarsi, trapassare, morire; *to — over to the enemy*, passare al nemico; *to — round*, *tr.* far circolare, *intr.* girare intorno a, superare; *to — through*, attraversare; *to — unnoticed (by)*, sfuggire (a).

**passabl-e** *adj.* (of road) praticabile; (of river) guadabile, navigabile; passabile, discreto, tollerabile. **-y** *adv.* passabilmente, discretamente, abbastanza bene.

**passage** *n.* passaggio, transito; *bird of* —, uccello di passo; viaggio, traversata; prezzo del biglietto; *to work one's* —, guadagnarsi la traversata lavorando a bordo; varco, passaggio; *to force a* —, aprirsi a forza un varco; (in building) passaggio, andito, corridoio; (in book) brano, passo; (mus.) passo, passaggio; approvazione, adozione; — *of words*, scambio di parole; — *of arms*, scontro.

**passageway** *n.* passaggio; *to leave a* —, lasciar libero il passaggio.

**passant** *adj.* (herald.) passante.

**pass-book** *n.* libretto di banca.

**passé** *adj.* antiquato, fuori moda.

**passementerie** *n.* passamaneria.

**passenger** *n.* viaggiatore; passeggiero. **-train** *n.* (rlwy.) treno viaggiatori; *to send a parcel by -train*, spedire un pacco come bagaglio.

**passer-by** *n.* passante *m.*, *f.*, viandante *m.*, *f.*

**passim** *adv.* passim, qua e là.

**passing** *adj.* che passa, passante; passeggiero; rapido; effimero, transitorio; fugace; casuale; — *events*, attualità *f.pl.*; *a — fancy*, un capriccio; *adv.* (poet.) — *fair*, assai bello; *n.* passaggio, transito; *in* —, di passaggio, tra parentesi; trapasso; (of law, etc.) approvazione; (of sentence) emissione; (schol. of candidate) promozione, amissione; — *away*, fine *f.*, trapasso; — *on*, trasmissione; (schol.) — *out*, promozione; — *out list*, elenco dei promossi; — *through*, attraversamento, traversata.

**passing-bell** *n.* rintocco funebre, campana a morto. **-place** *n.* (on river) guado; (on narrow road) baratto.

**passion** *n.* passione; (rel.) *the Passion of Christ*, la passione di Cristo; emozione; collera; entusiasmo; amore *m.*; *to have a — for*, essere appassionato di; *to fly*

*into a* –, andare su tutte le furie, arrabbiarsi, dare in eccessi. **-al** *adj.* passionale; *n.* (eccl.) passionario, passionale *m.* **-ate** *adj.* collerico, irascibile; ardente; appassionato; vivo; forte; veemente. **-ately** *adv.* appassionatamente; ardentemente; *to be -ately fond of*, essere appassionato di; con ira, irosamente.

**passion-flower** *n.* (bot.) passiflora.

**passionless** *adj.* impassibile; senza passione; calmo.

**passion-play** *n.* (theatr.) mistero della Passione; sacra rappresentazione. **-tide** *n.* settimana della Passione, settimana santa.

**passive** *adj.* passivo; – *resistance*, resistenza passiva; *n.* (gramm.) passivo. **-ness, passivity** *n.* passività; inerzia.

**pass-key** *n.* passe-partout *m.*, chiave universale. **-list** *n.* elenco degli ammessi, dei promossi. **-out** *adj.* di contromarca.

**Passover** *n.* Pasqua ebraica.

**pass-port** *n.* passaporto; *Nansen* –, passaporto apolide. **-word** *n.* parola d'ordine.

**past** *adj.* passato, andato, scorso, trascorso; *in times* –, nei tempi andati; *the* – *years*, gli anni passati; *the* – *week*, la settimana scorsa; *for some time* –, da qualche tempo; ex, già; – *chairman*, ex presidente; – *master*, esperto, campione *m.*, (pejor.) matricolato; (gramm.) – *tense*, tempo passato; *adv.* accanto, davanti, oltre; *to go* –, passare; *to run* –, passare di corsa; (mil.) *to march* –, sfilare; *n.* passato; *in the* –, nel passato, per l'addietro; *to be a thing of the* –, essere finito, non esistere più; *town with a* –, città con una storia; *woman with a* –, donna di dubbia reputazione.

**past** *prep.* al di là di, oltre, dopo; *a little* – *the bridge*, un poco al al di là del ponte; *she was out till* – *two o'clock*, essa rimase fuori fin dopo le due; *it is* – *eleven o'clock*, sono le undici passate; *half-past two*, le due e mezzo; *he is* – *seventy*, ha oltre settant'anni; – *bearing*, insopportabile; *he is* – *praying for*, è un caso disperato; *it is* – *all hope*, non c'è più speranza; *to be* – *one's work*, non essere più capace di lavorare.

**paste** *n.* (cul.) pasta; (techn.) impasto; colla; (jewellery) impasto, strasso; – *jewels*, gemme false; *tr.* impastare; incollare, appiccicare; *to* – (*up*) *a placard*, affissare un cartello; (pop.) *to* – *someone*, picchiare qualcuno. **-board** *n.* cartone *m.*; *attrib.* di cartone.

**pastel** *n.* (art) pastello; – *drawing*, pastello; *in* –, a pastello; – *painter*, pastellista *m.*, *f.*

**pastern** *n.* (of horse) pasturale *m.*

**pasteuriz-e** *tr.* pastorizzare. **-ation** *n.* pastorizzazione.

**pastiche** *n.* zibaldone *m.*; accozzaglia.

**pastille** *n.* pastiglia, pasticca.

**pastime** *n.* passatempo; divertimento.

**pastiness** *n.* pastosità; (fam.) pallore *m.*

**pasting** *n.* incollamento; (pop.) batosta.

**pastor** *n.* (rel.) pastore *m.*; (Protestant) ministro. **-al** *adj.* pastorale; *-al land*, pascolo; (eccl.) *-al letter*, pastorale *f.*; *-al staff*, pastorale *m.*; *n.* (lit.; mus.) pastorale *m.*, idillio.

**pastry** *n.* pasticceria, paste *f.pl.*, dolci *m.pl.* **-board** *n.* spianatoia. **-cook** *n.* pasticciere *m.*; *-cook's shop*, pasticceria.

**pasturage** *n.* see **pasture.**

**pasture** *n.* pastura, pascolo; *Alpine* –, malga; *tr.* condurre al pascolo; *intr.* pascere, pascolare. **-land** *n.* terreno da pascolo.

**pasty** *adj.* pastoso, di pasta; *n.* (cul.) pasticcio. **-faced** *adj.* pallido, dal viso pallido.

**Pat**[1] *pr.n.m.* (dimin. of **Patrick**) Patrizio; *f.* (dimin. of **Patricia**) Patrizia.

**pat**[2] *adj.* apposito, opportuno, pronto per l'occasione; *he always has an excuse* –, ha sempre la scusa pronta; *adv.* esattamente, a punto, a proposito; *to answer someone* –, rispondere a proposito; *to learn something off* –, imparare qualcosa a memoria.

**pat**[3] *n.* colpetto, buffetto; carezza; *to give someone a* – *on the back*, battere qualcuno affettuosamente sulla spalla, (fig.) lodare qualcuno; (fam.) *to give oneself a* – *on the back*, felicitarsi, essere contento di se stesso; – *of butter*, pane di burro; (sound) scalpiccio, ticchettio; *tr.* dare un buffetto a; accarezzare; *to* – *someone on the back*, battere qualcuno affettuosamente sulla spalla; *to* – *oneself on the back for having done something*, felicitarsi di aver fatto qualcosa.

**patch** *n.* pezza, toppa; *to put a* – *on a garment*, rappezzare un vestito; (on tyre) rappezzatura, (or inner tube) impiastro di gomma; (fam.) *not to be a* – *on*, essere molto inferiore a; (of land) pezzo, appezzamento; macchia, gruppo; *-es of trees*, macchie di alberi; *a* – *of blue sky*, una striscia di cielo azzurro; *good in -es*, buono in parte; (fam.) *to strike a bad* –, attraversare un momento brutto; (on face) neo.

**patch** *tr.* rappezzare, rattoppare, rammendare, accomodare; (fig.) *-ed with*, macchiato di; *to* – *up*, accomodare, aggiustare, raffazzonare; *to* – *up a quarrel*, comporre una lite; *a -ed up peace*, una pace aggiustata alla meglio; *a -ed up job*, una raffazzonatura.

**patchiness** *n.* ineguaglianza; mancanza di armonia; condizione macchiata; profusione di toppe; irregolarità; raffazzonamento; disposizione a macchie.

**patchouli** *n.* pasciulì *m.*

**patchwork** *n.* rappezzatura, rappezzamento; raffazzonatura; (needlew.) lavoro di cucito formato da pezze di diversi colori, trapunta; (fig.) miscuglio, mosaico.

**patchy** *adj.* rappezzato, rattoppato; a macchie, variegato; (fig.) irregolare, non uniforme.

**pate** *n.* (fam.) testa, zucca.

**patency** *n.* evidenza.

**patent** *adj.* manifesto, ovvio, chiaro, patente; (comm.) brevettato, patentato; *letters* –, brevetto; – *medicine*, specialità medicinale; – *food*, specialità alimentare; – *leather*, pelle verniciata, (fam.) copale *f.*; *n.* brevetto, titolo, diploma *m.*; – *office*, ufficio brevetti; *to take out a* – *for*, brevettare; – *of nobility*, patente di nobiltà; *tr.* brevettare. **-ee** *n.* concessionario di brevetto, esclusivista *m.*, *f.*

**paterfamilias** *n.* padre *m.* di famiglia, capo famiglia.

**patern-al** *adj.* paterno; (fig.) paternalistico. **-ity** *n.* paternità.

**paternoster** *n.* padrenostro; grano di rosario.

**path** *n.* sentiero; viottola; (fig.) via, strada; (astron., *etc.*) cammino, orbita, traiettoria; (sport) pista; *beaten* –, sentiero battuto; *the* – *of glory*, la via della gloria.

**pathetic** *adj.* patetico, commovente, pietoso.

**pathfinder** *n.* pioniere, esploratore; (aeron.) ricognitore.

**pathless** *adj.* senza vie, senza sentieri; inesplorato; impenetrabile.

**pathogenesis** *n.* patogenesi *f.*

**patholog-y** *n.* patologia. **-ical** *adj.* patologico. **-ist** *n.* patologo.

**pathos** *n.* pathos *m.*, patetico.

**pathway** *n.* sentiero; (in a street) marciapiede *m.*

**patience** *n.* pazienza; *to lose* –, perdere la pazienza; *to try someone's* –, mettere alla prova la pazienza di qualcuno; *to possess one's soul in* –, munirsi di pazienza; (game) pazienza, solitario.

**patient** *adj.* paziente; tollerante; diligente; perseverante; *to be* –, pazientare; *to be* – *with someone*, aver pazienza con qualcuno; *n.* paziente *m.*, *f.*, malato; (in hospital) degente *m.*, *f.*

**patina** *n.* patina.
**patness** *n.* esattezza, prontezza.
**patois** *n.* dialetto; gergo.
**patriarch** *n.* patriarca *m.* **-al** *adj.* patriarcale. **-ate** *n.* patriarcato.
**Patricia** *pr.n.* Patrizia.
**patrici-an** *adj.*, *n.* patrizio; nobile *m.* **-ate** *n.* patriziato; nobiltà.
**Patrick** *pr.n.* Patrizio.
**patrimon-y** *n.* patrimonio, beni ereditari; (eccl.) patrimonio. **-ial** *adj.* patrimoniale, ereditario.
**patriot** *n.* patriota *m.*, *f.* **-ic** *adj.* patriottico. **-ism** *n.* patriottismo.
**patristic** *adj.* patristico. **-s** *n.* (eccl.) patristica.
**patrol** *n.* pattuglia; ronda; *to go on —*, pattugliare, fare la ronda; (aeron.) volo di ricognizione; *tr.* perlustrare; controllare; *intr.* fare la ronda, andare di pattuglia, pattugliare.
**patron** *n.* protettore; patrono; mecenate *m.*; *— saint*, santo patrono; (eccl.) *— of a benefice*, collatore; cliente abituale, avventore; *the -s of the drama*, il pubblico del teatro. **-age** *n.* protezione, patronato; patrocinio; (eccl.) giuspatronato; (of shop, *etc.*) clientela; *under the -age of*, sotto gli auspici di. **-al** *adj.* patronale. **-ess** *n.* patronessa, patrona; protettrice.
**patroniz-e** *tr.* patrocinare; proteggere; favorire; frequentare; (pejor.) trattare con degnazione, darsi delle arie di protezione nei confronti di. **-er** *n.* protettore; patrocinatore. **-ing** *adj.* protettivo, protettore; (pejor.) condiscendente, con aria di protezione.
**patronymic** *adj.*, *n.* patronimico.
**patten** *n.* soprascarpa di legno, zoccolo; (archit.) zoccolo.
**patter**[1] *n.* gergo; recitativo; cicalio; (of showman, *etc.*) bonimento; *intr.* cicalare, recitare meccanicamente.
**patter**[2] *n.* ticchettìo, picchiettìo; *intr.* picchiettare; camminare a piccoli passi, sgambettare.
**pattern** *n.* modello; tipo; campione *m.*; esempio; disegno; (fig.) ideale *m.*; modello; *tr.* modellare; eseguire sulla base di un modello; *to — on something*, modellare su; *-ed stuffs*, stoffe decorate con disegni. **-book** *n.* campionario.
**patty** *n.* (cul.) pasticcino.
**paucity** *n.* pochezza, scarsità; insufficienza.
**Paul** *pr.n.* Paolo; *— Pry*, ficcanaso.
**Paula** *pr.n.* Paola.
**Pauline**[1] *pr.n.* Paolina.
**Pauline**[2] *adj.* di San Paolo, paolino.
**paunch** *n.* pancia, ventre *m.*; (anat.) rumine *m.*; *tr.* sviscerare. **-ed, -y** *adj.* panciuto.
**pauper** *n.* povero, indigente *m.*, *f.*, mendicante *m.*, *f.*; (pop.) morto di fame. **-ism** *n.* povertà, indigenza: i poveri.
**pauperiz-e** *tr.* impoverire, ridurre alla povertà. **-ation** *n.* impoverimento.
**pause** *n.* pausa; intervallo; sosta; (mus.) pausa; (prosod.) cesura; *intr.* fare una pausa; esitare.
**pavan(e)** *n.* (dance) pavana.
**pave** *tr.* lastricare, pavimentare; (fig.) *to — the way*, preparare il terreno, aprire la via.
**pavement** *n.* lastrico, selciato, pavimentazione, pavimento; (of brick) ammattonato; (sidewalk) marciapiede *m.*; (outside a café) terrazza. **-glass, -light** *n.* lucernario.
**pavilion** *n.* padiglione *m.*; tenda.
**paving** *n.* pavimentazione; pavimento, selciato, lastricato. **-stone** *n.* pietra da selciato, lastra. **-tile** *n.* mattonella.
**paviour, paver** *n.* lastricatore, selciatore.
**paw** *n.* zampa; *tr.* toccare con la zampa; (of horse) scalpitare, raspare; (fam.) maneggiare goffamente. **-ing** *n.* (of horses) scalpitìo.
**pawk-y** *adj.* (Scot.) scaltro; furbo; astuto. **-iness** *n.* (Scot.) furberia; malizia.
**pawn** *n.* pegno; garanzia; *in —*, in pegno; *to take out of —*, riscattare; (chess) pedina; *tr.* impegnare, dare in pegno, pignorare. **-broker** *n.* prestatore su pegno, commissionario del Monte di Pietà. **-shop** *n.* agenzia di prestiti su pegno, (in Italy) Monte di Pietà.
**pawn-ticket** *n.* ricevuta di pegno.
**pay** *n.* paga; salario; stipendio; rimunerazione; retribuzione; compenso, ricompensa; *full —*, paga intera; *half —*, mezza paga; *back —*, arretrati di paga; *holidays with —*, ferie retribuite; *to draw one's —*, toccare la paga; *to be in the — of*, essere al servizio di, (pejor.) essere al soldo di; (min.) prodotto.
**pay** *tr.* pagare, versare, saldare; *to — someone for something*, pagare qualcosa a qualcuno; *to — someone to do something*, pagare qualcuno per fare qualcosa; *to — in advance*, pagare in anticipo; *to — in arrear*, pagare posticipatamente; *to — cash down*, pagare in contanti; *to — by instalments*, pagare a rate; *to — a sum into someone's account*, versare una somma sul conto di qualcuno; *to — a bill*, saldare un conto; *to — one's way*, tirare avanti, sbarcare il lunario; *to — through the nose*, pagare profumatamente; *P.A.Y.E.*, trattenuta di ricchezza mobile sugli stipendi; rimunerare, ricompensare, retribuire; (fig.) *to — attention to*, fare attenzione a; *to — court to*, far la corte a; *to — homage to* rendere omaggio a; *to — the piper*, far le spese; *to — respect to*, stimare, rispettare; *to — one's respects to* presentare gli ossequi a; *to — a tribute to*, riconoscere il merito di, rendere omaggio a; *to — a visit*, fare una visita; *tr.*, *intr.* rendere, fruttare; *it -s to advertise*, la pubblicità rende; *crime doesn't pay*, il delitto non rende; *it wouldn't — me to go*, non mi varrebbe la pena di andare. FOLLOW. BY ADV. OR PREP.: *to — away*, sborsare, spendere, (naut.) allascare; *to — back*, rimborsare, restituire; (fig.) *to — someone back*, vendicarsi di qualcuno; *to — someone back in his own coin*, rendere pan per focaccia; *to — a sum down*, versare un acconto; *to — for*, pagare, espiare, pagare caro; *I'll make him — for it!*, glielo farò pagare!; *to — in*, versare; *to — off a debt*, estinguere un debito; *to — off an employee*, liquidare un impiegato; *to — out*, sborsare, (naut.) allascare; *to — someone out*, vendicarsi di qualcuno; *to — over*, versare; *to — up*, pagare.
**payable** *adj.* pagabile; *— to bearer*, pagabile al portatore; (min.) redditizio.
**paybook** *n.* (industr.) libretto di lavoro; (mil.; naval) libretto personale.
**pay-box** *n.* cassa; (theatr.) botteghino. **-day** *n.* giorno di paga. **-desk** *n.* cassa.
**payee** *n.* beneficiario, creditore.
**pay-envelope** *n.* busta paga.
**payer** *n.* pagatore; (fam.) *he is a good —*, paga bene.
**paying** *adj.* fruittifero, lucrativo, produttivo; che paga; *— guest*, pensionante *m.*, *f.*, dozzinante *m.*, *f.*; *n.* pagamento, versamento; *paying-in slip*, cedola, distinta di versamento.
**pay-load** *n.* (aeron.; comm.) carico pagante. **-master** *n.* (naval) ufficiale pagatore.
**payment** *n.* pagamento; versamento; ricompensa; *cash —*, pagamento in contanti; *part —*, acconto; *on — of ten pounds*, dietro pagamento di dieci sterline; *work against —*, lavoro pagato; *without —*, gratis; *— on account*, acconto; *— in full*, pagamento a saldo.
**paynim** *n.* (hist.) pagano, saraceno.
**pay-office** *n.* cassa, ufficio paga. **-packet** *n.* pacchetto della paga.
**pay-roll, -sheet,** *n.* libro paga.
**P.B.I.** *n.* (mil. slang) la Buffa.
**pea** *n.* pisello; *green -s*, piselli freschi; *sweet —*, pisello odoroso; *chick —*, cece *m.*; (fam.) *to be as like as two -s*, rassomigliarsi come due gocce d'acqua.
**peace** *n.* pace *f.*; tranquillità; calma, quiete *f.*; *to make —*,

fare la pace; — *treaty*, trattato di pace; *at* —, in pace; — *of mind*, tranquillità di animo; *to keep the — between two persons*, far vivere in pace due persone; *to make one's — with*, riconciliarsi con; *to hold one's* —, star zitto; (leg.) ordine pubblico; *breach of the* —, violazione dell'ordine pubblico, disturbo della pubblica quiete; *bound over to keep the* —, rilasciato dietro ammonimento di non disturbare la pubblica quiete; *justice of the* —, (in England) magistrato, (Ital., equiv.) pretore *m.*

**peace-loving** *adj.* pacifico, che ama la tranquillità. **-offering** *n.* dono propiziatorio.

**peaceable** *adj.* pacifico, tranquillo. **-ness** *n.* disposizione alla pace; pacatezza; tranquillità.

**peaceful** *adj.* pacifico; quieto; tranquillo. **-ness** *n.* tranquillità; quiete *f.*; pace *f.*

**peacemaker** *n.* pacificatore; paciere *m.*; *to act as* —, fare il paciere.

**peach**[1] *n.* pesca; (tree) pesco; (pop.) *she's a regular* —, che bella figliuola!

**peach**[2] *intr.* (lit.) denunciare i propri complici, cantare.

**peacock** *n.* (orn.) pavone; (fig.) persona vanitosa; *to strut like a* —, pavoneggiarsi. **-blue** *adj.*, *n.* blu pavone.

**pea-green** *n.*, *adj.* verde pisello.

**peahen** *n.* (orn.) femmina del pavone.

**pea-jacket** *n.* giaccotto da marinaio.

**peak** *n.* cima; picco; vetta; (fig.) massimo, punta; *at its* —, al massimo; — *hours*, ore di punta; (mech.) — *load*, carico massimo; (of cap) visiera; (naut.) penna, gavone *m.* **-ed** *adj.* appuntito, a punta; affilato; (of cap) con visiera.

**peal** *n.* scampanìo; suono di campane; suono d'organo; (artill.) salva; (fam., of laughter, applause) scoppio, scroscio; *intr.* (of bells) suonare, risuonare, scampanare; suonare a distesa; (of thunder) rimbombare, tuonare; *tr.* far risuonare.

**peanut** *n.* arachide *f.*, babbagigi *m.pl.*

**pea-pod, -shell,** *n.* baccello.

**pear** *n.* pera; (tree) pero; *prickly* —, fico d'India. **-shaped** *adj.* a forma di pera.

**pearl** *n.* perla; *a string of -s*, un filo di perle; *cultured -s*, perle coltivate; *to cast -s before swine*, gettare le perle ai porci; — *button*, bottone di madreperla; (lacem.) picot *m.*; *intr.* imperlarsi, ridursi in forma di perle; pescare perle; *tr.* imperlare, ornare di perle; (barley, *etc.*) perlare.

**pearl-ash** *n.* (chem.) carbonato di potassio. **-barley** *n.* orzo perlato. **-diver** *n.* pescatore di perle. **-fishery** *n.* pesca di perle. **-grey** *adj.*, *n.* grigio perla. **-shell** *n.* madreperla greggia.

**pearly** *adj.* perlato, di perla; perlaceo, simile a perla.

**peasant** *n.* contadino, campagnuolo, colono. **-ry** *n.* contadini *m.pl.*, gente di campagna, contadiname *m.*

**pease-pudding** *n.* (cul.) passato di piselli secchi.

**pea-shooter** *n.* cerbottana. **-soup** *n.* (cul.) passato di piselli, consommé di piselli. **-souper** *n.* (fam.) nebbione giallastro.

**peat** *n.* torba. **-y** *adj.* torboso. **-bog** *n.* torbiera.

**pebbl-e** *n.* ciottolo; sassolino, sasso; — *paving*, acciottolato; (fam.) *she's not the only — on the beach*, ce ne sono tante ragazze a questo mondo. **-estone** *n.* ciottolo. **-ing** *n.* (bldg.) lapidazione; (leatherm.) zigrinatura. **-y** *adj.* ciottoloso; (of leather) zigrinato.

**peccadillo** *n.* peccatuccio.

**pecc-ancy** *n.* colpevolezza, peccato. **-ant** *adj.* peccaminoso, difettoso; malsalubre.

**peccary** *n.* (zool.) pecari *m.*

**peck**[1] *n.* beccata; (joc.) baciucchio; *tr.* beccare; *to — a hole*, fare un buco; *to — at*, beccucchiare, (fig.) dare un bacetto a; *to — at one's food*, mangiucchiare, dar di becco; *to — out*, beccare (in modo di formare un buco), levare beccando.

**peck**[2] *n.* (meas. = 9.092 litri) peck *m.*; (fig.) *a — of troubles*, un sacco di guai.

**pecker** *n.* (orn.) picchio; (tool) piccone *m.*; (slang) naso, becco.

**peckish** *adj.* (fam.) famelico, affamato; *to feel* —, avere appetito.

**Pecksniff** *pr.n.* bacchettone *m.* Tartufo, ipocrita *m.*

**pectoral** *adj.*, *n.* pettorale *m.*

**peculat-e** *tr.* appropriarsi (di denaro); *intr.* fare del peculato. **-ion** *n.* (leg.) peculato, malversazione.

**peculiar** *adj.* peculiare, particolare, speciale; singolare, strano, bizzarro; *how —!*, che strano!; personale, individuale. **-ity** *n.* particolarità; singolarità, caratteristica, idiosincrasia; stranezza.

**pecuniary** *adj.* pecuniario.

**pedagogue** *n.* pedagogo; (pejor.) pedante *m.*, *f.*

**pedagog-y** *n.* pedagogia. **-ic(al)** *adj.* pedagogico. **-ics** *n.*, *pl.* pedagogia.

**pedal** *adj.* pedale, del piede; *n.* (mech.) pedale *m.*; (mus.) *loud* —, pedale del forte; *soft* —, smorzo; pedalare; (mus.) pedaleggiare.

**pedant** *n.* pedante *m.*, *f.*, pedagogo. **-ic** *adj.* (of person) pedante; (of thing) pedantesco. **-ry** *n.* pedanteria.

**peddle** *intr.* fare il venditore ambulante; (fam.) vendere.

**pederasty** *n.* See **paederasty**.

**pedestal** *n.* (archit.; sculpt.) piedistallo, basamento, piede *m.*, piedritto, zoccolo; (fam.) *to put someone on a* —, mettere qualcuno su un piedistallo.

**pedestrian** *adj.* pedestre, a piedi, pedonale; (fig.) prosaico, pedestre; *n.* pedone *m.*; — *crossing*, passaggio pedonale; (sport) podista *m.* **-ism** *n.* (sport) podismo; (fig.) stile prosaico.

**pediatr-ic** *adj.* (med.) pediatrico. **-ician, -ist** *n.* (med.) pediatra *m.*, *f.* **-ics** *n.* (med.) pediatria.

**pedicure** *n.* pedicure *m.*, *f.*, callista *m.*, *f.*; cura dei piedi.

**pedigree** *n.* genealogia, albero genealogico; (of dog) pedigree *m.*; — *dog*, cane di razza; (fig.) stirpe *f.*, origine *f.*

**pediment** *n.* (archit.) frontone *m.*; timpano.

**pedlar** *n.* venditore ambulante; (fig.) — *of gossip*, chiacchierone *m.*

**pedometer** *n.* pedometro, passimetro.

**peduncle** *n.* (bot.; zool.) peduncolo.

**pee** *intr.* (fam.) far pipì; *n.* pipì, *m. indecl.*, piscia.

**peek** *intr.* See **peep.**

**peel** *n.* buccia, scorza, corteccia; *candied* —, frutta candita; *tr.* sbucciare, scortecciare, mondare; (fig.) *to keep one's eyes -ed*, tenere gli occhi ben aperti; *to — off the bark from*, scortecciare; (fam.) *to — off one's clothes*, spogliarsi; *intr. to — off*, spellarsi, squamarsi, scorticarsi; (of paint, skin) staccarsi.

**peeler**[1] *n.* scorticatore, sbucciatore.

**peeler**[2] (slang) poliziotto, rame *m.*

**peeling** *n.* sbucciatura, sbucciamento; *potato -s*, bucce di patate.

**peep**[1] *n.* (of birds) pigolìo; *intr.* pigolare.

**peep**[2] sguardo furtivo; occhiata; sbirciata; *to take a — at*, guardare rapidamente, dare un'occhiatina a; *at — of day*, allo spuntare del giorno; *intr.* gettare un'occhiata furtiva, spiare, far capolino; *to — through the keyhole*, guardare dal buco della serratura; *to — at*, gettare una occhiata furtiva a; *to — out*, mostrarsi appena, lasciarsi intravvedere; (of stars) affacciarsi appena; (of sunflower) spuntare.

**peep-hole** *n.* spiraglio.

**peeping** *adj.* curioso; — *Tom*, curiosone *m.*

**peep-show** *n.* stereoscopio; (Punch & Judy) teatrino di burattini.

**peer**[1] *n.* (of the realm) pari *m.*; (fig.) uguale, simile; *you will not find his* —, non troverete

il suo pari; *tr.* uguagliare, pareggiare.

**peer**[2] *intr.* guardare; *to — at*, guardare da presso, scrutare; spuntare, far capolino.

**peerage** *n.* dignità di pari, i pari *n.pl.*, nobiltà, aristocrazia; *to confer a — on*, nobilitare; almanacco nobiliare.

**peeress** *n.* moglie di un pari, nobildonna; (in own right) paressa.

**peering** *adj.* curioso, scrutatore, penetrante.

**peerless** *adj.* senza pari, impareggiabile. **-ness** *n.* incomparabilità.

**peev-e** *tr.* (fam.) irritare, stizzire; *to be -d*, irritarsi. **-ish** *adj.* querulo, permaloso, irritabile; bisbetico, stizzoso. **-ishness** *n.* permalosità, irritabilità, stizza.

**peewit** *n.* (orn.) pavoncella.

**peg** *n.* caviglia, cavicchio, piuolo; (for hats, etc.) attaccapanni *m.*; zaffo, zipolo; (in violin) bischero; (of whisky, *etc.*) bicchierino; (fig.) *off the —*, bello e fatto; *a square — in a round hole*, un pesce fuor d'acqua; *to take someone down a —*, far abbassare la cresta a qualcuno; *tr.* incavigliare, mettere un piuolo a; (comm.) fissare, stabilire (prezzi). FOLLOW. BY ADV. OR PREP.: *to — away*, lavorare sodo, perseverare; *to — down*, fissare (con caviglie), incavicchiare; *to — someone down to*, obbligare qualcuno a; *to — out*, *tr.* segnare il limite di, *intr.* (slang) cessare, crepare.

**Pegasus** *pr.n.* (myth.; astron.) Pegaso.

**peg-top** *n.* (toy) trottola; (cost.) *— trousers*, calzoni a sbuffo.

**peignoir** *n.* (cost.) accappatoio, mantellina.

**pejorative** *adj.*, *n.* peggiorativo.

**Pekin-g** *pr.n.* (geog.) Pechino. **-(g)ese** *adj.*, *n.* (of Peking) pechinese *m.*, *f.*; cane pechinese.

**pelag-ic, -ian** *adj.* pelagico, oceanico.

**pelerine** *n.* (cost.) pellegrina, mantellina.

**pelf** *n.* (pejor.) denaro, lucro.

**pellet** *n.* pallottola (di carta, di mollica di pane); pallina; pillola; (for firearms) pallottola.

**pellic-le, -ule** *n.* pellicola; membrana.

**pell-mell** *adv.* alla rinfusa, in confusione.

**pellucid** *adj.* pellucido, trasparente; (fig.) limpidissimo, chiaro. **-ity, -ness** *n.* trasparenza, limpidezza.

**pelmet** *n.* (furn.) mantovana.

**pelt**[1] *n.* pelle greggia, pelle col pelo.

**pelt**[2] *n.* (of rain) colpo, rovescio di pioggia; *adv. phr.* (*at*) *full —*, a gambe levate, a piena velocità, a spron battuto; *tr.* assalire a colpi, colpire con proiettili; *to — someone with stones*, lanciare sassi contro qualcuno, lapidare qualcuno; *intr.* (of rain) battere con violenza; *the rain is -ing down*, piove dirottamente; affrettarsi; *he was off as fast as he could —*, scappò a gambe levate. **-er** *n.* chi colpisce con proiettili, lanciatore di sassi; (pop.) *a regular -er*, una pioggia dirotta.

**pelv-is** *n.* pelvi *f.*, bacino. **-ic** *adj.* pelvico.

**pemmican** *n.* pemmican *m.*, carne secca.

**pen**[1] *n.* recinto; pollaio; porcile *m.*; ovile, pecorile *m.*; adiaccio; (slang, prison) carcere *m.*; *tr.* rinchiudere, chiudere; *to — in*, rinchiudere; (fam.) *to feel -ned up*, sentirsi rinchiuso come una bestia.

**pen**[2] *n.* penna; *ball-point —*, penna a sfera, biro *f.*; *fountain-pen*, penna stilografica; *quill —*, penna d'oca; *a stroke of the —*, un tratto di penna; *to put — to paper*, scrivere, mettere il nero sul bianco; *tr.* scrivere.

**pen**[3] *n.* (orn.) femmina del cigno.

**penal** *adj.* penale; *— code*, codice penale; *— servitude*, lavori forzati.

**penaliz-e** *tr.* (leg.; sport) penalizzare. **-ation** *n.* penalizzazione.

**penalty** *n.* pena, penalità; punizione; *death —*, pena di morte; (fig.) *to pay the —*, pagare il fio; (football) calcio di rigore, *— area*, area di rigore.

**penance** *n.* penitenza; *to do —*, far penitenza; *tr.* dare una penitenza a.

**pen-and-ink** *attrib. adj.* *— drawing*, schizzo a penna, disegno a penna.

**Penates** *pr.n.pl.* Penati *m.pl.*

**pence** *n.pl.* of **penny**, *q.v.*; (eccl.) *Peter's —*, obolo di San Pietro.

**penchant** *n.* inclinazione; simpatia.

**pencil** *n.* lapis *m.*, matita; (art) *lead —*, piombino; *indelible —*, matita copiativa; *propelling —*, matita automatica; *to draw in —*, disegnare a matita; (optics) pennello; (geom.) raggiera; *tr.* scrivere a matita, disegnare a matita; abbozzare, tratteggiare; *to — one's eyebrows*, dipingere le sopracciglia.

**pencil-case** *n.* portalapis, portamatite *m.*

**pencilled** *adj.* scritto a matita, segnato a matita; *— eyebrows*, sopracciglia segnate a matita.

**pencil-mark** *n.* tratto a matita, segno a matita. **-point** *n.* punta di matita. **-sharpener** *n.* temperamatite *m. indecl.*

**pendant** *n.* pendente *m.*, pendaglio, ciondolo.

**pending** *adj.* pendente, non deciso, non risolto, in sospeso; *prep.* in attesa di, fino a, durante; *— further news*, in attesa di altre notizie.

**pendular** *adj.* pendolare.

**pendulous** *adj.* pendulo, pendente, sospeso; oscillante; (fig.) vacillante, incerto.

**pendulum** *n.* pendolo; *the swing of the —*, il moto del pendolo. **-clock** *n.* pendola; orologio a pendolo.

**Penelope** *pr.n.* Penelope; *-'s web*, la tela di Penelope.

**penetrab-le** *adj.* penetrabile. **-ility** *n.* penetrabilità.

**penetrat-e** *tr.* penetrare, entrare in; (fig.) capire, risolvere; *intr. to — into*, penetrare, addentrarsi in, diffondersi. **-ing** *adj.* penetrante, acuto. **-ion** *n.* penetrazione; acume *m.*; discernimento. **-ive** *adj.* penetrativo, penetrante.

**pen-friend** *n.* corrispondente *m.*, *f.*, pen-friend *m.*, *f.*

**penguin** *n.* (orn.) pinguino.

**penicillin** *n.* (pharm.) penicillina.

**peninsul-a** *n.* (geog.) penisola. **-ar** *adj.* peninsulare; (hist.) *the -ar War*, la guerra di Spagna (1808).

**penis** *n.* (anat.) pene *m.*

**penit-ence** *n.* penitenza, pentimento. **-ent** *adj.*, *n.* penitente *m.*, *f.* **-ential** *adj.* penitenziale. **-entiary** *adj.* penitenziale; *n.* penitenziario, bagno; (eccl.) penitenziere *m.*, penitenziaria. **-ently** *adv.* da penitente.

**pen-knife** *n.* temperino. **-man** *n.* calligrafo, scrivano, scrittore. **-manship** *n.* calligrafia, l'arte dello scrivere.

**pen-name** *n.* pseudonimo.

**pennant** *n.* (naut.) fiamma; pennello; bandiera da segnalazione.

**penniless** *adj.* senza quattrini, senza un soldo; (pop.) al verde, squattrinato.

**Pennines** *pr.n.* (geog.) Pennini *m.pl.*

**pennon** *n.* bandiera triangolare, stendardo, (ori)fiamma; (on lance) drappo; (naut.) guidone *m.*

**Pennsylvania** *pr.n.* (geog.) Pennsilvania.

**penny** penny *m.*; *old —*, la dodicesima parte di uno scellino; (fig.) due soldi; palanca; *a pretty —*, una bella sommetta; *a — for your thoughts*, pagherei per sapere a che cosa pensi; *to turn an honest —*, guadagnarsi onestamente da vivere; *they haven't a — to their name*, non hanno neanche un soldo; *— wise and pound foolish*, taccagno nelle piccole e prodigo nelle grandi spese; *to be not a — the worse*, stare meglio di prima; (euphem.) *to spend a —*, andare al gabinetto; (provb.) *in for a — in for a pound*, chi è in ballo deve ballare; *take care of the pence and the pounds will take care of them-*

*selves*, badare al centesimo, e il resto verrà da sè.
**penny-a-liner** *n.* (fam.) giornalista da strapazzo. **-dreadful** *n.* giallo da pochi soldi. **-farthing** *n.* (hist.) biciclo, biruota.
**penny-royal** *n.* (bot.) puleggio, menta romana. **-wort** *n.* (bot.) soldinella acquatica.
**pennyworth** *n.* (fig.) quanto si può comprare con due soldi; quantità insignificante, inezia; *a good* —, un buon affare.
**penology** *n.* criminologia.
**pen-pusher** *n.* (fam.) scrivano, piccolo impiegato. **-rack, -rest** *n.* portapenne *m.*
**pension** *n.* pensione; vitalizio; *old-age* —, *retirement* —, pensione di vecchiaia; *to retire on a* —, andare in pensione; (boarding-house) pensione; *tr.* pensionare, assegnare una pensione a; *to* — *off*, mettere in pensione, collocare a riposo. **-able** *adj.* avente diritto a pensione; *-able age*, età di collocamento a riposo. **-er** *n.* pensionato *m.*; pensionata *f.*
**pensive** *adj.* pensoso, pensieroso; cogitabondo; preoccupato. **-ness** *n.* pensosità.
**pent** *adj.* rinchiuso; *pent-up feelings*, sentimenti repressi.
**pentachord** *n.* (mus.) pentacordo.
**pentagon** *n.* pentagono. **-al** *adj.* pentagonale.
**pentameter** *n.* (prosod.) pentametro.
**pentasyllabic** *adj.* pentasillabo, quinquesillabo.
**Pentateuch** *pr.n.* Pentateuco.
**pentathlon** *n.* pentatlon *m.*
**Pentecost** *pr.n.* Pentecoste *f.* **-al** *adj.* di Pentecoste.
**penthouse** *n.* (bldg.) tettoia (addossata a un muro); appartamento sulla copertura di un edifizio.
**penultimate** *adj.* penultimo.
**penumbra** *n.* penombra.
**penurious** *adj.* gretto, parsimonioso; povero, indigente. **-ness** *n.* parsimonia; povertà, bisogno; penuria, insufficienza.
**penury** *n.* penuria, indigenza; miseria; (fig.) scarsità, penuria; — *of ideas*, scarsità d'idee.
**pen-wiper** *n.* nettapenne *m.*
**peon** *n.* (in Latin America) peone *m.*; (in India) soldato di fanteria, poliziotto indigeno.
**peony** *n.* (bot.) peonia.
**people** *n.* popolo; *the English-speaking -s*, i popoli di lingua inglese; *the Italian* —, il popolo italiano; *government by the* —, governo popolare; (collect.) gente *f.*; *Italian* —, gli italiani; *good* —, buona gente; *young* —, i giovani; *poor* —, i poveri; — *at large*, il pubblico; — *say*, si dice; *many* — *say*, molti dicono; (fam.) *my* —, i miei, la mia famiglia; *who are these* —*?*, chi sono questi?; *those* — *over there*, quelli lì; *he is one of those* — *who . . .*, è una di quelle persone che; *a thousand* —, mille persone; *tr.* popolare.
**pep** *n.* (pop.) vigore *m.*, forza, vivacità, energia; *to put some* — *into someone*, rinvigorire qualcuno; *full of* —, pieno di energia; — *talk*, discorso di incoraggiamento; — *pill*, pillola eccitante; *tr.* (pop.) rinvigorire, animare; *to* — *up a dance*, dare più vivacità ad un ballo.
**pepper** *n.* pepe *m.*; *tr.* impepare, cospargere di pepe, condire con pepe; (fig.) crivellare, mitragliare; *page -ed with blots*, pagina macchiettata d'inchiostro.
**pepper-and-salt** *attrib. adj.* color pepe e sale, grigiastro; (of hair) brizzolato. **-box, -castor** *n.* pepaiola.
**peppercorn** *n.* grano di pepe.
**pepperiness** *n.* gusto pepato; (fig.) irascibilità.
**pepper-mill** *n.* macinapepe *m.*
**peppermint** *n.* (bot.) menta peperita; (sweet) caramella di menta, duro di menta.
**pepper-pot** *n.* pepaiola.
**peppery** *adj.* pepato, acre, pungente; (fig.) irascibile, collerico.
**pepsin** *n.* (chem.) pepsina.
**per** *prep.* per, per mezzo di, per tramite di; — *annum*, all'anno, per ogni anno; — *cent*, per cento; — *head*, per ciascuno, a testa; *as* — *invoice*, come da fattura; *as* — *sample*, secondo campione; — *parcel post*, a mezzo pacco postale.
**per-adventure** *adv.* forse, per avventura, caso mai.
**perambulat-e** *tr.* percorrere (a piedi), girare, visitare; *intr.* passeggiare. **-ion** *n.* giro; passeggiata; ispezione. **-or** carrozzina, carrozzella per bambini.
**perceiv-e** *tr.* scorgere, accorgersi di, vedere, notare, rilevare; (philos.) percepire. **-able** *adj.* percettibile, sensibile.
**percentage** *n.* percentuale *f.*; un tanto per cento.
**percept** *n.* (philos.) oggetto di percezione.
**perceptib-le** *adj.* percettibile, sensibile; — *to the eye*, visibile. **-ility** *n.* percettibilità.
**perception** *n.* percezione; accorgimento; intuizione; (leg.) riscossione.
**perceptive** *adj.* percettivo. **-ness, perceptivity** *n.* percettività.
**perch**[1] *n.* posatoio, pertica, bastoncino, cannuccia; (fam.) *to knock someone off his* —, spodestare qualcuno, umiliare qualcuno; *come off your* —, smetti di darti delle arie; (meas.) pertica (= 5.0292 m.); *intr.* posarsi, appollaiarsi; *to be -ed on*, essere appollaiato su; *tr.* posare in alto.
**perch**[2] *n.* (ichth.) pesce persico.
**perchance** *adv.* (poet.) forse, per caso.
**percipi-ence** *n.* percezione; sensibilità. **-ent** *adj.* percettivo, intelligente; *n.* telepatico.
**percolat-e** *tr.* filtrare, colare; *to* — *the coffee*, filtrare il caffè; *intr.* infiltrarsi, penetrare. **-ion** *n.* filtrazione, infiltrazione. **-or** *n.* filtro, macchinetta per il caffè.
**percussion** *n.* percussione; percossa; (mus.) — *instruments*, strumenti a percussione, batteria. **-cap** *n.* capsula di percussione.
**perdition** *n.* perdizione; rovina; danno; (fam.) — *take him!*, che il diavolo lo prenda!
**peregrinat-e** *intr.* peregrinare. **-ion** *n.* peregrinazione.
**peregrine** *n.* (orn.) falcone pellegrino.
**peremptor-y** *adj.* perentorio, imperioso, autoritario; — *refusal*, rifiuto netto. **-iness** *n.* perentorietà; imperiosità.
**perennial** *adj.* perenne; perpetuo; eterno; *n.* pianta perenne.
**per·fect** *adj.* perfetto; compiuto, completo, intero; assoluto; pretto, vero; *in* — *silence*, fra un silenzio completo; *a* — *stranger*, completamente sconosciuto; — *weather*, tempo ideale; *a* — *gentleman*, un vero gentiluomo; *a* — *nuisance*, una vera seccatura; (theatr.) *to be word-perfect*, sapere a memoria la parte; (gramm.) *adj.*, *n.* perfetto; (mus.) giusto; (bot.) tipico.
**perfect** *tr.* perfezionare, rendere perfetto; *to* — *oneself*, perfezionarsi; terminare, dare l'ultimo tocco a.
**perfectib-le** *adj.* perfettibile. **-ility** *n.* perfettibilità.
**perfection** *n.* perfezione; *to do something to* —, fare qualcosa alla perfezione; — *itself*, la perfezione stessa; perfezionamento; personificazione; (bot.) maturità.
**perfidious** *adj.* perfido; infido; sleale; — *Albion*, la perfida Albione. **-ness, perfidy** *n.* perfidia; slealtà.
**perforat-e** *tr.* perforare; forare, bucare; (med.) perforare; *intr.* penetrare. **-ion** *n.* perforamento, perforazione; foro, buco. **-or** *n.* (person) perforatore; (machine) perforatrice.
**perforce** *adv.* per forza, per necessità, giocoforza.
**perform** *tr.* compiere, adempiere, fare, disimpegnare, eseguire; *to* — *one's duties*, disimpegnare i propri compiti; *to* — *miracles*, far miracoli, compiere prodigi; (surg.) *to* — *an operation* (*on*), eseguire un'operazione, operare; (theatr.) *to* — *a play*, rappresentare, recitare una commedia; *to* — *again*, replicare; *to* — *a part*,

sostenere, interpretare una parte; *-ing animals*, animali ammaestrati; (absol.) *to* —, dar spettacolo; *to — on the piano*, suonare il pianoforte. **-able** *adj.* adempibile, eseguibile, fattibile; (theatr.) rappresentabile.

**performance** *n.* compimento, adempimento; esecuzione; osservanza; azione; prestazione; *a creditable* —, una prestazione notevole; — *of one's duties*, adempimento delle proprie mansioni; (theatr.) rappresentazione, recita; *repeat* —, replica; *afternoon* —, mattinata; *evening* —, serata; *farewell* —, serata d'addio; *no — tonight*, questa sera riposo; interpretazione; (cinem.) spettacolo; *continuous* —, spettacolo continuo.

**performer** *n.* esecutore; (theatr.) attore, artista *m., f.*; (of part) interprete *m., f.*; (mus.) musicista *m., f.*, suonatore, concertista *m., f.*; cantante *m., f.*

**perfum-e** *n.* profumo; odore *m.*, fragranza; *tr.* profumare. **-er, -ier** *n.* profumiere *m.* **-ery** *n.* profumeria.

**perfunctor-y** *adj.* fatto alla buona, sbrigativo; superficiale; meccanico; noncurante, negligente. **-iness** *n.* noncuranza, negligenza; mancanza di zelo.

**perfus-e** *tr.* cospargere, aspergere; inondare. **-ion** *n.* cospargimento; aspersione; (med.) perfusione.

**pergola** *n.* pergola, pergolato.

**perhaps** *adv.* forse; per avventura; magari; può darsi (che); — *so — not*, forse che sì, forse che no.

**peri** *n.* (myth.) fata, peri *f. indecl.*

**pericardium** *n.* (anat.) pericardio.

**Pericles** *pr.n.* Pericle.

**peri-gee** *n.* (astron.) perigeo. **-helion** *n.* (geog.; astron.) perielio.

**peril** *n.* pericolo, rischio; *in — of one's life*, in pericolo di morte; *at your* —, a vostro rischio e pericolo. **-ous** *adj.* pericoloso; rischioso. **-ousness** *n.* pericolosità, pericolo; rischio.

**perimeter** *n.* perimetro.

**period** *n.* periodo; epoca; spazio di tempo; limite *m.*, termine *m.*; — *of availability*, validità; *at stated -s*, a momenti prestabiliti; (astron.; geol.) periodo, ciclo; (gramm.) periodo, frase *f.*; punto fermo; (med.) fase *f.*; stadio; mestruazione; *attrib.* caratteristico di un periodo; — *furniture*, mobili antichi; — *piece*, oggetto antico; anticaglia; (theatr.) dramma storico. **-ic(al)** *adj.* periodico; *n.* giornale *m.*, rivista. **-ically** *adv.* periodicamente; ad intervalli. **-icity** *n.* periodicità.

**peripatetic** *adj., n.* peripatetico. **-ism** *n.* peripateticismo.

**peripher-y** *n.* periferia; perimetro; circonferenza. **-al, -ic** *adj.* periferico.

**periphras-e, -is** *n.* perifrasi *f.*, circonlocuzione. **-tic** *adj.* perifrastico.

**periscope** *n.* periscopio.

**perish** *intr.* perire; morire; deperire, deteriorare, gustarsi; (fig.) *to — with hunger*, sentirsi morire di fame; — *the thought!*, via questo brutto pensiero!; *tr.* far perire, rovinare. **-able** *adj.* deperibile, che si guasta presto; *-able goods*, merci deperibili; *n.pl.* merce deperibile. **-ableness** *n.* deperibilità. **-ed** *adj.* guastato, rovinato; (fam.) *my feet are -ed*, i miei piedi sono intirizziti dal freddo. **-er** *n.* (pop.) tipo noioso. **-ing** *adj.* assiderante, da (far) morire; *n.* deperimento.

**peri-stalsis** *n.* peristalsi *f.* **-style** *n.* (archit.) peristilio. **-tonitis** *n.* (med.) peritonite *f.*

**periwig** *n.* parrucca.

**periwinkle** *n.* (bot.) pervinca.

**perjur-e** *tr.* spergiurare, rendersi spergiuro. **-ed** *adj.* spergiuro. **-er** *n.* spergiuro. **-y** *n.* spergiuro, giuramento falso.

**perk** *tr.* (fam.) *to — up one's ears*, drizzare le orecchie; *intr. to — up*, riprendere coraggio, animarsi. **-iness** *n.* vivacità; disinvoltura.

**perks** *n.pl.* (fam.) abbrev. of **perquisites**, *q.v.*

**perky** *adj.* vispo; impertinente.

**perm** *n.* (fam.) permanente *f.*; *tr. to have one's hair -ed*, farsi fare la permanente.

**perman-ent** *adj.* permanente; stabile; fisso; duraturo, durevole; (rlwy.) — *way*, strada rotabile; (hairdr.) — *wave*, ondulazione permanente, permanente *f.* **-ence, -ency** *n.* permanenza; cosa che rimane; posto fisso.

**permanganate** *n.* (chem.) permanganato.

**permeability** *n.* permeabilità.

**permeat-e** *tr.* permeare; penetrare; *intr.* permeare, percolare; (fig.) diffondersi. **-ion** *n.* permeazione, penetrazione, infiltrazione.

**permissible** *adj.* permissibile; ammissibile; tollerabile.

**permission** *n.* permesso; autorizzazione; *with your* —, con permesso; *to ask for* —, chiedere il permesso; *to give someone — to do something*, autorizzare qualcuno a far qualcosa.

**permissive** *adj.* permissivo; lecito.

**per'mit** *n.* permesso; autorizzazione; licenza; lasciapassare *m.*; *export* —, licenza di esportazione.

**permit** *tr.* permettere; lasciare; autorizzare; tollerare; concedere; *to — someone to do something*, permettere a qualcuno di far qualcosa; *to — something to be done*, permettere che si faccia qualcosa; *intr. to — of*, ammettere; *weather -ting*, se il tempo lo permette.

**permut-e** *tr.* (math.; ling.) permutare. **-ation** *n.* permutazione.

**pernicious** *adj.* pernicioso; nocivo; malefico; venefico; — *anaemia*, anemia perniciosa. **-ness** *n.* perniciosità.

**pernickety** *adj.* (fam.) meticoloso, pignolo.

**perorat-e** *intr.* perorare. **-ion** *n.* perorazione.

**peroxide** *n.* (chem.) perossido; *hydrogen* —, acqua ossigenata; (fam.) — *blonde*, bionda ossigenata.

**perpendicular** *adj.* perpendicolare; (archit.) — *style*, gotico fiammeggiante; *n.* perpendicolare *f.*; *to drop a* —, abbassare una perpendicolare; *to be out of* —, posare in falso. **-ity** *n.* perpendicolarità.

**perpetrat-e** *tr.* perpetrare, commettere; *to — a crime*, commettere un delitto. **-ion** *n.* perpetrazione. **-or** *n.* perpetratore; autore.

**perpetual** *adj.* perpetuo; eterno; continuo, incessante; — *motion*, moto perpetuo.

**perpetuat-e** *tr.* perpetuare, eternare. **-ion** *n.* perpetuazione.

**perpetuity** *n.* perpetuità; *in* —, in perpetuo, per sempre.

**perplex** *tr.* confondere, rendere perplesso; mettere in imbarazzo. **-ed** *adj.* perplesso; imbarazzato; incerto. **-ing** *adj.* imbarazzante; preoccupante; che rende perplesso. **-ingly** *adv.* in modo imbarazzante; in modo da rendere perplessi. **-ity** *n.* perplessità; imbarazzo.

**perquisite** *n.* guadagno occasionale; provento; spigolatura; *pl.* mancie *f.pl.*

**perry** *n.* sidro di pere.

**persecut-e** *tr.* perseguitare, vessare, molestare; (fig.) importunare. **-ion** *n.* persecuzione; *-ion mania*, mania di persecuzione. **-or** *n.* persecutore.

**Persephone** *pr.n.* (myth.) Persefone *f.*

**Perseus** *pr.n.* (myth.) Perseo.

**persever-e** *intr.* perseverare; durare. **-ance** *n.* perseveranza; assiduità; costanza. **-ing** *adj.* perseverante.

**Persia** *pr.n.* (geog.) Persia, Iran *m.* **-n** *adj.* persiano, persico, iraniano; *-n blind*, persiana, gelosia; *-n cat*, gatto d'Angora; *Persian Gulf*, Golfo Persico; *n.* persiano, iraniano; (language) il persiano.

**persiflage** *n.* canzonatura, ironia.

**persimmon** *n.* (bot.) cachi *m.*

**persist** *intr.* persistere;

continuare; ostinarsi, tornare alla carica; *to — in doing something*, ostinarsi a fare qualcosa. **-ence, -ency** *n.* ostinazione; tenacia; accanimento; sopravvivenza. **-ent** *adj.* persistente; continuo; tenace; ostinato; accanito; caparbio.

**person** *n.* persona; individuo; *pl.* gente *f.*; *in —*, personalmente, di persona; *young -s*, i giovani; *to be no respecter of -s*, non rispettare nessuno; *an important —*, un personaggio, una personalità; presenza; (pejor.) *who is that — ?*, chi è quel tizio?; (gramm.) persona; *to address in the second — singular*, dare del tu a. **-able** *adj.* bello, di bella presenza, di bell'aspetto, ben fatto.

**personage** *n.* personaggio; personalità; *a very important —*, una personalità, un pezzo grosso; (theatr.) personaggio.

**personal** *adj.* personale; individuale; *a — matter*, un affare privato; *— liberty*, la libertà della persona; *for — use*, per uso personale; *to make a — application*, presentarsi in persona; *to make a — statement*, fare una comunicazione a titolo personale; (gramm.) *— pronoun*, pronome personale; (journ.) *— column*, avvisi personali; (leg.) *— estate*, beni mobili; (fam.) *don't be so —*, non dire delle impertinenze.

**personalia** *n.* oggetti personali; pettegolezze *f. pl.*

**personality** *n.* personalità; carattere *m.*; presenza; *to be lacking in —*, mancare di personalità; *— cult*, culto della personalità; (fam.) allusione personale; *to indulge in personalities*, fare delle osservazioni sulla vita privata di una persona.

**personaliz-e** *tr.* personificare. **-ation** *n.* personificazione.

**personalty** *n.* (leg.) beni mobili.

**personate** *tr.* impersonare, rappresentare, farsi passare per.

**personif-y** *tr.* personificare. **-ication** *n.* personificazione.

**personnel** *n.* personale *m.*, effettivi *m.pl.*

**perspective** *n.* (art; geom.) prospettiva; scorcio; veduta; (fig.) prospettiva; (fam.) *to see a matter in its true —*, vedere una cosa nelle giuste proporzioni; *attrib.* in prospettiva; *— glass*, cannocchiale *m.*

**perspicac-ious** *adj.* perspicace; chiaroveggente; sagace. **-ity** *n.* perspicacia; chiaroveggenza; sagacità.

**perspicu-ity** *n.* perspicuità; chiarezza. **-ous** *adj.* perspicuo; chiaro; evidente.

**perspir-e** *intr.* sudare, traspirare. **-ation** *n.* sudore *m.*; traspirazione; *to be bathed in -ation*, essere madido di sudore. **-ing** *adj.* sudato, che suda.

**persuad-e** *tr.* persuadere; indurre; convincere; *to — someone into doing...*, persuadere qualcuno a fare...; *to be -ed of*, essere persuaso di; *to be easily -ed*, lasciarsi persuadere facilmente. **-able** *adj.* persuadibile, persuasibile.

**persuasion** *n.* persuasione; convinzione; *the art of —*, l'arte di persuadere; credenza, fede *f.*, confessione; *of the same —*, correligionario, (joc.) della stessa razza.

**persuasive** *adj.* persuasivo. **-ness** *n.* capacità persuasiva, forza di persuasione.

**pert** *adj.* impertinente, insolente, sfacciato.

**pertain** *intr. to — to*, appartenere a, riguardare, riferirsi a, spettare a; *this does not — to my office*, questo non è di mia competenza; *-ing to*, proprio di, che riguarda.

**pertinacious** *adj* pertinace, ostinato, caparbio. **-ness, pertinacity** *n.* pertinacia; ostinazione; caparbietà.

**pertin-ent** *adj.* pertinente; a proposito; opportuno; appropriato. **-ence, -ency** *n.* pertinenza; convenienza.

**pertness** *n.* impertinenza; vivacità.

**perturb** *tr.* perturbare, turbare; sconvolgere; sconcertare; *to be -ed*, turbarsi. **-ation** *n.* perturbazione, turbamento; agitazione, confusione. **-ing** *adj.* allarmante, che turba.

**Peru** *pr.n.* (geog.) Perù *m.*

**perus-e** *tr.* leggere attentamente, esaminare con cura. **-al** *n.* lettura; esame *m.*

**Peruvian** *adj.*, *n.* peruviano; *— bark*, china.

**pervad-e** *tr.* pervadere; permeare; compenetrare; diffondersi in, spargersi per; *to be -ed with*, compenetrarsi di, essere pervaso di. **-ing** *adj.* invadente; dominante; *all-pervading*, che si spande dappertutto, onnipresente.

**pervasion** *n.* penetrazione; diffusione.

**pervasive** *adj.* penetrante, invadente; diffuso. **-ness** *n.* diffusione, invadenza, penetrazione.

**perverse** *adj.* perverso, cattivo, malvagio; ostinato, capriccioso, intrattabile; (leg.) erroneo. **-ness, perversity** *n.* perversità, cattiveria; ostinatezza; capricciosità.

**pervers-ion** *n.* perversione, pervertimento; svisamento. **-ive** *adj.* che tende a pervertire.

**per'vert** *n.* pervertito; (rel.) apostata *m.*; *sexual —*, pervertito.

**pervert** *tr.* pervertire, corrompere; svisare, sviare, snaturare.

**pessim-ism** *n.* pessimismo. **-ist** *n.* pessimista *m., f.* **-istic(al)** *adj.* pessimistico, pessimista.

**pest** *n.* peste *f.*, pestilenza; (fig.) flagello; (joc., of person) seccatore; (insect, animal) insetto nocivo, animale nocivo; *— control*, eliminazione degli insetti nocivi, disinfestazione.

**pester** *tr.* infastidire, importunare, seccare, tormentare, molestare.

**pestiferous** *adj.* pestifero; (fig.) noioso, molesto; pernicioso.

**pestil-ence** *n.* peste *f.*, pestilenza. **-ent** *adj.* pestilente, nocivo, pernicioso; (fig.) noioso, molesto, fastidioso. **-ential** *adj.* pestilenziale, pernicioso, dannoso; (fig.) detestabile.

**pestle** *n.* pestello; *tr.* pestare, polverizzare.

**pet**[1] *n.* animale prediletto; favorito, cocco, beniamino; *to make a — of*, voler molto bene a, addomesticare; *attrib. he's my — aversion*, è persona per la quale provo un'avversione spiccata; *— dog*, cane prediletto; *— name*, vezzeggiativo; *— subject*, argomento prediletto, cavallo di battaglia; *— theory*, fissazione; *tr.* accarezzare, vezzeggiare, coccolare; allevare nella bambagia; *intr.* (fam.) abbandonarsi alle carezze amorose.

**pet**[2] *n.* malumore *m.*; stizza; *to be in a —*, essere arrabbiato, tenere il broncio.

**petal** *n.* (bot.) petalo; *without -s*, apetalo.

**petard** *n.* petardo; *to be hoist with one's own —*, darsi la zappa sui piedi.

**Peter**[1] *pr.n.* Pietro; *-'s pence*, l'obolo di San Pietro; *St. -'s*, (Rome), (la basilica di) San Pietro; *to rob — to pay Paul*, scoprire un altare per coprirne un altro; (naut.) *blue —*, pennello di partenza.

**peter**[2] *intr. to — out*, esaurirsi, finire gradatamente.

**petite** *adj.* (of woman) piccolina, carina.

**petition** *n.* petizione; supplica; istanza; ricorso; *tr.* presentare una supplica a; rivolgere un'istanza a; supplicare. **-er** *n.* supplicante *m.*, *f.*, postulante *m.*, *f.*

**Petrarch** *pr.n.* Petrarca. **-ism** *n.* Petrarchismo. **-ist** *n.* Petrarchista *m.*, *f.*

**petrel** *n.* (orn.) procellaria.

**petrif-y** *tr.* pietrificare; (fig.) impietrire; *intr.* pietrificarsi. **-action, -ication** *n.* pietrificazione; mineralizzazione. **-ied** *adj.* pietrificato; (fig.) impietrito, allibito. **-ying** *adj.* pietrificante; (fam., fig.) spaventevole.

**petrography** *n.* petrografia.

**petrol** *n.* benzina, petrolio raffinato. **-can** *n.* latta per benzina.

**petrol-eum** *n.* petrolio grezzo. **-iferous** *adj.* petrolifero.
**petrol-pump** *n.* distributore (di benzina). **-tank** *n.* serbatoio (di benzina).
**petrous** *adj.* pietroso.
**petticoat** *n.* sottana, sottogonna, sottoveste *f.*; — *government*, matriarcato, governo delle donne.
**pettifogging** *adj.* cavilloso, sofistico; — *lawyer*, azzeccagarbugli *m.*
**pettiness** *n.* piccolezza; meschinità.
**petting** *n.* (fam.) carezze amorose.
**pettish** *adj.* irritabile, permaloso, di cattivo umore. **-ness** *n.* irritabilità; permalosità; cattivo umore.
**petty** *adj.* piccolo, di poca importanza; insignificante, meschino; (comm.) — *cash*, piccola cassa; (leg.) — *sessions*, tribunale di prima istanza. **-mindedness** *n.* See **pettiness.**
**petty-officer** *n.* (naval) sottufficiale *m.*, capo.
**petul-ance** *n.* petulanza; irritabilità; scontrosità. **-ant** *adj.* petulante; scontroso; irritabile; dispettoso.
**petunia** *n.* (bot.) petunia.
**pew** *n.* banco (di chiesa); *family* —, banco di famiglia; (pop.) *take a* —, siediti.
**pewter** *n.* peltro; oggetti di peltro. **-er** *n.* fabbricante di oggetti di peltro.
**Phaedra** *pr.n.* (myth.) Fedra.
**Phaethon** *pr.n.* (myth.) Fetonte *m.*
**phagocyte** *n.* (biol.) fagocita *m.*
**phalanx** *n.* falange *f.*
**phall-us** *n.* fallo. **-ic** *adj.* fallico.
**phantasm** *n.* fantasma *m.*, spettro; (fig.) visione, illusione.
**phantasmagor-ia** *n.* fantasmagoria. **-ic** *adj.* fantasmagorico.
**phantasmal** *adj.* spettrale; di fantasma; fantasmagorico.
**phantasy** *n.* See **fantasy.**
**phantom** *n* .fantasma *m.*, spettro, ombra; *attrib.* fantasma, spettrale; — *ship*, vascello fantasma.
**Pharaoh** *n.* (hist.) Faraone.
**Pharis-ee** *n.* Fariseo. **-aic(al)** *adj.* farisaico. **-aism, -eism** *n.* fariseismo.
**pharmaceutic-(al)** *adj.* farmaceutico. **-s** *n.* farmaceutica.
**pharmaceutist, pharmacist** *n.* farmacista *m.*, *f.*
**pharmacolog-y** *n.* farmacologia. **-ical** *adj.* farmacologico. **-ist** *n.* farmacologo.
**pharmacopoeia** *n.* farmacopea.
**pharmacy** *n.* farmacia; scienza farmaceutica.
**pharyn-x** *n.* (anat.) faringe *f.* **-geal** *adj.* (anat.) faringeo.
**phase** *n.* fase *f.*, stadio, periodo; (electr.) fase.
**pheasant** *n.* (orn.) fagiano.
**phenacetin** *n.* (chem.) fenacetina.
**phenomen-on** *n.* fenomeno. **-al** *adj.* fenomenale; (fam.) straordinario, prodigioso. **-ology** *n.* (philos.) fenomenologia.
**phial** *n.* fiala, ampolla, boccetta, provetta.
**Phidias** *pr.n.* (art hist.) Fidia *m.*
**Philadelphia** *pr.n.* (geog.) Filadelfia.
**philander** *intr.* amoreggiare, fare il cascamorto. **-er** *n.* donnaiuolo, galante *m.*, cascamorto.
**philanthrop-y** *n.* filantropia. **-ic(al)** *adj.* filantropico. **-ism** *n.* filantropismo. **-ist** *n.* filantropo.
**philatel-y** *n.* filatelia. **-ic(al)** *adj.* filatelico. **-ist** *n.* filatelico.
**philharmonic** *adj.* filarmonico.
**philhellen-e** *adj.*, *n.* filelleno. **-ic** *adj.* filellenico. **-ism** *n.* filellenismo.
**Philip** *pr.n.* Filippo.
**Philippa** *pr.n.* Filippa.
**Philippi** *pr.n.* (geog.) Filippi *f.*
**philippic** *n.* filippica, invettiva.
**Philippines** *pr.n.* (geog.) (Isole) Filippine.
**Philistin-e** *n.* (bibl.) filisteo; (fig.) volgare *m.*, *f.*, persona incolta; barbaro di giudizio; *to fall among -es*, capitare tra gente ostile. **-ism** *n.* filisteismo; volgarità.
**philolog-y** *n.* filologia. **-ical** *adj.* filologico. **-ist** *n.* filologo.
**Philomel** *pr.n.* Filomela; (poet.) usignolo.
**philosopher** *n.* filosofo; *natural* —, scienziato; *the -'s stone*, la pietra filosofale.
**philosophic(al)** *adj.* filosofico.
**philosophize** *intr.* filosofare, fare il filosofo.
**philosophy** *n.* filosofia; *moral* —, filosofia morale, etica; *natural* —, fisica.
**philtre** *n.* filtro.
**phiz** *n.* (pop.) fisionomia, muso.
**phleb-itic** *adj.* (med.) flebitico. **-itis** *n.* (med.) flebite *f.* **-otomist** *n.* flebotomo. **-otomy** *n.* flebotomia, salasso.
**Phlegethon** *pr.n.* (myth.) Flegetonte *m.*
**phlegm** *n.* (med.) muco, pituita; (fig.) flemma, calma, apatia, sangue freddo. **-atic** *adj.* flemmatico, apatico, calmo.
**phlox** *n.* (bot.) flogo.
**phobia** *n.* fobia.
**Phoebe** *pr.n.* Febe *f.*; (myth.) Febe, Artemide *f.*; (poet.) la luna.
**Phoebus** *pr.n.* (myth.) Febo, Apollo; (poet.) il sole.
**phoenix** *n.* fenice *f.*
**phone** *n.* (ling.) suono; (fam.) telefono; *to be on the* —, avere il telefono; *he's on the — at the moment*, sta parlando al telefono in questo momento; *tr.* (fam.) chiamare al telefono; *intr.* telefonare.
**phoneme** *n.* (ling.) fonema *m.*
**phonetic(al)** *adj.* fonetico. **-s** *n.* fonetica.
**phoney** *adj.* (fam.) falso, fittizio; strano; (hist., fam.), *the — war* (1939–40), la guerra strampalata.
**phonic** *adj.* fonico.
**phonogram** *n.* fonogramma *m.*
**phonograph** *n.* fonografo. **-ic** *adj.* fonografico, stenografico. **-y** *n.* fonografia, stenografia.
**phonolog-y** *n.* fonologia. **-ic(al)** *adj.* fonologico.
**phosph-ate** *n.* fosfato. **-ide** *n.* (chem.) fosfuro. **-ite** *n.* (chem.) fosfito.
**phosphor** *n.* See **phosphorus.**
**phosphor-esce** *intr.* fosforeggiare. **-escence** *n.* fosforescenza. **-escent, phosphorus** *adj.* fosforoso, fosforescente.
**phosphorus** *n.* fosforo.
**photo** *n.* (fam.) for **photograph,** *q.v.*
**photochemistry** *n.* fotochimica.
**photo-electric(al)** *adj.* fotoelettrico. **-engraving** *n.* fotoincisione.
**photogen(e)tic** *adj.* fotogenico.
**photograph** *n.* fotografia, (fam.) foto *f.*; *to take a — of*, fotografare; *to have one's — taken*, farsi fotografare; *tr.* fotografare; *intr.* fare il fotografo; *I always — badly*, riesco sempre male in fotografia. **-er** *n.* fotografo; *press -er*, fotocronista *m.* **-ic(al)** *adj.* fotografico.
**photography** *n.* fotografia; *colour* —, fotografia a colori; *air* —, aerofotografia.
**photo-gravure** *n.* foto incisione. **-lithograph, -lithography** *n.* fotolitografia. **-meter** *n.* fotometro. **-metric(al)** *adj.* fotometrico. **-metry** *n.* fotometria. **-montage** *n.* fotomontaggio.
**photo-reconnaissance** *n.* (mil.) ricognizione fotografica.
**photo-sphere** *n.* (astron.) fotosfera. **-stat** *n.* riproduzione fotostatica.
**phrase** *n.* locuzione; espressione; modo di dire; frase fatta; *as the — goes*, come si dice, come si suol dire; (mus.) frase, diastole *f.*
**phrase** *tr.* esprimere, formulare; *intr.* (mus.) fraseggiare. **-book** *n.* libro di fraseologia.
**phraseo-gram** *m.* simbolo (stenografico) che rappresenta una espressione. **-logical** *adj.* fraseologico. **-logy** *n.* fraseologia.
**phrenesis** *n.* (med.) frenite, *f.*, frenesia.
**phrenolog-y** *n.* frenologia. **-ical** *adj.* frenologico. **-ist** *n.* frenologo.
**Phrygia** *pr.n.* (geog.) Frigia. **-n** *adj.* frigio.
**Phryne** *pr.n.* Frine.
**phthis-is** *n.* (med.) tisi *f.* **-ic(al)** *adj.* (med.) tisico.
**phut** *n.* sibilo (di vescica che si sgonfia); (pop.) *to go* —, andare in

fumo, andare in pezzi, guastarsi; (of electric bulb) bruciare.

**phylactery** *n.* (rel.) filatterio; amuleto, talismano.

**Phyllis** *pr.n.* Fillide.

**phylloxera** *n.* (ent.) fillossera.

**physic** *n.* medicina; farmaco; (fig.) rimedio; *tr.* somministrare una medicina a, curare.

**physical** *adj.* fisico; naturale; — *drill*, — *training*, ginnastica; — *strength*, forza fisica; sensuale; (fig.) *a* — *impossibility*, un'impossibilità materiale.

**physician** *n.* medico.

**physicism** *n.* (philos.) fisicismo, materialismo, naturalismo.

**physicist** *n.* fisico.

**physico-** *pref.* fisico-.

**physics** *n.* fisica.

**physiognom-y** *n.* fisiognomia, fisionomia; (fig.) aspetto; (fam.) viso; cf. **phiz**.

**physiography** *n.* fisiografia.

**physiolog-y** *n.* fisiologia; (bot.) *plant* —, fitofisiologia. **-ical** *adj.* fisiologico. **-ist** *n.* fisiologo.

**physiotherapy** *n.* fisioterapia.

**physique** *n.* fisico, costituzione fisica; *of poor* —, poco robusto.

**phytozoa** *n.* (zool.) fitozoi *m.pl.*

**pi**[1] *adj.* (fam.) pio, devoto.

**pi**[2] *n.* (geom.) pi greca ($\pi$).

**pianist** *n.* pianista *m., f.*

**piano, pianoforte** *n.* piano, pianoforte *m.*; *grand* —, piano(forte) a coda; *baby-grand* —, piano a mezza coda; *upright* —, piano verticale; *to play* (*on*) *the* —, suonare il pianoforte.

**piano-accordion** *n.* (mus.) fisarmonica. **-action** *n.* meccanismo del piano.

**pianola** *n.* pianola.

**piano-organ** *n.* (mus.) pianino, organino. **-player** *n.* (person) pianista *m., f.*; (instrument) pianola.

**piano(forte)-playing** *n.* pianismo.

**piano-stool** *n.* sgabello per pianoforte. **-tuner** *n.* accordatore. **-wire** *n.* corda, filo armonico.

**piastre, piaster** *n.* piastra.

**piazza** *n.* (in Italy) piazza; (USA) veranda.

**pibroch** *n.* (Scot.) variazioni per cornamusa scozzese.

**pica** *n.* (typ.) corpo dodici; *small* —, corpo undici.

**Picardy** *pr.n.* (geog.) Piccardia.

**picaresque** *adj.* picaresco.

**picaroon** *n.* manigoldo, furfante *m.*, pirata *m.*

**piccalilli** *n.* (cul.) sottaceti drogati.

**piccaninny** *n.* (fam.) piccino; negretto.

**piccolo** *n.* (mus.) ottavino, flautino.

**pick** *n.* piccone *m.*; colpo di piccone; — *and shovel man*, sterratore, terrazziere; *tooth-pick*, stuzzicadenti *m.*; scelta; *the* — *of the basket*, *the* — *of the bunch*, il fior fiore, la parte migliore; *take your* —, scegli quel che vuoi.

**pick** *tr.* scavare, rompere col piccone; cogliere, mondare; scegliere; *to* — *and choose*, fare il difficile; *to* — *acquaintance with someone*, fare la conoscenza di qualcuno; *to* — *a bone*, spolpare un osso; *to have a bone to* — *with someone*, avere qualcosa da rimproverare a qualcuno; *to* — *the brains of*, sfruttare il sapere di; *to* — *flowers*, cogliere dei fiori; *to* — *holes in*, trovare qualcosa da ridire su; *to* — *a lock*, forzare una serratura; *to* — *one's teeth*, stuzzicarsi i denti; *to* — *one's nose*, mettersi le dita nel naso; *to* — *oakum*, fare stoppa; *to* — *to pieces*, fare a pezzi, separare, (fig.) criticare aspramente, stroncare; *to* — *someone's pocket*, borseggiare qualcuno; *to* — *a quarrel*, attaccare briga; *to* — *one's way*, camminare con cautela, aprirsi un varco. FOLLOW. BY ADV. OR PREP.: *to* — *at one's food*, mangiucchiare; *to* — *off*, cogliere, togliere, (shoot) abbattere uno dopo l'altro; *to* — *out*, scegliere, distinguere; *to* — *out a tune*, (on piano) accennare un motivo; *to* — *out in red*, campire in rosso; *to* — *up*, raccogliere; trovare, scovare, (language) imparare rapidamente, (passenger) far salire; (radio) *to* — *up a station*, captare una stazione; *to* — *up a girl*, fare la conoscenza informale di una ragazza; *to* — *up a livelihood*, guadagnarsi da vivere; *rfl. to* — *oneself up*, rialzarsi; *intr.* migliorare.

**pick-a-back** *adv.* sulle spalle, sul dorso; *to ride* — *on*, montare sulle spalle di.

**pickaxe** *n.* piccone *m.*, gravina.

**picker** *n.* raccoglitore, spigolatore; *grape-picker*, vendemmiatore; *picker of quarrels*, attaccabrighe *m.*; (text.) lancianavetta.

**pickerel** *n.* (ichth.) piccolo luccio, luccioperca.

**picket** *n.* palo, piolo, picchetto; (mil.) picchetto; (police) pattuglia; picchetto; *tr.* circondare con pali; legare a un palo; (mil.) mettere di picchetto; *intr.* essere di picchetto; (of strikers) picchettare, organizzare picchetti.

**picket-boat** *n.* (naut.) lancia. **-fence** *n.* palizzata.

**picking** *n.* raccolta, raccolto; (of rice) mondatura; — *and stealing*, latrocinio; avanzi *m.pl.*; guadagni occasionali, spigolature *f.pl.*

**pickle** *n.* salamoia; (fam.) imbroglio, pasticcio; *pl.* sottaceti *m.pl.*; *tr.* salare, mettere sott'aceto, marinare, conservare in salamoia; (fam.) *to be* -*d*, essere ubriaco

**picklock** *n.* (person) scassinatore; grimaldello.

**pick-me-up** *n.* cordiale ristorativo.

**pickpocket** *n.* borsaiuolo.

**pick-up** *n.* il raccogliere; la cosa raccolta; (vehicle) furgoncino; (fam.) — *girl*, conoscenza fortuita, ragazza di facili costumi; (mech.) accelerazione, ripresa; (electr.) fonorivelatore; (radio) amplifono.

**picnic** *n.* picnic *m.*, scampagnatura, colazione sull'erba; (fig.) *life is no* —, la vita non è uno scherzo; *intr.* fare una scampagnatura. **-ker** *n.* gitante *m., f.*

**picot** *n.* (needlew.) — *stitch*, picò *m.*, festoncino.

**Pict** *pr. n.* (hist.) Pitto.

**pictograph** *n.* ideogramma *m.*

**pictorial** *adj.* pittorico, pittoresco; della pittura; illustrato; figurato; *n.* giornale illustrato.

**picture** *n.* dipinto, pittura, quadro; (on canvas) tela, (on wood) tavola; ritratto; (in book) illustrazione; film *m.*; (television) immagine *f.*; *to paint a* —, dipingere un quadro; (fig.) descrizione; *to draw a* — *of*, descrivere; (fam.) *she's a* —, è bellissima; *to be in the* —, essere ben informato; *to be out of the* —, non sapere niente; *to put someone in the* —, rendere qualcuno edotto; *pl.* (*motion*) -*s*, il cinema; *tr.* dipingere, fare un quadro di (also fig.); *to* — *to oneself*, figurarsi, immaginarsi.

**picture-book** *n.* libro illustrato. **-frame** *n.* cornice *f.* **-gallery** *n.* pinacoteca, galleria (di quadri). **-goer** *n.* assiduo frequentatore del cinema. **-palace** *n.* cinematografo, cinema *m.* **-postcard** *n.* cartolina illustrata. **-puzzle** *n.* rebus *m.* **-restorer** *n.* restauratore di quadri.

**picturesque** *adj.* pittoresco. **-ness** *n.* il pittoresco.

**piddl-e** *intr.* (pop.) orinare, far pipì. **-ing** *adj.* (pop.) meschino, insignificante, futile.

**pidgin** *n.* (Chinese corruption of **business**) affare *m.*; gergo anglo-cinese; *adj.* — *English* (or *n.* pidgin), miscuglio dell'inglese con qualunque altra lingua straniera.

**pie**[1] *n.* (orn.) pica, gazza.

**pie**[2] *n.* (cul.) pasticcio, torta; (fig.) *to have a finger in the* —, avere le mani in pasta; *to eat humble* —, andare a Canossa; (typ.) rifuso.

**piebald** *adj.* (of horse) pezzato, pomellato.

**piece** *n.* pezzo; frammento; parte *f.*; (coin) moneta; (text.) pezza; (mus.) pezzo; *a* — *of advice*, un consiglio; *a* — *of bread*, un tozzo di pane; *a* — *of business*, un affare; *a* — *of furniture*, un mobile; *a* — *of impudence*, una bella sfacciataggine; *a* — *of kindness*, un atto

di gentilezza; *a — of land*, un appezzamento di terra; *a — of luck*, un colpo di fortuna; *a — of news*, una notizia; *a — of nonsense*, una sciocchezza; *a — of ordnance*, un pezzo d'artiglieria, una bocca da fuoco; *a — of paper*, un pezzo di carta; *a — of poetry*, un brano di poesia; *a — of water*, uno specchio d'acqua; *a fine — of work*, un bel lavoro; *all of a —*. tutto d'un pezzo; *two pounds a —*, due sterline cadauno; *by the —*, al pezzo, a cottimo; *— by —*, pezzo per pezzo, un pezzo alla volta; *in ~s*, a pezzi, *to break to ~s*, fare a pezzi, rompere; *to fall to ~s*, andare in pezzi; (fig.) *to give someone a — of one's mind*, cantare il vespro a qualcuno; *to go all to ~s*, andare a catafascio; *to take to ~s*, smontare; *to tear to ~s*, fare a brani, ridurre a pezzi; (fig.) demolire, stroncare.

**piece** *tr.* rappezzare, rattoppare, raggiustare, rabberciare; *to — together*, mettere insieme; (fig.) coordinare.

**piece-goods** *n.* tessuti in pezza.

**piecemeal** *adj.* frammentario, fatto pezzo per pezzo; *adv.* a pezzi, pezzo per pezzo, a poco a poco.

**piece-work** *n.* lavoro a cottimo; *to do —*, lavorare a cottimo. **-worker** *n.* lavoratore a cottimo, cottimista *m., f.*

**pied** *adj.* screziato, variegato, variopinto, pezzato, pomellato.

**pie-dish** *n.* terrina.

**Piedmont** *pr.n.* (geog.) Piemonte. **~ese** *adj., n.* piemontese *m., f.*

**pie-eyed** *adj.* (slang) sbronzo.

**pier** *n.* molo, banchina; gettata; imbarcadero, pontile *m.*; (archit.) pilastro; (of bridge) pila, piliere *m.*, pilone *m.*; (of dome) pilone. **~age** *n.* diritto di banchina.

**pierc~e** *tr.* forare, perforare, traforare; attraversare; *to — a hole in*, fare un buco in; (fig.) trafiggere, squarciare, penetrare. **~ing** *adj.* penetrante; (of wind) pungente; (of sound) acuto, lacerante; *n.* perforamento, traforo, punzonatura.

**pier-glass** *n.* specchiera. **-head** *n.* testa di molo; (of bridge-pier) antibecco; (archit.) sprone *m.* di pila.

**Pierides** *pr.n.* Pieridi, Muse *f.pl.*

**pierrot** *n.* pagliaccio; cantambanco.

**pier-table** *n.* (archit.) mensola.

**piet~ism** *n.* pietismo. **~ist** *n.* pietista *m., f.*; (pejor.) bacchettone *m.* **~istic** *adj.* pietista. **~y** *n.* devozione, religiosità; pietà, riverenza.

**piffl~e** *n.* (fam.) inezie *f.pl.*, balle *f.pl.*; *to talk —*, dire delle sciocchezze; *intr.* (fam.) dire delle sciocchezze. **~ing** *adj.* (fam.) futile, assurdo.

**pig** *n.* (zool.) porco, maiale *m.*, suino; *wild —*, cinghiale *m.*; *sucking —*, porcellino da latte; (fig.) persona ghiotta, porco; *to make a — of oneself*, mangiare ingordamente; *to stare like a stuck —*, rimanere di stucco; *to buy a — in a poke*, comprare la gatta nel sacco; *to bring one's ~s to the wrong market*, pigliare un granchio, fare un cattivo affare; *when ~s fly*, quando gli asini voleranno; *to sleep like a —*, dormire come un ghiro; *you're a dirty —*, sei uno sporcaccione; *an obstinate —*, testardo come un mulo; (slang) poliziotto; (metall.) pane *m.*; *intr.* (of sow) figliare; (fam.) *to — it*, vivacchiare, vivere come porci; (metall.) colare in pani.

**pig-breeding** *n.* allevamento di suini.

**pigeon** *n.* piccione *m.*, colombo; *fantail —*, piccione pavonino; *homing —*, *carrier —*, piccione viaggiatore; *pouter —*, piccione gozzato; *wood —*, piccione selvatico; *clay —*, piattello; (fam.) *that's not my —*, non è affar mio, non tocca a me.

**pigeon-breasted, -chested** *adj.* dal petto sporgente. **-fancier** *n.* colombofilo. **-hearted** *adj.* pauroso, timido. **-hole** *n.* casella; *tr.* incasellare, mettere in casella; (fig.) accantonare, archiviare. **-loft** *n.* colombaia, piccionaia. **-toed** *adj.* dal piede varo.

**piggery** *n.* porcile *m.*; porcheria.

**piggish** *adj.* porcino, di porco; sudicio, sporco; goloso. **~ness** *n.* sudiciume *m.*; golosità; testardaggine *f.*

**pig-headed** *adj.* ostinato, caparbio, testardo, cocciuto. **~ness** *n.* ostinatezza, caparbietà, testardaggine *f.*, zucconaggine *f.*

**pig-iron** *n.* ghisa in pani, ghisa grezza.

**piglet, pigling** *n.* porcellino.

**pigment** *n.* colore *m.*, pigmento. **~ary** *adj.* pigmentario.

**pigmy** *n.* pigmeo.

**pigskin** *n.* pelle di porco.

**pigstick~er** *n.* (hunt.) cacciatore di cinghiali; macellaio; (knife) coltellaccio. **~ing** *n.* caccia al cinghiale.

**pig-sty** *n.* porcile *m.* **-swill** *n.* avanzi di cucina per i porci.

**pigtail** *n.* (of Chinese) codino; (of tobacco) treccia.

**pig-trough** *n.* truogolo.

**pike**[1] *n.* (ichth.) luccio.

**pike**[2] *n.* (tool) piccone *m.*, gravina; (weapon) picca. **~man** *n.* (hist.) picchiere *m.* **~staff** *n.* asta di picca; (fig.) *as plain as a ~staff*, chiaro come la luce del sole.

**pilaster** *n.* (archit.) pilastro, colonna piana, lesena.

**Pilate** *pr.n.* Pilato; *Pontius —*, Ponzio Pilato.

**pilchard** *n.* (ichth.) sarda.

**pile**[1] *n.* (bldg; eng.) palo, palafitta; *to drive ~s into*, palafittare; (herald.) pila; *tr.* (civ. eng.) conficcare pali in.

**pile**[2] *n.* (heap) ammasso, mucchio; catasta, accatastamento, monticello; (of wood) catasta; (of arms) fascio; *funeral —*, pira, rogo; (fam.) *to make one's —*, fare fortuna, far soldi; fabbricato, edifizio; (electr.) pila; *atomic —*, pila atomica; *voltaic —*, pila di Volta; *tr. to — (up)*, ammucchiare, ammassare, ammonticchiare, accatastare; *to — arms*, mettere le armi in fascio; (fam.) *to — on the expenses*, far salire le spese; *to — it on*, esagerare; *intr. to — up*, accumularsi, ammucchiarsi; (fam.) *to — into a car*, stiparsi dentro una macchina.

**pile**[3] *n.* (text.) pelo.

**pile**[4] *n.* (med.) nodulo emorroidario; *pl.* emorroidi *f.pl.*

**pile-driver** *n.* battipalo, berta. **-driving** *n.* conficcamento di pali. **-dwelling** *n.* abitazione su palafitte. **-work** *n.* palafitta.

**pilfer** *tr., intr.* rubacchiare. **~age** *n.* furterello. **~er** *n.* ladruncolo.

**pilgrim** *n.* pellegrino; *~'s staff*, bordone *m.* (also herald.); *the Pilgrim Fathers*, i Padri Pellegrini. **~age** *n.* pellegrinaggio; *to go on (a) ~age*, andare in pellegrinaggio.

**pill** *n.* pillola; (fig.) *to swallow a bitter —*, ingoiare una pillola amara; *to gild the —*, indorare la pillola; (fam.) pallottola; (in games) palla; (med.) *the —*, la pillolola.

**pillage** *n.* saccheggio; *tr.* saccheggiare, dare il sacco a. **~r** *n.* saccheggiatore, predone *m.*

**pillar** *n.* (archit.) colonna; pilastro; piliere *m.*; (fig.) sostegno, appoggio; *the Pillars of Hercules*, le colonne d'Ercole; (fam.) *to drive from — to post*, mandare da Erode a Pilato; *tr.* rinforzare con pilastri; (fig.) sostenere.

**pillar-box** *n.* buca delle lettere, cassetta postale.

**pill-box** *n.* scatoletta per pillole; (mil.) casamatta.

**pillion** *n.* (equit.) sella da donna, da amazzone; (on motor-cycle) sellino posteriore; *— rider*, passeggero.

**pillory** *n.* berlina; gogna; *tr.* (hist.) mettere alla berlina; (fig.) denunciare.

**pillow** *n.* guanciale *m.*, cuscino; capezzale *m.*; (fig.) *to take counsel of one's —*, dormirci sopra; (lacem.) tombolo; (mech.) cuscinetto; *tr.* posare, appoggiare, adagiare; *to — one's head on one's*

*arms*, reclinare la testa sulle braccia.
**pillow-case, -slip** *n.* federa.
**pilot** *n.* (naut.; aeron.) pilota *m.*; (fig.) guida, consigliere; *to drop the* —, (naut.) sbarcare il pilota, (fig.) non badare a chi dà buoni consigli; (R.A.F.) *pilot-officer*, tenente dell'aeronautica; *air-line* —, pilota di linea; *tr.* guidare, pilotare.
**pilotage** *n.* pilotaggio.
**pilot-balloon** *n.* pallone di prova. **-boat** *n.* battello pilota. **-burner** *n.* accenditoio. **-fish** (ichth.) pesce pilota. **-lamp** *n.* (electr.) lampada spia.
**pilotless** *adj.* senza pilota; radiocomandato.
**pil(l)ule** *n.* piccola pillola.
**pimento** *n.* (cul.) pimento, pepe di Giamaica.
**pimp** *n.* mezzano, ruffiano.
**pimpernel** *n.* (bot.) mordigallina, anagallide *f.*; (lit.) *the Scarlet Pimpernel*, Primula Rossa.
**pimpl-e** *n.* pustoletta, pustola, vescichetta, foruncolo. **-ed, -y** *adj.* foruncoloso, pustoloso.
**pin** *n.* spillo, spilla; *safety* —, spilla da balia, spilla di sicurezza, spilla inglese; (drawing-pin) puntina; (mech.) cavicchio, perno, piolo; (violin) pallone *m.*; (fam.) *-s and needles*, formicolìo; *to be on -s and needles*, essere sulle spine; *I don't care a* —, non me n'importa un bel niente, me n'infischio; *you might have heard a* — *drop*, non si sentiva volare una mosca; *pl.* (slang) gambe *f.pl.*; *to be quick on one's -s*, essere vispo.
**pin** *tr.* fissare con spilli, puntare, appuntare; *to* — *on*, attaccare con uno spillo, appuntare; *to* — *up*, fissare con uno spillo; (fig.) fissare; *to* — *down*, inchiodare; *to* — *someone down to a bargain*, costringere qualcuno a mantenere una promessa; *to* — *one's faith on*, riporre fiducia in, fidarsi di.
**pinafore** *n.* grembiulino.
**pince-nez** *n.* occhiali a molla, (pop.) stringinaso.
**pincer** *n.* tenaglia, pinza; *a pair of -s*, tenaglie, pinze; (zool.) chela; (mil.) — *movement*, movimento a tenaglia.
**pinch** *n.* pizzicotto; *to give someone a* —, dare un pizzicotto a qualcuno; pizzico; *a* — *of salt*, un pizzico di sale; *a* — *of snuff*, una presa di tabacco da fiuto; (fig.) morso; *the* — *of hunger*, il morso della fame; (fam.) *at a* —, caso mai; *when it comes to the* —, al momento critico.
**pinch** *tr.* pizzicare, dare un pizzicotto a, stringere, serrare; *to* — *one's finger in the door*, schiacciarsi il dito nella porta; *to* — *oneself*, pizzicarsi, (fig.) privarsi del necessario; (slang) rubare, alzare; *to get -ed*, essere colto in flagrante, farsi acchiappare; *intr.* far male, dolere; *where the shoe -es*, il punto doloroso, il punto difficile.
**pinchbeck** *n.* (metall.) similoro, princisbecco; (fig.) fasullo, falso, surrogato.
**pinched** *adv.* schiacciato, serrato; (of face) striminzito.
**pincushion** *n.* portaspilli *m. indecl.*
**Pindar** *pr.n.* Pindaro. **-ic** *adj.* pindarico, di Pindaro.
**pine**[1] *n.* pino; legno di pino; — *forest*, pineta.
**pine**[2] *intr. to* — (*away*), languire, deperire, struggersi, consumarsi; *to* — *for*, desiderare ardentemente, anelare, bramare.
**pineapple** *n.* ananasso, ananas *m.*
**pine-cone** *n.* pigna, pina, pinocchio. **-kernel** *n.* pignolo. **-needle** *n.* ago di pino.
**pin-feather** *n.* penna nascente.
**ping-pong** *n.* tennis da tavola.
**pin-head** *n.* capocchia di spillo.
**pinion** *n.* (orn.) sommolo, penna remigante; (poet.) ala; (mech.) pignone *m.*; *tr.* (orn.) tarpare le ali a; (fig.) legare, immobilizzare.
**pink**[1] *adj.* rosa, roseo; *n.* colore rosa; (bot.) garofano; (fig.) modello, quintessenza; *the* — *of perfection*, la perfezione stessa; *in the* — *of condition*, florido, in ottima forma; (fam.) *strike me* — *!*, accidenti!
**pink**[2] *tr.* trafiggere, bucare; (dressm., etc.) traforare, decorare con trafori.
**pink**[3] *intr.* (motor.) battere in testa, detonare.
**pink-eye** *n.* (med.) congiuntivite *f.*
**pin-money** *n.* denaro per le piccole spese personali; (leg.) spillatico.
**pinnace** *n.* (naut.) scialuppa.
**pinnacle** *n.* (archit.) pinnacolo, guglietta, cuspide *f.*; (fig.) colmo, culmine *m.*, cima, apogeo.
**pinnate** *adj.* (bot.) pennato.
**pin-point** *n.* capocchia di spillo.
**pinpoint** *tr.* fissare con esattezza la posizione di.
**pin-prick** *n.* puntura di spillo; (fig.) seccatura, piccolo fastidio.
**pint** *n.* pinta (= 0.568 l.); (approx. Ital. equiv.) mezzo litro.
**pin-table** *n.* biliardino.
**pintail** *n.* (orn.) anitra di coda lunga.
**pin-up** *adj.* — *girl*, ragazza da copertina.
**pioneer** *n.* pioniere, antesignano; (mil.) pioniere; *to be a* —, essere all'avanguardia; — *work*, lavoro sperimentale; *tr.* aprire la strada a, fare da pioniere a.
**pious** *adj.* pio, devoto, religioso; (fam.) — *humbug*, pinzochero.
**pip**[1] *n.* (bot.) seme di frutta, acino, chicco.
**pip**[2] *n.* (vet.) pipita; (fam.) *to have the* —, essere di cattivo umore, fare il broncio; *to give someone the* —, seccare qualcuno.
**pip**[3] *n.* (cards, dice) puntino, macchia; (mil., badge of rank) stelletta.
**pip**[4] *n.* (teleph.) suono breve; (radio) segnale orario.
**pip**[5] *tr.* (fam.) colpire con una fucilata; (schol.) bocciare.
**pipage** *n.* tubatura, canalizzazione; trasporto per tubatura.
**pipe** *n.* tubo, condotto, conduttura; *rainwater* —, tubo di scarico; (of organ) canna; (mus.) piffero, zufolo, fistola; (bagpipe) zampogna, cornamusa; *oaten* —, avena; (naval) *boatswain's* —, fischietto del nostromo; (for smoking) pipa; *to smoke a* —, fumare la pipa; *to fill one's* —, caricare la pipa; (fam.) *put that in your* — *and smoke it!*, e con ciò sei servito!.
**pipe**[2] *n.* (of wine) barile *m.* da centocinque galloni.
**pipe** *tr.* convogliare per mezzo di tubazioni; fornire di tubi; (mus.) suonare (sul piffero); (cul.) decorare di zucchero filato; (dressm.) ornare con cordoncini; (naval) chiamare col fischietto; (Scot.) *to* — *in the haggis*, far entrare lo haggis al suono della cornamusa; *intr.* suonare (il piffero); (of birds) cinguettare, cantare; (of person) parlare con voce esile; (fam.) *to* — *up*, farsi sentire; (naval) — *!*, alla banda!; (pop.) — *down!*, sta zitto!, basta!
**pipeclay** *n.* terra da pipa; *tr.* imbiancare con terra da pipa.
**pipe-cleaner** *n.* nettapipe *m.* **-dream** *n.* sogno (di fumatore di oppio); illusione.
**pipeful** *n.* pipata.
**pipe-line** *n.* (for oil) oleodotto; (for natural gas) metanodotto.
**pipe-major** *n.* (mil.) sottufficiale capobanda.
**piper** *n.* suonatore (di piffero), pifferaio; (fam.) *to pay the* —, saldare il conto, sostenere le spese; (provb.) *he who pays the* — *calls the tune*, chi paga comanda.
**pipe-rack** *n.* rastrelliera per pipe; (of organ) crivello. **-smoker** *n.* fumatore di pipa; *to be a -smoker*, fumare la pipa. **-stem** *n.* cannuccia di pipa.
**pipette** *n.* (chem.) pipetta.
**piping** *adj.* flebile, acuto, penetrante; — *hot*, caldo bollente; (fig.) *the* — *times of peace*, i bei tempi della pace; *n.* tubazione; (of birds) cinguettìo, canto; (mus.) il suonare (piffero); fischio; (cul.) decorazione di zucchero filato; (dressm.) cordoncino (per abiti).
**pipit** *n.* (orn.) pispola, calandro.
**pippin** *n.* (bot.) mela ranetta.
**pip-squeak** *n.* (pop.) tizio.

**piqu-ancy** *n.* gusto piccante; (fam.) il bello, il più bello. **-ant** *adj.* piccante, pungente, frizzante; arguto, mordace.
**pique** *n.* picca; ripicco; puntiglio; risentimento; animosità; *out of* —, per ripicco; *tr.* offendere; irritare, ferire l'orgoglio di; *to feel -d*, piccarsi, risentirsi; eccitare, stimolare, svegliare; *to — oneself on*, piccarsi di, vantarsi di.
**piqué** *n.* (text.) picchè *m.*
**piquet** *n.* (cards) picchetto.
**piracy** *n.* pirateria; (fig.) plagio.
**Piraeus** *pr.n.* (geog.) Pireo.
**pirat-e** *n.* pirata *m.*, corsaro; (fig.) plagiario. **-ed** *adj.* plagiato; *-ed edition*, edizione stampata senza il permesso dell'autore, edizione spuria. **-ical** *adj.* piratico, piratesco, da pirata.
**pirogue** *n.* piroga.
**pirouette** *n.* piroetta; *intr.* fare una piroetta, piroettare.
**Pisan** *adj.*, *n.* pisano; di Pisa.
**piscatorial, piscatory** *adj.* piscatorio, pescatorio.
**Pisces** *pr.n.* (astron.) Pesci *m.pl.*
**piscine** *adj.* di pesce.
**piscivorous** *adj.* ittiofago.
**piss** *n.* (slang) piscia; *intr.* pisciare. **-ed** *adj.* (pop.) sborniato.
**pistachio** *n.* (bot.) pistacchio.
**pistil** *n.* (bot.) pistillo.
**pistol** *n.* pistola.
**piston** *n.* pistone *m.*, stantuffo. **-rod** *n.* biella.
**pit** *n.* fossa, fosso; (for repairing cars) buca; (for wild animals) fossa; (for cockfights) arena; *the bottomless* —, l'inferno, l'abisso; (fig.) *to dig a — for someone*, stendere un tranello a qualcuno; (min.) miniera, pozzo, cava; (tan.) vasca; (anat.) cavo, cavità; — *of the stomach*, bocca dello stomaco, anticardio; (theatr.) platea; (med.) buttero.
**pit** *tr.* mettere in una fossa, collocare in un buco; (fig.) *to — one against another*, opporre l'uno all'altro; (med.) butterare.
**pit-a-pat** *n.* batticuore, palpitazione; ticchiettio, tic-tac *m.*, scalpiccio; *to go* —, palpitare, fare tic-tac, scalpicciare, picchierellare.
**pitch**[1] *n.* (miner.) pece *f.*, bitume *m.*; (fig.) *black as* —, nero come la pece; *tr.* impeciare, incatramare.
**pitch**[2] *n.* lancio, tiro; caduta; (archit.) grado di elevazione, altezza; pendenza, falda; (fig.) grado; *to the highest* —, al massimo grado; *to such a — that*, a tal punto che; (mus.) tono, tonalità, diapason *m.*; timbro; *to drop in* —, calare; *to rise in* —, crescere; (street-vendor's, *etc.*) posteggio; (aeron.; naut.) beccheggio; (of propeller) passo; (sport) campo; (cricket) terreno tra le due porte.
**pitch**[2] *tr.* gettare, lanciare, scagliare; *to be -ed off one's horse*, essere disarcionato; piantare, ficcare; *to — a tent*, piantare una tenda, attendarsi; *to — a camp*, impiantare un accampamento, accamparsi; (mus.) intonare, dare il tono a; (fig.) *to — a long story*, raccontare una lunga storia; (fam.) *to — it strong*, esagerare; *intr.* cadere, precipitare; *to — on one's head*, cadere a capofitto; (of ship) beccheggiare; (fam.) *to — into someone*, dare addosso a qualcuno; *to — over*, far capitombolo, rovesciarsi; *to — upon*, scegliere, trovare per caso.
**pitch-and-toss** *n.* giuoco di testa e croce.
**pitch-black** *adj.* nero come la pece.
**pitchblende** *n.* pechblenda.
**pitch-dark** *adj.* nero come la pece, buio pesto. **-ness** *n.* buio pesto.
**pitched** *p.def.* of **pitch**, *q.v.*; *adj.* — *battle*, battaglia campale.
**pitcher**[1] *n.* brocca; (provb.) *little -s have long ears*, i bambini hanno le orecchie lunghe; *the — goes so often to the well that at last it breaks*, tanto va la gatta al lardo che ci lascia lo zampino.
**pitcher**[2] *n.* (baseball) lanciatore.
**pitchfork**[1] *n.* forcone *m.*; *tr.* lanciare col forcone; (fig.) *to be -ed into a job*, essere costretto volente o nolente ad accettare un impiego.
**pitchfork**[2] *n.* (mus.) diapason *m.*
**pitching** *adj.* beccheggiante, che beccheggia; *n.* lancio; (of ship) beccheggio.
**pitch-pine** *n.* (bot.) pino rosso americano; (timber) pitch-pine *m.*
**pitchy** *adj.* pecioso, impeciato; buio pesto.
**piteous** *adj.* pietoso, miserando, commovente. **-ness** *n.* l'essere pietoso, aspetto pietoso.
**pitfall** *n.* trappola, fossa coperta; (fig.) tranello, insidia, inganno.
**pith** midollo; (fig.) succo, quintessenza; *n. attrib.* — *helmet*, casco coloniale.
**pithead** *n.* bocca di un pozzo minerario.
**pith-y** *adj.* pieno di midollo; (fig.) conciso, succinto, succoso, vigoroso. **-ily** *adv.* concisamente, succintamente; energicamente, efficacemente. **-iness** *n.* abbondanza di midollo; (fig.) concisione; vigoria.
**pitiable** *adj.* pietoso, degno di pietà, misero. **-ness** *n.* stato pietoso.
**pitiful** *adj.* pietoso, misericordioso, compassionevole; miserando, degno di pietà; (fig.) meschino. **-ness** *n.* pietà, compassione; stato pietoso.
**pitiless** *adj.* spietato, senza pietà; crudele. **-ness** *n.* mancanza di pietà; spietatezza, crudeltà.
**pitman** *n.* minatore.
**pit-prop** *n.* (min.) puntello. **-stall** *n.* (theatr.) poltroncina.
**pittance** *n.* elemosina; (fig.) magro salario, somma irrisoria, miseria.
**pitted** *adj.* butterato; (of metal) forato, punteggiato, vaiolato.
**pitter-patter** *n.* (fam.) picchiettiò.
**pituitary** *adj.* (anat.) pituitario.
**pity** *n.* compassione, pietà, misericordia; carità; *to feel — for*, provar pietà per; *to move to* —, destare la compassione di, commuovere; *to take — on*, aver compassione di; *have —!*, misericordia!; *for -'s sake!*, per carità!; (fam.) *it's a* —, è peccato, è un guaio; *what a —!*, che peccato!; *the more's the —!*, tanto peggio!; *tr.* compatire, provare pietà per, avere pietà di; *I — you*, ti compatisco; *he is to be pitied*, bisogna avere pietà di lui. **-ing** *adj.* compassionevole, pietoso.
**Pius** *pr.n.* Pio.
**pivot** *n.* perno, pernio; (fig.) cardine *m.*; *tr.* impernare, imperniare; *intr.* girare su un pernio, imperniarsi.
**pixie, pixy** *n.* fata, folletto.
**placab-le** *adj.* placabile. **-ility, -leness** *n.* placabilità.
**placard** *n.* affisso, cartellone *m.*, manifesto; *tr.* affiggere, attaccare (cartelli); coprire di affissi, annunciare con manifesti.
**placat-e** *tr.* placare, calmare, pacificare; conciliare, abbonacciare, ammansire, acquietare; *to be -d*, ammansirsi, abbonirsi. **-ion** *n.* placamento; conciliazione. **-ory** *n.*, *adj.* placatore; conciliatore.
**place** *n.* luogo; posto; — *of amusement*, luogo di svago; — *of birth*, *native* —, luogo di nascita, paese natio; — *of business*, ufficio; — *of residence*, luogo di residenza, domicilio, dimora; — *of worship*, luogo di culto, chiesa; *this is the* —, è qui; *in another* —, altrove; *in — of*, invece di, in luogo di; *in the first* —, in primo luogo, anzitutto; *in -s*, qua e là; *from — to* —, da un luogo all'altro; *all over the* —, dappertutto, dovunque; *out of* —, spostato, (fig.) male a proposito; *in his* —, (instead of him) invece di lui, a posto di lui, (in his position) nei suoi panni; *if I were in your* —, se io fossi in te; (fam.) *my* —, casa mia, da me, (in country) la mia villa; (provb.) *there's no — like home*, casa mia, casa mia, per piccina che tu sia, tu mi sembri una badia; piazza; *market* —, piazza del mercato; *fortified* —, piazzaforte; *a sore — on one's arm*, una zona dolente sul braccio; posto; *is this — taken?*, è occupato (*or* è libero) questo posto?; (at table) posto, coperto; *to change -s with*,

cambiare di posto con; *to find one's — in a book*, trovare il posto in un libro; *to find a — for someone*, collocare qualcuno; *to give — to*, cedere il posto a; *to keep someone in his —*, tenere qualcuno al suo posto; *to know one's —*, saper stare al proprio posto, saper comportarsi come si deve; *to lay a —* (at table), mettere un coperto; *to lose one's —* (in book), perdere il segno, (job) perdere l'impiego; *to take —*, aver luogo, accadere; *take your -s!*, accomodatevi! sedetevi!; *to take one's — at table*, sedersi a tavola; *to take someone's —*, occupare il posto di qualcuno, sostituire; (sport) *to get a —*, essere piazzato; *to back a horse for a —*, giuocare un cavallo piazzato.

**place** *tr.* collocare, mettere, posare, porre; *to — a book on the table*, mettere un libro sul tavolo; *to — an order with a firm*, collocare un ordine presso una ditta; *to — oneself at someone's service*, mettersi a disposizione di qualcuno; *to be -d in command*, essere posto al comando; *to — one's money*, collocare il denaro; *to — money in a bank*, depositare denaro presso una banca; (fig., hopes, faith) riporre; *to be awkwardly -d*, trovarsi in una situazione difficile; (fam.) *I cannot — him*, non mi ricordo chi sia; (mil.) *to — a gun*, postare un cannone; (sport) *to be -d*, essere piazzato.

**place-kick** *n.* (rugby) calcio piazzato. **-name** *n.* nome di luogo, toponimo; *study of -names*, toponimia, toponomastica.

**placenta** *n.* (anat.; bot.) placenta.

**placer** *n.* collocatore; (geol.) giacimento alluvionale.

**placet** *n.* beneplacito.

**placid** *adj.* placido, tranquillo, sereno, calmo. **-ity** *n.* placidità, tranquillità, serenità, calma.

**placket** *n.* (dressm.) apertura (in una gonna).

**plagiar-ism** *n.* plagio. **-ist** *n.* plagiario. **-ize** *tr.* plagiare, copiare.

**plague** *n.* peste *f.*, pestilenza; (fig.) flagello, afflizione, piaga; (pop.) *a — on it!*, accidenti!; *tr.* appestare; (fig.) tormentare, affliggere, vessare, importunare. **-spot** *n.* macchia sulla pelle caratteristica della peste; (fig.) focolare d'infezione, fonte di corruzione.

**plaice** *n.* (ichth.) pianuzza, passerino.

**plaid** *n.* (cost.) mantello scozzese a scacchi, plaid *m.*; coperta da viaggio.

**plain**[1] *adj.* chiaro, evidente; *as — as daylight*, chiaro come il sole; *it's as — as a pikestaff*, salta agli occhi; *to make —*, mettere in chiaro; *to make one's meaning —*, spiegarsi; comune, ordinario; (of looks) bruttino; semplice, schietto, puro; *in — English*, a dirla schietto, in buon italiano; *to be — with you*, per parlar chiaro; *— speaking*, schiettezza, sincerità; *the — truth*, la pura verità; *— dealing*, schiettezza, onestà; *a — diet*, un regime semplice; *— cooking*, cucina casalinga; disadorno, semplice; *— paper*, carta semplice; (of one colour) unito; piano, liscio; *in — clothes*, in borghese; (fig.) *all is now — sailing*, andiamo col vento in poppa; (herald.) pieno; *adv.* chiaramente, schiettamente.

**plain**[2] *n.* pianura, piano; *the Lombard —*, la pianura padana.

**plainchant** *n.* (mus.) corale *m.*, canto fermo.

**plain-clothes** *adj. attrib. — policeman*, poliziotto in borghese.

**plainness** *n.* chiarezza, evidenza; semplicità; schiettezza, franchezza; (of looks) bruttezza.

**plainsman** *n.* uomo della pianura.

**plainsong** *n.* (mus.) canto piano.

**plain-spoken** *adj.* franco, schietto, sincero.

**plaint** *n.* (poet.) lamento, compianto; (leg.) querela.

**plaintiff** *n.* querelante *m.*, *f.*, attore.

**plaintive** *adj.* lamentoso, flebile, querulo. **-ness** *n.* tono lamentoso, tristezza.

**plait** *n.* piega, pieghetta; cf. **pleat**; (of hair) treccia; *tr.* pieghare, pieghettare; cf. **pleat**; (hair) intrecciare.

**plan** *n.* piano; disegno; progetto; schema *m.*; *five-year —*, piano quinquennale; *according to —*, secondo il previsto; *to change one's -s*, cambiare proposito; *what are your -s?*, quali sono le tue intenzioni?; *the best — would be*, il meglio sarebbe; *it's not a bad — to . . .*, non sarebbe una cattiva idea . . .; (archit.) pianta, disegno, planimetria; *tr.* progettare; *-ned economy*, economia pianificata; (archit.) fare la pianta di, disegnare.

**planchette** *n.* tavoletta per sedute spiritistiche.

**plane**[1] *adj.* piano, piatto, livellato; *n.* piano, superficie piana; (fig.) livello; (mech.; paint.) piano; (aeron.) piano alare, ala; (fam.) see **aeroplane**; *intr.* (of birds, *etc.*) volare, planare; (aeron.) *to — down*, planare.

**plane**[2] *n.* (bot.) platano.

**plane**[3] *n.* (tool) pialla; *tr.* piallare, livellare; (fig.) spianare. **-r** *n.* (man) piallatore; (machine) piallatrice; (typ.) battitoio.

**planet** *n.* (astron.; eccl.) pianeta *m.* **-arium** *n.* planetario. **-ary** *adj.* planetario.

**plangent** *adj.* (lit.) rumoroso, risonante; (of wave) che s'infrange.

**planing** *n.* piallatura.

**planisphere** *n.* planisfero.

**plank** *n.* tavola, asse *f.*; *attrib. — partition*, assito; *— bed*, tavolaccio; (pol.) caposaldo; (naut.) *to walk the —*, camminare lungo un'asse fino a cadere in mare, (fig.) essere condannato a un supplizio grave; *tr.* rivestire di tavole, pavimentare; (fam.) buttare sul tavolo. **-ing** *n.* impalcatura, tavolato, assito.

**plankton** *n.* (biol.) plancton *m.*

**plann-er** *n.* progettista *m.*; (of towns) urbanista *m.* **-ing** *n.* progettazione; (pol.) pianificazione; (of town) piano regolatore, urbanistica; (fig.) concezione.

**plant** *n.* (bot.) pianta; *— biology*, fitobiologia; *— life*, vita vegetale, flora; (mech.) impianto, macchinario; *electric power —*, centrale elettrica; (factory) stabilimento, fabbrica; (fam.) inganno, falsificazione.

**plant** *tr.* (bot.) piantare, seminare; *to — out*, trapiantare; (fig.) infiggere, (con)ficcare; *to — an idea in someone's mind*, ficcare un'idea nella mente di qualcuno; fondare; (fam.) *to — oneself in front of*, piantarsi di fronte a; *to — oneself on someone*, stabilirsi in casa di qualcuno senza invito; *to — a blow*, assestare un colpo; (fam.) *to — evidence*, fabbricare una prova falsa.

**Plantagenet** *pr.n.* (hist.) Plantageneto.

**plaintain** *n.* (bot.) piantaggine *f.*, petacciuola; (banana) musa, fico banano; plantano.

**plantation** *n.* piantagione *f.*

**planter** *n.* piantatore, proprietario di una piantagione; (machine) piantatrice.

**plaqu-e** *n.* placca, lastra, piastra; *commemorative —*, targa. **-ette** *n.* piccola placca, piastrina.

**plash** *n.* rumore di corpo che cade nell'acqua; rumore dell'acqua che cade; *tr.* spruzzare, schizzare; sguazzare.

**plasma** *n.* plasma *m.*

**plaster** *n.* impiastro, cerotto, cataplasma; (bldg.) intonaco, gesso, stucco, calcina; *— cast*, calco, modello in gesso; (med.) *to put into —*, ingessare; *— setting*, ingessatura; *tr.* applicare un cerotto a; (bldg.) intonacare, ammaltare, ingessare; (fig.) ricoprire; *to — down one's hair*, impomatare i capelli; *to — up*, riparare; (fam.) *to be -ed*, essere sbronzo. **-ing** *n.* intonacatura; (med.) ingessatura.

**plastic** *adj.* plastico; *the — arts*, le arti plastiche; *— surgery*, anaplasti(c)a, chirurgia plastica; (fig.) malleabile, plasmatico; *n.pl.* materie plastiche.

-**ity** *n.* plasticità, malleabilità; (cinem.) rilievo.
**plastron** *n.* piastrone *m.*; (cost.) sparato inamidato.
**plat** *n.*, *tr.* (of hair), see **plait.**
**plate** *n.* lamina, lamiera, lastra, foglio, placca, piastra; (motor.) targa; (cul.) piatto; (for soup) fondina; *-s and dishes*, vasellame *m.*; (gold and silver ware) vasellame, argenteria; (in book) tavola fuori testo; *collection* —, piattino; (dentistry) dentiera, apparecchio, placca; (anat.) rotula; (armour) corazza; (rlwy.) piastrina; (prize for sporting event) coppa; (typ.) matrice *f.*
**plate** *tr.* rivestire di piastre, placcare; (with gold) dorare; (with lead) piombare; (with silver) inargentare; (with tin) stagnare; (with zinc) zincare; (with armour) corazzare, blindare; (typ.) preparare le matrici di.
**plateau** *n.* (geog.) altipiano, acrocoro.
**plated** *adj.* placcato; (with armour) blindato, corazzato.
**plateful** *n.* piatto.
**plate-glass** *n.* cristallo, vetro in lastre, vetro per specchi.
**platelayer** *n.* (rlwy.) operaio addetto alle rotaie, guardalinee *m.*
**platen** *n.* (typ.) platina; (mech.) piastra metallica; (of typewriter) rullo.
**plate-rack** *n.* portapiatti, scolapiatti *m.* **-warmer** *n.* scaldapiatti *m.*
**platform** *n.* (archit.) piattaforma, piano, terrazza; (in hall, etc.) tribuna, palco, impalcatura; (rlwy.) marciapiede *m.*, banchina, binario; *the train for Milan leaves from — three*, il treno per Milano è in partenza dal binario numero tre; — *ticket*, biglietto d'ingresso; (fig., pol.) piattaforma, programma *m.*
**plating** *n.* placcatura, placcaggio; preparazione delle lamiere; rivestimento metallico.
**platinum** *n.* platino. **-blonde** *n.* (fam.) bionda ossigenata.
**platitud-e** *n.* banalità; luogo comune; insulsaggine *f.* **-inarian** *n.* chi si compiace di banalità. **-inize** *intr.* dire banalità. **-inous** *adj.* banale, piatto, trito, comune.
**Plato** *pr.n.* Platone **-nic** *adj.* platonico. **-ism** *n.* platonismo. **-ist** *n.* platonico.
**platoon** *n.* (mil.) plotone *m.*, squadra.
**platter** *n.* piatto.
**platypus** *n.* (zool.) ornitorinco.
**plaudit** *n.* applauso, acclamazione.
**plausib-le** *adj.* plausibile, credibile. **-ility, -leness** *n.* plausibilità.
**Plautus** *pr.n.* Plauto.
**play** *n.* giuoco, divertimento, ricreazione, spasso; *it's child's* —, è facilissimo, è giuoco da bambini; *fair* —, giuoco leale, (justice) giustizia, equità; *foul* —, (murder) omicidio, (sport) giuoco falloso; *rough* —, giuoco scatenato; *in* —, per scherzo, (sport) in giuoco, (fig.) in ballo; — *will begin at three*, la partita avrà inizio alle ore tre; (provb.) *all work and no — makes Jack a dull boy*, meglio un asino vivo che un dottore morto; (gambling) giuoco d'azzardo; *the — was high*, si giuocava forte; (mus.) esecuzione; (theatr.) dramma *m.*, commedia, spettacolo; (collect.) *the -s of Goldoni*, il teatro di Goldoni; (fam.) *it's as good as a* —, è una commedia; (fig.) azione, movimento, corso; *to be in full* —, essere in azione; *to give full — to*, dare libero sfogo a; *to come into* —, entrare in azione; (mech.) giuoco, spostamento; *the — of light*, il giuoco della luce; *a — on words*, un giuoco di parole, una zeppa.
**play** *tr.*, *intr.* giuocare (a), divertirsi (di), trastullarsi (con); *to — cards*, giuocare a carte; *to — a game of football*, giuocare una partita di calcio; *to — a stroke*, fare un colpo; *the children are -ing in the garden*, i bambini giuocano nel giardino; *the little girl is -ing with her dolls*, la bambina si trastulla con le sue bambole; (gamble) giuocare d'azzardo; (mus.) suonare; *to — the piano*, suonare il pianoforte; (theatr.) *to — a part*, interpretare una parte; *to — well*, recitare bene; *to — to the gallery*, cercare di incontrare il gusto del grosso pubblico; (fig.) *to — one's cards well*, giuocare bene le proprie carte; *to — the devil*, fare il diavolo a quattro; *to — fair*, comportarsi lealmente; *to — someone false*, tradire qualcuno; *to — fast and loose*, giuocare a pari e caffo, comportarsi da irresponsabile; *to — second fiddle*, avere una parte secondaria; *to — with fire*, scherzare col fuoco; *to — a fish*, stancare un pesce dandogli corda; *to — the fool*, fare il buffone, scherzare; *to — the game*, stare al giuoco, comportarsi lealmente; *to — into someone's hands*, fare il giuoco di qualcuno; *to — a hose on the fire*, dirigere un getto d'acqua sull'incendio; *to — jokes*, scherzare, far scherzi; *to — a joke on someone*, beffarsi di qualcuno; *to — the man*, comportarsi da uomo; *to — one's part well*, recitare bene la propria parte, fare quel che si deve; *to — a dirty trick on someone*, giuocare un brutto tiro a qualcuno; *to — truant*, marinare la scuola, andare a zonzo. FOLLOW. BY ADV. OR PREP.: *to — at*, giuocare a, fare; *to — away*, *tr.* (lose) perdere al giuoco, *intr.* (sport) giuocare fuori casa; *to — down*, *tr.* minimizzare, fare poco caso di; *intr. to — down to the crowd*, adeguarsi al gusto del grosso pubblico; *to — one person off against another*, opporre una persona all'altra; *to — off*, (sport) rigiuocare (un incontro nullo); *to — on*, continuare a giuocare, (mus.) continuare a suonare; *to — out*, giuocare fino in fondo; (fam.) *to be -ed out*, essere finito; *to — up*, *tr.* fare dei capricci con; *intr.* fare del proprio meglio; (sport) — *up !*, forza!; *to — up to*, adulare; *to — upon*, approfittare di.
**playable** *adj.* (mus.) suonabile; (theatr.) recitabile; (sport, of ground) praticabile.
**play-acting** *gerund* (iron.) *he's only* —, fa la commedia; *n.* commedia.
**playbill** *n.* cartellone teatrale.
**playbox** *n.* cassetta per giocattoli.
**playboy** *m.* (fam.) giovane gaudente, buontempone *m.*; (Ireland) buffone *m.*
**player** *n.* (cards, sport) giuocatore; (mus.) suonatore; professore d'orchestra; (theatr.) attore, interprete *m.*, *f.*; *strolling* —, attore girovago.
**playfellow** *n.* compagno di giuoco; *old* —, amico d'infanzia.
**playful** *adj.* scherzoso, gaio, allegro, giocoso, spiritoso. **-ness** *n.* giocosità, gaiezza, allegria.
**playgoer** *n.* frequentatore di teatro, appassionato degli spettacoli.
**playground** *n.* (schol.) terreno usato per la ricreazione, cortile di scuola; (fig.) luogo di svago.
**playhouse** *n.* teatro.
**playing** *n.* il giuocare, il modo di giuocare; (mus.) il suonare, esecuzione; (theatr.) rappresentazione, interpretazione. **-card** *n.* carta da giuoco. **-field** *n.* campo sportivo.
**play-pen** *n.* recinto per bambini.
**playmate** *n.* See **playfellow.**
**playlet** *n.* commediola.
**play-room** *n.* stanza dei bambini. **-thing** *n.* giocattolo, balocco. **-time** *n.* ora della ricreazione.
**playwright** *n.* drammaturgo, commediografo.
**plea** *n.* (leg.) allegazione, eccezione, difesa; istanza, supplica; scusa, giustificazione.
**pleach** *tr.* (hortic.) intrecciare.
**plead** *tr.* (leg.) perorare, patrocinare, difendere; addurre, allegare, eccepire; *to — a cause*, perorare una causa; *intr.* (leg.) protestarsi, far valere le proprie ragioni in giudizio; *to — guilty*, dichiararsi colpevole, confessarsi reo; *to — not guilty*, dichiararsi innocente, protestare la propria innocenza; *to — for mercy*, implorare pietà, far domanda di

grazia; *to — for someone*, perorare a favore di qualcuno; *to — with someone*, intercedere presso qualcuno; *to — against*, deprecare. **-er** *n.* patrocinatore, avvocato difensore, intercessore. **-ing** *adj.* supplichevole, implorante; *n.* dichiarazione, difesa, patrocinio; arringa, perorazione.

**pleasant** *adj.* piacevole, grato, gradevole, ameno; amabile, simpatico, gentile, compiacente, affabile; *to make oneself — to*, mostrarsi amabile verso. **-ry** *n.* facezia, frizzo, amenità.

**please** *tr.*, *intr.* piacere (a), far piacere (a), soddisfare, contentare, accontentare; *to be -ed*, compiacersi (di), essere lieto (di); *to — oneself*, fare il proprio comodo; *as you —*, come ti piace, come vuoi; *(if you) please*, per piacere, per favore, per cortesia; (emphatic) per carità!

**pleased** *adj.* contento, lieto, soddisfatto; *— to meet you!*, lieto di fare la Sua conoscenza!, piacere!; *to be anything but —*, essere tutt'altro che lieto; (fam.) *— as Punch*, contento come una pasqua.

**pleasing** *adj.* piacevole, gradevole, dilettevole, simpatico. **-ness** *n.* piacevolezza, amenità, gradevolezza.

**pleasurable** *adj.* gradevole, piacevole. **-ness** *n.* gradevolezza, piacevolezza.

**pleasure** *n.* piacere, piacimento; diletto; *to have the — of*, avere il piacere di, dilettarsi di; *it gives me real —*, mi fa veramente piacere; *with —!*, ben volentieri!, con piacere!; *the — is mine!*, prego!; divertimento spasso, svago, diporto; *to travel for —*, viaggiare per diporto.

**pleasure-boat** *n.* battello da diporto. **-ground** *n.* parco, giardino pubblico. **-loving** *adj.* che ama divertirsi, gaudente.

**pleat** *n.* (dressm.) piega, pieghetta.

**plebeian** *adj.* plebeo, popolare, proletario.

**plebiscit-e** *n.* plebiscito. **-ary** *adj.* plebiscitario.

**plebs** *n.* plebe *f.*, proletariato.

**plectrum** *n.* (mus.) plettro.

**pledge** *n.* pegno, impegno; garanzia; promessa; voto; *under — of secrecy*, con impegno di segretezza, sotto il vincolo del segreto; (fam.) *to take the —*, promettere di astenersi dall'alcool; *tr.* dare in pegno, impegnare; (pawn) impegnare; *to — oneself*, garantire, promettere; brindare alla salute di.

**Pleiad** *pr.n.* (myth.; astron.) Pleiade *f.*

**pleistocene** *adj.* (geol.) pleistocenico; *n.* pleistocene *m.*

**plenary** *adj.* plenario, completo.

**plenipotentiary** *adj.*, *n.* plenipotenziario.

**plenitude** *n.* pienezza, completezza, abbondanza, dovizia.

**plenteous** *adj.* abbondante, copioso. **-ness** *n.* (poet.) abbondanza, copiosità, dovizia.

**plentiful** *adj.* abbondante, copioso; *to be —*, abbondare. **-ness** *n.* abbondanza, copia.

**plenty** *n.* abbondanza, copia; *horn of —*, cornucopia; *land of —*, paese di cuccagna; *to have — of*, abbondare di, avere in abbondanza, avere abbastanza; (fam.) *— of*, moltissimo, tanto, *in —*, a iosa; *adv.* abbastanza, abbondantemente.

**pleon-asm** *n.* pleonasmo. **-astic** *adj.* pleonastico.

**plethor-a** *n.* pletora, sovrabbondanza. **-ic** *adj.* pletorico, sovrabbondante; (med.) congesto.

**pleurisy** *n.* (med.) pleurite *f.*

**plexus** *n.* (anat.) plesso; *solar —*, plesso solare.

**pliab-le, pliant** *adj.* pieghevole, flessibile; (fig.) arrendevole, compiacente. **-ility, -leness** *n.* pieghevolezza, flessibilità; (fig.) arrendevolezza.

**pliers** *n.* pinze, tenaglie *f.pl.*

**plight** *n.* stato, condizione, situazione; *to be in a sorry —*, essere in uno stato pietoso; *what a — you are in!*, come sei ridotto!; *tr.* impegnare, promettere solennemente; *to — one's troth*, impegnarsi, dare la parola d'onore, giurare fedeltà.

**Plimsoll** *n.* *— line*, linea Plimsoll, linea di carica, bagnasciuga.

**plimsolls** *n.* scarpe di tela con suola di gomma.

**plinth** *n.* (archit.) plinto, zoccolo, piattabanda.

**Pliny** *pr.n.* Plinio.

**pliocene** *adj.* (geol.) pliocenico; *n.* pliocene *m.*

**plod** *tr.*, *intr.* camminare faticosamente, avanzare lentamente; *to — along*, tirare avanti; *to — away*, sgobbare, lavorare assiduamente; *to — on*, perseverare, proseguire. **-der** *n.* sgobbone, lavoratore assiduo.

**plop** *n.* rumore sordo, tonfo; *intr.* cadere nell'acqua, cadere con un tonfo; *to — down in an armchair*, lasciarsi cadere in una poltrona.

**plot** *n.* appezzamento, lotto; congiura, complotto, cospirazione; *to hatch a —*, ordire una congiura; intreccio, trama; *the — thickens*, l'intreccio si complica; (fig.) *to unravel the —*, dipanare la matassa; *tr.* tracciare, fare la pianta di; *to — a graph*, tracciare un grafico; *tr.*, *intr.* tramare, cospirare, complottare, macchinare. **-ter** *n.* cospiratore, congiurato, congiuratore.

**plough** *n.* aratro; (astron.) Orsa Maggiore; (fig.) *to set one's hand to the —*, por mano all'opera; *tr.* arare; (fig.) solcare, fendere; *to — one's way*, avanzare faticosamente; (schol.) bocciare; *to get -ed*, essere bocciato; *intr.* arare, usare un aratro; *to — in*, coprire arando; *to — up*, dissodare; (fig.) *to — through*, solcare, fendere, aprirsi un varco attraverso; *to — through a book*, leggere faticosamente un libro. **-ing** *n.* aratura. **-land** *n.* terreno arabile. **-man** *n.* aratore, bifolco. **-share** *n.* vomere *m.*, coltro.

**plover** *n.* (orn.) piviere *m.*

**pluck** *n.* tirata, strappo; *he gave my sleeve a —*, mi tirò la manica; (fam.) coraggio, fegato; (cul.) frattaglie *f.pl.*, ventraia; (schol. slang) bocciatura; *tr.* cogliere, strappare, tirare; *to — off*, cogliere, staccare; *to — up*, sradicare, svellere; *to — up courage*, farsi animo, prendere il coraggio a due mani; spennare, spiumare; *to have one's eyebrows -ed*, farsi depilare le sopracciglia; (mus.) pizzicare; (schol. slang) bocciare.

**pluck-y** *adj.* coraggioso, ardito; (fam.) di fegato, fegatoso; (photog.) ben definito. **-iness** *n.* coraggio, ardimento; (fam.) fegato.

**plug** *n.* tappo; (of wood) zaffo; (electr.) spina; (med.) tampone *m.*; (motor.) candela; (naut.) aleggio; (of tobacco) tavoletta, pezzo; *tr.* tappare, turare, tamponare; (electr.) *to — in*, attaccare, inserire la spina; *intr.* (fam.) *to — along*, avanzare faticosamente, tirare avanti; *to — away*, perseverare; sgobbare.

**plum** *n.* prugna, susina; (tree) prugno, susino; (fam.) il meglio; *the -s of office*, i migliori posti.

**plumage** *n.* penne *f.pl.*, piume *f.pl.*, piumaggio.

**plumb** *adj.* verticale, perpendicolare, a piombo; *adv.* a piombo; (fig.) assolutamente, proprio; *— in the centre*, proprio al centro; *n.* filo a piombo, piombino; *out of —*, non verticale; (naut.) scandaglio; *tr.* misurare la profondità di, verificare la verticalità di; (seal with lead) piombare; (naut.) scandagliare; (fig.) sondare.

**plumbago** *n.* piombaggine *f.*

**plumber** *n.* idraulico.

**plumbing** gerund of **plumb**, *q.v.*; *n.* lavori idraulici; impianto idraulico.

**plumb-line** *n.* filo a piombo; (fig.) linea verticale. **-rule** *n.* regolo da muratore, livella.

**plum-cake** *n.* panfrutto.

**plume** *n.* penna, piuma; (fig.) *borrowed -s*, penne di pavone; (on helmet) pennacchio; (fig.) palma, trofeo; *tr.* ornare di piume; *rfl.* (of bird) ripulirsi le penne; (of person) vantarsi, piccarsi.

**plummet** *n.* piombino, filo a piombo; (naut.) scandaglio.

**plump**[1] *adj.* grassoccio,

grassotto, grasso, pienotto, paffuto; *tr.* far ingrassare; *intr.* ingrassare; *adj.* schietto, brusco, categorico, netto; *a — refusal*, un netto rifiuto; *adv.* di peso, pesantemente, con un tonfo; *n.* tonfo, caduta pesante; *tr.* buttare giù; *intr.* cadere pesantemente, lasciarsi cadere con un tonfo; (fam.) *to — for*, scegliere, (pol.) votare in massa per.

**plumpness** *n.* grassezza, rotondità, paffutezza.

**plum-pudding** *n.* budino natalizio; (geol.) *— stone*, puddinga.

**plunder** *n.* bottino, spoglie *f.pl.*, saccheggio; *tr.* saccheggiare, spogliare, mettere a sacco, depredare. **~er** *n.* saccheggiatore, predatore, predone *m.*, spogliatore.

**plung-e** *n.* tuffo; immersione; sbalzo; (fig.) *to take the —*, rompere gl'indugi, saltare il fosso; *tr.* tuffare, immergere, lanciare; (fig.) *to be ~ed in darkness*, piombare nell'oscurità, essere immerso nelle tenebre; *to — the country into war*, trascinare il paese nella guerra; *intr.* tuffarsi, immergersi; (fig.) lanciarsi, precipitarsi; (of ship) beccheggiare; (of horse) slanciarsi in avanti; (pop.) giuocare forte, puntare l'ultimo soldo. **~er** *n.* tuffatore; (mech.) stantuffo, pistone *m.*

**plunk** *adv.* (pop.) proprio, esattamente; *tr.* scagliare; *to — down*, buttare giù; *intr.* cadere pesantemente.

**pluperfect** *adj.*, *n.* (gramm.) piuccheperfetto, trapassato.

**plural** *adj.*, *n.* (gramm.) plurale *m.*; *in the —*, al plurale; (pol.) *— vote*, voto plurimo. **~ism** *n.* pluralismo. **~ity** *n.* pluralità, molteplicità; *~ity of votes*, maggioranza relativa.

**plus** *adj.* in più, addizionale; (electr.; math.) positivo; (pol. econ.) *— value*, plusvalore *m.*; *n.* più *m.*, il segno $+$; quantità addizionale.

**plus** *prep.* più, con l'aggiunta di; (schol.) *eleven —*, esame da sostenere all'età di undici anni e più.

**plus-fours** *n.* (cost.) calzoni alla zuava.

**plush** *n.* (text.) felpa, peluche *f.*; *adj.* (fam.) alla moda, chic.

**Plutarch** *pr.n.* Plutarco.

**plutarchy** *n.* plutocrazia.

**Pluto** *pr.n.* (myth.) Plutone.

**plutocr-acy** *n.* plutocrazia. **~at** *n.* plutocrate *m.* **~atic** *adj.* plutocratico.

**Pluton-ian, ~ic** *adj.* plutoniano, di Plutone, infernale; (geol.) plutoniano, plutonico.

**pluvial** *adj.* pluviale, alluvionale; *n.* (eccl.) piviale *m.*

**ply** *n.* piega; (fig.) tendenza; (of thread, wool) capo, filo; (naut.) trefolo; (in plywood) strato; *tr.* adoperare, maneggiare; *to — the oars*, remare; *to — a trade*, esercitare un mestiere; (fig.) *to — with questions*, assediare di domande; *to — with drink*, spingere al bere, far bere; *intr.* fare servizio (fra ... e), fare la spola (da ... a); *to — for hire*, darsi a nolo.

**plywood** *n.* legno compensato.

**pneumatic** *adj.* pneumatico; *— tyre*, pneumatico, gomma. **~s** *n.* pneumatica.

**pneumoni-a** *n.* (fam.) polmonite *f.*, (med.) pneumonia. **~c** *adj.* (med.) pneumonico, polmonare.

**Po** *pr.n.* (river) Po, (poet.) Eridano; *attrib.* padano; *— delta*, delta padano, Polesine *m.*

**poach**[1] *tr.* (cul.) cuocere (uova senza guscio); *~ed eggs*, uova affogate, uova in camicia.

**poach**[2] *tr.* calpestare; (game) cacciare di frodo; (fish) pescare di frodo; *intr.* fare il bracconiere, cacciare, pescare di frodo; (fig.) *to — on someone's preserves*, usurpare i diritti di qualcuno. **~er** *n.* cacciatore di frodo, pescatore di frodo, bracconiere *m.* **~ing** *n.* caccia di frodo, pesca di frodo.

**pocket** *n.* tasca, taschino; *to keep one's hands in one's ~s*, tenere le mani in tasca; *he paid out of his own —*, ha pagato di tasca sua; *to put one's hand in one's —*, mettere mano alla borsa; *to pick someone's —*, borseggiare qualcuno; (fig.) *I am out of — by it*, ci rimetto del mio; *to be in —*, aver guadagnato; *to line one's ~s*, guadagnare, farsi il gruzzolo; *to put one's pride in one's —*, soffocare il proprio orgoglio; *to have someone in one's —*, poter far ciò che si vuole di qualcuno; *to have ~s under one's eyes*, avere le borse sotto gli occhi; (aeron.) vuoto d'aria; (billiards) buca; (geol.) sacca; (mil.) sacca, zona isolata; *attrib.* tascabile; *— dictionary*, dizionario tascabile. **~ful** *n.* tascata, tasca piena.

**pocket** *tr.* intascare, mettere in tasca; appropriarsi di, involare; (fig.) incassare, ingoiare, sopportare, subire senza reagire; *to — one's pride*, soffocare il proprio orgoglio; (billiards) mandare in buca.

**pocket-book** *n.* portafogli *m.*, taccuino, agenda. **-handkerchief** *n.* fazzoletto (da tasca). **-knife** *n.* temperino. **-money** *n.* denaro per le piccole spese, spillatico, argent-de-poche; (small change) spiccioli *m.pl.* **-picking** *n.* borseggio.

**pockmark** *n.* buttero. **~ed** *adj.* butterato.

**pod** *n.* (bot.) baccello, guscio, alveolo, siliqua; bozzolo; (for catching eels) nassa; *tr.* sbaccellare, sgusciare; *intr.* mettere baccelli.

**podg-y** *adj.* grassotto, tondo, tozzo; (of cheek) paffuto. **~iness** *n.* grassezza, l'essere piccolo e tozzo; (of cheeks) paffutezza.

**podium** *n.* (archit.) podio.

**poem** *n.* poesia; composizione poetica; versi *m.pl.*; (if long) poema *m.*

**poesy** *n.* (poet.) poesia.

**poet** *n.* poeta *m.*; *Poet Laureate*, (hist.) poeta laureato, (in Britain) poeta di corte. **~aster** *n.* poetastro. **~ess** *n.* poetessa.

**poetic(al)** *adj.* poetico; *poetic licence*, licenza poetica; *— works of*, opere in versi di.

**poeticize** *tr.* rendere poetico; *intr.* scrivere come un poeta.

**poetics** *n.* poetica.

**poetry** *n.* poesia; *a piece of —*, una poesia; *to write —*, comporre versi, scrivere versi; *Horace's 'Art of —'*, *l'Arte poetica* di Orazio.

**pogrom** *n.* 'pogrom' *m.*, massacro di ebrei.

**poign-ancy** *n.* acutezza; (fig.) intensità. **~ant** *adj.* cocente, acuto, vivo; (fig.) intenso; pungente, mordace, piccante.

**point** *n.* (in space, time) punto; *— of departure*, punto di partenza; *— of contact*, punto di contatto; *— of intersection*, punto di intersezione; *at the — of death*, in punto di morte; *boiling —*, punto di ebollizione; (math.) *decimal —*, virgola decimale; *six — five*, sei virgola cinque; *cardinal —*, punto cardinale; *the ~s of the compass*, le quarte della bussola; (degree) grado, punto; *the temperature has gone up five ~s*, il termometro è salito di cinque gradi; (sport) punto; *full ~s*, punteggio massimo; *to beat on ~s*, battere ai punti; *to give ~s to*, dare dei punti a; (mus.; typ.) punto; (sharp end) punta; *at the — of the sword*, sulla punta della spada, (fig.) a mano armata; *to sharpen to a —*, fare la punta a; (geog.) capo, promontorio; (of dog) il puntare; (electr.) presa, puntina; (rlwy.) *~s*, scambi; (lacem.) merletto a punto ago; (fig.) *up to a —*, fino a un certo punto; *a — of conscience*, una questione di coscienza; *a — of honour*, un punto d'onore; *a — of law*, una questione di diritto; *it is a sore — with him*, ciò lo tocca sul vivo; *— of view*, punto di vista, opinione; *from every — of view*, sotto tutti gli aspetti; *a turning-point*, una svolta; *~s to be remembered*, punti da tenere a mente; *his strong —*, il suo forte; *he has many good ~s*, ha molti meriti; *his weak —*, il suo lato debole; *the — of a joke*, l'arguzia di una storiella; *that is just the —!*, ecco il punto!; *what is the — of?*, a che cosa serve di?; *there is no — in*, non è il caso di; *armed at all ~s*, armato di tutto punto; *beside the —*, fuori argo-

mento, non pertinente; *a case in —*, un esempio tipico; *in — of fact*, in realtà; *on this —*, a questo proposito; *to the —*, a proposito, opportuno; *short and to the —*, breve e a proposito; *to be on the — of*, essere sul punto di, stare per; *to come to the —*, venire al sodo; *to gain one's —*, far prevalere la propria opinione, raggiungere lo scopo; *to give — to*, dare di peso a; *to insist on a —*, insistere su un punto, battere il chiodo; *to keep to the —*, non divagare; *to make a —*, far prevalere le proprie ragioni; *to make a — of*, farsi un dovere di; *to miss the —*, non cogliere l'essenziale; *not to put too fine a — on it*, senza essere troppo meticoloso; *to raise a — of order*, sollevare una questione di procedura; *to see the —*, cogliere l'essenziale; *to stretch a —*, fare un'eccezione, lasciar correre; *to wander from the —*, divagare; (provb.) *possession is nine -s of the law*, ci stiamo e ci staremo.

**point** *tr.* additare, indicare, mostrare; *to — a finger at*, additare; *to — the way*, indicare la strada; fare la punta a, aguzzare; *to — a pencil*, fare la punta a una matita; puntare; *to — a gun*, puntare un cannone; *to — a telescope*, orientare un telescopio; punteggiare; *to — a moral*, essere di lezione; (bldg.) affilettare, riempire di calce e cemento; *intr.* indicare col dito; (of dog) puntare; *to — at*, indicare col dito, additare; *to — to*, indicare, essere rivolto verso, provare, essere una prova di; *to — out*, indicare, accennare (a), far notare, far rilevare, porre in rilievo; *I would — out that*, faccio notare che; *to — out mistakes*, segnare gli errori.

**point-blank** *adj.* diretto, categorico, netto; *a — refusal*, un rifiuto categorico; *adv.* a bruciapelo, di punto in bianco, chiaro e tondo, categoricamente; *to fire —*, sparare a bruciapelo. **-duty** *n.* (of police) *to be on -duty*, essere addetto alla circolazione, regolare il traffico.

**pointed** *adj.* appuntito, acuminato, acuto, aguzzo, affilato; (fig.) arguto, pungente, mordace; chiaro, evidente, esplicito; (archit.) ogivale; *— arch*, arco a sesto acuto. **-ness** *n.* acutezza, mordacità; (fig.) chiarezza, evidenza; carattere esplicito.

**pointer** *n.* indicatore; indice *m.*; (of watch, *etc.*) lancetta; (dog) pointer *m.*, cane *m.* da ferma; (artill.) puntatore.

**pointill-ism** *n.* (paint.) divisionismo; scuola dei macchiaioli. **-ist** *adj.*, *n.* (paint.) divisionista *m.*; macchiaiolo.

**pointing** *n.* indicazione; additamento; (gramm.) punteggiatura; (sharpening) affilatura; (bldg.) affilettatura.

**point-lace** *n.* merletto a punto ago.

**pointless** *adj.* spuntato, smussato, senza punta; (fig.) inutile, senza scopo, futile; (sport) che non ha segnato punti; *— draw*, pareggio zero a zero. **-ness** *n.* inutilità, futilità.

**pointsman** *n.* (rlwy.) deviatore, scambista *m.*; (police) vigile addetto alla circolazione.

**point-to-point** *n.* (sport) cross *m.*

**poise** *n.* equilibrio; (of head) portamento; peso, contrappeso; (fig.) ponderatezza; *tr.* bilanciare, equilibrare; pesare, soppesare; (fig.) ponderare; sospendere; (of birds) *to be -d*, volteggiare, librarsi; *intr.* essere in equilibrio, essere sospeso, librarsi. **-d** *adj.* equilibrato, sospeso; *delicately -d*, in bilico.

**poison** *n.* veleno, tossico; *to take —*, avvelenarsi; *to get the — out of one's system*, disintossicarsi; (fig.) *to hate someone like —*, avere del veleno contro qualcuno; *tr.* avvelenare, attossicare, intossicare; (fig.) corrompere; *to — someone's mind*, corrompere l'anima di qualcuno, istillare odio nella mente di qualcuno. **-er** *n.* avvelenatore *m.*

**poison-gas** *n.* gas avvelenatrice *f.* asfissiante, gas intossicante.

**poisoning** *n.* avvelenamento; *blood-poisoning*, setticemia.

**poisonous** *adj.* velenoso, venefico; (fig.) pernicioso, malefico; *a — tongue*, una linguaccia; *— stuff*, veleno. **-ness** *n.* velenosità.

**poke**[1] *n.* cartoccio; sacco; *to buy a pig in a —*, comprare la gatta nel sacco, comprare a occhi chiusi.

**poke**[2] *n.* spinta, spintone *m.*; gomitata; (fam.) *to give the fire a —*, attizzare il fuoco; *tr.* spingere, urtare, cacciare innanzi; *to — the fire*, attizzare il fuoco; *to — someone in the ribs*, dare una gomitata amichevole a qualcuno; *to — one's head out*, cacciar fuori la testa; *to — something up the chimney*, cacciare qualcosa nel camino; *to — one's nose into other people's business*, ficcare il naso negli affari altrui; *to — fun at*, mettere in ridicolo, beffarsi di; *to — holes in*, bucherellare; *intr.* *to — about*, frugare, rovistare; *to — at something with one's umbrella*, tastare qualcosa coll'ombrello.

**poke-bonnet** *n.* cuffia a visiera.

**poker**[1] *n.* attizzatoio; (fig.) *as stiff as a —*, rigido come un palo. **-work** *n.* pirografia.

**poker**[2] *n.* (cards) poker *m.* **-face** *n.* viso impassibile.

**poking** *adj.* *— out*, sporgente; *n.* attizzamento; (fig.) intromissione negli affari altrui.

**poky** *adj.* piccolo, ristretto, meschino; *a — little room*, una stanzuccia.

**Poland** *pr.n.* (geog.) Polonia.

**polar** *adj.* polare; (fig.) antitetico, opposto. **-ity** *n.* polarità.

**polariz-e** *tr.* polarizzare; *intr.* polarizzarsi. **-ation** *n.* polarizzazione.

**pole**[1] *n.* palo, asta, pertica; *telegraph-pole*, palo telegrafico; *scaffold-pole*, abetella; *greasy —*, albero della cuccagna; (of wagon) timone *m.*; (meas. of length = 5.0292 m.) pertica; (fam.) *to be up the —*, essere matto; *tr.* sostenere con pali, mettere pali a; spingere con la pertica.

**pole**[2] *n.* (geog.) polo; *North —*, Polo Nord; *the — star*, la stella polare; (electr.) polo; (fig.) *to be as far apart as the -s, to be -s apart*, essere agli antipodi, essere antitetici.

**Pole**[3] *n.* Polacco *m.*; Polacca *f.*

**poleaxe** *n.* (hist.) ascia; (butcher.) scure *f.*, ascia; *tr.* macellare con la scure.

**polecat** *n.* (zool.) puzzola.

**pole-jump(ing)** *n.* salto con l'asta.

**polemic** *adj.* polemico; *n.* polemica. **-al** *adj.* polemico. **-ist, polemist** *n.* polemista *m.*, *f.*

**polemize** *intr.* polemizzare.

**police** *n.* polizia (N.B. In Italy the police force consists of [1] carabinieri, who deal with serious crimes and, as part of the armed forces, also act as military police; [2] agenti di pubblica sicurezza (questurini), who maintain order and investigate crimes; [3] vigili urbani, who deal with minor offences, control of traffic, *etc.*); *— headquarters*, questura; *railway —*, polizia ferroviaria; *road —*, polizia stradale; *— records*, casellario giudiziario; *tr.* mantenere l'ordine (per mezzo di agenti), fornire di agenti; (fig.) sorvegliare, vigilare.

**police-constable** *n.* poliziotto; appuntato dei carabinieri; agente di pubblica sicurezza; vigile *m.* **-court** *n.* tribunale *m.* di polizia, pretura. **-dog** *n.* cane poliziotto. **-force** *n.* corpo di polizia. **-inspector** *n.* ispettore di polizia, commissario di pubblica sicurezza. **-magistrate** *n.* pretore *m.*

**policeman** *n.* poliziotto, agente *m.*, vigile *m.*

**police-station** *n.* commissariato di pubblica sicurezza; *central — of town*, questura. **-van** *n.* furgone della polizia, furgone cellulare.

**policewoman** *n.* donna poliziotto.

**policy** *n.* (pol.) politica; *wait-and-see —*, politica temporeggiatrice; (fig.) linea di condotta, direttiva; sagacia, accortezza; (provb.)

*honesty is the best* —, l'onestà è la miglior politica; polizza (di assicurazione); *to take out a* —, assicurarsi. **-holder** *n.* assicurato.

**poliomyelitis** *n.* (med.) poliomielite *f.*

**Polish**[1] *adj.* polacco; *n.* (language) polacco, la lingua polacca.

**polish**[2] *n.* vernice *f.*, lustro; (for floor) cera; (for shoes) lucido, crema; (for nails) smalto; lucentezza, brillantezza; (fig.) raffinatezza, eleganza, finezza; (fam.) *to give something a* —, lucidare qualcosa; *tr.* lucidare, pulire, lustrare, verniciare, brillare; lisciare, levigare; (fig.) raffinare, rendere elegante; ingentilire, dirozzare; *intr.* prendere la vernice, lisciarsi; *to — off*, sbrigare, portare a termine; *to — off a meal*, divorare un pasto, mangiarsi un intero pasto; *to — off the enemy*, liquidare il nemico; *to — up*, pulire; ravvivare; (fig.) perfezionare, ripassare, rivedere. **-ed** *adj.* lucido, lucente, ripulito, levigato; (fig.) raffinato, distinto. **-er** *n.* (person) lucidatore; *French* —, lucidatore di mobili; (substance) liquido, pasta per lucidare, (for floors) cera; (cloth, rag) strofinaccio; (machine) lucidatrice. **-ing** *n.* lucidatura, lustratura, verniciatura, brillantatura.

**polite** *adj.* cortese, gentile, garbato; educato, colto, raffinato; — *society*, il bel mondo, la gente colta. **-ness** *n.* cortesia, gentilezza, garbo, belle maniere *f.pl.*

**Politian** *pr.n.* Poliziano.

**politic** *adj.* sagace, prudente, accorto, abile; utile; *the body* —, lo Stato, la Nazione sotto l'aspetto politico. **-al** *adj.* politico; *-al party*, partito politico.

**politician** *n.* uomo politico, statista *m., f.*; (derog.) politicante *m., f.*

**politics** *n.* politica; *foreign* —, la politica estera; *to go into* —, fare la carriera politica; *to go in for* —, dedicarsi alla politica; *to talk* —, parlare di politica; *to dabble in* —, fare della politica; *what are his* —?, quali sono le sue idee politiche?

**polity** *n.* regime politico, organizzazione di governo, lo Stato.

**polka** *n.* (dance) polca. **-dot** *n.* *blue polka-dot tie*, cravatta blu a pallini.

**poll**[1] *n.* (lit.) testa; (pol.) votazione; voti *m.pl.*; *heavy* —, alta percentuale di votanti; *to declare the result of the* —, proclamare i risultati della votazione; *to go to the* —, recarsi a votare, andare alle urne; *to head the* —, riscuotere il maggior numero di voti; *to be bottom of the* —, riscuotere il minor numero di voti, (pop.) reggere il fanale di coda; *opinion — survey*, indagine demoscopica; *Gallup* —, sondaggio Gallup (Ital. equiv., Istituto Doxa); *tr.* raccogliere (voti).

**poll**[2] *tr.* tosare; svettare, cimare, potare.

**pollack** *n.* (ichth.) pollacchio.

**pollard** *n.* albero cimato, capitozza; (zool.) animale senza corna; *tr.* cimare, capitozzare, svettare.

**pollen** *n.* (bot.) polline *m.*, polverina, pulviscolo.

**pollinat-e** *tr.* (bot.) impollinare, fecondare. **-ion** *n.* (bot.) impollinazione, fecondazione.

**polling** *n.* votazione, elezione. **-booth** *n.* cabina elettorale. **-district, -station** *n.* sezione elettorale.

**poll-tax** *n.* testatico.

**pollut-e** *tr.* contaminare, sporcare, inquinare; (fig.) corrompere, violare, profanare. **-er** *n.* contaminatore, corruttore, profanatore. **-ion** *n.* contaminazione, corruzione; inquinamento; (fig.) profanazione.

**Pollux** *pr.n.* (myth.; astron.) Polluce.

**Polly** *pr.n.f.* (dimin. of **Mary**) Marietta; (fam.) nomignolo di un pappagallo.

**polo** *n.* polo; *water* —, palla a nuoto.

**polonaise** *n.* (cost.; mus.) polacca.

**poltroon** *n.* codardo, vigliacco. **-ery** *n.* codardia, vigliaccheria.

**poly-** *pref.* poli-, multi-.

**poly-andry** *n.* poliandria. **-anthus** *n.* (bot.) tazzetta. **-archy** *n.* poliarchia. **-chromatic, -chrome, -chromic** *adj.* policromatico, policromo, multicolore. **-gamist** *n.* poligamo. **-gamous** *adj.* poligamo. **-gamy** *n.* poligamia. **-glot** *adj., n.* poliglotta *m., f.* **-gon** *n.* (geom.) poligono. **-gonal** *adj.* (geom.) poligonale. **-graph** *n.* poligrafo. **-graphy** *n.* poligrafia. **-hedral** *adj.* (geom.) poliedrico. **-hedron** *n.* (geom.) poliedro.

**Polynesia** *n.* (geog.) Polinesia. **-n** *adj.* polinesiano.

**Polyphemus** *pr.n.* Polifemo.

**poly-phonic** *adj.* polifonico. **-phony** *n.* polifonia. **-ptych** *n.* (paint.) polittico. **-style** *adj., n.* (archit.) polistilo. **-syllabic** *adj.* polisillabo, polisillabico. **-syllable** *n.* polisillabo. **-technic** *adj.* politecnico; *n.* (scuola) politecnica. **-theism** *n.* politeismo. **-theist** *n.* politeista *m., f.* **-thene** *n.* (chem.) politene *m.*

**pomace** *n.* (cidermaking) polpa di mele; (industr.) residui, sansa *f.*

**pomade, pomatum** *n.* pomata.

**pome** *n.* (bot.) pomo; (poet.) mela; (herald.) globo.

**pomegranate** *n.* melagrana; — *tree*, melagrano.

**Pomeranian** *adj.* della Pomerania; *n.* (dog) cane *m.* della Pomerania, (fam.) pomer *m. indecl.*

**pommel** *n.* pomo; *tr.* (fam.) picchiare.

**pomp** *n.* pompa, fasto, sfarzo, sfoggio; ostentazione.

**Pompei** *pr.n.* (geog.) Pompei *f.* **-an** *adj.* pompeiano.

**Pompey** *pr.n.* Pompeo.

**pompon** *n.* (cost.) pompon *m.*, fiocco.

**pomposity** *n.* pomposità, pompa; (of style) ampollosità; enfasi *f.*

**pompous** *adj.* pomposo; altisonante; gonfio; ampolloso; enfatico. **-ness** *n.* See **pomposity.**

**ponce** *n.* (slang) ruffiano.

**poncho** *n.* poncio.

**pond** *n.* stagno, laghetto, specchio d'acqua; (horse-pond) abbeveratoio; (fish nursery) vivaio, peschiera.

**ponder** *tr., intr.* meditare, ponderare, riflettere.

**ponderab-le** *adj.* ponderabile. **-ility, -leness** *n.* ponderabilità.

**ponderation** *n.* ponderazione.

**ponderingly** *adv.* ponderatamente.

**ponderosity** *n.* ponderosità; (of style) pesantezza, ampollosità.

**ponderous** *adj.* ponderoso, pesante, massiccio; (of style) pesante, ampolloso. **-ness** *n.* See **ponderosity.**

**pond-lily** *n.* See **water-lily.**

**pondweed** *n.* (bot.) erba tinca, lingua d'acqua.

**poniard** *n.* pugnale *m.*

**Pontic** *adj.* pontico; *the — Sea*, il Ponto Eusino.

**pontifex** *n.* (Rom. hist.) pontefice *m.*

**pontiff** *n.* pontefice *m.*, papa *m.*; *Sovereign* —, Sommo Pontefice.

**pontific-al** *adj.* (of the Pope) pontificio; (of a bishop) pontificale; *n.* (book) pontificale; *pl.* paramenti pontificali. **-ate** *n.* pontificato; *intr.* pontificare.

**Pontine Marshes** *pr.n.* (geog.) le Paludi Pontine.

**Pontius Pilate** *pr.n.* Ponzio Pilato.

**pontoon**[1] *n.* pontone *m.*; chiatta; — *bridge*, ponte *m.* di barche.

**pontoon**[2] *n.* (cards) tressette *m.*

**pony** *n.* puledro; pony *m.*, cavallino; (pop.) *Shank's* —, cavallo di San Francesco; (slang) venticinque sterline *f.pl.*

**poodle** *n.* cane *m.* barbone; *miniature* —, barboncino.

**poof** *n.* (slang, derog.) omosessuale.

**pooh** *excl.* poh!; oibo! **-pooh** *tr.* prendere alla leggera, mettere in ridicolo, disdegnare.

**pool**[1] *n.* laghetto, stagno, specchio d'acqua; pozzanghera; (London) il Tamigi a valle del Ponte di Londra; (for bathing) piscina; (bibl.) — *of Bethesda*, piscina probatica.

**pool**[2] *n.* banco, insieme delle

poste; *football* —, totocalcio; (comm.) fondo comune, pool *m.*; *typing* —, servizio di dattilografia; sindacato, cartello; *tr.* mettere in comune; *to — resources* fare borsa comune.

**poop** *n.* (naut.) poppa, cassero di poppa.

**poor** *adj.* povero, indigente, bisognoso; *the* —, i poveri; *the -er classes,* il popolo; — *as a church mouse,* povero in canna; — *in natural resources,* povero di risorse naturali; (fig.) scarso, meschino, misero, gretto, mediocre, modesto; (of soil) magro; — *me!,* povero me!; — *fellow!,* — *man!,* poverino!; — *thing!,* poverino! *m.*, poverina *f.*, (of animal) povera bestiola!; *a — consolation,* una magra consolazione; *a — crop,* un magro raccolto; *a — digestion,* una cattiva digestione; *a — driver,* un guidatore mediocre; *a — excuse,* una scusa meschina; — *health,* salute cagionevole; — *food,* cibo poco appetitoso; *a — memory,* una memoria labile; — *quality,* qualità scadente; *a — speaker,* un oratore mediocre; (theatr.) *a — attendance,* un pubblico scarso; (USA, colonies) — *whites,* bianchi poveri; *to be — at mathematics,* essere debole in matematica; *to cut a — figure,* fare brutta figura; *to have a — opinion of someone,* stimare poco qualcuno; *in my — opinion,* secondo il mio modesto parere.

**poor-box** *n.* cassetta per l'elemosina.

**poorhouse** *n.* albergo dei poveri.

**poor-law** *n.* legge per l'assistenza ai poveri.

**poorly** *adj.* malaticcio, indisposto; *to feel* —, star male, non sentirsi troppo bene; *adv.* male, poveramente, scarsamente.

**poorness** *n.* povertà, miseria; scarsezza, mediocrità

**poor-spirited** *adj.* pusillanime, timido.

**pop**[1] *adj.* (fam.) popolare; — *singer,* cantante yé-yé. *m., f.*

**pop**[2] *n.* (fam.) babbo, papà.

**pop**[3] *n.* gassosa, bevanda effervescente.

**pop**[4] *adv., excl.* crac!, pum!, pam!; *to go* —, schioccare, esplodere, far pam, scattare.

**pop**[4] *intr.* schioccare, scoccare; (of cork) saltare, saltare via; (fam.) *to — in,* fare una visitina; *I've just -ped in,* sono venuto a farti una visitina; *to — off,* scappare, (slang) crepare; *to — out,* uscire improvvisamente, saltar fuori; *to — up,* saltare su, saltar fuori; *to — up to London,* fare un salto a Londra; *tr.* ficcare, mettere; *to — something into a drawer,* ficcare qualcosa in una cassetta; *to — one's head out of the window,* sporgere la testa dalla finestra; *to — something down,* mettere qualcosa per iscritto; (fam.) *to — the question,* chiedere in sposa, fare la dichiarazione; (slang) impegnare, portare al Monte di Pietà.

**popcorn** *n.* granturco soffiato.

**pope** *n.* (eccl.) papa *m.*, pontefice *m.*; il Santo Padre; *Pope Joan,* Papessa Giovanna; (Orthodox priest) pope *m.*, papasso.

**popery** *n.* (pejor.) papismo.

**pop-gun** *n.* (toy) pistola ad aria compressa, scacciacani *m.*

**popinjay** *n.* damerino, zerbinotto.

**poplar** *n.* (bot.) pioppo; *silver* —, albaro, alberello.

**poplin** *n.* (text.) popeline *f.*

**poppet** *n.* (fam.) piccina, pupazzola; *what a —!,* che bella bambola!; *listen* —, senti, cara.

**poppy** *n.* (bot.) papavero.

**poppycock** *n.* (fam.) sciocchezze *f.pl.*, balle *f.pl.*

**poppy-coloured, poppy-red** *adj.* rosso papavero.

**populace** *n.* popolo; (pejor.) plebaglia, popolaccio.

**popular** *adj.* popolare, del popolo, del volgo, popolano, popolaresco; ben voluto, ben visto, popolare; alla moda, in voga; — *error,* errore comune; — *government,* governo democratico; — *manual,* libro divulgativo; — *opinion,* opinione generale; — *prices,* prezzi popolari; *to make oneself* —, farsi benvolere, farsi conoscere.

**popularity** *n.* popolarità, favore *m.* popolare.

**populariz-e** *tr.* popolarizzare, volgarizzare, divulgare. **-ation** *n.* popolarizzazione, volgarizzazione, divulgazione.

**populate** *tr.* popolare; *thickly -d district,* zona densamente popolata.

**population** *n.* popolazione; stato d'anime; *increase in* —, incremento demografico; *fall in* —, diminuzione della popolazione, spopolamento; abitanti *m.pl.*; popolo.

**populous** *adj.* densamente popolato, popoloso. **-ness** *n.* densità di popolazione.

**porcelain** *n.* porcellana; *attrib.* di porcellana. **-clay** *n.* caolino.

**porch** *n.* portico.

**porcine** *adj.* porcino, suino.

**porcupine** *n.* porcospino.

**pore**[1] *n.* (anat.; bot.) poro.

**pore**[2] *intr. to — over,* meditare (su), studiare; *to — over a book,* essere assorto nella lettura di un libro.

**pork** *n.* (cul.) carne di maiale, carne suina. **-butcher** *n.* salumaio, salumiere, pizzicagnolo.

**porker** *n.* giovane maiale *m.*, porco.

**pork-pie** *n.* pasticcio di carne di maiale.

**porn** *n.* (fam.) abbrev. of **pornography,** *q.v.*

**pornograph-y** *n.* pornografia. **-ic** *adj.* pornografico.

**porous** *adj.* poroso, permeabile. **-ness, porosity** *n.* porosità.

**porphyry** *n.* porfido.

**porpoise** *n.* marsovino, focena, porco marino.

**porridge** *n.* pappa di fiocchi d'avena.

**porringer** *n.* scodella.

**port**[1] *n.* porto; — *of call,* scalo, approdo; — *of registry,* porto di immatricolazione; — *charges,* tasse portuali; *naval* —, porto militare; — *admiral,* comandante di porto; (naut.) babordo, sinistra; *hard to* —, tutto a sinistra; *tr.* (naut.) girare a sinistra; — *your helm!,* accosta sinistra!

**port**[2] *n.* vino di Porto.

**port**[3] *n.* portello, foro, apertura; (Scot.) porta.

**port**[4] *tr.* (mil.) portare ad armacollo; — *arms!,* portat'arm!

**portab-le** *adj.* portabile, portatile, trasportabile; — *typewriter,* macchina per scrivere portatile. **-ility** *n.* l'essere portatile.

**portage** *n.* porto, trasporto; trasporto di una barca oltre una rapida; *tr.* trasportare (battelli) via terra.

**portal** *n.* (archit.) portale *m.*, portone *m.*

**portative** *adj.* portativo, atto a portare.

**portcullis** *n.* saracinesca.

**portend** *tr.* presagire, preannunciare, predire.

**portent** *n.* presagio, pronostico; (fig.) prodigio, portento. **-ous** *adj.* presago, funesto, di cattivo augurio; (fig.) prodigioso, portentoso.

**porter**[1] *n.* portinaio, portiere, custode *m.*; *-'s lodge,* portineria; (rlwy.) portabagagli *m.*; (at market, etc.) facchino, portatore; **-age** *n.* porto, trasporto; facchinaggio.

**porter**[2] *n.* birra scura.

**portfolio** *n.* cartella, busta; (of shares) portafoglio; (pol.) portafoglio, dicastero.

**porthole** *n.* (naut.) oblò *m.*, portella.

**portico** *n.* (archit.) portico, colonnato, pronao.

**portion** *n.* porzione; parte *f.*; *marriage* —, dote *f.*; (fig.) destino, sorte *f.*; *tr.* ripartire, dividere, assegnare; *to — out,* spartire, distribuire.

**portl-y** *adj.* corpulento, grassoccio; dignitoso, imponente. **-iness** *n.* grassezza, corpulenza; portamento distinto; prestanza, presenza.

**portmanteau** *n.* valigia; baule *m.*; (fig.) — *word,* parola macedonia.

**portrait** *n.* ritratto; effigie *f.*; *full-length* —, (ritratto a) figura intera; *half-length* —, mezzobusto; *to have one's — taken,*

farsi fare il ritratto; *to sit for one's —*, posare per un ritratto; (fig.) descrizione.

**portrait-gallery** *n.* galleria di ritratti. **-painter, portraitist** *n.* ritrattista *m., f.* **-painting** *n.* ritrattistica.

**portraiture** *n.* ritratto, pittura; arte di ritrarre, ritrattistica; (fig.) descrizione.

**portray** *tr.* ritrarre, fare il ritratto di, effigiare; dipingere, descrivere, rappresentare. **~al** *n.* ritratto, pittura, descrizione, rappresentazione. **~er** *n.* ritrattista *m., f.*, pittore, descrittore.

**Portug~al** *pr.n.* (geog.) Portogallo. **~uese** *adj., n.* portoghese *m., f.*; (zool.) *~uese man-of-war*, fisalia; (language) il portoghese.

**pose** *n.* posa; atteggiamento; affettazione; *tr.* far posare, mettere in posa; *to — a question*, proporre un quesito, fare una domanda; *intr.* posare, mettersi in posa; assumere una posa; *to — as*, atteggiarsi a, fingere di essere; *to — as a martyr*, atteggiarsi a martire.

**Poseidon** *pr.n.* (myth.) Poseidone *m.*

**poser** *n.* domanda imbarazzante, problema *m.* insolubile.

**poseur** *n.* posatore.

**posh** *adj.* (fam.) elegante; chic, snob; *tr.* (fam.) *to — oneself up*, mettersi in ghingheri.

**posing** *n.* atteggiamento, il posare.

**posit** *tr.* (log.) affermare, enunciare un postulato, premettere; collocare.

**position** *n.* posizione; situazione; posto; posa; posto, impiego; condizione, rango, grado; (mil.) posizione; (sport) posto in classifica; (fig.) atteggiamento, punto di vista; *in —*, a posto; *out of —*, fuori posto; *to be in a — to*, essere in grado di; *tr.* collocare, mettere in posizione; (mil.) piazzare.

**positive** *adj.* positivo, affermativo, esplicito; (fig.) certo, sicuro, convinto; (gramm.; photog.) positivo; *to be — that*, essere sicuro che; (fam.) *he's a — nuisance*, è proprio un seccatore; *n.* (gramm.) positivo; (photog.) positiva. **~ly** *adv.* positivamente, assolutamente, addirittura. **~ness** *n.* positività, certezza, sicurezza; tono perentorio.

**positiv~ism** *n.* (philos.) positivismo. **~ist** *n.* positivista *m., f.*

**posse** *n.* drappello (di agenti di polizia).

**possess** *tr.* possedere, avere, essere possessore di, tenere; *all I —*, tutti i miei averi, tutto quello che ho; *to be ~ed of a quality*, essere dotato di una qualità; *to — one's soul in patience*, armarsi di pazienza; *what ~ed you to do this?*, che cosa ti spinse a far questo?; *to — oneself of something*, impadronirsi di qualcosa; *to be ~ed by*, essere ossesso da; *one ~ed*, un ossesso.

**possession** *n.* possesso; *to take — of*, prendere possesso di; *to be in — of*, possedere, essere in possesso di; (of house, etc.) *with vacant —*, libero subito; *pl. personal ~s*, beni personali; *British ~s overseas*, possedimenti britannici d'oltremare; (fig.) ossessione.

**possessive** *adj.* (gramm.) possessivo; (fig.) possessivo, soffocante, opprimente; *n.* (gramm.) possessivo. **~ness** *n.* senso di possesso.

**possessor** *n.* possessore, possessore, proprietario, possidente *m., f.*

**possibility** *n.* possibilità; eventualità; *— of success*, possibilità di successo; *to foresee all possibilities*, prevedere tutte le eventualità; (fam.) *it's a —*, è possibile.

**possibl~e** *adj.* possible, eventuale; *it's — that*, può darsi che, forse (che), è possibile che; *as much as —*, quanto possibile; *as early as —*, quanto prima; effettuabile; *to do one's —*, far tutto il possibile; (sport) *to score a —*, fare il massimo. **~y** *adv.* possibilmente, può darsi, forse, eventualmente; *I cannot ~y*, non posso assolutamente; *it can't ~y be!*, impossibile!

**possum** *n.* see **opossum**; (fam.) *to play —*, fare il morto, star fermo.

**post**[1] *n.* palo, pilastro, colonna; (of door, *etc.*) stipite *m.*, montante *m.*; sostegno, puntello; (naut.) dritto; (fig.) *deaf as a —*, sordo come una campana; *from pillar to —*, da Erode a Pilato; (sport) punto di partenza; *to go to the —*, prendere parte alla corsa, correre; *to be left at the —*, mancare la partenza, non partire; traguardo, arrivo; *to be first past the —*, vincere, arrivare primo; *tr.* affissare, affiggere; *— no bills*, divieto d'affissione; *to — a notice on the board*, esporre un avviso sull'albo, affiggere un avviso sul tabellone.

**post**[2] *n.* posta, corrispondenza; corriere *m.*; vettura postale; posta, servizio postale; posta, ufficio postale; distribuzione; *parcel —*, servizio pacchi postali; *to send by parcel —*, spedire come pacco postale; *by return of —*, a volta di corriere, a giro di posta; *to miss the —*, impostare troppo tardi; *to take a letter to the —*, portare una lettera alla posta, impostare una lettera; (journ.) *the Evening Post*, il Corriere della Sera; (game) *general —*, (fig.) rimpasto, rimaneggiamento; *tr.* impostare, imbucare, spedire per posta; (comm.) registrare, trascrivere (sul libro mastro); (fig.) *to keep someone ~ed*, tenere qualcuno al corrente; *intr.* (hist.) viaggiare con cavalli di posta; (fig.) andare in fretta, affrettarsi.

**post**[3] *n.* posto; *to remain at one's —*, rimanere al proprio posto; (mil.) postazione posto; *trading —*, stazione commerciale; *tr.* mettere, collocare; postare, appostare; (mil.) *to — a sentry*, mettere una sentinella; *to be ~ed to a unit*, essere assegnato ad un reparto.

**post**[4]**-** *prep., pref.* post-, dopo-; *— bellum*, dopo la guerra; *— meridiem* (p.m.), pomeridiano, dopo pranzo.

**postage** *n.* porto; affrancatura; spese postali; *additional —*, soprattassa postale; *— paid*, porto pagato; *rates of —*, tariffa postale.

**postage-stamp** *n.* francobollo.

**postal** *adj.* postale; *error in — delivery*, disguido postale; *— order*, vaglia *m.* postale.

**post-bag** *n.* sacco postale.

**postcard** *n.* cartolina postale; *picture —*, cartolina illustrata.

**post-chaise** *n.* corriera, diligenza.

**postdate** *tr.* posdatare, datare con data posteriore.

**poster** *n.* affisso, cartellone *m.*, manifesto pubblicitario.

**poste restante** *n.* fermo posta, fermo in posta.

**posterior** *adj.* posteriore; *n.* (fam.) deretano. **~ity** *n.* posteriorità.

**posterity** *n.* posterità, i posteri *m.pl.*, discendenza.

**postern** *n.* pusterla, porta posteriore.

**postfix** *n.* (ling.) suffisso.

**post-free** *adj.* franco di porto.

**post-graduate** *adj.* (studi) dopo la laurea; *n.* laureato che continua a studiare.

**post-haste** *adv.* in gran fretta. **-horn** *n.* cornetto.

**posthumous** *adj.* postumo. **~ly** *adv.* dopo la morte; *published ~ly*, pubblicato postumo.

**postillion** *n.* postiglione *m.*

**post-impressionism** *n.* (art) postimpressionismo.

**posting** *n.* (ger. of **post**[1]) affissione; (ger. of **post**[2]) il viaggiare con cavalli di posta; (mailing) spedizione per posta, impostazione; (comm.) registrazione, trascrizione; (ger. of **post**[3]) postazione, collocamento; (mil.) assegnazione.

**postman** *n.* portalettere *m.* postino. **~mark** *n.* timbro postale, bollo della posta; *tr.* timbrare.

**postmaster** *n.* direttore di ufficio postale; *— General*, direttore generale delle poste, ministro delle Poste e Telecomunicazioni.

**postmeridian** *adj.* pomeridiano, del pomeriggio.

**postmistress** *n.* direttrice di ufficio postale.

**post-mortem** *adj., adv.* dopo

la morte; *n.* autopsia; (fig.) discussione dopo l'avvenimento.
**post-natal** *adj.* posteriore alla nascita; (med.) acquisito. **-nuptial** *adj.* posteriore alle nozze.
**post(-)office** *n.* posta, ufficio postale; *general —* posta centrale; *sub —, branch —,* succursale *f.* postale; *— box,* casella postale; *— clerk,* impiegato postale; *— savings bank,* cassa di risparmio postale.
**postpon-e** *tr.* posporre, rinviare, rimandare, differire; *to — a decision,* soprassedere ad una decisione; *intr.* (med.) tardare. **-able** *adj.* rinviabile, che si può rimandare, posponibile. **-ement** *n.* rinvio, posposizione; differimento; dilazione; (leg.) deroga.
**postprandial** *adj.* dopo un pranzo, posteriore al pranzo; *— eloquence,* eloquenza conviviale; *— nap,* siesta.
**postscript** *n.* poscritto.
**postulant** *n.* (eccl.) postulante *m., f.*
**postulat-e** *n.* (geom.; leg.) postulato; *tr., intr.* (eccl.) postulare; (geom.; log.) porre come postulato; chiedere, domandare. **-ion** *n.* postulazione.
**postur-e** *n.* positura, posizione, postura, posa, atteggiamento, stato, condizione; *tr.* posare, atteggiare, mettere in posa; *intr.* assumere un atteggiamento, assumere una posizione; *to — as,* fare, fingere di essere. **-ing** *n.* posa.
**post-war** *adj.* del dopoguerra, pos(t)bellico; *the — period,* il dopoguerra.
**posy** *n.* mazzetto di fiori.
**pot** *n.* vaso; brocca, boccale *m.*; (coffee-) caffettiera; (tea-) teiera; (cul.) pentola, marmitta, pignatta; *to keep the — boiling,* far bollire la pentola, (fig.) procurarsi il necessario per vivere, tirare avanti; *-s and pans,* batteria da cucina; (for jam, *etc.*) barattolo, recipiente *m.*; *melting-pot,* crogiuolo; *chamber-pot,* vaso da notte; (provb.) *the — calls the kettle black,* il ciuco dà del bue all'asino, da che pulpito viene la predica!; (fam.) *a big —,* un pezzo grosso; *-s of money,* un sacco di soldi; *to go to —,* andare in malora; *to take a — at,* sparare contro, (fig.) provare; (billiards) colpo che manda in buca, biglia; (slang) droga; *tr.* conservare in vaso; (hortic.) piantare in vaso; (billiards) *to — the red,* mandare la palla rossa in buca, far biglia; *intr.* (fam.) *to — at,* sparare contro.
**potable** *adj.* potabile, bevibile.
**potash** *n.* (miner.) potassa; *carbonate of —,* carbonato di potassio.
**potassium** *n.* (chem.) potassio.
**potation** *n.* bevuta, libazione.
**potato** *n.* patata; (bot.) pomo di terra; *sweet —,* batata, patata americana; (cul.) *boiled -es,* patate lesse; *chip(ped) -es, fried -es,* patatine fritte; *- chips,* chips *m.pl.*; *mashed -es, creamed -es,* purè di patate; *— salad,* patate all'olio. **-spirit** *n.* alcool di patate. **-starch** *n.* fecola di patate.
**pot-bell-y** *n.* pancione *m.* **-ied** *adj.* panciuto, corpacciuto.
**pot-boiler** *n.* libro scritto per far quattrini; (fam.) romanzo da serva; (person) scriba *m.* **-boy** *n.* garzone di osteria.
**poteen, potheen** *n.* whisky irlandese di contrabbando.
**pot-ency** *n.* potenza, forza, efficacia. **-ent** *adj.* potente, forte, efficace; (herald.) potenziato.
**potentate** *n.* potentato.
**potential** *adj.* potenziale, latente, eventuale; *n.* potenziale *m.*, rendimento. **-ity** *n.* potenzialità; *situation full of -ities,* situazione promettente.
**pothanger** *n.* see **pothook.**
**pother** *n.* polverone *m.*; (fig.) chiasso, confusione; *to make a —,* fare un gran chiasso, far tante storie; *to be in a —,* essere agitato; *tr.* infastidire, far arrabbiare; *intr.* far confusione, far chiasso, far storie.
**pot-herbs** *n.* ortaggi *m.pl.*
**pot-hole** *n.* (geol.) marmitta; (cave) spelonca, caverna; (in road) buca, pozzanghera.
**pothol-er** *n.* speleologo. **-ing** *n.* speleologia.
**pothook** *n.* gancio (del camino); (fig. of letter) asta.
**pothouse** *n.* bettola, osteria.
**pot-hunter** *n.* (fam.) cacciatore di premi.
**potion** *n.* pozione, bevanda; *love-potion,* filtro d'amore.
**Potiphar** *pr.n.* (bibl.) Putifarre.
**pot-luck** *n.* pasto alla buona, quello che c'è; *to take —,* mangiare alla buona, mangiare un boccone.
**pot-pourri** *n.* mescolanza, miscellanea; zibaldone *m.*; (mus.) selezione.
**potsherd** *n.* coccio, frammento.
**pot-shot** *n. to take a — at,* sparare a casaccio contro; (fig.) provare, tentare il colpo.
**pottage** *n.* minestra; (bibl.) *a mess of —,* un piatto di lenticchie.
**potted** *adj.* in scatola, inscatolato, conservato; (hortic.) in vaso, invasato.
**potter**[1] *n.* vasaio, stovigliaio, pentolaio; *-'s wheel,* tornio da vasaio.
**potter**[2] *intr. to — about,* gingillarsi, perdersi in bagatelle, baloccarsi; *to — away one's time,* perdere il tempo in inezie.
**pottery** *n.* ceramica, terraglie *f.pl.*, vasellame *m.*, stoviglie *f.pl.*; *the Potteries,* zone dove si fabbricano ceramiche.
**potty**[1] *adj.* (fam.) matto.
**potty**[2] *n.* (infant.) orinale *m.*
**pouch** *n.* borsa, sacchetto, tasca; (mil.) giberna; (zool.) marsupio; *tr.* intascare; gonfiare. **-ed, -y** *adj.* a forma di borsa; paffuto, gonfio.
**pouffe** *n.* (furn.) puf, sgabello imbottito.
**poulterer** *n.* pollivendolo, pollaiuolo; *-'s shop,* polleria.
**poultice** *n.* cataplasma *m.*, impiastro; (fam.) polentina; *tr.* applicare un cataplasma a.
**poultry** *n.* pollame *m.*, volatili *m.pl.*, gallinacei *m.pl.* domestici. **-farm** *n.* allevamento di gallinacei. **-yard** *n.* pollaio, bassa corte, cortile *m.* di pollaio.
**pounce** *n.* sbalzo, salto; *to make a —,* piombare (su), saltare (addosso a); artiglio; (art) spolvero; *tr.* (art) spolverare, spolverizzare; *intr.* piombare (su), saltare (addosso a); (fig.) *to — on,* cogliere al volo.
**pound**[1] *n.* (weight) libbra, (avoirdupois) 453·6 grammi, (troy) 373·248 grammi; (sterling), sterlina; *ten -s,* dieci sterline; *a five-pound note,* un biglietto da cinque sterline; *a question of -s, shillings and pence,* una questione di soldi; *intr.* (at mint) controllare il peso.
**pound**[2] *n.* recinto, chiuso; (for fish) camera della morte; (hydr. eng.) serbatoio; *tr.* rinchiudere, chiudere in un recinto, rinserrare.
**pound**[3] *n.* tonfo, colpo; (cider-m.) torchio da sidro; *tr.* pestare, battere, stritolare, frantumare, polverizzare; *-ed sugar,* zucchero in polvere; (fig.) *to — the piano,* pestare sul piano; *intr. to — along,* camminare faticosamente; *to — away at,* continuare a battere su; (of ship) *to — on the rocks,* schiantarsi sugli scogli, accasciare.
**poundage**[1] *n.* percentuale *f.*, commissione; (for postal order) tassa di emissione.
**poundage**[2] *n.* tassa per tenere il bestiame in recinto.
**pounder**[1] *n.* (of fish, *etc.*) *three-pounder,* del peso di tre libbre, da tre libbre; (artill.) *thirty-pounder,* pezzo da trenta, pezzo che lancia proiettili da trenta libbre.
**pounder**[2] *n.* pestello, mortaio; (person) pestatore.
**pound-foolish** *adj.* taccagno nelle piccole spese e prodigo nelle grandi.
**pounding** ger. of **pound**[3], *q.v.*; *n.* pestatura; (of feet, etc.) pestìo; (of ship) l'accasciare, schianto.
**pour** *tr.* versare, riversare; mescere; (metall.) colare; *to — cold water on something,* versare

acqua fredda su qualcosa; (fig.) dare una doccia fredda a qualcosa, scoraggiare qualcosa; *to — oil on troubled waters*, (fig.) mettere acqua sul fuoco, placare la tempesta; *intr.* riversarsi, scorrere; (of rain) scrosciare; *it is ~ing*, piove dirottamente; *it never rains but it ~s*, o troppo o niente, le disgrazie non vengono mai sole; (of sun) *to — through the window*, entrare a fiotti dalla finestra; *to — down*, *tr.* versare, *intr.* riversarsi, diluviare, (of rain) piovere a dirotto, (of sun) risplendere; *tears ~ed down her cheeks*, le lagrime le rigavano le gote; *to — forth*, *tr.* emettere, spandere, effondere, (fig.) esprimere, *intr.* sgorgare, (of people) riversarsi fuori; *to — in*, *tr.* versare, *intr.* entrare a fiotti, affluire, arrivare in massa; *to — in from all quarters*, affluire da tutte le parti; *to — off*, *tr.* travasare, *intr.* riversarsi, uscire a fiotti; *to — out*, *tr.* versare, mescere, effondere, (fig.) *to — out gifts*, elargire doni, *intr.* uscire, riversarsi fuori.

**pour-boire** *n.* mancia. **~parler** *n.* trattative *f.pl.* **~point** *n.* farsetto imbottito.

**pout**[1] *n.* (ichth.) gado, merlango.

**pout**[2] *n.* broncio, grugno; *intr.* fare il broncio, fare il grugno, ammusare, sporgere le labbra. **~er** *n.* chi fa il broncio; *~er pigeon*, piccione gozzuto. **~ing** *adj.* (of lip) sporgente.

**poverty** *n.* povertà; miseria; indigenza; angustia; (fig.) penuria, mancanza, scarsità; (of style) meschinità, scipitezza.

**poverty-stricken** *adj.* caduto in miseria; d'aspetto miserabile, misero.

**powder** *n.* polvere *f.*; *to reduce to —*, ridurre in polvere, polverizzare; (mil.; hunt.) polvere da sparo; (pharm.) polvere, polverina; (cosmetic) cipria; *baking —*, lievito artificiale; *tooth —*, dentifricio in polvere; *tr.* polverizzare; (cul.) spolverizzare, cospargere di polvere; (cosmetic) incipriare; *to — one's face*, incipriarsi; *intr.* polverizzarsi.

**powder-blue** *n.* blu chiaro. **-box** *n.* scatola per cipria. **~compact** *n.* portacipria *m. indecl.*

**powdered** *adj.* in polvere, cosparso di polvere; (of face, wig) incipriato; (herald.) seminato.

**powder-flash, -horn** *n.* fiaschetta per polvere da sparo.

**powderiness** *n.* friabilità; stato polveroso.

**powder-magazine** *n.* polveriera, santabarbara. **-mill** *n.* polverificio. **-puff** *n.* piumino per la cipria. **-room** *n.* (naval) santabarbara; gabinetto per signore.

**powdery** *adj.* polveroso, coperto di polvere; friabile, polverizzabile.

**power** *n.* potenza; potere *m.*; (theol.) potestà; facoltà, capacità; potenza; autorità; *the ~s that be*, l'autorità costituita; *discretionary ~s*, poteri discrezionali; *full ~s*, pieni poteri; *— behind the throne*, eminenza grigia; (leg.) *— of attorney*, procura; (pol.) *to be in —*, essere al potere; *to come into —*, giungere al potere; *balance of —*, equilibrio politico; (fig.) *to do all in one's —*, fare tutto il possibile; *it is not in my —*, non mi è possibile, non mi'è dato; (fam.) *it will do you a — of good*, ti farà un gran bene; *more — to your elbow*, auguri!, buona fortuna!; (mech.; electr.) forza, energia; *water —*, energia idraulica; *motive —*, forza motrice; *horse-power*, cavallo vapore; corrente *f.* industriale; rendimento; (fig.) *staying —*, resistenza; (math.) potenza; *tr.* fornire di energia; motorizzare.

**power-driven** *adj.* azionato da motore.

**powered** *adj.* che ha potenza; *high-powered*, di grande potenza, ad alta potenza; *high-powered car*, macchina potente.

**powerful** *adj.* potente, possente, poderoso; forte; efficace. **~ness** *n.* potenza; vigore *m.*; efficacia.

**power-house** *n.* See **power-station.**

**powerless** *adj.* impotente, incapace, debole, inefficace; *to be — to do something*, non poter far qualcosa, essere incapace di far qualcosa; *they are — in the matter*, non ci possono fare niente. **~ness** *n.* impotenza, incapacità, inefficacia.

**power-loom** *n.* telaio meccanico. **-station** *n.* centrale elettrica.

**pow-wow** *n.* stregone *m.* (fra i pellirosse); (fam.) riunione amichevole, colloquio.

**pox** *n.* (lit.) peste *f.*; *excl. a — on you!*, che ti venga un cancro!; (slang) sifilide *f.*

**practicab-le** *adj.* praticabile, fattibile. **~ility, ~leness** *n.* praticabilità, possibilità.

**practical** *adj.* pratico, fattibile, possibile; (of person) pratico, esperto, realista; *for — purposes*, in pratica; effettivo, vero; *— joke*, beffa, tiro birbone. **~ity, ~ness** *n.* praticità. **~ly** *adv.* praticamente, in effetto, effettivamente; quasi, virtualmente.

**practice** *n.* pratica; *in —*, in pratica, in effetti, effettivamente; *to put into —*, mettere in pratica, attuare; esercizio; clientela, clienti *m.pl.*; *to have a large —*, avere una vasta clientela; consuetudine *f.*, abitudine *f.*, uso, regola; *normal —*, uso comune, regola; *to make a — of*, avere l'abitudine di, usare, solere; *out of —*, fuori esercizio, disabituato, disavvezzo; (provb.) *— makes perfect*, con l'esercizio si raggiunge la perfezione, il fare insegna fare; (mus.) esercizio, studio; (sport) *— game*, allenamento; (fig.) *sharp —*, trucco, modo di fare poco onesto.

**practis-e** *tr.* esercitare, esercitarsi in, fare esercizio di; *to — speaking Italian*, esercitarsi in italiano; *to — medicine*, esercitare la medicina; praticare, mettere in pratica; *— what you preach*, metti in pratica ciò che predichi; *to — a shot*, esercitarsi (nel fare un colpo); *to — the same method*, usare lo stesso modo; *to — deceit on*, ingannare; *intr.* esercitarsi, fare esercizio, addestrarsi, impratichirsi; *to — on the piano*, fare esercizi di pianoforte; *where does he — ?*, dove esercita la sua professione?; (sport) allenarsi. **~ed** *adj.* esperto, pratico, abile per lunga pratica, perito. **~er** *n.* praticante *m.*, *f.* **~ing** *adj.* che esercita la professione, professionista; (rel.) praticante; *n.* pratica, esercizio; (sport) allenamento.

**practitioner** *n.* professionista *m.*; (med.) *general —*, medico generico.

**praetor** *n.* (Rom. hist.) pretore *m.* **~ial** *adj.* pretoriale, pretorio. **~ian** *adj.*, *n.* pretoriano.

**pragmatic** *adj.* prammatico; (hist.) *— sanction*, prammatica sanzione; (fig.) dogmatico; (pejor.) presuntuoso. **~al** *adj.* (philos.) prammatico; (fig.) dogmatico, presuntuoso.

**pragmat-ism** *n.* pragmatismo; (fig.) pedanteria. **~ist** *n.* pragmatista *m.* **~ize** *tr.* razionalizzare, rappresentare come reale.

**Prague** *pr.n.* (geog.) Praga.

**prairie** *n.* prateria; (orn.) *— chicken*, tetraone *m.*; *— oyster*, uovo all'ostrica.

**praise** *n.* lode *f.*; encomio, elogio; *— be to God!*, Dio sia lodato!; *hymn of —*, laude *f.*; *his conduct is beyond all —*, la sua condotta è al di sopra di ogni elogio; *he was loud in his ~s*, egli fece alte lodi; *to sing the ~s of*, lodare al cielo, portare alle stelle; *to damn with faint —*, lodare in modo maligno; *tr.* lodare, fare l'elogio di, elogiare, encomiare; *to — to the skies*, alzare al cielo, portare alle stelle. **~worthiness** *n.* lodevolezza. **~worthy** *adj.* lodevole, degno di lode, encomiabile.

**pram** *n.* carrozzina per bambini, carrozzella.

**pranc-e** *intr.* (horse) impennarsi; (of child) saltellare, balzellare; (of adult) camminare pavoneggiandosi, saltellare. **~ing** *adj.* (of horse) che si impenna; (of person) saltellante.

**prandial** *adj.* (joc.) del pranzo.

**prank** *n.* monelleria, birichinata, burla; *to play a — on someone*

fare un tiro a qualcuno; *to play all sorts of -s*, farne di tutti i colori.

**prat-e** *intr.* ciarlare, cianciare, fare discorsi oziosi. **-ing** *adj.* chiacchierone, loquace.

**prattl-e** *n.* ciarla, ciancia, cicaleccio; (of child) balbettìo, cinguettìo; *intr.* chiacchierare fanciullescamente, cianciare, ciarlare; (of child) balbettare, cinguettare; (fig.) mormorare. **-er** *n.* chiacchierone *m.* **-ing** *adj.* loquace, ciarliero, chiacchierone; *n.* ciarle *f.pl.*, chiacchierìo, cinguettìo; (fig.) mormorìo.

**prawn** *n.* gambero delle rocce, palemone *m.*; *Dublin Bay -s*, scampi *m.pl.*

**praxis** *n.* prassi *f.*; (gramm.) raccolta di esempi.

**pray** *tr.* pregare, implorare, impetrare, supplicare; *to — to God for someone*, pregar Dio affinchè aiuti qualcuno; *— tell me*, mi dica di grazia; *— be seated!*, si accomodi!; *intr.* pregare; *let us —*, preghiamo; *to — for*, pregare, impetrare; (fam.) *he is past -ing for*, è incorreggibile.

**prayer**[1] *n.* preghiera; orazione; (lit.) prece *f.*; *pl.* preghiere, devozioni *f.pl.*; *to say one's -s*, dire le proprie devozioni; *-s for the dying*, raccomandazione dell'anima; *-s for the dead*, suffragi *m.pl.*; *the Lord's Prayer*, la preghiera domenicale, il paternostro; *the Book of Common Prayer*, il rituale della Chiesa Anglicana; desiderio, supplica, petizione.

**prayer**[2] (person) pregante *m., f.*, pregatore, fedele *m., f.*

**prayer-book** *n.* libro di preghiere; (RC) messale *m.*

**prayerful** *adj.* fervente, pio, devoto. **-ness** *n.* devozione.

**prayer-mat** *n.* tappeto da preghiera. **-stool** *n.* inginnocchiatoio, predella.

**praying** *adj.* che prega, pio, devoto; (ent.) *— mantis*, pregadio; il pregare, devozioni *f.pl.*

**preach** *tr., intr.* predicare; *to — a sermon*, predicare, fare una predica; *to — the Gospel*, predicare il vangelo; *not to practise what one -es*, predicare bene e razzolare male. **-er** *n.* predicatore, pastore. **-ify** *intr.* (pejor.) sermoneggiare, moraleggiare, fare predicozze. **-ing** *n.* predicazione, predica; (joc.) il moraleggiare.

**pre-acquaintance** *n.* conoscenza anteriore.

**pre-adamic, pre-adamite, pre-adamitic** *adj.* preadamitico; *n.* preadamita *m.*

**preadmon-ish** *tr.* preavvertire, preammonire. **-ition** *n.* preammonizione; preavviso.

**Pre-Alps** *pr.n.* (geog.) Prealpi *f.pl.*

**preamble** *n.* preambolo, proemio.

**preannounce** *tr.* preannunciare. **-ment** *n.* preannuncio.

**prearrange** *tr.* predisporre. **-ment** *n.* predisposizione; *by -ment*, secondo quanto disposto in precedenza.

**prebend** *n.* prebenda. **-ary** *n.* prebendario, prebendato.

**precarious** *adj.* precario, incerto, aleatorio; pericoloso, rischioso; *to make a — living*, vivere alla giornata. **-ness** *n.* precarietà.

**precaution** *n.* precauzione; *to take -s against*, prendere precauzioni contro; *with due —*, con la debita cautela. **-ary** *adj.* precauzionale, cautelativo, preventivo.

**precede** *tr.* precedere; antecedere.

**precedence** *n.* precedenza, priorità; *order of —*, ordine di precedenza; protocollo; *to give — to*, dare la precedenza a, cedere il passo a; (of things) anteporre; *to take — over*, avere la precedenza su.

**precedent** *n.* precedente *m.*; *to create a —*, creare un precedente; *without —*, senza precedenti.

**preceding** *adj.* anteriore; antecedente; *prep.* prima di.

**precentor** *n.* precentore *m.*, maestro del coro.

**precept** *n.* precetto, massima, ammaestramento. **-or** *n.* precettore, istitutore.

**pre-christian** *adj.* precristiano.

**precinct** *n.* recinto; *pl.* paraggi *m.pl.*; (fig.) ambito; (USA) collegio elettorale.

**preciosity** *n.* preziosità, ricercatezza, affettazione.

**precious** *adj.* prezioso; *— metals*, metalli preziosi; *— stone*, gemma, pietra preziosa; costoso, ricercato, raro; (lit.) affettato, ricercato; (fam.) bello, famoso; *a — mess*, proprio un bel pasticcio; *adv.* ben; *— few*, ben pochi; *— little*, ben poco; *n. my —!*, tesoro!, carissimo! **-ness** *n.* preziosità; pregio; valore *m.*; see also **preciosity.**

**precipice** *n.* precipizio; dirupo; *to fall over a —*, cadere in un precipizio.

**precipit-ance, -ancy** *n.* precipitazione.

**precipitat-e** *adj.* precipitoso, affrettato, avventato; *n.* (chem.) precipitato; *tr.* precipitare (also chem.); spingere, affrettare; *to — matters*, agire con troppa fretta. **-ion** *n.* (chem.; meteor.) precipitazione; (fig.) fretta, avventatezza.

**precipitous** *adj.* precipitoso, dirupato, ripido, erto, a picco. **-ness** *n.* ripidezza.

**précis** *n.* sommario, sunto, riassunto.

**precise** *adj.* preciso, esatto; puntiglioso, meticoloso, pignolo. **-ly** *adv.* precisamente, esattamente; *at six o'clock -ly*, alle sei precise; *to state -ly*, precisare, specificare; *more -ly*, (più) propriamente. **-ness** *n.* precisione, esattezza; meticolosità, scrupolosità.

**precision** *n.* precisione, esattezza; *— instruments*, apparecchi di precisione.

**pre-classical** *adj.* preclassico.

**preclude** *tr.* precludere, impedire, evitare, rendere impossibile; *to be -d from doing something*, trovarsi nell'impossibilità di fare qualcosa.

**precocious** *adj.* precoce. **-ness, precocity** *n.* precocità.

**precognition** *n.* precognizione, preconoscenza, prescienza.

**preconceive** *tr.* concepire in anticipo, avere preconcetti su, pregiudicare; *-d idea*, preconcetto.

**preconception** *m.* preconcetto, pregiudizio.

**preconcerted** *adj.* predisposto, preordinato, prestabilito.

**preconiz-e** *tr.* preconizzare, proclamare; (eccl.) preconizzare. **-ation** *n.* (eccl.) preconio, preconizzazione.

**precordium** *n.* (anat.) anticardio.

**precursor** *n.* precursore, predecessore; anticursore; antesignano. **-y** *adj.* precursore; *-y remarks*, osservazioni preliminari.

**predate** *tr.* predatare, antidatare; antecedere, avvenire prima di, precedere.

**predator** *n.* predatore. **-y** *adj.* predatore, rapace; *— animal*, rapace *m.*

**predecease** *tr.* morire prima di, premorire a.

**predecessor** *n.* predecessore, antecessore; anticursore, antesignano; antenato.

**predella** *n.* predella.

**predestinat-e** *tr.* predestinare. **-ion** *n.* predestinazione.

**predestine** *tr.* predestinare, preordinare.

**predetermin-e** *tr.* predeterminare, preordinare; (theol.) predestinare. **-ation** *n.* predeterminazione; (theol.) predestinazione.

**predicament** *n.* (log.) predicato, categoria; situazione difficile, impiccio, pasticcio.

**predicat-e** *n.* (log.; gramm.) predicato; attributo; *tr.* predicare, affermare. **-ive** *adj.* predicativo, affermativo.

**predict** *tr.* predire, presagire, pronosticare. **-able** *adj.* che si può predire, probabile. **-ion** *n.* predizione, profezia; pronostico.

**predigest** *tr.* predigerire.

**predilection** *n.* predilezione.

**predispos-e** *tr.* predisporre. **-ed**

*adj.* predisposto. **-ition** *n.* predisposizione.
**predomin-ance** *n.* predominio; ascendente *m.*; preponderanza. **-ant** *adj.* predominante, prevalente. **-ate** *intr.* predominare, prevalere.
**pre-emin-ence** *n.* preminenza. **-ent** *adj.* preminente, per eccellenza; *to be -ent*, eccellere.
**pre-empt** *tr.* (leg.) acquistare per diritto di prelazione; (fig.) prevenire; (bridge) fare un'apertura preventiva. **-ion** *n.* prelazione, priorità. **-ive** *adj.* (leg.) di prelazione; (bridge) *-ive bid*, apertura preventiva.
**preen** *tr.* *to — oneself*, (of bird) lisciarsi (le penne), (of person) agghindarsi, azzimarsi, (fam.) leccarsi i baffi; (fig.) *to — oneself on*, vantarsi di.
**pre-engage** *tr.* prenotare, impegnare in anticipo. **-ment** *n.* impegno precedente.
**pre-establish** *tr.* prestabilire. **-existence** *n.* preesistenza. **-existent** *adj.* preesistente.
**prefab** *n.* casa prefabbricata.
**preface** *n.* prefazione, proemio, preambolo; (eccl.) prefazio; *tr.* fare la prefazione a; (fig.) premettere; *I will — my remarks by saying that*, premetto che.
**prefatory** *adj.* di prefazione, introduttivo, preliminare.
**prefect** *n.* (Rom. hist.; eccl.; admin.) prefetto; (schol., in Britain) studente *m.*, *f.* con funzioni disciplinari, (Ital. equiv.) capoclasse *m.*, *f.*
**prefector(i)al** *adj.* prefettizio, di prefetto.
**prefecture** *n.* prefettura.
**prefer** *tr.* preferire; *gentlemen — blondes*, gli uomini preferiscono le bionde; *I — working*, preferisco lavorare; *I — red wine to white*, mi piace di più il vino rosso che (non) il bianco; anteporre, preporre; promuovere, elevare; (eccl.) *to — to a living*, nominare a un beneficio; (leg.) *to — a charge against*, citare in giudizio; *to — a complaint*, presentare un reclamo, sporgere querela. **-able** *adj.* preferibile. **-ence** *n.* preferenza; (finan.) *-ence shares*, azioni privilegiate. **-ential** *adj.* preferenziale, privilegiato, di favore; *-ential treatment*, trattamento di favore. **-ment** *n.* avanzamento, promozione; (eccl.) nomina.
**prefigure** *tr.* prefigurare.
**prefix** *n.* (gramm.) prefisso; titolo; *tr.* premettere, anteporre, far precedere; mettere come prefisso. **-ed** *adj.* (gramm.) prefisso.
**pregn-able** *adj.* espugnabile, prendibile. **-ancy** *n.* gravidanza, gestazione; (fig.) significato, importanza. **-ant** *adj.* (of woman) incinta, gravida, grossa; (of animal) gravida; (fig.) fecondo, fertile, pregno, pieno, ricco.
**prehensile** *adj.* prensile.
**prehistor-y** *n.* preistoria. **-ic** *adj.* preistorico.
**prejudg-e** *tr.* pregiudicare, condannare prematuramente. **-ment** *n.* giudizio prematuro.
**prejudice** *n.* pregiudizio, prevenzione, preconcetto; *pride and —*, orgoglio e pregiudizio; (leg.) danno; *without —*, senza pregiudizio; *to have a — against something*, essere prevenuto contro qualcosa; *tr.* pregiudicare, compromettere; (fig.) nuocere a, danneggiare; *to — someone against something*, mettere qualcuno contro qualcosa. **-d** *adj.* prevenuto, diffidente, mal disposto.
**prejudicial** *adj.* pregiudizievole, dannoso, nocivo; *to be — to*, nuocere a.
**pre-judicial** *adj.* pregiudiziale. **-knowledge** *n.* (philos.) prescienza.
**prelacy** *n.* prelatura.
**prelat-e** *n.* prelato; antistite *m.*; presule *m.* **-ure** *n.* prelatura.
**preliminary** *adj.* preliminare, introduttivo; *n.* premessa; preliminare *m.*; *by way of —*, *as a —*, per primo, anzitutto; *preliminaries to peace*, preliminari della pace.
**prelude** *n.* preludio; *intr.* preludere, servire da preludio; (mus.) preludiare; *tr.* preludere a, preannunziare.
**premature** *adj.* prematuro; *— birth*, parto prematuro; (fig.) precoce, intempestivo. **-ly** *adv.* prematuramente; troppo presto.
**premeditat-e** *tr.* premeditare. **-ion** *n.* premeditazione.
**premier** *adj.* primo, primario, primiero; *n.* (Britain) primo ministro, capo del governo, presidente *m.* del consiglio. **-ship** *n.* carica di primo ministro; permanenza al potere.
**première** *n.* (theatr.) prima (rappresentazione).
**premise** *n.* (leg.) premessa; *pl.* locali stabile immobile *m.*; *to be consumed on the -s*, da bersi sul posto; *off the -s*, fuori dello stabile; *tr.* premettere, far precedere a.
**premiss** *n.* (leg.) see **premise.**
**premium** *n.* premio, ricompensa; (finan.) aggio, premio; *at a —*, sopra la pari; (fig.) *to be at a —*, costare caro, essere difficilmente trovabile; *to put a — on*, incoraggiare, favorire.
**premonition** *n.* premonizione, presentimento.
**premonitory** *adj.* premonitorio.
**prenatal** *adj.* prenatale, antenatale.
**prenotion** *n.* prenozione, preconcetto.
**preoccup-y** *tr.* preoccupare; *to be preoccupied with*, preoccuparsi di. **-ation** *n.* preoccupazione. **-ied** *adj.* preoccupato, assorto.
**pre-ordain** *tr.* preordinare, prestabilire.
**prepaid** *adj.* (comm.) pagato anticipatamente, franco di porto; (of telegram) *reply —*, risposta pagata; (of letter) affrancato.
**prepar-ation** *n.* preparazione, preparativo; (med.) preparato; (schol.) compiti *m.pl.* **-ative** *adj.* preparativo, preparatorio; *n.* preparativo. **-atory** *adj.* preparatorio; *-atory school*, scuola elementare privata; *adv. -atory to leaving*, prima di partire.
**prepare** *tr.* preparare, allestire, disporre; *to — someone for a piece of bad news*, preparare qualcuno ad una brutta notizia; *to — a house for occupation*, allestire una casa; *to — the table*, allestire la tavola; *to be -d for the worst*, aspettarsi il peggio; (eccl.) *to — the altar*, assettare l'altare; (schol.) *to — a lesson*, studiare la lezione, prepararsi; *intr.* prepararsi, fare preparativi; *to — for*, prepararsi a.
**prepared** *adj.* preparato; pronto; disposto; *be —!*, tenetevi pronti! **-ness** *n.* l'essere pronto; *to be in a state of -ness*, essere predisposto.
**prepar-er** *n.* preparatore. **-ing** preparazione.
**prepay** *tr.* pagare anticipatamente. **-ment** *n.* pagamento anticipato.
**prepense** *adj.* (leg.) premeditato.
**preponder-ance** *n.* preponderanza. **-ant** *adj.* preponderante, predominante. **-ate** *intr.* preponderare, predominare, prevalere, avere la prevalenza.
**preposition** *n.* (gramm.) preposizione.
**prepossess** *tr.* predisporre, influire, prevenire, impressionare. **-ing** *adj.* attraente, simpatico, di bella presenza. **-ion** *n.* buona predisposizione; prevenzione; pregiudizio.
**preposterous** *adj.* assurdo, ridicolo, sciocco, strampalato. **-ness** *n.* assurdità.
**prepuce** *n.* (anat.) prepuzio.
**pre-Raphael-ite** *adj.*, *n.* preraffaellita *m.*, *f.* **-(it)ism** *n.* (art) preraffaellismo.
**pre-release** *n.* (cinem.) anteprima.
**prerequisite** *n.* requisito primo, predisposto, essenziale.
**prerogative** *n.* prerogativa, privilegio.
**presage** *n.* presagio, pronostico, presentimento; *tr.* presagire, pronosticare, augurare; *intr.* essere presago, augurare.
**Presbyterian** *adj.*, *n.* presbiteriano. **-ism** *n.* presbiterianismo.
**presbytery** *n.* presbiterio, canonica.
**presci-ence** *n.* prescienza, previsione. **-ent** *adj.* presciente, previdente.

**prescind** *tr. intr.* prescindere, fare astrazione (da).

**prescribe** *tr., intr.* prescrivere, ordinare; (med.) prescrivere, fare una prescrizione (di), dare una ricetta (per).

**prescript** *n.* prescritto, precetto; ordinanza, ordine *m.* **-ion** *n.* prescrizione, ordine; (med.) ricetta; *can you make up this -ion?*, può spedirmi questa ricetta?; *to write (out) a -ion for someone*, dare una ricetta a qualcuno.

**presence** *n.* presenza; *in the — of*, alla presenza di; *— of mind*, presenza di spirito; *your — is requested at*, Ella è invitata ad assistere a; *saving your —*, con rispetto parlando.

**presence-chamber** *n.* sala di udienza.

**pre·sent**[1] *adj.* presente, attuale; questo; corrente; *— to the mind*, presente allo spirito, in mente; *my — address*, il mio indirizzo attuale; *in the — case*, in questo caso; *the — volume*, questo volume; *the — writer*, l'autore; *the — year*, l'anno corrente; *at the — time*, oggigiorno; (gramm.) presente; *to be — at*, assistere a, essere presente a; *all those —*, tutti i presenti; *no one else was —*, non c'era nessun altro; (comm.) *in the — letter*, con la presente (lettera); *n.* presente *m.*; *at —*, attualmente, al momento; *for the —*, per ora; *up to the —*, finora, sinora, fino ad oggi; (leg.) *by these -s*, con la presente.

**pre·sent**[2] *n.* dono, regalo; *to make a — of something*, regalare qualcosa, far dono di qualcosa; *to give as a —*, dare in regalo.

**present**[3] *tr.* presentare, offrire; donare, regalare, fare omaggio di, porgere; *to — something to*, regalare, offrire in omaggio qualcosa a; *to be -ed with something*, ricevere qualcosa in omaggio; (iron.) *to be -ed with a bill*, vedersi porgere il conto; (fig.) presentare; *to — someone to someone*, presentare qualcuno a qualcuno; *to — a cheque for payment*, presentare un assegno all'incasso; *to be -ed at court*, essere presentato a corte; *to — one's apologies*, offrire le proprie scuse; *to — one's compliments*, presentare i propri ossequi; (theatr.) (rap)presentare; (mil.) *to — arms*, presentare le armi; *— arms!*, presentat'arm'!; (pol.) *to — a bill*, introdurre un progetto di legge.

**presentable** *adj.* presentabile, di bella presenza; *to be —*, avere bella presenza; *to make oneself —*, ravviarsi gli abiti, fare un po' di toletta.

**presentation** *n.* presentazione, rappresentazione; dono, omaggio; *— copy*, esemplare *m.* in omaggio; (theatr.) rappresentazione; (eccl., of Virgin Mary) Presentazione, (of Christ) Purificazione, Candelora; (of benefice) collazione.

**present-ee** *n.* persona che riceve un dono; raccomandato; (eccl.) beneficiario. **-er** *n.* presentatore; (of débutante) madrina; (of gift) donatore.

**presentient** *adj.* presciente, che presagisce.

**presentiment** *n.* presentimento; *to have a — of*, presentire.

**presently** *adv.* fra poco, a momenti, subito, presto, quanto prima.

**presentment** *n.* rappresentazione, modo di presentarsi; (leg.) dichiarazione sotto giuramento; (eccl.) esposto al vescovo.

**preserv-ation** *n.* conservazione, preservazione, mantenimento; (fig.) salvezza, scampo. **-ative** *adj., n.* preservativo; antisettico.

**preserv-e** *n.* conserva; marmellata, conserva di frutta; *game —*, riserva; (fig.) *to poach on someone's -s*, cacciare nelle riserve di qualcuno; *tr.* conservare, preservare, salvare, proteggere; conservare, mettere in conserva; allevare in riserva; (fig.) *to — appearances*, salvare le apparenze. **-ed** *adj.* conservato, in conserva; *-ed fruit*, frutta candita; *-ed meat*, carne in conserva; *well -ed*, in buon stato di conservazione, (fig., of person) ben portante. **-er** *n.* (person) salvatore, preservatore; *life-preserver*, sfollagente *m.*, manganello.

**preside** *intr.* presiedere; *to — over*, presiedere a.

**presiden-t** *n.* (of State, company) presidente *m.*; (of trade union) segretario generale; (of Board of Trade) Ministro dell'Industria e del Commercio; (eccl.) presule *m.*; (schol.) preside *m.* **-cy** *n.* presidenza. **-tial** *adj.* presidenziale.

**presiding** *adj.* che presiede, presidente; *— judge*, presidente *m.*

**press** *n.* pressione, stretta; folla, calca, ressa; (fig.) premura, urgenza, incalzare *m.*, attività febbrile; armadio; (naut.) forza, sforzo; (machine) torchio, pressa, strettoio; (printing) macchina per stampare; *in the —*, in corso di stampa; *to go to —*, andare in macchina; *copying —*, copialettere *m.*; (for racket) pressa; (journ.) stampa, giornalismo; *the Press*, la stampa; *national —*, i grandi giornali; *local —*, i giornali locali; *stop —*, recentissime *f.pl.*, ultimissime *f.pl.*; *freedom of the —*, libertà di stampa; *— campaign*, campagna giornalistica; *to give a — conference*, tenere una conferenza stampa; *to write for the —*, scrivere per i giornali, fare il giornalista; *a good —*, una buona stampa; casa editrice; tipografia, stamperia; *Cambridge University Press*, casa editrice, tipografia dell'Università di Cambridge.

**press** *tr.* premere, comprimere, stringere, schiacciare, spingere; *she -ed his hand*, essa gli strinse la mano; *to — the button*, premere il bottone; pressare, pigiare; (fig.) fare pressione su, insistere, costringere; *to — someone to come*, insistere perchè qualcuno venga; *to — money upon someone*, costringere qualcuno ad accettare denaro; *to — the point*, insistere su un punto; *to — someone with questions*, incalzare qualcuno di domande; *to be hard -ed*, essere a corto (di), essere in difficoltà, essere incalzato; *to — the enemy hard*, incalzare il nemico; *to be -ed for time*, avere fretta; stirare; *intr.* urgere, stringere, incalzare; *time -es*, il tempo stringe; *to — against*, spingersi contro, affollarsi intorno a; *to — back*, *tr.* respingere, ricacciare, *intr.* spingersi indietro, indietreggiare; *to — down*, spingere giù, schiacciare, deprimere; *to — for*, insistere su; *to — forward*, *tr.* spingere innanzi, *intr.* spingersi avanti; *to — in*, far entrare premendo; *to — into service*, arruolare forzatamente; *to — on*, *tr.* imprimere, *intr.* affrettarsi, forzare il passo; *to — on with one's work*, affrettarsi nel proprio lavoro; *it -es on my mind*, mi pesa; *to — out*, spremere, esprimere, (creases) eliminare stirando; *to — round*, accalcarsi intorno; *to — upon*, pesare su, aggravare.

**press-agency** *n.* agenzia d'informazioni, agenzia pubblicitaria. **-agent** *n.* agente pubblicitario. **-box** *n.* tribuna della stampa.

**press-button** *n.* pulsante *m.*

**press-cutting** *n.* ritaglio di giornale.

**pressed** *adj.* premuto, compresso; *— beef*, manzo in scatola.

**presser** *n.* compressore; pressa; (on sewing-machine) premistoffa *m.*

**press-gallery** *n.* galleria della stampa.

**pressing** *adj.* urgente, pressante, incalzante; (fig.) insistente, importuno; insistenza; *he needs no —*, non si fa pregare; (mech.) stampaggio.

**pressman** *n.* (journ.) giornalista *m.*, cronista *m.*; (typ.) macchinista *m.*, stampatore.

**press-mark** *n.* segnatura.

**press-proof, press-revise** *n.* (typ.) bozza finale. **-room** *n.* (journ.) sala redazione; (typ.) sala macchine.

**press-stud** *n.* pulsante *m.*

**pressure** *n.* pressione; (fig.) peso, insistenza; *blood —*, pressione sanguigna; *to bring — to bear on*

*someone*, far pressione su qualcuno; *to yield to* —, cedere; *under* —, sotto pressione; *to work at high* —, lavorare febbrilmente; — *of business*, cumulo di lavoro.

**pressure-cabin** *n.* (aeron.) cabina pressurizzata. **-cooker** *n.* (cul.) pentola a pressione. **-gauge** *n.* manometro. **-head** *n.* (hydr. eng.) altezza manometrica.

**pressurize** *tr.* pressurizzare.

**presswork** *n.* (typ.) avviamento, messa in macchina.

**Prester John** *pr.n.* Prete Gianni.

**prestidigitat-ion** *n.* prestidigitazione. **-or** *n.* prestidigitatore, prestigiatore.

**prestige** *n.* prestigio, decoro; *loss of* —, disdoro; *having* — *value*, decoroso; — *symbol*, simbolo di prestigio.

**presto** *adv.* (mus.) presto; *excl. hey* —*!*, ecco!

**presum-e** *tr.* presumere, supporre, ritenere; *Dr. Livingstone, I* —, il dottor Livingstone, se non mi sbaglio; (fam.) permettersi (di); (pejor.) avere la presunzione (di); *let us* — *that*, supponiamo che; *you* — *too much*, ti aspetti troppo, sei troppo presuntuoso; *intr. to* — *upon*, abusare di, approfittare di. **-able** *adj.* presumibile. **-ed** *adj.* presunto, presumibile; *missing*, *-ed dead*, disperso. **-ing** *adj.* presuntuoso, arrogante; *n.* supposizione; (as *conj.*) *-ing that*, supposto che.

**presumpt-ion** *n.* presunzione; supposizione, congettura; — *in favour of*, pregiudizio a favore di; *the* — *is that*, si suppone che; (pejor.) arroganza, prepotenza. **-ive** *adj.* presuntivo, presunto; *heir -ive*, erede presunto.

**presumptuous** *adj.* presuntuoso, arrogante, prepotente. **-ness** *n.* presunzione, arroganza, prepotenza.

**presuppos-e** *tr.* presupporre. **-ition** *n.* presupposizione, presupposto.

**pretence** *n.* pretesa, pretensione; *devoid of all* —, senza pretese; *to make no* — *to*, non avere alcuna pretesa di, non pretendere a; finta, finzione, pretesto, falsa apparenza; *to make a* — *of*, far finta di; *under the* — *of*, col pretesto di; (leg.) *false -s*, millantato credito, frode *f.*, dolo.

**pretend** *tr.* pretendere di, avere pretensioni a, vantarsi di; fingere, far finta di, far mostra di, simulare, far vista di; *to* — *to do something*, fingere di far qualcosa; *to* — *ignorance*, fingere l'ignoranza; *to* — *to be a king*, far finta di essere re; *intr. to* — *to*, pretendere a, aspirare a, rivendicare. **-ed** *adj.* preteso, supposto; finto, simulato; sedicente. **-er** *n.* pretendente *m.*, *f.*; simulatore.

**pretension** *n.* pretensione, pretesa, ambizione; *to have -s to*, aver molte pretese a, pretendere di; *man of no -s*, uomo senza pretese.

**pretentious** *adj.* pretenzioso, ambizioso, arrogante, prepotente. **-ness** *n.* ostentazione, prepotenza, arroganza.

**preterite** *adj.*, *n.* (gramm.) preterito, passato remoto.

**preter-mission** *n.* pretermissione, omissione; *without* —, senza cessare, senza requie. **-natural** *adj.* preternaturale, soprannaturale.

**pretext** *n.* pretesto, scusa; *under* (*the*) — *of*, sotto pretesto di; *to give as a* —, addurre a pretesto; *tr.* addurre a pretesto.

**prett-ify** *tr.* illeggiadrire, rendere grazioso. **-ily** *adv.* leggiadramente, graziosamente; gentilmente.

**prettiness** *n.* leggiadria, grazia, graziosità; eleganza.

**pretty** *adj.* leggiadro; bello, bellino; grazioso; carino; (iron.) bello; *a* — *wit*, un bello spirito; *a* — *penny*, una bella sommetta; *adv.* (fam.) abbastanza, piuttosto, discretamente; — *nearly*, quasi, pressappoco; — *much the same*, quasi lo stesso; (fam.) *to sit* —, starsene zitto, leccarsi i baffi; *n.* gingillo, bordo lavorato; (golf) percorso libero; *pl. pretties*, biancheria intima.

**pretzel** *n.* (cul.) ciambellina salata.

**prevail** *intr.* prevalere, persistere; predominare, regnare, vincere; *to* — *upon*, persuadere, convincere, indurre; *to* — *over*, vincere, soverchiare. **-ing, prevalent** *adj.* prevalente, dominante, predominante, regnante; generale; in voga, alla moda, del momento.

**prevalence, prevalency** *n.* prevalenza, predominanza.

**prevaricat-e** *intr.* equivocare, tergiversare, mentire. **-ion** *n.* menzogna, tergiversazione.

**prevent** *tr.* impedire, ostacolare, evitare; *to* — *from doing something*, impedire di fare qualcosa; *what is to* — *you?*, che ti impedisce?; *to be unavoidably -ed from doing something*, trovarsi nell'impossibilità di far qualcosa. **-able, -ible** *adj.* evitabile, preventibile, impedibile. **-ion** *n.* prevenzione, l'impedire; misura preventiva; (med.) profilassi *f.*; *society for the -ion of cruelty to animals*, società protettrice degli animali; (provb.) *-ion is better than cure*, è meglio prevenire che curare. **-ive** *adj.* preventivo; *n.* misura preventiva; (med.) medicina profilattica.

**preview** *n.* (cinem.; theatr.) anteprima.

**previous** *adj.* che precede, precedente, antecedente, previo, anteriore; — *to*, prima di; — *history*, antefatto; (fam.) *to be* —, anticipare; impulsivo, precipitoso. **-ly** *adv.* precedentemente, antecedentemente, anteriormente; prima, addietro. **-ness** *n.* precedenza, antecedenza, priorità; (fam.) precipitazione, fretta.

**prevision** *n.* previsione, pronostico.

**pre-war** *adj.* di anteguerra, prebellico; *adv.* prima della guerra.

**prey** *n.* preda, rapina; *beast of* —, animale da preda; *bird of* —, uccello rapace; (fig.) *to be a* — *to*, essere in preda a; *to fall a* — *to*, cadere in preda a, cadere vittima di; *intr. to* — *on*, (of animals) far preda di, predare, divorare; (hunt) cacciare; (fig.) depredare, rubare; *something is -ing on his mind*, qualcosa lo rode; *to* — *on one's family*, vivere alle spalle dei parenti; (provb.) *the strong* — *upon the weak*, i pesci grossi mangiano i piccoli.

**Priam** *n.* (Gk. lit.) Priamo.

**priapism** *n.* libidine *f.*, lascivia; (med.) priapismo.

**price** *n.* prezzo; *cost* —, prezzo di costo; *below cost* —, sottocosto; *fair* —, prezzo equo, prezzo di concorrenza; *fixed -s*, prezzi fissi; *half-price*, metà prezzo; *purchase* —, prezzo di acquisto; *retail* —, prezzo al minuto; *sale* —, prezzo venale; *trade* —, prezzo di fabbrica, sconto; *wholesale* —, prezzo all'ingrosso; *what is the* — *of this book?*, quanto costa questo libro?; *the* — *is . . .*, costa . . .; *to pay a high* — *for*, pagare caro; *to quote a* —, fare un prezzo; *to rise in* —, rincarare; *the* — *is too high*, costa troppo; *the* — *is low*, costa poco; *at the* — *of*, al prezzo di; *at any* —, a qualunque prezzo, ad ogni costo; *not at any* —, a nessun costo, (fig.) mai; *you can buy it at a* —, lo troverai, ma dovrai pagarlo caro!; *to set a* — *on someone's head*, mettere una taglia sulla testa di qualcuno; *beyond all* —, di valore inestimabile; (fam.) *what* — *my hat?*, cosa ne pensi del mio cappello?; *tr.* fare il prezzo di; *to be -d at*, vendersi a; valutare, stimare; *to* — *high*, attribuire un alto valore a.

**price-current** *n.* listino (dei) prezzi correnti. **-cutting** *n.* riduzione dei prezzi, concorrenza.

**priced** *adj.* col prezzo segnato, che ha il suo prezzo; *high-priced*, dal prezzo elevato.

**priceless** *adj.* di valore inestimabile, senza prezzo; (fam.) *you're* —*!*, sei impagabile!; *a* — *story*, una barzelletta divertentissima. **-ness** *n.* valore inestimabile; (fam.) l'essere impagabile.

**price-list** *n.* listino (dei) prezzi, tariffa; catalogo. **-ring** *n.* (finan.) cartello, sindacato.

**prick** *n.* puntura, pungolo, punta,

pungiglione *m.*; rimorso; (fig.) *it's no use kicking against the ~s*, è inutile ribellarsi; pene *m.*; *tr.* pungere, punzecchiare; (fig.) *his conscience is ~ing him*, la coscienza lo rimorde; *to — a bubble*, far scoppiare una bolla d'aria, (fig.) sgonfiare; *to — a hole in*, forare, bucare, fare un buco in; *to — up one's ears*, drizzare gli orecchi; *to — off names on a list*, contrassegnare dei nomi su un elenco; (hortic.) *to — in*, piantare; *to — out*, trapiantare; *intr.* pungere, formicolare, pizzicare.

**prick-eared** *adj.* (of dog) con orecchie appuntite; (of person) con gli orecchi tesi; (hist.) *— rascal*, puritano.

**pricking** *adj.* pungente, che punge; *— sensation*, formicolìo; *n.* puntura; pizzicore; punzecchiatura; *~s of conscience*, rimorsi di coscienza.

**prickl-e** *n.* aculeo, spina, pungiglione *m.*; *tr.* pungere, leggermente; *intr.* essere spinoso; formicolare. **-iness** *n.* spinosità. **-ing** *n.* formicolìo. **-y** *adj.* spinoso, pungente; *to be ~y*, pungere; (fig.) difficile, scabroso; *~y pear*, fico d'India; (med.) *~y heat*, lichen dei tropici.

**pride** *n.* orgoglio, superbia, alterigia, boria, fierezza, amor proprio; *false —*, vanità; *puffed up with —*, gonfio d'orgoglio; *to be the — of*, essere l'orgoglio di; *to take a — in*, gloriarsi di; *to wound someone's —*, ferire l'amor proprio di qualcuno; (fig.) *in the — of*, nel fiore di; (provb.) *— goes before a fall*, la superbia andò a cavallo e tornò a piedi, chi si vanta si spianta; (herald.) *in its —* (of peacock), roteante; *rfl. to — oneself on*, gloriarsi di, vantarsi di, essere orgoglioso di inorgoglirsi di.

**pride²** *n.* (of lions) branca.

**pride³** *n.* (ichth.) lampreda.

**prier** *n.* curioso, ficcanaso.

**priest** *n.* prete *m.*, sacerdote *m.*; (of Eastern rite) papasso; *High —*, sommo sacerdote; *parish —*, parroco, curato, pievano; *assistant —*, vicario; *—'s house*, canonica, cura, presbiterio; *to become a —*, farsi prete; (fishing) mazza, maglio. **-craft** *n.* (pej.) clericalismo. **-ess** *n.* sacerdotessa. **-hood** *n.* sacerdozio, presbiterato; (collect.) clero; *to enter the ~hood*, farsi prete. **-ling** *n.* pretino; (pejor.) pretucolo. **-ly** *adj.* sacerdotale, pretesco, di prete.

**priest-ridden** *adj.* dominato dai preti, pretaiuolo.

**prig** *n.* saccentone *m.*, saputello, vanesio. **-gish** *adj.* saccente, saputello, presuntuoso, borioso. **-gishness** *n.* saccenteria, presuntuosità, boria.

**prim** *adj.* affettato, smorfioso, compito; *a — appearance*, un aspetto di educanda.

**primacy** *n.* primato, supremazia; (eccl.) primazia.

**primaeval** *adj.* See **primeval.**

**prima facie** *adv.* prima facie, a prima vista.

**primal** *adj.* primitivo, primo, originale.

**primar-y** *adj.* primo, primario, primitivo, originale, originario; *the — meaning*, il significato originario, *— colours*, colori fondamentali; *— school*, scuola elementare; (geol.) primario, paleozoico. **-ily** *adv.* in primo luogo, originalmente.

**primate** *n.* (eccl.) primate *m.*; *— of all England*, l'arcivescovo di Canterbury; (zool.) primato.

**prime** *adj.* primo, primario; di prima qualità, di prima scelta, eccellente; *of — importance*, di prima importanza; *— cost*, prezzo di costo; *— mover*, promotore, causa prima; *— necessity*, necessità prima; *— number*, numero primo; *Prime Minister*, (Britain) Primo Ministro, (elsewhere) Presidente del Consiglio; primordio; (fig.) perfezione, primavera; *in the — of life*, nel fiore degli anni; *fruit in its —*, frutta di piena stagione; *to be past one's —*, non essere più come prima; (liturg.) prima; (paint.) mestica; *tr.* (gun) innescare, caricare; (pump) adescare; (text.) apprettare: (paint.) mesticare, dare la mestica a, ammannire; (fig.) *to — with information*, preparare, istruire, mettere al corrente, dare l'imbeccata a; (fam.) *to — with drink*, far bere; *to be well ~d*, (with liquor), essere brillo. **-ness** *n.* eccellenza, buona qualità.

**primer¹** *n.* (for gun, mine) innesco; (person) innescatore; (paint.) impregnante *m.*, mestica, imprimitura.

**primer²** *n.* primo libro, sillabario, abbecedario, testo elementare; manuale *m.*; (eccl.) libro di preghiere; (typ.) *great —*, corpo sedici; *long —*, corpo dieci.

**primeval** *adj.* primevo, primordiale; *— forests*, foreste vergini.

**priming** *n.* innesco, polverino; (of pump) adescamento; (text.) appretto; (paint.) mestica, prima mano; ammannitura, imprimatura; (fig.) preparazione, imbeccata, insegnamento frettoloso.

**primipara** *n.* (med.) primipara.

**primitive** *adj.* primitivo, rozzo; *n.* (art) primitivo. **-ness** *n.* stato primitivo, rozzezza.

**primness** *n.* compitezza; affettazione; disposizione regolare.

**primogenit-or** *n.* primogenitore, progenitore. **-ure** *n.* primogenitura.

**primordial** *adj.* primordiale.

**primrose** *adj.* (colour) giallo pallido, color primula; *n.* (bot.) primula, primavera; (fig.) *the — path*, la via del peccato.

**primus** *adj.* primo (in ordine di età); *n. — stove*, stufetta a petrolio.

**prince** *n.* principe *m.*; *— of the Church*, cardinale *m.*, principe della chiesa; *Prince Consort*, principe consorte; *Prince of Wales*, Principe di Galles; *Prince Charming*, Il Principe Azzurro. **-dom** *n.* See **principality.** **-let, -ling** *n.* principino; (pejor.) principotto. **-ly** *adj.* principesco.

**princess** *n.* principessa.

**principal** *adj.* principale, capitale, più importante; (cul.) *— dish*, secondo (piatto); (theatr.) *— part*, parte del primo attore; *n.* (of firm) capo, direttore, gerente *m.*, (fam.) padrone *m.*; (schol.) preside, rettore, direttore, direttrice; (in duel) duellante *m.*; (comm.) committente *m.*, mandante *m.*; (finan.) capitale *m.*; (mus.) ottava, registro d'organo; (bldg.) trave maestra. **-ity** *n.* principato. **-ly** *adv.* principalmente.

**principle** *n.* principio; *first ~s*, principi; legge morale; *on —, as a matter of —*, per principio; *man of no —*, uomo senza principi, uomo di dubbia moralità; *to object in —*, sollevare un'obbiezione di principio; (fig.) *as a general —*, in genere; *on the same —*, nello stesso modo, in base allo stesso sistema. **-d** *adj.* che ha principi; *high-principled*, di principi elevati, retto; *low-principled*, di dubbia moralità.

**prink** *tr.* adornare, rendere elegante; *rfl. to — oneself up*, attillarsi; *intr.* (of birds) lisciarsi le penne.

**print** *n.* impronta, impressione; segno, traccia; orma; (typ.) caratteri *m.pl.*; *large —*, caratteri grandi; *small —*, caratteri piccoli; *in —*, stampato, in vendita, ancora trovabile; *out of —*, esaurito; *to appear in —*, essere stampato; *to rush into —*, far stampare senza pensare alle conseguenze; stampa, incisione, riproduzione; (photog.) prova, copia; (text.) tessuto stampato; stampo.

**print** *tr.* imprimere, stampare; *to — a book*, stampare un libro; *to have a book ~ed*, far stampare un libro; *the book is ~ing*, il libro è in corso di stampa; *to —* (in capitals), scrivere a stampatello; *~ed matter*, stampati *m.pl.*, stampe *f.pl.*; *to — (off) 5000 copies*, tirare cinquemila copie; (photog.) *to — a negative*, stampare una copia da una negativa; *~ed fabric*, tessuto stampato; *intr.* fare lo stampatore. **-able** *adj.* stampabile, imprimibile. **-er** *n.* tipografo,

stampatore; poligrafico; *-'s devil*, fattorino di tipografia, apprendista *m.*; *-'s error*, rifuso, errore tipografico; *-'s ink*, inchiostro da stampa; *-'s reader*, correttore di bozze.

**printing** *n.* tipografia, l'arte tipografica, stampa; *— operative*, poligrafico; *— operatives' trade union*, sindacato dei poligrafici; *first —*, prima tiratura; *second —*, prima ristampa, seconda tiratura.

**printing-house** *n.* tipografia, stamperia. **-ink** *n.* inchiostro da stampa. **-press** *n.* macchina stampatrice, torchio; *rotary-press*, rotativa. **-works** *n.* tipografia, stabilimento tipografico, stamperia.

**print-room** *n.* gabinetto (delle) stampe. **-seller** *n.* venditore di stampe. **-shop** *n.* negozio di stampe. **-works** *n.pl.* stamperia di stoffe.

**prior**[1] *adj.* antecedente, precedente, anteriore; *to have a — claim*, avere la precedenza, avere il primo diritto; *adv. — to*, prima di.

**prior**[2] *n.* (eccl.) priore *m.* **-ate** *m.* priorato, prioria. **-ess** *n.* priora, superiora, badessa.

**priority** *n.* priorità; precedenza, anteriorità; *top —*, precedenza assoluta.

**priorship** *n.* priorato, prioria.

**priory** *n.* prioria, monastero retto da priore; (Dominican, Franciscan) convento.

**prise** *tr.* far leva su; *to — open*, forzare, scoperchiare.

**prism** *n.* prisma *m.* **-atic** *adj.* prismatico.

**prison** *n.* prigione *f.*, carcere *m.*, reclusorio; (pop.) galera; *— for life*, ergastolo; *convict —*, bagno penale. **-er** *n.* prigioniero, incarcerato; ergastolano; *-er at the bar*, accusato, imputato; *-er of war*, prigioniero di guerra; *to take -er*, far prigioniero, catturare.

**prison-van** *n.* furgone cellulare.

**pristine** *adj.* pristino, primitivo.

**privacy** *n.* intimità; *the — of one's home*, l'intimità della casa; *lack of —*, mancanza di libertà personale, di vita privata; segretezza, riserbo.

**private** *adj.* privato, particolare; confidenziale, riservato, segreto; appartato, isolato; (on envelope) personale; confidenziale; (on door), —, vietato l'ingresso; *— citizen*, privato, particolare *m.*, *f.*, semplice cittadino; *— car*, automobile privata; *a — conversation*, una conversazione a quattr'occhi; *— income*, redditi *m.pl.*; *— interview*, abboccamento personale; *— lesson*, lezione privata; *— life*, vita privata, intimità; *— parts*, organi *m.pl.* sessuali, pudenda *f. pl.*; *— property*, proprietà privata; *— reasons*, ragioni personali; *— secretary*, segretaria privata; *— soldier*, semplice soldato; *— view*, anteprima; *by — arrangement*, all'amichevole; *in — clothes*, in borghese; *in my — opinion*, a parer mio, secondo me; *to keep —*, tenere segreto; *the funeral will be strictly —*, le esequie si celebreranno nella più stretta intimità; *n. in —*, in privato, in segreto, a porte chiuse; (mil.) soldato semplice; *pl.* (fam.) pudenda *f.pl.*

**privateer** *n.* (ship) nave corsara; capitano di nave corsara, corsaro. **-ing** *n.* pirateria; guerra di corsa.

**privately** *adv.* in forma privata, privatamente, personalmente; in segreto, segretamente; *— owned*, proprietà privata.

**privation** *n.* privazione; *pl.* stenti *m.pl.*

**privative** *adj.* negativo; (gramm.) privativo.

**privet** *n.* (bot.) ligustro, ruschio.

**privilege** *n.* privilegio, prerogativa; *breach of —*, infrazione di privilegio; *to enjoy a —*, godere di un privilegio, essere privilegiato; *it is my —*, mi spetta; *it is a — for me*, per me è un piacere; *tr.* privilegiare, accordare privilegi a; *I am -d to*, ho il privilegio di, mi spetta.

**privy** *adj.* privato, segreto, nascosto; *Privy Council*, consiglio privato; *Privy Councillor*, consigliere privato; *Privy Purse*, appannaggio reale; *— to*, a conoscenza di, partecipe di; *n.* cesso, ritirata.

**prize** *n.* premio, ricompensa; *to win a —*, vincere un premio, essere premiato; *the Nobel Prize*, il Premio Nobel; *— bull*, toro premiato; (naut.) presa, preda, nave catturata; *tr.* apprezzare, stimare, valutare; far caso di.

**prize-court** *n.* tribunale *m.* delle prese. **-crew** *n.* (naut.) equipaggio a bordo di una nave catturata. **-fight** *n.* gara di pugilato. **-fighter** *n.* pugile *m.* **-giving** *n.* distribuzione dei premi, premiazione. **-money** *n.* premio in denaro, taglia; (naut.) decima di preda. **-packet** *n.* (fam.) sorpresa. **-ring** *n.* (boxing) ring *m.*, quadrato; (fig.) arena. **-winner** *n.* premiato, vincitore.

**pro** *n.* (theatr., sport, fam.) professionista *m.*, *f.*

**probab-le** *adj.* probabile, verosimile. **-ility** *n.* probabilità; *in all -ility*, probabilmente, con tutta probabilità.

**probate** *n.* (leg.) omologazione, verificazione; *to obtain — of a will*, far omologare un testamento.

**probation** *n.* prova; *on —*, in prova; (eccl.) noviziato; (leg.) libertà condizionata; *— officer*, sorvegliante di condannati in libertà condizionata. **-ary** *adj.* probatorio, di prova. **-er** *n.* novizio; apprendista *m.*, *f.*, tirocinista *m.*, *f.*; (eccl.) novizio. **-ership** *n.* tirocinio, apprendistato; (eccl.) noviziato.

**probative** *adj.* probativo.

**probe** *n.* sonda, specillo, tentativo; (fig.) investigazione, inchiesta; *tr.* (surg.) sondare, specillare; (fig.) sondare, scandagliare, esplorare; *intr. to — into*, esaminare a fondo.

**probity** *n.* probità, integrità, onestà.

**problem** *n.* problema *m.*; *the housing —*, la crisi degli alloggi; *— child*, bambino difficile; (theatr.) *— play*, dramma *m.* a tesi. **-atic(al)** *adj.* problematico.

**proboscis** *n.* proboscide *f.*

**pro-British** *adj.* pro-Britannico.

**procedure** *n.* procedimento; (leg.) procedura.

**proceed** *intr.* procedere, avanzare; andare, recarsi; proseguire, continuare, andare avanti; *—!*, avanti!; proseguire, venire a dire; agire; *to — from*, provenire da, emanare da; *to — with*, proseguire, continuare; *the negotiations now -ing*, le trattative in corso; *how shall we —?*, che cosa faremo adesso?; *let us — to the dining-room*, passiamo nella sala da pranzo; (leg.) *to — against*, intentare causa contro.

**proceeding** *n.* procedimento, azione, modo di procedere, condotta; *pl. -s*, atti *m.pl.*, verbale *m.*; *the -s of the Royal Society*, gli atti della Società Reale; (leg.) causa, dibattito, deliberazione; *to take legal -s*, procedere per vie legali, intentare causa (contro).

**proceeds** *n.pl.* provento, ricavo, ricavato, profitto, incasso.

**process** *n.* processo, sviluppo, corso, andamento; *in — of time*, col passare del tempo, in seguito; *in — of construction*, in corso di costruzione; (fam.) *it's a long —*, ci vuole tempo; (techn.) procedimento; *tr.* (techn.) lavorare, trattare, sottoporre a procedimento; *intr.* (fam.) camminare in processione.

**process-engraving** *n.* zincografia.

**procession** *n.* processione, corteo, sfilata, accompagnamento. **-al** *adj.* processionale, di corteo; *n.* inno solenne.

**proclaim** *tr.* proclamare, dichiarare, promulgare, bandire, rendere pubblico; (fig.) rivelare.

**proclamation** *n.* proclama *m.*, proclamazione, promulgazione; bando, decreto, editto.

**proclitic** *adj.* (gramm.) proclitico; *n.* particella proclitica.

**proclivity** *n.* inclinazione, propensione, tendenza; *anglophile proclivities*, sentimenti anglofili.

**Procne** *pr.n.* (myth.) Progne.

**proconsul** *n.* (hist.) proconsole *m.*

**-ar** *adj.* proconsolare. **-ate, -ship** *n.* proconsolato.

**procrastinat-e** *intr.* procrastinare, temporeggiare, indugiare. **-ion** *n.* procrastinazione, temporeggiamento, indugio.

**procreat-e** *tr.* procreare, generare. **-ion** *n.* procreazione, generazione.

**Procrust-es** *pr.n.* (myth.) Procruste **-ean** *adj.* di Procruste; (fig.) drastico.

**proctor** *n.* (hist.) censore; (leg.; eccl.) procuratore *m.*; *Queen's Proctor*, procuratore generale (nelle cause di divorzio). (There is no Italian equiv. of a 'proctor' in a university.)

**procurable** *adj.* procurabile, trovabile.

**procurat-ion** *n.* (eccl.) procurazione; (comm.; leg.) procura; (pejor.) lenocinio. **-or** *n.* (leg.; eccl.) procuratore; (Scot.) Pubblico Ministero.

**procur-e** *tr.* procurare, procurarsi, acquistare, ottenere, procacciare; (leg.) adescare a scopo di prostituzione. **-ement** *n.* ottenimento, conseguimento; (leg.) lenocinio.

**procur-er** *n.* lenone *m.*, mezzano, (pop.) ruffiano. **-ess** *n.* mezzana, (pop.) ruffiana.

**prod** *n.* pungolo; (fig.) stimolo; *to give someone a —*, punzecchiare qualcuno; *tr.* pungolare, frugare; (fig.) stimolare, punzecchiare; *to — in the ribs*, dare una gomitata a.

**prodigal** *adj.* prodigo, scialacquatore; generoso, largo, liberale; *— son*, figliuol prodigo; *n.* scialacquatore. **-ity** *n.* prodigalità.

**prodigious** *adj.* prodigioso, portentoso, miracoloso; (fam.) enorme. **-ness** *n.* prodigiosità.

**prodigy** *n.* prodigio, portento, miracolo, fenomeno; *infant —*, bambino prodigio.

**pro·duce** *n.* prodotto, (collect.) prodotti, generi *m.pl.*; *farm —*, prodotti agricoli.

**produc-e** *tr.* produrre, estrarre, esibire, tirar fuori; *to — witnesses*, produrre testimoni; *to — something from one's pocket*, tirar fuori qualcosa dalla tasca; *to — one's passport*, esibire il passaporto; (of land, plant) produrre, generare; (industr.) fabbricare; fare, arrecare; *to — a sensation*, fare sensazione; *to — a book*, pubblicare un libro; (theatr.) presentare, mettere in scena; *-ed by*, regia di; (cinem.) presentare; (geom.) prolungare. **-er** *n.* (agric.; industr.) produttore; fabbricante *m.*; generatore; *-er gas*, gasogeno; (theatr.) impresario; (cinem.) regista *m.* **-ible** *adj.* producibile; (geom.) prolungabile.

**product** *n.* prodotto; (fig.) effetto, frutto.

**production** *n.* esibizione; (leg.) produzione; (industr.) produzione, prodotto, fabbricazione; *— costs*, spese di fabbricazione; *cost of —*, costo di fabbricazione; *— line*, trasportatore a cinghia; rendimento; (lit.) opera, produzione letteraria; (theatr.) messinscena, allestimento scenico, realizzazione scenica; (cinem.) regia; (mus.) *voice —*, emissione della voce.

**productiv-e** *adj.* produttivo, ad alto rendimento; fertile, fecondo;*— of great annoyance*, causa di gran fastidio. **-eness, -ity** *n.* produttività rendimento, potenzialità.

**proem** *n.* proemio.

**pro-English** *adj.* anglofilo.

**prof.** *n.* (fam.) professore.

**profan-e** *adj.* profano, empio; (heathen) pagano; *things sacred and —*, il sacro e il profano; *— language*, turpiloquio, linguaggio sacrilego; *tr.* profanare, violare; (rel.) profanare, sconsacrare. **-ation** *n.* profanazione, atto profano; (rel.) sconsacrazione. **-eness** *n.* profanità. **-er** *n.* profanatore; violatore. **-ity** *n.* profanità; irriverenza; bestemmia.

**profess** *tr.*, *intr.* professare, fare professione di, dichiarare, esprimere; pretendere, manifestare falsamente; confessare; esercitare; insegnare. **-ed** *adj.* dichiarato; preteso, sedicente; (eccl.) professo.

**profession** *n.* professione; mestiere *m.*; *by —*, di professione; dichiarazione, professione; *to make — of*, dichiarare, professare; (eccl.) il pronunciare voti.

**professional** *adj.* professionale, di professione, di mestiere; *a — man*, un professionista; *the — classes*, i professionisti; *— footballer*, calciatore di professione; *— jealousy*, gelosia di mestiere; *— practice*, usi della professione; *to take — advice*, consultare un esperto; *n.* professionista *m.*, *f*, esperto. **-ism** *n.* professionalismo.

**professor** *n.* professore *m.*, professoressa *f.*; (of doctrine) adepto. **-ate** *n.* professorato, cattedra; corpo dei professori. **-ial** *adj.* professorale, di professore. **-ship** *n.* professorato, cattedra; *to be appointed to a -ship*, essere nominato a una cattedra, essere nominato professore.

**proffer** *tr.* offrire, proferire.

**profici-ency** *n.* abilità, perizia, competenza; *— in Italian*, una buona conoscenza della lingua italiana; *to attain —*, arrivare a una buona competenza; (mil.) *— pay*, premio di specialità. **-ent** *adj.* abile, capace, esperto, versato, provetto, competente, forte; *to be -ent in*, essere forte in, avere una buona conoscenza di.

**profile** *n.* profilo, contorno; *in —*, di profilo; (archit.) sezione; (industr.) sagoma; *tr.* ritrarre in profilo; *to be -d against*, staccarsi da; (industr.) sagomare, profilare.

**profit** *n.* profitto; frutto, vantaggio, beneficio; *with — to*, con vantaggio di; *there is no — in*, è inutile; *to turn to —*, trarre profitto da; (comm.) utile *m.*, guadagno; *to make a— on*, guadagnare su; *— and loss account*, conto profitti e perdite; *to work for —*, lavorare per guadagnare; *the — motive*, il motivo del guadagno; *tr.* giovare (a), essere di vantaggio (a); *what will it — him?*, che vantaggio ne avrà?; *intr.* approfittare (di), trarre vantaggio (da), guadagnare.

**profitab-le** *adj.* utile, vantaggioso, lucroso, fruttuoso. **-leness** *n.* utilità, vantaggio, profitto. **-ly** *adv.* vantaggiosamente, con profitto.

**profiteer** *n.* profittatore, affarista *m.*; *war —*, pescecane *m.*, arricchito di guerra; *intr.* realizzare enormi guadagni, guadagnare illecitamente. **-ing** *n.* guadagni illeciti, realizzazione di grossi profitti.

**profitless** *adj.* senza profitto, inutile.

**profit-seeking** *adj.* interessato, a scopo di lucro. **-sharing** *n.* compartecipazione agli utili. **-taking** *n.* (finan.) realizzazione degli utili.

**proflig-acy** *n.* dissolutezza, sregolatezza; libertinaggio, licenziosità; sperpero. **-ate** *adj.* dissoluto, sregolato; *n.* libertino; scialacquatore.

**profound** *adj.* profondo; (fig.) approfondito, intenso; grande, immenso; *a — secret*, un segreto assoluto. **-ness, profundity** *n.* profondità.

**profus-e** *adj.* esuberante, copioso, abbondante; (fig.) prodigo; *to be — in one's apologies*, sprofondarsi in scuse. **-eness** *n.* profusione, abbondanza. **-ion** *n.* profusione, abbondanza, copia; *in -ion*, a profusione, in abbondanza.

**progenit-or** *n.* progenitore, antenato, capostipite *m.*; (MS.) originale *m.* **-ress, -rix** *n.* progenitrice.

**progeny** *n.* progenie *f.*, prole *f.*, discendenza, figli *m.pl.*, figliuolanza; (fig.) conseguenza.

**prognathous** *adj.* (anthrop.) prognato.

**prognos-is** *n.* prognosi *f.* **-tic** *adj.* profetico, di pronostico; (med.) rivelatore, sintomatico; *n.* pronostico; (med.) sintomo. **-ticate** *tr.* pronosticare. **-tication** *n.* pronostico.

**programme** *n.* programma *m.*;

*to draw up a* —, stabilire un programma. **-seller** *n.* maschera.

**pro·gress** *n.* progresso, progressi *m.pl.*, sviluppo, avanzata; corso, andamento; *in* —, in corso; *to make* —, fare progressi, progredire; *to make slow* —, progredire lentamente; *to make no* —, restare addietro; *the* — *of civilization*, il progresso della civiltà; *in the* — *of time*, nel corso degli anni; *to report* —, riferire sull'andamento; *the* — *of events*, l'andamento degli avvenimenti; *the* — *of the enemy*, l'avanzata del nemico; (hist.) viaggio ufficiale (di un sovrano); *Pilgrim's Progress*, 'Il viaggio del pellegrino'.

**progress** *intr.* progredire, far progressi, avanzare, andare avanti, svilupparsi, migliorare; *the patient is -ing satisfactorily*, il malato sta migliorando; *how is your work -ing?*, come va il lavoro? **-ion** *n.* (math.; mus.) progressione. **-ional** *adj.* progressivo. **-ive** *adj.* progressivo, crescente; (pol.) *-ive party*, partito progressista; *by -ive stages*, per gradi; *n.* (pol.) progressista *m.*, *f.*

**prohibit** *tr.* proibire, vietare, interdire; *smoking -ed*, vietato fumare.

**prohibition** *n.* proibizione, divieto; (USA) proibizionismo. **-ist** *adj.*, *n.* proibizionista *m.*, *f.*

**prohibit-ive** *adj.* proibitivo; *-ive prices*, prezzi esagerati. **-ory** *adj.* (leg.) proibitivo, coercitivo.

**pro·ject** *n.* progetto, disegno, piano.

**project** *tr.* proiettare, gettare, lanciare; *to* — *a picture on the screen*, proiettare un'immagine sullo schermo; progettare; *intr.* sporgere, aggettare. **-ile** *n.* proiettile *m.*, missile *m.* **-ion** *n.* proiezione; sporgenza; risalto, aggetto; (cinem.) proiezione. **-ive** *adj.* proiettivo. **-or** *n.* (person) progettista *m.*, promotore; (instrument, cinem.) proiettore.

**prolapse** *n.* (med.) prolasso.

**prolegomena** *n.pl.* prolegomini *m.pl.*

**prolepsis** *n.* (rhet.) prolessi *f.*

**proletari-an** *adj.*, *n.* proletario. **-at** *n.* proletariato; plebe *f.*

**proliferat-e** *tr.* proliferare, prolificare; *intr.* moltiplicarsi. **-ion** *n.* proliferazione.

**prolific** *adj.* prolifico, fecondo, fertile. **-ness** *n.* fecondità, fertilità, prolificità.

**prolix** *adj.* prolisso, diffuso. **-ity** *n.* prolissità.

**prologue** *n.* prologo, proemio; introduzione.

**prolong** *tr.* prolungare, allungare; prorogare. **-ation** *n.* prolungamento; proroga. **-ed** *adj.* lungo; *-ed applause*, applauso nutrito.

**promenade** *n.* passeggiata, passeggio pubblico; (sea-front) lungomare *m.*, passeggiata a mare; — *concert*, concerto popolare; — *deck*, ponte *m.* di passeggio; *intr.* passeggiare su e giù, fare una passeggiata; *tr.* condurre a passeggio. **-r** *n.* passeggiatore.

**Prometheus** *pr.n.* (myth.) Prometeo.

**promin-ence** *n.* prominenza, sporgenza, risalto; eminenza, importanza, evidenza; *to come into* —, distinguersi; *to give* — *to something*, dar risalto a qualcosa. **-ent** *adj.* prominente, sporgente, che risalta, che si distacca; cospicuo, notevole, eminente.

**promiscu-ous** *adj.* promiscuo, confuso, indiscriminato. **-ity**, **-ousness** *n.* promiscuità; confusione.

**promis-e** *n.* promessa; *to make a* —, promettere, fare una promessa; *to keep a* —, mantenere una promessa; *to break a* —, mancare a una promessa; *to put off with -s*, pascere di promesse; (leg.) *breach of* —, mancata promessa (di matrimonio); (fig.) *of great* —, di grandi speranze; *to show great* —, promettere bene; *tr.* promettere, assicurare; *to* — *someone something*, promettere qualcosa a qualcuno; *to* — *oneself something*, ripromettersi qualcosa; *to* — *the moon*, promettere mari e monti; *intr. to* — *well*, promettere bene. **-ing** *adj.* promettente, che promette bene; *to look -ing*, promettere bene. **-ory** *adj.* promettente; (comm.) *-ory note*, pagherò cambiario.

**promontory** *n.* promontorio, capo.

**promot-e** *tr.* promuovere, favorire, incoraggiare, dare impulso a; (mil.) *to be -ed*, essere promosso, passare. **-er** *n.* promotore, fautore; *company -er*, fondatore di società, (pejor.) affarista *m.* **-ion** *n.* promozione; avanzamento; *to get -ion*, essere promosso; (of a company) lancio.

**prompt** *adj.* pronto, sollecito, lesto, alacre; — *reply*, risposta sollecita, risposta a volta di corriere; — *payment*, pagamento in contanti, pronta cassa; *at six o'clock* —, alle sei precise; *tr.* ispirare, incitare, spingere, consigliare; (pejor.) istigare, soffiare; *to be -ed by*, essere spinto da; *to* — *a witness*, subornare un testimonio; (theatr.) suggerire, rammentare. **-er** *n.* istigatore; (theatr.) suggeritore; *-er's box*, buca del suggeritore.

**prompt-itude, promptness** *n.* prontezza, sollecitudine.

**prompt-note** *n.* (comm.) promemoria del termine di pagamento.

**promulgat-e** *tr.* promulgare; (fig.) propagare, diffondere. **-ion** *n.* promulgazione, propagazione, diffusione. **-or** *n.* promulgatore.

**pronaos** *n.* pronao.

**prone** *adj.* prono, disteso; (fig.) disposto, incline, proclive, propenso; *adv.* bocconi, lungo disteso. **-ness** *n.* inclinazione, propensione, proclività.

**prong** *n.* rebbio, dente *m.*, punta; forca; *tr.* infilzare con la forca. **-ed** *adj.* munito di rebbi; *three-pronged fork*, tridente *m.*

**pronominal** *adj.* (gramm.) pronominale.

**pronoun** *n.* (gramm.) pronome *m.*

**pronounc-e** *tr.* pronunciare, pronunziare; *to* — *clearly*, enunciare; *to* — *every syllable*, sillabare, scandire; proferire, dire; (leg.) *to* — *sentence*, proferire la sentenza, condannare; dichiarare; esprimere; *intr.* dichiararsi, pronunciarsi. **-eable** *adj.* pronunciabile. **-ed** *adj.* pronunziato, marcato, forte, spiccato; *to become more -ed*, accentuarsi. **-ement** *n.* dichiarazione, asserzione.

**pronunciamento** *n.* pronunciamento.

**pronunciation** *n.* pronuncia, pronunzia; accento.

**proof** *adj.* resistente (a), a prova di, impenetrabile, impermeabile; (against disease) immune; (fig.) *to be* — *against flattery*, essere indifferente alle lusinghe; (techn.) — *spirit*, liquore spiritoso contenente il 57% di alcool puro, alcool a 57 gradi; *n.* prova, dimostrazione, evidenza; (photog.) prova; *cast-iron* —, prova assoluta; *as a* — *of*, a prova di; *capable of* —, suscettibile di prova; *the onus of* —, l'onere *m.* della prova; *to give* — *of*, dare prova di, provare; *to put to the* —, mettere alla prova; *to stand the* —, reggere alla prova; (provb.) *the* — *of the pudding is in the eating*, alla prova si scortica l'asino; (typ.) bozza (di stampa); *clean* —, seconda bozza; *foul* —, prima bozza; *galley* —, bozza in colonna; *page* —, bozza impaginata.

**proof** *tr.* rendere resistente, rendere impermeabile; (typ.) tirare una bozza di.

**proof-press** *n.* (typ.) tirabozze *m.* **-reader** *n.* (typ.) correttore di bozze, revisore. **-reading** *n.* correzione delle bozze. **-sheet** *n.* (typ.) bozza (di stampa).

**prop** *n.* (bldg.; min.) puntello, rinforzo; (fig.) appoggio, sostegno; *tr. to* — (*up*), puntellare, rinforzare; (fig.) sostenere, sorreggere, appoggiare; *to* — (*up*) *a ladder against a wall*, appoggiare una scala contro il muro; *to* — *up an invalid with pillows*, sostenere un malato con guanciali; *intr.* (of horse) fermarsi improvvisamente.

**propagand-a** *n.* propaganda, réclame *f.* **-ist** *n.* propagandista *m.*; (pol.) attivista *m., f.*
**propagat-e** *tr.* riprodurre, propagare, diffondere, spargere; *intr.* (of animals, plants) riprodursi. **-ion** *n.* riproduzione, propagazione, diffusione. **-or** *n.* propagatore.
**propane** *n.* (chem.) propano.
**propel** *tr.* spingere avanti, lanciare, muovere, impellere, propulsare; (mech.) azionare; *mechanically -led*, a propulsione meccanica; (aeron.) *jet-propelled plane*, aviogetto. **-lent** *adj., n.* propulsore. **-ler** *n.* propulsore; (naut.; aeron.) elica.
**propeller-blade** *n.* pala di elica. **-shaft** *n.* albero dell'elica, albero di trasmissione.
**propelling** *adj.* propulsivo; — *force*, forza motrice; — *pencil*, matita automatica.
**propense** *adj.* (liter.) propenso, incline.
**propensity** *n.* propensione, inclinazione, tendenza.
**proper** *adj.* proprio, appropriato, particolare; *the — sense of the word*, il senso particolare della parola; — *to*, proprio di; propriamento detto, vero e proprio; *literature —*, la letteratura propriamente detta; confacente, appropriato, adatto; giusto, corretto, esatto; *at the — time*, al momento giusto; *to think — to*, ritenere giusto di; *in — condition*, in buono stato; *to have recourse to the — authorities*, ricorrere a chi di ragione; conveniente, convenevole, decoroso; *to be —*, convenire, essere conveniente; — *behaviour*, contegno decoroso; (math.) proprio; (gramm.) — *noun*, — *name*, nome proprio. **-ly** *adv.* bene, a modo, correttamente, come si deve; *to do something -ly*, fare bene qualcosa; *to be -ly dressed*, essere vestito correttamente; *to behave -ly*, comportarsi bene; propriamente, per essere esatti, effettivamente, a rigore; *-ly speaking*, a rigore di termini, a dire il vero; completamente.
**propertied** *adj.* possidente, benestante.
**property** *n.* proprietà; beni *m.pl.*, averi *m.pl.*; *personal —*, beni mobili; *real —*, beni immobili; *public —*, proprietà pubblica, di dominio pubblico; *a man of —*, un possidente; *to be the — of*, appartenere a; tenuta, possedimento; proprietà, qualità, caratteristica, virtù, attributo; (math.) affezione; *pl.* (theatr.) *properties*, *props*, fabbisogno, dotazione.
**property-man** (theatr.) trovarobe *m.* **-tax** *n.* imposta fondiaria.
**prophecy** *n.* profezia, predizione.
**prophesy** *tr.* profetare, profetizzare, predire, annunziare; *intr.* profetare, fare il profeta.
**prophet** *n.* profeta *m.*; *a — is not without honour save in his own country*, nessun profeta è nella patria caro. **-ess** *n.* profetessa. **-ic(al)** *adj.* profetico; *-ic skill*, arte divinatoria.
**prophyl-axis** *n.* (med.) profilassi *f.* **-actic** *adj., n.* (med.) profilattico.
**propinquity** *n.* propinquità, vicinanza, prossimità; parentela, affinità.
**propitiat-e** *tr.* propiziare, rendere propizio; (fig.) placare, calmare, rabbonire. **-ion** *n.* propiziazione, espiazione. **-ory** *adj.* propiziatorio, espiatorio.
**propitious** *adj.* propizio, favorevole, amico. **-ly** *adv.* propiziamente, favorevolmente. **-ness** *n.* disposizione propizia, l'essere propizio, buon augurio.
**proponent** *n.* proponente *m.*
**proportion** *n.* proporzione; *in — to*, in proporzione a; *out of (all) —*, sproporzionato, smisurato, a dismisura; parte *f.*; *pl.* dimensioni *f.pl.*, misure *f.pl.*; *tr.* proporzionare, dividere in parti proporzionate, adeguare. **-al** *adj.* proporzionale. **-ate** *adj.* proporzionato, adeguato, conforme.
**proposal** *n.* proposta, offerta; offerta di matrimonio, dichiarazione; progetto.
**propos-e** *tr.* proporre; *to — someone's health*, brindare alla salute di qualcuno; intendere, divisare, proporsi; *intr. to — (marriage) to*, fare un'offerta di matrimonio a, domandare la mano a, dichiararsi; (provb.) *man -s, God disposes*, l'uomo propone e Dio dispone. **-er** *n.* proponitore, proponente *m., f.* **-ition** *n.* proposta, asserzione; (gramm.) proposizione; (math.) teorema *m.*; (fam.) affare *m.*, progetto.
**propound** *tr.* proporre, porre.
**proprietary** *adj.* proprietario; — *rights*, diritti di proprietà; brevettato; — *medicines*, specialità medicinali.
**proprietor** *n.*proprietario, possessore; (of dog, *etc.*) padrone *m.*; *joint —*, comproprietario; *landed —*, proprietario terriero, possidente *m.* **-ship** *n.* diritto di proprietario, proprietà, possesso.
**proprietress** *n.* proprietaria, padrona.
**propriety** *n.* convenienza, decenza, decoro, opportunità; *pl. the proprieties*, le buone creanze.
**propuls-ion** *n.* propulsione, forza motrice; *jet —*, propulsione a reazione. **-ive** *adj.* propulsivo.
**prorogation** *n.* proroga; rinvio.
**prorogue** *tr.* prorogare, differire, rimandare, rinviare.
**prosaic** *adj.* prosaico, prosastico, banale. **-ness** *n.* prosaicità, banalità.
**prosaist** *n.* prosatore.
**proscenium** *n.* proscenio.
**proscribe** *tr.* proscrivere, proibire; bandire, esiliare.
**proscription** *n.* proscrizione; bando, esilio; proibizione.
**prose** *n.* prosa; *attrib.* in prosa; prosaicità.
**prosecut-e** *tr.* proseguire, continuare; esercitare; (leg.) accusare, citare in giudizio, processare, querelare; *to be -ed for*, (a crime) essere accusato di, (civil offence) essere querelato per; *trespassers will be -ed*, i contravventori verranno processati a termine di legge; *to — the charge*, sostenere l'accusa. **-able** *adj.* perseguitabile.
**prosecution** *n.* proseguimento, prosecuzione, continuazione; esercizio; (leg., for crime) accusa, (for civil offence) querela; processo; *to start a — against*, intentare processo contro, citare in giudizio; (prosecuting lawyers) accusa; *witness for the —*, testimone d'accusa.
**prosecutor** *n.* prosecutore; continuatore; (leg., in criminal action) accusatore, (in civil action) querelante *m.*, attore; *public —*, (Britain) procuratore della regina, (Italy) procuratore della Repubblica, pubblico ministero.
**prosecutrix** *n.* (leg.) querelante *f.*, attrice *f.*
**proselyt-e** *n.* proselito. **-ize** *tr.* convertire; *intr.* fare proseliti.
**Proserpine** *pr.n.* (myth.) Proserpina.
**prose-writer** *n.* prosatore.
**prosiness** *n.* prosaicità; banalità.
**prosod-y** *n.* prosodia, metrica. **-ic(al)** *adj.* prosodico.
**prosopopoeia** *n.* (rhet.) prosopopea.
**pro'spect** *n.* prospetto, vista, panorama *m.*; esposizione; (fig.) prospettiva, aspettativa, speranza; *to have something in —*, avere qualcosa in vista; *to open up new -s*, aprire nuove prospettive; *-s of success*, speranze di successo; *the -s of success are good*, si prevede un successo; *to have good -s*, avere un brillante avvenire; *to have no — of*, non avere speranza di.
**prospect** *intr.* esplorare. **-ing** *n.* ricerca, esplorazione. **-ive** *adj.* probabile, eventuale, futuro, previsto; (leg.) che riguarda il futuro. **-or** *n.* esploratore, cercatore. **-us** *n.* prospetto, programma *m.*, manifesto.
**prosper** *intr.* prosperare, fiorire, riuscire; (bot.) allignare, attecchire; *tr.* far riuscire, favorire. **-ity, -ousness** *n.* prosperità, ricchezza.

**prosperous** *adj.* prospero, fiorente benestante, abbiente; (fig.) favorevole, propizio.
**prostate** *n.* (anat.) prostata; — *gland*, prostata.
**prosthesis** *n.* (gramm.) prostesi *f.*; (surg.) protesi *f.*
**prostitut-e** *n.* meretrice *f.*, prostituta; (fam.) passeggiatrice; (vulg.) puttana; *tr.* prostituire. **-ion** *n.* prostituzione.
**pro·strat-e** *adj.* prostrato, prosternato, bocconi; (fig.) abbattuto, affranto, accasciato.
**prostrat-e** *tr.* prostrare, prosternare, distendere (per terra); (fig.) abbattere, accasciare. **-ion** *n.* prostrazione, prosternazione; (fig.) abbattimento, costernazione.
**prosy** *adj.* prosaico; noioso, tedioso; banale.
**protagonist** *n.* protagonista *m.*, *f.*
**protean** *adj.* proteiforme; (fig.) variabile, versatile.
**protect** *tr.* proteggere, difendere, tutelare, salvaguardare, riparare. **-ing** *adj.* protettivo. **-ion** *n.* protezione, difesa, tutela; patrocinio, egida; salvacondotto; *under the -ion of*, sotto la protezione di; *to afford -ion against*, proteggere da, riparare da. **-ionism** *n.* (econ.) protezionismo. **-ionist** *adj.*, *n.* (econ.) protezionista *m.*, *f.* **-ive** *adj.* protettivo, protettore, difensivo; *-ive colouring*, mimetismo; *-ive custody*, carcere preventivo.
**protector** *n.* protettore, difensore; (of arts) mecenate *m.* **-ate** *n.* protettorato. **-ship** *n.* patrocinio, protettorato.
**protectress** *n.* protettrice, patrona.
**protégé** *n.* protetto.
**proteiform** *adj.* proteiforme.
**protein** *n.* proteina.
**pro·test** *n.* protesta; *under* —, sotto riserva; *to make a* —, protestare, elevare una protesta; (comm.) protesto; *ship's* —, dichiarazione d'avaria.
**protest** *tr.* protestare, dichiarare; *intr.* protestare, reclamare.
**Protestant** *adj.*, *n.* (rel.) protestante *m.*, *f.*; evangelico. **-ism** *n.* protestantesimo.
**protestation** *n.* protesta, dichiarazione.
**protestingly** *adv.* in tono di protesta, per protesta.
**prothalamion** *n.* (lit.) epitalamio.
**protocol** *n.* protocollo.
**prototyp-e** *n.* prototipo; archetipo. **-ic(al)** *adj.* prototipo.
**protract** *tr.* protrarre, prolungare; (surv.) riprodurre in scala, rilevare. **-ion** *n.* protrazione; prolungazione. **-or** *n.* (geom.) rapportatore, goniometro; (anat.) muscolo estensore.
**protrud-e** *tr.* sporgere, spingere avanti, mettere fuori; *intr.* sporgere, sporgersi. **-ing** *adj.* sporgente.
**protuber-ance** *n.* protuberanza. **-ant** *adj.* protuberante; prominente.
**proud** *adj.* orgoglioso, fiero; superbo, altero, altezzoso, arrogante; (fig.) magnifico, grande, nobile; *house-proud*, orgoglioso della propria casa; *to be — of*, essere orgoglioso di, vantarsi di; (pop.) *to do oneself* —, non privarsi di nulla; (med.) — *flesh*, granulazione esuberante, (fam.) cicciolo.
**prov-e** *tr.* dimostrare, provare; mettere alla prova, verificare; (fig.) confermare; (provb.) *the exception -s the rule*, l'eccezione conferma la regola; *to — oneself*, affermarsi, mostrarsi; (leg.) *to — a will*, omologare un testamento; *intr.* mostrarsi, rivelarsi; *to — to be*, risultare. **-able** *adj.* provabile, dimostrabile.
**provenance** *n.* provenienza, origine *f.*
**Provençal** *adj.*, *n.* provenzale *m.*, *f.*
**Provence** *pr.n.* (geog.) Provenza.
**provender** *n.* (agric.) foraggio, biada; (fam.) cibo, vettovaglie *f.pl.*
**proverb** *n.* proverbio, adagio. **-ial** *adj.* proverbiale.
**provid-e** *tr.* provvedere, fornire, procurare; *to — an excuse*, fornire una scusa; *to — an opportunity*, procurare l'occasione; *the country was well -d with corn*, il paese era ben provvisto di grano; *to — oneself with*, provvedersi di, munirsi di; stabilire, stipulare; *intr.* provvedere, premunirsi; *to — for*, provvedere a; *to — against*, premunirsi contro. **-ed** *adj.* provvisto, munito; *conj.* *-ed* (*that*), purchè, a patto che.
**provid-ence** *n.* provvidenza; previdenza, prudenza; *divine* —, la Provvidenza. **-ent** *adj.* provvido, provvidente, previdente, prudente, economo; *-ent society*, società di mutuo soccorso. **-ential** *adj.* provvidenziale.
**provider** *n.* provveditore, fornitore; *universal -s*, grande magazzino.
**providing** *conj.* purchè, a patto che.
**province** *n.* provincia; *in the -s*, in provincia; (fig.) sfera d'azione, campo, competenza; *it was not within my* —, non era di mia competenza; (eccl.) diocesi *f.*; (leg.) giurisdizione.
**provincial** *adj.*, *n.* provinciale *m.*, *f.*; di provincia; (eccl.) padre provinciale. **-ism** *n.* provincialismo; (pejor.) campanilismo.
**provision** *n.* provvedimento, preparativo, disposizione; fornitura, raccolta; *to make — for something*, provvedere a; *to make — against*, premunirsi contro; condizione, disposizione, articolo; *to come within the -s of the law*, rientrare negli articoli della legge; *pl.* provviste *f.pl.*, provvigioni *f.pl.*, viveri *m.pl.*; — *dealer*, negoziante di generi alimentari; *tr.* approvvigionare, rifornire. **-al** *adj.* provvisorio, temporaneo; (leg.) provvisionale. **-ally** *adv.* provvisoriamente, in via provvisoria. **-ing, -ment** *n.* approvvigionamento.
**proviso** *n.* stipulazione, clausola condizionale. **-ry** *adj.* provvisorio, condizionale.
**provocat-ion** *n.* provocazione. **-ive** *adj.* provocativo, provocante; (med.) stimolante.
**provok-e** *tr.* provocare, eccitare, stimolare; (fam.) irritare, aizzare, esasperare. **-ing** *adj.* provocante, irritante, esasperante, fastidioso; *how -ing!*, che seccatura!
**provost** *n.* (eccl.) prevosto, preposto; (schol.) rettore; sindaco; (mil.) — *marshal*, capo della polizia militare.
**prow** *n.* (naut.) prora, prua.
**prowess** *n.* prodezza; valore *m.*
**prowl** *intr.* vagare in cerca di preda; (fig.) gironzolare, girare, andare furtivamente; *n.* *to go on the* —, andare in cerca di preda, (fig.) vagare, (pejor.) spiare. **-er** *n.* predone, girellone.
**proximate** *adj.* prossimo, vicino, approssimativo.
**proximity** *n.* prossimità, vicinanza.
**proximo** *adv.* (comm.) del mese venturo, prossimo.
**proxy** *n.* procura; mandato; *by* —, per procura; procuratore.
**prude** *n.* donna eccessivamente pudica, ritrosetta, puritana.
**prud-ence** *n.* prudenza, avvedutezza; circospezione. **-ent** *adj.* prudente, avveduto, cauto, circospetto. **-ential** *adj.* prudenziale.
**prud-ery** *n.* pudicizia affettata, ritrosia, schifiltà. **-ish** *adj.* ritrosetto, pudibondo, schifiltoso. **-ishness** *n.* See **prudery**.
**prune**[1] *n.* prugna secca (colour) color prugna.
**prun-e**[2] *tr.* (bot.) potare, discapezzare, accecare; (fig.) sfrondare, tagliare. **-er** *n.* potatore. **-ing** *n.* potatura.
**pruning-hook** *n.* potatoio.
**pruri-ence** *n.* prurito, pizzicore; libidine *f.* **-ent** *adj.* che pizzica, pruriginoso; (*m.*) lascivo, lubrico, libidinoso.
**Prussian** *adj.*, *n.* prussiano; — *blue*, blu *m.* di Prussia, ferrocianuro di potassio.
**prussic** *adj.* (chem.) prussico.
**pry** *intr.* curiosare, spiare, ficcare il naso (in); scrutare, indagare; *Paul Pry*, ficcanaso. **-ing** *adj.* curioso, indiscreto, scrutatore.
**psalm** *n.* salmo, cantico; *to sing -s*, salmodiare. **-ist** *n.* salmista *m.* **-ody** *n.* salmodia.

**psalter** *n.* salterio, libro dei salmi. **-y** *n.* (mus.) salterio.
**pseudo-** *pref.* pseudo-, falso.
**pseudonym** *n.* pseudonimo; (fam.) nome di battaglia. **-ous** *adj.* pseudonimo.
**pshaw** *interj.* puah!, uff!, oibò!
**psittacosis** *n.* (med.) psittacosi *f.*
**Psyche** *pr.n.* Psiche *f.*; *n.* anima, spirito; (ent.) psiche.
**psychiatr-y** *n.* psichiatria. **-ic** *adj.* psichiatrico. **-ist** *n.* psichiatra *m.*, alienista *m.,f.*
**psychic(al)** *adj.* psichico, medianico; *n.* medium *m. indecl.*
**psychoan-alysis** *n.* psicanalisi *f.* **-alyse** *tr.* psicanalizzare. **-alyst** *n.* psicanalista *m., f.* **-alytic(al)** *adj.* psicanalitico.
**psycholog-y** *n.* psicologia. **-ical** *adj.* psicologico; (fam.) *the -ical moment*, il momento opportuno. **-ist** *n.* psicologo.
**psychopath** *n.* psicopatico. **-y** *n.* psicopatia.
**psycho-sis** *n.* psicosi *f.* **-tic** *adj., n.* psicopatico.
**ptarmigan** *n.* (orn.) pernice bianca, roncaso.
**pterodactyl** *n.* (palaeont.) pterodattilo.
**Ptolem-y** *pr.n.* Tolomeo. **-aic** *adj.* tolemaico.
**ptomaine** *n.* (chem.) ptomaina; (fam.) — *poisoning*, intossicazione intestinale.
**pub** *n.* osteria, bar *m.*
**puberty** *n.* pubertà.
**pub-is** *n.* (anat.) pube *m.* **-ic** *adj.* pubico.
**public** *adj.* pubblico, noto, di pubblica ragione; — *assistance*, assistenza sociale; — *convenience*, — *lavatory*, albergo diurno, gabinetti pubblici; — *holiday*, festa civile; — *house*, osteria, bar *m. indecl.*; — *library*, biblioteca comunale; — *property*, proprietà statale, (fig.) *to be — property*, essere di dominio pubblico; — *prosecutor*, ministro pubblico, procuratore; — *school*, (Britain, Italy) collegio privato, (USA) scuola governativa; — *spirit*, civismo; — *utility*, servizio pubblico; *in* —, in pubblico, pubblicamente; *to make* —, rendere noto, pubblicare; *n.* pubblico; *the reading* —, il pubblico dei lettori, i lettori.
**publican** *n.* oste *m.*; (bibl.) pubblicano.
**public-ation** *n.* pubblicazione. **-ist** *n.* pubblicista *m.*, pubblicitario. **-ity** *n.* pubblicità. **-ize** *tr.* fare la pubblicità a, pubblicare, rendere noto.
**public-spirited** *adj.* dotato di senso civico. **-ness** *n.* civismo.
**publish** *tr.* pubblicare; *-ed by*, edito da; *to be -ed*, venire fuori, uscire; *just -ed*, appena uscito; divulgare, rivelare, rendere noto; promulgare. **-er** *n.* editore, casa editrice; (USA) proprietario di giornale. **-ing** *n.* il pubblicare; pubblicazione; il mondo editoriale, l'editoria; *-ing firm*, casa editrice; (fam.) *he's in -ing*, lavora per una casa editrice.
**puce** *adj., n.* (di) color pulce.
**Puck** *n.* il folletto Puck; demonietto; (ice-hockey) disco.
**pucker** *n.* grinza, ruga; piega; *tr.* raggrinzare, corrugare; *to — (up) one's brow*, corrugare la fronte; (clothing) pieghettare; *intr.* raggrinzarsi, corrugarsi.
**puckish** *adj.* da folletto, furbo, maliziosetto.
**pudding** *n.* budino; pasticcio; *Christmas* —, budino di Natale; *milk* —, budino al latte; *black* —, sanguinaccio; (provb.) *the proof of the — is in the eating*, alla prova si scortica l'asino. **-faced** *adj.* (fam.) dal viso grassoccio, paffuto. **-stone** *n.* (geol.) puddinga, conglomerato.
**puddle** *n.* pozzanghera; (bldg.) malta; *intr.* sguazzare, impantanarsi; *tr.* (metall.) pudellare.
**pudicity** *n.* pudicizia, modestia.
**pueril-e** *adj.* puerile, fanciullesco, infantile. **-eness, -ity** *n.* puerilità.
**puff** *n.* sbuffo, buffata; (from pipe) boccata; (of wind) soffio; (of breath) alito; (dressm.) sboffo; (of false hair) ciuffo; (for powder) piumino; (cul.) sfogliatella; (advt.) reclame *f.*, montatura, gonfiatura; *tr., intr.* sbuffare, soffiare, ansare, ansimare; *to — at one's pipe*, tirare boccate dalla pipa; *to be -ed*, ansimare; *to — out*, gonfiare, far gonfiare; *to be -ed up with pride*, insuperbire, alzare la cresta; (slang) fare pubblicità esagerata a, esaltare, lodare al cielo.
**puff-adder** *n.* vipera sudafricana. **-ball** *n.* (bot.) vescia di lupo.
**puffed** *adj.* gonfio, gonfiato; ansimante; (dressm.) a sboffi.
**puffin** *n.* (orn.) puffino.
**puffiness** *n.* gonfiezza, paffutezza.
**puff-pastry** *n.* (cul.) pasta sfogliata.
**puff-puff** *n.* (infant.) ciuf-ciuf *m.*
**puffy** *adj.* gonfiato, paffuto.
**pug** *n.* (dog) carlino, cane bolognese; (clay) impasto; (slang) pugile *m.*
**pugil-ism** *n.* pugilato, pugilistica; (pop.) boxe *m.* **-ist** *n.* pugile *m.*, pugilatore.
**pugnacious** *adj.* pugnace, combattivo, litigioso. **-ness, pugnacity** *n.* combattività, litigiosità.
**pug-nosed** *adj.* dal naso ricagnato.
**puissant** *adj.* potente, possente.
**puke** *tr., intr.* vomitare.
**pukka** *adj.* (anglo-Ind.) vero, autentico; *a — sahib*, un vero signore.
**pulchritude** *n.* (lit., joc.) bellezza.
**pul-e** *intr.* piagnucolare; (of chicken) pigolare. **-er** *n.* piagnucolone *m.*; uccellino. **-ing** *adj.* piagnucoloso, pigolante; *n.* piagnucolìo, pigolìo.
**pull** *n.* tiro, tirata, strappo, strappata; *to give something a* —, tirare qualcosa; (of drink) sorsata; *to take a — at*, bere una sorsata di; (of smoke) boccata; (fig.) forza di attrazione; *a stiff* —, un vero sforzo, una salita faticosa; (rowing) vogata; (of bell) cordone *m.*; *to have a — over*, avere il vantaggio su; *to have a — with*, avere una grande influenza su; (mech.) trazione, tensione; (typ.) tiratura.
**pull** *tr.* tirare; trascinare; strappare; cavare, estrarre, trarre; (typ.) tirare; (sport) battere (la palla) mandando da una parte; *intr.* tirare; *to — to pieces*, strappare, fare a pezzi, (fig.) demolire, stroncare; *to — someone's ears*, tirare gli orecchi a qualcuno; *to — a long face*, allungare il muso; *to — faces*, fare smorfie; *to — one's hair*, strappare i capelli; *to — someone's leg*, prendere in giro qualcuno; *to — a muscle*, stirarsi un muscolo; *to — a lone oar*, fare da solo, essere il solo a far qualcosa; *to — one's punches*, non picchiare troppo forte, (fig.) trattare con riguardo; *to — strings*, intrigare, reggere le fila; *to — one's weight*, mettercela tutta; *to — about*, trascinare qua e là, maltrattare; *to — apart*, dividere, separare; *to — away*, staccare, tirar via, strappare, *intr.* (rowing) vogare forte; *to — away from the shore*, remare al largo; *to — back*, tirare indietro, trattenere, *intr.* indietreggiare, esitare; *to — down*, abbassare, tirare giù, calare; *to — one's hat down over one's eyes*, rincalcarsi il cappello fin sugli occhi; abbattere, demolire; *to — in*, far entrare, *intr.* (of train) entrare in stazione; *to — off*, tirare via, strappare, levare, togliere; *the lid -s off*, si può levare il coperchio; (fig.) *to — something off*, riuscire a far qualcosa, vincere; *to — off a deal*, concludere un affare; *to — on*, tirare su, mettere, (clothes) infilare, (stockings) calzare; *to — open*, aprire, spalancare; *to — out*, far uscire, tirar fuori, strappare, cavare, estrarre, (fig.) *to — out of the fire*, salvare, *intr.* (of ship) partire, salpare, allontanarsi, (of train) uscire dalla stazione, (motor.) uscire dalla fila per sorpassare; *to — over*, rovesciare tirando, *intr. to — over to one side*, tirarsi da una parte; *to — round*, tirare intorno a, (fig.) ravvivare, rianimare, *intr.* rimettersi; *to — through*, tirare attraverso, tirare d'imbarazzo, *intr.* rimettersi, guarire; *to* —

*to*, chiudere; *to — together*, congiungere, *to — oneself together* riprendere animo, farsi coraggio, *intr.* agire in armonia, collaborare; *to — up*, tirare su, sradicare, strappare, fermare, rimproverare; *intr.* fermarsi.

**pullet** *n.* pollastro, pollastrella.

**pulley** *n.* puleggia, carrucola.

**pulley-block** *n.* paranco.

**pullman** *n.* (rlwy.) carrozza Pullman, vettura di lusso.

**pullover** *n.* pullover *m.*

**pull-through** *n.* (mil.) scovolo.

**pullulate** *intr.* (bot.) germogliare, germinare; (zool.) moltiplicarsi; (fig.) pullulare, brulicare, formicolare.

**pulmonary** *adj.* polmonare.

**pulp** *n.* polpa; (paperm.) pasta; (paper) carta di legno; (fig.) *crushed to a —*, stritolato; *tr.* ridurre in polpa, spolpare; (paperm.) ridurre in pasta.

**pulpit** *n.* pulpito, pergamo.

**pulpy** *adj.* polposo, molle.

**pulsat-e** *intr.* pulsare, battere, palpitare. **-ion** *n.* pulsazione, battito, vibrazione.

**pulse**[1] *n.* polso; battito; *to feel someone's —*, sentire il polso a qualcuno; (radio) impulso; (mus., fig.) ritmo; *intr.* pulsare, battere.

**pulse**[2] *n.* (agric.) legumi, semileguminosi *m.pl.*

**pulveriz-e** *tr.* polverizzare, vaporizzare; (fig.) demolire, abbattere; *intr.* polverizzarsi, vaporizzarsi. **-ation** *n.* polverizzazione. **-ator, -er** *n.* polverizzatore, vaporizzatore.

**puma** *n.* (zool.) puma *m.*, coguaro.

**pumice** *n.* — (*stone*), pomice *f.*, pietra pomice; *tr.* impomiciare.

**pummel** *tr.* picchiare, prendere a pugni.

**pump**[1] *n.* (cost.) scarpa da ballo, scarpa scollata.

**pump**[2] *n.* pompa; *petrol —*, distributore (di benzina); *lubrication —*, pompa oliatrice; *tr.* pompare, azionare (una pompa); *to — dry*, asciugare (pompando); *to — up a tyre*, gonfiare un pneumatico; *intr.* palpitare, pulsare; (fig.) interrogare, cavare informazioni da; *to — a secret out of someone*, strappare un segreto a qualcuno; *to — someone's hand*, stringere la mano a qualcuno con effusione; *to — bullets into*, sparare raffiche su.

**pumpernickel** *n.* pane *m.* di segala.

**pumpkin** *n.* zucca; popone *m.*

**pun** *n.* bisticcio, giuoco di parole; *intr.* fare giuochi di parole, equivocare.

**punch**[1] *n.* punzone *m.*, stampo; *tr.* punzonare, perforare; *to — a ticket*, perforare un biglietto.

**punch**[2] *n.* colpo di pugno; (fam., fig.) forza, energia; *with a — in it*, mordace, forte, piccante; *tr.* dar un colpo di pugno a, picchiare.

**punch**[3] *n.* ponce *m.*

**Punch**[4] *pr.n.* Pulcinella *m.*; *— and Judy show*, teatrino di Pulcinella; *as pleased as —*, contento come una pasqua.

**punch-bowl** *n.* coppa da ponce. **-drunk** *adj.* stordito; (med.) affetto da encefalopatia cronica da pugilato.

**Punchinello** *pr.n.* Pulcinella *m.*

**punch(ing)-ball** *n.* (boxing) sacco.

**punch-mark** *n.* punzione.

**punctilio** *n.* puntiglio; correttezza, formalismo.

**punctilious** *adj.* puntiglioso, scrupoloso, meticoloso, cerimonioso. **-ness** *n.* formalismo, puntigliosità, correttezza.

**punctual** *adj.* puntuale, esatto, regolare; (of train) in orario. **-ity** *n.* puntualità; esattezza.

**punctuat-e** *tr.* punteggiare; (fig.) dare enfasi a. **-ion** *n.* punteggiatura, interpunzione; *-ion marks*, segni d'interpunzione.

**puncture** *n.* (surg.) puntura; perforazione; (tyre) bucatura, foratura; *tr.* pungere; (tyre) forare, bucare.

**pundit** *n.* indù colto; (fig.) sapientone, dotto.

**pung-ency** *n.* asprezza, acrimonia; gusto piccante; odore forte. **-ent** *adj.* pungente, acre, aspro; piccante; forte, acre; (fig.) caustico, mordace, sarcastico.

**Punic** *adj.* (hist.) punico, cartaginese.

**puniness** *n.* piccolezza; sparutezza; meschinità.

**punish** *tr.* punire, castigare; (leg.) *to — with a fine*, infliggere una multa a; (fam.) picchiare, bastonare; (boxing) *to be -ed*, incassare. **-able** *adj.* punibile. **-ing** *adj.* che punisce; (of work) spossante; (sport) duro. **-ment** *n.* punizione, pena, castigo; *capital -ment*, pena capitale.

**punit-ive, -ory** *adj.* punitivo.

**punka(h)** *n.* (Anglo-Ind.) ventola.

**punnet** *n.* cestino per frutta, canestro.

**punt** *n.* barchino, sandalo, chiatta; *tr.* spingere un sandalo con la pertica.

**punter** *n.* (cards, sport) puntatore, scommettitore.

**punt-pole** *n.* pertica.

**puny** *adj.* piccino, sparuto, malaticcio, meschino.

**pup, puppy** *n.* cucciolo, cagnolino; (of bitch) *to be in pup*, essere pregna; (fig.) giovanotto vanesio, damerino; (fam.) *to sell someone a —*, vendere fumo a qualcuno; *tr., intr.* (of bitch) figliare, partorire.

**pupa** *n.* (ent.) crisalide *f.*

**pupil**[1] *n.* allievo, alluno, scolaro; (in convent school) educanda; (leg.) pupillo; discepolo.

**pupil**[2] *n.* (anat.) pupilla.

**puppet** *n.* burattino, marionetta, fantoccio; *— government*, governo di fantocci. **-player** *n.* burattinaio. **-show** *n.* teatrino di burattini.

**puppy** *n.* See **pup.** **-ish** *adj.* (fam.) impertinente, vanitoso, fatuo.

**purblind** *adj.* miope, mezzo orbo, cieco; (fig.) ottuso.

**purchas-e** *n.* compra; acquisto; (leg.) acquisizione; *to buy at twenty years —*, comprare a prezzo equivalente al reddito di venti anni; *hire-purchase*, acquisto rateale; (mech.) presa, punto d'appoggio; paranco; *tr.* acquistare, comprare. **-able** *adj.* acquistabile, trovabile.

**purchase-block** *n.* paranco di puleggia.

**purchaser** *n.* acquirente *m., f.*, compratore.

**purchasing** *n.* acquisizione, acquisto; (econ.) *— power*, potere di acquisto.

**pure** *adj.* puro, schietto; casto, puro, illibato; (fig.) mero, semplice, puro. **-ness** *n.* See **purity.**

**purgat-ion** *n.* purgazione, purificazione. **-ive** *adj.* purgativo; *n.* purgante *m.*, purga.

**purgator-y** *n.* purgatorio. **-ial** *adj.* del purgatorio.

**purge** *n.* purga purgante *m.*; (pol.) epurazione; *tr.* purgare, purificare; (pol.) epurare.

**purif-y** *tr.* purificare; (chem.) depurare, rettificare. **-ication** *n.* purificazione; (chem.) depurazione. **-ier** *n.* purificatore; (chem.) depuratore.

**pur-ism** *n.* purismo. **-ist** *n.* purista *m., f.*

**puritan** *adj., n.* puritano. **-ical** *adj.* da puritano; rigido; austero. **-ism** *n.* puritanismo, rigidezza.

**purity** *n.* purità, purezza; castità; illibatezza.

**purl**[1] *n.* (needlew.) smerlo, lavoro a punto rovescio; *tr.* smerlare, lavorare a punto rovescio.

**purl**[2] *n.* (of brook) mormorio.

**purlieu** *n.* confine *m.*; *pl.* vicinanze *f.pl.*, dintorni *m.pl.*, periferia.

**purloin** *tr.* sottrarre, rubare. **-ing** *n.* sottrazione; furto.

**purple** *adj.* purpureo, porporino, violaceo; (of face) paonazzo; (bot.) *— loosestrife*, salcerella; (fig.) *— passages*, passi (di un libro) troppo elaborati; *n.* porpora; (eccl.) veste cardinalizia, porpora; *to be raised to the —*, essere innalzato alla porpora; *intr.* tingere color porpora; (fig.) imporporare; imporporarsi.

**pur'port** *n.* tenore; senso, significato.

**purport** *tr.* significare; mostrare; far apparire; implicare; avere la pretesa di.

**purpose** *n.* mira, scopo, fine; intenzione; *he did it on —*, l'ha fatto apposta; *a novel with a —*, un romanzo a tesi; *not to the —*, non a proposito; *to no —*, con nessun risultato; fermezza, proposito; *infirm of —*, irresoluto, senza carattere; *tr.* proporre, proporsi. **-ful** *adj.* pieno di significato; tenace. **-fulness** *n.* intenzione; tenacia. **-less** *adj.* inutile; senza scopo; senza intenzione. **-lessness** *n.* inutilità; mancanza di scopo; mancanza di intenzione. **-ly** *adv.* di proposito, volutamente, intenzionalmente.

**purposive** *adj.* premeditato, intenzionale; utile, risoluto.

**purr** *n.* fusa; *intr.* fare le fusa; (fig.) esprimere soddisfazione. **-ing** *n.* il far le fusa.

**purse**[1] *n.* borsellino, borsa; (sport) premio in denaro; *public —*, tesoro pubblico. **-proud** *adj.* orgoglioso delle proprie ricchezze. **-strings** *n.pl.* cordoni della borsa; *to hold the -strings*, controllare le spese.

**purse**[2] *intr.* contrarre (le labbra); increspare, incresparsi; raggrinzirsi.

**pursu-ance** *n.* continuazione, proseguimento; esecuzione; perseguimento. **-ant** *adj.* che persegue; *-ant to*, conforme a, in seguito a.

**pursu-e** *intr.* seguire, inseguire; perseguitare; ricercare, aspirare a, perseguire; continuare. **-er** *n.* inseguitore, continuatore.

**pursuit** *n.* inseguimento; caccia; ricerca; occupazione, impiego; carriera.

**purul-ence, -ency** *n.* purulenza, suppurazione. **-ent** *adj.* purulento, marcio.

**purvey** *tr.* provvedere, approvvigionare; far provvigioni. **-ance** *n.* approvvigionamento; provvigioni. **-or** *n.* approvvigionatore.

**purview** *n.* (leg.) testo, dispositivo; limite; scopo; intenzione; vista; (fig.) campo, sfera.

**pus** *n.* pus *m.*

**push** *n.* spinta; cozzo, urto; botta; colpo; influenza; pressione; sforzo; operosità, energia; iniziativa; bisogno, momento critico; *at a —*, in caso di emergenza; *when it came to the —*, quando arrivò il momento critico; *he has plenty of —*, è un vero arrivista; *tr.*, *intr.* spingere; spingersi, avanzare; farsi strada; *to — one's way*, introdursi a forza; (fig.) incalzare, spingere, fare pressioni; *he was -ed for time*, gli mancava il tempo; *to be -ed for money*, essere a corto di denaro; rivendicare; *to — one's advantage*, perseguire il proprio vantaggio; lanciare; attivare; *to — aside*, scostare, mettere da parte; *to — away*, allontanare, respingere; *to — back*, respingere, spingere indietro; indietreggiare; *to — down*, far cadere; spingere giù; *to — forward*, aprirsi una strada, spingersi avanti; (far) avanzare; *to — on*, spingersi avanti; (far) avanzare; spronare, incitare; accelerare; affrettarsi; *to — out*, cacciare, espellere; *to — a boat out*, mettere in acqua un'imbarcazione; *to — over*, far cadere; *to — through*, (far) passare attraverso; condurre a termine; far accettare; *to — to*, chiudere, accostare con una spinta; *to — up*, far salire.

**push-bike** *n.* bicicletta. **-button** *n.* pulsante. **-button switch** *n.* interruttore.

**pushcart** *n.* carretto a mano; passeggino.

**pusher** *n.* chi spinge; (fig.) chi fa strada nel mondo; arrivista *m.,f.*; chi lancia.

**pushful** *adj.* energico; intraprendente; aggressivo. **-ness** *n.* energia; intraprendenza; aggressività.

**pushing** *adj.* operoso, energico; intraprendente; che si fa strada nel mondo; indiscreto; *n.* spinta; *— of oneself forward*, indiscrezione, intrusione.

**pushover** *n.* (fam.) vittima facile; problema *m.* senza difficoltà; *she's a —*, è una ragazza di facili costumi.

**pusillanim-ity** *n.* pusillanimità. **-ous** *adj.* pusillanime. **-ousness** *n.* pusillanimità.

**puss** *n.* micio, micino; *excl.* *—!*, *—!*, muci! muci!; *Puss in Boots*, il Gatto con gli stivali; *— in the corner*, i quattro cantoni. **-y** *n.* micino; (slang) fica.

**pustul-ar, -ate** *adj.* pustoloso. **-ate** *intr.* coprire, coprirsi di pustole. **-ation** *n.* formazione di pustole.

**pustule** *n.* pustola.

**put** *tr.* mettere, porre, posare; *to — a matter right*, sistemare per bene una faccenda; *to — right*, correggere; *to — to death*, mandare a morte; *to — to flight*, mettere in fuga; *to be hard — to it*, essere messo in imbarazzo; apporre; sottoporre, esporre; *to — a question to*, rivolgere una domanda a; esprimere, esporre; tradurre; stimare, valutare; indurre; obbligare; dirigere; *to — to sea*, prendere il mare; indirizzare; investire (denaro); puntare, scommettere; conficcare; *he — a bullet through his brains*, si fece saltare le cervella; (sport) *to — the weight*, lanciare il peso; *to — aside*, mettere da parte, accantonare; mettere in serbo; *to — back*, rimettere a posto; ostacolare, rallentare; mettere indietro (le lancette di un orologio); (naut.) rientrare in porto; *to — down*, deporre, posare; reprimere, abbattere; sopprimere; ridurre al silenzio; umiliare; mettere per iscritto; *to — forth*, metter fuori; buttare; *to — forward*, proporre, avanzare; *to — oneself forward*, mettersi in evidenza; *to — in*, immettere; introdurre; interporre (parola); installare, collocare; *to — in for*, presentare la propria candidatura per; *to — off*, rimandare, rinviare, differire, aggiornare; togliere, sconcertare, sviare; dissuadere, scoraggiare; *to — on*, indossare; assumere; fingere; aumentare; *to — on airs*, darsi delle arie; *to — out*, stendere, allungare; espellere, cacciare; spegnere; *to — oneself out for*, farsi in quattro per; *to — through*, portare a termine; mettere in comunicazione telefonica; *to — together*, mettere insieme, unire, riunire; *to — two and two together*, arrivare ad una conclusione; *to — up*, *tr.* alzare, sollevare; innalzare; offrire; alloggiare; mettere in scena, rappresentare; attaccare, affiggere; *intr.* prendere alloggio.

**putative** *adj.* putativo, apparente.

**putref-y** *intr.* putrefare; putrefarsi. **-action** *n.* putrefazione.

**putrid** *adj.* putrido; (fig.) corrotto; (slang) di cattiva qualità.

**putter** *n.* (golf) putter *m.*; giocatore che dà alla palla il colpo che deve portarla alla buca.

**putting** *n.* (golf) pratica del put(t); *— green*, spazio erboso intorno alla buca.

**putty** *n.* mastice *m.*; stucco; intonachino a gesso; *tr.* stuccare.

**puzzl-e** *n.* imbarazzo; confusione; perplessità; problema; intrigo; enigma; *crossword —*, parole incrociate; *jig-saw —*, giuoco di pazienza a incastro; *tr.*, *intr.* imbarazzare, confondere, imbrogliare; rendere perplesso. **-ement** *n.* perplessità; imbarazzo. **-er** *n.* chi, ciò che rende perplessi; chi si interessa di giuochi di pazienza. **-ing** *adj.* imbarazzante.

**pygmy** *adj.*, *n.* pigmeo.

**pyjamas** *n.pl.* pigiama *m.*

**pylon** *n.* pilone *m.*, traliccio.

**pyorrh(o)ea** *n.* (med.) piorrea.

**pyramid** *n.* (archit.; geom.) piramide *f.*; mucchio. **-ic(al)** *adj.* piramidale, a forma di piramide.

**pyre** *n.* pira, rogo.

**pyretic** *adj.* piretico, febbrile.

**pyrite** *n.* (min.) pirite *f.*

**pyrotechn-y** *n.* pirotecnica. **-ic(al)** *adj.* pirotecnico. **-ics** *n.* pirotecnica. **-ist** *n.* pirotecnico.

**Pyrrhic** *adj.* pirrico, di Pirro; (fig.) *— victory*, vittoria di Pirro.

**Pythagor-ean** *adj.* pitagorico. **-ism** *n.* pitagorismo.

**python** *n.* (zool.) pitone *m.*

**pyx** *n.* coppella (per monete di metalli preziosi; (eccl.) pisside *f.*

**Q, q** *n.* q (cu) *m., f.*; (teleph.) — *for Queenie*, q come Quarto; *on the q.t.*, tra quattr'occhi, segretamente, di nascosto.

**qua** *adv.* in qualità di; come; in quanto.

**quack**[1] *excl. qua qua qua!*; *n.* schiamazzo delle anitre; qua qua *m.*; (infant.) *quack-quack*, anitra; *intr. fare qua qua qua*, schiamazzare, anatrare.

**quack**[2] *n.* ciarlatano; — *doctor*, medicastro, dottoraccio; — *lawyer*, azzeccagarbugli *m.*; — *remedy*, rimedio da ciarlatano. **-ery** *n.* ciarlataneria; empirismo.

**quad** *n. abbrev.* of **quadrangle**, *q.v.*; *abbrev.* of **quadruplet**, *q.v.*; (typ.) quadratino, riga.

**quadrang-le** *n.* quadrangolo; corte quadrangolare interna. **-ular** *adj.* quadrangolare.

**quadrant** *n.* quadrante *m.*; quarto di cerchio; (techn.) settore *m.*

**quadrature** *n.* quadratura.

**quadrennial** *adj.* quadriennale.

**quadrilateral** *adj., n.* quadrilatero.

**quadrille** *n.* (cards) quadriglio; (dance) quadriglia.

**quadrisyllab-le** *n.* quadrisillabo. **-ic** *adj.* quadrisillabo.

**quadroon** *adj., n.* quarterone *m.*

**quadruped** *adj., n.* quadrupede *m.*

**quadruple** *adj.* quadruplo, quadruplice; *n.* quadruplo; *tr.* quadruplicare; *intr.* quadruplicarsi.

**quadruplet** *n.* gruppo di quattro; nato di parto quadrigemino; *pl.* quattro nati in un solo parto.

**quadruplicat-e** *adj.* quadruplo, quadruplice; *in* —, in quattro copie; *tr.* quadruplicare; fare quattro copie di. **-ion** *n.* quadruplicazione.

**quaestor** *n.* (Rom. hist.) questore *m.*

**quaff** *tr.* bere a gran sorsi; tracannare.

**quagmire** *n.* pantano; palude *f.*; acquitrino.

**quail**[1] *n.* (orn.) quaglia.

**quail**[2] *intr.* aver paura; sgomentarsi; tremare; indietreggiare.

**quaint** *adj.* strano; bizzarro; curioso; buffo; (fam.) *isn't she —!*, che buffa!, che macchietta! **-ness** *n.* bizzarria; singolarità, stranezza.

**quake** *n.* tremito; scossa; (fam.) terremoto; *intr.* tremare; rabbrividire; fremere.

**quaker** *n.* quacchero. **-ess** *n.* quacchera.

**qualificat-ion** *n.* riserva, condizione; *without -s*, senza riserve, incondizionatamente; *the statement requires —*, occorre precisare; requisito, titolo; *academic -s*, titoli di studio; diploma *m.*; *property* —, censo eletetoral; competenza, attitudine, capacità; qualifica. **-ive** *adj., n.* (gramm.) qualificativo. **-ory** *adj.* qualificativo.

**qualified** *adj.* competente; idoneo; *to be fully — to*, avere tutte le qualità necessarie per, essere capace di; abilitato, diplomato; — *accountant*, ragioniere *m.*; condizionato, con riserve.

**qualify** *tr.* qualificare; rendere idoneo; abilitare; qualificare (come); *to — someone as a rascal*, dare del mascalzone a qualcuno; limitare, avanzare riserve in merito a, modificare; diluire, correggere; *intr.* rendersi idoneo; abilitarsi, diplomarsi; essere ammesso; *to — as a pilot*, prendere il brevetto di pilota. **-ing** *adj.* qualificativo; di abilitazione; (sport) *-ing round*, eliminatoria.

**qualitative** *adj.* qualitativo.

**quality** *n.* qualità; grado di eccellenza; caratteristica; proprietà; attributo; pregio; dote *f.*; capacità; stato; rango; (chem.; techn.) potere *m.*

**qualm** *n.* nausea; malessere *m.*; (fig.) scrupolo di coscienza; inquietudine *f.*; preoccupazione.

**quandary** *n.* imbarazzo; impaccio; perplessità; situazione difficile; *to be in a* —, trovarsi in imbarazzo, essere perplesso.

**quantitative** *adj.* quantitativo.

**quantity** *n.* quantità; *in quantities*, in gran quantità, in abbondanza; *negligible* —, quantità trascurabile; (of person) nullità *f.*; (math.) *unknown* —, incognita; (phon.) quantità, lunghezza.

**quantum** *n.* quanto; sufficienza; (phys.) — *theory*, teoria dei quanti.

**quarantine** *n.* quarantena.

**quarrel** *n.* lite *f.*; controversia; bisticcio; baruffa; alterco; disputa; dissidio; *to pick a — with*, attaccare briga con; *to make up a* —, appianare le divergenze, riconciliarsi; *to have no — with*, non avere motivo di lagnanza contro; *intr.* litigare; bisticciare; attaccar brighe; altercare; disputare; venire a discussione; abbaruffars; (fig.) trovare a ridire.

**quarrel**[2] *n.* (archery) quadrello; (archit.) quadrato; (diamond-cutting) diamante da vetraio; (techn.) bulino.

**quarrelling** *n.* litigio; baruffa; alterco.

**quarrelsome** *adj.* litigioso, rissoso; — *fellow*, attaccabrighe *m.* **-ness** *n.* umore litigioso; irascibilità.

**quarry**[1] *n.* preda, selvaggina.

**quarry**[2] *n.* cava; pietraia; *marble* —, cava di marmo; *tr.* (s)cavare; (fig.) ricavare. **-man** *n.* cavatore.

**quart** *n.* quarto di gallone, due pinte *f.pl.* (= 1.136 litri); (cards) serie di quattro.

**quartan** *adj.* — *fever*, febbre quartana.

**quarter** *n.* quarto, quarta parte; *a — of an hour*, un quarto d'ora; *it's a — to ten*, sono le dieci meno un quarto, manca un quarto alle dieci; *a — past six*, le sei e un quarto; *a — full*, un quarto pieno; trimestre *m.*; — *day*, giorno della pigione; (weight) ventotto libbre (= 12.7 chili); (dry meas.) otto stai (= 2.908 ettolitri); (of town) quartiere *m.*, rione *m.*, (in Venice) sestiere *m.*; *residential* —, quartiere residenziale; direzione, parte *f.*, regione, ambiente *m.*; *the four -s of the globe*, le quattro parti del mondo; *the four -s of heaven*, le regioni del cielo; *from all -s*, da tutte le parti; *in high -s*, nelle alte sfere; *to apply to the proper* —, rivolgersi all'autorità competente; (herald.) quarto, quartiere; (naut.) anca, quartiere di poppa; *wind on the* —, vento al largo di poppa; grazia; *to ask for* —, chiedere grazia; *to give no* —, non dare quartiere, non concedere la grazia, essere spietato; (leg.) — *sessions*, tribunale che si riunisce trimestralmente; *pl.* alloggio, appartamento; *living -s*, stanze d'abitazione; *to take up one's -s*, prendere alloggio, sistemarsi; *at close -s*, da vicino; *to come to close -s*, venire ai ferri corti; (mil.) alloggiamento, accantonamento, acquartieramento, caserma; *to take up -s*, acquartierarsi; (naval, battle stations) posti di combattimento.

**quarter** *tr.* dividere in quattro parti; squartare, smembrare; alloggiare; *to — oneself on*, sistemarsi presso; (mil.) acquartierare, accasermare; (herald.) inquartare; (fig.) *to — a piece of land*, battere un terreno; *intr.* (of moon) entrare in un nuovo quarto.

**quarter-binding** *n.* rilegatura con dorso in pelle.

**quarterdeck** *n.* (naval) cassero; (fig.) *the* —, gli ufficiali.

**quartered** *adj.* diviso in quattro parti; (herald.) inquartato.

**quarter-face** *adj.* (of portrait) di profilo. **-hourly** *adj.* ad ogni quarto d'ora; *adv.* ogni quarto d'ora, ogni quindici minuto.

**quartering** *n.* divisione in quattro parti; squartamento; (herald.) inquartamento; (mil.) acquartieramento, alloggiamento.

**quarterly** *adj.* trimestrale; *adv.* trimestralmente, ogni tre mesi; *n.* pubblicazione trimestrale.

**quartermaster** *n.* commissario, furiere *m.*; (hist.) quartiermastro; — *general*, capo del dipartimento amministrazione e alloggi; (naval) secondo capo

timoniere. **-sergeant** *n.* (mil.) sergente furiere.
**quartern** *n.* quarto; *— loaf*, pagnotta di quattro libbre.
**quartet(te)** *n.* quartetto; *string —*, quartetto d'archi; (prosod.) quartina.
**quarto** *adj.*, *n.* in quarto.
**quartz** *n.* quarzo.
**quash** *tr.* sopprimere; schiacciare; (leg.) cassare; annullare; invalidare.
**quasi** *pref.* semi-, quasi; *adv.*, *conj.* come se fosse, in un certo senso, cioè.
**quatercentenary** *n.* quarto centenario.
**quaternary** *adj.* (geol.) quaternario.
**quatrain** *n.* (prosod.) quartina.
**quatrefoil** *n.* (archit.; bot.) quadrifoglio; (herald.) quattrofoglie.
**quaver** *n.* tremolio; voce tremula; (mus.) croma; *intr.* tremolare; parlare con voce tremula. **-ing** *adj.* tremolante; tremulo.
**quay** *n.* banchina; ponte *m.*; calata. **-side** *adj.* portuale; del porto; *-side worker*, portuale *m.*; *n.* banchina.
**quean** *n.* (lit.) sgualdrina.
**queas-y** *adj.* nauseante, nauseabondo; delicato di stomaco. **-iness** *n.* malessere *m.*; nausea.
**queen** *n.* regina; (cards) dama; *beauty —*, reginetta di bellezza, Miss *f.*; *— bee*, ape regina; (cat-breeding) gatta madre; (slang, derog.) omosessuale; *tr.* fare regina; (fam.) *to — it*, fare come se fosse la regina; regnare. **-like**, **-ly** *adj.* da regina, regale, reale.
**queen-mother** *n.* regina madre.
**queer** *adj.* strambo; bizzarro; strano; eccentrico; originale; *a — fellow*, un tipo strano, un originale; indisposto, male; *to feel —*, sentirsi male; *— in the head*, matto; (fig.) *Queer Street*, difficoltà finanziarie, guai *m.pl.*; *n.* (slang, derog.) omosessuale, finocchio; *tr.* guastare; rovinare; *to — the pitch for*, rompere le uova nel paniere a. **-ness** *n.* stranezza; bizzarria.
**quell** *tr.* reprimere; sopprimere; domare; soffocare.
**quench** *tr.* spegnere; estinguere; smorzare; *to — one's thirst*, dissetarsi. **-er** *n.* spegnitore; estintore; bibita dissetante.
**quern** *n.* macina a mano; *pepper —*, macinapepe *m. indecl.*
**querulous** *adj.* querulo; lamentoso; dolente. **-ness** *n.* querimonia; tono dolente.
**query** *n.* domanda; quesito; punto interrogativo; *to raise a —*, porre un quesito; *to settle a —*, decidere una questione; *tr.* indagare; chiedersi; contestare; mettere in dubbio, mettere un punto interrogativo su.
**quest** *n.* ricerca; (eccl.) questua; *to go in — of*, andare alla ricerca di, seguire le tracce di.
**question** *n.* questione; quesito; domanda interrogativa; interrogazione; problema *m.*; argomento materia; *a burning —*, un problema scottante; *the Eastern —*, la questione d'Oriente; *a — of time*, una questione di tempo; *rhetorical —*, interrogazione retorica; *indirect —*, interrogazione indiretta; *the book in —*, il libro di cui si tratta; *the — is*, la questione è, si tratta di sapere se; *that is the —*, ecco il problema; *to be or not to be, that is the —*, essere o non essere, ecco il dilemma; *that is not the —*, non si tratta di questo; *out of the —*, fuori questione; *beyond all —*, indubbio, certo; *to put a — to*, fare una domanda a, domandare a, interrogare; *to make no — about*, non sollevare obiezioni a; *tr.* interrogare, esaminare; mettere in dubbio, dubitare di, contestare. **-able** *adj.* dubbio, incerto, discutibile; *in -able taste*, in dubbio gusto; (pejor.) sospetto, equivoco, ambiguo. **-ableness** *n.* incertezza; contestabilità; ambiguità; dubbio gusto. **-er** *n.* interrogatore; interrogante *m.*, *f.*, esaminatore. **-ing** *adj.* interrogativo; dubbioso; *n.* interrogazione.
**question-mark** *n.* punto interrogativo.
**questionnaire** *n.* questionario.
**queue** *n.* coda; *to form a —*, fare la coda, accodarsi; (of hair) coda, codino; *intr.* fare la coda; *to — up*, mettersi in coda.
**quibbl-e** *n.* cavillo; sotterfugio; giuoco di parole; bisticcio; *intr.* cavillare; sofisticare; fare storie. **-ing** *adj.* cavilloso; pignolo; *n.* equivocazione; cavillo.
**quick** *adj.* rapido, veloce, celere; serrato; vivace, pronto, sveglio, desto; svelto, lesto, sbrigativo, agile; *be —!*, sbrigati!, presto!; *to be — to take offence*, essere facile ad offendersi; *to be — off the mark*, cogliere la palla al balzo, capire al volo; *to grow -er*, accelerarsi; (mus.) allegro; (living) vivo; *the — and the dead*, i vivi e i morti; *adv.* rapidamente, velocemente, presto, subito; (mil.) *— march!*, avanti marsch!; *n.* carne viva; (fig.) *to cut to the —*, toccare sul vivo, pungere nel vivo.
**quick-change** *adj.* (theatr.) *— artist*, trasformista *m.*, *f.* **-eared** *adj.* dall'orecchio fino.
**quicken** *tr.* accelerare; affrettare; (mus.) accelerare; *to — one's pace*, allungare il passo; (fig.) animare; ravvivare; dare vita a; stimolare; vivificare; *intr.* accelerarsi; (fig.) animarsi, vivificarsi. **-er** *n.* stimolante *m.*, eccitante *m.* **-ing** *adj.* che si accelera; più celere; stimolante, eccitante; *n.* accelerazione; ravvivamento; rinascita.
**quick-eyed** *adj.* dagli occhi acuti, sveglio. **-firer** *n.* fucile a ripetizione; cannone a tiro rapido. **-firing** *adj.* a tiro rapido.
**quicklime** *n.* calce viva.
**quick-lunch** *adj.* *— counter*, tavola calda, snack-bar *m.*
**quick-ly** *adv.* presto, subito, tosto; rapidamente, prontamente; senza indugio. **-ness** *n.* rapidità; celerità; prestezza; (fig.) svegliatezza; sveltezza; vivacità.
**quick-sand** *n.* sabbia mobile. **-set** *adj.* (bot.) siepe viva.
**quick-sighted** *adj.* dalla vista acuta; perspicace; intelligente. **-ness** *n.* vista acuta; perspicacità.
**quicksilver** *n.* argento vivo; mercurio.
**quick-tempered** *adj.* vivace; impulsivo; irascibile. **-witted** *adj.* di spirito pronto; sveglio; vivo; intelligente. **-wittedness** *n.* prontezza di spirito; intelligenza viva.
**quid** *n.* (of tobacco) cicca; (slang) sterlina.
**quiddity** *n.* (philos.) quiddità, essenza; (fam.) giuoco di parole, sottigliezza.
**quiesc-ence** *n.* quiescenza; inerzia; riposo. **-ent** *adj.* quiescente; tranquillo; a riposo.
**quiet** *adj.* tranquillo, quieto, calmo, placido; sereno; silenzioso, zitto, cheto; tenue, pallido, sobrio; dolce, mansueto; *be —!*, sta zitto!, taci!; *to grow —*, calmarsi, acchetarsi; *to keep —*, tacere, star zitto; *to keep something —*, tenere nascosto qualcosa; *— as a mouse*, mogio mogio; *all — on the western front*, niente di nuovo sul fronte occidentale; *n.* quiete *f.*; tranquillità; pace *f.*; calma; serenità; silenzio; (fam.) *on the —*, di nascosto, clandestinamente; *to tell somebody something on the —*, dire qualcosa a qualcuno a quattr'occhi; *tr.* acquietare, acchetare; calmare; tranquillizzare; far tacere.
**quieten** *tr.* acquietare; calmare; acchetare; tranquillizzare; *intr.* *to — down*, calmarsi; acchetarsi; rasserenarsi; placarsi.
**quiet-ism** *n.* (eccl. hist.) quietismo. **-ist** *n.* quietista *m.*, *f.*
**quietness, quietude** *n.* quiete *f.*; calma, tranquillità; pace *f.*; riposo; silenzio.
**quietus** *n.* colpo di grazia.
**quiff** *n.* ciuffo.
**quill** *n.* penna; spina; aculeo; *— pen*, penna d'oca, cannuccia; (mus.) penna, plettro.
**quill-driver** *n.* (fam.) imbrattacarte *m. indecl.*
**quilt** *n.* trapunta; coltre *f.*; *eiderdown —*, piumino. **-ed** *adj.* a trapunta, imbottito.
**quince** *n.* cotogna.

**quincentenary** *n.* quinto centenario.
**quinine** *n.* chinino, china.
**quinquagenarian** *adj.*, *n.* cinquantenne *m.*, *f.*
**quinquagesima** *pr.n.* (eccl.) (domenica di) quinquagesima.
**quinquenni-um** *n.* quinquennio. **-al** *adj.* quinquennale.
**quins** *n.* (fam.) see **quintuplets.**
**quinsy** *n.* (med.) angina.
**quintal** *n.* (meas.) quintale *m.*
**quintessence** *n.* quintessenza.
**quint-et** *n.* quintetto. **-uple** *adj.*, *n.* quintuplo; *tr.* quintuplicare; *intr.* quintuplicarsi. **-uplet** *n.* serie di cinque; *pl.* cinque nati da un medesimo parto.
**quip** *n.* frizzo; motteggio; battuta.
**quire** *n.* quinterno; (of paper) ventiquattro fogli.
**Quirinal** *pr.n.* Quirinale *m.*
**quirk** *n.* frizzo; arguzia; ticchio; vezzo; ghirigoro, svolazzo.
**quisling** *n.* collaborazionista *m.*; traditore.
**quit** *adj.* libero, liberato; sbarazzato; sdebitato.
**quit** *tr.* lasciare; abbandonare; smettere; *to — hold of*, lasciar andare; (fig.) *to — oneself*, comportarsi; *to — office*, dimettersi, dare le dimissioni; *intr.* andarsene; *notice to —*, disdetta.
**quite** *adv.* perfettamente; completamente; bene; del tutto, affatto, proprio, veramente; often rendered by -issimo form of *adj.*, e.g. *— young*, giovanissimo; *— right!*, giustissimo!, hai ragione!; *— so*, già, proprio così; *— late*, ben tardi; *to be — well*, star proprio bene; piuttosto, abbastanza; vero, proprio; *— a success*, un vero successo.
**quits** *adj.* pari, pari e patta; *to be —*, essere pari; *to cry —*, rinunciare; *double or —*, lascia o raddoppia.
**quittance** *n.* ricevuta, quietanza.
**quiver**[1] *n.* (archery) faretra; turcasso.
**quiver**[2] *n.* brivido; fremito; tremito; *intr.* tremare; avere i brividi; fremere; palpitare; (of voice) tremare; *tr.* agitare. **-ing** *adj.* tremolante, tremante; fremente; *n.* fremito; brivido; tremolìo.
**qui vive** *n. to be on the —.* stare all'erta, essere sul chi va là.
**Quixot-e** *pr.n.* (Don) Chisciotte. **-ic** *adj.* donchisciottesco, stravagante.
**quiz** *n.* scherzo; beffa; *n.* questionario; indovinello; (esame) orale *m.*; (radio) quiz *m.*; *tr.* burlarsi di, canzonare. **-zical** *adj.* beffardo; canzonatorio; curioso, strambo.
**quod** *n.* (pop.) gattabuia; fresco.
**quoin** *n.* (bldg.) cantone *m.*; spigolo; (typ.) cuneo; serraforme *m.*
**quoit** *n.* anello; *pl.* giuoco degli anelli.
**quondam** *adj.* antico, già, d'altre volte.
**quorum** *n.* numero legale.
**quota** *n.* quota, rata; (comm.) contingentamento; *to contribute one's —*, fare il proprio contributo.
**quotation** *n.* citazione; brano citato; (comm.; fin.) quotazione; corso. **-marks** *n.* virgolette; *to put in -marks*, mettere fra virgolette.
**quote** *n.* (fam.) citazione; *pl.* (typ.) virgolette; *end of -s*, chiuse le virgolette; *tr.* citare; addurre; allegare; (comm.) quotare, fare un prezzo (per); *in reply please — this number*, nella risposta si prega di riferirsi al numero; *intr. to — from a book*, citare da un libro.
**quoth** *defect. vb. — I*, dissi io; *— he*, disse egli.
**quotidian** *adj.* quotidiano, giornaliero.
**quotient** *n.* quoziente *m.*
**Q-ship** *n.* nave *f.* civetta.

**R, r** *n.* erre *m.*, *f.*; *to roll one's -'s*, parlare con l'erre; *the three R's*, leggere, scrivere e far di conto; (teleph.) *— for Robert*, erre come Roma.
**rabbet** *n.* (carpent.) scanalatura incastro; *tr.* scanalare, addocciare, incastrare. **-joint** *n.* giunto a maschio e femmina. **-plane** *n.* pialletto per scanalare, sponderuola.
**rabb-i** *n.* rabbino; *chief —*, gran rabbino. **-inical** *adj.* rabbinico.
**rabbit** *n.* (zool.; cul.) coniglio; (fig.) schiappa; fifone *m.*; *to go -ing*, dare la caccia ai conigli. **-hutch** *n.* conigliera. **-warren** *n.* garenna, conigliera.
**rabble** *n.* canaglia, plebaglia.
**Rabelaisian** *adj.* (lit.) rabelesiano.
**rabid** *adj.* rabbioso, furioso, violento; (med.) idrofobo; (fig.) fanatico, arrabbiato.
**rabies** *n.* (med.; vet.) idrofobia; (pop.) rabbia.
**raccoon** *n.* see **racoon.**
**race**[1] *n.* corsa, gara di velocità; *pl. the -s*, le corse, concorso ippico; (fig.) corso; *his — is nearly run*, è quasi alla fine dei suoi giorni; corrente *f.*; (of mill) gora; (mech.) gola di scorrimento, pista; (of ball-bearing) anello; *intr.* gareggiare (in velocità), andare a tutta velocità, correre; *to — along*, divorare la strada; (of engine) imballarsi; *tr.* far correre; *to — someone*, gareggiare con qualcuno; *he used to — me off my feet*, mi faceva correre troppo.
**race**[2] *n.* (ethn.) razza; schiatta, stirpe *f.*; lignaggio; *the human —*, il genere umano; *the white -s*, le razze bianche.
**race-card** *n.* programma *m.* delle corse.
**race-course** *n.* ippodromo, campo delle corse. **-goer** *n.* frequentatore delle corse di cavalli.
**race-hatred** *n.* odio di razza.
**racehorse** *n.* cavallo di corsa.
**raceme** *n.* (bot.) racemo.
**race-meeting** *n.* concorso ippico.
**racer** *n.* (person) corridore; (horse) cavallo da corsa; (motor.) macchina da corsa.
**race-track** *n.* pista.
**Rachel** *pr.n.* Rachele.
**rachit-is** *n.* (med.) rachitismo. **-ic** *adj.* (med.) rachitico.
**racial** *adj.* di razza, di stirpe; (pejor.) razziale. **-ist** *n.* razzista *m.*, *f.* **-ism** *n.* razzismo.
**raciness** *n.* brio, vivacità; vigore *m.*
**racing** *adj.* rapido, da corsa; *n.* le corse *f.pl.*; *horse-racing*, ippica; *— stable*, scuderia di cavalli da corsa; *motor-racing*, corse automobilistiche; *track-racing*, corse su pista.
**rack**[1] *n.* rastrelliera; (for letters) casellario; (for pipes) portapipe *m.*; (for plates) scolapiatti *m.*; (rlwy. for luggage) reticella; *— railway*, ferrovia a cremagliera.
**rack**[2] *n.* (torture) ruota; (fig.) *to be on the —*, essere sulle spine; *tr.* (hist.) mettere alla tortura, tormentare; dare gli stratti a; (fig.) *to — one's brains*, lambiccarsi il cervello; (of wine) filtrare.
**rack**[3] *n.* rovina; *to go to — and ruin*, andare in malora.
**racket**[1] *n.* (sport) racchetta.
**racket**[2] *n.* chiasso, baccano, fracasso, schiamazzo; (fam.) *to kick up a —*, far baccano; *to stand the —*, accettare le conseguenze, pagare il fio; affare losco, scandalo; truffa, ricatto; *intr. to — (about)*, far chiasso, far baccano. **-eer** *n.* ricattatore; truffatore; affarista *m.* **-eering** *n.* ricatto. **-y** *adj.* chiassoso, rumoroso; sgangherato, sconquassato.
**rack-rent** *n.* affitto esorbitante.
**-wheel** *n.* ruota dentata.
**racoon** *n.* (zool.) procione *m.*
**racquet** *n.* see **racket**[1]**.**
**racy** *adj.* brioso, piccante, vigoroso, vivace; *— anecdote*, aneddoto piccante, barzelletta; caratteristico.
**radar** *n.* radar *m.*
**raddle** *n.* ocra rossa, cinabrese *m.*; *tr.* dipingere con ocra rossa; imbellettare.

**radial** *adj.* radiale.
**radi-ance** *n.* irradiamento, irradiazione; (fig.) splendore *m.*, fulgore *m.* **-ant** *adj.* raggiante, radioso; splendido, fulgido, sfavillante, brillante; (phys.) radiante.
**radiat-e** *tr.* irradiare, diffondere; *intr.* irradiarsi, emettere raggi; (fig.) brillare, raggiare, emanare. **-ion** *n.* irraggiamento; (ir)radiazione. **-or** *n.* (mech.) radiatore *m.*; (for heating) termosifone *m.*, calorifero.
**radical** *adj.* radicale; *n.* radicale *m.*, *f.*
**radio** *n.* radiotelegrafia, radiofonia; (fam.) radio *f.*; — *beacon*, radiofaro; — (*set*), apparecchio radio; *tr.* radiotelegrafare, mandare (un messaggio) per radio.
**radioactiv-e** *adj.* radioattivo. **-ity** *n.* radioattività.
**radiogram** *n.* radiogramma *m.*, marconigramma *m.*; (fam.) radiogrammofono. **-ophone** *n.* radiogrammofono.
**radiography** *n.* radiografia.
**radiolog-y** *n.* radiologia. **-ical** *adj.* radiologico. **-ist** *n.* radiologo.
**radiotherapy** *n.* radioterapia.
**radish** *n.* (bot.) rafano, radice *f.*, ravanello.
**radium** *n.* (chem.) radio.
**radius** *n.* raggio; *within a — of ten miles*, entro un raggio di dieci miglia.
**raffia** *n.* (bot.) rafia.
**raffish** *adj.* dissipato, dissoluto.
**raffle** *n.* lotteria privata, riffa; *intr.* vendere per mezzo di una lotteria.
**raft** *n.* zattera, chiatta.
**rafter** *n.* (bldg.) trave *f.*, travetto, puntone *m.*
**rag**[1] *n.* cencio, straccio, brandello; *in -s*, a brandelli; *without a — to one's back*, nudo bruco; — *doll*, bamboccio, bambola di stracci; (pejor.) giornalaccio.
**rag**[2] *n.* (schol.) baccano, baldoria (di studenti); *tr.* (schol., fam.) prendere in giro, fare un tiro birbone a; *intr.* far baccano.
**ragamuffin** *n.* pezzente *m.*, straccione *m.*; monello, biricchino.
**rag-and-bone** *adj.* — *man*, cenciaiolo. **-bag** *n.* sacchetto per gli stracci.
**rage** *n.* rabbia, collera, ira, furia, furore *m.*; *to be in a —*, essere arrabbiato; *to fly into a —*, montare su tutte le furie, andare in bestia; *to be beside oneself with —*, non poterne più dalla rabbia; (fig.) mania, passione; *to be all the —*, essere di gran moda, far furore; *intr.* essere furioso, infuriarsi, andare in collera, montare su tutte le furie, smaniare; *to — against someone*, inveire contro qualcuno; (of elements) infierire, infuriare, imperversare.
**ragged** *adj.* stracciato, lacero, logoro, a brandelli; cencioso; aspro, ruvido, scabroso, frastagliato; (fig.) rozzo, imperfetto; (bot.) — *robin*, fiore *m.* cuculo. **-ness** *n.* asprezza, ruvidezza, scabrosità; (fig.) imperfezione, imcompiutezza.
**raging** *adj.* furioso, furibondo, rabbioso, violento, tempestoso, bollente; *n.* furia, furore *m.*, impeto, violenza.
**ragman** *n.* cenciaiolo, straccivendolo.
**ragout** *n.* (cul.) intingolo; ragù *m. indecl.*
**rag-paper** *n.* carta di stracci. **-tag** *n.* (fam.) *-tag and bob-tail*, plebaglia, canaglia.
**ragtime** *n.*, *adj.* (mus. hist.) tipo di ritmo sincopato.
**ragwort** *n.* (bot.) erba San Jacopo, erba chitarra.
**raid** *n.* razzia, scorreria, incursione, irruzione; *air-raid*, incursione aerea; *tr.* razziare, fare una incursione in, invadere, attacare. **-er** *n.* razziatore *m.*; invasore *m.*; predone *m.*
**rail**[1] *n.* sbarra, cancello, inferriata; balustrata, ringhiera, corrimano; (naut.) battagliola; (rlwy.) rotaia, binario; *British Rail*, le ferrovie britanniche; *by —*, per ferrovia, col treno; *to go off the -s*, deragliare, uscire dalle rotaie, (fig.) sviarsi, perdere le staffe, uscire dai gangheri; *tr.* provvedere di sbarre; *to — in*, rinchiudere con inferriate; *to — off*, delimitare con inferriate.
**rail**[2] *intr. to — against*, inveire contro, prendersela con.
**rail**[3] *n.* (orn.) rallo.
**rail-car** *n.* (rlwy.) automotrice.
**railhead** *n.* capolinea *m.*
**railing(s)** *n.* cancellata, inferriata, ringhiera; balustrata.
**raillery** *n.* canzonatura, motteggio, derisione.
**rail-way, -road** *n.* ferrovia, strada ferrata; *branch —*, diramazione ferroviaria; *light —*, ferrovia a scartamento ridotto; *underground —*, ferrovia sotterranea, metropolitana; *Italian State —*(*s*), Ferrovie dello Stato (FS) — *accident*, disastro ferroviario; — *carriage*, vagone ferroviario; — *engine*, locomotiva; — *line*, binario, linea ferroviaria; — *signal*, disco; — *station*, stazione ferroviaria; — *system*, rete ferroviaria. **-wayman** *n.* ferroviere *m.*
**raiment** *n.* abbigliamento; vestiti *m.pl.*
**rain** *n.* pioggia, acqua; *driving —*, pioggia dirotta; *pelting —*, pioggia scrosciante; *shower of —*, acquazzone *m.*; *in the —*, sotto la pioggia; *it looks like —*, vuol piovere; *to get caught in the —*, prendere dell'acqua, essere sorpreso dalla pioggia; (fig.) *right as —*, sano come un pesce; *intr.* piovere; *it is -ing cats and dogs*, piove a catinelle, diluvia; *it is -ing hard*, l'acqua viene giù; *it is -ing in torrents*, piove a dirotto; *it has -ed itself out*, la pioggia è cessata; (provb.) *it never -s but it pours*, le disgrazie non vengono mai sole, o niente o troppo; (fig.) *tears -ed down her cheeks*, le lacrime scorrevano copiose sulle sue guance; (fig.) far piovere, far cadere, riversare.
**rainbow** *n.* arcobaleno.
**rain-cloud** *n.* nembo, nube tempestosa. **-coat** *n.* impermeabile *m.*
**rain-drop** *n.* goccia di pioggia. **-fall** *n.* pioggia, precipitazione atmosferica, piovosità; (geol.) *-fall divide*, displuvio.
**rain-gauge** *n.* pluviometro.
**raininess** *n.* piovosità.
**rain-proof** *adj.* impermeabile. **-water** *n.* acqua piovana.
**rainy** *adj.* piovoso, di pioggia, umido; — *day*, giornata di pioggia; (fig.) *to provide against a — day*, assicurarsi il necessario per i momenti di bisogno.
**raise** *tr.* alzare, levare, sollevare, innalzare, elevare; drizzare, erigere, tirar su; aumentare; allevare; coltivare, produrre; suscitare, evocare, far nascere; *to — one's eyes*, alzare gli occhi; *to — one's eyebrows*, aggrottare le sopracciglia; *to — one's glass to someone*, brindare alla salute di qualcuno, *to — one's hat*, levarsi il cappello; *to — one's voice*, alzar la voce; *to — an army*, raccogliere un esercito; *to — cattle*, allevare bestiame; *to — a cloud of dust*, sollevare una nuvola di polvere; *to — the dead*, risuscitare i morti; *to — a family*, allevare una famiglia; *to — a flag*, issare una bandiera; *to — hopes*, suscitare speranze; *to — a laugh*, suscitare una risata; *to — money*, procurarsi denaro; *to — a monument*, erigere un monumento; (mus.) *to — the pitch of*, inacutire; *to — prices*, aumentare i prezzi; *to — an objection*, sollevare un'obiezione; *to — a question*, sollevare una questione; *to — the siege*, togliere l'assedio, *to — to the throne*, elevare al trono; *to — Cain*, far baccano, suscitare un pandemonio; (fam.) *to — the wind*, trovar soldi.
**raisin(s)** *n.* uva passa, uva secca; *one raisin*, un chicco d'uva passa.
**raising** *n.* innalzamento; elevazione, il sollevare; aumento; (of taxes) riscossione; allevamento; educazione; (of siege) il togliere (l'assedio); (of troops) leva; arruolamento; (of spirits) evocazione.
**raison d'être** *n.* scopo; giustificazione.
**rajah** *n.* raia *m.*, ragia *m.*
**rake**[1] *n.* rastrello; (fig.) *lean as a —*, magro come un chiodo;

*tr.* rastrellare, ammassare (con rastrello); raccogliere; (fig.) passare in rassegna, scrutare; (mil., with fire) battere d'infilata; *to — away*, togliere con rastrello; (fig.) *to — up*, ravvivare, risvegliare; *to — up the past*, rivangare il passato; *intr. to — about in*, frugare tra.

**rake**[2] *n.* libertino, scapestrato; *-'s progress*, carriera del libertino.

**rake**[3] *n.* (naut.) slancio; (mech.) angolo d'inclinazione; (fig.) inclinazione.

**rake-off** *n.* (fam.) percentuale *f.*, quota; (slang) bustarella.

**rakish**[1] *adj.* dissoluto, libertino, scapestrato.

**rakish**[2] *adj.* (naut.) slanciato; (fig.) *to wear one's hat at a — angle*, portare il cappello sulle ventitrè.

**rally**[1] *n.* raccolta, riunione, adunata; ricupero di forze; ripresa; (sport) scambio di colpi; (motor.) corsa; *the Monte Carlo —*, la corsa di Montecarlo; *tr.* radunare, riunire, (mil.) chiamare a raccolta; riprendere, ricuperare; *to — one's strength*, fare appello a tutte le proprie forze; *intr.* riunirsi, raccogliersi; riprendersi, rimettersi.

**rally**[2] *tr.* prendere in giro, canzonare, motteggiare, beffeggiare. **-ing** *adj.* motteggiante.

**Ralph** *pr.n.* Rodolfo.

**ram** *n.* (zool.) montone *m.*, ariete *m.*; (astron.) ariete; (of ship) sperone *m.*; (mech.) berta, battipalo; *battering-ram*, ariete; *tr.* (con)ficcare; *to — one's hat on one's head*, ficcarsi il cappello in testa; *to — something into someone's head*, conficcare qualcosa in testa a qualcuno; *to — one's head against the wall*, sbattere la testa contro il muro; *to — things into a cupboard*, ficcare la roba nell'armadio; (naut.) speronare.

**rambl-e** *n.* passeggiata senza meta, giro, gita; *intr.* vagare, girare, vagabondare, gironzolare; (in speech) divagare, vaneggiare; delirare. **-er** *n.* chi passeggia senza meta, girovago, vagabondo; (bot.) rosa rampiccante. **-ing** *adj.* errante, errabondo, vagabondo; sconnesso, incoerente, sconclusionato; *-ing thoughts*, divagazioni *f.pl.*

**ramif-y** *tr.* ramificare; ramificarsi. **-ication** *n.* ramificazione.

**ramp**[1] *n.* salita, rampa; pendìo, piano inclinato; (archit.) cordonata; (aeron.) scaletta.

**ramp**[2] *n.* (fam.) truffa, inganno; scandalo.

**rampage** *n.* (fam.) furia, irruenza; *to be on the —*, essere scalmanato, prendersela con tutti; *intr.* (fam.) smaniare, andare su tutte le furie. **-ous** *adj.* (fam.) violento, furioso, chiassoso.

**rampant** *adj.* violento, sfrenato, aggressivo; (fig.) predominante, prevalente; *to be —*, dilagare, imperversare; (herald.) rampante.

**rampart** *n.* bastione *m.*; (fig.) baluardo; difesa.

**rampion** *n.* (bot.) raperonzolo.

**ramrod** *n.* bacchetta; (artill.) scovolo; *straight as a —*, diritto come un fuso.

**ramshackle** *adj.* sgangherato, dirocato, cadente.

**ranch** *n.* podere *m.*, grande fattoria.

**rancid** *adj.* rancido, stantio. **-ity, -ness** *n.* rancidezza, rancidità, rancidume *m.*

**rancorous** *adj.* acrimonioso, pieno di rancora.

**rancour** *n.* rancore *m.*, acrimonia, amarezza.

**rand** *n.* (bootm.) soletta.

**randiness** *n.* libidine *f.*, foia.

**Randolph** *pr.n.* Rodolfo.

**random** *adj.* a caso, a casaccio, fortuito; *n. at —*, a casaccio, alla cieca.

**randy** *adj.* lascivo. libidinoso, foioso.

**rang** *p.def.* of **ring**[2], *q.v.*

**range** *n.* fila, serie *f.*; catena; gamma; distesa, estensione; campo, sfera, ambito; portata, tiro; *at close —*, a bruciapelo; *out of —*, fuori tiro; *within — of*, a portata di; *shooting —*, poligono di tiro; (aeron.; naut.) autonomia; (cul.) fornello, cucina economica; *tr.* ordinare, disporre, schierare; (fig.) *to — oneself*, schierarsi; (typ.) allineare; *intr.* estendersi; variare, oscillare; (fig.) errare, vagare; *to — over*, percorrere; (artill.) avere la portata di; dare l'alzo a.

**range-finder** *n.* telemetro.

**Rangoon** *pr.n.* (geog.) Rangun *f.*

**rank**[1] *adj.* rigoglioso, lussureggiante; (agric.) *too — to grow corn*, troppo grasso per la coltivazione del grano; (of smell) puzzolente, forte; (fig.) grossolano, osceno; (fam.) inconfondibile; flagrante; (horse-racing) *a — outsider*, un cavallo che vince inaspettatamente; (fig.) un tipo impossibile, un estraneo.

**rank**[2] *n.* fila; *front —*, prima fila; *rear —*, ultima fila; posteggio; grado, ordine *m.* ceto, condizione, piano; *of the first —*, di primo piano; (mil.; naval) grado; *— and file*, (mil.) bassa forza, truppa, (fig.) la gran massa, l'uomo qualunque; *to be promoted from the -s*, essere promosso ufficiale, (fam.) venire su dalla gavetta; *to be reduced to the -s*, essere degradato; *to serve in the -s*, essere semplice soldato; *tr.* mettere in fila, schierare, ordinare; (fig.) classificare, collocare, annoverare; *intr.* schierarsi, prendere posto; *to — above*, essere al di sopra di; *to — among*, essere nel numero di; *to — before*, avere la precedenza su; *to — next to*, essere inferiore solo a.

**ranker** *n.* (mil.) ufficiale venuto su dalla gavetta.

**rankle** *intr.* bruciare, infiammarsi; dolere, far male, inasprirsi, esacerbarsi.

**rankness** *n.* esuberanza, rigoglio; grossolanità, oscenità; rancidità; puzza.

**ransack** *tr.* saccheggiare; (fig.) frugare, rovistare.

**ransom** *n.* riscatto, prezzo del riscatto; *to hold to —*, tenere prigioniero fino al pagamento del riscatto; (fig.) *worth a king's —*, di grandissimo valore; *tr.* riscattare; (fig.) redimere.

**rant** *intr.* declamare, smaniare. **-er** *n.* declamatore *m.*, chiacchierone *m.* **-ing** *adj.* ampolloso, declamatorio, altisonante.

**ranunculus** *n.* (bot.) ranuncolo.

**rap** *n.* colpo leggero e secco, colpetto, bussa; (fig.) *to give someone a — on the knuckles*, lavare la testa a qualcuno; *it isn't worth a —*, non vale un cavolo; *to take the —*, accollarsi il biasimo, (fam.) pigliarne; *tr.* colpire, battere, picchiare su; (fig.) *to — out an oath*, lasciarsi scappare una bestemmia; *intr.* picchiare, bussare.

**rapacious** *adj.* rapace, vorace. **-ness, rapacity** *n.* rapacità, voracità, avidità.

**rape**[1] *n.* (bot.) colza, rapa, ravizzone *m.*

**rape**[2] *n.* (leg.) violenza carnale, violentamento, stupro; ratto, rapimento; *the Rape of the Sabines*, il ratto delle Sabine; *tr.* (leg.) usare violenza carnale a, violentare, stuprare.

**Raphael** *pr.n.* Raffaello. **-esque** *adj.* (art) raffaellesco.

**rapid** *adj.* rapido, celere, veloce; *n.* rapida, cascata. **-ity** *n.* rapidità, celerità, velocità.

**rapier** *n.* stocco, spadino. **-thrust** *n.* stoccata.

**rapine** *n.* rapina, saccheggio.

**rapping** *n.* colpo, picchiata.

**rapporteur** *n.* relatore *m.*

**rapscallion** *n.* furfante *m.*, mascalzone *m.*

**rapt** *adj.* rapito, estatico, assorto.

**raptur-e** *n.* estasi *f.*, rapimento, trasporto, ebrezza; *to go into -es*, andare in estasi, entusiasmarsi. **-ous** *adj.* estatico, rapito, entusiastico, frenetico.

**rare** *adj.* raro, eccezionale, poco comune, insolito; (of meat) poco cotto, al sangue.

**raref-y** *tr.* rarefare, (fig.) raffinare; *intr.* rarefarsi. **-action** *n.* rarefazione. **-ied** *adj.* rarefatto, sottile.

**rarely** *adv.* raramente, di rado, rade volte.

**rareness, rarity** *n.* rarità, rarezza,

eccezionalità; *to be a rarity*, essere raro.
**rascal** *n.* briccone *m.*, furfante *m.*, mascalzone *m.*; *an out-and-out* —, un briccone matricolato. **-ly** *adj.* bricconesco, furfantesco; (fig.) birbone *m.*
**rase** *tr.* see **raze.**
**rash**[1] *adj.* temerario, imprudente; avventato; sconsiderato.
**rash**[2] *n.* eruzione (cutanea); (med.) esantema *m.*
**rasher** *n.* (cul.) fetta sottile.
**rashness** *n.* temerità, imprudenza; sconsideratezza; avventatezza.
**rasp** *n.* raspa, raschietto; stridio; *tr.* raspare, raschiare, grattare; (fig.) offendere, irritare; *intr.* stridere, scricchiolare.
**raspberry** *n.* (bot.) lampone *m.*; (fam.) *to blow a* —, fare una pernacchia.
**rasping** *adj.* stridente, aspro, rauco.
**rat** *n.* topo, ratto; *like a drowned* —, come un pulcino bagnato; *to be caught like a — in a trap*, essere preso come un topo in trappola; *to die like a — in a hole*, morire come un cane; *to smell a* —, subodorare qualche inganno; traditore, rinnegato; crumiro; *intr.* andare a caccia di topi, uccidere topi; (pol.) cambiare bandiera, voltar casacca; (of workman) far il crumiro.
**rat-catcher** *n.* acchiappatopi *m.* **-catching** *n.* caccia ai topi.
**ratchet** *n.* dente *m.* di arresto, nottolino.
**rate**[1] *n.* aliquota, proporzione, percentuale *f.*; tasso; *bank* —, tasso di sconto; prezzo, tariffa; imposta, tassa; *pl.* (on house) imposta sul valore locativo, (pop.) tassa di famiglia; velocità, andamento, passo, ritmo; *birth-rate*, natalità; *death-rate*, mortalità; ordine *m.*; *third-rate*, di terz'ordine, (pejor.) scadente, pessimo; (fig.) *at any* —, comunque, in ogni caso; *at that* —, se è così; *at this* —, così; *at the — of*, in ragione di, al prezzo di.
**rate**[1] *tr.* stimare, valutare; considerare, riguardare; annoverare; classificare; *intr.* essere classificato.
**rate**[2] *tr.* (scold) sgridare, rimproverare, dare una lavata di capo a.
**rateable** *adj.* tassabile, imponibile; — *value*, valore *m.* imponibile.
**ratepayer** *n.* contribuente *m.*, *f.*
**rather** *adv.* piuttosto, alquanto, un po', un pochino, discretamente, abbastanza; *or* —, anzi; — *than*, (foll. by *n.*) piuttosto di, (foll. by *adj.* or *verb*) piuttosto che, anzi che; *I would* —, preferirei (di); *I would — not*, preferisco di no, non ci tengo; (foll. by verb) preferirei (di) non; (fam.) — *a lot*, abbastanza; (excl.) —*!*, sicuro!, eccome!, sfido!, altro che!
**ratif-y** *tr.* ratificare. **-ication** *n.* ratifica.
**rating** *n.* valutazione, stima, classifica; categoria, classe *f.*; (naut.) marinaio semplice, marò *m. indecl.*
**ratio** *n.* rapporto, proporzione, ragione.
**ratiocinat-e** *intr.* raziocinare, ragionare. **-ion** *n.* raziocinio, ragionamento.
**ration** *n.* razione, porzione; (mil.) rancio; *emergency* —, *iron* —, viveri *m.pl.* di riserva; *short -s*, razione ridotta; *to put on short -s*, dare poco da mangiare a; *tr.* razionare, mettere a razione. **-al** *adj.* razionale, ragionevole; (fig.) pratico. **-ale** *n.* ragione effettiva, base logica.
**rational-ism** *n.* (philos.) razionalismo. **-ist** *n.* (philos.) razionalista *m.*, *f.*, libero pensatore. **-ity** *n.* razionalità, ragionevolezza.
**rationaliz-e** *tr.* razionalizzare, rendere razionale. **-ation** *n.* razionalizzazione; (industr.) organizzazione razionale.
**rationing** *n.* razionamento.
**ration-book, -card** *n.* carta annonaria, tessera di razionamento.
**ratlines, ratlings** *n.* (naut.) griselle *f.pl.*
**rattan** malacca *m.*, rotang *m.*
**rattle** *n.* sonaglio; (baby's) raganella, sonaglino; rumore *m.*, strepito, tintinnìo; (in throat) rantolo; *tr.* scuotere, far risuonare, far tintinnare; (fig.) spaventare, mettere la fifa addosso a; *to get -d*, innervosirsi, avere la fifa; *to — off*, recitare rapidamente, snocciolare; *intr.* sbatacchiare, risuonare, tintinnare; *to — away*, (of vehicle) partire strepitosamente; (of person) chiacchierare, ciarlare; *to — on*, continuare a chiacchierare. **-snake** *n.* (zool.) crotalo, (fam.) serpente *m.* a sonagli. **-trap** *n.* macchina traballante, vetturaccia; *pl.* cianfrusaglia.
**rattling** *adj.* rumoroso, traballante.
**rat-trap** *n.* trappola per topi.
**ratty** *adj.* infestato dai topi; (fam.) furibondo; *to get* —, arrabbiarsi.
**raucous** *adj.* rauco, roco; chioccio, aspro. **-ness** *n.* raucedine *f.*
**ravage** *n.* strage *f.*, devastazione; (fig.) danno; *tr.* devastare; saccheggiare.
**rave** *intr.* delirare, vaneggiare, farneticare; (fig.) infuriare; *to — at*, inveire contro; (fam.) *to — about*, andare pazzo per.
**ravel** *n.* groviglio, nodo, garbuglio; lembo sfilacciato; *tr.* imbrogliare, ingarbugliare, avviluppare; confondere, complicare; *intr.* sfilacciarsi, sfrangiarsi.
**raven** *n.* (orn.) corvo; — *black*, corvino.
**ravening, ravenous** *adj.* vorace, insaziabile, ingordo; affamato; *to be* —, avere una fame da lupo
**Ravenna** *pr.n.* (geog.) Ravenna; *native of* —, ravennate *m.*, *f.*
**ravenousness** *n.* voracità, ingordigia, insaziabilità.
**ravine** *n.* burrone *m.*, gola.
**raving** *adj.* delirante, frenetico; furioso, furibondo; — *mad*, pazzo furioso, matto da legare.
**ravish** *tr.* rapire; violentare, stuprare; (fig.) estasiare, incantare; *to be -ed*, andare in estasi, estasiarsi. **-er** *n.* rapitore, violatore, stupratore. **-ing** *adj.* (fig.) che rapisce, affascinante, incantevole.
**raw** *adj.* greggio, grezzo, naturale; — *materials*, materie prime; crudo; (fig.) immaturo, inesperto, rozzo; scoperto, infiammato; freddo e umido; (fam.) *a — deal*, il peggio; *n.* (fig.) vivo; *to touch on the* —, toccare sul vivo.
**raw-boned** *adj.* scarno, ossuto.
**rawness** *n.* crudezza; escoriazione, scalfittura; (fig.) inesperienza, rozzezza.
**ray**[1] *n.* raggio *m.*; *X-rays*, raggi X; (fig.) barlume *m.*, filo.
**ray**[2] *n.* (ichth.) razza.
**rayon** *n.* raion *m.*, seta artificiale.
**raze** *tr.* radere al suolo, abbattere, spianare; (fig.) cancellare.
**razor** *n.* rasoio; *safety-razor*, rasoio di sicurezza; *as sharp as a* —, tagliente come un rasoio; *to be on the -'s edge*, camminare sul filo del rasoio.
**razor-back** *n.* (rorqual) fisalo. **-bill** *n.* (orn.) smergo minore. **-blade** *n.* lametta da rasoio. **-strop** *n.* coramella.
**razzle(-dazzle)** *n.* (fam.) *to go on the* —, far baldoria.
**re** *prep.* riguardo a, con riferimento a, in merito a.
**reabsorb** *tr.* riassorbire.
**reabsorption** *n.* riassorbimento.
**reach** *n.* portata; distanza; tratto; (fig.) capacità, possibilità; *within* —, a portata di mano, vicino; *within easy — (of)*, a breve distanza (da); *out of* —, distante, fuori mano; irraggiungibile; *tr.* arrivare a, pervenire a, raggiungere, giungere a, toccare; *to — out*, (s)tendere, porgere, allungare; *intr.* estendersi, allungarsi; *as far as the eye can* —, fin dove l'occhio può spaziare; *to — out for something*, stendere la mano per prendere qualcosa.
**reacquire** *tr.* riacquistare.
**react** *intr.* reagire; (fig.) *to — upon*, ripercuotersi su.
**re-act** *tr.* (theatr.) rappresentare di nuovo, replicare.
**reaction** *n.* reazione; (fig.) ripercussione. **-ary** *adj.*, *n.* reazionario; passatista *m.*, *f.*
**reactor** *n.* (phys.) reattore.

**read**[1] *n.* lettura; (fam.) *he was having a quiet —*, stava leggendo tranquillamente.

**read**[1] *tr., intr.* leggere; *to — a book*, leggere un libro; *I like -ing*, mi piace leggere; *to — of someone's wedding in the paper*, leggere sul giornale che qualcuno si è sposato; *to — between the lines*, leggere tra le righe; *to — someone's thoughts*, leggere nei pensieri di qualcuno; *we have received your telegram -ing . . .*, abbiamo ricevuto il Suo telegramma così concepito . . .; *for 'Indies' — 'India'*, per 'Indie' leggasi 'India'; *one can — him like a book*, è un libro aperto; *to — someone a lesson*, fare la predica a qualcuno; *to — aloud*, leggere ad alta voce; *to — oneself to sleep*, leggere fino a addormentarsi; *to — more into something than what is intended*, leggere in qualcosa quello che non c'è; *to — on*, continuare a leggere; *to — out*, leggere ad alta voce; *to — over and over*, leggere e rileggere; *to — through*, leggere fino alla fine; *to — through rapidly*, scorrere; *to — up*, studiare a fondi, documentarsi su.

**read**[2] *p.def., part.* of **read,** *q.v.*; letto; *well —*, istruito, colto; *to be well — in*, essere versato in, avere una profonda conoscenza di; *to hear something — out*, ascoltare la lettura di qualcosa.

**readab-le** *adj.* leggibile; (fig.) interessante; *it's —*, si può leggere. **-ility** *n.* leggibilità.

**readdress** *tr.* cambiare l'indirizzo su, rispedire.

**reader** *n.* lettore *m.*, lettrice *f.*; *an avid —*, un divoratore di libri; *he is a great —*, legge molto; (univ.) vice-professore; *publisher's —*, lettore di manoscritti; *proof-reader*, correttore di bozze; libro di lettura, antologia.

**readily** *adv.* prontamente, sollecitamente; volentieri; facilmente.

**readiness** *n.* prontezza, prestezza; sollecitudine *f.*; *in —*, pronto; buona volontà, premura; facilità.

**reading** *n.* lettura; *a man of vast —*, un uomo di vasta conoscenza letteraria; lezione, versione; interpretazione; *gerund* il leggere; (pol.) *second — of a bill*, seconda lettura di un progetto di legge; *attrib. the — public*, il pubblico dei lettori.

**reading-book** *n.* libro di lettura. **-desk** *n.* leggìo. **-lamp** *n.* lampada da tavolino. **-room** *n.* sala di lettura.

**readjust** *tr.* raggiustare, riassettare, riordinare. **-ment** *n.* riassestamento, riordinamento.

**readmission, readmittance** *n.* riammissione.

**readmit** *tr.* riammettere.

**ready** *adj.* pronto, preparato, a portata di mano; (fig.) disposto, pronto; *— for anything*, deciso a tutto; *— money*, contanti *m.pl.*; *to be — to*, essere disposto a; *to get —*, *tr.* preparare, allestire, *intr.* prepararsi; *tr. to make —*, preparare, (typ.) avviare; *n.* (mil.) *at the —*, in posizione di puntamento.

**ready-made, ready-to-wear** *adj.* fatto, confezionato. **-reckoner** *n.* prontuario. **-witted** *adj.* dallo spirito pronto, dall'ingegno vivace.

**reaffirm** *tr.* riaffermare. **-ation** *n.* riaffermazione.

**reafforestation** *n.* rimboschimento.

**reagent** *n.* (chem.) reagente *m.*

**real**[1] *adj.* reale, vero, genuino, autentico, effettivo; *— value*, valore effettivo; *in — earnest*, proprio sul serio; (leg.) *— estate*, beni immobili.

**real**[2] *n.* (coin) reale *m.*

**real-ism** *n.* realismo. **-ist** *n.* realista *m., f.* **-istic** *adj.* realistico.

**reality** *n.* realtà, verità; *in —*, in realtà, veramente; realismo.

**realiz-e** *tr.* realizzare, effettuare, attuare; capire, accorgersi di, rendersi conto di; *to be -ed*, verificarsi. **-able** *adj.* realizzabile. **-ation** *n.* realizzazione; percezione; (comm.; finan.) realizzo.

**really** *adv.* realmente, veramente, effettivamente, in realtà; (foll. by *adj.*) proprio; *— and truly*, davvero davvero; *excl. —?*, davvero?

**realm** *n.* reame *m.*, regno; (fig.) campo.

**ream**[1] *n.* risma.

**ream**[2] *tr.* (eng.) alesare. **-er** *n.* (eng.) alesatore.

**reanimate** *tr.* rianimare, ravvivare; rincuorare.

**reannex** *tr.* riannettere.

**reap** *tr.* mietere; (fig.) raccogliere. **-er** *n.* mietitore *m.*, mietitrice *f.* **-ing** *n.* mietitura, messe *f.*; *-ing machine*, mietitrice.

**reaping-hook** *n.* falce *f.*

**reappear** *intr.* ricomparire, riapparire, ripresentarsi. **-ance** *n.* riapparizione, ricomparsa.

**reappoint** *tr.* nominare di nuovo, reintegrare nelle proprie funzioni.

**re-appointment** *n.* reintegrazione.

**rear**[1] *adj.* posteriore, ultimo, di coda; *— rank*, ultima fila; *n.* parte posteriore, retro; *at the — of*, dietro a; (mil.) retroguardia, (area behind lines) retrovie *f.pl.*; *to bring up the —*, (mil.) formare la retroguardia, (fam.) essere il fanalino di coda.

**rear**[2] *tr.* innalzare, levare, erigere; allevare; educare, allevare; coltivare; *intr.* (of horse) impennarsi.

**rear-admiral** *n.* contrammiraglio di divisione. **-arch** *n.* (archit.) arco interno.

**rear-er** *n.* allevatore coltivatore; cavallo che si impenna. **-ing** *n.* allevamento; educazione; (of a horse) l'impennarsi.

**rearm** *tr.* riarmare. **-ament** *n* riarmo, riarmamento.

**rearmost** *adj.* ultimo, il più arretrato.

**rearrange** *tr.* riordinare. **-ment** *n.* riordinamento; nuova sistemazione.

**rearward** *adj.* posteriore. **-s** *adv.* indietro.

**reascend** *tr., intr.* risalire.

**reason** *n.* ragione *f.*, causa, motivo; ragionevolezza, buon senso; raziocinio, ragione, logica; *by — of*, a causa di; *with good —*, a ragione; *the — why he came*, la ragione per cui è venuto, il motivo della sua venuta; *there is — to believe*, c'è motivo di credere; *there's neither rhyme nor — in it*, non ha nè capo nè coda; *it stands to — that*, è evidente che; *to give -s for*, addurre motivi per, motivare; *to have — to*, avere motivo per; *to listen to —*, lasciarsi persuadere; *she has lost her —*, essa ha perduto la ragione; *intr.* ragionare, argomentare, discorrere; *to — about a subject*, ragionare su un argomento; *to — with someone*, far intendere ragione a qualcuno; *tr.* persuadere.

**reasonable** *adj.* ragionevole, logico; conveniente, modico; *— hour*, ora da cristiani, **-ness** *n.* ragionevolezza; moderazione, convenienza.

**reasoning** *adj.* ragionale, ragionativo; *n.* ragionamento, raziocinio, modo di ragionare; *there is no — with him*, non si può fargli intendere ragione.

**reassemble** *tr.* riunire, radunare; (fig.) ricomporre; (mech.) rimontare; *intr.* riunirsi.

**reassert** *tr.* riaffermare, riasserire.

**reassess** *tr.* valutare di nuovo; fare una nuova stima di.

**reassur-e** *tr.* rassicurare, confortare, tranquillizzare; (leg.) riassicurare; *to feel -ed*, rassicurarsi. **-ance** *n.* (leg.) riassicurazione; rassicurazione. **-ing** *adj.* rassicurante, confortante.

**reawaken** *tr.* risvegliare; *intr.* risvegliarsi.

**rebate** *n.* (comm.) riduzione; sconto; abbuono; rimborso.

**re·bel**[1] *adj., n.* ribelle *m., f.*

**rebel**[2] *intr.* ribellarsi, sollevarsi, rivoltarsi, insorgere.

**rebellion** *n.* ribellione, rivolta, insurrezione.

**rebellious** *adj.* ribelle, refrattario. **-ness** *n.* carattere *m.* ribelle, indisciplina, insubordinazione.

**rebind** *tr.* rilegare.

**rebirth** *n.* rinascita, reincarnazione, palingenesi *f.*
**reborn** *adj.* rinato.
**re'bound**[1] *n.* rimbalzo; (fig.) reazione, ripercussione; (fam.) *to catch someone on the* —, approfittare dalla reazione di qualcuno.
**rebound**[2] *intr.* rimbalzare; (fig.) ricadere.
**rebound**[3] *p.def., part.* of **rebind,** *q.v.*
**rebuff** *n.* rifiuto, ripulso, scacco, mortificazione; *tr.* respingere; mortificare.
**rebuild** *tr.* ricostruire, riedificare. **-ing** *n.* ricostruzione, rifattura, riedificazione.
**rebuke** *n.* rimprovero, riprensione, sgridata; *tr.* rimproverare, riprendere, sgridare.
**rebus** *n.* rebus *m. indecl.*
**rebut** *tr.* rifiutare, ribattere, respingere; (leg.) confutare. **-ment, -tal** *n.* rifiuto; (leg.) confutazione.
**recalcitr-ance** *n.* recalcitramento; (fig.) ostinata opposizione, riluttanza. **-ant** *adj.* ricalcitrante, riluttante, restìo.
**recall** *n.* richiamo; (of law) revoca; *past* —, irrevocabile; *tr.* richiamare, far ritornare; far rimpatriare; revocare, annullare; ricordare, richiamare alla mente; rammentarsi di, rievocare.
**recant** *tr.* ritrattare, rinnegare, ripudiare, sconfessare; *intr.* abiurare. **-ation** *n.* ritrattazione; abiura.
**recapitulat-e** *tr.* ricapitolare, riassumere, riepilogare. **-ion** *n.* ricapitolazione, riassunto, riepilogo. **-ory** *adj.* riassuntivo.
**recapture** *n.* riconquista, ripresa; *tr.* riconquistare, riprendere, ricatturare; (fig.) richiamare alla memoria.
**recast** *tr.* (metall.) rifondere, (fig.) dare nuova forma a, rimaneggiare, ricomporre; (theatr.) allestire con nuovi attori. **-ing** *n.* (metall.) rifusione; (fig.) rimaneggiamento.
**reced-e** *intr.* recedere, indietreggiare, ritirarsi, allontanarsi, rientrare; diminuire, rimpicciolire, restringersi. **-ing** che si allontana, rientrante; sfuggente; rifluente.
**receipt** *n.* ricevimento, ricezione, ricevuta; *to be in — of*, ricevere, (comm.) aver ricevuto; *to acknowledge — of*, accusare ricevuta di; ricevuta, quietanza; ricetta; *pl.* incasso, introiti *m.pl.*, entrate *f.pl.*; *tr.* quietanzare.
**receivable** *adj.* ricevibile, accettabile; (comm.) esigibile.
**receiv-e** *tr.* ricevere; accogliere; accettare; subire, soffrire, riportare; (leg.) *to — a sentence of*, essere condannato a; *to — stolen goods*, ricettare merci rubate; (radio) *to — a station*, captare una stazione; *to — a degree*, laurearsi; *intr.* ricevere, dare un ricevimento. **-er** *n.* chi riceve; destinatario; (leg.) ricettatore; (of bankruptcy) curatore fallimentare; (teleph.) ricevitore; (radio) ricevente *m.* **-ing** *adj.* ricevente; *n.* ricezione; (leg.) ricettazione; *-ing order*, nomina di un curatore fallimentare, dichiarazione di fallimento.
**recent** *adj.* recente, nuovo, moderno, attuale, fresco. **-ly** *adv.* recentemente, di recente, poco fa; *as -ly as yesterday*, solo ieri.
**receptacle** *n.* recipiente *m.*, ricettacolo; (bot.) talamo.
**reception** *n.* il ricevere, ricevuta; ricevimento; accoglienza; — *committee*, comitato per l'ospitalità; (radio) ricezione.
**reception-office** *n.* ufficio ricevimento, direzione. **-room** *n.* sala di ricevimento.
**receptive** *adj.* ricettivo. **-ness, receptivity** *n.* ricettività.
**recess** *n.* rientranza, nicchia, alcova; (fig.) recesso, ripostiglio, luogo appartato; vacanze *f.pl.*; (pol.) tregua; (geol.) retrocessione; (of water) decrescenza. **-ed** *adj.* rientrante; (archit.) sfondato. **-ion** *n.* retrocessione, recessione, arretramento; (comm.) crisi economica, crollo dei prezzi.
**recharge** *tr.* ricaricare, caricare di nuovo; (leg.) accusare di nuovo; *intr.* (mil.) tornare alla carica.
**recherché** *adj.* ricercato, raffinato.
**rechristen** *tr.* ribattezzare.
**recidiv-ism** *n.* recidività. **-ist** *n.* recidivo.
**recipe** *n.* (cul.) ricetta; (pharm.) formula; (fig.) chiave *f.*
**recipient** *n.* chi riceve, ricevente *m.*, *f.*, destinatario; (chem.) recipiente *m.*, *f.*
**reciproc-al** *adj.* reciproco, scambievole, bilaterale; (math.) inverso. **-ate** *tr.* ricambiare, contraccambiare, scambiare; *intr.* (mech.) alternarsi, muoversi alternativamente. **-ity** *n.* reciprocità.
**recital** *n.* racconto, narrazione, relazione; esposto; *organ* —, concerto d'organo.
**recit-e** *tr.* recitare, declamare, dire, raccontare, enumerare, esporre. **-ation** *n.* recitazione, recita. **-ative** *n.* (mus.) recitativo. **-er** *n.* recitatore, dicitore.
**reckless** *adj.* incauto, noncurante, avventato, insensato, temerario. **-ness** *n.* noncuranza, avventatezza, temerarietà.
**reckon** *tr.* contare, calcolare, computare, enumerare; (fig.) stimare, reputare, considerare; (fam.) pensare, credere; *intr.* fare i conti, calcolare; *to — on*, contare su, fare assegnamento su; *to — without one's host*, fare i conti senza l'oste, **-er** *n.* calcolatore, computista, enumeratore; *ready -er*, prontuario. **-ing** *n.* conto, calcolo, computo; (naut.) determinazione della posizione; (fig.) resa dei conti; *the day of -ing*, il Giudizio Universale, il dies irae.
**reclaim** *tr.* reclamare, rivendicare; redimere, richiamare al dovere; bonificare, prosciugare; (industr.) rigenerare, ricuperare. **-able** *adj.* redimibile, correggibile; bonificabile.
**reclamation** *n.* redenzione; rivendicazione; (of land) bonifica.
**recline** *tr.* appoggiare, posare, inclinare; *intr.* appoggiarsi, inclinarsi, sdraiarsi, giacere.
**reclothe** *tr.* rivestire.
**reclus-e** *n.* solitario, eremita *m.*, anacoreta *m.* **-ion** *n.* reclusione, solitudine *f.*
**recoal** *intr.* rifornirsi di carbone.
**recock** *tr.* riarmare (un fucile).
**recognition** *n.* (ri)conoscimento; ammissione; *to change beyond* —, diventare irriconoscibile.
**recogniz-e** *tr.* riconoscere, ravvisare; *to — by*, riconoscere da; ammettere, riconoscere; *to refuse to* —, disconoscere. **-able** *adj.* (ri)conoscibile.
**recoil** *n.* rinculo; rimbalzo; (fig.) movimento di orrore; *intr.* rinculare; rimbalzare; (fig.) ritirarsi, indietreggiare; *I — from the thought*, mi ripugna il pensiero; *to — on*, ricadere su.
**recollect** *tr.* ricordare, ricordarsi di, rammentarsi di; *to — doing something*, ricordare di aver fatto qualcosa; *as far as I* —, se ricordo bene; *to — oneself*, riprendersi, riaversi. **-ion** *n.* ricordo, memoria, reminiscenza; *a dim -ion*, un ricordo confuso; *to the best of my -ion*, per quanto io ricordi; riflessione, raccoglimento.
**recolour** *tr.* ricolorire, ritingere.
**recombine** *tr.* ricombinare, ricomporre.
**recommence** *tr.*, *intr.* ricominciare, rimettersi (a).
**recommend** *tr.* raccomandare; consigliare. **-able** *adj.* raccomandabile. **-ation** *n.* raccomandazione. **-atory** *adj.* di raccomandazione, commendatizio.
**recommission** *tr.* dare un nuovo incarico a, incaricare di nuovo; riarmare.
**recompense** *n.* ricompensa, compenso, rimunerazione; risarcimento, indennizzo; *tr.* (ri)compensare, rimunerare; risarcire, indennizzare.
**recompose** *tr.* ricomporre.
**reconcil-e** *tr.* (ri)conciliare, rappacificare, mettere d'accordo; *to become -ed*, riconciliarsi, rappacificarsi, mettersi d'accordo; *to — differences*, comporre dissensi; *to — oneself to something*, rassegnarsi a qualcosa. **-able** *adj.* (ri)conciliabile. **-ement,**

-**iation** *n.* (ri)conciliazione, riavvicinamento; rassegnazione.
**recondite** *adj.* recondito, astruso, oscuro.
**recondition** *tr.* rimettere in efficienza, ripristinare. -**ing** ripristino, revisione.
**reconnaissance** *n.* (mil.) ricognizione, esplorazione; sopraluogo, esame *m.* preliminare.
**reconnoitre** *tr.* fare una ricognizione, perlustrare, esplorare; (fig.) esaminare.
**reconquer** *tr.* riconquistare.
**reconquest** *n.* riconquista.
**reconsecrate** *tr.* riconsecrare; (eccl.) ribenedire.
**reconsider** *tr.* riconsiderare, riesaminare, rivedere, ritornare su. -**ation** *n.* riconsiderazione; riesame *m.*
**reconstitut-e** *tr.* ricostituire. -**ion** *n.* ricostituzione.
**reconstruct** *tr.* ricostruire. -**ion** *n.* ricostruzione.
**reconvert** *tr.* riconvertire.
**recopy** *tr.* ricopiare.
**re·cord**[1] *n.* registro; nota; documento; documentazione; verbale *m.*, resoconto, atti *m.pl.*; *to be on* —, essere a registro, essere noto; *the worst earthquake on* —, il più grande terremoto che mai si ricordi; *the earliest* -*s*, i più antichi documenti; *to keep a* — *of*, prendere nota di; *to put oneself on* — *as*, assicurarsi un posto nella storia come; *off the* —, ufficiosamente, (fam.) in confidenza; passato; (comm.) stato di servizio; *police* —, fedina penale; *to have a clean* —, avere la fedina pulita; archivio; *Record Office*, Archivio di Stato; (gramophone) disco; *long-playing* —, microsolco; — *library*, discoteca; (sport) primato, record *m. indecl.*; *speed* —, primato di velocità; *world* —, record mondiale; (industr.) — *output*, produzione che costituisce un primato.
**record**[2] *tr.* registrare, prendere nota di, mettere per iscritto, mettere a verbale, segnalare; ricordare, raccontare, dire, narrare; ricordare; segnare, marcare; incidere, registrare, riprodurre; *to* — *on tape*, registrare su nastro.
**recorder** *n.* registratore; archivista *m.*, *f.*, cancelliere *m.*; (leg.) giudice *m.*, consigliere giudiziario; (mus.) flautino.
**record-holder** *n.* (sport) detentore *m.* di un primato.
**recording** *adj.* registrante; registrazione; — *apparatus*, registratore; *gramophone* —, incisione.
**record-player** *n.* (mus.) giradischi *m. indecl.*, grammofono.
**re-count**[1] *tr.* contare di nuovo.
**re·count**[2] *n.* nuovo computo; (pol.) secondo scrutinio.
**recount**[3] *tr.* raccontare, narrare, riferire.
**recoup** *tr.* ricuperare, rifarsi di; compensare, indennizzare, risarcire.
**recourse** *n.* ricorso; *to have* — *to*, ricorrere a, far ricorso a; (comm.) *without* —, senza rivalsa; risorsa, espediente *m.*
**recover**[1] *tr.* ricuperare, riacquistare, riavere, riprendere; ritrovare, riscoprire; *to* — *one's balance*, rimettersi in equilibrio; *to* — *one's breath*, riprendere fiato; *to* — *consciousness*, riprendere coscienza; *to* — *damages*, ottenere il risarcimento dei danni; *to* — *one's health*, riacquistare la salute, rimettersi; *to* — *one's senses*, rientrare in sè; *intr.* riacquistare la salute, guarire, rimettersi, riaversi, riprendersi.
**re-cover**[2] *tr.* coprire di nuovo; ricoprire; (of book) rilegare.
**recoverable** *adj.* ricuperabile, ritrovabile.
**recovery** *n.* ricupero, riacquisto, ritrovamento; guarigione; *on the way to* —, in via di guarigione; *past* —, incurabile, in condizioni disperate; *to make a good* —, riaversi, rimettersi; (comm.; finan.) ripresa; (of debt) ricupero; (industr.) ricupero.
**recreant** *adj.*, *n.* vile *m.*, codardo; (rel.) ricredente *m.*, *f.*
**re-create**[1] *tr.* creare di nuovo, ricreare.
**recreat-e**[2] *tr.* divertire. -**ion** *n.* ricreazione, divertimento, passatempo, diporto, svago; (schol.) ricreazione, pausa. -**ional** *adj.* ricreativo. -**ion-ground** *n.* cortile *m.* per la ricreazione, terreno da giuoco.
**recrimin-ation** *n.* recriminazione. -**ative**, -**atory** *adj.* recriminatorio.
**recross** *tr.* riattraversare.
**recrudesc-ence** *n.* recrudescenza. -**ent** *adj.* recrudescente, che rincrudisce.
**recruit** *n.* (mil.) recluta *f.*; (fig.) novizio, principiante *m.*; *a raw* —, un novellino; *tr.* (mil.) reclutere, arruolare; *to* — *one's strength*, riprendere le forze; *intr.* rimettersi in salute, riacquistare la salute. -**ment**, -**ing** *n.* reclutamento; (mil.) *recruiting office*, Distretto; (of health) ricupero, riacquisto.
**rectang-le** *n.* rettangolo. -**ular** *adj.* rettangolare.
**rectif-y** *tr.* rettificare, correggere; (electr.; radio) raddrizzare. -**iable** *adj.* rettificabile. -**ication** *n.* rettificazione, rettifica.
**rectilin-eal**, -**ear** *adj.* rettilineo.
**rectitude** *n.* rettitudine *f.*, dirittura.
**recto** *n.* recto; (typ.) bivanco.
**rector** *n.* (eccl.) parroco, pievano; curato; (Univ.) rettore; (of school) preside *m.*, direttore. -**ate**, -**ship** *n.* rettorato.
**rectory** *n.* presbiterio, cannonica.
**rectum** *n.* (anat.) retto.
**recumbent** *adj.* supino, sdraiato, coricato, adagiato; (art) giacente.
**recuperat-e** *tr.* ricuperare; *intr.* ricuperare (le forze), rimettersi, ristabilirsi. -**ion** *n.* ricupero. -**ive** *adj.* ricuperativo, rigeneratore.
**recur** *intr.* ricorrere; ripresentarsi; ritornare. -**rence** *n.* ricorrenza, ricorso, ritorno; (of illness) ricaduta. -**rent** *adj.* ricorrente; periodico; abituale. -**ring** *adj.* ricorrente; periodico; (math.) -*ring decimal*, frazione periodica.
**recusant** *adj.*, *n.* (rel.) dissidente, dissenziente *m.*, *f.*
**recut** *tr.* ritagliare.
**red** *adj.* rosso; *dark* —, *deep* —, rosso cupo, rosso scuro; *blood* —, rosso sangue; — *hair*, capelli rossi; *the* — *flag*, la bandiera rossa; (art) — *pencil*, — *crayon*, sanguigna; — *lead*, minio; (cul.) — *pepper*, pepe *m.* di Caienna; (eccl.) *the* — *hat*, il cappello cardinalizio; *the Red Cross*, la Croce Rossa; *the Red Ensign*, la bandiera della marina mercantile britannica; *Red Indian*, pellerossa *m.*, *f.*; *the Red Sea*, il Mar Rosso; *to go* —, (of person) arrossire, (of thing) diventar rosso; (fig.) *to see* —, vedere rosso; *it's like a* — *rag to a bull*, fa vedere rosso; — *tape*, burocrazia; — *light*, segnale *m.* di pericolo; *to see the* — *light*, rendersi conto del pericolo, andar cauto; — *light district*, quartiere dove ci sono dei bordelli; *to paint the town* —, far baldoria; — *herring*, diversivo; *to draw a* — *herring across the track*, sviare la conversazione; (ent.) — *admiral*, vanessa atalanta; (bot.) — *currant*, ribes *m. indecl.*; (ichth.) — *mullet*, triglia; *n.* rosso; *the* — *white and blue*, la bandiera britannica; (pol.) rosso, comunista *m.*, *f.*; (billards) palla rossa; (fam.) *to be in the* —, essere scoperto.
**redbreast** *n.* (orn.) pettirosso.
**red-brick** *adj.* — *University*, università di recente formazione. -**cap** *n.* (mil.) soldato della polizia militare; (USA) facchino della ferrovia.
**redcoat** *n.* (hist.) soldato inglese.
**redden** *tr.* arrossare, rendere rosso; *intr.* (of person) arrossire, (of thing) diventare rosso.
**reddish** *adj.* rossiccio, rossastro.
**redeem** *tr.* redimere, riscattare, salvare, liberare, affrancare, svincolare; estinguere; (from pawn) riscattare; mantenere; -*ing feature*, particolare *m.* che salva. -**able** *adj.* (finan.) redimibile, riscattabile, rimborsabile. -**er** *n.* (rel.) *the Redeemer*, il Redentore; (fig.) liberatore.
**redemption** *n.* (rel.) redenzione,

salvezza; (fig.) liberazione, riscatto, salvezza; (finan.) rimborso, estinzione, ammortamento.
**redevelop** *tr.* risviluppare; **-ment** *n.* sviluppo ulteriore; *-ment plan*, piano regolatore.
**red-faced** *adj.* rubicondo. **-haired** *adj.* dai capelli rossi. **-handed** *adj.* con le mani insanguinate; (fig.) in flagrante.
**redhead** *n.* persona dai capelli rossi.
**red-hot** *adj.* rovente; (fig.) ardente; (news) ultimissimo, nuovissimo.
**redirect** *tr.* indirizzare di nuovo; (letter) far seguire.
**rediscover** *tr.* riscoprire, ritrovare. **-y** *n.* riscoperta.
**red-letter** *adj.* memorabile; *-letter day*, giorno festivo, (fig.) giorno di particolare importanza.
**redness** *n.* rossore *m.*, rossezza.
**redol-ence** *n.* profumo, fragranza. **-ent** *adj.* odoroso, profumato, fragrante, olezzante; (fig.) suggestivo.
**redouble** *tr.* raddoppiare, intensificare, aumentare; (bridge) surcontrare; *intr.* raddoppiarsi, intensificarsi.
**redoubt** *n.* (mil.) ridotto. **-able** *adj.* formidabile, temibile.
**redound** *intr.* ridondare; tornare; risultare; contribuire.
**redraft** *tr.* redigere di nuovo.
**redress**[1] *n.* riparazione, soddisfazione; *tr.* riparare, rettificare, rimediare a, porre rimedio a; *to — the balance*, ristabilire l'equilibrio.
**redress**[2] *tr.* rivestire di nuovo; *intr.* rivestirsi.
**redskin** *n.* pellerossa *m.*, *f.*
**reduc-e** *tr.* ridurre; diminuire; (mil.) degradare; *to — to the ranks*, degradare a soldato semplice. **-ed** *adj.* ridotto, diminuito; *-ed prices*, prezzi ridotti; *-ed scale*, scala ridotta; *in -ed circumstances*, in strettezze; *to be -ed to*, essere costretto a, essere ridotto a. **-ible** *adj.* riducibile.
**reduction** *n.* riduzione, diminuzione; abbassamento, sconto; riproduzione su piccola scala; (mus.) riduzione.
**redund-ant** *adj.* sovrabbondante, superfluo, ridondante; (lit.) pleonastico; (econ.) *to be made —*, essere messo in cassa integrazione. **-ance, -ancy** *n.* sovrabbondanza, ridondanza; (lit.) pleonasmo.
**reduplicat-e** *tr.* raddoppiare. **-ion** *n.* raddoppiamento, ripetizione.
**redwood** *n.* (bot.) sequoia.
**re-echo** *intr.* riecheggiare, risuonare; *tr.* (fig.) ripetere, riecheggiare.
**reed** *n.* (bot.) canna, giunco; (fig.) *broken —*, canna fessa; (poet.) zampogna; (mus.) ancia, linguetta. **-bed** *n.* canneto.
**re-edit** *tr.* ripubblicare, curare una nuova edizione di.
**reedmace** *n.* (bot.) mazza sorda, stiancia.
**reed-pipe** *n.* (mus.) canna a lingua, zampogna.
**reef**[1] *n.* (geog.) scoglio, scogliere; (coral) banco; (coral island) atollo; (min.) filone *m.*, vena.
**reef**[2] *n.* (naut.) terzaruolo; (fig.) *to take in a —*, andare piano. **-knot** *n.* nodo piano, nodo di terzaruolo.
**reefer**[1] *n.* giacca corta a doppio petto.
**reefer**[2] *n.* cigaretta che contiene della canapa indiana.
**reek** *n.* puzzo, fetore *m.*; fumo; *intr.* puzzare; emettere fumo.
**reel**[1] *n.* (text.) bobina, rocchetto; (fishing) mulinello; (fam.) *straight off the —*, tutto d'un fiato; (cinem.) rotolo, bobina; *tr.* annaspare, avvolgere, aggomitolare; *to — off*, sdipanare; (fig.) snocciolare, rinfilare; *intr.* (of grasshopper) frinire.
**reel**[2] *n.* vacillamento, barcollamento, giro vorticoso; *intr.* barcollare, andare barcollando, vacillare, girare; *my head -s*, mi gira la testa.
**reel**[3] *n.* trescone scozzese; *intr.* ballare un reel.
**re-elect** *tr.* rieleggere. **-ion** *n.* rielezione.
**reeling** *adj.* vacillante, barcollante.
**re-embarcation** *n.* rimbarco.
**re-embark** *tr.* rimbarcare; *intr.* rimbarcarsi.
**re-emerge** *intr.* riemergere.
**re-enact** *tr.* rimettere in vigore; (theatr.) riprodurre (una scena).
**re-enter** *intr.* rientrare (fig.) presentarsi di nuovo; *tr.* rientrare in; (fig.) riprendere; (comm.) registrare di nuovo.
**re-entrance** *n.* rientrata.
**re-entrant** *adj.* rientrante; *n.* angolo rientrante; (geog.) insenatura.
**re-entry** *n.* rientrata, rientro; (comm.) nuova registrazione.
**re-establish** *tr.* ristabilire, restaurare. **-ment** *n.* ristabilimento, restaurazione.
**re-examin-e** *tr.* riesaminare, rivedere; (leg.) interrogare di nuovo. **-ation** *n.* nuovo esame, riesame *m.*; (leg.) nuovo interrogatorio.
**re-export** *tr.* riesportare. **-ation** *n.* riesportazione.
**reface** *tr.* rinnovare la facciata di, riparare.
**re-fashion** *tr.* rimodernare, rifoggiare.
**refectory** *n.* refettorio.
**refer** *tr.* riferire, rimandare, rinviare, rimettere; attribuire, assegnare; *intr.* riferirsi, alludere, rimettersi; rivolgersi, ricorrere; (comm.) *— to drawer*, rivolgersi al traente; *-ring to*, con riferimento a. **-able** *adj.* riferibile, attribuibile.
**referee** *n.* (leg.; sport) arbito; (comm.) garante *m.*, *f.*; *tr.* arbitrare; *intr.* fare da arbitro.
**reference** *n.* riferimento; relazione; riguardo; *with — to*, con riferimento a, in merito a, riguardo a; allusione, accenno; riferimento; citazione; rimando, rinvio, richiamo; referenza, benservito; raccomandazione; garante *m.*, *f.*; (leg.) il deferire; *— library*, sala di consultazione (di una biblioteca); *map —*, coordinate *f.pl.*; *terms of —*, mandato, competenza.
**referend-ary** *n.* referendario. **-um** *n.* (pol.) referendum, plebiscito.
**re'fill**[1] *n.* rifornimento, ricambio.
**refill**[2] *tr.* riempire, rifornire, ricaricare; *intr.* riempirsi.
**refin-e** *tr.* (r)affinare, purificare, (fig.) raffinare, perfezionare; *intr.* raffinarsi, affinarsi; *to — upon a question*, sottilizzare su una questione. **-ed** *adj.* raffinato, fino; ricercato, squisito; (of person) distinto; raffinato. **-ement** *n.* (industr.) raffinamento, raffinazione; (fig.) raffinatezza, finezza, squisitezza; ricercatezza, sottigliezza. **-ery** *n.* raffineria.
**refit** *n.* riattamento; riparazione; (naut.) raddobbo; *tr.* riattare; riparare; (naut.) raddobbare.
**reflect** *tr.* riflettere, riverberare, rispecchiare; (fig.) *to — credit on*, tornare a credito di; *intr.* riflettere, pondere, pensare, meditare; *to — upon*, considerare, (pejor.) gettare biasimo su. **-ed** *adj.* riflesso; *to be -ed*, rispecchiarsi. **-ion, reflexion** *n.* immagine riflessa; (phys.) riflessione, riverbero, riflesso; (fig.) meditazione, riflessione; *on —*, riflettendovi, pensandovi; (pejor.) censura; critica; *to cast -ions on*, criticare, biasimare; *pl.* considerazioni *f.pl.*, pensieri *m.pl.* **-ive** *adj.* riflessivo, meditabondo, meditativo; (phys.) riflettente, che riflette. **-or** *n.* (phys.) riflettore *m.*; (bicycle) catarifrangente *m.*; (fig.) specchio.
**reflex** *adj.* riflesso, indiretto; *n.* (med.) riflesso. **-ible** *adj.* riflessibile. **-ive** *adj.* (gramm.) riflessivo.
**refloat** *tr.* rimettere a galla. **-ing** rimessa a galla.
**reflorescence** *n.* rifioritura.
**reflux** *n.* riflusso.
**reform**[1] *n.* riforma; *— school*, riformatorio; *tr.* riformare; emendare, correggere; *intr.* correggersi, emendarsi.
**re-form**[2] *tr.* formare di nuovo, riformare, rimodellare; *intr.* formarsi di nuovo.
**reformation** *n.* riforma, emendamento; (hist.) *the Reformation*, la Riforma.

**re-formation** *n.* nuova formazione.
**reform-ative** *adj.* riformativo, riformatore. **-atory** *n.* casa di correzione, riformatorio. **-er** *n.* riformatore *m.*
**refract** *tr.* rifrangere. **-ive** *adj.* rifrangente, rifrattivo. **-or** *n.* rifrattore *m.*
**refractor-y** *adj.* indocile, caparbio, ostinato; (med.; chem.) refrattario. **-iness** *n.* indocilità, caparbietà, ostinazione; (med.; chem.) reffrattarietà.
**refrain**[1] *n.* ritornello, ripresa.
**refrain**[2] *intr.* astenersi (da), trattenersi (da), fare a meno (di).
**refresh** *tr.* rinfrescare, ristorare, rinvigorire, ravvivare. **-er** *n.* (leg.) onorario supplementare; (fam.) rinfresco; *-er course*, corso di aggiornamento. **-ing** *adj.* rinfrescante, ristoratore; (fig.) che fa piacere, che incanta. **-ingly** *adv.* piacevolmente. **-ment** *n.* rinfresco, ristoro; riposo; *light -ments*, rinfresco; *to take some -ment*, rifocillarsi; *-ment room*, ristorante *m.*, buffet, caffè *m. indecl.*
**refrigerat-e** *tr.* refrigerare, raffreddare, congelare. **-ion** *n.* refrigerazione. **-or** *n.* frigorifero, refrigerante *m.*; *attrib.* frigorifero.
**refuel** *tr.* rifornire di carburante; *intr.* rifornirsi di combustibile.
**refuge** *n.* rifugio; asilo; riparo; *to seek —*, cercare rifugio; *to take —*, rifugiarsi; (for pedestrians) salvagente, spartitraffico.
**refugee** *n.* profugo, rifugiato.
**refulg-ence** *n.* fulgore *m.*, splendore *m.* **-ent** *adj.* rifulgente, fulgente, splendente.
**refund** *n.* rimborso, rifusione; *tr.* rimborsare, rifondere, restituire.
**refurbish** *tr.* riforbire, lustrare di nuovo; (fig.) rimettere a nuovo.
**refurnish** *tr.* rifornire; riammobiliare, rifare la mobilia di.
**refusal** *n.* rifiuto; *flat —*, rifiuto netto; *to have the — of*, avere il diritto di opzione su.
**re·fuse**[1] *n.* rifiuti, scarti *m.pl.*; immondizie *f.pl.*; *— collection*, nettezza urbana; *— dump*, immondezzaio.
**refuṣ-e**[2] *tr.* rifiutare, ricusare; *to — to*, rifiutare di; *to — admittance*, vietare l'entrata; *to — a request*, respingere una domanda; non volere; *he was -d a hearing*, non volevano sentirlo; *intr.* dire di no, rifiutarsi.
**refut-e** *tr.* confutare. **-able** *adj.* confutabile. **-al, -ation** *n.* confutazione.
**regain** *tr.* riguadagnare, riacquistare, ricuperare, riprendere, *to — one's health*, ricuperare la salute; *to — consciousness*, riprendere conoscenza; *to — possession*, rientrare in possesso; *Paradise -ed*, 'Il Paradiso riconquistato'; raggiungere di nuovo.
**regal** *adj.* regale, reale, regio; (fig.) principesco.
**regale** *tr.* rallegrare, deliziare; *to — with*, intrattenere piacevolmente con; *to — oneself with*, concedersi il piacere di; cibarsi di, gustarsi di.
**regalia** *n.pl.* insegne *f.pl.* reali; (Freemasonry) insegne; (fig.) distintivi *m.pl.*, decorazioni *f.pl.*
**regality** *n.* regalità.
**regard** *n.* sguardo, occhiata; riguardo, rispetto, considerazione, osservanza, deferenza; *with — to*, relativamente a, in relazione a, riguardo a, in merito a; *pl.* complimenti, saluti, ossequi *m.pl.*; *with best -s*, con i migliori saluti; *with kind -s*, con ossequi, (fam.) cordialmente.
**regard** *tr.* guardare; osservare, fare attenzione a; considerare, stimare, tenere conto di, prendere in considerazione; *to — someone kindly*, voler bene a qualcuno; riguardare, riferirsi a, concernere; *as -s, -ing*, per quanto riguarda, quanto a.
**regardant** *adj.* (herald.) guardante.
**regardful** *adj.* riguardoso, rispettoso, attento.
**regardless** *adj.* indifferente (a), noncurante (di), senza riguardo (a), senza badare (a). **-ness** *n.* indifferenza, non curanza, mancanza di riguardo.
**regatta** *n.* regata.
**regency** *n.* reggenza.
**regenerat-e** *adj.* rigenerato; *tr.* rigenerare; riformare; (industr.) ricuperare; *intr.* riprodursi, rigenerarsi, ricrescere. **-ion** *n.* rigenerazione; (industr.) ricupero. **-or** *n.* rigeneratore.
**Regensburg** *pr.n.* (geog.) Ratisbona.
**regent** *n.* reggente *m.*, luogotenente *m.* del regno; *Prince Regent*, Principe Reggente.
**regicid-e** *n.* regicida *m.*, *f.*; regicidio. **-al** *adj.* regicida.
**regime** *n.* regime *m.*, governo.
**regimen** *n.* (med.) regime *m.*, dieta; (gramm.) reggenza.
**regiment** *n.* (mil.) reggimento; (fig.) folla, gran numero; governo; *tr.* irreggimentare; (fig.) disciplinare. **-al** *adj.* reggimentale, di un reggimento; *n.pl.* alta uniforme. **-ation** *n.* irreggimentazione.
**Reginald** *pr.n.m.* Rinaldo, Reginaldo.
**region** *n.* (geog.) regione, zona; *the nether -s*, gli inferi. **-al** *adj.* regionale. **-alism** *n.* regionalismo.
**register** *n.* registro; elenco, lista; (med.; leg.) albo; *to be struck off the —*, essere radiato dall'albo; *— of births, marriages and deaths*, registro dello stato civile, anagrafe *f.*; *parish —*, vacchetta; *— of voters*, lista elettorale.
**register** *tr.* registrare, (far) iscrivere, allibrare; (car) immatricolare; (letter) raccomandare; (luggage) assicurare; (trademark) depositare; (of instrument) segnare, indicare; (fig.) esprimere; *intr.* (mech.) coincidere, essere in corrispondenza; (at hotel) scrivere il proprio nome sul registro; (pol.) farsi iscrivere nella lista elettorale. **-ed** *adj.* registrato, iscritto, immatricolato; *-ed letter*, lettera raccomandata; *-ed luggage*, bagagli assicurati; *-ed nurse*, infermiera diplomata; (comm.) *-ed office*, domicilio legale, sede *f.*; *-ed trade-mark*, marchio di fabbrica depositato; (finan.) *-ed capital*, capitale *m.* sociale; (finan.) *-ed stock*, titolo nominativo.
**registrable** *adj.* registrabile.
**registrar** *n.* segretario, cancelliere *m.*, archivista *m.*; ufficiale *m.* di stato civile; *— general*, capo dell'ufficio anagrafe.
**registration** *n.* registrazione, iscrizione, allibramento; (of letter) raccomandazione; (of luggage) assicurazione; (motor.) *— plate*, targa.
**registry (office)** *n.* ufficio d'anagrafe, ufficio di stato civile; *married at a — office*, sposati civilmente; (naut.) certificato d'immatricolazione.
**regnant** *adj.* regnante; (fig.) predominante, prevalente.
**regrade** *tr.* riclassificare.
**regress** *intr.* regredire, retrocedere; (astron.) retrogradare. **-ion** *n.* regresso, regressione. **-ive** *adj.* regressivo.
**regret** *n.* rammarico, rimpianto, rincrescimento; dispiacere *m.*; *tr.* rimpiangere, rammaricarsi di, addolorarsi di; *I —*, mi rincresce, mi duole, mi dispiace, sono spiacente; *to my great —*, con mio grande rincrescimento; *I have no -s*, non ho rimorsi; *please accept my -s*, prego di accettare le mie scuse.
**regretful** *adj.* dolente, addolorato, spiacente, pieno di rincrescimento. **-ly** *adv.* con rincrescimento, con dispiacere.
**regrettabl-e** *adj.* spiacevole, increscioso, deplorevole, doloroso. **-y** *adv.* deplorevolmente, incresciosamente.
**regroup** *tr.* raggruppare di nuovo.
**regular** *adj.* regolare; normale; *— habits*, abitudini regolate; *he has no — work*, non ha un lavoro regolare; *as — as clockwork*, preciso come un orologio; armonioso; formale; qualificato; vero e proprio, completo; perfetto; *he is a — rascal*, è un briccone matricolato; *n.* soldato regolare; (fam.) cliente abituale. **-ity** *n.* regolarità. **-ize** *tr.* regolarizzare.
**regulat-e** *tr.* regolare. **-ion** *n.*

regolamento; regola; ordine *m.*; (mech.) regolazione; *-ion speed*, velocità regolamentare. **-or** *n.* regolatore *m.*; (mech.) bilanciere *m.*

**regurgitat-e** *tr.*, *intr.* rigurgitare; rigettare, gettare fuori. **-ion** *n.* rigurgito.

**rehabilitat-e** *tr.* riabilitare; ripristinare. **-ion** *n.* riabilitazione; ripristino.

**rehash** *n.* rimaneggiamento; rifacimento; *tr.* rimaneggiare; rifare.

**rehear** *tr.* (leg.) riesaminare. **-ing** *n.* nuova udienza.

**rehearsal** *n.* ripetizione; narrazione; enumerazione; recitazione; (theatr.) prova; *dress —*, prova generale.

**rehearse** *tr.* ripetere; raccontare; enumerare; recitare; (theatr.) provare; fare le prove di.

**reign** *n.* regno (also fig.); *in the — of*, sotto il regno di; *the Reign of Terror*, il regno del Terrore; dominio, influenza; *the — of fashion*, l'influenza della moda; *intr.* regnare; (fig.) dominare; prevalere. **-ing** *adj.* regnante, dominante.

**reimburse** *tr.* rimborsare. **-ment** *n.* rimborso.

**rein** redine *f.*, briglia; *to draw —*, tirare le redini; *to give —*, dare libero corso a; *to give a horse free —*, dare briglia sciolta al cavallo; *tr.*, *intr.* guidare con le redini; (fig.) governare, controllare, guidare; frenare, trattenere; *to — in*, rimettere al passo.

**reincarnat-e** *tr.* reincarnare. **-ion** *n.* reincarnazione; metempsicosi *f.*

**reindeer** *n.* renna.

**reinforce** *tr.* rinforzare, rafforzare, consolidare; ristabilire; (fig.) avvalorare. **-ment** *n.* rinforzo; *pl.* (mil.) rinforzi.

**reins** *n.* (poet.) *pl.* reni, lombi *m.pl.*

**reinstate** *tr.* ristabilire; ripristinare; reintegrare. **-ment** *n.* ristabilimento; ripristino; reintegrazione.

**reinsure** *tr.* (finan.) riassicurare.

**reinvest** *tr.* rinvestire, investire di nuovo; impiegare, convertire di nuovo. **-ment** *n.* rinvestimento.

**reiterat-e** *tr.* ripetere, reiterare. **-ion** *n.* ripetizione insistente; reiterazione.

**re·ject**[1] *n.* persona, cosa rifiutata; (mil.) persona riformata; *export —*, articolo difettoso, non adatto per l'esportazione.

**reject**[2] *tr.* rigettare; rifiutare; respingere; (mil.) riformare; vomitare; evacuare. **-ed** *part. adj.*, rigettato; respinto. **-ion** *n.* rigetto; rifiuto; scarto; *-ion slip*, biglietto di rifiuto.

**rejoic-e** *intr.* rallegrare; allietare; gioire, godere; far festa, celebrare un evento. **-ing** *n.* allegria; gioia; giubilo; esultanza.

**rejoin**[1] *intr.* replicare; rispondere (ad un'accusa). **-der** *n.* risposta; replica (ad accusa).

**rejoin**[2] *intr.* ricongiungere, ricongiungersi; raggiungere.

**rejuvenat-e** *intr.* ringiovanire. **-ion** *n.* ringiovanimento.

**rekindle** *tr.*, *intr.* riaccendere; riaccendersi.

**relapse** *n.* ricaduta; recidiva; *intr.* ricadere; (med.) avere una ricaduta.

**relat-e** *tr.*, *intr.* narrare, raccontare; riferire; mettere in relazione; avere rapporto, avere attinenza. **-ed** *part. adj.* narrato; riferito; imparentato; *to be closely -ed to*, essere parente prossimo di. **-edness** *n.* relazione; parentela. **-er** *n.* chi narra, chi racconta. **-ing** *adj.* relativo; *-ing to*, concernente.

**relation** *n.* narrazione; racconto; relazione, rapporto, connessione, attinenza; parente, *m.*, *f.*, congiunto, consanguineo; *is he any — to you?*, è imparentato con voi? **-ship** *n.* relazione; rapporto; parentela.

**relative** *adj.* relativo; pertinente; *with — coolness*, con relativo sangue freddo; *— to*, in relazione a; *supply is — to demand*, l'offerta è in relazione alla domanda; *n.* parente *m.*, *f.*; (gramm.) relativo. **-ly** *adv.* relativamente. **-ness** *n.* relatività.

**relativism** *n.* relativismo.

**relativity** *n.* relatività; *theory of —*, teoria della relatività.

**relax** *tr.* rilassare; riposare; *intr.* rilassarsi; allentare; mitigare, moderare; ridurre; rendere meno severo; diminuire. **-ation** *n.* rilassamento; distensione; riposo; divertimento; svago; mitigazione; moderazione; diminuzione. **-ing** *adj.* rilassante, distensivo.

**re·lay**[1] *n.* squadra di operai che dà il cambio; *to work by -s*, lavorare a turni; materiale di ricambio; (electr.) relè *m. indecl.*, soccorritore; (radio) collegamento; *tr.*, *intr.* fornire, fornirsi di ricambio; (electr.) controllare a mezzo di soccorritore, di relè; (radio) collegare.

**relay**[2] *tr.* porre di nuovo.

**re·lay-race** *n.* (sport) corsa a staffetta.

**release** *n.* liberazione; scarcerazione; *— on bail*, libertà provvisoria; quietanza; cessione; *— of a film*, distribuzione di un film; *— of a speech*, autorizzazione di pubblicare un discorso; (mech.) scarico, scappamento; (photog.) scatto; *tr.* liberare, rilasciare, scarcerare; (leg.) cedere; autorizzare; (mech.) sganciare; liberare; *to — the brake*, allentare il freno; *to — a spring*, scaricare una molla; (photog.) *to — the shutter*, far scattare l'otturatore.

**relegat-e** *tr.* relegare; esiliare, bandire; rimettere, rimandare; (football) mandare in serie inferiore; *to be -ed*, essere retrocesso. **-ion** *n.* relegazione, esilio; rinvio.

**relent** *intr.* addolcirsi; diventare meno severo; intenerirsi.

**relentless** *adj.* inflessibile; inesorabile, implacabile; spietato. **-ly** *adv.* inflessibilmente; inesorabilmente, implacabilmente; spietatamente. **-ness** *n.* inflessibilità; inesorabilità, implacabilità; spietatezza.

**relev-ance, -ancy** *n.* relazione, rapporto; pertinenza; attinenza. **-ant** *adj.* relativo; pertinente; attinente. **-antly** *adv.* con attinenza.

**reliab-le** *adj.* fidato, degno di fiducia; attendibile; *a — source*, una fonte attendibile. **-ility** *n.* attendibilità; fidatezza; regolarità; *-ility trials*, prove di collaudo; prove di resistenza. **-leness.** See **reliability**. **-ly** *adv.* in modo degno di fiducia; in modo attendibile.

**reli-ance** *n.* fiducia, fede; *to place — upon*, riporre la propria fiducia in; sostegno, appoggio. **-ant** *adj.* fiducioso; fidente; che fa assegnamento.

**relic** *n.* reliquia; resto, vestigio; *-s of the past*, vestigi del passato.

**relict** *n.* vedova.

**relief**[1] *n.* sollievo, conforto, ristoro; *he gave a sigh of —*, ebbe un sospiro di sollievo; *to my great —*, con mio gran sollievo; soccorso, aiuto; sussidio; *— of old people*, assistenza ai vecchi; (mil.) liberazione; soccorso; esenzione; *the — of a sentry*, il cambio della sentinella; *by way of —*, come diversivo; *— fund*, fondo di soccorso; *— train*, treno sussidiario; *— troops*, truppe di soccorso.

**relief**[2] *n.* relievo; *it stands out in —*, spicca, ha rilievo; (painting) prospettiva; *— map*, plastico; carta fisica; *high —*, alto rilievo; *low —*, basso rilievo.

**reliev-e** *tr.* alleviare, mitigare, sollevare; *to — one's feelings*, sfogarsi; aiutare, soccorrere; liberare; alleggerire; rendere meno monotono; *to — the tedium of the journey*, ingannare la noia del viaggio; (mil.) dare il cambio a. **-er** *n.* chi conforta; soccorritore; liberatore. **-ing** *adj.* che allevia, che soccorre; di opere assistenziali.

**religion** *n.* religione *f.*; confessione religiosa; dovere; passione; *established —*, religione di stato.

**religious** *adj.* religioso, pio, devoto; scrupoloso; *n.* monaco; *— book*, libro di devozione; —

*exercises*, esercizi spirituali; — *wars*, guerre di religione. **-ly** *adv.* religiosamente. **-ness** *n.* religiosità.

**reline** *tr.* rinnovare la fodera di.

**relinquish** *tr.* abbandonare, lasciare; cedere, rinunziare a, desistere da; allentare la presa su. **-ment** *n.* abbandono; rinuncia.

**reliquary** *n.* reliquiario.

**reliques** *n.pl.* resti, reliquie.

**relish** *n.* gusto; piacere *m.*; attrattiva; sapore *m.*; profumo, aroma *m.*, fragranza; condimento, salsa, spezia; piccola dose, pizzico; *tr.* gustare, godere; apprezzare; mangiare con appetito, assaporare.

**relive** *intr.* rivivere.

**reload** *tr.* caricare di nuovo, ricaricare.

**reluct-ance, -ancy** *n.* riluttanza; ripugnanza; *to affect* —, fare lo smorfioso; *to show — to*, mostrarsi poco disposto a. **-ant** *adj.* riluttante; che agisce a malincuore; difficile da trattare. **-antly** *adv.* con riluttanza; con ripugnanza; a malincuore, di mala voglia.

**rely** *intr.* fare assegnamento; fidarsi, aver fiducia; *you can — upon me*, potete contare su di me.

**remain** *intr.* rimanere, restare; avanzare; *I — yours truly*, sono il vostro devotissimo.

**remainder** *n.* resto, residuo, avanzo; rimanenza; persone rimanenti; (leg.) riversione; (math.) resto; *tr.* liquidare (un'edizione); *a -ed copy*, un esemplare liquidato.

**remaining** *adj.* restante, che resta; *his — days*, il resto dei suoi giorni.

**remains** *n.pl.* avanzi; reliquie; spoglie mortali, cadavere *m.*; *pl.* opere postume.

**remake** *tr.* rifare.

**remand** *n.* (leg.) rinvio in carcere; *to be on* —, essere trattenuto a disposizione della legge; — *home*, carcere preventivo; *tr.* (leg.) rinviare in carcere per un supplemento d'istruttoria.

**remark** *n.* nota, attenzione; *worthy of* —, degno di nota; osservazione, appunto; commento; *to make -s about*, fare delle osservazioni su; *intr.* osservare; considerare con attenzione; notare; far notare; far rimarcare; fare osservazioni, fare commenti. **-able** *adj.* notevole; ragguardevole; eccezionale, straordinario; sorprendente.

**remarriage** *n.* nuovo matrimonio; seconde nozze.

**remarry** *intr.* unirsi di nuovo in matrimonio; risposarsi.

**remediable** *adj.* rimediabile.

**remedial** *adj.* atto a rimediare; riparatore. **-ly** *adv.* in modo da rimediare; come rimedio.

**remedy** *n.* rimedio, riparo; cura; medicina; *past* —, irrimediabile, irreparabile; incurabile; *tr.* rimediare, porre rimedio a; correggere.

**remember** *tr.*, *intr.* ricordare, ricordarsi; rammentare, rammentarsi; — *me to your parents*, ricordami ai tuoi genitori; — *to tell him*, ricordati di dirglielo; *do you — me?*, mi riconosci?, ti ricordi di me?; ricordare, sapere a memoria.

**remembrance** *n.* ricordo, memoria; *in — of*, in ricordo di, alla memoria di; *within my* —, per quanto io ricordi; *it escapes my* —, sfugge alla mia memoria; *to call to* —, richiamare alla memoria; *pl.* saluti.

**remind** *tr.* ricordare a, far ricordare a, rammentare a; fare venire in mente a; *you — me of your father*, mi ricordi tuo padre. **-er** ricordo, promemoria; (comm.) lettera di sollecitazione.

**reminisc-e** *intr.* raccontare i propri ricordi; abbandonarsi ai propri ricordi. **-ence** *n.* reminiscenza; rimembranza; ricordo; *pl.* memorie. **-ent** *adj.* che richiama alla mente; rammentare.

**remiss** *adj.* negligente, trascurato; lento, fiacco, svogliato.

**remission** *n.* remissione, perdono; (leg.) condono; *to grant — of*, assolvere da; annullamento; esonero (da tasse); abbassamento, diminuzione; (med.) remittenza.

**remissive** *adj.* remissivo, che perdona.

**remissness** *n.* negligenza, trascuratezza; lentezza, svogliatezza.

**remit** rimettere, perdonare; condonare; (leg.) diminuire; mitigare; rallentare; rimettere, sottomettere; (comm.) rimettere; *kindly — by cheque*, favorite effettuare il pagamento con assegno; rimandare; differire; rinviare. **-tal** *n.* remissione, perdono; (leg.) condono; rinvio di processo. **-tance** *n.* (comm.) rimessa; *-tance of balance*, invio del saldo; *to send someone a -tance*, fare una rimessa.

**remnant** *n.* avanzo, resto, residuo; scampolo; frammento; rimanenza; — *sale*, liquidazione, saldo.

**remodel** *tr.* rimodellare; ricomporre, rimaneggiare.

**remonstrance** *n.* rimostranza.

**remonstrate** *tr.*, *intr.* fare rimostranze; obiettare; protestare.

**remonstration** See **remonstrance.**

**remorse** *n.* rimorso. **-ful** *adj.* tormentato dal rimorso. **-fully** *adv.* con rimorso. **-fulness** *n.* rimorso. **-less** *adj.* spietato; senza rimorsi; crudele. **-lessness** *n.* assenza di rimorso; mancanza di pietà; crudeltà.

**remote** *adj.* remoto; distante; lontano; (fig.) estraneo, alieno; appartato; *a — resemblance*, una vaga rassomiglianza; *he had not the remotest idea*, non aveva la più pallida idea. **-ness** *n.* distanza; lontananza.

**remould** *tr.* riplasmare; rimodellare.

**remount** *tr.*, *intr.* rimontare; risalire; (mil.) rifornire di cavalli freschi.

**removable** *adj.* amovibile; rimovibile; trasportabile.

**removal** *n.* rimozione; allontanamento; (surg.) ablazione; trasferimento; trasloco; — *expenses*, spese di trasferta.

**remove** *n.* grado di parentela; trasferimento; *tr.* eliminare; ritirare; *intr.* rimuovere, spostare; togliere, levare; congedare, traslocare, trasferirsi; allontanarsi.

**removed** *adj.* lontano; estraneo; *first cousin once* —, cugino di secondo.

**remover** *n.* chi, cosa che rimuove, allontana, toglie; *varnish* —, acqua ragia, solvente per vernice.

**remunerat-e** *tr.* rimunerare, ricompensare. **-ion** *n.* rimunerazione, ricompensa. **-ive** *adj.* rimunerativo. **-or** *n.* rinumeratore.

**Renaissance** *pr.n.* Rinascimento; *Renaissance painter*, pittore del Rinascimento.

**renal** *adj.* (anat.) renale.

**rename** *tr.* rinominare; dare un nome nuovo a.

**renasc-ence** *n.* rinascita, rinascenza; rinascimento; rinnovamento; *the Renascence*, il Rinascimento. **-ent** *adj.* rinascente.

**rencontre** *n.* scontro; scaramuccia; battaglia; duello; incontro.

**rend** *tr.* strappare, lacerare; squarciare; dividere; *my heart is rent*, il mio cuore è a pezzi; *the shouts rent the air*, le urle squarciavano l'aria; *to — one's garments*, strapparsi le vesti.

**render**[1] *n.* chi squarcia, lacera.

**render**[2] *tr.* rendere, restituire; *to — good for evil*, rendere bene per male; — *(un)to Caesar the things that are Caesar's*, date a Cesare quello che è di Cesare; pagare; mostrare; far diventare; rappresentare; tradurre; sciogliere; raffinare.

**rendering** *n.* restituzione; resa; traduzione; interpretazione; fusione; raffinazione.

**rendezvous** *n.* luogo di raduno; luogo di convegno; appuntamento; convegno.

**rending** *n.* strappo; lacerazione, spaccatura.

**rendition** *n.* traduzione; interpretazione.

**renegade** *n.* (rel.) rinnegato, apostata *m.*; traditore; disertore.

**renegation** *n.* abiura, apostasia; rinnegamento; diserzione.

**renege** *tr.* (rel.) abiurare, rinnegare; *intr.* (*aux.* essere) apostatare.
**renew** *tr.*, *intr.* rinnovare; rinvigorire; *to — one's attention*, raddoppiare l'attenzione; sostituire. **-able** *adj.* rinnovabile. **-al** *n.* rinnovo; rinnovamento; ripresa; sostituzione. **-edly** *adv.* di nuovo; ripetutamente. **-er** *n.* rinnovatore.
**rennet** *n.* presame *m.*, caglio.
**renominate** *tr.* nominare di nuovo; riproporre come candidato.
**renounce** *tr.*, *intr.* rinunciare a; *to — the world*, rinunciare alla vita mondana, rinnegare, ripudiare; *to — one's faith*, rinnegare la propria fede. **-ment** *n.* rinuncia.
**renovat-e** *tr.* rinnovare, ripristinare, rinvigorire. **-ion** *n.* rinnovazione, rinnovamento. **-or** *n.* rinnovatore.
**renown** *n.* rinomanza, celebrità, fama. **-ed** *adj.* rinomato, celebre, famoso.
**rent**[1] *n.* pigione, affitto; nolo; *for —*, affittasi; reddito, entrata; rendita; *tr.*, *intr.* affittare, prendere in affitto; dare in affitto.
**rent**[2] *n.* strappo; laceramento, squarcio; spaccatura, fessura; scoscendimento; (fig.) rottura, scisma *m.*
**rentable** *adj.* affittabile.
**rental** *n.* introito derivante da affitti; affitto.
**renumber** *tr.* contare di nuovo; rinumerare, rifare la numerazione di.
**renunciation** *n.* rinuncia; abbandono; ripudio, rinnegamento; *— on oath*, abiura.
**reoccup-y** *tr.* rioccupare. **-ation** *n.* rioccupazione.
**reopen** *tr.* riaprire; *intr.* riaprirsi. **-ing** *n.* riapertura.
**reorganiz-e** *tr.*, *intr.* riorganizzare. **-ation** *n.* riorganizzazione; riassetto.
**repaint** *tr.* ridipingere.
**repair**[1] *intr.* rifugiarsi; riparare, trovare rifugio in un luogo.
**repair**[2] *n.* riparazione, restauro; *beyond —*, irreparabile; *out of —*, guasto; *under —*, in riparazione; *-s done while you wait*, riparazioni rapide; *in bad —*, in cattivo stato; *in good —*, in buono stato; *tr.* riparare; restaurare; fare riparazioni a; (fig.) rimediare a. **-able** *adj.* riparabile. **-er** *n.* riparatore. **-ing.** riparazione.
**repaper** *tr.* ritappezzare.
**repar-able** *adj.* riparabile. **-ation** *n.* riparazione; risarcimento.
**repartee** *n.* risposta spiritosa e pronta; replica arguta; abilità nel dare risposte spiritose.
**repass** *intr.* ripassare; riattraversare.
**repast** *n.* pasto; *a rich —*, un ricco pasto.
**repatriat-e** *n.* rimpatriato; *intr.* rimpatriare. **-ion** *n.* rimpatrio.
**repay** *tr.* ripagare; restituire; *to — a visit*, restituire una visita; ricompensare **-able** *adj.* rimborsabile, restituibile; ricompensabile. **-ment** *n.* rimborso; restituzione; ricompensa.
**repeal** *n.* revoca, abrogazione; annullamento; *tr.* revocare, abrogare; abolire, annullare.
**repeat** *n.* ripetizione; (mus.) ripresa; *— order*, ordine successivo; *tr.*, *intr.* ripetere; studiare, recitare a memoria; ricorrere; ritornare; (of food) tornare su; suonare a ripetizione (di orologio); (math.) ripetersi all'infinito. **-able** *adj.* ripetibile. **-ed** *part. adj.* ripetuto; ritornato. **-edly** *adv.* ripetutamente. **-er** *n.* ripetitore; arma da fuoco a ripetizione; orologio a ripetizione; bussola ripetitrice; (math.) numero periodico. **-ing** *adj.* a ripetizione; *-ing decimal*, decimale periodico; *-ing rifle*, fucile a ripetizione; *-ing watch*, orologio a ripetizione; *n.* ripetizione.
**repel** *tr.* respingere; (chem.) respingere; essere incapace a combinarsi con; ripugnare a; ispirare ripugnanza a **-lent** *adj.* repellente, ripulsivo, ripugnante.
**repent** *intr.* pentirsi; pentirsi di. **-ance** *n.* pentimento; resipiscenza. **-ant** *adj.* pentito; contrito. **-antly** *adv.* con pentimento; con compunzione, contritamente. **-er** *n.* penitente.
**repeople** *tr.* ripopolare.
**repercuss-ion** *n.* ripercussione. **-ive** *adj.* ripercussivo.
**repertoire** *n.* (theatr.) repertorio.
**repertory** *n.* repertorio; lista, catalogo; (theatr.) repertorio.
**repetit-ion** *n.* ripetizione; copia; replica; lezione da impararsi a memoria. **-ious** *adj.* che (si) ripete; noioso. **-ive** *adj.* che ripete, caratterizzato da una ripetizione.
**rephrase** *tr.* esprimere, formulare di nuovo.
**repin-e** *intr.* (poet.) dolersi; lamentarsi; lagnarsi; affliggersi. **-ing** *adj.* lamentoso, afflitto. **-ingly** *adv.* lamentosamente, con tono scontento, insoddisfatto.
**replace** *tr.* ricollocare; rimettere a posto; restituire; rimpiazzare; sostituire; prendere il posto di; succedere a; *to be -d by*, essere sostituito da.
**replace-able** *adj.* sostituibile. **-ment** *n.* ricollocamento; sostituzione.
**replant** *tr.* ripiantare; trapiantare. **-ation** *n.* nuova piantagione *f.*; trapianto.
**replay** *n.* partita ripetuta, di spareggio; *tr.* rigiocare (una partita).
**replenish** *tr.* riempire. **-ing**, **-ment** *n.* riempimento; rifornimento.
**replet-e** *adj.* pieno; ripieno; zeppo, colmo; sazio, satollo. **-eness**, **-ion** *n.* pienezza, sazietà; *full to -ion*, satollo.
**replicat-e** *tr.* replicare, ripetere. **-ion** *n.* risposta; (leg.) replica; riproduzione, copia.
**reply** *n.* risposta; (leg.) replica; (comm.) riscontro; *in — to your letter*, facendo riscontro alla vostra lettera; *intr.* rispondere, replicare; *-ing to your letter*, in risposta alla vostra lettera; *to — in the affirmative*, rispondere di sì.
**repopulat-e** *tr.* ripopolare. **-ion** *n.* ripopolamento.
**report** *n.* voce pubblica; rumore, notizia, diceria; *idle -s*, chiacchiere inutili; *the — goes*, si dice; fama; rapporto, relazione; servizio giornalistico; scoppio, rimbombo, detonazione; *a loud —*, una forte detonazione; *law reports*, cronaca giudiziaria; *weather-report*, bollettino meteorologico.
**report** *intr.* riportare, riferire, raccontare; *it is -ed that*, si dice che; *-ed speech*, discorso indiretto; fare la relazione di; render conto di; presentare, stendere rapporto; *to — a trial*, fare la cronaca di un processo; essere corrispondente, cronista; presentarsi; denunciare. **-able** *adj.* riferibile. **-age** *n.* 'reportage', servizio giornalistico; stile giornalistico.
**reporter** *n.* cronista *m.*; corrispondente di giornale; *the Reporters' Gallery*, tribuna della Stampa (in Parlamento); stenografo (al Parlamento); *crime —*, cronista di cronaca nera; *sports —*, cronista sportivo.
**repose** *n.* riposo; quiete *f.*, tranquillità; armonia; serenità; *intr.* posare; riposare; *rfl.* riposarsi; *tr.* porre, riporre; *to — one's trust in*, riporre la propria fiducia in. **-ful** *adj.* riposante; tranquillo.
**repository** *n.* deposito; magazzino; ripostiglio; museo, collezione; (fig.) miniera; confidente *m.*, *f.*
**repot** *tr.* rinvasare.
**reprehend** *tr.* riprendere, rimproverare; biasimare; censurare.
**reprehensible** *adj.* riprensibile, biasimevole.
**reprehension** *n.* biasimo, critica; rimprovero.
**represent** *tr.* rappresentare; descrivere; *exactly as -ed*, conforme alla descrizione; *picture -ing a hunting scene*, quadro raffigurante una scena di caccia; far notare, far presente;

dichiarare; significare, avere valore di; recitare (una parte); simboleggiare; sostituire, fare le veci di; spiegare.

**representation** *n.* rappresentazione; raffigurazione; immagine; rappresentanza; interpretazione; instanza; rimostranza, protesta. **-al** *adj.* relativo a rappresentanza; di rappresentazione; (art) rappresentativo.

**representative** *adj.* rappresentativo; *allegory — of charity*, allegoria che rappresenta la carità; tipico, caratteristico; *n.* delegato; rappresentante; deputato; esempio tipico.

**repress** *tr.* reprimere; frenare. **-ed** *adj.* represso; contenuto. **-ible** *adj.* reprimibile. **-ion** *n.* repressione.

**repressive** *adj.* repressivo. **-ness** *n.* carattere repressivo.

**reprieve** *n.* dilazione; sospensione, commutazione di pena capitale; *tr.* accordare una dilazione a; concedere una tregua a; sospendere l'esecuzione di; commutare la pena capitale a.

**reprimand** *n.* rimprovero; sgridata; *tr.* rimproverare; riprendere; sgridare.

**reprint** *n.* ristampa; nuova tiratura; *tr.* ristampare.

**reprisal** *n.* rappresaglia; *to make -s*, compiere rappresaglie; *pl.* compenso.

**reproach** *n.* rimprovero; biasimo; *to heap -es on*, coprire di improperi; vituperio, obbrobrio; vergogna, disonore; *tr.* rimproverare, biasimare, censurare. **-able** *adj.* riprovevole. **-ful** *adj.* di rimprovero; riprovevole; vergognoso. **-fulness** *n.* aria, tono di rimprovero. **-less** *adj.* irreprensibile.

**reprobat-e** *adj., n.* empio, reprobo, dannato; *tr.* riprovare; biasimare; censurare; dannare. **-ion** *n.* riprovazione; biasimo; condanna, dannazione.

**reproduce** *intr.* riprodurre.

**reproduction** *n.* riproduzione; generazione; copia, imitazione.

**reproductive** *adj.* riproduttivo; riproduttore. **-ness** *n.* riproduttività, fertilità.

**reproof**[1] *n.* rimprovero; biasimo.

**reproof**[2] *tr.* rendere nuovamente impermeabile.

**reprove** *tr.* rimproverare; biasimare; riprendere.

**reprovingly** *adj.* in tono di rimprovero.

**reptil-e** *adj.* (zool.) strisciante; *n.* rettile *m.* **-ian** *adj.* di rettile; simile a rettile; (fig.) servile, strisciante; *n.* rettile *m.*

**republic** *n.* repubblica. **-an** *adj., n.* repubblicano. **-anism** *n.* repubblicanesimo.

**republication** *n.* nuova edizione; (leg.) nuova pubblicazione (di legge, decreto); nuova stesura (di testamento).

**republish** *tr.* ripubblicare, preparare una nuova edizione di; emanare nuovamente (una legge); cambiare (un testamento).

**repudiat-e** *tr.* ripudiare; disconoscere; rinnegare; rifiutarsi di. **-ion** *n.* ripudio, disconoscimento, rinnegazione; rifiuto. **-or** *n.* chi ripudia.

**repugn** *tr., intr.* ripugnare; essere ripugnante.

**repugn-ance** *n.* ripugnanza, antipatia; incompatibilità. **-ant** *adj.* ripugnante; *it is -ant to me*, mi ripugna; incompatibile contrario; opposto, antagonistico.

**repulse** *n.* rifiuto; sconfitta; scacco; *tr.* respingere; ricusare; sconfiggere.

**repulsion** *n.* repulsione; ripugnanza, avversione.

**repulsive** *adj.* ripulsivo; repellente; ributtante. **-ness** *n.* l'essere ripulsivo, repellente, ributtante; (phys.) forza di ripulsione.

**repurchase** *n.* riacquisto, riscatto; *tr.* riacquistare, riscattare.

**reputable** *adj.* rispettabile; onorato; onorevole.

**reputation** *n.* reputazione; rispettabilità; fama; *person of —*, persona onorata; *I know him only by —*, lo conosco solo di fama; *to acquire a — for oneself*, farsi un gran nome; *to have a — for integrity*, goder fama di essere integro; *to have the — of being*, aver fama di essere.

**reput-e** *n.* reputazione; fama; *a place of ill —*, un luogo malfamato; *of —*, di fama; *in high —*, molto rinomato; *to know by —*, conoscere di fama; *tr.* reputare; stimare; giudicare; *to be reputed wealthy*, aver fama di essere ricco. **-ed** *adj.* supposto, presunto, ipoteco; (leg.) putativo. **-edly** *adv.* presumibilmente; secondo l'opinione generale; (leg.) putativamente.

**request** *n.* domanda; richiesta; petizione; preghiera; *by —*, su richiesta; *to grant a —*, accogliere una preghiera; (leg.) instanza; *in great —*, molto richiesto; *tr.* richiedere; domandare; sollecitare; pregare; *your presence is -ed*, si richiede la vostra presenza.

**requir-e** *intr.* richiedere; esigere; pretendere; ordinare, costringere, obbligare; domandare, chiedere; aver bisogno di; *the development of industry -es the construction of new factories*, lo sviluppo dell'industria rende necessaria la costruzione di nuove fabbriche; *it -es a lot of work to do it*, ci vuole molto lavoro per farlo; *this machine -es little care*, questa macchina non ha bisogno di molta manutenzione; *twenty workers are -ed*, occorrono venti operai. **-ed** *adj.* richiesto, domandato; necessario; obbligatorio.

**requirement** *n.* richiesta; esigenza; bisogno; necessità; *to meet all -s*, rispondere a tutte le esigenze; fabbisogno; requisito.

**requisite** *adj.* richiesto; necessario; indispensabile; *n.* requisito; oggetto, cosa necessaria.

**requisition** *n.* richiesta, istanza, domanda; ordine; (mil.) requisizione; *to call into —*, requisire; ricorrere a; requisito; domanda di estradizione; *tr.* requisire.

**requital** *n.* ricambio, contraccambio; *as a — for*, in contraccambio di; ricompensa; vendetta, rappresaglia.

**requite** *tr.* ricompensare; contraccambiare; vendicare.

**reread** *tr.* rileggere.

**reredos** *n.* (archit.) dossale *m.*

**resaleable** *adj.* rivendibile.

**rescind** *tr.* rescindere; abrogare; annullare; revocare.

**rescission** *n.* rescissione; abrogazione; revoca; annullamento.

**rescuable** *adj.* salvabile.

**rescue** *n.* liberazione; salvezza; scampo; salvataggio, soccorso; *to come to the —*, venire in soccorso; (leg.) liberazione illegale (di prigioniero); il recuperare (beni) con la violenza; *— corps*, squadra di salvataggio; *tr.* liberare; salvare; ricuperare. **-r** *n.* liberatore; salvatore; soccorritore.

**research** *n.* ricerca; indagine *f.*; *— department*, ufficio, servizio ricerche; *— work*, lavori di ricerca; *intr.* fare ricerche. **-er** *n.* ricercatore; investigatore.

**resell** *tr.* rivendere.

**resemblance** *n.* rassomiglianza, somiglianza; *to bear a strong — to*, avere una forte rassomiglianza con.

**resemble** *tr.* assomigliare a; *rfl.* assomigliarsi.

**resent** *tr.* risentirsi di; offendersi per; irritarsi per. **-ful** *adj.* pieno di risentimento, risentito; offeso; sdegnato; permaloso. **-fully** *adv.* con risentimento. **-ment** *n.* risentimento; rancore; *to bear -ment against*, serbare rancore a.

**reservation** *n.* riserva; restrizione; *with -s*, con riserve; prenotazione.

**reserve** *n.* riserva; limitazione, restrizione; *without —*, senza riserve; riserbo, riservatezza; discrezione; *an attitude of —*, un atteggiamento riservato; (comm.) riserva; *under —*, salvo buon fine; *— capital*, capitale autorizzato ma non emesso; *— price*, prezzo di riserva; *cash —*, riserva di cassa; *gold —*, riserva aurea.

**reserve** *tr.* riservare; *to — for*

*oneself*, riservare per sè; prenotare; serbare, mettere da parte; destinare. **-ed** *adj.* riservato, prenotato; *-ed seats*, posti riservati; (fig.) riservato; contegnoso. **-edly** *adv.* con riservatezza. **-edness** *n.* riservatezza. **-ist** *n.* (mil.) riservista *m.*

**reservoir** *n.* serbatoio, cisterna; bacino di riserva; (fig.) riserva, raccolta; *a great — of facts*, una miniera di fatti.

**reset** *n.* riordinamento, risistemazione; messa a punto; *tr.* incastonare di nuovo; regolare; ripreparare, ripiantare; rimettere a posto, aggiustare; (med.) *to — a limb*, aggiustare, ingessare un arto; (typ.) ricomporre.

**resettle** *tr.* risistemare; colonizzare di nuovo; *intr.* risistemarsi; depositarsi di nuovo. **-ment** *n.* risistemazione; ristabilimento; nuova colonizzazione.

**reshape** *tr.* dare nuova forma a, rifoggiare.

**reshuffle** *n.* (of cards) il mescolare di nuovo; (pol. fam.) rimaneggiamento; *tr.* (of cards) rimescolare; (pol., fam.) rimaneggiare.

**reside** *intr.* risiedere, dimorare, abitare; trovarsi, essere presente.

**residenc-e** *n.* residenza, soggiorno; *in —*, in residenza; *to take up one's —*, prendere residenza; dimora, abitazione, casa signorile; *— permit*, permesso di soggiorno. **-y** *n.* residenza ufficiale.

**resident** *adj.* residente; *to be — in a place*, risiedere in un luogo; inerente; localizzato; *privileges — in a class*, privilegi pertinenti ad una classe; *n.* residente, abitante; membro interno. **-ial** *adj.* occupato da abitazioni, residenziale; *-ial quarter*, quartiere residenziale.

**residual** *adj.* residuo; restante; *— oil*, olio pesante, nafta.

**residuary** *adj.* rimanente, restante, residuo; *— legatee*, legatario universale.

**resid-ue** *n.* residuo, resto; (chem.) sostanza residua; (leg.) residuo, attivo netto. **-uum** *n.* residuo, avanzo; errore residuo.

**re-sign** *intr.* firmare di nuovo.

**resign** *intr.* dimettersi, rassegnare le dimissioni; *he -ed from the cabinet*, si dimise dalla carica di ministro; *tr.* rinunciare a; consegnare, affidare; *rfl. to — oneself*, rassegnarsi, sottomettersi. **-ation** *n.* dimissioni *f.pl.*; abbandono, rinuncia; rassegnazione. **-ed** *adj.* rassegnato; dimissionario. **-edly** *adv.* rassegnatamente.

**resili-ence, -ency** *n.* rimbalzo; elasticità; resilienza; capacità di ricupero; *to have —*, avere capacità di ripresa. **-ent** *adj.* rimbalzante; elastico; resiliente; che ha capacità di ricupero.

**resin** *n.* resina. **-ous** *adj.* resinoso.

**resist** *tr.* resistere a; opporsi a; trattenersi dal; fare a meno di. **-ance** *n.* resistenza; *to take the line of least -ance*, prendere la via più facile. **-ant** *adj.* resistente. **-er** *n.* chi resiste; oppositore; forza resistente. **-ible** *adj.* a cui si può resistere. **-less** *adj.* irresistibile; inevitabile; incapace di; senza resistenza.

**resole** *tr.* risolare.

**resolute** *adj.* risoluto, deciso; *a — man*, un uomo deciso. **-ly** *adv.* risolutamente, con decisione. **-ness** *n.* risolutezza, fermezza, decisione.

**resolution** *n.* risolutezza, fermezza, decisione; risoluzione; (admin.) deliberazione, ordine del giorno; soluzione, risposta; scomposizione, analisi *f. indecl.*

**resolv-e** *n.* risoluzione; decisione; *he kept his —*, mantenne la sua decisione; *tr.*, *intr.* risolvere; decidere; deliberare; *to — to*, risolversi a; *to — upon*, decidersi; spiegare, chiarire; scomporre; analizzare. **-ed** *adj.* risoluto, deciso.

**reson-ance** *n.* risonanza. **-ant** *adj.* risonante; **-antly** *adv.* con risonanza. **-ator** *n.* (electr.) risonatore.

**resort** *n.* ricorso; *to have — to*, ricorrere a; *the last —*, l'ultima risorsa; convegno; luogo di soggiorno; *holiday —*, luogo di villeggiatura; *summer —*, stazione balneare; *intr.* ricorrere, far ricorso; recarsi, andare; affluire.

**re-sort²** *tr.* scegliere di nuovo, selezionare di nuovo.

**resound** *intr.* risonare; echeggiare; riecheggiare; far risonare, proclamare. **-ing** *adj.* resonante. **-ingly** *adv.* con risonanza.

**resource** *n.* risorse *f.pl.*; mezzi *m.pl.*; *a nation's -s*, i mezzi finanziari di una nazione; espediente, ripiego, rimedio; passatempo, distrazione; (fig.) risorsa; ingegnosità; abilità. **-ful** *adj.* pieno di risorse; ingegnoso; disinvolto. **-fully** *adv.* con molte risorse. **-fulness** *n.* abbondanza di risorse ingegnosità. **-less** *adj.* senza risorse. **-lessness** *n.* mancanza di risorse.

**respect** *n.* rispetto, stima, riguardo; *to hold in —*, tenere in considerazione; *to win the — of*, guadagnarsi la stima di; *pl.* saluti, ossequi; *to pay one's -s to*, ossequiare, rendere omaggio a; attenzione; considerazione; *with — to*, in riferimento a; *in all -s*, da tutti i punti di vista; *in every —*, sotto ogni aspetto; *tr.* rispettare, considerare, avere riguardo per.

**respectab-le** *adj.* rispettabile; degno di rispetto, discreto; abbastanza buono; passabile; ragguardevole, considerevole; onesto, decoroso. **-ility** *n.* rispettabilità; convenzioni sociali. **-ly** *adv.* rispettabilmente; discretamente; onestamente, decentemente.

**respecter** *n.* chi, che rispetta; *to be no — of*, non tener conto di; non aver parzialità per.

**respectful** *adj.* rispettoso; deferente; sottomesso. **-ly** *adv.* rispettosamente, con deferenza. **-ness** *n.* deferenza, rispetto.

**respecting** *prep.* rispetto a, riguardo a, relativamente a.

**respective** *adj.* rispettivo, relativo. **-ly** *adv.* rispettivamente.

**respirat-ion** *n.* respirazione; respiro. **-or** *n.* (med.) respiratore; maschera respiratoria; (mil.) maschera antigas. **-ory** *adj.* respiratorio; (anat.) *-ory tract*, vie aeree.

**respire** *intr.* respirare; (fig.) prender fiato.

**respite** *n.* dilazione, proroga, rinvio; tregua, pausa; respiro, sollievo.

**resplend-ence, -ency** *n.* splendore, fulgore. **-ent** *adj.* splendente, risplendente, brillante; smagliante.

**respond** *intr.* rispondere, replicare; (eccl.) cantare il responsorio; *to — to music*, essere sensibile alla musica. **-ent** *adj.* che risponde; rispondente; sensibile; che reagisce; *n.* (leg.) convenuto, imputato.

**response** *n.* risposta, replica; *the -s of the oracles*, i responsi degli oracoli; reazione; corrispondenza; (eccl.) responsorio.

**responsib-le** *adj.* responsabile; di, che comporta responsabilità; competente; capace; degno di fiducia. **-ility** *n.* responsibilità; *on one's own -ility*, sotto la propria responsabilità; *to assume -ility for*, assumersi la responsabilità di. **-ly** *adv.* in modo responsabile.

**responsive** *adj.* rispondente; sensibile; impressionabile, facile alle emozioni; *they are — to affection*, sono sensibili all'affetto. **-ly** *adv.* in maniera rispondente; con simpatia. **-ness** *n.* rispondenza; sensibilità; prontezza a simpatizzare.

**rest¹** *n.* riposo; sonno; *to have a —*, riposare, riposarsi; *at —*, in stato di riposo; in pace; *to lay to —*, seppellire; alloggio, ricovero; supporto, appoggio; (mus.) pausa; *intr.* riposare, riposarsi; *let him — in peace*, lasciatelo riposare in pace; *lie down and —*, sdràiati e riposa; *to — on one's laurels*, riposarsi sugli allori; *tr.* appoggiare; posare; basare; *God — his soul*, Dio dia pace alla sua anima; fare riposare.

**rest²** *n.* resto, residuo; *for the —*,

quanto al resto; *pl.* i rimanenti, gli altri; (comm.) saldo, chiusura; *intr.* restare, rimanere; *to — assured,* essere sicuro; *to — with,* toccare a, dipendare da.

**rest**[3] *n.* resta; *lance in —,* lancia in resta.

**restart** *tr.*, *intr.* ricominciare; riprendere; rimettere in moto.

**restate** *tr.* riesporre, enunciare di nuovo; esprimere in altra forma. **-ment** *n.* riaffermazione.

**restaurant** *n.* ristorante; **-car,** vagone *m.* ristorante.

**rest-cure** *n.* cura del riposo. **-day** *n.* giorno di riposo. **-house** *n.* ospizio.

**restful** *adj.* riposante; tranquillo, quieto. **-ly** *adv.* in modo riposante, tranquillamente. **-ness** *n.* riposo, tranquillità, quiete, pace.

**resting** *adj.* in riposo; *n.* riposo. **-place,** luogo di riposo, rifugio.

**restitution** *n.* restituzione; risarcimento; *to make —,* fare ammenda.

**restive** *adj.* restio, ricalcitrante; caparbio, indocile; intrattabile. **-ly** *adv.* in modo restio, caparbiamente; intrattabilmente. **-ness** *n.* caparbietà, ostinazione; irrequietezza; nervosismo.

**restless** *adj.* irrequieto; inquieto, agitato; incessante. **-ly** *adj.* irrequietamente; incessantemente; senza riposo. **-ness** *n.* *n.* irrequietezza, inquietudine; agitazione; nervosismo; insonnia.

**restock** *tr.* rifornire; ripopolare (vivaio, stagno); *intr.* rifornirsi.

**restoration** *n.* restituzione; restauro; ricostruzione; ripristino, reintegrazione; (hist.) restaurazione.

**restorative** *adj.* ristorativo, corroborante; *n.* ricostituente, tonico; cordiale.

**restor-e** *tr.* restituire; rendere; rimettere; restaurare, riparare, ripristinare; ricostruire; reintegrare; ristabilire; restaurare (una dinastia); *to — a king (to the throne),* rimettere un re sul trono; ristorare, rinvigorire. **-er** *n.* restauratore; ripristinatore.

**restrain**[1] *tr.* reprimere, frenare, trattenere; limitare, restringere; confinare, imprigionare; *intr.* trattenersi. **-ed** *adj.* trattenuto; limitato. **-edly** *adv.* con ritegno.

**restrain**[2] *tr.* forzare di nuovo; filtrare di nuovo.

**restraint** *n.* freno; controllo; misura; ritegno; limitazione, restrizione; relegamento; detenzione.

**restrict(ed)** *adj.* ristretto; limitato, *tr.* restringere, limitare. **-ion** *n.* restrizione, limitazione.

**restuff** *tr.* imbottire, rimpinzare di nuovo.

**result** *n.* risultato, esito; conseguenza; *intr.* derivare, risultare; risolversi, concludersi; *it may — in,* potrebbe risolversi in.

**resultant** *adj.*, *n.* risultante.

**resume** *tr.* riprendere, ricuperare; *to — the thread of one's discourse,* riprendere il filo del discorso; ricominciare; riassumere; ricapitolare.

**résumé** *n.* riassunto, sunto, sommario.

**resumption** *n.* ripresa.

**resurg-ence** *n.* risurrezione; rinascita. **-ent** *adj.* risorgente.

**resurrect** *tr.* far risorgere, far rivivere; esumare. **-tion** *n.* risurrezione; (rel.) *the Resurrection,* la Resurrezione; (fig.) rinascita, ripresa.

**resuscitat-e** *tr.* risuscitare. **-ion** *n.* risuscitamento, richiamo in vita. **-or** *n.* risuscitatore.

**re·tail** *n.* vendita al minuto, al dettaglio; *adv. to sell —,* vendere al minuto. **-dealer,** dettagliante. **— price,** prezzo al minuto. **— trade,** commercio al minuto.

**retail** *tr.* vendere al minuto, al dettaglio; raccontare dettagliatamente; *intr.* essere venduto al minuto. **-er** *n.* dettagliante; (colloq.) divulgatore.

**retain** *tr.* ritenere, trattenere, mantenere; conservare, serbare; prendere, fissare; *to — the services of,* assicurarsi i servizi di. **-able** *adj.* che si può ritenere. **-er** *n.* (leg.) diritto di ritenzione; onorario versato ad un avvocato; chi, che conserva, dipendente, seguace di un signore. **-ing** *adj.* che ritiene; *-ing fee,* onorario anticipato ad un avvocato; *-ing wall,* muro di sostegno.

**re·take** *n.* (cinema replica di una ripresa.

**retake** *tr.* riprendere, riconquistare; (cinema) ripetere la ripresa di.

**retaliat-e** *tr.*, *intr.* ricambiare (insulto, offesa); *to — an accusation upon someone,* ritorcere un'accusa su qualcuno; rendere la pariglia; far rappresaglie; (econ.; pol.) imporre dazi di rappresaglia su merci importate. **-ion** *n.* pariglia; rappresaglia; (leg.) ritorsione; *law of -ion,* legge del taglione. **-ive, -ory** *adj.* di rappresaglia; vendicativo.

**retard** *tr.* ritardare; rallentare; *intr.* tardare; indugiare. **-ation** *n.* ritardo; rallentamento; indugio.

**retch** *intr.* avere conati di vomito, recere.

**retell** *tr.* ripetere; raccontare di nuovo.

**retent-ion** *n.* conservazione; facoltà di ritenere; memoria; (med.) ritenzione, tenace. **-ive** *adj.* ritentivo, che trattiene, che conserva. **-iveness** *n.* capacità di ritenere; tenacità di memoria.

**retic-ence, -ency** *n.* reticenza; riservatezza; taciturnità. **-ent** *adj.* reticente; riservato; taciturno. **-ently** *adv.* con reticenza; con riservatezza.

**reticul-ar** *adj.* reticolare. **-ate** *adj.* reticolato; retiforme.

**reticule** *n.* borsetta a rete. (opt.) reticolo.

**retina** *n.* (anat.) retina.

**retinue** *n.* seguito; corteo; scorta.

**retire** *intr.* ritirarsi; *to — into oneself,* rinchiudersi in se stesso; dare le dimissioni, andare in pensione; (mil.) battere in ritirata; *tr.* far ritirare; (comm.) togliere dalla circolazione.

**retired** *adj.* ritirato; appartato, solitario; nascosto; a riposo, in pensione; *— list,* lista degli ufficiali in pensione; *— pay,* pensione; *— pension,* pensionato.

**retirement** *n.* ritiro; collocamento a riposo; (mil.) ritirata; (comm.) ritiro dalla circolazione; isolamento; solitudine; luogo appartato; dimora solitaria.

**retiring** *adj.* riservato; discreto; schivo; timido; (mil.) che batte in ritirata.

**retort**[1] *n.* ritorsione; risposta; *intr.* ritorcere; ribattere; ricambiare; replicare; rispondere.

**retort**[2] *n.* (chem.) storta.

**retouch** *n.* ritocco; *tr.* ritoccare.

**retrace** *tr.* rintracciare; analizzare minuziosamente; ripercorrere, rifare il cammino di; *to — one's steps,* ritornare sui propri passi; rievocare, risalire alle origini di; tracciare di nuovo. **-able** *adj.* rintracciabile.

**retract** *tr.* ritrarre, tirare indietro, far rientrare; riconoscere l'errore, la falsità di; *intr.* disdirsi; ritirarsi. **-ion** *n.* ritiro, azione del ritrarre; ritrazione, contrazione; revoca.

**retread** *tr.* ripercorrere, calpestare di nuovo; (motor.) ricostruire (un copertone).

**retreat** *n.* (mil.) ritirata; *to be in full —,* essere in rotta; *to beat a —,* battere in ritirata; ritiro; nascondiglio; asilo; *intr.* ritirarsi, indietreggiare; battere in ritirata. **-ing** *adj.* che si ritira; in ritirata; sfuggente, rientrante.

**retrench** *tr.* togliere; tagliar via; diminuire. **-ment** *n.* soppressione; restrizione; riduzione di spese.

**retrial** *n.* (leg.) giudizio di seconda istanza.

**retribu-tion** *n.* castigo, punizione; (rel.) *the Day of Retribution,* il Giorno del Giudizio; ricompensa. **-tive** *adj.* punitivo; retributivo.

**retriev-e** *n.* ricupero, riparazione; *beyond —,* irricuperabile, irreparabile; *tr.* rintracciare e riportare; ricuperare; ripristinare; riparare; rimediare a; salvare. **-able** *adj.* ricuperabile; riparabile,

rimediabile. **-al** *n.* ricupero; riparazione, rimedio; *information -al*, informazione di ritorno. **-er** *n.* cane da presa.
**retroactive** *adj.* (leg.) retroattivo.
**retrograde** *adj.* retrogrado; inverso; contrario.
**retrogress** *intr.* regredire; retrocedere; deteriorarsi. **-ive** *adj.* regressivo; retrogrado.
**retrospect** *n.* sguardo retrospettivo; visione retrospettiva. **-ion** *n.* retrospezione; sguardo retrospettivo. **-ive** *adj.* retrospettivo; (leg.) retroattivo.
**return** *n.* ritorno; *on my —*, al mio ritorno; *by — of post*, a giro di posta; restituzione, rinvio; ricompensa; *in — for*, in cambio di; *pl.* provento, profitto, guadagno; relazione, rapporto; — *(ticket)*, biglietto di andata e ritorno; — *journey*, viaggio di ritorno; (sport) — *match*, rivincita; *election -s*, risultati elettorali.
**return** *intr.* tornare; rispondere; restituire, rendere, rimettere, rimandare; *to — a compliment*, ricambiare un complimento; *to — someone's love*, contraccambiare l'amore di qualcuno; *to — like for like*, rendere pan per focaccia; produrre, rendere, dare; (pol.) eleggere; *-ed soldier*, reduce *m.*; *-ing officer*, membro di seggio elettorale. **-able** *adj.* restituibile; da restituirsi.
**reunion** *n.* riunione.
**reunite** *tr.* riunire; riconciliare.
**revalu-e** *tr.* rivalutare. **-ation** *n.* rivalutazione.
**reveal** *tr.* rivelare; scoprire.
**reveille** *n.* (mil.) sveglia, diana.
**revel** *n.* festa; baldoria, orgia, gozzoviglia; *usu. pl.* festeggiamenti; *intr.* divertirsi; far baldoria, fare delle orge; gozzovigliare; festeggiare; banchettare; trovare diletto.
**revelation** *n.* rivelazione; *the Revelation*, l'Apocalisse.
**revell-ed** *p.def.*, *part.* of **revel**, *q.v.* **-er** *n.* chi si dà a piaceri. **-ing, revelry** *n.* baldoria, orgia, gozzoviglia.
**revenant** *n.* spettro, fantasma *m.*, ombra.
**revendication** *n.* rivendicazione.
**revenge** *n.* vendetta; spirito di vendetta; *to take — for*, vendicarsi di; (sport) rivincita; *intr.* vendicare; *to — oneself upon someone*, vendicarsi su qualcuno; trarre vendetta. **-ful** *adj.* vendicativo; vendicatore. **-fully** *adv.* vendicativamente; per vendetta. **-fulness** *n.* animo vendicativo; spirito di vendetta.
**revenger** *n.* vendicatore.
**revenue** *n.* entrata, entrate; reddito; — *and expenditure*, entrate e spese in bilancio; entrate dello Stato; fisco; erario.
**reverberat-e** *intr.* riverberare; risuonare; riecheggiare. **-ion** *n.* riverbero; riverberazione; coda sonora. **-or** *n.* riflettore.
**revere** *tr.* riverire; venerare.
**rever-ence** *n.* riverenza; venerazione; rispetto; *to pay — to*, rendere onore a; *tr.* riverire, considerare con riverenza. **-end** *adj.* venerando; (eccl.) reverendo; *n.* ecclesiastico, prete. **-ent** *adj.* riverente; pieno di venerazione; rispettoso. **-ential** *adj.* riverente; reverenziale. **-ently** *adv.* con riverenza; con venerazione; con rispetto.
**reverer** *n.* veneratore.
**reverie** *n.* sogno a occhi aperti; fantasticheria.
**revers** *n.pl.* risvolto (di abito).
**reversal** *n.* rovesciamento; inversione; (leg.) annullamento, revoca.
**reverse** *adj.* rovescio, inverso; opposto, contrario; *n.* il rovescio, l'inverso; l'opposto, il contrario; disgrazia; rovescio finanziario; disfatta militare; (motor.) retromarcia; *tr.* rovesciare, ribaltare, capovolgere; *intr.* (motor.) innestare la retromarcia.
**reversible** *adj.* reversibile; rovesciabile; ribaltabile; (leg.) revocabile; a due diritti (di stoffa).
**reversion** *n.* reversione, ritorno a stato precedente; riversione; (biol.) regressione.
**revert** *intr.* ritornare; *to — to a topic*, ritornare su un argomento; *tr.* volgere indietro.
**review** *n.* esame *m.*, analisi *f.*; revisione; sguardo retrospettivo; ripasso; recensione, critica, rassegna; rivista, periodico; (mil.) rivista; (theatr.) rivista; *tr.* rivedere; riesaminare; dare une sguardo retrospettivo a; recensire, fare la rassegna di; fare recensioni; *to — a novel*, recensire un romanzo; (mil.) passare in rivista; (leg.) sottoporre a revisione. **-er** *n.* recensore; critico.
**revil-e** *tr.*, *intr.* ingiuriare, insultare; servirsi di linguaggio oltraggioso. **-er** *n.* oltraggiatore, offensore. **-ing** *n.* ingiuria.
**revise** *tr.* rivedere; riesaminare; correggere; *n.* seconda bozza.
**revision** *n.* revisione; correzione; **-al** *adj.* di revisione. **-ist** *n.* (pol.) revisionista *m.*
**revitalize** *tr.* dare nuova vita a.
**revival** *n.* ripristino; riesumazione; (theatr.) ripresa; risveglio; rifiorimento; rinascita, rinascimento; ritorno alla vita; ripresa dei sensi. **-ism** *n.* revivalismo, movimento promotore di un risveglio religioso.
**revive** *tr.* resuscitare, far rinascere; ritornare in vita; ravvivare; rimettere in uso; *intr.* rivivere; ritornare in vita; rianimarsi; rinvigorirsi.
**revivify** *tr.* ravvivare; rianimare; rinvigorire.
**revocation** *n.* revoca, abrogazione; annullamento; ritiro.
**revoke** *tr.* revocare; abrogare; annullare; ritirare; (carte) rifiutare.
**revolt** *n.* rivolta; ribellione; *in —*, in rivolta; disgusto; ripugnanza; *intr.* rivoltarsi, ribellarsi; provare orrore; rifuggire; *tr.* rivoltare, disgustare. **-ing** *adj.* rivoltante; disgustoso, ributtante; in rivolta.
**revolution** *n.* rivoluzione; ribellione; trasformazione; rivolgimento; giro, rotazione. **-ary** *adj.* rivoluzionario; (mech.) rotatorio; *n.* rivoluzionario. **-ize** *tr.* rivoluzionare; mutare radicalmente.
**revolve** *intr.* rivolgere; ponderare; *to — a problem*, esaminare un problema; rotare, girare, muoversi in giro; ricorrere, ritornare; avvicendarsi.
**revolver** *n.* rivoltella.
**revolving** *adj.* rotante; che gira intorno; ricorrente; (mech.) girevole; (comm.) rotativo; — *door*, porta girevole.
**revue** *n.* (theatr.) rivista.
**revulsion** *n.* mutamento improvviso; reazione; (med.) revulsione.
**reward** *n.* ricompensa; rimunerazione; compenso; *tr.* ricompensare, rimunerare; compensare. **-ing** *adj.* rimunerativo; rimunerazione.
**reword** *tr.* formulare con nuove parole.
**rewrite** *tr.* riscrivere; rimaneggiare.
**rhapsod-y** *n.* rapsodia; (colloq.) entusiasmo. **-ist** *n.* rapsodo. **-ize** *intr.* recitare come un rapsodo; *to -ize about*, andare in estasi per.
**rhetoric** *n.* retorica; enfasi. **-al** *adj.* retorico. **-ian** *n.* retore.
**rheumat-ic** *adj.* reumatico; *n.* reumatico; *pl.* reumatismi. **-ism** *n.* reumatismo.
**Rhine** *pr.n.* (geog.) Reno; *attrib.* — *wine*, vino del Reno; *the -land*, la Renania.
**rhino, rhinoceros** *n.* rinoceronte *m.*
**rhizome** *n.* (bot.) rizoma.
**rhododendron** *n.* (bot.) rododendro.
**rhomboid** *adj.*, *n.* (geom.) romboide *m.*
**rhubarb** *n.* rabarbaro; (theatr., joc.) — —, le chiacchiere di attori quando fanno finta di parlare insieme.
**rhyme** *n.* rima; *without — or reason*, senza senso, assurdo; versi; poesia; *nursery —*, poesia per bambini; *tr.* metter in rima; far rimare; *intr.* rimare, far rima. **-ster** *n.* poetastro.
**rhythm** *n.* ritmo. **-ic(al)** *adj.* ritmico.

**rib** *n.* (anat.) costola; *to poke in the ~s,* dar di gomito a; costa (di tessuto); costola, dorso (di libro); stecca (di ombrello, di violino); (archit.) costolone, nervatura; (naut.) costa, corba.

**ribald** *adj.* osceno, licenzioso. **~ry** *n.* oscenità; linguaggio sboccato; scherzo volgare.

**ribb~ed** *adj.* munito di coste; scanalato; — *fabric,* tessuto a coste; (archit.) a nervature. **~ing** *n.* armatura (di volta); nervature, coste, rigature.

**ribbon** *n.* nastro; fettuccia; cordone di decorazione; *to tear to ~s,* ridurre a brandelli; *typewriter —,* nastro per macchina da scrivere.

**ribwork** *n.* struttura nervata.

**rice** *n.* (bot.) riso; *husked —,* riso brillato. **-field** *n.,* **-paddy** *n.* risaia.

**rich** *adj.* ricco; — *in,* ricco di; *to make —,* arricchire; costoso; sontuoso; abbondante; fertile; — *soil,* terreno fertile; nutriente, sostanzioso; — *cream,* crema grassa; vivido, smagliante, intenso (di colore); pieno (di voce); (slang) divertente, comico. **~es** *n.pl.* ricchezza, ricchezze. **~ly** *adv.* riccamente, sontuosamente; abbondantemente; ampiamente; *he ~ly deserves punishment,* merita bene una punizione. **~ness** *n.* ricchezza; sontuosità, magnificenza; lusso; abbondanza.

**rick**[1] *n.* mucchio di fieno; bica; *tr.* formare mucchi di fieno; accatastare.

**rick**[2] *n.* storta, distorsione; *to have a — in the neck,* avere il torcicollo; *tr.* storcere; stortare; lussare.

**rickety** *adj.* (med.) rachitico; fragile, traballante; malsicuro.

**ricochet** *n.* rimbalzo (di proiettile); *intr.* rimbalzare.

**rid** *tr.* liberare, sbarazzare; *to get — of,* liberarsi da, sbarazzarsi di.

**rideable** *adj.* cavalcabile.

**riddance** *n.* liberazione; *good —!,* che liberazione!

**riddle**[1] *n.* indovinello; enigma *m.*; persona, cosa, fatto enigmatico; *intr.* proporre indovinelli; *tr. to — out,* risolvere, spiegare.

**riddle**[2] *n.* vaglio; crivello; *tr.* vagliare, setacciare; crivellare, perforare (con pallottole).

**ride** *n.* cavalcata, passeggiata a cavallo; scarrozzata, corsa su un veicolo; un giro con l'automobile; *to go for a —,* fare una passeggiata a cavallo; (slang) *to take someone for a —,* prendere in giro; tragitto, percorso; pista, sentiero per cavalcare.

**ride** *tr.* cavalcare; montare; *intr.* andare a cavallo; *to — astride,* montare a cavalcioni; *to — side-saddle,* montare all'amazzone; percorrere; *the moon is riding high,* la luna è alta nel cielo; *to — the high horse,* darsi delle arie; andare, correre (su veicoli); *the ship ~s at anchor,* la nave è ancorata; *to — out the storm,* uscire illesi da una burrasca; accavallarsi, sovrapporsi (di ossa, funi); (fig.) opprimere, dominare; *to be ridden by fear,* essere oppresso, dominato dalla paura; *to — down,* travolgere; calpestare; caricare; *to — over,* compiere un tragitto (a cavallo); *to — over to,* andare a cavallo a, verso.

**rider** *n.* cavallerizzo; viaggiatore (in veicolo); ciclista; motociclista; cavaliere; fantino; (leg.) codicillo; correttivo di una formola. **~less** *adj.* senza cavaliere.

**ridge** *n.* spigolo; colmo (del tetto); cresta (di monti), vetta; crinale, spartiacque; giogaia; linea di scogli affioranti; *tr.* corrugare; *intr.* corrugarsi; incresparsi.

**ridicule** *tr.* mettere in ridicolo; beffare, canzonare, schernire.

**ridiculous** *adj.* ridicolo; assurdo; irrisorio. **~ness** *n.* ridicolaggine *f.*; assurdità.

**riding** *n.* cavalcata; maneggio; equitazione; *to go in for —,* montare a cavallo; rada, ancoraggio. **-habit** *n.* abito da amazzone; — *light,* lanterna di naviglio all'ancora; — *school,* scuola d'equitazione; — *whip,* frustino.

**rife** *adj.* comune; diffuso.

**riff-raff** *n.* canaglia; plebaglia.

**riffle** *tr.* sfogliare.

**rifle**[1] *n.* fucile a palla, carabina; *pl.* fucilieri; *rifle-corps,* corpo di fucilieri volontari; *rifle-pit,* trincea per fucilieri; *rifle-range,* portata di un fucile; campo di tiro a segno, poligono; *rifle-shot,* portata, colpo di fucile; tiratore (di fucile). **~man** *n.* fuciliere.

**rifl~e**[2] *tr.* svaligiare; saccheggiare; rapinare; *intr.* commettere rapine. **~er** *n.* predone, ladrone; saccheggiatore.

**rifling**[1] *n.* rigatura (di fucile).

**rifling**[2] *n.* saccheggio.

**rift** *n.* crepa; crepaccio; spaccatura; fessura; fenditura; incrinatura; *a — in the fog,* una schiarita nella nebbia; *tr.* spaccare, fendere.

**rig** *n.* (naut.) attrezzatura; (industr.) impianto; *oil —,* impianto petrolifero; modo di vestire, tenuta, abbigliamento; *to be in full —,* essere in gran tenuta, essere in ghingheri; *tr.* (naut.) attrezzare; (fam.) vestire; *to — oneself out,* abbigliarsi in modo inconsueto; (fam.) arrangiare, sistemare; *to — an election,* commettere un broglio elettorale; *to — the markets,* provocare dei rialzi o dei ribassi artificiosi sul mercato. **~ged** *part. adj.* (naut.) attrezzato, con velatura; (fam.) arrangiato, sistemato. **~ging** *n.* (naut.) attrezzatura, attrezzi *m.pl.*, sartiame *m.*, incappellaggio; tenuta, abbigliamento, (fam.) manovre *f.pl.*

**right** *adj.* retto; giusto; onesto; corretto, esatto; *to put —,* mettere a posto, sistemare; *all —!,* benissimo!; *quite —!,* perfettamente!; *that's —,* va bene, d'accordo; *to be —,* avere ragione; adatto, appropriato, conveniente; *he is the — man in the — place,* è proprio l'uomo che ci vuole; *this is the — moment,* questo è il momento adatto; *the — side of a fabric,* il diritto di un tessuto; *to be on the — side of forty,* essere al di sotto della quarantina; *to get on the — side of,* insinuarsi nelle buone grazie di; (geom.) retto; rettangolo; destro; sano, in buone condizioni (fisiche, mentali); *he is not — in his head,* non ha la testa a posto; *she is not in her — mind,* non è in possesso delle sue facoltà mentali; *this medicine will put you — again,* questa medicina vi rimetterà in forze; (pol.) conservatore.

**right** *n.* il giusto, il bene; — *and wrong,* il giusto e l'ingiusto, il bene e il male; *to be in the —,* essere dalla parte della ragione; *to do —,* fare il bene; diritto; *~s and duties,* i diritti e i doveri; — *of way,* servitù di passaggio; *by —,* di, per diritto; destra, mano destra; lato destro; *from left to —,* da sinistra a destra; dritto (di tessuto); (pol.) la destra; i conservatori.

**right** *tr.* drizzare; raddrizzare; *intr.* raddrizzarsi, ricuperare l'equilibrio; rendere giustizia; riparare; vendicare; correggere; mettere in ordine.

**right** *adv.* rettamente, giustamente, bene; correttamente, esattamente; *—!, — ho!, — oh!,* bene!, va bene!, capito!; *it serves him —!,* gli sta bene!, se lo merita!; appropriatamente, convenientemente; come si deve; in linea retta; direttamente; *he was — behind us,* era proprio alle nostre spalle; — *in the middle,* proprio nel mezzo; — *round,* tutt'intorno a; *turn —,* voltate a destra; — *away,* immediatamente.

**right** (in compounds) (mil.) *right-about,* dietro front!; *right-and-left,* bilaterale; (geom.) *right-angled,* che ha un angolo retto; *right-hand,* situato a destra; *his right-hand man,* il suo uomo di fiducia, il suo braccio destro; *right-handed,* che usa di preferenza la destra; di destra; *right-thinking,* benpensante, saggio, giudizioso; *right-wing,* di ala destra, (pol.) di estrema destra.

**righteous** *adj.* retto; virtuoso; giusto; giustificato. **~ness** *n.*

rettitudine *f.*; giustizia; integrità; virtù *f.*; meriti *m.pl.*; legittimità.

**rightful** *adj.* legittimo; vero, giusto; retto, equo, virtuoso. **-ness** *n.* legittimità; giustizia; equità.

**right-ly** *adv.* rettamente, giustamente; correttamente; *I don't — know,* non so esattamente. **-ness** *n.* dirittura, rettitudine; correttezza, esattezza; giustezza.

**rigid** *adj.* rigido; severo; inflessibile, intransigente; rigoroso. **-ity** *n.* rigidità; inflessibilità; severità, intransigenza; rigore.

**rigmarole** *n.* lungagnata, tiritera.

**rigor** *n.* (med.) brivido; rigidità; *— mortis,* irrigidimento cadaverico. **-ist** *n.* rigorista; persona austera. **-ous** *adj.* rigoroso; rigido; severo; preciso, esatto; scrupoloso; inclemente.

**rigour** *n.* rigore; severità; austerità; rigorismo; esattezza, precisione; carestia; rigore, inclemenza (di tempo).

**rile** *intr.* annoiare; irritare.

**rill** *n.* rigagnolo, ruscello.

**rim** *n.* bordo, orlo, margine *m.*; cerchio; cerchione. **-less** *adj.* senza bordo; senza montatura (di occhiali); *tr.* bordare, orlare; cerchiare. **-med** *part. adj.* bordato, orlato, cerchiato; *gold-rimmed spectacles,* occhiali montati in oro.

**rime** *n.* (poet.) brina.

**rind** *n.* corteccia; scorza; buccia; *cheese —,* crosta di formaggio.

**ring**[1] *n.* anello; cerchio, bordo; circolo; movimento circolare; (comm.) sindacato; (sport) pista; recinto degli allibratori; *— master,* direttore di circo equestre; *boxing-ring,* quadrato; *engagement-ring,* anello di fidanzamento; *wedding-ring,* anello nuziale; *key-ring,* portachiavi *m.*

**ring**[1] *tr.* accerchiare, circondare; ornare di anello; mettere un anello a. **-ed** *adj.* inanellato (di dita); cerchiato (di occhi); dal collare (di uccello): ad anelli; circondato da anello; a forma di anello.

**ring**[2] *n.* scampanìo; scampanellata; squillo; timbro (di voce); (fig.) accento; tintinnìo; (colloq.) telefonata; squillo del telefono; *give me a —,* dammi un colpo di telefono; *intr.* suonare, squillare; *tr. to — the bell,* suonare il campanello; *to — the changes,* cantarla su tutti i toni; tintinnare; risuonare; riecheggiare; vibrare; *to — false, true,* risuonare falsa, vera; *to — down,* (theatr.) far calare (il sipario); *to — in,* celebrare al suono di campane l'entrata di; *to — off,* togliere la comunicazione teelfonica; *to — out,* celebrare al suono di campane l'uscita di; *to — up,* (theatr.) far alzare il sipario, (colloq.) dare un colpo di telefono a. **-er** *n.* chi suona; campanaro; (mech.) suoneria. **-ing** *adj.* risonante; sonoro; *n.* suono, tintinnìo; scampanìo.

**ringleader** *n.* capo di rivoltosi; capobanda.

**ringless** *adj.* senza anello.

**ringlet** *n.* anellino; cerchietto; ricciolo. **-ed** *adj.* ricciuto, inanellato.

**ringworm** *n.* (med.) tricofizia.

**rink** *n.* pista per pattinaggio sul ghiaccio; pista di schettinaggio; campo di ghiaccio.

**rins-e** *n.* risciacquata; (hairdr.) cachet *m. indecl.*; *tr.* risciacquare, sciacquare; *to — away,* pulire risciacquando. **-ing** *n.* risciacquamento.

**riot** *n.* rivolta, sommossa; disordine; tumulto; licenza, sregolatezza; *to run —,* abbandonarsi ad eccessi; abbondanza; *the fields were a — of colour,* i campi erano una profusione di colori; *— squad,* (polizia) volante; *to 'read the — act',* cantare la solfa; *intr.* fare chiasso; tumultuare; gozzovigliare; darsi ai piaceri. **-er** *n.* rivoltoso; chi si dà a orge e piaceri. **-ous** *adj.* tumultuante, sedizioso; sregolato, intemperante, dissoluto, licenzioso, sfrenato. **-ousness** *n.* sregolatezza, intemperanza, dissolutezza. **-ry** *n.* disordine, tumulto.

**rip**[2] *n.* lacerazione; strappo; scucitura; *tr.* strappare; lacerare; scucire; squarciare; *to — open,* aprire lacerandolo; *let her —!,* lasciate che vada a tutta velocità!; *to — off,* strappar via.

**rip**[2] *n.* vecchio ronzino; libertino.

**riparian** *adj.* rivierasco.

**rip-e** *adj.* maturo; stagionato; (fig.) pronto. **-en** *intr.* maturare; *tr.* far maturare; far stagionare. **-ening** *n.* maturazione. **-eness** *n.* maturità; (fig.) perfezione.

**ripost(e)** *n.* (sport.) replica; (fig.) risposta incisiva; replica; *intr.* (sport) rispondere, eseguire una risposta; (fig.) dare una risposta incisiva; fare una ritorsione.

**ripple** *n.* increspamento, increspatura; ondulazione; gorgoglio, mormorìo; *intr.* increspare; ondulare; incresparsi; gorgogliare, mormorare.

**rise** *n.* levata, alzata; *the — of day,* alba; *to get a — out of,* canzonare; salita; rampa; altura; ascesa; progresso; promozione, avanzamento; aumento di paga; rialzo, rincaro; crescita, innalzamento di livello; *the — of the tide,* il flusso della marea; *a sudden — of temperature,* un improvviso aumento di temperatura; sorgente; origine, principio; *to give — to,* dare origine a.

**rise** *intr.* sorgere, levarsi, alzarsi; (fig.) risorgere; *Christ is risen,* Cristo è risorto; *the sun -s,* sorge il sole; *the wind rose,* si levò il vento; *to — from table,* alzarsi da tavola; *to — to one's feet,* alzarsi in piedi; salire; crescere; aumentare; (of a river) crescere; elevarsi; erigersi; *to — above mediocrity,* essere al disopra della mediocrità; *to — in the world,* farsi strada nel mondo; *to — to greatness,* assurgere a grandezza; *to — to the occasion,* mostrarsi all'altezza della situazione; gonfiarsi, lievitare; sollevarsi, insorgere; *to — in arms,* sollevarsi in armi; *my gorge -s,* mi si rivolta lo stomaco; aver origine, nascere, provenire.

**riser** *n.* chi si alza (da letto); *I'm an early —,* sono mattiniero; alzata (di gradino).

**risible** *adj.* risibile, ridicolo.

**rising** *adj.* sorgente, nascente; *the — generation,* la nuova generazione; ascendente; in salita; crescente, in aumento; che avanza, che progredisce; che migliora; *— twenty,* vicino ai vent'anni; *n.* il sorgere; il levarsi; l'alzarsi; *he doesn't like early —,* non gli piace alzarsi presto; salita; ascesa; crescita; aumento; miglioramento; elevazione; innalzamento di livello; sollevamento, insurrezione, rivolta; sommossa popolare.

**risk** *n.* rischio, pericolo imprevisto; *at the — of,* a rischio di; *at customer's own —,* a rischio e pericolo del cliente; *to run the — of,* correre il rischio di; *to take -s,* correre dei rischi; *tr.* rischiare; arrischiare; mettere a repentaglio; *let's — it!,* tentiamo!; *to — one's reputation,* porre a repentaglio la propria reputazione. **-ily** *adv.* arrischiatamente; *adj.* rischioso, arrischiato.

**risqué** *adj.* azzardato, audace, ardito.

**rissole** *n.* (cul.) polpetta, crocchetta.

**rite** *n.* rito; cerimonia.

**ritual** *adj.*, rituale; *n.* rituale *m.*; riti *m.pl.*, cerimonie *f.pl.* **-ism** *n.* ritualismo. **-ist** *n.* ritualista *m.* **-istic** *adj.* relativo, conforme al rituale.

**rival** *adj.* rivale; che compete; *n.* rivale; competitore; *without a —,* senza pari; *intr.* rivaleggiare (con), gareggiare (con); emulare. **-ry** *n.* rivalità; concorrenza; emulazione.

**rive** *tr.* spaccare; lacerare; (fig.) spezzare.

**river** *n.* fiume *m.*; *down —,* a valle; *up —,* a monte. **-bank** riva, sponda di fiume. **-bed** alveo di fiume. **-god** divinità fluviale. **-head** sorgente *f.* di fiume. **-side**

*adj.* lungo il fiume, rivierasco; *n.* lungofiume *m.*; sponda, riva.

**rivet** *n.* chiodo, rivetto, ribattino; bullone; *tr.* inchiodare, ribadire; fissare, concentrare. **-(t)ing** *n.* chiodatura; ribaditura; *adj.* (colloq.) affascinante.

**rivulet** *n.* fiumicello, ruscelletto.

**road** *n.* strada; via; *across the —*, dall'altra parte della strada; *on the —*, per strada; cammino, percorso; strada, via; *to be on the right —*, essere sulla buona strada *the — to success*, la via del successo; (naut.) rada; *in the -s*, nella rada; *— sign*, cartello stradale; *country —*, strada di campagna; *main —*, strada principale. **-house** *n.* locanda, trattoria. **-side** *adj.* sul bordo della strada; *n.* bordo della strada. **-stead** *n.* (naut.) rada. **-way** *n.* carreggiata, piano stradale.

**roam** *n.* vagabondaggio; passeggiatina; *intr.* percorrere; errare, vagabondare, vagare per; *to — the seas*, solcare i mari. **-er** *n.* vagabondo, nomade *m.*

**roar** *n.* ruggito; muggito; urlo; scoppio; scroscio; rombo, rimbombo, boato; frastuono; strepito; il mugghiare (del vento, del mare).

**roar** *intr.* ruggire, muggire; urlare, gridare a squarciagola; vociare; strepitare; *to — oneself hoarse*, diventare rauco a furia di urlare; *to — with laughter* scoppiare delle risa; tuonare; rumoreggiare, mugghiare. **-er** *n.* sbraitone. **-ing** *adj.* rugghiante; mugghiante; urlante; rumoroso, fragoroso; scrosciante; tumultuoso; *a -ing fire*, un fuoco crepitante; (colloq.) prospero; *we did -ing business*, abbiamo fatto affari d'oro; *to be in -ing health*, scoppiare di salute.

**roast** *adj.* arrosto, arrostito; *n.* arrosto; arrostitura; arrostimento (di metalli); tostatura (di caffè); *tr.* arrostire; *to — on a spit*, arrostire allo spiedo; cuocere; tostare (caffè); *intr.* arrostirsi. **-er** *n.* rosticciere; girarrosto; tostino, macchina per tostare il caffè. **-ing** *adj.* rovente, cocente; torrido; *a -ing fowl*, un pollo da arrostire; *n.* arrostimento; arrostitura; torrefazione; (slang) beffa, canzonatura; lavata di capo, ramanzina.

**rob** *intr.* derubare; *to — Peter to pay Paul*, fare un buco per tapparne un altro; saccheggiare; *to — a bank*, svaligiare una banca; spogliare; rubare, commettere furti, rapine.

**robber** *n.* ladro; rapinatore; ladrone, predone, brigante. **-y** furto; rapina; estorsione; *armed -y*, rapina a mano armata; *highway -y*, brigantaggio.

**robe** *n.* abito lungo e sciolto; toga; abito; *tr.* vestire; rivestire; *intr.* vestirsi.

**robot** *n.* robot *m.*, automa *m.*; dispositivo automatico; *— pilot*, pilota automatico.

**robust** *adj.* robusto; sano; gagliardo; vigoroso. **-ness** *n.* robustezza.

**rock**[1] *n.* roccia; rupe *f.*, scoglio; *to run upon the -s*, naufragare; *on the -s*, al verde; rocca; *the Rock (of Gibraltar)*, (la Rocca di) Gibilterra; macigno, masso. **-bottom** *n.* minimo (di prezzo); *adj.* bassissimo. **-crystal** cristallo di rocca. **-fish** pesce di scoglio. **-salt** *n.* salgemma.

**rock**[2] *n.* dondollo; oscillazione; *tr.* dondolare; cullare; far vibrare; scuotere; *intr.* dondolarsi, oscillare; tremare. **-er** *n.* chi dondola, culla; dondolo (di sedia, cavallo); (slang) *to be off one's -er*, essere un po' tocco.

**rockery** *n.* giardino roccioso.

**rocket**[1] *n.* (bot.) ruca, ruchetta.

**rocket**[2] *n.* razzo; missile; *— propulsion*, propulsione a razzo; (fam.) lavata di testa, cicchetto; *intr.* dare un balzo in aria; elevarsi come un razzo; salire vertiginosamente.

**rocking** *adj.* a dondolo; vacillante, barcollane; traballante. oscillazione; scosse *f.pl.* **-chair** *n.* sedia a dondolo. **-horse** *n.* cavallo a dondolo.

**rocky**[1] *adj.* roccioso.

**rocky**[2] *adj.* malfermo, traballante.

**rococo** *adj.* (art) rococò.

**rod** *n.* bastone *m.*; mazza; verga, bacchetta; punizione, castigo; *to make a — for one's own back*, scavarsi la fossa sotto i piedi; *fishing —*, canna da pesca; pertica; *piston —*, biella.

**rodent** *adj.*, *n.* (zool.) roditore.

**roe**[1] *n.* capriolo. **-buck** *n.* capriolo maschio.

**roe**[2] *n.* uova dei pesci; *soft —*, sperma di pesce.

**rogue** *n.* mariuolo, briccone, furfante; (joc.) bricconcello, birbante *m.*; elefante, solitario. **-ry** *n.* bricconeria, furfanteria; birbonata, bricconata; birichinata, marachella.

**roguish** *adj.* bricconesco, furfantesco; (joc.) furbo, smaliziato; *— eyes*, occhi furbi. **-ness** *n.* bricconeria, furfanteria; malizia, furberia.

**roister** *intr.* fare il diavolo a quattro; far baldoria. **-er** *n.* chiassone, buontempone. **-ing** *adj.* chiassoso, rumoroso; chiasso; baldoria.

**role** *n.* (theatr.) ruolo; funzione, ufficio.

**roll**[1] *n.* rotolo; *a — of bread*, un panino; *a — of butter*, un rotolino di burro; ruolo, registro, lista, elenco; rullo; cilindro. **-call** *n.* appello.

**roll**[2] *n.* rotolamento; rollio; ondeggiamento; rullo di tamburo; rombo; ondulazione; *intr.* rotolare; correre; *tr.* arrotolare; avvolgere; appallottolare; *to — wool into a ball*, fare un gomitolo di lana; roteare, ruotare; (naut.) rollare; dondolare; rullare, spianare; *to — out*, stendere; *o — a road*, cilindrare una strada; *to — one's r's*, arrotare la erre; ondulare; *to be -ing in money*, guazzare nell'oro; *to — by*, passare; scorrere; *to — down*, ruzzolare; *the tears -ed down her face*, le lacrime le rigavano il volto; *to — over*, rivoltare; rovesciare, rotolare.

**roller** *n.* (naut.) rullo; cilindro, rotella; maroso, cavallone *m.* **-skates** *n.pl.* pattini a rotelle. **-towel** *n.* bandinella.

**rollick** *intr.* essere gioviale, oltre misura; far baldoria. **-ing** *adj.* gioviale, allegro oltre misura; *n.* allegria.

**rolling** *adj.* rotolante; *a — stone*, un sasso che rotola; ondulato; oscillante, barcollante; ruotante, roteante; ricorrente; *n.* rotolamento, arrotolamento. **-pin** *n.* matterello. **-stock** *n.* (rlwy.) materiale *m.* rotabile.

**roly-poly** *adj.* grassoccio, pienotto; sfoglia arrotolata con marmellata.

**Roman** *adj.* romano; *— Catholic*, cattolico romano; *— Catholic Church*, Chiesa Cattolica Apostolica Romana; *the Holy — Empire*, il Sacro Romano Impero; *— nose*, naso aquilino; *— numerals*, numeri romani; *n.* romano.

**Romance**[1] *adj.* romanzo, neolatino; *— languages*, lingue romanze; *n.* romanzo, lingua romanza.

**romance**[2] *n.* romanzo cavalleresco; racconto, sentimentale; avventura romanzesca, episodio romanzesco; *our meeting was quite a —*, il nostro incontro fu romanzesco; idillio; esagerazione fantasiosa; poesia; (mus.) romanza; *intr.* romanzare, esagerare, alterare la verità.

**Romanesque** *adj.* (archit.) romanico.

**Romansch** *adj.*, *n.* (ling.) romanico, retico romano.

**romantic** *adj.* romantico; sentimentale; romanzesco; fantastico; irreale; (art, etc.) romantico; *n.* persona romantica. **-ism** *n.* romanticismo. **-ize** *intr.* romanzare; assumere atteggiamenti romantici.

**Rome** *pr.n.* (geog.) Roma; *all roads lead to —*, tutte le strade conducono a Roma; (provb.) *when in —, do as the Romans do*, paese che vai usanze che trovi.

**romp** *n.* giuoco violento rumoroso; andatura veloce; *to win in a —*, vincere con facilità; *intr.*

giocare in modo rumoroso; correre velocemente; *to — home*, vincere facilmente; *to — through an examination*, passare un esame con il minimo sforzo.

**rood** *n.* croce *f.*; crocifisso. **-screen** *n.* (archit.) parete divisoria tra la navata e il coro.

**roof**[1] *n.* tetto, volta; *— of heaven*, volta celeste; *— of the mouth*, palato duro; (fig.) *to lift the —*, applaudire fragorosamente; *tr.* ricoprire con tetto. **-ing** *adj.* da tetto; *n.* costruzione di tetto; materiale da costruzione per tetti.

**roof-garden** *n.* giardino pensile.

**rook**[1] *n.* (orn.) cornacchia. **-ery** *n.* colonia di cornacchie.

**rook**[2] *tr.* (colloq.) truffare; far pagare prezzi esorbitanti.

**rook**[3] *n.* (chess) torre *f.*

**room** *n.* spazio, posto, luogo; *to leave — for*, far posto a; camera, stanza, locale; *pl.* appartamento occasione, possibilità; *-mate*, compagno di stanza; *dining-room*, sala da pranzo; *drawing-room*, salotto; *living-room*, soggiorno; *spare —*, stanza disponibile; *waiting-room*, sala d'aspetto; *intr.* alloggiare. **-y** *adj.* spazioso, ampio.

**roost** *n.* posatoio; *at —*, appollaiato; pollaio; (fig.) giaciglio, letto; *intr.* appollaiarsi; (colloq.) andare a dormire. **-er** *n.* (USA) gallo domestico.

**root** *n.* radice *f.*; *to pull up by the -s*, sradicare; *to take —*, prender radice; (fig.) causa; origine; fondamento, base *f.*; sorgente *f.*; *tr.* radicare; (fig.) inchiodare; *intr.* mettere radice, attecchire; (fig.) radicarsi, allignare; stabilirsi; grufolare, razzolare; (fig.) frugare; *to — among papers*, frugare tra le carte; (slang, USA) *to — for*, sostenere, fare il tifo per; *to — for a candidate*, sostenere un candidato; *to — out*, *to — up*, snidare, trovare.

**rope** *n.* fune, canapo; capestro; (naut.) cavo; *to know the -s*, saperla lunga; *-'s end*, sferza; *tr.* legare con fune; rimorchiare con fune; *to — in*, cintare con corde.

**rope-ladder** *n.* scala di corda.

**ropeway** *n.* teleferica.

**rosary** *n.* (eccl.) rosario.

**rose** *adj.* rosa, di color rosa; *n.* rosa; *bed of -s*, roseto; *no — without a thorn*, non c'è rosa senza spine; rosetta (di inaffiatoio); *-bud*, bocciolo di rosa; *-bush*, rosaio; cespuglio di rose. **-coloured** *adj.* di color rosa; (fig.) roseo ottimista. **-window** *n.* rosone. *m.*

**Rose** *pr.n.* Rosa.

**roseate** *adj.* roseo, rosato.

**Rosemary**[1] *pr.n.* Rosa Maria.

**rosemary**[2] *n.* (bot.) rosmarino.

**rosette** *n.* rosetta, coccarda.

**rosewood** *n.* palissandro.

**rosin** *n.* resina; colofonia, pece greca.

**rosiness** *n.* color roseo.

**roster** *n.* ruolino, turno di servizio; lista, elenco, ruolo; *duty —*, ruolino di servizio.

**rostrum** *n.* rostro; becco.

**rosy** *adj.* roseo, rosato, di color rosa; *to paint everything in — colours*, vedere tutto rosa; *to turn —*, diventar roseo; cosparso di rose.

**rot** *n.* putrefazione; marciume *m.*; (slang) stupidaggine *f.*; *dry-rot*, carie secca del legno; *intr.* imputridire, marcire; putrefarsi, corrompersi; *tr.* far imputridire.

**rota** *n.* orario dei turni (di lavoro, studio); lista; ruolo.

**rotary** *adj.* rotante, rotatorio; a rotazione.

**rotate** *intr.* rotare; far rotare; coltivare a rotazione.

**rotation** *n.* rotazione; successione; *— of crops*, rotazione delle colture; *the — of seasons*, la successione delle stagioni; *by —*, a rotazione; *clockwise —*, rotazione a destra.

**rote** *n.* abitudine meccanica; memoria meccanica; *by —*, a memoria.

**rotten** *adj.* marcio, putrido, putrefatto; (fig.) corrotto; (slang) sgradevole, disgustoso; abominevole; *what — luck!*, che scalogna! **-ness** *n.* marciume *m.*, putrefazione; (fig.) corruzione.

**rotter** *n.* (slang) farabutto, mascalzone.

**rotund** *adj.* paffuto, rotondetto; profondo (di voce); enfatico, magniloquente. **-ity** *n.* rotondità.

**roué** *n.* libertino.

**rouge** *adj.* rosso; *n.* belletto; rossetto; *tr.* dare il rossetto a.

**rough** *adj.* irregolare, disuguale; ruvido, scabro; *— road*, strada accidentata; tempestoso, burrascoso; violento, impetuoso; *— sea*, mare grosso; *— weather*, tempo burrascoso; rudimentale, approssimativo; *a — translation*, una traduzione approssimativa; rude, sgarbato; rozzo, zotico; *— manners*, modi bruschi; aspro acre; disagevole, scomodo; difficile; *n.* terreno accidentato; giovinastro; teppista; stato grezzo; *in the —*, allo stato grezzo; *he explained his ideas in the —*, espose le sue idee per sommi capi; lato spiacevole delle cose; *to take the — with the smooth*, prendere le cose come vengono; *adv.* rudemente; grossolanamente.

**rough** *tr.* rendere ruvido; increspare; arruffare; *to — it*, (colloq.) vivere primitivamente; *to — in, out*, abbozzare; schizzare.

**rough** (compounds) *-and-ready*, non elaborato, improvvisato; *-hewn*, grossolano; appena sbozzato; *-house*, rissa; *-shod*, ferrato a ramponi; *-and-tumble*, irregolare, disordinato; *n.* zuffa, mischia; *-cast* *n.* intonaco; *tr.* intonacare.

**roughage** *n.* crusca di cereali.

**roughen** *intr.* irruvidire, irruvidirsi; rendere, diventare grossolano.

**roughness** *n.* ruvidezza; anfrattuosità, scabrosità; violenza, agitazione; inclemenza, rigidità; rudezza, sgarbatezza.

**R(o)umania** *pr.n.* (geog.) Rumania. **-n** *adj.*, *n.* rumeno.

**round** *adj.* rotondo; circolare; sferico; cilindrico; tondo, paffuto; *as — as a ball*, tondo come una palla; intero, completo; *— dozen*, una buona dozzina; *in — figures*, in cifre tonde; franco, sincero; sonoro, pieno; *to go at a good — pace*, camminare di buon passo.

**round** *n.* cerchio; sfera, globo; corso, ciclo, serie *f.*; giro; (mil.) ronda; (fig.) ambito; *statue in the —*, statua a tutto rilievo; (cards) mano, giro; *— of applause*, scroscio di applausi; (mil.) carica, colpo, salva, scarica; *tr.* arrotondare; girare, ruotare; (naut.) doppiare; completare; perfezionare; *to — on*, rivoltarsi irosamente contro.

**round** *adv.* intorno, attorno; in giro, all'intorno; *they didn't have enough cake to go —*, non avevano abbastanza torta per tutti; *to hand —*, distribuire, dare in giro; *to turn — and —*, continuare a girare; *all the year —*, tutto l'anno; *come — and see us this evening*, vieni a trovarci questa sera; *he brought us a long way —*, ci fece fare un lungo giro; *to show a person —*, fare da guida a una persona; *to sleep the clock —*, dormire per dodici ore.

**round** *prep.* intorno a, tutto intorno a; *— the corner*, dietro l'angolo; *snow was falling all — me*, la neve mi cadeva tutt'intorno; *to argue — a subject*, girare intorno a un argomento; *to travel — the world*, fare il giro del mondo.

**round** (compounds) *-game*, giuoco in circolo; *-shouldered*, dalla schiena curva; *-trip*, viaggio di andata e ritorno. **-about** *adj.* indiretto; obliquo; tortuoso; giostra; via traversa.

**roundel** *n.* tondo, medaglione decorativo; (mus.) rondò *m.*

**round-ly** *adv.* severamente; vigorosamente; francamente. **-ness** *n.* rotondità, sfericità; scorrevolezza; franchezza. **-sman** *n.* fattorino.

**rous-e** *tr.* svegliare, destare; scuotere; *he wants rousing*, è indolente; *I was -ed by the ringing of a bell*, fui svegliato dal suono di un

campanello; sollevare, agitare, provocare; agitare; *intr.* svegliarsi, destarsi. **-ing** *adj.* eccitante, stimolante.
**rout**[1] *n.* folla tumultuante; plebaglia; tumulto, sommossa.
**rout**[2] *n.* (mil.) sconfitta, disfatta; rotta; *to put to —*, mettere in rotta; *tr.* mettere in rotta, sconfiggere.
**route** *n.* via, rotta, itinerario; cammino, strada; *en —*, in cammino, per strada; *map*, carta stradale; *march*, marcia di addestramento; *air —*, rotta aerea; *tr.* spedire, instradare; *to — goods*, spedire merci.
**routine** *n.* pratica, abitudine meccanica; *— treatment*, terapia comune; *— work*, lavoro quotidiano.
**rov-e** *intr.* errare, vagare; vagabondare, percorrere, attraversare; *to — over sea and land*, vagare per mare e per terra.
**rov-er** *n.* vagabondo, giramondo. **-ing** *n.* viaggio senza meta; vagabondaggio.
**row**[1] *n.* baruffa, rissa, zuffa, tafferuglio; schiamazzo; *intr.* (slang) sgridare, rimproverare; azzuffarsi.
**row**[2] *n.* fila, linea; filare; *in the first —*, in prima fila; *sitting in a —*, seduti in fila.
**row**[3] *tr.* remare; vogare; trasportare a forza di remi; essere canottiere; *n.* giro in barca; remata.
**rowan** *n.* (bot.) sorbo selvatico; *-berry*, sorba selvatica.
**rowd-y** *adj.* chiassoso; tumultuoso; attaccabrighe; persona turbolenta. **-iness** *n.* turbolenza. **-yism** *n.* turbolenza; baccano.
**rowel** *n.* stella di sperone.
**rower** *n.* rematore; canottiere; vogatore.
**rowlock** *n.* (naut.) scalmo; scalmiera.
**royal** *adj.* reale, regale; regio; *His Royal Highness*, Sua Altezza Reale; degno di re; splendido, maestoso; *a — welcome*, una accoglienza splendida; *n.* membro di famiglia reale; *— blue*, blu savoia; *blood —*, la famiglia reale. **-ist** *n.* realista, monarchico. **-ly** *adv.* regalmente, da re; (fam.) splendidamente. **-ty** *n.* dignità di re, regalità, sovranità; membro di famiglia reale; i reali; *pl.* prerogative, privilegi reali; pagamento di una percentuale sugli utili; diritti d'autore.
**rub** *n.* fregata; grattata; frizione; impedimento; ostacolo, difficoltà; *tr.* fregare; frizionare; strofinare; *to — one's hands*, fregarsi le mani; *to — shoulders with*, entrare in contatto con; *to — the wrong way*, prendere per il verso sbagliato; pulire, asciugare, lustrare, lucidare; scorticare, logorare; (colloq.) *to — along*, arrangiarsi, cavarsela; *to — down*, strofinare, pulire fregando; strigliare (un cavallo); *to — in*, far penetrare frizionando; *don't — it in!*, (colloq.) non insistere, ho capito!; *to — out*, togliere, cancellare con la gomma; *to — up*, fregare, levigare; lucidare.
**rubber**[1] *n.* gomma da cancellare; *India —*, caucciù; *— gloves*, guanti di gomma; *-plant*, albero della gomma; *— tyre*, pneumatico.
**rubber**[2] *n.* (cards) insieme di tre partite successive; *to have a —*, fare una partita; *the —*, la bella, la partita decisiva.
**rubber-stamp** *tr.* timbrare; (fig.) approvare senza riflettere.
**rubbish** *n.* macerie *f.pl.*, calcinacci *m.pl.*; immondizie *f.pl.*; rifiuti, scarti *m.pl.*; roba di poco conto; robaccia; (fig.) idee assurde; *—!*, sciocchezze!; *to talk —*, dire delle stupidaggini. **-y** *adj.* di scarto; senza valore; senza senso.
**rubbish-bin** *n.* pattumiera. **-heap** *n.* mucchio di spazzatura.
**rubble** *n.* pietrisco; frantumi *m.pl.* di pietra grezza; macerie *f.pl.*; (geol.) breccia.
**rubdown** *n.* massaggio (dopo il bagno).
**rubella** *n.* (med.) rosolia.
**rubicund** *adj.* rubicondo.
**rubric** *n.* rubrica; ocra rossa.
**ruby** *adj.* di color rubino, rosso rubino; *n.* color rubino; bitorzolo rosso.
**ruck**[1] *n.* mucchio; moltitudine, folla; (fig.) massa.
**ruck**[2] *intr.* appollaiarsi; raggomitolarsi.
**ruck**[3] *n.* piega; arricciatura; increspatura; *tr.* arricciare; increspare; spiegazzare.
**rucksack** *n.* sacco da montagna.
**ruction** *n.* tumulto, disordine; lite.
**rudder** *n.* (naut.; aeron.) timone *m.*; (fig.) guida. **-less** *adj.* senza timone; senza guida; alla deriva.
**ruddiness** *n.* aspetto rubicondo; colorito rosso.
**ruddle** *n.* sinopia, argilla rossa, ocra rossa; *tr.* marcare; colorare con ocra rossa.
**ruddy** *adj.* rubicondo; rosso; rosato, roseo; (slang) maledetto, odioso.
**rude** *adj.* rude, grossolano, rustico; primitivo, incolto; incivile, ineducato; *— people*, gente rozza, senza educazione; grezzo, rudimentale; violento, aspro, brusco; sgarbato; impertinente; offensivo; *don't be —*, non essere scortese; *to be — to*, insultare; vigoroso, florido; *— health*, salute ottima. **-ness** *n.* rozzezza; ineducazione; violenza; scortesia; intrattabilità, asprezza, insolenza, impertinenza.
**rudiment** *n.pl.* rudimenti, elementi fondamentali. **-al** *adj.* rudimentale. **-ary** *adj.* rudimentale.
**rue**[1] *tr.* pentirsi di; rammaricarsi di; rimpiangere; lamentare, deplorare. **-ful** *adj.* lamentevole, miserando, doloroso, pietoso. **-fulness** *n.* tono lamentevole; tristezza; pietà.
**rue**[2] *n.* (bot.) ruta.
**ruff** *n.* gorgiera, lattuga; collare di uccello.
**ruffian** *adj.* brutale, crudele; ribaldo. **-ism** *n.* scelleratezza; brutalità. **-ly** *adj.* scellerato, brutale.
**ruffle** *n.* colletto, polso, guarnizione pieghettata; increspatura di acqua, superficie; sconvolgimento, turbamento; tumulto, rissa; schermaglia; *tr.* increspare; pieghettare; ornare di pieghettature; arruffare; scompigliare, disordinare; agitare, irritare; conturbare; sfogliare affrettatamente.
**rug** *n.* coperta; tappetino, pedana; *bedside —*, scendiletto; *hearth-rug*, tappetino da camino.
**rugged** *adj.* ruvido, scabro, irregolare; *— features*, lineamenti irregolari; ispido, irsuto; rugoso; austero, inflessibile; scontroso; rozzo, rude, incivile, sgarbato. **-ness** *n.* ruvidezza, scabrosità, irregolarità; austerità; durezza, asprezza; rudezza.
**ruin** *n.* rovina; *to go to —*, andare in rovina; *to lay in -s*, distruggere completamente; *tr.* rovinare; distruggere; far fallire. **-ation** *n.* rovina; perdita completa. **-ed** *adj.* rovinato; in rovina. **-ous** *adj.* rovinoso, dannoso; in rovina, in stato di rovina. **-ousness** *n.* rovina; stato rovinoso.
**rule** *n.* regola, regolamento, norma, precetto; *the — of the road*, il codice della strada; *— of three*, regola del tre; *by —*, secondo le regole; *to make it a — to*, farsi un dovere di; *— of thumb*, regola empirica approssimativa; *hard and fast —*, regola fissa; *the exception proves the rule*, l'eccezione conferma la regola; regola, abitudine; *as a —*, di regola, generalmente; governo, regime *m.*, dominio, autorità; *slide —*, regolo calcolatore.
**rule** *tr.* governare, reggere; dominare; guidare, consigliare; dirigere; regolare; (leg.) decidere, decretare; rigare, fare righe; (comm.) *prices are ruling high*, i prezzi restano elevati; *to — out*, scartare, escludere; *possibility that cannot be -d out*, possibilità che non si può escludere.
**ruler** *n.* governatore; dominatore; sovrano; signore, padrone, riga, regolo.
**ruling** *adj.* dominante, dirigente;

predominante; — *prices*, prezzi correnti; *n.* governo, dominio.
**rum**[1] *n.* rum. **-runner** *n.* contrabbandiere di alcoolici.
**rum**[2] *adj.* (slang) strano, strambo, originale; curioso; *a — customer*, un individuo, un tipo bizzarro.
**Rumania** *pr.n.* see **Roumania**.
**rumbl-e**[1] *n.* rombo di tuono; brontolìo, rumore sordo; *intr.* rombare; rumoreggiare; brontolare; borbottare. **-ing** *adj.* rumoreggiante; brontolante; *n.* rumoreggiamento; brontolìo.
**rumble**[2] *tr.* (fam.) scoprire.
**ruminant** *adj.* ruminante; meditativo; *n.* ruminante.
**rumin-ate** *intr.* ruminare; (fig.) riconsiderare; meditare, ponderare. **-ation** *n.* ruminazione; (fig.) meditazione. **-ative** *adj.* ruminante; (fig.) meditativo.
**rummage**[1] *n.* perquisizione doganale; ricerca, rovistìo; insieme di oggetti, cianfrusaglie; *intr.* frugare; rovistare; cercare buttando all'aria.
**rummer** *n.* grosso bicchiere da cognac.
**rumour** *n.* chiacchiera, diceria, voce; *tr.* far correre voce, spargere la voce, vociferare; *it is rumoured that . . .*, corre voce che . . .; *they are rumoured to be*, si dice che essi siano.
**rump** *n.* groppone *m.*, groppa, posteriore *m.*; — *steak*, bistecca di filetto; (fig.) gruppo supersite di un partito.
**rumple** *tr.* spiegazzare; sciupare; sgualcire; arruffare, scompigliare i capelli.
**rumpus** *n.* (fam.) chiasso; scompiglio; tumulto; rissa.
**run** *n.* corsa; *to go for a —*, fare una corsa; *at a —*, di corsa; *on the —*, in fuga; gita; breve viaggio; giro; traversata; tragitto; percorso; *the — of the market*, l'andamento del mercato; serie, sequela; periodo; sequenza; *a — of luck*, una serie di eventi fortunati; *in the long —*, a lungo andare; *a great — on a book*, una forte richiesta di un libro; (theatr.) *to have a long —*, tenere a lungo il cartellone; *a — on the bank*, un forte afflusso agli sportelli della banca; orientamento, direzione; categoria, classe; *the common — of men*, la media degli uomini; recinto; pascolo; pista (di animali); *I had the — of their house*, avevo libero accesso in casa loro; (of stockings, etc.) smagliatura; (mus.) volata; *trial —*, giro di prova.
**run** **1.** *intr.* correre; affrettarsi; fuggire, scappare; passare; partire; *buses — every two minutes*, gli autobus passano, partono, ogni due minuti; *trains running between Rome and Milan*, treni che fanno servizio tra Roma e Milano; scorrere, fluire; spandersi, diffondersi, versarsi; colare, gocciolare; *his nose was running*, gli gocciolava il naso; liquefarsi; fondersi; *money -s through his fingers like water through a sieve*, ha le mani bucate; *the coast -s north and south*, la costa si estende da nord a sud; *a hedge -s round the villa*, una siepe circonda la villa; funzionare; *the lift is running*, l'ascensore funziona; (theatr.) tenere il cartellone; diventare, trasformarsi in; *my blood ran cold*, mi si agghiacciò il sangue; *the river is running dry*, il fiume sta asciugandosi; *to — riot*, scatenarsi, dare in eccessi. **2.** *tr.* far muovere, guidare, mettere in servizio; dirigere, governare; gestire, amministrare; *to — a blockade*, forzare un blocco; *to — a candidate*, appoggiare un candidato; *to — a chance*, avere buone probabilità; *to — errands*, fare commissioni; *to — a high temperature*, avere la febbre alta; *to — a risk*, correre un rischio; (slang) *to — the show*, essere il capo. **3.** FOLL. BY PREP. OR ADV.: *to — across*, traversare di corsa; imbattersi in, incontrarsi con; *to — after*, correre dietro a; fare la corte a; *to — against*, andare contro, urtare; *to — one's head against a wall*, battere il capo contro il muro; *to — at*, precipitarsi contro, assalire; *to — away*, correre via, scappare; *to — away with*, fuggire con; rubare; *to — away with an idea*, mettersi in testa un'idea; *his imagination -s away with him*, la sua fantasia gli prende la mano; *to — by*, passare vicino (a), passare davanti correndo; *to — down*, scaricarsi; indebolirsi; cessare di funzionare; scoprire, catturare; calunniare, gettare il discredito su; investire; *to get — down*, essere investito da un'automobile; esaurirsi, subire una crisi nervosa; *to — into*, incorrere in; raggiungere; entrare in collisione con; fondersi in; *to — into debt*, indebitarsi, incorrere in debito; *to — into five editions*, toccare la quinta edizione; *to — off*, fuggire, scappare via; scrivere di getto, (typ.) tirare; *to — on*, continuare di corsa; parlare senza pausa; (of time) passare; *to — out*, correre fuori; esaurirsi; scadere, terminare; scacciare fuori; *to — over*, dare una scorsa; (with an iron) ripassare; ricapitolare; investire; *he was — over by a car*, fu investito da un'automobile; *to — past*, sorpassare correndo; passare davanti correndo; traboccare; *to — through*, sperperare; trapassare con la spada; esaminare rapidamente, sfogliare; *he ran through his notes*, diede un'occhiata ai suoi appunti; *to — to*, correre a, raggiungere di corsa; bastare, essere sufficiente per; tendere a; *to — to seed*, andare in seme; *I'll — you to the station*, ti accompagno in macchina alla stazione; *to — up*, salire di corsa; accumulare; addizionare; *to — up against*, urtare; incontrare, imbattersi in.
**runaway** *adj. attrib.* fuggiasco, fuggitivo; (of horse) che prende la mano; fatto fuggendo; di corsa; *n.* fuggitivo, disertore; cavallo che ha preso la mano; fuga; — *speed*, velocità di fuga.
**run-e** *n.* runa, carattere runico. **-ic** *adj.* runico.
**rung** *n.* piuolo; raggio di ruota.
**runnel** *n.* ruscelletto, rigagnolo; scolatoio, canaletto.
**runner** *n.* corridore *m.*; fattorino; messo; (mil.) staffetta; (comm.) collettore; procuratore; passatoia; striscia ornamentale. **-up** *n.* (sport) finalista *m.*, *f.*
**running** *adj.* che corre, in corsa; da corsa; fluente, scorrevole; continuo; regolare; consecutivo; *he won three times —*, vinse per tre volte consecutive; funzionante; — *sore*, ferita purulente; *n.* il correre; corsa; durata; *to be in the —*, avere probabilità di vittoria; *to make the —*, dare l'andatura; esercizio, direzione amministrativa; scolo, flusso, scorrimento; marcia, funzionamento; suppurazione; contrabbando; — *commentary*, radiocronaca; — *cost*, costo di esercizio. **-in** *n.* (motor.) rodaggio. **-speed** *n.* velocità di funzionamento. **-track** *n.* pista.
**runt** *n.* animale più piccolo del normale; nano.
**runway** *n.* pista, sentiero; passerella; (aeron.) pista di decollo, di atterraggio.
**rupture** *n.* rottura; (med.) ernia; rottura; *tr.* rompere; scoppiare; rompere; *to — a ligament*, strappare un legamento; *intr.* rompersi; spezzarsi.
**rural** *adj.* rurale, campestre; rustico; — *occupations*, lavori campestri. **-ize** *tr.* ruralizzare.
**ruse** *n.* stratagemma *m.*; astuzia; trucco; frode *f.*
**rush**[1] *n.* giunco, festuca.
**rush**[2] *n.* corsa precipitosa; impeto; — *of blood to the head*, flusso di sangue alla testa; (comm.) grande richiesta; *gold-rush*, la febbre dell'oro; *intr.* precipitarsi; avventarsi; scagliarsi; *tr.* far muovere, spostare, velocemente; forzare, trascinare; *to — up*, costruire in fretta.
**rush-hour** *n.* ore *f.pl.* di punta.
**rusk** *n.* fetta di pane dolce biscottato.
**russet** *adj.* ruggine; rosso bruno; *n.* color ruggine; mela ruggine.
**Russia** *pr.n.* (geog.) Russia. **-n** *adj.*, *n.* russo; (language) il russo.

**rust** *n.* ruggine *f.*; (fig.) *to rub the — off*, aggiornarsi. *tr.* arrugginire; corrodere; deteriorare; *intr.* arruginirsi; (fig.) diventare inattivo; *better to wear out than — out*, è meglio esaurirsi lavorando che languire oziando. **-coloured** *adj.* color ruggine. **-proof** *adj.* inossidabile. **-red** color ruggine.
**rustic** *adj.* rustico, campestre; semplice; rozzo, grossolano; *n.* capagnuolo; zotico. **-ate** *intr.* vivere in campagna; condurre una vita rustica; *tr.* (Univ.) escludere temporaneamente.
**rustiness** *n.* rugginosità; ruggine *f.*
**rustle** *n.* fruscìo; stormire; picchiettìo; mormorìo; *intr.* far frusciare; *to — cattle*, rubare del bestiame.
**rustless** *adj.* senza ruggine; inossidabile.
**rustling** *adj.* frusciante; mormorante; *n.* fruscìo; mormorìo.
**rusty** *adj.* rugginoso, arrugginito; di color ruggine; *to get —*, arrugginirsi; *to go —*, fare la ruggine; antiquato; vecchio; rauco di voce; (fig.) a chi manca l'abitudine; *my Latin is —*, mi manca l'abitudine del latino, il mio latino è arrugginito.
**rut**[1] (of animals) *n.* fregola; *intr.* essere in fugola.
**rut**[2] *n.* rotaia, carreggiata; solco; (fig.) abitudine inveterata; *to settle into a —*, fossilizzarsi.
**ruth** *n.* pietà, compassione. **-less** *adj.* spietato, crudele, duro, inumano. **-lessness** *n.* crudeltà.
**rye** *n.* (bot.) segale *f.* **-bread** *n.* pane di segale.

**S, s** *n.* esse *m., f.*; *— for sugar*, esse come Savona; *S-shaped*, a forma di s.
**sabbatarian** *adj.* sabatino; *n.* sabatario.
**sabbath** *n.* il settimo giorno della settimana dedicato al riposo (sabato per gli Ebrei, domenica per i Cristiani); *to keep the —*, osservare il sabato; *witches' —*, sabba *m.*
**sabbatic(al)** *adj.* sabatico; *— year*, anno sabatico; *— leave*, congedo concesso ogni sette anni.
**sable** *adj.* di zibellino; *n.* zibellino; pelliccia di zibellino; (art) pennello (di martora); (herald.) colore nero.
**sabot** *n.* zoccolo.
**sabot-age** *n.* sabotaggio; *tr., intr.* sabotare; compiere atti di sabotaggio. **-eur** *n.* sabotatore.
**sabre** *n.* sciabola.
**saccharin(e)** *n.* saccarina; *adj.* saccarino, zuccherino.
**sacerdotal** *adj.* sacerdotale.
**sachet** *n.* sacchetto profumato.
**sack**[1] *n.* sacco; *— race*, corsa degli insaccati; (slang) congedo, licenziamento; *to get the —*, essere licenziato, congedato; *tr.* insaccare; (fam.) licenziare, congedare; silurare.
**sack**[2] *n.* (mil.) sacco, saccheggio; *tr.* (mil.) saccheggiare, mettere a sacco; spogliare dei beni.
**sack**[3] *n.* (poet.) vino bianco secco.
**sackcloth** *n.* tela da sacco; panno ruvido; (fig.) *in — and ashes*, vestito di sacco e col capo cosparso di cenere (di chi fa atto di penitenza).
**sackful** *n.* saccata.
**sacking**[1] *n.* tela da sacco, iuta.
**sacking**[2] *n.* saccheggio.
**sacrament** *n.* sacramento; *to administer the last Sacraments*, somministrare gli ultimi Sacramenti; *to receive the Sacraments*, ricevere i Sacramenti. **-al** *adj.* sacramentale.
**sacred** *adj.* sacro; religioso; inviolabile; sacrosanto; *a — duty*, un dovere sacro; consacrato, dedicato; *— to the memory of*, dedicato alla memoria di. **-ness** *n.* santità; carattere sacro; inviolabilità.
**sacrifice** *n.* sacrificio; olocausto; *offered up as a —*, offerto in sacrificio; rinuncia, abnegazione; *the last —*, il sacrificio della vita; (comm.) perdita, svendita; *intr.* sacrificare; immolare; rinunziare a; (comm.) svendere.
**sacrificial** *adj.* propiziatorio; espiatorio; (comm.) *at — prices*, (comm.) a prezzi molto sottocosto. **-ly** *adv.* in modo espiatorio; (fig.) eroicamente; facendo sacrificio.
**sacrileg-e** *n.* sacrilegio. **-ious** *adj.* sacrilegio.
**sacristy** *n.* (eccl.) sagrestia.
**sacrosanct** *adj.* sacrosanto; inviolabile.
**sad** *adj.* triste; mesto; lugubre; fosco; grave; deplorevole; *to become —*, rattristarsi; *to make —*, rattristare.
**sadden** *tr.* rattristare.
**sad-eyed** *adj.* dallo sguardo triste.
**saddle**[1] *n.* sella; sellino (di bicicletta); *to be in the —*, essere in sella; (geog.) giogaia, sella (di monte); (mech.) cannello; bilanciere *m.*; *hunting-saddle*, sella all'inglese; *side-saddle*, sella da donna; *to ride side-saddle*, cavalcare all'amazzone; *tr.* sellare; mettere la sella a; (fig.) *to — with*, (fig.) gravare, caricare, di.
**saddleback** *n.* (geog.) sella; (eng.) tetto a schiena d'asino. **-ed** *adj.* a schiena d'asino.
**saddle-bag** *n.* bisaccia da sella. **-cloth** *n.* gualdrappa. **-horse** *n.* cavallo da sella.
**saddl-ery** *n.* selleria; arte del sellaio. **-ing** *n.* sellatura.
**Sadducee** *pr.n.* (bibl.) Sadduceo.
**sad-ism** *n.* sadismo. **-ist** *n.* sadista *m., f.* **-istic** *adj.* sadico.
**sadly** *adv.* tristemente; mestamente; deplorevolemente; miseramente; meschinamente; gravemente; sfortunatamente, purtroppo.
**sadness** *n.* tristezza; mestizia; melanconia.
**safe**[1] *adj.* sicuro; al riparo; salvo; intatto; *— and sound*, sano e salvo; innocuo; cauto, prudente; *at a — distance from*, a una rispettosa distanza da; *to be on the — side*, tenere un margine di sicurezza; fido, fidato; certo; *n.* cassaforte *f.*; scrigno; credenza; *rifle (set) at —*, carabina in posizione di sicura.
**safe-conduct** *n.* salvacondotto. **-deposit** *n.* cassetta di sicurezza. **-keeping** *n.* buona guardia, custodia.
**safeguard** *n.* salvaguardia; scorta; *tr.* salvaguardare; difendere; proteggere; *-ed against*, al riparo da.
**safely** *adv.* sicuramente; senza pericolo; senza incidenti; in salvo; in luogo sicuro.
**safeness** *n.* sicurezza; certezza.
**safety** *n.* sicurezza; salvezza; scampo; *for -'s sake*, per maggior sicurezza; *in —*, in salvo; *to seek — in flight*, cercar scampo nella fuga; *— first !*, prudenza innanzitutto!; *— device*, dispositivo di sicurezza; *— factor*, coefficiente di sicurezza.
**safety-belt** *n.* cintura di sicurezza. **-catch** *n.* arresto di sicurezza. **-lock** *n.* serratura di sicurezza. **-match** *n.* fiammifero svedese. **-pin** *n.* spilla di sicurezza. **-valve** *n.* valvola di sicurezza.
**saffron** *n.* zafferano; *adj.* di color zafferano.
**sag** *n.* abbassamento; ripiegamento; (comm.) diminuzione, flessione dei prezzi; (eng.) cedimento; *intr.* piegarsi; chinarsi; curvarsi; abbassarsi; cedere sotto il peso; (comm.) cedere (di prezzi).
**saga** *n.* saga; epica medievale; romanzo fiume.
**sagacious** *adj.* acuto, perspicace;

sagace. **-ness, sagacity** *n.* sagacia; perspicacia.
**sage**[1] *n.* (bot.) salvia. **-green** *n.* color grigio-verde.
**sage**[2] *adj.* saggio; sapiente; colto; esperto; *n.* saggio; dotto; *the Seven Sages*, i Sette Savi. **-ness** *n.* saggezza; prudenza; discrezione.
**sagging** *n.* cedimento; abbassamento; curvatura; inclinazione; (comm.) diminuzione di prezzi.
**sago** *n.* sago, sagù *m.*
**sail** *n.* (naut.) vela; velatura; *to set —*, spiegare le vele, salpare, partire; *full —*, a vele spiegate; *to crowd all —*, far forza di vele; *to hoist —*, issare una vela; *to lower —*, abbassare una vela; *to strike —*, ammainare le vele; *— ho!*, nave in vista!; (of a mill) ala, pala; *to go for a —*, fare un'escursione su nave a vela.
**sail** *intr.* veleggiare; navigare; costeggiare; *to — against the wind*, andar contro corrente; *to — before the wind*, navigare col vento in poppa; *to — close to the wind*, navigare contro vento, orzare, (fig.) rasentare il precipizio; salpare, far vela; iniziare un viaggio; *we — next week*, salpiamo la settimana prossima; (aeron.) *to — over*, sorvolare; *tr.* percorrere; attraversare.
**sailable** *adj.* navigabile.
**sail-cloth** *n.* tela di olona, tela per vele.
**sailer** *n.* veliero.
**sailing** *n.* navigazione, traversata; (fam.) *it's plain —*, la cosa va da sè, la faccenda non fa una grinza; partenza; *list of -s*, elenco delle partenze; *— orders*, istruzioni per le partenze.
**sailor** *n.* marinaio; navigatore; *—'s knot*, nodo da marinaio; *are you a good or a bad —?*, soffri o no il mal di mare?
**sailor-hat** *n.* cappello alla marinara.
**sailorly** *adj.* da marinaio, alla marinara.
**saint** *adj.* San, Santo; *St Bernard*, cane San Bernardo; santo; sacro; *n.* santo; santa; *the blessed -s in Heaven*, i benedetti santi del cielo; *to live like a —*, vivere da santo; *to provoke the patience of a —*, far scappare la pazienza ad un santo; *All Saints' Day*, Ognissanti; *patron —*, santo patrono. **-ed** *adj.* santo; canonizzato, santificato; consacrato; sacro; (iron.) benedetto, santo. **-hood** *n.* santità; *the -hood*, i santi. **-like** *adj.* da santo, simile a santo. **-liness** *n.* santità. **-ly** *adj.* santo; *a -ly expression*, un viso di santo; *he lived a -ly life*, visse da santo; *a -ly air*, arie *f.pl.* da santarellina.
**sake** *n.* interesse *m.*; beneficio; causa; bene *m.*; riguardo; rispetto; *for his own —*, nel suo interesse; *for the — of*, per il bene di; *art for art's —*, l'arte per l'arte; *for God's —*, per l'amor di Dio; *for old times' —*, in ricordo del passato.
**salacious** *adj.* salace; lascivo. **-ness, salacity** *n.* salacità; lubricità; lascivia.
**salad** *n.* insalata; *fruit-salad*, macedonia di frutta; *— days*, inesperienza giovanile.
**salad-bowl** *n.* insalatiera. **-dressing** *n.* salsa per condire l'insalata.
**salamander** *n.* (zool.) salamandra.
**salar-y** *n.* stipendio; mensile *m.* **-ied** *adj.* stipendiato.
**sale** *n.* vendita; *bill of —*, fattura; *on —, for —*, in vendita; *to put up for —*, mettere in vendita; *— by auction*, vendita all'asta; liquidazione, svendita; saldo; *— price*, prezzo di liquidazione; *bargain —*, liquidazione.
**saleab-le** *adj.* vendibile, che si vende, commerciabile. **-ility** *n.* facilità di smercio.
**sale-room** *n.* sala di vendite all'asta.
**sales-girl** *n.* commessa. **-man** *n.* venditore, commesso. **-manship** *n.* l'arte del vendere; l'abilità nel vendere. **-woman** *n.* commessa, venditrice.
**sali-ence, -ency** *n.* prominenza; superiorità; cospicuità; importanza.
**sali-ent** *adj.* sporgente, prominente; saliente; notevole; principale; cospicuo.
**salin-e** *adj.* salino, salso; salato; *— drip*, fleboclise *f.* **-ity** *n.* salsedine *f.*, salinità.
**saliv-a** *n.* saliva. **-ary** *adj.* salivare. **-ate** *intr.* salivare. **-ation** *n.* salivazione.
**sallow** *adj.* giallastro; olivastro; terreo. **-ness** *n.* colorito giallastro.
**Sally**[1] *pr.n.* Sara.
**sally**[2] *n.* (mil.) sortita; escursione, gita; slancio, impeto; (fig.) motto di spirito; facezia; *intr.* (mil.) fare una sortita; *to — forth*, balzare fuori; mettersi in viaggio.
**sally**[3] *n.* impugnatura di corda di campana.
**salmon** *n.* salmone *m.*; *adj.* di color salmone.
**salon** *n.* salone *m.*, salotto; ricevimento.
**Salonica** *pr.n.* (geog.) Salonicco *f.*
**saloon** *n.* salone *m.*, sala da ricevimento; (naut.) cabina di lusso; ritrovo per passegeri.
**salt** *n.* sale *m.*; *the — of the earth*, il sale della terra; *a pinch of —*, un pizzico di sale; *common —*, sale grosso; *rock —*, salgemma; (fig.) frizzo, spirito; (colloq.) *an old —*, un lupo di mare; *pl.* (med.) sali; *a dose of -s*, una dose di sali, un purgante; *Epsom -s*, sale inglese; *adj.* salato; *— water*, acqua salata; amaro; piccante; *tr.* salare; cospargere di sale; condire, rendere piccante; *to — down*, conservare sotto sale; (colloq.) *to — away*, mettere da parte. **-ing** *n.* insalatura, salatura.
**salt-cellar** *n.* saliera. **-marsh** *n.* palude salata. **-mine** *n.* salina, miniera di sale. **-spoon** *n.* cucchiaino per il sale.
**saltpetre** *n.* salnitro.
**salty** *adj.* salato; salmastro, incrostato di sale; piccante; (fig.) mordace, arguto.
**salubrious** *adj.* salubre, sano. **-ness, salubrity** *n.* salubrità.
**salutary** *adj.* salutare.
**salutation** *n.* saluto.
**salute** *n.* saluto; gesto di saluto; (naut.; mil.) saluto; salva; *to take the —*, rispondere al saluto; *tr.* salutare; dare il benvenuto a; colpire l'orecchio a; offrirsi allo sguardo.
**salvage** *n.* indennità di ricupero; salvataggio, ricupero; merci ricuperate; *— operation*, operazione di ricupero; *tr.* ricuperare, salvare.
**salvation** *n.* salvezza; salute eterna; redenzione; *to work out one's —*, assicurarsi la salvezza eterna.
**salve**[1] *n.* unguento, balsamo; pomata; (fig.) rimedio; *tr.* ungere con balsamo; (fig.) lenire.
**salve**[2] *tr.* salvare.
**salver** *n.* vassoio, piatto; *a silver —*, un vassoio d'argento.
**salvo** *n.* (mil.) salva; *— of applause*, scroscio di applausi.
**salvolatile** *n.* (chem.) sali di carbonato di ammonio; sali odorosi.
**Salzburg** *pr.n.* (geog.) Salisburgo *f.*
**Samaritan** *pr.n., adj.* samaritano.
**same** *adj.* stesso, medesimo; uguale; invariato; *at the — time*, nello stesso tempo; tuttavia; nondimeno; *it comes to the — thing*, fa lo stesso; *prn.* lo stesso, il medesimo; *the — to you!*, altrettanto!; la stessa cosa; *adv.* nello stesso modo; *all the —*, non di meno, malgrado tutto. **-ness** *n.* identità; somiglianza; uniformità; monotonia.
**samphire** *n.* (bot.) salicornia.
**sampl-e** *n.* campione *m.*; modello; saggio, esemplare *m.*; (statistics) campione; *tr.* campionare; saggiare; provare. **-ing** *gerund* (comm.) campionatura.
**sample-book** *n.* campionario.
**Samson** *pr.n.* Sansone.
**sanatorium** *n.* sanatorio; infermeria.
**sanctif-y** *tr.* santificare, consacrare, purificare. **-ication** *n.* santificazione; canonizzazione. **-ied** *adj.* santificato; santo, sacro; consacrato.
**sanctimonious** *adj.* santarello, che affetta devozione. **-ness** *n.* santocchieria, aria di santità.

**sanction** *n.* autorizzazione, approvazione; permesso; (leg.) ratifica, decreto; pena; *punitive* —, sanzione punitiva; *tr.* autorizzare, approvare; ratificare, decretare.
**sanctity** *n.* santità; religiosità; carattere sacro; inviolabilità.
**sanctuary** *n.* santuario, tempio, chiesa; asilo, rifugio; riserva.
**sanctum** *n.* luogo sacro, santuario.
**sand** *n.* sabbia; rena; granelli di sabbia; spiaggia; banco di sabbia; *tr.* cospargere di sabbia; insabbiare, arenare; smerigliare.
**sandal** *n.* sandalo; *n.* legno di sandalo.
**sand-bag** *n.* sacchetto di sabbia; *tr.* munire, zavorrare con sacchetti di sabbia; colpire con un sacchetto di sabbia. **-bank** *n.* banco di sabbia. **-glass** *n.* clessida. **-hill** *n.* duna. **-paper** *n.* carta vetrata. **-pit** *n.* cava di sabbia. **-shoes** *n.pl.* scarpe da spiaggia. **-stone** *n.* (min.) arenaria.
**sandwich** *n.* panino imbottito; *attrib.* (fig.) *a — course*, un corso di studi che si alterna ogni due anni con un impiego industriale; *tr.* (fig.) serrare; intercalare; inserire.
**sandy** *adj.* sabbioso, arenoso; (colour) biondo rosso.
**sane** *adj.* sano di mente; sensato; equilibrato. **-ly** *adv.* sensatamente; ragionevolmente. **-ness, sanity** *n.* sanità di mente; equilibrio.
**sanguinary** *adj.* sanguinario; crudele.
**sanguine** *adj.* sanguigno; ottimistico; fiducioso; *to be of a — disposition*, essere portato all'ottimismo; *to feel — about the future*, aver fiducia nell'avvenire. **-ness** *n.* ottimismo; fiducia; speranza; temperamento sanguigno.
**sanitary** *adj.* igienico; sanitario; *— inspector*, ufficiale sanitario.
**sanitation** *n.* condizioni igieniche; costruzioni e materiale sanitari.
**sanitorium** *n.* sanatorio, casa di cura.
**sanity** *n.* sanità di mente; equilibrio; ragionevolezza, buon senso.
**Santa Claus** *pr.n.* San Niccolò (*Ital. equiv.:* Befana).
**sap**[1] *n.* (bot.) linfa; succo; (fig.) vigore *m.*, energia; *tr.* essiccare.
**sap**[2] *tr.* minare le fondamenta di; (fig.) insidiare; sfiaccare, svigorire.
**sapid** *adj.* sapido; gustoso. **-ity, sapidness** *n.* sapidità; gustosità.
**sapi-ent** *adj.* sapiente, savio; pedante. **-ence** *n.* sapienza, saggezza; pedanteria.
**sapling** *n.* alberello.
**sapper** *n.* zappatore; (mil.) geniere.
**sapphire** *n.* zaffiro; *adj.* di colore blu zaffiro.
**sarc-asm** *n.* sarcasmo. **-astic** *adj.* sarcastico.
**sarcophagus** *n.* sarcofago.
**sardine** *n.* sardina.
**Sardinia** *pr.n.* (geog.) Sardegna. **-n** *adj.*, *n.* sardo; (language) il sardo.
**sardonic** *adj.* sardonico.
**sartorial** *adj.* di sarto; di sartoria.
**sash** *n.* fascia, cintura, sciarpa; telaio scorrevole di finestra; *sash-cord*, corda del contrappeso. **-window** *n.* finestra a ghigliottina.
**Satan** *pr.n.* Satana *m.* **-ic(al)** *adj.* satanico. **-ism** *n.* satanismo.
**satchel** *n.* cartella da scolaro.
**sate** *tr.* saziare, satollare; soddisfare.
**satellite** *n.* (astr.) satellite *f.*; (fig.) seguace *m.*, *f.*; *attrib.* — *town*, città satellite.
**satiable** *adj.* saziabile, appagabile.
**satiat-e** *adj.* sazio, satollo; *tr.* saziare, satollare. **-ion, satiety** *n.* sazietà.
**satin** *adj.* di raso; simile a raso; *n.* raso. **-stitch** *n.* punto raso.
**satir-e** *n.* satira; sarcasmo. **-ic(al)** *adj.* satirico.
**satir-ist** *n.* autore di satire. **-ize** *tr.* satireggiare.
**satisfaction** *n.* soddisfazione; appagamento; (leg.) pagamento.
**satisfactory** *adj.* soddisfacente; esauriente; *not* —, che lascia a desiderare.
**satisfy** *tr.* soddisfare; appagare; accontentare; convincere, persuadere; assicurare; (leg.) pagare, compensare; fare ammenda a. **-ing** *adj.* soddisfacente.
**saturat-e** *adj.* saturo; intenso di colore; *tr.* saturare; imbeverare; impregnare; *to become -ed with*, impregnarsi di. **-ion** *n.* saturazione.
**Saturday** *pr.n.* sabato; — *to Monday*, fine settimana.
**saturnalian** *adj.* saturnale; licenzioso.
**saturnine** *adj.* triste, mesto; (med.) saturnino.
**satyr** *n.* satiro. **-ic** *adj.* di satiro, da satiro, satiresco.
**sauce** *n.* salsa; intingolo; condimento; (colloq.) impertinenza, impudenza; *none of your —!*, niente impertinenze!; *tr.* condire; rendere piccante; (colloq.) dire impertinenze a.
**sauce-boat** *n.* salsiera.
**saucepan** *n.* casseruola, pentolino.
**saucer** *n.* piattino.
**sauc-y** *adj.* sfacciato, insolente; impertinente; vivace, arguto. **-iness** *n.* sfacciataggine *f.*; insolenza; impertinenza.
**saunter** *n.* passeggiatina, giretto; *intr.* bighellonare; andare a zonzo. **-er** *n.* bighellone *m.*, girandolone *m.* **-ingly** *adv.* bighellonando.
**sausage** *n.* salsiccia, salame *m.* **-meat** *n.* carne trita per ripieni. **-roll** *n.* salatino di pasta arrotolata, ripiena di carne.
**sauté** *adj.* (cul.) saltato, fritto in padella.
**savage** *adj.* selvaggio, barbaro; feroce, crudele; *a — dog*, un cane feroce; (colloq.) furioso, arrabbiato; *n.* selvaggio, barbaro; persona crudele; *tr.* attaccare; mordere; (fig.) assalire. **-ness, savagery** *n.* stato selvaggio; selvatichezza; ferocia; crudeltà.
**savant** *n.* dotto, erudito.
**save** *tr.* salvare; difendere, proteggere; guardare; conservare, mettere in serbo, risparmiare; *intr.* fare risparmi, fare economie; evitare perdite; *prep.* salvo, eccetto, fuorchè, ad eccezione di.
**saver** *n.* salvatore; liberatore; risparmiatore, economizzatore.
**saving** *adj.* che salva; che redime; economico; (leg.) — *clause*, clausola restrittiva; *n.* salvezza; *pl.* risparmio; economia; *labour-saving*, che risparmia fatica; pratico.
**savings-bank** *n.* cassa di risparmio.
**saviour** *n.* salvatore; *the Saviour*, il Redentore.
**savour** *n.* sapore *m.*; gusto; aroma; *tr.* gustare; assaporare, sentire il sapore di; *intr.* sapere. **-iness** *n.* sapidità, gustosità. **-y** *adj.* saporito, piccante; delizioso, squisito; *n.* salatino; pietanza appetitosa.
**Savoy**[1] *pr.n.* (geog.) Savoia.
**savoy**[2] *n.* cavolo cappuccio.
**saw**[1] *n.* sega; *tr.* segare; *to — the air*, gesticolare.
**saw**[2] *n.* massima; detto; proverbio.
**sawdust** *n.* segatura.
**saw-mill** *n.* segheria.
**saxhorn** *n.* (mus.) basso tuba.
**saxifrage** *n.* (bot.) sassifraga.
**Saxon** *adj.*, *n.* sassone *m.*, *f.*; *n.* lingua sassone.
**saxophone** *n.* (mus.) sassofono.
**say** *n.* il dire; detto; parola; *he said his* —, disse la sua; *to have no — in the matter*, non avere voce in capitolo; *tr.*, *intr.* dire; affermare; *I have heard it said that*, ho sentito dire che; *what do you — ?*, cosa dici?, cosa ne pensi?; *I — !*, senti!, scusa!, davvero?; *it goes without -ing*, è evidente; *how many would you like?*, — *ten*, quanti ne vuoi? facciamo dieci; *you don't — so?*, davvero?, mi sembra impossibile; pronunciare, recitare; credere, ritenere; *and so — all of us*, la pensiamo anche noi così.
**sayer** *n.* dicitore.
**saying** *n.* proverbio, detto, massima; *as the — goes*, come dice il proverbio; *the doings and -s of*, vita, morte e miracoli di.
**scab** *n.* crosta; (vet.) rogna, scabbia; (pol.) crumiro.
**scabbard** *n.* fodero, guaina.
**scabies** *n.* (med.) scabbia.

**scabious** *n.* (bot.) scabbiosa.
**scabrous** *adj.* scabro; scabroso.
**scaffold** *n.* impalcatura; tribuna; patibolo, forca. **-ing** impalcatura, incastellatura, ponteggio.
**scald** *n.* scottatura; *tr.*, *intr.* scottare; ustionare; bruciare; sterilizzare con acqua bollente. **-ing** *adj.* bollente; bruciante, scottante; *gerund* lo scottare; *n.* scottatura.
**scale**[1] *n.* piatto di bilancia; *pl.* bilancia; bascula; *to tip the -s*, fare appendere la bilancia; (astron.) *the Scales*, la Libra, La Bilancia; *to hold the -s even*, mantenere l'equilibrio; essere imparziali; *tr.* pesare; soppesare; bilanciar ; (hor e-racing) venir pesato.
**scale**[2] *n.* scaglia, squama, lamella; (on metals) scoria, incrostazione, ossido; (fig.) *to remove the -s from someone's eyes*, togliere il velo dagli occhi di qualcuno; *tr.* squamare; crostare; *intr.* squamarsi; incrostarsi; *to — off*, scrostarsi.
**scale**[3] *n.* scala, misura, gradazione; *in —*, in gradazione; *to —*, secondo le proporzioni; (phys.; geog.; math.; mus.) scala; *to practise -s on the piano*, fare esercizi di scale al pianoforte; *sliding —*, scala mobile; *tr.* assalire con scale; (fig.) raggiungere il sommo di; *to — down*, diminuire.
**scalene** *adj.*, *n.* (geom.; anat.) scaleno.
**scaliness** *n.* squamosità.
**scallop** *n.* (zool.) pettine *m.*; conchiglia; (cul.) conchiglia; (needlew.) dentellatura, festone *m.*, smerlo.
**scallywag** *n.* fannullone *m.*, mascalzone *m.*
**scalp** *n.* (anat.) cuoio capelluto; (fig.) cotenna, trofeo.
**scalpel** *n.* (surg.) scalpello, bisturi *m indecl.*
**scaly** *adj.* squamoso.
**scamp** *n.* farabutto, furfante *m.*, mascalzone *m.*; (of child) birichino, furfantello; *tr.* abborracciare; *-ed work*, lavoro fatto in modo inadeguato.
**scamper** *n.* corsa rapida; galoppata; *intr.* correre, sgambettare, scorrazzare; *to — away*, darsela a gambe.
**scan** *tr.* misurare, scandire; esaminare, scrutare, sondare; *to — the horizon*, scrutare l'orizzonte; *to — someone's face*, scrutare il viso di qualcuno; *to — the newspaper*, scorrere velocemente il giornale; *intr.* essere metricamente esatto; *this line doesn't —*, questo verso non si può scandire.
**scandal** *n.* scandalo; onta, vergogna; *to create a —*, provocare uno scandalo; *to talk —*, fare della maldicenza; *The School for Scandal*, La Scuola della Maldicenza. **-monger** *n.* maldicente *m.*, *f.*, mala lingua.
**scandalize** *intr.* scandalizzare; disgustare; *to be -d*, scandalizzarsi.
**scandalous** *adj.* scandaloso, vergognoso.
**Scandinavia** *pr.n.* (geog.) Scandinavia. **-n** *adj.*, *n.* scandinavo.
**scanner** *n.* (telev.) dispositivo di esplorazione.
**scanning** *gerund* lo scrutare; l'esplorare; *n.* (prosod.) scansione.
**scansion** *n.* (prosod.) scansione.
**scant** *adj.* scarso, insufficiente; magro, povero. **-ily** *adv.* scarsamente; sommariamente; *-ily dressed*, vestito succintamente. **-iness** *n.* insufficienza; scarsezza; ristrettezza. **-y** *adj.* scarso, insufficiente; esiguo; *-y meal*, pasto frugale; *in -y attire*, in tenuta succinta.
**scape-goat** *n.* capro espiatorio. **-grace** *n.* scapestrato, cattivo soggetto; monello incorreggibile.
**scapul-a** *n.* (anat.) scapola. **-ar, -ary** *adj.* (anat.) scapolare; *n.* (eccl.) scapolare.
**scar** *n.* cicatrice; sfregio; *tr.* cicatrizzare; sfregiare; butterare; *intr.* cicatrizzarsi.
**scarab** *n.* (entom.; archeol.) scarabeo.
**scarce** *adj.* scarso; insufficiente; raro; (fam.) *to make oneself —*, tagliare la corda; *adv.* appena, a fatica.
**scarcely** *adv.* appena; a fatica, a mala pena; *— anyone*, quasi nessuno; *— ever*, raramente, quasi mai; *he could — speak*, poteva a mala pena parlare; *he is — fifteen years old*, non ha più di quindici anni. *n.* **scarceness, scarcity** *n.* scarsezza, penuria, carestia; rarità.
**scare** *n.* sgomento, spavento, panico; *to raise a —*, provocare panico; (fam.) *you did give me a —!*, che spaghetto mi hai fatto prendere!; *tr.* spaventare, sgomentare; *to be -d to death*, avere una fifa da morire; *to be -d stiff of*, avere una paura matta di. **-crow** *n.* spaventapasseri *m.*; (fig.) spauracchio. **-monger** *n.* allarmista *m.*, *f.*
**scarf** *n.* sciarpa; fascia; cravattone *m.*; (eccl.) stola.
**scarif-y** *tr.* (surg.) scarificare. smuovere; (colloq.) intimorire, **-ication** *n.* (surg.) scarificazione.
**scarlatina** *n.* (med.) scarlattina.
**scarlet** *adj.* scarlatto, porporino; *to blush —*, arrossire; *n.* color scarlatto; (med.) *— fever*, scarlattina; (bot.) *— runner*, fagiuolo di Spagna.
**scarp** *n.* scarpata; declivio.
**scarred** *adj.* segnato di cicatrici; (fig.) sfregiato.
**scatheless** *adj.* indenne; illeso; sano e salvo; *he did not get away —*, vi ha lasciato le penne.
**scathing** *adj.* sarcastico, mordace, caustico; *— criticism*, critica purgente.
**scatter** *tr.* spargere; sparpagliare; disseminare; *to — seeds*, seminare; mettere in fuga, disperdere; *the police -ed the crowd*, la polizia disperse la folla; *intr.* disperdersi; sfollarsi. **-brained** *adj.* scervellato; distratto. **-ed** *adj.* sparso, disseminato, disperso, sparpagliato.
**scavenge** *tr.* spazzare; raccogliere spazzatura. **-r** *n.* (zool.) animale che si ciba di rifiuti; (fig.) spazzino.
**scenario** *n.* (cinem.) sceneggiatura, scenario.
**scene** *n.* (theatr.) scena; *the — is laid in Venice*, la scena è ambientata a Venezia; (fig.) scena, episodio; *to appear on the —*, entrare in scena; *behind the -s*, dietro le quinte; vista, veduta; panorama *m.*, spettacolo; colpo d'occhio; *a change of —*, un cambiamento d'ambiente; (fam.) *don't make a —!*, non fare una scenata!
**scene-painter** *n.* scenografo. **-shifter** *n.* macchinista di scena.
**scenery** *n.* (theatr.) scena, scenario; prospettiva, veduta; panorama *m.*; *mountain —*, paesaggi di montagna.
**scenic** *adj.* scenico; teatrale.
**scent** *n.* odore *m.*, profumo, essenza; traccia, pista; *to get the — of*, aver sentore di; *to throw off the —*, far perdere la traccia, deviare i sospetti; *tr.* fiutare, annusare, seguire la traccia di; (fig.) sospettare, subodorare; *— out*, scoprire. **-ed** *adj.* profumato; odorante.
**sceptic** *n.* scettico. **-al** *adj.* scettico. **-ism** *n.* scetticismo.
**sceptre** *n.* scettro.
**schedule** *n.* catalogo, distinta, elenco, lista; (fig.) *according to —*, secondo il previsto; *tr.* comporre un catalogo di; elencare.
**Scheldt** *pr.n.* (geog.) Scelda.
**schema** *n.* schema *m.* **-tic(al)** *adj.* schematico.
**scheme** *n.* schema *m.*; *n.* piano, progetto, disegno, sistema *m.*; *to draw up a — of work*, tracciare un piano di lavoro; *colour-scheme*, combinazione di colore; *tr.* progettare, fare il piano di; (pejor.) macchinare, tramare. **-r** *n.* chi fa dei piani; (pejor.) affarista *m.*, *f.*, intrigante *m.*, *f.*
**schism** *n.* scisma *m.* **-atic** *adj.*, *n.* scismatico.
**schist** *n.* (geol.) schisto.
**schizoid** *adj.*, *n.* (med.) schizoide *m.*, *f.*
**schizophren-ia** *n.* (med.) schizofrenia. **-ic** *adj.*, *n.* (med.) schizofrenico.
**scholar** *n.* scolaro; borsista *m.*, *f.*;

(Univ.) studioso, dotto, erudito. **-ly** *adj.* dotto, erudito. **-ship** *n.* dottrina, sapere, erudizione; (school, Univ.) borsa di studio.
**scholastic** *adj.*, *n.* scolastico. **-ism** scolasticismo.
**scholiast** *n.* scoliaste *m.*, chiosatore.
**school**[1] *n.* scuola; *boarding-school*, collegio, convitto; *day-school*, scuola diurna; *primary* —, scuola elementare; *secondary* —, scuola media; *high* —, *grammar* —, *comprehensive* —, scuola media superiore, liceo; *infant* —, asilo; (in England) *preparatory* —, scuola che prepara alla 'public school'; (in England) *public* —, scuola privata, collegio per l'insegnamento secondario; (in England) *Sunday* —, scuola domenicale per l'insegnamento religioso; *attrib.* — *report*, pagella; — *term*, trimestre *m.*; (fig.) *of the old* —, di vecchio stampo; *tr.* istruire; addestrare, ammaestrare.
**school**[2] *n.* (of fish) banco.
**school-book** *n.* libro di testo. **-boy** *n.* scolaro, collegiale *m.* **-fellow, -friend** *n.* compagno di scuola. **-girl** *n.* scolara, collegiale *f.*
**schooling** *n.* istruzione, educazione, disciplina scolastica.
**school-master** *n.* maestro, insegnante *m.* **-mistress** *n.* maestra, insegnante *f.* **-room** *n.* aula scolastica. **-teacher** *n.* insegnante *m.*, *f.* **-teaching** *n.* insegnamento.
**schooner** *n.* goletta.
**schottische** *n.* danza scozzese.
**sciatica** *n.* (med.) sciatica.
**science** *n.* scienza; *man of* —, scienzato; tecnica, abilità; — *fiction*, letteratura di fantascienza.
**scientific** *adj.* scientifico.
**scientist** *n.* scienziato; scienziata.
**Scilly Isles** *pr.n.* (geog.) Isole Sorlinghe.
**scimitar** *n.* scimitarra.
**scintillat-e** *intr.* scintillare, brillare. **-ion** *n.* scintillo; sfavillìo.
**scion** *n.* rampollo; discendente *m.*
**scission** *n.* scissione; divisione.
**scissors** *n.pl.* forbici *f.pl.*, cesoie *f.pl.*; *nail-scissors*, forbicine da unghie.
**scissors-grinder** *n.* arrotino.
**sclero-sis** *n.* (med.) sclerosi *f.* **-tic** *adj.* sclerotico.
**scoff** *tr.* beffare; deridere, schernire; *intr.* *to* — *at*, farsi beffe di; *to be -ed at*, essere deriso. **-er** *n.* schernitore. **-ing** *adj.* derisorio; beffardo; *n.* derisione, scherno.
**scold** *n.* (donna) bisbetica, brontolona; *tr.* sgridare; rimproverare; *intr.* parlare in tono adirato. **-ing** *n.* sgridata; rimprovero; *to give someone a -ing*, dare una lavata di testa a qualcuno.
**sconce**[1] *n.* candeliere *m.* con manico, candelabro a muro.
**sconce**[2] *n.* (Oxford) penalità di birra imposta per infrazione alle regole d'etichetta a tavola; *tr.* (Oxford) multare di un boccale di birra; *to be -ed*, essere costretto a pagare da bere.
**scon(e)** *n.* pasticcino.
**scoop** *n.* pala, paletta; ramaiuolo, mestolo; palettata, mestolata; (fig.) colpo; notizia in esclusiva; *tr.* scavare; — *up*, raccogliere con la pala; (journ.) procacciarsi una notizia in esclusiva.
**scoot** *intr.* (fam.) andarsene rapidamente, guizzar via.
**scooter** *n.* monopattino; scooter *m. indecl.*, motoretta.
**scope** *n.* possibilità, opportunità; portata; *to be beyond the* — *of*, esulare dalla possibilità di; prospettiva, sfera, campo; *to extend one's* —, allargare il proprio campo d'azione; *to give free* —, dare piena libertà d'azione.
**scorbutic** *adj.*, *n.* (med.) scorbutico.
**scorch** *n.* bruciatura, scottatura superficiale; *tr.* bruciacchare; riardere; *intr.* bruciacchiarsi; (fam.) andare a forte velocità; bruciare le tappe. **-er** *n.* che brucia; (slang) giornata caldissima. **-ing** *adj.* bruciante, ardente; (fig.) caustico, mordace, pungente.
**score** *n.* tacca, scanalatura, sfregio; conto, debito; *death pays all -s*, la morte salda tutti i conti; *he paid his* —, pagò i debiti; *he paid off old -s*, regolò vecchi conti; ragione, causa, motivo; *on that* —, a questo riguardo; *to be excused on the* — *of illness*, essere scusato a causa di malattia; ventina; *half a* —, una decina; *two* —, quaranta; *three* — (*years*) *and ten*, settanta anni; *-s of*, una gran quantità di; (sport) punti, *what's the* —?, qual è il punteggio?; *to keep the* —, segnare il punteggio; (mus.) spartito, partitura.
**score** *tr.* intaccare, intagliare, segnare; (sport) *they -d five points*, fecero cinque punti; *to* — *a goal*, segnare una rete; (mus.) orchestrare, arrangiare; (fig.) assicurarsi; *to* — *a success*, riportare un successo; *intr.* (sport) fare dei punti; (of a scorer) segnare il punteggio; (slang) *to* — *off*, avere la meglio su.
**scorer** *n.* (sport) segnatore.
**scoria** *n.* scoria.
**scoring** *n.* (mus.) orchestrazione, arrangiamento; (sport) punteggio.
**scorn** *n.* disprezzo, disdegno, scherno; *to laugh to* —, deridere, schernire; *tr.* disprezzare, disdegnare; *to* — *to do something*, disdegnare di fare qualcosa.
**scornful** *adj.* sprezzante; sdegnoso; *to be* — *of*, disprezzare. **-ness** *n.* sdegnosità, disdegno, disprezzo.
**scorpion** *n.* (zool.) scorpione *m.*
**Scot**[1] *n.* scozzese *m.*, *f.*; (hist.) scoto; *Mary, Queen of Scots*, Maria Stuarda; *the Picts and the Scots*, i Pitti e gli Scoti.
**scot**[2] *n.* (bill) scotto, tassa. **-free** *adj.* impunito; *to go -free*, scavarsela bene, passarla liscia.
**Scotch** *adj.* scozzese; — *broth*, zuppa di orzo e verdura; — *egg*, uovo sodo circondato da salsiccia; — *fir*, pino silvestre; — *mist*, pioggerella; — *whisky*, whisky scozzese.
**Scots** *adj.* scozzese. **-man** *n.* scozzese *m.* **-woman** *n.* scozzese *f.*
**Scottish** *adj.* scozzese; *he is* —, è scozzese.
**scoundrel** *n.* furfante *m.*, farabutto, mascalzone *m.* **-ly** *adj.* furfante, ribaldo, infame.
**scour**[1] *tr.* fregare, sfregare, stropicciare, strofinare, lucidare, pulire; (fig.) spazzar via.
**scour**[2] *intr.* correre velocemente, muoversi rapidamente; *tr.* percorrere, perlustrare.
**scourge** *n.* flagello, castigo, punizione; *the* — *of war*, il flagello della guerra; sferza; *tr.* castigare, punire; sferzare.
**scout**[1] *n.* esploratore, ricognitore; *boy* —, giovane esploratore; (fam.) individuo, tipo; (Oxford) inserviente *m.*, *f.*; *intr.* andare in ricognizione.
**scout**[2] *tr.* respingere con disprezzo; *to* — *a suggestion*, respingere sdegnosamente un suggerimento.
**scouting** *n.* esplorazione; scoutismo.
**scow** *n.* zattera, chiatta.
**scowl** *n.* cipiglio, sguardo torvo; *intr.* aggrottare le ciglia, lanciare occhiate torve; *to* — *at*, guardare di sbieco. **-ing** *adj.* torvo, accigliato.
**scrabble**[1] *tr.* raschiare, grattare.
**Scrabble**[2] *n.* (trademark) nome di un giuoco di tavolo.
**scrag** *n.* (cul.) collottola; *tr.* (slang) torcere il collo a, strangolare; (rugby) afferrare per il collo.
**scragg-y** *adj.* ossuto, scarno, scheletrico; (cul.) magro. **-iness** *n.* magrezza scheletrica.
**scramble** *n.* arrampicata, scalata; gara, lotta; tafferuglio, parapiglia; *intr.* arrampicarsi con mani e piedi, inerpicarsi; *to* — *up the hill*, arrampicarsi su per la collina; *to* — *for*, affannarsi per; *tr.* (cul.) *to* — *eggs*, strapazzare delle uova.
**scrap**[1] *n.* pezzetto; *not a* —, niente affatto; scarti *m.pl.*, rottame *m.*; *-book*, album *m.*; *tr.* scartare, mettere fuori servizio, smantellare.

**scrap**[2] *n.* (slang) litigio, baruffa; *intr.* litigare.
**scrap-heap** *n.* mucchio di rifiuti. **-iron** *n.* rottame di ferro.
**scrape** *n.* graffio, scalfittura; suono prodotto da una raschiatura; (fig.) impiccio, imbroglio; *he is always getting into -s,* si mette sempre nei guai; *to get out of a —,* togliersi da impiccio; *tr.* grattare, scrostare, raschiare; *to — one's plate,* leccare il piatto; *to — a ship's bottom,* raschiare la carena di una nave; *the boat -d her side against a rock,* la barca strisciò il fianco contro una roccia; *to — together a few pounds,* raggranellare alcune sterline; *to — acquaintance with,* riuscire ad introdursi presso; *to — a living,* sbarcare il lunario; *to — a violin,* strimpellare il violino; *to — out,* scavare; *to — up,* raccogliere, racimolare; *intr. to bow and —,* fare salamecchi; *to — through,* cavarsela; *to — through an examination,* passare ad un esame per il buco della serratura.
**scraper** *n.* raschiatoio, raschietto.
**scrapp-y** *adj.* frammentario. **-iness** *n.* frammentarietà.
**scratch**[1] *adj.* messo insieme in fretta; *— team,* squadra eterogenea.
**scratch**[2] *n.* graffiatura; graffio, leggera ferita, scalfittura; grattata, grattatina; (sport) zero; *to start from —,* partire da zero; *to come up to —,* mostrarsi all'altezza della situazione; *tr.* graffiare; *to — out,* cancellare; (fig.) *to — the surface of,* sfiorare appena; *to — one's head,* grattarsi la testa; *intr.* essere spinoso; (sport) ritirarsi da una gara.
**scrawl** *n.* scarabocchio, sgorbio; *tr., intr.* scarabocchiare, imbrattare; scribacchiare, scrivere in modo illegibile.
**scrawny** *adj.* magro, scarno.
**scream** *n.* grido acuto, strillo, urlo; (fam.) *what a — !,* che buffo!; *tr., intr.* gridare, strillare, urlare; ridere senza ritegno.
**scree** *n.* (geol.) ghiaione *m.*
**screech** *n.* grido, strillo acuto; (fig.) stridio, stridore *m.*; *tr., intr.* gridare; strillare; (fig.) stridore.
**screech-owl** *n.* (orn.) barbagianni.
**screed** *n.* lunga filastrocca.
**screen** *n.* paravento; (archit.) transenna, parete divisoria; (mech.) vaglio, crivello; (fig.) riparo, protezione, cortina, schermo; *under the — of night,* col favore della notte; (mil.) truppe di copertura; (naut.) scorta (di convoglio); (cinem.; telev.) schermo; *smoke —,* cortina di fumo; *tr.* riparare, proteggere; fornire di schermo; (fig.) mettere al coperto, nascondere; selezionare, vagliare; *to — off,* separare con paravento.
**screenings** *n.pl.* materiale vagliato, scarti di vagliatura.
**screw** *n.* vite *f.*; *a turn of the —,* un giro di vite; (fam.) *to have a — loose,* avere una rotella fuori posto; *to put the — on,* esercitare pressione su; (naut.) elica; vapore ad elica; (billiards) effetto; (horse) ronzino; *tr.* avvitare, stringere, serrare; *to — tight,* avvitare ben stretto; (fam.) *to have one's head -ed on the right way,* avere la testa a posto; *to — back,* rimbalzare all'indietro; *to — in,* avvitare, fare entrare a forza; *to — up,* serrare con vite; (fig.) torcere, contorcere, chiudere rapidamente; *she -ed up her eyes,* strizzò gli occhi; *to — up one's courage,* prendere il coraggio a due mani; (slang) possedere sessualmente. **-driver** *n.* caccivite *m.* **-ed** *adj.* a vite, avvitato.
**scribble** *n.* sgorbio, scarabocchio; *tr., intr.* sgorbiare, scarabocchiare, scribacchiare. **-r** *n.* scribacchino, imbrattacarte *m.*
**scribe** *n.* copista *m.*, amanuense *m.*; (bibl.) scriba *m.*; (hist.) scrivano pubblico.
**scrimmage** *n.* baruffa, schermaglia.
**scrimshanker** *n.* (mil. slang) scansafatiche *m. indecl.*
**scrip**[1] *n.* biscaccia.
**scrip**[2] pezzo di carta; (finan.) certificato provvisorio; azioni *f.pl.*; titoli *m.pl.*
**script** *n.* scrittura a mano; (theatr.) testo, copione *m.*
**Scriptur-e** *n.* la Sacra Scrittura, la Bibbia. **-al** *adj.* concernente la Sacra Scrittura; biblico.
**scrivener** *n.* scrivano pubblico; notaio.
**scroful-a** *n.* (med.) scrofola. **-ous** *adj.* scrofuloso.
**scroll** *n.* rotolo; (archit.) decorazione a spirale; voluta; cartoccio; (of violin) chiocciola.
**scrot-um** *n.* (anat.) scroto. **-al** *adj.* scrotale.
**scrounge** *tr.* (slang) rubacchiare; scroccare; *intr.* scroccare; (fam.) *to — around for,* andare alla ricerca di. **-r** *n.* ladruncolo, scroccone *m.*, scroccona.
**scrub**[1] *n.* (bot.) sottobosco, macchia.
**scrub**[2] *n.* spazzolata, lavata, pulitura a fondo; *tr.* pulire fregando forte, fregare; (fam.) biffare; (chem.) lavare. **-ber** *n.* chi pulisce fregando forte; (slang) donnaccia squallida. **-bing** *n.* fregamento; lavaggio energico; una buona lavata. **scrubbing-brush** *n.* spazzola dura.
**scruff** *n.* nuca, collottola; *to take by the — of the neck,* prendere per la collottola; (fam.) monello. **-y** *adj.* trasandato, malmesso.
**scrum(mage)** *n.* (rugby) mischia.
**scrumptious** *adj.* (fam.) delizioso.
**scrunch** *n.* scricchiolìo, il cricchiare; *tr.* schiacciare rumorosamente; *intr.* scricchiolare.
**scruple** *n.* scrupolo; dubbio; incertezza; *to have -s about,* farsi scrupolo di; *intr.* avere scrupoli, esitare, farsi scrupolo (di).
**scrupulous** *adj.* scrupoloso; meticoloso; pignolo. **-ness, scrupulosity** *n.* scrupolosità; meticolosità; pedanteria.
**scrutator** *n.* investigatore.
**scrutineer** *n.* scrutatore.
**scrutiniz-e** *tr.* scrutinare, scrutare; esaminare minuziosamente.
**scrutiniz-er** *n.* scrutatore. **-ing** *adj.* scrutinatore, inquisitivo; *n.* esame minuzioso.
**scrutiny** *n.* esame minuzioso, esame critico; *to bear —,* essere ineccepibile.
**scud** *intr.* correre velocemente, guizzar via, fuggir via; (naut.) *to — along,* navigare (in direzione del vento).
**scuff** *tr., intr.* strascicare (i piedi).
**scuffle** *n.* zuffa, tafferuglio, rissa, mischia; strascichìo; *intr.* azzuffarsi; picchiarsi.
**scull** *n.* palella, bratto; *intr.* vogare con remi a palella.
**scullery** *n.* retrocucina, acquaio. **-boy** *n.* (hist.) sguattero. **-maid** *n.* (hist.) sguattera.
**scullion** *n.* (hist.) sguattero.
**sculptor** *n.* scultore *m.*, scultrice *f.*
**sculptur-e** *n.* scultura; *tr.* scolpire. **-al** *adj.* scultoreo, di scultura; *-al beauty,* bellezza scultorea. **-esque** *adj.* scutoreo, statuario.
**scum** *n.* schiuma, spuma; feccia; (metall.) scoria.
**scumble** *n.* (paint.) smorzatura di tinte, sfumatura di contorni; *tr.* smorzare; sfumare.
**scupper** *n.* (naut.) ombrinale *m.*; *tr.* (naut.) affondare; (fig.) annientare.
**scurf** *n.* forfora. **-iness** *n.* tendenza alla formazione di forfora. **-y** *adj.* forforoso.
**scurrilous** *adj.* scurrile; triviale. **-ness** *n.* scurrilità; trivialità.
**scurry** *intr.* affrettarsi a piccoli passi, sgambettare.
**scurv-y** *adj.* spregevole, meschino, basso; *n.* scorbuto. **-iness** *n.* bassezza, meschinità, piccineria.
**scut** *n.* (of rabbit) codino.
**scutcheon** *see* **escutcheon.**
**scuttle**[1] *n.* secchio per carbone.
**scuttle**[2] *n.* (naut.) portellino, boccaportella; *tr.* produrre falle in una nave per affondarla; (fig.) *intr. to — away,* fuggire, eclissarsi.
**scythe** *n.* falce *f.*; *tr.* falciare.
**sea** *n.* mare *m.*; oceano; *at the bottom of the —,* in fondo al mare;

*at* —, in mare; *far out to* —, in alto mare; *Brighton is on the* —, Brighton è sul mare; (fig.) *to be all at* —, perdere la bussola; *to travel by* —, viaggiare per mare; *to be between the devil and the deep blue* —, essere fra l'incudine e il martello; *to put out to* —, prendere il largo; *to go to* —, diventar marinaio; *the Black Sea*, il Mar Nero; *the Caspian Sea*, il Mar Caspio; *the Dead Sea*, il Mar Morto; *the Mediterranean Sea*, il Mare Mediterraneo; *the North Sea*, il Mare del Nord; *inland* —, mare interno; onda, ondata, cavallone *m.*; (fig.) *a — of faces*, un mare di facce; *a — of troubles*, un mare di guai; (fam.) *half -s over*, alquanto brillo.

**sea-bathing** *n.* bagni di mare. **-breeze** *n.* brezza marina. **-food** *n.* frutti di mare, pesce. **-front** *n.* lungomare *m.* **-girt** *adj.* circondato dal mare. **-going** *adj.* che veleggia in alto mare, adatto per le grandi traversate. **-green** *adj.* verde mare. **-gull** *n.* gabbiano. **-kale** *n.* cavolo di mare. **-legs** *n.pl.* capacità di tenersi in equilibrio; *to find one's -legs*, acquistare la capacità di mantenersi in equilibrio (su una nave). **-level** *n.* livello del mare. **-lion** *n.* (zool.) otaria, leone marino. **-mew** *n.* gabbiano. **-mile** *n.* miglio marittimo. **-monster** *n.* mostro marino. **-power** *n.* potenza navale. **-scout** *n.* giovane esploratore di mare. **-urchin** *n.* (zool.) riccio di mare. **-wall** *n.* diga marittima. **-water** *n.* acqua di mare.

**sea-bird** *n.* uccello marino. **-board** *n.* costa, litorale *m.* **-coast** *n.* costa.

**seafar-er** *n.* navigante *m.*, navigatore, uomo di mare. **-ing** *adj.* di mare, marinaro; *n.* viaggi per mare.

**seahorse** *n.* (ichth.) ippocampo, cavalluccio marino; (zool.) tricheco.

**seal**[1] *n.* (zool.) foca.

**seal**[2] *n.* sigillo; timbro; *removal of the -s*, rimozione dei sigilli; *to affix the* —, apporre il sigillo; *Great Seal of England*, Gran Sigillo d'Inghilterra; *Keeper of the Seals*, Guardasigilli *m.*; *Privy Seal*, Sigillo Reale; *given under my hand and* —, da me sottoscritto e sigillato; *to set one's — on*, autorizzare, dare la propria approvazione a; (fig.) sigillo, suggello; vincolo; marchio; *under the — of privacy*, sotto il vincolo del segreto; *tr.* sigillare; chiudere ermeticamente; *to — an envelope*, sigillare una busta; *to — a bargain*, suggellare un patto. **-ed** *part. adj.* sigillato; (fig.) ermetico, misterioso; *-ed book*, mistero.

**sealing**[1] *n.* caccia alla foca.

**sealing**[2] *n.* suggellamento, impronta del sigillo, piombatura. **-tape** *n.* nastro di carta gommata. **-wax** *n.* ceralacca.

**sealskin** *n.* pelle di foca.

**seam**[1] *n.* cucitura, costura, giuntura, linea di giunzione; (miner.; geol.) strato, vana, banco, filone *m.*; *tr.* unire con cucitura; (fig.) rigare, segnare.

**seaman** *n.* marinaio, uomo di mare; *able* —, marinaio scelto. **-like** *adj.* marinesco, proprio di marinaio. **-ship** *n.* arte della navigazione nautica; *piece of -ship*, manovra.

**seamless** *adj.* senza giunzioni; senza cuciture; — *stockings*, calze senza cucitura.

**seamstress** *n.* cucitrice.

**seamy** *adj.* provvisto di cuciture; (fig.) *the — side*, il lato meno attraente, il rovescio della medaglia.

**séance** *n.* seduta; seduta spiritica.

**sea-plane** *n.* idroplano, idrovolante. **-port** *n.* porto marittimo. **-scape** *n.* (paint.) marina.

**sear** *adj.* (poet.) dissecato, inaridito, appassito; *tr.* disseccare, inaridire; bruciare, cauterizzare, marcare a fuoco.

**search** *n.* ricerca, indagine *f.*; *to be in — of*, essere in cerca di; (customs) perquisizione *f.*; visita doganale; *right of* —, diritto di perquisizione; *tr.* perlustrare, perquisire, frugare; *to — a house*, perquisire una casa; (fig.) ricercare, frugare; *to — one's memory*, frugare nella memoria; (fam.) *— me!*, chi lo sa!; *to — after*, andare in cerca di, ricercare; *to — for*, cercare; *to — out*, scovare.

**searcher** *n.* ricercatore, ricercatrice; *a — after truth*, un ricercatore della verità.

**searching** *adj.* indagatore, inquisitorio, scrutatore; *a — glance*, uno sguardo indagatore; *a — examination*, un esame minuzioso; *n.* ricerca; esame *m.*; perlustrazione.

**searchlight** *n.* riflettore.

**search-warrant** *n.* mandato di perquisizione.

**seashore** *n.* spiaggia, lido, litorale *m.*

**seasick** *adj.* *to be* —, avere il mal di mare. **-ness** *n.* mal di mare.

**seaside** *n.* spiaggia, riva del mare, marina; *to go to the* —, andare al mare; — *resort*, stazione balneare.

**season** *n.* stagione *f.*; *the four -s*, le quattro stagioni; *compliments of the* —, auguri stagionali; *peaches are now in* —, ora è la stagione delle pesche; *out of* —, fuori stagione; (fig.) a sproposito, intempestivo; *a word in* —, un consiglio dato al momento opportuno; *tr.* stagionare; condire; rendere piccante; *highly-seasoned*, assai piccante. **-able** *adj.* di stagione; *-able weather*, clima di stagione; (fig.) *-able advice*, consiglio opportuno. **-al** *adj.* stagionale, di stagione. **-ed** *adj.* stagionato; (fig.) esperto. **-ing** *n.* stagionatura; (cul.) condimento.

**season-ticket** *n.* biglietto in abbonamento; — *holder*, abbonato *m.*, abbonata *f.*

**seat** *n.* sedile *m.*; posto; sedia; *corner* —, posto d'angolo; *keep your -s*, rimanete seduti, state al vostro posto; *to take a* —, accomodarsi; (rlwy.) *take your -s!*, in vettura!; *to win a — in Parliament*, vincere un seggio; residenza di campagna, villa, castello; (equit.) modo di stare in sella; (fig.) sede *f.*, centro; sedere *m.*, deretano; (of trousers) fondo.

**seat** *tr.* mettere a sedere, far sedere; *how many people can this theatre —?*, di quanti posti è fornito questo teatro?; *rfl.* mettersi a sedere; accomodarsi; *please be -ed*, s'accomodi, accomodatevi.

**seating** *n.* provvisione di posti; — *capacity*, numero di posti a sedere; (mech.) sede *f.*

**seaward** *adj.* che va verso il mare; *adv. to* —, in direzione del mare.

**seaward(s)** *adv.* verso il mare.

**seaweed** *n.* alga marina, fuco; varecchi *m.pl.*

**seaworth-y** *adj.* atto a tenere il mare. **-iness** *n.* capacità di tenere il mare.

**sebacious** *adj.* sebaceo.

**seborrh(o)ea** *n.* (med.) seborrea.

**secant** *adj.*, *n.* (geom.) secante *m.*

**secede** *intr.* separarsi; ritirarsi.

**secession** *n.* separazione. **-ism** *n.* separatismo. **-ist** *n.* secessionista *m.*, *f.*, separatista *m.*, *f.*

**seclud-e** *tr.* appartare; isolare. **-ed** *adj.* appartato; isolato; solitario; *a -ed life*, una vita ritirata.

**seclusion** *n.* isolamento; solitudine; *to live in* —, vivere in solitudine *f.*

**second**[1] *n.* secondo; istante *m.*

**second**[2] *adj.* secondo; *the — day of the month*, il due del mese; *the — of July*, il due luglio; *Charles the Second*, Carlo Secondo; *in the — place*, in secondo luogo; *on — thoughts*, ripensandoci meglio; (pol.) — *chamber*, camera alta; (motor.) — *gear*, la seconda marcia; (mus.) — *violin*, secondo violino; — *lieutenant*, sottotenente *m.*; *n.* secondo; *a good* —, un buon secondo; — *in command*, vicecomandante *m.*; (naval) ufficiale in seconda; (in duel) secondo, padrino; (boxing) secondo.

**second**[2] *tr.* assecondare; *to — a motion*, appoggiare una mozione.

**seco·nd**[3] *tr.* (mil.) distaccare dal regimento; trasferire temporaneamente.

**secondary** *adj.* secondario; — *school*, scuola media.
**second-best** *adj.* secondo per qualità; *to come off* —, avere la peggio.
**second-hand**[1] *adj.* di seconda mano.
**second-hand**[2] *n.* lancetta dei secondi.
**second-rate** *adj.* di seconda categoria, mediocre.
**secrecy** *n.* segretezza; *to bind to* —, impegnare al segreto.
**secret** *adj.* segreto; *n.* segreto; *to keep a* —, mantenere un segreto; *an open* —, il segreto di Pulcinella; *top* —, riservatissimo.
**secretaire** *n.* scrittoio, scrivania.
**secretarial** *adj.* segretariale.
**secretariat** *n.* segretariato, segreteria.
**secretary** *n.* segretario *m.*; segretaria; *Secretary of State*, Ministro Segretario di Stato; *Home Secretary*, Ministro degli Interni; (orn.) — *bird*, serpentario. **-ship** *n.* segretariato.
**secrete**[1] *tr.* (phys.) secernere.
**secrete**[2] *tr.* occultare; nascondere.
**secretion** *n.* (phys.) secrezione.
**secretive** *adj.* riservato; reticente. **-ness** *n.* riservatezza; reticenza.
**secretness** *n.* segretezza.
**secretory** *adj.* (phys.) secretorio; *n.* organo secretore.
**sect** *n.* setta. **-arian** *adj.*, *n.* settario. **-arianism** *n.* spirito di setta.
**section** *n.* sezione; parte *f.*; porzione; tratto; (geom.) sezione, spaccato; (bot.; zool.) suddivisione; (mil.) plotone *m.*; *tr.* sezionare.
**sector** *n.* settore *m.*
**secular** *adj.* secolare; laico; mondano; profano. **-ism** *n.* secolarismo; laicismo.
**seculariz-e** *tr.* secolarizzare, laicizzare. **-ation** *n.* secolarizzazione.
**securable** *adj.* assicurabile.
**secure** *adj.* sicuro; assicurato; *tr.* assicurare; salvaguardare; proteggere; rafforzare; (comm.) garantire; chiudere saldamente; (fig.) procurarsi.
**security** *n.* sicurezza; protezione; senso di sicurezza; garanzia, cauzione; (finan.) titoli *m.pl.*; — *device*, dispositivo di sicurezza; *social* —, previdenza sociale.
**sedan-chair** *n.* portantina.
**sedate** *adj.* posato; pacato; sereno; grave, serio. **-ness** *n.* posatezza; pacatezza; gravità, serietà.
**sedative** *adj.*, *n.* sedativo.
**sedentary** *adj.* sedentario.
**sedge** *n.* (bot.) carice *m.*, giunco. **-warbler** *n.* (orn.) forapaglie *m.*
**sediment** *n.* sedimento, deposito; (chem.) residuo. **-ary** *adj.* sedimentario. **-ation** *n.* sedimentazione.
**sedition** *n.* sedizione.
**seditious** *adj.* sedizioso. **-ness** *n.* spirito sedizioso.
**seduc-e** *tr.* sedurre; corrompere. **-er** *n.* seduttore *m.*, seduttrice *f.*
**seduction** *n.* seduzione.
**seductive** *adj.* seducente; allettante. **-ness** *n.* attrattiva.
**sedulous** *adj.* assiduo; diligente. **-ness** *n.* assiduità; diligenza.
**see**[1] *tr.*, *intr.* vedere; *as far as the eye can* —, a perdita d'occhio; *I saw him go*, l'ho visto partire; *they wonder what he sees in her*, si domandano cosa veda in lei; *she is not fit to be seen*, non è presentabile; *she will never* — *thirty again*, ha trent'anni suonati; *to have seen better days*, aver visto giorni migliori; capire, afferrare, rendersi conto di; *I* — *what you mean*, capisco quello che vuoi dire; *I saw that he didn't understand me*, mi resi conto che non mi capiva; *do you* — ?, vedi ?, capisci ?; *I* —, capisco; *to* — *daylight*, cominciare a vederci chiaro; *you can* — *for yourself*, puoi vedere da te; *let me* — *now*, mi lasci riflettere; *to* — *differently*, pensare diversamente; *to* — *eye to eye*, essere della stessa opinione; *to* — *fit to do something*, ritenere giusto fare qualcosa; — *that he comes in time*, fate in modo che arrivi in tempo; visitare, frequentare; — *you on Friday*, a venerdì; *come and* — *me next week*, venga a trovarmi la settimana ventura; accompagnare; *to* — *home*, accompagnare a casa; *to* — *about*, occuparsi di; esaminare, studiare; *to* — *through*, vedere attraverso, (fig.) penetrare, indovinare; *to* — *it through*, perseverare fino alla fine; *to* — *a person through*, essere d'appoggio a qualcuno, proteggere, aiutare; *to* — *to*, badare a, occuparsi di; *to* — *the New Year in*, aspettare l'anno nuovo; *to* — *off*, accompagnare; *to* — *out*, accompagnare alla porta, (fig.) vedere la fine di; *to* — *over*, ispezionare, esaminare, visitare.
**see**[2] *n.* (eccl.) diocesi *f.*; vescovato; arcivescovato; *the Holy See*, la Santa Sede.
**seed** *n.* seme *m.*; semenza; *to go to* —, inselvatichirsi; (fig.) lasciarsi andare, logorarsi; *to sow the* — *of rebellion*, seminare il germe della rivolta; (tennis) testa di serie; *tr.* togliere i semi da, sgranare; (sport) selezionare; *intr.* sementire.
**seedbed** *n.* semenzaio, vivaio.
**seeded** *adj.* (tennis) — *player*, testa di serie.
**seediness** *n.* abbondanza di semi; (fam.) malessere *m.*
**seeding** *n.* seminagione, semina.
**seedless** *adj.* senza semi.
**seedling** *n.* (bot.) pianticella, alberello.
**seedsman** *n.* venditore di semi.
**seedy** *adj.* pieno di semi; (fam.) sofferente, indisposto; *I feel* —, non mi sento in forma; scadente.
**seek** *tr.* cercare, andare alla ricerca di; *to* — *employment*, cercare un impiego; *the reason is not far to* —, il motivo è facile da scoprire; chiedere, domandare; tentare, cercare di; inseguire, aspirare a; *she is much sought after*, è molto corteggiata; *to* — *out*, scovare. **-er** *n.* cercatore *m.*, cercatrice *f.* **-ing** *n.* ricerca.
**seem** *intr.* sembrare; parere; aver l'aria di; *he -s to be happy*, sembra felice; *you* — *tired*, hai l'aria stanca. **-ing** *adj.* apparente; *n.* il sembrare. **-ingly** *adv.* apparentemente.
**seeml-y** *adj.* decoroso, decente, che si addice. **-iness** *n.* decenza, decoro.
**seen** *part.* of **see**, *q.v.*
**seep** *intr.* gocciolare, colare. **-age** *n.* gocciolamento, infiltrazione; colatura.
**seer** *n.* veggente *m.*, *f.*; profeta *m.*
**seesaw** *n.* altalena; *attrib.* fluttuante, ondeggiante; — *motion*, moto alternativo; *intr.* andare su e giù; (fig.) vacillare, esitare.
**seeth-e** *tr.*, *intr.* bollire, lessare; (fig.) ribollire, essere in subbuglio. **-ing** *adj.* in ebollizione; (fig.) in agitazione, in fermento.
**see-through** *adj.* trasparente.
**seg'ment** *n.* segmento; sezione; spicchio.
**segment** *tr.* dividere in segmenti. **-al, -ary** *adj.* a segmenti, segmentale. **-ation** *n.* (geom.; zool.) segmentazione; (physiol.) riproduzione per scissione.
**segregat-e** *tr.* segregare; separare. **-ion** *n.* segregazione; separazione. **-ionist** *n.* segregazionista *m.*, *f.*
**Seidlitz powder** *n.* (chem.) polvere di Seidlitz.
**seigneur** *n.* feudatorio; signore. **-ial** *adj.* da feudatorio; signorile.
**Seine**[1] *pr.n.* (geog.) Senna.
**seine**[2] *n.* (fishing) scorticaria.
**seisin** *n.* (leg.) presa di possesso.
**seismic(al)** *adj.* sismico.
**seismograph** *n.* sismografo. **-ic** *adj.* sismografico. **-y** *n.* sismografia.
**seismolog-y** *n.* sismologia. **-ic(al)** *adj.* sismologico. **-ist** *n.* sismologo.
**seizable** *adj.* afferabile; (leg.) sequestrabile, confiscabile.
**seize** *tr.* afferrare, prendere, impadronirsi di; *to* — *an opportunity*, afferrare un'occasione; *to* — *the throne*, impadronirsi del trono; *to be -d with terror*, essere preso da terrore; *to* — *upon an excuse*, prendere una scusa; (leg.) confiscare, pignorare, sequestrare; *intr.* (techn.; mech.) *to* — *up*, bloccarsi, grippare.
**seizing** *n.* atto dell'afferrare; conquista; cattura; sequestro,

confisca; (techn.; mech.) — *up*, bloccaggio, grippaggio, ingranamento.

**seizure** *n.* (leg.) confisca, sequestro; presa di processo, conquista, cattura; (med.) attacco, colpo apoplettico; (techn.; mech.) bloccaggio, grippaggio, ingranamento.

**sejant** *adj.* (herald.) sedente.

**seldom** *adv.* raramente, di rado.

**select** *adj.* scelto, selezionato; distinto; — *committee*, commissione d'inchiesta; *tr.* scegliere, eleggere. **-ion** *n.* selezione, scelta; *-ions from*, brani scelti da.

**selectiv-e** *adj.* selettivo. **-ity** *n.* capacità di scegliere; (radio) selettività.

**selectness** *n.* distinzione; raffinatezza.

**selector** *n.* sceglitore; (techn.) selettore.

**self** *n.* persona; individuo; l'io; *his second* —, il suo 'alter ego'; *now I feel my old — again*, ora ho ritrovato me stesso; *prn.* (sè) stesso; (comm.) *payable to* —, pagabile al firmatorio.

**self-** (in compounds) **-abasement** *n.* autoumiliazione. **-adjusting** *adj.* ad autoregolazione. **-appointed** *adj.* autonominato. **-assertive** *adj.* arrogante, borioso. **-assurance** *n.* sicurezza di sè. **-centred** *adj.* egocentrico. **-confidence** *n.* fiducia in sè. **-confident** *adj.* che ha fiducia in sè. **-conscious** *adj.* impacciato, imbarazzato, vergognoso. **-consciousness** *n.* imbarazzo. **-contained** *adj.* (of person) riservato, circospetto, (of thing) indipendente. **-contradictory** *adj.* che si contraddice. **-control** *n.* autocontrollo, padronanza di sè, sangue freddo. **-defence** *n.* autodifesa; **-denial** *n.* abnegazione, rinuncia a se stesso, frugalità. **-determination** *n.* autodeterminazione, autodecisione; (pol.) *right of self-determination*, diritto (di un popolo) di scegliere il proprio ordinamento. **-educated** *adj.* autodidatta. **-esteem** *n.* stima di sè, amor proprio. **-evident** *adj.* evidente, lampante, lapalissiano. **-examination** *n.* esame di coscienza, introspezione. **-explanatory** *adj.* autoesplicativo; ovvio; **-expression** *n.* autoespressione. **-governing** *adj.* indipendente, autonomo. **-government** *n.* indipendenza, autonomia. **-help** *n.* il fare da sè. **-importance** *n.* presunzione, prosopopea. **-important** *adj.* presuntuoso, arrogante. **-indulgence** *n.* intemperanza. **-inflicted** *adj.* causato da sè; *-inflicted wound*, autolesione. **-interest** *n.* interesse *m.* personale. **-loading** *adj.* (mech.) a caricamento automatico. **-opinionated** *adj.* caparbio, ostinato. **-pity** *n.* autocommiserazione. **-portrait** *n.* autoritratto. **-possessed** *adj.* padrone di sè, calmo, flemmatico. **-possession** *n.* padronanza di sè; calma, flemma. **-preservation** *n.* autoconservazione; *instinct of self-preservation*, istinto di conservazione. **-propelled** *adj.* a propulsione autonoma, semovente. **-raising** *adj.* (di farina) che contiene una certa percentuale di lievito. **-regulating** *adj.* (mech.) autoregolatore. **-respect** *n.* rispetto di sè, amor proprio. **-righteous** *adj.* farisaico. **-sacrificing** *adj.* che si sacrifica per gli altri. **-same** *adj.* assolutamente lo stesso. **-satisfaction** *n.* autocompiacimento, fatuità. **-satisfied** *adj.* contento di sè, vanesio. **-seeking** *adj.* egoista. **-service** *n.* il servirsi da sè. **-starter** *n.* avviatore automatico, motorino di avviamento. **-styled** *adj.* sedicente. **-sufficiency** *n.* autosufficenza; vanità, presunzione. **-supporting** *adj.* che si mantiene da sè, indipendente. **-taught** *adj.* autodidatta. **-willed** *adj.* ostinato, caparbio.

**selfish** *adj.* egoistico; interessato. **-ness** *n.* egoismo.

**selfless** *adj.* disinteressato; altruistico. **-ness** *n.* altruismo.

**sell**[1] *n.* (fam.) trucco, inganno; delusione, disappunto.

**sell**[2] *tr.* vendere, promuovere la vendita di, smerciare; *intr.* vendersi, avere smercio; *this book -s well*, questo libro si vende bene; *to — at a loss*, svendere, vendere in perdita; *to — by auction*, vendere all'asta; *to — by instalments*, vendere a rate; *to — on commission*, vendere a provvigione; *to — wholesale*, vendere all'ingrosso; *to — like hot cakes*, andare a ruba; *to — one's life dearly*, vendere a caro prezzo la propria vita; (slang) *sold again!*, me l'hanno fatto ancora!; *to — someone a pup*, raggirare qualcuno; (comm.) *to — off*, liquidare; *to — out*, vendere completamente; (fam.) tradire i propri principi; *to be sold out*, essere esaurito.

**seller** *n.* venditore *m.*, venditrice *f.*; *best* —, libro di successo.

**selling** *n.* vendita, smercio; — *off*, liquidazione; — *price*, prezzo di vendita.

**sell-out** *n.* (fam.) tradimento.

**selv-age, -edge** *n.* cimosa; bordo; vivagno; (geol.) salbanda.

**selves** *pl.* of **self**, *q.v.*

**semantic** *adj.* semantico. **-s** *n.* semantica.

**semaphore** *n.* semaforo.

**semblance** *n.* aspetto, apparenza, parvenza; *without the — of an excuse*, senza un gesto di scusa; somiglianza; immagine *f.*

**semé** *adj.* (herald.) seminato, punteggiato.

**semen** *n.* sperma.

**semester** *n.* semestre *m.*

**semi-** *pref.* semi-, mezzo-, metà. **-automatic**, *adj.* semiautomatico. **-darkness**, *n.* penombra, semioscurità. **-detached** *adj.* appaiato. **-grand** *adj.* a mezza coda (pianoforte) **-military**, *adj.* paramilitare. **-monthly**, *adj.* bimensile, quidicinale (di pubblicazione). **-official**, *adj.* semiufficiale, ufficioso. **-profile**, *n.* a tre quarti (di ritratto).

**semi-breve** *n.* (mus.) semibreve. **-circle** *n.* semicerchio. **-circular** *adj.* semicircolare; *-circular arch*, arco a tutto sesto. **-colon** *n.* punto e virgola. **-final** *adj.*, *n.* semifinale *f.* **-finalist** *n.* semifinalista *m.*, *f.*

**seminal** *adj.* seminale; riproduttivo.

**seminar** *n.* seminario.

**seminar-y** *n.* (eccl.) seminario. **-ist** *n.* seminarista *m.*

**semination** *n.* (bot.) seminatura, spargimento di seme.

**semi-quaver** *n.* semicroma. **-tone** *n.* semitono. **-tonic** *adj.* semitonico; *-tonic scale*, scala cromatica.

**semi-vowel** *n.* semivocale.

**semolina** *n.* semolino.

**sempiternal** *adj.* sempiterno, eterno, perpetuo.

**sempstress** *n.* cucitrice, sarta.

**senate** *n.* senato.

**senator** *n.* senatore. **-ial** *adj.* senatoriale; senatorio; *-ial dignity*, dignità senatoriale.

**send** *tr.*, *intr.* mandare, inviare, spedire; *to — coals to Newcastle*, mandare acqua al mare; (fam.) *to — someone about his business*, mandare qualcuno a quel paese; *to — flying*, scaraventare via; *to — word*, mandare un messaggio; *to — for*, (person) mandare a chiamare, (thing) mandare a prendere; *to — away*, congedare, mandar via; *to — back*, rinviare, mandare indietro; riflettere; *to — down*, far scendere, (from Univ.) espellere, (slang) mandare in carcere; *to — forth*, esalare, spandere; lanciare, gettare, emettere; *to — in*, far entrare; far pervenire; *to — in one's resignation*, inviare le proprie dimissioni; *to — off*, spedire; *to — on*, inoltrare; *to — out*, mandar fuori, far uscire, emettere; *to — round*, far circolare; *to — up*, far salire; lanciare; (slang) beffarsi di, burlare.

**sendal** *n.* zendale *m.*, zendado.

**sender** *n.* mittente *m.*, *f.*; *returned to* —, respinto al mittente.

**sending** *n.* invio; (comm.) spedizione.

**send-off** *n.* (fam.) festa d'addio. **-up** *n.* (slang) beffa, burla.
**senesc-ence** *n.* senescenza. **-ent** *adj.* senescente.
**seneschal** *n.* (hist.) siniscalco, maggiordomo.
**senil-e** *adj.* senile; — *decay*, decadimento senile. **-ity** *n.* senilità.
**senior** *adj.* più vecchio, più anziano; seniore; — *officer*, ufficiale superiore; *n.* anziano; superiore *m.*; — *clerk*, capo ufficio; — *partner*, socio dirigente. **-ity** *n.* anzianità.
**senna** *n.* (pharm.) senna; — *tea*, infuso di senna.
**sensation** *n.* senso; sensazione; impressione; colpo; *to create a* —, creare un effetto. **-al** *adj.* che dipende dai sensi; sensazionale, di grande effetto, impressionante; che fa colpo. **-alism** *n.* ricerca del sensazionale.
**sense** *n.* senso; *the five -s*, i cinque sensi; *to have a keen — of hearing*, avere l'udito fine; (fig.) facoltà mentali; *have you taken leave of your -s?*, hai perso la testa?; *to bring someone to his -s*, far rinsavire qualcuno; *common* —, buon senso, saggezza; *to talk* —, parlare con saggezza; *he has more — than to do that*, è troppo avveduto per fare ciò; senso, significato; *figurative* —, senso figurato; *in a* —, in un certo senso; *to take a common-sense view of things*, vedere il lato pratico delle cose; *tr.* intuire, avere la sensazione di; capire. **-less** *adj.* inanimato, senza conoscenza, privo di sensi; insensato, senza senno, stupido, assurdo. **-lessness** *n.* stupidità.
**sensible** *adj.* sensato; giudizioso; assennato; saggio; razionale; pratico; *a — person*, una persona giudiziosa; *be* —, sii ragionevole; — *people*, i saggi; sensibile, percettibile, che può essere percepito attraverso i sensi; notevole, considerevole; rilevante; consapevole, conscio. **-ness** *n.* buon senso; giudizio.
**sensism** *n.* (philos.) sensismo.
**sensitive** *adj.* sensibile; delicato sensorio; — *skin*, pelle delicata; *to be — to cold*, essere freddoloso; suscettibile; impressionabile. **-ness, sensitivity** *n.* sensibilità; delicatezza; *lack of sensitivity*, mancanza di sensibilità; suscettibilità, emotività.
**sensitiz-e** *tr.* sensibilizzare, rendere sensibile. **-er** *n.* (photog.) sensibilizzatore. **-ing** *n.* sensibilizzazione; (photog.) *-ing bath*, bagno sensibilizzatore.
**sensory** *adj.* sensoriale.
**sensual** *adj.* sensuale; voluttuoso; carnale; libidinoso. **-ity** *n.* sensualità; lascivia.
**sensuous** *adj.* voluttuoso; dei sensi; inebriante. **-ness** *n.* sensualità; voluttà.
**sent** *p.def., part.* of **send,** *q.v.*
**sentence** *n.* (leg.) giudizio, sentenza; condanna; pena; — *of death*, condanna a morte; *to pass (a)* —, pronunciare una condanna, condannare; *life* —, ergastolo; (grammar) frase *f.*; *tr.* pronunciare una condanna contro, condannare; *to — to two months' imprisonment*, condannare a due mesi di carcere.
**sententious** *adj.* sentenzioso; aforistico. **-ness** *n.* sentenziosità; tono sentenzioso.
**senti-ence** *n.* sensibilità, facoltà di sentire. **-ent** *adj.* senziente; sensibile; cosciente.
**sentiment** *n.* sentimento; *noble -s*, sentimenti nobili; opinione, parere, idea; sentimentalità, sentimentalismo.
**sentimental** *adj.* sentimentale; tenero; patetico; romantico; sentimentale, lacrimoso. **-ism** *n.* sentimentalismo. **-ity** *n.* sentimentalità.
**sentinel** *n.* sentinella, guardia, vedetta.
**sentry** *n.* (mil.) sentinella, guardia; (naut.) vedetta, gabbiere; *to relieve a* —, dare il cambio a una sentinella.
**sentry-box** *n.* garitta. **sentry-go** *n.* guardia.
**separable** *adj.* separabile.
**separate** *adj.* separato, staccato, isolato, individuale, distinto; indipendente; a parte; *tr.* separare; staccare; dividere; spartire; *intr.* separarsi; dividersi; lasciarsi. **-ness** *n.* separazione; isolamento.
**separation** *n.* separazione, divisione; rottura; *judicial* —, separazione legale. **-ism** *n.* (pol.) separatismo. **-ist** *n.* (pol.) separatista *m., f.*; (rel.) scismatico.
**separat-ism** *n.* (pol.) separatismo; (rel.) tendenza scismatica. **-ist** *adj., n.* (pol.) separatista *m., f.*; (rel.) scismatico.
**separator** *n.* separatore.
**sepia** *n.* seppia; — *drawing*, disegno a nero di seppia.
**sepsis** *n.* (med.) sepsi *f.*
**septangular** *adj.* ettagonale.
**Septemb-er** *pr.n.* settembre *m.*; *attrib.* di settembre, settembrino. **-rist** *n.* (hist.) settembrista *m.*
**sept-emvir** *n.* (Rom. hist.) settemviro. **-enary** *adj., n.* settenario. **-ennial** *adj.* settennale. **-entrional** *adj.* settentrionale. **-et** *n.* (mus.) settimino.
**septic** *adj.* (med.) settico. **-aemia** *n.* (med.) setticemia.
**sept-uagenarian** *n.* settuagenario, settuagenaria. **-ugesima** *n.* (eccl.) Settuagesima. **-uagint** *n.* (bibl.) versione dei settanta. **-uple** *adj.* settuplo.
**sepulchr-e** *n.* sepolcro; *the Holy Sepulchre*, Il Santo Sepolcro; *whited* —, sepolcro imbiancato. **-al** *adj.* sepolcrale; funereo.
**sepulture** *n.* sepoltura.
**sequel** *n.* conseguenza; seguito; continuazione.
**sequence** *n.* successione, sequela; (cards) sequenza; (gramm.) sintassi dei tempi; (eccl.; mus.; cinem.) sequenza.
**sequest-er** *tr.* isolare, appartare; *to live a -ed life*, vivere una vita appartata; (leg.) sequestare, confiscare. **-rable** *adj.* sequestrabile.
**sequestrat-e** *tr., intr.* sequestrare, confiscare. **-ion** *n.* (leg.) sequestro, confisca. **-or** *n.* (leg.) sequestrario.
**sequin** *n.* lustrino; zecchino.
**seraglio** *n.* serraglio, harem *m.*
**seraph** *n.* (rel.) serafino. **-ic(al)** *adj.* serafico; (fig.) dolce, angelico, celestiale; *-ic smile*, sorriso serafico.
**Serbia** *pr.n.* (geog.) Serbia. **-n** *adj., n.* serbo; (language) il serbo.
**sere** *adj.* dissecato, avvizzito, appassito.
**serenade** *n.* serenata; *intr.* (mus.) fare una serenata; *tr.* fare una serenata a.
**serendipity** *n.* (lit., joc.) capacità di fare delle trovate fortuite e geniali.
**seren-e** *adj.* sereno, senza nubi; (fig.) calmo, tranquillo; *a — old age*, una vecchiaia tranquilla; *all —!*, va bene!; *His (Her) Serene Highness*, Sua Altezza Serenissima. **-ity** *n.* serenità; tranquillità; calma.
**serf** *n.* (hist.) servo della gleba; (fig.) servo. **-dom** *n.* (hist.) servitù della gleba; (fig.) servaggio; schiavitù.
**serge** *n.* (text.) saia.
**sergeant** *n.* (police) brigadiere; (mil.) sergente *m.*; *quartermaster-sergeant*, sergente di fureria. **-major** *n.* (mil.) sergente maggiore.
**serial** *adj.* di serie, d'ordine; *n.* romanzo a puntate; pubblicazione periodica; — *rights*, diritti di riproduzione sui giornali.
**seriatim** *adv.* successivamente, in ordine regolare.
**sericulture** *n.* sericoltura.
**series** *n.* serie *f.*; sequela; successione.
**serio-comic** *adj.* semiserio.
**serious** *adj.* grave; serio; importante; *a — illness*, una malattia grave. **-ly** *adv.* sul serio, seriamente; *but -ly what will you do?*, ma, scherzi a parte, cosa vuoi fare?; gravemente.
**serious-minded** *adj.* riflessivo; serio.
**seriousness** *n.* serietà; *in all* —, in tutta serietà, seriamente; gravità.
**serjeant** *n.* (hist.) avvocato di ordine superiore.
**sermon** *n.* sermone *m.*; predica; *the Sermon on the Mount*, il Discorso della Montagna; (fam.) predicozzo, ramanzina. **-ize**

*intr.* (fam.) predicare, tenere un sermone; fare un predicozzo.
**serpent** *n.* serpente *m.* **-ine** *adj.* serpentino; serpeggiante; sinuoso; *-ine windings*, sinuosità *f.pl.* **-like** *adj.* serpentino.
**serrat-ed** *adj.* dentellato, seghettato. **-ion** *n.* dentellatura.
**serried** *adj.* serrato, compatto, fitto.
**serum** *n.* siero.
**servant** *n.* servo, servitore; serva domestica, domestica; *a large staff of -s*, una servitù numerosa; *your humble —*, servitor vostro umilissimo; *your obedient —*, vostro devotissimo; *civil —*, impiegato statale.
**serve** *n.* (sport) servizio.
**serve** *tr.* servire; prestar servizio a, essere al servizio di; *to — one's apprenticeship*, far tirocinio; *if my memory -s me right*, se la memoria non mi inganna; *to — a sentence*, scontare una pena; *dinner is -d*, il pranzo è servito; (leg.) *to — a summons on*, notificare una citazione a; *to — out*, distribuire; *to — up*, servire, mettere in tavola; *intr. to — on a committee*, far parte di un comitato; *to — at table*, servire a tavola; *to — in the armed forces*, prestare servizio nelle forze armate; (sport) servire.
**server** *n.* chi serve; *n.* vassoio; (eccl.) chierico; (sport) chi ha il servizio.
**service** *n.* servizio; *On His (Her) Majesty's Service* (abbrev. O.H.M.S.), Servizio di Stato; *to have seen —*, essere veterano; favore *m.*; utilità; *-s to science*, servigi in favore della scienza; *will you do me a —?*, mi vuoi fare un piacere?; (leg.) notificazione; (eccl.) ufficio divino, funzione religiosa; *burial —*, servizio funebre; *civil —*, pubblica amministrazione; *fighting -s*, forze armate; *merchant —*, marina mercantile; *tea —*, servizio da tè; *telephone —*, servizio telefonico; *train —*, servizio ferroviario.
**service** *tr.* servire; mantenere in buone condizioni; controllare, revisionare.
**serviceable** *adj.* utile, pratico.
**serviette** *n.* tovagliolo.
**servil-e** *adj.* servile, di servo; abbietto, meschino. **-ity** *n.* servilità; avvilimento; bassezza.
**serving** *adj.* che serve, che è al servizio di, (mil.) che è in servizio; *n.* servizio, il servire; (leg.) *the — of a writ*, la notifica di un decreto.
**servitor** *n.* servitore, servo.
**servitude** *n.* servitù *f.*, servaggio; schiavitù *f.*, asservimento; (leg.) servitù; *penal — for life*, lavori *m.pl.* forzati a vita.
**sesame** *n.* (bot.) sesamo; *open —!*, apriti, sesamo!
**sesquipedalian** *adj.* sesquipedale.
**sessile** *adj.* (bot.; zool.) sessile.
**session** *n.* sessione, seduta, assemblea, riunione; (pol.) *the House is in —*, la Camera è in seduta; *to go into secret —*, convocare una seduta segreta; (Univ.) anno accademico; *pl.* (leg.) udienza; *petty -s*, udienze dei giudici di pace per reati minori; (Scot.) *the Court of Sessions*, l'Alta Corte, la Corte Suprema.
**set**[1] *adj.* fermo, fisso, immobile; rigido; stabilito; prestabilito; prescritto; *— task*, compito assegnato; *at a — time*, ad un'ora fissata; *n.* posizione, atteggiamento; (of a dog) puntata; (colloq.) *to make a dead — at*, cercare di cattivarsi l'amicizia di; (of badger) tana; (tennis) set *m.*, partita; (theatr.; cinem.; telev.) set *m. indecl.*, scena.
**set**[2] *tr.* mettere, porre, collocare; *to — one's hand to a document*, apporre la propria firma ad un documento; *to — eyes on*, vedere; *to — foot in*, mettere piede in; *to — free*, liberare; *to — going*, mettere in moto; *to — on fire*, applicare fuoco a; *to — one's mind at rest*, togliersi una preoccupazione; *to — one's heart on*, rivolgere i desideri a; *to — at ease*, mettere ad agio; *to — someone on his feet*, aiutare qualcuno a sistemarsi; *to — someone's doubts at rest*, risolvere i dubbi di qualcuno; *to — someone's teeth on edge*, fare allegare i denti a qualcuno; *to — store by*, tenere in gran conto; *to — the table*, apparecchiare la tavola; (typ.) *to — type*, comporre; *to — to music*, musicare; mettere a punto, regolare; (med.) *to — a fracture*, mettere a posto una frattura; *to — sail*, spiegare le vele; *to — a trap*, tendere una trappola; *to — one's hair*, mettersi in piega i capelli; *to — an example*, dare un esempio; *to — the fashion*, lanciare la moda; *to — the pace*, segnare il passo; *to — a date*, fissare una data; *to — limits*, stabilire limiti; *to — a diamond*, incastonare un diamante; *intr.* coagularsi; (of sum, etc.) tramontare. Follow. by Adv. or Prep.: *to — about*, accingersi a; (fam.) colpire, assalire; *to — apart*, separare, mettere da parte; *to — aside*, mettere da parte; respingere; (leg.) annullare; *to — back*, mettere indietro; impedire; ritardare; *to — by*, mettere da parte; *to — down*, metter giù; far scendere; mettere per iscritto; *to — forth*, dichiarare; esporre; *intr.* avviarsi, partire; *to — in*, inserire; *intr.* incominciare; *to — off*, far esplodere, scaricare, far cominciare; *intr.* avviarsi, partire; mettere in risalto, sottolineare; *to — off a gain against a loss*, compensare una perdita con un guadagno; *to — on*, incitare; istigare; *tr. to — out*, esporre, spiegare; adornare, valorizzare; *intr.* avviarsi, partire; *to — to*, incominciare, accingersi a, (fam.) venire alle mani, discutere; *to — up*, (typ.) comporre; *to — up for oneself*, mettersi a lavorare per conto proprio.
**set**[3] *n.* serie completa; insieme *m.*; collezione; servizio; batteria; *— of furniture*, mobilia; gruppo; circolo; classe *f.*; ambiente *m.*; *the smart —*, il bel mondo; *the jet —*, la jet society, l'alta società; (radio) apparecchio ricevente; *television —*, televisore *m.*
**set-back** *n.* contratempo; regresso; ricalata. **-square** *n.* squadra (da disegno). **-to** *n.* incontro pugilistico; zuffa; disputa. **-up** *n.* portamento; sistemazione, messa a punto; trucco.
**setaceous** *adj.* setoloso, a forma di setola.
**sett** *n.* (techn.) pietra rettangolare per lastricati.
**settee** *n.* divano.
**setter** *n.* chi pone; chi mette in opera; cane da ferma.
**setting** *n.* messa in opera, montaggio; adattamento; (mech.) messa a punto; (mus.) messa in muscia; ambiente; (theatr.) messa in scena, scenario; (of jewel) montatura, incastonatura; (typ.) composizione; (of sun) tramonto; (mus.) arrangiamento.
**settle**[1] *n.* panca, cassapanca.
**settle**[2] *tr.* fissare; decidere, determinare, risolvere; *everything is -d*, l'affare è fatto; saldare, regolare, liquidare; sistemare; stabilire; mettere a posto; accomodare; calmare; comporre; (leg.) legare (a); *intr.* accomodarsi; sistemarsi; calmarsi; *dust -d on everything*, la polvere si depositò su ogni cosa; (leg.) *to — down*, stabilirsi; *as soon as the market -s down*, non appena il mercato si stabilizza; *they are now married and -d down*, sono sposati e sistemati.
**settled** *adj.* fissato, stabilito; permanente; (of weather) stabile; (of bill) saldato.
**settlement** *n.* risoluzione, saldo, liquidazione; *in —*, a saldo; lo stabilirsi; colonizzazione; colonia; *legal —*, concordato; *marriage —*, dote *f.*; *penal —*, colonia penale; (comm.) *yearly —*, liquidazione di fine d'anno.
**settler** *n.* chi stabilisce; chi decide; colono.
**settling** *n.* stabilizzazione; (of account) saldo, liquidazione, pagamento; (bldg.) cedimento;

sedimentazione, deposito; — *tank*, vasca di sedimentazione.
**seven** *card. num.* sette; *in -s*, a sette a sette, in gruppi di sette; *at sixes and -s*, in gran confusione. **-fold** *adj.* settuplo; *adv.* sette volte tanto.
**seventeen** *card. num. n.* diciasette; *sweet -teen*, la bella età dei diciasette anni. **-th** *n. ord. num.* diciasettesimo; *the -th of June*, il diciasette giugno.
**seventh** *ord. num.* settimo; *in one's — heaven*, al settimo cielo; *n.* settima parte; (mus.) settima; *dominant* —, settima dominante.
**seventieth** *ord. num.* settantesimo.
**seventy** *card. num.* settanta; *in the seventies*, tra il 70 e l'80.
**sever** *tr.* staccare; dividere; separare; *to — one's connections with*, cessare ogni relazione con.
**several** *adj.* parecchi; diversi; separato; distinto; *they went their — ways*, se ne andarono ognuno per la sua strada; *prn. pl.* parecchi, diversi; *I already have* —, ne ho già parecchi. **-ly** *adv.* separatamente; distintamente.
**severance** *n.* separazione; disgiunzione; distacco.
**severe** *adj.* severo, austero; duro; rigoroso; — *discipline*, disciplina rigorosa; violento, forte, grave; *a — cold*, un forte raffreddore; *a — illness*, una malattia grave; *a — storm*, una tempesta violenta; *a — winter*, un inverno rigido. **-ness, severity** *n.* severità; durezza; rigore *m.*; violenza, intensità, gravità; sobrietà.
**Seville** *pr.n.* (geog.) Siviglia; *The Barber of* —, 'Il Barbiere di Siviglia'; *attrib.* — *orange*, arancia amara.
**sew** *tr.*, *intr.* cucire; *to — on*, attaccare; *to — up*, cucire, ricucire.
**sewage** *n.* acque di scoloratura.
**sewer**[1] *n.* cucitore *m.*, cucitrice *f.*
**sewer**[2] *n.* canale *m.* di drenaggio, fogna, cloaca.
**sewing** *n.* il cucire; cucito; lavoro di cucito.
**sewing-machine** *n.* macchina da cucire. **-thread** *n.* cucirino.
**sewn** *part.* of **sew**, *q.v.*
**sex** *n.* sesso; *the fair* —, il bel sesso. **-appeal** *n.* attrazione del sesso.
**sexagenarian** *adj.* sessagenario; *n.* sessantenne *m.*, *f.*
**Sexagesima** *n.* (eccl.) sessagesima.
**sexennial** *adj.* sessennale.
**sexless** *adj.* asessuale. **-ness** *n.* asessualità.
**sextant** *n.* (astr.) sestante.
**sextet(te)** *n.* (mus.) sestetto, gruppo di sei.
**sextile** *adj.* (astron.) sestile.
**sexton** *n.* sagrestano, becchino.
**sextuple** *adj.*, *n.* sestuplo.
**sexual** *adj.* sessuale; — *organs*, organi genitali. **-ism** *n.* erotismo. **-ity** *n.* sessualità.
**sexy** *adj.* (slang) erotico, conturbante.
**shabb-y** *adj.* male in arnese; cencioso; stracciato; logoro; — *clothes*, vestiti frusti; — *room*, stanza squallida; spregevole, meschino, gretto; *a — trick*, un brutto tiro. **-iness** *n.* l'esser male in arnese; straccioneria; piccineria, meschinità; grettezza.
**shackle** *n.* manetta; ceppo; gambo (di lucchetto); (naut.) lunghezza (di catena); maniglia (di catena di ancora); *pl.* (fig.) impedimenti, restrizioni; *tr.* mettere in catene; ammanettare; inceppare.
**shad** *n.* (ichth.) alosa.
**shade**[1] *n.* ombra; *in the* —, all'ombra; (fig.) *he is a — better*, sta un pochino meglio; sfumatura; spirito, ombra; *the — of Anchises*, l'ombra di Anchise; *the -s of night*, le ombre della notte; *tr.* ombreggiare; proteggere; *to — one's eyes from the sun*, ripararsi gli occhi dal sole; (paint.) ombreggiare; *to — off*, sfumare.
**shading** *n.* l'ombreggiare, il dare ombra; ombreggiatura, gradazione di colori.
**shadow** *n.* ombra; immagine *f.*; spettro; *he is a mere — of his former self*, è solo l'ombra di se stesso; *tr.* pedinare; seguire come un'ombra; *to — forth*, rappresentare, suggerire.
**shadowy** *adj.* ombroso, ombreggiato; indistinto, vago; chimerico, irreale.
**shady** *adj.* ombreggiato, all'ombra; (pejor.) disonesto, infido, losco.
**shaft**[1] *n.* lancia; giavellotto; freccia; dardo; strale *m.*; *the -s of Cupid*, gli strali di Cupido; fulmine *m.*; raggio di luce; gambo; stelo; fusto; (archit.) — *of a column*, colonnina, scapo di una colonna; comignolo; fumaiolo; asta, bastone *m.*; pertica, palo; manico; (mech.) albero; (text.) liccio; (naut.) albero dell'elica; (aeron.) albero portaelica.
**shaft**[2] *n.* sfilatoio; condotto; (miner.) pozzo; *ventilating* —, condotto di ventilazione.
**shag** *n.* pelo ispido; tessuto peloso, ruvido; tabacco forte trinciato.
**shaggy** *adj.* di pelo lungo, ispido, irsuto; incolto, arruffato; peloso, ruvido; incolto, coperto di sterpi; folto, intonso; (bot.) vellutato, peloso.
**shagreen** *n.* zigrino.
**shah** *n.* scià.
**shake** *n.* scossa, scuotimento; urto; *a — of the hand*, una stretta di mano; *a — of the head*, una scrollata di capo; tremore *m.*, tremito, tremolio; *with a — in his voice*, con voce tremula; (mus.) trillo; (fam.) *in two -s of a lamb's tail*, in un batter d'occhio; *he's no great -s*, è un uomo di poco conto; frullato.
**shake** *tr.* scuotere; scrollare; — *the bottle*, agitare il flacone; *to — a carpet*, sbattere un tappeto; *to — hands with*, stringere la mano a; *to — one's fist at*, minacciare col pugno; far tremare; far vacillare; turbare; indebolire, infermare; *to be badly -n*, ricevere una brusca scossa; *intr.* fremere; tremare; turbarsi; (mus.) trillare. FOLLOW. BY ADV. OR PREP.: *to — down*, *tr.* far cadere scuotendo; *intr.* installarsi; assuedarsi; *to — off*, *tr.* scuotere da; liberarsi di; *to — off a cold*, liberarsi da un raffreddore; *to — off the yoke*, liberarsi dal giogo; (fam.) *to — off the dust from one's feet*, allontanarsi con sdegno; *to — out*, *tr.* far uscire scuotendo; vuotare; *intr.* (naut.) spiegare (vele, bandiere); *to — up*, *tr.* sprimacciare; agitare, mescolare scuotendo.
**shakedown** *n.* letto di fortuna.
**shake-out** *n.* (finan.) crisi *f.*; svendita; (metall.) sformatura.
**shake-up** *n.* rimaneggiamento; riorganizzazione.
**shaker** *n.* scotitore, shaker *m.* (per cocktail).
**Shakespearian** *adj.* scespiriano.
**shakiness** *n.* instabilità; vacillamento; tremore *m.*; debolezza.
**shaking** *adj.* tremante; vacillante; tremulo; *a — voice*, una voce tremula; scossa; scuotimento; sballottamento; *to get a* —, essere scosso, essere sballottato; tremore *m.*; tremolio.
**shaky** *adj.* instabile, tremolante, vacillante; precario; *a — hand*, una mano tremolante; *a — table*, una tavola vacillante; malsicuro, incerto; debole; *his English is* —, il suo inglese è traballante.
**shale** *n.* schisto.
**shall** *aux.vb.* denoting futurity, promise, obligation, intention, command, sometimes expressed in Italian by future tense of **dovere, volere.**
**shallot** *n.* (bot.) scaiogno.
**shallow** *adj.* poco profondo; basso; — *water*, acqua poco profonda; (fig.) leggero, superficiale; *n.pl.* bassofondo, secca. **-brained** *adj.* di poco cervello, sciocco, frivolo. **-minded** *adj.* superficiale, leggero. **-ness** *n.* poca profondità; (fig.) superficialità; futilità.
**shalt** see **shall.**
**shaly** *adj.* schistoso.
**sham** *adj.* finto, falso, simulato; fittizio; — *fight*, finto combatti-

mento; — *pearls*, perle false; *n.* finta; inganno; impostatura; mistificazione; imitazione; ipocrita *m.*; *tr.*, *intr.* fingere; simulare; *to — illness*, simulare una malattia; *to — sleep*, fingere di dormire; *to — dead*, far finta d'essere morto.

**shaman** *n.* sciamano.

**shamble** *intr.* camminare con passo strascicato.

**shambles** *n.pl.* mattatoio; (fig.) carneficina, scena di sangue, macello; (slang) confusione, disordine.

**shambling** *adj.* dinoccolato, strascicato; zoppicante; *a — gait*, un'andatura dinoccolata.

**shame** *n.* vergogna; pudore *m.*; *he is quite without —*, è un vero svergognato; — *on you!*, vergògnati!; *for —!*, vergogna!; disonore *m.*; infamia; *child of —*, figlio del disonore; *to cry —*, gridare allo scandalo; *to put to —*, svergognare, fare arrossire; (fam.) peccato, vergogna; *what a —!*, che peccato!

**shame** *tr.* svergognare; far arrossire di vergogna; disonorare; indurre, costringere.

**shamefaced** *adj.* vergogoso; confuso.

**shameful** *adj.* vergognoso; disonorevole.

**shameless** *adj.* svergognato; sfacciato, sfrontato; impudico; vergognoso, indecente. **-ly** *adv.* sfacciatamente; impudentemente; senza vergogna. **-ness** *n.* impudenza; sfacciatamente; immodestia.

**shammer** *n.* simulatore.

**shammy (-leather)** *n.* pelle di camoscio.

**shampoo** *n.* shampoo *m.*; lavatura dei capelli; *dry —*, shampoo secco; *tr.* lavare (i capelli); *to — one's hair*, lavarsi i capelli.

**shamrock** *n.* (bot.) trifoglio d'Irlanda.

**shandy(gaff)** *n.* bevanda composta di birra e zenzero.

**Shanghai** *pr.n.* (geog.) Sciangai *f.*; *tr.* portare inconscio a bordo come marinaio.

**shank** *n.* gamba; tibia, stinco; (joc.) *to go on Shank's pony*, viaggiare col cavallo di San Francesco; bambo, stelo; fusto (di colonna); manico; codolo; canna, fusto (di chiave); fuso (di ancora).

**shanty** *n.* (USA) capanna, baracca; (slang) bettola, osteria.

**shape** *n.* forma; figura; struttura; modello; *in the — of*, sotto forma di; *in any —*, di qualsiasi tipo; *to put an article into —*, metter a punto un articolo; forma, concretezza; *ideas that take — in action*, idee che si concretizzano nell'azione; *the — of things to come*, il profilo dell'avvenire; ombra, apparizione, spettro; stampo; (fam., USA) condizione, stato; *to be in good —*, essere in gran forma.

**shape**[2] *tr.* creare; dar forma a; formulare; modellare; dirigere, regolare; *to — the destiny of*, dirigere il destino di; (naut.) *to — a course*, far rotta; (mech.) limare; sagomare.

**shapeless** *adj.* informe; confuso. **-ness** *n.* mancanza di forma; deformità; (fig.) goffaggine *f.*

**shapel-y** *adj.* ben fatto; di bell'aspetto e proporzione. **-iness** *n.* bellezza; simmetria; proporzione di forme.

**shard** *n.* coccio; *to break into -s*, ridurre in frammenti.

**share**[1] *n.* parte *f.*; porzione; quota; *a fair —*, una parte equa; — *and — alike*, in parti uguali; *lion's —*, la parte del leone; *to go -s*, dividere equamente; (comm.) azione, titolo; *deferred —*, azione differita; *ordinary —*, azione ordinaria; *paid-up —*, azione interamente versata; *preference —*, azione preferenziale; *transferable —*, azione al portatore.

**share**[1] *tr.* dividere, spartire; *to — the opinion of*, condividere l'opinione di; *to — out*, distribuire; *intr. to — in*, prendere parte a.

**share**[1] (in compounds); **-capital,** *n.* capitale azionario. **-certificate** *n.* certificato azionario. **-cropper** *n.* mezzadro. **-cropping** *n.* mezzadria. **-holder** *n.* azionista *m.* **-list** *n.* listino valori. **-out** *n.* distribuzione. **-pusher** *n.* (pejor.) venditore di azioni.

**share**[2] *n.* vomere *m.*

**sharer** *n.* partecipante *m.*, *f.*, compartecipe *m.*, *f.*

**shark** *n.* squalo; pescecane *m.*; (fig.) profittatore; truffatore.

**sharkskin** *n.* zigrino, sagrì *m.*

**sharp** *adj.* tagliente, affilato; aguzzo; ad angolo acuto; — *edge*, spigolo acuto; — *features*, lineamenti angolosi; *a — turn*, una curva brusca; scosceso, ripido; *a — descent*, una discesa ripida; netto, chiaro, distinto; *a — difference*, una netta differenza; *a — outline*, un profilo netto; acuto, penetrante; acre; *a — appetite*, un appetito robusto; *a — cry*, un grido penetrante; — *flavour*, sapore aspro; — *frost*, gelo pungente; *a — pain*, un dolore acuto; (fig.) severo; tagliente, mordace; — *criticism*, critica severa; — *temper*, temperamento irascibile; — *tongue*, lingua caustica; intelligente, acuto, vivace, sveglio; *to keep a — look-out*, star bene in guardia; scaltro; disonesto; poco scrupoloso; — *practice(s)*, procedimenti poco onesti; trufferie *f.pl.*; *he was too — for me*, mi ha raggirato; lesto; impetuoso; *a — struggle*, una lotta accanita; *a — walk*, una rapida passeggiata.

**sharp** *n.* (mus.) diesis *m*; *adv.* con un tono troppo acuto.

**sharp** *adv.* puntualmente, in punto; *at ten o'clock —*, alle dieci in punto; presto, rapidamente; bruscamente; *the road turns — right*, la strada svolta bruscamente a destra; *look —!*, svelto!, fate presto!

**sharp** (in compounds). **-cut** *adj.* chiaro, netto. **-edged** *adj.* tagliente. **-set** *adj.* famelico; bramoso. **-shooter** *n.* tiratore scelto. **-sighted, -witted** *adj.* dalla vista, dall'intelligenza acuta.

**sharpen** *tr.*, *intr.* affilare; aguzzare; *to — a pencil*, far la punta a una matita; (fig.) rendere più acuto; affinare, affinarsi; inasprire, inasprirsi; (mus.) diesare.

**sharpener** *n.* arrotino; (mech.) affilatoio; affilatrice per lame.

**sharper**[1] *adj. comp.* of **sharp,** *adj.*

**sharper**[2] *n.* imbroglione *m.*; baro.

**sharpness** *n.* filo, affilatura; punta; acutezza; asprezza; vivacità.

**shatter** *tr.* fracassare; *to be -ed*, andare in frantumi; (fig.) distruggere; infrangere; *-ed hopes*, speranze infrante; rovinare; sconvolgere; *-ed nerves*, nervi in pezzi, scossi; *intr.* fracassarsi. **-ing** *adj.* (slang) schiacciante, massacrante.

**shave** *n.* rasatura; — *and haircut*, barba e capelli; sfioramento; *to have a narrow —*, cavarsela per un pelo; *tr.* radere; rasentare, sfiorare; (eccl.) tonsurare; *intr.* radersi, farsi la barba.

**shaven** *adj.* rasato; (eccl.) tonsurato.

**shaver** *n.* barbiere *m.*; (fam.) giovinetto.

**shaving** *n.* il radersi, il farsi la barba. **-brush** *n.* pennello da barba. **-cream** *n.* crema da barba. **-soap** *n.* sapone da barba. **-stick** *n.* bastoncino di sapone da barba.

**shawl** *n.* scialle *m.*

**shawn** *n.* (mus.) cennamella.

**shay** *n.* calesse *m.*, biroccino; carrozza da nolo.

**she** *prn.*, 3rd pers., *f.* ella, lei, colei; — *who sings*, colei che canta; *a she-bear*, un'orsa; *a she-devil*, un'orsa; una diavolessa; *n.* femmina.

**sheaf** *n.* fascio; covone *m.*

**shear** *tr.* cesoiare; tranciare; recidere; tosare; tagliare (capelli); falciare (erba); cimare (lana); (fig.) spennare.

**shearing** *n.* recisione; taglio; *pl.* i resti della tonsatura.
**shears** *n.pl.* cesoie, forbici *f.pl.*; *a pair of* —, un paio di cesoie; (naut.) biga, capra; *garden* —, forbici da giardino; *hedge* —, cesoie per le siepi; *pruning* —, cesoie per potatura.
**shearwater** *n.* (orn.) berta.
**sheath** *n.* guaina; fodero; astuccio; (ent.) elitra. **-knife** *n.* coltello a lama fissa con fodero.
**sheathe** *tr.* inguainare; mettere nel fodero; rivestire, ricoprire di.
**sheathing** *n.* inguainamento; rivestimento, copertura; (mech.) fasciame *m.*; fodera.
**sheave** *n.* carrucola.
**shed**[1] *tr.* versare, spandere; spargere; diffondere; *to — tears*, versare lacrime; *to — (a) light on*, far luce su; lasciar cadere, disfarsi di, perdere.
**shed**[2] *n.* tettoia; capannone *m.*; hangar *m.*; ripostiglio; riparo.
**shedding** *n.* spargimento, versamento; perdita; caduta (di foglie); muda (di animali).
**sheen** *n.* splendore; lucentezza.
**sheep** *n.* pecora; *a wolf in -'s clothing*, un lupo in veste di agnello; *to cast -'s eyes at*, fare l'occhio di triglia a; *to separate the — from the goats*, separare i buoni dai cattivi; (fig.) persona debole e timida. **-dog** *n.* cane da pastore. **-faced** *adj.* timido, impacciato. **-farmer** *n.* allevatore di pecore. **-fold** *n.* ovile *m.*, chiuso. **-shearing** *n.* tosatura. **-station** *n.* (Australia), azienda per l'allevamento degli ovini.
**sheepish** *adj.* timido, vergognoso; impacciato; sbigottito, confuso, sconcertato; sciocco.
**sheepskin** *n.* pelle *f.* di pecora; pergamena, cartapecora; giaccone foderato di pecora.
**sheer**[1] *adj.* puro, semplice, mero; assoluto; *a — waste of time*, una semplice perdita di tempo; *by — accident*, per un mero caso; — *madness*, pura follia; (of material) sottile, leggero, trasparente; perpendicolare, a piombo, a picco; *adv.* del tutto, assolutamente, completamente; a piombo, perpendicolariamente, a picco.
**sheer**[2] *intr.* (naut.) deviare; cambiar rotta; *to — off*, scostarsi, allagarsi; (fig.) svignarsela, fuggire, prendere il largo; *n.* virata, cambio di rotta; insellatura, curvatura del ponte (della nave).
**sheet** *n.* lenzuolo; foglio, pagina; giornale, quotidiano; lamina, lamiera; lastra, distesa (di ghiaccio, di neve); specchio (d'acqua); *winding* —, sudario; — *lightning*, battilastra, lattoniere *m.*; (comm.) *balance* —, bilancio; (naut.) scotta; *to let a — fly*, mollare una scotta; (naut.) — *anchor*, ancora di tonneggio; (fig.) ancora di salvezza; (fam.) *three -s in the wind*, ubriaco; *tr.* coprire con lenzuola; foderare, rivestire; *river -ed with ice*, fiume ricoperto di ghiaccio.
**sheik(h)** *n.* sceicco.
**shekel** *n.* siclo.
**shel-drake** *n.* (orn.) volpoca (maschio). **-duck** *n.* (orn.) volpoca (femmina).
**shelf** *n.* palchetto, ripiano; mensola; scaffale, scansia; *to be on the* —, essere messo in disparte; non aver prospettive matrimoniali; (geog.) secca, bassofondo.
**shell** *n.* conchiglia; guscio; crosta; squama, scaglia; *to retire into one's* —, ritirarsi nel proprio guscio; involucro; carcassa; ossatura; (artill.) proiettile *m.*; bomba; granata; bara interna; bara provvisoria; leggera imbarcazione da corsa, schifo; *tr.* sgusciare, sgranare; (artill.) bombardare; (fam.) *to — out*, tirar fuori del danaro.
**shellfire** *n.* bombardamento.
**shellfish** *n.* mollusco; crostaceo.
**shelling** *n.* sbuciatura, sgranamento; bombardamento, cannoneggiamento.
**shell-proof** *adj.* a prova di bomba. **-shock** *n.* (med.) psicosi traumatica dovuta a bombardamento.
**shelly** *adj.* ricoperto di conchiglie; pieno di conchiglie.
**shelter** *n.* riparo; tettoia; rifugio; (fig.) difesa, protezione; *to take* —, ripararsi, rifugiarsi; *air-raid* —, rifugio anti aereo; *tr.* riparare; mettere al coperto; dar asilo a; proteggere; *intr.* ripararsi, rifugiarsi. **-er** *n.* chi offre un asilo; protettore; chi cerca rifugio.
**shelv-e** *tr.* provvedere di scaffali; mettere negli scaffali; (fig.) differire, rinviare; *intr.* digradare. **-ed** *part. adj.* provvisto di scaffali; (fig.) rinviato; insabbiato. **-ing** *n.* scaffalatura, sistemazione a ripiani; disposizione negli scaffali; (fig.) differimento, rinvio; licenziamento; *adj.* digradante, in pendìo; *n.* pendìo, pendenza.
**shepherd** *n.* pastore, pecoraio; *the Good Shepherd*, il Buon Pastore; *-'s crook*, bastone da pastore; (bot.) *-'s purse*, borsa di pastore; *tr.* guardare, custodire; (fig.) guidare; aver cura di. **-ess** *n.* pastora, pecoraia; *young -ess*, pastorella.
**sherbet** *n.* succo di frutta.
**sherd** *n.* coccio.
**sheriff** *n.* sceriffo.
**sherry** *n.* sherry *m.*, vino di Xeres.
**shew** see **show**.
**shibboleth** *n.* parola; atteggiamento comprovante l'appartenenza a una particolare classe; formula, parola d'ordine; dottrina antiquata e screditata.
**shield** *n.* scudo; (fig.) protezione, difesa; (herald.) stemma *m.*, scudo; *tr.* proteggere, difendere; salvare; (mech.) schermare.
**shift** *n.* cambiamento; sostituzione; avvicendamento; (agric.) rotazione; — *of wind*, cambiamento di vento; risorsa; espediente *m.*; sotterfugio; *to make — with*, accontentarsi di; turno, squadra; *to work in -s*, lavorare a squadre; (cost.) camicia da donna; — *work*, lavoro a turni; *day* —, turno di giorno; *night* —, turno di notte.
**shift** *tr.* spostare; trasferire; cambiare; sostituire; *to — responsibility on to*, riversare la responsibilità su; *to — a load*, liberarsi da un peso; *to — one's ground*, prendere un nuovo atteggiamento; *intr.* spostarsi; trasferirsi; *the scene -ed*, la scena si cambiò; arrangiarsi, ricorrere ad espedienti; *to — for oneself*, cavarsela da solo; *to — a load*, liberarsi da un peso. **-er** *n.* chi cambia, chi sposta; (theatr.) machinista *m.* **-ing** *adj.* mutevole; mobile; astuto, scaltro; ambiguo; *n.* cambiamento, spostamento; *-ing sands*, sabbie mobili.
**shift-key** *n.* (typewriter) tasto maiuscolo.
**shiftless** *adj.* senza risorse, incapace, inabile; insufficiente; inefficace. **-ness** *n.* inettitudine *f.*; incapacità; inefficacia, insufficienza.
**shifty** *adj.* volubile; mutevole; malfido, ambiguo; astuto.
**shilling** *n.* scellino; *to be cut off with a* —, essere diseredato; *to take the King's (or Queen's)* —, arruolarsi nell'esercito.
**shilly-shally** *intr.* esitare, tentennare; *adj.* titubante.
**shimmer** *n.* lucchichìo, bagliore *m.*; scintillìo; *intr.* luccicare, mandare bagliori.
**shin** *n.* (anat.) cresta tibiale; (fam.) stinco; garretto di bue; *intr. to — up*, arrampicarsi a forza di braccia e gambe. **-bone** *n.* (anat.) tibia. **-guard** *n.* parastinchi *m. indecl.*
**shindy** *n.* (fam.) chiasso, baccano; *to kick up a* —, fare il diavolo a quattro.
**shine** *n.* splendore *m.*; luminosità, lucentezza; *come rain come* —, qualunque sia il tempo; *to give one's shoes a good* —, dare una buona lucidata alle scarpe; *intr.* splendere, brillare; emettere luce; *the sun is shining*, il sole brilla; essere brillante, eccellere; *tr.* lucidare.

**shiner** *n.* cosa che splende; (fam.) occhio pesto.

**shingle** *n.* assicella di copertura; taglio dei capelli 'a la garçonne'; *tr.* ciottoli; greto ciottoloso.

**shingles** *n.pl.* (med.) fuoco di Sant'Antonio.

**shining** *adj.* risplendente, brillante; luminoso.

**shinto, -ism** *n.* (rel.) scintoismo. **-ist** *n.* scintoista *m., f.*

**shiny** *adj.* rilucente; splendente; scintillante; lustro, lucido.

**ship** *n.* nave *f.*; bastimento; vascello; *to take —*, imbarcarsi; *— of the desert*, cammello; *when his — comes home*, quando farà fortuna; *-'s papers*, documenti di bordo.

**ship** *tr.* imbarcare; caricare; prendere a bordo; *to — a crew for a voyage*, ingaggiare un equipaggio per un viaggio; spedire; partire per nave; montare, mettere in posizione; *to — the oars*, disarmare i remi; *intr.* imbarcarsi; partire.

**ship-board** *n.* bordo; *on —*, a bordo. **-builder** *n.* construttore navale; ingegnere navale. **-building** *n.* costruzione navale. **-load** *n.* carico; numero di passeggeri. **-mate** *n.* compagno di bordo. **-ment** *n.* imbarco, carico; spedizione.

**ship-broker** *n.* agente di navigazione; agente di assicurazione marittima.

**shipper** *n.* spedizioniere marittimo.

**shipping** *n.* forze navali; marina mercantile; imbarco; *— company*, compagnia di navigazione; *— office*, agenzia di navigazione.

**shipshape** *adj.* ordinato; pulito; *adv.* in perfetto ordine.

**shipwreck** *n.* naufragio; *to suffer —*, far naufragio; (fig.) rovina, distruzione; *the — of one's hopes*, il crollo delle speranze; *intr.* naufragare; colare; *tr.* far naufragare.

**ship-wright** *n.* maestro d'ascia. **-yard** *n.* arsenale *m.*; cantiere navale.

**shire** *n.* contea; *the Shires*, le contee dell'Inghilterra centrale. **-horse** *n.* grosso cavallo da tiro.

**shirk** *tr.* schivare, evitare; eludere; sottrarsi a; *to — the question*, evadere alla domanda; *to — responsibility*, sottrarsi alla responsabilità. **-er** *n.* scansafatiche *m. indecl.*

**shirt** *n.* camicia; *— sleeves*, maniche da camicia; *— collar*, colletto da camicia; *to put one's — on, to put on one's —*, mettersi la camicia; (fig.) *to put one's — on*, (*e.g.* a horse), scommettere fino all'ultimo soldo su; (fam.) *to keep one's — on*, mantenersi calmo. **-ing** *n.* tela per camicie.

**shirt-front** *n.* sparata di camicia.

**shirtwaist** *n.* camicietta da donna. **-er** *n.* vestito da donna a foggia di *tailleur*.

**shirty** *adj.* (fam.) irascibile, irritabile; incollerito.

**shit** *n.* cacata; *excl.* merda; *you — !*, sei una merda; stronzo, puzzone *m.*; *intr.* cacare.

**shiver**[1] *n.* scheggia; frammento; *to break into -s*, andare in frantumi; *tr.* frantumare; fracassare; mandare in pezzi; (joc.) *— my timbers !*, alla malora!

**shiver**[2] *n.* brivido, fremito; *the -s*, febbre malarica; (fam.) brivido di raccapriccio; *intr.* rabbrividire; (naut.) fileggiare; ralingare. **-y** *adj.* tremante; in preda ai brividi; *to feel -y*, avere i brividi, sentirsi febbricitante.

**shoal**[1] *n.* secca, bassofondo.

**shoal**[2] *n.* moltitudine *f.*, gran quantità; banco (di pesci); *in -s*, in gran quantità; *intr.* (of fish) affollarsi, riunirsi in banchi.

**shock**[1] *n.* collisione; cozzo; colpo; shock *m.*, forte impressione, violenta emozione; *it gave me a dreadful —*, mi diede una forte emozione; (med.) collasso, colpo, sincope *f.*; (geol.) sismo; (electr.) scossa; (mil.) scontro, assalto; *— tactics*, tattica d'urto; *— troops*, truppe d'assalto.

**shock**[1] *tr.* colpire; disgustare; scandalizzare; *to be easily -ed*, scandalizzarsi con facilità; dare una scossa elettrica a; collidere, scontrarsi con.

**shock**[2] *n.* bica, mucchio di covoni di grano; folta chioma.

**shock-absorber** *n.* ammortizzatore *m.*

**shocker** *n.* chi colpisce; cosa che colpisce; romanzo giallo.

**shock-headed** *n.* dai capelli folti.

**shocking** *adj.* che colpisce; disgustoso, sconveniente; (fam.) pessimo, abominevole; orribile; *— weather*, un tempo infame.

**shod** *part.* of **shoe,** *q.v.*; *adj.* calzato; ferrato; rivestito, ricoperto.

**shoddy** *adj.* scadente; pretenzioso; falso; *n.* lana rigenerata; cascame *m.*; roba scadente e appariscente.

**shoe** *n.* scarpa; calzatura; *that's where the — pinches*; ecco la difficoltà, ecco gli svantaggi; *to be in someone's -s*, essere nei panni di qualcuno; *to shake in one's -s*, tremare di paura; ferro di cavallo; (electr.) pattino; (mech.) ceppo; *— brake*, freno ai ceppi; *— cream*, lucido da scarpe; *— leather*, cuoio per calzature; *tr.* calzare, mettere le scarpe a; *to — a horse*, ferrare un cavallo.

**shoe-black** *n.* lustrascarpe *m.* **-horn** *n.* corno da scarpa.

**shoe-lace** *n.* stringa.

**shoe-maker** *n.* calzolaio, ciabattino. **-making** *n.* calzoleria, arte del calzolaio. **-string** *n.* stringa.

**shoer** *n.* maniscalco.

**shoo** *excl.* sciò; *tr.* spaventare facendo sciò-sciò.

**shoot** *n.* partita, spedizione di caccia; riserva di caccia; germoglio, virgulto; rapida; condotto inclinato, scivolo; *tr.* lanciare; gettare; *to — an arrow*, scoccare una freccia; *to — dice*, gettare i dadi; *to — a glance*, lanciare un'occhiata; scaricare; sparare, tirare; *he -s well*, tira bene; *to — at*, far fuoco su; *to — straight*, mirar bene; *to — one's bolt*, sparare le cartucce; *to — wide of the mark*, mirar male; (fam.) *to — a line*, mettere una facciata; *to — dead*, uccidere sparando; versare; *to — coal into the cellar*, rovesciare carbone in cantina; fotografare; *to — a film*, girare un film; (football) sparare in rete; *intr.* lanciarsi; passare rapidamente; scendere, precipitare. FOLLOW. BY ADV. OR PREP.: *to — off*, sfrecciar via; *to — out*, protendersi; *to — up*, salire, guizzare, crescere rapidamente; *tr.* fucilare.

**shooter** *n.* cacciatore; tiratore; *n.* cannoniere; arciere; rivoltella; *six-shooter*, rivoltella a sei colpi.

**shooting** *n.* tiro, sparo; scarica (di fucile); caccia; riserva di caccia; spasimo, fitta; il fotografare; il girare un film; *adj.* lancinante. **-box** *n.* casino di caccia. **-jacket** *n.* giacca da cacciatore. **-gallery** *n.* sala di tiro al bersaglio. **-range** *n.* tiro a segno. **-star** *n.* stella cadente, meteora.

**shop** *n.* bottega, negozio; magazzino, fondaco; *chemist's —*, farmacia; officina, laboratorio, fucina; *to shut up —*, ritirarsi dagli affari; *to talk —*, parlare del proprio mestiere; *— hours*, orario di negozio; *— steward*, rappresentante *m.* sindacale di officina.

**shop** *intr.* far acquisiti; *to go -ping*, andare a far le spese; *tr.* (fam.) tradire.

**shop-assistant** *n.* commesso di negozio. **-front** *n.* facciata di negozio.

**shop-keeper** *n.* negoziante. **-keeping** *n.* commercio al minuto. **-lifter** *n.* taccheggiatore *m.*, taccheggiatrice *f.* **-lifting** *n.* taccheggio.

**shopper** *n.* chi gira per i negozi, chi fa compere.

**shopping** *n.* compere, acquisti; visita al negozio; *to go —*, fare acquisti; visita al negozio;

— *bag*, borsa per la spesa; — *centre*, zona degli acquisti.
**shop-soiled** *adj.* sciupato; scolorito; (fig.) danneggiato. **-window** *n.* vetrina; *in the shop-window*, in vetrina; (fig.) esibizione, mostra.
**shore**[1] *n.* spiaggia (fig.) esibizione, mostra, lido; riva, sponda; terra; *on* —, a terra; *to set foot on* —, sbarcare, scendere a terra; *to hug the* —, costeggiare; (poet.) paese *m.*
**shore**[2] *tr.* (bldg.) puntellare; *to* — *(up) a wall*, puntellare un muro.
**shore-leave** *n.* (naut.) permesso di scendere a terra.
**shoreward** *adj.* diretto verso la spiaggia.
**shoreward(s)** *adv.* verso la spiaggia.
**shorn** *part.* of **shear**, *q.v.*; *adj.* tosato, rasato.
**short** *adj.* corto; breve; — *steps*, piccoli passi; *a* — *time ago*, poco tempo fa; *a* — *way off*, poco lontano; *at* — *notice*, con breve preavviso; basso, piccolo di statura; conciso, breve, serrato; — *drink*, qualcosa di forte; — *list*, selezione; *to short-list*, selezionare per l'intervista; — *pastry*, — *crust*, pasta frolla; *in* —, in breve; *he is called Jim for* —, il suo diminutivo è Gino; *to cut* —, tagliar corto; *to cut a long story* —, a farla breve; brusco, rude. sgarbato; *he was very* — *with me*, è stato molto breve nei miei riguardi; scarso, insufficiente; mancante; *he never gives* — *weight*, non fa mai peso scarso; *we are four sheets* —, ci mancano quattro lenzuola; — *of money*, a corte di denaro; *he is* — *of breath*, è senza fiato; *to fall* —, essere insufficiente; *to run* —, scarseggiare; *our coffee is running* —, il nostro caffè sta finendo; (radio) — *waves*, onde corte; *n.* vocabolo, sillaba breve; *longs and -s*, le lunghe e le brevi; cortometraggio; (fig.) *the long and the* — *of it*, per riassumere; (short drink) qualcosa di forte; *adv.* bruscamente; improvvisamente; *he pulled up* —, si fermò di botte; *she took him up* —, lo interruppe; *to stop* —, fermarsi bruscamente; (fam.) *to be taken* —, essere sul punto di farsela addosso; (comm.) *to sell* —, vendere allo scoperto, (slang) ingannare, truffare; *adv phr.* — *of*, tranne, eccetto, fuorchè.
**short-** (in compounds). **-circuit** *n.* (electr.) corto circuito; *tr.*, *intr.* provocare un corto circuito (a); (fig.) prevenire. **-cut** *n.* scorciatoia. **-dated** *adj.* (comm.) a breve scadenza. **-handed** *adj.* a corto di personale, scarso di mano d'opera. **-lived** *adj.* di breve durata, di breve vita. **-sighted** *adj.* miope. **-tempered** *adj.* irascibile. **-winded** *adj.* dal fiato corto.
**shortage** *n.* deficienza, mancanza, carenza; — *of food*, carenza di cibo; — *of staff*, mancanza di personale.
**short-bread, -cake** *n.* torta, biscotti di pasta frolla. **-coming** *n.* mancanza, insufficienza; *pl.* difetti *m.pl.*, imperfezioni *f.pl.*
**shorten** *tr.*, *intr.* accorciare, accorciarsi; diminuire, abbreviare; (naut.) *to* — *sails*, ridurre le vele; (mil.) *to* — *step*, accorciare il passo; (cul.) rendere friabile. **-ing** *adj.* che diminuisce; che si accorcia; *n.* accorciamento, abbreviazione; diminuzione; grasso usato in pasticceria.
**shorthand** *n.* stenografia; *to take down in* —, stenografare; — *typist*, stenodattilografo; — *writer*, stenografo.
**shorthanded** *adj.* See under **short-.**
**shortly** *adv.* presto, fra breve; concisamente; brevemente; seccamente, bruscamente.
**shortness** *n.* brevità, cortezza; — *of sight*, miopia; asprezza (di carattere); mancanza, insufficienza; (cul.) friabilità, fragilità.
**shot**[1] *n.* sparo, colpo; scarica; *without firing a* —, senza colpo ferire; *to fire a* —, sparare un colpo; *blank* —, colpo a salve, in bianco; tiro, portata; proiettile *m.*, granata, pallottola; mina; *pl.* pallini di piombo; (fig.) *to be off like a* —, partire come una palla di schioppo; colpo, mossa; *at the first* —, alla prima mossa; *good* —*!*, bel colpo!; *I'll have a* — *at it*, tenterò il colpo; *it is your* —, tocca a te giocare; *to make a bad* —, fallire, mancare il colpo; *to be a good* —, essere un abile tiratore; (cinem.) ripresa; sequenza; inquadratura; piano; (photog.) istantanea; (sport) tiro; lancio; colpo; tiro in porta; (slang) presa, dose di cocaina, iniezione di morfina; (cinem.); *angle* —, ripresa inclinata; angolazione (di presa); *close* —, mezzo primopiano; *exterior* —, esterno; *high* —, colpo in aria; *long* —, campo lungo; *panning* —, panoramica; *running* —, carrellata, presa mobile.
**shot**[2] *adj.* — *silk*, seta cangiante.
**shot-gun** *n.* fucile da caccia. **-proof** *adj.* a prova di proiettile.
**should** *p.def.*, *cond.* of **shall**, *q.v.*; *I* — *be very happy to see you*, sarei felicissimo di vederti; *I* — *think so*, penso, penserei di sì; (emph.) *I* — *think so!*, certo!, senz'altro!; *he* — *arrive at any moment*, dovrebbe arrivare da un momento all'altro; — *it rain*, se dovesse piovere.
**shoulder** *n.* spalla; — *to* —, spalla a spalla; *slung over one's* —, a tracolla; *to have round -s*, avere le spalle curve; *old head on young -s*, giovane assennato; *to give the cold* — *to*, trattare con freddezza; *to hit out straight from the* —, colpire in pieno; *to put one's* — *to the wheel*, mettersi all'opera, darci dentro; (of road) bordo, margine *m.*, (of hill) spalla; *tr.*, *intr.* spingere con le spalle; portare sulle spalle, caricarsi di; (fig.) sobbarcarsi, addossarsi; (mil.) — *arms!*, spall'arm!
**shoulder-blade** *n.* (anat.) scapola. **-knot** *n. m.* cordone *m.* **-strap** *n.* spallina.
**shout** *n.* grido; grida, chiasso; clamore *m.*
**shout** *tr.*, *intr.* gridare; urlare; schiamazzare; strepitare; chiamare ad alta voce; *to* — *at*, aggredire con urla; *to* — *down*, far tacere a forza di grida, fischiare. **-ing** *n.* grido; acclamazione; vocìo.
**shove** *n.* spinta; urto; colpo; *tr.* spingere; far avanzare; (fam.) ficcare; *to* — *one's nose into*, ficcare il naso in; *to* — *away*, allontanare; respingere; (naut.) — *off*, spingere (una barca) al largo, *intr.* (fam.) allontanarsi, partire.
**shovel** *n.* pala; *tr.* spalare; (fam.) *to* — *food into one's mouth*, mangiare a quattro palmenti. **-ful** *n.* palata, palettata. **-hat** *n.* cappello a larghe tese.
**show** *n.* mostra, esibizione; esposizione; *Lord Mayor's* —, processione solenne del sindaco di Londra; *to vote by* — *of hands*, votare per alzata di mano; apparenza, sembiante *m.*; *he made a* — *of going out*, fece finta di uscire; parata, pompa, ostentazione; *to make a fine* —, fare un bell'effetto; parvenza, segno, traccia; (fam.) spettacolo teatrale; *they put on a good* —, recitarono abbastanza bene; (slang) affare; *to boss the* —, assumere il controllo di un affare; *to give the whole* — *away*, rivelare a tutti i difetti; *excl. good* —*!*, bravo!; *tr.* mostrare, far vedere; esporre; *to* — *a clean pair of heels*, darsela a gambe; *to* — *one's hand*, mettere le carte in tavola, (fig.) giocare a carte scoperte; *to* — *the white feather*, mostrarsi codardo; rappresentare, figurare, indicare; *to* — *to the door*, mettere alla porta; dimostrare, provare; rivelare; *she -s her age*, dimostra la sua età; (provb.) *time will* —, chi vivrà vedrà; condurre, accompagnare; *to* — *round*, accompagnare in giro; (theatr.)

dare una rappresentazione; *intr.* apparire; farsi vedere; essere visibile; *to — in*, fare entrare; *to — off*, *tr.* mettere in valore; *intr.* darsi delle arie, posare, mettersi in mostra; *to — out*, accompagnare alla porta; *to — up*, *tr.* svelare, smascherare; *intr.* disdegnarsi (su uno sfondo), stagliarsi; (fam.) fare atto di presenza. **-bill**, cartellone, manifesto. **-boat** *n.* battello su cui si danno spettacoli teatrali. **-card** *n.* manifesto, cartello (in vetrina). **-case** *n.* bacheca; vetrina di museo. **-down** *n.* chiarificazione, spiegazione. **-girl** *n.* generica di varietà. **-ring** *n.* arena di vendita. **-room** *n.* salone per esposizioni.

**shower** *n.* acquazzone *m.*; rovescio, scroscio; tempesta passeggera; *a heavy —*, un diluvio; doccia; *to have a —*, fare la doccia; (fig.) pioggia, grande quantità; *a — of blows*, una grandine di colpi; *tr.*, *intr.* versare, far cadere; (fig.) far piovere; coprire; *to — blows on*, far grandinare colpi su; *to — with kisses*, tempestare di baci.

**shower-bath** *n.* doccia.

**shred** *n.* brandello; *tr.* stracciare, lacerare, fare a brandelli; tagliuzzare.

**shrew** *n.* donna brontolona, pettegola, bisbetica; '*The Taming of the Shrew*', 'La Bisbetica domata'; (zool.) toporagno.

**shrewd** *adj.* sagace, accorto, astuto, perspicace; pungente, tagliente. **-ness** *n.* accortezza, perspicacia, sagacia; astuzia.

**shrewish** *adj.* brontolone; petulante; bisbetico. **-ness** *n.* acrimonia, petulanza.

**shriek** *n.* grido; strillo; fischio suono lacerante; *tr.*, *intr.* gridare; strillare; stridere; *to — with laughter*, ridere in modo isterico. **-ing** *n.* grida, urla *f.pl.*; stridore *m.*

**shrift** *n.* (rel.) confessione e assoluzione; (hist.) *short —*, breve periodo di tempo concesso al condannato a morte per confessarsi; (fig.) *to get short —*, rimanere a denti asciutti.

**shrike** *n.* (orn.) averla.

**shrill** *adj.* stridulo; acuto; penetrante; *tr.*, *intr.* strillare, stridere; emettere un suono acuto; cantare con voce stridula. **-ness** *n.* acutezza di suono; stridore *m.*; (fig.) inopportunità, insistenza.

**shrimp** *n.* (zool.) gamberetto (di mare); granchiolino; (fig.) omiciattolo, nano, pigmeo; *intr.* pescare gamberetti. **-er** *n.* pescatore di gamberetti. **-ing** *gerund* il pescare gamberetti; *adj.* *-ing net*, gamberana.

**shrine** *n.* reliquario; tomba di santo; altare *m.*; tempio; santuario; (fig.) *— of knowledge*, culla del sapere.

**shrink** *intr.* restringersi; contrarsi; ritirarsi; accorciarsi; *this cloth does not —*, questa stoffa è irrestringibile; *to — with cold*, essere rattrappito per il freddo; *to — with pain*, contorcersi dal dolore; indietreggiare; (fig.) rifuggire, evitare; *tr.* far restringere; (techn.) *to — on*, calettare a caldo, sottozero; *to — on a tyre*, calettare un cerchione; *n.* restringimento; contrazione; (techn.) ritiro. **-able** *adj.* restringibile. **-age** *n.* diminuzione; restringimento; rimpicciolimento; contrazione; (comm.) deprezzamento; calo, contrazione. **-er** *n.* (mech.) macchina per calettare; operaio addetto alla calettatura. **-ing** *adj.* che si restringe, che si contrae; timido; riluttante; *n.* contrazione; diminuzione; ritiro.

**shrink-fitting** *n.* (metall.) montaggio a caldo, sottozero. **-proof** *adj.* irrestringibile.

**shrive** *tr.* (rel.) confessare e assolvere; *to — oneself*, confessarsi.

**shrivel** *tr.*, *intr.* accartocciare, accartocciarsi; aggrinzare, aggrinzarsi; corrugare, corrugarsi; far avvizzire.

**shriving** *n.* confessione e assoluzione.

**shroud** *n.* sudario, lenzuolo funebre; (fig.) velo; schermo, riparo; *in a — of mystery*, in un velo di mistero; (naut.) sartia; *tr.* avvolgere nel sudario; nascondere, velare; *the country was -ed in mist*, la campagna era avvolta nella nebbia.

**Shrove-tide** *n.* gli ultimi tre giorni di carnevale.

**Shrove Tuesday** *n.* martedì grasso.

**shrub**[1] *n.* arbusto, cespuglio.

**shrub**[2] cordiale fatto di succo di agrumi e liquore; (USA) bibita di succo di frutta con aceto.

**shrubbery** *n.* macchia, boscaglia d'arbusti.

**shrubby** *adj.* coperto di arbusti.

**shrug** *n.* spallucciata; *intr.* scrollare le spalle, alzare le spalle, stringersi nelle spalle, fare spallucce; *tr.* *to — one's shoulders at*, infischiarsi di. **-ging** *n.* scrollata, alzata di spalle.

**shudder** *n.* brivido; tremito; *intr.* rabbrividire, avere i brividi; fremere, tremare; provare disgusto. **-ing** *adj.* tremante, rabbrividente; *n.* brivido; tremito; fremito.

**shuffl-e** *n.* passo strascicato; passo di danza; scompiglio, confusione; tramestio; il mescolare (le carte da giuoco); *it's your —*, tocca a te mescolare le carte; sotterfugio, artificio, inganno; equivoco; *intr.* trascinarsi, muoversi a fatica; *to — out*, uscire furtivamente, sgattaiolare; tergiversare; agire in modo equivoco; *to — off*, liberarsi di, sottrarsi a; *tr.* mescolare; confondere; scompigliare; *to — cards*, mescolare le carte; *to — off responsibility onto*, riversare la responsabilità su. **-ing** *adj.* strascicante; (fig.) evasivo; *n.* passo strascicato; (fig.) confusione; tergiversazione.

**shun** *tr.* sfuggire, scansare, evitare, schivare.

**shunt** *n.* (electr.) derivazione; (rlwy.) scambio; *tr.*, *intr.* (electr.) inserire in derivazione; derivare; (rlwy.) smistare; smistarsi; proporre, mettere da parte. **-er** *n.* (rlwy.) deviatore, manovratore di scambi; piccola locomotiva da smistamento. **-ing** *n.* (electr.) derivazione; (rlwy.) smistamento; intrastradamento.

**shut** *adj.* chiuso; (phon.) occlusivo; *n.* atto del chiudere; (techn.) linea di saldatura; (metall.) sovrapposizione, piega, sovradosso.

**shut** *tr.* chiudere; serrare; *to — one's eyes*, chiudere gli occhi; *to — one's heart to pity*, essere inaccessibile alla pietà; *to — one's mouth*, tacere; *intr.* chiudersi; serrarsi; FOLLOW. BY ADV. OR PREP.: *to — down*, sospendere l'attività; (aeron.) fermare il motore; *to — off*, separare, escludere, isolare; chiudere (l'acqua, il gas); *to — out*, serrare fuori; escludere; *to — up*, sbarrare; rinchiudere; *to — up shop*, chiudere bottega, ritirarsi dagli affari; (fam.) *— up!*, taci!, smettila!

**shutdown** *n.* interruzione, sospensione; chiusura temporanea.

**shutter** *n.* imposta; persiana; saracinesca; *to put up the -s*, abbassare la sarcinesca, (fig.) chiudere bottega; (photog.) otturatore; *to wind up the —*, caricare l'otturatore; *folding —*, persiana pieghevole; *rolling —*, serranda avvolgibile; *sliding —*, persiana scorrevole; *tr.* provvedere di imposte; chiudere le imposte di.

**shutting** *n.* il chiudere; chiusura.

**shuttle** *n.* spola, navetta; *— mechanism*, meccanismo alternativo; (techn.) *— movement*, movimento alternativo; (text.) lancio della navetta; *— service*, servizio di spola; *— train*, treno di collegamento; *tr.* muovere alternativamente; *intr.* fare la spola; andare avanti e indietro.

**shuttlecock** *n.* volano; giuoco del volano; (fig.) persona volubile.

**shy** *adj.* riservato, timido, schivo; timoroso; *a — child*, un bimbo scontroso; *a — person*, una persona timida, schiva; *he makes me —*, mi intimidisce; ombroso; *a — horse*, un cavallo ombroso; diffidente; *to fight — of*, tenersi alla larga da; (bot.) poco produttivo, sterile; *intr.* spaventarsi; esitare a fare qualche cosa; fare uno scarto; (of horse) impennarsi; *to — off*, schivare; (fig.) trovare un mezzo di evasione; (fam.) gettare, lanciare; *n.* (of horse) scarto; (fam.) getto, lancio; *to have a — at*, tentare di colpire.

**Shylock** *pr.n.* (fig.) usuraio.

**shyness** *n.* timidezza, riservatezza; ritrosia; scontrosità; diffidenza.

**si** *n.* (mus.) si.

**Siam** *pr.n.* (geog.) Siam *m.* **-ese** *adj.*, *n.* siamese *m.*, *f.*; *n.* lingua siamese; *— cat*, gatto siamese; *— twins*, fratelli siamesi, (fig.) amici inseparabili.

**Siberia** *pr.n.* (geog.) Siberia. **-n** *adj.*, *n.* siberiano.

**sibil-ant** *adj.*, *n.* (gram.) sibilante *f.* **-ance, sibilancy** *n.* sibilo. **-ate** *tr.*, *intr.* sibilare; pronunciare sibilando. **-ation** *n.* sibilo; fischio.

**sibling** *n.* (psych.) fratello; sorella; fratellastro; sorellastra.

**sibyl** *n.* sibilla; fatucchiera; strega. **-line** *adj.* sibillino; *the -line books*, i libri sibillini.

**Sicil-y** *pr.n.* (geog.) Sicilia. **-ian** *adj.*, *n.* siciliano; (language) il siciliano.

**sick** *adj.* malato, ammalato; indisposto, sofferente; *to fall —*, ammalarsi; (mil.) *to report —*, darsi ammalato; nauseato; (fig.) disgustato; stanco; depresso; *I am — of it*, non ne posso più; *it makes me —*, mi dà la nausea; *to be — at heart*, essere abbattuto.

**sick-bay** *n.* infermeria. **-bed** *n.* letto di un ammalato. **-benefit** *n.* indennità di malattia. **-leave** *n.* licenza per malattia. **-list** *n.* lista dei malati.

**sicken** *intr.* ammalarsi; (of plants) sfiorire, ingiallire; sentir nausea; *to — at the sight of blood*, sentir nausea alla vista del sangue; essere sazio; annoiarsi; *tr.* far ammalare; disgustare; dare noia a. **-ing** *adj.* nauseabondo, stomachevole; rivoltante; sgradevole; *to be -ing for something*, stare per ammalarsi di qualcosa.

**sickish** *adj.* malaticcio; indisposto.

**sickle** *n.* falcetto.

**sickl-y** *adj.* malaticcio; debole; pallido, delicato; *a — pink*, un rosa pallido; nauseante; *a — smell*, un odore nauseante. **-iness** *n.* salute delicata; pallore; scipitezza; nausea.

**sick-making** *adj.* (fam.) nauseante, rivoltante.

**sickness** *n.* malattia; nausea; *falling —*, epilessia; *sleepy —*, encefalite letargica.

**sickroom** *n.* camera per ammalati.

**side**[1] *n.* lato, fianco; *— by —*, fianco a fianco; *I have a pain in my right —*, ho un dolore al fianco destro; *to split one's -s with laughing*, ridere a crepapelle; versante *f.*; sponda, riva; margine; *by the — of the river*, sulla sponda del fiume; lato; parte *f.*; (fig.) aspetto; *on the other —*, d'altra parte; *the other — of the picture*, il rovescio della medaglia; *— of a gramophone record*, faccia di un disco; *the right, wrong —*, il lato buono, cattivo; il diritto, rovescio (di stoffa); *on the wrong — of the blanket*, di nascita illegittima; *to get out of bed on the wrong —*, alzarsi colla luna storta; partito, parte, fazione; *he is on our —*, è dei nostri, del nostro partito; *to change -s*, cambiare partito; *to take -s with*, prendere partito per; discendenza, lato, parte; *on his mother's —*, da parte di madre.

**side**[1] *intr.* essere dalla parte di; parteggiare; *we found out he -ed with the opposite party*, scoprimmo che parteggiava per il partito avversario; camminare a lato di.

**side**[2] *n.* (fam.) boria, arroganza; *to put on —*, darsi troppe arie.

**side-arms** *n.pl.* armi bianche. **-board** *n.* credenza. **-burns** *n.pl.* basette. **-car** *n.* side-car *m.*, motocarrozzetta.

**side-comb** *n.* pettine laterale; **-dish** *n.* portata extra. **-door** *n.* porta laterale, di servizio. **-face** *n.* profilo. **-glance** *n.* occhiata in tralice. **-issue** *n.* questione secondaria. **-line** *n.* (comm.) articolo secondario; (rlwy.) linea secondaria. **-lines** *n.pl.* (sport) linee laterali. **-saddle** *n.* sella da amazzone. **-show** *n.* mostra secondaria. **-slip** *n.* slittamento; (aeron.) scivolata d'ala; (motor.) sbandata. **-splitting** *adj.* che fa ridere a crepapelle. **-stroke** *n.* colpo laterale; nuoto alla marinara; (rlwy.) binario di raccordo. **-view** *n.* veduta di fianco. **-whiskers** *n.pl.* favoriti, basette. **-wind** *n.* vento di traverso.

**sided** *adj.* a lati, a facce; *twelve-sided polyhedron*, dodecaedro.

**side-light** *n.* luce *f.* laterale; riflesso; (fig.) spiegazione, informazione fortuita; (naut.) fanale *m.* di posizione; *pl.* fanali di via. **-lock** *n.* tirabaci *m.* **-long** *adj.* laterale; obliquo; *to cast -long glances at*, guardare con la coda dell'occhio.

**sidereal** *adj.* sidereo, siderale.

**siderite** *n.* (min.) siderite *f.*

**siderography** *n.* siderografia.

**sidesman** *n.* (eccl.) fabbriciero aggiunto.

**sidewalk** *n.* (USA) merciapiede *m.*

**sideward** *adj.* laterale. **-s** *adv.* lateralmente.

**side-ways, -wise** *adv.* lateralmente; obliquamente; a sghembo.

**siding** *n.* (rlwy.) binario di raccordo.

**sidle** *intr.* camminare di fianco; andare a sghembo; *to — along the wall*, camminare rasente il muro; *to — up to*, accostarsi con esitazione a.

**siege** *n.* assedio; *state of —*, stato d'assedio; *to lay — to a town*, assediare, cingere d'assedio una città; *to raise the —*, togliere l'assedio; *to stand a —*, sostenere un assedio.

**Sienna** *pr.n.* (geog.) Siena; (art) terra di Siena.

**sierra** *n.* sierra.

**siesta** *n.* siesta; *to take a —*, fare la siesta.

**sieve** *n.* setaccio, crivello, vaglio; *tr.* setacciare, crivellare.

**sift** *tr.* setacciare, vagliare; (fig.) esaminare minuziosamente; distinguere, separare; filtrare. **-er** *n.* chi setaccia, chi vaglia; (fig.) chi esamina minuziosamente; setaccio; buratto. **-ing** *n.* setacciatura, vagliatura; (fig.) esame minuzioso; *pl.* residui, mondiglia.

**sigh** *n.* sospiro; *intr.* sospirare; *to — with relief*, respirare di sollievo; *to — with grief*, sospirare per il dolore; *to — after*, desiderare, bramare; *to — for home*, avere la nostalgia del focolare; *tr.* esprimere sospirando; sibilare; soffiare. **-ing** *n.* il sospirare; sospiri.

**sight** *n.* vista; visione; *at first —*, a prima vista; *out of —*, fuori di vista; *to catch — of*, intravedere; *to have good —*, avere una buona vista; *to know by —*, conoscere di vista; *to lose — of*, perdere di vista; (provb.) *out of —, out of mind*, lontano dagli occhi, lontano dal cuore; veduta, panorama *m.*; spettacolo; *a fine —*, una bella vista; *what a —!*, che spettacolo!; *to make a — of oneself*, rendersi ridicolo; occhiata; sguardo; *to take a — at*, dare un'occhiata a; mira; *to take a — before shooting*, prendere la mira prima di sparare; mirino; *pl.* cose notevoli (da vedere); *to see the -s*, visitare i monumenti; (fam.) grande quantità; *it costs a — of money*, costa un sacco di soldi; *tr.* avvistare; osservare; *to —*, fornire di mirino; *intr.* prendere la mira. **-finder** mirino. **-reader** *n.* chi legge musica a prima vista. **-seeing** *n.* visita

turistica, turismo. **-seer** *n.* turista *m., f.*
**sighted** *adj.* fornito di vista; fornito di mirino (di arma da guoco); *long-sighted, far-sighted,* presbite; (fig.) previdente; *quick-sighted,* oculato; *short-sighted,* miope; (fig.) imprevidente.
**sightless** *adj.* che non vede, cieco; (poet.) invisibile. **-ness** *n.* cecità.
**sigil** *n.* suggello, sigillo; segno occulto.
**sign** *n.* segno, cenno; *to make -s to,* far cenni a; *to make the — of the cross,* fare il segno della croce; indicazione; indizio; traccia; presagio; *a — of the times,* un segno dei tempi; *— language,* mimica; insegna; *at the — of the Red Lion,* all'insegna del Leone Rosso; simbolo; (math.) *negative, positive —,* segno negativo, positivo; *radical —,* segno di radice.
**sign** *tr.* segnare; firmare; sottoscrivere; *to — one's name,* fare la propria firma; *to — away,* cedere per iscritto; *to — on,* assumere (un operaio), ingaggiare (un marinaio); *intr.* impegnarsi; (USA) *to — up,* arruolarsi, iscriversi.
**signal** *adj.* notevole; cospicuo; esemplare; *n.* segnale *m.,* segno; *distress —,* segnale di soccorso; *tr., intr.* far segnali; segnalare. **-box** *n.* (rlwy.) cabina di segnalazione.
**signalize** *tr.* segnalare; *to — oneself,* distinguersi.
**signaller** *n.* segnalatore.
**signally** *adv.* segnalatamente, notevolmente.
**signalman** *n.* segnalatore.
**signatory** *n.* firmatario.
**signature** *n.* firma, autografo; sigla; (typ.) segnatura; (mus.) indicazione (del tono, del tempo); *— tune,* sigla musicale; (mus.) segno di chiave.
**signer** *n.* firmatario.
**signet** *n.* sigillo. **-ring** *n.* anello con sigillo.
**signific-ance** *n.* espressione; significato, senso; importanza; *incident of no —,* incidente *m.* di nessuna importanza.
**significant** *adj.* espressivo, significativo; importante. **-ly** *adv.* in modo significativo.
**signification** *n.* significato, senso.
**signify** *tr.* significare, voler dire; *what does this word —?,* cosa significa questa parola?; denotare, indicare; preannunziare, presagire; essere segno di; far conoscere, far sapere; *intr.* importare, essere importante; *it does not —,* non ha importanza.
**signing** *n.* firma, sottoscrizione.
**signior, signor** *n.* signore *m.*; *The Grand —,* il Sultano di Turchia.
**sign-painter** *n.* pittore di insegne.
**signpost** *n.* palo indicatore.
**silage** *n.* conservazione di foraggio in silos; foraggio conservato in silos; *tr.* riporre in silos.
**silenc-e** *n.* silenzio; *a dead —,* un silenzio di tomba; *to put to —,* ridurre al silenzio, imporre il silenzio; (provb.) *— gives consent,* chi tace acconsente; *— is golden,* il silenzio è d'oro; *tr.* far tacere, imporre il silenzio a; far cessare. **-er** *n.* silenziatore.
**silent** *adj.* silenzioso, taciturno; quieto, tranquillo; *he kept —,* rimase zitto; muto; *a — h,* un'acca muta; *history is — on these things,* la storia tace questi fatti; *— film,* film muto.
**Silesia** *pr.n.* (geog.) Slesia. **-n** *adj.* slesiano.
**silhouette** *n.* siluetta; profilo; contorno; *in —,* di profilo; *tr.* fare la siluetta di; ritrarre di profilo.
**silic-a** *n.* (min.) silice *f.* **-ate** *n.* (min.; chem.) silicato. **-eous** *adj.* siliceo. **-ic** *adj.* silicico.
**silicon** *n.* (chem.) silicio.
**silicosis** *n.* (med.) silicosi *f.*
**silk** *adj.* di seta; serico; *n.* seta, tessuto di seta; *to take —,* essere nominato consigliere del re; *pl.* articoli di seta; *— hat,* cilindro; *artificial —,* seta artificiale; *raw —,* seta grezza; *shot —,* seta cangiante.
**silken** *adj.* serico, di seta; vestito di seta; morbido; lucente; (fig.) dolce; gentile; insinuante.
**silkgrower** *n.* sericoltore.
**silkiness** *n.* natura serica; morbidezza; lucentezza; (fig.) dolcezza, delicatezza; insinuazione.
**silk-mill** *n.* filanda.
**silkworm** *n.* baco da seta; *— breeder,* sericoltore; *— breeding,* sericoltura; *— nursery,* bachicoltura.
**silky** *adj.* di seta, serico; morbido, lucente; (fig.) dolce, delicato; insinuante.
**sill** *n.* (bldg.) soglia; davanzale *m.*; (min.) soletta (di galleria); (geol.) 'sill' *m.,* filone-strato.
**sillabub** *n.* quagliata con zucchero e vino.
**sill-y** *adj.* sciocco, stupido: *don't be —,* non fare lo stupido; *a Silly-Billy,* uno sciocchino; *n.* persona sciocca. **-iness** *n.* stupidità, sciocchezza.
**silo** *n.* silos *m.*; *tr.* conservare, mettere in silos.
**silt** *n.* fango, melma; *tr., intr. to —, to — up,* ostruire (con melma, fango); ostruirsi.
**silurian** *adj., n.* (geol.) siluriano, silurico.
**silvan** *adj.* silvano.
**silver** *adj.* d'argento; argento; argentino; *to be born with a — spoon in one's mouth,* essere nato con la camicia; (provb.) *every cloud has a — lining,* dopo il brutto viene il bello; *n.* argento; argenteria; moneta d'argento; *— fox,* volpe argentata; *German —,* argentone *m.*; *tr.* inargentare; *intr.* inargentarsi; diventare argenteo.
**silver** (in compounds). **-gilt** *n.* argento dorato. **-grey** grigio argento. **-haired,** dai capelli d'argento. **-plate** *n.* argenteria. **-plating** *n.* argentatura.
**silver-ed** *adj.* argentato. **-ing** *n.* argentatura.
**silvern** *adj.* (poet.) d'argento, argenteo.
**silver-smith** *n.* argentiere. **-ware** *n.* argenteria.
**silvery** *adj.* d'argento; argenteo; argentino.
**simian** *adj.* scimmiesco; *n.* scimmia.
**similar** *adj.* simile; somigliante; analogo; *n.* cosa simile, cosa analoga. **-ity** *n.* somiglianza, rassomiglianza.
**simile** *n.* similitudine *f.*; paragone *m.*
**similitude** *n.* similitudine *f.*; paragone *m.*; immagine *f.*; somiglianza.
**simmer** *intr.* incominciare a bollire; (fig.) essere sul punto di scoppiare; *to — with rage,* ribollire d'ira; *tr.* far bollire lentamente; *n.* stato di lenta ebollizione; *on the —,* al punto di ebollizione.
**simon-y** *n.* simonia. **-iacal** *adj.* simoniaco.
**simper** *n.* sorriso affettato; smorfia; *tr., intr.* sorridere, parlare in modo affettato; esprimere sorridendo in modo lezioso. **-er** *n.* persona leziosa, persona affettata. **-ing** *gerund* affettazione; il fare smorfie.
**simple** *adj.* semplice, elementare, facile; sincero; naturale, non sofisticato; autentico; vero e proprio; ignorante, senza esperienza; ingenuo; credulone; umile; di basso rango; *a — peasant,* un umile contadino; *n.pl.* semplici *f.pl.,* erbe medicinali *f.pl.*
**simpleton** *n.* sempliciotto.
**simplicity** *n.* semplicità; candore *m.*; ingenuità; chiarezza; facilità.
**simplif-y** *tr.* semplificare. **-ication** *n.* semplificazione.
**simplism** *n.* affettazione di semplicità.
**Simplon** *pr.n.* (geog.) Sempione *m.*
**simply** *adv.* semplicemente; solamente; facilmente; chiaramente.
**simulacrum** *n.* simulacro.
**simulat-e** *tr.* simulare, fingere; imitare l'apparenza di, prendere l'aspetto di; imitare. **-ion** *n.*

simulazione, finzione. **-or** *n.* simulatore *m.*, simulatrice *f.*

**simultan-eity** *n.* simultaneità. **-eous** *adj.* simultaneo. **-eously** *adv.* simultaneamente. **-eousness** *n.* simultaneità.

**sin** *n.* peccato, colpa; *deadly, capital* —, peccato mortale, capitale; *the forgiveness of -s*, la remissione dei peccati; *original* —, peccato originale; *the seven deadly -s*, i sette peccati capitali; *as ugly as* —, brutto come il peccato; *it is raining like* —, piove a dirotto; offesa; *it is a* — *against good taste*, è un'offesa al buon gusto; *intr.* peccare; *to — against propriety*, trasgredire le convenienze.

**since** *adv.* da allora, da allora in poi; *long* —, molto tempo fa; *many years* —, molti anni fa; (conj.) da quando, dal tempo in cui; — *I have known them*, da quando li conosco; poichè, dal momento che; — *we cannot go, you'd better stay with us*, dal momento che non possiamo andare, fareste meglio a trattenervi con noi; *prep.* da; — *that time*, — *then*, da allora; — *when have you been waiting for us?*, da quando ci aspetti?; *I have not seen her — last Sunday*, non la vedo da domenica scorsa.

**sincer-e** *adj.* sincero, schietto, franco. **-ely** *adv.* sinceramente; *yours -ely*, cordialmente vostro. **-ity** *n.* sincerità, buona fede.

**sine** *n.* (trig.) seno.

**sinecur-e** *n.* sinecura. **-ism** *n.* (eccl.) concessione, godimento di sinecure. **-ist** *n.* (eccl.) chi ha una sinecura.

**sinew** *n.* tendine *m.*, nervo; *pl.* (fig.) nerbo, forza, vigore *m.*; *the -s of war*, il nerbo della guerra.

**sinew-y** *adj.* tendinoso, fibroso; (fig.) nerboruto, muscoloso; vigoroso, energico; terso (di stile). **-iness** *n.* muscolosità; vigore *m.*; forza.

**sinful** *adj.* peccaminoso; colpevole; corrotto. **-ly** *adv.* peccaminosamente. **-ness** *n.* iniquità; colpevolezza.

**sing** *tr.*, *intr.* cantare; intonare; *to — in tune, out of tune*, cantare intonato, stonato; *to — to sleep*, fare addormentare cantando; (fig.) *to — another tune*, cambiar modo d'agire; (fig.) *to — for one's supper*, guadagnarsi la cena; lodare, celebrare le lodi di; *to — the praises of*, decantare i meriti di; poetare, celebrare in versi; *arms and the man I* —, canto le armi e l'eroe; accompagnare con canti; *to — the harvest home*, trasportare al chiuso il raccolto cantando; (of wind) fischiare, (of insects); ronzare; (of kettle) borbottare; *my ears are -ing*, mi ronzano le orecchie; *to — out*, cantare a voce spiegata, gridare. **-able** *adj.* cantabile; facile da cantare.

**singe** *n.* bruciacchiatura; strinatura; *tr.*, *intr.* bruciacchiare, bruciacchiarsi, strinare; *to — one's wings*, bruciarsi le ali.

**singer** *n.* cantante *m.*, *f.*; cantore; poeta *m.*

**singing** *adj.* che canta; canoro; *n.* canto; fischio; ronzio. **-bird** *n.* uccello canoro. **-lesson** *n.* lezione di canto. **-master** *n.* maestro di canto.

**single** *adj.* solo, unico; semplice; *he did not know a — soul*, non conosceva anima viva; *every — day*, tutti i giorni; individuale, particolare; *a — room*, una stanza singola; celibe, nubile; *are you married or —?*, sei sposato o celibe?; sincero, semplice, onesto; — *ticket*, biglietto di andata solo, biglietto semplice; *a — heart*, un cuore sincero; *n.* (tennis) singolo; *the — blessedness*, l'essere scapolo; *tr.* separare; distinguere; scegliere; *to — (out)*, scegliere. **-breasted** *adj.* a un petto. **-handed** *adj.* con una mano sola; (fig.) solo, senza aiuto. **-hearted** *adj.* **-minded** *adj.* sincero. **-seater** *n.* monoposto.

**singleness** *n.* unicità; sincerità; onestà.

**singlet** *n.* camiciola, maglia.

**singleton** *n.* (cards) carta unica di una serie; unico nato.

**singly** *adv.* separatamente, ad uno; da solo; senza aiuto.

**singsong** *adj.* monotono, noioso; *n.* canto monotono; cantilena; (fam.) riunione tenuta per cantare; concerto improvvisato.

**singular** *adj.* singolare; solo; sorprendente; eccezionale; bizzarro, strano; eccentrico; (gramm.) singolare; *n.* (gramm.) singolare.

**singularity** *n.* singolarità; rarità; particolarità; stranezza; eccentricità.

**singulariz-e** *tr.* distinguere; particolarizzare. **-ation** *n.* singolarizzazione.

**singularly** *adv.* singolarmente.

**sinister** *adj.* sinistro, funesto; di cattivo augurio; disonesto; (herald.) sinistro.

**sinistral** *adj.* sinistro; che gira a sinistra (di spirale).

**sink** *n.* lavandino, acquaio; scolo; fogna, sentina, (geol.) foiba, voragine *f.*; *intr.* andare a fondo; *to — like a stone*, colare a picco; immergersi; conficcarsi; *the car sank into the mud*, l'automobile sprofondò nel fango; *to — into decay*, andare in rovina; *to — into a deep sleep*, sprofondare in un sonno profondo; discendere; abbassare, abbassarsi; calare; diminuire; *the ground -s abruptly*, il terreno scende di colpo; *his voice sank*, la sua voce si abbassò; *prices are -ing*, i prezzi calano; *the river has sunk*, il fiume si è abbassato; *the sun is -ing*, il sole sta calando; cadere; cedere; crollare, abbattersi; *my heart sank at the news*, a quella notizia il mio cuore mancò; *to — to one's knees*, cadere in ginocchio; scavare; *tr.* mandare a fondo, affondare; *they sank their differences*, dimenticarono le loro divergenze; (finan.) investire denaro a fondo perduto.

**sinkable** *adj.* affondabile.

**sinker** *n.* scavatore; (fishing) piombo, peso.

**sinking** *n.* affondamento; cedimento, abbassamento; abbatimento; (finan.) — *fund*, fondo di ammortamento.

**sinless** *adj.* senza peccato, innocente, puro. **-ness** *n.* innocenza, purezza.

**sinner** *n.* peccatore *m.*, peccatrice *f.*

**Sinn Fein** *n.* (Irish) 'Sinn Fein' (movimento repubblicano irlandese, fondato nel 1905).

**sinologue** *n.* sinologo.

**sinology** *n.* sinologia.

**sinuat-e** *adj.* sinuoso, serpeggiante; (bot.) dentellato, frastagliato; *intr.* serpeggiare; essere sinuoso, serpeggiante. **-ion** *n.* sinuosità.

**sinuosity** *n.* sinuosità.

**sinuous** *adj.* sinuoso, tortuoso.

**sinus** *n.* (bot.) sinuosità (tra due lobi di foglie); (anat.) seno, cavità; (med.) fistola. **-itis** *n.* (med.) sinusite *f.*

**sip** *n.* sorso; *tr.*, *intr.* sorseggiare, centellinare.

**siphon** *n.* (phys.; zool.) sifone *m.*; sifone da selz; *tr.*, *intr.* travasare con un sifone; fluire attraverso un sifone. **-age** *n.* il travasare con un sifone.

**Sir** *n.* signore *m.*; *thank you*, —, grazie, signore; *Dear Sir*, Egregio Signore; *Dear Sirs*, Spettabile Ditta; 'Sir' (titolo premesso al nome di battesimo di un cavaliere, di un baronetto); *tr.* dare il 'Sir' a.

**sire** *n.* genitore (di animali); stallione *m.*; (poet.) padre; antenato; Sire *m.*, Maestà; *tr.* generare.

**siren** *n.* (myth.) sirena; (fig.) donna affascinante, incantatrice; (techn.) sirena.

**sirloin** *n.* lombo di manzo.

**sirocco** *n.* scirocco.

**sirup** *n.* sciroppo. **-y** *adj.* sciropposo.

**sisal** *n.* (bot.) agave sisaliana; fibra d'agave.

**sissy** *n.* (fam.) effeminato; timido.

**sister** *n.* sorella; amica intima; suora; — *of Mercy*, suora di carità; infermiera capo-reparto; *sister-in-law*, cognata; *half-sister*,

sorellastra. **-hood** *n.* sorellanza; congregazione religiosa; comunità di donne. **-ly** *adj.* di sorella; amorevole.

**sit** *intr.* sedere, essere seduto, stare seduto; *he was sitting on a chair*, era seduto su una sedia; *to — for a constituency*, rappresentare un collegio elettorale; *to — for an examination*, dare un esame; *to — for a portrait*, posare per un ritratto; *to — tight*, tenersi saldo, (fig.) tener duro; essere in seduta; tener seduta, riunirsi in seduta; *Parliament is sitting*, il Parlamento è in seduta; (of birds) apollaiarsi, posare, stare appollaiato; (of hens) covare; (of animals) accovacciarsi; covare; *sit!*, cuccia!; stare, cadere; *this skirt -s well*, questa gonna cade bene; (admin.) *to — on*, condurre un'inchiesta su, esaminare; *his losses — lightly upon him*, le sue perdite non gli pesano molto; *to — on the fence*, non prendere partito; *to — on a jury*, far parte di una giuria; *to — down*, mettersi a sedere; prendere posto; *to — down to table*, mettersi a tavola; *to — out*, sedere all'aperto; non prender parte a; *to — up*, stare eretto; mettersi in posizione eretta; rizzarsi (sul letto); vegliare; rimanere alzato; *to — up with a sick person*, vegliare un malato; *the news made him — up*, la notizia lo colse di sorpresa, lo fece sussultare; *to — up and take notice*, drizzare le orecchie.

**sitdown** *attrib. adj.* — *lunch*, colazione a tavola; — *strike*, sciopero bianco; *n.* il sedersi; (fam.) *let's have a —*, sediamoci un momento.

**site** *n.* sito, luogo; posizione; area fabbricabile; *tr.*, *intr.* porre; situare, essere situato; trovarsi.

**sit-in** *n.* l'occupazione.

**sitter** *n.* chi sta seduto; (art) modello, modella; *n.* chioccia; (sport) occasione fortunata per segnare un punto; colpo facile.

**sitting** *adj.* seduto; presente ad una seduta; *n.* posa; seduta; breve periodo di tempo; *in one —*, in una volta; adunanza, riunione; covata.

**sitting-room** *n.* stanza di soggiorno.

**situate** *adj.* situato, posto, collocato.

**situated** *adj.* situato, collocato, posto; in una certa posizione, situazione; *this is how I am —*, questa è la situazione in cui mi trovo.

**situation** *n.* situazione, posizione, ubicazione; stato, situazione, circostanza; impiego, posto; *to apply for a —*, fare una domanda d'impiego; *-s wanted*, richieste d'impiego; *-s vacant*, offerte di lavoro, lavori, impieghi offerti.

**six** *card. num.* sei; *— of one and half a dozen of the other*, se non è zuppa è pan bagnato; *to be at -es and sevens*, essere in disordine. **-fold** *adj.* sestuplo; *adv.* sei volte tanto.

**six-footer** *n.* persona alta sei piedi. **-shooter** *n.* rivoltella a sei colpi.

**six-pence** *n.* moneta da sei vecchi 'pennies', mezzo scellino. **-penny** *adj.* che vale mezzo scellino.

**sixte** *n.* (fencing) posizione di sesta.

**sixteen** *card. num.* sedici. **-th** *ord. num.* sedicesimo.

**sixth** *ord. num.* sesto.

**sixtieth** *ord. num.* sessantesimo.

**sixty** *card. num.* sessanta.

**sizable** *adj.* piuttosto grande.

**sizar** *n.* studente universitario che usufruisce di una 'sizarship'. **-ship** *n.* borsa di studio, (a Cambridge e a Dublin).

**size**[1] *n.* grandezza, misura, dimensione, taglia; statura; *all of a —*, tutti della stessa grandezza; *what is your —?*, che taglia hai?; formato; *tr.* (fam.), classificare secondo la misura; *to — up*, misurare la capacità di; valutare.

**size**[2] *n.* (techn.) turapori *m. indecl.*; (text.) bozzima *tr.* (techn.) preparare (una superficie) con turapori; (text.) bozzimare.

**sizeable** *adj.* see **sizable**.

**sized** *adj.* di una certa statura, grandezza, dimensione; classificato in ordine di grandezza, statura, dimensione.

**sizzle** *n.* (fam.) sfrigolio; *intr.* sfrigolare.

**skate**[1] *n.* pattino; *intr.* pattinare; (fig.) *to — on thin ice*, camminare sul filo del rasoio.

**skate**[2] *n.* (ichth.) razza.

**skater** *n.* pattinatore, pattinatrice.

**skating** *n.* pattinaggio. **-rink** *n.* pista per pattinaggio.

**skedaddle** *n.* (fam.) corsa sfrenata; fuga precipitosa; *there was a general —*, ci fu un fuggi-fuggi generale; *intr.* (fam.) scappare; svignarsela.

**skein** *n.* matassa; (fig.) confusione; scompiglio; stormo di oche selvatiche.

**skeletal** *adj.* scheletrico.

**skeleton** *n.* scheletro; *— at the feast*, un guastafesta *m.*; *a — in the cupboard*, un fatto che si vuol celare per vergogna; ossatura; intelaiatura; (bot.) venatura; canovaccio; schema *m.*; abbozzo. **-key** *n.* chiave madre.

**sketch** *n.* (paint.) schizzo; abbozzo; descrizione sommaria; profilo generale; bozzetto; (theatr.) sketch *m.*, scenetta; *first —*, primo getto. *tr.* abbozzare; schizzare; *to — in*, disegnare sommariamente; *to — out*, impostare il canovaccio di, delineare; *abs.* fari degli schizzi, disegnare.

**sketch-album, -book** *n.* album per schizzi.

**sketcher** *n.* disegnatore.

**sketchily** *adv.* in modo impreciso, in modo incompleto; per sommi capi.

**sketchiness** *n.* mancanza di finitura, di dettagli; superficialità.

**sketching** *n.* l'abbozzare; lo schizzare.

**sketchy** *adj.* abbozzato, non rifinito; impreciso; incompleto.

**skew** *adj.* obliquo; sbieco; sghembo; *tr.*, *intr.* mettere, mettersi di traverso; *to — at*, guardare di traverso; deviare, far deviare.

**skewer** *n.* spiedo; *tr.* infilare sullo spiedo.

**ski** *n.* sci *m.*; *intr.* sciare.

**skid** *n.* slittamento; (techn.) scivolo; pattino; (aeron.) pattino di coda; (motor.) *side —*, sbandamento; *tr.*, *intr.* scivolare, far scivolare; (motor.) slittare; (aeron.) derapare. **-chain** *n.* catena antisdrucciolevole.

**skier** *n.* sciatore *m.*, sciatrice *f.*

**skiff** *n.* (naut.) schifo, palischermo; scialuppa.

**ski-ing** *gerund* lo sciare.

**skilful** *adj.* abile, esperto, destro. **-ness** *n.* abilità, destrezza.

**ski-lift** *n.* sciovia.

**skill** *n.* abilità, destrezza, capacità. **-ed** *adj.* esperto, versato, abile; *-ed labour*, mano d'opera specializzata; *-ed worker*, operaio specializzato; (leg.) *-ed witness*, perito.

**skim** *adj.* schiumato; scremato; *n.* schiuma; coltello superiore dell'aratro; *— milk*, latte scremato; *tr.* schiumare; *to — the cream off*, scremare; sfiorare, rasentare; *to — over*, volare raso terra; sfiorare; (fig.) trattare con superficialità; scorrere, sfogliare, leggere superficialmente.

**skimmer** *n.* schiumaiuola, schiumarola, schiumatoio; chi legge superficialmente.

**skimming** *n.* scrematura; *pl.* scorie levate dal metallo fuso.

**skimp** *tr.*, *intr.* lesinare; limitare; tenere a corto, a stecchetto; razionare il cibo; risparmiare, essere parsimonioso, essere tirchio. **-iness** *n.* ristrettezza; razionamento; spilorceria. **-y** *adj.* scarso; tirchio, meschino.

**skin**[1] *n.* pelle, cute *f.*; pellame *m.*; *inner —*, derma; *outer —*, epidermide *f.*; *to have fair —*, avere una carnagione chiara; *wet to the —*, bagnato fino alle ossa; *I would not be in his —*, non vorrei essere

nei suoi panni; *to escape by the — of one's teeth*, cavarsela per il rotto della cuffia; (fig.) *to have a thick* —, essere insensibile; *to jump out of one's — for joy*, non star più nella pelle dalla gioia; *raw -s*, pelli grezze; *tanned -s*, pelli conciate, cuoio; otre *m.*; buccia, scorza; involucro; (on milk) pellicola; — *disease*, dermatosi *f.*, malattia della pelle; *tr.* scuoiare, scorticare, spellare; sbucciare; (fam.) *to — a flint*, essere spilorcio; (slang) *to keep one's eyes -ned*, tenere gli occhi bene aperti; truffare, frodare, pelare; *intr.* (med.) *to — over*, cicatrizzarsi, rimarginarsi.

**skin-dresser** *n.* conciatore di pelli.

**skinflint** *n.* taccagno, spilorcio.

**skin-game** *n.* (slang) truffo. **-grafting** *n.* innesto epidermico.

**skinner** *n.* conciapelli *m.*, cuoiaio.

**skinny** *adj.* magro; scarno; macilento; avaro, taccagno.

**skip** *n.* salto, balzo; omissione; *intr.* saltare; saltare la corda; muoversi a balzi; *tr.* omettere, saltare.

**skipper**[1] *n.* saltatore; chi omette qualcosa leggendo.

**skipper**[2] *n.* capitano, comandante di nave mercantile; (sport, fam.) capitano di squadra.

**skipping** *n.* salti *m.pl.*; omissione; (typ.) salto di uno spazio; **-rope** *n.* corda per saltare.

**skirmish** *n.* scaramuccia; schermaglia; *intr.* scaramucciare. **-ing** *n.* scaramuccia.

**skirt** *n.* sottana; gonna; orlo, lembo; falda (di vestito); (fam.) *to be fond of a bit of* —, essere sempre a caccia di gonnelle; (fig.) *pl.* estremità; periferia; *tr.* orlare; circondare; confinare; costeggiare. **-ing** *n.* orlo, bordo; fascia; stoffa per gonne; zoccolatura, bordatura; (bldg.) *-ing board*, zoccolo di legno.

**skit** *n.* scherzo, burla; *tr.*, *intr.* motteggiare; satireggiare; saltare, balzellare.

**skittish** *adj.* capricioso; frivolo; volubile, incostante; (of horse) ombroso. **-ness** *n.* volubilità; frivolezza; ombrosità.

**skittle** *n.* birillo; *pl.* giuoco dei birilli; *life is not all beer and -s*, la vita non è tutta rose e fiori.

**skive** *tr.*, *intr.* (mil. slang) evadere (al turno di dovere). **-r** *n.* (mil. slang) marmittore *m.*

**skivvy** *n.* (fam.) squattera, serva.

**skua** *n.* (orn.) stercorario.

**skulk** *intr.* stare nascosti; imboscarsi; (fig.) sottrarsi al proprio dovere; muoversi furtivamente. **-er** *n.* imboscato; codardo. **-ing** *adj.* brontolone; furtivo.

**skull** *n.* cranio, teschio; — *and crossbones*, teschio e tibie incrociate; *-cap*, papalina.

**skunk** *n.* (zool.) moffetta; pellicia di moffetta; (fam.) persona ignobile, farabutto.

**sky** *n.* cielo; volta celeste, firmamento; *clear* —, cielo sereno; *overcast* —, cielo coperto; *to praise to the skies*, portare alle stelle; *to sleep under the open* —, dormire all'addiaccio. **-blue** *adj.* azzurro cielo. **-high** *adj.* altissimo.

**sky-lark** *n.* allodola; *tr.*, *intr.* (slang) gabbare, prendersi giuoco di; far chiasso, baldoria. **-light** *n.* lucernario; lanterna di lucenario. **-line** *n.* linea, profilo; orizzonte *m.*

**sky-pilot** *n.* (slang.) prete *m.* **-rocket** *n.* razzo. **-scraper** *n.* grattacielo.

**slab** *n.* lastra, piastra; fetta, pezzo; (metall.) slebo.

**slack**[1] *adj.* molle, allentato; debole, fiacco; indolente; negligente; inerte; — *rope*, fune lenta; (comm.) debole, fiacco; morto; calmo; stagnante; *business is* —, gli affari languono; *the market is* —, il mercato è fiacco; *n.* (naut.) imbando; inattività; — *water*, bassa marea; *pl.* calzoni sportivi o da donna; *tr.* allentare; rallentare; trascurare, *intr.* (fam.) rilassarsi, riposarsi; (comm.) ristagnare; languire; spegnersi; *to — off*, allentare; rilassarsi.

**slack**[2] *n.* polvere di carbone.

**slacken** *intr.* allentarsi; diminuire; smorzarsi; ristagnare; *tr.* *to — speed*, diminuire la velocità. **-ing** *n.* allentamento, rallentamento; ristagno; diminuzione.

**slacker** *n.* fannullone *m.*, fannullona *f.*; scansafatiche *m.*, *f. indecl.*

**slackness** *n.* fiacchezza; rilassamento; trascuratezza, negligenza; (comm.) ristagno.

**slag** *n.* scoria, loppa.

**slake** *tr.* estinguere; smorzare; *to — one's thirst*, estinguere la sete; (fig.) appagare, soddisfare; spegnere; *intr.* estinguersi; spegnersi; *slaked lime*, calce spenta.

**slalom** *n.* (sport) slalom *m.*

**slam** *n.* sbatacchiamento; *to shut with a* —, chiudersi sbatacchiando; *tr.* sbattere, sbatacchiare; *intr.* chiudersi violentemente; *n.* (bridge) slam *m.*; *grand* —, grande slam, cappotto; *little* —, stramazzo.

**slander** *n.* calunnia, maldicenza; (leg.) diffamazione; *action for* —, querela per diffamazione; *tr.* calunniare; (leg.) diffamare. **-er** *n.* calunniatore *m.*, calunniatrice *f.*; maldicente *m.*, *f.*; (leg.) diffamatore *m.*, diffamatrice *f.*

**-ous** *adj.* calunnioso, maldicente; (leg.) diffamatorio.

**slang**[1] *n.* gergo; *to use* —, parlare in gergo.

**slang**[2] *tr.* vituperare, ingiuriare; sgridare; *to have a -ing match*, dirsene di cotte e di crude.

**slant** *adj.* sghembo; inclinato; *n.* inclinazione, pendenza; piano inclinato; china; punto di vista; (cinem.) prospettiva; *intr.* essere in pendenza; inclinarsi; *tr.* far deviare obliquamente. **-ed** *part. adj.* inclinato; (fig.) parziale, tendenzioso; *articles -ed for the foreign press*, articoli adattati, modificati, per la stampa estera. **-ing** *adj.* inclinato; obliquo; sghembo; *-ing eyes*, occhi a mandorla. **-wise** *adj.* obliquo, traversale; *adv.* obliquamente, di traverso.

**slap** *n.* pacca; schiaffo, ceffone *m.*; (fig.) affronto; rabuffo; rimprovero; (fam.) *a — in the eye*, uno schiaffo in pieno viso; *tr.* schiaffeggiare; dare una pacca a; sbattere; *to — down*, buttar giù con forza; (fig., fam.) sopprimere, stroncare.

**slap-bang** *adv.* (fam.) violentemente; rumorosamente. **-up** *adj.* (slang) di prim'ordine; all'ultima moda.

**slap-dash** *adj.* impetuoso; affrettato; noncurante; *n.* cosa fatta a casaccio; lavoro affrettato. **-stick** *n.* spatola d'Arlecchino; (fig.) farsa grossolana.

**slash** *n.* taglio, apertura; frustata, sferzata, scudisciata; *tr.* tagliare; fendere; sfregiare; frustare, sferzare, criticare aspramente. **-ed** *part. adj.* tagliato; sfregiato; con fenditure; *-ed sleeves*, maniche con aperture.

**slat** *n.* assicella; stecca; *tr.* fornire di assicelle.

**slate**[1] *n.* ardesia; tegola d'ardesia; lavagna; (fig.) *to clean the* —, cominciare una nuova vita; *tr.* coprire con tegole d'ardesia.

**slate**[2] *tr.* (fam.) sgridare; punire; criticare severamente.

**slater** *n.* conciatetti *m. indecl.*

**slating**[1] *n.* tegole d'ardesia; copertura con tegole d'ardesia.

**slating**[2] *n.* rimbrotto; lavata di testa; critica severa; stroncatura.

**slatted** *adj.* fornito di, fatto con assicelle.

**slattern** *n.* sudiciona, sciattona. **-liness** *n.* sporcizia; sciatteria. **-ly** *adj.* sudicio; sciatto; *adv.* sudiciamente; sciattamente.

**slaty** *adj.* di ardesia; color ardesia; schistoso.

**slaughter** *n.* macello; carneficina; massacro; strage *f.*; *tr.* macellare; massacrare; far strage di. **-er** *n.* macellatore; uccisore; massacratura. **-house** *n.* mattatoio.

**Slav** *adj.* slavo; *n.* slavo, slava; lingua slava.
**slave** *n.* schiavo, schiava; *a — of prejudices,* schiavo di pregiudizi; persona meschina, abietta; *intr.* lavorare come uno schiavo; sgobbare; *to — at,* logorarsi per.
**slave-driver** *n.* negriero. **-labour** *n.* lavoro di schiavi.
**slaver**[1] *n.* schiavista *m.*; negriero; nave negriera.
**slaver**[2] *n.* saliva; bava; (fig.) adulazione servile; *tr., intr.* imbavare; far bava, sbavare.
**slavery** *n.* schiavitù; lavoro faticoso.
**slave-ship** *n.* nave negriera. **-trade** *n.* tratta degli schiavi. **-trader** *n.* commerciante di schiavi.
**slavish** *adj.* di schiavo; servile; *a — imitation,* una imitazione servile; abietto. **-ly** *adv.* da schiavo; servilmente; bassamente.
**Slavonic** *adj.* slavo; *n.* slavo; slava; *n.* lingua slava.
**slavophil, slavophile** *adj., n.* slavofilo.
**slay** *tr.* ammazzare; trucidare. **-er** *n.* uccisore. **-ing** *n.* uccisione; massacro.
**sled** *n.* slitta.
**sledge**[1] *n.* slitta; *tr.* trasportare su slitta; *intr.* andare su slitta.
**sledge**[2] *n.* martello da fabbro; maglio.
**sleek** *adj.* liscio; levigato; lustro; soffice, morbido; sdolcinato; mellifluo; *tr.* lisciare; lustrare. **-ness** *n.* lucentezza; levigatezza; (fig.) untuosità.
**sleep** *n.* sonno (fig.) quiete *f.*; riposo; *broken —,* sonno interrotto; *restless —,* sonno inquieto; *to go to —,* addormentarsi (euphem.) morire; *to put to —,* fare una puntura a, addormentare, fare uccidere dal veterinario; *to rouse from —,* svegliare; *to walk in one's —,* essere sonnambulo; periodo di riposo; *beauty —,* primo sonno; *intr.* dormire; riposare; *to — on it,* dormirci sopra; *I did not — a wink all night,* non ho chiuso occhio tutta la notte; (euphem.) *to — with,* andare a letto con; *to — together,* andare a letto insieme; *tr. to — the clock round,* dormire dodici ore filate; *to — the sleep of the just,* dormire il sonno del giusto; (fam.) dare da dormire a; *this hotel -s 100 people,* questo albergo ha 100 letti.
**sleeper** *n.* dormiente *m., f.*; dormiglione *m.,* dormigliona *f.*; *n.* travetto; (rlwy.) traversina; (rlwy.) vagone letto.
**sleepiness** *n.* sopore *m.*; sonnolenza, pesantezza; languore *m.*; apatia.
**sleeping** *adj.* dormiente; addormentato; assopito; (provb.) *let — dogs lie,* non svegliare il can che dorme; *n.* sonno; riposo. **-bag** *n.* sacco a pelo. **-berth** *n.* cuccetta. **-car** *n.* vagone letto. **-draught** *n.* narcotico; sonnifero. **-partner** *n.* (comm.) socio accomandante. **-quarters** *n.pl.* dormitorio; camerata. **-sickness** *n.* malattia del sonno. **-suit** *n.* pigiama *m.*
**sleepless** *adj.* insonne; agitato; tormentato; *a — night,* una notte bianca. **-ness** *n.* insonnia.
**sleep-walker** *n.* sonnambulo. **-walking** *n.* sonnambulismo.
**sleepy** *adj.* assonnato, sonnolento; *a — look,* un'aria addormentata; *to be —,* aver sonno; apatico; indolente; molle.
**sleepy-head** *n.* (fam.) dormiglione *m.,* pigro; dormigliona *f.,* pigra. **-sickness** *n.* encefalite letargica.
**sleet** *n.* nevischio; nevischiare; *it is -ing,* vien giù nevischio.
**sleeve** *n.* manica; *to roll up one's -s,* rimboccarsi le maniche; (fig.) *to have a card up one's —,* avere un asso nella manica; *to laugh up one's —,* ridere sotto i baffi *to wear one's heart on one's —,* avere il cuore in mano; busta (di un disco); (techn.) manicotto; (electr.) lanterna; bussola; (aeron.) manica a vento.
**sleeve-board** *n.* stiramaniche *m*
**sleigh** *n.* slitta; *intr.* andare in slitta.
**sleight** *n.* abilità, destrezza; giuoco di abilità; furberia. **-of-hand** *n.* giuoco di prestigio.
**slender** *adj.* magro; snello, esile, sottile; *she has a very — waist,* ha la vita molto sottile; debole, fiacco, esiguo; scarso; *— hopes,* deboli speranze; *— income,* rendita esigua; *— means,* mezzi insufficienti. **-ness** *n.* magrezza; snellezza; delicatezza; esiguità; modicità.
**sleuth** *tr., intr.* pedinare; fare l'investigatore; *n.* investigatore.
**sleuth-hound** *n.* segugio; cane poliziotto; (fam.) agente investigativo.
**slew** *tr., intr.* girare, far girare; rotare; volgere, volgersi.
**slice** *n.* pezzo, parte; fetta, porzione; spicchio; spatola, paletta; *tr.* affettare, tagliare, dividere in parti.
**slick** *adj.* liscio, levigato; scorrevole; abile, svelto; *tr.* lisciare, levigare; lucidare.
**slide** *n.* scivolata; (mech.) scorrimento; piano, superficie *f.* di scorrimento; scivolo, sdrucciolo; piano inclinato; pista in discesa; (techn.) pattino; slitta; carrello; cursore; vetrino (per microscopio); (photog.) dispositiva, lastra; *intr.* scivolare; sdrucciolare; scorrere; *to le things —,* lasciar correre le cose; allontanarsi, sfuggire; *to — out of a room,* uscire da una stanza alla chetichella; *tr.* far scivolare; far scorrere.
**slider** *n.* chi sdrucciola, scivola; (techn.) corsoio, cursore.
**slide-rule** *n.* regolo calcolatore.
**sliding** *gerund* lo scivolare; *adj.* scorrevole; mobile; *— door,* porta scorrevole; *— roof,* soffietto, capote *f.*; *— scale,* scala mobile; *— seat,* sedile scorrevole.
**slight** *adj.* magro; minuto; esile; smilzo; *a — girl,* una ragazza esile; leggero; scarso; inadeguato; *we had a — lunch,* facemmo una colazione leggera; superficiale; *n.* disprezzo; affronto; trascuratezza; mancanza di riguardo; *tr.* disprezzare; guardare dall'alto in basso; mancare di riguardo a; trascurare; trattare con ostentata indifferenza.
**slightingly** *adv.* sprezzatamente, sdegnosamente; con noncuranza; negligentemente.
**slightly** *adv.* leggermente, lievemente; scarsamente; in modo insignificante; un poco.
**slightness** *n.* magrezza; leggerezza; debolezza; tenuità.
**slim** *adj.* magro, sottile, esile; snello; smilzo; *— fingers,* dita affusolate; leggero; scarso; *intr.* dimagrire; stare a regime.
**slime** *n.* melma, limo; fanghiglia; bava; umore viscoso; bitume *m.*
**sliminess** *n.* viscosità; melmosità; (fig.) servilità, ossequiosità.
**slimming** *adj.* che fa dimagrire.
**slimness** *n.* sottigliezza; snellezza; gracilità; astuzia, scaltrezza.
**slimy** *adj.* limaccioso; fangoso; viscoso; (fig.) servile, ossequioso.
**sling**[1] *n.* fionda, frombola; (hist.) balista; *tr.* scagliare con la fionda; gettare, lanciare; *to — a stone,* lanciare un sasso con la fionda; (colloq.) *to — one's hook,* borseggiare.
**sling**[2] *n.* cinghia; (med.) bendaggio a fionda; *he had his arm in a —,* portava il braccio al collo; *tr.* sospendere; appendere; *to — a hammock,* sospendere un'amaca; *to — over one's shoulder,* portare ad armacollo; (naut.) imbracare; tirar su, issare.
**slinger** *n.* fromboliere *m.*; lanciatore di pietre.
**slink** *intr.* sgattaiolare, svignarsela; muoversi furtivamente; *adj.* (of an animal) nato prematuramente; *n.* aborto; vitello nato prematuramente.
**slip**[1] *n.* innesto; persona giovane e snella; striscia; (typ.) bozza in colonna; (ichth.) piccola sogliola; *intr.* tagliare rami per innesto.
**slip**[2] (naut.) scalo, molo, ponte *m.* d'approdo, imbarcadero; guinzaglio; federa; scivolata, scivolone *m.*; (provb.) *there's many a — 'twixt the cup and the lip,* tra il dire e il fare c'è di mezzo il mare; errore *m.*; svista; passo falso; scontrino; (cost.) sottana, sottoveste *f.*;

*pl.* (theatr.) quinte *f.pl.* calzoncini da bagno; (ceram.) argilla semiliquida.

**slip**[2] *intr.* scivolare; inciampare, perdere l'equilibrio; scorrere; (fam.) *it -s my memory*, mi sfugge; *to — into bed*, infilarsi a letto; sgusciare, liberarsi; (naut.) filare, infilare; *to — away*, scorrere; eclissarsi; *to — up*, sbagliare, fare una gaffe; fallire, far fiasco (di progetto); *tr.* (naut.) *to — an anchor*, filare l'ancora; (of a dog) *to — its chain*, liberarsi dalla catena. **-coach** *n.* (rlwy.) vagone sganciabile in corsa. **-galley** *n.* (typ.) vantaggio per colonne. **-hook** *n.* scatto. **-knot** *n.* nodo scorsoio. **-proof** *n.* (typ.) prima bozza. **-ring** *n.* (electr.) anello di contatto.

**slipper** *n.* pantofola; pianella; ciabatta; (techn.) pattino; (rlwy.) freno sulla rotaia.

**slipper-y** *adj.* sdrucciolevole; viscido; (fig.) *as — as an eel*, viscido come un'anguilla; incerto, instabile; evasivo; non scrupoloso; infido. **-iness** *n.* sdrucciolevolezza; scaltrezza, astuzia.

**slippy** *adj.* (fam.) veloce, attivo, rapido; *to look —*, muoversi rapidamente, essere svelto.

**slipshod** *adj.* in ciabatte; disordinato; trasandato; trascurato; scorretto.

**slipslop** *adj.* insipido; incoerente; *n.* brodo, brodaglia; bevanda analcoolica; risciacquatura di piatti; (fig.) discorso incoerente; scritto sdolcinato.

**slipware** *n.* ceramica vetrificata.

**slipway** *n.* (naut.) invasatura.

**slit** *n.* fessura; crepa, fenditura; incisione; *tr.* fendere; spaccare; tagliare a strisce.

**slit-eyed** *adj.* dagli occhi a mandorla.

**slither** *intr.* (fam.) scivolare; sdrucciolare.

**slit-pocket** *n.* finta tasca.

**sliver** *n.* scheggia; frammento.

**slobber** *n.* bava; sdolcinatura; *intr.* sbavare; comportarsi in modo sdolcinato; *to — over*, soffocare di tenerezze. **-y** *adj.* bavoso.

**sloe** *n.* (bot.) prugnolo; prugnola; *— gin*, liquore di prugnole.

**slog** *n.* (fam.) colpo violento; lavoro faticoso; *tr.* colpire fortemente; *intr.* (fig.) lavorare tenacemente; sgobbare; *to — along*, avanzare a fatica.

**slogan** *n.* motto pubblicitario; frase fatta di propaganda.

**sloop** *n.* corvetta.

**slop** *n.* brodo, brodaglia; *pl.* liquidi sporchi; risciacquatura di piatti; *tr.* versare, rovesciare; spruzzare, schizzare; camminare nella fanghiglia; *intr.* essere rovesciato; *to — over*, traboccare; (fam.) *to — about*, andare in ciabatte, andar trasandato.

**slop-basin** *n.* scodella per i fondi del tè lasciati nelle tazze.

**slope** *n.* pendenza; pendìo, declivio; (rlwy.) scarpata; *intr.* essere in pendenza, pendere, inclinarsi; (slang) *to — off*, sparire, svignarsela; *tr.* declinare; inclinare, dare pendenza a.

**sloping** *adj.* inclinato; obliquo; in pendenza.

**sloppily** *adv.* disordinatamente; trasuratamente; sdolcinatamente.

**sloppiness** *n.* l'essere bagnato; trascuratezza, sciatteria; sdolcinatura; sentimentalismo.

**slop-pail** *n.* secchio per l'acqua sporca.

**sloppy** *adj.* bagnato di pioggia; fangoso; pieno di pozzanghere; bagnato; disordinato; trascurato, sciatto; sdolcinato; *— sentimentality*, sentimentalismo sdolcinato.

**slosh** *n.* fango, poltiglia; brodaglia; *intr.* diguazzare, sguazzare; *tr.* scuotere, (slang) battere, colpire.

**slot** *n.* fessura; scanalatura; automatico a gettoni; *tr.* fare una fessura in; scanalare; introdurre in un distributore automatico.

**sloth** *n.* pigrizia; indolenza; infingardaggine *f.*; (zool.) bradipo. **-ful** *adj.* pigro, indolente; infingardo. **-fulness** *n.* infingardaggine *f.*; pigrizia; indolenza.

**slot-machine** *n.* macchina a gettoni. **-meter** *n.* contatore a gettoni.

**slouch** *n.* andatura dinoccolata; *tr.*, *intr.* muoversi goffamente; camminare pigramente.

**slouch-hat** *n.* cappello a cencio.

**slouching** *gerund* il muoversi goffamente; *adj.* goffo, dinoccolato.

**slough**[1] *n.* pozzanghera; pantano.

**slough**[2] *n.* spoglia; crosta; (fig.) abitudine *f.*; vizio di cui ci si libera; *intr.* cambiare pelle; squamarsi; spogliarsi; (fig.) *to — off*, liberarsi di.

**Slovak** *adj.* slovacco; *n.* slovacco, slovacca; *n.* lingua slovacca.

**sloven** *n.* sudicione *m.*, sudiciona *f.*; sciattone *m.*, sciattona *f.*; pigrone *m.*, pigrona *f.*

**Sloven-e** *adj.* sloveno; *n.* sloveno, slovena. **-ian** *adj.* sloveno; *n.* sloveno, slovena; lingua slovena.

**slovenl-y** *adj.* sciatto; sudicio; negligente. **-iness** *n.* sciatteria; trascuratezza; negligenza, sporcizia.

**slow** *adj.* lento; *goods of — sale*, merci che si vendono poco; *plants of — growth*, piante tardive; *to cook in a — oven*, cuocere a fuoco lento; *he was — to answer*, non aveva la risposta pronta; *she is — to anger*, non si arrabbia facilmente; tardo, ottuso; noioso; in ritardo, indietro; *the guests were — in arriving*, gli ospiti erano in ritardo; *my watch is always ten minutes —*, il mio orologio è sempre indietro dieci minuti; (photog.) lento (di pellicola); *tr.*, *intr.* *to — up*, rallentare, ritardare; *the train was -ing down*, il treno rallentava; *to — down in speaking*, parlare più adagio; *adv.* lentamente, adagio; *go —*, va' piano, (fig.) sii cauto; *a go-slow strike*, uno sciopero bianco.

**slowcoach** *n.* (fam.) posapiano, trottapiano; persona ottusa, tarda di mente; persona retrograda.

**slowness** *n.* lentezza; pigrizia, indolenza, ignavia; ottusità mentale; ritardo (d'orologio).

**slow-worm** *n.* (zool.) orbettino.

**sludge** *n.* fango, melma; acque di scolo; (naut.) ghiaccio galleggiante; morchia; *intr.* camminare faticosamente nel fango.

**slug**[1] *n.* lumaca; *n.* persona pigra; fannullone *m.*, fannullona *f.*

**slug**[2] *n.* pallottola; proiettile *m.*; gettone *m.*; (typ.) lingotto; *tr.* caricare; (slang) colpire con una pallottola.

**sluggard** *adj.* indolente; pigro; *n.* persona indolente; fannullone *m.*, fannullona *f.*

**sluggish** *adj.* pigro, tardo, indolente; lento; pigro; *a — river*, un fiume dal corso lento. **-ness** *n.* pigrizia; indolenza; lentezza.

**sluice** *n.* chiusa, cateratta; canale con chiusa; *inlet —*, paratoia di presa; *tr.* munire di chiusa; inondare; allagare per mezzo di chiuse; risciacquare; *intr.* scorrere violentemente, riversarsi (come da una chiusa).

**sluice-gate** *n.* saracinesca. **-head** *n.* testa di chiusa.

**slum** *n.* viuzza, vicolo; *pl.* bassifondi *m.pl.*; *intr.* visitare i quartieri poveri di una città; *to go -ming*, fare un giro nei bassifondi.

**slumber** *n.* dormiveglia *m.*; assopimento; (fig.) stato di inattività; *intr.* dormire, sonnecchiare; essere in uno stato di inattività. **-er** *n.* chi dorme, sonnecchia. **-ing** *adj.* addormentato, sonnecchiante, assopito; dormiveglia **-ous** *adj.* che dorme; assopito; calmo, tranquillo; soporifero.

**slump** *n.* (comm.) crollo, caduta dei prezzi; crisi economica; *intr.* crollare; cadere.

**slur** *n.* insulto, affronto, accusa; macchia; *to cast a — on*, macchiare la reputazione di; (mus.) legatura; dizione indistinta; *tr.*

sorvolare, passar sopra a; *to — one's words*, biascicare le parole; *to — over details*, sorvolare sui particolari; pronunciare difettosamente, in maniera confusa; calunniare, denigrare; (mus.) legare.

**slurring** *gerund* il biascicare; calunnia, maldicenza; (mus.) legatura; pronuncia indistinta; difettosa; (typ.) doppieggiatura.

**slush** *n.* poltiglia, fango, melma; neve sciolta; (fig.) sdolcinatezza; *tr.* schizzare di fango. **-y** *adj.* fangoso, melmoso; (fig.) sentimentale, sdolcinante.

**slut** *n.* sudiciona, sciattona; cagna.

**sluttish** *adj.* sporco, sudicio; trascurato. **-ness** *n.* sporcizia; sudiciume *m.*; disordine *m.*

**sly** *adj.* astuto, accorto, malizioso; *a — dog*, un sornione, un furbacchione; infido, insincero, sleale; segreto; furtivo; *on the —*, furtivamente, in sordina.

**slyboots** *n.* (joc.) sornione *m.*; furbaccione *m.*

**sly-ly** *adv.* scaltramente, astutamente; slealmente; furtivamente. **-ness** *n.* astuzia, furberia, malizia, scaltrezza; ipocrisia, slealtà.

**smack**[1] *n.* sapore *m.*; aroma, fragranza; sentore *m.*; traccia; *intr. to — of*, sapere di, avere il gusto di; (fig.) far pensare a, ricordare.

**smack**[2] schiocco; bacione *m.*; schiaffo, colpo; *a — in the face*, uno schiaffo in faccia; (fig.) un severo rimprovero; *a — in the eye*, una delusione inaspettata; *tr.* schioccare; schiaffeggiare; andare a sbattere; *adv.* (slang) in pieno; direttamente; con un tonfo.

**smack**[3] *n.* (naut.) peschereccio.

**smacker** *n.* schiaffo sonoro; bacio con lo schiocco; esemplare notevole; (USA, slang) dollaro.

**small** *adj.* piccolo, minuto; leggero; debole; *the still — voice*, la coscienza; poco, scarso; limitato, ristretto; di poca importanza; insignificante; *a — tradesman*, un piccolo commerciante; umile, oscuro; povero; *to feel —*, sentirsi umiliato; *to look —*, aver l'aspetto dimesso; *to live in a — way*, vivere modestamente; *— beer*, birra leggiera; (fig.) di poca importanza; *— hours*, ore piccole; meschino; gretto; *n.* la parte più piccola; *— of the back*, le reni; *pl.* biancheria intima; *adv.* poco; in piccola quantità; *to sing —*, cantare a bassa voce, (fig.) abbassare la cresta.

**smallage** *n.* (bot.) appio, sedano.

**small-arms** *n.pl.* (in compounds) armi *f.pl.* portatili.

**small-holder** *n.* proprietario di una piccola fattoria. **-holding** *n.* piccola fattoria di campagna.

**small-minded** *adj.* dalla mentalità ristretta.

**smallness** *n.* piccolezza, esiguità, scarsità; meschinità.

**smallpox** *n.* (med.) vaiolo.

**small-talk** *n.* conversazione piacevole.

**smalt** *n.* smalto.

**smarm** *tr.* (fam.) impiastrare; *to — one's hair down*, impomatarsi i capelli; (fig.) adulare; *to — over*, adulare, lisciare. **-y** *adj.* (fam.) untuoso, strisciante.

**smart** *adj.* acuto, pungente; aspro; forte; severo, mordace; doloroso; *a — pain*, un dolore lancinante; *a — saying*, una battuta mordace; vivace; sveglio, intelligente, abile; attivo; brillante, spiritoso; *a — pace*, un'andatura veloce; *a — pupil*, un allievo sveglio; elegante, attillato, alla moda; (fam.) saccente; *n.* dolore acuto; bruciore *m.*; sofferenza.

**smart** *intr.* dolere, far male; bruciare; *to — under an insult*, soffrire per un insulto; *you shall — for this!*, questa me la pagherai!

**smarten** *tr.*, *intr.* abbellire; riordinare.

**smarting** *adj.* doloroso; cocente; pungente, acuto; bruciore *m.*

**smartness** *n.* acutezza; abilità; vivacità; brio; spirito; arguzia; eleganza.

**smash** *n.* forte colpo; urto; scontro; collisone (fig.) rovina; bancarotta, fallimento; *tr.* frantumare; fracassare; sfasciare; colpire violentemente; sbattere; urtare; *to — a door open*, sfondare una porta; sconfiggere, annientare; *intr.* andare a sbattere; fracassarsi; *the car -ed into a wall*, l'automobile si sfasciò contro un muro; (fam.) fallire, far bancarotta.

**smash-and-grab** *n.* furto compiuto infrangendo una vetrina.

**smasher** *n.* chi frantuma; (techn.) pressatoio; (slang) persona affascinante, giovanotto attraente, ragazza bellissima.

**smashing** *adj.* che fracassa, che rompe tutto; (slang) magnifico, bellissimo.

**smash-up** *n.* rovina completa.

**smatter** *n.* conoscenza superficiale. **-ing** *n.* infarinatura.

**smear** *n.* macchia imbrattatura; (fig.) calunnia; *tr.* macchiare; insudiciare; imbrattare; (fig.) calunniare; *intr.* imbrattarsi, velarsi. **-y** *adj.* grasso, untuoso, vischioso; macchiato; imbrattato.

**smell** *n.* odorato, olfatto; fiuto; cattivo odore; puzzo; *a sweet —*, un buon profumo; atto dell'annusare; *to take a — at*, annusare, fiutare; *tr.* fiutare, annusare; sentire l'odore di; *to — something burning*, sentir odore di bruciato; (fig.) *to — out*, scovare; *to — a rat*, fiutare un imbroglio; *intr.* avere odore di; *the milk smelt sour*, il latte aveva odore di acido; *these flowers don't —*, questi fiori non hanno profumo; *to — of*, sapere di.

**smelling** *gerund* atto dell'odorare; il fiutare; *adj.* odorifero, odoroso. **-bottle** *n.* boccetta dei sali. **-salts** *n.pl.* sali odorosi.

**smelly** *adj.* (fam.) che manda cattivo odore; puzzolente.

**smelt**[1] *p.def.*, *part.* of **smell**, *q.v.*

**smelt**[2] *n.* (ichth.) sperlano.

**smelt**[3] *tr.* (metall.) fondere (minerale); estrarre (il metallo) per fusione. **-er** *n.* fonditore. **-ing** *n.* fusione; *attrib.* *-ing furnace*, forno di fusione; *-ing house*, fonderia.

**smilax** *n.* (bot.) salsapariglia, smilace *f.*

**smil-e** *n.* sorriso; *intr.* sorridere; *to — at*, sorridere di; *to — on*, favorire, essere favorevole; *tr.* *to — consent*, approvare con un sorriso. **-er** *n.* chi sorride.

**smirch** *n.* macchia; *tr.* macchiare.

**smirk** *n.* sorriso affettato; *intr.* sorridere affettatamente. **-ing** *adj.* lezioso, affettato.

**smite** *tr.* colpire; percuotere; battere con violenza; *he was smitten with a serious disease*, fu colpito da una grave malattia; *the idea smote him*, gli venne un lampo di genio; (fam.) *to be smitten with*, essere innamorato di; sconfiggere, sgominare; distruggere; *to — the enemy hip and thigh*, sconfiggere definitivamente il nemico; affliggere, castigare; *his conscience -s him*, gli rimorde la coscienza; *n.* colpo; percossa.

**smith** *n.* fabbro.

**smithereens** *n.pl.* (fam.) frammenti, pezzetti; *to smash to —*, ridurre a pezzetti.

**smithy** *n.* forgia, fucina.

**smock** *n.* (hist. cost.) grembiule *m.* da contadino; blusa. **-ing** *n.* (needlew.) punto smock; crespe *f.pl.*

**smog** *n.* smog *m.* (miscela di fumo e nebbia).

**smoke** *n.* fumo; *to go up in —*, finire in fumo, sfumare; (provb.) *there is no — without a fire*, dove c'è fumo c'è fuoco; fumata; (fam.) sigaro, sigaretta; *let's have a —*, facciamoci una fumatina; *tr.* fumare; (fam.) *put that in your pipe and — it*, prendi e metti in tasca; affumicare; annerire di fumo; *-d haddock*, merluzzo affumicato; *to — out*, cacciare col fumo; *intr.* emettere fumo; fumigare.

**smoke-bomb** *n.* bomba fumogena. **-dried** *adj.* affumicato. **-hole** *n.* (geol.) fumarola.

**smokeproof** *adj.* a prova di fumo.
**smoker** *n.* fumatore *m.*, fumatrice *f.*; *n.* (rlwy.) carrozza, scompartimento per fumatori.
**smoke-screen** *n.* cortina di fumo. **-stack** *n.* fumaiolo; cimiera.
**smokiness** *n.* fumosità.
**smoking** *adj.* fumante, che fuma; *n.* fumo; il fumare; — *compartment*, scompartimento per fumatori; — *mixture*, miscela di tabacco da pipa. **-jacket** *n.* giacca da casa.
**smoky** *adj.* fumoso, che fa fumo; affumicato, annerito dal fumo; pieno di fumo; che sa di fumo.
**smooth** *adj.* liscio, levigato; piano; ben amalgamato, omogeneo; armonioso; scorrevole; gradevole; *a — wine*, un vino gradevole; dolce, affabile; mellifluo, subdolo; — *manners*, modi poco sinceri; calmo, tranquillo; *a — crossing*, una traversata tranquilla; (fig.) *to be in — waters*, essere al sicuro; (artill.) — *bore*, a canna liscia; *n.* lisciata; parte liscia; terreno uniforme; *to take the rough with the —*, far buon viso a cattiva sorte. **-faced** *adj.* imberbe; (fig.) dall'espressione melliflua. **-tongued** *adj.* dalle parole adulatrici.
**smooth(e)** *tr.* lisciare; spianare; levigare; (fig.) facilitare; appianare; *to — away differences*, attenuare le differenze; (fig.) *to — the way for*, appianare la strada a; *to — down*, calmare.
**smoothey** *n.* (fam.) adulatore.
**smoothing** *n.* lisciatura; spianatura; levigatura.
**smoothness** *n.* levigatezza; regolarità; scorrevolezza, armonia; dolcezza, affabilità; calma, tranquillità.
**smother** *tr.* soffocare; opprimere; sopprimere; reprimere; *to — a yawn*, reprimere uno sbadiglio; ricoprire; *intr.* morire soffocato.
**smothering** *adj.* soffocante; asfissiante; (fig.) opprimente; *n.* soffocamento; oppressione; soppressione; repressione.
**smoulder** *intr.* bruciare sotto la cenere; bruciare senza fiamma; (fig.) covare. **-ing** *n.* combustione lenta; *adj.* che brucia lentamente o di nascosto.
**smudg-e** *n.* macchia; imbrattatura; sgorbio; *tr.* macchiare, insudiciare; scarabocchiare. **-iness** *n.* sporcizia; imbrattatura. **-y** *adj.* macchiato, imbrattato.
**smug** *adj.* soddisfatto di sè; presuntuoso.
**smuggl-e** *tr.* contrabbandare; *to — something out of the country*, far uscire dal paese merce di contrabbando; *intr.* fare il contrabbando. **-er** *n.* contrabbandiere *m.*; nave usata da contrabbandieri. **-ing** *n.* contrabbando.
**smug-ly** *adv.* con aria di sufficienza, con piena soddisfazione di sè stesso. **-ness** *n.* mediocrità compiaciuta di sè.
**smut** *n.* macchia prodotta da fuliggine; linguaggio osceno; (agric.) golpe *f.*
**smutt-y** *adj.* annerito; sporco; fuligginoso; sboccato, osceno, sconcio; (agric.) che ha la golpe. **-iness** *n.* sporcizia; nerume *m.*; oscenità, sconcezza.
**snack** *n.* boccone *m.*; porzione; parte *f.*; merenda, spuntino. **-bar** *n.* tavola calda.
**snaffle**[1] *n.* morso snodato.
**snaffle**[2] *tr.* rubacchiare.
**snag**[1] *n.* sporgenza; protruberanza; (text.) smagliatura; (fig.) intoppo; difficoltà imprevista; *tr.* far urtare (una nave) contro un ostacolo nascosto; tagliare in modo imperfetto lasciando sporgenze; *to — one's stockings*, smagliarsi le calze.
**snail** *n.* chiocciola; lumaca; *to go at a -'s pace*, avanzare a passo di lumaca.
**snake** *n.* serpente *m.*; serpe *m.*; biscia; *a — in the grass*, il serpente fra l'erbe; *to cherish a — in one's bosom*, allevare una serpe in seno; (fig.) sleale.
**snake-charming** *n.* incantatore di serpenti.
**snakelike** *adj.* simile a serpente; anguiforme.
**snaky** *adj.* serpentino; serpeggiante; sinuoso, tortuoso.
**snap** *n.* colpo secco di denti; morso, morsicata; schiocco; *to make a — at*, cercare di afferrare, addentare; rottura improvvisa; fermaglio, fibbia; bottone automatico; (fam.) energia; vigore *m.*; brio; giuoco di carte infantile; — *vote*, votazione improvvisa; *cold —*, ondata di freddo intenso.
**snap** *tr.*, *intr.* schioccare, far schioccare; aprirsi di colpo; spezzare, spezzarsi con un colpo secco; *to — one's fingers at*, infischiarsi di; (photog.) scattare un'istantanea a; *to — at*, azzannare, tentare di mordere, ghermire; (fig.) investire, parlare aspramente a; *to — off*, portar via con un morso; (fig.) interrompere bruscamente; *to — off someone's head*, dare un rabbuffo a qualcuno; *to — up*, afferrare.
**snapdragon** *n.* (bot.) bocca di leone.
**snappish** *adj.* stizzoso; ringhioso; mordace, caustico; che scatta facilmente. **-ness** *n.* asprezza, tono stizzoso; viso arcigno.
**snappy** *adj.* stizzoso, irritabile, iroso; aspro, brusco; vivace, brillante (di stile); (fam.) elegante.
**snapshot** *n.* (photog.) istantanea; *to take a —*, scattare una istantanea; *tr.* prendere un'istantanea di.
**snare** *n.* trappola; rete *f.*; laccio; *to lay a —*, tendere una trappola; tentazione; *tr.* prendere al laccio.
**snarl**[1] *n.* intrico, viluppo, ginepraio; groviglio; arruffatura, nodo; arricciatura; *tr.* aggrovigliare; *intr.* aggrovigliarsi; annodarsi, arruffarsi.
**snarl**[2] *n.* ringhio; voce irosa; brontolamento; *intr.* ringhiare; parlare con acredine; pronunciare parole irose; brontolare.
**snatch** *n.* strappo, strattone *m.*; presa; *to make a — at*, ghermire; brano, frammento; breve periodo; *to work in -es*, lavorare saltuariamente; *tr.* afferrare; ghermire; agguantare; acchiappare; *to — at*, cercare di prendere; *to — away*, rapire, portar via; *to — up*, tirar su, raccogliere in fretta. **-er** *n.* ladro; rapinatore; *body-snatcher*, dissotterratore di cadaveri.
**sneak** *n.* persona vile, abietta, codarda; (school slang) spia; *intr.* insinuarsi; introdursi furtivamente; strisciare; *intr. to — away*, andar via di soppiatto; *to — in*, entrare furtivamente; (school slang) fare la spia; *tr.* rubare.
**sneakers** *pl.n.* scarpette *f.pl.* per ginnastica (in tela, con suole di gomma).
**sneaking** *adj.* servile; abietto; vile; furtivo; nascosto; celato; *to have a — affection for*, nutrire un affetto inconfessato per.
**sneck** *tr.*, *n.* chiavistello; saliscendi *m. indecl.*; boncinello; chiudere a chiavistello.
**sneer** *n.* sogghigno beffardo; tono canzonatorio; motteggio, canzonatura; *intr.* sorridere beffardamente, sogghignare; *to — at*, schernire, canzonare, burlarsi di. **-ing** *adj.* beffardo; canzonatorio; sarcastico; *n.* sarcasmo; beffa.
**sneez-e** *n.* starnuto; *intr.* starnutire; (fig.) *to — at*, disprezzare; *it is not to be -d at*, non è da sprezzare. **-ing** *n.* lo starnutire.
**snick** *n.* taglietto, piccola incisione; tacca; (sport) colpo che fa deviare la palla; *tr.* incidere; fare piccole intaccature in; (sport) far deviare leggermente (la palla) con la mazza.
**snicker** *n.* nitrito; risata repressa; *intr.* nitrire; reprimere il riso.
**sniff** *n.* l'annusare, il fiutare; annusata, fiutata; *tr.*, *intr.* aspirare rumorosamente col naso; fiutare; presagire, prevedere; *to — at*, annusare; (fig.) dimostrare disapprovazione per; *to — up*, fiutare; inspirare.
**snifting-valve** *n.* (techn.) valvola di scappamento.

**snigger** *n.* risolino malizioso, cinico; *intr.* ridere sotto i baffi; ridacchiare.
**snip** *n.* forbiciata; scampolo, ritaglio; occasione; (racing slang) certezza, vincitore sicuro; *tr.*, *intr.* tagliuzzare, fare dei tagli (con forbici, cesoie); *to — off the ends of*, spuntare.
**snipe**[1] *n.* (orn.) beccaccino; (fig.) sciocco, stupido.
**snip-e**[2] *n.* colpo sparato da luogo nascosto; *tr.*, *intr.* (mil.) sparare da luogo nascosto. **-r** *n.* (mil.) chi spara di soppiatto; franco tiratore.
**snippet** *n.* pezzetto; ritaglio; *pl.* frammenti *m.pl.*
**snip-snap** *n.* colpo di forbici.
**snivel** *intr.* moccicare, avere il moccio; piagnucolare, frignare; simular commozione. **-ler** *n.* piagnucolone *m.*, piagnucolona *f.* **-ling** *adj.* moccioso; piagnucoloso.
**snob** *n.* snob *m.* **-bery** *n.* snobismo; sussiego. **-bish** *adj.* snobistico; affettato. **-bishness, -bism** *n.* snobismo; sussiego.
**snood** *n.* nastro per i capelli; reticella da tuppè; lenza.
**snook** *n.* maramao; *to cock a —*, fare maramao.
**snoop** *intr.* interessarsi dei fatti altrui, ficcare il naso; spiare.
**snooty** *adj.* (fam.) sdegnoso.
**snooze** *n.* pisolino, sonnellino; *intr.* sonnecchiare, fare un pisolino.
**snor-e** *intr.* russare. **-ing** *gerund* il russare.
**snort** *n.* sbuffo; sbuffata; rumore sbuffante; *intr.* sbuffare; *tr.* esprimere sbuffando. **-er** *n.* chi sbuffa; (slang) forte vento; cosa strabiliante, eccezionale, violenta; risposta mordente.
**snot** *n.* muco, moccio, caccola. **-rag** *n.* (slang) fazzoletto.
**snotty**[1] *n.* (naut. slang) aspirante *m.* di marina.
**snot-ty**[2] *adj.* moccioso, caccoloso; (slang) arrogante; di cattivo umore, sdegnoso. **-nosed** *adj.* moccioso; (fig.) spregevole.
**snout** *n.* muso; grugno; ceffo; grifo; naso; (techn.) becco; cannello.
**snow** *n.* neve *f.*; tempesta, bufera di neve; nevicata; *eternal —*, nevi perenni; *a fall of —*, una nevicata; (fig.) bianchezza, candore *m.*; (slang) cocaina; (USA) eroina; *impers.* nevicare; *it is -ing*, nevica; *to be -ed up*, essere bloccato dalla neve; *-ed under*, sopraffatto.
**snow-ball** *n.* palla di neve; *tr.*, *intr.* lanciare palle di neve (a); (fig.) accumularsi. **-blindness** *n.* (med.) ambliopia. **-boot** *n.* soprascarpa per neve. **-bound** *adj.* bloccato dalla neve.
**snow-capped** *adj.* nevoso, incappucciato di neve.
**snow-drift** *n.* cumulo di neve; raffica di neve. **-drop** *n.* (bot.) bucaneve *m.* **-fall** *n.* nevicata. **-flake** *n.* fiocco di neve. **-line** *n.* limite *m.* delle nevi perenni.
**snow-leopard** *n.* lince *f.* **-like** *adj.* niveo; come la neve.
**snowman** *n.* pupazzo di neve.
**snow-plough** *n.* spazzaneve *m.* **-shoe** *n.* racchetta per la neve.
**snowstorm** *n.* bufera di neve.
**snow-white** *adj.* niveo.
**snowy** *adj.* nevoso, di neve, coperto di neve; niveo; *— hair*, capelli candidi; (fig.) puro, candido.
**snub**[1] *adj.* canuso, ricagnato; *n.* *— nose*, naso camuso.
**snub**[2] *n.* rimprovero, rabbuffo umiliante; mortificazione, affronto; *tr.* rimproverare, umiliare, riprendere; trattare con disprezzo; mozzar la parola a.
**snub-nosed** *adj.* dal naso ricagnato.
**snuff** *n.* aspirazione, l'aspirare col naso; tabacco da fiuto; *a pinch of —*, una presa di tabacco; *to take —*, fiutare il tabacco; (slang) *to be up to —*, essere accorto; *tr.*, *intr.* annusare, aspirare col naso; fiutare tabacco.
**snuff**[2] *n.* moccolaia, lucignolo (di candela); smoccolatura; *tr.* smoccolare (una candela); *to — out*, spegnere (una candela) con le dita; (fam.) spegnere, soffocare (una speranza, un progetto); (slang) *to — it*, crepare.
**snuff-box** *n.* tabacchiera. **-brown** *adj.* marrone scuro. **-coloured** *adj.* color tabacco.
**snuffers** *pl.n.* smoccolatoio.
**snuffing**[1] *n.* l'annusare, il fiutare, l'aspirare col naso.
**snuffing**[2] *n.* smoccolatura.
**snuffl-e** *n.* lo sbuffare, l'annusare, il respirare rumorosamente col naso; catarro nasale; *to have the -s*, avere il naso chiuso, essere raffreddato. **-ing** *gerund* il fiutare; il respirare rumorosamente dal naso; il parlare col naso; *adj.* che fiuta, che annusa.
**snuffy** *adj.* tabaccoso; che ha odor di tabacco.
**snug** *adj.* comodo; caldo; tranquillo; *to lie — in bed*, stare al calduccio sotto le coperte; ordinato; (of clothes) adatto, ben fatto; non esposto; nascosto; *to lie —*, rimanere nascosto; abbastanza buono; *a — little income*, una discreta rendita; (naut.) preparato a ogni evenienza; *intr.* (naut.) preparare una nave ad affrontare il cattivo tempo.
**snug** *n.*, **snuggery** *n.* cameretta, luogo, cantuccio comodo e tranquillo (specialmente in un bar).
**snuggle** *intr.* rannicchiarsi, accovacciarsi; *tr.* abbracciare, stringere, coccolare.
**so** *adv.* così, tanto; in tal modo; nello stesso modo; *— good*, così buono; *I'm not — bad as you think*, non sono tanto cattivo quanto credi; *I told him to do —*, gli dissi di fare così; *it is — kind of you*, è molto gentile da parte tua; *she is going to England and — is he*, lei va in Inghilterra ed anche lui; *they are — good*, sono talmente buoni; *— as to . . .*, così da . . .; *would you be — kind as to give me that book ?*, vorresti per gentilezza darmi quel libro ?; *— far*, fino ad ora, fino ad oggi; *in — far as*, per quanto; *— long as*, a patto che; *— much*, tanto; altrettanto; *— much that*, a tal punto che; *— many*, altrettanti; (provb.) *— many men, — many minds*, tante teste, tanti pareri; *— that*, affinchè; cosicchè; *— to say*, per così dire; *and — on*, eccetera, e così via dicendo; *how — ?*, come mai ?; *why — ?*, perchè mai ?; *if —*, in tal caso; *two or three or —*, circa due o tre; *I believe —*, credo di sì; *I hope —*, lo spero; *is that — ?*, davvero ?; *conj.* perciò.
**soak** *n.* immersione, bagnatura; inzuppamento, imbevimento; (of laundry) *to be in —*, essere a bagno; (slang) bevuta, sbornia; ubriacone *m.*; *tr.* immergere; bagnare; imbevere; inzuppare; macerare; saturare; *to — out*, estrarre per macerazione; smacchiare mediante immersione; *to — through*, penetrare; *I was -ed through*, ero tutto inzuppato; *to get -ed to the skin*, essere bagnato fino alle ossa; *to — up*, assorbire; impregnarsi di; (slang) tassare fortemente; estorcere denaro a; *intr.* *to — away*, sparire per infiltrazione; *to — in*, essere assorbito; penetrare.
**soaker** *n.* (slang); ubriacone *m.*, ubriacona *f.*; acquazzone *m.*; (of downpour) diluvio.
**soaking** *adj.* che bagna, inzuppa; bagnato, inzuppato; *— wet*, bagnato fradicio; *n.* immersione, bagnatura; assorbimento.
**so-and-so** *n.* (fam.) *he tells me to do —*, mi dice di fare così e cosà; *Mr. So-and-so*, Il Signor Tal dei Tali.
**soap**[1] *n.* sapone *m.*; *cake of —*, pezzo di sapone, saponetta; *soap-suds*, saponata; *soap-works*, saponificio; *soft —*, sapone liquido; (fig.) adulazione; *tr.* insaponare; *rfl.* insaponarsi.
**soapbox** *n.* cassa per sapone; (pop.) palco improvvisato per un oratore; *— oratory*, retorica da strada.
**soap-dish** *n.* portasapone *m.* **-flakes** *n.pl.* sapone in scaglie.

**soapiness** *n.* saponosità; (fig.) adulazione, untuosità.
**soaping** *n.* insaponatura.
**soap-suds** *n.pl.* saponata. **-works** *n.* saponificio.
**soapwort** *n.* (bot.) saponaria.
**soapy** *adj.* saponoso; impregnato di sapone; che sa di sapone; (bot.) saponaceo; (fig.) adulatore, insinuante, untuoso.
**soar** *intr.* librarsi in aria; spiccare il volo; elevarsi; veleggiare. **-ing** *gerund* il librarsi in aria; (fig.) volo, slancio; aumento, rialzo; elevazione; volo a vela, volo planato; *adj.* che spicca il volo; che aumenta incessantemente.
**sob** *n.* singhizzo; *intr.* singhiozzare; *to — out*, dire singhiozzando. **-bing** *gerund* il singhiozzare; *adj.* singhiozzante.
**sob-stuff** *n.* (USA) sentimentalità; *cut out the —!*, basta con quella sentimentalità!
**sober** *adj.* sobrio; equilibrato, assennato; calmo, composto; misurato; *in — fact*, in realtà, stando ai fatti; sobrio, discreto; *intr. to — down*, diventare sobrio; smaltire la sbornia; calmarsi; *tr.* far rinsavire.
**sober-minded** *adj.* saggio, serio.
**soberness, sobriety** *n.* sobrietà, moderazione, temperanza; calma; assennatezza, equilibrio.
**sobriquet** *n.* soprannome *m.*, nomignolo.
**so-called** *adj.* cosiddetto, così chiamato.
**soccer** *n.* football *m.*, calcio.
**sociab-le** *adj.* socievole; comunicativo; amichevole. **-ility, -leness** *n.* socievolezza.
**social** *adj.* sociale, della società; socievole; *man is an essentially — animal*, l'uomo è essenzialmente un animale socievole; *— evening*, serata mondana; *the — good*, il bene comune; *— science*, sociologia; *the — system*, la società; *n.* riunione sociale.
**social-ism** *n.* socialismo. **-ist** *adj.*, *n.* socialista *m.*, *f.* **-istic** *adj.* socialistico, socialista.
**society** *n.* società; compagnia; *fashionable —*, il bel mondo; confraternità; *Society of Friends*, associazione dei quacqueri; *Society of Jesus*, Compagnia di Jesù; *the Royal Society*, l'accademia reale fondata nel 1668 in Inghilterra per l'incremento degli studi scientifici e delle arti; *attrib. — gossip*, notizie mondane, pettegolezzi del bel mondo.
**sociolog-y** *n.* sociologia. **-ical** *adj.* sociologico. **-ist** *n.* sociologo.
**sock**[1] *n.* calza corta, calzino; *to pull up one's -s*, darsi da fare; soletta; socco; *— and buskin*, socco e coturno.
**sock**[2] *n.* (slang) colpo, pugno; *tr.* picchiare; percuotere.
**socket** *n.* cavità; (electr.) portalampada *m.*; bocciuolo; presa di corrente; (anat.) orbita, cavità; *— joint* (anat.) enartrosi *f.*; (techn.) manicotto, giunto ad incastri; (electr.) *bayonet-socket*, portalampada con attacco a baionetta; *eye-socket*, orbita (dell'occhio).
**socle** *n.* (arch.) zoccolo, piedistallo.
**Socrates** *pr.n.*, *m.* Socrate.
**Socratic** *adj.* (philos.) socratico.
**sod**[1] *n.* piota; zolla erbosa; tappeto erboso; *tr.* coprire di zolle.
**sod**[2] *n.* (abbrev. of **sodomite**) sodomita *m.*; (term of abuse or kindliness) compare *m.*
**soda** *n.* soda, carbonato di sodio; acqua di soda; *baking —*, bicarbonato di sodio; *caustic —*, (chem.) soda caustica; *washing —*, soda per lavare.
**sodality** *n.* congregazione, confraternità; sodalizio.
**soda-water** *n.* acqua di seltz.
**sodden** *adj.* inzuppato d'acqua; fradicio; mal cotto; molle; pesante (fig.) istupidito, abbrutito (per il troppo bere). **-ness** *n.* umidità; l'essere inzuppato, impregnato; (fig.) stupidità, ottusità.
**sodium** *n.* (chem.) sodio; *— carbonate*, carbonato di sodio; *— chloride*, cloruro di sodio, salgemma.
**sodom-y** *n.* sodomia. **-ite** *n.* sodomita *m.*
**sofa** *n.* divano; sofa *m. indecl.*
**soft** *adj.* molle; tenero; malleabile; liscio; morbido; soffice; dolce, mite; quieto, tranquillo; delicato; amabile; gentile; *— answer*, risposta gentile; tenue, attenuato; *— soap*, sapone molle, (fig.) lusinghe *f.pl.*; *— light*, luce *f.* tenue; *— music*, musica in sordina; *— pedal*, sordina; *— rain*, pioggia fine; *— voice*, voce *f.* tenue; *— palate*, palato molle; *— coal*, carbone bituminoso; (phon.) dolce; debole; effeminato; rammollito; semplice, sciocco; (slang) facile, agevole; *excl.* piano!, adagio!
**soft-** (in compounds). **-boiled** *adj.* (of eggs) 'à la coque'. **-footed** *adj.* dal passo felpato. **-hearted** *adj.* dal cuore tenero.
**soften** *tr.* ammollire, ammorbidire; calmare; raddolcire; intenerire; attenuare; *intr.* ammorbidirsi; calmarsi; raddolcirsi; intenerirsi; commuoversi. **-er** *n.* emolliente *m.*; (chem.) *water -er*, depuratore, addolcitore d'acqua. **-ing** *adj.* che rende molle, dolce; emolliente; *n.* mollificazione; ammorbidimento; rammollimento; *-ing of the brain*, rammollimento cerebrale; intenerimento, addolcimento; attenuazione.
**softly** *adv.* teneramente; dolcemente, delicatamente; sommessamente; pian piano; adagio.
**softness** *n.* morbidezza, delicatezza; dolcezza, mitezza; stupidità; debolezza, effeminatezza.
**softwood** *n.* legno dolce.
**softy** *n.* (slang) persona debole, sciocca.
**sogg-y** *adj.* umido; bagnato; saturo d'umidità; mal cotto. **-iness** *n.* umidità.
**soil**[1] *n.* suolo, terra, terreno; *native —*, paese natio.
**soil**[2] *tr.* macchiare; sporcare; concimare; *rfl.* macchiarsi; sporcarsi. **-ed** *adj.* sporco, macchiato.
**soirée** *n.* serata.
**sojourn** *n.* soggiorno; *intr.* soggiornare. **-er** *n.* ospite di passaggio. **-ing** *n.* soggiorno; dimora temporanea.
**sol** *n.* (mus.) sol.
**solace** *n.* sollievo, conforto, consolazione; *tr.* consolare; confortare; alleviare.
**solar** *adj.* solare; del sole; (anat.) *— plexus*, plesso solare; *— system*, sistema *m.* solare. **-ium** *n.* solario, stabilimento elioterapico.
**soldan** *n.* soldano, sultano.
**solder** *n.* lega per saldatura; *tr.* saldare; (fig.) unire, congiungere. **-ing** *n.* saldatura; *-ing iron*, saldatore di rame saldatoio.
**soldier** *n.* soldato, militare; *to play at -s*, giocare alla guerra; *the Unknown Soldier*, il Milite Ignoto; (ent.) formica, termite soldato; *common —*, soldato semplice; *fellow —*, commilitone *m.*; *foot-soldier*, soldato di fanteria; *horse-soldier*, soldato di cavalleria; *to go for a —*, andare soldato; *old —*, veterano, (fig.) uomo di molte risorse; *tin —, toy —*, soldatino di piombo; *intr.* fare il soldato; (fig.) *to — on*, mandare avanti la baracca, lavorare con assiduità. **-like, -ly** *adj.* marziale, militare; militaresco; *-ly bearing*, portamento marziale. **-y** *n.* soldatesca.
**sole**[1] *adj.* solo; unico; esclusivo; non accompagnato; *— heir*, unico erede; *— agent*, agente esclusivo.
**sole**[2] *n.* pianta (del piede); suola; fondo, base *f.*; *inner —*, soletta; *tr.* risolare; *to — and heel*, rifar suola e tacchi.
**sole**[3] *n.* (ichth.) sogliola.
**solecism** *n.* (gramm.) solecismo; comportamento scorretto; sconvenienza.
**solely** *adv.* solamente, unicamente; interamente, esclusivamente.
**solemn** *adj.* solenne; grave; serio. **-ity** *n.* solennità, gravità; rito solenne; festa solenne.

**solemniz-e** *tr.* solennizzare, celebrare con solennità; rendere solenne. **-ation** *n.* celebrazione.
**sol-fa** *n.* (mus.) solfeggio; *intr.* (mus.) solfeggiare.
**solfeggio** *n.* (mus.) solfeggio.
**solicit** *tr., intr.* sollecitare, fare una sollecitazione; richiedere; importunare; adescare. **-ing** *n.* adescamento.
**solicitation** *n.* sollecitazione, richiesta insistente; invito, adescamento.
**solicitor** *n.* (leg.) avvocato (con facoltà di discutere cause presso le corti di grado inferiore); *Solicitor General*, avvocato erariale.
**solicitous** *adj.* sollecito, premuroso; desideroso, ansioso; preoccupato. **-ness** premura.
**solicitude** *n.* sollecitudine *f.*; premura; ansia; preoccupazione.
**solid** *adj.* solido; consistente, compatto; tutto d'un pezzo; omogeneo; solido; reale; fondato; serio; posato; *a — vote*, un voto unanime; masiccio; *— wall*, muro pieno; (comm.) solvibile; (math.) intero; *n.* corpo solido; (geom.) solido; (math.) *— number*, numero intero.
**solidarity** *n.* solidarietà.
**solidification** *n.* solidificazione; condensazione.
**solidify** *tr., intr.* solidificare, solidificarsi; congelare, congelarsi; coagulare, coagularsi.
**solidity** *n.* solidità; (comm.) solvenza.
**solidness** *n.* solidità; compatezza; unanimità.
**solidus** *n.* solidus (antica moneta aurea romana); (typ.) barra trasversale.
**soliloqu-y** *n.* soliloquio; monologo. **-ize** *intr.* fare un soliloquio, recitare monologhi; parlare con se stesso.
**soling** *n.* solatura, risolatura.
**solitaire** *n.* (game) solitario; un diamante incastonato solo.
**solitar-y** *adj.* solo, unico; *not a — one*, nemmeno uno; solitario, solingo; isolato, romito, deserto, non frequentato; *n.* solitario; anacoreta *m.*, eremita *m.* **-iness** *n.* solitudine *f.*; isolamento.
**solitude** *n.* solitudine *f.*; isolamento; luogo solitario.
**solo** *adj.* solo, non accompagnato; *n.* (mus.) a solo; *to play —*, suonare un assolo; giuoco di carte; *to go —*, giocare a solo, (aeron.) volo solitario; *adv.* da solo. **-ist** *n.* (mus.) solista *m., f.*
**solomon** *n.* persona saggia; (bot.) *—'s seal*, sigillo di Salomone.
**so-long** (fam.) ciao, addio, arrivederci, a presto.
**solst-ice** *n.* (astron.) solstizio. **-itial** *adj.* solstiziale, solstiziario.
**solub-le** *adj.* (chem.) solubile; (fig.) solubile, risolvibile. **-ility** (chem.) solubilità; (fig.) risolvibilità.
**solution** *n.* (chem.) soluzione; processo di dissolvimento; interruzione; risoluzione; spegazione.
**solvab-le** *adj.* (comm.) solvibile; (chem.) solubile; (fig.) risolvibile. **-ility** *n.* (comm.) solvibilità; (chem.) solubilità; (fig.) risolvibilità.
**solve** *tr.* risolvere; chiarire; spiegare; *to — an equation*, risolvere un'equazione; *to — many doubts*, chiarire molti dubbi.
**solv-ency** *n.* (comm.) solvibilità; (chem.) capacità solvente. **-ent** *adj.* (comm.) solvibile; (chem.) solvente, dissolvente.
**solv-er** *n.* chi risolve, risolutore. **-ing** *n.* soluzione.
**somatic(al)** *adj.* somatico.
**somatolog-y** *n.* somatologia. **-ic(al)** *adj.* somatologico.
**sombre** *adj.* fosco, scuro; (fig.) tetro, triste. **-ness** *n.* oscurità; tetraggine *f.*; tristezza.
**sombrero** *n.* sombrero.
**some** *adj.* qualche; alcuni; certi; *at — distance*, a una certa distanza; *come and see me — day*, vieni a trovarmi un giorno o l'altro; *he will arrive — day*, arriverà uno di questi giorni; *she has been waiting (for) — time*, attende già da un po'; (partitive) del, della, dei, degli, delle; un po' di; ne; *pron.* alcuni, alcune; gli uni . . . gli altri . . .; chi . . . chi . . .; *— stayed and — went away*, alcuni rimasero là, gli altri se ne andarono; un po', una parte, una porzione; *— three hours*, circa tre ore.
**somebody** *indef. pron.* qualcuno; *— else*, qualcun altro; *n.* qualcuno, una persona famosa.
**somehow** *adv.* in qualche modo, in un modo o nell'altro; per una ragione o per l'altra.
**someone** *indef. prn.* qualcuno; *— else*, qualcun altro.
**somersault** *n.* salto mortale; capitombolo; capriola; *double —*, doppio salto mortale; *to turn a —*, fare un salto mortale, fare una capriola; (aeron.) capottamento; (motor.) ribaltamento; *intr.* far salti mortali; (aeron.) capottare; (motor.) ribaltare.
**something** *indef. pron.* qualche cosa; qualcosa; *— or other*, una cosa o l'altra; *we have — else to do*, abbiamo altro da fare; *or —*, o qualcosa di simile; *there was — of an improvement*, ci fu un certo miglioramento; *adv.* un poco; *— impatient*, un po' impaziente; circa pressappoco; *he left — like a million*, lasciò circa un millione; *this is — like a book!*, questo è veramente un buon libro!
**sometime** *adj.* di un tempo, precedente; *my — teacher*, il mio antico insegnante; *adv.* un tempo, già, altre volte; presto o tardi, un giorno o l'altro, *— soon*, uno di questi giorni.
**sometimes** *adv.* qualche volta, alcune volte, di quando in quando, talvolta; *it is — good, — bad*, è ora buono, ora cattivo.
**someway** *adv.* in un modo o nell'altro, in qualche modo.
**somewhat** *indef. prn.* un poco; *he is — of a miser*, è piuttosto avaro; *adv.* alquanto, un po', piuttosto.
**somewhere** *adv.* in qualche luogo; *— else*, in qualche altro luogo, altrove.
**somnambul-ism** *n.* sonnambulismo. **-ist** *n.* sonnambulo, sonnambula.
**somniferous** *adj.* soporifero, sonnifero.
**somnol-ence, -ency** *n.* sonnolenza, sopore *m.* **-ent** *adj.* sonnolento, sonnacchioso; assopito.
**son** *n.* figlio, figli(u)olo; *son-in-law*, genero.
**sonat-a** *n.* (mus.) sonata. **-ina** *n.* (mus.) sonatina.
**song** *n.* canto; canzone; aria; *to sell for a —*, (fam.) vendere per una schiocchezza; *nothing to make a — about*, niente d'importante; (poet.) poesia, componimento poetico; (eccl.) cantico; *the Song of Songs*, il Cantico dei Cantici; *love-song*, romanza.
**song-bird** *n.* uccello canterino. **-book** *n.* canzoniere *m.*
**songful** *adj.* melodioso, armonioso.
**songster** *n.* cantante *m., f.*, poeta *m.*; uccello canterino.
**songstress** *n.* cantante *f.*; poetessa.
**song-thrush** *n.* (orn.) tordo. **-writer** *n.* compositore di canzoni.
**sonic** *adj.* sonico; *— bang, boom*, (aeron.) scoppio sonico, esplosione sonica; *— barrier*, barriera, muro del suono; *— depth-finder*, (naut.) scandaglio acustico; *— mine*, (naut.) mina acustica.
**soniferous** *adj.* sonoro, risonante.
**sonnet** *n.* sonetto. **-eer** *n.* compositore di sonetti.
**sonny** *n.* (fam.) figliolino, piccino mio.
**sonometer** *n.* (phys.) sonometro.
**sonorific** *adj.* sonoro, risonante.
**sonority** *n.* sonorità, risonanza.
**sonorous** *adj.* sonoro, risonante; (fig.) altisonante. **-ness** *n.* sonorità, risonanza.
**sonship** *n.* condizione di figlio.
**soon, sooner** *adv.* presto, tosto, tra poco; *— after*, non molto dopo, subito dopo; *he arrived an hour too —*, arrivò con un'ora d'anticipo; *very —*, ben presto, quanto prima; *how — can you be ready?*, fra quanto tempo

sarai pronto?; *as — as,* (non) appena che, tosto che; *as — as possible,* il più presto possibile; *sooner or later,* presto o tardi, prima o poi; *no sooner said than done,* detto fatto; piuttosto; volentieri; *I would as — stay here,* starei qui volentieri.

**soot** *n.* fuliggine *f.*; *tr.* macchiare, sporcare di fuliggine; fertilizzare con cenere.

**sooth-e** *tr.* calmare, placare; blandire, lenire, addolcire; adulare, lusingare. **-ing** *adj.* lenitivo, calmante; *-ing draught,* calmante. **-ingly** *adv.* dolcemente, con dolcezza.

**soothsay-er** *n.* divinatore *m.*, divinatrice *f.*; indovino *m.*, indovina *f.* **-ing** *n.* divinazione, predizione.

**soot-y** *adj.* fuligginoso, coperto di fuliggine. **-iness** *n.* l'essere fuligginoso.

**sop** *n.* pezzo di pane, biscotto inzuppato; (fig.) dono propiziatorio; *tr.* intingere; inzuppare.

**soph-ism** *n.* sofisma *m.*; cavillo. **-ist** *n.* sofista *m.*; cavillatore.

**sophistic(al)** *adj.* sofistico; pedante, capzioso.

**sophisticat-e** *intr.* sofisticare; privare della semplicità; fare il sofistico; alterare; adulterare. **-ed** *adj.* sofisticato; raffinato; *-ed taste,* gusto eccessivamente raffinato; sofisticato, adulterato. **-ion** *n.* ragionamento sofisticato, sofisma *m.*; gusti complicati, raffinati; sofisticazione, adulterazione. **-or** *n.* falsificatore.

**sophistry** *n.* sofisma *m.*; sofisticheria; cavillo.

**sophomore** *n.* (USA) studente del secondo anno di università.

**soporific** *adj.* soporifico, soporifero; *n.* sonnifero, narcotico.

**soppy** *adj.* inzuppato; (slang) sentimental, svenevole.

**soprano** *n.* (mus.) soprano.

**sorb** *n.* (bot.) sorbo; (apple) sorba, sorbo.

**sorbet** *n.* sorbetto.

**sorbic** *adj.* (chem.) sorbico.

**sorcer-er** *n.* stregone *m.*, mago, incantatore. **-ess** *n.* strega, maga, incantatrice, fattucchiera. **-y** *n.* stregoneria, sortilegio, malia, fattura, incantesimo.

**sordid** *adj.* sordido, avaro, taccagno, spilorcio; vile, ignobile, meschino; opaco, scuro; infetto; squallido, miserabile; sudicio, sozzo. **-ness** *n.* sordidezza, spilorceria; viltà, meschinità; sporcizia, sudiciume *m.*

**sore** *adj.* doloroso; dolorante, inflammato, irritato; ulcerato; *to be — all over,* essere tutto indolenzito; *like a bear with a — head,* di umore nero; *you are a sight for — eyes,* vederti è un vero piacere; addolorato, triste, afflitto, desolato; depresso; estremo, intenso, grave, grande; *I was in — need of money,* mi trovavo in estrema necessità di danaro; (USA) seccato; *n.* piaga, ulcera; ferita; *— throat,* mal di gola, faringite *f.*; *adv.* dolorosamente; amaramente; crudelmente; gravemente.

**sorel** see **sorrel.**

**sore-ly** *adv.* dolorosamente; amaramente; crudelmente; gravemente, grandemente. **-ness** *n.* dolore *m.*; male *m.*; pena; dispiacere *m.*; rancore *m.*; irritazione.

**sorrel**[1] *n.* (bot.) acetosa.

**sorrel**[2] *adj.* di color sauro; *n.* sauro, cavallo sauro.

**sorrow** *n.* dispiacere *m.*, dolore *m.*, pena; tristezza; *to my great —,* con mio grande dolore; rincrescimento; pentimento; *pl.* sventure *f.pl.*; *intr.* affliggersi, addolorarsi; lamentarsi. **-er** *n.* chi soffre; persona addolorata. **-ful** *adj.* triste, infelice; addolorato, afflitto; melanconico, triste, penoso, doloroso. **-ing** *adj.* afflitto, addolorato; *n.* afflizione, dolore *m.*

**sorry** *adj.* dispiacente, dolente, addolorato; triste; *I am — to say that...,* mi rincresce dire che...; *—!,* scusate!; meschino, miserabile, povero; pietoso; *a — excuse,* una scusa meschina; *to cut a — figure,* fare una magra figura.

**sort** *n.* sorta; genere *m.*; specie *f.*; ordine *m.*; classe *f.*; *nothing of the —,* niente di simile; (fam.) *a good —,* una brava persona; *to be out of -s,* essere in cattive condizioni di salute; *in some —,* in un certo modo, fino ad un certo punto.

**sort** *tr.* raggruppare, classificare; scegliere, selezionare; distribuire; smistare; separare; accordarsi; adattarsi; frequentare; *to — with,* andar d'accordo con. **-able** *adj.* classificabile, selezionabile; conveniente, adatto, acconcio.

**sorter** *n.* selezionatore; classificatore.

**sortie** *n.* (mil.) sortita.

**sortilege** *n.* divinazione; sortilegio.

**sorting** *n.* classificazione; selezione.

**so-so** *adj.* mediocre, passabile; *adv.* così, così.

**sot** *n.* ubriacone, ubriacona; persona abbrutita dall'alcool.

**sottish** *adj.* istupidito, abbrutito dall'alcool; da ubriacone. **-ness** *n.* ubriachezza; alcoolismo, abbrutimento.

**sou** *n.* soldo; *he hasn't a —,* non ha il becco d'un quattrino.

**soubriquet** *n.* soprannome *m.*, nomignolo.

**soufflé** *n.* (cul.) soufflé *m.*, sformato.

**sough** *n.* (poet.) mormorìo, sussurro; sospiro profondo; *intr.* mormorare, sussurrare; sospirare profondamente.

**soul** *n.* anima; animo, spirito; *the life and — of the party,* l'anima della compagnia; *upon my —!,* parola mia!; essere *m.*; creatura, persona; *many -s were lost,* morirono molti uomini; *the poor — didn't know where to go,* la povera creatura non sapeva dove andare; personificazione, essenza; *she is the — of charity,* è la carità in persona; coraggio; forza spirituale.

**soul-destroying** *adj.* che abbrutisce; monotono; scoraggiante.

**soulful** *adj.* pieno di sentimento. **-ness** *n.* sentimento, espressione.

**soulless** *adj.* senz'anima; inespressivo; prosaico. **-ness** *n.* mancanza d'anima; inespressività; prosaicità.

**soul-searching** *n.* esame di coscienza; *adj.* che va in fondo all'anima. **-stirring** *adj.* commovente, emozionante.

**sound**[1] *adj.* sano; intero; in buono stato; *as — as a bell,* sano come un pesce; buono; solido; valido, legittimo; giudizioso; *— views,* vedute equilibrate; profondo; totale, completo; *a — sleep,* un sonno profondo; sincero, leale, onesto; *adv.* profondamente; *to be — asleep,* dormire profondamente.

**sound**[2] *n.* suono, rumore *m.*; rimbombo; tocco, rintocco; tono, intonazione; *intr.* suonare, risuonare; rimbombare; echeggiare; sembrare, dare l'impressione di, aver l'aria di; far suonare, far risuonare; far sentire; far risapere; *to — an alarm,* dare l'allarme; *to — the retreat,* suonare la ritirata; *to — the praises of,* cantare le lodi di; (med.) auscultare.

**sound**[3] *n.* (naut.) sondaggio; (surg.) sonda; *intr.* (naut.) sondare, scandagliare; fare dei sondaggi; (surg.) sondare; *n.* braccio di mare; stretto.

**sound** (in compounds) **-absorption** *n.* assorbimento acustico. **-barrier** *n.* barriera del suono. **-board** *n.* (of pianoforte) tavola. **-box** *n.* cassa di risonanza. **-effects** *n.pl.* (cinem.) effetti sonori. **-film** *n.* film sonoro. **-hole** *n.* esse (di violino). **-post** *n.* anima (di violino). **-projector** *n.* (cinem.) proiettore sonoro. **-proof** *adj.* impenetrabile al suono. **-shift** *n.* (phon.) rotazione consonantica. **-track** *n.* (cinem.) colonna sonora. **-truck** (cinem.) carro sonoro. **-wave** *n.* onda sonora.

**sounder** *n.* ricevitore telegrafico acustico; (teleph.) manipolatore fonico; *echo —,* (naut.) scandaglio acustico.

**sounding**[1] *adj.* sonoro, sonante, risonante; (fig.) pomposo, ridondante; *n.* suono, risonanza; seniorità; rimbombo; segnale *m.*; (med.) auscultazione.
**sounding**[2] *n.* (naut.) scandaglio; *pl.* (naut.) fondali scandagliabili; *to be in -s*, essere in acque poco profonde; *to strike -s*, toccare il fondo; (surg.) sondaggio.
**sounding-board** *n.* (mus.) tavola armonica.
**soundless**[1] *adj.* muto, senza suono, senza rumore.
**soundless**[2] *adj.* (naut.) insondabile, non scandagliabile; senza fondo.
**soundly** *adv.* sanamente; solidamente; giudiziosamente; fortemente, profondamente; *to sleep* —, dormire saporitamente.
**soundness** *n.* stato sano, buona condizione, buono stato; solidità; vigore *m.*; sicurezza; rettitudine *f.*, ortodossia; — *of judgement*, sicurezza di giudizio; (comm.) solidità, solvibilità.
**soup** *n.* zuppa, minestra; brodo; (fam.) *clear* —, consommé *m.*, *pea* —, passato di piselli; *to be in the* —, trovarsi nei pasticci. **-kitchen** *n.* mensa gratuita per i poveri. **-ladle** *n.* cucchiaione, mestolo. **-plate** *n.* fondina, scodella. **-tureen** *n.* zuppiera.
**soupy** *adj.* simile a zuppa, come zuppa; spesso, denso.
**sour** *adj.* agro, aspro; acerbo; acido, fermentato; — *milk*, latte acido; *to turn* —, inacidire; bisbetico, arcigno, amaro; umido, fangoso; (of soil) poco fecondo; *n.* sostanza, soluzione acida; acqua acidulata; *tr.* rendere agro; inacidire; acidificare; (fig.) esacerbare, inasprire.
**source** *n.* fonte *f.*, sorgente *f.*, (fig.) fonte, origine *f.*; principio; causa; documenti, libri, materiale di consultazione. **-book** *n.* raccolta di documenti.
**sour-ing** *n.* inasprimento; inacidimento. **-ish** *adj.* acidulo; asprigno. **-ness** *n.* acidità; acerbità; asprezza; (fig.) acrimonia; asprezza.
**sour-sweet** *adj.* agro-dolce.
**sous-e** *n.* vivande marinate; salamoia; *tr.* (cul.) marinare, mettere in salamoia; immergere, tuffare; inzuppare; rovesciare; *intr.* (slang) ubriacarsi; *n.* tuffo, immersione; (slang) ubriacatura.
**sous-ed** *adj.* marinato; (slang) ubriaco. **-ing** *adj.* marinato; immerso; inzuppato; *n.* (cul.) marinatura, il mettere in salamoia; immersione.
**soutane** *n.* (eccl.) tonaca, sottana dei preti.
**South** *adj.* del sud, del mezzogiorno, meridionale; — *coast*, costa meridionale; — *wind*, vento del sud; *South Sea*, il Pacifico; *n.* sud, mezzogiorno, mezzodì; *in the* —, al sud; *adv.* a sud, verso sud; *to travel* —, viaggiare verso il sud.
**south-east** *adj.* di sud-est; *n.* sud-est; *adv.* verso sud-est. **-er** *n.* vento di sud-est. **-erly** *adj.* di sud-est; *adv.* verso sud-est. **-ern** *adj.* di sud-est.
**south-eastward** *adj.* a, di sud-est.
**south-eastward(s)** *adv.* verso sud-est.
**southerly** *adj.* del sud, che viene dal sud; meridionale, australe; — *latitude*, latitudine australe; *adv.* verso sud; dal sud.
**southern** *adj.* del sud, del mezzo giorno, meridionale, australe; *n.* abitante del sud, meridionale; — *lights*, aurora australe. **-er** *n.* abitante del sud, meridionale; (USA) sudista *m.*, *f.*
**southernmost** *adj.* il più a sud, il più meridionale.
**southernwood** *n.* (bot.) artemisia.
**south-most** *adj.* il più a sud; il più meridionale. **-ward** *adj.* verso sud; *n.* sud. **-ward(s)** *adv.* verso sud.
**south-west** *adj.* di sud-ovest; *n.* sud-ovest; *adv.* verso sud-ovest. **-er** *n.* vento di sud-ovest; libeccio, garbino; cappellaccio a gronda. **-erly** *adj.* a sud-ovest, di sud-ovest, verso sud-ovest; *adv.* verso sud-ovest.
**south-westward** *adj.* verso sud-ovest; *n.* sud-ovest.
**souvenir** *n.* ricordo.
**sovereign** *adj.* sovrano, supremo, superiore; estremo, sommo; *the — good*, il sommo bene; *n.* sovrano *m.*, sovrana *f.*; re *m.*, regina *f.*; monarca *m.*; principe *m.*; sovrana, sterlina d'oro. **-ty** *n.* sovranità.
**soviet** *n.* soviet *m.*; *adj.* sovietico; *the Union of Socialist Soviet Republics* (*U.S.S.R.*), l'Unione delle Repubbliche Socialiste Sovietiche (U.R.S.S.).
**sow** *n.* scrofa; (metall.) canale di colata per lingotti; metallo solidificato nei canali di colata.
**sow** *tr.* seminare; piantare, disseminare; spargere; *to — land with corn*, seminare un terreno a grano. **-er** *n.* seminatore. **-ing** *n.* seminagione *f.*
**sowing-machine** *n.* macchina seminatrice. **-seed** *n.* semenza.
**soy, soya** *n.* (cul.) soi *m.* (salsa piccante cinese e giapponese fatta con la soia); — *bean*, soia.
**spa** *n.* sorgente d'acqua minerale; stazione termale.
**space** *n.* spazio, intervallo; momento; istante *m.*; *after a short* —, dopo breve tempo; posto; distesa; superficie *f.*; estensione; *blank* —, spazio in bianco; *tr.* spaziare; scaglionare, disporre ad intervalli; dividere, suddividere; (typ.) *to — out*, allargare gli spazi. **-bar** *n.* barra spaziatrice. **-capsule** *n.* capsula spaziale.
**spaceman** *n.* (neol.) astronauta *m.*
**space-pilot,** pilota *m.* spaziale; **-probe,** sonda spaziale.
**spacer** *n.* spaziatore (di macchina per scrivere).
**space-ship** *n.* astronave *f.* **-travel** *n.* astronautica. **-traveller** *n.* astronauta *m.* **-writer,** giornalista pagato un tanto per riga.
**spacing** *n.* (typ.) spaziatura, interlineatura; scaglionamento; suddivisione.
**spacious** *adj.* spazioso; ampio; vasto. **-ness** *n.* spaziosità; vastità.
**spade**[1] *n.* vanga; badile *m.*; *to call a — a* —, dire pane al pane; *tr.* vangare.
**spade**[2] *n.* (cards) picche; (slang, derog.) negro.
**spadeful** *n.* palata, vangata.
**spade-work** *n.* vangatura; lavoro preliminare.
**spaghetti** *n.* (cul.) spaghetti *m.pl.*; *this — is good*, questi spaghetti sono buoni; *this — is terrible*, questi spaghetti sono pestiferi.
**Spain** *pr.n.* (geog.) Spagna.
**spam** *n.* carne suina in scatola.
**span** *n.* spanna, palmo; breve spazio di tempo; *our life is but a* —, la vita non è che un breve passo di tempo; larghezza, apertura; *single-span bridge*, ponte ad una sola arcata; *wing-span*, apertura d'ala; *tr.* misurare a spanne; circondare; abbracciare; formare un arco con, estendersi attraverso; attraversare.
**spandrel** *n.* pennacchio (di un arco); altezza dei portali.
**spangle** *n.* lustrino, piccolo oggetto scintillante; *tr.*, *intr.* coprire, ornare di lustrini; brillare, risplendere.
**Spaniard** *adj.*, *n.* spagnuolo.
**spaniel** *n.* spaniel *m.*, cane spagnolo; (fig.) persona strisciante, servile; leccapiedi *m. indecl.*
**Spanish** *adj.* di Spagna, spagnuolo; — *fly*, (entom.) cantaride *f.*; — *influenza*, spagnola; — *onion*, cipolla dolce; *n.* lo spagnuolo.
**spank** *tr.*, (fam.) sculacciare; dare le botte a; schiaffeggiare.
**spanking**[1] *n.* sculacciata.
**spanking**[2] *adj.* di prim'ordine, eccellente; gagliardo, vigoroso; *a — trot*, un trotto rapido.
**spanner** *n.* chiave *f.* inglese.
**spar**[1] *n.* trave *f.*; palo, pertica; bastone *m.*; (naut.) alberatura; *tr.* munire di pali; (naut.) fornire di alberatura.
**spar**[2] *intr.* combattersi, battersi, esercitarsi al pugilato; *sparring*

*partner*, compagno per allenarsi.
**spare** *adj.* parco, frugale, sobrio; *a — meal*, un pasto frugale; magro, smilzo, sparuto; d'avanzo, disponibile, superfluo, in più; di riserva, di ricambio; *— room*, camera in più; *— time*, tempo disponibile; *— parts*, pezzi di ricambio; *— wheel*, ruota di scorta; *n.* pezzo di ricambio.
**spare** *tr.*, *intr.* essere frugale, economico; risparmiare, risparmiarsi; economizzare, far economia; *to — no expense*, non badare a spese; privarsi, fare a meno di; *to have enough and to —*, avere più del necessario; fare grazia di; evitare.
**spare-ly** *adv.* parcamente, frugalmente, stentatamente. **-ness** *n.* magrezza, sparutezza.
**sparing** *adj.* parco, frugale; sobrio; economo, parsimonioso; *— of words*, sobrio di parole, di poche parole; limitato, moderato, ristretto; *n.* risparmio, economia. **-ness** *n.* frugalità; sobrietà; parsimonia, economia.
**spark**[1] *n.* scintilla, favilla; (fig.) lampo, barlume *m.*; battuta, motto di spirito; (electr.) scintilla; *pl.* (naut. slang) radiotelegrafista *m.*; *intr.* emettere scintille, scintillare; *tr.* (electr.) fare esplodere, accendere.
**spark**[2] *n.* uomo galante, damerino; (iron.) *you're a bright —!*, sei brillante!
**sparking** *n.* (electr.) emissione di scintille; accensione mediante scintilla elettrica; *adj.* acceso; scintillante.
**sparking-plug** *n.* (motor.) candela (d'accensione).
**sparkl-e** *n.* scintilla, favilla; scintillio; splendore *m.*; vivacità di spirito; *intr.* emettere scintille (di fuoco); scintillare, sfavillare; brillare, risplendere; (of wine) spumeggiare, mussare. **-er** *n.* persona, cosa brillante; diamante *m.* **-et** *n.* piccola scintilla. **-ing** *adj.* scintillante, brillante; (of wine) spumante.
**sparrow** *n.* (orn.) passero. **-hawk** *n.* sparviero.
**sparse** *adj.* rado, poco denso; che si trova, che avviene ad intervalli irregolari. **-ly** *adv.* scarsamente; *-ly populated*, poco popolato; ad intervalli irregolari. **-ness** *n.* radezza, scarsità.
**spartan** *adj.*, *n.* spartano.
**spasm** *n.* spasimo; crampo; accesso, attacco. **-odic(al)** *adj.* spasmodico; intermittente; saltuario.
**spastic** *adj.*, *n.* spastico.
**spat**[1] *n.* uova di mollusco; *tr.*, *intr.* deporre uova (di molluschi).
**spat**[2] *n.* ghettina.
**spatchcock** *n.* (cul.) pollo, uccello alla griglia; *tr.* (cul.) cuocere (un volatile) alla griglia.
**spate** *n.* piena; inondazione; *in —*, in piena.
**spatial** *adj.* spaziale.
**spatter** *n.* schizzo, spruzzatura; macchia; gocciolio; *tr.*, *intr.* schizzare, inzaccherare; macchiare; gocciolare.
**spatul-a** *n.* spatola. **-ar, -ate** *adj.* a forma di spatola.
**spavin** *n.* (vet.) spavenio.
**spawn** *n.* (of fish) uova; (bot.) micelio; (pejor.) razza, progenie *f.*; *tr.*, *intr.* (of fish) deporre uova; (pejor.) generare, produrre; moltiplicare. **-er** *n.* pesce, mollusco che depone uova. **-ing** *n.* fecondazione.
**spay** *tr.* (vet.) asportare le ovaie a.
**speak** *intr.*, *tr.* parlare; *honestly -ing*, per parlare francamente; *roughly -ing*, approssimativamente; *so to —*, per così dire; *-ing for myself*, per quel che mi riguarda; *do you — English?*, parlate l'inglese?; esprimere; rivelare, far conoscere, manifestare; *to — one's mind*, parlare liberamente, dire la propria opinione; *the trumpets spoke*, le trombe suonarono; *to — for*, parlare per?, essere il portavoce di; testimoniare per; *speaking of ...*, a proposito di ...; *to — out*, parlare ad alta voce; parlare francamente; *to — up*, parlare più forte; *— up!*, alza la voce!; *to — up for*, parlare a favore di.
**speakeasy** *n.* (USA, hist.) bar clandestino.
**speaker** *n.* parlatore; interlocutore, oratore; annunciatore; *the Speaker of the House of Commons*, il presidente della Camera dei Comuni; (radio) altoparlante magnetodinamico.
**speaking** *adj.* parlante, che parla; espressivo, eloquente; *— likeness*, somiglianza parlante; *they were no longer on — terms*, non si rivolgevano più la parola; *n.* eloquenza, declamazione, arte oratoria. **-tube** *n.* tubo acustico, portavoce *m. indecl.* a tubo.
**spear** *n.* lancia; alabarda; asta; giavellotto; lanciere *m.*; fiocina; *tr.* pungere, trafiggere con lancia. **-head** *n.* ferro di lancia; punta di lancia; (fig.) avanguardia. **-man** *n.* lanciere *m.* **-mint** *n.* menta da giardino.
**spec** *abbrev.* of **speculation**; *on spec*, per provare.
**special** *adj.* speciale, particolare; apposito; *nothing —*, niente di particolare; *to make a — study of*, specializzarsi in; eccezionale; straordinario; *— mission*, missione straordinaria; intimo, preferito, amato; *my — friend*, il mio amico intimo; *— correspondent*, inviato speciale; *— edition*, edizione straordinaria; *— train*, treno speciale. **-ist** *n.* specialista *m.*, *f.*
**speciality** *n.* specialità; particolarità; caratteristica; *that is not my —*, non è il mio forte.
**specializ-e** *tr.*, *intr.* specializzare, specializzarsi; limitare; modificare; (biol.) differenziare. **-ation** *n.* specializzazione. **-ing** *n.* specializzazione.
**speciality** *n.* (comm.) specialità, articolo speciale; (leg.) contratto sigillato; documento legale sotto sigillo.
**specially** *adv.* specialmente, particolarmente; soprattutto.
**specie** *n.* denaro contante.
**species** *n.* (bot.; zool.) specie *f.*, classe *f.*; sorta, genere *m.*, tipo; (philos.; theol.) specie, apparenza; immagine *f.*; forma.
**specifiable** *adj.* specificabile, determinabile; distinguibile.
**specific** *adj.* specifico; particolare; preciso, determinato; *— aim*, scopo preciso; *n.* (pharm.) (rimedio) specifico; (phys.) *— weight*, *— gravity*, peso specifico. **-ally** *adv.* specificamente; particolarmente; precisamente.
**specification** *n.* specificazione; (leg.) *— of charge*, capo d'accusa; descrizione dettagliata.
**specify** *tr.* specificare, precisare; determinare; *unless otherwise specified*, salvo indicazione contraria.
**specimen** *n.* modello, esemplare, saggio, campione *m.*; *to take a — of blood*, prelevare un campione di sangue; (fam.) tipo, individuo; *what a —!*, che tipo!; *— copy*, libro in esame.
**specious** *adj.* specioso; capzioso. **-ness** *n.* speciosità.
**speck**[1] *n.* macchiolina, punto; chiazza; granello, atomo; briciola, filo; difetto, macchia; *tr.* macchiare; chiazzare.
**speckle** *n.* macchiolina; *tr.* macchiare; screziare. **-d** *adj.* macchiato; screziato.
**specs** *n.pl.* (*abbrev.* **spectacles**) (fam.) occhiali *m.pl.*
**spectacle** *n.* spettacolo; vista; *to make a — of oneself*, (fam.) dare spettacolo di sè; *pl.* occhiali; *to put on one's -s*, mettersi gli occhiali; *to see life through rose-coloured -s*, vedere la vita in rosa.
**spectacled** *adj.* che porta gli occhiali, occhialuto; (zool.) avente macchie a forma di occhiali.
**spectacles-case** *n.* astuccio per occhiali. **-frame** *n.* montatura per occhiali.
**spectacular** *adj.* spettacolare, grandioso; teatrale; *n.* (cinem.) film spettacoloso.
**spectator** *n.* spettatore.
**spectral**[1] *adj.* spettrale, fantomatico; *— ship*, nave fantasma; (phys.) spettrale.
**spectral**[2] *adj.* spettrale; *the — colours*, i colori dello spettro.

**spectre** *n.* spettro, fantasma *m.*; apparizione.
**spectro-graph** *n.* (phys.) spettrografo. **-graphy** *n.* (phys.) spettrografia. **-heliograph** *n.* (astr.) spettroeliografo. **-meter** *n.* (phys.) spettrometro. **-scope** *n.* (phys.) spettroscopio. **-scopy** *n.* (phys.) spettroscopia.
**spectrum** *n.* (phys.) spettro.
**specular** *adj.* speculare; — *surface*, superficie *f.* speculare.
**speculat-e** *tr.*, *intr.* speculare, meditare, considerare; congetturare; *to — on*, meditare su; (comm.) speculare. **-ion** *n.* speculazione, contemplazione, (comm.) speculazione. **-ive** *adj.* speculativo, contemplativo, meditativo; congetturale; *-ive philosophy*, filosofia speculativa; (comm.) speculativo. **-or** *n.* spirito speculativo, pensatore; osservatore; (comm.) speculatore.
**speculum** *n.* (med.) specolo; (of telescope) specchio.
**speech** *n.* parola, favella; modo di parlare; *to be slow of —*, essere lento nel parlare; *to lose the power of —*, perdere l'uso della parola; discorso, ragionamento; osservazione; lingua, linguaggio; discorso; arranga; *King's, Queen's —, — from the throne*, discorso della Corona; *maiden —*, primo discorso (di un membro del Parlamento); (gramm.) discorso; *direct —*, discorso diretto; *indirect —*, discorso indiretto; *parts of —*, parti del discorso; *— day*, giorno della premiazione.
**speechify** *intr.* (pejor.) fare discorsi; arringare. **-ing** *gerund* l'arringare; il fare discorsi.
**speechless** *adj.* senza parole, muto. **-ness** *n.* mutismo.
**speed** *n.* velocità, rapidità, celerità; fretta; passo rapido; *at full —*, a tutta velocità; a briglia sciolta; a gambe levate; *— trial*, prova di velocità; *top —*, velocità massima; (mus.) tempo; (provb.) *more haste less —*, chi ha fretta vada adagio; *God send you good —*, Dio ti mandi buona fortuna; (slang) droga stimolante; *intr.*, *tr.* affrettarsi, andare in fretta; prosperare, aver successo; far prosperare, aiutare; *God — you!*, che Dio ti aiuti; accomiatare, salutare; *to — the parting guest*, salutare l'ospite in partenza; *to — an arrow from the bow*, scoccare una freccia; regolare la velocità di una macchina; *to — up*, accelerare, affrettare.
**speed-boat** *n.* (naut.) fuoribordo. **-cop** *n.* (USA) agente della Polizia Stradale.
**speedily** *adv.* rapidamente, prontamente, affrettatamente, presto.
**speediness** *n.* celerità, rapidità, velocità; prontezza; sollecitudine.
**speed-limit** *n.* limite di velocità.
**speedometer** *n.* tachimetro, indicatore di velocità.
**speedway** *n.* pista, circuito (di autodromo); (USA) autostrada.
**speedwell** *n.* (bot.) veronica.
**speedy** *adj.* rapido, pronto, spedito, veloce, celere; *a — answer*, una risposta pronta.
**spelaeolog-y** *n.* speleologia. **-ist** *n.* speleologo.
**spell**[1] *n.* formula magica; incanto, incantesimo, malia; fascino, attrattiva, seduzione; *to be under the — of*, subire il fascino di; *to cast a — over*, gettare un incantesimo su; *tr.* affascinare, incantare; investire di poteri magici.
**spell**[2] *n.* turno (di lavoro); cambio (di sentinella); spazio di tempo; breve periodo; momento; *to do a — of duty*, fare un turno di servizio; (fam.) breve distanza.
**spell**[3] *tr.* compitare, sillabare, scrivere; *what does L.O.V.E. —?*, che parola formano le lettere L.O.V.E.?; *how do you — it?*, come si scrive?; *she couldn't —*, non sapeva l'ortografia; (fig.) significare, implicare; *to — ruin*, significare la rovina.
**spell-bind** *tr.* affascinare, incantare. **-binder** *n.* oratore affascinante. **-bound** *adj.* affascinato, incantato, ammaliato; sotto l'influenza di un incantesimo.
**speller** *n. to be a good —*, conoscere bene l'ortografia; sillabario.
**spelling** *n.* compitazione; ortografia; *to be good at —*, essere forte in ortografia.
**spelling-bee** *n.* gara di ortografia. **-book** *n.* abbecedario.
**spelt** *n.* (bot.) spelta, grano farro.
**spend** *tr.* spendere, sborsare; dedicare, impiegare; consumare; esaurire; passare, trascorrere.
**spendable** *adj.* spendibile.
**spender** *n.* chi spende.
**spending** *n.* lo spendere; spesa.
**spendthrift** *n.* dissipatore, prodigo.
**spent** *adj.* consumato; esausto, esaurito; *— cartridge*, cartuccia vuota; *— volcano*, vulcano spento.
**sperm** *n.* (biol.) sperma *m.*; spermatozoo.
**spermaceti** *n.pl.* spermaceti *n.pl.*, bianco di balena.
**spermatozoon** *n.* (biol.) spermatozoo.
**sperm-oil** *n.* olio di balena. **-whale** *n.* (zool.) capidoglio.
**spew** *n.* vomito; *tr.* vomitare. **-ing** *n.* vomito.
**sphagnum** *n.* (bot.) sfagno.
**sphere** *n.* sfera, globo; *the celestial —*, la sfera celeste; (fig.) ambiente *m.*; *— of action*, sfera, campo d'azione.
**spheric(al)** *adj.* sferico. **-ity** *n.* sfericità.
**spheriform** *adj.* a forma di sfera.
**spheroid** *n.* (geom.) sferoide *m.*
**sphincter** *n.* (anat.) sfintere *m.*
**sphinx** *n.* sfinge *f.*; *the Sphinx*, la Sfinge; (fig.) persona enigmatica.
**spice**[1] *n.* spezie *f.*; aroma; (fig.) sapore *m.*; gusto; sfumatura; *tr.* condire con spezie, aromatizzare; (fig.) dar sapore, gusto a; rendere interessante, aggiungere un pizzico di arguzia a.
**spiced** *adj.* condito con spezie, aromatizzato; (fig.) gustoso, saporoso.
**spiciness** *n.* gusto aromatico; aroma, profumo; (fam.) arguzia; salacità.
**spick-and-span** *adj.* (fam.) lindo; accurato; fresco; lucente; *their house is always —*, la loro casa è sempre pulita come uno specchio.
**spicy** *adj.* aromatico; piccante; pepato; (fig.) arguto, mordace; alquanto salace.
**spider** *n.* ragno; *-s web*, ragnatela; (USA) treppiedi *m.*, trespolo; (techn.) crociera; (electr.) sistema di bracci; (metall.) armatura.
**spider-crab** *n.* (zool.) ragno di mare. **-monkey** *n.* (zool.) atele *m.*
**spiderwort** *n.* (bot.) tradescanzia, erba miseria.
**spidery** *adj.* simile a ragno; infestato da ragni.
**spigot** *n.* zipolo, cavicchio, piuolo; (USA) rubinetto.
**spike**[1] *n.* punta, aculeo; (techn.) grosso chiodo a becco; *tr.* inchiodare; fermare con punte; munire di aculei; (mil.) rendere inservibile (un cannone); (fig.) *to — someone's guns*, guastare i piani di qualcuno.
**spike**[2] *n.* spiga; inflorescenza a spiga; *— lavender*, spigo di lavanda; *— oil*, essenza di lavanda.
**spike**[3] *n.* ministro della chiesa anglicana che ha delle tendenze ultramontane.
**spiked** *adj.* fornito di aculei.
**spikenard** *n.* (bot.) spigonardo.
**spiky** *adj.* aguzzo, irto; munito di punte; (fam.) stizzoso.
**spill**[2] *n.* rovesciamento; caduta, capitombolo; *tr.* versare; spandere; rovesciare; (provb.) *it is no use crying over spilt milk*, è inutile piangere sul latte versato; (naut.) sventare; (fam.) *to — the beans*, svelare le magagne, fare delle indiscrezioni; *intr.* versarsi; traboccare.
**spill**[2] *n.* scheggia; legnetto; carta arrotolata per accendere candele, pipe: zipolo.
**spillikin** *n.* stecco di legno, o

di osso; *pl.* giuoco fatto con stecchi.
**spillway** *n.* sfioratore (di diga).
**spin**[1] *n.* movimento rotatorio, rotazione; breve corsa (in bicicletta, auto); *to go for a —*, andare a fare una passeggiata (in bicicletta, macchina); (aeron.) avvitamento; *tr.* filare; imbutire, lavorare al tornio; (fig.) produrre, comporre, stendere; *to — a yarn*, raccontare una storia; far girare; far ruotare; *to — out*, prolungare, tirare in lungo; *to — out the time*, ingannare il tempo; *to — along*, andare a tutta velocità.
**spinach** *n.* spinaci *m.pl.*
**spinal** *adj.* (anat.) spinale, vertebrale; *— column*, colonna vertebrale; *— cord*, midollo spinale.
**spindle** *n.* fuso, fusello; perno, asse *m.*; mandrino; (aeron.) aerometro; (naut.) asse *m.*; albero; *tr.* (techn.) dar forma fusiforme a. **-shanks** *n.* persona lunga e magra dalle gambe affusolate. **-shaped** *adj.* fusiforme.
**spindly** *adj.* sottile, affusolato.
**spine** *n.* spino, spina; lisca; spina dorsale, colonna vertebrale; (of a book) dorso. **-less** *adj.* senza spina dorsale; (fam.) debole, molle, senza carattere.
**spinet** *n.* (mus.) spinetta.
**spinnaker** *n.* (naut.) controranda.
**spinner** *n.* filatore, filatrice; macchina filatrice; (zool.) ragno filatore.
**spinney** *n.* boschetto, sottobosco.
**spinning** *n.* filatura; filato; movimento rotatorio, rotazione. **-frame** *n.* filatoio. **-jenny** *n.* gianetta. **-mill** *n.* stabilimento di filatura, filanda. **-wheel** *n.* filatoio.
**spinster** *n.* filatrice; (leg.) donna nubile; (fam.) zitella. **-hood** *n.* l'essere nubile; condizione di zitella.
**spiny** *adj.* pieno di spine, spinoso; (fig.) difficile; imbarazzante.
**spiraea** *n.* (bot.) spirea.
**spiral** *adj.* spirale, a spirale, elicoidale; *n.* (geom.) spirale *f.*, elica; *tr.*, *intr.* formare una spirale; girare a spirale; dar forma spirale a.
**spire**[1] *n.* guglia; cuspide *f.*
**spire**[2] *n.* spira; spirale *f.*
**spirit**[1] *n.* spirito; anima; folletto; fantasma *m.*; essere incorporeo; genio, intelletto; coraggio; vigore *m.*; vivacità, brio; *a young man of —*, un giovane pieno di energia; *pl.* umore *m.*, disposizione, stato d'animo; intendimento, significato; *he obeyed the true — of the law*, si attenne al vero spirito della legge; *to take something in the wrong —*, prendere qualcosa in mala parte; *pl.* umore *m.*; disposizione; *in low -s*, depresso; *to be in high -s*, avere il morale alto; liquori alcoolici; *tr. to — away*, rapire; *to — off*, portare via in circostanze misteriose.
**spirited** *adj.* brioso, vivace; animoso; ardente, focoso; *high-spirited*, fiero, ardente; *mean-spirited*, meschino; *poor-spirited*, fiacco; vile; *public-spirited*, dotato di senso di civismo.
**spiritless** *adj.* inanimato, esanime; monotono; insulso; pusillanime; abbattuto, avvilito; fiacco, apatico. **-ness** *n.* apatia; monotonia; pusillanimità; abbattimento, avvilimento.
**spirit-level** *n.* livella a bolla d'aria.
**spiritual** *adj.* spirituale, dello spirito; *Lords Spiritual*, vescovi membri del Parlamento inglese; *n.* (USA) canto religioso negro.
**spiritual-ism** *n.* spiritismo. **-ist** *n.* spiritista *m.*, *f.*
**spirituality** *n.* spiritualità; *pl.* (hist.) beni ecclesiastici.
**spiritualiz-e** *tr.* spiritualizzare. **-ation** *n.* spiritualizzazione.
**spirituous** *adj.* alcoolico, spiritoso.
**spirt** see **spurt**[2].
**spit**[1] *n.* (cul.) spiedo, schidione; (geog.) lingua di terra; banco lungo e stretto; *tr.* mettere allo spiedo, schidionare; trafiggere.
**spit**[2] *n.* sputo; saliva; (fam.) *the very — of*, il ritratto parlante di; (mil. slang) *— and polish*, il pulire a pomice; *intr.* sputare; (of rain) cadere lievemente; (of candle) mandar faville; (of pen) spruzzare inchiostro; (of a cat) soffiare; *to — at, upon*, trattare con disprezzo; *tr. to — out*, sputare; pronunciare con violenza; *— it out!*, sputa fuori!
**spit**[3] *n.* vangata; profondità raggiunta con una vangata.
**spite** *n.* dispetto; rancore *m.*; malevolenza; *in — of*, nonostante, malgrado, a dispetto di; *tr.* far dispetto a, importunare, vessare, contrariare.
**spiteful** *adj.* dispettoso; vendicativo; malevolo; malintenzionato. **-ly** *adv.* per dispetto; con rancore; in modo vendicativo. **-ness** *n.* rancore *m.*; malevolenza.
**spitfire** *n.* persona collerica; (aeron.) tipo di aereo da caccia.
**spitting** *n.* sputo; espettorazione; lo sputare; *no — !*, vietato sputare!
**spittle** *n.* sputo; saliva, bava.
**spittoon** *n.* sputacchiera.
**splash** *n.* schizzo, spruzzo; *whisky and a —*, whisky al seltz; (fig.) *to make a —*, far colpo, attrarre l'attenzione; tonfo; pillacchera; macchia, chiazza; (journ.) *— headline*, titolo sensazionale; *tr.* schizzare, spruzzare; macchiare; *to — ink on*, macchiare d'inchiostro; (fig.) *to — one's money about*, scialacquare il denaro; inzaccherare, infangare; *intr.* impantanarsi; cadere con un tonfo; diguazzare; *to — through the river*, attraversare il fiume diguazzando.
**splash-board** *n.* parafango.
**splashing** *n. gerund* lo schizzare; *n.* schizzata, spruzzata; spruzzamento.
**splatter** *tr.*, *intr.* schizzare, spruzzare; sciabordare; barbugliare.
**splatterdash** *n.* chiasso, clamore *m.*; *pl.* uose *f.pl.*, ghette *f.pl.*
**splay** *adj.* largo e piatto; obliquo; storto; (bldg.) strombato; *n.* sguancio, strombo; svasatura; *tr.*, *intr.* svasare; (bldg.) strombare, sguanciare; essere in posizione obliqua; slogare; spallare. **-foot** *n.* piede piatto volto all'infuori.
**spleen** *n.* (anat.) milza; (fig.) malumore *m.*, umore nero; bile *f.*, collera; *to vent one's — on*, scaricare la propria stizza su.
**splendid** *adj.* splendido, magnifico, stupendo; sfarzoso; eccellente, ottimo; *that's — !*, fantastico!
**splendour** *n.* splendore *m.*; lustro; magnificenza; pompa.
**splenetic** *adj.*, *n.* (pathol.) splenetico, bilioso; (fig.) collerico, irritabile; stizzoso.
**splice**[1] (naut.) impiombatura; (carpen.) giunto a ganasce, giunto assiale.
**splice**[2] *tr.* (naut.) impiombare; (carpen.) calettare; (cinem.) montare (un film); (fam.) unire in matrimonio; *to get -d*, sposarsi; (naut. slang) *to — the mainbrace*, distribuire una razione supplementare di rum.
**splicing** *n.* (naut.) impiombatura; (carpen.) calettatura, giuntura; (cinem.) montaggio.
**splint** *n.* (med.) assicella, stecca; scheggia; *tr.* (med.) steccare, fissare con assicelle (un arto fratturato).
**splinter** *n.* scheggia, frantume *m.*; (med.) stecca; *tr.* scheggiare; *intr.* scheggiarsi. **-y** *adj.* pieno di schegge; scheggiabile.
**split**[1] *adj.* spaccato, diviso; *— peas*, piselli secchi; *— personality*, tendenza alla schizofrenia; *— second*, frazione di secondo; *n.* fessura; spaccatura; crepaccio; strappo (di tessuto); divisione, separazione; rottura; scissione; *pl.* (ginnastica) *to do the -s*, fare la spaccata.
**split**[2] *tr.* fendere; spaccare; scheggiare; *my head is splitting*, mi scoppia la testa; (fig.) *to — hairs*, spaccare un capello in quattro; *to — one's sides*, ridere a crepapelle; strappare; stracciare; dividere; ripartire; frazionare; (phys.) *to — the atom*, scindere l'atomo; (slang) *to — on*, de-

nunciare, tradire; *to — off*, distaccare; separare; *to — up*, frazionare; suddividere; *intr.* fendersi, spaccarsi; frazionarsi.
**split-pin** *n.* chiavetta. **-ring** *n.* anello doppio.
**splitting** *adj.* che si fende, che fende; (fig.) acuto; *a — headache*, un acuto mal di testa; *n.* fessura, spaccatura; scheggiamento; divisione; separazione; *gerund* (phys.) *the — of the atom*, la scissione dell'atomo.
**splodge, splotch** *n.* (fam.) macchia, chiazza.
**splurge** *n.* (fam.) ostentazione, esibizionismo; *intr.* (fam.) darsi arie; scialacquare.
**splutter** *tr.*, *intr.* barbugliare, parlare in modo confuso; sputacchiare; (of pen) spruzzare, crepitare.
**spoil** *n.* spoglia, preda; bottino; (fig.) profitto, vantaggio; (of snake) spoglia; carcame *m.*; (miner.) detrito; *the -s of war*, le spoglie della guerra; *tr.* rovinare, danneggiare; alterare; sciupare, deturpare; viziare; *to — a child*, viziare un bambino; saccheggiare, predare; rubare; *intr.* (of food) guastarsi, avariarsi, alterarsi. **-er** *n.* saccheggiatore; predatore. **-ing** *n.* deterioramento, avaria.
**spoilt** *adj.* guasto, avariato, rovinato; *a — child*, un bambino viziato.
**spoke**[1] *n.* razza, raggio (di ruota); piuolo (di scala); (naut.) impugnatura del timone; maniglia; bastone per arrestare le ruote di un carro; *to put a — in someone's wheel*, mettere un bastone fra le ruote a qualcuno.
**spoke**[2] *p.def.* of **speak**, *q.v.*
**spokesman** *n.* portavoce *m. indecl.*
**spondee** *n.* (poet.) spondeo.
**sponge**[1] *n.* spugna; (boxing) *to throw up the —*, gettare la spugna, abbandonare il combattimento; colpo di spugna; spugnatura; (med.) compressa, batuffolo; (artill.) scovolo; (fig.) spugna, scroccone *m.*, parassita *m.*; *tr.*, *intr.* pulire, lavare con la spugna; *to — down*, passare con la spugna il corpo di; (med.) fare spugnature a; (fam., pejor.) scroccare; *to — on*, vivere alle spalle di; *to — out*, cancellare (also fig.); *— up*, assorbire con spugna.
**sponge-bath** *n.* spugnatura. **-cake** *n.* pan di Spagna; savoiardo. **-cloth** *n.* (text.) spugna.
**sponger** *n.* parassita *m.*, scroccone *m.*
**sponginess** *n.* spugnosità.
**sponging** *n.* lavatura con la spugna; (text.) decatizzazione; (fam.) parassitismo.
**spongy** *adj.* spugnoso, poroso; elastico; assorbente; (fam.) tirchio.
**sponsor** *n.* (eccl.) padrino, madrina; *to stand — to a child*, tenere a battesimo un bambino; *n.* (leg.) garante *m.*, *f.*, mallevadore; (comm.) chi offre un programma radiofonico (a scopo pubblicitario); *to be — to a programme*, offrire un programma; *tr.* rendersi responsabile di; essere garante di; offrire (un programma radiofonico). **-ship** *n.* garanzia; condizione di padrino, di madrina.
**spontane-ous** *adj.* spontaneo; involontario; automatico. **-ity** *n.* spontaneità.
**spoof** *n.* (fam.) truffa, imbroglio, frode *f.*, *tr.* truffare, imbrogliare, frodare.
**spook** *n.* (fam.) spettro, apparizione.
**spool**[1] *n.* rocchetto, bobina; *delivery —*, bobina svolgitrice; (cinem.) *take-up —*, bobina ricevitrice; *tr.* avvolgere su rocchetto, incannare; *to — off*, svolgere.
**spoon** *n.* cucchiaio; *to be born with a silver — in one's mouth*, essere nato con la camicia; (golf) mazza; *table —*, cucchiaio da tavola; *tr.* prendere con un cucchiaio; *intr.* (fam.) baciucchiare.
**spoonbill** *n.* (orn.) spatola.
**spoon-feed** *tr.* nutrire col cucchiaio; (fig.) far la pappa a, coccolare. **-fed** *part. adj.* nutrito col cucchiaio; (fig.) coccolato.
**spoonful** *n.* cucchiaiata.
**spoor** *n.* traccia, pista.
**sporadic(al)** *adj.* sporadico; isolato, raro.
**spore** *n.* (biol.) spora. **-case** *n.* sporangio.
**sporran** *n.* borsa coperta di pelo (accessorio del costume scozzese).
**sport** *n.* giuoco; divertimento; passatempo; sport *m.*; *to be the — of fortune*, essere lo zimbello della fortuna; *to spoil the —*, guastare la festa; scherzo, burla; *to make — of*, farsi giuoco di; *to go in for —*, darsi agli sport; (biol.) specie anomala; (slang) persona sportiva; *he is a real —*, è un tipo chic; *come on, be a —!*, orsù, sii sportivo!, prendila con spirito!; *pl.* gare, incontri.
**sport** *intr.* giocare; scherzare; burlarsi; trastullarsi; baloccarsi; (biol.) produrre una specie anomala; *tr.* ostentare, mettere in mostra; *he was -ing a new coat*, si pavoneggiava con una giacca nuova; (Univ., Oxford and Cambridge) *to — one's oak*, tenere la porta chiusa per non essere disturbato.
**sporting** *adj.* sportivo; *— spirit*, spirito sportivo; *gerund* il burlarsi, lo scherzare; (biol.) produzione di specie anomala. **-dog** *n.* cane da caccia. **-gun** *n.* fucile da caccia.
**sportive** *adj.* gioviale; sportivo.
**sports-edition,** edizione sportiva. **-ground** *n.* terreno da giuoco; stadio. **-model** *n.* automobile da corsa. **-suit** *n.* tenuta sportiva.
**sportsman** *n.* sportivo; uomo animato da spirito sportivo; uomo leale; *he is a real —*, è un giocatore leale. **-like** *adj.* caratteristico di uno sportivo; leale. **-ship** *n.* abilità sportiva; spirito sportivo; lealtà.
**sportswear** *n.* abiti sportivi.
**sportswoman** *n.* donna sportiva.
**spot** *n.* luogo, località, posto; *a pretty —*, un bel posticino; *to arrive on the —*, arrivare sul posto; *on the —*, sul colpo; immediatamente sveglio, all'altezza della situazione; *they were killed on the —*, furono uccisi sul colpo; *this is his weak —*, questo è il suo punto debole; (slang) *to put on the —*, mettere in imbarazzo; chiazza della pelle; *a white dress with blue spots*, un vestito bianco a pallini azzurri; *— remover*, smacchiatore; goccia; (fam.) goccio; *a — of whisky*, un goccio di whisky; (comm.) *— cash*, denaro contante; *— market*, (comm.) mercato del disponibile.
**spot** *tr.* macchiare; punteggiare; infamare, tacciare; individuare, distinguere, riconoscere; scoprire; indovinare; (mil.) localizzare; *intr. to — with rain*, piovere leggermente, piovigginare.
**spotless** *adj.* senza macchia; immacolato; puro; *— conscience*, coscienza pulita.
**spotlight** *n.* (theatr.; cinem.) luce della ribalta; proiettore, riflettore; *to hold the —*, essere al centro della scena; *tr.* puntare i riflettori su; (fig.) mettere in evidenza, illuminare.
**spotted** *adj.* macchiato, chiazzato; picchiettato; maculato; a pallini.
**spotter** *n.* ricognitore.
**spotty** *adj.* chiazzato, macchiato; foruncoloso; irregolare, ineguale, non uniforme.
**spouse** *n.* sposo, sposa; coniuge *m.*, *f.*
**spout** *n.* tubo di scarico; grondaia; beccuccio; getto, colonna; cascata; *water —*, tromba marina; (slang) *to be up the —*, essere in pegno; essere sfinito, perduto, rotto; *intr.* scaricare; gettare; zampillare; scaturire, sgorgare; (slang) declamare; parlare a getto continuo. **-er** *n.* (slang) declamatore, oratore *m.* **-ing** *n.* zampillo, getto; (fig.) declamazione.
**sprain** *n.* distorsione; strappo muscolare; *tr.* distorcere; storcere; *to — one's ankle*, slogarsi la caviglia.

**sprat** *n.* (ichth.) spratto; *to throw a — to catch a mackerel,* dare poco per aver molto; (joc.) bimbo mingherlino.
**sprawl** *intr.* adagiarsi in modo scomposto; *to — on the bed,* sdraiarsi sul letto; *to send -ing,* mandar a gambe all'aria; allargarsi, estendersi; *n.* stiracchiamento. **-ing** *adj.* sdraiato.
**spray**[1] *n.* rametto, frasca.
**spray**[2] *n.* spruzzo, schiuma; getto vaporizzato liquido per vaporizzazioni; vaporizzatore, polverizzatore, spruzzatore; *tr.* polverizzare, vaporizzare, atomizzare; aspergere, spruzzare; innaffiare. **-er** *n.* spruzzatore, vaporizzatore; (agric.) irroratrice. **-ing** *n.* polverizzazione, vaporizzazione; irrorazione, annaffiamento; *-ing machine,* macchinetta vaporizzatrice.
**spread** *adj.* steso; aperto; spiegato; *n.* crescita; espansione; estensione; *middle-aged —,* apertura; la ciccia (di mezza età); *— of wings,* apertura d'ali; diffusione, divulgazione, propagazione; coperta; (fam.) festino, banchetto.
**spread** *tr.* stendere; spargere; spiegare; spalmare; coprire; *to — butter on bread,* spalmare il burro sul pane; (fig.) spargere; diffondere; propagare; disseminare; *flies — disease,* le mosche propagano le malattie; (fam.) *to — oneself,* farsi in quattro; avere mille attività; darsi delle arie, pavoneggiarsi; tendere, protendere; *intr.* spendersi; spargersi; diffondersi.
**spread-eagle** *tr.* mettere in posizione di aquila spiegata; *n.* (herald.) aquila spiegata; figura del pattinaggio artistico.
**spreader** *n.* chi propaga; spruzzatore; (agric.) concimatrice.
**spreading** *adj.* che si propaga; che si estende; folto, frondoso; *a — tree,* un albero frondoso; *gerund* lo stendersi; *n.* estensione, sviluppo; (fig.) propagazione, diffusione.
**spree** *n.* baldoria; *to be on the —,* far baldoria.
**sprig** *n.* ramoscello, rametto; disegno, lavoro a fiorami, a foglie; puntina; chiodino; (fig.) rampollo; giovincello; *tr.* ornare a fiorami, a foglie. **-ged** *adj.* a fiori, a ramoscelli; *-ged muslin,* mussola a fiorami.
**spright** *n.* see **sprite.**
**sprightl-y** *adj.* allegro, brioso, gaio, vivace. **-iness** *n.* allegria, brio, vivacità.
**Spring**[1] *n.* primavera; *attrib.* di primavera, primaverile; *— cleaning,* pulizia di primavera; *— tide,* marea equinoziale.
**spring**[2] *n.* sorgente *f.*, fonte *f.*; *pl.* terme *f.pl.*; (fig.) principio, origine *f.*; causa; salto, balzo; slancio; elasticità; molla; *spiral —,* molla a elica cilindrica.
**spring**[3] *intr.* nascere, discendere, derivare, procedere; scaturire; spuntare; spiccare; balzare; scattare; *the door sprang open,* la porta si spalancò di scatto; munire di sospensioni (una vettura); (naut.) fendersi, incrinarsi; *to — at,* gettarsi su; *to — at the enemy,* balzare sul nemico; *to — up,* saltare su; spuntare, crescere; *to — up into the air,* fare un balzo in aria. **-balance** *n.* bilancia a molla. **-board** *n.* trampolino. **-clip** *n.* staffa della balestra. **-lock** *n.* serratura a scatto. **-water** *n.* acqua di sorgente, acqua viva; *tr. to — a leak,* aprire una falla; *to — a mine,* far brillare una mina; (fam.) proporre; *to — a new theory,* proporre una nuova teoria.
**springbok** *n.* (zool.) antidorcade *f.*; (sport) *the Springboks,* i sud-africani, la squadra di calcio sud-africana.
**springer** *n.* saltatore; *n.* (zool.) antilope sud-africana; varietà di cane Spaniel; grampo; (archit.) chiave dell'arco; nervatura.
**springiness** *n.* elasticità, forza elastica.
**springing** *n.* principio; origine *f.*; nascita; zampillamento; il balzare, il saltare; (motor.) sospensione; (archit.) linea di imposta.
**spring-like** *adj.* primaverile, di primavera. **-tide** *n.* tempo di primavera. **-time** *n.* tempo di primavera.
**springy** *adj.* pieno di sorgenti; elastico; svelto, agile.
**sprinkl-e** *n.* aspersione, spruzzatina; pizzico; *tr.* spargere; spruzzare, aspergere, irrorare; *intr.* (of rain) piovigginare. **-er** *n.* spruzzatore; innaffiatoio; (eccl.) aspersorio. **-ing** *n.* spruzzamento, aspersione, spruzzo; (fig.) pizzico; infarinatura.
**sprint** *n.* (sport) sprint *m.*, scatto finale; *intr.* percorrere (una distanza) alla massima velocità; correre a tutta velocità. **-er** *n.* (sport) velocista *m.*
**sprit** *n.* (naut.) pennoncino.
**sprite** *n.* folletto, elfo, spirito.
**sprocket** *n.* rocchetto, rullo dentato. **-chain** *n.* catena articolata. **-hole** *n.* perforazione (di pellicola cinematografica). **-hum** *n.* (cinem.) ronzio. **-wheel** ruota dentata.
**sprout** *n.* germoglio; tallo; *pl.* (Brussels) sprouts, cavolini di Bruxelles; *tr.*, *intr.* germogliare, far germogliare; spuntare; crescere, far crescere. **-ing** *gerund* il germogliare, il crescere; *adj.* che germoglia, in germe.
**spruce**[1] *adj.* attillato; azzimato; lindo; elegante; *tr.* adornare, agghindare; *to — oneself up,* azzimarsi, agghindarsi.
**spruce**[2] *n.* (bot.) abete rosso.
**spruceness** *n.* lindezza; ricercatezza; eleganza.
**sprung** *p. def.*, *part. of* **spring,** *q.v.*, *adj.* a sospensione, a molla; spaccato, rotto.
**spry** *adj.* attivo, vivace, agile.
**spud** *n.* (agric.) sarchio; (fam.) patata; (mil. slang) *— bashing,* il pelar patate; *tr.* sarchiare, rimuovere (erbacce) col sarchio.
**spume** *n.* spuma, schiuma; *tr.* spumare, schiumare.
**spunk** *n.* (slang) coraggio, audacia, fegato; ira, collera. **-y** *adj.* audace, coraggioso; irato.
**spur** *n.* sperone *m.*; *to win one's spurs,* (hist.) essere investito cavaliere, (fig.) distinguersi, farsi un nome; (fig.) sprone *m.*, stimolo, impulso; *on the — of the moment,* di impulso, lì per lì; (geog.) contrafforte *m.*; *tr.* spronare; fornire di speroni; (fig.) stimolare, incitare; *to — on,* cavalcare a spron battuto.
**spurge** *n.* (bot.) euforbia.
**spurious** *adj.* spurio, falso; apocrifo; *— coin,* moneta falsa; illegittimo, bastardo. **-ness** *n.* falsità, contraffazione; carattere apocrifo; illegittimità.
**spurn** *tr.*, *intr.* disprezzare, disdegnare; rifiutare sdegnosamente; respingere.
**spurt**[1] *n.* breve sforzio improvviso; scatto di velocità; *intr.* fare un breve sforzo improvviso; scattare.
**spurt**[2] *n.* zampillo, getto improvviso; *tr.*, *intr.* schizzare, far schizzare; spuzzare; zampillare.
**sputter** *n.* barbugliamento; discorso rapido e confuso; spruzzo di penna; crepitìo, scoppiettìo; *tr.*, *intr.* barbugliare, parlare in modo confuso; sputacchiare; spruzzare; crepitare. **-er** *n.* barbuglione *m.*
**sputum** *n.* sputo; espettorato.
**spy** *n.* spia, spione, delatore; *tr.* spiare; notare; osservare, scrutare; *to — out,* indagare segretamente; scoprire; *intr.* fare la spia, spiare.
**spy-glass** *n.* cannocchiale *m.* **-hole** *n.* (techn.) spia, foro di vista.
**spying** *n.* spionaggio.
**squab** *adj.* tozzo; tarchiato; grassoccio; implume; timido; *n.* persona tozza; piccione implume.
**squabbl-e** *n.* battibecco; lite *f.*; alterco; zuffa; *intr.* venire a parole; accapigliarsi; altercare. **-er** *n.* attaccabrighe *m.*, *f.*
**squad** *n.* (mil.) squadra; plotone *m.*; drappello; banda, cricca.
**squadron** (naut.; aeron.) squadra, squadriglia; (mil.) squadrone *m.* (di cavalleria); battaglione (di fanteria).

**squalid** *adj.* squallido, miserabile; sordido.

**squall** *n.* urlo; schiamazzo; strepito; turbine *m.*, bufera; burrasca; (fig.) litigio; *intr.* urlare; vociare; schiamazzare; strepitare. **-ing** *adj.* schiamazzante; *n.* grido; schiamazzo. **-y** *adj.* tempestoso, burrascoso.

**squalor** *n.* squallore *m.*; miseria; sudiciume *m.*

**squander** *tr.* sciupare, sprecare; sperperare, scialacquare. **-er** *n.* sciupone *m.*; sperperatore. **-ing** *gerund* lo sciupare; *n.* spreco; sperperamento.

**square** *adj.* quadro, quadrato; *to be a — peg in a round hole*, non essere adatto ad un lavoro; robusto, massiccio, tozzo; ad angolo retto, perpendicolare; (fig.) sistemato, pareggiato; ordinato; *to be — with*, sdebitarsi con; esatto; netto, deciso; giusto, leale, onesto; (math.) quadrato, al quadrato; (math.) — *root*, radice quadrata; (golf) pari; (fam.) *a — meal*, un pasto sostanzioso; (pop.) integrato, antiquato conformista.

**square** *n.* quadrato, oggetto di forma quadrata; (mil.) quadrato, disposizione a quadrato; piazza; blocco; squadra; (math.) quadrato; quadretto; (metall.) barra quadra; (slang) *to be a —*, essere conformista *m.*, *f.*, essere un Matusa.

**square** *tr.* quadrare, squadrare, riquadrare; *to — the circle*, trovare la quadratura del circolo; *to — the account*, pareggiare, sistemare il conto; (fig.) *to — accounts with*, fare i conti con; conformare; accordare; adattare; (math.) elevare al quadrato; (fam.) corrompere; *to be -d*, essere comprato; (techn.) regolare, mettere a punto; *to — off*, quadrettare (un foglio); *to — up*, squadrare; *intr.* accordarsi; adattarsi; *to — up to*, assumere un atteggiamento bellicoso verso.

**square** *adv.* ad angolo retto; in forma quadrata; in squadra; direttamente; esattamente; *he was hit — in the face*, fu colpito proprio in faccia; (fam.) onestamente, con lealtà.

**square-built** *adj.* tarchiato.

**squared** *adj.* squadrato, quadrato; (math.) elevato al quadrato; quadrettato.

**squarely** *adv.* a forma di quadrato; direttamente; *to face —*, affrontare con coraggio; lealmente, onestamente.

**squash**[1] *n.* schiacchiamento; spremitura; spremuta; ressa, calca, pigia pigia *m.*; (fam.) ricevimento affollato; *tr.* schiacciare, spiaccicare; spremere; (fam.) sopprimere, stroncare; soffocare; (fig.) ridurre al silenzio; sconcertare; *intr. to — into a place*, accalcarsi in un luogo.

**squash**[2], **squash-rackets** *n.* (sport) squash *m.*, giuoco praticato con racchette e palla in un campo cintato.

**squash**[3] *n.* (bot.) melopopone *m.*

**squashy** *adj.* molle, molliccio; tenero; acquitrinoso; pantanoso.

**squat** *adj.* rannicchiato, accoccolato, seduto sui calcagni; tozzo, corto; tarchiato; schiacciato; *n.* posizione accoccolata, accucciata; persona tozza; *intr.* accovacciarsi, accoccolarsi; acquattarsi (di animali in pericolo); (fam.) sedersi, far sedere; impossessarsi abusivamente di un terreno pubblico; occupare un terreno pubblico per farne pascolo.

**squatt-er** *n.* persona che si accovaccia; animale accovacciato, acquattato; chi occupa abusivamente uno stabile, un terreno; chi occupa una proprietà per acquistare il diritto di tenerlo; *-s' rights*, diritti di occupazione abusiva. **-ing** *gerund* il rannicchiarsi, l'accovacciarsi, l'accoccolarsi; l'impossessarsi abusivamente di una proprietà pubblica; occupazione di un terreno pubblico per farne pascolo; *adj.* rannicchiato, accovacciato.

**squaw** *n.* squaw *f.*, moglie, donna dei pellirosse; (USA, joc.) donna.

**squawk** *n.* grido rauco e aspro; richiamo; *intr.* emettere un grido rauco, spezzato; gridare raucamente; (fam.) lamentare, lamentarsi con voce piagnucolosa. **-er** *n.* chi grida raucamente; chi si lamenta, chi protesta con voce aspra e rauca.

**squeak** *n.* grido acuto, strillo; grido, pigolio, squittio, guaito; cigolio, scricchilio; suono acuto; (slang) *to have a narrow —*, scamparla bella, scamparla per un filo; *intr.* strillare in tono acuto; dire con voce stridula; squittire, guaire; stridere, cigolare, scricchiolare; (slang) cantare. **-er** *n.* chi, ciò che emette un suono acuto. **-y** *adj.* che grida, che strilla con voce acuta; che guaisce; che squittisce; cigolante, scricchiolante, stridente.

**squeal** *n.* grido forte ed acuto, strillo; *intr.* strillare, gridare; (slang) protestare vivacemente; fare la spia, tradire. **-er** *n.* chi strilla, grida; (slang) chi si lamenta e protesta; spia, traditore. **-ing** *adj.* che strilla, che grida; *n.* grido forte ed acuto, strillo.

**squeamish** *adj.* soggetto a nausee; — *stomach*, stomaco delicato; schizzinoso, schifiltoso, di gusti difficili; scrupoloso. **-ness** *n.* disposizione alle nausee, delicatezza di stomaco; l'essere schizzinoso, di gusti difficili.

**squeez-e** *n.* compressione, pressione; schiacciamento, spremitura; restrizione; *a — of lemon*, poche gocce di limone; stretta; abbraccio; pizzicotto; calca, affollamento; *it was a tight —*, si era pigiati come sardine; estorsione di denaro; (econ.) estringimento; *tr.* spremere; stringere; abbracciare; spingere; estorcere (denaro); *intr.* accalcarsi; *please — up a little*, per favore stringetevi un pochino. **-er** *n.* chi, ciò che preme, spreme, strizza, schiaccia; (techn.) strettoio, torchio. **-ing** *n.* compressione, pressione; estorsione.

**squelch** *n.* rumore di chi sguazza nel fango; tonfo; *intr.* spiaccicare; fare ciac ciac; *tr.* (fam.) soffocare, sopprimere.

**squib** *n.* petardo; razzo; miccia; *to let off a —*, far partire un petardo; (fig.) *a damp —*, un affare mancato, un fiasco; satira, pasquinata.

**squid** *n.* (zool.) calamaro, seppia; seppia usata come esca.

**squiffy** *adj.* (sl.) brillo, alticcio.

**squill** *n.* (bot.) scilla, cipolla marittima; (zool.) squilla, cannocchia.

**squint** *adj.* strabico; *n.* strabismo; *he has a fearful —*, è tremendamente strabico; sguardo furtivo; occhiata furtiva; *I had a — at his letter*, gettai uno sguardo furtivo alla sua lettera; (archit.) finestrella obliqua; *intr.* essere strabico; (fig.) *to — at*, guardare di traverso; lanciare un'occhiata furtiva a.

**squint-eyed** *adj.* strabico.

**squinting** *n.* strabismo.

**squirarchy** see **squirearchy.**

**squire** *n.* gentiluomo, nobiluomo di campagna, castellano; *the —*, il principale possidente della contea, il signore del villaggio; (hist.) scudiero; cavalier servente; — *of dames*, cicisbeo; *tr.* accompagnare, scortare; fare da scorta a; dominare, governare.

**squirearchy** *n.* i proprietari terrieri, i gentiluomini di campagna; (Eng. hist.) governo dei proprietari terrieri.

**squirm** *n.* contorsione, contorcimento; attorcigliamento; *intr.* contorcersi; dimenarsi; attorcigliarsi; (fig.) mostrare imbarazzo; essere sulle spine; aversela a male; impazientirsi. **-ing** *adj.* contorto; dimenandosi.

**squirrel** *n.* scoiattolo.

**squirt** *n.* siringa; estintore d'incendi; zampillo, schizzo, piccolo getto d'acqua; (slang) *a little —*, un ometto, un tizio; *tr.* schizzare; zampillare; stringare; iniettare.

**squit** *n.* (slang) persona insignificante, nullità.

**stab** *n.* coltellata, pugnalata; fitta, dolore acuto; *tr.*, *intr.* pugnalare, accoltellare; ferire; martellare, dar colpi con la martellina a. **-bing** *gerund* il colpire con pugnale, l'accoltellare; *adj.* lancinante.

**stability** *n.* stabilità, fermezza; equilibrio; solidità; *man of no* —, uomo incostante.

**stabiliz-e** *tr.* stabilizzare, dare stabilità a. **-ation** *n.* stabilizzazione. **-er** *n.* (chem.; aeron.) stabilizzatore.

**stable**[1] *adj.* stabile, fermo, saldo; permanente; equilibrato; *to become* —, consolidarsi; *a* — *man*, una persona costante; *a* — *job*, un'occupazione permanente.

**stable**[2] *n.* scuderia, stalla; (provb.) *to shut the* — *door after the horse is gone*, chiudere la stalla quando i buoi sono fuggiti; allevamento di cavalli da corsa; personale di scuderia; *pl.* (mil.) servizio di stalla; *livery* —, stallaggio con noleggio di cavalli; *racing* —, scuderia di cavalli da corsa; *tr.* tenere in stalla; mettere in stalla.

**stable-boy** *n.* mozzo di stalla. **-companion** *n.* cavallo della stessa scuderia; (fam.) compagno.

**stabling** *n.* stallaggio; stalle, scuderie *f.pl.*

**staccato** *adj.*, *n.* (mus.) staccato.

**stack** *n.* mucchio, cumulo, ammasso; catasta; bica; pagliaio; fascio; *-s of money*, un sacco di soldi, soldi a palate; gruppo di camini; fumaiolo; *tr.* ammucchiare, accatastare, fare un mucchio di; abbicare; *to* — *the cards*, barare.

**stadium** *n.* stadio, campo sportivo.

**staff**[1] *n.* bastone *m.*; *pastoral* —, pastorale *m.*; *pilgrim's* —, bordone *m.*; (fig.) sostegno; *bread is the* — *of life*, il pane è il sostegno della vita; asta di bandiera; (naut.) albero, alberetto; (mil.) stato maggiore; personale *m.*; paletto graduato; biffa; (mus.) sistema *m.*; *diplomatic* —, corpo diplomatico; *domestic* —, personale di servizio; *editorial* —, corpo redazionale; *tr.* fornire di personale; *over-staffed*, con eccedenza di personale.

**stag** *n.* cervo.

**stag-** (in compounds). **-beetle** *n.* (entom.) cervo volante. **-hunt(ing)** *n.* caccia al cervo. **-party** *n.* riunione per soli uomini.

**stage** *n.* piattaforma; impalcatura; palcoscenico; teatro; *the English* —, il teatro inglese; *to come on the* —, entrare in scena; *to go on the* —, diventare attore, calcare le scene; *revolving* —, palcoscenico girevole; (fig.) campo d'azione, scena, teatro; grado, stadio, momento, periodo; *at that* — *an interruption occurred*, in quel momento ci fu un'interruzione; tappa; distanza tra due tappe; *tr.* mettere in scena, rappresentare; inscenare.

**stage-** (in compounds). **-box** *n.* (theatr.), palco di proscenio. **-coach** *n.* diligenza. **-direction** *n.* (theatr.) didascalie *f.pl.* **-door** *n.* porta di servizio (di teatro). **-fright** *n.* timore panico prima del debutto. **-hand** *n.* macchinista *m.* **-manager** *n.* regista *m.* **-name** *n.* nome d'arte. **-whisper** *n.* (theatr.) a parte.

**stagecraft** *n.* scenotecnica.

**stager** *n. an old* —, persona esperta, scaltrita.

**stagger** *n.* barcollamento, ondeggiamento, andatura a zig-zag; *pl.* vertigini *f.pl.*; (vet.) capogatto.

**stagger** *intr.* vacillare; barcollare; brancolare; ondeggiare; *tr.* sconcertare; scuotere; impressionare; *I was -ed by the news*, fui scosso dalla notizia; distribuire in turni; scaglionare; *to* — *the working hours of the staff*, stabilire dei turni di lavoro per il personale. **-ing** *adj.* sconcertante, sbalorditivo.

**staghound** *n.* grosso cane da caccia, specialmente per la caccia ai cervi.

**staging** *n.* (theatr.) messa in scena, allestimento scenico; (bldg.) impalcatura, ponteggio; viaggio in diligenza; guida di una diligenza.

**stagn-ant** *adj.* stagnante, fermo; — *water*, acqua stagnante, acqua morta; *business is* —, c'è un ristagno negli affari. **-ancy** *n.* ristagno, stasi *f.*

**stagnat-e** *intr.* ristagnare, fermarsi, cessare di scorrere; intorpidirsi; essere inattivo. **-ion** *n.* ristagno; stasi *f.*; inattività; torpore *m.*

**stagy** *adj.* (pejor.) teatrale, istrionico; artificioso.

**staid** *adj.* grave, posato, serio, sobrio. **-ness** *n.* compostezza, serietà; saggezza, ponderazione.

**stain** *n.* macchia; scolorimento; (fig.) taccia, macchia, onta, vergogna; colore *m.*, tinta; *tr.* macchiare; sporcare; stingere. **-ed** *adj.* macchiato; sporco; scolorito; colorato; tinto; *-ed glass window*, vetrata colorata, istoriata. **-ing** *n.* tintura; colorazione; (chem.) *-ing agent*, agente rivelatore; *-ing test*, prova con rivelatore.

**stainless** *adj.* senza macchia, immacolato; — *reputation*, reputazione senza macchia; che non scolorisce, non stinge; che non arrugginisce, inossidabile; — *steel*, acciaio inossidabile.

**stain-remover** *n.* smacchiatore.

**stair** *n.* scalino, gradino; scale *f.pl.*; *below -s*, nel seminterrato, nelle stanze della servitù; *flight of -s*, rampa di scale; gradinata.

**stair-carpet** *n.* passatoia.

**staircase** *n.* scala; scalone *m.*; tromba delle scale; *moving* —, scala mobile; *winding* —, scala a chiocciola.

**stairhead** *n.* pianerottolo.

**stair-rail** *n.* ringhiera delle scale. **-rod** *n.* bacchetta per fissare il tappeto alla scala.

**stairway** *n.* scala, scalone *m.*

**staith(e)** *n.* molo; scalo per il carbone.

**stake**[1] *n.* palo; piuolo, picchetto; paletto; rogo; *to be condemned to the* —, essere condannato al rogo; *tr.* sostenere con pali; palare; infrascare; legare a piuolo; trafiggere; *to* — *out*, cintare, chiudere con una palizzata; circoscrivere, delimitare con picchetti; (topogr.) palinare, picchettare; biffare; *to* — *out a claim*, reclamare, pretendere, rivendicare.

**stake**[2] *n.* posta, scommessa, puntata; *to play one's last* —, giocare l'ultima carta; *at* —, in giuoco; *to have a* — *in*, avere degli interessi in; (equestr.) premio; corsa; *tr.* mettere in giuoco, scommettere, giocare, rischiare; *I'd* — *my life on it*, ci scommetterei l'osso del collo.

**stake-money** *n.* posta, scommessa.

**stalactit-e** *n.* stalattite *f.* **-form** *adj.* stalattiforme.

**stalagmit-e** *n.* stalagmite *f.* **-ic** *adj.* stalagmitico.

**stale** *adj.* vecchio, stantio; — *air*, aria viziata; — *beer*, birra vecchia; — *bread*, pane raffermo; *to smell* —, sapere di vecchio, di stantio, di rinchiuso; (fig.) trito; — *joke*, barzelletta vecchia; esaurito, spossato; *intr.* diventare stantio; (fig.) perdere sapore.

**stalemate** *n.* (chess) stallo; (fig.) punto morto; *tr.* (chess) fare stallo a, tenere in scacco; (fig.) portare a un punto morto.

**staleness** *n.* l'essere raffermo; l'odorar di stantio, di chiuso; scipitezza, banalità.

**stalk** *n.* (bot.) stelo, gambo; peduncolo; andatura rigida e maestosa; passo altero; caccia furtiva alla preda; pedinamento silenzioso; *intr.* camminare con andatura rigida e maestosa; camminare a passi misurati; *tr.* inseguire furtivamente. **-ed** *adj.* (bot.) fornito di gambo, di peduncolo. **-er** *n.* persona che cammina a passi lunghi; cacciatore; cacciatore in agguato.

**stalking-horse** *n.* cavallo dietro a cui si apposta il cacciatore; (fig.) pretesto, maschera.

**stall**[1] *n.* stalla; banco di vendita; bancarella; chiosco; reparto; (eccl.) stallo, scanno; *a canon's* —,

stallo canonico; (fig.) canonicato; (theatr.) poltrona (di platea); *tr.* mettere in stalla; *intr.* (motor.) fermarsi; (aeron.) stallare.

**stall**[2] *intr.* (USA) parlare, agire evasivamente; *quit -ing!*, smettila di menare il can per l'aia!; *tr.* ritardare; *to — off*, tenere a bada.

**stallion** *n.* stallone *m.*

**stalwart** *adj.* robusto, forte, gagliardo; prode, valente, coraggioso; risoluto; *n.* persona coraggiosa; sostenitore; *one of the old -s*, uno della vecchia guardia. **-ness** *n.* vigoria, robustezza; risolutezza, coraggio.

**stamen** *n.* (bot.) stame *m.*

**stamina** *n.* capacità di resistenza, forza vitale, vigore *m.*; *man of great —*, uomo di fibra robusta; *young man who lacks —*, giovanotto senza spina dorsale.

**stammer** *n.* balbettamento; balbuzie *f.pl.*; *tr.*, *intr.* balbettare, tartagliare; farfugliare, parlare confusamente. **-er** *n.* balbuziente *m.*, *f.* **-ing** *gerund* il balbettare; *adj.* balbuziente, balbettante; *n.* balbuzie *f.pl.*; balbettìo.

**stamp** *n.* impronta; segno; bollo, francobollo; marchio; stampigliatura; timbro; *official —*, marchio officiale; (techn.) mazza battente; (metall.) stampo; (fig.) tipo, sorta, stampo, genere *m.*; *man of that —*, uomo di tal tempra; colpo (di piede).

**stamp** *tr.* imprimere, incidere, stampare; lasciare una impronta di; (fig.) marcare, dare l'impronta a; caratterizzare; timbrare; apporre un visto a; stampigliare; bollare; affrancare; pestare, battere i piedi; *to — the snow from one's feet*, scrollarsi la neve dalle scarpe; *to — with rage*, pestare i piedi per la rabbia; (metall.) stampare, punzonare; *to — out*, soffocare, domare; annientare.

**stamp-** (in compounds). **-album** *n.* album per francobolli. **-collector** *n.* filatelico. **-duty** *n.* tassa di bollo. **-paper** *n.* carta da bollo.

**stampede** *n.* fuga disordinata e precipitosa (di massa di animali); fuggi-fuggi *m.*; *intr.* fuggire in disordine; essere presi dal panico; *tr.* far fuggire, causare panico a.

**stamper** *n.* timbratore; punzonatore; (techn.) stampo; timbratrice; punzone; frantumatrice.

**stamping** *n.* scalpitìo; timbratura, bollatura; affrancatura; (techn.) stampaggio; (miner.) polverizzazione, sbriciolamento; frantumatura. **-ground** *n.* luogo di ritrovo molto frequentato. **-machine** *n.* affrancatrice postale.

**stance** *n.* atteggiamento del corpo.

**stanchion** *n.* sostegno, puntello; (techn.) montante *m.*; *tr.* puntellare, rinforzare con sostegni.

**stand** *n.* pausa, fermata, arresto; ristagno; (theatr.) tappa (di compagnia); *one-day —*, tappa di un giorno; presa di posizione; resistenza; *to make a — against*, opporre resistenza a; posizione, posto; luogo d'appostamento; palco, tribuna, piattaforma; posteggio; banco di vendita, bancarella; chiosco; piedistallo, sostegno; scaffale, leggìo; *three-legged —*, treppiedi *m. indecl.*; (techn.) supporto.

**stand** *intr.* stare in piedi; (mil.) *— at ease!*, riposo!; *— to attention!*, attenti!; stare, trovarsi; *not to have a leg to — on*, non avere nessuna scusa; *to — fast*, tener duro; fermarsi, trattenersi, indugiare; *— and deliver!*, o la borsa o la vita!; durare, rimaner valido; conservarsi; sopravvivere; *how do you — for money?*, come stanno le tue finanze?; *how do you — with him?*, in che rapporti sei con lui?; (pol.) *to — as a candidate*, presentarsi come candidato; *he made my hair — on end*, mi fece rizzare i capelli dalla paura; ristagnare; depositare; *to allow a liquid to —*, lasciar depositare un liquido; *to let tea —*, lasciare il tè in infusione; *tr.* mettere in piedi; collocare in posizione eretta; sopportare, resistere; *she can't — him*, non lo può soffrire; (fam.) pagare, sostenere le spese di; offrire; FOLLOW BY ADV. OR PREP.: *to — by*, stare accanto a; aiutare, sostenere; restare fedele a; assistere, essere spettatore; tenersi pronto; *to — down* (of witness), lasciare la barra; *to — for*, voler dire, significare; implicare; (pol.) essere candidato a; (USA), sopportare, tollerare; *to — off*, mantenersi distante; *tr.* sospendere temporaneamente; *to — on*, insistere su, osservare scrupolosamente; *don't — on ceremony*, non far complimenti; *to — to*, aderire a, essere fedele a, mantenere; *to — out*, resistere, tener duro; spiccare, predominare; far contrasto; *to — over*, essere differito; restare in sospeso; *to — up*, alzarsi in piedi; *to — up for*, prendere le difese di; *to — up to*, affrontare coraggiosamente.

**stand-** (in compounds). **-by** *n.* partigiano, sostenitore; riserva. **-in** *n.* (cinem.) controfigura. **-offish** *adj.* riservato, altero. **-up collar** *n.* colletto montante. **-up fight** *n.* combattimento in perfetta regola. **-up lunch** *n.* colazione in piedi.

**standard** *n.* stendardo, bandiera, insegna; *to raise the —*, iniziare una rivolta; modello, campione *m.*; tipo; misura; norma; *up to —*, secondo campione; grado di eccellenza; livello, qualità; *the — of living*, il tenore di vita; supporto; base *f.*; piedistallo; (bot.) arbusto tagliato ad alberello; *attrib. adj.* *— edition*, edizione normale; di serie; *— English*, l'inglese colto; (rlwy.) *— gauge*, scartamento normale; *— lamp*, lampada a stelo.

**standard-bearer** *n.* alfiere *m.*; (fig.) capo di partito.

**standardiz-e** *tr.* standardizzare, uniformare, normalizzare; *-ed production*, produzione in serie. **-ation** *n.* standardizzazione, uniformità, livellamento.

**standing** *adj.* che sta in piedi, eretto; verticale; *to be left —*, essere abbandonato sul posto; fermo; inattivo, inoperoso; fisso, immutabile, invariabile, permanente; radicata; *— invitation*, invito permanente; *— army*, esercito permanente; *— joke*, scherzo abituale; *— jump!*, salto da fermo; *— orders*, regole permanenti di condotta; *— room*, posto in piedi; *— rule*, regola fissa.

**standing** *n.* lo stare in piedi; luogo di fermata, arresto; posizione; rango, importanza; reputazione; *of good —*, attendibile, serio; durata, periodo di tempo.

**standpoint** *n.* posizione, luogo di osservazione; punto di vista.

**standstill** *n.* arresto, fermata, pausa; *at a —*, inattivo.

**stanza** *n.* (poet.) stanza, strofa.

**staple**[1] *adj.* principale; *— commodities*, generi di consumo; *n.* prodotto principale; materia prima, materiale grezzo.

**staple**[2] *n.* (techn.) cavallottino, cambretta; ponticello, forcella; supporto di formatura; serratura; (typ.) graffetta, punto metallico; *tr.* fissare, unire con graffetta; (typ.) cucire a macchina.

**staple**[3] *n.* (text.) fibra; fiocco; *— thread*, filo di fibra selezionata; *tr.* cernere, classificare i fiocchi di.

**stapler**[1] *n.* classificatore, cernitore di lana.

**stapler**[2] *n.* macchina cucitrice.

**stapling** *n.* cucitura con punti metallici; *stapling-machine*, macchina cucitrice.

**star** *n.* stella; astro; *falling —*, stella filante; *north —*, stella polare; *morning —*, stella del mattino; *evening —*, stella della sera; decorazione, medaglia; (mil.) stelletta; *the Stars and Stripes*, la bandiera degli Stati Uniti d'America; (typ.) asterisco; stella, diva, divo, celebrità; *attrib.* (theatr.) *— turn*, numero principale.

**star** *tr.* adornare di stelle;

costellare; tempestare di stelle; (typ.) segnare con asterisco, mettere un asterisco; (cinem.; theatr.) mettere in primo ruolo; *intr.* (cinem.; theatr.) primeggiare; avere il ruolo di protagonista.

**star-** (in compounds). **-cluster** *n.* gruppo di stelle. **-gazer** *n.* astronomo. **-shell** *n.* (mil.) bengala *m.*; razzo illuminante. **-spangled** *adj.* stellato.

**starboard** *adj.* (naut.) di tribordo; *n.* (naut.) tribordo, dritta, destra.

**starch** *n.* amido; (fig.) rigidezza, formalismo; *tr.* inamidare, incollare. **~ed** *adj.* inamidato.

**starching** *n.* inamidatura; apprettatura.

**starchy** *adj.* (chem.) amidaceo; — *foods*, cibi ricchi d'amido; amidoso; inamidato; (fig.) rigido; formale.

**stardom** *n.* (theatr.; cinem.) divismo, celebrità.

**stare** *n.* sguardo fisso; *intr.* sgranare gli occhi; *to — into the distance*, guardare lontano; *it's staring you in the face*, salta agli occhi, è evidente; *to — at*, fissare; squadrare.

**starfish** *n.* stella di mare.

**staring** *adj.* fisso; stupefatto; sbalordito; — *eyes*, occhi spalancati; chiassoso, sgargiante, vistoso; *stark — mad*, pazzo da legare; *n.* sguardo fisso; sguardo sfrontato.

**stark** *adj.* rigido, duro; (of landscape) brullo; (poet.) vigoroso; inflessibile; *adv.* completamente, interamente; — *mad*, matto da legare; — *naked*, completamente nudo. **~ness** *n.* rigidità, durezza; nudità.

**starlet** *n.* piccola stella; (cinem.) stellina.

**starlight** *n.* luce stellare; *by —*, al chiarore delle stelle.

**starlike** *adj.* simile a stella; lucente.

**starling** *n.* (orn.) storno, stornello.

**starlit** *adj.* illuminato dalle stelle; stellato.

**starred** *adj.* stellato, adorno di stelle; a stella; influenzato dalle stelle; (typ.) segnato con asterisco; (of glass) incrinato a raggiera; *ill-starred*, nato sotto una cattiva stella, sfortunato.

**starry** *adj.* stellato, trapunto di stelle; brillante, lucente come stella; — *eyes*, occhi splendenti.

**starry-eyed** *adj.* ingenuo.

**start** *n.* inizio; partenza; luogo di partenza; *at the —*, all'inizio; *for a —*, tanto per cominciare; *to make an early —*, cominciare di buon'ora; sobbalzo, soprassalto; *to give a —*, sobbalzare; *to wake with a —*, svegliarsi di soprassalto; *by fits and ~s*, irregolarmente; a sprazzi; posizione vantaggiosa; vantaggio dato all'inizio di una corsa; (techn.) avviamento; *kick —*, avviamento a pedale.

**start** *intr.* partire; mettersi in viaggio; (aeron.) decollare; (naut.) levare le ancore; *to — back*, riprendere la via; cominciare, iniziare, aver inizio; *~ing from*, prendendo spunto da; sobbalzare; sussultare; trasalire; alzarsi bruscamente; *his eyes were ~ing out of his head*, aveva gli occhi fuori dell'orbita; *to — out*, cominciare; *to — out to*, avere intenzione di; *to — up*, nascere, sorgere; *to — up from one's sleep*, svegliarsi di colpo, di soprassalto; *tr.* cominciare, iniziare, dare l'avvio a; far partire; mettere in moto; *to — a conversation*, intavolare una conversazione.

**starter** *n.* iniziatore; autore; fondatore; *n.* (horse-racing) partente *m.*, 'starter' *m.*; (shooting) cane che stana la selvaggina.

**starting** *n.* inizio, partenza; debutto; lancio; (techn.) messa in moto; avviamento; sussulto; sobbalzo; soprassalto. **-handle** *n.* manovella di avviamento. **-point** *n.* punto di partenza. **-post** *n.* palo di partenza. **-price** *n.* prezzo iniziale; (sport) ultima puntata (su un cavallo) prima della partenza.

**startl~e** *tr.*, *intr.* spaventare, spaventarsi; far trasalire; allarmare; *to — someone out of his sleep*, svegliare qualcuno di soprassalto. **~ed** *adj.* spaventato, allarmato. **~ing** *adj.* allarmante, impressionante; sensazionale; sorprendente.

**starvation** *n.* inedia, fame; *to die of —*, morire di fame; estrema povertà; — *wages*, salario da fame.

**starve** *tr.*, *intr.* soffrire la fame, far soffrire la fame; morire di fame, far morire di fame; *I am simply starving*, muoio di fame; (of plants) deperire, intristire; *to — for*, bramare; desiderare vivamente; (mil.) *to — out*, prendere per fame.

**starveling** *n.* affamato.

**stasis** *n.* (pathol.) stasi *f.*; ristagno; interruzione nello sviluppo.

**state**[1] *n.* stato, condizione, situazione, posizione; — *of mind*, disposizione d'animo; *a nice — of affairs*, un bel pasticcio; *State*, stato, nazione; governo; *affairs of State*, affari di stato; *Secretary of State*, segretario di stato, ministro degli Esteri; *the States of the Church*, gli Stati Pontifici; *the States*, gli Stati Uniti; rango, dignità; pompa, parata; splendore *m.*, magnificenza; *robes of —*, l'uniforme di gala; *to live in —*, vivere in gran pompa; (archit.) trono **baldacchino** sul trono.

**state-** (in compounds). **-aided** *adj.* sovvenzionato dallo Stato. **-apartments** *n.pl.* appartamenti di rappresentanza. **-carriage, -coach** *n.* carrozza di gala. **-control** *n.* (econ.) controllo di Stato. **-prisoner,** prigioniero politico. **-reception** *n.* ricevimento ufficiale. **-room** *n.* salone di rappresentanza. **-trial,** processo politico. **-visit** *n.* visita ufficiale.

**state**[2] *tr.* affermare, asserire; dichiarare, enunciare; specificare; *please — below*, pregasi annotare qui sotto; (leg.) *to — one's case*, esporre i fatti; fissare, stabilire; (math.) enunciare, esprimere con formule.

**statecraft** see **statesmanship.**

**stated** *part. adj.* dichiarato; *above —*, sopraccitato; *as —*, come sopra; stabilito; fisso; *at — intervals*, a intervalli fissi; *on — days*, a giorni fissi.

**stateless** *adj.* senza patria; senza nazionalità; apolide.

**statel~y** *adj.* nobile, signorile; maestoso, magnifico, sontuoso; altero; elevato; (joc.) *the — homes of England*, le sontuouse dimore d'Inghilterra. **~iness** *n.* aspetto imponente; grandiosità, imponenza, magnificenza, maestosità.

**statement** *n.* rapporto, relazione; *official —*, comunicato ufficiale; (leg.) deposizione; esposto, esposizione; asserzione, affermazione; (comm.; admin.) denunzia, dichiarazione; — *of expenses* conto spese; *monthly —*, bilancio mensile.

**stateroom** *n.* (naut.) cabina del capitano; cabina di lusso per passeggeri.

**statesman** *n.* uomo di Stato; statista *m.* **~like** *adj.* da uomo di Stato, da statista. **~ship** *n.* arte di governo; scienza politica.

**static** *adj.* statico; — *friction*, attrito di primo distacco. **~s** *n.pl.* (radio) statica; disturbi atmosferici; perturbazioni atmosferiche.

**station** *n.* posto, luogo; posto assegnato; stazione; base *f.*; posto di operazione; *action —*, posto di combattimento; *naval —*, porto militare; *broadcasting —*, stazione emittente; condizione sociale, rango; classe sociale; *tr.* assegnare un posto a, collocare, piazzare; (mil.) *to — troops*, postare truppe; *to be ~ed at . . .*, essere di guarnigione a . . .; (naut.) essere ormeggiato a . . .

**stationary** *adj.* stazionario; fermo, immoto; permanente, fisso; — *car*, automobile in sosta; (mil.) sedentario; — *troops*, truppe sedentarie.

**stationer** *n.* cartolaio; *—'s (shop)*, cartoleria.

**stationery** *n.* cartoleria; articoli

di cancelleria; *H.M. Stationery Office*, Istituto Poligrafico dello Stato.
**station-master** *n.* capostazione *m.* **-waggon** *n.* giardinetta.
**statist** *n.* statista *m.*, uomo di Stato; esperto in statistica.
**statistic-(al)** *adj.* statistico. **-ian** *n.* esperto, studioso di statistica. **-s** *n.* statistica.
**statuary** *adj.* statuario, scultorio; scolpito; *n.* scultura.
**statue** *n.* statua.
**statuesque** *adj.* statuario, scultoreo; plastico.
**statuette** *n.* statuetta, statuina.
**stature** *n.* statura; *to be of short —*, esser di bassa statura.
**status** *n.* stato; condizione sociale; rango; titolo ufficiale; situazione, condizione; *legal —*, condizione giuridica; *social —*, posizione sociale.
**statute** *n.* statuto, regolamento, ordinamento. **-book** *n.* raccolta di leggi approvate dal Parlamento. **-law** *n.* legge statutaria.
**statutory** *adj.* statutario, imposto dalla legge; regolamentare, conforme alla legge; riconosciuto dalla legge.
**staunch** *adj.* fedele, leale; sicuro; *— faith*, fede incrollabile; *— friend*, amico fedele; solido, saldo; massiccio; *tr.* arrestare, fermare l'uscita di; arrestare l'emorragia di. **-ly** *adv.* fedelmente, lealmente; fermamente, con fermezza. **-ness** *n.* fedeltà, lealtà; impermeabilità; solidità, stabilità.
**stave** *n.* doga (di botte); piuolo (di scala); (poet.) stanza, strofa; verso; (mus.) pentagramma *m.*; *tr.* cambiare le doghe a (un barile); *to — in*, fare un foro in, sfondare; *to — off*, stornare, allontanare; ritardare, differire; evitare.
**stay**[1] *n.* soggiorno, periodo di permanenza; pausa, fermata; (leg.) sospensione; *— of execution*, sospensione dell'esecuzione di una sentenza; *— of proceedings*, procedura sospesa; resistenza; controllo; freno.
**stay** *intr.* fermarsi, sostare, trattenersi; soggiornare; *shall I — with you ?*, mi volete con voi ?; *to — at a hotel*, alloggiare in un albergo; *to — in bed*, restare a letto; *— put !*, fermati dove sei!; *tr.* fermare, arrestare; trattenere; resistere; sopportare; (leg.) differire, sospendere; frenare; calmare; FOLLOW. BY ADV. OR PREP.: *to — away*, essere assente, non partecipare; *to — in*, non uscire, stare in casa; *to — up*, vegliare, stare alzato; *to — up late*, coricarsi tardi.
**stay**[2] *n.* sostegno; supporto; piedistallo; (techn.) puntello; supporto di lunetta; tubo montante; *pl.* corsetto, busto; *tr.* (techn.) puntellare, armare di puntelli.
**stay**[3] *n.* (naut.) straglio; *slack in -s*, lento a virare; *to miss -s*, non riuscire a virare; fune *f.*; *tr.* (naut.) sostenere con gli stragli; far virare di bordo.
**stay-at-home** *adj.* casalingo; *n.* persona casalinga.
**stayer** *n.* chi resta, chi rimane; *n.* (sport) atleta fondista *m.*, *f.*; cavallo di fondo.
**staying** *n.* soggiorno, visita; resistenza; arresto; interruzione; (leg.) aggiornamento, rinvio; *— power*, capacità di resistenza.
**staysail** *n.* (naut.) vela di straglio.
**stead** *n.* vece, posto, luogo; *to act in someone's —*, fare le veci di qualcuno; *to stand someone in good —*, essere di aiuto a qualcuno.
**steadfast** *adj.* fermo; risoluto; costante; incrollabile. **-ness** *n.* fermezza; tenacia; costanza.
**steadily** *adv.* saldamente; fermamente; regolarmente, costantemente; assiduamente, diligentemente; *to work —*, lavorare sodo.
**steadiness** *n.* fermezza; sicurezza; fissità; assiduità; perseveranza; diligenza; applicazione; regolarità; stabilità; condotta equilibrata; saggezza.
**steady** *adj.* fermo, saldo, fisso, rigido; *as — as a rock*, saldo come una roccia; calmo, equilibrato; disciplinato, controllato; continuo, regolare, costante, persistente; (med.) *— pulse*, polso regolare; (comm.) *— demand*, fedele, assiduo; serio; richiesta costante; attento!, fermo!, calmo!; *— (the helm) !*, (naut.) barra dritta !; *n.* (techn.) supporto, lunetta fissa; (USA, slang) amico, amica, amante *m.*, *f.*; *tr.* rafforzare, rinforzare; rendere fermo; consolidare; stabilizzare; *intr.* ritrovare l'equilibrio.
**steak** *n.* fetta; *fillet —*, bistecca di filetto.
**steal** *tr.* rubare; sottrarre; *to — a march on*, prevenire; *intr.* muoversi furtivamente; *to — into*, entrare di nascosto; *to — upon*, avvicinarsi pian piano a; *to — away*, svignarsela; *to — out*, uscire di soppiatto.
**stealing** *n.* furto; ruberia.
**stealth** *n.* procedimento segreto; segretezza; *by —*, di nascosto. **-ily** *adv.* furtivamente, di soppiatto; *to creep in -ily*, entrare di soppiatto. **-iness** *n.* carattere furtivo. **-y** *adj.* furtivo; *-y glance*, sguardo furtivo.
**steam** *n.* vapore; (naut.) *at full —*, a tutto vapore; *full — ahead !*, avanti a tutto vapore!; *to get up —*, aumentare la pressione, alzare il vapore; *to let off —*, lasciare andare il vapore; (fam.) energia; spirito; *to let off —*, sfogarsi.
**steam** *tr.* esporre al vapore; passare al vapore; cuocere a vapore; *intr.* emettere, esalare vapore; fumare; funzionare vapore; *to — ahead*, avanzare a vapore; *to — away*, partire; evaporare; *to — up*, aumentare la pressione del vapore; *-ed up*, coperto di vapore condensato; (fig., fam.) *to get -ed up*, agitarsi.
**steamboat** *n.* battello a vapore.
**steam-engine** *n.* macchina a vapore; locomotivo.
**steamer** *n.* battello, vaporetto; macchina a vapore; pentola a vapore.
**steaminess** *n.* esalazione di vapore; vaporosità; appannamento.
**steamship** *n.* piroscafo, nave a vapore.
**steamy** *adj.* che esala vapore; fumante; pieno di vapore, vaporoso; appannato; umido.
**steed** *n.* (lit.; joc.) corsiero, destriero.
**steel**[1] *n.* acciaio; arma, spada, lama, arma bianca; *to fight with cold —*, battersi all'arma bianca; acciarino; cote *f.*; (pharm.) ferro; (metall.) *— casting*, getto d'acciaio; *— company*, acciaieria; *— wool*, lana d'acciaio; *electro-plated —*, acciaio argentato; *stainless —*, acciaio inossidabile.
**steel**[2] *tr.* coprire d'acciaio, armare con acciaio; (fig.) rendere duro come l'acciaio; indurire; *rfl.* *to — oneself*, corazzarsi.
**steeliness** *n.* durezza; inflessibilità; insensibilità.
**steelwork** *n.* lavoro in acciaio; struttura di acciaio; *pl.* acciaierie *f.pl.*
**steely** *adj.* di acciaio; simile ad acciaio; (fig.) insensibile; severissimo; inflessibile.
**steep**[1] *adj.* ripido, scosceso, erto; (fig., fam.) esorbitante; irragionevole; incredibile; (fig.) arduo, ambizioso; *n.* luogo erto; pendio ripido; erta.
**steep**[2] *n.* macerazione; l'inzuppare, l'impregnare; liquido impregnante, bagno di macerazione; infusione; *tr.* immergere; impregnare; inzuppare; macerare; *steeped in*, imbevuto di. **-ing** *n.* immersione prolungata; macerazione; infusione.
**steeple** *n.* guglia; campanile *m.*
**steeplechase** *n.* (equestr.) corsa ad ostacoli; *intr.* partecipare a corse ad ostacoli.
**steeplejack** *n.* chi compie riparazioni sui campanili o sui camini.
**steeply** *adv.* a picco, ripidamente.
**steepness** *n.* pendenza, ripidezza; inclinazione.
**steer**[1] *n.* bue *m.* giovane, manzo.
**steer**[2] *tr.* guidare, governare; manovrare; dirigere; *to — north*, fare rotta verso nord; *to — clear of*,

evitare. **-age** *n.* (naut.) governo del timone. **-ing** *n.* direzione; guida; governo dello sterzo.
**steering-column** *n.* albero di sterzo; piantone di guida. **-gear** *n.* dispositivo comando di sterzo, di timone. **-wheel** *n.* (motor.) volante *m.*; (naut.) ruota del timone.
**steersman** *n.* timoniere, pilota *m.* **-ship** *n.* (naut.) abilità, mestiere di timoniere.
**stellar** *adj.* stellare, astrale.
**stellate** *adj.* (poet.) stellato; a forma di stella; disposto a stella (bot.) — *leaves*, foglie radiate.
**stelliform** *adj.* stelliforme.
**stem**[1] *n.* (bot.) tronco; gamba; (of glass) stelo; (of pipe) cannello; (mus.) gamba: ceppo, ramo; (gramm.) radice *f.*; *intr.* derivare; *to — from*, avere origine in.
**stem**[2] *n.* (naut.) prua; *from — to stern*, da prua a poppa.
**stem**[3] *tr.* arrestare; controllare; arginare, contenere.
**stench** *n.* puzzo, tanfo.
**stencil** *n.* stampino; decorazione, riproduzione fatta con stampino; marchio; — *copy*, copia a ciclostile; *tr.* stampinare; riprodurre mediante stampini; ciclostilare.
**stenograph-er** *n.* stenografo, stenografa. **-y** *n.* stenografia.
**stentorian** *adj.* stentoreo.
**step** *n.* passo; andatura; cadenza; tratto; *watch your —!*, attenzione!, guarda dove metti i piedi!; *to break —*, rompere il passo; *to fall into —*, mettersi al passo; *to keep —*, tenere il tempo; *to retrace one's -s*, tornare sui propri passi; — *by —*, gradualmente, un poco alla volta; (electr.) *in —*, in fase; orma, impronta; provvedimento; gradino, piolo (di scala); *pl.* scaletta; *flight of -s*, scalinata; grado; (mus.) intervallo; (naut.) scassa.
**step** *intr.* camminare, andare, venire; *please — this way*, venga di qua, per favore, s'accomodi; *tr. to — the mast*, inalzare l'albero; FOLLOW. BY ADV. OR PREP.: *to — across*, attraversare; *to — aside*, farsi da parte, fare una digressione; *to — back*, indietreggiare; *to — down*, discendere; (electr.) ridurre, diminuire (tensione); *to — forward*, avanzare; *to — in*, entrare; montare, salire su (un veicolo); (fig.) intervenire, frapporsi, intromettersi; *to — off*, partire; iniziare; scendere; *to — out*, uscire; affrettare il passo; *to — up*, *intr.* salire; *tr.* aumentare.
**step-brother** *n.* fratellastro. **-child** *n.* figliastro, figliastra. **-daughter** *n.* figliastra. **-father** *n.* patrigno. **-mother** *n.* matrigna.
**steppe** *n.* (geog.) steppa.
**stepping** *n.* andatura. **-stone** *n.* pietra per guadare; (fig.) passo.
**step-sister** *n.* sorellastra. **-son** *n.* figliastro.
**stereo** *adj.* (abbrev. of **stereoscopic, stereophonic**) stereoscopico; stereofonico.
**stereo-phonic** *adj.* stereofonico. **-scope** *n.* (opt.) stereoscopio. **-scopic(al)** *adj.* stereoscopico. **-scopy** *n.* stereoscopia. **-type** *n.* (typ.) stereotipo; cliché *m.*; *tr.* (typ.) sterotipare, stampare per mezzo di stereotipia.
**steril-e** *adj.* sterile. **-ity** *n.* sterilità. **-ization** *n.* sterilizzazione. **-ize** *tr.* rendere sterile, isterilire; sterilizzare. **-izer** *n.* sterilizzatore *m.*
**sterling** *adj.* di buona lega, genuino; — *silver*, argento puro; *10 pounds —*, 10 lire sterline; schietto, sincero; solido; puro; *n.* moneta legale inglese.
**stern**[1] *adj.* severo, austero; rigido, rigoroso.
**stern**[2] *n.* (naut.) poppa; *from stem to —*, da prua a poppa; deretano; (of animal) coda.
**sternness** *n.* severità, austerità, rigidezza.
**sternsheets** *n.pl.* (naut.) poppa.
**sternum** *n.* (anat.) sterno.
**stet** *n.* (in the correction of proofs) vive; *tr.* mettere la versione originale di.
**stethoscope** *n.* (med.) stetoscopio.
**stevedore** *n.* (naut.) stivatore.
**stew**[1] *n.* umido; stufato; (fig.) ansietà, agitazione; *Irish —*, spezzatino di montone; (slang) sgobbone *m.*; *tr.* cuocere in umido, stufare; *to let someone — in his own juice*, lasciar cuocere qualcuno nel proprio brodo; *intr.* (fig.) soffocare; (slang) sgobbare.
**steward** *n.* amministratore, intendente *m.*, castaldo; *the estate —*, l'amministratore della tenuta; dispensiere *m.*; (mil.) capo furiere; (aeron.; naut.) cameriere di bordo; sovrintendente incaricato; commissario di gara; *Lord Steward of the Household*, Siniscalco di Corte; *Lord High Steward of England*, cerimoniere per l'incoronazione di un re; giudice del tribunale che deve giudicare i Pari.
**stewardess** *n.* dispensiera; (naut.; aeron.) cameriera di bordo.
**stewardship** *n.* amministrazione, gestione; carica di gerente.
**stewing** *n.* stufato, umido; — *beef*, carne di manzo per stufato; — *plums*, prugne *f.pl.* da cuocere.
**stewpan** *n.* tegame *m.*
**stews** *n.pl.* bordello.
**stick**[1] *n.* bastone *m.*; bastone da passeggio; manico; *to get the —*, ricevere delle bastonate; *to be in a cleft —*, essere tra due fuochi; bastoncino; barra, stecca; (fig.) allocco, barbogio, persona poco intelligente; (mus.) bacchetta; (mil.) grappolo di bombe; (cul.) gambo, stelo; *a — of asparagus*, un asparago; *a — of celery*, un gambo di sedano.
**stick**[2] *tr.* ficcare; conficcare; incollare; appiccicare; attaccare; (fam.) sopportare; *I can't — him*, non lo posso vedere; *intr.* rimanere incollato; appiccicarsi; (fig.) *to — to one's opinions*, difendere le proprie convinzioni; *to — to one's word*, mantenere la parola; (fam.) — *to it!*, non mollare!; *to be stuck*, rimanere bloccato, essere nell'imbarazzo; FOLLOW. BY ADV. OR PREP.: *to — at nothing*, non avere scrupoli; *to — at a task*, lavorare indefessamente; *to — on*, incollare; *to — it on*, esagerare, fare delle frange; *to — out*, sporgere; tirar fuori, fare uscire; (fam.) *to — it out*, persistere, resistere fino alla fine; *to — out for*, non cedere nelle proprie richieste per; *to — up*, sporgersi; far penetrare in su; — *'em up!*, mani in alto!
**sticker** *n.* attacchino; gaffa; arpione *m.*, etichetta gommata; (fig.); persona noiosa, attaccabottone *m.*; persona assidua.
**stickiness** *n.* viscosità, adesività; tenacità.
**sticking** *adj.* appiccicoso, adesivo; colloso; *n.* aderenza, adesività; incollatura; (techn.) arresto; bloccaggio; grippaggio.
**sticking-plaster** *n.* cerotto. **-point** *n.* punto d'arresto.
**stick-in-the-mud** *adj.*, *n.* (persona) lenta, senza iniziativa.
**stickleback** *n.* (ichth.) spinarello.
**stickler** *n.* accanito sostenitore; persona pignola, intransigente.
**sticky** *adj.* appiccicaticcio; adesivo; viscoso; viscido; (fig., fam.) poco accomodante; sgradevole; rigido; *to come to a — end*, finire male; *to have — fingers*, essere svelto di mano.
**stiff** *adj.* rigido, duro; (fig.) inflessibile, ostinato; *to keep a — upper lip*, mostrare fermezza di carattere; indolenzito, intorpidito; irrigidito; freddo; riservato, contenuto; affettato; — *bow*, saluto freddo; che funziona male; difficile, duro, faticoso; *a — price*, un prezzo salato; *a — drink*, una forte bevanda; — *collar*, colletto duro; *bored —*, annoiato a morte; *frozen —*, indolenzito per il freddo; *scared —*, fifoso; *n.* (USA, slang) cadavere *m.*; un buono a nulla.
**stiffen** *tr.* indurire; irrigidire; inamidare; apprettare; indolenzire; intorpidire; rassodare; rinforzare; rendere più severo; *intr.* irrigidirsi; intorpidirsi.
**stiffener** *n.* (techn.) elemento di

rinforzo; (slang) bevanda alcoolica; tonico, stimolante *m.*
**stiffening** *gerund* l'indurire; *n.* indurimento; rafforzamento; consolidamento; (text.) appretto, inamidatura.
**stiffly** *adv.* rigidamente; inflessibilmente; ostinatamente; affettatamente.
**stiffness** *n.* durezza; rigidezza; (fig.) ostinazione; sostenutezza; intorpidimento; indolenzimento; consistenza; solidità.
**stifle** *tr.* soffocare; (fig.) *to — a sneeze,* trattenere uno starnuto; *to — a yawn,* reprimere uno sbadiglio; *intr.* sentirsi soffocare.
**stifling** *adj.* soffocante; *it's — here!,* qui si soffoca!; *n.* soffocamento.
**stigma** *n.* marchio, segno; (fig.) marchio d'infamia.
**stigmata** *n.pl.* stimmate *f.pl.*
**stigmatist** *n.* chi porta le stimmate.
**stigmatiz-e** *tr.* marchiare; stigmatizzare; bollare, disonorare. **-ation** *n.* lo stigmatizzare; il marchiare d'infamia; il segnare con stimmate.
**stile** *n.* scaletta fissa.
**stiletto** *n.* stiletto, piccolo pugnale, (artill.) punteruolo; *— heels,* tacchi a spillo.
**still**[1] *adj.* tranquillo, calmo; immobile; silenzioso; *to stand —,* non muoversi; *to keep a — tongue in one's head,* tacere; (provb.) *— waters run deep,* le acque chete rovinano i ponti; *n.* (poet.) silenzio, quiete *f.*, calma; *in the — of night,* nel silenzio della notte; (photog.) posa; *tr.* acquietare; calmare; placare.
**still**[2] *adv.* ancora, tuttora; *— more,* ancor più; tuttavia, nondimeno, pure.
**still**[3] *n.* alambicco.
**still-born** *adj.* nato-morto. **-life** *n.* (art) natura morta.
**stillness** *n.* calma, quiete *f.*, tranquillità; silenzio.
**still-room** *n.* laboratorio di distilleria; dispensa.
**stilly** *adj.* (poet.) calmo, tranquillo; silenzioso.
**stilt** *n.* trampolo; *on -s,* sui trampoli.
**stilted** *adj.* montato sui trampoli; pomposo, roboante, ampolloso. **-ness** *n.* ampollosità, pomposità, magniloquenza.
**stimulant** *adj., n.* stimolante, eccitante *m.*
**stimulat-e** *tr.* stimolare; incitare, spronare. **-ing** *adj.* stimolante, eccitante. **-ion** *n.* stimolo. **-or** *n.* stimolatore, stimolante, eccitante.
**stimulus** *n.* stimolo; pungolo, incentivo; impulso.
**sting** *n.* pungiglione *m.*, aculeo; puntura d'insetto; punzecchiatura; dolore acuto; pungolo, stimolo, morso; frizzo, frecciata; *a jest with a — in it,* uno scherzo maligno; *tr.* pungere; ferire; bruciare; (slang) truffare; derubare; *intr.* pizzicare, bruciare, essere pungente.
**stinginess** *n.* avarizia, spilorceria; meschinità; grettezza.
**stinging** *adj.* pungente; (fig.) mordace; *n.* puntura.
**stingy** *adj.* avaro, taccagno, spilorcio.
**stink** *n.* puzzo, fetore *m.*; *tr., intr.* puzzare; riempire di puzzo; (fig.) essere ripugnante. **-er** *n.* persona che emana cattivo odore; (slang) grosso problema; persona difficile.
**stinking** *adj.* puzzolente, fetido.
**stint** *n.* limite *m.*; restrizione; porzione, quantità di lavoro assegnato, compito; *one's daily —,* il proprio lavoro quotidiano; *tr.* limitare, razionare; *to — oneself,* sottoporsi a privazioni. **-ed** *adj.* limitato, scarso; ristretto; misurato. **-ing** *n.* restrizione, limitazione; risparmio.
**stipend** *n.* stipendio, salario. **-iary** *adj., n.* stipendiato, salariato.
**stipple** *n.* (paint.) puntinismo; (typ.) tecnica dell'incisione a retino; *tr.* (paint.) punteggiare; (typ.) incidere a retino.
**stipulat-e** *tr., intr.* stipulare, pattuire; convenire; accordarsi; stabilire. **-ion** *n.* (leg.) stipulazione, convenzione, patto, accordo. **-or** *n.* (leg.) stipulante *m., f.*
**stir**[1] *n.* il rimescolare; l'attizzare; rimescolata; moto, movimento; animazione; tumulto, subbuglio; commozione; *to make a —,* far sensazione; *tr.* muovere; agitare; rimescolare; agitare; commuovere, appassionare; eccitare; *to — up,* stimolare; eccitare; *to — up hatred,* fomentare odio; *to — up the fire,* attizzare il fuoco; *intr.* muoversi; agitarsi.
**stir**[2] *n.* (slang) prigione *f.*
**stirrer** *n.* incitatore; istigatore; chi si muove.
**stirring** *adj.* commovente; eccitante.
**stirrup** *n.* staffa; (naut.) corda a staffa. **-cup** *n.* bicchiere *m.* della staffa.
**stitch** *n.* punto; (provb.) *a — in time saves nine,* un punto a tempo ne risparmia cento; maglia; *to drop a —,* lasciar cadere una maglia; *to take up a —,* riprendere una maglia; fitta, trafitta; *tr.* cucire; (surg.) suturare; *to — on,* applicare con cucitura; *to — up,* rammendare. **-er** *n.* cucitore *m.*, cucitrice *f.*
**stitching** *n.* cucitura; impuntura; (surg.) sutura; *back —,* punto indietro; *ornamental —,* ricamo.
**stoat** *n.* ermellino.
**stock** *n.* tronco, ceppo; fusto da innesto; razza, famiglia, stirpe *f.*; base *f.*, sostegno; (of gun) calcio; ceppo; rifornimento, approvvigionamento, provvista; (comm.) riserva; *in —,* in magazzino; *to be out of —,* essere sprovvisto; *to lay in a — of,* far provvista di; *to take —,* far l'inventario; *— in hand,* merce in magazzino; (finan.) titoli, azioni, obbligazioni *f.pl.*; *-s and shares,* valori di borsa, titoli; (fam.) *his — is going up,* le sue azioni sono in rialzo; materia prima; (cul.) brodo da minestra; *pl.* (hist.) gogna, berlina; *to put in the -s,* mettere alla berlina; *to have a piece of work on the -s,* avere qualcosa in lavorazione.
**stock** *tr.* approvvigionare, fornire, rifornire; tenere in magazzino; (naut.) inceppare (un'ancora).
**stock** (in compounds). **-book** *n.* (comm.) libro magazzino. **-company** *n.* (comm.) società per azioni. **-exchange** *n.* (comm.) borsa valori. **-in-trade** *n.* tutti gli strumenti di un commercio. **-jobber** *n.* speculatore di Borsa. **-list** *n.* (comm.) listino di Borsa. **-market** *n.* (comm.) mercato finanziario; Borsa valori. **-raising** *n.* allevamento di bestiame. **-size** *n.* taglia corrente. **-still** *adj.* completamente immobile. **-taking** *n.* il fare l'inventario.
**stockade** *n.* stecconata, palizzata; *tr.* cingere con palizzata.
**stock-broker** *n.* (comm.) agente di cambio. **-broking** *n.* professione dell'agente di cambio.
**stockfish** *n.* stoccafisso.
**stockholder** *n.* (comm.) azionista *m., f.*
**stocking** *n.* calza; (fig.) *blue-stocking,* donna intellettuale. **-frame, -loom, -machine** *n.* telaio per calze. **-stitch** *n.* punto calza.
**stockist** *n.* (comm.) grossista *m.*
**stockman** *n.* guardiano di bestiame.
**stockpile** riserva di materiali; *tr.* far riserve di materiali.
**stockpot** *n.* pentola per il brodo; marmitta.
**stocky** *adj.* tarchiato.
**stodg-e** *n.* (slang) cibo pesante; *tr., intr.* (slang) ingozzare, ingozzarsi; rimpinzare, rimpinzarsi. **-iness** *n.* (fam.) pesantezza. **-y** *adj.* (fam.) pesante, indigesto.
**Stoic-(al)** *adj., n.* stoico. **-alness, -ism** *n.* stoicismo.
**stok-e** *tr., intr.* alimentare; fare il fuochista; sorvegliare le caldaie. **-er** *n.* fuochista *m.* **-ing** *n.* sorveglianza, cura, alimentazione di forni.
**stole**[1] *n.* stola, sciarpa, scialle *m.*
**stole**[2] *p.def.* of **steal,** *q.v.*

**stolid** *adj.* imperturbabile; flemmatico; calmo, non precipitoso. **-ity, -ness** *n.* flemma, lentezza.

**stomach** *n.* stomaco; ventre *m.*; — *ache*, mal di stomaco, mal di pancia; (fig.) desiderio, inclinazione; coraggio; *tr.* digerire; sopportare; ingoiare.

**stomach-pump** *n.* sonda per lavaggio gastrico.

**stone** *n.* pietra, roccia; *the Stone Age*, l'età della pietra; ciottolo, sasso; *at a stone's throw*, a un tiro di schioppo; *to kill two birds with one* —, prendere due piccioni con una fava; (of fruit) nocciolo; (med.) calcolo; (meas.) pietra (equiv. to 6.350 kg); *adj.* di pietra, in pietra; — *blind*, completamente cieco; *stone-break*, (bot.) sassifraga; *stone-breaker*, spaccapietre, tagliapietre *m.*; frantoio; — *coal*, antracite *f.*; — *curlew* (or — *plover*), (ornith.) gran piviere; *stone-cutter*, tagliapietre; *stone-deaf*, sordo come una campana, completamente sordo; (mech.) — *hammer*, mazzetta; — *mason*, scalpellino, tagliapietre; — *mason's disease*, silicosi *f.*; (ornith.) *stone-snipe*, piviere americano; *stone-work*, lavoro in muratura; scultura, lavoro di scultura; *tr.* lapidare; colpire a sassate; snocciolare, togliere il nocciolo a; affilare, molare, arrotare. **-d** *part. adj.* (pop.) ubbriaco; drogato.

**stonechat** *n.* (orn.) saltimpalo.

**stonewall** *n.* (cricket) giuoco di difesa; (Austral. pol.) ostruzionismo parlamentare; *intr.* (cricket) giocare in difesa; (fig.) fare un giuoco prudente; (pol.) fare dell'ostruzionismo parlamentare. **-er** *n.* (cricket) giuocatore prudente, che non rischia; (Austral. pol.) ostruzionista *m.*

**stoneware** *n.* ceramica.

**ston-y** *adj.* pietroso, sassoso; di pietra; (fig.) duro, freddo, insensibile; *a — stare*, uno sguardo gelido. **-iness** *n.* natura pietrosa; (fig.) insensibilità, durezza di cuore.

**stony-broke,** *adj.* al verde. **-hearted,** *adj.* dal cuore di pietra.

**stool** *n.* sgabello, seggiolino; panchetto; scanno; *to fall between two -s*, lasciarsi sfuggire ambedue le occasioni per indecisione; feci *f.pl.*; (bot.) radice *f.*; tronco da cui spuntano polloni; *foot* —, posapiedi *m. indecl.*

**stool-pigeon** *n.* piccione *m.* da richiamo; (fig.) persona che fa da esca.

**stoop**[1] *n.* curvatura; inchino; (fig.) condiscendenza; atto di umiltà; *intr.* curvarsi, chinarsi, piegarsi; (fig.) accondiscendere; abbassarsi; umiliarsi; degradarsi; *to — to conquer*, umiliarsi per conquistare.

**stoop**[2] *n.* (USA) terrazza sopraelevata sul fronte della casa; veranda.

**stop** *n.* sosta, arresto, interruzione; fermata; (naut.; aeron.) scalo; *do you get off at this —?*, scende a questa fermata?; *to put a — to*, porre termine a; *full* —, punto; (mus.) registro d'organo; (fig.) *to pull out all the -s*, non risparmiarsi, agire con molto vigore e risolutezza esagerata; (techn.) dispositivo di bloccaggio, (opt.; photog.) diaframma *m.* dell'obbiettivo.

**stop-** (in compounds). **-cock** *n.* (techn.) rubinetto di arresto. **-dowel** *n.* (techn.) grano di arresto. **-gap** *n.* rimedio temporaneo; (fam.) tappa buchi. **-press** *n.* (journ.) ultimissime *f.pl.* **-watch** *n.* cronometro a scatto.

**stop** *tr.* turare, tamponare; *to — a tooth*, otturare un dente; fermare; arrestare; far cessare; — *that noise!*, basta con questo rumore!; *to — the game*, porre fine al giuoco; *to — talking*, smettere di parlare; impedire, trattenere; (comm.) cessare (i pagamenti); (fam.) tagliare; (techn.) bloccare; (mus.) *to — a flute*, tappare i buchi di un flauto; *to — a string*, premere una corda; (gramm.) punteggiare; (naut.) abbozzare; *intr.* fermarsi; arrestarsi; cessare; *how long are you -ping?*, quanto tempo si trattiene Lei?

**stoppage** *n.* fermata; sosta, pausa; arresto; interruzione; sospensione; cessazione; (mil.) — *of leave*, consegna; — *of traffic*, interruzione del traffico; ostruzione, ingombro; intasatura; (comm.) giacenza; diritti di giacenza.

**stopper** *n.* chi arresta, chi ferma; tappo, turacciolo; otturatore; zaffo; (naut.) bozza; *screw* —, tappo a vite; *tr.* tappare, turare; tamponare.

**stopping** *gerund* il fermare, l'arrestare; *n.* otturazione, tamponamento; — *of a tooth*, otturazione di un dente; (comm.) cessazione, sospensione.

**storage** *n.* immagazzinamento; deposito, magazzino; (comm.) magazzinaggio; (electr.) carica (di energia); — *battery*, batteria di accumulatori; *cold* — conservazione in frigorifero.

**store** *n.* provvista, riserva; quantità, abbondanza; *to set great — by*, tenere in gran conto; magazzino, deposito; (USA) negozio; *pl.* depositi di magazzino, scorte di materie prime; rifornimenti; munizioni; (naut.) provviste di bordo; *pl.* grandi magazzini, cooperativa.

**store** *tr.* fornire, rifornire; immagazzinare, accumulare; mettere da parte; depositare in magazzino; contenere.

**storehouse** *n.* magazzino, deposito; (fig.) miniera.

**store-keeper** *n.* magazziniere *m.*; (USA) negoziante *m.*

**storeroom** *n.* magazzino.

**storey** *n.* piano; *on the first* —, al primo piano; *lower* —, piano inferiore; *upper* —, piano superiore; (fig.) *not quite all there in the upper* —, un po' strambo.

**storied**[1] *adj.* istoriato, ornato con figure, decorato; — *windows*, vetrate, finestre a vetri istoriati; celebrato in storie.

**storied**[2] *adj.* (bldg.) a piani; *two-storied*, a due piani.

**stork** *n.* cicogna.

**storm** *n.* tempesta; temporale *m.*; bufera; burrasca; fortunale *m.*; uragano; *hail-storm*, grandinata; *snow-storm*, tempesta di neve, tormenta; *a — of applause*, uno scroscio di applausi; *to take by* —, assalire, trascinare; *a — in a teacup*, molto rumore per nulla, una tempesta in un bicchier d'acqua; tumulto, agitazione; guerra; disputa; — *and stress*, disordine ed agitazione; (mil.) assalto; *intr.* infuriare, scatenarsi; (fam.) adirarsi; rimproverare; *to — at*, fare una scenata a; (mil.) prendere d'assalto.

**storm-** (in compounds). **-centre** *n.* centro dell'uragano; (fig.) focolaio d'agitazione. **-cloud** *n.* nube tempestosa. **-sail** *n.* (naut.) vela di fortuna. **-tossed** *adj.* sballottato dalla tempesta. **-troops** *n.pl.* (mil.) truppe d'assalto.

**stormer** *n.* (mil.) assalitore.

**storming** *n.* violenza, furia; (mil.) assalto; *storming-party*, truppe d'assalto.

**stormproof** *adj.* resistente alla tempesta; (mil.) inespugnabile.

**stormy** *adj.* burrascoso, tempestoso, procelloso; violento; — *sea*, mare in burrasca; *it is* —, fa tempo di burrasca; (orn.) — *petrel*, procellaria.

**story** *n.* storia; racconto; *according to her* —, stando a quel che dice lei; *funny* —, storiella, aneddoto; barzelletta; *that's quite another* —, è un altro paio di maniche; *the — goes . . .*, si dice che . . .; *to make a long — short*, per farla breve; novella; favola; intreccio; (fam.) menzogna, bugia; *to tell stories*, contar frottole; (USA) articolo di giornale; spunto interessante per un servizio giornalistico; *film* —, fotoromanzo; *short* —, novella.

**story-teller** *n.* novelliere, narratore; cantastorie *m.*; (fam.) bugiardo.

**stoup** *n.* acquasantiera.

**stout**[1] *n.* birra scura.

**stout**[2] *adj* forte, robusto, vigoroso; fermo, risoluto; coraggioso, intrepido; solido, resistente; —

*ship*, nave solida; grosso; tozzo, corpulento; *to grow* —, ingrassare. **-ly** *adv.* fortemente, vigorosamente; fermamente, risolutamente; *to deny -ly*, negare fermamente; solidamente; robustamente. **-ness** *n.* corpulenza, pinguedine *f.*; fermezza, risolutezza; durezza, resistenza.

**stove** *n.* stufa; (industr.) — *enamel*, vernice *f.* a fuoco; *gas-stove*, stufa, cucina a gas; *slow-combustion* —, stufa a fuoco continuo.

**stovepipe** *n.* tubo da stufa; (USA) — *hat*, cappello a cilindro.

**stow** *tr.* mettere a posto, ordinare, collocare accuratamente in un luogo; *to — away*, ascondere, mettere via; (fam.) mangiare; (naut.) *to — the anchor*, traversare l'ancora; *to — the sails*, ammainare le vele; stivare, mettere nella stiva; (fam.) — *that nonsense*, smettila di dire sciocchezze. **-age** *n.* (naut.) stivaggio; *-age in bulk*, stivaggio alla rinfusa; spese di stivaggio; (techn.) sistemazione. **-away** *n.* passaggero clandestino; nascondiglio; *intr.* imbarcarsi clandestinamente.

**straddle** *n.* posizione a gambe divaricate; (fig.) incertezza, indecisione sulla scelta fra due linee di condotta; *straddle-legged*, che sta a cavalcioni; *tr.* cavalcare, stare a cavalcioni; *intr.* divaricare; stare a gambe divaricate; (artill.) fare forcella.

**strafe** *n.* (mil. slang) bombardamento; assalto furioso; bastonata; punizione; sgridata; *tr.* bombardare (con artiglieria di grosso calibro); bastonare di santa ragione; sgridare.

**straggl-e** *intr.* disperdersi, sparpagliarsi; sbandarsi, muoversi disordinatamente; andare alla spicciolata; (fig.) divagare. **-er** *n.* chi rimane indietro, ritardatario; (mil.) soldato sbandato. **-ing** *adj.* sparso, disperso; isolato; *-ing beard*, barba rada; *-ing houses*, case sparse; *-ing plants*, piante rampicanti; *gerund*, *n.* andatura, marcia sbandata; vagabondaggio. **-y** *adj.* sparso, sparpagliato.

**straight** *adj.* diritto; rettilineo; — *line*, linea retta; — *as a die*, diritto come un fuso; onesto, retto; leale, franco; — *speaking*, il parlar franco; *to be — with*, agire lealmente verso; netto, ordinato; accurato, lindo; *to put everything* —, riordinare ogni cosa; diritto, perpendicolare; simmetrico; *your tie is not* —, hai la cravatta storta; *to get* —, rimettersi in sesto; autorevole, attendibile; esatto, esatta; (USA) non diluito, non mescolato; *a — whisky*, un whisky liscio.

**straight** *n.* posizone diritta; *to cut a cloth on the* —, tagliare della stoffa in dritto filo; (sport) il rettilineo d'arrivo.

**straight** *adv.* diritto, in linea retta; — *on*, sempre diritto; *to shoot* —, mirare dritto; *to read a book — through*, leggere un libro dal principio alla fine; *he does not see* —, non vede bene; direttamente; senza interruzione, senza deviazione; *to come — from school*, venire direttamente da scuola; — *out*, chiaro e tondo; *to stand* —, stare eretto; — *off*, senza esitazione, immediatamente.

**straightaway** *adv.* See **straightway.**

**straighten** *tr.* drizzare; raddrizzare; mettere in ordine, rassettare; regolare; (techn.) spianare; lisciare; *intr.* drizzarsi; (aeron.) *to — out*, raddrizzarsi, riprendere il volo orizzontale; *to — up*, rassettare; *intr.* raddrizzarsi. **-er** *n.* raddrizzatore.

**straightforward** *adj.* diritto; diretto; schietto, franco, leale; *to give a — answer*, dare una risposta franca; semplice, chiaro. **-ly** *adv.* francamente; apertamente. **-ness** *n.* onestà; schiettezza, franchezza; dirittura morale; semplicità, chiarezza.

**straightness** *n.* l'esser rettilineo; onestà, lealtà, rettitudine *f.*

**straightway** *adv.* immediatamente, subito.

**strain** *n.* tensione; sforzo; fatica; distorsione, strappo muscolare; (techn.) tensione; deformazione; tono; stile; *he spoke in a dismal* —, parlò in tono cupo; disposizione mentale; *a — of melancholy*, una tendenza alla melanconia; (poet.) poesia, canto; melodia, aria musicale.

**strain** *tr.* sottoporre a tensione, tendere fino a limite; *to — to breaking-point*, tirare al massimo; sforzare; affaticare; *to — one's ear*, tendere l'orecchio; *to — off*, filtrare, colare; esigere troppo da; forzare il significato di; danneggiare, deformare; *rfl.* sforzarsi; *to — one's ankle*, storcere una caviglia; *intr. to — after*, cercare di raggiungere; *that writer -s after effect*, cercare di fare effetto.

**strain** *n.* stirpe *f.*, lignaggio; famiglia; origini *f.pl.*; *he is of noble* —, è di nobile famiglia; carattere ereditario; costituzione; (of animals) razza.

**strained** *adj.* teso; — *relations*, rapporti tesi; danneggiato, indebolito; — *heart*, cuore debole; forzato, non spontaneo, artificiale; filtrato, colato.

**strainer** *n.* colino, filtro, depuratore; (industr.) trafila; *tea-strainer*, colino da tè.

**straining** *n.* ipertensione, sforzo, fatica; interpretazione forzata, esagerazione; filtratura.

**strait** *adj.* stretto, angusto; rigoroso; pieno di scrupoli; *-s n.pl.* (geog.) stretto; (fig.) posizione critica; ristrettezze *f.pl.*; *to be in -s*, essere in grande difficoltà.

**straitened** *adj.* difficile; precario; misero, povero; — *circumstances*, precarie situazioni economiche.

**strait-jacket** *n.* camicia di forza. **-laced** *adj.* pieno di scrupoli; rigoroso; puritano.

**strake** *n.* (naut.) corso di fasciame; sezione del cerchione; striscia di colore diverso dal resto della superficie.

**strand**[1] *n.* filo; fune *f.*, cavo; treccia; (naut.) legnolo.

**strand**[2] *n.* sponda; spiaggia, lido; *the Strand*, lo Strand (famosa strada di Londra); *tr.* arenare; *intr.* arenarsi, incagliarsi. **-ed** *adj.* (naut.) arenato, incagliato, insabbiato; (fig.) in difficoltà; (fam.) rimasto al verde.

**strange** *adj.* strano; bizzarro, singolare, insolito; misterioso; straordinario; eccentrico; strambo; — *to say*, strano a dire; estraneo, sconosciuto; nuovo; *in a — land*, in terra straniera; senza esperienza; non abituato; *I am — to this job*, sono nuovo a questo lavoro. **-ly** *adv.* stranamente, misteriosamente. **-ness** *n.* stranezza; singolarità; bizzarria; novità.

**stranger** *n.* estraneo *m.*, estranea *f.*; sconosciuto *m.*, sconosciuta *f.*, forestiero *m.*, forestiera *f.*; *he is no — to me*, lo conosco bene; *they were -s*, non erano pratici del luogo; (joc.) *a little* —, un neonato; *I spy -s*, formula usata alla Camera dei Comuni per richiedere che la discussione avvenga a porte chiuse.

**strangl-e** *tr.* strangolare; soffocare; (fig.) reprimere, sopprimere; *to — a laugh*, soffocare una risata. **-ehold** *n.* stretta mortale; (fig.) pol., comm. controllo paralizzante. **-er** *n.* strangolatore, strangolatrice. **-es** *n.pl.* (vet.) stranguglioni *m.pl.* **-ing** *n.* strangolamento.

**strangulat-e** *tr.* (pathol.; surg.) strozzare; fermare la circolazione a; *-ed hernia*, ernia strozzata. **-ion** *n.* strangolamento; (pathol.; surg.) strozzatura.

**strap** *n.* cinghia; correggia; maniglia a pendaglio; (techn.) nastro; cinghia; moletta; (naut.) stroppo; (bot.) linguetta; *shoulder-strap* spallina; *watch-strap*, cinturino da orologio; *tr.* percuotere con una cinghia; assicurare con cinghie; (naut.) stroppare.

**strap-hang** *intr.* viaggiare in

piedi (in autobus, ecc.) sostenendosi a una maniglia.
**strapping**[1] *adj.* vigoroso, gagliardo, robusto.
**strapping**[2] *n.* chiusura per mezzo di cinghie; colpo di cinghia, staffilata; bande *f.pl.*; nastri *m.pl.*; cerotto; (techn.) moietta, reggetta.
**Strasburg** *pr.n.* Strasburgo *f.*
**stratagem** *n.* stratagemma *m.*
**strateg-y** *n.* strategia. **-ic(al)** *adj.* strategico. **-ics** *n.* strategia. **-ist** *n.* stratega *m.*
**stratif-y** *tr.* disporre a strati, stratificare; *intr.* stratificarsi. **-ication** *n.* (geol.) stratificazione.
**stratum** *n.* (geol.) strato; giacimento; (fig.) strato sociale; classe *f.*
**straw** *adj.* di paglia; *n.* paglia; fuscello, festuca, cannuccia; (fig.) cosa da nulla; *to drink through a* —, bere con una cannuccia; *I don't care a* —, non me ne importa nulla; *it is not worth a* —, non vale un fico secco; *to catch at a* —, attaccarsi ad una pagliuzza; (provb.) *it is the last — that breaks the camel's back*, è l'ultima goccia che fa traboccare il vaso; — *hat*, paglietta; — *colour*, giallo paglierino; — *vote*, votazione esplorativa.
**strawberry** *n.* fragola; — *leaves*, corona ducale; — *mark*, neo angiomatoso.
**stray** *adj.* smarrito; sviato; randagio; errante; *a — dog*, un cane randagio; casuale, fortuito, accidentale; *a few — visitors*, alcuni visitatori casuali; isolato, staccato; — *thoughts*, pensieri isolati; *n.* animale domestico smarritosi; fanciullo abbandonato; *waifs and -s*, fanciulli abbandonati; *intr.* vagare, vagabondare; deviare; perdersi, smarrirsi; (electr.) disperdersi.
**streak** *n.* linea, riga, striscia, striatura; banda; *a — of lightning*, un lampo; *white with black -s*, bianco a righe nere; vena; *a — of eccentricity*, una punta d'eccentricità; *a — of gold*, una vena d'oro; *tr.* striare; rigare; venare; *intr.* muoversi velocemente, andare svelto come un lampo.
**streak-ed** *adj.* a strisce, striato, screziato; venato. **-iness** *n.* striatura, screziatura; venatura. **-y** *adj.* striato, screziato; lardellato.
**stream** *n.* corso d'acqua, ruscello; fiume *m.*; torrente; flusso, flotto, getto continuo; colata; corrente *f.*; *against the* —, controcorrente; *to go up* —, risalire un fiume, andar contro corrente; *to move down* —, scendere un fiume, seguire la corrente; *the Gulf Stream*, La Corrente del Golfo; (schol.) classifica, gruppo; *intr.* scorrere; fluire; sgorgare; scaturire; *to — in the wind*, ondeggiare al vento; *to — forth*, uscire a fiotti; *the crowd -ed in through the gates*, la fiumana di gente penetrò attraverso i cancelli; *to — out*, effondersi, riversarsi fuori; *tr.* (schol.) classificare, dividere secondo l'abilità.
**streamer** *n.* pennone *m.*; (naut.) fiamma, banderuola; nastro; (USA, journ.) titolo su tutta la larghezza della pagina.
**streamlet** *n.* ruscelletto; rivolo d'acqua.
**streamline** *n.* (hydraulic) linea di flusso; linea di corrente; (autom.; aeron.) linea aerodinamica; *tr.* (autom.; aeron.) dare linea affusolata a; *a -d car*, una macchina dalla carrozzeria aerodinamica.
**street** *n.* via, strada; *the man in the* —, l'uomo qualunque; (fam.) *not in the same — as*, di molto inferiore a; *this is right up your* —, questo è pane per i tuoi denti; *to be in Queer Street*, essere in cattive acque; *to be on the -s*, vivere di prostituzione; *to turn into the -s*, buttare sul lastrico; *to walk the -s*, battere il marciapiede, (or) vivere di prostituzione; *one-way* —, strada a senso unico; *side* —, via laterale.
**street-car** *n.* (USA) tram *m. indecl.* **-door** *n.* portone *m.* **-level** *n.* pianterreno. **-walker** *n.* prostituta.
**strength** *n.* forza, vigore *m.*, energia; — *of mind*, forza di volontà; *it is too much for my* —, è al di sopra delle mie forze; *by sheer* —, a viva forza; *I did it on the — of your promise*, lo feci basandomi sulla tua promessa; solidità; rigidezza, tenacia; resistenza; efficacia; intensità; (chem.) densità; (electr.) intensità; — *of a wine*, grado alcoolico di un vino; sostegno spirituale; *God is our* —, Dio è la nostra forza; quantità, numero; *to be present in great* —, esser presenti in gran numero; (mil.) truppe, forze effettive; *fighting* —, effettivi mobilitabili; *to be on the* —, figurare nei ruoli; *to bring a regiment up to* —, completare i ranghi di un reggimento; *breaking* —, resistenza alla rottura.
**strengthen** *tr.* dar forza a; fortificare; rafforzare; irrobustire; consolidare; (chem.) aumentare la concentrazione di; (mil.) potenziare. **-er** *n.* cosa che dà forza; (med.) corroborante *m.* **-ing** *adj.* fortificante; rafforzante; *gerund* il rafforzare; *n.* rafforzamento, irrobustimento, consolidamento.
**strenuous** *adj.* strenuo, energico; attivo; accanito; — *game*, giuoco molto combattuto; arduo; duro; — *life*, vita attiva e dura. **-ness** *n.* vigore *m.*, energia; ardore *m.*, zelo; accanimento.
**streptococcus** *n.* streptococco.
**streptomycin** *n.* (pharm.) streptomicina.
**stress** *n.* spinta; pressione; costrizione; tensione; *in times of* —, in periodi di difficoltà; *under the — of anger*, sotto l'impulso dell'ira; importanza; insistenza; *to lay special — on*, porre in rilievo; (gramm.) accento tonico; (bldg.) sollecitazione, sforzo, tensione; *to be under* —, essere soggetto a sforzo; *breaking* —, resistenza alla rottura; *maximum* —, carico di rottura; *torsional* —, sollecitazione di torsione.
**stress** *tr.* forzare, sottoporre a tensione; (gramm.) accentare; *to — a syllable*, mettere l'accento su una sillaba; porre in rilievo, sottolineare, accentuare; mettere in risalto. **-ing** *n.* insistenza; accentazione; (bldg.) sforzo, tensione.
**stretch** *n.* stiramento; tensione; sforzo; (fig.) abuso; *by a — of the imagination*, facendo uno sforzo d'immaginazione; periodo, spazio di tempo; *at a* —, tutto d'un fiato; *three hours at a* —, tre ore di seguito; distesa; estensione di spazio; *a — of road*, un bel tratto di strada; (slang) periodo di detensione; *to do a* —, scontare la pena.
**stretch** *tr.* tirare; tendere; stendere; *the bird stretched its wings*, l'uccello allargò le ali; esagerare, abusare di; *intr.* estendersi; sdraiarsi; *to — out*, allungarsi.
**stretcher** *n.* tenditore, stenditore; lettiga, barella; (techn.) allargatore; (naut.) traversino puntapiedi *m.*, pedagna; (bldg.) mattone per piano. **-bearer** *n.* barelliere *m.*
**stretching** *n.* stiramento; allungamento, allargamento; (techn.) tensione.
**strew** *tr.* spargere, sparpagliare; cospargere, coprire; disseminare. **-ing** *n.* sparpagliamento; cospargimento.
**striation** *n.* striatura.
**stricken** *adj.* colpito, ferito; *the — deer*, il cervo ferito; — *heart*, cuore afflitto; — *with paralysis*, colpito da paralisi; *panic-stricken*, atterrito.
**strict** *adj.* stretto; preciso, esatto; (fig.) severo, rigido, rigoroso; scrupoloso; — *parents*, genitori severi; *in — confidence*, in gran segretezza. **-ly** *adv.* esattamente, con precisione; *-ly speaking*, a rigor di termini; rigorosamente, severamente. **-ness** *n.* precisione, esattezza; rigore *n.*; severità.
**stricture** *n.* (pathol.) stenosi *f.*, restringimento; (fig.) critica,

biasimo; *to pass -s on*, far delle critiche severe a.
**stride** *n.* passo; andatura; *to make great -s*, avanzare a grandi passi; (fig.) fare grandi progressi; *to take an obstacle in one's —*, (fig.) superare facilmente un ostacolo; *intr.* camminare a grandi passi; *to — across*, attraversare a grandi passi.
**strident** *adj.* stridente, stridulo.
**stridulat-e** *intr.* stridulare. **-ion** *n.* stridulazione.
**stridulous** *adj.* stridulo.
**strife** *n.* contessa, lotta, conflitto; (poet.) *to cease from —*, deporre le armi.
**strike** *tr.* battere, colpire, percuotere, picchiare; *to — a bargain*, concludere un affare; (provb.) *— while the iron is hot*, batti il ferro finchè è caldo; (fig.) colpire, impressionare; *how does it — you ?*, che cosa ne pensi ?; battere, suonare; toccare; *the clock has just struck twelve*, l'orologio ha appena battuto le dodici; accendere; *to — a light*, accendere un fiammifero; scoprire; *to — oil*, scoprire un giacimento di petrolio, (fig.) fare un buon affare; *to — camp*, levare il campo; *to — tents*, smontare le tende; *intr.* scioperare, fare scioperi; FOLLOW. BY ADV. OR PREP.: *to — back*, rispondere all'attacco (di); *to — down*, abbattere, mandare a terra con un colpo; *to — home*, colpire nel segno; *to — off*, far cadere, abbattere; tagliare; cancellare; radiare; (comm.) dedurre, scontare; (typ.) tirare delle copie; *they struck off his head*, lo decapitarono; *to — off a name from a list*, radiare un nome da una lista; *to — out*, progettare, inventare; cancellare; tracciare, aprire; *intr.* allungare un pugno; *to — through*, cancellare con un tratto di penna; *to — up*, intonare, attaccare.
**strike** *n.* scoperta; *lucky —*, fortunata speculazione; sciopero; *— breaker*, crumiro; *— pay*, indennità di sciopero; *sit-down —*, sciopero bianco; *sympathetic —*, sciopero di solidarietà.
**striker** *n.* scioperante *m.*, *f.*; (techn.) percussore, batacchio.
**striking** *adj.* sorprendente, straordinario, singolare, sensazionale, impressionante; *— news*, notizie sensazionali; *n.* colpo, battitura; (electr.) innesco; *— clock*, orologio a suoneria.
**string** *n.* spago cordicella; corda, (fig.) *to pull every —*, giocare ogni carta; *to pull -s*, tenere in mano le fila, agire dietro le quinte; laccio, legaccio, stringa; *apron -s*, legacci di grembiule; (mus.) corda; *the -s*, gli strumenti a corda; *string-quartet*, quartetto d'archi; (fig.) *to harp on the same —*, insistere sullo stesso tasto; fibra, filamento; fila, filza; rosario; successione; (anat.) tendine *m.*, nervo, legamento.
**string** *tr.* legare con corde; munire di corde; *to — a tennis racket*, mettere le corde a una racchetta da tennis; *to — an instrument*, accordare uno strumento; *to — a bow*, tendere un arco; congiungere con corda; *to — beads*, infilare perline; (cul.) togliere i fili a; *to — up*, impiccare.
**stringency** *n.* rigore *m.*; severità; carenza, mancanza.
**stringent** *adj.* stretto, preciso; rigoroso, severo; incontestabile; *— argument*, argomento irrefutabile; scarso, mancante.
**stringer** *n.* chi infila; accordatore; (archit.) longarina; (autom.; aeron.) longarone *m.*
**stringy** *adj.* fibroso; filoso; filamentoso; viscoso.
**strip**[1] *n.* striscia, nastro; *comic —*, racconto a fumetti; *tr.* tagliare a strisce.
**strip**[2] *tr.* svestire; denudare; spogliare; *to — a tree of its bark*, scortecciare un albero; (fig.) privare (di titoli di proprietà); (mil.) esautorare; (techn.) spanare; *intr.* svestirsi, spogliarsi.
**stripe** *n.* striscia, lista; riga; banda; (mil.) gallone *m.*; *to lose one's —*, essere degradato; *tr.* rigare, listare, striare.
**striped** *adj.* a strisce, a righe; rigato, striato, zebrato; (anat.) striato; gallonato.
**strip-iness, -ing** *n.* rigatura; striatura.
**stripling** *n.* giovanetto.
**stripper** *n.* (chem.) estrattore *m.*; (paint.) sverniciatore *m.*; (entertainer) spogliarellista *f.*
**strip-tease** *n.* spogliarello.
**stripy** *adj.* rigato, striato; a strisce, a righe.
**strive** *intr.* sforzarsi; ingegnarsi; *to — against*, combattere contro.
**stroke**[1] *n.* colpo, percossa, botta; *— of lightning*, fulmine *m.*; *at a —*, d'un sol colpo; movimento; (swimming) bracciata; (rowing) vogata, remata; (person) primo rematore; (tennis) battuta; *to be off one's —*, essere fuori tempo, (fam.) essere sconcertato; *to keep —*, tenere il tempo, vogare in cadenza; *a — of genius*, un lampo di genio; *a — of good luck*, un colpo di fortuna; *not to do a — of work*, non far nulla, non alzare un dito; *with a — of the pen*, con un tratto di penna; *to give the finishing -s to*, dare gli ultimi ritocchi a; rintocco; *it is on the — of six*, stanno per suonare le sei; (med.) colpo, attacco.
**stroke**[1] *intr.* (naut.) vogare in cadenza; *tr. to — a boat*, fare da primo rematore.
**stroke**[2] *n.* carezza; lisciata; *tr.* accarezzare; lisciare; *to — the cat the wrong way*, accarezzare il gatto contropelo.
**stroll** *n.* passeggiatina, quattro passi; *to go for a —*, andare a fare quattro passi; *intr.* passeggiare; andare a zonzo; girovagare, vagabondare. **-er** *n.* vagabondo; attore girovago. **-ing** *adj.* errante, girovogo, ambulante; (theatr. hist.) *— company*, compagnia ambulante; *— player*, attore girovago.
**strong** *adj.* forte, robusto, resistente; *are you quite — again ?*, ti sei rimesso del tutto ?; *as — as a horse*, forte come un toro; energico, potente; violento; impetuoso; *— candidate*, candidato con molte probabilità di successo; *— measures*, misure energiche; *— wind*, vento impetuoso; *to have a — hold on*, avere un forte ascendente su; numeroso; *how — are they ?*, in quanti sono ?; *they are ten thousand —*, sono dieci mila; deciso; ardente; zelante; piccante, forte; (comm.) in rialzo; (gramm.) forte.
**strong-box** *n.* cassaforte *f.* **-minded** *adj.* risoluto, deciso. **-room** *n.* camera blindata.
**stronghold** *n.* roccaforte *f.*, fortezza; cittadella.
**stront-ia** *n.* (chem.) stronziana. **-ian** *adj.* (chem.) stronzianico; *n.* stronziana. **-ium** *n.* (chem.) stronzio.
**strop** *n.* coramella per rasoio; (naut.) stroppo; *tr.* affilare sulla coramella.
**stroph-e** *n.* strofa. **-ic** *adj.* strofico.
**struck** *part.* of **strike**, *q.v.*; (fam.) *— on*, innamorato di; *not very — on*, non molto entusiasta di.
**structur-e** *n.* struttura; costruzione; fabbricato; edificio. **-al** *adj.* strutturale, di struttura; (geol.) tettonico. **-alism** *n.* (ling.) strutturalismo. **-alist** *n.* (ling.) strutturalista *m.*, *f.*
**struggl-e** *n.* lotta, combattimento; sforzo; *class —*, lotta di classe; *intr.* lottare; cercare di liberarsi; divincolarsi; dibattersi; (fig.) lottare; sforzarsi, fare sforzi, cercare di; *to — for*, contendersi (qualcosa); *to — against destiny*, lottare contro il destino; *to — along*, avanzare a stento, (fig.) vivere alla peggio, sopravvivere; *to — in*, aprirsi un varco, penetrare a fatica; *we succeeded in struggling through*, ce l'abbiamo fatta. **-ing** *gerund* il lottare; *n.* combattimento; *adj.* penoso, stentato.
**strum** *n.* strimpellamento; *intr.* strimpellare; *tr. to — a tune*, accennare un motivo.

**strumpet** *n.* sgualdrina; prostituta.

**strut**[1] *n.* andatura affettata; *intr.* incedere con sussiego, camminare impettito.

**strut**[2] *n.* (bldg.) puntone *m.*; contropalo; (aeron.) montante *m.*; *tr.* sostenere con puntoni.

**strychnine** *n.* (pharm.) stricnina.

**stub** *n.* troncone *m.*; ceppo; (of cigar) mozzicone *m.*, rimanenza; (of tooth) radice *f.*; (of tail) moncherino; (of cheque book) matrice *f.*; *tr.* inciampare; urtare; *to — out*, spegnere, estinguere.

**stubbl-e** *n.* stoppia; barba corta e ispida. **-y** *adj.* coperto di stoppie; ispido.

**stubborn** *adj.* ostinato, cocciuto, caparbio, testardo; tenace, ribelle; refrattario; *— soil*, terreno ingrato. **-ness** *n.* ostinazione, caparbietà; tenacia; inflessibilità.

**stubby** *adj.* troncato; tozzo; tarchiato; ispido.

**stucco** *n.* stucco; *— decorator*, stucchinaio, stuccatore; *tr.* stuccare; decorare a stucco.

**stuck-up** *adj.* (fam.) presuntuoso; borioso; arrogante.

**stud**[1] *n.* chiodo a capocchia larga pomo; borchia; *collar —*, bottoncino; (techn.) colonnetta, perno sporgente; *— bolt*, vite prigioniera; (naut.) *— chain*, catena rinforzata; *tr.* guarnire di borchie; imbullettare; costellare; tempestare; *crown -ded with diamonds*, corona tempestata di diamanti.

**stud**[2] *n.* scuderia, allevamento di cavalli; (slang) giovanotto che si prostituta a donne.

**stud-book** *n.* registro della genealogia dei purosangue. **-farm** *n.* campo di allevamento di cavalli di razza. **-horse** *n.* stallone *m.* **-mare** *n.* cavalla fattriee.

**studding-sail** *n.* (naut.) coltellaccio.

**student** *n.* studente *m.*, studentessa *f.*; *medical —*, studente in medicina; studioso; *to be a — of*, studiare, essere uno studioso di. **-ship** *n.* borsa di studio.

**studied** *adj.* studiato, ricercato; premeditato, intenzionale.

**studio** *n.* studio; (cinem.) teatro di posa; (radio) auditorio.

**studious** *adj.* studioso; diligente, attento; premuroso, sollecito; **-ness** *n.* amore dello studio, passione per lo studio; diligenza, premura, zelo.

**study** *n.* studio; (room) studio, ufficio; esame attento; investigazione; *to make a — of*, indagare su; cura, attenzione, premura; riflessione, meditazione; *he is in a brown —*, è immerso nei propri pensieri; (paint.; sculpt.) studio, abbozzo, bozzetto; (mus.) studio; *a — by Chopin*, uno studio di Chopin; dissertazione, saggio; (theatr.) *to be a good —*, imparare facilmente; *tr.* studiare; esaminare attentamente; investigare; *intr. to — for an examination*, prepararsi a un esame; *to — hard*, sgobbare.

**stuff** *n.* sostanza; materia prima; essenza; cosa, roba; *funny —*, roba da ridere, cosa buffa; *what —!*, che roba!; *that's the —!*, bravo!, questa è roba buona!; stoffa, tessuto; sciocchezza, cosa di nessun valore; *— and nonsense!*, sciocchezze!

**stuff** *tr.* imbottire, riempire; (cul.) farcire; rimpinzare; ingozzare; *to — a goose*, fare ingrassare un'oca; impagliare; imbalsamare; *a -ed lion*, un leone imbalsamato; (fam.) *a -ed shirt*, impallone gonfiato; turare; ostruire; stivare, stipare; *intr.* rimpinzarsi

**stuffiness** *n.* mancanza d'aria; odore di chiuso, di stantio; l'avere il naso chiuso per il raffreddore; (fig., fam.) vecchi pregiudizi.

**stuffing** *n.* imbottitura; (cul.) ripieno; imbalsamazione; impagliatura; (fam.) *to take the — out of*, sgonfiare; ingrasso.

**stuffy** *adj.* senz'aria, mal ventilato; *it is very — in here*, qui dentro ci si soffoca; afoso, soffocante; *— air*, aria viziata; (fam.) conservatore, rigido; noioso.

**stultif-y** *tr.* togliere valore a; infirmare; rendere ridicolo; confondere; rendere vano; rendere stupido, rallentare. **-ication** *n.* il rendere ridicolo; l'infirmare; il privare di dignità, di valore, d'efficacia.

**stumbl-e** *n.* passo falso; (fig.) errore *m.*; *intr.* inciampare, incespicare; (fig.) fare un passo falso, fare errori; impaperarsi, impappinarsi; *to — across*, imbattersi in, trovare per caso; *to — at*, provare scrupoli di fronte a; *to — over*, tentennare di fronte a; *to — (up)on*, imbattersi in. **-ing** *n.* incespicamento; (fig.) errore *m.*; *-ing-block*, scoglio, ostacolo.

**stump**[1] *n.* ceppo, tronco (of tooth); radice *f.*; (of limb) moncherino, moncone *m.*; (of cigar) mozzicone; *pl.* (joc.) gambe; (fig.) *to stir one's -s*, muovere le gambe; (cricket) paletto.

**stump**[2] *tr.* mozzare, ridurre a ceppi; estirpare ceppi da (un terreno); (USA) imbarazzare; *I am -ed*, sono perplesso; (cricket) mettere fuori gara abbattendo i paletti; *intr.* camminare pesantemente; urtare contro.

**stump**[3] *n.* (art) sfumino; *tr.* sfumare.

**stumpy** *adj.* tarchiato, tozzo; pieno di ceppi.

**stun** *tr.* stordire; assordare; intronare; far perdere i sensi a; tramortire; sbalordire, far stupire. **-ner** *n.* chi assorda; chi fa sbalordire, stupire; (fam.) persona meravigliosa. **-ning** *adj.* assordante; (fam.) sbalorditivo; meraviglioso; magnifico; fenomenale.

**stunsail, stuns'l** *n.* (naut.) coltellaccio.

**stunt**[1] *n.* bravata; ostentazione; dimostrazione di forza; destrezza; trovata pubblicitaria; (journ.) montatura; (aeron.) acrobazia; *— flying*, volo acrobatico; (cinem.) *stunt-man*, controfigura acrobata.

**stunt**[2] *tr.* arrestare lo sviluppo di. **-ed** *adj.* striminzito; stentato; machitico.

**stupefacient** *adj.*, *n.* (med.) stupefacente *m.*

**stupef-y** *tr.* istupidire; inebituare; abbrutire, stordire, sbalordire. **-action** *n.* torpore provocato da stupefacenti; stupore *m.*

**stupendous** *adj.* splendido, stupendo, magnifico; prodigioso; formidabile. **-ness** *n.* mirabilità; prodigiosità; magnificenza.

**stupid** *adj.* stupido, ottuso; tardo, stolto; *n.* (fam.) stupido. **-ity** *n.* stupidità, ottusità; stolidità.

**stupor** *n.* stupore *m.*; meraviglia; (med.) torpore *m.*, incoscienza.

**sturd-y** *adj.* vigoroso, forte, robusto; risoluto, fermo. **-iness** *n.* vigoria, forza; risolutezza, fermezza.

**sturgeon** *n.* (ichth.) storione *m.*

**stutter** *n.* balbuzie *f.pl.*; tartagliamento; *to have a terrible —*, soffrire di balbuzie accentuate; *tr.*, *intr.* balbettare, tartagliare; essere balbuziente. **-er** *n.* balbuziente *m.*, *f.*; tartaglione *m.*, tartagliona *f.* **-ing** *adj.* balbuziente; *n.* balbuzie *f.pl.*

**sty**[1] *n.* porcile *m.*; (fig.) luogo sudicio e misero; luogo di corruzione.

**sty**[2], **stye** *n.* orzaiolo.

**style** *n.* stile *m.*; modello; genere *m.*, tipo; modo; maniera; *a gentleman of the old —*, un gentiluomo di vecchio stampo; *their — of living*, il loro tenore di vita; tono, distinzione; classe *f.*; moda; *in the latest —*, all'ultima moda; titolo, nome *m.*; (pen) stilo; (bot.; med.) stilo; (of sundial) gnomone *m.*; puntina del grammofono; (hist.) *old — (O.S.)*, vecchio sistema (secondo il calendario Giuliano); *new — (N.S.)*, sistema nuovo (secondo il calendario Gregoriano).

**style** *tr.* chiamare; nominare; denominare; designare; *to be -d*, avere il titolo di.

**stylish** *adj.* che ha distinzione; di classe; elegante. **-ness** *n.* eleganza; buon gusto; distinzione; stile *m.*

**stylist** *n.* stilista *m.*, *f.* **-ic** *adj.* stilistico; di stile.

**styliz-e** *tr.* stilizzare. **-ation** *n.* stilizzazione.

**stylographic** *adj.* stilografico.

**stylus** *n.* stile *m.*; puntina per grammofono; (of sun-dial) gnomone *m.*; (bot.) stilo.

**stymie** *n.* (golf) palla che ostacola l'entrata in buca.

**stymie** *tr.* ostacolare buche a; (fig.) mettere nell'imbarazzo, ostacolare.

**styptic** *adj.* (med.) astringente; anti-emorragico.

**suav-e** *adj.* soave; dolce; affabile, cortese. **-ity** *n.* soavità; dolcezza; affabilità, cortesia.

**sub-**[1] *pref.* sub-, sotto-.

**sub**[2] *n.* (fam.) subalterno; sottomarino; sottoscrizione; sostituto; *intr.* fare da sostituto; *to — for*, sostituire.

**subacid** *adj.* acidulo; agrodolce.

**subalpine** *adj.* subalpino.

**subaltern** *adj.* inferiore, sottoposto; *n.* (mil.) subalterno.

**subaquatic, subaqueous** *adj.* subacqueo.

**subclass** *n.* (bot.; zool.) sottoclasse *f.* **-ify** *tr.* dividere in sottoclassi. **-ification** *n.* sottoclassificazione.

**sub-committee** *n.* sottocomitato. **-conscious** *adj.*, *n.* subcosciente. **-contract** *n.* subappalto; *tr.*, *intr.* subappaltare. **-cutaneous** *adj.* (med.) sottocutaneo. **-deacon** *n.* (eccl.) suddiacono. **-dean** *n.* sottodecano. **-delegate** *n.* vicedelegato. **-divide** *tr.*, *intr.* suddividere, suddividersi. **-divisible** *adj.* suddivisibile. **-division** *n.* suddivisione, ripartizione; spezzettamento. **-dominant** *n.* (mus.) sottodominante *m.*

**subdu-e** *tr.* conquistare; soggiogare, sottomettere; domare; controllare; ridurre, attenuare; addolcire, mitigare. **-ed** *part. adj.* soggiogato, sottomesso; represso; controllato; attenuato; addolcito; *-ed colours*, colori attenuati; *in a -ed voice* sottovoce. **-er** *n.* soggiogatore; vincitore; conquistatore.

**subedit** *tr.* (journ.) redigere. **-ing** *n.* lavoro redazionale. **-or** *n.* redattore aggiunto.

**sub-family** *n.* (bot.; zool.) sottofamiglia, sottogruppo. **-genus** *n.* sottospecie *f.* **-group** *n.* sottogruppo. **-heading** *n.* sottotitolo. **-human** *adj.* al di sotto del genere umano; quasi umano.

**sub·ject** *adj.* soggetto, assoggettato, sottoposto; *— to discount*, suscettibile di uno sconto; *— to colds*, soggetto al raffreddore; *— to your consent*, salvo la tua approvazione; *n.* argomento; soggetto; tema *m.*; materia; contenuto; (gramm.) soggetto; *British —*, cittadino britannico; (med.) soggetto.

**subject** *tr.* assoggettare, sottomettere, soggiogare; esporre, sottoporre. **-ion** *n.* assoggettamento; conquista; sottomissione; cattività; *to bring into —*, soggiogare.

**subjective** *adj.* soggettivo; individuale; (gram.) soggettivo; *the — case*, il nominativo. **-ness** *n.* soggettività. **-ism** *n.* soggettivismo.

**sub-join** *tr.* unire; aggiungere; soggiungere. **-jugate** *tr.* soggiogare; asservire; vincere; domare. **-junctive** *adj.*, *n.* (gram.) congiuntivo, soggiuntivo **-lease** *n.* subaffitto. **-lessee** *n.* subaffittuario; subappaltatore. **-lessor** *n.* subaffittante *m.*, *f.* **-let** *n.* subaffitto; *tr.* subaffittare; subappaltare. **-librarian** *n.* vicebibliotecario. **-lieutenant** *n.* (mil.) sottotenente; (naut.) sottotenente di vascello. **-limate** *adj.*, *n.* (chem.) sublimato; *tr.* (chem.; psych.) sublimare. **-limation** *n.* sublimazione.

**sublime** *adj.* sublime; eccelso; supremo, perfetto, senza pari; (anat.) superficiale; a fior di pelle.

**subliminal** *adj.* (psych.) subliminale.

**sublimity** *n.* sublimità; (anat., superfialità.

**submarin-e** *adj.* subacqueo, sottomarino; *n.* sommergibile *n.*; *— earthquake*, maremoto; *— plants*, piante subacquee; *minelaying —*, sommergibile posamine *m.* **-er** *n.* (naut.) sommergibilista *m.*

**submerge** *tr.*, *intr.* sommergere; affondare; (of submarine) immergersi.

**submersion** *n.* sommersione; immersione.

**submission** *n.* sottomissione; rassegnazione; rispetto, docilità, umiltà; tesi *f.*, teoria.

**submissive** *adj.* remissivo; docile; umile; sottomesso. **-ness** *n.* sottomissione; docilità; umiltà.

**submit** *intr.* sottomettersi, sottoporsi; cedere, piegarsi; rassegnarsi; rassegnarsi; *tr.* sottoporre, rimettere (leg.) *to — a case to a court*, deferire un caso al tribunale.

**subnormal** *adj.* al di sotto della norma; *n.* (geom.) sottonormale.

**subordinacy** *n.* subordinazione.

**subordinate** *adj.* subordinato; secondario; di ordine inferiore; in sott'ordine; (gramm.) *— clause*, proposizione subordinata; *n.* subalterno; inferiore *m.*; *tr.* subordinare, considerare men importante; far dipendere; assoggettare.

**subordination** *n.* subordinazione; sottomissione; inferiorità di rango, di posizione; (gram.) subordinazione.

**suborn** *tr.* subornare, corrompere; sobillare; *to — witnesses*, corrompere dei testimoni. **-ation** *n.* subornazione; corruzione. **-er** *n.* chi suborna, corrompe.

**subplot** *n.* intreccio secondario.

**subpoena** *n.* (leg.) citazione, mandato di comparizione; *tr.* (leg.) citare (un testimonio); notificare l'ordine di comparizione in tribunale a.

**sub-prefect** *n.* sottoprefetto, viceprefetto. **-prefecture** *n.* sottoprefettura. **-prior** *n.* sottopriore *m.*

**sub-rogation** *n.* (leg.) surrogazione.

**subscrib-e** *tr.*, *intr.* sottoscrivere, sottoscriversi; firmare; aderire a; impegnarsi; trovarsi d'accordo, approvare: abbonarsi. **-er** *n.* chi sottoscrive, firma; *the -er*, il sottoscritto; (comm.) il contraente; abbonato, abbonata.

**subscript** *adj.* (Gk. gramm.; typ.) sottoscritto; *iota —*, iota sottoscritta.

**subscription** *n.* sottoscrizione; firma; abbonamento; consenso, approvazione; *— form*, modulo di abbonamento.

**sub-section** *n.* sottosezione. **-sequent** *adj.* successivo; ulteriore; seguente. **-serve** *tr.* promuovere; giovare a; favorire. **-servience, -serviency** *n.* subordinazione; remissività; servilismo. **-servient** *adj.* dipendente; ossequente; servile; soggetto; che serve a promuovere.

**subsid-e** *intr.* calare; decrescere; abbassarsi; cadere; sprofondere; cedere. **-ence** *n.* abbassamento; cedimento; crollo; il calmarsi.

**subsidiary** *adj.* sussidiario; supplementare; di riserva; ausiliario; accessorio; secondario; *— company*, società consociata; *— stream*, fiume tributario.

**subsid-y** *n.* sussidio; sovvenzione. **-ize** *tr.* sussidiare; sovvenzionare.

**subsist** *intr.* sussistere, continuare a esistere; tenersi in vita. **-ence** *n.* esistenza, sussistenza; mantenimento; *-ence money*, acconto paga. **-ent** *adj.* sussistente; esistente.

**sub-soil** *n.* (agric.) sottosuolo. **-species** *n.* sottospecie *f.*

**substance** *n.* sostanza; essenza; materia; *the Son is of one — with the Father*, (theol.) il Figlio è consostanziale al Padre; contenuto; solidità; nerbo; fondamento; sostanze *f.pl.*, beni *m.pl.*, ricchezze *f.pl.*; (chem.) sostanza; elemento.

**substantial** *adj.* sostanzioso; solido; resistente; importante; notevole; effettivo; ricco; reale; grosso. **-ly** *adv.* sostanzialmente; sostanziosamente; notevolmente; realmente, effettivamente.

**substantiat-e** *tr.* dimostrare la verità di; provare; dare fondamento a; convalidare; *to — a charge*, dimostrare la fondatezza di un'accusa; dare sostanza a; rendere sostanziale. **-ion** *n.* prova; giustificazione; materializzazione.

**substantive** *adj.* indipendente, autosufficiente; considerevole; *a — share*, una parte considerevole; reale; essenziale; *n.* (gram.) sostantivato.

**substation** *n.* stazione sussidiaria.

**substitut-e** *n.* sostituto; rappresentante *m., f.*; delegato; *as a — for*, in sostituzione di, al posto di; surrogato; imitazione; *beware of substitutes!*, attenti alle imitazioni!; supplente *m., f.*; *tr., intr.* sostituire, agire come sostituto; rimpiazzare, supplire a. **-ion** *n.* sostituzione; (leg.) surrogazione.

**sub-stratum** *n.* strato, substrato; (fig.) base *f.*; fondo; sottosuolo. **-structure** *n.* base *f.*; piano di posa; fondamento, sottostruttura. **-sume** *tr.* includere in una regola, classe; classificare. **-tenancy** *n.* subaffitto. **-tenant** *n.* subaffittuario. **-tend** *tr.* (geom.) sottendere. **-terfuge** *n.* sotterfugio; pretesto; raggiro. **-terranean** *adj.* sotterraneo; nascosto; segreto. **-title** *n.* sottotitolo; (cinem.) didascalia.

**subtle** *adj.* indefinibile, elusivo, misterioso; penetrante, acuto; ingegnoso, sottile; astuto, scaltro; tenue, sottile; rarefatto. **-ness, -ty** *n.* carattere elusivo; acutezza, sagacia, sottigliezza; astuzia.

**subtract** *tr.* detrarre, dedurre, defalcare; (math.) sottrarre. **-ion** *n.* sottrazione.

**subtropic(al)** *adj.* subtropicale.

**suburb** *n.* sobborgo; *pl.* periferia. **-an** *adj.* suburbano; della periferia; (pejor.) limitato, ristretto.

**sub-vention** *n.* sovvenzione, sussidio. **-version** *n.* sovversione; mutamento, sconvolgimento radicale. **-versive** *adj.* sovversivo, sovvertitore. **-vert** *tr.* sovvertire, rovesciare. **-way** *n.* sottopassaggio, pasaggio sotterraneo; (USA) metropolitana.

**succeed** *tr., intr.* aver successo, riuscire (a); succedere a, prendere il posto di; ereditare; *to — to the throne* (*or to the Crown*), salire al trono; succedersi, seguire in ordine; susseguirsi. **-ing** *adj.* susseguente, seguente; *n.* successo.

**success** *n.* successo; buon esito, buona riuscita; ricchezza, posizione; persona che ha buona riuscita; cosa ben riuscita; *the book was a great —*, il libro ebbe un grande successo. **-ful** *adj.* che ha successo; *the -ful candidate*, il candidato eletto. **-fully** *adv.* con successo; felicemente; favorevolmente.

**succession** *n.* successione; serie *f.*; *in close —*, a brevi intervalli; eredi, discendenti *m.pl.*; eredità; *apostolic —*, eredità apostolica.

**successive** *adj.* successivo, seguente; consecutivo.

**successor** *n.* successore.

**succinct** *adj.* succinto; conciso, terso. **-ness** *n.* concisione, brevità.

**succour** *n.* soccorso, aiuto, assistenza; *tr.* soccorrere, aiutare, correre in aiuto di.

**succubus** *n.* succubo; demonio.

**succul-ence** *n.* succosità. **-ent** *adj.* succulento.

**succumb** *intr.* soccombere; soggiacere; *to — to pneumonia*, morire di polmonite; *to — to temptation*, cedere alla tentazione.

**such** *adj.* tale, simile, siffatto; *he got — a fright*, provò una tale paura; *— people as you*, gente come te; *in — cases*, in casi del genere; *in — weather*, con un tempo simile; *there are no — things as fairies*, le fate non esistono; *— as*, come; *— as it is*, così com'è, anche se non vale un gran che; *— that*, *— as to*, tale che, tale da; così, tanto; *— a clever girl*, una ragazza così intelligente; *to — an extent*, talmente; *it was — a long time ago*, fu tanto tempo fa; *he was in — a hurry*, aveva una tale fretta.

**such** *prn.* tale, tali; questo, questa, questi, queste; quello, quella, quelli, quelle.

**such-and-such** *adj.* tale, così e così, tal dei tali; *— a person*, un tale, uno così e così; *prn.* il tale, la tale (dei tali).

**suchlike** *adj.* simile, dello stesso genere; di tal genere; *prn.* cose, persone simili; gente di tal fatta.

**suck** *n.* succhiata; poppata; *to give —*, allattare; sorso; risucchio; *tr., intr.* succhiare; poppare; *to — dry*, succhiare completamente; assorbire; sorbire sfruttare; *to — in*, inghiottire; aspirare; (fam.) truffare; *to — up*, assorbire; (slang) fare il leccapiedi. **-er** *n.* chi succhia; (slang) persona sempliciotta; *don't be a -er!*, non essere uno stupido!; *to be a -er for*, avere un debole per; (bot.) pollone *m.* **-ing** *adj.* lattante, poppante; *n.* succhiamento; *a -ing child*, un lattante.

**sucking-pig** *n.* porcellino da latte.

**suckl-e** *tr.* allattare. **-ing** *n.* lattante *m., f.*; *babes and -lings*, gli innocenti.

**suction** *n.* succhiamento; (techn.) aspirazione; *— pump*, pompa aspirante.

**sudden** *adj.* improvviso, inaspettato, repentino; *adv. phr. all of a —*, all'improvviso. **-ly** *adv.* improvvisamente, d'un tratto; bruscamente, di colpo. **-ness** *n.* subitaneità.

**suds** *n.pl.* schiuma di sapone, saponata.

**sue** *tr., intr.* ricorrere in giudizio; citare in giudizio; far processare; intentare un processo a; *to — for damages*, far causa per danni; *to — for peace*, chiedere la pace.

**suede** *n.* pelle scamosciata.

**suet** *n.* sugna, grasso di bue.

**suffer** *tr., intr.* soffrire; patire; tollerare; subire; *to — for*, scontare; essere danneggiato; risentire le conseguenze. **-ance** *n.* sofferenza; tacito assenso; rassegnazione; tolleranza; *on -ance*, per tacita tolleranza. **-er** *n.* chi soffre, chi patisce; *fellow-sufferer*, compagno di sventura. **-ing** *n.* sofferenza; pena, dolore *m.*; tolleranza.

**suffice** *tr., intr.* bastare, essere sufficiente; *— it to say that . . .*, basti dire che . . .; soddisfare i bisogni di.

**sufficiency** *n.* sufficienza; l'essere sufficiente; quantità sufficiente; competenza; efficienza.

**sufficient** *adj.* sufficiente, bastevole; competente; *n.* quantità sufficiente; *have you had —?*, hai mangiato abbastanza? **-ly** *adv.* sufficientemente, a sufficienza; abbastanza.

**suffix** *n.* (gramm.) suffisso.

**suffocat-e** *tr., intr.* soffocare; asfissiare. **-ing** *adj.* soffocante; asfissiante. **-ion** *n.* soffocazione, soffocamento; asfissia.

**suffrag-e** *n.* suffragio; diritto di voto. **-ette** *n.* suffragetta. **-ist** *n.* suffragista *m., f.*

**suffus-e** *tr.* coprire; cospargere. **-ion** *n.* spargimento.

**sugar** *n.* zucchero; *brown —*, zucchero greggio; *caster —*, zucchero in polvere; *granulated —*, zucchero cristalizzato; *— and water*, acqua zuccherata; *— almond*, confetto; (fig.) atteggiamento mellifluo; lusinghe; adulazione; parole melate; *tr., intr.* inzuccherare; addolcire; spolverare di zucchero; (fig.) addolcire; adulare; *to — the pill*, indorare la pillola. **-basin, -bowl** *n.* zuccheriera. **-beet** *n.* barbabietola da zucchero. **-candy** *n.* zucchero candito. **-cane** *n.* canna da zucchero.

**-refinery** *n.* raffineria di zucchero. **-tongs** *n.pl.* mollette per zucchero.

**sugar-y** *adj.* zuccheroso, zuccherino; (fig.) mellifluo, insinuante. **-iness** *n.* dolcezza; (fig.) mellifluità.

**suggest** *tr.* proporre; suggerire; ispirare; insinuare; fare pensare a; esprimere; richiamare alla mente; (leg.) contestare.

**suggestib-le** *adj.* suggeribile; suggestionabile. **-ility** *n.* suggestionabilità.

**suggestion** *n.* suggerimento; consiglio; proposta; ispirazione; associazione di idee; lieve traccia; *hypnotic* —, suggestione ipnotica.

**suggestive** *adj.* allusivo; — *of*, che fa pensare a; (pejor.) audace, rischiato. **-ness** *n.* carattere allusivo.

**suicid-e** *n.* suicidio; *to commit* —, suicidarsi; suicida *m., f.* **-al** *adj.* suicida; che ha tendenze al suicidio; *-al mania*, mania suicida; (fig.) fatale, rovinoso.

**suing** *n.* (leg.) citazione.

**suit[1]** *n.* domanda, richiesta; preghiera; *to press one's* —, insistere con la propria richiesta; domanda di matrimonio; (leg.) causa; *to bring a — against*, intentar causa a; (cost.) abito completo; *dress-suit*, abito da sera; (woman's) tailleur *m.*; — *of armour*, armatura completa; (cards) seme *m.*, colore *m.*; *to follow* —, rispondere a colore, (fig.) seguire l'esempio, imitare.

**suit[2]** *tr., intr.* soddisfare, andar bene a, convenire a; accontentare; confarsi a, andare a genio a; — *yourself*, fa' come ti pare; far bene a, giovare a; addirsi, accordarsi, intonarsi a; *he is not -ed to be a teacher*, non è tagliato per l'insegnamento.

**suitab-le** *adj.* adatto, idoneo; conveniente; adeguato; *as you think* —, come meglio credi. **-ility** *n.* convenienza; opportunità. **-ly** *adv.* appropriatamente; convenientemente.

**suit-case** *n.* valigia.

**suite** *n.* seguito, corteo; serie; *a — of rooms*, una serie di stanze; appartamento; — *of furniture*, mobilia per una stanza; (mus.) suite; seguenza.

**suitings** *n.pl.* tessuti per confezione.

**suitor** *n.* postulante *m.*; corteggiatore; (leg.) attore.

**sulk** *intr.* fare il broncio, tenere il broncio, essere di malumore; *n.* malumore *m.*, broncio.

**sulk-y** *adj.* imbronciato; scontroso, poco socievole; tetro, cupo. **-iness** *n.* malumore *m.*

**sullen** *adj.* accigliato, imbronciato; astioso; tetro, cupo, lugubre.

**sullen-ly** *adv.* con astio, con risentimento; di malumore. **-ness** *n.* cattivo umore; tetraggine *f.*; risentimento.

**sully** *tr.* macchiare, sporcare; (fig.) offuscare, macchiare, disonorare.

**sulph-ide** *n.* (chem.) solfuro. **-ite** *n.* (chem.) solfito.

**sulphur** *n.* (chem.) zolfo. **-eous** *adj.* sulfureo; (bot.) del colore dello zolfo. **-ic** *adj.* (chem.) solforico. **-ize** *tr.* (chem.; industr.) solforare. **-ous** *adj.* (chem.) solforoso; (fig.) focoso, infiammabile.

**sultan** *n.* sultano. **-a** *n.* sultana; chicco di uva sultanina.

**sultr-y** *adj.* afoso, soffocante; (fig.) infocato, appassionato. **-iness** *n.* afa, caldo soffocante.

**sum** *n.* somma; quantità di denaro; (math.) somma, addizione; operazione aritmetica; *to do -s*, far calcoli; (fig.) somma, totale; *in* —, in breve; *tr.* sommare; *to — up*, riassumere, ricapitolare; *intr.* (leg.) ricapitolare i fatti.

**sumach** *n.* (bot.) sommacco.

**summarily** *adv.* sommariamente.

**summarize** *tr.* riassumere, compendiare.

**summary** *adj.* sommario, conciso; *n.* sommario, compendio, ricapitolazione.

**summer** *n.* estate *f.*; *in* —, d'estate; *Indian* —, l'estate di S. Martino; *pl.* (poet.) anni; *intr.* trascorrere l'estate; *tr.* far pascolare in estate. **-house** *n.* bersò *indecl.* **-like** *adj.* come d'estate; estivo. **-school** *n.* corso estivo. **-time** *n.* ora legale.

**summersault,** see **somersault.**

**summertime** *n.* stagione estiva, estate *f.*

**summery** *adj.* estivo.

**summing** *n.* somma. **-up** *n.* (leg.) ricapitolazione dei fatti.

**summit** *n.* cima, vetta; (fig.) culmine *m.*, apice *m.*; colmo.

**summon** *tr.* chiamare, mandare a chiamare; convocare; (leg.) citare, chiamare in giudizio; intimare a; (fig.) raccogliere; fare appello a. **-er** *n.* chi convoca; (leg.) usciere *m.*

**summons** *n.* (leg.) citazione, ingiunzione; convocazione; chiamata; — *to arms*, chiamata alle armi; *tr.* citare in giudizio.

**sump** *n.* pozzo nero; (miner.) bacino di pompaggio.

**sumptuary** *adj.* suntuario; — *law*, legge suntuaria.

**sumptuous** *adj.* sontuoso, fastoso, imponente. **-ness** *n.* sontuosità, fasto, imponenza.

**sun** *n.* sole *m.*; raggi solari; *to sit in the* —, sedersi al sole; — *treatment*, elioterapia; (provb.) *to make hay while the — shines*, battere il ferro finchè è caldo; (fig.) astro; *his — is set*, il suo momento è passato; *tr.* esporre al sole; *to — oneself*, prendere il sole.

**sun-** (in compounds). **-blind** *n.* persiana, veneziana. **-bonnet** *n.* cappellino da sole. **-dial** *n.* meridiana. **-glasses** *n.pl.* occhiali da sole. **-parlour** *n.* veranda.

**sun-bathe** *intr.* fare i bagni di sole. **-beam** *n.* raggio di sole. **-burn** *n.* abbronzatura; scottatura scolare. **-burnt** *adj.* abbronzato; scottato dal sole.

**sundae** *n.* (USA) porzione di gelato misto con frutta e nocciole.

**Sunday** *pr.n.* domenica; *he comes on -s*, viene la domenica; *a month of -s*, un lungo periodo.

**sunder** *tr.* separare; dividere.

**sundown** *n.* tramonto.

**sundowner** *n.* (Austral.) vagabondo (che arriva al calar del sole ad una fattoria solo per scroccare cibo e letto); (Commonwealth) aperitivo serale.

**sundr-y** *adj.* parecchi, vari, diversi; *he showed us — samples*, ci mostrò diversi campioni; *all and* —, ciascuno e tutti, tutti quanti. **-ies** *n.pl.* generi diversi, cose diverse; cianfrusaglie *f.pl.*; (comm.) spese varie.

**sun-flower** *n.* (bot.) girasole *m.* **-hat** *n.* cappello a larghe tese. **-helmet** *n.* casco coloniale.

**sunken** *adj.* affondato; sommerso; cavo, incavato; sprofondato.

**sun-less** *adj.* senza sole; tetro. **-light** *n.* luce del sole. **-lit** *adj.* illuminato dal sole, soleggiato.

**sunny** *adj.* luminoso; esposto al sole, soleggiato; (fig.) ridente, allegro, gioioso; ottimista; *to be on the — side of forty*, essere sotto ai quaranta.

**sun-proof** *adj.* inalterabile al sole. **-rise** *n.* il sorger del sole; *at -rise*, all'alba. **-set** *n.* tramonto; (fig.) declino. **-shade** *n.* parasole *m.*

**sunshine** *n.* sole, luce del sole; bel tempo; splendore *m.*; (fig.) gioia, gaiezza, felicità; (motor.) — *roof*, tetto scorrevole. **-spot** *n.* macchia solare. **-stroke** *n.* colpo di sole, insolazione. **-struck** *adj.* sofferente per un colpo di sole.

**sup** *n.* sorso; *a — of wine*, una goccia di vino; *intr.* cenare; *tr.* (poet.) offrire la cena a.

**super-[1]** *pref.* sopra-, sovra-.

**super[2]** *adj.* (comm.) sopraffino, finissimo; (fam.) ottimo, magnifico.

**superabund-ance** *n.* sovrabbondanza. **-ant** *adj.* sovrabbondante, copioso.

**superannuat-ion** *n.* collocamento a riposo; pensione per vecchiaia. **-ed** *adj.* che ha raggiunto il limite di età; sorpassato.

**superb** *adj.* superbo, eccellente, magnifico, splendido.
**super-charger** *n.* (techn.) compressore *m.*; sovralimentatore *m.* **-ciliary** *adj.* sopraccigliare. **-cilious** *adj.* altero, arrogante. **-conductivity** *n.* (electr.) superconduttività, superconduzione. **-dominant** *n.* (mus.) sopradominante *m.* **-elevation** *n.* sopraelevazione. **-erogation** *n.* supererogazione. **-erogatory** *adj.* supererogatorio.
**superficial** *adj.* di superficie; poco profondo; *a — knowledge of*, un'infarinatura di. **-ity** *n.* superficialità.
**superfine** *adj.* sopraffino, eccellente; molto fine, raffinato
**super-fluity** *n.* superfluità; eccesso, sovrabbondanza. **-fluous** *adj.* superfluo; inutile. **-human** *adj.* sovrumano. **-impose** *tr.* sovrimporre, sovrapporre. **-intend** *tr.*, *intr.* sovraintendere a, sorvegliare; controllare; fare il sovraintendente. **-intendence** *n.* sovrintendenza; sorveglianza, controllo. **-intendent** *n.* sovrintendente *m.*, *f.*; sorvegliante *m.*, *f.*
**superior** *adj.* superiore; *— rank*, grado superiore; migliore; maggiore; *— to*, superiore a, migliore di; al di sopra di; superbo, sprezzante; *to put on a — air*, darsi delle arie; *n.* superiore *m.*, *f.*; *Mother Superior*, Madre Superiora; (math.) *— number*, esponente algebraico. **-ity** *n.* superiorità.
**superlative** *adj.* superlativo; eccellente; (gramm.) superlativo; *adjective in the —*, aggettivo superlativo; *n.* superlativo; *to speak in -s*, lodare al cielo.
**super-lunar, -lunary** *adj.* che è al di là della luna; celestiale, ultraterreno. **-man** *n.* superuomo. **-mundane** *adj.* ultraterreno.
**supernal** *adj.* (poet.) superno, sommo; celeste, divino.
**super-natural** *adj.* soprannaturale, straordinario; miracoloso; *the —*, il soprannaturale. **-numerary** *adj.* in soprannumero, superfluo; straordinario; aggiunto; *n.* soprannumerario; (theatr.) comparsa.
**super-phosphate** *n.* (chem.) perfosfato. **-pose** *tr.* sovrapporre; disporre a piani; (geom.) sovrapporre, far coincidere. **-saturate** *tr.* (chem.) soprasaturare. **-script** *adj.*, *n.* soprascritto. **-scription** *n.* soprascritta; iscrizione; intestazione. **-sede** *tr.* rimpiazzare, sostituire; prendere il posto di. **-sensitive** *adj.* ipersensibile; di una sensibilità morbosa. **-sensual** *adj.* soprasensibile; spirituale. **-sonic** *adj.* ultrasonoro; (aeron.) supersonico.
**superstit-ion** *n.* superstizione. **-ious** *adj.* superstizioso.
**super-stratum** *n.* (geol.) strato superiore. **-structure** *n.* (philos.; econ.; pol.) sovrastruttura; (rlwy.) armamento. **-tax** *n.* soprattassa; imposta supplementare. **-terrestrial** *adj.* sulla crosta terrestre; ultraterreno.
**super-vene** *intr.* sopraggiungere; sopravvenire. **-vention** *n.* sopravvenienza.
**supervis-e** *tr.* sovrintendere a; sorvegliare. **-ion** *n.* sorveglianza; *to be under police -ion*, essere sorvegliato dalla polizia; sovrintendenza. **-or** *n.* sovrintendente *m.*, *f.*; ispettore; sorvegliante *m.*, *f.*. **-ory** *adj.* di sorveglianza, di controllo.
**supine** *adj.* supino, sdraiato; passivo, indifferente; indolente; *n.* (Lat. gramm.) supino. **-ness** *n.* posizione supina; inerzia; passività.
**supper** *n.* cena; *the Last Supper*, l'ultima Cena; *the Lord's Supper*, l'Eucarestia.
**supplant** *tr.* soppiantare; prendere il posto di, rimpiazzare.
**supple** *adj.* pieghevole, flessibile; agile, elastico; (fig.) docile, arrendevole, compiacente.
**sup·plement** *n.* supplemento; appendice *f.*
**supplement** *tr.* fare aggiunte a, completare, integrare; *to — one's income*, arrotondare i propri guadagni. **-al, -ary** *adj.* supplementare. **-ation** *n.* integrazione; aggiuta.
**suppleness** *n.* flessibilità; agilità; elasticità; (fig.) compiacenza, arrendevolezza.
**suppliant** *adj.* supplichevole; *n.* supplicante *m.*, *f.*; chi implora.
**supplicat-e** *tr.*, *intr.* supplicare, implorare. **-ion** *n.* supplica. **-ory** *adj.* supplicatorio.
**supplier** *n.* fornitore.
**supply** *n.* rifornimento; approvvigionamento; fornitura; provvista; *to lay in a — of*, fare provvista di; (econ.) offerta; *— and demand*, domanda e offerta; *pl.* (mil.) approvvigionamenti; viveri *m.pl.*; *food —*, vettovaglie *f.pl.*; *tr.*, *intr.* fornire, provvedere, rifornire; supplire a; soddisfare a; fare supplenza a.
**support** *n.* sostegno, appoggio; aiuto; assistenza; *in — of*, in favore di; mantenimento; *to be without means of —*, essere senza mezzi di sostentamento; (techn.) supporto; mensola; *tr.* sostenere, reggere; dare appoggio a; incoraggiare; convalidare; fare da spalla a; mantenere; (theatr.) sostenere adeguatamente; (mil.) rincalzare; mandar rinforzi a. **-er** *n.* sostegno, appoggio; fautore, partigiano, sostenitore; (herald.) sostegno, supporto. **-ing** *gerund* il sostenere; *adj.* di sostegno; portante.
**suppos-e** *tr.*, *intr.* supporre; immaginare; presupporre; presumere; credere, pensare; *I — so*, lo penso; *I am not -ed to do it*, non dovrei farlo. **-ed** *adj.* presunto, supposto. **-edly** *adv* per supposizione.
**supposition** *n.* supposizione; ipotesi *f.*; congettura; *unfounded —*, supposizione gratuita.
**suppository** *n.* (pharm.) supposta.
**suppress** *tr.* sopprimere; reprimere; sedare, far cessare; *to — a yawn*, soffocare uno sbadiglio; (fig.) trattenere; nascondere, tener nascosto. **-ion** *n.* soppressione; repressione; il soffocare.
**suppurat-e** *intr.* suppurare, venire a suppurazione. **-ion** *n.* suppurazione.
**supranatural** See **supernatural.**
**supremacy** *n.* supremazia.
**supreme** *adj.* sommo, supremo; *the Supreme Being*, L'Ente Supremo; *the Supreme Pontiff*, il Sommo Pontefice; supremo, massimo, eccelso.
**surcease** *n.* (poet.) cessazione.
**surcharge** *n.* sovraccarico; soprattassa; penalità; soprapprezzo.
**surcingle** *n.* sopraccinghia (della sella); cintura (di veste talare).
**surcoat** *n.* sopravveste *f.*
**surd** *adj.* (math.) irrazionale; (phon.) sordo; *n.* (math.) numero irrazionale; (phon.) consonante sorda.
**sure** *adj.* sicuro, certo; inevitabile; *to be — to*, non mancare di, essere destinato a; *to make —*, essere sicuro, accertarsi; fidato; attendibile; indubbio; saldo, fermo; *adv.* sicuro; (USA) certamente, sicuramente, davvero; senz'altro.
**sure-footed** *adj.* dal piede fermo.
**sure-ly** *adv.* sicuramente, certamente; senza dubbio; con sicurezza; bene. **-ness** *n.* sicurezza; certezza. **-ty** *n.* certezza; garanzia; pegno; *n.* garante *m.*, *f.*; *to stand -ty for*, farsi garante per.
**surf** *n.* frangente *m.*; spuma dei marosi; risacca; *intr.* (sport) praticare l'acquaplano. **-bathing** *n.* bagni tra i frangenti. **-riding** *n.* sport dell'acquaplano.
**surface** *n.* superficie *f.*; faccia; piano stradale; *— of the water*, pelo dell'acqua; *tr.*, *intr.* (far) salire alla superficie; rifinire, sfiorare la superficie di.
**surfeit** *n.* eccesso, sovrabbondanza; rimpinzamento; sazietà; *tr.* rimpinzare; saziare.
**surge** *n.* ondata; flutto; *the — of the sea*, i flutti del mare; (fig.) impeto; *intr.* ondeggiare, fluttu-

are; agitarsi; montare, sollevarsi; affluire.
**surgeon** *n.* chirurgo; (naut.; mil.) medico; *dental* —, medico dentista.
**surgery** *n.* chirurgia; gabinetto medico; dispensario; — (*hours*), ore di consultazione (also fig.).
**surgical** *adj.* chirurgico.
**surloin** *n.* lombo di manzo.
**surl-y** *adj.* arcigno, burbero; sgarbato. **-iness** *n.* scontrosità, sgarberia; umore nero.
**sur·mise** *n.* supposizione, congettura.
**surmise** *tr.*, *intr.* supporre, congetturare; sospettare.
**surmount** *tr.* sormontare, coprire; superare, vincere. **-able** *adj.* sormontabile, superabile.
**surname** *n.* soprannome *m.*; cognome *m.*; *tr.* soprannominare, chiamare per soprannome; dare il cognome a.
**surpass** *tr.* sorpassare, superare; vincere. **-ing** *adj.* superiore, eccellente, incomparabile; estremo.
**surplice** *n.* (eccl.) cotta.
**surplus** *n.* sovrappiù, eccedenza, avanzo; *to have a — of*, avere in sovrappiù; residuati *m.pl.*; — *population*, eccesso di popolazione; (comm.) — *account*, fondo residui; — *stock*, rimanenze *f.pl.*
**surprisal** *n.* sorpresa.
**surprise** *n.* sorpresa; *to give someone a* —, fare una sorpresa a qualcuno; stupore *m.*, meraviglia; *much to my* —, (*or to my great* —), con mia grande meraviglia; *I watched them in* —, meravigliato li guardai; — *visit*, visita inaspettata.
**surpris-e** *tr.* sorprendere, cogliere all'improvviso; stupire; *to be -ed at*, stupirsi di; *I should not be -ed if . . .*, non mi stupirei se . . . **-edly** *adv.* con sorpresa. **-ing** *adj.* sorprendente. **-ingly** *adv.* sorprendentemente; in modo straordinario.
**surreal-ism** *n.* (art) surrealismo. **-ist** *adj.*, *n.* surrealista *m.*, *f.*
**surrender** *n.* (mil.) resa, capitolazione; abbandono, cessione, consegna; (comm.) — *value*, riscatto; *tr.*, *intr.* cedere, consegnare, abbandonare; arrendersi; darsi per vinto; *to — oneself to justice*, consegnarsi alla giustizia; (fig.) abbandonare, rinunciare a.
**surreptitious** *adj.* clandestino, furtivo, segreto.
**surrogate** *n.* sostituto; delegato.
**surround** *tr.* circondare, cingere, attorniare; (mil.) accerchiare, assediare; *n.* bordura, bordo. **-ing** *adj.* circostante; vicino. **-ings** *n.pl.* dintorni *m.pl.*; ambiente *m.*; condizioni ambientali.
**sur-** *pref.* sopra-, sovra-.
**sur-tax** *n.* soprattassa; imposta complementare. **-veillance** *n.* sorveglianza; ispezione.
**sur·vey** *n.* esame *m.*; indagine *f.*; quadro generale; *to make a* —, fare una perizia; rapporto; valutazione; studio ufficiale; misurazioni topografiche, rilievo topografico; — *map*, mappa catastale.
**survey** *tr.*, *intr.* esaminare, ispezionare; contemplare; guardare; compiere uno studio generale su; preparare un rapporto su; fare una perizia di; misurare, rilevare; fare rilevazioni. **-ing** *n.* ispezione; esame *m.*; sorveglianza; misurazione topografica; agrimensura. **-or** *n.* ispettore; sovraintendente *m.*; geometra *m.*; agrimensore; topografo; *-or of roads*, ispettore stradale; *-or of weights and measures*, controllore dei pesi e delle misure.
**survival** *n.* sopravvivenza; *the — of the fittest*, la sopravvivenza del più adatto; avanzo; vestigio; reliquia.
**surviv-e** *tr.*, *intr.* sopravvivere a; vivere più a lungo di; (leg.) passare. **-or** *n.* superstite *m.*, *f.*
**susceptib-le** *adj.* suscettibile; sensibile; impressionabile; permaloso; soggetto, predisposto. **-ility** *n.* suscettibilità; sensibilità; predisposizione.
**sus·pect**[1] *adj.* sospetto; *to hold* —, sospettare; *n.* persona sospetta.
**suspect** *tr.*, *intr.* aver l'impressione che; sospettare di; essere sospettoso; dubitare.
**suspend** *tr.* appendere, tenere sospeso; sospendere; posporre, differire; ritirare; differire.
**suspender** *n.* giarrettiera; *suspender-belt*, cintura portabretelle *f.*; *pl.* (USA) bretelle *f.pl.*
**suspense** *n.* sospensione d'animo; indecisione, incertezza; attesa ansiosa; (leg.) sospensione.
**suspension** *n.* sospensione; interruzione; dilazione; ritiro temporaneo.
**suspension-bridge** *n.* ponte sospeso.
**suspicion** *n.* sospetto; dubbio; diffidenza; piccolissima quantità, pizzico; accenno.
**suspicious** *adj.* sospettoso, diffidente; ambiguo. **-ly** *adv.* sospettosamente; sospettamente. **-ness** *n.* diffidenza; carattere sospettoso; natura sospetta.
**sustain** *tr.* mantenere; provvedere; sostenere; prolungare; reggere, sopportare; sorreggere, incoraggiare; subire, soffrire; confermare, convalidare; (mus.) *to — a note*, sostenene una nota. **-ing** *adj.* che sostiere; (of food) nutriente.
**sustenance** *n.* mezzi di sussistenza; vitto, sostentamento; mantenimento.
**sutler** *n.* (mil. hist.) vivandiere *m.*, cantiniere *m.*
**suture** *n.* (surg.) sutura; materiale usato per le suture; *tr.* suturare.
**suzerain** *n.* sovrano feudatario. **-ty** *n.* sovranità.
**svelte** *adj.* snello, sottile; agile.
**swab** *n.* strofinaccio; (naut.) radazza; (med.) tampone *m.*, zaffo; campione prelevato per esame batteriologico; *tr.* passare lo strofinaccio su; (naut.) radazzare; *to — up*, detergere; spugnare.
**swaddle** *tr.* fasciare (un bambino); bendare; (fig.) coccolare.
**swaddling** *n.* fasciatura. **-bands, -clothes** *n.pl.* fasce per bambini; (fig.) restrizioni, impedimenti.
**swag** *n.* movimento ondeggiante; (archit.) festone *m.*; (slang) bottino ladresco, guadagni illegali.
**swagger** *tr.*, *intr.* camminare con sussiego; pavoneggiarsi; vantarsi, gloriarsi; fare lo spavaldo; *n.* fanfaronata; boria; spavalderia; andatura spavalda; *to walk with a* —, pavoneggiarsi; (slang) vistoso; sgargiante. **-cane, -stick** *n.* frustino da ufficiale.
**swain** *n.* (poet.) contadinotto, villico; pastore innamorato; (joc.) innamorato, corteggiatore *m.*
**swallow**[1] *n.* rondine *f.*; (provb.) *one — does not make a summer*, una rondine non fa primavera.
**swallow**[2] *tr.*, *intr.* inghiottire; ingoiare (fig.) assorbire; esaurire; divorare; *to — the bait*, abboccare l'amo; sopportare, subire; ritrattare; soffocare, reprimere.
**swallow-dive** *n.* (sport) tuffo a rondine. **-tail** *n.* (abito) a coda di rondine; frac *m.* marsina.
**swamp** *n.* palude *f.*, acquitrino, pantano; *tr.*, *intr.* inondare; sommergere; (fig.) mandare in rovina, schiacciare. **-ed** *part. adj.* sommerso; che affoga. **-y** *adj.* paludoso, acquitrinoso.
**swan** *n.* cigno; poeta *m.*, cantore; *the Swan of Avon*, il Cigno dell'Avon; (fig.) — *song*, canto del cigno; (fig.) *black* —, mosca bianca.
**swank** *intr.* (slang) darsi delle arie; *n.* pretenziosità; eleganza vistosa; ostentazione, boria.
**swank-y** *adj.* borioso. **-iness** *n.* eleganza vistosa.
**swannery** *n.* allevamento di cigni.
**swap** *n.* (fam.) scambio, baratto; *tr.* scambiare; (slang) *wife -ping*, scambio di mogli.
**sward** *n.* (poet.) zolla erbosa; terreno erboso.
**swarm** *n.* sciame *m.*; folla,

frotta; *tr.*, *intr.* sciamare; muoversi in frotte; affollarsi; pullulare, brulicare; arrampicarsi.
**swarth-y** *adj.* dalla carnagione scura; scuro; bruno. **-iness** *n.* carnagione *f.*; colore scuro.
**swashbuckl-er** *n.* fanfarone *m.*, rodomonte *m.* **-ing** *adj.* borioso, spavaldo.
**swastika** *n.* svastica, croce uncinata.
**swat** *tr.* schiacciare d'un colpo; *n.* colpo; scacciamosche *m. indecl.*
**swatch** *n.* (of cloth) campione *m.*
**swathe** *n.* falciata; grano falciato; striscia; benda, fascia; *tr.* fasciare, bendare; avvolgere.
**sway** *n.* oscillazione; spinta; preponderanza; impero, dominio; *to hold — over*, esercitare podere su; *tr.*, *intr.* oscillare, far oscillare; inclinare, inclinarsi, piegare; *to — in the wind*, oscillare al vento; governare, influenzare; *to refuse to be swayed*, essere inflessibile.
**swear** *tr.*, *intr.* giurare; prestare giuramento; promettere solennemente; bestemmiare; imprecare; *to — like a trooper*, bestemmiare come un turco; *to — at*, maledire, ingiuriare; *to — blind*, credere ciecamente; *to — to*, attestare, certificare sotto giuramento; *to — in*, insediare in una carica facendo prestare giuramento; *n.* bestemmia; imprecazione.
**sweat** *n.* sudore *m.*; traspirazione; (fig.) sudata, lavoro duro, fatica; (mil. slang) *an old —*, un veterano; *tr.*, *intr.* traspirare, sudare; far sudare; trasudare, (fig.) penare, affaticarsi; sfacchinare; *to — blood*, sudar sangue; sfruttare; sottoporre a fermentazione; (metall.) saldare a stagno, unir per fusione parziale; *to — out*, trasudare, far trasudare; curare con sudoriferi.
**sweater** *n.* maglione *m.* di lana.
**sweat-gland** *n.* ghiandola sudoripara.
**sweatiness** *n.* traspirazione; trasudamento.
**sweating** *n.* sudore *m.*; traspirazione; trasudamento; sfruttamento (di dipendenti).
**sweaty** *adj.* sudato, coperto di sudore.
**Swed-e** *n.* sevedese *m.*, *f.*; rapa svedese. **-ish** *adj.* svedese; *-ish drill*, la ginnastica svedese; *n.* lo svedese.
**sweep** *n.* scopata; spazzata; movimento circolare; curva, linea curva; distesa; raggio, cerchio d'azione; portata; movimento rapido; *tr.* spazzare, scopare, ramazzare; sfiorare, toccare leggermente; percorrere con lo sguardo; (artill.) battere (col tiro); (naut.) dragare; *to — along*, trasportare; trascinare; *to — away*, spazzar via; *intr.* muoversi rapidamente; *to — down*, abbattersi; dilagarsi.
**sweeper** *n.* chi scopa; (techn.) spazzatrice meccanica; (naut.) dragamine *n.*; *carpet-sweeper*, aspirapolvere per tappeti; *street-sweeper*, spazzino, (machine) spazzatrice stradale.
**sweeping** *adj.* largo, esteso; vasto, illimitato; completo; assoluto; *— changes*, cambiamenti radicali; *n.* scopatura; *pl.* rifiuti.
**sweepstake(s)** *n.* lotteria.
**sweet** *adj.* dolce; zuccherino; *to have a — tooth*, avere un debole per i dolci; fresco; profumato, fragrante; armonioso, musicale, soave; (fig.) piacevole, gradevole; gentile, amabile, grazioso, carino; *to be — on*, essere innamorato di; *— nothings*, paroline dolci; *n.* caramella; dolce *m.*; torta; *pl.* (fig.) piaceri, delizie.
**sweet-** (in compounds). **-pea** *n.* (bot.) pisello odoroso. **-potato** *n.* patata americana. **-William** *n.* (bot.) garofano dei poeti.
**sweet-bread** *n.* (cul.) animella. **-brier** *n.* rosa selvatica.
**sweeten** *tr.* zuccherare, aggiungere zucchero a; addolcire; rendere piacevole mitigare, alleviare; depurare, purificare. **-er** *n.* chi addolcisce; ciò che addolcisce. **-ing** *n.* sostanza che addolcisce; addolcimento; alleviamento; purificazione.
**sweetheart** *n.* innamorato, innamorata; tesoro, amore.
**sweetish** *adj.* dolciastro, dolcigno.
**sweetly** *adv.* dolcemente, soavemente; amabilmente; gradevolmente; (techn.) in modo regolare, regolarmente.
**sweetmeat** *n.* dolce *m.*; frutta candita.
**sweetness** *n.* sapore *m.* dolce; dolcezza; soavità; amabilità; fragranza.
**swell** *n.* rigonfiamento; protuberanza; il gonfiarsi; (mus.) crescendo; crescendo seguito da diminuendo; organo espressivo, organo recitativo; (slang) elegantone *m.*; *adj.* (slang) benone; magnifico; *tr.*, *intr.* gonfiare, gonfiarsi; dilatare, dilatarsi; ingrossare, ingrossarsi; crescere; aumentare. **-ing** *adj.* ondulato; curvo; *n.* rigonfiamento; ingrossamento; protuberanza; tumefazione, edema *m.*
**swelter** *intr.* soffocare per l'afa; essere oppresso dal caldo; trasudare. **-ing** *adj.* soffocante; opprimente, afoso.
**swerve** *n.* deviazione; scarto improvviso; *tr.*, *intr.* deviare, far deviare; fare uno scarto; (fig.) scostarsi.
**swift**[1] *n.* (orn.) rondore *m.*
**swift**[2] *adj.* rapido, lesto, veloce; agile; svelto, pronto; *— to anger*, facile ad adirarsi; (techn.) *n.* rocchetto; aspo. **-footed** *adj.* dal piede veloce.
**swift-ly** *adv.* rapidamente, velocemente; prontamente. **-ness** *n.* rapidità, velocità; prontezza.
**swig** *n.* (slang) sorsata, sorso; bevuta; *tr.*, *intr.* (slang) tracannare, bere a lunghi sorsi, bere d'un sol fiato.
**swill** *n.* risciacquatura; rifiuti *m.pl.*; *pig —*, intruglio per i maiali; *tr.* sciacquare; sbevazzare. **-er** *n.* ubriacone *m.* **-ing** *n.* risciacquatura.
**swim** *n.* nuotata; (fig.) *to be in the —*, essere al corrente, essere all'avanguardia; *intr.* nuotare; *to — for one's life*, salvarsi a nuoto; (fig.) *to be swimming in money*, nuotare nell'oro; *to — with the tide*, seguire la corrente; galleggiare; essere inondato; *to be swimming with*, traboccare di; *his head was swimming*, gli girava la testa; *tr.* attraversare nuotando; *to — a river*, pasare a nuoto un fiume.
**swimmer** *n.* nuotatore, nuotatrice.
**swimming** *adj.* che nuota; affetto da capogiro; *n.* nuoto. **-bath** *n.* piscina coperta. **-belt** *n.* salvagente *m.* **-pool,** piscina all'aperto.
**swimmingly** *adv.* agevolmente; a meraviglia.
**swim-suit** *n.* costume *m.* da bagno. **-wear** *n.* indumenti *m.pl.* da nuoto.
**swindl-e** *n.* truffa; frode *f.*; raggiro; *tr.*, *intr.* truffare; raggirare; *I have been -ed out of it*, me l'hanno truffato. **-er** *n.* truffatore; imbroglione *m.* **-ing** *n.* truffa; imbroglio; raggiro.
**swine** *n.* maiale *m.*, porco; *to behave like a —*, comportarsi da animale; *to throw pearls before —*, gettar perle ai porci. **-fever** *n.* colera dei suini.
**swineherd** *n.* porcaro.
**swing** *n.* altalena; *what you lose on the -s you gain on the roundabouts*, quello che perdi da una parte guadagni dall'altra; oscillazione; movimento oscillatorio; ampiezza dell'oscillazione; (fig.) *the — of a pendulum*, l'alternarsi di vicende, l'alternarsi dei partiti al potere; *to be in full —*, essere in piena attività; ritmo; *to go with a —*, avere un ritmo scorrevole, procedere bene; (mus.) tipo di jazz.
**swing** *tr.*, *intr.* dondolare, dondolarsi; oscillare, fare oscillare; *room to — a cat in*, spazio per girarsi; ruotare, far ruotare; girare, far girare; *to — open*, spalancarsi; *to — to*, chiudersi; brandire, agitare, vibrare; (mil. slang) *to — the lead*, marcare visita, evadere al lavoro, battere fiacca; (slang) essere impiccato; essere all'ultimo guado.

**swing-bridge** *n.* ponte *m.* girevole. **-door** *n.* porta a vento.
**swingeing** *adj.* forte; violento; *a — blow*, un colpo durissimo; (fam.) enorme; schiacciante.
**swinging** *adj.* oscillante, dondolante; ritmico, cadenzato; *n.* dondolìo, oscillamento; (radio) fluttuazione di frequenza.
**swingle** *n.* (text.) gramola, maciulla; *tr.* battere.
**swinish** *adj.* bestiale; sozzo, sudicio; schifoso. **-ness** *n.* bestialità; sudiceria.
**swipe** *n.* (slang) colpo violento; *tr.*, *intr.* dare un colpo violento (a); (slang) fregare, sgrafignare.
**swirl** *n.* vortice *m.*; turbine *m.*; *tr.*, *intr.* turbinare; girare, far girare vorticosamente.
**swish** *n.* sibilo; fruscìo; mormorìo; forte getto di acqua; sferza, sferzata; *tr.*, *intr.* fischiare, far fischiare; sibilare, far sibilare; frusciare; frustare; *adj.* (pop.) elegante.
**Swiss** *adj.*, *n.* svizzero; *— guard*, guardia svizzera.
**switch** *n.* verga; frustino, frusta; colpo di frusta; capelli posticci, treccia falsa; (electr.) interruttore; commutatore; (rlwy.) scambio.
**switch** *tr.*, *intr.* colpire, battere, percuotere con un frustino; muovere bruscamente, agitare; smistare, deviare, far deviare; (fig.) mutare; sviare; (electr.) *to — off*, interrompere; *to — off the light*, spegnere la luce; *to — on*, inserire; *to — on the ignition*, inserire l'accensione; *to — on the light*, accendere la luce; *to — over*, commutare.
**switch-back** *n.* ferrovia a zigzag; montagne russe. **-board** *n.* quadro di controllo; (teleph.) tavolo di commutazione.
**Switzerland** *pr.n.* (geog.) Svizzera.
**swivel** *n.* perno; anello girevole; piccola spola; navetta; *tr.*, *intr.* ruotare, far ruotare su un perno; spostare mediante parte girevole. **-eyed** *adj.* strabico.
**swizz** *n.* (slang) inganno.
**swollen** *adj.* gonfio; rigonfio; (fig.) enfatico; *to suffer from a — head*, essere vanitoso.
**swoon** *n.* svenimento, deliquio; *intr.* svenire, venir meno; (of music) smorzarsi dolcemente.
**swoop** *n.* calata improvvisa; attacco; *at one fell —*, in un sol colpo; *tr.*, *intr. to — down*, piombare; calare improvvisamente, abbattersi.
**swop** *n.* (slang) scambio; baratto; *tr.*, *intr.* (slang) scambiare; barattare; *to — places with*, cambiar posto con.
**sword** *n.* spada; *to cross swords with*, battersi con; *to be put to the —*, essere passato a fil di spada.
**sword-** (in compounds). **-arm** *n.* braccio destro. **-bearer,** portatore di spada, spadaro. **-cut** *n.* fendente *m.*, sciabolata. **-knot** *n.* dragona. **-stick** *n.* stocco.
**sword-fish** *n.* (ichth.) pesce spada. **-like** *adj.* spadiforme. **-play** *n.* scherma.
**swordsman** *n.* spadaccino. **-ship** *n.* arte di maneggiare la spada.
**sworn** *adj.* giurato; *a — enemy*, un acerrimo nemico; *a — friend*, un amico fidato; (leg.) che ha giurato; sotto giuramento; *a — statement*, dichiarazione sotto giuramento.
**swot** *n.* (slang) secchione *m.*, secchiona *f.*; studio accanito; *tr.*, *intr.* sgobbare; *to — a subject up*, sgobbare su una materia.
**sybarit-e** *n.* sibarita *m.* **-ic(al)** *adj.* sibaritico; molle, lussuoso. **-ism** *n.* vita da sibarita.
**Sybil** *pr.n.*, *n.* Sibilla.
**sycamore** *n.* (bot.) sicomoro.
**sycoph-ancy** *n.* adulazione servile. **-ant** *n.* sicofante *m.*; adulatore, adulatrice; parassita *m.* **-antic** *adj.* adulatorio, servile.
**syllabic(al)** *adj.* sillabico.
**syllable** *n.* sillaba; *tr.* sillabare; (poet.) proferire, dire.
**syllabub** *n.* quagliata con zucchero e vino.
**syllabus** *n.* sommario; programma *m.*; prospetto.
**syllogism** *n.* (log.) sillogismo.
**sylph** *n.* silfo, silfide *f.* **-like** *adj.* leggera e graziosa come una silfide.
**sylvan** *adj.* silvano, silvestre; *n.* abitatore dei boschi; (myth.) silvano, divinità dei boschi.
**symbio-sis** *n.* simbiosi *f.* **-tic** *adj.* in stato di simbiosi.
**symbol** *n.* simbolo, emblema *m.* **-ic(al)** *adj.* simbolico. **-ism** *n.* simbolismo. **-ist** *n.* simbolista *m.*
**symboliz-e** *tr.* simboleggiare. **-ation** *n.* simbolizzazione.
**symmetr-y** *n.* simmetria. **-ic(al)** *adj.* simmetrico.
**sympathetic** *adj.* sensibile, comprensivo; che mostra simpatia; *— heart*, cuore comprensivo; congeniale, adatto; (anat.) simpatico; *— strike*, sciopero di solidarietà; *— string*, corda che vibra in simpatia; *n.* nervo simpatico; persona facilmente ipnotizzabile.
**sympathiz-e** *intr.* sentire comprensione; aver compassione; *to — with*, condividere i sentimenti di; essere d'accordo; considerare favorevolmente. **-er** *n.* chi è comprensivo; chi condivide i sentimenti altrui; fautore, fautrice; simpatizzante *m.*, *f.*
**sympathy** *n.* comprensione; partecipazione; compassione; *to have wide sympathies*, essere molto comprensivo; *a letter of —*, una lettera di condoglianze; armonia, accordo; comunità, affinità; attrazione; (med.) simpatia.
**symphonic** *adj.* (mus.) sinfonico.
**symphony** *n.* (mus.) sinfonia; *— orchestra*, orchestra sinfonica.
**symposium** *n.* simposio; discussione accademica; raccolta di articoli sullo stesso argomento.
**symptom** *n.* (med.) sintomo; indizio, segno. **-atic(al)** *adj.* sintomatico.
**synagogue** *n.* sinagoga.
**synchro-mesh** *n.* (motor.) cambio di velocità sincronizzato.
**synchron-ism** *n.* sincronismo. **-istic** *adj.* sincronistico.
**synchroniz-e** *tr.*, *intr.* sincronizzare; muoversi sincronicamente. **-ation** *n.* sincronizzazione. **-ed** *adj.* sincronizzato.
**syncopat-e** *tr.* (gramm.; mus.) sincopare. **-ion** *n.* sincopatura.
**syncope** *n.* (gramm.; mus.; med.) sincope *f.*
**syndic** *n.* sindaco, magistrato, alto funzionario; rappresentante *m.*, *f.*
**syndical-ism** *n.* sindacalismo. **-ist** *n.* sindacalista *m.*
**syndicat-e** *n.* sindacato; ufficio di sindaco; *tr.*, *intr.* dirigere a mezzo di sindacato; riunirsi in sindacato. **-ion** *n.* costituzione in sindacato.
**syndrome** *n.* sindroma, sindrome *f.*
**syne** *adv.* (Scot.) fin da; *auld lang —*, i vecchi tempi, i giorni lontani.
**syn-ecdoche** *n.* (rhet.) sineddoche *f.* **-eresis** *n.* (rhet.) sineresi *f.*
**synod** *n.* (eccl.; astron.) sinodo; *oecumenical —*, sinodo ecumenico; riunione, convegno.
**synodic(al)** *adj.* (eccl.) sinodale; (astron.) sinodico; *— month*, lunazione.
**synonym** *n.* sinonimo. **-ity** *n.* sinonimia. **-ous** *adj.* sinonimo. **-y** *n.* studio dei sinonimi; uso dei sinonimi; sinonimia.
**synop-sis** *n.* sinossi *f.* **-tic(al)** *adj.* sinottico.
**synovitis** *n.* (path.) sinovite *f.*
**synt-ax** *n.* (gramm.) sintassi *f.* **-actic(al)** *adj.* (gramm.) sintattico.
**synthe-sis** *n.* sintesi *f.* **-size** *tr.* sintetizzare. **-tic(al)** *adj.* sintetico. **-tize** *tr.* sintetizzare.
**synton-y** *n.* (radio) sintonia. **-ize** *tr.* sintonizzare.
**syphil-is** *n.* (path.) sifilide *f.* **-itic, -ous** *adj.* sifilitico.
**syphon** see **siphon.**
**Syracuse** *pr.n.* (geog.) Siracusa.
**syren** see **siren.**
**Syria** *pr.n.* (geog.) Siria. **-c** *n.* lingua siriaca. **-n** *adj.*, *n.* siriano.
**syringa** *n.* (bot.) siringa.
**syringe** *n.* siringa; *hypodermic —*,

siringa ipodermica; *garden* —, siringa nebulizzatrice; *tr.* siringare; iniettare; spruzzare con siringa.
**syrinx** *n.* zampogna, siringa; (anat.) tromba d'Eustachio.
**syrup** *n.* sciroppo; *golden* —, melassa. **-y** *adj.* sciropposo.
**system** *n.* sistema *m.*; metodo; organizzazione; organismo; *decimal* —, sistema decimale; *railway* —, rete ferroviaria; *solar* —, sistema solare. **-atic** *adj.* sistematico, metodico.
**systematiz-e** *tr.* ridurre a sistema. **-ation** *n.* sistemazione.
**syzygy** *n.* (astron.) sizigia.

**T, t** *n.* ti *m.*, *f.*; (teleph.) *T for Tommy*, t come Torino; *to a* — a pennello, perfettamente; (cul.) *done to a* —, perfetto, squisito; *to cross one's* —*'s*, mettere i punti sugli i.
**ta** *excl.* (fam.) grazie.
**tab** *n.* (of shoe) linguetta; (of belt, etc.) passante *m.*; etichetta *f.*, cartellino, portaindirizzi *m.*, *indecl.*; (fam.) *to keep -s on*, sorvegliare attentamente; (mil.) mostrina; (slang) *red* —, ufficiale *m.* di Stato Maggiore.
**tabard** *n.* cotta d'arme; (hist.) tabarro.
**tabby** *adj.* marezzato, tigrato; *n.* gatto soriano, gatto tigrato; (fam.) vecchia pettegola.
**tabernacle** *n.* tabernacolo, ciborio; tempio, cappella; (archit.) nicchia.
**tabes** *n.* (med.) tabe *f.*
**Tabitha** *pr.n.* Tabita.
**table** *n.* tavolo, tavola, tavolino; mensa; *high* —, tavola dei professori, tavola d'onore; *the Round Table*, la Tavola Rotonda; *to keep a good* —, mangiare bene, tenere una buona tavola; *to lay the* —, apparecchiare (la tavola); *to clear the* —, sparecchiare (la tavola); *to sit down to* —, mettersi a tavola; *to rise from* —, alzarsi da tavola; *to wait at* —, servire a tavola; tavolata, commensali *m.pl.*; (fig.) *to lay one's cards on the* —, mettere le carte in tavola; *to turn the -s*, rovesciare le posizioni; tabella, elenco; — *of contents*, indice *m.*, sommario; (math.) *multiplication* —, tavola pitagorica; tavoletta, lastra; (geog.) tavolato, altipiano, tavoliere *m.*; (techn.) piano, tavola, banco.
**table** *tr.* porre sul tavolo, intavolare; (pol.) *to — a bill*, depositare un progetto di legge.
**tableau** *n.* quadro plastico tablò *m.*, scena drammatica.
**table-centre** *n.* centro ornamentale da tavola, centrino, trionfo, alzata.
**tablecloth** *n.* tovaglia.
**table-companion** *n.* commensale *m.*, *f.*
**table d'hôte** *n.* pasto a prezzo fisso.
**table-flap** *n.* ribalta da tavola. **-fork** *n.* forchetta da tavola. **-knife** *n.* coltello da tavola.
**tableland** *n.* (geog.) altipiano, tavolato, tavoliere *m.*
**table-leaf** *n.* allungo di tavola, ribalta. **-linen** *n.* biancheria da tavola. **-mat** *n.* sottopiatto. **-napkin** *n.* tovagliolo.
**tablespoon** *n.* cucchiaio da tavola. **-ful** *n.* cucchiaiata.
**tablet** *n.* tavoletta; (pharm.) compressa, pastiglia; (commemorative) targa, lapide *f.*; (votive) ex voto *m.*, tabella.
**table-talk** *n.* conversazione a tavola. **-tennis** *n.* tennis da tavola, ping-pong *m.* **-turning** *n.* seduta spiritica a tavolino.
**tableware** *n.* vasellame *m.*, stoviglie *f.pl.* da tavola.
**table-water** *n.* acqua minerale.
**tabloid** *n.* (pharm.) compressa, pastiglia; *adj.* (fig.) conciso, succinto; (of newspaper) sensazionale.
**taboo** *n.* tabù *m.*; *attrib.* proibito; *tr.* mettere al bando, proibire, vietare.
**tabor** *n.* (mus.) tamburello.
**tabouret** *n.* sgabello; (needlew.) telaio da ricamo.
**tabular** *adj.* tabulare, a forma di tabella; sinottico, ordinato in tabelle; piatto, piano; (miner.) a strati sottili.
**tabulat-e** *tr.* disporre in tabelle, incolonnare; (fig.) elencare, classificare, presentare in forma sinottica. **-or** *n.* (mech.) tabulatore; (typewriter) tasto incolonnatore.
**tacheomet-er** *n.* (surveying) tacheometro. **-ry** *n.* (surveying) tacheometria.
**tachomet-er** *n.* (mech.) tachimetro, contagiri *m.* **-ry** *n.* (eng.) tachimetria.
**tachymeter** *n.* (survey.) tacheometro; (mech.) tachimetro.
**tacit** *adj.* tacito, implicito, sottinteso; silenzioso.
**taciturn** *adj.* taciturno. **-ity** *n.* taciturnità.
**Tacitus** *pr.n.* Tacito.
**tack**[1] *n.* chiodetto, bulletta; (fig.) *to get down to brass -s*, venire ai fatti, considerare il lato pratico; (needlew.) punto lungo, imbastitura; (naut.) bordata; (rope) mura; *to make a* —, virare; *to sail on the starboard* —, virare a tribordo; (fig.) *to be on the right* —, essere sulla strada giusta; *to be on the wrong* —, essere sulla strada sbagliata; *tr.* inchiodare, imbullettare; (needlew.) imbastire; (fig.) *to — on to a story*, aggiungere ad un racconto; *intr.* (naut.) bordeggiare, virare di bordo, (fig.) cambiare tattica.
**tack**[2] *n.* (fam.) cibo; *hard* —, gallette *f.pl.*, biscotti *m.pl.*; *soft* —, pane *m.*
**tackl-e** *n.* attrezzatura, arnesi *m.pl.*; *fishing* —, arnesi da pesca; (naut.) paranco; (eng.) taglia; (rugby) placcaggio; (soccer) intervento, arresto; *tr.* afferrare, trattenere; *to — a thief*, affrontare un ladro; venire alle prese con; *to — a job*, affrontare un lavoro; (fam.) *to — one's food*, mettersi a mangiare con appetito; (rugby) placcare; (soccer) fermare, intervenire su. **-ing** *n.* afferramento; (naut.) paranco; (rugby) placcaggio; (soccer) arresto, intervento.
**tact** *n.* tatto, riguardo; *to be wanting in* —, mancare di riguardo. **-ful** *adj.* pieno di tatto, diplomatico, riguardoso, accorto. **-fully** *adv.* con tatto, diplomaticamente.
**tactic-al** *adj.* (mil.) tattico; — *exercise*, esercizio tattico; (fig.) abile. **-ian** *n.* (mil.) tattico; (fig.) persona abile. **-s** *n.* (mil.) tattica.
**tactile** *adj.* tattile, tangibile.
**tactless** *adj.* senza tatto, che manca di tatto, indiscreto, malaccorto. **-ness** *n.* mancanza di tatto.
**tadpole** *n.* (zool.) girino.
**taffeta** *n.* taffetà *m.*
**taffrail** *n.* (naut.) coronamento, ringhiera di poppa.
**Taffy** *pr.n.* (Welsh) Davide *m.*; (fam.) gallese *m.*, *f.*
**tag** *n.* lembo; etichetta, cartellino; (of shoelace) aghetto, puntale *m.*; (of boot) tirante *m.*; luogo comune, frase fatta, cliché *m.*; battuta; (of animal) estremità della coda.
**tag** *tr.* mettere il puntale a; mettere l'etichetta a; aggiungere; (fam.) seguire, pedinare; *intr.* (fam.) *to — behind*, stare alle calcagna di; *to — along behind*, essere il fanalino di coda.
**tag-end** *n.* estremità, fin fine *f.*
**Tagus** *pr.n.* (geog.) Tago.
**Tahiti** *pr.n.* (geog.) Taiti *f.* **-an** *adj.*, *n.* di Taiti.
**tail**[1] *n.* coda; estremità; (of violin) codolo; *the — of the eye*, la coda dell'occhio; *with his — between his legs*, con la coda tra le gambe, (of person) mogio mogio; *the dog wags his* —, il cane dimena la coda, il cane scodin-

zola; (fig.) *to keep one's — up*, non lasciarsi abbattere, stare allegro; *to turn —*, scappare, squagliarsi; (of coin) rovescio, croce *f.*; *heads or ~s*, testa o croce; *I can't make head or — of this*, non ci raccapezzo nulla, non ci capisco niente; (of coat) coda, falda; *pl.* (evening dress) frac *m.*; (sport) i giuocatori più deboli.

**tail**[2] *n.* (leg.) vincolo; *tr.* see **entail**.

**tail**[1] *tr.* pedinare, seguire da vicino, *to — after*, seguire da vicino, accodarsi a; *to — off*, diminuire poco a poco, assottigliarsi.

**tail-board** *n.* (of cart, etc.) ribalta. **-coat** *n.* (evening dress) frac *m.*, marsina *f.*; (morning coat) tight *m.*, abito a coda. **-dive** *n.* (aeron.) scivolata di coda. **-end** *n.* estremità, fine *f.*, fin fine, coda. **-fin** *n.* (ichth.) pinna caudale; (aeron.) piano di deriva. **-light** *n.* (motor.) fanalino di coda.

**tailor** *n.* sarto; *~'s shop*, sartoria; *intr.* fare il sarto; *tr.* confezionare (abiti), vestire (un cliente). **-ing** *n.* mestiere del sarto; confezione di vestiti.

**tailor-made** *adj.* fatto su misura; *n.* tailleur *m. indecl.*

**tailpiece** *n.* coda; (typ.) finalino, cul de lampe *m.*; (mus.) cordiera.

**taint** *n.* contaminazione, corruzione, infezione; tara, vizio ereditario; (fig.) marchio, segno, traccia; *tr.* guastare, viziare; infettare, inquinare; ammorbare; *intr.* guastarsi.

**take** *n.* il prendere; incasso; (hunt.) presa; (of fish) pesca; (cinem.) ripresa; *give and —*, compromesso, concessione reciproca.

**take** *tr.* 1. prendere, pigliare, afferrare, cogliere, impadronirsi di, togliere; scegliere; accompagnare, condurre, menare; interpretare, intendere; *as I — it*, secondo me; pigliare, acchiappare; volerci, richiedere; *how long will it —?*, quanto tempo ci vorrà?; *it ~s a clever man to do that*, ci vuole un uomo intelligente per fare questo; *it ~s some doing*, ce ne vuole. 2. FOLLOW. BY NOUN OR PRN. *to — someone in the act*, cogliere qualcuno sul fatto; *to — advantage of*, abusare di, approfittare di; *to — at a disadvantage*, cogliere in posizione di svantaggio; *to — by the arm*, prendere per il braccio; *to — a bath*, fare un bagno; *to — breath*, prendere fiato; *to — the bull by the horns*, prendere il toro per le corna; *to — care of*, aver cura di; *to — the chair*, assumere la presidenza, presiedere; *to — a chance*, rischiare; *to — one's chances*, tentare la propria sorte; *to — cover*, rifugiarsi, *to — a degree*, laurearsi; *to — delight in*, dilettarsi di; *to — delight in doing something*, provare piacere nel fare qualcosa; *to — an examination*, dare un esame; *to — exception to*, opporre eccezione a, trovare a ridire su; *to — a fancy to*, (*a person*) prendere in simpatia, provare simpatia per, (*a thing*) provare piacere a, dilettarsi di; *to — fire*, prendere fuoco, incendiarsi; *to — in one's hand*, prendere in mano; *to — in hand*, intraprendere, occuparsi di; *to — hold of*, afferrare, aggrapparsi a; *to — holy orders*, ricevere gli ordini sacri; *to — it amiss*, aversela a male; *to — it easy*, prendersela con comodo; *to — it upon oneself* (*to*), incaricarsi (di); *to — leave*, prendere congedo; *to — leave to do something*, permettersi di fare qualcosa; *to — French leave*, andarsene all'inglese; *to — a meal*, mangiare; *to — the opportunity of*, cogliere l'occasione di; *to — a photograph of*, fotografare; *to — to pieces*, smontare, fare a pezzi; *to — place*, aver luogo, accadere; *to — one's place*, sedersi, accomodarsi; *to — possession of*, entrare in possesso di, impadronirsi di; *to — a prize*, vincere un premio; *to — a room*, affittare una camera; *to — root*, attecchire, prendere radice; *to — a seat*, prendere posto, sedersi; *please — a seat*, s'accomodi; (rlwy.) — *your seats!*, in vettura!; *to — shape*, prendere forma, delinearsi; *to — shelter*, rifugiarsi; *to — by storm*, prendere d'assalto; *to — to task*, rimproverare, fare una paternale a; *to — time by the forelock*, afferrare la fortuna per i capelli; *to — (the) trouble to*, prendersi la briga di, darsi da fare per; *to — the veil*, prendere il velo; *to — a walk*, fare una passeggiata. 3. TO BE TAKEN: *not to be ~n*, per uso esterno; *to be ~n aback*, essere sorpreso, essere preso alla sprovvista; (of book, etc.) *not to be ~n away*, da consultarsi sul posto; *to be ~n in*, abboccare, cascarci; *to be ~n ill*, ammalarsi, cadere malato, sentirsi male; *to be ~n by*, essere attratto da, essere colpito da; *I was ~n by the idea that*, mi sorrideva l'idea che; *to be ~n by surprise*, essere colto di sorpresa. 4. INTR. (of plants, vaccine, etc.) attecchire, appiccare; riuscire, aver successo; (photog.) *he does not — well*, non è fotogenico. 5. FOLLOW. BY ADV. OR PREP.: *to — about*, portare a spasso, portare in giro; *to — across*, far attraversare; *to — after*, assomigliare a; *to — again*, riprendere; *to — away*, portare via, (math.) sottrarre; *to — back*, riprendere, portare indietro, riportare, riaccompagnare; *to — down*, tirare giù, far scendere, abbassare; (*machine*) smontare, (fig.) prendere nota di, trascrivere; *to — down a peg or two*, far abbassare la cresta a; *to — for*, scambiare per, prendere per; *to — for granted*, accettare come vero; *to — in*, portare dentro, tirare dentro, far entrare, (naut.) imbarcare, (give lodging to) ospitare, dare alloggio a, accogliere in casa; *to — a lady in to dinner*, essere cavaliere di una signora a tavola, *to — in washing*, fare il bucato a domicilio; ingannare, dare a bere a; capire, afferrare, *to — in at a glance*, abbracciare con lo sguardo; (dressm.) stringere, ridurre (naut., sail) serrare, ammainare; *to — off*, *tr.* portare via, togliere, levare, staccare; *to — off one's hat*, cavarsi il cappello; (teleph.) *to — off the receiver*, staccare il ricevitore; (from price, bill) defalcare, dedurre, fare uno sconto di; *to — off a train*, sopprimere un treno; (fig.) *to — oneself off*, andarsene; scimmiottare, contraffare, fare il verso a, parodiare; *intr.* spiccare un salto; (aeron.) decollare; *to — on*, *tr.* intraprendere; *to — on personnel*, assumere dipendenti; addossarsi, assumere; *to — on a job*, accettare un lavoro; *to — on at tennis*, fare una partita di tennis con; *intr.* (fam.) prendersela a male; *to — out*, tirare fuori, portare fuori, portare a spasso, ritirare, levare, togliere, cavare; *to have a tooth ~n out*, farsi levare un dente; farsi rilasciare, prendere, ottenere; (dressm.) allargare; (fam.) *to — it out of*, estenuare; *it ~s it out of you!*, ti riduce un cencio; *to — it out on someone*, sfogarsi su; *to — over*, *tr.* portare; *will you — me over in your car?*, mi porterai in macchina?; acquistare; *to — over a firm*, rilevare un'azienda; *to — over the management from someone*, succedere a qualcuno nella direzione di un'azienda; *to — someone over a house*, far visitare una casa a qualcuno; *intr. to — over from*, succedere a; *to — round*, far girare, far visitare, accompagnare nella visita (a); *to — to*, darsi a, affezionarsi a; *to — to drink*, darsi al bere; *to — to flight*, fuggire, darsi alla fuga; *to — to one's heels*, alzare il tacco, scappare a gambe levate; *to — up*, prendere su, raccogliere, prendere a bordo, assorbire, *to — up too much space*, occupare troppo spazio; *the bus stops to — up passengers*, l'autobus si ferma a raccogliere passeggieri; *to — up Italian*, mettersi a studiare l'italiano; (dressm.) raccorciare; (fig.) *to — up a cause*, abbracciare una causa; *to — up a challenge*,

raccogliere una sfida; *to — a matter up*, occuparsi di una faccenda; *to be wholly ~n up with*, essere dedito a; *intr.* (fam.) *to — up with someone*, legarsi d'amicizia con qualcuno.
**take-in** *n.* (fam.) inganno, tranello. **-off** *n.* caricatura, parodia, imitazione; (aeron.) decollo; (sport) punto di partenza, linea di partenza. **-out** *n.* (cards) cambiamento di colore dopo la dichiarazione del partner.
**takeover** *n.* (comm.) rilievo, acquisto; — *bid*, offerta di acquisto.
**taker** *n.* prenditore; acquirente *m.*, *f.*; accettante *m.*, *f.*; (of option) optante *m.*, *f.*
**taking** *adj.* attraente, simpatico, seducente, contagioso; *n.* presa; cattura, arresto; (med., of blood) prelevamento; (leg.) sottrazione; — *back*, ripresa; — *down*, distacco, (in writing) trascrizione, (techn.) smontaggio; — *off*, imitazione, (aeron.) decollo; — *out*, rilascio, estrazione; — *over*, presa di possesso, accettazione, (of business) rilievo; — *up*, il tirar su, il sollevare; (text.; cinem.) avvolgimento; (fig.) l'occuparsi di; *pl.* incasso, introito; (theatr.) borderò *m.*
**takingly** *adv.* in modo attraente, in modo simpatico.
**takingness** *n.* attrattiva, fascino, incanto.
**talc** *n.* (miner.) talco, silicato di magnesio; (comm.) mica.
**talcum** *n.* talco; — *powder*, talco in polvere, talco borato.
**tale** *n.* racconto, storia, favola, leggenda, novella; *old wives' ~s*, racconti di vecchie comari; *The Winter's Tale*, 'Il racconto d'inverno'; *to tell a —*, raccontare una favola; *to tell ~s*, raccontare chiacchiere, spifferare segreti; *it tells its own —*, parla da sè; (iron.) *I've heard that — before*, non me la dai a bere, raccontalo al gatto. **~bearer** *n.* rapportatore di maldicenze, rifischione *m.*; chiacchierone *m.*, chiacchierona *f.* **~bearing** *adj.* maldicente; *n.* maldicenza.
**talent** *n.* talento, attitudine, dono, dote *f.*, ingegno, capacità naturale; *a man of —*, un uomo d'ingegno; *to have a — for languages*, avere attitudine alle lingue; *to have a — for doing the right thing*, avere il dono di fare quel che occorre, saper regolarsi; *to have a — for doing the wrong thing*, sembrare nato per sbagliare; (hist., coin) talento. **~ed** *adj.* di talento, che ha talento, valente, abile, molto dotato; *a ~ed writer*, uno scrittore di valore.
**talion** *n.* (hist.) taglione *m.*
**talisman** *n.* talismano, amuleto; palladio; abraxeo.
**talk** *n.* colloquio, conversazione, dialogo, discorso, discussione; parole *f.pl.*, (fam.) chiacchierata; *he is all —*, è un fanfarone; *it's nothing but —!*, è una parola!; *there is — of*, si dice che, corre voce che; *the — of the town*, la favola della città; *small —*, chiacchiere *f.pl.*, pettegolezzi *m.pl.*, voce frivola; *to have a — with*, intrattenersi con; *to engage in —*, attaccare discorso con; *to give a — on*, fare un discorso su; *pl.* discussione, trattative *f.pl.*
**talk** *tr.* parlare; *to — Italian*, parlare italiano; *to — slang*, parlare in gergo; *to — business*, parlare di affari, (fam.) *now you're ~ing business*, ora veniamo al sodo; *to — politics*, parlare di politica; *to — nonsense*, dire sciocchezze; (fam.) *to — rot*, raccontare balle; *to — sense*, parlare con saggezza; *to — treason*, fare discorsi sediziosi; (fam.) *to — the hind-leg off a donkey*, chiacchierare a non finire più; *to — oneself hoarse*, parlare tanto da diventare rauco; *to get onself ~ed about*, far parlare di sè; *to — down*, ridurre al silenzio, far tacere; *to — things out*, discutere a fondo; (pol.) *to — a bill out*, prolungare il dibattito per far aggiornare un progetto di legge; *to — something over*, discutere qualcosa; *we'll — it over*, ne parleremo; *to — someone round*, persuadere qualcuno; *intr.* parlare, discorrere, intrattenersi, conversare; chiacchierare, dire sciocchezze; *let him —!*, lascialo dire!; *people will —*, la gente mormorerà; *you can't — to him*, non ci si discorre; *I'm ~ing to you* dico a te, sai!; *to — for the sake of ~ing*, parlare per il gusto di parlare, parlare tanto per parlare; (fam.) *to — big*, vantarsi; *to — through one's hat*, parlare a vanvera; *to make someone —*, far cantare qualcuno; *to — back*, replicare, rispondere per le rime; *to — down to*, accondiscendere; *to — on*, continuare a parlare; *to — on and on*, parlare come un mulino a vento; *to — to*, intrattenersi con, (fam.) *who do you think you're ~ing to?*, con chi credi di parlare?; *to — to oneself*, parlare tra sè e sè.
**talkative** *adj.* loquace, garrulo, linguacciuto; eloquente; chiacchierone. **~ness** *n.* loquacità, parlantina, eloquenza.
**talker** *n.* parlatore, conversatore, chiacchierone *m.*; *a great —*, una persona eloquente.
**talkie** *n.* (cinem.) film parlato, film sonoro.
**talking** *adj.* parlante, che parla; (cinem.) — *picture*, film parlato, film sonoro; *n.* il parlare, conversazione; discorsi *m.pl.*; chiacchiere *f.pl.*; — *is allowed*, si dispensa dal silenzio; *have done with —*, basta con questi discorsi; *there was a lot of —*, si parlò molto; *no — please!*, silenzio!; *to do all the —*, far le spese della conversazione.
**talking-to** *n.* (fam.) ramanzina, predichetta; *to give someone a good —*, lavare la testa a qualcuno.
**tall** *adj.* alto; grande; *to be six feet —*, essere alto due metri; *she is ~er than I*, è più alta di me; *to grow —*, crescere, ingrandire, allungarsi; (fig.) *a — order*, un'impresa difficile; — *hat*, cappello a cilindro, tuba; *a — story*, una storia incredibile; *to tell — stories*, raccontare delle balle, spararle grosse.
**tallboy** *n.* canterano, cassettone.
**tallness** *n.* (of person) grandezza, altezza, statura; (of thing) altezza.
**tallow** *n.* sego; *attrib.* di sego, segoso. **-faced** *adj.* dal viso pallido, terreo.
**tally** *n.* tacca, taglia di contrassegno, piastrina indicatrice; etichetta, cartellino; *to keep — of*, controllare; *tr.* segnare con una tacca; mettere etichette a; *to — up*, calcolare, sommare; *intr.* corrispondere, concordare; combaciare (con); quadrare.
**tally-clerk, -keeper** *n.* controllore, impiegato che controlla la consegna di merci. **-sheet** *n.* foglio di controllo, borderò *m.*, registro di vendite rateali. **-stick** *n.* taglia.
**talon** *n.* artiglio; (comm.) matrice *f.*, talloncino; (archit.) modanatura a S; (of lock) dente *m.* **~ed** *adj.* provvisto di artigli.
**tamarind** *n.* (bot.) tamarindo.
**tamarisk** *n.* (bot.) tamarice *f.*; tamarisco, cipressino.
**tambour** *n.* (archit.; mil.) tamburo; (needlew.) telaio da ricamo; (mus.) grancassa, tamburo; (ichth.) pesce tamburo. **~ine** *n.* tamburello, tamburino.
**tame** *adj.* (of animal) domestico, addomesticato, ammaestrato, addestrato; *to become —*, addomesticarsi, ammansirsi; (of person) ammansito, mansueto, docile, sottomesso, servizievole; (fig.) montono, insipido, incolore, scialbo, meschino, piatto, banale.
**tame** *tr.* addomesticare, domare, addestrare, ammansire, ammaestrare, sottomettere; (fig.) imbrigliare, domare, sopprimere, reprimere; (fam.) *to — down*, attenuare. **~able** *adj.* addomesticabile, domabile. **~ly** *adv.* docilmente, senza opporre resistenza, servilmente; (fig.) banalmente. **~ness** *n.* docilità, mansuetudine *f.*; mancanza di coraggio, pusillanimità, mollezza; (fig.) monotonia, banalità, insipidità, mancanza di originalità.

**tamer** *n.* domatore, ammaestratore.
**taming** *n.* addomesticamento, ammansimento, addestramento, ammaestramento; *The Taming of the Shrew*, 'La bisbetica domata'.
**tammy** *n.* abbrev. of **tam-o'-shanter,** *q.v.*
**tam-o'-shanter** *n.* berretto scozzese.
**tamp** *tr.* (bldg.) pigiare, comprimere, pestare, calcare; (soil) costipare; (min.) intasare.
**tamper** *n.* pestello, mazzeranga.
**tamper** *intr. to — with*, manomettere, alterare, falsificare; immischiarsi di; corrompere, subornare. **-er** *n.* falsificatore, corruttore; ficcanaso *m.* **-ing** *n.* manomissione, falsificazione, alterazione; corruzione, subornazione.
**tamping** *n.* (bldg.) pigiatura, battitura; (of soil) costipamento.
**tampon** *n.* (surg.) tampone *m.*
**tan** *n.* (tan.) concia, corteccia di quercia; (fig.) abbronzatura, abbronzata; (colour) marrone rossiccio; *tr.* (tan.) conciare; (fig.) abbronzare, annerire, abbrunire; (slang) picchiare, conciare per le feste; *intr.* abbronzarsi, annerirsi.
**tandem** *n.* tandem *m.*; *attrib.* a tandem, uno dietro l'altro; (electr.) — *system*, cascata.
**tang**[1] *n.* (of knife) punta; (bot.) aculeo, puntiglione *m.*; calcio; sapore piccante; odore penetrante; (of sea-air) salsedine *f.*; *tr.* munire di punta; dare sapore a; dare odore a.
**tang**[2] (of bell) tintinnìo, suono acuto, trillare *m.*; (fig.) accento, vibrazione; *tr.* far tintinnare, far suonare, far vibrare; *intr.* tintinnare, trillare, vibrare, suonare.
**tang**[3] *n.* (bot.) laminaria.
**tangent** *adj.* tangenziale, tangente; *n.* (geom.) tangente *f.*; (mus.) linguetta; *at a —*, (geom.) tangenzialmente, (fig.) *to fly off at a —*, partire per la tangente, prendere un dirizzone. **-ial** *adj.* (geom.) tangenziale.
**tangerine** *adj., n.* di Tangeri, tangerino; (orange) mandarino.
**tangib-le** *adj.* tangibile; palpabile; (fig.) sensibile; manifesto; reale; realizzabile. **-ility, -leness** *n.* tangibilità, palpabilità.
**Tangiers** *pr.n.* (geog.) Tangeri *f.*
**tangle**[1] *n.* groviglio; viluppo; garbuglio; intreccio; *to get in a —*, aggrovigliarsi, ingarbugliarsi, abbindolarsi, intrecciarsi; (fig.) impiccio, pasticcio, confusione, imbroglio; *tr.* aggrovigliare, intrecciare, ingarbugliare, abbindolare; *intr.* aggrovigliarsi, ingarbugliarsi, abbindolarsi; *to get -d up*, imbrogliarsi, complicarsi.
**tangle**[2] *n.* (bot.) fellandrio; millefoglie acquatico.
**tangy** *adj.* (of taste) piccante; (of smell) penetrante, acuto, acre.
**tank** *n.* vasca, serbatoio, cisterna; (motor.) serbatoio; (mil.) carro armato; (naut.) cassone *m.*; *tr.* mettere in serbatoio; *intr.* (motor.) *to — up*, fare il pieno.
**tankard** *n.* boccale *m.*, bicchierone *m.*
**tank-engine** *n.* (rlwy.) locomotiva autonoma.
**tanker** *n.* (ship) nave cisterna, petroliera; (barge) battello cisterna; (lorry) autocisterna, autobotte *f.*; (rlwy.) carro cisterna; (aeron.) aerocisterna.
**tanned** *adj.* (tan.) conciato; (of skin) abbronzato, annerito.
**tanner**[1] *n.* conciatore *m.*
**tanner**[2] *n.* (fam.) moneta da sei vecchi 'pennies'.
**tannery** *n.* conceria.
**tannic** *adj.* (chem.) tannico.
**tannin** *n.* (chem.) tannino.
**tanning** *n.* concia, conciatura; (slang) *to give someone a —*, conciare qualcuno per le feste.
**tanning-bark** *n.* corteccia di quercia.
**tansy** *n.* (bot.) tanaceto.
**tantaliz-e** *tr.* infliggere il supplizio di Tantalo a; tormentare; lusingare con promesse. **-ing** *adj.* che tormenta; provocante, allettante, stuzzicante.
**Tantalus** *pr.n.* (myth.) Tantalo.
**tantamount** *adj.* equivalente; *to be — to*, equivalere a, essere come; *that is — to saying*, è come dire.
**tantrum(s)** *n.* accesso d'ira, capriccio; *to be in a —*, fare la bizza, fare la tarantella, avere un diavolo per capello, uscire dai gangheri.
**tap**[1] *n.* rubinetto; zipolo, chiavetta; cannella; (in cask) spina, tappo; (mech.) maschio (per filettare); (electr.) presa; *to turn on the —*, aprire il rubinetto; *to turn off the —*, chiudere il rubinetto; *to wash under the —*, lavarsi alla cannella; *on —*, alla spina, (fig.) a disposizione.
**tap**[1] *tr.* munire di rubinetto, munire di spina; spillare; forare, bucare; (surg.) drenare; (trees) incidere (per estrarne la linfa); (fig.) spillare, *to — resources*, sfruttare le risorse; (teleph.) intercettare, ascoltare; *to — a telephone*, intercettare una comunicazione telefonica.
**tap**[2] *n.* colpetto, buffetto, colpo leggero; (of heels) ticchettìo; *I heard a — on the door*, ho sentito bussare alla porta; (mil., of drums) rullo.
**tap**[2] *tr.* battere leggermente, picchiare, dare un colpetto a; *intr.* bussare; (drum) tambureggiare, picchiettare; *he was -ping away on his typewriter*, stava scrivendo a macchina; *to — out one's pipe*, svuotare la pipa battendola.
**tap-dance, -dancing** *n.* tip-tap *m.*
**tape** *n.* nastro; fettuccia; *adhesive —*, nastro gommato; *insulating —*, nastro isolante; *measuring —*, nastro metrico; *recording —*, nastro magnetico; *steel —*, nastro d'acciaio; *red —*, nastro rosso, (fig.) burocrazia, burocratismo; *ticker —*, nastro di telescrivente; (sport) nastro del traguardo; *to breast the —*, tagliare il traguardo.
**tape** *tr* applicare un nastro a; misurare con un nastro; registrare a nastro; (fig.) *I've got him -d*, l'ho giudicato, so con chi ho da fare.
**tape-measure** *n.* nastro metrico, misura, rotella metrica, metro.
**taper** *n.* diminuzione graduale, assottigliamento, conicità; (archit.) rastremazione; candela, moccolo, stoppino, lucignolo; (eccl.) cero.
**taper** *tr.* affilare, restringere; (archit.) rastremare, assottigliare; *intr.* affilarsi, restringersi; (archit.) rastremarsi, assottigliarsi; *to — off*, finire a punta, (fig.) finire gradualmente. **-ed** *adj.* conico, affilato, rastremato.
**tape-recorder** *n.* magnetofono, registratore a nastro, registratore magnetico. **-recording** *n.* registrazione a nastro, registrazione magnetica.
**tapering** *adj.* affilato, affusolato, rastremato, a punta, conico, acuminato; *n.* diminuzione graduale, rastremazione, conicità.
**tapestry** *n.* arazzo, tappezzeria, paramento; addobbo; — *work*, tappezzeria; *tr.* tappezzare, coprire di arazzi, parare; addobbare.
**tapestry-weaver, -worker** *n.* tappezziere, arazziere *m.*
**tapeworm** *n.* (zool.) tenia *m.*, verme solitario.
**taphouse** *n.* osteria, bettola.
**tapioca** *n.* (bot.; cul.) tapioca.
**tapir** *n.* (zool.) tapiro.
**tapping**[1] *n.* (of cask) spillatura; (surg.) drenaggio, puntura; (of tree) incisione della corteccia; (electr.) presa, derivazione; (mech.) maschiatura; (of teleph.) intercettazione, ascolto.
**tapping**[2] *n.* colpetto; ticchettìo; tambureggiamento.
**taproom** *n.* bar *m.*; osteria.
**tap-water** *n.* acqua di rubinetto.
**tar** *n.* catrame *m.*, bitume *m.*, pece liquida; *coal —*, catrame minerale; *wood —*, catrame vegetale; (sailor) marinaio, (fam.) marò *m.*, lupo di mare.
**tar** *tr.* incatramare, impeciare; *to — and feather*, spalmare di pece e coprire di penne; *to be -red*

*with the same brush*, essere gente della stessa risma.
**tarantula** *n.* (ent.) tarantola.
**tardiness** *n.* lentezza, noncuranza, indolenza; malavoglia, riluttanza; ritardo; tardezza.
**tardy** *adj.* lento, pigro, tardo, indolente; svogliato, riluttante; tardivo, in ritardo.
**tare**[1] *n.* (bot.) veccia; (bibl.) zizzania; (fig.) loglio.
**tare**[2] *n.* (comm.) tara; *tr.* tarare, fare la tara a.
**Tarent-um** *pr.n.* (hist.; geog.) Taranto. **-ine** *adj.*, *n.* tarantino.
**targe** *n.* (hist.) scudo, targa.
**target** *n.* bersaglio; (fig.) mira; oggetto; *to hit the —*, colpire il bersaglio; *to miss the —*, mancare il bersaglio; *to be a — for scorn*, essere oggetto di scherno; (mil.) *— practice*, tiro al bersaglio; (hist.) scudetto, targhetta, rotella.
**tariff** *n.* tariffa; *customs —*, tariffa doganale; *— reform*, riforma delle tariffe doganali, (hist.; pol.) protezionismo.
**tarmac** *n.* macadam al catrame, (pop.) asfalto; zona di decollo e di atterraggio, pista, area di stazionamento.
**tarn** *n.* laghetto montano.
**tarnish** *n.* appannamento; (of metals) ossidazione; *tr.* appannare, offuscare, annerire; (fig.) macchiare; *-ed reputation*, disdoro, reputazione macchiata; *intr.* appannarsi, offuscarsi, annerirsi; (of metals) ossidarsi.
**taroc, tarot** *n.* (cards) tarocchi *m.pl.*
**tarpaulin** *n.* incerata, copertone *m.*, tela incatramata.
**Tarpeian** *adj.* (hist.) *the — Rock*, la Rupe Tarpea.
**Tarquin** *pr.n.* (hist.) Tarquinio.
**tarragon** *n.* (bot.) dragoncello, targone *m.*; *— vinegar*, aceto aromatico.
**tarr-ed** *adj.* (in)catramato. **-ing** *n.* (in)catramatura, incatramazione.
**tarry** *adj.* catramoso; catramato, ricoperto di catrame.
**tarry** *intr.* indugiare, sostare, tardare; rimanere indietro, restare; *to — for someone*, attendere qualcuno. **-ing** *n.* indugio, sosta.
**tart**[1] *adj.* acerbo, agro, agrigno; (fig.) aspro, mordace.
**tart**[2] *n.* (cul.) torta, crostata; (slang) passeggiatrice, puttana.
**tartan** *n.* (text.) tessuto di lana a quadri, tessuto scozzese, tartan *m.*
**tartar**[1] *adj.*, *n.* tartaro, della Tartaria; (fig.) persona violenta, brutto tipo; megera.
**tartar**[2] *n.* (chem.) tartaro; *cream of —*, cremore *m.* di tartaro.
**tartlet** *n.* (cul.) piccola torta.
**tartness** *n.* acerbità, asprezza; (fig.) mordacità.
**Tartu(f)fe** *pr.n.* (lit.) Tartufo; (fig.) ipocrita *m.*, bacchettone *m.*
**task** *n.* compito, lavoro, incarico; dovere *m.*, mansione *f.*; *an endless —*, una tela di Penelope, un lavoro che non finisce mai; *no easy —*, un compito difficile; *to apply oneself to a —*, dedicarsi ad un lavoro, assumere un incarico; *to set someone a —*, assegnare un compito a qualcuno; *to take someone to — for*, rimproverare qualcuno per; (mil.) *— force*, gruppo d'assalto in missione speciale.
**task** *tr.* assegnare un compito a, imporre un lavoro a; affaticare, mettere a dura prova; *it -s my powers*, mi costa un grande sforzo.
**taskmaster** *n.* sorvegliante *m.*, maestro; *a hard —*, un padrone duro, un vero tiranno, (fig.) un maestro inflessibile.
**task-work** *n.* lavoro a cottimo.
**tassel** *n.* nappa, nappina, fiocco; nastrino segnalibro; (bot.) barba.
**tasselled** *adj.* infiocchettato.
**taste** *n.* gusto; sapore *m.*; *the sense of —*, il senso del gusto; *the — of cheese*, il sapore del formaggio; *to have a — of*, avere un gusto di, sapere di; *to have a nasty —*, avere un sapore sgradevole; *to have a bad — in one's mouth*, avere la bocca amara; *just a —*, un pezzettino, un bocconcino, (of liquid) una sorsatina; (fig.) gusto, predilezione, inclinazione; *in good —*, di buon gusto; *in bad —*, di cattivo gusto; *acquired -s*, gusti acquisiti; *-s differ*, i gusti son gusti; *to follow one's natural -s*, seguire i propri gusti; *to have a — for*, essere appassionato di gustare; *to have no — for*, non amare, non gustare; *not to my —*, non di mio gusto; *to give someone a — of the whip*, far assaggiare la frusta a qualcuno.
**taste** *tr.* assaggiare, gustare, sentire il sapore di; *to — the soup*, assaggiare la minestra; assaggiare, degustare; assaporare, apprezzare, gustare; *he hasn't tasted food for three days*, da tre giorni non mangia; *intr.* aver gusto, aver sapore, sentire; *to — good*, avere un buon sapore, essere buono; *to — like*, avere un gusto che ricorda, saper di; *to — of*, saper di; *to make something — bitter*, dare un gusto amaro a qualcosa.
**tasteful** *adj.* di buon gusto, fine, raffinato, squisito, fatto con buon gusto, elegante. **-ness** *n.* buon gusto; eleganza, raffinatezza.
**tasteless** *adj.* senza sapore, insipido, scipito; (fig.) di cattivo gusto, di pessimo gusto. **-ness** *n.* scipitezza, insipidità; (fig.) mancanza di gusto, cattivo gusto.
**tast-er** *n.* assaggiatore, degustatore. **-ing** *n.* il gustare; (comm.) degustazione, assaggio, assagiatura. **-y** *adj.* gustoso, saporito; (fig.) elegante, fine, raffinato, di buon gusto.
**tat** *n.* *tit for —*, pan per focaccia, occhio per occhio; *to give someone tit for —*, rendere la pariglia a qualcuno.
**ta-ta** *excl.* (pop.) ciao!, arrivederci!
**tatar** *adj.*, *n.* See **tartar.**
**tatler** *n.* See **tattler.**
**tatter** *n.* cencio, brandello, straccio; *in -s*, a brandelli.
**tatterdemalion** *n.* straccione *m.*, pezzente *m.*
**tattered** *adj.* stracciato, sfilato, a brandelli; *all — and torn*, tutto cenci e brandelli; (fig.) *a — reputation*, una pessima reputazione.
**tatting** *n.* (needlew.) chiacchierino *m.*
**tattle** *n.* chiacchiera, pettegolezzo, ciarla; *intr.* chiacchierare, spettegolare, ciarlare.
**tattler** *n.* chiacchierone, pettegolo, ciarlone.
**tattoo**[1] *n.* (mil.) ritirata; *to sound the —*, suonare la ritirata; carosello militare; (mus.) taratatà *m.*; (fig.) *to beat a —*, batter all'impazzata, tamburellare; *intr.* tamburellare con le dita.
**tattoo**[2] *n.* tatuaggio; *tr.* tatuare; *to have oneself -ed*, farsi tatuare. **-ing** *n.* tatuaggio.
**tatty** *adj.* (fam.) stantio; disordinato.
**taught** *p.def.*, *part.* of **teach** *q.v.*
**taunt** *n.* rinfaccio, sarcasmo; insulto, ingiuria; sfida; *tr.* rinfacciare, colmare di sarcasmi, rimproverare aspramente; ingiuriare; sfidare; *to — with cowardice*, dare del vigliacco a; dileggiare, schernire, canzonare, motteggiare. **-ing** *adj.* sarcastico, beffardo, schernitore, provocante, canzonatorio; *n.* rimprovero sarcastico, scherno, canzonatura; motteggio.
**Taurus** *pr.n.* (astron.) Toro; (geog.) Tauro.
**taut** *adj.* teso, tirato, rigido; (fig.) teso; *to stretch —*, tendere.
**tauten** *tr.* tendere; (fig.) irrigidire; *intr.* tendersi, diventare più teso; (of person) irrigidirsi.
**tautness** *n.* tensione, rigidità, rigidezza.
**tautolog-y** *n.* tautologia, ripetizione inutile. **-ical** *adj.* tautologico.
**tavern** *n.* taverna, osteria, trattoria; mescita; (pejor.) bettola. **-keeper** *n.* oste *m.*
**taw** *n.* pallina, biglia di vetro; giuoco delle biglie.
**tawdr-y** *adj.* vistoso, appariscente, d'orpello, pretenzioso; *— finery*, orpello. **-iness** *n.* aspetto

vistoso, falso splendore, sfoggio volgare, orpellatura.

**tawny** *adj.* abbronzato, bronzeo, bruno fulvo; — *mane*, criniera fulva; (orn.) — *owl*, gufo selvatico; — *old port*, vino di Porto ingiallitosi nel fusto.

**tawse** *n.* cor(r)eggia.

**tax** *n.* tassa, imposta, contribuzione; *direct -es*, imposte dirette; *indirect -es*, imposte indirette; *value added* — (*VAT*), imposta valore aggiunta (IVA); *income* —, imposta sul reddito; *land* —, imposta fondiaria; *luxury* —, tassa di lusso; *purchase* —, tassa di scambio; *road fund* —, tassa di circolazione; *turnover* —, imposta generale sulle entrate; *visitor's* —, imposta di soggiorno; *free of* —, esente da tasse; — *avoidance*, modi legali di ridurre la contribuzione fiscale; — *evasion*, evasione fiscale; (fig.) peso, onere *m.*; *to be a — on one's time*, portare via molto tempo.

**tax** *tr.* tassare, imporre una tassa su, mettere un'imposta su; (leg.) tassare, fissare, stabilire; (fig.) mettere alla prova; tacciare, accusare, rimproverare, rifarsela; *why do you — me with it?*, perchè se la rifà con me?

**taxable** *adj.* tassabile; imponibile; — *income*, reddito imponibile; (leg.) *costs — to*, spese a carico di.

**taxation** *n.* tassazione, tasse *f.pl.*, imposte *f.pl.*, fiscalità.

**tax-collector** *n.* esattore delle imposte, agente *m.* del fisco. **-dodger** *n.* evasore *m.* fiscale. **-evasion** *n.* evasione *f.* fiscale. **-farmer** *n.* (hist.) appaltatore *m.* delle tasse.

**taxi, taxi-cab** *n.* tassì *m.*, auto pubblica, automobile *f.* di piazza; andare in tassì; (aeron.) rullare.

**taxiderm-y** *n.* tassidermia. **-ist** *n.* tassidermista *m.*, impagliatore *m.*

**taxi-driver, taximan** *n.* tassista *m.*, autista *m.* di tassì.

**taximeter** *n.* tassimetro.

**taxi-rank** *n.* posteggio per tassì.

**tax-office** *n.* esattoria, agenzia delle tasse, ufficio delle imposte dirette.

**taxpayer** *n.* contribuente *m.*, *f.*

**tax-relief** *n.* abbattimento, deduzione dalle tasse, abbuono; esenzione.

**tea** *n.* tè *m.*; *a cup of* —, una tazza di tè; *strong* —, tè forte, tè carico; *weak* —, tè chiaro, tè leggero; *afternoon* —, tè delle cinque; *high* —, cena fredda, tè delle sette; *to ask someone to* —, invitare qualcuno a prendere il tè; (fam.) *that's not your cup of* —, non è cibo per i tuoi denti; — *up!*, ecco fatto il tè!

**tea-bag** *n.* bustina di tè. **-blending** *n.* miscela di tè. **-caddy** *n.* scatola per il tè. **-cloth** *n.* tovaglia da tè; canovaccio. **-cosy** *n.* copriteiera *m.* **-cake** *n.* pasticcino da tè.

**teach** *tr.* insegnare, far imparare, istruire; — *me how to do it*, vuoi mostrarmi come si fa; *he is being taught to speak three languages*, gli si insegna a parlare tre lingue; *to — oneself something*, imparare qualcosa da solo; (fam.) *that will — him!*, così imparerà!; *to — one's grandmother to suck eggs*, voler insegnare a volare agli uccelli; *intr.* insegnare, fare l'insegnante; (Univ.) professare, essere professore, fare il docente.

**teachable** *adj.* insegnabile; (of thing) che si può insegnare facilmente, (of person) che impara facilmente, intelligente, svelto.

**teacher** *n.* insegnante *m.*, *f.*, precettore; professore, professoressa; (at primary school) maestro, maestra; (at secondary school) professore, professoressa; (at University), docente *m.*, *f.*; (of music) maestro; (fig.) maestro, maestra; *to be a* —, insegnare, fare l'insegnante; *training college for -s*, istituto magistrale.

**tea-chest** *n.* cassa di tè.

**teach-in** *n.* seminario, dibattito.

**teaching** *adj.* che insegna; *attrib.* magistrale; *the — staff*, il corpo insegnante, il corpo dei professori; *n.* insegnamento, istruzione; — *method*, metodo insegnativo, sistema didattico; — *programme*, programma didattico; *pl.* dottrina, disciplina, precetti *m.pl.* (fig.) ammaestramento.

**teacup** *n.* tazza da tè; (fig.) *a storm in a* —, una tempesta in un bicchier d'acqua.

**teak** *n.* te(a)k *m.*, teck *m.*

**tea-kettle** *n.* bollitore.

**teal** *n.* (orn.) alzavola, arzavola.

**tea-leaf** *n.* foglio di tè.

**team** *n.* (of draught animals) tiro, pariglia; collaboratori *m.pl.*; (sport, etc.) squadra; *the home* —, gli ospitanti; *the visiting* —, gli ospiti; *football* —, squadra di calcio; *members of the first* —, titolari *m.pl.*; *reserve* —, riserve *f.pl.*

**team** *tr.* (draught animals) attaccare, aggiogare; *intr. to — up*, unirsi, collaborare, (joc.) sposarsi; *to — up with*, mettersi a lavorare insieme con.

**team-spirit** *n.* spirito di collaborazione; (sport) spirito di squadra, spirito di corpo. **-work** *n.* lavoro fatto in collaborazione, lavoro di squadra, affiatamento.

**tea-party** *n.* tè *m.*, ricevimento all'ora del tè; *to give a* —, offrire un tè.

**tea-planter** *n.* coltivatore di tè, conduttore di una piantagione.

**teapot** *n.* teiera.

**tear**[1] *n.* lacrima, lagrima; *pl.*, lacrime, pianto; *to burst into -s*, scoppiare in lacrime; *to shed -s*, versare lacrime, piangere; *to shed -s for*, piangere; *this vale of -s*, questa valle di lacrime.

**tear**[2] *n.* squarcio, strappo, stracciatura, lacerazione; (fam.) fretta, impeto; *tr.* stracciare, strappare, squarciare, lacerare; (fig.) straziare; *to — one's trousers*, farsi uno strappo nei calzoni; *to — one's hair*, strapparsi i capelli; *to — open*, aprire lacerando; *to — to pieces*, stracciare, fare a pezzi, (of animal) dilaniare; (fig.) demolire; *to — away*, *to — off*, strappare, staccare; *to — oneself away*, staccarsi; *to — down*, strappare, (fig.) demolire, smontare; *to — out*, strappare; *to — up*, strappare, sradicare, stracciare; (fig.) *to be torn between*, dibattersi fra; *to be torn by remorse*, essere straziato dal rimorso; *to be torn by factions*, essere dilaniato dalle fazioni; (fam.) *that's torn it!*, non ci mancava altro!; *intr.* strapparsi, stracciarsi, lacerarsi; (fam.) correre, precipitarsi; *to — along*, correre all'impazzata; *to — about*, correre dappertutto; *to — downstairs*, precipitarsi giù dalle scale; *to — off*, scappare.

**tear-dimmed** *adj.* velato dalle lacrime. **-drop** *n.* lacrima, goccia. **-duct** *n.* (anat.) condotto lacrimale.

**tearful** *adj.* lacrimoso, lacrimevole, piangente; piagnucoloso; triste. **-ly** *adv.* piangendo, con le lacrime agli occhi. **-ness** *n.* stato lacrimevole, l'avere le lacrime agli occhi; l'essere piagnucoloso.

**tear-gas** *n.* gas lacrimogeno.

**tearing** *adj.* lacerante, violento; (fig.) impetuoso; *a — wind*, un vento impetuoso; (fam.) *to be in a — hurry*, avere una fretta terribile; *to be in a — rage*, avere la rabbia addosso; *n.* lacerazione, strappo; — *of a muscle*, strappo muscolare.

**tearless** *n.* senza lacrime, a ciglio asciutto.

**tear-off** *adj.* perforato, da staccarsi.

**tea-room** *n.* sala da tè. **-rose** *n.* (bot.) rosa tea, tè *m.*

**tear-stained** *adj.* rigato di lacrime.

**tease** *n.* (fam.) stuzzichino, seccatore; *tr.* stuzzicare, far dispetti a, annoiare, molestare, tormentare, irritare, canzonare; (text.) cardare, pettinare, *to — out*, sfilacciare, sfilare.

**teasel** *n.* (bot.) scardaccio, stoppione *m.*, labbro di Venere; (text.) garzatrice.

**teaser** *n.* seccatore, stuzzichino, tormentatore; (fig.) rompicapo,

domanda imbarazzante; (text.) cardatrice, pettinatrice.
**tea-service, -set** *n.* servizio da tè. **-shop** *n.* pasticceria dove si serve il tè, sala da tè.
**teasing** *adj.* stuzzicante, dispettoso, molesto, irritante, canzonatorio, malizioso; *n.* il far dispetti, seccatura, molestamento, malizia; (text.) cardatura, pettinatura, — *machine*, cardatrice, lupo carda. **-ly** *adv.* con tono dispettoso, per far dispetti, dispettosamente.
**teaspoon** *n.* cucchiaino. **-ful** *n.* cucchiaino; *heaped -ful*, cucchiaino abbondante; *level -ful*, cucchiaino raso.
**tea-strainer** *n.* colino da tè.
**teat** *n.* (anat.) capezzolo, mammella, tetta; poppatoio, tettarina, tettarella.
**tea-table** *n.* tavola da tè. **-things** *n.* servizio da tè.
**teatime** *n.* l'ora del tè.
**tea-tray** *n.* vassoio (da tè). **-urn** *n.* samovar *m. indecl.*
**tec** *n. dimin.* (fam.) of **detective,** *q.v.*
**technical** *adj.* tecnico, di ordine tecnico; — *institute*, scuola professionale, istituto tecnico; — *difficulty*, difficoltà di ordine tecnico, (leg.) questione di procedura; — *offence*, quasi-delitto; — *assault*, quasi-aggressione; *on a — point*, su una questione di termini; *judgment quashed on a — point*, sentenza cassata per vizio di procedura. **-ity** *n.* tecnicismo, questione di ordine tecnico; termine tecnico.
**technician** *n.* tecnico, perito.
**technicolour** *n.* (cinem.) tecnicolore *m.*
**techn-ics** *n.* tecnica, tecnologia. **-ique** *n.* tecnica; arte *f.*, meccanismo.
**technolog-y** *n.* tecnologia. **-ical** *adj.* tecnologico. **-ist** *n.* tecnologo, tecnico.
**Ted, Teddy** *pr.n. dimin.* of **Edward,** *q.v.*; *Teddy bear*, orsacchiotto di pezza, orso di felpa; *Teddy boy*, giovane teppista *m.*
**tedious** *adj.* noioso, tedioso, faticoso, uggioso. **-ness, tedium** *n.* noia, tedio, uggia, mancanza d'interesse, afa.
**tee** *n.* (golf) monticello di rena per la palla, tee *m.*; piazzuola di partenza; (curling, *etc.*) bersaglio; *tr.* (golf) mettere la palla sul tee; *to — off*, dare la mazzata iniziale.
**teem** *intr. to — with*, formicolare di, brulicare di, abbondare in; (fig.) essere fertile di, generare, essere un vivaio di. **-ing** *adj.* formicolante, brulicante, rigurgitante, fertile; *-ing rain*, pioggia torrenziale.
**teen** *num. suff.* -dici.
**teenager** *n., adj.* adolescente *m., f.*, non ancora ventenne.
**teens** *n.* adolescenza, età da tredici a diciannove anni; *to be in one's —*, essere adolescente, aver meno di vent'anni; *to be just out of one's —*, avere appena vent'anni.
**teeny** *adj.* (fam.) piccino, minuscolo. **-bopper** *n.* (slang) giovane ammiratrice. **-weeny** *adj.* (fam.) piccolissimo, piccino piccino.
**teeter** *intr.* bilanciarsi; (fig.) esitare, vacillare.
**teeth** *n.pl.* of **tooth,** *q.v.*
**teeth-e** *intr.* (of child) mettere i denti. **-ing** *n.* dentizione; *-ing troubles*, disturbi di crescita; *-ing ring*, dentaruolo; *-ing rash*, strofolo.
**teetotal** *adj.* astemio, antialcoolico; (pop.) acquatile. **-ism** *n.* astinenza completa dall'alcool; lotta contro l'alcoolismo. **-ler** *n.* astemio, antialcoolico; (pop.) bevilacqua *m., f.*, acquatile *m., f.*
**teetotum** *n.* trottola.
**tegument** *n.* (anat.) tegumento. **-al, -ary** *adj.* tegumentale, tegumentario.
**tehee** *n.* risolino, risata affettata; *intr.* ridacchiare, ridere con affettazione.
**telamon** *n.* (archit.) telamone *m.*, atlante *m.*
**tele-** *pref.* tele-.
**tele-camera** *n.* telecamera, apparecchio per telefotografia. **-cast** *n.* trasmissione televisiva, teletrasmissione, telediffusione; *tr.* teletrasmettere, telediffondere. **-caster** *n.* apparecchio teletrasmittente; (person) telecronista *m., f.* **-communication** *n.* telecomunicazione; *pl.* servizio postelegrafonico.
**tele-gram** *n.* telegramma *m.*; *reply-paid —*, telegramma con risposta pagata; *wireless —*, radiotelegramma *m.* **-graph** *n.* telegrafo; semaforo; *-graph form*, modulo per telegrammi; *-graph office*, ufficio telegrafico; *-graph operator*, telegrafista *m., f.*; (naut.) *ship's -grapher*, trasmettitore d'ordini; *engine-room -grapher*, quadrante del trasmettitore d'ordini; (anthrop.; fig.) *bush -graph*, il tam tam della giungla; *tr.* telegrafare; telegrafare a, mandare un telegramma a; *he was -graphed for*, gli si telegrafò di venire; *intr.* telegrafare. **-graphic** *adj.* telegrafico; *-graphic address*, indirizzo telegrafico.
**telegraph-board** *n.* (sport) indicatore *m.* **-boy, -messenger** *n.* fattorino del telegrafo. **-pole, -post** *n.* palo telegrafico. **-wire** *n.* filo telegrafico.
**telegraph-ist** *n.* telegrafista *m., f.* **-y** *n.* telegrafia; *wireless -y*, radiotelegrafia.
**telelens** *n.* (photog.) teleobiettivo.
**Telemachus** *pr.n.* Telemaco.
**telemark** *n.* (skiing) telemark *m.*, manovra di rallentamento.
**telepath-y** *n.* telepatia. **-ic** *adj.* telepatico.
**telephone** *n.* telefono, apparecchio telefonico; *automatic —*, telefono automatico; *party-line —*, duplex *m.*; *— directory*, elenco telefonico; *— exchange*, centrale telefonica; *internal — exchange*, centralino; *— extension*, derivazione, telefono interno; *by —*, per telefono, telefonicamente; *to be on the —*, avere il telefono, essere abbonato al telefono; *to be wanted on the —*, essere chiamato al telefono; *tr.* telefonare; telefonare a, dare un colpo di telefono a, chiamare al telefono; *intr.* telefonare, fare una telefonata.
**telephone-bell** *n.* campanello del telefono. **-box, -booth, -kiosk** *n.* cabina telefonica. **-call** *n.* telefonata, colpo di telefono, chiamata; *long-distance trunk-call*, telefonata interurbana; *local -call*, telefonata urbana. **-dial** *n.* disco. **-girl** *n.* telefonista *f.*, centralinista *f.* **-line** *n.* linea telefonica. **-number** *n.* numero di telefono; *what is your -number ?*, che numero ha ?; *my -number is 245672*, il mio numero è ventiquattro cinquantasei settantadue. (N.B. In Italy teleph. numbers are always given in pairs, except when a pair contains a 0; e.g. 2420, ventiquattro due zero, 2402, ventiquattro zero due.) **-operator** *n.* telefonista *m., f.* **-receiver** *n.* ricevitore. **-wire** *n.* filo telefonico.
**telephon-y** *n.* telefonia. **-ic** *adj.* telefonico. **-ist** *n.* telefonista *m., f.*
**telephoto(graph)** *n.* telefoto *f.*, telefotografia.
**telephotography** *n.* telefotografia.
**teleprinter** *n.* telescrivente *m., f.*
**telescop-e** *n.* telescopio, cannocchiale *m.*; *tr.* incastrare, infilare; (fig.) condensare; *intr.* incastrarsi, infilarsi, commettersi, chiudersi a telescopio, rientrare; (of rlwy. carriages, *etc.*) incastrarsi. **-ic** *adj.* telescopico, a telescopio, a incastro; (photog.) *-ic finder*, mirino telescopico; *-ic lens*, teleobiettivo; (on rifle) *-ic sight*, mirino telescopico.
**tele-selection** *n.* (teleph.) teleselezione. **-type** *n.* telescrivente *m.* **-typesetter** *n.* (typ.) telecompositrice. **-viewer** *n.* telespettatore.
**televise** *tr.* teletrasmettere, trasmettere per televisione.
**television** *n.* televisione; *colour —*, televisione a colori; *— set*, televisore, apparecchio televisivo; *— screen*, video, schermo

televisivo, teleschermo; — *news-bulletin*, telecronaca, telegiornale *m.*; — *announcer*, telecronista *m.*, *f.*, annunciatore.

**tell** *tr.* raccontare, narrare, dire, riferire, contare; *he told me that he had seen you*, mi disse di averti visto; *I am told that*, mi dicono che; *I cannot — you how glad I am*, non so dirti quanto (io) sia felice; *how could I —?*, come avrei potuto sapere?; *one never can —*, non si può mai sapere; *who can —?*, chi lo sa?, va a indovinarlo!; *to — a story*, raccontare una storia; — *that to the marines!*, contala ai gonzi!, va a raccontarlo al gatto!; *dead men — no tales*, i morti non parlano; *to — one's beads*, dire il rosario; *to — fortunes*, predire l'avvenire; *to — tales about someone*, spargere chiacchiere sul conto di qualcuno; *to — the truth*, dire la verità; *to — a lie*, raccontare una bugia; *I — you*, ti dico; — *me*, dimmi, dica; *let me — you*, permetti ch'io ti dica; *I — you what!*, senti!; *I told you so!*, te l'avevo detto!; (fam.) *you're -ing me!*, lo dici a me!; *all told*, in tutto, tutto sommato; *to — truth from falsehood*, distinguere il vero dal falso; *I can — him by his voice*, lo riconosco dalla voce; rivelare, rendere noto, divulgare; *to — a secret to someone*, rivelare un segreto a qualcuno; *his face told me everything*, la sua espressione mi rivelò tutto; *to — off*, (mil.) designare, dare un compito a, fare una ramanzina a, sgridare; *I got told off because I arrived late*, mi hanno sgridato perchè sono giunto in ritardo; *intr.* aver effetto, incidere; *his years are beginning to —*, gli anni cominciano a pesargli; *to — in favour of*, deporre a favore di; *one can — by*, si capisce da; *to — against*, nuocere a, militare contro; *to — on*, pesare su; *the strain is beginning to — on him*, comincia a risentire dello sforzo; (slang) *to — on someone*, tradire qualcuno, spifferare, cantare.

**tellable** *adj.* raccontabile, narrabile.

**teller** *n.* raccontatore, narratore; (in bank) cassiere; (of votes) scrutatore.

**telling** *adj.* efficace, che colpisce, espressivo, impressionante; rivelatore; *n.* racconto, raccontare, narrazione; rivelazione; (fam.) *there's no —*, non si può sapere. **-ly** *adv.* efficacemente, vividamente, in modo impressionante.

**telltale** *adj.* rivelatore; pettegolo, indiscreto; *n.* chiacchierone, rivelatore di segreti, spifferone, rifischione, bisbiglione; (mech.) controllare; — *light*, lampada spia.

**telluric** *adj.* terrestre; (chem.) tellurico.

**telly** *n.* (fam.) televisore; TV (tivì) *f.*

**temerarious** *adj.* temerario, audace.

**temerity** *n.* temerarietà, temerità, audacia.

**temper** *n.* (metall.) tempra, coefficiente *m.* di durezza; (steel) rinvenimento; (fig.) umore, indole *f.*, carattere *m.*, disposizione; *of even —*, calmo, placido; *of uncertain —*, di umore vario; *in a good —*, di buon umore; *in a bad —*, di cattivo umore; collera, rabbia, stizza; *a fit of —*, un impeto di collera; *to control one's —*, contenersi, mantenere la padronanza di se stesso; *to keep one's —*, mantenersi calmo; *to fly into a —*, montare in collera, andare su tutte le furie; *to lose one's —*, arrabbiarsi, andare in collera, (fam.) perdere le staffe; *to get someone's — up*, arrabbiare qualcuno, far uscire qualcuno dai gangheri.

**temper** *tr.* (metall.) temperare, addolcire, far rinvenire; (mortar) stemperare; (fig.) moderare, temperare, annacquare, affinare; (mus.) attemperare, modulare; (provb.) *God -s the wind to the shorn lamb*, Dio manda il freddo secondo i panni; *intr.* (of steel) rinvenire; (fig.) temperarsi.

**tempera** *n.* (art) tempera.

**temperament** *n.* temperamento; indole *f.*; disposizione, carattere *m.*, umore *m.*; complessione; (mus.) temperamento; (pejor.) carattere capriccioso, impulsività. **-al** *adj.* capriccioso, impulsivo, impressionabile, instabile; (sport) incostante, incerto.

**temperance** *n.* moderazione, temperanza, sobrietà; astinenza, antialcoolismo; — *hotel*, albergo in cui è proibita la vendita delle bevande alcooliche; — *movement*, lega contro l'alcoolismo.

**temperate** *adj.* moderato, sobrio, temperato; (of climate) temperato, mite, dolce. **-ness** *n.* moderazione, sobrietà, temperanza; (of climate) mitezza, dolcezza.

**temperature** *n.* temperatura; *room —*, temperatura ambiente; *normal —*, temperatura normale; *to have a —*, avere la febbre; *to take someone's —*, prendere la temperatura a qualcuno.

**tempered** *adj.* (metall.) temperato; (of steel) rinvenuto; (fig.) moderato, sobrio; temperato; *justice — with mercy*, la giustizia temperata con la clemenza; *bad-tempered*, di cattivo umore, di cattiva disposizione; *quick-tempered*, irascibile, irritabile; *short-tempered*, impulsivo.

**tempest** *n.* tempesta, burrasca; procella; (fig.) agitazione, commozione.

**tempestuous** *adj.* tempestoso, burrascoso, procelloso; (fig.) violento, impulsivo, focoso, agitato, irruente. **-ness** *n.* violenza; irruenza.

**templar** *n.* (hist.) (cavaliere) templare.

**template** *n.* See **templet.**

**temple**[1] *n.* (archit.; rel.) tempio; (poet.) delubro; tempietto, edicola; (fig.) tempio, santuario.

**temple**[2] *n.* (anat.) tempia.

**temple**[3] *n.* (text.) tempiale *m.*

**templet**[1] *n.* (archit.) architrave *f.*; (mech.) sagoma, maschera, calibro sagomato; (bldg.) cuscino d'appoggio, piastra di ripartizione del carico.

**templet**[2] *n.* (text.) tempiale *m.*

**tempo** *n.* andamento, ritmo, movimento; (mus.) tempo.

**temporal** *adj.* (rel.; gramm.) temporale; — *power*, potere temporale; — *affairs*, affari secolari; *lords spiritual and —*, vescovi e pari della Gran Bretagna.

**temporar-y** *adj.* temporaneo, provvisorio, transitorio, per interim; momentaneo, passeggero; — *measures*, misure provvisorie; (comm.) — *importation*, importazione temporanea. **-iness** *n.* temporaneità, provvisorietà.

**temporiz-e** *intr.* temporeggiare, indugiare; cercare di guadagnare tempo, procrastinare. **-ation** *n.* temporeggiamento; procrastinazione. **-er** *n.* temporeggiatore; procrastinatore.

**tempt** *tr.* tentare, allettare, indurre; cercare di sedurre; (bibl.) tentare, mettere alla prova; (fig.) *to be -ed to*, aver voglia di, essere incline a. **-ation** *n.* tentazione; seduzione; *to lead into -ation*, indurre in tentazione, sviare; *to yield to -ation*, cedere alla tentazione. **-er** *n.* tentatore *m.*, seduttore *m.* **-ing** *adj.* che tenta, seducente, allettante, attraente; (of food) appetitoso. **-ress** *n.* tentatrice; seduttrice.

**ten** *card. num.* dieci; *about —*, una d(i)ecina(di); *a hundred and —*, centodieci; *a thousand and —*, mille (e) dieci; *-thousand*, diecimila; *the — Commandments*, il Decalogo, i dieci Comandamenti; — *o'clock*, le dieci; — *per cent*, il dieci per cento; *to be — years old*, avere dieci anni, essere decenne; *some — years back*, una diecina di anni fa; *one out of (every) —*, uno su dieci; — *times as much*, dieci volte tanto, il decuplo; — *to one he'll find it out*, (scommetto) dieci contro uno che lo scoprirà; *n.* il numero dieci, una serie di dieci; *to arrange in -s*, disporre a gruppi di dieci; *to count by -s*, contare a dieci; (fig.) *the upper —*,

l'aristocrazia, l'alta società, il gran mondo.
**tenab-le** *adj.* sostensibile, difendibile, difensibile, tenibile; *post — for five years*, impiego che si può tenere per cinque anni. **-ility, -leness** *n.* sostenibilità.
**tenacious** *adj.* tenace, ostinato, duro, accanito; (fig.) *to be — of*, essere attaccato a; (of glue, *etc.*) viscoso, adesivo. **-ness, tenacity** *n.* tenacia, ostinazione, accanimento, tenacità; (of memory) sicurezza; (of glue, *etc.*) tenacità, forza adesiva.
**tenancy** *n.* (of house) locazione, affittanza; (leg.) usufrutto; (of office) permanenza.
**tenant** *n.* inquilino, locatario, affittuario, fittaiuolo, pigionale *m.*, tenutario; (leg.) usufruttuario; *-'s repairs*, riparazioni locative; *tr.* tenere in affitto, occupare come inquilino, abitare come locatario.
**tenant-farmer** *n.* affittuario, fittaiuolo, mezzadro.
**tenantless** *adj.* senza inquilini, sfitto, disabitato.
**tench** *n.* (ichth.) tinca.
**tend**[1] *tr.* curare, soccorrere, assistere; *to — to*, curare, badare a, attendere a, sorvegliare; *to — the fire*, badare al fuoco.
**tend**[2] *intr.* tendere, dirigersi (verso); (fig.) tendere, aver tendenza, essere soggetto (a); aiutare a, contribuire a; *blue -ing to green*, blu che tende al verde.
**tendency** *n.* tendenza, disposizione; inclinazione; *to have a — to*, tendere a, essere suscettibile di.
**tend-ential, -entious** *adj.* tendenzioso, a tendenza. **-entiousness** *n.* tendenziosità.
**tender**[1] *adj.* tenero, frollo; *a — steak*, una bistecca tenera; *a — spot*, un punto dolorante, un punto sensitivo, una questione delicata; delicato; *a — skin*, una pelle delicata; sensibile; *a — heart*, un cuore sensibile; tenero, affettuoso, sollecito, sensibile; giovane, immaturo; *— age*, giovane età, età tenera; dolce, grato; *a — recollection*, un dolce ricordo.
**tender**[2] *n.* custode *m.*, guardiano; barista *m.*; (rlwy.) carro scorta, tender *m.*; (naut.) nave appoggio.
**tender**[3] *n.* (comm.) offerta, preventivo, appalto; (leg.) offerta reale; (of money) *legal —*, valuta legale; *tr.* offrire, presentare; *to — one's excuses*, presentare le proprie scuse; *to — evidence*, avanzare delle prove, presentare una difesa, produrre testimoni; *to — one's resignation*, dare le dimissioni, dimettersi; (leg.) *to — money in discharge of a debt*, fare una offerta reale; *intr.* concorrere per un appalto, fare un'offerta, proporre un prezzo.
**tender-hearted** *adj.* dal cuore sensibile, affettuoso.
**tenderloin** *n.* (cul.) filetto di carne.
**tenderness** *n.* tenerezza; affettuosità; delicatezza; sensibilità; (of food) l'essere tenero.
**tending**[1] *n.* cura, assistenza, sorveglianza.
**tending**[2] *gerund* of **tend**[2], *q.v.*; *adj.* tendente, incline.
**tendon** *n.* (anat.) tendine *m.*; *Achilles —*, tendine d'Achille.
**tendril** *n.* viticcio, cirro, capreolo.
**tenement** *n.* (leg.) tenuta; podere *m.*; possesso, godimento; casa operaia, casa popolare, casamento.
**Teneriffe** *pr.n.* (geog.) Teneriffa.
**tenet** *n.* dogma *m.*, dottrina; principio; (fam.) credenza, opinione.
**tenfold** *adj.* decuplo; *adv.* dieci volte tanto, al decuplo; *to increase —*, decuplicare, rendere dieci volte tanto.
**tenner** *n.* (fam.) biglietto da dieci (sterline).
**tennis** *n.* giuoco della palla; (*lawn-*) —, tennis *m.* **-arm, -elbow** *n.* crampo da tennis. **-ball** *n.* palla da tennis. **-court** *n.* campo da tennis. **-player** *n.* giuocatore di tennis, tennista *m.*, *f.* **-racket** *n.* racchetta da tennis.
**tenon** *n.* (carpent.) tenone *m.*; (metall.) aletta.
**tenon** *tr.* (carpent.) congiungere con tenone.
**tenor** *n.* tenore di vita, sistema di vita; andamento; (leg.) copia conforme; (comm.) scadenza; (mus.) tenore *m.*, *attrib.* tenorile; *to sing —*, tenoreggiare.
**ten-pounder** *n.* che pesa dieci libbre, dal peso di dieci libbre.
**tense**[1] *n.* (gramm.) tempo *m.*; *in the future —*, al futuro; *in the present —*, al presente; *in the past —*, al passato.
**tense**[2] *adj.* teso; tirato; rigido; *— moment*, momento critico; *— silence*, silenzio drammatico; *— situation*, situazione tesa; *voice — with emotion*, voce strozzata dall'emozione; *to be — with expectancy*, essere teso nell'aspettativa. **-ness** *n.* rigidità, tensione.
**tensile** *adj.* estensibile, elastico; (of metal) duttile; (mech.) relativo alla tensione; *— force*, forza di trazione.
**tension** *n.* tensione; rigidità; *easing of —*, distensione; (phys.) pressione, tensione; (electr.) tensione, potenziale *m.*; *high —*, alta tensione; (mech.) trazione.
**tent** *n.* tenda; padiglione *m.*; *to pitch -s*, piantare le tende; *to strike -s*, levare le tende; (med.) *oxygen —*, tenda ad ossigeno; *tr.* coprire con una tenda; *intr.* attendarsi, vivere sotto le tende.
**tentac-le** *n.* tentacolo; (bot.) cirro, viticcio. **-ular** *adj.* tentacolare, tentacolato.
**tentative** *adj.* di prova, sperimentale, a titolo di prova; *— effort*, tentativo; *— offer*, offerta tentativa, una semplice proposta; *n.* prova, tentativo.
**tenter** *n.* (text.) stenditoio; (person) stenditore.
**tenterhook** *n.* (text.) uncino di stenditoio; (fig.) *to be on -s*, essere sulle spine; *to keep someone on -s*, far morire qualcuno dalla curiosità.
**tenth** *ord. num.* decimo; *the — of November*, il dieci novembre; *n.* decimo, decima parte; (eccl.; mus.) decima. **-ly** *adv.* in decimo luogo.
**tent-peg** *n.* picchetto per tenda.
**tenu-ous** *adj.* tenue, sottile; debole; scarso; fluido; rarefatto; (fig.) semplice, esile. **-ity** *n.* tenuità, finezza, sottigliezza; rarefazione; (of light) debolezza; (of liquid) fluidità; (fig.) semplicità.
**tenure** *n.* (leg.) possesso, godimento, usufrutto; (fig.) periodo di possesso, occupazione, tenuta; *during his — of office*, durante l'esercizio delle sue funzioni.
**ten-year-old** *adj. n.* decenne *m.*, *f.*
**tepid** *adj.* tiepido, tepente, tepefatto; *to become —*, intiepidirsi. **-ity, -ness** *n.* t(i)epidezza, tepore *m.*, tepidità.
**tercent-enary** *adj.*, *n.* trecentenario. **-ennial** *adj.* trecentenario.
**tercet** *n.* (poet.) terzina.
**Terence** *pr.n.* Terenzio.
**tergal** *adj.* dorsale, tergale.
**tergiversat-e** *intr.* tergiversare. **-ion** *n.* tergiversazione. **-or** *n.* tergiversatore.
**term** *n.* termine *m.*; periodo di tempo; limite *m.*, estremo; (schol.) trimestre *m.*; (leg.) sessione; durata; *— of delivery*, termine di consegna; *— of office*, periodo di carica, mandato; *attrib. long-term*, a lunga durata; *short-term*, a breve durata; (math.; logic) termine; parola, termine; *technical —*, termine tecnico; *in the stricter sense of the —*, a rigore di termini; *in the wider sense of the —*, nel senso lato della parola; *contradiction in -s*, contraddizione in termini; *to use the proper —*, usare la parola giusta; *in the strongest -s*, con parole molto energiche; termine, condizione; *pl. -s and conditions*, condizioni e modalità; *-s of contract*, termini del contratto; *-s of reference*, mandato, attribuzioni *f.pl.*; *-s of sale*, condizioni di vendita; (of hotel) condizioni *f.pl.*, prezzi *m.pl.*; *-s for board and lodging*, retta;

*inclusive -s*, (prezzo) tutto compreso; *name your own -s*, stabilite voi le condizioni; *on easy -s*, con facilitazioni di pagamento; (fig.) *to come to -s with*, venire a patti con, venire ad un accomodamento con; *to be on good -s with*, essere in buoni rapporti con; *to be on friendly -s with*, essere amico di, essere in rapporti di amicizia con; *to be on bad -s with*, essere in cattivi rapporti con; *to be on speaking -s with*, conoscere abbastanza bene; *not to be on speaking -s with*, essere in rotta con; *on equal -s*, a parità di condizioni, sopra un piede di uguaglianza.

**term** *tr.* chiamare, nominare, definire, qualificare; *to be -ed*, chiamarsi; *to — oneself*, qualificarsi come, chiamarsi.

**termagant** *n.* (of woman) magera, virago *f.*; (of child) cattivello.

**terminable** *adj.* terminabile; (of contract) risolvibile.

**terminal** *adj.* estremo, terminale, ultimo; (schol.) trimestrale; (gramm.) finale; *— point (of line)*, capolinea *m.*; *n.* estremità, punta estrema; (rlwy.) stazione di testa; *air —*, aerostazione, terminal *m.*; (electr.) terminale *m.*, morsetto.

**terminat-e** *tr.* terminare, portare a termine, porre fine a, finire, stare alla fine di; limitare, delimitare; *intr.* finire, terminare; (gramm.) *to — in*, terminare per. **-ion** *n.* termine *m.* fine *f.*; cessazione; conclusione; (gramm.) desinenza, terminazione.

**terminolog-y** *n.* terminologia *f.* **-ical** *adj.* terminologico, di terminologia; *-ical inexactitude*, inesattezza di terminologia, (joc.) bugia.

**terminus** *n.* termine *m.*; fine *f.*; meta; (of buses, *etc.*) capolinea *m.*; (rlwy.) stazione di testa.

**termite** *n.* (ent.) termite *f.*

**term-time** *n.* (schol.) periodo dei corsi, trimestre *n.*

**tern** *n.* (orn.) sterna, rondine *f.* di mare.

**ternary** *adj.* ternario.

**Terpsichore** *pr.n.* Tersicore.

**terrace** *n.* (on hillside) terrazzo, ripiano, terrapieno, balza; (bldg.) terrazza, tetto a terrazza; (levelled ground) spianata; (on football ground) spalto; (row of houses) fila di case. **-d** *adj.* a terrazze, a ripiani; *-d vineyard*, vigna a balze; *-d houses*, case attigue in fila.

**terracotta** *n.* terracotta; *attrib.* di terracotta.

**terra firma** *n.* terraferma.

**terrain** *n.* terreno.

**terrapin** *n.* (zool.) tartaruga acquatica.

**terrestrial** *adj.* terrestre, terreno, di questo mondo.

**terrible** *adj.* terribile, spaventoso, atroce, orribile; (fam.) tremendo; formidabile; *he's a — bore*, è un gran seccatore. **-ness** *n.* spaventevolezza, spaventosità; (of Michelangelo) terribilità.

**terribly** *adv.* terribilmente, spaventosamente; (fam.) *it's — cold*, fa un freddo birbone; *I'm — hungry*, ho una fame da lupo; *I'm — sorry*, mi spiace tanto.

**terrier** *n.* (dog) terrier *m. indecl.*; (fam.) membro della milizia territoriale; *the -s*, la milizia territoriale.

**terrific** *adj.* spaventoso, terrificante, terribile; (fam.) tremendo, magnifico; (of speed) vertiginoso.

**terrify** *tr.* terrificare, atterrire, spaventare, far paura a; *to be terrified*, aver paura, atterrirsi, allibire, impaurirsi, (fam.) avere una paura matta. **-ing** *adj.* terrificante, spaventoso.

**territorial** *adj.* territoriale, proprio d'un territorio, nazionale; *— waters*, acque territoriali; (mil.) *— army*, milizia territoriale; *n.* membro della milizia territoriale.

**territory** *n.* territorio; terreno; distretto; zona.

**terror** *n.* terrore *m.*; paura; spavento; *reign of —*, regime terroristico; (Fr. hist.) *the Reign of Terror*, il Terrore; *to be in — of*, temere, avere paura di; *to be in — of one's life*, temere per la propria vita; *to strike — into*, incutere terrore a; *to go in — of*, avere una paura matta di; (fam.) *a holy —*, un'ira di Dio; (of child) *a little —*, un diavoletto. **-ism** *a.* terrorismo. **-ist** *n.* terrorista *m.*, *f.*

**terroriz-e** *tr.* terrorizzare; incutere terrore a, intimorire. **-ation** *n.* terrorizzazione; intimidazione.

**terror-struck, -stricken** *adj.* terrorizzato, allibito, atterrito.

**terse** *adj.* conciso, incisivo; brusco, terso, stringato. **-ness** *n.* concisione; stringatezza, tersezza.

**tertiary** *adj.* terziario; *n.* (eccl.) terziario, terziaria; (geol.) *lower —*, paleogene; *upper —*, neogene.

**tessellat-ed** *adj.* tessellato, a mosaico, a scacchiera. **-ion** *n.* tessellatura, decorazione a mosaico.

**tessera** *n.* (in mosaic) tessera.

**test** *n.* prova, esperimento, saggio, assaggio; (chem.) analisi *f.*; (med.) test *m.*, analisi, saggio reattivo; *Wassermann —*, reazione Wassermann; (cinem.) provino; (industr.) prova collaudo, controllo; *crucial —*, prova decisiva; *endurance —*, (sport) prova di resistenza, (mech.) prova di durata; *to put to the —*, mettere alla prova, provare; *to stand the —*, superare la prova; *to fail to pass the —*, fallire la prova; *to undergo a —*, subire una prova; (fig.) criterio, pietra di paragone; (metall.) coppella, saggio; (cricket) *— (match)*, incontro internazionale di cricket; *— case*, (leg.) processo di cui la soluzione farà legge, (fig.) prova decisiva.

**test** *tr.* provare, mettere alla prova, esaminare, controllare, verificare; saggiare, assaggiare; (industr.) collaudare; (chem.) analizzare; (metall.) passare dalla coppella, coppellare.

**testament** *n.* (leg.) testamento, ultime volontà *f.pl.*; *to make one's —*, fare il testamento, testare; *Old —*, Vecchio Testamento; *New —*, Nuovo Testamento. **-ary** *adj.* testamentario.

**testat-e** *adj.*, *n.* (leg.) testante *m.*, *f.* **-or** *n.* (leg.) testatore, testante *m.*, *f.* **-rix** *n.* (leg.) testatrice.

**test-bench** *n.* (industr.) banco di prova.

**tester**[1] *n.* (of bed) cielo, baldacchino *m.*

**tester**[2] *n.* (person) saggiatore, (industr.) collaudatore; (machine) apparecchio di prova, verificatore.

**testicle** *n.* (anat.) testicolo.

**testif-y** *tr.* testimoniare, testificare, attestare; dimostrare, provare; (leg.) testimoniare, dichiarare sotto giuramento, deporre, affermare; *intr. to — in someone's favour*, deporre a favore di qualcuno; *to — to*, testimoniare, affermare; provare, dimostrare, essere prova di. **-ier** *n.* testimone *m.*, *f.*; attestatore.

**testimonial** *n.* certificato di servizio, benservito, attestato; referenza, lettera di raccomandazione; (fig.) dono in segno di stima, omaggio.

**testimony** *n.* testimonianza, attestazione, affermazione; (leg.) dichiarazione sotto giuramento, deposizione; *to produce — of*, allegare prove di; *in — of*, a prova di; *to be a — to*, provare, dimostrare; (rel.) *to give —*, affermare pubblicamente la propria fede; (bibl.) *the tables of the Testimony*, le tavole della Legge, il Decalogo.

**testiness** *n.* irritabilità, suscettibilità, scontrosità.

**testing** *n.* prova, il provare; saggio, assaggio; (industr.) collaudo.

**testing-bench** *n.* banco di prova. **-ground** *n.* campo sperimentale.

**test-paper** *n.* (chem.) carta reattiva; (schol.) compito (in preparazione per gli esami). **-pilot** *n.* (aeron.) pilota collaudatore. **-tube** *n.* (chem.) provetta.

**testy** *adj.* irritabile, irascibile, suscettibile, bilioso, scontroso.

**tetanus** *n.* (med.) tetano.

**tetchiness** *n.*, **tetchy** *adj.* See **testiness, testy.**

**tête-à-tête** *adv.* a quattr'occhi; *n.* colloquio a quattr'occhi, tête-à-tête *m.*

**tether** *n.* pastoia; (fig.) vincolo, legame *m.*; *to be at the end of one's* —, essere all'estremo delle proprie risorse, non potere più; *tr.* impastoiare, attaccare; (fig.) vincolare, legare.

**tetra-** *pref.* tetra-.

**tetra-gon** *n.* (geom.) tetragono. **-hedron** *n.* (geom.) tetraedro. **-pod** *adj.*, *n.* (zool.) tetrapodo.

**tetrarch** *n.* (hist.) tetrarca *m.* **-ate** *n.* (hist.) tetrarcato. **-y** *n.* tetrarchia.

**Teuton** *n.* teutone *m.*, germano. **-ic** *adj.* teutonico, germanico.

**Texan** *adj.*, *n.* del Texas.

**text** *n.* testo; *to stick to one's* —, non allontanarsi dalla propria tesi. **-book** *n.* manuale *m.*, trattato, libro di testo.

**textile** *adj.* tessile; *n.* tessuto, stoffa.

**textual** *adj.* testuale, di testo; — *error*, errore di testo; — *criticism*, critica dei testi. **-ly** *adv.* testualmente, alla lettera.

**texture** *n.* (techn.) trama; (biol.) tessuto; (fig.) struttura, natura.

**Thaddeus** *pr.n.* Taddeo.

**Thai** *n.*, *adj.* siamese *m.*, *f.* **-land** *pr.n.* (geog.) Tailandia.

**Thames** *pr.n.* Tamigi *m.*; — *Embankment*, Lungotamigi *m.*; *he'll never set the — on fire*, non è mica un'aquila.

**than** *conj.* (after *comp.*) di, che, di quello che, di quello che non, di quanto, di quanto non; (after *hardly*, *no sooner*, *scarcely*): quando, che; *rather* —, piuttosto che; *other* —, oltre che; *no other* —, nessun altro che; *more — once*, più di una volta; *I have more — you*, ne ho più di te; *more — I am*, *more — I do*, più di me; *I know him better — you do*, lo conosco meglio di te, lo conosco meglio di quanto non lo conosci tu; *I know him better — I know his brother*, lo conosco meglio di quanto non conosco suo fratello; *no sooner said — done*, detto fatto; (as quasi-*prep.*): *a man — whom none was more respected*, un uomo più rispettato di qualsiasi altro.

**thane** *n* (hist.) conte *m.*, signorotto.

**thank** *tr.* ringraziare, dire grazie a, esprimere riconoscenza a; — *you*, grazie, ti ringrazio, La ringrazio, gradisca i miei migliori ringraziamenti; *no — you*, no grazie; — *you for your letter*, grazie della lettera; — *you so much*, tante grazie; — *you ever so much*, mille grazie; (iron.) — *you for nothing!*, tante grazie!; *I'll — you to mind your own business*, ti prego di badare ai fatti tuoi; *you can — your lucky stars*, puoi ringraziare il cielo; — *God!*, grazie a Dio!; — *goodness!*, grazie al cielo!; *he has only himself to* —, deve ringraziare solo se stesso, la colpa è tutta sua.

**thankful** *adj.* grato, riconoscente, lieto; — *to*, grato a; — *for*, grato di; — *that*, lieto che. **-ly** *adv.* con gratitudine, con riconoscenza, lietamente. **-ness** *n.* gratitudine, riconoscenza.

**thankless** *adj.* ingrato; *a — task*, un lavoro ingrato. **-ness** *n.* (of person) ingratitudine; (of work, *etc.*) l'essere ingrato, futilità.

**thank-offering** *n.* regalo in segno di riconoscenza; (rel.) offerta votiva, ex voto *m.*

**thanks** *n.* ringraziamenti *m.pl.*, grazie *f.pl.*; — *!*, grazie!; *many — !*, tante grazie!, grazie mille!; *no — !*, grazie no!, no grazie!; *please accept my* —, gradisca i miei ringraziamenti; — *to*, grazie a; *small — I got!*, bel ringraziamento ne ho avuto!; *vote of* —, ringraziamento dell'assemblea; *to express one's — to someone for something*, ringraziare qualcuno di qualcosa; *to give — for*, rendere grazie di.

**thanksgiving** *n.* (eccl.) rendimento di grazie, azioni di grazie; — *festival*, rendimento di grazie per il raccolto.

**that** *dem. adj.*, *m.* quel, quello, quell'; *f.* quella; cf. **this**; (lit.) cotesto, codesto; — *book*, quel libro (là); *at — hour*, a quell'ora; — *book of yours*, quel tuo libro; — *one*, quello (là), quella (là); — *fool of a gardener*, quell'imbecille di un giardiniere; *adv.* (fam.) così, quanto, talmente; — *far*, così tanto; — *stupid*, talmente stupido.

**that** *conj.* che (never omitted in Italian); *I hope — it is true*, spero che sia vero; *in order* —, affinchè, perchè; *provided* —, purchè; *in* —, in quanto che; *but for the fact* —, *except* —, senonchè.

**that** *dem. prn.* quello, questo, ciò; *who's — ?*, chi è quello?; *—'s my cousin*, (quello) è mio cugino; *what's — ?*, che è questo?; *—'s my book*, (questo) è il mio libro; *is — you?*, sei tu?; — *is*, cioè; — *is to say*, vale a dire; — *is how*, ecco come; — *is why*, ecco perchè; *—'s all*, ecco tutto, basta; *—'s enough*, basta; *—'s — !*, ecco fatto!; *I'm going to do it, —'s — !*, lo faccio e basta!; *like* —, così, in quel modo; *but for* —, se non fosse per quello, altrimenti; *—'s right*, è proprio così, è giusto; *he's a writer and a good one at* —, è uno scrittore e per di più bravissimo; — *I will!*, ben volentieri!, sicuro!; *has it come to — ?*, siamo a questo punto?; *what do you mean by — ?*, cosa intendi dire con ciò?; FOLLOW. BY REL. PRN.: quello, ciò; *—'s what I wanted to tell you*, ecco quello che volevo dirti.

**that** *rel. prn.* che, il quale, la quale; N.B. never omitted in Italian, *e.g. the book (that) I am reading*, il libro che sto leggendo; (with *prep.*) cui, il quale; *the book — we are talking about*, il libro di cui stiamo parlando; (in expressions of time) in cui, nel quale; *the day — I arrived*, il giorno in cui sono arrivato.

**thatch** *n.* copertura di paglia, stoppia; (fam.) capelli *m.pl.*, capigliatura; *tr.* coprire di paglia. **-ed** *adj.* coperto di paglia; *-ed cottage*, casetta con tetto di paglia, pagliereccio. **-er** *n.* impagliatore, chi fa coperture di paglia.

**thaumaturg-y** *n.* taumaturgia. **-e, -ist** *n.* taumaturgo. **-ic(al)** *adj.* taumaturgico.

**thaw** *n.* sgelo, disgelo; *tr.* disgelare, fondere, sciogliere; *intr.* disgelarsi, sciogliersi; (fam.) *to — (oneself)*, riscaldarsi; (fig.) diventare più cordiale. **-ing** *n.* disgelo; scioglimento.

**the** *def. art. sing.m.* il, lo l'; *f.* la, l'; *pl.m.* i, gli; *f.* le; *at* —, *to* —, *sing.m.* al, allo, all'; *f.* alla, all'; *pl.m.* ai, agli; *f.* alle; *of* —, *sing.m.* del, dello, dell'; *f.* della, dell'; *pl.m.* dei, degli; *f.* delle; *in* —, *sing.m.* nel, nello, nell'; *f.* nella nell'; *pl.m.* nei, negli; *f.* nelle; *from (or by)* —, *sing.m.* dal, dallo, dall'; *f.* dalla, dall'; *pl.m.* dai, dagli; *f.* dalle; *with* —, *sing.m.* col, con il, con lo, collo, con l', coll'; *f.* con la, colla; *pl.m.* coi, con i, con gli, cogli; *f.* con le, colle; (N.B. collo, coll', colla, cogli, colle are now becoming obsolete); (in titles of monarchs omitted in Ital.) *Elizabeth the Second*, Elisabetta seconda; *all — better*, tanto meglio; *so much — worse*, tanto peggio; — *more* . . . — *more*, (quanto) più . . . (tanto) più; — *sooner — better*, più presto e meglio è; (emphatic) il grande, il celebre, il noto, il migliore; *a certain Charles Dickens, not* 'the' *Dickens*, un certo Carlo Dickens, non il grande Dickens.

**theatre** *n.* teatro; *to go to the* —, andare a teatro; *open-air* —, teatro all'aperto; *picture* —, cinematografo, cinema *m.*; *news* —, cineattualità *m.*; (the drama) teatro, arte drammatica; (fig.) teatro, scena, luogo; — *of war*, teatro di guerra, (mil.) zona di guerra; (med.) *operating* —, sala operatoria.

**theatre-bill** *n.* cartellone.

**theatre-goer** *n.* frequent tore di teatri, appassionato del teatro. **-land** *n.* quartiere *m.* dei teatri.

**theatrical** *adj.* teatrale, del teatro, scenico; — *works*, opere drammatiche, teatro; *n.pl.* spet-

tacoli drammatici, rappresentazioni teatrali; *amateur -s*, spettacoli filodrammatici; (fig.) teatrale, melodrammatico, istrionico; pomposo affettato. **-ity, -ness** *n.* teatralità.

**Thebes** *pr.n.* (geog.) Tebe; *The Seven against —*, I sette a Tebe.

**thee** *prn.* ti, te; (after *prep.*) te.

**theft** *n.* furto, latrocinio, sottrazione; *to commit a —*, commettere un furto, rubare.

**their** *poss. adj.* il loro, la loro, i loro, le loro; *— brother*, (il) loro fratello; *— mother*, (la) loro madre; *they have hurt — hands*, si sono fatti male alle mani; (loosely = his) suo, sua, suoi, sue; *if everybody minded — own business*, se ognuno badasse ai suoi affari; *Their Majesties*, Loro Maiestà.

**theirs** *poss. prn.* il loro, la loro, i loro, le loro; di loro; *a friend of —*, un loro amico; *it's no business of —*, non è affare loro.

**the-ism** *n.* (theol.) teismo. **-ist** *n.* teista *m., f.*

**them** *pr.n. m.* li, *f.* le; *m., f.* loro; (after *prep.*) *m.* essi, *f.* esse, *m., f.* loro; *one of —*, uno di loro, uno di essi, uno dei due; *neither of —*, nè l'uno nè l'altro; *none of —*, nessuno di loro; *both of — saw me*, tutti e due (*or* entrambi) mi hanno visto; (with *rfl.* sense) sè; *they have taken the keys with —*, hanno portato le chiavi con sè; (fam.) *it's —*, sono loro.

**thematic** *adj.* (gramm.; mus.) tematico.

**theme** *n.* tema *m.*, soggetto, argomento, materia; (schol.) tema, composizione; (mus.) tema, motivo, aria; (gramm.) tema, radice *f.*

**theme-song** *n.* sigla.

**themselves** *prn. rfl.* si, se stessi; *they asked — why*, si domandarono perchè; *by —*, da soli; *they are masters of —*, sono padroni di se stessi; (provb.) *God helps those who help —*, chi si aiuta il ciel l'aiuta; (emph.) *they —*, essi stessi; *the professors —*, gli stessi professori.

**then** *adj.* di allora, di quel tempo; *the — Prime Minister*, il Primo Ministro di allora, l'allora Presidente del Consiglio; as a *n.* allora *m.*, quel tempo; *before —*, prima di allora; *between now and —*, di qui ad allora; *by —*, a quel tempo, a quell'epoca; *from — on*, *since —*, da allora, d'allora in poi; *till —*, *until —*, fino allora, fino a quel tempo; *every now and —*, ogni tanto, di quando in quando, di tanto in tanto; *adv.* allora, a quel tempo, a quell'epoca; *there and —*, subito, immediatamente; *now and —*, ogni tanto; dopo, poi, quindi; *what —?*, e poi?, e allora?; *I went to Turin and — to Milan*, sono andato a Torino e poi a Milano; poi, inoltre, anche; *conj.* dunque, allora, in questo caso; *you knew all the while, —?*, dunque lo sapevi già?; *well —?*, dunque?, ebbene?; *if he doesn't come, — ring him up*, se non viene, allora dagli un colpo di telefono; *but —*, però, tuttavia.

**thence** *adv.* di là, quindi; perciò, quindi, pertanto. **-forth, -forward** *adv.* da allora in poi, quindi.

**Theobald** *pr.n.* Teobaldo, Tebaldo.

**theocr-acy** *n.* teocrazia. **-at** *n.* teocratico, teocrate *m.* **-atic** *adj.* teocratico.

**Theocritus** *pr.n.* Teocrito.

**theodolite** *n.* teodolito, teodolite *m.*

**Theodora** *pr.n.* Teodora.

**Theodore** *pr.n.* Teodoro.

**Theodoric** *pr.n.* (hist.) Teodorico.

**theogony** *n.* teogonia.

**theologian** *n.* teologo.

**theolog-y** *n.* teologia. **-ical** *adj.* teologico; *the -ical virtues*, le virtù teologali; *-ical college*, seminario.

**Theophilus** *pr.n.* Teofilo.

**theorem** *n.* teorema *m.*

**theoretic-(al)** *adj.* teoretico, teorico, accademico. **-ian** *n.* teorico. **-s** *n.* teorica, parte teorica.

**theorist** *n.* teorico.

**theoriz-e** *tr., intr.* teorizzare, formulare delle teorie. **-ing** *n.* formulazione di teorie, ideologia, speculazione.

**theory** *n.* teoria, dottrina, tesi *f.*; *in —*, in teoria, teoricamente; *the — that*, la teoria secondo la quale; (fam.) idea, nozione.

**theosoph-y** *n.* teosofia. **-ist** *n.* teosofista *m., f.*

**therapeut-ic(al)** *adj.* terapeutico. **-ics** *n.* terapeutica. **-ist** *n.* terapeuta *m.*

**therapy** *n.* terapia; *occupational —*, terapia di rieducazione.

**there** *adv.* lì, là, laggiù, di là, da quella parte, in quel luogo; (lit.) colà; *in —*, là dentro; *from —*, di là, quindi; *on —*, là sopra, lassù; *over —*, di là, laggiù; *under —*, là sotto, laggiù; *up —*, lassù, là sopra; *here and —*, qua e là; *— and back*, andata e ritorno; *— and then*, subito, lì per lì; seduta stante; *pass along —!*, avanti signori!, circolate per favore!; (fam.) *he is not quite all —*, gli manca un venerdì; *he's all —*, è un tipo sveglio, è in gamba; (with *aux. verb*) ci, vi; *— is*, c'è, vi è; *— are*, ci sono, vi sono; *who's —?*, chi c'è?, chi è là?; *is anybody —?*, c'è qualcuno?, non c'è nessuno?; *— he is*, eccolo; *— you are*, eccoti; *— we are*, eccoci; *— is some*, ce n'è; *— are some*, ce ne sono; *— are none*, non ce ne sono; *— will be*, ci sarà; *— may be*, ci può essere, può darsi che ci sia; *— must be*, ci deve essere; *— was no stopping her*, non ci fu modo di fermarla; *— he goes again*, eccolo che ricomincia; *there's the rub!*, qui sta il difficile!, ecco il guaio!; *—'s a dear!*, su bravo!; *excl.* ecco!, su!; *— now!*, ecco!; *so —!*, e basta!, ecco fatto!

**there-about(s)** *adv.* là vicino, là intorno, da quelle parti; all'incirca, circa, pressappoco. **-after** *adj.* dopo di ciò, in seguito, indi, quindi, poscia. **-at** *adv.* a quel proposito, di ciò, di questo; *they wondered greatly -at*, ci si meravigliarono molto. **-by** *adv.* perciò, da ciò, così? in tal modo, quindi; *-by hangs a tale*, a questo proposito c'è tutta una storia. **-fore** *adv.* dunque, perciò, per questa ragione, per conseguenza, quindi, onde, laonde. **-from** *adv.* da ciò, da questo; *it follows -from that*, ne consegue che. **-in** *adv.* in ciò, in questo, a questo proposito; (là) dentro; entro; ci, vi; in merito. **-of** *adv.* di ciò, di questo; ne; *they ate -of*, ne mangiarono; *in lieu -of*, invece (di questo). **-on** *adv.* su di ciò, sopra di esso.

**Theresa** *pr.n.* Teresa.

**there-to** *adv.* a ciò, ivi, vi; (moreover) inoltre. **-tofore** *adv.* prima di allora, precedentemente. **-under** *adv.* là sotto, a tal proposito. **-upon** *adv.* su di ciò, al che, quindi, subito dopo; (lit.) a questo proposito. **-with** *adv.* con ciò, con questo; in più; subito dopo, quindi; (comm.) *enclosed -with*, ivi allegato. **-withal** *n.* con tutto ciò, inoltre, in più.

**therm** *n.* (phys.) caloria; (industr.) unità di calore.

**therm-al** *adj.* termale; *-al baths*, terme *f.pl.*; (phys.) termico, termale, calorifico; *-al unit*, unità di misura del calore. **-ic** *adj.* (phys.) termico, termale, calorifico.

**Thermidor** *n.* (Fr. hist.) termidoro.

**thermogene** *n.* ouatta termogena.

**thermometer** *n.* termometro.

**Thermopylae** *pr.n.* (geog.) Termopili *f.*

**thermos** *n.* *— flask*, termos *m.*, bottiglia termos.

**thermostat** *n.* termostato, termoregolatore. **-ic** *adj.* termostatico.

**thesaurus** *n.* tesoro, florilegio, repertorio lessicale.

**these** *dem. adj. prn. m.* questi, queste; cf. **this**.

**Theseus** *pr.n.* (myth.) Teseo.

**thesis** *n.* tesi *f.*; dissertazione; *degree —*, tesi di laurea.

**Thespian** *adj.* di Tespi, drammatico; *the — art*, il dramma, il teatro.

**Thessalonica** *pr.n.* (geog.) Tessalonica.
**Thessaly** *pr.n.* (geog.) Tessaglia.
**theta** *n.* (Gk.) teta.
**Thetis** *pr.n.* (myth.) Teti, Tetide.
**theurg-ic(al)** *adj.* teurgico. **-ist** *n.* teurgo.
**thews** *n.* muscoli *m.pl.*, tendini *m.pl.*, nervi *m.pl.*; (fig.) forza muscolare; *all — and sinews*, tutto nervi e muscoli.
**they** *pers. prn.* essi *m.*, esse *f.*, loro *m.*, *f.*, coloro *m.*, *f.*, costoro, quelli; (N.B. Normally omitted in Ital. except when emphatic; *e.g. — did it*, l'hanno fatto loro); *here — are*, eccoli; *do you know who — are ?*, sai chi sono ?; *— who*, coloro che, quelli che; *indef.* si; *— say that*, si dice che, dicono che; *— told me that*, mi si disse che.
**thick** *adj.* spesso; *three feet —*, dello spessore di tre piedi; *how — is the ice ?*, quanto è spesso il ghiaccio ?; grosso; pesante; folto, fitto, denso; serrato, compatto, consistente, viscoso; torbido; (of voice) rauco, velato; (of weather) coperto, nebbioso, brumoso, fosco; (of fog) denso, fitto; ottuso, stupido, intontito; *— or clear soup*, minestra o brodo; *to grow thick(er)*, diventare (più) spesso, inspessirsi, addensarsi, affittirsi, affoltire; (fig.) *to have a — skin*, essere insensibile, essere duro; (fam.) *that's a bit — !*, questa è grossa, questo è un po' troppo; *— as thieves*, amici per la pelle; *to be very — with*, essere molto intimo con, andare molto d'accordo con; (fam.) *to give someone a — ear*, conciare qualcuno per le feste; *adv.* a strati spessi; *to cut the bread —*, tagliare il pane a fette grosse; *snow is lying — on the ground*, uno spesso strato di neve copre il suolo; *bodies were lying — on the ground*, il terreno era sparso di cadaveri; *to lay it on —*, rincarare la dose; *n. in the — of the battle*, nel folto della mischia; *through — and thin*, nella buona e nella cattiva sorte, fedelissimamente.
**thicken** *tr.* ispessire, addensare, affittire, ingrossare; *intr.* ispessirsi, addensarsi, affittirsi, ingrossarsi, affoltire; (fig.) *the plot -s*, la trama si complica. **-er** *n.* (chem.) concentratore, condensatore; (cul.) sostanza che lega, legante *m.* **-ing** *n.* ispessimento, ingrossamento, il diventare più fitto; (cul.) legamento.
**thicket** *n.* boschetto, macchia folta, gruppo di alberi.
**thick-headed** *adj.* (fam.) ottuso, tonto, stupido, duro. **-lipped** *adj.* dalle labbra grosse.
**thickness** *n.* spessore *m.*, altezza, grossezza; densità; nebbiosità, foschia, oscurità; strato.
**thickset** *adj.* folto, fitto; (fig.) tarchiato, tozzo, atticciato.
**thick-skinned** *adj.* dalla pelle dura; insensibile, non suscettibile, indifferente, duro.
**thick-skulled, thick-witted** *adj.* See **thick-headed.**
**thief** *n.* ladro, ladruncolo, ladrone *m.*; *stop — !*, al ladro!; *hotel —*, topo d'albergo; *set a — to catch a —*, per conoscere un furbo ci vuole un furbo e mezzo; *thick as thieves*, amici per la pelle; *there is honour among thieves*, cane non mangia cane; *thieves' kitchen*, covo di ladri.
**thiev-e** *tr.* rubare; *intr.* fare il ladro. **-ing** *adj.* ladro, che ruba, ladresco; *n.* il rubare, ruberia, latrocinio, ladroneria.
**thievery** *n.* see **thieving.**
**thigh** *n.* (anat.) coscia; *to smite someone hip and —*, bastonare qualcuno di santa ragione.
**thigh-bone** *n.* (anat.) femore *m.*; *— socket*, acetabolo. **-boots** *n.* cosciali *m.pl.*
**thimble** *n.* ditale *m.* **-ful** *n.* quanto sta in un ditale, dito.
**thin** *adj.* sottile, fine; *— as a wafer*, sottile come un velo di cipolla; magro, snello; *— as a lath*, magro come un chiodo; *to grow —*, (of person) dimagrire, (of thing) rassottigliarsi; rarefatto; *to vanish into — air*, dileguarsi, svanire senza lasciar traccia; rado, scarso, sparso; (fam.) *he is growing — on top*, gli si diradano i capelli; diluito, esile; povero, impoverito; debole, fievole; *to cut the bread —*, tagliare il pane a fette sottili; *a — slice*, una fettuccina; *— soup*, brodino; (fig.) *to be on — ice*, toccare un argomento delicato; (fam.) *to have a — time*, passarsela piuttosto brutta; *a — excuse*, una magra scusa.
**thin** *tr.* assottigliare, diradare, sfoltire, affinare; allungare; *to — out*, diradare, dicioccare; *intr.* assottigliarsi, dimagrire, diradarsi, sfoltire.
**thine** *poss. prn.* il tuo, la tua; *pl.* i tuoi, le tue; cf. **thy**; *what is mine is —*, quel che è mio è tuo.
**thing** *n.* cosa, oggetto; affare *m.*; *a — of beauty*, una bellissima cosa, una bellezza; *give me that —*, dammi quella cosa; *there's a — I want to talk to you about*, c'è una cosa di cui voglio parlarti; *for one —*, in primo luogo; *for another —*, d'altra parte; *to know a — or two*, saperla lunga; *what with one — and another*, con tutte queste faccende; *that's the very — I wanted*, è proprio quel che volevo; *to make a good — out of*, fare un bell'affare con; *it's the latest —*, è l'ultima moda; *the most important — is*, l'importante è; *the — is to find a way out*, l'essenziale è di trovare una via d'uscita; *it isn't the —*, non si fa così, non conviene; *how could you do such a — ?*, come hai potuto fare una cosa simile ?; *that was a silly — to do*, è stata una stupidaggine; (pejor.) *what's that — you're reading?*, che razza di libro stai leggendo ?; *here's a nice — !*, che bell'affare!; (fam.) *poor — !*, povera creatura!; *she's a dear little — !*, è un tesoro!; *I'm not feeling quite the —*, mi sento un po' giù di corda; *pl.* roba; *where can I put my -s ?*, dove posso mettere la mia roba ?; *to take off one's -s*, spogliarsi, svestirsi; *-s for writing*, il necessario per scrivere; *tea -s*, servizio da tè; *to clear away the —*, sparecchiare (la tavola); *-s are going badly*, le cose stanno prendendo una brutta piega; *to keep -s going*, mandare avanti la baracca; *well, of all -s !*, chi l'avrebbe mai detto!; *to expect great -s*, avere grandi speranze; *as -s are*, come stanno le cose; *how are -s with you ?*, come va la vita ?.
**thingamy, thingamabob, thingummy** *n.* (fam.) coso, affare *m.*; (of person) quel tale, quel tizio.
**think** *n.* (fam.) *to have a quiet —*, pensarci, rifletterci.
**think** *tr.*, *intr.* pensare, riflettere, ragionare; *I — therefore I am*, penso dunque sono; *to — aloud*, pensare a voce alta; *to — hard*, pensarci bene, riflettere a lungo, (fam.) rompersi la testa; *to — no harm*, non pensare di fare male; *let me —*, lasciami pensare; *I — she is very nice*, lo trovo simpatica; *I have been -ing that*, mi è venuto in mente che; credere, pensare, ritenere, giudicare; *do you — you can manage it ?*, credi di poterlo fare ?; *to — so*, pensare di sì; *I think so*, mi pare, mi sembra; *I can hardly — so*, mi sembra poco probabile; *to — not*, pensare di no; *to — well of*, pensare bene di; *to — ill of*, pensare male di; *it makes you —*, fa pensare, dà da pensare; *he always -s he's right*, crede sempre di aver ragione; credere, figurarsi, dire; *just — !*, figurati!; *you might — we were in Italy*, si direbbe che siamo in Italia; *one would have thought that*, si avrebbe detto che; *who would have thought it ?*, chi l'avrebbe detto ?; *I wouldn't — of doing it*, non c'è nemmeno da pensarci, non mi sogno di farlo; *you can't — how sorry I am*, non puoi figurarti quanto sia spiacente; *I little thought to see you again*, non mi aspettavo di rivederti; *to — a lot of oneself*, avere una grande opinione di sè, ritenersi chissà chi; *to — about*,

*to — of*, pensare a; *I have other things to — about*, ho altre cose a cui pensare; *I was -ing of you*, pensavo a te; *— of the time it would take*, pensa al tempo che ci vorrebbe; *what do you — of him?*, cosa pensi di lui?, come lo trovi?; *— of my surprise*, figurati la mia sorpresa; *I can't — of her name*, non mi ricordo il suo nome, mi sfugge il suo nome; *when you come to — of it*, quando ci si pensa; *it isn't worth -ing about*, non vale la pena di pensarci; *to — of doing something*, pensare di fare qualcosa; *to be well thought of*, essere ben visto; *to — out*, escogitare, trovare; *to — over*, riflettere, ripensare, ponderare; *after -ing it over*, dopo averci ripensato; *to — up*, escogitare.

**thinkable** *adj.* pensabile, concepibile, immaginabile, credibile, ammissibile.

**thinker** *n.* pensatore; *free-thinker*, libero pensatore.

**thinking** *adj.* pensante, ragionevole; *n.* pensiero, il pensare, meditazione, riflessione; *way of —*, avviso, modo di vedere; *to my way of —*, a mio avviso, secondo me; *to do some hard —*, riflettere bene, pensarci seriamente.

**thin-lipped** *adj.* dalle labbra sottili; (fig.) severo, austero.

**thinner** *adj.* comp. of **thin**, *q.v.*

**thinner** *n.* (usu. *pl.*) (chem.; techn.) diluente *m.*, solvente *m.*

**thinness** *n.* sottigliezza, tenuità, finezza; (of person) magrezza, esilità; (of hair, *etc.*) radezza (of air, *etc.*) rarefazione, leggerezza; (of liquid) fluidità; (fig.) debolezza.

**thinning** *n.* assottigliamento, dimagrimento; *— out*, diradamento.

**thinnish** *adj.* piuttosto sottile; magrolino, magretto; piuttosto rado.

**thin-skinned** *adj.* dalla pelle delicata; (fig.) sensibile, permaloso, suscettibile.

**third** *ord. num.* terzo; *Edward the Third*, Edoardo terzo; (*on*) *the — of December*, il tre dicembre; *every — year*, ogni tre anni; *on the — floor*, al terzo piano; (gramm.) *— person*, terza persona; (leg.) *— party*, terzi *m.pl.*; *— party insurance*, assicurazione per danni contro terzi; *— degree*, interrogatorio di terzo grado; *— finger*, (dito) anulare *m.*; (pol.) *the Third Estate*, il Terzo Stato; *the Third World*, il Terzo Mondo; (motor.) *— gear*, terza marcia, terza velocità; *n.* terzo, terza parte; *two -s*, due terzi; (mus.) terza. **-ly** *adv.* in terzo luogo.

**third-class** *adj.* di terza classe; (of hotel) di terza categoria; (pejor.) scadente, di qualità inferiore. **-hand** *adj.* di terza mano. **-rate** *adj.* scadente, di pessima qualità, da strapazzo, mediocre.

**thirst** *n.* sete *f.* arsura; (fig.) *— for*, sete di, smania di, bramosia di, avidità di; *intr.* aver sete, soffrire la sete; *to — after*, avere sete di, aver voglia di bere, bramare, ambire. **-iness** *n.* sete *f.*, arsura. **-ing** *adj.* assetato, avido, bramoso, sitibondo. **-y** *adj.* assetato; (fig.) avido, bramoso; *to be -y*, aver sete; (fig.) *to be -y for*, aver sete di, essere assetato di, bramare, aver voglia di, ambire; (of soil) arido, secco, arso, sitibondo.

**thirteen** *card. num.* tredici; *to be — (years old)*, essere tredicenne, aver tredici anni; *to be — (at table)*, essere in tredici (a tavola); (fam.) *to talk — to the dozen*, parlare a vanvera, fare una lungagnata. **-th** *ord. num.* tredicesimo, decimoterzo; (*on*) *the -th of December*, il tredici dicembre; *the -th century*, il secolo decimoterzo, il duecento, il dugento; *of the -th century*, duecentesco, dugentesco; *n.* tredicesimo, tredicesima parte; (mus.) decimaterza.

**thirtieth** *ord. num.* trentesimo; (*on*) *the — of December*, il trenta dicembre.

**thirty** *card. num.* trenta; *about —*, una trentina; *to be — (years old)*, essere trentenne, aver trent'anni; *to be over —*, aver superato la trentina, aver più di trent'anni; *in the thirties*, fra il 'trenta e il 'quaranta, nella quarta decade del secolo; (of person) *to be in one's early thirties*, essere sulla trentina; *to be in one's late thirties*, essere sulla quarantina; (provb. phr.) *— pieces of silver*, i trenta denari.

**thirty-first** *ord. num.* trentunesimo, trentesimo primo; (*on*) *the — of December*, il trentun dicembre. **-one** *card. num. adj.* trentuno. **-second** *ord. num. adj.* trentaduesimo, trentesimo secondo. **-two** *card. num.* trentadue.

**this** *dem. adj.* questo *m.*, questa, (lit.) codesto *m.*, codesta *f.*; *— morning*, questa mattina, stamattina, stamane; *— afternoon*, questo pomeriggio, oggi nel pomeriggio; *— evening*, questa sera, stasera; *— day week*, oggi a otto; *— day last year*, un anno fa come oggi, oggi un anno; *in — country*, qui (in Inghilterra), nel nostro paese, da noi; *— way!*, di qui!, di qua!; *— way and that*, di qua e di là; (comm.) *— letter*, la presente (lettera); (fam.) *— here book*, questo libro qui; *prn.* questo *m.*, questa *f.*; (referring to persons) questi *m.*, *f.*; (lit. and pejot.) costui *m.*, costei *f.*; *— is what he said*, questo è (*or* ecco) ciò che disse; *— is what I mean*, ecco quello che voglio dire; *to talk of — and that*, parlare del più e del meno; *to put — and that together*, trarre le conclusioni da sè.

**Thisbe** *pr.n.* Tisbe.

**thistl-e** *n.* (bot.) cardo selvatico, cardone *m.*, stoppione *m.* **-edown** *n.* carduccio, lanuggine del cardo. **-y** *adj.* pieno di cardi, spinoso, pungente.

**thither** *adj.* ulteriore, più lontano; *adv.* colà, là, da quella parte; *hither and —*, qua e là, di qua e di là.

**tho'** *conj.* see **though**.

**Thomas** *pr.n.* Tommaso; *St. — Aquinas*, San Tommaso d'Aquino, il Dottor Angelico; *to be a doubting —*, fare come San Tommaso.

**Thom-ism** *n.* (philos.) tomismo, scolasticismo tomistico. **-ist** *n.* tomista *m.*, *f.* **-istic(al)** *adj.* tomistico.

**thong** *n.* correggia, cinghia, striscia di cuoio; sferzino; *tr.* fornire di correggia, assicurare con cinghia.

**thor-ax** *n.* (anat.) torace *m.* **-acic** *adj.* toracico, del torace.

**thorn** *n.* spina, spino, aculeo, pungiglione *m.*; *no rose without a —*, non c'è rosa senza spine; *to be on -s*, stare sulle spine; *a — in the flesh*, una spina nel cuore. **-bush** *n.* spineto, biancospino.

**thorn-hedge** *n.* siepe di biancospino.

**thorn-y** *adj.* spinoso; dumoso. **-iness** *n.* spinosità.

**thorough** *adj.* minuzioso, accurato; profondo, completo; *a — change*, un cambiamento radicale; coscienzioso, diligente, preciso; *to be — in one's work*, lavorare coscienziosamente; *to give a room a — cleaning*, pulire ben bene una stanza; (fig.) *a — scoundrel*, un briccone matricolato. **-bred** *adj.* di puro sangue, di razza; *n.* purosangue *m.*, *f.* **-fare** *n.* via pubblica, via di transito, arteria di grande traffico, via principale; *no -fare!*, divieto di transito!, vicolo cieco. **-going** *adj.* coscienzioso, meticoloso; completo, radicale, accurato. **-ness** *n.* accuratezza, meticolosità, coscienziosità; perfezione.

**those** *dem. adj. prn. m.* quei, quegli, quelli; *f.* quelle; *cf.* **that**.

**thou** *prn.* tu.

**though** *adv.* però, tuttavia, comunque; *conj.* benchè, sebbene, quantunque, ancorchè, tuttochè, per quanto; *as —*, come se, che; *even —*, anche se; *what —*, che importa se; *it looks as —*, sembra che; *strange — it may seem*, per quanto strano sembri.

**thought** *n.* pensiero; medita-

zione, riflessione; idea; parere *m.*, opinione; *a happy —*, una buona idea, una trovata; *the mere — of it*, solo a pensarci; *on second -s*, ripensandoci; *second -s are best*, è sempre meglio riflettere; *his one — is*, non pensa che a; *have you ever given it a —?*, ci hai mai pensato?; *to collect one's -s*, raccogliere le proprie idee, ripensarci; *to give up all — of*, rinunciare all'idea di; *to keep one's -s to oneself*, non fiatare, star zitto, non rivelare il proprio pensiero; *to be lost in —*, starsene meditabondo; *to read someone's -s*, leggere nel pensiero di qualcuno; *to take — how to do something*, riflettere sul come fare qualcosa; *to take no — for the morrow*, non preoccuparsi del domani; (fam.) *a —*, (*foll.* by *adj.* or *adv.*) un tantino, un pochino.

**thought** *p.def.*, *part.* of **think**, *q.v.*; *well — of*, ben visto.

**thoughtful** *adj.* pensieroso, pensoso, meditabondo, riflessivo; prudente; premuroso, sollecito, gentile, riguardoso, pieno di riguardi; *it was very — of him to do that*, era molto gentile da parte sua di fare così; profondo, ricco di pensiero. **-ly** *adv.* pensosamente; premurosamente, gentilmente. **-ness** *n.* meditazione, riflessione, raccoglimento; premura, sollecitudine *f.*, gentilezza, riguardo.

**thoughtless** *adj.* spensierato, sconsiderato, sventato; imprudente, avventato, irriflessivo, senza riflessione, noncurante; poco riguardoso, poco gentile, senza riguardo. **-ness** *n.* spensieratezza, sconsideratezza, sventatezza, noncuranza, leggerezza, mancanza di riguardo.

**thought-reading** *n.* lettura del pensiero, telepatia.

**thousand** *card. num.* mille; *one —*, mille; *two —*, duemila; *one — and one*, milleuno; *1972*, millenovecentosettantadue; *n.* migliaio; *pl.* migliaia *f.pl.*; *a — pounds*, mille sterline, un migliaio di sterline; *-s of pounds*, migliaia di sterline; *a thousand-lire note*, un biglietto da mille; *by -s*, a migliaia; (fam.) *I've told you -s of times*, ti ho detto mille volte. **-fold** *adj.* moltiplicato per mille; *adv.* mille volte tanto. **-th** *ord. num.* millesimo; *n.* millesimo, millesima parte; *for the -th time*, per l'ennesima volta.

**thraldom** *n.* servitù, servaggio, schiavitù.

**thrall** *n.* servo, schiavo; *to be kept in —*, essere schiavo, essere asservito.

**thrash** *tr.* battere, percuotere; bastonare, sferzare; (agric.) see **thresh**; *to — someone soundly*, bastonare qualcuno a santa ragione; (swimming) *to — the water*, battere l'acqua; *intr.* battere; (mech.) vibrare; (fig.) *to — out*, discutere a fondo; *to — out the truth*, scoprire la verità. **-ing** *n.* bastonatura, legnata; *to give someone a good -ing*, bastonare qualcuno a santa ragione; (sport) sconfitta, batosta; (of waves, rain) battito.

**thread** *n.* filo; refe *m.*; filato, filamento; (of screw) filetto; *darning —*, filo da rammendo; (fig.) *the — of an argument*, il filo di un discorso; *the — of life*, la trama della vita; *to hold on to life by a —*, reggere l'anima con i denti; *to gather up the -s*, raccogliere i fili; *to hang by a —*, essere sospeso da un filo; (fam.) *not to have a — to wear*, non avere nulla da indossare; *tr.* infilare; (screw, etc.) filettare; (fig.) *to — one's way through the crowd*, farsi strada tra la folla; (of hair) *to be -ed with white*, essere striato di bianco. **-bare** *adj.* logoro, liso, consumato, consunto, frusto; (fig.) trito, banale. **-ed** *adj.* infilato; (of screw) filettato. **-like** *adj.* filiforme. **-y** *adj.* filamentoso, filaccioso, fibroso; (of voice) esile, sottile; (med.) filiforme.

**threat** *n.* minaccia; *a — to*, una minaccia per; *empty -s*, minacce vane; *to carry out a —*, mettere in atto una minaccia; *to utter a —*, profferire una minaccia, minacciare.

**threaten** *tr.*, *intr.* minacciare, profferire minacce, fare delle minacce; *to — someone with something*, minacciare qualcuno di qualcosa. **-ing** *adj.* minaccioso, minacciante, minatorio; incombente, imminente; *a -ing letter*, una lettera minatoria.

**three** *card. num.* tre; *— o'clock*, le tre; *— times as much*, tre volte tanto; *3 per cent War Loan*, prestito di guerra al tre per cento; *to be — (in number)*, essere in (numero di) tre.

**three-act** *adj.* (theatr.) in tre atti. **-cornered** *adj.* triangolare (also fig.); *-cornered hat*, tricorno, cappello a tre punte, (eccl.) nicchio. **-dimensional** *adj.* tridimensionale. **-engined** *adj.* (aeron.) *-engined aeroplane*, trimotore *m.*

**threefold** *adj.* triplice, triplo; *adv.* tre volte tanto, in modo triplice.

**three-handed** *adj.* *— game*, partita a tre. **-legged** *adj.* a tre gambe, a tre piedi; *-legged stool*, treppiedi *m.* **-phase** *adj.* (electr.) trifase. **-ply** *adj.* a tre spessori, a tre fili; *-ply wood*, legno compensato a tre strati; *-ply wool*, lana a tre capi. **-pointed** *adj.* a tre punte, tridentato, tricuspide. **-quarter** *adj.* a tre quarti; (art) *-quarter face portrait*, ritratto da tre quarti; *n.* (rugby) trequarti *m.* **-quarters** *adv.* a tre quarti, al settantacinque per cento; *-quarters full*, a tre quarti pieno.

**threescore** *adj.* sessanta; *— and ten*, settanta.

**three-speed** *adj.* a tre velocità. **-storied, -story** *adj.* a tre piani. **-wheeled** *adj.* a tre ruote, triciclo.

**threnody** *n.* trenodia, epicedio.

**thresh** *tr.* (agric.) trebbiare, battere; (fig.) battere, sferzare. **-er** *n.* (agric.) battitore; (machine) trebbiatrice; (ichth.) *-er whale*, alopia, volpe *f.* di mare. **-ing** *n.* (agric.) trebbiatura, battitura.

**threshing-floor** *n.* aia.

**threshold** *n.* soglia, entrata, porta; (fig.) inizio, esordio, orlo.

**threw** *p.def.* of **throw**, *q.v.*

**thrice** *adv.* tre volte; *— as much*, tre volte tanto; (fig.) *— told*, detto e ridetto.

**thrift** *n.* frugalità; economia, risparmio; (bot.) statice *f.*; *sea —*, armeria marittima, spilli *m.pl.* di dama.

**thriftless** *adj.* prodigo, spendereccio, scialacquatore; noncurante, imprevidente. **-ness** *n.* prodigalità, scialacquo; spreco.

**thrifty** *adj.* frugale, parco, parsimonioso, previdente; *to be —* fare economia.

**thrill** *n.* brivido, fremito, palpito; emozione; *it gave me quite a —*, mi ha proprio elettrizzato; *tr.* far rabbrividire, far fremere, far trasalire; emozionare, elettrizzare, entusiasmare; *to be -ed*, fremere, trasalire; *to be -ed with something*, essere entusiasta di qualcosa; *intr.* fremere, trasalire, vibrare, tremare. **-er** *n.* romanzo poliziesco, (pop.) giallo; film sensazionale, dramma *m.* sensazionale. **-ing** *adj.* che fa rabbrividire; emozionante, sensazionale, impressionante, appassionante; vibrante, squillante.

**thrive** *intr.* fiorire, prosperare; aver successo, riuscire, far fortuna; *to — on*, crescere vigorosamente; (fig.) approfittare da; (bot.) allignare, dilettare, lussureggiare.

**thriving** *adj.* fiorente, florido; rigoglioso, lussureggiante; prospero, prosperoso.

**throat** *n.* gola, strozza; collo; (of chimney) gola; (of tube) strozzatura; *a lump in one's —*, un nodo alla gola; *sore —*, mal di gola; *to clear one's —*, schiarirsi la gola; *to seize by the —*, prendere per il collo; *to thrust something down someone's —*, imporre una opinione a qualcuno.

**throat-y** *adj.* (of voice) gutturale, di gola. **-iness** *n.* qualità gutturale.

**throb** *n.* battito, pulsare *m.*, pulsazione, vibrazione; rombo; (fig.) fremito, palpito; *to give a —*, palpitare, fremere; *intr.* battere; pulsare; vibrare; rombare; (fig.) fremere; palpitare. **-bing** *adj.* palpitante, pulsante; vibrante; fremente.

**throes** *n.* doglie *f.pl.*, spasimi *m.pl.*; (of death) agonia; (fig.) *to be in the — of*, essere nel travaglio di, essere alle prese con.

**thrombosis** *n.* (med.) trombosi *f.*

**throne** *n.* trono; *to ascend the —*, salire al trono. **-ed** *adj.* seduto sul trono, troneggiante.

**throng** *n.* folla, calca, ressa, turba; moltitudine *f.*; *tr.* affollare, riempire, ingombrare; *intr.* affollarsi, accalcarsi, stiparsi, accorrere. **-ing** *adj.* compatto, serrato.

**throstle** *m.* (poet.) tordo bottaccio.

**throttle** *n.* (anat.) gola, trachea, strozza; valvola regolatrice di flusso, valvola a farfalla; (aeron.; motor.; rlwy.) leva di controllo (del flusso); *tr.* strozzare, strangolare, soffocare; (techn.) strozzare, controllare, regolare; *intr. to — down*, rallentare.

**through** *adj.* diretto; *— ticket*, biglietto di corrispondenza; *— carriage*, vettura diretta; *— traffic*, transito, veicoli in transito; *no — road!*, vicolo cieco!; (fam.) finito; *adv.* attraverso, da una parte all'altra, da banda a banda, sino alla fine; *to be wet —*, essere bagnato fino alle ossa; *to be — with*, averne abbastanza di; *I'm —*, basta!, ho finito!; *to book — to Milan*, prendere un biglietto diretto per Milano; *to book one's luggage — to Rome*, spedire i bagagli direttamente a Roma; *to carry —*, portare a termine; *to let —*, lasciare passare; *to pour —*, passare; *to read —*, leggere fino in fondo; *to read — and —*, leggere e rileggere; *to run someone —*, trafiggere qualcuno; *I'll see you —*, ti aiuterò io; (fam.) *to see it —*, andare fino in fondo; (teleph.) *to get —*, ottenere la comunicazione; *to put — to*, mettere in comunicazione con; *please put me — to Mr. X*, mi faccia parlare col signor X; *I'll put you — to Mr. X's secretary*, Le dò la segretaria del signor X.

**through** *prep.* attraverso, da una parte all'altra di, fra, per, sino alla fine di; durante, per tutta la durata di; per, per mezzo di, a causa di, per tramite di, grazie a; *— illness*, per malattia; *— fear*, per paura; *— a misunderstanding*, per un malinteso; *— the ages*, da sempre, attraverso i secoli; *all — the day*, per tutta la giornata, da mattina a sera; *— thick and thin*, nella buona e nella cattiva sorte, in qualsiasi caso, in ogni circostanza; *to be halfway — something*, essere a metà di qualcosa; *to be on one's way — London*, essere di passaggio a Londra; (fam.) *to have been — a lot*, averne passato di tutti i colori; *to go — something*, andare attraverso qualcosa; *to go — someone's papers*, frugare fra le carte di qualcuno; *to get — one's work*, portare a termine, sbrigare, il lavoro; sbrigare qualcosa; *to get — a fortune*, dissipare una fortuna; *to look — a letter*, scorrere una lettera; *to look — a telescope*, guardare attraverso un cannochiale; *to pass — a town*, attraversare una città; *to pay — the nose for*, pagare profumatamente; *to put one's pen —*, cancellare con la penna; (fam.) *to put someone — it*, mettere qualcuno alle strette, far passare un brutto quarto d'ora a qualcuno; *to read — something*, leggere qualcosa sino alla fine; *to run —*, percorrere; *to run — with a sword*, trafiggere colla spada; *to run — a fortune*, dissipare una fortuna; (fig.) *to see —*, capire benissimo; *to sleep — a lecture*, dormire durante tutta una conferenza; *to walk — the fields*, camminare fra i campi; *to walk — a gate*, passare attraverso un cancello; *to wander — the woods*, vagare per i boschi.

**throughout** *adv.* completamente, interamente, da un capo all'altro; dappertutto; *to be wrong —*, aver torto su tutti i punti; per tutto il tempo, ininterrottamente, dal principio alla fine; *prep.* per tutto, durante tutto, in ogni parte di, da un capo all'altro di; *— the country*, in tutto il paese; *— his life*, durante tutta la sua vita, vita durante; *— the year*, per tutto l'anno.

**throve** *p.def.* of **thrive**, *q.v.*

**throw** *n.* lancio, tiro, colpo; gittata; *a — of dice*, un colpo di dadi; *your —!*, tocca a te!; *a long —*, un tiro lungo, *within a stone's —*, vicinissimo, a breve distanza, a un tiro di sasso; (fishing) colpo; *at the first —*, al primo colpo; (wrestling) messa a terra, l'atterrare (l'avversario); (geol.) rigetto, spostamento.

**throw** *tr.* gettare, lanciare, buttare, scagliare; tirare; (of horse) disarcionare, sbalzare di sella; (equit.) *to be -n*, essere disarcionato; (fam.) sconcertare; (vet.) figliare, partorire; (wrestling) *to — one's opponent*, atterrare l'avversario; (text.) torcere; (ceram.) tornire (vasi); *to — oneself on someone's generosity*, affidarsi alla generosità di qualcuno; *to — oneself into the fray*, lanciarsi nella mischia; *to — oneself at someone's head*, buttarsi fra le braccia di qualcuno; *to be -n on one's resources*, essere abbandonato a se stesso; *to be -n together*, incontrarsi spesso; *to — the blame on*, gettare la colpa su; *to — a bridge over a river*, gettare un ponte attraverso un fiume; *to — cold water on*, dare una doccia fredda a, scoraggiare; *to — into confusion*, confondere, sbaragliare; *to — dice*, gettare dadi; *to — a six*, fare un sei; *to — dust in someone's eyes*, gettare polvere negli occhi a qualcuno; *to — a fit*, cadere in convulsioni; *to — a glance at*, lanciare uno sguardo a; *to — someone a kiss*, gettare un bacio a qualcuno; *to — light on*, fare luce su; *to — a picture on the screen*, proiettare un'immagine sullo schermo; (fam.) *to — a party*, dare una festicciuola; *to — into prison*, mettere in prigione, incarcerare; *to — two rooms into one*, ridurre due stanze a una; *to — a shawl over one's shoulders*, buttarsi uno scialle sulle spalle; (fam.) *to — a spanner into the works*, mettere il bastone fra le ruote; *to — stones*, scagliare sassi; (provb.) *people who live in glass houses shouldn't — stones*, chi ha tegoli di vetro non tiri sassi al vicino; *to — temptation in someone's way*, esporre qualcuno alla tentazione. FOLLOW. BY ADV. OR PREP.: *to — about*, buttare qua e là, sparpagliare, seminare; *to — one's arms about*, agitare le braccia; *to — one's money about*, spendere a piene mani; *to — one's weight about*, darsi delle arie; *to be -n about*, essere sballottato; *to — aside*, buttar via; *to — away*, (cards) scartare; (of girl) *to — herself away*, sposare un uomo indegno di lei; *to — back*, rilanciare, (of mirror) riflettere, (mil.) respingere (il nemico); (fig.) *to be -n back on*, doversi accontentare di; *intr.* (biol.) regredire, essere soggetto a riversione; *to — down*, buttar giù, abbandonare, abbattere; *to — in*, buttar dentro, (sport) rimettere in giuoco, aggiungere, comprendere; *a room at three pounds with breakfast -n in*, una camera che costa tre sterline compresa la prima colazione; *to — in one's hand*, buttare le carte sulla tavola, (fig.) smettere, dare partita vinta; *to — one's lot in with*, unire la propria sorte a quella di, far causa comune con; (boxing) *to — in the towel*, gettare la spugna; *to — off*, emettere, mandare fuori, emanare; *to — off a cold*, liberarsi da un raffreddore; *to — off one's clothes*, svestirsi rapidamente; *to — off a bad habit*, liberarsi da una brutta abitudine; *to — off the scent*, far perdere la traccia a; *to be -n off one's*

*balance*, perdere l'equilibrio; *to — out*, mettere alla porta, espellere; *to — out a challenge*, lanciare una sfida; *to — out one's chest*, mettere il petto in fuori; *to — out a suggestion*, dare un consiglio; (motor.) *to — out the clutch*, disinnestare la frizione; (pol.) *to — out a bill*, respingere una proposta di legge; *to — over*, buttare sopra, abbandonare, (fam.) piantare, (mech.) rovesciare, invertire; *to — together*, riunire in fretta; *to — up*, lanciare in aria; rigettare, vomitare; dare risalto a, mettere in rilievo; *to — up one's job*, dare le dimissioni; (boxing) *to — up the sponge*, gettare la spugna, (fig.) smettere.

**throwaway** *n.* dépliant *m. indecl.*; avviso; foglietto; foglio volante; *adj.* (theatr.) *— line*, battuta (comm., of goods) disponibile.

**throwback** *n.* (biol.) regressione; ritorno atavico.

**thrower** *n.* lanciatore, scagliatore; (ceram.) vasaio; (text.) torcitore.

**throw-in** *n.* (sport) rimessa in giuoco laterale.

**throwing** *n.* lancio, scagliamento; (of rider from horse) sbalzamento, l'essere disarcionato; (wrestling) atterramento; (text.) torcitura; *— machine*, torcitoio; *— about*, spreco, sparpagliamento, disseminazione; *— aside*, scarto, il buttare da parte; *— away*, il buttar via, spreco, perdita, abbandono, (cards) scarto; *— back*, rinvio (della palla), il rilanciare; (of image) riflessione; (of light, heat) riverberazione, riverberamento; *— down*, il buttar giù, abbattimento, (of arms) abbandono; *— out*, lancio, emissione, (of bill) respingimento; *— over*, abbandono.

**thrown** *part.* of **throw**, *q.v.*; *adj.* (ceram.) modellato; (text.) ritorto; *— silk*, organzino.

**throw-off** *n.* inizio; (mech.) dispositivo di arresto. **-out** *n.* (comm.) scarto, articolo difettoso; (mech.) dispositivo di disinnesto; (electr.) interruttore automatico.

**thrum** *n.* tambureggiamento, suono monotono; (mus.) strimpellata, strimpellio; *tr.* tamburellare; (mus.) strimpellare, scarabillare; *intr. to — on the table*, tamburellare con le dita sulla tavola; (mus.) schitarrare.

**thrush**[1] *n.* (orn.) tordo; *missel —* tordela.

**thrush**[2] *n.* (med.) afta; (vet.) tigna, irritazione della forchetta.

**thrust** *n.* spinta; botta; *cut and —*, botta e risposta; *to make a — at*, dare una botta a; *negative —*, reazione; (mil.) attacco, offensiva; (fig.) battuta, osservazione acuta.

**thrust** *tr.* spingere, ficcare, cacciare; *to — through with a sword*, trafiggere con la spada; *to — one's nose into everything*, ficcare il naso dappertutto; *to — into one's pocket*, cacciare in tasca; *to — a word in here and there*, frapporre una parola ogni tanto; *to — one's way through the crowd*, farsi strada attraverso la folla; (fig.) *to — oneself into*, intromettersi in; *to — oneself on*, imporre la propria compagnia a; *it was — upon him*, gli fu imposto; *to — away*, allontanare, scartare, parare; *to — back*, respingere, cacciare indietro; *to — down*, cacciare giù, spingere in basso; *to — forward*, spingere avanti; *to — oneself forward*, farsi avanti, mettersi in vista; *to — in*, spingere dentro, conficcare, addentrare, affondare; *to — out*, spingere fuori, cacciar fuori, sporgere; *to — out one's hand*, tendere la mano; *to — up*, alzare, spingere in alto; *intr.* lanciarsi, farsi avanti; *to — at with a dagger*, dare colpi di pugnale a; *to — past*, spingere per passare.

**thrust-er** *n.* (fencing) tiratore; (fam.) arrivista *m.*, *f.* **-ing** *adj.* che spinge; *n.* spinta, lo spingere.

**Thucydides** *pr.n.* Tucidide.

**thud** *n.* tonfo, rumore sordo; *intr.* fare un rumore sordo, cadere con un tonfo.

**thug** *n.* (fam.) teppista *m.*; delinquente *m.*, malvivente *m.*; (hist., India) membro di una fraternità di strangolatori. **-gery** *n.* teppismo, malavita.

**Thule** *pr.n.* Tule; *ultima —*, ultima Tule, (fig.) terra remota.

**thumb** *n.* pollice *m.*; *rule of —*, regola basata sulla pratica, empirismo; *-s up!*, evviva!, benone!; *-s down!*, a morte!, abbasso!; *Tom Thumb*, Pollicino; *to be under someone's —*, essere dominato da qualcuno; *to be all -s*, essere goffo, essere maldestro; *to hold between finger and —*, tenere fra il pollice e l'indice; *to keep under one's —*, tenere basso, comandare a bacchetta a; *to twiddle one's -s*, star con le mani alla cintola; *tr.* toccare col pollice; (fig.) maneggiare maldestramente; lasciare l'impronta del pollice su; (pop.) *to — one's nose at*, fare maramao a; (slang) *to — a lift*, fare l'autostop chiedere un passaggio facendo l'autostop. **-ed** *part. adj.* coperto d'impronte del pollice.

**thumb-index** *n.* indice a rubrica.

**thumb-mark** *n.* ditata, impronta di pollice. **-marked** *adj.* pieno di ditate, sciupato. **-nail** *n.* unghia del pollice; *-nail sketch*, schizzo in miniatura, schizzetto. **-screw** *n.* (mech.) vite ad alette, vite a farfalla; (fam.) *to put the -screws on*, dare un tratto di corda (a), dare un giro di vite (a).

**thumb-stall** *n.* ditale *m.*

**thump** *n.* tonfo, rumore sordo; (fam.) toc-toc *m.*; *to go —*, fare toc-toc; colpo, pugno, botta; *tr.*, *intr.* battere, percuotere, picchiare, martellare, pestare; *to — on the table*, battere gran pugni sul tavolo; *my heart is -ing*, mi batte il cuore tumultuosamente; *to — out a tune*, strimpellare una melodia; *to — the big drum*, suonare la grancassa. **-ing** *adj.* che batte; (fam.) grosso, enorme; *a -ing great lie*, una grossa bugia; *n.* rumore sordo, tonfo; battito; bastonata.

**thunder** *n.* tuono; *a peal of —*, un colpo di tuono; rombo, tambureggiamento; *the -s of Jove*, i fulmini di Giove; (fig.) *a voice of —*, una voce tonante; *to steal someone's —*, impadronirsi della trovata di qualcuno; *blood and — story*, racconto sensazionale, giallo; (fam.) *why in the name of — didn't you tell me?*, ma santo Dio perchè non me l'hai detto?

**thunder** *intr.* tuonare; (fig.) rimbombare, rombare; minacciare, parlare con voce tonante; *to — against*, scagliare invettive contro. **-bolt** *n.* meteorite *f.*; colpo di tuono; (fig.) fulmine *m.* **-clap** *n.* scoppio di tuono; (fig.) fulmine *m.* **-cloud** *n.* nube temporalesca.

**thundering** *adj.* tonante, fulminante; (fig.) *to be in a — rage*, essere fuori di sè per la rabbia; (fam.) formidabile, grosso; *a — lie*, una grossa bugia; *adv.* (fam.) enormemente; *n.* tuono; (fig.) rumore fragoroso.

**thunderous** *adj.* temporalesco, minaccioso; (of sound) fragoroso; (of voice) tonante.

**thunder-storm** *n.* temporale *m.* **-struck** *adj.* fulminato, folgorato; (fig.) stupito, attonito. **-y** *adj.* temporalesco, minaccioso.

**thur-ible** *n.* (eccl.) turibolo, incensiere. *m.* **-ifer** *n.* (eccl.) turiferario.

**Thursday** *pr.n.* giovedì *m.*; *on —*, (il) giovedì; *every —*, tutti i giovedì; *Maundy —*, giovedì santo; *last — of Carnival*, giovedì grasso.

**thus** *adv.* così, in questo modo; *— far*, sin qui, fino a questo punto; così, perciò, quindi.

**thwart** *n.* (naut.) traversino, banco; *to fit with -s*, abbancare; *tr.* contrastare, frustrare, ostacolare, opporsi a; *to be -ed*, essere frustrato, (fam.) rimanere a denti asciutti.

**thy** *poss. adj.* (il) tuo, (la) tua, i tuoi, le tue.

**thyme** *n.* (bot.) timo; *wild —*, sermollino selvatico, serpellino.

**thymol** *n.* (pharm.) timolo.

**thyroid** *adj.* tiroideo; *n.* tiroide *f.*; *— gland extract*, tiroidina.
**thyself** *rfl. prn.* te stesso *m.*, te stessa *f.*; (with *rfl. vb.*) ti, te.
**tiara** *n.* tiara; diadema *m.*; (of Pope) tiara, triregno.
**Tiber** *pr.n.* (geog.) Tevere *m.*
**Tiberius** *pr.n.* (hist.) Tiberio.
**Tibet** *pr.n.* (geog.) Tibet *m.* **-an** *adj.*, *n.* tibetano.
**tibia** *n.* (anat.; mus.) tibia.
**tic** *n.* (med.) tic nervoso.
**Ticino** *pr.n.* (geog.) Ticino, Svizzera italiana; *of the —*, *adj.*, *n.* ticinese *m.*, *f.*
**tick**[1] *n.* tictac *m.*, tictoc *m.*, ticchettìo; scatto; (fam.) *on the —*, in punto, in perfetto orario; *in two -s*, subito, in un attimo; *half a —!*, un momento!, un attimo!; segno, contrassegno tratto, punto, (to signify approval) visto; *to mark with a —*, contrassegnare; *to put a — against a name*, segnare un nome.
**tick**[2] *intr.* ticchettare, far tictac; scattare; (motor.) *to — over*, girare in folle, rallentare al massimo; *tr.* segnare, contrassegnare, spuntare; *to — off*, segnare, contrassegnare, (fam.) fare una ramanzina a; *to get -ed off*, prendere una lavata di testa, non passarla liscia.
**tick**[2] *n.* (of bedstead) traliccio; (of mattress) fodera.
**tick**[3] *n.* (fam. = credit) credito; *to buy on —*, comprare a credito.
**tick**[4] *n.* (ent.) acaro, zecca.
**ticker** *n.* (fam.) orologio, tictoc *m.*; cuore *m.*; (teleprinter) telescrivente *f.* **-tape** *n.* nastro di telescrivente.
**ticket** *n.* biglietto; scontrino; buono; *-s please!*, (favoriscano i) biglietti!; *to take one's —*, fare il biglietto; (rlwy.) *single —*, biglietto di sola andata, biglietto semplice; *return —*, biglietto di andata e ritorno; *week-end return —*, biglietto festivo; *through —*, biglietto di corrispondenza; *group —*, biglietto cumulativo; *landing —*, contrassegno per lo sbarco; *luggage —*, scontrino di bagaglio; *season —*, abbonamento; *platform —*, biglietto d'ingresso; *entrance —*, (biglietto d') ingresso; *complimentary —*, biglietto di favore; (fam.) *that's the —!*, benone!, benissimo!; (mil.) *to get one's —*, essere congedato; etichetta cartellino; (aeron.) *pilot's —*, brevetto di pilota; *tr.* mettere l'etichetta a, segnare con cartellino; (fig.) classificare, definire, qualificare.
**ticket-agency** *n.* agenzia per la vendita dei biglietti. **-collector** *n.* bigliettario, controllore. **-holder** *n.* (rlwy.) viaggiatore munito di biglietto; *season -holder*, abbonato (sport; theatr.) spettatore munito di biglietto. **-inspector** *n.* controllore. **-office** *n.* biglietteria, sportello. **-of-leave** *n.* *— man*, vigilato.
**ticking** *n.* (of clock) ticchettìo; (of mechanism) scatto.
**ticking-off** *n.* (of names, *etc.*) il contrassegnare; (fam.) lavata di testa, ramanzina. **-over** *n.* (motor.) marcia in folle.
**tickl-e** *tr.* solleticare, fare il solletico a, titillare; (fig.) stuzzicare, stimolare; lusingare; divertire; *to be -ed by an idea*, divertirsi dell'idea; (fam.) *to be -ed to death by*, torcersi dalle risa per; *to — up*, risvegliare, eccitare; *intr.* fare solletico, prurito; *my hand -es*, sento solletico a una mano **-ing** *adj.* solleticante, stuzzicante; *-ing cough*, tosse *f.* per irritazione; *n.* solletico, prurito. **-ish** *adj.* sensibile allo solletico; (fig.) suscettibile, permaloso; difficile, imbarazzante, delicato, scabroso. **-ishness** *n.* sensibilità allo solletico; (fig.) suscettibilità, permalosità; difficoltà, scabrosità, delicatezza.
**tick-tack, tick-tock** *n.* tictac *m.*, ticchettìo.
**tidal** *adj.* della marea, dipendente dalla marea; *— basin*, bacino di marea; *— harbour*, porto accessibile solo con alta marea; *— river*, fiume *m.* soggetto a marea; *— wave*, onda di marea, (fig.) impulso travolgente.
**tiddly** *adj.* (pop.) brillo, sbronzo.
**tiddlywinks** *n.* giuoco della pulce.
**tide** *n.* marea; *flood —*, flusso, marea montante; *ebb —*, riflusso, marea colante; *high —*, alta marea, acqua alta; *low —*, bassa marea, acqua bassa; *spring —*, marea massima sigiziale *neap —*, marea minima sigiziale, marea quadraturale; (fig.) ondata; *a — of enthusiasm*, un'ondata di entusiasmo; *in the full — of his glory*, all'apice della gloria; *the — of battle*, la fortuna della battaglia; *to swim with the —*, andare con la corrente; *to stem the —*, navigare contro corrente; stagione, periodo; *tr.* portare, trasportare; *intr.* navigare con l'aiuto della marea; (fig.) *to — over*, superare, sormontare. **-less** *adj.* senza marea, stabile. **-mark** *n.* battigia, linea di alta marea. **-way** *n.* tratto di fiume a regime di marea; (on Thames) il Tamigi a valle di Richmond.
**tidiness** *n.* ordine *m.*, pulitezza.
**tidy** *adj.* ordinato, accurato, preciso; in ordine, pulito; lindo; (of hair) ben pettinato, ben lisciato; *to keep —*, tenere in ordine; (fam.) *a — sum*, una bella scommessa; *n.* astuccio, busta; *tr.* mettere in ordine, riordinare, rassettare; *to — one's hair*, pettinarsi, ravviarsi i capelli; *to — oneself up*, fare un po' di toletta, ravviarsi; *intr.* *to — up*, mettere tutto in ordine, fare un po' di pulizia.
**tie** *n.* legame *m.*; vincolo; *family -s*, legami familiari; *the -s of blood*, il vincolo del sangue; nodo; cravatta; *bow-tie*, cravatta a farfalla; *to straighten one's —*, raccomodarsi la cravatta; *to tie one's —*, annodarsi la cravatta; (archit.) chiavarda, legatura, asticciola; (rlwy.) traversina; (pol., in voting) parità di voti; (sport) parità di punti, partita nulla; *cup-tie*, eliminatoria di torneo.
**tie** *tr.* legare; attaccare; annodare; allacciare; *to — one's shoes*, allacciarsi le scarpe; *to be -d*, essere legato, (fig.) *to be -d to one's bed*, essere costretto a letto; *to be -d to one's mother's apron-strings*, essere attaccato alle gonnelle della mamma; *to be -d to one's work*, essere schiavo del dovere; *to — down*, immobilizzare (legando), (fig.) imporre condizioni a; *to — on*, attaccare; *to — up*, legare, fasciare, bendare; *to — up a parcel*, fare un pacco; *to — up one's estate*, vincolare i propri beni; *intr.* uguagliare; (pol.) ottenere la parità dei voti, (sport) pareggiare, raggiungere lo stesso punteggio; *to — with someone for first place*, essere primo ed equo con qualcuno; (fam.) *to — up with*, associarsi a, unirsi a.
**tie-bar, -beam, -bolt** *n.* (bldg.) tirante *m.* **-clip** *n.* (cost.) fermacravatta *m.*
**tied** *part.* of **tie**, *q.v.*; *adj.* legato, stretto; (fig.) vincolato, costretto; *to be — for time*, aver poco tempo, essere molto impegnato; *— house*, locale *m.* che vende solo la birra di una determinata birreria.
**tie-on** *adj.* *— label*, cartellino. **-pin** *n.* (cost.) spillo per cravatta. **-plate** *n.* (rlwy.) piastra di fissaggio.
**tier** *n.* (archit.) ordine *m.*, serie *f.*, gradino; (of seats) fila.
**tierce** *n.* sequenza di tre (carte dello stesso seme); (fencing; eccl.; herald.; mus.) terza.
**tie-rod** *n.* (bldg.) tirante *m.*, barra di accoppiamento.
**Tierra del Fuego** *pr.n.* (geog.) la Terra del Fuoco.
**tiff** *n.* (fam.) bisticcio, battibecco, diverbio; *to have a — with*, bisticciarsi con.
**tig** *n.* (game) acchiappino; *to play —*, giuocare ad acchiappino, fare a rincorrersi.
**tiger** *n.* tigre *f.*; *sabre-toothed —*, tigre sciabola; *American —*, giaguaro; *red —*, coguaro; *striped like a —*, tigrato. **-cub** *n.* tigrotto, tigrino.
**tigerish** *adj.* tigresco, da tigre;

(of colour) tigrato. **-ness** *n.* ferocia; crudeltà da tigre.
**tiger-lily** *n.* (bot.) giglio tigrino.
**tight** *adj.* impermeabile; impenetrabile; ermetico; stagno; stretto, aderente, attillato; *to take a — hold of*, stringere; teso, tirato; avaro, taccagno, tirchio; *to be —*, scarseggiare; (fam.) ubriaco, alticcio, brillo; *to get —*, ubriacarsi; (fig.) conciso, serrato, terso; (fam.) *to be in a — spot*, trovarsi con le spalle al muro; *to drive into a — corner*, mettere alle strette; *adv.* strettamente, ermeticamente, forte; *to shut —*, chiudere bene; *to squeeze —*, stringere forte; *to hold —*, tenere stretto; *hold —!*, tenetevi ben saldi!, tenetevi aggrappati!; *to sit —*, non mollare, stare tranquillo; *to screw up —*, avvitare bene; *to blow a tyre up —*, gonfiare un pneumatico fino a renderlo duro.
**tighten** *tr.* stringere, serrare, rinserrare, stringare; (fig.) rinforzare, rendere più severo; *to — one's belt*, tirare la cinghia, (fig.) saltare qualche pasto; *to — a screw*, stringere una vite; tendere, tirare; (fig.) *to — up discipline*, rinforzare la disciplina; *intr.* stringersi, serrarsi, rinserrarsi, tendersi, diventare teso, irrigidirsi.
**tight-fisted** *adj.* taccagno, tirchio. **-fitting** *adj.* stretto, aderente, attillato. **-laced** *adj.* strettamente allacciato; (fig.) rigido, austero, bigotto, da puritano.
**tightly** *adv.* See **tight** *adv.*
**tightness** *n.* impermeabilità, ermeticità, strettezza; tensione; scarsità, mancanza; (fig.) rigidezza, irrigidimento; severità.
**tight-packed** *adj.* serrato, stretto, pigiato, fitto; pigiati come acciughe. **-rope** *n.* corda tesa (per funamboli); *-rope walker*, funambolo, equilibrista *m., f.*
**tights** *n.* (cost.) calzamaglia; *flesh-coloured —*, calzamaglia color carne.
**tigress** *n.* tigre femmina.
**Tigris** *pr.n.* (geog.) Tigri *m.*
**tile** *n.* tegola; *curved —*, tegolo; *flat —*, embrice *m.*; (for wall) mattonella; (for paving) piastrella, formella; (slang) zucca; (fam.) *to have a — loose*, avere una rotella fuori posto; *to have spent a night on the -s*, aver fatto una notte di baldoria; *tr.* (roof) coprire di tegole, accoppare; (floor) pavimentare con piastrelle; (wall) rivestire con piastrelle.
**tiler** *n.* tegolaio.
**till**[1] *conj., prep.* See **until**.
**till**[2] *n.* (comm.) cassetto, cassa, cassetta, registratore di cassa; *to be caught with one's hand in the —*, essere colto in flagrante.
**till**[3] *n.* (geol.) argilla morenica, masso erratico; *tr.* (agric.) dissodare, arare, lavorare, coltivare. **-age** *n.* dissodamento, aratura, coltivazione; terreno coltivato.
**tiller**[1] *n.* (agric.) aratore, agricoltore.
**tiller**[2] *n.* (naut.) barra del timone, timone *m.*
**tilt** *n.* inclinazione, pendenza, piano inclinato; *to give a — to*, far inclinare; (geol.) sollevamento; (hist.) giostra, torneo, colpo di lancia; (fig.) *full —*, a tutta velocità; *to run full — into*, scontrarsi a grande velocità con; *to have a — at*, spezzare una lancia con.
**tilt** *tr.* inclinare, far inclinare, ribaltare; *to — one's hat over one's eyes*, calarsi il cappello sugli occhi; *intr.* inclinarsi, pendere; *to — over*, rovesciare; *intr.* rovesciarsi; *to — up*, ribaltare; *intr.* ribaltarsi; (hist.) giostrare, torneare; *to — at windmills*, combattere contro i mulini a vento. **-ed** *adj.* inclinato, a sghembo. **-ing** *adj.* inclinato; inclinazione, pendenza; (hist.) il giostrare.
**tilth** *n.* coltivazione, coltura, terreno coltivato; profondità del suolo.
**timber** *n.* legname *m.* da costruzione; travi *f.pl.*; alberi *m.pl.*, bosco da legname, boscaglia; (naut.) costola; (joc.) *shiver my -s!*, tuoni e fulmini!; *attrib.* di legno; *tr.* (land) piantare alberi in, imboschire; (bldg.) rivestire di legno. **-ed** *adj.* di legno, rivestito con legno; alberato, boschereccio; *half-timbered*, costruita a casse.
**timber-yard** *n.* deposito di legname, cantiere *m.*
**timbre** *n.* (mus.) timbro, tono.
**timbrel** *n.* (mus.) tamburello, timpanello, cembalo.
**Timbuctoo** *pr.n.* (geog.) Timbuktù *f.*
**time** *n.* tempo; *— is money*, il tempo è denaro; *the good old -s*, i bei tempi antichi; *hard -s*, tempi difficili; *in our —(s)*, al giorno d'oggi, oggigiorno; *after a long —*, molto tempo dopo; *after a short —*, dopo qualche tempo; *ahead of —*, in anticipo; *behind —*, in ritardo; *as — goes on*, col passare del tempo; *at the — of Queen Victoria*, all'epoca della regina Vittoria, regnante Vittoria; *at no —*, mai; *for a long — past*, da qualche tempo; *for a long — to come*, per molto tempo ancora; *from — to —*, ogni tanto, di tanto in tanto; *in good —*, per tempo, tempestivamente; *in less than no —*, in un batter d'occhio, subito; *in a week's —*, fra otto giorni; *at this — of year*, in questa stagione; *to be ahead of one's -s*, essere all'avanguardia; *to be in —*, essere in tempo, arrivare tempestivamente; *to be on —*, essere in orario; *to have an easy —*, passarsela bene; *to have a good —*, divertirsi; *to have the — of one's life*, divertirsi un mondo, stare come il papa; *to have a bad —*, passare un brutto quarto d'ora; *to have no — to*, non avere tempo per; *to have plenty of —*, avere del tempo d'avanzo; *to make up for lost —*, ricuperare il tempo perso; *to waste —*, perdere tempo; *to be doing one's —*, (in prison) stare scontando la pena, (as apprentice) stare facendo il tirocinio; ora, momento; *standard —*, ora legale; *—, gentlemen, please!*, signori, si chiude!; *ship's —*, ora di bordo; *what — is it?*, che ora è?; *excuse me, could you tell me the —?*, scusi, signore, può dirmi che ora sia?; *the — is four o'clock*, sono le quattro; *to look at the —*, guardare l'ora; *at a given —*, a un dato momento; *at the same —*, nello stesso tempo, allo stesso momento, (fig.) però; (industr.) *short —*, orario ridotto; *full —*, orario normale; *the -s of the trains for Venice*, l'orario dei treni per Venezia; volta; *how many -s?*, quante volte; *four -s*, quattro volte; *at one —*, una volta; *at -s*, delle volte, a volte; *one at a —*, uno per volta; *once upon a —*, c'era una volta; (mus.) tempo, ritmo, cadenza; *in —*, a tempo; *out of —*, fuori tempo; *to keep —*, tenere il tempo; (mil.) passo; *quick —*, passo regolare.
**time** *tr.* fissare l'ora di, scegliere il momento giusto per; *to be -d for*, essere fissato per; *to be -d to arrive at*, dover arrivare a; calcolare il tempo di, (sport) cronometrare; (mus.) eseguire in tempo, tenere il tempo; *to — one's steps to the music*, ritmare il passo secondo la musica; (photog.) fissare, regolare.
**time-bomb** *n.* bomba a orologeria. **-exposure** *n.* (photog.) posa. **-fuse** *n.* (mil.; min.) spoletta a tempo. **-honoured** *adj.* consacrato dal tempo; venerando.
**timekeeper** *n.* (sport) cronometrista *m.*; (watch) cronometro, orologio che va bene; (fam.) *a good —*, chi arriva sempre puntuale al lavoro.
**time-lag** *n.* ritardo, differimento, intervallo di tempo.
**timeless** *adj.* infinito, eterno, senza fine; che ha valore permanente.
**time-limit** *n.* termine *m.*
**timel-y** *adj.* opportuno, tempestivo, a proposito; *your arrival was —*, sei arrivato proprio al momento giusto. **-iness** *n.* opportunità, tempestività.

**timepiece** *n.* orologio; cronometro; pendola.
**timer** *n.* cronometrista *m.*; cronometro; *old-timer*, vecchio del mestiere, praticone, anziano.
**time-saving** *adj.* che fa risparmiare tempo. **-server** *n.* opportunista *m.*, *f.* **-serving** *n.* opportunismo. **-sheet** *n.* foglio di presenza. **-signal** *n.* segnale orario. **-table** *n.* orario. **-worn** *adj.* logorato dal tempo, vecchio.
**timid** *adj.* timido, pauroso, timoroso, dubitoso. **-ity** *n.* timidezza, timore *m.*, paura.
**timing** *n.* calcolo del tempo; (sport) cronometraggio; (mech.) regolazione, sincronizzazione.
**timorous** *adj.* timoroso, timido, pauroso.
**Timothy** *pr.n.* Timoteo.
**tin** *n.* (metal) stagno; bidone *m.*; scatola; *attrib.* — *hat*, elmetto di acciaio; — *soldier*, soldatino di piombo; (slang) schei *m.pl.*, palanche *f.pl.*; *tr.* (metall.) stagnare, rivestire di stagno; conservare in scatola, inscatolare.
**tincture** *n.* (pharm.) tintura, estratto; (fig.) infarinatura, impronta; *tr.* tingere, colorare; (fig.) improntare.
**tinder** *n.* esca.
**tinfoil** *n.* stagn(u)ola, stagno battuto.
**ting** *n.* tintinnìo; *intr.* tintinnare.
**ting-a-ling** *n.* dindin *m.*, drindrin *m.*
**tinge** *n.* tinta; sfumatura tocco; (fig.) pizzico, punta, traccia; *tr.* tingere, dare una sfumatura a; *-d with*, misto a, colorato di, venato di.
**tingl-e** *intr.* pizzicare, prudere; (fig.) vibrare, fremere; bruciare; (of ears) ronzare. **-ing** *adj.* che pizzica, che pruisce; (fig.) sonoro; *n.* formicolìo, prurito; (of sound) see **tinkling**.
**tininess** *n.* piccolezza estrema, minutezza, esiguità.
**tinker** *n.* stagnino, calderaio ambulante; (Scots.) vagabondo; (fam.) rabberciatore *m.*, guastamestieri *m. indecl.*; *tr. to — up*, rabberciare, riparare alla meglio; *intr. to — with*, armeggiare con; (fig.) svisare.
**tin-kettle** *n.* bollitore di stagno.
**tinkl-e** *n.* tintinnìo, suono argentino; *tr.* far tintinnare; *intr.* tintinnare. **-ing** *n.* tintinnante.
**tin-mine** *n.* miniera di stagno.
**tinned** *adj.* (metall.) stagnato, rivestito di stagno; conservato in scatola, inscatolato, in scatola.
**tinniness** *n.* suono metallico.
**tinning** *n.* stagnatura; inscatolamento.
**tinny** *adj.* (of sound) metallico; (of earth) ricco di stagno.
**tin-opener** *n.* apriscatole *m.* **-plate** *n.* latta, ferro stagnato, lamiera stagnata; *tr.* stagnare, rivestire di stagno. **-pot** *adj.* (fam.) meschino, sgangherato.
**tinsel** *n.* (dressm.) lamé *m.*; (fig.) orpello, falso splendore.
**tinsmith** *n.* stagnaio, stagnino, lattaio, lattoniere *m.*
**tint** *n.* tinta, sfumatura; tono; colorito; (eng.) ombreggiatura, tratteggio; *tr.* tinteggiare; tingere; colorire; (eng.) ombreggiare, tratteggiare.
**tin-tack** *n.* chiodo da tappezziere, bulletta.
**tintinnabulate** *intr.* tintinnare.
**tiny** *adj.* piccino, minuscolo, microscopico; *a — bit*, un pochino; pochino pochino, un tantino, un pezzettino; — *tot*, piccino, bimbetto.
**tip**[1] *n.* punta; estremità; cima, puntale *m.*; *from — to toe*, dalla testa ai piedi, da capo a piedi; *at the -s of one's fingers*, sulla punta delle dita; *on the — of one's tongue*, sulla punta della lingua; (cigarette) filtro; (of umbrella, *etc.*) puntale *m.*, ghiera; *tr.* mettere un puntale a; (fig.) orlare, ornare la punta di.
**tip**[2] *n.* inclinazione; colpetto, buffetto, tocco; deposito, scarico; *rubbish* —, immondezzaio; mancia; accenno, consiglio, suggerimento; notizia confidenziale; *if you take my* —, se segui il mio consiglio.
**tip**[2] *tr.* rovesciare, far ribaltare; *to — rubbish*, scaricare immondizie; *to — the scales*, dare il tracollo alla bilancia; dare la mancia a; *to — someone the wink*, avvertire qualcuno; *he is -ped for the job*, si fa il suo nome per il posto; *to — off*, avvisare, avvertire; *to — over*, rovesciare, capovolgere, *intr.* rovesciarsi, capovolgersi; *to — up*, inclinare, ribaltare, *intr.* inclinarsi, ribaltarsi.
**tip-off** *n. to give someone the* —, avvertire tempestivamente qualcuno.
**tipped** *adj.* con la punta; (of cigarette) con filtro.
**tippet** *n.* (cost.) pellegrina, mantellina; (eccl.) stola.
**tipping** *n.* ribaltamento, rovesciamento; meccanismo di ribaltamento; l'usanza di dare la mancia.
**tippl-e** *n.*(fam.) bevanda alcoolica; *what's your —?*, cosa prendi?; *intr.* bere, ubriacarsi, (fam.) alzare il gomito. **-er** *n.* beone *m.*, ubriacone *m.* **-ing** *gerund* il bere troppo.
**tipsiness** *n.* ubriachezza.
**tipstaff** *n.* (leg.) usciere *m.*, aiutante *m.* di sceriffo.
**tipster** *n.* chi consiglia i puntatori.
**tipsy** *adj.* brillo, alticcio, allegro, da ubriaco.
**tip-tilted** *adj.* (of nose) all'insù.
**tiptoe** *adv. n.* sulla punta dei piedi; (fig.) *to be on* —, bruciare d'impazienza; *intr.* camminare sulla punta dei piedi.
**tiptop** *adj.* magnifico, eccellente, meraviglioso, superlativo.
**tip-up** *adj.* ribaltabile; — *seat*, strapuntino.
**tirade** *n.* diatriba, filippica, tirata, arringa.
**tire**[1] *n.* see **tyre.**
**tire**[2] *tr.* stancare, affaticare, annoiare; *intr.* stancarsi, affaticarsi; *to — out*, stancare, spossare.
**tired** *adj.* stanco, affaticato, esaurito; — *out*, stanco morto; stufo, annoiato; *she has grown — of him*, le è venuto a noia. **-ness** *n.* stanchezza, fatica.
**tire-less** *adj.* instancabile, infaticabile. **-lessness** *n.* instancabilità. **-some** *adj.* fastidioso, noioso, seccante, importuno, tedioso; *how -some!*, che seccatura!; *how -some you are!*, quanto sei noioso! **-someness** *n.* fastidio, noia.
**tiring** *adj.* faticoso, che stanca, che stufa.
**tisane** *n.* tisana, infuso.
**tissue** *n.* (biol.; text.) tessuto; *adipose* —, tessuto adiposo; (fig.) *a — of lies*, un tessuto di menzogne; — *paper*, carta velina, (photog.) carta al carbone.
**tit**[1] *n.* (orn.) cinciallegra.
**tit**[2] *n.* (fam.) capezzolo, tettarella.
**tit**[3] *n.* — *for tat*, occhio per occhio, pan per focaccia; *to give — for tat*, rendere la pariglia, rispondere per le rime.
**Titan** *pr.n.* (myth.) Titano; *n.* (fig.) titano, gigante *m.* **-ic** *adj.* titanico, gigantesco, colossale; (chem.) titanico.
**titbit** *n.* bocconcino, leccornia.
**tithe** *n.* (hist.; eccl.) decima; *register of -s*, decimario; (fig.) decimo, decima parte, minima parte, iota *m.*; *tr.* imporre le decime su; pagare le decime su.
**tithe-barn** *n.* granaio in cui veniva depositato il grano delle decime.
**Titian** *pr.n.* Tiziano; — *red*, rosso Tiziano. **-esque** *adv.* tizianesco, nello stile di Tiziano.
**titillat-e** *tr.* stuzzicare, solleticare, titillare. **-ing** *adj.* stuzzicante, solleticante, piccante. **-ion** *n.* solletico, titillamento.
**titivate** *tr.* abbellire, fare più bello; *intr.* farsi bello, azzimarsi, fare un po' di toletta, ravviarsi.
**titlark** *n.* (orn.) pispola, calandro; *meadow* —, mattolina.
**title** *n.* titolo; grado; diritto; (eccl.) benefizio di chierico, (of church) invocazione; (chem.) titolo; (cinem.) didascalia; (theatr.) — *role*, ruolo del protagonista; *tr.* intitolare, chiamare, denominare. **-d** *adj.* titolato, nobile.
**title-page** *n.* (typ.) frontespizio.

**titmouse** *n.* (orn.) cinciallegra, cincia.
**titter** *n.* risolino, risatina sciocca, riso da gallina; *intr.* ridacchiare, ridere in modo sciocco, ridere come una gallina.
**tittle** *n.* puntino, trattino di penna; (fig.) iota *m.*, ette *m.*, nonulla.
**tittle-tattle** *n.* chiacchiere *f.pl.*, pettegolezzi *m.pl.*
**titular** *adj.* titolare; nominale; *– head*, titolare *m.*
**Titus** *pr.n.* Tito.
**to** *prep.* (motion towards) a, verso, in, per; (with dative sense) (before noun) a, (before prn.) rendered by dative form, (before inf.) a, da, per (but frequently omitted); *– be or not – be*, essere o non essere; per, onde; (before inf. with passive sense) da, *to have something – do*, avere qualcosa da fare; (with pass. inf.) *– be taken*, da prendersi; in acc. and inf. phrases rendered by 'che' foll. by conjunct.: *I want him – go*, voglio ch'egli vada; *adv.* *– and fro*, avanti e indietro, su e giù; *– pull the window –*, chiudere la finestra.
**toad** *n.* rospo, bufone *m.*, botta.
**toadflax** *n.* (bot.) linaiola.
**toad-in-the-hole** *n.* (cul.) pasticcio di salsiccia.
**toadstool** *n.* fungo.
**toady** *n.* adulatore, sicofante *m.*, *f.*; leccapiedi *m.*; *tr.* adulare, leccare i piedi a. **-ism** *n.* adulazione, servilismo.
**toast** *n.* (cul.) pane abbrustolito, crostino, (neol.) tosto; *mushrooms on –*, funghi serviti su crostini, tosto ai funghi; (fig.) *to be warm as –*, avere un bel caldo, starsene al calduccio; *to have someone on –*, mettere qualcuno nel sacco; brindisi *m.*, alzabicchieri *m.*; *to drink a – to*, brindare a, fare un brindisi a, bere alla salute di; *tr.* abbrustolire, tostare, riscaldare; brindare a, fare un brindisi a, bere alla salute di. **-er** *n.* abbruschino, tostapane *m.*, graticola.
**toasting-fork** *n.* forchettone per tostare.
**toast-master** *n.* annunciatore di brindisi.
**toast-rack** *n.* portacrostini *m.*
**tobacco** *n.* tabacco; *Virginia –*, tabacco della Virginia; *Turkish –*, tabacco Macedonia; *cut –*, trinciato; *twist –*, tabacco in corda; *pipe –*, tabacco da pipa; *chewing –*, tabacco da masticare; (bot.) *– plant*, tabacco, erba della regina, nicoziana; *mountain –*, arnica.
**tobacco-box, -jar** *n.* tabacchiera.
**tobacconist** *n.* tabaccaio; *-'s shop*, tabaccheria, spaccio di generi di monopolio.
**tobacco-pipe** *n.* pipa. **-poisoning** *n.* nicotinismo. **-pouch** *n.* borsa da tabacco. **-shop** *n.* tabaccheria, spaccio di generi di monopolio.
**Tobiah, Tobias** *pr.n.* Tobia.
**toboggan** *n.* toboga *m.*; *intr.* andare in toboga. **-ing** *n.* sport del toboga.
**toboggan-run** *n.* pista per toboga.
**Toby** *pr.n.* Tobiolo; cane sapiente (negli spettaccoli dei burattini); *– jug*, boccale da birra (raffigurante un vecchio).
**tocsin** *n.* segnale d'allarme, rintocco; *to sound the –*, suonare le campane a martello.
**today** *adv.*, *n.* oggi, il giorno d'oggi, oggidì, quest'oggi; *of -'s date*, di oggi, odierno; *what is – ?*, che giorno è oggi?; *– is Wednesday the 16th February*, oggi è mercoledì (il) sedici febbraio; *– week*, oggi a otto; *– fortnight*, oggi a quindici; *a week ago –*, otto giorni fa.
**toddle** *intr.* camminare a passi incerti, trotterellare, fare i primi passi; *to – into the room*, entrare trotterellando nella stanza; *to – about*, trottolare; (fam.) *to – along*, andare passo passo; *to – off*, andarsene, squagliarsi; *to – round to someone's house*, fare una capatina in casa di qualcuno. **-r** *n.* bambino ai primi passi, piccino.
**toddy** *n.* toddi *m.*, ponce *m.*
**to-do** *n.* trambusto, tam-tam *m.*; *to make a great – about*, darsi un gran daffare per.
**toe** *n.* dito del piede; *big –*, alluce *m.*; *little –*, mignolo del piede; (of shoe) punta, puntale *m.*; *the – of Italy*, la punta dello stivale; *from top to –*, dalla testa ai piedi; *to keep someone on his -s*, far rigar dritto qualcuno; *to stand on the tips of one's -s*, alzarsi sulla punta dei piedi; *to tread on someone's -s*, pestare i piedi a qualcuno; (fam.) *to turn one's -s up*, crepare.
**toe** *tr.* *to – a shoe*, mettere la punta ad una scarpa; (fig.) *to – the line*, rigar dritto, conformarsi alle regole, stare in binario.
**toe-cap** *n.* mascherina. **-clip** *n.* (on bicycle) fermapiede *m.*
**toenail** *n.* unghia (di dito del piede); *ingrowing –*, unghia incarnita.
**toff** *n.* elegantone, signore; *to act the –*, darsi delle arie.
**toffee** *n.* caramella al burro.
**toffee-nosed** *adj.* (fam.) disdegnoso, altero.
**tog** *tr.* (fam.) *to – oneself up*, agghindarsi, farsi bello.
**toga** *n.* (hist.) toga.
**together** *adv.* insieme, assieme, in compagnia, d'accordo, di conserva; *– with*, insieme con, assieme a, unitamente a; contemporaneamente; *for twelve hours –*, per dodici ore consecutive; *to get –*, riunirsi, far brigata; (euphem.) *to sleep –*, andare a letto insieme; *to pull oneself –*, raccogliersi, ricomporsi, calmarsi; *to stand –*, essere solidali; *to rub two things –*, sfregare due cose l'una contro l'altra; *to put two and two –*, trarre le conclusioni.
**toggle** *n.* (naut.) coccinello; (eng.) ginocchiera.
**togs** *n.* (fam.) abiti *m.pl.*, tenuta.
**toil** *n.* duro lavoro, fatica, travaglio, affanno; *intr.* lavorare duramente, faticare, affaticarsi, affannarsi, penare; *to – along*, avanzare faticosamente; *to – up*, salire faticosamente. **-er** *n.* lavoratore indefesso.
**toilet** *n.* toletta, pulizia; *to make one's –*, far toletta; gabinetto, toletta. **-case** *n.* necessario da toletta. **-cover** *n.* tovaglia da toletta. **-paper** *n.* carta igienica. **-powder** *n.* talco, borotalco. **-table** *n.* tavolo da toletta, tavolino.
**toiling** *adj.* laborioso.
**toils** *n.* (hunt.) rete *f.*, laccio; (fig.) *to be caught in the -s*, cadere nella trappola, essere preso al laccio.
**toilsome** *adj.* laborioso, faticoso, penoso, affannoso.
**toil-worn** *adj.* logorato dal lavoro, spossato, sfinito.
**tokay** *n.* (wine) toccai *m.*, tokay *m.*
**token** *n.* simbolo, emblema *m.*, insegna; (fig.) segno, prova, pegno, attestato; *in – of*, in attestato di, in segno di, a titolo di; *– payment*, pagamento simbolico; *book –*, buono per l'acquisto di un libro; *gift –*, buono d'acquisto.
**Tokyo** *pr.n.* (geog.) Tokio.
**tolbooth** *n.* (Scot.) casello del dazio; (town hall) municipio; (prison) carcere *m.*
**told** *p.def.*, *part.* of **tell**, *q.v.*; *all –*, tutto compreso.
**tolerab-le** *adj.* tollerabile, sopportabile; (fig.) discreto, passabile. **-ility, -leness** *n.* tollerabilità, sopportabilità.
**toler-ance** *n.* tolleranza, sopportazione, indulgenza. **-ant** *adj.* tollerante, indulgente; *to be -ant of*, sopportare con pazienza, tollerare.
**tolerat-e** *tr.* tollerare, sopportare, soffrire; *inability to –*, intolleranza (di). **-ion** *n.* tolleranza. sopportazione.
**toll**[1] *n.* diritto di passaggio, pedaggio; dazio, gabella; (fig.) *to take a heavy – of human lives*, mietere molte vittime, costare molto sangue; *the – of the roads* la mortalità sulle strade.
**toll**[2] *n.* rintocco; *tr.*, *intr.* suonare, rintoccare; *to – a knell*, suonare a morto.

**toll-bar, -gate** *n.* barriera di pedaggio. **-bridge** *n.* ponte a pedaggio.
**tolling** *adj.* che suona; *n.* suono, rintocco.
**Tom** *pr.n. dimin.* of **Thomas**; —, *Dick and Harry*, Tizio, Caio e Sempronio; *every —, Dick and Harry*, chiunque, un tizio qualsiasi; — *Thumb*, Pollicino; *m. Tiddler's ground*, terra di nessuno; *n.* gatto maschio, gattone *m.*
**tomahawk** *n.* ascia di guerra (dei pellirosse).
**tomato** *n.* pomodoro; (bot.) licopersico; — *ketchup*, salsa rubra; — *sauce*, salsa di pomodoro. **-juice** *n.* succo di pomodoro.
**tomb** *n.* tomba, sepolcro, mausoleo, avello; *to rifle a —*, violare una tomba.
**tomboy** *n.* maschietta, maschiotta.
**tombstone** *n.* pietra tombale, pietra sepolcrale, lapide *f.*
**tom-cat** *n.* gattone, gatto maschio.
**tome** *n.* tomo, volume grosso.
**tomfool** *adj.* stupido, scemo, cretino; *n. to play the —*, fare lo stupido. **-ery** *n.* stupidaggini *f.pl.*, sciocchezze *f.pl.*, alloccheria.
**Tommy** *pr.n. dimin.* of **Thomas**; Tommasino *m.*; — *Atkins*, soldato privato. **-gun** *n.* fucile mitragliatore, mitra *m.*, *f.* **-rot** *n.* sciocchezze *f.pl.*, stupidaggini *f.pl.*, balle *f.pl.*
**tomorrow** *adv.*, *n.* domani *m.*, l'indomani *m.*; — *morning*, domattina, domani presto; — *week*, domani a otto; *the day after —*, dopodomani, posdomani; *see you —!*, a domani; *never put off till — what you can do today*, non rimandare mai a domani ciò che puoi fare oggi.
**tom-tit** *n.* (orn.) cinciazzurra.
**tomtom** *n.* tam-tam *m.*
**ton** *n.* tonnellata, mille chili *m.pl.*; *English —*, *long —*, millesedici chili; *metric —*, tonnellata metrica, mille chili, dieci quintali; (fam.) *-s of*, un sacco di.
**tonal** *adj.* (mus.) tonale. **-ity** *n.* tonalità.
**tone** *n.* tono, timbro, accento, intonazione, inflessione; (mus.) tono; *uniform —*, omofonia; (paint.) tono, tinta, sfumatura; (comm.) tendenza; (phon.) accento tonico; (teleph.) suono, segnale *m.*; *to change one's —*, cambiar tono; *to set the — of the conversation*, dare il la.
**tone** *tr.* dare il tono a, accordare, intonare, armonizzare; (photog.) virare; *intr.* armonizzare, accordarsi, intonarsi; *to — down*, *tr.* addolcire, abbonacciare, attenuare, abbagliare, digradare, ammorzare, *intr.* (fig., fam.) calmarsi; *to — up*, tonificare, rafforzare, ritemprare.
**toned** *adj.* intonato, accordato, tonificato; (paint.) sfumato, colorato; — *down*, addolcito, ammortito.
**toneless** *adj.* senza tono, atono, sordo, inespressivo. **-ness** *n.* mancanza di tono, atonia, inespressività.
**tongs** *n.pl.* pinza, tenaglia, molle *f.pl.*; *curling —*, ferro da ricci; *sugar-tongs*, mollette *f.pl.*; (fig., fam.) *hammer and —*, con tutte le forze, a santa ragione; *I wouldn't touch it with a pair of —*, non lo toccherei nemmeno con le molle.
**tongue** *n.* lingua; favella; *mother —*, lingua madre, lingua materna; (cul.) lingua salmistrata; *smoked —*, lingua affumicata; (mech.) linguetta, flangia, aletta; (of balance) ago; (of bell) battaglio; (of buckle) puntale *m.*, ardiglione *m.*; *a sharp —*, una lingua tagliente; *a ready —*, una lingua pronta; *to give —*, parlare, farsi sentire, (of hounds) latrare; *to have a glib —*, aver la lingua sciolta; *to have a smooth —*, aver la lingua facile; *to have something on the tip of one's —*, aver qualcosa sulla punta della lingua; *to hold one's —*, star zitto, non fiatare; *to keep a civil — in one's head*, tenere un linguaggio educato, (fam.) tenere la lingua a casa; *to put out one's —*, tirar fuori la lingua, mostrare la lingua; *to speak with one's — in one's cheek*, parlare ironicamente; (provb.) — *ever turns to aching tooth*, la lingua batte dove il dente duole.
**tongued** *adj.* munito di lingua, a lingua, dalla lingua, a linguetta.
**tongue-tied** *adj.* muto, interdetto, ammutolito, silenzioso; (fam.) *he was —*, gli si annodò la lingua in bocca. **-twister** *n.* scioglilingua *m.*
**tonic** *adj.* tonico; (med.) energetico, corroborante; *n.* (phon.) accento tonico; (mus.) tonica; (med.) ricostituente *m.*
**tonight** *adv.* stanotte, stasera, questa notte, questa sera.
**toning** *n.* intonazione, accordatura; — *down*, addolcimento, attenuazione.
**tonnage** *n.* tonnellaggio, stazza; *gross —*, stazza lorda; *net —*, stazza netta; *register —*, stazza di registro.
**tonsil** *n.* (anat.) tonsilla, amigdala. **-litis** *n.* (med.) tonsillite *f.*, amigdalite *f.*
**tonsorial** *adj.* di barbiere.
**tonsure** *n.* tonsura, chierica. **-d** *adj.* tonsurato, chiercuto.
**Tony** *pr.n. dimin.* of **Anthony, Antony**; Antonino, Tonio.
**too** *adv.* troppo; — *kind*, troppo gentile; — *much*, troppo, di troppo, — *many*, troppi; — *little*, troppo poco; anche, inoltre, pure, per di più, altresì; proprio, veramente; *to go — far*, eccedere; *to drink — much*, abusare nel bere, bere troppo; *this is — much of a good thing!*, questo è troppo!
**took** *p.def.* of **take**, *q.v.*
**tool** *n.* utensile *m.*, strumento, arnese *m.*, attrezzo; (slang) pene *m.*; (bookb.) ferro; *machine —* macchina utensile; *gardening -s*, arnesi da giardino; *the -s of one's trade*, i ferri del mestiere; (fig.) strumento, fantoccio, burattino, creatura, uomo di paglia; *to make a — of*, sfruttare, servirsi di.
**tool** *tr.* (bookb.) decorare (una rilegatura), bulinare; dorare, indorare; (industr.) lavorare; (bldg.) martellinare.
**tool-bag** *n.* borsa attrezzi.
**tooled** *adj.* (bookb.) dorato, bulinato.
**tooling** *n.* (bookb.) doratura, decorazione; (bldg.) martellinatura.
**tool-shed,** *n.* ripostiglio per attrezzi.
**toot** *n.* suono di corno; (motor.) colpo di clacson; (naut.) fischio di sirena; *tr.*, *intr.* suonare; (motor.) *to — the horn*, dare un colpo di clacson.
**tooth** *n.* dente *m.*; zanna; (mech.) dente d'ingranaggio; (of fork, comb) dente; *set of teeth*, dentatura; *set of false teeth*, dentiera; *wisdom —*, dente del giudizio; *cutting of teeth*, dentizione; *to cut one's teeth*, mettere i denti; *his teeth were chattering*, batteva la diana; — *and nail*, con accanimento, accanitamente; *armed to the teeth*, armato fino ai denti; *in the teeth of*, a dispetto di, nonostante, malgrado; *an eye for a eye, a — for a —*, occhio per occhio, dente per dente; *to be long in the —*, non essere più giovane; *to cast something in someone's teeth*, rinfacciare qualcosa a qualcuno; *to escape by the skin of one's teeth*, cavarsela per il rotto della cuffia; *to get one's teeth into*, addentare; *to have a — out*, farsi cavare un dente; *to have a — stopped*, farsi otturare un dente; *to have a sweet —*, essere ghiotto di dolci; *to grind one's teeth*, digrignare i denti; *to set one's teeth*, stringere i denti; *to set one's teeth on edge*, far allegare i denti; *to show one's teeth*, mostrare i denti; *to take the bit between one's teeth*, impennarsi, ribellarsi.
**tooth-ache** *n.* mal di denti; (med.) odontalgia. **-brush** *n.* spazzolino da denti; *-brush moustache*, baffi all'americana, baffi tagliati a spazzola.
**toothed** *adj.* dentato, a denti; (archit.) addentellato; (eng.) ad ingranaggi; — *wheel*, ruota dentata.

**tooth-less** *adj.* senza denti, sdentato. **-mark** *n.* dentata. **-paste** *n.* dentrifricio, pasta dentifricia. **-pick** *n.* stuzzicadenti *m.*
**tooth-powder** *n.* polvere dentifricia.
**toothsome** *adj.* gustoso, saporito.
**toothy** *adj.* dentato, dai denti sporgenti; gustoso, saporito.
**top**[1] *n.* cima, vetta; sommità; alto; (fig.) apice *m.*, apogeo; (of bus) imperiale *m.*; *turnip -s*, cime di rapa; *attrib.* superiore, di sopra, sommo, ultimo, ottimo; — *floor*, ultimo piano; — *secret*, segretissimo, riservatissimo; — *side*, parte superiore; — *speed*, massima velocità; (mus.) — *note*, acuto; — *part*, soprano; (motor.) — *gear*, quarta velocità; (naut.) coffa, gabbia; *at the — of the page*, in testa alla pagina; *at the — of his voice*, con tutta la voce che aveva in corpo, a squarciagola; *at the — of the tree*, in cima all'albero, (fig.) all'apice, al primo posto; *from — to bottom*, da cima in fondo; *from — to toe*, da capo a piedi; *on — of*, sopra, in cima a, in testa a; *to be at the — of one's form*, essere in ottima forma; *to be — dog*, essere dappiù di tutti; *to come out on —*, riuscire primo, vincere; (mil.) *to go over the —*, andare all'assalto.
**top**[1] *tr.* coprire, essere sopra di; raggiungere la sommità di, essere sulla cima di; (fig.) essere all'apice di; superare, essere più alto di, misurare di più di; *to — a tree*, svettare un albero; (slang) impiccare; *to — off*, terminare, dare l'ultimo tocco a; *to — up*, riempire completamente.
**top**[2] *n.* (toy) trottola; *to sleep like a —*, dormire come un ghiro.
**topaz** *n.* topazio.
**top-boots** *n.* stivali *m.pl.* con risvolto.
**topcoat** *n.* soprabito.
**topee** *n.* casca coloniale.
**toper** *n.* beone *m.*, ubriacone *m.*
**topgallant** *adj.*, *n.* (naut.) — *mast*, albero di pappafico; *main — sail*, velaccio.
**top-hat** *n.* cilindro.
**topheav-y** *adj.* sovraccarico; poco stabile. **-iness** *n.* l'essere sovraccarico, mancanza di stabilità; (fig.) elefantiasi *f.*
**topiary** *adj.* (hortic.) di taglio ornamentale; — *work*, arte *f.* di tosare le piante.
**topic** *n.* tema *m.*; argomento; — *of the day*, argomento del giorno; (rhet.) topica.
**topical** *adj.* d'attualità; — *allusion*, allusione ai fatti del giorno; — *film*, film d'attualità; (rhet.) topico; (med.) topico, locale.
**topknot** *n.* ciuffo, cresta; nastro da capelli; (slang) zucca.
**topless** *adj.* svettato; (fig.) altissimo, irraggiungibile; (neol.) — *dress*, vestito che lascia scoperto il petto, topless *m.*
**top-light** *n.* (naut.) fanale di gabbia.
**topmast** *n.* (naut.) albero di gabbia.
**topmost** *adj.* il più alto, il più elevato; — *height*, cima, sommità.
**topo-graphy** *n.* topografia. **-logy** *n.* topologia. **-nymy** *n.* toponomastica.
**topper** *n.* cilindro.
**topping** *adj.* (fam.) eccellente, ottimo, primissimo; *n.* svettamento; (chem.) predistillazione.
**toppl-e** *tr.* *to — down*, far cadere, far crollare; *intr.* traballare; *to — over*, crollare, cadere. **-ing** *adj.* traballante, vacillante, che minaccia di crollare.
**topsail** *n.* (naut.) gabbia, seconda vela.
**topsy-turvy** *adj.*, *adv.* sottosopra.
**tor** *n.* picco, sommità rocciosa, collina.
**torch** *n.* fiaccola, torcia; *electric —*, lampadina tascabile; (fig.) *to hand on the —*, tener viva la fiaccola. **-light** *n.* luce di fiaccola, illuminazione con fiaccole; *-light procession*, fiaccolata.
**tore** *p.def.* of **tear**, *q.v.*
**toreador** *n.* torero.
**tor·ment** *n.* supplizio, strazio, tormento, tortura; agonia, afflizione; *the — of Tantalus*, il supplizio di Tantalo; *to suffer -s*, patire, angosciarsi, affliggersi.
**torment** *tr.* tormentare, affliggere, angosciare; *to be -ed by*, patire. **-or** *n.* tormentatore.
**torn** *part.* of **tear**, *q.v.*
**tornado** *n.* turbine *m.*, tromba d'aria, uragano, bufera, ciclone *m.*; (fig.) scroscio; uragano.
**torpedo** *n.* (naut.) siluro, torpedine *f.*; — *factory*, silurificio; — *firing-range*, siluripedio; (ichth.) torpedine; *tr.* silurare.
**torpedo-boat** *n.* torpediniera, silurante *f.*; — *destroyer*, cacciatorpediniere *m.* **-man** *n.* (naut.) silurista *m.* **-net** *n.* rete di protezione contro i siluri. **-plane** *n.* aerosilurante *m.* **-tube** *n.* lanciasiluri *m.*
**torpid** *adj.* torpido, intorpidito, inerte; (fig.) apatico, indifferente. **-ity**, **-ness**, **torpor** *n.* torpore *m.*, inerzia; (fig.) apatia.
**torque** *n.* (mech.) coppia, torsione; — *stress*, sollecitazione di torsione.
**torrefaction** *n.* torrefazione.
**torrent** *n.* torrente *m.*, fiume *m.*, fiumara; (fig.) torrente, diluvio; *in -s*, a diluvio, a dirotto, dirottamente. **-ial** *adj.* torrenziale; (of stream) torrentizio.
**torrid** *adj.* torrido, tropicale.
**torsion** *n.* torsione.
**torso** *n.* (anat.; art) torso, tronco.
**tort** *n.* (leg.) torto, danno.
**tortoise** *n.* (zool.) tartaruga; *water —*, chelidro; (mil. hist.) testuggine *f.* **-shell** *n.* tartaruga; *-shell cat*, gatto di Spagna; *-shell butterfly*, vanessa.
**tortuous** *adj.* tortuoso, serpeggiante, sinuoso. **-ness** *n.* tortuosità.
**torture** *n.* tortura, supplizio; (fig.) tormento; *tr.* torturare, sottoporre alla tortura; (fig.) tormentare, affliggere; distorcere, svisare il senso di, snaturare. **-r** *n.* (hist.) aguzzino, boia *m.*; (fig.) tormentatore.
**Tory** *n.* (pol.) conservatore; *the — Party*, il partito conservatore. **-ism** *n.* (pol.) conservatorismo.
**tosh** *n.* sciocchezze *f.pl.*, balle *f.pl.*
**toss** *n.* azione di lanciare in aria, lancio; *pitch and —*, testa e croce; (sport) lancio in aria (di una moneta), sorteggio; *to win the —*, vincere (a testa e croce), essere vittorioso nel sorteggio; (fig.) *a — of the head*, una scrollata del capo; *to take a —*, (from horse) essere sbalzato di sella, (fig.) subire una batosta.
**toss** *tr.* lanciare, gettare in aria; scuotere, agitare, sbattere, sballottare; (of horse) sbalzare di sella; *to — money about*, sperperare denaro; *to — aside*, buttare da parte; *to — back (a ball)*, rilanciare (una palla); *to — off*, buttare giù, (slang, of a man) masturbarsi; *to — up*, lanciare in aria; *intr.* agitarsi, dimenarsi; *to — about in bed*, rivoltarsi nel letto; (of ship) *to pitch and —*, beccheggiare; (sport) tirare a sorte, sorteggiare.
**toss-up** *n.* lancio in aria di moneta; (fig.) cosa incerta; *it's a —!*, chissà!
**tot**[1] *n.* piccino, *a tiny —*, un bimbetto; (of liquor) sorso, bicchierino.
**tot**[2] *tr.* sommare, addizionare; *to — up*, fare la somma di; *intr.* ammontare.
**total** *adj.* totale; completo; assoluto; globale; *to be in — ignorance of*, ignorare completamente; — *warfare*, guerra totale; *n.* totale *m.*, ammontare *m.*, cifra globale; *to reach a — of*, ammontare a; *tr.* fare la somma di, sommare; *intr.* ammontare a, essere in tutto.
**totalitarian** *adj.* totalitario. **-ism** *n.* totalitarismo.
**totality** *n.* totalità.
**totaliz-e** *tr.*, *intr.* totalizzare. **-ator** *n.* (racing) totalizzatore.
**tote** *n.* See **totalizator**.
**totem** *n.* totem *m.* **-ism** *n.* totemismo.
**totem-pole** *n.* palo totemico.
**totter** *intr.* barcollare, traballare, vacillare, essere pericolante; *to — in*, entrare barcollando. **-ing**, **-y** *adj.* barcollante, traballante,

pericolante; malsicuro, malfermo, incerto.

**toucan** *n.* (orn.) tucano.

**touch** *n.* tatto; *the sense of —*, il senso del tatto; *to recognize by the —*, riconoscere al tatto; (mus.) tocco, tatto; tocco, colpetto; *he felt a — on his arm*, si sentì toccare il braccio; *finishing —*, ultimo tocco; (fam.) *that's the finishing —!*, ecco fatto il becco all'oca; contatto, rapporto; *to be in — with*, essere in contatto con; *to be in — with the situation*, essere al corrente della situazione; *to get into — with*, mettersi in contatto con; *to lose — with*, perdere i contatti con; pizzico, che, punta; *a — of salt*, un pizzico di sale; *a — of irony*, un che d'ironia; *a — of influence*, una leggera influenza; *a — of fever*, un filo di febbre; (sport) linea, limite del campo di giuoco; *to kick into —*, calciar fuori (la palla).

**touch** *tr.* toccare, tastare, tasteggiare; palpare, maneggiare; *to — lightly*, sfiorare; *to — one's hat*, portare la mano al cappello; *don't —!*, non toccare!; (fam.) *— wood!*, tocca ferro!; (fig.) *there's no one to — him*, è un fuoriclasse, non c'è nessuno che lo eguagli; *yesterday the thermometer -ed 30°*, ieri il termometro ha raggiunto i trenta gradi; commuovere, intenerire, toccare; *I was deeply -ed*, fui molto commosso; *to — to the quick*, toccare sul vivo; (fam.) *to — someone for money*, spillare denaro a; (art) *to — in*, aggiungere; *to — off*, far esplodere, far scoppiare; *to — up*, ritoccare, dare l'ultimo ritocco a, ripassare, (slang) toccare sessualmente; *intr.* toccarsi, combaciare; *to — on a subject*, toccare un argomento; (of ship) *to — at*, fare scalo a, approdare a; *to — down*, (aeron., on land) atterrare, (on water) ammarare, (rugby) mandare (la palla) in touche, annullare (la palla).

**touchable** *adj.* toccabile; tangibile, palpabile.

**touch-and-go** *n.* cosa rischiosa, un affare problematico, una cosa incerta; *it was — that*, quasi quasi, ci è mancato poco che. **-down** *n.* (aeron.) atterraggio, (on water) ammaraggio; (rugby) messa in touche, calcio annullato.

**touched** *p.def.*, *part.* of **touch**, *q.v.*; *adj.* commosso; (fam.) *to be a bit —*, essere un po' tocco.

**touchiness** *n.* suscettibilità, permalosità; angolosità.

**touching** *adj.* a contatto, che si toccano; commovente, patetico; (as *prep.*) circa, a proposito di, per quanto riguarda; *n.* il toccare, tocco, contatto; *— up*, ritocchi *m.pl.*, il ritoccare. **-ly** *adv.* in modo commovente, pateticamente. **-ness** *n.* il commovente, carattere patetico.

**touch-line** *n.* (sport) linea, limite del campo. **-me-not** *n.* (bot.) balsamina, impaziente *m.*, noli me tangere *m.*

**touchstone** *n.* (miner.) diaspro nero; (fig.) pietra di paragone, criterio.

**touchwood** *n.* esca.

**touchy** *adj.* suscettibile; permaloso, angoloso; irascibile; *to be —*, adombrarsi facilmente, prendersela per nulla.

**tough** *adj.* duro; forte, robusto, solido, resistente; tenace, duro, inflessibile; *to have a — constitution*, avere la pelle dura; duro, difficile; *a — customer*, un tipo poco accomodante, un tipo difficile; (slang) *a — guy*, un duro; *— luck!*, che scarogna!; *n.* teppista *m.*, malvivente *m.*, duro. **-en** *tr.* indurire, rinforzare, compensare; *intr.* indurirsi, irrigidirsi, diventare duro. **-ness** *n.* durezza; solidità; robustezza; inflessibilità; tenacia.

**Toulouse** *pr.n.* (geog.) Tolosa.

**toupee, toupet** *n.* tuppè *n.*

**tour** *n.* giro; circuito; viaggio circolare; *a — round the world*, un viaggio intorno al mondo; *to be on a —*, star viaggiando; (theatr.) tournée *f.*; *to be on —*, star facendo il giro delle provincie; (mil.) turno; *tr.*, *intr.* fare il giro (di), viaggiare (attraverso). **-ing** *adj.* che sta facendo un viaggio; turistico.

**touring-car** *n.* vettura da turismo, torpedone *m.*, pullman *m.*

**tourism** *n.* turismo.

**tourist** *n.* turista *m.*, *f.*; *— agency*, agenzia turistica, ufficio turismo; *— ticket*, biglietto turistico. **-ic** *adj.* turistico, di turismo.

**tournament** *n.* (hist.) torneo, giostra; (sport) torneo, concorso.

**tourniquet** *n.* (surg.) pinza emostatica, tornichetto.

**tousled** *adj.* scompigliato, arruffato, spettinato.

**tout** *n.* sollecitatore; ruffiano; (on racecourse) informatore; *ticket —*, bagarino; *tr.* sollecitare, rivendere alla borsa nera; *to — for*, sollecitare; *intr.* fare il bagarino. **-ing** *n.* sollecitazione, bagarinaggio.

**tow**[1] *n.* stoppa, filaccia; *hank of —*, matassa di stoppa.

**tow**[2] *n.* rimorchio; (naut.) alaggio; *in —*, a rimorchio; *to have in —*, rimorchiare; *tr.* rimorchiare, prendere a rimorchio; (naut.) alare. **-age** *n.* diritti di rimorchio; (naut.) alaggio.

**toward** *adj.* prossimo, che sta per accadere, che si sta svolgendo; *prep.* see **towards**.

**towards** *prep.* verso, in direzione di, verso di, incontro; *— the mountains*, verso le montagne; *he came — me*, mi venne incontro; *his attitude — me*, il suo atteggiamento verso di me; *to save — the children's education*, risparmiare per far studiare i figli.

**towel** *n.* asciugamano; *bath-towel*, asciugamano da bagno; *roller —*, bandinella; *sanitary —*, assorbente igienico; (boxing) *to throw in the —*, gettare la spugna; *tr.* asciugare; *to — oneself*, asciugarsi.

**towel-horse, -rail** *n.* porta-asciugamano.

**towelling** *n.* asciugatura; (text.) tessuto spugnoso per asciugamano.

**tower**[1] *n.* torre *f.*; *the Tower of London*, la Torre di Londra; *church —*, campanile *m.*; *clock —*, torre dell'orologio; *observation —*, belvedere *m.*; *water —*, torre serbatoio, castello d'acqua; (aeron.) *control —*, torre di controllo; (fig.) *ivory —*, torre d'avorio; *a — of strength*, un paladino, un valido appoggio; *intr.* torreggiare, elevarsi; *to — above*, torreggiare su, dominare.

**tower**[2] *n.* rimorchiatore.

**towered** *adj.* turrito, difeso da torri; (herald.) cimato.

**towering** *adj.* torreggiante; dominante; sublime; altissimo; (fig.) *— ambition*, ambizione smisurata; *— rage*, collera violenta, furia.

**towing** *n.* rimorchio, il rimorchiare; (naut.) alaggio.

**tow-line** *n.* cavo da rimorchio.

**town** *n.* città, comune *m.*; *country —*, cittadina; *county —*, capoluogo di provincia; *to go to —*, andare in città, (fig.) far le cose per bene; *to be out of —*, essere fuori città; *— house*, residenza in città; *a flat in —*, un recapito in città, un pied-à-terre; *attrib.* municipale, comunale, cittadino; *— clerk*, segretario comunale; *— council*, consiglio municipale, giunta; *— hall*, palazzo del municipio, palazzo comunale; *a man about —*, un uomo di mondo; *the talk of the —*, i pettegolezzi della città, la cronaca cittadina; *he's the talk of the —*, l'intera cittadinanza ne parla; *to paint the — red*, far baldoria.

**town-crier** *n.* banditore municipale. **-major** *n.* (mil.) comandante *m.* di piazza. **-planner** *n.* urbanista *m.* **-planning** *n.* urbanistica; *-planning scheme*, piano regolatore.

**township** *n.* borgata.

**towns-man** *n.* cittadino; *fellow-townsman*, concittadino. **-folk -people** *n.* cittadinanza, gente di città.

**townward(s)** *adv.* verso la città.

**towpath** *n.* alzaia.

**toxic** *adj.* tossico, intossicante. **-ity** *n.* tossicità. **-ologist** *n.*

tossicologo. **-ology** *n.* tossicologia.
**toxin** *n.* tossina.
**toy** *n.* giocattolo; balocco, trastullo; bagatella; — *soldier*, soldatino di piombo; *attrib.* minuscolo, per bambini; — *dog*, cagnolino; *intr.* giocherellare; trastullarsi; divertirsi; dilettarsi; *to — with one's food*, mangiucchiare; *to — with an idea*, accarezzare un'idea.
**toyshop** *n.* negozio di giocattoli.
**trabeation** *n.* (archit.) trabeazione.
**trace**[1] *n.* traccia, orma, impronta; tracciato; residuo, resti *m.pl.*; *pl.* resti; vestigie *f.pl.*, tracce *f.pl.*; ricordi *m.pl.*; *tr.* seguire le tracce di, rintracciare; scoprire, trovare; tracciare, ricalcare; (with tracing-paper) lucidare; (fig.) *to — one's descent back to*, far risalire le proprie origini a.
**trace**[2] *n.* tirella; (fig.) *to kick over the -s*, impennarsi, ribellarsi.
**traceable** *adj.* rintracciabile; che si può tracciare.
**tracer** *n.* chi rintraccia, scopritore; chi ricalca, lucidatore; (mil.) — *bullet*, pallottola tracciante; — *shell*, proiettile tracciante.
**tracery** *n.* (archit.) decorazione ad intaglio, ornamento a rete, traforo, nervatura.
**trachea** *n.* (anat.) trachea.
**tracing** *n.* rintracciamento; tracciato; (art) calco, ricalco, lucidamento, lucido. **-paper** *n.* carta da ricalco, carta lucida.
**track** *n.* traccia, orma, impronta, pista; *to be on the — of*, essere sulle piste di; *to keep — of*, seguire il corso di, tenersi aggiornato sul corso di; *to lose — of*, perdere le tracce di; *to throw off the —*, far perdere la traccia a; sentiero, via; mulattiera; *the beaten —*, il sentiero battuto, (fig.) la norma; *off the beaten —*, fuori mano, remoto; *to be on the right —*, essere sulla buona strada; (fam.) *to make -s*, svignarsela; *to make -s for*, dirigersi verso; (of ship) scia, rotta; (astron.) orbita, corso; (rlwy.) binari *m.pl.*, strada ferrata; (mech., of tank) cingolo; (gramoph.) banda; (cinem.) *sound —*, banda sonora; (sport) pista; *dirt —*, pista di cenere; *racing —*, stadio; *cycle —*, velodromo; *motor-racing —*, autodromo; — *racing*, corse su pista.
**track** *tr.* inseguire, seguire le tracce di, pedinare; tracciare; *to — down*, raggiungere, catturare, (fig.) scoprire; *to — out*, scoprire, scovare, stanare.
**tracked** *adj.* (mech.) cingolato.
**tracker** *n.* inseguitore, battitore, perlustratore; — *dog*, cane poliziotto.
**track-gauge** *n.* (rlwy.) scartamento.
**tracklayer** *n.* (rlwy.) posatore di binari.
**trackless** *adj.* senza strade, senza sentieri, impraticabile, impervio; — *forest*, foresta vergine.
**track-shoes** *n.* scarpe a punte da corsa.
**tract**[1] *n.* (of land) zona, distesa, regione; (anat.) apparato.
**tract**[2] *n.* trattatello; opuscolo; foglio volante; manifesto; (mus.) tratto.
**tractab-le** *adj.* docile, mansueto; facile da maneggiare. **-ility, -leness** *n.* docilità, mansuetudine *f.*
**tractarian** *n.* (rel.) puseista *m.* **-ism** *n.* (rel.) puseismo.
**traction** *n.* trazione; *steam —*, trazione a vapore; *electric —*, trazione elettrica. **-engine** *n.* locomotore stradale, locomobile.
**tractor** *n.* (agric.) trattrice, trattore; *caterpillar —*, trattore a cingoli.
**trade** *n.* mestiere *m.*, occupazione; *to ply a —*, esercitare un mestiere; *to be a tailor by —*, essere di mestiere sarto; *everyone to his —*, a ciascuno il suo mestiere; *slave —*, tratta degli schiavi; (pol.) *free —*, libero scambio; commercio, affari *m.pl.*, traffico; *retail —*, commercio al minuto; *wholesale —*, commercio all'ingrosso; *the Board of Trade*, il Ministero del Commercio e dell'Industria; *to be in —*, essere in commercio, fare il commerciante; — *discount*, sconto ai rivenditori; — *name*, nome depositato; — *price*, prezzo del fabbricante al rivenditore; — *union*, sindacato; *Trades Union Congress* (*T.U.C.*), Confederazione Generale del Lavoro (C.G.I.L.); (meteor.) — *winds*, (i venti) alisei.
**trade** *tr.* vendere, commerciare in, scambiare; *intr.* commerciare, trafficare, fare il commercio; *to — on*, approfittare di, speculare su; *to — in*, essere commerciante di.
**trademark** *n.* marchio di fabbrica, marca depositata.
**trader** *n.* commerciante *m.*, mercante *m.*, trafficante *m.*; *small —*, negoziante *m.*, esercente *m.*; (pol.) *free-trader*, liberoscambista *m.*
**trade-sign** *n.* insegna commerciale.
**trades-man** *n.* negoziante *m.*, esercente *m.*, bottegaio, fornitore; artigiano. **-people** *n.* i negozianti, gli esercenti.
**trade-unionist** *n.* sindacalista *m.* **-unionism** *n.* sindacalismo.
**trading** *adj.* commerciale, mercantile; *n.* commercio, traffico; — *stamp*, buono premio.
**tradition** *n.* tradizione. **-al** *adj.* tradizionale. **-alism** *n.* tradizionalismo, conformismo. **-alist** *n.* tradizionalista *m.*, *f.*; conformista *m.* *f.*; (art) passatista *m.*, *f.*
**traduce** *tr.* diffamare, calunniare, denigrare, sparlare di. **-r** *n.* diffamatore, calunniatore.
**traffic** *n.* commercio, traffico; (on road) traffico, circolazione, movimento; — *police*, corpo dei vigili, polizia stradale; — *policeman*, vigile addetto alla circolazione; *one-way —*, circolazione a senso unico; — *regulations*, codice stradale; *intr.* commerciare; *to — in*, vendere, essere commerciante di.
**traffic-island** *n.* spartitraffico. **-jam** *n.* ingorgo stradale. **-lights** *n.* semaforo. **-manager** *n.* (rlwy.) direttore dell'ufficio movimento.
**tragedian** *n.* attore tragico, tragediante *m.*; tragediografo, tragedo.
**tragedienne** *n.* attrice tragica, tragediante *f.*
**tragedy** *n.* tragedia.
**tragic(al)** *adj.* tragico, fatale; *how tragic!*, che tragedia!
**tragi-comedy** *n.* tragicommedia. **-comic(al)** *adj.* tragicomico.
**trail** *n.* pista, traccia, orma; sentiero; *to be on the — of*, essere sulle tracce di; striscia; *a — of smoke*, un pennacchio di fumo; (astron.) — *of a meteor*, coda di una meteora.
**trail** *tr.* trascinare; inseguire, pedinare, seguire le tracce di; (mil.) *to — arms*, bilanciare i fucili; *intr.* trascinarsi, strascicare, strisciare; *to — along behind*, seguire faticosamente, camminare lentamente dietro a; (fig.) *to — off*, degenerare (in).
**trailer** *n.* inseguitore; (motor.) rimorchio; (caravan) roulotte *f.*
**train**[1] *n.* (cost.) strascico, coda; traccia; seguito; *to be in the — of*, essere al seguito di; serie *f.*, fila; corso, svolgimento; — *of events*, corso degli avvenimenti; (fig.) tenore *m.*, concatenamento; (rlwy.) treno, convoglio, *excursion —*, treno popolare; *express —*, rapido, direttissimo; *goods —*, treno merci; *slow —*, accelerato; *to go by —*, andare in treno; *to get into the —*, salire in treno; *to get out of the —*, scendere dal treno; *to miss the —*, perdere il treno; (artill.) treno.
**train**[2] *tr.* allevare, addestrare, educare, formare; ammaestrare, addomesticare; agguerrire, esercitare; (gun) d(i)rizzare, puntare, brandeggiare; (plants) far crescere, far arrampicare, (vinestems) accollare; (sport) allenare; *intr.* addestrarsi, abilitarsi, esercitarsi; (for war) agguerrirsi; (sport) allenarsi.
**train-bearer** *n.* paggio; (eccl.) caudatario.
**trainee** *n.* allievo, novizio; (mil.) recluta.
**trainer** *n.* istruttore, ammaestra-

tore, maestro; domatore; (sport) allenatore, accompagnatore.
**train-ferry** *n.* nave traghetto, ferry-boat *m.*
**training** *n.* addestramento, ammaestramento; educazione; esercitazione; apprendistato, tirocinio; *physical* —, educazione fisica, ginnastica; (sport) allenamento; *to be in* —, essere in forma; *to be out of* —, essere giù di forma; *to go into* —, allenarsi.
**training-ship** *n.* (naut.) nave scuola.
**train-sickness** *n.* mal di treno, malessere provocato dal treno.
**traipse** *n.* (fam.) trascinarsi, strascicarsi.
**trait** *n.* tratto, caratteristica.
**trait-or** *n.* traditore; rinnegato, (pop.) venduto; *to turn* —, passare al nemico, vendersi. **-ress** *n.* traditrice.
**Trajan** *pr.n.* Traiano.
**trajectory** *n.* traiettoria.
**tram** *n.* see **tram-car.**
**tram-car** *n.* tram *m.*, vettura tranviaria. **-conductor** *n.* controllare, tranviere. **-driver** *n.* tranviere, manovratore, conduttore. **-line** *n.* linea tranviaria; binario del tram.
**trammel** *tr.* (equit.) mettere le pastoie a; (fig.) inceppare, ostacolare, imbarazzare.
**tramp** *n.* calpestìo, scalpiccìo, rumore di passi; passeggiata a piedi; vagabondo, barbone *m.*; (naut.) — *steamer*, nave mercantile che non ha linea regolare, bastimento da carico, outsider *m.*
**tramp** *intr.* camminare pesantemente; andare a piedi; *to — up and down*, camminare su e giù; *tr. to — the streets*, vagabondare in cerca di lavoro, battere il selciato.
**trample, trampling** *n.* scalpiccìo, rumore di passi.
**trample** *tr. to — under foot*, calpestare, camminare su, pestare; *intr. to — on*, calpestare, pestare, conculcare; (fig.) offendere, trattare con disprezzo.
**tramway** *n.* tranvia, tram, linea tranviaria.
**trance** *n.* estasi *f.*, rapimento; (med.) catalassi ipnotica; *to send into a* —, mettere in trance.
**tranquil** *adj.* tranquillo, calmo, quieto, sereno. **-lity** *n.* tranquillità, calma, serenità; pace *f.* **-lize** *tr.* tranquillizzare, calmare, rasserenare; acchetare, acquietare. **-lizer** *n.* (pharm.) tranquillante *m.*, sedativo, calmante *m.*
**trans-** *pref.* trans-, tra-, tras-.
**transact** *tr.* trattare, fare (affari), sbrigare; *to — business with*, trattare con, entrare in trattativa con, negoziare con; *intr.* transigere. **-ion** *n.* affare *m.*, trattativa, operazione; *pl.* (of society) atti *m.pl.*, verbali *m.pl.*
**transatlantic** *adj.* transatlantico; — *liner*, transatlantico.
**transcend** *tr.* trascendere, superare, oltrepassare. **-ent** *adj.* preminente, superiore; (philos.) trascendente. **-ental** *adj.* (philos.) trascendentale; (math.) trascendente. **-entalism** *n.* (philos.) trascendentalismo.
**transcribe** *tr.* trascrivere, copiare.
**transcript** *n.* copia, trascritto; *typewritten* —, dattiloscritto. **-ion** *n.* trascrizione; copia; *to make a -ion of*, trascrivere.
**transept** *n.* (archit.) transetto; crociera.
**transfer** *n.* trasferimento; trasporto; trasbordo, trasferta; (leg.) cessione, trapasso, alienazione; atto di cessione; (comm.) storno, rimessa, devoluzione, accantonamento; (art) trasporto; ricalcatura, decalco; (soccer) cessione.
**transfer** *tr.* trasferire, trasportare, riportare; (comm.) stornare, devolvere, accantonare, girare; (leg.) cedere, alienare; (art) trasportare, ricalcare, riportare; (soccer) cedere. **-able** *adj.* trasferibile; (leg.) alienabile. **-ee** *n.* cessionario, alienatario. **-ence** *n.* trasferimento; trasporto. **-er, -or** *n.* cedente *m.*, *f.*, alienante *m.*, *f.*
**transfigur-e** *tr.* trasfigurare; *to be -d*, trasfigurarsi. **-ation** *n.* trasfigurazione.
**transfix** *tr.* trafiggere, trapassare; (fig.) paralizzare, inchiodare, petrificare.
**transform** *tr.* trasformare, convertire, cambiare. **-ation** *n.* trasformazione; convertimento; metamorfosi *f.*, conversione; (theatr.) *-ation scene*, trasformazione a vista, apoteosi *f.* **-er** *n.* trasformatore.
**transfus-e** *tr.* travasare; (fig.) trasfondere; (surg.) fare una trasfusione di sangue a. **-ion** *n.* travaso; trasfusione; trasfondimento; *blood -ion*, trasfusione di sangue.
**transgress** *tr.* trasgredire a, violare, infrangere, contravvenire a; (fig.) oltrepassare; *intr.* trasgredire, peccare. **-ion** *n.* trasgressione, trasgredimento; violazione, infrazione, contravvenzione; peccato. **-or** *n.* trasgressore; violatore; peccatore.
**tranship** *tr.*, *intr.* trasbordare. **-ment** *n.* trasbordo.
**transi-ent** *adj.* transitorio, fugace, effimero, momentaneo, passeggero, transeunte. **-ence, -ency** *n.* transitorietà, fugacità.
**transistor** *n.* (radio) transistor(e), radiolina.
**transit** *n.* transito; passaggio; viaggio; *in* —, in transito, transitante, di passaggio; durante il trasporto.
**transition** *n.* transizione, passaggio; — *stage*, fase di transizione; (mus.) modulazione, transizione.
**transitive** *adj.* (gramm.) transitivo.
**transitor-y** *adj.* transitorio, passaggero, momentaneo, fugace. **-iness** *n.* transitorietà, fugacità.
**translate** *tr.* tradurre; rendere; ridurre; volgere; *-d from English into Italian*, tradotto dall'inglese in italiano; *-d by*, traduzione, versione di; (fig.) interpretare, spiegare; (eccl.) trasferire, traslocare; *to be -d into Heaven*, essere assunto al Cielo.
**translation** *n.* traduzione; versione; *to make a — of*, fare una traduzione di, tradurre, volgere; (eccl.) traslazione, (into Heaven) assunzione.
**translator** *n.* traduttore, traduttrice.
**transliterat-e** *tr.* trascrivere, traslitterare. **-ion** *n.* trascrizione, traslitterazione.
**translocation** *n.* trasloco.
**transluc-ent** *adj.* traslucido; trasparente; diafano. **-ence, -ency** *n.* traslucidità, trasparenza.
**transmigr-ant** *adj.*, *n.* trasmigrante *m.*, *f.*, emigrante *m.*, *f.* **-ation** *n.* trasmigrazione, emigrazione; *-ation of souls*, trasmigrazione delle anime, metempsicosi *f.*
**transmission** *n.* (phys.; radio; electr.) trasmissione, emissione; (motor.) cambio, trasmissione.
**transmit** *tr.*, *intr.* trasmettere; (mech.; phys.) trasmettere, condurre; *tr.*, *intr.* (radio) emettere, trasmettere. **-ter** *n.* trasmettitore; (radio sets) trasmittente *m.*, (station) emittente *f.*, trasmittente *f.* **-ting** *adj.* trasmettitore, trasmittente, emittente; *n.* trasmissione, emissione.
**transmogrify** *tr.* trasformare, cambiare.
**transmut-e** *tr.* trasmutare, cambiare, trasformare. **-able** *adj.* trasmutabile, trasmutevole. **-ation** *n.* trasmutazione, trasformazione.
**transom** *n.* (archit.) traversa, architrave *m.*, *f.*
**transpadane** *adj.* transpadano.
**transpar-ent** *adj.* trasparente, diafano, limpido; (fig.) ovvio, evidente, chiaro. **-ence** *n.* trasparenza. **-ency** *n.* trasparenza; (of water) limpidezza; (picture) trasparente *m.*; (photog.) diapositiva.
**transpire** *tr.* traspirare, esalare; *intr.* (fig.) trapelare; accadere, succedere.
**trans'plant** *n.* trapianto.
**transplant** *tr.* trapiantare. **-ation, -ing** *n.* trapianto.

**trans'port** *n.* trasporto, porto; — *charges*, spese di porto; *Minister of* —, Ministro dei Trasporti; mezzo di trasporto; (mil.) carriaggio, treno; (naut.) nave da trasporto; (fig.) trasporto, slancio; estasi *f.*; accesso.
**transport** *tr.* trasportare, portare; deportare; (fig.) trasportare, rapire; *to be -ed with joy*, essere fuori di sè dalla gioia. **-able** *adj.* trasportabile, amovibile. **-ation** *n.* trasportazione, trasporto; (hist.) deportazione, relegazione. **-er** *n.* trasportatore.
**transpos-e** *tr.* trasporre, spostare; (mus.) trasporre, trasportare; *to — to a lower key*, abbassare il tono di. **-ition** *n.* trasposizione; spostamento; (mus.) trasposizione, trasporto di tono.
**transteverine** *adj.* trasteverino.
**transubstantiat-e** *tr.* (theol.) transustanziare. **-ion** *n.* (theol.) transustanziazione.
**transude** *intr.* trasudare, traspirare.
**transversal** *adj.* trasversale; *n.* trasversale *f.*
**Transylvania** *pr.n.* (geog.) Transilvania.
**trap** *n.* trappola; tagliola; (fig.) tranello, trabocchetto; insidia; agguato; *to set a* —, tendere un agguato, caricare una trappola; botola, ribalta; carrozzetta; calesse *m.*; (in drain) collo d'oca, sifone *m.*; (fam.) bocca, muso; (vulg.) *shut your —!*, chiudi la bocca!
**trap** *tr.* prendere in trappola, accalappiare, tendere una trappola a; *to be -ped*, essere preso, cadere in una trappola; (fig.) ingannare.
**trap-door** *n.* botola, ribalta.
**trapeze** *n.* trapezio.
**trapezoid** *adj.*, *n.* trapezoide *m.*
**trapper** *n.* chi tende trappole; accalappiatore, cacciatore.
**trappings** *n.* bardatura, gualdrappa.
**trappist** *n.* (eccl.) trappista *m.*
**traps** *n.* (fam.) bagaglio, roba, oggetti personali.
**trash** *n.* vecchiume *m.*, rifiuti *m.pl.*, immondizie *f.pl.*; robaccia; ciarpame *m.*, roba di nessun valore. **-y** *adj.* senza valore, di scarto, spregevole, pessimo.
**Trasimene** *pr.n.* (geog.) Trasimeno.
**traum-a** *n.* (med.) trauma *m.* **-atic** *adj.* traumatico. **-atology** *n.* traumatologia.
**tra'vail** *n.* sforzo penoso, travaglio, angoscia; doglie del parto, travaglio; *woman in* —, partoriente *f.*
**travail** *intr.* affaticarsi.
**travel** *n.* viaggi, il viaggiare; *to be fond of* —, essere appassionato del viaggiare, amare i viaggi; *on my -s*, durante i miei viaggi, in viaggio; — *agency*, agenzia di viaggi; — *books*, libri di viaggio.
**travel** *intr.* viaggiare, fare viaggi, girare; *to — by train*, viaggiare in treno; *to — by air*, viaggiare in aeroplano, volare; *to — on foot*, viaggiare a piedi; *to — at sixty miles an hour*, camminare a sessanta miglia all'ora; (comm.) viaggiare, fare il commesso viaggiatore; (mech.) scorrere; (fig.) *to — over in one's mind*, riandare con la mente a, percorrere; (phys.) propagarsi.
**travelled** *adj.* che ha viaggiato.
**traveller** *n.* viaggiatore, viaggiatrice; turista *m.*, *f.*; *to be a great* —, viaggiare molto; *commercial* —, commesso viaggiatore, piazzista *m.*; *-'s cheques*, assegni per viaggiatori; *fellow-travellers*, compagni di viaggio.
**travelling** *adj.* che viaggia; viaggiante, ambulante, circolante, mobile; *n.* il viaggiare; — *expenses*, spese di viaggio.
**travelogue** *n.* conferenza su un viaggio.
**traversable** *adj.* attraversabile; (leg.) contestabile.
**traverse** *n.* via trasversale, traversa; (geom.) linea trasversale; (mount.) traversata; (mil.) traversa, paraschegge *m.*; (artill.) brandeggio, spostamento di tiro; — *arc*, arco di tiro; (survey.) topografia poligonale; (mech.) spostamento laterale, movimento trasversale; (leg.) contestazione.
**traverse** *tr.*, *intr.* attraversare, traversare, passare, percorrere; fare una traversata; (artill.) brandeggiare; (mech.) spostarsi lateralmente; (leg.) contestare.
**travertine** *n.* (miner.) travertino tiburtino.
**travesty** *n.* parodia, travestimento, travisamento; *tr.* parodiare, travestire, travisare.
**trawl** *n.* rete a strascico, sciabica, sciabicone *m.*; (for mines) draga; *tr.*, *intr.* pescare con strascico, sciabicare; dragare. **-er** *n.* (boat) peschereccio a strascico; (man) sciabigoto. **-ling** *n.* pesca con strascico; dragaggio.
**trawl-line** *n.* palamite *m.*
**tray** *n.* vassoio; (photog.) bacinella; *tea-tray*, vassoio da tè; *ash-tray*, portacenere *m.*; scompartimento.
**tray-cloth** *n.* tovagliolino per vassoio.
**treacherous** *adj.* traditore; perfido; sleale, infido, proditorio; doppio; malsicuro, poco sicuro, pericoloso, incerto. **-ly** *adv.* slealmente; perfidamente; da traditore. **-ness** *n.* perfidia; slealtà; doppiezza; l'essere pericoloso; incertezza.
**treachery** *n.* perfidia; slealtà; doppiezza; tradimento.
**treacl-e** *n.* melassa. **-y** *adj.* simile a melassa; (fig.) melato.
**tread** *n.* passo, incesso; andatura; rumore di passi, scalpiccio, calpestio; (of stair) pedata, scaglione *m.*; piuolo; superficie di contatto; (of tyre) battistrada *m.*; (of shoe) suola.
**tread** *tr.* calpestare, pigiare, calcare, pestare; *to — a measure*, fare un passo di danza; ballare, *to — grapes*, pigiare l'uva, ammostare; *to — water*, nuotare in piedi; *to — under foot*, calpestare, schiacciare, (fig.) opprimere, sottomettere; (theatr.) *to — the boards*, calcare le scene; *to — in*, calcare dentro, far entrare camminando sopra; *intr.* camminare, mettere il piede; *to — lightly*, camminare con passo leggero, (fig.) trattare con prudenza un argomento scabroso; *to — in someone's footsteps*, seguire le orme di qualcuno; *to — on someone's heels*, seguire da presso qualcuno; *to — on someone's toes*, pestare i piedi a qualcuno.
**treadle** *n.* pedale *m.*
**treadmill** *n.* cilindro azionante un mulino, gabbia di scoiattolo; (fig.) lavoro ingrato, sfacchinata.
**treason** *n.* tradimento; *high* —, alto tradimento; *to talk* —, fare dei discorsi sediziosi. **-able** *adj.* traditore, infido, perfido, sedizioso.
**treasure** *n.* tesoro; *tr.* accumulare, tesoreggiare; (fig.) custodire gelosamente, considerare un tesoro, attribuire gran valore a.
**treasure-hunt** *n.* caccia al tesoro.
**treasurer** *n.* tesoriere, cassiere, economo; *-'s office*, economato, tesoreria.
**treasure-trove** *n.* (leg.) tesoro trovato.
**treasury** *n.* tesoreria, erario, dicastro delle finanze; *the Treasury*, il Ministero del Tesoro; — *bill*, buono del Tesoro; — *note*, banconota; — *bench*, banco ministeriale; (eccl.) tesoro; (bibl.; hist.) donario.
**treat** *n.* regalo; piacere fuori del comune; *school* —, festa scolastica, trattenimento scolastico; *a — in store*, un piacere da venire, (iron.) *you've got a — in store!*, povero te!; *to stand* —, pagare le spese; (fam.) *it's a — to listen to him*, fa piacere ascoltarlo.
**treat** *tr.* trattare; (med.) curare, medicare; *to — someone to a good dinner*, offrire a qualcuno un buon pranzo; offrire da bere; *intr. to — of*, trattare di; *to — for peace*, trattare la pace; *to — with*, venire a trattative con.
**treatise** *n.* trattato; dissertazione; tesi *f.*
**treatment** *n.* trattamento, modo di trattare; (med.) cura; *he complains of his* —, si lamenta del

modo in cui viene trattato; *I didn't expect such — at your hands*, non mi aspettavo che mi trattassi così; *to undergo — for*, farsi curare di, sottoporsi a una cura per; (art, music) esecuzione.

**treaty** *n.* trattato; patto; convenzione; *peace —*, trattato di pace; (comm.) contratto, trattativa; *by private —*, all'amichevole; *party to a —*, contraente *m., f.*

**trebl-e** *adj.* triplice, triplo; (mus.) *— voice*, voce bianca; *— clef*, chiave di sol; *adv.* tre volte tanto; *hs earns — my salary*, guadagna tre volte quanto me; *n.* triplo; (mus.) soprano; *tr.* triplicare, rinterzare, moltiplicare per tre; *intr.* triplicarsi. **-ing** *n.* moltiplicazione per tre, triplicazione.

**tree** *n.* albero; *timber —*, albero d'alto fusto; *Christmas —*, albero di Natale; *clump of -s*, boschetto; *grove of -s*, alberato; *attrib.* arboreo; *to climb a —*, arrampicarsi su un albero; *to plant with -s*, alberare; *to be at the top of the —*, essere in cima all'albero, (fig.) essere al culmine della carriera; *to be up a —*, essere perplesso, trovarsi nei guai; (fig.) *family —*, albero genealogico; (for shoes) forma.

**tree** *tr.* far rifugiarsi negli alberi; (shoes) mettere in forma; (fig.) *to be -d*, essere nell'imbarazzo, trovarsi in scacco.

**tree-creeper** *n.* (orn.) abbricagnolo, rampichino. **-frog** *n.* (zool.) raganella. **-shaped** *adj.* arboriforme. **-trunk** *n.* fusto, caudice *m.*

**treetop** *n.* cima d'albero.

**trefoil** *n.* (bot.) trifoglio, citiso; (archit.) ornamento trilobato, trilobo.

**trek** *n.* (S. Africa) viaggio in carro trainato da buoi; (fig.) migrazione, lungo viaggio; *intr.* (S. Africa) viaggiare su carro trainato da buoi; (fig.) viaggiare, andare.

**trellis** *n.* traliccio, graticolato, graticciata, pergolato; *tr.* ingraticciare, fornire di graticci.

**trembl-e** *n.* tremito, tremolìo, fremito, brivido, tremarella; (fam.) *to be all of a —*, tremare come una foglia, avere la tremarella; *intr.* tremare, fremere; (fig.) vibrare; *I — to think what may happen*, tremo al pensiero di ciò che possa accadere. **-ing** *adj.* tremante, tremolante, fremente; *n.* tremito, tremolìo, fremito; (fig.) vibrazione; *in fear and —*, tutto tremante, tremante di paura, tremebondo.

**tremendous** *adj.* terribile, spaventoso, pauroso; (fam.) tremendo, formidabile, straordinario, enorme.

**tremolo** *n.* (mus.) vibrato, tremolo.

**tremor** *n.* tremore *m.*, tremito, fremito, brivido; *earth —*, scossa sismica, terremoto.

**tremulous** *adj.* tremulo, tremante, fremente; (fig.) timido. **-ness** *n.* tremolamento, tremolìo; (fig.) timidezza.

**trench** *n.* (agric.) fosso, canale *m.*; affossatura; (mil.) trincea, trincera; *— warfare*, guerra di trincea; *communication —*, camminamento; *to fortify with -es*, vallare; (geol.) fossa; *tr., intr.* scavare fossi (in), solcare, affossare, divellare; (hortic.) piantare in trincea; (fig.) *to — (up)on*, rasentare, (leg.) usurpare.

**trench-ant** *adj.* tagliente, affilato; acuto, penetrante; (fig.) mordace, caustico, incisivo, energico. **-ancy** *n.* mordacità, causticità; (fig.) energia.

**trench-coat** *n.* impermeabile *m.* di tipo militare.

**trencher**[1] *n.* tagliere *m.*, piatto.

**trencher**[2] *n.* scavatore di fossi.

**trencherman** *n.* mangiatore, buona forchetta.

**trench-mortar** *n.* (mil.) mortaio.

**trend** *n.* direzione; (fig.) tendenza, orientamento, andamento, corso; *intr.* dirigersi, volgere; (fig.) tendere, orientarsi; *to — towards*, tendere a; *to — away from*, allontanarsi da. **-y** *adj.* (neol.) di moda.

**Trent** *pr.n.* (geog.) Trento; (hist.) *the Council of —*, il Consiglio di Trento, il Buon Consiglio.

**trepan** *n.* (surg.) trapano; (min.) trivella; *tr.* (surg.) trapanare. **-ning, -ation** *n.* (surg.) trapanazione.

**trepidation** *n.* trepidanza, trepidazione, ansietà; emozione; (med.) tremito.

**trespass** *n.* trasgressione; infrazione della legge; (on land) violazione di proprietà; (theol.) peccato, offesa.

**trespass** *intr. to — (up)on*, violare, trasgredire, (fig.) abusare di; (theol.) peccare; *to — against*, offendere; *forgive us our -es, as we forgive them that — against us*, perdona i nostri peccati come noi perdoniamo coloro che ci hanno offeso. **-er** *n.* trasgressore; violatore; intruso; *-ers will be prosecuted*, i trasgressori saranno puniti a termini di legge, vietato entrare, proprietà privata.

**tress** *n.* treccia, ricciolo; *pl.* capigliatura, chioma.

**trestle** *n.* cavalletto, trespolo; (bldg.) capra; intelaiatura, traliccio.

**trestle-bridge** *n.* ponte a trespolo. **-table** *n.* tavolo su cavaletti.

**Trèves** *pr.n.* (geog.) Treviri *f.*

**trews** *n.* calzoni stretti, specialmente di stoffa scozzese.

**triad** *n.* triade *f.*; (chem.) elemento trivalente.

**trial** *n.* prova; esperimento; saggio; *on —*, a titolo di prova; *attrib.* di prova, esperimentale; *— flight*, volo di prova; *to give someone a —*, assumere qualcuno in prova; (leg.) processo giudizio, causa; *famous -s*, cause celebri; *summary —*, procedura sommaria; *to be sent for —*, essere rinviato a giudizio; *to bring to —*, portare in giudizio; *to commit for — at the assizes*, rinviare alle assise; *to stand —*, essere processato; (sport) partita di prova, allenamento; (fig.) croce *f.*; *pl.* tribolazioni *f.pl.*, sofferenze *f.pl.*, peripezie *f.pl.*; *to proceed by — and error*, andare a tastoni.

**triangle** *n.* triangolo.

**triangular** *adj.* triangolare, triangolato, a triangolo. **-ity** *n.* triangolarità.

**tribadism** *n.* tribadismo, lesbianismo.

**tribal** *adj.* tribale, di tribù. **-ism** *n.* organizzazione in tribù.

**tribe** *n.* tribù *f.*; (fig.) stuolo. **-sman** *n.* membro di tribù.

**tribulation** *n.* tribolazione; afflizione, acciacco; (fig.) calvario.

**tribunal** *n.* tribunale *m.*; corte *f.* di giustizia.

**tribune**[1] *n.* (hist., person) tribuno.

**tribune**[2] *n.* (of orator) tribuna, rostro; (of bishop) trono; (archit.) tribuna, coretto.

**tributary** *adj.* tributario; *n.* tributario; (geog.) affluente *m.*

**tribute** *n.* tributo; *to pay —*, pagare tributo; *to lay under —*, imporre un tributo a; (fig.) tributo, omaggio; *to pay a — to*, rendere omaggio a; *floral -s*, omaggi floreali, (at funeral) corone *f.pl.*

**trice** *n. in a —*, in un batter d'occhio, a volo.

**tricentenary** *adj., n.* trecentenario *m.*

**trichology** *n.* tricologia.

**trichosis** *n.* (med.) tricosi *f.*

**trichromatic** *adj.* (photog.) tricromico.

**trick** *n.* trucco; truffa; artificio; espediente *m.*, stratagemma *m.*; astuzia; tiro, scherzo, raggiro, gherminella; mistificazione, imbroglio; *confidence —*, truffa all'americana; *a dirty —*, un brutto scherzo; *one of his -s*, una delle sue; *the -s of the trade*, i trucchi del mestiere; *to play a — on*, giuocare un brutto tiro a; *he knows a — or two*, la sa lunga; *the whole bag of -s*, tutto quanto; vezzo, mania, abitudine, ticchio; illusione, artifizio; giuoco di prestigio, (pop.) psichiatra; *acrobatic —*, acrobazia; *— cyclist*, ciclista acrobata; *— photography*, fotografia truccata;

— *riding*, volteggio; (cards) presa, levata, alzata.
**trick** *tr.* gabbare, ingannare, imbrogliare, giuocare un brutto tiro a; mistificare, abbindolare, raggirare, turlupinare; *to — someone into doing something*, indurre qualcuno con l'inganno a fare qualcosa; *I've been -ed!*, mi hanno raggirato!; *to — something out of someone*, scroccare qualcosa a qualcuno; *to — out*, truccare, agghindare.
**trickery** *n.* inganno, ravvolgimento; mistificazione; furberia; soperchieria.
**trickiness** *n.* furberia; malizia; (fig.) difficoltà, natura complicata; scabrosità; delicatezza; complessità.
**trickle** *n.* gocciolìo, gocciolamento; filo d'acqua, ruscelletto; (fig.) stillicidio; *intr.* colare, gocciolare, stillare; *to — out*, colare, gocciolare, (fig.) trapelare; (sport) rotolare; *tr.* palleggiare (la palla); *to — the ball into the net*, mandare la palla in rete con un colpetto.
**tricklet** *n.* filo d'acqua, ruscelletto.
**trickster** *n.* briccone, imbroglione; abbindolatore; furbo; barone; *confidence —*, truffatore all'americana.
**tricky** *adj.* astuto, furbo, scaltro; difficile, complicato, rischioso, pericoloso, delicato.
**tricolour** *adj.* tricolore; *n.* tricolore *m.*, bandiera tricolore.
**tricorn** *adj.*, *n.* tricorno.
**tricycle** *n.* triciclo; *motor —*, mototriciclo.
**trident** *n.* tridente *m.*
**Tridentine** *adj.* (geog.) tridentino, di Trento.
**tried** *p.def.*, *part.* of **try**, *q.v.*
**triennial** *adj.* triennale; *n.* terzo anniversario; avvenimento che ricorre ogni tre anni; triennale *f.* **-ly** *adv.* ogni tre anni.
**triennium** *n.* triennio.
**trier** *n.* saggiatore, esperimentatore; lavoratore indefesso; assiduo, diligente *m.*, persona tenace, persona che non si scoraggia; (leg.) giudice *m.*
**Trieste** *pr.n.* (geog.) Trieste *f.*; *of —*, triestino.
**trifle** *n.* bagattella, inezia, bazzeccola, nonnulla *m.*, sciocchezza; (small quantity) dito; (cul.) zuppa inglese; *a —* (*foll.* by *adj.*) un po', un pochino, alquanto, leggermente.
**trifl-e** *intr.* frivoleggiare, baloccarsi, gingillarsi, scherzare, perdere tempo in inezie, divertirsi; *to — with*, prendersi giuoco di, farsi beffe di, scherzare con; *to — with a girl's affections*, amoreggiare con una ragazza; *not to be -ed with*, con cui non si può scherzare; *to — away*, perdere, buttar via, sprecare, divertirsi di. **-er** *n.* persona frivola, baloccone, dilettante *m.*; dongiovanni *m.* **-ing** *adj.* insignificante, di poca importanza, trascurabile, futile, minimo; frivolo, leggero, poco serio.
**triforium** *n.* (archit.) triforio.
**trigger** *n.* grilletto; *quick on the —*, pronto a sparare; *to pull the —*, premere il grilletto; (mech.) levetta di comando; (photog.) scatto; *tr.* premere (il grilletto); (fig.) *to — off*, far scattare, far scoppiare.
**trigger-finger** *n.* indice *m.*; *to be -fingered*, sparare a casaccio. **-guard** *n.* guardamano, ponticello.
**triglyph** *n.* (archit.) triglifo, corrente *m.*
**trigonometry** *n.* trigonometria; *plane —*, trigonometria rettilinea.
**trilateral** *adj.* trilatero, trilaterale.
**trilby** *n.* cappello floscio di feltro.
**trilinear** *adj.* (geom.) trilineo, trilineare.
**trilingual** *adj.* trilingue.
**trill** *n.* trillo, gorgheggìo; (phon.) consonante vibrata; *tr.*, *intr.* trillare, trilleggiare; (mus.) gorgheggiare, gargarizzare; (phon.) vibrare. **-ing** *n.* gorgheggìo, trillo, trillìo.
**trillion** *n.* trilione; *m.* (USA) bilione *m.*
**trilogy** *n.* trilogia.
**trim** *adj.* ordinato, ben tenuto, lindo, attillato, ben curato; *n.* ordine *m.*, stato, condizione; (hairdr.) spuntatina; (naut.; aeron.) assetto; *in fighting —*, in assetto di guerra; (fig.) *to be in good —*, essere in forma; *to be in no — for doing something*, non sentirsi di far qualcosa.
**trim** *tr.* assettare, aggiustare, ordinare, ripulire, tagliare; sgrossare, digrossare; (candle) smoccolare; raffilare, ritagliare, tosare; (stones) accapezzare; (bookb.) sbavare; (dressm.) ornare, guarnire; (hairdr.) spuntare; (animal's coat) tosare; (hortic.) potare, dirappare, arroncare; (naut.) assettare, orientare, aggiustare, equilibrare; *to — sails*, orientare le vele; (fig.) barcamenarsi, navigare secondo il vento, temporeggiare; *to — away*, ritagliare, raffilare.
**trimest-er** *n.* trimestre *m.* **-rial** *adj.* trimestrale.
**trimmer** *n.* decoratore; (mech.) sbavatore, raffilatoio, tagliatrice; (naut.) stivatore, facchino del porto; (fig.) opportunista *m.*
**trimming** *n.* guarnizione, ornamento, rifinitura; (of edges) raffilatura; (hortic.) potatura, arroncamento, dicioccatura; (naut.) equilibrazione; *pl.* (cul.) guarnizioni *f.pl.*, contorno.
**trimness** *n.* ordine *m.*; lindezza; assetto; l'essere ben tenuto.
**trine** *adj.* triplice, trino; *n.* triade *f.*; (astrol.) aspetto trino.
**Trinidad** *pr.n.* (geog.) Trinidad *f.*; la Trinità.
**Trinitarian** *adj.*, *n.* (rel.) trinitario.
**Trinity** *n.* Trinità.
**trinket** *n.* ninnolo, ciondolo, gioiellino, gingillo.
**trinomial** *adj.* (math.) trinomiale; *n.* trinomio.
**trio** *n.* terzetto, trio.
**trip** *n.* gita, giro, viaggio, viaggetto, escursione; *round —*, viaggio di andata e ritorno, giro; *to take a —*, fare una gita; passo falso; (football) sgambetto; disinnesto a scatto; (neol.) effetto allucinante del drogarsi; *to take a —*, drogarsi.
**trip** *tr.*, *intr.* *to — along*, camminare con passo leggero, saltellare, sgambettare; *to — over*, inciampare, incespicare in; *to — up*, *tr.* far inciampare, (fig.) cogliere in fallo, *intr.* inciampare, mettere il piede in fallo, (fig.) sbagliare.
**tripartite** *adj.* tripartito.
**tripe** *n.* (cul.) trippa; (fig.) robaccia; sciocchezze *f.pl.*, balle *f.pl.*
**trip-gear** *n.* (mech.) dispositivo a scatto.
**triphase** *adj.* (electr.) trifase, trifasico.
**triphthong** *n.* (ling.) trittongo.
**triple** *adj.* triplo, triplice; *— crown*, triregno, tiara pontificia; (rugby) campionato internazionale di rugby; (hist.) the *Triple Alliance*, la Triplice (Alleanza); (aeron.) *— fin*, impennaggio verticale triplo; *tr.* triplicarsi.
**triplet** *n.* terzetto, terzine, serie di tre; *pl.* nati da parto trigemino, trigemini *m.pl.*
**triplex** *adj.* triplice, a tre spessori, a tre fili; *— glass*, vetro infrangibile.
**triplicat-e** *adj.* triplicato, triplo, triplice; *in —*, in triplice copia; *tr.* triplicare; redigere in triplice copia. **-ion** *n.* triplicazione; il redigere in triplice copia.
**tripod** *n.* treppiedi *m.*; (photog.) calvalletto.
**Tripoli** *pr.n.* (N. Africa) Tripoli *f.*; (Syria) Tripoli di Soria.
**tripper** *n.* gitante *m.*, *f.*, escursionista *m.*, *f.*
**tripping** *gerund* of **trip**, *q.v.*; *adj.* (of step) leggero, lesto, saltellante.
**triptych** *n.* (art) trittico.
**trip-wire** *n.* filo teso.
**trireme** *n.* (hist.) trireme *f.*
**trisect** *tr.* tripartire, dividere in tre parti uguali.
**Tristan, Tristram** *pr.n.* Tristano.
**trisyllab-le** *n.* trisillabo. **-ic** *adj.* trisillabo, trisillabico.
**trite** *adj.* banale, trito, comune, consumato. **-ness** *n.* banalità.
**Triton** *pr.n.* (myth.) Tritone;

(fig.) *a — among the minnows*, un gigante fra i pigmei.

**triturate** *tr.* triturare, tritare, polverizzare, trituzzare.

**triumph** *n.* trionfo; gran successo, vincita clamorosa; (hist.) trionfo; (fig.) esultazione, aria di trionfo, gioia, giubilo; *intr.* trionfare, riportare un gran successo, vincere; (hist.) celebrare il trionfo; *to — over*, trionfare su, vincere, superare; (fig.) esultare, giubilare. **-al** *adj.* trionfale; *-al arch*, arco di trionfo; *-al success*, successo clamoroso. **-ant** *adj.* trionfale, trionfante, vittorioso.

**triumvir** *n.* triumviro. **-ate** *n.* triumvirato.

**triune** *adj.* (theol.) uno e triuno, uno e trino.

**trivet** *n.* treppiedi *m. indecl.*

**trivial** *adj.* insignificante, senza importanza, da nulla, futile, banale, superficiale; frivolo, leggero; *the — round*, il solito tran-tran. **-ity, -ness** *n.* poca importanza; futilità; banalità; superficialità.

**trivium** *n.* (hist.) trivio.

**triweekly** *adj.* di ogni tre settimane; trisettimanale; *adv.* ogni tre settimane; tre volte ogni settimana.

**troch-ee** *n.* (prosod.) trocheo. **-aic** *adj.* trocaico.

**trod, trodden** *p.def.*, *part.* of **tread**, *q.v.*

**troglodyte** *n.* troglodita *m.*

**Troilus** *pr.n.* Troilo.

**Trojan** *adj.* troiano, di Troia; *n.* troiano; *the — Women*, le Troade; *to work like a —*, lavorare come un cane.

**troll**[1] *n.* (Norse myth.) gnomo, spiritello.

**troll**[2] *tr.* cantare in canone; *to — forth*, cantare a voce spiegata; *intr.* (fishing) pescare con il cucchiaino.

**trolley** *n.* carrello, carretto, vagoncino; *dinner —*, carrello; (electr. eng.) antenna, trolle *m.*

**trolley-bus** *n.* filovia, filobus *m.* **-pole** *n.* asta di presa, antenna.

**trolling** *n.* (fishing) pesca con il cucchiaino.

**trollop** *n.* sudiciona, sgualdrina; puttana, bagascia.

**trombone** *n.* (mus.) trombone *m.*

**troop** *n.* banda, frotta, gruppo, branco; (artill.) batteria; (cavalry) squadrone di cavalleria; *pl.* frotte; (mil.) truppa, truppe *f.pl.*, soldati *m.pl.*; (rank and file) bassa forza; (theatr.) see **troupe.**

**troop** *intr. to — along*, camminare in gruppo, sfilare; *to — in*, entrare a frotte; *to — off*, partire in gruppo; *to — out*, uscire tutti insieme.

**troop-carrier** *n.* aero per trasporto di truppe.

**trooper** *n.* (mil.) soldato di cavalleria; (fam.) *to swear like a —*, bestemmiare come un turco; nave per trasporto di truppe.

**trooping** *n.* il raggrupparsi, il radunarsi; *— of the colour*, presentazione della bandiera.

**troopship** *n.* nave per trasporto di truppe.

**troop-train** *n.* tradotta militare.

**trope** *n.* (rhet.; mus.) tropo.

**trophy** *n.* trofeo; panoplia; (sport) premio, trofeo, coppa.

**tropic** *n.* tropico; *— of Cancer*, tropico del Cancro; *— of Capricorn*, tropico del Capricorno; *pl. the -s*, le regioni tropicali. **-al** *adj.* tropicale; (fig.) caldissimo, ardente; *-al vegetation*, vegetazione lussureggiante.

**trot** *n.* trotto, trottata; (fig.) trottatina; *slow —*, piccolo trotto; *to break into a —*, mettersi al trotto; (fam.) *on the —*, di seguito; *tr.* mettere al trotto, far trottare; *intr.* trottare, andare al trotto; trotterellare; (fam.) *I must — along*, devo scappare; *to — round to the pub*, fare una capatina all'osteria; (fig.) *to — out*, uscire con, allegare, far mostra di, sfoggiare.

**troth** *n.* fede *f.*; *to plight one's —*, giurare, impegnarsi; fidanzarsi.

**trotter** *n.* trottatore; (joc.) piede *m.*, zampa; (cul.) *pig's -s*, zampetti di maiale.

**trotting** *adj.* che trotta; *n.* il trottare, trotto; *— race*, corsa al trotto.

**troubadour** *n.* (lit. hist.) trovatore, troviero.

**trouble** *n.* disturbo; pena, noia, fastidio, seccatura; imbarazzo; dispiacere *m.*; molestia; (difficulty) guaio, difficoltà; pasticcio; imbroglio; bega; disgrazia; male *m.*; *family -s*, dispiaceri domestici; (fam.) *to get a girl into —*, fare incinta una ragazza; *-s never come singly*, i mali vengono insieme; *the — is that*, il guaio è che; *it isn't worth the —*, non vale la pena; *what shall I give him for his —?*, che cosa gli devo dare per il disturbo?; *what's the —?*, cosa c'è?, che cosa hai?; *it's no —!*, niente affatto!, s'immagini!, prego!, non c'è di che!; *to be in —*, trovarsi nei guai, avere delle beghe; *to get into —*, cacciarsi nei guai; *to get into — with the police*, avere da fare con la polizia; *to get out of —*, togliersi dai pasticci; *to get someone into —*, creare delle difficoltà a qualcuno, dare del filo da torcere a qualcuno; *to give — to*, recare disturbo a; *to go to great — to*, darsi briga di, darsi da fare per; *to have — with*, avere delle seccature con; *to look for —*, cercare i guai; *to make —*, seminare discordia; *to take —*, darsi da fare, affaccendarsi; *to put to a lot of —*, procurare molto disturbo a; (med.) disturbo, malattia, male *m.*; *heart —*, disturbi di cuore; disordine *m.*, conflitto, sommossa; (mech.) guasto; *engine —*, guasto al motore.

**trouble** *tr.* disturbare, incomodare, importunare, infastidire, seccare; *sorry to have -d you*, scusi il disturbo, mi dispiace se sia disturbato; *may I — you for the salt?*, vuol passarmi il sale?; *to be -d with*, essere tormentato da; *to be -d about*, preoccuparsi di; *don't — your head about it*, non te ne preoccupare; *I shall not — you with the details*, non ti importunerò con i particolari; affliggere, far soffrire; *intr.* disturbarsi, incomodarsi; *please don't —*, non si disturbi; *don't — to write*, non ti dare la pena di scrivere; preoccuparsi.

**troubled** *adj.* agitato, turbato, inquieto, preoccupato; *— sleep*, sonno agitato; *a — soul*, un'anima inquieta; affannoso; *— waters*, acque torbide; (fig.) *to fish in — waters*, pescare nel torbido; *to pour oil on — waters*, versare acqua sul fuoco, calmare i dissensi.

**trouble-maker** *n.* attaccabrighe *m.*, seminatore di zizzania; (pol.) agitatore *m.* **-shooter** *n.* conciliatore, paciere *m.*

**troublesome** *adj.* fastidioso, noioso, seccante, importuno, penoso, doloroso, molesto; *how —!*, che seccatura!, che barba! **-ness** *n.* molestia, noia, fastidiosaggine *f.*

**troublous** *adj.* turbato, agitato, burrascoso; *— times*, tempi difficili.

**trough** *n.* tr(u)ogolo, mastello; (industr.) vasca; *drinking —*, abbreveratoio; *feeding —*, trogolo, mangiatoia; *kneading —*, madia; (archit.) padiglione *m.*; (meteor.) depressione, avvallamento; (between waves) cavo fra le onde.

**trounc-e** *tr.* castigare, picchiare, conciare per le feste; (sport) battere facilmente, stravincere. **-ing** *n.* castigo; busse *f.pl.*; batosta.

**troupe** *n.* (theatr.) compagnia di attori, troupe *f.*

**trouser-button** *n.* bottone dei calzoni. **-clip** *n.* molletta per calzoni. **-hanger** *n.* gruccia per calzoni.

**trousering** *n.* stoffa per calzoni.

**trouser-pocket** *n.* tasca dei calzoni. **-press, -stretcher** *n.* stiracalzoni *m.*

**trousers** *n.* calzoni *m.pl.*, pantaloni *m.pl.*; *a pair of —*, un paio di calzoni.

**trousseau** *n.* corredo da sposa.

**trout** *n.* (ichth.) trota, trotella; *salmon-trout*, *sea-trout*, trota salmonata; *L. Garda —*, carpione *m.*

**-fishing** *n.* pesca delle trote. **-stream** *n.* torrente *m.* da trote.

**trow** *tr.* (poet.) credere, pensare.

**trowel** *n.* (bldg.) cazzuola, mestola, frattazzo; (hortic.) *gardening* —, paletta, vanghetto, trapiantatoio; (fig.) *to lay it on with a* —, caricarla, adulare grossolanamente.

**Troy**[1] *pr.n.* (geog.) Troia.

**troy**[2] *n.* sistema di pesi troy; *ounce* —, oncia troy (=gr. 31.10).

**tru-ant** *n.* chi trascura il proprio lavoro, pigrone; (schol.) allievo che marina la scuola; *to play* —, marinare la scuola, bigiare, far forca; *adj.* (fig.) vagabondo, assente, ozioso. **-ancy** *n.* svogliatezza; (schol.) assenza ingiustificata, il marinare la scuola.

**truce** *n.* tregua, armistizio; *flag of* —, bandiera bianca; (fig.) tregua, pausa, riposo.

**truck**[1] *n.* traffico, scambio, baratto; (hist.) — *system*, pagamento in natura; (fig.) rapporti *m.pl.*; *to have no — with*, non avere rapporti con, non avere nulla a che fare con; (fam.) articoli vari, merce scadente, robaccia.

**truck**[2] *n.* (rlwy.) carro; vagone *m.*; *goods-truck*, carro merci; *hand* —, carrello; *porter's luggage* —, carrello portabagagli; camion *m.*, autocarro; *tank* —, autobotte *f.*, autocisterna; *fork-lift* —, carrello a forcella; (naut., of mast) pomo, varea.

**truck-driver** *n.* camionista *m.*

**truckful, truckload** *n.* (rlwy.) vagone completo; (motor.) camion completo.

**truckle** *intr.* umiliarsi, avvilirsi, strisciare.

**truckle-bed** *n.* letto basso con rotelle; brandina.

**trucul-ent** *adj.* truculento, brutale, feroce, prepotente. **-ence, -ency** *n.* truculenza; prepotenza.

**trudge** *intr.* camminare faticosamente, trascinarsi.

**true** *adj.* vero; veritiero, verace, conforme a verità; esatto; *only too* —, più che vero; reale, autentico; fedele, leale, sincero; *as — as steel*, a tutta prova; — *to life*, al naturale; — *to type*, (biol.) conforme al genere, (fig.) conforme al proprio temperamento; —*!*, precisamente!, è vero!, hai ragione!; —, *I don't know him very well*, è vero che non lo conosco tanto bene; (iron.) *if he says so it must be —!*, se lo dice lui!; *to come* —, avverarsi, realizzarsi, verificarsi; *to hold — for*, valere per; *to ring* —, (of coin) risuonare vero, (fig.) sembrare vero; *to show one's — colours*, rivelare il proprio vero carattere; (comm.) — *copy*, copia conforme; — *to sample*, conforme a campione; (mech.) centrato, allineato, diritto; orizzontale, perfettamente liscio; *n.* (mech.) centratura, allineamento; *to be out of* —, aberrare, essere fuori squadra.

**true-blue** *adj.* fedele, leale, a tutta prova; *n.* (pol.) conservatore convinto. **-born** *adj.* vero, autentico, di marca, genuino. **-bred** *adj.* purosangue, di razza. **-hearted** *adj.* fedele, leale, sincero. **-heartedness** *n.* sincerità, lealtà.

**trueness** *n.* verità, veracità; fedeltà, sincerità; esattezza.

**truffle** *n.* tartufo.

**trug** *n.* (hortic.) cestino di vimini, panierino.

**truism** *n.* truismo; verità lapalissiana.

**truly** *adv.* veramente, davvero, in verità; fedelmente, sinceramente; *well and* —, ben bene; *really and* —, davvero davvero; giustamente; esattamente, precisamente; *yours (very)* —, (formal) suo devotissimo, con ossequi, (comm.) Vostro, distinti saluti; *yours* —, (fam.) io stesso, chi scrive.

**trump**[1] *n.* (poet., joc.) tromba, trombetta; *the last* —, la tromba del giudizio universale.

**trump**[2] *n.* (cards) trionfo, briscola; (bridge) atout *m.*; *spades are -s*, atout sono le picche; *no -s*, senza (atout); *three no -s*, tre senza; (fig., person) brav'uomo, bravo ragazzo; *to turn up -s*, riuscire, aver fortuna; *tr., intr.* (cards) giuocare una briscola; vincere con una briscola; (bridge) tagliare, giuocare un atout; (fig.) *to — up*, fabbricare, inventare.

**trump-card** *n.* trionfo, briscola; (bridge) atout; (fig.) cavallo di battaglia, forte *m.*

**trumpery** *adj.* che non ha valore; meschino; insignificante.

**trumpet** *n.* (mus.) tromba, trombetta; (poet.) oricalco; megafono, portavoce *m.*; trombettiere, araldo; *to blow a* —, suonare la tromba; (fig.) *to blow one's own* —, vantare i propri meriti, tessere le proprie lodi; *tr.* proclamare a suon di tromba; (fig.) strombazzare, strombettare, gridare sui tetti; *intr.* suonare la tromba; (of elephant) barrire.

**trumpet-call** *n.* squillo di tromba.

**trumpeter** *n.* suonatore di tromba; (mil.) trombettiere; (orn.) agami *m.*

**trumpeting** *n.* trombata; (of elephant) barrito.

**trumpet-major** *n.* (mil.) primo trombettiere.

**truncat-e** *tr.* troncare; mozzare. **-ed** *adj.* tronco, troncato; *-ed cone*, tronco di cono. **-ion** *n.* troncamento.

**truncheon** *n.* randello, manganello, sfollagente *m.*

**trundle** *tr.* far rotolare, far scorrere, abbambinare; *to — a hoop*, far ruzzolare un cerchio; spingere; *intr.* rotolare; *to — along*, camminare lentamente.

**trunk** *n.* (anat.) tronco, torso, busto; (of tree) fusto, tronco; — *road*, strada maestra, arteria, strada di grande comunicazione, strada nazionale; (archit.) troncone *m.*; baule *m.*, valigia, cassa; *cabin* —, baule da cabina; *wardrobe* —, baule armadio; (of elephant) proboscide *f.*; (min.) vasca di sedimentazione; *pl.* (cost.) calzoncini *m.pl.*

**trunk-call** *n.* (teleph.) chiamata interurbana.

**trunkful** *n.* baule pieno.

**trunk-line** *n.* (rlwy.) linea principale; (teleph.) linea interurbana, circuito di collegamento.

**trunnion** *n.* (artill.; mech.) orecchione *m.* **-bearing** *n.* (artill.) orecchioniera.

**truss** *n.* fastello, fascio, fagotto; (archit.) capriata, travatura, armatura; (med.) cinto erniario; (naut.) trozza; *tr.* affastellare; legare le ali di; *to — up*, legare saldamente; (archit.) armare, puntellare.

**trust** *n.* fiducia, fede *f.*, confidenza; *breach of* —, abuso di fiducia; *position of* —, incarico di fiducia; speranza; *to put one's — in*, aver fiducia in, affidarsi a; *to take on* —, accettare senza esitazione, credere a; (leg.) fidecommesso; — *deed*, atto di fidecommesso; *to hold in* —, tenere per fidecommesso; (comm.) credito; *on* —, a credito; (finan.) consorzio, cartello, trust *m.*; — *company*, società finanziaria; *investment* —, società finanziaria di investimento; *Trust House*, albergo gestito dalla Società 'Trust Houses' (alberghi di fiducia).

**trust** *tr.* fidarsi di, aver fiducia in, affidarsi a, credere a; *he is not to be -ed*, non si può fidarsi di lui, non è degno di fiducia; (fam.) — *him!*, lascia fare a lui!; (comm.) far credito a; *intr. to — to one's memory*, fidarsi della memoria; *to — in*, aver fede in, affidarsi a, credere a; sperare, augurarsi; *I — you will soon be better*, mi auguro che presto starai meglio.

**trusted** *adj.* di fiducia.

**trustee** *n.* fiduciario, curatore; fidecommissario; *board of -s*, consiglio di amministrazione; *Public Trustee*, curatore statale dei lasciti testamentari; — *in bankruptcy*, curatore di fallimento; (fig.) depositario. **-ship** *n.* carica di fiducia; (leg.) fidecommesso.

**trustful** *adj.* fiducioso, pieno di

fiducia, confidente. **-ly** *adv.* fiduciosamente; ad occhi chiusi. **-ness** *n.* fiducia, fede *f.*, confidenza; l'essere fiducioso.

**trusting** *adj.* fiducioso; ingenuo, semplice.

**trustworth-y** *adj.* fido, fidato, degno di fiducia; leale, onesto; credibile, verosimile, attendibile. **-iness** *n.* l'essere degno di fiducia, fedeltà, lealtà, fidatezza; credibilità, veracità, attendibilità, verosimiglianza.

**trusty** *adj.* fedele, leale, bravo; *n.* (in prison) carcerato che si comporta bene; informatore.

**truth** *n.* verità; vero; *the soul of —*, la bocca della verità; *gospel —*, vangelo; *the honest —*, la verità pura e semplice; *home -s*, verità spiacevoli; *— to tell, in —*, a dire il vero; *— will out*, la verità viene sempre a galla, le bugie hanno le gambe corte; *there is some — in what you say*, c'è del vero in ciò che dici; *there is no — in it*, non c'è nulla di vero; *this is nothing but the —*, questa non è che la pura verità; *to get at the — of the matter*, chiarire una faccenda; *to know for a —*, avere per vero; *to speak the —*, dire la verità.

**truthful** *adj.* verace, sincero, schietto, veritiero; vero, veridico, esatto; fedele. **-ness** *n.* veracità, sincerità, buona fede; verità, veridicità, esattezza; fedeltà.

**truth-drug, -serum** *n.* siero della verità.

**try** *n.* tentativo, prova; *to have a —*, tentare, provare; (rugby) meta; *to convert a —*, trasformare una meta.

**try** *tr.* provare, tentare, sperimentare; cercare, sforzarsi; *to — to*, provare a, tentare di; *to — hard to*, sforzarsi di, cercare con ogni mezzo di; saggiare; verificare, controllare, collaudare; (fig.) provare, mettere alla prova; *it's worth -ing*, vale la pena di provare; *to — one's best to*, fare tutto il possibile per, cercare con ogni mezzo di; *to — one's eyes*, affaticarsi gli occhi; *to — one's hand at*, provarsi a, tentare di fare; *to — someone's patience*, mettere alla prova la pazienza di qualcuno; *to — one's strength*, misurare le proprie forze; *to be sorely tried*, essere duramente provato; (leg.) processare, giudicare; *to be tried for manslaughter*, essere processato per omicidio colposo; *intr.* provare; *to — and — again*, provare e riprovare; *to — for*, cercare di ottenere, concorrere a, competere per; *to — on*, provare, misurare; (fam.) *to — it on, to — it on with*, cercare di imbrogliare; *to — out*, provare, sottoporre a prova, sperimentare, collaudare; *to — over*, provare.

**trying** *adj.* difficile, duro, penoso, che mette a dura prova, che affatica, seccante, snervante; *a — experience*, un incidente snervante; *a — time*, un brutto quarto d'ora, un momento critico; *— times*, tempi difficili; *a — winter*, un inverno rigido; insopportabile, difficile; *n.* prova, il provare, collaudo; (leg.) il processare, giudizio.

**try-on** *n.* tentativo d'inganno, imbroglio. **-out** *n.* prova, collaudo; (theatr.) rappresentazione in provincia.

**tryst** *n.* (poet.) appuntamento, convegno.

**tsar** *n.* zar *m.* **-evich** *n.* zarevic *m.* **-ina** *n.* zarina.

**tsetse** *n. — fly*, mosca tsè-tsè.

**t-square** *n.* riga a T, squadra a T.

**tub** *n.* tino, tinozza; mastello; conca; vasca da bagno; (fig.) *a tale of a —*, una fantasticheria; (min.) carrello, vagoncino; (rowing) barcaccia; (naut.) *old —*, vecchia carcassa.

**tuba** *n.* (mus.) tuba.

**tubbing** *n.* messa in tinozza; bagno in vasca.

**tubby** *adj.* a forma di tinozza; (fig.) grassoccio, corpulento, panciuto.

**tube** *n.* tubo; tubetto; *inner —*, camera d'aria; *speaking-tube*, citofono; *test-tube*, provetta; *bronchial -s*, bronchi; (bot.) tubulo, tubo pollinico; (underground rlwy.) ferrovia sotterranea, metropolitana.

**tuber** *n.* (bot.) tubero, tubercolo, radice tuberizzata.

**tubercle** *n.* (anat., med.) tubercolo.

**tubercular** *adj.* (bot.) a tubercoli, tubercolare; (med.) tubercolare, tubercoloso.

**tuberculosis** *n.* (med.) tubercolosi *f.*, tisi *f.*

**tuberose** *n.* (bot.) tuberosa.

**tube-station** *n.* stazione della metropolitana.

**tubing** *n.* tubazione, tubatura, tubi *m.pl.*; *rubber —*, tubo di gomma.

**Tübingen** *pr.n.* (geog.) Tubinga.

**tub-thumper** *n.* arringatore, oratore da strapazzo, demagogo. **-thumping** *n.* eloquenza ampollosa, oratoria da strapazzo.

**tubular** *adj.* tubolare, tubiforme; cavo; *— scaffolding*, ponteggio tubolare; *— furniture*, mobili metallici.

**tuck** *n.* (cost.) piega, basta, rimbocco; *to put a — in*, fare una basta a; (fam.) dolci *m.pl.*, leccornie *f.pl.* dolciumi *m.pl.*

**tuck** *tr.* (cost.) fare pieghe a; (fig.) stipare, far entrare; *to — away in a drawer*, chiudere in un cassetto; *a village -ed away in the mountains*, un paesino seminascosto tra i monti; ripiegare; mettere; *to — one's legs under one*, ripiegare le gambe sotto di sè; *the bird -ed its head under its wing*, l'uccello ripiegò il capo sotto l'ala; *to — a napkin under one's chin*, mettere un tovagliolo sotto il mento; *to — a rug around*, avvolgere in una coperta; *to — in*, ripiegare, piegare in dentro, rincalzare; *to — the sides of a bed in*, rincalzare un letto; *intr.* fare una scorpacciata; (fam.) *— in!*, buon appetito!; *to — up one's sleeves*, rimboccarsi le maniche; *to — someone up in bed*, rimboccare le coltri a.

**tucker** *n.* scialletto, fazzoletto; (fam.) *to put on one's best bib and —*, indossare gli abiti migliori, farsi bello.

**tuck-in** *n.* (fam.) scorpacciata. **-shop** *n.* (fam.) spaccio di dolciumi.

**Tudor** *adj.* dell'epoca Tudor, di stile Tudor, elisabettiano.

**Tuesday** *pr.n.* martedì *m.*; *on —*, (il) martedì; *Shrove —*, martedì grasso.

**tufa** *n.* (geol.) tufo.

**tuft** *n.* ciuffo, ciuffetto; ciocca; pennacchio; macchia; fiocco, nappa; barbetta; (anat.) glomerulo *m.* **-ed** *adj.* ornato di fiocchi; (bot.) acciocco; (orn.) crestato; *-ed lark*, cappellaccia.

**tug** *n.* strappo, tirata, strappata; (fig.) sforzo, strazio; (naut.) rimorchiatore; *tr.* tirare, strappare, trascinare, dare strattoni a; *to — along*, trascinare; (naut.) rimorchiare; *intr. to — at*, tirare, dare uno strappo a.

**tug-of-war** *n.* tiro alla fune.

**tuition** *n.* istruzione, insegnamento, lezioni *f.pl.*

**tulip** *n.* (bot.) tulipano.

**tulle** *n.* (text.) tulle *m.*, velo.

**Tully** *pr.n.* Tullio (Cicerone).

**tumble** *n.* capitombolo; caduta, cascata; *intr.* cascare, cadere, ruzzolare, fare un capitombolo; precipitarsi, buttarsi; *to — downstairs*, cascare giù per le scale; *to — into one's clothes*, vestirsi in tutta fretta; *to — into bed*, buttarsi sotto le coltri; *to — out of bed*, saltar giù dal letto; *to — down*, crollare, sfasciarsi, rovinare; *to — on*, imbattersi in, trovare per caso; *to — to*, afferrare il significato di, arrivarci; *to — over*, rovesciarsi, cadere; inciampare in; *tr.* scompigliare, rovesciare, mettere in disordine, disfare; *to — everything into a box*, buttare ogni cosa alla rinfusa in una scatola.

**tumbledown** *adj.* che sta per crollare, traballante, diroccato, sgangherato, cadente, rovinante.

**tumbled** *adj.* arruffato, scompigliato, in disordine.

**tumbler** *n.* saltimbanco, acrobata *m.*, giocoliere; bicchiere

(largo), calice *m.*, (hist.) bicchiere senza piede; (toy) misirizzi *m.*, sempreinpiedi *m.*; (orn.) — *pigeon*, piccione tomboliere; (mech.) cilindro, tamburo, barilatrice *f.*; (electr.) invertitore; — *switch*, commutatore oscillante.
**tumbrel, tumbril** *n.* carro ribaltabile, carro per trasporto letame; (Fr. hist.) carretta per il trasporto dei condannati a morte.
**tumef-y** *tr.* tumefare; *intr.* tumefarsi. **-action** *n.* tumefazione, gonfiore *m.*
**tumescent** *adj.* tumescente.
**tumid** *adj.* tumido, gonfio; (fig.) ampolloso. **-ity, -ness** *n.* tumidezza, gonfiore *m*; (fig.) ampollosità.
**tummy** *n.* (fam.) pancia, stomaco; pancione *m.*
**tummy-trouble** *n.* (fam.) mal di pancia.
**tumour** *n.* (med.) tumore, fibroma; *malignant* —, tumore maligno.
**tumult** *n.* tumulto; clamore *m*; fracasso, agitazione; disordine *m.*; sommossa; sconvolgimento. **-uous** *adj.* tumultuoso, clamoroso, burrascoso.
**tumulus** *n.* tumulo; dolmen *m.*
**tun** *n.* botte *f.*, barile *m.*
**tuna** *n.* (ichth.) tonno.
**tune** *n.* aria, motivo, melodia, cadenza; canzone *f.*; *to play a* —, suonare un motivo; *give us a* —*!*, suona qualcosa!; *to change* —, mutar registro; tono; *in*—, in tono, intonato, accordato, (fig.) d'accordo; *to be in* —, accordare; *out of* —, fuori tono, discordato, falso, stonato; *to be out of* —, (mus.) disaccordare, (fig.) stonare, scordare, non essere d'accordo; *to play* (*or sing*) *out of* —, stonare; armonia, accordo, consonanza; (fig.) *to pay to the* — *of*, pagare la bellezza di.
**tune** *tr.* (mus.) concordare, accordare, intonare; (radio) accordare, sintonizzare; (fig.) accordare, adattare, mettere d'accordo; *intr.* essere d'accordo, armonizzare; (radio) *to* — *in to another station*, cambiare stazione, trovare un'altra stazione; *to* — *up*, (mus.) accordarsi, (mech.) mettere a punto, regolare.
**tuneful** *adj.* melodioso, armonioso, arioso, melodico.
**tuner** *n.* accordatore; (text.) apparecchiatore; (radio) sintonizzatore.
**tungsten** *n.* (chem.) volframio, tungsteno.
**tunic** *n.* (cost.) tunica; (bot.) membrana, tunica.
**tunicate(d)** *adj.* (bot.; zool.) tunicato.
**tuning** *n.* (mus.) accordatura, temperamento, intonazione; — *device*, dispositivo per l'intonazione, (radio) sintonia, sintonizzazione, accordo; (mech.) messa a punto, regolazione.
**tuning-fork** *n.* (mus.) diapason *m.*, corista *m.* **-indicator** *n.* (radio) indicatore di sintonia. **-hammer, -key** *n.* (mus.) chiave per l'accordatura, accordatoio. **-knob** *n.* (radio) manopola di sintonia. **-scale** *n.* (radio) scala graduata. **-up** *n.* (mus.) accordatura, accordamento.
**Tunis** *pr.n.* (geog.) Tunisi *f.* **-ia** *pr.n.* (geog.) Tunisia. **-ian** *adj.*, *n.* tunisino.
**tunnel** *n.* galleria, traforo; *to drive a* — *through*, costruire una galleria sotto, traforare; *wind-tunnel*, tunnel aerodinamico; (archit.) — *vault*, volta a botte; *tr.*, *intr.* scavare una galleria (sotto), traforare; *to* — *into*, traforare. **-ling** *n.* traforo, costruzione di una galleria.
**tunny (-fish)** *n.* (ichth.) tonno.
**tuppence, tuppenny** see **twopence, twopenny.**
**turban** *n.* turbante *m.*
**turbid** *adj.* torbido, ammorchiato; (fig.) confuso, vago. **-ity** *n.* torbidezza; (fig.) confusione.
**turbine** *n.* turbina; *steam* —, turbina a vapore; *water* —, turbina idraulica; — *engine*, turbomotore.
**turbo-electric** *adj.* turboelettrico.
**turbo-generator** *n.* turbogeneratore. **-jet** *n.* (aeron.) turbogetto, turboreattore.
**turbot** *n.* (ichth.) rombo chiodato, rombo maggiore.
**turbul-ent** *adj.* turbolent; riottoso; tumultuoso; indisciplinato; (of wind) variabile; (of sea) grosso, burrascoso, agitato. **-ence** *n.* turbolenza, agitazione; indisciplina.
**turcoman** *n.* (hist.) turcomanno.
**turd** *n.* escrementi *m.pl.*, (vulg.) stronzo.
**tureen** *n.* zuppiera, terrina; (for sauce) salsiera.
**turf** *n.* piota, zolla erbosa, zoccolo; tappeto erboso; *the Turf*, il mondo ippico, ippica; *tr.* coprire di zolle erbose, piotare; (fam.) *to* — *out*, buttar fuori.
**Turf-accountant** *n.* allibratore.
**turgesc-ent** *n.* (bot.; med.) turgescente, turgido. **-ence** *n.* (bot.; med.) turgescenza, turgidezza.
**turgid** *adj.* turgido, gonfio; (fig.) pomposo, ampolloso, enfatico.
**Turin** *pr.n.* (geog.) Torino. **-ese** *adj.*, *n.* di Torino; torinese *m.*, *f.*
**turk** *n.* (ethn.) turco, (pop.) moro; (fig.) tiranno.
**turkey**[1] *n.* (orn.) tacchino; (USA) *to talk* —, parlare chiaro, non aver peli sulla lingua.
**Turkey**[2] *pr.n.* (geog.) Turchia; — *carpet*, tappeto orientale; — *red*, rosso turco. **-cock** *n.* (orn.) tacchino; *red as a -cock*, rosso come un tacchino. **-hen** *n.* tacchina.
**Turkish** *adj.* turco, della Turchia; (derog.) turchesco; — *bath*, bagno turco; — *tobacco*, tabacco Macedonia; — *towel*, asciugatoio turco, di spugna; *n.* turco, lingua turca.
**Turkoman** *n.* turcomanno.
**turmoil** *n.* tumulto, fermento; tormenta, burrasca; *in a* —, in agitazione.
**turn** *n.* giro, rotazione, rivoluzione; *a* — *of the screw*, un giro di vite; (cul.) *done to a* —, cotto a puntino; *a car with a good* — *of speed*, una macchina velocissima; svolta, curva, piega, cambiamento di direzione; (aeron.; naut.) virata; *a sharp* —, una svolta brusca; *to take a* — *to the right*, svoltare a destra; *the* — *of the tide*, il cambiamento della marea; *the tide is on the* —, la marea sta cambiando; *things are taking a bad* —, le cose stanno prendendo una brutta piega; *to take a* — *for the better*, volgere per il meglio, migliorare; *to take a* — *for the worse*, peggiorare, guastarsi; *the milk is on the* —, il latte sta diventando acido; *to give a new* — *to the conversation*, cambiare discorso; passeggiatina, due passi *m.pl.*; (fig.) *a* — *of phrase*, un modo di dire; colpo, effetto, spavento, crisi; *it gave me quite a* —, mi fece effetto, sono rimasto male; *yesterday she had one of her -s*, ieri ha avuto una delle sue solite crisi; volta, turno; *whose* — *is it?*, a chi tocca?; *it's his* —, tocca a lui; *in* —, *by -s*, uno alla volta, a vicenda, uno dopo l'altro; *out of* —, fuori turno; — *and* — *about*, a turni, a vicenda; *she laughed and cried by -s*, ora rideva, ora piangeva; *rising in his* —, alzandosi a sua volta; *to take -s in*, avvicendarsi in; *to do someone a good* —, rendere un servizio a qualcuno; *to do someone a bad* —, giuocare un brutto tiro a qualcuno; *it serves my* —, fa al caso mio; (provb.) *one good* — *deserves another*, chi semina raccoglie; (mus.) gruppetto, (of trill) terminazione; (theatr.) numero; (typ.) lettera rovesciata.
**turn** *tr.* girare, far girare, voltare, volgere, rivoltare; cambiare, trasformare, convertire, far diventare; (techn.) tornire; *to* — *one's back on*, volgere le spalle a, (fig.) abbandonare, piantare; *to* — *the corner*, voltar l'angolo, (fig.) superare il momento critico; *to* — *a deaf ear*, far orecchi da mercante; *to* — *the flank of an army*, aggirare un esercito; *to* — *someone's head*, far perdere la testa a

qualcuno; *to — the key in the lock*, girare la chiave nella serratura; *to — the pages of a book*, sfogliare un libro; *to — an honest penny*, guadagnarsi la vita onestamente; *to — the scale*, far traboccare la bilancia; *to — a ship from its course*, invertire la rotta di una nave; *to — the cold shoulder on*, trattare con freddezza; *to — a somersault*, fare una capriola; *to — one's steps homeward*, dirigere i propri passi verso casa; *to — the stomach*, dare la nausea, alterare lo stomaco; *to — the tables*, rovesciare le posizioni; *to — tail*, scappare, darsela a gambe, squagliarsi; *to — traitor*, passare al nemico; *it has -ed eight o'clock*, sono le otto passate; *to have -ed fifty*, aver cinquant'anni suonati; *intr.* girare, girarsi, (ri)voltarsi, voltare, prendere; cambiare, cambiarsi; *to toss and — in bed*, rivoltarsi nel letto; *to — right*, voltare a destra; (mil.) *right —!*, a destr'!; *left —!*, a sinistr'!; *about —!*, dietro front'!; *he doesn't know which way to —*, non sa a che santo votarsi; diventare, farsi, trasformarsi in; *to — Catholic*, farsi cattolico; *to — nasty*, andare in bestia; *to — red*, diventare rosso, arrossire; *to — sour*, cagliarsi; FOLLOW. BY ADV. OR PREP.: *to — about*, *intr.* girare, (ri)girarsi, (mil.) far dietro front; *to — against*, *tr.* alienare; *he has -ed everyone against him*, si è alienato l'affetto di tutti; *intr.* ribellarsi a, rivoltarsi contro; *to — aside*, *tr.* scartare, allontanare, respingere, sviare, *intr.* scostarsi, voltarsi da parte; *to — away*, *tr.* cacciare, congedare, rimandare, *intr.* voltarsi da parte; *to — away from*, voltare le spalle a; *to — back*, *tr.* far ritornare, respingere, *intr.* tornare indietro, rifare il cammino; *to — down*, *tr.* (ri)piegare, (light, *etc.*) abbassare, (fig.) respingere; *to — in*, *tr.* ripiegare, far rientrare; *to — one's job in*, dare le demissioni, abbandonare il lavoro; restituire, riconsegnare; *intr.* andare a letto; *his toes — in*, ha i piedi vari; *to — inside out*, *tr.* rivoltare, rovesciare; *to — into*, *tr.* cambiare in, trasformare in, trasmutare in, convertire in, ridurre a; *to — water into wine*, cambiare acqua in vino; *to — something into money*, convertire qualcosa in denaro; *to — English into Italian*, tradurre dall'inglese in italiano; *intr.* diventare, cambiarsi in, trasformarsi in, ridursi a; (of car, pedestrian) *to — into a street*, svoltare in una via; *to — off*, *tr.* (light, radio) spegnere, (tap) chiudere, (water) tagliare, chiudere; *to — someone off the premises*, cacciar qualcuno dallo stabile; *intr.* svoltare, cambiare stada, imboccare una via laterale; *to — on*, *tr.* (light, radio) accendere, (tap) aprire; (pop.) eccitare; *intr.* dipendere da; *to — on someone*, aggredire, rivoltarsi contro qualcuno; *to — out*, *tr.* scacciare, buttar fuori, mettere alla porta; (mil.) *to — out the guard*, far uscire la guardia; (gas, *etc.*) spegnere; produrre, fabbricare; vuotare; pulire a fondo; *to be well -ed out*, essere molto elegante, essere vestito impeccabilmente; *intr.* uscire; *to — out on strike*, mettersi in sciopero; accadere, risultare, finire, andare; (fam.) *let's hope it -s out all right!*, Dio ce la mandi buona!; *to — out to the advantage of*, tornare a vantaggio di; *to — out to be*, dimostrarsi, risultare; diventare; *to — over*, *tr.* voltare, rivoltare; *to — over the page*, voltare la pagina; *please — over!* (*p.t.o.*), voltare!, vedi retro!; (fig.) *to — over a new leaf*, cambiare vita; trasferire; rovesciare, capovolgere; (fig.) *to — over in one's mind*, riflettere su; *intr.* (ri)voltarsi, rivoltolarsi, rovesciarsi, capovolgersi, (of car) capotare; *to — round*, *tr.* (far) girare, voltare, *intr.* girare, voltarsi, volgersi; *to — to*, *intr.* mettersi al lavoro, (become) diventare, andare in; *the weather is -ing to rain*, sta per piovere; *to — to the dictionary*, consultare il dizionario; *to — to another matter*, cambiare argomento; *to — to someone*, ricorrere all'aiuto di qualcuno; *to — something to account*, trar vantaggio da qualcosa; *to — one's attention to*, rivolgere l'attenzione a; *to be able to — one's hand to any kind of work*, essere capace di fare qualsiasi genere di lavoro; *to — one's thoughts to God*, rivolgere i pensieri a Dio; *to — towards*, voltarsi verso; *to — up*, *tr.* alzare, rivoltare, rimboccare, (card) scoprire, (gas, *etc.*) alzare; *to — up one's nose*, arricciare il naso; *to — up the whites of one's eyes*, mostrare il bianco degli occhi; *to — up a word in the dictionary*, cercare una parola nel dizionario; (slang) *to — up one's toes*, crepare; *intr.* (ri)voltarsi in su, capitare, arrivare all'improvviso; accadere, succedere, (of card, *etc.*) uscire; *to — up again*, ripresentarsi, ricomparire, capitare ancora una volta; *to — upside down*, *tr.* capovolgere, *intr.* capovolgersi, (of car, *etc.*) capotare.

**turncoat** *n.* voltagabbana *m.*, rinnegato, ricreduto, traditore, voltabandiera *m.*

**turncock** *n.* fontaniere *m.*

**turner** *n.* tornitore. **-y** *n.* arte del tornitore; tornitura, officina di tornitore.

**turning** *adj.* girevole, che gira, ruotante; (of road) a svolte, sinuoso, tortuoso, serpeggiante; *n.* rotazione, giro, il girare; (in road) svolta, curva, svoltata, gomito, (off main street) traversa, via laterale; *the second — to the right*, la seconda (svolta) a destra; *— back*, ritorno; *— out*, uscita, sfratto; *— of the tide*, cambiamento della marea, (fig.) rovesciamento della situazione; (mech.) tornitura; *pl.* (mech.) trucioli *m.pl.*

**turning-lathe** *n.* (mech.) tornio. **-point** *n.* svolta decisiva, crisi *f.*, momento critico; (survey.) vertice *m.* **-radius** *n.* (motor.) raggio di sterzo.

**turnip** *n.* (bot.) rapa, navone *m.* **-tops** *n.* cime di rapa. **-watch** *n.* (fam.) cipolla.

**turnkey** *n.* secondino, carciere *m.*

**turnout** *n.* concorso, pubblico numeroso, affluenza; sciopero; (mil.) tenuta, uniforme *f.*; equipaggio; (fam.) *to have a good —*, far pulizia, mettere un po' d'ordine.

**turnover** *n.* rovesciamento, ribaltamento; (comm.) giro d'affari, movimento, entrate e uscite *f.pl.*; *— tax*, imposta generale sulle entrate (abbrev. I.G.E.), tassa di scambio; (cul.) torta, pasticcio; (typ.) *— word*, richiamo; (pol.), spostamento di voti.

**turn-pike** *n.* barriera (dove si paga il pedaggio); (hist.) *— road*, strada a pedaggio. **-spit** *n.* (person) girarrosto *m.*; (instrument) spiedo. **-stile** *n.* tornichetto, arganello, cancelletto girevole. **-table** *n.* (rlwy.) piattaforma girevole, voltacarro; (on gramophone) giradischi *m.*

**turn-up** *n.* risvolto, rimboccatura, rimbocco.

**turpentine** *n.* trementina, acquaragia.

**turpitude** *n.* turpitudine *f.*

**turps** *n.* (fam.) essenza di trementina.

**turquoise** *n.* turchese *f.*

**turret** *n.* torretta; (rlwy.) lanternino, lucernario. **-ed** *adj.* turrito, con torrette.

**turtle** *n.* tartaruga, testuggine *f.* di mare; (cul.) *— soup*, zuppa di tartaruga; *mock-turtle soup*, finto brodo di tartaruga; *to turn —*, capovolgersi, (of car) capotare.

**turtle-dove** *n.* (orn.) tortora.

**Tuscan** *adj.*, *n.* toscano; (ancient hist.) tosco.

**Tuscany** *pr.n.* (geog.) Toscana.

**tush** *excl.* oibò!, macchè!

**tusk** *n.* zanna. **-ed** *adj.* zannuto. **-er** *n.* animale zannuto; (elephant) elefante maschio; (boar) cinghiale *m.*

**tussle** *n.* zuffa, rissa, mischia, battibecco; lotta; *intr.* azzuffarsi, venire alle mani; lottare.
**tussock** *n.* ciuffo d'erba. **-y** *adj.* erboso, coperto di ciuffi d'erba.
**tussore** *n.* (text.) tussor *m.*
**tut** *excl.* — — *!*, là là!, ohimè!
**tutee** *n.* (Univ.) allievo, allieva.
**tutel-age** *n.* tutela. **-ar(y)** *adj.* tutelare.
**tutor** *n.* precettore; ripetitore; istitutore; insegnante privato; (leg.) tutore (di minorenne); *tr.* istruire; ammaestrare; (fig.) disciplinare; (fig.) *to — oneself*, padroneggiarsi. **-ial** *adj.* di precettore, di ripetitore; (leg.) tutorio, tutelare; *n.* lezione privata. **-ing** *n.* insegnamento; lezioni private; istruzione.
**tu-whit tu-whoo** *n.* squittìo della civetta; uh uh!
**tuxedo** *n.* smoking *m.*
**twaddle** *n.* (fam.) sciocchezze *f.pl.*, frottole *f.pl.*, ciarle *f.pl.*; vaniloquio, sproloquio.
**twain** *n., adj.* (poet.) due; *these —*, questi due; *to cut in —*, tagliare in due.
**twang** *n.* stridore *m.*, suono acuto; suono nasale, nasaggine *f.*; *to speak with a —*, parlare con voce nasale, naseggiare; *tr.* lasciar andare la corda di un arco; (mus.) far vibrare, far risuonare, pizzicare le corde di; *intr.* vibrare, risuonare, schitarrare; naseggiare, parlare con voce nasale.
**twat** *n.* (vulg.) fica.
**tweak** *n.* pizzicotto; *tr.* pizzicare; tirare.
**tweed** *n.* tessuto di lana scozzese; — *cap*, berretto sportivo; (woman's) — *suit*, tailleur sportivo.
**Tweedledum** *n. — and Tweedledee*, due persone simili; *it's a case of — and Tweedledee*, se non è zuppa è pan bagnato.
**'tween** *prep.* see **between.**
**'tweendecks** *n.* (naut.) falso ponte, interponte *m.*, intercapedine *f.*; *adv.* nell'interponte, sottocoperta.
**tweeny, Tweeny-maid** *n.* (hist.; joc.) servetta.
**tweet** *n.* cinguettìo, pigolìo; *intr.* cinguettare, pigolare.
**tweezers** *n.* pinzette *f.pl.*
**twelfth** *ord. num.* dodicesimo, duodecimo; *(on) the — of March*, il dodici marzo; *Louis the Twelfth*, Luigi dodicesimo; *Twelfth Day*, l'Epifania; *Twelfth Night*, la notte dell'Epifania; *n.* dodicesimo, dodicesima parte; (mus.) duodecima.
**twelve** *card. num.* dodici; una dozzina di; — *o'clock*, le dodici, (midday) mezzogiorno, mezzodì, (midnight) mezzanotte; *a boy of —*, un ragazzo dodicenne; *to be — years old*, essere dodicenne, aver dodici anni; *in -s*, dodici alla volta, (typ.) indodicesimo. **-month** *n.* anno, annata; *this day -month*, fra un anno, (a year ago) un anno fa.
**twelve-note, -tone** *adj.* (mus.) dodecafonico; — *system*, dodecafonia. **-point** *adj., n.* (typ.) corpo dodici. **-year-old** *adj., n.* dodicenne *m., f.*
**twentieth** *ord. num.* ventesimo, vigesimo; *(on) the — of March*, il venti marzo; *the — century*, il ventesimo secolo, il novecento; *n.* ventesimo; ventesima parte.
**twentieth-century** *adj.* novecentesco.
**twenty** *card. num.* venti; *about — people*, una ventina di persone; *period of — years*, ventennio; — *thousand*, ventimila; *the twenties*, gli anni dal 'venti al 'trenta, la terza decade del secolo; *to be in one's early twenties*, avere poco più di vent'anni; *to be in one's late twenties*, essere vicino alla trentina.
**twenty-first** *ord. num. n.* ventunesimo, ventesimo primo.
**twenty-five** *card. num.* venticinque; *n.* (rugby) la linea dei ventidue metri.
**twentyfold** *adj.* ventuplo; *adv.* venti volte tanto.
**twenty-year-old** *adj., n.* ventenne *m., f.*
**twerp** *n.* (pop.) mascalzone *m.*
**twice** *adv.* due volte, il doppio di, doppiamente; — *as big as*, due volte più grande di; *I am — your age*, ho il doppio della tua età; — *over*, a due riprese, due volte; *to think — before doing something*, pensarci due volte prima di fare qualcosa; *he did not have to be asked —*, non si fece pregare due volte; *that made him think —*, ciò gli ha dato da pensare.
**twiddle** *tr., intr.* (far) girare, (far) roteare; *to — one's moustache*, attorcigliarsi i baffi; (fig.) *to — one's thumbs*, gingillarsi, grattarsi la pancia.
**twig**[1] *n.* ramoscello, ramo, fraschetta; verga; *dry —*, stecco; (bot.) sarmento; (water-diviner's) bacchetta.
**twig**[2] *tr.* (fam.) capire, arrivarci.
**twi-light** *n.* crepuscolo; penombra; luce crepuscolare; (fig.) tramonto, fine *f.* **-lit** *adj.* crepuscolare; illuminato dal tramonto; fioco, diffuso.
**twill** *n.* (text.) tessuto diagonale, spigato, saia.
**twin** *adj., n.* gemello; — *brother*, fratello gemello; — *sister*, sorella gemella; *pl.* gemelli; *to have -s*, dare alla luce gemelli; *a pair of -s*, una coppia di gemelli; *Siamese -s*, gemelli siamesi, (fig.) amici inseparabili; (astron.) *the Twins*, i Gemelli, i Gemini; — *beds*, letti gemelli; (fig.) — *souls*, anime gemelle; *attrib.* gemello, geminato, doppio, a due, bi-; (archit.) (ab)binato; (bot.) doppio. **-barrelled** *adj.* a due canne. **-cylinder** *adj.* (motor.) a due cilindri.
**twine** *n.* spago; refe *m.*; corda; filo ritorto; *tr.* torcere, attorcigliare, intrecciare; *to — one's arms round*, prendere tra le braccia, abbracciare; *intr.* attorcigliarsi; serpeggiare.
**twin-engined** *adj.* (aeron.) a due motori; — *aircraft*, bimotore *m.*
**twinge** *n.* fitta, contrazione dolorosa, spasimo; (fig.) — *of conscience*, rimorso di coscienza; *intr.* far male, causare dolore acuto.
**twining** *adj.* sinuoso, serpeggiante; (bot.) volubile, rampicante.
**twin-jet** *adj. — plane*, bireattore *m.*
**twinkl-e** *n.* luccichìo, scintillìo, balenìo, battito, movimento rapido; ammicco, strizzata d'occhio; *in the — of an eye*, in un batter d'occhio, in men di un baleno; *a mischievous —*, una strizzatina d'occhio maliziosa; *intr.* luccicare, scintillare, balenare; ammiccare, strizzare l'occhio. **-ing** *adj.* luccicante, scintillante; *n.* see **twinkle.**
**twin-screw** *adj.* (naut.) vite *f.* a due eliche.
**twirl** *n.* giro; mulinello; piroetta; (archit.) voluta, spirale *f.*; spira; ghirigoro, svolazzo; *tr.* girare, roteare, brillare, fare il mulinello con; *to — one's moustache*, attorcigliarsi i baffi; *intr.* girare, ruotare, avere il brillo; piroettare, brillare.
**twist** *n.* (text.) filo ritorto, cordoncino, tessuto a spire; (of tobacco, *etc.*) treccia, rotolo; torsione, torcimento, avvitamento; *to give a — to*, torcere; svolta, curva, gomito; *to give one's ankle a —*, slogarsi la caviglia; (billiards) effetto; (dance) twist *m.*; (fig.) deformazione, perversione, alterazione, travisamento; (of character) stramberia, eccentricità.
**twist** *tr.* torcere, contorcere; attorcigliare; intrecciare; avvolgere; abbindolare; *to become -ed*, attorcigliarsi, avvolgersi, abbindolarsi; *to — one's ankle*, slogarsi la caviglia; *to — one's mouth*, torcere la bocca, fare una smorfia; *to — the tail of*, torcere la coda a; (text.) ritorcere, accordellare; imbrogliare, abbindolare, agguindolare; *to — someone round one's little finger*, far ciò che si vuole con qualcuno; *to — someone's arm*, convincere; travisare, svisare, alterare; *intr.* torcersi, contorcersi, attorcigliarsi, divincolarsi; serpeggiare, insinuarsi; ballare il twist.
**twister** *n.* (text.) (ri)torcitoio, (ri)torcitrice; (fig.) imbroglione *m.*, truffatore, raggiratore; prob-

lema difficile, enigma *m.*; *tongue-twister*, scioglilingua *m.*
**twisting** *adj.* tortuoso, sinuoso, serpeggiante; *n.* (con)torcimento, avvolgimento; contrazione; (text.) torcitura, accordonatura, svergolamento.
**twit** *tr.* rimbrottare, rimproverare; dileggiare, beffarsi di; *n.* (slang) imbecille *m.*, *f.*
**twitch** *n.* contrazione spasmodica, tic *m.*, movimento convulsivo; (fig.) — *of conscience*, rimorso di conscienza; (tug) strattone *m.*, tirata; *tr.* tirare, dare uno strappo a; (of animal) *to — its ears*, rizzare gli orecchi; *to — something out of someone's hand*, far saltare qualcosa dalla mano di qualcuno; *intr.* contrarsi, avere un tic nervoso, contorcersi, palpitare; (of eyes) ammiccare.
**twitching** *n.* contrazione, tic nervoso, movimento convulsivo.
**twitter** *n.* cinguettìo, pigolìo; (fig.) *to be all of a —*, essere scombussolato, avere la fifa addosso; *intr.* cinguettare.
**'twixt** *prep.* (poet.) see **betwixt, between.**
**two** *card. num.* due; — *hundred*, duecento, dugento; — *thousand*, duemila; *the — of them*, entrambi, tutti e due; *one or —*, uno o due, qualche, parecchi; — *by —*, *in -s*, a due a due; *in -s*, in un attimo; — *into four goes twice*, il due nel quattro sta due volte; — *out of ten*, due su dieci; — *deep*, in due file; (cards) — *no trumps*, due senza; *the — of spades*, il due di picche; — *can play at that game*, non sei il solo a saperlo; *-'s company, three's none*, poca brigata vita beata; *to add — and — together*, tirare le conclusioni; *you can't add — and — together*, ti ci vuol l'abbaco; *to divide into —*, dimezzare; *to eat enough for —*, mangiare per due; *to fold in —*, piegare in due; *to walk — abreast*, camminare per due. **-fold** *adj.* doppio, duplice; *adv.* doppiamente, due volte.
**two-barrelled** *adj.* a due canne; — *gun*, doppietta. **-chamber** *adj.* (pol.) *the -chamber system*, il sistema bicamerale. **-colour(ed)** *adj.* a due colori, bicolore. **-decker** *n.* (ship) nave a due ponti; (bus) autobus a imperiale. **-edged** *adj.* a doppio taglio. **-engined** *adj.* bimotore; *-engined plane*, bimotore; *-engined jet plane*, bireattore. **-faced** *adj.* see **double-faced, -footed** *adj.* bipede. **-handed** *adj.* ambidestro; con due mani; *-handed saw*, segone a quattro mani; (of game) che si giuoca in due. **-headed** *adj.* bicipite. **-horse** *adj.* a due cavalli; *-horse carriage*, tiro a due, carrozza a due cavalli. **-legged** *adj.* bipede. **-master** *n.* (naut.) duealberi *m.* **-oar** *adj.* a due remi; *n.* un due di punta.
**two-pence** *n.* due vecchi penny; (fig.) *he doesn't care — about it*, non gliene importa un corno; *it isn't worth —*, non vale niente. **-penny** *adj.* da due penny, da quattro soldi.
**twopenny-halfpenny** *adj.* (hist.) da due penny e mezzo; (fig.) da quattro soldi, che non vale niente.
**twopennyworth** *n.* (per un valore di) quattro soldi.
**two-phase** *adj.* (electr.) bifase. **-piece** *adj.* in due pezzi; *a -piece suit*, un due-pezzi. **-seater** *n.* macchina a due posti, biposto, coupé *m.*; *-seater sports car*, vettura sportiva a due posti. **-sided** *adj.* bilaterale, ambilaterale; (fig.) ambiguo, che ha due aspetti.
**twostep** *n.* (dance) passo doppio.
**two-storied** *adj.* a due piani. **-stroke** *adj.* (of motor) a due tempi. **-way** *adj.* (of road, traffic) a due sensi; (of tap) a due vie; (electr., of switch), bipolare; *-way radio*, radio trasmittente-ricevente. **-winged** *adj.* (ent.) dittero. **-yearly** *adj.* biennale, duennale. **-year-old** *adj.* di due anni; *n.* due-anni *m.*; *three two-year-olds*, tre due-anni.
**tycoon** *n.* taicun *m.*; (fig.) affarista *m.*, magnate *m.*
**tying** *adj.* impegnativo, che non lascia libero, che vincola; *n.* allacciamento, annodatura, legatura; (surg., of artery) compressione, emostasi *f.*
**tyke** *n.* cagnaccio.
**tympanum** *n.* timpano.
**type** *n.* tipo; genere *m.*; sorta; categoria, modello; *a queer —*, un tipo strano; (typ.) carattere tipografico; caratteri, tipi; *in 12-point —*, in (carattere) corpo dodici; *bold —*, neretto; *to keep the — standing*, lasciar in piede la composizione; *to print from —*, stampare dal piombo; *to set (in) —*, comporre; *tr.*, *intr.* see **typewriter**; (med.) determinare il gruppo sanguigno.
**type-area** *n.* (typ.) giustezza. **-bar** *n.* (typ.) compositoio, (slang) riga di composizione. **-caster, -founder** *n.* fonditore di caratteri; (machine) macchina fonditrice. **-casting** *n.* fusione di caratteri; (theatr.) distribuzione dei ruoli a seconda delle caratteristiche personali degli attori. **-face** *n.* (typ.) occhio del carattere; carattere *m.*, serie *f.* **-foundry** *n.* fonderia di caratteri. **-height** *n.* (typ.) altezza, corpo. **-metal** *n.* lega tipografica; (fam.) piombo.
**typescript** *adj.*, *n.* dattiloscritto.
**typesett-er** *n.* compositore. **-ing** *n.* composizione; *-ing machine*, macchina compositrice; (Monotype, Linotype) tastiera.
**type-write** *tr.*, *intr.* dattilografare, scrivere a macchina. **-writer** *n.* macchina da scrivere. **-writer-ribbon** *n.* nastro inchiostrato per macchina da scrivere. **-writing** *n.* dattilografia, lo scrivere a macchina; *-writing pool*, servizio di dattilografia. **-written** *adj.* dattiloscritto.
**typhoid** *adj.* (med.) tifoideo; *n.* febbre tifoidea, tifoide *f.*
**typhoon** *n.* tifone *m.*
**typhus** *n.* (med.) tifo.
**typical** *adj.* tipico, caratteristico, rappresentativo.
**typify** *tr.* rappresentare, figurare, incarnare, esemplificare, essere caratteristico di; (of person) essere il tipo di.
**typing** *n.* see **typewriting.**
**typist** *n.* dattilografo, dattilografa; *shorthand —*, stenodattilografo, stenodattilografa.
**typo-** *pref.* tipo-.
**typograph-y** *n.* arte tipografica, tipografia. **-er** *n.* tipografo. **-ic(al)** *adj.* tipografico.
**tyrannical** *adj.* tirannico, dispotico, tirannesco.
**tyrannicide** *n.* (crime) tirannicidio; (criminal) tirannicida *m.*, *f.*
**tyrannize** *tr.*, *intr.* tiranneggiare, fare il tiranno, regnare dispoticamente; *to — over*, tiranneggiare, opprimere.
**tyrannous** *adj.* tirannico, dispotico, tirannesco.
**tyranny** *n.* tirannia, tirannide *f.*, dispotismo.
**tyrant** *n.* tiranno, despota *m.*; *petty —*, tirannello; *to play the —*, tiranneggiare, fare il tiranno.
**tyre**[1] *n.* gomma, pneumatico; *flat —*, gomma a terra; *anti-skid —*, gomma antisdrucciolevole; (of cartwheel) cerchione *m.*
**Tyre**[2] *pr.n.* (geog.) Tiro.
**tyre-chains** *n.* catene antineve. **-cover** *n.* copertone *m.* **-lever** *n.* leva smontapneumatici *m.* **-tread** *n.* battistrada *m.*
**Tyrian** *adj.* tirio, di Tiro.
**tyro** *n.* novizio, principiante *m.*, *f.*, apprendista *m.*, *f.*, neofito.
**Tyrol** *pr.n.* (geog.) Tirolo; *South —*, Alto Adige. **-ese** *adj.*, *n.* tirolese *m.*, *f.*; *South -ese*, atesino, sudtirolese *m.*, *f.*
**Tyrrhenian** *adj.* tirreno; — *Sea*, (Mar) Tirreno.
**Tzar, Tzarina** See **tsar, tsarina.**
**tzigane** *adj.*, *n.* tzigano, zingaro.

**U, u** *n. m., f.* (pron. oo); (teleph.) — *for uncle,* U come Udine; (gramm.; joc.) *U and non-U,* usato dalle classi superiori e non usato dalle classi superiori.
**ubiquitous** *adj.* dotato di ubiquità, che si trova ovunque, onnipresente. **-ness, ubiquity** *n.* ubiquità; (theol.) onnipresenza.
**U-boat** *n.* sommergibile tedesco.
**udder** *n.* mammella.
**Udine** *pr.n.* (geog.) Udine *f.*; *inhabitant of —,* Udinese *m., f.*
**ugh** *excl.* uh!
**uglif-y** *tr.* imbruttire, rendere brutto. **-ication** *n.* imbruttimento.
**ugliness** *n.* bruttezza; laidezza.
**ugly** *adj.* brutto; laido; *as — as sin,* brutto come il peccato; *rather —,* bruttino; (slang) *an — mug,* un brutto ceffo; turpe, vile, abietto; (fig.) brutto, minaccioso, pericoloso, *an — customer,* un tipo pericoloso.
**Ukrain-e** *pr.n.* (geog.) Ucraina. **-ian** *adj., n.* ucraino.
**ulcer** *n.* ulcera; *gastric —,* ulcera gastrica; *duodenal —,* ulcera duodenale; (fig.) piaga morale. **-ate** *tr.* ulcerare; *intr.* ulcerarsi. **-ation** *n.* ulcerazione. **-ous** *adj.* ulceroso.
**ult.** *adv.* (comm.) ultimo, scorso mese, ultimo scorso; *your letter of the 3rd ult.,* vostra lettera del tre s.m.
**ulterior** *adj.* ulteriore, più lontano; (fig.) segreto, nascosto; *an — motive,* un motivo segreto; *without — motives,* senza secondi fini.
**ultimate** *adj.* ultimo, finale, definitivo; *— result,* risultato definitivo; *— success,* successo finale; *— destination,* destinazione finale; (fig.) fondamentale, basilare; *— truth,* verità fondamentale; *— cause,* causa prima; (chem.) *— analysis,* analisi *f.* elementare; (math.) *— ratio,* rapporto assoluto; *n.* assoluto; *the quest for an —,* la ricerca dell'assoluto. **-ly** *adv.* alla fine, in definitiva; fondamentalmente.
**ultimatum** *n.* ultimatum; *to deliver an —,* presentare un ultimatum; *in the nature of an —,* equivalente ad un ultimatum.
**ultimo** *adv.* (comm.) dello scorso mese, ultimo scorso.
**ultra** *adj.* estremo, eccessivo; *n.* (pol.) estremista *m.,* oltranzista *m.*; (fig.) *a non plus —,* un nonplusultra *m.*
**ultra-fashionable** *adj.* all'ultima moda; (fam.) molto snob.
**ultramarine** *adj.* d'oltremare; *adj., n.* (colour) oltremare *m.,* oltremarino.
**ultramontan-e** *adj.* oltremontano, subalpino, italiano; (rel. hist.) *adj., n.* oltremontano. **-ism** *n.* (rel. hist.) oltramontanismo *m.* **-ist** *n.* (rel. hist.) oltremontano *m.,* sostenitore *m.* dell'oltremontanismo.
**ultramundane** *adj.* oltremondano; non compreso nel sistema solare.
**ultra-red** *adj.* (phys.) ultrarosso, infrarosso. **-short** *adj.* (radio) ultracorto; *-short waves,* onde cortissime. **-sonic** *adj.* (phys.) ultrasonico, ultrasonoro. **-violet** *adj.* (phys.) ultravioletto.
**ultra vires** *adv.* (leg.) *action —,* eccesso di potere; *to act —,* commettere un eccesso di potere.
**ululat-e** *intr.* ululare, urlare; (fig.) lamentarsi. **-ion** *n.* ululato.
**Ulysses** *pr.n.* Ulisse.
**umbellifer** *n.* (bot.) ombrellifero. **-ous** *adj.* (bot.) ombrellifero.
**umber** *n.* (paint.) terra d'ombra, terra di Siena; *burnt —,* terra d'ombra bruciata; *adj.* di color terra d'ombra; fosco, scuro.
**umbilic-us** *n.* (anat.) ombelico, umbilico; (geom.) ombilico. **-al** *adj.* (anat.) ombelicale, umbilicale; *-al cord,* cordone umbilicale.
**umbrage** *n.* ombra, sospetto; (fig.) dispiacere *m.,* risentimento; *to take — at,* adombrarsi per, risentirsi.
**umbrella** *n.* ombrello, parapioggia *m.*; *beach —,* ombrellone da spiaggia; *to put up one's —,* aprire l'ombrello; *to fold up one's —,* chiudere l'ombrello; (zool.) ombrello; (bot.) ombrella. **-frame** *n.* intelaiatura dell'ombrello. **-maker, -mender, -seller** *n.* ombrellaio. **-ribs** *n.pl.* stecche *f.pl.* d'ombrello **-shaped** *adj.* a forma d'ombrello, ombrelliforme **-stand** *n.* portaombrelli *m.* **-tree** *n.* (bot.) magnolia tripetala.
**Umbria** *pr.n.* (geog.) Umbria. **-n** *adj., n.* (geog.) umbro, umbra.
**umlaut** *n.* dieresi tedesca.
**umpir-e** *n.* arbitro; giudice *m.* di gara; *tr., intr.* arbitrare, fare l'arbitro. **-ing** *n.* arbitraggio.
**umpteen** *adj.* (fam.) moltissimi, mille, un numero imprecisato. **-th** *adj.* (slang) ennesimo.
**un-** *neg. pref.* in-, non, senza; for words beginning with **un-** not listed below see under unprefixed word.
**unabashed** *adj.* imperturbato, impassibile; senza batter ciglio.
**unabat-ed** *adj.* che non diminuisce, costante, senza sosta. **-ing** *adj.* persistente, sostenuto.
**unable** *adj.* incapace, inabile, incompetente; *to be — to . . .,* non potere . . .
**unabridged** *adj.* non abbreviato, senza tagli, completo; *— edition,* edizione integrale.
**unacademic** *adj.* non accademico.
**unaccented** *adj.* non accentato, atono; (mus.) *— beat,* battuta debole.
**unacceptable** *adj.* inaccettabile, non accetto, sgradito.
**unaccommodating** *adj.* poco condiscendente, poco accomodante; scortese, sgarbato.
**unaccompanied** *adj.* non accompagnato, solo; *ladies — by a gentleman are not admitted,* non sono ammesse le signore non accompagnate; (mus.) senza accompagnamento; *passage for — violin,* passo per solo violino.
**unaccountable** *adj.* inesplicabile, inspiegabile, strano.
**unaccounted** *adj.* *— for,* inesplicato, inspiegato; mancante; *this sum is — for in the balance-sheet,* questa somma non figura nel bilancio; *seven of the passengers are still — for,* sulla sorte di sette passeggeri mancano tuttora notizie.
**unaccustomed** *adj.* insolito, non abituale, dissueto; *— to,* poco abituato a.
**unacknowledged** *adj.* non riconosciuto, non confessato, non ammesso; rimasto senza risposta, senza riscontro, inevaso.
**unacquainted** *adj.* ignaro, non al corrente; *to be — with the facts,* ignorare i fatti; non presentato, che non ha fatto conoscenza; *to be — with,* non conoscere.
**unadaptable** *adj.* inadattabile; poco socievole.
**unadopted** *adj.* non adottato; *— road,* strada privata, la cui manutenzione spetta ai proprietari del terreno.
**unadorned** *adj.* disadorno; *the — truth,* la pura verità.
**unadulterated** *adj.* non adulterato, non sofisticato, sincero; *— praise,* lode sincera; *— wine,* vino sincero.
**unadvised** *adj.* non consigliato; imprudente, sconsiderato.
**unaffected** *adj.* semplice, genuino, sincero; senza affettazione; impassibile; imperturbabile; (chem.) inalterabile, che resiste; *metal — by acids,* metallo che resiste agli acidi. **-ness** *n.* assenza di affettazione, semplicità, naturalezza.
**unafraid** *adj.* impavido, senza paura.
**unaided** *adj.* senza aiuto, da solo.
**unalarmed** *adj.* tranquillo, non allarmato.
**unalloyed** *adj.* (of metal) senza lega; (fig.) puro, perfetto, esente.
**unalter-able** *adj.* immutabile, invariabile. **-ed** *adj.* tale quale, immutato.
**unambiguous** *adj.* inequivocabile, chiaro, evidente; *— terms,* termini precisi.
**unambitious** *adj.* senza ambizione, modesto.
**unamended** *adj.* senza modifiche, non emendato, non corretto; (pol.) *to pass a bill —,* approvare

un progetto di legge senza emendamenti.

**un-American** *adj.* non americano; contrario ai costumi o interessi americani; — *activities*, attività giudicate pregiudiziali alla sicurezza degli Stati Uniti.

**unamiable** *adj.* poco amabile, poco affabile; burbero, sgarbato.

**unamusing** *adj.* poco divertente, noioso.

**unanimity** *n.* unanimità; accordo; *with* —, all'unanimità, di comune accordo, unanimemente.

**unanimous** *adj.* unanime. **-ly** *adv.* all'unanimità, di comune accordo; unanimemente.

**unanswer-able** *adj.* cui non si può rispondere; irrefutabile, incontestabile. **-ed** *adj.* senza risposta, inevaso; non refutato.

**unanticipated** *adj.* imprevisto, inatteso.

**unappeasable** *adj.* implacabile; insaziabile.

**unappetizing** *adj.* poco appetitoso, sgradevole.

**unappreciat-ed** *adj.* incompreso, non apprezzato. **-ive** *adj.* insensibile, indifferente.

**unapproachable** *adj.* inaccessibile, irraggiungibile, inavvicinabile; riservato. **-ness** *n.* inaccessibilità.

**unapprov-ed** *adj.* non approvato. **-ing** *adj.* poco favorevole, disapprovante.

**unarmed** *adj.* inerme, disarmato.

**unascertainable** *adj.* non verificabile, indeterminabile.

**unashamed** *adj.* senza vergogna, svergognato, spudorato, sfacciato; *to be* — *of*, non vergognarsi di.

**unasked** *adj.* non richiesto, non sollecitato; non invitato; *adv.* *to do something* —, fare qualcosa spontaneamente.

**unassailable** *adj.* inattaccabile, irrefutabile; (fig.) irreprensibile.

**unassisted** *adj.* see **unaided.**

**unassuaged** *adj.* non placato.

**unassuming** *adj.* senza pretese, modesto, semplice.

**unassured** *adj.* incerto, dubbio; diffidente, dubbioso; (comm.) non assicurato.

**unaton-able** *adj.* inespiabile. **-ed** *adj.* inespiato.

**unattached** *adj.* indipendente, libero; (mil.) in disponibilità, non aggregato a nessun reparto; (fam., of girl) non fidanzata; (of man) celibe.

**unattainable** *adj.* irraggiungibile, inaccessibile.

**unattempted** *adj.* intentato.

**unattended** *adj.* solo, non accompagnato, senza seguito; non custodito, senza sorveglianza.

**unattractive** *adj.* poco attraente, che non attrae; antipatico.

**unauthentic** *adj.* non autentico, apocrifo.

**unauthorized** *adj.* non autorizzato, illecito.

**unavailab-le** *adj.* non disponibile, indisponibile. **-ility, -leness** *n.* indisponibilità.

**unavailing** *adj.* inutile, vano, inefficace, infruttuoso.

**unavoidable** *adj.* inevitabile, ineluttabile. **-ness** *n.* inevitabilità, ineluttabilità.

**unaware** *adj.* ignaro, inconsapevole, incosciente; *to be* — *of*, ignorare. **-ness** *n.* inconsapevolezza.

**unawares** *adv.* inconsapevolmente, inconsciamente; inavvertitamente; di sorpresa.

**unbacked** *adj.* senza appoggi, senza sostenitori; (cavallo) sul quale nessuno vuol scommettere; (bldg.) non rinforzato.

**unbalance** *n.* equilibrio, mancanza di equilibrio; *tr.* sbilanciare. **-d** *adj.* sbilanciato, non equilibrato (comm.) non pareggiato.

**unbandage** *tr.* sbendare, togliere le bende a.

**unbar** *tr.* aprire, disserrare, levare le sbarre. **-red** *adj.* aperto, non sbarrato; senza barra; senza barriere; (mus.) non diviso in battute.

**unbearabl-e** *adj.* insopportabile, intollerabile. **-y** *adv.* insopportabilmente, intollerabilmente; *it is -y hot*, fa un caldo insopportabile.

**unbeat-able** *adj.* imbattibile, invincibile, insuperabile; (sport) fuoriclasse. **-en** *adj.* insuperato, mai battuto.

**unbecoming** *adj.* sconveniente, disdicevole, incongruo; (of clothing) che non si addice, inadatto. **-ness** *n.* sconvenienza, disdicevolezza; incongruità.

**unbeknown** *adj.* (lit.) sconosciuto; *adv.* — *to*, all'insaputa di.

**unbelief** *n.* incredulità, scetticismo; (theol.) miscredenza.

**unbeliev-able** *adj.* incredibile. **-er** *n.* persona incredula, scettico; (theol.) miscredente *m., f.* **-ing** *adj.* incredulo; miscredente.

**unbend** *tr.* raddrizzare; (fig.) rilassare, distendere; *intr.* raddrizzarsi; (fig.) lasciarsi andare, perdere il sussiego, farsi affabile. **-ing** *adj.* rigido, non pieghevole; (fig.) inflessibile, austero, intransigente.

**unbiased** *adj.* imparziale, spregiudicato, non prevenuto; (boccia) senza peso eccedente.

**unbidden** *adj.* non invitato; non richiesto, non sollecitato, spontaneo.

**unbind** *tr.* sciogliere, slegare; togliere le bende a, sbendare.

**unblemished** *adj.* puro, senza macchia, immacolato; (fig.) irreprensibile.

**unblock** *tr.* sbloccare, sgombrare; (cards) *to* — *a suit*, sbloccare un colore.

**unblushing** *adj.* che non arrossisce; (fig.) sfacciato, senza vergogna. **-ly** *adv.* senza arrossire, sfacciatamente.

**unboiled** *adj.* non bollito, crudo.

**unbolt** *tr.* aprire, togliere il chiavistello a.

**unborn** *adj.* non ancora nato, nascituro; (fig.) futuro, da venire.

**unbosom** *tr.* scoprire, rivelare; *rfl.* sbottonarsi, sfogarsi.

**unbound** *p.def.*, *part.* of **unbind,** *q.v.*; *adj.* slegato, sciolto, liberato; (of book) non rilegato, in brossura.

**unbounded** *adj.* illimitato, sconfinato; (fig.) smisurato.

**unbowed** *adj.* indomito, tenuto sempre insù.

**unbreakable** *adj.* infrangibile.

**unbreathable** *adj.* irrespirabile.

**unbribable** *adj.* incorruttibile.

**unbridle** *tr.* sbrigliare (un cavallo); (fig.) dare libero corso a, sfogare. **-d** *adj.* senza briglia, sbrigliato; (fig.) sfrenato, scatenato.

**unbroached** *adj.* (of cask) non spillato; (fig.) non affrontato.

**unbroken** *adj.* intatto, intero, non rotto; inviolato, vergine; — *soil*, terreno mai arato, terreno vergine; continuo, ininterrotto; indomito, invitto; — *spirit*, spirito indomito; (of horse) non ammansito, brado; (mil.) — *front*, fronte intatta, fronte non infranta; — *record*, record imbattuto.

**unbrotherly** *adj.* poco fraterno, indegno di un fratello; non amichevole.

**unbuckle** *tr.* slacciare, sfibbiare; *rfl.* (fig.) uscire dal riserbo.

**unbuilt** *adj.* non ancora costruito; (of ground) — *on*, fabbricabile.

**unburden** *tr.* scaricare, alleggerire; (fig.) sollevare, alleviare, liberare; *to* — *the mind*, alleggerire lo spirito; *rfl.* sfogarsi; *to* — *oneself of a secret*, liberarsi dal peso di un segreto.

**unburied** *adj.* insepolto, senza sepoltura.

**unbusinesslike** *adj.* poco pratico, non portato per gli affari; *in an* — *way*, senza metodo; *to be* —, mancare di metodo, mancare di senso pratico.

**unbutton** *tr.* sbottonare; *rfl.* *to* — *oneself*, sbottonarsi (also fig.).

**uncalled** *adj.* non chiamato, non invitato; — *for*, non necessario, gratuito, superfluo; immeritato, ingiustificato.

**uncannily** *adv.* stranamente, misteriosamente; straordinariamente.

**uncanny** *adj.* strano, misterioso, soprannaturale; inquietante.

**uncared-for** *adj.* trascurato, negletto, abbandonato.

**uncaught** *adj.*, inafferrato, libero; (of criminal) latitante.
**unceasing** *adj.* incessante, continuo. **-ly** *adv.* incessantemente, senza tregua.
**unceremonious** *adj.* poco cerimonioso, brusco; semplice, alla buona. **-ly** *adv.* senza cerimonie, senza complimenti, alla buona; (pejor.) bruscamente, sgarbatamente.
**uncertain** *adj.* incerto; indeterminato; dubbio, aleatorio; *of — origin*, di origine incerta; *— light*, luce incerta; *— outline*, contorno mal definito; *— temper*, umore incerto, umore ineguale; *— health*, salute vacillante; irresoluto; *to be — what to do*, non sapere che cosa fare; (of weather) instabile, mutevole. **-ty** *n.* incertezza; incerto; *pl. the -ties of life*, gl'incerti della vita.
**unchain** *tr.* scatenare, sciogliere da catene, liberare; (fig.) dare libero corso a.
**unchallengeable** *adj.* indiscutibile, indisputabile; (leg.) irrecusabile.
**unchallenged** *adj.* non sfidato, non provocato; non chiamato in questione, incontestato; (leg.) non ricusato.
**unchangeable** *adj.* immutabile, invariabile, inalterabile. **-ness** *n.* immutabilità, invariabilità, inalterabilità.
**unchang-ed** *adj.* immutato, invariato; sempre lo stesso. **-ing** *adj.* immutabile, invariabile; che non cambia mai.
**uncharged** *adj.* non carico, scarico; (leg.) non accusato; (electr.) scarico; (comm.) non addebitato, non fatturato; *— for*, gratuito, gratis.
**uncharitable** *adj.* poco caritatevole, poco indulgente. **-ness** *n.* mancanza di carità.
**uncharted** *adj.* non segnato sulle carte geografiche; (fig.) inesplorato.
**unchaste** *adj.* impudico, impuro, incontinente.
**unchastened** *adj.* non castigato; (fig.) impenitente.
**unchecked** *adj.* non represso, sfrenato, indisciplinato; non ostacolato; (comm.) non controllato, non verificato.
**unchivalrous** *adj.* poco cavalleresco, poco cortese; ingeneroso.
**unchoke** *tr.* (techn.) sbloccare.
**unchristian** *adj.* non cristiano, pagano; indegno di un cristiano; (fig.) poco comodo, assurdo; *at this — hour*, a quest'ora impossibile.
**uncial** *adj.* onciale.
**uncircumcised** *adj.* non circonciso; non ebreo.
**uncircumscribed** *adj.* incircoscritto, illimitato.
**uncivil** *adj.* incivile, maleducato, scortese.
**uncivilized** *adj.* barbaro, non civilizzato.
**unclad** *adj.* non vestito, svestito, nudo; (fig.) spoglio.
**unclasp** *tr.* slacciare, sfibbiare; (fig.) allentare la stretta di.
**uncle** *n.* zio; *Uncle John*, lo zio Giovanni; *great-uncle*, prozio; (fam.) prestatore su pegno.
**unclean** *adj.* impuro; immondo; sporco, sudicio. **-ly** *adj.* impuro; immondo; sporco; *adv.* in modo poco pulito; sporcamente. **-liness** *n.* impurità; sporchezza; sudiceria; sudicezza. **-ness** *n.* impurità; mancanza di pulizia; (rel). immondizia.
**uncleansed** *adj.* non purificato; non pulito.
**unclench** *tr.* aprire, rilassare.
**unclinch** *tr.* disserrare, schiudere.
**uncloak** *tr.* togliere il mantello a; (fig.) smascharare, svelare.
**unclog** *tr.* liberare da impedimenti, sbloccare.
**unclothe** *tr.* svestire, spogliare; *intr.* svestirsi, spogliarsi.
**unclouded** *adj.* senza nuvole, sereno; (of fluid) limpido.
**uncloyed** *adj.* insaziato, non satollato.
**uncoil** *tr.* svolgere, srotolare, sgomitolare; *intr.* svolgersi, srotolarsi.
**uncoloured** *adj.* incolore, non colorato; (fig.) imparziale.
**uncomely** *adj.* sgraziato, brutto; (fig.) sconveniente.
**uncomfortable** *adj.* scomodo, disagevole; *to feel —*, sentirsi a disagio; *an — feeling*, una sensazione inquietante; fastidioso, spiacevole.
**uncommitted** *adj.* non commesso; non impegnato; (pol.) neutrale.
**uncommon** *adj.* poco comune, raro, insolito. **-ly** *adv.* insolitamente, raramente; *not -ly*, assai spesso; singolarmente, straordinariamente; *-ly good*, eccellente; *-ly well done*, eseguito a meraviglia. **-ness** *n.* rarità, singolarità.
**uncommunicative** *adj.* riservato, taciturno, poco comunicativo.
**uncomplaining** *adj.* che non si lamenta; paziente, rassegnato.
**uncompleted** *adj.* incompiuto, incompleto; non finito.
**uncomplimentary** *adj.* poco lusinghiero.
**uncomprehending** *adj.* che manca di comprensione, non comprensivo.
**uncompromising** *adj.* intrattabile, intransigente; assoluto; rigido.
**unconcern** *n.* noncuranza, indifferenza. **-ed** *adj.* noncurante, indifferente, distaccato, impassibile; *he went on speaking quite -ed*, senza commuoversi continuò a parlare; neutrale, imparziale, estraneo. **-edly** *adv.* con noncuranza, con aria indifferente; senza commuoversi.
**unconditional** *adj.* senza riserve, senza condizioni; incondizionato, assoluto; *— acceptance*, approvazione senza riserve; *— refusal*, rifiuto categorico; *— surrender*, resa incondizionata.
**uncongenial** *adj.* poco simpatico, antipatico; poco favorevole; spiacevole, sgradito; *— job*, lavoro ingrato; (fig.) *— atmosphere*, ambiente *m.* ostile.
**unconnected** *adj.* non collegato, disgiunto; (fig.) sconnesso, sconclusionato; senza legami di parentela; senza rapporti, senza relazioni, senza amicizie.
**unconquerable** *adj.* invincibile, indomabile, insuperabile, irresistibile; incorreggibile; insuperabile; insaziabile.
**unconquered** *adj.* invitto, indomito; insormontabile; non conquistato.
**unconscionab-le** *adj.* (fig.) irragionevole; eccessivo, enorme, smisurato; esorbitante, esagerato. **-ly** *adv.* poco coscienziosamente; eccessivamente. **-leness** *n.* irragionevolezza; enormità.
**unconscious** *adj.* inconscio; inconsapevole; *to be — of*, non accorgersi di, essere ignaro di, non rendersi conto di; *to be not — of*, non essere insensibile a; privo di sensi, svenuto, insensibile; *to become —*, svenire, perdere conoscenza, perdere i sensi; *n.* (psych.) *the —*, l'inconscio. **-ly** *adv.* inconsciamente, inconsapevolmente; senza saperlo, senza rendersene conto. **-ness** *n.* inconsapevolezza; incoscienza; svenimento, stato di incoscienza.
**unconsidered** *adj.* inconsiderato, sconsiderato; avventato.
**unconsol-able** *adj.* inconsolabile. **-ed** *adj.* inconsolato.
**unconstitutional** *adj.* incostituzionale, anticostituzionale.
**unconstrained** *adj.* non costretto, senza costrizione, libero; (fig.) spontaneo, naturale, disinvolto; *— laughter*, ilarità spontanea; *— manner*, aria disinvolta.
**unconstraint** *n.* assenza di costrizione; libertà, disinvoltura.
**unconsummated** *adj.* (of marriage) inconsumato.
**uncontainable** *adj.* irreprimibile, irrefrenabile.
**uncontested** *adj.* incontestato, pacifico; *— election*, elezione alla quale si presenta un solo candidato.
**uncontrollab-le** *adj.* incontrollabile, irrefrenabile, irreprimibile, irresistibile; indocile, ingovernabile, indisciplinato; assoluto; *— temper*, esplosione d'ira. **-ility** *n.* incontrollabilità, indocilità, indisciplina.

**uncontrolled** *adj.* non controllato, indipendente; senza freno, sfrenato; — *liberty*, libertà assoluta; — *passions*, passioni sfrenate.

**unconventional** *adj.* non convenzionale; anticonformista; — *dress*, costume originale; *to lead an — life*, fare una vita irregolare, fare una vita di boemme. **-ity** *n.* anticonvenzionalismo; anticonformismo, originalità. **-ly** *adv.* in modo non convenzionale, in modo anticonformista; senza badare alle convenzioni.

**unconversant** *adj.* — *with*, poco pratico di, non al corrente di, poco versato in.

**unconvertibile** *adj.* inconvertibile.

**unconvicted** *adj.* non condannato, non riconosciuto colpevole; (leg.) *previously* —, incensurato.

**unconvinc-ed** *adj.* non convinto, scettico, poco persuaso. **-ing** *adj.* poco convincente, poco verosimile.

**unco-ordinated** *adj.* non coordinato, che manca di coordinazione; (fig.) incoerente, scucito.

**uncork** *tr.* sturare, stappare; (fig.) *to — one's feelings*, sfogarsi.

**uncorrupted** *adj.* incorrotto, incontaminato, integro.

**uncounted** *adj.* non contato; innumerevole.

**uncoupl-e** *tr.* scoppiare, spaiare; sguinzagliare, lasciar liberi; (rlwy.) sganciare; (eng.) staccare. **-ing** *n.* scoppiamento, spaiamento; lo sguinzagliare; (rlwy.) sganciamento; (eng.) distacco.

**uncouth** *adj.* rozzo, grossolano; goffo, sgraziato; selvatico, rustico; strano, bizzarro. **-ness** *n.* goffaggine *f.*, rozzezza.

**uncover** *tr.* scoprire, spogliare; (fig.) rivelare, svelare; smascherare, palesare; scoperchiare; esporre; mettere allo scoperto; *intr.* scoprirsi, scappellarsi, togliersi il cappello. **-ed** *adj.* scoperto, spogliato, nudo; scoperchiato; senza tetto; senza cappello, a capo scoperto; (comm.) allo scoperto.

**uncritical** *adj.* non critico, privo di senso critico; *an — audience*, un pubblico poco esigente.

**uncross** *tr.* disincrociare.

**uncrossed** *adj.* mai attraversato, mai valicato; non incrociati; (of cheque) non sbarrato; (fig.) non ostacolato.

**unction** *n.* unzione; l'ungere; *extreme* —, estrema unzione, olio santo; (fig.) unzione, mellifluità; *to speak with* —, parlare con compiacimento.

**unctuous** *adj.* untuoso, oleoso, grasso; (fig.) untuoso; mellifluo. **-ness** *n.* untuosità; mellifluità.

**uncultivated** *adj.* non coltivato; (fig.) senza cultura.

**uncultured** *adj.* incolto, senza cultura.

**uncurbed** *adj.* libero, senza costrizione; sfrenato; (of horse) senza barbazzale *m.*

**uncurl** *tr.* disfare (i riccioli); sgomitolare; svolgere; *intr.* svolgersi, sgomitolarsi, srotolarsi.

**uncurtailed** *adj.* non abbreviato; per esteso, integrale; senza restrizione.

**uncustomary** *adj.* insolito, inconsueto.

**uncut** *adj.* non tagliato, senza tagli, intatto, integro; — *pages*, pagine intonse.

**undamaged** *adj.* non avariato, non danneggiato; intatto, in buone condizioni; (fig.) — *reputation*, reputazione intatta.

**undated** *adj.* non datato, senza data.

**undaunt-able** *adj.* indomabile, imperturbabile. **-ed** *adj.* intrepido, impavido, imperterrito.

**undeceive** *tr.* disingannare, disilludere; aprire gli occhi a.

**undecided** *adj.* indeciso, irresoluto; non risolto; (leg.) vertente.

**undecipherable** *adj.* indecifrabile; illeggibile.

**undefaced** *adj.* non deturpato, non sfigurato, non mutilato; intatto; (of stamp) non timbrato, non cancellato; *landscape — by posters*, paesaggio non deturpato dalle insegne pubblicitarie.

**undefeated** *adj.* invitto, indomito, insuperato.

**undefended** *adj.* indifeso, senza difesa, privo di protezione; (leg.) non assistito da un avvocato; — *suit*, causa in cui il convenuto si astiene dal comparire.

**undefiled** *adj.* puro, senza macchia, immacolato; non deturpato, non profanato.

**undefined** *adj.* non precisato, indeterminato, vago.

**undeliver-able** *adj.* (of letter) che non può essere recapitata; (comm.) non disponibile. **-ed** *adj.* non liberato, non sgravato; (comm.) non consegnato; (of letter) non recapitata; *if -ed return to sender*, in caso di mancata consegna rispedire al mittente.

**undemonstr-able** *adj.* indimostrabile. **-ative** *adj.* poco espansivo, riservato.

**undeniable** *adj.* innegabile, irrefutabile, incontestabile; (leg.) irrecusabile.

**undenominational** *adj.* non appartenente ad alcuna setta religiosa; laico, aconfessionale; — *schools*, scuole laiche.

**undependable** *adj.* poco fidato; poco attendibile.

**under** *adv.* sotto, al di sotto; *children of ten years and* —, bambini di dieci anni e al di sotto; *to keep someone* —, tenere qualcuno in soggezione; (fam.) *down* —, agli antipodi, in Australia e nella Nuova Zelanda; *prep.* sotto, al di sotto di; — *water*, sott'acqua; — *the table*, sotto la tavola; — *one's breath*, sottovoce; — *lock and key*, sotto chiave; — *the counter*, sottobanco; (mil.) — *the rank of captain*, al di sotto del grado di capitano; (fam.) *to be — the weather*, sentirsi poco bene; — *construction*, in costruzione; — *the circumstances*, in queste circostanze; — *these conditions*, in queste condizioni; *to be — the necessity of*, essere nella necessità di; secondo, in virtù di; meno di; *to be — forty*, avere meno di quarant'anni; *to be — age*, essere minorenne; inferiore a.

**under-** *pref.* sotto-, sub-, vice-; inferiore, insufficiente.

**under-arm** *adj.* ascillare; *adv.* (sport) con la mano al di sotto del gomito o della spalla.

**underact** *tr.* (theatr.) interpretare con scarsa efficacia.

**underbid** *tr.* praticare prezzi meno cari di, offrire condizioni più vantaggiose di; *intr.* (cards) fare una dichiarazione inferiore al valore della mano.

**under-body** *n.* (motor.) telaio.

**undercall** *tr.* (cards) See **underbid.**

**under-carriage** *n.* (aeron.) carrello di atterraggio.

**undercharge** *tr.*, *intr.* (artill.; electr.) sottocaricare; (comm.) far pagare meno del dovuto.

**under-clothes, -clothing** *n.* biancheria intima, biancheria personale; indumenti intimi.

**undercoat** *n.* (of animals) peluria; (paint.) fondo, imprimatura.

**undercurrent** *n.* corrente sottomarina; sottocorrente *f.*; (fig.) tendenza nascosta, fondo.

**undercut** *n.* (cul.) filetto di manzo; (boxing) undercut *m.*; colpo di taglio; *tr.* minare, erodere, scalzare; (comm.) offrire a prezzo più basso di, fare condizioni più vantaggiose di. **-ting** *n.* erosione, scalzatura; (comm.) vendita a prezzi inferiori a quelli della concorrenza.

**under-developed** *adj.* sottosviluppato; *the — countries*, i paesi sottosviluppati.

**underdog** *n.* (fam.) persona che ha la peggio; gli oppressi, i poveri.

**underdone** *adj.* (cul.) poco cotto, al sangue; (fig.) fatto in modo inefficace.

**underestimat-e** *tr.* sottovalutare, stimare al di sotto del valore, calcolare troppo basso. **-ion** *n.* sottovalutazione, stima inferiore al valore.

**under-exposure** *n.* (photog.) sottoesposizione.

**underfed** *adj.* malnutrito, denutrito; (eng.) sottoalimentato.
**underfeed** *tr.* nutrire insufficientemente; (eng.) alimentare insufficientemente. **-ing** *n.* denutrizione; (eng.) sottoalimentazione.
**underflow** *n.* corrente subacquea, corrente sottomarina.
**underfoot** *adv.* sotto i piedi, tra i piedi; (fig.) in posizione d'inferiorità.
**under-garment** *n.* indumento intimo.
**undergo** *tr.* subire; sottoporsi a; *to — an operation*, sottoporsi a un intervento chirurgico; *to — a prison sentence*, scontare una condanna; patire, soffrire, sopportare; *-ing repairs*, in riparazione.
**undergraduate** *n.* 'studente *m.*, studentessa (all'Università di Oxford o di Cambridge).
**underground** *adj.* sotterraneo; *— railway*, ferrovia sotterranea, metropolitana; *— passage*, passaggio sotterraneo, sottopassaggio; (min.) *— worker*, minatore; (fig.) clandestino, segreto; (pol.) *— movement*, movimento clandestino, resistenza, macchia; *to go —*, darsi alla macchia; *adv.* nel sottosuolo, sotto terra, sotterra; (pol.) clandestinamente; *n.* sottosuolo; (pol.) resistenza; (rlwy.) *The Underground*, la ferrovia sotterranea (londinese).
**undergrown** *adj.* poco sviluppato.
**undergrowth** *n.* sterpaglia, sottobosco, boscaglia, macchia; (med.) crescita ritardata.
**underhand** *adj.* clandestino, segreto; *— dealings*, mene segrete; (pejor.) losco, mancino; *— trick*, tiro mancino.
**under-jaw** *n.* mascella inferiore, mandibola.
**underlay** *n.* (typ.) tacco; feltro (posto sotto il tappeto); *tr.* mettere sotto; (typ.) taccheggiare.
**underlie** *tr.* giacere sotto, essere al di sotto di; (fig.) essere alla base di; *intr.* (geol.) inclinarsi.
**underline** *tr.* sottolineare.
**underlinen** *n.* biancheria personale.
**underling** *n.* subordinato, subaltero; (pejor.) tirapiedi *m.*
**underlying** *adj.* sottostante, che giace sotto; (fig.) fondamentale, che serve di base a.
**undermanned** *adj.* a corto di mano d'opera, con personale insufficiente; (naut.) insufficientemente equipaggiato.
**undermentioned** *adj.* sottoindicato, sottocitato.
**undermine** *tr.* minare, sottominare; (fig.) insidiare.
**underneath** *adj.* più basso, inferiore; *adv.* di sotto, al di sotto, in basso; *from —*, da sotto; *n.* la parte più bassa; *prep.* sotto, al di sotto di.
**under-nourished** *adj.* malnutrito. **-nourishment** *n.* malnutrizione.
**underpaid** *adj.* mal pagato, mal retribuito.
**underpants** *n.* mutande *f.pl.*, slip *m.*
**underpart** *n.* parte inferiore, parte più bassa.
**underpass** *n.* sottopassaggio.
**underpin** *tr.* (bldg.) puntellare, sottomurare.
**underpopulated** *adj.* sottopopolato, scarsamente popolato.
**underprivileged** *adj. the —*, i mal pagati; i non abbienti.
**underproduction** *n.* sottoproduzione, produzione inferiore al rendimento normale.
**underquote** *tr.* (comm.) quotare prezzi più bassi di.
**underrate** *tr.* sottovalutare, stimare troppo poco, fare troppo poco caso di, attribuire poca importanza a; sprezzare.
**underscor-e** *tr.* sottolineare. **-ing** *n.* sottolineatura.
**under-secretary** *n.* sottosegretario; *permanent —*, direttore generale di un ministero.
**undersell** *tr.* svendere, vendere a minor prezzo di, vendere sottocosto.
**under-sheriff** *n.* viceceriffo.
**undershirt** *n.* maglia, camiciola.
**undershoot** *tr.* (aeron.) *to — the runway*, fare un atterraggio corto, atterrare corto.
**undershor-e** *tr.* (bldg.) puntellare, sostenere. **-ing** *n.* puntellamento.
**underside** *n.* parte inferiore, parte più bassa.
**undersigned** *adj.* sottoscritto, firmato; (*I*) *the —*, io sottoscritto, il sottoscritto, chi scrive; *pl.* i sottoscritti.
**under-sized** *adj.* di misura inferiore al normale; troppo piccolo; di dimensioni insufficienti.
**under-skirt** *n.* sottana. **-slip** *n.* sottogonna.
**understaffed** *adj.* che ha personale insufficiente, a corto di manodopera.
**understand** *tr.* capire; comprendere; intendere; *to make oneself understood*, farsi capire; rendersi conto (che); *I — (that) he wants to leave tomorrow*, mi risulta che vuol partire domani; *to — one's business*, conoscere bene il proprio mestiere; *to — horses*, intendersi di cavalli; *to give someone to — that . . .*, far credere a qualcuno che . . ., dare a divedere che; *I was given to — that you would help us*, mi si diceva che tu ci avresti aiutato; *it is understood that you too are invited*, è sottinteso che anche tu sei invitato; *I am at a loss to —*, non ci capisco niente; *to — how to drive a car*, saper guidare una macchina.
**understandable** *adj.* comprensibile.
**understanding** *adj.* comprensivo, intelligente; *n.* comprensione; *the age of —*, l'età della ragione; *beyond our —*, al di là della nostra comprensione; *he has a good — of philosophy*, conosce bene la filosofia; accordo, intesa; *on this —*, a queste condizioni; *on the — that*, alla condizione che, premesso che.
**understate** *tr.* minimizzare; attenuare. **-ment** *n.* attenuazione del vero, eufemismo.
**understudy** *n.* (theatr.) sostituto (di un attore), pertichino; *tr.* (theatr.) sostituire (un attore), studiare per sostituire.
**under-subscribed** *adj.* (finan.) non interamente assorbito dal mercato, non coperto.
**undertake** *tr.* intraprendere, incaricarsi di, impegnarsi a; *to — a journey*, intraprendere un viaggio; *to — a task*, intraprendere un lavoro; *to — responsibility*, assumersi la responsabilità, promettere, garantire.
**undertaker** *n.* imprenditore di pompe funebri; *-'s mute*, impiegato di pompe funebri, (pop.) beccamorti *m.*
**undertaking** *n.* impresa, l'intraprendere; (comm.) impresa, intrapresa; impegno, promessa; *a written —*, un impegno scritto.
**underthrust** *n.* (geol.) spinta (di una faglia).
**undertimed** *adj.* (photog.) sottoesposto.
**undertone** *n.* tono sommesso, bisbiglio, bassa voce; *to speak in an —*, parlare a bassa voce; (fig.) *an — of discontent*, una corrente sorda di malcontento.
**undertrump** *tr.* (cards) tagliare con atout troppo debole.
**undervalu-e** *tr.* sottovalutare. **-ation** *n.* sottovalutazione, valutazione inferiore al dovuto; (fig.) scarsa stima.
**underwater** *adj.* subacqueo, sottomarino; *— fishing*, pesca subacquea.
**underwear** *n.* indumenti intimi.
**underwent** *p.def.* of **undergo**, *q.v.*
**underwood** *n.* sottobosco, sterpaglia.
**underworld** *n.* inferno, inferi *m.pl.*; (of crime) malavita, bassi fondi *m.pl.*
**underwrite** *tr.* sottoscrivere, firmare; (finan.) garantire (una emissione); (insurance) assicurare, riassicurare, dividere il rischio. **-r** *n.* firmatario; (finan.) garante *m.* di una emissione; riassicuratore.
**undeserved** *adj.* immeritato, ingiusto.

**undeserving** *adj.* immeritevole; — *of*, che non merita.
**undesign-ed** *adj.* involontario, accidentale, non premeditato; imprevisto, inatteso. **-ing** *adj.* candido, schietto, sincero.
**undesirable** *adj.* indesiderabile; inopportuno; *n.* persona non grata; — *alien*, straniero raccomandato per la deportazione. **-ness** *n.* l'essere indesiderabile; inopportunità.
**undesirous** *adj.* non desideroso; *to be — of*, aver poca voglia di.
**undetected** *adj.* non scoperto.
**undetermined** *adj.* indeterminato, indefinito, indeciso; irresoluto, indeciso.
**undeterred** *adj.* non scoraggiato, non distolto.
**undeveloped** *adj.* non sviluppato; (of land) non sfruttato; — *area*, area fabbricabile; — *mind*, mente incolta; (photog.) — *image*, immagine *f.* latente.
**undeviating** *adj.* diritto, che non devia; (fig.) costante, rigido.
**undid** *p.def.* of **undo**, *q.v.*
**undies** *n.pl.* (fam.) biancheria intima (per donna).
**undignified** *adj.* senza dignità poco dignitoso; *to be* —, mancare di dignità.
**undiluted** *adj.* non diluito, liscio; concentrato.
**undine** *n.* (myth.) ondina.
**undisbanded** *adj.* (mil.) ancora in servizio, non congedato.
**undiscern-ible** *adj.* impercettibile, invisibile. **-ing** *adj.* senza discernimento, poco accorto, poco perspicace.
**undisciplined** *adj.* indisciplinato.
**undiscoverable** *adj.* introvabile, irreperibile, non scopribile.
**undiscriminating** *adj.* indiscriminato; che non fa distinzioni, senza discernimento; poco fine, poco raffinato.
**undisguised** *adj.* non mascherato, non dissimulato, schietto, sincero; evidente; *with — pleasure*, con evidente piacere; — *satisfaction*, soddisfazione sincera.
**undismayed** *adj.* senza paura, imperterrito; non spaventato.
**undisposed** *adj.* non disposto; — *to do something*, non disposto a fare qualcosa; (comm.) — *of*, non venduto.
**undisputed** *adj.* incontestato, indiscusso, incontrastato.
**undistinguished** *adj.* indistinto, confuso; (fig.) mediocre, banale.
**undisturbed** *adj.* indisturbato, non toccato; tale quale; calmo, tranquillo.
**undivided** *adj.* indiviso, intero; (finan.) — *profits*, utile non ripartito; *give me your — attention*, datemi tutta la vostra attenzione; non separato (da); — *opinion*, opinione unanime.
**undo** *tr.* slacciare, disfare, sciogliere, slegare; *to — a knot*, disfare un nodo; (provb.) *what is done cannot be undone*, cosa fatta capo ha; distruggere, rovinare; — *the mischief*, riparare il male. **-er** *n.* distruttore, rovinatore; seduttore. **-ing** *n.* disfacimento, scioglimento; (fig.) sfacelo, rovina.
**undomestic, undomesticated** *adj.* poco amante della casa.
**undone** *adj.* sfatto; slacciato; slegato; snodato; rovinato, perso; *to leave work* —, lasciare un lavoro incompiuto; *to leave nothing* —, non lasciar nulla di intentato; *we have left — those things which we ought to have done*, non abbiamo fatto le cose che avremmo dovuto fare.
**undoubt-able** *adj.* indubitabile. **-ed** *adj.* indubbio, indubitato; certo, incontestato. **-edly** *adv.* indubbiamente, certamente. **-ing** *adj.* che non dubita; sicuro, convinto.
**undraped** *adj.* non drappeggiato; (art) nudo.
**undreamed, undreamt** *adj.* non sognato, impensato, inatteso; — *of*, mai sognato.
**undress** *n.* veste *f.* da camera; — *uniform*, tenuta piccola; *tr.* svestire, spogliare; *to — a wound*, togliere le bende da una ferita; *intr.* svestirsi, spogliarsi. **-ed** *adj.* svestito, in veste da camera; (industr.) greggio, non levigato; (cul.) non guarnito, non condito; (of wound) non bendato, non medicato.
**undrinkable** *adj.* imbevibile; non potabile.
**undue** *adj.* non dovuto, indebito; inadatto; sproporzionato, eccessivo; (leg.) illegittimo, illecito; *use of — authority*, abuso di autorità; — *influence*, intimidazione, (on testator) captazione.
**undulant** *adj.* ondeggiante; (med.) — *fever*, febbre *f.* maltese.
**undulat-e** *tr., intr.* ondeggiare, ondulare. **-ing** *adj.* ondeggiante, ondulato; (of road) a saliscendi. **-ion** *n.* ondulazione; (phys.) movimento ondulatorio.
**unduly** *adv.* indebitamente; senza ragione, a torto, ingiustamente; eccessivamente, esageratamente, troppo; (leg.) illegalmente, illecitamente.
**undutiful** *adj.* che manca ai propri doveri; poco filiale. **-ness** *n.* mancanza ai propri doveri; irreverenza.
**undying** *adj.* imperituro, immortale; — *hatred*, odio eterno.
**unearned** *adj.* non guadagnato col lavoro; immeritato.
**unearth** *tr.* dissotterrare, esumare; (fig.) scoprire; (hunt.) stanare. **-ing** *n.* dissotterramento, esumazione; (fig.) scoperta. **-ly** *adj.* che non è di questa terra, soprannaturale; *-ly pallor*, pallore *m.* mortale; *-ly light*, luce sinistra; (fam.) assurdo, impossibile; *at this -ly hour!*, a quest'ora impossibile!; *an -ly din*, un rumore infernale.
**uneas-y** *adj.* a disagio; inquieto, ansioso; *an — feeling*, una sensazione d'inquietudine; *an — smile*, un sorriso imbarazzato; — *sleep*, sonno agitato; *to pass an — night*, agitarsi tutta la motte; *an — silence*, un silenzio significativo; *he has an — conscience*, gli morde la coscienza; *to feel — about*, preoccuparsi di; *to be — in one's mind about*, inquietarsi per. **-ily** *adv.* a disagio; ansiosamente, con inquietudine; con difficoltà. **-iness** *n.* disagio; inquietudine *f.*; ansia.
**uneat-able** *adj.* immangiabile; non commestibile. **-en** *adj.* non mangiato; *-en food*, cibi non consumati.
**uneconomic** *adj.* non economico, contrario alle leggi dell'economia; poco rimunerativo. **-al** *adj.* poco economo, scialacquatore, prodigo.
**unedifying** *adj.* poco edificante.
**unedited** *adj.* che non è stato riveduto, non corretto; inedito.
**uneducated** *adj.* senza coltura, senza istruzione, ignorante; volgare.
**unembarrassed** *adj.* non imbarazzato, disinvolto; libero.
**unembellished** *adj.* non abbellito, non ornato; semplice; crudo, rozzo.
**unembodied** *adj.* incorporeo, immateriale; non incorporato.
**unemotional** *adj.* freddo; non impressionabile.
**unemployable** *adj.* non impiegabile; non adatto ad assumere un impiego.
**unemployed** *adj.* disoccupato, senza lavoro; *the* —, i disoccupati; in aspettativa; non utilizzato, non impiegato; — *capital*, capitale *m.* giacente.
**unemployment** *n.* disoccupazione, mancanza di lavoro; — *benefit*, sussidio di disoccupazione.
**unencumbered** *adj.* non ingombro, libero; — *estate*, proprietà non gravata da ipoteche.
**unending** *adj.* interminabile, che non finisce più, eterno, senza fine.
**unendurable** *adj.* insopportabile, intollerabile.
**unenforceable** *adj.* ineseguibile, che non può essere applicato.
**unenforced** *adj.* non applicato, non in vigore.
**unengaged** *adj.* libero, non impegnato; non fidanzato; non prenotato, libero, disponibile; (of taxi) libero.
**un-English** *adj.* non tipicamente

inglese, indegno di un Inglese; (sport) poco sportivo.
**unenterprising** *adj.* poco intraprendente.
**unequal** *adj.* ineguale, disuguale; incapace, inadeguato; *to be — to*, non essere all'altezza di; (med.) *— pulse*, polso irregolare; (sport) *an — contest*, una lotta impari. **-led** *adj.* ineguagliato, senza pari.
**unequivocal** *adj.* non equivoco, inequivocabile; chiaro, non ambiguo.
**unerring** *adj.* infallibile, sicuro. **-ness** *n.* infallibilità, precisione.
**unescapable** *adj.* ineluttabile, inevitabile.
**Unesco** *pr.n.* (pol.) Unesco *f.*
**unescorted** *adj.* senza scorta, senza seguito.
**unessential** *adj.* non essenziale, poco importante.
**unestablished** *adj.* non stabilito, non accertato; (of Church) separato dallo Stato.
**uneven** *adj.* ineguale, irregolare, non uniforme; (of ground) accidentato; (math.) dispari; *— numbers*, numeri dispari; *parking on — dates*, è permesso il posteggio nei giorni dispari. **-ly** *adv.* irregolarmente; (math.) in modo dispari. **-ness** *n.* disuguaglianza, irregolarità; (of ground) anfrattuosità, accidentalità.
**uneventful** *adj.* tranquillo, normale, senza avvenimenti sensazionali; senza incidenti.
**unexampled** *adj.* senza precedenti; senza pari, unico.
**unexcelled** *adj.* insuperato, senza pari.
**unexceptionable** *adj.* ineccepibile, irreprensibile. **-ness** *n.* ineccepibilità, irreprensibilità.
**unexceptional** *adj.* senza eccezioni, che non ammette eccezioni.
**unexcit-ed** *adj.* calmo, tranquillo; (electr.) non eccitato.
**unexciting** *adj.* non emozionante, noioso, privo d'interesse.
**unexemplified** *adj.* senza esempi, non illustrato da esempi.
**unexpansive** *adj.* poco espansivo, riservato.
**unexpected** *adj.* inatteso, imprevisto, inopinato; intempestivo, improvviso; *to allow for the —*, tenere in debito conto l'imprevidibile. **-ness** *n.* subitaneità; carattere inatteso.
**unexpired** *adj.* non scaduto, ancora valido; non ancora scontato.
**unexplainable** *adj.* inspiegabile, inesplicabile.
**unexpounded** *adj.* non esposto; non spiegato; misterioso.
**unexpressed** *adj.* inespresso; (gramm.) sottinteso.
**unexpurgated** *adj.* non espurgato; *— edition*, edizione integrale.
**unextinguishable** *adj.* inestinguibile.
**unfading** *adj.* che non appassisce, che non sbiadisce; (fig.) imperituro, immortale; *— memories*, ricordi ancora vivi.
**unfailing** *adj.* infallibile, immancabile; indefesso, indefettibile; *to be — in one's duty*, non mancare mai ai propri doveri; inesauribile.
**unfair** *adj.* ingiusto, non equo; sleale, disonesto; *that's —!*, non è giusto!; (comm.) *— competition*, concorrenza sleale; (sport) poco sportivo. **-ly** *adv.* ingiustamente, non equamente, slealmente; *he has been -ly treated*, è stato vittima di una ingiustizia. **-ness** *n.* ingiustizia; parzialità; slealtà; malafede *f.*
**unfaithful** *adj.* infedele, sleale; impreciso, inesatto; *n.* (eccl.) *the —*, gli infedeli. **-ness** *n.* infedeltà, slealtà; inesattezza.
**unfaltering** *adj.* fermo, risoluto; indefesso, indefettibile.
**unfamiliar** *adj.* poco conosciuto, strano; *to be — with*, non conoscere, non essere al corrente di. **-ity** *n.* novità, carattere strano; ignoranza, mancanza di familiarità.
**unfashionable** *adj.* fuori moda, non di moda; che non si porta più.
**unfasten** *tr.* slacciare, slegare, sciogliere; sbottonare, disfare. **-ed** *adj.* mal chiuso, socchiuso; sbottonato, disfatto; *to come -ed*, sbottonarsi, disfarsi.
**unfather-ed** *adj.* senza padre, illegittimo, (fam.) figlio di N.N.; (of rumour) poco attendibile; (of theory) non riconosciuto dall'autore, di cui non si conosce l'autore. **-ly** *adj.* poco paterno, indegno di un padre.
**unfathomable** *adj.* che non si può scandagliare, insondabile, senza fondo; impenetrabile; smisurato, infinito; inscrutabile. **-ness** *n.* insondabilità; (fig.) impenetrabilità.
**unfathomed** *adj.* non scandagliato, non misurato; (fig.) impenetrabile, smisurato.
**unfavourable** *adj.* sfavorevole, poco vantaggioso; *— criticism*, critica avversa; (of wind) contrario, non propizio. **-ness** *n.* l'essere sfavorevole.
**unfeasible** *adj.* non fattibile, non attuabile, non pratico, irrelizzabile.
**unfed** *adj.* a digiuno, non nutrito; (mech.) non alimentato.
**unfeeling** *adj.* insensibile; spietato, inflessibile, duro; (fig.) freddo, arido. **-ness** *n.* insensibilità; mancanza di cuore, durezza.
**unfeigned** *adj.* non finto, sincero, genuino; non simulato. **-ness** *n.* sincerità.
**unfermented** *adj.* non fermentato; (of bread) azzimo, non lievitato.
**unfertile** *adj.* infertile, infruttifero; sterile.
**unfetter** *tr.* liberare, slegare; sciogliere da catene, scatenare. **-ed** *adj.* libero, senza ceppi; (fig.) senza restrizioni, senza impacci.
**unfilial** *adj.* poco filiale, indegno di un figlio; irreverente.
**unfinished** *adj.* incompiuto, incompleto; non finito, non terminato; (industr.) non rifinito, greggio; *— products*, prodotti semilavorati; (mus.) *the — Symphony*, l'Incompiuta.
**unfit** *adj.* inadatto, improprio, non idoneo; *— to drink*, non potabile, imbevibile; *— to eat*, immangiabile; *— to rule*, indegno di governare; indisposto, inabile al lavoro; *to be —*, essere indisposto, sentirsi poco bene; (mil.) *to be — for military service*, essere inabile al servizio militare; *to be discharged as —*, essere riformato; (sport) giù di forma, insufficientemente allenato; *tr.* rendere inabile, rendere incapace. **-ness** *n.* improprietà; inidoneità; inettitudine; incapacità; l'essere giù di forma, mancanza di allenamento.
**unfitted** *adj.* disadatto, non idoneo, incapace; *to be — for*, non essere buono a.
**unfitting** *adj.* poco adatto, sconveniente, inopportuno. **-ly** *adv.* in modo non adatto, inopportunamente. **-ness** *n.* inadattabilità; sconvenienza, inopportunità.
**unfix** *tr.* staccare; *intr.* staccarsi; (mil.) *to — bayonets*, togliere le baionette. **-ed** *adj.* non fisso, non fissato; mobile; (fig.) variabile, non stabilito; irresoluto, instabile; (photog.) non fissato.
**unflagging** *adj.* instancabile, infaticabile, indefesso; sostenuto, costante.
**unflattering** *adj.* poco lusinghiero.
**unfledged** *adj.* implume; (fig.) immaturo, poco sviluppato.
**unflinching** *adj.* che non indietreggia, che non batte ciglio; (fig.) stoico, impassibile, rigido.
**unfold** *tr.* aprire, schiudere, spiegare; (fig.) rivelare, esporre, divulgare; *intr.* aprirsi, schiudersi, spiegarsi, svilupparsi; (fig.) rivelarsi, scoprirsi.
**unforeseeable** *adj.* imprevedibile. **-ness** *n.* imprevedibilità.
**unforeseeing** *adj.* imprevidente, miope.
**unforeseen** *adj.* imprevisto, inatteso, inaspettato, inopinato; *unless something — occurs*, salvo imprevisti; (leg.) *— circumstances*, forza maggiore.

**unforgettable** *adj.* indimenticabile.

**unforgivable** *adj.* imperdonabile.

**unfor-given** *adj.* imperdonato, non perdonato. **-giving** *adj.* che non perdona mai; implacabile, inesorabile, senza misericordia.

**unforgotten** *adj.* indimenticato, sempre presente.

**unfortified** *adj.* non fortificato, senza difese; — *town*, città aperta.

**unfortunate** *adj.* sfortunato, disgraziato, infelice; spiacevole, rincrescevole; *an — incident*, un incidente spiacevole; *an — remark*, un'osservazione infelice; *an — joke*, uno scherzo inopportuno; *it is — that . . .*, purtroppo, è peccato che . . .; *how —*, che peccato!; *n.* infelice *m.*, *f.*, disgraziato; *pl. the —*, i disgraziati, gli infelici, i diseredati. **-ly** *adv.* purtroppo, sfortunatamente, disgraziatamente, per disgrazia; *-ly for him*, per sua disgrazia.

**unfounded** *adj.* infondato, senza fondamento; *an — rumour*, una voce priva di fondamento; *an — supposition*, una supposizione gratuita.

**unframed** *adj.* non inquadrato, senza cornice.

**unfreeze** *tr.* disgelare, sgelare; *intr.* disgelarsi, sgelarsi.

**unfrequented** *adj.* poco frequentato, poco praticato.

**unfriendliness** *n.* mancanza di cordialità, freddezza, riservatezza, ostilità.

**unfriendly** *adj.* poco cordiale, freddo; poco gentile; riservato; ostile; (of weather) poco propizio, minaccioso; (of wind) contrario, sfavorevole.

**unfrock** *tr.* spretare (priest), sfratare (monk or friar); (eccl.) schiericare.

**unfruitful** *adj.* infruttuoso, infruttifero; sterile; infertile, infecondo. **-ness** *n.* infruttuosità, infecondità, sterilità.

**unfulfilled** *adj.* inadempiuto, non esaudito, mancato; — *promise*, promessa mancata.

**unfulfilment** *n.* (psychol.) non-esaudimento; (leg.) inadempienza.

**unfurl** *tr.* spiegare, sventolare; sciogliere; *to — an umbrella*, aprire un ombrello; *intr.* spiegarsi.

**unfurnished** *adj.* smobiliato, senza mobili, non ammobiliato; sguarnito, sprovvisto.

**unfurrowed** *adj.* non solcato; senza rughe; sereno.

**ungainl-y** *adj.* goffo, sgraziato. **-liness** *n.* goffaggine *f.*

**ungainsayable** *adj.* irrefutabile.

**ungallant** *adj.* poco galante, poco cavalleresco.

**ungarbled** *adj.* (of text) non mutilo, integrale; *the — truth*, la verità pura e semplice, la verità nuda.

**ungarnished** *adj.* privo di ornamenti, non abbellito; semplice.

**ungenerous** *adj.* poco generoso, ingeneroso; meschino, avaro.

**ungentleman-like, -ly** *adj.* poco signorile; maleducato, non da gentiluomo.

**un-get-at-able** *adj.* inaccessibile.

**ungird** *tr.* togliere la cintura a, scingere, discingere.

**unglazed** *adj.* (ceram.) non verniciato, poroso; (of window) senza vetri; (of paper) non gelatinato; (photog.) opaco.

**ungloved** *adj.* senza guanti.

**unglue** *tr.* scollare.

**ungodl-y** *adj.* empio; (slang) tremendo; maledetto. **-iness** *n.* empietà.

**ungovernable** *adj.* incontrollabile, refrattario alla disciplina; sfrenato, violento.

**ungraced** *adj.* sgraziato; — *with*, sprovvisto di.

**ungraceful** *adj.* sgraziato, senza grazia, goffo. **-ness** *n.* goffaggine *f.*

**ungracious** *adj.* sgraziato, poco cortese, aspro; *to meet with an — reception*, essere accolto poco cordialmente; *it would be — to*, sarebbe poco gentile. **-ness** *n.* asprezza, malagrazia, mancanza di cordialità.

**ungrammatical** *adj.* sgrammaticato, incorretto.

**ungrateful** *adj.* ingrato, poco riconoscente; *an — task*, un compito ingrato; *to be — to*, essere ingrato verso; *to be — for*, non essere grato di; *to be — for benefits*, pagare d'ingratitudine i benefizi. **-ness** *n.* ingratitudine *f.*

**ungrounded** *adj.* infondato, privo di fondamento; poco preparato.

**ungrudging** *adj.* concesso di buon grado, non lesinato; generoso, liberale. **-ly** *adv.* di buon grado, senza lesinare.

**unguarded** *adj.* non guardato, senza difesa; non protetto, non scortato, senza scorta; (chess) senza guardia; (fig.) incauto, imprudente, indiscreto, inavvertito, irreflessivo; sconsiderato, indiscreto; *in an — moment*, in un momento d'inavvertenza; (mech.) senza dispositivo di protezione; (rlwy.) — *level-crossing*, passaggio a livello non sorvegliato. **-ly** *adv.* innavvertitamente, per inavvertenza; senza riflettere, sconsideratamente. **-ness** *n.* inavvertenza; imprudenza; disattenzione.

**unguent** *n.* unguento.

**unguided** *adj.* senza guida; *in an — moment*, in un momento d'inavvertenza.

**ungulate** *adj.*, *n.* ungulato.

**ungum** *tr.* scollare, distaccare.

**unhallowed** *adj.* non consacrato; empio.

**unhampered** *adj.* non impedito, non impacciato; libero; — *by rules*, senza badare al regolamento.

**unhandy** *adj.* maldestro; poco maneggiabile, scomodo.

**unhappily** *adv.* infelicemente, tristemente; purtroppo, sfortunatamente, per disgrazia.

**unhappiness** *n.* infelicità, tristezza, mestizia; inopportunità.

**unhappy** *adj.* infelice, triste, mesto; *to look —*, aver l'aria triste; (fig.) poco felice, inopportuno; *an — remark*, un'osservazione poco felice; *to be — in one's choice of words*, scegliere male le proprie parole.

**unharmed** *adj.* illeso, indenne, sano e salvo.

**unharmful** *adj.* innocuo.

**unharness** *tr.* staccare, togliere i finimenti a (un cavallo).

**unhealthiness** *n.* insalubrità; carattere poco igienico; salute malferma; (fig.) morbosità.

**unhealthy** *adj.* malsano, insalubre; malaticcio, non in buona salute; — *complexion*, brutta cera, cera terrosa; poco igienico; malsicuro, pericoloso; (fig.) morboso, malsano; — *curiosity*, curiosità morbosa; — *influence*, influenza nociva.

**unheard** *adj.* non udito, non ascoltato; non esaudito; *to condemn someone —*, condannare qualcuno senza averlo ascoltato; — *of*, inaudito, senza precedenti, finora sconosciuto, (of person) ignoto, sconosciuto.

**unheated** *adj.* non riscaldato, senza riscaldamento.

**unheed-ed** *adj.* cui non si presta attenzione; inascoltato, trascurato, negletto. **-ful** *adj.* disattento, sbadato, sventato; noncurante, imprudente; *-ful of*, senza badare a. **-ing** *adj.* distratto, noncurante, disattento.

**unhelpful** *adj.* inutile, non costruttivo; vano; poco volonteroso.

**unhesitating** *adj.* che non esita; fermo, deciso; *an — reply*, una risposta pronta. **-ly** *adv.* senza esitazioni, senza esitare; subito, senza por tempo in mezzo, senz'altro; *I say -ly that . . .*, dico senz'altro che . . .

**unhing-e** *tr.* scardinare, smontare; (fig.) sconvolgere. **-ed** *adj.* scardinato, smontato; (fig.) sconvolto; *his mind is -ed*, è infermo di mente. **-ing** *n.* smontaggio; (fig.) sconvolgimento (di mente).

**unhitch** *tr.* staccare. **-ing** *n.* distacco.

**unhol-y** *adj.* non sacro, profano, empio; — *desires*, cupidigia; (fam.) spaventoso, infernale; *an — muddle*, un bel pasticcio,

una confusione spaventosa. **-iness** *n.* empietà; carattere profano.
**unhonoured** *adj.* inonorato; disprezzato.
**unhook** *tr.* sganciare, staccare; (teleph.) *to — the receiver*, staccare il ricevitore; slacciare; *to come -ed*, sganciarsi.
**unhoped** *adj.* insperato, inatteso.
**unhorse** *tr.* disarcionare, smontare, sbalzare di sella.
**unhoused** *adj.* senza tetto, senza alloggio.
**unhurried** *adj.* senza fretta, fatto con comodo; calmo, tranquillo. **-ly** *adv.* senza fretta, tranquillamente.
**unhurt** *adj.* illeso, indenne, sano e salvo, incolume; *to escape —*, cavarsene senza danno; intatto.
**uni-** *pref.* uni-, mono-.
**unicorn** *adj.* unicorno; *n.* (myth.) unicorno, locorno; (astron.) unicorno.
**unidentified** *adj.* non identificato; sconosciuto.
**unification** *n.* unificazione.
**unifier** *n.* unificatore.
**uniform** *adj.* uniforme, costante; *— temperature*, temperatura costante; *to make —*, uniformare; *to become —*, uniformarsi; *n.* (mil.) divisa, uniforme *f.*, tenuta; *in —*, in divisa; *out of —*, in borghese. **-ed** *adj.* uniformato; (mil.) in divisa.
**uniformity** *n.* uniformità; unità; (electr., of current) costanza; regolarità; (rel.) conformismo.
**unify** *tr.* unificare; unire; dare unità a.
**uni-lateral** *adj.* unilaterale. **-lingual** *adj.* monoglotto, monolingua.
**unimagin-able** *adj.* inimmaginabile; inconcepibile. **-ative** *adj.* privo di immaginazione; poco immaginativo. **-ativeness** *n.* mancanza d'immaginazione.
**unimpaired** *adj.* non danneggiato, non minato, non affievolito, non indebolito; intatto; *with faculties —*, in pieno possesso delle proprie facoltà.
**unimpeachable** *adj.* irreprensibile, incontestabile, incensurabile. **-ness** *n.* incontestabilità.
**unimpeded** *adj.* non impedito, libero; senza ostacoli.
**unimport-ance** *n.* mancanza d'importanza; futilità; insignificanza. **-ant** *adj.* poco importante; privo d'importanza, insignificante; trascurabile; *that is -ant*, ciò non importa.
**unimposing** *adj.* poco imponente, insignificante.
**unimpressed** *adj.* non impressionato; *I was — by his speech*, il suo discorso non mi ha fatto molta impressione.
**unimpressionable** *adj.* poco impressionabile, freddo, impassibile.
**unimpressive** *adj.* poco impressionante, poco emozionante; che non colpisce, che non fa impressione.
**uninflammable** *adj.* ininfiammabile, incombustibile.
**uninfluenced** *adj.* non influenzato, spregiudicato; *to remain —*, non lasciarsi influenzare.
**uninfluential** *adj.* senza influenza, non autorevole, non influente; che conta poco, di nessun conto.
**uninformed** *adj.* non informato, ignaro; *to be — of*, ignorare; *to be — on*, conoscere poco; ignorante, poco colto.
**uninhabit-able** *adj.* inabitabile. **-ed** *adj.* disabitato; deserto, senza abitanti, abbandonato.
**uninitiated** *adj.* non iniziato, non introdotto; *the —*, i profani, quelli che non sanno i segreti.
**uninjured** *adj.* illeso, incolume, indenne; non danneggiato, intatto.
**uninquisitive** *adj.* non curioso, che non indaga; indifferente.
**uninspir-ed** *adj.* non ispirato, poco entusiasmante; trito, banale. **-ing** *adj.* senza ispirazione; poco emozionante.
**unintelligent** *adj.* inintelligente, non intelligente, poco perspicace; stupido.
**unintelligib-le** *adj.* inintelligible. **-ility, -leness** *n.* inintelligibilità.
**unintended** *adj.* non premeditato, involontario, non intenzionale.
**unintentional** *adj.* non intenzionale, involontario.
**uninterest-ed** *adj.* non interessato, indifferente. **-ing** *adj.* poco interessante, privo di interesse; noioso.
**uninterrupted** *adj.* ininterrotto, senza interruzione; continuo.
**uninventive** *adj.* poco inventivo, poco geniale.
**uninvit-ed** *adj.* non invitato, senza invito; *— guest*, ospite non invitato, intruso; *to come —*, venire senza essere stato invitato. **-ing** *adj.* poco attraente, poco allettante; poco appetitoso.
**uninvolved** *adj.* non coinvolto, non implicato, non compromesso; semplice, non involuto.
**union** *n.* unione, unificazione, confederazione di stati; (hist.) *the Union*, l'unione dell'Inghilterra e della Scozia (1603); l'unione della Gran Bretagna e dell'Irlanda (1801); (USA) gli Stati Uniti d'America; (geog.) *the Soviet Union*, l'Unione Sovietica; *the Union of Soviet Socialist Republics* (*U.S.S.R.*), l'Unione delle Repubbliche Socialisti Sovietiche (U.R.S.S.); *the South African Union*, l'Unione Sudafricana; associazione, lega, sindacato; *— regulations*, regolamenti sindacali; *— hours*, orario stabilito dal sindacato; *— rates*, tabella base delle paghe approvata dal sindacato; *— men*, operai iscritti al sindacato; *non-union men*, operai non iscritti a nessun sindacato; *Students' —*, associazione studentesca; concordia, armonia; *to live in perfect —*, vivere in perfetta armonia; matrimonio; *a happy —*, un matrimonio felice.
**union-ism** *n.* tendenza ad unirsi; *trade —*, sindacalismo **-ist** *n.* unionista *m.*; sindacalista, *m.* membro di un sindacato; (hist.) *-ist party*, gli avversari dell'indipendenza irlandese.
**unique** *adj.* unico; *— of its kind*, unico nel suo genere; eccezionale; singolare, particolare, straordinario. **-ly** *adv.* unicamente; in modo eccezionale. **-ness**, *n.* unicità, carattere unico; singolarità, rarità.
**unison** *n.* (mus.) unisono; accordo; *in perfect —*, di perfetto accordo; *in — with*, all'unisono con, d'accordo con.
**unit** *n.* unità; *— of measure*, unità di misurà; *— of weight*, unità di peso; *— of heat*, unità di calore; *monetary —*, unità monetaria; *standard —*, modulo; (comm.) *— price*, prezzo unitario; (mil.) reparto, unità; *infantry —*, reparto di fanteria; (mech.) complesso, insieme *m.*, gruppo, elemento.
**un-Italian** *adj.* non tipicamente italiano.
**unitary** *adj.* unitario.
**unite** *tr.* unire, riunire; congiungere; combinare, collegare; *to become -d*, unirsi; *to — in marriage*, unire in matrimonio; *intr.* unirsi, riunirsi, congiungersi, combinarsi, collegarsi; mettersi d'accordo, allearsi; (pol.) *to — against*, fare blocco contro; *workers of the world —!*, lavoratori di tutto il mondo riunitevi!; (of companies) amalgamarsi, fondersi.
**united** *adj.* unito; riunito, congiunto, confederato; *— we stand, divided we fall*, l'unione fa la forza; *— efforts*, sforzi riuniti; *— front*, fronte unita; *the United Kingdom of Great Britain and Northern Ireland*, il Regno Unito della Gran Bretagna e dell'Irlanda settentrionale; *the United States of America*, gli Stati Uniti d'America, *attrib.* statunitense; *the United Arab Republics*, la Repubbliche Arabe Unite.
**uniting** *adj.* unitivo, che unisce; *n.* unione, collegamento.
**unity** *n.* unità; *to lack —*, mancare di unità; (math.) unità, il numero uno; (fig.) armonia, concordia, accordo; *to live together*

*in perfect* —, vivere in perfetto accordo.
**universal** *adj.* universale; totale, generale; — *suffrage*, suffragio universale; *to make* —, universalizzare. **-ity** *n.* universalità.
**universally** *adv.* universalmente; generalmente; *it is known — that*, tutti sanno che.
**universe** *n.* universo.
**university** *n.* università; *red-brick universities*, le università britanniche all'infuori di quelle di Oxford e di Cambridge; — *degree*, laurea; *to take a — degree*, laurearsi, conseguire la laurea, addottorarsi; — *man*, laureato, universitario; — *professor*, (professore) cattedrante *m.*, professore universitario, titolare di una cattedra; — *town*, città sede *f.* di un'università; — *boat-race*, gara di canottaggio tra squadre universitarie.
**univocal** *adj.* univoco, non ambiguo; avente un solo significato.
**unjust** *adj.* ingiusto; ingiustificato; infondato.
**unjustifi-able** *adj.* ingiustificabile. **-ed** *adj.* ingiustificato.
**unkempt** *adj.* trascurato, sciatto, irsuto; arruffato, scarmigliato, spettinato; mal tenuto.
**unkind** *adj.* duro, crudele; poco gentile, poco benevolo; *to be — to*, trattar male; *to say — things about*, parlare male di qualcuno; *that's very — of you!*, sei poco gentile!; (of weather) inclemente, poco favorevole.
**unkindly** *adv.* poco gentilmente, duramente, crudelmente; *adj.* poco gentile.
**unkindness** *n.* durezza, crudeltà; malevolenza; (of climate) rudezza.
**unknot** *tr.* disfare i nodi di, districare; *to — two ropes*, staccare una corda dall'altra.
**unknow-able** *adj.* inconoscibile, inaccessibile. **-ing** *adj.* inconsapevole, ignaro, inconscio. **-ingly** *adv.* inconsapevolmente, senza saperlo.
**unknown** *adj.* sconosciuto, ignoto; poco conosciuto, oscuro; (math.) incognito; — *to me*, a mia insaputa; (leg.) *warrant against a person* —, mandato contro ignoto; *Unknown Warrior*, Milite Ignoto; *n.* ignoto; *towards the* —, verso l'ignoto; (math.) incognita.
**unlabelled** *adj.* senza etichetta.
**unlace** *tr.* slacciare; sciogliere.
**unladderable** *adj.* indemagliabile.
**unlad-e** *tr.* scaricare; togliere la soma da. **-ing** *n.* scaricamento.
**unladylike** *adj.* indegno di una signora o di una signorina; poco signorile; volgare.
**unlatch** *tr.* tirare il saliscendi (di una porta), aprire.
**unlawful** *adj.* illecito, illegale, contrario alla legge; (leg.) — *assembly*, adunanza illecita. **-ness** *n.* illegalità.
**unlearn** *tr.* disimparare; dimenticare; disfarsi di.
**unlearne·d** *adj.* ignorante, incolto, indotto; poco versato (in).
**unlearned, unlearnt** *adj.* non imparato.
**unleash** *tr.* sguinzagliare; (fig.) liberare, scatenare.
**unleavened** *adj.* non lievitato, senza lievito; (fig.) non temperato; — *bread*, pane azzimo, (bibl.) *the feast of — bread*, gli azzimi.
**unless** *conj.* a meno che, salvo che, se non che, eccetto se, tranne quando; — *he comes*, a meno che non venga; — *I am mistaken*, se non (mi) sbaglio; — *otherwise stated*, — *I hear to the contrary*, salvo avviso contrario; — *and until*, sinchè non; — *it be for*, salvo, all'infuori di.
**unlettered** *adj.* ignorante, incolto; analfabeta, illetterato.
**unlicensed** *adj.* non autorizzato, senza licenza; — *premises*, locale *m.* dove la vendita di alcoolici non è autorizzata.
**unlighted** *adj.* non acceso; non illuminato.
**unlike** *adj.* dissimile (da), diverso (da), differente; (math.) — *quantities*, quantità dissimili; (electr.) — *poles*, poli opposti; *to be* —, non rassomigliare a; *not* —, assai simile a; *that is — him*, non è il suo solito modo di fare; a differenza di, diversamente da.
**unlik(e)able** *adj.* antipatico, poco simpatico.
**unlikel-y** *adj.* inverosimile, improbabile, poco probabile; *he is — to come*, è poco probabile che venga; *an — story*, una storia inverosimile; *most* —, quasi da escludere; *it is not at all — that*, è ben possibile che; poco adatto; poco da aspettarsi. **-ihood, -iness** *n.* inverosimiglianza, improbabilità, poca probabilità.
**unlikeness** *n.* dissomiglianza, differenza.
**unlimited** *adj.* illimitato, sconfinato; *with — wine*, vino a discrezione; (finan.) — *liability*, responsabilità illimitata.
**unlined** *adj.* sfoderato, senza fodera; (of face) senza rughe.
**unlink** *tr.* sciogliere, slegare, svincolare; smagliare, disfare gli anelli di; staccare; *to — hands*, lasciar la presa, cessare di far catena.
**unlisted** *adj.* non elencato, non segnato; (finan.) — *stocks*, azioni non quotate.
**unlit** *adj.* non acceso; non illuminato.
**unlive** *tr. to — the past*, cancellare il passato.
**unliv(e)able** *adj.* (of life) impossibile, insopportabile; — *in*, inabitabile.
**unload** *tr.* scaricare; disfarsi di; (fig.) liberare da un peso, alleggerire; (aeron.) *to — bombs*, sganciare bombe. **-ed** *adj.* scarico. **-ing** *n.* scaricamento, scarico.
**unlock** *tr.* aprire (con chiave), disserrare; (fig.) rivelare, scoprire; (finan.) liberare (fondi); (typ.) aprire (la forma); (motor.) *to — the steering-gear*, sbloccare lo sterzo. **-ed** *adj.* non chiuso a chiave, non serrato, aperto.
**unlooked** *adj.* — *at*, trascurato, dimenticato; non guardato; non letto; — *for*, imprevisto, inatteso, insperato.
**unloose(n)** *tr.* slegare, staccare, allentare, sciogliere; *to — one's tongue*, sciogliere la lingua; *to — one's shoes*, slacciare le scarpe.
**unlov-(e)able** *adj.* poco amabile, poco simpatico. **-ed** *adj.* non amato; impopolare. **-ely** *adj.* sgraziato, senza fascino, poco attraente; brutto. **-ing** *adj.* poco affettuoso, freddo.
**unluck-y** *adj.* sfortunato, sventurato, disgraziato; *to be* —, non aver fortuna, essere sfortunato; *the — ones*, i disgraziati, gli sfortunati; *how —!*, che sfortuna!; (provb.) *lucky at cards, — in love*, fortunato al giuoco, sfortunato in amore; di cattivo augurio, malaugurato; sinistro, malefico; che porta sfortuna. **-ily** *adv.* sfortunatamente, per sfortuna; per disgrazia, disgraziatamente, sventuratamente, purtroppo; *-ily for me*, per mia sventura. **-iness** *n.* sfortuna, sventura; (slang) scarogna.
**unmade** *adj.* non ancora fatto; disfatto, sfatto; non confezionato; — *bed*, letto sfatto.
**unmaidenly, unmaidenlike** *adj.* che non si addice a una fanciulla; immodesto.
**unmaintainable** *adj.* insostenibile, indifendibile; (leg.) inammissibile.
**unmak-e** *tr.* disfare; distruggere; (fig.) causare la rovina di. **-ing** *n.* il disfare; (fig.) rovina.
**unmalleable** *adj.* poco malleabile; (fig.) indocile, indisciplinato.
**unman** *tr.* evirare, castrare; (fig.) commuovere, togliere forza a, togliere coraggio a; (naut.) disarmare, privare dell'equipaggio; (mil.) *-ned trenches*, trincee non presidiate.
**unmanageable** *adj.* incontrollabile, intrattabile; indocile, ricalcitrante; (of ship) ingovernabile; poco maneggevole, scomodo.
**unmanl-y** *adj.* indegno di un uomo; poco virile, effem(m)inato;

pusillanime. **-iness** *n.* mancanza di virilità; effem(m)inatezza, pusillanimità.

**unmannerl-y** *adj.* sgarbato; incivile; rozzo. **-iness** *n.* sgarbatezza, sgarbataggine *f.*, inciviltà.

**unmarketable** *adj.* invendibile, non commerciabile; (comm.) — *assets*, attivo immobilizzato.

**unmarred** *adj.* non guasto, non sciupato; perfetto.

**unmarriageable** *adj.* non ancora di età nubile; (figlia) che i genitori non riescono ad accasare; non adatto al matrimonio.

**unmarried** *adj.* non sposato, non coniugato; (man) celibe, scapolo; (woman) nubile, ragazza; *to remain* —, non sposarsi, restar celibe; *the — state*, il celibato; — *mother*, ragazza madre.

**unmask** *tr.* smascherare, togliere la maschera a; *intr.* togliersi la maschera, smascherarsi, mostrarsi come si è. **-ed** *adj.* senza maschera, smascherato.

**unmatch-able** *adj.* (of colour) che non si può armonizzare, che non si può assortire; (fig.) impareggiabile, senza pari, incomparabile. **-ed** *adj.* impareggiabile, senza pari, senza rivali, incomparabile; scompagnato.

**unmeaning** *adj.* senza significato, che non significa niente, inintelligibile; inespressivo.

**unmeant** *adj.* involontario, fatto senza intenzione.

**unmendable** *adj.* che non si può rammendare; irreparabile.

**unmention-able** *adj.* innominabile, irripetibile; di cui non si deve parlare, non riferibile. **-ed** *adj.* non menzionato, non riferito; *to leave -ed*, passare sotto silenzio.

**unmerciful** *adj.* senza misericordia, spietato, senza pietà, inumano. **-ly** *adv.* spietatamente, senza misericordia. **-ness** *n.* mancanza di misericordia; spietatezza.

**unmerited** *adj.* immeritato.

**unmetalled** *adj.* non macadamizzato, senza massicciata, in terra battuta.

**unmethodical** *adj.* non metodico, non sistematico, senza metodo, disordinato. **-ness** *n.* mancanza di metodo; disordine *m.*

**unmindful** *adj.* immemore, dimentico; — *of his duty*, immemore del suo dovere; *to be — of*, dimenticare, fare poco caso di; *to be not — of*, non trascurare; disattento, noncurante; — *of warnings*, incurante degli avvertimenti.

**unmissed** *adj.* di cui non si sente la mancanza, non rimpianto.

**unmistakabl-e** *adj.* indubbio, inequivocabile; chiaro, evidente; facilmente riconoscibile. **-y** *adv.* senza alcun dubbio, senza possibilità di errore; chiaramente, evidentemente.

**unmitigated** *adj.* non mitigato, non attenuato; (fam.) *an — ass*, un perfetto imbecille; *an — scoundrel*, un briccone matricolato.

**unmixed** *adj.* non mescolato; puro, genuino, scevro; *it is not an — blessing*, non è senza inconvenienti.

**unmolested** *adj.* indisturbato, non molestato; in pace, senza ostacoli.

**unmoor** *tr.* (naut.) disormeggiare, disafforcare.

**unmounted** *adj.* (of photo) non montato; (of gem) non incastonato; (mil.) a piedi, non a cavallo.

**unmourned** *adj.* incompianto, illacrimato; non rimpianto.

**unmoved** *adj.* non rimosso; fisso, immobile; senza emozione, senza commuoversi, impassibile, insensibile; indifferente, inflessibile, inesorabile; *to listen* —, ascoltare senza alcuna emozione.

**unmusical** *adj.* poco melodioso, cacofonico; non musicale; che non ama la musica.

**unmuzzle** *tr.* togliere la museruola a; (fig.) permettere di parlare. **-d** *adj.* senza museruola; (fig.) libero, non controllato.

**unnamed** *adj.* innominato, non nominato; anonimo, senza nome.

**unnatural** *adj.* non naturale, innaturale; anormale, contro natura; crudele, disumano, snaturato; pervertito; artificiale, affettato; forzato, amaro. **-ly** *adv.* snaturatamente; artificialmente; *not -ly*, naturalmente. **-ness** *n.* mancanza di naturalezza, artificiosita; snaturatezza.

**unnecessar-y** *adj.* non necessario, inutile; superfluo; *it is — to say that . . .*, non occorre dire che . . .; *to do without — things*, fare a meno del superfluo. **-ily** *adv.* senza necessità, inutilmente, eccessivamente.

**unneeded** *adj.* non necessario; di cui non si ha bisogno.

**unneighbourl-y** *adj.* non amichevole, da cattivo vicino, poco cortese. **-iness** *n.* atteggiamento scortese verso un vicino.

**unnerv-e** *tr.* snervare, indebolire, fiaccare; far perdere il sangue freddo a. **-ing** *adj.* che fa paura; sconcertante.

**unnoticeable** *adj.* che sfugge all'attenzione; impercettibile.

**unnoticed** *adj.* inosservato, inavvertito, che sfugge all'attenzione; *to let a remark pass* —, non rilevare un'osservazione, (fam.) far l'orecchio di mercante.

**unnumbered** *adj.* non numerato, senza numero; innumerevole.

**unobjectionable** *adj.* irreprensibile, inoffensivo; non sgradevole, non ripugnante, non molesto, irreclamabile.

**unobliging** *adj.* poco compiacente, poco gentile, non servizievole.

**unobserv-ance** *n.* inosservanza, inadempimento; disattenzione, inattenzione. **-ant, -ing** *adj.* inosservante; inattento, disattento; che vede poco.

**unobtainable** *adj.* non ottenibile, introvabile; irreperibile.

**unobtrusive** *adj.* discreto, modesto; che non si fa notare; *to be* —, non dare nell'occhio.

**unoccupied** *adj.* non occupato, senza occupazione, inoccupato; libero, vuoto, vacante; (mil.) — *zone*, zona non presidiata.

**unoffending** *adj.* inoffensivo; innocente.

**unofficial** *adj.* non ufficiale; non confermato. **-ly** *adv.* senza conferma; non in qualità di funzionario.

**unopposed** *adj.* incontrastato, senza opposizione; *to be* —, non incontrare opposizione; (pol.) — *candidate*, candidato unico; *to be returned* —, essere eletto senza opposizione.

**unorganized** *adj.* non organizzato, disorganizzato.

**unoriginal** *adj.* senza originalità, poco originale; banale.

**unorthodox** *adj.* inortodosso, poco ortodosso, eterodosso.

**unostentatious** *adj.* semplice, senza pretese, che non si dà delle arie, che non si mette in mostra; modesto, non vistoso, non fastoso. **-ness** *n.* mancanza di ostentazione; modestia; semplicità.

**unpack** *tr.* disimballare; disfare; scassare; spacchettare; togliere da una balla; *to — a suitcase*, disfare una valigia; *intr.* disfare le valige. **-ing** *n.* disimballamento, scassatura; il disfare le valige.

**unpaid** *adj.* non retribuito, non rimunerato, che non riceve stipendio; — *secretary*, segretario onorifico; — *services*, servizi a titolo gratuito; non saldato, non pagato; (of capital) non versato; (of letter) non affrancato.

**unpalatable** *adj.* di gusto sgradevole, inappetitoso; (fig.) spiacevole, sgradevole.

**unparalleled** *adj.* senza pari, imparagonabile, senza paragone; inaudito; senza precedenti.

**unpardon-able** *adj.* imperdonabile, inescusabile; (eccl.) irremissibile. **-ableness** *n.* imperdonabilità, inescusabilità; (eccl.) irremissibilità **-ed** *adj.* non perdonato, imperdonato; (of criminal) non graziato; (eccl.) non assolto.

**unparliamentary** *adj.* non parlamentare, contrario alle usanze parlamentari; (fig.) grossolano.

**unpatriotic** *adj.* non patriottico, antipatriottico.

**unpeg** *tr.* togliere i piuoli da, togliere le caviglie da; togliere giù dai piuoli.

**unpen** *tr.* far uscire dal recinto.

**unperceived** *adj.* non percepito, inavvertito, inosservato.

**unpermitted** *adj.* non autorizzato, non permesso; illecito; *to do something* —, fare qualcosa senza autorizzazione.

**unperturbed** *adj.* imperturbato, impassibile; calmo.

**unpick** *tr.* scucire; disfare.

**unpicked** *adj.* non scelto, non prescelto; (of fruit) non ancora raccolto.

**unpigmented** *adj.* (zool.) albino.

**unpin** *tr.* togliere gli spilli a, spuntare; (eng.) togliere i cavicchi da.

**unplaced** *adj.* privo di posto, senza impiego; non classificato; (sport) non piazzato.

**unplayable** *adj.* che non si può giuocare; (of football pitch, *etc.*) impraticabile; (theatr.) non rappresentabile; (mus.) ineseguibile.

**unpleasant** *adj.* sgradevole, spiacevole; antipatico; — *weather*, brutto tempo. **-ness** *n.* spiacevolezza; carattere *m.* sgradevole; carattere antipatico; dissapore *m.*, dissenso, bisticcio.

**unpleasing** *adj.* poco gradevole, sgradevole.

**unpliable, unpliant** *adj.* inflessibile, non pieghevole; poco arrendevole, poco compiacente; rigido.

**unplug** *tr.* togliere il tampone a, stappare, sturare; (electr.; radio) disinserire, staccare, togliere la spina dalla presa.

**unplumbed** *adj.* non scandagliato; (fig.) inesplorato; — *depths*, profondità inesplorate.

**unpoetic(al)** *adj.* poco poetico, non poetico; prosaico, trito.

**unpointed** *adj.* spuntato, smussato; (typ.) senza punteggiatura, senza segni diacritici; (bldg.) — *brickwork*, mattoni non cementati.

**unpolished** *adj.* non lucidato, non pulito; grezzo, non levigato; (fig.) rozzo, grossolano.

**unpolite** *adj.* see **impolite**.

**unpopular** *adj.* impopolare; mal visto; poco amato; malvoluto; *to make oneself* — *with*, farsi malvolere da. **-ity** *n.* impopolarità.

**unpopulated** *adj.* poco popolato, disabitato, senza abitanti.

**unpot** *tr.* togliere dal vaso, trapiantare, svasare. **-ting** *n.* (of plant) trapianto, svasamento.

**unpractical** *adj.* poco pratico, inesperto, non dotato di spirito pratico; inattuabile.

**unprecedented** *adj.* senza precedenti, inaudito.

**unpredictable** *adj.* che non può essere predetto; imprevedibile.

**unprejudiced** *adj.* spregiudicato, senza prevenzioni; imparziale, disinteressato.

**unpremeditated** *adj.* impremeditato, non premeditato.

**unprepared** *adj.* impreparato, senza preparazione; improvvisato; estemporaneo; *to be* — *for*, essere colto alla sprovvista da. **-ness** *n.* impreparatezza, impreparazione; mancanza di preparativi.

**unprepossessing** *adj.* poco attraente, poco seducente; *a man of* — *appearance*, un uomo dall'aspetto poco rassicurante, (fam.) un brutto ceffo.

**unpresentable** *adj.* impresentabile, poco presentabile.

**unpresuming, unpresumptuous** *adj.* modesto, senza presunzione, senza pretese.

**unpretending, unpretentious** *adj.* senza pretese, modesto, semplice; non pretenzioso.

**unpretentiousness** *n.* mancanza di pretese; semplicità.

**unpreventable** *adj.* inevitabile, che non si può impedire.

**unpriced** *adj.* senza indicazione del prezzo; di valore inestimabile.

**unprincipled** *adj.* senza principi, amorale; senza scrupoli.

**unprint-able** *adj.* non adatto ad essere stampato, non stampabile; che la legge vieta di stampare. **-ed** *adj.* non stampato; esistente solo in manoscritto; inedito.

**unprivileged** *adj.* senza privilegi.

**unprocurable** *adj.* non procurabile, introvabile, irreperibile.

**unproductive** *adj.* improduttivo, sterile; (finan.) infruttifero, non utilizzato; — *land*, terreno che non rende niente, terreno ingrato. **-ness** *n.* improduttività.

**unprofessional** *adj.* non professionale; — *conduct*, condotta contraria agli usi della professione, scorrettezza professionale; non autorizzato ad esercitare una professione; da dilettante.

**unprofitable** *adj.* poco lucrativo; poco vantaggioso; inutile; che non rende, poco redditizio; infruttuoso, sterile. **-ness** *n.* inutilità, sterilità; infruttuosità.

**unprogressive** *adj.* non progressivo; retrogrado, reazionario.

**unpromising** *adj.* che non promette niente di buono; non promettente.

**unprompted** *adj.* di propria iniziativa, senza farsi pregare; spontaneo, non suggerito.

**unpronounceable** *adj.* impronunciabile; (fam.) *an* — *name*, un nome ostrogotico.

**unpropertied** *adj.* senza beni, senza proprietà immobiliare; che non è proprietario.

**unprotected** *adj.* non protetto, senza protezione, senza difesa; senza appoggi, senza protettori; (industr.) senza dispositivi di sicurezza.

**unprov-able** *adj.* indimostrabile, che non si può provare. **-ed, -en** *adj.* (leg.) non provato, senza prova; (fig.) non messo alla prova.

**unprovided** *adj.* sprovvisto, non fornito, sfornito; *to be* — *with*, essere sprovvisto di; *to be left* — *for*, essere lasciato senza mezzi; *contingencies* — *for*, casi imprevisti.

**unprovoked** *adj.* non provocato, senza provocazione; — *insults*, insulti ingiustificati, insulti gratuiti; *to remain* —, mantenere la calma, non arrabbiarsi.

**unpublished** *adj.* inedito, non pubblicato; non reso pubblico.

**unpunctual** *adj.* non puntuale; spesso in ritardo. **-ity, -ness** *n.* mancanza di puntualità; imprecisione.

**unpunctuated** *adj.* non punteggiato, senza punteggiatura, senza interpunzione.

**unpuncturable** *adj.* (of tyre) inforabile, a prova di bucature, a prova di forature.

**unpunished** *adj.* impunito; *to go* —, sfuggire alla pena; (of crime) restare impunito.

**unqualified** *adj.* non qualificato, non abilitato, non autorizzato, inabile, senza diploma, senza titoli di studio; (fig.) incompetente; categorico, assoluto; — *denial*, diniego categorico; — *praise*, elogio senza riserve; — *statement*, dichiarazione in termini generici; — *success*, successo assoluto, successo incontrastato.

**unquestionabl-e** *adj.* incontestabile, indiscutibile, indubitabile, fuori questione. **-y** *adv.* indiscutibilmente, indubbiamente; senza alcun dubbio, senz'altro.

**unquestion-ed** *adj.* indiscusso, incontestato; non interpellato, non interrogato; *to let a statement pass* —, lasciar passare un'affermazione senza porla in dubbio. **-ing** *adj.* che non fa domande, che non solleva dubbi; (fig.) *-ing obedience*, ubbidienza cieca.

**unquotable** *adj.* non citabile, irripetibile.

**unrationed** *adj.* non soggetto a razionamento, in vendita libera; libero a tutti.

**unravel** *tr.* districare, sbrogliare, disfare; (fig.) sciogliere, chiarire; *to* — *a plot*, sciogliere un intreccio; *intr.* sfilacciarsi. **-led** *part. adj.* sfilacciato. **-ling** *n.* sfilacciatura; districamento; (fig.) scioglimento.

**unread** *adj.* non letto, che nessuno legge; senza coltura, illetterato. **-able** *adj.* noioso, che nessuno riesce a leggere

fino alla fine; illeggibile, indecifrabile. **-ableness** *n.* illeggibilità.
**unread-y**[1] *adj.* impreparato; non pronto, lento, irresoluto. **-iness** *n.* impreparazione, impreparatezza; mancanza di prontezza.
**unready**[2] *adj.* (hist.) *Ethelred the Unready*, Etelred il malavvisato.
**unreal** *adj.* irreale, senza realtà; immaginario, chimerico. **-istic** *adj.* poco realistico. **-ity** *n.* irrealtà, carattere illusorio; illusione.
**unrealiz-able** *adj.* irrealizzabile; (finan.) inutilizzabile. **-ed** *adj.* non realizzato; (fam.) di cui non ci si rende conto.
**unreason** *n.* irrazionalità.
**unreasonable** *adj.* irragionevole, stravagante, assurdo, eccessivo; esagerato; troppo esigente. **-ness** *n.* irragionevolezza; stravaganza; assurdità.
**unreason-ed** *adj.* non ragionato, non ponderato. **-ing** *adj.* che non ragiona, irragionevole; (fig.) *-ing hatred*, odio cieco.
**unreclaimed** *adj.* non redento, irredento; non civilizzato, barbaro; (of land) non bonificato.
**unrecogniz-able** *adj.* irriconoscibile. **-ed** *adj.* non riconosciuto; misconosciuto.
**unreconciled** *adj.* non riconciliato; non rassegnato.
**unrecoverable** *adj.* irrecuperabile.
**unrectified** *adj.* (chem.) non rettificato, grezzo; (electr.) non raddrizzato; (of error) non corretto, non rettificato.
**unredeem-able** *adj.* irredimibile, non riscattabile; (finan.) non rimborsabile. **-ed** *adj.* irredento, non redento; (fig.) non compensato, non controbilanciato; non mantenuto; (finan.) inestinto, non ammortizzato, non rimborsato.
**unreel** *tr.* svolgere, sgomitolare; *intr.* svolgersi.
**unrefined** *adj.* non raffinato, grezzo; (fig.) rozzo, sgarbato, grossolano.
**unreflecting** *adj.* irriflessivo; non riflettente, non rifrangente.
**unreformed** *adj.* non riformato; incorreggibile.
**unregistered** *adj.* non registrato, non iscritto; non segnato; (of trade-mark) non deposto; (of letter, parcel) non raccomandato.
**unrehearsed** *adj.* non preparato, improvvisato; impremeditato; improvviso, inaspettato; (theatr.) non provato, senza prove preliminari.
**unrelated** *adj.* senza rapporti, senza legami; non imparentato, senza alcun legame di parentela; non raccontato, passato sotto silenzio.
**unrelenting** *adj.* inesorabile, implacabile; irremovibile; inflessibile; accanito.
**unreliab-le** *adj.* malfido, inattendibile, su cui non si può fare affidamento, poco attendibile, da non fidarsene; inesatto; (of weather) instabile, incerto; *an — memory*, una memoria labile. **-ility** *n.* inattendibilità, incertezza; (of character) instabilità.
**unrelieved** *adj.* non soccorso, privo di soccorso; non alleviato; uniforme, monotono, senza alcun rilievo; *— monotony*, monotonia ininterrotta; *— poverty*, miseria nera.
**unremark-able** *adj.* irrilevante, poco notevole. **-ed** *adj.* inosservato, non visto.
**unremitting** *adj.* ininterrotto, senza intermissione; assiduo, instancabile.
**unremunerat-ed** *adj.* non rimunerato, irremunerato; a titolo gratuito. **-ive** *adj.* poco rimunerativo, poco lucrativo; infruttifero.
**unrepeatable** *adj.* irripetibile.
**unrepent-ant, -ing** *adj.* impenitente, incorreggibile; *to die -ant*, morire senza essersi pentito.
**unrepresentative** *adj.* non rappresentativo, non tipico.
**unrequested** *adj.* non richiesto, non invitato; di propria iniziativa.
**unrequired** *adj.* non necessario, superfluo; non richiesto.
**unrequited** *adj.* non ricambiato, non corrisposto; *— love*, amore non corrisposto.
**unresent-ful, -ing** *adj.* senza risentimento, non risentito; che non si offende facilmente.
**unreserved** *adj.* non riservato; franco, schietto, aperto, espansivo; illimitato, senza condizioni, incondizionato; *— confidence*, fiducia illimitata; completo, intero; (of seat) non prenotato. **-ly** *adv.* senza riserbo, francamente; incondizionatamente; senza fare riserve. **-ness** *n.* mancanza di riserbo; franchezza, schiettezza.
**unresolved** *adj.* non risolto, insoluto, senza soluzione.
**unresponsive** *adj.* freddo, insensibile, che non si lascia commuovere; che difficilmente si lascia convincere.
**unrest** *n.* inquietudine *f.*, agitazione; discontento, malcontento; malumore *m.*; *social —*, fermento generale.
**unrestored** *adj.* non restituito; non restaurato; non reintegrato; non ripristinato.
**unrestrain-able** *adj.* irrefrenabile, non reprimibile, sfrenato. **-ed** *adj.* non represso, non impacciato; sfrenato, irrefrenabile, senza ritegno.
**unrestricted** *adj.* senza limitazioni, senza restrizioni; libero; assoluto; (sport) *— race*, corsa a formula libre; (motor.) *— road*, strada senza limitazioni di velocità.
**unretentive** *adj.* che non ritiene; *— memory*, memoria labile.
**unrevealed** *adj.* non rivelato, non divulgato.
**unrewarded** *adj.* non ricompensato, senza ricompensa.
**unrhymed** *adj.* non rimato; *— verse*, versi sciolti.
**unrighteous** *adj.* empio, iniquo, ingiusto, malvagio. **-ness** *n.* empietà, iniquità, malvagità.
**unrip** *tr.* lacerare, scucire, strappare.
**unrip-e, -ened** *adj.* immaturo; acerbo, verde. **-eness** *n.* immaturità.
**unrippled** *adj.* liscio, senza crespe, senza increspature, non crespato.
**unrivalled** *adj.* impareggiabile; senza rivali, senza pari, incomparabile; senza concorrenti, fuori concorso; (comm.) *our goods are —*, la nostra merce non teme concorrenza.
**unroadworthy** *adj.* (motor.) non atto a circolare.
**unrobe** *tr.* svestire, spogliare; *intr.* svestirsi, spogliarsi.
**unroll** *tr.* svolgere, spiegare, sviluppare; *intr.* svolgersi, spiegarsi, svilupparsi.
**unromantic** *adj.* poco romantico, prosaico.
**unruffled** *adj.* sereno, calmo, imperturbabile; (of sea) liscio.
**unrul-y** *adj.* indisciplinato, facinoroso, insubordinato, turbolento, ribelle, sregolato; (of horse) focoso. **-iness** *n.* indisciplinatezza, insubordinazione, turbolenza, sregolatezza; (of horse) carattere focoso.
**unsaddle** *tr.* (horse) dissellare, levare la sella a; (rider) disarcionare.
**unsafe** *adj.* malsicuro, poco sicuro, pericoloso, rischioso; arrischiato, azzardato, azzardoso; (naut.) *— anchorage*, rada aperta; (finan.) di dubbio valore, rischioso.
**unsaid** *adj.* non detto, taciuto; *to leave —*, passare sotto silenzio, tacere; *consider that —*, passiamo sopra.
**unsalaried** *adj.* non stipendiato, non retribuito.
**unsaleable** *adj.* invendibile. **-ness** *n.* invendibilità.
**unsatisfactor-y** *adj.* poco soddisfacente, manchevole, che lascia desiderare; poco convincente; difettoso; mediocre. **-iness** *n.* carattere *m.* non soddisfacente; manchevolezza, insufficienza.
**unsatisfied** *adj.* insoddisfatto, malcontento; non saziato; non convinto; *to be — about*, avere dei dubbi su.

**unsavour-y** *adj.* scipito; di gusto sgradevole; (fig.) ripugnante, losco, poco pulito, equivoco, nauseante, disgustoso. **-iness** *n.* scipitezza, gusto sgradevole; (fig.) disgustevolezza.
**unscarred** *adj.* senza cicatrici, indenne; non sfregiato.
**unscathed** *adj.* illeso, indenne, incolume, sano e salvo.
**unscholarly** *adj.* indegno di un letterato, non erudito.
**unschooled** *adj.* senza istruzione, illetterato; naturale, spontaneo; (fig.) non avvezzo, inesperto.
**unscientific** *adj.* poco scientifico, non scientifico.
**unscreened** *adj.* esposto, non riparato, senza schermo; non vagliato; (electr.) non schermato.
**unscrew** *tr.* svitare; allentare; *intr.* svitarsi; allentarsi. **-ing** *n.* svitatura; allentamento.
**unscrupulosity, unscrupulousness** *n.* mancanza di scrupoli; indelicatezza.
**unscrupulous** *adj.* poco scrupoloso, senza scrupoli; indelicato, incosciente; *man of — ambition*, arrivista *m.*
**unseal** *tr.* dissigillare, dissuggellare; aprire; (fig.) rivelare; *to — someone's lips*, rendere a qualcuno la libertà di parlare.
**unseamanlike** *adj.* non degno di un marinaio, non da marinaio, non marinaresco.
**unseasonable** *adj.* fuori stagione; insolito per la stagione; inopportuno, intempestivo. **-ness** *n.* l'essere fuori stagione; (fig.) inopportunità, intempestività.
**unseasoned** *adj.* immaturo; (cul.) non condito; non stagionato; (mil.) — *troops*, reparti senza esperienza di guerra, truppe non agguerrite.
**unseat** *tr.* disarcionare; far cadere; (pol.) privare del seggio.
**unseaworth-y** *adj.* non idoneo alla navigazione, incapace di tenere il mare. **-iness** *n.* (naut.) non idoneità alla navigazione, innavigabilità.
**unsecured** *adj.* malsicuro; non ammarrato, non assicurato; non garantito; (of debt) scoperto.
**unseeded** *adj.* privo di semi; (tennis) non selezionato, non seminato.
**unseeing** *adj.* che non vede, da cieco; *to look at with — eyes*, guardare senza vederlo.
**unseeml-y** *adj.* sconveniente, indecoroso, inopportuno, disdicevole. **-iness** *n.* sconvenienza, contegno indecoroso, inopportunità.
**unseen** *adj.* non visto, inosservato; *n.* traduzione a prima vista; *the —*, l'altro mondo, l'al di là *m.*
**unselfconscious** *adj.* disinvolto, naturale. **-ness** *n.* disinvoltura, naturalezza.
**unselfish** *adj.* altruistico, altruista; disinteressato; *— life*, vita di abnegazione. **-ness** *n.* altruismo; abnegazione; disinteresse *m.*
**unsensitized** *adj.* (photog.) non sensibilizzato.
**unsent** *adj.* non inviato; non spedito; — *for*, non richiesto, (of person) senza essere chiamato, non convocato.
**unserviceable** *adj.* inservibile, inutilizzabile; poco pratico. **-ness** *n.* inservibilità; inutilità.
**unset** *adj.* (surg., of fracture) che non è stato messo a posto, non steccato; (of gun) non incastonato; (of trap) non armato; (of cement, *etc.*) non solidificato, che non ha preso; (typ.) non ancora composto; *tr.* smontare; disincastonare, disarmare.
**unsettl-e** *tr.* sconvolgere, disturbare, turbare. **-ed** *part. adj.* sconvolto, turbato, agitato; instabile, mutevole, incerto; indeciso, non risolto; senza fissa dimora, che non è riuscito a sistemarsi; non ancora colonizzato, senza abitanti, disabitato; (comm.) non pagato, non soldato, non regolato; (leg.) non costituito, non assegnato; (bldg.) non assestato. **-ing** *adj.* inquietante, che turba.
**unsew** *tr.* scucire; *to come -n*, scucirsi.
**unshackle** *tr.* togliere dai ceppi, liberare. **-d** *adj.* liberato dai ceppi; libero.
**unshaded** *adj.* senz'ombra, non ombreggiato, esposto al sole; senza persiana, senza imposte; senza paralume; (art) non ombreggiato, senza ombreggiatura, senza tratteggio.
**unshadowed** *adj.* non ombreggiato; (fig.) non rattristato.
**unshak-able** *adj.* incrollabile, fermo. **-en** *adj.* non scosso, non agitato; (fig.) incrollabile, irremovibile.
**unshapely** *adj.* senza forma, informe; deforme, sgraziato, malfatto.
**unshav-ed, -en** *adj.* non rasato, non sbarbato.
**unsheath(e)** *tr.* sguainare.
**unsheltered** *adj.* non riparato, esposto.
**unship** *tr.* (naut.) sbarcare, scaricare; *to — the mast*, smontare l'albero; — *oars!*, armate i remi!
**unshod** *adj.* senza scarpe, scalzo; (of horse) non ferrato.
**unshrink-able** *adj.* irrestringibile. **-ing** *adj.* intrepido, impavido; che non indietreggia.
**unshriven** *adj. to die —*, morire senza essersi confessato.
**unsightl-y** *adj.* spiacevole a vedere, che offende gli occhi. **-iness** *n.* squallidezza, spiacevolezza.
**unsinkable** *adj.* insommergibile.
**unsinning** *adj.* senza peccato, innocente.
**unskilful** *adj.* maldestro, inesperto, imperito, malaccorto, inetto. **-ness** *n.* imperizia; inabilità, incapacità.
**unskilled** *adj.* inesperto, imperito, inabile; *— labour*, lavoro manuale, manovalanza; — *worker*, manovale *m.*, operaio non specializzato.
**unsleeping** *adj.* che non dorme, desto; (fig.) guardingo, vigilante.
**unsmiling** *adj.* che non sorride, grave.
**unsnap** *tr.* sfibbiare, aprire (un fermaglio).
**unsociab-le** *adj.* poco socievole, scontroso, burbero. **-ility, -leness** *n.* insocievolezza, scontrosità
**unsocial** *adj.* antisociale, asociale; poco socievole.
**unsoiled** *adj.* non insudiciato, pulito; incontaminato, immacolato.
**unsold** *adj.* invenduto.
**unsoldier-like, -ly** *adj.* indegno di un soldato; poco marziale, poco militare.
**unsolicited** *adj.* non sollecitato, non richiesto; gratuito, spontaneo.
**unsolicitous** *adj.* incurante, non sollecito, indifferente.
**unsolv-able** *adj.* insolubile; impenetrabile. **-ed** *adj.* insoluto, non risolto.
**unsophisticated** *adj.* puro, non adulterato, non sofisticato; ingenuo, candido, semplice; (of wine) sincero.
**unsought** *adj.* non ricercato, non richiesto; spontaneo.
**unsound** *adj.* malsano, malaticcio; *of — mind*, infermo di mente; vizioso, corrotto; fallace, erroneo, eterodosso; (of material) guasto, avariato; (of knowledge) poco profondo. **-ness** *n.* infermità, cattiva salute; *-ness of mind*, infermità di mente; fallacia, erroneità; viziosità.
**unsparing** *adj.* zelante, che non si risparmia; indefesso, instancabile; prodigo, liberale, largo.
**unspeakable** *adj.* inesprimibile, indicibile; — *joy*, gioia ineffabile; — *torments*, tormenti inenarrabili; (fig.) detestabile, inqualificabile; — *manners*, modo di fare odioso.
**unspent** *adj.* non speso, non sborsato; non esaurito, inesausto.
**unsplinterable** *adj.* — *glass*, vetro antischeggia, vetro di sicurezza.
**unspoiled, unspoilt** *adj.* non guasto, non deteriorato, non contaminato; non viziato; (of countryside) non contaminato dal progresso, non invaso dai turisti.
**unspoken** *adj.* non profferito, non detto; tacito.
**unsporting, unsportsmanlike**

*adj.* poco sportivo, antisportivo; sleale.

**unspotted** *adj.* non macchiato, immacolato, senza macchia; (bot.; zool.) non maculato, non chiazzato; non visto, inosservato.

**unstable** *adj.* instabile; poco sicuro, malfermo; vacillante; incostante, mutevole; (geol.) franoso.

**unstated** *adj.* non specificato; passato sotto silenzio, taciuto.

**unstead-y** *adj.* vacillante, barcollante, malfermo, malsicuro; *to be — on one's legs*, avere un'andatura barcollante; (of light, *etc.*) traballante, intermittente; (irresolute) irresoluto, indeciso, titubante; (of wind, *etc.*) instabile, variabile, irregolare. **-iness** *n.* instabilità, incostanza, irregolarità, variabilità; (fig.) irresolutezza, indecisione.

**unstick** *tr.* staccare, scollare; (slang) *to come unstuck*, far fiasco; *intr.* (aeron.) decollare.

**unstint-ed** *adj.* abbondante, copioso, illimitato, non lesinato; (fig.) senza riserve, non lesinato, di tutto cuore. **-ing** *adj.* generoso, liberale.

**unstitch** *tr.* scucire, togliere i punti da; *to come -ed*, scucirsi.

**unstrap** *tr.* togliere la cinghia da, disfare le cinghie di.

**unstressed** *adj.* (gramm.) non accentato, atono; (fig.) non posto in rilievo, non sottolineato.

**unstring** *tr.* sciogliere, slegare; *to — a violin*, allentare le corde di un violino; (of beads) sfilare; (fig.) snervare.

**unstruck** *adj.* (of tent) non smontato; (of match) non acceso; (of coin) non coniato.

**unstrung** *adj.*, *p.def.*, *part.* of **unstring**, *q.v.*; (of instrument) con le corde allentate, senza corde; sfilato; nervoso, giù di corda; *his nerves are —*, ha i nervi scoperti.

**unstudied** *adj.* non studiato; (of style) facile, naturale, spontaneo.

**unsubdued** *adj.* non soggiogato, indomito; non domato.

**unsubmissive** *adj.* non sottomesso, indocile, ribelle, insubordinato.

**unsubsidized** *adj.* non sovvenzionato.

**unsubstantial** *adj.* non sostanziale, poco importante, immateriale; poco sostanzioso; privo di fondamento; (fig.) effimero, chimerico.

**unsubstantiated** *adj.* non provato; non confermato; non dimostrato, non stabilito.

**unsuccessful** *adj.* mal riuscito, vano, sfortunato; *an — attempt*, un tentativo mal riuscito, un colpo mancato; *— efforts*, sforzi inutili; che non riesce, che non ha fortuna; *to be —*, non riuscire, fallire; (in exam.) respinto, (fam.) bocciato; non eletto; congedato. **-ly** *adv.* senza successo, invano.

**unsugared** *adj.* senza zucchero, non zuccherato.

**unsuitab-le** *adj.* inadatto, non idoneo, che non va; inopportuno, non appropriato, incongruo, sconveniente; *an — marriage*, un matrimonio mal assortito. **-ility, -leness** *n.* inadeguatezza; inettitudine *f.*; inopportunità, impropriet à.

**unsuited** *adj.* inadatto, non idoneo; inopportuno, non appropriato; incongruo; incompatibile; non accontentato; *to be still —*, non aver ancora trovato ciò che conviene.

**unsullied** *adj.* pulito, senza macchia, immacolato.

**unsung** *adj.* non cantato; non celebrato.

**unsupported** *adj.* non confermato; senza appoggi, solo; non appoggiato; (bldg.) non puntellato; (mil.) scoperto.

**unsuppressed** *adj.* non soppresso, non messo a tacere; non represso.

**unsure** *adj.* poco sicuro, malsicuro, precario; inconsistente, che dà poco affidamento, sul quale non si può contare; incerto, indeterminato; dubbioso.

**unsuspect-ed** *adj.* insospettato, non sospetto; di cui nessuno sospettava l'esistenza. **-ing** *adj.* non sospettoso, che non sospetta niente, non diffidente.

**unsuspicious** *adj.* non sospettoso, che non desta sospetti.

**unswathe** *tr.* sbendare, sfasciare.

**unsweetened** *adj.* non zuccherato, senza zucchero; (fig.) non addolcito.

**unswerving** *adj.* diritto, rettilineo, che non devia; (fig.) irremovibile, inflessibile, fermo, costante.

**unsworn** *adj.* (of witness) che non ha prestato giuramento; (of evidence) che non è stato prestato sotto giuramento.

**unsymmetrical** *adj.* asimmetrico, senza simmetria.

**unsympathetic** *adj.* insensibile; indifferente; freddo, duro; non simpatico.

**unsystematic** *adj.* non sistematico, non metodico; disordinato.

**untack** *tr.* (needlew.) levare l'imbastitura; staccare; scucire.

**untam(e)-able** *adj.* indomabile; ribelle, riottoso. **-ed** *adj.* indomito; selvaggio.

**untapped** *adj.* non spillato; (fig.) non ancora sfruttato, non utilizzato; *— resources*, risorse non ancora utilizzate; (mech.) non tarato, non filettato; (bot.) non gemmato.

**untarnished** *adj.* non appannato, non offuscato, lucente; non ossidato; (fig.) immacolato, illibato, senza macchia.

**untasted** *adj.* non assaggiato; *to send a dish away —*, rinviare un piatto senza averlo gustato.

**untaught** *adj.* poco istruito, ignorante; innato, spontaneo; autodidatto.

**untax-able** *adj.* non imponibile, non soggetto ad imposte, non tassabile. **-ed** *adj.* non tassato; esente da imposte.

**unteachable** *adj.* non educabile, incapace d'imparare; incorreggibile; difficile da insegnare.

**untempered** *adj.* non temperato, non rivenuto; stemperato; non temprato.

**untempting** *adj.* che non tenta, che non alletta; poco appetitoso.

**untenable** *adj.* insostenibile, indifendibile, non tenibile.

**untenanted** *adj.* disabitato, non occupato, non affittato.

**untended** *adj.* incustodito; non curato, trascurato.

**untether** *tr.* togliere le pastoie a (un cavallo); slegare, sciogliere.

**unthankful** *adj.* ingrato. **-ness** *n.* ingratitudine *f.*, mancanza di riconoscenza; (of job) l'essere ingrato.

**unthink-able** *adj.* impensabile, inconcepibile; inammissibile. **-ing** *adj.* irriflessivo, spensierato, sconsiderato, sventato.

**unthought** *adj.* impensato; *— of*, inaspettato, a cui non si è pensato; imprevisto; (fig.) inaudito, impossibile.

**unthread** *tr.* sfilare, togliere il filo a; (fig.) sciogliere, abrogliare.

**unthrifty** *adj.* prodigo, dissipatore, sperperatore, scialacquatore.

**untid-y** *adj.* disordinato, trascurato, sciatto; *an — person*, una persona trasandata; arruffato, mal pettinato. **-iness** *n.* disordine *m.*; trascuratezza, sciatteria, mancanza d'ordine.

**untie** *tr.* sciogliere, slacciare; disfare, snodare; slegare, lasciar libero; sguinzagliare; (naut.) disormeggiare; *intr.* sciogliersi, slegarsi; *to come untied*, snodarsi, slacciarsi.

**until** *prep.* fino a; *not —*, non prima di; *conj.* finchè non, fino a che (non), fintanto che, fino al momento in cui.

**untilled** *adj.* incolto, non coltivato; a maggese.

**untimel-y** *adj.* prematuro; *— death*, morte prematura; *to come to an — end*, morire prematuramente, inopportuno, intempestivo; *at an — hour*, ad ora scomoda. **-iness** *n.* l'essere prematuro; inopportunità, intempestività; precocità.

**untinged** *adj.* senza tinta; (fig.) senz'ombra, senza traccia.

**untiring** *adj.* instancabile, infaticabile; indefesso; assiduo.

**unto** *prep.* (poet.) a, verso; *to come near* —, avvicinarsi a; *to turn* —, girarsi verso; fino a; — *this day*, fino ad oggi.

**untold** *adj.* non detto, non raccontato; incalcolabile, innumerevole; — *wealth*, ricchezza incalcolabile; — *suffering*, immense sofferenze *f.pl.*

**untouch-able** *adj.* insuperabile, irraggiungibile; *n.* (in India) intoccabile *m.*, *f.* **-ed** *adj.* non toccato; intatto; *-ed by human hand*, non maneggiato; *to leave -ed*, lasciare intatto; illeso, indenne; immacolato; non trattato, non discusso, non menzionato; insensibile, indifferente.

**untoward** *adj.* restio, caparbio, indocile; infausto, funesto, sfortunato; sconveniente.

**untrace-able** *adj.* introvabile, irreperibile. **-d** *adj.* mai trovato, perduto.

**untrained** *adj.* inesperto, non esercitato, senza pratica; (sport) non allenato.

**untrammelled** *adj.* non inceppato, non impacciato; — *by conventions*, incurante delle convenzioni.

**untransferable** *adj.* non trasferibile, inalienabile.

**untranslat-able** *adj.* intraducibile. **-ed** *adj.* non (ancora) tradotto.

**untravelled** *adj.* che non ha viaggiato.

**untried** *adj.* non provato; non sperimentato; intentato; non toccato; *to leave no remedy* —, non lasciare intentato nessun rimedio; (leg., of accused) non ancora processato.

**untrimmed** *adj.* non tagliato; (of tree) non potato; (of hat, *etc.*) non ornato.

**untrodden** *adj.* non calpestato, non frequentato, non battuto; inesplorato; — *snow*, neve immacolata; — *paths*, sentieri poco battuti.

**untroubled** *adj.* imperturbato, sereno, tranquillo, calmo; limpido.

**untrue** *adj.* non vero, falso, erroneo, contrario alla verità; infedele; (mech.) inesatto, non centrato; (sport) — *to form*, giù di forma, contrariamente all'aspettativa.

**untrustworth-y** *adj.* indegno di fiducia, infido; poco attendibile, poco sicuro; — *memory*, memoria labile. **-iness** *n.* slealtà; inattendibilità.

**untruth** *n.* menzogna, bugia; *to tell an* —, dire una bugia. **-ful** *adj.* falso, menzognero, poco veritiero; inesatto. **-fulness** *n.* falsità; carattere menzognero; mancanza di veridicità.

**untuck** *tr.* (bed) tirar giù le lenzuola di; (fam.) *to* — *one's legs*, allungare le gambe.

**untuned** *adj.* (mus.) scordato, stonato.

**unturned** *adj.* non rivoltato, non rovesciato; *to leave no stone* —, non lasciare nulla di intentato.

**untutored** *adj.* poco istruito, senza istruzione; — *taste*, gusto non formato; naturale, spontaneo.

**untwine** *tr.* svolgere, districare; *intr.* svolgersi, districarsi.

**untwist** *tr.* sbrogliare, districare; *to come -ed*, districarsi.

**ununderstandable** *adj.* incomprensibile.

**unusable** *adj.* inutilizzabile.

**unused** *adj.* non usato, non adoperato, nuovo; non utilizzato, fuori uso; non abituato.

**unusual** *adj.* insolito, inusitato; eccezionale; singolare, straordinario; fuori del comune; che si vede raramente, che non si usa; *nothing* —, niente di strano; *of* — *interest*, d'interesse eccezionale. **-ness** *n.* rarità, carattere eccezionale; singolarità.

**unutter-able** *adj.* indescrivibile, indicibile, inesprimibile; impronunciabile. **-ed** *adj.* non pronunciato; inespresso, taciuto.

**unvalued** *adj.* poco stimato, disprezzato; di cui non si fa caso; non valutato, non stimato.

**unvanquished** *adj.* invitto.

**unvaried** *adj.* invariato, uniforme, monotono; che manca di varietà.

**unvarnished** *adj.* non verniciato; (fig.) semplice, disadorno, senza abbellimenti; *the* — *truth*, la pura verità.

**unvarying** *adj.* invariabile, costante, uniforme.

**unveil** *tr.* togliere il velo; *to* — *a statue*, scoprire una statua; (fig.) svelare. **-ing** *n.* scoprimento, inaugurazione.

**unversed** *adj.* non versato (in), poco pratico (di); ignorante, inesperto (di).

**unviolated** *adj.* inviolato, intatto.

**unvisited** *adj.* non visitato, non frequentato.

**unvoiced** *adj.* non espresso, non pronunciato; (ling.) sordo, non sonoro.

**unwanted** *adj.* non desiderato, non richiesto; superfluo.

**unwariness** *n.* imprudenza.

**unwarlike** *adj.* poco bellicoso, poco marziale; pacifico.

**unwarrant-ed** *adj.* non garantito; non autorizzato, ingiustificabile; — *remark*, osservazione gratuita; — *intervention*, ingerenza; — *proceedings*, atti illeggitimi; — *familiarity*, familiarità esagerata. **-able** *adj.* che non può essere garantito; (fig.) ingiustificabile; insostenibile.

**unwary** *adj.* imprudente, incauto, indiscreto.

**unwashed** *adj.* non lavato; sporco.

**unwatered** *adj.* non innaffiato; non irrigato, senz'acqua; (of wine) non annacquato, sincero; (finan.) non diluito; (of horse) non abbrevato; (of silk) non marezzato.

**unwavering** *adj.* costante, fermo; incrollabile, che non vacilla.

**unwearable** *adj.* non indossabile.

**unwear-ied** *adj.* non stanco; indefesso, instancabile. **-ying** *adj.* instancabile, indefesso; tenace.

**unwedded, unwed** *adj.* non sposato; celibe *m.*, nubile *f.*

**unwelcome** *adj.* non benvenuto; male accolto; sgradito; inopportuno; — *news*, notizie sgradevoli. **-d** *adj.* male accolto, non festeggiato.

**unwell** *adj.* poco bene, indisposto; ammalato.

**unwholesome** *adj.* malsano, insalubre; corrotto, nocivo, morboso; (fig.) pernicioso. **-ness** *n.* insalubrità; morbosità.

**unwield-y** *adj.* pesante, lento, impacciato; poco maneggevole, ingombrante. **-iness** *n.* pesantezza, difficoltà di movimento; peso, l'essere ingombrante.

**unwilling** *adj.* riluttante; poco propenso; restio; svogliato; *to be* —, aver poca voglia; *to be* — *that*, non volere che; involontario, non voluto, fatto controvoglia. **-ly** *adv.* malvolentieri, controvoglia, svogliatamente; involontariamente. **-ness** *n.* riluttanza; cattiva volontà, malavoglia.

**unwind** *tr.* svolgere, srotolare, districare; *intr.* srotolarsi, districarsi; (fig.) rilassarsi.

**unwinking** *adj.* senza batter ciglio, impassibile; — *attention*, attenzione fissa.

**unwise** *adj.* imprudente, malaccorto; senza discernimento; poco circospetto; contrario al buon senso, insensato. **-ly** *adv.* con poca prudenza.

**unwished** *adj.* — (*for*), non desiderato, non voluto.

**unwitnessed** *adj.* senza testimoni; — *signature*, firma non certificata da testimoni.

**unwitting** *adj.* inconsapevole, involontario. **-ly** *adv.* senza saperlo; involontariamente.

**unwomanly** *adj.* poco femminile, che non si addice ad una donna.

**unwonted** *adj.* insolito, non abituale; singolare. **-ness** *n.* rarità; singolarità; novità.

**unworkable** *adj.* ineseguibile, impraticabile; che non può funzionare; innavigabile; (min.) che non si può sfruttare.

**unworkmanlike** *adj.* indegno di un buon operaio; non eseguito a regola d'arte, mal fatto.

**unworldl-y** *adj.* non terreno, non di questo mondo; semplice, candido. **-iness** *n.* distacca-

mento da questo mondo; disinteresse nelle cose terrene; semplicità; candore *m.*
**unworn** *adj.* non indossato, nuovo; non logoro, non sciupato.
**unworried** *adj.* non preoccupato; non disturbato; sereno.
**unworthiness** *n.* indegnità.
**unworthy** *adj.* indegno; *— of notice*, che non merita considerazione, spregevole; poco meritevole.
**unwounded** *adj.* non ferito; illeso, incolume; (mil.) valido.
**unwrap** *tr.* disfare, svolgere, aprire; *to come ~ped*, disfarsi.
**unwritten** *adj.* non scritto, tradizionale, tramandato oralmente; *— law*, legge *f.* d'onore; *— on*, in bianco.
**unyielding** *adj.* inflessibile, che non cede; fermo, rigido, ostinato. **~ness** *n.* inflessibilità, ostinatezza, rigidità.
**unyoke** *tr.* togliere il giogo a, staccare dal giogo; (fig.) liberare.
**up** *adj.* ascendente, in salita; *the — train*, il treno per Londra, il treno per la città; *the — platform*, il binario per i treni che vanno a Londra; *n.pl. the ~s and downs of life*, gli alti e bassi della vita; *the ~s and downs of the market*, le oscillazioni del mercato; *a road all ~s and downs*, una strada a saliscendi.
**up** *adv.* su, in su, in alto; *— here*, quassù; *— above*, *— there*, lassù; *further —*, più in su; *all the way —*, fino in cima (a); (to dog, etc.) *— !*, oplà!; *— and down*, su e giù, dall'alto in basso; *to look someone — and down*, guardare qualcuno dall'alto in basso; *— to*, fino a; *— to now*, finora; *— to then*, fino ad allora; *— to five pounds*, fino a cinque sterline; *— to three months*, non più di tre mesi; *from my youth —*, sin da giovane; *it's all — !*, è finito!, non c'è niente da fare!; *it's all — with him*, è spacciato; *it's — to you*, tocca a te; *it isn't — to me*, non tocca a me, non è affar mio; *hold yourself —*, tienti dritto; *speak —*, parla più forte; *is there something —?*, succede qualcosa?; *what's — with you?*, che cosa hai?; *hurry — !*, presto!, spicciatevi!; *his blood is —*, gli è montato il sangue alla testa, gli ribolle il sangue; *hands — !*, mani in alto!; *time's —*, è l'ora, si chiude; *— with the monarchy!*, evviva la monarchia!; *this side —*, non capovolgere; *to be — against*, essere alle prese con; *to be — from the country*, essere venuto in città dalla provincia; *to be — in arms*, essere in armi, essere in rivolta; *to be well — in*, conoscere a fondo; *let's be — and doing*, mettiamoci al lavoro; *to be — to anything*, essere capace di tutto, essere pronto a tutto; *to be — to something*, star tramando qualcosa; *to be — to one's work*, essere all'altezza del proprio lavoro; *he is not — to the journey*, non è in istato di fare il viaggio; *to be — to one's neck in something*, essere dentro fino al collo in qualcosa; *to be not — to much*, non valere gran che; *I don't feel — to much*, non mi sento troppo bene; *I don't feel — to going out*, non mi sento di uscire; *to be — to date*, essere aggiornato; *we were — to our knees in water*, eravamo nell'acqua fino ai ginocchi; *to blush — to one's hair*, arrossire fino alla radice dei capelli; *to get —*, alzarsi; *to be — all night*, star su tutta la notte; *to get — to mischief*, combinare una delle sue, meditare un brutto tiro; *to give someone a leg —*, aiutare qualcuno a montare in sella, (fig.) dare una mano a qualcuno; *to live — to one's income*, spendere tutto quello che si guadagna; *to praise someone —*, portare alle stelle qualcuno; (sport) *to be two goals —*, condurre per due gol; (golf) *three holes —*, tre buchi di vantaggio.
**up** *prep.* su, su per, in cima di; *to climb — a hill*, salire su una collina; *— the street*, più in là sulla strada; *to walk — and down the street*, andare avanti e dietro per la strada; *— (the) river*, a monte, risalendo il fiume.
**up** *tr.* (fam.) balzare su, saltare in piedi; (slang) *he ~s and says to me*, salta su e mi dice; *to — swans*, fare il censimento e contrassegnare i cigni di proprietà della famiglia reale.
**up-anchor** *intr.* (naut.) levare l'ancora, salpare; (fig.) partire, scappare.
**up-and-down** *adj.* che va in su e in giù; variabile, oscillante; (of road) a saliscendi.
**upas** *n.* (bot.) albero del veleno di Giava, antiaride *f.*
**upbraid** *tr.* rimproverare, riprendere, sgridare, rampognare, apostrofare, biasimare.
**upbringing** *n.* allevamento, educazione, ammaestramento; *what sort of an — has he had?*, che razza di educazione ha avuto?
**up-country** *adj.* dell'interno di una regione, della retroterra; *adv.* all'interno; *to travel —*, spingersi nell'interno, addentrarsi in una regione.
**up-end** *tr.* (fam.) mettere dritto, rizzare.
**up-grade** *n.* salita, pendio ascendente; *on the —*, in salita, che cresce, (fig.) che migliora, che progredisce; *tr.* promuovere a grado superiore.
**upheaval** *n.* sollevamento; (fig.) commozione, sconvolgimento, scompiglio.
**uphill** *adj.* che sale, in salita, ascendente, ripido; (fig.) arduo, difficile, faticoso; *an — task*, un compito difficile; *adv.* in salita, in su; *to go —*, salire.
**uphold** *tr.* sostenere, sorreggere, appoggiare; *to — the law*, far rispettare la legge; (fig.) mantenere, confermare. **~er** *n.* sostegno, appoggio; sostenitore, partigiano, defensore; *~er of the law*, guardiano della legge, difensore dell'ordine pubblico.
**upholster** *tr.* tappezzare, ricoprire; imbottire. **~er** *n.* tappezziere *m.*, decoratore. **~ing, ~y** *n.* tappezzeria; imbottitura.
**upkeep** *n.* mantenimento, manutenzione; *expenses of —*, spese di manutenzione.
**upland** *n.* regione montagnosa, altipiano; *pl.* la zona alta; *adj.* montano, alpino.
**uplift** *n.* sollevamento, elevazione; (fig.) elevatezza; *moral —*, elevatezza morale, ispirazione. **~ed** *adj.* sollevato, elevato; alzato; alto; (fig.) esaltato, ispirato.
**upmost** *adj.* see **uppermost.**
**upon** *prep.* see **on.**
**upper** *adj.* superiore, più alto, più elevato; *— part*, parte *f.* superiore; (pol.) *the Upper House*, la Camera Alta; (theatr.) *— circle*, seconda galleria; *to get the — hand*, avere la prevalenza, prevalere, prendere il disopra; (fam.) *to keep a stiff — lip*, tenere duro; *the — dog*, chi ha il predominio; (geog.) alto, superiore; *the Upper Adige*, l'Alto Adige; *Upper Egypt*, l'Alto Egitto; (typ.) *— case*, alta cassa; *— case letters*, maiuscole *f.pl.*
**upper** *n.* (shoem.) tomaia, gambale *m.*; (fam.) *to be on one's ~s*, essere al verde.
**upper-cut** *n.* (boxing) upper-cut *m.*, colpo dal basso in alto.
**uppermost** *adj.* il più alto, il più elevato; (fig.) il più importante, principale; *to be —*, prevalere, predominare; *adv.* in alto, al di sopra, più in alto di tutto.
**upping** *n.* (of swans) censimento e contrassegnatura dei cigni di proprietà della Corona.
**uppish** *adj.* (fam.) altezzoso, prepotente, arrogante. **~ness** *n.* prepotenza, arroganza, boria.
**upraised** *adj.* alzato; sollevato.
**upright** *adj.* verticale, perpendicolare, ritto, dritto, eretto; in piedi; *to hold oneself —*, tenersi dritto; *to set —*, raddrizzare; *— piano*, piano verticale, pianino; (fig.) retto, integro, onesto, per bene; *adv.* verticalmente, perpendicolarmente; dritto, in piedi.
**upright** *n.* stipite *m.*, montante *m.*; palo verticale, montante *m.*; *out of —*, fuori del perpendicolare;

piano verticale. **-ness** *n.* verticalità, perpendicolarità; (fig.) rettitudine *f.*, integrità, onestà.

**uprising** *n.* il sorgere; rivolta, insurrezione.

**up-river** *adj.* a monte, verso la sorgente.

**uproar** *n.* tumulto, subbuglio, chiasso, trambusto; *to be in an —*, essere in tumulto; *to make an —*, far chiasso. **-ious** *adj.* tumultuoso, chiassoso, rumoroso; *an -ious meeting*, un'adunanza burrascosa; *-ious applause*, applausi scroscianti; *-ious laughter*, risata sonora. **-iousness** *n.* tumultuosità, rumorosità.

**uproot** *tr.* sradicare, divellere, estirpare; (fig.) strappare. **-ing** *n.* sradicamento; estirpazione.

**uprush** *n.* il sorgere bruscamente, lo scaturire; buffata.

**up'set** *n.* rovesciamento, ribaltamento; (fig.) disordine *m.*, confusione; seccatura, disturbo; disgrazia, contrattempo; indisposizione.

**upset** *adj.* rovesciato, capovolto; sconvolto, turbato, emozionato; indisposto; disturbato; *to be —*, turbarsi, emozionarsi, rimanere male, (in health) essere indisposto; *he looks —*, sembra emozionato; *tr.* rovesciare, capovolgere; (fig.) sconvolgere, turbare, emozionare, disturbare; disordinare, gettare in confusione; *rfl.* emozionarsi, inquietarsi; *don't — yourself*, non ti lasciar emozionare, calmati; *intr.* rovesciarsi, capovolgersi.

**upsetting** *adj.* turbante, inquietante, sconvolgente; *n.* rovesciamento, sconvolgimento.

**upshot** *n.* esito, risultato; conclusione, quintessenza; *what will be the —?*, come andrà a finire?

**upside-down** *adv.* capovolto, sottosopra, sossopra, a rovescio; (fig.) in disordine, in confusione; *to turn everything —*, mettere tutto sossopra.

**upstairs** *adj.* situato al piano superiore; *adv.* di sopra, al piano superiore; *to go —*, salire le scale.

**upstanding** *adj.* dritto, eretto; *a fine — lad*, un ragazzo robusto.

**upstart** *n.* nuovo ricco, persona venuta dal nulla, villano rifatto.

**up-stream** *adv.* a monte, controcorrente.

**upsurge** *n.* spinta in alto.

**uptake** *n.* (fam.) comprensione, intelligenza; *to be quick in the —*, afferrare a volo; *to be slow in the —*, essere duro di comprensione.

**upthrust** *n.* spinta in alto; (geol.) sollevamento; (phys.) pressione idrostatica.

**uptilted** *adj.* rivolto in su.

**up-to-date** *adj.* aggiornato, bene informato; moderno, di moda; *— model*, ultimo modello. **-ness** *n.* l'essere aggiornato, modernità, attualità.

**upturn** *tr.* volgere verso l'alto, rivolgere in alto; rivoltare.

**upward** *adj.* ascendente, ascensionale, rivolto in alto, diretto verso l'alto; in salita; *— gradient*, rampa; *— glance*, sguardo rivolto verso l'alto; *— movement*, movimento ascensionale, fase ascendente, tendenza al rialzo, ascesa; (aeron.) *— motion*, cabrata, impennata.

**upward(s)** *adv.* in su, in alto, verso l'alto; all'insù; *— of*, al di sopra di, più di; *the road runs —*, la strada sale; *face —*, col viso all'insù, (of book, *etc.*) dalla parte diritta; *to look —*, guardare in su; *from twenty —*, dai venti in su; *fifteen years and —*, quindici anni e più; *— of fifteen*, al di sopra dei quindici.

**up-welling** *n.* lo scaturire in su, zampillio; (fig.) sgorgamento, impeto.

**uraemi-a** *n.* (med.) uremia. **-c** *adj.* (med.) uremico.

**Ural** *pr.n.* (geog.) *the — Mountains*, gli Urali, i Monti Urali.

**uranium** *n.* (chem.) uranio.

**Uranus** *pr.n.* (myth.; astron.) Urano.

**Urban**[1] *pr.n.* Urbano.

**urban**[2] *adj.* urbano, di città. **-e** *adj.* urbano, cortese, civile. **-ism** *n.* urbanismo, urbanesimo. **-ity** *n.* urbanità, cortesia, civiltà. **-ization** *n.* urbanismo, urbanizzazione. **-ize** *tr.* urbanizzare.

**urchin** *n.* monello; *sea-urchin* *n.* (zool.) riccio di mare.

**ureter** *n.* (anat.) uretere *m.*

**urethra** *n.* (anat.) uretra *f.*

**urge** *n.* stimolo, sprone *m.*; bisogno imperioso; *tr.* spingere, spronare; incitare, esortare; (fig.) insistere su, raccomandare; *intr.* urgere.

**urgency** *n.* urgenza, premura; bisogno, necessità pressante; imminenza; istanza.

**urgent** *adj.* urgente; pressante, incalzante; insistente; *to be —*, urgere; *at his — request*, alla sua richiesta pressante; *— business*, affari urgenti; *an — need*, un bisogno urgente. **-ly** *adv.* urgentemente, di urgenza, insistentemente; *help is -ly needed*, urge aiuto.

**Uriah** *pr.n.* Uria.

**uric** *adj.* (chem.) urico.

**urin-e** *n.* orina. **-al** *n.* orinale *m.*, orinatoio, vespasiano; (vulg.) pisciatoio. **-ary** *adj.* (anat.) orinario, orinatorio; (med.) *-ary calculus*, urolito. **-ate** *intr.* orinare; (fam.) pisciare, fare acqua. **-ation** *n.* orinazione

**urn** *n.* urna; *funeral —*, urna cineraria; olla cineraria; *— burial*, seppellimento in urne; *tea-urn*, samovar *m.*

**urolog-y** *n.* (med.) urologia. **-ical** *adj.* (med.) urologico. **-ist** *n.* (med.) urologo.

**Ursa** *pr.n.* (astron.) Orsa; *— Major*, Orsa Maggiore; *— Minor*, Orsa Minore.

**ursine** *adj.* orsino.

**Ursul-a** *pr.n.* Orsola. **-ine** *adj.*, *n.* (eccl.) Orsolina.

**urticaria** *n.* (med.) orticaria, orticaia.

**Uruguay** *pr.n.* (geog.) Uruguay. **-an** *adj.*, *n.* uruguaiano.

**us** *pers. prn.* ci; (after *prep.*) noi; (fam.) *— two*, noi due; *it's —*, siamo noi.

**usable** *adj.* usabile, utilizzabile; utile.

**usage** *n.* uso, usanza; costume *m.*; abitudine *f.*; impiego; usura; trattamento; *common —*, uso corrente; *in modern —*, nell'uso moderno; *sanctified by —*, consacrato dall'uso.

**use** *n.* uso; impiego; utilità, vantaggio; usanza, costume *m.*; (leg.) godimento, usufrutto; *in —*, in uso, d'uso; *out of —*, fuori uso, in disuso, disusato, non usato; *directions for —*, istruzioni per l'uso; *to make — of*, adoperare, impiegare, far uso di; *to put something to good —*, impiegare bene qualcosa; *what's the —?*, a che pro?, a che serve?; *it's no —*, è inutile; *I haven't much — for it*, non so che farmene; *to have the — of*, avere il diritto di servirsi di; (provb.) *it's no — crying over spilt milk*, è inutile piangere sul latte versato.

**uṣe** *tr.* usare, adoperare, servirsi di, impiegare, far uso di, utilizzare; *to — violence*, usare violenza; *to — the railway regularly*, far uso regolare della ferrovia; *to — money to buy something*, impiegare denaro per acquistare qualcosa; *he -s his wife badly*, tratta male sua moglie; *to — up*, consumare, esaurire, usare completamente; *intr.* solere, essere abituato a; (in *p.def.* only, followed by to + *inf.*), generally rendered in Italian by *imperf. indic.* of follow. verb); *it -d to be said that ...*, si soleva dire che ...; *I -d to go to the cinema once a week*, andavo al cinema una volta la settimana.

**used** *adj.* solito; abituato; *to get — to*, abituarsi a.

**uṣed** *adj.* non nuovo, usato, adoperato; di seconda mano; logorato; *hardly —*, quasi nuovo; *— cars*, macchine d'occasione; *— stamp*, francobollo usato.

**useful** *adj.* utile, servizievole, pratico; proficuo, vantaggioso; *to be —*, essere utile; *to come in very —*, essere di grande utilità; *to make oneself —*, rendersi utile. **-ness** *n.* utilità; vantaggio.

**useless** *adj.* inutile; vano, super-

fluo, infruttuoso; *to be —*, non servire a nulla.

**user** *n.* utente *m., f.*; (leg.) usufruttuario, usuario.

**usher** *n.* usciere *m.*; (schol.) assistente *m.*, ripetitore, bidello; *tr.* introdurre; *to — in*, introdurre, far entrare, (fig.) dare inizio, inaugurare; *to — out*, ricondurre alla porta, far uscire.

**usherette** *n.* (fam., cinem.) maschera, inserviente *f.* di cinema.

**using** *n.* impiego, uso, l'usare.

**usual** *adj.* usuale, solito, consueto, abituale; *as —*, come al solito, come sempre; *on the — terms*, alle solite condizioni; *at the — time*, alla solita ora; *with his — kindness*, con la sua gentilezza abituale; *the — practice*, l'usanza normale. **-ly** *adv.* di solito, solitamente; abitualmente, usualmente; generalmente; *more than -ly*, più del solito. **-ness** *n.* consuetudine *f.*; frequenza; mancanza di originalità, banalità.

**usufruct** *n.* (leg.) usufrutto. **-uary** *adj., n.* (leg.) usufruttuario.

**usurer** *n.* usuraio, prestatore di denaro; (pop.) strozzino.

**usurp** *tr.* usurpare; (fig.) rubare. **-ation** *n.* usurpazione, usurpamento. **-er** *n.* usurpatore.

**usury** *n.* usura; interessi esorbitanti; (fig.) *with —*, ad usura.

**utensil** *n.* utensile *m.*, arnese *m.*; vaso, recipiente *m.*; *pl.* utensileria; *household -s*, arnesi casalinghi; *set of kitchen -s*, batteria da cucina.

**uterine** *adj.* (med.) uterino; (leg.) *— brother*, fratello uterino.

**uterus** *n.* (anat.) utero.

**utilitarian** *adj.* utilitario; (philos.) utilitaristico; *n.* (philos.) utilitario, utilitarista. **-ism** *n.* (philos.) utilitarismo.

**utility** *n.* utilità; vantaggio, profitto; *public —*, servizio pubblico, ente *m.* parastatale che gestisce un servizio pubblico; (motor.) *— car*, utilitaria, giardiniera; (theatr.) *— man*, generico.

**utiliz-e** *tr.* utilizzare, adoperare, servirsi di, sfruttare. **-a·ble** *adj.* adoperabile. **-ation** *n.* utilizzazione.

**utmost** *adj.* ultimo, sommo, estremo, massimo; *with the — care*, con la massima cura; *of the — importance*, della massima importanza; *the — ends of the earth*, gli estremi confini della terra; *the — bliss*, la somma beatitudine; *n.* il massimo, il possibile; *to the —*, il più possibile; *at the —*, al più; *to do one's —*, fare il possibile, fare del proprio meglio; *that's the — I can do*, di più non posso fare.

**Utopia** *pr.n.* Utopia; (fig.) utopia. **-n** *adj.* di Utopia; (fig.) utopistico, utopista; *n.* (lit.) utopiano; (fig.) utopista *m., f.*

**utter**[1] *adj.* completo, totale, assoluto, sommo; *in — darkness*, nell'oscurità più completa; *he is an — stranger to me*, mi è completamente sconosciuto; *to our — astonishment*, con nostro sommo stupore; (pejor.) perfetto, matricolato; *an — scoundrel*, un perfetto mascalzone.

**utter**[2] *tr.* emettere, pronunciare, proferire; *to — a groan*, emettere un gemito; *not to — a word*, non aprire bocca; mettere in circolazione, spacciare; *to — a forged cheque*, presentare per l'incasso un assegno a firma falsificata.

**utterance** *n.* espressione; emissione, articolazione; *to give — to*, esprimere, pronunciare, proferire.

**utterer** *n.* dicitore, (persona) che pronuncia, che proferisce.

**utterly** *adv.* completamente, assolutamente, totalmente.

**uttermost** *adj., n.* see **utmost.**

**utterness** *n.* assolutezza, completezza, totalità.

**uvula** *n.* (anat.) ugola, uvola. **-r** *adj.* di ugola.

**uxori-al** *adj.* di moglie. **-cide** *n.* (crime) uxoricidio; (killer) uxoricida. **-ous** *adj.* eccessivamente affezionata alla moglie, dominato dalla moglie. **-ousness** *n.* amore eccessivo per la moglie.

**V, v** *n.* vu *m., f.* (pop.) vi *m., f.*; (teleph.) *— for Victor*, vu come Venezia; (dressm.) *V-neck*, scollatura a punta; (neol.) *V-sign*, segno di vittoria; (mil.) *backsight —*, tacca di mira.

**vacancy** *n.* vuoto; vacuità; l'essere vacante; (fig.) mancanza d'intelligenza; posto libero, posto disponibile; *to fill a —*, coprire un posto vacante; camera libera; *no vacancies*, pieno, tutto esaurito.

**vacant** *adj.* vacante, vuoto; libero, disponibile; *a — seat*, un posto libero; *a — house*, una casa non occupata; *— possession*, immobile libero subito; (fig.) senza espressione, vuoto, vacuo; *a — stare*, uno sguardo vacuo.

**vacate** *tr.* lasciare libero, lasciare vacante; sgomberare; (leg.) vacare, rendere inoperante, invalidare.

**vacation** *n.* vacanza, vacanze *f.pl.*, ferie *f.pl.*; *long —*, vacanze estive.

**vaccinat-e** *tr.* (med.) vaccinare; *to get -ed*, farsi vaccinare. **-ion** *n.* vaccinazione.

**vaccine** *adj.* vaccino, di vacca; (vet.) *— virus*, virus del vaiolo; *n.* vaccino; *— inoculation*, vaccinazione.

**vacillat-e** *intr.* vacillare; esitare, tentennare, titubare. **-ing** *adj.* vacillante; esitante, irresoluto, titubante. **-ion** *n.* vacillazione, vacillamento, esitazione, titubazione, tentennamento. **-ory** *adj.* vacillante, esitante, irresoluto.

**vacuity** *n.* vacuità; vuoto, spazio vuoto; (fig.) mancanza di idee.

**vacuous** *adj.* vacuo, vuoto; (fig.) senza espressione, ozioso. **-ness** *n.* see **vacuity.**

**vacuum** *n.* vuoto, vuoto pneumatico, vacuo.

**vacuum-bottle** *n.* termos *m.*, bottiglia isolante. **-brake** *n.* (rlwy.) freno a depressione. **-cleaning** *n.* pulitura a mezzo aspirapolvere. **-cleaner** *n.* aspirapolvere *m.* **-flask** *n.* termos *m.* **-pump** *n.* pompa a vuoto; (aeron.) depressore. **-tube** *n.* tubo a vuoto; (radio) audion *m.*

**vademecum** *n.* vademecum *m.*, prontuario, manuale *m.*

**vagabond** *adj.* vagabondo, errabondo, nomade; *n.* vagabondo; (pejor.) barbone *m.*, lazzarone *m.*, buono a nulla. **-age, -ism** *n.* vagabondaggio.

**vagary** *n.* capriccio; idea stravagante; eccentricità; *the vagaries of fashion*, i capricci della moda.

**vagin-a** *n.* (anat.) vagina; (bot.) guaina. **-al** *adj.* (anat.) vaginale. **-itis** *n.* (med.) vaginite *f.*

**vagitus** *n.* vagito.

**vagr-ant** *adj., n.* vagabondo; nomade *m.*; accattone *m.*; *— tribes*, tribù *f.pl.* nomadi; *— musicians*, suonatori ambulanti. **-ancy** *n.* (leg.) vagabondaggio, accattonaggio; (fig.) vita errante.

**vague** *adj.* vago, impreciso, indistinto; indeterminato; (fam.) *I haven't the -st idea*, non ho la minima idea. **-ness** *n.* indeterminatezza; imprecisione.

**vain** *adj.* vano, inutile; *— efforts*, sforzi inutili; *a — pretext*, un pretesto frivolo; *a — hope*, una speranza vana; *in —*, invano; *to take the name of God in —*, pronunciare il nome di Dio in vano; vanitoso, orgoglioso; *as — as a peacock*, vanitoso come un pavone.

**vainglorious** *adj.* vanaglorioso, vanitoso. **-ness, vainglory** *n.* vanagloria; vanità.

**vainly** *adv.* vanamente, invano, inutilmente; vanitosamente, orgogliosamente.
**vainness** *n.* vanità, inutilità, futilità; vanità, orgoglio.
**vair** *n.* (herald.) vaio.
**valance** *n.* (of bed) cortina; (for window) mantovana.
**vale** *n.* valle *f.*, vallata; (poet.) vallea; (fig.) *this — of tears*, questa valle di lacrime.
**valedict-ion** *n.* commiato, addio. **-ory** *adj.* di saluto, d'addio; *a -ory speech*, un discorso di commiato.
**Valencia** *pr.n.* (geog.) Valencia.
**valency** *n.* (chem.) valenza; atomicità.
**Valentine** *pr.n.* Valentino; *St. -'s day*, giorno di San Valentino; *n.* biglietto amoroso che si invia il giorno di San Valentino.
**Valerian**[1] *pr.n.* (Rom. hist.) Valeriano.
**valerian**[2] (bot.) valeriana.
**valet** *n.* valletto, cameriere; *tr.* servire come valletto, servire come cameriere. **-ing** *n.* servizio come valletto, il fare il valletto; (comm.) *-ing service*, ditta che cura la pulitura e rammendatura dei vestiti.
**valetudinar-ian** *adj.* valetudinario; *n.* valetudinario, ipocondriaco, malato immaginario. **-ianism** *n.* valetudinarianismo, ipocondria. **-y** *adj.* valetudinario.
**Valhalla** *n.* (myth.) Valalla *m.*; (fig.) luogo che accoglie le tombe di persone illustri, panteon *m.*
**valiant** *adj.* valoroso, coraggioso, prode.
**valid** *adj.* valido, valevole; legittimo, valido a tutti gli effetti, regolare, in regola; *a — argument*, un argomento valido; (rlwy. ticket) *— three months*, valevole tre mesi; *a — passport*, un passaporto in regola; *no longer —*, scaduto. **-ate** *tr.* rendere valido, convalidare, vidimare. **-ation** *n.* convalidazione, vidimazione. **-ity** *n.* validità; legittimità.
**valise** *n.* valigia, borsa da viaggio.
**Valkyrie** *n.* (myth.) Valchiria.
**valley** *n.* valle *f.*, vallata; (poet.) vallea; (when forming part of *pr.n.*, often Val, *e.g.* Val d'Aosta); *— dweller*, valligiano; *small —*, vallecola, vallicella; *deep —*, vallone *m.*; (bldg.) compluvio; *— tile*, conversa. **-bottom** *n.* fondovalle *m.*
**vallum** *n.* (hist.) vallo; (anat.) vallo.
**Valois** *pr.n.* (geog.; hist.) Valesia.
**valorous** *adj.* valoroso, coraggioso, prode.
**valour** *n.* valore; coraggio; prodezza.
**valse** *n.* valzer *m.*; *intr.* ballare il valzer.
**valuable** *adj.* costoso, prezioso, di (gran) valore; *not — in terms of money*, non valutabile in denaro; *n.pl. -s* oggetti di valore, valori *m.pl.* **-ness** *n.* valore *m.*; valutabilità.
**valuat-ion** *n.* valutazione, stima, perizia. **-or** *n.* stimatore; perito.
**value** *n.* valore *m.*; prezzo, costo; *of great —*, di gran valore; *of little —*, di poco valore, di scarso valore; *market —*, valore commerciale; *taxable —*, valore imponibile; *rateable —*, valore locativo; *face —*, valore nominale; *gross —*, valore lordo; *net —*, valore netto; *to set — on*, attribuire valore a; *to be good — for money*, valere il prezzo; (fig.) valore, importanza, utilità; *the — of education*, l'importanza dell'insegnamento; (chem.) indice *m.*, numero; (math.) valore *m.*; (phys.) potere *m.*
**value** *tr.* valutare; stimare, fare la stima di; computare, calcolare; (fig.) dare importanza a, tenere in gran conto, apprezzare, aver caro, tenere in considerazione.
**valued** *adj.* valutato, stimato, apprezzato; (comm.) *your — orders*, i Vostri stimati ordini.
**valueless** *adj.* senza valore, di nessun valore. **-ness** *n.* mancanza di valore.
**valuer** *n.* stimatore, perito.
**valuing** *n.* valutazione, stima; (banking) valorizzazione.
**valve** *n.* (anat.) valvola; (bot.; zool.) valva; (mech.) valvola; *amplifying —*, valvola amplificatrice; *ball —*, valvola a sfera; *check —*, valvola di ritegno; *exhaust —*, valvola di scarico; *inlet —*, valvola di ammissione; *safety —*, valvola di sicurezza; *stop —*, valvola di arresto.
**valvular** *adj.* (anat.; mech.) valvolare; (bot.; zool.) di valva.
**vamoose, vamose** *intr.* (slang) filarsela, squagliarsi.
**vamp**[1] *n.* (shoem.) tomaia, rabberciamento, rappezzamento; (mus.) improvvisazione; *tr.* (shoem.) rappezzare, mettere la tomaia a, raffazonare, rabberciare; (mus.) improvvisare.
**vamp**[2] *n.* (slang) avventuriera, maliarda, donna fatale; *tr.* (slang) ammaliare, adescare; sfruttare.
**vampire** *n.* vampiro; (fig.) sfruttatore, succiasangue *m.*; (theatr.) botola a molle.
**van**[1] *n.* (mil.) avanguardia; *to be in the —*, essere alla testa.
**van**[2] *n.* vaglio, crivello; (of windmill) vela.
**van**[3] *n.* (vehicle) furgone *m.*, carrozzone *m.*; *delivery —*, furgoncino; *removal-van*, furgone per mobilia, furgone per traslochi; (rlwy.) *luggage —*, bagagliaio; *guard's —*, vettura di coda, scompartimento del capotreno.
**vandal** *n.* vandalo, barbaro; (hist.) *the Vandals*, i Vandali. **-ism** *n.* vandalismo, devastazione insensata; *an act of -ism*, un atto di vandalismo. **-istic** *adj.* vandalistico.
**vane** *n.* banderuola, mostravento; pala; (eng.) aletta; (naut.; aeron.) manica a vento; (aeron., of bomb) governale *m.*; (survey.) mirino; (of bird's feather) lama.
**vanguard** *n.* (mil.) avanguardia (also fig.).
**van-guard** *n.* guardamerci *m.*, fattorino.
**vanilla** *n.* (bot.; cul.) vaniglia; *— ice*, gelato alla vaniglia.
**vanish** *intr.* svanire, sparire, dileguarsi, scomparire; *to — without leaving trace*, sparire senza lasciar traccia; *to — into thin air*, dileguarsi; (math.) diventare zero.
**vanishing** *adj.* che svanisce, che sparisce, evanescente; *— point*, punto di fuga; *— cream*, crema evanescente; *n.* scomparsa, sparizione, il dileguarsi.
**vanity** *n.* vanità; futilità, inutilità; *Vanity Fair*, 'La Fiera delle vanità'. **-bag** *n.* borsetta da signora.
**vanquish** *tr.* vincere, conquistare; *the -ed*, i vinti. **-er** *n.* vincitore, conquistatore. **-ing** *n.* conquista; soggiogazione.
**vantage** *n.* vantaggio, profitto; *— ground*, terreno favorevole; (tennis) *— in*, vantaggio interno; *— out*, vantaggio esterno.
**vapid** *adj.* svaporato; insignificante; insulso; insipido. **-ity, -ness** *n.* insulsaggine *f.*; futilità; insipidezza.
**vaporiz-e** *tr.* vaporizzare, far evaporare; *intr.* evaporare, volatilizzarsi. **-ation** *n.* vaporizzazione, evaporazione. **-er** *n.* vaporizzatore.
**vaporous** *adj.* vaporoso, nebbioso; (fig.) chimerico.
**vapour** *n.* vapore *m.*; esalazione; *water —*, vapore acqueo. **-y** *adj.* vaporoso; (fig.) vago, indefinito.
**variab-le** *adj.* variabile, mutevole; incostante, instabile; (eng.) regolabile; *— weather*, tempo instabile; (mech.) *— motion*, moto vario; (math.) *— quantity*, quantità variabile; *n.* (math.) quantità variabile; (naut.) vento variabile. **-ility, -leness** *n.* variabilità; mutevolezza; (biol.) incostanza.
**variance** *n.* variazione; disaccordo, disputa; *at —*, in disaccordo, in attrito, in contraddizione; *at — with the facts*, incompatibile con i fatti; (leg.) discordanza.
**variant** *adj.* diverso (da), differente; *n.* variante *f.*; *two -s of the same story*, due versioni della medesima storia.
**variation** *n.* variazione; oscillazione; cambiamento; *— of speed*, variazione di velocità; *— of*

*temperature*, oscillazione di temperatura; (mus.) variazione; *theme with -s*, tema con variazioni; (naut.; astron.) declinazione; *magnetic —*, declinazione magnetica; *— compass*, bussola di declinazione, declinometro.

**vari-coloured** *adj.* variopinto, variegato, multicolore, policromatico.

**varicose** *adj.* (med.) varicoso; *— veins*, vene varicose.

**varied** *adj.* vario, variato, svariato, diverso; *— interests*, interessi svariati; *— opinions*, pareri diversi; *— style*, stile accidentato. **-ness** *n.* varietà, diversità.

**variegat-e** *tr.* variegare; screziare. **-ed** *adj.* variegato, diverso; vario, multiforme. **-ion** *n.* varietà di colori; screziatura.

**variety** *n.* varietà; diversità; molteplicità; *a — of patterns*, un assortimento di campioni; *a — of reasons*, ragioni varie; (theatr.) varietà; *— artist*, artista di varietà; *— show*, spettacolo di varietà.

**variform** *adj.* di varie forme, multiforme, variforme.

**variola** *n.* (med.) vaiuolo.

**various** *adj.* vario; diverso; disparato; *of — types*, di vari tipi; *under — names*, sotto diversi nomi; *at — times*, a diverse riprese; parecchi, alcuni.

**varlet** *n.* (hist.) paggio, valletto; (joc.) furfante *m.*, briccone *m.*

**varmint** *n.* (fam.) furfante *m.*, briccone *m.*

**varnish** *n.* vernice *f.*; lacca; *nail —*, smalto per unghie; *oil —*, vernice grassa; (fig.) verniciatura, apparenza, aspetto esteriore; *tr.* verniciare; laccare; (fig.) abbellire, adornare; (fig.) *to — (over)*, mascherare, velare, nascondere, scivolare su. **-er** *n.* verniciatore. **-ing** *n.* verniciatura; laccatura.

**varnishing-day** *n.* (paint.) vernice *f.*, vernissage *m.*

**vary** *tr.* variare, cambiare, modificare; *to — the menu*, variare il menu; (mus.) fare variazioni a; *intr.* cambiarsi, modificarsi; differire; *opinions —*, i pareri differiscono; *to — from*, differire da; (math.) variare. **-ing** *adj.* che varia, variabile, mutevole, diverso; *n.* variazione, cambiamento. **-ingly** *adv.* in vari modi, variamente.

**vascular** *adj.* (phys.; bot.) vascolare.

**vase** *n.* vaso; *flower —*, vaso da fiori, portafiori *m.*; (archit.) vaso (di capitello). **-shaped** *adj.* a forma di vaso, vasiforme.

**vassal** *adj.* (hist.) di vassallo, feudatario; (fig.) servile; *n.* (hist.) vassallo; (fig.) suddito, soggetto; (pejor.) servo. **-age** *n.* (hist.) vassallaggio; (fig.) soggezione.

**vast** *adj.* vasto; immenso, enorme, ampio, grande; *on a — scale*, su vasta scala; *a — sum of money*, una grande quantità di denaro. **-ness** *n.* vastezza, vastità; immensità, ampiezza.

**vat** *n.* tino, tinozza; vasca.

**Vatican** *n.* Vaticano; (geog.) *the — City*, la Città del Vaticano; (hist.) *the — State*, lo Stato Pontificio; *the — Council*, il Consiglio Ecumenico del Vaticano; *the — Library*, la Biblioteca apostolica vaticana.

**vaticinat-e** *intr.* vaticinare; profetizzare. **-ion** *n.* vaticinazione, vaticinio; profezia. **-or** *n.* vaticinatore; profeta *m.*

**Vaucluse** *pr.n.* (geog.) Valchiusa.

**Vaud** *pr.n.* (geog.) Vaud *m.*, Valdesia.

**vaudeville** *n.* (theatr.) vaudeville *m.*, rivista, spettacolo di varietà.

**Vaudois** *adj.*, *n.* (geog.) valdese *m.*, *f.*

**vault**[1] *n.* (archit.) volta, soffitto a volta; *barrel —*, volta a botte; (tomb) sepolcro, tomba, cripta; *family —*, tomba di famiglia; cantina, sotterraneo a volte; (of bank) camera di sicurezza; (anat.) volta; *cranial —*, volta cranica; *tr.* (archit.) coprire con una volta, costruire a forma di volta; *intr.* curvarsi a volta.

**vault**[2] *n.* (sport) salto, volteggio; (with pole) salto con l'asta; *intr.* (sport) saltare, volteggiare; *to — into the saddle*, balzare in sella; *tr. to — a fence*, saltare uno steccato.

**vaulted** *adj.* (archit.) a volta, centinato.

**vaulter** *n.* (sport) saltatore.

**vaulting**[1] *n.* (archit.) costruzione a volta; il costruire volte, centinatura; *cross-vaulting*, volta a crociera.

**vaulting**[2] *adj.* che salta, che supera gli ostacoli; (fig.) *— ambition*, ambizione che non conosce ostacoli; *n.* salto, volteggio; (gymn.) *vaulting-horse*, cavalletto.

**vaunt** *n.* vanto, vanteria, millanteria; *tr.* lodare; *to — the beauties of London*, decantare le bellezze di Londra; *intr.* vantarsi, gloriarsi. **-er** *n.* vantatore. **-ing** *adj.* da vantatore; vanitoso, vanaglorioso; *n.* vanto, vanteria.

**veal** *n.* (cul.) vitello; *— cutlet*, costoletta di vitello.

**vector** *n.* (math.) vettore *m.*; (astron.) *radius —*, raggio vettore.

**vedette** *n.* (mil.) vedetta; (naut.) *— boat*, vedetta.

**Ved-ic** *adj.* vedico. **-ism** *n.* vedismo, dottrina dei Veda.

**veer** *n.* cambiamento di direzione; (naut.) virata, viramento.

**veer** *intr.* cambiare direzione; girare; (naut.) virare, cambiare rotta; *tr.* (naut.) filare; *to — and haul*, filare e tesare.

**vegetable** *adj.* vegetale; *the — kingdom*, il regno vegetale; *— diet*, regime vegetariano; *n.* (bot.) vegetale *m.*; *pl.* ortaggi *m.pl.* verdura; (cul.) verdura, contorno, legumi *m.pl.*; *— garden*, ortaglia, orto; *— marrow*, zucca; *— soup*, minestra di verdura; *early -s*, primizie *f.pl.* **-dish** *n.* legumiera.

**vegetal** *adj.* vegetale, vegetativo; *n.* vegetale *m.*

**vegetarian** *adj.* vegetariano; *— restaurant*, ristorante vegetariano; *n.* vegetariano. **-ism** *n.* vegetarianismo.

**vegetat-e** *intr.* vegetare. **-ion** *n.* vegetazione; *luxuriant -ion*, vegetazione lussureggiante; *natural -ion*, vegetazione spontanea; (fig.) il vegetare. **-ive** *adj.* vegetativo.

**vehem-ence** *n.* veemenza; impeto. **-ent** *adj.* veemente; impetuoso; appassionato; violento.

**vehic-le** *n.* veicolo, mezzo di trasporto; *a jolting —*, un veicolo traballante; (fig.) mezzo di trasmissione, mezzo di propagazione; (med.) veicolo; (pharm.) eccipiente *m.*; (paint.) veicolo (legante). **-ular** *adj.* dei veicoli, veicolare.

**veil** *n.* velo, velame *m.*; (eccl.) *to take the —*, prendere il velo, farsi monaca; (bibl.) *the — of the Temple*, il velo del Tempio; (fig.) velo, cortina; *to draw a — over the past*, stendere un velo sul passato; *a fine — of mist*, un velo di nebbia; *beyond the —*, nell'al di là; maschera, apparenza, pretesto; *under the — of religion*, sotto la maschera della religione.

**veil** *tr.* velare, coprire; (fig.) nascondere, mascherare, dissimulare; *to — one's resentment*, nascondere il proprio risentimento.

**veiledly** *adv.* velatamente.

**veiling** *n.* il velare, il coprire con un velo; (fig.) schermo; (comm.) *nun's —*, flanella, mussola di lana.

**vein** *n.* (anat.) vena; *jugular —*, vena giugulare; *varicose —*, vena varicosa; (bot.; ent.) venatura, nervatura; (min.) vena; *a — of gold*, un filone d'oro; (fig.) umore *m.*, disposizione, vena; *he is not in the —*, non è in vena; *the poetic —*, la vena poetica.

**vein** *tr.* (paint.) venare, marmorizzare. **-ed** *adj.* venato, a vene; (bot.; ent.) con venature, con nervature. **-ing** *n.* (bot.; ent.) venatura, nervatura; (collect.) le vene *f.pl.* **-ous** *adj.* venoso, attraversato da vene.

**velar** *adj.*, *n.* (phon.) velare *f.*

**velleity** *n.* velleità.

**vellum** *n.* (bookb.) pergamena; *Japanese —*, carta Giappone; *bound in —*, rilegato in perga-

mena; *printed on —*, stampato su pergamena.
**velocipede** *n.* velocipede *m.*, bicicletta.
**velocity** *n.* velocità.
**velour(s)** *n.* velluto; felpa, feltro.
**velum** *n.* (anat.; bot.; zool.) velo, membrana; (of the palate) velo palatino.
**velvet** *n.* velluto; *as soft as —, like —*, come velluto; (fig.) *to be on —*, riposare sul velluto; *attrib.* vellutato; (fig.) *with — tread*, con passo felpato; *an iron hand in a — glove*, pugno di ferro e guanto di velluto.
**velvet-eyed** *adj.* dagli occhi dolci.
**velvetiness** *n.* vellutatura; morbidezza.
**velvet-pile** *n.* (text.) tessuto peloso.
**velvety** *adj.* vellutato, morbido; *— black*, nero vellutato.
**venal** *adj.* venale, corruttibile, mercenario, vendereccio. **-ity** *n.* venalità; corruttibilità.
**vend** *tr.* vendere. **-er** *n.* venditore; venditore ambulante.
**Vendée (la)** *pr.n.* (geog.) Valdea.
**vendetta** *n.* vendetta, faida.
**vending-machine** *n.* distributrice automatica.
**vendor** *n.* venditore.
**veneer** *n.* impiallacciatura, foglio per impiallacciatura; (fig.) vernice *f.*; maschera; *under a — of politeness*, sotto una vernice di cortesia; *tr.* impiallacciare; (fig.) mascherare, nascondere sotto una apparenza attraente. **-ing** *n.* impiallacciatura; (fig.) vernice *f.*; maschera.
**venerab-le** *adj.* venerabile, venerando; (eccl.) *the — Bede*, il venerabile Beda. **-ility** *n.* venerabilità.
**venerat-e** *tr.* venerare; riverire. **-ion** *n.* venerazione, veneramento; *to hold in -ion*, venerare. **-or** *n.* veneratore.
**venereal** *adj.* (med.) venereo; *— diseases*, malattie *f.pl.* veneree.
**venery**[1] *n.* (la) caccia.
**venery**[2] *n.* piaceri venerei *m.pl.*
**Venetia** *pr.n.* (geog.) Veneto; *the three -s*, le tre Venezie (Veneto, Venezia Tridentina, Venezia Giulia).
**Venetian** *adj.*, *n.* (of Venice) veneziano; (of Venetia) veneto; *— blind*, persiana alla veneziana; *— glass*, vetri di Murano, cristalli di Venezia.
**vengeance** *n.* vendetta; *the — of God*, la giustizia di Dio; *to take — upon*, vendicarsi di, fare vendetta su; *to cry —*, gridare vendetta; (fam.) *with a —* ad oltranza.
**vengeful** *adj.* vendicativo, vendicatore, vendichevole. **-ness** *n.* carattere vendicativo, spirito di vendetta.
**venial** *adj.* veniale, perdonabile; *— sin*, peccato veniale. **-ity** *n.* venialità.
**Venice** *pr.n.* (geog.) Venezia.
**venison** *n.* (cul.) carne di daino, carne di capriolo.
**venom** *n.* veleno; (fig.) cattiveria, malignità.
**venomous** *adj.* velenoso, velenifero; (fig.) cattivo, maligno, che schizza veleno. **-ness** *n* velenosità; (fig.) malignità.
**venous** *adj.* (anat.) venoso; (bot.; zool.) con nervature.
**vent** *n.* sbocco, orifizio, foro, buco; (anat.) ano; (cost.) spacco (di un vestito); (mech.) scarico; (fig.) sfogo, espressione; *to give — to*, sfogare; *to give — to a sigh*, lasciare scappare un sospiro; *tr.* scaricare, sfogare, evacuare, esalare; (fig.) sfogare, dare libero corso a, esprimere; *to — one's rage*, sfogare la rabbia.
**vent-hole** *n.* apertura di sfogo; (of volcano) camino.
**ventilate** *tr.* ventilare, aerare; (phys.) ossigenare; (fig.) discutere; esprimere.
**ventilating** *adj.* aerante, aeratore, ventilatore; *n.* see **ventilation.**
**ventilating-cowl** *n.* (industr.; naut.) manica di ventilazione. **-fan** *n.* ventilatore.
**ventilation** *n.* ventilazione, aerazione; (fig.) *the question needs —*, il problema richiede chiarificazione. **-shaft** *n.* pozzo di ventilazione.
**ventilator** *n.* ventilatore, aeratore.
**vent-plug** *n.* zipolo; (artill.) tampone *m.*
**ventral** *adj.* (anat.) ventrale, addominale.
**ventric-le** *n.* (anat.) ventricolo, ventriglio; cavità addominale. **-ular** *adj.* (anat.) ventricolare, addominale.
**ventriloqu-ism, -y** *n.* ventriloquio. **-ist** *n.* ventriloquo. **-istic** *adj.* ventriloquo.
**venture** *n.* avventura; azzardo; impresa rischiosa; *a desperate —*, un tentativo disperato; (comm.) speculazione, iniziativa, affare speculativo; *at a —*, a caso, a casaccio, alla ventura; *to answer at a —*, rispondere a caso.
**venture** *tr.* avventurare, arrischiare, osare, azzardare; *to — a few words*, arrischiarsi a dire due parole; *to — a guess*, azzardare un'ipotesi; *intr.* avventurarsi, arrischiarsi; *I — to write to you*, mi permetto di scriverle; *I — to say that . . .*, oso dire che . . .; *to — forth*, arrischiarsi ad uscire; *to — too far*, andare troppo lontano; (provb.) *nothing —, nothing gain*, chi non risica non rosica.
**venturesome, venturous** *adj.* ardito, temerario; rischioso; *a — act*, un atto rischioso.
**venue** *n.* (leg.) giurisdizione; sede *f.* di un processo; *to change the — of a trial*, rinviare la causa ad altra sede per legittimo sospetto; (fam.) luogo di ritrovo, luogo di convegno.
**Venus** *pr.n.* (myth.) Venere *f.*, Afrodite *f.*; (astron.) Venere; (fig.) amore *m.*, voluttà; donna bellissima; (anat.) *mount of —*, monte *m.* di Venere.
**veracious** *adj.* verace, veritiero, veridico. **-ness, veracity** *n.* veracità, veridicità.
**veranda(h)** *n.* veranda.
**verb** *n.* (gramm.) verbo.
**verbal** *adj.* verbale, orale; (gramm.) verbale; *a — communication*, una comunicazione verbale; letterale, testuale. **-ism** *n.* vocabolo, locuzione verbale; (fig.) verbalismo, ricercatezza nel parlare.
**verbaliz-e** *tr.* rendere un'idea in parole; (gramm.) impiegare come verbo; *intr.* essere verboso, essere prolisso. **-ation** *n.* il rendere un'idea in parole.
**verbatim** *adv.* parola per parola, testualmente.
**verbena** *n.* (bot.) verbena.
**verbiage** *n.* verbosità.
**verbose** *adj.* verboso, prolisso. **-ness, verbosity** *n.* verbosità, prolissità.
**verdant** *adj.* verde, verdeggiante; (fig.) immaturo, ingenuo.
**verdict** *n.* (leg.) verdetto; *a — of not guilty*, un verdetto di non colpevolezza, un verdetto di assoluzione; (fig.) giudizio, parere *m.*; *the popular —*, l'opinione popolare.
**verdigris** *n.* verderame *m.*; (agric.) verdetto, grigio-verde *m.*
**verdure** *n.* verzura, vegetazione; il verde, verdura; (fig.) freschezza, giovinezza.
**verge** *n.* orlo; limite *m.*; estremità; bordo; *on the — of*, sull'orlo di, (fig.) sul punto di; *to be on the — of forty*, essere sulla soglia dei quaranta; *on the — of war*, alla vigilia della guerra; *on the — of tears*, sul punto di scoppiare in lacrime.
**verge** *intr.* tendere, volgere, declinare; *the sun -s towards the horizon*, il sole declina verso l'orizzonte; *to — towards old age*, avvincinarsi alla vecchiaia; *to — on*, essere vicino a, confinare con, rasentare, costeggiare; *colour that -s on red*, colore vicino al rosso; *that -s on madness*, ciò rasenta la follia.
**verger** *n.* (eccl.) sagrestano.
**veridical** *adj.* veridico, veritiero.
**verifiable** *adj.* verificabile, constatabile.
**verification** *n.* verifica, verificazione; autenticazione; accertamento; controllo.
**verify** *tr.* verificare, controllare; (leg.) confermare.
**verily** *adv.* (bibl.) in verità.
**verisimilar** *adj.* verosimile.

**verisimilitude** *n.* verosimiglianza; *beyond the bounds of* —, al di là del verosimile.
**veritab-le** *adj.* vero; autentico; *a — deluge*, un vero diluvio. **-ly** *adv.* veramente.
**verity** *n.* verità; realtà; *the eternal verities*, le verità eterne.
**verjuice** *n.* agresto, agrestata; succo di frutta acerba.
**vermi-cide** *n.* vermifugo. **-cular** *adj.* vermicolare, vermiforme; (anat.) *the -cular appendix*, l'appendice vermicolare. **-culation** *n.* l'essere infestato dai vermi; (phys.) peristalsi *f.*; (archit.) disegno vermicolato. **-fuge** *adj.*, *n.* vermifugo.
**vermilion** *n.* vermiglio, vermiglione, cinabro.
**vermin** *n.* insetti parassiti *m.pl.*, insetti nocivi; verminaia; (fig.) persone nocive *f.pl.*, feccia della società. **-ous** *adj.* verminoso, infestato da parassiti; (pop.) pidocchioso.
**verm(o)uth** *n.* vermut *m.*, vino vermutato.
**vernacular** *adj.* vernacolo, nativo, indigeno; — *languages*, lingue indigene; *a — poet*, un poeta dialettale; (med.) endemico; *n.* vernacolo, dialetto nativo; volgare *m.*, lingua volgare; *in the* —, in volgare; *translated into the* —, volgarizzato; gergo.
**vernal** *adj.* primaverile, vernale; *the — equinox*, l'equinozio di primavera.
**Veron-a** *pr.n.* (geog.) Verona. **-ese** *adj.*, *n.* veronese *m.*, *f.*, di Verona.
**veronal** *n.* (pharm.) veronale *m.*
**Veronica**[1] *pr.n.* Veronica.
**veronica**[2] *n.* (bot.) veronica; (eccl.) veronica, sudario.
**Versailles** *pr.n.* (geog.) Versaglia.
**versatil-e** *adj.* versatile; dotato di molti talenti; multilaterale; *a — genius*, un genio universale; (bot.; zool.) mobile; (mech.) girevole; (fig.) incostante, volubile. **-ity** *n.* versatilità; universalità; (bot.; zool.) mobilità; (fig.) incostanza, volubilità.
**verse** *n.* verso; *in* —, in versi; *iambic* —, verso iambico; *blank* —, versi sciolti; poesia, componimento in versi; *he writes very good* —, scrive ottime poesie; *light* —, poesia leggera; stanza, strofe *f.*; *to give chapter and* —, citare capitolo e verso; (bibl.) versetto.
**versed** *adj.* versato, istruito, abile; *well — in*, molto versato in.
**versification** *n.* versificazione, metrica; stile poetico; riduzione in versi.
**versifier** *n.* versificatore, poeta *m.*; (pejor.) poetastro.
**versify** *tr.* versificare, volgere in versi. **-ing** *n.* versificazione.
**version** *n.* versione; traduzione; *the Authorized Version*, la versione anglicana della Bibbia (1611); *the Revised Version*, la versione anglicana della Bibbia riveduta nel 1884; descrizione; *according to his* —, secondo lui; *this is quite a different* —, questa è un'altra storia.
**verso** *n.* (of page) verso; (of medal) rovescio; (typ., of forme) volta.
**versus** *prep.* (generally abbreviated to v.) (leg.; sport) contro.
**vert** *adj.* (herald.) verde.
**vertebr-a** *n.* (anat.) vertebre *f.pl.* **-al** *adj.* (anat.) vertebrale; *-al column*, colonna vertebrale, spina dorsale; *-al ribs*, coste fluttuanti. **-ate** *adj.*, *n.* vertebrato.
**vertex** *n.* vertice *m.*, sommità, apice *m.*; (astron.) zenit *m.*
**vertical** *adj.* verticale, perpendicolare, situato al vertice, situato allo zenit; — *line*, linea perpendicolare all'orizzonte; (astron.) — *circle*, azimut *m.*; (techn.) — *engine*, motore verticale; (aeron.) — *rudder*, timone di direzione; *n.* verticale *m.*, piano verticale. **-ly** *adv.* verticalmente, a perpendicolo, a piombo. **-ity** *n.* verticalità, posizione verticale, perpendicolarità.
**vertiginous** *adj.* vertiginoso, vorticoso.
**vertigo** *n.* capogiro; (med.) vertigine *f.*
**vervain** *n.* (bot.) verbena.
**verve** *n.* brio vigore *m.*
**very**[1] *adj.* vero, vero e proprio, autentico; *this is my — son*, questo è veramente mio figlio; *the veriest fool*, il più gran cretino; *for — shame*, proprio per la vergogna; proprio, esatto, stesso, medesimo; *in this — place*, proprio qui; *at the — beginning*, proprio all'inizio; *at that — moment*, in quello stesso momento; *you're the — man for the job*, sei proprio l'uomo che ci vuole per questo lavoro; *the — children know it*, perfino i bambini lo sanno; *this — day*, oggi stesso; *a year ago to the — day*, proprio un anno fa; *the — thought terrifies me*, il solo pensiero mi fa paura; *in the — act*, proprio nell'atto, in flagrante; *those were his — words*, queste furono le sue precise parole; *this is my — own*, questo è proprio mio; *adv.* molto, assai, moltissimo (N.B. in Italian often rendered by the superlative form of the adjective in -issimo); — *rich*, molto ricco, assai ricco, ricchissimo; — *pleased*, molto lieto, lietissimo; — *well known*, molto conosciuto, conosciutissimo; *that's — nice of you*, è molto gentile da parte tua; — *much*, moltissimo; — *little*, pochissimo; — *well*, molto bene, benissimo; *are you hungry?*, *Yes*, —, hai fame?, Sì, molta; *the — first*, il primissimo; *the — last*, proprio l'ultimo; *at the — most*, tutt'al più; *at the — latest*, al più tardi; *the — same*, proprio lo stesso; *I did the — best I could*, ho fatto tutto il possibile; *the — next day*, il giorno immediatamente successivo.
**Very**[2] *pr.n.* (mil.) — *light*, very *m.*; — *pistol*, pistola very.
**vesicle** *n.* (med.) vescicola, vescichetta.
**vesicul-ar** *adj.* (anat.; med.) vescicolare. **-ation** *n.* (med.) vescicolazione.
**Vesper**[1] *pr.n.* (astron.) Vespero, Espero.
**vesper**[2] *n.* (poet.) sera, vespro; stella vespertina; (astron.) vespero; *pl.* (eccl.) i vespri; — *bell*, campana che chiama ai vespri; (hist.) *the Sicilian Vespers*, i Vespri Siciliani.
**vessel** *n.* vaso, recipiente *m.*; ricettacolo; (bibl.) *chosen* —, vaso d'elezione, anima eletta; *the weaker* —, il sesso debole; (anat.; bot.) vaso; (bot.) trachea; (naut.) nave *f.*, vascello, bastimento.
**vest**[1] *n.* panciotto; maglia; (for women) camiciola; (sport) maglietta, canottiera.
**vest**[2] *tr.* investire, conferire; *to — with authority*, conferire autorità a; (leg.) assegnare, passare a; *to — property in*, assegnare dei beni a; (poet.) vestire, indossare.
**Vesta**[1] *pr.n.* (myth.; astron.) Vesta.
**vesta**[2] *n.* (match) fiammifero; *wax* —, cerino.
**Vestal** *adj.* vestale, di Vesta; *Vestal Virgin*, vergine vestale.
**vested** *adj.* vestito; (leg.) — *rights*, diritti acquisiti; — *interests*, interessi acquisiti; (eccl.) vestito con paramenti.
**vestibule** *n.* vestibolo, anticamera, entrata; (of church) portico, antiporto.
**vestig-e** *n.* vestigio; traccia, orma; (biol.) residuo; *not a — of ...*, neppure una traccia di ...; *you have not a — of evidence*, non hai la minima prova. **-ial** *adj.* (biol.) rudimentale, residuale.
**vestment** *n.* abito da cerimonia; (eccl.) pianeta *f.*; (altar-cloth) tovaglia d'altare.
**vest-pocket** *n.* taschetta del panciotto; (photog.) — *camera*, apparecchio tascabile.
**vestry** *n.* (eccl.) sagrestia; — *meeting*, assemblea parrocchiale.
**Vesuvi-us** *pr.n.* (geog.) Vesuvio. **-an** *adj.* vesuviano, del Vesuvio.
**vet**[1] *n.* (abbrev. of **veterinary surgeon**). See under **veterinary**.
**vet**[2] *tr.* controllare; esaminare criticamente; (mil.) interrogare sommariamente (prigionieri di guerra).
**vetch** *n.* (bot.) veccia; *milk* —,

vecciarini *m.pl.*; *bitter* —, vecciola.

**veteran** *n.* veterano; (mil.) reduce *m.*; *attrib.* vecchio, esperto; *a — cricketer*, un veterano del cricket.

**veterinary** *adj.*, *n.* veterinario; — *surgeon*, (medico) veterinario; — *science*, veterinaria.

**veto** *n.* veto, interdizione, proibizione; *right of* —, diritto di veto; *to put a — upon*, porre il veto a, proibire; *tr.* opporre il veto a, vietare, proibire, interdire.

**vetting** *n.* (mil.) controllo; interrogazione sommaria dei prigionieri di guerra.

**vex** *tr.* vessare; stizzire; irritare, seccare, infastidire, contrariare; affliggere, addolorare; (poet.) agitare, sconvolgere. **-ation** *n.* vessazione; fastidio; irritazione, seccatura. **-atious** *adj.* vessatorio; spiacevole, noioso, fastidioso, seccante. **-ed** *adj.* vessato; stizzito, seccato, infastidito; *to get -ed*, seccarsi, infastidirsi; *a -ed question*, una questione dibattuta, una questione vessata. **-ing** *adj.* vessante; seccante, fastidioso, irritante.

**vexillum** *n.* (hist.) vessillo; (eccl.; bot.) stendardo; (orn.) vessillo, barba (di penna).

**via**[1] *n.* (astron.) via; *the Via Lactea*, la Via Lattea; (logic) — *media*, termine medio.

**via**[2] *prep.* via, per, attraverso; — *the usual diplomatic channels*, attraverso le solite vie diplomatiche.

**viab-le** *adj.* (of a road) transitabile, viabile; (med.) vitale, viabile, atto a vivere. **-ility** *n.* (of a road) viabilità, transitabilità; (med.) viabilità, vitalità, capacità di vivere.

**viaduct** *n.* viadotto; cavalcavia.

**vial** *n.* fiala; *to pour out the -s of one's wrath*, dar sfogo alla propria collera.

**viand** *n.* vivanda, cibo; *pl.* alimenti *m.pl.*; *choice -s*, cibi *m.pl.* scelti.

**viaticum** *n.* (eccl.) viatico; (fig.) provvigioni *f.pl.*; viatico.

**vibr-ant** *adj.* vibrante; palpitante. **-ancy** *n.* vibrazione; risonanza; sonorità.

**vibraphone** *n.* (mus.) vibrafono.

**vibrat-e** *intr.* vibrare; risuonare; oscillare; *tr.* far vibrare, far oscillare. **-ing** *adj.* vibrante; risonante; sonoro; oscillante. **-ion** *n.* vibrazione; oscillazione; tremolio. **-or** *n.* (electr.) vibratore; (radio) oscillatore. **-ory** *adj.* vibratorio; oscillatorio.

**vibro-massage** *n.* (med.) massaggio vibratorio, vibromassaggio, sismoterapia.

**vicar** *n.* (R.C.) vicario; (Anglican) curato, parroco. **-age** *n.* canonica, casa del parroco, presbiterio.

**vicar-general** *n.* vicario generale.

**vicarious** *adj.* vicario; delegato.

**vice**[1] *n.* vizio; immoralità; depravazione; difetto; imperfezione; pecca.

**vice**[2] *n.* (mech.) morsa, tenaglia; *bench* —, morsa da banco; *the jaws of a* —, le ganasce di una morsa; *a grip like a* —, una stretta come una morsa.

**vice**[3] *n.* (fam.) vicepresidente *m.*

**vice-**[3] *pref.* vice.

**vice-admiral** *n.* viceammiraglio, ammiraglio di squadra. **-chairman** *n.* vicepresidente *m.* **-chairmanship** *n.* vicepresidenza. **-chancellor** *n.* vicecancelliere; (of University) rettore magnifico. **-chancellorship** *n.* vicecancellierato; (of University) rettorato. **-consul** *n.* viceconsole. **-consular** *adj.* viceconsolare. **-consulate, -consulship** *n.* viceconsolato, **-manager** *n.* vicegerente *m.*, vicedirettore. **-marshal** *n.* (aeron.) *Air Vice-Marshal*, generale di divisione dell'Aeronautica.

**Vicenza** *pr.n.* (geog.) Vicenza; *native of* —, vicentino; *relating to* —, vicentino.

**vice-presidency** *n.* vicepresidenza. **-president** *n.* vicepresidente *m.*

**viceregal** *adj.* vicereale.

**vice-reine** *n.* viceregina, consorte del vicerè.

**vice-roy** *n.* vicerè *m.* **-royalty** *n.* vicereggenza; vicereame *m.*

**vice-squad** *n.* (police) squadra del buon costume.

**vice-versa** *adv.* viceversa.

**vicinity** *n.* vicinanza; prossimità; vicinanze *f.pl.*, dintorni *m.pl.*; *in the — of*, vicino a.

**vicious** *adj.* vizioso; *a — circle*, un circolo vizioso; immorale, depravato; *a — life*, una vita immorale; — *tastes*, gusti depravati; cattivo, maligno, dispettoso; difettoso, imperfetto. **-ness** *n.* viziosità, malignità, cattiveria; imperfezione.

**vicissitude** *n.* vicissitudine *f.*; vicenda; peripezia; *the -s of life*, gli alti e bassi della vita; *the -s of fortune*, i rovesci della fortuna.

**victim** *n.* vittima; *a — of an accident*, un infortunato, un sinistrato; *to fall a — to*, soccombere a; (fig.) *to fall an easy — to*, essere facile preda di.

**victimiz-e** *tr.* vittimizzare, offrire come vittima; (fig.) ingannare, truffare. **-ation** *n.* vittimismo, oppressione; sacrificio; (after strike) rappresaglie *f.pl.*

**Victor**[1] *pr.n.* Vittore, Vittorio.

**victor**[2] *n.* vincitore, conquistatore, trionfatore.

**Victoria** *pr.n.* Vittoria; (hist.) *Queen* —, la regina Vittoria; (geog.) Vittoria; (vehicle) vittoria; — *Cross*, la Croce della Regina Vittoria (Italian equiv.: medaglia d'oro al valore militare).

**victorian** *adj.* (hist.) vittoriano, dell'epoca vittoriana. **-ism** *n.* vittorianismo; gusto dell'epoca vittoriana.

**victorious** *adj.* vittorioso; di vittoria.

**victory** *n.* vittoria; vincita; *a Pyrrhic* —, una vittoria di Pirro; *to gain a* —, riportare una vittoria, essere vittorioso, vincere; *an overwhelming* —, una vittoria schiacciante.

**victual** *tr.* vettovagliare, approvvigionare, fornire di viveri; *intr.* rifornirsi, approvvigionarsi. **-ler** *n.* incaricato dei rifornimenti; negoziante in viveri, fornitore di viveri; *licensed -ler* gestore di locale autorizzato a vendere alcoolici. **-ling** *n.* vettovagliamento, approvvigionamento. **-s** *n.pl.* viveri *m.pl.*, vivande *f.pl.*, vettovaglie *f.pl.*, provviste *f.pl.*; (fam.) il mangiare, il vitto.

**vide** (abbrev. v.) vedi.

**video** *n.* (telev.) video; (USA) televisione; — *signal*, segnale *m.* video, segnale d'immagine; — *tape*, nastro video.

**vie** *intr.* gareggiare; rivaleggiare; scendere in lizza; lottare.

**Vienn-a** *pr.n.* (Austria) Vienna. **-ese** *adj.*, *n.* viennese *m.*, *f.*; di Vienna.

**Vienne** *pr.n.* (France) Vienne.

**Vietnam** *pr.n.* (geog.) Vietnam *m.* **-ese** *adj.*, *n.* Vietnamese *m.*, *f.*

**view** *n.* vista; *in* —, in vista; *out of* —, fuori di vista; *on* —, esposto al pubblico; *point of* —, punto di vista; *angle of* —, angolo visuale; (fig.) *to have something in* —, avere qualcosa in vista; *to keep in* —, tenere in vista, tenere in mente; veduta, panorama *m.*; *a front — of the hotel*, l'albergo visto di fronte; *a side* —, una veduta laterale; *what a lovely — !*, che bel panorama!, che bella vista!; *a bird's-eye* —, una veduta a volo d'uccello; *a comprehensive — of Italian literature*, un panorama della letteratura italiana; *in — of the circumstances*, date le circostanze; *with a — to*, allo scopo di, col proposito di; opinione, giudizio, veduta; *in my* —, secondo me, secondo il mio avviso; *to meet a person's -s*, andare incontro ai desideri di una persona; visione; *field of* —, campo visivo; (leg.) sopralluogo.

**view** *tr.* vedere; osservare, guardare; ispezionare; visitare; (leg.) fare un sopralluogo; (hunt.) *to — the fox*, avvistare la volpe; (fig.) considerare, vedere.

**viewer** *n.* persona che guarda, spettatore; (telev.) telespettatore; ispettore; (leg.) funzionario

che deve compiere un sopralluogo.

**view-finder** *n.* (photog.) mirino. **-halloo** *n.* (hunt.) visto!

**viewing** *n.* esame *m.*, ispezione.

**view-lens** *n.* (photog.) obiettivo semplice.

**viewpoint** *n.* punto di vista; belvedere *m.*

**vigil** *n.* veglia, vigilia; *to keep —*, vegliare; *pl.* (eccl.) preghiere notturne.

**vigil-ant** *adj.* vigilante, vigile. **-ance** *n.* vigilanza.

**vignette** *n.* (art) vignetta; (photog.) ritratto a mezzo busto con sfondo sfumato.

**vigorous** *adj.* vigoroso, robusto, forte; vivace. **-ness** *n.* vigorosità, vigoria.

**vigour** *n.* vigore *m.*, energia, vitalità; vigoria; (mus.) brio; *wanting in —*, molle, fiacco.

**viking** *n.* (hist.) vichingo; *attrib.* dei vichinghi.

**vile** *adj.* vile, spregevole, ignobile, abietto, infame, tristo; *to render —*, avvilire; *a — calumny*, una vile calunnia; *a — song*, una canzone ignobile; *a — hovel*, un tugurio; *— language*, turpiloquio; (fam.) esecrabile, schifoso; *— weather*, tempo schifoso; *in a — temper*, di pessimo umore; (poet.) *in durance —*, in prigionia. **-ness** *n.* viltà, bassezza, abiezione.

**vilif-y** *tr.* vilipendere, denigrare, diffamare. **-ication** *n.* denigrazione, vilipendio; avvilimento, deteriorazione. **-ier** *n.* denigratore, diffamatore.

**villa** *n.* (country house) villa; (suburban) villino.

**village** *n.* villaggio, paese *m.*, borgata; frazione di un comune; *native —*, paese natio; *the — idiot*, il cretino del paese; *— inn*, albergo di campagna; *— green*, prato comunale. **-r** *n.* abitante di un villaggio; paesano, contadino, campagnuolo.

**villain** *n.* scellerato; furfante *m.*; anima nera; (joc.) mascalzone *m.*; (of a child) biricchino. **-ous** *adj.* scellerato, infame; *a -ous action*, una scelleratezza; *what a -ous face!*, che brutta faccia!; (fig.) pessimo, schifoso, esecrabile. **-y** *n.* scelleratezza; infamia; (fam.) brutto tiro.

**villanelle** *n.* (mus.) villanella.

**Villefranche** *pr.n.* (geog.) Villafranca.

**villein** *n.* (hist.) vassallo, servo, villano.

**villose, villous** *adj.* (anat.; bot.) villoso.

**vim** *n.* (fam.) forza, energia; impegno; *to put plenty of — into it*, darci sotto.

**vinaigrette** *n.* boccetta di sali aromatici; (cul.) salsa verde.

**Vincent** *pr.n.* Vincenzo.

**vindicat-e** *tr.* rivendicare, sostenere; *to — one's right*, rivendicare i propri diritti; giustificare; *to — one's character*, giustificarsi. **-ion** *n.* giustificazione; apologia; *in -ion of his conduct*, per giustificare la sua condotta; rivendicazione, asserzione. **-or** *n.* rivendicatore; difensore; assertore. **-ory** *adj.* vindice.

**vindictive** *adj.* vendicativo, vindice; malevolo, maligno; (leg.) punitivo. **-ly** *adv.* in modo vendicativo, per vendetta; malignamente. **-ness** *n.* carattere vendicativo, spirito di vendetta.

**vine** *n.* vite *f.*, vigna; *wild —*, vite selvatica; *to prune -s*, potare le viti; *planted with -s*, vignato.

**vine-arbour** *n.* pergola. **-branch** *n.* tralcio, sarmento. **-culture** *n.* viticoltura. **-dresser** *n.* vignaiuolo, vignarolo.

**vinegar** *n.* aceto; *wine —*, aceto di vino; *to turn to —*, *tr.* acetare, *intr.* pigliare l'aceto. **-ish, -y** *adj.* acetino, acetoso; (fig.) agro, acido.

**vine-grower** *n.* viticoltore. **-harvest** *n.* vendemmia. **-leaf** *n.* pampino. **-mildew** *n.* oidio. **-pest** *n.* fillossera. **-plant, -stock** *n.* ceppo di vite.

**vinery** *n.* serra per viti.

**vineyard** *n.* vigna, vigneto.

**vinous** *adj.* vinoso.

**vintag-e** *n.* vendemmia, raccolta dell'uva; produzione vinicola di un'annata; *— wine*, vino di marca, vino di una buona annata; *— year*, buona annata; (fig.) di vecchio tipo; *a — car*, automobile di vecchio modello. **-er** *n.* vendemmiatore. **-ing** *n.* vendemmia, raccolta dell'uva.

**vintner** *n.* vinaio, commerciante di vini.

**vinyl** *n.* (chem.) vinile *m.*; *— resin*, resina vinilica.

**viol** *n.* viola (antica).

**viola** *n.* viola (moderna).

**violate** *tr.* violare, trasgredire, infrangere; *to — the law*, violare la legge; profanare; (leg.) violentare, stuprare; (fig.) turbare, violare.

**violation** *n.* violazione; trasgressione, infrazione; profanazione; (leg., of woman) violentamento, stupro; (fig., of privacy) turbamento, interruzione.

**violator** *n.* violatore; trasgressore; profanatore; (leg., of woman) violentatore; (of privacy) perturbatore.

**violence** *n.* violenza; veemenza; forza; (leg.) *robbery with —*, rapina.

**violent** *adj.* violento, impetuoso; *a — temper*, un carattere violento; *to die a — death*, morire di morte violenta; *to lay — hands upon oneself*, attentare alla propria vita; *to become —*, abbandonarsi ad atti di violenza; (fig.) intenso, acuto, forte; *a — toothache*, un acuto mal di denti; *to have a — cold*, essere fortemente raffreddato; *a — red*, un rosso squillante. **-ly** *adv.* violentemente, con violenza; acutamente; *to fall -ly in love*, innamorarsi pazzamente.

**violet** *adj.* violetto, di color viola; *ultra-violet rays*, raggi ultravioletti; *n.* (bot.) viola, violetta, viola mammola; (colour) viola, violetto.

**violin** *n.* (mus.) violino; *first —*, primo violino, violino da spalla; *second —*, violino secondo.

**violinist, violin-player** *n.* (mus.) violinista *m.*, *f.*

**violist** *n.* (mus.) violista *m.*, *f.*, suonatore di viola.

**violoncell-o** *n.* (mus.) violoncello. **-ist** *n.* (mus.) violoncellista *m.*, *f.*

**viper** *n.* (zool.) vipera; *that woman is a —*, quella donna è una vipera; *a nest of -s*, un viperaio; *to nourish a — in one's bosom*, scaldarsi una vipera in seno. **-ish, -ous** *adj.* di vipera, vipereo; *a -ish brood*, una generazione di vipere; *a -ish tongue*, una lingua velenosa.

**virago** *n.* virago *f.*, viragine *f.*; donna sfacciata.

**virelay** *n.* virelai *m.*

**virescence** *n.* verdezza; (bot.) virescenza.

**Virgil** *pr.n.* Virgilio. **-ian** *adj.* virgiliano, di Virgilio.

**virgin** *n.* vergine *f.*; donna casta; *the Blessed Virgin*, la Beata Vergine; *male —*, vergine *m.*; *attrib.* vergine, vergineo, puro, casto; *— modesty*, modestia verginea; *the Virgin Queen*, la regina vergine; (fig.) vergine, non coltivato, inviolato; *— forest*, foresta vergine; *a — peak*, una vetta inviolata; *— snow*, neve vergine, neve fresca; *— gold*, oro puro; (geog.) *the Virgin Islands*, le Isole Vergini. **-al** *adj.* verginale, puro, casto; *n.* (mus.) virginal *m.*

**Virginia** *pr.n.* Virginia; (geog.) Virginia; (bot.) *— creeper*, vite *f.* del Canadà. **-n** *adj.*, *n.* della Virginia.

**virginity** *n.* verginità.

**Virgo** *pr.n.* (astron.) la Vergine.

**viril-e** *adj.* virile, maschio; *a — old age*, una vecchiaia robusta; *— strength*, forza virile; *the — member*, il membro virile. **-ity** *n.* virilità.

**virtual** *adj.* effettivo; *a — promise*, quasi una promessa; *he is the — head of the firm*, è il capo effettivo dell'azienda; *this was a — confession of guilt*, effettivamente era una confessione. **-ly** *adv.* effettivamente, praticamente; *I am -ly certain that . . .*, sono quasi sicuro che . . . **-ity** *n.* virtualità; potenzialità.

**virtue** *n.* virtù *f.*; (theol.) *the Virtues*, le Virtù; (philos.) *the cardinal -s*, le virtù cardinali;

*the theological -s,* le virtù teologali; castità; moralità; *a woman of —,* una donna casta, una donna virtuosa; *a woman of easy —,* una donna di facili costumi; *in — of,* in virtù di, in forza di, a titolo di; *— is its own reward,* la virtù è premio a se stessa; *to make a — of necessity,* fare di necessità virtù; (fig.) vantaggio; qualità; *it has the — of being unbreakable,* ha il vantaggio di essere infrangibile; *the healing -s of plants,* le proprietà curative delle piante.

**virtuos-o** *n.* amatore delle arti; conoscitore intenditore; (mus.) virtuoso. **-ity** *n.* virtuosismo, virtuosità.

**virtuous** *adj.* virtuoso, morale, casto; (iron.) ipocrita, farisaico. **-ness** *n.* virtù *f.,* virtuosità; (iron.) ipocrisia.

**virul-ent** *adj.* virulento; (fig.) velenoso, feroce. **-ence** *n.* virulenza.

**visa** *n.* visto consolare; *customs —,* visto doganale; *tr.* vistare (un passaporto).

**visage** *n.* volto, viso, faccia.

**vis-à-vis** *pref.* di faccia (a), dirimpetto (a), di fronte (a).

**visceral** *adj.* (med.) viscerale.

**viscid** *adj.* viscoso, viscido. **-ity** *n.* viscosità, viscidità, viscidezza.

**viscos-e** *n.* (text.) viscosa, viscosio. **-ity** *n.* viscosità.

**viscount** *n.* visconte *m.* **-cy, -ship** *n.* viscontado, viscontea, visconteria. **-ess** *n.* viscontessa.

**viscous** *adj.* viscoso, viscido.

**visib-le** *adj.* visibile; evidente, manifesto, palese; *to become —,* diventare percettibile; manifestarsi, apparire; *without any — cause,* senza alcuna causa manifesta; *he spoke with — satisfaction,* parlò con evidente soddisfazione. **-ility** *n.* visibilità; campo di visione; *-ility nil,* visibilità zero. **-leness** *n.* l'essere visibile.

**Visigoth** *pr.n.* (hist.) Visigoto. **-ic** *adj.* (hist.) visigotico.

**vision** *n.* vista; capacità visiva; *the field of —,* il campo visivo; *within the range of —,* a portata di vista; *beyond our —,* al di là della nostra capacità visiva, fuori di vista; *a man of —,* un uomo perspicace, un uomo che vede lontano; *the accident has impaired his —,* l'incidente ha recato danno alla sua vista; visione, immaginazione, intuizione; *prophetic —,* visione profetica; allucinazione, sogno; *he sees -s,* ha delle allucinazioni; apparizione; spettro; (fig.) *I had -s of being arrested by the police,* mi vedevo arrestato dalla polizia. **-al** *adj.* immaginario, chimerico; fondato su una visione.

**visionar-y** *adj.* visionario; fantastico; chimerico; immaginario; *n.* visionario; ideologo; utopista *m., f.* **-iness** *n.* carattere visionario, irrealtà.

**visit** *n.* visita; *to pay a — to,* fare una visita a; *to receive a — from,* ricevere la visita di; *to return a —,* restituire una visita; *to exchange -s,* scambiarsi visite; *a doctor's round of -s,* il giro di visite di un medico; soggiorno; *we have been on a — to friends,* siamo stati in visita presso amici; (leg.) *— to the scene,* sopralluogo; *domiciliary —,* visita domiciliare; (naut.) *right of — and search,* diritto di visita.

**visit** *tr.* visitare; fare una visita a; andare a trovare; *to — regularly,* frequentare; *come and — us one day,* vieni a trovarci un giorno; *to — the museums,* fare il giro dei musei; ispezionare; (fig.) *to be -ed by a disease,* essere colpito da una malattia; *the sins of the fathers shall be -ed on the children,* ricadranno sui figli le colpe dei genitori; *intr.* fare un giro di visite.

**visitant** *adj.* che visita; *n.* (poet.) visitatore; (orn.) uccello di passo; *ghostly —,* apparizione soprannaturale, spettro; *Visitant (nun),* Visitandina.

**visitation** *n.* visita ufficiale; (fam., iron) visita troppo lunga; (eccl.) *bishop's —,* visita pastorale; *Visitation nuns,* Visitandine *f.pl.*; (bibl.) *the Visitation,* la Visitazione, visita della Madonna a Santa Elisabetta; *— of God,* visita di Dio; (comm.) ispezione, esame *m.*; (fig.) calamità; apparizione.

**visiting** *adj.* in visita, visitante; *a — lecturer,* un conferenziere esterno; (sport) *the — team,* gli ospiti, la squadra ospite; *n.* il far visite, visita; *— hours,* ore delle visite; ore di apertura; *— list,* lista degli amici; *he is not on my — list,* non è un mio amico, non lo conosco; *to be on — terms,* essere in termini di amicizia (tali da scambiarsi visite).

**visiting-book** *n.* album dei visitatori, libro degli ospiti. **-card** *n.* biglietto da visita.

**visitor** *n.* visitatore; (guest) ospite *m., f.*; turista *m., f.,* forestiero; *summer —,* villeggiante estivo; *winter —,* svernante *m., f.*; ispettore, verificatore; (orn.) uccello di passo.

**visor** *n.* visiera; (motor.) parasole *m.*

**vista** *n.* scorcio panoramico, prospettiva; radura; viale *m.* d'alberi; (fig.) visione; *to open up new -s,* aprire nuovi orizzonti.

**visual** *adj.* visivo, visuale; percepibile, percettibile; *— angle,* angolo visivo; (anat.) *— nerve,* nervo ottico; *— organ,* organo visivo; (radio) *— tuning indicator,* indicatore ottico di sintonia, occhio magico.

**visualiz-e** *tr.* concepire, evocare l'immagine di, farsi un'immagine di; rendere visibile. **-ation** *n.* evocazione mentale, immagine mentale, il rendere visibile.

**vital** *adj.* vitale; essenziale; capitale; *of — importance,* di importanza capitale; *— organs,* organi *m.pl.* vitali; *secrecy is —,* la segretezza è una condizione essenziale; fatale, mortale; (admin.) *— statistics,* statistiche demografiche, anagrafiche; (joc.) le misure *f.pl.* del personale femminile.

**vitality** *n.* vitalità; vigore *m.*; (fig.) dinamismo, vivacità; forza.

**vitalize** *tr.* vivificare, animare, infondere vita a.

**vitally** *adv.* vitalmente, in modo essenziale; *— important,* di importanza capitale.

**vitamin** *n.* (biol.) vitamina; (med.) *— deficiency,* avitaminosi *f.* **-ized** *adj.* vitaminizzato.

**vitiat-e** *tr.* viziare, corrompere, guastare; (leg.) viziare, invalidare. **-ion** *n.* viziatura, viziosità; (leg.) invalidazione, l'invalidare.

**viticultur-e** *n.* viticoltura. **-al** *adj.* viticolo, vitifero. **-ist** *n.* viticoltore.

**vitreous** *adj.* vitreo, vetroso; (anat.) *— humour,* umore vitreo.

**vitrif-y** *tr.* vetrificare; *intr.* vetrificarsi. **-ication** *n.* vetrificazione.

**vitriol** *n.* (chem.) vetriolo; *to throw — at someone,* vetrioleggiare qualcuno, lanciare vetriolo su qualcuno; (fig.) *a pen dipped in —,* una penna intinta nel vetriolo. **-ic** *adj.* (chem.) vetriolico; (fig.) pungente, sarcastico; *a -ic pen,* una penna intinta nel vetriolo.

**vituperat-e** *tr.* vituperare; oltraggiare, vilipendere, inveire contro. **-ion** *n.* vituperio; vilipendio, invettiva. **-ive** *adj.* vituperativo, vituperoso; oltraggioso.

**Vitus** *pr.n.* Vito; (med.) *St. -'s dance,* ballo di San Vito, corea.

**viva** *n.* (schol., abbrev. of **viva voce**) esame orale, orale *m.*; (fam.) *to be ploughed in the —,* essere bocciato all'orale.

**vivacious** *adj.* vivace, vispo, animato, vivo, allegro, movimentato; *a — discussion,* una discussione animata. **-ness, vivacity** *n.* vivacità; animazione; brio.

**viva voce** *adv.* a viva voce, oralmente; *n.* (esame) orale *m.*

**Vivian** *pr.n.* Viviano *m.,* Viviana *f.*

**vivid** *adj.* vivido; intenso, brillante, acceso; *a — blue,* un blu intenso; (fig.) vivace, vivo, vigoroso; *a — imagination,* una immaginazione vivace; *to have a — recollection of one's childhood,* avere vivi ricordi dell'infanzia.

**-ness** *n.* vivezza; vivacità; intensità; (fig.) vigore *m.*
**vivify** *tr.* vivificare; animare; rinvigorire, dare nuova vita a.
**viviparous** *adj.* (bot.; zool.) viviparo.
**vivisect** *tr.* vivisezionare, praticare la vivisezione su. **-ion** *n.* vivisezione. **-ionist** *n.* chi pratica la vivisezione, vivisettore; sostenitore della vivisezione.
**vixen** *n.* (zool.) volpe femmina; (fig.) megera, donna litigiosa, bisbetica. **-ish** *adj.* volpino, volpigno; (fig.) litigioso, bisbetico.
**viz.** *adv.* cioè.
**vizier** *n.* visir *m.*; *Grand —*, gran visir.
**vocable** *n.* parola.
**vocabulary** *n.* vocabolario; glossario, elenco di voci; nomenclatura; dizionarietto; lessico.
**vocal** *adj.* vocale; espresso con la voce; canoro; *— music*, musica vocale; *— concert*, concerto vocale; (anat.) *— chords*, corde *f.pl.* vocali; *— organs*, organi *m.pl.* vocali; orale; *a — communication*, una comunicazione orale; loquace; *to become —*, farsi sentire; *the most — member of the audience*, il membro dell'uditorio che più degli altri ha fatto sentire la voce; (phon.) avente carattere di vocale, vocalico, sonoro.
**vocal-ic** *adj.* (phon.) vocalico, di vocale. **-ism** *n.* (phon.) vocalismo; (mus.) vocalizzo, gorgheggio.
**vocalist** *n.* cantante *m., f.*
**vocaliz-e** *tr.* vocalizzare (una consonante); (mus.) cantare; *intr.* (mus.) vocalizzare; (fam.) cantare, farsi sentire. **-ation** *n.* vocalizzazione.
**vocally** *adv.* a voce, oralmente; (mus.) cantando.
**vocation** *n.* vocazione, chiamata divina; *the — of the Gentiles*, la vocazione dei Gentili; (fig.) inclinazione, attitudine *f.*; professione, impiego, mestiere *m.*; *to change one's —*, cambiar mestiere; *to mistake one's —*, scegliere la carriera sbagliata. **-al** *adj.* professionale; *-al training*, istruzione professionale.
**vocative** *adj., n.* (gramm.) vocativo; *in the —*, al vocativo.
**vociferat-e** *intr.* vociferare; gridare, vociare. **-ion** *n.* vociferazione; clamore *m.*
**vociferous** *adj.* vociferante, rumoroso, clamoroso.
**vodka** *n.* vodka, vodca.
**vogue** *n.* voga; moda; *to be in —*, essere in voga, essere di moda; *to come into —*, entrare in voga, diventare di moda; *war novels have had their —*, i romanzi di guerra non sono più di moda.
**voice** *n.* voce *f.*; *in a loud —*, ad alta voce; *in a low —*, bassa voce; *to raise one's —*, alzare la voce; *to lower one's —*, abbassare la voce; *to lose one's —*, perdere la voce; *he is not in good —*, è giù di voce; *he likes to hear his own —*, gli piace sentirsi parlare; *at the top of his —*, a squarciagola; *a cracked —*, una voce fessa; *a mellow —*, una voce pastosa; *a muffled —*, una voce affogata; *to give — to one's feelings*, sfogarsi; *with one —*, all'unanimità; *to have no — in a matter*, non aver voce in capitolo; (of bird, animal) verso, grido; (gramm.) *active —*, voce attiva; *passive —*, voce passiva; (theatr.) *voice-trial*, provino, audizione; *voice-production*, formazione della voce.
**voice** *tr.* esprimere, dire, dare espressione a; *to — the general feeling*, esprimere l'opinione popolare; (phon.) rendere sonoro, vocalizzare.
**voiceless** *adj.* senza voce, muto, silenzioso; (phon.) muto, sordo; (med.) afono, afonico. **-ness** *n.* mancanza di voce; mutismo; (phon.) carattere sordo di una consonante; (med.) afonia.
**voice-pipe** *n.* (aeron.) aerofono. **-tube** *n.* citofono; portavoce *m.*
**void** *adj.* vuoto; vacante; *to fall —*, diventar vacante, diventare libero; (leg.) nullo, non valido; *— ballot-paper*, scheda di votazione nulla; (poet.) vano, inutile; (fig.) privo di, libero da, senza; *— of interest*, senza interesse; *— of common sense*, privo di senso comune; *n.* vuoto; *to fill the —*, colmare il vuoto; *to disappear into the —*, sparire nel vuoto; (fig.) mancanza; *to feel a —*, sentire la mancanza; *an aching —*, un vuoto doloroso.
**void** *tr.* vuotare, liberare, sgombrare; (leg.) annullare, abrogare; (med.) defecare, evacuare. **-ance** *n.* svuotamento; (leg.) annullamento.
**voile** *n.* (text.) voile *m.*, mussola.
**volatile** *adj.* (chem.) volatile; (fig.) volubile, incostante, instabile. **-ness** *n.* (chem.) volatilità; (fig.) volubilità, incostanza, instabilità.
**volatility** *n.* (chem.) volatilità.
**volatiliz-e** *tr.* (chem.) volatilizzare; *intr.* (chem.) volatilizzarsi; (fig.) sparire nel vuoto, evaporare. **-ation** *n.* (chem.) volatilizzazione.
**volcanic** *adj.* vulcanico; *a — eruption*, una eruzione vulcanica; *— ash*, ceneri vulcaniche; *— glass*, ossidiana; *— tufa*, tufo vulcanico; (fig.) focoso, impetuoso.
**volcano** *n.* vulcano; *active —*, vulcano attivo; *dormant —*, vulcano inattivo; *extinct —*, vulcano estinto, vulcano spento; *mud —*, vulcano di fango, soffione *m.*; (fig.) *to be sitting on the edge of a —*, essere sopra un vulcano.
**vole** *n.* (zool.) arvicola; *— rat*, topo campagnolo; *water —*, topo d'acqua.
**volet** *n.* (art) tavola (di trittico).
**volition** *n.* volizione; volontà. **-al, -ary** *adj.* volitivo.
**volitive** *adj.* (gramm.) desiderativo.
**volley** *n.* salva, raffica, scarica; *to fire a —*, sparare una salva; *a — of stones*, una scarica di pietre; (fig.) *a — of oaths*, un profluvio di bestemmie; (tennis) volata; *on the —*, di volata.
**volley** *tr.* sparare, lanciare; (fig.) *to — forth abuse*, investire con un profluvio di bestemmie; (tennis) colpire a volo.
**volplane** *n.* (aeron.) volo planato; *intr.* (aeron.) planare.
**volt** *n.* (electr.) volta *m.*, volt *m.*
**voltage** *n.* tensione, voltaggio; *high —*, alta tensione; *mains —*, tensione della rete; *no-load —*, tensione a vuoto; *line —*, tensione di linea.
**voltaic** *adj.* voltaico; *— pile*, pila voltaica.
**Voltairean, Voltairian** *adj., n.* volterriano.
**Voltair(ian)ism** *n.* volterrianismo.
**volte-face** *n.* voltafaccia.
**voltmeter** *n.* (electr.) voltometro.
**volub-le** *adj.* mobile, mutevole; loquace, garrulo, veemente; *to be a — talker*, parlare spedito. **-ility** *n.* loquacità; speditezza, scioltezza.
**volume** *n.* (phys.) volume *m.*; massa, mole *f.*; *the — of a sphere*, il volume di una sfera; *a — of water*, una massa d'acqua; *to calculate the —*, calcolare la mole; volume, tomo, libro; *a work in six -s*, un'opera in sei volumi; *— I, part II*, volume primo, tomo secondo; (fig.) *it speaks -s for your generosity*, è una chiara manifestazione della tua generosità, (hist.) papiro, rotolo (di pergamena); (mus.) volume, ampiezza; (radio) volume.
**volumetric(al)** *adj.* volumetrico; (chem.) *— analysis*, analisi volumetrica; (mech.) *— efficiency*, rendimento volumetrico.
**voluminous** *adj.* voluminoso; di grande mole; in molti volumi; *a — correspondence*, una corrispondenza voluminosa; (fig.) *a — writer*, uno scrittore fecondo. **-ness** *n.* voluminosità.
**voluntary** *adj.* volontario; spontaneo; *— contributions*, contributi volontari; *a — offer*, un'offerta spontanea; (comm.) *— liquidation*, liquidazione volontaria; (mil.) *— service*, servizio volontario; facoltativo; *— organization*, opera di beneficenza; *— worker*,

volontario; (fig.) *to be a — agent in a matter*, agire liberamente in un affare; *n.* (mus.) assolo di organo.

**volunteer** *n.* (mil.) volontario; *to call for -s*, chiedere volontari; *tr.* offrire volontariamente; *to — information*, dare spontaneamente delle informazioni; *to — to do something*, offrire volontariamente di far qualcosa; *intr.* (mil.) arruolarsi come volontario; (fig.) offrirsi spontaneamente.

**voluptuary** *adj.* voluttuario; sibaritico; voluttuoso, sensuale; *n.* epicureo, sibarita *m.*, *f.*; libertino, persona sensuale.

**voluptuous** *adj.* voluttuoso; sensuale. **-ness** *n.* voluttà; sensualità.

**volut-e** *n.* (archit.) voluta; rivolta; cartoccio; (mech.) spira, spirale *f.* **-ed** *adj.* avvolto a spirale; (archit.) provvisto di voluta, a voluta. **-ion** *n.* attorcigliamento, avvolgimento a spirale; (anat.) circonvoluzione; (zool.) spira (di conchiglia).

**vomica** *n.* (med.) vomica; (pharm.) *nux —*, noce vomica.

**vomit** *n.* vomito; ciò che è stato vomitato; (pharm.) emetico, vomitorio; *tr.*, *intr.* vomitare; (fig.) *to — smoke*, vomitare fumo; (of volcano) eruttare. **-ing** *n.* vomito; il vomitare. **-ory** *adj.* (pharm.) emetico; *n.* (Rom. hist.) vomitorio.

**voracious** *adj.* vorace; ingordo; goloso; *a — appetite*, un appetito da lupo; (fig.) *a — reader*, un lettore insaziabile, un divoratore di libri.

**voraciousness, voracity** *n.* voracità; ingordigia; golosità.

**vortex** *n.* vortice *m.*; turbine *m.*; gorgo; (fig.) *the — of war*, il vortice della guerra.

**vortical, vortiginous** *adj.* vorticoso, vortiginoso, turbinoso.

**votaress** *n.* devota, adoratrice.

**votary** *n.* devoto; seguace *m.*; adoratore; *a — of art*, un amante dell'arte; *to be a — of a saint*, essere devoto a un santo.

**vote** *n.* voto; suffragio; votazione; mozione; *to cast a —*, votare; *to put to the —*, mettere ai voti, porre in votazione; *to proceed to a —*, passare alla votazione; *open —*, voto palese; *secret —*, voto segreto; *— by show of hands*, votazione per alzata di mano; *popular —*, suffragio popolare; *the right to a —*, il diritto di suffragio; *— of censure*, voto di censura, mozione di censura; *— of confidence*, voto di fiducia, mozione di fiducia; *— of thanks*, ringraziamento dell'assemblea; *to give a casting —*, emettere un voto preponderante; *by a unanimous —*, con votazione unanime; *to poll ten thousand -s*, ottenere diecimila voti; *to count the -s*, contare i voti, procedere allo scrutinio; *counting of the -s*, scrutinio, spoglio delle schede.

**vote** *tr. intr.* votare; *to — for*, votare in favore di; *to — against*, votare contro; *to — in*, eleggere; *to — a sum of money*, stanziare una somma; *to — a bill through Parliament*, far passare una legge dal parlamento; (fig.) *they -d him the best sportsman of the year*, lo dichiararono il miglior sportivo dell'anno; *I — that we go*, propongo che andiamo.

**voter** *n.* persona che vota; elettore.

**voting** *adj.* votante; *n.* votazione, il votare; *manner of —*, sistema di votazione; *— slip*, scheda di votazione; *to abstain from —*, astenersi dalla votazione; *to declare the — open*, dichiarare aperta la votazione.

**votive** *adj.* (rel.) votivo; *— offering*, offerta votiva, ex voto *m.*; *— mass*, messa votiva.

**vouch** *tr.* affermare, attestare, garantire; (leg.) citare come garante; *intr. to — for*, garantire, rispondere di; *to — for*, rendersi garante per; *without -ing for it*, con le debite riserve.

**voucher** *n.* testimone *m.*; documento giustificativo, pezzo giustificativo, certificato; (comm.) ricevuta; buono, tagliando; *delivery —*, buono di consegna.

**vouchsafe** *tr.* accordare, concedere; *he -d no reply*, non degnò di rispondere.

**voussoir** *n.* (archit.) cuneo; *centre —*, chiave *f.* di volta.

**vow** *n.* voto; giuramento; promessa solenne; *to make a —*, fare un voto; *he made a — to give up smoking*, ha fatto il voto di non fumare più; (eccl.) *to take the -s*, pronunciare i voti; *baptismal -s*, voti battesimali; *marriage -s*, voti matrimoniali; *lovers' -s*, giuramenti di amorosi; *empty -s*, voti di marinari; *— of chastity*, voto di castità; *to fulfil a —*, mantenere un voto; *to break a —*, rompere un voto; *to release from a —*, sciogliere da un voto; *to be under a —*, aver fatto voto.

**vow** *tr.* fare voto di, giurare, promettere; *to — obedience*, giurare ubbidienza; *to — vengeance*, giurare vendetta.

**vowel** *n.* (gramm.) vocale *f.*

**voyag-e** *n.* viaggio (per mare); traversata; *maiden —*, primo viaggio (di una nave), viaggio inaugurale; *— out*, viaggio di andata; *— home*, viaggio di ritorno; *to go on a —*, intraprendere un viaggio; *intr.* viaggiare (per mare); attraversare il mare; navigare; percorrere il mare. **-er** *n.* viaggiatore (per mare); passagero (di nave), navigatore. **-ing** *gerund* il viaggiare; *she likes -ing*, le piace viaggiare per mare.

**Vulcan** *pr.n.* (myth.; astron.) Vulcano; *-'s forge*, la fucina di Vulcano.

**vulcan-ite** *n.* vulcanite *f.*, ebanite *f.* **-ize** *tr.* vulcanizzare. **-izer** *n.* vulcanizzatore.

**vulgar** *adj.* volgare; triviale; plebeo; ordinario; grossolano; di pessimo gusto; *there is something — about him*, ha qualcosa di volgare; *a — expression*, un'espressione triviale; *the — herd*, il popolino, la plebe, il volgo; *a — display of wealth*, uno sfoggio vulgare di ricchezza; *— Latin*, il latino volgare; *in the — tongue*, nel volgare, (hist.) *the — era*, l'era volgare, l'era cristiana; (math.) *— fractions*, frazioni ordinarie, frazioni comuni; *the —*, il volgo. **-ian** *n.* persona volgare; nuovo ricco. **-ism** *n.* volgarismo; espressione triviale; volgarità; trivialità. **-ity** *n.* volgarità; trivialità; cattivo gusto; *to lapse into -ity*, cadere nel cattivo gusto.

**vulgariz-e** *tr.* volgarizzare; divulgare, rendere volgare. **-ation** *n.* volgarizzazione; divulgazione, volgarizzamento.

**Vulgate** *pr.n.* (bibl.) Volgata.

**vulnerab-le** *adj.* vulnerabile; (fig.) *the — spot*, il tallone d'Achille; (bridge) vulnerabile, in zona. **-ility** *n.* vulnerabilità.

**vulpine** *adj.* volpino, di volpe; (fig.) furbo.

**vulture** *n.* (orn.) avvoltoio; *bearded —*, gipeto; (fig.) persona rapace, persona avida; (joc.) *culture —*, persona avida di cultura.

**vulv-a** *n.* (anat.) vulva. **-itis** *n.* (med.) vulvite *f.*

**vying** *n. gerund* il gareggiare; gareggiamento, (cf. **vie**).

**W, w** *n.* vu doppio; (teleph.) — *for William*, vu doppio come Washington.

**wad** *n.* batuffolo, tampone *m.*, stoppaccio; (firearms) borra; *a — of notes*, un rotolo di banconote; (fam.) *a — of money*, un sacco di soldi; (mil. slang) fetta di focaccia; *tr.* comprimere in batuffolo; tamponare, tappare; (of clothing) foderare. **-ded** *adj.* tamponato; foderato. **-ding** *n.* ovatta, bambagia, stoppaccio; (firearms) borra; (clothing) fodera.

**waddle** *n.* andatura ondeggiante; *intr.* camminare ondeggiando, dimenare i fianchi; *to — off*, andarsene dimenando i fianchi.

**wade** *tr.* guadare, passare a guado; *intr. to — in the sea*, sguazzare nel mare; (fig.) *to — through a book*, leggere laboriosamente un libro; (fam.) *to — into*, attaccare ferocemente. **-r** *n.* chi passa a guado; bambino che sguazza nell'acqua; (orn.) trampoliere *m.*; *pl.* stivaloni *m.pl.* impermeabili.

**wafer** *n.* (cul.) cialda; (eccl.) ostia; (fig.) *thin as a —*, magrissimo, sottilissimo.

**waffle**[1] *n.* (cul., USA), cialda.

**waffl-e**[2] *intr.* (fam.) fare una lungagnata, parlare a vanvera, chiacchierare. **-ing** *n.* sproloquio, lungagnata.

**waffle-iron** *n.* ferro da cialda.

**waft** *n.* soffio; (of perfume) zaffata; *tr.* (poet.) sospingere (attraverso l'aria, sull'acqua); diffondere, spandere; soffiare blandamente; *music -ed on the breeze*, musica diffusa dalla brezza.

**wag**[1] *n.* burlone *m.*, bontempone *m.*

**wag**[2] *n.* cenno del capo; (of dog's tail), scodinzolamento; *with a — of his finger*, con un cenno del dito.

**wag**[2] *tr.* agitare, dimenare, scuotere; *intr.* muoversi, agitarsi; *the dog -ged his tail*, il cane dimenò la coda; *tongues are -ging*, le male lingue si sono messe in moto; *to set chins -ging*, suscitare pettegolezzi; *your tongue -s too freely*, chiacchieri troppo; *he -ged his finger at me*, mi ammonì col dito.

**wage**[1] *n.* salario, paga, rimunerazione; *a living —*, una paga che basta per vivere; *starvation -s*, paga da fame; *the -s of sin is death*, il prezzo del peccato è la morte. **-earner** *n.* salariato, sostegno della famiglia.

**wage**[2] *tr.* intraprendere; *to — war against*, muovere guerra contro.

**wager** *n.* scommessa; *to lay a —*, fare uno scommessa, scommettere; *to take up a —*, accettare una scommessa; *tr.* scommettere, fare una scommessa, puntare. **-er** *n.* scommettitore *m.*, puntatore *m.* **-ing** *gerund* lo scommettere, il puntare; le scommesse *f.pl.*

**wage-scale** *n.* tabella base delle paghe. **-sheet** *n.* foglio paga.

**waggery** *n.* lepidezza, argutezza, buon umore.

**wagging** *adj.* che si agita, che si dimena; *n.* agitazione, scuotimento; (of dog's tail) scondinzolio.

**waggish** *adj.* faceto, arguto, lepido; *— remarks*, facezie *f.pl.* **-ness** *n.* gusto per le facezie, argutezza.

**waggle** see **wag.**

**waggon** see **wagon.**

**Wagnerian** *n.*, *adj.* wagneriano, vagneriano.

**wagon** *n.* carro, vagone *m.*, vettura, carrozza, carrozzone *m.*; (rlwy.) carrozza, (goods) carro; (mil.) furgone *m.*; (astron.) Orsa maggiore; (fig.) *to hitch one's — to a star*, avere dei progetti ambiziosi; (fam.) *to be on the (water) —*, dover astenersi dalle bevande alcooliche. **-er** *n.* carrettiere; (astron.) l'Auriga *m.* **-ette** *n.* wagonette *m.*, carrozza con sedili laterali.

**wagon-load** *n.* carico di un vagone, carrettata.

**wagtail** *n.* (orn.) cutrettola, batticoda, coditremola; *grey —*, codinzinzola.

**waif** *n.* trovatello; *home for -s and strays*, brefotrofio; (fig.) vagabondo, senzatetto.

**wail** *n.* gemito, lamento; (of newborn child) vagito; *intr.* gemere; lamentarsi; (of newborn child) vagire. **-ing** *adj.* lamentoso; (fig.) triste, straziante; *gerund* il gemere; *n.* lamento, gemito; *the Wailing Wall*, il muro del pianto.

**wain** *n.* (poet.; agric.) carro; (astron.) *the Wain, Charles's Wain*, l'Orsa maggiore.

**wainscot, wainscoting** *n.* (of a wall) zoccolo; (of a room) rivestimento a pannelli di legno, intavolato.

**wainwright** *n.* carraio, carradore.

**waist** *n.* vita; cintola, cintura; (naut.) passavanti *m.* **-band** *n.* cintura, fascia.

**waist-belt** *n.* cintura; (mil.) cinturone *m.* **-cloth** *n.* perizoma *m.* **-deep, -high** *adj.*, *adv.* (che arriva) fino alla cintola.

**waistcoat** *n.* panciotto, gilè *m.*; *double-breasted —*, gilè a doppio petto; *sleeved —*, gilè a maniche.

**waistline** *n.* vita; altezza della vita; misura della vita.

**wait** *n.* attesa; *to have a long —*, attendere a lungo; agguato; imboscata; *to lie in — (for)*, stare in agguato, tendere un'imboscata(a); *pl.* cantori *m.pl.* che a Natale vanno di casa in casa cantando degli inni.

**wait** *intr.* aspettare; attendere; (at table); *to — for*, aspettare; *ask him to — a minute*, gli dica di aspettare un momento; *they kept me -ing for an hour*, mi fecero aspettare un'ora; *he didn't — to be told twice*, non se lo fece dire due volte; *this can —*, questo non è urgente; *— and see!*, aspetta e vedrai!; *— and see policy*, attendismo; *you just —!*, aspetta che ti accomodo io!; *— here!*, attendi qui!; *everything comes to those who —*, basta avere pazienza; *time and tide — for no man*, la marea non aspetta nessuno; *to — at table*, servire a tavola; *tr.* aspettare, attendere; *he is -ing his opportunity*, aspetta il momento buono; *we -ed dinner for him*, ritardammo il pranzo per lui; *to — it out*, aspettare sino alla fine; *to — (up)on*, servire, essere al servizio di; *to — on someone hand and foot*, essere schiavo di qualcuno; *to be -ed (up)on by servants*, essere servito da domestici; visitare, andare a trovare; *to — on*, *intr.* aspettare ancora; *to — up for someone*, restare alzato in attesa di qualcuno.

**waiter** *n.* chi aspetta; (in cafés, restaurants) cameriere *m.*; *—!*, cameriere!; *head —*, capocameriere, maître d'hôtel; *dumb-waiter*, carrello.

**waiting** *gerund.* l'aspettare; (motor.) *no —*, divieto di sosta; *n.* attesa; *adj. a — attitude*, un atteggiamento d'attesa; *to play a — game*, aspettare il momento giusto.

**waiting-list** *n.* elenco di candidati (di riserva); *to be on the —*, essere in aspettativa. **-room** *n.* anticamera; (rlwy.) sala di attesa.

**waitress** *n.* cameriera; *—!*, Signorina!

**waiv-e** *tr.* rinunciare a, desistere da, tralasciare; *to — a condition*, non insistere su una condizione. **-ing** *gerund* il rinunciare; *n.* rinuncia, deroga; *-ing of age-limit*, deroga al limite di età; *-ing all other considerations*, tralasciando ogni altra considerazione.

**wake**[1] *n.* orma; (of ship) scia; (naut.) rotta; *to follow in the — of*, seguire le orme di, mettersi a rimorchio di; *crises follow in the — of a war*, le crisi sono una conseguenza della guerra.

**wake**[2] *n.* (Ireland) veglia funebre.

**wake**[3] *tr.* svegliare, destare; (fig.) animare, provocare; *it woke an echo in the valley*, fece risuonare la vallata; *intr.* svegliarsi, destarsi; (fig.) animarsi, rendersi conto; *— up!*, svegliati!, (fig.) sta' attento!; *at last he woke up to the truth*, finalmente si è reso conto della verità.

**wakeful** *adj.* sveglio, insonne; (fig.) vigile, attento; *a — night,* una notte insonne. **-ness** *n.* insonnia; (fig.) vigilanza.

**waken** *tr.* svegliare; (fig.) risuscitare, ridestare; *intr.* svegliarsi. **-ing** *n.* risveglio.

**waker** *n.* persona che si sveglia; *to be an early —,* svegliarsi abitualmente di buon'ora, essere mattinero.

**waking** *gerund* lo svegliare; *the sleep that knows no —,* l'ultimo sonno; *adj.* sveglio, desto, insonne; *— hours,* le ore della giornata, le ore di sveglia; *— state,* stato di veglia; *n.* risveglio, veglia; *between sleeping and —,* tra il sonno e la veglia.

**Waldens-es** *n.* (rel.) valdesi *m.pl.* **-ian** *adj., n.* (rel.) valdese *m., f.*

**waldgrave** *n.* (hist.) valgravio.

**Wales** *pr.n.* (geog.) Galles *m.*, il paese di Galles; *North Wales,* Galles settentrionale; *South Wales,* Galles meridionale; *New South Wales,* Nuova Galles del Sud; *the Prince of Wales,* il principe di Galles.

**walk** *n.* passeggiata; cammino; *an hour's — from here,* a un'ora di cammino da qui; *to go for a —,* fare una passeggiata, andare a fare un giro, (fam.) fare due passi; *to take a dog for a —,* portar fuori il cane; viale *m.*; marciapiede *m.*; andatura, passo; (of horse) *to go at a —,* andare al passo; rango, condizione; *people in the humbler -s of life,* gente di umile condizione; mestiere *m.*; (sport) corsa podistica; *intr.* andare a piedi, camminare, passeggiare; *shall we — or drive?,* andiamo a piedi o in macchina?; *you can — there in a few minutes,* ci si va a piedi in pochi minuti; *you — faster than I do,* cammini più presto di me; *to — up and down,* passeggiare su e giù; *to — in one's sleep,* essere sonnambulo; FOLLOW. BY ADV. OR PREP.: *to — about,* passeggiare, andare in giro; *to — along, tr.* seguire, *intr.* circolare, andare avanti; *to — away,* andarsene a piedi, partire; *he -ed away with it,* ha vinto facilmente; *to — back,* ritornare a piedi; *to — down,* scendere a piedi; *to — in,* entrare; *please — in,* entrare (senza bussare); *to — into,* entrare in, penetrare in, (fig.) imbattersi in, incontrare per caso; *to — off,* andarsene, partire, squagliarsi; *to — off with,* rubare; *to — off one's anger,* far sbollire la rabbia a forza di camminare; *to — off one's dinner,* camminare per digerire; *to — off the stage,* abbandonare il palcoscenico, uscire; *to — on,* andare avanti, proseguire, (theatr.) fare la comparsa; *to — out,* uscire (a piedi), scioperare senza preavviso; *to — out with a girl,* uscire con una ragazza; (fam.) *to — out on,* piantare, abbandonare; *to — over,* camminare su; *to — up,* salire a piedi; *to — up to,* avvicinarsi a; *tr.* far andare, condurre, percorrere; *to — a horse,* mettere un cavallo al passo; *to — the wards,* seguire le lezioni in clinica; *to — the streets,* girare per le strade, gironzolare, (of prostitute) fare la passeggiatrice; *to — someone off his feet,* stancare qualcuno camminando; (theatr.) *to — the boards,* calcare le scene; (fam.) *to — the plank,* essere condannato a buttarsi in mare.

**walkaway** *n.* (fam.) vittoria facilissima.

**walker** *n.* camminatore; (sport) podista *m.*

**walkie-talkie** *n.* radio portabile trasmittente-ricevente, radiotelefono da passeggio.

**walking** *adj.* che cammina, ambulante; (sport) podistico; *— encyclopaedia,* enciclopedia ambulante; (med.) *— case,* ammalato che può camminare; *gerund: do you like —?,* ti piace camminare?; *n.* (sport) podistica; *attrib. — race,* gara podistica; *— tour,* escursione a piedi; *it is within — distance,* ci si può andare a piedi.

**walking-boots** *n.pl.* stivali da passeggio. **-on** *adj.* (theatr.) *to have a -on part,* fare la comparsa. **-out** *adj.* (mil.) *-out dress,* tenuta piccola, tenuta di uscita. **-pace** *n.* passo d'uomo; *to drive at a -pace,* andare a passo d'uomo. **-stick** *n.* bastone da passeggio.

**walk-out** *n.* sciopero lampo; *to stage a —,* organizzare uno sciopero lampo. **-over** *n.* vittoria per mancanza di altri concorrenti; (fig.) successo sicuro, vittoria facilissima.

**wall** *n.* muro, muraglia, muraglione *m.*; (of room) parete *f.*; *within the -s,* entro le mura; *outside the -s,* fuori le mura; *the Great Wall of China,* la Grande Muraglia; (provb.) *-s have ears,* i muri hanno orecchia; (fig.) *to have one's back to the —,* essere con le spalle al muro; *to go to the —,* fallire, avere la peggio; *to run one's head against a —,* urtare contro ostacoli insuperabili, arrampicarsi sui vetri; *to see through a brick —,* avere un grande intuito; (bldg.) *dead —,* muro cieco, muro pieno; *boundary —,* muro di cinta; *front —,* muro anteriore; *party —,* muro comune, muro divisorio; *partition —,* parete divisoria; (anat.) parete *f.*

**wall** *tr.* murare, circondare di mura; *to — (in) a garden,* murare un giardino; *to — off,* separare a mezzo di un muro, cintare; *to — up, tr.* murare, immurare, ostruire, (fig.) murare vivo; *to have a window -ed up,* far murare una finestra.

**wallaby** *n.* (zool.) piccolo canguro dell'Australia; (fam.) australiano.

**wall-bracket** *n.* mensola da muro, sopporto a mensola, consol(l)e *f.* **-clock** *n.* orologio da muro. **-creeper** *n.* (orn.) picchio muraiuolo; (bot.) muraiuolo.

**walled** *adj.* murato, cinto da mura, circondato di mura; *double-walled,* a doppia parete; *brick-walled,* a muro di mattoni; *— off,* separato da un muro, diviso da una parete.

**wallet** *n.* portafogli *m.*, saccoccia; (of pilgrim) bisaccia; (of workman) borsetta per attrezzi; (mil.; mus.) giberna.

**wall-eye** *n.* (med.; vet.) strabismo, glaucoma *m.*, leucoma *m.* corneale. **-eyed** *adj.* strabico, affetto da glaucoma. **-fitting** *n.* attrezzo murale.

**wallflower** *n.* (bot.) viola ciocca gialla; (fig.) ragazza che fa da tappezzeria ad un ballo.

**walling** *n.* muratura, opera in muratura; *rough —,* muratura a secco. **-up** *n.* muratura.

**wall-lamp** *n.* lampada da muro. **-map** *n.* carta geografica murale.

**Walloon** *adj., n.* vallone *m., f.*

**wallop** *n.* (fam.) percossa, colpo violento; *to go down with a —,* cadere con un tonfo; *tr.* percuotere; (sport) battere facilmente; (fam.) bastonare a santa ragione. **-ing** *adj.* (fam.) enorme, grandissimo; *n.* bastonatura, legnata; (fig.) *our team got a -ing,* la nostra squadra ha preso una batosta.

**wallow** *intr.* voltolarsi, rotolarsi, guazzare nel brago; sguazzare; (of ship) rullare, rollare.

**wall-painting** *n.* pittura murale; affresco.

**wallpaper** *n.* carta da parato, tappezzeria.

**walnut** *n.* (tree) noce *m.*; (nut) noce *f.*; (wood) noce *m.*, legno di noce; *— suite,* mobilio in noce. **-brown** *adj.* color noce. **-grove** *n.* noceto.

**Walpurgis** *pr.n. — night,* notte di Valpurga (vigilia del primo maggio).

**walrus** *n.* (zool.) trichecho; (fig.) *— moustache,* baffi *m.pl.* spioventi.

**Walter** *pr.n.* Gualtiero, Walter.

**waltz** *n.* valzer *m.*; *hesitation —,* boston *m.*; *to dance a —,* fare un giro di valzer; *intr.* ballare il valzer; (fam.) *to — off with something,* squagliarsi portando via qualche cosa; *to — along,* andare a passo di valzer; *tr. he -ed her round,* le fece fare un giro di valzer.

**wan** *adj.* esangue, pallido, smorto, smunto; *to grow* —, impallidire; (fig.) languido, debole; — *light*, luce debole; — *smile*, debole sorriso.

**wand** *n.* bacchetta, verga; *conjurer's* —, bacchetta di prestigiatore; (dowser's) *hazel* —, bacchetta divinatoria; (usher's) —, mazza; (myth.) *Mercury's* —, caduceo.

**wander** *n.* passeggiata senza meta, giro, vagabondaggio; *intr.* vagare, errare, vagabondare; (fig.) deviare, smarrirsi, vaneggiare; gironzolare; *his eyes* ~*ed over the landscape*, il suo sguardo percorse il paesaggio; *the sheep have* ~*ed away*, le pecore si sono smarrite; *his mind is* ~*ing*, vaneggia; *to* — *from the subject*, fare una digressione, divagare; *to let one's thoughts* —, lasciar vagare i propri pensieri; *to* — *from the right path*, uscire dalla retta via. **~er** *n.* vagabondo; (fam.) girandolone *m.*; (fig.) persona che si smarrisce; *a* ~*er from the fold*, una pecorella smarrita.

**wandering** *adj.* errante, vagabondo, vagante, ambulante, nomade, migrante; (fig.) distratto; *the* — *Jew*, l'Ebreo errante; — *tribes*, tribù *f.pl.* nomadi; — *eyes*, occhi *m.pl.* distratti; (orn.) — *albatross*, diomedea; (med.) — *kidney*, rene *m.* migrante; *n.* vagabondaggio, nomadismo; (fig.) smarrimento; (med.) delirio; (techn.) spostamento.

**wanderlust** *n.* voglia di vagabondare, voglia di viaggiare.

**wane** *n.* calare *m.*; declino; decrescenza; *on the* —, decrescente, calante; (fig.) in declino; *intr.* (of moon) calare, decrescere; *the moon is waning*, la luna è in fase calante; (fig.) declinare, decadere; *his strength is slowly waning*, sta perdendo lentamente le forze.

**wangle** *n.* trucco, maneggio, intrigo, traffico; *tr.* ottenere per sotterfugio, accomodare; *intr.* brigare, darsi da fare; *to* — *money out of someone*, far allentare i cordoni della borsa; *to* — *the accounts*, imbrogliare la contabilità; (mil.) *to* — *a week's leave*, farsi accordare una licenza di otto giorni. **~r** *n.* imbroglione *m.*, intrigante *m.*, *f.*

**waning** *adj.* calante, declinante, decrescente; — *light*, luce che sta venendo meno; — *glory*, gloria in declino; *n.* decrescenza, declino, calo, calata, decadenza.

**wank** *intr.*, *tr.* (vulg.) masturbarsi, masturbare; *n.* atto di masturbazione.

**wanness** *n.* pallidezza, pallore *m.*

**want** *n.* mancanza, difetto, deficienza; bisogno, necessità, (fig.) povertà; — *of tact*, mancanza di tatto; *for* — *of anything better*, in difetto di meglio; — *of funds*, deficienza di fondi; *he has few* ~*s*, ha pochi bisogni; *we can supply all your* ~*s*, possiamo fornire tutto quello che vi occorre; *to live in* —, vivere nel bisogno; *to die of* —, morire di fame.

**want** *tr.* mancare di, essere senza; *he* ~*s the ability to do it*, gli manca l'abilità di farlo; aver bisogno di, richiedere, esigere; *I* — *your address*, mi occorre il tuo indirizzo; *this* ~*s careful study*, questo esige uno studio accurato; volere, desiderare, aver voglia di; *what do you* — *?*, che cosa desidera ?; *whom do you* — *to see ?*, con chi vuol parlare ?; *I* — *you to come at once*, voglio che venga subito; *I* — *some money*, mi occorre un po' di denaro; *how much does he* — *for this book ?*, quanto chiede per questo libro ?; (provb.) *the more a man has the more he* ~*s*, l'appetito viene mangiando.

**wanted** *adj.* desiderato, richiesto, ricercato; cercasi; *a* — *man*, un uomo ricercato (dalla polizia); — *for murder*, ricercato per omicidio; *these goods are not* — *nowadays*, oggi non c'è piu richiesta di questi articoli.

**wanting** *adj.* mancante, che manca; senza; (fig.) *he was tried but found* —, la prova dimostrò che non era all'altezza del compito; (fam.) deficiente.

**wanton** *adj.* licenzioso, lascivo, impudico; — *thoughts*, pensieri impudichi; (fig.) capriccioso, gratuito, senza motivo; — *breezes*, brezze capricciose; — *insult*, offesa gratuita; — *destruction*, vandalismo; — *misbehaviour*, grave indisciplina; (lit.) lussureggiante, selvatico; *n.* persona dissoluta, donna impudica; *intr.* folleggiare, scherzare. **~ly** *adv.* lascivamente, capricciosamente; senza scopo; *he did it* ~*ly*, lo fece senza motivo. **~ness** *n.* libertinaggio, dissolutezza, leggerezza; allegria sfrenata, capriccio; *he did it out of sheer* ~*ness*, lo fece per leggerezza.

**war** *n.* guerra; (fig.) lotta; *to wage* — *on*, fare guerra a, guerreggiare con; *to go to* —, dichiarare la guerra, entrare in guerra; *to be at* — *with*, essere in guerra con; *to be on a* — *footing*, essere sul piede di guerra; *to carry the* — *into the enemy's country*, portare la guerra in territorio nemico, (fig.) passare all'attacco; *to let loose the dogs of* —, scatenare i furori della guerra; — *of nerves*, guerra dei nervi; — *of movement*, guerra di movimento; — *to the knife*, guerra ad oltranza, lotta sino alla morte; *civil* —, guerra civile; *class* —, guerra sociale; *cold* —, guerra fredda; *hot* — guerra guerreggiata; *holy* —, guerra santa; *private* —, guerra tra famiglie, faida *f.*, (pol.) guerra privata; *world* —, guerra mondiale; *tariff* —, guerra delle tariffe, guerra doganale; *the Trojan* —, la guerra di Troia; *the Punic Wars*, le guerre puniche; *the Wars of the Roses*, le guerre delle due rose; *the Boer* —, la guerra dei Boeri; (fig.) *the* — *of the elements*, la furia degli elementi; *the* — *against disease*, la lotta contro le malattie; — *of words*, guerra di parole, battibecco; (fam.) *you look as if you'd been in the* ~*s*, hai l'aria malconcia, sei ridotto un ecce homo; (provb.) *all's fair in love and* —, tutto è lecito in amore e in guerra.

**war** *intr.* fare la guerra, guerreggiare, lottare; *to* — *against* lanciare un attacco contro.

**war-baby** *n.* figlio di guerra.

**warble**[1] *n.* trillo, gorgheggio, modulazione; mormorio; *intr.* trillare, gorgheggiare, modulare; (of water, voices) mormorare; *tr.* *to* — *a song*, gorgheggiare una canzone.

**warble**[2] *n.* (vet.) indurimento (prodotto dalla sella), sclerosi *f.*, tumore *m.*

**warbler** *n.* (orn.) uccello canoro; beccafico, capinera, silvia.

**warbling** *adj.* melodioso, trillante, gorgheggiante; *n.* see **warble**[1].

**war-cloud** *n.* minaccia di guerra. **-correspondent** *n.* corrispondente di guerra.

**warcraft** *n.*, arte militare, arte della guerra; (naut.) bastimenti di guerra; (aeron.), aeroplani di guerra.

**war-crime** *n.* delitto di guerra. **-criminal** *n.* criminale di guerra. **-cry** *n.* grido di guerra.

**ward** *n.* minorenne *m.*, *f.*, pupillo; *a* — *in Chancery*, un minorenne sotto tutela della corte; (fencing) guardia, parata; (of a hospital) sala, corsia; (of a prison) reparto, cella; (of a town) rione *m.*, circoscrizione comunale, parrocchia; *electoral* —, circoscrizione elettorale; *casual* —, sala di un ospizio dei poveri; (fig.) *to keep watch and* —, vigilare; *pl.* (of a key) seghettatture *f.pl.*

**ward** *tr.* proteggere, vigilare; *to* — *off a blow*, parare un colpo; *to* — *off illness*, schivare una malattia.

**warden** *n.* custode *m.*, guardiano, portiere *m.*; direttore, direttrice; rettore; *game-warden*, guardacaccia *m. indecl.*; *traffic* —, assistente *m.*, *f.*, ufficiale che controlla il parcheggio.

**warder** *n.* carceriere *m.*, guardia carceraria, secondino; (fig., joc.) cerbero; *chief* —, capocarceriere *m.*; *female* —, see **wardress**.

**wardress** *n.* carceriera.

**wardrobe** *n.* armadio, guardaroba; (fig.) vestiti *m.pl.*; — *trunk*, baule *m.* armadio.
**wardroom** *n.* (naut.) quadrato degli ufficiali.
**wardship** *n.* tutela; *to be under* —, essere sotto tutela.
**ware**[1] *n.* manufatto; vasellame *m.*; *pl.* merce *f.*, merci *f.pl.*
**ware**[2] *tr.* (*imp.* only, poet.; joc.) stare attento, evitare; — *wire!*, attenti al filo spinato!
**warehouse** *n.* deposito, magazzino; negozio; *bonded* —, magazzino doganale, magazzini generali; *furniture* —, deposito mobili; *tr.* immagazzinare, depositare (in magazzino). **-man** *n.* magazziniere *m.*
**warfar-e** *n.* guerra; stato di guerra; *chemical* —, guerra chimica; *trench* —, guerra di trincea; *field* —, *open* —, guerra di campagna. **-ing** *adj.* belligerante, contendente, guerriero.
**war-fever** *n.* psicosi della guerra. **-game** *n.* kriegspiel *m.*; esercitazione tattica su mappa.
**warhead** *n.* (naut.) testata carica (di un siluro).
**warhorse** *n.* cavallo da battaglia, destriero; (fig.) *an old* —, un veterano (della guerra), (pol.) un uomo che vanta molte battaglie politiche.
**wariness** *n.* circospezione, cautela, avvedutezza.
**warlike** *adj.* guerriero, bellicoso, marziale; battagliero.
**war-loan** *n.* prestito di guerra.
**warlock** *n.* mago, stregone *m.*
**war-lord** *n.* generalissimo, capo supremo (delle Forze Armate).
**warm** *adj.* caldo; che tien caldo; *to be* —, (of persons) avere caldo, sentirsi caldo, (of things) essere caldo; *to get* —, riscaldarsi; — *clothes*, abiti che tengono caldo; — *water*, acqua calda; *barely* —, tiepido; (fig.) cordiale, caloroso; generoso; animato, violento; *a* — *heart*, un cuore generoso; *a* — *contest*, una lotta accanita; *a* — *reception*, un'accoglienza cordiale; *the argument was getting* —, la discussione diventava animata; (fig.) difficile, faticoso, pericoloso; (of colours) caldo; — *tints*, tinte calde; — *red*, rosso caldo; (of weather) caldo; *it is* — *today*, oggi fa caldo; (of tracks of animals) fresco, recente; (fam., in games) *you're getting* —, ci sei vicino, fuoco, fuochino!; *n.* (fam.) atto di scaldare, atto di scaldarsi; *to have a good* — *by the fire*, scaldarsi al fuoco; *to give something a* —, scaldare qualcosa.
**warm** *tr.* scaldare, riscaldare; *the sun has -ed the air*, il sole riscaldato l'aria; *to* — *one's hands*, scaldarsi le mani; *intr.* animarsi, entusiasmarsi; *to* — *to someone*, provare simpatia per qualcuno; *my heart -ed when I heard the news*, il mio cuore s'entusiasmò sentendo la notizia; *to* — *to one's work*, appassionarsi al lavoro; *to* — *up*, *tr.* riscaldare, (fig.) animare; *to* — *up the coffee*, riscaldare il caffè; *the wine will* — *you up*, il vino ti riscalderà; *intr.* riscaldarsi, animarsi, eccitarsi; *the game -ed up after half-time*, dopo la ripresa il giuoco si è riscaldato.
**war-memorial** *n.* monumento ai caduti.
**warm-hearted** *adj.* affettuoso, espansivo, cordiale, caloroso. **-ness** *n.* affetuosità, cordialità, calorosità.
**warming** *adj.* riscaldante, che riscalda; *n.* riscaldamento.
**warming-pan** *n.* scaldaletto, scaldino.
**warmonger** *n.* guerrafondaio. **-ing** *n.* propaganda di guerra.
**warmth** *n.* calore *m.*, caldo; (fig.) ardore *m.*, zelo; risentimento; (art, of colours) intensità; *his style lacks* —, il suo stile manca di calore; *he replied with* —, rispose con risentimento.
**warn** *tr.* avvertire, mettere in guardia, ammonire, dare l'allarme, informare; (leg.) diffidare; (mil.) designare; *I* — *you not to do it again*, ti ammonisco di non farlo un'altra volta; *he -ed me against smoking*, mi mise in guardia contro il pericolo di fumare; *you have been -ed!*, siete avvertiti!; *you should* — *the police*, dovresti informare la polizia; *the court -ed him*, la corte lo diffidò; (mil.) *to* — *a soldier for guard duty*, designare un soldato per la guardia; *to* — *off*, *tr.* diffidare, intimare di allontanarsi; (racing) *to* — *someone off the course*, vietare a qualcuno di partecipare alle corse.
**warning** *adj.* che avverte; *a* — *look*, uno sguardo di avvertimento; — *light*, spia luminosa; *n.* avvertimento, ammonimento, preavviso, diffida; *to give* — *of danger*, avvertire del pericolo; *let this be a* —, che questo serva di lezione; *without* —, senza preavviso; *to sound a note of* —, mettere in guardia, raccomandare prudenza; *air-raid* —, allarme aereo.
**warp** *n.* (text.) ordito, catena; (fig.) deformazione, curvatura; (naut.) tonneggio, ormeggio; (agric.) deposito alluvionale.
**warp** *tr.* (text.) ordire; piegare, curvare; (fig.) deformare, alterare; (naut.) tonneggiare, rimorchiare; (agric.) bonificare; (aeron.) svergolare; *intr.* deformarsi, imbarcarsi.
**war-paint** *n.* pittura di guerra (dei pellirosse); (fig.) assetto di guerra, alta tenuta, abito di gala.
**warpath** *n.* sentiero della guerra (dei pellirosse); (fig.) *to be on the* —, essere pronto a scendere in lizza.
**warping** *n.* (text.) orditura; (of wood) curvatura; (metall.) deformazione; (fig.) alterazione, perversione; (naut.) tonneggio; (agric.) bonifica; (aeron.) svergolamento.
**warrant** *n.* garanzia; (person) garante *m.*, *f.*; *I will be your* —, sarò il vostro garante; (leg.) mandato, autorizzazione, ordine *m.*; — *of arrest*, mandato di cattura; *search* —, mandato di perquisizione; *distress* —, ordine di sequestro; — *of attorney*, procura; (comm.) certificato, ordine; — *for delivery*, ordine di consegna; *stock* —, certificato di azione al portatore; *dividend* —, ordine per la riscossione del dividendo; *travelling* —, foglio di via.
**warrant** *tr.* garantire, attestare; giustificare; *I* — *you it won't happen again*, non succederà una seconda volta, ve lo garantisco io!; *this might* — *his behaviour*, questo potrebbe giustificare il suo comportamento.
**warranted** *adj.* garantito; (leg.) autorizzato; — *pure silk*, seta pura garantita; *we are* — *in assuming*, siamo autorizzati a pensare.
**warrant-officer** *n.* (mil.) sottufficiale *m.*; (naval) capo.
**warrantor** *n.* garante *m.*, *f.*
**warranty** *n.* garanzia, autorizzazione; (fig.) giustificazione; *breach of* —, rottura di garanzia.
**warren** *n.* conigliera, garenna; (fig.) *that house is a (rabbit)* —, quella casa è un formicaio.
**warring** *adj.* guerreggiante, belligerante, contrastante, in stato di guerra; *the* — *nations*, le nazioni contendenti; — *interests*, interessi contrastanti.
**warrior** *n.* guerriero, soldato; *the Unknown Warrior*, il Milite Ignoto; *female* —, guerriera, amazzone *f.*
**Warsaw** *pr.n.* (geog.) Varsavia.
**warship** *n.* nave *f.* da guerra.
**wart** *n.* verruca, porro, bitorzolo, neo; protuberanza, escrescenza; *to paint someone -s and all*, fare un ritratto fedele di qualcuno.
**wart-hog** *n.* (zool.) facocero.
**wartime** *n.* tempo di guerra; *attrib.* — *regulations*, regolamenti emessi in tempo di guerra.
**warty** *adj.* verrucoso, bitorzoluto; (fig.) pieno di escrescenze, simile a verruca.
**war-wear-y** *adj.* stanco della guerra. **-iness** *n.* stanchezza della guerra.
**war-widow** *n.* vedova di guerra. **-worn** *adj.* logorato dalla guerra; devastato dalla guerra.
**wary** *adj.* diffidente, acuto, guardingo, circospetto, accorto; *they are* — *of strangers*, diffidano dei forestieri; *to keep a* —

*eye on*, diffidare di, stare ben attento a.

**was** *p.def.* of **be**, *q.v.*

**wash** *n.* lavaggio, lavatura, abluzione; *to give something a* —, lavare qualcosa; *to have a* —, lavarsi (le mani); *to have a — and brush-up*, farsi un po' di toilette; (laundry), bucato, lavanderia; (fam.) *it will all come out in the* —, tutto si aggiusterà; lozione, liquido cosmetico; sciacquìo, sciabordìo; (of a ship) scia, rotta; (for pigs) brodaglia; intonaco, mano di colore, coloritura; (art) guazzo, acquerello; *pen and — drawing*, disegno a penna acquerellato.

**wash** *tr.* lavare, bagnare; (laundry) *to — a few things*, fare un bucatino; (metals) depurare; (walls) tinteggiare; (electr.) galvanizzare, metallizzare; (of river, sea) lambire, bagnare, spazzare, portare via; *a sailor was ~ed overboard*, un marinaio fu spazzato via dalle onde; (poet.) inumidire; *flowers ~ed with dew*, fiori imperlati di rugiada; (art) *to — a drawing*, acquerellare un disegno; (fig.) *to — one's dirty linen in public*, lavare i propri panni sporchi in pubblico; *intr.* lavarsi, lavare; *this material won't* —, questa stoffa non è lavabile; (fig.) *that story won't* —, questa non la bevo, non ci credo. FOLLOW. BY ADV.: *to — away, tr.* lavar via, eliminare, (fig.) purificare, corrodere, erodere; *to — away one's sins*, lavare i peccati; *~ed away by the tide*, trascinato via dalla marea; *~ed away by the sea*, eroso dal mare; *to — down, tr.* lavare con getti d'acqua, (of rain) trascinare a valle; (fig.) *to — down one's dinner with a glass of wine*, annaffiare il pranzo con un bicchiere di vino; *to — off, tr.* eliminare lavando, togliere; *to — off a stain*, eliminare una macchia; *intr. it will — off*, si può togliere con l'acqua; *to — out, tr.* risciacquare, eliminare lavando, ripulire, (fig.) cancellare; *to — out an insult in blood*, lavare un affronto col sangue; *you can — that out*, puoi escludere questo; *we must — the whole business out*, è meglio dimenticare tutto; (min.) *to — out the gold*, estrarre l'oro; *to — up, tr.* (dishes), rigovernare (stoviglie); (of sea) rigettare; *intr.* (of sea, river) rifluire.

**washable** *adj.* lavabile.

**wash-bag** *n.* sacchetto per biancheria. **-basin** *n.* lavabo, lavandino.

**washboard** *n.* asse *f.* per lavare; (naut.) battente *m.* di boccaporto, falchetta, battimare *m.*; (bldg.) zoccolo di legno.

**washed** *adj.* lavato; (chem.) purificato; (art) — *drawing*, disegno a guazzo; (min.) — *coal*, carbone lavato; (of colour) *~ed out*, slavato, scolorito; (fig.) *to feel ~ed out*, sentirsi sfinito, essere giù di corda; *a ~ed-out complexion*, un colorito scialbo.

**washer**[1] *n.* lavatore, addetto al lavaggio; (chem.) gorgogliatore di lavaggio.

**washer**[2] *n.* (eng.) rondella, ranella, rosetta; *spring* —, rondella elastica, rosetta elastica; *tab* —, rondella di sicurezza; *thrust* —, rondella di spinta; *packing* —, guarnizione, rondella di guarnizione.

**washer-man** *n.* lavandaio; (min.) addetto al lavaggio di minerali. **-woman** *n.* lavandaia.

**wash-hand** *adj.* — *basin*, lavandino; — *stand*, lavabo, portacatino. **-house** *n.* lavatoio, lavanderia.

**washing** *adj.* lavabile, che si può lavare; *n.* lavaggio; (eccl.) abluzione; *the — of feet*, il lavaggio dei piedi; bucato, biancheria; *to hang out the* —, stendere il bucato; *who does your — ?*, chi ti lava la biancheria ?, chi ti fa il bucato ?; *she takes in* —, fa la lavandaia; *we do our own* —, facciamo il bucato in casa; (industr.) depurazione.

**washing-day** *n.* giorno di bucato. **-machine** *n.* (for clothes) lavatrice automatica; (slot) lavatrice a gettoni; (bldg.) lavatrice per pietrame. **-soda** *n.* soda commerciale. **-up** *n.* rigovernatura delle stoviglie; *to do the -up*, rigovernare le stoviglie, lavare i piatti.

**wash-leather** *n.* pelle scamosciata. **-out** *n.* lavaggio; (rlwy.) cedimento della strada ferrata causato dalla pioggia; (fam.) fiasco, fallimento; *it was a complete -out*, era un fiasco completo. **-room** *n.* gabinetto; (USA) lavanderia.

**washstand** *n.* lavabo, lavandino, portacatino.

**wash-tank** *n.* tinozza, vasca di lavaggio. **-tub** *n.* tinozza, mastello, vasca; conca del bucato.

**washy** *adj.* (of food) insipido, acquoso; (of style) fiacco; (of colour) scialbo, smorto.

**wasp** *n.* (ent.) vespa; *~s' nest*, vespaio. **-waist** *n.* vitino di vespa. **-waisted** *adj.* dal vitino di vespa.

**waspish** *adj.* cattivo, molesto come una vespa; (fig.) acre, pungente; (of a woman) bisbetica. **-ness** *n.* irascibilità, acredine *f.*

**wastage** *n.* perdita; disspendio esagerato; deperimento; (industr.) scarto.

**waste** *adj.* (of land) incolto, arido, brullo; *to lie* —, rimanere incolto; devastato; *to lay* —, devastare, saccheggiare; (comm.; industr.) inutilizzabile, di scarto; — *paper*, carta straccia; — *products*, rifiuti *m.pl.*, prodotti di scarto.

**waste** *n.* spreco, sciupìo; *a — of energy*, uno spreco di energia; *what a — of time !*, quanto tempo sprecato!; zona incolta, deserto; *the ~s of Africa*, il deserto africano; *a — of waters*, una immensa distesa di acqua; *to let the garden go to* —, lasciare inselvatichire il giardino; (industr.) rifiuti *m.pl.*, scarto, cascame *m.*; *cotton* —, cascami di cotone; — *yarn*, filato di cascame; *to throw the — away*, buttare via lo scarto; (leg.) deteriorazione, usura; (techn.) perdita, usura, dissipazione.

**waste** *tr.* sprecare, sciupare, sperperare; (fig.) perdere; *to — money*, sprecare denaro; *to — time*, perdere tempo; *to — one's breath*, sprecare il fiato; (provb.) — *not, want not*, chi risparmia si arricchisce; *intr.* consumarsi, logorarsi, sciuparsi, deperire; *he is wasting away*, si consuma lentamente, deperisce a poco a poco.

**waste-basket** *n.* cestino per rifiuti. **-cock** *n.* (mech.) rubinetto di scarico.

**wasted** *adj.* (of country) devastato; (fig.) sciupato, sprecato; (of an invalid) scarno, indebolito, deperito; (electr.) — *output*, potenza perduta.

**wasteful** *adj.* prodigo, spendereccio; rovinoso; — *expenditure*, spese inutili. **-ness** *n.* prodigalità, sciupìo, sperpero.

**waste-heap** *n.* mucchio di rifiuti, immondezzaio; (min.) scorie *f.pl.* **-paper** *attrib.* *-paper basket*, cestino; *to throw into the -paper basket*, cestinare. **-pipe** *n.* (hydr. eng.) tubazione di scarico, tubo di scarico, scolo, sfogo, tubo d'emissione.

**wast-er** *n.* dissipatore; (fam.) fannullone *m.*, buono a nulla. **-ing** *adj.* logorante, assillante; *a -ing disease* una malattia logorante; *n.* sciupìo, spreco; deperimento, consunzione; (of a limb) atrofia. **-rel** *n.* fannullone *m.*, discolo, sprecone *m.*, buono a nulla.

**watch** *n.* orologio; *wrist-watch*, orologio da polso; *pocket* —, orologio da tasca; *stop-watch*, cronometro, orologio a scatto; *to set a* —, regolare un orologio; *what time is it by your — ?*, che ora fai ?; *my — is fast*, il mio orologio va avanti; *your — is ten minutes slow*, il tuo orologio va indietro dieci minuti; *his — is right*, il suo orologio va bene; (hist.) polizia, corpo dei vigili; *the night* —, la ronda notturna; veglia; *in the -es of the night*, nelle veglie della notte; guardia; sorveglianza, attenzione; *to be on*

*the* —, stare attento, stare in guardia, essere in attesa; *to keep a close — on*, sorvegliare da vicino; (naut.) guardia, quarto; *officer of the* —, ufficiale di guardia; *to set the -es*, regolare i quarti; *to be on* —, essere di guardia; (ent.) *death-watch beetle*, orologio dei morti.

**watch** *tr.* osservare, guardare, tener d'occhio; badare a, assistere a; *to — a game of football*, assistere a una partita di calcio; (fig.) *to — one's time*, attendere il momento opportuno; *to — the expense*, badare alle spese; *— your step!*, sta attento!; (leg.) *to — a case*, seguire una causa per conto di terzi; *to — for*, attendere, aspettare; *to — after*, seguire con gli occhi; *to — over*, sorvegliare; *intr.* vegliare, star sveglio; guardare.

**watch-bracelet** *n.* orologio-braccialetto, cinturino da orologio. **-case** *n.* astuccio da orologio. **-chain** *n.* catena da orologio. **-dog** *n.* cane *m.* da guardia.

**watcher** *n.* che veglia; spettatore; osservatore; *bird* —, osservatore della vita degli uccelli.

**watchful** *adj.* vigile, vigilante; attento; (fig.) guardingo, cauto; *to keep a — eye on*, sorvegliare attentamente; *to be — of*, osservare con diffidenza; (poet.) *— nights*, notti insonni. **-ness** *n.* vigilanza; circospezione.

**watching** *adj.* (leg.) *a — brief*, incarico (dato ad un avvocato) di sorvegliare l'andamento di una causa per conto di terzi; *n.* veglia, osservazione, vigilanza, sorveglianza; *she needs* —, bisogna sorvegliarla; *bird* —, osservazione degli uccelli.

**watchmak-er** *n.* orologiaio. **-ing** *n.* orologeria.

**watch-man** *n.* guardiano, sorvegliante *m.*; *night* —, guardiano notturno; (rlwy.) *track*—, guardalinee *m.*, cantoniere *m.* **-word** *n.* parola d'ordine.

**water** *n.* acqua; *salt* —, acqua salsa, acqua salata; *fresh* —, acqua dolce; *brackish* —, acqua salmastra; *hot* —, acqua calda; *cold* —, acqua fredda, acqua fresca; *h. & c. — in every room*, acqua corrente calda e fredda in tutte le camere; *lukewarm* —, acqua tiepida; *sea-water*, acqua di mare; *drinking* —, acqua potabile; *— unfit for drinking*, acqua non potabile; *spring* —, acqua di fonte, acqua viva; *main* —, acqua di conduttura; *tap* —, acqua dal rubinetto; *stagnant* —, acqua morta; *mineral* —, acqua minerale; *fizzy* —, acqua effervescente; (rel.) *holy* —, acqua benedetta; *lustral* —, acqua lustrale; *rain* —, acqua piovana; *flood* —, acqua di piena; *slack* —, acqua stanca; *high* —, alta marea; *low* —, bassa marea; (chem.) *heavy* —, acqua pesante; (med.) *— on the brain*, idrocefalia; *— on the knee*, sinovite *f.*; *the -s*, il mare, le acque; acque termali; *territorial -s*, acque territoriali; *to take the -s*, fare una cura di acque termali; (obstet.) *the -s*, le acque; (fig.) *to get into hot* —, cacciarsi nei guai; *to throw cold — on a scheme*, gettare acqua sul fuoco; *to keep one's head above* —, tenersi a galla; *like a fish out of* —, come un pesce fuor d'acqua; *to be in deep* —, essere in cattive acque; *this won't hold* —, questo non è logico; *to cast one's bread upon the -s*, far del bene senza aspettarsi ricompensa; *to pour oil on troubled -s*, gettar acqua sul fuoco, calmare i dissensi; (provb.) *still -s run deep*, le acque chete rovinano i ponti; *a lot of — has flowed under the bridge*, è passata molt'acqua sotto i ponti; *blood is thicker than* —, il sangue non è acqua; (of precious stones) trasparenza; *of the first* —, della più bell'acqua.

**water** *tr.* inaffiare, bagnare, irrigare; aggiungere acqua a, diluire, annacquare; (animals) abbeverare, menare a bere; (text.) marezzare; *to — the plants*, inaffiare le piante; *-ed by the Po*, bagnato dal Po; *to — one's wine*, mettere acqua nel vino; *to — down*, diluire, annacquare, (fig.) attenuare; *intr.* inumidirsi, lacrimare; rifornirsi d'acqua; *it makes my mouth* —, mi fa venire l'acquolina in bocca; *the ship -ed at Naples*, la nave si è rifornita d'acqua a Napoli.

**water-bath** *n.* (chem.; cul.) bagnomaria. **-beetle** *n.* (ent.) idrofilo. **-borne** *adj.* galleggiante; (of goods) trasportato via acqua; (of disease) propagato da acqua inquinata. **-bottle** *n.* bottiglia per acqua; brocca, caraffa; (mil.) borraccia; *hot-water bottle*, borsa per acqua, borsa d'acqua calda. **-butt** *n.* botte *f.* per acqua piovana. **-carrier** *n.* portatore d'acqua; (astron.) Acquario. **-cart** *n.* annaffiatrice, carretta da inaffiare. **-cask** *n.* botte *f.* **-chute** *n.* scivolo a canale. **-closet** *n.* gabinetto, ritirata, toletta; water *m.*, cesso. **-colour** *n.* acquerello; *to paint in -colour*, acquerellare. **-colourist** *n.* acquerellista *m.*, *f.*

**watercourse** *n.* corso d'acqua; ruscello; canale *m.*

**watercress** *n.* crescione *m.* d'acqua, agretto.

**water-cure** *n.* (med.) idroterapia, cura idrica. **-diviner** *n.* rabdomante *m.*

**watered** *adj.* bagnato, inaffiato, irrigato; annacquato, diluito; (text.) marezzato.

**waterfall** *n.* cascata, cateratta; salto caduta d'acqua.

**water-fern** *n.* (bot.) felce florida.

**waterfowl** *n.* uccello acquatico; selvaggina acquatica.

**water-front** *n.* banchina; quartiere del porto, zona portuale; lungomare *m.* **-gauge** *n.* indicatore del livello dell'acqua; (hydr. eng.) idrometro, idrostato *m.* **-glass** *n.* idroscopio; clessidra; (chem.) tetrasilicato di soda. **-hole** *n.* (geol.) pozza, stagno. **-ice** *n.* (cul.) sorbetto.

**wateriness** *n.* acquosità; (fig.) insipidezza, scipitezza; (med.) sierosità.

**watering** *adj.* lacrimante; *n.* annaffiamento, bagnatura; (of animals) abbeveramento, abbeverata; (of ship) rifornimento d'acqua; (text.) marezzatura; (med.) *— of the eyes*, lacrimazione.

**watering-can** *n.* annaffiatoio.

**watering-place** *n.* luogo di rifornimento d'acqua; abbeveratoio; stazione termale, stazione balneare; spiaggia.

**water-jug** *n.* brocca, caraffa. **-jump** *n.* (sport) riviera; arginello. **-level** *n.* livello dell'acqua, altezza dell'acqua, piano dell'acqua; livello ad acqua.

**waterless** *adj.* privo d'acqua, arido.

**water-lily** *n.* (bot.) ninfea, nenufaro; *royal* —, vittoria regia; *white* —, ninfea degli stagni, giglio degli stagni; *yellow* —, giglio d'acqua.

**water-line** *n.* livello dell'acqua; (naut.) linea di galleggiamento, linea d'immersione; battigia, battima; (paperm.) linea di filigrana.

**water-logged** *adj.* saturo d'acqua, pieno d'acqua; (fig.) imbevuto.

**water-main** *n.* acquedotto, conduttura d'acqua.

**waterman** *n.* barcaiolo; traghettatore; (fig.) *a good* —, un canottiere esperto.

**watermark** *n.* (=tidemark) battigia, battima; (naut.) linea d'immersione; (paperm.) filigrana. **-ed** *adj.* (paperm.) filigranato.

**water-meadow** *n.* (agric.) marcita, prateria irrigabile. **-melon** *n.* (bot.) cocomero, anguria. **-mill** *n.* mulino ad acqua. **-nymph** *n.* (myth.) naiade *f.*; (bot.) nenufaro bianco, ninfea. **-pipe** *n.* conduttura d'acqua, condotto, tubo di scarico. **-polo** *n.* (sport) pallanuoto. **-power** *n.* forza idraulica, forza idrica, energia idraulica, acqua motrice; (fig.) carbone bianco.

**waterproof** *adj.* impermeabile; idrofugo, imbrifugo; *n.* impermeabile *m.*; *tr.* impermeabilizzare; (text.) cerare.

**water-rat** *n.* (zool.) topo acquaiolo, topo d'acqua. **-rate** *n.* imposta comunale per il consumo dell'acqua. **-resisting** *adj.* idrofugo, acqua-resistente, idrorepellente.

**watershed** *n.* (geog.) spartiacque *m.*, crinale *m.*, displuvio, linea divisoria delle acque, bacino idrografico.

**waterside** *n.* sponda, riva; *attrib.* rivierasco, littoraneo.

**water-skiing** *n.* sci nautico. **-softener** *n.* depuratore d'acqua, addolcitore d'acqua, anticalcareo. **-softening** *adj.* idrodepurante; *n.* depurazione dell'acqua. **-spaniel** *n.* tipo di bracco spagnolo addestrato per la caccia in palude. **-spider** *n.* (ent.) idrometra *m.*; (zool.) argironeta *m.*

**waterspout** *n.* (meteor.) tromba marina; (bldg.) pluviale *m.*

**water-sprite** *n.* ondina. **-supply** *n.* provvista d'acqua, approvvigionmento d'acqua, alimentazione idraulica. **-system** *n.* impianto idrico, canalizzazione. **-tank** *n.* serbatoio d'acqua, cisterna.

**watertight** *adj.* stagno, impermeabile, a tenuta d'acqua; — *bulkheads*, paratie stagne; — *compartments*, compartimenti stagni (also fig.); — *regulations*, regolamenti che non offrono nessuna scappatoia. **-ness** *n.* impermeabilità.

**water-tower** *n.* (hydr. eng.) torre serbatoio, castello d'acqua. **-vole** *n.* (zool.) topo acquaiolo, topo d'acqua. **-wag(g)on** *n.* vagone *m.* cisterna; (fig., joc.) *to be on the -waggon*, essere acquatico, essere astemio.

**waterway** *n.* idrovia, canale *m.* navigabile; (eng.) cunetta.

**water-wings** *n.pl.* salvagente *m.* per imparare a nuotare.

**waterworks** *n.pl.* impianto idrico, acquedotto, castello d'acqua; (fam.) *to turn on the* —, piangere come una vacca.

**watery** *adj.* acquoso, umido, acquitrinoso; piovoso; (fig.) insipido; (of colour) stinto, slavato; — *eyes*, occhi pieni di lacrime; — *moon*, luna offuscata; (poet.) *the — plain*, il mare; *to find a — grave*, morire annegato.

**watt** *n.* (electr.) watt *m.* **-hour** *n.* (electr. eng.) watt ora; *-hour meter*, contatore elettrico, wattorametro, wattimetro.

**wattage** *n.* (electr. eng.) wattaggio.

**wattle**[1] *n.* canniccio, graticcio, graticciata, canne *f.pl.*, vimini *m.pl.*; (bot.) acacia australiana, mimosa; *wattle-and-daub wall*, muro a cannicchiata ricoperto di fango; (mil.) — *hut*, baracca di vimini.

**wattle**[2] *n.* (of birds) barbiglio, caruncola; (of fish) barbetta.

**wattmeter** *n.* (electr. eng.) wattimetro.

**wave** *n.* onda, flutto, ondata; *a — of enthusiasm*, un'ondata di entusiasmo; *a — of anger*, un impeto d'ira; (mil.) *to attack in -s*, attaccare a ondate successive; (meteor.) *a heat-wave*, un'ondata di caldo; *tidal* —, onda di marea, mareggiata; cenno, gesto, saluto; *with a — of his hand*, con un cenno della mano; *he greeted her with a — of his hat*, la salutò agitando il cappello; (hairdr.) ondulazione; *permanent* —, permanente *f.*; (radio) onda; *long* —, onda lunga; *short* —, onda corta; *ultra-short* —, onda cortissima; *medium* —, onda media.

**wave** *tr.* sventolare, agitare; (weapon) brandire; fare segno con; (hairdr.) ondulare; *to — a handkerchief*, sventolare un fazzoletto; *the policeman -d us on*, il vigile ci fece segno di proseguire; *to — aside*, scartare, far segno di scostarsi; *to — goodbye*, fare un cenno d'addio; *intr.* ondeggiare, sventolare, fluttuare, ondulare; fare segno; *flags waving in the wind*, bandiere *f.pl.* ondeggianti al vento; (of hair) *to — naturally*, avere onde *f.pl.* naturali.

**wave-band** *n.* (radio) gamma di lunghezza d'onda.

**waved** *adj.* ondulato, increspato.

**wave-length** *n.* (radio) lunghezza d'onda.

**wavelet** *n.* piccola onda, ondicina; increspatura.

**waver** *intr.* vacillare, oscillare, ondeggiare; (of flame) guizzare; (fig.) esitare, titubare, tentennare; (of voice) tremare, titubare; (of courage) mancare; cedere. **-er** *n.* uomo indeciso, irresoluto, vacillante. **-ing** *adj.* vacillante, guizzante; (fig.) titubante, irresoluto; *n.* ondeggiamento, vacillazione, guizzo; (fig.) esitazione.

**wave-setting** *n.* (hairdr.) messa in piega.

**waviness** *n.* ondulazione, ondosità.

**waving** *n.* ondeggiamento; (of flags) sventolio; (with hand) cenno; (of hair) ondulazione.

**wavy** *adj.* ondulato, ondoso, ondeggiante; *—hair*, capelli ondulati; — *line*, linea ondeggiante.

**wax**[1] *n.* cera; cera vegetale, pece *f.*, ceralacca; (mineral) paraffina, ozocerite *f.*; *sealing-wax*, ceralacca; *cobbler's* —, pece da calzolai; — *modelling*, ceroplastica; — *plaster*, cerotto; *ear* —, cerume *m.*; *tr.* incerare, dare la cera a, lucidare; (shoemaking) impeciare.

**wax**[2] *intr.* (of moon) crescere; *to — and wane*, crescere e calare; (fig.) diventare, farsi; *to — fat*, diventare grasso, (fig.) diventare ricco; *to — sentimental*, cadere nel sentimentalismo.

**wax-candle** *n.* candela di cera, cero. **-chandler** *n.* ceraiuolo, candelaio; mercante di candele.

**waxcloth** *n.* tela cerata.

**waxen** *adj.* di cera, cereo, come cera; plasmabile come cera; — *complexion*, colorito cereo.

**waxing**[1] *n.* inceratura, lucidatura a cera.

**waxing**[2] *n.* (of moon) crescita.

**wax-paper** *n.* carta paraffinata, carta cerata. **-taper** *n.* cero, candela di cera, cerino. **-vesta** *n.* cerino.

**waxwing** *n.* (orn.) beccofrosone, beccofrusone *m.*

**waxwork** *n.* modello di cera, figura di cera; modellamento in cera; *pl.* museo di riproduzioni in cera.

**waxy** *adj.* cereo, di cera, simile a cera.

**way** *adv.* — *back in 1914*, nel lontano 1914; — *down in Tennessee*, laggiù nel Tennessee; — *up in the sky*, lassù nel cielo.

**way** *n.* via, strada; cammino; passaggio; *to ask one's* —, chiedere la strada; *to start on one's* —, mettersi in cammino; *the right* —, la strada giusta, (fig.) la retta via; *the wrong* —, la strada sbagliata, (fig.) la via dell'errore; *which — did you come?*, quale via hai preso?; *to lead the* —, far strada, fare da guida; *to make* —, farsi largo, aprire un varco; *make —!*, indietro!; *to make — for*, cedere il passo a; *to make one's — in the world*, farsi strada nel mondo; *to go one's* —, andarsene; *to go one's own* —, andare per la propria strada, fare di testa propria; *to know one's — about*, essere pratico di, sapersi orientare; (fig.) *he knows his — about*, è furbo, sa cavarsi d'impiccio; *to work one's — up*, farsi una posizione, (fam.) venire dalla gavetta; *to pave the* —, preparare il terreno; *to pay one's* —, coprire le spese dalla propria tasca; *to be in the* —, essere un ostacolo, essere di troppo; *he is always in my* —, mi sta sempre fra i piedi; *to get out of the* —, togliersi di mezzo; *get out of my —!*, levati di qua!, via!; *to keep out of the* —, tenersi nascosto; *to keep out of the — of*, scansare, schivare, evitare; *out of the* —, fuori mano, remoto, (fig.) fuori del comune; *it was nothing out of the* —, non era nulla di eccezionale; — *in*, entrata, ingresso; — *out*, uscita; — *up*, salita; — *down*, discesa; *this is the — down*, si scende di qua; — *through*, passaggio; *no through —!*, vicolo cieco!; *on the — to London*, tra qui e Londra; *on my — home*, andando a casa; *on the* —, strada facendo; *across*

*the* —, dall'altra parte della strada, dirimpetto; (leg.) *right of* —, diritto di passaggio; (rlwy.) *permanent* —, strada ferrata, massicciata; distanza, percorso, tragitto; *it's a long* —, è molto lontano; *it's a short* —, è vicino; *all the* —, per tutto il cammino; *he'll go a long* —, andrà lontano; *his name goes a long* —, il suo nome apre tutte le porte; *you are a long — out*, sbagli di grosso; *not by a long* —, neppure approssimativamente; direzione, lato, senso; *the wrong — up*, a rovescio; *I didn't know which — to look*, non sapevo da che parte guardare; *you should look both -s before crossing the street*, dovresti guardare nei due sensi prima di attraversare la strada; *to look the other* —, guardare altrove; *the wind is now blowing the other* —, ora il vento soffia in senso contrario; *one — street*, senso unico; modo, maniera, usanza; *the Italian — of life*, il modo di vivere degli Italiani; *the — things are nowadays*, dato l'andamento delle cose in questi tempi; *she has a — with people*, sa come trattare la gente; *I don't like his -s*, non mi piacciono le sue maniere; *to change one's -s*, mutare vita; *to learn the hard* —, imparare a proprie spese; *to get one's own* —, far valere la propria volontà; (provb.) *where there's a will there's a* —, volere è potere; *to my — of thinking*, secondo me; *to get into the — of*, prendere l'abitudine di; *there are no two -s about it*, non c'è da discutere; senso, punto di vista; *in one* —, in un certo senso; *in every* —, sotto ogni aspetto; *to be in a bad* —, star male, trovarsi in cattive acque; *he's in a terrible* —, è agitatissimo, è fuori di sè; *to be in a large — of business*, commerciare in grande; (fam.) *she's in the family* —, aspetta un bambino, è incinta; *by the* —, sul bordo della strada, (fig.) a proposito, tra parentesi, incidentalmente; *by — of explanation*, a titolo di spiegazione; *by — of contrast*, in via di contrapposto; *to go to Milan by — of Chiasso*, andare a Milano via Chiasso; *on the* —, imminente, in arrivo; *once in a* —, ogni tanto; (techn.) superficie *f.* di scorrimento, guida; (naut.) *to gather* —, prendere velocità; *to get under* —, salpare.

**way-bill** *n.* (comm.) nota di spedizione, lettera di vettura; (list) elenco di passeggeri, lista merci.

**wayfar-er** *n.* viandante *m.*, *f.*, passante *m.*, *f.* **-ing** *adj.* viaggiante.

**way-lay** *tr.* appostare, tendere un agguato a; (fig.) attendere al varco, abbordare. **-out** *adj.* (pop.) strambo. **-side** *adj.* stradale; *a -side inn*, un'osteria al margine della strada; *n.* margine della strada.

**wayward** *adj.* capriccioso, indocile, ribelle, di carattere difficile, caparbio. **-ness** *n.* caparbietà, carattere capriccioso.

**w.c.** *n.* (fam.) See **water-closet**; (West Central), centro-occidentale (di una città).

**we** *pers. prn., nom. pl.*; noi; — *are here*, noi siamo qui; *here — are!*, eccoci!; (*follow. by n.*) noialtri; — *Italians*, noialtri *Italiani*; *indef.* si; *in England — say*, in Inghilterra si dice.

**weak** *adj.* debole; gracile; fragile; fievole; *the -er sex*, il sesso debole; *the — point*, il lato debole; — *tea*, tè leggero; (gramm.) — *verb*, verbo debole.

**weaken** *tr.* indebolire, infiacchire, ammortire; *intr.* indebolirsi, infiacchirsi; scemare. **-ing** *adj.* che indebolisce, che infiacchisce, enervante; *n.* indebolimento, infiacchimento, infievolimento.

**weakling** *n.* persona debole, di carattere debole; bambino gracile, malaticcio.

**weakly** *adj.* malaticcio, poco robusto.

**weak-minded** *adj.* debole di carattere; irresoluto.

**weakness** *n.* debolezza, fiacchezza, spossatezza; (fig.) lato debole; *he has a — for cats*, ha un debole per i gatti.

**weal**[1] *n.* bene *m.*, benessere *m.*; felicità, prosperità; *the common* —, il bene pubblico; *in — and woe*, nella buona e nella cattiva sorte, nella fortuna come nella disgrazia.

**weal**[2] *n.* striscia sulla pelle causata da una sferzata.

**wealth** *n.* ricchezza; opulenza; (fig.) abbondanza; dovizia; lusso; *to achieve* —, fare fortuna; *a — of illustrations*, una grande profusione di illustrazioni; *he is rolling in* —, sguazza nell'oro. **-y** *adj.* ricco, opulento; dovizioso; benestante; *the -y classes*, le classi benestanti; *n.pl. the -y*, i ricchi.

**wean** *tr.* slattare, spoppare, svezzare; (fig.) togliere il vezzo.

**weapon** *n.* arme *f.*; arma; *steel* —, arme bianca; *-s of offence and defence*, mezzi di offesa e difesa; *ordeal by -s*, prova delle armi; *to beat someone with his own -s*, controbattere qualcuno con le sue stesse armi; (fig.) *the — of fear*, l'arma del terrore.

**wear** *n.* abbigliamento; abito; *children's* —, articoli di vestiario per bambini; *evening* —, abito da sera; *no longer in* —, fuori moda, fuori uso; logorìo, consumo, usura; — *and tear*, logoramento; (leg.) *fair — and tear*, usura legittima; (mech.) *negligible* —, usura trascurabile; uso; *material of good* —, stoffa di lunga durata; *the worse for* —, essere sgualcito, (fig.) decrepito, malandato.

**wear** *tr.* portare, indossare; (shoes) calzare; (fig.) *to — a melancholy look*, avere l'aria triste; *to — one's heart upon one's sleeve*, non saper nascondere i propri sentimenti; logorare, consumare; *worn by time*, consumato dal tempo; *to — holes in carpets*, formare buchi nei tappeti; *to — oneself to death*, esaurirsi; *intr.* durare, resistere; *this cloth will — for years*, questa stoffa durerà anni; (fig.) *he -s well*, non dimostra la sua età; FOLLOW. BY ADV.: *to — away*, *tr.* consumare, logorare, *intr.* consumarsi, logorarsi; *to — down*, *tr.* consumare, logorare, (fig.) abbattere; *to — off*, *intr.* consumarsi, (fig.) passare, svanire, dissiparsi; *to — on*, *intr.* passare lentamente; *to — out*, *tr.* logorare, esaurire, (fig.) stancare, *intr.* logorarsi, esaurirsi, (fig.) stancarsi; *to — through*, *tr.* fare un buco in, forare.

**wearable** *adj.* portabile, che si può indossare.

**wearer** *n.* persona che porta, che indossa; *clothes too big for the* —, vestiti troppo larghi per chi li porta.

**wearied** *adj.* stanco, affaticato; annoiato.

**weariness** *n.* stanchezza, fatica; (fig.) noia, tedio.

**wearing** *adj.* da portare, da indossare; — *apparel*, vestiario, abbigliamento; che logora, che consuma; faticoso; *gerund* il portare, l'indossare; uso; logorìo, usura.

**wearisome** *adj.* noioso, fastidioso, tedioso, pesante; *a — task*, un compito noioso. **-ness** *n.* fatica; tedio.

**weary** *adj.* stanco, affaticato; (fig.) disgustato, annoiato, (fam.) stufo; (fam.) *a — Willie*, un fannullone, un Michelaccio; — *of life*, stanco della vita; — *of writing*, stufo di scrivere; *a — day*, una giornata noiosa; *to get* —, stancarsi, annoiarsi; *tr.* affaticare, stancare, annoiare; *intr.* affaticarsi, stancarsi, annoiarsi.

**wearying** *adj.* affaticante; noioso, fastidioso.

**weasel** *n.* (zool.) donnola.

**weather** *n.* tempo; *good* —, bel tempo; *beautiful* —, tempo bellissimo; *bad* —, brutto tempo; *rainy* —, tempo piovoso; *stormy* —, tempo burrascoso; *heavy* —, mare grosso; *settled* —, tempo stabile; *changeable* —, tempo instabile; *in such* —, col tempo che fa; *what awful —!*, che tempaccio!; *what sort of — did you have?*, che tempo hai

trovato?; — *permitting*, se il tempo lo permette; *if the — breaks*, se il tempo si guasta; (fam.) *to be under the* —, essere indisposto; *attrib.* — *expert*, esperto del tempo, meteorologo; — *report*, bollettino meteorologico; — *side*, soppravvento.

**weather** *tr.* esporre all'aria, scolorire; (fig.) superare, resistere a; *to — a storm*, uscire incolume da una tempesta, (fig.) superare una crisi; *intr.* alterarsi; (of metals) patinarsi, prendere una patina.

**weather-beaten** *adj.* rovinato dalle intemperie; abbronzato, ruvido, scabro.

**weatherboard** *n.* asse *f.* a sgrondo; asse per rivestimento esterno; (naut.) lato di sopravvento, orza; tavola di copertura, paraonda.

**weather-bound** *adj.* confinato dal cattivo tempo; (of ship) costretto a rimanere in porto. **-chart** *n.* carta meteorologica.

**weathercock** *n.* ventaruola, banderuola, girondino, segnavento; (fig.) voltagabbana *m.*, girella.

**weather-forecast** *n.* previsione del tempo, bollettino meteorologico. **-gauge** *n.* (naut.) sopravvento; *tr.* (naut.) prendere il sopravvento di. **-glass** *n.* barometro a quadrante; (bot.) *poor man's -glass*, mordigallina, primula rossa, anagallide *f.*

**weathering** *n.* effetto dell'aria; deteriorazione, sgretolamento.

**weather-proof** *adj.* che resiste alle intemperie; impermeabile; (bldg.) stagno. **-side** *n.* lato esposto al vento; (naut.) sopravvento, sopravventame *m.*, lato di sopravvento. **-station** *n.* stazione meteorologica. **-wise** *adj.* esperto del tempo, che sa prevedere il tempo. **-worn** *adj.* logorato dalle intemperie.

**weave** *n.* (text.) tessuto, tessitura; armatura; *plain* —, armatura semplice.

**weave** *tr.* tessere, fare il tessitore; *to — thread into cloth*, trasformare il filo in tessuto; (fig.) intrecciare, inserire, ordire; *to — a wreath*, intrecciare una ghirlanda; *to — a plot*, ordire un complotto; *intr.* serpeggiare, insinuarsi; *to — through the traffic*, sgusciare in mezzo al traffico.

**weaver** *n.* (text.) tessitore, tessitrice; (orn.) — *bird*, tessitore; (ent.) psiche *f.*

**weaving** *n.* (text.) tessitura; *hand* —, tessitura a mano; *power-loom* —, tessitura meccanica; — *mill*, tessitoria; (fig.) intreccio, orditura; serpeggiamento.

**web** *n.* tessuto, tela; (fig.) trama, rete *f.*; *a — of lies*, un tessuto di menzogne; *the — of life*, la trama della vita; *spider's* —, ragnatela; (orn.) membrana connettiva (of palmipeds); (of wing) barba di piuma.

**webbing** *n.* (text.) tessuto ritorto; (industr.) tela da cinghia; (zool.) membrana connettiva.

**web-footed** *adj.* (zool.) palmipede, dal piede palmato.

**wed** *tr.* sposare; unire in matrimonio; (fig.) unire, combinare; *intr.* sposarsi, unirsi in matrimonio; (of man) ammogliarsi; (of woman) maritarsi. **-ded** *adj.* sposato, unito in matrimonio; *a newly -ded couple*, una coppia di sposini; *my -ded wife*, la mia legittima sposa; coniugale; *-ded life*, la vita coniugale; (fig.) unito, combinato; attaccato, legato.

**wedding** *n.* nozze *f.pl.*; sposalizio, sponsali *m.pl.*, matrimonio; *silver* —, nozze d'argento; *golden* —, nozze d'oro; *attrib.* nuziale; *to attend a* —, assistere ad un matrimonio; — *procession*, corteo nuziale; — *dress*, abito nuziale.

**wedding-bells** *n.pl.* (not rung in Italy) campane *f.pl.* di nozze; (fig.) *to be as merry as a wedding-bell*, essere allegro e contento come una Pasqua. **-breakfast** *n.* pranzo nuziale, rinfresco nuziale. **-cake** *n.* torta nuziale. **-card** *n.* partecipazione di nozze. **-day** *n.* giorno di nozze; anniversario di nozze. **-guest** *n.* invitato alle nozze. **-march** *n.* marcia nuziale. **-present** *n.* regalo di nozze. **-ring** *n.* fede *f.* nuziale, anello matrimoniale.

**wedge** *n.* cuneo; conio, bietta, zeppa, lingotto; *to drive in a* —, mettere una bietta; *the thin edge of the* —, un primo tentativo destinato a successivo sviluppo; (aeron.) — *formation*, formazione a v.

**wedge** *tr.* incuneare, imbiettare, rincalzare con una zeppa; (fig.) conficcare, incastrare, serrare; *to — oneself into the crowd*, inserirsi tra la folla; *to — something apart*, forzare qualcosa per mezzo di un cuneo.

**wedged** *adj.* cuneiforme; *part. adj.* incastrato, serrato.

**wedlock** *n.* matrimonio; stato coniugale; (leg.) vincolo matrimoniale; *born in* —, legittimo; *out of* —, illegittimo; *holy* —, il santo matrimonio; *the bonds of* —, il vincolo matrimoniale, i legami matrimoniali.

**Wednesday** *pr.n.* mercoledì *m.*; *I'll come on* —, verrò mercoledì; *Ash* —, le Ceneri, mercoledì delle Ceneri.

**wee** *adj.* piccolino, piccino; *a — drop*, un goccio; *a — bit jealous*, un tantino geloso.

**weed** *n.* (bot.) erbaccia, malerba, gramigna; (fig., of person) magro, sparuto; (fam.) *the* —, il tabacco; *tr.* sarchiare, sradicare; (fig.) *to — out*, estirpare, eliminare. **-er** *n.* (person) sarchiatore; (tool) sarchio, sarchiello. **-ing** *n.* sarchiatura.

**weed-killer** *n.* diserbante *m.*, erbicida *m.*

**weeds** *n.* (widow's) —, gramaglie *f.pl.*, lutto vedovile, bruno di vedova.

**weedy** *adj.* coperto di erbacce, pieno di erbacce; (fig.) sparuto, magro, allampanato.

**week** *n.* settimana, otto giorni; *a — ago*, otto giorni fa; *this* —, la settimana corrente; *today* —, oggi a otto; *tomorrow* —, domani a otto, otto giorni domani; *the days of the* —, i giorni della settimana; *next* —, settimana entrante; — *in — out*, una settimana dopo l'altra; *Holy Week*, la Settimana Santa; *a — of Sundays*, sette settimane, (fam.) un'eternità; *to be paid by the* —, essere pagato a settimana.

**weekday** *n.* giorno feriale, giorno lavorativo; *on -s*, *-s only*, solo nei giorni feriali.

**week-end** *n.* vacanza di fine settimana, week-end *m.*; *a long* —, da venerdì a martedì; *I stayed over the — with friends*, ho passato il week-end presso amici; (rlwy.) — *return* (*ticket*), biglietto festivo; *intr. to — in the country*, trascorrere la fine settimana in campagna.

**weekly** *adj.* settimanale, ebdomadario; *n.* settimanale *m.*, ebdomadario; *adv.* settimanalmente, ogni otto giorni; *twice* —, due volte alla settimana.

**week-old** *adj.* (of children, animals) nato otto giorni fa, dell'età di otto giorni; (of newspaper) di otto giorni fa.

**weeny** *adj.* (fam.) piccolino, piccino.

**weep** *n.* pianto, sfogo di pianto; *to have a good* —, piangere a calde lacrime; *to have a little* —, versare qualche lacrimuccia; *intr.* piangere, versare lacrime; *to — for joy*, piangere di gioia; *that's nothing to — about*, non c'è da piangere; *I could have wept to see them*, a vederli mi veniva voglia di piangere; (of wall) trasudare; (med.) essudare; *tr. to — oneself to sleep*, addormentarsi piangendo; *to — one's heart out*, piangere fino a spezzarsi il cuore.

**weeping** *adj.* piangente; (med.) essudante; — *willow*, salice *m.* piangente; — *ash*, frassino pendulo; *n.* pianto; lacrime *f.pl.*; *a fit of* —, una crisi di lacrime; (fig.) trasudamento; (med.) essudazione.

**weepy** *adj.* (fam.) lacrimoso.

**weevil** *n.* (ent.) curculione *m.*, punteruolo; *grain* —, calandra.

**weft** *n.* (text.) trama.

**weigh** *tr.* pesare; soppesare; (fig.) calcolare, considerare, valutare; *to — the consequences*, riflettere sulle conseguenze; *to — one's words*, soppesare le proprie parole; (naut.) *to — anchor*, levare l'ancora, salpare; *intr.* pesare, aver peso; *to — heavy*, pesare molto; *it doesn't — much*, pesa poco; (fig.) *it -ed on his conscience*, gli pesò sulla coscienza; *personal interests ought not to — at all*, gli interessi personali non dovrebbero aver alcun peso; FOLLOW. BY ADV.: *to — down*, *tr.* pesare più di (qualcosa); (fig.) far piegare, piegare; opprimere; *to — down the scales*, dare il tracollo alla bilancia; *trees -ed down by fruit*, alberi piegati dal peso dei frutti; *-ed down by grief*, oppresso dal dolore; *to — in*, *intr.* (jockeys, boxers) pesarsi prima della gara; *to — in with an argument*, intervenire con un argomento; *to — out*, *intr.* misurare pesando, (of jockeys) pesarsi dopo la corsa; *to — up*, calcolare.

**weigh-beam** *n.* stadera, braccio di stadera.

**weighbridge** *n.* pesatrice a ponte, stadera a ponte, basculla.

**weighing** *gerund, n.* pesatura, pesata, pesaggio; (naut.) levata dell'ancora, partenza. **-in** *n.* (of jockeys) pesaggio prima della corsa; *-n room*, pesaggio. **-machine** *n.* pesa, pesatrice; basculla, bilancia automatica.

**weight** *n.* peso; *to sell by —*, vendere a peso; *to put on —*, aumentare di peso, ingrassare; *to lose —*, dimagrire; *to carry —*, essere handicappato; *to be worth one's — in gold*, valere tanto oro quanto si pesa; *to pull one's —*, mettercela tutta; *to throw one's — about*, darsi delle arie; *-s and measures*, pesi e misure; (comm.) *gross —*, peso lordo; *net —*, peso netto; *to give short —*, rubare sul peso; (sport) *putting the —*, lancio del peso; (chem.) *atomic —*, peso atomico; *molecular —*, peso molecolare; *specific —*, peso specifico; (fig.) peso, responsabilità, influenza, importanza; *to have great —*, avere grande peso; *a person of —*, una persona importante; *that's a great — off my mind!*, mi sono levato un bel peso!

**weight** *tr.* caricare con un peso; appesantire.

**weightiness** *n.* pesantezza; (fig.) gravità; importanza; influenza, autorità.

**weightless** *adj.* senza peso; (fig.) senza importanza. **-ness** *n.* (aeron.) perdita di gravità.

**weight-lifting** *n.* (sport) sollevamento pesi.

**weighty** *adj.* pesante, gravoso; (fig.) importante, ponderato; influente.

**weir** *n.* sbarramento, scaricatoio, chiusa a stramazzo, traversa, paratoia.

**weird** *adj.* soprannaturale, misterioso, fatidico; (fam.) bizzarro, strano; (myth.) *the — sisters*, le Parche, (in *Macbeth*) le streghe. **-ness** *n.* carattere *m.* soprannaturale; (fam.) stranezza, bizzarria.

**welcome** *adj.* benvenuto, grato, gradito, benaccetto; *— home!*, ben tornato!; *— news*, lieta notizia; *you are — to do what you like*, sei libero di fare ciò che vuoi; *you are — to my books*, i miei libri sono a tua disposizione; (USA) *you're —*, prego, non c'è di che!; *n.* buona accoglienza, benvenuto; *a warm —*, un'accoglienza cordiale; *to meet with a cold —*, essere male accolto; *to outstay one's —*, abusare dell'ospitalità altrui.

**welcome** *tr.* accogliere, dare il benvenuto a, fare buona accoglienza a; (fig.) gradire, accettare con piacere; *I — your suggestion*, gradisco la tua proposta; *discussion will be -d*, tutti sono invitati a intervenire nella discussione.

**welcoming** *adj.* accogliente; *n.* buona accoglienza, benvenuto.

**weld** *n.* (mech.) saldatura, saldamento, giuntura saldata; *tr.* saldare; *intr.* saldarsi; (fig.) fondere. **-ing** *n.* saldatura; (fig.) fusione.

**welfare** *n.* benessere *m.*; prosperità; *public —*, la salute pubblica; *child —*, puericultura; *— work*, assistenza sociale; *— worker*, assistente sociale; *— institution*, opera di assistenza, opera pia; *the Welfare State*, lo Stato assistenziale.

**welkin** *n.* cielo, volta celeste; (poet.) *to make the — ring*, far risuonare la volta celeste.

**well**[1] *adv.* bene; a fondo; *very —*, benissimo; *not very —*, non troppo bene; *they speak English —*, parlano bene l'inglese; *— done!*, bravo!; *that boy will do —*, quel ragazzo si farà strada; *to do oneself —*, viver bene, passarsela bene, godersela; *it speaks — for him that . . .*, gli fa onore che . . .; *she deserves — of you*, merita la tua gratitudine; *you are — out of it*, te ne sei cavato a buon mercato; *to get on — together*, andare d'accordo; *to be — in with*, essere pane e cacio con; *I am — on in years*, sono bene in là con gli anni; *— off*, benestante; *to be — up in*, essere ben informato di; *pretty — everything*, quasi tutto; *I will do it as — as I can*, farò del mio meglio; *as —*, anche; *you might as — say*, protresti dire ugualmente bene; *you can come this evening as — as tomorrow*, puoi venire tanto stasera che domani; *he accepted, as — he might*, ha accettato, e ci mancava altro; *oh —, —, —, such is life!*, insomma la vita è così; *— then, why worry?*, e allora! perchè preoccuparsi?; *— and good!*, alla buon'ora!, sta bene!; *to be —*, star bene (di salute); *to feel —*, sentirsi bene; *to get —*, guarire, ristabilirsi, rimettersi; (mil.) *all's —!*, tutto bene!; *that's all very — but . . .*, sta bene, ma . . .; *to let — alone*, lasciar stare; *to wish someone —*, augurar bene a qualcuno; *if he comes tonight, — and good!*, se viene stasera, tanto meglio!; (provb.) *all's — that ends —*, tutto è bene ciò che finisce bene; *n.pl. the sick and the —*, i malati e i sani.

**well**[2] *n.* pozzo; fontana, fonte *f.*; *to sink a —*, scavare un pozzo; (of staircase) vano, tromba.

**well**[2] *intr.* sgorgare; scaturire; *to — up*, zampillare, pullulare.

**well-advised** *adj.* avvisato, saggio, prudente. **-appointed** *adj.* (of hotel) ben arredato, ben equipaggiato. **-balanced** *adj.* equilibrato. **-behaved** *adj.* (ben) educato, saggio, ben costumato. **-being** *n.* benessere *m.*, prosperità; buona salute. **-beloved** *adj.* benamato, amatissimo, adorato. **-born** *adj.* di buona famiglia, bennato. **-bred** *adj.* educato, cortese, bennato; (of animals) purosangue. **-conducted** *adj.* (person) educato, saggio; ben tenuto, ben condotto, ben organizzato. **-connected** *adj.* di buona famiglia, di buon parentado; che ha buone relazioni sociali. **-earned** *adj.* meritato. **-educated** *adj.* colto, istruito, di buona coltura. **-found** *adj.* (of ship) ben provvisto, ben equipaggiato. **-founded** *adj.* ben fondato, attendibile; *-founded fears*, timori legittimi. **-grounded** *adj.* competente; ben preparato.

**well-head** *n.* (of river) sorgente *f.*; (fig.) *the — of knowledge*, la fonte della sapienza; vera da pozzo.

**well-informed** *adj.* ben informato, istruito; (journ.) *a — source*, una fonte ben informata; *to keep oneself —*, tenersi al corrente.

**welling** *adj.* sgorgante, zampillante; *n.* sgorgamento, zampillio.

**wellingtons** *n.pl.* soprascarpe di gomma a gambale.

**well-knit** *adj.* robusto, solido, compatto; (fig.) ben congegnato. **-known** *adj.* rinomato, noto. **-mannered** *adj.* gentile, cortese, educato. **-marked** *adj.* evidente, ben segnato, chiaramente indicato; (fig.) pronunciato, fortemente accusato. **-meaning** *adj.* ben intenzionato, benevolo, animato da buoni sentimenti.

**well-meant** *adj.* detto, fatto a

fin di bene. **-nigh** *adv.* quasi, pressappoco. **-off** *adj.* agiato, benestante, discretamente ricco; (fig.) fortunato. **-oiled** *adj.* ben lubrificato; (fig.) mellifluo; (slang) brillo, alticcio, sbronzo. **-preserved** *adj.* (of person) ben portante; (of thing) ben conservato. **-read** *adj.* colto, istruito, versato (in). **-rounded** *adj.* ben finito; ben tornito.

**Wellsian** *adj.* di H. G. Wells, alla maniera di H. G. Wells.

**well-spoken** *adj.* che parla bene, raffinato nel parlare, facondo; che parla correttamente, che parla senza accento popolare.

**well-spring** *n.* (poet.) fonte *f.* perenne.

**well-timbered** *adj.* ben costruito; (of country) alberato boscoso, boschereccio. **-timed** *adj.* tempestivo, opportuno. **-to-do** *adj.* agiato, benestante, abbiente; *n.pl. the -to-do*, le classi benestanti. **-tried** *adj.* provato, sperimentato con successo, attendibile.

**well-water** *n.* acqua di pozzo.

**well-wisher** *n.* amico, persona che vuol bene; sostenitore. **-worn** *adj.* logorato, consunto; (fig.) banale, trito.

**Welsh**[1] *adj.* gallese, del Galles; *the* —, i Gallesi; (cul.) — *rabbit*, — *rarebit*, tosto con formaggio fuso; *n.* il gallese, la lingua gallese.

**welsh**[2] *tr.*, *intr.* andarsene senza pagare i debiti, squagliarsi; (pop.) bruciare il paglione. **-er** *n.* allibratore che scappa senza pagare le vincite; truffatore. **-ing** *n.* truffa commessa ai danni dei vincitori di scommesse.

**Welsh-man** *n.* Gallese *m.* **-woman** *n.* Gallese *f.*

**welt** *n.* (shoem.) guardone *m.*, tramezza; rinforzo; (mech.) coprigiunto; (fig.) colpo violento, sferzata; lividore, striscia causata da un colpo.

**welt** *tr.* (shoem.) mettere il guardone, mettere la tramezza; (mech.) mettere il coprigiunto; (fig.) colpire violentemente, staffilare.

**welter** *n.* confusione; disordine *m.*; tumulto; (fig.) sballottamento; fuga disordinata; *a — of words*, una babele di parole; *intr.* avvoltolarsi; guazzare.

**wen** *n.* (med.) cisti *f.* sebacea, natta, porro; (fam.) gozzo.

**Wenceslaus** *pr.n.* Venceslao.

**wench** *n.* popolana; *a strapping* —, una ragazza gagliarda, un pezzo di figliuola; *serving* —, servetta; *intr.* (fam.) correre dietro le donne. **-er** *n.* (fam.) donnaiuolo, dongiovanni.

**wend** *intr.*, *tr.* proseguire (il cammino), dirigersi lentamente; *to — one's way home*, tornare lentamente a casa.

**went** *p.def.* of **go**, *q.v.*

**wept** *p.def.*, *part.* of **weep**, *q.v.*

**were** *p.def.* of **be**, *q.v.*

**werewolf** *n.* licantropo, lupo mannaro.

**west** *adj.* occidentale, a ovest, dell'ovest, di ponente; *the — wind*, il vento dell'ovest, il vento di ponente; *the — coast*, la costa occidentale; — *aspect*, esposto all'ovest; *West Germany*, la Germania Occidentale; *West Country*, il sud-ovest dell'Inghilterra (le contee di Cornovaglia, Devon, Somerset e Dorset); *West Indian*, delle Indie Occidentali, delle Antille, caraibico; *West Indies*, le Indie Occidentali, le Antille, le isole del mar caraibico; *adv.* verso ovest, a occidente, a ponente; *to travel* —, viaggiare verso l'ovest; *to go* —, andare all'ovest, (fig.) morire, (fam.) crepare; *gone* —, via.

**west** *n.* ovest *m.*, occidente, ponente *m.*; (fig., poet.) tramonto; *the West*, l'Occidente; *the Middle West* (*USA*), regione *f.* tra gli Allegani e le Montagne Rocciose; *the Far West* (*USA*), regione a ovest delle Montagne Rocciose; *houses facing* —, case esposte a ponente; *to the* —, verso ovest; *to the — of*, a ponente di.

**west-bound** *adj.* diretto all'ovest.

**westering** *adj.* che muove verso ovest; (fig.) che volge al tramonto.

**westerly** *adj.* verso ovest; dall'ovest; *the most — point*, il punto più a ovest; — *current*, corrente *f.* che si dirige verso ovest; — *wind*, vento dall'ovest, vento di ponente.

**western** *adj.* occidentale, dell'ovest; (hist.) *the Western Empire*, l'Impero Romano d'Occidente; *the Western Church*, la Chiesa Romana; *the Western Powers*, le potenze occidentali; *the Western States*, gli stati occidentali (dell'USA); (geog.) *the Western Isles*, le Isole Ebridee; *n.* occidentale; abitante *m.*, *f.* dell'occidente; (eccl.) membro della Chiesa Romana; (cinem.) western *m.*, film western. **-er** *n.* occidentale, abitante *m.*, *f.* dell'occidente. **-ize** *tr.* occidentalizzare, apportare la civiltà occidentale a.

**westernmost** *adj.* il più occidentale, all'estremo occidente.

**west-north-west** *n.* ovest-nord-ovest *m.*; *adv.* (verso) ovest-nord-ovest. **-north-westerly** *adj.* (vento) che soffia dal l'ovest-nord-ovest. **-south-west** *n.* ovest-sud-ovest *m.*; *adv.* (verso) ovest-sud-ovest. **-south-westerly** *adj.* (vento) che soffia dall'ovest-sud-ovest.

**Westphalia** *pr.n.* (geog.) Vestfalia.

**westward** *n.*, *adj.* volto a occidente, occidentale; *adv.* see **westwards.**

**westwards** *adv.* verso l'ovest, all'ovest, a ponente.

**wet** *adj.* bagnato, umido, fradicio, zuppo; *to get* —, bagnarsi; *her eyes were* —, aveva gli occhi umidi; — *as a drowned rat*, bagnato come un pulcino; — *through*, bagnato fradicio; *soaking* —, bagnato fino all'osso; *wringing* —, bagnato da torcere; piovoso, umido; *a — day*, una giornata di pioggia; — *weather*, tempo piovoso, tempo umido; *it's going to be* —, sta per piovere; *it is turning* —, il tempo si guasta; fresco, non ancora asciutto; — *paint*, vernice fresca; (fam.) — *dream*, emissione notturna; (fig., pop.) molle; — *blanket*, guastafeste *m.*; — *nurse*, balia; *n.* umidità; pioggia, tempo piovoso; *tr.* bagnare, inumidire, inzuppare; *to — the bed*, bagnare il letto; *to — one's whistle*, bagnarsi l'ugola.

**wether** *n.* castrato, montone castrato; *bell-wether*, montone che guida il gregge, (fig.) capobanda *m.*, caporione *m.*

**wetness** *n.* umidità.

**wetting** *adj.* inumidente, che inumidisce; *n.* bagnatura; *to get a* —, bagnarsi; (med.) *bed-wetting*, enuresi *f.*

**whack** *n.* percossa, bussa, bastonata; (fam.) *to have a — at something*, tentare una impresa difficile, dare l'assalto a qualcosa; (fam.) parte *f.*, porzione, fetta; *excl.* —*!*, to'!, pum!, pam!; *tr.* percuotere, battere, bastonare, picchiare; sculacciare; (sport) battere, sconfiggere. **-ing** *adj.* (fam.) enorme, colossale; *a -ing lie*, una colossale bugia; *n.* bastonata, legnata, bastonatura; sculacciata; (sport) sconfitta, batosta.

**whale** *n.* (zool.) balena *blue* —, balenottera; *sperm* —, capodoglio; *a school of -s*, un banco di balene; (astron.) *the Whale*, la Balena; (geog.) *Bay of Whales*, Baia delle Balene; (slang) *to have a — of a time*, godersela.

**whalebone** *n.* (zool.) fanone *m.*; (dressm.) stecca di balena.

**whale-fishing** *n.* caccia alla balena.

**whaler** *n.* (man) baleniere; (craft) baleniera.

**whaling** *n.* caccia alla balena; — *ship*, baleniera.

**whaling-ground** *n.* zona frequentata dalle balene. **-gun** *n.* fucile-arpione *m.* **-master** *n.* capitano di una baleniera.

**whang** *n.* (fam.) rimbombo; *tr.* (fam.) bastonare, picchiare; *intr.* rimbombare.

**wharf** *n.* (naut.) pontile *m.*, banchina, calata, scalo; (techn.) spalto. **-age** *n.* diritto di banchina; scarico a banchina; le banchine, le calate. **-inger** *n.* proprietario di una banchina; guardiano di banchina.

**what** *rel. adj.*, *m.* quel(lo) che, *f.*, quella che; *m.pl.* quelli che, *f.pl.*, quelle che; *he has spent — little money he had*, ha speso quel poco denaro che aveva; *— few friends he had were away*, quelli pochi amici che aveva erano assenti; *wear — shoes you like*, metti le scarpe che vuoi; *interr. adj.* quale, che; *— books do you want?*, quali libri vuoi?; *— prices do you charge?*, che prezzi fate?; *— time is it?*, che ora è?, che ore sono?; *— train do you want to catch?*, con quale treno vuoi partire?; *— use is it?*, a che serve?, a che pro?; *excl. — a pity!*, che peccato!; *— fun!*, che spasso!; *— an idea!*, che idea!; *— a shame!*, che vergogna!; *rel. prn.* ciò che, quel che, la cosa che; *— he thinks doesn't matter*, ciò che pensa non importa; *say — you will*, di' quel che ti pare; *— we need is a new government*, quello che ci occorre è un nuovo governo; *not but — . . .*, non già che . . .; *interr. prn.* che, che cosa; *— can I do for you?*, in che cosa posso esserLe utile?; *-'s happened?*, che cosa è successo?; *-'s the matter with you?*, che cosa hai?; *— does it matter if . . .?*, che importa se . . .?; *— else?*, che altro?; *— then?*, e allora?; *— for?*, perchè?, a che scopo?; *-'s it for?*, a che cosa serve?; *— if it isn't true?*, ebbene, e se non fosse vero?; *— is he?*, che cosa fa?, che mestiere fa?; *— is he like?*, che tipo è?; *— about a game of bridge?*, che cosa ne dici di una partita di bridge?; *he knows -'s —*, la sa lunga; *— if he doesn't come?*, e se non viene?; *I'll tell you —*, ti dirò io che cosa fare; (slang) *so —?*, chi se ne infischia?, (vulg.) chi se ne frega?; *excl. — I have suffered!*, quanto ho sofferto!; —, *here already!*, come (*or* ma come), già qui!

**what-d'ye-call-it (-him, -her, 'em)** *prn. phrase*, (fam.) quel-l'affare, quella cosa, come si chiama; *pass me the —*, dammi quell'affare lì; *that Mr. what-d'ye-call-him*, quel signore, come si chiama.

**whatever** (poet. **whate'er**) *rel. prn.* qualunque cosa, qualsiasi cosa, quello che; *— happens*, qualunque cosa accada; *— it may be*, qualunque cosa sia; *— he does he will certainly be wrong*, qualsiasi cosa faccia avrà certamente torto; *do — you like*, fa' quel che vuoi; *adj.* qualunque, qualsiasi; *— crime he may have committed . . .*, qualunque reato abbia commesso . . .; *at — price*, a qualsiasi prezzo; *none —*, neppure uno, nessuno; *nothing —*, proprio niente; *I have no intention — of doing it*, non ho nessuna intenzione di farlo.

**what-ho!** *excl.* diamine!, ma guarda!, guarda un po'!; (as greeting) *— James!*, ciao Giacomo!

**what-not** *n.* nonnulla *m.*, bagattella; scaffaletto, scansia.

**what's-his-name** see **what-d'ye-call-it** *etc.*

**whatsoever** (poet. **whatsoe'er**) *prn.*, *adj.* see **whatever**.

**wheat** *n.* grano, frumento; *the — crop*, la raccolta del grano. **-ear** *n.* spiga di grano; (orn.) culbianco. **-en** *adj.* di grano, fatto con frumento. **-meal** *n.* farina di frumento. **-sheaf** *n.* covone *m.* di grano.

**wheedl-e** *tr.* adulare, lusingare, persuadere, blandire, ingannare con lusinghe; *to — money out of*, farsi dare del denaro da, spillare denaro da. **-ing** *adj.* lusinghiero, mellifluo, allettante; *n.* lusinga, adulazione, blandizia. **-er** *n.* adulatore; lusingatore.

**wheel** *n.* ruota, rotella; *front —*, ruota anteriore; *back —*, ruota posteriore; *spare —*, ruota di ricambio; *driving —*, ruota motrice; *cog —*, ruota dentata; *gear —*, ruota d'ingranaggio; *paddle —*, ruota a palette; *potter's —*, tornio da vasaio; *spinning —*, rocchetto, filatoio; *water —*, ruota idraulica; *to put one's shoulder to the —*, darci dentro, mettersi sotto; *the -s of a watch*, il meccanismo di un orologio, il roteggio; *Catherine —*, girandola; (of ship) timone *m.*, ruota di governo, barra del timone, (of car) volante *m.*; *don't speak to the man at the —*, non parlare al guidatore; (fig.) rotazione, movimento circolare; (mil.) *left —*, conversione a sinistra; *right —!*, per fila destr!; *left —!*, per fila sinistr!

**wheel** *tr.* far ruotare; spingere un veicolo a ruote; *to — a bicycle*, spingere a mano una bicicletta; *intr.* ruotare, girare, roteare, svolazzare; *to — about*, fare voltafaccia; (mil.) fare una conversione.

**wheelbarrow** *n.* carriuola, carriola, carretta.

**wheel-base** *n.* distanza tra gli assi. **-chair** *n.* sedia a rotelle per invalidi. **-clearance** *n.* distanza tra le ruote, scartamento. **-drag** *n.* martinicca.

**wheeled** *adj.* con ruota, a ruote; rotato.

**wheel-house** *n.* (naut.) timoniera.

**wheeling** *adj.* rotativo, roteante, rotatorio; *n.* rotazione, roteamento; (mil.) conversione.

**wheel-spin** *n.* (motor.) spostamento delle ruote. **-track** *n.* impronta delle ruote, solco; rotaia, carreggiata.

**wheelwright** *n.* carraio, carradore.

**wheez-e** *n.* respiro affannoso, sibilo; (fam.) trucco; *a good —*, una buon'idea; *intr.* ansare, ansimare, parlare affannosamente; *to — out*, emettere affannosamente. **-iness** *n.* respiro affannoso, ansamento. **-y** *adj.* affannoso, ansante, ansimante.

**whelk** *n.* (zool.) buccino, bollicina.

**whelp** *n.* cucciolo; lupacchiotto; (fig.) giovanotto maleducato, ragazzaccio; *intr.* (of a bitch) figliare.

**when** *adv.*, *interr.* quando?; *— is he coming?*, quando viene?; *till —?*, fino a quando?; *since —?*, da quando?, da quanto tempo?; *conj.* quando, allorchè, nel momento in cui, mentre, appena; *— I was young*, quando ero giovane; *— I entered the room*, nel momento in cui entrai nella stanza; *call me — you are ready*, chiamami appena sei pronto; *just — we were going out*, proprio mentre stavamo uscendo; in cui, nel quale; *the day — I first met you*, il giorno in cui ti incontrai per la prima volta; sebbene; *why does he walk — he's got a car?*, perchè va a piedi sebbene abbia una macchina?; se, qualora; *what is the good of my talking — you won't listen?*, è inutile ch'io parli se non vuoi ascoltarmi; *— translating, you need a dictionary*, qualora traduca, ti occorre un vocabolario; *come tomorrow, — I shall tell you everything*, vieni domani e ti dirò tutto; *since — I haven't seen him*, da allora non l'ho più visto; *— all's said and done*, alla fine dei conti, insomma; *n. tell me the — and the how of it*, dimmi quando e come è successo.

**whence** *adv.*, *interr.* donde?, da dove?, da che cosa?; *— are we and why are we?*, donde veniamo e perchè siamo?; *conj.* donde, da dove, da che cosa, da cui; *he asked me — I came*, mi chiese da dove venivo; *rel.* da dove, da cui; *the source — these evils spring*, la fonte da cui provengono questi mali; *— it is clear that . . .*, da cui risulta che . . . .

**whenever** (poet. **whene'er**) *adv.* ogni volta che, tutte le volte che, a qualsiasi ora (che), quando; *— I think of you*, ogni volta che penso a te; *come — you like*, vieni a qualsiasi ora, vieni quando ti piace.

**where** *adv.*, *interr.* dove?; (poet.)

ove?; da che parte?; — *are you?*, dove sei?; — *did we leave off?*, dove siamo rimasti?; *from* —, di dove; — *are the snows of yesteryear?*, ove sono le nevi dell'altr'anno?; *rel.* dove, (nel luogo) in cui, ove, da che parte; *we shall stay — we are*, rimarremo dove siamo; *go — you like*, va dove ti piace; *we ran to — the car was waiting*, accorremmo nel luogo in cui la macchina aspettava; *the hotel — I stayed*, l'albergo in cui alloggiai; *I don't know — he lives*, non so da che parte abita; *the house — I was born*, la casa ove nacqui; *n.* il luogo; *the — and the when of his birth are unknown*, il luogo e la data della sua nascita sono sconosciuti.

**whereabouts** *adv.*, *interr.* dove (all'incirca)?, da che parte?; — *do you live?*, da che parte abiti?; *rel.* dove, da che parte, in che posto; *n.* luogo, locazione; *his present — are unknown*, non si sa dove si trovi attualmente.

**whereafter** *rel. adv.* dopo di cui, in seguito a cui.

**whereas** *conj.* poichè, siccome, quando invece, dal momento che, dato che; — *it has seemed good* . . ., poichè è sembrato opportuno . . .; mentre, laddove; *he is always ill, — she is the picture of health*, lui è sempre ammalato, mentre lei è il ritratto della salute.

**whereby** *adv.*, *rel.* onde, per lo che.

**wherefore** *adv.*, *interr.* (poet.) perchè?; — *do you weep?*, perchè piangi?; *rel.* perciò, quindi; *he was angry, — he forgot it*; era in collera, perciò lo dimenticò; cf. **therefore**; *n. the whys and the -s*, i perchè ed i percome.

**wherein** *adv.*, *interr.* in che cosa?; — *have I offended you?*, in che cosa ti ho offeso?; *rel.* in cui, nel quale, in che; dove; *the month — it took place*, il mese in cui avvenne.

**whereof** *adv.*, *interr.* (poet.) di che?, di che cosa?; *rel.* di che, da che, di cui, di che cosa; *materials — clothes are made*, stoffe di cui sono fatti i vestiti.

**whereon** *adv.*, *interr.* su che?, su che cosa?; *rel.* su cui; *the ground — the house was built*, il terreno su cui la casa fu costruita; cf. **whereupon.**

**wheresoever** (poet. **wheresoe'er**) see **wherever**.

**whereupon** *adv.*, *rel.* dopo di che, su che; — *he left the house*, dopo di che uscì dalla casa.

**wherever** *adv.*, *interr.* (fam., emphatic) dove mai?; — *did I leave my pencil?*, dove mai è andata a finire la mia matita?; *rel.* dovunque, ovunque, in qualunque luogo, dove; — *I go I feel at home*, dovunque vado mi sento come a casa mia; *sit — you like*, siediti dove vuoi.

**wherewith** *adv.*, *interr.* (poet.) con che?, con che cosa?; — *shall they be fed?*, con che cosa si devono nutrire?; *rel.* con cui; *we have nothing — to feed them*, non abbiamo nulla con cui sfamarli.

**wherewithal** *n.* il necessario, i mezzi, il denaro; *I hadn't the — to pay the bill*, non avevo la somma necessaria per saldare il conto.

**wherry** *n.* barca leggera da passeggeri; barca-traghetto, battello, barchino.

**whet** *tr.* affilare, arrotare, appuntare, ripassare; (fig.) stimolare, eccitare, aguzzare; *to — the appetite*, stimolare l'appetito.

**whether** *conj.* se, secondo che; *he asked me — it was true*, mi chiese se fosse vero; *it depends on — he comes*, secondo che venga o no; *I want to know — you have told the truth or — you are lying*, voglio sapere se hai detto la verità o se dici delle bugie; — *today or tomorrow it is bound to happen*, o oggi o domani accadrà; — *he is guilty or not*, sia egli colpevole o no; — *or not*, in ogni caso; — *it rains or snows*, che piova o nevichi.

**whetstone** *n.* cote *f.*, mola; pietra per affilare a umido.

**whetting** *n.* affilatura, affilamento; (fig.) stimolazione.

**whew** *excl.* uffa!

**whey** *n.* siero di latte, acqua di latte. **-faced** *adj.* pallido; (fig., fam.) pusillanime, vigliacco.

**which** *adj.*, *interr.* quale, *pl.* quali; — *colour do you prefer?*, quale colore preferisci?; — *one?*, quale?; — *way?*, da che parte?; *rel.* il quale, la quale, *pl.* i quali, le quali; *for — reason*, per la quale ragione; *look at it — way you will*, da qualunque punto di vista; *interr.*, *prn.* (person) chi?; (thing) quale?, quali?; — *of you is coming?*, chi di voi viene?; — *do you prefer, tea or coffee?*, quale preferisci, tè o caffè?; — *is —?*, qual'è l'uno e qual'è l'altro?; *rel. prn.* che, il che, il quale, la quale cosa, cui; *he gave me a present, — was nice of him*, mi ha fatto un regalo, il che era molto gentile; *he drinks too much, — is bad for his health*, beve troppo la quale cosa nuoce alla sua salute; (fam.) *the house — we live in*, la casa nella quale abitiamo; *I don't mind* —, non mi importa quale.

**whichever** *rel. adj.* qualunque, qualsiasi; — *way you turn*, da qualunque parte ti volti; *take — book you like*, prendi qualsiasi libro ti piaccia; *rel. prn.* (person) chiunque; (thing) qualunque cosa; — *of them comes will be welcome*, chiunque di loro venga sarà il benvenuto; — *you choose, it doesn't matter*, qualunque cosa scegliate, non importa.

**whiff** *n.* soffio, alito, sbuffo, boccata; (of bad smell) zaffata; *to go out for a — of fresh air*, andare a prendere una boccata d'aria; (hist.) *a — of grapeshot*, una raffica di mitraglia; *intr.* soffiare, emettere sbuffi di fumo. **-y** *adj.* (fam.) puzzolente, di odore sgradevole.

**Whig** *n.* (pol. hist.) liberale *m.* (di vecchia stampa); *the — party*, il partito liberale.

**while** *conj.* mentre, allorchè; sinchè, finchè; — *I was in Italy*, mentre ero in Italia, durante il mio soggiorno in Italia; — *there's life there's hope*, finchè c'è vita c'è speranza; sebbene, seppure, quantunque, nel mentre; — *I admit that it is true* . . ., pure ammettendo che sia vero . . .; mentre; *one of them wore white, — the other was in black*, l'una vestiva di bianco, mentre l'altra vestiva di nero.

**while** *n.* momento, spazio di tempo; *a long — ago*, molto tempo fa; *all the* —, (per) tutto il tempo; *once in a* —, una volta ogni tanto; *to be worth* —, valere la pena; *I shall make it worth your* —, ti ricompenserò per il disturbo; *the* —, (nel) mentre.

**while** *tr.* far passare (il tempo) piacevolmente; *to — away the time*, ingannare il tempo.

**whilst** *conj.* see **while.**

**whim** *n.* capriccio; ghiribizzo; fantasia; *a passing* —, un capriccio fugace.

**whimper** *n.* piagnisteo, piagnucolìo; (of dog) uggiolìo; *intr.* piagnucolare, gemere, pigolare, vagire; (fig.) lagnarsi; (of dog) uggiolare. **-er** *n.* piagnone, piagnucolone, pigolone *m.* **-ing** *adj.* piagnucoloso, piagnoloso; lagnoso, lamentoso; *n.* see **whimper.**

**whimsical** *adj.* fantastico, fantasioso, capriccioso; eccentrico, bizzarro. **-ity** *n.* fantasticheria, stravaganza, capriccio, bizzarria. **-ness** *n.* carattere fantastico; bizzarria, eccentricità.

**whin** *n.* (bot.) ginestra spinosa, ginestrone *m.*

**whin-e** *n.* piagnucolìo; (of dog) uggiolìo; (of missiles) fischio, ronzìo; *intr.* piagnucolare, lamentarsi, gemere; *you've nothing to — about*, non hai nulla di cui lamentarti; (of dog) uggiolare; fischiare, ronzare. **-ing** *adj.* piagnucoloso, lamentoso; *n.* piagnucolìo, piagnisteo; (of dog) uggiolìo; fischio, ronzìo.

**whinny** *n.* nitrito; *intr.* (of horse) nitrire.

**whip** *n.* frusta, scudiscio, staffile *m.*, sferza, flagello; (hunt.)

bracchiere; (Parliament) deputato che mantiene la disciplina nel suo partito; (biglietto di) convocazione (ad intervenire a una seduta); sbattimento, colpo di frusta, frustata.

**whip** *tr.* frustare, battere, fustigare; (fig.) criticare aspramente, fustigare; (cul.) sbattere, montare, frullare; *to — eggs*, sbattere le uova; *-ped cream*, panna montata; (sport) vincere, sconfiggere; (needlew.) cucire a sopraggitto; (naut.) issare; (fig.) avvolgere strettamente; tirare fuori bruscamente; *intr.* (fig.) precipitarsi, buttarsi, slanciarsi; (mech.) oscillare, spostarsi, scattare come una frusta, schioccare; FOLLOW. BY ADV.: *to — away*, *tr.* cacciare a colpi di frusta, (fig.) portar via bruscamente, *intr.* partire improvvisamente, squagliarsi; *to — back*, *intr.* scattare indietro come una frusta, schioccare, (motor., of steering-wheel) reagire; *to — in*, *tr.* (hunt.) riunire i cani, rimenare i cani, *intr.* entrare bruscamente, (hunt.) fare il bracchiere; *to — off*, *tr.* togliere bruscamente, (hunt.) scacciare (i cani) a frustate, *intr.* andarsene di punto in bianco, squagliarsi; *to — on*, *tr.* costringere a proseguire con la frusta, (clothes) indossare in fretta; *to — out*, *tr.* tirar fuori, estrarre, (of a sword) sguainare; (fig.) *he -ped out an oath*, cacciò fuori una bestemmia; *intr.* uscire bruscamente; *to — round*, *intr.* girarsi bruscamente; *to — up*, *tr.* frustare, toccare con la frusta; *to — up one's friends*, radunare i propri amici.

**whipcord** *n.* corda per fruste; (text.) saia a righe marcate, whipcord *m.*

**whip-hand** *n.* mano che tiene la frusta; (fig.) vantaggio; *to have the — of*, essere in posizione di vantaggio su.

**whiplash** *n.* parte *f.* flessibile della frusta; frustino, sferza, sferzino; (fig.) *a tongue like a —*, una lingua sferzante.

**whipper** *n.* frustatore, sferzatore, flagellatore.

**whipper-in** *n.* (hunt.) bracchiere.

**whipper-snapper** *n.* bellimbusto, vanerello, giovanotto prepotente.

**whippet** *n.* piccolo levriero, cane da corsa.

**whipping** *n.* frustata, scudisciata, fustigazione; (leg.) pena della flagellazione; (cul.) il frullare; (sport) sconfitta, batosta; (mech.) scatto, oscillazione; (needlew.) sopraggitto; (naut.) ghia.

**whipping-top** *n.* trottola.

**whip-poor-will** *n.* (orn.) caprimulgo della Virginia.

**whippy** *adj.* flessibile.

**whip-round** *n.* (fam.) colletta. **-stitch** *n.* (needlw.) sopraggitto, punto a sopraggitto.

**whirl** *n.* giro rapido; turbine *m.*; ridda, vortice *m.*, mulinello; (fig.) dinamismo; confusione, smarrimento; *my head is in a —*, mi gira la testa; *intr.* girare rapidamente, roteare, turbinare; volteggiare, piroettare; *tr.* far girare, far roteare, far turbinare; trascinare via rapidamente.

**whirligig** *n.* carosello, giostra; girella; (fig.) l'avvicendarsi degli avvenimenti.

**whirling** *adj.* turbinante, vorticoso, volteggiante; girante, roteante, rotatorio; *n.* turbinio, volteggiamento, rotazione, roteazione.

**whirlpool** *n.* vortice *m.*; gorgo; mulinello.

**whirlwind** *n.* turbine *m.*, vortice *m.* di vento, tromba d'aria, tifone *m.*; (provb.) *sow the wind and reap the —*, chi semina vento raccoglie tempesta.

**whir(r)** *n.* ronzìo *m.*; frullìo, frullo *m.*; rombo; fischio; *intr.* ronzare; frullare; rombare; girare a grande velocità.

**whisk** *n.* spolveraccio, piumino per la polvere, scopino; cacciamosche *m.*; (cul.) frusta, frullino; (fig.) movimento rapido; *with a — of the tail*, con uno scodinzollo; *in a —*, in un lampo, in un baleno.

**whisk** *tr.* spolverare, spazzolare; (cul.) sbattere; (fig.) agitare; *intr.* guizzare via, muoversi bruscamente; *to — away*, sparire a tutta velocità; *to — past*, passare come una freccia.

**whiskered** *adj.* baffuto, fornito di basette.

**whiskers** *n.pl.* (of a man) fedine *f.pl.*, basette *f.pl.*, favoriti *m.pl.*; (moustache) baffi *m.pl.*; (of animals) vibrisse *f.pl.*; (of cat) baffi.

**whiskey** *n.* whisky *m.* (irlandese) cf. **whisky**.

**whisky** *n.* whisky *m.* (scozzese); *— and soda*, whisky con seltz.

**whisper** *n.* bisbiglio, sussurro, mormorìo; *in a —*, sottovoce, a bassa voce; *stage —*, a parte; (fig.) diceria, eco, insinuazione.

**whisper** *intr.* bisbigliare, sussurrare, parlare a bassa voce, mormorare; (of leaves) stormire; (fig.) riferire una diceria, dir male; *it is -ed that . . .*, corre voce che . . ., si dice che . . . **-er** *n.* bisbigliatore, sussurratore. **-ing** *adj.* che bisbiglia, che parla sottovoce; *n.* (of water) sussurrìo, mormorìo, stormire; (fig.) maldicenza.

**whispering-dome** *n.* volta acustica. **-gallery** *n.* galleria acustica.

**whist** *n.* (cards) whist *m.*; *dummy —*, whist a tre, whist col morto. **-drive** *n.* torneo di whist.

**whistle** *n.* fischio, sibilo; (instrument) fischietto, zufolo; *to blow a —*, dare un colpo di fischietto; (fam.) *to wet one's —*, bagnarsi l'ugola, bagnarsi il becco.

**whistle** *intr.* fischiare, fischiettare, zufolare; chiamare con un fischio; *to — between one's teeth*, fischierellare; *to — for*, chiamare con un fischio; (fig.) *you may — for your money*, aspetta pure il tuo denaro; (of wind) muggire, mugghiare; *tr.* fischiare, chiamare con un fischio; *to — a dog back*, richiamare un cane con un fischio; *to — a tune*, fischiare un'aria.

**whistler** *n.* (person) fischiatore; (horse) cavallo bolso; (bird) uccello canoro; (zool.) marmotta canadese.

**whistling** *adj.* fischiante, sibilante; *n.* fischiata, fischiettìo, fischiamento.

**Whit**[1] *adj.* di Pentecoste; *— Sunday*, domenica di Pentecoste; *— Monday*, lunedì di Pentecoste; *— week*, la settimana di Pentecoste.

**whit**[2] *n.* particella, iota *m.*, ette *m.*, mica; *every —*, sotto ogni aspetto; *not a —*, niente affatto.

**white** *adj.* bianco; candido; chiaro; incolore; (fig.) pallido; puro, innocente; *— bread*, pane bianco; *— coffee*, cappuccino, caffelatte *m.*, caffè macchiato; *— friar*, carmelitano; *— frost*, brina; *— glass*, vetro incolore; *— hair*, canizie *f.*, capelli bianchi; *— heat*, calore bianco, incandescenza; *— horses*, (waves) cavalloni *m.pl.*; *— lie*, bugia pietosa; *— magic*, magia bianca; *— man*, uomo bianco; *— paper*, carta bianca, (admin.) libro bianco, relazione governativa; *— sale*, vendita di biancheria; *— slave traffic*, tratta delle bianche; *— wine*, vino bianco; *the — races*, le razze bianche, i bianchi; *the White House*, la Casa Bianca; *the White Sea*, il Mar Bianco; *to go —*, diventare bianco, imbiancare, imbianchire; mettere i capelli bianchi; *— as a sheet*, bianco come un lenzuolo; *as — as snow*, bianco come la neve; *— with terror*, pallido per il terrore; (industr.) *— alloy*, metallo antifrizione; *— iron*, ghisa bianca; *n.* bianco; *to be dressed in —*, essere vestito di bianco; (chem.) albume *m.*; *— of egg*, chiara d'uovo; (anat.) cornea; *to turn up the -s of one's eyes*, mostrare il bianco degli occhi; *tr.* imbiancare; (fig.) *-d sepulchre*, sepolcro imbiancato, ipocrita *m.*

**whitebait** *n.* (cul.) bianchetti *m.pl.*, pesciolini *m.pl.*

**white-collar** *adj.* *— workers*, la

categoria degli impiegati, (fam.) le mezze maniche. **-faced** *adj.* dal volto pallido; (of animal) dal muso bianco. **-haired** *adj.* dai capelli bianchi, canuto. **-headed** *adj.* (of person) dai capelli bianchi; (of animal) dalla testa bianca; (fam.) *-headed boy*, beniamino, figlio di papà. **-hot** *adj.* a calore bianco, incandescente.

**whiten** *tr.* imbiancare, sbiancare; (fig.) discolpare, far apparire senza colpa; intonacare; *intr.* impallidire, sbiancarsi. **-ing** *n.* imbiancamento, candeggiamento; (of hair) imbianchimento; (of sky at dawn) albescenza.

**white-horn** *n.* (bot.) biancospino, uva spina bianca. **-throat** *n.* (orn.) silvia comune, capinera grigia.

**whiteness** *n.* bianchezza, biancore *m.*, candore *m.*, pallore *m.*; (of hair) canizie *f.*; (fig.) purezza, innocenza.

**whitewash** *n* calce *f.* per imbiancare, intonaco; (fig.) riabilitazione; apologia; *tr.* imbiancare, intonacare; (fig.) scolpare, riabilitare; nascondere i difetti di. **-ing** *n.* imbiancatura, intonacatura; (fig.) riabilitazione, apologia.

**whither** *adv.*, *interr.* (poet.) dove?, verso che parte?; *rel.* dove, ove. **-soever** *adv.* (poet.) in qualunque luogo, ovunque, dovunque.

**whiting** *n.* (ichth.) merlango, merlano.

**whitish** *adj.* biancastro, bianchiccio.

**whitlow** *n.* (med.) patereccio, paronichia, panariccio.

**Whitsun(tide)** *n.* settimana della Pentecoste.

**whittl-e** *tr.* tagliuzzare, aguzzare; (fig.) *to — down, to — away,* ridurre tagliuzzando, attenuare, assottigliare, ridurre rosicchiando, sgrossare. **-ing** *n. — down,* riduzione, rosicchiamento, tagliuzzamento.

**whizz** *intr.* ronzare; sibilare; (mech.) asciugare con una macchina centrifuga; (slang) muoversi rapidamente.

**who** *prn.* (of persons), *interr.* chi?; *-'s that?*, chi è; *— does he think he is?*, cosa si crede di essere?; *— knows?*, chissà?; (mil.) *— goes there?*, chi vive?, chi va là?; *— is your friend?*, come si chiama quel tuo amico?; *Who's Who?*, annuario delle personalità; (corresponding Italian publication) Chi è?; *rel.* che, il quale, la quale, i quali, le quali; *he —*, colui che; *she —*, colei che; *they —*, coloro che; (without antecedent) chi; *it is I — have done it*, sono io che l'ho fatto; *a writer —, I am told, is still read*, un autore il quale, mi dicono, viene ancora letto; (*he*) *— eats, must pay*, chi mangia paga; *as — should say that ...*, come a dire che ...; *anybody —*, chiunque; *all —*, tutti quelli che.

**whoa** *excl.* (to a horse) ferma!

**whoever** (poet. **whoe'er**) *prn.* chiunque, colui che; *— finds it may keep it*, chiunque lo trova può tenerlo; (emphatic) *— did it?*, ma chi l'ha fatto?

**whole** *adj.* intero, integrale, tutto; *he swallowed it —*, l'ha ingoiato intero; *the — year*, tutto l'anno; *tell me the — truth*, dimmi tutta la verità; *a — holiday*, un'intera giornata libera; (fam.) *to go the — hog*, andare fino in fondo, rischiare tutto; sano, di buona salute, intatto, incolume; *with a — skin*, sano e salvo; (provb.) *they that are — need not a physician*, chi è sano non ha bisogno del medico.

**whole** *n.* (il) tutto, l'intero, il totale, il complesso; *the — of my money*, tutto il mio denaro; *he spent the — of September in Italy*, ha passato tutto il mese di settembre in Italia; *the — amounts to £100*, il totale ammonta a cento sterline; *a homogeneous —*, un complesso omogeneo; *two halves make a —*, due metà fanno un intero; *as a —*, nell'insieme; *on the —*, nel complesso, insomma.

**whole-hearted** *adj.* generoso, espansivo, sincero. **-heartedly** *adv.* di tutto cuore. **-hogger** *n.* (slang) estremista *m.*, *f.*, fanatico. **-length** *n.* (of portrait) a tutta figura.

**wholemeal** *adj.* pane *m.* integrale.

**wholeness** *n.* totalità, interezza.

**wholesale** *n.* vendita all'ingrosso; *— and retail*, commercio all'ingrosso e al minuto; *— price*, prezzo all'ingrosso; *they are produced —*, sono prodotti in serie; (fig.) *— slaughter*, uccisione in massa; *adv.* all'ingrosso; *to buy —*, comprare all'ingrosso; (fig.) su vasta scala. **-r** *n.* grossista *m.*, commerciante *m.* all'ingrosso.

**wholesome** *adj.* (of food) sano; (of air) salubre; (of remedy, *etc.*) salutare; (fig.) *— reading matter*, letture morali. **-ness** *n.* natura sana; salubrità; (fig.) bontà.

**whole-time** *adj. — job*, lavoro a giornata intera, a tutta giornata; stabile, fisso. **-timer** *n.* lavoratore fisso, impiegato fisso.

**wholly** *adv.* interamente, completamente, totalmente, del tutto.

**whom** *prn.* (*acc.* of **who**) *interr.* chi?; *— did you see?*, chi hai visto? *— did you speak to?*, a chi hai parlato?; *rel.* che, il quale, la quale, i quali, le quali; (after a *prep.*) cui; colui che, colei che, coloro che; *the boy — you saw*, il ragazzo che hai visto; *the men between — I was sitting*, gli uomini tra i quali sedevo; *the man — I was speaking about*, l'uomo di cui stavo parlando; (without antecedent) chi; (provb). *— the gods love die young*, muor giovane chi al cielo è caro.

**whomever** *prn.* (*acc.* of **whoever**) chiunque; *she smiled at — she met*, sorrideva a chiunque incontrasse.

**whomsoever** (poet. **whomsoe'er**), emphatic form of **whomever**, *q.v.*

**whoop** *n.* urlo, grido; (med.) urlo della pertosse.

**whoop** *intr.* gridare, urlare, schiamazzare; (med.) fare il grido caratteristico della pertosse.

**whoopee** *n.* (fam.) baldoria, schiamazzo; *to make —*, far baldoria.

**whooping** *n.* urlo, urlatìo, schiamazzo; (med.) urlo della pertosse. **-cough** *n.* (med.) pertosse *f.*; (fam.) tosse asinina, tosse canina.

**whop** *tr.* battere, bastonare, picchiare; (sport) sconfiggere, sbaragliare. **-per** *n.* (fam.) cosa enorme; grossa bugia.

**whore** *n.* prostituta, puttana, meretrice; (slang) passeggiatrice, peripatetica; *to play the —*, fare la puttana; *— house*, bordello; *intr.* (of men) fornicare, bazzicare donne di malaffare; (of women) fare la prostituta, prostituirsi. **-dom** *n.* prostituzione, meretricio; (bibl., fig.) idolatria. **-monger** *n.* mezzano, ruffiano, lenone *m.*; frequentatore di prostitute. **-mongering** *n.* lenocinio; frequentazione di prostitute.

**whoring** *n.* prostituzione; (bibl.) *to go a — after strange gods*, prostituirsi agli dei stranieri.

**whorl** *n.* spira, giro di spirale; voluta, vortice *m.*; (bot.) verticillo; (text.) disco che regola il movimento di un fuso. **-ed** *adj.* (bot.) disposto a spirale; verticillato; (archit.) volutato, a voluta.

**whortleberry** *n.* (bot.) mirtillo.

**whose** *poss. prn.* (of persons) *interr.* di chi?; *— seat is this?*, di chi è questo posto?; *— fault is it?*, di chi è la colpa?; *rel.* di chi, del quale, della quale, dei quali, delle quali, il cui, i cui, le cui; *the author — books you dislike*, l'autore i cui libri non ti piacciono; *the man for — sake I did it*, l'uomo per cui lo feci; *the girl to — sister I am writing*, la ragazza alla cui sorella, alla sorella della quale, sto scrivendo.

**whosever** *rel. prn.* di chiunque; *take that book — it is*, prendi quel libro, di chiunque esso sia.

**whoso, whosoever** *prn.* see **whoever.**

**why** *adv., interr.* perchè?, per quale ragione?; — *did you do it?*, perchè l'hai fatto?; — *not?*, perchè no?; — *so?*, per quale ragione?; *rel.* per cui; *the reason* —, la ragione per cui; *conj.* perchè; *I don't know — he's come*, non so perchè sia venuto; *excl.* ebbene!, perbacco!, diamine!; —, *I think so*, ebbene!, così mi pare; —, *can't you see it?*, perbacco, non lo vedi?; *n. the -s and the wherefores*, i perchè e i percome.

**wick** *n.* lucignolo, stoppino; (surg.) stuello.

**wicked** *adj.* malvagio, scellerato, cattivo, empio, maligno, iniquo, perverso; crudele; peccaminoso, vizioso; *it's a — thing that ...*, è un delitto che...; *a — lie*, un'iniqua menzogna; *pl. the* —, i malvagi.

**wickedness** *n.* malvagità, malignità, empietà, scelleratezza, cattiveria, perversità, iniquità.

**wicker** *n.* vimine *m.*; *attrib.* di vimini, in vimini. **-work** *n.* lavoro in vimini.

**wicket** *n.* portello, cancellino; porta pedonale; sportello; (croquet) archetto; (cricket) porta, sbarre *f.pl.*; campo, spazio tra le porte; *the — was in perfect condition*, il campo era in condizione perfetta; (fig.) *a sticky* —, una brutta situazione. **-gate** *n.* portello, cancellino. **-keeper** *n.* (cricket) guardaporta *m.*

**widdershins** *adv.* in senso contrario, a rovescio, da destra a sinistra.

**wide** *adj.* largo, vasto, spazioso; (fig.) ampio, esteso, immenso; *how — is it?*, quanto è largo?; *two metres* —, largo due metri; *to become -r*, allargarsi; (of roll of cloth) alto; *18 inches* —, alto diciotto pollici; *the — world*, l'universo; *to have — powers*, avere ampi poteri; *to have — interests*, avere vasti interessi; *to stare with — eyes*, fissare ad occhi spalancati; (fam.) scaltro; (cricket) — *ball*, palla scartata, palla che cade lontano dal battitore; *adv.* lontano; *to fall* —, cadere lontano (da); *far and* —, in lungo e in largo; — *apart*, distanziati, spaziati, ad intervallo; *to open* —, spalancare; — *open*, spalancato; *the blow went* —, il colpo andò a vuoto; lontano; — *of the truth*, lontano dalla verità; fuori posto, fuori proposito; *to give a — berth to*, stare alla larga da.

**wide** *n.* (poet.) ampiezza, estensione; (cricket) palla scartata, palla che cade lontano dal battitore; (fam.) *to be broke to the* —, essere al verde; *to be done to the* —, essere sfinito.

**wide-awake** *adj.* completamente sveglio, ad occhi aperti; (fig.) vigilante, guardingo; (cunning) furbo.

**widely** *adv.* largamente, molto, ampiamente, diffusamente; — *known*, largamente conosciuto, conosciutissimo; — *travelled*, che ha molto viaggiato; *to be — read*, essere molto letto, (reader) aver molto letto, essere un uomo di molta lettura.

**widen** *tr.* allargare; ampliare; dilatare; estendere; *intr.* allargarsi, ampliarsi; *to — out*, allargarsi, estendersi. **-ing** *n.* allargamento, allargatura; ingrandimento; punto dove una cosa si allarga; estensione.

**wide-ranging** *adj.* ampio, di grand estensione; (fig.) lungimirante.

**widespread** *adj.* esteso, diffuso; generale.

**widgeon** *n.* (orn.) fischione *m.*, anitra selvatica.

**widow** *n.* vedova; *to be left a* —, essere rimasta vedova; *grass* —, donna il cui marito è assente; *-'s weeds*, gramaglie *f.pl.*, lutto vedovile, abiti vedovili; (bibl.) *the -'s mite*, l'obolo della vedova; *tr.* rendere vedova; privare del compagno. **-ed** *adj.* vedovo, vedova; *his -ed mother*, sua madre che è vedova. **-er** *n.* vedovo. **-hood** *n.* vedovanza.

**width** *n.* larghezza, ampiezza; (of rolls of cloth) altezza; (of an arch) apertura; (of tyres) grossezza; *four feet in* —, quattro piedi di larghezza, largo quattro piedi.

**wield** *tr.* maneggiare, tenere; (weapon) brandire; (power) esercitare. **-er** *n.* (persona) che maneggia, che brandisce; che esercita; *the -er of power*, colui che esercita il potere.

**wife** *n.* moglie *f.*, sposa, coniuge *f.*, consorte *f.*; signora; *my* —, mia moglie; *remember me to your* —, (fam.) saluti a tua moglie, (formal) i miei saluti alla Signora; *to take a* —, sposarsi, ammogliarsi, accasarsi; *to take for* —, sposare, prendere in moglie; (fig.) comare *f.*; *The Merry Wives of Windsor*, le allegre comari di Windsor; (joc.) *all the world and his* —, tutti quanti, uomini e donne. **-hood** *n.* condizione di moglie, stato coniugale.

**wifie** *n.* (fam.) mogliettina.

**wifely** *adj.* (qualità, doveri) di una moglie, che convengono ad una donna sposata; — *virtues*, le virtù coniugali.

**wig** *n.* parrucca; capelli posticci; *theatrical* —, parrucca da scena; *powdered* —, parrucca incipriata. **-ging** *n.* (fam.) sgridata, ramanzina, lavata di testa.

**wiggle** *tr.* (fam.) dimenare, muovere da una parte all'altra; *intr.* dimenarsi, contorcersi; *n.* ancheggio.

**wigwam** *n.* tenda dei pellirosse.

**wild** *adj.* selvatico, selvaggio; deserto, incolto; feroce; timido, pauroso; (of weather) tempestoso, tumultuoso, burrascoso; (of wind) violento; (fig.) furibondo, eccitato, frenetico, sfrenato, folle; malaccorto, fatto a casaccio; disordinato, arruffato; — *animals*, animali selvatici; — *beasts*, animali feroci, fiere *f.pl.*, belve *f.pl.*; — *ass*, onagro; — *boar*, cinghiale *m.*; — *cat*, gatto selvatico; — *goose*, oca selvatica; (fig.) *a — goose chase*, un inseguimento vano, un'impresa sbagliata; — *life*, selvaticume *m.*; — *flowers*, fiori *m.pl.* di campo, fiori dei prati; *to run* —, inselvatichire; *to let children run* —, lasciar crescere i figli senza disciplina; *a — young man*, un giovane sfrenato; *to sow one's — oats*, correre la cavallina; *to make someone* —, far arrabbiare qualcuno; — *with joy*, folle di gioia; *to be — with anger*, essere fuori di sè dalla rabbia; *it makes me — when I think of it*, quando ci penso mi viene la rabbia; — *exaggeration*, esagerazione insensata; — *ideas*, nozioni assurde, roba da matti, idee fantastiche; *a — rumour*, una voce infondata; — *shooting*, sparatoria a casaccio; — *talk*, dicerie assurde, discorsi imprudenti; *n.* regione selvatica; *the call of the* —, il richiamo della foresta; *the -s of Africa*, le regioni selvagge dell'Africa; *to take to the -s*, darsi alla macchia.

**wild-cat** *adj.* (fig.) — *scheme*, idea assurda, impresa rischiosa; — *strike*, sciopero irregolare.

**wildebeest** *n.* (zool.) gnu *m.*

**wilderness** *n.* deserto; (fig.) solitudine *f.*; (bibl.) *the voice of one crying in the* —, la voce di uno che grida nel deserto; (pol.) *a wanderer in the* —, deputato che non appartiene a nessun partito; (fig.) distesa desolata.

**wildfire** *n.* conflagrazione estesa e furibonda; lampo senza tuoni; (hist.) fuoco greco; (fig.) *to spread like* —, diffondersi in un lampo; (med.) risipola, fuoco di Sant'Antonio.

**wildfowl** *n.* selvaggina alata.

**wildly** *adv.* selvaggiamente, ferocemente, violentemente; (fig.) follemente, freneticamente; a casaccio, a vanvera, alla disperata.

**wile**[1] *n.* stratagemma *m.*, astuzia, trucco; *the -s of the Devil*, le astuzie del diavolo; *to fall a victim to the -s of*, cader vittima delle seduzioni di.

**wile**[1] *tr.* allettare, adescare, ingannare; *to — someone into a trap*, attirare qualcuno in una trappola.

**wile**[2] *tr.* see **while.**
**Wilfred** *pr.n.* Vilfredo.
**wilful** *adj.* caparbio, ostinato, volitivo; volontario, intenzionale, fatto apposta; (leg.) premeditato; — *murder*, omicidio doloso, omicidio premeditato; — *damage*, danneggiamento doloso; — *intent*, dolo. **-ness** *n.* ostinazione, testardaggine *f.*, caparbietà; premeditazione, intenzione.
**Wilhelmina** *pr.n.* Guglielmina.
**wili-ly** *adv.* astutamente, scaltramente. **-ness** *n.* astuzia, scaltrezza.
**Will** *pr.n.* (abbrev. of **William**) Guglielmo.
**will** *n.* volontà, volere; *good* —, buona volontà; *ill* —, cattiva volontà; *to bear someone ill* —, avercela con qualcuno; *free* —, libero arbitrio; *iron* —, volontà di ferro; *lack of* —, mancanza di volontà; *at* —, a volontà, a piacere; *God's* —, la volontà di Dio; *Thy — be done*, sia fatta la Tua volontá, (provb.) *where there' a — there's a way*, volere è potere; buona volontà, lena; *to work with a* —, lavorare di buona lena; di buona voglia; *he went at it with a* —, ci si mise con buona volontà; piacimento, beneplacito, desiderio; *you may come and go at* —, puoi andare e venire a tuo piacimento; *it is our — that*, è il nostro desiderio che . . .; *at your — and pleasure*, a tua discrezione; (leg.) *tenant at* —, usufruttuario a tempo indeterminato; testamento, ultime volontà *f.pl.*; *to make one's* —, fare testamento; *the last — and testament of . . .*, le ultime volontà di . . .; *to witness a* —, firmare un testamento come testimone; *executor of a* —, esecutore testamentario.
**will** *tr.* volere, disporre; *God -ed that we should be happy*, Dio dispose che fossimo felici; *those who -ed the war*, quelli che vollero la guerra; costringere, suggestionare; lasciare (per testamento), legare; *intr.* volere; *as God -s*, come Dio vuole.
**will** *aux.* **1.** volere, desiderare; *do as you* —, fate come volete; *I won't do it*, non voglio farlo; *I would rather*, preferirei . . .; *would to God . . .*, piaccia a Dio (che) . . .; *would it were true!*, vorrei che fosse vero!; (in marriage service) *I* —, sì; *wait a moment, — you?*, vuoi aspettare un momento?; *he — have none of it*, non vuole sentirne parlare; (emphatic) *he — have it that I was wrong*, persiste nell'affermare ch'io avevo torto; *I — not have it said*, non permetto che si dica così; *accidents — happen*, le disgrazie non si possono escludere, non si può cambiare il corso degli avvenimenti; **2.** (simply futurity) expressed in Italian by the future or conditional tense.
**willed** *adj.* voluto, volontario; (of person) sotto l'influenza d'altrui, suggestionato; legato, lasciato per testamento; disposto; *even if I had been so* —, anche se fossi stato disposto; *strong-willed*, tenace, di forte volontà.
**William** *pr.n.* Guglielmo; (hist.) — *the Conqueror*, Guglielmo il Conquistatore; — *Rufus*, Guglielmo il Rosso; — *the Silent*, Guglielmo il Taciturno, — *Tell*, Guglielmo Tell.
**Willie** *pr.n.* (dimin. of **William**) Guglielmino.
**willies** *n.* (fam.) *to have the* —, avere la fifa; *it gives me the* —, mi dà sui nervi.
**willing** *adj.* volenteroso, compiacente, alacre, ben disposto; *a — worker*, un lavoratore volonteroso; *a — horse*, un cavallo generoso; — *or not*, volente o nolente; *to be — to . . .*, essere pronto a . . ., essere disposto a . . .; *I am quite* —, sono d'accordo. **-ly** *adv.* (ben) volentieri, di buon grado; prontamente. **-ness** *n.* buona volontà, impegno; *with the utmost -ness*, ben volentieri; compiacenza; *to express one's -ness*, dichiararsi pronto.
**will-o'-the-wisp** *n.* fuoco fatuo; (fig.) fantasma *m.*, persona inafferrabile.
**willow** *n.* (bot.) salice *m.*, salcio; *purple* —, salicella; *weeping* —, salice piangente; (cricket, joc.) mazza; *attrib.* salcigno.
**willow-warbler, willow-wren** *n.* (orn.) luì grosso.
**willowy** *adj.* coperto di salici, fiancheggiato da salici; (fig.) sottile, pieghevole.
**willy-nilly** *adv.* volente o nolente, giocoforza, buon grado mal grado, per amore o per forza.
**wilt** *intr.* appassire, avvizzire; deperire, consumarsi, languire; (fig., fam.) crollare, sgonfiarsi; *tr.* far appassire, far avvizzire.
**wily** *adj.* astuto, scabro, furbo; *a — old bird*, un vecchiotto furbo.
**wimple** *n.* soggolo, velo.
**win** *n.* vincita, vittoria; *last month we had three -s*, il mese scorso abbiamo vinto tre volte; *a — on points*, una vincita ai punti; *tr.* vincere, conquistare, guadagnare, ottenere; *to — a battle*, vincere una battaglia; *to — fame*, conquistare la fama; *to — a reputation*, farsi una reputazione; *to — the day*, essere vittorioso; *to — a game*, vincere una partita; *to — ten pounds at the races*, vincere dieci sterline alle corse; *to — all hearts*, ottenere il favore di tutti; *to — one's spurs*, guadagnarsi gli speroni; *to — someone's confidence*, ottenere la fiducia di qualcuno; guadagnare, meritare; *to — one's daily bread*, guadagnarsi il pane quotidiano; *his gallantry won him a medal*, il suo coraggio gli ha meritato una decorazione; *intr.* vincere, essere vittorioso; *who won?*, chi ha vinto?; *to — hands down*, vincere senza fatica, stravincere; *to — free*, liberarsi, districarsi; FOLLOW. BY ADV.: *to — away*, *tr.* togliere, staccare; *he tried to — her away from her husband*, cercò di staccarla dal marito; *intr.* (sport) vincere fuori casa; *to — back*, *tr.* riconquistare, riguadagnare, rifarsi (di); *to — back ground*, riconquistare terreno; *to — back money*, riguadagnarsi il denaro perduto; *to — over*, *to — round*, *tr.* captare, guadagnare, riconciliarsi, convertire; *he won me round*, mi ha persuaso; *to — through*, *intr.* raggiungere il traguardo, (fig.) superare gli ultimi ostacoli; *to — upon*, *intr. the idea is -ning upon him*, si sta convincendo.
**wince** *n.* sussulto, trasalimento; *intr.* sussultare, trasalire, ritrarsi trasalendo; *he -d at the insult*, trasalì all'insulto.
**winch** *n.* (eng.) argano, verricello, martinello, burbera, molinello; *tr. to — (up)*, (eng.) sollevare col verricello.
**wind**[1] *n.* vento; *north* —, vento del nord, tramontana, aquilone *m.*, ventavolo, borea *m.*, vento boreale, vento polare; *north-east* —, vento del nord-est, greco, grecale *m.*, (in Trieste area) bora; *north-west* —, vento del nord-ovest, (in Trieste area) bora; *east* —, vento dell'est, levante *m.*; *south-east* —, vento del sud-est, scirocco; *south* —, vento del sud, australe *m.*; *south-west* —, vento del sudovest, libeccio, affrico, garbino; *west* —, vento dell'ovest, ponente *m.*; *prevailing* —, vento dominante; *a gust of* —, una raffica di vento; *fair* —, vento favorevole; *head* —, vento di prua, vento contrario; *following* —, vento in poppa; *trade -s*, venti alisei, venti costanti; *Etesian -s*, venti etesii; (fig.) *gone with the* —, via col vento; *to cast prudence to the -s*, abbandonare ogni prudenza; *to find out how the — blows*, sentire da che parte tira il vento; (slang) *to get the — up*, avere la fifa; *to put the — up*, mettere la fifa addosso a; (fam.) *to raise the* —, trovare i soldi; *to sail close to the* —, (naut.) navigare stretto al vento, andare all'orza, (fig.) sfiorare l'indecenza; (med.) vento, flatulenza; *to break* —, trullare, (vulg.) tirare un peto, scoreggiare; fiato, respiro; *he soon lost his* —,

gli mancò presto il fiato; *to get one's second —*, ripigliar fiato; *sound in — and limb*, sano come un pesce; sentore *m.*, odore *m.*; *the stag got — of the hunter*, il cervo fiutò l'odore del cacciatore; *to get — of a plot*, aver sentore di un complotto; (mus.) *the —*, gli strumenti a fiato, i fiati.

**wind**[1] *tr.* (fam.) sfiatare, far perdere il fiato a; *the climb -ed him*, la salita l'ha sfiatato.

**wind** *tr.* (poet., of instruments) see under **wind**[2] *tr.*

**wind**[2] *tr.* avvolgere, circondare, cingere; *he wound a blanket round her*, l'avvolse in una coperta; *the mother wound her arms round the child*, la madre cinse il bambino con le braccia; (text.) arrotolare, avvolgere, bobinare, incannare, aggomitolare; *to — wool into a ball*, avvolgere la lana in gomitolo; (watch, spring) caricare, rimontare; *to — a handle*, girare una manovella; (poet.) suonare (strumento a fiato); *to — the horn*, suonare il corno; (naut.) virare di bordo; (fig.) *to — someone round one's little finger*, fare di qualcuno ciò che si vuole; *rfl. to — oneself into someone's heart*, insinuarsi nel cuore di qualcuno; *intr.* serpeggiare, salire a spirale; *the river -s down to the sea*, il fiume scorre serpeggiando verso il mare; avvolgersi, arrotolarsi, attorcigliarsi; *the snake -s round its victim*, il serpente si attorciglia intorno alla sua vittima; *to — up*, *tr.* arrotolare, avvolgere, (spring, clock) caricare; (fig.) *to — oneself up*, raccogliere tutte le proprie forze; *wound up to a fury*, al parossismo della collera; terminare, chiudere, finire; *to — up a debate*, chiudere un dibattito; *to — up the evening*, terminare la serata; (comm.) *to — up a business*, liquidare una ditta; *intr.* finire.

**windbag** *n.* camera d'aria, serbatoio d'aria; (of bagpipe) otre *m.*; (fig., derog.) parolaio, chiacchierone *m.*, chiacchierona *f.*, testa vuota.

**wind-break, -brake** *n.* frangivento. **-cheater** *n.* giacca a vento.

**winded** *adj.* sfiatato; *long-winded*, dal fiato lungo, (fig.) verboso, *short-winded*, dal respiro corto.

**winder** *n.* (text.) bobinatore, incannatore, (machine) bobinatrice; (of watch) caricatore; (bot.) pianta volubile.

**windfall** *n.* legna abbattuta dal vento, frutto fatto cadere dal vento; (fig.) fortuna inaspettata, bazza.

**wind-flower** *n.* (bot.) anemone *m.* **-gauge** *n.* anemoscopio, anemometro, indicatore di pressione del vento; (aeron.) derivometro.

**windiness** *n.* tempo burrascoso, clima *m.* ventoso; (fig.) verbosità, loquacità.

**winding**[1] *n.* suonatura (di corno).

**winding**[2] *adj.* serpeggiante, sinuoso, tortuoso; *— streets*, vie tortuose; *— stairs*, scala a chiocciola; *n.* movimento tortuoso, serpeggiamento, meandro; (industr.) avvolgimento, bobinaggio; (electr.), avvolgimento; (text.) incannaggio *m.*, incannatura.; (of watch, spring) caricamento.

**winding-frame** *n.* (text.) incannatoio, spolatrice. **-gear** *n.* (of a lift) verricello. **-key** *n.* manovella; (of watch) chiavetta da orologio. **-tackle** *n.* (naut.) paranco, calorna, caliorna. **-sheet** *n.* sudario, lenzuolo funebre. **-up** *n.* (comm.) liquidazione, scioglimento; (of meeting) chiusura; (of watch) caricamento.

**wind-instrument** *n.* (mus.) istrumento a fiato, istrumento a vento.

**windjammer** *n.* (naut.) veliero.

**windlass** *n.* argano, verricello; (naut.) guindaste *m.*, cabestano orizzontale; *tr.* issare con un argano.

**windless** *adj.* senza vento, calmo.

**windmill** *n.* mulino a vento; (fig.) *to tilt at -s*, combattere contro i mulini a vento.

**window** *n.* finestra; sportello; (rlwy.) finestrino; (motor.) cristallo; (of shop) vetrina; *casement —*, finestra a due battenti, finestra a gangheri; *French —*, porta finestra; *plate-glass —* cristallo; *sash-window*, finestra a ghigliottina; *stained-glass —*, vetrata a colori, invetriata.

**window-box** *n.* cassetta per i fiori (per davanzali), giardino di finestra. **-display** *n.* mostra (in vetrina). **-dresser** *n.* vetrinista *m.*, *f.* **-dressing** *n.* l'arredamento di una vetrina; (fig.) l'arte di mettere in mostra, camuffamento, truccatura; *his achievements were all -dressing*, le sue imprese servivano solo a far bella mostra. **-frame** *n.* telaio di finestra, cornice *f.*, incorniciatura. **-ledge** *n.* davanzale *m.* **-pane** *n.* vetro di finestra, cristallo, lastra di vetro. **-sash** *n.* telaio di finestra a ghigliottina. **-seat** *n.* banco nel vano della finestra; (rlwy.) posto vicino alla finestra. **-sill** *n.* davanzale *m.*

**windpipe** *n.* (anat.) trachea.

**windscreen** *n.* riparo contro il vento; (agric.) frangivento; (motor.) parabrezza *m.*; *— wiper*, tergicristallo, *-wiper blade*, spazzola del tergicristallo.

**wind-shield** *n.* (motor.) parabrezza *m.* **-sleeve, -sock, -stocking** *n.* (meteor.; aeron.) manica a vento, mostravento. **-swept** *adj.* ventoso, esposto al vento, spazzato dal vento; (fig.) aerodinamico, affusolato. **-tight** *adj.* impermeabile all'aria. **-tunnel** *n.* (aeron.) tunnel aerodinamico.

**wind-up**[1] *n.* (slang) *to get the —*, avere la fifa.

**wind-up**[2] *n.* fine *f.*, terminazione; finale *m.*

**wind-valve** *n.* (of chimney) valvola di tiraggio. **-vane** *n.* ventaruola, mostravento segnavento.

**windward** *adj.* situato verso la parte da cui soffia il vento; che si muove contro vento; *n.* (naut.) sopravvento; (geog.) *the Windward Islands*, le Isole Sopravvento.

**windy** *adj.* ventoso, esposto al vento; *to be —*, far vento; (fam., of speaker) ampolloso, verboso; (slang) che ha la fifa, pauroso; (med.) flatulente.

**wine** *n.* vino; *red —*, vino rosso, vino nero; *white —*, vino bianco; *sparkling —*, spumante *m.*; *rose —*, vino rosato; *— of low alcoholic content*, vinello; *muscat —*, moscato; *Rhine —*, vino del Reno; *Port —*, vino di Porto; *dry —*, vino secco; *sweet —*, vino dolce, vino amabile; *pure —*, vino sincero; *— made from fruit other than grapes*, succo fermentato; *— of the district*, vino nostrano; *— from the wood*, vino dal fusto; *table —*, vino da pasto; *bottled —*, vino in bottiglia; *the — trade*, l'industria vinicola, l'industria enologica; (provb.) *good — needs no bush*, buon vino non vuole frasca; *intr.* offrire vino a; *to dine and — someone*, festeggiare qualcuno.

**winebag** *n.* otre *m.*; (fig.) beone *m.*, ubriacone *m.*

**wine-basket** *n.* cesta per il vino. **-bibber** *n.* bevitore di vino; beone *m.*, ubriacone *m.* **-bibbing** *n.* il bere, ubriachezza. **-bin** *n.* ripostiglio per vino in bottiglia. **-bottle** *n.* bottiglia da vino; fiasco. **-butler** *n.* maggiordomo, cameriere addetto ai vini, cantiniere; (hist.) siniscalco. **-cellar** *n.* cantina per vini, cella vinaria. **-coloured** *adj.* (di colore) vinoso. **-cooler** *n.* cantinetta, secchiello. **-glass** *n.* bicchiere da vino, calice *m.* **-grower** *n.* viticultore, enofilo, vignaiolo, vinificatore; proprietario di una vigna. **-growing** *adj.* vinicolo, vinifero, viticolo, *n.* viticoltura, enologia; l'industria vinicola. **-list** *n.* carta dei vini, lista dei vini. **-merchant** *n.* mercante di vino. **-party** *n.* bicchierata; trattenimento in cui si offre vino. **-press** *n.* torchio da vino, torchio da uva, torcolo.

**-producing** *adj.* vinicolo, vinifero, viticolo. **-shop** *n.* bettola, spaccio di vini, bottega dei vini, taverna. **-skin** *n.* otre *m.* **-vat** *n.* tino. **-vault** *n.* cantina per vini.

**wing** *n.* ala; *the -s of a bird*, le ali di un uccello; *on the -s of the wind*, sulle ali del vento; *to clip the -s of*, tarpare le ali a; *fear lent him -s*, la paura gli dava le ali; *he took me under his —*, mi prese sotto la sua protezione; *the new — of the hospital*, l'ala nuova dell'ospedale; *on the —*, in volo; *to take —*, prendere il volo; distintivo di pilota; (of a door) battente *m.*; (mil.; aeron.) ala; (soccer) *right —*, ala destra; *left —*, ala sinistra; (rugby) *— forward*, terza linea ala; *— three-quarter*, tre quarti ala; (theatr.) *in the -s*, tra le quinte.

**wing** *tr.* dare ali a; (fig.) accelerare; ferire all'ala; *to — one's way*, andare velocemente, volare; *intr.* volare, prendere il volo. **-beat** *n.* colpo d'ala, battito d'ala, alata, remeggio.

**wing-bolt** *n.* bullone ad alette. **-case** *n.* (ent.) elitra. **-commander** *n.* tenente colonello dell'aeronautica. **-compass(es)** *n.* compasso quarto di cerchio.

**winged** *adj.* alato; (poet.) aligero; (myth.) *the — god*, Mercurio; *the — horse*, Pegaso; (of wounded bird) ferito all'ala.

**winger** *n.* (soccer) ala.

**wingless** *adj.* senza ali; (zool.) aptero; *the — Victory*, la Nike aptera.

**wing-span, -spread** *n.* (orn.; aeron.) apertura alare. **-tip** *n.* (orn.) estremità dell'ala; (aeron.) alettone *m.*

**Winifred** *pr.n.* Ginevra, Vinifrida.

**wink** *n.* ammicco, strizzatina d'occhio; occhiata; (med.) battimento delle palpebre; *without a — of the eyelid*, senza battere ciglio; *to tip the — to*, far cenno con gli occhi a, (fig.) mettere in guardia, *in a —*, in un attimo; *to have forty -s*, schiacciare un pisolino; *I haven't slept a —*, non ho chiuso occhio.

**wink** *intr.* ammiccare, sbattere le palpebre, strizzare l'occhio; (fig.) *to — at*, chiudere gli occhi a; scintillare, brillare.

**winking** *adj.* scintillante, brillante; intermittente; *n.* sbattimento delle palpebre, ammicco, strizzata; scintillìo, brillìo.

**winkle** *n.* (zool.) chiocciola di mare, lumaca di mare; *tr.* (fam.) estrarre con difficoltà.

**winner** *n.* vincitore *m.*; (cards) *to hold all the -s*, avere in mano tutte le carte migliori; (fig.) qualcosa di gran successo; *bread-winner*, sostegno economico della famiglia.

**winning** *adj.* vittorioso, vincente, vincitore; *the — side*, la squadra vittoriosa; *the — horse*, il cavallo vincente; (fig.) simpatico, attraente, avvincente, seducente; *a — smile*, un sorriso simpatico; *— ways*, modi seducenti; (cards) *the — game*, la bella; *n.* vittoria, conquista, vincita; (cards) vincita. **-ly** *adv.* in modo avvincente, in modo seducente.

**winning-post** *n.* traguardo; (fig.) meta.

**winnow** *tr.* (agric.) vagliare, spulare, ventilare; *to — out the chaff from the grain*, separare la loppa dal grano; (fig.) vagliare, scegliere. **-er** *n.* (agric.) (person) che vaglia, che spula; (machine) macchina vagliatrice. **-ing** *n.* (agric.) vagliatura, spulatura; *-ing machine*, vagliatrice; (fig.) scelta, scernita.

**winsome** *adj.* attraente, cattivante, seducente, amabile; *a — girl*, una ragazza cattivante; *a — face*, una faccia simpatica. **-ness** *n.* amabilità; fascino.

**winter** *n.* inverno; invernata, stagione invernale; *a hard —*, un inverno rigido; *a mild —*, un inverno mite; *a man of 80 -s*, un uomo d'ottant'anni; *attrib.* invernale, d'inverno; *— clothing*, abiti pesanti; *— resort*, stazione invernale; *— visitors*, ibernanti *m.pl.*, svernanti *m.pl.*; (mil.) *— quarters*, quartieri d'inverno; *intr.* passare l'inverno, svernare, ibernare.

**wintering** *n.* svernamento; ibernazione.

**winter-time** *n.* inverno, stagione invernale.

**wintry** *adj.* invernale, rigido; (fig.) triste, senza calore; *a — smile*, un sorriso freddo; *a — reception* un'accoglienza glaciale.

**wipe** *tr.* asciugare, pulire, strofinare; spolverare; *to — one's eyes*, asciugarsi gli occhi; *to — the dishes*, asciugare i piatti; *to — one's nose*, pulirsi il naso; (slang) *to — the floor with*, infliggere una batosta sonora a; FOLLOW. BY ADV.: *to — away*, *tr.* allontanare asciugando, eliminare strofinando; *to — off*, *tr.* eliminare strofinando, cancellare; *to — off one's debts*, liquidare tutti i propri debiti; (fam.) *I'll soon — that smile off his face*, penserò io a spegnere quel suo sorriso; *to — out*, *tr.* eliminare, cancellare, (debts.) liquidare, saldare; *to — out an insult*, vendicare un affronto; *he has -d out his past*, ha liquidato il suo passato; sterminare, annientare; *the army was -d out*, l'esercito fu annientato; *to — up*, *tr.* pulire, togliere (una sporcizia); *n.* asciugatura, strofinata; spolverata; *to give something a —*, asciugare qualcosa.

**wiper** *n.* strofinaccio, straccio; asciugamani *m.*; (motor.) *windscreen —*, tergicristallo.

**wiping** *n.* asciugatura, pulitura; *— out*, annientamento, eliminazione.

**wire** *n.* filo metallico; *barbed —*, filo spinato; *copper —*, filo di rame; *drawn —*, filo trafilato; *live —*, filo carico, (fig.) uomo in gamba, persona dinamica; *high-tension -s*, fili ad alta tensione; *telegraph -s*, fili telegrafici; *attrib.* metallico; *— sieve*, crivello di rete metallica; *— entanglement*, reticolato di filo spinato; *to pull the -s*, manovrare i fili (di marionette), (fig.) tenere le fila, intrigare; (fam.) *to be on -s*, avere i nervi tesi; telegramma *m.*

**wire** *tr.* legare con fili metallici; *to — the cork of a bottle*, assicurare il tappo di una bottiglia con un filo metallico; (electr.) *to — a house*, installare l'impianto elettrico in una casa; *intr.* *to — in*, *tr.* circondare con rete metallica, recintare; *to — off*, *tr.* isolare a mezzo di reticolato, recintare; *to — up*, *tr.* (electr.) montare (una pila), collegare con fili; telegrafare.

**wire-cutter(s)** *n.* pinza tagliafili, forbici tagliafili.

**wired** *adj.* rinforzato con filo metallico, circondato da rete metallica; (electr.) collegato, munito d'impianto elettrico; *— glass*, vetro retinato.

**wire-drawing** *n.* (metall.) trafilatura in fili. **-gauge** *n.* calibro per fili metallici, palmer. **-glass** *n.* vetro retinato. **-haired** *adj.* (of dogs) a pelo ruvido.

**wireless** *adj.* senza fili; *— telegraphy*, radiotelegrafia; *— telephony*, radiotelefonia, radiofonia; *— (set)*, radio *f.*, apparecchio radio; *portable — set*, radiolina transistore; *— operator*, radiotelegrafista *m.*; *— commentator*, radiocronista *m.*; *— engineer*, radiotecnico; *tr.*, *intr.* radiotelegrafare.

**wire-netting** *n.* rete metallica, reticolato, traliccio metallico, graticcio di rete, inferriata. **-pull** *intr.* reggere le fila; intrigare. **-puller** *n.* (of marionettes) burattinaio; (fig.) intrigante *m.*, *f.* **-pulling** *n.* l'arte di reggere le fila, intrighi *m.pl.* **-stitch** *tr.* (bookb.) cucire (un libro), incartonare, brossare. **-strainer** *n.* colino metallico, colatoio; (industr.) trafila. **-tapping** *n.* intercettazione di messaggi telegrafici e telefonici; servizio d'ascolto delle comunicazioni telefoniche.

**wirework** *n.* trafilatura; (fence) traliccio metallico, reticolato.

**wireworm** *n.* (ent.) enteride *m.*, elatore, millepiedi *m.*, iulo.

**wiriness** *n.* qualità metallica; (med.) carattere filiforme; (fig.) vigoria.
**wiring** *n.* fili metallici; (electr.) installazione di un impianto elettrico, complesso di linee telegrafiche, cablaggio; spedizione di un telegramma.
**wiry** *adj.* simile a filo metallico; — *hair*, capelli ispidi; (med.) filiforme; (fig.) asciutto, nerboruto, tenace.
**wisdom** *n.* saggezza, sapienza; giudizio, senno, buon senso; — *after the event*, il senno del poi; — *tooth*, dente del giudizio; *the Book of Wisdom*, (il libro della) Sapienza.
**wise**[1] *adj.* saggio, sagace, savio; prudente, avveduto; *it wouldn't be — to do that*, non sarebbe prudente di farlo; *after the meeting I was none the -r*, dopo la riunione ne sapevo meno di prima; *to do something without anyone being the -r*, fare qualcosa all'insaputa di tutti; (fam.) *to get — to*, rendersi conto di; *to put someone — to a fact*, mettere qualcuno al corrente di un fatto; *the Wise Men of the East*, i Re Magi; (soothsayer) — *man*, indovino, mago; — *woman*, indovina, strega, (Scot.) levatrice.
**wise**[2] *n.* modo, maniera, sorta, guisa; *in no —*, in nessun modo; *in some —*, in qualche modo.
**-wise**[2] *suffix.* (neol.) in quanto riguarda.
**wiseacre** *n.* saccente *m.* sapientone *m.*, pedante *m.*, barbassoro.
**wisecrack** *n.* spiritosaggine *f.*, battuta; *intr.* dire spiritosaggini.
**wish** *n.* desiderio, voglia, voto; *I have no — to go*, non ho nessuna voglia di andare; *I cannot grant your —*, non posso darti ciò che desideri; *to meet the -es of*, accontentare; *the — is father to the thought*, i desideri guidano i pensieri; *the -es of the people*, i voti del popolo; *my best -es*, i miei migliori auguri; *New Year's -es*, auguri di capodanno; (in will) volontà; *last -es*, ultime volontà.
**wish** *tr.*, *intr.* desiderare, volere; *to — for something*, desiderare una cosa; *to have everything one can — for*, avere tutto ciò che si possa desiderare; *do you — me to go?*, vuoi che me ne vada?; *I — I were in Italy*, vorrei essere in Italia, se fossi in Italia!; *I — it to be known*, voglio che tutti sappiano; *I do not — it*, non lo voglio, non ci tengo; *how I — I could help you!*, mi piacerebbe tanto aiutarti!; augurare; *to — good night to*, augurare la buona notte a.
**wishbone** *n.* forchetta dello sterno; (fig.) portafortuna *m.*
**wisher** *n.* persona che desidera, che augura; *well-wisher*, amico, sostenitore *m.*
**wishful** *adj.* pieno di desiderio, desideroso, bramoso; — *thinking*, il credere vero qualcosa perchè lo si desidera, pio desiderio. **-ly** *adv.* con desiderio, ardentemente, fervidamente.
**wishing** *n.* desideri *m.pl.*, il desiderare.
**wishing-bone** *n.* see **wishbone**.
**wishy-washy** *adj.* (fam.) insipido, annacquato; (fig.) di poco spirito.
**wisp** *n.* ciuffo, ciocca; manata, manciata, piccolo fascio; *a — of hair*, una ciocca di capelli; *a — of smoke*, un filo di fumo; *will-o'-the-wisp*, fuoco fatuo, (fig.) cosa inafferrabile; (orn.) *a — of snipe*, uno stormo di beccaccini.
**wistaria, wisteria** *n.* (bot.) glicine *m.*
**wistful** *adj.* pieno di desiderio, ansioso; pensoso, un po' triste, pieno di vaghe speranze. **-ness** *n.* desiderio, ansia, tristezza.
**wit** *n.* intelligenza, spirito, ingegno; arguzia, argutezza; *he has not the — to see it*, non ha l'intelligenza di capirlo; *a flash of —*, un tratto di spirito; *the — of man*, l'intelletto umano; *a man of —*, un uomo spiritoso; *pl.* mente *f.*, ingegno; *to have quick -s*, essere d'ingegno vivace; *to be out of one's -s*, essere fuori di sè, essere pazzo; *to be at one's -s' end*, non sapere a che santo votarsi; *to have one's -s about one*, avere prontezza di spirito; *to set one's -s to work*, ingegnarsi; *to live by one's -s*, vivere di espedienti; (person) uomo di spirito; persona arguta, persona spiritosa, bello spirito; *the university -s*, i begli ingegni universitari.
**wit** *tr.* sapere; *God wot*, Dio la sa; *to —*, vale a dire, cioè.
**witch** *n.* strega, maga, fattucchiera; (fig.) donna affascinante, donna seducente; *an old —*, una vecchia megera, una vecchiaccia; *-es' sabbath*, sabba *m.* delle streghe. **-craft** *n.* stregoneria, arti magiche.
**witch-doctor** *n.* stregone *m.*, mago. **-elm** *n.* (bot.) olmo riccio.
**witchery** *n.* stregoneria, incantesimo; (fig.) fascino.
**witch-hazel** *n.* (bot.) 1. See **witch-elm**; 2. avellano, nocciolo delle streghe; (pharm.) tintura di hamamelis. **-hunting** *n.* caccia alle streghe; (fig.) persecuzione dei presunti sovversivi; ricerca affannata di un capro espiatorio.
**witching** *adj.* che ha potere magico; (fig.) affascinante, incantevole, malioso; *the — hour*, l'ora propizia alle pratiche magiche; *n.* stregoneria; (fig.) fascino.
**with** *prep.* con; insieme a; presso; *come — me*, vieni con me; *yesterday I had dinner — a friend*, ieri ho pranzato con un amico; *I saw him — two friends*, l'ho visto insieme a due amici; *I am staying — my brother*, abito presso mio fratello; *complete —*, completo di; con, per mezzo di; *to cut — a knife*, tagliare con un coltello; *we see — our eyes*, vediamo per mezzo degli occhi; da, a causa di; *he was trembling — fear*, tremava dalla paura; — *all this noise I can't hear what you're saying*, a causa del rumore non capisco quello che dici; da, con, munito di; *a man — grey hair*, un uomo dai capelli grigi; *a man — four children*, un uomo con quattro figli; *you must go to the office — the necessary documents*, devi presentarti in ufficio munito dei documenti necessari; con, contro; *he has quarrelled — his father*, ha litigato con suo padre; *to be angry — someone*, essere adirato contro qualcuno; *to be at war — a country*, essere in guerra con una nazione; *to fight — someone*, lottare contro qualcuno; con, nonostante; *England — all thy faults I love thee still*, Inghilterra!, con, nonostante, tutti i tuoi difetti, ti amo sempre; nel caso di, quanto a, riguardo a, per; — *him it's money that counts*, nel suo caso, quanto a lui, è il denaro che conta; — *art it's a different matter*, riguardo all'arte la cosa è diversa; — *ease*, facilmente; — *an eye to*, tenendo d'occhio, tenendo conto di; — *one accord*, unanimemente; — *reference to*, in riferimento a; — *all due respect*, con tutto il rispetto dovuto; *to begin —*, per cominciare; *filled —*, pieno di; *down — the King!*, abbasso il re!, morte al re!; *away — him*, portatelo via!; *be off — you!*, vattene!; *get along — you!*, muoviti!, (fam.) ma cosa mi racconti!; *bear — me!*, scusami!, abbi paziena!; *I am — you there*, sono perfettamente d'accordo con te su questo punto; *I could do — a glass of wine*, mi andrebbe un bicchiere di vino; *I have done — it*, non ne voglio più sentire parlare; *it is pouring — rain*, piove a catinelle; *the book deals — philosophy*, il libro tratta di filosofia; *to be — child*, essere incinta, essere gravida; (of animal) *to be — young*, essere pregna; (neol.) *to be — it*, essere al corrente.
**withal** *adv.* per di più, inoltre, con tutto ciò.
**withdraw** *tr.* ritirare, tirare

indietro, levare; (money) prelevare; *intr.* ritirarsi, allontanarsi, eclissarsi; (mil.) ripiegare. **-al, -ing** *n.* ritiro; (mil.) ritirata; (of money) prelevamento.

**withe** *n.* vimine *m.*, vinco.

**wither** *intr.* appassirsi, avvizzirsi, disseccarsi, inaridirsi, sfiorire; deperire; (med.) atrofizzarsi; *tr.* far sfiorire, far appassire, far disseccare; (fig., joc.) agghiacciare, fulminare; *she -ed him with a look*, lo fulminò con una occhiata. **-ed** *part. adj.* appassito, disseccato; sfiorito, inaridito; (med.) atrofizzato. **-ing** *adj.* che fa appassire, che fa inaridire, languente, deporito; (bot.) marcescente; (fig., joc.) fulminante, sprezzante; *-ing contempt*, disprezzo che annienta; *n.* appassimento, avvizzimento; sfioritura; (of person) deperimento; (med.) atrofia.

**withers** *n.* garrese *m.*; (fig.) *to wring one's —*, fare un appello fortissimo alla emozione.

**withhold** *tr.* trattenere, ritirare, detenere; rifiutare, negare; (fig.) nascondere, dissimulare; *to — payment*, trattenere il pagamento; *to — consent*, negare il consenso; *to — the truth*, nascondere la verità. **-er** *n.* detentore. **-ing** *n.* trattenimento; (of pay) trattenuta; rifiuto; *-ing of the truth*, dissimulazione della verità.

**within** *adv.* all'interno, dentro; *— and without*, dentro e fuori; (fig.) in sè, nell'animo; *prep.* entro, dentro, in, all'interno di; (this side of) al di qua di; *— the walls*, entro le mura; *— doors*, in casa; *— fixed limits*, entro i limiti prestabiliti; *— the frontier*, al di qua della frontiera; *— two miles*, in un raggio di due miglia; *— call*, a portata di voce; *— hearing*, fin dove si può udire; *— sight*, in vista; *— someone's reach*, a portata di qualcuno; *to keep — the law*, mantenersi nella legalità; *dissensions — the party*, dissensi in seno al partito; *to live — one's income*, vivere secondo le proprie possibilità; entro, fra, in meno di, non oltre; *— a week*, entro una settimana, in meno di otto giorni; *— twenty-four hours*, entro ventiquattro ore; *— a year of his death*, non oltre un anno dopo la sua morte; *— the memory of man*, a memoria d'uomo; *— an inch of . . .*, a un pelo di . . .

**without** *adv.* fuori, al di fuori; *the noise —*, il rumore fuori; *from —*, da fuori, dall'esterno; *within and —*, dentro e fuori; *conj.* See **unless**; *prep.* senza, senza di; *— fail*, senza fallo; *— doubt*, senza dubbio, indubbiamente; *— him*, senza di lui; *— speaking*, senza parlare; *— your saying so*, senza che tu lo dica; *that goes — saying*, va da sè, è ovvio; *— so much as apologizing*, senza nemmeno scusarsi; *to do —*, fare a meno di, sopportare la mancanza di; *to be —*, essere senza, essere privo di; *times — number*, innumerevoli volte; (poet.) fuori, fuori di, al di fuori di; *there is no life — Verona's walls*, non c'è vita fuori delle mura di Verona.

**withstand** *tr.* resistere a, opporre resistenza a, sostenere; *to — temptation*, resistere alla tentazione; *to — hard wear*, resistere all'usura; (mil.) *to — a siege*, sostenere un assedio.

**withstood** *p.def., part.* of **withstand**, *q.v.*

**withy** *n.* vimine *m.*, vinco; *cf.* **osier.**

**witless** *adj.* senza spirito, sciocco, privo d'intelligenza.

**witness** *n.* testimone *m.*, teste *m.*; *— for the prosecution*, testimone a carico; *— for the defence*, testimone a discarico; *eye-witness*, testimone oculare; *God is my —*, Dio mi è testimone; testimonianza, testimonio; *in — whereof*, a testimonianza di cui, in fede di cui; *to bear —*, deporre, testimoniare; *to act as —*, fare testimonio; *the — states. . .*, il teste dichiara . . .; *to sign as —*, firmare come testimonio; (fig.) prova, dimostrazione; *a — to his skill*, una prova della sua abilità.

**witness** *tr., intr.* testimoniare, essere testimone di, attestare; *to — in favour of . . .*, testimoniare a favore di . . .; *to — an accident*, essere testimone di un incidente; *to — a document*, firmare un documento come testimone, attestare un documento; (fig.) mostrare, tradire. **-box** *n.* banco dei testimoni.

**witnessing** *n.* testimonianza; (of a signature) vidimazione, legalizzazione.

**witticism** *n.* motto di spirito, battuta, frizzo, arguzia.

**wittily** *adv.* spiritosamente, argutamente.

**wittiness** *n.* spirito, argutezza.

**wittingly** *adv.* consapevolmente, di proposito, intenzionalmente.

**witty** *adj.* spiritoso, arguto, intelligente; *a — remark*, un'osservazione arguta; *to be —*, aver spirito.

**wizard** *n.* mago, stregone *m.*; *adj.* (neol.) ottimo, magnifico. **-ry** *n.* stregoneria.

**wizened** *adj.* raggrinzito, rugoso, avvizzito, secco.

**wo! whoa!** *excl.* oh!, fermo!; *— back!*, indietro!

**woad** (bot.) guado, pastello; (hist.) tintura blu di cui si tingevano i britanni.

**wobbl-e** *n.* dondolio, oscillazione; (fig.) incertezza, esitazione; (mech.) rotazione fuori piano; (motor., of wheels) sfarfallamento; *intr.* dondolare, oscillare; (fig.) tentennare, esitare, barcollare; (mech.) girare fuori piano; (motor., of wheels) sfarfallare; (cul., of jelly) tremolare. **-er** *n.* persona che vacilla, che oscilla; (fig.) persona che esita, che tentenna; (pol.) elettore indeciso. **-y** *adj.* vacillante, barcollante, malsicuro; (fig.) esitante, titubante; (slang) *to feel -y*, sentirsi male, essere giù di corda.

**woe** *n.* guaio, sventura, calamità; *a tale of —*, un racconto di sventura; *in weal and —*, nella prosperità e nella miseria; *to tell all one's -s*, raccontare tutti i propri guai; *excl.* guai!; *— unto you!*, guai a voi!; *— is me!*, povero me!, ahimè; *— to the vanquished!*, guai ai vinti!, vae victis! **-begone** *adj.* triste, abbattuto; addolorato; (fig.) inconsolabile.

**wo(e)ful** *adj.* pieno di guai, triste, afflitto; *a — day*, una mesta giornata, una giornata funesta; (fig.) deplorevole; *a — lack of tact*, una deplorevole mancanza di tatto. **-ly** *adv.* in modo triste, mestamente; (fig.) deplorevolmente.

**wog** *n.* (derog.) persona di razza bruna, specialmente del levante.

**woke** *p.def.* of **wake**, *q.v.*

**wold** *n.* pianura ondeggiante, landa; (geog.) *the Wolds*, zone dell'Inghilterra centrale.

**wolf** (zool.) *n.* lupo; *she-wolf*, lupa; *timber —*, lupo grigio dell'America; *prairie —*, lupo delle praterie, coiote *m.*; (fig.) persona avida, persona rapace; (fam.) donnaiuolo; *a — in sheep's clothing*, un lupo in veste di agnello; *to be as hungry as a —*, avere una fame da lupo; *to cry —*, gridare al lupo, dare falsi allarmi; *to keep the — from the door*, tener lontana la miseria; (mus.) dissonanza.

**wolf** *tr.* divorare avidamente; *to — down one's food*, ingozzare il cibo.

**wolf-cub** *n.* (zool.) lupacchiotto, lupacchino. **-dog** *n.* canelupo, cane da pastore tedesco; *cf.* **alsatian**; (hunt.) cane addestrato alla caccia al lupo. **-hound** *n.* alano.

**wolfish** *adj.* lupesco, da lupo, simile a un lupo; *a — appetite*, un appetito da lupo; (fig.) rapace, crudele.

**wolfram** *n.* (miner.) volframio, tungsteno.

**wolfsbane** *n.* (bot.) aconito europeo, nappello.

**wolverine** *n.* (zool.) ghittone *m.*

**woman** *n.* donna; femmina. N.B. After an *adj.* or with a noun, usually expressed in

Italian by the feminine form of the *adj.* or *noun*, *e.g.*: *an Italian* —, un'Italiana; *single* —, nubile; — *friend*, amica; — *servant*, serva, cameriera; — *writer*, scrittrice; — *doctor*, dottoressa, medichessa; — *teacher*, maestra, professoressa; — *student*, studentessa; *young* —, giovane; *old* —, vecchia, vecchia comare; (fam.) *my old* —, mia moglie, mia vecchia, (derog. of man) femminuccia; donna di servizio, cameriera; donna ad ore; (hist.) dama di compagnia; *-'s wit*, intuito femminile; *women's movement*, movimento femminile; *women's rights*, i diritti della donna; *women's suffrage*, suffragio femminile; *Women's Lib*, Movimento di Liberazione della Donna; (in compounds) *apple-woman*, venditrice di mele; *milk-woman*, lattaia, lattivendola; (hist.) *women's apartments*, gineceo; (med.) *hospital for women*, ginecomio; *specialist in women's diseases*, ginecologo.

**woman-hater** *n.* misogino, nemico delle donne.

**woman-hood** *n.* condizione di donna; maturità fisica (della donna); (collect.) le donne, il sesso femminile. **-ish** *adj.* femminile, donnesco; (of a man) effeminato. **-ize** *tr.* rendere effeminato, effeminare; *intr.* correre dietro le donne. **-izer** *n.* donnaiuolo. **-kind** *n.* le donne, il sesso femminile. **-like** *adj.* femminile, femmineo; *adv.* da donna. **-liness** *n.* femminintà, qualità femminili. **-ly** *adj.* femminile, femmineo; di donna, degno di donna.

**womb** *n.* (med.) utero; ventre *m.*; grembo; seno.

**wombat** *n.* (zool.) vombato.

**womenfolk** *n.* donne *f.pl.*; *my* —, le mie parenti.

**won** *p.def.*, *part.* of **win** *q.v.*

**wonder** *n.* meraviglia, prodigio, portento, miracolo; persona (o cosa) che suscita meraviglia; *what a* —*!*, che miracolo!; *you're a* —, sei un prodigio, sei un portento; *the seven -s of the world*, le sette meraviglie del mondo; *a nine days'* —, un fuoco di paglia; *for a* —, strano a dirsi; stupore *m.*, sorpresa, meraviglia; *no — he refused*, non c'è da stupirsi che abbia rifiutato.

**wonder** *intr.* meravigliarsi, stupirsi; *I don't* —, non mi stupisco, non c'è da stupirsi; (fig.) domandarsi, chiedersi, essere curioso di sapere; *I — what time it is*, mi domando che ora sia; *we -ed who he was*, ci siamo chiesti chi fosse; *I — why*, vorrei sapere perchè; *to — at*, ammirare, stupirsi di.

**wonderful** *adj.* meraviglioso, stupendo, prodigioso, sorprendente, stupefacente; *what a — day!*, che bella giornata!; *a — sight*, uno spettacolo stupendo; *a — likeness*, una rassomiglianza che colpisce; *how —!*, che bello!, ma questo è meraviglioso! **-ly** *adv.* meravigliosamente, stupendamente, prodigiosamente; *he has been -ly kind to me*, è stato tanto gentile con me; *I feel -ly well*, mi sento proprio bene. **-ness** *n.* carattere stupefacente, carrattere meraviglioso.

**wondering** *adj.* stupito, meravigliato. **-ly** *adv.* con stupore, con meraviglia, con sorpresa.

**wonderland** *n.* paese delle meraviglie; regno delle fate; *Alice's Adventures in* —, 'Alice nel paese delle meraviglie'.

**wonderment** *n.* stupore *m.*, meraviglia.

**wonder-struck** *adj.* stupefatto, trasecolato, meravigliato. **-worker** *n.* operatore *m.* di miracoli, taumaturgo. **-working** *adj.* che fa miracoli, miracoloso, prodigioso.

**wondrous** *adj.* meraviglioso, mirabile, stupendo.

**wonky** *adj.* (fam.) traballante, sgangherato; *to feel* —, sentirsi giù di corda.

**wont** *adj.* solito, abituato; *to be — to*, avere l'abitudine di; *people are — to believe that* . . ., la gente crede facilmente che . . .; *n.* uso, abitudine *f.*, costume *m.*, solito; *according to his* —, secondo il suo solito.

**won't** = **will not**, see **will**.

**wonted** *adj.* solito, abituale.

**woo** *tr.* corteggiare, fare la corte a, chiedere la mano a, chiedere in matrimonio; (fig.) cercare di ottenere, sollecitare.

**wood**[1] *n.* legno; (firewood) legna; (timber) legname *m.*; *a box made of* —, una scatola di legno; *put some — on the fire*, metti della legna sul fuoco; *a pile of* —, una catasta di legname; *touch —!*, tocca ferro!; — *alcohol*, alcool metilico.

**wood**[2] *n.* bosco, boschetto; foresta, selva; *attrib.* silvestre, selvatico; (fig.) *we are not yet out of the* —, siamo sempre nei guai; *not to see the — for the trees*, perdere di vista il tutto per il particolare, perdersi in quisquiglie; *to take to the -s*, darsi alla macchia; barile *m.*; fusto, botte *f.*; *whisky matured in the* —, whisky invecchiato nel fusto; *wine from the* —, vino dal fusto; (mus.) i legni, gli istrumenti a fiato; (paint.) tavola; (bowls) boccia.

**wood-anemone** *n.* (bot.) silvia. **-ant** *n.* (ent.) formica fulva.

**woodbine** *n.* (bot.) caprifoglio; (USA) vite *f.* del Canadà.

**wood-carver** *n.* intagliatore, scultore in legno. **-carving** *n.* intaglio, scultura in legno.

**woodchat** *n.* (orn.) averla capirossa.

**wood-chopper** *n.* ascia, asciuolo, scuretta.

**woodchuck** *n.* (zool.) marmotta dell'America settentrionale.

**woodcock** *n.* (orn.) beccaccia; (cul.) *Scotch* —, uova strapazzate con filetti d'acciuga su tosto.

**woodcraft** *n.* conoscenza dei boschi; arte di lavorare il legno.

**woodcut** *n.* incisione su legno, xilografia, silografia; vignetta.

**wood-cutter** *n.* legnaiolo, boscaiolo, tagliatore di legna, tagliabosco; (art), xilografo, silografo.

**wood-cutting** *n.* taglio di legna; (art) incisione su legno, xilografia, silografia.

**wooded** *adj.* boscoso, coperto di alberi, alberato.

**wooden** *adj.* di legno, legnoso; (fig.) rigido, inespressivo; *a — smile*, un sorriso stereotipato; — *horse*, cavallo di Troia; (gymn.) cavalletto; — *spoon*, cucchiaio di legno; (sport) *to get the — spoon*, arrivare ultimo; *the — walls of old England*, le vecchie navi da guerra inglesi.

**wooden-headed** *adj.* stupido, ottuso, testone. **-headedness** *n.* stupidità.

**woodenness** *n.* legnosità; (fig.) rigidità; stupidità.

**woodland** *n.* boscaglia, zona boschiva; *attrib.* boschereccio.

**wood-lark** *n.* (orn.) calandra. **-louse** *n.* (zool.) onisco, porcellino di terra. **-moth** *n.* (ent.) anobio. **-notes** *n.pl.* il canto dei boschi, il canto degli uccelli. **-nymph** *n.* (myth.) driade *f.*, ninfa dei boschi, amadriade *f.*

**woodpecker** *n.* (orn.) picchio.

**wood-pigeon** *n.* (orn.) colombo selvatico, palombo, colombaccio. **-pile** *n.* catasta di legna. **-pulp** *n.* pasta di legno, cellulosa.

**woodruff** *n.* (bot.) stellina odorosa, epatica dei boschi.

**woodsman** cacciatore, abitatore dei boschi.

**wood-sorrel** *n.* (bot.) acetosella, pane di cuculo. **-spirit** *n.* alcool metilico, spirito di legno. **-stack** *n.* catasta di legname. **-warbler** *n.* (orn.) luí verde. **-wind** *n.* (mus.) (i)strumenti di legno, (i)strumenti a fiato.

**woodwork** *n.* lavoro in legno, ebanisteria; (motor.) carrozzeria.

**wood-worm** *n.* (ent.) tarlo.

**woody** *adj.* boscoso, boschivo, alberato; (bot.) legnoso, ligneo; (fig.) silvestre, silvano.

**wooer** *n.* corteggiatore; (fam.) spasimante *m.*

**woof**[1] *n.* (text.) trama.

**woof**[2] (onom.) bau bau.

**wooing** *adj.* che corteggia, corteggiante; *n.* corteggiamento.

**wool** *n.* lana; tessuto di lana; *carding —*, lana da carda; *pulled —*, lana da concia; *cotton —*, bambagia, ovatta; *wood —*, lana di legno; *steel —*, lana d'acciaio; *glass —*, lana di vetro; *hand-knitting —*, lana per maglieria; *a skein of —*, una matassa di lana; *the — industry*, l'industria laniera; (hist.) *the — guild*, l'arte della lana; *— mill*, *— factory*, lanificio; *to wear —*, portare indumenti di lana; *dyed in the —*, tinto in lana, lana tinta; (fig.) *a dyed-in-the-— liberal*, un liberale purosangue, un liberale convinto; (fig.) *against the —*, contropelo; *to pull — over someone's eyes*, gettar fumo negli occhi di qualcuno; vello; (of animal) lana, peluria; (fam., human hair) capigliatura riccia e lanosa; (joc.) *keep your — on*, non ti arrabbiare.

**wool-bearing** *adj.* lanigero, lanifero. **-carding** *n.* cardatura della lana.

**wool-comber** *n.* (person) pettinatore, pettinatrice; (machine) pettinatrice *f.* **-combing** *n.* pettinatura della lana; *-combing machine*, pettinatrice.

**wool-fat** *n.* lanolina. **-fell** *n.* pelle *f.* di pecora, vello.

**woolgathering** *n.* (fam.) distrazione, sbadataggine *f.*, sogno ad occhi aperti; *to be —*, sognare ad occhi aperti.

**woollen** *adj.* di lana; *— cloth*, panno di lana; *— goods*, articoli di lana; *n.pl.* articoli di lana; indumenti di lana.

**woolliness** *n.* lanosità; (fig.) confusione mentale; (radio) mancanza di chiarezza; (art) *— of outline*, nebulosità dei contorni.

**woolly** *adj.* di lana, lanoso, lanuto; *— hair*, capelli lanosi; (fig.) indistinto, impreciso; *a — mind*, una mente annebbiata; *n.pl. woollies*, biancheria intima di lana; maglieria di lana.

**woolsack** *n.* sacco di lana; (pol.) il cuscino del saggio del Lord Cancelliere d'Inghilterra nella Camera dei Lordi; (fig.) carica del Lord Cancelliere.

**wool-waste** *n.* cascami *m.pl.* di lana. **-winder** *n.* (text.) matassatrice; gomitolaio, aggomitolatrice *f.*

**wop** *n.* guappo; (derog.) Italiano; (USA) immigrato italiano.

**word** *n.* parola; termine *m.*; vocabolo; *in a —*, in una parola, in breve; *that isn't the right —*, non è il termine giusto; *in other -s*, in altri termini, vale a dire, altrimenti detto; *I can't find this — in the dictionary*, non trovo questo vocabolo sul lessico; *a play upon -s*, un giuoco di parole; *to take the -s out of someone's mouth*, anticipare le parole di qualcuno; *to eat one's -s*, ritrattare le proprie parole; *to put in a good — for*, dire una buona parola per; *to suit the action to the -s*, passare dalle parole ai fatti; *deeds, not -s*, fatti, non parole; *to have the last —*, avere l'ultima parola; *the last — in*, l'ultima novità nel campo di; (provb.) *a — to the wise*, a buon intenditore poche parole; (excl.) *my —!*, accidenti!; *— for —*, alla lettera, testualmente; *he never says a —*, non apre mai bocca; *to waste -s*, sprecare fiato; *a — in season*, un consiglio opportuno; *don't say a —!*, non dire niente a nessuno!; *I can't get a — out of him*, non riesco a farlo parlare; *by — of mouth*, oralmente, a voce; (fam.) *mum's the —!*, acqua in bocca!; *I want to have a — with you*, vorrei dirti una cosa; *to come to -s with*, litigare con; *you are too kind for -s*, sei troppo gentile; *book of -s*, (of opera), libretto; *here is your book of -s*, ecco le tue istruzioni in iscritto; parola (d'onore), promessa; *I give you my —*, ti dò la mia parola; *he is a man of his —*, è uomo di parola; *to take someone at his —*, prendere qualcuno in parola; *he is as good as his —*, mantiene ciò che promette; *to break one's —*, mancare alla parola data; ordine *m.*, comando; *to give the —*, dare ordine; *— was given to cease fire*, fu dato ordine di cessare il fuoco; (password) parola d'ordine; notizia, informazione; *— came that he was dead*, giunse la notizia che era morto; *to send — of*, far sapere; *— is going round that . . .*, circola la voce che . . .; (rel.) verbo; *the — of God*, il Verbo di Dio; *in the beginning was the —*, nel principio fu il Verbo.

**word** *tr.* mettere in parole, redigere, esprimere, formulare; *to — a message*, redigere un messaggio.

**wordiness** *n.* verbosità, prolissità.

**wording** *n.* espressione, formulazione; redazione.

**wordless** *adj.* senza parole; muto.

**word-painting** *n.* descrizione pittoresca, ritratto vivace.

**word-perfect** *adj.* (persona) che conosce a memoria il testo (di una poesia, *etc.*); (allievo) che ha imparato a perfezione la lezione; (theatr.) (attore) che sa a memoria la parte.

**wordy** *adj.* verboso, prolisso; diffuso, ampolloso.

**wore** *p.def.* of **wear**, *q.v.*

**work** *n.* lavoro; fatica; *hard —*, lavoro pesante, dura fatica; *to set to —*, *tr.* far lavorare, *intr.* mettersi al lavoro; *to be out of —*, essere disoccupato; *to stop —*, smettere di lavorare; *to go the right way to —*, fare come si deve; *to have one's — cut out*, aver di che lavorare; *to make short — of it*, sbrigarsela; *a maid of all —*, una domestica tutto fare; (provb.) *all — and no play makes Jack a dull boy*, meglio un asino vivo che un dottore morto; opera; oggetto lavorato; *a — of art*, un'opera d'arte; *the complete -s of Petrarch*, le opere complete di Petrarca; *this book is your best —*, questo libro è la tua opera migliore; *-s of mercy*, opere di misericordia; *what a beautiful piece of —!*, che bell'oggetto; *the villagers sell their — to tourists*, gli abitanti del paese vendono oggetti lavorati ai turisti; *engineering —*, lavori di costruzione; (mil.) *defensive -s*, fortificazioni *f.pl.*, opere di difesa; *the Office of Works*, il Ministero dei Lavori Pubblici; *road -s*, lavori stradali; meccanismo; *the -s of a clock*, il meccanismo di un orologio; fabbrica, stabilimento, officina.

**work** *intr.* lavorare; *to — hard*, lavorare sodo; *to — twice as hard as anyone else*, lavorare per due; *to — like a Trojan*, sgobbare, lavorare come un bue; *to — overtime*, fare lo straordinario; *to — to rule*, fare lo sciopero del regolamento; *to — at Italian*, studiare l'italiano; *to — for a firm*, lavorare presso una ditta, essere alle dipendenze di una ditta; funzionare; *the bell doesn't —*, il campanello non funziona; *I can't get this machine to —*, non riesco a far funzionare questa macchina; *to start -ing*, entrare in funzionamento; *the screw has -ed loose*, la vite si è allentata; fermentare, germogliare; *the yeast is beginning to —*, il lievito comincia a fermentare; (fig.) *drop him a hint and let it —*, dàgli un consiglio e lascia che germogli; *to — upstream*, risalire la corrente; (naut.) *to — southwards*, navigare verso il sud contro il vento; *his mouth was -ing*, torceva la bocca; *tr.* far lavorare, far funzionare, azionare, operare; *he -s me hard*, mi fa lavorare sodo; *to — a crane*, azionare una gru; *do you know how to — the brakes?*, sei capace di far funzionare i freni?; *time -s many changes*, il tempo opera molti cambiamenti; *to — oneself into a rage*, montare in furia; *to — oneself to death*, ammazzarsi col lavoro; *the current -s the mill*, il mulino è azionato dalla corrente; *flowers -ed in silk*, fiori ricamati in seta; *to — a nail into a hole*, introdurre un chiodo in un buco; dirigere, amministrare; *he is -ing a farm*, dirige una fattoria; *to — one's passage*, pagarsi la traversata

lavorando; *to — one's hands free*, liberarsi le mani; *to — one's way*, aprirsi il cammino lavorando; plasmare, modellare; *to — clay into a statue*, modellare una statua in argilla; *iron is easily -ed*, il ferro è molto malleabile; (fig.) *to — the audience into a frenzy*, sollevare l'entusiasmo frenetico dell'uditorio; sfruttare; FOLLOW. BY ADV.: *to — away*, *intr.* continuare a lavorare, lavorare con diligenza; *to — down*, *intr.* scendere poco a poco, *tr.* *to — one's way down*, scendere cautamente; (industr.) *to — a piece down to shape*, lavorare un pezzo fino a farlo prendere la forma desiderata; *to — in*, *tr.* far entrare poco a poco, introdurre, far penetrare; *try to — in a few jokes*, prova di introdurre qualche battuta umoristica; *intr.* andare d'accordo, adattarsi; *the plan won't — in with yours*, il piano non si adatterà al vostro; *to — off*, *tr.* liberarsi di, sfogare, smaltire; (typ.) tirare (i fogli); *to — off one's anger*, sfogare la rabbia; *intr.* staccarsi; *to — on*, *intr.* continuare a lavorare; (fig.) influenzare; *we have no data to — on*, non abbiamo dati su cui basarci; *to — out*, *tr.* elaborare, progettare, calcolare; (math.) *to — out a problem*, risolvere un problema; (of a prisoner) *to — out his time*, espiare la pena; (of a mine) esaurire; *the mine is -ed out*, la miniera è esaurita; *intr.* uscire poco a poco; (fig.) *I don't know how it will —*, non so come andrà a finire; *the price works out at . . .*, il prezzo ammonta a . . .; *to — round*, *intr.* girare, cambiare direzione; *the wind is -ing round*, il vento sta girando; *tr.* *to — round a hill*, girare una collina; *to — up*, *intr.* aumentare a poco a poco, salire; *to — up to a crisis*, culminare in una crisi; *it's -ing up for a storm*, viene una burrasca; *what are you -ing up to?*, dove vuoi arrivare?, che cosa intendi dire?; *tr.* preparare, formare, lavorare; *to — up a connection*, farsi una clientela; (fig.) eccitare, fomentare, suscitare; *to — oneself up*, riscaldarsi, eccitarsi; *he was all -ed up*, era agitatissimo; *to — one's way up*, fare strada, salire a poco a poco.

**workable** *adj.* lavorabile; manovrabile; sfruttabile, redditizio; realizzabile, praticabile.

**workaday** *adj.* di ogni giorno, quotidiano, comune; *— clothes*, abiti da lavoro; (fig.) *this — world*, questo mondo noioso.

**work-bag** *n.* borsa da lavoro. **-basket** *n.* cestino da lavoro.

**worker** *n.* lavoratore, lavoratrice; operaio, operaia; *to be a good —*, lavorare bene; *the -s*, la categoria degli operai, la classe lavoratrice, il proletariato; *-s of the world unite!*, lavoratori di tutto il mondo riunitevi!; *the firm employs 200 -s*, la ditta dà lavoro a duecento fra impiegati e operai; *fellow -s*, compagni di lavoro; (fig.) *a — of miracles*, taumaturgo, mago; *social —*, assistente *m.* sociale; *unskilled —*, manovale *m.*; *skilled —*, operaio di categoria; *black-coated —*, *white-collar —*, impiegato.

**workhouse** *n.* (hist.) asilo dei poveri, albergo dei poveri, ospizio di mendicità; *— inmate*, ricoverato all'asilo dei poveri; *to end one's days in the —*, finire all'asilo dei poveri, (fig.) rovinarsi, fallire; (USA) riformatorio per minorenni.

**working** *adj.* che lavora; che funziona; operante; lavorativo; *a — man*, un operaio; *the — classes*, la classe operaia, il proletariato; *a hard-working man*, un uomo che lavora molto; *the — parts of a machine*, le parti funzionanti di una macchina; *— days*, giorni lavorativi; (comm.) *— capital*, capitale circolante; *a — agreement*, un modus vivendi; *a — theory*, una teoria praticabile; *not —*, non funziona, guasto; (pol.) *a — majority*, una maggioranza sufficiente; *— party*, gruppo di lavoro, (mil.) corvè *f.*; *n.* lavoro, lavorìo; *— hours*, ore *f.pl.* di lavoro, orario; *— day*, giornata lavorativa; *— to rule*, sciopero del regolamento; (fig.) *the -s of conscience*, il lavorìo della coscienza; funzionamento; *to put a machine in — order*, mettere una macchina in stato di efficienza; (industr.) lavorazione; (min.) galleria; *disused -s*, gallerie abbandonate; (math.) calcolo; (of beer, *etc.*) fermentazione; *— out*, esecuzione; (of a plan) elaborazione, calcolo; (of a problem) soluzione; *— round*, cambiamento di direzione.

**workless** *adj.* senza lavoro, disoccupato; *the —*, i disoccupati.

**workman** *n.* operaio, lavoratore, salariato; *the workmen (of a factory)*, la maestranza; *skilled —*, operaio specializzato, operaio di prima categoria. **-like** *adj.* ben fatto, eseguito a regola d'arte; (of person) competente, abile, capace. **-ship** *n.* esecuzione, lavorazione, fattura; *a fine example of -ship*, un articolo di buona fattura; *sound -ship*, esecuzione accurata.

**work-out** *n.* esercizi ginnastici.

**workpeople** *n.* lavoratori *m.pl.*, operai *m.pl.*, maestranza.

**work-room** *n.* stanza da lavoro, studio, laboratorio, officina.

**workshop** *n.* officina, laboratorio, bottega.

**work-shy** *adj.* pigro, neghittoso, indolente, avverso al lavoro. **-table** *n.* tavolo da lavoro.

**workwoman** *n.* operaia, lavoratrice.

**world** *n.* mondo, universo; *this —*, questo mondo, questa vita, quaggiù; *the other —*, *the next —*, *the — to come*, l'altro mondo, l'oltretomba *m.*, l'al di là *m.*; *the end of the —*, la fine del mondo, (rel.) la consumazione dei secoli; *at the other end of the —*, agli antipodi; *the Old World*, il Vecchio Mondo; *the New World*, il Nuovo Mondo, l'America; *all over the —*, dappertutto, in tutto il mondo; *that's the way of the —*, così va il mondo; *out of the —*, fuori mondo; *he's gone down in the —*, ha conosciuto giorni migliori; *to go round the —*, fare il giro del mondo; *a — of troubles*, un mare di guai; *— without end*, in saecula saeculorum, per sempre; *he is not long for this —*, non ha molto da vivere; *to make the best of both -s*, conciliare i piaceri del mondo con la salute spirituale; (fam.) *what in the — is happening?*, che diavolo succede?; *where in the — is my purse?*, dove mai è andata a finire la mia borsetta?; (astron.) mondo, pianeta *m.*, terra; mondo, vita mondana, società; secolo; *a man of the —*, un uomo del mondo; *the — of letters*, il mondo letterario; *the publishing —*, il mondo editoriale; *the English-speaking —*, i popoli di lingua inglese; *the animal —*, il regno animale; la gente; *what will the — say*, che cosa ne dirà la gente?; *attrib.* mondiale, del mondo, universale; *the second — war*, la seconda guerra mondiale.

**world-famous** *adj.* di fama mondiale, rinomato. **-history** *n.* storia universale, storia del mondo.

**worldliness** *n.* temporalità; (fig.) mondanità, attaccamento ai piaceri di questo mondo.

**worldling** *n.* persona mondana, amante dei piaceri di questo mondo, bontempone *m.*

**worldly** *adj.* terreno, temporale, di questo mondo; (rel.) secolare; *— goods*, beni temporali; *— wisdom*, buon senso, saggezza; (fam.) *all my — goods*, tutta la mia roba; (fig.) mondano, dedicato ai piaceri materiali; *a — cleric*, un prete mondano.

**worldly-minded** *adj.* mondano, attaccato alle cose di questo mondo. **-mindedness** *n.* attaccamento alle cose materiali.

**world(ly)-wise** *adj.* che conosce la vita, che conosce il mondo; pratico, oculato, esperimentato, esperto.

**world-power** *n.* potere secolare;

potere temporale; (pol.) potenza mondiale, grande potenza. **-weary** *adj.* stanco della vita, stufo di vivere. **-wide** *adj.* mondiale, universale, diffuso in tutto il mondo.

**worm** *n.* verme *m.*; baco; bruco; (fig.) tarlo; *earth-worm*, lombrico; *book-worm*, tarma, (fig.) topo di biblioteca; arenicola, lombrico della sabbia; (med.) *to have -s*, avere i vermi; *one day the — will turn*, anche la pazienza ha un limite; (derog.) persona spregevole, poltrone *m.*; (mech.) filetto; vite *f.* senza fine; (chem.) serpentino, storta.

**worm** *tr.* strisciare; (fig.) insinuarsi, intrufolarsi; *to — one's way through the bushes*, passare strisciando attraverso i cespugli; (fig.) carpire; *to — a secret out of*, carpire un segreto a; (mech.) filettare (una vite); liberare dai vermi; estrarre i vermi.

**worm-auger** *n.* succhiello a vite, trivella. **-bit** *n.* morso a vite. **-cast** *n.* terra sollevata dal lombrico. **-eaten** *adj.* roso dai vermi; tarlato, bucherellato; mangiato dai vermi.

**wormwood** *n.* (bot.) assenzio, artemisia amara; (fig.) amarezza, mortificazione.

**worn** *p. part.* of **wear**², *q.v.*; *adj.* liso, usato, sciupato, già portato; logorato, corroso; (fig.) consumato, esausto, sfinito, ridotto a un cencio; *he is — to a shadow*, è solo l'ombra di se stesso.

**worried** *adj.* preoccupato, inquieto, vessato; *to look —*, sembrare preoccupato.

**worrier** *n.* persona sempre preoccupata; seccatore *m.*; (dog) cane *m.* che attacca le pecore.

**worry** *n.* inquietudine *f.*, ansia, preoccupazione; dispiacere *m.*; (fig.) fastidio, molestia.

**worry** *tr.* preoccupare; *something is -ing him*, c'è qualche cosa che lo preoccupa; *don't — your head about it*, non ti preoccupare di questo; infastidire, importunare, molestare, vessare; seccare; *don't — him*, non lo infastidire; lasciatelo tranquillo; *to — to death*, far disperare; (of animals) azzannare, lacerare, tormentare; *intr.* preoccuparsi, tormentarsi, essere in ansia; *he is always -ing*, è sempre preoccupato; *what's the use of -ing?*, perchè preoccuparsi?; *to — along*, tirare avanti (nonostante le preoccupazioni); *to — out a problem*, risolvere faticosamente un problema.

**worrying** *adj.* preoccupante; fastidioso, molesto, vessatorio; *n.* preoccupazione, ansia; vessazione.

**worse** *adj.* (comp. of **bad**) peggiore; *the weather couldn't be —*, il tempo non potrebbe essere peggiore; *it might have been —*, sarebbe potuto andare peggio; *— luck!*, purtroppo!; *so much the —!*, tanto peggio!; *the — for wear*, logorato a forze di portarlo; *she's looking the — for wear*, ha l'aria un po' malandata, (joc., drunk) sembra un po' brilla; *he's feeling none the — for the accident*, non ha risentito per nulla dell'incidente; *he's getting —*, (in health) sta peggiorando, (in conduct) diventa sempre più cattivo; *adv.* (comp. of **badly**) peggio; *— still*, peggio ancora; *— off*, in situazione peggiore, meno ricco; *— than ever*, peggio che mai; *a hundred times —*, cento volte peggio; *— educated*, meno istruito; *n.* peggio; *there is — to follow*, il peggio deve ancora venire; *a change for the —*, un peggioramento; *to change for the —*, peggiorare, cambiare in peggio; *things are going from bad to —*, le cose vanno di male in peggio; *for better or for —*, nella buona e nell'aversa fortuna.

**worsen** *tr.* aggravare, peggiorare, rendere peggiore; *intr.* peggiorare, deteriorare, aggravarsi, diventare peggiore. **-ing** *n.* peggioramento, deterioramento.

**worship** *n.* culto; adorazione; venerazione; (fig.) adulazione; *public —*, ufficio in chiesa, servizio religioso; *divine —*, l'ufficio religioso, la messa; *place of —*, luogo sacro; *the — of images*, l'iconolatria; *the — of success*, il culto del successo; *hero-worship*, il culto degli eroi; eccellenza, signoria; *His Worship the Mayor*, il Signor Sindaco; *your -s*, le Signorie Vostre; (to magistrate) *yes, your —*, sí, signor giudice.

**worship** *tr.* adorare; venerare; (fig.) idolatrare; *to — sport*, avere un culto per lo sport; *intr.* assistere alla messa, ascoltare la messa, andare in chiesa, assistere a un ufficio religioso.

**worshipful** *adj.* (title) eccellente, eccellentissimo; onorevole, venerabile.

**worshipp-er** *n.* adoratore; veneratore; (rel.) praticante *m.*, *f.*; *pl. the -s*, i fedeli. **-ing** *adj.* adorante, adoratore; *n.* culto; adorazione; venerazione.

**worst** *adj. superl.* of **bad**, peggiore, pessimo, il più brutto; *the — time of year*, la stagione peggiore di tutto l'anno; *the — book I have ever read*, il più brutto libro che abbia mai letto; *adv.* peggio; *— of all*, peggio di tutto; *the — organized*, il meno organizzato; *n.* il peggio; *the — is over*, il peggio è ormai passato; *the — of it is that . . .*, il peggio è che . . .; *to be prepared for the —*, essere preparato al peggio; *if the — comes to the —*, nella peggiore delle ipotesi, a peggio andare; *to do one's —*, fare il peggior male possibile; *he got the — of it*, ne ha avuto il peggio; *to be at one's —*, essere in pessima forma, fare bruttissima figura; *the — has happened*, è successa una catastrofe, è la fine!

**worst** *tr.* sconfiggere, battere, avere la meglio su.

**worsted**¹ *part. adj.* sconfitto; *to be —*, avere la peggio.

**worsted**² *n.* (text.) worsted *m.*, tessuto di lana pettinata.

**worth** *adj.* del valore di, valente, (che) vale; *to be —*, valere; *it is — nothing*, non vale niente; *is it — while?*, vale la pena?; *whatever it may be —*, valga che valga; *he is — a lot of money*, ha un sacco di soldi, è ricchissimo; *the game isn't — the candle*, il giuoco non vale la candela; (provb.) *a bird in the hand is — two in the bush*, meglio un uovo oggi che una gallina domani; degno, meritevole; *— attention*, degno di considerazione; *this book is — reading*, questo libro merita di essere letto; *n.* valore *m.*; prezzo; (fig.) merito; *of great —*, di grande valore; *a man of —*, un uomo di merito; *to want one's money's —*, volere una cosa che vale il prezzo.

**worthiness** *n.* merito, valore *m.*; rispettabilità; capacità, attitudine *f.*

**worth-while** *adj.* che vale la pena; *a — job*, un lavoro che rende.

**worthless** *adj.* senza valore, di nessun valore; (fig.) immeritevole; indegno; *a — cheque*, un assegno a vuoto. **-ness** *n.* mancanza di valore; (fig.) indegnità.

**worthy** *adj.* degno; meritevole; *— of respect*, degno di rispetto; *it is — of note*, vale la pena di notare, conviene notare; (iron.) bravo; *n.* personalità, notabile *m.*; *the village worthies*, i pezzi grossi del paese.

**would** see **will** *aux.*

**would-be** *adj.* sedicente, preteso, aspirante.

**wound**¹ *n.* ferita, piaga; (fig.) offesa; *to dress a —*, medicare una ferita; *tr.* ferire; (fig.) offendere; *to — the feelings of*, urtare la suscettibilità di.

**wound**² *p. part.* of **wind**², *q.v.*

**wound-ed** *part. adj.* ferito; *a — man*, un ferito; *n.pl. the —*, i feriti. **-ing** *gerund* il ferire; *adj.* che ferisce, che offende; offensivo, insultante.

**wove** *p.def.*, **woven** *part.* of **weave**, *q.v.*

**wow** *excl.* uh!; (slang) *it was a —!*, è stato un successone!; (cinema)

*-s*, difetti della riproduzione sonora.

**wrack** *n.* alghe *f.pl.*; relitti di mare.

**wraith** *n.* spettro, fantasma *m.*

**wrangl-e** *n.* lite *f.*; litigio, bisticcio; alterco; baruffa; *intr.* litigare, bisticciare. **-er** *n.* attaccabrighe *m.*; (Cambridge) studente classificato tra i primi all'esame del tripos di matematica. **-ing** *adj.* litigioso; *n.* litigio, alterco, bisticcio.

**wrap** *n.* scialle *m.*, sciarpa; accappatoio, vestaglia; mantello; coperta da viaggio; (comm.) involucro, imballo.

**wrap** *tr.* avvolgere, coprire, rivestire; *to — oneself up*, coprirsi bene; confezionare, incartare.

**wrapped** *adj.* avvolto; incartato, imballato; (fig.) *to be — up in someone*, vivere per qualcuno; *to be — up in one's work*, essere completamente assorbito dal lavoro.

**wrapper** *n.* involucro, copertina, fascia, fascetta; (post) *stamped —*, sottofascia affrancata; (dressing-gown) vestaglia, veste da camera; (techn.) rivestimento.

**wrapping** *gerund* l'avvolgere, il fare pacchi; *n.* involucro, imballo; carta da impacco.

**wrath** *n.* ira, collera; indignazione; *slow to —*, non facile alla collera; *to bottle up one's —*, reprimere la collera. **-ful** *adj.* adirato, iroso, collerico, incollerito. **-fulness** *n.* ira, collera.

**wreak** *tr.* sfogare, dare sfogo a, dare libero corso a; *to — vengeance on*, vendicarsi di; *to — one's anger*, dar sfogo alla collera. **-ing** *n.* sfogo.

**wreath** *n.* ghirlanda; (poet.) serto; corona; *funeral —*, corona mortuaria; *to lay a —*, deporre una corona; *laurel —*, corona d'alloro; (fig.) anello, cerchio; *a — of smoke*, un anello di fumo.

**wreath-e** *tr.* inghirlandare, incoronare; intrecciare; attorcigliare; *the snake -d itself round the tree*, il serpente si attorcigliò attorno all'albero; *intr.* innalzarsi in volute. **-ed** *adj.* inghirlandato, coronato; intrecciato; *a face -ed in smiles*, un viso raggiante. **-ing** *n.* intreccio; attorcigliamento.

**wreck** *n.* naufragio; nave che ha subito un naufragio, relitto; (fig.) rovina, relitto, rottame *m.*, rudere *m.*; *my car is a —*, la mia macchina è ridotta a un rottame; *to be a nervous —*, avere i nervi a pezzi; *he is only a — of his former self*, non è più che l'ombra di se stesso.

**wreck** *tr.* far naufragare; (a train) far deragliare; (pol.) sabotare, ostruire, silurare; (fig.) rovinare; demolire; distruggere. **-age** *n.* naufragio; rovina; rottami *m.pl.*, relitti *m.pl.*, resti di un naufragio. **-er** *n.* persona che causa naufragi a scopo di saccheggio, naufragatore; (pol.) ostruzionista *m.* **-ing** *n.* il far naufragare; il far rovinare, distruzione; (pol.) *-ing policy*, politica di sabotaggio, ostruzionismo.

**wren** *n.* (orn.) scricciolo, scriccio, troglodite *m.*

**wrench** *n.* strappo, torsione, tirata; (fig.) strazio, dolore *m.*; (med.) strappo muscolare, slogatura; (mech.) chiave fissa; *monkey-wrench*, chiave inglese.

**wrench** *tr.* strappare, torcere; (fig.) forzare, aprire con uno strappo; *to — off*, strappare via; *to — oneself free*, liberarsi con uno strappo; alterare, svisare.

**wrest** *tr.* strappare, togliere con violenza; estorcere; *to — a confession from*, estorcere una confessione a.

**wrestl-e** *n.* lotta; (sport) lotta libera; (fig.) sforzo, lotta dura; *intr.* lottare, combattere; *to — with a problem*, applicarsi con accanimento alla soluzione di un problema; (sport) fare la lotta. **-er** *n.* lottatore. **-ing** *n.* (sport) lotta; *all-in-wrestling*, catch *m. indecl.*, lotta libera; *-ing match*, incontro di lotta; (fig.) lotta, combattimento.

**wretch** *n.* delinquente *m.*, *f.*; (fig.) disgraziato, poveretto, meschino, infelice *m.*, sciagurato; *that poor —*, quel povero diavolo; (derog.) vigliacco; incosciente *m.*, *f.*

**wretched** *adj.* infelice, miserabile, disgraziato; *to lead a — life*, trascinare una vita miserabile; *that — woman has lost everything*, quella poveretta ha perso tutto; *to look —*, avere l'aria sofferente; *to feel —*, sentirsi male, essere infelice; pietoso, pessimo, di pessima qualità, misero, squallido, meschino; *a — performance*, uno spettacolo pietoso; *a — little room*, un bugigattolo; *a — little house*, una stamberga; *they gave us — food*, ci hanno fatto un trattamento pessimo; *— weather*, brutto tempo, tempo infame; (joc.) maledetto. **-ness** *n.* miseria, povertà; (fig.) tristezza, depressione.

**wrick** *n.* strappo, storta, slogatura; *— in the neck*, torcicollo; *tr.* storcere, slogare; *to — one's ankle*, slogarsi la caviglia.

**wriggl-e** *n.* contorsione, contorcimento, (fig.) tergiversazione, equivocità; *intr.* contorcersi; dimenarsi; storcersi; insinuarsi, intrufolarsi; (fig.) tergiversare, equivocare, dare risposte evasive; *to — out*, sgusciar fuori; *to — out of an awkward situation*, cavarsi d'impaccio; *tr.* contorcere, dimenare. **-er** *n.* che si contorce; che sguscia; che non vuole star seduto; (fig.) tergiversatore *m.* **-ing** *n.* contorcimento, dimenamento; (fig.) tergiversazione; *adj.* che si contorce.

**wring** *n.* stretta, torsione; *a — of the hand*, una stretta di mano; *tr.* torcere, contorcere; strizzare; stringere, serrare; spremere, strappare; (joc.) *I'll — his neck!*, gli torcerò il collo!; *to — a bird's neck*, tirare il collo a un volatile; *he wrung his hands*, si torse le mani; *it -s my heart*, mi si stringe il cuore; *to — (out) the washing*, strizzare la biancheria; *to — out a confession*, estorcere una confessione; *to — money out of*, spillare denaro a; *to — out a tear*, spremere una lacrima. **-er** *n.* torcitoio; asciugatrice meccanica. **-ing** *gerund* il torcere; *adj.* *-ing wet*, bagnato fradicio, bagnato da torcere; *n.* torcitura, asciugatura meccanica.

**wrinkl-e** *n.* ruga, crespa; piega, grinza; rugosità; crespa, increspatura (fam.) espediente *m.*, trovata astuta, consiglio utile; *tr.* corrugare; raggrinzire; increspare; spiegazzare; *intr.* corrugarsi; raggrinzirsi; incresparsi. **-ing** *n.* rugosità; increspamento, increspatura; raggrinzimento; contrazione. **-y** *adj.* corrugato; rugoso; raggrinzito; increspato.

**wrist** *n.* polso; *to feel someone's —*, tastare il polso a qualcuno. **-band** *n.* polsino da camicia, manichino.

**wrist-bone** *n.* carpo, osso del carpo.

**wristlet** *n.* braccialetto; *— watch*, orologio da polso.

**wrist-watch** *n.* orologio da polso.

**writ** *n.* (leg.) mandato, ordine *m.*, mandato esecutivo; *— of summons*, mandato di comparizione, citazione; *to serve a — on*, consegnare un mandato a; (pol.) ordine *m.* di procedere all'elezione di un membro del parlamento; *Holy Writ*, la Sacra Scrittura; (poet.) *part. adj.* of **write.**

**write** *tr.* scrivere; *to — a good hand*, avere una bella calligrafia; *I have written ten pages*, ho riempito dieci fogli; *that's nothing to — home about*, non è niente di speciale; (fig.) *surprise was written all over his face*, lo stupore era dipinto sul suo volto; *intr.* scrivere; *he -s*, fa lo scrittore; *he -s for the papers*, fa il giornalista; *— as soon as you can*, scrivimi non appena possibile; FOLLOW. BY ADV.: *to — back*, *tr.*, *intr.* rispondere per iscritto, *to — down*, *tr.* trascrivere, annotare, registrare (in iscritto), mettere su carta, (fig.) definire, (derog.) denigrare; (comm.) *to — down*

*capital*, ridurre il capitale; *to — for*, *tr.* scrivere per far venire; *to — in*, *tr.* inserire, *intr.* rivolgersi per iscritto; *to — off*, scrivere in fretta, buttare giù rapidamente, (debts) cancellare, annullare, (capital) ridurre, ammortare, ammortizzare; *to — out*, *tr.* trascrivere, copiare, fare una bella copia di; formulare, redigere; *to — out a cheque*, scrivere un assegno; *to — oneself out*, esaurirsi, esaurire la propria vena, (fam.) vuotare il sacco; *to — up*, *tr.* aggiornare, (journ.) redigere, fare un resoconto di, (fig.) scrivere un elogio esagerato di, fare la pubblicità di.

**write-off** *n.* annullamento per iscritto; (fam.) *it's a —!*, non c'è nulla da fare!; *he's a —* non si può più contare su di lui; *the car's a —*, la macchina è ridotta a un rottame.

**writer** *n.* scrittore, scrittrice, autore, autrice; *the — of this letter*, lo scrivente, chi scrive; *he is one of the best -s in Italy*, è una delle migliori penne d'Italia; scrivano, copista *m.*; *letter-writer*, scrivano pubblico; *-'s cramp*, crampo degli scrivani; (cinem.) *script-writer*, sceneggiatore; (Scot.) avvocato, legale *m.*, procuratore *m.*; *— to the Signet*, procuratore.

**write-up** *n.* pubblicità elogiativa.

**writh-e** *intr.* contorcersi, dimenarsi convulsamente, dibattersi; (fig.) fremere. **-ing** *n.* contorsione, contorcimento; convulsione.

**writing** *pres. part.* of **write**, *q.v.*; *cannot come*, —, impossibile venire, segue lettera; *gerund* lo scrivere; *I like —*, mi piace scrivere; *at the time of —*, in questo momento, (journ.) nel mentre andiamo in macchina; *n. to put into —*, trascrivere; *to answer in —*, rispondere per iscritto; calligrafia, scrittura; *illegible —*, calligrafia indecifrabile; scritto, scritta; *a fine piece of —*, un bel brano, un pezzo buono; (fig.) *the — on the wall*, un presagio infausto; *pl.* gli scritti, le opere (letterarie); *— down*, annotazione, registrazione, (comm.) riduzione del capitale; *— off*, (comm.) ammortamento, ammortizzazione.

**writing-block** *n.* blocco (di carta da scrivere). **-book** *n.* quaderno; manuale di calligrafia. **-cabinet** *n.* scrivania. **-case** *n.* astuccio con il necessario per scrivere. **-desk** *n.* scrivania. **-pad** *n.* notes *m.*, taccuino, blocco (di carta da scrivere), cartello da scrivere. **-paper** *n.* carta da lettera, carta da scrivere. **-table** *n.* tavolino, scrittoio, scrivania.

**written** *p. part.* of **write**, *q.v.*; *adj.* messo per iscritto, scritto, in iscritto; *a — apology*, scusa per iscritto; (leg.) *— evidence*, prova scritta.

**wrong** *adj.* cattivo; immorale; peccaminoso; illegale; *it is — to steal*, rubare è peccato; *that was very — of you*, hai fatto molto male; (fam.) *he's a — 'un*, è un farabutto; sbagliato, erroneo, inesatto; *my watch is —*, il mio orologio va male; *the — way up*, capovolto, a rovescio; *the — side out*, a rovescio; *to be —*, avere torto; essere sbagliato; *you are quite —*, ti sbagli; *to take the — train*, salire sul treno sbagliato; *— ideas*, idee sbagliate; *to drive on the — side of the road*, circolare in senso vietato; *to do the — thing*, fare ciò che non si dovrebbe fare; *to be born on the — side of the blanket*, essere figlio illegittimo; *to be on the — side of forty*, aver oltrepassato la quarantina; *to get out of bed on the — side*, alzarsi di cattivo umore; *he has got hold of the — end of the stick*, ha capito male; *what is — with you?*, che cosa hai?; (fam.) *what's — with that?*, che cosa trovi da ridire?; *I hope nothing is —*, spero che non sia successo niente.

**wrong** *adv.* male; *everything is going —*, tutto va male; *to go —*, cadere in peccato, deviare dal retto cammino; (of machines) fallire; *to choose —*, scegliere male; (typ.) *— fount*, refuso.

**wrong** *n.* torto; ingiustizia; danno; *to be in the —*, essere dalla parte del torto; *to put someone in the —*, dare torto a qualcuno, (leg.) dimostrare la colpevolezza di qualcuno; *he is not wholly in the —*, non ha tutti i torti; *the — I have suffered*, le ingustizie che ho sofferte; *two -s do not make a right*, due neri non fanno un bianco; *to labour under a sense of —*, nutrire un sentimento d'ingiustizia; male *m.*; *to know right from —*, distinguere il bene dal male; (leg.) danno; *private —*, violazione del diritto privato; *public —*, violazione del diritto pubblico.

**wrong** *tr.* fare torto a, trattare ingiustamente, maltrattare.

**wrong-doer** *n.* peccatore, peccatrice; trasgressore, malfattore. **-doing** *n.* peccato; malfatti *m.pl.*; trasgressione, infrazione.

**wrongful** *adj.* ingiusto, ingiustificato, abusivo; *— dismissal*, licenziamento ingiustificato; (leg.) illegale, pregiudiziale, risarcibile. **-ness** *n.* ingiustizia; iniquità.

**wrong-headed** *adj.* ostinato nell'errore; perverso. **-headedness** *n.* ostinatezza; perversità.

**wrong-ly** *adv.* a torto; ingiustamente; male; erroneamente; *rightly or —*, a torto o a ragione. **-ness** *n.* see **wrongfulness**; inesattezza; erroneità.

**wrote** *p.def.* of **write**, *q.v.*

**wroth** *adj.* adirato, iroso, sdegnato, arrabbiato; (poet.) *to wax —*, adirarsi, arrabbiarsi, sdegnarsi.

**wrought** *p.def.*, *part.* of **work**; *adj.* lavorato, elaborato; (of metals) battuto, saldato, fucinato; *— iron*, ferro battuto; *— silver*, argento battuto; *— steel*, acciaio saldato; (fig.) *— up*, teso, agitato, perturbato; *his nerves are — up*, ha i nervi tesi.

**wrung** *p.def.*, *part.* of **wring**, *q.v.*

**wry** *adj.* storto, obliquo, sbieco; *a — smile*, un sorriso sbieco; *to make a — face*, fare una smorfia; (fig.) svisato, falso; ironico. **-faced** *adj.* con il viso storto, sbieco. **-ly** *adv.* per traverso, di sbieco, obliquamente; (fig.) ironicamente. **-neck** *n.* (orn.) torcicollo; (med.) torcicollo, torcicolite *f.* **-ness** *n.* l'essere storto, mancanza di simmetria, mancanza di regolarità; contorsione.

**wulfenite** *n.* (miner.) wulfenite *m.*, molibdato di piombo.

**Württemberg** *pr.n.* (geog.) Virtemberga Svevia.

**Wuthering Heights** *pr.n.* 'Cime tempestose' (romanzo di Emily Brontë).

**wych-elm** *n.* (bot.) olmo riccio, olmo di montagna.

**wyvern** *n.* (herald.) dragone alato.

**X, x** *n.* (in Italian found only in foreign words) ics *m.*, *f.*; (teleph.) *— for Xmas*, ics come Xantia; (math.) x, prima incognita; (Roman numeral) dieci, decimo; *Charles X*, Carlo Decimo.

**Xanthippe** *pr.n.* (Gk. hist.) Santippe; (fig.) moglie bisbetica.

**Xavier** *pr.n.* Saverio.

**xebec** *n.* (naut.) sciabecco.

**Xenocrates** *pr.n.* (Gk. philos.) Senocrate.

**xenophile** *adj.*, *n.* xenofilo, senofilo.

**xenophob-e** *adj.*, *n.* xenofobo, senofobo. **-ia** *n.* xenofobia, senofobia.

**Xenophon** *pr.n.* (Gk. lit.) Senofonte.

**xero-** *pref.* (med., *etc.*) xero-.
**xerox** *n.* macchina xerografica.
**Xerxes** *pr.n.* (hist.) Serse.
**Xmas** *n.* (fam.) Natale *m.*; *attrib.* natalizio.
**xylo-** *pref.* xilo-, silo-.
**xylograph** *n.* xilografia, silografia; incisione su legno. **-er** *n.* xilografo, silografo; incisore. **-ic** *adj.* xilografico, silografico. **-y** *n.* xilografia, silografia; l'arte dell'incisione su legno.
**xyloid** *adj.* xiloide, legnoso.
**xylonite** *n.* xilonite, celluloide *f.*
**xylophon-e** *n.* (mus.) xilofono, silofono. **-ist** *n.* (mus.) xilofonista, silofonista *m.*
**X-ray** *adj.* (med.; phys.) di raggi X, radioscopico, radiografico; *X-ray examination*, esame radioscopico; *X-ray photograph*, radiografia; *n.* *X-rays*, raggi X *m.pl.*, radiografia, radioscopia.
**X-ray** *tr.* sottoporre a raggi X, radiografare.
**xyster** *n.* (surg.) raschiatoio.

**Y, y** *n.*; (in Italian found only in foreign words) ipsilon *m.*, i greco; (teleph.) — *for yellow*, i greco come York; (math.) *y*, seconda incognita.
**yacht** *n.* yacht *m.*, panfilo; nave da diporto, imbarcazione da diporto, barca a vela; *sailing* —, panfilo a vela; *steam* —, panfilo a vapore; *seagoing* —, panfilo d'alto mare; *racing* —, yacht da corsa, yacht da regata; *schooner-rigged* —, yacht armato a goletta; *intr.* viaggiare su panfilo, prendere parte a gare di panfili.
**yacht-club** *n.* yacht-club *m.*, circolo nautico.
**yachting** *adj.* da panfilo; — *cruise*, crociera in panfilo *n.* il viaggiare su panfilo; il prendere parte a gare di panfilo; la nautica, lo sport nautico.
**yachts-man** *n.* proprietario di un panfilo; persona che si dedica allo sport nautico. **-manship** *n.* l'arte di governare un panfilo. **-woman** *n.* donna che si dedica allo sport nautico.
**yack-yack, yackety-yackety** (fam.) il parlare a vanvera.
**yaffle** *n.* (orn., fam.) picchio verde.
**yah** *excl.* (disgust) puah!; (derision) là là!
**yahoo** *n.* yahoo *m.*; (fig.) bruto, uomo maleducato; (USA) zoticone *m.*, ignorante *m.*
**Yahveh** *pr.n.* (bibl.) Geova.
**yak** *n.* (zool.) yak *m.*, bue tibetano.
**Yale** *pr.n.* (geog.) (l'università di) Yale; — *key*, chiave all'inglese, chiave Yale; — *lock*, serratura Yale.
**yam** *n.* (bot.) igname *m.*; (USA) patata dolce.
**yammer** *intr.* lamentarsi, piagnucolare.
**yank**[1] *n.* (fam.) strattone *m.*, strappo; *tr.* (fam.) dare uno strattone a, strappare, tirare con violenza.
**yank**[2], **yank-ee, yankee** *n.* (derog.) Yankee *m.*, americano (degli Stati Uniti); (USA) nativo della Nuova Inghilterra. **-eefied** *adj.* (derog.) americanizzato. **-eeism** *n.* (derog.) americanismo.
**yap** *n.* guaito; uggiolìo di un cagnolino; (fig.) chiacchierìo; *intr.* guaire, guaiolare; uggiolare; (fig.) gridare; chiacchierare; parlare a vanvera; *what are you -ping about?*, di che cosa vai chiacchierando?
**yapp** *n.* (bookb.) rilegatura in cuoio soffice.
**Yarborough** *n.* (bridge) Yarborough *m.*; mano che non contiene carte di valore superiore a nove.
**yard**[1] (measure) iarda (=91·4399 cm.); (loosely) metro; braccio; *square* —, iarda quadrata (=0·8631 m.²); *cubic* —, iarda cubica (=0·7645 m.³); *how many -s do you want?*, che metraggio desiderate?; *I can't see a — in front of me*, non vedo più in là del naso; *a — long*, lungo un metro; (fig.) lunghissimo; *a face a — long*, un muso lunghissimo; *-s of words, words by the* —, parole a non finire più; (naut.) pennone *m.*
**yard**[2] *n.* cortile.; *m* piazzale *m.*; recinto; terreno cintato; (industr.) cantiere *m.*, deposito di materiali; (naut.) *navy* —, arsenale della marina di guerra; *refitting* —, cantiere di raddobbo; *shipbuilding* —, cantiere navale, cantiere di costruzioni navali; (rlwy.) *goods* —, *freight* —, scalo merci, stazione merci; *marshalling* —, stazione di smistamento.
**yardage**[1] *n.* metraggio; misurazione in iarde; (civil eng.) materiale di sterro in iarde cubiche.
**yardage**[2] *n.* (bldg.) spese di sosta in un recinto; (rlwy.) manovra, smistamento.
**yard-arm** *n.* (naut.) *n.* pennone *m.*
**yard-measure** *n.* strumento di misura di una iarda, metro.
**yardstick** *n.* stecca di una iarda di lunghezza, metro; (fig.) pietra di paragone.
**yard(s)man** *n.* manovale *m.*; guardiano di un cantiere; (rlwy.) manovale, manovratore ferroviario.
**yarn** *n.* (text.) filo, filato; (fig.) storia, storiella, filastrocca; *to spin -s*, raccontar storie, (fam.) spararle grosse, tirarle per le lunghe; *to pitch a long* —, fare un lungo discorso, raccontare a lunga i propri guai; *intr.* (fam.) raccontare storie, spararle grosse.
**yarrow** *n.* (bot.) achillea, millefoglie *m.*; *Alpine* —, achillea muscosa, genepì *m.*
**yashmak** *n.* velo delle donne arabe.
**yatter** *intr.* (Scot.) schiacchierare, far pettegolezze.
**yaw** *n.* (naut.) straorzata, imbardata; (aeron.) imbardata; (fig.) deviazione; *intr.* (naut.) straorzare, imbardare; (aeron.) imbardare; (fig.) deviare, virare.
**yawl** *n.* (naut.) iola, yole *f.*, iolla; (jollyboat) barca a remi.
**yawn** *n.* sbadiglio, sbadigliamento; *to stifle a* —, reprimere uno sbadiglio; (fig.) apertura; voragine *f.*; *intr.* sbadigliare; parlare sbadigliando; rimanere a bocca aperta; *to — one's head off*, sbadigliare di fila; (fig.) spalancarsi, aprirsi. **-ing** *adj.* sbadigliante; sonnolento; (fig.) spalancato; *m.* sbadigliamento; *a fit of -ing*, sbadigliella.
**ye**[1] *pers. prn.* (poet.) voi; (fam.) *how d'ye do?*, come va?
**ye**[2] *def. art.* (archaic) see **the.**
**yea** *adv.* (bibl.; lit.) sì; (emphatic) sì, anche, persino; *it is useless, — harmful*, è inutile, anche nocivo; *n.* sì *m.*; affermazione; *the -s and the nays*, i voti favorevoli e sfavorevoli.
**yeah** *adv.* (USA) sì; (iron.) *oh —!*, davvero!
**year** *n.* anno; annata; *calendar* —, anno civile; *commercial* —, anno di gestione; *financial* —, esercizio sociale; *holy* —, anno santo; — *of grace*, anno di grazia; — *of Our Lord*, anno di Nostro Signore, anno domini; *leap* —, anno bisestile; *lunar* —, anno lunare; *solar* —, anno solare; *school* —, anno scolastico; *university* —, anno accademico; *half-year*, semestre *m.*; *quarter-year*, trimestre *m.*; — *of drought*, anno di siccità; — *of plenty*, annata buona; — *of office*, anno di carica; *the New Year*, l'anno nuovo, il nuovo anno; *at the end of the* —, in capo all'anno; *New Year's Day*, Capodanno, il primo dell'anno; *New Year's Eve*, il San Silvestro; *New Year's gift*, strenna; *to wish someone a happy New Year*, augurare a qualcuno buon anno; *every* —, ogni anno, tutti gli anni;

*every other* —, un anno sì e l'altro no, ogni due anni; *every third* —, ogni tre anni; — *by* —, *from* — *to* —, di anno in anno; — *in* — *out*, un anno dopo l'altro; *all the* — *round*, per tutto l'anno; *twice a* —, due volte all'anno; *this day* —, oggi a un anno; *a* — *ago*, un anno fa; *last* —, l'anno scorso, l'anno passato; *this day last* —, un anno a quest'oggi; *next* —, l'anno venturo, l'anno prossimo; *in three* ~*s' time*, fra tre anni; *for a number of* ~*s*, per un numero determinato di anni; *by the* —, all'anno; *to earn a thousand a* —, guadagnare mille sterline all'anno, avere uno stipendio annuo di mille sterline; *he is twenty* ~*s old*, ha vent'anni; *he is young for his* ~*s*, è giovane per la sua età, non dimostra la sua età; *from his earliest* ~*s*, dall'età più tenera, dall'infanzia; *childhood* ~*s*, infanzia; ~*s of discretion*, maggior età, l'età della ragione; ~*s of manhood*, l'età virile; *advanced in* ~*s*, anziano; *to grow old in* ~*s*, invecchiare; *stricken with* ~*s*, carico d'anni; *to die full of* ~*s*, morire pieno d'anni; *in after* ~*s*, in seguito; *I've known him for* ~*s*, lo conosco da anni; *I haven't seen him for donkey's* ~*s*, non lo vedo da tanti anni; *disparity in* ~*s*, differenza d'età; *I've had a good* —, per me è stata una buona annata; *a good* — *for wine*, una buona annata per il raccolto del vino; *I've been in this job for twenty* ~*s*, sono vent'anni che faccio questo lavoro; *to be sentenced to ten* ~*s' imprisonment*, essere condannato a dieci anni di carcere; (industr.) — *of manufacture*, anno di costruzione; (bot.) — *ring* (*on trees*), anello annuale di crescita; (hist.) *the Hundred Years' War*, la guerra dei cent'anni; *hundreds of* ~*s old*, secolare.

**year-book** *n.* annuario, almanacco.

**yearling** *n.* animale che ha un anno, di un anno di età.

**year-long** *adj.* che dura un anno, che dura degli anni.

**yearly** *adj.* annuo, annuale; *half-yearly*, semestrale, ogni sei mesi; *quarter-yearly*, trimestrale, ogni tre mesi; — *instalments*, annualità; *adv.* annualmente, ogni anno.

**yearn** *intr.* languire; struggersi; *tr. to* — *for*, agognare, anelare, bramare, desiderare ardentemente; (fam.) non vedere l'ora di. **~ing** *adj.* desideroso; bramoso; languente; *n.* desiderio ardente; brama; struggimento; tenerezza; vivo desiderio; aspirazione.

**year-old** *adj.* di un anno di età; di un anno fa.

**yeast** *n.* lievito; fermento; luppolina; *intr.* fermentare; lievitare. **~y** *adj.* (from **yeast**) di lievito; (fig.) spumeggiante, schiumante, schiumoso; (of style) verboso, gonfio.

**yell** *n.* urlo; grido; strillo; *to utter* ~*s*, urlare; (USA) grido d'incitamento (di studenti); (USA) persona, cosa buffa; *intr.* urlare; gridare; strillare; *to* — *with pain*, urlare dal dolore; *to* — *with laughter*, ridere a crepapelle. **~ing** *adj.* urlante, strillante; *n.* urlata; clamore *m.*; strillata.

**yellow** *adj.*, *n.* giallo; *pale* —, gialletto, gialliccio; *light* —, giallino; *dirty* —, giallognolo, gialloso; *sickly* —, gialluccio giallume; *saffron* —, giallo zafferano; — *complexion*, giallore; — *fever*, (fam.) — *jack*, febbre gialla; — *soap*, sapone di Marsiglia; — *ochre*, giallo ocra, terra gialla; (geog.) *the Yellow Sea*, il Mar Giallo; (of races) giallo, di pelle gialla; (hist.) '*the* — *peril*', il pericolo giallo; (fig.) geloso, sospettoso; (slang) vile, codardo; *the* — *press*, la stampa scandalistica.

**yellow** *tr.* ingiallire, rendere giallo; *paper* ~*ed with age*, carta ingiallita dal tempo; *intr.* diventare giallo, ingiallire.

**yellow-back** *n.* romanzo francese dalla copertina gialla. **-bill** *n.* (orn.) macrosa nera. **-hammer** *n.* (orn.) zigolo giallo; (geog.) *Yellowhammer State* (USA), Alabama.

**yellow~ing** *adj.* che diventa giallo, gialleggiante; *n.* ingiallimento. **~ish** *adj.* giallastro, gialligno, giallognolo; tendente al giallo. **~ness** *n.* giallore, giallura.

**yellowthroat** *n.* (orn.) silvia gialla.

**yellowy** *adj.* giallastro.

**yelp** *n.* guaito; *intr.* guaire; uggiolare; squittire. **~er** *n.* cucciolo che guaisce; (fig.) persona che guaisce. **~ing** *adj.* che guaisce; *n.* guaito; uggiolio.

**Yemen** *pr.n.* Iemen.

**yeoman** *n.* (hist.) piccolo proprietario terriero che aveva l'obbligo di prestare servizio militare in tempo di guerra; (mil.) volontario di un reggimento di cavalleria; — *of the guard*, alabardiere del corpo di guardia che presta servizio alla Torre di Londra; (fig.) — *service*, aiuto valoroso; (naut.) sottufficiale della marina di guerra, magazziniere; — *of signals*, segnalatore. **~ry** *n.* (hist.) classe dei piccoli proprietari terrieri; (mil.) corpo volontario di cavalleria.

**yes** *adv.* sì; perfettamente, davvero; (interr.) e allora?; (emphatic) non solo, e per di più; *to say* —, dire di sì; — *or no?*, sì o no?; *yes sir*, sì signore, (mil.) signorsì; — *of course*, ma sì!; — *please*, sì grazie, con piacere, volentieri.

**yes-man** *n.* persona accondiscente, uomo senza carattere, fantoccio.

**yesterday** *adv.*, *n.* ieri *m.*; — *afternoon*, ieri pomeriggio; — *evening*, ieri sera; — *morning*, ieri mattina; *the day before* —, ieri l'altro, avantieri; — *week*, ieri otto; *all our* ~*s*, tutto il nostro passato; (iron.) *I wasn't born* —, non sono nato ieri.

**yester~morn** *adv.*, *n.* (poet.) iermattina. **~night** *adv.*, *n.* (poet.) iersera, l'altra notte. **~year** *adv.*, *n.* l'anno passato, l'anno scorso, l'altr'anno.

**yet** *adv.* ancora; tuttora; in più; già, finora; *I can see her* —, la vedo ancora; *work* — *to be done*, lavoro ancora da fare; *not* —, non ancora; — *again*, ancora una volta; — *more*, ancor più; *need you go* —?, devi già andare?; *as* —, finora; *he will win* —, malgrado tutto vincerà; ma, eppure; *nor* —, neppure; *conj.* ma, però tuttavia; *he seems honest*, — *I don't trust him*, sembra onesto, tuttavia non mi fido di lui; *and* — *I like him*, però mi è simpatico; (poet.) *ere* —, prima che.

**yew** *n.* (bot.) tasso; (poet., archery) *the* —, l'arco, la balestra.

**yid** *n.* (slang., derog.) ebreo.

**Yiddish** *adj.* Yiddish, dialetto germanico-slavo parlato dagli ebrei.

**yield** *n.* produzione; prodotto; ricavo; (of taxes) gettito; (agric.) raccolto; (industr.) resa, rendimento, produzione; (finan.) rendimento, frutto, reddito; (bldg.) cedimento; *tr.* produrre; rendere, fruttare; cedere, concedere; *to* — *up the ghost*, rendere l'anima; *to* — *ground*, cedere terreno; esalare, emettere; *intr.* cedere, arrendersi, acconsentire; *to* — *to force*, cedere alla forza; *to refuse to* —, tener duro; (fig.) *I* — *to none*, non sono secondo a nessuno.

**yield-capacity** *n.* produttività; potenziale *m.*; produttivo.

**yielding** *adj.* cedente, cedevole; flessibile; poco resistente; (fig.) condiscendente, compiacente, rendevole; che rende bene; *n.* rendimento; cedimento; resa; (fig.) abbandono.

**yield-point** *n.* (mech.) limite di snervamento, limite di resistenza; (bldg.) punto di cedimento.

**yodel** *intr.* jodellare, cantare alla maniera dei montanari tirolesi.

**yoga** *n.* yoga *m.*, ioga *m.*

**yogurt** *n.* yog(h)urt *m.*

**yoho, yo-heave-ho** *excl.* (naut.; joc.) issa!

**yoke** *n.* giogo; pariglia, paio; coppia; — *oxen*, buoi da tiro; *a — of oxen*, una coppia di buoi, una pariglia di buoi; (fig.) giogo; schiavitù *f.*; *to cast off the —*, liberarsi dal giogo, scuotere il giogo; (dressm.) busto; *tr.* aggiogare, soggiogare, mettere il giogo a; (fig.) asservire; accoppiare; unire.

**yokel** *n.* bifolco; zoticone *m.*; villano.

**yolk** *n.* (of egg) tuorlo, rosso d'uovo, giallo d'uovo; (of wool) grasso naturale, lanolina; (biol.) vitello.

**yon, yonder** *adj.* situato laggiù, ontano, distante; — *tree*, quell'albero laggiù; *adv.* laggiù, lassù.

**yore** *n. of —, in times of —*, una volta di un tempo, nei tempi antichi.

**York** *pr.n.* (geog.) York (sometimes written Jork); *New —*, Nuova York.

**yorker** *n.* (cricket) palla lanciata in modo che rimbalza sulla linea bianca davanti al battitore; (fig.) cosa contro la quale ogni difesa è inutile.

**you** *pers. prn.* (nom. sing.) tu, (formal) Lei, Ella; (acc. sing.) ti, (after prep.) te, (formal) La, (after prep.) Lei; (dat. sing.) te, (formal) Le; (nom. pl.) voi, (formal) Loro; (acc. pl.) vi, ve, (formal) Loro; (dat. pl.) vi, ve; (formal) Loro; — *and I*, tu ed io, noi due; — *Italians*, voialtri Italiani; *away with —!*, (sing.) vattene, (pl.) andatevene!; — *silly boy!*, sciocco che sei; — *darling!*, cara!; *if I were —*, se fossi te, se fossi al tuo posto, se fossi nei tuoi panni; *indef. prn.* si; *how do — say this in Italian?*, come si dice questo in italiano?; — *never know*, non si sa mai.

**young** *adj.* giovane, giovine; (fig.) nuovo, inesperto; *a — man*, un giovane, un giovanotto; *a — woman*, una giovane, una giovane donna; *a — gentleman*, un giovane signore, un signorino; *a — lady*, una signorina; *a — boy*, un giovanetto, un ragazzo; *a — girl*, una giovinetta, una ragazza; *-er son*, cadetto, figlio minore; *-est son*, figlio ultimogenito; — *people*, i giovani, la gioventù; (fam.) — *'un*, giovinotto; *the -er generation*, la gioventù di oggi, i giovani, i nostri figli; *he is -er than I am*, è piu giovane di me; *in his -er days*, in gioventù, nei suoi verdi anni; *when I was twenty years -er*, quando avevo vent'anni di meno; *he is — for his years*, porta bene la sua età; — *in mind*, giovane di spirito; *to grow — again*, ringiovanire; *to look —*, sembrare più giovane; — *moon*, luna nuova; *n.pl. the —*, i giovani, la gioventù; *old and —*, i grandi e i piccoli; (of animals) i piccoli, la prole; *to be with —*, essere gravida; *to bring forth —*, figliare; (fig.) *a lake like a — sea*, un lago grande quanto un piccolo mare. **-ish** *adj.* piuttosto giovane. **-ling** *n.* (poet.) giovane *m.*, *f.*; piccolo *m.*, piccola *f.* **-ness** *n.* aspetto giovanile; inesperienza. **-ster** *n.* giovane *m.*; giovincello; ragazzo; *my -ster*, mio figlio.

**your** *poss. adj.* (sing.) il tuo, la tua, i tuoi, le tue; (formal) il Suo, la Sua, i Suoi, le Sue; (pl.) il vostro, la vostra, i vostri, le vostre, (formal) il Loro, la Loro, i Loro, le Loro; *Your Majesty*, Maestà, Sua Maestà; *Your Excellency*, Eccellenza, Sua Eccellenza; *Your Worship*, Signor Giudice; (comm.) — *good selves*, Voi Signori, la Vostra spettabile ditta.

**yours** *poss. prn.* (sing.) il tuo, la tua, i tuoi, le tue; (formal, now more usually lower case) il Suo, la Sua, i Suoi, le Sue; (pl.) il vostro, la Vostra, i vostri, le vostre, (formal) il Loro, la Loro, i Loro, le Loro; *is this book —?, Yes, it's mine*, è tuo questo libro? Sì, è mio; *is this a book of —?*, non è un tuo libro questo?; *you and —*, tu e i tuoi cari; *it's no business of —*, non ti riguarda, non è affar tuo; (in a bar) *what's —?*, cosa prendi?; (comm.) — *of the 10th inst.*, la vostra del dieci c.m. (*or* del corrente mese); — *truly*, distinti saluti; — *faithfully*, vostro devotissimo; — (*sincerely*), Suo, cordialmente Suo.

**yourself** *rfl. prn.* (nom.) tu stesso, Lei stesso, voi stessi, Loro stessi; (acc.) te stesso, Lei stesso, voi stessi, Loro stessi; (with rfl. verbs) ti, si, vi, si; *you —*, tu stesso, Lei stesso; *you yourselves*, voi stessi; *you were not — yesterday*, ieri non eri tu, ieri eri di diverso umore; *be —!*, cerca di ricomporti!

**youth** *n.* gioventù; giovinezza; adolescenza, giovane; giovanotto; adolescente *m.*; *in the days of my —*, in gioventù, quand'ero giovane; *from — upwards*, sin dalla gioventù; — *will have its way*, beata gioventù!; — *hostel*, ostello della gioventù. **-ful** *adj.* giovane, giovanile, di gioventù; *-ful ambitions*, ambizioni giovanili; *-ful appearance*, aspetto giovanile. **-fulness** *n.* giovanilità; aspetto giovanile.

**yowl** *n.* (of dog) ululato; (of cat) miagolìo; *intr.* (of dog) ululare; (of cat) miagolare.

**yo-yo** *n.* girella.

**Yugoslav** *adj.*, *n.* iugoslavo, jugoslavo. **-ia** *pr.n.* (geog.) Iugoslavia, Jugoslavia.

**Yule** *n.* Natale *m.*; feste natalizie.

**yule-log** *n.* ceppo natalizio.

**yuletide** *n.* periodo natalizio.

**Z, z** *n.* zeta; *from A to —*, dall'a alla zeta; (teleph.) — *for zebra*, zeta come Zara.

**Zacchaeus** *pr.n.* (bibl.) Zaccheo.

**Zachariah, Zacharias** *pr.n.* Zaccaria.

**Zagreb** *pr.n.* (geog.) Zagabria.

**Zambesi** *pr.n.* (geog.) Zambesi.

**zany** *n.* zanni *m.*; buffone *m.*; semplicione *m.*; *adj.* da buffone.

**zeal** *n.* zelo; ardore *m.*; fervore *m.*; premura; *misguided —*, falso zelo; *excess of —*, eccesso di zelo, zelanteria; *bustling —*, affaccendamento; premura.

**Zealand** *pr.n.* (geog.) Zelanda; *New —*, la Nuova Zelanda. **-er** *n.* zelandese *m.*, *f.*; *New -er*, nuovazelandese *m.*, *f.*

**zealot** *n.* (hist.) zelote *m.*; (fig.) zelatore, fanatico. **-ism** *n.* (hist.) zelotismo; (fig.) fanatismo; fervore *m.* **-ry** *n.* (hist.) zelotismo; (fig.) zelanteria; fanatismo. **-ous** *adj.* zelante, zeloso; ardente; fanatico; premuroso; *to be -ous*, fare lo zelante.

**Zebadiah** *pr.n.* (bibl.) Zebadia.

**Zebedee** *pr.n.* (bibl.) Zebedeo.

**zebra** *n.* (zool.) zebra; (motor.) — *crossing*, zebrata, passaggio pedonale zebrato, zebratura con strisce parallele; (USA) — *suit*, pigiama a strisce dei forzati; — *markings*, zebratura, striatura.

**zed** *n.* zeta, la lettera z.

**Zedekiah** *pr.n.* (bibl.) Sedecia *m.*

**zedoary** *n.* (bot.) zedoaria.

**zenith** *n.* (astron.) zenit *m.*; (fig.) zenit, culmine *m.*; apogeo.

**Zeno** *pr.n.* Zeno; (Gk. philos.) Zenone.

**zephyr** *n.* zeffiro; (sport) canottiera, maglietta.

**zero** *n.* zero; *ten degrees above —*, dieci gradi sopra zero; *ten degrees below —*, dieci gradi sotto zero; (aeron.) *at —*, sotto i trecento metri; *absolute —*, zero assoluto; — *point*, punto nullo; — *point energy*, energia al punto zero; (electr.) — *potential*, potenziale nullo; (mech.) — *setting*, messa a zero, azzeramento; (mil.) — *hour*, ora zero; *to fire with — degree of elevation*, sparare a zero; (fig.) *to start from —*, partire da zero.

**zest** *n.* aroma *m.*; gusto, sapore piccante; *to add* —, aggiungere una nota piccante; (fig.) entusiasmo, impegno, premura; *to eat with* —, mangiare con appetito.
**zeugm-a** *n.* (rhet.) zeugma *m.* **-atic** *adj.* (rhet.) zeugmatico.
**Zeus** *pr.n.* (myth.) Zeus, Giove; (ichth.) pesce di San Pietro.
**zibet(h)** *n.* (zool.) zibetto, civetta indiana.
**zigzag** *n.* zigzag *m.*; — *road*, strada a zigzag; (naut.) *to steer a — course*, far rotta a zigzag; *tr.* disporre in zigzag; *intr.* andare a zigzag, camminare a zigzag. **-ging** *n.* lo zigzagare; disposizione in zigzag. **-gy** *adj.* a zigzag.
**zinc** *n.* zinco; — *white*, bianco di zinco, ossido di zinco; *tr.* zincare, rivestire di zinco, galvanizzare.
**zinc-coating** *n.* zincatura. **-engraver** *n.* zincografo. **-engraving** *n.* zincografia; incisione su zinco.
**zincograph** *n.* zincografia, incisione su zinco; clichè *m.*; *tr.* zincografare; imprimere su lastre di zinco. **-er** *n.* zincografo. **-y** *n.* zincografia.
**zincotype** *n.* zincotipia.
**zinc-white** *n.* (paint.) bianco di zinco.
**zinnia** *n.* (bot.) zinnia.
**Zion** *pr.n.* Sion, Sionne. **-ism** *n.* sionismo. **-ist** *adj.*, *n.* sionista *m.*, *f.*
**zip** *n.* sibilo; fischio; (fig.) energia; vigore *m.*; — *fastener*, chiusura lampo, cerniera, 'zip' *m.*; *intr.* sibilare; fischiare; *to — past*, passare come un lampo. **-per** *n.* cerniera; chiusura lampo, zip *m.* **-py** *adj.* pieno di energia; svelto.
**zircon** *n.* (miner.) zircone *m.*
**zither(n)** *n.* (mus.) cetra, chitarra tirolese.
**zizania** *n.* (bot.) zizzania.
**zoanthropy** *n.* (med.) zoantropia.
**zodiac** *n.* (astron.) zodiaco; *the signs of the* —, i segni dello zodiaco. **-al** *adj.* zodiacale.
**zoic** *adj.* zoico; degli animali.
**Zolaesque** *adj.* alla maniera di Zola, zolaesco, zoliano.
**zombie** *n.* (West Indies) morto risuscitato per magia (fig.) persona inerte.
**zonal** *adj.* zonale.
**zon-e** *n.* zona; (geog.) *temperate* —, zona temperata; *torrid* —, zona torrida; *frigid* —, zona glaciale; *danger* —, zona di pericolo; *free* —, zona franca; *war* —, zona di guerra; *business* —, centro degli affari; — *system*, divisione in zone, (admin.) zonizzazione; (poet.) cintura, fascia; *tr.* (admin.) dividere in zone, zonizzare. **-ing** *n.* (admin.) divisione in zone, zonizzazione.
**zoo** *n.* zoo *m.*; giardino zoologico; *open-air* —, parco zoologico; *the Zoo*, il giardino zoologico di Londra.
**zoo-** *pref.* zoo-.
**zoo-biology** *n.* zoobiologia. **-chemistry** *n.* zoochimica. **-genic** *adj.* zoogenico. **-graphy** *n.* zoografia.
**zoolog-y** *n.* zoologia. **-ical** *adj.* zoologico. **-ist** *n.* zoologo.
**zoom** *n.* rombo; ronzìo; (aeron.) salita in candela; *intr.* rombare, ronzare; (aeron.) salire in candela.
**zoo-morphy** *m.* (biol.) zoomorfia. **-phile** *n.* zoofilo. **-phily** *n.* zoofilia. **-phobe** *n.* zoofobo. **-phyte** *n.* zoofito. **-sperm** *n.* (physiol.) spermatozoo.
**Zoroaster** *pr.n.* Zoroastro.
**Zouave** *n.* (mil.) zuavo *m.*; (cost.) — *jacket*, zuava; — *breeches*, pantaloni alla zuava.
**Zulu** *adj.*, *n.* zulù; *the — War*, la guerra degli zulù. **-land** *pr.n.* (geog.) Zululand; il paese degli Zulù.
**Zürich** *pr.n.* (geog.) Zurigo.
**zygo-** *pref.* zigo-.
**zygoma** *n.* (anat.) zigomo.
**zygo-morphic, -morphous** *adj.* (bot.) zigomorfo.
**zygosis** *n.* (biol.) zigosi *f.*
**zygot-e** *n.* (biol.) zigote *m.* **-ic** *adj.* zigotico.
**zymase** *n.* (chem.) zimasi *f.*
**zym-e** *n.* (med.) enzima *m.* **-ology** *n.* (chem.) zimologia. **-osis** *n.* zimosi *f.*; fermentazione. **-otic** *adj.* zimotico, enzimatico.

# ENGLISH IRREGULAR VERBS

**abide** abode (*sometimes* abided).
**awake** awoke; awoke, awaked.

**be** *pr. indicative* am, art, is, *pl.* are; *p. ind.* was, wast *or* wert, was, *pl.* were, *pr. subjunctive* be; *p. subj.* were *except* 2 *sing.* wert; *imperative* be; *p.pr.* being; *p.p.* been. *Contractions*: 'm (am), 's (is), 're (are).
**bear** bore; borne.
**beat** beat; beaten (*sometimes* beat).
**beget** begot; begotten.
**begin** began; begun.
**bend** bent; bent.
**bereave** bereaved (*or* bereft).
**beseech** besought.
**bid** bad, bade, bid; bidden, bid.
**bind** bound.
**bite** bit; bitten (*sometimes* bit).
**bleed** bled; bled.
**blend** blended (*sometimes* blent).
**blow** blew; blown.
**break** broke; broken (*sometimes* broke).
**breed** bred.
**bring** brought.
**build** built.
**burn** burnt (*sometimes* burned).
**burst** burst.
**buy** bought.

**can** *pr.* I, he, etc., can, thou canst, *neg.* cannot, can't. *p.* etc., *conditional*, I, he, etc., could, thou could(e)st. *i.*, *p.pr.* etc., *p.p. wanting*; *defective parts supplied from* be able to.
**cast** cast.
**catch** caught.
**chide** chid; chidden (*sometimes* chid).
**choose** chose; chosen.
**cleave** clove *or* cleft; cloven *or* cleft.
**cling** clung.
**clothe** clothed *or* clad.
**come** came; come.
**cost** cost.
**could.** See *can.*
**creep** crept.
**crow** crew *or* crowed; crowed.
**cut** cut.

**dare** dared, durst; dared.
**deal** dealt.
**die** died; *p.pr.* dying; died.
**dig** dug.
**do** *pr. indicative* do, doest (*as auxiliary* dost), does, *pl.* do; *p.* did, didst, did, *pl.* did; *p.p.* done. *Contractions*: don't (do not), doesn't (does not), didn't (did not).
**draw** drew; drawn.
**dream** dreamt *or* dreamed.
**drink** drank; drunk.
**drive** drove; driven.
**dwell** dwelt.

**eat** ate *or* eat; eaten.

**fall** fell; fallen.
**feed** fed.
**feel** felt.
**fight** fought.
**find** found.
**flee** fled.
**fling** flung.
**fly** flew; flown.
**forbear** forbore; forborne.
**forbid** forbad *or* -bade; forbidden.
**forget** forgot; forgotten.
**forsake** forsook; forsaken.
**freeze** froze; frozen.

**get** got; got, *also* -gotten *in combination as* ill-gotten.
**gild** gilded *or* gilt.
**gird** *p. & p.p.* girt, *poet.* girded.

**give** gave; given.
**go** *pr.* I go, thou goest, he goes, we, etc., go; *p.* went; *p.p.* gone.
**grave** graved; graven *or* graved.
**grind** ground; ground.
**grow** grew; grown.

**hang** hung *or* hanged.
**have** *pr.* I have, *archaic* thou hast, he has, we, you, they, have; *p.* had. *archaic* thou hadst; *p.p.* had; *abb.* I've, we've, etc.; I'd, we'd, etc.; 's (has); *colloq. neg.* haven't, hasn't; hadn't.
**hear** heard.
**heave** heaved *or* hove.
**hew** hewed; hewn *or* hewed.
**hide** hid; hidden *or* hid.
**hit** hit.
**hold** held.
**hurt** hurt.

**keep** kept; kept.
**kneel** knelt.
**knit** knitted *or* knit.
**know** knew; known.

**lade** laded; laden.
**lay** laid.
**lead** led.
**lean** leaned *or* leant.
**leap** leapt *or* leaped.
**learn** learnt *or* learned.
**leave** left.
**lend** lent.
**let** let.
**lie** lay; *p.pr.* lying; *p.p.* lain.
**light** lit *or* lighted.
**lose** lost.

**make** made.
*pr.* **I may,** he may; *p.* might.
**mean** meant, meant.
**meet** met.
**melt** melted; melted, molten.
**mow** mowed; mown.
*pr.* **I must,** he must; *p.* must.

*pr.* **I ought** *p.* ought.
**outbid** outbid *or* -bade; outbid *or* -bidden.
**overhang** overhung.

**pay** paid.
**put** put.

**read** read.
**rend** rent.
**rid** ridded, rid; rid.
**ride** rode; ridden.
**ring** rang; rung.
**rise** rose; risen.
**rive** rived; riven.
**run** ran; run.

**saw** sawed; sawn.
**say** said.
**see** saw; seen.
**seek** sought.
**sell** sold.
**send** sent.
**set** set.
**sew** sewed; sewed *or* sewn.
**shake** shook; shaken.
*pr.* **I shall,** thou shalt, he, etc., shall; *p. and conditional* I should, though should(e)st, he, etc., should; *neg.* shall not *or* shan't; should not *or* shouldn't.
**shear** sheared; shorn.
**shed** shed.
**shew** shewed; shewn.
**shine** shone.
**shoe** shod.
**shoot** shot.
**should.** See *shall.*
**show** showed; shown.
**shrink** shrank; shrunk.
**shut** shut.
**sing** sang; sung.
**sink** sank; sunk.
**sit** sat.
**slay** slew; slain.
**sleep** slept.
**slide** slid.
**sling** slung.

**slink** slunk.
**slit** slit.
**smell** smelt.
**smite** smote; smitten.
**sow** sowed; sown *or* sowed.
**speak** spoke; spoken.
**speed** sped.
**spell** spelt *or* spelled.
**spend** spent.
**spill** spilt *or* spilled.
**spin** spun *or* span; spun.
**spit** spat.
**split** split.
**spread** spread.
**spring** sprang; sprung.
**stand** stood.
**stave** staved *or* stove.
**steal** stole; stolen.
**stick** stuck.
**sting** stung.
**stink** stank *or* stunk; stunk.
**strew** strewed; strewn, strewed.
**stride** strode.
**strike** struck; struck *or* stricken.
**string** strung.
**strive** strove; striven.
**swear** swore; sworn.
**sweep** swept.
**swell** swelled; swollen.
**swim** swam; swum.
**swing** swung.

**take** took; taken.
**teach** taught.
**tear** tore; torn.
**tell** told.
**think** thought.
**thrive** throve; thriven.
**throw** threw; thrown.
**thrust** thrust.
**tie** tied; *p.pr.* tying; tied.
**tread** trod; trodden.

**wake** woke, waked; waked, woken, woke.
**wear** wore; worn.
**weave** wove; woven *or* wove.
**weep** wept.
*pr.* **I**, he, etc., **will** *or* 'll, thou wilt *or* 'lt; *p. and conditional* I, he, etc., would *or* 'd, thou would(e)st *or* 'dst; *neg.* will not *or* won't; would not *or* wouldn't *or* 'd not.
**win** won.
**wind** wound.
**would**. See *will.*
**wring** wrung.
**write** wrote; written.

# ABBREVIATIONS COMMONLY USED IN ITALIAN

**A.** autore – author; (title) Altezza – Highness; (electr.) ampère; (theatr.) atto – act; (rlwy.) automotrice – diesel-propelled rail-car.

**AA.** autori – authors; (motor.) Assistenza Automobilistica – ACI (q.v.) organization for assisting motorists; (mil.) Arma Aeronautica – (Italian) Air Force.

**ab.** abitanti – population; (eccl.) abate – abbé.

**abbr.** abbreviazione – abbreviation.

**a.c.** anno corrente – current year; (typ.) a capo – new paragraph.

**a.C.** avanti Cristo – before Christ, B.C.

**a.c.** (comm.) assegno circolare – banker's cheque.

**Acc.** accademia – academy; (rlwy.) accelerato – slow train (i.e. faster than a 'treno omnibus').

**A.C.D.G.** Associazione Cristiana dei Giovani: *see* Y.M.C.A.

**ACI** Azione Cattolica Italiana – Catholic Action Party; Automobile Club d'Italia – Italian Automobile Club.

**ACLI** Associazioni Cristiane dei Lavoratori Italiani – Christian Workers' (welfare) Societies.

**A.D.** Anno Domini.

**ag.** agosto – August.

**agg.** (gramm.) aggettivo – adjective.

**AGIP** Azienda Generale Italiana dei Petroli – National Italian Oil Company.

**ALITALIA** Aerolinee Italiane Internazionali – Italian Air Lines.

**a.m.** antemeridiano – before mid-day, a.m.

**AMIG** Associazione Mutilati e Invalidi di Guerra – Association of Disabled Servicemen.

**ANA** Associazione Nazionale Alpini – National Association of former members of Alpine Regiments.

**ANAS** Azienda Nazionale Autonoma della Strada – National Road Board.

**ANB** Associazione Nazionale Bersaglieri – National Association of former members of Bersaglieri Regiments.

**ANC** Associazione Nazionale Combattenti – Ex-Soldiers' Association.

**ANSA** Agenzia Nazionale Stampa Associata – Italian News Agency.

**ant.** antemeridiano – a.m.

**apr.** aprile – April.

**A.R.** Altezza Reale – Royal Highness.

**AA.RR.** Altezze Reali – Royal Highnesses; (rlwy.) (biglietti d') andata e ritorno – return tickets.

**ARAR** Azienda Rilievo e Alienazione Residuati – Organization for the Resale of Army Surplus Stores.

**Arc.** (eccl.) arcivescovo – archbishop.

**arch.** architetto – architect.

**art.** (gramm.) articolo – article.

**A.S.** Altezza Serenissima – Serene Highness.

**ASCI** Associazione Scoutistica Cattolica Italiana – Catholic Boy Scouts.

**AT** (telegrams) a – to.

**A.T.** Antico Testamento – Old Testament.

**AUT** (telegrams) o – or.

**a.v.** (in bibliogr. references) ad vocem – s.v.

**AVIS** Associazione Volontari Italiani del Sangue – Association of Voluntary Italian Blood-donors.

**avv.** avvocato – solicitor or barrister; (gramm.) avverbio – adverb.

**B.** (eccl.) Beato – Blessed.

**B.A.** Belle Arti – Fine Arts.

**bar.** (title) barone – baron.

**B.F.** (mil.) Bassa Forza – Other Ranks.

**B.M.** Buona Memoria – of blessed memory.

**B.U.** Bollettino Ufficiale – Official Bulletin.

**B.V.** (eccl.) Beata Vergine – the Blessed Virgin Mary.

**c.** (manuscripts) carta – folio; (books) capitolo – chapter; (leg.) codice – code; (eccl.) (after names of saints) confessore – confessor; (comm.) conto – account; (typ.) corpo – type-size (*e.g.* c. 8 = 8-point).

**C.A.** (electr.) corrente alternata – alternating current.

**CAI** Club Alpino Italiano – Italian Alpine Club.

**cap.** (mil.) caporale – corporal.

**Cap.** (mil.) capitano – captain.

**CAR** (mil.) Centro Addestramento Reclute – Recruit Training Centre.

**Card.** (eccl.) cardinale; (gramm.) cardinale (number).

**cav.** cavaliere (decoration, corresponding approximately to O.B.E.).

**CC** Carabinieri (Italian gendarmerie).

**c.c., c/c** (comm.) conto corrente – current account.

**C.C.** (leg.) codice civile – civil code; (electr.) corrente continua – direct current; (comm.) Camera di Commercio – Chamber of Commerce; Corpo consolare – Consular Corps.

**CCI** Camera di Commercio Internazionale – International Chamber of Commerce.

**C.Co.** (leg.) Codice di Commercio – Commercial Code.

**c.c.p.** (comm.) conto corrente, postale – current postal account.

**C.C.p.** Codice di procedura civile. Code of Civil Procedure.

**C.D.** Corpo Diplomatico–Diplomatic Corps; (comm.) Consigliere Delegato – Managing Director.

**C.d.A.** (mil.) Corpo d'Armata – Army Corps.

**c.d.d.** (math.) come dovevasi dimostrare – Q.E.D., quod erat demonstrandum, which was to be demonstrated.

**C.d.G.** (eccl.) Compagnia di Gesù – Society of Jesus (Jesuits).

**C.d.L.** Camera del Lavoro – Trade Union H.Q.

**C.d.R.** Cassa di Risparmio – Savings Bank.

**C.E.** Comitato Esecutivo – Executive Committee.

**ced.** (comm.) cedola – (dividend or interest) coupon.

**C.E.R.N.** Consiglio Europeo per le Ricerche Nucleari – European Council for Nuclear Research.

**cfr.** confronta – cf.

**C.G.** Console Generale – Consul-General.

**C.G.I.L.** Confederazione Generale Italiana di Lavoro – Federation of Italian Trade Unions with extreme-left-wing political trend, cf. C.I.S.L., C.I.S.Na.L., U.I.L.

**chiar.mo** chiarissimo – form of address used when writing to distinguished persons.

**Cia** Compagnia – Company.

**C.I.O.** Comitato Internazionale Olimpico – International Olympics Committee.

**C.I.P.** Comitato Interministeriale dei Prezzi – Interdepartmental Committee on Prices.

**C.I.S.L.** Confederazione Italiana Sindacati Liberi – Federation of Italian Trade Unions, officially non-party, but with moderate Socialist–Christian Democrat trend; cf. C.G.I.L., C.I.S.Na.L., U.I.L.

**C.I.S.Na.L.** Confederazione Italiana Sindacati Nazionali Liberi – Federation of Italian Trade Unions with right-wing tendency.

**CIT** Compagnia Italiana Turismo – Italian Travel Agency.

**CITOM** Compagnia Italiana Trasporto Olii Minerali, Italian Oil Transport Company.

**CLN** Comitato di Liberazione Nazionale – organizers of Resistance Movement during Second World War.

**c.m.** corrente mese – inst.

**C.M.** Circolare Ministeriale –Ministerial Circular.

**CNR** Consiglio Nazionale delle Ricerche – National Research Council.

**cod.** codice – code, codex.

**Col.** (mil.) Colonel.

**com.** (mil. and naval) comandante – commanding officer.

**comm.** commendatore – decoration, corresponding approximately to C.B.E.

**cond.** (gramm.) condizionale – conditional.

**cong.** (gramm.) congiunzione – conjunction.

**compar.** (gramm.) comparativo – comparative.

**CONI** Comitato Olimpionico Nazionale Italiano – Italian Olympic Games Committee (also controls football pools).

**cons.** consigliere – member of a municipal council or of a board of directors.

**corr.** corrente – current.

**cors.** (typ.) corsivo – italic.

**c.p.** cartolina postale – postcard.

**C.P.** Casella Postale – (Private) Post Box; Consiglio Provinciale – District Council; (leg.) Codice Penale – Penal Code.

**C.P.p.** Codice di Procedura Penale, Code of Criminal Procedure.

**CRAL** Circolo Ricreativo Assistenza Lavoratori – Recreational Clubs organized by National Assistance Board.

**C.R.I.** Croce Rossa Italiana – Italian Red Cross.

**C.S.** Codice della Strada – Highway Code.

**c.s.** come sopra – as above.

**C.S.di C.** Centro Sperimentale di Cinematografia – Experimental Film Studios, Rome.

**c.ssa** contessa – countess.

**cte** conte – count (title).

**cto** (comm.) conto – account.

**C.V.** cavallo vapore – H.P. (horse power).

**C.X.** (Venice) Consiglio de Dieci – Council of Ten.

**d.** don – (eccl.) rev.; also used as courtesy title for members of the nobility; (bibliogr.) data – date.

**D** (rlwy.) diretto – fast train; (typ.) Didot.

**d.c.** (mus.) da capo; (typ.) new para.

**d.C.** dopo Cristo – after Christ, A.D.

**D.C.** Democrazia Cristiana – Christian Democrat Party.

**DD** (rlwy.) direttissimo – express train.

**DDT** Dicloro-Difenil-Tricloruroetano – insecticide.

**dev., dev.mo** devotissimo – (in letters) yours truly.

**D.G.** Direzione Generale – Managing Director's Office.

**dic.** (or **10bre**) dicembre – December.

**dis.** disegno – drawing, design.

**D.L.** Decreto Legge – decree promulgating a law.

**doc.** documenti – documents.

**dott.** or **dr.** doctor (of medicine, etc.); first university degree, corresponding approximately to B.A.

**D.P.R.** Decreto del Presidente della Repubblica – Decree of President of the Republic.

**E** (geog.) est – East.

**E.A.** Ente autonomo – Independent Committee.

**ECA** Ente Comunale di Assistenza (formerly Congregazione di Carità) – Municipal Public Assistance Board.

**ecc.** eccetera – etc.

**Ecc.** Eccellenza – Excellency (ambassador, minister, etc.); Lordship (bishop).

**ed.** edito, editore – edited by, editor, publisher.

**EFTA** Associazione europea di libero scambio – European Free Trade Association (cf. Z.C.L.).

**Eg.** (or **Egr.**) **Sig.** Egregio Signore – (in addresses) Mr.

**Em.** (eccl.) Eminenza – Eminence.

**ENAL** Ente Nazionale Assistenza Lavoratori – National Association for Assistance to Workers.

**ENAPI** Ente Nazionale per l'Artigianato e le Piccole Industrie – National Association of Artisans and Owners of Small Factories.

**ENI** Ente Nazionale Idrocarburi – National Hydrocarbon Corporation.

**ENIC** Ente Nazionale Industrie Cinematografiche – National Association of Film Producers.

**ENIT** Ente Nazionale Industrie Turistiche – National Institution for the Promotion of Tourist Industry.

**ENPI** Ente Nazionale per la Prevenzione degli Infortuni – National Institution for the Prevention of Accidents.

**E.P.T.** Ente Provinciale per il turismo – Provincial Board for promotion of Tourist Industry.

**es.** esempio – example.

**E.V.** Era Volgare – Anno Domini; Eccellenza Vostra – Your Excellency.

**f., ff.** (mus.) forte, fortissimo.

**fatt.** (comm.) fattura – invoice.

**f.c.** (boxing) fuori combattimento – knockout.

**f.co** franco – free.

**f.c.t.** (boxing) fuori combattimento tecnico – technical knockout.

**febb.** febbraio – February.

**fem.** (gramm.) femminile – feminine.

**FERT** motto of the House of Savoy and of the Order of the Annunziata, traditionally supposed to denote 'Fortitudo Eius Rhodum Tenuit' (its valour saved the island of Rhodes), but other interpretations have been suggested.

**FF.SS.** Ferrovie dello Stato – Italian State Railways.

**FGC** Federazione Giovanile Comunista – Association of Young Communists.

**F.I.A.** Federazione Internazionale dell'Automobile – International Automobile Federation.

**FIDAL** Federazione Italiana di Atletica Leggera – Italian Light Athletics Association.

**F.I.E.** Fondazione Figli Italiani all'Estero – Foundation of Sons of Italy abroad.

**FIFA** Federazione Internazionale – Football Association.

**F.I.G.C.** Federazione Italiana Gioco Calcio – Italian Football Association.

**FILM** Federazione Italiana Lavoratori del Mare – Italian Seamen's Union.

**FIP** Federazione Italiana Pallacanestro – Italian Basketball Association.

**FIR** Federazione Italiana Rugby – Italian Rugby Association.

**FIS** Federazione Italiana Scherma – Italian Fencing Association; Fédération Internationale de Ski.

**FISI** Federazione Italiana Sports Invernali – Italian Winter Sports Association.

**FIT** Federazione Italiana Tennis – Italian Lawn Tennis Association.

**FITAV** Federazione Italiana Tiro a Volo – Italian Pigeon-Shooting Association.

**fob** (comm.) franco a bordo – free on board.

**F.P.I.** Federazione Pugilistica Italiana – Italian Boxing Association.

**fr.** (comm.) franco – French or Swiss franc.

**F.S.** Ferrovie dello Stato – Italian State Railways.

**f.to** (comm.) firmato – signed.

**FUCI** Federazione Universitaria Cattolica Italiana – Italian Catholic University Association.

**g.** giorno – day; (med.) grani – grains.

**G.A.** Giunta Amministrativa – Municipal Council.

**G.B.** (name) Giovanni Battista; (geog.) Gran Bretagna – Gt Britain.

**G.C.** (eccl.) Gesù Cristo – Jesus Christ; (decoration) Gran Croce – Grand Cross.

**G.D.** Granduca – Grand Duke.

**G.d.F.** Guardia di Finanza – Revenue Guard.

**GEI** Giovani Esploratori Italiani – Italian Boy Scouts.

**Gen.** (mil.) Generale.

**genn.** gennaio – January.

**G.G.** (name) Gian Giacomo.

**G.I.A.C.** Gioventù Italiana di Azione Cattolica – Catholic Youth Association.

**giugn., giu.** giugno – June.

**G.M.** (mil.) Genio Militare – Corps of Engineers; (Masonic title) Gran Maestro – Grand Master.

**G.N.** Genio Navale – Engineer Branch of Italian Navy.

**G.P.** (sport) Gran Premio – Grand Prix.

**G.P.A.** Giunta Provinciale Amministrativa – County Council.

**gr.** grammo – gramme.

**GR.EST** Gruppo Estivo – Church organization which arranges games, etc., for children during summer holidays.

**Gr.Uff.** (decoration) Grande Ufficiale – corresponds approximately to K.B.E.

**G.U.** Gazzetta Ufficiale – Official Gazette.

**G.V.** (rlwy.) Grande Velocità – express goods service.

**ICE** Istituto Nazionale per il Commercio Estero – National Institute for Foreign Trade.

**I.C.S.** Istituto Centrale di Statistica – National Statistics Office.

**I.G.E.** Imposta Generale Entrate – turnover tax, generally 3% charged on all invoices, unless goods are intended for export.

**I.G.M.** Istituto Geografico Militare – Military Survey Office.

**Ill., Ill.mo.** Illustre, Illustrissimo – courtesy forms of address.

**IMEO** Istituto Italiano per il Medio ed Estremo Oriente – Italian Near and Far East Association.

**INA** Istituto Nazionale Assicurazioni – National Insurance Service.

**INA Casa** Department of INA which finances building of houses for the working classes.

**INAM** Istituto Nazionale Assicurazione Malattie – National Health Insurance Service.

**INCIS** Istituto Nazionale Case per gli Impiegati di Stato – Institute for providing houses for Civil Servants.

**INE** Istituto Nazionale per l'Esportazione – National Export Institute.

**ing.** ingegnere – engineer.

**INPI** Istituto Nazionale per la Prevenzione degli Infortuni – National Institution for the Prevention of Accidents.

**int.** (comm.) interessi – interest.

**INT** Istituto Nazionale Trasporti – National Transport Institute.

**I.R.** Imperiale Regio – Imperial and Royal.

**IRI** Istituto Nazionale per la Ricostruzione Industriale – National Institute for the Reconstruction of Industry.

**ISPI** Istituto per gli Studi di Politica Internazionale.

**I.T.C.** Compagnia Italiana Cavi Telegrafici Sottomarini (Italcable) – Italian Cable Company.

**kg.** chilogramma – kilogram.

**km.** chilometro – kilometre.

**km/h** chilometri all'ora – kilometres per hour.

**kmq.** chilometro quadrato – square kilometre.

**lat.** latitudine – latitude.

**Lit.** (comm.) Lire Italiane – Italian lire.

**lit.** (measure of capacity) litro – litre.

**LL.AA** Loro Altezze – Their Highnesses.

**LL.EE** Loro Eccellenze – Their Excellencies.

**LL.PP** Lavori Pubblici – (Ministry of) Public Works.

**LL.MM** Loro Maestà – Their Majesties.

**L.N.I.** Lega Navale Italiana – Italian Navy League.

**long.** longitudine – longitude.

**L.st.** (comm.) Lire sterline – pounds sterling (usu. written £ not £ in Italian).

**lu., lugl.** luglio – July.

**m.** metro – metre; (comm.) mio – my; morto – died.

**M.A.E.** Ministero degli Affari Esteri – Ministry of Foreign Affairs.

**magg.** maggio – May.

**Magg.** (mil.) Maggiore – Major.

**marz.** marzo – March.

**MAS** (naval) Motoscafo Antisommergibile – MTB (Motor Torpedo Boat).

**masc.** (gramm.) maschile – masculine.

**M.C.** (eccl.) Minore Conventuale; (hist.) Maggior Consiglio – Grand Council.

**m.c.d.** (math.) massimo comune divisore – highest common factor.

**m.c.m.** (math.) minimo comune multiplo – lowest common multiple.

**m.coli** (typ.) maiuscoli – caps.

**m.coletti** (typ.) maiuscoletti – small caps.

**M.E.** (hist.) Medio Evo – Middle Ages.

**M.E.C.** Mercato Europeo Comune, European Common Market.

**M.F.E.** Movimento Federalista Europeo.

**min.** (typ.) minuscoli – lower-case letters.

**mitt.** (on envelopes) mittente – sender.

**M.L.** (name) Maria Luisa.

**M.M.** Marina Militare – Italian Navy (formerly known as R.M., q.v.).

**Mn.** Motonave – Motor Vessel.

**Mo** Maestro.

**M.O.** Minori Osservanti.

**mons.** (eccl.) monsignore.

**M.P.** (hist.) manu propria (in documents, after king's signature).

**mq.** metro quadrato – square metre.

**M.R.** Molto Reverendo (a courteous variant of 'Reverendo') – Reverend.

**ms.** or **MS.** manoscritto – manuscript.

**M.S.** Mutuo Soccorso – Mutual Aid.

**M.S.I.** Movimento Sociale Italiano – neo-Fascist Party.

**mss.** manoscritti – manuscripts.

**Mv.** Motoveliero – sailing-boat or fishing-boat with auxiliary motor.

**n.** nota – note; nato – born.

**no.** numero – number.

**N** Nord – North.

**NATO** (pronounced as in Italian) North Atlantic Treaty Organization.

**N.B.** nota bene.

**N.D.** (eccl.) Nostra Donna – Our Lady; (title) Nobil Donna – member of a noble family.

**N.d.A.** Nota dell'autore – author's note.

**N.d.D.** Nota della Direzione – note by the editor (of a newspaper.)

**N.d.E.** Nota dell'editore – publisher's or editor's note.

**N.d.R.** Nota della redazione – editor's note (newspapers).

**N.d.T.** Nota del Traduttore – translator's note.

**NE** (geog.) Nord-est – North-east, NE.

**N.H.** Nobil Uomo (Homo) – member of a noble family.

**N.N.** Nescio nomen – (on birth certificates, etc.) name (of father) unknown.

**NNE** (geog.) Nord-nord-est – North-north-east, NNE.

**NNO** (geog.) Nord-nord-ovest – North-north-west, NNW.

**NO** (geog.) Nord-ovest – North-west, NW.

**nob.** nobile – nobleman.

**nov.** (or **9bre**) novembre – November.

**ns.** (comm.) nostro – our.

**N.S.** (eccl.) Nostro Signore – Our Lord.

**N.S.G.C.** (eccl.) Nostro Signore Gesù Cristo – Our Lord Jesus Christ.

**N.T.** Nuovo Testamento – New Testament.

**N.U.** Nettezza Urbana – Municipal service for collecting rubbish, cleaning streets, etc.

**O** Ovest (cf. W) – West.

**obb.mo** obbligatissimo – your obedient servant.

**O.C.S.** (decoration) Ordine Civile di Savoia.

**O.d.G.** (mil.) Ordine del Giorno, dispatches; (pol.) parliamentary motion; (admin.) agenda; order of the day, resolution.

**O.F.M.** Ordine del Frati Minori.

**O.M.S.** (decoration) Ordine Militare di Savoia.

**on.** onorevole – honourable (prefixed to names of members of the Chamber of Deputies).

**ONO** (geog.) Ovest-nord-ovest – West-north-west, WNW.

**ONU** Organizzazione Nazioni Unite – United Nations Organization (UNO).

**OO.PP** Opere Pubbliche – Public Works.

**O.P.** Ordine dei Predicatori (i.e. Dominicans).

**OSO** (geog.) Ovest-sud-ovest – West-south-west, WSW.

**O.S.SS.A.** (decoration) Ordine Supremo della Santissima Annunziata.

**ott.** (or **8bre**) ottobre – October.

**OVRA** (hist.) Opera Volontaria per la Repressione dell'Antifascismo – Fascist Secret Police.

**p., pp.** (mus.) piano, pianissimo.

**p.** pagina – page; (eccl.) padre – Father.

**p.a.** per auguri – used on visiting cards to express congratulations, birthday wishes, etc.

**pag.** pagina – page.

**pagg.** pagine – pages.

**par.** paragrafo – paragraph.

**pass.** passim.

**p.c.** per condoglianza – used on visiting cards to express condolence; per cortesia – please.

**P.C.A.** Pontificia Commissione di Assistenza.

**p.c.c.** per copia conforme – certified true copy.

**P.C.I.** Partito Comunista Italiano – Italian Communist Party.

**P.D.C.** Partito della Democrazia Cristiana (cf. D.C.).

**P.D.I.** Partito Democratico Italiano – new name (1960) of Monarchist Party in Italy (cf. P.N.M.).

**P.D.O.** (eccl.) Prete dell'Oratorio.

**p.es.** per esempio – for example.

**p.f.** (comm.) prossimo futuro – prox.

**P.G.** (leg.) Procuratore Generale – Attorney General; (eccl.) Padre Generale.

**P.I.** Pubblica Istruzione – (Ministry of) Public Education.

**P.L.I.** Partito Liberale Italiano – Italian Liberal Party.

**p.m.** pomeridiano – after midday, p.m.

**P.M.** Pontifex Maximus; (leg.) Pubblico Ministero – Public Prosecutor.

**P.M.P.** Partito Monarchico Popolare – Popular Monarchist Party.

**P.N.** (after names of rlwy. stations) Porta Nuova.

**P.N.F.** (hist.) Partito Nazione Fascista – National Fascist Party.

**P.N.M.** Partito Nazionale Monarchico – National Monarchist Party (now P.D.I., q.v.).

**pp.** pagine – pages.

**p.p.** (comm.) per procura – by proxy; per pro, through... for...; prossimo passato – ult.

**PP.** (comm.) porto pagato – carriage paid; (eccl.) Padri – Fathers.

**P.P., P.P.I.** (on packages) posa piano – handle with care; (hist.) Partito Popolare founded in 1919 by Don Sturzo, reformed in 1943 as P.D.C., q.v.

**p.r.** (on visiting cards) per ringraziamento – with thanks.

**PRA** Pubblico Registro Automobilistico – office where cars and other motor vehicles are registered and numbers allotted.

**P.R.I.** Partito Repubblicano Italiano.

**prof.** Professore – Professor.

**PS.** Post-scriptum.

**P.S.** Publica Sicurezza – Police.

**P.S.D.I.** Partito Socialista Democratico Italiano – right-wing Socialist Party.

**P.S.I.** Partito Socialista Italiano – left-wing Socialist Party.

**P.T.** Poste e Telegrafi – Post and Telegraph Service.

**P.T.P.** Posto telefonico pubblico – public telephone.

**P.T.T.** Poste, Telegrafi e Telefoni – Post, Telegraph and Telephone Services.

**p.v.** (comm.) prossimo venturo – prox.

**P.V.** (rlwy.) Piccola Velocità – ordinary goods service.

**q.** quadrato – square.

**q.e.d.** quod erat demonstrandum.

**r.** (bibliogr.) recto.

**R.** (rlwy.) rapido – express train; (eccl.) Rev(erend).

**rag.** ragioniere – accountant.

**RAI** Radio Audizioni Italiane – Italian Broadcasting Corporation, formerly EIAR.

**rc.** (math.) radice cubica – cube root.

**R.C.** Rotary Club.

**R.D.** (hist.) Regio Decreto – Royal Decree.

**R.D.L.** (hist.) Regio Decreto Legge – Law promulgated by Royal Decree.

**Rev.mo** *see* R.mo.

**R.I.** Repubblica Italiana – Republic of Italy.

**ric.** ricevuta – received, receipt.

**R.M.** Ricchezza Mobile – (tax on) income; (hist.) Regia Marina – Royal (Italian) Navy, now Marina Militare, M.M., q.v.

**R.mo., Rev.mo** Reverendissimo – Most Reverend, Right Rev(erend), Very Rev(erend).

**R.N.** Riserva Navale – Naval Reserve; Regia Nave – Royal Ship

**RR.CC.** (hist.) Reali Carabinieri, now CC, q.v.

**RP** (post) risposta pagata – reply paid.

**R.S.I.** (hist.) Repubblica Sociale Italiana (also known as Repubblica di Salò), founded by Mussolini after his escape from the Gran Sasso (1943–5).

**R.T.** Radiotelegrafia – wireless; radiotelegrafista – wireless operator; radiotelegrafo – wireless telegraph.

**s.** san, santo, santa – St (before names of saints); (mus.) solo, soli.

**S.** San, Santo, Santa – St (before names of churches and places); (geog.) Sud – South.

**S.A.** Sua Altezza – His (or Her) Highness; (comm.) Società Anonima – Limited Company.

**S.A.R.** Sua Altezza Reale – His (or Her) Royal Highness.

**S.a.r.l.** Società a responsabilità limitata – (private) limited company.

**s.b.f.** salvo buon fine – under usual reserve (formula used when acknowledging receipt of cheque).

**S.C.** (on restaurant menus) Secondo consumo – according to amount eaten; (comm.) Sede Centrale – Head Office.

**S.C.V.** Stato della Città del Vaticano – Vatican City; (joc.) Se Cristo vedesse – If Christ could only see it!

**S.D.N.** (hist.) Società delle Nazioni – League of Nations.

**s.d.** (bibliogr.) senza data – no date.

**s.d.l.** (bibliogr.) senza data o luogo – no date or place of publication.

**SE** (geog.) Sud-est – South-east, SE.

**S.E.** Sua Eccellenza – His Excellency; (eccl.) His Grace; His Lordship.

**S.E.A.T.** Società Elenchi Ufficiali Abbonati al Telefono – Official Telephone Directory Company.

**Sec.** secolo – century.

**S.E. & O.** (comm.) Salvo errori ed omissioni – E. and O.E.

**seg.** seguente – following.

**S.Em.** (eccl.) Sua Eminenza – His Eminence.

**Sen.** Senatore – Senator.

**Serg.** (mil.) Sergente – Sergeant.

**SET** Società Esercizi Telefoni – Telephone Company.

**SETAF** Southern European Task Forces – Nato Powers H.Q. in Italy.

**sett.** (or **7bre**) settembre – September.

**sfr** (post) sotto fascia raccomandata – registered printed matter; franco svizzero – Swiss franc.

**sfs** (post) sotto fascia semplice – unregistered printed matter.

**S.G.** (on restaurant menus) Secondo grandezza – according to size of portion; (title) Sua Grazia – His Grace.

**SIA** Servizio Informazioni Aeronautiche – (Italian) Air Intelligence.

**S.I.A.E.** Società Italiana Autori ed Editori – Italian Authors' and Publishers' Association.

**Sig.** Signore – Mr.

**Sig.a., Sig.ra** Signora – Mrs.

**Sigg.** Signori – Messrs.

**Sig.na** Signorina – Miss.

**SIM** Servizio Informazioni Militari – (Italian) Military Intelligence.

**SIN** Servizio Informazioni Navali – (Italian) Naval Intelligence.

**SISAL** Sport Italiana Società a responsabilità limitata – original founders of football pools in Italy, now administered by CONI (q.v.).

**s.l.m.** sul livello del mare – above sea level.

**S.M.** Sua Maestà – Hiss (or Her) Majesty; (mil.) Stato Maggiore – Staff; (naut.) submarine (also S.M.G.).

**S.M.G.** (mil.) Stato Maggiore Generale – General Staff; (naut.) sommergibile – submarine.

**S.M.O.M.** Sovrano Militare Ordine di Malta – Sovereign Military Order of Malta (Knights of Malta).

**S.N.D.A.** Società Nazionale Dante Alighieri.

**sost.** (gramm.) sostantivo – substantive.

**sp.** specie – species.

**S.P.** (eccl.) Santo Padre – His Holiness (the Pope).

**SPA** Società Protettrice degli Animali – (Italian) Society for the Protection of Animals.

**S.p.a.** Società per azioni – Limited Company.

**S.P.E.** (mil.) Servizio Permanente Effettivo – Service in regular army qualifying for pension.

**sped.** (on envelopes) spedisce-sender.

**Spett.** Spettabile – (in letters addressed to firms) Messrs.

**s.p.m.** sua propria mano – personal for addressee.

**S.P.Q.R.** Senatus Populusque Romanus – still used on proclamations, etc. by Rome City Council.

**S.Q.** (on bill of fare) secondo quantità – price according to quantity consumed.

**S.R.C.** Santa Romana Chiesa – Holy Roman Church.

**S.R.I.** Sacro Romano Impero – Holy Roman Empire.

**s.r.l.** società a responsabilità limitata – (private) limited company.

**S.S.** (eccl.) Sua Santità – His Holiness; Santa Sede – Holy See.

**SS.** Piroscafo – Steamship; (eccl.) Santi – Saints; Santissim-o, -a, Blessed.

**SS.A.** Santissima Annunziata – Order of the Holy Annunciation.

**SSE** (geog.) Sud-sud-est – South-south-east, SSE.

**SS.M.e L.** Santi Maurizio e Lazzaro – Order of knighthood.

**SSO** (geog.) Sud-sud-ovest – South-south-west, SSW.

**SS.PP.** (eccl.) Santi Padri – Holy Fathers (esp. the 'Fathers of the Church').

**S.Ten.** (mil.) Sottotenente – 2nd Lieutenant – Sub-Lieutenant.

**STET** Società Torinese Esercizio Telefoni – Turin Telephone Co.

**STIPEL** Società Telefonica Interregionale Piemonte e Lombardia – Company controlling telephone services in Piedmont and Lombardy.

**S.T.V.** Societá Tiro a Volo – Pigeon-Shooting Association.

**S.U.C.A.I.** Sezione Universitarii Club Alpino Italiano – Italian Universities Alpine Club.

**succ.** successori – successors.

**s.v.** (bibliogr.) sub voce.

**S.V.** Signoria Vostra – Your Lordship, but also used in official communications to ordinary citizens.

**S.V.P.** Südtiroler Volkspartei – Party of the Germany-speaking minority in Alto Adige; *s'il vous plaît* – please.

**T.** (mus.) tutti; *or* trillo – trill (more usually TR).

**tbc.** (med.) tuberculosi – tuberculosis.

**tang.** (math.) tangente – tangent.

**T.C.I.** Touring Club Italiano – Italian Touring Club.

**T.E.** (rlwy.) Trazione elettrica – electrified line.

**TELVE** Società Telefoni delle Venezie – Company controlling telephone services in the Three Venetias.

**Ten.** (mil.) Tenente – Lieutenant.

**TETI** Telefoni del Tirreno – Company controlling telephone services along the Tyrrhenian Coast.

**TIMO** (Società) Telefoni Italiani Medio-Orientali – Company controlling telephone services in Central and Eastern Italy.

**tit.** titolare – owner; titolo – title, share certificate.

**tom.** (bibliogr.) tomo – volume.

**TOTIP** Totalizzatore Ippico – Company controlling totalizators on racecourses and also pools on the same lines as football pools.

**tr.** traduzione – translation; (mus.) trillo – trill.

**Tr.** (comm.) tratta – bill of exchange.

**T.S.F.** Telegrafo senza fili – wireless.

**T.U.** (leg.) Testo Unico – Consolidation Act.

**T.V.** Televisione.

**U.C.** (mil.) Ufficiale di Complemento – Territorial Army Officer.

**U.C.D.G.** Unione Cristiana delle Giovani – Italian branch of the Y.W.C.A.

**U.D.I.** Unione Donne Italiana – Association of Italian Women.

**UFAC** Unione Femminile di Azione Cattolica – Catholic Women's Association.

**U.I.** Utile Idiota – useful idiot (said of well-known personages who lend their names to a political party).

**U.I.L.** Ufficio Internazionale del Lavoro – International Labour Office; Unione Italiana del La-

**U.I.L.** (*cont.*) voro – Italian Federation of Trade Unions with moderate Socialist and Republican trend (cf. C.G.I.L., C.I.S.L., C.I.S. Na.L.).

**U.R.S.S.** Unione Repubbliche Socialisti Sovietiche – U.S.S.R.

**u.s.** (comm.) ultimo scorso – ult.

**U.T.E.** Ufficio Tecnico Erariale, Inland Revenue Surveyors' Office.

**U.T.E.** Ufficio Tecnico Erariale, Inland Revenue Surveyors' Office.

**v.** vedi – see; (bibliogr.) verso – verse, verso.

**val.** (comm.) valuta – value; currency; foreign exchange; effective date.

**V.C.** Vice-Console – Vice-Consul; Valore Civile – used after decorations awarded for non-military services (cf. V.M.).

**V.E.** Vostra Eccellenza – Your Excellency; (eccl.) Your Grace; Your Lordship; (name) Vittorio Emanuele.

**V.Em.** Vostra Eminenza – Your Eminence.

**ver.** (comm.) versamento – payment, remittance.

**V.E.R.D.I.** Vittorio Emanuele Re d'Italia – (hist.) slogan of Italian patriots during Risorgimento; now name of a monarchist students' association.

**VF** Vigili di Fuoco – Fire Brigade.

**V.M.** Vostra Maiestà – Your Majesty; Valore Militare – used after military decorations, cf. V.C.

**vol.** (bibliogr.) volume – volume.

**vs.** (comm.) vostro – your.

**V.S.** Vostra Signoria – cf. S.V.; (mus.) volti subito, turn over quickly.

**VV** (usually written W) viva!, long live!

**W** West – often used instead of O (Ovest).

**W.C.** Water-Closet.

**WL** Wagon Lits, Carrozza con letti – sleeping-car.

**X Mas** Decima Flottiglia Mas (q.v.) – Naval unit which during 1939–45 War controlled 'secret weapons' such as human torpedoes, frogmen, etc. Subsequently expanded to include Commando units (Battaglioni San Marco).

**Y.C.I.** Yacht Club Italia – Italian Yacht Club.

**Y.C.N.** Yacht Club Napoli – Neapolitan Yacht Club.

**Y.M.C.A.** Associazione Cristiana dei Giovani, Young Men's Christian Association (initials as English, to distinguish it from U.C.D.G., q.v.).

**Z.C.L.** Zona di Commercio Libero – European Free Trade Area (cf. EFTA).

# ABBREVIATIONS COMMONLY USED IN ENGLISH

**A...** Associate...
**A** Amateur; Academician; ampere; atomic (in *A-bomb*); denoting the first, of a high-class (*A-road*); advanced (in *A-level*); adult – used to mark a film at a showing of which a child should be accompanied by an adult.
**a.** accepted; acre; active; afternoon; *annus*, year; *ante*, before.
**AA** Automobile Association; Anti-aircraft; used to mark a film to which no child may be admitted.
**AAA** Amateur Athletic Association.
**AAM** air-to-air missile.
**A and M** (Hymns) Ancient and Modern.
**AB** Able-bodied seaman.
**ABA** Amateur Boxing Association.
**Abb.** Abbess; Abbot; Abbey.
**abbr., abbrev.** abbreviated; abbreviation.
**abl.** ablative.
**Abp.** Archbishop.
**abr.** abridged; abridgment.
**abs., absol.** absolutely.
**abs., abstr.** abstract.
**AC** Aircraftman; Aero Club; Alpine Club.
**a.c.** alternating current.
**ACA** Associate of the Institute of Chartered Accountants.
**acc.** account (also acct., a/c); accountant; accusative (also accus.) according.
**ACGB** Arts Council of Great Britain.
**act.** active.
**ACTH** adrenocorticotrophin.
**ACW** Aircraftwoman.
**A.D.** *anno Domini*, in the year of the Lord.
**a.d.** after date; *ante diem*, before the day.
**ad.** advertisement.
**ADC** Aide-de-camp.
**adj.** adjective; adjourned; adjustment.
**Adjt.** Adjutant.
**Adjt.-Gen.** Adjutant-General.
**ad lib.** *ad libitum*, at pleasure.
**Adm.** Admiral.
**a.d.p.** automatic data processing.
**adv.** advent; adverb; *adversus*, against; advocate; advisory.
**advt.** advertisement.
**ae., aet.** *aetatis*, of his age, aged (so many years).
**AEA** Atomic Energy Authority (UK).
**AEC** Army Educational Corps (now RAEC); Atomic Energy Commission (US).
**AET** Associated Electrical Industries.
**AEU** Amalgamated Engineering Union (now A.U.E.W.).
**AF...** Associate Fellow...
**A.F.** Admiral of the Fleet; Army Form; (or **a.f.**) audio frequency.
**AFA** Amateur Football Association.
**AFC** Air Force Cross.
**AFL** American Federation of Labour.
**AFM** Air Force Medal.
**A.G.** Adjutant-General; (or A.-G.) Attorney-General.
**agr., agric.** agriculture
**Agt.** Agent.
**A.I.** artificial insemination.
**AID** artificial insemination donor.
**Ald.** Alderman.
**alg.** algebra.
**alt.** alternate; altitude; alto.

**A.M...** Associate Member...; (also a.m.) *ante meridiem*, before noon; amplitude modulation.
**Am., Amer.** America; American.
**AMA** Assistant Masters' Association.
**amp.** ampere.
**amt.** amount.
**a.m.t.** air mail transfer.
**amu** atomic mass unit.
**an.** *anno*, in the year; anonymous; *ante*, before.
**anal.** analysis; analogy.
**anat.** anatomy; anatomical.
**anc.** ancient; anciently.
**Ang.** *Anglice*, in English.
**anon.** anonymous.
**ans.** answer.
**antiq.** antiquities; antiquarian.
**A.O.** Army Order.
**A.O.C.-in-C.** Air Officer Commanding-in-Chief.
**AOF** Ancient Order of Foresters.
**aor.** aorist.
**AP** Associated Press.
**Ap., Apl., Apr.** April.
**apo.** apogee.
**Apoc.** Apocalypse; Apocrypha, Apocryphal.
**app.** appendix; apparent, apparently; apprentice.
**appro.** approval, approbation.
**approx.** approximate; approximately.
**AQ** achievement quotient.
**aq.** *aqua*, water.
**Ar., Arab.** Arabic.
**ar., arr.** arrive or arrives; arrival.
**ARA** Associate of the Royal Academy.
**ARC** Agricultural Research Council.
**arch.** archaic.
**arch., archit.** architecture.
**archaeol.,** archaeology.
**Archd.** Archdeacon; Archduke.
**arith.** arithmetic; arithmetical.
**ARP** Air Raid Precautions.
**arr.** arranged; arrival.
**art.** article; artificial; (also arty.) artillery.
**A.S.** Anglo-Saxon; Assistant Secretary.
**ASA** Amateur Swimming Association.
**ASE** Amalgamated Society of Engineers.
**ASF** Associate of the Institute of Shipping and Forwarding Agents.
**ASLEF** Associated Society of Locomotive Engineers and Firemen.
**ASM** air-to-surface missile.
**Ass., Assoc.** Association.
**Asst.** Assistant.
**AST** Atlantic Standard Time.
**ASTMS** Association of Scientific, Technical and Managerial Staffs.
**astr., astron.** astronomer; astronomy.
**astrol.** astrology.
**ATC** Air Training Corps; automatic train control.
**atm.** atmosphere.
**at. no., at. numb.** atomic number.
**ATS** Auxiliary Territorial Service (superseded by WRAC).
**Att.** Attic (Greek); Attorney.
**Att.-Gen.** Attorney-General.
**attrib.** attribute(d); attributive; attributively.
**Atty.** Attorney.
**ATV** Associated Television.
**at. wt.** atomic weight.
**A.U.E.W.** Amalgamated Union of Engineering Workers.
**Aug.** August.
**aug.** augmentative.
**AUT** Association of University Teachers.
**aut., auto.** automatic.
**Auth. Ver., A.V.** Authorized Version.
**av.** avenue; average.
**ave.** avenue.

**A.V.M.** Air Vice-Marshal.
**avoir., avdp.** avoirdupois.
**AWOL** absent, or absence, without official leave.
**AWRE** Atomic Weapons Research Establishment.
**ax.** axiom.
**az.** azimuth.

**B.** Baron; British; Bachelor.
**B** (on lead pencils) black.
***B*** magnetic flux density.
***b*** breadth.
**b.** born; book.
**B.A.** *Baccalaureus Artiam*, Bachelor of Arts; British Association (for the Advancement of Science) British Academy; British Airways.
**BAA** British Airports Authority.
**BABS** beam, or blind, approach beacon system.
**Bach.** Bachelor.
**BACIE** British Association for Commercial and Industrial Education.
**B.Agr., B.Agric.** Bachelor of Agriculture.
**B.A.I.** *Baccalaureus in Arte Ingeniaria*, Bachelor of Engineering.
**bal.** balance.
**BALPA.** British Airline Pilots' Association.
**B and B.** bed and breakfast.
**B and FBS** British and Foreign Bible Society.
**BAOR** British Army of the Rhine.
**Bap., Bapt.** Baptist.
**bap., bapt.** baptized.
**Bar.** Barrister.
**Bart.** Baronet.
**bat, batt** battalion; battery.
**B.B.** Boys' Brigade.
**BB** (on lead pencils) very black.
**bb.** books.
**BBB** (on lead pencils) triple black.
**BBC** British Broadcasting Corporation.
**BBFC** British Board of Film Censors.
**B.C.** Before Christ; Board of Control; British Columbia; Battery Commander.
**B. Comm., B.Com.** Bachelor of Commerce.
**BCS** British Computer Society.
**B.D.** Bachelor of Divinity.
**bd.** bound.
**BDA** British Dental Association.
**Bde.** Brigade.
**bds.** boards.
**B.E.** Bachelor of Engineering; Board of Education.
**b.e.** bill of exchange.
**BEA** British European Airways (now incorporated in British Airways).
**BEAMA** British Electrical and Allied Manufacturers Association.
**B.Ed.** Bachelor of Education.
**Beds** Bedfordshire.
**BEF** British Expeditionary Force.
**bef.** before.
**BEM** British Empire Medal.
**B.Eng.** Bachelor of Engineering.
**Berks** Berkshire.
**bet.** between.
**bf** brought forward.
**Bib.** Bible.
**Bibl.** Biblical.
**bibl.** bibliotheca.
**bibliog.** bibliographer; bibliography.
**BIM** British Institute of Management.
**biog.** biographer; biography, biographical.
**biol.** biology; biological.
**BIR** British Institute of Radiology.
**BIS** Bank for International Settlements.
**bis.** bissextile.

**bk** book; bank.
**bkg.** banking.
**bkt.** basket.
**B.L., BL** Bachelor of Law; Bachelor of Letters.
**bl.** barrel; bale.
**b.l.** bill of lading.
**bldg.** building.
**B.Litt., B.Lit.** *Baccalaureus Lit(t)erarum*, Bachelor of Literature or Letters.
**B.M.** Bachelor of Medicine; British Museum; Brigade Major.
**BMA** British Medical Association.
**BMEWS** Ballistic Missile Early Warning System.
**BMJ** British Medical Journal.
**B.Mus.** Bachelor of Music.
**Bn.** Baron.
**bn.** battalion.
**BNEC** British National Export Council.
**b.o.** branch office; buyer's option; body odour (also B.O.).
**BOAC** British Overseas Airways Corporation (now incorporated in British Airways).
**Boh.** Bohemia, Bohemian.
**bor.** borough.
**B.o.T.** Board of Trade.
**bot.** botany; botanical; bought.
**Bp.** Bishop.
**BP** British Pharmacopoeia; British Petroleum.
**b.p.** boiling-point (or bp); bills payable; birthplace (also b.pl.).
**B.Pharm.** Bachelor of Pharmacy.
**B.Phil.** *Baccalaureus Philosophiae*, Bachelor of Philosophy.
**Br.** Brother.
**b.r.** bank rate.
**br.** branch; brig; brown.
**B.R.** British Rail.
**BRCS** British Red Cross Society.
**b. rec.** bills receivable.
**brev.** brevet; breveted.
**Brig.** Brigadier.
**Brig.-Gen.** Brigadier-General.
**Brit.** Britain; Britannia; British; Briton.
**Bro.** Brother.
**Bros.** Brothers.
**BRS** British Road Services.
**b.s.** bill of sale.
**B.S.** Bachelor of Science or of Surgery (or BS); Blessed Sacrament; Balance Sheet; Bill of Sale.
**BSA** Building Societies Association; Birmingham Small Arms.
**BSC** British Steel Corporation; British Sugar Corporation.
**B.Sc.** Bachelor of Science.
**BSI** British Standards Institution; Building Societies Institute.
**BS(S)** British Standards (Specification).
**BST** British Summer Time; British Standard Time.
**Bt.** Baronet.
**BTU** Board of Trade Unit.
**Btu** British Thermal Unit.
**bu.** bushel(s).
**BUA** British United Airways.
**Bucks** Buckinghamshire.
**BUP** British United Press.
**BUPA** British United Provident Association.
**bus., bush.** bushel(s).
**B.V.M.** The Blessed Virgin Mary.
**B.V.M.(&)S.** Bachelor of Veterinary Medicine & Surgery.
**bvt.** brevet, breveted.

**C.** Conservative.
**°C** degree(s) Celsius, centigrade.
**c.** *caput*, chapter; cent; centime; *circa*, about.
**c** centi-.
**c** cent(s); (Ghanean) cedi(s).
**CA** Chartered Accountant (Scotland); County Alderman.
**ca.** cases; *circa*, about.
**CAB** Citizens' Advice Bureau.
**Cam., Camb.** Cambridge.

**Cambs** Cambridgeshire.
**Can.** Canon; Canto.
**Cantab.** *Cantabrigiensis*, of Cambridge.
**Cantuar.** *Cantuaria*, Canterbury; *Cantuariensis*, of Canterbury.
**cap.** *caput*, chapter; capital; *capitulum*, head, chapter.
**caps** capitals.
**Capt.** Captain.
**Car.** *Carolus*, Charles,
**car.** carat.
**Card.** Cardinal.
**CARD** Campaign Against Racial Discrimination.
**Cards** Cardiganshire.
**carp.** carpentry.
**Cash.** Cashier.
**CAT** College of Advanced Technology.
**cat.** catechism; catalogue.
**Cath.** Catholic.
**C.B.** Companion of the Order of the Bath; confined to barracks; County Borough.
**CBE** Commander of the Order of the British Empire.
**CBI** Confederation of British Industry.
**CC** County Council; Cricket Club; closed circuit (transmission).
**cc.** *capita*, chapters.
**cc** cubic centimetre(s).
**CD** *Corps Diplomatique*, Diplomatic Corps; Civil Defence.
**Cdr.** Commander.
**CDSO** Companion of the Distinguished Service Order.
**CE** Civil Engineer; Council of Europe.
**CEGB** Central Electricity Generating Board.
**CEI** Council of Engineering Institutions.
**Celt.** Celtic.
**cen.** central; century.
**C.Eng.** Chartered Engineer.
**cent., cent** *centum*, a hundred; century; central.
**cert.** certainty; certificate; certificated; certify.
**CET** Central European Time.
**CETS** Church of England Temperance Society.
**CF** Chaplain to the Forces.
**cf.** *confer*, compare; calf (bookbinding).
**c.f.** (and) **i.** cost, freight, and insurance.
**cg** centigram(me)(s).
**c.g.** centre of gravity.
**CGH** Cape of Good Hope.
**CG(L)I** City and Guilds (of London) Institute.
**C.G.S.** Chief of the General Staff.
**C.H.** Companion of Honour.
**Ch.** Chief; China; Church; Champion.
**ch.** chaldron; chapter; child.
**c.h.** central heating.
**Chamb.** Chamberlain.
**Chanc.** Chancellor; Chancery.
**Chap.** Chaplain; Chapter.
**Chas.** Charles.
**Ch.B.** *Chirurgiae Baccalaureus* Bachelor of Surgery.
**chem.** chemistry; chemical.
**Ch. Hist.** Church History.
**Chin.** China; Chinese.
**Ch.J.** Chief-Justice.
**Ch.M.** *Chirurgiae Magister*, Master of Surgery.
**Chr.** Christ; Christian.
**Chron.** Chronicles.
**chron.** chronicle; chronology; chronological.
**CI** Channel Islands.
**Cic.** Cicero.
**CID** Criminal Investigation Department; Council of Industrial Design; *Cambridge Italian Dictionary*.
**c.i.f.** cost, insurance, freight.
**C.-in-C.** Commander-in-Chief.

**cir., circ.** *circa, circiter, circum,* about.
**circs.** circumstances.
**CIS** Chartered Institute of Secretaries.
**cit.** citation; citizen.
**civ.** civil; civilian.
**CJ** Chief-Justice.
**cl.** class; clause.
**c.l.** *cum laude,* with praise.
**class.** classical; classification.
**C.Litt.** Companion of Literature.
**C.M.** Certificated Master; Corresponding Member; Common Metre; *Chirurgiae Magister,* Master of Surgery.
**cm** centimetre(s).
**CMG** Companion of the Order of St Michael and St George.
**CMS** Church Missionary Society.
**CND** Campaign for Nuclear Disarmament.
**CO** Commonwealth Office; Commanding Officer; Criminal Office; Crown Office; conscientious objector.
**Co.** Company; County.
**c/o** care of.
**Cod.** Codex.
**c.o.d.** cash on delivery.
**C. of E.** Church of England; Council of Europe.
**C. of I.** Church of Ireland.
**C. of S.** Chief of Staff; Church of Scotland.
**cog.** cognate.
**c.o.g.** centre of gravity.
**COI** Central Office of Information.
**Col.** Colonel; Colossians.
**col.** column.
**coll.** college; colleague; collector; colloquial.
**collat.** collateral; collaterally.
**colloq.** colloquial; colloquially.
**Coloss.** Colossians.
**Com.** Commander; Commodore; Committee; Commissioner; Commonwealth; Communist.
**com.** common; comedy; commerce; committee; commune.
**Comdr** Commander.
**Comdt** Commandant.
**comm.** commentary; commander.
**Commy** Communist.
**comp.** comparative; compositor; compare; compound; compounded.
**compar.** comparative; comparison.
**Con.** Consul.
**con.** *contra,* against; convenience.
**conj.** conjunction; conjunctive.
**conn.** connection, connected; connotation.
**cons.** consonant.
**con. sec.** conic section.
**Consols.** Consolidated Funds.
**cont., contd** continued.
**contr.** contracted; contraction.
**conv.** conventional.
**co-op.** co-operative.
**Cop., Copt.** Coptic.
**Cor.** Corinthians; Coroner.
**Cor. Mem.** Corresponding Member.
**Corn.** Cornish; Cornwall.
**corol., coroll.** corollary.
**Corp.** Corporation; Corporal.
**corr.** corrupted; corruption; correspond.
**Cor. Sec.** Corresponding Secretary.
**cos** cosine.
**cosec** cosecant.
**cosmog.** cosmography.
**cot** cotangent.
**cp.** compare.
**CP** Clerk of the Peace; Carriage Paid; College of Preceptors; Cape Province (S. Africa); Communist Party.
**c.p.** candle power.
**C.P.C.** Clerk of the Privy Council.
**Cpl.** Corporal.
**C.P.S.** *Custos Privati Sigillii,* Keeper of the Privy Seal.
**cr** credit; creditor; crown.

**cres., cresc.** crescendo; crescent.
**CS** Court of Session; Civil Service; Christian Science; Chemical Society.
**c/s** cycles per second (hertz).
**CSE** Certificate of Secondary Education.
**CSM** Company Sergeant Major.
**CST** Central Standard Time.
**ct** cent; carat.
**CTC** Cyclists' Touring Club.
**cu., cub.** cubic.
**cur., curt** current (this month).
**cusec** cubic feet per second.
**CVO** Commander of the (Royal) Victorian Order.
**c.w.o.** cash with order.
**CWS** Co-operative Wholesale Society.
**cwt** hundredweight(s).

*D* electric flux or displacement.
**3-D** three-dimensional.
**d.** *dele*, delete; dead; died; degree; a penny, pence (before 1971).
**d** day; diameter.
**DA** District Attorney; Diploma of Art.
**D.(A.)A.G.** Deputy (Assistant) Adjutant-General.
**Dan.** Daniel.
**D and C** dilatation and curettage (surgical scraping of tissue from the womb for examination).
**dat.** dative.
**dau.** daughter.
**db** decibel.
**DBE** Dame Commander of the Order of the British Empire.
**DC** *Da capo* (It.), return to the beginning (*mus.*); District of Columbia; District Commissioner.
**d.c.** direct current.
**D.C.L.** Doctor of Civil Law; Distillers Company, Limited.
**DCM** Distinguished Conduct Medal.
**DCMG** Dame Commander of the Order of St Michael and St George.
**DCVO** Dame Commander of the (Royal) Victorian Order.
**D.D.** *Divinitatis Doctor*, Doctor of Divinity.
**d.d., D/D, d/d** days after date; day's date.
**D.D.S.** Doctor of Dental Surgery.
**DDT** Dichlorodiphenyltrichloroethane (insecticide).
**DEA** Department of Economic Affairs.
**Dec.** December.
**dec.** deceased.
**dec., decl.** declaration; declension.
**D.Ed.** Doctor of Education.
**def.** definition; defendant.
**deg.** degree(s).
**del.** delegate; *delineavit*, drew it (after the draughtsman's name).
**demon., demons.** demonstrative.
**D.Eng.** Doctor of Engineering.
**dent.** dental; dentist; dentistry.
**Dep., Dept., dep., dept.** department; deputy.
**dep.** deposed.
**der., deriv.** derivation; derived.
**derv** Diesel Oil (from *D*iesel-*E*ngine *R*oad *V*ehicle).
**DES** Department of Education and Science.
**Deut.** Deuteronomy.
**D.F.** Defender of the Faith.
**DFC** Distinguished Flying Cross.
**DFM** Distinguished Flying Medal.
**dft.** defendant; draft.
**dg** decigram(s).
**DHSS** Department of Health and Social Services.
**dial.** dialect.
**diam.** diameter.
**D.I.C.** Diploma of the Imperial College.
**dict.** dictator; dictionary.
**diff.** different; difference.
**dil.** dilute.

**D.Ing.** *Doctor Ingeniariae*, Doctor of Engineering.

**Dip.** Diploma.

**Dir.** Director.

**dis.** discontinued.

**disc.** discount; discoverer.

**diss.** dissertation.

**dist.** distance; distinguish; district; distilled.

**div.** divide; division; divine; divorced.

**D.I.Y.** Do-it-yourself.

**D.J.** dee-jay, disk-jockey.

**dl** decilitre(s).

**D.L.** Deputy Lieutenant.

**D.Lit.** or **Litt., D Lit**(**t**) *Doctor litterarum* or *litteraturae*, Doctor of Letters or Literature.

**dm** decimetre(s).

**DM** deutsche mark.

**D.Mus.** Doctor of Music.

**DNA** dexoyribonucleic acids.

**DNB** Dictionary of National Biography.

**do.** *ditto*, the same.

**D.O.A.** dead on arrival.

**dols.** dollars.

**Dom.** *Dominus*; Dominion.

**dom.** domestic.

**doz.** dozen.

**DP** Displaced Person; data processing.

**D.Phil.** *Doctor Philosophiae*, Doctor of Philosophy.

**dpt.** department.

**Dr** Doctor; Debtor; Driver.

**dr** drawer.

**d.r.** dead reckoning.

**D.Sc.** *Scientiae Doctor*, Doctor of Science.

**DSC** Distinguished Service Cross.

**DSM** Distinguished Service Medal.

**DSO** Distinguished Service Order.

**dsp** *decessit sine prole*, died without issue.

**DT** data transmission; DT's, delirium tremens.

**D.Th.** *Doctor Theologiae*, Doctor of Theology.

**dyn** dyne; dynamo; dynamometer.

**E.** East; English.

*E* energy.

**E. and O.E.** errors and omissions excepted.

**e.a.o.n.** except as otherwise noted.

**Ebor.** *Eboracum*, York; *Eboracensis*, of York.

**EC** East Central; Established Church.

**Eccl., Eccles.** Ecclesiastes; Ecclesiastical.

**Ecclus.** Ecclesiasticus.

**ECG** electrocardiogram (-graph).

**ECT** Electroconvulsive therapy.

**Ed.** Editor.

**ed., edit.** edited; edition.

**EDC** European Defence Community.

**Edin.** Edinburgh.

**EDS** English Dialect Society.

**E.E.** Errors Excepted.

**EEC** European Economic Community.

**EEG** electroencephalogram (-graph).

**EETS** Early English Text Society.

**EFTA** European Free Trade Association.

**e.g., eg, ex. gr.** *exempli gratia*, for example.

**EI** East Indies.

**elec., elect**(**r**). electric; electricity.

**emf** electromotive force.

**Emp.** Emperor, Empress.

**emu** electromagnetic unit.

**Ency., Encyc.** Encyclopaedia.

**E.N.E.** East-north-east.

**Eng.** England; English.

**eng.** engineer; engraver; engraving.

**Ens.** Ensign.

**ENSA** Entertainments National Services Association (World War II).
**E.N.T.** Ear, Nose and Throat.
**ent., entom.** entomology.
**e.o.d.** every other day.
**Ep.** Epistle.
**EP** Extended play.
**Eph.** Ephesians.
**Epiph.** Epiphany.
**Epis(c).** Episcopal.
**EPNS** electroplated nickel silver; English Place-Name Society.
**ER** East Riding (Yorks); *Elisabeth Regina*, Elizabeth, Queen.
**E.S.E.** East-south-east.
**ESN** Educationally subnormal.
**esp., espec.** especially.
**ESP** extra-sensory perception.
**Esq., Esqr.** Esquire.
**est.** established; estimated.
**Esth.** Esther.
**ESU** English Speaking Union.
**esu** electrostatic unit.
**ETA** (or **D**) Estimated time of arrival (or departure).
**et al.** *et alibi*, and elsewhere; *et alii*, *aliae*, or *alia*, and others.
**etc., &c.** *et ceteri* or *cetera*, and the others, and so forth.
**et seq.** or **sq.** (sing.) *et sequens*, **et sqq.** (pl.), *et sequentes* or *sequentia*, and the following.
**ETU** Electrical Trades Union.
**ety., etym.** etymology; etymological.
**EU** Evangelical Union.
**eV** electron-volt.
**Ex., Exod.** Exodus.
**ex.** examined; example; exception; excursus; executive; export.
**Exc.** Excellency.
**exc.** except; exception.
**ex. div.** *extra dividendum*, without dividend.
**ex lib.** *ex libris*, from the books (of) (on book-plates).
**exp.** export: exponential.
**Ez.** Ezra.
**Ezek.** Ezekiel.

**F...** Fellow...
**F** Fahrenheit; farad.
*F* force.
**f** following; feminine; fathom; foot; forte.
*f* frequency.
**FA** Football Association.
**fam.** familiar; family.
**f.a.s.** free alongside ship.
**FAS** Fellow of the Society of Arts; Fellow of the Antiquarian Society.
**FBA** Fellow of the British Academy.
**FBI** Federal Bureau of Investigation.
**FCA** Fellow of the Institute of Chartered Accountants.
**FCO** Foreign and Commonwealth Office.
**fcp., fcap.** foolscap.
**F.D.** *Fidei Defensor*, Defender of the Faith.
**Feb.** February.
**fem.** feminine.
**feud.** feudal.
**ff.** *fecerunt*, did it or made it (pl.); folios; (or ff) following (pl.); (or ff) fortissimo.
**FH** Fire hydrant.
**Fid. Def.** *Fidei Defensor*, Defender of the Faith.
**fig.** figure; figuratively.
**FJI** Fellow of The Institute of Journalists.
**fl.** *floruit*, flourished; florin (before 1971, two shillings).
**fl. oz.** fluid ounce.
**fm** fathom.
**F.M.** Field-Marshal.
**FM** frequency modulation.
**F.O.** Field-Officer; Flying Officer; Full Organ. Foreign Office.
**fo., fol.** folio.

**f.o.b.** free on board.
**f.o.r.** free on rail.
**fp** forte-piano.
**f.p.** freezing-point.
**FPA** Family Planning Association.
**FPS** foot-pound-second.
**Fr.** Father; France, French; Friar; Friday.
**fr.** fragment; franc; frequently.
**FRCP** Fellow of the Royal College of Physicians.
**FRCS** Fellow of the Royal College of Surgeons.
**FRS** Fellow of the Royal Society.
**ft** foot, feet; fort.
**fth, fthm** fathom.
**fur** furlong(s).
**fut.** future.
**fz.** forzando or forzato.

**G** Gauss; constant of gravitation.
**g** gram(me); gravity, acceleration of gravity.
**GA** General Assembly.
**Gael.** Gaelic.
**Gal.** Galatians.
**gal, gall** gallon(s).
**gam.** gamut.
**gaz.** gazette; gazetteer.
**GB** Great Britain.
**GBE** (Knight or Dame) Grand Cross of the British Empire.
**g.b.h.** grievous bodily harm (legal and police usage).
**GBS** George Bernard Shaw.
**GC** George Cross.
**GCB** (Knight) Grand Cross of the Bath.
**GCE** General Certificate of Education.
**GCMG** (Knight) Grand Cross of the Order of St Michael and St George.
**GCVO** (Knight or Dame) Grand Cross of the (Royal) Victorian Order.
**Gdns.** gardens (in street-names).
**Gen.** Genesis; General.
**gen.** gender; genitive; genus.
**gent.** gentleman.
**geog.** geography.
**geol.** geology.
**geom.** geometry.
**Ger.** German.
**ger.** gerund.
**GFS** Girls' Friendly Society.
**GHQ** General Headquarters.
**GI** (US Army) government (or general) issue; hence, common soldier.
**Gib.** Gibraltar.
**Gk** Greek.
**Glam.** Glamorganshire.
**GLC** Greater London Council.
**Glos.** Gloucestershire.
**GM** George Medal; Geiger-Müller counter (also G-M).
**gm** gram(me).
**GMC** General Medical Council.
**GMT** Greenwich Mean Time.
**G.O.C.** General Officer Commanding.
**G.O.M.** Grand Old Man (orig. W. E. Gladstone).
**Gov.** Governor; Government (also Govt.).
**GP** General Practitioner; Gallup Poll.
**GPI** general paralysis of the insane.
**GPO** General Post Office.
**Gr.** Greek.
**gr.** grain; grammar; gross; gunner.
**GS** General Staff; General Service; Geological Society.
**gs** guineas.
**GSM** Guildhall School of Music and Drama.
**G.S.O.** General Staff Officer.
**GSP** Good Service Pension.
**GT** gran turismo.
**GTC** General Teaching Council (Scotland).
**gu.** guinea; gules.
**guin.** guinea.

**G.W.(R.).** Great Western (Railway) (formerly).

**H** hydrant; hospital; hard (on lead pencils).
**h** hecto-; hour.
*h* height.
**H.A.** Heavy Artillery.
**ha.** hectare.
**Hab.** Habakkuk.
**h and c** hot and cold (water laid on).
**Hants.** Hampshire.
**Hb** haemoglobin.
**HB** hard black (on lead pencils).
**hbar** hectobar.
**HBM** His (or Her) Britannic Majesty.
**HC** Heralds' College; House of Commons; Holy Communion.
**HCF** Honorary Chaplain to the Forces; highest common factor.
**HE** His Excellency; His Eminence; High Explosive; Horizontal Equivalent.
**Heb., Hebr.** Hebrew; Hebrews.
**her.** heraldry; *heres*, heir.
**Herts** Hertfordshire.
**hf.** half. **hf.-bd.** half-bound. **hf.cf.** half-calf. **hf.-mor.** half-morocco.
**HF** high frequency.
**HG** His (or Her) Grace.
**HGV** Heavy goods vehicle.
**HH** His (or Her) Highness; very hard (on lead pencils).
**hhd.** hogshead.
**Hi-Fi, hi-fi** high fidelity.
**HIM** His (or Her) Imperial Majesty.
**hist.** historian; history.
**HK** House of Keys (Isle of Man).
**hl.** hectolitre(s).
**HM** His (or Her) Majesty.
**HMC** His (or Her) Majesty's Customs.
**HMI** His (or Her) Majesty's Inspector, Inspectorate.
**HMS** His (or Her) Majesty's Ship or Service.
**HMSO** His (or Her) Majesty's Stationery Office.
**HNC** Higher National Certificate.
**ho.** house.
**Hon.** Honourable, Honorary.
**hor.** horizon; horology.
**hort., hortic.** horticulture; horticultural.
**Hos.** Hosea.
**HP** hire-purchase; half-pay; horse-power (also h.p.).
**HQ** headquarters.
**hr** hour.
**HRH** His (or Her) Royal Highness.
**HSS** *Historiae Societatis Socius*, Fellow of the Historical Society.
**HT** High tension.
**Hunts** Huntingdonshire.
**HWM** high water mark.
**Hz** hertz (cycles per second).

*I* electric current.
**IA** Institute of Actuaries.
**IB** Institute of Bankers.
**IBA** Independent Broadcasting Authority.
**ib., ibid.** *ibidem*, in the same place.
**IBRD** International Bank for Reconstruction and Development (World Bank).
**i/c** in charge.
**ICA** Institute of Contemporary Arts.
**ICAO** International Civil Aviation Organization.
**ICBM** intercontinental ballistic missile.
**ICE** Institution of Civil Engineers; internal combustion engine.
**IAFTU** International Conference of Free Trade Unions.
**ich., ichth.** ichthyology.
**IChemE** Institution of Chemical Engineers.
**ICI** Imperial Chemical Industries.

**ICJ** International Court of Justice.
**icon.** iconography, iconographic.
**id.** *idem*, the same.
**ID** Intelligence Department.
**i.e., ie** *id est*, that is.
**IEE** Institution of Electrical Engineers.
**IFC** International Finance Corporation.
**ihp** indicated horse-power.
**IL** Institute of Linguists.
**ILEA** Inner London Education Authority.
**ill.** illustration; illustrated.
**ILO** International Labour Organisation; International Labour Office.
**ILP** Independent Labour Party.
**IMF** International Monetary Fund.
**imit.** imitative.
**Imp.** Imperial; *Imperator*, Emperor.
**imp.** (also **imperf.**) imperfect; (also **imper.**) imperative; *imprimatur*, let it be printed; (also **impers.**) impersonal.
**in.** inch(es).
**inc., incorp.** incorporated.
**incl.** including; included.
**incog.** *incognito* (It.), unknown, avoiding publicity.
**Ind.** Independent.
**ind., indic.** indicative.
**indecl.** indeclinable.
**indef.** indefinite.
**indic.** indicative.
**indiv.** individual.
**inf.** *infra*, below; infantry; infinitive.
**infra dig.** *infra dignitatem*, beneath one's dignity.
**inst.** instant – the present month; institute.
**Inst.** Institute.
**int.** interest; interior; interpreter; international; integral.
**Interpol** International Criminal Police Commission.
**interrog.** interrogation; interrogative; interrogatively.
**in trans.** *in transitu*, in transit.
**intrans.** intransitive.
**intro., introd.** introduction.
**inv.** invoice; inventor; invented.
**IOM** Isle of Man.
**IOU** I owe you.
**IOW** Isle of Wight.
**I.P.A.** Institute of Practitioners in Advertising; India Pale Ale.
**IQ** Intelligence Quotient.
**i.q.** *idem quod*, the same as.
**IRA** Irish Republican Army.
**IRBM** intermediate range ballistic missile.
**Irel.** Ireland.
**Is., Isa.** Isaiah.
**It.** Italian.
**ITA** Independent Television Authority (since 1972 IBA).
**ita** initial teaching alphabet.
**ital.** italic; Italian.
**ITO** International Trade Organisation.
**ITU** International Telecommunications Union.
**IU** international unit.
**I.U.(C.)D.** Intra-uterine (contraceptive) device.
**IW** Isle of Wight.
**IWW** Industrial Workers of the World (U.S.A., Labour history).

**J.** Judge, Justice.
**Jan.** January.
**Jas.** James.
**JC** *Juris Consultus*, Jurisconsult; Jesus Christ; Justice Clerk.
**J.C.D.** *Juris Civilis Doctor*, Doctor of Civil Law.
**Jer.** Jeremiah.
**Jno.** John.
**Jo.** Joel.
**Josh.** Joshua.
**JP** Justice of the Peace.
**Jr., Jun., Junr.** Junior.

**J.U.D.** *Juris Utriusque Doctor*, Doctor both of Canon and of Civil Law.
**Jud., Judg.** Judges.
**Jul.** July.
**Jun.** June.
**Junc.** Junction.
**jurisp.** jurisprudence.

**K** Kelvin (thermometer scale); kelvin; (Mozart's works) number assigned by Köchel, musicologist who arranged them chronologically.
**k** kilo-.
**KB** Knight of the Bath; Knight Bachelor; King's Bench.
**KBE** Knight Commander of the Order of the British Empire.
**KC** King's Counsel; King's College.
**kc** kilocycle(s).
**KCB** Knight Commander of the Bath.
**KCMG** Knight Commander of Order of St Michael and St George.
**KCVO** Knight Commander of the Royal Victorian Order.
**kg** kilogram(me)(s).
**KG** Knight of the Order of the Garter.
**KGB** Komitet Gosudarstvennoi Bezopasnosti (Russian Committee of State Security).
**KGCB** Knight of the Grand Cross of the Bath.
**KGF** Knight of the Golden Fleece.
**kHz** hilohertz.
**kilo** kilogram(me); kilometre.
**KKK** Ku Klux Klan.
**KLH** Knight of the Legion of Honour.
**KLM** Koninklijke Luchtvaart Maatschappij (Royal Dutch Airlines).
**KM** Knight of Malta.
**km** kilometre(s).
**kn** (*naut.*) knot.
**KO, ko** knock out.
**kr.** kreutzer; krone.
**KT** Knight of the Thistle.
**Kt** Knight.
**Kt Bach.** Knight Bachelor.
**κ.τ.λ., k.t.l.** *kai ta leipomena* or *kai ta loipa*, and the rest, and so forth.
**kW** kilowatt.
**kWh** kilowatt-hour.

**L** Lake; Latin; Liberal; learner (driver); *libra*, pound (sterling).
*L* symbol for inductance; luminance.
**l.** latitude; league; long; *libra*, pound (sterling).
*l* length.
**LA** Law Agent; Los Angeles; Library Association; Local Authority.
**Lab.** Labour.
**lab.** laboratory.
**Lam.** Lamentations.
**LAMDA** London Academy of Music and Dramatic Art.
**Lancs** Lancashire.
**lang.** language.
**Lat.** Latin.
**lat.** latitude.
**lb.** *libra*, pound (weight).
**l.b., l.b.w.** leg before wicket (in cricket).
**l.c.** lower-case (in printing); *loco citato*, in the place cited; left centre; letter of credit.
**LCC** London County Council (now GLC).
**L.Ch., LCh, LChir** *Licentiatus Chirurgiae*, Licentiate in Surgery.
**LCJ** Lord Chief-Justice.
**LCM, lcm** least common multiple.
**Ld** Lord.
**LD** Lady Day.

**Ldp, Lp** Lordship.
**LEA** Local Education Authority.
**lect.** lecture.
**leg.** legal; legate; legislature.
**Leics** Leicestershire.
**Lev., Levit.** Leviticus.
**lex.** lexicon.
**LF** low frequency.
**l.h.** left hand.
**LI** Light Infantry.
**lib.** *liber*, book.
**lib. cat.** library catalogue.
**Lieut.** Lieutenant.
**Lincs** Lincolnshire.
**Linn.** Linnaean, Linnaeus.
**liq.** liquid.
**lit.** literally; literature.
**lith., litho., lithog.** lithograph; lithography.
**Lit. Hum.** *litterae humaniores*, humane letters, the humanists.
**Lit(t).D.** *Litterarum Doctor*, Doctor of Letters.
**LJ** Lord Justice.
**LL.B.** *Legum Baccalaureus*, Bachelor of Laws.
**L.L.C.M.** Licentiate of the London College of Music.
**LL.D.** *Legum Doctor*, Doctor of Laws.
**LL.M.** *Legum Magister*, Master of Laws.
**L.M., l.m.** long metre.
**lm** lumen.
**loc. cit.** *loco citato*, at the place quoted.
**L of C** line of communication.
**log** logarithm.
**lon., long.** longitude.
**Lond.** London.
**loq.** *loquitur*, speaks.
**L.P.** Lord Provost; long-playing; low pressure.
**L.R.A.M.** Licentiate of the Royal Academy of Music.
**L.R.C.P.** Licentiate of the Royal College of Physicians (**E**, of Edinburgh).
**L.R.C.S.** Licentiate of the Royal College of Surgeons.
**L.S.** Linnaean Society; *loco. sigilli*, in the place of the seal.
**l.s.** left side.
**LSD** lysergic acid diethylamide.
**L.S.D.** *librae*, *solidi*, *denarii*, pounds, shillings, pence (before 1971).
**LSE** London School of Economics.
**Lt.** Lieutenant.
**LTA** Lawn Tennis Association.
**Lt.-Col.** Lieutenant-Colonel.
**Ltd.** Limited Liability.
**Lt.-Gen.** Leieutenant-General.
**lx** lux.

**μ** mu; micron; micro-.
**M...** Member...
**M** mega-.
**M.** *Monsieur* (Fr.), Mr (pl. MM.).
**M. or m.** *mille*, a thousand.
**m.** married; masculine; *meridiem*, noon.
**m** milli- metre; mile.
***m*** mass.
**M.A.** *Magister Artium*, Master of Arts.
**Mac., Macc.** Maccabees.
**mach.** machinery.
**Mad.** Madam.
**mag.** magazine.
**Maj.** Major.
**Mal.** Malachi.
**Man., Manit.** Manitoba.
**M & B** May and Baker (sulphonamides prepared by this firm and others).
**Mar.** March.
**marg.** margin; marginal.
**Marq.** Marquis.
**mas., masc.** masculine.
**math., maths** mathematics.
**Matt.** Matthew.
**max.** maximum.
**mb** millibar.

**M.B.** *Medicinae Baccalaureus*, Bachelor of Medicine.
**MBE** Member of the Order of the British Empire.
**MC** Member of Congress; Master of Ceremonies; Member of Council; Military Cross.
**MCC** Marylebone Cricket Club; Member of the County Council.
**M.Ch.** *Magister Chirurgiae*, Master of Surgery.
**MCP**(**A**) methyl-chloro-phenozy-acetic acid (methoxone; used as selective weedkiller).
**Mc/s** megacycles per second.
**M.D.** *Medicinae Doctor*, Doctor of Medicine; mentally deficient.
**Mdlle, Mlle** *Mademoiselle* (Fr.), Miss.
**Mdm** Madam.
**M.D.S.** Master of Dental Surgery.
**M.E.** Most Excellent; Middle English.
**ME** Mining or Mechanical Engineer.
**MEC** Member of the Executive Council.
**mech.** mechanic; mechanical.
**med.** medical; medicine; mediaeval; *medius*, *-a*, *-um*, middle.
**Mem.** Member.
**mem.** memorandum; *memento*, remember.
**memo.** memorandum.
**Messrs** *Messieurs* (Fr.), Sirs, Gentlemen; used as pl. of Mr.
**met., metaph.** metaphysics; metaphor; metaphorical.
**met., meteor.** meteorology.
**metal., metall.** metallurgy.
**meteor.** meteorology.
**meth**(**s**). methylated spirits.
**MeV** million electron-volt(s).
**Mex.** Mexico; Mexican.
**μF** microfarad.
**mf** mezzo-forte.
**mfd** manufactured.
**MFH** Master of Foxhounds.
**mfrs** manufacturers.
**mg** milligram(me)(s).
**MG** machine-gun.
**Mgr** Monseigneur; Monsignor.
**M.H.G.** Middle High German.
**MI** Military Intelligence; MI5 Security Services, MI6 Secret Intelligence Service.
**Mic.** Micah.
**Middx** Middlesex.
**mil., milit.** military.
**min** minute.
**min.** mineralogy; minimum.
**Min.** Ministry.
**misc.** miscellaneous; miscellany.
**MIT** Massachusetts Institute of Technology.
**MJI** Member of the Institute of Journalists.
**Mk** mark.
**MKS, mks** metre-kilogram-second unit, or system.
**MKSA** metre-kilogram-second-ampere unit, or system.
**ml** millilitre(s).
**MLA** Member of Legislative Assembly.
**MLC** Member of Legislative Council.
**Mlle** *Mademoiselle*, pl. Mlles, *Mesdemoiselles*.
**MM.** *Messieurs* (Fr.), Gentlemen or Sirs.
**MM** (Their) Majesties; Martyrs; Military Medal.
**mm** millimetre(s).
**mμ** millimicron.
**Mme** *Madame* (Fr.), pl. *Mmes*, *Mesdames*.
**mmf** magnetomotive force.
**MN** Merchant Navy.
**MO** Medical Officer.
**mo.** month.
**MOD** Ministry of Defence.
**mod.** modern; moderato.
**mod. cons.** modern conveniences.
**Mods** moderations (Oxford University).

**MOH** Medical Officer of Health.
**mol** mole (unit).
**mol wt** molecular weight.
**Mon.** Monmouthshire; Monday.
**Monsig.** Monsignor.
**Mont.** Montgomeryshire.
**Mor.** Morocco.
**morn.** morning.
**mos** months.
**mp** mezzo-piano (rather soft); (or m.p.) melting-point.
**MP** Member of Parliament; Military Police; Metropolitan Police.
**mpg** miles per gallon.
**mph** miles per hour.
**M.Pharm.** Master of Pharmacy.
**MR** Master of the Rolls.
**Mr** Master or Mister.
**MRA** Moral Rearmament.
**mrad** millirad.
**μrad** microrad.
**MRC** Medical Research Council.
**Mrs** Mistress.
**MS** manuscript.
**M.S.** Master of Surgery; *Memoriae Sacrum* Sacred to the Memory; milestone; multiple sclerosis.
**Ms** title of woman (mod. equiv. of Mr).
**ms** millisecond(s).
**μs** microsecond(s).
**M.Sc.** Master of Science.
**msec** millisecond(s).
**MSF** Medium standard frequency.
**m.s.l.** mean sea-level.
**MST** Mountain standard time.
**MT** Mechanical Transport; Mean time.
**Mt, mt** mount.
**MTB** motor torpedo-boat.
**mth** month.
**Mts, mts** mountains.
**mus.** music; museum.
**Mus.B(ac)** Bachelor of Music.
**Mus.D., Doc., MusD, Doc** Doctor of Music.
**Mus.M.** Master of Music.
**mv** merchant vessel; motor vessel; muzzle velocity; *mezza voce*, with medium fullness of sound.
**MVO** Member of the Royal Victorian Order.
**MW** medium wave.
**MWGM** Most Worshipful (or Worthy) Grand Master (Freemasonry).
**Mx** Middlesex.
**myst.** mysteries.
**myth.** mythology.

**N.** North, Northern.
**N** newton; Avogadro number; neper.
**n.** name; noun; *natus*, born; neuter; noon.
**n** nano-.
**N.A.** North America.
**NAAFI** Navy, Army and Air Force Institutes.
**N and Q** Notes and Queries.
**Nap.** Napoleon.
**NASA** National Aeronautics and Space Administration (USA).
**nat.** *natus*, born.
**Nat.** National.
**nat. hist.** natural history.
**NATO** North Atlantic Treaty Organization.
**naut.** nautical.
**nav.** naval; navigation.
**NB** North Britain; North British.
**NB, nb** *nota bene*, note well, or take notice.
**nbg** no bloody good.
**NBL** National Book League.
**NCB** National Coal Board.
**NCCL** National Council for Civil Liberties.
**NCO** non-commissioned officer.
**NCR** no carbon required.
**n.c.v.** no commercial value.
**n.d.** no date, not dated.
**NDPS** National Data Processing Service.

**N.E., NE** North-east; New England.

**NEB** New English Bible.

**NEDC** National Economic Development Council (Neddy).

**neg.** negative.

**Neh.** Nehemiah.

**N.E.I.** *non est inventus*, has not been found.

**nem. con.** *nemine contradicente*, no one contradicting.

**nem. diss.** *nemine dissentiente*, no one dissenting.

**Neth.** Netherlands.

**neut.** neuter.

**New M.** New Mexico.

**N.F.** Norman French; Northern French; (or NF, or Nfd.) Newfoundland.

**NFS** National Fire Service.

**NFU** National Farmers' Union.

**NFWI** National Federation of Women's Institutes.

**NHS** National Health Service.

**NI** Northern Ireland.

**NIC** National Incomes Commission (Nicky).

**n.l.** *non licet*, it is not permitted; *non liquet*, it is not clear; *non longe*, not far.

**N.M., N.Mex.** New Mexico.

**n mile** international nautical mile.

**N.N.E.** North-north-east.

**NNI** noise and number index.

**N.N.W.** North-north-west.

**No., no.** *numero*, (in) number.

**nom., nomin.** nominative.

**noncom.** noncommissioned.

**Noncon.** Nonconformist.

**n.o.p.** not otherwise provided.

**Northants** Northamptonshire.

**Northumb.** Northumberland.

**Nos., nos.** numbers.

**Notts** Nottinghamshire.

**Nov.** November.

**NP** Notary Public; (also n.p.) new paragraph.

**n.p.** no place (of publication).

**NPFA** National Playing Fields Association.

**nr** near.

**NS** New Style; Nova Scotia.

**n.s.** not specified.

**ns** nanosecond(s).

**NSPCC** National Society for Prevention of Cruelty to Children.

**NSW** New South Wales.

**NT** New Testament; Northern Territory.

**ntp** normal temperature and pressure.

**NU** name unknown.

**NUJ** National Union of Journalists.

**NUM** National Union of Mineworkers.

**Num., Numb.** Numbers.

**NUPE** National Union of Public Employees.

**NUR** National Union of Railwaymen.

**NUS** National Union of Students.

**NUT** National Union of Teachers.

**NUTG** National Union of Townswomen's Guilds.

**NV** New Version.

**n.v.d.** no valued declared.

**N.W.** North-west.

**NZ** New Zealand.

**o/a** on account of.

**OAP** Old Age Pension or Pensioner.

**OAS** on active service.

**ob. obiit**, died.

**Ob., Obad.** Obadiah.

**obdt** obedient.

**OBE** Officer of the Order of the British Empire.

**obj.** object; objective.

**obl.** oblique; oblong.

**obs.** observation; obsolete.

**o/c** overcharge.

**OC** Officer Commanding.

**Oct.** October.

**oct.** octavo.

**OCTU** Officer Cadet Training Unit.
**OD** Ordnance Datum or Data.
**O.E.** Old English.
**OED** Oxford English Dictionary.
**O.F.** Old French.
**off.** official; officinal.
**OFM** Order of Friars Minor.
**O.F.S.** Orange Free State (province of Rep. of South Africa).
**O.H.G.** Old High German.
**O.H.M.S.** On His (or Her) Majesty's Service.
**Old Test.** Old Testament.
**OM** Order of Merit; Old Measurement.
**o.n.o.** or near offer.
**Op.** Opera; *Opus*, work.
**O.P.** *Ordinis Praedicatorum*, of the Order of Preachers (or Dominicans); opposite prompt (*theatr.*).
**o.p.** out of print.
**op.** opposite; *opus*; operation.
**op. cit.** *opere citato*, in the work cited.
**opp.** opposed; opposite.
**Ops** Operations; Operations Officer; Operations room.
**opt.** optative; *optime*, very well indeed.
**ord.** ordained; order; ordinary; ordnance.
**orig.** origin; original; originally.
**OS** Old Style; Ordinary Seaman; outsize (dressm.).
**osp** *obiit sine prole*, died without issue.
**OT** Old Testament; occupational therapy.
**OTC** Officers' Training Corps.
**OUDS** Oxford University Dramatic Society.
**Oxf.** Oxford.
**Oxon.** *Oxonia*, Oxford; *Oxoniensis*, of Oxford.
**oz** ounce(s).
**P.** President; Prince; pedal.
**P** phosphorus; parking.
*P* power.
**p.** page; participle.
**p** new penny; new pence; piano.
**pa.** past.
**p.a.** per annum; participial adjective.
**PA** Press Association; Publishers Association.
**paint.** painting.
**Pal.** Palestine.
**pam.** pamphlet.
**Pan.** Panama.
**Pan Am** Pan-American (World Airways Incorporated).
**P. and O.** Peninsular and Oriental (Steamship Co.).
**pa.p.** past participle.
**par.** paragraph; parallel; parish.
**pass.** passive.
**pa.t.** past tense.
**Pat. Off.** Patent Office.
**PAYE** Pay As You Earn (Income Tax).
**PB** Pharmacopoeia Britannica; Plymouth Brethren.
**PBI** poor bloody infantry.
**PC** *Patres Conscripti*, Conscript Fathers; Privy Councillor; Police Constable.
**pc** postcard.
**pd.** paid.
**PDSA** People's Dispensary for Sick Animals.
**PE** physical education.
**PEC, pec** photoelectric cell.
**ped.** pedal.
**P.E.N.** Poets, Playwrights, Editors, Essayists, and Novelists (International Association of).
**Pen.** Peninsula.
**Pent.** Pentecost.
**PEP** Political and Economic Planning (research organization).
**per.** period; person.
**per an.** *per annum*, per year, by the year.

**per cent** *per centum*, by the hundred.

**perf.** perfect.

**perh.** perhaps.

**per pro.** *per procurationem*, by the agency (of).

**Pers.** Persian.

**pers.** person; personal.

**PF** Procurator Fiscal.

**pf** piano-forte.

**PG** paying guest.

**P.G.M.** Past Grand Master (*Freemasonry*).

**Phar., Pharm.** pharmaceutical; pharmacopoeia; pharmacy.

**Ph.B.** *Philosophiae Baccalaureus*, Bachelor of Philosophy.

**Ph.D.** *Philosophiae Doctor*, Doctor of Philosophy.

**Phil.** Philippians; Philemon; Philadelphia; philology; philological; philosophy; philosophical.

**phon., phonet.** phonetics.

**phot.** photography.

**phr.** phrase.

**phys.** physiology; physics; physician.

**PIB** Prices and Incomes Board.

**PK** psychokinesis.

**PL** Primrose League; Poet Laureate; Public Library.

**PLA** Port of London Authority.

**PLP** Parliamentary Labour Party.

**plu., plur.** plural.

**plup.** pluperfect.

**pm.** premium.

**PM** Past Master; *post meridiem*, after noon; Postmaster; *post mortem*, after death; Prime Minister; Provost-Marshal.

**PMG** Postmaster-General.

**PMO** Principal Medical Officer.

**Pmr.** Paymaster.

**p.n.** promissory note.

**PNdb** perceived noise decibel.

**PNEU** Parents' National Educational Union.

**po.** pole.

**P.O.** post-office; postal order; Petty Officer; Pilot Officer.

**p.o.d.** pay on delivery.

**pop.** population; popular.

**pos., posit.** positive.

**POW** prisoner of war.

**pp** pianissimo.

**p.p.** past participle.

**pp.** pages; *per procurationem*, by proxy.

**PPS** *post postscriptum*, an additional postscript; Parliamentary Private Secretary.

**Pr.** Prince; priest; Provençal.

**pr.** pair; per; present; price.

**PRA** President of the Royal Academy.

**PRB** Pre-Raphaelite Brotherhood.

**Preb.** Prebend; Prebendary.

**pref.** preface.

**prep.** preparation; preparatory; preposition.

**Pres.** President.

**pret.** preterite.

**PRIBA** President of the Royal Institute of British Architects.

**Prin.** Principal.

**Pro.** Professional.

**PRO** Public Relations Officer; Public Record Office.

**prob.** probably.

**Prof.** Professor.

**prop.** proper; properly; proposition; property.

**pro tem.** *pro tempore*, for the time being.

**Prov.** Proverbs; Provincial; Provost.

**prox.** *proximo* (*mense*), next (month).

**prox. acc.** *proxime accessit*, next (in order of merit) to the winner.

**PRS** President of the Royal Society.

**PRSA** President of the Royal Scottish Academy.

**P.S.** *post scriptum*, written after, postscript.
**Ps., Psa.** Psalm(s).
**PS** Philological Society; Pharmaceutical Society.
**pseud.** pseudonym.
**pt** part; pint(s).
**PT** physical training; purchase tax.
**PTA** Parent/Teacher Association.
**Pte.** private (military).
**PTFE** polytetrafluoroethylene.
**PTO** Please turn over.
**pty, Pty** proprietary.
**PU** pick-up.
**PWD** Public Works Department.

*Q* symbol for electric charge.
**Q.** (or **Qu.**) query, question.
**Q** queue; Sir Arthur Quiller-Couch.
**q.** query; quintal.
**QAB** Queen Anne's Bounty
**QB** Queen's Bench.
**QC** Queen's Counsel; Queens' College.
**Q.M.** Quartermaster.
**Q.M.G.** Quartermaster-General.
**Q.M.S.** Quartermaster-Sergeant.
**Qq.** (or **qq.**) quartos.
**qq.v.** *quae vide*, which (pl.) see (sing. **q.v.**).
**qr.** quarter.
**Q.S.** Quarter-Sessions.
**q.s., quant. suff.** *quantum sufficit*, a sufficient quantity.
**QSO** quasi-stellar object (quasar).
**qt.** quantity; quart(s).
**q.t.** quiet.
**qto.** quarto.
**qts.** quarts.
**qty.** quantity.
**Qu.** Queen; question.
**qu., quar.** quart; quarter, quarterly.
**q.v.** *quod vide*, which (sing.) see (pl. **qq.v.**); *quant umvis*, as much as you will.

**R.** *rex, regina*, King, Queen; rand.
*R* symbol for electric resistance.
**r.** right; radius; *recipe*, take.
**r** Röntgen unit.
**R., Réau** Réaumur's thermometric scale.
**RA** Royal Academy or Academician; Royal Artillery; Rear Admiral.
**RAAF** Royal Australian Air Force.
**Rabb.** Rabbinical.
**RAC** Royal Automobile Club; Royal Armoured Corps.
**Rad.** Radical.
**rad.** *radix*, root.
**rad** radian.
**RADA** Royal Academy of Dramatic Art.
**RAEC** Royal Army Educational Corps.
**RAF** Royal Air Force.
**RAM** Royal Academy of Music.
**RAMC** Royal Army Medical Corps.
**RAOC** Royal Army Ordnance Corps.
**RAPC** Royal Army Pay Corps.
**RAS** Royal Astronomical Society; Royal Asiatic Society.
**RAVC** Royal Army Veterinary Corps.
**RB** Rifle Brigade.
**R.B.L.** Royal British Legion.
**RBA** Royal Society of British Artists.
**RC** Roman Catholic; Red Cross; Royal College of Art.
**RCAF** Royal Canadian Air Force.
**RCM** Royal College of Music; Regimental Court-martial.
**RCO** Royal College of Organists.
**RCOG** Royal College of Obstetricians and Gynaecologists.
**RCP** Royal College of Preceptors; Royal College of Physicians.
**RCS** Royal College of Surgeons; Royal Corps of Signals; Royal College of Science.

**RCT** Royal Corps of Transport.
**RCVS** Royal College of Veterinary Surgeons.
**RD** Rural Dean; Naval Reserve Decoration; refer to drawer.
**Rd.** Road.
**rd** rutherford.
**RDC** Rural District Council.
**RDS** Royal Dublin Society.
**RE** Royal Engineers; Royal Society of Etchers and Engravers; Royal Exchange.
**Rec.** *recipe*, take.
**recd.** received.
**REconS** Royal Economic Society.
**recpt.** receipt.
**Rect.** Rector; Rectory.
**ref.** referee; reference.
**Reg. Prof.** Regius Professor.
**regt.** regiment.
**rel.** relating; relation; relative.
**REME** Royal Electrical and Mechanical Engineers.
**Rep.** representative; republic; report; reporter.
**rept.** receipt.
**retd.** returned; retired.
**Rev.** revise; revision; Revelation; (or Revd.) Reverend.
**rev.** revolution.
**Rev. Ver.** Revised Version.
**Rf.** rinforzando (*mus.*).
**R.F.** *République française*, French Republic; radio frequency.
**RFC** Royal Flying Corps (now RAF); Rugby Football Club.
**RGG** Royal Grenadier Guards.
**RGN** Registered General Nurse.
**RGS** Royal Geographical Society.
**Rgt.** Regiment.
**Rh** rhodium; rhesus.
**RH** Royal Highness.
**r.h.** right hand.
**RHA** Royal Horse Artillery; Royal Hibernian Academy.
**rhet.** rhetoric.
**RHF** Royal Highland Fusiliers.
**RHG** Royal Horse Guards.
**RHistS** Royal Historical Society.
**RHS** Royal Humane Society; Royal Horticultural Society; Royal Historical Society.
**RIA** Royal Irish Academy.
**RIAM** Royal Irish Academy of Music.
**RIBA** Royal Institute of British Architects.
**RICS** Royal Institution of Chartered Surveyors.
**RIGB** Royal Institution of Great Britain.
**R.I.P.** *requiescat in pace*, may he (or she) rest in peace.
**RLO** Returned letter office.
**RLS** Robert Louis Stevenson.
**Rly, rly** railway.
**RM** Royal Mail; Royal Marines; resident magistrate; riding master.
**RMA** Royal Military Academy, Sandhurst; Royal Marine Artillery.
**RN** Royal Navy.
**RNA** ribonucleic acids.
**RNIB** Royal National Institute for the Blind.
**RNLI** Royal National Lifeboat Institution.
**RNR** Royal Naval Reserve.
**RNVR** Royal Naval Volunteer Reserve.
**RNZAF** Royal New Zealand Air Force.
**Ro.** *recto*, on the right-hand page.
**ROC** Royal Observer Corps.
**Rom.** Romans.
**Rom. Cath.** Roman Catholic.
**Ro-Ro** roll-on-roll-off.
**rpm, rps** revolutions per minute, second.
**RPS** Royal Photographic Society.
**RR** Right Reverend.
**RRE** Radar Research Establishment.
**Rs** Rupees.
**RS** Royal Society.

**RSA** Royal Society of Antiquaries; Royal Society of Arts; Royal Scottish Academy or Academician.

**RSE** Royal Society of Edinburgh.

**RSL** Royal Society of Literature.

**RSM** Regimental Sergeant-Major; Royal Society of Medicine; Royal School of Music.

**RSO** railway sub-office; railway sorting office; rural sub-office; Resident Surgical Officer.

**RSPA** (**Rospa**) Royal Society for the Prevention of Accidents.

**RSPB** Royal Society for the Protection of Birds.

**RSPCA** Royal Society for the Prevention of Cruelty to Animals.

**RSV** Revised Standard Version.

**RSVP** *répondez s'il vous plaît*, reply, if you please.

**RT** radiotelephone, -phony.

**Rt Hon.** Right Honourable.

**RTO** Railway Transportation (or Traffic) Officer.

**Rt Rev.** Right Reverend.

**RU** Rugby Union.

**r-unit** Röntgen unit – unit of measurement of X-ray radiation.

**RV** Revised Version.

**R.W.** Right Worthy.

**Rx** tens of rupees.

**Ry, ry** railway.

**RYS** Royal Yacht Squadron.

**RZS** Royal Zoological Society.

**S.** South; Sabbath; Saint; society; sun.

**S** square; strokes.

**s** second(s).

**SA** South Africa; South America; South Australia; Salvation Army; sex-appeal; *Societé Anonyme* (Fr.), limited liability company; Society of Arts; Society of Antiquaries.

**SAA** Small Arms Ammunition; South African Airways; Society of Incorporated Accountants (formerly and Auditors).

**s.a.e.** stamped addressed envelope.

**Salop** Shropshire.

**SALT** Strategic Arms Limitation Talks.

**SAM** surface-to-air missile.

**Sam.** Samuel.

**SARAH** Search and rescue and homing.

**Sarum** Salisbury.

**SAS** *Societatis Antiquariorum Socius*, Fellow of the Society of Antiquaries; Scandinavian Airlines System.

**Sat.** Saturday.

**SBN** Standard Book Number.

**SC** Special Constable; Supreme Court; Staff College; Staff Corps.

**s.c., s. caps, sm. caps** small capitals.

**sc., sc** *scilicet*, that is to say.

**Sc.B.** *Scientiae Baccalaureus*, Bachelor of Science.

**Sc.D.** *Scientiae Doctor*, Doctor of Science.

**sci.fi.** science fiction.

**SCL** Student of Civil Law.

**SCM** Student Christian Movement; State Certified Midwife.

**Scot.** Scotland; Scottish.

**Script.** Scripture.

**sculp.** sculpture; sculptor.

**s.d.** *sine die*, without a day (fixed).

**SDC** single data converter.

**SDF** Social Democratic Federation (Labour history).

**SDLP** Social Democratic and Labour Party (in Northern Ireland).

**S.E., SE** South-east.

**SE** Society of Engineers.

**SEATO** South-East Asia Treaty Organization.

**Sec., Secy** Secretary.

**sec.** *secundum*, in accordance with; second; section.

**sec** secant.

**sec. leg.** *secundum legem*, according to law.

**sec. reg.** *secundum regulam*, according to rule.

**sect.** section.

**Sem.** seminary; Semitic.

**Sen.** Senator; senior.

**SEN** State Enrolled Nurse.

**Sep., Sept.** September; Septuagint.

**seq.** *sequens* (sing.), **seqq.**, *sequentes* or *sequentia* (pl.), following.

**ser.** series; sermon.

**Serg., Sergt** Sergeant.

**Serj., Serjt** Serjeant.

**Sess.** Session.

**SET** Selective Employment Tax.

**S.F.** Sinn Fein; science fiction; (or SF) signal frequency.

**SFA** Scottish Football Association.

**sfz.** sforzando (*mus.*).

**SG** Solicitor-General.

**s.g.** specific gravity.

**SHAEF** Supreme Headquarters of the Allied Expeditionary Force.

**SHAPE** Supreme Headquarters Allied Powers Europe.

**sig.** signature.

**sin** sine.

**sing.** singular.

**sinh** hyperbolic sine.

**SIS** Secret Intelligence Service.

**SJ** Society of Jesus.

**SL** Solicitor at Law; Sergeant-at-Law.

**SL., S.Lat.** South latitude.

**sld** sailed.

**s.l.p.** *sine legitima prole*, without lawful issue.

**S.M.** Short Metre; Sergeant-Major; *Sa Majesté*, His (or Her) Majesty.

**Smith. Inst.** Smithsonian Institution.

**SMO** Senior Medical Officer.

**s.m.p.** *sine mascula prole*, without male issue.

**SNP** Scottish National Party.

**s.o.** seller's option.

**SO** Staff Officer; Signal Officer; standing order; special order.

**s.o.b.** son of a bitch.

**Soc.** Society.

**sol.** solution.

**Sol., Solr.** Solicitor.

**Sol.-Gen.** Solicitor-General.

**sop.** soprano.

**sp.** spelling; species.

**s.p.** *sine prole*, without issue.

**SPCK** Society for Promoting Christian Knowledge.

**sp.gr.** specific gravity.

**SPR** Society for Psychical Research.

**s.p.s.** *sine prole superstite*, without surviving issue.

**spt** seaport.

**sp.vol.** specific volume.

**sq., Sq.** square; *sequens*, following; **sqq.** (pl.), *sequentes* or *sequentia*).

**sqn** squadron.

**Sr** senior; Sir.

**SR** Southern Railway; Southern Region.

**SRC** Science Research Council; Student Representative Council.

**SRN** State Registered Nurse.

**SRS** *Societatis Regiae Socius*, Fellow of the Royal Society; also RSS; *cf.* FRS.

**SRU** Scottish Rugby Union.

**SS** Saints; Santa Stamina.

**s.s.** steamship; screw steamer.

**SSAFA** Soldiers', Sailors' and Airmen's Families Association.

**S.S.E.** South-south-east.

**SSM** surface-to-surface missile.

**SST** supersonic transport.

**S.S.W.** South-south-west.

**St** Saint; Strait; Street.

**st.** stone (weight).

**Staffs** Staffordshire.
**STD** subscriber trunk dialling.
**std** standard.
**ster.** (or **stereo.**) stereotype; (or **stg.**) sterling.
**STOL** Short Take-off and Landing.
**stp** standard temperature and pressure.
**STS** Scottish Text Society.
**STUC** Scottish Trades Union Congress.
**STV** Scottish Television.
**SU** strontium unit – unit of measurement of strontium radiation.
**sub.** subject.
**subj.** subject; subjunctive.
**subst.** substitute; substantive.
**suf., suff.** suffix.
**sup.** superfine; superior; (also superl.) superlative; supreme; *supra*; supine; supplement.
**Sup. Ct** Superior Court; Supreme Court.
**superl.** superlative.
**supp., suppl.** supplement.
**Supr.** Supreme.
**Supt** Superintendent.
**Surg.** surgeon; surgery.
**Surv.-Gen.** Surveyor-General.
**s.v.** *sub voce*, *sub verba*, under the word.
**S.W.** South-west; small women('s); short wave.
**SYHA** Scottish Youth Hostels Association.
**sym.** symbol.
**syn.** synonym.
**synop.** synopsis.
**syr.** *syrupus*, syrup.
**syst.** system.

*t* time.
**TA** Territorial Army (from 1967 T and AVR *q.v.*).
**tal. qual.** *talis qualis*, just as it comes; average quantity.
**Tam.** Tamil.
**tan** tangent.
**T and AVR** Territorial and Army Volunteer Reserve.
**tanh** hyperbolic tangent.
**TB** tuberculosis.
**TBD** torpedo-boat destroyer.
**tc.** tierce.
**TCD** Trinity College, Dublin.
**TCL** Trinity College of Music, London.
**TCP, t.c.p.** trichlorophenylmethyliodosalicyl (proprietary germicide).
**TD** Territorial Decoration.
**tech.** technical; technology.
**tel., teleg.** telegram, telegraph.
**temp.** temporal; *tempore*, in the time of; temperature; temporary.
**Ten., Tenn.** Tennessee.
**ten.** tenor; tenuto.
**Ter., Terr.** Territory; terrace.
**term.** termination.
**Test.** Testament.
**Teut.** Teutonic.
**Tex.** Texas.
**Text. Rec.** *textus receptus*, the received text.
**TF** Territorial Force.
**t.f.** till forbidden.
**TFR** Territorial Force Reserve.
**TGWU** Transport and General Workers' Union.
**Th.** Thursday.
**theat(r.)** theatrical.
**theol.** theology; theologian.
**theor.** theorem.
**Thess.** Thessalonians.
**Tho., Thos** Thomas.
**THWM** Trinity High-water Mark.
**t.i.d.** *ter in die*, thrice a day.
**Tim.** Timothy.
**TIROS** Television and Infra-red Observation Satellite.
**Tit.** Titus.
**TLS** *The Times Literary Supplement.*
**TNT** trinitrotoluene.

**T.O.** turn over; Telegraph Office; Transport Officer.
**Toc H** Talbot House.
**tom.** *tomus*, tome or volume.
**tp.** township; troop.
**TPI** Town Planning Institute.
**tpr** teleprinter.
**tr.** transpose; transactions; translator; trustee.
**trans.** transitive; translated; translation.
**transf.** transferred.
**treas.** treasurer.
**TRH** Their Royal Highnesses.
**trig.** trigonometry.
**Trin.** Trinity.
**TT** teetotal; teetotaller; Tourist Trophy; tuberculin tested.
**tty** teletypewriter.
**Tu., Tues.** Tuesday.
**TUC** Trades Union Congress.
**TV** television.
**typ., typo.** typographer; typography.

**U** universal (film certificate); Unionist.
**UAR** United Arab Republic.
**UCCA** Universities Central Council on Admissions.
**UDC** Urban District Council; Universal Decimal Classification.
**UDI** Unilateral Declaration of Independence.
**UDT** United Dominions Trust.
**UFO** Unidentified flying object.
**UGC** University Grants Committee.
**UHF** Ultra high frequency.
**UJD** *Utriusque Juris Doctor*, Doctor of both Laws (Canon and Civil).
**UK** United Kingdom.
**UKAEA** United Kingdom Atomic Energy Authority.
**ult., ulto.** *ultimo*, last; ultimate; ultimately.
**UN** United Nations.
**UNA** United Nations Association.
**UNESCO** United Nations Educational, Scientific and Cultural Organisation.
**UNICEF** United Nations International Children's Emergency Fund – now United Nations Children's Fund, but still known as UNICEF.
**Unit.** Unitarian.
**Univ.** University.
**UNO** United Nations Organisation.
**UNRRA** United Nations Relief and Rehabilitation Administration.
**UP** United Presbyterian; United Press; United Provinces (British India); Uttar Pradesh (Republic of India).
**US** United States; United Service(s); Under-secretary.
**u.s.** *ut supra*, as above.
**USA** United States of America; United States Army.
**USN** United States Navy.
**USPG** United Society for the Propagation of the Gospel.
**USSR** Union of Soviet Socialist Republics.
**usu.** usually.
**USW** ultrasonic waves; ultrashort waves.
**UT** Universal Time.
**ut dict.** *ut dictum*, as said.
**ut sup.** *ut supra*, as above.
**UU** Ulster Unionist.
**uv** ultraviolet.
**ux.** *uxor*, wife.

**V** volt.
*V* symbol for electric potential difference.
**v** velocity; *versus*, against; *vide*, see; verb; verse; volume.
$\nu$ symbol for frequency.

**V1** *Vergeltungswaffe* 1, German flying bomb (World War II).
**V2** German rocket weapon (World War II).
**VA** Royal Order of Victoria and Albert; Vicar Apostolic.
**vac.** vacuum.
**val.** value.
**V and A** Victoria and Albert Museum.
**var.** variant; variety; variable.
**var. lect.** *varia lectio*, variant reading.
**VAT** Value-added Tax.
**Vat.** Vatican.
**vb** verb.
**VC** Vice-Chancellor; Vice-Consul; Victoria Cross.
**VD** venereal disease(s).
**v.d.** various dates; vapour density.
**VDC** Volunteer Defence Corps.
**VE** Victory in Europe (World War II).
**veg.** vegetable(s).
**vel.** velocity.
**Ven.** Venerable.
**Venet.** Venetian.
**VERA** Versatile reactor assembly; vision electronic recording apparatus.
**Vert.** Vertebrata.
**ves.** vessel.
**Vet., Veter.** Veterinary.
**Vet. Surg.** Veterinary Surgeon.
**VF** voice frequency; video frequency.
**VG** Vicar-General.
**v.g.** *verbigratia*, for example; (or **V.G.**) very good.
**VHF** very high frequency.
**v.i.** verb intransitive.
**Vic.** Vicar; Vicarage.
**Vict.** Victoria.
**vid.** *vide*, see.
**vil.** village.
**VIP** Very Important Person.
**Vis., Visc.** Viscount.
**viz.** *videlicet*, namely (z = mediaeval Latin symbol of contraction).
**VJ** Victory over Japan (World War II).
**VLF** very low frequency.
**vo.** *verso*, on the left-hand page.
**voc.** vocative.
**vocab.** vocabulary.
**Vol.** Volunteer.
**vol.** volume.
**VP** Vice-President.
**VR** *Victoria Regina*, Queen Victoria.
**VRI** *Victoria Regina et Imperatrix*, Victoria, Queen and Empress.
**V.S.** Veterinary Surgeon.
**V.S.O.** Voluntary Service Overseas.
**v.t.** verb transitive.
**VTO** Vertical Take-off (**L**, and Landing).
**Vul., Vulg.** Vulgate.
**vul., vulg.** vulgar.
**vv. ll.** *variae lectiones*, various readings
**v.y.** various years

**W.** West; Welsh; women('s).
**W** watt.
**w.** weak.
**WA** West Africa; Western Australia.
**WAAC** Women's Army Auxiliary Corps.
**WAAF** Women's Auxiliary Air Force (now WRAF).
**Wal.** Walloon.
**WC** water-closet; Western Central; Wesleyan Chapel.
**W./Cdr.** Wing Commander.
**WD** War Department.
**WEA** Workers' Educational Association.
**Wed.** Wednesday.
**WEU** Western European Union.
**w.f.** wrong fount (*typ.*).
**WFTU** World Federation of Trade Unions.
**w.g.** wire gauge.
**WHO** World Health Organisation.

**Wilts** Wiltshire.
**wk.** week.
**Wm** William.
**WNP** Welsh Nationalist Party.
**W.N.W.** West-north-west.
**WO** War Office (1964 absorbed in Ministry of Defence); Warrant Officer.
**Worcs** Worcestershire.
**Wp., Wpfl.** Worshipful.
**w.p.** weather permitting.
**wpm** words per minute.
**WR** West Riding; Western Region.
**WRAC** Women's Royal Army Corps.
**WRAF** Women's Royal Air Force.
**WRI** Women's Rural Institute.
**WRNS** Women's Royal Naval Service.
**WRVS** Women's Royal Voluntary Service (previously WVS).
**ws.** women's (*dressm.*).
**W.S.W.** West-south-west.
**wt** weight.
**WVS** Women's Voluntary Service (now WRVS).
**wx** women's extra (*dressm.*).

**X** Used to mark films to which persons under eighteen will not be admitted.
**x.** *ex*, without; x.d., ex dividend.
**X.** or **Xt.** Christ (*X* = Gr. *Ch*).
**XD** ex-directory (of telephone numbers).
**Xm., Xmas.** Christmas.
**Xn., Xtian.** Christian.

**y.** year; yard.
**yd** yard.
**Yeo.** Yeomanry.
**YHA** Youth Hostels Association.
**YMCA** Young Men's Christian Association.
**Yorks** Yorkshire.
**yr.** your; younger; year.
**YWCA** Young Women's Christian Association.

**Zech.** Zechariah.
**Zeph.** Zephaniah.